Who'sWho in America®

Who's Who in America®

2004

MARQUIS
Who'sWho
21st
Since 1899
Century Editions
The Chronicle of Human Achievement

58th Edition
Volume 3
Indexes

MARQUIS
Who'sWho® 121 Chanlon Road
New Providence, NJ 07974 U.S.A.
www.marquiswhoswho.com

Who's Who in America®
Marquis Who's Who®

Chief Executive Officer	Gene M. McGovern
President	James A. Finkelstein
Senior Managing Director	Fred Marks
Director, Editorial & Product Development	Robert Docherty
Research Director	Lisa Weissbard

Editorial

Managing Editor	Karen Chassie
Senior Editor	Danielle Netta
Associate Editor	Kate Spirito
Assistant Editors	Patricia Delli Santi
	Ryan Karwell
	Deanna Richmond
	Sandy Sauchelli

Editorial Services

Director	Debby Nowicki
Production Manager	Paul Zema
Production Editors	Daniel D. Crawford
	Jeffrey Uthaichai
Freelance Manager	Mary SanGiovanni
Editorial Services Assistant	Ann Chavis
Special Projects Supervisor	Sola Osofisan
Mail Processing Manager	Kara A. Seitz
Mail Processing Staff	Betty Gray
	Hattie Walker

Creative Services

Director, Marketing & Creative Services	Michael Noerr
Creative Services Manager	Rose Butkiewicz
Production Manager	Jeanne Danzig
Marketing Specialist	Jill Tarbell

Research

Managing Editor	Kerry Nugent Morrison
Senior Research Editors	Maria L. Izzo
	Jennifer Podolsky
Associate Research Editor	Todd Kineavy

Editorial Systems

Director	Jack Zimmerman
Technical Project Leader	Ben Loh
Composition Programmer	Tom Haggerty
Database Programmer	Latha Shankar
Senior Quality Assurance Analyst	Angela Sorrenti

Published by Marquis Who's Who LLC.

For information, contact:
  Marquis Who's Who
  121 Chanlon Road
  New Providence, New Jersey 07974
  1-908-673-1001
  www.marquiswhoswho.com

WHO'S WHO IN AMERICA is a registered trademark of Marquis Who's Who LLC.

International Standard Book Number	0-8379-6974-3	(Set, Classic Edition)
	0-8379-6977-8	(Volume 3, Classic Edition)
	0-8379-6978-6	(Set, Deluxe Edition)
	0-8379-6981-6	(Volume 3, Deluxe Edition)
International Standard Serial Number	0083-9841	

Manufactured in the United States of America.

Table of Contents

Introduction

The *Who's Who in America* Geographic and Professional Indexes provide access to biographical information in the 58th Edition through two avenues in alphabetical form—geography and profession. Each Biographee entry contains name and occupational description. A dagger symbol (†) indicates a new name first appearing in the 58th Edition.

The Geographic Index lists names in the United States under state and city designations, as well as Biographees in American territories. Canadian listings include provinces and cities. Names in Mexico and other countries appear by city. Biographees whose addresses are not published in their sketches are found under Address Unpublished.

The Professional Index includes thirty-eight categories ranging alphabetically from Agriculture to Social Science. Within each area, the names appear under geographic subheadings. Names without published addresses appear at the end of each professional area listing under Address Unpublished. If the occupation does not fall within one of the specified areas, the name is listed under Unclassified.

Some Biographees have professions encompassing more than one area; each of these appears under the field best suited to the Biographee's occupation. Thus, while most bankers are listed under Finance: Banking Services, investment bankers are found in Finance: Investment Services. A Biographee with two or more diverse occupations is found under the area that best fits his or her professional profile.

The Retiree Index lists the names of those individuals whose biographical sketches last appeared in the 55th, 56th, or 57th Edition of *Who's Who in America.*

The Necrology lists Biographees of the 57th Edition whose deaths were reported to Marquis prior to the close of the compilation of this edition of *Who's Who in America.*

Alphabetical Practices

Names are arranged alphabetically according to the surnames and under identical surnames according to the first given name. If both surname and the first given name are identical, names are arranged alphabetically according to the second given name.

Surnames beginning with De, Des, Du (however capitalized or spaced) are recorded with the prefix preceding the surname and arranged alphabetically under the letter D.

Surnames beginning with Mac and Mc are arranged alphabetically under M.

Surnames beginning with Saint or St. appear after names that begin Sains, and are arranged according to the second part of the name, e.g., St. Clair before Saint Dennis.

Surnames beginning with Van, Von, or von are arranged alphabetically under the letter V.

Compound surnames are arranged according to the first member of the compound.

Many hyphenated Arabic names begin Al-, El-, or al-. These names are alphabetized according to each Biographee's designation of last name. Thus Al-Bahar, Neta may be listed either under Al- or under Bahar, depending on the preference of the listee.

Also, Arabic names have a variety of possible spellings when transposed to English. Spelling of these names is always based on the practice of the Biographee. Some Biographees use a Western form of word order, while others prefer the Arabic word sequence.

Similarly, Asian names may have no comma between family and given names, but some Biographees have chosen to add the comma. In each case, punctuation follows the preference of the Biographee.

Parentheses used in connection with a name indicate which part of the full name is usually deleted in common usage. Hence Chambers, E(lizabeth) Anne indicates that the usual form of the given name is E. Anne. In such a case, the parentheses are ignored in alphabetizing and the name would be arranged as Chambers, Elizabeth Anne. However, if the name is recorded Chambers, (Elizabeth) Anne, signifying that the entire name Elizabeth is not commonly used, the alphabetizing would be arranged as though the name were Chambers, Anne. If an entire middle or last name is enclosed in parentheses, that portion of the name is used in the alphabetical arrangement. Hence Chambers, Elizabeth (Anne) would be arranged as Chambers, Elizabeth Anne.

Where more than one spelling, word order, or name of an individual is frequently encountered, the sketch has been entered under the form preferred by the Biographee, with cross-references under alternate forms.

Geographic Index

†New name in *Who's Who in America*, 58th Edition

UNITED STATES

ALABAMA

Abbeville
Anderson, Ruth T. *retired air traffic controller*

Albertville
Johnson, Clark Everette, Jr., *judge*
Rice, Fuhrman D. (Runt Rice) *retired paper company executive*

Alexander City
Shuler, Ellie Givan, Jr., *retired military officer, military museum administrator*
Tyler, Eric Owen *pediatrician*

Alexandria
Conaway, Charles Alan *music educator*

Alpine
Abbott, Benjamin Edward, Jr., *corporate executive*
Hartman, Donald Dewayne *retired secondary education educator, writer*

Andalusia
Cross, Charlotte Lord *retired social worker, artist*
Fuller, William Sidney *lawyer*
†Lanier, Grady Oliver, III, *lawyer*
Patterson, Edwin *minister*
Taylor, James Marion, II, *automotive wholesale executive*

Anniston
Ayers, Harry Brandt *editor, publisher, columnist*
Comfort, Kenneth A. *court official*
Currie, Larry Lamar *insurance agent*
Harwell, Edwin Whitley *judge*
Klinefelter, James Louis *lawyer*
Umling, David Arthur *urban planner*

Arab
Black, Daniel Hugh *retired secondary school educator*
Hammond, Ralph Charles *real estate executive*

Ashland
Ingram, Kenneth Frank *retired state supreme court justice*

Athens
Gatlin, Tony Franklin *electrical engineer*
Hodson, Roy Goode, Jr., *retired logistician*
Ruf, Donnie Lee *delivery service provider, fashion model, clothing designer*

Atmore
Garrard, John, Jr., *bank executive, city councilman*

Auburn
Amacher, Richard Earl *literature educator*
Andelson, Robert Vernon *social philosopher, educator*
Ball, Donald Maury *agronomist, consultant*
†Baskiyar, Sanjeev *engineering educator*
†Brewer, Jesse Wayne *education educator, entomologist*
Cicci, David Allen *aerospace engineer, educator*
Cochran, John Euell, Jr., *aerospace engineer, educator, lawyer*
Dobson, F. Stephen *ecologist*
†Eaves, Ronald Clark *special education educator*
Flynt, James Wayne *history educator, researcher*
Galbraith, Ruth Legg *retired university dean, home economist*
Govil, Narendra Kumar *mathematics educator*
Gropper, Daniel Michael *college assistant dean, business educator*
Haneman, Vincent Siering, Jr., *consulting engineer, educator, university dean*
Harrell, David Edwin, Jr., *history educator*
Havens, Carolyn Clarice *librarian*
Irwin, John David *electrical engineering educator*
Jaeger, Richard Charles *electrical engineer, educator, science center director*
Jardine, Murray Donald *political science educator*
†Jenda, Overtoun Malandula *mathematician, educator, mathematician, researcher, dean*
Kam, Frederick Anthony *internist, physician*
Kandhal, Prithvi Singh *civil engineer, manager*
Lechner, Norbert Manfred *architect educator*
Littleton, Taylor Dowe *humanities educator*
Miller, Wilbur Randolph *university educator and administrator*
Millman, Richard George *architect, educator*
Morrow, Patrick David *English educator*
Neely, William Charles *chemistry educator, consultant, research scientist*
Niu, Guofu *electrical engineer, educator*
Noe, Kenneth William *historian, educator*
†Osei, Joseph *education educator, minister*
Parsons, Daniel Lankester *pharmaceutics educator*
Philpott, Harry Melvin *former university president*
Powell, William Clayton *music educator*
Rainer, Rex Kelly *civil engineer, educator*
Samford, Thomas Drake, III, *lawyer*
†Samoylova, Tatiana I *biochemist, researcher*
Seroka, James Henry *social sciences educator, university administrator*

†Sforzini, Richard Henry *aerospace engineer, educator*
Straiton, T(homas) Harmon, Jr., *librarian*
Tolbert, Clinton Jame *army officer, machinist*
Tullier, Michael Joseph *communications and industrial relations executive*
Turnquist, Paul Kenneth *agricultural engineer, educator*
Vazsonyi, Alexander Thomas *education educator*
Vodyanoy, Vitaly Jacob *biophysicist, educator*
Voitle, Robert Allen *college dean, physiologist*
†Wehrs, Donald Roger *English educator*
Whitten, David Owen *economics educator*
Yoo, Chai Hong *civil engineering educator*
Zallen, Harold *corporate executive, scientist, former university official*
Zhang, Daowei *forest economist, researcher, educator*

Auburn University
†Boosinger, Timothy R. *dean*
†Chen, An-Ban *physicist, educator*
†Dodge, Timothy de K. *college librarian*
†Winn, John Emmett *education educator*

Bay Minette
Granade, Fred King *lawyer*

Berry
Moore, Elizabeth Ann Davis *home fashion products specialist*

Bessemer
Stephens, Betsy Bain *retired elementary school educator*

Birmingham
Acker, William Marsh, Jr., *federal judge*
Albritton, William Harold, IV, *lawyer*
Allen, Lee Norcross *historian, educator*
Allen, Maryon Pittman *former senator, journalist, lecturer, interior and clothing designer*
Allinder, David Randall *musician, educator*
Allman, Richard Mark *physician, gerontologist*
Avant, Grady, Jr., *lawyer*
Avent, Charles Kirk *medical educator*
Bailey, Jeffrey Wayne *law enforcement educator, consultant*
Bailey, Kelly Frank *occupational health company executive*
Bains, David Ralph *religious studies educator*
Baker, David Remember *lawyer*
Balch, Samuel Eason *lawyer*
Ball, Laurence Andrew *microbiologist, educator, researcher*
Bashir, Khurram *neurologist*
†Beard, Craig Wyeth *librarian*
Bell, David Samuel Henry *medical educator*
Benditt, Theodore Matthew *humanities educator, educator*
Bennett, Joe Claude *pharmaceutical executive*
Bennett, Thomas B. *federal judge*
Berte, Neal Richard *academic administrator*
Bird, John Commons *arbitrator, educator*
Blackburn, Sharon Lovelace *federal judge*
Blair, Ludie Mae Riley *retired furniture company executive*
Blan, Ollie Lionel, Jr., *retired lawyer*
Boardman, Mark Seymour *lawyer*
Boliek, Robert Gerald, Jr., *writer, lawyer*
Bonfield, Barbara Goldstein *non-profit organization administrator*
Boomershine, Donald Eugene *bureau executive, development official*
Booth, Rachel Zonelle *nursing educator*
Bowron, Lee Matthews *actuary, consultant*
Bradley, Laurence Alan *psychologist*
Branham, Grady Eugene *principal*
Brannan, Stephen E. *health services administrator*
†Bray, Gerald Lewis *minister, educator*
Bridgers, William Frank *retired physician*
Brooke, William Wade *business executive, lawyer*
Brown, Ephraim Taylor, Jr., *lawyer*
Brown, Stephen Edward *lawyer*
Bueschen, Anton Joslyn *physician, educator*
†Bunchman, Timothy Edward *nephrologist, educator*
Bunt, Randolph Cedric *mechanical engineer*
Burden, Cedric Jerome, Sr., *English educator*
Callahan, Alston *physician, author*
Campbell, Charles Alton *business executive*
Carlo, Waldemar A. *neonatologist*
Carmichael, Mary Alice *artist, genealogist*
†Carmody, Richard Patrick *lawyer*
Carruthers, Thomas Neely *lawyer*
Carter, Frances Tunnell (Fran Carter) *fraternal organization administrator*
Carter, John Thomas *retired educational administrator, writer*
Chapman, Wes *dancer, performing company executive*
Chrencik, Frank *chemical company executive*
Christ, Chris Steve *lawyer*
†Christian, Thomas William *lawyer*
Cicio, Anthony Lee *lawyer*
Clayton, Orville Woolford *surgeon*
Clemmons, Nancy Washington *library administrator, educator*
†Cleveland, Edwin Pittman *music educator*
Cohen-DeMarco, Gale Maureen *pharmaceutical executive*
Cole, Charles DuBose, II, *law educator*

Coleman, Brittin Turner *lawyer*
Coleman, John James, III, *lawyer, educator*
Comer, Donald, III, *investment company executive*
Connors, Marty *political party administrator, small business owner*
Cook, Ralph D. *lawyer, retired state supreme court justice*
Cooper, Jerome A. *lawyer*
Cooper, Max Dale *pediatrician, researcher*
Cooper, N. Lee *lawyer*
Corts, Thomas Edward *university president*
Coyne, Edward James, Sr., *international business educator*
Crawford, Edwin Mac *health facilities executive*
Crichton, Douglas Bentley *editor, writer*
Crittenden, Martha A. *disability specialist*
†Crump, Michael David *electrical engineer*
Cullen, William Zachary *lawyer*
Daniel, Kenneth Rule *former iron and steel manufacturing company executive*
Davenport, Horace Willard *physiologist, science educator*
Davis, Gwendolyn Louise *air force officer, English educator*
Davis, Julian Mason, Jr., *lawyer*
Davis, Richard Oliver *obstetrician-gynecologist, educator*
Deal, William Brown *physician, educator, author, medical school dean*
de la Torre, Jorge Ignacio *plastic surgeon, educator*
Del Greco, Albert Louis, Jr., *former football player*
†Denaburg, Charles L(eon) *lawyer*
Denson, William Frank, III, *lawyer*
Devane, Denis James *health care company executive*
Diasio, Ilse Wolfartsberger *volunteer*
Diethelm, Arnold Gillespie *surgeon*
†Dobbs, Carney H. *retired lawyer, retired insurance company executive*
†Donahue, Timothy Patrick *lawyer*
Dougherty, Dana Dean Lesley *television producer, educator*
†Drentea, Patricia *educator, researcher*
Edmonds, William Fleming *retired engineering and construction company executive*
Elewski, Boni Elizabeth *dermatologist, educator*
†El-Galley, Rizk *urologist, educator*
Elgavish, Ada *molecular and cellular biologist*
Elgavish, Gabriel Andreas *physical biochemistry educator*
†Eloubeidi, Mohamad Ali *gastroenterologist, internist*
Etterer, Sepp *industrial relations specialist, consultant, application developer*
Falkson, Carla Isadora *medical oncologist*
Farley, Joseph McConnell *lawyer*
†Ferguson, Harold Laverne, Jr., *lawyer*
Finley, Sara Crews *medical geneticist, educator*
Finney, James Owen, Jr., *cardiologist*
Fix, R. Jobe *plastic surgeon, reconstructive hand surgeon*
Flakes, Larry Joseph *civil engineer*
†Flowers, Vonetta *Olympic athlete*
Floyd, John Alex, Jr., *marketing executive, editor, horticulturist*
†Foley, David E. *bishop*
Foster, Arthur Key, Jr., *retired lawyer*
Francavilla, Donna T. *journalist*
Franklin, H. Allen *electric company executive*
Friend, Edward Malcolm, III, *lawyer, educator*
Fullmer, Harold Milton *dentist, educator*
Furman, Howard *mediator, arbitrator, lawyer*
†Gale, Fournier Joseph, III, *lawyer*
Galloway, Catherine Black *publishing executive*
Gamble, Joseph Graham, Jr., *lawyer*
Garner, Robert Edward Lee *lawyer*
Geer, Jack Charles *retired pathology educator*
George, Frank Wade *small business owner, antiquarian book dealer*
Gibbs, Sydney Royston *health facility administrator*
Gilchrist, William Aaron *architect*
Givhan, Robert Marcus *lawyer*
Goldberg, Edward Jay *general contractor*
Goldman, Jay *industrial engineer, educator, former dean*
Goldman, Renitta Librach *special education educator, consultant*
Goodrich, Thomas Michael *engineering and construction executive, lawyer*
Grantham, Charles Edward *broadcast engineer*
Greene, Ernest Rinaldo, Jr., *anesthesiologist, chemical engineer*
†Griffin, Eleanor *magazine editor*
Guin, Junius Foy, Jr., *federal judge*
Haddox, Jeffrey Lynn *vision scientist*
Hall, Robert Alan *construction company executive*
Hamilton, Virginia Van der Veer *historian, educator*
Hanson, Victor Henry, II, *newspaper publisher*
Harbert, Bill Lebold *retired construction corporation executive*
Harris, Aaron *management consultant*
†Haskell, Wyatt Rushton *lawyer*
Haworth, Michael Elliott, Jr., *aerospace company executive*
Hendley, Dan Lunsford *retired finance executive*
Hickson, Marcus Lafayette, III, *communication educator, consultant*
Hilliard, Earl Frederick *congressman, lawyer*

Hinton, James Forrest, Jr., *lawyer*
Hirschowitz, Basil Isaac *physician*
Holmes, Suzanne McRae *nursing supervisor*
Holton, J(erry) Thomas *concrete company executive*
Honan, Michael Benjamin *cardiologist*
Hooper, Dawn M. *accountant*
†Horsley, Richard David *banker*
Howell, William Ashley, III, *lawyer*
Hull, William Edward *theology educator*
Hutchins, William Bruce, III, *utility company executive*
Jackson, Keith *law educator*
Janes, Clarence Harrison, Jr., *music educator*
Jones, Albert Cecil *consulting engineer*
†Jones, Carl E., Jr., *bank executive*
Jones, D. Paul, Jr., *banker, lawyer*
Jones, Moniaree Parker *legal nurse consultant*
Jones, Warren Thomas *computer science educator*
Kassouf, Gerard Joseph *accountant*
Keller, Armor *artist, arts advocate*
Kennedy, Joe David, Jr., (Joey Kennedy) *editor*
†Kiefe, Catarina Isabel *medical educator*
King, Charles Mark *dentist, educator*
Kirby, Russell Stephen *epidemiologist, statistician, geographer*
Kirkley, D. Christine *non-profit organization administrator*
†Kirklin, John Webster *surgeon*
Koopman, William James *medical educator, internist, immunologist*
Kracke, Robert Russell *lawyer*
Krishna, N(epalli) Rama *biochemist*
Lacy, Alexander Shelton *lawyer*
†Langum, David John *law educator, historian*
†Lide, Neoma Jewell Lawhon (Mrs. Martin James Lide Jr.) *poet*
Lochridge, Stanley Keith *cardiovascular and thoracic surgeon*
Lockamy, Archie, III, *operations management educator*
Logan, J. Patrick *lawyer*
Long, Thad Gladden *lawyer*
Luckie, Robert Ervin, Jr., *advertising executive*
Marchase, Richard Banfield *cell biologist, educator*
Marks, Charles Caldwell *retired investment banker, retired industrial distribution company executive*
Martin, Arthur Lee, Jr., *lawyer*
Martin, R. Brad *retail executive*
Martin, Roy Clayton *clinical neuropsychologist*
Massey, Richard Walter, Jr., *retired investment counselor*
Masters, Jeffrey D. *association executive*
†Mayne, Richard *educator*
Mc Callum, Charles Alexander *university official*
†McMahon, John J., Jr., *metal processing company executive*
Mc Millan, George Duncan Hastie, Jr., *lawyer, former state official*
McWhorter, Hobart Amory, Jr., *lawyer*
Meezan, Elias *pharmacologist, educator*
Meredith, Ruby Frances *radiation oncologist, researcher, educator*
Mills, William Hayes *lawyer*
Mishra, Digambar *political science educator*
Miyagawa, Ichiro *physicist*
Molen, John Klauminzer *lawyer*
Moran, Mary Shanks *hydrogeologist*
Morgan, Hugh Jackson, Jr., *bank executive*
Morris, Florence Henderson *auditor*
Morrisey, Michael A. *health economics educator*
Morrison, Gregg Scott *theology educator, college administrator*
†Morros, Stephen Vincent *marketing professional, educator*
Morton, Marilyn Miller *retired genealogy and history educator, lecturer, researcher, travel executive, director*
Mowry, Robert Wilbur *pathologist, educator*
Mueller, Robin Sue *biology educator*
Murrell, Susan DeBrecht *librarian*
Neal, Phil Hudson, Jr., *manufacturing company executive*
†Nelson, Leonard John, III, *lawyer, educator*
Nepomuceno, Cecil Santos *physician*
Nettelbeck, Dirk Manfred *biomedical researcher*
Nettles, Bert Sheffield *lawyer*
Newton, Alexander Worthy *lawyer*
Newton, Don Allen *real estate broker, economic development consultant*
Norris, Robert Wheeler *military officer*
North, James Little *lawyer*
†Northen, Charles Swift, III, *retired banker*
Nunn, Grady Harrison *political science educator emeritus*
Oakes, Walter Jerry *pediatric neurosurgeon*
O'Connor, Stephen James *healthcare educator*
Omura, Emily Fowler *dermatologist, educator*
Omura, George Adolf *medical oncologist*
Oparil, Suzanne *cardiologist, educator, cardiologist, researcher*
Pacifico, Albert Dominick *cardiovascular surgeon*
Page, John Gardner *research administrator, scientist*
Palmer, Robert Leslie *lawyer*
Parker, John Malcolm *management and financial consultant*
†Parma, Edward Scott *engineer, surgeon*
Peeples, William Dewey, Jr., *mathematics educator*

Perry, Helen *medical/surgical nurse, secondary school educator*
†Peti-Peterdi, Janos *physiologist*
Pittman, James Allen, Jr., *physician, educator*
Pizitz, Richard Alan *retail and real estate group executive*
Pointer, Sam Clyde, Jr., *retired federal judge, lawyer*
Potter, John Leith *mechanical and aerospace engineer, educator, consultant*
†Powell, Larry *communications educator*
Powell, William Arnold, Jr., *retired bank executive*
Price, Rosalie Pettus *artist*
Privett, Caryl Penney *judge*
Quintana, Jose Booth *health care executive*
†Read, Russell W. *ophthalmology educator*
Redden, Lawrence Drew *lawyer*
†Reilly, Kevin Denis *computer scientist, educator*
†Reynolds, W. Ann *academic administrator*
Reynolds, W(ynetka) Ann *academic administrator, educator*
Robinson, Edward Lee *retired physics educator, consultant*
Roby, Jasper *bishop*
Rogers, Ernest Mabry *lawyer*
Rotch, James E. *lawyer*
Roth, William Stanley *hospital foundation executive*
Rountree, Asa *lawyer*
Rousso, Daniel Elliott *facial plastic surgeon, educator*
Russell, Richard Olney, Jr., *cardiologist, educator*
†Rynearson, W. John *foundation administrator*
Sain, Charles (Hack Sain) *civil engineer, surveyor*
Sansbury, Michael Todd *lawyer*
†Sathiakumar, Nalini *public health educator, researcher, epidemiologist, pediatrician*
Savage, Laura L. *ministry consultant, author, speaker*
†Scales, William Clinton, Sr., *minister, small business owner*
Schroeder, Harry William, Jr., *physician, scientist*
†Schwacha, Martin G. *biomedical researcher*
†Schwebel, David Charles *psychologist, educator*
Scott, Owen Myers, Jr., *nuclear engineer*
Segner, Edmund Peter, Jr., *civil engineer, educator*
Seitz, Karl Raymond *editor*
Selfe, Edward Milton *lawyer*
Sellers, Fred Wilson *accountant*
†Shaneyfelt, Terrence M *physician, researcher*
†Shanks, William Ennis, Jr., *lawyer*
†Sheppard, Scott *magazine publisher*
Shoemaker, Richard L. *retired physiologist*
Siegal, Gene Philip *pathology educator*
Skalka, Harold Walter *ophthalmologist, educator*
Sklenar, Herbert Anthony *industrial products manufacturing company executive*
Sloan, Albert *college president*
†Smith, Carol Ann *lawyer*
Spahn, James Francis *marketing professional*
Spence, Paul Herbert *librarian*
Stabler, Lewis Vastine, Jr., *lawyer*
Stephens, Deborah Lynn *health company executive*
†Stephens, James T. *publishing executive*
Stephens, Jerry Wayne *librarian, library director*
Stevenson, Edward Ward *retired physician, surgeon, otolaryngologist*
†Stewart, Donald W. *lawyer*
Stewart, Joseph Grier *lawyer*
Stone, Edmund Crispen, III, *banker*
Strickler, Howard Martin *physician*
Styslinger, Lee Joseph, Jr., *manufacturing company executive*
Taub, Edward *psychology researcher*
Tent, James Foster *historian*
Theibert, Richard Wilder *lawyer, educator*
Thompson, Charles Amos *lawyer*
Tieszen, Ralph Leland, Sr., *hospital administrator*
†Trimmier, Charles Stephen, Jr., *lawyer*
Tucker, Thomas James *retired investment manager*
Uddin, Nasim *civil engineer, educator*
Vargas, Pilar *physician, consultant*
Vinson, Laurence Duncan, Jr., *lawyer*
Vyazovkin, Sergey *chemist, educator*
Weatherly, Robert Stone, Jr., *banker*
Weeks, Arthur Andrew *lawyer, law educator*
†Wells, Alan Hilary *biomedical researcher*
Westerfield, Richard *music director*
Wheeler, Cathy Jo *government official*
Wheeler, Ruric E. *educator*
Whigham, Mark Anthony *computer scientist*
†Whiteside, David Powers, Jr., *lawyer*
†Wienhold, Lisa J. *musician, educator*
Wilson, James Charles, Jr., *lawyer*
Wood, Clinton Wayne *middle school educator*
†Wright, Allison Marshall *lawyer*
Wright, Amos Jasper, III, *medical librarian*
Wrinkle, John Newton *lawyer*
†Wyatt, Charles Herbert, Jr., *lawyer*
Young, Thomas Richard *sales management professional*
Zahl, Paul Francis Matthew *dean*

Bremen
Weathersby, Cecil Jerry *accounting and finance manager*

Brewton
Reynolds, Harold Mark *language educator*

Camden
Lewis, Robert Henry *lay worker*

Camp Hill
Melzer, John T.S. *translator, editor*

Centre
Ellis, Joanne Hammonds *computer consultant*

Chapman
Miller, James Rumrill, III, *finance educator*

Chelsea
Culpepper, Michael Irving *researcher, educator*

Clanton
Jackson, John Hollis, Jr., *lawyer*

Collinsville
Beasley, Mary Catherine *home economics educator, administrator, researcher*

Columbiana
Pizzitola, Patricia Gallman *music educator*

Cordova
Anthony, Yancey Lamar *minister*

Coy
Zinnermon, Susan *writer*

Cullman
†Brunck, Terri Lee *journalist*
Freeman, Chester Willie *small business owner*
Key, Randall Don *band director, musician*
Lott, Roger Richard Stanley *priest*
Munger, James Guy *protective services executive*
Poston, Beverly Paschal *lawyer*
Silvey, Tony Lee *music educator*
Taylor, Garry Lance *music educator*
†Thornton, Nancy Freebairn *psychotherapist, consultant, military officer*

Dadeville
Adair, Charles Robert, Jr., *lawyer*

Daleville
†Burkett, Trenton Shane *music educator*
†Turner, Chad Wesley *music educator*

Daphne
Curreri, Peter William *health policy consultant*
Henson, Pamela Taylor *secondary education educator*
†Jeffreys, Elystan Geoffrey *geological engineer, petroleum consultant and appraiser, gemologist*
Neese, Kristal Ann *comptroller*
Nelson, David Herman *biologist, educator, researcher*
†Spybey, Amanda N. *mortgage company executive*

Dauphin Island
Levenson, Maria Nijole *retired medical technologist*

Deatsville
Owen, Larry Lesli *management educator, retired military officer, small business owner*

Decatur
Belser, Howard McGriff, Jr., *lawyer*
Caddell, John A. *lawyer*
Cooper, John Burton *band director*
Cummins, David Loyal *mission director*
Mardis, Elizabeth Williams *occupational health nurse*
Mason, Loretta Ann *accountant assistant*
O'Brien, Richard Alan *research scientist*
Sandlin, Anathalee Gray *writer, music company owner*
Sims, William Arthur *orthopedist*
†Smith, Trina *academic administrator*
Smith, Troy Alvin *aerospace research engineer*
Talley, Richard Woodrow *accountant*

Demopolis
Dinning, Woodford Wyndham, Jr., *lawyer*
Lloyd, Hugh Adams *lawyer*

Dothan
†Bailey, Chip *investment advisor, former state senator*
Cross, Steven Jasper *finance educator*
†Fell, Elizabeth P. *education educator*
Fletcher, Sarah Lee *retired elementary school educator*
Flowers, V. Anne *academic administrator emerita*
†Huskey, Dow Thobern *lawyer*
Mocker, Hans Walter *physicist*
Peterson, M. Roger *community bank executive, retired international investment banker, retired manufacturing executive, retired Air Force officer*
Rabon, Ronald Ray *retail jewelry store chain executive*
†Turkoski, William Steve *workforce development consultant*
Wright, Burton *sociologist*

Duncanville
Prescott, Perry Don *psychology educator, counselor*

Eclectic
†Morris, George Hoey *writer*

Elmore
Williams, Glenda Carlene *writer*

Enterprise
†Grice, Robert E., Jr., *music educator, composer*
Holdman, Bettie *retired elementary school educator*
Parker, Ellis D. *retired career officer, aviation executive*
Stagliano, James Joseph *physical science educator, scientist*

Eufaula
Twitchell, E(rvin) Eugene *lawyer*
Vandenberg, Donald *retired education educator, philosopher*

Evergreen
†Ausby, Kenneth Lavon *criminologist*

Fairhope
Gwin, John Michael *emeritus educator, consultant*
Hart, Eric Mullins *finance company executive*
McBrearty, Michael Leigh *family physician*
Mozley, Paul David *retired obstetrics and gynecology educator*
Ottensmeyer, David Joseph *retired neurosurgeon, retired healthcare executive*
Radtke, Dawn Eleanor *clinical social worker*

Florence
Badger, Phillip Charles *agricultural engineer*
Barfield, Kenny Dale *religious school administrator*
Barrier, John Wayne *engineer, management consultant*
†Foote, Avon Edward *web developer/producer, communications educator*
Johnson, Johnny Ray *mathematics educator*
Potts, Robert Leslie *academic administrator*
Schuessler, Cindy Sandlin *lawyer, judge*
Tease, James Edward *judge*
†Woodford, Martha Haddock *retired music educator*

Foley
Kingston, George Willis *retired naval officer, small business owner*
Leatherbury, Gregory Luce, Jr., *lawyer*
Russell, Ralph Timothy *insurance company executive, mayor*
St. John, Henry Sewell, Jr., *utility company executive*

Fort Payne
†Helton, Thomas Charles *mental health services professional*

Fort Rucker
†Jones, Anthony Ray *military career officer*
Koach, Stephen Francis *flight instructor, retired army officer*

Gadsden
Brown, Andrew M. *otolaryngologist, allergist*
Coakley, Deirdre *writer*
Cornett, Bradley Williams *lawyer*
Grimm, James R. (Ronald Grimm) *multi-industry executive*
Massaro, Traci Lynn *special education educator*
Sledge, James Scott *judge*
Smothers, Jimmy *editor, sportswriter*

Gilbertown
†Ross, Cecil Brandt *literature educator*

Gordo
McKnight, William Baldwin *physics educator*

Greensboro
Massey, James Earl *clergyman, educator*

Gulf Shores
Appelt, Glenn David *pharmacologist, consultant, medical educator*
McCanless, Christel Ludewig *library consultant, researcher*
Wallace, John Loys *aviation services executive*

Guntersville
Patterson, Harold Dean *retired superintendent of schools*
Sparkman, Brandon Buster *educator, writer, consultant*
Zahn, Allan Lee *emergency physician*

Hamilton
Vinson, Leila Terry Walker *retired gerontological social worker*

Hanceville
Galin, Jerry Dean *college dean*

Hartselle
Slate, Joe Hutson *psychologist, educator*
Smith, Pamela Rodgers *elementary education educator*

Hayden
Berry, Chris David *artist, writer*
Standridge, Jean *real estate executive, real estate broker*

Homewood
†Pence, Ronald Kaylor *music educator*

Hoover
Bishop, Joan H. *health facility administrator*
Kennon, Rozmond Herron *retired physical therapist*
Schaffhausen, Robert Joseph *retired structural engineer*
Sobhan, Tanveer *physician*

Houston
Lafontaine, Diane Elaine *retired elementary education educator, computer specialist*

Huntsville
Allan, Barry David *research chemist, government official*
Balint, David Lee *engineering company executive*
Baxter, James Thomas, III, *lawyer*
†Bearden, Thomas Eugene *research scientist, researcher*
Bounds, Sarah Etheline *historian*
Bowden, Charles Malcolm *research physicist, educator*
Brandon, Walter Wiley, Jr., *retired physicist, retired aerospace engineer*
Buckelew, Robin Browne *aerospace engineer*
Burg, Fredric David *physician, university dean*
Campbell, Jonathan Wesley *astrophysicist, aerospace engineer*
†Carney, Horace R., Jr., *performing arts educator*
Chassay, Roger Paul, Jr., *engineering executive*
Childs, Rand Hampton *data processing executive, consultant*
Componation, Paul Joseph *industrial and systems engineer, educator*
Corman, Lourdes C. *physician, educator*
Cornatzer, William Eugene *retired biochemistry educator*
Costes, Nicholas Constantine *aerospace technologist, university educator, retired government official*
Daussman, Grover Frederick *electrical engineer, consultant*
Decher, Rudolf *physicist, researcher*
Dimmock, John Oliver *university research center director*
Dobson, Christopher Calvin *physicist*
†Durnya, Louis Richard *lawyer*
Evans, Darrell J. *higher education educator*
†Francis, Herbert Edward, Jr., *writer*
Franz, Frank Andrew *university president, physics educator*
Freas, George Wilson, II, *computer consultant*
Freeman, Paula S. *social worker*
Gabig, Jerome S., Jr., *lawyer*
Gawronski, Elizabeth Ann *retired army officer*
Gillani, Noor Velshi *atmospheric scientist, researcher, educator*
Giroir, Michael James *software analyst*
Graves, Benjamin Barnes *business administration educator*
Hammond, Walter Edward *aerospace engineer*
†Hartline, Thomas William *aerospace engineer*
Hawley, Harold Patrick *educational consultant*
Heidish, Louise Oridge-Schwallie *transportation specialist, marketing professional*
Hoppe, Lea Ann *elementary education educator*
Huber, Donald Simon *physician*
Huckaby, Gary Carlton *lawyer*
Hughes, Kaylene *historian, educator*
Hunter, Herbert Erwin *aerospace engineer*
Ingram, Shirley Jean *social worker*
Kim, Young Kil *aerospace engineer*
†Liu, Jiwen *research scientist*
London, John Rutherford, III, *aerospace program administrator*
Lundquist, Charles Arthur *university official*
†Madewell, Charles David *aerospace engineer*
Mathews, Fred Leroy *librarian*
Mazumder, Sandip *engineer, researcher*
†McAuley, Van Alfon *aerospace mathematician*
†McCaleb, John E. *public health environmentalist, biologist*
Mc Donough, George Francis, Jr., *retired aerospace engineer, consultant*
McIntyre-Ivy, Joan Carol *data processing executive*
Miller, Walter Edward *physical scientist, researcher*
Mohan, Annette Imelda *producer, educator*
Mohan, Tungesh Nath *television and film producer, film educator*
Moore, Fletcher Brooks *retired engineering company executive*
Morgan, Beverly Hammersley *middle school educator, artist*
Morgan, John Derald *electrical engineer*
Motz, Kenneth Lee *former farm organization official*
†Muth, William Donald *aeronautical engineer*
Norman, Ralph Louis *physicist, consultant*
Nuessle, William Raymond *surgeon*
Osterman, Eurydice V. *music educator*
Parnell, Thomas Alfred *physicist*
Pastrick, Harold Lee *aeronautical engineer*
Pittman, William Claude *electrical engineer*
Preston, Robert Kevin *software quality engineer*
Pruitt, Alice Fay *mathematician, engineer*
Quick, Jerry Ray *academic administrator, retired*
†Reddy, Chintareddy Vidya Sagar *electrical engineer*
Richardson, Patrick William *lawyer*
Robinson, Helen Margaret *emergency physician, internist*
†Sapp, A. Eugene, Jr., *former electronics executive*
Schroer, Bernard Jon *industrial engineering educator*
Schumann, J. Paul *federal agency administrator*
†Simpson, Debra Brashear *artist*
Smith, Robert Earl *space scientist*
Steinbuchel, Carla Faye *pediatrics nurse, nursing educator*
†Stephenson, Arthur G. *aerospace engineer*
Stevens, Dale Marlin *civil engineer*
Stewart, Verlindsey Laquetta *accounting educator*
Stuhlinger, Ernst *physicist*
Theisen, Russell Eugene *electrical engineer*
Tietke, Wilhelm *gastroenterologist, educator*
†Tolbert, Timothy Ray *systems analyst, military officer*
Traylor, Orba Forest *economist, lawyer, educator*
Urias, John M. *military officer, government agency administrator*
†Vargo, Robert Frank *lawyer*
Vaughan, Otha H., Jr., *retired aerospace engineer*
Vaughan, William Walton *atmospheric scientist*
Vinz, Frank Louis *electrical engineer*
†Ward, Elaine Pamplin *social worker*
Watson, Raymond Coke, Jr., *engineering executive, academic administrator*
Watts, William Park *naval officer*
Wieland, Paul Otto *environmental control systems engineer*
Williamson, Donald Ray *retired career Army officer*
Wilson, Timothy Wayne *music educator, musician*
Wright, John Collins *retired chemistry educator*
Wu, Susan Ying Chu Lin (Ying-chu Lin) *engineering company executive, engineer*
Yarbrough, Isabel Miles *dentist, educator*

Hurtsboro
Bouilliant-Linet, Francis Jacques *global management consultant*

Jacksonville
Boswell, Rupert Dean, Jr., *retired academic administrator, math educator*
Dunaway, Carolyn Bennett *retired sociology educator*
Dunaway, William Preston *retired educator*
Hubbard, William James *library director*
†Jackson, Harvey Hardaway, III, *history educator, columnist*
McCrary, Judy Hale *education educator*
Merrill, Martha *library media educator*
†Smith, Matthew DuBose *personnel director*
Spector, Daniel Earl *historian, educator*

Jasper
†Bevill, Tom *retired congressman, lawyer*
†Rowland, David Jack *academic administrator*

Lillian
Burnette, Ollen Lawrence, Jr., *historian*

Lineville
†Creed, Wayne J. *writer*

Livingston
Green, Asa Norman *university president*
Wenger, Jay Lamar *psychology educator*

Loachapoka
Schafer, Elizabeth Diane *historian, writer*
Schafer, Robert Louis *agricultural engineer, researcher*

Locust Fork
Edwards, Sheila M. *banker, educator*

Madison
Adams, Gary Lee *systems engineering supervisor*
†Brown, Daniel Morris *lens designer, consultant*
Cazavan, Larry O. *television executive*
Dannenberg, Konrad K. *aeronautical engineer*
Emerson, William Kary *engineering company executive*
†Johnson, Kathy Virginia Lockhart *art educator*
Lilly, Julius Quentin *engineering researcher*
Maladkar, Madan Ananda Rao *internist*
Vo, Hieu N. *intern architect*

Maplesville
Nichols, J Hugh *economic development consultant*

Marion
†Faurot, Ellen F. *librarian*
Street, Deborra Lynn *director of fine arts*

Maxwell AFB
†MacGhee, David F. *military officer*
†Timmerman, Thomas J. *military planner, operations analyst*
Winton, Harold Raymond *historian*

Mc Calla
Kes, Vicki Paulette *museum director*

Meridianville
Oberhausen, Joyce Ann Wynn *aircraft company executive, artist*

Mobile
Agapos, Michael Angelo *economics educator*
Armbrecht, William Henry, III, *retired lawyer*
Atkinson, William James, Jr., *retired cardiologist*
Booker, Larry Frank *accountant*
Bostwick, Robert Otis *municipal staff member*
Brandon, Jeffrey Campbell *physician, interventional radiologist, educator*
Braswell, Louis Erskine *lawyer*
Brigance, Marcelena *critical care nurse*
Brock, Glen Porter, Jr., *lawyer*
Brogdon, Byron Gilliam *physician, radiology educator*
Butler, Charles Randolph, Jr., *federal judge*
Byrd, Mary Jane *education educator*
Clark, Jack *retired hospital company executive, accountant*
Clark, Veronica Ann Wilds (Ronni Patriquin Clark) *journalist*
Clausell, Deborah Deloris *artist, songwriter*
Cohen, Michael Victor *cardiologist*
Coker, Donald William *economic, management, banking, evaluation, healthcare, international business and real estate consultant, stock trader*
Coley, F(ranklin) Luke, Jr., *lawyer*
†Cox, Emmett Ripley *judge*
Cunningham, Julian Antonia *retired protective services official*
DeBakey, Ernest George *physician, surgeon*
Donalson, Malcolm Drew *classics educator*
Edwards, Jack *former congressman, lawyer*
Eichold, Samuel *medical educator, medical museum curator*
Finkbohner, George Wheeler, Jr., *lawyer*
French, Elizabeth Irene *biology educator, violinist*
Gandy, Maurice Edward *English language educator, writer*
Graddick, Charles Allen *lawyer*
†Gremse, David Albert *pediatrician, educator*
Guarino, Anthony Michael *pharmacologist, educator, consultant, counselor*
†Habib, Thomas Mark *musician, educator*
Hamid, Michael *electrical engineering educator, consultant*
Hamner, Eugenie Lambert *English educator*
†Harpen, Michael Dennis *physicist, educator*
Harris, Benjamin Harte, Jr., *lawyer*
Helmsing, Frederick George *lawyer*
Higginbotham, Prieur Jay *city official*
Holland, Lyman Faith, Jr., *lawyer*
Holmes, Broox Garrett *lawyer*
Horenstein, Marcelo Gabriel *pathologist, educator*
†Hsiao, Kuang-Ting *mechanical engineer educator, researcher*
†Hutchens, Dennis Wade *anesthesiologist*
Johnston, Neil Chunn *lawyer*
Jones, Joseph Seymour *small business owner, poet*
†Kargleder, Charles Leonard *language educator*
Kreisberg, Robert A. *dean, medical educator*
Langley, Barry Lynn *dentist*
†Lee, Ron Rafael, Jr., *physician, medical educator, researcher*
Lipscomb, Oscar Hugh *archbishop*
Littleton, Jesse Talbot, III, *radiology educator*
Livers, Thomas Henry *fundraiser for nonprofit organizations*
†LoCicero, Joseph *thoracic surgeon, researcher*
Mahoney, Margaret A. *federal judge*
McCann, Clarence David, Jr., *special events coordinator, museum curator and director, artist*
McCleery, Winston Theodore *computer consulting company executive*
†Meigs, Walter Ralph *lawyer, dry dock and shipbuilding company executive*
Milling, Bert William, Jr., *magistrate judge*
†Moore, Richard Wayne *prosecutor*
†Mosley-Hill, Charvon Lashell *physical therapist*
Murchison, David Roderick *lawyer*
Outlaw, Kitti Kiattikunvivat *plastic surgeon*
†Parker, James Courtney *physiologist, researcher*
Parsley, Brantley Hamilton *librarian*
Peebles, E(mory) B(ush), III, *lawyer*
†Pennington, Al *lawyer*
Peplowski, Celia Ceslawa *librarian*
Perry, Nelson Allen *retired radiation safety engineer, radiological consultant*
†Phan, Anh-Vu *adult education educator, researcher*
Philips, Abe L., Jr., *lawyer*
Rewak, William John *former academic administrator, clergyman*
Richelson, Paul William *curator*
Robinson, Kenneth Larry *insurance company executive*
Rodning, Charles Bernard *surgeon*
Roedder, William Chapman, Jr., *lawyer*
Rye, Scott Cairney *advertising executive, author*
Sawyer, Ana Maria Ramirez *clinical psychologist*
Smith, Jesse Graham, Jr., *dermatologist, educator*
Spake, Deborah Foster *marketing professional, educator*
Steadman, John Marcellus, III, *English educator*
Stevens, Gail Lavine *community health nurse, educator*
Suess, James Francis *clinical psychologist*
Talley, Beverly M. *music educator*
†Taylor, Cecil Ray *religious studies educator, minister*
†Tidwell, William C., III, *lawyer*
†Trippe, Annette Guy *music educator*
Vitulli, William Francis *psychology educator, retired*
Vulevich, Edward, Jr., *prosecutor*
Waldrop, Norman Erskine, Jr., *lawyer*
Winter, Arch Reese *retired architect*
†Wisner, Pamela L. *social worker*
†Xu, Yu *nursing educator*
Zoghby, James Francis *priest*

Montevallo
Jarrett, Cynthia S. *accountant*
McChesney, Robert Michael, Sr., *educator*

Montgomery
Adams, Robert Barry *pathologist*
Aleinikov, Andrei Grigoryevich *science administrator, researcher, consultant*
†Banning, Kevin Charles *finance educator, department chairman*
Barnes, Harrey McGwinn, III, *internist, oncologist*
†Barron, Lowell Ray *state legislator*
†Baxley, Lucy *lieutenant governor*
Bennett, James Ronald *state official*
Bigham, Wanda Durrett *college president*
Black, Robert Coleman *judge, lawyer*
Blount, Winton Malcolm, III, *investment executive*
Boston, Hollis Buford, Jr., *retired military officer*
Brannan, Eulie Ross *educational consultant*
†Bright, Bobby *mayor*
Byars, Walter Ryland, Jr., *lawyer*
Campbell, Maria Bouchelle *state official*
Carnes, Edward E. *federal judge*
†Carter, Gordon Thomas *lawyer*
Cassels, Martha Beasley *realtor, developer*
Cornett, Lloyd Harvey, Jr., *retired historian*
†Dees, Morris Seligman, Jr., *lawyer*
De Ment, Ira *judge*
Dillon, Jean Katherine *executive secretary, small business owner*
Dixon, Larry Dean *state legislator*
Dubina, Joel Fredrick *federal judge*
†Dybczak, Zbigniew Wladyslaw *dean, educator, mechanical engineer*
†Elrod, Stephen Roy *theater educator*
Ely, Robert Eugene *lawyer, author, educator*
Frazer, David Hugh, Jr., *allergist*
Frazer, Nimrod Thompson *financial services company executive*
Frazer, Stuart Harrison, III, *cotton merchant*
Fry, Donna Marie *military officer, educator*
†Gerard, William Blake *literature educator*
†Givhan, Edgar Gilmore *physician, writer*
Godbold, John Cooper *judge*
†Greenhaw, Harold Wayne *writer*
Gribben, Alan *English language educator, research consultant*
†Griffin, Broderick DeVond *science educator, political consultant*
Hammett, Seth *state legislator*
Hamner, Reginald Turner *lawyer*
Harris, Joseph Lamar *state official*
Harwood, Robert Bernard, Jr., *state supreme court justice*
Hertenstein, Myrna Lynn *publishing executive*
Hester, Douglas Benjamin *lawyer, federal official*
Hilliard, Lil *sales executive*
Hobbs, Truman McGill *federal judge*
Hoffman, Richard William *banker*
†Holifield, Leonard Cleve *security firm executive, educator*
†Honey, William Chipman *lawyer, educator*
Hooper, Perry Ollie *retired state supreme court judge*
Houston, James Gorman, Jr., *state supreme court justice*
Hunker, Fred Dominic *internist, medical educator*
Johnson, Mark Matthew *museum administrator*
†Kim, Ki Hang *mathematician*
Kirschenfeld, J. J. *retired physician, educator*
Kline, John Alvin *academic administrator*
Kloess, Lawrence Herman, Jr., *retired lawyer*
Laurie, Robin Garrett *lawyer*
Lawson, Thomas Seay, Jr., *lawyer*
Lee, Harry Antonius *allergist, immunologist*
Leslie, Henry Arthur *lawyer, retired banker*
Lewis, Joseph Brady (Jay Lewis) *lawyer*
Lyons, Champ, Jr., *state supreme court justice*
Maddox, Alva Hugh *retired state supreme court justice*
Mandry, Christine M. *public adminstator*
Mathew, Tom *economics educator*
May, Cecil Richard, Jr., *academic administrator*
Maya, Ivan Dario *internist*
McFadden, Frank Hampton *lawyer, business executive, former judge*
Medina, Sue O'Neal *librarian*
Moore, Roy S. *state supreme court chief justice*
Murkett, Philip Tillotson *human resource executive*
Myers, Ira Lee *physician*
Nachman, Merton Roland, Jr., *lawyer*
Napier, Cameron Mayson Freeman *historic preservationist*
Pan, Chai-Fu *engineering educator*
Pitt, Redding *political organization administrator*
Prestwood, Alvin Tennyson *lawyer*
Pryor, William Holcombe, Jr., *state attorney general*
†Reilly, Erin Rene *education educator*
Riley, Robert *governor*
Ritvo, Roger Alan *vice chancellor, health management-policy educator*
Robinson, Ella Scales *language educator*
Rowan, John Robert *retired medical center director*
Salmon, Joseph Thaddeus *lawyer*
Sass, Neil Leslie *toxicologist*
Schloss, Samuel Leopold, Jr., *retired food service executive, consultant*
Shashy, Paul Moses *urologist*
†Singleton, Patricia Moore *librarian*
Smith, Larry Steven *financial analyst, farmer, accountant*
Smith, Maury Drane *lawyer*
Smitherman, David Conrad *medical marketing professional*
†Stakely, Charles Averett *lawyer*
Steele, Rodney Redfearn *judge*
Tan, Boen Hie *analytical biochemist, biomedical scientist*
Taylor, Watson Robbins, Jr., *investment banker*
Taylor, Watson Robbins *construction company executive*
Volz, Charles Harvie, Jr., *lawyer*
Walker, Annette *retired counseling administrator*
Wendzel, Robert Leroy *political science educator*
Whitt, Mary F. *reading educator, consultant*
Williamson, Donald Ellis *state official*
Wood, James Jerry *lawyer*
Woodall, Thomas A. *state supreme court justice*
†Worley, Nancy L. *secretary of state*
†Young, Caron L *county official*

Montrose
†Haynie, Betty Jo Gillmore *personal property appraiser, antiques dealer*

Mooresville
Reeder, Edward Cameron *association executive, clergyman*

Moulton
Dutton, Mark Anthony *lawyer*

Muskogee
†Hearn, William Charles *music educator, music minister*

New Market
†Kearns, Nancy J. *language educator*

Normal
Dawkins, Jimmie Angela *art educator*
†Edwards, Matthew E. *physicist, educator*
†Hall, Doris Spooner *educator*
Jarrett, Alfred A. *social policy analyst*
†Lane, Rosalie Middleton *extension specialist*
Wesley, Arthur Bernell, II, *music educator, musician*
Yates, Derrick K. *music educator, director*

Northport
Allen, Randy Lee *lawyer*
Lawley, Esther Gminder Smith *mental health counselor*

Odenville
Whitten, Joseph Lee *retired school librarian, elementary educator*

Ohatchee
Ellis, Bernice Allred *personnel executive*

Oneonta
Turner, Jeff Neal *minister*

Opelika
†Hand, Benny Charles, Jr., *lawyer, judge*
Jenkins, Richard Lee *manufacturing company executive*
Samford, Yetta Glenn, Jr., *lawyer, director*
Smith-Sanders, Carol Ann *music therapist, psychologist*

Orange Beach
Adams, Daniel Fenton *law educator*
Conrad, Marcel Edward *hematologist, educator*
Gordon, Beth N. *real estate appraiser*
Loveless, Ralph Peyton *lawyer*
Owens, Marsha *library director*

Owens Cross Roads
Williams, Lowell Craig *lawyer, employee relations executive*

Ozark
Covin, Theron Michael *psychotherapist*
DuBose, Elizabeth (Bettye DuBose) *community health nurse*
Hennies, Clyde Albert (Lou Hennies) *military officer, state official, military academy administrator*

Pelham
Harvey, James Mathews, Jr., *communications specialist*
Johnson, Frank William *marketing professional*
Lee, James A. *health facility finance executive*
Nuckols, Frank Joseph *psychiatrist*
Turner, Malcolm Elijah *biomathematician, educator*

Pell City
Passey, George Edward *psychology educator*

Phenix City
Jinright, Noah Franklin *vocational school educator, security executive*

Pike Road
Schuetzenduebel, Wolfram Gerhard *retired engineering executive*

Point Clear
Englund, Gage Bush *dancer, educator*

Prattville
Burrows, Henry Peter, III, *secondary education educator*

Ramer
Napier, John Hawkins, III, *historian*

Redstone Arsenal
†Parlier, Greg H. *military officer, engineer*

Remlap
Mathews, Clayton Jerome *trucking executive*
Peoples, Linda Erwin *psychotherapist*

Scottsboro
McGill, Judy Annell McGee *early childhood and elementary educator*

Seale
Lishak, Lisa Anne *secondary education educator*

Selma
Klein, Deborah Rae *health facility administrator*

Semmes
Laxton, Judy Brinkley *social work services administrator*
Phelps, James Franklin *retired county official*

Sheffield
Hamby, Gene Malcolm, Jr., *lawyer*

Shoal Creek
Ahearn, John Francis, Jr., *retired oil and gas company executive*

Spanish Fort
van Aken, John Henry *retired marine surveyor, engineer, consultant*

Talladega
Jeffers, Trellie Lee James *language educator, dean*
†Schwinghamer, Mary Denise *veterinarian*
†Swain, Mary Madgalene *pediatrics nurse*

Theodore
Hollis, Julia Ann Roshto *critical care, medical, and surgical nurse*

Thomasville
†Corzealious, Forrest Lee *entrepreneur*
Davis, Gene *retired civil engineer*

Troy
Davidson, Barry Sheldon *academic administrator, education educator*
Jinright, John William *music educator*
McPherson, Milton Monroe *history educator*
Mitchell, Norma Taylor *history educator*
Moffett, Thomas Delano *music educator*

Trussville
Best, Frederick Napier *artist, designer, educator*

Tuscaloosa
Aldridge, Kenneth William *physician*
Axel, Bernard *finance executive*
Baklanoff, Eric Nicholas *economist, educator*
Barfield, Robert F. *retired mechanical engineer, educator, dean*
†Beito, David Timothy *humanities educator*
Bickley, John S. *insurance association executive, educator, writer*
Bills, Robert E(dgar) *emeritus psychology educator*
Bindon, James Robert *anthropology educator*

Blackburn, John Leslie *small business owner*
Bryan, Colgan Hobson *aerospace engineering educator*
Bunker, Matthew D. *humanities educator*
Cava, Michael Patrick *chemist, educator*
†Chalmers, Jon D. *director*
†Chou, Kevin *mechanical engineer, educator*
Cook, Camille Wright *retired law educator*
Cramer, Dale Lewis *retired economics educator*
Crowley, John W(illiam) *English language educator*
Dalton, Margaret Stieg *library and information sciences educator*
†Delpar, Helen *historian*
Edgeworth, Emily *retired insurance agency executive-antique dealer*
England, John Henry, Jr., *judge*
†Filler, Daniel M. *law educator*
Fish, Mary Martha *economics educator*
Fonseca, Daniel J. *engineering educator*
Fowler, Conrad Murphree *retired manufacturing company executive*
†Freyer, Tony Allan *historian, educator*
†Greene, Timothy James *industrial engineering educator*
†Griffin, Marvin Anthony *industrial engineer, educator*
Gup, Benton Eugene *banking educator*
Hocutt, Max Oliver *philosophy educator*
†Hoff, Timothy *law educator, priest*
†Hubbard, Perry *lawyer, educator*
†Janiga-Perkins, Constance Gabrielle *language educator*
Keeton, J. E. *retired psychiatrist*
Koger, Michael Pigott *physician, writer*
LaMoreaux, Philip Elmer *geologist, hydrogeologist, consultant*
Lockett, James *history educator*
Lumpkin, Thomas Riley *physician, educator*
Mancini, Ernest Anthony *geologist, educator, researcher*
Martone, Michael *writer*
Mayer, Morris Lehman *marketing educator*
McFarland, James William *real estate development company executive*
Moody, Maxwell, Jr., *retired physician*
Morley, Lloyd Albert *electrical engineering educator*
Moynihan, Gary Peter *industrial engineering educator*
†Mysore, Shrikanth Bhaskar *operations research specialist*
Newsom, Barry Douglas *cardiovascular and thoracic surgeon*
Oltz, Donald Frederick *research mineral resources executive*
Orcutt, Ben Avis *retired social work educator*
†Parsons, Laura Elizabeth *music educator, freelance/self-employed musician*
†Peles, Stephen Victor *composer*
Pieroni, Robert Edward *internist, educator, military officer*
†Pittman, Kathleen M. *education educator, consultant*
Polites, Michael Edward *aerospace engineer, educator*
†Raines, Michael Carl *language educator*
Reinhart, Kellee Connely *journalist*
Ross, Daniel J.J. *publishing executive*
Ruiz-Fornells, Enrique *history and Spanish educator*
Searcy, Jane Berry *retired educational administrator, counselor*
Southern, James Terry *secondary education educator*
†Spurlin, Adam Corey *music educator*
†Temimi, Akram *education educator*
Thomas, Joab Langston *retired university president, biology educator*
Thomson, H. Bailey *editor, educator*
Turner, Daniel Shelton *civil engineering educator*
Vincent, John Bertram *chemist, educator*
Warren, Garry Wilbur *engineering educator*
Williams, Roger Courtland *lawyer*

Tuscumbia
Heflin, Howell Thomas *former senator, lawyer, former state supreme court chief justice*
Hutchens, Eugene Garlington *college administrator*
†Munsey, Stanley Edward *lawyer*

Tuskegee
Green, Elbert P. *retired university official*
Payton, Benjamin Franklin *college president*

Tuskegee Institute
Ahl, Alwynelle Self *zoology, ecology and veterinary medical executive*
Cooley, Fannie Richardson *emeritus educator, consultant*
Hill, Walter A. *agricultural sciences educator, researcher*
†Madison, Willie Clarence *park administrator*
†Olson, Mary *language educator, writer*

Union Grove
Drew, Thomas Paul *chaplain*
Roberts, Lynn Novak *government employee*

Valley
Striblin, Lori Ann *critical care nurse, Medicare coordinator, nursing educator*

Vestavia Hills
†Coleman, Travis Brent *music educator*

Vina
†Cayson, Joyce Scallorn *editor, small business owner*

Wadley
†Caldwell, Ann B. *music educator*

Wetumpka
Bush, John B. *circuit judge*

Wilmer
Nelson, Linda Benefield *writer, secretary*

Wilsonville
Copeland, David A. *software engineer*

Woodstock
†Downs, Bernard Boozer, Jr., *lawyer*

ALASKA

Anchorage
†Allingham, Lynn Marie *lawyer*
†Alsua, Carlos J. *educator*
Anderson, Kathleen Gay *mediator, hearing officer, arbitrator, trainer*
Baker, Grant Cody *civil engineering educator*
†Ballew, Carol *epidemiologist, researcher*
†Bankston, William Marcus *lawyer*
Behrend, Donald Fraser *environmental educator, university administrator*
Bond, Marc Douglas *lawyer*
Brady, Carl Franklin *retired aircraft charter company executive*
Branson, Albert Harold (Harry Branson) *judge, educator*
†Braund-Allen, Julianna Elise *librarian*
Breckberg, Robert Lee *lawyer*
Breinig, Jeane M. *English educator, consultant*
†Britton, Emily Maddox *sales executive*
Brown, Dean Naomi *state official, geologist*
†Brown, Harold MacVane *lawyer*
Burke, Marianne King *state agency administrator, financial executive, consultant*
Butler, Rex Lamont *lawyer*
Byrd, Milton Bruce *college president, former business executive*
Cantor, James Elliot *lawyer*
†Charles, George P. *religious studies educator*
Cohn, Gary Dennis *journalist*
Collins, Michael Paul *secondary school educator, earth science educator, consultant*
†Comeau, Carol Smith *educator*
†Coran, Joshua D. *mechanical engineer*
Cuddy, Daniel Hon *bank executive*
Davies, Garry *biology educator*
De Lisio, Stephen Scott *lawyer, director, pastor*
†DeTerra, Sandra Lee Shivers *secondary school educator*
Dickson, Robert Jay *lawyer*
Ealy, Jonathan Bruce *lawyer*
Eastaugh, Robert L. *state supreme court justice*
Ebell, C(ecil) Walter *lawyer*
Ennis, William Lee *physics educator*
Erving, Claude Moore, Jr., *career officer, pilot*
Fabe, Dana Anderson *state supreme court chief justice*
†Feldman, Jeffrey Marc *lawyer*
Finley, John Clifford *cardiologist*
Fisher, Margaret Eleanor *psychologist, lawyer, arbitrator, mediator, educator*
Fleming, Carolyn Elizabeth *religious organization administrator, interior designer*
Flynn, Charles P. *lawyer*
Fortier, Samuel John *lawyer*
Gamble, Patrick K. *retired military officer, rail transportation executive*
Gier, Karan Hancock *psychologist*
Gorsuch, Edward Lee *chancellor*
Gottstein, Barnard Jacob *retail and wholesale food company executive, real estate executive*
Harris, Jan Caplan *health care administrator*
Hickel, Walter Joseph *investment firm executive, forum administrator*
Hill, Erik Bryan *newspaper photographer*
Hong, Patricia Anne *nursing educator*
Hughes, Mary Katherine *lawyer*
†Ippolito, Maria F. *psychologist, educator*
Jones, Jewel *social services administrator*
Jones, Mark Logan *educational association executive, educator*
Jones, Thomas Brooks *lawyer, educator*
†Katzke, Mary Rosanne *filmmaker, scriptwriter*
Keffer, Maria Jean *environmental auditor*
Kelly, Maxine Ann *retired property developer*
†Kim, Taesoo *language educator*
†Kline, Daniel Thomas *English educator*
Knowles, Tony *former governor*
Lacy, Gregory Lawrence *protective services official*
†Leman, Loren Dwight *lieutenant governor, civil engineer*
†Maki, Alan Walter *biologist, environmental scientist*
Mandell, Gordon Keith *aerospace engineer*
Mann, Lester Perry *mathematics educator*
Marx, Donald Lee *statistician, educator*
Matsui, Dorothy Nobuko *elementary education educator*
Metzger, Yale Hyder *lawyer, educator*
Miller, Kevin Clark *heavy equipment operator, writer*
Mitchell, Michael Kiehl *elementary and secondary education educator, minister*
Molinari, Carol V. *writer, investment company executive, educator*
†Narang, Deborah Lynn *education educator*
Nielsen, Jennifer Lee *molecular ecologist, researcher*
North, Douglas McKay *academic administrator*
Nosek, Francis John *lawyer, diplomat*
Obermeyer, Theresa Nangle *sociology educator*
†Oesting, David W. *lawyer*
†Olivares, Walter G. *music educator*
Owens, Robert Patrick *lawyer*
Park, Gloria *family physician, consultant*
Parker, Walter Bruce *arctic research specialist, consultant*
Patrick, Leslie Dayle *hydrologist*
Pearson, Larry Lester *journalism educator, internet presence provider*
†Pfiffner, Frank Albert *lawyer*
Porcaro, Michael Francis *advertising agency executive*
Pressley, James Ray *electrical engineer*
Rasmuson, Edward Bernard *banker*
†Reed, Frank Metcalf *bank executive, director*
Rentschler, Carl Thomas *real estate executive, consultant*
†Richmond, Robert Lawrence *lawyer*
Riendl, Robin Wendy *financial consultant*
Roberts, John Derham *lawyer*
Rogers, Donald Robert *retired pathologist*
Rollins, Alden Milton *documents librarian*
Rose, David Allan *investment manager*
Ross, Wayne Anthony *lawyer*
Ruedrich, Randy *political party official*
Rylander, Robert Allan *financial service executive*
Schnell, Roger Thomas *business owner, retired state official and career officer*
Sells, Colin David *meteorologist*
Shadrach, Jean Hawkins (Martha Shadrach) *artist*
Shively, John Terry *business executive*
Singleton, James Keith *federal judge*
Skladal, Elizabeth Lee *retired elementary school educator*
Smith, Isaac Danial *artist*
†Sneed, Spencer Craig *lawyer*
Sterling, Scott *political party official*
Strohmeyer, John *writer, former editor*
Suddock, Frances Suter Thorson *grief educator, writer*
Sullivan, George Murray *transportation consultant, former mayor*
Teague, Bruce Williams *chiropractor*
Thomas, Howard Paul *civil engineer, consultant*
Thomas, Lowell, Jr., *writer, lecturer, former lieutenant governor, former state senator*
Thorsness, Julia Marie *hospice administrator*
Thrasher-Livingston, Kara Scott *program director*
Trevithick, Ronald James *underwriter*
von der Heydt, James Arnold *federal judge*
†Walther, Dale Jay *lawyer*
Wedel-Cowgill, Millie Redmond *secondary school educator, performing arts educator*
Weinig, Richard Arthur *lawyer*
Widdicombe, Richard Toby *educator*
Wilkniss, Peter E. *foundation administrator, researcher*
†Willard-Jones, Donna C. *lawyer*
†Williams, Deborah Lee *foundation administrator*
Williams, Eleanor Joyce *retired government air traffic control specialist*
Wohlforth, Eric Evans *lawyer*
†Wood, Darryl Scott *criminologist, educator*
Zeiger, Maria Theresia *music educator*

Arctic Village
Tritt (Gwich'in), Lincoln C. *writer, educator, musician*

Bethel
Cooke, Christopher Robert *former state judge, lawyer*
McMahon, Craig Roger *lawyer*
Selby, Naomi Ardean *women's health nurse, medical/surgical nurse*

Big Lake
†DeLoach, Robert Edgar *corporate executive*

Delta Junction
†Noble, Alice L. *writer, researcher*

Eagle River
Cotten, Samuel Richard *fisheries consultant, former state legislator*

Ester
Ragan, John David *writer, historian*

Fairbanks
Alexander, Vera *dean, marine science educator*
Beistline, Earl Hoover *mining consultant*
Bergeson, Marvin Ernest *pediatrician*
Berry Bertram, Kathryn *editor in chief science publication*
†Bird, Roy Kennedy *literature educator, director*
†Bowyer, R. Terry *science educator*
†Cole, Terrence M. *historian, educator*
Corti, Lillian Zell *humanities educator, writer*
Crawford, Sarah Carter (Sally Carter Crawford) *broadcast executive*
Doran, Timothy Patrick *educational administrator*
Duffy, Lawrence Kevin *biochemist, educator*
Falk, Marvin William *historian, bibliographer*
Fathauer, Theodore Frederick *meteorologist*
Gianni, Keith Brian Michael *internist*
Hamilton, Mark R. *academic administrator*
Hess, Richard Christian, Jr., *obstetrician/gynecologist, educator*
Johnson, Diane *educator*
Kessel, Brina *ornithologist, educator, researcher*
Kleinfeld, Andrew J. *federal judge*
†Lan, Ping *business educator*
Lewis, Carol E. *academic administrator, management consultant*
Lind, Marshall L. *academic administrator*
Lingle, Craig Stanley *glaciologist, educator*
Ma, Zhongguo (John Ma) *engineering educator, researcher*
McBeath, Gerald Alan *political science educator, researcher*
Milne, Clark Roger *civil engineer*
Murakami, Gael Baxley *artist*
Nakoneczny, Michael Martin *artist*
Odom, David Malcolm *natural hormone replacement therapist*
Reichardt, Paul Bernard *provost, chemistry educator*
Roederer, Juan Gualterio *physics educator*
†Schamel, Douglas L. *science educator, researcher*
Schendel, William Burnett *lawyer*
Simon, James Johnson Koffroth *anthropologist*
Thompson, Daniel Emerson *vending machine service company executive*
Tilsworth, Timothy *retired environmental/civil engineering educator*
Wackerbauer, Renate Anna *physicist*
Weller, Gunter Ernst *geophysics educator*
Wichmann, Henry, Jr., *accounting educator, researcher*

Fort Wainwright
Lubbers, Alice Dianne *operating room nurse*

Girdwood
Trautner, John James *real estate executive*

Gustavus
Burgess, Marilyn K. *science educator*

Haines
Kaufman, David Graham *construction executive*

Homer
Beach, Geo *journalist, poet*
Gillon, Stephen John *business educator, consultant*
Oberstein, Sally *entrepreneur, not-for-profit fundraiser*

Indian
Wright, Gordon Brooks *musician, conductor, educator*

Juneau
†Blitz, Brian G. *mathematician, educator*
Carpeneti, Walter L. *judge*
Crane, Karen R. *retired library director*
DeRoux, Daniel Grady *artist*
†Eastaugh, Frederick Orlebar *lawyer*
Kohring, Victor H. *state legislator*
Kolkhorst, Kathryn Mackay *lawyer*
†Kott, Pete *state representative*
Meacham, Charles P. *president, capital consulting*
Murkowski, Frank Hughes *governor*
Pugh, John Robert *chancellor, former state health administrator*
†Renkes, Gregg *state attorney general*
Ruotsala, James Alfred *historian, writer*
Schorr, Alan Edward *librarian, publisher*
Shepard, Beatrice L. *retired microbiologist, historian*
Smith, Charles Anthony *business executive*
†Smith, Winston Paul *wildlife scientist, forest service*
Sonneman, Joseph Abram *lawyer, researcher, mediator, photographer*
†Tangen, Jon Paul *lawyer*
†Therriault, Gene *state senator*
Ulmer, Frances Ann *former lieutenant governor*
Whistler, Bradley James *state government official*

Kenai
Means, Lane Lewis *entertainer*

Kodiak
Jamin, Matthew Daniel *lawyer, magistrate judge*
Ott, Andrew Eduard *lawyer*
Selby, Jerome M. *mayor*

Kotzebue
†Dakai, Steven Henry *alcohol/drug abuse services professional*
O'Brien, Annmarie *education educator, educator*

Nondalton
Gay, Sarah Elizabeth *lawyer*

North Pole
James, Jeannette Adeline *state legislator, accountant*
†McGee, Michael Venhook *writer*

Palmer
†Holbert, Carolyn D. *education educator, writer*
Kent, E(verett) Allen *performing arts administrator, theatrical producer*
Lambert, Tobias P. *music educator*
Lawler, Marita A. *addiction therapist*

Salcha
Alsip, Cheryl Ann *small business owner*

Sitka
Ross, Dona Ruth *education program director, retired*

Soldotna
Franzmann, Albert Wilhelm *wildlife veterinarian, consultant*
†Moore, Hubert J. *addictions counselor, consultant*
Petersen, Lance W. *fine arts educator*

Tuntutuliak
Daniel, Barbara Ann *retired elementary school educator*

Valdez
Devens, John Searle *natural resources administrator*

Wasilla
†Brunke, Dawn Baumann *writer, editor*

Willow
White, Gwendolyn A. *recreational facility executive*

Wrangell
†Clarke, Laurence B. *retired real estate broker, writer*

ARIZONA

Apache Junction
Bracken, Harry McFarland *philosophy educator*
†Campbell, John Carl *retired engineering educator*

GEOGRAPHICAL INDEX 5795 ARIZONA

Ransom, Evelyn Naill language educator, linguist

Arizona City
Donovan, Willard Patrick retired elementary education educator

Avondale
Jaeger, Kenneth John music educator
Manning-Weber, Claudia Joy medical education consultant, author

Bisbee
Arrowsmith, Nancy journalist
Behney, Charles Augustus, Jr., veterinarian
Eppele, David Louis columnist, author
Holland, Robert Dale retired judge
Milton, John P. ecologist, educator, author, photographer

Bullhead City
†Jones, Vernon Quentin surveyor
Shervheim, Lloyd Oliver insurance company executive, lawyer

Camp Verde
Bell, Daniel Carroll realtor, community association, ranch and land manager
†Wagner, Gary Wayne educational administrator

Carefree
Alexander, Judd Harris retired paper company executive
Chase, James Keller retired artist, museum director, educator
Galda, Dwight William financial company executive
Garr, Carl Robert manufacturing company executive
Hook, William Franklin locum tenens radiologist

Casa Grande
Kapsos, Philip John anesthesiologist
Khan, Habib Urrehman neurologist
Landers, Patricia Glover reading specialist
McGillicuddy, Joan Marie psychotherapist, consultant
Wendt, Steven William business educator

Cave Creek
O'Reilly, Thomas Eugene human resources consultant, retired

Chandler
Barnard, Annette Williamson elementary school principal
†Basha, Edward N., Jr., grocery chain owner
Brunello-McCay, Rosanne sales executive
†Carpenter, Ron D. music educator
Devi, Talluri S. retired obstetrician/gynecologist
Dunn, Boyd mayor, lawyer
Eckstat, Arthur Gene consultant
Farley, James Newton manufacturing executive, engineer
†Faust, Donny D. music educator
Fordemwalt, James Newton microelectronics engineering educator, consultant
Goyer, Robert Stanton communication educator
Joyce, Kenneth Thomas electronics company executive
Mönkemüller, Klaus Erik physician, researcher, clinician
Myers, Gregory Edwin aerospace engineer
†Rossi, Mark Antony political consultant, writer
Rowe, Ernest Ras education educator, academic administrator
Simon, Diane Rose music educator, writer, poet
Stewart, Nancy Sue Spurlock educator
VanderVeen, Joseph Richard special education administrator
Zinman, David Joel conductor

Chinle
†Quell, Margaret Anne special education educator
Reed, Leonard Newton secondary school educator

Chino Valley
†Casey, Bonnie Mae artist, educator

Clarkdale
Eide, Joel Sylvester art consultant, appraiser

Cornville
White, Judith Louise social worker, counselor

Cortaro
Fossland, Joeann Jones professional speaker, personal coach

Cottonwood
Gorriaz, Mary Alice real estate broker

Davis Monthan AFB
†Barksdale, Barry W. career officer
†Foglesong, Robert H. lieutenant general United States Air Force
Miller, Charles Wallace historian, environmental geologist, educator
Woods, Sharhonda Michele military officer

Davis Monthan Afb
Smail, Leslie Anne librarian

Douglas
†Britton, Ruth Ann Wright elementary educator
Burgess Flores, Elsa Marie counselor, health educator, advocate

Duncan
Ouzts, Eugene Thomas minister, secondary education educator

Eloy
O'Leary, Thomas Michael lawyer

Flagstaff
Barlow, Nadine Gail planetary geoscientist
†Baron, Patricia Burrell university director
Bolin, Richard Luddington industrial development consultant
Braunstein, Ethan Malcolm skeletal radiologist, paleopathologist, educator
Brown, Frederick Lee health care executive
Collins, Galen Robert technology educator
Cortner, Hanna Joan research scientist, educator
†Cothran, Dan Allen political scientist, educator
Cowser, Danny Lee lawyer, mental health specialist
Edgerton, Debra artist, educator
Gliege, John Gerhardt lawyer
Gunderson, Margaret Steeble music educator
Haeger, John Denis academic administrator
Hammond, Howard David retired botanist, editor
Lacey, Henry Bernard lawyer
Lewicky, Roman Taras orthopedic surgeon
Lovely, Cynthia Jane reading educator
Marcus, Karen Melissa foreign language educator
McDonald, Craydon Dean psychologist
†Motschman, Keith Allen health products executive
Pavlik, William Bruce psychologist, educator
Phillips, Arthur Morton, III, botanist, consultant
Price, Peter Wilfrid ecology educator, researcher
Putnam, William Lowell science association administrator
Reyhner, Jon Allan education educator
†Schlosberg, David political scientist, educator
Shoemaker, Carolyn Spellman planetary astronomer
Smith, Zachary Alden political science and public administration educator
Stoops, Daniel J. lawyer
†Swann, Gloria S. music educator
†Weidenaar, Gary Alan music educator
Wetzel, Wendy Sue women's health nurse practitioner, holistic health nurse
Wolf, Arthur Henry museum administrator
Young, Robert Donald physicist, educator

Florence
Puglia, Frank Alan academic administrator

Fort Defiance
Livingston, Alfred James archaeologist, consultant

Fort Huachuca
Adams, Frank education specialist
Clark, Brian Thomas mathematical statistician, operations research analyst
†Howdeshell, Daniel Thomas music educator

Fort Smith
†Detary, Timothy James banking and health care executive

Fountain Hills
Gifford, Ray Wallace, Jr., retired physician, educator
Humes, Charles Warren counselor, educator
Israel, Robert Allan statistician
Lacy, Herman Edgar management consultant
Tyl, Noel Jan baritone, astrologer, writer
Wright, C. T. Enus former academic administrator

Fredonia
Pickett-Trudell, Catherine psychotherapist

Gilbert
Bennett, Kevin Ray music educator, musician
Duran, Michael Carl bank executive
†Earnhardt, Hal J., III, automotive executive
Eitner, James William physician, medical consultant, administrator
†Figueroa, Yile Margaret Hannah writer, educator
Kenney, Thomas Frederick broadcasting executive
Larson, Dorothy Ann business educator
Metcalf, Virgil Alonzo economics educator
Pendleton, Winston Kent, III, aerospace engineer, physics educator
Peoples, Esther Lorraine elementary education educator, writer, publisher
Stith, Joseph computer infosystems specialist, author

Glendale
†Avila, Lidia D. principal
Baum, Phyllis Gardner travel management consultant
Brewer, William E. city materials manager
Chavez, Mary Lynn pharmacy educator
Cole, James W. academic administrator
Collins, Richard Francis microbiologist, educator
Edwards, Vicki Ann elementary school principal
Goforth, Nathan Dan protective services official
Hanhila, Matt Oscar, Jr., orthodontist
Heathcotte, Toby Fesler writer, retired educator
Joseph, Gregory Nelson media critic, writer, actor
Lack, Larry Henry small business owner
†Lysik, Melanie Alison pharmacologist, educator
Mathis, F. John economist, educator
McDonald, Barbara Ann retired psychotherapist
Michael, Cecil Francis, Jr., pediatrician
Mosley, Shelley Elizabeth library administrator
†Riales, Ron O. custodian
Schabow, John William accountant
Scruggs, Elaine M. mayor
Shimek, John Anton legal investigation business owner, educator
†Staczek, John Joseph academic administrator, consultant
Stauffer, Thomas Michael former university president
†Strom, April Dawn mathematician, educator
†Sweat, Lynda Sue cooking instructor, catering company owner, deaconess

Woods, Cyndy Jones secondary educator, researcher
Zinn, Dennis Bradley magician, actor, comedian

Golden Valley
Davis, Richard Ernest engineer

Goodyear
Bailey, Thomas Everett engineering company executive
Carlson, Norman A. government official
Eppen, Gary Dean business educator

Green Valley
Bates, Charles Carpenter oceanographer
Bennett, Bradley Frederick retired military officer, science association director
Brewington, Arthur William retired English language educator
Brissman, Bernard Gustave retired insurance company executive
de Soto, Ernest Frank artist, publisher
Dingle, Albert Nelson meteorology educator
Gilliam, Mary travel executive
Greenwood, Helen Maxine retired office manager, executive assistant
Leege, David Calhoun political scientist, educator
Macafee, Susan Diane reporter
McDonough, Russell Charles retired state supreme court justice
Moser, Robert Harlan physician, educator, writer
Page, John Henry, Jr., artist, educator
Pike, George Harold, Jr., religious organization executive, clergyman
Shafer, Susan Wright retired elementary school educator
Smith, Raymond Lloyd former university president, consultant
Turner, Harold Edward education educator
Vanderspek, Peter George management consultant, writer

Hereford
Hirth, John Price metallurgical engineering educator
Schenk, Quentin Frederick retired social work educator, mayor, psychologist
†Seeland, Arthur David bishop, psychotherapist

Holbrook
Eiler, Jason E music educator
Passer, Gary Louis college president

Kingman
Basinger, Richard Lee lawyer
Jones, Barbara Christine educator, linguist, creative arts designer
McAfee, Susan Jacqueline educator

Kykotsmovi
†Honan, Raena writer

Lake Havasu City
Brydon, Ruth Vickery history educator

Lake Montezuma
Burkee, Irvin artist

Litchfield Park
McKeighen, Ronald Eugene physicist

Mesa
Baxter, Gene Kenneth mechanical engineer, company executive
Berger, James Charles computer consultant and systems educator
Boren, Kenneth Ray endocrinologist, nephrologist
Boyd, Leona Potter retired social worker
Brown, Wayne J. former mayor
Bunchman, Herbert Harry, II, plastic surgeon
†Burgess, Robert Kingsley aeronautical engineer
Carter, Sally Packlett elementary education educator
†Christiansen, Larry K. college president
DeRosa, Francis Dominic chemical company executive
Dorland, Elizabeth M. chemistry educator
Estabrook, Brooke Kendell instructional technologist
Fiorino, John Wayne podiatrist
Garwood, John Delvert former college administrator
Gunderson, Brent Merrill lawyer
Hagen, Nicholas Steward medical educator, consultant
Hawker, Keno mayor, trucking company executive
Hicks, Bethany Gribben judge, commissioner, lawyer
Horne, Jeremy consultant, writer, research executive
Johnson, Doug advertising and public relations executive
†Kent, Sherie Lynn music educator
†Kiefer, Don Russell writer, researcher
Lingle, Muriel Ellen retired elementary education educator
Loose, Mary Ellen musician
Luth, William Clair retired research manager
Mason, Marshall W. theater director, educator
Mason, Terence K. critical care nurse, emergency nurse
McCollum, Alvin August consultant, real estate company executive
McGill, John J. radiologist
McIlray, John Frederick organist
McKinnon, Elizabeth Longo musician, educator
Mead, Linda McCullough secondary education educator, adult education specialist
Murphy, Edward Francis executive
†Nielson, Theo Gilbert protective services official, university official
†Ohl, John Kennedy history educator
†Raymond, Robert Joseph mechanical engineer

Rummel, Robert Wiland aeronautical engineer, writer
†Skoldberg, Phyllis Linnea music educator, musician
Thompson, Ronald MacKinnon former family physician, artist, writer
Trejos, Franklin Anthony physician assistant
†Tudor-Locke, Catrine Elizabeth research scientist, educator, research scientist, consultant
†Wong, Willie former mayor, automotive executive
†Yates, Cheryl Ann home economist, educator

Morristown
Cortright, Inga Ann accountant

Nogales
Percious, Jacquelin Marlyn musician, travel writer
†Robertson, Leon S retired sociologist, retired social sciences educator

Oracle
Rush, Andrew Wilson artist

Oro Valley
†Hodge, Mark Louis music educator, conductor
McConnell, Robert Eastwood architect, educator
Scoville, Lynda Sue special education educator, writer

Paradise Valley
Burkholder, Peter Miller physician, educator
Calkins, Jerry Milan anesthesiologist, educator, administrator, biomedical engineer
Chrisman, William Herring property tax consultant
Day, Richard Putnam marketing, strategic planning and employee benefits consultant, arbitrator
Doede, John Henry investment company executive
Harnett, Lila retired publisher
Hazard, Robert Culver, Jr., hotel executive
Lorenzen, Robert Frederick ophthalmologist
Maxey, Diane Meadows artist
McCall, Louise Harrup artist
McKennon, Keith Robert chemical company executive
Moya, Sara Dreier educator
North, Gerald David William lawyer
Ratkowski, Donald J. mechanical engineer, consultant
Russell, Paul Edgar electrical engineering educator
Targovnik, Selma E. Kaplan physician
Tubman, William Charles lawyer
Unruh, James Arlen banking executive

Parker
Carnicom, Gene E. health services administrator
†Grazier, Diana Lynn community health nurse, medical/surgical nurse, writer

Patagonia
Bonner, Herbert Dwight construction management educator
La Noue, Terence David artist, educator

Payson
Brown, James Carrington, III, (Bing Brown) public relations and communications executive
Crom, Thomas LeRoy, III, venture capitalist, accountant
Hegarty, Christopher Joseph management and financial consultant
Hershberger, Robert Glen architect, educator
Lasys, Joan medical nurse, writer, educator, publisher
Salomon, Marilyn artist

Pearce
Malone, Paul Scott writer, artist

Peoria
Bailey, Claudia Jean retired professor, librarian, artist
Dapples, Edward Charles retired geologist, educator
Engelhardt, Thomas Francis lawyer, consultant
†Gould, Dorothy Mae executive secretary, soprano
Lichtenberg, Larry Ray chemist, consultant, researcher
McMahon, Maribeth Lovette physicist
Molinsky, Bert tax consultant
Morrison, Manley Glenn real estate investor, former army officer
Schindler, William Stanley retired public relations executive, consultant
Willard, Garcia Lou artist

Phoenix
Allen, Janice Faye Clement nursing administrator
Allen, Robert Eugene Barton lawyer
†Allison, Rebecca Anne cardiologist, writer
Alsentzer, William James, Jr., lawyer
†Ammon, John Richard anesthesiologist
†Andersen, Ronald Meredith lawyer
Anderson, Gary Gene music educator
†Anderson, Ib performing company executive
Anderson, Lawrence Ohaco magistrate judge, lawyer
Anderson, Milada Filko manufacturing company executive
†Anderson, Vicki retired librarian
†Avilez, Victoria Marie lawyer
Bachus, Benson Floyd mechanical engineer, consultant
Bain, C. Randall lawyer
Baker, William Dunlap lawyer
Bakker, Thomas Gordon lawyer
Ballinger, James K. art museum executive
Banerjee, Ajoy Kumar engineer, constructor, executive

Barclay, Steven Calder *lawyer*
Begam, Robert George *lawyer*
Bellus, Ronald Joseph *marketing and communications executive*
Beltrán, Anthony Natalicio *non-commissioned officer, deacon*
Bentheim, Wendy J. *municipal official*
Berch, Rebecca White *state supreme court justice, lawyer*
Bergamo, Ron *marketing executive*
†Beshears, Robert Gene *lawyer*
Bickford, David Lawrence *librarian, educator*
Bidwill, William V. *professional football executive*
Bildhauer, W. Mathias *philosophy educator, real estate broker*
Binnie, Nancy Catherine *retired nurse, educator*
Bivens, Donald Wayne *lawyer, judge*
Blanchard, Charles Alan *lawyer, former state senator*
Blevins, Willard Ahart *electrical engineer*
Bodensteiner, John Burton *neurologist*
Bodney, David Jeremy *lawyer*
Bolin, Vernon Spencer *microbiologist, consultant*
Borel, James David *anesthesiologist*
Bostwick, Todd William *city archaeologist*
†Bouma, John Jacob *lawyer*
Brenly, Bob *professional sports team executive, broadcaster*
†Brewer, Janice Kay *state official*
†Brewer, Stephanie L. *lawyer*
Broomfield, Robert Cameron *federal judge*
†Brunacini, Alan Vincent *protective services official*
Buffmire, Donald K. *internist*
Burke, Timothy John *lawyer*
Burns, Brenda *state senator*
†Bushee, Ward *newspaper editor*
Cai, Weizhong (Will Cai) *electronics engineer, researcher, physicist*
Canby, William Cameron, Jr., *judge*
Carroll, Earl Hamblin *federal judge*
Carter, Ronald Martin, Sr., *pharmaceutical company executive*
Case, David Leon *lawyer*
†Castleberry, W. Thomas *financial company executive*
Chanen, Steven Robert *lawyer*
†Chang, Gail Cathryn May *music educator*
Charlton, John Kipp *pediatrician*
Chenal, Thomas Kevin *lawyer*
Clark-Johnson, Susan *publishing executive*
Clements, John Robert *real estate professional*
Coghill, William Thomas, Jr., *retired lawyer*
Cohen, Jon Stephan *lawyer*
†Colangelo, Jerry John *professional sports team executive*
Cole, Daniel John *anesthesiologist, educator*
Cole, George Thomas *lawyer*
Coleman, George Joseph, III, (Jay Coleman) *lawyer*
†Comus, Louis Francis, Jr., *lawyer*
Condo, James Robert *lawyer*
Conrad, John Regis *lawyer, engineering executive, consultant*
Cooledge, Richard Calvin *lawyer*
Coor, Lattie Finch *university president*
Coppersmith, Sam *lawyer*
†Crawford, Neil Robert *mechanical engineer, researcher*
Cristiano, Marilyn Jean *speech communication educator*
Crockett, Clyll Webb *lawyer*
Culnon, Sharon Darlene *reading specialist, special education educator*
Cunningham, James Patrick *lawyer*
Curcio, Christopher Frank *city official*
†Cure, Carol Campbell *lawyer*
Curzon, Thomas Henry *lawyer*
Daily-Washington, Joyce Marie (Joyce Marie Jackson) *utilization management nurse*
Daniel, James Richard *accountant, computer company financial executive*
Darnell, Yolanda (Yolanda Darnell) *videomaker, filmmaker, writer*
Davies, David George *lawyer, educator*
†Dawson, John Joseph *lawyer*
†DelParigi, Angelo *research scientist*
deMatties, Nicholas Frank *artist, art educator*
De Michele, O. Mark *utility company executive*
Denning, Michael Marion *marketing professional, educator*
Derouin, James Gilbert *lawyer*
Dewane, John Richard *retired manufacturing company executive, consultant, business owner*
†Dib, Nabil *cardiologist, researcher*
Dignac, Geny (Eugenia M. Bermudez) *sculptor*
Dinner, Janice Marie *lawyer*
Dorland, Byrl Brown *retired civic worker*
Doto, Irene Louise *statistician*
†Downey, Janet Marion *anthropologist, educator*
Drain, Albert Sterling *business management consultant*
Drnjevic, Jonathan Mark *language educator*
Dunipace, Ian Douglas *lawyer*
Duyck, Kathleen Marie *poet, musician, retired social worker*
Edens, Gary Denton *broadcasting executive*
Ehmann, Anthony Valentine *lawyer*
Ellison, Cyril Lee *literary agent, retired publisher*
Elmore, James Walter *architect, retired university dean*
Esahak, George Michael *lawyer*
Everett, James Joseph *lawyer*
Everett, Paul Marvin *physicist*
Fannin, Paul Robert *political party official*
Feinstein, Allen Lewis *lawyer*
Felicetta, James Vincent *endocrinologist, educator*
†Fernandez, Helen Agnes *municipal official*
Ferreira, Donna Blair *interior designer*
Fishburne, John Ingram, Jr., *obstetrician/gynecologist, educator*
Fleenor, Geneva Lucille *retired elementary school educator*
Flickinger, Don Jacob *patent agent*
Florence, Henry John *lawyer*
†Foley, William Patrick, II, *title insurance company executive*
Franke, William Augustus *corporate executive*
Freyermuth, Clifford L. *structural engineering consultant*
Fugiel, Frank Paul *insurance company executive*
Fullmer, Steven Mark *engineering executive*
Gaffney, Donald Lee *lawyer*
Gaines, Francis Pendleton, III, *judge*
Galbut, Martin Richard *lawyer*
Gall, Donald Alan *data processing executive*
†Gallagher, Michael L. *lawyer*
†Garagiola, Joe, Jr., *baseball team executive*
Genrich, Mark L. *foundation administrator*
Geraghty, Patrick James *organ recovery manager*
Gerber, Rudolph Joseph *lawyer, educator*
Giedt, Bruce Alan *paper company executive*
Gilbert, Donald Roy *lawyer*
Gillom, Jennifer *professional basketball player*
Gladner, Marc Stefan *lawyer*
†Goddard, Terry *state attorney general*
Godfrey, John William *retired music educator*
Goldberg, Morris *internist*
Gomez, David Frederick *lawyer*
Grafe, Warren Blair *broadcast executive*
†Graham, LeRoy Cullen *retired electrical engineer*
†Grant, Merwin Darwin *lawyer*
Griller, Gordon Moore *court administrator*
Gunty, Christopher James *newspaper editor*
Hagan, Judith Ann *social worker*
Halpern, Barry David *lawyer*
Hamilton, Gillian *geriatrician*
†Hammond, Larry Austin *lawyer*
Hanley, Fred William *librarian, educator*
Hardaway, Penny (Anfernee Deon Hardaway) *professional basketball player*
Harris, Ray Kendall *lawyer*
Harrison, Mark Isaac *lawyer*
Hawkins, Jasper Stillwell, Jr., *architect*
Hay, John Leonard *lawyer*
Hayden, William Robert *lawyer*
Hays, E. Earl *youth organization administrator*
Hedberg, John Charles *investor*
Helling, Ricky Allen *professional baseball player*
Henderson, James Forney *lawyer*
Hicks, William Albert, III, *lawyer*
Hienton, James Robert *lawyer*
Hiller, Neil Howard *lawyer*
†Hirsch, Steven A. *lawyer*
Hoecker, Thomas Ralph *lawyer*
Holman, John Foster *investment banker*
Holman, Paul David *plastic surgeon*
Horner, Harry Charles, Jr., *sales executive, theatrical and film consultant*
Hotz, Jeffrey Alan *anesthesiologist, educator*
Houseworth, Richard Court *state agency administrator*
Howard, William Matthew *arbitrator, writer, lawyer*
Huffman, Edgar Joseph *oil company executive*
Huntwork, James Roden *lawyer*
Hutchinson, Ann *management consultant*
Inman, William Peter *lawyer*
Jacobson, Edward (Julian Edward Jacobson) *lawyer*
†Jacques, Raoul Thomas *lawyer*
James, Charles E., Jr., *lawyer*
Jirauch, Charles W. *lawyer*
Johnson, Frank *professional basketball coach*
Johnson, Kevin Maurice *professional basketball player*
Johnson, Randy (Randall David Johnson) *professional baseball player*
Johnston, Logan Truax, III, *lawyer*
Jones, Charles E. *chief justice supreme court*
Jungbluth, Connie Carlson *wealth strategist*
Karabatsos, Elizabeth Ann *career counseling services executive*
Karnas, Fred G., Jr., *non-profit organization executive*
†Kasarjian, Levon, Jr., *lawyer*
Khan, Ahmed Mohiuddin *finance, insurance executive*
Kimball, Bruce Arnold *soil scientist*
Kitzman, Jerry Matson *pharmaceutical executive*
†Klahr, Gary Peter *retired lawyer*
Klausner, Jack Daniel *lawyer*
†Klein, R. Kent *lawyer*
Klepinger, John William *trailer manufacturing company executive*
†Klor de Alva, Jorge *education company executive*
Knoller, Guy David *lawyer*
Koester, Berthold Karl *lawyer, law educator, retired honorary German consul*
Koffman, Martha Alice *communications and training executive, ergonomist*
Koppenbrink, Walter Edwin, III, *internist*
†Kramer, Kevin William *aerospace engineer*
Krietor, David *airport authority executive*
Kurn, Neal *lawyer*
†Kuzma, George Martin *retired bishop*
Laufer, Nathan *cardiologist*
LaValle, Jennifer Suzette *marketing communications specialist, consultant*
Lawlis, Patricia Kite *air force officer, computer consultant*
Lawrence, Steven Thomas *lawyer*
Lawrence, William Henry, Jr., *neurologist*
Leach, John F. *editor, journalism educator*
Lemon, Leslie Gene *retired diversified services company executive*
†Leshner, Stephen I. *lawyer*
†Levetown, Robert Alexander *lawyer*
Lewis, Carl Edwin *artist, photographer, designer*
Lewis, Orme, Jr., *real estate company executive, land use adviser*
Liaw, Hang Ming *engineer*
Linde, Ronald Keith *corporate executive, private investor*
Linxwiler, Louis Major, Jr., *retired finance company executive*
Long, Michael Alan *musician, writer*
Lubin, Stanley *lawyer*
Lyon, William James *sociology educator*
†Lyons, George Harris *lawyer*
Maimon, Elaine Plaskow *English educator, university provost, campus chief executive officer*
Marbury, Stephon *professional basketball player*
Martone, Frederick J. *judge*
Martori, Joseph Peter *lawyer*
Maxson, Barbara Kinzie *clinical social worker, educator*
McCarthy, M. Juliann *school psychologist*
†McClelland, Norman P. *food products executive*
McClennen, Crane *judge*
Mc Clennen, Louis *lawyer, educator*
McClennen, Miriam J. *former state official*
McConnell, Albert Lynn *dean*
†McCormick, Kathryn Ellen *prosecutor*
McGrath, Jane Lee *education educator, writer*
McGregor, Ruth Van Roekel *state supreme court justice*
McLoone, James Brian *psychiatrist, educator*
McRae, Hamilton Eugene, III, *lawyer*
McWhorter, Ruth Alice *counselor, marriage and family therapist*
Melner, Sinclair Lewis *retired military officer*
Meridith, Denise Patricia *business consultant*
Merlin Kearfott, DuVal *health consultant*
Merritt, Nancy-Jo *lawyer*
Meschkow, Jordan M. *lawyer*
Metzler, Jerry Don *retired nursing administrator*
Meyers, Howard Craig *lawyer*
Miel, Vicky Ann *city official*
Miller, Beatrice Ellen *communications executive*
Miller, Michael Jon *survey engineer, local government manager*
Minor, Willie *college department chair*
Mitchell, Wayne Lee *health care administrator*
Moriarty, Karen *state agency administrator*
Morrison, John Haddow, Jr., *engineering company executive*
Moyer, Alan Dean *retired newspaper editor*
Mullen, Daniel Robert *finance executive*
Murnane, George, III, *business executive*
†Murray, Vincent Smith *network technician, historian*
Myers, Robert David *judge*
Napoliello, Daniel Andrew *nursing administrator*
Napolitano, Janet Ann *governor*
Newman, Lois Mae *marketing executive*
Nijinsky, Tamara *actress, puppeteer, author, librarian, educator*
Nilsen, Laurance Beckwith *retired endocrinologist*
Noone, Palmer *academic administrator*
Norris, John Steven *healthcare company executive*
Olsen, Alfred Jon *lawyer*
Olson, Kevin Lory *lawyer*
O'Neal, Steven G. *chemist, educator*
O'Steen, Van *lawyer*
Parrington, Diane J. *nutritionist*
Pederson, Jim *political party official*
†Perry, Barbara Mitchell *retired librarian*
Petitti, Michael Joseph, Jr., *lawyer*
†Phillips, James Harold *lawyer*
Pidgeon, Steven D. *lawyer*
Pietzsch, Michael Edward *lawyer*
†Pillalamarri, Seshasayi *computer scientist and engineer, researcher*
Pittman, Hal Watson *neurosurgeon*
†Pittman, Timona Miller *arts adminstrator*
Platt, Warren E. *lawyer*
Plattner, Richard Serber *lawyer*
Pogson, Stephen Walter *lawyer*
Powell, Suzanne K. *nurse, consultant*
Preston, Bruce Marshall *lawyer, educator*
Price, Charles Steven *lawyer*
Pyle, Thomas Alton *instructional television and motion picture executive*
†Quayle, Dan (James Danforth Quayle) *former vice president United States, entrepreneur*
Quddus, Mohammed Tanvir *electrical engineer, researcher*
Rajyaguru, Mahesh Shantilal *education educator*
Rathwell, Peter John *lawyer*
Reed, Wallace Allison *anesthesiologist*
Refo, Patricia Lee *lawyer*
Reiff, A.E. *writer, artist*
Revie, Jean E. *science educator*
†Riikola, Michael Edward *lawyer*
Rimsza, Skip *mayor*
Rister, Gene Arnold *humanities educator*
Rivera, Jose de Jesus *lawyer*
Rodriguez, Leonard *foundation and nonprofit administrator*
Rodriguez-Lopez, Julio Arnaldo *surgeon, researcher*
Rose, David L. *lawyer*
†Rose, Scott A. *lawyer*
†Roselle, Ann *school librarian*
Rosen, Sidney Marvin *lawyer*
Rosenblatt, Paul Gerhardt *judge*
Roth, Sanford Harold *rheumatologist, health care administrator, educator*
Rudd, Gerald Patrick *ophthalmologist*
Rudolph, Gilbert Lawrence *lawyer*
Ryan, D. Jay *lawyer*
Ryan, Michael D. *state supreme court justice*
Sage, Webster LeGene, Jr., *ophthalmologist*
Salmonson, Marty Lee *stockbroker, consulting engineer*
Savage, Stephen Michael *lawyer*
Scarbrough, Ernest Earl *stockbroker, financial planner*
Schatt, Paul *newspaper editor*
Schaumburg, Donald Roland *art educator, ceramic artist*
Schiffner, Charles Robert *architect*
Schilling, Curtis Montague *professional baseball player*
†Schneider, Elizabeth Kelley *law librarian*
Schroeder, Mary Murphy *federal judge*
Scozzari, Albert *portfolio manager, inventor*
Sertich, Kelli Ann *land use planner*
†Shaffer, Dennis Michael *psychology educator*
Sharp, Linda *professional basketball coach*
Sherk, Kenneth John *lawyer*
Shultz, Susan F *executive search and corporate governance executive*
Silver, Roslyn O. *federal judge*
Silverman, Alan Henry *lawyer*
Silverman, Barry G. *federal judge*
Singer, Jeffrey Alan *surgeon*
Smith, James Parker *accountant*
†Smith, Susan Kimsey *lawyer*
Snell, Richard *holding company executive*
Sochacki, Andrzej *mechanical engineer, researcher, tourism educator*
Song Ong, Roxanne Kay *lawyer, judge*
Sourbrine, Richard Don, II, *architect*
†Spencer, Roger Keith *lawyer*
†Spraggins, Robert Lee *organic chemist, research scientist*
†Squire, Bruce M. *lawyer*
Steckler, Phyllis Betty *publishing company executive*
Stegmayer, Joseph Henry *housing industry executive*
Stern, Richard David *investment company executive*
Stern, Stanley *psychiatrist*
†Sterns, Patricia Margaret *lawyer, consultant*
Stone, Hazel Anne Decker *artist*
Storey, Lee A. *lawyer*
Storey, Norman C. *lawyer*
Strand, Roger Gordon *federal judge*
Subach, James Alan *information systems company executive, consultant*
Swafford, Leslie Eugene *physician assistant, consultant*
Swann, Eric Jerrod *professional football player*
Swartz, Jack *chamber of commerce executive*
Swartz, Melvin Jay *lawyer, writer*
Taylor, Elizabeth Jane *investment consultant, real estate and international marketing executive*
†Tennen, Leslie Irwin *lawyer, consultant, inventor*
Theobald, Scott M. *lawyer*
Thomas, Jim Gus *music educator*
Thompson, Bonnie Ransa *education consultant*
Thompson, Herbert Ernest *tool and die company executive*
Thompson, Joel Erik *lawyer*
Thompson, Terence William *lawyer*
†Thorne, Ann LaRayne *secondary school educator*
Thumma, Samuel Anderson *lawyer*
Tomback, Jay Loren *lawyer*
Torrens, Daniel *lawyer*
Tribble, Richard Walter *brokerage executive*
Turi, Louis *publishing executive*
Udall, Calvin Hunt *lawyer*
†Udall, Vesta Hammond *special education educator*
Ulrich, Paul Graham *lawyer, writer, editor*
†Underwood, Paul Lester *cardiologist*
Upson, Donald V. *financial executive, retired*
Vallee, Roy *electronics company executive*
Van Fleet, David Dominic *finance educator*
Van Horssen, Charles Arden *manufacturing executive*
Van Sittert, Barbara C. *retired classics educator, writer*
Vu, Eric Tin *neurobiologist, researcher*
Waas, Andrea Sue *nonprofit foundation administrator*
Walker, Richard K. *lawyer*
Wall, Donald Arthur *lawyer*
Walters, Carrie Lou *neurosurgeon*
Weiers, Jim *state representative*
Weil, Louis Arthur, III, *retired newspaper publishing executive*
Weisenburger, Theodore Maurice *retired judge, poet, educator, writer*
Wells, GladysAnn *library director*
Wheaton, Marilyn *music educator, pianist, organist*
Wheeler, Steven M. *lawyer*
Whisler, James Steven *lawyer, mining and manufacturing executive*
White, Edward Allen *electronics company executive*
Wiley, William David *engineer, hydrologist*
Williams, Quinn Patrick *lawyer*
Winslow, Paul David *architect*
Winthrop, Lawrence Fredrick *judge*
†Wirken, Charles William *lawyer*
Wolf, G. Van Velsor, Jr., *lawyer*
Wolf, Irna Lynn *psychologist*
Wright, Richard Oscar, III, *pathologist, educator, clinical ethicist*
†Yamamoto, Alice M. *educator*
†Yu, Angie *auditor, music educator*
Zepeda, Guillermo *language educator, speech professional*
Zerella, Joseph T. *retired pediatric surgeon*

Picacho

Cortright, Lewis Stephen *elementary educator*

Pima

Shafer, James Albert *health care administrator*

Portal

Zweifel, Richard George *curator*

Prescott

Anderson, Parker Lynn *editorial columnist, playwright*
Anderson, Walter Lee *environmental educator, artist, photographer*
†Bennett, Kenneth R. *oil company executive, state legislator*
Bieniawski, Zdzislaw Tadeusz Richard *engineering educator emeritus, writer, consultant*
Chesson, Eugene *civil engineering educator, consultant*
Clancy, Lynn Roger, Jr., *retired educational administrator, educator*
†Fleischner, Thomas Lowe *conservation biologist, educator*
Forbes, Judie *university official*
Garvey, Daniel Edward *foundation administrator, educator, academic administrator*

Goodman, Mark N. *lawyer*
Gose, Richard Vernie *lawyer*
Halvorson, Mary Ellen *education educator, writer*
Huard, Donald V. *psychologist, educator*
Kahne, Stephen James *systems engineer, educator, academic administrator, engineering executive*
Lorant, John Herman *retired economist, health policy analyst*
Madden, Paul Robert *lawyer, director*
Martinez, Anthony Joseph *real estate appraiser*
Mayol, Richard Thomas *advertising executive, political consultant*
Osborn, DeVerle Ross *insurance company executive*
Palmer, Robert Arthur *private investigator*
Parkhurst, Charles Lloyd *electronics company executive*
†Perry, John Richard, Jr., *lawyer, mediator*
Rheinish, Robert Kent *university administrator*
Schaeffer, Reiner Horst *military officer, foreign language professional*
†Sloan, Marjorie Hawkins *science educator, retired advertising executive*
Stasack, Edward Armen *artist*
Stuart, Spencer Raymond *management consultant*
Waldock, William David *aeronautical science and aviation safety educator*
Waterer, Bonnie Clausing *retired high school educator*
Welna, Jerome Sheldon *agriculturist, consultant*

Prescott Valley
Beck, Doris Olson *retired library media director*
Decil, Stella Walters (Del Decil) *artist*

Rio Rico
Ryan, John Duncan *lawyer*

Rio Verde
Ramsey, David Selmer *retired hospital executive*
Scott, Louis Edward *advertising agency executive*
Vanselow, Neal Arthur *university administrator, physician*

Sacaton
Stephenson, Larry Kirk *stategic planner, management, geography educator*

Saint Johns
DuBoise, Aaron T. *music educator*

San Manuel
Hawk, Dawn Davah *secondary education educator*
Hawk, Floyd Russell *secondary school educator*

San Simon
Burke, Ruth *writer*

Scottsdale
Ailloni-Charas, Miriam Clara *interior designer, consultant*
Amonte, Anthony Lewis *hockey player*
Amrozowicz, Paul Douglas *lawyer, electrical engineer*
Ash, Fayola Foltz *musician, music educator*
†Baack, Paula D. *music educator*
Baum, Herbert Merrill *consumer products company executive*
Berry, Charles Richard *lawyer*
†Berry, Kenneth Jay, Jr., *aerospace engineer, consultant*
Biglin, Karen Eileen *library director*
†Birkelbach, Albert Ottmar *retired oil company executive*
Blinder, Martin S. *business consultant, art dealer*
Braun, Stephen Hughes *psychologist*
Brown, Shirley Margaret Kern (Peggy Brown) *interior designer*
Bullerdick, Kim H. *petroleum executive*
Burke, Sean *professional hockey player*
Burr, Edward Benjamin *life insurance company executive, financial executive*
Carpenter, Betty O. *writer*
Carpenter, Peter Rockefeller *retired bank executive*
Carr, M(ary) L(ois) *mental health professional*
Carter, Carla Cifelli *management consultant*
†Case, Stephen Shevlin *lawyer*
Cassidy, Barry Allen *physician assistant, clinical medical ethicist*
†Cawley, Leo Patrick *pathologist, immunologist*
Cazier, Barry James *electrical engineer, software developer*
Chaurasia, Vishal *physician, writer, computer programmer*
Churchill, William DeLee *retired education educator, psychologist*
Coffinger, Maralin Katharyne *retired career officer, consultant*
Comfort, Clifton C. *fraud examiner, management consultant*
Coutts, Lawrence Robert *publisher*
Crossen, Rev. Mr. John F. *writer, researcher*
†Dahl, Mark Victor *dermatologist, educator*
Dalton, Phyllis Irene *library consultant*
Dean, Leslie Alan (Cap Dean) *economist, consultant*
Dlugie, Paul David *physician*
Doglione, Arthur George *data processing executive*
Donaldson, Scott *English language educator, writer*
Donnelly, Richard E. *physician assistant, educator*
Drake, Albert Estern *retired statistics educator, farming administrator*
Ellis, Frank Russell *retired pathologist*
Esquer, Deborah Anne *elementary school educator*
Evans, Tommy Nicholas *obstetrician/gynecologist, educator*
Faer, A.M. *magazine publishing consultant, poet*
Ferree, John Newton, Jr., *fundraising specialist, consultant*
Fisher, John Richard *engineering consultant, former naval officer*
Fosgate Heggli, Julie Denise *producer*
Francis, Robert *professional hockey coach*
Fratt, Dorothy *artist*
Freedman, Stanley Marvin *manufacturing company executive*
French, Lyle Albert *surgeon*
Friedman, Shelly Arnold *cosmetic surgeon*
Gans, Eugene Howard *cosmetic and pharmaceutical company executive, consultant*
Garcia-Buñuel, Luis *neurologist*
Garfield, Ernest *bank consultant*
George, Frank Richard *science and technoloty officer*
Getz, Bert Atwater *investment company executive*
Gilson, Arnold Leslie *retired engineering executive, consultant*
Gookin, Thomas Allen Jaudon *civil engineer*
Gray, Don *artist*
Grenell, James Henry *retired manufacturing company executive*
†Gretzky, Wayne Douglas *retired hockey player, businessman*
Grier, James Edward *hotel company executive, lawyer*
Gwinn, Mary Dolores *business developer, organizational theorist, philosopher, writer, speaker*
Handy, Robert Maxwell *lawyer*
Hansen, Donald W. *insurance and financial services executive*
Haupt, Adrienne Lynn *nurse administrator*
Heigh, Russell Irwin *gastroenterologist*
Hepler, Kenneth Russel *manufacturing executive*
Hill, Louis Allen, Jr., *former university dean, consultant*
Hockmuth, Joseph Frank *physicist, psychotherapist*
Howard, William Gates, Jr., *electronics company executive*
Huston, Christopher Worth *rehabilitation medicine physician*
Hutchison, Stanley Philip *retired lawyer*
Jackson, Donald Frank *organizational development consultant*
Jacobson, Frank Joel *cultural organization administrator*
Jeffe, Sidney David *automotive engineer*
Jensen, Dale Finnlay *accountant*
Jesky, T. J. *pharmaceutical products executive*
Jorden, Douglas Allen *lawyer, zoning hearing officer*
Kandell, Howard Noel *pediatrician*
Kane, Grace McNelly *maternal, women's health and pediatrics nurse*
Kaufman, Jeffrey Allen *publisher*
Kiehn, Mogens Hans *aviation engineer, consultant*
Kilgore, L(eRoy) Wilson *minister*
Kinsinger, Jack Burl *chemist, educator*
Kleppe, Shirley R. Klein *artist*
Krupp, Clarence William *lawyer, personnel and hospital administrator*
Kübler-Ross, Elisabeth *physician*
†Kuschell, Daniel J *radio personality*
Land, George A. *philosopher, writer, educator, consultant, speaker*
Lang, Margo Terzian *artist*
Lavenson, Susan Barker *hotel corporate executive, consultant*
La Vista, Frank William *author, educator, speaker*
Lee, Dennis Turner *civil engineer, construction executive*
Leighton, William D. *plastic and reconstructive surgeon*
Lemieux, Claude *hockey player*
Leonard, George Edmund *real estate, bank, high tech and consulting executive*
Lillestol, Jane Brush *development consultant*
†Lillo, Joseph Leonard *osteopath, family practice physician*
Linderman, William Earl *elementary school educator, writer*
Lindgren, D(erbin) Kenneth, Jr., *retired lawyer*
Lloyd, Eugene Walter *retired construction company executive*
Lloyd, Sally-Heath Fahnestock *artist*
Lorrance, Arleen *foundation administrator*
Lowry, Edward Francis, Jr., *lawyer*
Luke, David Kevin *investment company executive*
MacKinnon, Sally Anne *retired fast food company executive*
Maggard, Woodrow Wilson, Jr., *management consultant*
Manross, Mary *mayor*
Marks, Merton Eleazer *lawyer, international arbitrator, mediator, consultant*
Marshall, Jonathan *charitable foundation administrator, journalist*
Mayer, Robert Anthony *retired college president*
McCabe, Mary Williamson *computer systems analyst*
Milanovich, Norma JoAnne *training and development company executive*
Miller, Harry *mechanical engineer*
Mohraz, Judy Jolley *foundation administrator*
Monyak, Wendell Peter *pharmacist*
Morrison, James William, Jr., *lobbyist, government relations consultant*
Mousseux, Renate *language educator*
Murian, Richard Miller *book company executive*
Nadler, Henry Louis *pediatrician, geneticist, medical educator*
Nelson, Florence Ely *civic leader*
Nelson, Mary Kathryn *bilingual counselor, artist, singer, comedienne*
Newman, Marc Alan *electrical engineer*
†Newman, Ursula Irene *music educator*
†Northey, William Thomas *microbiologist, educator*
Novicki, Donald Edward *urologic surgeon*
Numminen, Teppo *professional hockey player*
O'Donnell, William Thomas *management consultant*
O'Meara, Sara *nonprofit organization executive*
Orford, Robert Raymond *consulting physician*
†Overgaard, Cordell Jersild *lawyer, business executive*
Parsons, Cynthia *writer, educational consultant*
Peterson, John Willard *composer, music publisher*
Prisbrey, Rex Prince *retired insurance agent, underwriter, consultant*
Quigley, Jerome Harold *management consultant*
Reidy, Richard Robert *publishing company executive*
Rethore, Bernard Gabriel *retired manufacturing and mining company executive*
Reznick, Richard Howard *pediatrician*
†Roberts, Joan Ila *psychologist, educator*
Root, Laura Lee *personal care industry executive*
Rosenfeld, Edward *travel company executive*
Salmon, Matt *former congressman, communications company executive*
Sanderson, David R. *physician*
Sapp, Donald Gene *retired minister*
Schleifer, Thomas C. *management consultant, author, lecturer*
Schmitz, Shirley Gertrude *marketing and sales executive*
Scholder, Fritz *artist*
Starr, Phillip Henry *psychiatrist, educator*
Stone, Alan Jay *retired college administrator*
Stott, Brian *software company executive, consultant*
Swanson, Robert Killen *management consultant*
†Taylor, James C. *writer*
Timmons, Evelyn Deering *pharmacist*
Tyner, Neal Edward *retired insurance company executive*
Vairo, Robert John *insurance company executive*
†Van Brunt, Gary T. *consumer products company executive*
Vanier, Jerre Lynn *art director*
Van Weelden, Thomas H. *waste industry company executive*
Walsh, Edward Joseph *toiletries and food company executive*
Washburn, Jerry Martin *accountant, corporate executive*
Watkins, Eugene Leonard *surgeon, educator*
Weil, John David *financial executive*
Weisman, Avery *psychiatrist*
Wesbury, Stuart Arnold, Jr., *health administration and policy executive, educator*
†Whitaker, Michael D. *endocrinologist, consultant*
White, Alexander B. *retired internist*
†Whittington, Thomas Lee *lawyer*
Wise, Paul Schuyler *insurance company executive*
†Wong, Joe Bing *retired architect*

Sedona
Bell, Robert Matthew *pharmaceutical company consultant*
Briney, Allan King *retired radiologist*
Catterton, Marianne Rose *occupational therapist*
Chicorel, Marietta Eva *publishing company executive, consultant*
Copeland, Suzanne Johnson *real estate executive*
Dansby, John Walter *retired oil company executive*
Darrow, Jane *artist*
Felsted, Carla Martindell *librarian, writer, editor*
Frankel, Jennie Louise *writer, composer, playwright, publisher*
Frankel, Terrie Maxine *writer, composer, playwright, publisher, producer*
†French, Richard Edmund *insurance company executive*
Garrison, Gene Kirby *artist, writer, photographer*
Griffin, Jean (Alva Jean Griffin) *entertainer*
Hawkins, David Ramon *psychiatrist, writer, researcher, religious studies educator*
†Mastor, Helen *career planning administrator, educator*
Metzner, Richard Joel *psychiatrist, psychopharmacologist, educator*
Mikles, Devin Alaric *physician, educator*
Prather, Richard Scott *author*
Reno, Joseph Harry *retired orthopedic surgeon*
Rhines, Marie Louise *composer, violinist*
Sasmor, James Cecil *publishing representative, educator*
Sasmor, Jeannette Louise *educational consulting company executive*
Shors, Clayton Marion *cardiologist*
Vayanian, Solara Zakeli *artist, educator*
Wolfe, Al *marketing and advertising consultant*

Sierra Vista
†Boughan, Zanetta Louise *music educator*
†Childers, John R. *education educator*
Cowger, Phyllis *nurse*
Hasney, Christopher William *retired investment company executive, educator*
Hessler, Thomas John *community activist*
Lutes, Todd Oakley *political science educator*
†Plummer, Val J. *education educator, chaplain*
Rumler, Diana Gale *retired geriatrics nurse*
Sizemore, Nicky Lee *computer scientist*
Smith, Donna Nadine *army noncommissioned officer*
†Townsend, Lawrence Ray *paramedic, nurse*

Sonoita
Cook, William Howard *architect*
Scott, William Coryell *medical executive*

Sun City
Black, Robert Frederick *former oil company executive*
Blanchet, Jeanne Ellene Maxant *artist, educator, performer*
Buchman, Elwood *internist, pharmaceutical company medical director*
†Coffman, Harold Emerson *retired agricultural products supplier, retail merchant*
Davies, Percy (Pete) Charles *mechanical engineer*
Davis, Virginia *trade show producer*
Filek, Allan August *physician*
Hamilton, Ronald Ray *minister*
Hauer, James Albert *lawyer*
Keesling, Karen Ruth *lawyer*
Lackey, James Franklin, Jr., *retired civil engineer*
Lapsley, James Norvell, Jr., *minister, pastoral theology educator*
Larkin, Mary Sue *financial planner*
Meade, Kenneth John *realty company owner, broker*
Oppenheimer, Max, Jr., *foreign language educator, consultant*
Randall, Claire *church executive*
Thompson, Betty Jane *small business owner*
Treece, James Lyle *lawyer*

Sun City West
Berkenkamp, Fred Julius *management consultant*
Brown, Ruth Geisler *engineering supervisor*
Cohen, Abraham J. (Al Cohen) *educational administrator*
Coté, Ralph Warren, Jr., *mining engineer, nuclear engineer*
Dementis, Katharine Hopkins *retired interior designer*
Forti, Lenore Steimle *business consultant*
Hartzog, Ira Barnes *aviation executive*
Hernly, Sharon Kelley *geriatrics nurse practitioner, consultant, educator*
Holloway, Diane Elaine *psychological consultant, psychotherapist, writer*
Nordin, John Algot *economist, educator*
O'Brien, Gerald James *utilities executive*
Person, Robert John *financial management consultant*
Schlabach, Leland A. *electrical engineer*
Schmitz, Charles Edison *evangelist*
Schrag, Adele Frisbie *business education educator*
Stevens, George Richard *business consultant, public policy commentator*
Vision, Blanche Stein *retired judge*
†Wasmuth, Carl Erwin *physician, lawyer*
Williams, William Harrison *retired librarian*
Woodruff, Neil Parker *agricultural engineer*

Sun Lakes
Cantor, David Jules *economist*
Johnson, Marian Ilene *education educator*
Sharpless, Joseph Benjamin *retired county official*
Smith, Eleanor Jane *university chancellor, retired, consultant*
Thompson, Loring Moore *retired college administrator, writer*

Sun Valley
Hamilton, Jimmy Ray *secondary education educator*

Sunsites
Datcu, Ioana *visual artist*

Surprise
Clark, Lloyd *historian, writer, educator*
Fennelly, Jane Corey *lawyer*
Jackson, Randy *information technology executive*
Koessel, Donald Ray *retired banker*
Lazar, Max Seymour *pharmaceutical company executive, retired*
Lowe, Robert Charles *lawyer, banker*
Mitsui, James Masao *retired language educator, poet, consultant*
Raat, William Dirk *history educator*
Steffan, Wallace Allan *entomologist, educator, museum director*
Veigel, Jon Michael *science administrator*
Wargo, Andrea Ann *retired public health official, commissioned officer*
Ybarra, Kathryn Watrous *systems engineer*

Taylor
Kerr, Barbara Prosser *research scientist, educator*

Tempe
Adelson, Roger Dean *history educator, editor, historian*
Alisky, Marvin Howard *political science educator*
Amin, Omar Mohamed *parasitologist*
Anand, Suresh Chandra *physician*
Anchie, Toby Levine *health facility administrator*
Asadi, Robert Samir *insurance company executive*
†Askland, Andrew *academic administrator, educator*
Balanis, Constantine Apostle *electrical engineering educator*
Bauer, Ernst Georg *physicist, educator*
Bender, Paul *lawyer, educator*
Berman, Neil Sheldon *chemical engineering educator*
Bjork, Robert Eric *language professional educator*
Black, Kristine Mary *physicist*
Blankenship, Robert Eugene *biochemistry educator*
Brack, O. M., Jr., *English language educator*
Bristol, Stanley David *mathematician, educator*
Bucklin, Leonard Herbert *lawyer*
Buseck, Peter R. *geochemistry educator*
Chamberlin, Ralph Vary *physicist, educator*
Chawla, Nikhilesh *engineering educator*
†Ching, Anthony Bartholomew *lawyer, educator, consultant*
Chiriac, Victor Adrian *aerospace engineer, researcher*
Codell, Julie Francia *academic administrator, educator*
Collins, Richard Augustine *mechanical engineer*

Cortright, Barbara Jean *writer*
Cowley, John Maxwell *physics educator*
Crow, Michael *academic administrator*
†Crown, Eric J. *information systems executive*
†Dagger, Richard Keith *political science and philosphy educator*
†Doherty, Brian James *musicologist*
Duhnke, Robert Emmet, Jr., *retired aerospace engineer*
Ferry, David Keane *electrical engineering educator*
†Foster, David William *language educator, humanities educator*
†Freeman, Gary Eugene *civil engineer, researcher*
†Furnish, Dale Beck *lawyer, educator*
†Garzon, Amalia *Spanish educator, translator*
†Gilfillan, Daniel David *language educator, consultant*
Giuliano, Neil Gerard *mayor, academic administrator*
Glick, Milton Don *chemist, university administrator*
Golshani, Forouzan *computer science and engineering educator*
Gordon, Leonard *retired sociology educator*
Goronkin, Herbert *physicist*
Gruzinska, Aleksandra *language educator*
Guinouard, Donald Edgar *psychologist*
Haggerson, Nelson Lionel, Jr., *education educator*
Harris, Warren Lynn *computer engineer*
Haygood, Robert Collins *industrial psychologist, educator, consultant*
Herbert, Christopher Jay *marketing professional, management consultant*
Hoke, Judy Ann *physical education educator*
Hoza, Steven Paul *museum curator, consultant, educator, conservator*
Iverson, Peter James *historian, educator*
†James, L. Ward *medical/surgical nurse, consultant*
Johanson, Donald Carl *physical anthropologist*
Jones, Owen Donald *law educator*
Jungbluth, Kirk E.
Juvet, Richard Spalding, Jr., *chemistry educator*
Karady, George Gyorgy *electrical engineering educator, consultant*
Kaufman, Herbert Mark *finance educator*
Knox, Robert Lee *educator*
Krahenbuhl, Gary Stuart *university administrator*
†Kronenfeld, Jennie Jacobs *medical sociologist, health care researcher*
Laananen, David Horton *mechanical engineer, educator*
LaFaro, Angelo John *small business owner*
†Lang, Scott M. *music educator*
†Lockard, Joseph Franklin *literature educator, writer*
†Lohr, Dennis E. *research scientist, education educator*
Lombardi, Eugene Patsy *retired orchestra conductor, violinist, educator*
Lounsbury, John Frederick *geographer, educator*
MacKinnon, Stephen R. *Asian studies administrator, educator*
Major, Roy Coleman *language educator*
†Makri, Marianna *finance educator, researcher*
Matheson, Alan Adams *law educator*
Matthias, Judson Stillman *civil engineering educator, consultant*
Maynard, Michael *librarian*
Mays, Larry W. *civil engineering educator, hydrologist*
McCormack, Brian Jerome *political science educator*
McGinnis, Dave *professional football coach*
McKelvy, Michael John *materials chemist, research scientist*
Meehan, Robert Henry *human resources executive, electronics company executive, business educator*
Meissinger, Ellen Murray *artist, educator*
Metros, Mary Teresa *librarian*
Missimer, Denise Louise *mental health nurse*
Moore, Carleton Bryant *geochemistry educator*
Moya, Patrick Robert *lawyer*
Ortiz, Andrew Flores *management consultant*
Pany, Kurt Joseph *accounting educator, consultant*
Pasqualetti, Martin J. *geography educator*
Perry, Ronald William *public affairs educator*
Peterson, Michael R. *music company executive*
Pettit, George Robert *cancer researcher*
Playford, Nancy Jean *medical staff administrator*
Poe, Jerry B. *financial educator*
Raby, William Louis *writer, consultant*
Rankin, William Parkman *educator, former publishing company executive*
†Razdan, Anshuman *computer scientist, researcher*
†Reckers, Philip Merle *accounting and business educator*
Richards, Gale Lee *communication educator*
Rivers, Patrick A. *education educator, researcher*
Robertson, Samuel Harry, III, *transportation safety research engineer, educator*
Rowley, Beverley Davies *medical sociologist*
Roy, Asim *business educator*
Russell, Timothy Wells *music educator, researcher, conductor*
Sabine, Gordon Arthur *educator, writer*
Sackton, Frank Joseph *public affairs educator*
Schatzki, George *law educator*
Schroder, Dieter Karl *electrical engineering educator*
Shah, Jami J. *mechanical engineering educator, researcher*
Shaw, Milton Clayton *mechanical engineering educator*
Shimpock, Kathy Elizabeth *lawyer, writer*
Shoemaker, Scott David *network consultant, educator*
†Sigler, Mary Elizabeth *law educator*
Simon, Sheldon Weiss *political science educator*
Smith, Carol Estes *retired city councilman*
Smith, David John *physicist, educator*
Smith, Harvey Alvin *mathematics educator, consultant*
†Snyder, Lester M. *sports association executive*
Spritzer, Ralph Simon *lawyer, educator*
Starrfield, Sumner Grosby *astrophysics educator, researcher*
Stephenson, Frank Alex *engineer, consultant*
Strom, Robert Duane *psychologist, educator*
†Theodore, David *research scientist*
†Tillman, Hoyt Cleveland *historian, educator, writer*
†Tohe, Laura *English educator*
Tseng, Ampere An-Pei *mechanical engineer, educator, administrator*
Uttal, William R(eichenstein) *psychology and engineering educator, research scientist*
Vandenberg, Edwin James *chemist, educator*
van Gelderen, Elly *linguistics educator, researcher*
†Velupillai Mani, Ramesh *research scientist*
Weigend, Guido Gustav *geographer, educator*
Weiler, Dorothy Esser *librarian*
Wentz, Richard Eugene *religious studies educator*
†Wetsel, William David *literature educator*
Williams, James Eugene *management consultant*
Wills, J. Robert *academic administrator, drama educator, writer*
Winicov, Ilga Butelis *biochemist, educator*
Wong, Timothy C. *language and literature educator*
†Wytko, Joseph Rudolph *music educator*
Yau, Stephen Sik-sang *computer science and engineering educator, computer scientist, researcher*
†Yazzie, Aaron Franklin *events laborer*

Tonopah

Brittingham, James Calvin *nuclear engineer*

Tubac

Brandon, Gary Kent *physician, health facility administrator*
Fey, John Theodore *retired insurance company executive*
Miller, Frederick Robeson *banker*

Tucson

Abrams, Herbert Kerman *physician, educator*
Acker, Loren Calvin *medical instrument company executive*
Acker, Robert Flint *microbiologist*
Acosta, Ruben *surgeon*
†Adjarian, Maude Madeleine *literature educator, researcher*
Ahern, Geoffrey Lawrence *behavioral neurologist*
Aiken, Susan Hardy *English language educator*
Alberts, David Samuel *physician, pharmacologist, educator*
Alexander, Edward Harrison *mathematician, educator*
†Alley, Steven E. *foundation administrator*
Alpert, Joseph Stephen *physician, educator*
Andersen, Luba *electrologist, electropigmentologist*
Angel, James Roger Prior *astronomer*
†Apel, Harry James *composer*
Arcus, Sam George *social worker, educator, writer*
Armstrong, R(obert) Dean *entertainer*
Arnell, Walter James William *engineering educator, consultant*
Arzoumanian, Linda Lee *early childhood educator*
Aurand, Charles Henry, Jr., *music educator, educator*
Axinn, George Harold *rural sociology educator*
Bainton, Denise Marlene *lawyer*
Barrett, Bruce Richard *physics educator*
Bartlett, David Carson *state legislator*
Barton, Stanley Faulkner *management consultant*
Basford, Robert Eugene *retired biochemistry educator, researcher*
†Batterbury, Simon Peregrine John *geographer, educator*
Bechtel, Robert Bernard *social sciences educator, consultant*
Bedford, Felice L. *psychologist, educator*
Ben-Asher, M. David *physician*
Besselsen, David Guy *veterinary pathologist, researcher*
Best, Gary Thorman *commercial real estate broker*
Betteridge, Frances Carpenter *retired lawyer, mediator*
†Biddulph, Dana Lee *research scientist*
Billings, Richard Bruce *economics educator, consultant*
Birdman, Jerome Moseley *drama educator, consultant*
Birkby, Walter Hudson *forensic anthropologist, consultant*
Birkinbine, John, II, *philatelist*
Bjorhovde, Reidar *civil engineer, educator, researcher, consultant*
Blackman, Jeffrey William *lawyer*
Bloembergen, Nicolaas *physicist, educator*
Bodinson, Holt *conservationist*
Boyle, Christopher George *English educator, counselor*
†Boyle, Michael Frederick *retired television producer, actor*
Bradley, Gilbert Francis *retired banker*
Brammer, J. William, Jr., *judge, lawyer*
Breckenridge, Klindt Duncan *architect*
†Breiger, Ronald Louis *social sciences educator*
Brewer, David L. *sociologist*
Broadfoot, Albert Lyle *physicist*
Brown, Howard Mark *physician*
Browning, Sinclair *writer*
Browning, William Docker *federal judge*
Brunton, Daniel William *mechanical engineer*
Brusca, Richard Charles *biologist, researcher, educator*
Buras, Nathan *hydrology and water resources educator*
Butcher, Russell Devereux *author, photographer*
Cain, Vernon *retired information services executive*
Cameron, Alastair Graham Walter *astrophysicist, educator*
Canfield, John Douglas *English educator, writer, consultant*
Capp, Michael Paul *physician, educator*
Carleton, Willard Tracy *retired finance educator*
Carter, L. Philip *neurosurgeon, consultant*
Chandola, Anoop C. *educator, writer*
Chapman, Richard Grady *engineer*
Chaves, Mark Alan *sociologist, educator*
†Cherrick, Ruth E. *medical researcher, researcher*
Childs, Richard Francis *retired scientist, educator*
Cisler, Theresa Ann *osteopath, former nurse*
Clarke, James Weston *political science educator, writer*
Coates, Wayne Evan *agricultural engineer*
Coleman, Dan *composer, arranger, recording engineer, educator*
†Comiter, Craig Vance *urologist*
Conant, Howard Somers *artist, educator*
Constantino, Valerie *artist, writer, art educator*
Contractor, Dinshaw N. *civil engineer, educator*
Cook, Paul Christopher *engineering psychologist*
Cope, Thom K. *lawyer*
Copeland, Jack G. *cardiac surgeon, researcher*
Corey, Barry Martin *lawyer*
Crawford, David L. *astronomer*
Crawford, Richard Eben, Jr., *former investment advisor*
Cuello, Joel L. *biosystems engineer, educator*
Dalen, James Eugene *cardiologist, educator*
Daley, Richard Halbert *museum director*
D'Antonio, James Joseph *lawyer*
Dave, Romeel *astronomer, educator, researcher*
Davis, Richard Calhoun *dentist*
Davis, Roswita Beate *architectural engineer*
Davis, Stanley Nelson *hydrologist, educator*
DeLuca, Dominick *medical educator, researcher*
Denney, Dwight Lee *engineer*
Dessler, Alexander Jack *astrophysicist, educator*
De Young, David Spencer *astrophysicist, educator*
Diáz, Elena R. *community health nurse*
Dinnerstein, Leonard *historian, educator*
Dobbs, Dan Byron *lawyer, educator*
Done, Robert Stacy *educator, consultant*
Donoghue, John Charles *software management consultant*
Dunn, Floyd *biophysics and biomedical engeering educator*
†Dyer, James Harrison *lawyer*
Dyer-Raffler, Joy Ann *special education diagnostician, educator*
Eckhardt, August Gottlieb *retired law educator*
Edwards, John Womer *aerospace systems engineer*
Eigel, James Anthony *environmental engineer*
†Elliott, Sean P. *pediatrician, infectious disease specialist*
†Ensign, John D. *retired military officer*
Erickson, Eric Herman, Jr., *entomologist, scientist*
Erickson, Robert Porter *genetics researcher, educator, clinician*
Esposito, Joseph Louis *lawyer*
Evans, Arthur Haines, Jr., *educational consultant, researcher*
Evans, Gay Goodwin *nurse*
Ewy, Gordon Allen *cardiologist, clinician, researcher, educator*
†Fajardo, Sarah Elizabeth Johnson *financial consultant*
†Falbaum, Bertram Seymour *law educator, investigator*
†Fass, Ronnie *gastroenterologist, director*
Feldman, Stanley George *lawyer*
Fink, James Brewster *geophysicist, consultant*
Flint, Willis Wolfschmidt (Willi Wolfschmidt) *artist, sculptor*
Fontana, Bernard Lee *retired anthropologist, writer, consultant*
Fortman, Marvin *law educator, consultant*
Fountain, Ellen Allgaier *artist, educator*
Franks, Sondra Lou *music educator, organist*
Fredericksen, Dick Hartman *retired computer programmer*
Fritts, Harold Clark *dendrochronology educator, researcher*
Froman, Sandra Sue *lawyer*
Gaines, Kendra Holly *English language educator, editorial and writing consultant*
Gaither, William Samuel *civil engineering executive, consultant*
Galloway, James Malcolm *cardiologist*
†Ganapol, Barry Douglas *nuclear engineering educator, consultant, aerospace engineer, mechanical engineer*
Gantz, David Alfred *lawyer, university official*
Gerba, Charles Peter *microbiologist, educator*
Gibbs, David N(eil) *history and political science educator*
Gill, Rebecca LaLosh *aerospace engineer*
Girardeau, Marvin Denham *physics educator*
Goldfarb, Robert Paul *neurological surgeon*
Gonzales, Richard Joseph *lawyer*
Graham, Anna Regina *pathologist, educator*
Grams, Theodore Carl William *librarian, educator*
Grand, Marcia *civic worker*
Green, Robert Scott *biotechnology company executive*
Griffen, Agnes Marthe *library administrator*
Grimes, James Cahill *retired publishing executive, advertising executive*
Gruhl, James *energy scientist, artist*
Gutsche, Carl David *chemistry educator*
Hale, William Bryan, Jr., *newspaper editor*
Hamilton, Allan J. *neurosurgeon*
Hamilton, Ruth Hellmann *design company owner*
Haney, Robert Locke *retired insurance company executive*
Harrington, Roger Fuller *electrical engineering educator, consultant*
Harris, David Thomas *immunology educator*
Harrison, Edward Robert *physicist, educator, science administrator*
Hartley, Roger Edward *political science educator*
Hatch, Kenneth Deroy *gynecologist, oncologist*
Hattery, Robert Ralph *radiologist, educator*
Hawke, Robert Francis *dentist*
Hay, Richard Le Roy *geology educator*
†Hayashi, Kim *music educator*
Haynes, Caleb Vance, Jr., *geology and archaeology educator*
Hays, James Fred *geologist, educator*
Heaphy, John Merrill *lawyer*
Hechler, Pauline Urbano King *fundraiser*
Heins, Marilyn *college dean, pediatrics educator, writer*
Heller, Frederick *retired mining company executive*
†Hellon, Michael Thomas *tax consultant, political party official*
Herrnstadt, Richard Lawrence *American literature educator*
Hildebrand, John G(rant) *neurobiologist, educator*
Hill, Henry Allen *physicist, educator*
Hirsh, Robert Joel *lawyer*
Horan, Mary Ann Theresa *retired medical/surgical nurse*
Horne, William McHenry *management educator*
Houser, Harold Byron *epidemiologist*
Hoyt, Charlee Van Cleve *management executive*
Hubbard, William Bogel *planetary sciences educator*
†Huestis, Douglas William *physician, pathologist*
Hull, Herbert Mitchell *plant physiologist, researcher*
Humphrey, John Julius *university program director, historian, writer*
Hunten, Donald Mount *planetary scientist, educator*
Hunter, Tim Bradshaw *radiologist, educator*
Hutchinson, Charles Smith, Jr., *book publisher*
Hyams, Harold *lawyer*
Ingram, Helen Moyer *political science educator*
Irwin, Mildred Lorine Warrick *library consultant, civic worker*
†Isaak, G. Eugene *lawyer*
†Ismael, Jenann T. *philosopher, educator*
Jackson, Kenneth Arthur *physicist, researcher*
Jaffe, Steven Alan *real estate investor and management executive*
Jamison, Harrison Clyde *oil company executive, retired*
Jefferies, John Trevor *astrophysicist, observatory administrator*
Jeter, Wayburn Stewart *retired microbiology educator, microbiologist*
Johnson, John Gray *retired university chancellor*
†Johnson, Robert Bruce *company director*
Jones, Frank Wyman *management consultant, mechanical engineer*
Jones, John Stanley *urban development executive*
Jurkowitz, Daniel S. *lawyer, prosecutor, judge*
Kaliher, Michael Dennis *historian, librarian*
Kaltenbach, C(arl) Colin *dean, educator*
Kamilli, Robert Joseph *geologist*
Karson, Catherine June *database administrator*
Kassman, Andrew Lance *orthodontist*
Kaszniak, Alfred Wayne *neuropsychologist*
Katakkar, Suresh Balaji *hematologist, oncologist*
Kaucher, James William *lawyer*
†Kay, Margarita *anthropologist, consultant, nurse*
Kearney, Joseph Laurence *retired athletic conference administrator*
Kececioglu, Dimitri Basil *reliability engineering educator, consultant*
Kellogg, Frederick *historian*
Kennicutt, Robert Charles, Jr., *astronomer*
†Kershner, Robert M. *ophthalmologist, educator, research scientist*
Kerwin, William James *electrical engineering educator, consultant*
†Khouzam, Rami Nadim *physician*
Kim, Jeong-Kyun *metallurgist, researcher*
Kimble, William Earl *lawyer*
King, James Edward *retired museum director, consultant*
King, Joseph Willet *child psychiatrist*
Kingsolver, Barbara Ellen *writer*
Kischer, Clayton Ward *human embryologist, educator*
Kitchen, Charles William *lawyer*
Kittredge, John Russell *physician*
Kleese, William Carl *genealogy research consultant, financial services representative*
Koshkarian, Gregory Merrill *physician*
Kozolchyk, Boris *law educator, consultant*
Lacagnina, Michael Anthony *judge*
Laird, Wilbur David, Jr., *bookseller, editor*
Lamb, Willis Eugene, Jr., *physicist, educator*
Lanham, Sandra *conservationist*
Larson, L. Jean *educational administrator*
Lascelles, Susan *artist*
Lauver, Edith Barbour *nonprofit organization administrator*
Lavu, Rana Pratap *engineer*
Law, John Harold *biochemistry educator*
†Leafgren, John Robert *education educator*
Leavitt, Jerome Edward *childhood educator*
Ledin, Patricia Ann *nurse, nurse legal consultant*
Lee, Joyce Ann *computer educator*
Lehrling, Terry James *real estate broker*
Lemley, Diane Claire Beers *principal*
Lesher, Stephen Harrison *lawyer*
Levenson, Alan Ira *psychiatrist, physician, educator*
Levine, Norman *physician*
Lewis, Wilbur H. *educational management consultant*
†Lien, Yeong-Hau Howard *nephrologist, researcher*
Likins, Peter William *university administrator*
†Liu, Si *language educator*
Lomicka, William Henry *investor*

Smith, Stephen Austin *communications educator*
Steele, Kenneth Franklin, Jr., *science educator, director*
Van Patten, James Jeffers *education educator*
Waters, H. Franklin *federal judge*
Webb, Lynne McGovern *communication scholar, consultant*
Wilkie, Brian Francis *English educator*
Wilkins, Charles L. *chemist, educator*
Williams, Doyle Z. *university dean, educator*
Williams, Miller *poet, fiction writer, translator*
Wilson, Charles Banks *artist*

Forrest City
Stipe, John Ryburn *bank executive*
†Warren, Charlene *music educator*

Fort Smith
Ashley, Ella Jane (Ella Jane Rader) *medical technologist*
†Buchanan, L A *band director, music educator*
Clark, Susan Glasson *economics educator*
†Coleman, Michael Dortch *nephrologist*
Craig, David Clarke *financial advisor*
Decker, Josephine I. *health clinic official*
Drolshagen, Leo Francis, III, *radiologist, physician*
Flanders, Donald Hargis *manufacturing company executive*
Floyd, William R. *health facility administrator*
Gooden, Benny L. *school system administrator*
Harper, S. Birnie *business brokerage company owner*
Hembree, Hugh Lawson, III, *diversified holding company executive*
Hinkle, Richard Allen, Jr., *internist*
Howard, Jeff David *volunteer, retired military officer*
Husarik, Stephen *music educator*
†Karr, Charles *lawyer*
Larson, Larry *librarian*
Martin, Deborah Ann *intensive care nurse, educator*
Pendergrass, Ewell Dean *communications executive*
Smith-Leins, Terri L. *mathematics educator*
Snider, James Rhodes *radiologist*
†Walker, Rosilee *music educator*
Young, Robert A., III, *freight systems executive*

Garfield
Campbell, Patricia Ann *artist*

Gillett
Copley, Stephen Jean *minister*

Greenbrier
Reed, James David *retired minister, social worker*

Greenwood
Walters, Bill *former state senator, lawyer*

Hardy
†Carithers, Jill Marie *speech pathology/audiology services professional*

Harrison
Mathis, Kevan Eugene *journalist*
McKelvy, Nikki Kay *nurse*
Pinson, Jerry D. *lawyer*
Street, Susan Lee *elementary school educator*

Hartford
Roller Hall, Gayle Aline *gifted and talented education educator*

Heber Springs
Niehaus, Sherry M. *social welfare administrator*
Rawlings, Paul C. *retired government official*

Helena
Roscopf, Charles Buford *lawyer*

Hope
LeJeune, J. Kenneth *respiratory therapist*

Hot Springs National Park
Brown, Dennis James *industrial engineer, consultant*
Brunner, John Harry *surgeon*
Counts, Mary Lou *retired telephone company executive*
Craft, Kay Stark *real estate company executive*
Farris, Jefferson Davis *university administrator*
McDaniel, Ola Jo Peterson *retired social worker, educator*
Plummer, Jack Moore *psychologist*
Ray, Arliss Dean *retired environmental consultant*
Schroeder, Donald Perry *retired food products company executive*
Stein, Karen Louise *elementary music education educator, composer*
Tanenbaum, Bernard Jerome, Jr., *corporate executive*

Hot Springs Village
Hanard, Patricia Ann *family nurse practitioner*
†Smith, Preston *minister*
Smith, W. Preston *publishing executive, educator, real estate broker*

Humphrey
Wilson, Victoria Jane Simpson *farmer, nurse*

Huntsville
Carr, Gerald Paul *former astronaut, retired business executive, former marine officer*

Jefferson
Casciano, Daniel Anthony *biologist, educator*
Hotchkiss, Charlotte Evans *veterinarian, researcher*

Jonesboro
†Allen, William Julius *art history educator*
†Bartee, Neale *music educator, musician, conductor*
Calaway, Dennis Louis *insurance company executive, real estate broker, financial executive*
†Deacon, John C. *lawyer*
Elkins, Francis Clark *history educator, university official*
Fair, Everett Neil *public administrator*
Hanners, G(ary) Dale *retired psychological mental health professional*
Jones, Kenneth Bruce *surgeon*
Smith, Eugene Wilson *retired university president and educator*
Tims, Robert Austin *data processing official, pilot*
Womack, Tom D. *lawyer*

Lakeview
Roe, Richard C. *industry consultant, former home furnishings manufacturing executive*

Little Rock
Adams, Rose Ann *nonprofit administrator*
†Afouna, Mohsen M.I. *pharmaceutical scientist, researcher*
†Anand, Kanwaljeet Singh *pediatrician, researcher*
†Anderson, Joel E., Jr., *university administrator*
Anderson, Philip Sidney *lawyer*
Arnold, Morris Sheppard *judge*
Arnold, Richard Sheppard *federal judge*
Arnold, W. H. (Dub Arnold) *state supreme court chief justice*
†Basnakian, Alexei G. *biochemist, researcher*
Bass, Evelyn Elizabeth *educator*
Bates, Joseph Henry *physician, educator*
Beebe, Mike *state attorney general*
Bell, James Winfred *retired publishing executive*
Bissada, Nabil Kaddis *urologist, educator, researcher, author*
Bohannon, Charles Tad *lawyer*
Bowen, William Harvey *banker, lawyer*
†Brack, Robert Louis *retired music educator*
Braithwaite, Wilfred John *physics educator*
Branon, M. Susan *school system administrator*
Briscoe, David Lloyd *academic sociologist, educator*
†Brodsky, Michael Carroll *ophthalmologist, educator*
Bruce, Thomas Allen *physician, educator*
Burruss, Terry Gene *architect*
Caldwell, Bettye McDonald *education educator, director*
Campbell, George Emerson *lawyer*
Campbell, Gilbert Sadler *surgery educator, surgeon*
†Carpenter, Thomas Milton *lawyer*
Casey, Paula Jean *former prosecutor*
†Castleberry, Crata Lee *librarian*
†Catlett, S. Graham *lawyer*
Cheek, James Richard *ambassador*
Chesser, Thelma Jo Sykes *early childhood educator, administrator*
†Chiang, Chia-Chu *computer scientist, educator*
Cone, John Baxter *trauma surgeon, medical researcher*
Corbin, Donald L. *state supreme court justice*
Cox, Frank *advertising executive*
Cross, J. Bruce *lawyer*
Culp, William Combs *radiologist*
Darsey, Jerome Anthony (Jerry Darsey) *chemistry educator, consultant*
Dillahunty, Wilbur Harris *lawyer*
Dillard, William, II, *department store chain executive*
Drummond, Winslow *lawyer*
DuBois, Alan Beekman *art museum curator*
Ferguson, John Lewis *state historian*
Ferrer, Thomas John *surgeon*
Flournoy, Jacob Wesley *internal audit director*
Fogleman, John Albert *lawyer, retired judge*
Ford, Joe Thomas *telephone company executive, former state senator*
Frank, Ben William *lawyer, administrator*
Franks, Candace Ann *bank executive*
Fribourgh, James Henry *university administrator*
Glaze, Thomas A. *state supreme court justice*
Good, Mary Lowe (Mrs. Billy Jewel Good) *investment company executive, educator*
Goodner, Norman Wesley *governmental relations specialist*
†Green, Johnnie D. *government agency administrator, finance educator*
Greenberg, Paul *editor*
Greene, Tristan Dorian *state agency administrator*
Griffin, William Mell, III, *lawyer*
Gulley, Wilbur Paul, Jr., *retired savings and loan association executive*
Gunter, Russell Allen *lawyer*
Haley, John Harvey *lawyer*
Hanson, Jeanne Sutley *accountant*
†Hargis, David Michael *lawyer*
Harmon, Kay Madelon *occupational therapist*
Hart, Ronald Wilson *radiobiologist, educator, toxicologist, researcher, government research executive*
Hathaway, Charles E. *academic administrator*
Haught, William Dixon *lawyer, writer*
†Hearne, Mary *retired legal secretary, artist*
Heath, Richard Raymond *investment company executive, retired*
Henderson, Victor Warren *behavioral and geriatric neurologist, researcher, educator*
†Heuer, Sam Tate *lawyer*
†Hill, Jim B. *state legislator*
Hinson, Jack Allsbrook *research toxicologist, educator*
†Holzer, Linda Ruth *education educator*
Huckabee, Michael Dale *governor*
Hussman, Walter E., Jr., *publishing executive*
Itkin, David *music director, conductor*
†Jacobi, Sandra E. *molecular biologist, researcher*
Jansen, G. Thomas *dermatologist*
Jennings, Alston *lawyer*
Jones, Stephen Witsell *lawyer*
Kaza, Greg John *economist, educator*
Kemp, Stephen Frank *pediatric endocrinologist, educator, composer*
†Kumar, Udaya *urologist*
Lang, Nicholas Paul *surgeon*
Ledbetter, Calvin Reville, Jr., (Cal Ledbetter) *political science educator, university dean, former legislator*
Light, Jo Knight *stockbroker*
†Light, Robert Vann *lawyer*
Lipe, Linda Bon *lawyer*
Logan, Charles Wilbur *urologist*
Logan, Michael J. *veterinary epidemiology officer*
Lucy, Dennis Durwood, Jr., *neurologist, educator*
†Machaca, Khaled *cell biologist, educator*
Mackey, Diane Stoakes *lawyer*
Malone, David Roy *educational association administrator, director*
Marshall, William Taylor *lawyer*
May, Ronald Alan *lawyer*
McCaleb, Annette Watts *executive secretary*
McCoy, Stuart Sherman *manufacturing executive*
McSwain, Byrdie Engle *laboratory scientist, immunohemotologist*
†Means, Kevin Michael *health facility administrator*
Mehta, Jawahar Lal *cardiologist*
†Miller, Peter Alexander *lawyer*
Moore, W. David *charitable foundation executive, minister*
Mrak, Robert Emil *neuropathologist, educator, electron microscopist*
Mulkey, Jack Clarendon *library director*
Munoz, Olivier *artistic director*
Murphey, Arthur Gage, Jr., *law educator*
Nagarajan, Radhakrishnan *medical researcher*
Nelson, Edward Sheffield *lawyer, former utility company executive*
Nelson, Rex *communications executive*
†Nunn, Patarica Dian *poet, telephone directory operator*
Oliver, Ron *political party official*
O'Neal, Nell Self *retired principal*
Peters, Phillip Joseph *endocrinologist, educator*
Portis, Charles McColl *reporter, writer*
†Price, Peter Michael *molecular biology researcher, educator*
Priest, Sharon Devlin *secretary of state*
Quick, Edward Raymond *museum director, educator, curator*
Raney, Miriam Day *actress*
Reece, E. Albert *dean, obstetrician, gynecologist, perinatologist*
Reeves, Rosser Scott, III, *retired investment company executive*
†Roaf, Andree Layton *judge*
†Robison, Judy A. *grants officer, research administrator*
†Rolland, Philip Dale *pharmacist*
†Rollefson, Aimar Andre *physicist, department chairman*
Ryall, Marty *political organization administrator*
Scivally, Bart Murnane *accountant, auditor*
†Scott, Isaac Alexander, Jr., *lawyer*
Sherman, Jerome Kalman *retired anatomy educator*
Sherman, William Farrar *lawyer, former state legislator*
Simmons, Caroline Jennermann *biomedical researcher, writer*
Simmons, Debra Lynn *physician, educator*
†Simpson, James Marlon, Jr., *lawyer*
Smith, Anne Orsi *lawyer*
Smith, Griffin *editor*
†Smith, Mary Scott *elementary school educator, education educator*
Stockburger, Jean Dawson *lawyer*
†Stowe, Cindy D. *pharmacologist, educator*
Strode, Steven Wayne *physician*
Stroud, John Fred, Jr., *judge*
Suen, James Yee *otolaryngologist, educator*
†Swepston, Gene Fain *small business owner*
Thomas, Lestene *nurse*
Thomas, Thorp *lawyer*
Thornton, Ray *state supreme court justice, former congressman*
Townsend, James Willis *computer scientist*
Truemper, John James, Jr., *retired architect*
Truex, Dorothy Adine *retired university administrator*
Tucker, Gary Edward *botanist, wetland scientist, ecologist*
Vickery, William *arts administrator*
Voss, Linda I. *automotive company executive*
Walden, Catherine Jane *not-for profit director, social worker, consultant*
Ward, Harry Pfeffer *physician, retired university chancellor*
†Wenger, Galen Rosenberger *pharmacology educator*
Westbrook, Kent Coleman *surgeon, educator*
Whiteside, Charles B., III, *investment company executive*
Wight, Patricia Anne *neuroscience educator*
†Wilson, I. Dodd *dean*
Witherspoon, Carolyn Brack *lawyer*
Wright, Robert Ross, III, *law educator*
Wright, Susan Webber *judge*
†Yarberry, Lonnie Stephen *information scientist, director*
Zhang, Xuming *microbiology educator*

Lonoke
Ross, Philip Rowland *retired library director*

Lowell
†Hunt, J. B. *transportation executive*

Magnolia
Avard, Joseph L. *mathematician, educator*
Barnard, Anna Marion *county official*
Campbell, Robert Gordon *music educator*
Juniker, Anthony Michael *economic developer, consultant*
Reppert, James Eugene *mass communications educator*

Malvern
†Carpenter, Virgie Mae *retired librarian*
Dodd, Jerry Lee *lawyer*
Schultz, Marvin E. *historian, educator*

Mammoth Spring
†Smith, Jo Kay *language educator, school librarian*

Marianna
Carroll, Stephen Douglas *chemist, researcher*

Marion
Fogleman, John Nelson *lawyer*
Hughes, Michael Randolph *evangelist*

Marked Tree
†Everett, Mike *lawyer*

Mena
Eddleman, Floyd Eugene *retired English language educator*
Thrailkill, Daniel B. *lawyer*
Wiles, Betty Jane *accountant*

Monticello
Babin, Claude Hunter *history educator*
Ball, William Kenneth *lawyer*
†Dupree, Sandra Kay *librarian*
Ficklin, Robert Lee *soil scientist, research scientist*
Webster, Linda Jean *communications educator, media consultant*

Morrilton
†Denniston, Jeannie L. *lawyer*
Johnson, Bob W. *state senator*

Mountain Home
Baker, Robert Leon *naval medical officer*
†Hatcher, Milton Wright *psychologist, educator*
†Strother, Lane Howard *lawyer*

Newport
Thaxton, Marvin Dell *lawyer*

North Little Rock
Bailey, Charles Michael *clinical data analyst, pharmacist*
Biondo, Raymond Vitus *retired dermatologist*
†Clothier, Jeffrey Lane *neuropsychiatrist, educator*
George, James Edward *accountant*
Givens, John Kenneth *manufacturing executive*
Harrison, Angela Eve *manufacturing executive*
Patty, Claibourne Watkins, Jr., *lawyer*
Paulsen, Darlyne Evelyn *artist, residential and commercial architectural designer, interior decorator*
†Pyne, Jeffrey Mark *psychiatrist, researcher*

Paragould
Humway, Ronald Jimmie *accountant, former state agency administrator*

Paris
†Cleveland, Herschel *state representative*

Pine Bluff
†Economos, Cora Matheny *librarian*
Engle, Carole Ruth *aquaculture economics educator*
Holmes, Claire Coleman *real estate broker*
Jacks, David Clinton *urologist*
Jones, John Harris *lawyer*
†Lakew, Dejenie Alemayehu *mathematics educator*
Long, Edward Arlo *business consultant, retired manufacturing company executive*
Perschbacher, Peter Wesley *environmental scientist, educator*
Ramsay, Louis Lafayette, Jr., *lawyer, banker*
Seawell, William Thomas *former airline executive*
Strode, Joseph Arlin *lawyer*
Tai, Chong-Soo Stephen *political scientist, educator*
Walker, Richard Brian *chemistry educator*

Rogers
Angleman, Sharon Ann *journalist*
Spainhower, James Ivan *retired college president*
Wood, Charles Earl *obstetrician, gynecologist*

Russellville
†Burris, Rebecca Frances *nursing educator*
†Finan, Marcel Bassil *mathematics educator, researcher*
Jenkins, Ellen Janet (Jan Jenkins) *historian, history educator*
Morris, Lois Lawson *education educator*
†Morrow, Hubert W. *retired minister, retired theology studies educator, writer, educator*
White, Donna Rae *English educator, writer*

Scranton
Uzman, Betty Ben Geren *pathologist, retired educator*

Searcy
†Allen, Jimmy R. *religious studies educator*
Hughes, Teresa Lee *lawyer, minister*
†Hughes, Thomas Morgan, III, *lawyer*
Simpson, James Albert *surgeon*

Sherwood
Keaton, Frances Marlene *insurance sales representative*

Siloam Springs
Hill, James Robert *accountant*
Lewis, Cecil Dwain *minister*
McMennamy, Roger Neal *automotive executive*
Oliver, Gary Jackson *psychologist, educator*
†Roby, Warren B. *humanities educator*

Springdale
Cordell, Beulah Faye *special education educator*
Hill, Peggy Sue *principal*
Phillips, Linda Lou *pharmacist*
Pirozzoli, Heather Jo *food company professional*
Tyson, John H. *food products executive*

State University
†Comeau, Matthew J. *athletic training program director, educator*
Crawford, Jerry Lee *economics educator*
†Darwin, John Scott *language educator*
Johnson, Warren *foreign language educator*
Lindquist, Evan *artist, educator*
Miao, Jie *mathematics educator*
Milner, Clyde A., II, *historian*
Power, Mary Susan *political scientist, educator*
Rutherford, Mary Jean *laboratory administrator, science educator*
Schichler, Robert Lawrence *English language educator*
†Wyatt, Leslie *academic administrator*

Stuttgart
†Ashley-Iverson, Mary E. *retired librarian*

Subiaco
†Pirrera, Aaron Charles *priest, headmaster*

Warren
Claycomb, Hugh Murray *lawyer, author*

West Memphis
†Fogleman, Julian Barton *lawyer*

White Hall
Scott, Vicki Sue *school system administrator*

Winslow
Burggraf, Frank Bernard, Jr., *landscape architect, retired educator*

CALIFORNIA

Acampo
Eger, Marilyn Rae *artist*

Acton
Butman, Harry Raymond *clergyman, writer*

Agoura Hills
Chagall, David *journalist, writer*
Currie, Malcolm Roderick *aerospace and automotive executive, scientist*
deCiutiis, Alfred Charles Maria *oncologist, television producer*
Gressak, Anthony Raymond, Jr., *sales executive*
Havlicek, Michael *medical association administrator*
Merchant, Roland Samuel, Sr., *hospital administrator, educator*
Teresi, Joseph *publishing executive*

Alameda
Acker, Cindy Sherlinda Bernice *preschool administrator*
Bartalini, C. Richard *judge*
Billings, Thomas Neal *computer and publishing executive, management consultant, entrepreneur, author, journalist, software designer and inventor*
Brown, Timothy Donell *professional football player*
Callahan, Bill *professional football coach*
Carter, Roberta Eccleston *therapist, counselor*
Dahlquist, John Paul *economics educator*
Davis, Allen *professional football team executive*
Gannon, Rich *football player*
Grzanka, Leonard Gerald *writer, consultant*
Harbaugh, James Joseph *former professional football player*
Herrera, John *professional football team executive*
Herrick, Sylvia Anne *health service administrator*
Hudkins, James Allen *accountant*
†Kohgadai, Shukrullah *foundation administrator, editor*
Liu, Zenghe *research scientist*
Luther, John Stafford *biology educator, consultant*
Ngo, Tung Thanh *writer, photographer*
Potash, Jeremy Warner *public relations executive*
Rice, Jerry Lee *professional football player*
Stonehouse, James Adam *lawyer*
†Vaughn, Donna Becker *retired social worker*
Whorton, M. Donald *occupational and environmental health physician, epidemiologist*

Alamo
†Baker, William P. (Bill Baker) *former congressman*
Bouret, Pierre George *brokerage house executive*
Fleisher, Steven M. *lawyer*
Liggett, Lawrence Melvin *vacuum equipment manufacturing company executive*
Madden, Palmer Brown *lawyer*
Reed, John Theodore *writer, publisher*
Shiffer, James David *retired utility executive, consultant*
†Thiessen, Brian David *lawyer*
Whalen, John Sydney *management consultant*

Albany
Boris, Ruthanna *dancer, choreographer, dance therapist, educator*
Eastwood, DeLyle *chemist*
Ginzberg, Abigail *video producer*
†Schonbrun, Rena *librarian*
Schwimmer, Sigmund *food enzymologist*
Thomsen, Peggy Jean *educator, mayor, council member*

Alhambra
†Birch, Tobeylynn *librarian*
Duke, Donald Norman *publishing executive*
†Im, Jaemo *research scientist*
Kilburn, Kaye Hatch *medical educator*
Knighton, Barbara McLeod *occupational health specialist, risk specialist*
Liu, Zhong-Ping (Peter Liu) *natural medicine specialist, actor*
Mabee, John Richard *physician assistant, educator*
†Schuster, Darleen Victoria *director*

Aliso Viejo
Boeckmann, Alan L. *engineering company executive*
†Carroll, Adeline F. *special education educator*
Collazo, Sergio I. *computer company executive*
Dascenzi, Hazel Marie *real estate broker*
Dunn, Dana-Lori *counselor*
Harder, Wendy Wetzel *communications executive*
†Hawkins, Gregory J. *consumer products company executive*
Jeung, Albert *secondary school educator*
Trivelpiece, Craig Evan *computer electronics executive*

Alpine
Doliber, Darrel Lee *retired engineering consultant, hotel executive*
Greenberg, Byron Stanley *newspaper and business executive, consultant*

Alta Loma
Bordner, Gregory Wilson *chemical engineer*
Haskvitz, Alan Paul *elementary education educator, consultant*

Altadena
Bockus, Herman William, Jr., *artist, educator, writer*
Branin, Joan Julia *health services management educator*
Burden, Jean Prussing *poet, writer, editor*
Coles, Donald Earl *retired aeronautics educator*
Davis, Christopher *writer, retired writing educator*
Dobbins, Maggie Sonne *real estate investment company executive*
Dutton, Pauline Mae *fine arts and reference librarian*
Eisen, Glenn Philip *management consultant, teacher*
Fairbanks, Mary Kathleen *computer scientist, researcher*
Mkryan, Sonya *geophysicist, educator, research scientist*
Montgomery, Cranston Parker *retired lawyer*
Stewart, Homer Joseph *engineering educator*
Webster, Jeffery Norman *engineer*
Willans, Jean Stone *bishop, religious organization executive*
Willans, Richard James *bishop, religious organization executive*

American Canyon
†Downer, Eugene Debs, Jr., *editor, publisher*

Anaheim
Anderson, Garret *baseball player*
†Barkemeijer de Wit, Jeanne Sandra *graphic artist, illustrator, writer, multimedia consultant*
Baumgartner, Anton Edward *automotive sales professional*
Bennett, Genevieve *artist*
Carvajal, Jorge Armando *endocrinologist, internist*
†Elchert, Kenneth Clarence *aerospace engineer*
Fenton, Donald Mason *retired oil company executive*
Gregg, James R. *optometrist, educator*
Guajardo, Elisa *counselor, educator*
†Hicks, Eva Fern *retired music educator*
Hill, Harry David *city official, human resources professional*
Kallay, Michael Frank, II, *medical devices company official*
Kariya, Paul *professional hockey player*
†Laderman, Kathleen Ann *magazine publisher*
Lano, Charles Jack *retired financial executive*
Lawton, Michael James *entomologist, pest management specialist*
Linhart, Eddie Gene *aerospace executive*
†Miller, Jean Ruth *retired librarian*
Murray, Bryan Clarence *professional sports team executive*
Nelipovich, Sandra Grassi *artist*
O'Berry, Carl Gerald *former career officer, electrical engineer*
Phelan, Patrick John *engineer*
†Pringle, Curt *mayor*
Puzder, Andrew F. *restaurant executive, lawyer*
Sorenson, Sandra Louise *merchandising manager*
†Stegemeier, Richard Joseph *oil company executive*
Strudwick, Ivan H. *archaeologist*
Sykora, Petr *hockey player*
Thompson-Kramer, Helen Amelia *retired librarian*
Torbat, Akbar Esfahani *investment advisor, economics educator, researcher*
Uyehara, Otto Arthur *mechanical engineering educator emeritus, consultant*
†Vidergar, Teresa *music educator, musician*
Warring, Jerome Thomas *management consultant*
Watson, Oliver Lee, III, *aerospace engineering manager*

Anaheim Hills
Orlow-Townsend, Dawn Michelle *personal care industry executive*
Searle, Peter J. *lawyer*

Anderson
†Wittmann, Jane Gordon *volunteer*

Angwin
Maxwell, Donald Malcolm *clergyman, religious educator*

Antioch
Adams, Liliana Osses *music performer, harpist*
Archuleta, Keith Anthony *entrepreneur, business and management consultant*
Granik, Vladimir *mechanics researcher, educator*
Richards, Gerald Thomas *lawyer, consultant, educator, writer*
†Thomson, Sondra K. *secondary school educator*

Apple Valley
Beller, Gerald Stephen *professional magician, former insurance company executive*
Fisher, Weston Joseph *economist*
Lavallee, Charles Phillip *music educator, musician*
Mays, George Walter, Jr., *educational technology educator, consultant, tutor*

Aptos
Bohn, Ralph Carl *educational consultant, retired educator*
Garcia, Louis Lawrence *financial executive*
Heron, David Winston *librarian*
Hirsch, Bette G(ross) *college administrator, foreign language educator*
†Kehoe, Dennis Joseph *lawyer*
Mechlin, George Francis *electrical manufacturing company executive*
Trounstine, Philip John *communications consultant, institute administrator*

Arcadia
Anderson, Holly Geis *women's health facility administrator, commentator, educator*
Baltz, Patricia Ann (Pann Baltz) *elementary education educator*
Belnap, David F. *journalist*
Berkus, David William *venture capitalist*
Coulombe, Charles Aquila *writer, educator*
Danziger, Louis *graphic designer, educator*
†DeFato, Joan *librarian*
†Endrusick, Rose Marie *secondary school educator*
Fisher, Alan J. *otolaryngologist, plastic surgeon*
Freedman, Gregg *real estate appraisal company executive*
Gamboa, George Charles *retired oral surgeon, educator*
Gelber, Louise C(arp) *lawyer*
Imbus, Sharon Haughey *neuroscience nurse*
Kalm, Arne *investment banker*
Kenvin, Roger Lee *writer, retired English educator*
Khoo-Zeng, May-Sze (Macy Khoo-Zeng) *music educator*
†Margett, Bob G. *state legislator*
Mc Cormack, Francis Xavier *lawyer, former oil company executive*
Meysenburg, Mary Ann *principal*
†Morris, Gary Wayne *lawyer*
†Samaan, Yvette *language and psychology educator*
†Seitz, Charles Lewis *computer scientist and engineer*
Sloane, Beverly LeBov *writer, consultant*
Talsania, Bharat Himatlal *sales and marketing executive*
†Tressel, Violet Manooshaq
Ulrich, Peter Henry *banker*
Yen, Wen-Hsiung *language and music professional, educator*
Zimmerman, Amy J. *television producer, television director*

Arcata
Bowker, Lee Harrington *sociologist, educator, writer*
Emenhiser, JeDon Allen *political science educator, academic administrator*
Janssen-Pellatz, Eunice Charlene *healthcare facility administrator*
†Lamberson, Roland H. *environmental scientist, educator, mathematician*
McCrone, Alistair William *retired academic administrator*
Meyer, John Mark *political scientist, educator*
Swanson, Carolyn Rae *news reporter, counselor*
Zoellner, Robert William *chemistry educator*

Arroyo Grande
Bekey, Shirley White *psychotherapist*
Hoffmann, Jon Arnold *retired aeronautical engineer, educator*
Mott, Robert Lewis *writer, sound effects artist*
Oseguera, Palma Marie *retired career officer*
Thiel, Robert James *nutrition researcher*

Artesia
Dhamija, Kailash Raj *physician, consultant*

Atascadero
†Locke, Virginia Otis *writer*
Meyer, Lois Kathryn *graphic artist*
Ogier, Walter Thomas *retired physics educator*
Rios, Evelyn Deerwester *columnist, musician, artist, writer*

Atherton
Alexander, Theron *behavioral scientist, psychologist, writer*
Bales, Royal Eugene *philosophy educator*
Baran, Paul *computer executive*
Barker, Robert Jeffery *financial executive*
Coleman, Robert Griffin *geology educator*
Ferris, Robert Albert *lawyer, venture capitalist*
Gill, Stephen Paschall *retired physicist, mathematician*
Goodman, Sam Richard *electronics company executive*
Hogan, Clarence Lester *retired electronics executive*
Lane, Joan Fletcher *educational administrator*
Levinthal, Elliott Charles *physicist, educator*
Lowry, Larry Lorn *management consulting company executive*
Morel-Seytoux, Hubert Jean *civil engineer, educator*
Oakes, David Duane *medical educator*
Ritter, Mary L. *interior decorator*
Sollman, George Henry *venture capitalist*
Starr, Chauncey *research institute executive*

Auburn
Aro, Glenn Scott *environmental and safety executive*
Henrikson, Donald Merle *forensic pathologist*
Hess, Patrick Henry *chemist, researcher*
Jeske, Howard Leigh *retired life insurance company executive, lawyer*
Rothwell, Elaine B. *artist*
†Werner, Terry Scott *otorhinolaryngologist*

Avila Beach
Dvora, Susan (Susan Bernstein) *non-profit organization professional*
McLaren, Archie Campbell, Jr., *marketing executive*

Azusa
Durbin, Timothy Terrell *music educator*
Gray, Paul Wesley *university dean*
Kostoulas, Ioannis Georgiou *physicist*
Lau, Henry *mechanical engineer, consultant*
Sambasivam, Samuel E. *computer science and mathematics educator*
†Vest, R. Lamar *church administrator*

Bakersfield
Abdou, Wafik Andrew *anesthesiologist*
Akers, Tom, Jr., *cotton broker, consultant*
Arciniega, Tomas Abel *university president*
†Ashburn, Roy *state senator*
Bacon, Leonard Anthony *accounting educator*
Barmann, Bernard Charles, Sr., *lawyer*
Bradley, Katherine *librarian*
Farr, G(ardner) Neil *retired lawyer*
†Fiedler, Joseph Robert *mathematician, educator*
†Florez, Dean R. *state senator*
†Frazier, Jo Frances *religious organization administrator*
Gilmore, Gordon Ray *engineering executive*
Hall, Harvey L. *mayor, medical transportation company executive*
Hancock, Tapp *elementary school educator*
Kegley, Jacquelyn Ann *philosophy educator*
Kind, Kenneth Wayne *lawyer, real estate broker*
Lundquist, Gene Alan *cotton company executive*
Martin, George Francis *lawyer*
McAlister, Michael H. *architect*
†Mc Quiston, Jonathan Alan *county official*
Mosby, Dorothea Susan *retired municipal official*
Myren, Richard Albert *criminal justice consultant*
†Provencio, Roberto Enrique *music educator, music minister*
†Prunes, Fernando *plastic surgeon, educator*
Reep, Edward Arnold *artist*
Sawyer, Nelson Baldwin, Jr., *credit union executive*
†Senining, Randolph Del Castillo *internist, infectious diseases consultant*
Singer, George Milton *clinical psychologist*
†Sio, Jimmy Ong *embryologist*
†Thomason, Scott *automobile executive*
Thornton, Pauline Cecilia Eve Marie Suzanne *special education educator*
Watkins, Judith Ann *nurse administrator*
Wong, Wayne D. *nutritionist*
Zarra, Ernest Joseph, III, *educator, researcher*

Banning
Finley, Margaret Mavis *retired elementary school educator*
Gladden, Garnett Lee *educator, health consultant, psychologist*

Barstow
Nyborg, Kenneth Wayne *retired social sciences educator, small business owner*

Bayside
Cocks, George Gosson *retired chemical microscopy educator*

Beale AFB
Cross, Coy Franklin, II, *historian*

Beaumont
Mayer, Harvey Ethan *educator*

Bell
†Jackman, Hugh *actor*

Bell Canyon
Labbett, John Edgar *senior financial executive*

Bellflower
†Bermudez, Rudy *state official*
Davis, W. Howard *retired oral and maxillofacial surgeon*
de Thouars, Victor Ivan Charles *professional martial artist, educator*
Kivuls, Juris *plastic surgeon*
Lee, Paul Yue-Yan *surgeon*
Martin, Melissa Carol *radiological physicist*

Belmont
Endriz, John Guiry *electronics executive, consultant*
Hollis, Mary Frances *aerospace educator*
†MacLennan, Amy Marie *poet*
Morris, Bruce D. *technical writer, test engineer, educator, literary historian*
Musmann, Klaus *librarian*
Pava, Esther Shub *artist, educator*
†Sansing, Lucille H. *academic administrator*

Belmont Shore
Fleming, Jane Williams *retired educator, writer*

Belvedere
Benet, Carol Ann Levin *journalist, teacher*
Gale, Daniel Bailey *architect*
Hugenberg, Patricia Ellen Petrie *product designer*
Wallerstein, Robert Solomon *psychiatrist*

Belvedere Tiburon
†Allan, Walter Robert *lawyer*
Behrman, Richard Elliot *pediatrician, neonatologist, university dean*
Bremer, William Richard *lawyer*
Buell, Edward Rick, II, *lawyer*
Collins, Dennis Arthur *foundation executive*
FitzGerald, Desmond J. *philosopher, educator*
Hudnut, David Beecher *retired leasing company executive, lawyer*
Kilgore, Eugene Sterling, Jr., *former surgeon*
Kline, Donna S. *musician, educator*
Rayner, Arno Alfred *investment company executive, consultant*
Rice, Edward Earl *former government official, author*
Widman, Gary Lee *lawyer, former government official*

Ben Lomond
Johnson-Grauer, Lois Eileen *artist*
Sikora, James Robert *educational business consultant, financial analyst*

Benicia
Farnham, Timothy *training and education administrator*
le Conge, Monique Anne *library director, consultant*
Nelson, Elmer Kingsholm, Jr., *educator, writer, mediator, consultant*
Szabo, Peter John *investment company executive, financial planner, mining engineer, lawyer*
von Studnitz, Gilbert Alfred *state official*

Berkeley
†Abbott, Myles Bruce *pediatrician*
Abel, Carlos Alberto *immunologist*
Akerlof, George Arthur *economics educator*
Alhadeff, David Albert *economics educator*
Alter, Robert Bernard *comparative literature educator, critic*
Anderson, John Richard *entomologist, educator*
Anderson, William Scovil *classics educator*
Arveson, William Barnes *mathematics educator*
Attwood, David Thomas *physicist, educator*
Auerbach, Alan Jeffrey *economist, educator*
Baas, Jacquelynn *museum consultant, art historian*
Bagdikian, Ben Haig *journalist, emeritus university educator*
†Bajcsy, Ruzena Kucerova *computer science educator*
Bakalov, Bojko Nentchev *mathematician*
†Baldocchi, Dennis David *micrometeorologist*
Baldwin, Bruce Gregg *botany educator, researcher*
†Barnes, Thomas G. *law educator*
Barnett, R(alph) Michael *theoretical physicist, educational agency administrator*
Barrett, Reginald Haughton *biology educator, wildlife management educator*
Bartlett, Neil *chemist, emeritus educator*
Barton, Babette B. *lawyer, educator*
Bastrenta, Brigitte Elisabeth *school administrator*
†Baumrind, Diana *research psychologist*
Bellah, Robert Neelly *sociologist, educator*
Bendix, Jane *artist, author, anthropological illustrator*
Benedict, Burton *retired museum director, anthropology educator*
†Berck, Peter *agricultural economics educator*
Berdahl, Robert Max *academic administrator, historian, educator*
Berger, Stanley Allan *mechanical and biomechanical engineering educator*
Bergman, George Mark *mathematician, educator*
Bergman, Robert George *chemist, educator*
Bern, Howard Alan *science educator, research biologist*
Berring, Robert Charles, Jr., *law educator, law librarian, former dean*
Bevir, William Mark *political science educator*
Bickel, Peter John *statistician, educator*
Birdsall, Charles Kennedy *electrical engineer*
Bloom, Robert *language professional educator*
Blume, James Beryl *financial advisor*
Bogy, David B(euregard) *mechanical engineering educator*
Bolt, Bruce Alan *seismologist*
Booth, Stephen Walter *English language educator*
Bowker, Albert Hosmer *retired university chancellor*
Bragg, Robert Henry *physicist, educator*
Brandes, Stanley Howard *anthropology educator, writer*
Brenner, Sydney *molecular biologist, researcher*
Breslauer, George William *political science educator*
Brocchini, Ronald Gene *architect*
Brooke, Tal (Robert Taliaferro) *writer*
Browne, G.M. Walter Shawn *journalist, publisher, organizer*
†Buchanan, Bob Branch *education educator*
Buckland, Michael Keeble *librarian, educator*
Bucklin, Louis Pierre *business educator, consultant*
Budaev, Bair V. *mathematician, researcher*
†Budinger, Thomas Francis *radiologist, educator*
Buffler, Patricia Ann *epidemiologist, educator, retired dean*
Burger, Edmund Ganes *architect*
Burnside, Mary Beth *biology educator, researcher*
Buxbaum, Richard M. *law educator, lawyer*
Cairns, Elton James *chemical engineering educator*
Callenbach, Ernest *writer, editor*
Canfield, Judy S. *psychologist*
Cantor, Rusty Sumner *artist*
Cardwell, Kenneth Harvey *architect, educator*
Carmichael, Ian Stuart Edward *geologist, educator*
Carpenter, Kenneth John *nutrition educator*
Casida, John Edward *entomology educator*
Casida, Kati *artist*
Cerny, Joseph, III, *chemistry educator, scientific laboratory administrator, university dean and official*
Chamberlain, Owen *nuclear physicist*
Chamberlin, Michael John *biochemistry educator*
Chandler, David *scientist, educator*
Cheit, Earl Frank *economist, educator*
†Chern, Shiing-Shen *mathematics educator*
Chew, Geoffrey Foucar *physicist*
Chew, Linda Lee *fundraising management executive*
Choper, Jesse Herbert *law educator, university dean*
Chopra, Anil Kumar *civil engineering educator*
Chorin, Alexandre Joel *mathematician, educator*
Cieslak, William *academic administrator*
Clarke, John *physics educator*
Cohn, Theodore Elliot *optometry educator, vision scientist , bioengineer*
Cole, Robert E. *sociologist, educator*
Colson, Elizabeth Florence *anthropologist*
†Consey, Kevin Edward *museum administrator*
Cook, Geoffrey Arthur *editor, writer*
Cooper, Michael David *information systems educator*
Cooper, William Secord *information science educator*
Costa, Gustavo *Italian studies scholar*
Craig, William *philosopher, educator*
Crews, Frederick Campbell *humanities educator, writer*
†Crocker, Richard Lincoln *retired music educator*
†Davis, Maggie L. *elementary teacher*
Day, Lucille Lang *museum administrator, educator, writer*
Deck, Richard Allen *political scientist, consultant, writer, human rights activist*
†De Jonghe, Lutgard C. *educator*
Diamond, Marian Cleeves *anatomy educator*
Diamond, Richard Martin *nuclear chemist*
Dickinson, Michael *physiologist*
†Dietrich, William E. *geophysicist, educator*
Dornfeld, David Alan *engineering educator*
Dresher, Paul Joseph *composer, music educator, performer*
Duhl, Leonard *psychiatrist, educator*
Dundes, Alan *writer, folklorist, educator*
†Edelman, Lauren B. *law educator, sociologist, educator*
Eisenberg, Melvin A. *law educator*
Eisenbud, David *mathematics educator*
Ellis, Ella Thorp *writer, retired educator*
Enoch, Jay Martin *optometrist, vision scientist*
Falkner, Frank Tardrew *physician, educator*
Feeley, Malcolm McCollum *law educator, political scientist*
Felix, Susan Duhan *consultant, community development specialist, artist*
Finnie, Iain *mechanical engineer, educator*
Fleming, Graham Richard *chemistry educator*
†Fletcher, Daniel A. *adult education educator*
Foster, George McClelland, Jr., *anthropologist, educator*
Fowler, Thomas Kenneth *physicist*
Fréchet, Jean Marie Joseph *chemistry educator*
Freedman, David Amiel *statistics educator, consultant*
Freedman, Mervin Burton *psychologist, educator*
Freeling, Michael Richard *genetics educator, researcher*
Frickey, Philip Paul *law educator*
Frisch, Joseph *mechanical engineer, educator, consultant*
Fuerstenau, Douglas Winston *mineral engineering educator*
Gaillard, Mary Katharine *physics educator*
Garrison, William Louis *civil engineering educator*
Gelpi, Donald Louis *theology studies educator*
Genn, Nancy *artist*
Getz, Wayne Marcus *biomathematician, researcher, educator*
Gifford, Barry Colby *writer*
Gilbert, Neil Robin *social work educator, writer, consultant*
Gilbert, Richard Joseph *economics educator*
Glaser, Donald Arthur *physicist*
Goldhaber, Gerson *physicist, educator*
Graham, Susan Lois *computer science educator, consultant*
Greif, Ralph *mechanical engineer, educator*
Grimes, Ruth Elaine *city planner*
Grossman, Elmer Roy *pediatrician*
Grossman, Lawrence Morton *nuclear engineering educator*
Guest, Barbara *author, poet*
Hack, Elizabeth *artist*
Hafey, Joseph Michael *health association executive*
Hahn, Erwin Louis *physicist, educator*
Halbach, Edward Christian, Jr., *law educator, educator*
Haley, George Patrick *lawyer*
Haller, Eugene Ernest *materials scientist, educator*
Hamilton, Randy Haskell *city manager*
Harlan, Robert Dale *information studies educator, academic administrator*
Harris, Michael Gene *optometrist, educator, lawyer*
Hartman, Robert Leroy *artist, educator*
Hazen, Terry Clyde *microbial ecologist, educator*
Heathcock, Clayton Howell *chemistry educator, researcher*
Helson, Henry Berge *publisher, retired mathematics educator*
Henkin, Leon Albert *mathematician, educator*
†Hermalin, Benjamin E. *economics educator*
Herr, Richard *history educator*
Hertelendy, Paul *critic, writer, poet*
Hill, Lorie Elizabeth *psychotherapist*
†Hinshaw, Stephen P. *education educator*
Hodges, David Albert *electrical engineering educator*
Hodges, Frederick Mansfield *historian*
Hoffman, Darleane Christian *chemistry educator*
Horvath, Arpad *engineering educator*
†Hout, Michael *sociologist, educator*
Howell, Francis Clark *paleo-anthropologist*
Hu, Teh-wei *economics educator*
Hyman, Edward Jay *forensic psychologist, cognitive and information scientist, consultant, educator, television news commentator*
Imbrie, Andrew Welsh *composer, educator*
Jackson, J(ohn) David *physicist, educator*
Jensen, Arthur Robert *psychology educator*
Johnson, Mary Katherine (Katie Johnson) *elementary education educator*
Johnston, Harold S(ledge) *chemistry educator*
Jones, Patricia Bengtson *sculptor*
Josephian, Jenny Adele *acupuncturist, artist*
Judge, George Garrett *economics educator*
Kadish, Sanford Harold *law educator*
Kaplansky, Irving *mathematician, educator, research institute director*
Karlinsky, Simon *language educator, writer*
Karp, Richard Manning *computer sciences educator*
Kasten, Karl Albert *painter, printmaker, educator*
Kastenberg, William Edward *engineering educator, science educator*
Kay, Herma Hill *education educator*
Kay, Paul de Young *linguist*
Kerman, Joseph Wilfred *musicologist, critic*
Kerr, Clark *academic administrator emeritus*
Kerth, Leroy T. *physics educator*
Kessler, Seymour *clinical psychologist, consultant*
Kirch, Patrick Vinton *anthropology educator, archaeologist*
Kleiman, Vivian Abbe *filmmaker*
Klinman, Judith Pollock *biochemist, educator*
Koshland, Daniel Edward, Jr., *biochemist, educator*
Kuh, Ernest Shiu-Jen *electrical engineering educator*
LaBelle, Thomas Jeffrey *academic administrator*
Lambert, Nadine Murphy *psychologist, educator*
Landau, Martin *political science educator*
Langridge, Robert *scientist, educator*
Lashof, Joyce Cohen *public health educator*
Lee, Ronald Demos *demographer, economist, educator*
Lehmann, Erich Leo *statistics educator*
Leitmann, George *mechanical engineer, educator*
Leonard, Thomas *dean, educator, librarian*
Leopold, Luna Bergere *geology educator*
Lesser, Wendy *editor, writer, consultant*
Lester, William Alexander, Jr., *chemist, educator*
Letiche, John Marion *economist, educator*
Levine, Mark David *science administrator, director*
Levine, Michael Steven *science educator*
Lewis, Edwin Reynolds *biomedical engineering educator*
Lichterman, Martin *history educator*
Lidicker, William Zander, Jr., *zoologist, educator*
Linn, Stuart Michael *biochemist, educator*
Lipps, Jere Henry *paleontology educator*
Little, Angela Capobianco *nutritional science educator*
Litwack, Leon Frank *historian, educator*
†Liu, Xin *education educator*
Long, Anthony Arthur *classics educator*
Lu, Adolph *physicist, researcher*
Lyons, Richard Kent *economics educator*
Ma, Chung-Pei Michelle *astronomer, educator*
Mace, Susan Lidgate *comparative literature educator, researcher*
Maisel, Sherman Joseph *economist, educator*
Margen, Sheldon *public health educator*
Marletta, Michael A. *biochemistry educator, researcher, protein chemist*
Marquard, Steven Sandel *economist, financial consultant*
Martin, G. Steven *biochemist, educator*
Maslach, Christina *psychology educator*
Maslach, George James *former university official*
†Mason, Mary Ann *college program director, lawyer, computer consultant*
Matsumura, Vera Yoshi *pianist*
Matthews, Mildred Shapley *scientific editor, freelance writer*
†Maughan, Patricia Davitt *librarian, consultant*
May, Adolf Darlington *civil engineering educator*
Mayer, Thomas *economics educator*
McCoy, Charles Sherwood *university president, former theology educator*
McFadden, Daniel Little *economist, educator*
McKee, Christopher Fulton *physicist, educator, astronomer, educator*
†McKown, Clark Atwater *psychologist*
McLaughlin, Sylvia Cranmer *community volunteer, environmentalist*
†McMains, Sara A. *engineering educator*
McNamara, John Stephen *artist, educator*
McNulty, John Kent *lawyer, educator*
McPhail-Geist, Karin Ruth *secondary education educator, realtor, musician*
†McWhorter, John Hamilton *linguist, educator*
Meltzer, David *author, musician, educator*
Merchant, Carolyn *environmental history educator*
Merrill, Richard James *educational director*
Messinger, Sheldon L(eopold) *law educator*
Middlekauff, Robert Lawrence *history educator, administrator*
Miles, Raymond Edward *former university dean, organizational behavior and industrial relations educator*
Miller, Adam David *poet, publishing executive*
Miller, William Hughes *theoretical chemist, educator*
†Milosz, Czeslaw *poet, writer, educator*
Minudri, Regina Ursula *librarian, consultant*
Mishkin, Paul J. *lawyer, educator*
Miyasaki, George Joji *artist*
Mohle-Boetani, Janet Carol *epidemiologist*
Monismith, Carl Leroy *civil engineering educator*
Moore, Frank James *artist, educator*
Moran, Rachel *lawyer, educator*
Mudge, Lewis Seymour *theologian, educator, university dean*
Muir, William Ker, Jr., *political science educator*
Muller, Richard Stephen *electrical engineer, educator*
Muscatine, Charles *English educator, author*
Myers, Miles Alvin *educator, educational association administrator*
Nader, Laura *anthropology educator*
†Nagler, Michael Nicholas *peace and conflict studies educator*
Nazaroff, William W. *engineering educator*
Newman, John Scott *chemical engineer, educator*
Norgaard, Richard Bruce *economist, educator, consultant*
†Norris, Carl William *psychologist*
†O'Brien, Kevin Joseph *political scientist, educator*
Odermatt, Diana B. *development consultant*
†Ogden, Dunbar Hunt *author, theatre educator*
Ogg, Wilson Reid *lawyer, judge, poet, lyricist, curator, publisher, educator, philosopher, social scientist, parapsychologist*
Osserman, Robert *mathematician, educator, writer*
Ott, David Michael *engineering company executive*
Pagni, Patrick John *mechanical and fire safety engineering science educator*
†Pakter, Walter Jay *legal scholar and educator, aviation lawyer*
Pavlath, Attila Endre *research chemist*
Pawsey, Stuart Frederick *structural engineer, retired*
Penzien, Joseph *structural engineering educator*
Perez-Mendez, Victor *physics educator*
Perloff, Jeffrey Mark *agricultural and resource economics educator*
Perry, Dale Lynn *chemist*
Peterson, Roland E. *business management company executive*
Pham, Quang Xuan *statistics educator*
Phillips, Norman Edgar *chemistry educator*
Pigford, Thomas Harrington *nuclear engineering educator*
Pister, Karl Stark *engineering educator*
Polak, Elijah *engineering educator, computer scientist*
Policoff, Leonard David *physician, educator*
†Polos, Iris Stephanie *artist, art educator*
Pope, Alexander H. *former lawyer, county assessor and non-profit administrator*
Post, Robert Charles *law educator*
†Poulos, Paige M. *public relations executive*
Prausnitz, John Michael *chemical engineer, educator*
†Price, Lynn Kauffman *environmental scientist*
Pyle, Walter K. *lawyer*
Quigley, John Michael *economist, educator*
Quinn, Nigel William Trevelyan *scientist, engineer*
Radke, Clayton J. *chemical engineer, educator*
†Rakas, Jasenka Milan *aerospace engineer, researcher, aerospace engineer, educator*
Ralston, Lenore Dale *academic policy and program analyst*
Ranney, Austin (Joseph Ranney) *political science educator*
Rapoport, Sonya *artist*
Rappaport, Stuart Ramon *lawyer*
Rasmussen, John Oscar *nuclear research scientist*
Ratch, Jerry *writer*
Rauch, Irmengard *linguist, educator*
Rausser, Gordon C(lyde) *agricultural and resource economics educator*
Raymond, Kenneth Norman *chemistry educator, research chemist*
Reich, Michael *economics educator*
†Reidhaar, Donald Laverne *lawyer*
Rex, Walter Edwin, III, *humanities educator*
Rice, Robert Arnot *school administrator*
†Richardson, John David *physicist*
Rippe, Lynn E. *contract administrator*
Ritchie, Robert Oliver *materials science educator*
Roland, Gerard *economics educator*
Rosenzweig, Mark Richard *psychology educator*
Ross, Julia *lawyer*
†Rudin, Norah *forensic DNA consultant, science writer*
Russell, Charlie L. *writer*
Schachman, Howard Kapnek *molecular biologist, educator*
Scheiber, Harry N. *law educator*
†Scheper-Hughes, Nancy Marie *anthropologist, writer, education educator*
Scott, Peter Dale *writer, retired English language educator*
Seitz, Walter Stanley *cardiovascular research consultant*
Selvin, David F. *retired editor, journalist*
Selz, Peter Howard *art historian, educator*
Séquin, Carlo H. *computer science educator*
†Shaffer, Juliet Popper *statistics educator*
†Shannon, Thomas Frederic *German language educator*
Shen, Yuen-Ron *physics educator*
Shortell, Stephen Michael *dean, health services researcher*
Shugart, Howard Alan *physicist, educator*
†Sim, Alexander *computer scientist, researcher*
Simpson, David William *artist, educator*
Sloane, Thomas O. *speech educator*
Smith, Alan Jay *computer science educator, consultant*
Smolensky, Eugene *economics educator*
Somorjai, Gabor Arpad *chemist, educator*
†Sorensen, Linda *lawyer*

Spacek, Sissy (Mary Elizabeth Spacek) *actress*
Spielberg, Steven *motion picture director, producer*
Spivak, Jacque R. *bank executive*
Stambler, Irwin *publishing executive*
Stefano, Joseph William *film and television producer, writer*
Stern, Sandor *film writer, director*
Stolinsky, David C. *physician*
Stowe, Madeleine *actress*
Streep, Meryl (Mary Louise Streep) *actress*
Sutherland, Donald *actor*
Sutherland, Kiefer *actor*
Tamkin, Curtis Sloane *real estate development company executive*
†Theron, Charlize *actress*
Thompson, Larry Angelo *motion picture and TV producer, lawyer, personal manager, writer*
†Thompson, Richard Dickson *lawyer*
†Toffel, Alvin Eugene *corporate executive, business and governmental consultant*
Travolta, John *actor*
Van Ark, Joan *actress*
Van Dyke, Dick *actor, comedian*
†Vaughn, Vince *actor*
†Verhoeven, Paul *film director*
Victor, Robert Eugene *real estate corporation executive, lawyer*
Walker, William Tidd, Jr., *investment banker*
Ward, David Schad *screenwriter, film director*
Ward, Sela *actress*
†Warren, Steve *lawyer*
Waters, John *film director, writer, actor*
Weaver, Sigourney (Susan Alexandra Weaver) *actress*
Weber, Jeffrey Randolph *record producer*
Weinstein, Irwin Marshall *internist, hematologist*
Weir, Peter Lindsay *film director*
Weisz, Rachel *actress*
Weitz, Bruce (Peter Weitz) *actor*
†Wiatt, James Anthony *theatrical agency executive*
Widaman, Gregory Alan *financial executive, accountant*
Williamson, Kevin *writer, producer, director*
†Willis, Walter Bruce *actor, singer, writer*
Willson, James Douglas *aerospace executive*
†Wilson, Luke *actor*
†Wilson, Owen *actor*
Winkler, Irwin *motion picture producer*
†Winningham, Mare *actress*
Winthrop, John *wines and spirits company executive*
†Wirtschafter, David *agent*
Witherspoon, Reese (Laura Jean Witherspoon) *actress*
Wolper, David Lloyd *motion picture and television executive*
†Wu, Yusen (John Woo) *film director*
Yaryan, Ruby Bell *psychologist*
†Yorn, Rick *talent agent*
Young, Robert Edward *computer company executive*
Yuan, Robin Tsu-Wang *plastic surgeon*
†Zanuck, Richard Darryl *motion picture company executive*
Zarem, Abe Mordecai *management consulting executive*
Zellweger, Renee *actress*
Zeta-Jones, Catherine *actress*

Big Bear City
Pipes, Doris Perry *secondary school educator, consultant*

Big Bear Lake
Brueske, Charlotte *poet, composer*
Prewoznik, Jerome Frank *lawyer*

Big Sur
Cross, Robert Louis *realtor, land use planner, writer, landscape architect, appraiser*
†Wong, Joseph H. *religious organization administrator, theology studies educator*

Bishop
Clark, D. Scott *surgeon*

Blue Jay
Gourley, James Walter, III, *airport executive*

Bodega
Hedrick, Wally Bill *artist*

Bodega Bay
Clegg, James Standish *physiologist, biochemist, educator*
Cohen, Anne Carolyn Constant *biologist*
Cohen, Daniel Morris *museum administrator, marine biology researcher*
†Freeman, Donna Cook *small business owner*
†Fruiht, Dolores Giustina *artist, educator, poet*
Hand, Cadet Hammond, Jr., *marine biologist, educator*
King, Leland W. *architect*

Bolinas
Harris, Paul *sculptor*
Okamura, Arthur Shinji *artist, educator, writer*
Remen, Rachel Naomi *pediatrician, integrative medicine physician*

Bonita
Covarrubias-Lugo, Irma *physician*
Curtis, Richard Earl *former naval officer, former company executive, business consultant*
Deane, Debbe *psychologist, journalist, editor, consultant*
†Kline, Paul Conley *lawyer*

Bonsall
Jeffredo, John Victor *aerospace engineer, manufacturing company executive, inventor*

Boonville
Hanes, John Ward *sculptor, civil engineer consultant*

Borrego Springs
†Scallen, Terence Joseph *retired medical educator*
†Strong, John Oliver *plastic surgeon, educator*

Boulevard
Charles, Blanche *retired elementary education educator*

Bradbury
Ackerman, Page *librarian, educator*

Brawley
Jaquith, George Oakes *ophthalmologist*

Brea
Brown, Ronald Malcolm *engineering corporation executive*
†Daucher, Lynn M. *state official*
†Ellis, Cynthia Bueker *musician, educator*
Hall, Linda Sue Bohannon *special education educator*
Oh, Tai Keun *business educator*
Painchaud, Phillip Andre *metrologist*
Pierpoint, Karen Ann *marriage, family and child therapist*
Schlose, William Timothy *health care executive*
Shen, Gene Giin-Yuan *organic chemist*
Tamura, Cary Kaoru *consultant*

Brentwood
Baker, Paul Thornell *anthropology educator*
Defield, Charleen K. *accountant*
Fridley, Saundra Lynn *private investigator*
Groseclose, Wanda Westman *retired elementary school educator*
†Houston, Guy Spencer *state legislator*
Peters, William Frank *art educator*
Rawson, Eric Gordon *optical engineer*

Brisbane
Daniels, Caroline *publishing company executive*
Orban, Kurt *foreign trade company executive*

Buellton
Porter, Bruce Jackman *military engineer, computer software engineer, application developer, investment broker, civil engineer*

Buena Park
Kristy, James E. *financial management consultant*
McClendon, Irvin Lee, Sr., *office services and computer consultant, writer and editor*
Turkus-Workman, Carol Ann *educator*
Wiersema, Harold LeRoy *aerospace engineer*

Burbank
Ajalat, Sol Peter *lawyer*
Ancier, Garth Richard Richard *television broadcast executive*
Bader, Diedrich *actor*
†Baker, Rick *make-up artist*
†Berman, Bruce *entertainment company executive, television producer*
†Bishop, Debbie *publishing executive, book designer, writer*
Bower, Richard James *minister*
Braverman, Alan N. *lawyer*
†Bright, Kevin S. *producer*
Brogliatti, Barbara Spencer *television and motion picture executive*
Chiarelli, Robert Charles *audio engineer*
†Clapton, Eric *musician*
†Cook, Richard W. *motion picture company executive*
†Costner, Kevin *actor*
†Crane, David *producer*
†Daniels, Susanne *broadcast executive*
†DiBonaventure, Lorenzo *film company executive*
†Donner, Richard *film director, producer*
Eisner, Michael Dammann *entertainment company executive*
†Fishburne, Laurence, III, *actor*
Franco, James *actor*
Frank, Amélie Lorraine *marketing professional*
†Gibson, Mel *actor, film director, producer*
Gold, Stanley Phillip *diversified investments executive*
Goldstein, Kenneth F. *entertainment executive, software publisher*
Ha, Chong Wan *information technology executive*
†Henley, Don *singer, drummer, songwriter*
Iger, Robert A. *broadcast executive*
Janney, Allison *actress*
†Jonas, Tony *television executive*
Joseff, Joan Castle *manufacturing executive*
†Kellner, Jamie *broadcasting executive*
†Kinney, Kathy *actress*
†Lee, Paulette Wang *lawyer*
†Leno, Jay (James Douglas Muir Leno) *television personality, comedian, writer*
Levinson, Barry L. *film director*
Marinace, Kenneth Anthony *financial advisor*
†Meyer, Barry Michael *motion picture executive*
Michel, Donald Charles *editor*
Miller, Clifford Albert *merchant banker, business consultant*
†Mitchell, Joni (Roberta Joan Anderson) *singer, songwriter*
Murphy, Peter E. *corporate financial officer*
Neill, Ve *make-up artist*
†Nevis, Tillam *lawyer*
Nielsen, Kenneth Ray *academic administrator*
Raulinaitis, Pranas Algis *electronics executive, consultant*
Rawlinson, Joseph Eli *foundation executive, lawyer*
Razouk, Rashad Elias *retired chemistry educator*
Renner, Andrew Ihor *surgeon*
†Robertson, Richard Trafton *entertainment company executive*
Roth, Joe *motion picture company executive*
Roth, Peter *broadcast executive*
†Samaha, Elie *producer, film company executive, business owner*
†Sassa, Scott M. *broadcast executive*

Schacter, David Martin *judge*
†Schneider, Peter *film company executive*
†Schumacher, Joel *director, writer*
†Schumacher, Thomas *film company executive*
Shriver, Maria Owings *news correspondent*
†Silver, Joel *film producer*
Steel, Shawn *political party official*
Stiles, Ryan *actor*
Thornton, Cameron Mitchell *financial planner*
†Thyret, Russ *recording industry executive*
Tran, Lawrence Delano *family physician, educator*
Wachowski, Andy *film director*
Wachowski, Larry *film director*
Walters, Kenneth C. *retired educator*
†Wells, John Marcum *producer, writer*
Wise, Woodrow Wilson, Jr., *retired small business owner*
†Wonder, Stevie (Stevland Morris) *singer, musician, composer*
†Zucker, Jeffrey *broadcast executive*

Burlingame
Cotchett, Joseph Winters *lawyer, author*
Denten, Christopher Peter *lawyer*
Diebel, Gary R. *architect*
Doyle, William B. *investment executive*
Hubbard, Gregory Scott *physicist*
Mendelson, Lee M. *film company executive, writer, producer, director*
Most, Nathan *mutual fund executive*
†Muller, Richard Forrest *information technology executive*
Ocheltree, Richard Lawrence *lawyer, retired forest products company executive*
Schwantes, Robert Sidney *international relations executive*

Calabasas
Andrews, Ralph Herrick *television producer*
Bursten, Stuart Lowell *physician, biochemist*
Christensen, Donn Wayne *insurance executive*
Goldfield, Emily Dawson *finance company executive, artist*
Grimwade, Richard Llewellyn *lawyer*
Isham, Mark *composer, jazz musician*
Landau, Martin *actor*
Laney, Michael L. *manufacturing executive*
Moule, William Nelson *electrical engineer, consultant*
Mozilo, Angelo R. *diversified financial services company executive*
Sloan, Michael Dana *information systems specialist*
Tennen, Ken *lawyer*

Caliente
de Fonville, Paul Bliss *monument and library administrator*

California City
Friedl, Rick *lawyer, former academic administrator*
Paiva, Clifford Anthony *physicist, consultant*

Calimesa
†McNulty, James Francis, Jr., *lawyer, industrial designer*

Calistoga
Ogg, Robert Danforth *corporate executive*

Camarillo
Alexander, John Charles *editor, writer*
Cobb, Roy Lampkin, Jr., *retired computer sciences corporation executive*
Cobb, Shirley Ann Dodson *public relations consultant, journalist*
†Ford, Paul Francis *theology studies educator, musician*
Hall, Cynthia Jean *music educator, author, composer, musician*
Halperin, Kristine Briggs *insurance sales and marketing professional*
Leerabhandh, Marjorie Bravo *chemist, educator*
Lingl, James Peter *lawyer*
MacAlister, Robert Stuart *petroleum engineer, consultant*
MacDonald, Norval (Norval Woodrow MacDonald) *safety engineer*
McConnel, Richard Appleton *aerospace company official*
Rieger, Elaine June *retired nursing administrator*
Rush, Richard R. *academic administrator*
Sullivan, Michael Evan *investment and management company executive*

Cambria
Harden, Marvin *artist, educator*
Morse, Richard Jay *human resources and organizational development consultant, manufacturers' representative company executive*
†Price, Stephen Earl *artist*
Salaverria, Helena Clara *retired language educator*
Stephens, John Richard *writer*
Stotter, James, II, *lawyer, legal consultant*

Camino
Van Klaveren, Nico *engineer, consultant*

Camp Pendleton
Prato, Kimberly *public affairs officer*

Campbell
Beizer, Lance Kurt *lawyer*
Kaipa, Prasad Lakshmi Narasimha *educational researcher and consultant*
Kendall, Burton Nathaniel *software designer*
Levy, Salomon *mechanical engineer*
Mizer, Richard Anthony *technology company executive*
Nicholson, Joseph Bruce *real estate developer*
Ross, Hugh Courtney *electrical engineer*
Tran, Nam Van *health education specialist*

Campo
Jermini, Ellen *educational administrator, philosopher*

Canoga Park
†Adams, Anne Claire *lawyer*
Brandenburg, Stanley C. *financial company executive*
Dickey, Gary Alan *minister*
†Egermeier, Robert Paul *retired engineer, retired lawyer*
Lederer, Marion Irvine *cultural administrator*
†Meier, Sue A. *marriage and family therapist, director*
Rosenfeld, Sarena Margaret *artist*

Canyon Country
Hawkins, Dale Cicero *aviator, educator, engineer*

Canyon Lake
Schilling, Frederick Augustus, Jr., *geologist, consultant*

Capistrano Beach
Sheedy, Evelyn Mardelle *nonprofit corporation executive*

Capitola
Peduto, Ralph *actor, author, producer*
Wolff, Jean Walton *writer, artist*

Carlsbad
Allison, Stephen Galender *broadcast executive*
Anderson, Paul Irving *management executive*
†Benjamin, Theresa Mary *psychotherapist, writer*
Chopra, Deepak *preventive medicine physician, writer*
Conway, Daniel Edward *management consultant*
Crooke, Rosanne M. *pharmacologist*
Crooke, Stanley Thomas *pharmaceutical company executive*
Duringer, David Robert *lawyer*
Farrell, Warren Thomas *author*
Halberg, Charles John August, Jr., *mathematics educator*
Hale, David Fredrick *biotechnologist*
Harrington-Lloyd, Jeanne Leigh *interior designer*
Howard, Robert Staples *newspaper publisher*
Kauderer, Bernard Marvin *retired naval officer, consultant*
Lange, Clifford E. *librarian*
Lu, Taijin *physical chemist, researcher*
Marx, Michael William *language educator, writer*
McNamara, Kevin Michael *floorcovering company executive*
†Muth, Dorothy Dudley *volunteer*
Nahavandi, Amir Nezameddin *retired engineering firm executive*
Pernasetti, Flavia Mercer *molecular biologist*
Plachno, Ronald John *electrical engineer*
Rodenhausen, John E. *sales executive*
†Smith, Benjamin Eric *venture capitalist*
Smith, Warren James *optical scientist, consultant, lecturer*
Somit, Albert *political educator*
Tompane, Mary Beth *management consultant*
†Turner, Lyle C. *biotechnology company executive*
Wilson, Donald Grey *management consultant*

Carmel
Adams, Tracey Linden *artist, educator*
Alich, John Arthur, Jr., *manufacturing executive*
Alsberg, Dietrich Anselm *electrical engineer, consultant*
Aurner, Robert Ray, II, *oil company, auto diagnostic, restaurant franchise and company development executive*
Barton, Hugh Perry *bank executive*
Bohannon-Kaplan, Margaret Anne *publisher, lawyer*
Chung, Kyung Cho *Korean specialist, educator, writer*
Creighton, John Wallis, Jr., *novelist, publisher, former management educator, consultant*
Dobey, James Kenneth *banker*
Epel, David *biologist, educator*
†Evans, Charlotte Mortimer *communications consultant, writer*
Faul, June Patricia *education specialist*
Felch, William Campbell *internist, editor*
Flanagan, Michael Brendan *obstetrician/gynecologist*
Hamilton, Lyman Critchfield, Jr., *telecommunications industry executive*
Hobbs, C. Fredric *artist, filmmaker, author*
†Jacobs, Ralph, Jr., *artist*
Janko, Albert Bela *physician*
†Jung, Glenn Harold *retired oceanographer educator, researcher*
Koeppel, Gary Merle *publisher, art gallery owner, writer*
Krugman, Stanley Lee *international management consultant*
Lockton, David Ballard *business executive*
Mollman, John Peter *book publisher, consultant electronic publishing*
Pasten, Laura Jean *veterinarian*
Robinson, John Minor *lawyer, retired business executive*
Smith, Gordon Paul *management consultant*
Vagnini, Livio Lee *chemist, forensic consultant*

Carmel Valley
Chapman, Robert Galbraith *retired hematologist, administrator*
Kasson, James Matthews *electronics executive*
Meckel, Peter Timothy *arts administrator, educator*
Sands, Sharon Louise *graphic design executive, art publisher, artist*
Wolfe, Maurice Raymond *retired museum director, educator*

Carmichael
Areen, Gordon E. *finance company executive*

Crabbe, John Crozier *telecommunications consultant*
Edgar, Marilyn Ruth *marriage and family therapist*
Halpenny, Diana Doris *lawyer*
Hellmuth, William Frederick, Jr., *economics educator*
Marino, Joseph Thomas *physician*
McHugh, James Joseph *retired naval officer, retired associate dean*
Wagner, Carruth John *physician*

Carpinteria
Fisher, John Crocker *physicist*
Hansen, Robert William *artist, educator*
Lovborg, Uffe *diagnostic research company manager*
†Morgan, Alfred Vance *management consulting company executive*
Schmidhauser, John Richard *political science educator*
Wheeler, John Harvey *political scientist, writer*

Carrboro
†Ferrán, Jaime M. *language educator*

Carson
†Ferrario, Larry *history and literature educator*
Garcia, Angélica María *elementary education educator*
Hirsch, Gilah Yelin *artist, writer*
Kowalski, Kazimierz *computer science educator, researcher*
†Moore, Jerry D. *anthropologist, educator*
Mori, Allen Anthony *academic administrator, consultant*
†Oropeza, Jenny *state official*
Palmer, Beverly Blazey *psychologist, educator*
†Rashkin, Elissa Joy *editor, writer*
Suchenek, Marek Andrzej *computer science educator*
Toh, Chai *information science educator*

Caspar
Schooley, Caroline Naus *retired laboratory supervisor*

Castaic
Ashton, Tamarah M. *special education educator, consultant*
†Burkhart, Stephanie Gloria *protective services official, writer*
†Holmes, Dale Arthur *optics scientist*
†Rouzbehani, Anousheh *engineering executive, consultant*

Castro Valley
Erwin, Frances Suzanne *artist*
Friesen, Janice A. *social worker*
Knight, Andrew Kong *visual artist, educator*
Lee, Joyce Y. *educational administrator*
McLean, Richard Thorpe *artist*
Morrison, Glenn Leslie *minister*
Palmer, James Daniel *protective services official*

Cathedral City
Berry, Ester Lorée *vocational nurse*
†Garcia, Bonnie *state official*
Hoffman, Jetha L. *piano and vocal teacher, musician*
Jackman, Robert Alan *retail executive*
Konwin, Thor Warner *financial executive*
Paul, Vivian *lawyer*
Satcher, Clement Michael *elementary school educator*

Cayucos
Shahan, Sherry Jean *writer, educator*
Theurer, Byron W. *aerospace engineer, business owner*

Cedar Ridge
Adams, Margaret Bernice *retired museum official*

Century City
†Braun, Lloyd *broadcast executive*

Ceres
Abbott, Dan-San *parachute designer*

Cerritos
El-Sayed, Khalil Mohamad *aerospace engineer*
Sarno, Maria Erlinda *lawyer, scientist*
Subramanya, Shiva *aerospace systems engineer*

Chatsworth
Dunwich, Gerina *writer, magazine editor, astrologer*
Henry, Carla L. *advertising executive*
Klein, Jeffrey S. *lawyer, media executive*
Schwab, Howard Joel *judge*
Stephenson, Irene Hamlen *biorhythm analyst, consultant, editor, educator*
Ulin, Samuel Alexander *computer systems developer*
Weisbrod, Ken (Joseph Louis Weisbrod) *marketing professional*
†Wimberly, Doug J. *design engineer, consultant*

Chico
Akimoto, Martin Wayne *mental health services professional*
Allen, Charles William *mechanical engineering educator*
Brislain, Judy Ann *psychologist*
Burks, Rocky Alan *independent living center executive, consultant*
Cooke, Ron Charles *science educator*
†Cooper, Erwin *writer*
Davidson, Robert G. *writer, English language educator*
Ediger, Robert Ike *botanist, educator*
Esteban, Manuel Antonio *academic administrator, language educator*
Etz, Jane (Helen Jane Etz) *hospital review analyst*
Fuller, David Ralph *lawyer*
Hanton, E. Michael *public and personnel relations consultant*
Hornaday, Richard H. *artist, retired art educator*
Houpis, James Louis Joseph *dean, biologist*
Houx, Mary Anne *investments executive*
†Keene, Rick *state legislator*
King, Claudia Louan *film producer, lecturer*
†Knudson, Duane Victor *kinesiology education educator, researcher*
Learned, Vincent Roy *electrical engineer, educator*
Lenzi, Albert James, Jr., *lawyer*
Lobosky, Jeffrey *physician, neurosurgeon*
†Loker, William Meverell *anthropologist, educator*
McNall, Scott Grant *sociologist, educator, academic administrator*
Moore, Everett LeRoy *library administrator*
Patton, Thomas Edward *artist, educator*
Ritter, Dale William *obstetrician, gynecologist*
Robinson, Beulah Lobdell *retired educator*
†Schmidt, Diane Ellen *political scientist*
Shahid-García, María de Lourdes *foreign language educator*
†Spear, Paul Stanley *psychology educator, musician*
Stout, Robert Joe *freelance journalist*
Thomas, Stafford Tutt *political scientist, educator*
Ward, Chester Lawrence *physician, consultant*

China Lake
Bennett, Jean Louise McPherson *physicist, research scientist*

Chino
Determan, John David *lawyer*
Forsyth, Barbara Jean *elementary reading specialist, writer, poet*
Goodman, Lindsey Alan *furniture manufacturing executive, architect*
Koestel, Mark Alfred *geologist, photographer*

Chino Hills
Burge, Willard, Jr., *software company executive*
Hemenway, Stephen James *record producer, author*
†Lascurain, Randolph *county official*
Ofner, William Bernard *investor*
Pearson, April Virginia *lawyer*

Chula Vista
Allen, Henry Wesley *biomedical researcher, consultant*
Blankfort, Lowell Arnold *newspaper publisher*
Briggs, Franklin Henry *retired naval officer*
Cohen, Elaine Helena *pediatrician, pediatric cardiologist, educator*
Gongora, Eduardo *plastic surgeon*
Kemery, William Elsworth *psychotherapist, hypnotherapist*
Manary, Richard Deane *manufacturing executive*
McGowan, Charlotte Acord *anthropologist*
†Moreno-Ducheny, Denise *state senator*
Otten, Richard Heuse *physician*
Reinhart, Roderick Lester *non-profit organization consultant*
Rusconi, Louis Joseph *marine engineer*
Santee, Dale William *lawyer, air force officer*
Smith, Peggy O'Doniel *physicist, educator*
Weiss-Cornwell, Amy *interior designer*
Wolk, Martin *physicist, electronics engineer*
Worthington, George Rhodes *retired naval officer*

Citrus Heights
†Daves, Sandra Lynn *poet, lyricist*
Knight, Arthur Winfield *English educator*
Knight, Kit Marie *poet, writer, movie critic*
Leisey, Donald Eugene *educational materials company executive, educator*
Osaki, Mark Stephen *writer, development administrator*

City Of Commerce
Johnson, Keith Liddell *chemical company executive*

City Of Industry
Churchill, James Allen *lawyer*
Ji, Qing *chemist, researcher*
†Pacheco, Robert *state official*
Perry, William Joseph *food processing company executive*

Claremont
Ackerman, Gerald Martin *art historian, consultant*
Acosta, Nelson John *civil engineer*
Albaum, Jean Stirling *psychologist, educator*
Alexander, John David, Jr., *college administrator*
Ansell, Edward Orin *lawyer*
Atlas, Jay David *philosopher, consultant, linguist*
Bekavac, Nancy Yavor *academic administrator, lawyer*
Benjamin, Karl Stanley *artist, art educator*
Berg, Barbara Ann Cowan *corporate workshops consultant, critical incident consultant*
Bjork, Gordon Carl *economist, educator*
Blizzard, Alan *artist*
†Bradley, Rochelle Elaine *music educator*
Burns, Richard Dean *history educator, publisher, writer*
Casanova, Aldo John *sculptor*
Christian, Suzanne Hall *financial planner*
Coleman, Courtney Stafford *mathematician, educator*
Cooke, Kenneth Lloyd *mathematician, educator*
†Csikszentmihalyi, Mihaly *psychology educator*
†Cumberbatch, Ellis *education educator, researcher*
Davis, Nathaniel *humanities educator*
†Dewey, Thomas Gregory *dean, physical chemist, educator*
Douglass, Enid Hart *educational program director*
†Dunye, Cheryl *artist, film maker*
Dym, Clive Lionel *engineering educator*
Ferguson, Cleve Robert *lawyer, educator*
Forti, William Bell *business executive, inventor*
Fossum, Robert H(eyerdahl) *retired English literature educator*
Gann, Pamela Brooks *academic administrator*
†Genung, Dan Baldwin *minister, writer*
Goodrich, Norma Lorre (Mrs. John H. Howard) *French and comparative literature educator*
Grabiner, Sandy *mathematics educator*
Gray, Paul Bryan *lawyer, historian, arbitrator*
Helliwell, Thomas McCaffree *physicist, educator*
Henriksen, Melvin *mathematician, educator*
Johnson, Jerome Linné *cardiologist, educator*
Kucheman, Clark Arthur *philosophy and religious studies educator*
†Kurita, Kyoko *education educator*
Lasswell, Marcia Lee *psychologist, educator*
Leeb, Charles Samuel *clinical psychologist*
Liggett, Thomas Jackson *retired seminary president*
Likens, James Dean *economics educator*
Lipman-Blumen, Jean *public policy and organizational behavior educator*
Lofgren, Charles Augustin *legal and constitutional historian, history educator*
Maguire, John David *academic administrator, educator, writer*
Martin, Jay Herbert *psychoanalyst, English and political science educator*
McKirahan, Richard Duncan *classics and philosophy educator*
Molinder, John Irving *engineering educator, consultant*
Monson, James Edward *electrical engineer, educator*
Moss, Myra Ellen (Myra Moss Rolle) *philosophy educator*
Myhre, Janet *mathematician, educator*
Neumann, Harry *philosophy educator*
Oxtoby, David William *college president, chemistry educator*
Pedersen, Richard Foote *diplomat and academic administrator*
Pendleton, Othniel Alsop *fundraiser, clergyman*
†Phelps, Orme Wheelock *economics educator emeritus*
Pinney, Thomas Clive *retired English language educator*
Pitney, John Joseph, Jr., *political science educator*
Platt, Joseph Beaven *former college president*
Presecan, Nicholas Lee *environmental and civil engineer, consultant*
Purves, William Kirkwood *biologist, educator*
Reynolds, Margaret Ann *minister, educator*
Riggs, Henry Earle *academic administrator, engineering educator*
Riley, Judith Merkle *writer, educator*
Rossum, Ralph Arthur *political science educator*
Roth, John King *philosopher, educator*
Sanders, James Alvin *minister, religious studies educator*
†Shahriari, Shahriar *mathematics educator*
Shimkhada, Deepak *art historian*
Smith, Gary Nance *economics educator*
Sontag, Frederick Earl *philosophy educator*
Stanley, Peter William *former academic administrator*
Strauss, Jon Calvert *academic administrator*
Tanenbaum, Basil Samuel *engineering educator*
Tengbom, Luverne Charles *retired religion educator*
Tilden, Wesley Roderick *writer, retired computer programmer*
†Wachtel, Albert *writer, educator*
Wents, Doris Roberta *psychologist*
†Wettack, F. Sheldon *academic administrator*
Wheeler, Geraldine Hartshorn *historian, essayist*
Woodress, James Leslie, Jr., *English language educator*
Young, Howard Thomas *foreign language educator*
Zornes, Milford *artist*

Clearlake
Alexander, Onnie Susan *clinical nurse specialist*

Clovis
†Brahma, Chandra Sekhar *civil engineering educator*
Chang, Stanley F. *gastroenterologist*
Kellam, Becky *business educator, consultant*
Shields, Allan Edwin *writer, photographer, retired educator*
†Smith, William Clarke *clergyman*

Coalinga
Frame, Ted Ronald *lawyer*
Russell, Beverly Ann *librarian, writer*

Coarsegold
Samuelson, William Allen *music educator*

Colton
†Brown, Jack H. *supermarket company executive*
Crowley, Diane Nita *home health administrator*
Greene, Gerald R. *pediatrician*
Jones, Thomas Edward *medical technologist*
†Seifert, Mark R. *pathologist*

Colusa
Carter, Jane Foster *agriculture industry executive*

Compton
Drew, Sharon Lee *sociologist*
Dymally, Mervyn Malcolm *retired congressman, international business executive*
†Maradiaga Kieffer-Aanonsen, Nora Ludmila *language educator*
Shiloh, Allen *writer, postal employee*
Wang, Charles Ping *engineering executive*

Concord
Albrecht, Donna G. *author*
†Christian, John Robert *music educator*
Crandall, Ira Carlton *consulting electrical engineer*
Fuld, Fred, III, *computer consultant, financial consultant*
Hearst, John Eugene *chemistry educator, researcher, consultant*
Jones, Gerald Edward *religion educator*
Jothi, Rishyur K. *surgeon*
Latner, Barry P. *pathologist*
Lee, Low Kee *electronics engineer, consultant*
Middleton, Michael John *civil engineer*
Miller, John Nelson *banker*
Misner, Charlotte Blanche Ruckman *retired community organization administrator*
Paterson, Bruce Foote *internist, allergist*
†Rohra, Srikrishin Assardas *cardiologist*
†Schwartz, Eric *lawyer*
Thompson, Jeremiah Beiseker *international medical business executive, sinologist*
Travers, Judith Lynnette *human resources executive*

Cool
Sheridan, George Groh *elementary education educator, teacher educator, English educator*
Trybul, Theodore Nicholas *engineering educator*

Copperopolis
†Ezell, Wayland L. *biologist, educator*
†Wooster, Kelly C. *lawyer*

Corcoran
Martines, Eugenia Belle *elementary school educator*

Corona
Alch, Mark Lee *organization executive, educator*
Amato, Carol Joy *writer, anthropologist*
Clark, Nanci *elementary education educator*
Everett Nollkamper, Pamela Irene *legal management company executive, educator*
Garrett, Thomas Monroe *chemist*
Hagmann, Lillian Sue *violin instructor*
Hall, Harlan *federal agency administrator*
Lamb, Mildred Shimonishi *retired administrative secretary*
Shaffer, Audrey Jeanne *health information administrator, educator*
Tillman, Joseph Nathaniel *engineering executive*
†Weisemann, Claus *pharmaceutical executive*

Corona Del Mar
Britten, Roy John *biophysicist*
Delap, Tony *artist*
†Dougherty, Jocelyn *retired neurologist*
Eaton, Barry David *retired city planner*
Freeman, Richard Dean *new business start-up service company executive*
Helphand, Ben J. *actuary, consultant*
Hinderaker, Ivan *political science educator*
Hochschild, Richard *medical instruments executive, researcher*
Karson, Burton Lewis *musician, educator*
†O'Brien, John William, Jr., *investment management company executive, finance educator*
Richmond, Ronald LeRoy *aerospace engineer*
Terrell, A. John *retired university telecommunications director*
Tobis, Jerome Sanford *physician*
Wolf, Karl Everett *aerospace and communications corporation executive*
Yeo, Ron *architect*

Coronado
†Adelson, Benedict James *retired lawyer*
Betts, Barbara Lang *lawyer, rancher, realtor*
Butcher, Bobby Gene *retired military officer*
Carrier, Lynne Thomson *journalist*
Crilly, Eugene Richard *engineering consultant*
Dalton, Matt *retired foundry executive*
†Edison, Thomas Robert *management educator, retired military officer*
Foster, Brian Duane *biologist, consultant*
†Heisner, John Richard *lawyer*
Hinsvark, Don George *social services agency professional*
Hostler, Charles Warren *former ambassador, international affairs consultant*
Hubbard, Donald *marine artist, writer*
Mock, David Clinton, Jr., *internist*
Neblett, Carol *soprano*
Plumb, Robert Thompson, II, *lawyer*
Sack, Edgar Albert *electronics company executive*
Smith, Albert Cromwell, Jr., *investments consultant*
Stames, William Alexander *realtor, cost management executive*
Stockdale, James Bond *writer, research scholar, retired naval officer*
Wagener, Hobart D. *retired architect*

Corralitos
Short, Harold Ashby *imaging engineer*

Corte Madera
Dalpino, Ida Jane *retired secondary education educator*
Epstein, William Louis *dermatologist, educator*
†Gajdusek, Robert Elemer *writer, retired language educator*
Serber, William *radiation oncologist, educator*

Costa Mesa
Alexiou, James *electronics executive*
Anderson, Jon David *lawyer*
†Angell, Susan L. *lawyer*
†Bartletti, Don *photographer, editor*
Brady, John Patrick, Jr., *electronics educator, consultant*
Buchtel, Michael Eugene *optical mechanical engineer*
Caldwell, Courtney Lynn *lawyer, real estate consultant*
Carpenter, Frank Charles, Jr., *retired electronics engineer*
Cohen, Stanley *commercial real estate developer*
†Connally, Michael W. *lawyer*

Currie, Robert Emil *lawyer*
Daniels, James Walter *lawyer*
Demille, Dianne Lynne *mathematics educator, administrator*
Dempster, Murray Wayne *academic administrator, religion educator, minister*
†Epstein, Susan Baerg *librarian, consultant*
Florey, Jerry Jay *aerospace and management consultant*
Frieden, Clifford E. *lawyer*
Gimple, W. Thomas *sales executive*
Guilford, Andrew John *lawyer*
Hay, Howard Clinton *lawyer*
Hazewinkel, Van *manufacturing executive*
Jones, H(arold) Gilbert, Jr., *lawyer*
Kiang, Assumpta (Amy Kiang) *brokerage house executive*
Klein, Eleanor (Mary Klein) *retired clinical social worker*
Kolanoski, Thomas Edwin *financial company executive*
†Kramer, Kenneth Scott *lawyer*
Labbe, Armand Joseph *curator, anthropologist*
Lattanzio, Stephen Paul *astronomy educator*
†Maddox, Ken *state official*
†Marshall, Ellen Ruth *lawyer*
McEnary, John Walter *music educator*
Medina-Puerta, Antonio *research scientist*
Metzger, Vernon Arthur *management educator, consultant*
Muller, Jerome Kenneth *photographer, art director, editor*
Okamoto, Vicki E. *orthodontist*
†Phelps, Aaron K(ay) *lawyer*
Rayner, Linda Calix *financial analyst*
†Rose, I. Nelson *lawyer, educator*
Schaaf, Douglas Allan *lawyer*
†Snowden, David L. *protective services official*
Steinberg, Russell Max *behavioral pediatrician, educator*
Tanner, R. Marshall *lawyer*
Tennyson, Peter Joseph *lawyer*
Tillman, Barbara Ann *education educator, consultant*
Williams, William Corey *theology educator, consultant*

Cotati
†Baker, Sarah E. *music educator, composer, writer*
Hill, Debora Elizabeth *writer, journalist, screenwriter*
James, Mary Spencer *nursing home health administrator*
Robertson, William Abbott *arbitrator, mediator, lawyer*

Coto De Caza
Bezar, Gilbert Edward *retired aerospace company executive, volunteer*
Sheehy, Jerome Joseph *electrical engineer*

Cottonwood
†Fernandez, Joseph Jacob *sportscaster, basketball announcer*

Covina
Aguilar, Gladys Maria *counselor, educator*
Cottrell, Janet Ann *controller*
Durham, Betty Louise *poet*
White, Rebecca E. *advocate*

Cowan Heights
Ruttencutter, Brian Boyle *manufacturing company executive*

Coyote
Keeshen, Kathleen Kearney *public relations consultant*

Crescent City
Carter, Neville Louis *geophysicist, educator*
Swart, Bonnie Blount *artist*

Crestline
Douglas, Cindy Holloway *consultant*
Merrill, Steven William *research and development executive*
Noble, Lawrence Alan *artist*

Crockett
Leporiere, Ralph Dennis *retired quality engineer*
Silverman, Mervyn F. *health science association administrator, consultant*

Cromberg
Kolb, Ken Lloyd *writer*

Culver City
Abarbanell, Gayola Havens *financial planner*
Binder, Bettye B. *author, lecturer*
Boonshaft, Hope Judith *public affairs executive*
†Brooks, James L. *writer, director, producer*
Brooks, Mel *producer, director, writer, actor*
†Calley, John *motion picture company executive, film producer*
†Chaffin, Cean *producer*
†Chow, Judy *library science and information sciences educator*
Clodius, Albert Howard *history educator*
†Coolio, (Artis Ivey Jr.) *popular musician*
†Crowe, Cameron *screenwriter, film director*
Eckel, James Robert, Jr., *financial planner*
Ewing, Michael Snyder *producer, film company executive*
†Feltheimer, Jon *entertainment company executive*
Fisher, Lucy *motion picture company executive*
Friedland, David L. *industrial and organizational psychologist*
†Gordon, Florence Irene *graphic artist, illustrator*
Grant, Joan Julien *artist, poet*
†Guber, Peter *executive producer*
†Harris, Mel *broadcast executive*
Jarmon, Lawrence *developmental communications educator*
†Johnson, Magic (Earvin Johnson) *professional sports team executive, former professional basketball coach*
†Kaufman, Richard Stuart *conductor, music director*
†Lenk, Edward C. (Toby) *Internet company executive*
Leve, Alan Donald *electronic materials manufacturing company owner, executive*
Maltzman, Irving Myron *psychology educator*
Marcus, Richard Andrew *accountant, mayor*
Mark, Laurence Maurice *film producer*
†Marshall, Penny (C. Marshall) *director, actress*
Maxwell-Brogdon, Florence Morency *school administrator, educational adviser*
†Michaels, Helene *broadcast executive*
Netzel, Paul Arthur *fund raising management executive, consultant*
Pascal, Amy *film company executive*
Richardson, John Edmon *marketing educator*
†Souza, Blase Camacho *librarian, educator*
Sussman, Deborah Evelyn *designer, company executive*
Tang, Yin Sheng *physicist*
†Tisch, Steven Elliot *TV and movie producer*
Wick, Douglas *producer*
†Wigan, Gareth *film company executive*
Wilson, David *artist*
†Ziskin, Laura *television producer, film producer*

Cupertino
Berg, Karl *real estate company executive*
Burg, John Parker *signal processing executive*
Carnie, Kay C. *artist, educator*
Cheeseman, Douglas Taylor, Jr., *wildlife tour executive, photographer, educator*
Chung, Jin Soo *ocean mining and ocean engineer*
Compton, Dale Leonard *retired space agency executive, consultant*
Edson, William Alden *electrical engineer, researcher*
Fan, Chien *aerospace engineer, researcher*
Fenn, Raymond Wolcott, Jr., *retired metallurgical engineer*
Finnemore, (Erhardt) John *civil engineer, educator*
Fletcher, Homer Lee *librarian*
Geddes, Barbara Sheryl *communications executive, consultant*
Haskell, Barry Geoffry *computer company researcher*
Jelinch, Frank Anthony *lawyer*
Knapp, George Griff Prather *retired insurance executive*
Lam, Cheung-Wei *electrical engineer*
†Lyon, Mary Lou *educator*
Mathias, Leslie Michael *electronic manufacturing company executive*
†McCormick, Yumi *language educator, translator*
Simon, Nancy Ruth *lawyer*
Sobrato, John A. *construction executive*
Svalya, Phillip Gordon *lawyer*
Szczerba, Victor Bogdan *electrical engineer, sales engineer*
Tice, Bradley Scott *humanities educator*
†Zhang, Ming *engineering researcher*
Zobel, Louise Purwin *author, educator, lecturer, writing consultant*

Cypress
Bloom, Julian *artist, editor*
Cao, Dac-Buu *software engineer*
Edmonds, Ivy Gordon *writer*
Friess, Donna Lewis *children's rights advocate*
†Henrickson, Leslie Ann *educational consultant, educator*
Olschwang, Alan Paul *lawyer*
Osgood, Frank William *urban and economic planner, writer*
Waite, Verner Stuart *surgeon, retired*

Daggett
Bailey, Katherine Christine *artist, writer*

Daly City
Batlin, Robert Alfred *retired newspaper editor*
†Gao, Luji *foreign language educator, columnist*
Hargrave, Sarah Quesenberry *consulting company executive*
Kennedy, Gwendolyn Debra *artist, scriptwriter, playwright*
†Malifrando, Frank *foundation executive director, theater producer, consultant*
Mobley, Clarence Fowler *retired civil engineer*

Dana Point
Camp, Joseph Shelton, Jr., *film producer, director, writer*
Easton, Richard Allen *electrical engineer*
Fabricant, Jill Diane *technology company executive*
Lang, George Frank *insurance executive, consultant, lawyer*
Mardian, Robert Charles, Jr., *restaurateur*
Milunas, J. Robert *health care organization executive*
Olvera, Carlos Nelson *mechanical engineer, executive*
Parker, John Marchbank *consulting geologist*
Walker, Doris Isaak *writer, historian, educator*

Danville
Bergsten, James Robert *computer technology architect*
Candland, D. Stuart *lawyer*
Cross, Christopher T. *education consultant*
Grager, Steven P. *investment consultant*
Levine, Michael *telecommunications industry executive, consultant*
Nothern, Marjorie Carol *nursing administrator*
†Raines, Richard Clifton *lawyer*
Reed, William Gerald *consulting firm executive*

Darwin
Palazzo, Robert Paul *lawyer, accountant*

Davis
Akesson, Norman Berndt *agricultural engineer, emeritus educator*
Allard, Robert Wayne *geneticist, educator*
Ardans, Alexander Andrew *veterinarian, laboratory director, educator*
Barbour, Michael G(eorge) *botany educator, ecological consultant*
Bartosic, Florian *law educator, lawyer, arbitrator*
Baskin, Ronald Joseph *cell biologist, physiologist, biophysicist educator, dean*
†Bernd, Clifford Albrecht *language educator*
†Bloom, Heather Lynn *physician*
†Boorkman, Jo Anne *librarian*
Brandt, Harry *mechanical engineering educator*
†Brody, David *history educator*
†Brower, Daniel Roberts *historian, educator, writer*
Bruch, Carol Sophie *lawyer, educator*
Bunch, Richard Alan *writer, educator*
†Burnett, Katharine Persis *art historian, educator*
Burri, Betty Jane *research chemist*
Cahill, Thomas Andrew *physicist, educator*
Cardiff, Robert Darrell *pathology educator*
Carey, James Robert *educator*
Carter, Colin Andre *education educator*
Chancellor, William Joseph *agricultural engineering educator*
Chander, Anupam *lawyer*
Chang, Daniel Pan Yih *environmental engineering educator*
Cheney, James Addison *civil engineering educator*
Cliver, Dean Otis *microbiologist, educator*
Cohen, Lawrence Edward *sociology educator, criminologist*
Colvin, Harry Walter, Jr., *physiology educator*
Conn, Eric Edward *plant biochemist*
Cook, Roberta Lynn *agricultural economist, educator*
Day, Howard Wilman *geology educator*
DePaoli, Geri M. (Joan DePaoli) *artist, art historian*
Dorf, Richard Carl *electrical engineering and management educator*
†Druzhnikov, Yuri Ilya *literature educator, writer*
†Duan, Ren-Guan *materials scientist*
Enders, Allen Coffin *anatomy educator*
Ennis, Michael Patrick *psychologist, educator*
Epstein, Emanuel *plant physiologist*
Ernst, Ralph Ambrose *poultry specialist*
†Fannjiang, Albert *mathematician, educator*
Feeney, Floyd Fulton *legal educator*
Franco, Elaine Adele *librarian*
Freedland, Richard Allan *retired biologist, educator*
Gardner, Murray Briggs *pathologist, educator*
Gates, Bruce Clark *chemical engineer, educator*
Ghausi, Mohammed Shuaib *electrical engineering educator, university dean*
Gifford, Ernest Milton *biologist, educator*
Goldstone, Jack Andrew *sociologist*
Grossman, George Stefan *library director, law eductor*
Groth, Alexander Jacob *political science educator*
†Hall, John Ross *educator*
Hance, Anthony James *retired pharmacologist, educator*
Handel, Darrell Dale *composer, retired music educator*
Hastings, Alan *environmental biology educator*
Hayden, John Olin *English literature educator, writer*
Hess, Charles Edward *environmental horticulture educator*
†Hess, Ronald Andrew *aerospace engineer, educator*
Hoffman, Michael Jerome *humanities educator, educator*
Hope, Hakon *research scientist*
Horwitz, Barbara Ann *physiologist, educator, consultant*
Hristova, Krassimira Radoykova *microbiologist, researcher*
Imwinkelried, Edward John *law educator*
Jensen, Hanne Margrete *pathology educator*
Johnson, Kevin Raymond *law educator*
Jones, Edward George *neuroscience professor*
Jungerman, John Albert *physics educator*
Kado, Clarence Isao *molecular biologist*
Kaplan, Douglas Allen *financial care company executive*
Kavvas, M. Levent *civil engineering educator*
Kester, Dale Emmert *pomologist, educator*
Klasing, Susan Allen *environmental toxicologist*
Kofranek, Anton Miles *floriculturist, educator*
†Korvatska, Elena *biologist, educator*
†Kraft, Rosemarie *dean, educator*
Lagunas-Solar, Manuel Claudio *research radiochemist*
Laidlaw, Harry Hyde, Jr., *entomology educator*
Larock, Bruce Edward *civil engineering educator*
Major, Clarence Lee *poet, novelist, educator, artist*
Marino, Miguel Angel *engineering educator*
Mason, William A(lvin) *psychologist, educator, researcher*
McHenry, Henry Malcolm *anthropologist, educator*
Meyer, Margaret Eleanor *microbiologist, educator*
Motley, Michael Tilden *communication educator*
Moyle, Peter Briggs *fisheries and biology educator*
Mukherjee, Amiya K. *metallurgy and materials science educator*
Mulase, Motohico *mathematics educator*
Murphy, Terence Martin *biology educator*
Musolf, Lloyd Daryl *political science educator, institute administrator*
Naik, Prasad Anand *marketing educator*
Nash, Charles Presley *chemistry educator*
Norton, Donald Alan *retired adult education educator*
Olsson, Ronald Arthur *computer science educator*
†Osburn, Bennie I. *dean*
Owings, Donald Henry *psychology educator*
Painter, Ruth Robbins *retired environmental biochemist*
Palmer, Philip Edward Stephen *radiologist*
†Pan, Ning *engineering educator*
†Powers, Gay Havens-Monteagle *artist*
Pritchard, William Roy *former university system administrator*
Qualset, Calvin O. *plant genetics and agronomy educator*
Rhode, Edward Albert *veterinary medicine educator, veterinary cardiologist*
Richman, David Paul *neurologist, educator, researcher*
Rodolfa, Emil Raymond *psychologist*
Rost, Thomas Lowell *plant biology educator*
Rothchild, Donald Sylvester *political science educator*
Saler, Michael Theodore *history educator*
†Sandoval, Jonathan Hough *education educator*
Savageau, Michael Antonio *science educator, engineering educator*
Schenker, Marc Benet *preventive medicine educator*
Schneeman, Barbara Olds *nutritionist, educator*
Schoener, Thomas William *zoology educator, researcher*
Shackelford, James Floyd *materials science educator, researcher*
Sharrow, Marilyn Jane *library administrator*
†Shimomura, Floyd Dudley *lawyer, educator*
Sillman, Arnold Joel *physiologist, educator*
Simonton, Dean Keith *psychology educator*
Skinner, G(eorge) William *anthropologist, educator*
Smith, Michael Peter *social science educator, researcher*
†Sperling, Daniel *engineering educator, transportation studies director*
Spindler, George Dearborn *anthropologist, educator, writer, editor*
Springer, Sally Pearl *university administrator*
Steffey, Eugene Paul *veterinary medicine educator*
Stern, Judith Schneider *nutritionist, researcher, educator*
Stewart, James Ian *agricultural water scientist, cropping system developer, consultant*
Stumpf, Paul Karl *biochemistry educator emeritus*
Sumner, Daniel Alan *economist, educator*
Swift, Richard G(ene) *composer, educator*
Tchobanoglous, George *civil engineering educator*
Tinney, Thomas Milton, Sr., *genealogical research specialist*
Traill, David Angus *classics educator*
Troy, Frederic Arthur, II, *medical biochemistry educator*
Tsai, Chih-Ling *management educator*
Tuma, Elias H. *economist, educator*
Turcotte, Donald Lawson *geophysical sciences educator*
Turnlund, Judith Rae *nutritionist*
Vanderhoef, Larry Neil *academic administrator*
†Villarejo, Don *industrial relations specialist, researcher*
Volman, David Herschel *chemistry educator*
Von Behren, Ruth Lechner *adult day health care specialist, retired*
Waddington, Raymond Bruce, Jr., *English language educator*
Walters, Richard Francis *computer science educator*
Wang, Shih-Ho *electrical engineer, educator*
Watt, Kenneth Edmund Ferguson *zoology educator*
Wegelin, Jacob Andreas *statistician*
Williams, Hibbard Earl *medical educator, physician*
Williams, William Arnold *agronomy educator*
Williamson, Alan Bacher *English literature educator, poet, writer*
Willis, Frank Roy *history educator*
Wooten, Frederick (Oliver Wooten) *applied science educator*
Wydick, Judith Brandli James *volunteer*
Wydick, Richard Crews *lawyer, educator*

Deer Park
Hodgkin, John E. *pulmonologist*

Del Mar
Boynton, Robert Merrill *retired psychology educator*
†Engler, Robert L. *retired cardiologist*
Farquhar, Marilyn Gist *cell biology and pathology educator*
Fricke, Martin Paul *science company executive*
†Johnson, Mary Evans *musicologist, musician*
Lesko, Ronald Michael *osteopathic physician*
Morton, Frederic *author*
†Mullen, George D. *artist*
Ogdon, Wilbur (Will Ogdon) *composer, music educator*
Randall, Chandler Corydon *church rector*
Seitman, John Michael *lawyer, arbitrator, mediator*
Smith, Robert Hamil *writer, fund raiser*
Wilkinson, Eugene Parks *nuclear engineer, director*

Delano
Salmassi, Sadegh *family practice physician*

Desert Hot Springs
Fulton, Norman Robert *credit manager*
Halasz, Stephen Joseph *retired electro-optical systems engineer*
†Laws, Maurice Wesley *set decorator, museum exhibit designer*

Diamond Bar
Johnson, Leonidas Alexander *optometrist, minister*
Mirisola, Lisa Heinemann *air quality engineer*
White, Joy Mieko *communications executive*

Dinuba
Leps, Thomas MacMaster *civil engineer, consultant*

Discovery Bay
Higgins, John Ralph *writer, educator*

Downey
Baumann, Theodore Robert *aerospace engineer, consultant, army officer*
Brooks, Lillian Drilling Ashton (Lillian Hazel Church) *adult education educator*
†Chui, Helena Chang *physician*
†Conwell, Virginia Donley *librarian*
†del Calvo, Alberto C. *educational association administrator, lawyer*
Duzey, Robert Lindsey *lawyer*
Gong, Henry, Jr., *physician, researcher*
Hackney, Jack Dean *physician*
Hart-Duling, Jean Macaulay *clinical social worker*
Mishal, Devadatt M. *obstetrician/gynecologist*
Ruecker, Martha Engels *retired special education educator*
Schauf, Carolyn Jane *lawyer*
Stormes, John Max *instructional systems developer*
Swyden, Robert Gene *family practice physician*
Tompkins, Dwight Edward *lawyer*
Wayman, Joseph McKelden *editor, researcher*

Downieville
Allen, Lawrence Richard *prosecutor*
Forbes, Cynthia Ann *small business owner, marketing educator*

Duarte
†Buckley, Cornelius Michael *priest, educator, chaplain*
Comings, David Edward *physician, medical genetics scientist*
Driskill, James Lawrence *minister*
Fung, Henry Chi-hang *physician, medical researcher*
Kabingue, Ken *biochemist*
†Li, Jian Jian *medical educator*
O'Donnell, John Patrick *journalist, photographer*
Probst, John Elwin *chaplain, minister*
†Riggs, Arthur D. *health facility administrator, research scientist*
Vaughn, James English, Jr., *neurobiologist*
Yoshida, Akira *biochemist*

Dublin
Ingram, Judith Elizabeth *writer, counselor*
Mettinger, Karl Lennart *pharmaceutical executive*
Nelson, Elinor S. *human resources consultant, labor arbitrator*
Whetten, John D. *food products executive*

Earlimart
†White, Kathleen *director*

East Palo Alto
Bates, William, III, *lawyer*
Furbush, David Malcolm *lawyer*

Edwards
Brand, Vance Devoe *astronaut*
Petersen, Kevin *federal agency administrator*
Smolka, James William *aerospace research pilot*

El Cajon
Cole, George Arthur *marketing professional*
Graf, Sheryl Susan *lawyer*
†Higgins, Janice *social worker, writer*
†Hollingsworth, Dennis *state senator*
†Jordan, Jack D. *art educator*
Ostermeyer, Maryann *secondary school educator, writer*
Pollock, Richard Edwin *former county official*
Silverberg, Lewis Henry *legal consultant*
†Swanson-Perrelet, Donna Kay *speech pathology/audiology services professional*
Thigpen, Mary Cecelia *city official, consultant*
Thomas, Esther Merlene *elementary education educator*
Turk, Robert Louis *radiologist*

El Centro
Kussman, Eleanor (Ellie Kussman) *retired educational superintendent*
Steensgaard, Anthony Harvey *federal agency administrator*
†Sutherland, Lowell Francis *lawyer*

El Cerrito
Alpen, Edward Lewis *biophysicist, educator*
Coyner, Eugene Casper *chemist, consultant, economist*
Doyle, William Thomas *retired newspaper editor*
Garbarino, Joseph William *labor arbitrator, economics and business educator*
Hargis, Barbara Louise *artist*
Herzberg, Dorothy Crews *secondary education educator*
Kao, Yasuko Watanabe *retired library administrator*
†Koenig, James Bennett *geologist, consultant*
Komatsu, Shigego Richard *architect*
Koths, Kirston Edward *biochemist*
Kuo, Ping-chia *historian, educator*
†Maxwell, John E. *priest, educator*
Mendoza, Lydia *vocalist*
Siri, William E. *physicist, consultant*
Smith, Eldred Reid *library educator*
Stenmark, Jean Kerr *mathematics educator*
Templeton, David Henry, Jr., *chemist, educator*

El Dorado Hills
Davies, William Ralph *service executive*
Schlachter, Gail Ann *publishing company executive*
Sparks, Robert Dean *medical administrator, physician*

El Granada
Tempesta, Michael Steven *pharmaceuticals company executive, chemist*

El Macero
Andrews, Neil Corbly *surgeon*
Stowell, Robert Eugene *pathologist, retired educator*

El Monte
Last, Marian Helen *social services administrator*

El Segundo
†Abbassian-Kashi, Mandana *industrial engineer, systems engineer*
†Agrawal, Suphal P. *engineering company executive*
Armstrong, Wallace Dowan, Jr., *data processor*
Bauer, Jerome Leo, Jr., *chemical engineer*
Brown, Lorraine Ann *event coordinator, minister, hypnotist*
Bryant, Kobe *professional basketball player*
†Carey, Chase *broadcast executive*
Chang, I-Shih *aerospace engineer*
Conrad, Paul Francis *editorial cartoonist*
Daughaday, Douglas Robert *computer engineer*
Eckert, Robert A. *manufacturing company executive*
Gambaro, Ernest Umberto *lawyer, consultant, engineer*
Harper, David Taylor *civilian military employee*
Hollander, Sidney *computer systems engineer*
Honeycutt, Van B. *computer company executive*
†Hunter, Larry Dean *lawyer*
Jacobs, Michael Moises *aerospace engineer, consultant*
†Kelble, Jack R. *electronics executive*
Lantz, Norman Foster *electrical engineer*
Leslie, Lisa DeShaun *professional basketball player*
McDonald, Rosa Nell *engineering executive*
McQuillin, Richard Ross *management consultant*
Muhlbach, Robert Arthur *lawyer*
Olson, Jeanne Innis *technology and technical management executive*
O'Neal, Shaquille Rashaun *professional basketball player*
†Pearce, Harry Jonathan *lawyer*
†Puckett, Allen Emerson *aeronautical engineer*
Richmond, Mitchell James *professional basketball player*
†Rosen, Harold A. *retired aeronautical engineer*
Rozman, James D. *military chaplain*
†Schimmenti, John Joseph *lawyer*
†Toler, Penny *former professional basketball player, sports team executive*
Williamson, Charles R. *energy company executive*
†Willis, Judy Ann *lawyer*
†Zucker, David Clark *lawyer*

El Sobrante
White, Nelson Henry *writer, publisher, realtor*

Eldridge
†Mason, William H. *podiatrist*

Elk Grove
Landon, JoJene Babbitt *special education educator*
McDavid, Douglas Warren *executive research consultant*
McIntyre, Mary Maureen *social services consultant*
†Moe, Janet Anne *elementary school educator, musician*
Romano, Sheila June *telecommunications industry executive, artist, writer*
Sparks, Jack Norman *college dean*
Vang, Timothy Teng *religious organization administrator*

Emeryville
†Blackburn, Robert Parker *lawyer*
†Bonci, Antonello *neurologist*
Choi, Doo-Sup *molecular biologist*
†Deeb, Rula Anselmo *environmental engineer*
Donnelly, John James, III, *immunologist*
Fineman, Jeanette Krulevitz *retired artist*
Finney, Lee *social worker, negotiator*
Goldstein, Jack *health science executive, microbiologist*
Gombocz, Erich Alfred *biochemist*
Howe, Drayton Ford, Jr., *lawyer*
Hurst, Deborah *pediatric hematologist*
Jobs, Steven Paul *computer company executive*
Lance, Sean P. *pharmaceutical executive*
Masri, Merle Sid *biochemist, consultant*
Nady, John *electronics company executive*
†Nenov, Ivo P. *mathematical and software researcher*
†Ostrach, Michael Sherwood *lawyer, business executive*
Penhoet, Edward *medical association administrator, biochemicals company executive, former dean*
†Reuter, William Charles *historian, educator*
Smith, Christopher Allen *technology company executive, finance professional*
Weaver, Velather Edwards *small business owner*
Zwoyer, Eugene Milton *retired consulting engineering executive*

Encinitas
Bartok, Michelle *cosmetic company executive*
Breslaw, Cathy Lee *artist, educator*
Chavez, Cesar T. *ophthalmologist, cosmetic surgeon*
Forrester, Kevin Kreg *lawyer*
Frank, Michael Victor *risk assessment engineer*
Goldberg, Edward Davidow *geochemist, educator*
Litvin, Inessa Elizabeth *piano educator*
Miller, Kerry Lee *city manager*
Nemeth, Valerie Ann *lawyer*
Payne, James Richard *environmental chemist*
Wigmore, John Grant *lawyer*
Williams, Michael Edward *lawyer*

Encino
Bach, Cynthia *educational program director, writer*
Baker, William Morris *cultural organization administrator*
†Dor, Yoram *accountant*
Dosik, Gary M. *internist, oncologist, hematologist, educator*
Ehrlich, Kenneth James *television producer*
Friedman, George Jerry *aerospace engineer, executive*
Gavin, Delane Michael *television writer, producer, director*
†Ginty, Robert *actor*
Greenberg, Allan *advertising and marketing research consultant*
Hawthorne, Marion Frederick *chemistry educator*
Hein, Jennifer Loomis *information technology consultant*
Holman, Harland Eugene *retired motion picture company executive*
House-Hendrick, Karen Sue *nursing consultant*
†Husain, Shujaat *music educator*
Ingels, Marty *theatrical agent, television and motion picture production executive*
Knuth, Eldon Luverne *engineering educator*
Laba, Marvin *management consultant*
La Cava, Donald Leon *communications executive*
Levine, Thomas Jeffrey Pello *lawyer*
Luna, Barbara Carole *financial analyst, accountant, appraiser*
Medak, Peter *film director*
Nicolosi, Joseph *psychologist, writer, researcher*
†O'Riley, Karen E. *principal*
Parrott, Dennis Beecher *retired insurance executive*
Phelps, Michael Edward *biophysics educator*
Pryor, Richard *actor, writer*
Rance, Quentin E. *interior designer*
Rawitch, Robert Joe *journalist, educator*
Ribac, Catalino Tagatac *retired accountant*
Saginor, Sidney V. *management consultant*
Seiden, Paul *insurance agent, consultant*
Semos, William *management consultant, educator, air transportation executive*
Shire, David Lee *composer*
Smith, Selma Moidel *lawyer, composer*
Thorpe, Gary Stephen *chemistry educator*
Vogel, Susan Carol *nursing administrator*
†Weissman, I. Donald *lawyer*
Weitzman, Bernard *film company executive, consultant*
Westmore, Michael George *make-up artist, writer*
Zsigmond, Vilmos *cinematographer, director*

Escalon
Barton, Gerald Lee *farming company executive*

Escondido
†Baugh, Steven Michael *theology studies educator*
Briggs, Edward Samuel *naval officer*
†Carey, Catherine Anita *artist, art educator*
Damsbo, Ann Marie *psychologist*
Daniels, Richard Martin *public relations executive*
Dotto, Peter Attilius *retired marine corps officer, defense consultant*
†Duguid, Iain Moir *education educator*
Ehrhart, Joseph Edward *retired television broadcast engineer*
Ellenberger, William Joseph *retired engineering consultant*
Everton, Marta Ve *retired ophthalmologist*
Friedman, Alan Howard *writer, educator*
†Garcia, Luis F. *social worker, photographer*
Gentile, Robert Dale *optometrist, consultant*
Ghandhi, Sorab Khushro *electrical engineering educator*
Godone-Maresca, Lillian *lawyer*
Grew, Raymond Edward *mechanical engineer*
†Hannam-Oosterbaan, Maria Gertrude *educator*
Huang, Kun Lien *software engineer, scientist*
Kelley, George Lorenze *psychologist, consultant*
†Kennedy, Robert Philip *civil engineer*
Linzey, Verna May *minister, writer*
Mayer, James Hock *mediator, lawyer*
Moore, Marc Anthony *university administrator, writer, retired military officer*
Newman, Barry Ingalls *retired banker, lawyer*
Niehoff, Arthur Herman *anthropologist, writer*
Pantos, William Pantazes *mechanical engineer, consultant*
Polesetsky, Harold H. *contractor*
Rich, Elizabeth Marie *nursing educator*
Rockwell, Elizabeth Goode *dance company director, consultant, educator*
Sanders, Adrian Lionel *educational consultant*
Steele, John Thomas *surgeon, military officer*
Tomomatsu, Hideo *chemist*
Ziegler, James Russell *computer consultant*

Etna
Auxentios, *clergyman*

Eureka
†Berg, Patty *state legislator*
†Clark, Dwight William *lawyer*
Marak, Louis Bernard, Jr., *artist, educator*

Fair Oaks
Agerbek, Sven *mechanical engineer*
Chernev, Melvin *retired beverage company executive*
Church, Bryan P. *business owner, educator*
Dorf, Eve Buckle *artist*
Jackson, Fred Lester *retired civil engineer*
Lemke, Herman Ernest Frederick, Jr., *retired elementary education educator, consultant*
Maskall, Martha Josephine *web site designer, publisher, health consultant*
Papa, Michael Joseph *real estate broker*
Stewart, William Thomas *communications educator*
Yarrigle, Charlene Sandra Shuey *realtor, investment advisor*

Fairfax
Delaney, Marion Patricia *retail executive*
Ryan, Kay Pedersen *poet*
Urquhart, Karin May *foundation administrator, environmentalist*

Fairfield
Kirkorian, Donald George *retired college official, management consultant*
Martin, Clyde Verne *psychiatrist*
Munn, William Charles, II, *psychiatrist*
Phelps, Joseph Alfred *social services administrator, small business owner*
Stevenson, James D(onald), Jr., *psychologist, counselor*

Fall River Mills
Caldwell, Walter Edward *editor, small business owner*
Reed, Eva Silver Star *chieftain*

Fallbrook
Bryant, Don Estes *economist, scientist*
David, Ward S. *bank officer, retired federal agency executive*
Freeman, Harry Lynwood *retired accountant*
†Higbee, Donald William *electronics company executive, lawyer*
Loeber, Thomas Stanton *retired biologist*
Ragland, Jack Whitney *artist*
†Seelye, Gloria Walls *retired newswriter, public relations executive*
Sorbello, Joseph Charles *retired lawyer*

Felicity
Istel, Jacques Andre *mayor*

Flintridge
Johnston, Oliver Martin, Jr., *animator*
Pickering, William Hayward *research scientist*

Folsom
Anderson, Jeffrey Lee *physician, anesthesiologist, consultant*
Campbell, Ann Marie *artist*
Ettlich, William F. *electrical engineer*
Ewing, Russell Charles, II, *physician*
†Goodwin, James Jeffries *lawyer*
Hennessey, David Patrick *banker*
Jantzen, J(ohn) Marc *retired education educator*
Jefferds, William John *military advisor*
†Munroe, Jeanette C. *music educator*
Peck, Ellie Enriquez *retired state administrator*
Peck, Raymond Charles, Sr., *driver behavior research specialist and research consultant*
Regan, William Joseph, Jr., *energy company executive*
†Ryu, Woong Hwan *electrical engineer*
†Sample, Winona Elliott *educational consultant*
†Sarraf, Shirley A. *secondary school educator*

Fontana
Atkinson, Donald D., Sr., *real estate broker*
Donica, Cheryl Marie *elementary education educator*
†Johna, Samir *surgeon*
†Mayse, Susan Galilee *music educator*
†Tong, Freda Madeline *writer*

Foothill Ranch
Sperling, Scott Edward *software consultant, Bible expositor*
Weiss, Sherman David *lawyer, consultant*

Forestville
Kielsmeier, Catherine Jane *school system administrator*

Fort Bragg
Galli, Darrell Joseph *management consultant*
Lehan, Jonathan Michael *judge*

Fort Irwin
Shuler, George Nixon, Jr., *social worker, writer*
†Webster, William G., Jr., *army officer*

Foster City
Barnett, David Hughes *software engineer, computer systems architect*
Berman, Daniel K(atzel) *educational consultant, university official*
†Denny, James M. *health care services company executive*
Hotz, Henry Palmer *retired physicist*
†Jeffrey, John Orval *lawyer*
†Kellogg, Deren Earl *historian*
Ladunga, Istvan (Steve Ladunga) *computational molecular biologist*
Lonnquist, George Eric *lawyer*
Lutvak, Mark Allen *computer company executive*
Nugent, Denise *holistic nurse consultant and educator*
Thomlinson, Ralph *demographer, educator*
Zaidi, Iqbal Mehdi *biochemist, scientist*

Fountain Valley
Berman, Steven Richard *computer company executive*
Bray, Ronald Lawrence *sales executive*
Curl, Wade, Jr., (Mack Curl Jr.) *health facility administrator, consultant*
Davis, Jeremy Matthew *chemist*
†de Jong-Pombo, Teresa Maria *concert pianist, educator*
Einstein, Stephen Jan *rabbi*
†Kalb, Virginia Grover *retired school library administrator, educator*
Le, Vinh Tu *language educator, translator*
†Olivadoti, Victoria Ruth *educational consultant*
Otto, Marie (Bertha Otto) *educational administrator, educational consulting company executive*
Penderghast, Thomas Frederick *business educator*

Purdy, Leslie *community college president*
Smith, Marie Edmonds *real estate agent, property manager*
Treadway-Dillmon, Linda Lee *athletic trainer, actress, stuntwoman*
†Tu, John *engineering executive*

Fremont
Buswell, Debra Sue *small business owner, programmer, analyst*
Cummings, John Patrick *lawyer*
†Dutra, John A. *state legislator*
Feinberg, Richard Alan *clinical psychologist*
Hsu, Gloria *piano teacher*
†Huang, Robert *electronics manufacturing executive*
Jensen, Paul Edward Tyson *business educator, consultant*
Kitta, John Noah *lawyer*
Ko, Hyunok *artist, sculptor*
Lane, Eric Jay *retail executive*
Le, Thuy Trong *educator, researcher*
Li, Fuhe *research scientist, science administrator*
Mah, Tina Lily *science administrator*
Maloney, Cheryl Ann *foundation, consultant, business executive*
Maurer, Robert Michael *medical company executive*
Mian, Guo *electrical engineer*
Morrison, Gus (Angus Hugh Morrison) *mayor, engineer*
Nguyen, Sam (Van Nguyen) *economist, researcher*
†Puri, Umesh Chandra *application developer*
Ramirez-Mireles, Fernando *electrical engineer*
Rusch, Thomas William *manufacturing executive*
Sahatjian, Manik *nurse, psychologist*
Saraf, Dilip Govind *management consultant*
Sarkar, Arindam *information technology executive*
Smith, Bernald Stephen *retired airline pilot, aviation consultant*
Squiers, Elizabeth C. *healthcare administrator*
Steinmetz, Seymour *pediatrician*
†Tang, John *network technician, information scientist, educator*
Tantra, Muljadi *corporate marketing professional*
Tribus, Myron *retired quality counselor, engineer, educator*
Unsal, Cem *electrical engineer, educator*
Wang, Huai-Liang William *mechanical engineer*
White, Raymond Leslie *geneticist*
Wood, Linda May *librarian*
Wu, James Chen-Yuan *aerospace engineering educator*

Fresno
Armey, Douglas Richard *investment consultant*
Autry, Alan *mayor, actor, former professional football player, film company executive*
Bundy-DeSoto, Teresa Mari *language educator, vocalist*
Chandler, Bruce Frederick *internist*
Chang, Sidney H. (Sidney H. Chang) *history educator*
†Cole, Jessie Mae *nursing assistant, writer*
Coleman, Donald Gene *education educator*
Coyle, Robert Everett *federal judge*
Dackawich, S. John *sociology educator*
Dandoy, Maxima Antonio *education educator emeritus*
Darden, Edwin Speight, Sr., *architect*
Dauer, Donald Dean *investment executive*
Epperson, Robert Dale *farmer*
Ewell, A. Ben, Jr., *lawyer, businessman*
Ezaki-Yamaguchi, Joyce Yayoi *dietitian*
†Fields, Jill S. *education educator*
Ganulin, Judy *public relations professional*
Garrison-Finderup, Ivadelle Dalton *writer, educator*
Garza, Alvaro *physician*
†Garza-Lozano, Nereyda *language educator*
Genini, Ronald Walter *history educator, historian*
Girvin, Shirley Eppinette *retired elementary education educator, journalist*
Gorman, Michael Joseph *library director, educator*
Holmes, Albert William, Jr., *physician*
Howe, Ronald Evans *lawyer, minister, small business owner*
Huffman, David George *electrical engineer*
†Ishigaki, Miles Mitsurn *musician, educator*
Jamison, Daniel Oliver *lawyer*
Joseph, James William *political analyst*
Kauffman, George Bernard *chemistry educator*
Khouzam, Hani Raoul *psychiatrist, physician, educator*
Klassen, Peter James *academic administrator, history educator*
Kouymjian, Dickran *art historian, Orientalist, educator*
†Kuhn, Rose Marie *language educator*
Lambe, James Patrick *lawyer*
†Lanter, Lanore *writer, educator*
Leigh, Hoyle *psychiatrist, educator, writer*
Levine, Philip *poet, retired educator*
McGregor, John Joseph *lawyer*
Michael, James Daniel *computer scientist*
†Ng, Franklin C.L. *historian, educator*
O'Brien, John Conway *economist, educator, writer*
O'Connor, Kevin John *psychologist, educator*
Patnaude, William Eugene *architect*
Patton, Jack Thomas *family practice physician*
Petrochilos, Elizabeth A. *writer, publisher*
Pings, Anthony Claude *architect*
Rank, Everett George *government official*
Renberg, Michael Loren *lawyer*
†Richter, Bertina *librarian*
Salzman, Barnett Seymour *psychiatrist*
†Saul, Walter Biddle, II, *music educator, composer*
Schroeder, Rita Molthen *retired chiropractor*
†Scott, David Allen *mental health services professional, writer*
Shigyo, Tetsuo Ted *emergency physician*
Shmavonian, Gerald S. *philanthropist, art collector*
Smith, Richard Howard *banker*
Smith, V. Roy *neurosurgeon*
Steinbock, John Thomas *bishop*
Stuart, Dorothy Mae *artist*
Tellier, Richard Davis *management educator*
Thompson, Leonard Russell *pediatrician*
van der Elst, Dirk Hendrik *cultural anthropologist, educator*
Wanger, Oliver Winston *federal judge*
Welch, Jack Hamill *retired internist*
Welty, John Donald *academic administrator*
Wilson, James Ross *communications educator, broadcasting executive*
Winslow, Norman Eldon *business executive*
Xiong, Tousu Saydangnmvang *minister*
†Zweifler, John Andrew *physician, educator*

Fullerton
†Ackerman, Richard Charles *lawyer, state legislator*
†Aston, Edward Ernest, IV, *dermatologist*
Ayala, John *librarian, dean*
Bell, Melodie Elizabeth *artist, massage therapist*
Bradburn, David Denison *engineer, retired air force officer*
†Bush, William Merritt *lawyer*
Carrithers, Joseph Edward *english composition and literature educator*
†Coronel, Raul Angulo *sculptor*
de Rios, Marlene Dobkin *medical anthropologist, educator*
Donoghue, Mildred Ransdorf *education educator*
†Elliott-Scheinberg, Wendy *history educator, genealogist*
Fearn, Heidi *physicist, educator*
Fischer, Robert Blanchard *university administrator, researcher*
Fleissig, Adrian R. *economics educator, consultant*
Goldstein, Edward David *lawyer, former glass company executive*
Gunness, Robert Charles *retired chemical engineer*
Hershey, Gerald Lee *psychologist, educator*
Jones, Claris Eugene, Jr., *botanist, educator*
Kaisch, Kenneth Burton *psychologist, priest*
Lupash, Lawrence Ovidiu *computer analyst, researcher*
Miller, Arnold *electronics executive*
Moerbeek, Stanley Leonard *lawyer*
Nitta, Douglas *family practice physician*
O'Donnell, Edith J. *educational and information technology consultant, writer, musician*
†Rao, Prasada *engineering educator*
Roberts, Mark Scott *lawyer*
†Sa, Julie *councilwoman*
Sadrudin, Moe *humanitarian organization executive*
Shapiro, Mark Howard *physicist, educator, academic dean, consultant*
†Smiley, Stanley Robert *lawyer*
Smith, Ephraim Philip *academic administrator, former university dean, educator*
Snider, Jane Ann *elementary school educator*
Steinmeyer, Robert Jay *lawyer*
Sugarman, Michael *physician, rheumatologist*
†Talmo, Ronald Victor *lawyer, law educator*
Tehrani, Fleur Taher *electrical engineer, educator, researcher*
Wan, Julia Chang *retired science educator*
Wiley, David Cole *producer*

Galt
Nunes, Judy Omai *artist*

Garden Grove
Broadwater, Bruce A. *mayor*
†Dornan, Robert Kenneth *former congressman*
Gandhi, Manish P. *microbiologist*
†Schuller, Robert Harold *minister, writer*
Sherrard, Raymond Henry *retired federal agent*
Virgo, Muriel Agnes *swimming school owner*
Williams, J(ohn) Tilman *insurance executive, real estate broker, city official*

Garden Valley
Price, Lew Paxton *writer, engineer, scientist*

Gardena
Hardison, Dee *former mayor*
†Harvey, Cyril Leslie *education educator*
Hu, Steve Seng-Chiu *scientific research company executive, academic administrator*
Kanner, Edwin Benjamin *electrical manufacturing company executive*
Morton, James Carnes, Jr., *automotive company executive*
†Stuart, Jay William *retired engineer*

Gilroy
Borton, George Robert *retired airline captain*
George, Marilyn L. *music educator, musician*
Hart, William Carl *retired civil engineer*

Glen Ellen
Berkland, James Omer *geologist*
Hurlbert, Roger William *information service industry executive*

Glendale
†Altman, Steven *financial consulting company executive*
Benedict, Chuck (Charles J. Benedict Jr.) *writer, broadcaster, editor, producer*
†Burr-Stienon, Elaine *writer, minister, private school educator*
Carley, Kurt *actor*
Cross, Richard John *banker*
Cutts, Stephen Paul *civil engineer, linguistics researcher*
†Davidson, Suzanne Mouron *lawyer*
de Grassi, Leonard *art historian, educator*
Dudash, Linda Christine *insurance executive*
Early, Alexander Rieman, III, *judge*
Ebert, Gerard (Gerry Ebert) *hypnotherapist, freelance/self-employed writer*
Edwards, Kathryn Inez *educational technology consultant*
Ferren, Bran *graphics designer*
†Fluharty, Jesse Ernest *lawyer*
†Gedjeyan, Hovannes John *real estate broker*
Green, Norman Harry *lawyer*
Hadley, Paul Ervin *international relations educator*
Hoffman, Donald M. *lawyer*
Hughes, B. Wayne *retail executive*
†Katzenberg, Jeffrey *motion picture studio executive*
Kaye, Jhani *radio station manager, owner production company*
Kazanjian, Phillip Carl *lawyer*
†Kazarian, Poghos F. *physicist, researcher, educator*
Kinney, Paul William *investment company executive*
Knoop, Vern Thomas *civil engineer, consultant*
MacDonald, Kirk Stewart *lawyer*
Martinetti, Ronald Anthony *lawyer*
Michelson, Lillian *librarian, researcher*
Misa, Kenneth Franklin *management consultant*
†Moorhead, Carlos J. *former congressman*
†O'Connor, (Robert) Patrick *editor*
Polley, Terry Lee *lawyer*
Renner, Marguerite *history educator*
Scott, A. Timothy *lawyer, business executive*
Shahshahani, Ahmad *economics educator*
Sherman, Eric *director, writer, educator*
Spring, Carl Chaffee, Jr., *medical writer*
Sprosty, Joseph Patrick *producer, writer, weapons specialist*
Stanfill, Latayne Colvett *non-fiction writer*
Toscano, Oscar Ernesto *lawyer*
†Trivison, Margaret Ann *librarian*
Wang, James K. *internist, medical administrator*
Whalen, Lucille *retired academic administrator*
†Young, George Walter *lawyer*

Glendora
Condiff, David Wesley *clinical psychologist*
Haile, Benjamin Carroll, Jr., *retired chemical engineer, retired mechanical engineer*
Harmsen, Mark Spaulding *legislative aide*
Lasko, Allen Howard *pharmacist*
O'Hagan, William Gordon *state agency administrator*
†Prukesatonkul, Kamol *music educator*
Schiele, Paul Ellsworth, Jr., *education business owner, writer*
†Solheim, Bruce Olav *education educator*
Walters, Matthew Paul *recreational facility executive, consultant*

Gold River
Andrew, John Henry *lawyer, retail corporation executive, author*
Gray, Myles McClure *retired insurance company executive*

Goleta
Cork, Donald Burl *electrical engineer*
Crowfoot, Betsy M. *writer*
Frech, Harry Edward, III, *economics educator, consultant*
Jammalamadaka, Vijaya Lakshmi *environmental specialist*
†Lea, Wayne Adair *electrical engineer, linguist*
Loomis, Edward Warren *writer, educator*
†Sullivan, Kevin Joseph *mechanical engineer*
Zuk, Gerald Harvey *psychologist, consultant*

Granada Hills
Aller, Wayne Kendall *psychology educator, researcher, computer education company executive, property manager*
Lehtihalme, Larry K. (Lauri Lehtihalme) *financial planner*
†O'Connor, Betty Lou *service executive*
Shoemaker, Harold Lloyd *infosystem specialist*
Stump, D. Michael *librarian*
†Weitkamp, Fredrick John *lawyer*

Granite Bay
Cornwell, Jimmy Lee *fundraising executive, retired air force officer*
†Findlay, Margery Waldo *retired librarian*
Hartmann, Frederick Howard *political science educator emeritus*
Holtz, Sara *consultant*
Hunnicutt, Richard Pearce *metallurgical engineer*
Kemper, Dorla Dean Eaton (Dorla Dean Eaton) *real estate broker*
†Reisman, Judith Ann Gelernter *media communications executive, educator*

Grass Valley
Bell, Joseph James *lawyer*
Bennison, Allan Parnell *geological consultant*
Cassella, Dennis Gene *retired county official*
†Connell, Will *financial consultant*
†Ely, Parry Haines *dermatologist, educator*
†Gillett, Annette Damron *retired speech and forensics educator*
Hawkins, Richard Michael *lawyer*
Lunde, Karen Tamm *real estate broker*
McDaniel, Carolyn Marie (Lynn) *secondary education educator*
Ozanich, Charles George *real estate broker*

Greenbrae
Bonapart, Alan David *lawyer*
Levy, S. William *dermatologist, educator*
Neuharth, Daniel J., II, *psychotherapist*
Parnell, Francis William, Jr., *otolaryngologist*
Ramirez, Archimedes *neurosurgeon, educator*

Greenfield
Munoz, John Joseph *retired transportation company executive*

Gualala
Ring, Alice Ruth Bishop *retired physician*

Guerneville
†Mannino, J. Davis *psychologist, educator, author*

Hacienda Heights
Love, Daniel Joseph *consulting engineer*

Half Moon Bay
Fennell, Diane Marie *marketing executive, process engineer*
Harris, David Jack *artist, painter, educator*
Hinthorn, Micky Terzagian *volunteer, retired*
Lambert, Frederick William *lawyer, educator*
Melvin, Jay Wayne *computer programmer*
Robertson, Abel L., Jr., *pathologist*

Hanford
Gamboa, Lucito G. *physician, pathologist*
Harris, Mildred Staeger *retired broadcast executive*
†Hazen, William A. *secondary school educator*
Park, Penny Sheran *elementary school educator, writer*

Happy Camp
Black, Barbara Ann *publisher*

Harbor City
Ackerson, Bradley Kent *physician*
Kwan, Benjamin Ching Kee *ophthalmologist*
Lee, Grace Tze *information services company executive*

Hat Creek
Shepard, David Haspel *film restoration specialist*

Hathaway Pines
Williams, Alan Keiser *management consultant*

Hawthorne
Brann, Donald Lewis, Jr., *school superintendent*
Fila, John Charles *psychoanalyst*
†McRuer, Duane Torrance *aerospace engineering executive*
†Perry, Lucinda B. *retired elementary school educator, writer*

Hayward
Bachicha, Joseph Alfred *physician, educator*
Cooper, Roberta *mayor*
†Deshpande, Deepa Suhas *research scientist*
Duncan, Doris Gottschalk *information systems educator*
Getz, Melissa B. *secondary education educator*
†Gleason, Ken Bell *historian, educator, journalist*
†Hammond, Marian Corleene *retired literature educator*
Jun, Jong Sup *public administration educator*
Kimbell, Marion Joel *retired engineer*
Laycock, Mary Chappell *gifted and talented education educator, consultant*
McCune, Ellis E. *retired university system chief administrator, higher education consultant*
Minzner, Dean Frederick *aviation company executive*
Perrizo, James David *art and sculpture educator, forestry pilot*
Rees, Norma S. *academic administrator*
Reevy-Manning, Gretchen Maria *psychology educator*
†Roby, Tom *mathematician, educator*
Sabharwal, Ranjit Singh *mathematician*
Smith, John Kerwin *lawyer*
Solé, Pedro *management consultant*
†Staudohar, Paul David *economics educator, labor arbitrator*
Stern, Ralph David *lawyer*
Waller, Marilyn Jean *podiatric surgeon, educator*
Yeliseev, Alexei Arkadievich *biochemist, researcher*

Healdsburg
Eade, George James *retired air force officer, research executive, defense consultant*
Erdman, Paul Emil *author*
Glad, Joan Bourne *retired clinical psychologist, educator*
Myers, Robert Eugene *writer, educator*
Vedros, Neylan Anthony *microbiologist, educator*

Hemet
†Berger, Lev Isaac *physicist, educator*
Culverwell, Albert Henry *historian*
Galletta, Joseph Leo *physician*
†Holley, Robert William *sales executive, minister*
Knapp, Lonnie Troy *elementary education educator*
Lawrence, Paula Denise *physical therapist*
Levine, Elaine Prado *school psychologist, musician, artist*
Mata, David Joseph *physician*
Rowe, Mary Sue *accounting executive*

Hermosa Beach
Barr, Warren Paul *optometrist*
Kokalj, James Edward *retired aerospace administrator*
Lay, Alfred Alan *recording engineer, musician*
Rowland, Christopher Lee *filmmaker, educator, artist*
Wickwire, Patricia Joanne Nellor *psychologist, educator*
Williams, Jack Jeff *realtor, retired executive administrator*
Winthrop, Kenneth Ray *insurance executive*

Hesperia
Butcher, Jack Robert (Jack Risin) *manufacturing executive, film producer, actor*
Taylor, Gary Jay *fire services professional*

Highland
Lee, Robert Erich *information technology consultant*
Miller, R. Warburton *psychologist, citrus farmer*
Tacal, Jose Vega, Jr., *retired public health official, veterinarian*

Hillsborough
Atwood, Mary Sanford *writer*
Kane, Steven Edward *human resources executive*
Keller, John Francis *retired wine company executive, mayor*
Komissarchik, Edward *computer scientist*
Kraft, Robert Arnold *retired medical educator, physician*
Packard, Peter *medical educator, retired internist*
Quigley, Philip J. *retired telecommunications industry executive*
Westerfield, Putney *management consulting executive*

Hollister
†Miller, Alisa Dorothy Norton *artist*
Smith, George Larry *analytical and environmental chemist*
Spencer, Douglas Lloyd *chemist, manufacturing executive*
Turpin, Calvin Coolidge *retired university administrator, educator*
†Zuniga, James R. *director, music educator, conductor, composer*

Hollywood
†Bird, Topanga *artist, writer*
†Calva, Robert Baraquiel *music educator*
Fisher, Joel Marshall *political scientist, legal consultant, educator*
Gould, Julian Saul *lawyer*
Marshall, Conrad Joseph *entrepreneur*
Melchior, Ib Jorgen *author, television and motion picture writer, director*
Milhous, David Matthew *film and television editor*
Mkhitarian, Marine *chemical engineer*
†Nyirenda, Vukani Gaskell *social sciences educator*
Parks, Robert Myers *appliance manufacturing company executive*
†Perth, Rod *network entertainment executive*
Powell, Leslie *poet*
Roberts, Mel (Melvin Richard Kells) *retired film editor*
Salzman, David Elliot *entertainment industry executive*
Shurtleff, C. Michael *writer*
Stepanov, Sergei Valentinovich *consultant, researcher*
Thomas, Tony *producer*

Hopland
Jones, Milton Bennion *retired agronomist, educator*

Huntington Beach
†Agadjanyan, Michael Grant *education educator*
Appelbaum, Bruce David *physician*
Armstrong, Alan Leigh *lawyer*
Berry, Kim Lauren *artist*
Botsko, Ronald Joseph *business and engineering consultant*
Canyon, Steven *financial officer*
Carey, Shirley Anne *nursing consultant*
Carter, Henrietta McKee *educator*
Cook, Debbie *lawyer, councilman*
Davidson-Shepard, Gay *secondary education educator*
De Massa, Jessie G. *media specialist*
De Veirman, Geert Adolf *engineer*
†Duong, Cong Nghiep *aeronautical engineer*
Flakes, Susan *playwright, screenwriter, director*
Grooms, Henry Randall *civil engineer*
Hamilton, Allen Philip *financial advisor*
†Harman, Thomas *state official*
Harsha, Philip Thomas *aerospace engineer*
†Isabelle, Beatrice Margaret *artist*
Jackle, Karen Dee *real estate company executive*
Jensen, Dennis Lowell *lawyer*
†Lans, Carl Gustav *architect, economist*
Lopata, Martin Barry *business executive*
MacCauley, Hugh Bournonville *banker*
Martin, Wilfred Wesley Finny *psychologist, property owner and manager*
McGuire, James Charles *aircraft company executive*
†Myles, Margaret Jean *real estate appraiser*
Nash, Richard Eugene *aerospace engineer*
Neal, Anita *artist*
Nguyen, Han Van *mechanical engineer*
Nichter, Larry Steven *medical educator, plastic surgeon*
Nikas, Richard John *lawyer*
Nowlan, Daniel Ralph *engineering executive*
†Pacino, Frank George *physician, educator*
Peters, Robert L(ouis) *retired English educator, poet, critic*
†Sebag, Jerry *ophthalmologist, surgeon*
Solomon, Susan Carol *hospital administrator, marketing specialist*
Stillman, Alfred William, Jr., *electrical engineer*
Strutzel, J(od) C(hristopher) *escrow company executive*
†Typaldos, Sylvia Joyce *musician, writer*
Welsh, William Daniel *geriatric medicine family practice physician*
Winterowd, Walter Ross *English educator*

Idyllwild
Smith, Robert Bruce *college administrator*

Imperial
Lokey, Frank Marion, Jr., *broadcast executive, consultant*

Imperial Beach
Merkin, William Leslie *retired lawyer*

Indian Wells
Biagi, Richard Charles *retail executive, real estate consultant*
Criste, Virginia Spiegel *lawyer*
Harding, James Warren *retired finance company executive*
Jorgensen, Gordon David *retired engineering company executive*

Kelley, John Paul *communications consultant*
†Trotter, F(rederick) Thomas *retired academic administrator*
†Weinberg, Steven Jay *lawyer*

Indio
De Salva, Christopher Joseph *lawyer, consultant*
Garra, Raymond Hamilton, II, *marketing executive*
†York, Douglas Arthur *manufacturing and construction company executive*
Zorick, Nancy Lee *artist, actress*

Inglewood
Alaniz, Miguel José Castañeda *library director*
†Cato, Gloria Maxine *retired secondary education educator, school program administrator*
†Dixon, Tamecka *professional basketball player*
Epstein, Marsha Ann *public health administrator, physician*
†Horton, Jerome E. *state official*
†Jackson, Philip Douglas *professional basketball coach*
Kierulff, Stephen Charles *psychologist*
Lewis, Roy Roosevelt *physicist*
Logan, Lynda Dianne *elementary education educator*
Sludikoff, Stanley Robert *publisher, writer*
Sukov, Richard Joel *radiologist*
†Vincent, Edward *state legislator*
Wakefield, Marie Cynthia *performing arts educator, playwright, poet*

Inverness
†Ciani, Judith Elaine *retired lawyer*
Welpott, Jack Warren *photographer, educator*

Inyokern
Norris, Lois Ann *elementary school educator*

Irvine
Abu-Mostafa, Ayman Said *computer consultant*
Agran, Larry *mayor, lawyer*
Alspach, Philip Halliday *manufacturing company executive*
Antonelli, G. Aldo *logic and philosophy of science educator*
Aswad, Dana William *biochemist, educator*
Ayala, Francisco José *geneticist, educator*
Back, Lloyd H. *mechanical engineer, researcher*
Bander, Myron *physics educator, university dean*
Bartkus, Richard Anthony *magazine publisher*
Bastiaanse, Gerard C. *lawyer*
Bean, Frank D(awson) *sociology and demography educator*
Beard, Ronald Stratton *lawyer*
Belić Weiss, Zoran *artist, designer, educator*
Bernal, Victoria *anthropologist, educator*
Black, William Rea *lawyer*
†Boris, James R. *investment company executive*
Boyd, Carolyn Patricia *history educator*
Bradshaw, Ralph Alden *biochemistry educator*
†Braunstein, Myron Lee *psychology educator*
Broadhurst, Norman Neil *food products executive*
Burton, Michael Ladd *anthropology educator*
†Campbell, John B. T., III, *state official*
Cesario, Thomas Charles *dean*
Chelapati, Chunduri Venkata *civil engineering educator*
Chen, Chuansheng *education educator*
Chen, Chungte William *optical engineer*
†Choi, Bernard *laser scientist, researcher*
Chronley, James Andrew *real estate executive*
Cicerone, Ralph John *academic administrator, geophysicist*
Clark, Bruce Robert *geologist, consultant*
Clark, Karen Heath *lawyer*
Cobianchi, Thomas Theodore *engineering and marketing executive, educator*
Craig, Karen Lynn *accountant, controller*
Curtis, Jesse William, Jr., *retired federal judge*
Danziger, James Norris *political science educator*
Davis, Clifton Duncan *actor, composer*
de la Maza, Luis M. *pathology educator*
Demetrescu, Mihai Constantin *research scientist, educator, computer company executive*
DeSipio, Louis *political science educator*
Dzyaloshinskii, Igor Ekhielievich *physicist*
Farrar, Donald Keith *retired financial executive*
Farrell, Teresa Joanning *lawyer*
Feldstein, Paul Joseph *management educator*
†Ferguson, James *anthropologist, educator*
Fleischer, Everly Borah *academic administrator*
Freeman, Linton Clarke *sociology educator*
Friedenberg, Richard Myron *radiology educator, physician*
Gehricke, Jean-Guido *psychologist, researcher*
Giannini, Valerio Louis *investment banker*
Godfrey, Raymond Michael *information systems educator*
†Goldman, Doris Toran *not-for-profit developer*
†Goldstock, Barry Philip *lawyer*
†Grandone-LLorente, Maria Elisa *dean, consultant*
Greenberger, Ellen *psychologist, educator*
Gupta, Sudhir *immunologist, educator*
Hancock, S. Lee *business executive*
Hensley, William Michael *lawyer*
Hilker, Walter Robert, Jr., *lawyer*
Hine, Robert Van Norden, Jr., *historian, educator*
Hoffman, Donald David *cognitive and computer science educator*
Hubbell, Floyd Allan *physician, educator*
Huff, C(larence) Ronald *public policy and criminology educator*
Hurst, Charles Wilson *lawyer*
Jamshidipour, Yousef *bank executive, economist, financial advisor*
Jones, Joie Pierce *entrepreneur, acoustician, educator, writer, scientist*
†Kaneda, Masayoshi *mathematics educator, researcher*
Kaplan, Arline Ray *editor, writer*
†Kempff, Juergen *language educator*

Key, Mary Ritchie (Mrs. Audley E. Patton) *linguist, writer, educator*
Khalessi, Mohammad R. *structural engineer, researcher*
Kim, Han Pyong *dentist, researcher*
Knobbe, Louis Joseph *lawyer, educator*
Kobsa, Alfred *computer scientist, educator*
Kraemer, Kenneth Leo *architect, educator, urban planner*
Kumar, Anil *nuclear engineer*
†Lafky, Deborah Beranek Palser *information scientist, researcher*
Lathrop, Richard Harold *computer science educator*
†Lave, Charles Arthur *economics educator*
Leets, Peter J. *consulting firm executive*
Lenhoff, Howard Maer *biological sciences educator, academic administrator, activist*
Lesonsky, Rieva *editor*
Li, Peter Wai-Kwong *mathematics educator*
Lillyman, William John *German language educator, academic administrator*
London, Ray William *consultant, mediator, arbitrator, researcher*
†Lorimer, Mark W. *transportation company executive*
Luce, R(obert) Duncan *psychology educator*
Manasson, Vladimir Alexandrovich *physicist*
Maradudin, Alexei A. *physics educator*
Margolis, Julius *economist, educator*
†Martens, Don Walter *lawyer*
Maybay, Duane Charles *recycling systems executive*
McCubbin, Sharon Anglin *elementary school educator*
McLaughlin, Calvin Sturgis *biochemistry educator*
Miledi, Ricardo *neurobiologist*
Monroe, Kristen Renwick *political scientist, educator*
†Mussey, Joseph Arthur *health and medical product executive*
Nalcioglu, Orhan *physics educator, radiological sciences educator*
Nowick, Arthur Stanley *metallurgy and materials science educator*
Olek, Michael Joseph *medical educator*
Olsson, Carmen *interior designer*
Orme, Melissa Emily *mechanical engineering educator*
Overman, Larry Eugene *chemistry educator*
Paine, David M. *public relations executive*
Pechmann, Cornelia Ann Rachel *marketing professional*
Peltason, Jack Walter *foundation executive, educator*
Petrasich, John Moris *lawyer*
Phalen, Robert Franklynn *environmental scientist*
Pirkle, Hubert Chaillé *pathologist, educator*
Power, Francis William *newspaper publisher*
Puhl, Jennifer Louise *music teacher, pianist, organist*
Pyott, David Edmund Ian *pharmaceutical executive*
Qin, Suofu *biochemist*
Quilligan, Edward James *obstetrician, gynecologist, educator*
Rachlis, Arnold Israel *rabbi, religion educator*
Rangel, Roger Henrique *mechanical and aerospace engineering educator*
Regener, Connie Sue *minister, religious commentator*
Reisman, Richard S. *publisher*
Ribak, Charles Eric *anatomy educator*
†Ristau, Kenneth Eugene, Jr., *lawyer*
†Rodríguez Ordoñez, Jaime Edmundo *historian, educator*
Rowland, Frank Sherwood *chemistry educator*
Ruttenberg, Susann I. *health sciences administrator*
Rynn, Nathan *physics educator, consultant*
Saari, Donald Gene *mathematician, economist*
Salesky, William Jeffrey *corporate executive*
Samueli, Henry *electrical engineering educator, entrepreneur*
Sandu, Constantine *process development engineer*
Schonfeld, William Rost *political science educator, researcher*
Seller, Gregory Erol *marketing executive, writer, consultant*
Sharbaugh, W(illiam) James *plastics engineer, consultant*
Shea, Christina *former mayor*
†Shen, Ba-Zhong *research scientist*
Shirilau, Mark Steven *utilities executive*
†Shirley, Robert Bryce *lawyer*
Shusterman, Neal Douglas *writer, screenwriter*
Silverman, Paul Hyman *science administrator, former university official*
Sirignano, William Alfonso *aerospace and mechanical engineer, educator*
†Skyrms, Brian *social science educator*
Small, Kenneth Alan *economics educator*
Smedley, Keyue Ma *engineering educator, researcher*
Smith, Harold Raymond *neurologist, sleep medicine specialist, educator*
Smith, Vincent C. *information technology executive*
Specter, Richard Bruce *lawyer*
Sperling, George *cognitive scientist, educator*
Stack, Geoffrey Lawrence *real estate developer*
Stein, M(eyer) L(ewis) *journalist, magazine editor, writer*
Stone, David Mark *plastic surgeon*
Stone, Samuel Beckner *lawyer*
†Suarez-Villa, Luis *innovation and technological change, economic and social development, regional analysis educator*
Sutton, Dana Ferrin *classics educator*
Tengs, Tammy Ora *educator*
Teta, Todd Nicholas *technology consultant, real estate developer*
Tetef, Merry Lynn *internist, oncologist*
Ting, Albert Chia *bioengineering researcher*
Treas, Judith Kay *sociology educator*

Tripoli, Masumi Hiroyasu *financial consultant*
Tumakov, Vladimir Leonidovich *physicist, researcher*
Villaverde, Roberto *civil engineer*
Vines, Henry Ellsworth, III, *accountant, lawyer, financial planner*
von Tilsit, Heidemarie *information management specialist*
Wallis, Richard Fisher *physicist, educator*
†Warble, Charles Edward *materials scientist*
Weinstein, Gerald D. *dermatology educator*
Werlin, Lawrence B. *obstetrician, gynecologist, reproductive endocrinologist*
†Wertheim, Jay Philip *lawyer*
West, Robert Lee, Jr., *marketing professional*
†Wetterau, Mark S. *food products/distributor executive*
White, Alyssa Milman *lawyer, educator*
White, Douglas Richie *anthropology educator*
White, Stephen Halley *biophysicist, educator*
Wintrode, Ralph Charles *lawyer*
Zabsky, John Mitchell *engineering executive*
Zhu, Peter Chaoquan *chemist*

Irwindale
Lu, Guiyang *electrical engineer*
Miao, Rongsheng *mechanical and thermal engineer*

Jacumba
Johnson, Crane *writer, lawyer*

Janesville
Lathrop, Lawrence Erwin, Jr., *retired business owner, retired state forest ranger*

Julian
Rice, Earle, Jr., (Earle Wilmont Rice Jr.) *writer*

Kaweah
Foster, Joseph Kevin, IV, *entertainer, scribe*

Keene
†Rodriguez, Arturo Salvador *labor union official*

Kelsey
Rankin, Graham M. *educator, consultant*

Kelseyville
Fletcher, Leland Vernon *artist*
Sandmeyer, E. E. *toxicologist, consultant*

Kensington
Appelman, Evan Hugh *retired chemist*
Connick, Robert Elwell *retired chemistry educator*
Kolenda, Pauline M. *anthropology educator, researcher*
Littlejohn, David *writer*
Oppenheim, Antoni Kazimierz *mechanical engineer*
Stent, Gunther Siegmund *molecular biologist, educator*

Kentfield
Blum, Joan Kurley *fundraising executive*
Bruyn, Henry Bicker *physician*
Edgar, James Macmillan, Jr., *management consultant*
Freed, Thomas Alexander *retired radiologist*
Halprin, Anna Schuman (Mrs. Lawrence Halprin) *dancer*

Kenwood
Podboy, John Watts *clinical, forensic psychologist*

Kingsburg
Quaday-Gray, Ailene Diann *retired speech pathologist*

La Canada
Baker, Althea Ross *court hearing officer, lawyer, mediator, arbitrator, educator*
Larsen, Traci Lyn *interior designer*
Ruskin, Arnold Milton *engineer, educator*
Sanchez, Victor David *computer scientist, educator*
Tookey, Robert Clarence *consulting actuary*

La Canada Flintridge
Baines, Kevin Hays *planetary scientist, astronomer*
Byrne, George Melvin *physician*
Costello, Francis William *lawyer*
Lamson, Robert Woodrow *retired school system administrator*
†Leko, Gabrielle M. *mathematician, educator*
Price, Humphrey Wallace *aerospace engineer*
Wallace, James Wendell *lawyer*

La Crescenta
Fisk, Irwin Wesley *financial investigator*
†Gray, Velma LeVan *medical surgical nurse*
Klint, Ronald Vernon *secondary school educator, financial consultant*
Phillips, Mary Linda *actress*

La Habra
Chase, Cochrane *advertising agency executive*
Cramer, Esther Ridgway *author, historian, retired supermarket executive*
†Hyslop, Richard Stewart *law educator*
Lundberg, Lois Ann *political consultant, property manager executive*
Schoppa, Elroy *accountant, financial planner*

La Habra Heights
Agajanian, Gilda *pianist*

La Jolla
Alvariño De Leira, Angeles (Angeles Alvariño) *biologist, oceanographer*
Andre, Michael Paul *physicist, educator*
Anthony, Harry Antoniades *city planner, architect, educator*
Antin, David *poet, critic*

Arnold, James Richard *chemist, educator*
Asmus, John Fredrich *physicist*
Attiyeh, Richard Eugene *economics educator*
Backus, George Edward *theoretical geophysicist*
Bailey, David Nelson *pathology educator, university official*
†Ball, Edward David *hematologist, oncologist*
Bardwick, Judith Marcia *management consultant*
Barlow, Carrolee *physician, scientist, educator*
Barrett-Connor, Elizabeth Louise *epidemiologist, educator*
Bastien, Jane Smisor *music educator*
Bavasi, Peter Joseph *sports management executive*
Beebe, Mary Livingstone *curator*
Berger, Wolfgang H. *oceanographer, marine geologist*
Beutler, Ernest *physician, research scientist*
†Blanchard, Daniel G. *cardiologist*
Block, Melvin August *surgeon, educator*
Bloom, Floyd Elliott *physician, research scientist*
Boger, Dale L. *chemistry educator*
Brimble, Alan *business executive*
Brooks, Charles Lee, III, *computational biophysicist, educator*
Brown, Stuart I. *ophthalmologist, educator*
Bruggeman, Terrance John *financial corporate executive*
Bryan, John Rodney *management consultant*
Buckingham, Michael John *oceanography educator*
†Bunch, James Raymond *mathematician, educator*
Burbidge, E. Margaret *astronomer, educator*
Burgin, George Hans *computer scientist, educator*
Buss, Samuel Rudolph Rudolph *mathematics educator, researcher*
Cain, William Stanley *experimental psychologist, educator, researcher*
Carmichael, David Burton *physician*
†Carson, Richard Taylor, Jr., *economics educator*
Carty, Heidi Marlene *educator, researcher*
Case, Kenneth Myron *physics educator*
Cavenee, Webster K. *director*
†Chandler, Marsha *academic administrator, professor*
Chang, William Shen Chie *electrical engineering educator*
Coburn, Marjorie Foster *psychologist, educator*
Coler, Myron A(braham) *chemical engineer, educator*
†Cometto-Muñiz, Jorge Enrique *biochemist, researcher*
Copley, David C. *newspaper publishing company executive*
†Cordova, Armando *chemist*
Corrigan, Mary Kathryn *theater educator*
Counts, Stanley Thomas *aerospace consultant, retired naval officer, retired electronics company executive*
Covington, Stephanie Stewart *psychotherapist, writer, educator*
Cowhey, Peter Francis *international relations educator, consultant*
Cox, Charles Shipley *oceanography researcher, educator*
†Crawford, Vincent Paul *economist, educator*
Cunningham, Bruce Arthur *biochemist, educator*
Dalessio, Donald John *internist, neurologist, educator*
Davies, Hugh Marlais *museum director*
†Degryse, Bernard *cell biologist*
Diamant, Joel Charles *internist*
Dixon, Frank James *medical scientist, educator*
Dorsey, Dolores Florence *retired corporate treasurer, business executive*
Drake, Hudson Billings *aerospace and electronics company executive*
Driscoll, Charles Frederick *physics educator*
Edelman, Gerald Maurice *biochemist, neuroscientist, educator*
†Edgington, Thomas S. *pathologist, educator, molecular biologist, vascular biologist*
Edwards, Charles Cornell *surgeon, research administrator*
Elander, Richard Paul *consultant, retired pharmaceutical executive*
†Elgamal, Ahmed *geotechnical and structural engineering educator*
†Ely, Kathryn R. *crystallographer*
†Esherick, Joseph Wharton *history educator*
Falk, Julia S. *linguist, educator*
†Fantino, Edmund *psychology educator*
Farson, Richard Evans *psychologist*
Fisher, Frederick Hendrick *oceanographer emeritus*
Fisher, Robert Lloyd *retired geologist, retired oceanographer*
Fokin, Valery Valerievich *chemistry educator, researcher*
Foley, L(ewis) Michael *real estate executive*
Freedman, David Noel *religious studies educator*
Freedman, Jonathan Borwick *journalist, writer, lecturer, educator*
Friedmann, Theodore *physician*
Fung, Yuan-Cheng Bertram *bioengineering educator, writer*
Garland, Cedric Frank *epidemiologist, educator*
Gascoigne, Nicholas Robert John *immunologist, researcher*
Geckler, Richard Delph *metal products company executive, retired*
Geiduschek, E(rnest) Peter *biophysics and molecular biology educator*
Gerber, Michael Lewis *cardiac surgeon*
Gill, Gordon N. *medical educator*
Gittes, Ruben Foster *urological surgeon*
†Glass, Christopher Kevin *physician*
Golomb, Beatrice Alexandra *physician, medical researcher*
Graham, Ronald Lewis *mathematician*
Granger, Clive William John *economist, educator*
Grave de Peralta, Armando Rene *venture capitalist*
†Grise, Mark Andrew *cardiologist*
Guillemin, Roger C. L. *physiologist*
†Gutierrez, Ramon A. *history educator*
Halkin, Hubert *mathematics educator, research mathematician*
Hall, Harold Robert *retired computer engineer*
Hall, TennieBee M. *editor*
†Hallin, Daniel Clark *communications educator*
†Han, Jiahuai *medical researcher*
Harris, Philip Robert *management and space psychologist*
Harris, T. George *editor*
Harvey, A. Raymond *mathematician, educator*
Havis, Allan Stuart *playwright, theatre educator*
Haxo, Francis Theodore *marine biologist*
Hazzard, Mary Elizabeth *nurse, educator*
Helinski, Donald Raymond *biologist, educator*
Hench, Philip Kahler *physician*
Hendler, Sheldon Saul *internist, educator, biochemist, writer*
Henig, Suzanne *retired educator, writer, editor*
Hofmann, Alan Frederick *biomedical researcher, educator*
Holland, Charles Edward *medical products corporate executive*
Holmes, Edward W. *dean, physician, medical educator*
Hornaday, Aline Grandier *publisher, independent scholar*
Hostetler, Karl Yoder *internist, endocrinologist, educator*
Hughes, Gordon F. *research scientist, electrical engineer*
Hujsak, Ruth Joy *musician, educator*
Hunter, Tony (Anthony Rex Hunter) *molecular biologist, educator*
Iddings, Kathleen *poet, editor, publisher, consultant*
Ideker, Trey *computational biologist, molecular biologist*
Imana, Jorge Garron *artist*
Itano, Harvey Akio *biochemistry educator*
Jeub, Michael Leonard *financial consultant*
Jones, Charlie *television sports announcer*
Joris-Quinton, Liesbet *internal medicine physician*
Kadonaga, James Takuro *biochemist*
Karin, Sidney *computer science and engineering educator*
Katzman, Robert *medical educator, neurologist*
Kent, Paula *public relations, marketing and management consultant, lecturer*
Kenyon, Karen Beth Smith *literature educator, writer*
Kirchheimer, Arthur E(dward) *lawyer, business executive*
Kitada, Shinichi *biochemist*
Knox, Elizabeth Louise *community volunteer, travel consultant*
Kolodner, Richard David *biochemist, educator, geneticist*
†Kripke, Daniel Frederick *psychiatrist, educator*
Lal, Devendra *nuclear geophysics educator*
†Lambrou, Peter Thomas *psychologist*
Lane, Sylvia *economist, educator*
Langacker, Ronald Wayne *linguistics educator*
†Lanza Di Scalea, Francesco *engineering educator*
Lauer, James Lothar *physicist, educator*
Levy, Ralph *engineering executive, consultant*
Lewin, Ralph Arnold *biologist*
†Lewis, George *music educator*
†Lindenberg, Katja *chemistry educator*
Low, Mary Louise (Molly Low) *documentary photographer*
†Machina, Mark Joseph *economist*
†Madsen, Richard Paul *sociology educator, writer*
†Majumdar, Amitava *computer scientist, educator, nuclear engineer*
Mandler, George *psychologist, educator*
Mandler, Jean Matter *psychologist, educator*
Martin, James John, Jr., *retired consulting research firm executive, systems analyst*
Masouredis, Serafeim Panagiotis *pathologist, educator*
Masys, Daniel Richard *medical school director*
†Mayer, John M *medical researcher, educator*
McCammon, James Andrew *chemistry educator*
McDonald, Marianne *classicist*
McIlwain, Carl Edwin *physicist*
Mendoza, Stanley Atran *pediatric nephrologist, educator*
Merrim, Louise Meyerowitz *artist, actress*
†Micciancio, Daniele *computer scientist*
Milstein, Laurence Bennett *electrical engineering educator, researcher*
Mirsky, Phyllis Simon *librarian*
Moon, Mona McTaggart *speaker, trainer, consultant, educator*
†Morrow, Esther M. *aerospace engineer, researcher*
Morse, Jack Hatton *management consultant*
†Munk, Walter Heinrich *geophysics educator*
Nakamura, Robert Motoharu *pathologist*
Nemat-Nasser, Sia *engineering educator, researcher*
Newmark, Leonard Daniel *linguistics educator*
North, Kathryn E. Keesey (Mrs. Eugene C. North) *retired educator*
Nyhan, William Leo *pediatrician, educator*
Olafson, Frederick Arlan *philosophy educator*
O'Neil, Thomas Michael *physicist, educator*
Oreskes, Naomi *science historian*
Patton, Stuart *biochemist, educator*
Peet, Raymond Edward *consultant*
Penner, Stanford Solomon *engineering educator*
Peterson, Paul Ames *lawyer, educator*
Phillips, David P. *sociologist, educator*
Pollok, Brian Andrew *biotechnology company executive*
Pratt, George Janes, Jr., *psychologist, author*
Purdy, Kevin Moore *estate planner*
Rapaport, Samuel I. *educator, physician*
Rearden, Carole Ann *clinical pathologist, educator*
Reed, James Anthony *hotel and restaurant industry executive and owner, consultant*
Resnik, Robert *medical educator*
Reynolds, Roger Lee *composer, educator*
Richard, Rae Linda *nurse practitioner, vascular access specialist*
Richman, Douglas Daniel *medical virologist, educator, internist*
Ride, Sally Kristen *physics educator, scientist, former astronaut*
Rinaker, Samuel Mayo, Jr., *retired utilities executive*
Ripley, Stuart McKinnon *real estate consultant*
Rosen, Judah Ben *computer scientist*
Rosenblatt, Adylin Isabelle *social worker*
Rosenblatt, Murray *mathematics educator*
Rosenbluth, Marshall Nicholas *physicist*
Rosenfeld, Michael G. *medical educator*
†Rubin, Lewis J *physician, researcher*
Rudee, Mervyn Lea *engineering educator, researcher*
Rudolph, Walter Paul *engineering research company executive*
†Saldivar, Enrique *bioengineer, researcher*
†Schiller, Anita Rosenbaum *librarian*
Schimmel, Cleo Ritz *civic worker*
Schimmel, Paul Reinhard *biochemist, biophysicist, educator*
Schmid-Schoenbein, Geert Wilfried Wilfried *biomedical engineer, educator*
†Schneider, Gerald L. *plastic surgeon*
Seslar, Patrick George *writer, artist*
Shakespeare, Frank *ambassador*
Sham, Lu Jeu *physics educator*
Shannahan, William Paul *lawyer*
Shapiro, William Maurice *emergency medicine physician, administrator, researcher*
Sharpless, K. Barry *chemist, educator*
†Shawver, Laura K. *biotechnology company executive*
Sherman, Wilson *poet*
Shor, George G., Jr., *geophysicist, oceanographic administrator, engineer*
Shuler, Kurt Egon *chemist, educator*
Simon, Ronald I. *financial executive*
†Singer, Robert *plastic surgeon*
†Sobel, Joel Kenneth *economist*
Somerville, Richard Chapin James *atmospheric scientist, educator*
Spiess, Fred Noel *oceanographer, educator*
Spiro, Melford Elliot *anthropology educator*
Starr, Ross Marc *economist, educator*
Stefan, Vladislav Alexander *academic administrator, educator, research scientist, writer*
†Stein, Murray Brent *psychiatrist, researcher*
Steinberg, Daniel *preventive medicine physician, educator*
Stevens, Paul Irving *manufacturing company executive*
Stone, Donald Diamond *investment and sales executive*
Stone, William Ross *research and development company executive, physicist*
Takabe, Kazuaki *gastroenterology surgeon, research scientist*
Tan, Eng Meng *immunologist, biomedical scientist*
Taur, Yuan *physicist, researcher*
Teirstein, Paul Shepherd *physician, health facility administrator*
Terras, Audrey Anne *mathematics educator*
Terry, Robert Davis *neuropathologist, educator*
Tietz, Norbert Wolfgang *clinical chemistry educator, administrator*
Timmermann, Allan Gilling *economics educator*
Trujillo, Solomon D. *telecommunications executive*
Tsien, Roger Yonchien *chemist, cell biologist*
Vale, Wylie W. *biochemist*
Vallbona-Freeman, Marisa Freeman *public relations counselor*
Van Lint, Victor Anton Jacobus *physicist*
Verma, Inder M. *biochemist*
Waddy, Lawrence Heber *religious writer*
Walker, Richard Hugh *orthopaedic surgeon*
Watson, Kenneth Marshall *physics educator*
Weiner, Ferne *psychologist*
Weiss, Egon Arthur *retired library administrator*
West, John Burnard *physiologist, physician, educator*
Whitaker, Eileen Monaghan (Eileen Monaghan) *artist*
White, Halbert Lynn, Jr., *economist, educator, consultant*
White, Michelle Jo *economics educator*
Wilkie, Donald Walter *biologist, aquarium museum director*
Wilkins, Floyd, Jr., *retired lawyer, consultant*
Williams, Forman Arthur *engineering science educator, combustion theorist*
†Wilson, Bonnie Jean *lawyer, educator, investor*
Wolynes, Peter Guy *chemistry researcher, educator*
Wright, Andrew *English literature educator*
Wulbert, Daniel Eliot *mathematician, educator*
Yen, Samuel S(how)-C(hih) *obstetrics and gynecology educator, reproductive endocrinologist*
York, Herbert Frank *physics educator, government official*
Youngstedt, Shawn Douglas *research scientist*
†ZoBell, Karl *lawyer*
Zyroff, Ellen Slotoroff *information scientist, classicist, educator*

La Mesa
Behrend, Albert James *surgeon*
Black, Eileen Mary *retired elementary school educator*
†Boghairi, Anoushiravan *cardiologist*
Charleton, Margaret Ann *child care administrator, consultant*
†Espinosa, Ruben *education educator, consultant*
Freeland, Robert Frederick *retired librarian*
Hansen, Grant Lewis *retired aerospace and information systems executive*
Kafka, John Abraham *pediatrician*
†La Suer, Jay *state official*
Mitry, Darryl Joseph *writer, educator*
Schlador, Paul Raymond, Jr., *insurance agent*
Schmidt, James Craig *retired bank executive*
Tansey, Lisa Rebecca *database administrator, dancer, masseuse, musician*
Threlkeld, Steven Wayne *civil/environmental engineer*

La Mirada
Graybill, Ruth Ann *social worker*
Kong, Xiangli (Charlie Kong) *mechanical and control engineer, educator*
Lewis, Frederick Thomas *property manager*
†Lingenfelter, Judith Elaine *social sciences educator*
Pike, Patricia Louise *psychology educator*
†Rhee, Victor Sung-yul *theology studies educator, minister*
Stone, Leland Edward *writer*

La Palma
Kreeger, Margaret Ryan *lawyer*
†Sinard, Gary *mortgage company executive*

La Puente
†Hitchcock, Frederick E. "Fritz", Jr., *automotive company executive*
Sheridan, Christopher Frederick *human resources executive*

La Quinta
Adolph, Diane Joyce *retired underwriter*
Calvin, James Willard *thoracic and vascular surgeon*
Farber, Patricia Ann *secondary education educator*
Holman, David Calvin *independent television and film producer and director*
Peden, Lynn Ellen *marketing executive*
Pitkin, Roy Macbeth *retired obstetrician, educator*
†Tebbs, Carol Ann *secondary education educator, academic administrator*

La Verne
†Driebe, Michael D. *corporate financial executive*
†Ebersole, Helen Brownsberger *elementary school educator*
Fleck, Raymond Anthony, Jr., *retired university administrator*
†Gabelich, Christopher James *environment specialist, researcher*
Gelm, Richard Joseph *political scientist, educator*
Hwang, Cordelia Jong *chemist*
Jones, Jay H. *biology and biochemistry educator*
Marcus, Kenneth Hearne *historian, educator*
Morgan, Stephen Charles *academic administrator*
Neher, Robert Trostle *biology educator*

Lafayette
Alexander, Kenneth Lewis *editorial cartoonist*
Cobb, George Edward *surgeon*
Davies, Paul Lewis, Jr., *retired lawyer*
Dethero, J. Hambright *banker*
James, Muriel Marshall *writer, lecturer, psychotherapist*
Krueger, Robert Edward *manufacturing executive, mechanical engineer*
Lewis, Sheldon Noah *technology consultant*
Michelsen, Diane *lawyer*
Monheit, Molly Jane *artist, writer*
Morehouse, Valerie Jeanne *librarian*
Peirano, Lawrence Edward *civil engineer*
Peters, Ray John *surveyor*

Laguna Beach
Arnold, John David *management counselor, catalyst*
Benford, Gregory Albert *physicist, writer*
Bent, Alan Edward *political science educator, administrator*
Castro, Charles Edward *chemist, consultant*
Dale, Leon Andrew *economist, educator*
Foltz, Eldon Leory *neurosurgeon, educator*
Frenzel, Frances Johnson *registered nurse, educator, lecturer, poet, real estate broker*
Fry, Edward Bernard *education educator, retired*
†Ghiselin, Brewster *author, English language educator emeritus*
Hanauer, Joe Franklin *real estate executive*
†Jensen, Gloria Veronica *adult nurse practitioner*
Pelton, Virginia Lue *small business owner*
Pories, Muriel H. *business executive, loan consultant*
Powers, Runa Skötte *artist*
Richard, Robert Max *cardiologist*
Solon, Deborah Epstein *curator*
Taylor, James Walter *business and management educator*
Taylor, Theodore Langhans *author*
Wong, Wallace *medical supplies company executive, real estate investor*

Laguna Hills
†Alva, Alejandro *psychiatrist*
Banuelos, Betty Lou *rehabilitation nurse*
Beck, Gregory Michael *lawyer*
Block, Amanda Roth *artist*
Hammond, R. Philip *chemical engineer*
†Mathews, Stanton Terry *lawyer*
Miller, Eldon Earl *corporate business publications consultant, retired manufacturing company executive*
Pelton, Harold Marcel *mortgage broker*
Powers, Janet F. *special education educator*
Reinglass, Michelle Annette *lawyer*
Rossiter, Bryant William *chemistry consultant*
†Tuohey, Conrad Gravier *lawyer*
Wheatley, Lucile Maris *civic worker*
Wheatley, Melvin Ernest, Jr., *retired bishop*
Widyolar, Sheila Gayle *dermatologist*
Wrobel, Lance J. *orthopedic surgeon*

Laguna Niguel
Axon, Donald Carlton *architect*

†Bates, Patricia C. *state official*
†Bauer, Barbara A. *financial consultant*
Carr, Bernard Francis *hospital administrator*
Chen, Shoei-Sheng *retired mechanical engineer*
Coleman, Roger Dixon *bacteriologist*
Freeland, Darryl Creighton *psychologist, educator*
Greenberg, Lenore *public relations professional*
King, Richard Maurice, Jr., *consultant*
Kursewicz, Lee Z. *marketing consultant*
Malott, John Raymond *writer, consultant*
McEvers, Duff Steven *lawyer*
Nelson, Alfred John *retired pharmaceutical company executive*
†Ricci, Robert Ronald *manufacturing company executive*
Smith, Leslie Roper *hospital and healthcare administrator*
Teitelbaum, Harry *English educator*
Teitelbaum, Marilyn Leah *special education educator*
York, James Orison *real estate executive*
Zagon, Laurie *artist, writer*

Laguna Woods
Batdorf, Samuel B(urbridge) *physicist*
Berk, Jack Edward *gastroenterologist, educator*
Green, Leon, Jr., *mechanical engineer*
Hussey, William Bertrand *retired foreign service officer*
Leonard, Elizabeth Adney *social worker*
McClure, Hal H.
Ross, Mathew *medical educator*
Strong, Winifred Hekker *educational counselor, consultant*

Lagunitas
Holman, Arthur Stearns *artist*

Lake Arrowhead
Asher, James Edward *forestry consultant, engineer, arborist, forensic expert*
Beckman, James Wallace Bim *economist, marketing executive, educator*
Fitzgerald, John Charles, Jr., *investment banker*
Tinturin, Noëlle Compinsky *pianist, music educator*

Lake Elsinore
Shears, Roger Hammond *investment company executive*
Young, Patricia Janean *speech pathologist*

Lake Forest
Ballard, Ronald Michael *lawyer, political consultant*
Larsen, Robert Ray *healthcare executive, surgeon*
Prior, Michelle *antiques dealer, caterer*

Lake View Terrace
McCraven, Eva Stewart Mapes *health service administrator*

Lakeport
†Jansen, Kathleen Mary *librarian*

Lakeside
Koski, Donna Faith *poet*
†Walker, Wanda Medora *retired elementary school educator, consultant*

Lakeview Terrace
Coolidge, Martha *film director*

Lakewood
Bogdan, Carolyn Louetta *financial specialist*
Bogdan, James Thomas *secondary education educator, electronics researcher and developer*
De Lorca, Luis E. *public school administrator, educator, speaker*
Woodson-Glenn, Yolanda *social worker*

Lancaster
Bell, Gary Lynn *owner production company, video and audio producer*
Bianchi, David Wayne *lawyer*
Dalrymple, Marilyn Anita *small business owner, photographer*
Ellsworth, Richard German *psychologist*
†Groom, Diane V. *not-for-profit developer*
Hodges, Vernon Wray *mechanical engineer*
Houck, John Dudley *investment adviser, educator*
Kiersch, George Alfred *geological consultant, retired educator*
Walsh, Patricia Maack *special education educator*

Landers
Landers, Vernette Trosper *writer, educator, association executive*

Larkspur
†Burke, Robert Thomas *lawyer*
Earley, Edward Joseph, Jr., *studio musician, composer, copyist, trombonist*
Greenberg, Myron Silver *lawyer*
Ramos, Charles Joseph (Joe Ramos) *wealth management consultant*
Ratner, David Louis *retired law educator*
†Saxe, Steven Louis *lawyer*
Saxton, Lloyd *psychologist, writer*

Lemon Grove
Denning, Eileen Bonar *management consultant*
Mott, June Marjorie *school system administrator*

Lincoln
Chiang, George Djia-Chee *retired engineer, educator*
Dorn, Mary Ann *retired auditor*
Helzer, James Dennis *retired hospital executive*
McKay, Thomas Frederick *retired radiologist*
Oscarson, Kathleen Dale *retired writing assessment coordinator, educator*

Linden
Smith, Donald Richard *editor, publisher*

Littleriver
Van Dyck, Wendy *dancer*

Littlerock
Haas, Sir Russell (Duke of Elbasan) *federal agency administrator*

Livermore
Alder, Berni Julian *physicist, researcher*
Ambrose, William Patrick *engineer*
Balasubramanian, Krishnan *research scientist, educator*
Bennett, Alan Jerome *electronics executive, physicist*
Brereton, Sandra Joy *engineer*
Chen, Er-Ping *engineering executive*
Christopher, Steven Lee *religious studies educator*
Cook, Robert Crossland *research chemist*
Darter, Thomas Eugene, Jr., *composer, musician, writer*
Deleray, Arthur Loyd *chemist, educator*
Ellsaesser, Hugh Walter *retired atmospheric scientist*
†Ezzedine, Souheil M. *physicist, researcher*
Fodor, Imola Katalin *mathematician, researcher*
Futch, Archer Hamner *retired physicist*
Glenzer, Siegfried Heinz *physicist, educator, researcher*
Grant, Alan J. *business executive, educator*
Haga, Enoch John *computer educator, author*
Hiskes, Dolores G. *educator*
Holzrichter, John F. *physicist*
Hooper, Edwin Bickford *physicist*
Johnson, Roy Ragnar *electrical engineer, researcher*
Judge, James Carl *quality assurance officer, information systems specialist*
Kidder, Ray Edward *physicist, consultant*
King, Ray John *electrical engineer, educator, business executive*
Kirkwood, Robert Keith *applied physicist*
†Lambert, Michael Allen *physicist*
Lau, Albert Man-Fai *physicist*
Leith, Cecil Eldon, Jr., *retired physicist*
Love, Sandra Rae *information specialist*
Martovetsky, Nicolai N. *mechanical engineer, researcher*
Nuckolls, John Hopkins *physicist, researcher*
O'Brien, Kevin Charles *business development executive*
Roshong, Dee Ann Daniels *dean, educator*
Schock, Robert Norman *geophysicist*
Seward, James Pickett *internist, educator*
Shotts, Wayne J. *nuclear scientist, federal agency administrator*
Spiller, Eberhard Adolf *physicist, researcher*
Tarter, Curtis Bruce *physicist, science administrator*
Tripodes, James G. *nuclear safety and environmental regulatory affairs professional*
†Zhu, Xinhai *computer scientist*

Livingston
†Carter, Paul *food products executive*
†Fox, Robert August *food company executive*

Lockeford
Walker, Nancy Anne *antiques importer*

Lodi
Bernhoft, Franklin Otto *psychotherapist, psychologist*
Bishop-Graham, Barbara *secondary school educator, journalist*
Nusz, Phyllis Jane *not-for-profit fundraiser, consultant, educational consultant*
Schulz, Laura Janet *writer, retired secretary*

Loleta
Schoenfeld, Diana Lindsay *photographer, educator*

Loma Linda
Aloia, Roland Craig *scientist, administrator, educator*
Armon, Carmel *neurologist*
†Ballard, Jeffrey Lawrence *surgeon, educator*
Behrens, Berel Lyn *physician, academic and healthcare administrator*
Bell, Denise Louise *newspaper reporter, photographer, paralegal, librarian, life agent*
Bleidt, Barry Anthony *pharmacy educator*
Bull, Brian Stanley *pathology educator, medical consultant, business executive*
Bullock, Weldon Kimball *health facility administrator, pathologist, pathology educator*
Bunnell, William Paul *orthopaedic surgery educator*
Coggin, Charlotte Joan *cardiologist, educator*
Condon, Stanley Charles *gastroenterologist*
†Dayes, Lloyd Albert *neurosurgeon, minister*
†Edwards, Lincoln Paul *pharmacologist, educator*
Fechter, Laurence David *toxicology educator, researcher*
†Fodor, Istvan *molecular biologist, researcher*
Goodacre, Charles J. *academic administrator*
Herrmann, Paul C. *physician, chemist*
Klooster, Judson *academic administrator, dentistry educator*
Krick, Edwin Harry, Sr., *medical educator, internal medicine physician*
†Lewis, Victor Wayne, I, *minister*
Llaurado, Josep G. *nuclear medicine physician, scientist*
Longo, Lawrence Daniel *physiologist, obstetrician-gynecologist*
Mace, John Weldon *pediatrician*
Pendergraft, Janice Gayle *volunteer*
†Razzouk, Anees Jacob *surgeon*
Reeve, Ivan Leon *physician*
Roberts, Walter Herbert Beatty *anatomist, educator*
†Rungcharassaeng, Kitichai *dentist*
†Schwab, Ernest Roe, III *physiology educator, researcher*
Slater, James Munro *radiation oncologist*
Slattery, Charles Wilbur *biochemistry educator*
†Smith, Aida Marissa *medical reference librarian*
Snyder, John Joseph *retired optometrist*
Strother, Allen *biochemical pharmacologist, researcher*
†Wareham, Ellsworth Edwin *cardiothoracic surgeon, educator*
Wilcox, Ronald Bruce *biochemistry educator, researcher*
Wong, Raymond Y. *physician, educator*
Worley, Margaret Ann *apparel designer, writer*

Lomita
Balcom, Orville *engineer*

Lompoc
Bongiorno, James William *electronics company executive*
Boone, Donna Clausen *physical therapist, biostatistician, researcher*
Brown, William Frederick, Jr., *protective services official*
Means, James Andrew *engineer*
Wagner, Geraldine Marie *nursing educator, consultant*

Long Beach
Adler, Jeffrey D. *political consultant, public affairs consultant, crisis management expert*
†Aguilar, Félix *public health physician, educator*
Aldrich, David Lawrence *public relations executive*
†Altman, Mimi Angster *business owner*
Anderson, Gerald Verne *retired aerospace company executive*
Bauer, Roger Duane *chemistry educator, science consultant*
Berke, Irving *obstetrician-gynecologist, military officer*
Blazey, Michael Alan *educator*
Boccia Rosado, Ann Marie *paralegal, legal association administrator*
Bond, Frances Curtis *retired editor*
Brown, Lester B. *social worker, educator*
†Brown, Roxanne (Jerene Roxanne Brown) *sales executive*
Button, Glenn Marshall *aeronautical engineer*
Calhoun, John R. *lawyer*
†Collins, Jr., Aristide J. *academic administrator*
Cook, Karla Joan *elementary education educator*
Cotner, Douglas Monroe *provost, mathematics and environmental science educator*
Culton, Paul Melvin *retired counselor, educator, interpreter*
Cummings, Darold Bernard *aircraft engineer*
†Davies, Grace Lucille *real estate broker, educator*
Davis, Mark Hezekiah, Jr., *electrical engineer*
Dawson, Dixie Tuttle *mathematics consultant*
Dawson, Norma Ann *lawyer*
†de Soto, Simon *mechanical engineer*
Deukmejian, George *lawyer, former governor*
Dillon, Michael Earl *engineering executive, mechanical engineer, educator*
Dublin, Stephen Louis *secondary school educator, singer, musician*
Duffy, Patrick Sean *events producer, real estate consultant*
Duran, Matias Martin *adult education educator*
Elliott, John Gregory *aerospace design engineer*
Ellis, Harriette Rothstein *editor, writer*
Fagan, Frederic *neurosurgeon*
Feinberg, Cheryl Lackman *lawyer, mediator*
Fiebert, Martin Stephen *psychology educator, psychologist*
Fischler, Sandy Lynn *event producer*
Friis, Robert Harold *epidemiologist, health science educator*
Gittleman, Arthur Paul *computer science and engineering educator*
Glenn, Constance White *art museum director, educator, consultant*
Haile, Lawrence Barclay *lawyer*
†Halili, Antonio Marquez *facilities maintenance mechanic*
Hancock, John Walker, III, *banker*
Hansell, Susan *writer, educator*
Hart, Peggy I. *small business owner*
†Heggeness, Julie Fay *foundation administrator, lawyer*
†Heiser, James S. *manufacturing company executive*
Hellmer, Lynne Beberman *education educator*
†Helwick, Christine *lawyer*
Herman, Elaine *non-profit theatre artistic director*
Higginson, John *retired career officer*
Hirshtal, Edith *concert pianist, educator, chamber musician*
Hu, Chi Yu *physicist, educator*
Hunt, Herbert Gage, III, *accounting and tax educator*
Jager, Merle LeRoy *aerospace engineer*
†Karnette, Betty *state senator*
Keller, J(ames) Wesley *credit union executive*
Kelly, Chuck H. *singer, writer, trombonist*
Kenigsberg, Martin Ira *psychologist*
Kingore, Edith Louise *retired geriatrics and rehabilitation nurse*
Knudson, Ruth Esther *education educator*
Kumar, Rajendra *electrical engineering educator*
Kwaan, Jack Hau Ming *retired physician*
Lathrop, Irvin Tunis *retired academic dean, educator*
Lauda, Donald Paul *university dean*
†Lazarowitz, Arlene *social sciences educator*
†Li, Lijuan *chemistry educator*
†Lofland, Patricia Lois *educator*
Loganbill, G. Bruce *logopedic pathologist*
†Lowenthal, Alan *state official*
Lowentrout, Peter Murray *religious studies educator*
Lunderville, Gerald Paul *bilingual ESL/social studies educator*
Macer, George Armen, Jr., *orthopedic hand surgeon*
†Madan, Ram Chand *aeronautical engineer*
†Mandarino, Candida Ann *education educator, consultant*
Marks, Melvin I. *physician, educator, health services consultant*
†Maxson, Robert C. *university president*
McAbee, Douglas DeWitt *biochemistry educator, researcher*
McClune, Michael Marlyn *real estate executive*
McGann, John Milton *real estate executive*
McGaughey, Charles Gilbert *retired research biochemist*
Mills, Don Harper *pathology and psychiatry educator, lawyer*
Moroso, Michael Joseph *aerospace engineer*
Mullins, Ruth Gladys *nurse*
Myers, John Wescott *aviation executive*
†Nageotte, Michael Patrick *obstetrician*
Nelson, Harold Bernhard *museum director*
Nielsen, Pamela Jeanne *artist, writer*
Nwokogba, Isaac *financial analyst*
O'Neill, Beverly Lewis *mayor, former college president*
Oviatt, Larry Andrew *retired secondary school educator*
†Proust, Joycelyn Ann *retired librarian*
†Quam-Wickham, Nancy Lynn *history educator*
†Reed, Charles Bass *chief academic administrator*
†Reichard, Gary Warren *university administrator, history educator*
Rosenberg, Jill *realtor, civic leader*
Sato, Eunice Noda *former mayor, consultant*
Schroeder, Arnold Leon *mathematics educator*
Schubel, Jerry Robert *marine science educator, scientist, university dean*
†Sinclitico, Dennis J. *lawyer*
†Singhal, Meena *education educator*
Snider, Clifton Mark *English educator, writer, poet*
Sosoka, John Richard *consulting firm executive, engineer*
Stemmer, Edward Alan *surgeon, educator*
Stevens, Tom Granville *psychologist, educator*
†Stolpman, Thomas Gerard *lawyer*
Swatek, Frank Edward *microbiology educator*
†Tai, Kwok-Keung *biologist, researcher*
Tang, Paul Chi Lung *philosophy educator*
Tikosh, Mark Axente *lawyer*
Tucker, Marcus Othello *judge*
VavRosky, Mark James *career officer, educator*
Vernon, Alejandra *artist*
Viola, Bill *artist, writer*
Walker, Linda Ann *financial planner*
Warder, Michael Young *non-profit executive*
†Welch, Ronnie Scott *health facility administrator*
White, Katherine Elizabeth *retired pediatrician*
Wise, George Edward *lawyer*
Wollmer, Richard Dietrich *statistics and operations research educator*
Worcester, Howard Lester *internist*
Yang, Xinjian (Sam Yang) *environmental engineer*

Los Alamitos
Aberman, Harold Mark *veterinarian*
Booth, John Nicholls *minister, writer, photographer*
Dunne, Donald Redmond *military officer*
Eckelman, Richard Joel *engineering specialist*
Nemirow, Lawrence H. *lawyer*
Rippo, Olga Alicia *art director*
Weinberger, Frank *information management consultant*

Los Altos
Abrams, Arthur Jay *physician*
Beer, Clara Louise Johnson *retired electronics executive*
Carlson, Warren Ore *civil engineer*
Carr, Jacquelyn B. *psychologist, educator*
Carsten, Jack Craig *venture capitalist*
Clark, Sondra *composer, musicologist, educator*
Collins, Gordon Dent *recording company executive*
Esber, Edward Michael, Jr., *software company executive*
Gough, William Cabot *engineer*
Hahn, Harold Thomas *physical chemist, chemical engineer*
Haines, Richard Foster *retired psychologist*
Ilstad, Geir Are *venture capitalist*
Keller, James Warren *college administrator*
King, Chi-Yu *research scientist*
Martin, Leonardo S.J. *urologist, surgeon*
McCreary, Deborah Dennis *oncology nurse*
Moll, John Lewis *electronics engineer, retired*
Nivison, David Shepherd *Chinese and philosophy educator*
Peterson, Victor Lowell *aerospace engineer, management consultant*
Poonja, Mohamed *business reorganization, financial and management consultant*
Riter, Bruce Douglas *lawyer*
Sharpe, Kathryn Peck *artist*
Sharpe, Roland Leonard *structural engineer, consultant*
Sherwood, Patricia Waring *artist, educator*
Spangler, Dorothy Benita *artist*
Spiller, Gene Alan *nutritionist, health facility administrator*
Thurber, Emily Forrest *political consultant*
Vickers, Roger Spencer *physicist, environmental mapping director*
Welsh, Doris McNeil *early childhood education specialist*
Wilbur, Colburn Sloan *foundation consultant and trustee, former executive*
†Yu, Oliver Shukiang *corporate executive, educator, technology strategist*
Zebroski, Edwin Leopold *risk management consultant*

Los Altos Hills
Alexander, Katharine Violet *lawyer*
Dyal, Palmer *retired physicist*

Fondahl, John Walker *civil engineering educator*
Wheeler, Frank Knowles Blasdell *retired military officer, business consultant*

Los Angeles

Aaron, Benjamin *law educator, arbitrator*
Abrams, Norman *law educator, university administrator*
Acosta, Frank Xavier *psychologist, educator*
Adamek, Charles Andrew *lawyer*
Adams, Thomas Merritt *lawyer*
Adamson, Arthur Wilson *chemistry educator*
Adell, Hirsch *lawyer*
Adler, Erwin Ellery *lawyer*
Adler, Fred Peter *retired electronics company executive*
†Adler, Michael I. *lawyer*
Adler, Sara *arbitrator, mediator*
†Agarwal, Sanjay Kumar *physician*
Agnew, John A. *education educator*
Aguas, Ruben Tech *otolaryngologist*
Agus, David Bernard *physician*
Alarcon, Arthur Lawrence *federal judge*
†Albright, Julie Marie *sociologist, educator*
Alden, John W. *lawyer*
†Alkalay, Arie L. *pediatrician, neonatologist*
Alkana, Ronald Lee *neuroscientist*
Alkon, Ellen Skillen *physician*
Alkon, Paul Kent *English language educator*
Allen, Michael John Bridgman *English educator*
Allen, Suzanne *financial planning executive, insurance agent, writer*
Allen, William Richard *retired economist*
Allerton, Samuel Ellsworth *biochemist*
Allison, Jason *hockey player*
Allison, Laird Burl *business educator*
†Allred, Gloria Rachel *lawyer*
Alpers, Edward Alter *history educator*
Alvarez, Rodolfo *sociology educator, consultant*
Amey, Rae *project management and development consultant*
Amos, Brice Allen *film company executive, writer*
†Anastos, Rosemary Park *retired higher education educator*
Anawalt, Patricia Rieff *anthropologist, researcher*
Andersen, Ronald Max *health services educator, researcher*
Anderson, Charles David *lawyer*
Anderson, John Edward *diversified holding company executive, lawyer*
Anderson, Kathryn D. *surgeon*
Anderson, Kenneth Jeffery *financial planner, accountant, lawyer*
Anderson, W. French *biochemist, physician*
Angel, Arthur Ronald *lawyer, consultant*
Angelo, Christopher Edmond *lawyer, consultant*
Angeloff, Dann Valentino *investment banking executive*
Aniston, Jennifer *actress*
Antin, Michael *lawyer*
Antonovich, Michael Dennis *county official*
Apfel, Gary *lawyer*
Apple, Jacki (Jacqueline B. Apple) *artist, writer, educator*
†Appleby, Joyce Oldham *historian, educator*
April, Rand Scott *lawyer*
Apt, Charles *artist*
Apt, Leonard *physician*
Arbib, Michael Anthony *neuroscientist, educator, computer scientist*
Arbit, Beryl Ellen *legal assistant*
Archie, Carol Louise *obstetrician and gynecologist, educator*
Ardehali, Abbas *physician, surgeon*
Aristei, J. Clark *lawyer, educator*
Armistead, Thomas Boyd, III, *television and film producer*
Armstrong, Lloyd, Jr., *university official, physics educator*
Armstrong, Orville *judge*
Arnold, Jeanne Eloise *anthropologist, educator*
Arpesella, Pietro *actor, writer*
Arzube, Juan Alfredo *bishop*
Ash, Lawrence Robert *public health educator, administrator*
Ash, Roy Lawrence *business executive*
Ashley, Sharon Anita *pediatric anesthesiologist*
Askanas-Engel, Valerie *neurologist, educator, researcher*
Askin, Richard Henry, Jr., *entertainment company executive*
Atchley, Raymond Deval *technology company executive*
†Auch Yellin, Barbara Ann *musician*
Bahr, Ehrhard *Germanic languages and literature educator*
†Bailey, Craig Bernard *lawyer*
Bailey, Julia Nancy *geneticist*
Bailey, Kenneth D. *sociology educator*
Bain, Conrad Stafford *actor*
Bakaly, Charles George, Jr., *lawyer, mediator*
Bakeman, Carol Ann *travel manager, singer*
Baker, Carolyn *non-profit executive, fundraiser*
†Baker, Donald P. *lawyer*
Baker, Robert Frank *molecular biologist, educator*
†Ballard, Glen *composer*
†Ballhaus, William Francis, Jr., *aerospace industry executive, research scientist*
†Ballsun, Kathryn Ann *lawyer*
†Banner, Lois Wendland *education educator, writer*
Barker, Robert William *television personality*
Barker, Wiley Franklin *surgeon, educator*
Baron, Melvin Farrell *pharmacy educator*
Barren, Bruce Willard *merchant banker*
Barrett, Jane Hayes *lawyer*
†Barron, Stephanie *curator*
†Barsugli, Jesse Benjamin *lab administrator*
Bartchy, S(tuart) Scott *history educator, researcher*
Barth, Karen Ann *lawyer*
Barton, Alan Joel *lawyer*
Barza, Harold A. *lawyer*
Basil, Douglas Constantine *writer, educator*
Basile, Paul Louis, Jr., *lawyer*
Bates, Marcia Jeanne *information scientist educator*
†Baum, Geoffrey Leo *director*
Baum, Michael Lin *lawyer*
Bauman, John Andrew *law educator*
Baumann, Richard Gordon *lawyer*
Baumgarten, Ronald Neal *lawyer*
Baxter, Frank Edward *brokerage executive*
Beam, William Washington, III, *data coordinator*
Beamon, Gena R. *human resources specialist*
Beart, Robert W., Jr., *surgeon, educator*
Beckson, Mace *psychiatrist*
Becraft, Stephen Jay *accountant*
Bekey, George Albert *computer scientist, educator, engineer*
Bell, Lee Phillip *television personality, television producer*
Beltramo, Michael Norman *management consultant*
Bender, Charles William *lawyer*
Bendix, Helen Irene *lawyer*
†Bennett, Bianca Cherie *lawyer*
Bennett, Charles Franklin, Jr., *biogeographer, educator*
Bennett, Fred Gilbert *lawyer*
Bennis, Warren Gameliel *business administration educator, writer, consultant*
Benson, Sidney William *chemistry researcher*
Berek, Jonathan Samuel *writer, educator, dean, surgeon, gynecologist*
Berenbaum, Michael Gary *theology educator*
†Bergman, Emily Anne *librarian*
Bergman, Marilyn Keith *lyricist, writer*
Berman, Geoffrey Louis *management company executive*
Berman, Myles Lee *lawyer*
†Berman, Richard Keith *television producer, film producer*
Bernacchi, Richard Lloyd *lawyer*
Bernhard, Herbert Ashley *lawyer*
Bernstein, Arthur Harold *venture capital executive*
Bernstein, Samuel *insurance company executive*
Bernstein, Sol *cardiologist, educator*
Bernstein, William *film company executive*
†Berry, Stephen Joseph *reporter*
Bessman, Samuel Paul *pediatrician, biochemist*
Beydoun, Said R. *physician, neurology educator*
Bharitkar, Sunil Ganpat *research scientist, technology specialist*
Bhaumik, Mani Lal *physicist*
†Bhidayasiri, Roongroj *neurologist, researcher*
Bice, Scott Haas *dean, lawyer, educator*
Biggs, Jason *actor*
Bilderback, James William, II, *lawyer*
Biles, John Alexander *pharmacology educator, chemistry educator*
Billig, Franklin Anthony *chemist*
Binder, Gordon M. *venture capitalist*
Birren, James Emmett *university research center executive*
Bishop, Sidney Willard *lawyer*
†Bitting, William M. *lawyer*
Blahd, William Henry *physician, nuclear medicine physician*
Blakeney, Karen Elizabeth *social service and community health program executive, consultant*
Blencowe, Paul Sherwood *lawyer, private investor*
Bloch, Saul K. *obstetrician-gynecologist*
†Bloomberg, Stu *broadcast executive*
Blumberg, Grace Ganz *law educator, lawyer*
Bodey, Bela *immunologist, pathologist, oncologist*
Bodkin, Henry Grattan, Jr., *lawyer*
Boehm, Barry William *computer science educator*
†Boehmer, Richard A. *lawyer*
†Bohle, Sue *public relations executive*
Boime, Albert Isaac *art history educator*
Bok, Dean *cell biologist, educator*
Bomes, Stephen D. *lawyer*
Bondareff, William *psychiatry educator*
Bonesteel, Michael John *lawyer*
Bordy, Michael Jeffrey *lawyer*
Borenstein, Daniel Bernard *psychiatrist, educator*
Borenstein, Mark A. *lawyer*
Borko, Harold *information scientist, psychologist, educator*
Borneman, John Paul *pharmaceutical executive*
Borsch, Frederick Houk *bishop*
Borsting, Jack Raymond *business administration educator*
Bortman, David *lawyer*
Bosl, Phillip L. *lawyer*
Bottjer, David John *earth scientist, biologist, educator*
†Bouju, Jean-Marc *photojournalist*
Bowers, David Paul *operations analyst*
†Boxer, Lester *lawyer*
Boyarsky, Igor *emergency physician*
Boyd, Malcolm *minister, writer*
Boyer, Paul D. *biochemist, educator*
†Brackmann, Derald E. *otolaryngologist*
Bradley, Lawrence D., Jr., *lawyer*
Bradshaw, Murray Charles *musicologist, educator*
Branca, John Gregory *lawyer, consultant*
Bratton, William J. *chief of police, former police commissioner*
Braun, David A(dlai) *lawyer*
Braunstein, Glenn David *physician, educator*
Bremond, Duane Benjamin *marketing professional*
Breslow, Lester *physician, educator*
Bressan, Paul Louis *lawyer*
Breuer, Stephen Ernest *religious organization administrator*
Bridges, B. Ried *lawyer*
Broad, Eli *financial services executive*
†Brodwin, Martin George *counselor, educator*
Brogan, Kevin H. *lawyer*
Brooks, Philip G. *obstetrician-gynecologist*
†Brooks, Robert Eugene *decision support software designer*
Broussard, Thomas Rollins *lawyer*
Brown, Carol *make-up artist*
Brown, James Kevin *professional baseball player*
†Brown, Robert Freeman *mathematics educator*
Browner, Carole Helen *anthropologist, educator*
Brubaker, William Rogers *sociology educator*
†Bruce, William A. *airport executive*
†Bryan, James Spencer *lawyer*
Brynes, Russell Kermit *pathologist, educator*
Buchman, Mark Edward *banker*
Buffington, Gary Lee Roy *safety engineer, construction executive*
Bufford, Samuel Lawrence *federal judge*
Burch, Robert Dale *lawyer*
Burgess, J. Wesley *neuropsychiatrist*
Burgin, Mark Semjonovich *mathematician, computer scientist, philosopher*
Burke, Robert Bertram *lawyer, political consultant, lobbyist*
†Burkle, Ronald W. *former food service executive, business investor*
Burns, Marcelline *psychologist, researcher*
Burns, Robert Ignatius *historian, educator, clergyman*
†Burrows, James *television and motion picture director, producer*
†Burton, Tim *film director*
Buzzi, Ruth *comedienne*
Byers, Nina *physics educator*
Byrd, Christine Waterman Swent *lawyer*
Byrnes, James Bernard *museum director, consultant*
Caine, Michael *actor*
Calman, Craig David *writer, actor, director*
Campbell, Kenneth Eugene, Jr., *vertebrate paleontologist, ornithologist*
Campion, Robert Thomas *manufacturing company executive*
Caram, Eve La Salle *English educator, writer*
Carman, Greg *mechanical engineer, educator*
Carnesale, Albert *academic administrator*
Caroompas, Carole Jean *artist, educator*
Carothers, A. J. *scriptwriter*
Carr, James Patrick *lawyer*
Carr, Willard Zeller, Jr., *lawyer*
Carrey, Neil *lawyer, educator*
Carroll, John Sawyer *newspaper editor*
†Carroll, Raoul Lord *lawyer, investment banker*
Carter, Bret Robert *lawyer*
Carter, Emily Ann *physical chemist, researcher, educator*
Cartwright, Brian Grant *lawyer*
Caryl, Naomi *artist*
Caskie, William Wirt *accountant, securities broker*
Castro, Leonard Edward *lawyer*
Cates, Gilbert *film, theater, television producer and director*
Cathcart, David Arthur *lawyer*
†Cedillo, Gilbert A. *state senator*
†Chacko, George Kuttickal *systems science educator, consultant*
†Chadwick, William Jordan *lawyer*
†Chambers, Mortimer Hardin, Jr., *retired history educator*
Champagne, Duane Willard *sociology educator*
Champlin, Charles Davenport *television host, book critic, writer*
Chan, David Ronald *tax specialist, lawyer*
Chan, Thomas Tak-Wah *lawyer*
Chandor, Stebbins Bryant *pathologist*
Chang, Edward H. *computer company executive*
Chang, Henry C. *library administrator*
Chapman, Carolyn *broadcasting director*
Chapman, Orville Lamar *chemist, educator*
†Charles, Ray (Ray Charles Robinson) *musician, singer, composer*
Chavez, Victor Edwin *judge*
Chazen, Stephen I. *oil company executive*
†Chedid, John G. *retired bishop*
Cheeseboro, Margrit *economics educator*
Chen, Peter Wei-Teh *mental health services administrator*
Cheng, Tsen-Chung *electrical engineering educator*
Cherkin, Adina *interpreter, writer, poet, translator*
†Chernin, Peter *motion picture company executive*
Cherry, James Donale *pediatrician*
Chiate, Kenneth Reed *lawyer*
†Chiklis, Michael *actor*
Chin, Llewellyn Philip *lawyer*
Chobotov, Vladimir Alexander *aerospace engineer, educator*
Chopra, Inder Jit *physician, endocrinologist*
Christol, Carl Q(uimby) *lawyer, political science educator*
Christopher, James Roy *executive director*
Chu, Morgan *lawyer*
†Churgin, Amy *publishing executive*
Cicciarelli, James Carl *immunology educator*
Ciccone, Amy Navratil *art librarian*
†Cislowski, Joseph A. *association executive*
Clark, Burton Robert *sociologist, educator*
Clark, R(ufus) Bradbury *lawyer, director*
Clark, William Arthur V. *geographer, demographer*
Clarke, Peter *communications and health educator*
Cleary, William Joseph, Jr., *lawyer*
Clemente, Carmine Domenic *anatomist, educator*
†Clow, Lee *advertising agency executive*
†Cochran, Johnnie L., Jr., *lawyer*
Cochran, Sachiko Tomie *radiologist, educator*
†Coget, Jean-Francois Axel Hugues *management researcher*
Cohen, Cynthia Marylyn *lawyer*
Cohen, S(tephen) Marshall *philosophy educator*
†Coker, Sybil Jane Thomas *counseling administrator*
†Colbert, James W., III, *lawyer*
Coleman, Charles Clyde *physicist, educator*
Coleman, Paul Jerome, Jr., *physicist, educator*
Coleman, Rexford Lee *lawyer, educator*
Collias, Nicholas Elias *zoology educator, ornithologist*
Collier, Charles Arthur, Jr., *lawyer*
Collins, Audrey B. *judge*
Conley, Darlene Ann *actress*
Conomikes, George Spero *management consultant executive, publisher*
Cook, Ian Ainsworth *psychiatrist, researcher, educator*
Coombs, Robert Holman *behavioral scientist, medical educator, therapist, writer*
†Cooper, Chris *actor*
Cooper, Edwin Lowell *anatomy educator*
†Copley, Ralph D., Jr., *lawyer*
Corman, Roger William *motion picture producer, director*
Cornwall, John Michael *physics educator, consultant, researcher*
Coroniti, Ferdinand Vincent *physics educator, consultant*
Cortinez, Veronica *literature educator*
Corwin, Norman *writer, director, producer*
†Cosgrove, Denis Edmund *geographer, writer*
Cosner, Christopher Mark *engineer*
Costello, Kelly Lynn *lawyer*
Costello, Kenneth R. *lawyer*
Cote, Richard James *pathologist, researcher*
†Cowan, Georgianne *dancer, educator, writer*
Craft, Cheryl Mae *neurobiologist, anatomist, researcher*
Crampon, Jean Elaine *librarian*
Crecelius, Daniel Neil *history educator*
Creim, William Benjamin *lawyer*
Crockett, Donald Harold *composer, university educator*
Crombie, Douglass Darnill *aerospace communications system engineer*
Crosby, Peter Alan *management consultant*
Crossley, John Parshley, Jr., *religous studies educator, researcher, consultant*
Crowell, Donald W. *diversified financial services company executive, financial consultant*
Cuadra, Carlos Albert *information scientist, management executive*
Curran, Darryl Joseph *photographer, educator*
Currie, Janet M. *economics educator*
Curry, Daniel Arthur *judge*
Dabrowska, Dorota Maria *statistician, educator*
D'Accone, Frank Anthony *music educator*
Dafter, Roger E. *psychologist*
Dallmeyer, Robert Frederick *exhibitions executive*
Dana, Lauren Elizabeth *lawyer*
Daniels, John Peter *lawyer*
†Danielson, Walter George *lawyer*
Danoff, Dudley Seth *surgeon, urologist*
Darby, G(eorge) Harrison *lawyer*
†Darby, Michael Rucker *economist, educator*
Darmstaetter, Jay Eugene *secondary education educator*
†Datar, Ram Hemant *pathologist, educator*
Davidson, Ezra C., Jr., *physician, educator*
Davidson, Herbert Alan *Near Eastern languages and cultures educator*
Davidson, Jeffrey H. *lawyer*
Davies, Kelvin James Anthony *research scientist, educator, consultant, author*
†Davis, Michael Rico *county official*
Davis, Terri Judith *television producer, writer*
Dawson, Adam *private investigator*
Daya Mata, Sri (Faye Wright) *clergywoman*
De Brier, Donald Paul *lawyer*
de Castro, Hugo Daniel *lawyer*
De Cherney, Alan Hersh *obstetrics and gynecology educator*
DeCherney, Deanna Saver *interior designer*
Dekmejian, Richard Hrair *political science educator*
Delaney, Matthew Sylvester *mathematics educator, academic administrator*
†De Larios, Dora *artist*
Del Giudice, Luisa *folklorist, ethnologist, historical institution administrator, educator*
Del Olmo, Frank *newspaper editor*
†DeLuca, Michael *film company executive*
Delugach, Albert Lawrence *journalist*
DeMartini, Frank Thomas *film company executive, lawyer*
Demoff, Marvin Alan *lawyer*
Demsetz, Harold *economist, educator*
†Denham, Robert Edwin *lawyer, investment company executive*
Dennison, Terry Alan *investment consultant*
†Derebery, Mary Jennifer *otolaryngologist*
Detels, Roger *epidemiologist, physician, former university dean*
Dewey, Donald Odell *dean, academic administrator*
†Diamond, Jared Mason *biologist*
Diamond, Lindy S. *financial executive*
Diamond, Stanley Jay *lawyer*
Diehl, Dolores *communication arts director*
Dignam, William Joseph *obstetrician, gynecologist, educator*
Dinel, Richard Henry *lawyer*
Dismukes, Valena Grace Broussard *photographer, former physical education educator*
Dixit, Vivek *biomedical scientist, medical educator*
Di XX Miglia, Gabriella *artist, conservationist*
Dobos, Erzsebet *language educator*
Doll, Lynne Marie *public relations agency executive*
Donaldson, Michael Cleaves *lawyer*
Donovan, Thomas B. *judge*
Dorman, Albert A. *consulting engineer executive, architect*
Douglas, Kirk (Issur Danielovitch) *actor, motion picture producer*
Dows, David Alan *chemistry educator*
Dragan, Feodor Feodorovich *research scientist*
†Dr. Dre, (Andre Young) *rapper, record producer*
†Dribin, Leland George *lawyer*
Drummond, Marshall Edward *business educator, university administrator*

Kleingartner, Archie *founding dean, educator*
Kline, Lee B. *retired architect*
Kline, Richard Stephen *public relations executive*
Klinger, Allen *engineering and applied science educator*
Klinger, Marilyn Sydney *lawyer*
Kloner, Robert A. *cardiologist, researcher, educator*
Knight, Henry L. *minister*
Knittle, William Joseph, Jr., *media executive, psychologist, religious leader, management and marketing consultant, educator*
Knopoff, Leon *geophysics educator*
Knox, Gertie R. *company executive, accountant*
Kobe, Lan *medical physicist*
Koch, Richard *retired pediatrician, educator*
Koffler, Stephen Alexander *investment banker*
Koga, Rokutaro (Rocky Koga) *physicist*
Kolber, Richard A. *lawyer*
†Kolesnik, Grigori *mathematician, educator, mathematician, researcher*
Kolve, V. A. *English literature educator*
†Koo, Eun-Hee *education educator*
Korsch, Barbara M. *pediatrician*
Krag, Olga *interior designer*
Kramer, Barry Alan *psychiatrist, educator*
Kranwinkle, Conrad Douglas *broadcast executive*
Kraus, Robert *physician*
Kresa, Kent *aerospace executive*
Kristof, Kathy M. *journalist*
Krueger, Robert William *management consultant*
†Krupka, Robert George *lawyer*
Krupp, Robin Rector *illustrator, author*
Kuechle, John Merrill *lawyer*
Kuehl, Hans Henry *electrical engineering educator*
†Kupietzky, Moshe J. *lawyer*
Kupper, Ketti *artist*
Kwon, Oh Chae *researcher*
La Force, James Clayburn, Jr., *economist, educator*
†Lagasse, Emeril *chef*
†Lagier, Christophe Philippe *language educator*
Laird, David *humanities educator emeritus*
Lamb, H. Richard *psychiatry educator*
Lamison, Eric Ross *lawyer*
Langguth, Arthur John *writer, journalism educator*
Lansing, Sherry Lee (Heimann) *motion picture executive*
Lapatin, Kenneth D.S. *archaeologist, art historian*
Lappen, Chester I. *lawyer*
Lappen, Timothy *lawyer, investor*
Lark, Raymond *artist, art scholar*
Larkin, Thomas Ernest, Jr., *investment management company executive*
Larson, Gary *cartoonist*
†Lasorda, Thomas Charles (Tommy Lasorda) *professional baseball team manager*
Latham, Joseph Al, Jr., *lawyer*
Lauchengco, Jose Yujuico, Jr., *lawyer*
Laudicina, Salvatore Anthony *film industry executive*
Lavin, Laurence Michael *lawyer*
†Lavin, Stephen Michael *university basketball coach*
Lawrence, Sanford Hull *physician, immunochemist, author*
Layton, Harry Christopher *artist, lecturer, consultant*
Lazareff, Jorge Antonio *neurosurgeon, researcher*
Lazarus, Mell *cartoonist*
†Le, Bach Trong *maxillofacial surgeon*
Leahy, T. Liam *business development, technology investor*
†LeBeau, Mary Delle *education educator, writer, dancer*
Le Berthon, Adam *lawyer*
Lechago, Juan *pathologist, educator*
†Lederman, Bruce Randolph *lawyer*
Ledger, Heath *actor*
Lee, Cecilia Hae-Jin *artist, writer*
Lee, Lance *theater and film educator, writer*
Lee, Robert Andrew *librarian*
Lee, William Bradley *education educator*
Leibow, Ronald Louis *lawyer*
Leijonhufvud, Axel Stig Bengt *economics educator*
Lem, Richard Douglas *painter*
Lenard, Michael Barry *merchant banker, lawyer*
Lesser, Ian O. *foreign affairs expert*
Lesser, Joan L. *lawyer*
Lettich, Sheldon Bernard *director, screenwriter*
Letwin, Leon *law educator*
Leung, Frankie Fook-Lun *lawyer*
Levey, Gerald Saul *dean, internist, educator*
†Levine, Jesse E. *publishing executive*
Levine, Meldon Edises *lawyer, former congressman*
Levine, Michael *public relations executive, writer, announcer*
Levine, Philip *classics educator*
Levine, Raphael David *chemistry educator*
†Levinsohn, Gary *producer*
Levy, Alan David *real estate executive*
Lew, Joycelyne Mae *actress*
Lewin, Klaus Jonathan *pathologist, educator*
Lewis, Basil *investment company executive*
Lewis, Charles Edwin *epidemiologist, educator*
Lewis, Mary Ann *nursing educator*
†Leyritz, James Joseph *professional baseball player*
Liberman, Robert Paul *psychiatry educator, researcher, writer*
Lieber, David Leo *university president*
Lim, Larry Kay *university official*
Lin, Thomas Wen-shyoung *accounting educator, researcher, consultant*
Lin, Tung Hua *civil engineering educator*
Lindholm, Dwight Henry *lawyer*
Lindley, F(rancis) Haynes, Jr., *foundation executive, lawyer*
Linsk, Michael Stephen *real estate executive*
Lionnet, Francoise *French and comparative literature educator*
Lipsig, Ethan *lawyer*
†Litvack, Sanford Martin *lawyer*
†Ljubimov, Alexander V. *molecular biologist, cell biologist, researcher*
Lloyd-Jones, Dadiva Bocobo *nursing assistant, writer*
†Loewy, Peter Henry *lawyer*
Löfstedt, Bengt Torkel Magnus *classics educator*
London, Andrew Barry *film editor*
Long, Gregory Alan *lawyer*
Looney, Claudia Arlene *healthcare administrator*
LoPucki, Lynn Michael *law educator*
Loukaitou-Sideris, Anastasia *urban planner, educator, urban planner, consultant*
Lowenthal, Abraham Frederic *international relations educator*
Lu, John Kuew-Hsiung *physiology educator, endocrinologist*
Lubman, Richard Levi *physician, educator, research scientist*
Lucente, Rosemary Dolores *retired educational administrator, consultant*
†Ludlam, James Edward *lawyer*
†Lumaroa, Joseph Matthew *foundation administrator*
†Luna, Dennis R. *lawyer*
Lund, James Louis *lawyer*
†Lurvey, Ira Harold *lawyer*
Lynch, Beverly Pfeifer *education and information studies educator*
Lynch, Patrick *lawyer*
†Macavinta-Tenazas, Gemorsita *family physician*
Mack, J. Curtis, II, *civic organization administrator*
MacKenzie, John Douglas *engineering educator*
†MacLaughlin, Francis Joseph *lawyer*
MacLeod, William Bentley *economics and law educator*
Maeder, Gary William *lawyer*
Mager, Artur *retired aerospace company executive, consultant*
Maguire, Tobey *actor*
Maher, William James *investment executive*
Mahony, Roger Michael *archbishop*
Maida, Carl Albert *anthropologist*
Main, Laurie (Laurence George Main) *actor*
Maizel, Samuel Ruven *lawyer*
Maker, Janet Anne *writer, retired literature educator*
Maki, Kazumi *physicist, educator*
Malamuth, Neil Moshe *psychology and communication educator*
Malden, Karl (Malden Sekulovich) *actor*
Malick, Terrence (David Whitney II) *film director*
Mall, William John, Jr., *aerospace executive, retired Air Force general*
Maloney, Robert Keller *ophthalmologist, medical educator*
Maltin, Leonard *television commentator, writer*
Man, Lawrence Kong *architect, entrepreneur, graphics, furniture and fashion designer*
†Manalo, Victor A. *social work educator*
Mancino, Douglas Michael *lawyer*
Mandal, Ashis K. *cardiothoracic surgeon*
Mandel, Joseph David *academic administrator, lawyer*
Mann, Delbert *film, theater, television director and producer*
Mann, Nancy Louise (Nancy Louise Robbins) *entrepreneur*
Mann, Wesley F. *editor, writer, reporter*
Maquet, Jacques Jerome Pierre *anthropologist, writer*
†Marciano, Maurice *apparel executive*
Marcus, Stephen Howard *lawyer*
Marder, Stephen R. *psychiatrist, educator*
Markham, Charles Henry *neurologist*
Markland, Francis Swaby, Jr., *biochemist, educator*
Marmarelis, Vasilis Zissis *engineering educator, writer, consultant*
Marmor, Judd *psychiatrist, educator*
Maronde, Robert Francis *internist, clinical pharmacologist, educator*
Marshall, Mary Jones *civic worker*
Marshall-Daniels, Meryl *telecommunications executive, lawyer, mediator*
Martin, J(ohn) Edward *architectural engineer*
Martin, Shane Patrick *education educator, consultant*
†Martinez, Dai'Quiriya S. *social studies educator*
Martinez, Miguel Acevedo *urologist, consultant, lecturer*
†Mason, Andrew *film producer*
Masri, Sami F(aiz) *civil and mechanical engineering educator, consultant*
Mass-Achs, Sharon *social worker, educator*
Mathias, Alice Irene *business management consultant*
Mayorkas, Alejandro *lawyer, former prosecutor*
McAniff, Edward John *lawyer*
McCabe, Edward R. B. *academic administrator, educator, physician*
McCloskey, Mark *educator*
†McCluggage, Kerry *television executive*
McClure, William Owen *biologist*
McCullagh, Grant Gibson *architect*
McGarry, Dorothy *librarian*
McGee, Lynda Plant *guidance counselor*
McGowen, Gerald Ellis *biologist*
McKinzie, Carl Wayne *lawyer*
McLane, Frederick Berg *lawyer*
McLean, Ian Small *astronomer, physics educator*
McLinn, Anna Ruth *educator*
McLurkin, Thomas Cornelius, Jr., *lawyer*
McNamara, Aida Shahid *insurance executive*
Mc Pherson, Rolf Kennedy *clergyman, religious organization administrator*
McQueen, Justice Ellis (L. Q. Jones) *actor, director*
†McWilliams, James C. *earth sciences educator*
Mears, Linda Shaw *artist*
Medearis, Miller *lawyer*
Meecham, William Coryell *engineering educator*
Meier, Stephen Charles *foundation executive*
†Meisinger, Louis M. *lawyer*
Mellinkoff, Sherman Mussoff *medical educator*
Mellor, Ronald John *history educator*
Melnick, Michael *geneticist, educator*
Memel, Sherwin Leonard *lawyer*
Mendel, Jerry Marc *electrical engineering educator*
Menefee, John William, III, *cinematographer, producer*
Merlis, George *television producer*
†Mersel, Marjorie Kathryn Pedersen *lawyer*
Messerli, Douglas *writer, publisher*
Mestres, Ricardo A., III, *motion picture company executive*
†Metheny, Patrick Bruce *musician*
Metzger, Robert Streicher *lawyer*
Meyer, Michael Edwin *lawyer*
Michael, William Burton *psychologist, educator*
Michelson, Sonia *music educator, author*
Mihan, Richard *retired dermatologist*
†Milchan, Arnon *film producer*
Miles, Jack (John Russiano) *journalist, educator*
Miles, Samuel I(srael) *psychiatrist, educator*
Millard, Neal Steven *lawyer, educator*
Miller, Bruce Norman *lawyer, retired podiatrist*
Miller, Eric *neuropsychologist*
Miller, Gary Douglas *business tax reform consultant, former aerospace company executive*
Miller, Milton Allen *lawyer*
†Miller, Timothy Alden *plastic and reconstructive surgeon*
Milligan, Sister Mary *theology educator, religious consultant*
†Mintz, Jim *psychiatrist, educator*
Mintz, Marshall Gary *lawyer*
Mintz, Ronald Steven *lawyer, photojournalist*
Mirza, Zakir Hussain *aerospace company consultant*
Mishell, Daniel R., Jr., *obstetrician, gynecologist, educator*
†Mitchell, Theodore Reed *academic administrator*
Mittenthal, Peter A. *lawyer*
Miyoshi, David Masao *lawyer, international investment consultant*
Moe, Stanley Allen *architect, consultant*
Mohr, Anthony James *judge*
Mohr, John Luther *biologist, environmental consultant*
Moloney, Stephen Michael *lawyer*
Money, Ruth Rowntree *infant development and care specialist, consultant*
Monforte-Muñoz, Hector L. *pathologist*
†Monkkonen, Eric H. *social sciences educator*
†Monorieff, Dorothy *retired paralegal*
Montgomery, James Issac, Jr., *lawyer*
Montoya, Velma *economist, policy consultant*
Moore, Donald Walter *academic administrator, school librarian*
Moore, Ronald Bruce *visual effects producer*
More, Philip Harvey Birnbaum *business administration educator*
Morgenthaler-Lever, Alisa *lawyer*
Morgner, Aurelius *economist, educator*
†Morisky, Donald E. *director, medical educator*
Morrison, Donald Graham *business educator, consultant*
Morrow, Winston Vaughan *financial executive*
Mortazavian, Harold *electrical engineer, researcher, mathematician*
Moshfegh, Moussa *surgeon*
Mosich, Anelis Nick *accountant, writer, educator, consultant*
Mosk, Richard Mitchell *judge*
Moskowitz, Joel Steven *lawyer*
Moxley, John Howard, III, *internist*
Moy, Ronald Leonard *dermatologist, surgeon*
Mracky, Ronald Sydney *marketing and media executive, tourism consultant*
Mueller, Carl Richard *theater arts educator, author*
Muldaur, Diana Charlton *actress*
Mulligan, Robert *film director, producer*
Mulryan, Lenore Hoag *art curator, author*
Munitz, Barry *arts and foundation administrator*
Muntz, Eric Phillip *aerospace and mechanical engineering and radiology educator, consultant*
Murray, Alice Pearl *data processing company executive*
Murray, Andy *professional hockey coach*
Nadler, Gerald *management consultant, educator*
Naqvi, Tasneem Zehra *cardiologist, researcher, consultant*
Nathanson, Theodore Herzl *aeronautical engineer, architect*
Nathwani, Bharat N. *pathologist, consultant*
†Nazario, Sonia *reporter*
†Neelin, J. David *meteorologist, educator*
Neely, Sally Schultz *lawyer*
Neiter, Gerald Irving *lawyer*
Nelligan, Kate (Patricia Colleen Nelligan) *actress*
Nelson, Bryce Eames *journalist, educator*
Nelson, Grant Steel *lawyer, educator*
Nelson, Howard Joseph *geographer, educator*
Nelson, Mark Bruce *interior designer*
Nelson, Marvin Dale, Jr., *radiologist, educator*
Neufeld, Elizabeth Fondal *biochemist, educator*
Neutra, Dion *architect*
Newhall, Eric Luther *American literature educator*
Newhart, Bob *entertainer*
Newman, Anita Nadine *surgeon*
Newman, Michael Rodney *lawyer*
Newman, Randy *singer, songwriter, musician*
†Newman, Richard G. *engineering company executive*
Nicholas, Frederick M. *lawyer*
Nicholas, William Richard *lawyer*
Nichols, Gerald *counselor, hypnotist*
†Nicholson, Jack *actor, director, producer*
Niemeth, Charles Frederick *lawyer*
Nilles, John Mathias (Jack Nilles) *futurist*
Nilles, Laila Padorr *musician, record producer*
†Nimni, Marcel Ephraim *biochemistry educator*
Nissenson, Allen Richard *physician, educator*
Nissman, Bonnie O'Brian *library services supervisor*
Nixon, John Harmon *retired economist*
Nobe, Ken *chemical engineering educator*
†Noble, Douglas *architecture educator*
Noble, Ernest Pascal *pharmacologist, biochemist, educator*
Noble, James Wilkes *actor*
Nochimson, David *lawyer*
Noel, Hans Christopher *political scientist*
Noguchi, Thomas Tsunetomi *author, forensic pathologist*
Nordlinger, Stephanie G. *lawyer*
†Norris, William Albert *lawyer, retired judge*
†Nosco, Peter Erling *humanities educator, consultant*
Nunez, Victor *film director, producer, writer*
†O'Brien, Rosanne P. *corporate financial executive*
†Ochoa, Arthur J. *lawyer, hospital administrator*
O'Connell, Kevin *lawyer*
O'Connell, Taaffe Cannon *actress, publishing executive*
O'Connor, Kevin Thomas *religious organization administrator*
O'Day, Anita Belle Colton *entertainer, singer*
Odell, John Stephen *political scientist*
O'Donnell, Pierce Henry *lawyer*
†Ogden, Devika *accounting executive*
†Ogilvie, Lloyd John *clergyman*
†Ohlgren, Joel R. *lawyer*
†Ohlmeyer, Donald Winfred, Jr., *film and television producer*
Okrent, David *engineering educator*
Olah, George Andrew *chemist*
Oldman, Gary *actor*
†O'Leary, Prentice Lee *lawyer*
Olivas, Daniel Anthony *lawyer*
†Oliver, Anthony Thomas, Jr., *lawyer*
Oliver, Dale Hugh *lawyer*
†Olivier, Kathy *college basketball coach*
Olsen, Frances Elisabeth *law educator, theorist*
†Olson, Ronald Leroy *lawyer*
O'Neill, Russell Richard *engineering educator*
†Orbach, Jerry *actor, singer*
Orchard, Henry John *electrical engineer*
Ordin, Andrea Sheridan *lawyer*
O'Reilly, Richard Brooks *journalist*
Orme, Antony Ronald *geography educator*
Orsatti, Alfred Kendall *organization executive*
Owen, Michael Lee *lawyer*
†Ownbey, Vance Scott *corporate financial executive*
Palevsky, Max *industrialist*
Palffy, Zigmund (Ziggy Palffy) *professional hockey player*
Palmieri, Victor Henry *lawyer, business executive*
Parham, Linda Diane *occupational therapist, researcher, educator*
†Park, Chan Ho *professional baseball player*
Park, Lee (Lee Parklee) *artist*
Park, No-Hee *academic administrator*
†Park, Sam-Koo *transportation executive*
Parker, Alice Cline *computer engineering educator, consultant*
Parks, Debora Ann *private school director*
Parks, Michael Christopher *journalist*
Parmelee, Arthur Hawley, Jr., *pediatric medical educator*
Parsky, Gerald Lawrence *lawyer*
Pasich, Kirk Alan *lawyer*
†Pastor, Jennifer *sculptor*
Patrick, Robert *playwright*
Patron, Susan Hall *librarian, writer*
†Patterson, Charles Ernest *lawyer*
Patzakis, Michael J. *orthopaedic surgeon, educator*
Paulson, Donald Robert *chemistry educator*
Pearce, Joan DeLap *research company executive*
Pearl, Judea *computer scientist, educator*
†Pearman, Robert Charles *lawyer*
Peck, Austin H., Jr., *lawyer*
Peña, Elizabeth *actress*
Perkins, William Clinton *company executive*
Perlmutter, Donna *music and dance critic*
Perrine, Richard Leroy *environmental engineering educator*
Perry, Antoinette Krueger *pianist, instructor*
Perry, Ralph Barton, III, *lawyer*
Pesta, Ben W., II, *lawyer, writer*
Petak, William John *systems management educator*
†Peterson, Linda S. *lawyer*
Peterson, Lowell *cinematographer*
†Pettibon, Raymond *video artist*
Pfaelzer, Mariana R. *federal judge*
†Pfatteicher, Linda E. *lawyer*
Phelps, Barton Chase *architect, educator*
†Phelps, Kathy Bazoian *lawyer*
Philips, Chuck *journalist*
Phillips, Geneva Ficker *academic editor*
†Phillips, Patricia Dominis *lawyer*
†Phillips-Oland, Pamela Barbara *lyricist, writer*
Phinney, Bernard O. *research scientist, educator*
Pieper, Darold D. *lawyer*
Pierskalla, William Peter *university dean, management-engineering educator*
Pircher, Leo Joseph *lawyer, director*
Pisegna, Joseph Rocco *gastroenterologist*
Plate, Thomas Gordon *newspaper columnist, educator*
Pleasants, Ben *writer, poet, playwright, educator*
Poindexter, William Mersereau *lawyer*
Pollock, John Phleger *lawyer*
†Ponty, Jean-Luc *violinist, composer, producer*
Poole, Robert William, Jr., *foundation executive*
Poole, Stafford *historian, priest*
Popek, Gerald John *computer software company executive, educator*
Port, Sidney Charles *mathematician, educator*
Porter, Bonnie *artist, photographer*
Porter, Verna Louise *lawyer*
†Potenza, Frank William *music educator*
Potvin, Felix *professional hockey player*
Powell, James Lawrence *museum director*
†Powell, Wonda A. *social studies educator, writer*

Withers, Hubert Rodney *radiotherapist, radiobiologist, educator*
Wittrock, Merlin Carl *educational psychologist*
Wlaschin, Ken *cultural organization administrator, writer*
Woessner, Frederick T. *composer, pianist*
Wohl, Robert *historian, educator*
Wolf, Lawrence *lawyer*
Wolfen, Werner F. *lawyer*
Wong, James Bok *economist, engineer, technologist*
Wong-McDonald, Ana *psychologist*
Woodland, Irwin Francis *lawyer*
Woodley, David Timothy *dermatology educator*
Woodruff, Fay *paleoceanographer, geological researcher*
†Woods, Daniel James *lawyer*
†Woods, Shirley *mathematics educator, writer*
Wortham, Thomas Richard *English language educator*
Woyt, James Charles (Jim Woyt) *actor*
Wright, Kenneth Brooks *lawyer*
Wu, Shi-Qi (Samuel Wu) *medical geneticist*
Wudl, Fred *chemistry educator*
Xiao, Guishan *research scientist*
Xue, Yongkang *science educator*
Yaffe, Sumner Jason *pediatrician, educator*
Yager, Thomas C. *retired judge*
Yanai, Michio *atmospheric scientist*
Yang, Fan *electrical engineering research scientist*
Yang, Henry S. (Hong Yang) *metallurgist, materials engineer*
Yang, Yang *science educator*
Yen, Teh Fu *civil and environmental engineering educator*
†Yip, Andy Ming-Ham *education educator, researcher*
Yoshiki-Kovinick, Marian Tsugie *author*
†Younai, Fariba Simhai *dental educator, researcher*
†Yu, Pauline Ruth *dean, East Asian languages educator*
†Yuan, Huidong *molecular biologist*
Zeitlin, Maurice *sociology educator, writer*
Zelikow, Howard Monroe *management and financial consultant*
Zelon, Laurie Dee *lawyer*
†Zemeckis, Robert L. *film director*
Zerunyan, Frank Vram *lawyer*
Zexter, Eleanor M. *secondary education educator*
†Ziane, Mohammed Boulanouar *mathematician, educator*
†Zobrist, Duane Herman *lawyer*
†Zone, Ray *writer*
Zucker, Lynne Goodman *sociology educator, consultant*
Zwick, Barry Stanley *newspaper editor, speechwriter*

Los Banos

†Ellington, Karen Renae *secondary education resource specialist*
Peterson, Stanley Lee *artist*
York, Courtney Carter *retired engineering executive, genealogist*

Los Gatos

Blasgen, Sharon Walther *lawyer*
†Carson, Sol Kent *artist, educator*
Cohen, James Robert *oncologist, hematologist*
Conaway, Margaret Grimes (Peggy Conaway) *library administrator*
Dahlberg, Thomas Robert *writer, lawyer, educator, software company executive*
†Ferrari, L. Katherine *speaker, consultant, entrepreneur*
Foy, Wade Hampton *research scientist*
Frugoli, Anthony Francis *priest, educator*
Kazan, Benjamin *research engineer*
Koomen, Cornelis Jan *telecommunications and electronics executive*
Lee, Alfred Theodore *research psychologist*
Mahmoudi, Massoud
Naughten, Robert Norman *pediatrician*
Naymark, Sherman *consulting nuclear engineer*
Rissanen, Jorma Johannes *computer scientist*
Rogers, Franklin Robert *former language and literature educator, writer, literary critic*
Rosenheim, Donald Edwin *electrical engineer*
Westendorf, Elaine Susan *social worker*

Los Olivos

†Battaglia, Philip Maher *lawyer*

Los Osos

Hampton, Anita *artist, writer*
Just, Faye Jordan *antique restoration company executive*
†Kreitzer, Jacalyn Bower *vocalist, voice educator*
Law, Orley Thomas *retired neuroscientist, educator, consultant, poet*
Moore, Walter Dengel *rapid transit system professional*
Topp, Alphonso Axel, Jr., *environmental scientist, consultant*

Lynwood

Dove, Donald Augustine *city planner, educator*
†Legesse, Solomon *technology executive*
Sterling, Arthur James *legal assistant*

Madera

Brashear, James Thomas *lawyer*
Glynn, James A. *sociology educator, author*

Malibu

Almond, Paul *film director, producer, screenwriter, novelist*
Ancker, Clinton James, Jr., *emeritus systems and industrial engineering educator*
Baskin, Otis Wayne *business educator*
Bedrosian, Edward *electrical engineer*
†Benton, Andrew Keith *university administrator, lawyer*
Bowman, Bruce *art educator, writer, artist*

†Cardoso, Dinora Caridad *education educator*
Carson, Johnny *television personality*
Dankanyin, Robert John *international business executive*
Darraby, Jessica L. *lawyer, educator, writer*
de la Rocha, Raquelle *lawyer, educator*
DeMieri, Joseph L. *retired bank executive*
Ensign, Richard Papworth *transportation executive*
†Flynn, Carl Frederick *religious studies educator*
Hanson, Gary A. *lawyer, legal educator, university administrator*
Harris, Ed(ward Allen) *actor*
Herschensohn, Bruce *film director, writer*
Hill, Lawrence Sidney *finance educator*
Hunt, Valerie Virginia *electrophysiologist, educator*
Jeffrey, Francis *software developer, forecaster*
Jenden, Donald James *pharmacologist, educator*
Keach, Stacy, Jr., *actor, director, producer, writer, musician, composer*
Liu, David Shiao-Kung *physical scientist*
Lloyd, Robert Baldwin *political science educator*
Lobel-Angel, Meredith Anne *lawyer*
Luft, Herbert *history educator, former dean and academic administrator*
Marshall, Donald Glenn *English language and literature educator*
Mataré, Herbert F. *physicist, consultant*
Monsma, Stephen Vos *political scientist, educator*
Moore, John George, Jr., *medical educator*
Morgenstern, Leon *surgeon*
Palacio, June Rose Payne *nutritional science educator*
Pepper, David M. *physicist, educator, writer, inventor*
Phillips, Ronald Frank *university administrator*
Raine, Melinda L. *library manager*
Smith, David Matthew *economist, educator*
Stalzer, Mark Anthony *computer scientist, technical director*
Tellem, Susan Mary *public relations executive*
Walla-Murphy, Meghan Anne *foundation administrator*
Zakian, Michael *museum director*

Mammoth Lakes

Fitzgerald, Timothy K. *writer, political organizer, non-profit administrator*
†Mager, Ingrid Irina *artist*

Manhattan Beach

Blanton, John Arthur *architect, writer*
Champion, David *music educator*
Deutsch, Barry Joseph *consulting and management development company executive*
Devitt-Grasso, Pauline Virginia *civic volunteer, nurse*
Di Massa, Ernani Vincenzo, Jr., *broadcast executive, television producer, writer*
†Magner, Rachel Harris *retired banker*
Pettersen, Thomas Morgan *accountant, finance executive*
Schoenfeld, Lawrence Jon *real estate developer, asset lender*

Manteca

Miller, Max William *emergency physician*
Talmage, Kenneth Kellogg *business executive*
Tonn, Elverne Meryl *pediatric dentist, dental benefits consultant, forensic odontologist*

Marina

Endsley, Daniel Steven *public administrator*
Hill, Karen Caecilia *education educator*
†Madsen, Roy I., Jr., *language educator*
Mettee-McCutchon, Ila *municipal official, retired career officer*
Shane, William Whitney *astronomer*

Marina Del Rey

Allmon, Michael Bryan *financial consultant*
Annotico, Richard Anthony *legal administrator, real estate investor*
Banks, Ernest (Ernie Banks) *retired professional baseball player*
Carter, Janice Joene *telecommunications executive*
†Coplan, Daniel Jonathan *lawyer, actor, writer, producer, director*
Fash, Michael William *cinematographer, director*
Gold, Carol Sapin *international management consultant, speaker*
Lindheim, Richard David *television company executive, university official*
†Neuman, Clifford *computer scientist, educator*
Nizze, Judith Anne *retired physician assistant*
Philpott, Lindsey *civil engineer, researcher, educator*
†Serena, C. David *lawyer*
Smolker, Gary Steven *lawyer*
Touch, Joseph Dean *computer scientist, educator*
Uretz, Michael Albert *health and fitness executive*

Mariposa

Rogers, Earl Leslie *artist, educator*
Sutherland, Gail Russell *retired industrial equipment manufacturing company executive*

Marshall

Evans, Robert James *architect*

Martinez

†Baird, Laurel Cohen *clinical nurse*
Barnard, William Marion *psychiatrist*
†Canciamilla, Joseph *state legislator*
McKnight, Lenore Ravin *child psychiatrist, educator*
†St. James, Holly (Saundra Manning) *social worker*
Thomas, Walter Dill, Jr., *retired forest pathologist, consultant*
Tong, Siu Wing *computer programmer*
†Torlakson, Tom A. *state senator*
Williams, Charles Judson *lawyer, writer*

Marysville

Gray, Katherine *marriage, family and child therapist, writer, educator*
†Larson, Billy Dell *finance company executive*
Myers, Elmer *psychiatric social worker*

McKinleyville

†Peithman, Roscoe Edward *physicist, educator*

Mcclellan AFB

Chong, Vernon *surgeon, physician, air force officer*

Mckinleyville

Berry, Glenn *educator, artist*
†Byrd, Joseph *composer*
LaPlantz, David Milton *artist, retired educator*
†Morris, Marjorie Hale *artist, writer*
Schoettger, Theodore Leo *city official*
Thueson, David Orel *pharmaceutical executive, researcher, educator, writer*

Mendocino

Alexander, Joyce Mary *illustrator*
†Bilas, Richard A. *economist*
Felton, Jean Spencer *physician*
Masterson, William A. *retired judge*

Menifee

Balow, Irving Henry *retired education educator*

Menlo Park

Abdou, Ikram Escandar *engineering consultant*
†Allison, Anthony Clifford *research scientist, consultant*
Bader, W(illiam) Reece *lawyer*
Baez, Joan Chandos *folk singer*
†Bales, Flossie Kathleen *retired librarian, systems analyst*
Bourne, Charles Percy *information scientist, educator*
Boyarski, Adam Michael *physicist*
Bremser, George, Jr., *electronics company executive*
Brest, Paul A. *law educator*
Bukry, John David *geologist*
Chapin, June Roediger *education educator*
Clair, Theodore Nat *educational psychologist*
†Collins, Nancy Whisnant *foundation administrator*
Coward, David Hand *physicist, researcher*
Craig, Gordon Alexander *historian, educator*
Crane, Hewitt David *science advisor*
Creswell, Donald Creston *business executive*
Davies, Paul Lewis, III, *venture capitalist*
†Deken, Jean Marie *librarian, archivist*
Dorset, Phyllis Flanders *technical writer, editor*
†Drell, Sidney David *physicist, educator*
Dusel-Bacon, Cynthia *geologist, researcher*
Dyer, Charles Arnold *lawyer*
†Edwards, John Wesley, II, *lawyer*
Ehrlich, Thomas *law educator*
Evans, Bob Overton *electronics executive, director*
†Exuzides, Alex *statistician, researcher*
Fenner, Peter David *communications executive*
Fenton, Noel John *venture capitalist*
Funkhouser, Lawrence William *retired geologist*
Goerz, Mary Elizabeth Larsen *civic worker*
Halluin, Albert Price *lawyer*
Haslam, Robert Thomas, III, *lawyer*
†Hazen, Paul Mandeville *banker*
Herrmannsfeldt, William Bernard *physicist*
Hoffman, Thomas Edward *dermatologist*
Holmquest, Donald Lee *physician, astronaut, lawyer*
Holzer, Thomas Lequear *geologist*
Honey, Richard Churchill *retired electrical engineer*
Jeffries, Robin *computer engineer*
Jorgensen, Paul J. *research company executive*
Kalinske, Thomas J. *education, video game and toy company executive*
Kamin, William Stephen *food company executive, photographer*
Kaufman, Christopher Lee *lawyer*
Keeley, Michael Clark *economist*
Kelly, Daniel Grady, Jr., *lawyer*
Kirk, Cassius Lamb, Jr., *retired lawyer, investor*
Kovachy, Edward Miklos, Jr., *psychiatrist, consultant*
Kuwabara, James Shigeru *research hydrologist*
†Kvamme, Mark D. *marketing professional*
Lachenbruch, Arthur Herold *geophysicist, researcher*
Lane, Laurence William, Jr., *retired ambassador, publisher*
Lindzey, Gardner *psychologist, educator*
Lucas, Donald Leo *investor*
Lynch, Charles Allen *investment executive, corporate director*
Lynch, Kevin J. *publishing executive, media planner*
Madison, James Raymond *lawyer*
Marton, Laurence Jay *researcher, educator, clinical pathologist*
McCarthy, Roger Lee *mechanical engineer*
†McCown, George E. *venture banking company executive*
McDonald, Warren George *accountant, former savings and loan executive*
†McGarr, Arthur Francis *geophysicist*
†McLain, Christopher M. *lawyer*
Mendelson, Alan Charles *lawyer*
†Messmer, Harold Maximilian, Jr., *financial services executive*
Middleton, Teresa Muir *Internet company executive, researcher*
†Montana, Joseph C., Jr., *former professional football player*
Mulgaonkar, Prasanna G. *computer scientist*
Neumann, Peter Gabriel *computer scientist*
Nichols, William Ford, Jr., *foundation executive, business executive*
O'Brien, Raymond Francis *transportation executive*
Pausa, Clements Edward *electronics company executive*

Penzias, Arno Allan *astrophysicist, technology consultant, research scientist, information systems specialist*
†Raab, Michael George *venture capital investor*
Raffo, Susan Henney *elementary education educator*
Reamy, Michaelin *marriage and family therapist, educator, consultant*
Richter, Burton *physicist*
Ross, Bernard *engineering consultant, educator*
Saifer, Mark Gary Pierce *pharmaceutical executive*
Santry, Barbara Lea *venture capitalist*
Schmidt, Chauncey Everett *banker*
Shah, Haresh Chandulal *civil engineering educator*
Smith, Marshall Savidge *foundation executive*
Studley, Jamienne Shayne *former academic administrator, lawyer*
Sweeney, Lawrence Earl, Jr., *computer company executive*
Taft, David Dakin *chemical executive*
Taylor, Richard Edward *physicist, educator*
Taylor, Robert P. *lawyer*
†Terman, Donna Lea *lawyer, foundation administrator*
†Tiet, Quyen Q. *clinical psychologist, researcher*
Tokheim, Robert Edward *physicist*
Vane, Sylvia Brakke *anthropologist, publisher, cultural resource management company executive, writer*
Wachtel, John Steven *obstetrician, gynecologist*
†Walker, George Edward *academic administrator, physicist*
Walsh, William Desmond *investor*
Westcott, Brian John *manufacturing executive*
White, Cecil Ray *librarian, consultant*
Wolfson, Mark Alan *investor, business educator*
Woodrow, Kenneth M. *psychiatrist*
Zdeblick, Mark James *information technology executive*
†Zercher, Craig Allen *special education educator, researcher*

Merced

†Denham, Jeffrey *state senator*
†Dylina, Timothy Joseph *dentist, educator*
Elliott, Gordon Jefferson *retired English language educator*
LeCocq, Karen Elizabeth *artist*
Olsen, David Magnor *chemistry and astronomy educator*

Mi Wuk Village

Rainey, Barbara Ann *sensory evaluation consultant*

Middletown

Selandia, Elizabeth *acupuncturist, Oriental medicine physician*

Midway City

McCawley, William Dale, II, *accountant, writer, ethnohistorian*

Mill Valley

Burke, Kathleen J. *foundation administrator*
Cohn, Bruce *film and television company executive*
†Cole, Richard Charles *lawyer*
Crews, William Odell, Jr., *religious organization administrator*
D'Amico, Michael *architect, urban planner*
Dyer, Gregory Clark *lawyer, mediator*
†Fuller, Glenn R. *park ranger*
Harner, Michael James *anthropologist, educator, author*
Harris, Jeffrey Saul *physician, executive, consultant*
†Hoffman, John Douglas *lawyer, mediator*
Jones, Pirkle *photographer, educator*
Kettunen Zegart, Mar(garet) Jean *artist, art educator*
Kolb, Felix Oscar *physician*
Leslie, Jacques Robert, Jr., *journalist*
Maubert, Jacques Claude *retired school superintendent*
McNamara, Stephen *newspaper executive*
Mumford, Christopher Greene *corporate financial executive*
Nemir, Donald Philip *lawyer*
†Newman, Nancy Marilyn *ophthalmologist, educator*
Owings, Alison June *writer, journalist*
Padula, Fred David *filmmaker*
Premo, Paul Mark *oil company executive*
Selvig, Jettie Pierce *lawyer*
Taylor, Rose Perrin *social worker*
Ware, David Joseph *financial consultant*
Whiting, Christine Light *art librarian*
Winskill, Robert Wallace *manufacturing executive*

Millbrae

Chow, Eileen Siu-Ha *computer retailing, investment company executive*
Ferrer, Adelardo Manuel *physician*
Lande, James Avra *lawyer*
†Rosenthal, Herbert Marshall *lawyer*

Milpitas

Allen, Vicky *sales and marketing professional*
Brown, Michael A. *computer hardware company executive*
†Cannon, Michael R. *manufacturing executive*
Chiu, Peter Yee-Chew *physician*
Corrigan, Wilfred J. *computer company executive*
Nishimura, Koichi *former electronics manufacturing company executive*
Roddick, David Bruce *construction company executive*
Treichel, Helmuth W.A. *technology executive*
†Tufano, Paul *computer company executive*
†Wang, Shao *tribologist, senior hard disk drive engineer*

Mission Hills
Cramer, Frank Brown engineering executive, combustion engineer, systems consultant
†Weber, Francis Joseph archivist, museum director

Mission Viejo
Austin, Berit Synnove small business owner, central services specialist
†Brierre, Maud French and Spanish educator
†Burke, Kathleen J. music director, writer
Dergarabedian, Paul energy and environmental company executive
Dillon, Francis Patrick retired human resources executive, financial, insurance and tax consultant
Drozdowski, Miladin Peter Ljubicic consulting engineer
Faley, Robert Lawrence retired instruments company executive
Gilbert, Heather Campbell manufacturing company executive
Harris, Ruby Lee real estate agent
Hodge, Kathleen O'Connell academic administrator
McKinney, Monica Lorraine media/communications company executive, application developer
Mruthyunjaya, G.T. pediatrician
Ruben, Audrey H. Zweig lawyer, arbitrator, actress
Ruben, Robert Joseph lawyer
Shah, Shirish Anantlal pharmacist
Wilson, Eleanor McElroy county official

Modesto
Barnes, William David non-profit charities consultant, publisher
Berry, John Charles clinical psychologist, educational administrator
Blair, Jimmy minister, educator
Boyce, Dennis Wayne radiologist
Bucknam, Mary Olivia Caswell artist, educator
Cimino, Lewis R., Jr., surgeon
Cofer, Berdette Henry public management consulting company executive
†Gallo, Ernest vintner
†Gallo, Joseph E. vintner
Hardage, Darwin "Dar" Henry animal technologist
Harrison-Scott, Sharlene Marie elementary school educator
Khanna, Kanwal rheumatologist
Lewis, Marshall Edward psychiatrist, administrator, educator
Lipomi, Michael Joseph health facility executive
Mattos, William Harold trade association executive, newspaper publisher
Moe, Andrew Irving veterinarian
Morrison, Robert Lee physical scientist
†Murphy, John Thomas lawyer
Mussman, Carol Lynne lawyer
Mussman, William Edward, III, lawyer
Nash, Edgar Mason writer
†Piccinini, Robert M. grocery store chain executive
Sabatino, Carmen mayor
Smith, Chester broadcasting executive
Smith, Heather Lynn psychotherapist, recreational therapist
†Suntra, Charles Ratapol surgeon, educator
Tidball, Lee Falk elementary school educator, writer
Turner-Silvia, JoAnn writer, vocalist, actress, music producer
Whiteside, Carol Gordon foundation executive

Moffett Field
†Bernhard, Roberta research psychologist
†Bilimoria, Karl D. aerospace engineer
Biswas, Rupak computer scientist
†Caldwell, William Frank aerospace project manager, mechanical engineer
Cohen, Malcolm Martin psychologist, researcher
†Denery, Dallas G. aeronautical engineer, researcher
Dismukes, Robert Key medical scientist
Eodice, Michael Thomas aerospace engineer, biomedical engineer
Friedmann, E(merich) Imre biologist, educator
†Havelund, Klaus computer scientist
Kittel, Peter research scientist
Lissauer, Jack Jonathan astronomy educator
†Park, Chul aerospace engineer
Salerno, Louis J. research scientist
Statler, Irving Carl aerospace engineer
†Whiting, Ellis Eugene retired research scientist

Mojave
Shelby, Tim Otto secondary education educator

Mokelumne Hill
Testa, Stephen Michael geologist, consultant

Monarch Beach
Alexander, Barbara Toll investment banker
Dougherty, Elmer Lloyd, Jr., retired chemical engineering educator, consultant
Mackaig, Janet Brownlee artist, printmaker, educator

Monrovia
Andary, Thomas Joseph biochemist, researcher
Deliman, Robert Michael surgeon
Dobay, Susan Vilma artist
Edwards, Kenneth Neil chemical engineering executive
Jemelian, John Nazar management consultant
Kimnach, Myron William botanist, horticulturist
Lim, SallyJane insurance company executive, financial consultant, diversified financial services company executive
†Liu, Wenhai optical engineer
Mac Cready, Paul aeronautical engineer
†Miller, Karen clinical psychologist, neuropsychologist
†Mountjoy, Dennis Lee state official

Pray, Ralph Emerson metallurgical engineer
†Salaman, Maureen Kennedy nutritionist

Montague
Stone, Gwen visual artist

Montclair
Haage, Robert Mitchell retired history educator, organization leader
†Negrete McLeod, Gloria state official

Monte Nido
Brandewie, Richard Anthony laser and optics consultant

Monte Sereno
†Allan, Lionel Manning lawyer

Montebello
†Bucey, Constance Virginia Russell retired elementary school educator, education educator
†Calderon, Ronald state official
Dible, Rose Harpe McFee special education educator
Meeker, Arlene Dorothy Hallin (Mrs. William Maurice Meeker) manufacturing company executive
Orr, Stanley Chi-Hung financial executive

Monteca
Hoffmann, James Vernon, Jr., social studies educator, writer

Montecito
Brenken, Hanne Marie artist
Coln, William Alexander, III, retired pilot
Meghreblian, Robert Vartan manufacturing executive, physicist
Schwartz, Norman Benjamin theatre director
Wheelon, Albert Dewell physicist

Monterey
†Astore, William Joseph historian, dean
Bhaskar, Surindar Nath pathologist, periodontist
Black, Robert Lincoln pediatrician, educator
Boger, Dan Calvin statistical and economic consultant, educator
†Boger, Gail Lorraine Zivna reading specialist
Bomberger, Russell Branson lawyer, writer
†Browder, John Glen former congressman, educator
Butler, Jon Terry computer engineering educator, researcher
Caldwell, Joni psychology and women's studies educator, small business owner
Collins, Curtis Allan oceanographer
†Davis, Craig Alphin lawyer, manufacturing company executive
Denning, Peter James computer scientist, engineer
Di Girolamo, Rosina Elizabeth education educator
Dutta, Indranath metallurgical engineer, educator
Eckersley, Norman Chadwick bank executive
Fenton, Lewis Lowry lawyer
Franke, Jack Emil foreign language educator
†Goldstein, Lynn Meg language educator
Gotshall, Cordia Ann publishing company executive, distributing executive
Haddad, Louis Nicholas paralegal
Hanlon, James Allison confectionery company executive
Hoivik, Thomas Harry military educator, international consultant
Le, Ly Ngoc (Le Ngoc Ly) environmental physicist, educator, research scientist
Marto, Paul James retired mechanical engineering educator, consultant, researcher
Matthews, David Fort career officer
Mehrabian, Albert psychology educator, author, researcher
†Miller, Richard Connelly publishing executive, writer
Newberry, Conrad Floyde aerospace engineering educator
Oder, Broeck Newton school emergency management consultant
†Peet, Phyllis Irene women's studies educator
Rago, Thomas Ashton physical oceanographer
Reese, William Albert, III, psychologist, clinical neuropsychologist
Reneker, Maxine Hohman librarian
Rowe, Neil Charles science educator
Schneidewind, Norman Floyd computer scientist, educator
Schrady, David Alan civilian military employee, educator
Shull, Harrison chemist, educator
Sunde, Douglas plastic surgeon
von Drachenfels, Suzanne Hamilton writer

Monterey Park
Besen, Jane Phyllis Triptow retired civic worker
Chang, Jonathan Lee orthopedist, educator
†Ly, Allan Q. medical technician
Montag, David Moses telecommunications industry executive
†Singer-Frankes, Deborah lawyer
Smith, Betty Denny county official, administrator, fashion executive
Stapleton, Jean journalism educator
Szeto, Paul (Cheuk-Ching Szeto) religious mission executive
Wilson, Linda librarian
Zheng, Dawei process integration engineer, materials scientist

Montrose
Greenlaw, Roger Lee interior designer

Moorpark
Bahn, Gilbert Schuyler retired mechanical engineer, researcher, novelist
†Kessner, Dolly Eugenio music educator, musician

Young, Victoria E. occupational health and pediatrics nurse practitioner, lawyer

Moraga
Allen, Richard Garrett healthcare and education consultant
Brown, James Edward retired research scientist
Gerold, Charles McAdow real estate broker
Gordon, David Jamieson tenor
Haag, Carol Ann Gunderson marketing professional, consultant
Ittner, Helen Louise entrepreneur
Meisch, Lynn Ann anthropologist, educator
O'Brien, Bea Jae artist
Sestanovich, Molly Brown writer
Silcox, Frances Eleanor museum and exhibits planning consultant

Moreno Valley
Garcia, Ariel H. plastic surgeon
Gull, Paula Mae adult nurse practitioner
White, Charles R. former mayor
†Wittwer, Marc Wayne secondary school educator, football coach

Morgan Hill
Foster, John Robert lawyer
Freimark, Robert (Bob Freimark) artist
Kuster, Robert Kenneth former scientist
Tan, Lucas G. anesthesiologist

Morongo Valley
Lindley, Judith Morland cat registry administrator

Morro Bay
†Merzon, James Bert lawyer
Wagner, Peter Ewing physics and electrical engineering educator

Moss Landing
Brewer, Peter George ocean geochemist
Coale, Kenneth Hamilton biogeochemist, educator
Lange, Lester Henry mathematics educator

Mount Shasta
Mann, Karen consultant, educator
Mariner, William Martin chiropractor
Stienstra, Stephani Ann editor, writer

Mountain View
†Abel, Elizabeth A. dermatologist
Aron, Mohit software engineer
Bennett, Stephen M. computer company executive
Bills, Robert Howard political party executive
†Bull, Howard Livingston lawyer
Chandramouli, Ramamurti electrical engineer
Ching, Andy Kwok-yee minister
Clancey, William John computer scientist, researcher
Clark, Jonathan L. photographer, printer, publisher
Crawford, Walt systems analyst
de Geus, Aart J. computer software company executive
Di Muccio, Mary-Jo retired librarian
Fischman, Stanley Edwin psychiatrist
†Gluhovsky, Ilya statistician, researcher
Harrison, Wendy Jane Merrill insurance company executive
Ivy, Edward Joseph plastic surgeon
Johnson, Conor Deane mechanical engineer
Kobza, Dennis Jerome architect
Koo, George Ping Shan business consultant
Lee, Murlin E. software company executive
†Lowen, Robert Marshall plastic surgeon
Miller, Jon Philip marketing and business development professional, pharmaceutical executive
Pasahow, Lynn H(arold) lawyer
Perrella, Anthony Joseph electronics engineer
Piazza, Duane Eugene biomedical researcher
†Polese, Kim software company executive
Popovici, Alexander Mihai geophysicist, business executive
Qureishi, A. Salam computer software and services company executive
†Radlo, Edward John lawyer, mathematician
Salama, Farid astrophycicist, spectroscopist, research scientist
Savage, Thomas Warren engineering director
Serra, Patricia Janet social services administrator
†Sultanov, Namig, 2d Baronet, musician, music educator
Unangst, Gregory John aerospace engineer
Urman, Jeffrey David physician, educator
Warren, Richard Wayne obstetrician, gynecologist

Murrieta
†Cloud, Mark F. video producer, director, writer, musician
Geffe, Philip Reinhold electrical engineer, consultant
Lake, Bruce Meno applied physicist
McClellan, Barry Dean city manager

Napa
Anderson, Richard Elliott internist, educator
Battisti, Paul Oreste retired county supervisor
Brough, Bruce Alvin public relations and communications executive
Chiarella, Peter Ralph vintner
Gillespie, Marcia Lou accountant, tax preparer, musician
Glaser, Edwin Victor rare book dealer
Grambow, Richard F. construction engineer, consultant
Hennings, Dorothy Ann financial advisor
†Ianziti, Adelbert John industrial designer
Kuntz, Charles Powers lawyer
Lee, Margaret Anne psychotherapist, social worker
Leggett, John Ward writer

Loar, Peggy Ann foundation administrator, museum administrator
Meyers, David W. lawyer, writer, educator
Moore, Bonnie Lou biology educator, consultant
†Morgese, Vincent John neurosurgeon
Norman, Sheri Hanna artist, educator, cartographer
Savage, Michael John Kirkness oil company and arts management executive
Smith, Robert Bruce former security consultant, retired career officer
Snow, Tower Charles, Jr., lawyer
Strock, David Randolph brokerage house executive
Wahl, Howard Wayne retired construction company executive, engineer
Wilhelm-Hass, Elaine operating room nurse

National City
Beauchamp, Miles Philip newspaper editor, columnist, education consultant
Morgan, Jacob Richard cardiologist

Nevada City
†Aanestad, Samuel Mark state legislator
André Kildare, Michel Walter neurosurgeon
Symes, Peter David engineer
Whitsel, Richard Harry biologist, entomologist

New Orleans
Ford, Gerald J. finance company executive

Newark
†Balmuth, Michael A. retail executive
†Gupta, Anju risk management consultant
Nemenman, Mark Yefim mathematics and computers educator, consultant

Newbury Park
Bleiberg, Leon William surgical podiatrist
†Keller, James Robert business development director
Lichtenstein, Chase Walter retired management consultant
Lindsey, Joanne M. flight attendant, poet
Naulin, John Arthur entertainment company executive
Stadler, Katherine Loy advertising sales executive

Newhall
†Halstead, Thomas A. theology studies educator
†Stein, Karl N. plastic and reconstructive surgeon
†Stone, Susan Foster mental health services professional, psychologist

Newman
Carlsen, Janet Haws retired insurance company owner, mayor

Newport Beach
Adams, William Gillette lawyer
Allen, Russell G. lawyer
Amyes, Edwin Westby neurosurgeon
Anderson, Paul Scott architect
Baskin, Scott David lawyer
Becker, Juliette psychologist, marriage and family therapist
Bennett, Bruce W. construction company executive, civil engineer
Bissell, George Arthur architect
Blinder, Barton Jerome physician, psychiatrist, psychoanalyst, educator
†Brown, Ernest Christopher lawyer, engineer
Brown, Giles Tyler history educator, lecturer
Bryant, Thomas Lee magazine editor
Calcagnie, Kevin Frank lawyer
Cano, Kristin Maria lawyer
Cardin, Frederick investment banker
Carman, Ernest Day lawyer
Carmichael, David Richard lawyer
Casey, Thomas Clark trust company executive, investment advisor
Connolly, John Earle surgeon, educator
Cordova, Ron lawyer
Cosgrove, Cameron insurance company executive
Cranford, Steven L. lawyer
Dean, John F. retired school system administrator
Dean, Paul John magazine editor
Fawcett, John Scott real estate developer
Frederick, Dolliver H. merchant banker
Fries, Arthur Lawrence life health insurance broker, disability claim consultant
Gellman, Gloria Gae Seeburger Schick marketing professional
Gerken, Walter Bland insurance company executive
Glass, Geoffrey Theodore judge
Gross, William H. financial analyst, investment company executive
†Harlan, Nancy Margaret lawyer
Harley, Halvor Larson banker, lawyer
Hinshaw, Ernest Theodore, Jr., private investor, former Olympics executive, former finance company executive
Hoffman, George Bernard estate planner
Jeffers, Michael Bogue lawyer
Johnson, Thomas Webber, Jr., lawyer
Jones, Roger Wayne electronics executive
Jones, Sheldon Atwell lawyer
Kenney, William John, Jr., real estate development executive
†Kolyer, John McNaughton materials specialist, chemist
Kraus, John Walter former aerospace engineering company executive
†Lawless, William Burns lawyer, retired judge, academic administrator
Lawson, Thomas Cheney fraud examiner
Li, Shu electronics executive
Lipson, Melvin Alan technology and business management consultant
Lorti, Daniel Caesar engineer
Mallory, Frank Linus lawyer
Mandel, Maurice, II, lawyer, educator, mediator

Marcoux, Carl Henry *former insurance executive, writer, historian*
†Matsen, Jeffrey Robert *lawyer*
Matteucci, Dominick Vincent *real estate developer*
McCue, Dennis Michael *management consultant*
Mc Culloch, Samuel Clyde *history educator*
Millar, Richard William, Jr., *lawyer*
Mink, Maxine Mock *real estate company executive*
Mirams, William C. *construction executive*
Monaghan, Anne *public relations consultant*
Mortensen, Arvid LeGrande *lawyer*
†Otto, James Daniel *lawyer*
Pepe, Stephen Phillip *lawyer*
Phillips, Layn R. *lawyer*
Randolph, Steven *financial advisor*
Richardson, Walter John *architect*
Robinson, Hurley *surgeon*
†Schafer, Glenns *insurance company executive*
Schiff, Laurie *lawyer*
Schilling, John Russell *lawyer, retail executive*
Schnapp, Roger Herbert *lawyer, consultant*
Schumacher, Stephen Joseph *lawyer, educator*
Shohet, Jack A. *otolaryngologist*
Shonk, Albert Davenport, Jr., *advertising executive*
Spitz, Barbara Salomon *artist*
Sutton, Thomas C. *insurance company executive*
Thorp, Edward Oakley *investment management company executive*
Tracy, James Jared, Jr., *accountant, financial executive, law firm administrator*
Wadden, Christopher David *food products executive*
Wagner, John Leo *lawyer, former magistrate judge*
Webb, H. Lawrence *real estate executive*
Weber, Mark Edward *editor, historian*
Weissbard, Samuel Held *lawyer*
Wentworth, Diana von Welanetz *author*
Wentworth, Theodore Sumner *lawyer*
Whittemore, Paul Baxter *psychologist*
Williams, Donald Edward *endocrinologist*
Wolf, Alan Steven *lawyer*
Zubrin, Jay Ross *surgeon*

Newport Coast
Pavony, William H. *retail executive, consultant*
Swan, Peer Alden *public utility executive*

Nipomo
Schindler, Keith William *software engineer*
Stock, Kim H. *dance studio owner, choreographer*

Norco
Kromka, James Thomas Michael *designer, illustrator*

North Fork
Flanagan, James Henry, Jr., *lawyer, writer, business educator*

North Highlands
Emburg, Kathryn Maria *social worker, writer*

North Hills
†Boeckmann, Herbert F., II, *automotive executive*
†Clason, Richard Lewis *retired protective services official, writer*
†Deets, Richard M. *secondary school educator, consultant*
Squires, Norma Jean *artist, writer*

North Hollywood
Balmuth, Bernard Allen *retired film editor*
†Boulanger, Donald Richard *financial services executive*
Burman, Sheila Flexer Zola *special education educator*
Chang, Wung *business advisor, researcher, lecturer*
Charis, Barbara *nutritionist, consultant, health researcher*
de la Houssaye, Brette Angelo-Pepe *electronics engineer, researcher*
Downey, Roma *actress*
Gallardo, Sandra Silvana *producer*
Grasso, Mary Ann *theater association executive*
Kantor, Igo *film and television producer*
Kreger, Melvin Joseph *lawyer*
Kuter, Kay E. *writer, actor*
†Mallery, Sarah *folk artist, educator*
†Milliken, Susan *film director, human services administrator*
Price, Joe (Joe Allen) *artist, former educator, actor*
Reynolds, Debbie (Mary Frances Reynolds) *actress*
Schrier, Ruth *artist, educator*
†Shersher, Zinovy *artist, composer*
†Stone, Sharon *actress*
Toplitt, Gloria H. *voice educator, singer, actress*
Winogradsky, Steven *lawyer*
Zimring, Stuart David *lawyer*

Northridge
Barnard, Ian *writer, educator*
Bassler, Robert Covey *artist, educator*
Bekir, Nagwa Esmat *electrical engineer, educator, consultant*
Bradshaw, Richard Rotherwood *engineering executive*
Brotman, Carol Eileen *adult education educator, advocate*
Chen, Joseph Tao *historian, educator*
Curzon, Susan Carol *university administrator*
Dart, John Seward *journalist, author*
†Duran, Karin Jeanine *librarian*
Falk, Heinrich Richard *theater and humanities educator*
Garland, G(arfield) Garrett *sales executive, golf professional*
Harwick, Betty Corinne Burns *sociology educator*
†Hedge, Thomas Lyle, Jr., *rehabilitation services professional*
Kiddoo, Robert James *engineering service company executive*
†Koistinen, Paul Abraham Carl *historian, educator*
†Kranz, Jack *university librarian, educator*
Logan, Lee Robert *orthodontist*
Loudon, Craig Michael *video specialist*
†McHenry, Leemon Benton *education educator, writer*
Mitchell, James Andrew *education educator*
Mitchell, Rie Rogers *psychologist, counselor, educator*
Orenstein, Michael (Ian Orenstein) *philatelic dealer, columnist*
Reagan, Janet Thompson *psychologist, educator*
Roberts, Teri Alane *accountant, educator, civic activist*
Ross, Camille *photographer, art educator*
Ruley, Stanley Eugene *cost analyst*
Smathers, James Burton *medical physicist, educator*
Stampke, Stuart Reh *physicist, researcher*
Stout, Thomas Melville *control systems engineer*
Syms, Helen Maksym *educational administrator*
Torgow, Eugene N. *electrical engineer*
Weatherup, Wendy Gaines *graphic designer, writer*

Norwalk
Armstrong, David Ligon *psychiatrist*
Bao, Joseph Yue-Se *orthopedist, microsurgeon, educator*
Khajawall, Ali Mohamad *psychiatrist*
†Kiss, Boglarka *music educator*
Matsuura, Kenneth Ray *counselor, articulation officer*
Ori, Jerry Allen *management consultant*
†Pritchard, Gary Paul, Jr., *musicologist, educator*
†Schreiner, Gregory Lee *music educator*

Novato
†Batchelor, Robert Paul *corporate communications specialist, writer*
Bibeault, Donald Bertrand *business executive, investor*
Bugental, James Frederick Thomas *retired psychologist, educator*
Hanahan, Donald James *biochemist, educator*
Jaeger, Patsy Elaine *retired secondary education educator, artist*
Kratka-Schneider, Dorothy Maryjohanna *psychotherapist*
Lewin, Werner Siegfried, Jr., *lawyer*
Patterson, W. Morgan *college president*
Thompson, Peter Layard Hailey, Sr., *landscape and golf course architect, architectural firm executive*

Oak Park
Caldwell, Stratton Franklin *kinesiology educator*
Schulner, Keith Alan *lawyer, business owner*
Vinson, William Theodore *lawyer, diversified corporation executive*

Oakdale
Saletta, Mary Elizabeth (Betty Saletta) *sculptor, rancher*

Oakhurst
Cantwell, Christopher William *artist*

Oakland
Alba, Benny *artist*
Alford, Joan Franz *entrepreneur*
Allen, Jeffrey Michael *lawyer*
Al Malek, Amir Isa *entrepreneur, business consultant, musician*
Ames, Bruce N(athan) *biochemist, molecular biologist*
†Anderson, Doris Elaine *lawyer*
Anderson, Robert Thomas *anthropologist, researcher, physician*
Anderson, Brother Timothy Mel *academic administrator*
Arazi, Lorri Rosenberg *real estate broker*
Atkinson, Richard Chatham *university president*
†Bacon, Robert Dale *lawyer*
Baldwin, Mark Alan *communications consultant, writer*
Beasley, Bruce Miller *sculptor*
†Berry, Kathleen A. *English language educator*
Bewley, Peter David *lawyer*
Bjork, Robert David, Jr., *lawyer*
Brevetti, Francine Clelia *journalist*
Brown, Jerry (Edmund Gerald Brown Jr.) *mayor, former governor*
Brust, David *physicist*
Bryant, Arthur H. *lawyer*
†Buckley, Mike Clifford *lawyer*
Burns, Catherine Elizabeth *art dealer*
Buzaljko, Grace Wilson *retired editor*
Carwell, Hattie Virginia *health physicist*
Ching, Eric San Hing *health care and insurance administrator*
Cole, Joan Hays *social worker, clinical psychologist*
Collen, Morris Frank *medical association administrator, physician, medical researcher*
Collins, James Francis *toxicologist*
†Cowens, David William (Dave Cowens) *professional basketball coach, insurance executive, retired professional basketball player*
Crane, Robert Meredith *health care executive*
Crocker, Joy Laksmi *concert pianist and organist, composer*
†Crowley, Thomas B., Jr., *water transportation executive*
Dailey, Garrett Clark *publisher, lawyer*
DeFazio, Lynette Stevens *dancer, choreographer, educator, chiropractor, author, actress, musician*
Dell, Stephen Owen *neurosurgeon*
Delmain, Fred *industrial psychologist*
Deming, Willis Riley *lawyer*
De Vos, George Alphonse *psychologist, anthropologist*
Diaz, Sharon *education administrator*
Dibble, David Van Vlack *visually impaired educator, lawyer*
Drexel, Baron Jerome *lawyer*
Dunn, David Cameron *entrepreneur, business executive*
Dynes, Robert C. *academic administrator*
Earle, Sylvia Alice *research biologist, oceanographer*
†Elkin, Lynne Osman *science historian, educator*
†Elliott, Jack *folk musician*
Eykamp, Paul W. *academic administrator*
Farrell, Kenneth Royden *economist*
†Finkle, Bernard J *biochemist, researcher*
Foley, Jack (John Wayne Harold Foley) *poet, writer, editor*
Ford, Gail *library administrator*
Gaál, Violetta *retired social worker, massage therapist*
George, Donald Warner *online columnist and editor, freelance writer*
†Givant, Steven Roger *mathematician, computer scientist, educator*
Gomes, Wayne Reginald *academic administrator*
Gonzalez, Arthur Padilla *artist, educator*
Granoff, Dan Martin *research scientist*
Griffin, Betty Jo *elementary school educator*
Haiman, Franklyn Saul *author, communications educator*
†Halpern, Mark *writer*
Harper, Rob March *artist, educator*
Harpster, Robert Eugene *engineering geologist*
Haskell, Arthur Jacob *retired steamship company executive*
†Hawkins, Robert B. *think tank executive*
Hemmerich, Stefan *biomedical scientist, biotechnologist*
Heydman, Abby Maria *academic executive*
Hilsinger, Raymond L., Jr., *otolaryngologist*
†Holmgren, Janet L *college president*
†Horton, David Harrison *writer, educator*
Howatt, Sister Helen Clare *former human services director, former college library director*
†Hsu, John *physician scientist*
Hwang, Michael Tian-Chung *university president*
Isaac Nash, Eva Mae *educator*
Jackson, M. Leigh *analyst programmer, fine art photographer, graphic designer*
Jackson, Marjorie *musician*
Jakubowsky, Frank Raymond *religious writer*
Jedrzejas, Mark J. *microbiologist, researcher*
†Johnson, Kenneth F. *lawyer*
†Johnston, Gerald E. *manufacturing company executive*
Keeports, David Dale *physical science educator*
Kelso, David William *artist, fine arts publishing executive*
Killebrew, Ellen Jane (Mrs. Edward S. Graves) *cardiologist, educator*
†King, C. Judson *academic administrator*
King, Cary Judson, III, *chemical engineer, educator, university official*
King, Janet Carlson *nutrition educator, researcher*
†Knox, Helene Margrethe *writer*
Koplin, Donald Leroy *health products executive, consumer advocate*
Lake, Suzanne *singer, teacher*
Lazar, John Edward *administrator non-profit organization*
Lee, Jong Hyuk *accountant*
Lepowsky, William Leonard *mathematics and statistics educator*
Leslie, Robert Lorne *lawyer*
Levine, Marilyn Anne *artist*
Linford, Rulon Kesler *physicist, engineer*
Lomhoff, Peter George *lawyer*
Loving, Deborah June Pierre *lawyer, real estate broker*
Lowndes, David Alan *retired programmer analyst, application developer*
Lubliner, Irving *mathematics educator, consultant*
MacKay, Nancy *librarian, oral historian*
Macmeeken, John Peebles *foundation executive, educator*
†Massachi, Dalya Faith *writer, non-profit administrator*
Matsumoto, George *architect*
McCarthy, Steven Michael *lawyer*
McKeever, Michael Pierce, Sr., *economics and business educator*
McKinney, Judson Thad *broadcast executive*
Melchert, James Frederick *artist, educator*
Meyer, Carl Beat *chemical consultant, mediator, arbitrator, lawyer*
Michael, Gary G. *retired retail supermarket and drug chain executive, university administrator*
Miller, Barry *research administrator, psychologist*
Miller, Connie Joy *assistant real estate officer, broker*
†Miller, Kirk Edward *lawyer, health foundation executive*
†Miller, Steven Lamont *neuroscience company executive, researcher*
Miller, Thomas Robbins *lawyer, publisher*
Morris, Ronald Lew *oil and gas company executive*
Musihin, Konstantin K. *electrical engineer*
Musselman, Eric *professional basketball coach*
Narell, Irena *freelance writer, history educator*
Nebelkopf, Ethan *psychologist*
Neeley, Beverly Evon *sociologist, consultant*
†Nelson, Luella Eline *lawyer*
Newsome, Randall Jackson *judge*
Ng, Lawrence Ming-Loy *pediatrician*
O'Dwyer, Thomas Stephen *lawyer*
O'Hara, Delia Iglauer *family nurse practitioner*
Okazawa-Rey, Margo *social worker, educator*
†Osmond, Dennis Hubert *epidemiologist*
†Ostrander, Willis Frederick *real estate appraiser*
Patten, Bebe Harrison *minister, chancellor*
Perlmutter, Martin Lee *interactive media producer, consultant, writer, educator*
Potter, Beverly Ann *management psychologist, consultant, publisher*
Power, Dennis Michael *museum director*
Quinby, William Albert *lawyer, mediator, arbitrator*
Randisi, Elaine Marie *accountant, educator, writer*
Randle, Ellen Eugenia Foster *opera and classical singer, educator*
Rath, Alan T. *sculptor*
Raver, Miki (Mikala) *scriptwriter, film producer*
†Reese, Charles Woodrow, Jr., *lawyer*
Rice, Frances Mae *physician*
†Richmond, William O'Neal *retired music educator*
†Roesling, Marjorie Inez *interior designer*
Roster, Michael *lawyer*
†Rutherford, Constance Mary *lawyer*
Sample, Herbert Allan *reporter*
†Sandler, Herbert M. *savings and loan association executive*
†Sandler, Marion Osher
Saunders, Ward Bishop, Jr., *retired aluminum company executive*
Schacht, Henry Mevis *writer, consultant*
Schrag, Peter *editor, writer*
Sharpton, Thomas *physician*
Silverberg, Robert *author*
Skaff, Andrew Joseph *lawyer, public utilities, energy and transportation executive*
†Spencer, Carol Lynn *biologist, educator*
Steele, Richard Donald *researcher, linguist, physicist*
Stewart, John Lincoln *university administrator*
Stewart, Leslie Mueller *editor, writer*
Stromme, Gary L. *law librarian*
Sullivan, G. Craig *household products executive*
Sun, Peter P. *neurosurgeon*
Sutcliffe, Eric *lawyer*
Tennant, Roy *librarian*
Teufel, William Lockwood *emergency physician*
Tsztoo, David Fong *civil engineer*
†Turner, Tom *writer, editor*
Tyndall, David Gordon *business educator*
Vaux, Henry James, Jr., *economics educator*
†Victorino, Gregory Peter *trauma surgeon*
Warren, Fan Lee *artist, educator*
†Washington, Kaye *lawyer*
Webster, William Hodges *lawyer*
†Weinmann, Robert Lewis *neurologist*
†West, Natalie Elsa *lawyer*
Wiesenthal, Andrew Michael *physician*
Wilken, Claudia *judge*
Wills, John Arthur *computer programmer, analyst*
Willson, Clyde D. *biologist, educator*
Wong, Ivan Gynmun *seismologist*
Wood, James Michael *lawyer*
Wood, Larry (Mary Laird) *journalist, author, university educator, public relations executive, environmental consultant*
†Woodbury, Marda Liggett *librarian, writer*
Youngs, Robert Riggs *engineer*
Zelmanowitz, Julius Martin *mathematics educator, university administrator*

Oakley
Arai-Abramson, Lucy *artist, writer*

Occidental
Rumsey, Victor Henry *electrical engineering educator emeritus*

Oceano
Scott, Donald Michael *writer, educator*

Oceanside
Beck, Marilyn Mohr *columnist*
Bell, Sharon Kaye *small business owner*
Curtin, Thomas Lee *ophthalmologist*
†Doucette, Jodi Leazott *lawyer*
Downer, William John, Jr., *retired hospital administrator*
Eichman, Patricia *retired interior designer*
Garfin, Louis *retired actuary*
Haley, Thomas John *retired pharmacologist*
Hertweck, E. Romayne *psychology educator*
Humphrey, Phyllis A. *writer*
†LaRosa, John Paul *education educator*
Lyon, Richard *mayor emeritus, retired naval officer*
McLean, Arthur Frederick *mechanical engineer*
Munson, Lucille Marguerite (Mrs. Arthur E. Munson) *real estate broker*
†Ochoa Carlos, Sergio *language educator*
Peckham, Donald *computer company executive*
Pena, Maria Geges *academic services administrator*
Roberts, James McGregor *retired professional association executive*
Rosier, David Lewis *investment banker*
Sarkisian, Pamela Outlaw *artist*
Swoger, James Wesley *magician*
Taverna, Rodney Elward *financial services company executive*
Villasenor, Barbara *book publisher*
Yurist, Svetlan Joseph *mechanical engineer*

Ojai
Cusumano, James Anthony *filmmaker, retired pharmaceutical company executive, former recording artist*
Paxton, Glenn Gilbert *composer*
Shagam, Marvin Hückel-Berri *private school educator*

Ontario
Ariss, David William, Sr., *real estate developer, consultant*
Bernard, Alexander *protective services official*
Coney, Carole Anne *accountant*
Dunn, Donald Jack *law librarian, law educator, dean, lawyer*
Hull, Jane Laurel Leek *retired nurse, administrator*

Kennedy, Mark Alan *secondary school educator*
Ogbogu, Cecilia Ify *lawyer*
Ovitt, Gary C. *mayor*
Perri, Audrey Ann *lawyer*
Rappaport, Michael Paul *columnist*
Seagull, Helen Ann *paralegal, educator, writer, public relations consultant, medical assistant*
†Soto, Nell *state senator*

Orange

Avdeef, Thomas *lawyer*
Barr, Ronald Jeffrey *dermatologist, pathologist*
Batchelor, James Kent *lawyer*
Bennett, William Perry *lawyer*
Berman, Michael Leonard *gynecologic oncologist*
Blaser, Arthur Weston *political science educator, writer*
Booth, Donald Richard *economist, educator*
Brown, Tod David *bishop*
Calvert, Jay Wynn *plastic surgeon*
Chang, Jae Chan *hematologist, oncologist, educator*
†Cinat, Marianne Eva *surgeon*
†Cooper, Steven Harold *education educator*
Crumley, Roger Lee *surgeon, educator*
†Cumiford, William Lloyd *historian, educator, curator*
Demarchi, Ernest Nicholas *retired aerospace executive*
†Doti, Frank John *law educator, consultant*
Evans, Gregory Randolph Dean *plastic surgeon, educator*
Fischel, Richard Jeffrey *thoracic surgeon*
Fisher, Mark Jay *neurologist, neuroscientist, educator*
Fisk, Edward Ray *retired civil engineer, author, educator*
Godeke, Raymond Dwight Cook *insurance company executive, accountant*
Hamilton, Harry Lemuel, Jr., *educator*
†Harran, Marilyn Jean *historian, educator, consultant*
Hurley, Amy Elizabeth *human resources educator*
Jones, Cleon Boyd *research engineer*
Kaempen, Charles Edward *manufacturing company executive*
Kelley, Robert Paul, Jr., *management consultation executive*
Kim, Moon Hyun *endocrinologist, educator*
†Klassen, Henry John *ophthalmologist*
Korb, Lawrence John *metallurgist*
Lippa, Linda Susan Mottow *ophthalmologist*
Lott, Ira Totz *pediatric neurologist*
Martin, Mike W. *philosophy educator*
Mason, Naomi Ann *interior designer*
†Matthews, Joseph Virgil *pianist, music educator*
Mc Farland, Norman Francis *bishop*
Meshkinpour, Hooshang *gastroenterologist, educator*
Milliken, Jeffrey *cardiothoracic surgeon*
Monk, Bradley James *gynecologic oncologist, researcher, educator*
Morgan, Beverly Carver *pediatrician, educator*
Mosier, Harry David, Jr., *physician, educator*
Rowen, Marshall *radiologist*
Salenius, Sylvia Marja *environmental planner*
†Sanders, Gary Wayne *lawyer*
Schneider, Max Alexander *physician, educator*
Schoon, Doris Vivien *ophthalmologist*
Shirvani, Hamid *architect, educator, author, administrator, philosopher*
Simjee, Aisha *ophthalmologist, educator*
Smith, John LeRoy *mathematician, educator*
†Spitzer, Todd *state official*
Stamos, Michael Jerry *surgeon, educator*
†Stevens, Cherita Wyman *writer, educator*
†Stratton, Samuel Joe *emergency physician, researcher*
Sundine, Michael James *plastic surgeon*
Talbott, George Robert *physicist, mathematician, educator*
Todsen, Dana Rognar *health care executive*
Toeppe, William Joseph, Jr., *retired aerospace engineer*
Torres, Rudy Arnold *artist*
Tuggle, Francis Douglas *dean, consultant*
†Underwood, Vernon O., Jr., *grocery stores executive*
Vatcher, James Gordon *retired physician*
Vaziri, Nosratola Dabir *internist, nephrologist, educator*
Vice, Charles Loren *electromechanical engineer, consultant*
†Weissberg-Ortiz, Judith Lee *lawyer*
Wilson, Archie Fredric *medical educator*
Wilson, Samuel Eric *vascular and general surgeon*
Yeager, Myron Dean *English language educator, business writing consultant*
Yu, Jen *medical educator*

Orinda

Amoroso, Richard Louis *cosmologist, educator*
†Anderson, Barbara Jeanne *music educator*
Baker, Don Robert *chemist, inventor, writer*
†Casey, Kathleen Heirich *lawyer, educator*
Danvers, David Bell *equity broker*
Dorn, Virginia Alice *artist, art gallery director*
Epperson, Stella Marie *artist*
Fisher, Robert Morton *foundation administrator, university administrator*
Glasser, Charles Edward *university president*
Graber, William Raymond *pharmaceutical executive*
Heftmann, Erich *biochemist*
Hetland, John Robert *lawyer, educator*
Sohnen, Harvey *lawyer*
Somerset, Harold Richard *retail executive*
Strong, Susan Clancey *writer, communication consultant, editor*
Trowbridge, Thomas, Jr., *mortgage banking company executive*
Woolsey, David Arthur *leasing company executive*

Oroville

Chandy, Mammen G. *surgeon*
Curry, William Sims *county official*
Davis, Frederick Charles *county official*
Gordon, Daniel Seth *business executive, consultant*
Sincoff, Steven Lawrence *chemistry educator*

Oxnard

Auston, David Henry *former academic administrator, electrical engineer, educator*
Bacin, Mark Stephen *museum director, retired naval officer*
Gerber, David A. *lawyer*
Hayashi, Alan T. *mathematics educator*
Hill, Alice Lorraine *history, genealogy and social researcher, educator*
Kavli, Fred *retired manufacturing executive, retired engineering executive*
Kirschbaum, Alan Ira *air force officer, systems integration specialist*
Lopez, Manuel M. *mayor*
†Neilson, Jane Scott *mathematics educator*
O'Connell, Hugh Mellen, Jr., *retired architect*
Perrier, Barbara Sue *artist*
Poole, Henry Joe, Jr., *business executive*
Rosales, Sandra Johnson *school system administrator*
Sweet, Harvey *theatrical set designer, lighting designer*
Takasugi, Nao *state official, business developer*
Tolmach, Jane Louise *community activist, municipal official*
Young, Ronald Frederick *neurosurgeon*
Zhou, Sophia Huai *biomedical engineering scientist*

Pacific Grove

†Adamson, Kathleen Frances *not-for-profit developer, educator*
Bailey, Stephen Fairchild *museum director and curator, ornithologist*
Davis, Robert Edward *retired communication educator*
Elinson, Henry David *artist, language educator*
Flury, Jane Madawg *artist, educator*
Longman, Anne Strickland *special education educator, consultant*

Pacific Palisades

Anwyl-Davies, Marcus John *judge, arbitrator*
Beck, John Christian
Bilson, Wesley *healthcare company executive*
Cale, Charles Griffin *lawyer, private investor*
Casady, Dorothea Jane *artist, educator, sculptor*
Chesney, Lee Roy, Jr., *artist*
Claes, Daniel John *physician*
Dean, Ronald Glenn *lawyer*
Dickson, Robert Lee *lawyer*
Diehl, Richard Kurth *retail business consultant*
Flattery, Thomas Long *lawyer, legal administrator*
Garwood, Victor Paul *retired speech communication educator, audiology*
Georges, Robert Augustus *emeritus educator, researcher, writer*
Gregor, Eduard *laser physicist, consultant*
Hadges, Thomas Richard *media consultant, consultant*
Hagenbuch, Rodney Dale *consulting principal, financial consultant*
Herman, Elvin E. *retired consulting electronic engineer*
Hoffenberg, Marvin *retired political science educator, consultant*
Holberg, Eva Maria *volunteer*
Horowitz, Edward Jay *lawyer*
Jennings, Marcella Grady *rancher, investor*
†Jones, Edgar Allan, Jr., *law educator, arbitrator, lawyer*
Katz, George Gershon *psychologist*
Kaufer, Shirley Helen *artist, painter*
Kirkgaard, Valerie Anne *retired media group executive, syndicated talk radio host, writer, producer, consultant*
Klein, Joseph Mark *retired mining company executive*
Lagle, John Franklin *lawyer*
†Lebrecht, Henry Alexander *graphics designer*
Longaker, Richard Pancoast *political science educator emeritus*
McGinn, James Thomas *writer, producer*
†Mendel, Dennis D. *lawyer*
Middleton, James Arthur *oil and gas company executive*
Mulryan, Henry Trist *mineral company executive, consultant*
Newmark, Harris, III, *diagnostic radiologist*
Price, Frank *motion picture and television company executive*
Sevilla, Stanley *lawyer*
Share, Richard Hudson *lawyer*
Tourtellotte, Wallace William *neurologist, educator*
Verrone, Patric Miller *lawyer, writer*

Pacifica

Brooks-Korn, Lynne Vivian *artist*
Kelly, Kevin *editor*

Palm Desert

Ayling, Henry Faithful *writer, editor, consultant*
†Bass, Betty Zoe Passmore (Mrs. Eric Bass) *artist*
†Battin, James F., Jr., *state legislator, sales executive*
Baxter, Betty Carpenter *educational administrator*
Cedar, Paul Arnold *church executive, minister*
Copperman, William H. *value engineer, consultant*
Dugan, Robert Perry, Jr., *retired minister, religious organization administrator*
Epstein, Marvin Morris *retired construction company executive*
Friesz, Mary Lee *freelance/self-employed poet*
Godfrey, Alden Newell *communications educator*
Goldberg, Martin Stanford *retired lawyer*
Hixon, Donald L. *librarian, musician*
Hoffmann, Joan Carol *retired academic dean*
Joseph, Jerry
Krallinger, Joseph Charles *entrepreneur, business advisor, author*
†Kubiak, Andrea Celeste *language educator*
Miller, Donald Ross *management consultant*
Morrison, Robert Thomas *aerospace engineering and marketing consultant*
Olson, Phillip David LeRoy *agriculturist, chemist*
Osborne, Bartley Porter, Jr., *aeronautical engineer*
†Pierno, Anthony Robert *lawyer*
Ponder, Catherine *clergywoman, author*
Porter, Priscilla *elementary education educator*
†Reordan, Beverly Jean *artist*
Ryan, Allyn Cauagas *writer, educator*
Sausman, Karen *zoological park administrator*
Sexson, Stephen Bruce *education writer, educator*
Stenhouse, Everett Ray *clergy administrator*
Vander Naald Egenes, Joan Elizabeth *business owner, educator*
Warren, Joan Leigh *pediatrician*
†Wheeler, William Chamberlain, Jr., *association administrator, lawyer*

Palm Springs

Alameda, Russell Raymond, Jr., *radiologic technologist*
Arnold, Stanley Norman *manufacturing consultant*
Boyajian, Timothy Edward *public health officer, educator, consultant*
†Brain, Jesse *manufacturing executive*
Coffey, Nancy Ann *real estate broker*
Diodosio, Charles Joseph *lawyer*
Dupree, Stanley M. *lawyer*
†Fitzgerald, Jack Lyon *education educator, writer*
FitzGerald, John Edward, III, *lawyer*
Gaede, James Ernest *physician, medical educator*
Gerard, James Wilson *publishing consultant*
Gill, Jo Anne Martha *middle school educator*
Gordon, Stewart Lynell *musician, educator*
†Harris, Michael David *lawyer*
Hartman, Rosemary Jane *retired special education educator*
Holtz-Borders, Karen Lynn *police officer*
†Ingelson, Brian Charles *music educator, director*
Jones, Milton Wakefield *publisher*
Jumonville, Felix Joseph, Jr., *physical education educator, realtor*
Kern, Donald Michael *internist*
Mann, Zane Boyd *editor, publisher*
Motto, Geralyn *multi-media artist*
†Munyon, William Harry, Jr., *architect*
†Philip, Michel Henri *classicist, writer*
Racina, Thom (Thomas Frank Raucina) *television writer, editor*
Rupracht, William George *chaplain*
Salometo, Peter James Morgan *marketing professional, lawyer*
Scott, Walter, Jr., *business consultant*
Seale, Robert McMillan *office services company executive*
Sheffield, Simone *business executive*
Streeto, Joseph Michael *catering company official*
Underwood, Thomas Woodbrook *communications company executive*
Wilson, Myron Robert, Jr., *retired psychiatrist*

Palmdale

Anderson, R(obert) Gregg *real estate company executive*
†Farley, Margaret Wilhelmina *librarian*
Finch, Susan Chloë *mediator, educator*
Kilanowski, Dana Marcotte *historian, writer, filmmaker, archaeologist*
Kinzell, La Moyne B. *school health services administrator, educator*
Luther, Amanda Lisa *producer*
Smith, Maureen McBride *laboratory administrator*

Palo Alto

Adamson, Geoffrey David *reproductive endocrinologist, surgeon*
Alexander, Steven Roy *pediatric nephrology educator*
Allen, Louis Alexander *management consultant*
Andersen, Torben Brender *optical researcher, astronomer, software engineer*
Anderson, Charles Arthur *former research institute administrator*
Bagshaw, Malcolm A. *radiation oncologist, educator*
Balzhiser, Richard Earl *research and development company executive*
Barnholt, Edward W. *computer company executive*
†Baron, Frederick David *lawyer*
†Baum, Brandon *lawyer, law educator*
Bebb, Richard S. *lawyer*
Bensch, Klaus George *pathology educator*
†Benton, Lee F. *lawyer*
Beutler, Larry Edward *psychology educator*
†Bohrnstedt, George William *educational researcher*
Botstein, David *geneticist, educator*
Bradley, Donald Edward *lawyer*
Briggs, Winslow Russell *plant biologist, educator*
Bright, Peter Bowman *scientist, engineer, researcher*
Briskin, Mae *writer*
Britton, M(elvin) C(reed), Jr., *physician, rheumatologist*
†Brown, Charles Dickson *not-for-profit fundraiser, consultant*
Brown, David Randolph *electrical engineer*
Brown, H. William *urban economist, private banker*
Byrd, Thomas Russell *medical educator*
Calvin, Allen David *psychologist, educator*
†Casati, Fabio *engineer*
Casillas, Mark *lawyer*
†Castro, Cynthia M *clinical psychologist, researcher*
Chen, Stephen Shi-hua *pathologist, biochemist*
Climan, Richard Elliot *lawyer*
Cohen, Karl Paley *nuclear energy consultant*
Cohen, Nancy Mahoney *lawyer*
†Coughran, William M., Jr., *management consultant, researcher*
†Cunningham, Brian C. *lawyer, corporate executive*
Cutler, Leonard Samuel *physicist*
†Dabbagh, Karim *research scientist*
†Dement, William Charles *medical researcher, medical educator*
†Diamond, Diana Louise *editor, graphic artist*
Dong, Xuzhu *information technology manager*
†Druyan, Lara Catherine *financial consultant*
Dwyer, John Charles *lawyer*
Early, James Michael *electronics research consultant*
Efird, Jimmy Thomas *statistician*
Eggers, Alfred John, Jr., *research corporation executive*
Eng, Lawrence Fook *biochemistry educator, neurochemist*
Ernst, Wallace Gary *geology educator*
Farquhar, John William *physician, educator*
Fiorina, Carleton S. (Carly Fiorina) *computer company executive*
Flanagan, Robert Joseph *economics educator*
Flory, Curt Alan *research physicist*
Forbes, Alfred Dean *religious studies researcher*
†Forno, Lysia S. *neuropathologist*
Fortmann, Stephen Paul *medical educator, researcher, epidemiologist*
Fried, Louis Lester *information technology and management consultant*
Fries, James Franklin *internal medicine educator*
Gabashvili, Irene *biophysicist*
Gaither, James C. *lawyer*
Gerety, Robert John *microbiologist, pharmaceutical company executive, pediatrician, vaccinologist*
Glauthier, T. J. *non-profit executive*
Gliner, Erast Boris *theoretical physicist*
Goff, Harry Russell *retired manufacturing company executive*
Goldstein, Mary Kane *physician*
Gong, Mamie Poggio *elementary education educator*
Hahn, Gordon Martin *political scientist, writer*
Halamek, Louis Patrick *neonatologist*
Hamilton, David Mike *publishing company executive*
Hammett, Benjamin Cowles *psychologist*
Harris, Edward Day, Jr., *physician*
Hays, Marguerite Thompson *nuclear medicine physician, educator*
Herrick, Tracy Grant *fiduciary*
†Hinckley, Robert Craig *lawyer*
Hodge, Philip Gibson, Jr., *mechanical and aerospace engineering educator*
Holman, Halsted Reid *medical educator, physician*
Huberman, Bernardo A *physicist*
Hubert, Helen Betty *epidemiologist*
†Illes, Judy *medical researcher, radiologist*
Ivy, Benjamin Franklin, III, *financial and real estate investment advisor*
†Jackson, Cynthia L. *lawyer*
Johnson, Noble Marshall *research scientist*
†Johnston, Alan Cope *lawyer*
Jung, Henry Hung *mechanical engineer*
†Kapoor, Ashok Kumar *engineer*
Karlsson, Magnus *computer engineer/scientist, researcher*
Keller, Arthur Michael *computer science researcher*
Kim, Wan Hee *electrical engineering educator, business executive*
Kincaid, Judith Wells *electronics company executive*
Kirk, Carmen Zetler *data processing executive*
Kiser, Stephen *artist, educator*
Klay, Anna Nettie *lawyer*
Kott, Joseph *transportation executive, consultant, educator*
Kung, Frank F. *biotechnology and life sciences investor, venture capitalist*
†Lacovara, Michael *lawyer*
Lane, Alfred Thomas *medical educator*
Laurie, Ronald Sheldon *lawyer*
Lee, Virginia Fern *community volunteer*
Linna, Timo Juhani *immunologist, researcher, educator*
Loewenstein, Walter Bernard *nuclear power technologist*
Love, Brenda Zejdl *writer*
Loveless, Edward Eugene *education educator, musician*
Luh, Howard H. *aerospace engineer*
Maffly, Roy Herrick *medical educator, retired*
Mahmood, Aamer *computer system architect*
Massey, Henry P., Jr., *lawyer*
Mayo, Robert N. *computer science researcher*
McCluskey, Lois Thornhill *photographer*
McHugh, Stuart Lawrence *materials engineer*
Miller, Michael Patiky *lawyer*
†Moffitt, Donald Eugene *transportation company executive*
Mommsen, Katharina *retired German language and literature educator*
Moore, Cassandra Chrones *real estate broker and policy analyst*
Moos, Rudolf H. *psychologist, researcher*
†Moran, Amanda Marie *acquisitons editor*
†Mosher, Roger L. *lawyer*
Murovic, Judith Ann *neurosurgeon*
Murray, Dave *marketing professional, editor*
Mutch, James Donald *health therapist*
Neale-May, Donovan *marketing professional*
Nopar, Alan Scott *lawyer*
Nordlund, Donald Craig *lawyer*
Nycum, Susan Hubbell *lawyer*
†O'Brien, Bradford Carl *lawyer*

†O'Brien, Christina Maria *lawyer*
†Omana-Zapata, Imelda *research scientist*
O'Rourke, C. Larry *lawyer*
†Pake, George Edward *research executive, physicist*
Parker, James Wesley *former career naval officer, investment company executive*
Patterson, Robert Edward *lawyer*
Perl, Martin Lewis *physicist, educator, chemical engineer*
Phair, Joseph Baschon *lawyer*
Pizzo, Philip A. *pediatrics educator, university administrator*
Rehman, Saifur *business executive*
Renda, Patrick Blake *investment company executive*
Rich, Lesley Mosher *artist*
Richardson, Tom (Edward Thompson Richardson) *artist*
†Rinsky, Arthur C. *lawyer*
Robinson, Agnes Claflin *educational administrator*
Rosaldo, Renato Ignacio, Jr., *cultural anthropology educator*
Salvatierra, Oscar, Jr., *transplant surgeon, urologist, educator*
Sanders, William John *research scientist*
Saxena, Arjun Nath *physicist*
Schrier, Stanley Leonard *hematologist, educator*
Schulz, Michael *physicist*
†Schutt, Geoff *writer, performance artist*
Scitovsky, Anne Aickelin *economist, researcher*
†Seethaler, William Charles *international business executive, consultant*
Sharma, Bhavender Paul *biotechnologist*
Shuer, Lawrence Mendel *neurosurgery educator*
Silverman, Norman Henry *cardiologist, educator*
Simon, James Lowell *lawyer*
Skoog, Douglas Arvid *retired chemistry educator, writer*
Smith, Glenn A. *lawyer*
†Spanner, Robert Alan *lawyer*
Staprans, Armand *electronics executive*
†Steer, Reginald David *lawyer*
Strober, Samuel *immunologist, educator*
Sullivan, Patrick Henry *management consultant*
Survilo, Francine Marion *painter, sculptor*
Sweitzer, Michael Cook *healthcare product executive*
†Ta, Christopher Nguyen *performing arts educator*
Taimuty, Samuel Isaac *physicist*
Tanner, Douglas Alan *lawyer*
Tart, Charles Theodore *psychologist, educator*
Taylor, John Joseph *nuclear engineer, researcher*
Tiffany, Joseph Raymond, II, *lawyer*
Tirschwell-Newby, Kathy Ann *events production company executive*
†Trumbull, Terry ALan *energy and environmental consultant, lawyer*
†Tsien, Richard Winyu *biology educator*
†Tucker, Brian *seismologist*
†Tune, Bruce Malcolm *pediatrics educator, renal toxicologist*
Urquhart, John *medical researcher, educator*
Van Atta, David Murray *lawyer*
Varney, Robert Nathan *retired physicist, researcher*
†Vassar, Richard Holt *aerospace engineer*
Walker, Carolyn Peyton *English language educator*
Waller, Peter William *public relations executive*
Watson, David Colquitt *electrical engineer, educator*
Weng, Wen-Kai *physician, medical researcher*
Wheeler, Raymond Louis *lawyer*
Wong, Michael Anthony *financial analyst*
Wong, Nancy L. *dermatologist*
Wong, Y(ing) Wood *real estate investment company executive, real estate development company executive, venture capital investment company executive*
†Wren, Sherry M. *surgeon*
Wright, Kirby Michael *writer, editor*
Youngdahl, Paul Frederick *mechanical engineer*
Yu, Jiun-Der *mechanics researcher*
Zarins, Christopher Kristaps *surgery educator, vascular surgeon*
Zwicky, Arnold Melchior, Jr., *linguistics educator*

Palos Verdes Estates

Abbott, A. Dwight *retired astronautical engineer*
Blackman, Lee L. *lawyer*
Chary, Erika M. *music educator*
DeLuce, Richard David *lawyer*
Joshi, Satish Devdas *organic chemist*
Lazzaro, Anthony Derek *university administrator*
Loether, Herman John *sociologist, educator*
Mackenbach, Frederick W. *welding products manufacturing company executive*
Mennis, Edmund Addi *investment management consultant*
Paulikas, George Algis *retired physicist*
Perry, Robert Michael *engineering company executive*
Raue, Jorg Emil *electrical engineer*
Rubenstein, Leonard Samuel *communications executive, ceramist, painter, sculptor, photographer*
†Sharp, Jane Shriver *artist*
Toftness, Cecil Gillman *lawyer, consultant*
Yarbrough, Allyson Debra *electrical engineer*

Palos Verdes Peninsula

Barab, Marvin *financial consultant*
Berg, Kathy Rae *public relations consultant*
Christie, Hans Frederick *retired utility company subsidiaries executive, consultant*
Cubillos, Robert Hernan *church administrator, philosophy educator*
Denke, Paul Herman *retired aircraft engineer*
Grant, Robert Ulysses *retired manufacturing company executive*
Haynes, Moses Alfred *physician*
Leone, William Charles *retired manufacturing executive*
Manning, Christopher Ashley *finance educator, consultant*
Mirels, Harold *aerospace engineer*
Seide, Paul *civil engineering educator*
Slayden, James Bragdon *retired department store executive*
Slusser, Robert Wyman *aerospace company executive*
Thomas, Claudewell Sidney *psychiatry educator*
Thomas, Hayward *manufacturing company executive*
Unger, Ken R. *writer*
†Vanderlip, Elin Brekke *philanthropic executive*
Wilson, Theodore Henry *retired electronics company executive, aerospace engineer*

Panorama City

Jacob, Peter James *obstetrician-gynecologist*

Paradise

Barr, Donald Roy *statistics and operations research educator, statistician*
Bernstein, Elizabeth Ann *retired executive secretary*
Haws, Hale Louis *medical consultant*
Wilder, James D. *geology and mining administrator*

Paramount

Cohn, Lawrence Steven *physician, educator*
Hall, Howard Harry *lawyer*
Williams, Vivian Lewie *retired counseling administrator*

Pasadena

†Abelson, John Norman *biology educator*
Albee, Arden Leroy *geologist, educator*
Allen, Clarence Roderic *geologist, educator*
Almore-Randle, Allie Louise *special education educator*
Anderson, Don Lynn *geophysicist*
Arik, Baha Engin *engineering executive*
Armour, George Porter *lawyer*
Arnott, Robert Douglas *investment company executive*
Arrieta, Marcia *poet, editor, publishing executive, educator*
Ashley-Farrand, Margalo *lawyer, mediator, private judge*
Axelson, Charles Frederic *retired accounting educator*
†Azinfar, Fatemeh *financial analyst, writer, finance educator*
Baltimore, David *academic administrator, microbiologist, educator*
Barnes, Charles Andrew *physicist, educator*
Bean, Maurice Darrow *retired diplomat*
Beer, Reinhard *atmospheric scientist*
Bejczy, Antal Károly *research scientist, research facility administrator*
Bertani, Lillian Elizabeth Teegarden *biologist, researcher, educator*
†Bishop, Robert Calvin *pharmaceutical company executive*
Bjorck, Jeffrey Paul *psychology educator, clinical psychologist*
Blandford, Roger David *astronomy educator*
†Bobba, Kumar Manoj *engineer, researcher*
Boehm, Felix Hans *physicist, educator*
Bogaard, William Joseph *mayor, lawyer, educator*
Boochever, Robert *judge*
†Borodin, Alexei *mathematician*
Braverman, Amy Joan *statistician, researcher*
†Breen, David Edward *physicist, researcher*
Brenner, Anita Susan *lawyer*
Bridges, William Bruce *electrical engineer, researcher, engineering educator*
Brogden-Stirbl, Shona Marie *writer, researcher*
Brooks, Edward Howard *college administrator*
Brotman, Richard Dennis *counselor*
Buck, Francis Scott *pathologist, educator*
Bunting, Anne Evelyn (Eve Bunting) *author*
Bunt Smith, Helen Marguerite *lawyer*
Caine, Stephen Howard *data processing executive*
Call, Merlin Wendell *lawyer*
Calleton, Theodore Edward *lawyer, educator*
Carey, Keith Grant *editor, publishing executive*
Carregal, Enrique J. *anesthesiologist, educator*
Chahine, Moustafa Toufic *atmospheric scientist*
Chan, Sunney Ignatius *chemist, educator*
Chiang, Wen-Li *hydrodynamicist*
†Choi-Yim, Haein *research scientist*
†Cienfuegos, Mauricio *professional soccer player*
†Cooray, Asantha Roshan *astrophysicist, researcher*
Corby, John Meade *investment company executive*
Crowley, John Crane *real estate developer*
Culick, Fred Ellsworth Clow *physics and engineering educator*
Dallas, Saterios (Sam Dallas) *aerospace engineer, researcher, consultant*
D'Angelo, Robert William *lawyer*
Davidson, Eric Harris *molecular and developmental biologist, educator*
Davis, Edmond Ray *lawyer*
Davis, Lance Edwin *economics educator*
†Del Prado, Sergio *professional soccer team executive*
Dervan, Peter Brendan *chemistry educator*
Dressler, Alan Michael *astronomer*
Drutchas, Gerrick Gilbert (Baron Khabarovsky) *investigator*
Duxbury, Thomas Carl *planetary scientist*
†Eckford, Wendel *historian, educator*
†Elachi, Charles *aerospace engineer*
Elliot, David Clephan *historian, educator*
Ellis, Richard Salisbury *astronomer, educator*
Epstein, Bruce Howard *lawyer*
Everhart, Thomas Eugene *retired university president, engineering educator*
Farr, Donald Eugene *engineering scientist*
Ferber, Robert Rudolf *physics researcher, educator, science administrator*
Fernandez, Ferdinand Francis *federal judge*
Fisher, Raymond Corley *judge*
Franklin, Joel Nicholas *mathematician, educator*
Frautschi, Steven Clark *physicist, educator*
Fredericks, Ward Arthur *venture capitalist, food industry consultant*
Friedl, Randall Raymond *environmental scientist*
Fu, Lee-Lueng *oceanographer*
Fu, Li Min *biomedical and computer science educator*
Fultz, Brent Thomas *materials scientist, educator, researcher*
Gill, Gene *artist*
Gillis, Christine Diest-Lorgion *financial planner, stockbroker*
Gilman, Richard Carleton *retired college president*
Girod, Erwin Ernest *internist*
Goei, Bernard Thwan-Poo (Bert Goei) *architectural and engineering firm executive*
†Goldreich, Peter Martin *astrophysics and planetary physics educator*
Goodstein, David Louis *physics educator*
Goodwin, Alfred Theodore *federal judge*
Gray, Harry Barkus *chemistry educator*
Gref, Lynn G. *mathematician*
Grether, David Maclay *economics educator*
Grubbs, Robert Howard *chemistry educator*
Gurnis, Michael Christopher *geological sciences educator*
Haight, James Theron *lawyer, corporate executive*
Hall, Cynthia Holcomb *federal judge*
Harmsen, Tyrus George *librarian*
Harvey, Joseph Paul, Jr., *orthopedist, educator*
Hatheway, Alson Earle *mechanical engineer*
Heindl, Clifford Joseph *physicist, researcher*
Hemann, Raymond Glenn *research company executive*
Hicklin, Ronald Lee *music production company executive*
Hilbert, Robert S(aul) *optical engineer*
Hitlin, David George *physicist, educator*
Hoffman, Philip Thomas *university educator*
Holmes, Louis Ira *physician assistant, educator, photojournalist*
Horak, Jan-Christopher *film studies educator, curator*
Horner, Althea Jane *psychologist*
Hornung, Hans Georg *aeronautical engineering educator, science facility administrator*
†Housner, George William *retired civil engineering educator, consultant*
Hunt, Gordon *lawyer*
Hussein, Ziad A. *electromagnetics scientist, researcher*
Ingersoll, Andrew Perry *planetary science educator*
†Iturbide, Graciela *photographer*
Jacobs, Joseph John *engineering company executive*
†Jalbert, Janelle Jennifer *financial consultant, educator*
Janssen, Michael Allen *astronomer*
Jastrow, Robert *physicist, educator*
Jennings, Paul Christian *civil engineering educator, academic administrator*
Johnson, Barbara Jean *retired judge, lawyer*
Johnson, Kristen Marie *art director*
†Judd, Stephen Alan *biomedical researcher, educator, marketing professional*
†Jun, Insoo *nuclear scientist, researcher*
†Kahle, Anne B. *geophysicist*
Kaplan, Gary *executive recruiter*
Kathol, Anthony Louis *real estate executive*
Kimbrough, Lorelei *elementary education educator*
Knowles, James Kenyon *applied mechanics educator*
Koelzer, George Joseph *lawyer*
Koenig, Marie Harriet King *public relations director, fund raising executive*
†Koon, Wang-Sang *mathematician, researcher*
Koonin, Steven Elliot *physicist, educator, academic administrator*
Kousser, J(oseph) Morgan *history educator*
Kozinski, Alex *federal judge*
Kuppermann, Aron *physical chemist, educator*
Lake, Kevin Bruce *medical association administrator*
†Lamassoure, Elisabeth Sylvie *aerospace engineer*
Ledyard, John Odell *economics educator, consultant*
Lee, Fred Arthur *radiologist, educator*
Leonard, Nelson Jordan *chemistry educator*
Lewis, Edward B. *biology educator*
Lewis, Nathan Saul *chemistry educator*
Liebau, Frederic Jack, Jr., *investment manager*
†Liebe, Carl Christian *aerospace engineer, researcher*
Liepmann, Hans Wolfgang *physicist, educator*
Lingenfelter, Sherwood Galen *university provost, anthropology educator*
List, Ericson John *environmental engineering science educator, engineering consultant*
†Littke, Lael Jensen *author*
Logan, Francis Dummer *retired lawyer*
Losh, Samuel Johnston *engineering administrator*
Magnes, Harry Alan *physician*
Mandel, Oscar *literature educator, writer*
Marcus, Rudolph Arthur *chemist*
Marien, Robert *producer, director, naturalist, photographer, designer*
Marlen, James S. *chemical, plastics and building materials manufacturing company executive*
Mc Carthy, Frank Martin *oral surgeon, surgical sciences educator*
Mc Koy, Basil Vincent Charles *theoretical chemist, educator*
†McNulty, James F. *engineering, construction company executive*
Means, Tina *police officer, consultant*
Meye, Robert Paul *retired seminary educator, administrator, writer*
Meyerowitz, Elliot Martin *biologist, educator*
Miklusak, Thomas Alan *psychiatrist, psychoanalyst*
†Mosher, Sally Ekenberg *lawyer, musician*
Mueth, Joseph Edward *lawyer*
Myers, R(alph) Chandler *lawyer*
Nackel, John George *technology executive*
Neal, Philip Mark *diversified manufacturing executive*
Nelson, Dorothy Wright (Mrs. James F. Nelson) *federal judge*
Newell, Michael Alfred *electrical engineer*
†Newman, Marjorie Yospin *psychiatrist*
Njoku, Eni Gerald *research scientist*
Olson, Diana Craft *image and etiquette consultant*
Otoshi, Tom Yasuo *electrical engineer, consultant*
Owen, Ray David *biology educator*
Paez, Richard A. *federal judge*
†Parilis, Edward S. *physicist, researcher, consultant*
Parker, Robert Allan Ridley *federal agency administrator, astronaut*
†Parr, James Allan *literature professor*
Pashgian, Margaret Helen *artist*
Patton, Richard Weston *retired mortgage company executive*
Perez, Reinaldo Joseph *electrical engineer*
Pfeiffer, Edward J. *public and economic affairs specialist, presidential historian, research scientist*
Pings, Cornelius John *educational consultant, director*
†Pleasants, John *online services company executive*
Politzer, Hugh David *physicist, educator*
Poon, Peter Tin-Yau *engineer, physicist*
Reimer, Jennifer Ann *computer scientist*
Roberts, John D. *chemist, educator*
Rosenfeld, Harold Lee *plastic surgeon*
Roshko, Anatol *aeronautic engineer*
Rymer, Pamela Ann *federal judge*
Sabersky, Rolf Heinrich *mechanical engineer*
Sackmann, Inge-Juliana *astrophysicist*
Saffman, Philip G. *mathematician, educator*
Salandra, Helen E. *volunteer, retired nurse*
Sanders, Gary Hilton *physicist*
Sargent, Wallace Leslie William *astronomer, educator*
Schander, Mary Lea *retired protective services official*
Schlinger, Warren Gleason *retired chemical engineer*
†Schmid, Sigi *professional soccer coach*
Schmidt, Maarten *astronomy educator*
†Scoonover, Frank Miller, Jr., *retired secondary school educator*
Scott, David Clinton *research scientist*
†Scott, Jack Alan *state senator*
†Scott, Ronald Fraser *civil engineering educator, engineering consultant*
Scudder, Thayer *anthropologist, educator*
Seinfeld, John Hersh *chemical engineering educator*
Sekanina, Zdenek *astronomer*
Sharp, Robert Phillip *geology educator*
Shaw, Anthony *physician, pediatric surgeon*
Shimada, Katsunori *retired electrical engineer*
Short, Elizabeth M. *physician, educator, federal agency administrator*
Shuster, Marguerite *minister, educator*
Siemon-Burgeson, Marilyn M. (Marilyn Burgeson) *education administrator*
†Silver, Leon Theodore *geologist, educator*
Smith, Howard Russell *manufacturing company executive*
Smith, Michael Robert *electro-optical engineer, physicist*
Soleimani, Massoud *internist, rheumatologist*
Staehle, Robert L. *foundation executive*
Stelzried, Charles Thomas *engineer*
†Sterling, Thomas L. *research scientist, educator*
Stevens, Roy W. *sales and marketing executive*
Stolper, Edward Manin *secondary education educator*
†Stoltz, Brian Mark *chemist, educator*
†Stolzberg, Michael Meyer *lawyer*
Stone, Edward C. *physicist, educator*
Tanner, Dee Boshard *retired lawyer*
Tappan, Janice Ruth Vogel *animal behavior researcher*
Tashima, Atsushi Wallace *federal judge*
†Taylor, John David *lawyer*
Tekippe, Rudy Joseph *civil engineer*
Thomas, Joseph Fleshman *retired architect*
Thorne, Kip Stephen *physicist, educator*
Tollenaere, Lawrence Robert *retired industrial products company executive*
Tombrello, Thomas Anthony, Jr., *physics educator, consultant*
Ubovich, Ben A. *music educator*
Varshavsky, Alexander Jacob *molecular biologist*
Vogt, Rochus Eugen *physicist, educator*
Wang, Jin-Chen Camilla *physician, geneticist*
Wasserburg, Gerald Joseph *geology and geophysics educator*
Watkins, John Francis *management consultant*
†Watson, Noel G. *construction executive*
Webster, Christopher R. *chemist, physicist, research scientist*
Weisbin, Charles Richard *nuclear engineer*
Weiswasser, Stephen *electronics manufacturing executive*
†Wennberg, Paul *chemist*
White-Thomson, Ian leonard *retired mining executive*
Wilcox, Roberta Moat *music educator*
Wong, Raymond Shiu-Loong *radiologist*
Wood, Lincoln Jackson *aerospace engineer*
Worby, Rachael Beth *conductor*
Wyatt, Joseph Lucian, Jr., *lawyer, writer*
Wyllie, F(rances) Rosemary (Romy Wyllie) *interior designer, educator*
Yariv, Amnon *electrical engineering educator, scientist*
Yau, Kevin Kam-ching *astronomer*

Yazami, Rachid *research scientist, consultant, editor*
Yeh, Paul Pao *electrical and electronics engineer, educator*
Yeomans, Donald Keith *astronomer*
Yohalem, Harry Morton *lawyer*
Yorke, Harold W. *astrophysicist*
Zewail, Ahmed Hassan *chemistry and physics educator, editor, consultant*
Zuetel, Kenneth Roy, Jr., *lawyer*

Paso Robles
Allison, Ralph Brewster *psychiatrist*
Boxer, Jerome Harvey *computer and management consultant, vintner, accountant*
Brown, Benjamin Andrew *journalist*
Gruner, George Richard *retired secondary education educator*
Knecht, James Herbert *lawyer*
Rocha, Marilyn Eva *retired clinical psychologist*
Spencer, Editha Mary (Editha Hayes) *artist*
Spencer, Harold Edwin *retired art educator, art historian, painter*
Webster, David Arthur *retired life insurance company executive*

Pearblossom
Benedict, Lawrence Neal *foreign service officer*

Pebble Beach
†Dallmann, William Charles *speech educator, writer*
Ference, Helen Marie *nursing consultant, consultant*
Mauz, Henry Herrward, Jr., *retired naval officer*
Mortensen, Gordon Louis *artist, printmaker*
Robinson, William Adams *lawyer*
Sanford-Hugus, Barbara *geneticist, consultant*

Penn Valley
Hodgson, Peter John *author, composer, lecturer*
†Holmes, Genta Hawkins *diplomat*
†Longan, Suzanne M. *retired elementary school educator*
Morgenthaler, John Herbert *chemical engineer*
Nehls, Robert Louis, Jr., *school system financial consultant*
Nix, Barbara Lois *real estate broker*
Throner, Guy Charles, Jr., *engineering executive, scientist, engineer, inventor, consultant*

Penngrove
Chadwick, Cydney Marie *writer, art projects executive*
Elliott, Virgil Irl, Jr., *artist, writer*
Ellison, Robert W. *sculptor*

Penryn
Bryson, Vern Elrick *nuclear engineer*

Perris
Zimmer, Paul Gerald, II, *retired community care licensing professional*

Petaluma
Angress, Dina Dasberg *retired social worker*
Castagnola, George Joseph, Jr., *lawyer, mediator, secondary education educator*
Frederickson, Arman Frederick *minerals and petroleum company executive*
Fuller-McChesney, Mary Ellen *sculptor, writer, publisher*
†Hass, Robert L. *writer, educator*
†Immel, Barbara K. *management consultant*
McChesney, Robert Pearson *artist*
McKibben, James Denis *marketing and sales executive*
Pronzini, Bill John (William Pronzini) *writer*
Reichek, Jesse *artist*
Skalagard, Hans Martin *artist*
†Spiegelman, Art *author, cartoonist*
Stubblefield, Jerry Mason *religious educator, minister*

Phelan
Erwin, Joan Lenore *artist, educator*

Piedmont
Hughes, James Paul *physician*
Martin, Hosea L. *public relations and marketing professional*
Mayeri, Beverly *artist, ceramic sculptor, educator*
Putter, Irving *French language educator*
Reich, Stanley Benjamin *radiologist, medical educator*
Schell, Farrel Loy *transportation engineer*
†Weil, Arthur J. *real estate broker, poet*
Willrich, Mason *energy industry executive*

Pine Mountain
Edwards, Sarah Anne *radio, cable TV personality, clinical social worker*

Pinedale
Falcone, Patricia Jeanne Lalim *investor, foundation administrator*

Pinole
Grogan, Stanley Joseph *educational and security consultant*
Naughton, James Lee *internist*

Pismo Beach
Brisbin, Robert Edward *insurance agency executive*

Pittsburg
†Kaiper, Donald Dixon *historian, educator*
Schmalenberger, Jerry Lew *pastor, religious studies educator*
Williams, Elizabeth A. *financial planner, business consultant*
†Williscroft-Barcus, Beverly Ruth *lawyer*

Pixely
†Golden, Raymond Lee *retired theology studies educator, retired minister*

Placentia
†Ambrose, Henry Bartlett *real estate broker, writer*
Evans, Winthrop Shattuck *retired lawyer*
Gobar, Alfred Julian *retired economic consultant, educator*
Zweifel, Donald Edwin *newspaper editor, lobbyist, consultant*

Placerville
Bonser, Quentin *retired surgeon*
Fitzgerrell Smith, Lee *artist, illustrator*
Masson, Knute Andrew *artist*
†Miller, Edna Rae Atkins *educator*
Vandenberg, Byron F. *cardiologist*
Wall, Sonja Eloise *nurse administrator*
†Winkler, Jack Richmond *lawyer, writer*

Playa Del Rey
McNeill, Daniel Richard *writer*
Mishelevich, David Jacob *medical company executive, consultant*
Weir, Alexander, Jr., *utility consultant, inventor*

Playa Vista
Mikesell, Richard Hugh *writer*

Pleasant Hill
Gearheart, Mark Edwin *lawyer*
Hassid, Sami *architect, educator*
Hollister, Arthur Clair, Jr., *epidemiologist, public health officer*
Hopkins, Robert Arthur *retired industrial engineer*
Otis, Roy James *lawyer*
Richard, Robert Carter *psychologist*
Schrank, Shirley Ann *artist*

Pleasanton
†Auker, Todd Alan *ophthalmologist, surgeon*
Bjorkholm, John Ernst *retired physicist*
Burd, Steve *food service executive*
†Cheng, Shide *engineer, researcher*
Choy, Clement Kin-Man *research scientist*
Denavit, Jacques *retired physicist*
Edwards, Traci Van Arsdale *drug company official*
Erbskorn, Amy Gordon *healthcare executive*
Fehlberg, Robert Erick *architect*
Fine, Marjorie Lynn *lawyer*
†Goddard, John Wesley *cable television company executive*
Hearey, Elizabeth Berle *lawyer*
Jarnagan, Harry William, Jr., *project manager*
June, David Harold *information technology specialist*
Lawson, J(enice) Evelyn *quality assurance professional, pharmacist*
Lucas, Linda Lucille *dean*
MacDonald, Peter David *lawyer*
Novak, Randi Ruth *engineer, computer scientist*
Opperwall, Stephen Gabriel *lawyer*
†Payack, Paul JJ *marketing executive*
Scott, G. Judson, Jr., *lawyer*
Shen, Mason Ming-Sun *medical center administrator*
Staley, John Fredric *lawyer*
Stallings, Charles Henry *retired physicist*
†Sundgren, Donald E. *construction executive*
Van Dreser, Merton Lawrence *ceramic engineer*
Whisnand, Rex James *association housing executive*
†Wu, Jia Hao *transportation executive, researcher, consultant*

Plymouth
Andreason, John Christian *lawyer*

Point Mugu
Fisk, Charles John *meteorologist, researcher, consultant*

Point Reyes Station
Temple, Lee Brett *architect, songwriter*

Point Richmond
Edginton, John Arthur *lawyer*

Pollock Pines
Johnson, Stanford Leland *marketing, international business educator*
Rickard, Margaret Lynn *library and grants consultant, former library director*

Pomona
†Agvanian, Youri *mathematician, educator, physicist*
Ambrose, William Wright, Jr., *dean, academic administrator*
Aurilia, Antonio *physicist, educator*
Bernau, Simon John *mathematics educator*
Bidlack, Wayne Ross *nutritional biochemist, toxicologist, food scientist*
†Callaway, Linda Marie *special education educator*
Cortez, Edward S. *mayor*
Cosgrove, William James *business educator, researcher*
Cranston, John Welch *historian, educator*
Demery, Dorothy Jean *secondary school educator*
†Evans, William McKee *historian, educator*
†Fremont, Ronald H., II, *academic administrator, consultant*
Garrity, Rodman Fox *psychologist, educator*
Keating, Eugene Kneeland *animal scientist, educator*
†Kim, Hoon *statistician, educator*
†Kinsey, Gary W. *education educator*
†Kopplin, David F. *music educator, composer*
Lenz, Craig *academic administrator*
Lin, Lianlian *management educator, researcher*
McClelland, Harold Franklin *economics educator*
Palmer, Robert Alan *lawyer, educator*
†Partritz, Joan Elizabeth *lawyer, educator*
Patten, Thomas Henry, Jr., *management, human resources educator*

Rhodes, Rhonda Lynn *business educator*
Singer-Chang, Gail Leslie *social sciences educator, dean*
Teague, Lavette Cox, Jr., *systems educator, consultant*
Tunison, Elizabeth Lamb *education educator*
Wirsig, Woodrow *magazine editor, trade organization executive, business executive*
Young, Norman Gregory *law educator, lawyer*

Port Hueneme
Schneider, Arthur Paul *retired videotape and film editor, author*

Porterville
Golightly, Douglas Raymond *artist*
Hayes, Shirley Ann *special education educator*
Mullen, Rod *nonprofit organization executive*

Portola Valley
Arnold, Maxwell *adveristing executive, writer*
Carnochan, Walter Bliss *retired humanities educator*
Cooper, John Joseph *lawyer*
Garsh, Thomas Burton *publisher*
Harper, Elizabeth A. *retired occupational therapist*
Kuo, Franklin F. *computer scientist, electrical engineer*
Purl, O. Thomas *retired electronics company executive*
Ward, Robert Edward *retired political science educator and university administrator*

Poway
Conrad, Alan John *internist*
Mueller, Gerhard G(ottlob) *retired financial accounting standard setter, retired educator*
Pugay, Jeffrey Ibanez *mechanical engineer*
Turner, David G. *information technology executive*
Uke, Alan Kurt *company executive*
Waitt, Theodore W. *computer company executive*

Prather
Coren, Lance Scott *consulting firm executive*

Quartz Hill
Nettelhorst, Robin Paul *academic administrator, writer*

Ramona
Cooper, James Melvin *healthcare executive, consultant*
Hoffman, Wayne Melvin *retired airline official*

Rancho Cordova
Alenius, John Todd *retired insurance executive*
Carleone, Joseph *business executive*
Hendrickson, Elizabeth Ann *retired secondary education educator*
Ling, Robert Malcolm *banker, publishing executive*

Rancho Cucamonga
Alvarez, Tirso Reyes, Jr., *engineer*
Deppisch, Paul Vincent *data communications executive*
†Dutton, Robert D. *state official*
†Rodriguez, Juan Antonio *literature educator*

Rancho Dominguez
Collopy, Christopher Stephen *clothing company executive*
Janura, Jan Arol *apparel manufacturing executive*

Rancho Mirage
Abel, Michael L. *marketing executive*
†Ausman, James I. *neurosurgeon, educator*
Ford, Betty Bloomer (Elizabeth Ford) *former First Lady of United States, health facility executive*
†Ford, Gerald Rudolph, Jr., *38th President of the United States*
Foster, David Ramsey *soap company executive*
Fromm, Erwin Frederick *retired insurance company executive*
Greenbaum, James Richard *liquor distributing company executive, real estate developer*
Kiser, Roberta Katherine *medical records administrator, education educator*
Kramer, Gordon *mechanical engineer*
Lacey, John Irving *psychologist, physiologist, educator*
Leydorf, Frederick Leroy *lawyer*
Masotti, Louis Henry *real estate educator, consultant*
Olderman, Murray *columnist, cartoonist*
Reuben, Don Harold *lawyer*
Shaeffer, Charlie Willard, Jr., *cardiologist*
Sheldon, Deena Lynn *television camera operator*
Steele, Charles Glen *retired accountant*
Wyatt, Lenore *civic worker*

Rancho Murieta
Irelan, Robert Withers *retired metal products executive*

Rancho Palos Verdes
Frassinelli, Guido Joseph *retired aerospace engineer*
Hillinger, Charles *journalist, writer*
Hughs, Mary Geraldine *accountant, social service specialist*
Savage, Terry Richard *information systems executive*
Smirnov, Alexei Vladimirovich *research scientist, consultant*
Swank, Damon Raynard *lawyer*
Yassin, Robert Alan *museum administrator, curator*
†Zar, Judith L. (Mickey McBride) *writer*

Rancho Santa Fe
Affeldt, John Ellsworth *retired physician*
Baker, Charles Lynn *management consultant*
Best, Jacob Hilmer, Jr., (Jerry Best Jr.) *retired hotel chain executive*
Bestwick, Warren William *retired construction company executive*
Byrd, Betty Rantze *writer*
Carr, David Turner *physician*
Creutz, Edward Chester *physicist, museum consultant*
Dieffenbach, Otto Weaver, III, *real estate company executive*
Gruenwald, George Henry Henry *new products development management consultant, writer*
Jordan, Charles Morrell *retired automotive designer*
Kessler, A. D. *business, financial, investment and real estate advisor, consultant, lecturer, author, broadcaster, producer*
LaBonté, C(larence) Joseph *financial and marketing executive*
Matthews, Leonard Sarver *advertising and marketing executive*
McNally, Connie Benson *magazine editor, publisher, antiques dealer*
Peterson, Nad A. *retired lawyer*
Polster, Leonard H. *investment company executive*
Robinson, Lawrence Brandon *investment company executive*
Rockoff, S. David *radiologist, physician, educator*
Ruiz, Ramon Eduardo *history educator*
Simon, William Leonard *film and television writer and producer, writer*
Step, Eugene Lee *retired pharmaceutical company executive*

Rancho Santa Margarita
Aguilera, Donna Conant *psychologist, researcher*
Curtis, John Joseph *lawyer*
Parth, Frank R. *consulting company executive, educator*

Red Bluff
†Felthouse, Patricia Mae Avrit *librarian*
Hoofard, Jane Mahan Decker *retired elementary school educator*
Kennedy, James William, Jr., (Sarge Kennedy) *special education administrator, consultant*
†Peters, Michael Morgan *playwright, consultant, theater director, theater critic, educator*
Purdy, Carol Ann *psychotherapist*

Redding
Drake, Patricia Evelyn *psychologist*
†Emmerson, Archie Aldis (Red Emmerson) *sawmill owner*
†La Malfa, Doug *state representative*
Nicholas, David Robert *minister, college president*
Peterson, Robyn Gayle *museum curator*
Potter, James Vincent *association executive*
Shadish, William Raymond *retired plastic surgeon*
Stone, William Kenneth *surgeon*

Redlands
Adey, William Ross *physician*
†Auerbacher, Mary Jane *church organist*
Bangasser, Ronald Paul *physician*
Burgess, Charlotte Gaylord *academic administrator*
Burgess, Larry Eugene *library director, history educator*
Chandler, David Leslie *engineer*
Coleman, Arlene Florence *retired nurse practitioner*
Gogolin, Marilyn Tompkins *language pathologist, retired educational administrator*
Griesemer, Allan David *retired museum director*
Hanson, Gerald Warner *retired county official*
Healy, Daniel Thomas *secondary education educator*
Heiss, David James *editor*
Huntley, William Barney *educator*
Niks, Inessa *piano teacher*
Pick, James Block *finance educator*
Sagmeister, Edward Frank *retired military officer, business owner*
Skomal, Edward Nelson *aerospace company executive, electromagnetic environments consultant*
Skoog, William Arthur *former oncologist, educator*
Spee, James Curtis *management consultant, educator*

Redondo Beach
Abernethy, Robert John *real estate developer*
Barter, James Duncan *physicist*
Battles, Roxy Edith *novelist, consultant, educator*
Brodsky, Robert Fox *aerospace engineer, educator, author*
Cardin, Suzette *nursing educator*
Contescu, Cristian Ion *chemist, researcher*
Dennis, Helen Marion *gerontologist, educator*
Dockstader, Jack Lee *retired electronics executive*
Engstrom, Stephanie Cloes *wildlife artist, small business owner*
Foster, John Stuart, Jr., *physicist, former defense industry executive*
†Grzesik, Jan Alexander *electronics engineer, mathematician*
Harman, Jane *congresswoman*
Hollander, Michael Frederic *communications executive*
†Johnson, Dan R. *engineering executive*
Kagiwada, Reynold Shigeru *electronics executive*
†Kich, Rolf *communications scientist, consultant*
Mercant, Jon Jeffry *lawyer, educator, musician*
Mulvey, Gerald John *meteorologist*
Naples, Caesar Joseph *law and public policy educator, lawyer, consultant*
Ramstein, William Louis *manufacturing company executive*
Reed, John E. *producer, consultant*

Shellhorn, Ruth Patricia *landscape architect*
Sillman, George Douglas *computer programmer analyst*
Woike, Lynne Ann *computer scientist*

Redwood City

Bell, Frank Ouray, Jr., *lawyer*
Bertram, Jack Renard *information systems company executive*
Coddington, Clinton Hays *lawyer*
Cook, Paul Maxwell *technology company executive*
Ellis, Eldon Eugene *surgeon*
Ellison, Lawrence J. *computer company executive*
†Hagart-Alexander, Claud *software engineer*
†Hearst, William Randolph, III, *newspaper publisher*
Johnson, James Harding *advertising executive*
Jones, Brenda Gail *school district administrator*
Mandel, Martin Louis *lawyer*
Martone, Massimiliano Max *telecommunications consultant*
McFarland, Kevin John *foundation administrator*
Millard, Richard Steven *lawyer*
Miller, Anne Kathleen *training company executive, technical marketing consultant*
†Moore, Nicholas G. *finance company executive*
Nacht, Sergio *biochemist*
Neville, Roy Gerald *scientist, chemical management and environmental consultant*
†Nosler, Peter Cole *construction company executive*
Rohde, James Vincent *software systems company executive*
Shmagranoff, George L. *physician*
Spangler, Nita Reifschneider *volunteer*
Stone, Herbert Allen *management consultant*
Tight, Dexter Corwin *lawyer*
Wang, Chen Chi *electronics company, real estate, finance company, investment services, and international trade executive*
Wilhelm, Robert Oscar *lawyer, civil engineer, developer*

Redwood Shores

Chaudhry, Nauman Ahmed *computer scientist*

Reedley

Carey, Ernestine Gilbreth (Mrs. Charles E. Carey) *writer, lecturer*
Dick, Henry Henry *minister*
†Heise, Clarence Buddy *secondary school educator, real estate developer*
Walter Jr., Burl Leroy *retired music educator*

Rescue

Ackerly, Wendy Saunders *construction company executive*

Reseda

Chavez, Albert Blas *financial executive*
†Hoover, Pearl Rollings *nurse*
Turner, Lloyd Daniel *musician*

Rialto

Bauza, Christine Diane *special education educator*
Davis, David Earl *lawyer*
Jackson, Betty Eileen *music and elementary school educator*

Richmond

Anderson, Vera Strong *retired dentist*
†Arnon, Stephen Soulé *epidemiologist, research scientist*
Beall, Frank Carroll *science director and educator*
Birman, Alexander *physicist, researcher*
†Cohen, Abraham Ezekiel *retired health care company executive*
Dixon, Thelma Dunnebacke *research scientist*
Dolberg, David Spencer *business executive, marketing professional, lawyer, scientist, molecular biologist*
Forghani-Abkenari, Bagher *virologist, researcher*
Jenkins, Everett Wilbur, Jr., *lawyer, author, historian*
Kirk-Duggan, Cheryl Ann *religious studies educator*
Kirk-Duggan, Michael Allan *retired law, economics and computer sciences educator*
Lasseter, John P. *film director, computer animator*
†Mulder, Armand E.R. *protective services official, educator*
Robles, Eliodoro Gonzales *consulting company executive, educator*
†Shenoy, Surendra *internist*
Shladover, Steven Elliot *transportation research professional*
Svoboda, George Jiri *historian, librarian*
Terrill, Karen Stapleton *retired medical planning consultant*
Ward, Carl Edward *research chemist*
Wessel, Henry *photographer*

Ridgecrest

Bennett, Harold Earl *physicist, optics researcher*
Long, Andre Edwin *law educator, lawyer*
†Paik, Sun Hye *cell biologist, research scientist*

Riverside

†Aaron, Kathleen F. *librarian*
Adrian, Charles Raymond *political science educator*
Anderson, Jolene Slover *small business owner, publishing executive, consultant*
Balandin, Alexander A. *electrical engineer, educator*
†Bargmeyer, Brad D. *communications exectuve, advocate*
Bartnicki-Garcia, Salomon *microbiologist, educator*
Beni, Gerardo *electrical and computer engineering educator, robotics scientist*
†Benoit, John *state official*
†Bergman, Daniel Charles *county official, lawyer, environmental manager*
†Bielucke, Edward Anthony, III, *transportation executive, writer*
Bricker, Neal S. *physician, educator*
Bulloch, Kathleen Louise *educational professional*
Carpenter, Mark Warren *social sciences educator*
Chamberlain, Willard Thomas *retired metals company executive*
Chang, Janice May *lawyer, naturopathic doctor, psychologist*
Chang, Sylvia Tan *health facility administrator, educator*
Chen, Adam I. *physician*
Czekanski, James P. *military officer*
Darling, Scott Edward *lawyer*
†Deal, Kevin Paul *furniture designer*
†Deese, E(thel) Helen *English educator*
†d'Encarnacao-Bradley, Aja A. *supervisor*
Elliott, Emory Bernard *English language educator, educational administrator*
Embleton, Tom William *horticultural science educator*
Erwin, Donald Carroll *plant pathology educator*
†Farabelli, Stephen J. *accountant, finance educator*
Finan, Ellen Cranston *secondary education educator, consultant*
†Fischer, John Martin *education educator, researcher*
†Fontana, Sandra Ellen Frankel *special education educator*
Froehly, Bertram Martin, Jr., *neurologist*
Giroir, Leo Jean Jr. *accountant*
Goldberg, Sabine Ruth *soil scientist*
Green, Harry Western, II, *geology-geophysics educator*
Griffin, Keith Broadwell *economics educator*
Grimm, Reinhold *humanities educator*
Hackwood, Susan *electrical and computer engineering educator*
Hall, Anthony Elmitt *crop ecologist*
Hendrick, Irving Guilford *education educator*
†Holmes, Dallas Scott *judge, educator*
Jung, Timothy Tae Kun *otolaryngologist*
Korotkov, Alexander N. *physicist, educator, researcher*
Kronenfeld, Judy Zahler *humanities educator, writer*
Kummer, Glenn F. *retired manufacturing executive*
Lacy, Carolyn Jean *elementary education educator, secondary education educator*
†Lear, William H. *lawyer*
†Leifer, Gloria *pediatrics nurse, writer, educator*
Linaweaver, Walter Ellsworth, Jr., *physician*
Marlatt, Michael James *lawyer*
Martins-Green, Manuela *cell biologist*
Mc Cormac, Weston Arthur *retired educator, retired career officer*
McLaughlin, Leighton Bates, II, *journalism educator, former newspaperman*
McQuern, Marcia Alice *newspaper publishing executive*
Mulchandani, Ashok Kimatrai *chemical engineer, educator*
Oakes, Judy Dianne *real estate broker*
O'Reilly, Patrick James *public relations executive*
†Ozkan, Mihri *engineering educator*
Page, Albert Lee *soil science educator, researcher*
Petrinovich, Lewis Franklin *psychology educator*
Pratt, John Jackson *property manager, retired telephone installer*
Prosser, Michael Joseph *college librarian*
Rabenstein, Dallas Leroy *chemistry educator*
Ratliff, Louis Jackson, Jr., *mathematics educator*
Robbins, Karen Diane *editor*
Rosenthal, Robert *psychology educator*
Ross, Delmer Gerrard *historian, educator*
†Schaible, Siegfried *mathematician, educator*
Sheppard, Howard Reece *accountant*
Sherman, Irwin William *biological sciences educator*
Shoji, Hiromu *orthopedic surgeon, educator*
Sklar, Wilford Nathaniel *retired lawyer, real estate broker*
Smith, Dorothy Ottinger *jewelry designer, civic worker*
Smith, Richard Charles *not-for-profit administrator, educator*
Sokolsky, Robert Lawrence *journalist, entertainment writer*
Spencer, William Franklin, Sr., *soil scientist, researcher*
Stewart, Richard A. *former mayor*
Stone, Herman Hull *internist*
Taylor, R. Ervin, Jr., *archaeologist*
Timlin, Robert J. *judge*
Turk, Austin Theodore *sociology educator*
Van Gundy, Seymour Dean *nematologist, plant pathologist, educator*
Wild, Robert Lee *physics educator*
†Wilson, Jason *mathematician, educator*
Yacoub, Ignatius I. *university dean*
†Yount, Gwendolyn Audrey *humanities educator*
Zaera, Francisco *chemistry educator, consultant*
Zank, Gary Paul *phyicist*
Zentmyer, George Aubrey *plant pathology educator*

Rocklin

Dwyer, Darrell James *finance company executive*
Hyde, Geraldine Veola *retired secondary school educator*
Reilly, Christopher Patrick *artist*
Tal, Jacob *electronics executive*

Rodeo

Emmanuel, Jorge Agustin *chemical engineer, environmental consultant*

Rohnert Park

Arminana, Ruben *academic administrator, educator*
Babula, William *university dean*
†Brassington, Glenn Sidney *psychologist, educator*
Byrne, Noel Thomas *sociologist, educator*
Criswell, Eleanor Camp *psychologist*
Haslam, Gerald William *writer, educator*
Johnson, Herman Leonall *research nutritionist, retired*
Lord, Harold Wilbur *electrical engineer, electronics consultant*
Ochoa, Eduardo Martin *economics educator*
Phillips, Peter Martin *sociologist, educator, media researcher*
†Rosin, R. Thomas *anthropologist, educator*
Shinagawa, Larry Hatime *American studies educator*
Tenn, Joseph Simon *physics and astronomy educator*
Trowbridge, Dale Brian *educator*
Wautischer, Helmut *philosophy educator*

Rolling Hills

Rumbaugh, Charles Earl *arbitrator, mediator, educator, lawyer, speaker, judge*

Rolling Hills Estates

Allbee, Sandra Moll *real estate broker*
Bellis, Carroll Joseph *surgeon, educator*
Castor, Wilbur Wright *futurist, writer, consultant, playwright, actor*
Diaz-Zubieta, Agustin *nuclear engineer, engineering executive*
Ingerson, Nancy Nina Moore *special education educator*
Page, Phyllis Eleanor *physician*
Price, Lia Scott *writer*
Rechtin, Eberhardt *retired aerospace executive, retired educator*
Wong, Sun Yet *engineering consultant*

Rosemead

Bryson, John E. *utilities company executive*
†Danner, Bryant Craig *lawyer*
Rosenblum, Richard Mark *utility executive*

Roseville

French, Leura Parker *secondary educator*
Haugen, David Lee *surgeon*
Jacks, Bruce William *civil engineer*
Jammal, Joseph Jamil *cardiologist*
Nordman, Oether *security firm executive*
†Oller, Thomas R. *state senator*
Reichmann, Péter Iván *mathematician*
Wright, Carole Yvonne *chiropractor*

Ross

Godwin, Sara *writer*
Matan, Lillian Kathleen *educator, designer*
Nicholson, William Joseph *forest products consultant*
Rosenbaum, Michael Francis *securities dealer*

Rowland Heights

Hsu, John *anesthesiologist*

Running Springs

Fangerow, Kay Elizabeth *nurse*
Liddle, Sidney George *retired mechanical engineer, researcher*

Rutherford

Staglin, Garen Kent *computer service company executive, venture capitalist*

Sacramento

†Adelman, Rick *professional basketball coach*
†Aghazarian, Greg G. *state representative*
Alberson, Barbara *health services professional*
Aldrich, Thomas Albert *former brewing executive, consultant*
†Allen, Sonny *professional basketball coach*
Alpert, Deirdre Whittleton (Dede Alpert) *state legislator*
Arkin, Michael Barry *lawyer, arbitrator, writer*
†Avendaño, Fausto *language educator, writer*
Baccigaluppi, Roger John *agricultural company executive*
Baltake, Joe *film critic*
†Barilla, Frank (Rocky Barilla) *lawyer, consultant, educator*
†Battistella, Felix D. *physician, educator*
†Behrman, Bruce Ward *social sciences educator*
Bell, Wayne S. *lawyer, state agency official*
Belyn, David Neves *journalist, editor*
Bennett, Lawrence Allen *psychologist, criminal justice researcher*
Betts, Bert A. *former state treasurer, accountant*
Birney, Philip Ripley *lawyer*
†Blake, D. Steven *lawyer*
Block, Alvin Gilbert *publishing executive*
Bobrow, Susan Lukin *lawyer*
Boekhoudt-Cannon, Gloria Lydia *business education educator*
Bogren, Hugo Gunnar *radiology educator*
Bolton-Holifield, Alice Ruth *basketball player*
Booze, Thomas Franklin *toxicologist*
†Bowen, Debra Lynn *lawyer, state legislator*
Boylan, Richard John *psychologist, psychotherapist, researcher, anthropologist, educator*
Brazier, John Richard *lawyer, physician*
Brewer, Roy Edward *lawyer*
Briscoe, Agatha Donatto *data processing executive, instructor*
†Brittan, Martin R. *biologist, educator*
Brookman, Anthony Raymond *lawyer*
Bruce, Thomas Edward *psychology educator, thanatologist*
†Brulte, James L. *state legislator*
Burns, John Francis *state official, educator*
†Burton, John *state official*
Burton, Randall James *lawyer*
Bustamante, Cruz M. *lieutenant governor*
†Byears, Latasha *professional basketball player*
Cahill, Virginia Arnoldy *lawyer*
Carr, Gerald Francis *German educator*
Carrel, Marc Louis *lawyer, public affairs consultant*
Cavigli, Henry James *petroleum engineer*
Chandramouli, Srinivasan (Chandra Chandramouli) *management and systems consultant*
Chapman, Michael William *orthopedist, educator*
Childress, Dori Elizabeth *nursing consultant*
†Cogdill, David *state representative*
†Cohn, Rebecca *state representative*
Cole, Glen David *minister*
†Cox, Dave *state legislator*
Crimmins, Philip Patrick *metallurgical engineer, lawyer*
Cunningham, Mary Elizabeth (Mary Cunningham-Lusby) *physician*
†Dager, William Erling *pharmacist specialist, educator*
Dahlin, Dennis John *landscape architect, environmental consultant*
Davis, Brian Adam *physician*
Davis, Gray (Joseph Graham Davis) *governor*
Day, James McAdam, Jr., *lawyer*
Dedrick, Kent Gentry *retired physicist, researcher*
Detwiler, Peter Murray *legislative staff member, educator*
DeYoung, David Jeffrey *state official*
†Diaz, Manny *state representative*
Dobie, Robert Alan *otologist*
Doyel, Cindy Marie *information systems specialist*
Drachnik, Catherine Meldyn *recreational therapist, artist, counselor*
†Dunn, Joseph *state legislator*
Dunnett, Dennis George *retired state official*
Edwards, Michael Steven Brent
†Ellis, William Gene *neuropathologist*
Enomoto, Jerry Jiro *protective services official*
†Escutia, Martha *state senator*
Evans, David Alun *otolaryngologist*
Evrigenis, John Basil *obstetrician/gynecologist*
Fargo, Heather *mayor*
Farrell, Francine Annette *psychotherapist, educator, author*
†Figueroa, Liz *state senator*
Forsyth, Raymond Arthur *civil engineer, consultant*
Foster, Douglas Taylor *lawyer, investor*
Franz, Jennifer Danton *public opinion and marketing researcher*
Friedman, Morton Lee *lawyer*
†Frommer, Dario F. *state representative*
Gardner, Jerry Lee *financial consultant*
Garth-Lewis, Kimberley *state official, political scientist*
Geiken, Alan Richard *contractor*
Gerringer, Elizabeth (The Marchioness de Roe Devon) *writer, lawyer*
Gerth, Donald Rogers *university president*
Gibson, Patrice Vandegrift *anthropologist, educator*
Giguiere, Michele Louise *lawyer*
Glackin, William Charles *arts critic, editor*
†Goode, Barry Paul *lawyer*
Gray, Walter P., III, *archivist, consultant*
Grimes, Pamela Rae *retired elementary school educator*
Hackney, Robert Ward *plant pathologist, nematologist, parasitologist, molecular geneticist, commercial arbitrator*
†Hall, Terry L. *aerospace executive*
Harris, Wilson *psychiatrist, research scientist*
Hayward, Fredric Mark *social reformer*
Heaphy, Janis Besler *newspaper executive*
†Hilty, Donald M *psychiatrist, educator*
Hodgkins, Francis Irving (Butch Hodgkins) *county official*
Holmes, Robert Eugene *legislative staff member, journalist*
Horton, Shirley A. *state legislator, former mayor*
Houpt, James Edward *lawyer*
Hull, Frederick Albert *artist*
Hunter, Patricia Rae (Tricia Hunter) *state official*
Janigian, Bruce Jasper *lawyer, educator*
†Jasperson, John Arthur *public health service educator, consultant*
†Johnson, Ross *state legislator*
Johnson, Van R. *health facility administrator*
Jones, Mark Alan *broadcast technician*
†Kawamoto, Walter *family life educator, consultant*
Keiner, Christian Mark *lawyer*
Kerri, Kenneth Donald *civil engineering educator*
Kho, James Wang *computer scientist*
Knight, William J. (Pete Knight) *state legislator, retired air force officer*
†Knudson, Thomas Jeffery *journalist*
Kolkey, Daniel Miles *judge*
†Koretz, Paul *state representative*
†Kuehl, Sheila James *state legislator*
Kumar, B. Preetham *engineering educator, researcher*
†Lam, Siuwa Monica *education educator, consultant*
Landsberg, Brian Keith *law educator*
LaVally, Rebecca Jean *research editor, journalist*
Levi, David F. *federal judge*
†Levine, Lloyd E. *state representative*
†Lieber, Sally J. *state representative*
†Lilla, James A. *plastic surgeon*
†Lim, Alan Young *plastic surgeon*
Lionakis, George *architect*
Lippold, Roland Will *surgeon*
†Liu, Carol *state representative*
†Locker, Raymond Duncan *editor*
Lockyer, Bill *state attorney general*
†Loewy, Erich H. *bioethicist*
Lundstrom, Marjie *newspaper editor and columnist*
Lynch, Peter John *former dermatologist*
†Machado, Michael J(ohn) *state legislator, farmer*
Mack, Edward Gibson *retired business executive*
†Madden, Kenneth Robert *mining executive*
Majesty, Melvin Sidney *psychologist, consultant*

Malkin, Harold Marshall *medical researcher*
Malloy, Michael Patrick *law educator, consultant*
†Maze, Bill *state representative*
Mazzaferro, James Joseph *music educator*
†McCarthy, Kevin *state representative*
McElroy, Leo Francis *communications consultant, journalist*
†McGrath, William Arthur *arbitrator, mediator*
†McPherson, Bruce *state legislator*
Meindl, Robert James *English language educator*
Menebroker, Ann *special education educator, writer*
Merwin, Edwin Preston *healthcare educator, consultant*
Meyer, Rachel Abijah *foundation director, artist, theorist, poet*
Mogull, Robert G. *educator, researcher*
†Montanez, Cindy *state representative*
†Morrow, Bill *state legislator*
Moulds, John F. *federal judge*
Muehleisen, Gene *retired protective services administrator, state official*
Mueller, Virginia Schwartz *lawyer*
†Murray, Kevin *state legislator*
Newland, Chester Albert *public administration educator*
Nice, Carter *conductor, music director*
†Norman, Ben Eric *mathematician, educator*
†Nunez, Fabian *state representative*
Nye, Gene Warren *retired art educator*
O'Leary, Marion Hugh *university dean, chemist*
Oliva, Stephen Edward *resource conservationist, lawyer*
Olson, Timothy Allan *state official*
†Ortiz, Deborah V. *state legislator*
Oseas, Nannette N. *industrial hygienist, toxicologist, educator*
†Parra, Nicole M. *state representative*
†Parsons, Gibbe Hull *medical educator*
Patino, Douglas Xavier *foundation, government agency, and university administrator*
†Pavley, Fran J. *state representative*
Penicheiro, Ticha Nunes *professional basketball player*
†Perata, Don *state legislator*
†Peterson, Roy Martin, Jr., *environmental scientist*
Pettite, William Clinton *public affairs consultant*
†Piper, Jami Kathleen *music educator, composer*
†Poochigian, Charles *state legislator*
Post, August Alan *economist, artist*
Proud, Robert Donald (Robert Payton) *broadcast executive*
Quinn, Francis A. *bishop*
Radford, R. S. *lawyer, law educator*
Ramey, Felicenne Houston *dean*
Reed, Nancy Boyd *English language and elementary education educator*
Reed-Graham, Lois L. *eeducation consultant, author, management organizer*
†Reyes, Sarah *state representative*
†Reynolds, Jerry Owen *sports team executive*
Rich, Ben Arthur *lawyer, educator*
Richards, John Ray *emergency physician, educator*
†Richman, Keith Stuart *state representative*
Robbins, Stephen J. M. *lawyer*
†Roberts, James E. *civil engineer*
Roberts, Paul Dale *state agency administrator, writer*
Rodriguez, Miquel *prosecutor*
Rodriguez, Rick *newspaper executive editor*
†Romero, Gloria *state senator*
Root, Gerald Edward *legal administrator*
Rosenberg, Dan Yale *retired plant pathologist*
Ross, Terence William *architect*
†Rowland, Shirley K. *alcohol/drug abuse services professional, educator, mental health services professional, consultant*
†Runner, Sharon *state representative*
Russell, David E. *judge*
Ryan, Patricia Ellen *healthcare executive*
Sanborn, Kathy *career planning administrator, consultant*
Sato-Viacrucis, Kiyo *nurse, inventor, entrepreneur, consultant*
†Sciammarella, Maria Graciela *internist, cardiologist*
†Scott, Windie Olivia *lawyer*
†Severaid, Ronald Harold *lawyer*
Shapero, Harris Joel *pediatrician*
Sharma, Arjun Dutta *cardiologist*
Shaw, Eleanor Jane *newspaper editor*
Sherwood, Robert Petersen *retired sociology educator*
Shirey, John Frederick *local government administrator, lecturer, consultant*
Shoemaker, Cameron David James *dean, educator*
Silva, Joseph, Jr., *dean, medical educator*
Simeroth, Dean Conrad *chemical engineer*
†Simitian, Joe *state representative*
Spann, Lawrence Henry (Chip Spann) *physician associate*
†Speier, Jackie *state senator*
Starr, Kevin *librarian, educator*
†Steinberg, Darrell S. *state legislator*
Stenzel, Larry Gene *writer*
Stevenson, Thomas Ray *plastic surgeon*
†Strickland, Anthony *state representative*
Styne, Dennis Michael *physician, educator*
Swatt, Stephen Benton *communications executive, consultant*
†Tarrant, Kevin Theodore *music educator*
Taylor, Walter Wallace *retired lawyer*
†Teel, Michael J. *supermarket chain executive*
Thomas, Laura Marlene *artist, retired private antique dealer*
Torres, Art *former state legislator*
Tranum, Jean Lorraine *freelance writer*
Tubbs, William Reid, Jr., *public service administrator*
†Tung, Prabhas *plastic surgeon*
Twiss, Robert Manning *prosecutor*
Ubaldi, Michael Vincent *lawyer*
†Ueda, Kara Kimiko *lawyer*
Van Camp, Brian Ralph *judge*
Venosdel, Daniel Paul *agricultural association administrator*
Walsh, Denny Jay *reporter*
†Ward, Ruth Ellen *language educator*
Wasserman, Barry L(ee) *architect*
Wassmer, Robert William *economics educator*
Watson, Robert D. *allergist, immunologist, pediatric rheumatologist*
Webber, Chris, III, (Mayce Edward Christopher Webber) *professional basketball player*
Wesson, Herb J. *state representative*
West, Irma Marie *retired occupational health physician*
Wile, Philip Hodges *law educator*
Willis, Dawn Louise *legal assistant, small business owner*
Willis, Edward Oliver *management consultant, state official*
Wilson, E. Dotson *legislative staff member*
Wishek, Michael Bradley *lawyer*
†Wisner, David Hamilton *surgeon, educator*
Wolfe, Bruce McLaren *surgery educator*
Wolfman, Earl Frank, Jr., *surgeon, educator*
Wolkov, Harvey Brian *oncologist, researcher*
Woo, Karen *physician*
Wunder, Haroldene Fowler *taxation educator*
†Yang, Yung Y. *economics educator, consultant*
Yousif, Salah M. *electrical engineer, educator, electrical engineer, consultant*
Zaidi, Emily Louise *retired elementary school educator*
†Zhou, Jian-zhong (Joe) *librarian*
Zil, J. S. *psychiatrist, physiologist*

Saint Helena
Marvin, Monica Louise Wolf *lawyer*
†Wiggins, Rita Cassidy *poet*
Yates, Donald Alfred *retired literature educator*

Salinas
Bolles, Donald Scott *lawyer*
Chester, Lynne *foundation executive, artist*
†Collins, Judith Ann *librarian*
†Fink, Joseph E. *purchasing agent, finance educator*
†Jeffries, Russell Morden *communications company official*
Lewellen, Robert Thomas *research geneticist*
Liebersbach, Norbert John *protective services official*
Loose, Stephanie Joy *accountant*
Mercurio, Edward Peter *natural science educator*
†Michener, John Russell *electrical engineer*
†Phillips, John P(aul) *retired neurosurgeon*
Puckett, Richard Edward *artist, consultant, retired recreation executive*
Solis, Gilberto, Jr., *county official*
Wong, Walter Foo *county official*
Wu, Wayne Wen-Yau *artist*

San Andreas
Breed, Allen Forbes *correctional administrator*
†Cretan, Donna *neonatal nurse, lactation consultant*

San Anselmo
Chiaverini, John Edward *construction company executive*
Ellenberger, Diane Marie *nurse, consultant*
†Harpham, Heather Elise *educator*
Motz, Julie Ann *energy healer, author*
Murphy, Barry Ames *lawyer*
Torbet, Laura *writer, artist, photographer, graphic designer*
Truett, Harold Joseph, III, (Tim Truett) *lawyer*

San Bernardino
Bauer, Steven Michael *cost containment engineer*
Burgess, Mary Alice (Mary Alice Wickizer) *publisher*
Burgess, Michael *library director, writer*
Caballero, Sharon *academic administrator*
Crowell, Samuel Marvin, Jr., *education educator*
Curry, Paul Russell *law enforcement official, lobbyist*
De Haas, David Dana *emergency physician*
Eskin, Barry Sanford *court investigator*
Estes, James Paul *financial services company executive*
Farmer, Wesley Steven *police officer*
†Fenelon, James V. *sociologist, educator, poet, advocate*
Fullerton, Robert Victor *lawyer*
Golondzinier, Theodore Matthew *civil engineer*
Kirkland, Bertha Theresa *project engineer*
Maul, Terry Lee *psychologist, educator*
Mian, Lal Shah *entomologist, educator*
†Mills, Denise Yvonne *librarian*
Neighbors, Ira Arthell *social work educator*
Norton, Ruth Ann *education educator*
Prince, Timothy Peter *lawyer*
Roberts, Katharine Adair *retired bookkeeper*
Seitz, Victoria Ann *marketing educator*
Traynor, Gary Edward *association administrator*
Turpin, Joseph Ovila *counselor, educator*
Valles, Judith *mayor, former academic administrator*
Willis, Harold Wendt, Sr., *real estate developer*

San Bruno
Amick, Collin Hal *civil engineer, consultant*
Bradley, Charles William *podiatrist, educator*
Mattathil, George Paul *strategic advisor communication technology*
†White, Frances LaVonne *academic administrator*

San Carlos
Dafforn, Geoffrey Alan *biochemist*
Eby, Michael John *marketing research and technology consultant*
Gutow, Bernard Sidney *packaging manufacturing company executive*
Hoffman, Paul Jerome *psychologist, statistician*
Lee, John Jin *lawyer*
†Mitchell, Sally E. *lawyer, city official, former mayor*
Oliver, Nancy Lebkicher *artist, retired elementary education educator*
Patnode, Darwin Nicholas *retired academic administrator, professional parliamentarian*
Schumacher, Henry Jerold *museum administrator, former career officer, business executive*
Symons, Robert Spencer *electronic engineer*
Taniere, Romain Andre *pharmaceutical company scientist*

San Clemente
Clark, Earnest Hubert, Jr., *tool company executive*
Fisher, Myron R. *lawyer*
Geyser, Lynne M. *lawyer, writer*
Gialamas, Gus G. *orthopedic surgeon*
Halamandaris, Harry *aerospace executive*
Kim, Edward William *ophthalmic surgeon*
Nguyen, Ky Duc *electrical engineer*
Petrone, Joseph Anthony *business consultant, writer*
†Petruzzi, Christopher Robert *business educator, consultant*
†Steinberg, Howard *chemical company executive, consultant*
White, Stanley Archibald *research electrical engineer*
Wolfram, Thomas *physicist, educator*

San Diego
Aaron, Cynthia G. *judge*
Addis, Thomas Homer, III, *professional golfer*
Adler, Louise DeCarl *judge*
†Alksne, John F. *medical educator, former dean*
†Amstadt, Nancy Hollis *retired language educator*
†Anderson, Karl Richard *aerospace engineer, consultant*
Anderson, Paul Maurice *electrical engineering educator, researcher, consultant*
†Angyal, Charles *architect*
Auld, Robert Henry, Jr., *biomedical engineer, educator, consultant, author*
Backer, Matthias, Jr., *obstetrician, gynecologist*
†Backes, Jack Abraham *application developer*
Bakko, Orville Edwin *retired health care executive, consultant*
Bales, Dorothy Johnson *violinist, educator*
Bales, Robert Freed *social psychologist, educator*
†bar-Lev, Zev *linguist, educator*
Barone, Angela Maria *artist, researcher*
†Barton, Thomas Donald *lawyer, educator*
Bartus, Raymond Thomas *neuroscientist, pharmaceutical executive, writer*
Batey, Sharyn Rebecca *clinical research scientist*
Bauer, Judy Marie *minister*
Baum, Stephen L. *utilities company executive*
Baxter, Robert Hampton *insurance executive*
†Bayer, Richard Stewart *lawyer*
Beattie, Geraldine Alice (Geri Beattie) *advocate*
†Bell, Gene *newspaper publishing executive*
†Benedyk, Mika Ono *editor, writer*
Berger, Newell James, Jr., *retired security professional*
Bernstein, Sanford Irwin *biology educator*
†Besada, Hany Gamil *international affairs administrator, researcher*
Beyster, John Robert *engineering company executive*
†Bird, Charles Albert *lawyer*
Blade, Melinda Kim *archaeologist, educator, researcher*
Blakemore, Claude Coulehan *banker*
Bleiler, Charles Arthur *lawyer*
Bliesner, James Douglas *municipal/county official, consultant*
†Bochy, Bruce *professional sports team manager, coach*
Boersma, June Elaine (Jalma Barrett) *writer, photographer*
Boersma, Lawrence Allan (Larry Allan) *animal welfare administrator, photographer*
†Boggs, William S. *lawyer*
Bonn, Ronald Sheldon *TV news producer, journalism educator*
†Bookstein, Joseph J. *radiologist, educator*
Borden, Diane Lynn *communications educator*
Boston, David *football player*
Bot, Adrian Ion *immunologist*
Bowie, Peter Wentworth *judge, educator*
†Boyle, Michael Fabian *lawyer*
Brandes, Raymond Stewart *history educator*
†Brennan-Sparks, Jennifer Anne *writer*
Brewster, Rudi Milton *judge*
Brierton, Cheryl Lynn *lawyer*
†Brom, Robert H. *bishop*
Brooks, John White *lawyer*
Brown, Barbara Sproul *retired librarian, consultant, writer*
Brown, LaMar Bevan *lawyer*
Burge, David Russell *concert pianist, composer, piano educator*
Burns, Larry Alan *judge*
Bussard, Robert William *physicist*
Buzunis, Constantine Dino *lawyer*
Cabrera, Quincy Rodolfo *minister, educator*
Callahan, LeeAnn Lucille *psychologist*
Campbell, Ian David *opera company director*
Cantor, Charles Robert *biochemistry educator*
Carsola, Alfred James *oceanographer, geologist, educator*
Cassady, Marsh G. *writer, editor*
†Caughlin, Stephenie Jane *organic farmer*
Chambers, Henry George *orthopedic surgeon*
Chen, Carlson S. *mechanical engineer*
Christensen, Charles Brophy *lawyer*
†Chun Fat, George *writer*
Cianciolo-Carney, Rossana *investigative analyst*
†Claus, Laurence Paul *law educator*
Cobble, James Wikle *chemistry educator*
†Cobbs Hoffman, Elizabeth Anne *history educator*
Cogan, Mary Jo Gleber *lawyer*
Comrie, Sandra Melton *human resource executive*
Conly, John Franklin *engineering educator, researcher*
Contreras, Thomas J., Jr., *career officer*
†Cook, Stephen Barton *art educator, artist*
Copeland, Robert Glenn *lawyer*
Cosman, Bard Clifford *surgeon, educator*
Cota, John Francis *utility executive*
Covert, Michael Henri *healthcare facility administrator*
Crick, Francis Harry Compton *science educator, researcher*
Crisci, Mathew G. *marketing executive, writer*
Crocker, Valerie Marian *mechanical engineer*
Crook, Sean Paul *aerospace systems division director*
Crumpler, Hugh Allan *author*
†Crute, James John *biochemist, researcher*
†Dai, Liang *electrical engineer*
Daley, Arthur Stuart *retired humanities educator*
Damoose, George Lynn *lawyer*
Darby, Joanne Tyndale (Jaye Darby) *arts and humanities educator*
Darmstandler, Harry Max *real estate executive, retired air force officer*
Davenport, Roger Lee *research engineer*
Davies, Thomas Mockett, Jr., *history educator*
Davis, James McCoy *retired real estate executive*
Davis, John Warren *real estate broker*
Dawe, James Robert *lawyer*
Day, Robert William *geotechnical engineer*
Dean, Richard Anthony *mechanical engineer, engineering executive*
Delawie, Homer Torrence *retired architect*
DeMaria, Anthony Nicholas *cardiologist, educator*
Demeter, Steven *neurologist, medical publishing company executive*
Dershem, Larry Douglas *lawyer, author*
Devine, Brian Kiernan *pet food and supplies company executive*
Dintrone, Charles Vincent *librarian*
DiRuscio, Lawrence William *advertising executive*
†Doan, Tai Danh *social worker, director*
Doll, Linda A. *artist, educator*
Donley, Dennis Lee *school librarian*
†Dorne, David J. *lawyer*
Dostart, Paul Joseph *lawyer, investor and director*
Downing, David Charles *retired minister*
Drummond, John C. *anesthesiologist, educator*
Dulbecco, Renato *biologist, educator*
Dunlop, Marianne *retired English as second language educator*
Dunn, David Joseph *financial executive*
Dyer, Charles Richard *law librarian, law educator*
Early, Teri Wilson (Denise Wilson) *elementary education educator*
Eastham, John Howard *pharmacist, educator*
Eckhart, Walter *molecular biologist, educator*
Edwards, Darrel *psychologist*
†Edwards, James Richard *lawyer*
Edwards-Tate, Laurie Ellen *human services administrator, educator*
Eigner, William Whitling *lawyer*
†Elliott, Graham *science educator*
Ellsworth, Robert Fred *investment executive, former government official*
Emerick, Robert Earl *sociologist, educator*
Engle, Robert Irwin *music educator, musician, composer, writer, translator*
†Engle, Steven B. *biotechnology company executive*
Estep, Arthur Lee *lawyer*
†Eulert, Corneaux H *drama therapist, educator*
Evans, Ersel Arthur *consulting engineer executive*
Evans, John Joseph *management consultant, executive, educator, writer*
†Everett, Hobart Ray, Jr., *engineer, naval officer, consultant, researcher*
Farmer, Janene Elizabeth *artist, educator*
Fauchier, Dan R(ay) *mediator, arbitrator, educator, construction management consultant*
Feinberg, Lawrence Bernard *university dean, psychologist*
Fellmeth, Robert Charles *law educator*
†Fellows, Christohper Charles *information scientist*
†Ferraro, Joanne M. *humanities educator*
Fike, Edward Lake *newspaper editor*
Fleischmann, Paul *religious organization administrator, minister*
Flettner, Marianne *opera administrator*
Flutie, Douglas Richard (Doug Flutie) *professional football player*
†Foerster, Barrett Jonathan *lawyer*
Foreman, John Patrick *electrical engineer*
Fraitag, Leonard Alan *product development engineer*
Frederick, Norman L., Jr., *electrical engineer*
Freeman, Myrna Faye *county schools official*
Friedman, Arthur Daniel *electrical engineering and computer science educator, investment management company executive*
Friedman, Barbara Bernstein *investor, money manager, glass artist, speaker*
†Friedman, Gary E. *lawyer*
Friedman, Lawrence Stuart *internist, pediatrician, educator*
Friedman, Paul Jay *radiologist, educator*
Gallison, H(arold) Bailey, Sr., *youth agency administrator, public relations and marketing consultant*
†Gamble, Lynn Hunter *anthropologist, educator*
Garfin, Steven R. *orthopedic surgeon*
Garrison, Betty Bernhardt *retired mathematics educator*
Gastil, Russell Gordon *geologist, educator*
Gazell, James Albert *public administration educator*
Gengor, Virginia Anderson *financial planning executive, educator*
†Genovese, Edgar Nicholas *humanities educator*
Georgakakos, Konstantine Peter *research hydrologist*
†German, G. Michael *lawyer*

Getis, Arthur *geography educator*
Gilbertson, Oswald Irving *marketing executive*
Gilleland, John Rogers *technology company executive*
Gillespie, George Hubert *physicist*
Gold, Steven Bruce *lawyer*
Golding, Brage *university president*
Golding, Susan *former mayor*
Goldstein, Mark Kingston Levin *information technology executive, researcher*
Goltz, Robert William *physician, educator*
Gonzalez, Irma Elsa *federal judge*
González-Trujillo, César Augusto *Chicano studies educator, writer*
Grant, Igor *psychiatrist*
Gray-Bussard, Dolly H. *energy company executive*
Gross, Jeffrey *software engineer*
Grossbard-Shechtman, Amyra *economist, educator, researcher*
Grosser, T.J. *administrator, developer, fundraiser*
Guinn, Stanley Willis *lawyer*
†Gundersen, Larry Edward *academic administrator*
Gupta, Madhu Sudan *electrical engineering educator*
Gwynn, Anthony Keith (Tony Gwynn) *former professional baseball player*
†Haener, Juan A. *physicist*
Hager, Michael W. *museum director*
Hales, Alfred Washington *mathematics educator, consultant*
Hamilton, James Douglas *economics educator*
Hansotte, Louis Bernard *retired lawyer*
†Harutunian, Albert T(heodore), III, *judge*
Hayes, Claude Quinten Christopher *research scientist, inventor*
Hayes, Robert Emmet *retired insurance company executive*
†Heer, David Macalpine *sociology educator*
†Heidrich, Robert Wesley *lawyer*
Heinemann, Stephen F. *molecular neurobiologist educator*
Henderson, John Drews *architect*
†Herring, Charles David *lawyer, educator*
†Higgs, Craig DeWitt *lawyer*
Hoffer, Michael E. *otolaryngologist, naval officer*
Hofflund, Paul *lawyer*
Hollingsworth, Margaret Camille *financial services administrator, consultant*
Hoston, Germaine Annette *political science educator*
Houston, Carol Olson *educator, accounting*
†Howard, Mildred *sculptor*
Huberman, Jonathan Serge *venture capitalist*
Hunt, Barnabas John *priest, religious organization administrator*
Hunt, Robert Gary *medical consultant, oral and maxillofacial surgeon*
†Idos, Rosalina Vejerano *secondary school educator*
Intriere, Anthony Donald *retired internist, gastroenterologist*
Iredale, Eugene Gerald *lawyer*
Ito, Carl Susumu *computer engineer*
†Iversen, Leslie Lars *pharmaceutical executive*
Jacobs, Irwin Mark *communications executive*
Jacobs, Paul E. *communications executive*
Jacoby, Irving *physician*
Jagoda, Barry Lionel *writer, media adviser, communications consultant*
James, Helen Foster *education director*
Jamieson, Stuart William *surgeon, educator*
Jeffers, Donald E. *retired insurance executive, consultant*
Jenson, Ronald Allen *religious executive, educator*
Johnson, Kenneth Owen *retired audiologist*
Jones, Clyde William *anesthesiologist*
Jones, Ronald H. *computer information systems executive*
Kaback, Michael *medical educator*
Kadous, Tamer Adel *research scientist*
†Kahan, David Michael *education educator*
Kaplan, George Willard *urologist*
†Kassel, Daniel Brian *biotechnologist, researcher*
Kaufman, Julian Mortimer *broadcasting company executive, consultant*
†Kehoe, Christine T. *state official*
†Keramati, Shahin *cardiologist*
Kiesler, Charles Adolphus *psychologist, academic administrator*
Kilmer, Maurice Douglas *marketing executive*
Klamerus, Karen Jean *pharmacist, researcher*
Klein, Herbert George *newspaper editor*
Klesko, Ryan *baseball player*
Klinedinst, John David *lawyer*
Koenig, Harold Martin *former United States Navy surgeon general*
Kovacic, Peter *chemistry educator*
†Kranzler, Jay D. *pharmaceutical executive*
Kraus, Pansy Daegling *gemology consultant, editor, writer*
Krejci, Robert Harry *non-profit organizations development consultant*
Kremer, Matthew Markus *lawyer, mediator, judge pro tem*
†Kronewitter, Frank Dell *software engineer, researcher*
Krulak, Victor Harold *newspaper executive*
Krupchak, Tamara *artist*
†Kubilus, Norbert John *information technology executive*
Kunkel, Scott William *strategic management and entrepreneurship educator*
†Kuntz, William Richard, Jr., *lawyer*
Kyle, Robert Campbell, II, *publishing executive*
Lakritz, Esther *retired English language educator*
Lane, Gloria Julian *foundation administrator*
Langer, Eva Marie *video specialist*
L'Annunziata, Michael Frank *chemist, consultant*
Lao, Lang Li *nuclear fusion research physicist*
Lapota, David *oceanographer, marine biologist*
Larson, Arvid Gunnar *electrical engineer*
Larson, Mark Devin *communications executive*
†Larson, Vernon Dale *audiologist, researcher*
Lathrop, Mitchell Lee *lawyer*
LeBeau, Charles Paul *lawyer*
Lederer, Richard Henry *writer, educator, columnist*
Legrand, Shawn Pierre *computer systems programmer*
Levi, Victor H. *retired electrical engineer*
Levy, Jerome *dermatologist, retired naval officer*
Levy, Michael Lee *neurosurgeon*
Lewis, Gerald Jorgensen *judge*
Lewis, Shirley Jeane *psychotherapist, educator*
Liber, Hillary Selese Jacobs *writer, educator*
Lindh, Patricia Sullivan *banker, former government official*
†Longstreth, Robert Christy *lawyer*
Loper, Warren Edward *computer scientist*
Lowenstam, Susan Guggenheim *lawyer*
Lundy-Slade, Bettie B. *retired electronics professional*
†Lustbader, Philip Lawrence *lawyer, stock brokerage executive*
Lynch, Frank P. *pediatric surgeon*
†Lyons, Mary E. *academic administrator*
Madhavan, Murugappa Chettiar *economics educator, international consultant*
Magadan, David Joseph *professional baseball player*
Mahdavi, Kamal B. *writer, researcher*
Manifold, Gregory Lee *sportswriter*
Margolis, Anita Joy *lawyer*
Markowitz, Harry M. *finance and economics educator*
Mayer, George Roy *educator*
McCarberg, Bill Harold *physician*
McClellan, Craig Rene *lawyer*
Mc Comic, Robert Barry *real estate development company executive, lawyer*
McDermott, Thomas John, Jr., *lawyer*
McDonough, Mark *neuropsychologist, forensic consultant*
McGinnis, Robert E. *lawyer*
McGraw, Donald Jesse *biologist, science historian, writer*
McKeown, Mary Margaret *federal judge*
McKeown, Michael Eugene *psychologist, consultant*
†McLeod, Douglas Bailey *mathematician, educator*
McLeod, John Hugh, Jr., *mechanical and electrical engineer*
†McVey, Lane Leroy *lawyer*
†Mebane, Julie Shaffer *lawyer*
Meerson, Felix Zalmanovich *cardiologist*
Mercola, Daniel A. *medical researcher*
Mercurio, Philip Joseph *computer programmer/analyst*
Merrill-Nach, Suzanne Marie *obstetrician, gynecologist*
Mestechkin, Mikhail Markovich *math physicist*
Milder, David Geoffrey *oral and maxillofacial surgeon*
Miller, William Charles *lawyer*
Mills, Paul J. *psychiatry educator*
Mittermiller, James Joseph *lawyer*
Mohan, Chandra *research biochemistry educator*
†Moos, Walter Hamilton *pharmaceutical company executive*
Moossa, A. R. *surgery educator*
Morgan, Mark Quenten *astrophysics educator*
Morgan, Neil *writer, newspaper editor, lecturer, columnist*
Morris, Grant Harold *law educator*
Morris, Sandra Joan *lawyer*
Moss, Barbara Gae *education educator*
Moss, Gene Richard *psychiatrist*
Mosteller, James Wilbur, III, *data processing executive*
Mulcahy, Robert Joseph *lawyer*
Murakami, Masanori *physicist*
Murphy, Dick *mayor, former superior court judge*
Myers, Douglas George *zoological society administrator*
Nagao, Norris Sadato *educator, consultant*
†Naslund, Eric *architectural firm executive*
†Naviaux, Robert *pediatrician, educator*
Nelson, Craig Alan *management consultant*
Nenner, Victoria Corich *nurse, educator*
Neuman, Tom S. *emergency medical physician, educator*
Neumann, Linda Kay *marketing executive*
Nevin, Phillip *baseball player*
Norling, Richard Arthur *health care executive*
†Ojeda, Norma *social sciences educator, researcher*
Olevsky, Eugene A. *research scientist, educator*
O'Malley, Edward *psychiatrist, consultant*
O'Malley, James Terence *lawyer*
Overton, Marcus Lee *performing arts administrator, actor, writer*
Owen, Charles Theodore *journalist, publisher*
Paderewski, Sir Clarence Joseph *architect*
Pagan, Keith Areatus *music educator, academic administrator*
Paget, John Arthur *mechanical engineer*
Panetta, Joseph Daniel *biotechnology executive*
Partida, Gilbert A. *executive*
Payne, Margaret Anne *lawyer*
Pecsok, Robert Louis *chemist, educator*
Peebles, Carol Lynn *immunology researcher*
Perlman, Richard Donald *orthopedic surgeon*
Perrault, Jacques *educator*
Peters, Richard *lawyer*
Petersen, Martin Eugene *curator*
Peterson, Richard Hermann *retired history educator*
Petix, Stephen Vincent *lawyer*
†Pfiffner, Patrick Meehan *musician, educator*
Pincus, Howard J. *geologist, engineer, educator*
Pincus, Robert Lawrence *art critic, cultural historian*
Pitt, William Alexander *cardiologist*
†Plescia, George A. *state official*
Plovanich, Patricia Ann *theologian, educator*
Poppendiek, Heinz Frank *engineering executive*
Pottenger, Mark McClelland *computer programmer*
†Potter-Hill, Lynne Ann *lawyer*
†Prado, Pablo Jose *physicist, researcher*
Prescott, Lawrence Malcolm *medical and health science writer*
Preston, David Raymond *lawyer*
†Price, Robert E. *manufacturing company executive*
Proehl, Gerald T. *pharmaceutical executive*
Pryde, Philip Rust *retired geography educator*
Pugh, Richard Crawford *lawyer*
Purcifull, Robert Otis *insurance company executive*
Pyatt, Kedar Davis, Jr., *research and development company executive*
Raczka, Tony Michael *artist*
†Ransom, Bryan Kenneth *music educator*
Ray, Albert *family physician*
Reading, James Edward *transportation executive*
†Reed, T. Michael *lawyer*
†Reid, Robert Tilden *medical association administrator, internist*
Reif, Louis Raymond *lawyer, utilities executive*
Reinhard, Christopher John *merchant banking, venture capital and biotechnology executive*
†Ren, Steven Shijun *chemist*
Repetti, Anamaria *healthcare foundation executive*
Rhoades, John Skylstead, Sr., *federal judge*
Rice, Clare I. *electronics company executive*
Riedy, Mark Joseph *finance educator*
†Riffenburgh, Gerrye H. *artist, educator*
†Riley, Kirk Holden *lawyer*
Risser, Arthur Crane, Jr., *zoo administrator*
Robbins, Arthur M. *retired aerospace engineer*
†Robbins, Eleanora Iberall *biogeologist, researcher*
Roberts-DeGennaro, Maria *social work educator*
Robinson, David Howard *lawyer*
Rodgers, Janet Ahalt *nursing educator, dean*
Roseman, Charles Sanford *lawyer*
†Ross, John, Jr., *cardiologist, educator*
Ross, Terry D. *lawyer*
Rossi, Norma J. *not-for-profit executive, advocate*
Ross-Serakos, Vonia P.
†Roth-Douquet, Kathryn Gaie *lawyer*
Rotter, Paul Talbott *retired insurance executive*
Rowe, Peter A. *newspaper columnist*
Rubin, Stuart Harvey *computer science educator, researcher*
Rymer, Thérèse Elizabeth *family practice nurse practitioner*
St. Clair, Hal Kay *electrical engineer*
Saito, Frank Kiyoji *import and export firm executive*
†Sakamoto, Kyoko *surgeon, educator*
Samuelson, Derrick William *lawyer*
†Sasaran, Laura Jeanne *humanities educator*
†Sasidharan, Vinod *travel and tourism educator, researcher*
Sauer, David Andrew *librarian, technical writer*
Sceper, Duane Harold *lawyer*
Schade, Charlene Joanne *adult and early childhood education educator*
Schechter, Clifford *financial executive, lawyer*
Schmidt, Joseph David *urologist*
Schmidt, Terry L. *health care executive*
†Schmidt, Thomas Charles *biomedical engineer, researcher*
†Schottenheimer, Martin Edward *former professional football coach, television analyst*
†Schoville, Dennis A(rnold) *lawyer*
Schrock, Donald E. *communications executive*
Schryver, Bruce John *safety engineer*
Schuckit, Marc Alan *psychiatry educator, researcher*
†Schultz, Kenneth Robert *nuclear engineer, researcher*
Schwartz, Alfred *university dean*
Schwartz, Jeffrey Scott *lawyer*
†Scott, Bonnie Kime *English literature educator*
Seagren, Stephen Linner *oncologist*
†Seidenwurm, Richard Lewis *lawyer*
Sejnowski, Terrence Joseph *science educator*
Sell, Robert Emerson *electrical engineer*
Shapiro, Philip Alan *lawyer*
†Shaw, Richard Allan *lawyer*
Shearer, William Kennedy *lawyer, publisher*
†Shedroff, Sharon D. *psychologist, researcher, anthropologist, consultant*
Sheldon, Lois Elizabeth *social services administrator*
Shelton, Dorothy Diehl Rees *lawyer*
†Shen, Larry Z. *pharmaceutical executive, researcher*
Shippey, Sandra Lee *lawyer*
Shneour, Elie Alexis *biophysicist, researcher, historian*
†Short, Jay Milton *biotechnology company executive*
Siegal, Barbara Leatrice *visual artist*
Silverstone, Leon Martin *neuroscientist, cardiologist, educator, researcher*
Skwara, Erich Wolfgang *novelist, poet, educator, literary critic*
Slate, John Butler *biomedical engineer*
Sledge, Reginald Leon *planner and consultant*
Smith, Raymond Edward *retired health care administrator*
Smith, Steven Ray *law educator*
Snaid, Leon Jeffrey *lawyer*
Snyder, David Richard *lawyer*
†Soria, Merja T. *music educator*
Sorrentino, Renate Maria *illustrator*
Spanos, Alexander Gus *construction company owner, professional sports team owner*
Spanos, Dean A. *professional sports team executive, business executive*
Spira, Patricia Goodsitt *association executive*
Springer, Wayne Richard *healthcare system official, research biochemist*
Steen, Paul Joseph *retired broadcasting executive*
Stein, Eleanor Benson (Ellie Stein) *playwright, writer*
Stein, Franklin Joseph *youth counselor*
Sterrett, James Kelley, II, *lawyer*
Stetson, Robert Francis *retired metallurgist*
Stevens, William C., Jr., *pharmaceutical executive*
Steward, Harold David (Hal Steward) *author, journalist, retired army officer*
Stewart, Jean Catherine *critical care and neuroscience emergency trauma nurse, educator*
†Stewart, Morgan Elizabeth *research scientist*
Stock, Lauri Jane *lawyer*
Stoessinger, John George *political science educator*
Storer, Norman William *sociologist, educator*
†Sturman, George *poet, volunteer*
†Sullivan, Patrick James *lawyer*
Sullivan, William Francis *lawyer*
Sutton, L. Paul *criminal justice educator*
Suycott, Mark Leland *systems engineer, retired naval flight officer*
Swank, William George *historian, writer*
Swanson, Mary Catherine *educational reform program founder*
Tartz, Robert Scott *engineering executive*
Taylor, George Allen *advertising agency executive*
Tennent, Valentine Leslie *accountant*
Thomas, Charles Allen, Jr., *molecular biologist, educator*
Thomas, Kevin Anthony *biomedical engineer*
Thompson, David Renwick *federal judge*
Thompson, Gordon, Jr., *federal judge*
Tidwell, Geoffrey Morgan *medical company executive*
Tillinghast, Charles Carpenter, III, *marketing company executive*
Tom, Lawrence *technology executive*
Tragen, Irving Glenne *consultant*
Travaglini, Joseph *educational consultant*
Trembley, Mark Michel *geographer, educator*
Tricoles, Gus Peter *electromagnetic engineer, physicist, consultant*
Tsybakov, Boris Solomon *information theory and communication networks researcher, educator*
Turcu, Ion Cristian Edmond *physicist*
Turner, B. Russell *tax accountant, real estate broker*
Turrentine, Howard Boyd *federal judge*
†Underwood, Anthony Paul *lawyer*
†Uribe, Jennie Ann *elementary school educator*
†Valdez, Jose Carbajal, Jr., *poet, lyricist*
Valliant, James Stevens *lawyer*
Vanderbilt, Kermit *English language educator*
Van Gorder, Chris *medical executive*
†Van Kirk, Jaye Frances *psychology educator*
Van Tassel, Lowell Thomas *mathematics educator*
†Vartanian, Pershing *education educator*
Vaughn, Billy Eldridge *psychology educator, publisher*
Vause, Edwin Hamilton *research foundation administrator*
Vazakas, Maura Fran *artist, music teacher*
†Velo, Ani Piro *mathematician, educator*
Wadlington, W. M. *retired commodity futures trader and financial engineer*
Walker, Donald Ezzell *retired academic administrator*
Wallace, Helen Margaret *physician, educator*
Wallace, J. Clifford *federal judge*
Ward, Charles Raymond *systems engineer*
Ward-Steinman, David *composer, music educator, pianist*
Warner, John Hilliard, Jr., *technical services, military and commercial systems and software company executive*
Wasserman, Stephen Ira *physician, educator*
†Wawrytko, Sandra Ann *humanities educator*
Weaver, Michael James *lawyer*
Weber, Stephen Lewis *university president*
Weeks, John Robert *geographer, sociology educator*
Weinrich, James Donald *psychobiologist, internet consultant*
Wertheim, Robert Halley *national security consultant*
Whittington, Anne Elizabeth *diabetes educator*
Wiesler, James Ballard *retired banker*
Willerding, Margaret Frances *mathematician, educator*
Willis, Norman Hunt *author, writer, director, producer*
†Wilson, Jerry Clark *language educator*
Wilson, Richard Allan *landscape architect*
Winner, Karin E. *editor*
Wojcik, Martin Henry *foundation development official*
Wostrel, Nancy Jo *painter, illustrator*
Wozniak, Joyce Marie *sales executive*
†Wyatt, Roland Gratts *music educator, voice educator, consultant*
Yamazaki, Shinji *research scientist*
Yarber, Robert Earl *writer, retired educator*
Yokley, Richard Clarence *protective services official*
Young, David Bradley *lawyer*
Youngs, Jack Marvin *cost engineer*
Yuan, Jason Xiao-Jian *medical researcher, educator*
Zyskind, Judith Weaver *molecular biology educator, entrepreneur*

San Dimas

†Cameron, Judith Lynne *secondary education educator, hypnotherapist*
Lindly, Douglas Dean *elementary/middle school educator, administrator*
Peters, Joseph Donald *filmmaker*

San Francisco

†Abbott, Barry Alexander *lawyer*
Achtenberg, Roberta *former federal official*
Adams, Donald Elwin *cultural and organization development administrator, consultant*
Adler, Nancy Elinor *psychologist, educator*
†Ahmed, Mahnaz *bank executive*
Albino, Judith Elaine Newsom *university president*

†Inman, Robert Anthony *writer*
Innes, Kenneth Frederick, III, *lawyer*
Jacobson, Lester Barry *cardiologist*
†Jacobson, Mark Andrew *epidemiologist, educator, physician*
Jaffe, Robert Benton *obstetrician, gynecologist, reproductive endocrinologist*
James, David Lee *lawyer, international advisor, author*
James, Thomas Larry *chemistry educator*
Jarvis, Donald Bertram *judge*
Jewett, George Frederick, Jr., *forest products company executive*
Johns, Richard Seth Ellis *lawyer*
Johns, Roy (Bud Johns) *publisher, writer*
†Johnson, Gardiner *lawyer*
Jones, J. Gilbert *private investigator*
Jones, Stanton William *management consultant*
Jonsen, Albert R(upert) *retired medical ethics educator*
Kahn, Linda McClure *actuary, consultant*
Kahn, Ronald N. *investment researcher*
†Kakar, Sanjay *gastrointestinal and liver pathologist*
Kalicki, Jan H. *economist, political scientist*
Kallet, Richard Hubbard *medical researcher*
Kammerer, Ann Marie *geotechnical engineer*
Kan, Yuet Wai *hematologist, educator*
Kane, Mary Kay *dean, law educator*
†Kao, John Sterling *mathematician, educator*
†Kari, Ross *banking executive*
Kasanin, Mark Owen *lawyer*
†Kashani-Sabet, Mohammed *physician*
Katz, Hilliard Joel *physician*
Katzung, Bertram George *pharmacologist*
Kaufman, Jonathan Allan (Jon Kaufman) *public relations executive*
Kazalia, Marie Ann *writer*
Keats, Jonathon *writer*
Keeney, Ralph Lyons *decision and risk analyst, educator*
Keller, Edward Lowell *electrical engineer, educator*
†Kelley, Michael Garhart Roosevelt *historian, educator, writer*
Kelly, Alan *public relations executive*
Kelly, J. Michael *lawyer*
Kelly, James Anthony *priest*
Kelly, Regis Baker *biochemistry educator, biophysics educator*
Kendall, Robert Daniel *priest, theology educator*
Kennard, Joyce L. *judge*
Kennedy, Matthew Lawry *film historian, anthropologist*
†Kenyon, Cynthia *medical researcher*
Kerman, Barry Martin *ophthalmologist, educator*
Kern, John McDougall *lawyer*
Khosla, Ved Mitter *oral and maxillofacial surgeon, educator*
Kielarowski, Henry Edward *marketing executive*
Kikukawa, Randall Hiroyuki *university administrator*
Kimport, David Lloyd *lawyer*
King, Alonzo *artistic director, choreographer*
King, Talmadge E. *physician*
Kinsell, Jeffrey Clift *investment banker*
Klammer, Joseph Francis *management consultant*
Kleinberg, David Lewis *education administrator*
†Kleinknecht, Jochen *management consultant*
Kline, Howard Jay *cardiologist, educator*
Kloos, Helmut *geographer*
Klott, David Lee *lawyer*
Knapp, Charles Lincoln *law educator*
Knebel, Jack Gillen *lawyer*
†Knutzen, Martha Lorraine *lawyer*
Koeppel, John A. *lawyer*
Koffel, Martin M. *engineering company executive*
Kong, Gail Mildred *foundation executive*
†Koo, John Ying Ming *dermatologist*
Kopel, Stephen *educator*
Kovacevich, Richard M. *bank executive*
Kozloff, Lloyd M. *university dean, educator, scientist*
Krempel, Ralf Hugo Bernhard *writer, artist, art gallery owner*
Kriken, John Lund *architect*
Krippner, Stanley Curtis *psychologist*
Kuhl, Paul Beach *lawyer*
Kuhns, Craig Shaffer *business educator*
Kuriloff, Effie Hannah *education educator*
†Kurtz, Larry *corporate communications executive*
Ladar, Jerrold Morton *lawyer*
La Farge, Timothy *retired plant geneticist*
Lamberson, John Roger *insurance company executive*
Landis, Richard Gordon *retired food company executive*
Lane, Fielding H. *lawyer*
†Lane, Mary B. *education educator, writer*
Langton, Daniel Joseph *English, writing educator, poet*
Laret, Mark R. *school system administrator*
Larson, John William *lawyer*
Lasky, Moses *lawyer*
Latta, Thomas Albert *lawyer*
Lauterbach, Michael Alan *artist*
La Vine, Robert L. *lawyer*
†Lawton, Michael Thomas *neurosurgeon*
LeBlanc, Tina *dancer*
†Leddy, William *architect*
Lee, Ivy, Jr., *public relations consultant*
Lee, Philip Randolph Randolph *medical educator*
LeFlore, John Lauzine *artist, historian*
†Leno, Mark *state legislator*
Leshy, John David *lawyer, legal educator, government official*
Leung, Kason Kai Ching *computer specialist*
†Levada, William Joseph *archbishop*
Leviton, Alan Edward *curator*
Libbin, Anne Edna *lawyer*
Lin, Robert Kwanhwan *language educator, consultant*
Lin, Tung Yen *civil engineer, educator*
†Liu, Samuel T. *economist, consultant*
Liu, Xiao *ophthalmologist, neurobiologist*
Livsey, Robert Callister *lawyer*
Lobdell, Frank *artist*
Lofton, Kenneth *professional baseball player*
†Lopes, James Louis *lawyer*
Lord, Mia W. *world peace and disarmament activist*
Low, Arnold Kinman *systems executive*
Low, Donald *diplomat, financial investor*
Low, Harry William *judge*
Low, Randall *internist, cardiologist*
Lu, Francis Gordon *psychiatrist, educator*
†Lu, Ying *statistician, educator*
Lucia, Marilyn Reed *physician*
†Luft, Harold S. *health economist*
Luft, Rene Wilfred *civil engineer*
Lull, Robert John *nuclear medicine physician, educator*
Lynch, Timothy Jeremiah-Mahoney *lawyer, educator, theologian, realtor, writer*
Lyon, David William *research executive*
MacGowan, Eugenia *lawyer*
†Mack, John Oscar *lawyer*
MacNaughton, Angus Athole *finance company executive*
Madson, David John *fundraising executive*
Magie, Gregory Alden *music educator*
Magowan, Peter Alden *professional baseball team executive, grocery chain executive*
Mahoney, David L. *pharmaceutical wholesale and healthcare management company executive*
Mahoney, Michael James *investment and software executive*
Maibach, Howard I. *dermatologist*
Maier, Peter Klaus *lawyer, business executive*
Maloney, James John *network administrator*
†Man, Yvonne *maritime company executive*
Mandra, York T. *geology educator*
Mann, Bruce Alan *lawyer, investment banker*
Mann, Charles Frederick *language educator, translator, author*
Manning, Jerome Alan *retired lawyer*
†Maracek, Leigh *association administrator*
Marcus, Richard Leon *lawyer, educator*
Marcus, Robert *aluminum company executive*
†Margolin, Frederick Ronald *radiologist, educator*
†Marineau, Philip Albert *apparel executive*
Márquez-Magaña, Leticia Maria *biology educator*
Marshall, Grayson William, Jr., *biomaterials scientist, health sciences educator*
†Marshall, Raymond Charles *lawyer*
†Marshall, Scott *advertising agency executive*
Marston, Michael *urban economist, asset management executive*
Martel, John Sheldon *lawyer, writer*
Martin, Fred *artist, college administrator*
Martin, John L. *airport executive*
†Martin, Stephen James *retired lawyer*
Martin-O'Neill, Mary Evelyn *advertising, marketing, business writing, sales training consultant*
Marzke, Ronald Oscar *physics and astronomy educator*
Mason, Dean Towle *cardiologist*
Mason, Greg *publishing executive*
Massie, Barry Michael *cardiologist*
Mattern, Douglas James *foundation administrator*
Mattes, Martin Anthony *lawyer*
Matthews, Gilbert Elliott *investment banker*
†Mattimore, Patrick *social sciences educator*
McAninch, Jack Weldon *urological surgeon, educator*
McClure, Thomas Allan *physician*
McCovey, Willie Lee *former professional baseball player*
†McDevitt, Ray Edward *lawyer*
McElhinny, Harold John *lawyer*
McGettigan, Charles Carroll, Jr., *investment banker*
McGrath, Mary Helena *plastic surgeon, educator*
McGuckin, John Hugh, Jr., *lawyer*
†McGuire, William Albert *humanities educator*
McIntyre, Robert Wheeler *retired conservation organization executive*
McKean, Kevin S. *editor-in-chief, editor, writer*
Mc Kee, Allen Page *investment company executive*
†McKenzie, John F. *lawyer*
Mc Laughlin, Jerome Michael *lawyer, shipping company executive*
McNally, Thomas Charles, III, *lawyer*
McQuown, Eloise *librarian*
Merrill, Harvie Martin *manufacturing executive, director*
†Messina, Louis Michael *vascular surgeon, educator*
Metz, Mary Seawell *foundation administrator, retired academic administrator*
†Meyerson, Ivan D. *lawyer, holding company executive*
†Miles, Donald F. *lawyer*
Miller, Walter Luther *pediatrician, educator*
Miller, William Napier Cripps *lawyer*
†Millner, Dianne Maxine *lawyer*
Millstein, David J. *lawyer*
Minar, Paul G. *design consultant*
Minnick, Malcolm David *lawyer*
†Minor, Halsey *multimedia company executive*
Mitchell, Bruce Tyson *lawyer*
Moore, Scott Michael *lawyer*
Moreno, Carlos R. *state supreme court justice*
Moris, Lamberto Giuliano *architect*
Morrison, Ellen M. *writer, researcher*
Morrissey, John Carroll, Sr., *lawyer*
†Muegge, Lyn *advertising executive*
†Murphy, Arthur John, Jr., *lawyer*
†Murray, Kathleen Anne *lawyer*
†Musfelt, Duane Clark *lawyer*
Musser, Sandra G. *retired lawyer*
Mustacchi, Piero *preventive medicine physician, educator*
Naegele, Carl Joseph *university academic administrator, educator*
Navarro, J. Renee *anesthesiologist*
Nee, D. Y. Bob *think tank executive, engineering consultant*
Needleman, Jacob *philosophy educator, writer*
†Nelson, Paul Douglas *lawyer*
†Neve, Victoria J *music educator*
†Newacheck, Paul W. *education educator, researcher*
Newirth, Richard Scott *cultural organization administrator*
Nguyen, Ann Cac Khue *pharmaceutical and medicinal chemist*
Nichols, Richard Alan *ecologist*
Nichols, William J. *film studies educator*
Nicolaï, Judithe *international business executive*
Noonan, John T., Jr., *judge, law educator*
†Norris, Cynthia Ann *lawyer*
O'Connor, Sheila Anne *freelance writer*
Odgers, Richard William *lawyer*
Offer, Stuart Jay *lawyer*
Oliver, John Edward *bank strategic management and training consultant*
Olsen, Steven Kent *dentist*
Olson, Robert Howard *lawyer*
Olson, Walter Gilbert *lawyer*
†O'Neill, Brian *national recreation area administrator*
O'Neill, Michael *management educator*
Oppel, Andrew John *computer systems consultant*
O'Reilly, David J. *oil company executive*
Owsley, John Quincy, III, *plastic surgeon, educator*
Palmer, Bonita Ann *physician, healing minister, marriage and family therapist*
Palmer, Venrice Romito *lawyer, educator*
†Pan, Edward *neuro-oncologist*
Papakonstantino, Stacy *English language educator*
†Parer, Julian Thomas *obstetrics and gynecology educator*
Parker, Diana Lynne *restaurant manager, special events director*
Parker, Harold Allen *lawyer, real estate executive*
Parker, Harry S., III, *museum director*
†Parry, Robert Troutt *bank executive, economist*
Paterson, Richard Denis *financial executive*
Patula, Rodney Richard *lawyer*
†Pazour, Don *publishing executive*
Pearlman, Amalia Cecile *artist, educator*
Penn, Lee *information technology consultant, journalist*
Penskar, Mark Howard *lawyer*
Perlman, David *science editor, journalist*
†Peterlin, Boris Matija *physician*
†Peterson, Wayne Turner *composer, pianist*
Petrakis, Nicholas Louis *epidemiologist, medical researcher, educator*
Petty, George Oliver *lawyer*
Pfau, George Harold, Jr., *investment advisor*
†Phillips, Richard Myron *lawyer, educator*
Phillips, Theodore Locke *radiation oncologist, educator*
†Pipes, Sally C. *think-tank executive*
Pollack, Jeffrey Lee *restaurateur*
Poole, Edward G. *attorney*
Poole, Gordon Leicester *lawyer*
†Pope, Carl *professional society administrator*
Popofsky, Melvin Laurence *lawyer*
†Porter, Dorothy Elizabeth *history educator*
Pottruck, David Steven *brokerage house executive*
Pratt, James Norwood *scholarly writer*
Presniakov, Alexander *painter, sculptor, inventor, novelist, writer*
†Pressler, Paul S. *retail executive*
Raciti, Cherie *artist*
Raeber, John Arthur *architect, construction consultant*
Ragan, Charles Ransom *lawyer*
Ralston, Henry James, III, *neurobiologist, anatomist, educator*
Rascón, Armando *artist*
Raskin, Neil Hugh *neurology educator*
Rather, Lee *psychologist, educator*
Raven, Robert Dunbar *lawyer*
†Rea, John Martin *lawyer, state official*
Ream, James Terrill *architect, sculptor*
Reding, John Anthony *lawyer*
Redo, David Lucien *investment company executive*
Reed, Robert Daniel *publisher*
Reese, John Robert *lawyer*
Reilly, Linda M. *surgeon*
Rembe, Toni *lawyer, director*
Renfrew, Charles Byron *lawyer*
†Rice, Denis Timlin *lawyer*
Rice, Dorothy Pechman (Mrs. John Donald Rice) *medical economist*
Richards, Norman Blanchard *lawyer*
Richardson, Daniel Ralph *lawyer*
†Riggenbach, Jeff *journalist*
Riney, Hal Patrick *advertising executive*
Risser, James Vaulx, Jr., *journalist, educator*
Ristow, Brunno *plastic surgeon*
Robertson, Armand James, II, *judge*
†Robinson, Effie *social worker, educator*
Rock, Arthur *venture capitalist*
Roe, Benson Bertheau *surgeon, educator*
†Rogan, Richard A. *lawyer*
Rogoff, Alice Elizabeth *writer, editor*
Rosales, Suzanne Marie *hospital coordinator*
Rosch, John Thomas *lawyer*
†Rose, Jordan Payman *lawyer*
†Rosen, Evan Mark *executive communication advisor, journalist*
Rosen, Joshua Nathan *lawyer*
Rosen, Moishe *religious organization founder*
Rosen, Sanford Jay *lawyer*
Rosenbaum, Ernest Harold *internist, oncologist, educator*
Rosenberg, Claude Newman, Jr., *investment adviser*
†Rosenberg, Pamela *conductor*
Rosenberg, Richard Morris *banker*
†Rosenthal, Philip *gastroenterologist*
Rosinski, Edwin Francis *medical educator*
Ross, David A. *art museum director*
Rossmann, Antonio *lawyer, educator*
Roth, Charles Philip *psychotherapist*
Rowe, Mary Ann Gunder *education educator*
†Rowland, John Arthur *lawyer*
Rubenstein, Steven Paul *newspaper columnist*
Rubin, Michael *lawyer*
Rubin, Seth Isaiah *psychologist*
†Rudebusch, Glenn D. *economist*
Rudolph, Abraham Morris *pediatrician, educator*
†Rumjahn, Diana *academic administrator*
†Runnicles, Donald *conductor*
Rusher, William Allen *writer, commentator*
†Russoniello, Joseph Pascal *lawyer*
†Ryan, Dennis *information technology executive*
Saavedra, Charles James *banker*
Sachs, Marilyn Stickle *author, lecturer, editor*
St. Louis, Nena *artist, performance artist*
Salomon, Darrell Joseph *lawyer*
Sano, Emily Joy *museum director*
Sassone, Marco Massimo *artist*
Satin, Joseph *language professional, university administrator*
Saunders, Joseph W. *financial services company executive*
Savage, Mark Randall *lawyer*
Savage, Thomas Joseph *executive development company executive, priest*
Sawyer, Frank Denzil *clergyman*
Scarlett, Randall H. *lawyer*
Schechter, Joel *magazine editor, writer, educator*
Schiller, Francis *neurologist, medical historian*
Schmid, Rudi (Rudolf Schmid) *internist, educator, academic administrator*
Schmidt, Robert Milton *physician, scientist, educator, administrator*
Schneider, Kirk J. *psychologist, writer*
†Schochet, Harvey S. *lawyer*
†Schon, Steven Eliot *lawyer*
Schrock, Theodore R. *surgeon*
Schroeder, Steven Alfred *medical educator*
Schwab, Charles R. *brokerage house executive*
Schwarz, Glenn Vernon *newspaper editor*
Schwarzer, William W *federal judge*
Seabolt, Richard L. *lawyer*
Seavey, William Arthur *lawyer, vintner*
Sedway, Lynn Massel *real estate economist*
Seebach, Lydia Marie *physician*
Seegal, John Franklin *lawyer*
Seelenfreund, Alan *retired pharmaceutical company executive*
Selover, William Charlton *corporate communications and governmental affairs executive*
†Seneker, Carl James, II, (Kim Seneker) *lawyer*
Shadwick, VirginiaAnn Greer *librarian*
Shansby, John Gary *investor*
Shapiro, Gary John *lawyer*
Sharp, Stefanie Teresa *lawyer*
Shaw, Richard Eugene *cardiovascular researcher*
Shenk, George H. *lawyer*
†Sherman, Martin Peter *lawyer*
†Shiffman, Michael A. *lawyer*
Shinefield, Henry Robert *pediatrician*
Shorenstein, Walter Herbert *commercial real estate development company executive*
Shvidler, Mark Joseph *mathematician*
Sias, John B. *former multi-media company executive, newspaper publisher, publishing executive*
Simini, Joseph Peter *accountant, financial consultant, author, former educator*
Singer, Allen Morris *lawyer*
†Siniscalco, Gary Richard *lawyer*
Small, Marshall Lee *lawyer*
Smegal, Thomas Frank, Jr., *lawyer*
Smith, David Elvin *physician*
Smith, Kerry Clark *lawyer*
Smith, Lloyd Hollingsworth *physician*
Smith, Robert Charles *political science educator, researcher*
Smith, Robert Michael *lawyer, mediator, arbitrator*
Smuin, Michael *choreographer, director, dancer*
Sneed, Joseph Tyree, III, *federal judge*
Soberon, Presentacion Zablan *state bar administrator*
Soh, Chunghee Sarah *anthropology educator*
Solday, Alidra (Linda Brown) *psychotherapist, psychoanalyst, filmmaker*
†Soler, Esta *foundation administrator*
†Solomon, Daniel *architectural firm executive*
Solomon, Neal Edward *management consultant, executive recruiter, social theorist, entrepreneur, author*
Sparks, Thomas E., Jr., *lawyer*
Speidel, John Joseph *obstetrician, educator*
†Spiegel, Hart Hunter *retired lawyer*
Spivey, Bruce E. *ophthalmologist, integrated healthcare delivery systems management executive*
Sproul, John Allan *retired public utility executive*
Stamper, Robert Lewis *ophthalmologist, educator*
Staring, Graydon Shaw *lawyer*
†Steinberg, David M. *securities analyst*
Stephens, Elisa *college president*
†Sterkina, Sofiya *writer*
Stermer, Dugald Robert *designer, illustrator, writer, consultant*
Stotter, Lawrence Henry *lawyer*
Stowell, Christopher R. *choreographer, retired dancer*
Straube, Barry Maynard *physician executive*
Strock, James Martin *management consultant, educator, mediator, writer*
Stromberg, Ross Ernest *lawyer*
Stroup, Stanley Stephenson *lawyer, educator*
†Suba, Eric John *physician*
Sugarman, Myron George *lawyer*
Sullivan, Robert Edward *lawyer*
Susskind, Teresa Gabriel *publishing executive*
Sutton, John Paul *lawyer*
Talbot, Stephen Henderson *television producer, documentary filmmaker, writer*
Tang, Man-Chung *engineer, administrator*

San Luis Rey
Melbourne, Robert Ernest *civil engineer*
Williams, Elizabeth Yahn *writer, lecturer, lawyer*

San Marcos
Ball, Betty Jewel *retired social worker, consultant*
Barnes, Howard G. *communications executive, film and video producer*
Berry, Dawn Bradley *writer, lawyer, jeweler*
†Cater, Judy Jerstad *librarian*
Christman, Albert Bernard *historian*
Ciurczak, Alexis *librarian*
DeMarco, Ralph John *real estate developer*
†Dovenbarger, Barbara *accountant*
†Glasson, Frank Michael *musician (classical and jazz), music educator*
Harmon, Harry William *architect, former university administrator*
Houk, Benjamin Noah *artistic director, choreographer*
†Jones, William Henry *retired military officer*
Knight, Edward Howden *retired hospital administrator*
Lilly, Martin Stephen *university dean*
Page, Leslie Andrew *disinfectant manufacturing company executive*
Purdy, Alan Harris *biomedical engineer*
Schon, Isabel *library science specialist, educator*
Tanner, John Douglas, Jr., *history educator, writer*
†Whitney, Stan *marriage and family therapist*
Winebrenner, Susan Kay *writer, educational consultant*
Wingert, Hannelore Christiane *real estate agent, chemical company executive*
Yuan, Yuan *English educator, translator*

San Marino
Benzer, Seymour *neuroscience educator*
Blodgett, Peter John *curator*
Cranston, Howard Stephen *lawyer, management consultant*
Footman, Gordon Elliott *educational administrator*
Galbraith, James Marshall *lawyer, business executive*
Grantham, Richard Robert *financial consultant*
Hull, Suzanne White *writer, retired administrator*
Lashley, Virginia Stephenson Hughes *retired computer science educator*
Mortimer, Wendell Reed, Jr., *judge*
Rolle, Andrew *historian, writer*
Sadun, Alfredo Arrigo *neuro-ophthalmologist, scientist, educator*
Terry, Roger *pathologist, consultant*
Tomich, Lillian *lawyer*
†Travis, Albert Hartman *retired ancient language educator*
Zall, Paul Maxwell *retired English language educator, consultant*

San Mateo
†Aadahl, Jorg *business executive*
Bell, Leo S. *retired physician*
Bhatnagar, Mary Elizabeth *lawyer*
Bresler, Michael Jay *emergency physician*
†Brzozowsky, Keith William *software consultant*
Castleberry, Arline Alrick *architect*
Chabra, Anand *public health physician, epidemiologist*
Chester, Sharon Rose *photographer, natural history educator, writer, illustrator*
Douglass, Donald Robert *banker*
†Dummer, William L *lawyer, writer*
Goyan, Jere Edwin *business executive, former university dean*
Grill, Lawrence J. *lawyer, accountant, corporate/banking executive*
Haisch, Bernard Michael *astronomer, researcher*
Halperin, Robert Milton *retired electrical machinery company executive*
Helfert, Erich Anton *management consultant, writer, educator*
Holmes, John Richard *physicist, educator*
Hoops, Alan R. *health care company executive*
Hopkins, Cecilia Ann *business educator*
Hur, Stephen Ponyi *civil engineer, management consultant, educator*
Huxley, Mary Atsuko *artist*
Johnson, Charles Bartlett *mutual fund executive*
†Johnson, Rupert Harris, Jr., *finance company executive*
Jones, Louis Worth *retired management analyst, journalist*
Kane, Robert Francis *lawyer, former ambassador, consultant*
Kenney, William Fitzgerald *lawyer*
Knight, Alexa Davey *real estate company executive, real estate broker*
Leong, Carol Jean *electrologist*
Monaco, Daniel Joseph *lawyer*
†Mullin, Gene *state legislator*
Nazzaro, David Alfred *sales executive*
†Nizard, Michael *editor-in-chief*
†O'Reilly, Terence John *lawyer*
Petit, Susan Yount *French and English language educator*
Richens, Muriel Whittaker *marriage and family therapist, educator*
Sadilek, Vladimir *architect*
Slabach, Stephen Hall *lawyer*
†Tormey, James Roland, Jr., *lawyer*
Trabitz, Eugene Leonard *aerospace company executive*
Van Kirk, John Ellsworth *retired cardiologist*
Wiefels, Paul Harold *management consultant*
Wong, Otto *epidemiologist*

San Pablo
Collier, Judith Brandes *elementary education educator*

San Pedro
Bowling, Lance Christopher *record producer, publishing executive*
Chamberlain, Thomas Eugene *mechanical engineer*
Crutchfield, William Richard *artist, educator*
Daniels, Kathleen Angela *educational administrator*
Ellis, George Edwin, Jr., *chemical engineer*
Gaines, Jerry Lee *retired secondary education educator*
Hoang, Thu-Anh *diagnostic radiologist*
Kline, Frank Menefee *psychiatrist*
McCarty, Frederick Briggs *electrical engineer, consultant*
McMullen, Sharon Joy Abel *marriage and family therapist*
†Montgomery, Thom Mathew *health program administrator, counselor*
Parkhurst, Violet Kinney *artist*
Plutchak, Noel Bernard *meteorologist, consultant*
Simmons, William *physicist, retired aerospace research executive*

San Rafael
Adcock, Muriel W. *special education educator*
Amada, Gerald *psychotherapist*
Badgley, John Roy *architect*
Barker, Celeste Arlette *computer scientist*
Brett, Peter D. *writer*
†Brubeck, David Warren *musician*
Chilvers, Robert Merritt *lawyer*
Clark, Charles Sutter *interior designer*
Djordjevich, Miroslav-Michael *bank executive*
Douglas, James *construction engineering educator*
Drexler, Kenneth *lawyer*
Duke, George F. *lawyer*
†Evenhuis, Henk J. *research company exxecutive*
Fairbairn, Sydney Elise *lawyer*
Fink, Joseph Richard *academic administrator*
Finkelstein, James Arthur *management consultant*
Follett, Carolyn Brown *poet, artist*
Freitas, David Prince *lawyer*
Friesecke, Raymond Francis *health company executive*
Greene, John Clifford *dentist, former university dean*
Gryson, Joseph Anthony *orthodontist*
Hanson, Rick *psychologist*
Henry, Joseph Louis *university dean*
Henry, Marie Elaine *poet*
Howley, Peter Anthony *communications executive*
†Hoyt, Michael F. *psychologist, writer*
†Kathrein, Reed Richard *lawyer*
Keegan, Jane Ann *insurance executive, consultant*
Latno, Arthur Clement, Jr., *telephone company executive*
Lucas, George W., Jr., *film director, producer, screenwriter*
Miller, Michael David *gynecologist, obstetrician*
Nelson, James Carmer, Jr., *writer, editor, advertising executive*
Pomerantz, Martin Arthur *astronomer, educator*
Purcell, Stuart McLeod, III, *financial planner*
Roth, Hadden Wing *lawyer*
Sachs, Freeman *retired management consultant, volunteer*
Sansweet, Stephen Jay *journalist, author, marketing executive*
†Santana, Carlos *guitarist*
Saunders, Kathryn A. *retired data processing administrator*
Tosti, Donald Thomas *psychologist, consultant*
Trepp, Leo *rabbi*
Turner, William Weyand *writer*
Wilson, Ian Holroyde *management consultant, futurist*
Wright, Frederick Herman Greene, II, *computer systems engineer*

San Ramon
Freed, Kenneth Alan *lawyer*
†Hossain, Tarique M. *marketing science analyst, educator*
Jue, Susan Lynne *interior designer*
Litman, Robert Barry *physician, writer, television and radio commentator*
Malani, Narendra *physician*
Moore, Justin Edward *data processing executive*
Morrison, Cheryl Lynn *petroleum engineer, project manager*
Schlitt, William Joseph, III, *metallurgical engineer*
Schofield, James Roy *computer programmer*
Solari, Paul Gregory *physician*
Su, George Shenghui (Sheng-Hui Su) *chemist, medical researcher, educator*
Vaughn, John Rolland *auditor*
†Welch, Thomas Andrew *retired lawyer, arbitrator*
Zamani, Saeed *gastroenterologist, consultant*

San Ysidro
Ortiz, Antonio Ignacio *public relations executive*

Sand City
†Coile, Russell Cleven *electrical engineer, consultant*

Sanger
Chynoweth, W. Edward *retired lawyer, farmer*

Santa Ana
Adams, John M. *library director*
Amoroso, Frank *retired communication system engineer, consultant*
†Anderson, James E., Jr., *lawyer*
Anderson, N. Christian, III, *newspaper publisher*
†Andres, Eugen Charles *lawyer*
†Austin, Marie A. *academic administrator*
†Balzer, Robert Lawrence *journalist*
Barr, James Norman *federal judge*
Bauer, Bruce F. *former aerospace engineer*
†Beal, Dennis *academic administrator*
Boynton, William Lewis *retired electronic manufacturing company official*
Capizzi, Michael Robert *prosecutor*
Chenhalls, Anne Marie *nurse, educator*
†Correa, Lou *state official*
Daly, Tom *county official, mayor*
Danoff-Kraus, Pamela Sue *real estate developer*
Dean, William Evans *aerospace industry executive*
Dillard, John Martin *lawyer, pilot*
Fay-Schmidt, Patricia Ann *paralegal*
Ferguson, Warren John *judge*
Foster, Kent B. *information technology executive*
Freeman, James Michael *musician, vocalist*
†Gudea, Darlene *publishing company executive*
Haldeman, Scott *neurology educator*
Harley, Robison Dooling, Jr., *lawyer, educator*
†Hukel, Dennis Randall *industrial designer, translator*
Ingalsbe, William James *lawyer*
Kato, Terri Emi *elementary school and gifted and talented educator*
Katz, Tonnie *newspaper editor*
Kelly, James Patrick, Jr., *retired engineering and construction executive*
Kinosian, Janet Marie *journalist*
†Kropp, William Rudolph *physicist*
†Lehrer, John *editor*
LeMaster, Susan M. *marketing executive, writer*
Madden, Thomas A. *automotive parts manufacturing executive*
†Mei, Tom Y. K. *lawyer*
Murai, Kevin *electronics company executive*
Myers, Marilyn Gladys *pediatric hematologist and oncologist*
Oberstein, Marydale *geriatric specialist*
Patt, Herbert Jacob *lawyer*
Phanstiel, Howard G. *health care system executive*
Pulido, Miguel Angel *mayor*
†Schmitz, Stephen E. *mental health specialist, writer*
Sethi, Sandeep *environmental engineer*
Storer, Maryruth *law librarian*
Stotler, Alicemarie Huber *judge*
Sudbeck, Robert Francis *music educator, philosophy educator*
Tanaka, Richard I. *computer products company executive*
Toledano, James *lawyer*
Waaland, Irving Theodore *retired aerospace design executive*
Washburn, Lawrence Robert *manufacturing executive*
Watts, Judith-Ann White *secondary school educator*
Whelan, Veronica *family practice physician, geriatrician*
Yuen, Andy Tak Sing *electronics executive*
Zepeda, Susan Ghozeil *foundation executive*

Santa Barbara
Ackerman, Marshall *publishing company executive*
Adizes, Ichak *management consultant, writer*
Adler, William F. *technology business development consultant*
Ahlers, Guenter *physicist, educator*
Ah-Tye, Kirk Thomas *lawyer*
Aigner, Dennis John *economics educator, consultant*
†Albanese, Catherine *religious studies educator*
Aldisert, Ruggero John *judge*
Allaway, William Harris *retired university official*
†Altschuler, Allan Bruce *society administrator*
Anderson, Donald Meredith *bank executive*
Austin, Joyce Caroline *cake decorator, artist*
Avalle-Arce, Juan Bautista *Spanish language educator*
Aylesworth, Owen Roy *firefighter*
Badash, Lawrence *science history educator*
†Baker, Gordon Edward *political science educator*
Barber, Jerry Randel *medical device company executive*
†Barry, Robert Michael *education educator*
Bartlett, James Lowell, III, *investment company executive*
Bauer, Marvin Agather *lawyer*
†Bermúdez, Silvia *literature educator*
Bischel, Margaret DeMeritt *physician, managed care consultant*
Blasingame, Benjamin Paul *electronics company executive*
Bock, Russell Samuel *writer*
Boehm, Eric Hartzell *information management executive*
Bohn, Henning *economist, educator*
Boyan, Norman J. *retired education educator*
†Brant, Henry *composer*
Brantingham, Barney *journalist, writer*
Breitweiser, Gary Charles *art dealer, appraiser*
Brilliant, Ashleigh Ellwood *writer, cartoonist, publisher, educator*
Brodhead, James E(aston) *actor, writer*
Brown, J'Amy Maroney *journalist, media relations consultant, investor*
Brownlee, Wilson Elliot, Jr., *history educator*
Bruch, John Clarence, Jr., *engineer, educator*
Burgee, John Henry *architect*
Campbell, Robert Charles *minister, theology educator*
Campbell, William Steen *publishing executive, writer, speaker*
Cavat, Irma *artist, educator*
Chafe, Wallace LeSeur *linguist, educator*
Christman, Arthur Castner, Jr., *scientific advisor*
Cirone, William Joseph *educational administrator*
Coffin, Dwight Clay *retired grain company executive*
Cohen, Peter Gray *artist*
Coldren, Larry Allen *engineering educator, consultant*
Collins, Robert Oakley *history educator*
Comanor, William S. *economist, educator*
Conklin, Hal (Harold Conklin) *public affairs director*
Conley, Philip James, Jr., *retired air force officer*
Cooper, Saul *film and TV producer, public relations executive*
Corbani, Candace Bedford *antiques broker, political campaign consultant*
†Cortijo, Antonio *education educator*
Crawford, Donald Wesley *philosophy educator, university official*
Crowell, John C(hambers) *geology educator, researcher*
†Culler, Glen *retired electrical engineer, electrical engineer, educator*
Cunningham, Julia Woolfolk *author*
Davidson, Roger H(arry) *political scientist, educator*
Del Chiaro, Mario Aldo *art historian, archeologist, etruscologist, educator*
†Dickey, Denise Ann *lawyer, arbitrator*
Dubroff, Henry Allen *newspaper editor, publisher*
Dunne, Thomas *geology educator*
Edebo, Ralph Bertil *engineer, economist*
Egenolf, Robert F. *lawyer*
Eguchi, Yasu *artist*
Elliott, Warren G. *lawyer*
Ellis, Eugene Joseph *cardiologist*
Emmeluth, Bruce Palmer *investment company executive, venture capitalist*
Enelow, Allen Jay *psychiatrist, educator*
Erasmus, Charles John *anthropologist, educator*
Evans, Thomas Edgar, Jr., *title insurance agency executive*
†Fetter, Trevor *healthcare industry executive*
Fingarette, Herbert *philosopher, educator*
Fisher, Steven Kay *neurobiology educator*
Focht, Michael Harrison *health care industry executive*
Ford, Anabel *research anthropologist, archaeologist*
Formby, Bent Clark *immunologist*
Freidell, Hugh Vernon *internist, nephrologist*
†Friedland, Roger *religious studies educator, writer*
Gibney, Frank Bray *publisher, editor, writer, foundation executive*
†Gibor, Aharon *biologist, educator*
Gilbert, Paul Thomas *chemical development engineer*
Gillquist, Peter Edward *church organization executive*
Gold, Calla Giselle *jewelry designer*
†Goldsmith, Melissa Ursula Dawn *musicologist*
Gordon, Helen Heightsman *English language educator, writer, publisher*
Gossard, Arthur Charles *physicist, researcher*
Gravitz, Herbert L. *clinical psychologist, writer*
Gunn, Giles Buckingham *language educator, religious studies educator, global and international studies educator*
Gutierrez-Jones, Carl Scott *English educator*
Hanley, Kevin Lance *maintenance manager*
†Hayward, Jean *artist, musician, interior designer, performance artist*
Heeger, Alan Jay *physicist, educator*
Helgerson, Richard *English literature educator*
Higgins, Isabelle Jeanette *librarian*
Hong, Sehee *education and psychology educator*
†Howell, Weldon U., Jr., *lawyer*
Howorth, David *producer, director*
Hsu, Immanuel Chung Yueh *history educator*
Hubbard, Arthur Thornton *chemistry educator, electro-surface chemist*
Iselin, Donald Grote *civil engineering and management consultant*
Israel, Barry John *lawyer*
Jackson, Beverley Joy Jacobson *columnist, lecturer*
Jochim, Michael Allan *archaeologist*
Johnsen, Eugene Carlyle *mathematician and educator*
Karpeles, David *museum director*
Kelliher, Richard James *psychologist*
Kelm, Bonnie G. *art museum director, educator*
Kendler, Howard H(arvard) *psychologist, educator*
Kennedy, John Harvey *chemistry educator*
Klakeg, Clayton Harold *cardiologist*
Kohn, Roger Alan *surgeon*
Kohn, Walter *educator, physicist*
Kokotovic, Petar V. *electrical and computer engineer, educator*
Kramer, Edward John *materials science and engineering educator*
Kroemer, Herbert *electrical engineering educator*
Kruger, Kenneth Charles *architect*
Kryter, Karl David *retired research scientist*
Kuczynski, John-Michael Maxime *humanities educator, writer*
Langer, James Stephen *physicist, educator*
Larsgaard, Mary Lynette *librarian, writer*
Latimer, Ronald Gordon *surgeon*
Lawrance, Charles Holway *retired civil and sanitary engineer*
Lee, Glen K. *dentist*
†Leedham, Clive Douglas *retired electrical engineer*
Leone, Frank Harrison *health care educator, consultant*
†Lewandowski, Leon Scott *elementary school educator*
Lifshitz, Fima *pediatrician, endocrinologist*
Lindemann, Albert S. *history educator*
Luyendyk, Bruce Peter *geophysicist, educator, institution administrator*
Macdonald, Ken Craig *geophysicist*
Mack, Judith Cole Schrim *political scientist, educator*
Mahoney, Tim J. *utility company executive*
Marcus, Marvin *mathematician, educator*
Martzen, Philip D. *physicist, software developer*
Mathews, Barbara Edith *gynecologist*
Mayer, Richard Edwin *psychology educator*
†McCollum, Susan Hill *lawyer*
McCoy, Lois Clark *emergency services professional, retired county official, magazine editor*
Mc Duffie, Malcolm *oil company executive*

McEwen, Willard Winfield, Jr., *lawyer, judge*
McGee, James Sears *historian, educator*
McKee, Kathryn Dian Grant *human resources consultant*
Meinel, Aden Baker *optics scientist*
Metzinger, Timothy Edward *lawyer*
Minc, Henryk *mathematics educator*
Mitchell, Shawne Maureen *author*
Mitra, Sanjit Kumar *electrical and computer engineering educator*
Newman, Morris *mathematician, educator*
O'Dowd, Donald Davy *retired university president*
†O'Jack, Justin *religious studies educator, researcher*
Parhami, Behrooz *engineering educator, consultant*
Perloff, Jean Marcosson *lawyer*
Pilgeram, Laurence Oscar *biochemist*
Pochini, Judy Hay *interior designer, writer, editor*
†Pointer, Richard Wayne *history educator*
Polívka, Jiří *physicist*
Potter, David Samuel *former automotive company executive*
Poynter, Dan *author, publisher, speaker*
Prindle, William Roscoe *retired glass company executive*
Pritchard, Sarah Margaret *library director*
Ramsay, William Charles *writer, composer*
Reed, Frank Fremont, II, *retired lawyer*
Reid, Robert Alfred *physician*
Renehan, Robert Francis Xavier *Greek and Latin educator*
Roads, Curtis *music educator, composer*
Roberts, Jerry *newspaper editor*
Robinson, William I. *sociologist, journalist*
Rockwell, Don Arthur *retired psychiatrist*
Rose, Mark Allen *humanities educator, educator*
Russell, Charles Roberts *chemical engineer*
Russell, Jeffrey Burton *historian, educator*
Scheff, Thomas Joel *sociologist, educator*
Scheinfeld, James David *travel agency executive*
Schneider, Edward Lee *botanic garden administrator*
Schultz, Arthur Warren *communications company executive*
Sebastian, Suzie *producer*
Sengupta, Jati Kumar *economics educator*
Sensiper, Samuel *electrical engineer*
Shackman, Daniel Robert *psychiatrist*
†Sharrer, Harvey L. *language educator*
Sherman, Alan Robert *psychologist, educator*
Shreeve, Susanna Seelye *educational planning facilitator*
Simons, Stephen *mathematics educator, researcher*
Sinsheimer, Robert Louis *retired university chancellor and educator*
Sipprelle, Dudley Gene *investor*
Slater, Paul Bernard *physicist*
Steckel, Richard J. *radiologist, academic administrator*
Steigerwald, Douglas Gardiner *economics educator*
Stirling, Clark Tillman *lawyer*
Sulzbach, Christi Rocovich *lawyer*
Swalley, Robert Farrell *retired structural engineer, consultant*
Theofanous, Theo G. *engineering educator, consultant*
Thomas, Bertram David *retired chemical engineer*
Tilton, David Lloyd *savings and loan association executive*
Tilton, George Robert *geochemistry educator*
†Tobin, Ronald William *French language educator*
Torbert, Meg Birch *artist, design and color consultant*
†Tu, Kuo-ch'ing *literature educator*
Tucker, Shirley Lois Cotter *botany educator, researcher*
Veigele, William John *physicist*
Wade, Glen *electrical engineer, educator*
Walker, Sally C. *fundraising consultant*
White, Robert Stephen *physics educator*
Wilkins, Burleigh Taylor *philosophy educator*
Wilson, Leslie *biochemist, cell biologist, biology educator*
Yang, Henry T. *academic administrator, educator*
Yankwich, Peter Ewald *chemistry educator*

Santa Clara
Aitken, Robert Campbell *engineer*
Alexander, George Jonathon *law educator, former dean*
Barrett, Craig R. *computer company executive*
Benhamou, Eric A. *computer company executive*
Blawie, James Louis *law educator*
Chakravarty, Sreejit *computer engineer, researcher*
Chan, Shu-Park *electrical engineering educator*
†Chastain, Brandi Denise *professional soccer player*
Chen, Deanford Frederick *software engineer*
Chen, Wai-Kai *electrical engineering and computer science educator, consultant*
†Chessman, Rebecca Lee *librarian*
DeBartolo-York, Denise *sports team executive*
†Dunlap, F. Thomas, Jr., *lawyer, electronics company executive*
Elkus, Richard J., Jr., *electronics company executive*
†Erickson, Dennis *professional football coach*
†Farris, Frank A. *mathematician, educator, editor*
Field, Alexander James *economics educator*
Garcia, Jeff *football player*
Gozani, Tsahi *nuclear physicist*
†Grove, Andrew S. *electronics company executive*
Hall, William Spencer *software engineer*
Halla, Brian L. *electronics company executive*
Halmos, Paul Richard *mathematician, educator*
Hearst, Garrison (Gerald Garrison Hearst) *professional football player*
Hoagland, Albert Smiley *electrical engineer, researcher*
†Hood, Mary Dullea *law librarian*
Hopkinson, Shirley Lois *library and information science educator*
Janis, Michael Jon *molecular biologist, entrepreneur*
Jo, Hoje *finance educator*
†Kamal, Abu Hena M. *electrical engineer, researcher*
Kaneda, David Ken *electrical engineering company executive*
Kelley, Robert Suma *network engineer*
Klosinski, Leonard Frank *mathematics educator*
Kwong, Donald *contracts administrator, consultant*
Lane, Holly Diana *artist*
Lau, John Hon Shing *electronics scientist*
Lawrence, Deborah Jean *quality assurance professional*
Le, Son Minh *philosophy educator*
Lee, Chan-Yun *physicist, process engineer, educator*
Ling, Nam *educator*
†Liu, Kevin *structural engineer*
Locatelli, Paul Leo *academic administrator*
Ludgus, Nancy Lucke *lawyer*
McNealy, Scott G. *computer company executive*
McNown, Cade *professional football player*
Meier, Matthias S(ebastian) *historian*
Miller, Guy M. *critical care physician and anesthesiologist*
Morgan, James C. *computer equipment company executive*
Mori, Maryellen Toman *language educator, translator, literature educator*
Nevins, Bryan Dexter *integrated circuit design engineer*
Nguyen, Luu Thanh *engineering executive*
†Ostwald, Venice Eloise Varner *librarian, educator, minister, writer*
Owens, Terrell *football player*
†Papadopoulos, Gregory Michael *computer company executive*
Parden, Robert James *engineering educator, management consultant*
†Pease, Robert Allen *electrical engineer*
Plante, Thomas Gerard *psychologist*
Reavis, Liza Anne *semiconductor executive*
†Ross, Peter *mathematician, educator*
Rudolph, Ronald Alvin *human resources specialist*
Simmons, Janet Bryant *writer, publisher*
Singh, Loren Chan *technical writing specialist*
†Smith, Ronald S. *online retail executive*
Smith, Stephen Allen *mathematician, educator*
†Splinter, Michael R. *corporate financial executive*
Tang, Xianmin *physicist, researcher*
†Tollini, Frederick Paul *priest, theater educator*
†Vakanas, George P. *process engineer, research scientist, consultant, entrepreneur*
Vincent, David Ridgely *management consulting executive*
Vu, Quat Thuong *electrical engineer*
Weinberg, William Henry *chemical engineer, chemical physicist, educator*
Weller, Douglas LaFontaine *patent lawyer*
†White, Fred Daniel *literature educator, writer*
Yan, Pei-Yang *electrical engineer*
Zecevic, Aleksandar I. *engineering educator*

Santa Clarita
†Boyer, Carl, III, *non-profit organization executive, former mayor, city official, secondary education educator*
Garcia, Andrew B. *chemical engineer*
Grishman, Lee Howard *college program administrator*
Lavine, Steven David *academic administrator*
†Mumford, Lawrence R. *composer, educator*
Ungar, Roselva May *primary and elementary educator*
Zuk, Carmen Veiga *psychiatrist*

Santa Cruz
Aschbacher, James Carl *artist, consultant*
Beecher, Jonathan French *history educator*
Beevers, Harry *biologist, educator*
Bridgeman, Bruce *psychobiology educator*
Brown, George Stephen *physics educator*
Bunnett, Joseph Frederick *chemist, educator*
Chinn, Menzie David *economics educator*
†Costello, Donald Fredric *lawyer*
Crosby, Faye Jacqueline *psychology educator, author*
Crow, Ben *sociologist, educator*
Dilbeck, Charles Stevens, Jr., *real estate company executive*
Epps, Harland Warren *astronomy educator, optical design consultant*
Faber, Sandra Moore *astronomer, educator*
Fan, Guangwei *seismologist*
Flatté, Stanley Martin *physicist, educator*
Goldbeck, Robert Arthur, Jr., *physical chemist*
Griggs, Gary Bruce *science administrator, oceanographer, geologist, educator*
Hersley, Dennis Charles *environmentalist, software systems consultant*
Hill, Terrell Leslie *chemist, biophysicist*
Houston, James D. *writer*
Huskey, Harry Douglas *information and computer science educator*
Jackson, Kingsbury Temple *educational contract consultant*
†Jansen, Virginia *art historian, educator*
Kang, Sung-Mo (Steve Kang) *electrical engineering educator*
Langenheim, Jean Harmon *biology educator*
Lay, Thorne *geosciences educator*
Leites, Barbara L. (Ara Leites) *artist, educator*
†Lenox, Catherine Corneau *volunteer*
Levinson, Robert Arlen *computer science educator, consultant*
Lieberman, Fredric *ethnomusicologist, educator, composer*
†Lindquist, Claude S. *technical consultant and executive, educator, researcher*
†Magid, Gail Avrum *neurosurgeon, neurosurgery educator*
†Males, Michael Arnold *sociologist, educator, writer, consultant*
†Mantey, Patrick Edward *engineering educator, consultant*
Martinez, Alma R. *actor, director, educator*
McLean, Hulda Hoover *volunteer, conservationist, naturalist, artist*
Miller, Ethan *computer science educator*
Mirk, Judy Ann *retired elementary educator*
Osterbrock, Donald E(dward) *astronomy educator*
Pettigrew, Thomas Fraser *social psychologist, educator*
†Pletsch, Marie Eleanor *plastic surgeon*
Podesta, Robert Edward *artist*
†Ritscher, Lee A *literature educator*
Roby, Pamela Ann *sociology educator*
Sands, Matthew Linzee *physicist, educator*
Schalk, Robert Partridge *lawyer*
Seligmann, William Robert *lawyer, author*
Sherman, Frieda Frances *writer*
Shorenstein, Rosalind Greenberg *internist*
†Smith, Darin Scott *marriage and family therapist*
Smith, M(ahlon) Brewster *psychologist, educator*
Stevens, Stanley David *historian, researcher, retired librarian, archivist*
Suckiel, Ellen Kappy *philosophy educator*
Summers, Carol *artist*
†Terdiman, Richard *literature educator*
Tharp, Roland George *psychology, education educator*
Wasson, Eleanor Walsh *volunteer*
Wiberg, Donald Martin *electrical engineering educator, consultant*
Williams, Quentin Christopher *geophysicist, educator*
Winston, George *solo pianist, guitarist, harmonica player*
Wipke, W. Todd *chemistry educator*
Wu, Ru-Shan *geophysicist*
Young, Gary Eugene *editor, poet*

Santa Fe Springs
Hammond, Judy McLain *business services executive*
Hanzel, Mimi S. *psychotherapist*
†Lovatt, Arthur Kingsbury, Jr., *manufacturing company executive*

Santa Maria
†Bowker, Margaret Sheard *artist*
Ellis, Emory Leon *former biochemist*
Everhart, Leon Eugene *retired career officer*
Frith, Anna Barbara *artist*
Kelly, Quentin Patrick *lawyer*
Moss, Elizabeth Lucille (Betty Moss) *transportation company executive*
Phillips, Dorothy Lowe *nursing educator*
Roadarmel, Stanley Bruce *civilian military employee*
†Walton, Maurine Isabel *social worker*

Santa Monica
Aaron, David L. *diplomat, author*
Abarbanel, Gail *social service administrator, educator*
Aghabegian, Diana E. Bortnowsky *English language educator, publisher*
Alpern, Harvey L. *cardiologist*
Angel, Steven *musician*
Angier, Joseph *television producer, writer*
Augenstein, Bruno W. *research scientist, researcher*
Baer, Walter S. *research executive*
†Block, Bill *film company executive*
Bohn, Paul Bradley *psychiatrist, psychoanalyst*
Boltz, Gerald Edmund *lawyer*
Bower, Allan Maxwell *lawyer*
Brenner, Richard James *physician*
Brook, Robert Henry *health services researcher, physician, educator*
Brosman, Stanley Allen *urologist*
Bruckheimer, Jerry *producer*
†Burrell, Orville Richard (Shaggy) *popular musician*
Bush, William Glenn *manufacturing company executive, engineer*
†Cameron, James *film director, screenwriter, producer*
†Carlson, Jeffery John *lawyer*
Chartoff, Robert Irwin *film producer*
Chow, Brian Gee-Yin *policy analyst, researcher*
Cooper, Jay Leslie *lawyer*
Costello, Edward J., Jr., *arbitrator, mediator, lawyer*
Cretin, Shan *activist*
Crichton, Michael (John Crichton) *author, film director*
†Custer, Barbara Ann *lawyer*
Dargan, John Henry *business executive*
†Deffry, Frank M. *retired marriage and family therapist*
Dreyfus, Edward A. *psychologist*
Eizenberg, Julie *architect*
Falender-Zohn, Carol Ann *psychologist*
Fenimore, George Wiley *management consultant*
Fine, Marjorie Blank *surgeon*
Fisher, Frances *actress*
Foley, Jane Deborah *foundation administrator*
Gabriel, Jeanette Hanisee *curator, art historian*
Gehry, Frank Owen *architect*
Genego, William Joseph *lawyer*
†Greene, C. Michael *art association administrator*
Griffith, Arnold Koons *computer consultant*
Gritton, Eugene Charles *nuclear engineer, director*
Halperin, Stuart *entertainment company executive*
Haroon, Nasreen *artist*
Hinerfeld, Robert Elliot *lawyer*
Hirsch, Richard Gary *lawyer*
Hofer, Stephen Robert *lawyer*
Honour, Lynda Charmaine *research scientist, educator, psychotherapist*
Hosie, Stanley William *foundation executive*
†Hsueh, Eddy C. *surgeon, oncologist*
Intriligator, Devrie Shapiro *physicist*
Israel, David *journalist, screenwriter, producer*
Jones, Janet Dulin *writer, film producer*
†Jones, William Allen *lawyer, entertainment company executive*
†Kaminski, Janusz *cinematographer*
†Kaplowitz, Karen (Jill) *lawyer, business consultant*
Kawamoto, Henry K. *plastic surgeon*
Kayton, Myron *engineering company executive*
Kessler, Robert Allen *data processing executive*
†Kinney, James Howard *lawyer*
Kirkland, John C. *lawyer*
Klowden, Michael Louis *think-tank executive*
Koning, Hendrik *architect*
†Kranzdorf, Jeffrey Paul *lawyer, recording company executive, television producer*
Kronenberg, S. Allyx *poet, writer, lyricist*
†LaBelle, Patti (Patricia Louise Holt) *singer*
Leaf, Paul *producer, director, writer*
Lempert, Philip *advertising executive, author, television correspondent, columnist*
†Levin, Marvin Eugene *lawyer*
†Lewis, Leslie Joy *music company executive, artist*
Lieber, Daniel Joel *oncologist*
Lincoln, Thomas L. *pathologist, educator*
†Littlefield, Warren *television executive*
†Lockhart, Sharon *artist, photographer*
†Lohner, Henning *composer, filmmaker*
Loo, Thomas S. *lawyer*
Magnabosco-Bower, Jennifer Lynn *mental health professional*
†Malin, Amir *film company executive*
†Mancuso, Frank G. *entertainment and communications company executive*
†Marin, Mindy *casting agent, entrepreneur, film producer, writer*
†Markoff, Steven C. *finance company executive*
†McGuire, Michael Francis *plastic and reconstructive surgeon*
McGuire, Michael John *environmental engineer*
†McGurk, Christopher *film company executive*
McMillan, M. Sean *lawyer*
†McNally, Susan Fowler *lawyer*
Monosson, Ira Howard *physician*
Mora, Philippe *screenwriter, producer, director, painter*
Morgan, Kermit Johnson *lawyer*
Morgan, Monroe *retired savings and loan executive*
Muller, Edward Robert *lawyer*
Palmatier, Malcolm Arthur *editor, consultant*
Park, Edward Cahill, Jr., *retired physicist*
Patel, Chandra Kumar Naranbhai *communications company executive, educator, researcher, entrepreneur*
Pieton, Richard *anesthesiologist*
Pizzulli, Francis Cosmo Joseph *lawyer, bioethicist*
†Postaer, Larry *advertising executive*
Preble, Laurence George *lawyer*
Rand, Robert Wheeler *neurosurgeon, educator*
Redford, Robert (Charles Robert Redford) *actor, director*
Reichmann, Susan Helene *psychotherapist*
Renetzky, Alvin *publisher*
†Resnick, Jeffrey I. *plastic surgeon*
Rhodes, Carl Anthony *engineer*
Rice, Donald Blessing R. *business executive, former secretary of air force*
Rich, Michael David *research corporation executive, lawyer*
†Rifkin, Arnold *film company executive*
Ringler, Jerome Lawrence *lawyer*
Risman, Michael *lawyer, business executive, securities company executive, real estate developer*
Roberts, Tony (David Anthony Roberts) *actor*
†Roberts, Virgil Patrick *lawyer, business executive*
Rodrigues, William Patrick, Jr., *city planner*
†Roney, Alice Lorraine Mann *poet*
Roney, Robert Kenneth *retired aerospace company executive*
Rose, Michael Leonard *film, television and video producer*
†Rubin, Gerrold Robert *advertising executive*
Rush, Herman E. *television executive*
Russell, Marlou *psychologist*
Ryan, Jane Frances *corporate communications executive*
Safa, Afshin Akhavan *oncologist, researcher*
†Schlei, Norbert Anthony *lawyer*
Schultz, Victor M. *physician*
Sherman, Zachary *civil and aerospace engineer, consultant*
†Shim, Elisabeth K. *dermatologist*
Shipbaugh, Calvin LeRoy *physicist*
Silbergeld, Carol A. *clinical social worker, psychotherapist*
Simon, Diane Meyer *environmental services administrator, consultant*
Singer, Frederick Raphael *medical researcher, educator*
Smith, James Patrick *economist*
†Spataro, Janie Dempsey Watts *writer*
†Stone, Arnold Joseph *lawyer*
Suschitzky, Peter *cinematographer*
Sussman, Peter Alan *entertainment company executive*
Tennant, John Randall *management advisory company executive*
Thirtle, Michael Robert *community activist, consultant*
Thompson, Dennis Peters *plastic surgeon*
Thomson, James Alan *research company executive*
Timmer, Barbara *state agency administrator*
†Tinturin, Peter *composer*
†Torres, Cynthia Ann *banker*
Toussaint, Christopher Andre *video producer, director, editor, writer*
Unterman, Thomas *venture capitalist, lawyer*
Vega, Benjamin Urbizo *retired judge, television producer*

Veit, Clairice Gene Tipton *measurement psychologist*
Ware, Willis Howard *computer scientist*
†Watson, Doc (Arthel Lane Watson) *vocalist, guitarist, banjoist, recording artist*
Weintraub, Bernard Stephen *chest physician*
Wexler, Haskell *film producer, cameraman*
†Whalley, Tom *recording industry executive*
Wilfert, Catherine M. *medical association administrator, medical educator*
Williams, Kenneth Scott *entertainment company executive*
Wolf, Charles, Jr., *economist, educator*
Wosk, Miriam *artist*
†Yemenidjian, Alex *film company executive*
York, Michael (Michael York-Johnson) *actor*
Zimmerman, Bill *political consultant*

Santa Paula
Edwards, Samuel Roger *internist*
Kay, Hazel T. *local commissioner*
Leeds-Horwitz, Susan Beth *director*

Santa Rosa
Adams, Delphine Szyndrowski *lawyer*
Aman, Reinhold Albert *philologist, publisher*
Andriano-Moore, Richard Count *retired military officer, secondary school educator, elementary school educator*
Biderman, Charles Israel *diversified financial services company executive*
Bowen, James Thomas *career officer*
Bozdech, Marek Jiri *physician, educator*
Brashear, Charles Ross *English educator, retired, writer*
Brigham, John Allen, Jr., *financial executive, environmentalist, polition*
Bruner-Welch, Ann S. *physician assistant*
Callum, Myles *magazine editor, writer*
Cavanagh, John Charles *advertising agency executive*
†Chesbro, Wesley *state senator*
Cheung, Judy Hardin *retired special education educator*
Clement, Clayton Emerson *lawyer*
Cohn, Joseph David *surgeon*
Conway, Lois Lorraine *piano teacher*
Cornett, Donna J. *counselor, alcohol moderation administrator*
Courteau, Girard Robert *retired prosecutor*
Daniel, Gary Wayne *motivation and behavior consultant*
Elam, John Richard *mortgage company executive*
Feissel, Gustave *former international organization official*
Foster, Lucille Caster *school system administrator, retired*
†Gack, Kenneth David *lawyer*
Gilger, Paul Douglass *architect*
Grundy, Richard David *engineer*
Howard, Victor *management consultant*
King, Gwendolyn Bair *former government staff member, public speaker*
King, Ruth Marie *artist, educator*
Leong, Stephanie Mei *financial planner*
Leuty, Gerald Johnston *osteopathic physician and surgeon*
Lewis, Alvin Edward *pathology educator*
†Mann, Jennifer E. *education development coordinator*
Monk, Diana Charla *artist, stable owner*
†Morris, Jack G. *architecture educator, writer*
Neuberg, Joel Gary *librarian*
Nickens, Catherine Arlene *retired nurse, freelance writer*
O'Connor, Paul Daniel *lawyer*
Pearson, Roger Lee *library director*
Person, Evert Bertil *newspaper and radio executive*
Provost, Rhonda Marie *nurse anesthetist*
Rabinowitsh, Steve *urban planner educator, city council member*
Root, Charles Joseph, Jr., *finance executive, consultant*
Schafer, John Francis *retired plant pathologist*
Schudel, Hansjoerg *international business consultant*
Smith, Betty L. *results coach, seminar leader*
Smith, Thomas Kent *retired radiologist, viticulturist*
Swofford, Robert Lee *newspaper editor, journalist*
Thistlethwaite, Aline McQuiston *artist*
Walsh, Daniel Francis *bishop*
Webb, Charles Richard *retired university president*
Yatsenko, Nikolai Afanasyevich *physics researcher, educator*

Santa Ynez
†Jensen, Regina Brunhild *psychotherapist*
Krug, Fred Roy *film and television director and producer*
O'Grady, Barbara Vinson *community health nurse, administrator, retired*
Palola, Harry Joel *international affairs executive, consultant*
Rymer, Ilona Suto *artist, retired art educator*
Walker, Burton Leith *psychotherapist, engineering writer*

Santee
Bourgeois, James Honoré *landscape company executive*
Kropotoff, George Alex *civil engineer*
Morris, Henry Madison, Jr., *education educator*
Morris, Henry Madison, III, *minister, speaker, writer, consultant*
Morris, John David *research institute administrator, geology educator*
Peters, Raymond Eugene *computer systems company executive*
Schenk, Susan Kirkpatrick *nurse educator, consultant, business owner*
Yang, Hsin-Ming *immunologist*

Saratoga
Baratta-Lorton, Robert *economics educator*
Brown, Paul Fremont *aerospace engineer, educator*
Chisholm, Margaret Elizabeth *retired library education administrator*
†deBarling, Ana Maria *language educator*
Greenleaf, John Edward *research physiologist*
Houston, Elizabeth Reece Manasco *correctional education consultant*
Houston, Joseph Brantley, Jr., *optical instrument company executive*
Johnson, Noel Lars *biomedical engineer*
Levy, Ruth J. *clinical psychologist, consultant*
Lynch, Milton Terrence *retired advertising agency executive*
Ogle, David William *art educator, sculptor, ceramist, printmaker*
Park, Joseph Chul Hui *computer scientist*
Reagan, Joseph Bernard *retired aerospace executive, management consultant*
†Rollo, F. David *hospital management company executive, health care educator*
Syvertson, Clarence Alfred *engineering and research management consultant*
Thelin, Peter Carl *economist, educator*

Sausalito
Apatoff, Michael John
Berkman, William Roger *lawyer, army reserve officer*
Casals, Rosemary *retired professional tennis player*
†Gordon, Robert Eugene *lawyer*
Groah, Linda Kay *nursing administrator, educator*
Hansen, Charles Morton *editor, retired military officer*
Klingensmith, Arthur Paul *industrial and organizational psychologist, consultant*
Ornish, Dean *medical educator, administrator*
Pryor, Lois Marie *management consultant*
Seymour, Richard Burt *health educator*

Scotia
Hise, Mark Allen *dentist*

Scotts Valley
Crandell, K(enneth) James *management and strategic planning consultant, entrepreneur*
Janssen, James Robert *consulting software engineer*
Luczo, Stephen J. *computer equipment company executive*
McClymonds, Jean Ellen *marketing professional*
Nitz, Frederic William *electronics company executive*

Seal Beach
Caesar, Vance Roy *newspaper executive*
Gaspar, Max R. *surgeon*
Harkey, Verna Rae *piano, educator*
†Hennen, Thomas Waldo *lawyer*
Mirick, Robert Allen *military officer*
Olechno-Huszcza, Czeslaw *retired translator and educator*
†Robinson, Michael R. *aeronautical engineer*
Rossi, Mario Alexander *architect*
Weitzman, Marc Herschel *lawyer*

Seaside
Gales, Samuel Joel *retired civilian military employee, counselor*
†May, James Harvey *communications educator*
†Mendoza, Ruben G. *anthropologist, educator, archaeologist*
†Paget, Ruth Lois *academic administrator, educator, writer*
Panetta, Leon Edward *federal official, former congressman*
Weingarten, Saul Myer *lawyer*

Sebastopol
Arnold, Marsha Diane *writer*
†Boatright, Ann Long *dancer, pianist, music educator, choreographer*
Dorr, Daniel Alan *personal and professional development facilitator*
Hillberg, Marylou Elin *lawyer*
†Marler, Joan *writer, educator*
Martin, Hugh *asset manager, securities dealer, natural medicine researcher/developer*
McCarthy, Thomas Edward *retired telecommunications executive*
Norman, Arnold McCallum, Jr., *engineer*
Sabsay, David *library consultant*
Yaswen, Gordon *artist, writer*

Selma
†Janian, Paulette *lawyer*
Rezac, Debra Dowell *bilingual educator*

Sepulveda
Burton, Paul Floyd *social worker*
†Fujikawa, Denson Gen *neurologist, researcher*
†Yano, Elizabeth Martin *epidemiologist, researcher*

Shasta Lake
Parsons, Debra Lea *elementary school educator*

Sherman Oaks
†Bergman, Alan *lyricist, writer*
Caren, Robert Poston *aerospace company executive*
Clark, Susan (Nora Goulding) *actress*
Crump, Gerald Franklin *retired lawyer*
Ellison, Harlan Jay *author, screenwriter*
Feldman, Phillip *lawyer*
Foldes, Lawrence David *film producer, director, writer*
Gibbs, Antony (Tony Gibbs) *film editor*
†Goldenthal, Elliot *composer*
Gross, Sharon Ruth *forensic psychologist, researcher*
Heffner, Daniel Jason *film producer*
Hein, Todd Jonathan *accountant*
Hershman, Jerome Marshall *endocrinologist*
Holden, William Willard *insurance executive*
†Hoover, Richard *set designer*
†Horner, James *composer*
Howe, Daniel Walker *historian, educator*
Joyce, Stephen Michael *lawyer*
†Kahn, Mario Santamaria *international marketing executive*
Karras, Alex *actor, former professional football player*
Kerr, Gib *financial planner*
Koonce, John Peter *investment company executive, educator*
Krueger, Kenneth John *nutritionist, educator*
†LeBlanc, Rena *writer*
Levin, Evanne Lynn *lawyer*
Lindgren, Timothy Joseph *supply company executive*
Milgrim, Darrow A. *insurance broker, recreation consultant*
†Montgomery, James Fischer *savings and loan association executive*
†Norwood, Brandy *singer, actress*
O'Neill, Sallie Boyd *educational consultant, business owner, sculptor*
Platus, Libby *artist, sculptor, speaker*
†Serova, Nina *music educator, accompanist*
Sertner, Robert Mark *producer*
†Tesoro, Robert Aaron White *vocalist, actor, photographer*
Weinstein, Charles David *psychologist*
Winkler, Lee B. *business consultant*
Yasnyi, Allan David *communications company executive*
Zemplenyi, Tibor Karol *cardiologist, educator*

Sierra Madre
Converse, Elizabeth *artist, writer*
Dewey, Donald William *magazine publisher, editor, writer*
Nation, Earl F. *retired urologist, educator*

Signal Hill
Schinnerer, Alan John *entrepreneur*
Vandament, William Eugene *retired academic administrator*

Silverado
Mamer, James Michael *secondary education educator*

Simi Valley
†de Castro, Brenda J. *artist, webmaster*
Hochheiser, Marilyn *author, actress*
Ritacco, Patsy Richard *sales executive*
Robison, Marsha Gail *career planning administration*
Shawn, Eric *author, artist, film director*
Slonaker, Dena Meckler *occupational therapist, rehabilitation consultant*
Trager, D. David *retired pharmacist, general consultant*
Vigdor, James Scott *distribution executive*

Skyforest
Wagner, Cheri J. *business owner*

Solana Beach
Agnew, Harold Melvin *physicist*
Arledge, Charles Stone *former aerospace executive, entrepreneur*
Beard, Ann Southard *diplomat, government official, travel company executive, oil company executive, consultant, event planner, writer, educator*
†Beck-von-Peccoz, Michele *retired secondary school educator, writer*
Beck-von-Peccoz, Stephen George Wolfgang *artist*
Brody, Arthur *industrial executive*
Derbes, Daniel William *manufacturing executive*
Friedman, Maurice Stanley *religious educator*
Gildred, Theodore E. *former diplomat, real estate developer*

Soledad
Zika, Bill *psychologist*

Somerset
Carr, Les *psychologist, educator*

Somis
Kehoe, Vincent Jeffré-Roux *photographer, author, cosmetic company executive*
Premack, Ann J. *writer*
Premack, David *psychologist*

Sonoma
Anderson, Gunnar Donald *artist*
Beckmann, Jon Michael *publishing company executive*
Bow, Stephen Tyler, Jr., *management consultant*
Clynes, Manfred *musician, neuroscientist, inventor*
Fellows, Alice Combs *artist*
Herron, Ellen Patricia *retired judge*
Hobart, Billie *education educator, consultant*
Kizer, Carolyn Ashley *poet, educator*
Markey, William Alan *health care administrator*
†Minelli, Helene Marie *artist*
Muchmore, Robert Boyer *engineering consultant executive*
Obninsky, Victor Peter *lawyer*
Sasaki, Y(asunaga) Tito *engineering executive*
Scott, John Walter *chemical engineer, research management executive*
Weinberger, Lilla Gilbrech *bookseller*
Woodbridge, John Marshall *architect, urban planner*

Sonora
†Carter, John Robert *music educator*
Chandler, E(dwin) Russell *clergyman, writer*
Clarke, Paula Katherine *anthropology educator, sociology educator*
Coffill, Marjorie Louise *civic leader*
Jones, Georgia Ann *publisher*
Mathias, Betty Jane *communications and community affairs consultant, writer, editor, lecturer*
Wheeler, Elton Samuel *financial executive*

Soquel
Bidelman, Mark *music educator*
Goodman, Charles Schaffner, Jr., *food product executive, consultant*

South Gate
†Firebaugh, Marco Antonio *state official*

South Lake Tahoe
Barr, Lois I. *personnel administrator*
Dean, John Randall *financial consultant, general building contractor*
Kingsbury, Suzanne Nelson *judge, educator*
Nason, Rochelle *conservation organization administrator*
†Williams, Mark Didrik *music educator, composer*

South Pasadena
Askin, Walter Miller *artist, educator*
Finnell, Michael Hartman *corporate executive*
†Fuller, Kathy J. *special education educator, consultant, researcher*
Girvigian, Raymond *architect*
Glad, Dain Sturgis *aerospace engineer, consultant*
Kopp, Eugene Howard *electrical engineer*
†Li, Songtao *research scientist*
Mantell, Suzanne Ruth *editor*
Remy, Ray *management and public affairs consultant*
Whang, Sukoo Jack *pathologist, microbiologist*
White, W. Robin *writer*
Yett, Sally Pugh *elementary school educator, art educator*
Zimmerman, William Robert *entrepreneur, engineering based manufacturing company executive*

South San Francisco
Caro, Ivor *dermatologist*
Glatt, Daniel J. *physician*
Goodman, Corey Scott *neurobiology educator, researcher, biotechnology company executive*
Hull, Cordell William *business executive*
Lewis, Jason Alvert, Jr., *communications executive*
Lipsky, Ian David *business executive*
†Rainey, Gerald Wayne *sales executive*
Salerno, Philip Adams *information systems specialist*
†Walsh, Gary L. *consumer products company executive*
Zhong, Min *chemist*

Spring Valley
Long, David Michael, Jr., *biomedical researcher, cardiothoracic surgeon*
†Roberts, Carolyn June *real estate broker*

Standish
Klaseen-Eagle, Virginia *retired volunteer*

Stanford
Abrams, Herbert LeRoy *radiologist, educator*
Allen, Matthew Arnold *physicist*
†Alter, Orly *theoretical physicist, geneticist*
†Amemiya, Takeshi *economist, statistician*
Anderson, Martin Carl *economist*
Anderson, Theodore Wilbur *statistics educator*
Andreopoulos, Spyros George *writer*
Anthony, Donald Bruce *humanities educator*
Arrow, Kenneth Joseph *economist, educator*
Aziz, Khalid *petroleum engineering educator*
Baker, Keith Michael *history educator*
Baker, Patricia Ann *publishing executive*
Baldwin, Robert Lesh *biochemist, educator*
Bandura, Albert *psychologist, educator*
Barton, John Hays *law educator*
Batygin, Yuri Konstantinovich *accelerator physicist*
Bauer, Eugene Andrew *dermatologist, educator*
Baylor, Denis Aristide *neurobiologist*
Befu, Harumi *anthropology educator*
†Belichenko, Pavel Vasilievich *neuroscientist, researcher*
Berg, Paul *biochemist, educator*
Berger, Joseph *author, educator, counselor*
Bienenstock, Arthur Irwin *physicist, educator, federal official*
Blaschke, Terrence Francis *medicine and molecular pharmacology educator*
Bocock, Maclin *writer*
Boudart, Michel *chemical engineer, chemist, educator, consultant*
Bracewell, Ronald Newbold *engineering educator*
Brauman, John I. *chemist, educator*
Breitrose, Henry S. *communications educator*
Brinegar, Claude Stout *retired oil company executive*
Brody, Richard Alan *political science educator, researcher*
Brown, Byron William, Jr., *biostatistician, educator*
Brunger, Axel Thomas *biophysicist, researcher, educator*
Bryson, Arthur Earl, Jr., *retired aerospace engineering educator*
Bube, Richard Howard *materials scientist, educator*
†Bueno de Mesquita, Bruce James *political science educator*
Bunzel, John Harvey *political science educator, researcher*
Byer, Robert Louis *applied physics educator, university dean*
Campbell, Allan McCulloch *bacteriology educator*
Cannon, Robert Hamilton, Jr., *aerospace engineering educator*
Carlsmith, James Merrill *psychologist, educator*
Carlson, Robert Wells *physician, educator*
Chang, Steven Daniel *neurosurgeon*
Chao, Alexander Wu *physicist, educator*
Chase, Robert Arthur *surgeon, educator*

Sutter Creek
Sanders, Elizabeth Anne Weaver (Betsy Sanders) *management consultant*

Sylmar
Bridges, Robert McSteen *mechanical engineer*
Corry, Dalila Boudjellal *internist, educator*
†Flippen, Charles Curtis *neurologist*
Foster, Dudley Edwards, Jr., *musician, educator*
Froelich, Beverly Lorraine *foundation director*
Hayes, Cynthia Ann (C.A. Hayes) *administrative assistant, writer*
Kroll, Mark William *electrical engineer*
†Liu, Paul Ishen *pathologist, educator*
Madni, Asad Mohamed *engineering executive*
Scheib, Gerald Paul *fine art educator, jeweler, metalsmith*
Tully, Susan Balsley *pediatrician, educator*
Yguado, Alex Rocco *economics educator*
Ziment, Irwin *medical educator*

Tahoe City
Hirshon, Jack Thomas *lawyer*

Tarzana
Firestone, Morton H. *business management executive*
Gentile, Joseph F. *lawyer, educator*
Goldberg, Harvey *financial executive*
Handelsman, Yehuda *endocrinologist, internal medicine physician*
Hansen, Robert Clinton *electrical engineering consultant*
Kamatoy, Lourdes Aguas *artist*
Larson, Edward William *civil engineering educator, aerospace engineer*
Lauter, James Donald *retired stockbroker*
Macmillan, Robert Smith *electronics engineer*
Meyers, Robert Allen *chemist, publisher*
Neece, Olivia Helene Ernst *investment company executive, consultant*
Portney, Joseph Nathaniel *retired aerospace executive, navigation consultant*
Richman, Peter Mark *actor, painter, writer, producer*
Rinsch, Maryann Elizabeth *occupational therapist*
Sklarin, Burton S. *endocrinologist*
Smith, Mark Lee *architect*
Weil, Leonard *banker*

Tehachapi
Melsheimer, Harold *obstetrician, gynecologist*
Mitchell, Betty Jo *writer, publisher*
Smith-Thompson, Patricia Ann *public relations consultant, educator*

Temecula
Angel, Michael Gonzalez *cultural organization administrator*
†Bathaee, Soussan *engineering technician*
Coram, David James *gaming industry professional*
Keenan, Retha Ellen Vornholt *retired nursing educator*
†May, Brian Thomas *mathematician, educator*
Minogue, Robert Brophy *retired nuclear engineer*
Petersen, Vernon Leroy *communications and engineering corporations executive*
Spjut, Richard Wayne *botanist, consultant*
Steiling, Daniel Paul *retired railroad conductor, writer, geographer*

Temple City
Lau, Bobby Wai-Man *marketing professional, investment and financial planner, business startup trainer*
Perkins, Floyd Jerry *retired theology educator*
Robbins, William Curtis, Jr., *television and motion picture producer, director, writer, news reporter, cameraman*
Weidaw, Kenneth Roe *musician, educator, consultant*

Templeton
Foster-Wells, Karen Margaret *artist*
Gandsey, Louis John *petroleum and environmental consultant*
Hale, Thomas Walter *emergency medicine physician*

Terra Bella
Gletne, Jeffrey Scott *forester*

The Sea Ranch
Hayflick, Leonard *microbiologist, cell biologist, gerontologist, educator, writer*

Thousand Oaks
†Allen, David Harlow *business educator, logistician, consultant*
Ames, Steven Edmund *journalist, educator*
†Brogden, Stephen Richard *library director*
Chang, Jie (Jay Chang) *power electronics and control specialist*
Conant, David Arthur *architectural acoustician, educator, consultant*
Donenfeld, Alice R. Greenbaum *producer, broadcast executive*
Emerson, Alton Calvin *retired physical therapist*
Farshidi, Ardeshir B. *cardiologist, educator*
Ferber, Samuel *publishing executive*
†Gaus, Clifton R. *healthcare executive*
Geiser, Thomas Christopher *lawyer*
Gillette, Dennis C. *academic administrator, mayor*
Gregory, Calvin *insurance service executive*
Herman, Joan Elizabeth *healthcare company executive*
Heyer, Carol Ann *illustrator*
Hudson, Barbara *religious writer, actor*
Knight, Jeffrey Richard *information technology specialist*
Kocen, Lorraine Ayral *accountant*
†Kuzmanovic, Jane Violet *director*
Lark, M. Ann *management consultant, strategic planner, naturalist*
Loren, Sophia *actress*
Malmuth, Norman David *research scientist, program manager*
†McClintock, Tom *state senator*
Mulkey, Sharon Renee *gerontology nurse*
Nanula, Richard *health products executive*
Noonan, Daniel Christopher *consultant*
†Pakula, Anita Susan *dermatologist*
Powe, Larry Kenneth *clinical researcher*
†Reaves, Michaela Crawford *history educator*
Relkin, Michele Weston *artist*
†Rooney, Mickey (Joe Yule Jr.) *actor*
Schaeffer, Leonard David *healthcare executive*
Sharer, Kevin W. *healthcare products company executive*
Shi, Zhi-Qing *endocrinologist*
Sladek, Lyle Virgil *mathematician, educator*
Sloane, J.P. *television producer, writer, entertainer, theologian*
Trover, Ellen Lloyd *lawyer*
Uellendahl, Gail Elizabeth *psychologist*
Urban, Gary Ross *computer and information processing consultant*
Walker, Lorenzo Giles *surgeon, educator*
Woodworth, Stephen Davis *investment banker*
Woolley, J(onathan) Michael *health economist, economic consultant*
Zhao, Sean Zixian *pharmaceutical company executive*

Toluca Lake
Bitting, Kevin Noel *pediatric craniofacial orthotist, researcher*
Litwack, Gerald *biochemistry researcher, educator, administrator*
Morton, Hugh Wesley *producer, director*
Ragan, Ann Talmadge *media and production consultant, actor*
Runquist, Lisa A. *lawyer*

Torrance
Algra, Ronald James *dermatologist*
†Ananth, Jambur *psychiatrist, educator*
Anderson, Marilyn Wheeler *English language educator*
Blumenfeld, Anita *community relations director*
Bryan, Sharon Ann *lawyer*
Burris, Bill Buchanan, Jr., *automotive marketing executive*
Carey, Kathryn Ann *foundation administrator, editor, consultant*
†Carlini, Piero Eliso *secondary school educator*
David, Guy Albert *electrical engineer*
†Donovan, Dennis Francis *lawyer*
Ebeling, Vicki *marriage and family therapist, psychotherapist, educational therapist*
Emmanouilides, George Christos *physician, educator*
Enright, Stephanie Veselich *investment company executive, financial consultant*
Everts, Connor *artist*
Grollman, Julius Harry, Jr., *cardiovascular and interventional radiologist*
Hammer, Terence Michael *physician*
Hicks, Jerry *retired systems engineer*
Horwich, Harvey *printer, publisher*
†Imbarus, Aura *language educator, consultant*
Jarc, Frank Robert *retail executive*
Kallman, Burton Jay *foods association director*
Kaufman, Sanford Paul *lawyer*
Keller, Margaret Anne Eikrem *pediatrician, educator*
†Kerstiens, Gene J. *mathemagenician, consultant*
Khorram, Omid Alexander *obstetrics-gynecology educator*
Kohan, Betsy Burns *lawyer*
Kram, Harry Bernard *surgeon*
Kuc, Joseph A. *education educator, consultant*
Kucij, Timothy Michael *engineer, minister, musician*
†Kuykendall, Steven Thomas *former congressman*
Lee, Francis Cho-Kuen *aerospace engineering analyst*
Lewis, Eric Stephen *elementary school educator*
Lieberman, Robert Arthur *physicist*
Ludwick, Jack Rydel *surgeon*
Matsunaga, Geoffrey Dean *lawyer*
McNamara, Brenda Norma *secondary school educator*
Medley, Nancy May *nurse*
Mehringer, Charles Mark *medical educator, educator*
Mende, Howard Shigeharu *mechanical engineer*
Mittal, Arun K. *physician*
Moore, Christopher M. *lawyer*
Moy, Gwendolyn C.I. *nursing administrator, nursing educator*
Myhre, Byron Arnold *pathologist, educator*
Nguyen, Tuan Huy *internist*
Parfenov, Alexander Vsevolodovitch *physicist, researcher*
Petillon, Lee Ritchey *lawyer*
Pi, Edmond Hsin-Tung *psychiatry educator*
Ringold, Joel *internist*
Rogers, Howard H. *retired chemist*
Roney, Raymond G. *educator, publisher*
Shitabata, Paul Kent *pathologist*
Signorovitch, Dennis J. *communications executive*
Sloves, Robert B. *obstetrician-gynecologist*
Sorstokke, Susan Eileen *systems engineer*
Sperling, Irene R. *publishing executive*
Stabile, Bruce Edward *surgeon*
†Stringer, William Warner *physician*
Sun, Nora Chi-Jun *pathologist*
Swerdloff, Ronald S. *medical educator, researcher*
Tanaka, Kouichi Robert *hematologist, educator*
†Ulrich, Vera Elizabeth *educator*
Walker, Dan *mayor, business consultant*
†Ward, Anthony John *lawyer*
Wylie, Richard Thornton *aerospace engineer*

Trabuco Canyon
Addy, Jo Alison Phears *economist*
Jessup, R. Judd *health care executive*

Tracy
†Harris, Kathleen Renee *information technology supervisor, fashion designer*
Hay, Dennis Lee *lawyer*

Travis AFB
†Kelly, Christopher A. *brigadier general United States air force*

Trinidad
Conant, Ralph Wendell *educator, consultant, author*
Green, Benjamin W. *poet*
Marshall, William Edward *historical association executive*

Truckee
Sanwick, James Arthur *international executive recruiter, management consultant*
Todd, Linda Marie *circulation manager, nutrition researcher, financial consultant, pilot, newspaper professional, pilot*
Turner, George Pearce *consulting company executive*

Tujunga
Bangs, Cate (Cathryn Margaret Bangs) *film production designer, interior designer*
Daly, Saralyn R. *retired humanities educator, writer*
Lathe, Robert Edward *management and financial consultant*
Loehwing, Rudi Charles, Jr., *publicist, radio broadcasting executive, journalist*

Tulare
Avila, John Santos *agricultural pilot*
Cooke, William Robert *minister, mayor*
†Speckman, Virginia Wilson *music educator*
Vickrey, Herta M. *microbiologist*

Turlock
Ahlem, Lloyd Harold *psychologist*
Klein, James Mikel *music educator, associate dean*
†Li, Peter Ping *management educator*
Parker, John Carlyle *retired librarian and archivist, editor*
Stensether, John Eldon *minister*
†Tereshchenko, Alexander Pavlovich *research scientist, educator*

Tustin
Clauson, Gary Lewis *chemist*
Greene, Wendy Segal *special education educator*
Hester, Norman Eric *chemical company technical executive, chemist*
Kollias, Jim Harry *music educator*
Kraft, Henry Robert *lawyer*
Lee, Patrick Kevin *dermatologist*
Madory, Richard Eugene *lawyer*
Poyer, Joseph John *writer, publisher*
Prasad, Birendra (Brian) *mechanical engineer*
Re Velle, Jack B(oyer) *statistician, consultant*
Rogers, Linda Gibbons *artist*
†Wang, Feng Kevin *application developer, computer company executive*

Twain Harte
Kinsinger, Robert Earl *property company executive, educational consultant*

Twentynine Palms
Fultz, Philip Nathaniel *management analyst*

Ukiah
Lohrli, Anne *retired English language educator, writer*
Martin-Gall, Jennie Marie *editor*
McClintock, Richard Polson *dermatologist*
†Newell, Barbara Ann *coatings company executive*
†Sager, Madeline Dean *lawyer*
Sakowicz, John *hedge fund administrator*
†Speed, Cynthia Agnes *retired mathematics educator*
†Van Dusen, Wilson M. *writer, psychologist*

Union City
Glueck, Mary Audrey *retired psychiatric and mental health nurse*
Velarde, Heide Marie *publisher, writer, lyricist*

Universal City
Crow, Sheryl *singer/songwriter, musician*
†Fleishman, Susan Nahley *media consultant*
Geffen, David *recording company executive, producer*
Kingi, Henry Masao *actor, stuntman*
Meyer, Ron *agent*
†Mulligan, Brian *film company executive*
†Rapke, Jack *agent*
†Reitman, Ivan *film director, producer*
Snider, Stacey *film company executive*
†Wolf, Dick (Richard A. Wolf) *television producer, film company executive*

Upland
Boswell, Dan Alan *health maintenance organization executive, health care consultant*
Doyle, Michael James *educator, organist*
†Goodman, John M. *construction executive*
Graw, LeRoy Harry *purchasing and contract management company executive*
Innes, William B. *chemist, consultant*
Jones, Nancy Langdon *financial planning practitioner*
Jordan, Charles Wesley *retired bishop*
Lewis, Goldy Sarah *real estate developer, corporation executive*
†Likens, John David *rehabilitation services professional*
Robertson, Carey Jane *musician, educator*
†Suh, Jung Sook Ky *management consultant, educator*

Upper Lake
Twitchell, Kent *artist*

Vacaville
Dedeaux, Paul J. *orthodontist*
Engle, Susan Ann *chemist*
Ford, John T., Jr., *art, film and video educator*
†Longoria, Steve *security firm executive, consultant*
Luther, Richard S. *music educator*
Suga, Steven Hidenori *neurologist*
Welton, Michael Peter *dentist*
†Wolk, Lois *state legislator*

Valencia
Anguiano, Lupe *business executive*
Fogel, Jennifer Lynn *technical associate, researcher*
Harvey, Rufus William *nonprofit organization administrator*
LeBaron, Alice Anne *musician*
Levy, Ezra Cesar *aerospace scientist, real estate broker*
Parks, Suzan Lori *playwright*
Pocrass, Richard Dale *management consultant*
Webb, Margot *writer*
Werkheiser, Steven Lawrence *financial executive*
Windsor, William Earl *consulting engineer, sales representative*

Vallejo
Apple, Daina Dravnieks *government agency official*
Brown, Earl Kent *historian, clergyman*
Crocker, Kenneth Franklin *data processing consultant*
†DeHaan, John David *forensic specialist*
Feil, Linda Mae *tax preparer*
Gunn, Alexander N., II, *surgeon*
Landauer, Elvie Ann Whitney *humanities educator, writer*
McGowan, Thomas Randolph *retired religious organization executive*
Murillo, Carol Ann *secondary school educator*
Purificacion, Dennis Torres *secondary school educator, lecturer, theologian*
†Smith, Frank Leonard, III, *lawyer*
Womack, Thomas Houston *manufacturing company executive*
Zeliger, Bernard *dean*

Valley Center
Andersen, Robert *health products, business executive*
Fry, Eva Margaret *entertainer, writer*

Valley Springs
Anema-Garten, Durlynn C. *communications educator, counselor, writer*
Vitrac, Jean-Jacques Charles *international business consultant*

Valley Village
Sandel, Randye Noreen *artist*

Van Nuys
†Alarcon, Richard *state legislator, former councilman*
Altshiller, Arthur Leonard *secondary education educator*
Arabian, Armand *arbitrator, mediator, lawyer*
†Becker, Frawley *film company executive*
Cook, Jenik Esterm (Jenik Esterm Cook Simonian) *artist, educator*
Ewing, Guin Porter *historian, art collector*
Farman, Richard Donald *energy company executive*
Fisher, Earl Monty *utilities executive*
Graham, Roger John *photography and journalism educator*
Greenberg, Daniel *electronics rental company executive*
Hertzberg, Robert M. *former state legislator*
Kagan, Stephen Bruce (Sandy Kagan) *chief financial officer*
Mikesell, Richard Lyon *lawyer, financial counselor*
Seymour, Jeffrey Alan *governmental relations consultant*
Solomon, Rhonda Hope *school and educational psychologist*
Tilkian, Ara Garabed *cardiologist*
Westall, Andrew Jon *legislative staff member, urban planner*
Zucker, Alfred John *English language educator, academic administrator*

Vandenberg AFB
Huggins, Elaine Jacqueline *nurse, retired army officer*
Miller, David Allen *air force officer*

Vandenberg Afb
Hamel, Michael A. *career officer*

Venice
Alf, Martha Joanne *artist*
Beal, Jason Eliot *architect*
Bengston, Billy Al *artist*
Bill, Tony *producer, director*
Chipman, Jack *artist*
Davis, Kimberly Brooke *art gallery director*
Eliot, Alexander *author, mythologist*
Eversley, Frederick John *sculptor, engineer*
Hester, Gail *receptionist, writer*
Katz, Brian Philip *language educator, writer*
Padilla, Mario René *literature educator, writer, actor*
Schanes, Christine *lawyer*

Ventura
Abul-Haj, Suleiman Kahil *pathologist*
Anderson, William *retail company executive, business education educator*
Bircher, Andrea Ursula *psychiatric nurse practitioner*
Bowles, Walter Donald *economist, educator*

Bray, Laurack Doyle *lawyer*
Downs, Floella McIntyre *civic worker, ferry pilot, instructor and flight examiner*
Gartner, Harold Henry, III, *lawyer*
Gay, Marilyn Fanelli Martin *television producer, writer, talk show hostess, journalist*
Gaynor, Joseph *chemical engineer, technical-management consultant*
Greene, Warren W. *anesthesiologist*
Greig, William Taber, II, *publishing company executive*
Kirman, Charles Gary *photojournalist*
†Kreissman, Starrett *librarian*
Kump, Kary Ronald *lawyer*
Lipinski, Barbara Janina *psychologist, psychotherapist, educator, writer*
Lovell, Frederick Warren *pathologist, medical legal consultant*
Moffatt, Mindy Ann *educator, educational training specialist*
Naurath, David Allison *engineering psychologist, researcher*
Ruebe, Bambi Lynn *interior, environmental designer*
Smith, Bill *city manager*
†Tamke, George William *printing/copying company executive*
Villaveces, James Walter *allergist, immunologist*
Werber, Fred Alan *dermatologist*
Zuber, Norma Keen *career counselor, educator*

Vernon
Kim, Ho Gill *poet*

Victorville
Dilliard, Maxine K. *retired school psychologist*
Hallworth, Robert Earl *anesthesiologist*
McGulpin, Elizabeth Jane *nurse*
Sedeño, Eugene Raymond *electronics engineer, consultant*
†Szasz, Lorant (ZAS) *industrial engineer, poet*
Umakanthan, Jeremiah *geriatrician*
Yochem, Barbara June (Runyan) *sales executive, lecturer*

Villa Park
Britton, Thomas Warren, Jr., *retired management consultant*
Buffington, Linda Brice *interior designer*
Hawe, David Lee *manufacturing consultant, venture capitalist*
†Murphy, Patrick Christopher *music educator*

Visalia
†Atkins, Thomas Jay *lawyer, missionary and pastor*
Crowe, Daniel Walston *lawyer*
Crowe, John T. *lawyer*
†Daniels, Joan Frances *private school educator*
Daniels, Madeline Marie *forensic psychologist, educator, author*
Goulart, Janell Ann *elementary education educator*
Hart, Timothy Ray *lawyer, dean*
Higgins, John Stuart, Jr., *lawyer*
Hsu, Shu-Dean *hematologist, oncologist*
Keenan, Robert Joseph *trade association executive*
Neeley, James Kame *credit agency executive*
Nevin, David Wright *real estate broker, mortgage broker*
†O'Leary, Deanna Kay *analyst, consultant*
Phillipe, Chester Tolleson *alcohol/drug abuse services professional, educator, substance abuse facility administrator*
Riegel, Byron William *ophthalmologist*
Ryan-Halley, Charlotte Muriel *oncology clinical specialist, family nurse practitioner*
Singh, Daljit *dean, business and public administration educator*
Taylor, Helen Shields *civic worker*

Vista
Cavanaugh, Kenneth Clinton *retired housing consultant*
Ferguson, Margaret Ann *tax consultant*
Fuhlrodt, Norman Theodore *retired insurance executive*
Hofmann, Frieder Karl *biotechnologist, consultant*
Linhart, Letty Lemon *editor*
Tadeo, Elvia *artist*
†Wyland, Mark *state official*

Walnut
McKee, Catherine Lynch *law educator, lawyer*
Muszynski, Jane *interior designer, colorist, space planner*
†Shea, John F. *construction executive, contractor*
Smith, Harry Mendell, Jr., *science educator*
Spencer, Constance Marilyn *secondary education educator*

Walnut Creek
Anderberg, Roy A. *journalist*
Anderson, Robert Leroy *lawyer*
Arnold, William Thomas *software developer, chemist*
Baker, Roy Gordon, Jr., *lawyer*
†Bicksler, Diana Guido *lawyer*
Borenstein, Daniel Asa *newspaper political editor*
†Bryant, Warren F. *retail executive*
Burnison, Boyd Edward *lawyer*
Burns, Francis Raymond *medical facility administrator, researcher*
Cannon, Grace Bert *immunologist*
Carson, Jay Wilmer *pathologist, educator*
Carver, Dorothy Lee Eskew (Mrs. John James Carver) *retired secondary education educator*
Cassidy, John Joseph *hydraulic and hydrologic engineer*
Chu, Valentin Yuan-ling *author*
Curtin, Daniel Joseph, Jr., *lawyer*
da Roza, Victoria Cecilia *human resources administrator*
Davis, Ron Lee *clergyman, author*
De Benedictis, Dario *lawyer, arbitrator, mediator*
Derby, Steven Leo *lawyer*
Everson, Martin Joseph *lawyer*
Fielding, Elizabeth Brown *education educator*
†Gardner, Trudi York *lawyer, insurance company executive*
Garlough, William Glenn *marketing executive*
Ginsburg, Gerald J. *lawyer, business executive*
Hallock, C. Wiles, Jr., *athletic official*
Hamlin, Kenneth Eldred, Jr., *retired pharmaceutical company executive*
Hammond, Charles Edgar *data processing executive*
Hanschen, Peter Walter *lawyer*
Hanson, Robert Duane *civil engineering educator*
Horner, Clifford R. *lawyer*
Keith, Bruce Edgar *political analyst, genealogist*
†Lederman, Henry David *lawyer*
†Lilly, Luella Jean *academic administrator*
Long, Robert Merrill *retail drug company executive*
McCauley, Bruce Gordon *financial consultant*
McGrath, Don John *banker*
Moore, John David *management consultant*
Nolan, Janiece Simmons *health care company executive*
Ogilby, Barry Ray *lawyer*
Pagter, Carl Richard *lawyer*
Palmer, William Joseph *accountant*
Pfeiffer, Phyllis Kramer *publishing executive*
Pinkerton, Albert Duane, II, *lawyer*
Polgar, Leslie George *venture executive*
Rainey, William Joel *lawyer*
†Reimann, Arline Lynn *artist*
Rhody, Ronald Edward *banker, communications executive*
Roath, Stephen D. *retired pharmaceutical company executive*
Rose, Joan L. *computer security specialist*
Satz, Louis K. *publishing executive*
Seaborg, David Michael *evolutionary biologist*
Shastid, Jon Barton *wine company executive*
Skaggs, Sanford Merle *lawyer*
Trousdale, Stephen Richard *newspaper editor*
Van Maerssen, Otto L. *aerospace engineer, consulting firm executive*
†Van Voorhis, Thomas *lawyer*
Wilkins, Sheila Scanlon *management consultant*
Willson, Prentiss, Jr., *lawyer*
Wolf, Harry *retired dean and educator*
Wu, Tse Cheng *research chemist*

Waterford
Reed, Thomas W. *secondary education educator*

Watsonville
Brown, Alan Charlton *retired aeronautical engineer*
Cane, William Earl *nonprofit organization executive*
Condon, Thomas Joseph *editor, writer*
Fields, Carl Victor *food company executive*
Hernandez, Jo Farb *music director, consultant*

Weed
Ryan, Daberath *chemistry educator*

Weimar
Ing, Clarence Sinn Fook *preventive medicine physician, ophthalmic surgeon*
Kerschner, Lee R(onald) *academic administrator, political science educator*

West Covina
Adams, Sarah Virginia *psychotherapist, family counselor*
†Ebiner, Robert Maurice *lawyer*
†Jee, James Rodney *statistician*
Krishnasamy, Bharath Kumar *physician*
Manners, Nancy *retired mayor*
McHale, Edward Robertson *retired lawyer*
Montooth, Sheila Christine *state agency administrator*
†Shanks, Sanford H. *sales executive, writer*
Shiershke, Nancy Fay *artist, educator, property manager*
Torres, Esteban Edward *former congressman, business executive*
Tuck, Edward Fenton *venture capitalist*
West, Edward Alan *graphics communications executive*

West Hills
Abdo, Lynda Lee *art director, designer*
Cheney, Anna Marie Jangula *retired medical-surgical nurse*
Struhl, Stanley Frederick *real estate developer*

West Hollywood
Annakin, Kenneth Cooper *film director, writer*
Bloom, Claire *actress*
†Cage, Nicolas (Nicolas Coppola) *actor*
†Chillida, Eduardo *sculptor*
†De Palma, Brian Russell *film director, writer*
Einstein, Clifford Jay *advertising executive*
Gates, Lisa *private chef, caterer*
Grasshoff, Alex *writer, producer, director*
Harper, Robert *actor*
Hoffenblum, Allan Ernest *political consultant*
Innes, Laura *actress*
Jaglom, Henry David *actor, director, writer*
†Kaplan, Andy *broadcast executive*
†Lyon, John David *lawyer, computer products company executive*
Madonna, (Madonna Louise Veronica Ciccone) *singer, actress, producer*
Perry, Troy D. *clergyman, religious organization administrator*
Prang, Jeffrey *mayor*
Santillan, Antonio *financial company executive*
Shaye, Robert Kenneth *cinema company executive*
Sherman, Robert B(ernard) *composer, lyricist, screenwriter*
Stein, Benjamin J. *television personality, writer, lawyer, economist*
Stern, James Coper *sales executive*
Stern, Ruth Szold *business executive, artist*
Thaw, Mort *writer*

West Sacramento
†Coyne, William J. *retail executive*
†Solomon, Russell M. *retail products executive*
†Teel, James E. *supermarket and drug store retail executive*
†Teel, Joyce Raley *supermarket and drugstore retail executive*

Westlake Village
Anastasi, Richard Joseph *computer software consultant*
†Baumheinrich, Thorsten Frank *electrical engineer*
Caligiuri, Joseph Frank *retired engineering executive*
Castrejon, Elizabeth Blackwell *artist*
Chuman, Frank Fujio *lawyer*
†Colburn, Keith W. *electronics executive*
Cucina, Vincent Robert *retired financial executive*
Dahl, Curtis Ray *photographer*
Detterman, Robert Linwood *financial planner*
Doerr, Patricia Marian *elementary and special education educator*
Erdelyi, Eileen Edith *financial planner and advisor*
Friedman, Collette Sweet *kitchen and interior designer*
Gibson, John Robert *software engineer*
Levine, Donald Arthur *anesthesiologist*
†Levinson, Christopher Gregory *legal administrator*
Munson, John Backus *computer systems consultant, retired computer engineering company executive*
Murdock, David H. *diversified company executive*
Nichols, Steven *shoe and clothing manufacturing executive*
†Pardau, Stuart Lloyd *market research company executive, lawyer, educator*
Richardson, Leatrice Joy *artist*
Smyth, Glen Miller *management consultant*
Steadman, Lydia Duff *symphony violinist, retired elementary school educator*
†Sullivan, Mark Francis *lawyer*
Troxell, Lucy Davis *management consultant*
Valentine, Gene C. *securities dealer*
Weisman, Martin Jerome *retired manufacturing company executive*
†Weiss, Barbara G. *artist*

Westminster
Allen, Merrill James *marine biologist*
Amalsad, Meher Dadabhoy *writer, speaker, seminar leader*
Armstrong, Gene Lee *systems engineering consultant, retired aerospace company executive*
Gylseth, Doris Hanson (Doris Lillian Gylseth) *retired librarian*
Hannah, JaNellyn Bender *public health nurse*
Luong, Khanh Vinh Quoc *nephrologist, researcher*
†Nguyen, Duoc Tan *small business owner*
Rupel, Daniel Patrick *protective services official, retail and consulting executive*
Salaymeh, Muhammad Tawfik *surgeon*

Whittier
Arenowitz, Albert Harold *psychiatrist*
Caro, Evelyn Inga Rouse *writer*
Drake, E. Maylon *academic administrator*
Hartling, Earle Charles *environmental engineer*
Harvey, Patricia Jean *special education administrator, retired*
Korf, Jean Prinz *retired theater educator*
Korf, Leonard Lee *theater arts educator*
Loughrin, Jay Richardson *mass communications educator, consultant*
Lowe, Oariona *dentist*
Meardy, William Herman *retired educational association administrator*
†Price, Joseph Llewellyn *religious educator*
Prickett, David Clinton *physician*
Renteria, Juana *community health educator*
Topjon, Ann Johnson *librarian*

Wildomar
Wells, James T. *development and brokerage executive, consultant*

Willits
Akins, George Charles *accountant*

Wilmington
Burlingame-Smith, June *English language educator, administrator*
†Farabi-Nance, Khadijah *writer*
Hamai, James Yutaka *business executive*
Hatch, Ronald Ray *engineer*

Wilton
Felts, Margaret "George" Clemen *environmental engineer, consultant*
Harrison, George Harry, III, (Hank Harrison) *publishing executive, author*

Windsor
Greiner, Robert Philip *lawyer, real estate broker*
Matkin, Judith Conway *jewelry designer and manufacturer*
Sparks, Bennett Sher *retired military officer*

Winnetka
Zinn, Alexander Nathan *retired surgeon*

Woodland
Clement, Katherine Robinson *retired social worker*
Melton, Barry *lawyer, musician*
Ramirez, Graciela *women's health nurse*
Squires, Richard Felt *research scientist*

Woodland Hills
Anastasi, Michael Anton *journalist*
Anaya, Richard Alfred, Jr., *accountant, investment banker*
Babayans, Emil *financial planner*
Barrett, Robert Matthew *law educator, lawyer*
†Berger, Phil *musician*
Brown, Michael R. *former defense industry executive*
Deters, Thomas C. *editor-in-chief, educator*
DeWitt, Barbara Jane *journalist*
Elperin, Louis Solomon *physician*
Ennis, Thomas Michael *management consultant*
†Even, Randolph M. *lawyer*
Feiman, Thomas E. *investment manager*
Fox, Stuart Ira *physiologist*
Fuld, Steven Alan *financial advisor, insurance specialist*
Funari, Robert Glenn *health care services executive*
Gellert, Jay M. *health and medical products executive*
Glick, Earl A. *retired lawyer*
Goldberg, Bruce Edward *hypnotherapist*
†Harmon, David *finance company executive*
†Harris, Barbara S. *publishing executive*
†Hayes, Troy Allyn *forensic scientist*
Herdeg, Howard Brian *physician*
Hokana, Gregory Howard *engineering executive*
Holland, Kathleen *political science educator*
Homer, Raymond Rodney *film producer, director*
Johnson-Champ, Debra Sue *lawyer, educator, writer, artist*
Katz, Cleo *real estate educator*
Kaufman, Albert I. *lawyer*
Koep, Richard Michael *lawyer*
Lax, Kathleen Thompson *judge*
Levy, Norman *motion picture company executive*
Lin, Lawrence Shuh Liang *lawyer*
†Maizels, Morris *physician*
Monteau, Norman Keith *gemologist*
Morishita, Akihiko *trading company executive*
Mund, Geraldine *judge*
Nierenberg, Norman *urban land economist, retired state official*
†O'Connor, Brian D.A. *music educator, musician*
Pettit, John W. *administrator*
Piersol, Allan Gerald *mechanical engineer*
Pohl, John Martin DeLand *archaeologist*
Pregerson, Harry *federal judge*
†Rolin, Christopher E(rnest) *lawyer*
Schueler, John R. *newspaper executive*
Shuster, Fred Todd *journalist, commentator*
Siever-Henderson, Patricia *history university educator*
†Stahlecker, Barbara Jean *marketing professional, consultant*
Stratton, Gregory Alexander *computer specialist, administrator, mayor*
Tuthill, Walter Warren *financial executive, international business consultant*
Weinman, Glenn Alan *lawyer*
†Wiesner, Carol A. *financial services company executive*
Yates, Gary L. *marriage and family therapist*
Zeitlin, Herbert Zakary *retired academic administrator, real estate consultant*

Woodside
Arthur, Greer Martin *maritime container leasing firm executive*
Ashley, Holt *aerospace scientist, educator*
Blum, Richard Hosmer Adams *educator, writer*
Freitas, Antoinette Juni *insurance company executive*
Gates, Milo Sedgwick *retired construction company executive*
Klein, August Stone *retired physicist*
Markkula, A.C., Jr., *entrepreneur, computer company executive*
Patterson, Francine G. P. *foundation administrator*

Wrightwood
Caudron, John Armand *accident reconstructionist, forensic examiner*
Frame, John Fayette *sculptor*
†LaMay-Abner, Julie Ann *English educator*

Yorba Linda
Loeblich, Helen Nina Tappan *paleontologist, educator*
Lunde, Dolores Benitez *retired secondary education educator*
Lynch, Frank Thomas *aeronautical engineer, consultant*
Medland, Maurice Blue *writer*
Naulty, Susan Louise *archivist*
Porcello, Leonard Joseph *engineering research and development executive*
Stavropoulos, Rose Mary Grant *community activist, volunteer*
Sternitzke-Holub, Ann *elementary school educator*
Vilardi, Agnes Francine *real estate broker*

Yosemite National Park
Best, Hollis Garber *judge*

Yountville
Bedell, Jay Dee *educator, writer*
Jones, Thomas Robert *social worker*
Sedlock, Joy *social worker*

Yreka
Nelson, Steven Leslie *surgeon*
Smith, Vin *sports editor, business owner, novelist*

Yuba City
Doscher, Richard John *protective services official*
Kemmerly, Jack Dale *retired state official, aviation consultant*
Sarringar, Michael Ray *manufacturing executive*

Yucaipa
†Bogh, Russell *state official*
Gomez, Louis Salazar *college president*

Horn, Paul Ervin *minister*
Lardy, Leonard Anthony *English educator*
Marks, Sharon Lea *primary school educator, nurse*
Matsuda, Stanley Kazuhiro *secondary education educator*
†Ramirez, Stephen John *mathematician, educator*

Yucca Valley
Dockendorff, Robert Lawrence *computer graphics designer*
Styles, Beverly (Juanita Robins Carpenter) *entertainer, composer, musician*

COLORADO

Alamosa
Garcia, Castelar Medardo *lawyer*
Stafford, George Timothy *surgeon*

Allenspark
†Newman, Dean Gordon *business consultant*

Arvada
Bert, Carol Lois *retired educational assistant*
Brown, Mark Steven *medical physicist*
Carney, T.J *lawyer*
Ferguson, Lloyd Elbert *retired manufacturing engineer*
†Glodava, Mila Garcia *entrepreneur, educator, consultant*
Halley, Diane Esther *artist*
Hancock, N(ewell) Les(lie) *accountant*
†Howard, Barry Christopher *minister*
Leafgreen, Lisa Diane *education coordinator*
Meiklejohn, Mindy June (Lorraine Meiklejohn) *political organizer, realtor*
†Peck, Kenneth E. *lawyer*
Pettit, Claud Martin *religious organization administrator*
Reed, Joan-Marie *special education educator*
Simon, Marvin B. *investment company executive, real estate broker*
Tingley, Walter Watson *computer systems manager*
Yamamoto, Kaoru *retired psychology and education educator*
Yang, In Che *hydrologist, researcher*

Aspen
Caudill, Samuel Jefferson *architect*
Clauson, F.L. Stan, Jr., *city planner, consultant*
Ewing, Wayne Hilley *film producer, director, writer*
Hansen, Steven Alan *construction executive*
Hayes, Mary Eshbaugh *editor, writer*
Jennings, Richard Milburn *resort developer*
Manosevitz, Martin *psychologist*
Mitchell, Karen Frances *artist, jewelry designer*
Oden, Robert Rudolph *surgeon*
Peirce, Frederick Fairbanks *lawyer*
Pullen, Margaret I. *genetics physicist*
Roth, Don *music executive*
Williams, Rhys A. *surgeon*

Aurora
As-Salaam, Jamaal (William Louis Williams Jr.) *poet, film producer, writer*
Battaglia, Frederick Camillo *physician*
Bauman, Earl William *accountant, government official*
Beckman, L. David *university chancellor*
Brown, Anne Sherwin *speech pathologist, educator*
Brown, Darmae Judd *librarian*
Dooley, J. Gordon *food scientist*
Durkop, Georgia F. *interior designer*
Fisk, Charles Carroll *retired civil engineer, consultant*
Gardner, Sandra Lee *nurse, outreach consultant*
Grace, William Pershing *petroleum geologist, real estate developer*
†Green, Larry Alton *physician, educator*
Groblebe, Jimmy Lee *graphics designer*
Halford, Sharon Lee *college administrator, advocate, educator*
†Hampton, Clyde Robert *lawyer, educator*
Hughes, Christopher Adam *conductor, educator*
†Jarvis, Mary Grace *principal*
Katz, Michael Jeffery *lawyer*
Kellogg Fain, Karen *retired history and geography educator*
Khanna, Kishanlal K. *lawyer, educator*
King Calkins, Carol Coleman *health sciences administrator*
Lassen, Betty Jane *educator*
†McKenney, Muriel Anita *art educator, engineer*
†Mellette, Julian Ramsey, Jr., *dermatologist, dermatologic surgeon*
Miller, Dorothea Helen *retired educator and librarian*
Nelson, Marvin Ray *retired life insurance company executive*
Newman, John Henry *educational researcher*
Nichols, Clyde Richard *clergyman, company executive*
Nora, Audrey Hart *physician*
Onyeuku, Alfred Eme *small business owner, consultant*
Osterberg, Jorj O. *retired civil engineer*
Robertson, James Mueller *civil engineer, educator*
Schwartz, Lawrence *aeronautical engineer*
Seybert, Janet Rose *lawyer, military officer*
Sheffield, Nancy *city agency administrator*
Sorenson, Katherine Ann *elementary school educator*
Staelin, Earl Hudson *lawyer*
Starr, Nancy Barber *pediatric nurse practitioner*
Stauffer, Scott William *lawyer, accountant*
Stifel, Frederick Benton *pastor, biochemist, nutritionist*
†Sun, Juan *biologist, immunologist*
Tauer, Paul E. *mayor, educator*
†Ton, Paul *investor, educator*
Vallado, David Anthony *aerospace engineer*
Walker, Joyce Marie *secondary school educator*
Wessler, Mary Hraha *real estate company executive*
Wiedel, Jerome D. *orthopedic surgeon*
Zuschlag, Nancy Hansen *environmental and nature resources educator*

Avon
Laub, David L. *music educator*
†Marks, Richard Samuel *lawyer, real estate development executive*

Bailey
Wright, Dixie Lee *special needs persons consultant*

Basalt
Shipp, Dan Shackelford *lawyer*

Bayfield
Haug, Edward Joseph, Jr., *retired mechanical engineering educator, simulation research engineer*

Berthoud
Davis, Donald Alan *news correspondent, writer, lecturer*

Beulah
Barton, Paul B. *artist, sculptor*

Black Hawk
Jones, Linda May *tour guide*

Boulder
Adler, Patricia Ann *sociologist, educator*
Albritton, Daniel Lee *atmospheric scientist*
Alldredge, Leroy Romney *retired geophysicist*
Anderson, Ronald Delaine *education educator*
Anuta, Karl Frederick *lawyer*
Armstrong, David Michael *biology educator*
Arnold, Janet Nina *health care consultant*
Balkin, David Bruce *management consultant, educator*
Bangs, F(rank) Kendrick *former business educator*
Barnes, Frank Stephenson *electrical engineer, educator*
Bartlett, David Farnham *physics educator*
Baugh, L. Darrell *financial executive*
Baughn, William Hubert *former business educator and academic administrator*
Beer, Francis Anthony *political science educator*
Begelman, Mitchell Craig *astrophysicist, educator, writer*
Bellac, Patricia Sharman *lawyer*
Beylkin, Gregory *mathematician*
†Bickman, Martin *literature educator, writer*
Bintliff, Barbara Ann *law librarian, educator*
Birosik, PJ *music company executive*
Bolomey, Roger Henry *sculptor*
Borysenko, Joan *psychologist, biologist*
Bourne, Lyle Eugene, Jr., *psychology educator*
Boydston, James Christopher *composer*
Braddock, David Lawrence *health science educator*
Breddan, Joe *systems engineering consultant*
Breed, Michael Dallam *environmental, population, organismic biology educator*
†Buchanan, Mary Estill *education trustee*
†Buechner, John C. *academic administrator*
Burge, Catherine Alice *musician, educator*
†Burke, Thomas Sebastian, Jr., *educator, writer*
Burns, Daniel Hobart *management consultant*
Byerly, Radford, Jr., *science policy official*
†Byyny, Richard Lee *academic administrator, physician*
Carlson, Devon McElvin *architect, educator*
Carlson, Rhonda *writer, law educator*
Cathey, Wade Thomas *retired electrical engineering educator*
Chappell, Charles Franklin *meteorologist, consultant*
Clark, Melvin Eugene *chemical company executive*
Clifford, Steven Francis *science research director*
Clos, Lynne Mobley *magazine publisher, paleontologist*
Conti, Peter Selby *astronomy educator*
†Conway, Robert Edward *corporate executive*
Cope, Joseph Adams *lawyer*
Cornell, Eric Allin *physics educator*
Corotis, Ross Barry *civil engineering educator, academic administrator*
Cristol, Stanley Jerome *chemistry educator*
Crites, Gayle *artist, educator*
†Danielson, Luke Jeffries *lawyer*
Danilov, Victor Joseph *museum management program director, consultant, author, educator*
Dawson, Roy Edward *academic advisor*
Deaktor, Darryl Barnett *lawyer*
De Fries, John Clarence *behavioral genetics educator, researcher*
Duckworth, Guy *musician, pianist, educator*
DuVivier, Katharine Keyes *lawyer, educator*
Echohawk, John Ernest *lawyer*
†Ellsworth, Oliver Bryant *music educator, writer*
Enarson, Harold L. *retired academic administrator*
Fenster, Herbert Lawrence *lawyer*
†Ferme, Valerio Cristiano *language educator*
Fiflis, Ted James *lawyer, educator*
Fink, Robert Russell *music theorist, former university dean*
Fleming, Rex James *meteorologist*
Flowers, William Harold, Jr., *lawyer*
†Forstrom, June Rochelle *professional society administrator*
Garstang, Roy Henry *astrophysicist, educator*
†Getches, David Harding *law educator, state environmental executive, lawyer*
Glasergreen, Lawson Scott *designer*
Glover, Fred William *artificial intelligence and optimization research director, educator*
†Goldstein, Tamara Beth *musician*
Gonzalez-del-Valle, Luis Tomas *Spanish language educator*
Grabowski, Wojciech W. *physicist, researcher*
Gralapp, Marcelee Gayl *librarian*
Greenberg, Edward Seymour *political science educator, writer*
Hakeem, Muhammad Abdul *artist, educator*
†Halpern, Alexander *lawyer*
Hanna, William Johnson *electrical engineering educator*
Hauser, Ray Louis *research engineer, entrepreneur*
Healy, Alice Fenvessy *psychology educator, researcher*
Heath, Josephine Ward *foundation administrator*
Hermann, Allen Max *physics educator*
Herring, Jackson Rea *physicist*
Hess, John Warren *professional society administrator*
Hill, David Allan *electrical engineer*
Hill, Melvin James *oil company executive*
Hoffman, Charles Fenno, III, *architect*
Hogg, David Clarence *physicist*
Holdsworth, Janet Nott *women's health nurse*
Horii, Naomi *editor*
†Huemer, Michael *philosophy educator*
Hurd, Jerrie *writer*
Jerritts, Stephen G. *management consultant*
Jessor, Richard *psychologist, educator*
Johnston, Laurance Scott *foundation director*
Johnston, Leland Mann, Jr., *physician*
Joselyn, Jo Ann *space scientist*
Joy, Edward Bennett *electrical engineer, educator*
†Jurafsky, Daniel *linguist*
Kapteyn, Henry Cornelius *physics and engineering educator*
Kelley, Bruce Dutton *pharmacist*
†Kellogg, Dale M *editor*
Kellogg, William Welch *meteorologist, researcher*
Kerr, Baine Perkins, Jr., *lawyer, writer*
Kilmer, Eve Ann *psychologist*
Kinder, Eugene J(oseph) *psychiatrist, psychoanalyst*
King, Edward Louis *retired chemistry educator*
Kintsch, Walter *psychology educator, director*
Kisslinger, Carl *geophysicist, educator*
Koch, Tad Harbison *chemistry educator, researcher*
Kompala, Dhinakar Sathyanathan *chemical engineering educator, biochemical engineering researcher*
†Korevaar, David *musician, educator*
Lally, Vincent Edward *atmospheric scientist*
LaVelle, Betty Sullivan Dougherty *legal professional*
LeMone, Margaret Anne *atmospheric scientist*
Lemp, John, Jr., *telecommunications engineer*
Lineberger, William Carl *chemistry educator*
Low, Boon Chye *physicist*
MacDonald, Alexander Edward *meteorologist*
†Mahajan, Roop L. *dean, engineering educator*
Mahanthappa, Kalyana Thipperudraiah *physicist, educator*
Mahlman, Jerry David *research meteorologist*
Malde, Harold Edwin *retired federal government geologist*
Mancino, John Gregory *software company executive*
Manka, Ronald Eugene *lawyer*
Marecaux, M. L. *consultant, writer*
Martinez, Jose Rafael *writer, educator, poet*
McCray, Richard Alan *astrophysicist, educator*
McGuinness, Aims Chamberlain, Jr., *higher education policy analyst*
Mehalchin, John Joseph *entrepreneur, finance executive*
Meier, Mark Frederick *research scientist, glaciologist, educator*
Melicher, Ronald William *finance educator*
Menken, Jane Ava *demographer, educator*
Menn, Lise *linguistics educator*
Meyer, Andrea Peroutka *small business owner*
Middleton-Downing, Laura *psychiatric social worker, artist, small business owner*
Miller, Harold William *nuclear geochemist*
Mitchell, David Spear *writer, editor, publisher, science educator*
Mitchell, Joan LaVerne *research scientist*
Monarchi, David Edward *management scientist, information scientist, educator*
Mooney, William Piatt *actor*
Moses, Raphael Jacob *lawyer*
Mulhern, Martin Robert *engineer*
Murino, Clifford John *atmospheric and oceanic research institute executive*
Mycielski, Jan *mathematician, educator*
†Nagel, Robert Forder *legal educator, lawyer*
O'Brien, Elmer John *librarian, educator*
†O'Connor, Heidi Roberts *federal appellate lawyer*
Ostashev, Vladimir E. *physicist, researcher*
†Owen-Riesch, Anna Lou *economics and history educator*
Pankove, Jacques Isaac *physicist, researcher*
†Park, Wounjhang *adult education educator*
Peters, Max Stone *chemical engineer, educator*
Peterson, Courtland Harry *law educator*
†Pierpont, Cortlandt *chemist, educator*
Porzak, Glenn E. *lawyer*
Prescott, David Marshall *biology educator*
Purvis, John Anderson *lawyer, educator*
Ramirez, W. Fred *chemical engineering educator*
Randa, James Paul *physicist, electrical engineer*
Rast, Mark Peter *research scientist*
†Reinhold, Karen *music educator*
Reitsema, Harold James *aerospace engineer*
Richardson, Donn Charles *business and marketing educator*
Ridley, Brian Ward *physics educator, researcher*
Rienner, Lynne Carol *publishing executive*
†Riis, Thomas Laurence *music educator*
Robba, William A. *research scientist, consultant*
Robinson, Peter *retired paleontology educator, consultant*
Rodriguez, Juan Alfonso *technology corporation executive*
Roellig, Leonard Oscar *physics educator*
Rood, David S. *linguistics educator*
Routson, Clell Dennis *manufacturing company executive*
Sable, Barbara Kinsey *former music educator*
Sani, Robert LeRoy *chemical engineering educator*
Sarson, John Christopher *television producer, director, writer*
Schneider, Nicholas McCord *planetary scientist, educator, textbook author*
Schnell, Russell Clifford *atmospheric scientist, researcher*
†Serreze, Mark Clifford *environmental scientist, researcher*
†Shankman, Paul Andrew *anthropologist, educator*
Shumick, Diana Lynn *computer executive*
Sirotkin, Phillip Leonard *education administrator*
Smith, Ernest Ketcham *electrical engineer*
†Smith, Joel B. *environmental scientist, consultant*
Snell, Esmond Emerson *biochemist*
Snow, Theodore Peck *astrophysics educator*
Sodal, Ingvar Edmund *electrical engineer, scientist*
Staehelin, Lucas Andrew *cell biology educator*
Stanton, William John, Jr., *marketing educator, author*
Stepanek, Joseph Edward *industrial development consultant*
Sture, Stein *civil engineering educator*
Swenson, Ann-Marie *education educator*
Tatarskii, Valerian Il'Ich *physics researcher*
Taylor, Allan Ross *linguist, educator*
Thomas, Daniel Foley *retired financial services company executive*
Timmerhaus, Klaus Dieter *chemical engineering educator*
Tolbert, Bert Mills *biochemist, educator*
Trenberth, Kevin Edward *atmospheric scientist*
Truce, William Everett *chemist, educator*
Uberoi, Mahinder Singh *aerospace engineer, educator*
Uhrik, Carl Thomas *computer scientist, educator*
†Valdovino, Luis Hector *art educator*
Vigil, Daniel Agustin *academic administrator*
†Waggoner, Michael James *law educator*
Walker, Deward Edgar, Jr., *anthropologist, educator*
†Wallace, Brett *music educator, musician*
Washington, Warren Morton *meteorologist*
White, Gilbert F(owler) *geographer, educator*
Wieman, Carl E. *physics educator*
Williams, James Franklin, II, *university dean, librarian*
†Wittemyer, John *lawyer*
†Ye, Jun *physicist, researcher*
†Zable, Jack Louis *mechanical engineer, educator*
Zax, Jeffrey Stephen *economist, educator*
Zhao, Cong Long *physicist*

Breckenridge
Ehrhorn, Richard William *electronics company executive*
Fromm, Jeffery Bernard *lawyer*

Brighton
Rinkenberger, Richard Krug *physical scientist, geologist, consultant*
Wagner, Samuel Albin Mar *records management executive, educator*

Broomfield
Andreiev, Yura (George Andreiev) *electronics engineer*
Arnesen, Tore Olav *structural engineer, inventor*
Bobrick, Steven Aaron *transportation executive*
Burns, James Scotte, II, *secondary school educator*
Crawford, Caren Lee *computer engineer*
†Hoffman, Marilyn Kay *psychologist*
†Hoover, R. David *packaging company executive*
†Hopper, Terry N. *pharmaceutical executive, consultant, research scientist*
Jonsen, Eric Richard *lawyer*
Lybarger, John Steven *human resources development consultant, trainer*
Lybarger, Marjorie Kathryn *nurse*
Williams, John James, Jr., *architect*

Buena Vista
Goddard, Hazel Bryan *religious organization administrator*
Herb, Edmund Michael *optometrist, educator*

Calhan
Henderson, Freda LaVerne *elementary education educator*

Canon City
Alexander, Arline *entrepreneur, writer, real estate consultant*
Cochran, Susan Mills *librarian*
Honaker, Charles Ray *health facility administrator*
McDermott, John Arthur *lawyer*
Mohr, Gary Alan *physician*
Rivera-Reyes, Gladys M. (Gladys Dalton) *retired stenographer, court reporter*
Watson, Carrie Ann *writer, artist*
Williamson, Edward Henry *chaplain, army officer*

Carbondale
Cowgill, Ursula Moser *biologist, educator, environmental consultant*
Wohl, Kenneth Allan *lawyer*

Cascade
Seger, Linda Sue *script consultant, lecturer, writer*

Castle Rock
Barnard, Rollin Dwight *retired financial executive*

Drake, Sylvie (Jurras Drake) theater critic
Driggs, Margaret educator
†Du, Yiping P. education educator
Ducker, Bruce novelist, lawyer
Dugan, Michael Joseph former career officer, health agency executive
Dunham, Joan Roberts administrative assistant
†Dunham, Stephen Sampson lawyer
†Durkin, Dennis John librarian
Eaton, Gareth Richard chemistry educator, university dean
Ebel, David M. federal judge
†Eberle, Donald Cramer lawyer, governmental relations consultant
†Ebert, Darlene Marie lawyer
†Eckstein, John Alan lawyer
Edelman, Joel medical center executive
Edwards, Daniel Walden lawyer
Ehret, Josephine Mary microbiologist, researcher
Eickhoff, Theodore Carl epidemiologist
Eklund, Carl Andrew lawyer
†Elliman, Donald M., Jr., magazine publisher and executive
Ellis, Sylvia D. Hall development and library education consultant
Emery, Henry Alfred petroleum engineer
Engdahl, Todd Philip editor
Enright, Cynthia Lee illustrator
Eppler, Jerome Cannon private financial advisor
†Estes, Mark Ernest law librarian
Evans, Mike professional basketball coach
Faatz, Jeanne Ryan councilperson
Fails, Thomas Glenn geologist
†Fanganello, Joseph Michael lawyer
Fasel, Ida English language educator, writer
Faxon, Thomas Baker retired lawyer
Fay, Richard James mechanical engineer, executive, educator
Felter, Edwin Lester, Jr., judge
Fevurly, Keith Robert educational administrator
Fielden, C. Franklin, III, early childhood education consultant
Filley, Christopher Mark neurologist, researcher
Finn, John Stephen lawyer
†Fletcher, Courtney Vance pharmacologist, educator
Forsberg, Peter professional hockey player
Fortune, Lowell lawyer
Frederick, Robert Allen history educator
Fredmann, Martin ballet artistic director, educator, choreographer
Freeman, Deborah Lynn lawyer
Freiheit, Clayton Fredric zoo director
Friedberg, Alan Charles lawyer
Fuller, Robert Kenneth architect, urban designer
Gabow, Patricia Anne internist
Gallagher, Dennis Joseph municipal official, state senator, educator
Galloway, Judy A. deputy commissioner
Gampel, Elaine Susan investment company executive, consultant
Garcia, June Marie librarian
Garnar, Martin Luther librarian
Gates, Charles Cassius rubber company executive
Gehres, James retired lawyer
George, Russell Lloyd lawyer, former state legislator
Gibson, Elisabeth Jane retired principal
†Gilbert, Alan Jay lawyer, educator
Gloss, Lawrence Robert fundraising executive
Goldberg, Gregory Eban lawyer
Goldman, L. Barton physician
Golitz, Loren Eugene dermatologist, pathologist, clinical administrator, educator
Graham, Pamela Smith artist, distributing company executive
†Grant, Patrick Alexander lawyer, association administrator
Grant, William West, III, banker
Gratiot, Robert B.R. artist, director
Green, Jersey Michael-Lee lawyer
†Greene, Kelly Elizabeth medical educator
Greyson, Clifford Russell internist
Grilly, Gerald E. publishing executive
Grimshaw, Thomas Tollin lawyer
Grissom, Garth Clyde lawyer, director
†Groff, JoAnn organization administrator
†Guo, James Chwen-Yuan civil engineer, educator
Gustus, Stacey A. legal secretary
Haase, Gerald Martin pediatric surgeon
Halgren, Lee A. academic administrator
†Haliw, Jerome Michael civil engineer
Hall, Larry Dean energy company executive, lawyer
Hall, Richard Murray, Jr., finance executive, consultant
Hamel, Fred Meade lawyer
†Hamman, Richard F. epidemiologist, educator
Hamrick, Joseph Eugene, Jr., information services specialist
†Hardaway, Timothy Duane basketball player
Harmon, Robert John child psychiatrist
Harmsen, Dorothy food products executive
Harris, Dale Ray lawyer
†Hartley, James Edward lawyer
†Hautzinger, James Edward lawyer
Havekost, Daniel John architect
†Hawley, Robert Cross lawyer
Heiserman, Robert Gifford lawyer
Helton, Todd professional baseball player
Hendrix, Lynn Parker lawyer
Hensen, Stephen Jerome lawyer
†Heppler, Robin Lee science administrator
Hetzel, Fredrick William biophysicist, educator
†Hickenlooper, John W. mayor
Hilbert, Otto Karl, II, lawyer
Hill, Robert F. lawyer
Himmelmann, William Charles municipal official
Hirschfeld, Arlene F. civic worker, homemaker
Hoagland, Donald Wright lawyer
Hobbs, Gregory James, Jr., state supreme court justice
Hoehn, Margaret Maier neurologist
†Hoehn, Robert J. plastic surgeon, educator
Hoffer, Philip Craig information technology manager, consultant
Hoffman, Daniel Steven lawyer, law educator
Hoffman, Murray Stanley internist, cardiologist, educator
Hogan, Curtis Jule union executive, industrial relations consultant
Hohner, Kenneth Dwayne retired fodder company executive
†Holder, Holly Irene lawyer
Holme, Richard Phillips lawyer
Holmes, Randall Kent microbiology educator, physician, university administrator
Holmquist, Darrel Vernon geotechnical engineer
Hopfenbeck, George Martin, Jr., lawyer
Hopkins, Donald J. lawyer
†Horton, Frank Elba university official, geography educator
†Hotchkiss, Heather A. social worker, consultant
†Houtsma, Peter C. lawyer
Hovland, Kenneth Roger ophthalmologist, educator
†Howard, W. Scott language educator
Howse, Cathy L. writer, researcher, entrepreneur
†Huang, Linda Chen plastic surgeon
Hughes, Bradley Richard business executive
Hughes, J(ohnson) Donald history educator, editor
Hunsaker, Jill Ann public health administrator
Hurdle, Clint professional athletics manager
†Husband, John Michael lawyer
Hynek, Frederick James architect
†Im, Kun Shin information scientist, educator
Imber, Richard Joseph physician, dermatologist
Imhoff, Walter Francis investment banker
Imig, William Graff lawyer, lobbyist
Iona, Mario retired physics educator
Irwin, R. Robert lawyer
†Jablonski, James Arthur lawyer
Jacobs, Paul Alan lawyer
Jafek, Bruce William otolaryngologist, educator
†Jarles, Ruth Sewell education educator
Jennett, Shirley Shimmick home care management executive, nurse
†Jibson, Randall Wade geologist
Johnson, Candice Elaine Brown pediatrics educator
†Johnson, Geraldine Esch language specialist
Johnson, Harold Earl human resources specialist
†Johnson, Philip Edward lawyer
Johnson, Walter Earl geophysicist
Johnston, Richard Boles, Jr., pediatrician, educator, biomedical researcher
Jones, Jean Correy organization administrator
Jones, M. Douglas, Jr., pediatrics educator
Jones, Richard Michael lawyer
Joyce, Mary Holt retired social worker
Judson, Franklyn Nevin physician, educator
Kahn, Benjamin Alexander lawyer
†Kahn, Edwin Sam lawyer
†Kanan, Gregory Brian lawyer
Kane, John Lawrence, Jr., judge
Kaplan, Marc J. lawyer
Kaplan, Sheila academic administrator
Karsh, Philip Howard advertising executive
Kauvar, Abraham J. gastroenterologist, medical administrator
Keatinge, Robert Reed lawyer
Keithley, Roger Lee judge
Keller, Glen Elven, Jr., lawyer
Kelly, William States data network engineer
Kintzele, John Alfred lawyer
Kirkpatrick, Charles Harvey physician, immunology researcher
Kirshbaum, Howard M. retired judge, arbiter
Klipping, Robert Samuel geophysicist
Kluck, Clarence Joseph physician, health facility administrator
Knaus, Tim political organization administrator
Knyazev, Andrew mathematician, consultant
Koh, Eunmee mathematician, educator, consultant
Koul, Hari Krishen research scientist, rights activist
Kourlis, Rebecca Love state supreme court justice
Kraizer, Sherryll A. child safety and interpersonal violence prevention educator
†Krendl, Cathy Stricklin lawyer
Krikos, George Alexander pathologist, educator
Krugman, Richard David pediatrician, university administrator, educator
Kurtz, Maxine personnel consultant, lawyer
Laird, Frank N. political science educator
LaMendola, Walter Franklin technology educator, business executive
†Lance, Keith Curry library and information scientist
Landesman, Howard M. academic administrator
Landon, Susan Melinda petroleum geologist
Lane, Peggy Lee educator
La Rosa, Francisco Guillermo pathologist, researcher, educator
Larsen, Gary Loy physician, researcher
Law, John Manning retired lawyer
Lazarus, Steven S. management consultant, marketing consultant
Lee, Hyunyoung computer scientist, educator
†Lee, Joo-Mee musician, music educator
Lefly, Dianne Louise research psychologist
Leitinger, Christiane educator
Lepoff, Ronald Bart physician
†Leprino, James G. food products executive
Leraaen, Allen Keith financial executive
Lerman, Eileen R. lawyer
Levine, Joel Seth medical school administrator, educator
Levinson, Shauna T. financial services executive
†Levis, William Herst lawyer
Lewallen, Elinor Kirby religious organization executive, lay church worker
Lillehei, Kevin Owen neurosurgeon, educator
Lincoln, Alexander, III, financier, lawyer, private investor
Lindenfeld, JoAnn physician, educator
Livingston, Johnston Redmond manufacturing executive
Lockspeiser, Nancy Flanders artist, designer
Lofton, Kevin Eugene medical facility administrator
Logan, James Scott, Sr., federal agency administrator
London, David L. lawyer
Long, Francis Mark retired electrical engineer
Long, Martin Edward lawyer
†Lothrop, Robert S. agricultural studies educator
Low, Andrew M. lawyer
Low, John Wayland lawyer
Low, Merry Cook civic worker
Lubeck, Marvin Jay ophthalmologist
Lucero, Carlos federal judge
Lundy, Barbara Jean training executive
†Lutz, John Shafroth lawyer
Lyons, Cherie Ann researcher, writer
Macey, William Blackmore oil company executive
MacGregor, George Lescher, Jr., freelance writer
†Major, Alice Jean lawyer
Malatesta, Mary Anne lawyer
Malone, Michael William electronics executive, software engineer
†Mandell, Mercedes Susan anesthesiologist, educator
Marcum, Walter Phillip manufacturing executive
Markovchick, Vincent J. surgeon
Marquess, Lawrence Wade lawyer
Martin, Dallas Rea lawyer
Martin, Richard Jay medical educator
Martin, Robert Burton management and marketing consultant
Martinez, Alex J. state supreme court justice
Martz, Clyde Ollen lawyer, educator
Maul, Carol Elaine small business owner
Mauro, Richard Frank lawyer, investment manager
Maurstad, David Ingolf federal agency administrator, insurance company executive
Maytham, Thomas Northrup art and museum consultant
McCabe, John L. lawyer
McCandless, Bruce, II, aerospace engineer, former astronaut
McConnell, Michael Theodore lawyer
†Mc Connell, Michael W. judge, law educator
McDowell, Karen Ann lawyer
†McDyess, Antonio professional basketball player
McElhinney, James Lancel artist, educator
McIntosh, Carolyn Leigh lawyer
McLain, William Allen lawyer
McManus, Richard Griswold, Jr., lawyer
McMichael, Donald Earl lawyer
†McMorris, Jerry transportation company executive, sports team executive
McWilliams, Robert Hugh federal judge
Meeks, Mark Anthony minister
Meiklejohn, Alvin J., Jr., state legislator, lawyer, accountant
Mendelsohn, Harold sociologist, educator
Mendez, Celestino Galo mathematics educator
Mendez, William Humbert family medicine physician
Merker, Steven Joseph lawyer
†Merrick, Glenn Warren lawyer
Messer, Donald Edward theological school president, theology educator
Meurlin, Keith W. airport manager
Miller, Gale Timothy lawyer
Miller, J. Kent lawyer, educator
Miller, Jill Marie psychoanalyst
Miller, Robert Nolen lawyer
Miller, Walker David judge
Milstead, John David reporter
†Mitchem, Allen P. lawyer
†Mitchem, James E. lawyer
Moeller, Richard Robert political science educator
†Mohebbi, Afshin telecommunications industry executive
Moody, Eric John psychologist, researcher
Moore, Ernest Eugene, Jr., surgeon, educator
Moore, Gregory L. editor
Moore, Steven Woodrow lawyer
†Moreno, Abel computer scientist, educator, director
Mouton, Andre Paul artist
Mowry, Frank Henry journalist, photojournalist
Moye, John Edward lawyer
Mueller, Kathryn Lucile occupational and environmental medicine educator
Mullarkey, Mary J. state supreme court chief justice
Mullineaux, Donal Ray geologist
Murane, William Edward lawyer
Murdock, Pamela Ervilla travel and advertising company executive
Murray, James Alan urban and environmental consultant, investor
†Myernick, Glenn professional soccer coach
Myhren, Trygve Edward communications company executive
Nanda, Ved Prakash law educator, university official
†Nelson, Bernard William foundation executive, educator, physician
Nelson, John Gustaf lawyer
Nelson, L. Bruce lawyer
Nelson, LeAnn Lindbeck small business owner
Nelson, Nevin Mary interior designer
Nelson, Sarah Milledge archaeology educator
Nemiro, Beverly Mirium Anderson author, educator
Neu, Carl Herbert, Jr., management consultant
Neumann, Herschel physics educator
Newberry, Elizabeth Carter greenhouse and floral company owner
Newcom, Jennings Jay lawyer
Nicholson, Will Faust, Jr., bank holding company executive
Nier, Harry Kaufman lawyer
Norman, John Edward petroleum landman
†Norton, Jane E. lieutenant governor
Notebaert, Richard C. telecommunications industry executive
Nottingham, Edward Willis, Jr., federal judge
†Nutting, Paul Albert medical educator, medical science administrator
Oakes, Terry Louis retail clothing store executive
O'Connell, Richard J. insurance adviser
†Oiso, Naoki dermatologist, researcher
O'Keefe, Edward Franklin lawyer
Olsen, M. Kent lawyer, educator
Orullian, B. LaRae bank executive
Otten, Arthur Edward, Jr., lawyer, corporate executive
Owen, Maureen A. poet
Owens, Bill governor
Owens, Marvin Franklin, Jr., oil company executive
†Oxman, Stephen Eliot lawyer
†Pahs, Stephen Walter pilot, real estate broker
Palmer, David Gilbert lawyer
Parker, Catherine Susanne psychotherapist
Parsell, Roger Edmund retired educator, civic worker
†Partrick, David Allen pediatrician, surgeon
†Pascoe, Donald Monte lawyer
Patterson, Daniel William dentist
Pear, Bertram Lincoln radiologist, educator
Petty, Thomas Lee physician, educator
Pfnister, Allan Orel humanities educator
Plummer, Ora Beatrice nursing educator, trainer
Pocs, Martin M. executive search consultant
†Pointer, Marsha G. principal
Poirot, James Wesley engineering company executive
Pomerantz, Marvin thoracic surgeon
Ponzi, James Doughlas police officer, computer specialist
Porfilio, John Carbone federal judge
Potter, Gary Thomas lawyer
†Pratt, Kevin Burton lawyer
Price, Kathleen McCormick book editor, writer
†Prichard, Vincent Marvin lawyer
Prochnow, James R. lawyer
Prosser, John Martin architect, educator, urban design consultant
Puck, Theodore Thomas geneticist, biophysicist, educator
Puckett, Paul Walter lawyer
Purcell, Kenneth psychology educator, university dean
Quiat, Gerald M. lawyer
Quiat, Marshall lawyer
Rael, Henry Sylvester, Sr., retired health administrator, financial and management consultant
Ragland, Bob artist, educator
Rainer, William Gerald cardiac surgeon
Raughton, Jimmie Leonard education consultant, public administrator, urban planner
Ray, Bruce David lawyer, writer
†Redondo Velasco, Maria Jose endocrinologist, researcher
Reece, Monique Elizabeth marketing, advertising and sales consultant
Rench, Stephen Charles lawyer
†Reynolds, Collins James, III, management consultant
Rich, Robert Stephen lawyer
Richardson, Elizabeth Hall retired ecologist
Ricklin, Elaine Paula artist, educator
†Rigg, John Brownlee, Jr., lawyer
Ritchie, Daniel Lee academic administrator
Robertson, Lawrence Marshall, Jr., neurosurgeon
Robins, Judy Roselyn interior designer
†Robinson, Charles Andrew audiology services professional
Robinson, Cleo Parker artistic director
Rockwell, Bruce McKee retired banker and foundation executive
Rockwood, Linda Lee lawyer
Roesler, John Bruce lawyer
Rogers, Joe former lieutenant governor
†Romer, Roy R. former governor
Rothman, Paul Alan publishing executive
Rovira, Luis Dario state supreme court justice
Roy, Arthur Putnam lawyer
Ruge, Daniel August retired neurosurgeon, educator
Ruppert, John Lawrence lawyer
Sadun, Alberto Carlo astrophysicist, educator
Sakic, Joseph Steve professional hockey player
Salazar, Kenneth L. state attorney general
Saltz, Howard Joel newspaper editor
Sandler, Thomas R. accountant
Sarney, Saul Richard lawyer
Satter, Raymond Nathan judge
†Sattler, Bruce Weimer lawyer
Sayre, John Marshall lawyer, former government official
Schiff, Donald Wilfred pediatrician, educator
Schmidt, L(ail) William, Jr., lawyer
Schoeneberger, Marlies Luise alcohol/drug abuse services professional, gerontologist, sociologist
Schwartz, Cherie Anne Karo storyteller, writer
Seawell, Donald Ray lawyer, publisher, arts center executive, producer
Shaddock, Paul Franklin, Sr., human resources executive
Shadrick, Dorothy Jo management consultant
Shaeffer, Thelma Jean primary school educator
†Shaffer, Oren George former manufacturing company executive
Sharp, Lewis I. museum director
Shawe, Daniel Reeves geologist
†Shea, Kevin Michael lawyer
Sheeran, Michael John Leo priest, college administrator
Sheldon Epstein, Vivian author, publisher
†Shepherd, John Frederic lawyer
Shindell, Sidney medical educator, physician
Shirkey, Linda Sue interior designer, film company executive, set designer
Shore, James H(enry) psychiatrist
Shreve, Theodore Norris construction company executive
†Shwayder, Elizabeth Yanish sculptor
Silverman, Arnold pediatrician, educator
Simoes, Eric Arun Francis pediatrics educator

GEOGRAPHICAL INDEX 5837 COLORADO

Simpson, Diane Jeannette *school social worker, counselor, adoption home study worker*
Singleton, Dean *publishing executive*
Skok, Paul Joseph *lawyer*
†Slavin, Howard Leslie *lawyer, real estate broker, law educator, judge*
Smith, Dwight Morrell *chemistry educator*
Smith, Sallye Wrye *librarian*
Smith, William French, II, *safety engineer, special projects administrator*
Snyder, Charles Royce *sociologist, educator*
†Solano, Henry L. *lawyer*
Solano, Janine T. *physician assistant*
Spilka, Bernard *psychology educator*
†Spradley, Lola *state representative*
Starrs, Elizabeth Anne *lawyer*
†Steefel, David Simon *lawyer*
Steele, Thomas Joseph *English language educator, writer*
Steenhagen, Robert Lewis *landscape architect, consultant*
Stephens, Larry Dean *engineer, consultant*
Stephenson, Arthur Emmet, Jr., *corporate and investment company executive*
Strand, Melford Lien *anesthesiologist*
†Strenski, Robert Francis *lawyer*
Sujansky, Eva Borska *pediatrician, geneticist, educator*
Sundel, Harvey H. *marketing research analyst, consultant*
†Švec, Jan G. *voice scientist, researcher*
Swihart, Steven Taylor *judge*
Szefler, Stanley James *pediatrics and pharmacology educator*
Takeda, Yasuhiko *pathologist*
†Talman, Louis A. *mathematician*
Taylor, Edward Stewart *physician, educator*
†Taylor, Julia Fisher *public relations executive*
Temple, John R. *publishing executive*
†Thomas, Enolia *nutritionist, educator*
Thomasch, Roger Paul *lawyer*
†Thompson, Cathy Joanne *nursing educator, consultant, acute care nurse practitioner*
†Thompson, Joseph Paul *retired systems administrator*
Timmins, Edward Patrick *lawyer*
Tisdale, Douglas Michael *lawyer*
Trueblood, Harry Albert, Jr., *oil company executive*
Tyler, Kenneth Laurence *neurologist, researcher*
†Tymkovich, Timothy *federal judge*
Ulrich, Theodore Albert *lawyer*
Van Arsdale, Kathy *music educator*
van Westrum, Anthony *lawyer, arbitrator, mediator*
Vickery, Robert Bruce *oil industry executive, consultant*
Vogel, Robert Lee *college administrator, clergyman*
Volpe, Richard Gerard *insurance accounts executive, consultant*
†Von Wald, Richard B. *lawyer*
Vosevich, Kathi Ann *writer, editor, scholar*
Wagner, Judith Buck *investment firm executive*
†Waits, Frankie A. *real estate broker*
†Walcher, Jennifer Lynne *city official*
†Waldstein, Gail P. *pediatric pathologist, writer*
Walker, Larry Kenneth Robert *professional baseball player*
Walker, Radford *computer system architect*
Walsh, John Francis *lawyer*
Ward, Lester Lowe, Jr., *arts executive, lawyer*
Weatherley-White, Roy Christopher Anthony *surgeon, consultant*
Webb, Wellington E. *former mayor*
Weihaupt, John George *geosciences educator, scientist, university administrator*
Weinberg, Hedy Leah *journalist*
Weiner, Norman *pharmacology educator*
Weinstein, David Akers *lawyer*
†Welch, Carol Mae *lawyer*
Welch, J(oan) Kathleen *entrepreneur*
Wetzel, Jodi (Joy Lynn Wetzel) *history and women's studies educator*
Wheeler, Malcolm Edward *lawyer, educator*
White, Joyce Louise *librarian*
Wilcox, Martha Anne *lawyer*
Wilkinson, Joan Kristine *nurse, pediatric clinical specialist*
Willbanks, Roger Paul *publishing and book distributing company executive*
†Williams, Andrea Irene *arbitrator, mediator, consultant*
Williams, Michael Anthony *lawyer*
Williams, Sue M. *corporate communications specialist, writer*
Wirkler, Norman Edward *architectural, engineering, construction management firm executive*
Witt, Catherine Lewis *neonatal nurse practitioner, writer*
Woerner, Robert Eugene *federal agency administrator, editor*
Wohlgenant, Richard Glen *lawyer, director*
Wollins, David Hart *lawyer*
Woodcock, Jonathan Hugh *neurologist*
Woodward, Lester Ray *lawyer*
Wunnicke, Brooke *lawyer*
Yegge, Robert Bernard *law educator, dean*
Yohannes, Daniel W. *banker*
Yuan, Shen-Chuan *civil and structural engineer, consultant*
Zanecchia, Thomas Edward *financial executive*
Zimet, Carl Norman *psychologist, educator*
Zimmer, Larry William, Jr., *sports announcer*

Dillon

Becker, Quinn Henderson *orthopedic surgeon, army officer*
Follett, Robert John Richard *publisher*
Roder, Hans Martin *retired physicist, consultant*

Dolores

Kreyche, Gerald Francis *retired philosophy educator*
Winterer, Barbara Jean *designer, author*

Dumont

Hudson, Miller Newton *public agency manager, consultant*

Durango

Ballantine, Morley Cowles (Mrs. Arthur Atwood Ballantine) *newspaper editor*
Burnham, Bryson Paine *retired lawyer*
Fogleman, Ronald Robert *retired air force officer, consultant*
Foster, James Henry *advertising and public relations executive*
Gulliford, Andrew Jellis *historian, photographer*
Korns, Leota Elsie *writer, mountain land developer, insurance broker*
Langoni, Richard Allen *civil engineer*
†Mann, Rochelle Gayl *education educator, writer*
Sherman, Lester Ivan Jerry *retired lawyer*
Smith, Duane Allan *history educator, researcher*
Thurston, William Richardson *oil and gas industry executive, geologist*
Van Mols, Brian *publishing executive*
Vogl, Laurel Covington *artist, educator*
Wigton, Chester Mahlon *family physician*
Zeller, Christopher Lee *archaeologist, preservationist*

Edwards

Bryson, Gary Spath *cable television and telephone company executive*
Chambers, Joan Louise *retired librarian, retired dean*

Englewood

Asarch, Elaine *interior designer, anthropologist*
Barbezat, Eugene LaVar *computer systems engineer, retired air force officer*
Bardsley, Kay *historian, archivist, dance professional*
Bartee, Roy McKinley, II, *anesthesiologist*
Barth, David Victor *computer systems designer, consultant*
Bayes, Marjorie Andress *psychologist*
Benson, Robert Craig, III, *business consultant*
Bondi, Bert Roger *accountant, financial planner*
Bowlen, Pat(rick)(Dennis) *professional sports team executive, holding company executive, lawyer*
Bradshaw, Beverly Jean *psychotherapist, consultant, educator*
Carroll, Kim Marie *nurse*
†Coffee, Melvin Arnold *retired lawyer*
Coffman, Penelope Dalton *judge*
Conroy, Thomas Francis *insurance company consultant*
Cooper, Sharon Marsha *marketing, advertising executive*
Cooper, Steven Jon *healthcare management consultant, educator*
Cowley, Gerald Dean *architect*
Davis, Mary Georgia *music educator*
Davis, Terrell *former professional football player*
†Deutsch, Harvey Elliot *lawyer*
†Epstein, Joseph Marc *lawyer*
Erickson, William Hurt *retired state supreme court justice*
Ervin, Patrick Franklin *nuclear engineer*
Figa, Phillip Sam *lawyer*
Gabel, Connie *chemist, educator*
Gertz, David Lee *homebuilding company executive*
Giesen, John William *advertising executive*
Greenagel, Debra *travel agency executive*
Griese, Brian *football player*
Hall, Michael L. *obstetrician-gynecologist*
Hardy, Wayne Russell *insurance and investment broker*
Haupenthal, Laura Ann *clinical psychologist*
Irwin, Mark *writer, educator*
Jessee, William Floyd *executive*
†Karstaedt, Arthur R., III, *lawyer*
Keegan, James Joseph *financial executive*
†Keesling, Ruth Morris *foundation administrator*
†Kepros, John Paul *trauma surgeon*
†Knize, David Maurice *plastic surgeon*
Kramer, Ronald E. *neurologist, neurophysiologist*
Kristin, Karen *artist*
Kuhn, Donald Marshall *marketing professional*
Lake, Stanley James *security consulting company executive, motel chain executive, locksmith*
Lamb, Darlis Carol *sculptor*
Lessey, Samuel Kenric, Jr., *foundation administrator*
Lidstone, Herrick Kenley, Jr., *lawyer*
†Magoun, Harold Ives, Jr., *osteopath*
Mahoney, Gerald Francis *manufacturing company executive*
†Malone, John C. *telecommunications executive*
Manley, Richard Walter *insurance executive*
McGlockton, Chester *professional football player*
McGraw, Jack Wilson *federal agency administrator*
Moran, Gregory Allan *real estate developer*
Neiser, Brent Allen *foundation executive, public affairs and personal finance consultant, speaker*
Nelson, Barbara Louise *secondary education educator*
†Oberhelman, Todd W. *aerospace engineer, consultant*
†Peterson, Ralph Randall *engineering executive*
Plummer, Jason Steven (Jake Plummer) *professional football player*
Reese, Monte Nelson *agricultural association executive*
Rosser, Edwin Michael *mortgage company executive*
Schwartz, Michael Lee *financial planner, consultant*
Shanahan, Mike *professional football coach*
Shannon, Malcolm Lloyd, Jr., *lawyer, educator*
Shields, Marlene Sue *elementary school educator*
Shimokubo, Janice Teruko *marketing professional*
Simendinger, Theodore John *writer, publishing executive*
Simmons, David Norman *lawyer*
†Smith, Neil *professional football player*
Smith, Rod *football player*
Spencer, Margaret Gilliam *lawyer*
Steinhauser, John William *retired lawyer*
Strauss, Eric L. *retired materials scientist*
†Surrey, Eric S. *reproductive endocrinologist*
Van Loucks, Mark Louis *venture capitalist, business advisor*
Wagner, David James *lawyer*
Wham, Dorothy Stonecipher *retired state legislator*
Whiteaker, Ruth Catherine *retired secondary education educator, counselor*
†Woodward, John Simpson, Jr., *orthopedic surgeon*
†Yukl, Richard Lester *surgeon*

Erie

Alpers, John Hardesty, Jr., *financial planning executive, retired military officer*
Dilly, Marian Jeanette *humanities educator*

Estes Park

Bridges, Douglas M. *musician, small business owner*
Cope, James Dudley *retired trade association executive*
†Easton, Lois Brown *educational consultant*
Guest, Linda Sand *education educator*
Marr, J(ames) Joseph *venture capitalist*
Moore, Omar Khayyam *experimental sociologist*
Ojalvo, Morris *civil engineer, educator*
Piper, Mark Harry *retired banker*
Webb, Richard C. *engineering company executive*

Evergreen

Dobbs, Gregory Allan *journalist*
Evans, David Lynn *management consultant*
Frobel, Ronald Kenneth *geosynthetic engineer, consultant*
Haun, John Daniel *petroleum geologist, educator*
Heyl, Allen Van, Jr., *geologist*
Jackson, William Richard *entrepreneur*
McEldowney, Roland Conant *gold mining company executive, photographer*
Rodolff, Dale Ward *engineer, sales executive, consultant*
Saxton, Mary Jane *management educator*
White, John David *composer, theorist, cellist*

Falcon AFB

†Dylewski, Gary R. *retired career officer*

Fleming

Nichols, Lee Ann *library media specialist*

Fort Collins

Abt, Steven R. *civil engineering educator, dean*
Anderson, John Albert *physician*
†Baldwin, Lionel Vernon *retired university president*
†Bartels, Randy A. *science educator, researcher*
Bennett, Jacqueline Beekman *school psychologist*
Bennett, Thomas LeRoy, Jr., *clinical neuropsychology educator*
Bernstein, Elliot Roy *chemistry educator*
Brockwell, Peter John *statistics educator*
†Buddenbaum, Judith M. *communications educator, writer*
Cermak, Jack Edward *engineer, educator*
Charlie, Wayne Alexander *civil engineering educator*
Chorpenning, H. R., III, *minister*
Christiansen, Norman Juhl *retired newspaper publisher*
†Cooperman, Matthew B. *language educator*
Cummings, Sharon Sue *state extension service youth specialist*
†Delgado, Jorge A. *soil scientist*
Downey, Arthur Harold, Jr., *lawyer, mediator*
Driscoll, Richard Stark *retired land evaluation and land use planner*
Eitzen, David Stanley *sociologist, educator*
Emslie, William Arthur *electrical engineer*
Ernest, Douglas Jerome *librarian*
Evans, Norman Allen *retired civil engineering educator*
Ewing, Jack Robert *accountant*
Fixman, Marshall *chemist, educator*
Follett, Ronald Francis *soil scientist*
Fotsch, Dan Robert *elementary education educator*
Frink, Eugene Hudson, Jr., *business and real estate consultant*
Gandy, H. Conway *retired judge, state official*
Gast, Richard Shaeffer *lawyer*
Gillette, Edward LeRoy *radiation oncology educator*
Gilmore, Timothy Jonathan *paralegal*
Grandin, Temple *industrial designer, science educator*
Gubler, Duane J. *research scientist, administrator*
Hallahan, Kirk Edward *journalism educator*
Halvorson, Ardell David *soil scientist, researcher*
Harper, Judson Morse *university administrator, consultant, educator*
Held, Royer Burnell *economics educator*
Hjelmfelt, David Charles *lawyer*
Hultgren, Glenn M. *chiropractor*
Jensen, Margaret *real estate broker*
Johnson, Bruce Allan *engineering executive*
†Johnson, Donald Edward, Jr., *lawyer*
Johnson, Neil Arthur *composer, educator*
Kaufman, Harold Richard *mechanical engineer and physics educator*
Keim, Wayne Franklin *retired genetics educator, plant geneticist*
†Ketcham, Sally Ann *historic site staff member, consultant*
Kinnison, Robert Wheelock *retired accountant*
Knopf, Fritz L. *biologist*
†Kosoy, Michael Y. *biomedical researcher*
†Kraus, David (Dirk) Bruce *musician, educator*
Ladanyi, Branka Maria *chemist, educator*
Linden, James Carl *educator, consultant*
†Loy, Ivan *mathematician, educator*
Lumb, William Valjean *veterinarian*
MacLauchlin, Robert Kerwin *communications artist, educator*
Mader, Douglas Paul *research administrator*
Maher, Thomas George *academic administrator, producer, media educator*
Marvel, M. Kim *psychologist, researcher*
Matthies, Frederick John *civil and environmental engineer*
May, Stephen James *communications educator, writer*
Mc Clellan, William Monson *library administrator, retired*
McComb, David Glendinning *history educator*
Mesloh, Warren Henry *civil and environmental engineer*
Meyers, Albert Irving *emeritus chemistry educator*
Mielke, Paul William, Jr., *statistician, consultant*
†Mister, William Gray *accountant, educator*
†Moorcroft, William Herbert *retired bio-psychologist, educator, researcher*
Moore, Charles E. *engineer*
Morgan, David Allen *electronic engineer*
Mortvedt, John Jacob *soil scientist, researcher*
Mosier, Arvin Ray *chemist, researcher*
Nassar, Carl Rudolph *engineering executive, psychotherapist*
Newlin, Douglas Randal *retired lead information engineer*
Ogg, James Elvis *microbiologist, educator*
Ozawa, Terutomo *economics educator, consultant*
Patton, Carl Elliott *physics educator*
†Perryman, Lance *dean*
Peterson, Gary Andrew *agronomics researcher*
Phemister, Robert David *veterinary medical educator*
Redder, Thomas Joseph *lawyer, judge, legislator, federal administrator, biotech executive*
Richardson, Everett Vern *hydraulic engineer, educator, administrator, consultant*
Roberts, Archibald Edward *retired career officer, writer*
Roesner, Larry August *civil engineer*
Rogers, Garth Winfield *lawyer*
Rollin, Bernard Elliot *philosophy educator, consultant on animal ethics*
Rolston, Holmes, III, *theologian, educator, philosopher*
Sandborn, Virgil Alvin *civil engineer, educator*
Schendel, Winfried George *insurance company executive*
Schumm, Stanley Alfred *geologist, educator*
Sedei Rodden, Pamela Jean *therapist*
Seidel, George Elias, Jr., *animal scientist, educator*
Shands, Henry Lee *plant geneticist, administrator*
Sloane, Sarah Jane *English educator*
Smith, Dwight Raymond *ecology and wildlife educator, writer*
Smith, Nina Maria *mental health nurse, administrator, consultant*
Smith, Ralph Earl *virologist*
Sons, Raymond William *journalist*
Sprague, Amaris Jeanne *real estate broker*
Stoaks, Ralph Duval *biotechnologist, consultant*
Suinn, Richard Michael *psychologist*
Terauds, Juris *retired science educator, research scientist*
Tremblay, William Andrew *English language educator, writer*
Tyler, Gail Madeleine *nurse*
Vonder Haar, Thomas H. *meteorology educator*
Watz, Martin Charles *brewery consultant*
Weiler, Stephan *economist, educator*
Wilber, Clare Marie *musician, educator*
Woolhiser, David Arthur *hydrologist*
Yates, Albert Carl *academic administrator, chemistry educator*

Fort Garland

Boyer, Lester Leroy, Jr., *architecture educator, consultant*
Moullette, John Brinkley *retired corporate trainer, consultant*

Fort Morgan

Higinbotham, Jacquelyn Joan *lawyer*
Raines, Louis Edward *school administrator*

Fowler

Fox, Jonathan Randall *banker, real estate broker, insurance agent*

Fraser

Hibbs, John David *software executive, engineer, business owner*

Frederick

Emlen, Warren Metz *computer-related services company owner*

Frisco

Helmer, David Alan *lawyer*
McElyea, Monica Sergent *lawyer*

Georgetown

Hildebrandt-Willard, Claudia Joan *banker*
Stern, Mort(imer) P(hillip) *journalism and communications educator, academic administrator, consultant*

Glenwood Springs

Karp, Sander Neil *lawyer*

Golden

Baron, Robert Charles *publishing executive*
Bickart, Theodore Albert *university president emeritus*
Carney, Deborah Leah Turner *lawyer*

Christensen, Robert Wayne *oral maxillofacial surgeon, minister*
†Contreras, Miguel Alberto *materials scientist, researcher*
†Coors, Peter Hanson *beverage company executive*
†Coors, William K. *brewery executive*
Eber, Kevin *science writer*
Eckley, Wilton Earl, Jr., *humanities educator, educator*
Eiberger, Carl Frederick *lawyer*
Ellsworth, Joseph Cordon *real estate executive, lawyer*
Fahey, Barbara Stewart Doe *public agency administrator*
Fanchi, John Richard *physicist, educator, industrial technologist*
Fleener, Terry Noel *marketing professional*
Hamilton, Warren Bell *geologist, researcher, geophysicist, educator*
Henderson, Sabrina Nicole *journalist*
Hu, Jian *physicist, researcher*
Hughes, Marcia Marie *lawyer, consultant, motivational speaker*
Illangasekare, Tissa Harischandra *engineering educator, researcher*
Klug, John Joseph *secondary education educator, director of dramatics*
Kopel, David Benjamin *lawyer*
Krauss, George *metallurgist*
Lane, William Lewis *civil engineer*
Lindsay, Nathan James *space systems consultant, retired military officer*
Loomis, Christopher Knapp *metallurgical engineer*
†Manion, Randolph Thomas *energy executive, consumer products company executive*
Mathews, E. Anne Jones *library educator and administrator, consultant*
Matthews, Thomas Michael *former energy company executive*
Moore, Michal Charles *land economist, educator*
Myers, Daryl Ronald *engineer*
Olson, Marian Katherine *management executive, consultant, publisher*
†Outerbridge, Cheryl *lawyer*
Petrick, Alfred, Jr., *mineral economics educator, consultant*
†Phillipson, Donald E. *lawyer*
Quirke, Terence Thomas, Jr., *genealogist, retired geologist*
Rodgers, Frederic Barker *judge*
Shea, Dion Warren Joseph *university official, fund raiser*
Sloan, Earle Dendy, Jr., *chemical engineering educator*
Snead, Kathleen Marie *lawyer*
†Speer, John Gordon *metallurgist, educator, materials scientist, educator*
Stewart, Frank Maurice, Jr., *federal agency administrator*
†Stoffel, Thomas *research scientist*
Trefny, John Ulric *college president*
†Truly, Richard H. *academic administrator, former federal agency administrator, former astronaut*
Van Dusen, Donna Bayne *communications consultant, educator, researcher*
Wei, Su-Huai *physicist, researcher*
Weimer, Robert Jay *geology educator, energy consultant, civic leader*
Wellisch, William Jeremiah *social psychology educator*
Yarar, Baki *mining and metallurgical engineering educator*
Zhang, Ruichong *civil and mechanical engineer, educator*
Zhong, Dalong *materials scientist, consultant*

Granby
Johnson, William Potter *newspaper publisher*

Grand Junction
Achen, Mark Kennedy *city administrator, management consultant*
Armstrong, Linda Jean (Gene Armstrong) *writer, artist*
Bacon, Phillip *geographer, author, consultant*
Bishop, Tilman Malcolm *retired state legislator, college administrator*
Bornmann, Lewis Joseph *computer scientist*
†Casebolt, James Stanton *lawyer*
Duray, John Robert *physicist*
†Elias, Carlos Enoc *music educator, conductor*
†Erickson, Mary Evelyn *artist, writer*
Freeman, Neil *accounting and computer consulting firm executive*
†Griff, Harry *lawyer*
†Janson, Richard Anthony *plastic surgeon*
†Lachance, Paul Arthur *legal educator, consultant*
Layton, Robert Glenn *radiologist*
Mallory, Elgin Albert *business educator, management consultant, small business owner, school system administrator*
McCarthy, Mary Frances *medical foundation administrator*
Moberly, Linden Emery *educational administrator*
†Nizalowski, John Anthony *writer, educator*
Pantenburg, Michel *hospital administrator, health educator, holistic health coordinator*
Rutz, Richard Frederick *physicist, researcher*
Rybak, James Patrick *engineering educator*
Skogen, Haven Sherman *investment company executive*
Van Horn, O. Frank *retired counselor, consultant*
†Woodworth, Sandra Sue *communications educator*

Greeley
Cook, Donald E. *pediatrician, educator*
Duff, William Leroy, Jr., *university dean emeritus, business educator*
Ebomoyi, William Ehigie *epidemiologist*
Gritts, Gerald Lee *home health nurse, AIDS care nurse, AIDS educator*
Hilgenkamp, Kathryn Darline *exercise and sport psychologist, health educator*
Houtchens, Barnard *retired lawyer*
Jenkins, Virginia *visual arts educator, artist*
Kelsey, Michael Loyal *geography educator*
†Knott, Alexander Waller *historian, educator*
Linde, Lucille Mae (Lucille Jacobson) *motor-perceptual specialist*
Longwell, Robert Leroy *writer*
Miller, Diane Wilmarth *retired human resources director*
Moore, Melanie *sociology educator*
†Morgensen, Jerry Lynn *construction company executive*
Rames, Douglas Dwight *civil engineer*
Ross, Rosann Mary *psychotherapist, educator*
Schrenk, Gary Dale *foundation executive*
Shadwick, Gerald *management educator*
†Simons, John S. *food products executive*
Smith, Jack Lee *bank executive*
Ursyn, Anna *computer graphics artist, educator*
Van Gorp, Gary Wayne *clergyman*
Willis, Connie (Constance E. Willis) *author*
†Woody, William Douglas *social sciences educator, researcher*
Worley, Lloyd Douglas *English language educator*

Greenwood Village
Arvizu, Dan Eliab *mechanical engineer*
†Aspinwall, David Charles *lawyer, insurance company executive*
Chesser, Al H. *union official*
Cocklin, Ruth Ellen *artist*
Corboy, James McNally *investment banker*
Davidson, John Robert (Jay) *banking executive*
Dymond, Lewis Wandell *lawyer, mediator, educator*
†Fierst, Bruce Philip *lawyer*
Gallegos, Larry Duayne *lawyer*
Hendrick, Hal Wilmans *human factors educator*
Karr, David Dean *lawyer*
†Klasco, Richard *emergency physician, information technology executive*
Lynn, Patricia Anne *student services representative*
Nixon, Scott Sherman *lawyer*
Poe, Robert Alan *lawyer*
Ramsey, John Arthur *lawyer*
Sims, Douglas D. *bank executive*
†Unruh, Kurt D. *lawyer, consultant*

Guffey
McCaslin, Kathleen Denise *child abuse educator*
Ward, Larry Thomas *social program administrator*

Gunnison
Venturo, Frank Angelo *communications educator, college offical*

Henderson
Thompson, Robert Frank, Jr., *career officer*

Highlands Ranch
Allen, Roberta Jane *social worker*
Brierley, James Alan *biohydrometallurgy consultant*
Bublitz, Deborah Keirstead *pediatrician*
Erickson, Linda Rae *educator*
Fiess, Stephen Charles Edward *musician, music educator*
Hagen, Glenn W. *lawyer*
Hoover, Gary Lynn *banker*
Krinsky, Fredda S. *clinical chemist, consultant*
†Mezey, Richard R. *music educator, organist*
Mierzwa, Joseph William *lawyer, legal communications consultant*
Sandoval, Lisa Ann *occupational therapist*
Townsend, James Douglas *accountant*

Hotchkiss
Blackstock, Virginia Harriett *artist*

Idledale
Brown, Gerri Ann *physical therapist*

Ignacio
Craig, Roy Phillip *writer, educator, rancher*

Jamestown
Craigo, Christina Ila *artist, educator*

Jefferson
Maatsch, Deborah Joan *financial company executive, tax advisor*

Johnstown
Williams, Matt Eugene *chiropractor, educator*

Kersey
Guttersen, Michael *ranching and investments professional*

La Junta
Williams, Ronald Lee *retired pharmacologist*

La Salle
Clausen, Bret Mark *industrial hygienist, safety professional*

Lafayette
Conrad, Kelley Allen *industrial and organizational psychologist*
Hasund, Svein Harald *mechanical engineer*
†Lutton, Cheri *small business owner, researcher*
McNeill, William *environmental scientist*
Middlebrooks, Eddie Joe *environmental engineer*
Short, Ray Everett *minister, sociology educator emeritus, author, lecturer*

Lake George
Norman, John Barstow, Jr., *designer, educator*

Lakewood
Barber, Larry Eugene *financial planner*
Barger, Louise Baldwin *religious organization administrator*
Berg Oram, Stephanie *music educator*
Bettinghaus, Erwin Paul *research scientist*
Binns, Cathleen Isabel *retired secondary school educator*
Brant, John Getty *lawyer*
Brinkmeyer, Dotty Stewart *maternal/child nurse*
Burkholder, Steve *mayor*
Burnett, Elizabeth (Betsy Burnett) *counselor*
Coakley, William Thomas *retired utilities executive*
Finnie, Doris Gould *investment company executive*
Fugate, Ivan Dee *banker, lawyer*
†Goolsby, Donald Allton *water resources scientist*
Guyton, Samuel Percy *retired lawyer*
Hansen, Richard Olaf *geophysicist, educator*
Heath, Gary Brian *manufacturing firm executive, engineer*
Hickman, Ruth Virginia *Bible educator*
Isely, Henry Philip *association executive, integrative engineer, writer, educator*
Jacobson, Dennis John *lawyer*
Joy, Carla Marie *history educator*
Keller, Shirley Inez *accountant*
Knott, William Alan *library director, management and building consultant*
Kulkarni, Kishore Ganesh *economics educator, consultant*
Lipson, Jonathan Mark *psychologist*
Lu, Paul Haihsing *mining engineer, geotechnical consultant*
Martinen, John A. *travel company executive*
McBride, Guy Thornton, Jr., *college president emeritus*
McElwee, Dennis John *lawyer, former pharmaceutical company executive*
Nichols, Vicki Anne *financial consultant, librarian*
O'Brien, Kathleen Ann *economist*
†Padilla, Francisco S. *language educator*
Quinn, John Michael *physicist, geophysicist*
Rosa, Fredric David *construction company executive*
Scott, Peter Bryan *lawyer*
Shannon, Richard Stoll, III, *financial executive*
Soeth, James Richard *forester*
Strain, Mac Burns *civil engineer*
Thome, Dennis Wesley *lawyer*
Walton, Roger Alan *public relations executive, mediator, writer*
Weskamp, Kelley S. *loan account manager, real estate company executive*
Wilson, James Robert *lawyer*
Woodruff, Kathryn Elaine *English language educator*
†Yuthas, George Anthony *lawyer*

Las Animas
DeKrey, Ramona *medical/surgical nurse, educator*

Leadville
Bellhouse, Carol *lawyer*
Watson, Jack Crozier *retired state supreme court justice*

Littleton
†Alykova, Valentina *musician, music educator*
Annandale, George William *engineer*
Battilega, John A. *research and development company executive*
Benkert, Mary Russell *pediatrics nurse, researcher*
Bennett, Janice Lynn *publisher, educator*
Bradley, James Alexander *software engineer, researcher*
Brega, Kerry Elizabeth *physician, researcher*
Burgess, Larry Lee *commercial investment executive*
Bush, Stanley Giltner *secondary school educator*
Cabell, Elizabeth Arlisse *psychologist*
Carleno, Harry Eugene *lawyer*
†Crum, Julie Wade *literature educator*
Cypser, Darlene Ann *lawyer, movie producer*
Doty, Della Corrine *organization administrator*
†Ergen, Charles *communications professional*
Estep, John Hayes *religious organization administrator, clergyman*
Fisher, Louis McLane, Jr., *management consultant*
Forstot, Stephan Lance *ophthalmologist*
Fryt, Monte Stanislaus *petroleum company executive, speaker, advisor*
Geringer, James E. *former governor*
Goebel, Kathryn Mary *nurse*
Grant, Newell M. *real estate investment manager*
Greenberg, Elinor Miller *university official, consultant*
Hadley, Marlin LeRoy *direct sales financial consultant*
Hagman, Sally Wingchong *physical therapist*
Harney, Patricia Rae *enviromental technical supervisor*
Hopping, William Russell *hospitality industry consultant and appraiser*
†Ingui, Nicolle Eileen *journalist*
Inzano, Karen Lee *advertising agency executive*
†Johansson, Alicia Barbara *musician*
Keats, Donald Howard *composer, educator*
Kennedy, Jack *secondary education journalism educator*
Keogh, Heidi Helen Dake *advocate*
Kielmeyer, William Henry *ceramic engineer, researcher*
Kleinknecht, Kenneth Samuel *retired aerospace company executive, former federal space agency official*
Kullas, Albert John *management and systems engineering consultant*
Lesh-Laurie, Georgia Elizabeth *university administrator, biology educator, researcher*
Lohman, Loretta Cecelia *social scientist, consultant*
Marion, John Martin *academic administrator*
Meyer, Milton Edward, Jr., *lawyer, artist*
Mielke, Donald Earl *lawyer, lobbyist*
Miller, Betty Sue *counselor*
Moore, Dan Sterling *insurance executive, sales trainer*
Nesheim, Dennis Warren *art educator, artist, writer, instructional materials producer, special education educator*
Newell, Michael Stephen *finance company executive, international finance, protective services consultant*
†Panetta, Sandra Jean *education coordinator*
Pardue, Karen Reiko *elementary education educator*
Paull, Richard Allen *geologist, educator*
Riley, Mary Jane *computer scientist*
Robinson, Warren A. (Rip Robinson) *lawyer*
Rockwell, Kay Anne *elementary education educator*
Rothenberg, Harvey David *educational administrator*
Rotherham, Larry Charles *insurance executive*
Shelton, Olga-Jean *school counselor*
Shepherd, Donna Lou *interior designer*
Strang, Sandra Lee *airline official*
Treybig, Edwina Hall *sales executive*
Truhlar, Doris Broaddus *lawyer*
Udevitz, Norman *publishing executive*
Unkelbach, L. Cary *lawyer*
Vail, Charles Daniel *veterinarian, consultant*
VanderLinden, Camilla Denice Dunn *telecommunications industry manager*
Vostiar, John *retired telecommunications industry executive*
Zwilling, Mark C. *music director*

Loma
Young, David Bennion *artist*

Lone Tree
Bauer, Randy Mark *management training firm executive*
Spelts, Richard John *lawyer*

Lonetree
Washington, Reginald Louis *pediatric cardiologist*

Longmont
†Bisgard, Eileen Bernice Reid *lawyer*
Blackwood, Lois Anne *elementary education educator*
Breuer, Werner Alfred *retired plastics company executive*
Dierks, Richard Ernest *veterinarian, educational administrator*
Flanders, Eleanor Carlson *community volunteer*
†Flanders, Laurence Burdette, Jr., *retired lawyer*
Jones, Beverly Ann Miller *nursing administrator, retired patient services administrator*
Kaminsky, Glenn Francis *retired protective services official, business owner, teacher*
Keene, Samuel James, Jr., *reliability engineer researcher, educator*
King, Jane Louise *artist*
Melendez, Joaquin *retired orthopedic assistant*
Pattyn, Sue *publishing executive*
Ralston Thompson, Paula Jane *nurse*
†Venrick, Kristie Lund *educator*

Louisville
Donze, Jerry Lynn *electrical engineer*
Jonsen, Richard Wiliam *retired educational administrator*
†Kenney, Alan Adams *lawyer*
Kenney, Belinda Jill Forseman *technology company executive*
Maddock, Jerome Torrence *information services specialist*
Raymond, Dorothy Gill *lawyer*
Schonbrun, Michael K. *real estate developer, director*
†Sontag, Peter Michael *travel management company executive*
Syed, Yasser Fouad Khaderi *electrical engineer*

Louviers
Murdock, John T., II, *academic organization administrator, publishing company executive*

Loveland
Balsiger, David Wayne *television-video director, researcher, producer, writer*
Bierbaum, J. Armin *petroleum company executive, consultant*
Carter, Laura Lee *academic librarian, psychotherapist*
Geisendorfer, Nancy Kay *mathematics educator*
Hartsock, Jane Marie *nurse, educator*
Jones, Janis Sue *women's health nurse*
Lee, Evelyn Marie *elementary and secondary education educator*
McKinley, Jeneal Ruth *computer company executive*
Nossaman, Marian Alecia *manufacturing engineering executive*
Rodman, Alpine C. *arts and crafts company executive, photographer*
Rodman, Sue A. *wholesale company executive, artist, writer*
†Rosa, Linda *advocate*
Weimer, Dawn *sculptor*
Weresh, Thelma Faye *sculptor, artist*

Lyons
Spring, Kathleen *writer*

Mancos
Brown, Joy Alice *social services administrator*

Monte Vista
Guadagnoli, Michael John *music educator*

Montrose
Boice, Judith Lynette *physician, writer, educator*
†Overholser, John W. *lawyer*
Pitcher, Helen Ione *advertising director*

Monument
Boggs, Steven Eugene *real estate broker, lawyer*

Breckner, William John, Jr., *retired air force officer, corporate executive, consultant*
Caine, Philip David *retired military officer, author*
De Francesco, John Blaze, Jr., *public relations consultant, artist, writer*
Karasa, Norman Lukas *home builder, developer, geologist*
Miele, Alfonse Ralph *former government official*

Morrison
Bowen, Peter Geoffrey *arbitrator, business educator*
†Dorn, Mark S. *music educator, musician*
Gentry, Donald William *engineering executive, mining engineer*
Myers, Harry J., Jr., *retired publisher*
†Neumann, Stephanie Tower *retired librarian*
Pettee, Daniel Starr *retired neurologist*

Nederland
Lutz, Frank Wenzel *education administration educator*
†Morrison, K. Jaydene *education counseling firm executive*
Sutton, Philip D(ietrich) *psychologist, educator*

New Castle
Spuhler, Jacilyn Erickson *librarian*

Niwot
†Buss, Kathleen E. *music educator*
Farrington, Helen Agnes *personnel director*

Northglenn
†Hemlock, Roberta Leigh *veterinary technician*
Winter, William Paul, Jr., *ministry director*

Pagosa Springs
Howard, Carole Margaret Munroe *retired public relations executive*

Palisade
Fay, Abbott Eastman *history educator*

Palmer Lake
Dixon, Robert Clyde *systems engineer, consultant*

Parker
Fedak, Barbara Kingry *retired technical center administrator*
Greenberg, Morton Paul *lawyer, consultant, life settlement broker*
Haas, Bradley Dean *pharmacy director, clinical pharmacist, consultant*
Pastore, Thomas Michael *telecommunications sales executive*

Peterson AFB
†Dekok, Roger Gregory *career officer*

Peyton
Ball, Jennifer Leigh *writer, editor*
†Dunn, Doris *retired critical care nurse, artist, rancher*

Pine
Jones, David Milton *economist, educator*

Placerville
Kickert, Juliana Arlene *investor*
Monferrato, Angela Maria *investor, writer, designer*
Reagan, Harry Edwin, III, *lawyer*
Treat, John Elting *entrepreneur*

Pritchett
†Hall, Carol Ann *music educator*

Pueblo
†Chi, Jacob *music educator*
Cress, Cecile Colleen *retired librarian*
Farley, Thomas T. *lawyer*
Farwell, Hermon Waldo, Jr., *parliamentarian, educator, former speech communication educator*
Giffin, Walter Charles *retired industrial engineer, educator, consultant*
Heizer, Ida Ann *retired real estate broker*
Humes, James Calhoun *lawyer, communications consultant, writer, educator*
†Keller, Robert L. *sociologist, educator*
Kogovsek, Daniel Charles *lawyer*
Kulkosky, Paul Joseph *psychology educator*
Lewallen, William Marvin, Jr., *ophthalmologist*
Mo, Suchoon *psychology educator*
Occhiato, Michael Anthony *city official*
O'Conner, Loretta Rae *lawyer*
Rawlings, Robert Hoag *newspaper publisher*
Sisson, Ray L. *retired dean, author*
Vega, Jose Guadalupe *neuropsychologist, clinical professional*
Vorpagel, Wilbur Charles *historical consultant*

Ridgway
Lathrop, Kaye Don *nuclear scientist, educator*

Rocky Ford
†Mendenhall, Harry Barton *lawyer*

Sedalia
Ewing, Mary *lawyer*
†Ewing, Robert Craig *lawyer, educator*
McKee, John Morrison *management consultant*

Silver Cliff
Weber, Kent *wildlife organization administrator*

Silverthorne
Nobe, Kenneth Charles *international agricultural and water resource economics consultant*

Silverton
Voorlas, Stephanie Katherine *freelance/self-employed writer, photographer*

Snowmass
Lovins, L. Hunter *public policy institute executive*

Snowmass Village
Casebeer, Douglas Kelley *artist, ceramist, consultant*
Neumann, Bruce Russell *emergency physician*

Springfield
Wessler, Melvin Dean *farmer, rancher*

Steamboat Springs
†Farmer, Debra *academic administrator, educator*
Zabel, Curtis Lee *artist, rancher*

Sterling
Christian, Roland Carl (Bud Christian) *retired English language and speech communications educator*
Jones, Laurie Ganong *sales and marketing executive*

Superior
†Carey, Stephanie L. *systems engineer, educator*
Forshee, Gladys Marie *writer, insurance agent*

Telluride
†Hadley, Paul Burrest, Jr., (Tabbit Hadley) *domestic engineer*
Tatum, Thomas Deskins *film and television producer, director*

Thornton
Johnson, Carole Jean
Sawyer, Michael E. *library director*
Sherk, George William *lawyer*
Siska, Robert John *softwre engineer*

Trinidad
Potter, William Bartlett *business executive*
†Veltri, Sandra Kay *education educator*

Twin Lakes
Homan, Ralph William *finance company executive*

U S A F Academy
†Casebeer, William D. *adult education educator*
†Dallager, John R. *career officer*
†DeBerry, Fisher *college football coach*
Krise, Thomas Warren *military officer, English language educator*
Newmiller, William Ernest *English educator*
Wells, Mark Kendall *military officer, educator*

United States Air Force Academy
†Heidler, Jeanne Twiggs *adult education educator*

Vail
Bevan, William Arnold, Jr., *emergency physician*
Chow, Franklin Szu-Chien *obstetrician, gynecologist*
Kelton, Arthur Marvin, Jr., *real estate developer*
Knight, Constance Bracken *writer, realtor, corporate executive*
McFadden, Joseph Tedford *retired neurosurgeon, writer*
McGee, Michael Jay *protective services official, educator*
Vosbeck, Robert Randall *architect*
†Wilroy, Jo Ann *librarian*

Walsenburg
†Mellott, George Kenneth *retired music educator*

Westcliffe
Jones, Daniel Edwin, Jr., *bishop*
Merfeld, Gerald Lydon *artist*
†Snyder, Paul *lawyer*

Westminster
†Bocock, Scott Gregory *historian*
Callier, Maria Cecile *writer, actress*
Campagna, Timothy Nicholas *institute executive*
†Carol Ann, *artist, educator*
Eaves, Stephen Douglas *educator, vocational administrator*
†Gaither, John Francis, Jr., *lawyer*
Lingle, JoLynn Fleishman *writer, educator*
Shirai, Scott *communications executive*
Wirkkala, John Lester *cable company executive*

Wheat Ridge
Barrett, Michael Henry *civil engineer*
Brown, Steven Brien *radiologist*
Leino, Deanna Rose *business educator*
Morriss, Frank *writer, educator*
†Parrish, Peter Trasel *retired civil engineer*
Scherich, Erwin Thomas *civil engineer, consultant*
Wilcox, Mary Marks *retired Christian education consultant, educator*

Wiggins
†Kammerzell, Susan Jane *elementary school educator, music educator*

Windsor
†Landon, Jack Leonard *music educator*

Winter Park
†Newberry, Hal D. *operations specialist*

Woodland Park
Cockrille, Stephen *art director, business owner*
Olson, Warren Kinley *operations research analyst, engineer, physicist*
Stewart, Robert Lee *retired career officer, astronaut*
Trench, William Frederick *mathematician, educator*

Woody Creek
Jenkins, Robert Berryman *real estate developer*

Yuma
Hertneky, Randy Lee *optometrist*
Pfalmer, Charles Elden *secondary school educator*

CONNECTICUT

Ansonia
Dvoretzky, Israel *dermatologist*

Avon
†Boucher, Louis Jack *retired dentist, educator*
†Coburn, Elizabeth Ann *librarian*
De Moura Castro, Luiz C. *musician, educator*
Drapeau, Suzanne Eva *art educator, artist*
†Fantozzi, Donald Robert *music educator*
Godbout, Arthur Richard, Jr., *lawyer*
Hinz, Carl Frederick, Jr., *physician, educator*
Kling, Phradie (Phradie Kling Gold) *small business owner, educator*
Mazur, Edward John, Jr., *financial planner*
Schatz, Norma H. *volunteer*
von Kutzleben, Bernd Eberhard *nuclear engineer*
Weiss, Robert Michael *dentist*
†Widing, Carol Scharfe *lawyer*

Bantam
Privitera, Joseph F. *retired foreign service officer, writer-researcher*

Barkhamsted
†Stokes, Susan *political science educator*

Beacon Falls
Holub, Barbara Ann *rehabilitation nurse*

Berlin
†Kelly, Robert A. *music educator*
Pulito, Francis N. *artist*

Bethany
Bergen, Robert Ludlum, Jr., *retired materials scientist*
Childs, Brevard Springs *religious educator*

Bethel
Cheh, Huk Yuk *electrochemist, battery company executive*
DeLugo, Ernest Mario, Jr., *electrical engineer*
Kurfehs, Harold Charles *real estate executive*
Schetky, Laurence McDonald *metallurgist, researcher*
Shepard, Jean Heck *publishing company consultant, author, agent*
Tomanic, Joseph P(aul) *retired research scientist*

Bloomfield
Coburn, Richard Joseph *company executive, electrical engineer*
D'Annolfo, Suzanne Cordier *educational administrator, educator*
De Maria, Anthony John *electrical engineer*
Foster, Benjamin, Jr., *educational administrator*
Goldenberg, Philip Theodore *physician*
Hamilton, Thomas Stewart *physician, hospital administrator*
Handel, Morton Emanuel *management consultation executive*
Ivey, Elizabeth S. *retired physicist, educator*
Kelly, John Michael *lawyer*
Kissa, Karl Martin *electrical engineer*
†Messemer, Glenn Matthew *lawyer*
Scheuch, Richard *economist, educator*
Schwoerer, John Arnold *mechanical engineer*
Thorpe, James *humanities researcher*

Bolton
Marshall, James Hilton *retired secondary education educator*

Branford
Blake, Peter Jost *architect*
Chapman, Roger Stevens, Jr., *construction company executive*
Cronin, Michael Thomas Ignatius *pathologist, educator*
DeSimone, Robert Walter *medicinal chemist, educator*
Frase, Lawrence Thomas *psychologist, science administrator*
Gejdenson, Sam *former congressman*
Glick, Marion Shepherd *psychology, educator*
Gordon, John Charles *forestry educator*
LeVasseur, Lee Allan *fine artist*
Milgram, Judith Lee *art educator, administrator, artist*
Milgram, Richard Myron *music school administrator*
Smith, Richard Emerson (Dick Smith) *make-up artist*
†Tchernev, Velizar Tzvetanov *biomedical scientist*
Thomas, Lisa Francine *secondary school educator, assistant principal*
Vietzke, Wesley Maunder *internist, educator*
Wegener, Peter Paul *engineering educator, author*
Wright, Nancy Howell *interior designer*

Bridgeport
Bernstein, Larry Howard *clinical pathologist*
Black, Hillel Moses *publisher*
Brenner, John G. *protective services official*
Byrd, Charles Everett *clergyman*
Dexter, Gregory Warren *real estate and financial investor*
Eginton, Warren William *federal judge*
Ettre, Leslie Stephen *chemist*
Gallagher, Joan Frances *business administration educator*
†Gerber, Frances Joyce *early childhood educator*
†Goldberger, Robert R. *lawyer*
†Graham, Kenneth Albert *lawyer*
Hanley, Hilda Christina *endocrinologist*
Henderson, Albert Kossack *publishing company executive, dairy executive, consultant*

Hendricks, Edward David *education director, consultant, speaker, trainer*
Hofbauer, Michele Pace *illustrator, writer*
Kantrowitz, Jonathan Daniel *educational publishing and services company executive, lawyer*
†Kern, Irving J. *lawyer*
Lanci, Janet Mead *academic administrator, educator*
Lobdell, David Hill *pathologist*
Lori, William E. *bishop*
†Maloney, Maureen Murphy *social sciences educator*
†McAuliffe, Catherine A. *counselor, psychology educator, psychotherapist*
Nijensohn, Daniel Edgardo *neurosurgeon*
Pagano, Celeste Ann *social services coordinator*
Payson, Norman C. *healthcare services company executive*
†Reed, Charles Eli *retired chemist, chemical engineer*
Rosenman, Stephen David *obstetrician and gynecologist*
†Salam, Adil *pulmonary critical care physician*
†Salyer, Douglas W *music educator*
Salzman, Beverly E. *behavioral and social sciences educator, consultant*
Schrandt, Curtis Leon *lawyer, securities analyst, financial advisor*
Schwartz, James Peter *real estate broker*
†Schwartz, Lawrence B. *lawyer, accountant, banker*
Semple, Cecil Snowdon *retired manufacturing company executive*
†Sheldon, Robert Ryel *lawyer*
Silvestri, Robert *electric company executive*
Simoneau, Cynthia Lambert *newspaper editor, journalism educator*
Skowron, Tadeusz Adam *physician*
Slepian, Jacob Zeiger *otolaryngologist*
Trefry, Robert J. *healthcare administrator*
Zeldes, Jacob Dean *lawyer*

Bridgewater
Crooke, Robert Andrew *media consultant, writer, educator*

Bristol
Barnes, Carlyle Fuller *manufacturing executive*
Barnes, Wallace *manufacturing executive*
†Bodenheimer, George *broadcast executive*
Copeland, Karin A. *training director*
Eisen, Rich *reporter*
LaGanga, Donna Brandeis *sales and marketing executive*
†Raymond, Kathy Ann *graphics designer, poet*
Roberts, Alida Jayne *elementary school educator*

Brookfield
Cohen, Mark Steven *dentist*
Lewis, Edwin Leonard, III, *lawyer*
Reynolds, Jean Edwards *publishing executive*
Rowe, Edward Lawrence, Jr., *graphic designer*
Secola, Joseph Paul *lawyer*

Brooklyn
Dune, Steve Charles *retired lawyer*

Burlington
Nelson, Linda Beatrice D'Andrea *volunteer worker*

Canaan
Capecelatro, Mark John *lawyer*
Kettenhofen, Gretchen Maria *development executive*
†Mercer, John Charles *veterinary technician, pharmacy technician*

Canterbury
Brown, Philip Henry *psychiatric social worker*

Canton Center
Humphrey, Samuel Stockwell *town official, physicist*

Chaplin
Gunn, Bert Dennis *social worker*
Wood, Wendy Deborah *filmmaker*

Cheshire
Bozzuto, Michael Adam *wholesale grocery company executive*
Eppler, Richard Andrew *chemical engineer, educator, consultant*
Keiser, David Wharton *biotechnology executive*
McKee, Margaret Jean *federal agency administrator*
Pettine, Linda Faye *physical therapist*
Rowland, Ralph Thomas *retired architect*
Saad, Edward Theodore *architect*
Sherman, Barbara Jane *social worker*
Tufte, Edward Rolf *writer, publisher, statistics educator*
Walter, Kenneth Gaines *library director*

Chester
Feldmann, Shirley Clark *psychology educator*
Frost-Knappman, Elizabeth (Linda Elizabeth Frost-Knappman) *editor, author, executive*
Harwood, Eleanor Cash *librarian*
Spencer, William Courtney *foundation executive, international business executive*
Stark, Evelyn Brill *poet, musician*

Clinton
Adler, Peggy Ann *writer, illustrator, investigator*
Douglas, Hope M. *psychotherapist, forensic hypnotist*
Friedmann, Paul Garson *control engineer, editor*
Harris, Doris Ann *medical/surgical nurse*
Kingsbury, Katherine Duffield *social worker*
†Panayotov, Christo Angelov *research scientist, consultant*
Zack, Steven Jeffrey *master automotive instructor*

Colchester
Broder, Joseph Arnold *lawyer*
Winter, John Dawson, III, *blues guitarist, singer*

Colebrook
Ash, Hiram Newton *graphic designer*
McNeill, William Hardy *retired history educator, writer*

Collinsville
Whitney, Carol Marie *securities sales professional*

Columbia
Vance, Carmen Lee *retired university official*

Cornwall Bridge
Leich, John Foster *political scientist, European languages educator*

Cos Cob
Barnard, Charles Nelson *editorial consultant, author*
Beliveau Muchnicki, Margaret Anne *television producer*
Duncalf, Deryck *retired anesthesiologist*
Hauptman, Michael *broadcasting company executive*
Kane, Jay Brassler *banker*
Kane, Margaret Brassler *sculptor*
Kucic, Joseph *management consultant, industrial engineer, network engineer, information security specialist*
†Leamy, Nancy M. *professional athletics coach*
McElwaine, Theresa Weedy *academic administrator, artist*
Murphy, Robert Blair *management consulting company executive*
Neal, Irene Collins *artist, educator*
Sorese, Denise Powers *reading and language arts consultant, educator*

Coventry
Ferguson, Ronald Max *chemistry educator, researcher*
Halvorson, Judith Anne (Judith Anne Devaud) *elementary education educator*

Cromwell
†Stiber, Julie Anne *social worker*

Danbury
Anderson, Alan Reinold *real estate executive, communications consultant*
Arbitelle, Ronald Alan *elementary school educator*
Aronson, Kristin Janina *philosopher, educator*
Baker, Leonard Morton *manufacturing company executive*
Bascom, Lionel Cyril *writer, educator*
Bernasconi, Stacey Christine *project data manager*
Bristol, Josephine Hart *psychiatrist*
Chaifetz, David Harvey *lawyer*
Cutsumpas, Lloyd *judge*
Edelstein, David Simeon *historian, educator*
Falkenstein, Ralph Jay *ophthalmologist*
Gogliettino, John Carmine *insurance broker*
Goldstein, Joel *finance and statistics educator, researcher*
Hartford, Kathleen Lischko *financial services company executive*
Hawkes, Carol Ann *academic administrator*
Hulnick, Donald H. *radiologist*
Humphreville, James Edwin *conductor*
Jennings, Alfred Higson, Jr., *music educator, actor, singer*
Jensen-Ruopp, Helga Spitko *school program administrator, consultant*
†Joyce, William H. *chemist*
Keenan, Linda Lee *paralegal*
Keller, Barry R. *physician*
Kurien, Santha T. *psychiatrist*
Kuther, Tara L. *psychology educator*
Layton, Howard Manton *electrical engineer*
†Lichtenberger, H(orst) William *chemical company executive*
Mashman, Jan Howard *neurologist, educator, rehabilitation administrator*
Meyers, Abbey S. *foundation administrator*
Miller, Jeffrey David *allergist*
Moskowitz, Stanley Alan *financial executive*
†Nair, Vijay *school librarian*
†Pastor, Stephen Daniel *chemistry educator, researcher*
Proctor, Richard Jerome, Jr., *business educator, accountant, expert witness*
†Reilley, Dennis H. *chemicals executive*
†Roach, James Richard *university president*
†Roman, Eric *humanities educator*
Saghir, Adel Jamil *artist, painter, sculptor*
†Stichnoth, John A. *corporate lawyer*
Taweh, Ziad Michael *internist*
Tolor, Alexander *psychologist, educator*
Upson, Thomas Fisher *judge, former state senator, lawyer*
Vossler, John Albert *civil engineer*
Walker, Michael James *surgeon*
Weiner, Patricia Hermann *performing arts administrator, concert manager, artist manager*
Wright, Marie Anne *management information systems educator*
Yamin, Dianne Elizabeth *judge*

Danielson
Jungeberg, Thomas Donald *lawyer*

Darien
Beach, Stephen Holbrook *lawyer*
Bigelow, Jonathan Lehr *editor, publishing executive*
Black, Lisa *artist*
Brooke, Avery Rogers *publisher, writer*
Brown, James Shelly *lawyer*
Burchenal, Joan Riley *science educator*
Cronk, Leonard *management consultant*
Dale, Erwin Randolph *lawyer, author*
Dordelman, William Forsyth *food company executive*
Forman, J(oseph) Charles *chemical engineer, consultant, writer*
Gushée-Molkenthin, Allison *financial advisor*
Hailey, Arthur *author*
Himmelreich, David Baker *lawyer*
Kobak, James Benedict *management consultant*
†Koontz, Carl Lennis, II, *investment counselor*
Kutz, Kenneth John *retired mining executive*
Mapel, William Marlen Raines *retired banking executive*
McIntire, William Tredick, II, *municipal official, investment banker*
Moltz, James Edward *investment brokerage company executive*
Morano, Gerard John *marketing executive*
Morse, Edmond Northrop *investment management executive*
Nava, Eloy Luis *financial planner, financial consultant*
Newman, Fredric Alan *plastic surgeon, educator*
Ossi, James Matthew *artist*
Peppet, Russell Frederick *accountant*
Prince, Kenneth Stephen *lawyer*
Rezek, Geoffrey Robert *management consultant*
Schell, James Munson *financial executive*
Sprole, Frank Arnott *retired pharmaceutical company executive, lawyer*
Swiggart, Carolyn Clay *lawyer*
Welsh, John Francis *retired advertising executive*
Ziegler, William, III, *diversified industry executive*

Deep River
Cobb, Hubbard Hanford *magazine editor, writer*
†Spallone, Jeanne Field *retired state judge*

Derby
Augusta, Judith Wood *librarian*
Jekel, James Franklin *physician, public health educator*
McEvoy, Sharlene Ann *law educator*

Durham
Holahan, John Michael *music educator, researcher*
Russell, Thomas James *critical care supervisor*

East Glastonbury
Smith, David Clark *research scientist*

East Granby
Scanlon, Lawrence Eugene *English language educator*

East Haddam
Borton, John Carter, Jr., (Terry Borton) *theatrical producer*
Clarke, Cordelia Kay Knight Mazuy *management consultant, artist*
Clarke, Logan, Jr., *management consultant*
Conant, Jan Royce *artist*

East Hampton
Jamieson, Leland *retired career management consultant*
Tucceri, Clive Knowles *science writer and educator, consultant*

East Hartford
Altman, Richard Lewis *aeronautical engineer*
Banas, Richard Frederick *geographer*
Barredo, Rita M. *auditor*
Cassidy, John Francis, Jr., *industrial technology executive*
Danko, Gene Andrew *materials scientist*
Dubin, Joseph William *federal mediator*
†Giardina, David Vincent *music educator*
Henry, Paul Eugene, Jr., *minister*
†Lien, Steven Kenneth *strategic planner*
Rivers, Loretta J. *film producer, film director, consultant*
Scholsky, Martin Joseph *priest*
Singh, Ripudaman *aerospace structure engineering researcher*
Soppelsa, George *artist*
Vacher, Clive Graham *aerospace executive*
Venkatesh, Prasana Krishnamurthi *oil industry executive, researcher*
†Wusatowska-Sarnek, Agnieszka M. *engineer, researcher*
†Young, Albert Frederick Antonio *grants coordinator*

East Haven
Conn, Harold O. *physician, educator*

East Lyme
Levin, Robert Earl *clinical rheumatologist*

Easton
Berry, Ronald George *marketing professional*
Enos, Randall *cartoonist, illustrator*
Lorenz, Lee Sharp *cartoonist*
Maloney, John Joseph *writer*
Meyer, Alice Virginia *state official*

Ellington
Edgar, Gregory T. *author*

Enfield
Berger, Robert Bertram *lawyer*
Folmsbee, Patricia Hurley *reading and language arts consultant*
Oliver, Bruce Lawrence *information systems specialist, educator*
Squires, William Allen *distribution company executive*

Essex
Burris, Harriet Louise *emergency physician*
Goff, Christopher Wallick *pediatrician*
Hieatt, Allen Kent *language professional, educator*
Hieatt, Constance Bartlett *English language educator*
Lyon, Rick (Richard Woodward) *water transportation professional, poet*
Miller, Elliott Cairns *retired bank executive, lawyer*
Miller, Walter Neal *insurance company consultant*
Thompson, George Lee *consulting and retailing company executive*

Fairfield
Barone, Rose Marie Pace *writer, retired educator, entertainer*
Booth, George Keefer *financial service executive*
Brett, Arthur Cushman, Jr., *banker*
Bryan, Barbara Day *retired librarian*
Bullard, Roger Perrin *artist*
Burd, Robert Meyer *hematologist, oncologist, educator*
Caruso, Daniel F. *lawyer, judge, former state legislator*
Clements, Hana Joan *physician*
Dean, George Alden *advertising executive*
Denniston, Brackett Badger, III, *lawyer*
Dunham, Christopher Scott *librarian*
Eigel, Edwin George, Jr., *mathematics educator, retired university president*
Eigel, Marcia Duffy *editor*
Eliasoph, Philip *art historian, gallery director*
Evans, Margaret A. *volunteer*
Everett, Wendy Ann *toy designer*
Fash, Victoria R. *healthcare company executive*
Ford, Maureen Morrissey *civic worker*
Gad, Lance Stewart *investment advisor, lawyer, private investor*
Harkrader, Milton Keene, Jr., *corporate executive*
Harris, Wiley Lee *financial services executive*
Hauck, Madeline (Agnes Hauck) *special and adult basic education educator*
†Heineman, Benjamin Walter, Jr., *lawyer*
Hergenhan, Joyce *public relations executive*
Hodgkinson, William James *publishing executive*
†Howell, Karen Jane *private school educator*
Huth, William Edward *lawyer*
†Hye, A. *electrical engineering educator*
Immelt, Jeffrey R. *diversified technology and services company executive*
Ingis, Gail *interior designer, educator, writer, photographer, artist*
Johnsen, Walter Craig *security firm executive*
Kaff, Albert Ernest *journalist, author*
Kalapos, Felicia Zera *elementary school educator, writer*
Kelley, Aloysius Paul *university administrator, priest*
Khachian, Elisa Arpenia *artist, educator*
†King, Ann Stockman *librarian, educator*
Kleine, Herman *economist*
Ladd, Louise *writer*
Leask, John McPhearson, II, *accountant*
Levinson, Stephen Ronald *retired otolaryngologist*
Levitt, Jesse *retired foreign language educator*
†Ligas, Mark Steven *business educator*
Luther, David Byron *management consultant*
†Mascia, Mark Joseph *language educator*
Mauer, Kenneth Ray *gastroenterologist, educator*
McCreight, John A. *management consultant*
McLaughlin, John Richardson *electric motor company executive*
Mead, Philomena *mental health nurse*
Miles, Leland Weber *university president*
Newton, Lisa Haenlein *philosopher, educator*
Orris-Modugno, Michele Marie *public relations, marketing and advertising consultant*
Osis, Daiga Guntra *lawyer*
Paolini, Claire Jacqueline *dean, educator*
Pinto, Edward Ralph *internist, cardiologist*
Reeves, Edmund Hoffman, III, *food products executive*
Rogers, Louis Jerome *writer, educator*
Shaffer, Dorothy Browne *retired mathematician, educator*
Spence, Barbara E. *publishing company executive*
Sutphen, Harold Amerman, Jr., *retired paper company executive*
Timmermann, Sandra *educational gerontologist, communication specialist*
†Trotter, Lloyd G. *electric power industry executive*
Turetsky, Judith *librarian, researcher*
†Weiss, Joan Wyzkoski *mathematics educator*
Wexler, Herbert Ira *retail company executive*
Whyte, Bruce Lincoln *management executive, marketing professional*
Wright, Robert *broadcasting executive*

Falls Village
Cronin, Robert Lawrence *sculptor, painter*
Purcell, Mary Louise Gerlinger *retired adult education educator*
Toomey, Jeanne Elizabeth *animal activist*

Farmington
†Arnold, Andrew *medical researcher, physician*
†Banya, Santonino Ku'Caya *science educator*
Bronner, Felix *physiologist, biophysicist, educator, painter*
Centofanti, Joseph *accountant*
Cone, Robert Edward *immunologist, educator*
Cooperstein, Sherwin Jerome *medical educator*
Cutler, Leslie Stuart *academic administrator and medical educator*
Deckers, Peter John *dean*
Dellaripa, Christine M. *nursing care administrator*
Donaldson, James Oswell, III, *neurology educator*
Goodson, Richard Carle, Jr., *chemist, consultant*
†Grafstein, Joel M. *lawyer*
Grunnet, Margaret Louise *pathology educator*
Halligan, Howard Ansel *investment management company executive*
Harvey, Elton Bartlett, III, *lawyer*
†Higgins-Biddle, John Charles *humanities educator, consultant*
Houchin, John Frederick, Sr., *human services administrator*
Jestin, Heimwarth B. *retired university administrator*
Jones, Mary Jeanne A. *investment adviser*
Klobutcher, Lawrence Anthony *molecular biologist, educator*
Liebowitz, Neil Robert *psychiatrist*
Mandell, Joel *lawyer*
McCawley, Austin *psychiatrist, educator*
†Metersky, Mark L. *physician*
Moskowitz, Harold *radiologist*
Muse, James Michael *bank executive, finance educator*
Osborn, Mary Jane Merten *biochemist, educator*
Paplauskas, Leonard Paul *academic administrator, health science educator*
†Riley, Deon *human resources specialist, consultant*
Rothfield, Lawrence I. *microbiology educator*
Rothfield, Naomi Fox *physician*
Schenkman, John Boris *pharmacologist, educator*
Slepchenko, Boris Moyseyevich *mathematical physicist, educator*
Spencer, Richard Paul *biochemist, educator, physician*
Walker, James Elliot Cabot *physician*
Wiechmann, Eric Watt *lawyer*

Gales Ferry
Wilson, Margaret Elizabeth *educator*

Georgetown
Einstein, Eric Brandt *internal medicine physician*
Roberts, Priscilla Warren *artist*

Glastonbury
Andrews, Bryant Aylesworth *software company executive*
Hilton, John David *business owner, infosystems specialist*
Juda, Richard John *anesthesiologist, critical care specialist*
Orr, Richard Clayton *financial modeler, futures trader*
Pudlo, Frances Theresa *human resources specialist*
Pudlo, Virginia Mary *medical surgical nurse*
Rintoul, David Skinner *lawyer*
Singer, Paul Richard *ophthalmologist*
†Stephan, George Peter *lawyer, international business consultant*

Granby
Pfeiffer, Edward Joseph *public relations consultant, photojournalist*

Greens Farms
Deford, Frank *sportswriter, television and radio commentator, author*
McManus, John Francis, III, *advertising executive*

Greenwich
Allen, Paul Howard *financial institutions investor*
Alonzo, Martin Vincent *mining and aluminum company executive, investor, financial consultant*
Anderson, Carolyn Ruth Hunt *interior designer, realtor*
Angel, Jack Easton *publishing executive*
Bachenheimer, Ralph James *merchant banker*
Badman, John, III, *real estate developer, architect*
Ball, John Fleming *advertising and film production executive*
Bam, Foster *lawyer*
Bara, Jean Marc *finance and communications executive, artist*
Bennett, Jack Franklin *oil company executive*
Bentley, Peter *lawyer*
Berk, Alan S. *law firm executive*
Berkley, William Robert *insurance holding company executive*
Birle, James Robb *investor*
Bjornson, Edith Cameron *foundation executive, communications consultant*
Blumberg, Joel Myron *cardiologist*
Bollman, Mark Brooks, Jr., *communications executive*
Brandrup, Douglas Warren *lawyer*
Broadhurst, Austin, Jr., *executive recruiter*
Camel, Mark Howard *neurological surgeon*
†Cameron, Dort *electronics executive*
Cantor, Samuel C. *lawyer, company executive*
Cantwell, Robert *lawyer*
Carmichael, William Daniel *consultant, educator*
Caruso, Victor Guy *investment banker*
Case, Richard Paul *electronics executive*
Clark, Harry Warren *public policy consultant*
Clark, Thomas Carlyle *banker*
Clements, Robert *insurance executive*
Coleman, Joel Clifford *lawyer*
Collins, Richard Lawrence *magazine editor, publisher, author*
Cook, Jay Michael *accounting company executive*
Davidson, Thomas Maxwell *international management company executive*
DeCrane, Alfred Charles, Jr., *petroleum company executive*
Dederick, Ronald Osburn *lawyer*
de Mar, Leoda Miller *designer*
DeNigris, Carole Dell Cato *artist*
Dettmer, Robert Gerhart *retired beverage company executive*
de Visscher, Francois Marie *investment banker*
Dickerson, Thomas Pasquali *investment banker, lawyer*
Donley, James Walton *management consultant*
Egbert, Richard Cook *retired banker*
Engstrom, Erik *private equity investor*
Erlanger, Richard Alan *investment executive*

Ewald, William Bragg, Jr., *author, consultant*
Farbish, Alfred B. *waterproofing materials executive*
Fleisher, Jerrilyn *financial planner*
Forrow, Brian Derek *lawyer, corporation executive*
Fuller, Theodore *retired insurance executive*
†Garg, Uday Ramakant *financial analyst*
Griggs, Nina M. *realtor*
Harrington, Robert Dudley, Jr., *retired printing company executive*
Hershaft, Elinor *space planner, interior designer*
Hess, Marilyn Ann *state legislator*
Hewitt, Dennis Edwin *financial executive*
Higgins, Jay F. *financial executive*
Hirschberg, Ruth *retired social worker*
Hoberman, Mary Ann *author*
†Hurwich, Robert Allan *lawyer, multimedia, manufacturing and services company executive*
Johnson, Herbert Michael *publisher*
Kalan, Gary Edward *anesthesiologist*
Kelly, David Austin *investment counselor*
Keogh, James *journalist*
Kestnbaum, Albert S. *advertising executive*
Kleinman, Noela MacGinn *family nurse practitioner*
Kolb, Jerry Wilbert *accountant*
Kopenhaver, Patricia Ellsworth *podiatrist*
Kovner, Kathleen Jane *civic worker, portrait artist*
Krauser, Robert Stanley *health care executive*
Langley, Patricia Coffroth *retired psychiatric social worker*
Lebec, Alain *investment banker*
Lewis, Audrey Gersh *financial marketing/public relations consultant*
Lochner, Philip Raymond *retired communications executive, consultant*
Lowenstein, Peter David *lawyer*
Lynch, William Redington *lawyer*
Mango, Wilfred Gilbert, Jr., *real estate and construction company executive*
Marks, Charles *architect*
Matthaei, Gay Humphrey *interior designer*
McDonald, Paul Kimball *lawyer, investment executive*
Mendenhall, John Ryan *retired lawyer, transportation executive*
Miller, Donald Keith *venture capitalist, asset management executive*
Mock, Robert Claude *architect*
Moffly, John Wesley, IV, *magazine publishing executive*
Moonie, Clyde Wickliffe *financial consultant*
Moore, John Plunkett Dennis *publisher*
More, Douglas McLochlan *lawyer*
Moreira-Caunedo, Debra *manufacturing executive*
Nelson, Don Harris *gas and oil industry executive*
Nevin, Crocker *investment banker*
Nimetz, Matthew *investment company executive*
Nockler, Linda A. *corporate financial executive*
Pascarella, Henry William *lawyer*
Paulson, Paul Joseph *advertising executive*
Perless, Ellen *advertising executive*
Perless, Robert L. *sculptor*
Pope, Ingrid Bloomquist *sculptor, poet*
†Putman, Linda Murray *lawyer*
Roach, John Handee, Jr., *bank executive, investment banker, financial service executive*
Roitsch, Paul Albert *pilot*
Rosenberg, Arthur Henry *internist*
Rudy, Kathleen Vermeulen *small business owner*
Rukeyser, Louis Richard *economic commentator*
Sandbank, Henry *photographer, film director*
Schlafly, Hubert Joseph, Jr., *communications executive*
Schmidt, Herman J. *former oil company executive*
Schneider, John Arnold *investor*
Schoonmaker, Samuel Vail, III, *lawyer*
Selby, Leland Clay *lawyer*
Shanks, Eugene Baylis, Jr., *banker*
Smith, Phillips Guy *banker*
Smith, Rodger Field *financial executive*
Srere, Benson M. *communications company executive, consultant*
Stauffer, John Eugene *engineering company executive*
Stauffer, Valerie Vilas *civic volunteer*
Stockman, David Alan *investment banker*
Storms, Clifford Beekman *lawyer*
Swarz, Jeffrey Robert *securities analyst, neuroscientist*
Sweeney, Michael Andrew *newspaper editor*
Tarantino, Dominic A. *retired professional services firm executive*
Tell, William Kirn, Jr., *retired oil company executive, lawyer*
Tomikawa, Soji *educational institute administrator*
Urstadt, Charles J. *real estate executive*
van Rosendaal, John *journalist*
von Braun, Peter Carl Moore Stewart *business executive*
von der Heyden, Karl Ingolf Mueller *retired manufacturing executive*
Walker, Robert Martin *writer, minister*
Wallach, Magdalena Falkenberg (Carla Wallach) *writer*
Wearly, William Levi *business executive*
Weppler, Jay Robert *merchant banking executive*
Whitmore, George Merle, Jr., *management consulting company executive*
Winkler, Charles Howard *investment company executive*
Wolfson, Ellen N. *physician*
Wyman, Ralph Mark *finance company executive*

Groton

†Bi, Honggang *pharmaceutical executive, researcher*
†Cocheo, John Frank *lawyer*
Colgan, Stephen Thomson *analytical chemist*

English, James Fairfield, Jr., *former college president*
†Fossa, Anthony Andrea *pharmacologist*
Harrigan, Edmund Patrick *physician, researcher*
Helm, John Leslie *retired mechanical engineer, company executive*
Huang, Liang Hsiung *microbiologist*
Kavarnos, George James *research chemist*
Kennedy, Evelyn Siefert *foundation executive, textile specialist*
†Kopchinski, Anita Francine *pharmaceutical executive*
Sheets, Herman Ernest *marine engineer*
†Smock, Steven Lee *cell biologist, molecular biologist*
Stoddard, Patrick Clare *retired military systems consultant, computer engineer*
†Stuart, Peter Fred *lawyer*
Swindell, Archie Calhoun, Jr., *research biochemist, statistician*
Tassinari, Melissa Sherman *toxicologist*
†Wallach, Morton L. *scientist*

Guilford

Chatt, Allen Barrett *psychologist, neuroscientist*
Colish, Marcia Lillian *history educator*
Handschumacher, Robert Edmund *biochemistry educator*
Langdon, Robert Colin *dermatologist, educator*
Macy, Terrence William *social services administrator*
Mick, Margaret Anne *communications executive*
Morgan, Leon Alford *retired utility executive*
Pâquin, Trudy *gerontological nurse*
Pease, David Gordon *artist, educator*
Peters, William *author, producer, director*
Speth, James Gustave *dean, environmental studies educator, lawyer*
Springgate, Clark Franklin *physician, researcher*

Hamden

Ballard, Terry Lee *librarian, educator*
Barberi, Matthew *physical education and health educator*
Bershtein, Herman Sammy *lawyer*
Brown, Jay Marshall *retired secondary school educator*
†Bulger, Carrie Ann *science educator*
Cofrancesco, Donald George *health facility administrator*
Cole-Schiraldi, Marilyn Bush *occupational therapy educator*
Culler, Arthur Dwight *English language educator*
Cunningham, Walter Jack *electrical engineering educator*
Davis, Lorraine Jensen *writer, editor*
Delehant, Raymond Leonard *botanist, educator*
Dittes, James Edward *psychology of religion educator*
†Eisner, Lawrence Brand *lawyer, real estate developer*
Forman, Charles William *religious studies educator*
Greenblatt, Morton Harold *retired assistant attorney general*
He, Xiaohong *finance educator*
†Lucas, Doina C. *librarian*
Margulies, Martin B. *lawyer, educator*
†McClellan, Edwin *Japanese literature educator*
Mintz, Max M. *historian*
Nuland, Sherwin *surgeon, author*
Pelikan, Jaroslav Jan *history educator*
Pisani, Lawrence Frank *sociology educator*
Ricard, Thomas Armand *electrical engineer*
Richardson, Dennis James *biologist, educator*
Roche, Eamonn Kevin *architect*
Smith, David Martyn *forestry educator*
Sola, Janet Elaine *secondary school educator*
Stankewich, Paul Joseph *lawyer*
St Aubyn, Frederic Chase *French language educator*
Strong, James Alan *architect*
Tomasko, Edward A. *financial planner*
Villano, Peter F. *state legislator*
Westerfield, Carolyn Elizabeth Hess *city planner*
Williams, Edward Gilman *retired banker*

Hanover

Cheney, Glenn Alan *writer, educator*

Hartford

Alfano, Charles Thomas, Sr., *lawyer*
Amatuli, Robert Alexander *architect*
Anthony, J(ulian) Danford, Jr., *lawyer*
Appel, Robert Eugene *lawyer, educator*
Ayer, Ramani *insurance company executive*
†Baldini, Laura Flynn *lawyer*
Banever, Thomas Clark *surgeon, educator*
†Bartolini, James Daniel *lawyer*
Behuniak, Peter *psychometrician, educational psychologist, educational consultant*
Bennett, Jessie F. *lawyer*
Berall, Frank Stewart *lawyer*
Bieluch, William Charles *judge*
Blair, Charles Lee *physician, educator*
Blumberg, Phillip Irvin *law educator*
Blumenthal, Richard *state attorney general*
Bonee, John Leon, III, *lawyer*
Borden, David M. *state supreme court justice*
†Borus, David Murray *college dean*
Brauer, Rima Lois *psychiatrist*
Brennan, Tracy Elizabeth *physician*
Bronzino, Joseph Daniel *electrical engineer*
†Buck, Gurdon Hall *lawyer, urban planner*
Bysiewicz, Susan *secretary of state*
Cain, George Harvey *lawyer, business executive*
Campbell, Timothy Reid *financial services company executive*
Cantor, Donald Jerome *lawyer*
Carey, Ellen *artist*
†Caspar, George J., III, *lawyer*
Chatigny, Robert Neil *judge*
Cibes, William Joseph, Jr., *chancellor, educator*
Cohn, Jan Kadetsky *American literature and American studies educator*
Cole, Solon Robert *pathologist, educator*

Cook, Catherine Welles *state legislator*
Coyle, Michael Lee *lawyer*
Craig, Joyce Krutick *judge*
†Cronin, Daniel Anthony *archbishop*
Cullina, William Michael *lawyer*
Curran, Ward Schenk *economist, educator*
David, George Alfred Lawrence *aerospace transportation executive*
Davis, Andrew Neil *lawyer, educator*
Davis, Jack Wayne, Jr., *publishing executive*
Decker, Robert Owen *history educator, clergyman*
†Decko, Kenneth Owen *trade association administrator*
Del Giudice, Leon Louis *auctioneer*
Del Negro, John Thomas *lawyer*
Dempsey, Edward Joseph *lawyer*
Dennis, Anthony James *lawyer*
Dobkin, Eric David *critical care surgeon, educator*
Donnell, Brian James *lawyer*
Droney, Christopher F. *judge*
Dworkin, Paul Howard *pediatrician*
Englehart, Robert Wayne, Jr., *cartoonist*
Fahrbach, Ruth C. *state legislator*
Fain, Joel Maurice *lawyer*
†Fiondella, Robert William *insurance company executive*
Fiszel, Geoffrey Lynn *investment banker, investment advisor*
Flaschen, Evan Daniel *lawyer*
Frost, James Arthur *former university president*
Gastmann, Albert Lodewijk *retired political science and language educator, writer*
Giannaros, Demetrios Spiros *economist, educator, politician*
Gibbons, John Martin, Jr., *physician, educator*
Gieras, Jacek Franciszek *electrical engineering educator, scientist*
Gillam, Linda Dawn *cardiologist, researcher*
Glasser, Joseph *manufacturing and marketing executive*
Godfrey, Robert Douglas *lawyer*
Gunderson, Gerald Axel *economics educator, administrator*
Hammer, Alfred Emil *artist, educator*
Harden, Jon Bixby *publishing executive*
Harrison, Thomas Flatley *lawyer*
Hedrick, Joan Doran *writer, university educator*
Hermann, Robert Jay *manufacturing company engineering executive, consultant*
Herzog, Alfred *psychiatrist, health facility executive*
†Hoim, Terje *mathematician, educator*
Huie, Georgette Lynn *social services administrator*
Humphrey, Chester Bowden *cardio-thoracic surgeon*
Inniss-Brewer, Yvonne *nurse, insurance company administrator*
Jahiel, Rene Ino *physician*
Jeresaty, Robert Michel *cardiologist, educator*
Johnson, Dwight Alan *lawyer*
Joshi, Vijay V. *pathologist, educator*
Jung, Betty Chin *epidemiologist, research analyst, educator, medical/surgical nurse*
Kaimowitz, Jeffrey Hugh *librarian*
Katz, Joette *state supreme court justice*
Keating, Christopher Patrick *reporter*
Kennedy, Jack Stanners *lawyer*
Killian, Robert Kenneth *former lieutenant governor*
Killian, Robert Kenneth, Jr., *judge, lawyer*
†Kirton, Orlando Cecilio *surgeon, educator*
Klimek, Joseph John *physician, educator*
Knickerbocker, Robert Platt, Jr., *lawyer*
Korzenik, Armand Alexander *lawyer*
Krause, Peter James *pediatrician, researcher, educator*
Leibin, Harvey Bruce *architect*
Leonhardt, Clifton Andrew *lawyer, public official*
Link, Henry *environmental engineer*
Lloyd, Alex *lawyer*
†Lloyd, James Hendrie, III, *lawyer*
Lotstein, James Irving *lawyer*
Lyman, Peggy *artistic director, dancer, choreographer, educator*
Lyon, James Burroughs *lawyer*
Lyons, Moira K. *state legislator*
Lyons, Robert William *medical educator, infectious disease consultant*
Margulies, Beth Zeldes *assistant attorney general*
†Markham, Ian Stephen *theology studies educator, dean*
Martin, Ionis B *artist, educator*
Martinez, Donna F. *federal judge*
McCormack, Katherine McGrath *nursing administrator*
†McCracken, Gregory William *lawyer*
Mc Lean, Jackie *jazz saxophonist, educator, composer, community activist*
Merriam, Dwight Haines *lawyer, land use planner*
Metzler, Robert J., II, *lawyer*
Middlebrook, Stephen Beach *lawyer*
Miller, Jeffrey Clark *lawyer*
Milliken, Charles Buckland *lawyer*
†Morawetz, Thomas H. *law educator*
Morgan, William Francis, Jr., *police chief*
†Morrison, Francis Henry *lawyer*
Mullane, Denis Francis *insurance executive*
Naples, Nancy A. *sociology and women's studies educator*
Newman, Jon O. *federal judge*
Nimirowski, Ramona Furphy *legal administrator*
Noel, Don Obert, Jr., *retired newspaper columnist*
Nolan, John Blanchard *lawyer*
Norcott, Flemming L., Jr., *state supreme court justice*
Ogden, Hugh *English literature educator, poet*
Orefice, Gary James *state legislator*
Orth, Paul William *retired lawyer*
Pach, Peter Barnard *newspaper columnist and editor*
Pachter, Lee M. *pediatrician*

Packard, Stephen Michael *lawyer*
†Painter, Borden W. *academic administrator*
Pastuszak, William Theodore *hematopathologist*
†Paul, Jeremy Ralph *law educator*
Pepe, Louis Robert *lawyer, educator*
Perez, Eddie A. *mayor*
Peters, Ellen Ash *judge, trial referee, retired state supreme court justice*
Pinney, Sidney Dillingham, Jr., *lawyer*
Posteraro, Catherine Hammond *librarian, gerontology educator*
Powers, Robert David *physician*
Raffay, Stephen Joseph *manufacturing company executive*
Rell, M. Jodi *lieutenant governor*
Reynolds, Scott Walton *academic administrator*
Reynolds, Stephen H. *insurance safety and loss prevention consultant*
Richter, Donald Paul *lawyer*
Robison, Julie Thompson *gerontologist, educator*
Rosa, Peter Manuel *university administrator, researcher, education educator*
Rosenberg, Eric Lee *internal medicine physician, educator*
Ross, Coleman DeVane *accountant, insurance company executive*
Rowe, John Wallis *health insurance executive, medical executive*
Rowland, John G. *governor, former congressman*
Ryan, David Thomas *lawyer*
Sargent, Joseph Denny *insurance executive*
Schaller, Barry R. *judge*
Schroth, Peter W(illiam) *lawyer, management and law educator*
Scully, John Carroll *life insurance marketing research company executive*
See, Edmund M. *lawyer*
Shaw, L. Edward, Jr., *lawyer*
Shea, David Michael *state supreme court justice*
Shuler, Scott Corbin *art education administrator*
Smith, Francis Xavier *nurse*
Smyth, Gerard A. *lawyer, administrator*
Sorokin, Ethel Silver *lawyer*
Space, Theodore Maxwell *lawyer*
Speziale, John Albert *lawyer*
Squatrito, Dominic J. *judge*
Stewart, James George *producer, director, video executive*
Stravalle-Schmidt, Ann Roberta *lawyer*
Sullivan, Kevin B. *state legislator*
Swyers, Donald G. *information scientist*
Sylvester, Kathryn Rose *lawyer*
Tancredi, James J. *lawyer*
Tanski, James Michael *lawyer*
Taylor, Allan Bert *lawyer*
Thomas, Calvert *lawyer*
Thompson, Alvin W. *judge*
Toolan, Brian Paul *newspaper editor*
Veale, John Edmond (Jack Veale) *business executive*
Voigt, Richard *lawyer*
Webster, Arthur Edward *lawyer*
†Weinberger, Steven *lawyer, educator*
Whaley, Charles Henry, IV, *communications company executive*
Wiggin, Kendall French *state librarian*
Wilde, Wilson *insurance company executive*
Wilson-Coker, Patricia Anne *lawyer, social service administrator, educator*
Winter, Miriam Therese (Gloria Frances Winter) *nun, religious education educator*
Wolf, Barry *genetics, pediatric educator*
Wolin, Neal Steven *lawyer*
Wolman, Martin *lawyer*
†Wood, Margaret *performing company executive*
Wright, Douglass Brownell *retired judge, lawyer*
Younessi, Houman *computer science educator*
Young, Roland Frederic, III, *lawyer*
Young, Sara Ann *women's health nurse*

Higganum

de Brigard, Emilie *anthropologist, consultant*
Franklin, Robert Richard *retired federal agency administrator, farmer*
Gillmor, Rogene Godding *retired medical technologist*

Ivoryton

Bendig, William Charles *editor, artist, publisher*
Jensen, Leo *artist*
Osborne, John Walter *historian, educator, author*
Osborne, Judith Barbour *artist, art educator*

Kent

Friedman, Frances *public relations executive*
White, Roger Bradley *priest*

Killingworth

Sampson, Edward Coolidge *humanities educator*

Lakeville

Cook, Charles David *international lawyer, arbitrator, consultant*
Estabrook, Robert Harley *journalist*
Jones, Ronald David *lawyer*
Nickerson, Bee Davis *social services executive, volunteer*
Restout, Denise *musician*
†Rout, Robert Howard *lawyer*

Ledyard

Chiang, Albert Chinfa *polymer chemist*
Hammond, Russell Paul *music educator*

Litchfield

Booth, John Thomas *investment banker*
Ellison, William Theodore *marine engineer*
Fiederowicz, Walter Michael *lawyer*
Kenagy, Robert Coffman *planning consulting company executive*
Sherva, Dennis G. *retired investment company executive*

Lyme

Bessie, Simon Michael *publisher*
Bloom, Barry Malcolm *pharmaceutical consultant*

Hoyt, Charles King *architect, editor*

Madison
Carlson, Dale Bick *writer*
Clendenen, William Herbert, Jr., *lawyer*
Egbert, Emerson Charles *retired publisher*
Evans, Evan *petroleum executive*
Falk, Peter Hastings *publishing company executive, author, art dealer*
Golembeski, Jerome John *wire and cable company executive*
Houghton, Alan Nourse *association executive, educator, consultant*
Kay, Herbert *retired natural resources company executive*
Kilbourne, Edwin Dennis *virologist, educator*
Lucas, Shari *musician, educator*
Nebel, Sara Drought *artist, poet*
Purcell, Bradford Moore *publishing company executive*
Snell, Richard Saxon *anatomist*

Manchester
Beauregard, Michael Raymond *engineering executive, consultant*
Brazeal, Earl Henry, Jr., *electrical engineer*
Galasso, Francis Salvatore *materials scientist*
Horwitz, Melvin *lawyer, physician*
Jacobson, Charles Edward, Jr., *urologist*
Klipstein, Arnold Lloyd *gastroenterologist*
McHaelen, Robin Passariello *executive*
†Salvio, Regina Eugenia *language educator*
Schwartz, Robert G. *physician*
Szymonik, Peter Ted *information scientist, consultant, systems analyst*

Mansfield
Katz, Leonard *psychology educator*

Mansfield Center
Petrus, Robert Thomas *internet business owner, real estate investor*

Marlborough
White, Harold R. *insurance and health care information company executive*

Mashantucket
Yale, John Paul *computer systems developer*

Meriden
Bertolli, Eugene Emil *sculptor, goldsmith, designer, consultant*
Brandt, Irene Hildegard *retired secondary education educator*
Chiarenza, Frank John *English language educator*
Combs, Jerome Thomas *pediatrician, consultant*
Frederick, Paul G. *financial services systems company executive*
Horton, Paul Chester *psychiatrist*
Kemp, Roger Lark *city manager, writer*
Lowry, Houston Putnam *lawyer*
Molder, Sybil Ailene *retired occupational health nurse*
†Perricone, Nicholas V. *dermatologist*
Reitz, H(oward) Wesley *construction company executive*
Trotta, Marcia Marie *librarian, consultant, education educator*

Middlebury
Arnold, William Parsons, Jr., *retired internist*
Calarco, Vincent Anthony *specialty chemicals company executive*
Fickenscher, Gerald H. *chemicals company executive*
Phillips, Walter Mills, III, *psychologist, educator*

Middlefield
†Lang, Edward Gerald *lawyer*
Rammler, Linda Hope *human services consultant*

Middletown
Balay, Robert Elmore *editor, reference librarian*
Barber, William Joseph *educator, economist*
Bennet, Douglas Joseph, Jr., *university president*
Blume, Ginger (Elaine Blume) *psychologist*
Brogan, Mary Rose *public mental health facility administrator, psychologist*
Buel, Richard Van Wyck, Jr., *history educator, writer, editor*
Cline, John Carroll *clinical psychologist*
Comfort, William Wistar *mathematics educator*
Crites, Stephen Decatur *religion educator*
Fry, Albert Joseph *chemistry educator*
Gillmor, Charles Stewart *history and science educator, researcher*
Hager, Anthony Wood *mathematics educator*
Heimann-Hast, Sybil Dorothea *language arts and literature educator*
†Hoffmann, Leonard A *church administrator, director*
Malkin, Moses Montefiore *employee benefits administration company executive*
†McAlister, Elizabeth *religious studies educator*
Meyer, Priscilla Ann *Russian language and literature educator*
Meyers, Arthur Solomon *library director*
Miel, Jan *humanities educator*
Miller, Donald Edwin *physician*
Miller, Richard Alan *economist, educator*
Narad, Joan Stern *psychiatrist*
Pomper, Philip *history educator*
Rabuffo, Jeffrey Vincent *urologist*
Reed, Joseph Wayne *American studies educator, artist*
Reid, James Dolan *mathematics educator, researcher*
Rockwood, Irving E., Jr., *publisher*
Sage, Elderia Franckling *social worker*
Scheibe, Karl Edward *psychology educator*
Schwarcz, Vera *history educator, poet*
Shapiro, Norman Richard *Romance languages and literatures educator*
Torop, Paul *psychiatrist*
Valentine, George Edward *dentist*
Wasch, William Karl *gerontologist, contractor*
Wensinger, Arthur Stevens *language and literature educator, writer*
Winston, Krishna *foreign language professional*
Yohe, Gary Wynn *economics educator*
Zito, Christopher Richard *molecular biologist, biochemist*

Milford
Berchem, Robert Lee, Sr., *lawyer*
Calabrese, Anthony *marine biologist*
Curt, Denise Morris *artist, limner, photographer*
Haigh, Charles *criminal justice educator*
Muth, Eric Peter *ophthalmic optician*
Myers, David Richard *youth organization financial executive*
Olson, Harold Roy *computer company executive*
†Palm, April H. *special education educator*
†Sullivan, Christine Anne *secondary school educator*
Taylor, Charles Henry *psychoanalyst, educator*
Turko, Alexander Anthony *biology educator, hypnotherapist*

Monroe
Cote-Beaupre, Camille Yvette *artist, educator*
Davis, Bobby J. *pastor, family therapist*
Gleason, Mary Rena *secondary education educator*
Hyman, Andrew Theodore *patent lawyer, physicist*
†Oliver, Milton McKinnon *lawyer, German translator, patent database searcher*
Paniccia, Mario Domenic *architect*
Siegel, Richard Allen *corporate management consultant*

Moodus
Cumming, Robert Emil *editor, writer*

Mystic
Antipas, Constantine George *lawyer, civil engineer*
Bobruff, Carole Marks *radio producer, radio personality*
Burlingame, Michael Ashton *historian, retired educator*
Burrow, Gerard Noel *physician, educator*
Lincoln, Walter Butler, Jr., *marine engineer, educator*
Nolf, David M. *financial consultant*
Rogers, Brian Deane *retired librarian*
Rooney, Maria Dewing *photographer*
Spakoski, Marcia *insurance agent*
Thompson, Robert Allan *aerospace engineer*
†Valentine, Garrison Norton *lawyer*

Naugatuck
†Chrzanowski, Rose-Ann Cannizzo *art educator*
Davis, Robert Glenn *research scientist*
Flannery, Joseph Patrick *manufacturing executive, director*
Mannweiler, Mary-Elizabeth *painter*
Stauffer, Elizabeth Clare *elementary education educator, music choral director, consultant*
Stott, Paul Edwin *chemist, research manager*
Suscovich, David J. *neuropsychologist, marriage and family therapist*

New Branford
Peterkin, Albert Gordon *retired education educator*

New Britain
Barnett, Stuart Adrian *English language educator*
Baskerville, Charles Alexander *geologist, educator*
Bernene, James Louis *physician*
†Chasse, Emily Schuder *librarian, educator, storyteller*
Czajkowski, Eva Anna *aerospace engineer, educator*
Detmar-Pines, Gina Louise *business strategy and policy educator*
Dimmick, Charles William *geology educator*
Emeagwali, Gloria Thomas *humanities educator*
†Foster, Walton Brown *political science educator*
†Heitner, John A. (Jack Heitner) *English language educator, writer*
Higgins, Jane Margaret *university official*
Iannone, Abel Pablo *philosophy educator*
Judd, Richard Louis *academic administrator*
Leeds, Barry Howard *English language educator*
†Lunn, Charles Paul *elementary school educator*
Margiotta, Mary-Lou Ann *software engineer*
†Martin, Vivian Bonita *journalist, educator*
Meskill, Thomas J. *federal judge*
Mitrano, John R. *sociology educator*
†O'Connell, Brian Michael *computer scientist, educator*
Owens, Guy *neurosurgeon*
†Packer, Joan Garrett *librarian*
Pearl, Helen Zalkan *lawyer*
Tomaiuolo, Nicholas Gregory *librarian, educator*

New Canaan
Ackerman, Sigurd Howard *psychiatrist*
Baker, George Walter *lawyer*
Bartlett, Dede Thompson *communications consultant*
Bisbee, Gerald Elftman, Jr., *investment company executive*
Burns, Ivan Alfred *grocery products and industrial company executive*
Christensen, Donna Radovich *needlecraft designer, consultant, educator*
Cohen, Richard Norman *insurance executive*
Coughlin, Francis Raymond, Jr., *surgeon, educator, lawyer*
Dean, Robert Bruce *architect*
Fredericks, Jeanne Maria Judson *literary agent*
Gilbert, Steven Jeffrey *venture capitalist, screenwriter*
Grace, Julianne Alice *investor relations firm executive*
Halverstadt, Robert Dale *mechanical engineer, metals manufacturing company*
Hedley, Robert Peveril *retired petroleum and chemical company executive*
Hodgson, Richard *electronics company executive*
Johansen, Barbara B. *social worker, consultant*
Kamerschen, Robert Jerome *consumer products executive, investor*
Kearns, Gary P. *finance company executive*
Kovatch, Jak Gene *artist*
Lindstrom, Janet Elena *non-profit executive*
Lione, Susan Garrett *consultant*
Lucas, Norman Arthur *retired town manager*
MacEwan, Nigel Savage *merchant banker*
Marcus, Edward *economist, educator*
McIvor, Donald Kenneth *retired petroleum company executive*
Mc Mennamin, George Barry *advertising agency executive*
McNamara, Francis Joseph, Jr., *retired foundation executive, lawyer*
Means, David Hammond *retired advertising executive*
Mountcastle, Kenneth Franklin, Jr., *retired stockbroker*
Penny, Susan Caroline Voelker *investment manager*
Pike, William Edward *business executive*
Rendl-Marcus, Mildred *artist, economist*
Richards, Walter DuBois *artist, illustrator*
Richardson, Dana Roland *technology consultant*
Risom, Jens *furniture designer, manufacturing executive*
Sachs, John Peter *carbon company executive*
Steinmetz, Richard Bird, Jr., *lawyer*
Suen, Tzeng-Jiueq *chemical enginner, researcher*
Sweeny, Kenneth S. *graphic design consultant*
Thomas, Marianne Gregory *school psychologist*
Vasta, Vincent Joseph, Jr., *lawyer*
Ward, Richard Vance, Jr., *management executive*
White, Richard Booth *management consultant*
Ylvisaker, James William *insurance executive*

New Fairfield
Daukshus, A. Joseph *systems engineer*
Lambrech, Régine M. *college program administrator, language educator*
Mann, Jean Adah *artist*

New Haven
Adair, Robert Kemp *physicist, educator*
Aghajanian, George Kevork *medical educator*
Ahern, Jo Ann *diabetes clinical nurse specialist*
Alexander, Bruce Donald *real estate executive, educator*
Altman, Sidney *biology educator*
Alwood, Edward McQueen *writer, journalist, media specialist*
Anderson, Carl Albert *association executive, lawyer*
Anderson, John Frederick *science administrator, entomologist, researcher*
†Andriole, Vincent Thomas *medical educator, researcher*
Armbruster, Paula *child mental health educator, university director*
Arons, Marvin Shield *plastic and hand surgeon*
Aronson, Peter Samuel *medical scientist, physiology educator*
Askenase, Philip William *medicine and pathology educator*
Bailey, William Harrison *artist, educator*
†Baltay, Charles *physicist, educator*
Baltayan, Ara M. *engineering executive*
Barash, Paul George *anesthesiologist, educator*
†Bartoshuk, Linda J. *otolaryngologist, educator*
†Bazzy-Asaad, Alia *pediatrician, pulmonologist, academic administrator*
Behrman, Harold Richard *endocrinologist, physiologist, educator*
Bell, Wendell *sociologist, educator, futurist*
Benfer, David William *hospital administrator*
Berdon, Robert Irwin *judge trial referee, retired state supreme court justice*
Berson, Jerome Abraham *chemistry educator*
†Bhayro, Siam *religious studies educator*
Birnbaum, Irwin Morton *lawyer*
Birnbaum, Jerome *pharmaceutical executive, consultant*
Blatt, Sidney Jules *psychology educator and investigator, psychoanalyst*
Bloom, Harold *humanities educator, writer*
Blum, John Morton *historian, educator*
Bly, Mark John *playwright, educator*
Borroff, Marie *English language educator*
Boyer, James Lorenzen *physician, educator*
Brainard, William Crittenden *economist, educator, university official*
Brantl, Sister Charlesmarie *economics educator*
Braverman, Irwin Merton *dermatologist, educator*
†Breny Bontempi, Jean M. *health educator*
†Brisman, Leslie *English language educator*
Bromley, David Allan *physicist, engineer, educator*
Brooks, Peter (Preston) *French and comparative literature educator*
Brown, Thomas Huntington *neuroscientist*
Brownell, Kelly David *psychologist, educator*
Brunson, Kenneth Wayne *cancer biologist*
Buck, Donald Tirrell *retired finance educator*
Buckley, Richard Bennett *asset management company executive*
†Burak, Eric Steven *pharmaceutical researcher*
Burger, Richard L. *museum director*
Burns, Ellen Bree *federal judge*
Burt, Robert Amsterdam *lawyer, educator*
Cabranes, José Alberto *judge*
Calabresi, Guido *judge, law educator*
Caplan, Lincoln *journalist*
†Carroll, Deirdre Holden *psychiatric nurse practitioner, clinical researcher, educator*
Casten, Richard Francis *physicist*
Chandler, William Knox *physiologist*
Chertow, Marian Ruth *industrial ecologist, educator*
Chilton, William David *architect*
Chupka, William Andrew *chemical physicist, educator*
†Ciuparu, Dragos Mihael *research scientist, educator*
Clarie, Thomas Cashin, II, *librarian*
Clark, Elias *law educator*
Clark, Susan Atkinson *clinical social worker, educator*
Clarke, Fred W., III, *architect, architectural firm executive*
†Coan, Richard Morton *lawyer*
Coe, Michael Douglas *anthropologist, educator*
Cohen, Donald Jay *pediatrics, psychiatry and psychology educator, administrator*
Cohen, Lawrence Baruch *neurobiologist, educator*
Cohen, Lawrence Sorel *physician, educator*
Cohen, Morris Leo *retired law librarian and educator*
†Coifman, Ronald R. *mathematician, educator*
†Cole, First Dana *computer scientist, educator*
Collins, William F., Jr., *neurosurgery educator*
Comer, James Pierpont *psychiatrist, educator*
Conklin, Harold Colyer *anthropologist, educator*
Cooke, Edward Strong, Jr., *art educator*
Cooper, Dennis Lawrence *oncologist, educator*
Cooper, Jack Ross *pharmacology educator, researcher*
Crakes, Gary Michael *economics educator*
Davey, Lycurgus Michael *neurosurgeon*
Days, Drew S., III, *lawyer, law educator*
De Lio, Anthony Peter *lawyer*
DePino, Chris Anthoney *state legislator*
De Rose, Sandra Michele *psychotherapist, educator, supervisor, administrator*
†Diaz, Sebastian R. *education educator*
†Dimitrov, Ivan Kolev *education educator, researcher*
†Donatich, John E *publishing executive, writer*
†Donnelly, Robert L. *lawyer, corporation executive*
†Dudley, Kathryn Marie *anthropology and American studies educator*
Duke, Steven Barry *law educator*
Dunkle, Lisa Marie *pharmaceutical research executive*
Dupré, Louis *retired philosopher, educator*
Dworski, Sylvia *modern languages educator*
Dyson, William R. *state legislator, educator*
Ellickson, Robert Chester *law educator*
Ember, Carol R. *anthropology educator, author*
Ember, Melvin Lawrence *anthropologist, educator*
Erikson, Kai *sociologist, educator*
Erlich, Victor *Slavic languages educator*
Evenson, Robert Eugene *economist, educator*
Fei, Yijian *ophthalmologist, biomedical researcher*
†Feinstein, Rochelle *artist, educator*
†Fikrig, Erol *rheumatologist, medical educator*
†Forster, Susan H. *ophthalmologist, educator*
Frank, Roberta *English language educator*
Freed, Daniel Josef *law educator*
Freedman, Gerald Stanley *radiologist, healthcare administrator, educator*
Freedman, Paul Harris *historian, educator*
Freeman, Joanne Barrie *history educator*
Fried, Charles A. *accountant, financial executive*
Friedlaender, Gary Elliott *orthopedist, educator*
Galston, Arthur William *biology educator*
Garvey, Sheila Hickey *theater educator*
Gastwirth, Donald Edward *lawyer, literary agent*
†Gaudiani, Claire Lynn *retired academic administrator*
Gaynor, Mark Leslie *clinical social worker*
Geisler, Thomas Milton, Jr., *lawyer*
Genel, Myron *pediatrician, educator*
Gewirtz, Paul D. *lawyer, legal educator*
Gilbert, Creighton Eddy *art historian*
Gildea, Brian Michael *lawyer*
†Gilliss, Catherine Lynch *nursing educator*
Gilman, Todd Seacrist *librarian, scholar, educator, musician*
Glaser, Gilbert Herbert *neuroscientist, physician, educator*
†Goetsch, Charles Carnahan *lawyer, legal historian*
Goffart, Walter André *history educator*
†Goldman-Rakic, Patricia Shoer *neuroscience educator*
Goldstein, Abraham Samuel *lawyer, educator*
Goodrich, Isaac *neurosurgeon, educator*
Gordon, Sarah Herbert *historian*
Graedel, Thomas Eldon *industrial ecology educator, researcher*
Grausman, Philip *sculptor*
Green, Donald Philip *education educator*
Greene, Liliane *French language and literature educator, editor*
Greenfield, James Robert *lawyer*
†Haddad, Gabriel G. *pediatrician, educator*
Hallo, William Wolfgang *Assyriologist*
Halvorsen, Per Helge *medical physicist, educator*
Harries, Karsten *philosophy educator, researcher*
Harrison, Henry Starin *real estate educator, entrepreneur*
Hartman, Geoffrey H. *language professional, educator*
Hayden, Dolores *author, architect, educator*
Heninger, George Robert *psychiatry educator, researcher*
†Hennah, Vivian Lisa *school system administrator*
†Hernandez-Rodriguez, Rafael *language educator, writer*
Hersey, George Leonard *art history educator, retired*
Herzenberg, Arvid *physicist, educator*
Hickey, Leo J(oseph) *museum curator, educator*
Hill, Gordon Charles, III, *company executive*
†Hockfield, Susan *medical educator*
Hoffman, Joseph Frederick *physiology educator*
Hoge, Michael Alan *psychologist*
Hollander, John *humanities educator, poet*
†Holmes, Frederic Lawrence *science historian*
Holquist, James Michael *Russian and comparative literature educator*
†Holt, Philetus Havens, IV, *lawyer, consultant*

Horváth, Csaba *chemical engineering educator, researcher*
†Horwich, Arthur L. *medical educator*
Howe, Roger Evans *mathematician, educator*
Inouye, Sharon K. *physician, educator*
Insler, Stanley *philologist, educator*
†Irwin, Melinda Liggett *healthcare educator, researcher*
†Jackson, Shirley Ann *sociology educator*
†Jarvin, Linda *research scientist*
Jatlow, Peter I. *pathologist, medical educator, researcher*
Johnson, Lester Fredrick *artist*
Johnstone, Quintin *law educator, writer*
Jordan, Paul *music director*
Kagan, Donald *historian, educator*
Kashgarian, Michael *pathologist, physician*
†Kaufman, Alan Stephen *psychologist, educator*
Kazdin, Alan E. *psychology educator*
Kennedy, Paul Michael *history educator*
Kernan, Walter Newberry *physician*
Kessler, David A. *dean, medical educator*
Kevles, Daniel Jerome *history educator, writer*
Kirchner, John Albert *retired otolaryngology educator*
Klein, Martin Jesse *physicist, educator, science historian*
Knag, Paul Everett *lawyer*
†Kosten, Thomas R. *psychiatrist, educator*
†Krasner, David *education educator*
Krauss, Judith Belliveau *nursing educator*
Kronman, Anthony Townsend *law educator, dean*
Kushlan, Samuel Daniel *physician, educator, hospital administrator*
Lamar, Howard Roberts *educational administrator, historian*
Langbein, John Harriss *lawyer, educator*
Langer, Lawrence Lee *English educator, writer*
Lannin, Donald Rowe *oncologist, surgeon*
LaPalombara, Joseph *political science and industrial management educator*
Laub, Dori *psychiatrist*
Lee, Sin Hang *pathologist, educator*
Leffell, David Joel *dermatologist, surgeon, health facility administrator, educator, writer*
Lentz, Thomas Lawrence *biomedical educator, dean, researcher*
Levin, Richard Charles *academic administrator, economist*
Levine, Robert John *physician, educator*
Lewis, Melvin *psychiatrist, pediatrician, psychoanalyst*
Lindroth, Linda (Linda Hammer) *artist, curator, writer*
Lord, George deForest *English educator*
Lytton, Bernard *urology educator*
MacAvoy, Paul Webster *economics, management educator, university dean*
MacMullen, Ramsay *retired history educator*
Madigan, Janet A. *psychiatrist, child psychiatrist, educator*
Malherbe, Abraham Johannes, VI, *religion educator, writer*
Mandelbrot, Benoit B. *mathematician, scientist, educator*
†Marchesi, Vincent T. *biochemist, educator*
Marcus, Ruth Barcan *philosopher, educator, writer, lecturer*
Margulis, Gregory A. *mathematics educator, researcher*
Mark, Harry Horst *ophthalmologist, researcher*
Marks, Lawrence Edward *psychologist, educator*
†Marmor, Theodore Richard *political science and public management educator*
†Martin, John C. *structural engineer, consultant*
Martin, Walter Francis, 3rd, *librarian*
†Martinsson, Per-Gunnar Johan *mathematician, mechanical engineer*
†Mason, Graeme Finlay *biophysicist, researcher, educator*
Massey, William S. *mathematician, educator*
†Matthay, Richard A. *pulmonary and critical care physician, educator*
Mayhew, David Raymond *political science educator*
McCarthy, Paul Louis *pediatrics educator*
McClatchy, J. D. *editor, writer, educator*
McGuire, William James *social psychology educator*
Meeks, Wayne A. *religious studies educator*
†Mehring, Christine *art historian*
Meyers, Amy *museum director*
Miller, Walter Richard, Jr., *banker*
†Mindell, Constance *social studies educator*
Moore, Peter Bartlett *biochemist, educator*
†Morgan, Robert P. *music theorist, educator*
†Mostaghimi, Mehdi *economist, educator*
Mostow, George Daniel *mathematics educator*
Mukherjee, Sandip Kumar *cardiologist*
Musto, David Franklin *physician, educator, historian, consultant*
Naftolin, Frederick *physician, reproductive biologist educator*
Narendra, Kumpati Subrahmanya *electrical engineer, educator*
Neisler, Otherine Johnson *education educator, consultant*
†Nelson, Alondra R. *social sciences educator*
Newick, Craig David *architect*
Niederman, James Corson *physician, educator*
Nolan, Victoria *theater director*
Nwangwu, John Tochukwu *epidemiologist, public health educator*
Ogbaa, Kalu *English literature educator*
Okerson, Ann Shumelda Lillian *librarian*
Oliver-Warren, Mary Elizabeth *retired library science educator*
†Orszag, Steven Alan *applied mathematician, educator*
Papageorge, Tod *photographer, educator*
Park, Jeffrey John *science educator*
Peck, Merton Joseph *economist, educator*
Pelli, Cesar *architect*
†Peralta, Rene Caupolican *cryptologist, educator*
Persing, John Arthur *surgeon*
Peterson, Linda H. *English language and literature educator*
†Peterson, Sandra Kay *librarian*
Phillips, Peter Charles Bonest *economist, educator, researcher*
Piehler, Wendell Howard *organist, choir director, fund raiser*
†Pierson, W. Lee *retired headmaster, foundation administrator*
Platner, Warren *architect*
†Podnar, Hrvoje *education educator*
Pollard, Thomas Dean *cell biologist, educator*
Pollitt, Jerome Jordan *art history educator*
†Porter, George Arthur, Jr., *pediatric cardiologist, researcher*
Pospisil, Leopold Jaroslav *anthropology and law educator*
†Powsner, Seth *psychiatry educator, medical computing researcher*
Priest, George L. *law educator*
Prown, Jules David *art historian educator*
Prusoff, William Herman *biochemical pharmacologist, educator*
†Quaglia, Jordano *language educator, writer*
†Rae, Douglas Whiting *management educator*
Rakic, Pasko *neuroscientist, educator*
Ranis, Gustav *economist, educator*
Rawson, Claude Julien *English educator*
Redmond, Donald Eugene, Jr., *neuroscientist, educator*
Reed, Mark Arthur *educator, researcher*
†Regan, Frederick E. *foundation administrator*
Reiner, Leona Hudak *consultant, attorney*
Reisman, William M. *lawyer, educator*
Reyes, Marcia Stygles *medical technologist*
Reynolds, Lloyd George *economist, educator*
Richards, Frederic Middlebrook *biochemist, educator*
†Richerson, George Bradley *neurologist, educator*
Ritchie, J. Murdoch *pharmacologist, educator*
Ritvo, Samuel *psychoanalyst, researcher, educator*
Robinson, Dorothy K. *lawyer*
Robinson, Fred Colson *English language educator*
Romero-González, Guido Mauricio *psychiatrist, educator, consultant*
Rose-Ackerman, Susan *law and political economy educator*
Roth, Harold *architect*
Rouse, Irving *anthropologist, emeritus educator*
Russett, Bruce Martin *political science educator*
Ryden, John Graham *publishing executive*
†Safriel, Yair *neuroradiologist*
Sartorelli, Alan Clayton *pharmacologist, educator*
Sasaki, Clarence Takashi *surgeon, medical educator*
Scarf, Herbert Eli *economics educator*
Scarf, Margaret (Maggie Scarf) *author*
Schloss, Irving Steven *lawyer*
Schlusberg, Julian Simon *theater educator, theater director, writer*
Schowalter, John Erwin *child and adolescent psychiatry educator*
Schultz, T. Paul *economics educator*
Schwartz, Peter Edward *physician, gynecologic oncology educator*
Seashore, Margretta Reed *physician*
Seligman, George Benham *mathematics educator*
†Shahar, Golan *psychologist, researcher, psychotherapist*
Shapiro, Ian *political science educator*
†Shaumyan, Alexander *poet, education educator*
Shaywitz, Bennett Arthur *medical educator*
Shubik, Martin *economics educator*
†Shulman, Gerald I. *physician, scientist, educator*
Shulman, Robert Gerson *biophysics educator*
Siegel, Norman Joseph *pediatrician, educator*
Silverstone, David Edward *ophthalmologist*
Singer, Jon Douglas *receptionist, writer*
Skalka, Douglas Scott *lawyer*
Skinner, Helen Catherine Wild *biomineralogist*
Slayman, Clifford Leroy *biophysicist, educator*
†Smith, Brian Richard *hematologist, oncologist, pathologist*
Smith, John Edwin *philosophy educator*
†Sobol, Alan J. *lawyer*
†Soderstrom, Edward Jonathan *academic administrator, consultant*
Sofia, Sabatino *astronomy educator*
Spataro, Sandra Elizabeth *business educator, consultant*
Spinner, Gary Frederick *physician assistant, healthcare administrator*
Spiro, Howard Marget *physician, educator*
†Stahl, Nanette *librarian, theologian*
†Staib, Lawrence Hamilton *biomedical engineer*
†Steitz, Joan Argetsinger *biochemistry educator*
Stern, Robert *psychiatrist*
†Sternberg, Robert Jeffrey *psychology educator, researcher*
Stevens, Joseph Charles *psychology educator*
Stolwijk, Jan Adrianus Jozef *physiologist, biophysicist*
Stuehrenberg, Paul Frederick *librarian*
Summers, William Cofield *science educator*
Sutterlin, James Smyrl *political science educator, researcher*
Sze, Gordon *neuroradiologist*
Tamborlane, William V., Jr., *physician, biomedical researcher, pediatrics educator*
Tirro, Frank Pascale *music educator, author, composer*
Totman, Conrad Davis *history educator*
Tully, John Charles *research chemical physicist*
Turekian, Karl Karekin *geochemistry educator*
†Udier-Blagovic, Marina *science educator, researcher*
Underdown, David Edward *historian, educator*
†Volkmar, Fred Robert *psychiatrist, educator*
Waggoner, Paul Edward *agricultural scientist*
Wagner, Günter Paul *biologist educator*
Walker, John Mercer, Jr., *federal judge*
†Wall, Joyce Elizabeth Maria *neuroscientist, educator*
Wallerstein, Immanuel *sociologist*
Wandycz, Piotr Stefan *history educator*
Warren, Graham Barry *cell biology educator*
†Warshaw, Marvin D. *conductor, educator, musician*
Waxman, Merle *dean*
†Waxman, Stephen George *neurologist, neuroscientist*
†Weiner, Susan E. *language educator*
Weinstein, Stanley *Buddhist studies educator*
Weiss, Robert M. *urologist, educator*
†Werdiger, Norman *neurologist*
Wessel, Morris Arthur *retired pediatrics educator*
Westerfield, Holt Bradford *political scientist, educator*
Wilson, Robert Rutherford *religious studies educator*
†Winter, Ralph Karl, Jr., *federal judge*
Wiznia, Carolann Kamens *lawyer*
Wolf, Werner Paul *physicist, educator*
Wright, Hastings Kemper *surgeon, educator*
Wrightson, Keith Edwin *historian*
Yanagisawa, Eiji *otolaryngologist, educator*
Yandle, Stephen Thomas *dean*
Yeager, Catherine Anne *research psychologist*
Yellis, Kenneth *museum administrator*
Zamfir, Nicolae Victor *physicist, researcher*
Zaret, Barry Lewis *cardiologist, medical educator*
Zeller, Michael Edward *physicist, educator*
†Zigler, Edward Frank *psychologist, educator*

New London
†Allen, Carol Marie *radiologic technologist*
Andrews, Constance Elaine *pharmaceutical executive*
Asselin, John Thomas *lawyer*
Bobruff, Jerome *physician*
†Bouchard, Jae Arlene *writer, poet, interior designer*
Dupont, Ralph Paul *lawyer, educator*
Dygert, James Lloyd, Jr., *music educator, musician*
Espinosa, Resurreccion *playwright, theater director, writer*
†Fainstein, Norman *college president*
Held, Dirk tomDieck *classics educator*
Johnson, Diana Atwood *business owner, innkeeper*
Johnstone, Philip MacLaren *lawyer*
Kalkstein, Joshua Adam *lawyer*
Larson, Richard Everett *lab technician*
Olsen, Robert C., Jr., *academic administrator, military officer*
Pinhey, Frances Louise *retired physical education educator*
Reardon, Robert Ignatius, Jr., *lawyer*
Santaniello, Angelo Gary *retired state supreme court justice*
Schoenberger, Steven Harris *physician, research consultant*
Thompson, Douglas Marshall *geomorphologist, educator*
Urbanetti, John Sutherland *internist, consultant*
Vinson, Danny Steve *musician, music educator*
Willauer, George Jacob *English literature educator*
Winter, Jerry Alan *sociology educator*

New Milford
Battista, John Robert *psychiatrist*
Edmondson, John Richard *lawyer, pharmaceutical manufacturing company executive*
Fabricand, Burton Paul *physicist, educator*
†Nadeau, Coni (Concetta) *editor, writer*
Page, Alice Cecilia *artist, educator*
Stalter, Richard Alan *museum administrator*
Tower, Roni Beth *psychologist*

New Preston Marble Dale
Biddle, Flora Miller *writer*
Grizzard, George *actor*
Myers, Robert Luther *architect, artist*

Newington
Foley, Patricia Jean *accountant*
Leeds, Robin Leigh *transportation executive*
Skwirut, John Laurence *computer company executive*
Vassar, Barbara Ellen *educational consultant*
Zeldes, Benjamin *optometrist*
Zeldes, Edith R. *freelance journalist*

Newtown
Briody, L(aurence) Patrick *journalist, consultant*
Carroll, Thomas Lawrence, Jr., *film and video producer*
Cayne, Bernard Stanley *editor*
Coates, John Peter *technical executive*
Cole, Richard John *marketing executive*
†Farrell, Edgar Henry *building components manufacturing executive, lawyer*
Geckle, Katherine L. *interior designer*
Goodwick, David Lee *advertising executive*
Wismar, Gregory Just *minister*

Niantic
Danos, Harry John *architect, educator, artist*
Deakyne, William John *library director, musician*
Douglas, Robert Gordon, Jr., *physician*
Hunt, Francis Howard *retired navy laboratory official*
†Morrill, Billie Alberta *librarian*
Mountzoures, Harry Louis *writer*

Norfolk
Burrows, John Edward *communications company executive*
Jessup, Philip Caryl, Jr.,
O'Malley, Margaret Parlin *marketing administrator*
Potter, Elizabeth Stone *academic administrator*
Rallo, Harry *architect, artist*
†Smith, Patrick Lawrence *journalist*

North Branford
Crossley, Francis Rendel Erskine *former engineering educator*
Logan, John Arthur, Jr., *retired foundation executive*
Mead, Lawrence Myers, Jr., *retired aerospace executive*
Ward, Frederick Champion *retired educator*
Womer, Charles Berry *retired hospital executive, management consultant*

North Canton
†Swibold, Gretchen Ann *librarian, writer*

North Granby
Riley, Christopher Sibley *museum supervisor*

North Grosvenordale
Kornbluth, Frances Helen Schachter *artist*
Murphy, Kathleen Jane *psychologist, educator*

North Haven
Bennett, Harry Louis *history educator*
Dahl, Robert Alan *political science educator*
Fuggi, Gretchen Miller *education educator*
Gradoville, Robert Thomas *lawyer*
Hogan, James Carroll, Jr., *public health administrator, research biologist*
Hudson, Richard L. *retired educator, clergyman*
Mahl, George Franklin *psychoanalyst, psychologist, educator*
Sawyer, Charles S. *environmental engineer, engineering educator*
Weaver, Kitra K. *sales and marketing executive*

North Stonington
Keane, John Patrick *retired secondary education educator*
Mills, Joshua Redmond *financial executive*
Neves-Elbaum, Stella Boudrias *design company representative*
Svengalis, Kendall Frayne *law librarian, educator, publishing executive*

Northford
Gregan, Edmund Robert *landscape architect*

Norwalk
Alderman, Rhenus Hoffard, III, *investment company executive*
Atlas, Ernest *physician*
Babcock, Catherine Evans *artist, educator*
Baylis, Robert Montague *investment banker*
Bays, John Theophanis *consulting engineer*
Bennett, Carl *retired discount department store executive*
Boles, Lenore Utal *nurse psychotherapist, educator*
Bortolot, Gary *writer, educator*
Brooks, Torrey Dexter *real estate executive*
Brown, Otha Nathaniel, Jr., *political official, retired educator*
†Cammaker, Sheldon Ira *lawyer*
Conoscenti, Craig Stephen *physician*
Crosbie, Michael James *architect, writer, educator*
Czajkowski-Barrett, Karen Angela *human resources management executive*
DeCesare, Donald E. *broadcasting executive*
Floch, Martin Herbert *physician*
Foster, John McNeely *accounting standards executive*
Freedman, Howard Martin *financial planner*
Greenberg, Sheldon Burt *plastic and reconstructive surgeon*
Harris, Holton Edwin *plastics machinery manufacturing executive*
Hathaway, Carl Emil *investment management company executive*
Hickey, Kevin Francis *healthcare executive*
Lang, Jules *lawyer*
Macdonald, Karen Crane *occupational therapist, geriatric counselor*
†MacInnis, Frank T. *construction company executive, holding company executive*
Maisano, Phillip Nicholas *investment company executive*
Mintz, Lenore Chaice (Lea Mintz) *consultant*
Mundt, Barry Maynard *management consultant*
Nightingale, William Joslyn *management consultant*
Pagano, Michael Pro *advertising executive*
Raikes, Charles FitzGerald *retired lawyer*
Ratchford, Roger Lionel *retired secondary education educator*
Rose, Gilbert Jacob *psychiatrist, writer, psychoanalyst*
†Ruggiero, Anthony William *chemical company executive*
Schmalzried, Marvin Eugene *financial consultant*
Sinclair, David Macowan *marine surveyor*
Tracey, Edward John *physician, surgeon*
†Weiner, Sandra Joan *computer catalog reseller company executive*
†White, Rick *publishing executive*
†Willcox, Roger *city planner, consultant*
Yeosock, Michael Michael *funeral director, civil engineer*
†York, Jerome B. *computer retail executive*

Norwich
Anderson, Carl Dennis *lawyer*
Chakrabarti, Jai *internist, cardiologist*
Cote, Michael Richard *bishop*
Hart, Daniel Anthony *bishop*
Masters, Barbara J. *lawyer*
Sherrard, James Robert *nuclear engineering educator*

Old Greenwich
†DeOrchis, Frankie Juanita *forester, writer*
Dixon, John Morris *magazine editor*
Hayden, Anthony *secondary and elementary educator*
Hittle, Richard Howard *corporate executive, international affairs consultant*
Levine, I. Robert *business executive*

Parris, Sally Nye *real estate agent*
Pursley, Carol Roberts *admissions director*
†Roca-de-Togores, Luis D. *writer*

Old Lyme

†Algiere, Scott G. *health facility administrator*
Bond, Niles Woodbridge *cultural institute executive, former foreign service officer*
Chandler, Elisabeth Gordon (Mrs. Laci De Gerenday) *sculptor, harpist*
Cook, Charles Davenport *pediatrician, educator*
Crandall, Oliver Perry *lawyer, poet*
Doersam, Charles Henry, Jr., *engineer, educator, entrepreneur*
Fairfield-Sonn, James Willed *management educator and consultant*
Johnson, James Myron *psychologist, educator*
Kraus, Janice *social worker, educator*
Mangin, Charles-Henri *electronics company executive*
Osborne, Frederick Spring, Jr., *academic administrator, artist*
Peagler, Owen Fair *retired college dean*
Pepe, Joy *art history educator*
St. George, Judith Alexander *author*

Old Saybrook

Narad, Richard M. *safety engineer*
Nuhn, Charles Kelsey *advertising executive*
Phillips, William E. *advertising agency executive*

Orange

Beringer, Michael Pennell *public relations executive*
Collier, Christopher *history educator, writer*
Davis, David Brion *historian, educator*
Dileone, Carmel Montano *dental hygienist*
Douskey, Theresa Kathryn *health facility administrator*
Granata, Attilio Vincent *medical educator, physician executive*
Gyorgyey, Clara M. *educator, writer*
Lobay, Ivan *mechanical engineering educator*
Phillips, Jeannette Veronica *management consultant, gerontologist*

Pawcatuck

Gualtieri, Joseph Peter *museum director*

Plainville

Anderson, William Carl *lawyer*
Glassman, Gerald Seymour *metal finishing company executive*
Petit, William Arthur, Jr., *endocrinologist*
†Zagorsky, Peter Joseph *lawyer*

Plantsville

Roy, Ralph Lord *clergyman*

Plymouth

Hall, William Smith, Jr., *land surveyor*

Portland

Chapman, Allen Floyd *management educator, college dean*
Rundle, Margaret *literary arts educator*

Preston

Gibson, Margaret Ferguson *poet, educator*

Prospect

Powell, Raymond William *financial planner, school administrator*
Thornley, Wendy Ann *retired educator, sculptor*

Putnam

Day, John Anthony, Jr., *pulmonologist*
Desaulniers, Rene Gerard Lesieur *retired optometrist*
†Osgood-Lemay, Sheri *child protective investigator, psychologist*

Rawayton

Parker, John Richard *mechanical engineer, consultant*

Redding

Benyei, Candace Reed *psychotherapist*
Binger, Wilson Valentine *civil engineer*
Gooch, Anthony Cushing *lawyer*
Isley, Alexander Max *graphic designer, lecturer*
McClure, Grover Benjamin *management consultant*
Russell, Allan David *lawyer*
Stack, J. William, Jr., *management consultant*
Wetzel, Edward Thomas *business executive*

Ridgefield

Bernstein, William Robert *banker*
†Bracken, Nanette Beattie *lawyer*
Brewster, Carroll Worcester *former academic administrator*
Clary, Alexia Barbara *management company executive*
Davie, Malcolm Henderson *city official*
†Egan, Kenneth J. *dermatologist*
Farrall, George William *marketing executive*
Fricke, Richard John *lawyer*
Hancock, Ellen Marie *communications executive*
Kantor, James Graham *music educator, composer*
Knortz, Herbert Charles *retired conglomerate company executive*
Kromer, Ann Marie *artist*
Leonard, Sister Anne C. *superintendent, education director*
Levine, Paul Michael *paper industry executive, consultant*
Lindsay, Dianna Marie *educational administrator*
Lodewick, Philip Hughes *equipment leasing company executive*
Lupia, David Thomas *corporate financial advisor, management consultant*
†Matteo, Martha R. *biochemist*
McConnell, John Edward *electrical engineering company executive*
Mesznik, Joel R. *investment banker*
†Pargellis, Christopher Allen *biologist, researcher*
Richard, David Dean *publishing executive*
Riche, Robert Savery *writer*
Sadow, Harvey S. *health care company executive*
Sen, Pabitra N. *physicist, researcher*
Sherman, Harold *lawyer*
Stoddard, William Bert, Jr., *economist*
†Tamsett, Susan O. *architect, artist*
Wang, Yuwen *chemist, researcher*

Riverside

Coulson, Robert *retired association executive, arbitrator, author*
Crawford, R. George *investment manager, educator*
Deering, Allan Brooks *retired soft drink company executive*
Dunn, Virginia *artist, community volunteer*
Geismar, Richard Lee *communications executive*
MacDonald, Gordon Chalmers *management consultant*
McSpadden, Peter Ford *retired advertising agency executive*
Powers, Claudia McKenna *state legislator*

Rocky Hill

Chu, Hsien-Kun *chemist, researcher*
Chuang, Frank Shiunn-Jea *engineering executive, consultant*
†Ettore, Joseph R. *discount department store chain executive*
†Lissy, David H. *corporate lawyer*
Olsen, John William *political organization administrator*
Roy, Thomas David *accountant*

Rogers

Kenworthy, Harry William *company executive*

Rowayton

Gold, Richard N. *management consultant*
Nelson, Paula Morrison Bronson *educator*
Piper, Thomas Laurence, III, *banker*

Roxbury

Friedman, John Maxwell, Jr., *lawyer*
Gurney, Albert Ramsdell *playwright, novelist, educator*
†Kelsey, Sterett-Gittings *sculptor*
Knutson, David Harry *retired lawyer, banker*

Salisbury

Block, Zenas *management consultant, educator*
Kilner, Ursula Blanche *genealogist, writer*
Levy, Ira Howard *marketing professional, real estate investor*
Magowan, Robin *writer*
White, Norval Crawford *architect*

Sandy Hook

†Hopkins, Homer Thawley *chemist, researcher, retired chemist*

Sharon

Chatfield, Judith Spencer *garden historian*
Gordon, Nicholas *broadcasting executive*
Gottlieb, Richard Matthew *psychiatrist, consultant*
Jensen, Philip Bailey *urologist*
Mesniaeff, Gregory *economist, securities analyst*
Nweeia, Martin Thomas *dentist, musician, composer, anthropologist*

Shelton

Asija, S(atya) Pal *lawyer*
Bonina, Sally Anne *secondary school educator*
Coverdale, Watson Shallcross, Jr., *communications company executive*
Fedornak, Mary *school counselor, educator*
Mariotti, Margaret *executive secretary*
Pagliaro, Frank Carl, Jr., *collection agency executive, city official*
†Ryan, William Joseph, Jr., *lawyer*
Wham, William Neil *publisher*
Zeller, Claude *physicist, researcher*

Sherman

Goodspeed, Barbara *artist*
Valeriani, Richard Gerard *news broadcaster*

Simsbury

Barnicle, Stephan Patrick *secondary school educator*
†Berberich, Patricia Louise *librarian*
Calvert, Lois Wilson *civic worker*
DiCosimo, Patricia Shields *secondary school educator*
Dumais, Arlene *psychiatric mental health and critical care nurse*
Long, Ann Marie *health facility administrator*
Main, Philip David *lawyer, probate judge*

South Kent

Keehner, Michael Arthur Miller *investment bank executive*
Samartini, James Rogers *retired appliance company executive*

South Windsor

Carman, Gary Olen *child welfare company executive*
Famiglietti, Nancy Zima *computer executive*
Gerlt, Wayne Christopher *lawyer*
Hobbs, David Ellis *mechanical engineer*
Saakvitne, Karen Winslow *psychologist*

Southbury

Atwood, Edward Charles *economist, educator*
Auerbach, Ernest Sigmund *lawyer, company executive, writer*
Barry, Edward William *retired publisher*
†Foxworth, Johnnie Hunter *state agency administrator*
Hopf, Frank Rudolph *retired dentist*
Leonard, John Harry *advertising executive*
Morehead, Frederick Ferguson *retired physical chemist*
†Normann, Margaret Ella *deacon, educator*
Rorick, William Calvin *librarian, educator, portrait artist*
Rubin, Jacob Carl *mechanical research engineer*
Vega, Marylois Purdy *journalist*
†Wolsch, Robert Allen *communication educator*

Southington

Burkhardt, Dolores Ann *library consultant*
Byeff, Peter David *hematologist, oncologist*
Carrington, Virginia Gail (Vee Carrington) *marketing professional, consultant*
Raymond, Gordon H. *engineering executive, consultant*
Rudolph, Kathleen Ann *insurance company executive*
Weichsel, John *town manager*

Southport

Damson, Barrie Morton *oil and gas exploration company executive*
Gryka, George Edwin *chemical company executive*
Hill, David Lawrence *research corporation executive*
Pickerstein, Harold James *lawyer*
Sanetti, Stephen Louis *lawyer*
Savage, Robert Heath *advertising executive*
Sheppard, William Stevens *investment banker*
Walker, Charles Dodsley *conductor, organist*
Wheeler, Wilmot Fitch, Jr., *diversified manufacturing company executive*
Wilbur, E. Packer *investment company executive*
†Williams, Michael Peter Anthony *lawyer*

Stamford

Allaire, Paul Arthur *office equipment company executive*
Anderson, Susan Leigh *philosophy educator*
Barker, James Rex *water transportation executive, director*
Barreca, Christopher Anthony *lawyer*
Beck, Angel C. *columnist, screenwriter, educator, film director*
†Benedict, Peter Behrends *lawyer*
†Besser, Gary Steven *obstetrician, gynecologist, surgeon*
Bijur, Peter I. *retired petroleum company executive*
Block, Ruth *retired insurance company executive*
Bobrow, Henry Bernard *lawyer*
Bostin, Marvin Jay *hospital and health services consultant*
Bowen, Patrick Harvey *lawyer, consultant*
†Braddock, Richard S. *internet company executive*
Brakeley, George Archibald, Jr., *fundraising consultant*
Britt, Glenn Alan *media company executive*
Burston, Richard Mervin *business executive*
Caldwell, Philip *retired automobile manufacturing company executive, retired financial services company executive*
Callahan, Robert Jeremiah *retired judge, mediator*
Chang, Ted T. *chemist*
Chickering, Howard Allen *insurance company executive, lawyer*
†Chisholm, Andrea Lynne *business association administrator, foundation administrator*
Chisholm, Colin Alexander Joseph, III, *media professional*
Coleman, Ernest Albert *plastics and materials consultant*
Cook, Colin Burford *psychiatrist*
Courter, Jeanne Lynn *materials scientist*
†Critelli, Michael J. *lawyer, manufacturing executive*
Daniels, Daniel Lloyd *lawyer*
deKoster, Heinz Adolph *retired technology consultant*
Dell, Warren Frank, II, *management consultant*
Della Rocco, Kenneth Anthony *lawyer*
Dennies, Sandra Lee *city official*
Duhov, Benjamin *consulting group executive*
Evans, James *engineer*
Fein, Ronnie *writer, journalist*
Ferguson, Ronald Eugene *reinsurance company executive*
Fiorino, Anthony Saverio (Tony Eitan) *research analyst*
Frank, Laura Jean *computer scientist*
†Friedman, Michael *pharmaceutical executive*
Frishkorn, David Loy *finance company executive*
Gardiner, Hobart Clive *petroleum company executive*
†Gilman, Kenneth B. *retail executive*
Gladstone, Herbert Jack *manufacturing company executive*
Godfrey, Robert R. *financial services executive*
Gold, Steven Michael *lawyer*
Goodhue, Peter Ames *obstetrician and gynecologist, educator*
Goodkin, Deborah Gay *mutual funds administrator*
Griffith, Katherine Scott *librarian*
Gross, Ronald Martin *forest products executive*
Grossman, Sanford Jay *economics educator*
Harrington, Richard J. *information business executive*
Hathaway, Lynn McDonald *education advocate, administrator*
Hawley, Frank Jordan, Jr., *venture capital executive*
Hollander, Milton Bernard *corporate executive*
Hollinger, Morton *business owner*
Hood, Edward Exum, Jr., *retired electrical manufacturing company executive*
†Hubschman, Henry A. *lawyer*
Hudson, Harold Jordon, Jr., *retired insurance executive*
Jacobson, Ishier *retired utility executive*
Jason, J. Julie *money manager, author, lawyer*
†Jensen, Frode, III, *lawyer*
Johnson, Dwayne Douglas (The Rock) *professional wrestler, actor*
Karp, Steve *producing director*
Kingsley, John McCall, Jr., *manufacturing company executive*
Kisseberth, Paul Barto *retired publishing executive*
Klein, Neil Charles *physician*
Kobrin, Jay Arthur *interior designer, fiber artist*
Koproski, Alexander Robert *real estate executive*
Kweskin, Edward Michael *lawyer*
Lalli, Michael Anthony *lawyer*
†Lennick, Robert Brent *rabbi*
Lewis, Perry Joshua *investment banker*
†Lieberman, Steven Paul *lawyer*
Liebeskind, David *business management consultant, educator*
†Ligelis, Gregory John *lawyer*
Loh, Arthur Tsung Yuan *finance company executive*
Maarbjerg, Mary Penzold *office equipment company executive*
Malloy, Dannel Patrick *mayor*
Margolis, Emanuel *lawyer, educator*
McDonald, Cassandra Burns *lawyer*
McGrath, Richard *lawyer*
Mc Kinley, John Key *retired oil company executive*
Merritt, William Alfred, Jr., *lawyer, telecommunications company executive*
Mersereau, Stephen Crocker *electronic commerce executive*
Miklovic, Daniel Thomas *research executive*
Miller, Wilbur Hobart *business diversification consultant*
†Mirsky, Ellis Richard *lawyer*
†Moore, Sharon Helen Scott *gerontological nurse*
Morgan, William J. *accounting company executive*
Motroni, Hector John *manufacturing executive*
Munera, Gerard Emmanuel *manufacturing company executive*
Nevans, Roy Norman *food products executive, producer*
Nichols, Ralph Arthur *lawyer*
†Novikova, Tatyana *music educator*
†Olson, Richard E. *paper company executive*
Pansini, Michael Samuel *tax and financial consultant*
Papp, Laszlo George *architect*
Patterson, Denis W. *economic development official*
Perle, Eugene Gabriel *lawyer*
Pollock, M. Duncan *advertising executive*
Popelyukhin, Aleksey *mathematician, educator, actuary, researcher*
Preiss-Harris, Patricia *music educator, composer, pianist*
†Rand, A. Barry *technology company executive*
Ried, Tessa *environmentalist*
Rizzuto, Leandro Peter *consumer products company executive*
Roberts, Victoria Lynn P. *antique expert*
Robins, Robert Sidwar *political science educator, administrator*
†Rohrer, Dean Cougill *lawyer*
†Romeril, Barry D. *office equipment company executive*
Rose, Richard Loomis *lawyer*
Rudman, Joan Eleanor *artist, educator*
Ryan, Theresa Ann Julia *accountant*
Sahota, Gurcharn Singh *mechanical engineer*
Sarner, Richard Alan *lawyer*
Schiff, Jayne Nemerow *underwriter*
Schnitzer, Robert C. *theater administrator*
Scott, Gregory Alan *pharmacist, writer*
Shanman, James Alan *lawyer*
Sharp, Daniel Asher *foundation executive*
Silver, Charles Morton *communications company executive*
†Silver, R. Philip *metal products executive*
Skidd, Thomas Patrick, Jr., *lawyer*
Smith-Young, Anne Victoria *health services coordinator*
Smolyar, Adam J. *business executive*
Spiegel, Merle Andrea *pharmaceutical company executive*
Stapleton, James Francis *lawyer*
†Stern, Arlene Helen *human resources specialist*
Stillings, Irene Ella Grace Cordiner *foundation executive*
†Swerdloff, David Alan *lawyer*
Teeters, Nancy Hays *economist, director*
Teitell, Conrad Laurence *lawyer, author*
†Tenaglia, Douglas Joseph *advertising copywriter*
Thomas, Dennis *paper company executive, former government official*
Tregurtha, Paul Richard *marine transportation company executive*
†Trivisonno, Nicholas Louis *communications company executive, accountant*
Valentine, Robert John (Bobby Valentine) *former professional baseball manager*
Wallfesh, Henry Maurice *business communications company executive, editor, writer*
Walsh, Thomas Joseph *neuro-ophthalmologist*
Waxberg, Jonathan Abel *urologic surgeon, oncologist*
Wenger, Derrick Eliot *securities analyst*
Wilensky, Julius M. *publishing company executive*
Williams, Derek, Jr., *pharmaceutical professional*
Willkie, Wendell Lewis, II, *lawyer*
Wilson, Robert Albert *communications consultant*
†Yap, Jesus F., Jr., *cardiologist*
Yonkman, Fredrick Albers *lawyer, management consultant*

Stonington

Elliott, Inger McCabe *designer, textile company executive, design consultant*
Elliott, Osborn *journalist, educator, urban activist, former dean*
Friedman, Malcolm *consultant*
Mantz, Arlan W. *physics educator*
Rees, Charles H. G. *retired finance company executive, investor, consultant*
Stoddard, Alexandra *designer, writer, lecturer*
Van Rees, Cornelius S. *lawyer*

Storrs

Bancroft, James Rogers *consulting engineer*
†Boggs, Steven A *electrical engineer*
Crow, Laura Jean *design educator, costume designer*
Gouwens, Kenneth Veld *history educator*
†Higonnet, Margaret Randolph *education educator*
†Langlois, Richard Normand *economist, educator*
†Leadbetter, Edward Renton *microbiologist, educator*
†Liu, Lanbo *adult education educator*
Millikan, Ruth Garrett *philosophy educator*
Shaw, Leon Lingang *engineering educator, materials researcher*
†Siegle, Del *education educator*

Storrs

Bagtzoglou, Amvrossios C. *civil engineering educator*

Storrs Mansfield

†Abikoff, William *mathematician, educator*
Abramson, Arthur Seymour *linguistics educator, researcher*
Aindow, Mark *engineering educator*
Austin, Philip Edward *university president*
Azaroff, Leonid Vladimirovitch *physics educator*
Bartram, Ralph Herbert *physicist*
Britner, Preston Arthur, IV, *developmental psychologist, educator*
Brown, Richard David *history educator*
Bzymek, Zbigniew Marian *educator*
Charters, Ann *biographer, editor, educator*
Coons, Ronald Edward *historian, educator*
Devereux, Owen Francis *metallurgy educator*
Dewar, Robert Earl, Jr., *anthropologist, educator*
DiBenedetto, Anthony Thomas *engineering educator*
Dussart, Francoise *anthropologist, educator*
Gell, Maurice *engineering executive, educator*
Gilbert, Margaret P. *university educator, researcher*
Gross, Robert Alan *history educator*
Hahn, Yukap *physics educator, researcher*
Jensen, Helene Wickstrom *retired nutritionist, educator*
Jensen, Robert Gordon *nutritionist, consultant*
Johnston, E. Russell, Jr., *civil engineer, educator*
Kerr, Kirklyn M. *university administrator, veterinary pathologist, researcher*
Klemens, Paul Gustav *physicist, educator*
Kotula, Anthony William *retired research food scientist*
Laufer, Hans *developmental biologist, educator*
Lederer, Herbert *foreign languages educator*
Lee, Tsoung-Chao *education educator*
Long, Richard Paul *civil engineering educator, geotechnical engineering consultant*
†MacDonald, Earl Murray *musician, educator*
MacDonald, John Thomas *educational administrator*
Maier, Romulus *journalist*
Marcus, Harris Leon *materials science educator*
Marcus, Philip Irving *virology educator, researcher*
Miller, Thomas William *psychologist*
Nieforth, Karl Allen *university dean, educator, retired*
†Orringer, Nelson Robert *Spanish and comparative literature educator*
Pitkin, Edward Thaddeus *aerospace engineer, consultant*
Reed, Howard Alexander *historian, educator*
Reiter, Howard Lee *political scientist, educator*
Rimland, Lisa Phillip *writer, composer, lyricist, artist*
Rosen, William *English language educator*
Sazama, Gerald Walter *economist, educator*
Shaffer, Jerome Arthur *philosophy educator*
Skauen, Donald Matthew *retired pharmaceutical educator*
Slater, James Alexander *entomologist, educator*
Stephens, Jack Edward *civil engineer, educator*
Stwalley, William Calvin *physics and chemistry educator*
Suib, Steven Lawrence *chemist*
Suits, Alice-Mae *retired school social worker*
Tian, Xiuchun *research scientist*
Tucker, Edwin Wallace *law educator*
Zhang, Bi *mechanical engineering educator*

Stratford

Cox, Richard Joseph *former broadcasting executive*
Feinberg, Dennis Lowell *dermatologist*
Kossl, Thomas Leonard *lawyer*
Murty, Hema S. *aerospace engineer, researcher*
O'Rourke, James Louis *lawyer*
Probert, Dorothy Wittman *retired social worker*
Rock, William Booth *producer, announcer*
†Schimpf, William Paul *university administrator*
Sipprell, George Sidney *engineering professional*
Trapasso, Robert Louis *surgical pathologist*
Walker, Gladys Lorraine *author*

Suffield

Bianchi, Maria *critical care specialist, adult and acute care nurse practitioner, nursing administration*
†Sullivan, Edmund Bertram *writer*

Thomaston

Mühlanger, Erich *ski manufacturing company executive*

Thompson

Fisher, William Thomas *business administration educator*

Tolland

Butterworth, Michael *computer programmer*
Feller, Winthrop Bruce *physicist*
Simons, Sir Barry *underwriter, insurance consultant*

Torrington

Di Russo, Terry *communications educator, writer*

Drobena, Thomas John *minister, educator*
Leard, David Carl *lawyer*
McKenzie, Kathleen Julianna *artist*
Wall, Robert Anthony, Jr., *lawyer*

Trumbull

Allen, Richard Stanley (Dick Allen) *English language educator, author*
Beres, Milan *surgeon*
†Berg, Charles G. *insurance company executive*
†Binder, Steven F. *publishing executive*
Czajkowski, Frank Henry *lawyer*
†Fox, Mitchell B. *magazine publisher*
Harty, Thomas H. *publishing executive*
†Lang, James Richard *education consultant*
†Linck, Joseph Charles *priest*
Liu, Donald C. *mechanical engineer*
London, Michael Jeffrey *public relations executive*
Nevins, Lyn (Carolyn A. Nevins) *educational supervisor, trainer, consultant*
Norcel, Jacqueline Joyce Casale *educational administrator*
Schmitt, William Howard *cosmetics company executive*
Seitz, Nicholas Joseph *magazine editor, journalist*
Sorbo, Allen Jon *actuary, consultant*
Watson, Donald Ralph *architect, artist, educator, author*
Wigsten, Paul Bradley, Jr., *computer and financial consultant*
Williams, Ronald Doherty *lawyer*

Vernon Rockville

Gallien, Sandra Jean *social worker*
McKeever, Brian Edward *general contractor*
Orr, Jim (James D. Orr) *editor, writer*
Purnell, Oliver James, III, *judge*
†Putnam, Richard *dentist, educator*
Roden, Jon-Paul *retired educator and labor union organizer, educational consultant*
Susi, Anthony J *music educator, composer*
Wolff, Gregory Steven *insurance company executive*

Voluntown

Caddell, Foster *artist*
Thevenet, Patricia Confrey *social studies educator*

Wallingford

Cohen, Gordon S. *health products executive*
Galligan, Matthew G. *lawyer*
Jia, Weitao *dental products executive, researcher*
Kailasam, Mala Trichur *physician*
Lauttenbach, Carol *artist*
†Odeshoo, Linda *biostatistician, mathematician, educator*
Poindexter, Graham S. *chemist*
†Romine, Jeffrey Lee *chemist*
†Sanchez, Ramiro, Jr., *pharmaceutical physician*
Spero, Barry Melvin *medical center executive*

Warren

Hill, May Brawley *art historian*

Washington

Fishman, Mitchell Steven *lawyer*
Grimes, Margaret Whitehurst *artist, educator*
Leab, Daniel Joseph *history educator*
Phillips, Laughlin *art museum chairman emeritus, former magazine editor*
Renouf, Edda *artist*
†Shay, Christopher King *music educator*
Strojny, Norman *analytical chemist*

Washington Depot

Tracy, Michael Cameron *choreographer, performer, educator*
Wolken, Jonathan *performing company executive*

Waterbury

Aucella, Laurence Frank *counseling administrator, educator*
Bachman, Carol Christine *trust company executive*
Bellemare, David John *architectural designer*
Bobowick, A. Roger *neurologist*
DeFrancesco, Mark Stephen *physician*
deLuise, Vincent Paul *ophthalmologist*
Dost, Mark W. *lawyer*
Dudrick, Stanley John *surgeon, scientist, educator*
Fischbein, Charles Alan *pediatrician*
Garsten, Joel Jay *gastroenterologist*
Getnick, Richard Alan *ophthalmologist*
Goettel, Gerard Louis *federal judge*
Harper, Barbara Clara *counselor, educational program administrator, counselor*
†Jacobs, Timothy Lester *sociologist, educator, genealogist*
Knight, David Clough *physician*
Luedke, Frederick Lee *manufacturing company executive*
MacLeod, Glen Gary *English language educator*
Marano, Richard Michael *lawyer*
McDonald, Francis Michael *judge trial referee, retired state supreme court justice*
McIntyre, Kaye *non-profit organization executive, consultant*
Ogrodnik, Lana Kathleen *real estate broker*
Pape, William James, II, *newspaper publisher*
Peterson, W(alter) Scott *ophthalmic surgeon*
Rosa, Domenico *mathematics educator*
Semple, Donita C. *nurse*
Shetty, Jayakara *surgeon*
†Wu, Zheng Y. *hydroinformatics engineer, hydrologist, consultant*

Waterford

Commire, Anne *playwright, writer, editor*
Hinkle, Janet *project leader*
†Hinkle, Muriel Ruth Nelson *naval warfare analysis company executive*
Johnson, Gary William *environmental scientist, consultant*

Patnode, Mark W. *artist, graphic designer*
Pierson, Anne Bingham *physician*
Walsh, Peter Joseph *multimedia marketing professional*
White, George Cooke *theater director, foundation executive*

Watertown

Bertrand, Robert Simeon *manufacturing engineer*
Sherwood, James Alan *physician, scientist, educator*
†Thompson, Thomas James *music educator*
Wuthrich, Paul *electrical engineer, researcher, consultant*

Weatogue

Wise, Richard Evans *corporate executive*

West Cornwall

Klaw, Spencer *writer, editor, educator*
Prentice, Tim *sculptor, architect*

West Hartford

Bigler, Harold Edwin, Jr., *retired investment company executive*
Calip, Roger *writer, educator*
Camp, J. Holden *history educator*
Clear, Albert F., Jr., *retired hardware manufacturing company executive*
Coleman, Winifred Ellen *academic administrator*
Collins, Alma Jones *English educator, writer*
Cornell, Robert Witherspoon *engineering consultant*
Doran, James Martin *retired food products company executive*
Dowling, Vincent John *retired lawyer*
Dunn, Robert Elbert *education consultant, principal*
Elliot, Ralph Gregory *lawyer*
Farnen, Russell Francis *political scientist, educator*
Faude, Wilson Hinsdale *museum director, consultant*
Gebo, Susan Claire *consulting nutritionist*
Gerjuoy, Herbert George *educator, psychologist, consultant, poet*
Gitterman, Alex *social work educator*
Gobes, Landy *psychotherapist*
Gryc, Stephen Michael *composer, music educator*
Guberman, Jayseth *financial analyst*
Harrison, Walter Lee *university president*
Hugg, Geraldine Bertha Novotny *retired gerontology specialist, journalist*
Katrichis, Jerome M. *business educator, consultant*
Leshem, Osnat Alice *healthcare administrator*
Liftig, S. Rick *dentist, author*
Malone, Thomas Francis *academic administrator, meteorologist*
Markham, Claire Agnes (M. Clare Markham) *retired chemistry educator, consultant*
Nereberg, Eliot Joel *lawyer*
Panik, Michael Joseph *economics educator*
†Schindelman, Sylvia *education educator*
†Shea, Thomas F. *literature educator*
Silver, Herbert *physician*
Spencer, Priscilla James *physical education educator*
Stavola, John Joseph *retired obstetrician-gynecologist*
Storm, Robert Warren *lawyer*
Swerdloff, Ileen Pollock *lawyer*
Swerdloff, Mark Harris *lawyer*
Thompson, Howard King, Jr., *retired physician, educator*
Tonkin, Humphrey Richard *academic administrator, educator*
Uccello, Vincenza Agatha *artist, director, educator emerita*
Welna, Cecilia *mathematics educator*
Yueh, Chai-Lun *voice educator, opera singer*

West Haven

Bowerman, Richard Henry *utility company executive, lawyer*
†Bryant, Matthew Scott *research scientist*
Carroll, Joseph Gregory *pharmaceutical company executive*
DeNardis, Lawrence J. *academic administrator*
Ellis, Lynn Webster *management educator, telecommunications consultant*
Farquharson, Patrice Ellen *primary school educator*
Glen, Robert Allan *history educator*
†Haley, Usha C.V. *international business educator*
Levinson Miller, Carolyn *mental health services professional, researcher*
Mendez, Angela M. *small business owner*
Onton, Ann Louise Reuther *chemist*
†Singh, Parbudyal *dean, educator*
†Song, James Xin *statistician, consultant*
Suster, Zeljan *business educator, dean*

West Mystic

Hoagland, Porter, Jr., *electrical and mechanical engineer, consultant*

West Simsbury

Morest, Donald Kent *neuroscientist, educator*

Westbrook

Hall, Jane Anna *writer, model, artist*
†Vogell, Connie *paralegal*

Weston

Aibel, Howard J. *lawyer, arbitrator, mediator*
Bleifeld, Stanley *sculptor*
Brodax, Albert Philip *writer, film producer and director*
Cohen, Fred Howard *lawyer, investment company executive*
Daniel, James *curator, business executive, writer, former editor,*
Diforio, Robert George *literary agent*
Fredrik, Burry *theatrical producer, director*
Harmon, James Allen *bank executive*

Kilty, Jerome Timothy *playwright, stage director, actor*
Miller, Christopher Edward *investment advisor*
Murray, Stephen James *lawyer*
Murray, Thomas J. *advertising executive*
Oliver, Sandra *art dealer, painter*
Reinker, Nancy Cooke *artist*
Strauss, Ellen Louise Feldman *lawyer*
Thompson, N(orman) David *insurance company executive*
Wayne, Neil Russell *investment management company executive*
Williams, Paul Alan *artist*
Wilson, Melissa Anne *sculptor*
Wiseman, Carter Sterling *editor, writer, educator*
Zimmerman, Bernard *investment banker*

Westport

Aasen, Lawrence Obert *public relations executive*
Abel, Alan Irwin *film company executive*
Altman, Lawrence Gene *biologist, educator*
†Amschler, James Ralph *lawyer, relocation company executive*
Axelson, Linda Rae *event planning specialist*
Barton, James Miller *lawyer, international business consultant*
Blau, Barry *marketing executive, financial investor*
Burns, John Joseph *pharmacology educator*
Carr, Cynthia *lawyer*
Chernow, Ann Levy *artist, art educator*
Clausman, Gilbert Joseph *retired medical librarian*
Cramer, Allan P. *lawyer*
Dakofsky, LaDonna Jung *radiation oncologist, educator*
Davis, Joel *publisher*
Daw, Harold John *lawyer, director*
Dimes, Edwin Kinsley *lawyer*
Donaldson, James Neill *banker*
Ferris, Roger Patrick *architect*
Fisher, Leonard Everett *artist, writer, educator*
Frese, Edward Scheer, Jr., *information technology executive, consultant*
Frey, Dale Franklin *financial investment company executive, manufacturing company executive*
Gallagher, Michael Robert *consumer products company executive*
Grodd, Leslie Eric *lawyer*
Hayden, Vern Clarence *financial planner*
Hedge, Arthur Joseph, Jr., *corporate executive*
Hotchner, Aaron Edward *author*
†Kanaga, Lawrence Wesley *lawyer*
Kelly, Paul Knox *investment banker*
Kosakow, James Matthew *lawyer*
Kramer, Sidney B. *publisher, lawyer, literary agent*
Lacouture, Peter George *medical researcher*
Levien, Roger Eli *strategy and innovation consultant*
Lindskog, David Richard *lawyer*
Lopker, Anita Mae *psychiatrist, researcher*
Losen, Stuart Melvin *clinical psychologist*
†Mallon, Thomas *writer*
†Malloy, Susan Rabinowitz *artist*
McCormack, Donald Paul *newspaper consultant*
McKane, David Bennett *business executive*
†McTague-Stock, Nancy A. *painter, printmaker*
Meinke, Alan Kurt *surgeon*
Murphy, Thomas John *publishing executive*
Nedom, H. Arthur *petroleum consultant*
O'Keefe, John David *investment specialist*
Paul, Roland Arthur *lawyer*
Razzano, Pasquale Angelo *lawyer*
Ready, Robert James *financial company executive*
Reilly, Nancy (Anne Caulfield Reilly) *painter*
Ross, John Michael *editor, magazine publisher*
Rothenberg, Abraham Joseph *architect*
Rudd, Nicholas *investor, consultant*
Sacks, Herbert Simeon *psychiatrist, educator, consultant*
Santoro, Charles William *investment banker*
Saxl, Richard Hildreth *lawyer*
Schriever, Fred Martin *management consultant, financial investor*
†Schwarz, Shirlee *library consultant*
Sheiman, Ronald Lee *lawyer*
Siff, Marlene Ida *artist, designer*
Smith, Peter Wolfgang *physicist, artist*
Solum, John Henry *flutist, educator, author*
Spitzer, Vlad Gerard *lawyer*
Stern, Robert D. *publishing executive*
Walton, Alan George *venture capitalist*
Weyher, Harry Frederick, III, *merchant banker*
Wilk, Barbara *artist, educator*
Woog, Dan *journalist*

Wethersfield

Bussiere, Bruce Emile *protective services official*
†DiCicco, Tony *soccer coach*
Franco, Carole Ann *international consultant*
Gallicchio, David Michael
Gaudreau, Gayle Glanert *computer resource educator*
†Jenks, Dennis *publishing executive*
Karwic, Richard A. *management consultant, educator*
†Osborne, Louise *publishing executive*
Terk, Glenn Thomas *lawyer*

Willimantic

Carter, David George, Sr., *university administrator*
Danforth, Jeffrey Scott *psychologist, educator*
Eshoo, Barbara Anne Rudolph *academic official*
Koirala, Hari Prasad *mathematics educator*
Lacey, James Francis *American studies educator*
Mann, Prem Singh *economics educator*
†Nilsson, Andrew Thorpe *social sciences educator*
†Schiller, Howard Barry *lawyer*
Stoloff, David L. *education educator, academic administrator, web site designer*
Williams, Neil Franklin *physical education educator*

Wilson, Margaret Sullivan *retired executive dean, consultant*

Willington
Chao, Yong-Sheng *physicist*

Wilton
Adams, Thomas Tilley *lawyer*
Bishop, William Wade *advertising executive*
Brown, James Thompson, Jr., *computer information scientist, logistics specialist*
Caravatt, Paul Joseph, Jr., *communications company executive*
Duke, Robert Dominick *lawyer*
Eriksen, Dan Oluf *film director*
Farley, James Parker *retired advertising agency executive*
Flesher, Margaret Covington *communications consultant, writer*
Forger, Robert Durkin *retired professional association administrator*
Frank, Robert Allen *advertising executive*
Healy, James Casey *lawyer*
Hersh, Ira Paul *tax and financial planning consultant*
Horgan, Susan Bedsow (Susan Merril Taylor) *producer, writer*
Juran, Joseph Moses *engineer, consultant*
Keenan, James Joseph *organizational consultant, communications educator*
McNear, Barbara Baxter *retired financial communications executive, consultant*
Mitchell, Richard Boyle *security consultant*
Nickel, Albert George *advertising agency executive*
†Nugent, Gordon Walker *writer*
Oberstar, Helen Elizabeth *retired cosmetics company executive*
Pethley, Lowell Sherman *retired management consultant*
Poundstone, Sally Hill *library director*
Schadt, James Phillip *investment and software executive*
Silverman, Melvin J. *lawyer*
Steinfeld, Thomas Albert *publisher*
†Tarde, Gerard (Jerry) *magazine executive*
Tedesco, Frank Mario *management consultant*
Weiland, Juliette Marie *public relations executive, freelance writer and photographer*

Windsor
Auten, Arthur Herbert *history educator*
Ferraro, John Francis *business executive, financier*
Lerman, Kenneth B. *lawyer*

Windsor Locks
Coelho, Sandra Signorelli *secondary school educator, consultant*

Winsted
Stawicki, Joseph John, Jr., *marketing executive*

Wolcott
Austin, Robert Brendon *civil engineer*

Woodbridge
Alvine, Robert *industrialist, entrepreneur*
Arnold, Philip Bruno *physician*
Bondy, Philip Kramer *physician, educator*
Ecklund, Constance Cryer *French language educator*
Just, Jennifer Ramsay *television and video producer, writer*
Yesner, Raymond *pathologist, consultant*

Woodbury
Dressler, David Michael *psychiatrist*
Martin, M. Gertrude *artist*
Moeckel, Henry Theodore *architect*
Skinner, Brian John *geologist, educator*
Whelan, William Paul *retired research scientist*

Woodstock
Susla, Jeffrey Jonathan *English language educator*

Woodstock Valley
Allaby, Stanley Reynolds *clergyman*

DELAWARE

Bear
Davis, Richard Frank *former state legislator, research scientist*
Golden, Kelly Paul *electronic engineer, computer scientist*
Longfellow, Charles Alfred *information officer*
McLain, William Tome *principal, educator*
Stewart, Shirley Anne *educational administrator*

Bethany Beach
Gale, Robert L. *educational association administrator, consultant*

Camden Wyoming
Porterfield, Craig Allen *psychologist, consultant*

Claymont
Johnson, Lois Ann *patient educator*

Dagsboro
Lally, Richard Francis *aviation security consultant, former association executive, former government official*

Dover
†Adams, Thurman G., Jr., *state legislator*
Amick, Steven Hammond *state legislator, lawyer*
†Babiarz, Francis Stanley *lawyer*
Beugre, Constant D. *management educator, researcher*
Braverman, Ray Howard *secondary school educator*
Britt, Maisha Dorrah *protective services official*
Broderick, Cyril Emery, Sr., *plant physiologist, educator*
Carney, John C., Jr., *lieutenant governor*
Coyle, Kevin Francis *planner*
†Dean, Thomas Eugene *music educator, consultant*
Delauder, William B. *academic administrator*
De Roche, Linda Lee *English language educator*
Deuble, Lottie Edwards *lay worker*
Ennis, Bruce Clifford *lawyer*
Friedland, Billie Louise *former human services administrator*
Gambardella, Robert Edward *retired medical social services consultant*
Gorum, Jacquelyne W. *dean, social work educator*
Hoff, Samuel Boyer *political science educator*
†Jones, Jay Paul *environmental engineer*
Kim, Dae Ryong *management information systems educator*
†Lewis, Larry *communications educator, video producer*
Masland, Charles Henry, IV, (Chad Masland) *financial services executive*
†McNulty, Mark Andrew *lawyer, state official*
Millon-Wisneski, Sharon Marie *critical care nurse, educator*
Minner, Ruth Ann *governor*
Ornauer, Richard Lewis *retired educational association administrator*
Pokrajac, Dragoljub Milos *engineering educator*
Sessoms, Allen Lee *academic administrator, former diplomat, physicist*
Smyth, Joel Douglas *newspaper executive*
Spence, Terry R. *state legislator*
Steele, Myron Thomas *lawyer*
Stone, F. L. Peter *lawyer*
Taylor, Stephen Craig *philosophy educator, researcher, lecturer*
Taylor, Suzonne Berry Stewart *real estate broker*
Twilley, Joshua Marion *lawyer*
Vaughn, James T. *state legislator, former state police officer*
Wagner, Nancy Hughes *secondary school educator, state legislator*
Wasfi, Sadiq Hassan *chemistry educator*
Wilson, Samuel Mayhew *surgeon*
†Windsor, Harriet Smith *state official*

Ellendale
Davis, Mark Lofland, II, *retired educator, farmer, photographer, financial consultant*

Elsmere
Shearin, K. Kay *procurator, legal and humor writer, freelance technical writer*

Frederica
†Cadogan, David Phillip *aerospace engineer, researcher*
†Miller, Mary-Emily *history educator*

Georgetown
Holland, Randy James *state supreme court justice*
Hook, Donald Dwight *humanities educator, writer*
Pippin, Kathryn Ann *state agency administrator*
†Tuman, Rhonda Helene *director, advocate*
Williams, William Henry *history educator, liberal arts coordinator*

Greenville
†Cooch, Nancy duPont (Mrs. Edward W. Cooch Jr.) *sculptor*
Daney, Bernard Joseph *accountant, consultant*
DeWees, Donald Charles *securities company executive*
Long, Linda Ann *lawyer*
Schroeder, Herman Elbert *scientific consultant*

Hockessin
Croyle, Barbara Ann *health care management executive*
Dombeck, Harold Arthur *insurance company executive*
†Faulcon, Clarence Augustus *musician*
Hounsell, Jillann Cusick *secondary education educator*
Kramer, Janet Phillips *physician*
†Mertz, Anne Morris *writer, researcher, freelance journalist, teacher, lecturer*
Mills, George Alexander *retired science administrator*

Lewes
Adams, John Pletch *orthopaedic surgeon*
Bookhammer, Eugene Donald *state government official*
†Buchert, Stephanie Nicole *music educator*
Chapman, Janet Carter Goodrich (Mrs. John William Chapman) *economist, educator*
Costigan, Constance Frances *artist, educator*
Fried, Jeffrey Michael *health care administrator*
Laub-Novak, Karen *artist, writer, sculptor*
Little, R. Donald *real estate entrepreneur*
Nehrling, Arno Herbert, Jr., *retired chemical company executive*
Spence, Sandra *retired professional administrator*
Visbal, Kristen Elizabeth *sculptor*
Warden, Richard Dana *government labor union official*

Milford
Bergmann, William J. *personnel director*
Konowitz, Herbert Henry *textile company executive*
Quinn, Edward Francis, III, *orthopedic surgeon*

Millsboro
Carter, William Allen *sales executive, insurance company executive*
Derrickson, Shirley Jean Baldwin *elementary school educator*
Kettinger, David John *broadcast executive*
Lasher, Hiram Nelson *international biological consultant, entrepreneur*
Tennov, Dorothy *psychologist*

Montchanin
Freytag, Richard Arthur *banker*
Hall, Robert Paul *social services administrator*
Olney, Robert C. *diversified products manufacturing executive*

New Castle
Almquist, Don *illustrator, artist*
Bayard, Richard H. *political party official*
Bellenger, George Collier, Jr., *physics educator*
Brownson, Kenneth C. *university dean*
Cansler, Leslie Ervin *retired newspaper editor*
Cope, Maurice Erwin *art history educator*
Curran, Barbara Sanson *lawyer*
†Fairchild, Edward Harold *chemist, researcher*
Henley, Deborah *newspaper editor*
Martin, Jean Ann *educator*
Zhu, Tulong *engineer*

Newark
Abrams, Burton A. *economics educator*
†Advani, Suresh G. *mechanical engineer, educator*
Allen, Herbert Ellis *environmental chemistry educator*
Barteau, Mark Alan *chemical engineering and chemistry educator*
Bilinsky, Yaroslav *political scientist*
Böer, Karl Wolfgang *physicist, educator*
Brams, Marvin Robert *economist, mental health counselor, interfaith minister*
Breslin, Nancy Ann *psychiatrist, photographer, educator*
Brockenbrough, Thomas William *civil engineer, educator*
Brown, Hilton *visual arts educator, artist, writer*
Bunkše, Edmunds Valdemārs *geographer, educator, consultant*
Burmeister, John Luther *chemistry educator, consultant*
Byrne, John Michael *energy and environmental policy educator, researcher*
Cairns, Sara Albertson *physical education educator*
Campbell, Linzy Leon *molecular biology researcher, educator*
†Carroll, Charles E. *electronics executive*
Carter, Mae Riedy *retired academic official, consultant*
Chester, Daniel Leon *computer scientist, educator, consultant*
Christy, Charles Wesley, III, *industrial engineering educator*
Clayton, John Middleton, Jr., *development officer*
†Collier, Virginia Upchurch *internist*
Colton, David Lem *mathematician, educator*
Connelly, Donald Preston *retired electric and gas utility company executive*
†Coulet du Gard, Donna M. *language educator*
Dadmarz, Kewmars Ebrahim *physician, educator*
†Davis, Darwin Jacob *finance educator*
Day, Robert Androus *English language educator, former library director, editor, publisher*
†DeLorme, Michael *toxicologist, researcher*
DiRenzo, Gordon James *sociologist, psychologist, educator*
Doberenz, Alexander R. *nutrition educator, chemist*
Elson, Charles Myer *law educator*
Esrey, Elizabeth Gove Goodier *chemist, biologist*
Esterly, Katherine Louise *pediatrician*
Evans, Dennis Hyde *chemist, educator*
Freel, Edward J. *former state official*
Garcia-Frias, Javier *engineering educator*
†Garland, Howard *psychology educator*
Gehrlein, William Vincent *business education educator*
Godwin, Ralph Edward *retired computer operator*
†Gore, Robert W. *electronics executive*
Gorski, Robert Alexander *chemist, consultant*
Graham, Frances Keesler (Mrs. David Tredway Graham) *psychologist, educator*
Gulick, Walter Lawrence *psychologist, former college president*
Halio, Jay Leon *language professional, educator*
Harik, Vasyl Michael *research scientist*
Hockersmith, Charles Edwin *information technology educator*
Holmes, Larry Wayne *artist, educator*
Homer, William Innes *art history educator, art expert, author*
†Huang, C. P. *engineering educator*
Igwe, Godwin Joseph *chemical engineer*
Isaacs, Diane Scharfeld *English educator*
†Jackson, M.(arvin) Dennis *journalism educator, writer*
Kamack, Harry Joseph *retired chemical engineer*
Karlsson, Anette M. *aerospace engineer, educator*
Kobayashi, Nobuhisa *civil and coastal engineer, educator*
Koford, Kenneth John *economics educator*
Krishnan, Palaniappa *agricultural engineering educator*
Lathrop, Thomas Albert *language educator, writer*
Lemay, J(oseph) A(lberic) Leo *American literature educator*
Lemole, Gerald Michael *surgeon*
Lieberman, Joseph Aloysius, III, *physician, educator*
Lomax, Kenneth Mitchell *agricultural engineering educator*
Mangone, Gerard J. *international and maritime law educator*
†Manrai, Ajay K. *marketing professional, educator*
Marrs, Barry Lee *executive director*
McCann, Richard Stephen *lawyer*
Molz, Robert Joseph *manufacturing company executive*
Murray, Richard Bennett *physics educator*
Neal, James Preston *state senator, project engineer*
Nelson, Marilyn (Marilyn Nelson Waniek) *education educator, poet*
Nelson, Robert R. *hotel, restaurant and tourism educator*
Ness, Norman Frederick *astrophysicist, educator, administrator*
Palley, Marian Lief *political science educator, author*
†Panda, Kenneth Bires *English educator*
Phoon, Wai Wor *physician*
Prodan, James Christian *university administrator*
Protokowicz, Nora Jane *nursing administrator*
Raffel, Jeffrey Allen *urban affairs educator*
Reider, Martha Crawford *industrial immunologist*
Ritter, William Frederick *civil and agricultural engineering educator*
†Roller, Cathy M. *educational association administrator*
Roselle, David Paul *university president, mathematics educator*
Rowe, Charles Alfred *artist, designer, educator*
Sandler, Stanley Irving *chemical engineering educator*
Sawyer, John Edward *management educator*
Schwartz, Norman B. *humanities educator, consultant*
Shapiro, Allan David *plant biology educator*
Shipman, Harry Longfellow *astrophysicist, educator*
†Silva, Luis M. *marketing professional*
†Snair, Roger Clifford *writer, comedian*
Solano, Paul (Paul Leonard Solano) *finance educator*
Sparks, Donald Lewis *soil chemistry educator*
Stark, Robert Martin *mathematician, civil engineer, educator*
Steiner, Roger Jacob *linguistics educator, writer, researcher*
Stick, Thomas Howard Fitchett *corporate architect, construction litigation consultant*
Szeri, Andras Z. *engineering educator*
Talbert, Dorothy Georgie Burkett *social worker*
Tannian, Francis Xavier *economist, educator*
Theopold, Klaus Hellmut *chemistry educator*
Tolles, Bryant Franklin, Jr., *history and art history educator*
Trofimenko, Swiatoslaw *chemist, researcher, consultant*
Vassiliou, Eustathios *chemist, consultant*
Venezky, Richard Lawrence *English language educator*
Walker, Jeanne Murray *English educator*
Wei, Tie-Quan *biochemist*
Weintraub, Stanley *arts and humanities educator, writer*
†Welsh, Paul Patrick *retired lawyer*
†Wilgen, Julie Mapes *family studies educator*
Williams, Evelyn Lois *chemical company executive, safety consultant*
Wolters, Raymond *historian, educator*
Woo, S. B. (Shien-Biau Woo) *former lieutenant governor, physics educator*
Yagoda, Ben James *author, English educator*
Yan, Xiao-Hai *science center director, educator*
Zuckerman, Marvin *psychologist*

Newport
†Karode, Sandeep Kishor *chemical engineer, researcher*

Rehoboth Beach
Bischoff, Kenneth Bruce *chemical engineer, educator*
Piklo, Charlene Lorraine *retail management executive*

Rockland
Burdick, Kim Rogers *historic preservation consultant*
Harvey, Andre *sculptor*
Levinson, John Milton *obstetrician, gynecologist*
Rubin, Alan A. *pharmaceutical and biotechnology consultant*

Seaford
Campbell, Eugene Paul *retired public health administrator*
Norton, Lilburn Lafayette *chemist, consultant*
Slater, Charles James *construction company executive*

Washington
†Diaz-Balart, Mario *congressman*
Hutchinson, Tim *former senator*

Wilmington
Ambro, Thomas L. *federal judge*
Bader, John Merwin *lawyer*
Balick, Helen Shaffer *retired judge*
Battaglia, Basil Richard *company executive, former political party official*
Baumann, Julian Henry, Jr., *lawyer*
Benes, Solomon *biomedical scientist, physician*
Berger, Carolyn *state supreme court justice*
Bettinger, Judith Pedersen *soprano, voice educator*
†Biondi, O. Francis *lawyer*
Bissell, Rolin Plumb *lawyer*
Blankenship, Roy *conservator, artist, writer*
Bounds-Seemans, Pamella J. *artist*
Brady, M. Jane *state attorney general*
Brown Leatherberry, Thomas Henry *gospel music company executive, clergy member*
Busche, Robert Marion *chemical engineer, consultant*
†Butterfield, Margaret Anne Davis *music educator, vocalist*
Carey, John Patrick, III, *lawyer*
†Carey, Robert George *lawyer*
Carpenter, Edmund Nelson, II, *retired lawyer*
Caruso, Nicholas Dominic *protective services official*
Cason, June Macnabb *musician, educator, arts administrator, fundraiser*

Bailey, Vicky A. *federal agency administrator*
Bainum, Peter Montgomery *aerospace engineer, consultant*
Bair, Sheila Colleen *federal agency administrator*
Baird, Brian N. *congressman*
†Baker, Nancy Kassebaum (Nancy Kassebaum) *former senator, foundation official*
†Baker, Pauline Halpern *political scientist, policy analyst*
Baker, Richard Hugh *congressman*
Baldi, Stéphane *education researcher, sociologist*
†Baldwin, Elizabeth Ann *academic administrator*
Baldwin, Tammy *congresswoman*
Baldyga, Leonard J. *retired diplomat, international consultant*
Bale, Judith R. *health science association administrator*
Ball, Markham (Robert Ball) *lawyer, arbitrator, educator*
†Ballance, Frank W., Jr., *congressman*
Ballenger, Cass Thomas (Thomas Ballenger) *congressman*
†Bandar, Prince bin Sultan bin Abd al-Aziz Al Saud *Saudi Arabian ambassador to United States*
Bandler, Donald K. *diplomat*
Bandow, Douglas Leighton *editor, columnist, policy consultant*
Banzhaf, John F., III, *legal association administrator, lawyer*
†Baran, Christine *systems analyst*
Baran, Jan Witold *lawyer, educator*
†Barbehenn, Elizabeth *research analyst*
Barber, Ben Bernard Andrew *journalist*
Barbosa, Rubens Antonio *Brazilian ambassador*
†Barcella, Ernest Lawrence, Jr., *lawyer*
Bardin, David J. *lawyer*
Barnes, Donald Michael *lawyer*
Barnes, Mark James *lawyer*
Barnes, Shirley Elizabeth *foreign service officer*
Barnet, Richard Jackson *author, educator*
Barnett, Robert Bruce *lawyer, educator*
Baroody, Judith Raine *federal official, educator*
Barr, Cyrilla Patricia *music educator*
Barr, Michael Blanton *lawyer*
Barr, Robert Laurence, Jr., *congressman, lawyer*
Barreto, Hector *federal agency administrator*
†Barrett, James Gresham *congressman*
Barrett, Laurence Irwin *public relations executive, writer*
Barrett, Richard David *university director, consultant, bank executive*
†Barrett, Thomas J. *military officer*
†Barrie, John Paul *lawyer, educator*
Barringer, Philip E. *retired government official*
Barr-Kumar, Raj *architect*
Barron, Jerome Aure *law educator*
†Barry, John J. *labor union leader*
†Barry, John L. *military officer*
Bartlett, Bruce Reeves *economist, columnist*
Bartlett, Charles Leffingwell *foundation executive, former newspaperman*
Bartlett, John Laurence *lawyer*
Bartlett, Michael John *lawyer*
Bartlett, Roscoe G. *congressman*
Bartnoff, Judith *judge*
Barton, Jean Marie *psychologist, educator*
Basa, Enikö Molnár *librarian*
Basch, Richard Vennard *photographer, producer, writer, director*
Baskir, Lawrence M. *chief judge*
Bass, Charles F. *congressman*
Basseches, Robert Treinis *lawyer*
Bassin, Jules *foreign service officer*
Basu, Sudeshna *mathematician, educator, researcher*
Batdorf, Lynn Robert *horticulturist*
Bateman, Paul William *government official, business executive*
Bath, Ronald J. *military officer*
Batla, Raymond John, Jr., *lawyer*
Battis, Emery John *actor*
Battle, Lucius Durham *retired educational institution administrator, former diplomat*
†Battle, Vincent M. *ambassador*
Baucus, Max S. *senator*
Baughman, J. Ross *photographer, writer, educator*
Bauleke, Howard Paul *lawyer*
†Baum, Alissa L. *lawyer*
Baumgart, Matthew *congressional aide*
†Baumgarten, Jonathan *flutist*
Baxter, Nathan Dwight *dean*
Baxter, Nevins Dennis *bank consultant*
Bayh, Evan *senator, former governor*
Bayly, John Henry, Jr., *judge*
Beach, Walter Eggert *retired publishing organization executive*
Beale, Betty (Mrs. George K. Graeber) *columnist, writer*
Beale, Susan Yates *social worker*
Beall, James Howard *physicist, educator, public policy analysis*
Beauprez, Bob *congressman*
Bebchick, Leonard Norman *lawyer*
Becerra, Xavier *congressman, lawyer*
Beck, Richard Thomas *scientific facility administrator*
Becker, Brenda L. *federal agency administrator*
Becker, Jerome David *writer*
Becker, Mary Louise *political scientist*
Beckham, Edgar Frederick *educational consultant*
Beckner, Everet Hess *federal agency administrator*
Beckwith, Edward Jay *lawyer*
Bedard, Emil R. *career officer*
Bedini, Silvio A. *historian, author*
†Bednar, Richard John *lawyer, law educator*
Bednash, Geraldine Polly *association executive*
Beecher, William Manuel *government official*
Beehler, Bruce McPherson *research zoologist, ornithologist, conservationist*
Beers, Charlotte Lenore *federal agency administrator*
Beghe, Renato *federal judge*

Beisner, John Herbert *lawyer*
†Beisner, Robert Lee *historian*
Beizer, Robert A. *lawyer*
Belak, Michael James *information systems executive*
Belinfante, Alexander Erik Ernst *economist, statistician*
Bell, Jeanne Viner *public relations counselor*
†Bell, Jerry Alan *science education association administrator*
†Bell, Robert Brooks *lawyer*
†Bell, Robert Christopher (Chris Bell) *congressman*
Bell, Stephen Robert *lawyer*
Beller, Herbert N. *lawyer*
Bellinger, Edgar Thomson *lawyer*
Bellinger, John Bellinger, III, *lawyer, government official*
Bello, Judith Hippler *lawyer*
Bellows, Michael Donald *foreign service officer*
Belman, Murray Joel *lawyer*
Belson, James Anthony *judge*
Beltz, William Albert *publisher*
Bender, David Ray *library association executive*
Benitez, Juan Carlos *federal agency administrator*
Benjamin, Georges Curtis *emergency physician, consultant*
Bennett, Alexander Elliot *lawyer*
Bennett, Betty T. *English literature educator, university dean, writer*
Bennett, Robert F. *senator*
†Benoh, Ibrahim *artist, art educator*
Bentsen, Kenneth E., Jr., *congressman*
Berendzen, Richard *astronomer, educator, author*
Beresford, Douglas Lincoln *lawyer*
Bereuter, Douglas Kent *congressman*
Berg, Patricia Elene *molecular biologist*
Berg, Stephen Warren *government official*
Bergmann, Barbara Rose *economics educator*
Bergner, Jane Cohen *lawyer*
Berkley, Burton *federal judge*
Berkley, Shelley *congresswoman*
Berl, Joseph M. *lawyer*
Berman, Ellen Sue *energy and telecommunications executive, theatre producer*
Berman, Howard Lawrence *congressman*
Berman, Marshall Fox *lawyer*
Bern, Paula Ruth *columnist*
Bernabei, Lynne Ann *lawyer*
Berner, Frederic George, Jr., *lawyer*
†Bernhardt, Barbara Izabela *language educator, writer*
Bernstein, Lionel M. *gastroenterologist, educator*
Bernstein, Mitchell Harris *lawyer*
†Bernstein, Stuart A. *ambassador*
Bernthal, Frederick Michael *association executive*
Berry, Marion *congressman*
Berry, Mary Frances *federal agency administrator, history and law educator*
†Berry, Morrell John *cultural organization administrator*
†Berz, David Richard *lawyer*
Besen, Stanley Martin *economist*
Besozzi, Paul Charles *lawyer*
Best, Judah *lawyer*
Betts, Kirk Howard *lawyer*
Bhattacharya, Rina *economist*
†Bickwit, Leonard, Jr., *lawyer*
Biddle, Catharina Baart *artist*
Biddle, Timothy Maurice *lawyer*
Biden, Joseph Robinette, Jr., *senator*
Biebuyck, Julien Francois *medical educator, administrator*
Bierman, James Norman *lawyer*
Bies, Susan Schmidt *federal agency administrator*
Bigelow, Donald Nevius *educational administrator, historian, consultant*
Biggert, Judith Borg *congresswoman, lawyer*
Biggs, Jeffrey Robert *educator*
Bilirakis, Michael *congressman, lawyer, business executive*
Billington, James Hadley *historian, librarian*
Bingaman, Anne K. *lawyer*
Bingaman, Jeff *senator*
Bingham, Jeff *federal agency administrator*
Binkley, Marilyn Rothman *educational research administrator*
Bird, Kai *journalist, historian*
†Birnbaum, Charles A. *landscape architect*
Birnbaum, Norman *author, humanities educator*
Birnbaum, S. Elizabeth *lawyer*
Birnkrant, Henry Joseph *lawyer*
†Bishop, James Dodson *lawyer, mediator*
†Bishop, Rob *congressman*
Bishop, Sanford Dixon, Jr., *congressman*
†Bishop, Timothy H. *congressman*
Bixler, John Mourer *lawyer*
†Black, Allida Mae *historian, educator, writer, consultant*
†Black, J. Cofer *government agency administrator*
Black, Stephen Franklin *lawyer*
†Blackburn, Marsha *congresswoman*
Blackwelder, Brent Francis *environmentalist*
†Blackwill, Robert D. *ambassador*
Blair, Dan Gregory *federal agency administrator, lawyer*
Blair, David Belmont *lawyer*
Blair, James Pease *retired freelance photographer*
Blair, Louis Helion *foundation executive*
Blair, Margaret Mendenhall *research economist, consultant, law educator*
Blair, Robert Allen *business executive, lawyer*
Blair, Thomas Delano *museum administrator*
Blair, William McCormick, Jr., *lawyer*
Blake, Jonathan Dewey *lawyer*
Blakey, Marion C. *federal agency administrator*
Blanchard, Bruce *civil engineer, government official*
†Blankenship, J. Richard *ambassador*
Blazek-White, Doris *lawyer*
Bleakley, Peter Kimberley *lawyer*

Bleicher, Samuel Abram *lawyer, government official*
†Bliley, Thomas Jerome, Jr., *former congressman*
Bliss, Donald Tiffany, Jr., *lawyer*
Bloch, Farrell Edward *economist, writer*
Bloch, Richard Isaac *labor arbitrator*
Bloch, Stuart Marshall *lawyer*
Block, John Rusling *former secretary of agriculture*
Blocker-Burnette, Maxine Peterson *social worker*
Bloomfield, Lincoln Palmer *federal agency administrator*
Bloomfield, Sara J. *museum director*
Blumenauer, Earl *congressman*
Blumenfeld, Jeffrey *lawyer, educator*
Blumenthal, Susan J. *physician*
†Blumenthal, Susan Jane *psychiatrist, educator, public health agent*
Blumer, Dennis Hull *lawyer, academic administrator*
Blunt, Roy D. *congressman*
†Blust, Steven R. *commissioner*
Bluth, B. J. (Elizabeth Jean Catherine Bluth) *sociologist, aerospace technologist*
Boaz, David Douglas *foundation executive*
Bodansky, Robert Lee *lawyer*
Bode, Barbara *Internet entrepreneur, foundation executive, freelance/self-employed writer*
Bodner, John, Jr., *lawyer*
†Boehler, Gabriel D. *aerospace company executive, educator*
Boehlert, Sherwood Louis *congressman*
Boehm, Peter Michael *ambassador, diplomat*
Boehm, Steven Bruce *lawyer*
Boehner, John A. *congressman*
Bogard, Lawrence Joseph *lawyer*
Boger, William Hanna *lawyer*
Boggs, George Robert *academic administrator*
Boggs, George Trenholm *lawyer*
Boggs, Judith Susan *lawyer, health policy expert*
Boggs, Thomas Hale, Jr., *lawyer, director*
Bohannon, Camille *news anchor*
Boisvert, Marc Edward *surgeon, researcher*
Boland, Christopher Thomas, II, *lawyer*
Bolino, August Constantino *economics educator*
†Bolten, Joshua Brewster *federal official*
Bolton, Claude M., Jr., *federal agency administrator, retired military officer*
Bolton, John Robert *lawyer, government official*
Bond, Christopher Samuel (Kit Bond) *senator, lawyer*
Bond, Phillip J. *federal agency administrator*
Bonde, Count Peder Carlsson *investment company executive*
Bonilla, Henry *congressman, broadcast executive*
†Bonner, Josiah Robins, Jr., (Jo Bonner) *congressman*
Bonner, Robert Cleve *federal agency administrator, lawyer*
Bono, Mary Whitaker *congresswoman*
Bonosaro, Carol Alessandra *professional association executive, former government official*
Bonvillian, William Boone *lawyer*
†Boo, Katherine *newswriter*
Bookbinder, Hyman H(arry) *public affairs counselor*
Boorstin, Daniel Joseph *historian, lecturer, educator, author, editor*
Boozman, John *congressman*
Bordeaux, Christi Renee *government agency administrator*
Borenstein, David Gilbert *physician, author*
Borgstrom, Howard Gustave *federal agency administrator*
Born, Brooksley Elizabeth *lawyer*
†Borod, Donald Lee *lawyer*
Borsari, George Robert, Jr., *lawyer, broadcaster*
Borski, Robert Anthony *former congressman*
Boskey, Bennett *lawyer*
Boss, Lenard Barrett *lawyer*
Bost, Eric M. *federal agency administrator*
Boswell, Leonard L. *congressman*
Boucher, Frederick C. *congressman, lawyer*
Boucher, Jack Edward *architectural photographer, writer*
Boucher, Richard A. *federal agency administrator*
Boughton, James Murray *economist*
Bourne, Peter Geoffrey *physician, educator, author*
†Bowen, Jose Antonio *music educator*
†Bowie, Darren A. *legal adviser*
Bowman, Dorothy Louise *artist*
Bowman, Frank Lee (Skip Bowman) *admiral and director naval nuclear propulsion*
Boxer, Barbara *senator*
Boyce, Clayton Winfred *magazine publisher, editor*
Boyd, Alan Martin *lawyer, legal administrator*
Boyd, F. Allen, Jr., *congressman, farmer*
Boyd, Ralph F., Jr., *federal agency administrator*
Boyd, Stephen Mather *arbitrator, mediator, lawyer*
†Boykin, Hamilton Haight *lawyer*
Boykin, Richard Renarda *legislative staff member, lawyer*
Boyle, Patrick Kevin *journalist*
Boza, Clara Brizeida *marketing and communications executive*
†Braceras, Jennifer C. *commissioner*
Bradlee, Benjamin Crowninshield *executive editor*
Bradley, Barbra Bailey *musician, educator, accompanist*
†Bradley, Jeb E. *U.S. Congressman*
Bradlow, Daniel David *law educator*
Bradshaw, Richard Eugene *government relations, energy and environment consultant*
Brady, Kevin *congressman*
Brady, Patricia G. *volunteer*
†Brady, Richard Alan *lawyer*
Brady, Robert A. *congressman*
Bragg, Lynn Munroe *federal commissioner*
Brahms, Thomas Walter *engineering institute executive*
Brame, Joseph Robert, III, *lawyer*

†Branch, Ronald Drewitt *lawyer*
Branegan, James Augustus, III, *journalist*
Brant, Donna Marie *journalist*
†Braverman, Burt Alan *lawyer*
Braverman, Jordan *columnist*
Bray, Sarah Hardesty *newspaper editor, writer*
Brazaitis, Thomas Joseph *journalist*
Brazeal, Aurelia Erskine *former ambassador*
Breaux, John B. *senator, former congressman*
†Bredhoff, Elliot *lawyer*
Bregman, Arthur Randolph *lawyer, educator*
†Bremer Martino, Juan Jose *ambassador*
Brenner, Janet Maybin Walker *lawyer*
Brenner, Robert David *federal agency administrator*
Bresee, James Collins *chemical engineer*
Bretzfelder, Deborah May *retired museum staff member*
Breul, Jonathan Dutro *consultant*
Brewster, Christopher Ralph *lawyer*
Brewster, Robert Charles *diplomat, consultant*
†Breyer, Stephen Gerald *United States supreme court justice*
Brick, Barrett Lee *lawyer*
†Bridgewater, Pamela E. *ambassador*
Briggs, Alan Leonard *lawyer*
Briggs, Ethel D. *federal agency administrator*
Brightup, Craig Steven *lobbyist*
Brimmer, Andrew Felton *economic and financial consultant*
Brinkmann, Robert Joseph *lawyer*
Brintnall, Michael Arthur *association executive, political scientist*
Briscuso, Raymond J. *biotechnologist*
Broad, Robin *political economist, educator, researcher*
Brobeck, Stephen James *consumer advocate*
Brockway, David Hunt *lawyer*
Broder, David Salzer *reporter, writer*
Brody, Kenneth David *investment banker*
Bromm, Susan Elizabeth *lawyer, government official*
†Bromwich, Michael Ray *lawyer*
Bronstein, Alvin J. *lawyer*
Brookins, Carole L. *federal agency administrator*
Brooks, Linton Forrestall *federal agency administrator*
Brouillette, Dan *federal agency administrator*
Broun, Elizabeth *art historian, museum administrator*
Brown, Ann W. *not-for-profit developer*
Brown, Charles Freeman, II, *lawyer*
Brown, Corrine *congresswoman*
Brown, Dale Susan *government administrator, educational program director, writer*
Brown, David Nelson *lawyer*
Brown, Donald Arthur *lawyer*
†Brown, Dorothy M. *academic administrator*
Brown, Elizabeth Ann *foreign service officer*
Brown, George Leslie *legislative affairs and business development consultant, former manufacturing company executive, former lieutenant governor*
Brown, Gordon Stewart *diplomat, business association administrator, writer*
Brown, Harold *former secretary of defense, corporate director*
Brown, Henry E., Jr., *congressman*
Brown, John Patrick *newspaper executive, financial consultant*
Brown, Lester Russell *research institute executive*
Brown, Louis *physicist, researcher*
Brown, Michael DeWayne *federal agency administrator, lawyer*
Brown, Pamela Wedd *artist*
Brown, Preston *lawyer*
Brown, Reginald Jude *federal agency administrator*
†Brown, Richard E., III, *military officer*
†Brown, Richard L. *lawyer*
Brown, Sherrod *congressman, former state official*
Brown, Thomas Philip, III, *lawyer*
Brownback, Sam *senator, lawyer*
Browne, Ray *congressman, insurance broker*
Browne, Richard Cullen *lawyer*
Brownell, Nora Mead *federal agency administrator*
Browner, Carol M. *former federal agency administrator*
†Brownfield, William R. *ambassador*
Brownlee, R. L. *federal agency administrator*
†Brownstein, Elizabeth Smith *writer*
Bruce, E(stel) Edward *lawyer*
Bruck, Nicholas *economist, educator*
Bruckman, Richard R. *aerospace engineer*
†Brunenkant, Jon Lodwick *lawyer*
Brunsvold, Brian Garrett *lawyer, educator*
Brustein, Michael Labe *lawyer*
Bruzelius, Nils Johan Axel *journalist*
Bryant, Daniel J. *federal agency administrator*
Bryant, Thomas Edward *physician, lawyer*
Bryson, Nancy S. *federal agency administrator*
Bryson, William Curtis *federal judge*
Brzezinski, Zbigniew *political science educator, author*
Buc, Nancy Lillian *lawyer*
Buchan, Douglas Charles *petroleum company executive, government official*
Bucholtz, Harold Ronald *lawyer*
Buck, Carolyn J. *federal official*
Buckberg, Albert *retired economist*
Buckley, Jeremiah Stephen *lawyer*
Buckley, John Joseph, Jr., *lawyer*
Bucklin, Donald Thomas *lawyer*
†Buffon, Charles Edward *lawyer*
Buhler, Leslie Lynn *museum director*
†Buist, Henry *economist*
†Bujon de L'Estang, Francois *diplomat*
Bulger, Roger James *academic health center executive*
†Bullett, Vicky *basketball player*
Bumpers, Dale L. *former senator, former governor, lawyer*

Dam, Kenneth W. *lawyer, law educator, federal agency administrator*
†Damelin, Harold *federal official*
Damgard, John Michael *trade association executive*
D'Amico, Carol *federal agency administrator*
Danas, Andrew Michael *lawyer*
Daniels, Deborah Jean *federal agency administrator*
Daniels, Diana M. *lawyer*
Daniels, Stephen M. *government official*
†Danzig, Richard Jeffrey *former government official, lawyer*
Danziger, Raphael *political scientist, researcher*
†Da Ponte, John Joseph, Jr., *lawyer*
Darman, Richard *investor, educator*
Daroff, William Clayton *political organization executive, lawyer*
Darr, Ann Russell *poet, educator*
Daschle, Thomas Andrew *senator*
†Dastoor, Minoo *biochemist*
Dave, Harish Pranlal *hematologist*
Davidow, Joel *lawyer*
Davidson, Dan Eugene *Russian language and area scholar, academic administrator*
Davidson, Daniel Ira *lawyer*
Davidson, Daniel Morton *lawyer*
Davidson, Eugene Abraham *biochemist, university administrator*
Davidson, Lee Howard *reporter*
Davidson, Richard J. *medical association administrator*
Davidson, Susan Bettina *editor, writer*
Davidson, Tom William *lawyer*
Davies, Charles R. *lawyer*
Davies, J. Clarence (Terry Davies) *government agency administrator*
†Davis, Artur *congressman*
Davis, David Oliver *radiologist, educator*
Davis, Donald Ray *entomologist*
Davis, Evelyn Y. *editor, writer, publisher, investor*
Davis, Garry (S. Gareth Davis)
Davis, Harley Cleo *retired career officer*
Davis, Jim *congressman, lawyer*
Davis, Jo Ann S. *congresswoman*
Davis, Lance Alan *research and development executive, metallurgical engineer*
†Davis, Lincoln *congressman*
Davis, Michele *federal agency administrator*
†Davis, Nathan Chilton *federal agency administrator*
Davis, Randy Lee *soil scientist*
Davis, Rex Darwin *business consultant*
Davis, Ruth A. *federal agency administrator*
†Davis, Shelton Harold *sociologist, educator*
Davis, Susan A. *congresswoman*
Davis, Thomas M., III, *congressman*
Davison, Calvin *retired lawyer*
Dawson, Horace Greeley, Jr., *former diplomat, government official*
Dawson, Howard Athalone, Jr., *federal judge*
Dawson, Mimi Weyforth *public policy consultant*
†Day, James MacDonald *lawyer, educator*
†Day, Lincoln Hubert *demographer, educator*
Day, Mary *artistic director, ballet company executive*
†Day, Melvin Sherman *information and telecommunications company executive*
Dayton, Deane Kraybill *translation company executive*
Dayton, Mark *senator*
Deal, Nathan J. *congressman, lawyer*
Deal, Timothy *association executive, former diplomat*
de Borchgrave, Arnaud *editor, writer, lecturer*
Decker, Michael H. *government agency administrator*
Deeb, Mary-Jane *editor, educator*
DeFazio, Peter A. *congressman*
DeGioia, John J. *university president*
DeGiovanni-Donnelly, Rosalie Frances *biology researcher, educator*
Deily, Linnet Frazier *federal agency administrator*
†deKieffer, Donald Eulette *lawyer*
DeKuyper, Mary Hundley *non-profit consultant*
Delahunt, William D. *congressman*
Deland, Michael Reeves *energy executive*
Delaney, Morgan D. *physician, educator*
DeLauro, Rosa L. *congresswoman*
DeLay, Thomas D. (Tom DeLay) *congressman*
†DeLeon, Patrick Henry *lawyer*
de Leon, Sylvia A. *lawyer*
Delgado, Jane *health executive, writer*
†Dell, Christopher William *ambassador*
Dellums, Ronald V. *former congressman, health facility administrator*
Dembling, Paul Gerald *lawyer, former government official*
Demetrion, James Thomas *art museum director*
†Deming, Rust M. *ambassador*
Dempsey, Joan *federal agency administrator*
Denger, Michael Louis *lawyer*
Denison, Mary Boney *lawyer*
Denlinger, John Kenneth *journalist*
Dennis, Gary C. *neurosurgeon, educator*
Dennis, Kimberly Ohnemus *philanthropy consultant*
Denny, Judith Ann *retired lawyer*
Denysyk, Bohdan *international consultant*
DeRocco, Emily Stover *federal agency administrator*
†Derrick, John Martin, Jr., *electric company executive*
Deso, Robert Edward, Jr., *lawyer*
Dessaso, Deborah Ann *freelance writer, online communications specialist, consultant*
†Determan, Sara-Ann *lawyer*
†DeThomas, Joseph Michael *ambassador*
Dettke, Dieter M. *foundation executive*
Detweiler, Richard Allen *college president*
Deutsch, Peter R. *congressman, lawyer*
Deutsch, Stanley *anesthesiologist, educator*
Devall, James Lee *lawyer*
Devaney, Earl E. *federal agency administrator*
DeVaul, Diane D. *policy director*
Devens, Richard Mather *publishing executive, economist*
Dewey, Arthur Eugene *federal agency administrator*
Dewey-Balzhiser, Anne Elizabeth Marie *lawyer*
DeWine, R. Michael *senator, lawyer*
Dey, Radheshyam Chandra *cytologist*
Diaz, Nils Juan *federal agency administrator*
Diaz-Balart, Lincoln *congressman, lawyer*
Dicello, Francis P. *lawyer*
Dicks, Norman De Valois *congressman*
DiConti, Michael Andrew *trade organization executive*
Diercks, Walter Elmer *lawyer*
Di Lella, Alexander Anthony *biblical studies educator*
Dillard, Todd W. *protective services official*
Dillin, John Woodward, Jr., *retired newspaper editor, correspondent*
Dillon, Wilton Sterling *anthropologist, foundation administrator*
Dils, Robert M. *military officer*
Dinan, Donald Robert *lawyer*
Dinerstein, Robert David *lawyer*
Dingell, John David *congressman*
Dinh, Viet D. *law educator*
Dinneen, Gerald Paul *electrical engineer, former government official*
DiPerna, Frank Paul *photographer, educator*
Disenhaus, Helen Elizabeth *lawyer*
Disheroon, Fred Russell *lawyer*
Dixon, Michel L. *educational administrator*
Dixson, Diane Elizabeth *acquisitions librarian, tax preparation business owner*
Dizard, Wilson Paul, Jr., *international affairs consultant, educator*
Doan, Michael Frederick *editor*
Dobriansky, Paula Jon *federal agency administrator*
Docter, Charles Alfred *lawyer, former state legislator*
Dodd, Christopher J. *senator*
Dodge, Judith C. *musician*
†Dodgen, Larry J. *career officer*
Doggett, Lloyd *congressman, former state supreme court justice*
Dolan, Michael William *lawyer*
†Dole, Elizabeth Hanford *senator, former charitable organization administrator, former federal official*
†Dole, Robert J. *lawyer, former senator*
Dolibois, Robert Joseph *trade association administrator*
Domenici, Pete V. (Vichi Domenici) *senator*
†Domingo, Placido *tenor*
Dominguez, Michael L. *federal agency administrator*
Dominiquez, Cari M. *federal agency administrator*
Domning, Daryl Paul *paleontologist, educator*
Donahue, Thomas Reilly *trade union official*
Donaldson, Samuel Andrew *journalist*
Donaldson, William Henry *financial executive, insurance company executive*
Donders, Joseph Gerard *priest*
Donegan, Charles Edward *lawyer, educator*
Donlan, Thomas Garrett *journalist*
Donnelly, Shaun Edward *government agency administrator*
Donohoe, Cathryn Murray *journalist*
Donohoe, Charles Richard *general patent counsel*
Donohue, Joyce Morrissey *biochemist, toxicologist, nutritionist, educator*
Donohue, Kenneth M. *federal agency administrator*
Donohue, Thomas Joseph *transportation association executive*
Donovan, George Joseph *industry executive, consultant*
Dooley, Betty Parsons *educational association administrator*
Dooley, Calvin Millard *congressman*
Doolittle, Jesse William, Jr., *lawyer*
Doolittle, John Taylor *congressman*
Dorgan, Byron Leslie *senator*
Dorn, James Andrew *editor*
Dorn, Jennifer L. *federal agency administrator*
Doroslovacki, Milos *engineering educator, consultant*
Dorsen, David M(ilton) *lawyer*
Dorsey, David Byard *non-profit executive*
Dougherty, Jude Patrick *philosophy educator, dean*
†Douglas, John Woolman *lawyer*
Douglas, Leslie *investment banker*
†Doumato, Lamia *librarian, art historian*
Dowd, Maureen *columnist*
Dowley, Joseph Kyran *lawyer, member congressional staff*
Downey, Arthur Thomas, III, *lawyer*
Downie, Leonard, Jr., *editor, writer*
Downs, Anthony *urban economist, real estate consultant*
Downs, Clark Evans *lawyer*
Doyle, Michael F. *congressman*
Dreier, David Timothy *congressman*
Dreisbach, Daniel Livingstone *lawyer, educator*
Drew, Elizabeth *television commentator, journalist, author*
Drinan, Robert Frederick *lawyer, former congressman, educator, clergyman*
Dritschilo, Anatoly *radiologist, educator*
Droms, William George *finance educator, investment advisor*
Dublin, Thomas David *retired physician*
DuBois, Paul Martin Joseph *non-profit organization executive*
Ducat, Suzanne Basha *television producer, communications specialist*
Duckworth, Walter Donald *museum executive, entomologist*
DuCran, Claudette Deloris *retired financial analyst*
Dudley, William Sheldon *historian*
Duelfer, Charles A. *diplomat*
Duemling, Robert Werner *diplomat, museum director*
Duffey, Joseph Daniel *academic administrator*
†Duffy, Brian *editor*
†Duffy, Michael F. *commissioner*
Duggan, Joseph Patrick *federal agency administrator*
Dugoff, Howard Jay *business consultant*
Dujack, Stephen Raymond *editor*
Dunbar, Leslie Wallace *writer, consultant*
Duncan, John J., Jr., *congressman*
Duncan, John M. *federal agency administrator*
Duncan, Richard Ray *history educator*
Dunn, Herbert Irvin *lawyer*
Dunn, James Milton *religious organization administrator*
Dunn, Jennifer Blackburn *congresswoman*
Dunn, Keith A. *government agency administrator*
Dunner, Donald Robert *lawyer*
Dunton, James Raynor *publisher*
†Durakovic, Asaf *nuclear medicine physician, consultant*
Durbin, Richard Joseph *senator*
Durney, Michael Cavalier *lawyer*
Durnil, Gordon Kay *lawyer, diplomat, arbitrator, political party official*
Dutro, John Thomas, Jr., *geologist, paleontologist*
†Dutton, Frederick Gary *lawyer*
Duvall, Henry Franklin, Jr., *public relations executive*
Dye, Alan Page *lawyer*
Dye, Stuart S. *lawyer*
Dyk, Timothy Belcher *federal judge, educator*
Eads, George Curtis *economic consultant*
Earll, Jerry Miller *internist, educator*
Eastham, Alan Walter, Jr., *foreign service officer, lawyer*
†Eastment, Thomas James *lawyer*
Easton, John Jay, Jr., *lawyer*
Eaton, Sabrina Catherine Elizabeth *journalist*
Eaton, William A. *federal agency administrator*
†Eberstadt, Nicholas Nash *social sciences educator, researcher*
Eby, Lloyd Martin *editor, writer, educator, filmmaker*
Eckenhoff, Edward Alvin *health care administrator*
Eddy, John Joseph *diplomat*
Edelman, Alan Irwin *lawyer*
Edelman, Marian Wright (Mrs. Peter B. Edelman) *lawyer*
Edsall, Thomas Byrne *reporter*
Edson, Charles Louis *lawyer, educator*
Edwards, Bob (Robert Alan Edwards) *radio news anchor*
Edwards, Chet *congressman*
Edwards, Harry T. *judge*
Edwards, John Reid *senator, lawyer*
Edwards, Steve *attorney, former political organization executive*
Effron, Andrew S. *federal judge*
Efros, Ellen Ann *lawyer*
Eggenberger, Andrew Jon *federal agency administrator*
†Eghbal, Morad *geologist, lawyer*
Ehlers, Vernon James *congressman*
Ehrenhaft, Peter David *lawyer*
Ehrenreich, Robert Marc *archaeologist, materials scientist, museum administrator*
Ein, Daniel *allergist*
Einaudi, Luigi Roberto *diplomat, educator*
Eisenberg, Meyer *lawyer*
Eisenberg, Pablo Samuel *non-profit organization executive*
Eisner, Howard *engineering educator, engineering executive*
Eizenstat, Stuart Elliot *ambassador, lawyer*
Ekman, Richard *association executive, educator*
Elcano, Mary S. *lawyer*
Elder, James Perry *management consultant*
†Eldridge, William Butler *lawyer*
Elfin, Mel *magazine editor*
El-Fishawy, Saad Samuel *lawyer*
Elias, Thomas Sam *botanist, author*
Eliasson, Jan K. *Swedish ambassador*
El Khadem, Hassan Saad *chemistry educator, researcher*
Ellicott, John LeMoyne *lawyer*
†Elliott, Emerson John *education consultant, policy analyst*
Elliott, Thomas Michael *retired association executive, educator, consultant*
Ellis, Courtenay *lawyer*
Ellison, Michael Scott *former financial executive, sailing coach*
Elmer, Brian Christian *lawyer*
†Elnakib, Hesham Moussa *diplomat*
Elrod, Eugene Richard *lawyer*
Elsasser, Glen Robert *journalist*
Elsberg, John William *editor-in-chief*
Elsey, George McKee *retired foundation administrator*
†Elson, Beverly Lynn *art educator*
Ely-Raphel, Nancy *diplomat*
†Emanuel, Rahm *congressman*
Emely, Mary Ann *association executive*
Emerson, Jo Ann *congresswoman*
Emery, Nancy Beth *lawyer*
Emmons, William Monroe, III, *business educator, consultant*
†Emperado, Mercedes Lopez *librarian*
Engel, Eliot L. *congressman*
Engel, Richard L. *career officer*
England, Gordon R. *civilian military employee*
Englar, Kenneth G. *aerospace engineer*
Engle, Jane *research nurse, artist*
Engleman, Ellen G. *federal agency administrator*
English, Philip Sheridan *congressman*
†English, Richard Allyn *sociologist, social work educator*
English, William Joseph *engineer*
Ennis, Michael E. *government agency administrator*
Ensenat, Donald Burnham *ambassador, lawyer*
Enzel, David Howard *lawyer*
Enzi, Michael Bradley *senator, accountant*
Epps, Roselyn Elizabeth Payne *pediatrician, educator*
Epstein, Gary Marvin *lawyer*
Epstein, Lionel Charles *lawyer*
Epstein, Sidney *retired editor*
Epstien, Jay Alan *lawyer*
†Ericsson, Neil R. *economist, consultant*
Ershler, William Baldwin *biogerontologist, educator*
†Ertel, Ruth Robinson *lawyer, government official*
Ervin, Clark Kent *federal agency administrator*
†Ervin, Susan Chadwick *lawyer*
Erwin, Douglas Hamilton *museum director, paleobiologist*
Esfandiary, Dara Sadigh *information technology executive*
Esfandiary, Mary S. *physical scientist, operations consultant*
Eshoo, Anna Georges *congresswoman*
Esslinger, John Thomas *lawyer*
Etheridge, Bob *congressman*
Etzioni, Amitai *sociologist, educator*
Evans, Charles Hawes, Jr., *immunologist, health science educator*
†Evans, Donald Charles, Jr., *lawyer*
Evans, Donald L. *secretary of commerce*
Evans, Joy *foundation administrator*
Evans, Lane *congressman*
Evans, Marsha Johnson *non-profit association administrator, former career officer*
Evans, Robert David *legal association executive*
Evelyn, Douglas Everett *museum director*
Everett, Ralph Bernard *lawyer*
Everett, Terry *congressman*
Everson, Mark W. *federal agency administrator*
Ewing, Ky Pepper, Jr., *lawyer*
Ewing, Patrick Aloysius *professional basketball coach*
Fabricant, Robert E. *federal agency administrator*
Faherty, Robert Louis *publishing executive*
†Fahey, John M., Jr., *book publishing executive*
Fahrenkopf, Frank Joseph, Jr., *lawyer*
Fai, Ghulam Nabi *cultural organization administrator*
Fain, Cheryl Ann *translator, editor*
Fairbanks, David Nathaniel Fox *physician, surgeon, educator*
Fairbanks, Richard Monroe, III, *lawyer, former ambassador at large*
Fajors, Nique *policy advisor*
†Faleomavaega, Eni Fa'auaa Hunkin *congressman*
Faley, R(ichard) Scott *lawyer*
Falk, Diane M. *research director, librarian, editor, writer*
Fallon, Harold Joseph *physician, pharmacology and biochemistry educator*
Fanone, Joseph Anthony *lawyer*
Farabow, Ford Franklin, Jr., *lawyer*
Farber, Donna Sylvie *marketing professional*
Farley, John Joseph, III, *federal judge*
Faron, Robert Steven *lawyer*
Farr, Michael Keogh *investment company executive*
Farr, Sam *congressman*
Farrelly, Mark John *retired theologian, priest*
Farrow, Robert Scott *economist, educator*
Fattah, Chaka *congressman, former state legislator*
Fauntleroy, Carma Cecil *arts administration executive*
Faux, Jeff (Geoffrey Peter Faux) *economist, writer*
†Fawell, Reed Marquette, III, *lawyer*
Fay, William Patrick *church administrator*
Fedders, John Michael *lawyer*
†Feder, David L. *lawyer*
Federspiel, Ulrik *diplomat*
†Feeney, Tom *congresswoman*
Feffer, Gerald Alan *lawyer*
Feierstein, Mark Barry *pollster*
Feigelson, Boris N. *physical chemist, researcher, materials scientist*
Feinberg, Kenneth Roy *lawyer, law educator*
Feingold, Russell Dana *senator, lawyer*
Feinstein, Dianne *senator*
Feinstein, Nathan B. *lawyer*
Feith, Douglas Jay *federal agency administrator*
Felbinger, Claire Louise *research administrator*
Feld, Karen Irma *columnist, journalist, broadcaster, public speaker*
Feldbaum, Carl *biotechnologist*
Feldhaus, Stephen Martin *lawyer*
Feldman, Clarice Rochelle *lawyer*
Feldman, Mark B. *lawyer*
Feldman, Roger David *lawyer*
Feldman, Sandra *labor union executive*
†Fels, Nicholas Wolff *lawyer*
Fennel, Melody H. *federal agency administrator*
Fenton, Wayne S. *psychiatrist*
Ferguson, Michael *congressman*
Ferguson, Roger W., Jr., *bank executive*
†Fernandes, Jane *academic administrator, educational consultant, sign language professional*
Ferrand, Louis George *lawyer*
Ferrara, Ralph C. *lawyer*
†Ferrell, James T. *sculptor*
Ferren, John Maxwell *judge*
†Ferretti, Maddalena F. *humanities educator*
Ferris, George Mallette, Jr., *investment banker*
Feshbach, Murray *demographer, educator*
Feuer, Marvin C. *political scientist, educator*
Feulner, Edwin John, Jr., *research foundation executive*
†Fex, Cecilia *lawyer*
Fhanks, Hershel *editor, writer*
Ficarra, Bernard Joseph *former surgeon, legal medicine and bioethics consultant*
Fielding, Fred Fisher *lawyer*
Fields, Suzanne Bregman *syndicated columnist*
†Fienberg, Linda Doris *lawyer*
Fifer Canby, Susan Melinda *library administrator*
Figueroa, Orlando *federal agency executive*
Filner, Bob *congressman*

Halsey, Ashley, III, *newspaper editor*
Halton, David Campbell *journalist*
Haltzel, Michael Harris *federal agency administrator, writer*
Halvorson, Newman Thorbus, Jr., *lawyer*
Hambel, John Joseph *lawyer*
Hamburg, Margaret Ann (Peggy Hamburg) *public health administrator*
Hamilton, Lee Herbert *educational organization administrator, former congressman*
Hamilton, Richard Clay *basketball player*
†Hamlisch, Marvin *composer, conductor, pianist, entertainer*
Hammerman, Edward Scott *lawyer*
Hammerschmidt, John Arthur *federal agency administrator*
†Hammond, Anthony *commissioner*
†Hammond, William Michael *historian, educator*
Hammonds, Timothy Merrill *association executive, economist*
Hand, John Oliver *museum curator*
Handel, Mark David *atmospheric scientist*
†Handleman, Aaron L. *lawyer*
†Handman, Bobbie (Barbara Handman) *foundation executive*
Hanford, John V., III, *federal agency administrator*
Hanley, Frank *labor union official*
Hannaford, Peter Dor *public relations executive, writer*
Hannett, Frederick James *healthcare consulting company executive*
Hansen, James Vear *former congressman*
Hansen, Mark Charles *lawyer*
Hansen, William *federal agency administrator*
Hanson, Jason David *lawyer*
Happel, Stephen P. *university dean*
Harding, Fann *health scientist, administrator*
Harkin, Thomas Richard *senator*
Harlem, Susan Lynn *librarian*
†Harman, Donna A. *lawyer*
Harman, William Boys, Jr., *lawyer*
†Harness, Gregory C. *Senate librarian*
Harper, Jennifer *journalist, entertainer*
Harper, Robert Allan *retired consulting psychologist*
Harpham, Virginia Ruth *violinist*
Harrington, Anthony Stephen *lawyer, diplomat*
Harrington, Kathleen M. *federal agency administrator*
Harris, Don Victor, Jr., *lawyer*
Harris, Jeffrey *lawyer*
Harris, Katherine *congresswoman*
†Harris, Patricia Flora *epidemiologist*
Harris, Scott Blake *lawyer*
Harris, Steven Brown *lawyer*
†Harrison, Donald *lawyer*
Harrison, Earl David *lawyer, real estate executive*
Harrison, Glennon Joseph *economist*
Harrison, Marion Edwyn *lawyer*
Harrison, Monika Edwards *business development executive*
Harrison, Patricia de Stacy *federal agency administrator*
Harrison, Ronald O. *association administrator*
Harrop, William Caldwell *retired ambassador, foreign service officer*
Hart, Christopher Alvin *lawyer*
†Hart, Clyde J., Jr., *federal agency administrator*
Hart, Katherine Marie *environmental scientist*
Hart, Melissa Anne *congresswoman*
Hart, Sarah V. *federal agency administrator*
Hart, William Lee, IV, *legislative staff member*
Harter, Donald Harry *neurologist, medical educator*
Hartman, Carl (Howard Carl Hartman) *reporter*
Hartman, Chester Warren *public interest organization executive*
Hartman, George Eitel *architect*
Hartmann, Robert Sankey *hospital administrator, communications and fundraising executive*
†Hartnett, Mary *lawyer*
Hartwell, Stephen *investment company executive*
Harvey, John Collins *physician, educator*
Harwit, Martin Otto *astrophysicist, writer, educator, museum director*
Hassett, Joseph Mark *lawyer*
Hastert, Dennis (J. Dennis Hastert) *congressman*
Hastings, Alcee Lamar *congressman, former federal judge*
Hastings, Richard Doc *congressman*
†Hathaway, Robert Morse *historian*
Hauser, Gabriel Jacob *pediatrician*
Hauser, Richard Alan *Federal Agency Administrator, Lawyer*
†Havens, Charles W., III, *retired lawyer*
Havlicek, Franklin J. *communications executive*
Hawke, John Daniel, Jr., *United States Comptroller of the Currency*
Hawke, Paul Henry *historian*
Hawkins, Monica Spann *environmental health scientist*
Hawkinson, Brian Patrick *professional association executive*
Hawks, William T. *federal agency administrator*
Hayden, John Carleton *priest, history educator*
Hayes, Allene Valerie Farmer *government executive*
Hayes, Kevin Gregory *university administrator*
Hayes, Paula Freda *governmental official*
Hayes, Robert (Robin Hayes) *congressman*
Haynes, R. Michael *lawyer*
Haynes, William J(ames), II, *lawyer*
Haythe, Winston McDonald *lawyer, educator, consultant, real estate investor*
Hayworth, J(ohn) D(avid), Jr., *congressman, former sportscaster*
Hazen, Robert Miller *research scientist, writer*
Hecht, Anthony Evan *poet*
Hecht, Marjorie Mazel *editor*
†Hecklinger, Richard E. *ambassador*
Heckman, Jerome Harold *lawyer*
Heddell, Gordon S. *federal agency administrator*
Hedges, Harry George *computer scientist, educator*
Hedges, Kamla King *library director*
Hedlund, Charles John *oil company executive, conservationist*
Heelan, Patrick Aidan *philosophy educator*
Heffernan, James Vincent *lawyer*
Hefley, Joel M. *congressman*
Hefter, Laurence Roy *lawyer*
Heineman, Heinz *chemist*
Heinemann, Heinz *chemist, educator, researcher, consultant*
Heintz, John Edward *lawyer*
Heinz, Teresa F. *foundation administrator*
Heinze, John Edward *microbiologist, industrial researcher/developer*
†Heise, Dorothy Hilbert *librarian, government official*
Heiss, Harry Glen *archivist*
Heivilin, Donna Mae *government executive*
Helfer, Ricki Tigert *banking consultant*
Helgerson, John Leonard *federal agency administrator*
Heller, (Douglas) Brian *human services administrator*
Heller, Jack Isaac *lawyer*
Heller, John Roderick, III, *lawyer, business executive*
Hellmuth, George William *architect*
†Helman, Donald Lee *physician, military officer*
Helmly, James R. *military officer*
Helms, Robert Brake *economist, research director*
Henck, Charles Seymour *lawyer*
Henderson, Douglas Boyd *lawyer*
Henderson, Karen LeCraft *federal judge*
Henderson, Thomas Henry, Jr., *lawyer, legal association executive*
Hendrickson, Constance C. *social worker*
Henke, Michael John *lawyer, educator*
Henkin, Robert Irwin *neurobiologist, internal medicine, nutrition and neurology educator, scientific products company executive, taste and smell disease physician*
Hennessy, Ellen Anne *lawyer, benefits compensation analyst, educator*
Henney, Jane Ellen *health administrator, oncologist*
Hennig, Bertrand Randy *journalist, commentator*
Henry, John Cooper *journalist*
†Hensarling, Jeb *congressman*
Hense, Donald Langford *educational association administrator*
Henshaw, John Lester *federal agency administrator*
Heravi, Mehdi *economist*
Herbert, James Charles *educational association administrator*
Herbert, John David *urban planner*
†Herbst, John Edward *diplomat*
Herdman, Roger C. *physician, policy analyst*
Herger, Wally W. *congressman*
Herman, Alexis M. *former labor secretary*
Herman, Andrea Maxine *newspaper editor*
Herman, George Edward *radio and television correspondent*
†Hernreich, Nancy *federal official*
Heron, Julian Briscoe, Jr., *lawyer*
†Herrera, Jessica Rae *lawyer, educator*
Herrett, Richard Allison *agricultural research institute administrator*
†Hershberg, James Gordon *historian, educator*
Hershey, Robert Lewis *mechanical engineer, management consultant*
Herzstein, Robert Erwin *lawyer*
Hess, Stephen *political scientist, author*
Hewitt, Emily Clark *judge, minister*
Hewitt, Paul Buck *lawyer*
Hezir, Joseph S. *energy and environmental company executive*
†Hiatt, Fred *editorial editor*
Hickey, Bruce William *lawyer*
Hickey, James Aloysius Cardinal *emeritus archbishop*
†Hickok, Eugene W. *federal agency administrator*
Hiebert, Ray Eldon *educator, author, consultant*
†Hiestand, O.S., Jr., *lawyer*
Higgins, James Henry, III, *marketing executive*
Higgins, Kathryn O'Leary *non-profit organization executive*
Higgins, Peter Thomas *technology consultant*
Higgins, Robin L. *federal agency administrator*
Higham, Scott *reporter*
†Highton, Richard Taylor *biologist, educator*
Hill, Baron P. *congressman*
†Hill, Edwin D. *trade association administrator*
Hill, Kent Richmond *federal agency administrator*
Hills, Carla Anderson *lawyer, former federal official*
Hills, John Merrill *educational administrator, consultant, former public policy research center executive*
Hills, Roderick M. *lawyer, business executive, former government official*
Hinchey, Maurice D. *congressman*
Hinden, Stanley Jay *newspaper editor*
Hinojosa, Ruben *congressman*
†Hirsch, Robert Allen *lawyer*
Hirschhorn, Eric Leonard *lawyer*
Hoagland, Jimmie Lee *newspaper editor*
†Hoak, Michael Shane *historian*
Hobbins, William T. *career officer*
†Hobbs, Caswell O., III, *lawyer*
Hobbs, J. Timothy, Sr., *lawyer*
Hobelman, Carl Donald *lawyer*
Hobson, David Lee *congressman, lawyer*
Hocker, John Robert *technical operations executive*
Hoeffel, Joseph M. *congressman, lawyer*
Hoehn, Richard Albert *association executive, clergyman*
Hoekstra, Peter *congressman, manufacturing executive*
Hoffa, James P. *labor union administrator*
†Hoffinger, Adam Steven *lawyer*
Hoffman, E. Leslie *lawyer*
Hoffman, Joel Elihu *lawyer*
Hoffmann, Robert Shaw *museum administrator, educator*
†Hogan, Howard *statistician, educator*
†Hoglander, Harry R. *legislative staff member*
Ho-Gonzalez, William *lawyer*
Hojo, Lawrence Matthew, Jr., *legislative director*
Holcomb, Lee *federal agency administrator*
Holden, Raymond Thomas *physician, educator*
Holden, Tim *congressman, protective official*
Holdsclaw, Chamique Shaunta *professional basketball player*
Holladay, Wilhelmina Cole *interior design and museum executive*
Holland, Christie Anna *biochemist, virologist*
Hollerbach, Paula Elizabeth *demographer, researcher*
Hollings, Ernest Frederick *senator*
Hollinshead, Ariel Cahill *research oncologist, educator*
Hollis, Nicholas Everett *trade association executive*
Hollis, Sheila Slocum *lawyer*
Holloway, John Thomas *physicist, consultant*
†Holman, John Clarke *lawyer*
Holmer, Alan Freeman *trade association executive, lawyer*
Holmstead, Jeffrey Ralph *federal agency administrator*
Holt, Rush Dew *congressman, physics educator, researcher, consultant*
†Holt, Thaddeus *lawyer*
Honda, Michael M. *congressman*
Honohan, Patrick *economist*
Hooley, Darlene *congresswoman*
Hooper, John David *coast guard officer*
†Hope, Karin *lawyer, legislative staff member*
Hope, William Duane *zoologist, curator*
Hoppe, John David *political organization worker*
Horahan, Edward Bernard, III, *lawyer*
Horinko, Marianne Lamant *federal agency administrator*
Horlick, Gary Norman *lawyer, legal educator*
Horn, Charles M. *lawyer*
Horn, Donald Herbert *lawyer*
†Horn, Stephen *lawyer*
Horn, Wade Frederick *federal agency administrator*
Horne, Michael Stewart *lawyer*
Horner, Constance Joan *federal agency administrator*
Horowitz, Herbert Eugene *retired diplomat*
Horwitz, Sari *reporter*
Hoskins, Carlton L. *legislative staff member*
Hostettler, John N. *congressman*
Houghton, Amory, Jr., (Amo Houghton) *congressman*
†Houlihan, David Paul *lawyer*
House, W(illiam) Michael *lawyer*
Houseman, Alan William *lawyer*
Howard, Glen Scott *foundation executive, lawyer*
†Howard, J. Timothy *finance company executive*
Howard, Jack *labor relations consultant*
Howard, Jeffrey Hjalmar *lawyer*
Howard, John *federal agency administrator*
Howard, Russell Alfred *astrophysicist, researcher*
Howe, Fisher *management consultant, former government official*
Howes, Theodore Clark *claims examiner*
Howland, Nina Davis *historian*
Howland, Richard Hubbard *architectural historian*
Hoyer, Steny Hamilton *congressman*
Hoyt, Clark Freeland *journalist, newspaper editor*
Hoyt, John Arthur *humane society executive*
Huband, Frank Louis *educational association executive*
Hubbard, Helen Mitchell *accountant, lawyer*
Huber, Richard Miller *American studies consultant*
Huberman, Benjamin *technology consultant*
†Huberman, Richard Lee *lawyer*
Huddleson, Edwin Emmett, III, *lawyer*
Hudnut, William Herbert, III, *senior resident fellow, political scientist*
Hudson, Michael Craig *political science educator*
Hudson, Timothy Leon *nursing educator*
Huebner, Emily Zug *judicial administrator*
Hufbauer, Gary Clyde *lawyer*
†Huffman, Walter B. *army officer*
Hug, James Edwin *religious organization executive*
†Huge, Harry *lawyer*
Huggins, James Bernard *corporate executive*
Hughes, Kent Higgon *economist*
Hughes, Marija Matich *law librarian*
Hughes, Sharon Mary *trade association executive*
Hughes, Thomas Lowe *foundation executive*
Hugler, Edward Charles *lawyer, federal and state government*
†Hull, Edmund J. *ambassador*
Hulshof, Kenny *congressman*
Hume, Brit (Alexander Britton Hume) *journalist*
Hungate, Joseph Irvin, III, *information technology executive*
Hunnicutt, Charles Alvin *lawyer*
†Hunt, Albert R. *newspaper executive*
†Hunt, David Wallingford *lawyer*
Hunt, Earl Stephen *federal agency administrator*
Hunter, Michael James *state government official, lawyer, educator*
†Hunter, Milton *army officer*
†Hunter, Stephen *film critic, writer*
Huntress, Wesley Theodore, Jr., *scientist*
Huntsman, Jon Meade, Jr., *federal agency administrator*
Hussain, Syed Taseer *biomedical educator, researcher*
Huston, John Wilson *air force officer, historian*
Hutchinson, Asa *federal agency administrator*
Hutchison, Claude B., Jr., *federal agency administrator*
Hutt, Peter Barton *lawyer*
Hyde, Henry John *congressman*
Hyde, Howard Laurence *lawyer*
Hyman, Lester Samuel *lawyer*
Iklé, Fred Charles *former federal agency administrator, policy advisor, defense expert*
†Ilkin, Baki *diplomat*
Imam, M. Ashraf *materials scientist, educator*
Indyk, Martin S. *diplomat*
Ingold, Catherine White *academic administrator*
Ingram, Richard Thomas *educational association executive*
Inhofe, James M. *senator*
†Inman, Harry Ansel *lawyer*
Innis, Pauline *writer, publishing company executive*
Inouye, Daniel Ken *senator*
Inslee, Jay R. *congressman*
Ireland, Patricia *not-for-profit developer*
Irvine, Reed John *media critic, corporation executive*
†Irwin, Paul Garfield *minister, social services executive*
Isakson, Johnny *congressman*
Isbell, David Bradford *lawyer, educator*
†Ishak, Kamal George *pathologist, consultant, pathologist, researcher, pathologist, educator*
Issa, Darrell E. *congressman*
Istook, Ernest James, Jr., (Jim Istook) *congressman, lawyer*
Ivers, Donald Louis *judge*
Iverson, Kristine Ann *federal agency administrator*
Ives, Stephen Bradshaw, Jr., *retired lawyer*
†Ivry, David *diplomat*
Jackson, Alphonso *federal agency administrator*
Jackson, Beverly Roberson *state agency administrator, consultant*
†Jackson, James Kinsey *lawyer*
Jackson, Jesse L., Jr., *congressman*
Jackson, John Howard *lawyer, educator*
Jackson, Mary Ellen *librarian, consultant*
Jackson, Michael P. *federal agency administrator*
Jackson, Neal A. *lawyer*
Jackson, Thomas Penfield *federal judge*
Jackson Lee, Sheila *congresswoman*
Jacobs, David Ernest *federal agency administrator*
Jacobs, Harvey S. *lawyer*
Jacobs, Julian I. *federal judge*
†Jacobs, Susan S. *ambassador*
Jacobsen, Hugh Newell *architect*
Jacobsen, Raymond Alfred, Jr., *lawyer*
Jacobson, Allen Howard *economist*
Jacobson, David Edward *lawyer*
Jacobson, Michael Faraday *consumer advocate, writer*
†Jagr, Jaromir *professional hockey player*
Jamar, Steven Dwight *law educator*
James, Bruce Richard *information specialist*
James, Kay Coles *federal agency administrator*
Janes, William Sargent *real estate corporation executive*
Jani, Sushma Niranjan *pediatric psychiatrist*
Janklow, William John *congressman, former governor*
†Jarboe, Kenan Patrick *think-tank executive, researcher*
†Jarque Uribe, Carlos *former federal official*
Jarrett, Jeffrey D. *federal agency administrator*
Jaschik, Scott P. *editor*
Jasper, John A. *writer, lawyer*
Jaspersen, Frederick Zarr *economist*
Jee, Justin Soonho *government official*
Jefferson, William J. (Jeff Jefferson) *congressman*
Jeffords, James Merrill *senator*
†Jeffress, D. Ames *prosecutor*
Jen, Joseph Jwu-Shan *federal agency administrator*
Jenkins, William L. (Bill Jenkins) *congressman*
Jennings, Jerry D. *federal agency administrator*
Jensen, Donald Norman *diplomat, writer*
†Jensen, James E. *director congressional and government affairs*
Jensen, Paul Rolf *lawyer, real estate investor*
Jenson, William G. *federal agency administrator*
Jepsen, Peter Lee *court reporter*
†Jeter, Howard F. *diplomat*
Jimenez, Emmanuel *economist*
Jochum, James J. *federal agency administrator*
John, Christopher *congressman*
John, Frank Herbert, Jr., *real estate appraiser, real estate investor, health products executive*
Johnson, Allen Frederick *federal agency administrator*
Johnson, Arlene Lytle *government agency official*
Johnson, Charles Minor *physicist*
Johnson, David Raymond *lawyer*
Johnson, Eddie Bernice *congresswoman*
†Johnson, Hansford Tillman *civilian military employee*
Johnson, James A. *financial organization executive*
†Johnson, Karen *legislation and congressional affairs secretary*
Johnson, Nancy Lee *congresswoman*
Johnson, Norma Holloway *federal judge*
Johnson, Oliver Thomas, Jr., *lawyer*
Johnson, Philip McBride *lawyer*
Johnson, Richard Kent *publishing executive*
Johnson, Robert Henry *political science educator*
†Johnson, Robert Louis *cable television company executive*
Johnson, Samuel (Sam Johnson) *congressman*
Johnson, Shirley Z. *lawyer*
Johnson, Stephen L. *federal agency administrator*
Johnson, Thomas Dale *management consultant*
Johnson, Timothy Peter *senator*
Johnson, Timothy Vincent *congressman*
Johnson, Victor Charles *association executive*
Johnston, Gerald Samuel *physician, educator*
†Johnston, John Bennett, Jr., *former senator, consultant*
Johnston, Kenneth John *astronomer, scientific director naval observatory*
Jones, A. Elizabeth *federal agency administrator*
Jones, Aidan Drexel *lawyer*
Jones, Allen, Jr., *lawyer*
Jones, Boisfeuillet, Jr., *publishing executive*

Lewis, William Henry, Jr., *lawyer*
Liberty, Arthur Andrew *judge*
Libutti, Frank *federal agency administrator*
Lichtman, Allan Jay *historian, educator, consultant*
Liebenson, Gloria Krasnow *interior design executive, freelance writer*
Liebenson, Herbert *economist, trade association executive*
Lieber, Robert James *political science educator, writer*
Lieberman, Joseph I. *senator*
Liebman, Ronald Stanley *lawyer*
†Liedquist, Robert Eric *lawyer*
Lietzau, William Kendall *career officer, lawyer*
†Lifschitz, Judah *lawyer*
†Light, Jeffrey Louis *lawyer*
Lightfoot, David William *linguistics educator*
Lilienthal, Alfred M(orton) *author, historian, editor*
Lilly, William Eldridge *government official*
Lincoln, Blanche Lambert *senator*
Lindberg, Tod Marshall *editor, writer*
Linder, John E. *congressman, dentist*
Lindsey, Seth Mark *lawyer, federal agency administrator*
Linowitz, Sol Myron *lawyer*
Lipinski, William Oliver *congressman*
Lipnic, Victoria A. *federal agency administrator*
Lipstein, Robert A. *lawyer*
Liroff, Richard Alan *environmental association executive*
Lisboa-Farrow, Elizabeth Oliver *public and government relations consultant*
Liss, Jeffrey F. *lawyer, educator*
Lister, Harry Joseph *finance company executive*
Litan, Robert Eli *lawyer, economist*
Littell, Richard Gregory *lawyer*
Littig, Lawrence William *psychologist, educator*
Liu, Michael Minoru Fawn *federal agency administrator*
Livingood, Wilson S. *law enforcement official*
Livingston, Bob (Robert Linlithgow Livingston Jr.) *lawyer, former congressman*
Livingston, Robert Gerald *historian, journalist*
Lloyd, James D. *federal agency administrator*
Lobel, Martin *lawyer*
LoBiondo, Frank A. *congressman*
Locke, Thomas Bernard *retired federal agency administrator, security firm executive*
Lockhart, James Bicknell, III, *federal agency administrator*
Loesberg, Jonathan *humanities educator*
Loevinger, Lee *lawyer, science writer*
Loewinger, Kenneth Jeffery *lawyer*
Lofgren, Zoe *congresswoman*
†Loftis, Robert G. *ambassador*
†Logan, Ann D. *financial company executive*
Loge, Peter Martin *organization administrator*
Logsdon, John Mortimer, III, *aerospace analyst, educator*
Logue-Kinder, Joan *consultant*
Lombardo, Fredric Alan *pharmacist, educator*
Long, Kerry Blair *lawyer*
Long, Pamela Olivia *historian*
Loots, James Mason *lawyer*
Lopatin, Alan G. *lawyer*
Lopez Calix, Jose Roberto *economist*
†Lorber, Lawrence Zel *lawyer*
Loren, Donald Patrick *naval officer*
Lorsung, Thomas Nicholas *news service editor*
Lott, Trent *senator*
Lourie, Alan David *federal judge*
Lovell, Malcolm Read, Jr., *public policy institute executive, educator, former government official, former trade association executive*
Lovett, Clara Maria *university administrator, historian*
Low, Stephen *foundation executive, educator, former diplomat*
†Lowe, Florence Segal *retired public relations executive*
Lowe, Harry *museum director*
Lowe, Mary Frances *federal government official*
Lowe, Randall Brian *lawyer*
Lowenstein, James Gordon *former diplomat, international consultant*
Lowey, Nita M. *congresswoman*
†Loyevsky, Mark Michael *biochemist, researcher*
Lozada, Jacob *federal agency administrator*
Lozansky, Edward Dmitry *physicist, author, consultant*
Lubar, Jeffrey Stuart *journalist, trade association executive*
Lubic, Robert Bennett *lawyer, arbitrator, law educator*
Lucas, C. Payne *development organization executive*
†Lucas, Frank D. *congressman*
Lucas, James Walter *federal government official*
†Lucas, Ken *congressman*
Luce, Gregory M. *lawyer*
Luck, Andrew Peter *federal agency administrator*
Luessenhop, Alfred John *neurosurgeon, educator*
Lugar, Richard Green *senator*
†Lukken, Walt *commissioner*
Lundergan, Conor Francis *cardiologist*
Lupo, Raphael V. *lawyer*
Lurensky, Marcia Adele *lawyer*
Lurton, Horace VanDeventer *brokerage house executive*
†Luskin, Robert David *lawyer*
Luther, Michael R. *federal agency administrator*
Lutterodt, Clement H. *mathematician, educator*
Luttwak, Edward Nicolae *academic administrator, educator, policy and business consultant*
Luxenberg, Steven Marc *newspaper editor*
Lybecker, Martin Earl *lawyer*
†Lyden, Jacki Lyn *journalist, writer*
Lynch, Robert L. *art association administrator*
Lynch, Stephen F. *congressman*
Lyons, Dennis Gerald *lawyer*
MacBeth, Angus *lawyer*
Macdonald, David Robert *lawyer, fund administrator*
†MacDonald, Purificacion O. *statistician, researcher*
MacDougall, Gordon Pier *lawyer*
Mack, Connie, III, (Cornelius Mack) *former senator*
Mack, Julia Cooper *retired judge*
†MacKay, Kenneth Hood, Jr., (Buddy MacKay) *federal official*
Mackay, Leo Sidney, Jr., *federal agency administrator*
Mackiewicz, Edward Robert *lawyer*
Macleod, John Amend *lawyer*
†MacLeod, William Cyrus *lawyer, economist*
Maco, Paul Stephen *securities and exchange administrator*
Macomber, John D. *investment company executive*
Madden, Jerome Anthony *lawyer*
Madden, Murdaugh Stuart *lawyer*
†Madden, Thomas James *lawyer, educator*
Madian, Alan Leonard *economist, management consultant*
†Madole, Donald Wilson *lawyer*
Maechling, Charles, Jr., *lawyer, diplomat, educator, writer*
Magaw, John W. *former federal agency administrator*
Magee, Charles Thomas *international consultant, retired diplomat*
Magielnicki, Robert L. *lawyer*
Magnee, Tom *federal agency administrator*
Magrath, C. Peter *educational association executive*
Mahaffey, Kathryn Rose *risk assessor*
Mahmood, M. F. *research scientist, educator*
Mahmoud, Hosam M. *statistics educator, academic administrator*
Mahone, Glenn *federal agency administrator*
Mailander, William Stephen *lawyer*
Mainella, Frances P. *federal agency administrator*
Maisto, John F. *ambassador*
Maizel, Roy *federal agency administrator*
Majd, Massoud *radiology and nuclear medicine educator*
†Majette, Denise *congresswoman*
Majev, Howard Rudolph *lawyer*
†Majors, Melynda Elizabeth *not-for-profit organization administrator*
Makalou, Oumar *economic advisor*
Makins, Christopher James *foreign policy institute administrator*
Makris, Andreas *composer*
†Malcolm, Mark Alan *military analyst*
Maldonado, F. César *priest, educator*
Malek, Frederic Vincent *finance company executive*
†Maletsky, Alfred F. *sculptor, engraver*
†Malinowski, Michael E. *ambassador*
†Mallon, William T. *education educator, researcher*
†Mallory, Charles King, III, *lawyer*
Maloney, Carolyn Bosher *congresswoman*
†Malott, Frank Stephen *foreign service officer*
Malveaux, Floyd Joseph *dean*
Manatos, Andrew E. *public relations executive*
Manatt, Charles Taylor *lawyer*
Manchester, Paul Brunson *economist*
Mandel, H(arold) George *pharmacologist, educator*
Mandula, Jeffrey Ellis *physicist*
†Mankiewicz, Frank F. *journalist, writer*
Manley, Audrey Forbes *retired academic administrator, pediatrician, military officer*
†Manley, James P *congressional press secretary*
Mann, Charles Roy *statistician*
Mann, Marion *physician, educator*
Mann, Oscar *retired physician, internist, educator*
†Mann, Thomas *reference librarian*
Mann, Thomas Edward *political scientist*
Mannina, George John, Jr., *lawyer*
†Manning, Michael J. *lawyer*
Mansfield, Edward Patrick, Jr., *advertising executive*
Mansfield, Gordon H. *federal agency administrator*
Mansfield, Jerry Wayne *librarian*
Manson, Harold Craig *federal agency administrator*
Manson, Joseph Lloyd, III, *lawyer*
Mantyla, Karen *distance learning consultant*
†Manwell, John Parker, II, *lawyer*
Manzullo, Donald A *congressman, lawyer*
Marans, J. Eugene *lawyer*
Marburger, John Harmen, III, *federal agency administrator*
Marburg-Goodman, Jeffrey Emil *lawyer*
Marchand, Michael J. *military officer*
Marcotte, Michael Steven *municipal administrator*
Marcum, Deanna Bowling *library administrator*
Marcus, Devra Joy Cohen *internist*
Marcuss, Rosemary Daly *economist*
Marcuss, Stanley Joseph *lawyer*
Margeton, Stephen George *law librarian*
Margolis, Doris May Rosenberg *editor, writer*
Margolis, Lawrence Stanley *federal judge*
Marin, Rosario *federal agency administrator*
Marinaccio, Charles Lindbergh *lawyer, consultant*
†Marinelli, Bonnie Jean Meacham *lawyer*
Mariotte, Michael Lee *environmental activist, environmental publication director*
Markey, Edward John *congressman*
Marks, Herbert Edward *lawyer*
Marks, Jonathan Bowles *mediator, arbitrator*
Marks, Leonard Harold *lawyer*
Marks, Richard Daniel *lawyer*
Marquez, Joaquin Alfredo *lawyer*
Marr, Phebe Ann *historian, educator*
Marriott, John Willard, Jr., *lodging and senior living executive*
Marshall, Ann Louise *pastoral counselor*
Marshall, Brian Laurence *trade association executive*
†Marshall, James Creel *congressman*
Marshall, John *federal agency administrator*
Marshall, Maryann Chorba *office administrator*
Martas, Julia Ann *special education administrator*
Martin, David O'Brien *congressman*
Martin, Guy *lawyer*
Martin, Jack *federal agency administrator*
Martin, Jerry Lee *organization executive, educator*
†Martin, Kate Abbott *lawyer*
Martin, Kevin J. *federal agency administrator*
Martin, Ralph Drury *lawyer, columnist*
Martin, Robert Sidney *federal agency administrator*
Martin, William J. *economist*
†Martinez, Carmen M. *ambassador*
Martinez, Herminia S. *economist, banker*
Martinez, Melquiades R. (Mel Martinez) *secretary of housing and urban development*
Martinez, Rose Marie *health facility administrator*
Martino, Peter Dominic *financial software company executive, real estate developer, real estate broker, federal agency administrator*
Marumoto, William Hideo *management consultant*
Marvel, L. Paige *federal judge*
Marvin, Charles Rodney, Jr., *lawyer*
Masi, Dale A. *research company executive, social work educator*
Mason, Eileen B. *federal administrator*
Massaro, Donald John *medical educator, medical researcher*
Massey, Jeanne Kelly *music festival producer*
Masters, Edward E. *association executive, former foreign service officer*
†Mather, Susan M. *humanities educator*
†Mathers, Peter Robert *lawyer*
Matheson, Jim *congressman*
Mathews, Jessica Tuchman *executive, foreign policy expert*
Mathias, Edward Joseph *merchant banker*
Mathis, John Prentiss *lawyer*
Matsui, Robert Takeo *congressman*
Mattingly, J. Virgil, Jr., *federal lawyer*
Mattsson, Ake *psychiatrist, physician*
†Maude, Timothy J. *career officer*
Maudlin, Robert V. *economics and government affairs consultant*
†Mauery, D. Richard *research scientist*
Maul, Kevin Jay *financial consultant*
Maxwell, David Ogden *former government official and financial executive*
†May, Gregory Evers *lawyer*
May, Stephen *writer, former government official*
May, Timothy James *lawyer*
†Mayeaux, Maxwell Hayden Edward *government agency administrator*
Mayer, Haldane Robert *federal chief judge*
Mayer, Neal Michael *lawyer*
Mayers, Daniel Kriegsman *lawyer*
Mayfield, Richard Heverin *lawyer*
Maynes, Charles William *foundation executive*
Mayo, George Washington, Jr., *lawyer*
Mazo, Mark Elliott *lawyer*
Mazzaferri, Katherine Aquino *lawyer, bar association executive*
Mc Afee, William *government official*
†McAleavey, David *English educator*
McAnaney, Kevin George *lawyer*
McAuliffe, Jane Dammen *religious studies and Islamic studies educator*
McAvoy, John Joseph *lawyer*
McBee, Susanna Barnes *retired journalist*
McBride, Jonathan Evans *executive search consultant*
†McBride, Michael Flynn *lawyer*
McCain, John Sidney, III, *senator*
McCaleb, Neal *federal agency administrator*
McCallum, Robert D., Jr., *federal agency administrator*
McCamman, John William *federal official*
†McCann, Clifton Everett *lawyer*
McCargar, James Goodrich *diplomat, writer*
McCarrick, Theodore Edgar Cardinal *archbishop*
McCarron, Douglas J. *labor union administrator*
McCarter, Katherine Sauter *association executive*
McCarthy, Carolyn *congresswoman*
McCarthy, Karen P. *congresswoman, former state legislator*
†McCartin, Joseph Anthony *historian, educator*
McCaslin, John Larson *political columnist*
McClain, Tim S. *federal agency administrator*
McClellan, Donald William, Jr., *lawyer*
McClintic, Howard Gresson *foundation executive*
McClure, William Pendleton *lawyer*
McCollam, William, Jr., *utility company executive*
McCollum, Betty *congresswoman*
McConnell, Bruce William *information technology executive*
McConnell, Mitchell, Jr., (Mitch McConnell Jr., Addison Mitchell McConnell Jr.) *senator, lawyer*
McCormick, Walter Bernard, Jr., *lawyer*
†McCotter, Thaddeus G. *congressman*
McCoy, Jerry Jack *lawyer*
†McCrabb, Donald Raymond *pastoral field educator*
†McCray, Nikki Kesangame *basketball player*
McCrery, James (Jim McCrery) *congressman*
McCrum, Robert Timothy *lawyer*
†McCulley, Helen Marie *mathematician*
McCutchen, Tommy Dee *federal agency administrator*
McDaniels, William E. *lawyer*
McDavid, Janet Louise *lawyer*
McDermott, James A. *congressman, psychiatrist*
McDiarmid, Robert Campbell *lawyer*
†McDonald, Jackson *ambassador*
McDonough, William J. *banker*
Mc Elroy, John Harley *electrical and industrial engineering educator*
McElveen, Junius Carlisle, Jr., *lawyer*
†McElveen-Hunter, Bonnie *ambassador*
†McElwee, Jerry W. *military career officer*
†McEnroe, John Patrick, Jr., *former professional tennis player, commentator*
McEntee, Gerald W. *labor union official*
McFarland, Patrick E. *federal agency administrator*
McFeatters, Ann Carey *journalist*
McGee, Robert Merrill *oil company executive*
Mc Giffert, David Eliot *lawyer, former government official*
McGill, Willis Alexander *anesthesiologist*
McGinn, Dennis Vincent *career officer*
McGinnies, Elliott Morse *psychologist, educator*
McGovern, James P. *congressman*
McGovern, Michael Barbot *lawyer*
McGrath, Kathryn Bradley *lawyer*
†McGrath, Kevin Michael *military analyst, civilian military employee, researcher*
McGraw, Lavinia Morgan *retired retail company executive*
†McGuire, Stephen J.J. *business educator*
McGuirl, Marlene Dana Callis *law librarian, educator*
†McHale, Paul F., Jr., *federal official, former congressman*
McHugh, James Lenahan, Jr., *lawyer*
McHugh, John Michael *congressman, former state senator*
McIlwain, John Knox *housing policy fellow*
McInerney, Joseph Aloysius *hotel executive*
McInnis, Scott Steve *congressman, lawyer*
McIntyre, Douglas Carmichael, II, (Mike McIntyre) *congressman*
Mc Kay, Emily Gantz *civil rights professional*
McKeever, Joseph Francis, III, *lawyer*
McKelvey, Virginia Maude *language educator*
McKeon, Howard P. (Buck McKeon) *congressman, former mayor*
†McKie, Edward Foss *lawyer*
McKinney, Cynthia Ann *former congresswoman*
McKinney, James DeVaine, Jr., *lawyer*
†McLarty, Thomas F., III, (Mack McLarty) *business executive*
†McLaughlin, David *foundation administrator*
McLaughlin, John E. *federal agency administrator*
McLaughlin, John J. *broadcast executive, television producer, political commentator, journalist*
McLean, Donna *federal agency administrator*
McLean, Ian William *ophthalmic pathologist, researcher*
McLean, R. Bruce *lawyer*
McMahon, Joseph Einar *lawyer, consultant*
McMichael, Guy H., III, *federal official*
McNamara, Robert M., Jr., *federal agency administrator, lawyer*
McNamara, Robert Strange *former banking executive, cabinet member*
McNicholas, Edward *lawyer*
McNulty, Michael Robert *congressman*
McNulty, Robert Holmes *non-profit executive*
Mc Phee, Henry Roemer *lawyer*
McPherson, Edward Russell *federal agency administrator*
Mc Pherson, Harry Cummings, Jr., *lawyer*
†McQueary, Charles E. *federal official*
McReynolds, Mary Armilda *lawyer*
McSlarrow, Kyle E. *federal agency administrator*
McTaggart, Timothy Robert *state agency administrator, lawyer*
Mead, Kenneth Minor *federal agency administrator*
Meadows, Vickers B. *federal agency administrator*
†Means, Marianne *political columnist*
Means, Thomas Cornell *lawyer*
Medaglia, Mary-Elizabeth *lawyer*
Medalie, Richard James *lawyer*
Medalie, Susan Diane *lawyer, management consultant*
Mederos, Carolina Luisa *management consultant*
†Meece, Roger A. *ambassador*
Meehan, Martin Thomas *congressman, lawyer*
†Meek, Kendrick B. *congressman*
Meeks, Gregory Weldon *congressman*
Meggers, Betty J(ane) *anthropologist, researcher*
Mehan, George Tracey, III, *federal agency administrator*
Mehlman, Bruce P. *federal agency administrator*
Meijer, Paul Herman Ernst *educator, physicist*
Melamed, Arthur Douglas *lawyer*
Melamed, Carol Drescher *lawyer*
Melanson, Richard Allen *political science educator*
Melendy, David Russell *broadcast journalist*
Mellor, John Williams *economist, policy consultant firm executive*
Melton, Carol A(nne) *corporate executive*
Melusky, Raymond Gabriel, Jr., *electrical engineer*
Mencher, Bruce Stephan *judge*
†Mendales, Richard Ephraim *lawyer*
Mendelowitz, Allan Irwin *federal agency administrator*
Mendelsohn, Martin *lawyer*
Mendis, Patrick *economist, geographer, educator*
Menendez, Robert *congressman, lawyer*
Menkel-Meadow, Carrie Joan *law educator*
†Mercanti, John M. *sculptor, engraver*
Merow, James F. *federal judge*
Merrell, Jesse Howard *writer*
Merrifield, Dudley Bruce *business educator, former government official*
Merry, Robert William *publishing executive*
Metcalf, Howard *military officer*
Metz, Helen Chapin *retired Middle East analyst*
†Metz, Thomas Fredric *military career officer*
†Metzger, James W. *military officer*
Mewani, Rajshree Ramchand *researcher*
Meyer, Alden Merrill *environmental association executive*
Meyer, Armin Henry *retired diplomat, author, educator*
Meyer, Dennis Irwin *lawyer*
Meyer, Laurence Harvey *former federal official*
Meyer, Margaret Vaughan *librarian, educator*

Meyers, Tedson Jay *lawyer*
Meyers, Wayne Marvin *microbiologist*
†Meyerson, Adam *foundation administrator*
Mezey, Robert
Mica, John L. *congressman*
Michael, Terry P. *foundation executive, educator*
Michaelson, Martin *lawyer*
†Michal-Smith, Susan *lawyer*
†Michaud, Michael Alan George *diplomat, writer*
Michel, Paul Redmond *federal judge*
Michnich, Marie E. *health facility administrator, consultant, educator*
†Mickalide, Angela Denise *public health educator*
†Mickum, George Brent, III, *lawyer*
Milam, William Bryant *former ambassador, economist*
Miles, David Michael *lawyer*
Millar, James Robert *economist, educator, university official*
Millender-McDonald, Juanita *congresswoman, school system administration*
†Miller, Alan *newswriter*
†Miller, Alan Stanley *ecology center administrator, law educator*
Miller, Andrew Pickens *lawyer*
Miller, Candice S. *former state official*
Miller, Charles A. *lawyer*
Miller, Christine Odell Cook *judge*
Miller, Dan *retired congressman*
Miller, David Christopher *psychologist, researcher*
Miller, Gary G. *congressman*
Miller, Gay Davis *lawyer*
Miller, George *congressman*
Miller, G(eorge) William *merchant banker, business executive*
Miller, H. Todd *lawyer*
Miller, Hope Ridings *author*
Miller, James Clifford, III, *economist*
Miller, Jeanne-Marie Anderson (Mrs. Nathan J. Miller) *English language educator, academic administrator*
Miller, Jeff *congressman*
Miller, John T., Jr., *lawyer, educator*
Miller, Judith Rosalind *mathematician, educator*
Miller, Kerry Lee *lawyer*
†Miller, Marcia E. *federal government official*
Miller, Margery Silberman *psychologist, speech pathologist, medical educator and administrator*
Miller, Marshall Lee *lawyer*
†Miller, Mary Rita *former college educator*
†Miller, Ralph Bradley *congressman*
Miller, Richard N. *medical association administrator*
Miller, Warren Lloyd *lawyer*
Miller, William Green *ambassador*
Miller, Zell Bryan *senator, former governor*
Millian, Kenneth Young *public policy consultant*
Millon, Henry Armand *fine arts educator, architectural historian*
Mills, Kevin Paul *lawyer*
†Millstein, Leo Lee *lawyer*
Milstein, Elliott Steven *law educator, academic administrator*
Mineta, Norman Yoshio *secretary of transportation*
Minor, William Henning *lawyer*
Mishkin, Barbara Friedman *lawyer*
Misner, Robert David *electronic warfare and magnetic recording consultant, electro-mechanical company executive*
Missar, Charles Donald *retired librarian*
†Mistral, Jacques *economist*
Mitchell, Andrea *journalist*
Mitchell, George John *former senator, lawyer*
Mitchell, Roy Shaw *lawyer*
Mixter, Christian John *lawyer*
Mlay, Marian *retired government official*
Moates, G. Paul *lawyer*
Modiano, Albert Louis *gas, oil industry executive*
Moe, Richard Palmer *lawyer*
Moe, Ronald Chesney *public administration researcher*
†Mohrman, Kathryn J *academic administrator*
Mok, Samuel T. *federal agency administrator*
Moler, Elizabeth Anne *lawyer*
Moll, Robert Henderson *lawyer*
Mollohan, Alan B. *congressman*
Monagan, John Stephen *retired congressman and lawyer, writer, lecturer*
Monaghan, Jessine Adrienne *lawyer*
Monk, Carl Colburn *lawyer, academic administrator*
Monroe, Robert Rawson *engineering construction executive*
Montedonico, Joseph *lawyer*
Montelongo, Michael *federal agency administrator, career officer*
†Montero, Mario F., Jr., *military career officer*
†Montgomery, George Cranwell *lawyer, former ambassador*
Moon, Marilyn Lee *economist*
Mooney, Marilyn *lawyer*
Moore, Amy Norwood *lawyer*
Moore, Bob Stahly *communications executive*
Moore, Dennis *congressman*
Moore, Jacquelyn Cornelia *labor union official, editor*
†Moore, Matthew David *religious studies educator*
Moore, Miles David *journalist*
Moore, Powell Allen *federal government official*
Moore, Robert Madison *food industry executive, lawyer*
†Moorefield, Kenneth P. *ambassador*
†Moorhead, Glen W., III, *career officer*
Moorhead, Thomas Burch *lawyer, corporation and government executive*
Mora, Alberto *federal agency administrator, councilman*
Morales, Diane K. *federal agency administrator*
Moran, James Patrick, Jr., *congressman, stockbroker*
Moran, Jerry *congressman*
Morehouse, David Frank *geologist*
Morello, Steven J. *federal agency administrator, lawyer*
Morgan, Bruce Ray *international consultant*
†Morgan, Daniel Louis *lawyer, educator*
Moring, John Frederick *lawyer*
Morris, Cynthia Taft *economics educator*
Morrissey, Elizabeth R. *investment company executive*
Morrissey, Patricia A. *commissioner*
Morse, Jerome Samuel *government administrator, trade specialist*
Morse, M. Howard *lawyer*
Mortenson, R. Stan *lawyer*
†Moschella, William Emil *state attorney general*
Moseley, James R. *federal agency administrator, farmer*
†Moser, Donald Bruce *magazine editor*
Moses, Alfred Henry *lawyer, writer, diplomat*
Mosettig, Michael David *television producer, writer*
Mosley, Everett L. *federal agency administrator*
Mosley, Raymond A. *federal agency administrator*
Mosley, William Harry, Jr., *public affairs specialist*
Moss, Madison Scott *editor*
Mosso, Lyle David *financial executive*
Mostoff, Allan Samuel *lawyer, consultant*
Moulton, David Aubin *library director*
Mowlana, Hamid *international relations and communication educator*
Moyer, Homer Edward, Jr., *lawyer*
Muckenfuss, Cantwell Faulkner, III, *lawyer*
Mueller, Robert Swan, III, *federal agency administrator, lawyer*
Mueller, Sharon Lee (Sherry Mueller) *educational organization executive*
Muir, J. Dapray *lawyer*
Muir, Patricia Allen *professional association administrator*
†Mujica, Barbara Louise *language educator, writer*
Muldrow, Tressie Wright *psychologist*
†Muller, Steven *international studies educator, academic administrator*
Mulloy, Patrick Aloysius *lawyer*
Mulville, Daniel R. *federal agency administrator*
Murano, Elsa A. *federal agency administrator*
Muravchik, Joshua *writer*
Muris, Timothy Joseph *federal agency administrator*
†Murkowski, Lisa *senator*
Murphy, Betty Southard (Mrs. Cornelius F. Murphy) *lawyer*
Murphy, Gerard Norris *trade association executive*
†Murphy, James Paul *lawyer*
Murphy, Joanne Becker *writer*
†Murphy, Joseph Albert, Jr., *lawyer*
Murphy, Terence Roche *lawyer*
†Murphy, Timothy F. *congressman*
Murray, Christopher Charles, III, *architect*
Murray, James Joseph, III, *association executive*
Murray, John Einar *lawyer, retired army officer, federal official*
Murray, Patty *senator*
Murray, Robert Fulton, Jr., *physician*
Murry, Harold David, Jr., *lawyer*
Murtha, John Patrick *congressman*
†Musgrave, Franklyn Garfield *obstetrician, gynecologist*
†Musgrave, Marilyn N. *congresswoman*
Musil, Robert Kirkland *professional society administrator*
Muth, William Henry Harrison, Jr., *medical/surgical nurse, nurse practitioner*
Mwenda, Kenneth Kaoma *legal consultant, advisor, educator*
Myers, Donald Lee *university chief financial officer*
†Myers, Richard B. *chairman Joint Chiefs of Staff*
Myers, William Gerry, III, *federal agency administrator*
Myrick, Bismarck *diplomat*
Nabholz, Joseph Vincent *biologist, ecologist*
Nace, Barry John *lawyer*
†Nader, Ralph *consumer advocate, lawyer, author*
Nadler, Jerrold Lewis *congressman, lawyer*
Nagorski, Zygmunt *political scientist, writer*
Nakhleh, Emile A. *political science educator*
Napolitano, Grace F. *congresswoman*
Nardi Riddle, Clarine *legislative staff member*
Nash, John Davidson, Jr., *economist*
Natalie, Ronald Bruce *lawyer*
Natarajan, Aruna *physician, educator, researcher*
Natsios, Andrew *federal agency administrator*
Nauheim, Stephen Alan *lawyer*
Navarro, Bruce Charles *lawyer*
Navas, William Antonio, Jr., *federal agency administrator, retired military officer*
Neal, Darwina Lee *government official*
Neal, Richard Edmund *congressman, former mayor*
Nedelkoff, Richard R. *federal agency administrator*
†Nelligan, Jeffrey Parnell *public information officer*
Nelsen, Hart Michael *sociologist, educator*
Nelson, Alan Ray *internist, medical association administrator*
Nelson, Benjamin *senator, former governor, lawyer*
Nelson, Bill *senator, former state treasurer*
Nelson, Candice Jean *political science educator*
Nelson, Gaylord Anton *former senator, association executive*
Nelson, Kimberly Terese *federal agency administrator*
Nelson, Larry Dean *telecommunications and computer systems company executive, consultant*
Nemeroff, Michael Alan *lawyer*
†Nemeth, Norman E. *sculptor, engraver*
Nesbitt, Veronica A. *management executive*
†Nesbitt, Wanda L. *ambassador*
†Nesmith, Jeff *journalist*
†Nesmith, Steven B. *congressional and intergovernment relations secretary*
Ness, Andrew David *lawyer*
Nethercutt, George Rector, Jr., *congressman, lawyer*
Nethery, John Jay *government official*
Neufeld, Michael John *curator, historian*
†Neugebauer, Randy *congressman*
Neuman, Susan B. *federal agency administrator*
Neverson, Norman Carl *political organization administrator*
Newhouse, Alan Russell *federal government executive*
Newkirk, Thomas Charles *lawyer*
Newman, Constance Berry *federal agency administrator*
Newman, Monroe *retired economist, educator*
Newman, Pauline *judge*
Newsome, James E. *federal agency administrator*
Ney, Robert W. *congressman*
Nguyen, Alex Thinh *internet company executive, aerospace engineer, consultant*
Nicely, Andrew Abbott *lawyer*
†Nicely, Olza M. (Tony) *insurance company executive*
Nichols, Henry Eliot *lawyer, savings and loan executive*
†Nicholson, Jim *political organization administrator*
†Nicholson, John W. *federal agency administrator*
Nicholson, Richard Selindh *educational association administrator*
Nickles, Don (Donald Nickles) *senator*
Niehuss, John Marvin *lawyer*
Nightingale, Elena Ottolenghi *geneticist, physician, administrator*
Nightingale, Stuart Lester *physician, public health officer*
Nilles, Kathleen Mary *lawyer*
Niskanen, William Arthur, Jr., *economist, think-tank executive*
Nitze, William Albert *government official, lawyer, not-for-profit developer*
Njie, Veronica P.S. *nurse educator, clinical nurse*
Noble, Lawrence Mark *lawyer, association administrator*
Nolan, John Edward *lawyer*
†Nolan, John Patrick *mathematician, educator*
Noland, Marcus *economist, educator*
Nordhaus, Robert Riggs *lawyer*
Nordlinger, Gerson *investor*
†Noriega, Roger Francisco *federal agency administrator*
Norland, Donald Richard *retired foreign service officer*
Norman, William Stanley *travel and tourism executive*
Norsworthy, Leonid A. *bank executive, educator*
Northup, Anne Meagher *congresswoman*
Norton, Eleanor Holmes *congresswoman, lawyer, educator*
Norton, Floyd Ligon, IV, *lawyer*
Norton, Gale Ann *secretary of interior*
Norton, Gerald Patrick *lawyer*
†Norton, Randell Hunt *lawyer*
Norwood, Charles W., Jr., *congressman*
Norwood, Deborah Anne *law librarian*
Novak, Michael (Michael John Novak) *religion educator, author, editor*
Novak, Michael John *government analyst*
Novak, Robert David Sanders *newspaper columnist, television commentator*
†Novins, Alan Slater *lawyer*
Novitch, Mark *physician, retired pharmaceutical executive*
Nowak, Judith Ann *psychiatrist*
†Nsouli, Talal Mounir *physician, allergist, immunologist*
†Nuland, Anthony C. J. *lawyer*
†Nunes, Devin *congressman*
Nurnberger, Ralph D. *public affairs executive*
Nussle, James Allen *congressman*
Nutter, Franklin Winston *lawyer*
Nutting, Wallace Hall *army officer*
Nwagbaraocha, Joel Onukwugha *academic administrator, educator*
†Oakley, Charles *professional basketball player*
Oakley, Diane *insurance executive, benefit consultant*
Oberdorfer, Louis F. *federal judge*
Oberstar, James L. *congressman*
Obey, David Ross *congressman*
Obrams, Gunta Iris *medical officer*
O'Brien, Edwin Frederick *archbishop*
O'Brien, Richard Francis *advertising agency association executive*
O'Brien, Soledad *newscaster, news anchor*
O'Brien, Timothy Andrew *writer, journalist, lawyer, educator*
O'Connor, Charles P. *lawyer*
O'Connor, Eileen J. *federal agency administrator*
O'Connor, John Jay, III, *lawyer*
O'Connor, Karen *political science educator, researcher, writer*
O'Connor, Sandra Day *United States supreme court justice*
O'Dell, Michael James *social sciences specialist*
Odle, Robert Charles, Jr., *lawyer*
Odom, William Eldridge *army officer, educator*
O'Donnell, Terrence *lawyer*
O'Donovan, Leo Jeremiah *former academic administrator, priest, theologian*
Oehme, Wolfgang Walter *landscape architect*
O'Flaherty, James Daniel *council executive*
Ogilvie, Donald Gordon *bankers association executive*
Ohl, Joan E. *federal agency administrator*
†Ohle, David H. *military career officer*
†Ohlke, Amanda Anne *museum association administrator, museum educator*
O'Hollaren, Sean B. *federal agency administrator*
Oka, Takashi *journalist, consultant, educator*
O'Kane, Margaret E. *non-profit organization executive*
O'Keefe, Sean Charles *federal agency administrator*
Olender, Jack Harvey *lawyer*
Oliver, LeAnn Michelle *government official*
Oliver, William Albert, Jr., *paleontologist, researcher*
Olmstead, Cecil Jay *lawyer*
Olsen, Josephine *federal agency administrator*
Olsen, Kathie Lynn *federal agency administrator*
†Olson, Lyndon Lowell, Jr., *ambassador*
Olson, Mark Walter *banker, federal agency administrator*
†Olson, Randy *photographer*
Olson, Theodore Bevry *federal agency administrator, lawyer*
Olver, John Walter *congressman*
Oman, Ralph *lawyer*
O'Neil, Thomas Francis, III, *lawyer, business executive*
†O'Neill, Brian Dennis *lawyer*
O'Neill, John H., Jr., *lawyer*
O'Neill, Joseph F. *health science association administrator*
Ongman, John Will *lawyer*
Ooms, Van Doorn *economist*
Oppenheimer, Franz Martin *lawyer*
Oran, Elaine Surick *physicist, engineer*
Orbach, Raymond Lee *physicist, educator*
†Ordway, John *ambassador*
Orlans, F(lora) Barbara *bioethics researcher*
Orr, Bobette Kay *diplomat*
Orszag, Jonathan Marc *economist, consultant*
Orszag, Peter Richard *economist*
†Ortiz, Ricardo L. *language educator*
Ortiz, Solomon P. *congressman*
Ortner, Donald J. *biological anthropologist, educator*
Osborne, Tom *congressman, former college football coach*
Ose, Douglas *congressman*
Osnos, David Marvin *lawyer, director*
Ostrov, Jerome *lawyer*
O'Sullivan, Judith Roberta *lawyer, author, artist*
O'Sullivan, Lynda Troutman *lawyer*
O'Toole, Francis J. *lawyer*
Ottaway, David Blackburne *journalist*
Otter, Clement Leroy (Butch Otter) *congressman*
Ottley, William Henry *professional association director, consultant*
Outman, William Dell, II, *lawyer*
Oweiss, Ibrahim Mohamed *economist, educator*
Owen, Henry *former ambassador, consultant*
Owen, Roberts Bishop *lawyer, arbitrator*
Owens, Major Robert Odell *congressman*
Oxley, Michael Garver *congressman*
Oxman, Mark *sculptor, educator*
†Oyarzabal, Antonio *diplomat*
Oyler, Gregory Kenneth *lawyer*
Ozer, Martha Ross *psychologist, counselor*
†Pace, Peter *military officer*
Padgett, Nancy Weeks *law librarian, consultant, lawyer*
†Page, Clarence E. *newspaper columnist*
Page, Robert Wesley *engineering and construction company executive, federal official*
Page, Tim *music critic, writer, producer*
Pahira, John Joseph *urology educator*
†Pahnke, Robert David *architect, interior designer*
Paige, Hilliard Wegner *corporate director, consultant*
Paige, Roderick R. *secretary of education*
Painter, William Hall *law educator*
Pallone, Frank, Jr., *congressman*
Palmer, R(obie) Mark (Robie Marcus Hooker Palmer) *banker*
†Palmeter, N. David *lawyer*
Palumbo, Benjamin Lewis *public affairs consulting company executive*
†Pamerleau, Susan L. *career officer*
Pannu, Sardul Singh *science educator, researcher*
Pape, Stuart M. *lawyer*
Paper, Lewis J. *lawyer, educator*
Papkin, Robert David *lawyer*
Paradis, Donald Edward *lawyer, arbitrator*
Pardavi-Horvath, Martha Maria *physicist, educator*
Parde, Duane Arthur *association executive*
†Park, Alice Mary Crandall *genealogist*
Parkel, James G. *health association administrator*
†Parker, Ché André *writer, journalist*
Parker, Michael (Mike Parker) *federal agency administrator*
Parker, Richard Bordeaux *writer, educator*
†Parris, Mark Robert *ambassador*
Parrish, Edgar Lee *financial services executive*
Pascrell, William J., Jr., *congressman*
Pascu, Dan *astronomer*
Passage, David *diplomat*
Pasternack, Robert Harry *school psychologist*
Pasternack, Stefan Alan *psychiatrist, psychoanalyst*
Pastor, Edward *congressman*
Pastorek, Paul G. *federal agency administrator*
Pasurka, Jr., Carl A. *economist*
Pate, Michael Lynn *lawyer*
Patron, June Eileen *former government official*
†Patterson, Eliza *lawyer*
†Patterson, James E. *agricultural economist, speech professional*
Patterson, Sally Jane *government affairs consultant*
†Patton, Frances Anne *lawyer*
Paul, William McCann *lawyer*
Paulhus, Norman Gerard, Jr., *aerospace engineer*
Paulson, Gwen O. Gampel *government relations consultant*
Paulson, Jerome Avrom *pediatrician*
Pawley, Carl John *laser engineer, physicist*
†Paxon, L. William *former congressman*
Payne, Donald M. *congressman*
Payne, Fred J. *physician, educator*
Payne, Michael Lee *association management executive*
Payne, Steven Lawrence *priest*

†Payton, John *lawyer*
†Pearce, Steve *congressman*
Pearlman, Ronald Alan *lawyer, educator*
Pearlstein, Paul Davis *lawyer*
Pearson, Roger *organization executive*
Peart, Laverne T. *retired nursing assistant, poet*
†Pease, Edward *former congressman*
Peck, Louis Moses *editor*
Peck, Malcolm Cameron *educational exchange specialist*
Peck, Robert Stephen *lawyer, educator*
Pedersen, Wesley Niels M. *public relations and public affairs executive*
Pedersen, William Francis *lawyer*
Peet, Richard Clayton *lawyer, consultant*
Peirce, Neal R. *journalist*
Pelavin, Diane Christine *small business owner*
Pelavin, Sol Herbert *research company executive*
Pellegrino, Edmund Daniel *physician, educator, academic administrator*
†Pellegrino, Stephen Charles *civilian military employee*
Pellmar, Terry C. *neurophysiologist, researcher*
Pelosi, Nancy *congresswoman*
†Peña, Maria Teresa *surgeon, educator, otolaryngologist*
Pence, Michael Richard *congressman*
Pendleton, Miles Stevens, Jr., *diplomat*
Penner, Rudolph Gerhard *economist, educator*
Perkins, Joseph S. *medical association administrator*
Perkins, Lucian *photographer*
Perle, Richard Norman *former government official*
Perlik, William R. *lawyer*
Perlman, Matthew Saul *lawyer*
Perper, Michael Joseph *federal agency administrator*
Perry, George Lewis *research economist, consultant*
Persinger, Del Louis *pharmaceutical company executive*
†Pestell, Richard G. *health facility administrator, medical educator*
Peters, Charles Given, Jr., *editor*
†Peters, F. Whitten *lawyer, former federal official*
Peters, Frederick Whitten *lawyer*
Peters, Mary E. *federal agency administrator*
Peterson, Charles Hayes *lawyer*
Peterson, Charles Buckley, III, *librarian, geographer*
Peterson, Collin C. *congressman*
Peterson, E. Anne *federal agency administrator*
Peterson, John E. *congressman*
†Petito, Christopher Salvatore *lawyer*
Petito, Margaret L. *foundation administrator*
Petrash, Jeffrey Michael *lawyer*
Petri, Thomas Evert *congressman*
Petrie, John Noel *career officer*
Pettis, Francis Joseph, Jr., *electrical engineer*
Pfeiffer, Leonard, IV, *executive recruiter, consultant*
Pfeiffer, Margaret Kolodny *lawyer*
Pfeiffer, Steven Bernard *lawyer*
Phelps, David D. *former congressman, government agency administrator*
Phemister, Thomas Alexander *lawyer*
†Philion, Norman Joseph, III, *lawyer*
Phillips, Carter Glasgow *lawyer*
Phillips, James D. *retired diplomat*
†Phillips, Jeanne L. *ambassador*
Phillips, Karen Borlaug *economist, railroad industry executive*
Phillips, Michael M. *gastroenterologist*
Phillips, Susan Meredith *financial economist, university administrator*
†Pibulsonggram, Nitya *diplomat*
†Piccininno, Anthony Ray *government administrative executive*
Pichard, Augusto D. *medical educator*
Pickenpaugh, Thomas Edward *archaeologist, anthropologist*
Pickering, Charles W., Jr., *congressman*
Pickering, John Harold *lawyer*
Pickholtz, Raymond Lee *electrical engineering educator, consultant*
Pierce, David R. *educational administrator*
Pierce, Margaret Hunter *government official*
Pincus, Jonathan Henry *neurologist, educator*
Pincus, Stephanie Hoyer *dermatologist, educator*
Pincus, Walter Haskell *editor*
Pines, Wayne Lloyd *public relations executive*
†Pinkerson, Alan Lee *physician*
Pionk, Jerome Lee *government official, association administrator*
Pireddu, Nicoletta *Italian and comparative literature educator*
Pittman, Lisa *lawyer*
Pittman, Steuart Lansing *lawyer*
Pitts, Joseph R. *congressman*
Pitts, Tyrone S. *reverend*
Pizzella, Patrick *federal agency administrator*
Placke, James A(nthony) *foreign service officer, international affairs consultant*
Plager, S. Jay *judge*
Plaine, Daniel J. *lawyer*
Plaine, Lloyd Leva *lawyer*
Plaisted, Joan M. *diplomat*
Platt, Laurence Eric *lawyer*
Platt, Roger *lawyer, lobbyist*
Platts, Howard Gregory *scientific, educational organization executive*
Platts, Todd Russell *congressman, state legislator*
Player, Thelma B. *librarian*
Plewes, Thomas Jeffrey *military officer*
Plusquellec, Herve Louis *irrigation and agricultural engineering consultant*
Pluta, Tom *lawyer*
Podberesky, Samuel *lawyer*
Poe, Luke Harvey, Jr., *lawyer*
Pogue, L(loyd) Welch *lawyer*
Pojeta, John, Jr., *geologist, researcher*
Polan, Annette Lewis *artist, educator*
Policy, Vincent Mark *lawyer*
Pollack, Murray Michael *physician, medical services administrator*
Pollak, Stephen John *lawyer*
Pollin, Abe *professional basketball team executive, builder*
†Polon, Ira H. *lawyer*
Pombo, Richard *congressman, rancher, farmer*
Pomeroy, Earl R. *congressman, former state insurance commissioner*
Poneman, Daniel Bruce *lawyer*
Pope, Andrew *medical organization administrator*
†Pope, Anne B. *government agency administrator, department chairman*
Pope, Michael Thor *chemistry educator*
†Pope, Nancy *historian, curator*
Popkin, Joel *economic consulting company executive*
Poppleton, Janet Waters *legislative staff member*
Porter, John Edward *former congressman*
Porter, John Weston *counselor, consultant, administrator*
†Porter, Jon Christopher *congressman*
Porter, Leah LeEarle *biological researcher, industry executive*
Portman, Rob *congressman*
Posey, Ada Louise *management consultant*
Posner, Paul Leonard *government official*
†Post, Robert Louis *research and development company executive*
Postol, Lawrence Philip *lawyer*
†Potenza, Joseph Michael *lawyer*
Potok, Nancy Ann Fagenson *federal agency administrator*
Potter, Barry M. *radiologist, medical educator*
Potter, Trevor Alexander McClurg *lawyer*
Potts, Ramsay Douglas *lawyer, aviator*
Potts, Stephen Deaderick *lawyer*
Povich, David *lawyer*
Powell, Colin Luther *secretary of state, retired military officer, author, public speaker*
Powell, Donald E. *federal agency administrator*
†Powell, Michael K. *federal agency administrator*
Powers, Richard Edward, Jr., *lawyer*
Press, Frank *geophysicist*
†Pressler, Larry *former senator*
Preston, Richard McKim *lawyer*
Prestowitz, Clyde Vincent *economist, researcher*
Prettyman, Elijah Barrett, Jr., *lawyer*
Price, Daniel Martin *lawyer*
Price, David Eugene *congressman, educator*
†Price, Donald Douglas *lawyer*
Price, Griffith Baley, Jr., *lawyer*
Price, Joseph Hubbard *lawyer*
Prigmore, Kathryn Bradford Tyler *architecture educator, architect*
Principi, Anthony Joseph *secretary of veterans affairs*
Pritzl, Kurt John *philosophy educator, university dean, priest*
Prosper, Pierre-Richard *federal agency administrator*
Prost, Sharon *federal judge*
Pryce, Deborah D. *congresswoman*
Pryor, Mark Lunsford *senator*
Przytycki, Jozef Henryk *mathematician, educator*
†Puchalski, Christina M. *physician, medical educator*
Pulley, Lewis Carl *lawyer*
Puryear, Jeffrey Merrill *cultural association administrator*
Pusey, William Anderson *lawyer*
Putnam, Adam Hughes *congressman, farmer, rancher*
Putzel, Michael *journalist, entrepreneur*
Pyke, Thomas Nicholas, Jr., *government science and engineering administrator*
Pyle, Robert Noble *government relations executive*
Quainton, Anthony Cecil Eden *diplomat*
Quale, John Carter *lawyer*
Quarles, James Linwood, III, *lawyer*
Quarles, Randal Keith *lawyer, federal official, bank executive*
Quarterman, Cynthia Louise *lawyer*
Quello, James Henry *government official*
Quinn, Jack *congressman, English language educator, sports coach*
†Quinn, Maureen E. *ambassador*
Quinn, Pat Maloy *engineering company executive*
Quint, Arnold Harris *lawyer*
Quintanilla-Villanueva, Rosalinda *economist*
Quintiere, Gary Gandolfo *lawyer*
Quivers, Eric Stanley *physician*
Rabecs, Robert Nicholas *lawyer*
Rabekoff, Elise Jane *lawyer*
†Rabin, David L. *medical educator*
Rabinowitz, Stanley Samuel *rabbi*
Racicot, Marc F. *lawyer, former governor*
Radanovich, George P. *congressman*
Rademaker, Stephen Geoffrey *lawyer*
Rader, Randall Ray *federal judge*
Radin, Alex *former association executive, consultant*
Rafferty, James Gerard *lawyer*
Rahall, Nick Joe, II, (Nick Rahall) *congressman*
Rahming, John Christopher *investment company executive, consultant*
Railton, William Scott *federal agency administrator*
Raimo, Bernard (Bernie Raimo) *lawyer*
Rainey, Jean Osgood *public relations executive*
Raley, Bennett W. *federal agency administrator*
Ramberg, Walter Dodd *architect*
†Ramos, Flavia Sales *education educator, consultant*
†Ramphele, Mamphela A. *medical educator*
Ramsey, Charles H. *protective services official*
Ramsey, Robert Leslie *oncologist*
Ramstad, James *congressman, lawyer*
Ranck, Edna Runnels *academic administrator, researcher*
Rand, Harry Zvi *art historian, poet*
Randall, Robert L(ee) *ecological economist*
Randell, Cortes W. *news service executive*
Randolph, A(rthur) Raymond *federal judge*
Rangel, Charles Bernard *congressman*
Rankin, Robert Arthur *journalist*
Ransom, David Michael *retired ambassador*
Raphael, Nan Helene *musician*
Rapp, Michael Thomas *emergency physician*
Raslear, Thomas Gregory *psychologist*
Rasmus, John Charles *trade association executive, lawyer*
†Rassam, Ghassan Noel *information scientist*
†Rauh, Carl Stephen *lawyer*
Raul, Alan Charles *lawyer*
Rausch, Howard *information service executive*
†Ravallion, Martin *economist*
†Ravenal, Carol Bird Myers *artist, art historian*
Ravenal, Earl Cedric *international relations educator, author*
†Ray, J. Ram *foundation administrator*
†Reade, Claire Elizabeth *lawyer*
Reaman, Gregory Harold *pediatric hematologist, oncologist*
Recchia, Christopher *state agency administrator*
Reddel, Carl Walter *educational administrator*
Redman, Robert Shelton *pathologist, dentist*
Reed, Berenice Anne *art historian, artist, government official*
Reed, John Francis (Jack Reed) *senator*
Reed, John Hathaway *former ambassador*
Reed, Travis Dean *public relations executive*
Reef, Grace *government official*
Reese, George W. *federal agency administrator*
†Reese, La Tanya Lynn *academic administrator*
Reger, Lawrence Lee *trade association administrator*
Regula, Ralph *congressman, lawyer*
Rehberg, Dennis R. *congressman*
Rehnquist, William Hubbs *United States supreme court chief justice*
Reich, Alan Anderson *executive*
Reich, Bernard *political science educator*
Reich, Otto Juan *political analyst, business consultant*
Reid, Inez Smith *lawyer, educator*
Reilly, John Marsden *English language educator*
Rein, Bert Walter *lawyer*
Reingold, David Ami *sociologist, educator*
Reingold, Janet Rose *corporate communications specialist*
Reinsch, William Alan *association executive, educator*
Relyea, Harold Clarence *political scientist*
†Rennert, Wolfgang Peter *pediatrician, educator*
Renninger, Mary Karen *librarian*
†Renzi, Rick *congressman*
Repa, Edward William *waste management association executive, hydrologist*
Replogle, Michael A. *civil engineer, urban planner, environmentalist*
Repper, George Robert *lawyer*
Resor, Stanley Rogers *lawyer*
Rey, Mark E. *federal agency administrator*
†Reyes Heroles, Jesus *former Mexican government official*
Reynolds, Gerald *federal agency administrator*
Reynolds, Thomas M. *congressman*
Rezneck, Daniel Albert *lawyer*
Rheintgen, Laura Dale *research center official*
Rhodes, Lee Ann *anesthesiologist*
Rhyne, Sidney White *lawyer*
†Ribaudo, Marc Owen *agricultural economist*
†Riccards, Michael Patrick *academic administrator*
Rice, Condoleezza *national security advisor*
Rice, Edmund Burke *trade association executive*
Rice, Lois Dickson *former computer company executive*
Rice, Paul Jackson *lawyer, educator*
Rich, Dorothy Kovitz *writer, educational administrator*
†Richards, Femi Soyinka *lawyer*
Richards, Suzanne V. *lawyer*
Richardson, Ann Bishop *foundation executive, lawyer*
Richardson, David B. *writer, journalist*
†Richardson, Donna Darlene *historian, consultant, researcher*
†Richardson, Henry Shattuck *philosophy educator*
Richert, John Rolin *neuroimmunologist, educator*
†Richeson, James G., Jr., *dentist*
Richlen, Scott Lane *federal government program administrator*
Richman, Joseph Herbert *retired public health services official*
Richmond, David Walker *lawyer*
Richmond, Marilyn Susan *lawyer*
Ridenour, Amy Moritz *research center administrator*
†Rider, James Lincoln *lawyer*
Ridge, Thomas Joseph *secretary of homeland security*
Ridgeway, James Fowler *journalist*
Ridings, Dorothy Sattes *association executive*
Ridley, Keith Alexander, IV, *funeral director*
Riegler, Guenter *federal agency administrator*
Riehle, B. Hudson *trade association executive*
Rieser, Joseph A., Jr., *lawyer*
Riley, Terry Zene *biologist, researcher*
Rill, James Franklin *lawyer*
†Rissetto, Harry A. *lawyer*
†Ritchie, Donald A. *historian*
Ritchie, Elisavietta *writer, poet, educator, editor, translator*
Ritter, Jeffrey Blake *lawyer, consultant*
†Rivers, Beverly D. *secretary of the district*
Rivers, Richard Robinson *lawyer*
Rives, Jack L. *military officer*
†Rivlin, Alice Mitchell *federal agency administrator, economist*
Rizzo, James Gerard *lawyer*
Robb, James Willis *Romance languages educator*
Robb, Lynda Johnson *writer*
Robbins, Robert Bernard *lawyer*
Roberson, Jessie Hill *federal agency administrator*
Roberts, Charles Patrick (Pat Roberts) *senator*
†Roberts, Edward Thomas *lawyer*
Roberts, James Harold, III, *lawyer*
Roberts, Jeanne Addison *retired literature educator*
†Roberts, John Glover, Jr., *federal judge*
Roberts, Markley *economist, educator*
Roberts, Walter Ronald *political science educator, former government official*
Robertson, James *judge*
Robinowitz, Carolyn Bauer *psychiatrist, educator*
Robinson, Davis Rowland *lawyer*
Robinson, Elaine *consultant*
Robinson, Robert Cribben *librarian, information company executive*
†Robinson, Stephanie *tax lawyer*
Robison, Victor James, Jr., *retired military officer*
Rocca, Christina B. *federal agency administrator*
†Roccograndi, Anthony Joseph *lawyer*
Rockefeller, Edwin Shaffer *lawyer*
Rockefeller, John Davison, IV, (Jay Rockefeller) *senator, former governor*
Rocque, Vincent Joseph *lawyer*
Rodemeyer, Michael Leonard, Jr., *lawyer*
Rodgers, Clifton Eugene, Jr., *trade association administrator, lobbyist*
Rodman, Peter Warren *government official*
†Rodriguez, Ciro Davis *congressman*
†Rodriguez, Rita Maria *economist*
Roemer, Timothy J. *former congressman, lawyer*
†Roessel, Faith *Indian arts and crafts administrator*
Roett, Riordan *political science educator, consultant*
Rogan, James E. *federal agency administrator, former congressman*
Rogers, Harold Dallas (Hal Rogers) *congressman*
Rogers, Judith W. *federal judge*
†Rogers, Mike *congressman*
Rogers, Paul Grant *lawyer, former congressman*
Rogers, Thomasina *federal commissioner*
Rogers, Warren Joseph, Jr., *journalist*
Rogers, William Dill *lawyer*
Rogovin, John A. *lawyer*
Rogowsky, Robert Arthur *trade commission operations director, professor*
Rohner, Ralph John *lawyer, educator, university dean*
Rohrabacher, Dana *congressman*
Roll, David Lee *lawyer*
Romani, Paul Nicholas *government official*
Romeo, Peter John *lawyer*
Romeo, Ross Victor *army officer*
†Romero, Jesse Charles *political organization worker*
Romig, Edgar Dutcher *clergyman*
Romig, Thomas J. *military officer*
Rooney, Kevin Davitt *lawyer*
Roos, Barbara Diane *association administrator*
Roper, Odean S. *environmentalist, researcher*
Roque, Francis Xavier *auxiliary bishop*
Rose, George Andrew *software developer, information systems specialist*
Rose, Jonathan Chapman *lawyer*
Roseboro, Brian Carlton *federal agency administrator*
Rosebush, James Scott *international management and public affairs consultant, former government official*
Rosen, Gerald Robert *editor*
Rosenau, James Nathan *political scientist, author*
Rosenberg, Jerome David *physicist*
Rosenberg, Joel Barry *government economist*
Rosenberg, Ruth Helen Borsuk *lawyer*
Rosenblatt, Jason Philip *English language educator*
Rosenblatt, Peter Ronald *lawyer, former ambassador*
Rosenbloom, David Harry *political science and law educator*
Rosenbloom, H. David *lawyer*
Rosendhal, Jeffrey David *federal science agency administrator, astronomer*
Rosenfeld, Arthur F. *federal agency administrator*
Rosenfeld, Ronald A. *federal agency administrator*
Rosenker, Mark Victor *federal agency administrator*
Rosenkrantz, Steven Jay *lawyer*
Rosenstein, Peter D. *educational association administrator*
Rosenthal, Aaron *management consultant*
Rosenthal, Douglas Eurico *lawyer, author*
Rosenthal, Ilene Goldstein *lawyer*
Rosenthal, Steven Siegmund *lawyer*
Ros-Lehtinen, Ileana *congresswoman*
Ross, Douglas *lawyer*
Ross, Malcolm *minerals consultant*
Ross, Mike *congressman*
Ross, Robinette Davis *publisher*
Ross, Stanford G. *lawyer, government official*
†Rossin, Lawrence G. *ambassador*
Rossotti, Barbara Jill Margulies *lawyer*
†Rostker, Bernard *federal official*
Roswell, Robert H. *federal agency administrator*
Rotberg, Eugene Harvey *investment banker, lawyer*
Roth, Stanley Owen *federal agency administrator*
†Rothberg, Loretta Sue *lawyer*
†Rothenberg, Gilbert Steven *lawyer, law educator*
Rothenberg, Marc *historian*
Rothman, Steven R. *congressman*
Rottman, Ellis *public information officer*
Rotunda, Donald Theodore *public relations consultant*
†Rove, Karl Christian
Rovelstad, Mathilde V(erner) *library science educator*
Rowden, Marcus Aubrey *lawyer, former government official*
Rowe, Richard Holmes *lawyer*
Rowson, Richard Cavanagh *publisher*
Roybal-Allard, Lucille *congresswoman*
Royce, Edward R. (Ed Royce) *congressman*
Royle, David Brian Layton *television producer, journalist*

†Rubin, Andrew N. *literature educator*
Rubin, Kenneth Allen *lawyer*
Ruckman, Roger Norris *pediatric cardiologist*
Ruddy, Frank *lawyer, former ambassador*
†Rudman, Warren Bruce *former senator, lawyer, think tank executive*
Ruehle, Charles Joseph *pathologist, military officer*
Ruiz, Vanessa *judge*
Rule, Charles Frederick (Rick Rule) *lawyer*
Rumsfeld, Donald Henry *secretary of defense*
Runge, Jeffrey William *federal agency administrator*
†Ruppersberger, Charles Albert, III, *congressman*
Rusch, Jonathan Jay *lawyer*
Ruser, John William *economist*
Rush, Bobby L. *congressman*
Rush, Jeffrey, Jr., *federal agency administrator*
Rushton, Harry Gil *pediatric urologist, educator*
Ruskin, Robert Sterling *association executive*
Russell, Mark *comedian*
Russell, Michael James *lawyer*
Russell, Richard M. *federal agency administrator*
Russell, William Joseph *educational association administrator*
Russert, Timothy John *broadcast journalist, executive*
Russin, Jonathan *lawyer, consultant*
Russo, Roy R. *lawyer*
Rust, William David, Jr., *retired structural engineer*
Rutledge, Peter J. *federal agency administrator*
Rutstein, David W. *lawyer, food products executive*
Ruttenberg, Charles Byron *lawyer*
Rutter, Alan *federal agency administrator*
Ruttinger, George David *lawyer*
†Rutzick, Mark Charles *lawyer*
Ruwe, Robert P. *federal judge*
Ryan, David Alan *computer specialist*
Ryan, Frederick Joseph, Jr., *lawyer, retired federal official, broadcast executive*
†Ryan, Joseph *lawyer*
Ryan, Mary A. *diplomat*
Ryan, Paul *congressman*
Ryan, Sheila A. *nursing educator, former dean*
†Ryan, Timothy *congressman*
Ryerson, Paul Sommer *lawyer*
Ryn, Claes Gösta *political science educator, author, research institute administrator*
Ryun, James Ronald *congressman*
†Sable, Craig *physician, cardiologist*
Sabo, Martin Olav *congressman*
†Sabshin, Melvin *psychiatrist, educator, medical association administrator*
Sacher, Seth Barry *economist*
Sacher, Steven Jay *lawyer*
†Sackler, Arthur Brian *lawyer*
Sacksteder, Frederick Henry *former foreign service officer*
Sáenz, Albert William *theoretical physicist, researcher, consultant*
†Safir, Peter Oliver *lawyer*
Safire, William *journalist, author*
Sagalkin, Sanford *lawyer*
St. Amand, Janet G. *government relations lawyer*
Sakoda, Robin (Sak Sakoda) *government administrator*
Salamon, Linda Bradley *English literature educator*
Salant, Jonathan D. *reporter*
Salas, Henry Joseph *environmental engineer*
Saleeba, David A. *federal agency administrator*
Saleh, Ali-Abdullah *state official*
Salem, George Richard *lawyer*
Salgado, Elizabeth M. R. *lawyer*
Saliba, George *Maltese government official*
Salisbury, Dallas L. *research institute executive*
†Salleo, Ferdinando *Italian diplomat*
†Salsbury, Michael H. *lawyer*
Saltzburg, Stephen Allan *law educator, consultant*
Sambur, Marvin *federal agency administrator*
Sampson, David Allan *federal agency administrator*
Samsot, Robert Louis *newspaper editor, consultant*
Samuelson, Kenneth Lee *lawyer*
†Sanchez, Linda T. *congresswoman*
Sanchez, Loretta *congresswoman*
Sanders, Bernard (Bernie Sanders) *congressman*
Sanders, Charles F. *dean*
†Sanderson, Janet A. *ambassador*
Sandler, Sumner Gerald *medical educator*
Sandlin, Max Allen, Jr., *congressman*
Sanford, Bruce William *lawyer*
†Sankaran, Shubha Silver *musician, music educator, consultant*
Sansonetti, Thomas L. *federal agency administrator*
†Santoro, Miléna *education educator*
Santorum, Rick *senator*
Santos, Leonard Ernest *lawyer*
Saperstein, Marc Eli *theology studies educator, rabbi*
Sarbanes, Paul Spyros *senator*
†Sargentich, Thomas Oliver *law educator, researcher*
†Sarring, Kevin Lee *architect, archaeologist*
Sarros, P. Peter *diplomat, consultant*
Satcher, David *public health service officer, federal official*
Satin, Mark *editor, lawyer*
†Satloff, Robert B. *think-tank executive*
Saunders, Harold Henry *foundation administrator*
Savukinas, Robert Steven *educator*
†Sawhill, Isabel Van Devanter *economist*
Sawin, Clark Timothy *endocrinologist*
Saworotnow, Parfeny Pavlovich *mathematician, educator*
Saxton, H. James *congressman*
Sayre, Edward Vale *chemist*
Sayre, Robert Marion *ambassador*
Scalia, Antonin *judge*
Scanlon, Terrence Maurice *public policy foundation administrator*
Scarbrough, Frank Edward *government official*
Scarlett, Patricia Lynn *federal agency administrator*
Schaal, Pamela Marguerite *program evaluation analyst*
Schachter, Myron Marvin *retired research chemist, engineer*
Schad, Theodore MacNeeve *science research administrator, civil engineer, consultant*
Schaffer, Robert (Bob Schaffer) *former congressman*
†Schaffner, Joan Elsa *law educator*
Schafrick, Frederick Craig *lawyer*
Schakowsky, Janice *congresswoman*
Schall, Alvin Anthony *federal judge*
†Schapiro, Mary *federal agency administrator, lawyer*
†Schaumber, Peter C. *government agency administrator*
Scheffman, David Theodore *economist, management educator, consultant*
Scheibel, Kenneth Maynard *journalist*
†Scheige, Steven Sheldon *lawyer*
Scheman, L. Ronald *lawyer, professional society administrator*
Schieck, Frederick W. *federal agency administrator*
Schieffer, Bob *broadcast journalist*
Schierow, Linda-Jo *environmental policy analyst*
Schiff, Adam Bennett *congressman, lawyer*
Schiffer, Lois Jane *lawyer*
Schildhaus, Sam *political scientist, researcher*
Schlesinger, B. Frank *architect, educator*
Schley, Wayne Arthur *political consultant*
Schlicht, James P. *pharmaceutical executive, lobbyist*
Schmeltzer, Edward *lawyer*
Schmidt, Edward Craig *lawyer*
Schmidt, Richard Marten, Jr., *lawyer*
Schmidt, William Arthur, Jr., *lawyer*
†Schmitt, John K. *army officer*
†Schmukler, Sergio L. *economist*
†Schneebaum, Steven Marc *lawyer*
Schneider, Mark Lewis *government official*
Schneider, Matthew Roger *lawyer*
†Scholl, Kathleen Kay *economist*
†Schoomaker, Peter J. *military officer*
Schor, Laurence *lawyer*
Schorr, Lisbeth Bamberger *child and family policy analyst, author, educator*
Schram, Martin Jay *journalist*
Schram, Susan Gale *agriculturist, consultant*
Schriever, Bernard Adolph *management consultant*
Schrock, Edward L. (Ed Schrock) *congressman, former state senator*
Schroeder, Patricia Scott *trade association administrator, retired congresswoman*
Schropp, James Howard *lawyer*
Schubert, Frank Nicholas *historian*
†Schubert, Richard D. *medical educator, physician*
Schubert, William G. *federal agency administrator*
Schulz, William Henry *transportation executive*
Schumer, Charles Ellis *senator*
Schwaab, Richard Lewis *lawyer, educator*
Schwartz, Daniel C. *lawyer*
Schwartz, Gregory John *lawyer, business and investments transactions specialist*
Schwartz, Herman *law educator*
†Schwartz, Norton A. *military officer*
Schwartz, Victor Elliot *lawyer, educator*
†Schwartzman, David William *chemist, educator*
Schwebel, Stephen Myron *mediator*
Schwelb, Frank Ernest *appellate judge*
†Sclafani, Frances Ann *lawyer, federal agency executive*
Scoblic, J. Peter *journalist*
Scolese, Christopher *federal agency administrator*
Scott, Betsy Sue *lawyer*
†Scott, Bruce K. *army officer*
†Scott, David Albert *congressman*
Scott, Gary Thomas *historian*
Scott, Robert Cortez *congressman, lawyer*
†Scott, Terry D. *military officer*
Scott, Thomas Jefferson, Jr., *lawyer, electrical engineer*
Scott-Finan, Nancy Isabella *government administrator*
Scowcroft, Brent *retired air force officer, government official*
Scruggs-Leftwich, Yvonne *association executive*
Scully, Thomas A. *federal agency administrator*
Sears, John Patrick *lawyer*
Sears, Mary Helen *lawyer*
Seats, Peggy Chisolm *marketing executive*
Sebejais, Melanie *federal agency administrator*
Seck, Mamadou Mansour *ambassador, career officer*
†Seeger, Edwin Howard *lawyer*
Seidman, L(ewis) William *television commentator, publisher*
Selin, Ivan *entrepreneur*
Selin, Nina Evvie *philanthropist*
Sellin, Theodore *foreign service officer, consultant*
Sensenbrenner, F(rank) James, Jr., *congressman*
Sentelle, David Bryan *federal judge*
Serrano, Jose E. *congressman*
Sessions, Jefferson Beauregard, III, *senator*
Sessions, William Steele *former government official, lawyer*
Severino, Roberto *foreign language educator, academic administration executive*
Sewell, John Williamson *research association executive*
Shadegg, John B. *congressman*
Shaffer, David James *lawyer*
†Shambaugh, David Leigh *political scientist, educator, writer*
Shamim, Mah Talat *chemist*
Shanahan, Sheila Ann *pediatrician, educator*
Shane, Jeffrey Neil *state agency administrator, lawyer*
Shanks, Judith Weil *editor*
Shanmugam, Kannon Kumar *lawyer*
Shannon, Donald Hawkins *retired editor*
Shanny, Ramy *physicist*
Shapiro, Michael Henry *government executive*
Shapiro, Paul Arnold *museum director*
Shapiro, Walter Elliot *political columnist*
†Sharpless, Mattie R. *ambassador*
Shaw, E. Clay, Jr., (Clay Shaw) *congressman*
Shaw, Russell Burnham *author, journalist*
Shaw, William Frederick *statistician*
†Shaw, William J. *hotel facility executive*
Shays, Christopher *congressman*
†Shea, Donald William *military officer*
Shear, Natalie Pickus *conference and event management executive*
Shearer, Paul Scott *government relations professional*
Sheavly, Robert Bruce *social worker*
Sheehan, Neil *reporter, scholarly writer*
Shelby, Richard Craig *senator, former congressman*
Shelby, Richard David *trade association executive*
Shelley, Herbert Carl *lawyer*
Shelly, Thaddeus Rubez, III, *trust company executive*
Shenon, Philip *journalist*
Shepherd, Mary Elizabeth *dermatologist*
Sherman, Bradley James *congressman*
Sherman, Gerald Howard *lawyer, educator*
Sherman, Jonathan Henry *lawyer*
Sherman, Lawrence Jay *lawyer*
Sherman, Nancy *philosophy educator*
†Sherrard, James E., III, *career officer*
Sherwood, Donald Lewis *congressman*
Shestack, Alan *museum administrator*
†Shieber, William J. *lawyer*
Shimkus, John Mondy *congressman*
†Shiner, Josette Sheeran *ambassador*
Shinn, David Hamilton *educator, former diplomat*
Shinolt, Eileen Thelma *artist*
Shipway, John Francis *career officer, retired*
Shosky, John Edwin *communications consultant, speechwriter*
Shrier, Adam Louis *investment firm executive, consultant*
Shrier, Diane Kesler *psychiatrist, educator*
Shriver, Robert Sargent, Jr., *lawyer*
Shriver, Sargent *sports association executive*
Shriver, Timothy P. *sports association executive*
Shroder, Mark Davis *economist*
Shuler, James Mannie *health physicist*
Shulman, Stephen Neal *lawyer*
†Shuman, Mark Patrick *lawyer, economist*
Shumate, John Page *diplomat*
Shuster, William (Bill Shuster) *congressman*
Sibley, Lynn M. *anthropologist, educator*
Sibolski, John Alfred, Jr., *educational association executive*
Sidey, Hugh Swanson *correspondent*
Siebert, Thomas L. *lawyer, diplomat*
Sieck, Robert *aerospace engineer*
Siegel, Frederic Richard *geology educator*
Siegel, Lloyd Harvey *architect, real estate developer, consultant*
Siegel, Michael Eric *judicial center official*
Siegel, Richard David *lawyer, former government official*
Siegel, Robert Charles *broadcast journalist*
†Siekman, Thomas Clement *lawyer*
Sieverts, Frank Arne *association executive*
Silver, Brian Quayle *broadcast journalist, musician, educator*
Silver, Harry R. *lawyer*
Silverman, Leslie E. *federal agency administrator*
Silverman, Lester Paul *economist, energy industry consultant*
†Silverstein, Martin J. *ambassador*
Simes, Dimitri Konstantin *international affairs expert and educator*
Simko, Jan *English, foreign language and literature educator*
Simmons, Anne L. *federal official*
Simmons, Caroline Thompson *civic worker*
Simmons, Edwin Howard *marine corps officer, historian*
Simmons, Emmy B *federal agency administrator*
Simmons, Robert Ruhl *congressman*
Simon, Gary Leonard *internist, educator*
Simon, James M. *federal agency administrator*
†Simons, Barbara M. *lawyer*
Simons, Carol Lenore *magazine editor*
Simons, Lawrence Brook *lawyer*
Simpson, Charles Reagan *retired judge*
Simpson, Jacqueline Angelia *legal administration*
Simpson, John M. *lawyer*
Simpson, Louis A. *insurance company executive*
Simpson, Michael K. *congressman*
Simpson, Michael Marcial *science specialist, consultant*
Singer, Daniel Morris *lawyer*
Singer, Maxine Frank *retired biochemist, scientific institute executive*
†Singh, Daljhit *science and technology conuselor, chemical engineer and technology educator*
Singleton, Harry Michael *lawyer*
†Singpurwalla, Nozer Darabsha *statistician, engineer, educator*
†Sinha, Phulgenda *small business owner*
Sinkford, Jeanne Craig *dental association administrator, dentist, retired dean, educator*
†Sinn, Jerry L. *army officer*
Sisco, Joseph John *management consultant, corporation director, educator, government official*
Skeen, Joseph Richard *congressman*
Skelton, Isaac Newton, IV, (Ike Skelton) *congressman*
Skinner, Robert Earle, Jr., *civil engineer, engineering executive*
†Skinner, William Polk *lawyer*
Sklarew, Myra *humanities educator, poet*
Skolfield, Melissa T. *public relations executive, former government official*
Skolnik, Merrill I. *electrical engineer*
Slade, John Danton *lobbyist*
†Slafka, Kristi Lynne *journalist*
Slagle, Larry B. *human resources specialist*
Slater, Doris Ernestine Wilke *business executive*
Slater, Eve *federal agency administrator*
Slater, Rodney E. *former federal official, lawyer*
†Slater, Valerie A. *lawyer*
†Slaughter, Louise McIntosh *congresswoman*
Sloame, Stuart C. *lawyer*
Sloboda, Brian William *economist*
†Slonim, Anthony Daniel *pediatrician, internist*
Sly, Ridge Michael *physician, educator*
†Small, Lawrence M. *museum executive*
Small, Sarah Mae *volunteer*
Smerling, Thomas Robert *think-tank executive, consultant*
Smith, Abbie Oliver *college administrator, educator*
†Smith, Brian William *lawyer, former government official*
Smith, Bruce David *archaeologist*
Smith, Carl Michael *federal agency administrator, lawyer*
Smith, Christopher Henry *congressman*
Smith, D. Adam *congressman*
Smith, Daniel Clifford *lawyer*
Smith, Dean *communications advisor, arbitrator*
†Smith, Duncan Campbell, III, *lawyer*
Smith, Dwight Chichester, III, *lawyer*
Smith, Elaine Diana *foreign service officer*
Smith, Elise Fiber *international non-profit development agency administrator*
Smith, Emory Clark *lawyer, financial advisor*
Smith, Gordon Harold *senator*
Smith, James Earl *astronautical engineer*
†Smith, Jessie P. Dowling *retired social services administrator*
Smith, Lamar Seeligson *congressman*
Smith, Lee Elton *surgery educator, retired military officer*
Smith, Lloyd David *community activist*
Smith, Loren Allan *federal judge*
Smith, Nancy Lee *communications official*
Smith, Nick *congressman, farmer*
†Smith, Pamela Hyde *ambassador*
Smith, Roy Philip *judge*
Smith, Stephanie Zaharoudis *producer*
Smith, Stephen Grant *communications executive*
Smith, Stuart Seaborne *writer, government official, union official*
†Smith, Turner Taliaferro, Jr., *lawyer*
†Smith, William S., Jr., *education association administrator*
Smoot, Oliver Reed, Jr., *lawyer, trade association administrator*
Smuckler, Ralph Herbert *dean, political scientist, educator*
Smyth, Paul Burton *lawyer*
Snider, Virginia L. *antitrust consultant*
Snow, John William *secretary of treasury*
Snow, Robert Anthony *journalist*
Snowbarger, Vince *former congressman*
Snowe, Olympia J. *senator*
Snyder, Jed C. *foreign affairs specialist*
Snyder, John Michael *lobbyist, public relations director*
Snyder, Vic *congressman, physician*
†Soapes, Thomas F. *archivist*
Sohn, Louis Bruno *lawyer, educator*
†Sokal, Allen Marcel *lawyer*
Sokolowski, Robert S. *priest, educator*
Solis, Hilda Lucia *congresswoman, educational administrator*
Solomon, Elinor Harris *economics educator*
†Solomon, Frederic *lawyer*
Solomon, Henry *university dean*
†Solomon, Lewis David *law educator*
Solomon, Richard Harvey *political scientist*
Solomon, Rodney Jeff *lawyer*
Solomon, Sean Carl *geophysicist, lab administrator*
Solomons, Mark Elliott *lawyer, art dealer, entrepreneur*
Soloway, Rose Ann Gould *clinical toxicologist*
Sombrotto, Vincent R. *postal union executive*
Somerville, Walter Raleigh, Jr., *government official*
Sommerfelt, Soren Christian *foreign affairs, international trade consultant, former Norwegian diplomat, lawyer*
Sonde, Theodore Irwin *lawyer*
Sonneborn, Daniel Atesh *composer, ethnomusicologist, producer, author*
Sonnenfeldt, Helmut *former government official, educator, consultant, author*
Sontag, Ed *federal agency administrator*
Sorrels, Carrie L. *federal agency administrator*
Souder, Mark Edward *congressman*
Soule, Jeffrey Lyn *urban planner, consultant*
Southerland, Derrick Theodore *microbiologist*
Spaeder, Roger Campbell *lawyer*
Spaeth, Steven Michael *lawyer*
Spagnolo, Samuel Vincent *internist, pulmonary specialist, educator*
Sparks, Kenneth R. *association executive*
Spear, Chris *federal agency administrator*
Spear, Scott Lawrence *plastic surgeon*
Specter, Arlen *senator*
Spector, Phillip Louis *lawyer*
†Spector, Ronald H. *historian, educator*
Spencer, George Henry *lawyer*
†Spencer, Harrison Clark, Jr., *public health administrator, educator*
Spencer, John Howard *radio astronomer*
Sperling, Godfrey, Jr., *journalist*
Spiegelman, James Michael *international affairs expert*
Spilhaus, Athelstan Frederick, Jr., *oceanographer, association executive*
Spinrad, Richard William *oceanographer, researcher*
Splete, Allen Peterjohn *association executive, educator*

Spratt, John McKee, Jr., *congressman, lawyer*
†Springer, Linda *portfolio manager, controller*
Springer, Michael Louis *federal agency administrator*
†Staats, Elmer Boyd *foundation executive, former government official*
Stabenow, Deborah Ann *senator, former congresswoman*
Stadd, Courtney *federal agency administrator*
†Stadtler, Walter Edward *diplomat*
Stanley, Jean-Daniel *geological oceanographer*
†Stanley, Keith Eugene *lawyer*
†Stapleton, Craig Roberts *ambassador*
Stark, Fortney Hillman (Pete Stark) *congressman*
Stark, Nathan J. *medical administrator, health policy consultant, lawyer*
Starrs, James Edward *law and forensics educator, consultant*
†Statland, Edward Morris *lawyer*
†Statom, Laurena Edith *retired special education educator*
Staton, Candi Maria *singer*
Stauffer, Ronald Eugene *lawyer*
Stauffer, Thomas George *retired hotel executive*
Stayin, Randolph John *lawyer*
Steadham, Richard Lynn *magazine art director*
Steadman, John Montague *appellate court judge*
Steadman, Stephen Geoffrey *physicist*
Stearns, Clifford Bundy *congressman, business executive*
Stebbins, Leroy Joseph (Lee Stebbins) *not-for-profit organization executive*
Steele, Ana Mercedes *former government official*
Steigman, Andrew L. *academic dean*
Stein, Daniel Alan *public interest lawyer*
Steinberg, David Isaac *economic development consultant, educator*
Steinberg, Donald Kenneth *diplomat*
Steinberg, Jonathan Robert *judge*
Steinberg, Paul Jay *psychiatrist*
Steiner, David Miller *lawyer*
†Steinwurtzel, Richard A. *lawyer*
Steitz, Philip Wakeford *research corporation owner*
Stekler, Herman O. *finance educator*
Stelzer, Irwin Mark *economist*
Stenbit, John Paul *federal agency administrator*
Stenholm, Charles W. *congressman*
Stent, Angela E. *political scientist, educator, director*
†Stephan, Dietrich A. *pediatrician, educator, geneticist*
Stephens, John Frank *association executive, researcher*
†Stephenson, Sherry Madeline *economist*
†Sterling, Christopher H. *telecommunications educator*
Stern, Andrew L. *labor union administrator*
Stern, Carl Leonard *former news correspondent, federal official*
Stern, Gerald Mann *lawyer*
†Stern, Paula *international trade advisor*
Stern, Samuel Alan *lawyer*
Sterner, Michael Edmund *international affairs consultant*
Sterrett, Samuel Black *lawyer, former judge*
Stevens, Herbert Francis *lawyer, law educator*
Stevens, John Paul *judge*
Stevens, Paul Schott *lawyer*
Stevens, Theodore Fulton *senator*
Stevenson, Frances Kellogg *museum program director*
Stevenson, Katherine Holler *federal agency administrator*
Stevenson, Nancy Nelson *museum executive*
Stewart, David Pentland *lawyer, educator*
†Stewart, Debra Wehrle *academic administrator*
Stewart, John Todd *economist, consultant*
†Stewart, Joseph D. *merchant marine officer*
Stillman, Robert Donald *government official*
†Stock, Stuart Chase *lawyer*
Stoiber, Susanne A. *health science organization administrator*
Stokes, Louis *former congressman, lawyer*
†Stoll, Richard G(iles) *lawyer*
Stolley, Paul David *medical educator, researcher*
Stollman, Israel *city planner*
Stone, Alec J. *healthcare lobbyist*
Stone, Donald Raymond *lawyer*
Stone, Florence Smith *film festival executive, consultant*
Stone, Roger David *environmentalist*
Stone, Russell A. *sociology educator*
Stoner, John Richard *federal government executive*
Stover, Mark Edward *economist*
Stowe, Alexis Mariani *accountant, consultant*
Straser, Richard Alan *lawyer*
Stratton, Kathleen R. *medical association administrator*
Strauss, Stanley Robert *lawyer*
Streb, Paul Gerard *arbitrator*
Strickland, Ted *congressman, clergyman, psychology educator, psychologist*
Stromberg, Clifford Douglas *lawyer*
Stromberg, Jean Wilbur Gleason *lawyer*
Strong, Carter *lawyer*
Strong, Henry *foundation executive*
Stroup, Sally *federal agency administrator*
Stuart, Pamela Bruce *lawyer*
Stucky, Jean Seibert *lawyer*
Stucky, Scott Wallace *lawyer*
Stump, E. Gordon *association administrator*
Stupak, Bart T. *congressman, lawyer*
†Sturgell, Robert A. *government agency administrator*
Styles, Angela B. *federal agency administrator*
Subramaniam, Suresh *electrical engineering educator*
Sullivan, Brendan V., Jr., *lawyer*
Sullivan, David Bryan *lawyer*
Sullivan, Eugene Raymond *federal judge*
Sullivan, John A. *congressman*
†Sullivan, John Fox *publisher*
†Sullivan, Kevin *editor-in-chief, reporter*
Sullivan, Thomas M. *federal agency administrator*
Sullivan, Timothy *lawyer*
Summerford, Ben Long *retired artist, educator*
Summers, Janis Lee *lawyer*
Sunderlin, Charles Eugene *consultant*
Sundermeyer, Michael S. *lawyer*
Sunley, Emil McKee *economist*
Sununu, John E. *senator*
Sutter, Eleanor Bly *retired diplomat*
Swain, Susan Marie *communications executive*
Swankin, David Arnold *lawyer, consumer advocate*
Swarthworth, Sharon T. *military officer*
Sweeney, John E. *congressman*
Sweeney, John Joseph *labor union administrator*
Sweeney, Richard James *economics educator*
†Swendiman, Alan Robert *lawyer*
Swenson, Sue *foundation administrator, former health and education administrator*
Swift, Stephen Jensen *federal judge*
†Swimmer, Ross Owen *federal agency administrator*
Swinton, Sonya DeVonne *government agency administrator*
†Swisher, Larry *newspaper executive*
Swygert, Haywood Patrick *university president, law educator*
Sypolt, Diane Gilbert *federal judge*
Szymanski, Christopher John *consulting company executive*
Tabackman, Steven Carl *lawyer*
Tabor, Mary Leeba
Tacha, Athena *sculptor, educator*
Taft, John Thomas *television producer, writer*
Taft, William Howard, IV, *federal agency administrator*
Taler, George Abraham *medical educator*
Tallent, Stephen Edison *lawyer*
Tamargo, Mauricio J. *federal agency administrator*
Tancredo, Thomas G. *congressman*
Tanham, George Kilpatrick *retired research company executive*
Tannenwald, Peter *lawyer*
Tanner, John S. *congressman, lawyer*
Tanous, Peter Joseph *banker*
Tarplin, Richard J. *federal agency administrator*
Tarrants, William Eugene *government official*
Tate, Sheila Burke *public relations executive*
Tatel, David Stephen *federal judge*
Tauber, Mark J. *lawyer*
†Taurman, John David *lawyer*
Tauzin, W. J. Billy, II, (Wilbert J. Tauzin) *congressman*
Tavassoli, Fattaneh Abbas-zadeh *pathologist, consultant*
Taylor, Charles H. *congressman*
Taylor, David Kerr *international business educator, consultant*
Taylor, Gene *congressman*
Taylor, Henry Splawn *literature educator, poet, writer*
Taylor, James, Jr., *lawyer*
Taylor, John Brian *federal agency administrator, economist, educator*
Taylor, Ralph Arthur, Jr., *lawyer*
Taylor, Richard Powell *lawyer*
Teague, Randal Cornell, Sr., *lawyer*
†Teal, Arabella W. *state attorney general*
†Teare, Richard Wallace *educational administrator*
Teets, Peter B. *federal agency administrator*
†Tefft, John *ambassador*
Teich, Albert Harris *professional society administrator*
Teichler, Stephen Lin *lawyer*
Temko, Stanley Leonard *lawyer*
Tenet, George John *government agency official*
†Tenorio, Pedro A. *resident representative*
†Terpeluk, Peter, Jr., *ambassador*
Terry, John Alfred *state supreme court judge*
Terry, Lee R. *congressman, lawyer*
Terzian, Philip Henry *journalist*
Tetelman, Alice Fran *small business owner*
Tether, Anthony J. *government agency administrator*
Tetzlaff, Charles Robert *lawyer*
Thawley, Michael *diplomat*
Theis, Paul Anthony *publishing executive*
Theiss. Patricia Kelley *public health researcher, educator*
Theodore, Eustace D. *educational advancement consultant, management consultant*
Theroux, Eugene *lawyer*
Thomas, Clarence *United States supreme court justice*
Thomas, Craig *senator*
†Thomas, Gerald E. *ambassador*
Thomas, Helen A. (Mrs. Douglas B. Cornell) *newspaper bureau executive*
Thomas, Mary Augusta *library administrator*
Thomas, Ralph Charles, III, *federal official*
Thomas, Ritchie Tucker *lawyer*
Thomas, Scott E. *federal government executive, lawyer*
Thomas, William Marshall *congressman*
Thompson, Bennie G. *congressman*
Thompson, Bernida Lamerle *principal, consultant, educator*
Thompson, C. Michael *congressman*
†Thompson, John C. *military career officer*
Thompson, Larry Dean *federal agency administrator, lawyer*
Thompson, Lawrence Hyde *federal agency official*
Thompson, Richard Leon *pharmaceutical company executive, lawyer*
Thompson, Tommy George *secretary of health and human services, former governor*
Thompson, Wayne Wray *historian*
Thompson, William Reid *public utility executive, lawyer*
Thompson-Curry, Dorothy *federal agency administrator*
Thornberry, Mac *congressman*
Thornburgh, Dick (Richard L. Thornburgh) *lawyer, former United Nations official, former United States attorney general, former governor*
†Thornton, Leslie *lawyer*
Thornton, Michael B. *federal judge*
Thura, Peter *emergency physician*
Thurman, Karen L. *congresswoman*
Tiahrt, W. Todd *congressman, former state senator*
Tiberi, Patrick J. *congressman, former state legislator*
Tidball, M. Elizabeth Peters *physiologist, educator, research director*
Tiede, Tom Robert *journalist*
Tiefel, William Reginald *hotel company executive*
Tierney, John F. *congressman, lawyer*
Tigar, Michael Edward *law educator*
†Tilley, Jack L. *military officer*
Timmons, William Evan *corporate executive*
Timpane, Philip Michael *education educator, policy analyst*
Tinsley, Nikki Lee *federal agency administrator*
Tipton, E. Linwood *trade association executive*
Tirana, Bardyl Rifat *lawyer*
Tobias, Robert Max *labor leader, lawyer*
Toder, Eric Jay *economist*
Todhunter, John Anthony *toxicologist, consultant*
Tolchin, Martin *retired newspaper reporter, author*
Toledano, Ralph De *columnist, author, poet*
Toles, Thomas Gregory *editorial cartoonist*
Tolson, John J. *writer, editor*
Tolu, Tolu *foundation administrator*
Tomb, Diane Lenegan *federal agency administrator*
Tomlinson, Alexander Cooper *investment banker, consultant*
Tomlinson, Margaret Lynch *lawyer*
Tompert, James Emil *lawyer*
Tompkins, Joseph Buford, Jr., *lawyer*
†Toner, Michael E. *commissioner*
Tong, Chiling *trade and commerce administrator*
Tonkin, Leo Sampson *educational foundation administrator*
Toomey, Patrick J. *congressman*
Topelius, Kathleen Ellis *lawyer*
†Topol, Allan Jerry *lawyer*
†Torain, Terri Lisa *writer, consultant*
Torrey, Barbara Boyle *research council administrator*
Tosi, Laura Lowe *orthopaedic surgeon*
Totenberg, Nina *journalist*
†Totushek, John B. *military officer, federal agency administrator*
Towns, Edolphus *congressman*
Townsend, Ann Van Devanter *foundation administrator, art historian*
†Townsend, Frances Fragos *federal agency administrator*
Townsend, John Michael *lawyer*
Townsend, Marjorie Rhodes *aerospace engineer, business executive*
Trachtenberg, Stephen Joel *university president*
Tracy, Alan Thomas *trade association administrator*
Trafford, Abigail *columnist, editor, writer*
Trager, Michael David *lawyer*
Train, Russell Errol *environmentalist*
†Trencher, William Mannes *lawyer*
†Trenkle, Amy Barba *secondary school educator*
Trimble, Kathleen Louise *library director*
Trimble, Sandra Ellingson *lawyer*
Trinder, Rachel Bandele *lawyer*
Trisco, Robert Frederick *church historian, educator*
†Trooboff, Peter Dennis *lawyer*
Trowbridge, Alexander Buel, Jr., *business consultant*
Troyer, Thomas Alfred *lawyer*
Truitt, Anne Dean *artist*
Truman, Edwin Malcolm *federal official*
†Trumka, Richard Louis *labor leader, lawyer*
Tse, Man-Chun Marina *educational association administrator*
Tuck, John Chatfield *former federal agency administrator, public policy advisor*
Tucker, Marc Stephen *education policy analyst, author*
Tufaro, Richard Chase *lawyer*
Tulumello, Andrew Santo *lawyer*
Tung, Ko-Yung *lawyer*
Tuohey, Mark Henry, III, *lawyer*
Turnage, Fred Douglas *lawyer*
Turner, Douglas Laird *writer, editor, columnist*
Turner, James *congressman*
Turner, James Thomas *judge*
Turner, John Andrew *economist*
Turner, John Freeland *federal agency administrator*
†Turner, Michael *congressman*
Turner, Ted (Robert Edward Turner) *former television executive, philanthropist*
Turtell, Neal Timothy *librarian*
Tushnet, Mark Victor *law educator*
Tylenda, Joseph N. *library director*
Tyler, Cecilia Kay *career officer*
Tyler, Peggy Lynne Bailey *lawyer*
Tyner, Lee Reichelderfer *lawyer*
Uberall, Herbert Michael Stefan *physicist, educator*
Ucko, David Alan *museum consultant*
Udall, Mark *congressman*
Udall, Thomas (Tom Udall) *congressman*
Uehlein, E(dward) Carl, Jr., *lawyer*
†Underwood, Robert Anacletus *former congressman, university official*
Unger, Laura S. *lawyer, commissioner*
Unger, Peter Van Buren *lawyer*
†Unlu, Tuba *diplomat, researcher*
Unsell, Lloyd Neal *energy organization executive, former journalist*
†Upshaw, Gene *sports association executive*
Upton, Frederick Stephen *congressman*
Ushakov, Yuri Viktorovich *diplomat*
Utley, Jon Basil *think tank director, journalist*
Vacketta, Carl Lee *lawyer, educator*
Vakerics, Thomas Vincent *lawyer*
†Valachovic, Richard W. *medical association administrator*
Valadez, Joseph James *epidemiologist, researcher*
†Valenti, Jack Joseph *motion picture executive*
Valentine, Debra A. *attorney*
Valentine, Steven Richards *lawyer*
†Valenzuela, Arturo Arms *political science educator, writer, consultant*
Van Allen, Barbara Martz *marketing professional*
Vance, Stephanie *consultant*
Vanderryn, Jack *philanthropic foundation administrator*
†Vanderstar, John *lawyer*
Vanderver, Timothy Arthur, Jr., *lawyer*
Van de Water, Read *federal agency administrator*
Vane, John Robert *pharmacologist*
†van Ee, Daun Roell *historian*
†Van Hollen, Christopher, Jr., *congressman*
Van Lare, Barry Lee *social welfare executive*
Van Tine, Kirk Kelso K. *federal agency administrator*
Van Ummersen, Claire A(nn) *academic administrator, biologist, educator*
Van Winkle, Hans A. *military officer*
Vardaman, John Wesley *lawyer*
Vasquez, Gaddi *federal agency administrator*
Vaughan, Kenneth Edward
†Vaughn, Robert Gene *law educator*
Vazirani-Fales, Heea *legislative staff member, lawyer*
Veatch, Elizabeth Wilson *educational administrator*
Veatch, Robert Marlin *philosophy educator, medical ethics researcher*
Velazquez, Nydia M. *congresswoman*
Veneman, Ann M. *secretary of agriculture*
Venneri, Samuel L. *federal agency administrator*
†Vernalis, Marina *osteopath*
Verner, James Melton *lawyer*
Verrill, Charles Owen, Jr., *lawyer*
Vertes, Akos *chemist, educator*
Verville, Elizabeth Giavani *federal official*
Vickery, Ann Morgan *lawyer*
Vickery, Raymond Ezekiel, Jr., *international business consultant, lawyer*
Victory, Nancy *federal agency administrator*
Viehe, Karl William *mathematics educator, lawyer, investment banker*
Vieth, Gifford Duane *lawyer*
Villa, John Kazar *lawyer*
Villarreal, June Patricia *sales consultant*
Vince, Clinton Andrew *lawyer*
†Vining, Margaret Simmons *historian, curator*
Violante, Joseph Anthony *lawyer*
Visclosky, Peter John *congressman, lawyer*
Vitter, David *congressman*
Vittone, Bernard John *psychiatrist, researcher*
†Vogelsong, Diana Louise *librarian*
Voinovich, George V. *senator, former mayor and governor*
Voll, John Obert *history educator*
Voll, Sarah Potts *economic consultant*
Vondracek, M. Jon *communications executive*
†von Kaenel, Howard J. *army officer*
von Kann, Clifton Ferdinand *aviation and space executive, software executive*
†Vos, Joris Michael *diplomat*
Votaw, Carmen Delgado *civic association executive*
Wagner, Annice McBryde *judge*
Wagner, Curtis Lee, Jr., *judge*
†Wagstaff, Grayson *musicologist, educator*
†Wahba, Marcelle M. *ambassador*
Wahlbeck, Paul J. *political science educator, lawyer*
Waits, John A. *lawyer*
Walcott, John L. *communications executive*
Wald, Patricia McGowan *retired federal judge*
Walden, Greg *congressman*
Walder, Debby Jean *program director, quality manager, nursing service administrator, nurse, educator*
Waldron, Jonathan Kent *lawyer*
†Walker, Barbara Dodson *cultural organization administrator, consultant, lecturer, researcher*
Walker, David A(lan) *finance educator, educator*
Walker, David Michael *federal official*
†Walker, Edward S., Jr., *diplomat*
Walker, Mary L. *federal agency administrator, lawyer*
Walker, Robert Smith *former congressman*
Walker, Savannah T. *retired executive assistant, legislative assistant*
Wallace, Don, Jr., *law educator*
Wallace, Hank *seminar speaker, lawyer*
Wallace, James Harold, Jr., *lawyer*
†Wallace, William Charles *science educator, neurobiologist*
Wallace Douglas, Jean *conservationist*
†Walsh, Dennis P. *government agency administrator*
Walsh, James Thomas *congressman*
†Walsh, John F. *government agency administrator*
Walsh, Michael J. *lawyer*
Walston, Roderick Eugene *federal official*
Walters, John P. *federal official*
†Walton, Reggie Barnett *judge*
Walton, Tracy Matthew, Jr., *radiologist*
Wamp, Zach *congressman*
Wang, John Cheng Hwai *communications engineer, researcher*
Ward, David *academic administrator, educator*
†Ward, Erica Anne *lawyer, educator*
Warner, John William *senator*
Warren, Albert *publishing executive*
Warren, Clay *communication educator*
Warren, David Liles *educational association executive*
Wartofsky, Leonard *medical educator*
Washburn, Abbott McConnell *government official*
Washburn, Kathryn Hazel *government agency executive*

Belle Glade
Clay, Irene Gibson *community activist, retired educational administrator, educator*

Belleair
Lasley, Charles Haden *cardiovascular surgeon, health and fitness consultant*

Belleair Beach
Ayers, Richard Wayne *electrical company official, writer, journalist*
Fuentes, Martha Ayers *playwright*

Belleair Bluffs
Alexander, Christina Anamaria *translator, performing company executive*

Belleview
Bellis, Arthur Albert *financial executive, government official*

Beverly Hills
Larsen, Erik *art history educator*

Big Pine Key
Harris, Douglas Clay *retired newspaper executive*

Boca Grande
Brock, Mitchell *lawyer*
de Saint Phalle, Thibaut *investment banker, educator, lawyer, financial consultant*
Dyche, David Bennett, Jr., *retired management consultant*
Heffernan, John William *retired journalist*
McInnes, Donald Gordon *railroad executive*
Winterer, Victoria Thompson *hospitality executive*

Boca Raton
Agler, Richard Dean *rabbi*
Allen, Barry Morgan *corporate communications consultant*
Arden, Eugene *retired university provost*
Arent, Albert Ezra *retired lawyer*
Balter, Murray *interior designer*
Barbarosh, Milton Harvey *merchant banking executive*
Barnett, Judy Jannette *healthcare technology company executive, consultant*
Batmasian, Marta Tersakian *investment company owner*
Beber, Robert H. *lawyer, financial services executive*
Bernstein, Edwin S. *judge*
Bloomberg, Judith *stockbroker*
Breakstone, Robert Albert *consumer products, e-commerce, information technology and consulting executive*
Brogan, Frank T. *former lieutenant governor*
Buckstein, Mark Aaron *lawyer, mediator, educator*
Camilleri, Michael *lawyer, educator*
Cannon, Herbert Seth *investment banker*
Collins, Robert Arnold *English language educator*
Connor, Frances Partridge *retired education educator*
Connor, Leo Edward *special education administrator*
Coz, Steve *editorial director*
Crossman, William Whittard *retired wire cable and communications executive*
†Decker, Larry E *education educator*
Dembowski, Frederick Lester *educational administrator, educator, consultant*
Deppe, Henry A. *insurance company executive*
Dorfman, Allen Bernard *international management consultant*
Dower Gold, Catherine Anne *music history educator*
Dunhill, Robert W. *advertising direct mail executive*
†Early, John D. *anthropologist, educator*
Eckelson, Robert Alan *orthodontist*
Eisenberg, Robin Ledgin *religious education administrator*
Erdman, Joseph *lawyer*
Feld, Joseph *construction executive*
Fels, Robert Alan *psychotherapist*
Fengler, John Peter *television producer, director, advertising executive*
†Ferrari, Roberto C. *librarian*
Fier, Elihu *lawyer, educator*
Finegold, Ronald *computer services executive*
Frankel, Charles James, III, *banker*
Friend, Harold Charles *neurologist*
Furman, Mark Evan *human performance scientist*
Garelick, Martin *retired transportation executive*
†Garlick, Michael *lawyer*
Godofsky, Stanley *lawyer*
Goldberger, Melvin Tobias *executive investment banker*
Golis, Paul Robert *lawyer*
Gralla, Eugene *natural gas company executive*
†Gutting, Gabrielle L. *literature educator, researcher*
Han, Chingping Jim *industrial engineer, educator*
†Hermann, Naomi Basel *librarian, interior decorator*
Hoppenstein, Abraham Solomon *investment and merchant banker, consultant*
Innes-Brown, Georgette Meyer *real estate broker, insurance broker*
†Jacobs, Joseph James *lawyer, communications company executive*
Jacobson, Susan Bogen *psychotherapist*
Jessup, Jan Amis *arts volunteer, writer*
Jessup, Joe Lee *business educator, management consultant*
Kaplan, Judith Helene *company executive*
Karmelin, Michael Allen *financial executive*
Kassner, Herbert Seymore *lawyer*
Katz, Richard Jon *marketing and advertising company executive*

Kaye, Barry *insurance company executive*
†Kenwood, Joel David *lawyer*
Kephart, Larry Robert *architect*
Kewley, Sharon Lynn *systems analyst, consultant*
Keyes, Daniel *author*
Kitzes, William Fredric *lawyer, safety analyst, consultant*
Klein, Peter William *lawyer, corporate officer, investment company executive*
Klein, Robert *manufacturing company executive*
Knudsen, Rudolph Edgar, Jr., *insurance company executive*
Konrad, Agnes Crossman *retired real estate agent, retired educator*
Kornberg, Joel Barry *lawyer, emergency physician*
Kramer, Cecile E. *retired medical librarian*
Laine, Iris Ruth *minister, public relations/advertising executive*
Land, Judith Broten *stockbroker*
Langbort, Polly *retired advertising executive*
Langfield, Raymond Lee *real estate developer*
Latané, Bibb *social psychologist*
Leary, William James *educational administrator*
Lee, Xiaoyang *scientist*
Lerner, Theodore Raphael *dentist*
Levenson, David Irwin *endocrinologist*
Levin, Marlene *human resources executive, educator*
Levine, Irving Raskin *news commentator, university dean, author, lecturer*
Levine, Richard A. *physician*
†Levy, Ralph *elementary school educator*
Lin, Yukweng M. *engineer, educator*
Litvak, Isaiah A. *business educator, consultant*
Marcus, Harold *retired physician, health facility administrator*
McFarland, Thomas *language educator, literature educator*
McNair, Russell Arthur, Jr., *lawyer*
McQueen, Scott Robert *broadcasting company executive*
Michel, Stephen Lewis *physician*
Miles, Jesse Mc Lane *retired accounting company executive*
Miller, Eugene *university official, business executive*
Miller, William *library administrator*
Monroe, William Lewis *human resources executive*
Narayanan, Ramaswamy *biomedical engineer*
O'Donnell, Joseph Michael *electronics executive*
Ortiz, Jaime *business educator*
Ortlip, Paul Daniel *artist*
Pajunen, Grazyna Anna *electrical engineer, educator*
Párkányi, Marie Hřebíček *real estate broker*
Peterson, Mark F. *business educator*
Plosker, Harvey *anesthesiologist*
Pradere, Sonia *accounting administrator*
Rabinowitz, Wilbur Melvin *manufacturing executive, consultant*
Reinstein, Joel *lawyer*
Resnick, Robert *physicist, educator*
Reynolds, George Anthony, Jr., *engineering executive*
†Ricciardi, Salvatore *wholesale distribution executive*
Richardson, R(oss) Fred(erick) *insurance executive*
†Rosen, Harriet R. *elementary school educator*
Rosenberg, Lee Evan *financial planner*
Rosenkranz, Herbert S. *public health educator*
Rosner, M. Norton *business systems and financial services company executive*
Ross, Fred Michael *organic chemist*
Rothberg-Blackman, June Simmonds *retired nursing educator, psychotherapist, psychoanalyst*
St. Clair, James Earl *music educator*
Samuels, William Mason *physiology association executive*
Sarna, Helen Horowitz *retired librarian, educator*
†Sax, Spencer Meridith *lawyer*
Schechterman, Lawrence *private chef, business consultant*
Schlager, Maynard M(orton) *psychologist, consultant*
†Siegel, Lisa Beth *lawyer, accountant*
Sigel, Marshall Elliot *financial consultant*
Silver, Barry Morris *lawyer*
Singer, Merle Elliot *rabbi*
Su, Tsung-Chow Joe *engineering educator*
Tata, Robert Joseph *retired geographer, educator*
Tennies, Robert Hunter *headmaster*
Turner, Hugh Joseph, Jr., *lawyer*
Turner, Lisa Phillips *human resources executive*
Vissicchio, Andrew John, Jr., *linen service company executive*
Wallach, Steven Ernst *lawyer, pilot*
†Warshaw, Carole Klein *education educator, consultant*
Weiner, Howard Marc *physician*
Weissbach, Herbert *biochemist, researcher*
Wertheimer, Esther *sculptor*
Wichinsky, Glenn Ellis *lawyer*
Wiesenfeld, John Richard *chemistry educator*
Willis, John Alexander *lawyer*
Wyatt, James Luther *drapery hardware company executive*
Yelin, Robert Bruce *musician, recording artist, composer, lyricist*
Yoder, Patricia Doherty *public relations executive*
Zaleznak, Bernard D. *physician*
Zhong, Dawn He *material engineer*
Zuckerman, Sidney *retired allergist, immunologist*

Bokeelia
Adams, Alfred Hugh *retired college president*
Grottanelli, Pamala N. *nursing administrator, educator*
Vilardi, Charles Ronald *principal*

Bonita Springs
Becker, Richard Charles *retired college president*

Brown, Theodore Lawrence *chemistry educator*
Dignan, Thomas Gregory, Jr., *lawyer*
Dougherty, James *orthopedic surgeon, educator, author*
Ericson, Alvin Charles *marketing professional, consultant*
Feldblum, Sandra Faye Neuman *communal worker, nurse*
Johnson, Franklyn Arthur *academic administrator*
Katzen, Raphael *consulting chemical engineer*
McNamara-Ringewald, Mary Ann Thérèse *artist, educator*
Megee, Geraldine Hess *social worker*
Mehuron, William Otto *government official*
Olander, Ray Gunnar *retired lawyer*
Powell, Robert Ellis *mathematics educator, college dean*
Rust, William James *retired steel company executive*
Sargent, Charles Lee *manufacturing company executive*

Boynton Beach
Allison, Dwight Leonard, Jr., *investor*
†Ashley, James MacGregor *management consultant*
Babler, Wayne E. *lawyer, retired telephone company executive*
Balis, Moses Earl *biochemist, educator*
Bartholomew, Arthur Peck, Jr., *accountant*
Bryant, Donald Loyd *insurance company executive*
Caras, Joseph Sheldon *life insurance company executive*
Charles, Joel *forensic audio and video tape analyst, voice identification consultant*
†Corbière, Paul *music educator*
Costa, Terry Ann *principal*
†Davant, James Waring *investment banker*
†Dembicer, Edwin Herbert *retired lawyer*
Gill, Milton Randall *minister, artist*
Glickman, Franklin Sheldon *dermatologist, educator*
Hermann, Philip J. *lawyer*
†Horowitz, Fedora Cohen *music educator, pianist*
Jensen, Reuben Rolland *former automotive company executive*
Kempner, Marvin A. *broadcasting corporation executive*
Klein, Bernard *publishing company executive*
Kobliner, Richard *secondary school educator*
Kronman, Joseph Henry *orthodontist, educator*
Lemanski, Larry Fredrick *medical educator, university administrator*
Machtiger, Harriet Gordon *retired psychoanalyst*
†Mark, Audra *small business owner, educator*
Mittel, John J. *economist, corporate executive*
Oppler, Ralph Leo *retired publishing executive, advertising executive*
Pataky, Paul Eric *ophthalmologist*
Polinsky, Janet Naboicheck *retired state official, former state legislator*
Rogers, John S. *retired union official*
Schneider, Paul *consultant*
Sondak, Arthur *retired management consultant*
Srinath, Latha *physician*
Stubbins, Hugh A(sher), Jr., *architect*
Van Den Brande, Rene Albert *retired accountant*
†Yudell, Barbara R. *science educator, writer*

Bradenton
Acs, Joseph Steven *transportation engineering consultant, civil engineer*
Aerts, Cindy Sue *nurse*
Bateman, John Jay *classics educator*
Beall, Robert Matthews, II, *retail chain executive*
†Becker, Nancy S. *retired real estate broker, retired shop owner*
Blanchard, Leonard Albert *educator, consultant, writer*
Boudreau, Alice Benjamin *artist, educator*
Brenner, Frank *lawyer*
Charlton, Gordon Randolph *physicist*
Clements, Allen, Jr., *retired lawyer*
Compton, Charles Daniel *chemistry educator*
Crouthamel, Thomas Grover, Sr., *editor, consultant*
†Dickie, George Thomas *philosopher, educator*
Doyle, William Jay, II, *business consultant*
Driscoll, Constance Fitzgerald *educator, writer*
†Dudley, Perry, Jr., *retired electronics executive*
†Ehde, Ava Louise *librarian, educator*
Ellman, Norman Kenneth *psychologist, psychoanalyst*
Engelhard, Arthur William *research scientist, consultant*
Engelman, Melvin Alkon *retired dentist, business executive, scientist*
Eppinger, James Edward *educational administrator*
Frederick, Nancy Ackerman *real estate broker*
†Howe, Carroll Victor *construction equipment company executive*
LaForest, Lana Jean *lawyer*
Lister, Thomas Mosie *composer, lyricist, publishing company executive, minister*
Long, Michael Eldon *government and history educator*
Lopacki, Edward Joseph, Jr., *lawyer*
Lorentzen, Robert Roy, Jr., *producer*
Maynard, Donald Nelson *horticulturist, educator*
McClish, Jerry Franklin *artist*
McFarland, Richard Macklin *retired journalist*
McMullan, Kathryn Oatman *watercolor painter, promotion specialist*
Nelson, Ralph Erwin *investment company executive, coin dealer*
Pedersen, Norman Arno, Jr., *retired headmaster, literary club director*
Phelan, John Densmore *insurance executive, consultant*
Price, Edgar Hilleary, Jr., *business consultant*
Rechcigl, Jack Edward *soil and environmental sciences educator*
Robinson, Hugh R. *retired marketing executive*

Rutstein, Stanley Harold *apparel retailing company executive*
†Sarakatsannis, Leonidas Nicholas *musician, music educator, composer, conductor*
Schuster, David J. *entomologist, researcher*
Stewart, Priscilla Ann Mabie *art historian, educator*
Taylor, Carol *rehabilitation nurse*
Thomas, Ella Cooper *lawyer*
Voorhees, Stephanie Robin Faught *retired art educator*
Watkins, William, Jr., *electric power industry executive*
Webb, Edsel Philip *retired textile engineer*
White, Dale Andrew *journalist*
Wolf, John Michael *adult education seminar consultant*

Brandenton
†Miles, Elizabeth Jane *social worker*

Brandon
Cartlidge, Edward Sutterley *mechanical engineer*
Curry, Clifton Conrad, Jr., *lawyer*
England, Lynne Lipton *lawyer, speech pathologist, audiologist*
Hirohata, Derek Kazuyoshi *air force officer, lawyer*
Holladay-Hicks, Sylvia A. *humanities educator*
†Jurch, George R., Jr., *retired science educator*
Mack, Arthur Neal *emergency medicine and family practice physician*
Mussenden, Gerald *psychologist*
Pomeroy, Wyman Burdette *business owner, consultant*
Thompson, Venita Brant *nutritionist, diet technician*
Tittsworth, Clayton (Clayton Magness Tittsworth) *lawyer*
Urka, Martin C. *soil scientist, retired*

Brooksville
Anderson, Richard Edmund *city manager, management consultant*
†Brown, James Milton *law educator*
Lauer, Harry Curtis *civil engineer*
Pylipow, Stanley Ross *retired manufacturing company executive*

Bushnell
Hagin, T. Richard *lawyer*

Cantonment
†Hoskins, John Royce, Jr., *organization program specialist*

Cape Canaveral
Field, Thomas Harold *software design engineer*
Hess, Terry Lee *writer, educator*

Cape Coral
Andert, Darlene (Darlene Andert-Schmidt) *management consultant in corporate governance*
Buthman, Nancy Smith *nurse practitioner, critical care nurse*
Croteau, Jack Randall *civil engineer*
†Driscoll, Dawn-Marie *lawyer*
Martin, Benjamin Gaufman *ophthalmologist*
McKinley, James Frank, Jr., *retired manufacturing executive*
Milaski, John Joseph *business transformation industry consultant*
Smith, Bruce William *safety engineer*
Stuart, Robert *container manufacturing executive*
Wendel, Joan Audrey *music educator*
West, John Merle *retired physicist, nuclear consultant*

Carrollwood
O'Keefe, Fredrick Rea *bishop, consultant, educator, writer*

Casselberry
†Homayssi, Ruby Lee *small business owner*
Lucas, Robert William *human resources consultant, writer*
Pantuso, Vincent Joseph *food service consultant*
†Sen, Pranab Kumar *statistics educator*

Cedar Key
Starnes, Earl Maxwell *urban and regional planner, architect*

Celebration
Crabtree, Valleri Jayne *real estate executive, lawyer*
O'Neal, Kathleen Len *communications executive, writer, management consultant*
Pollack, Robert William *psychiatrist*
Renard, Meredith Anne *marketing and advertising professional*

Chipley
Spangenberg, Theodore S. *retired civil engineer*

Citra
Parisi, Marita *artist, art gallery director*

Citrus Springs
Tillery, Billy Carey *writer, poet*

Clearwater
Bairstow, Frances Kanevsky *arbitrator, mediator, educator*
Barry, Joyce Alice *dietitian*
Bernsdorff, Oliver Thomas *social sciences educator*
Blumencranz, Peter William *surgeon*
Bramante, Pietro Ottavio *physiology educator, retired pathology specialist*
Brenner, Rena Claudy *communications executive*
Brown, Richard Christopher *retired epidemiologist*
Campolettano, Thomas Alfred *international contract manager*

Chisholm, William DeWayne *retired contract manager*
Coleman, Jeffrey Peters *lawyer*
Conwell, Theresa Gallo *financial services representative*
Crites, Richard Ray *financial planner, investment advisor, financial services company executive*
†Dougall-Sides, Leslie K. *lawyer*
†Falkner, William Carroll *lawyer*
Fenderson, Caroline Houston *psychotherapist*
Free, E. LeBron *lawyer, mediator*
†Glymph, Dianne Tyler *librarian*
Goldenfarb, Paul Bennett *internist, oncologist*
Grala, Jane M. *securities firm executive*
Heid, Michael Patrick *surgeon*
Henderson, Janet Lynn *city commissioner, real estate broker*
Hirzel, Charles K. *retired architect*
Hogan, Elwood *lawyer*
Hoornstra, Edward H. *retail company executive*
Horowitz, Harry I. *podiatrist*
Hunt, Peter James *management consultant, statistics educator*
†Kiehl, E. Robert *manufacturing executive, consultant*
Loos, Randolph Meade *financial planner*
Maxwell, Richard Anthony *retail executive*
McGann, Michael Geyer *martial arts instructor, protection expert*
Pathak, Sunit Rawly *business owner, consultant, journalist*
Peters, Robert Timothy *judge*
Peterson, James Robert *engineering psychologist*
Raymund, Steven A. *computer company executive*
Rogers, H. Dennis *lawyer*
Sandefer, G(eorge) Larry *lawyer*
Sassouni, Chris Garo *investment advisor*
Scarne, John *game company executive*
Slade, Roy *artist, college president, museum director*
Smith, Marion Pafford *avionics company executive, retired*
Stein, Roger Richard *microcomputer specialist, educator*
Stewart, Michael Ian *orthodontist*
Swope, Scott Paul *lawyer*
Thomas, Patrick Robert Maxwell *oncology educator, academic administrator*
Tragos, George Euripedes *lawyer*
Turley, Stewart *retired retail company executive*
VanMeer, Mary Ann *publisher, writer, researcher, webmaster*
†Warden, Jo Ann Griffith *retired journalist*
Weidemeyer, Carleton Lloyd *lawyer*
Werner, Elizabeth Helen *librarian, language educator*
Whedon, George Donald *medical administrator, researcher*
†Zbella, Edward Andrew *obstetrician, educator*
Zschau, Julius James *lawyer*

Clermont
Levy, David Walton *music educator*
Morris, Helen Julia *artist*

Clewiston
Griffith, Lonzo, Jr., *technology specialist, educator, farmer*

Cocoa
Baker, David Allen *protective services official*
Davis, Duane Lee *marketing educator*
†Dhere, Neelkanth G *research scientist*
Gamble, Thomas Ellsworth *academic administrator*
Malvey, Donna M. *health sciences educator*
McCluney, Ross (William Ross McCluney) *research physicist, education educator*
McLendon, Dorothy *school psychologist*
Muradov, Nazim Ziraddin *chemist, researcher*
Ollie, Pearl Lynn *artist, singer, songwriter*
†Pound, Frank R., Jr., *lawyer*

Cocoa Beach
Blum, June *artist, curator*
Burch, William Mark, II, *retired lawyer*
Church, Glenn J. *lawyer*
Coppola, Phyllis Gloria Cecire *retired special education educator*
Herbstman, Loretta *sculptor, painter*
Kennedy, Thomas Patrick *financial executive*
Wirtschafter, Irene Nerove *tax specialist, consultant*

Coconut Creek
Brenner, Egon *university official, education consultant*
†Marshak, Arthur *artist, sculptor*
Rogge, James Alan *education educator*

Coconut Grove
Arboleya, Carlos Joaquin *lawyer, broker*
Denaro, Gregory *lawyer*
†Dominguez, Ramon Emilio *composer, visual artist*
Freeman, Lewis Bernard *forensic accountant, lawyer*
Gorman, Michael Stephen *construction executive*
Martinez-Carbonell, Karelia *not-for-profit fundraiser*
McAmis, Edwin Earl *lawyer*
Softness, John *public relations executive*
Taylor, J(ames) Bennett *management consultant*
Turkel, Bruce *advertising executive*

Cooper City
Stabile, Christopher Michael *secondary school educator*

Coral Gables
†Anthony, Andrew John *lawyer*
Bacon, Lydia Leach *human resources professional*
†Barentyne-Truluck, Ross *musicologist, educator, voice educator*
Bolton, David *lawyer, educator*
Buchsbaum, Karen Fuson *public relations executive, consultant*
Burini, Sonia Montes de Oca *apparel manufacturing and public relations executive*
†Butterman, Steven Fred *language educator, researcher*
Cano, Mario Stephen *lawyer*
Criss, Cecil M. *chemistry educator*
Dady, Robert Edward *lawyer*
David, George A. *lawyer*
Einspruch, Norman Gerald *physicist, engineering educator*
Ely, John Hart *lawyer, university dean*
†Felder-Rodriguez, Monica Lee *lawyer*
Fitzgerald, John Thomas, Jr., *religious studies educator*
Fletcher, Paul Gerald *lawyer*
Fournaris, Theodore James *lawyer*
Friedman, Marvin Ross *lawyer*
Glaser, Luis *biochemistry educator*
Gould, Taffy *Internet company executive, real estate executive*
Green, Willie Harold *mathematician, physicist*
Gustafson, Anne-Lise Dirks *lawyer, foreign consul*
Haggard, William Andrew *lawyer*
†Herald, Sara Barli *bank executive*
Hertz, Arthur Herman *business executive*
Higginbottom, Samuel Logan *retired aerospace company executive*
Hoffman, Carl H. *lawyer*
Howard, Bernard Eufinger *mathematics and computer science educator*
Kearns, John W. *lawyer*
Landon, Robert Kirkwood *philanthropist, retired insurance company executive*
Leblanc, Roger Maurice *chemistry educator*
†Liu, Hongtan *engineering educator*
Lomonosoff, James Marc *marketing professional*
Lucà-Moretti, Maurizio *research scientist, nutrition researcher*
Lynch, Catherine Gores *social work administrator*
Manning, Elliott *lawyer, educator*
†Mantell, Murray I. *engineering educator*
Meyers, Stuart Irwin *real estate developer*
†Moreno, Fernando *lawyer, educator*
Moss, Ambler Holmes, Jr., *lawyer, former ambassador*
Nacknouck, James D. *management executive*
Nunez-Portuondo, Ricardo *investment company executive*
O'Donnell, Anthony Joseph, Jr., *lawyer, educator*
†Omer-Sherman, Ranen E *religious studies educator, researcher*
Paul, Robert *lawyer*
Perez, Josephine *psychiatrist, physician, educator*
Pettigrew, Richard A. *lawyer*
†Pilar, Nobleza G. *vocalist*
Polo, Richard Joseph *engineering executive*
Quillian, Warren Wilson, II, *pediatrician, educator*
†Regalado, Eloisa *lawyer*
Roberts, Samuel Smith *television news executive*
Rust, Robert Warren *retired lawyer*
†Sacasas, Rene *lawyer*
†Saffi, Clinia Mabell *language educator*
Saffir, Herbert Seymour *structural engineer, consultant*
Schmitt, Peter Harlan *educator*
Schwartztol, Holly Wechsler *psychologist*
Shalala, Donna E. *university administrator, former federal official, political scientist, educator*
Simpson, Russell Gordon *lawyer, former mayor, not-for-profit developer, consultant*
Steinberg, Alan Wolfe *investment company executive*
Stover, James Howard *retired real estate executive*
†Sugarman, Robert Alan *lawyer*
Sumanth, David Jonnakoty *industrial engineer, educator*
Van Vliet, Carolyne Marina *physicist, educator*
Warburton, Ralph Joseph *architect, engineer, planner, educator*
Weiner, Morton David *banker, insurance agent*
Weiner, Ruth Eileen Blower Kassewitz *retired public relations executive*
Yarger, Sam Jacob *dean, educator*
Young, Tzay Y. *electrical and computer engineering educator*
†Zavac, Nancy *librarian*

Coral Springs
Becker, Edward A. *accounting educator, consultant*
Bolene, Rosalie Steele (Margaret Bolene) *bacteriologist, civic worker*
Brown, Ted Leon, Jr., *investment company executive*
Burg, Ralph *art association executive*
Kotheimer, William Conrad *consulting engineer*
†MacDonald, Laurianne *accountant, poet*
†Medina-Salinas, Elizabeth *publishing executive, writer*
Miller, Karl Frederick *insurance professional*
Polin, Alan Jay *lawyer*
Sanders, Marc Andrew *computer technical consultant*
†Singh, Vijay *professional golfer*
Swiller, Randolph Jacob *internist*
Wise, Steven M. *lawyer, author*

Crawfordville
Black, B. R. *retired educational administrator, consultant*
†Brumby, James Remley, III, (Knox Brumby) *retired priest*

Crestview
Scott, George Gallmann *accountant*

Crystal River
Schlumberger, Robert Ernest *accountant*
Stone, Fred Lyndon *retired human resources administrator*

Dade City
Burdick, Glenn Arthur *physicist, engineering educator*
Currier, Douglas Gilfillan, II, *urban planner*
†Feld, Harvey Joel *pathologist*
Smith, Howell Jackson, III, *physician assistant*
†Wickersheim, Michael Edward *music educator*

Dania
Dozier, Eleanor Cameron *computer company executive, writer*
Fernander, Karen Geneine *secondary school educator*
Satin, Claire Jeanine *sculptor, book artist*

Davenport
†Vaughn, Rosalyn Mae *human resources specialist*

Davie
Childrey, John A., Jr., *literacy educator*
†Gailey, Thomas Chandler *professional football coach*
Labowitz, Shoni *writer, lecturer*
Madison, Sam A., Jr., *football player*
Mare, Olindo Franco *football player*
†Marino, Dan, Jr., *sports broadcaster, retired professional football player*
Martin, Tony Derrick *professional football player*
†McDuffie, Otis James (O.J. McDuffie) *professional football player*
Morris, Joseph Raymond *business and economics educator*
O'Farrill, Alan John *music educator*
†Pittle, Jeffrey Robert *artist*
†Richmond, Michael Lloyd *lawyer, educator*
Seau, Junior (Tiana Seau Jr.) *professional football player*
†Thomas, Thurman Lee *football player*
Thomas, Zach Michael *football player*
Upadhiaya, Umesh Chandra *engineer, consultant*
Williams, Ricky *professional football player*

Daytona
†Wilson, Neva June *psychologist, educator*

Daytona Beach
Adams, John Carter, Jr., *insurance executive*
Amick, William Walker *golf course architect*
Andrews Reeves, Donna *professional golfer*
Barker, Robert Osborne (Bob Barker) *educator, mediator*
Barrett, Tina *professional golfer*
Betancourt, Ralph Ernest *mayor*
†Bodine, Brett *race car driver*
†Bodine, Geoff *race car driver*
Bronson, Oswald Perry, Sr., *religious organization administrator, clergyman*
Brown, Benjamin Thomas *urologist, educator*
Cardwell, Harold Douglas, Sr., *retired rehabilitation specialist*
Carmona, José Antonio *Spanish language educator, English language educator*
Chesnut, Nondis Lorine *screenwriter, consultant, reading and language arts educator, instructor, counselor*
Cool, Mary L. *education specialist*
Davidson, Herbert M., Jr., (Tippen Davidson) *newspaper owner*
Di Nicolo, Roberto *allergist*
Duma, Richard Joseph *microbiologist, physician, pathologist, researcher, educator*
Ebbs, George Heberling, Jr., *university executive*
Erickson, Larry Ray *dermatologist*
France, William Clifton, Jr., *professional sports team executive*
Frank, Robert Edwin *artist*
Furstman, Shirley Elsie Daddow *advertising executive*
†Gordon, Jeff *race car driver*
Green, Betty Nielsen *education educator, consultant*
†Harrison, William D. *humanities educator*
Hartsell, Horace Ed *college president*
Helton, Mike *professional sports team executive*
†King, Betsy *professional golfer*
Libbey, James K. *education educator*
Libby, Gary Russell *museum director emeritus, writer*
Martin, Kimberly Sue *critical care nurse, educator*
Mc Collister, John Charles *writer, clergyman, educator, executive producer*
†Miller, Sanford *car rental company executive*
Neitzke, Eric Karl *lawyer*
Pagan Ortiz, Alex Omar *computer systems analyst, educator*
†Pak, Se Ri *professional golfer*
Palmer, William D. *judge*
Picott, Jr., Jerry Lee *music educator*
Rogers, Patricia June *clinical social worker*
†Rudd, Ricky *race car driver*
Schauer, Catharine Guberman *public affairs specialist*
†Schrader, Ken *race car driver*
Scott, John Brooks *retired research institute executive*
†Seenith, Sivasundaram *mathematician, educator*
Sharples, D. Kent *college administrator*
†Sigerson, Marjorie Lorraine *librarian*
Steinhauer, Sherri *professional golfer*
Swanson, Gerald Carl *chemistry educator*
Tiblier, Fernand Joseph, Jr., *municipal engineering administrator*
†Trocine, Linda *engineering educator, researcher*
†Votaw, Ty M. *golf association commissioner*
†Wallace, Rusty *race car driver*
Watts, C. Allen *lawyer*
Whitworth, Kathrynne Ann *professional golfer*
Xepapas, Anargyros *architect*
†Yarborough, William Caleb *retired race car driver*

Daytona Beach Shores
Dalia, Vesta Mayo *artist*

De Leon Springs
Price, Artis J. *retired secondary education educator*
Price, Harry Mackey *dentist*

DeLand
†ElAarag, Hala *adult education educator*

Debary
Barry, Wayne Stephen *physician, educator*
Pajama, Helen *advocate*
†Pelosi, Haydee *sculptor*

Deerfield Beach
Areskog, Donald Clinton *retired chiropractor*
†Bader, Robert S. *dermatologist*
†Brown, Colin *automotive executive*
Bruno, Andrew Felix *ophthalmologist*
Buck, Thomas Randolph *retired lawyer, financial services executive*
†Drucker, Lisa K. *editor*
†King, Don *boxing promoter*
Laser, Charles, Jr., *oil company executive*
Lenoff, Michele Malka *lawyer*
†Moran, James M. *automotive sales executive*
Moran, Patricia Genevieve *corporate executive*
Schaefer, Robert Joseph *counselor*
Siegel, Steven L. *finance company executive, consultant*
Solomon, Barry Jason *healthcare administrator*

Deland
Bear, Frederick Thomas *educator*
Brakeman, Louis Freeman *retired university official*
Caccamise, Alfred Edward *real estate executive*
Caccamise, Genevra Louise Ball (Mrs. Alfred E. Caccamise) *retired librarian*
Dascher, Paul Edward *university dean, accounting educator*
Gill, Donald George *education educator*
Goldberg, Paul Bernard *gastroenterologist, clinical researcher*
Horton, Thomas Roscoe *business advisor*
†Juusela, Kari Henrik *dean*
Langston, Paul T. *music educator, university dean, composer*
Lee, Howard Douglas *academic administrator*
Morland, Richard Boyd *retired educator*
†Musco, Lynn Ann *music educator*
†Robinson, Stephen A. *music educator*
Rouse, Robert Kelly, Jr., *judge*
Sanders, Edwin Perry Bartley *judge*
Sorensen, Jacki Faye *choreographer, aerobic dance company executive*
Wood, Richard Harvey, Jr., *economics educator*

Delray Beach
Armstrong, Jack Gilliland *lawyer*
Baine, Stuart Allan *cardiologist*
Beckman, Frank Samuel *computer science educator, researcher*
Bryan, Robert Fessler *former investment analyst*
Case, Manning Eugene, Jr., *retired food products executive*
Charyk, Joseph Vincent *retired satellite telecommunications executive*
Chavin, Walter *biological science educator and researcher*
Ehrlich, Geraldine Elizabeth *management consultant*
Ehrlich, S(aul) Paul, Jr., *physician, consultant, former government official*
†Ellsweig, Phyllis Leah *retired psychotherapist*
Erenstein, Alan *emergency room nurse, medical education consultant*
Fedder, Norman J. *retired theater educator, playwright*
Fitzpatrick, David J. *electronics executive*
Force, Elizabeth Elma *retired pharmaceutical executive, consultant*
Frazer, Vernon *writer, musician*
Goldenberg, George *retired pharmaceutical company executive*
Hegstrom, William Jean *mathematics educator*
Himmelright, Robert John, Jr., *rubber company executive*
Jacobson, Herbert Leonard *licensing executive*
Kronish, Jan Warren *ophthalmologist*
Larry, R. Heath *lawyer, director*
Levinson, Harry *psychologist, educator*
Love, Marsha Lynn *interior decorator*
Mavrides, Gregory *computer scientist, psychoanalyst, computer engineer, computer company executive*
Mills, Agnes Eunice Karlin *artist, printmaker, sculptor*
Murphy, Kevin George *novelist*
Nelson, Bruce *consumer products company executive*
Nikischer, Frank William, Sr., *retired restaurant owner and operator*
Pesses, Marvin *metal products executive, consultant*
Randall, Priscilla Richmond *travel executive*
Reichart, Stuart Richard *lawyer*
Rippeteau, Darrel Downing *retired architect*
Robinson, Brenda Kay *editor, public relations professional*
Robinson, Richard Francis *writer, author, geneaologist, historian*
Rosenfeld, Steven Ira *ophthalmologist*
Ross, Beatrice Brook *artist*
Saffer, Alfred *retired chemical company executive*
Salsberg, Arthur Philip *publishing company executive*
†Schaffer, Marvin W. *investor*
Schenkel, Suzanne Chance *retired natural resource specialist*
Schultz, Joel Sidney *architect*
Sherwood, Louis Maier *physician, scientist, pharmaceutical company executive*
Siegel, Ira T. *publishing executive*
Silberman, Charlotte Schatzberg *retired lawyer, artist*
Smith, Charles Oliver *engineer*

Smith, John Joseph, Jr., *textile company executive, educator*
Solon, Leonard R(aymond) *retired physicist, educator, consultant*
Sonnenblick, Bernard *obstetrician-gynecologist*
Spyker, Harry A., III, *music educator*
Stewart, Patricia Carry *foundation administrator*
Warshaw, Stanley Irving *policy advisor*
Weiner, Anne Lee *social worker*
Wells, Mary Elizabeth Thompson *minister*
Zarwyn, Berthold *physical scientist*
Zepnick, Seymour *civil engineer, consultant*

Deltona
Bondinell, Stephanie *counselor, academic administrator*
Neal, Dennis Melton *middle school administrator*
Zagnoli, Roland Candiano *management and marketing consultant, pharmacist*

Destin
Asher, Betty Turner *academic administrator*
Davis, Christopher Kevin *sales executive*
Deel, Frances Quinn *retired librarian*
De Revere, David Wilsen *retired professional society administrator*
Ferner, David Charles *non-profit management and development consultant*
†Giadrosich, Donald Louis *research scientist, retired electrical engineer*
†Harmuth, Henning F. *electrical engineer, educator*
Linn, James Eldon, II, *insurance company executive*
Robinson, Wilkes Coleman *retired federal judge*
Stansberry, James Wesley *air force officer*

Dover
Pearson, Walter Donald *editor, columnist*

Dunedin
Allison, Brooke Hastings *artist, educator*
†Banome, Lydia M. *elementary school educator*
Flemm, Eugene William *concert pianist, educator, conductor, chamber musician*
†Gamblin, Cynthia MacDonald *mathematics educator, loybbist*
Goodale, Arthur Worthington *civil engineer, researcher*
†Gurr, Jim R. *statistician*
Klingbiel, Paul Herman *retired information science consultant*
McIntosh, Roberta Eads *retired social worker*
Metcalf, Robert John Elmer *industrial consultant*
†O'Dea, J. David *psychologist, educator*
Rosa, Raymond Ulric *retired banker*
Samson, Jerome *communications executive, software engineer*
Tweedy, Robert Hugh *retired equipment company executive*

Dunnellon
Dixon, W(illiam) Robert *retired educational psychology educator*
Miller, Kenneth Edward *mechanical engineer, consultant*

Edgewater
Dunagan, Walter Benton *lawyer, educator*
Henderson, Janice Elizabeth Wilson *respiratory therapist*
†Lawson, Bonnie Hulsey *psychotherapist, consultant*

Ellenton
Edson, Herbert Robbins *retired foundation and hospital executive*

Englewood
Brainard, Paul Henry *musicologist, retired music educator*
Catterlin, Cindy Lou *English educator*
Curtis, Caroline A. S. *community health and oncology nurse*
Dickson, Katharine Hayland *dance educator*
Heintz, Mary Ethel *business owner*
Sanders, W(illiam) Eugene, Jr., *physician, educator*
Schultz, Arthur Joseph, Jr., *retired trade association executive*
Simis, Theodore Luckey *investment banker, information technology executive*

Estero
Barney, Charles Richard *retired transportation executive*
Brown, William Robert *association executive, consultant*
Brush, George W. *college president*
Routh, Donald K(ent) *psychology educator*

Eustis
Alfrey, Lydia Jean *musician educator*
Chorosinski, Eugene Conrad *writer, poet, author*
Welch, Jerry *oil company executive*

Fernandina Beach
Barlow, Anne Louise *pediatrician, medical research administrator*
D'Agnese, John Joseph *sanitation, public health and pest management consultant*
DelPesco Thornton, Nancy Rose *artist, educator*
Kurtz, Myers Richard *hospital administrator*
Lilly, Wesley Cooper *marine engineer, surveyor*
Rhodes, Robert Milford *management consultant*
Rogers, Robert Burnett *naval officer*
Smeeton, Thomas Rooney *governmental affairs consultant*

Flagler Beach
Cornelius, Aleta *artist, designer, restorer, educator, judge*
Stockton, Anderson Berrian *electronics company executive, consultant, genealogist*

Floral City
Williams, Nelson Garrett *retired lawyer, mediator*
Wise, Lawrence George *human resources executive*

Fort Lauderdale
†Abraham, Rebecca Jacob *finance educator*
†Adams, Daniel Lee *lawyer*
Adams, S. Charles *lawyer, speaker, writer, financial consultant, radio and television commentator*
Alpert, Martin Jeffrey *chiropractor*
Ambrose, Judith Ann *designer*
Austin, John Norman *classics educator*
Azrin, Nathan Harold *psychologist, educator*
†Ballot, Alissa E. *lawyer*
Bamberg, Louis Mark *wealth management specialist*
Barnard, George Smith *lawyer, former federal agency official*
Bartelstone, Rona Sue *gerontologist*
Baruch, Eduard *management consultant*
Beatty, Robert Clinton *religious studies educator*
Blumenfeld, Harry *retired social worker*
Bogenschutz, J. David *lawyer*
Bolanos, Michael Templeton *new media executive*
Bowen, Judith Reina *fundraising executive*
Bunnell, George Eli *lawyer*
Burleigh, A. Peter *ambassador*
Bustamante, Nestor *lawyer*
Calhoun, Peggy Joan *fundraising executive*
†Cane, Marilyn Blumberg *lawyer, educator*
Cantwell, John Walsh *advertising executive*
Carney, Dennis Joseph *former steel company executive, consulting company executive*
Cassidy, Terrence Patrick, Jr., *engineering consultant*
Castro, Stephanie L. *business management educator*
Chernow, Bart *critical care physician*
Clubb, Bruce Edwin *retired lawyer*
Cobb, David Keith *business executive*
†Cole, James Otis *lawyer*
Collins, Ronald William *psychologist, educator*
Costello, John H., III, *business and marketing executive*
Craib, Kenneth Bryden *resource development executive, physicist, economist*
Crikelair, George Francis *retired plastic surgeon, educator, researcher*
†Denman, James Burton *lawyer*
Dickens, Joyce Rebecca *addictions therapist, educator*
Di Giulian, Bruno L. *lawyer*
Dimitrouleas, William Peter *judge*
Donaldson, Lisa Miller *city administration*
Dorn, Samuel O. *endodontist*
Dressler, Robert A. *lawyer*
Duke, James T *art educator, consumer products company executive*
Dutko, Michael Edward *lawyer*
Easton, Robert Morrell, Jr., *optometric physician*
Edmund, Norman Wilson *educational researcher*
Eisner, Will *publishing company executive*
Etling, Terry Douglas *state agency administrator*
Eynon, Steven Scott *minister*
Feldman, Les J. *finance educator*
Fernandez, Bernardo B., Jr., *physician*
Fine, Howard Alan *travel industry executive*
Fischer, Carey Michael *lawyer*
Fischler, Abraham Saul *educator, retired university president*
Fitch, Mary Killeen *human resources specialist*
Fitzpatrick, George E. *research scientist, educator*
†Garcia-Godoy, Franklin *dental educator*
Gardner, Russell Menese *lawyer*
Geronemus, Diann Fox *social work consultant*
Ginn, Vera Walker *director*
Golden, E(dward) Scott *lawyer*
†Goldsten, Robert Emanuel *lawyer, investor*
Gonzalez, Jose Alejandro, Jr., *federal judge*
Gremillion, Robert *publishing executive*
Gude, Nancy Carlson *lawyer*
†Guest, Suzanne Mary *adult education educator, artist*
Haliczer, James Solomon *lawyer*
Hanbury, George Lafayette, II, *academic administrator*
Harbaugh, Joseph Delbert *legal educator, consultant*
Hargrove, John Russell *lawyer*
Harris, Jeffrey Mark *lawyer, educator*
Heath, Thomas Clark *lawyer*
Heidelberg, Paul *writer*
†Hennessy, David V. *literature educator*
Hershenson, Miriam Hannah Ratner *librarian*
Hess, George Franklin, II, *lawyer*
Hester, Julia A. *lawyer*
Hirsch, Jeffrey Allan *lawyer*
Hoines, David Alan *lawyer*
Holland, Beth *actress*
†Horowitz, Kenneth A. *communications executive, entrepreneur*
Huizenga, H. Wayne *entrepreneur, professional sports team executive*
Hull, Richard Franklin *insurance brokerage executive*
Jackson, Michael J. *automotive retail company executive*
James, Gordon, III, *lawyer*
Jarvis, Robert Mark *law educator*
Jotcham, Thomas Denis *marketing communications consultant*
Katz, Thomas Owen *lawyer*
†King, Donald Charles *fire rescue battalion chief*
King, Jenn L. *civil engineer*
King, Robert Lee *lawyer*
Knight, Kenneth Vincent *leisure company executive, entrepreneur, venture capitalist*
Kobert, Norman Noah *asset management consultant*
Koch, Katherine Rose *communications executive*
Kreizinger, Loreen I. *lawyer, nurse*
Kropp, Stacy Anne *small business owner*
Kubler, Frank Lawrence *lawyer*
Lampert, Wayne Morris *corporate financier*
Landry, Michael Gerard *investment company executive*
†Lassiter, Roy *soccer player*
Leach, Ralph F. *banker*
Leasher, Janet Louise *optometric physician*
Lerner, Lauren Lipshutz *physician*
LeRoy, Miss Joy *model, apparel designer*
Levant, Ronald F. *psychologist, educator*
†Levitt, Preston Curtis *lawyer*
†Levy, Michael *electronic manufacturing company executive*
Lilley, Mili Della *insurance company executive, entertainment management consultant*
Lister, Mark Wayne *clinical laboratory scientist*
Littman, Marlyn Kemper *information scientist, educator*
Lodwick, Gwilym Savage *radiologist, educator*
Loos, John Thompson *business owner*
Lundt, Eric L. *lawyer*
Marine, Michael R. *healthcare company executive*
Markos, Chris *retired real estate company executive*
Markus, Robert Michael *journalist, retired*
Maucker, Earl Robert *newspaper editor, newspaper executive*
Maxwell, Sara Elizabeth *psychologist, educator, speech pathologist, director*
McCan, James Lawton *education educator*
†McCarthy, James Peter *marine safety officer, management consultant*
Meeks, William Herman, III, *lawyer*
†Melo, Welton *professional soccer player*
Miller, Barry M. *child care administrator*
Moraitis, Karen Karl *real estate broker*
†Morse, Edward J. *automotive executive*
Moss, Stephen B. *lawyer*
Olen, Milton William, Jr., *marketing executive*
Oliet, Seymour *endodontics educator, dean, dentist*
†Oltman, John Harold *patent lawyer*
Pellet, Pedro Fernando *economist, educator, consultant*
Peltzer, Douglas Lea *semiconductor device manufacturing company executive*
Phillips, Linda Darnell Elaine Fredricks *retired psychiatric and geriatrics nurse*
Randi, James (Randall James Hamilton Zwinge) *magician, writer, educator*
Ray, Raymond B. *federal judge*
Rentoumis, Ann Mastroianni *psychotherapist*
Richmond, Gail Levin *law educator*
†Rieder, Christopher Anton *music educator*
Riggs, Donald Eugene *librarian, university official*
Robb, James Arthur *pathologist*
Roselli, Richard Joseph *lawyer*
Rough, Herbert Louis *insurance company executive*
Ruback, Alan Steven *lawyer*
Rubinson, Howard Alan *physician*
†Russell, Terrence Joseph *lawyer*
Sanders, Dale R. *lawyer*
†Sanderson, Rita Marye *history educator*
Sands, Roberta Alyse *real estate investor*
Scanlon, George Patrick *transportation services executive, accountant*
Schear, Betty Z. *engineering executive, consultant*
Schneider, Laz Levkoff *lawyer*
Schreiber, Alan Hickman *lawyer*
Searcy, Leon, Jr., *football player*
Seltzer, Barry S. *federal judge*
Sherman, Richard Allen, Sr., *lawyer*
Sherry, William F. *airport executive*
Shoemaker, William Edward *financial executive*
†Siegel, Michael Alan *dental educator*
Silva, Joanne Rizzo *family nurse practitioner*
Silvagni, Anthony Joseph *dean, osteopath*
Singer, Caren Bebchuck *physician*
Skellings, Edmund *communications educator, poet*
Sklar, Alexander *electric company executive*
†Spellacy, John Frederick *lawyer*
Spungin, Charlotte Isabelle *retired secondary education educator, writer*
Stankee, Glen Allen *lawyer*
†Stinson, Steven Arthur *lawyer*
Strickland, Wilton L. *lawyer*
Sundel, Sandra Stone *social worker*
Sutton, Douglas Hoyt *nurse*
Sydnor, William Andrew *special education educator, writer*
†Tacher, Robert Frederick *lawyer*
Taylor, Ralph Orien, Jr., *real estate developer, investor*
Thayer, Charles J. *investment banker*
Thomas, John Melvin *retired surgeon*
Tobias, Benjamin Alan *portfolio manager, financial planner*
†Tolchin, Karen Rebecca *adult education educator*
†Toothaker-Walker, Stephanie Jean *lawyer*
†Trubey, Lillian Priscilla *secondary education educator, retired*
Tsai, James H. *entomologist, educator*
van der Veur, Paul W. *humanities educator*
Vasquez, William Leroy *business educator, consultant*
Vladem, Paul Jay *investment advisor, broker*
†Wand, Paul Henry *neurologist, researcher*
†Weissman, Jeffrey Mark *lawyer*
Wich, Donald Anthony, Jr., *lawyer*
Williamson, William Paul, Jr., *journalist*
Zikakis, John P. *life scientist, biochemist, nutritionist, educator*
Zimmerman, Jordan *marketing professional*
Zloch, William J. *federal judge*

Fort Myers
Adams, Todd Porter *financial and investment advisor*
Antonic, James Paul *international marketing consultant*
Arnall, Robert Esric *physician, medical administrator*
Aron, Eve Glicka Serenson *personal care industry executive*
Barbour, William Rinehart, Jr., *retired book publisher*
Beever, Lisa Britt-Dodd *transportation and environmental planner, researcher*
†Blomquist, Robert Oscar *retired insurance company executive*
Canham, Pruella Cromartie Niver *retired educator*
Clarkson, Julian Derieux *lawyer*
Colasurd, Richard Michael *lawyer*
Colgate, Doris Eleanor *sailing school owner and administrator*
Courtney, James Edmond *real estate developer*
Dalton, Anne *lawyer*
Dean, Jean Beverly *artist*
Diers, Hank H. *drama educator, playwright, director*
Dockins, George Joel *retired insurance and securities company executive*
†Eccles, David Fitzgerald *conductor, educator*
†Elliott, Elizabeth Marie *education educator*
Elliott, Luella Lee *retired women's health nurse, educator*
Finman, Sheldon Eliot *lawyer, mediator*
Frank, Elizabeth Ahls (Betsy Frank) *art educator, artist*
Frank, Mary Lou *retired elementary education educator*
Fulker, Edmund Norman *management consultant*
Gauvey, Ralph Edward *educational consultant*
Giebels, Sharon J. *human services manager*
Goyak, Elizabeth Fairbairn *retired public relations executive*
Griffin, Jerry J. *chaplain*
†Harman, Joyce Elizabeth *humanities educator*
Harrison, Simon M. *mediator, lawyer, arbitrator*
Hartman, Earl Kenneth *writer*
Herriott, Donald Richard *optical physicist*
Horecker, Bernard Leonard *retired biochemistry educator*
Housel, Natalie Rae Norman *physical therapist*
Jenkins-Owen, Sharon *land use planner*
Johnson, Sally A. *nurse, educator*
Kiernan, Edwin A., Jr., *lawyer, corporation executive*
†Kleman, Charles J. *finance company executive*
Laboda, Gerald *oral and maxillofacial surgeon*
†Mair, Bruce Logan *interior designer, company executive*
Massa, Conrad Harry *religious studies educator*
McDonough, Joseph Corbett *former army officer, aviation consultant*
Mc Queen, Robert Charles *retired insurance executive*
Medvecky, Robert Stephen *lawyer*
Mergler, Harry Winston *engineering educator*
Miner, Thelma Smith *retired American literature educator*
Missimer, Thomas Michael *geologist*
Moeschl, Stanley Francis *electrical engineer, management consultant*
†Monear, Edwin Everett *writer*
Moore, Spencer Roneal *retired business owner, accounts receivable funder*
Morse, John Harleigh *lawyer, director*
Newland, Jane Lou *nursing educator*
†Nolan, Anne Maria *nursing educator, director*
†Nugent, Timothy Scott *alcohol/drug abuse services professional*
Oligario, Max *retired accountant*
Pascotto, Robert Daniel *cardiovascular/thoracic surgeon*
Pearson, Paul Holding *insurance company executive*
Peterson, Rodney Delos *mediator, forensic economist*
Pouliot, Assunta Gallucci *retired business school owner and director, consultant*
Ranney, Mary Elizabeth *business executive*
†Renfroe, W. Douglas *musician, conductor, music educator*
Schoonover, Jack Ronald *retired judge*
Schwartz, Carl Edward *artist, printmaker*
†Scott, George Alfred *advertising executive, writer*
Scott, Kenneth Elsner *mechanical engineering educator*
Sechrist, Chalmers Franklin, Jr., *electrical engineering educator*
Shafer, Robert Tinsley, Jr., *judge*
Simmons, Vaughan Pippen *medical consultant*
Smith, Paul Frederick *economist, former educator*
†Terry, T(aylor) Rankin, Jr., *lawyer*
†Van Vleck, Pamela Kay *real estate company officer*
Vera, Enrique *psychiatrist*
Wall, Robert J. *author, researcher*
Wassersug, Stephen Robert *environmental consultant*
Weiss, Susette Maré *technical and photographic consultant, mass communications and media relations specialist, investor*
Wendeborn, Richard Donald *retired manufacturing company executive*
Williams, Suzanne *pediatric nurse practitioner*
Woodbridge, Norma Jean *registered nurse, writer*
Zeldes, Ilya M. *forensic scientist, lawyer*

Fort Myers Beach
Tatarian, Mary Linda *retailer, real estate broker*

Fort Pierce
Arnold, Donna F. *business educator*
Belcher, Dorothy S. *state correctional department administrator*
Calvert, David Victor *soil science educator*
Cassens, Susan Forget *artist*
Eastmond-Robinson, June Patricia *public health nurse*
Eisenberg, Susan Mary *retired employment representative*

†Fuchs, Eran *oceanographer, researcher*
†Harris, Martha Jane *retired librarian*
Herman, Richard J. *marine life administrator*
Hurley, William Joseph *retired information systems executive*
Locklin, Wilbert Edwin *management consultant*
Norton, Robert Howard *entertainer, musical arranger, author*
Partenheimer, Robert Chapin *emergency physician*
Peterson, Barbara Owecke *artist, nurse, realtor*
Rice, Mary Esther *biologist*
Starner, Don Edward *radiologist, educator*
Stock, Grace Emma *civic volunteer*
Thoma, Richard William *chemical safety and waste management consultant*

Fort Walton Beach
Cooke, Fred Charles *real estate broker*
Fleischer, Leslie Raymond *cardiologist*
Hill, Carol Koelling *library director*
†Lindegren, Cecile Keyser *music educator*
†Register, Annette Rowan *reading educator*
Rogers, Steven Charles *electronics technician*
Sanders, Jimmy Devon *public administration and health services educator*
†Urquhart, Troy Alexander *language educator*
Villecco, Judy Diana *substance abuse, mental health counselor, director*

Ft Myers
†O'Donnell, Bernard Joseph, Jr., *lawyer*

Gainesville
Abbaschian, Reza *materials science and engineering educator*
†Albarracín, Dolores *psychologist, educator*
Anderson, Timothy J. *chemical engineering educator*
Antonelli, Patrick Joseph *otolaryngologist, educator*
†Aranda, Juan M., Jr., *cardiologist, medical educator*
Ardelt, Monika *sociologist, educator*
†Aydede, Murat *education educator*
†Balaban, Avraham *literature educator, poet, writer*
Balabanian, Norman *electrical engineering educator*
Bandarchi-Chamkhaleh, Bizhan *pathologist*
Barber, Charles Edward *newspaper executive, journalist*
Bedell, George Chester *retired publisher, educator, priest*
Bernard, H. Russell *anthropologist, educator, scientific editor*
Berns, Kenneth Ira *physician*
Besch, Emerson Louis *physiology educator, past academic administrator*
Bihorac, Azra *research scientist*
Bilgili, Ecevit Atalay *chemical engineer, researcher*
Black, David Joseph *physician*
†Bona, Miklos *mathematician, educator*
Boothroyd, Herbert J. *insurance company executive*
†Briones, Nick Alcantara *writer*
Brodeur, Michael Stephen *dean*
†Brown, Myra Suzanne *librarian*
Brown, William Samuel, Jr., *communication sciences and disorders educator*
Brushwood, David Benson *pharmacy educator, lawyer*
Bryan, Robert Armistead *university administrator, educator*
Burridge, Michael John *veterinarian, educator, research director*
Butler, George Bergen *chemistry educator*
†Cabrera-Trujillo, Remigio *research scientist*
Caffee, H. Hollis *plastic surgery educator*
†Calin, William *literature educator*
Cance, William George *surgery educator*
Cantliffe, Daniel James *horticulture educator*
Capehart, Barney Lee *industrial and systems engineer*
Carr, Glenna Dodson *retired economics educator*
Cassisi, Nicholas John *otolaryngologist, dean*
Cenzer, Douglas Alfred *mathematician, educator*
Challoner, David Reynolds *university official, physician*
Chambers, Robert Hunter, III, *college president, American studies educator, consultant*
Cheek, Jimmy Geary *university administrator, agricultural education and communications educator*
†Chmielewski, Terese Lynn *physical therapist, educator*
Clemmons, Roger Mayeda *veterinarian, educator*
Cluff, Leighton Eggertsen *physician*
Collins, Harvey Arnold *art educator, retired*
Conrad, Joseph Henry *animal nutrition educator*
Conway, M. Margaret *political science educator, consultant*
Copeland, Edward Meadors, III, *surgery educator*
Cousins, Robert John *nutritional biochemist, educator*
Criser, Marshall M. *lawyer, retired university president*
†Cristescu, Nicolaie Dan *engineering educator*
Davis, George Kelso *nutrition biochemist, educator*
†Davis, Richard Hunt, Jr., *historian*
Delfino, Joseph John *environmental engineering sciences educator*
Der-Houssikian, Haig *linguistics educator*
DeThomasis, Craig Constantine *lawyer, educator*
Detweiler, Nancy Logan *social worker*
Dewsbury, Donald Allen *historian of psychology, comparative psychologist*
Dickinson, Joshua Clifton, Jr., *museum director, educator*
Dilcher, David Leonard *paleobotany educator, research scholar*
Dinculeanu, Nicolae *mathematician, educator*
†DiPietro, Joseph A. *dean, educator*
†Doering, Paul Louis *pharmacist, educator*
Dolan, Teresa A. *dean, educator, researcher*
Donnelly, William Henry *pathology educator*
†Donovan, Billy *university basketball coach*
Doty, Leilani *geriatric neuropsychologist, administrator*
Drummond, Willa Hendricks *physiology and medical educator*
Drury, Kenneth Clayton *biological scientist*
†Dunn, William A., Jr., *cell biologist, educator*
Emch, Gerard Gustav *mathematics and physics educator*
†Emery, Kitty Frances *curator, educator*
Fan, Z. Hugh *chemist, biomedical engineer*
Fossum, Jerry George *electrical engineering educator*
Frazer, William Johnson, Jr., *economics educator*
Freund, Gerhard *medical educator*
Gamble, Kathryn *nurse*
Gets, Lispbeth Ella *educational administrator*
†Ginway, Mary Elizabeth *language educator*
Goggin, Margaret Enid (Knox) *librarian, educator*
Gold, Mark Stephen *psychopharmacologist, physician*
†Gordon, Michael Wallace *law educator*
Gossinger, Gary Thomas *physician, psychiatrist, educator*
Green, Eleanor Myers *veterinarian, educator*
Greenberg, Samuel I. *psychiatrist, psychoanalyst*
Greer, Melvin *medical educator*
Grobman, Hulda Gross (Mrs. Arnold B. Grobman) *retired health sciences educator*
Gutekunst, Richard Ralph *microbiology educator*
Hall, David Walter *botanist, consultant*
Hanrahan, Robert Joseph *chemist, educator*
Hanson, Harold Palmer *physicist, government official, editor, academic administrator*
†Hartigan, Karelisa Dorothy *classics educator*
Heflin, Martin Ganier *foreign service officer, international political economist*
Heuer, Marvin Arthur *physician, research and industry consultant*
†Hiers, Richard Hyde *lawyer, educator, writer*
Holland, Norman Norwood *literary critic*
Hollien, Harry Francis *speech and communications scientist, educator*
Hollien, Patricia Ann *small business owner, scientist*
Holloway, Paul Howard *materials science educator*
Hornberger, Robert Howard *psychologist*
Hoy, Marjorie Ann *entomology educator*
Huszar, Arlene Celia *lawyer, mediator*
Idris, Ahamed H. *emergency medicine physician*
Isaacs, Gerald William *retired agricultural engineering educator, consultant*
Israel, Jerold Harvey *law educator*
Jaeger, Marc Julius *physiology educator, researcher*
†Jones, Clifford Alan *lawyer*
Jones, David Alwyn *geneticist, botany educator*
Jones, Elizabeth Nordwall *county government official*
Jones, Richard Lamar *entomology educator*
Kaid, Lynda Lee *communications educator*
Kaimowitz, Gabe Hillel *lawyer*
Kaplan, John *photojournalist, educator, consultant*
Katritzky, Alan Roy *chemistry educator, consultant*
Kelly, Kathleen S(ue) *communications educator*
Kersey, Talana S. *mental health counselor*
Kerslake, Kenneth Alvin *artist, printmaker, art educator*
Kurrus, Thomas William *lawyer*
Kurzweg, Ulrich Hermann *engineering science educator*
†Langstaff, Margaret J. *writer and editor*
Law, Mark Edward *electrical engineer, educator*
Leahy, Thomas Melvin, Jr., *writer*
Leavitt, David Adam *writer, English educator*
Lee, Kyu-pil *electrical engineer, researcher*
LeVeen, Robert Frederick *radiologist*
†Li, Qin-Bao *biological scientist, laboratory manager*
†Li, Sheng-San *engineering educator*
†Li, Yue Irene *education educator*
Limacher, Marian Cecile *cardiologist*
Lowenstein, Ralph Lynn *university dean emeritus*
Malasanos, Lois Julanne Fosse *nursing educator*
Maple, Marilyn Jean *educational media coordinator*
†Mareci, Thomas Harold *biophysicist, educator*
Marohn, Ann Elizabeth *health information management professional*
Maurer, Virginia Gallaher *law educator*
Mazzaferri, Ernest Louis *physician, educator*
McClellan, Richard Augustus *small business owner*
†McCoy, Francis Tyrone *law educator*
McDougal, William George *civil engineering educator*
†McMahon, Martin James, Jr., *law educator, consultant*
Mead, Frank Waldreth *taxonomic entomologist*
†Meakin, Faith Anne *medical library diector*
Micha, David Allan *chemistry and physics educator*
Milanich, Jerald Thomas *archaeologist, museum curator*
Mills, Teheran L. (Terry Mills) *sociology educator*
Mitselmakher, Guenakh *physics educator, researcher*
Modell, Jerome Herbert *anesthesiologist, educator*
Moore, John Hartwell *anthropology educator, consultant*
†Morey, Timothy E. *anesthesiologist, medical researcher*
Morgan, Anne Margaret Barclay *artist, author, psychologist*
Murray, Kate Shakeshaft *artist*
Nair, Ramachandran P.K. *agroforestry educator, researcher*
Neims, Allen Howard *university dean, medical scientist*
Newman, Robert C. *urologist, educator*
Nguyen, Ru *entomologist*
Niblack, Nancy Lee Parham *insurance agent, financial consultant, social worker*
Nicoletti, Paul Lee *retired veterinarian, educator*
Nozzi, Dom *urban planner*
Oberlander, Herbert *retired physiologist*
Ohrn, Nils Yngve *chemistry and physics educator*
Palovcik, Reinhard Anton *research neurophysiologist*
Papila, Melih *aeronautical engineer, researcher, aerospace engineer*
Parker, Karen F. *sociology educator*
Paul, Ouida Fay *music educator*
Peebles, Peyton Zimmermann, Jr., *electrical engineer, educator*
†Perrone, Charles A. *humanities educator*
Perry, Vernon G. *research scientist, educator*
Pfaff, William Wallace *medical educator*
Phillips, Winfred Marshall *dean, biomedical research executive, mechanical engineer, educator*
Poe, Gerald Dean *music educator, consultant*
Polasek, Edward John *retired electrical engineer, consultant*
Popenoe, Hugh Llywelyn *soils educator*
Price, Donald Ray *university official, agricultural engineer*
Primack, Alice Lefler *librarian*
Proctor, Samuel *history educator*
Puckett, Ruby Parker *nutritionist, hospital administrator, consultant, author*
Purcifull, Dan Elwood *plant virologist, educator*
Quesenberry, Kenneth Hays *agronomy educator*
Rakov, Vladimir A. *electrical and computer engineering educator*
Randall, Malcom *health care administrator*
Ray, Timothy Britt *social worker, lawyer, administrator*
Renner, Richard Roy *education educator, educator*
Reynolds, Richard Clyde *physician, educator*
Rhoton, Albert Loren, Jr., *neurological surgery educator*
Robertson, James Cole *consultant*
Rosenberger, Margaret Adaline *retired elementary school educator, writer*
Rosenblatt, Howard Marshall *lawyer, financial professional*
Rosenbloom, Arlan Lee *physician, educator*
†Ross, Melanie Fridl *journalist, writer*
Rubin, Melvin Lynne *ophthalmologist, educator*
Ruth, Byron Edward *civil engineering educator*
Ryerson, Gene Grove *internist*
Sabin, John Rogers *physics educator*
†Saxonhouse, Matthew Adam *pediatrician, researcher*
Schelske, Claire L. *limnologist, educator*
Schmeling, Gareth *classics educator*
Schmertmann, John Henry *civil engineer, educator, consultant*
Schmidt-Nielsen, Bodil Mimi (Mrs. Roger G. Chagnon) *physiologist, educator*
Schwartz, Michael Averill *pharmacy educator, consultant*
†Seaberg, David Charles *emergency physician, educator*
Seale, James Lawrence, Jr., *agricultural economics educator, international trade researcher*
Seeger, James M. *vascular surgeon*
Severy, Lawrence James *psychologist, educator*
Sheng, Yea-Yi Peter *oceanographic engineer, educator, researcher*
Sherif, S. A. *mechanical engineering educator*
†Sheu, Jiunn-Jye *healthcare educator, researcher*
†Shih, Chuan-kang *anthropologist*
Shyy, Wei *aerospace and mechanical engineering researcher, educator*
Siegel, Robert James *communications executive*
†Sigmund, Wolfgang M. *materials scientist, educator*
Silas, Nancy *small business owner*
Singley, John Edward, Jr., *retired environmental scientist, consultant*
Sisler, Harry Hall *chemist, educator*
Small, Natalie Settimelli *pediatric mental health counselor*
Small, Parker Adams, Jr., *pediatrician, educator*
Smith, David Thornton *lawyer, educator*
Smith, Jo Anne *writer, retired educator*
Sommerville, Charles John *humanities educator*
Stansbury, James Patrick *anthropologist, researcher*
Stavrev, Krassimir K. *chemist, researcher*
Steele, Jere Randall *elementary school educator*
Stehli, Francis Greenough *geologist, educator*
Stern, William Louis *botanist, educator*
†Stipek, Kathleen *reference librarian*
Sugarman, Bahira *clinical social worker*
Suzuki, Howard Kazuro *retired anatomist, educator*
†Taylor, Grace Elizabeth Woodall (Betty Taylor) *law educator, law library administrator*
Taylor, James Daniel *consulting engineer*
Teitelbaum, Philip *psychologist*
Teixeira, Arthur Alves *food engineer, educator, consultant*
Thiele, Leslie Paul *political science educator*
Thompson, Neal Philip *food science and nutrition educator*
Tia, Mang *civil engineering educator*
Tomar, Scott Lance *dentist*
Trickey, Samuel Baldwin *physics educator, researcher, university administrator*
†Tsao, Jennie Ching-I *research scientist, educator*
Tulenko, James Stanley *nuclear engineer, educator*
Uthman, Basim Mohammad *neurologist, epileptologist, consultant*
Van Alstyne, W. Scott, Jr., *lawyer, educator*
Varnes, Jill Tutton *university official, health educator*
Verink, Ellis Daniel, Jr., *metallurgical engineering educator, consultant*
Victorica, Benjamin Eduardo *pediatrician, educator*
Vierck, Charles John, Jr., *neuroscience educator, scientist*
Viessman, Warren, Jr., *civil engineering educator emeritus, researcher*
von Mering, Otto Oswald *anthropology educator*
Wagner, Eric Armin *sociology educator*
Wass, Hannelore Lina *educational psychology educator*
Watson, Robert Joe *hospital administrator, retired career officer*
Weinrich, Brian Erwin *mathematician, computer scientist*
Westphal, Roger Allen *electrical engineer*
Weyrauch, Walter Otto *law educator*
White, Jill Carolyn *lawyer*
White, Susie Mae *school psychologist*
Widmer, Charles Glenn *dentist, researcher*
Wilcox, Charles Julian *geneticist, educator*
Willocks, Robert Max *retired librarian*
Willumson, Glenn Gardner *curator, art historian*
Wise, William R. *engineering educator*
Wyatt-Brown, Anne Marbury *linguistics educator*
Wyatt-Brown, Bertram *historian, educator*
†Yamamoto, Janet Kazuko *science educator*
Yarmola, Elena Georgiyevna *research scientist*
York, E. Travis *academic administrator, former university chancellor, consultant*
York, Vermelle Cardwell *real estate broker and developer*
Yost, Richard Alan *chemistry educator*
Young, Charles Edward *academic administrator*
Zapletal, Jindrich *mathematician*
†Zlotecki, Robert Alan *education educator*

Gonzalez
Plischke, Le Moyne Wilfred *research chemist*

Goulds
Cooper, Kenneth Stanley *principal, educator, finance company executive*

Graceville
Cox, Buford E. *music educator*
Kinchen, Thomas Alexander *college president*
Tilbe, Linda MacLauchlan *nursing administrator*

Grand Island
Johnson, Tesla Francis *data processing executive, educator*

Grassy Key
Mankowitz, Barry Joel *surgeon*

Green Cove Springs
Dasher, Bonita Ann *accountant*
Davidson, Joy Elaine *mezzo-soprano*

Greenacres
Goldfarb, Arthur A. *allergist and immunologist, educator*

Gulf Breeze
Burr, Timothy Fuller *lawyer*
Couch, John Alexander, Sr., *biomedical researcher*
DeBardeleben, John Thomas, Jr., *retired insurance company executive*
French, Jere Stuart *landscape architect*
Jester, William David *lawyer*
Menzer, Robert Everett *toxicologist, educator*
Pettyjohn, Frank Schmermund *cardiology and emergency medicine educator*
Rainwater, Freddie Barrett *volunteer worker*
Walker, Peggy Jean *retired social work agency administrator*

Gulf Stream
Nalen, Craig Anthony *government official*

Gulfport
Allen, John Thomas, Jr., *lawyer*
Bourke, Thomas Anthony *librarian, writer*
Davis, Ann Caldwell *history educator*
Smith, Catherine Louise *library administrator, consultant*

Haines City
Clement, Robert William *retired air force officer*
Kirk, Sherwood *librarian*
†Mc Dougall, Dugald Stewart *retired lawyer*

Hallandale
Glaubinger, Lawrence David *retired manufacturing company executive*
†Rose, Lucille Marie *retired writer*
Schatken, Nancy Leah *medical editor*
Sielczak, Marek Wlodzimierz *pathologist, researcher*
†Vaserstein, Ludmila *music educator*
Yigit, Nuyan *journalist*

Heathrow
Darbelnet, Robert Louis *automobile association executive*

Hernando
Park, Chung Il *retired librarian*
Saxe, Thelma Richards *secondary school educator, consultant*

Hialeah
Agrawal, Piyush C. *school system administrator*
Economides, Christopher George *pathologist*
Engler, Eva Kay *dental and veterinary products company executive*
Gil de Gibaja, Susana *artist, small business owner*
Grahm, Charles Morton *retired sales executive*
†Hernandez, Roland *broadcast executive*
Koreman, Dorothy Goldstein *physician, dermatologist*
†Palacios, Olga *director*

Perez, Leyanee C. *nutritionist, consultant*
Phelps, Dorothy Frink *civic worker*
Shaw, Steven John *retired marketing educator, academic administrator*

Hialeah Gardens
Tuninskaya, Galina M. *chemist, consultant*

Highland Beach
Frager, Albert S. *retired retail food company executive*
Haight, Carol Barbara *lawyer*
Lane, James McConkey *retired investment executive*
Schor, Stanley Sidney *mathematical sciences educator*
Settler, Eugene Brian *record company executive*
Tolf, Robert Walter *writer*
Zagoria, Sam D(avid) *reporter, government official, educator*

Hillsboro Beach
Donoho, Tim Mark *charity founder and executive, entrepreneur*
Gibbons, Celia Victoria Townsend (Mrs. John Sheldon) *editor, publisher*
Marshall, Jo Taylor *social worker*
McGarry, Carmen Racine *historian, artist*

Hobe Sound
Buetens, Eric D. *lawyer*
Casey, Edward Paul *manufacturing company executive*
Craig, David Jeoffrey *retired manufacturing company executive*
Gold, Kenneth R. *computer software consulting executive*
Hand, Peter James *neurobiologist, educator*
Houser, Jim (James Cowing Houser Jr., Jim Houser) *painter, art educator*
Markoe, Frank, Jr., *lawyer, business and hospital executive*
Matheson, William Lyon *lawyer*
Parker, H. Lawrence *investor, rancher, retired investment banker*
†Pierpoint, Paula Jean *music educator*

Holiday
Swatos, William Henry, Jr., *priest, sociologist*

Holly Hill
Perman, Carrie Lee *artist, educator*

Hollywood
†Alfano, Jorge *music company executive, counselor*
Angstrom, Wayne Raymond *communications executive*
Blakley, John Clyde *telecommunications consultant*
Border, Gladys Louise *piano educator*
Budnik, Patricia McNulty *retired elementary education educator*
Burton, John Jacob *retired real estate company executive appraiser*
Colbert, Dia Teresa *legal assistant*
Cowan, Irving *real estate owner, developer*
Duffner, Lee R. *ophthalmologist*
Engel, Tala *lawyer*
Fell, Frederick Victor *publisher*
Foreman, Edwin Francis *economist, real estate broker*
Giulianti, Mara Selena *mayor, civic worker*
†Harkin, Daniel John *controller*
Harringer, Olaf Carl *architect, museum consultant*
Hochberg, Victor I. *retired neurologist*
†Hollander, Bruce Lee *lawyer, business executive*
†Kelly, Cleo Parker *retired bank executive*
King, Alma Jean *former health and physical education educator*
Korthals, Candace Durbin *lawyer*
Krane, Jessica (Aida Jessica Kohnop-Krane) *writer, educator*
Ladin, Eugene *communications company executive*
†Martinez, Carlos *insurance adjuster, company manager*
Matasa, Claude George *researcher, science administrator, educator*
Mendelson, Laurans Adam *accountant*
Novak, Stephen Bruce *endocrinologist*
†Phillips, Gary Stephen *lawyer*
†Rogovin, Lawrence H. *lawyer*
†Rosenthal, Phyllis Karen *toxicologist, clinical chemist*
Sadowski, Carol Johnson *artist*
Schonfeld, Wayne Brent *gastroenterologist*
Shane, Doris Jean *respiratory therapist, administrator*
Sim, Robert Wilson *accountant*
Sundel, Martin *psychologist, educator, management consultant*
Vaicys, Ceslovas *neurosurgeon*
Valdes, Jacqueline Chehebar *psychologist, consultant, researcher*
Waganheim, Arthur Brian *marketing executive*
Zebersky, Edward Herbert *lawyer*

Holmes Beach
Anderson, Herbert G. *marine biologist, researcher*
Dunne, James Robert *academic administrator, management consultant, business educator*
Dunne, Nancy Anne *retired social services administrator*
Evanofski, Bernard Peter *Roman Catholic priest*
McCartney, James Harold *newspaper columnist, educator, journalist*

Homestead
Davis, Scott Michael *director, music educator*
Dong, Quan *ecologist, educator*
Horton, Thelma White *educational administrator, author*
Roberts, Larry Spurgeon *biological sciences educator, zoologist*

Willner, Eugene Burton *food and liquor company executive*

Homosassa
Carmichael, Roberta Kay *writer*

Homosassa Springs
Burch, Annetta Jane *writer*

Hudson
Hirschauer, David R. *physician*

Hutchinson Island
Wanzer, Mary Kathryn *computer company executive, consultant*
Wegman, Harold Hugh *management consultant*

Hypoluxo
Ferguson, Paula Irene *nursing administrator*

Indialantic
Krasny, Charlotte Althea *volunteer*
MacDonald, Stephen Hugh *physician, reserve naval officer*
MacNeill, John Harmon *mechanical engineer*
Rose, Peter Edward *former professional baseball player and manager*
†Rosenberg, Priscilla Elliott *lawyer*

Indian Harbor Beach
Tasker, Molly Jean *lawyer*
Traylor, Angelika *stained glass artist*

Indian Harbour Beach
†Rains, Baxter Smith *sculptor, consultant*

Indian River Shores
Ahrens, William Henry *architect*
Wiegner, Edward Alex *multi-industry executive*

Indian Rocks Beach
DeLucia, Gene Anthony *government administrator, computer company executive*
Sullivan, Paul William *communications specialist*

Inverness
Dowdell, Michael Francis *critical care nurse, forensic and anesthesia nurse practitioner*
Esquibel, Edward V. *psychiatrist, clinical medical program developer*
†Hawk, Pauletta Browning *student elementary school educator*
Mavros, George S. *clinical laboratory director*
Robinson, Charlene G. *mental health nurse, educator*

Jacksonville
†Achem, Sami Rene *internist, medical educator*
Adams, Scott Leslie *accountant*
Akers, James Eric *health facility administrator*
Aleschus, Justine Lawrence *retired real estate broker*
Alexander, Edna M. DeVeaux *elementary education educator*
Allen, Ronald Wesley *financial executive*
Arbogast, Gordon Wade *systems engineer, educator, consultant , retired military officer*
Ball, Haywood Moreland *lawyer*
Barrow, Sally Settle *media specialist, librarian*
Beattie, Donald A. *energy scientist, consultant*
Beytagh, Francis Xavier, Jr., *law educator*
Black, Susan Harrell *judge*
Bodkin, Lawrence Edward *research development company executive, gemologist, inventor, writer*
Bodkin, Ruby Pate *corporate executive, real estate broker, educator*
†Bosworth, William Posey *physician, physical education educator*
Boyer, Tyrie Alvis *lawyer*
Braddock, Donald Layton *lawyer, accountant, real estate broker, investor*
Bradford, Dana Gibson, II, *lawyer*
Brady, James Joseph *economics educator*
Brady, Kyle James *football player*
Bridgman, Mary Wood *lawyer*
Brown, Lloyd Harcourt, Jr., *newspaper editor*
Brunell, Mark Allen *professional football player*
Bryan, Joseph Shepard, Jr., *lawyer*
Bullock, Bruce Stanley *lawyer*
Burnett, Mary Parham *lawyer, airline captain*
Callender, John Francis *lawyer*
Camacho, George *internist*
Cangemi, John Richard *physician*
Carlson, Raymond Howard *retired military officer, prosecutor*
Carver, Joan Sacknitz *academic administrator*
Chalam, Kakarla Venkata *physician, educator*
Chambers, Jack Allen *educator*
Cherry, Barbara Waterman *speech and language pathologist, physical therapist*
Christian, Gary Irvin *lawyer*
†Claborn, David Merrell *entomologist*
Clark, Mark David *public relations consultant*
Clarkson, Charles Andrew *real estate investment executive*
Clifton, Rachel Letter *music educator, performing arts educator*
†Coffman, Daniel Ray, Jr., *lawyer*
Coker, Howard Coleman *lawyer*
Cole, Linda Sue *grant program planner, computer software professional*
Commander, Charles Edward *lawyer, real estate consultant*
Constantini, JoAnn M. *small business owner, consultant*
Cooke, Alexander Hamilton *lawyer*
Copley, William McKinley, III, *counselor, counseling administrator, consultant*
†Cornelius, Jacquelyn H. *high school principal, educator*
Corse, John Doggett *university official, lawyer*
Costin, Rea-Silvia *civil engineer*
Courtwright, David Todd *history educator, author*
Cramer, Jeffrey Allen *lawyer*
Crawford, Maria Lynn *technical support analyst*

†Davis, A. Dano *grocery store chain executive*
Davis, Fred *journalist, educator*
†Deen, Hugh Gordon *physician, neurological surgeon*
Delaney, John Adrian *mayor*
Delaney, Kevin Francis *retired naval officer, consulting firm executive*
†Del Rio, Jack *professional football coach, former professional football player*
†DeOrio, James Keith *orthopedic surgeon*
†Dumbleton, Duane Dean *college president, educator*
Dundon, Margo Elaine *museum director*
Earle, J.D. *physician*
Eden, F. Brown *artist*
Edwards, Marvin Raymond *investment counselor, economic consultant*
Ejimofor, Cornelius Ogu *political scientist, educator*
Enns, John Benjamin *polymer scientist*
Fahner, Harold Thomas *marketing executive*
Farkas, Andrew *library director emeritus, educator, writer*
Farmer, Guy Otto, II, *lawyer*
Feinglass, Neil Gordon *anesthesiologist*
†Fine, Cory R. *education educator, consultant*
Francis, James Delbert *oil company executive*
Fulton-Quindoza, Debra Ann *nurse practitioner*
Gabel, George DeSaussure, Jr., *lawyer*
†Gaston, Joseph *minister, educator*
Glocker, Theodore William *lawyer, accountant*
†Glover, Gene Alan *banking risk analyst*
†Glover, Nathaniel, Jr., *sheriff*
†Godfrey, John Munro *economic consultant*
Gonwa, Thomas Arthur *nephrologist, transplant physician, educator*
†Greene, Barry *music educator, writer*
Grogan, Michael Kevin *lawyer, negotiator*
†Grundig, John Patrick *director*
Hair, Mattox S. *mediator, arbitrator, former judge, lawyer*
†Haley, Donald Robert *health facility administrator*
Halverson, Steven Thomas *lawyer, construction executive*
Hamilton, Susan Owens *transportation company executive, lawyer*
Hartmann, Frederick William *newspaper editor*
Hecht, Frederick *physician, researcher, writer, educator, consultant*
Hill, James Clinkscales *federal judge*
Hodge, James Edward *lawyer*
Holliday, Patricia Ruth McKenzie *evangelist*
Hollon, John O(aks) *lawyer*
Houser, John Edward *lawyer*
†Huber, Mary Susan *music educator*
Jackson, Julian Ellis *food company executive*
Jamrich, John Xavier *retired university administrator*
Johnson, Douglas William *physician, radiation oncologist*
Jones, Herman Otto, Jr., *corporate professional*
Joyce, Edward Rowen *retired chemical engineer, educator*
†Kaunitz, Karen Rose Koppel *retired lawyer*
Kelalis, Panayotis *pediatric urologist*
†Kelso, Linda Yayoi *lawyer*
Kent, John Bradford *lawyer*
Kilbourne, Krystal Hewett *retired rail transportation executive*
Kimmich, Haydee Javier *orthopedist, consultant*
Kinne, Frances Bartlett *chancellor emeritus*
Koeppel, Mary Sue *communications educator*
Korn, Michael Jeffrey *lawyer*
Krueger, Ross T. *gastroenterologist*
Lane, Edward Wood, Jr., *retired banker*
Langford, Cecilia Motes *nurse educator*
†Lazaran, Frank *retail executive*
Lee, Lewis Swift *lawyer*
Legler, Mitchell Wooten *lawyer*
Leonard, Thomas Michael *university program director, educator*
Lestage, Daniel Barfield *retired naval officer, physician*
Lewis, Richard Harlow *urologist*
Libby, Ronald Theodore *political science educator, consultant, researcher*
Link, Robert James *lawyer, educator*
Longino, Theresa Childers *nurse*
Loucks, Terry Lee *writer, retired biosystems executive*
Lovett, Radford Dow *marine terminal real estate and investment company executive*
†Lurie, Jay Scott *Internet company executive*
Lyon, Wilford Charles, Jr., *insurance executive*
Mahaffy, Telfair *safety scientist*
Maier, William Ernst, Jr., *railroad executive*
Main, Edna Dewey (June Main) *education educator*
Margileth, Andrew Menges *physician, former naval officer*
Maxwell, W(ilbur) Richard *retired management consultant*
McBurney, Charles Walker, Jr., *lawyer*
McWilliams, John Lawrence, III, *lawyer*
Melton, Howell Webster, Sr., *federal judge*
Milbrath, Robert Henry *retired petroleum executive*
Mizrahi, Edward Alan *allergist*
Monsky, John Bertrand *investment banking executive*
Morgan, William Newton *architect, educator*
Moseley, James Francis *lawyer*
Moses, Daniel *writer, singer*
Motsett, Charles Bourke *sales, marketing and leadership executive*
†Mueller, Cherone *religious organization administrator, writer, minister*
Mueller, Edward Albert *retired transportation engineer executive*
Narayan, Vaduvur Srinivasan *preventive medicine physician*
Nuss, Robert Conrad *oncologist*
†Nutter, Wallace Lee *paper manufacturing executive*
Oldenburg, Warner Andrew *vascular surgeon*
O'Neal, Michael Scott, Sr., *lawyer*

Osborn, Marvin Griffing, Jr., *educational consultant*
Owusu, Akua *psychiatrist*
Paryani, Shyam Bhojraj *radiologist*
Pavlick, Pamela Kay *nurse, consultant*
Pearce, Jennifer Sue *real estate appraiser*
Pillans, Charles Palmer, III, *lawyer*
Posgay, Matthew Nichols *lawyer*
Rader, David *insurance company executive*
†Raynor, Eileen Margolies *otolaryngologist, educator*
Reagan, James Raymond *safety and ergonomics consultant*
Reed, Ronald Ernst *lawyer*
Rhatigan, Ronald Merlin *pathologist*
Rinaman, James Curtis, Jr., *lawyer*
Rinehart, Harry Elmer *retired sales executive*
Robinson, Christine Marie *mathematics educator*
Rowland, Allen R. *grocery company executive*
Rubens, Linda Marcia *home health services administrator*
Rumpel, Peter Loyd *architect, educator, artist*
†Rumrell, Richard Gary *lawyer*
Russell, David Emerson *mechanical engineer, consultant*
†Safford, Robert Eugene *cardiologist, health facility administrator, educator*
Sandercox, Robert Allen *college official, clergyman*
Sanders, Marion Yvonne *retired geriatrics nurse*
Scarborough, Marion Nichols *nutritionist, recreational facility executive*
Schlageter, Robert William *museum administrator*
Schlesinger, Harvey Erwin *judge*
Schramm, Bernard Charles, Jr., *retired advertising agency executive*
Schultz, Frederick Henry *investor, former government official*
Schultz, Nancy Reilly *artist*
†Schupp, Robert Warren *law educator*
Sederbaum, William *marketing executive*
Shoup, James Raymond *computer systems consultant*
†Simms, Jacqueline Kamp *secondary education educator*
Smallridge, Robert Christian *endocrinologist*
Smith, David A. *medical services executive*
Smith, Jimmy, Jr., *football player*
†Smith, Stephen Mark *special education educator, music educator*
Stanley, Helen Camille *composer, musician*
Stanton, Robert John, Jr., *English language educator*
Stephenson, Samuel Edward, Jr., *retired physician*
Sterman, Gail K. Mendelson *public relations specialist*
Stern, Steven Alan *sports development owner*
Stewart, Sandra Kay *music educator*
Surrency, Gary Lawrence *military officer, counselor, writer*
Swartz, Stephen Arthur *corporate financial executive*
Talbot, Peter Jennings *financial services executive*
Taylor, Fred *professional football player*
†Taylor, Gavin Hall *music educator*
Taylor, Robert M. *minister*
Thomas, Archibald Johns, III, *lawyer*
Thorsteinsson, Gudni *physiatrist*
Thrasher, John *lawyer, former state legislator*
Threlkel, Robert Hays *pediatrician*
Tjoflat, Gerald Bard *federal judge*
Tolford, Frank Stefan *bookstore executive*
Tomlinson, William Holmes *management educator, retired army officer*
Tucker, N(imrod) H(olt), III, *physician*
Urbina, Susana Patricia *psychology educator, consultant*
†Vadnal, John Louis *dean, mathematician, educator*
Van Cleve, Robert Baldwin *cardiologist*
Vane, Terence G., Jr., *finance company executive, lawyer*
Vincent, Norman Fuller *broadcasting executive*
Wallis, Donald Wills *lawyer*
Walters, John Sherwood *retired newspaperman*
†Ward, Michael J. *rail transportation executive*
Welch, Philip Burland *electronics and office products company executive*
Wharen, Robert Ellsworth, Jr., *neurosurgeon, educator*
White, Edward Alfred *lawyer*
Wiles, Jon W(hitney) *education educator, consultant*
Yamane, Stanley Joel *optometrist, consultant*
Younkin, Steven G. *neuroscientist*
Zbiegien, M. Andrea *chaplain, religious education educator, consultant, educational administrator*

Jacksonville Beach
Hearle, Edward F.R. *retired management consultant*
Mahorner, James M. *engineer*
Morris, Max King *foundation executive, former naval officer*
Saltzman, Irene Cameron *consumer products company executive*

Jasper
McCormick, John Hoyle *lawyer*

Jensen Beach
Blettner, James Donald *engineering company executive*
Gamble, Raymond Wesley *marriage and family therapist, clergyman*
Gruppe, Charles Camille *artist*
†Lowrie, Jean Elizabeth *librarian, educator*
McHale, Michael John *lawyer*
Peterson, David Frederick *government agency executive*
Stuart, Harold Cutliff *lawyer, business executive*
†Zuber, Shantung E., III, *physician, pastor*

Juno Beach
†Broadhead, James Lowell *electrical power industry executive*
Clark, David William *lawyer, councilman*
Holmes, Melvin Almont *insurance company executive*
Mathavan, Sudershan Kumar *nuclear power engineer*
McCloud, Paul Duane *chemical engineer*
Migliaro, Marco William *electrical engineer*
Penn, Sherry Eve *communication psychologist, educator*

Jupiter
Callahan, Edward William *chemical engineer, retired manufacturing executive*
Colucci, Jacqueline Strupp *interpreter, small business administration specialist, sculptor*
De George, Lawrence Joseph *diversified company executive*
del Russo, Alessandra Luini *retired law educator*
Elwell, Howard Andrew *safety engineer*
Feinberg, Herbert *apparel and beverage executive*
Garfinkel, Harmon Mark *retired specialty chemicals company executive*
Gerson, Irwin Conrad *advertising executive*
Jacobson, Jerry Irving *biophysicist, theoretical physicist*
Kulok, William Allan *entrepreneur, venture capitalist*
Malm, Rita H. *securities executive*
McGee, Lynne Kalavsky *principal*
Moseley, Karen Frances Flanigan *educational consultant, retired school system administrator, educator*
Mutters, David Ray *real estate broker*
Nessmith, H(erbert) Alva *dentist*
Small, Melvin D. *physician, educator*
Sproull, Robert Lamb *retired university president, physicist*
Wolff, Edward Alvin *electronics engineer*
†Wrist, Peter Ellis *retired pulp and paper company executive*
Yinh, Victor Marius *electrical engineer*

Kennedy Space Center
Banks, Lisa Jean *government official*
Darwood, John Joseph *physician*
Feldman, Stephen *academic administrator*
Myers, Kenneth Jeffrey *physician*

Key Biscayne
Aleniewski, Monica Irene *retired anesthesiologist*
Duffy, Earl Gavin *hotel executive*
Evans, Peter Kenneth *advertising executive*
Grey, Jerry *science educator*
Landis, Carolyn Press *corporate executive*
Palmer, Roger Farley *pharmacology educator*
†Pearson, John Edward *lawyer*
Ross, Marilyn J. *English and communications educator*
Smith, Harrison Harvey *journalism consultant*
Wilson, Robert Gordon *investment banker*
Zayas-Bazan, Eduardo *foreign language educator*

Key Colony Beach
Crenshaw, Patricia Shryack *sales executive, consultant*

Key Largo
Chevins, Anthony Charles *retired advertising agency executive*
Daenzer, Bernard John *insurance company executive, legal consultant*
Davidson, Thomas Noel *business executive*
Fundora, Thomas *artist, journalist, composer*
Kennedy, Mary Sussock *artist*
Mattson, James Stewart *lawyer, environmental scientist, educator*
Stern, Joanne Thrasher *elementary school educator*

Key West
†Braddock, Stephen E. *not-for-profit executive, priest*
Brihammar, B. Niklas *lawyer*
Burns, William Joseph *audiologist, speech-language pathologist*
Davila, Gregory David *lawyer*
Eden, Nathan E. *lawyer*
Elwood, William Norelli *medical educator*
Evans, John Derby *telecommunications company executive*
Haskell, Monica M. *art association administrator*
†Lawrence, Judith M. *writer, journalist*
MacDougall, Peter *lawyer*
McIntosh, Jon Charles *illustrator, graphic designer*
Mitchell, John Dietrich *theatre arts institute executive*
Murphy, S(usan) (Jane Murphy) *small business owner*
Smith, Wayne LaRue *lawyer, consultant*
†Taylor, Victoria *sculptor*
Trammell, Herbert Eugene *physicist, laboratory executive*

Keystone Heights
Ohanian, Mihran Jacob *nuclear engineering educator, research dean*

Kissimmee
Dean, James Wendell *military officer, nurse*
Evans-O'Connor, Norma Lee *secondary education educator, consultant*
Haynes, Ulric St. Clair, Jr., *dean*
Jablon, Elaine *education consultant*
Rajyaguru, Vrajlal Laljibhai *anesthesiologist*
Rattie, Margaret Elizabeth (Beth Rattie) *educator*
†Severance, Jeri-Lynne White *elementary school educator*
Toothe, Karen Lee *elementary and secondary school educator*

Lady Lake
Akins, Zane Vernon *association executive*
Dore, Stephen Edward, Jr., *retired civil engineer*
Granger, Robert Alan *mechanical and aerospace engineering educator*
Hartzler, Genevieve Lucille *physical education educator*
Langevin, Thomas Harvey *higher education consultant*
Rossbacher, John Robert *retired insurance broker, musician, writer*
Sligh, Gary Lee *English educator*

Lake Alfred
Kender, Walter John *horticulturist, educator*

Lake Buena Vista
Schmudde, Lee Gene *corporate lawyer*
†Sereno, Keala *musician*

Lake City
Freeby, Stephen John, Jr., *music educator*
†Montgomery, June C. *musician, composer*
Moore, Emma Sims *finance educator*
†Poplin, William L., Jr., *retired music educator*

Lake Forest
Ross, Jimmy Douglas *retired military officer*

Lake Helen
Finn, Stephen Martin *producer*

Lake Mary
Aparicio, Julio L. *systems analyst*
Bachmann, Bill *photographer*
†Reagan, Bettye Jean *artist*
Southward, Patricia C. *volunteer*

Lake Park
Portera, Alan A. *parochial school educator*

Lake Placid
Bohlen, Patrick Joseph *ecologist, researcher*
Rew, William Edmund *civil engineer*
Roberts, William B. *lawyer, business executive*

Lake Suzy
Ogan, Russell Griffith *business executive, retired air force officer*

Lake Wales
Adams, Paul Winfrey *lawyer, business executive*
Luing, Gary Alan *financial management educator*
Wales, Gwynne Huntington *retired lawyer*

Lake Worth
Asher, Kathleen May *communications educator*
Bell, Melvin *management consultant*
Cohen, Edward *civil engineer*
Goldstein, Jerome Charles *professional association executive, surgeon, otolaryngologist*
Gorman, Marcie Sothern *personal care industry franchise executive*
Gough, Carolyn Harley *library director*
Heessel, Eleanor Lucille Lea *retired state agency administrator*
Kieval, Joshua *cardiologist, educator*
Kreidler, Frank Allan *lawyer*
Levow, Judith L(ee) Holtz (Judi Levow) *interior designer*
Melvin, Pamela Lee *artist*
Rose, Norman *retired lawyer, retired accountant*
Saffir, Leonard *public relations executive*
Shepherd, Charles Clinton *real estate executive*
Stone, Ross Gluck *orthopedic surgeon*
Taylor, Clifford Otis *retired principal*
†Volkman, Barry M. *conductor, music educator*
Wilson, William J. *English language educator*
†Zeltzer, Jack *vascular surgeon*

Lakeland
Arndt, Melvin C. *writer*
Balish, Ruth Reitz *retired community health nurse*
Barber, Gerard Reno *pharmacist, writer*
Glotfelty, John William *ophthalmologist*
Harris, Christy Franklin *lawyer*
Hatten, William Seward *manufacturing company executive*
†Herron, Robert Wilburn, Jr., *academic administrator, educator*
Hixon, Andrea Kaye *healthcare quality specialist*
Jackson, Elijah, Jr., *communication executive*
†Jenkins, Charles H., Jr., *retail company executive*
Jenkins, Howard M. *supermarket executive*
Jennings, Ralph Henry, Jr., *physician*
Kittleson, Henry Marshall *lawyer*
Knowlton, Kevin Charles *lawyer*
Koren, Edward Franz *lawyer*
Luther, George Albert *truck brokerage executive*
†Manners, Malcolm M. *horticulturist, educator*
McFarlin, Richard Francis *retired industrial chemist, researcher*
Meads, Walter Frederick *communications executive, consultant*
Moffitt, Tony Lee *family practice nurse practitioner*
Mooney, Burton Lee *secondary school educator, editor*
Perez, Louis Michael *newspaper editor*
†Pranno, Arthur James *music educator*
Prince, Don David *automotive technician*
Ratliff, Charles Edward, Jr., *economics educator*
Reich, David Lee *library director*
†Rogers, James Gordon, Jr., *art educator*
Siedle, Robert Douglas *management consultant*
Sklenicka, Russell Charles *orthopaedic surgeon*
†Solberg, Daniel Arnold *language educator*
Spencer, Mary Miller *civic worker*
Spoto, Angelo Peter, Jr., *internist, allergist*
Stark, Bruce Gunsten *artist*
Tate, Robert Hale *academic administrator*
Tripi, Vincent James *physician*
Wade, Ben Frank *college administrator*
Waugaman, Richard William *sales executive*
†Wendel, John Fredric *lawyer, professional sports consultant*
Willoughby, Robert Earl *minister, writer*
Zucco, Ronda Kay *planning and marketing professional*

Lantana
Weeks, Charles, Jr., *real estate executive, retired publishing company executive*

Largo
Camara, Vincent Antonin Reginald *mathematician, educator, statistician, researcher*
Chambers, Ray Wayne *security and loss control consultant*
Christ, Earle L. *lawyer*
Dolan, John E. *consultant, retired utility executive*
Ellis, Susan Gottenberg *psychologist*
†Fedor, Allan John *lawyer*
†Gould, Glenn Hunting *marketing professional, consultant*
Grove, Jeffrey Scott *family practice physician*
†Hafling, Marilyn Elizabeth *lawyer*
Hamlin, Robert Henry *public health educator, management consultant*
Haumschild, Mark James *pharmacist*
†Klutho, Mark Paul *landscape architect, educator*
Loader, Jay Gordon *retired utility company executive*
Manty, Brian Alan *high technology company executive*
Meredith, Bradford L. *musician, educator*
Nixon, Wayne Robert *engineering manager*
Ray, Roger Buchanan *retired communications executive, lawyer*
Shillinglaw, Gordon *accounting educator, consultant*
Simmons, Deborah Jo *pharmacy executive*
Szep, Paul Michael *editorial cartoonist*
Trevena, John Harry *lawyer*
Wheat, Myron William, Jr., *cardiothoracic surgeon*

Lauderdale By The Sea
†Kennedy, Beverly (Kleban) Burris *financial advisor, tv and radio talk show host*
Wynne, Brian James *former association executive, consultant*

Lauderhill
†Swisher, Charles Francis *electrical engineer, consultant*

Lecanto
Corsi, Philip Donald *lawyer*
Dixon, Charles Sim *urban planner*
Fischer, Theodore David *retired lawyer*
Mathia, Mary Loyola *parochial school educator, nun*
Max, Buddy (Boris Max Pastuch) *musician*
Mchedlishvili, Gela *physician*

Leesburg
Austin, Robert Eugene, Jr., *lawyer*
Fechtel, Vincent John *legal administrator*
Talley, William Giles, Jr., *manufacturing company executive*
Thompson, Mary B. *writer, illustrator*
Twiss, Wanda May *interior designer*
†Whalen, Norma Jean *special education educator*

Lighthouse Point
Farho, James Henry, Jr., *mechanical engineer, consultant*
Friedrichs, Arthur Martin *manufacturing company executive, retired*
Gauthier, Doreen Ann *librarian*
Shein, Jay Lesing *financial planner*

Live Oak
Peters, Lee Ira, Jr., *public defender*

Longboat Key
Albee, George Wilson *psychology educator*
Dorsey, Eugene Carroll *former foundation and communications executive*
Freeman, Richard Merrell *lawyer, corporate director*
Gilbert, Hamlin Miller, Jr., *publishing executive*
Goldsmith, Jack Landman *former retail company executive*
Hazan, Marcella Maddalena *writer, educator, consultant*
Holcomb, Constance L. *sales and marketing management executive*
Jeglie, Jill A. *urban planner*
Levitt, Irving Francis *investment company executive*
Molles, Emily DeMartino *artist, real estate broker*
Morse, Marvin Henry *retired judge*
Stapleton, Harvey James *physics educator*
Van Dyke-Cooper, Anny Marion *retired financial company executive*
†Winfree, Charles Van *management consultant*
Workman, George Henry *structural engineering consultant*

Longwood
Andrews, Diane Randall *nursing administrator, critical care nurse*
†Bernabei, Raymond *management consultant*
Brown, Barbara Jean *special and secondary education educator*
Brown, Donald James, Jr., *insurance company executive*
Chernak, Jerald Lee *television executive*
Cirello, John *utility and engineering company executive*
Cordes, Alexander Charles *lawyer*
Dalles, John Allan *minister*
Faller, Donald E. *marketing and operations executive*
Gasperoni, Ellen Jean Lias *interior designer*
Gasperoni, Emil, Sr., *realtor, developer*
Goddard, Edward Dean *stockbroker, accountant*
†Johnson, Nancy Plattner *secondary education educator*
Laven, David Lawrence *nuclear and radiologic pharmacist, consultant*
Manjura, Bonnie Doreen *marketing professional, advertising executive, educator*
McIntosh, John Osborn *engineering consultant*
O'Keefe, Maurice Timothy *editor, author, photographer, educator*
Smyth, Joseph Patrick *retired naval officer, physician*
Tomasulo, Virginia Merrills *retired lawyer*
Walters, Philip Raymond *foundation executive*

Loxahatchee
Foucauld, Jean *cardiologist*

Lutz
Bedke, Ernest Alford *retired air force officer*
Corbitt, Doris Orene *retired real estate agent, dietician*
†Cualing, Hernani Del Mundo *physician, researcher*
Fritzsche, R(obert) Wayne *corporate executive*
Hayes, Timothy George *lawyer, consultant*
Koff, Fred William *retired research chemist*
Kolb, Richard Maurice *sports writer, sportscaster*
Learn, Doris Lynn *application developer*
McNeely, David John *computer programmer*
Miller, Bonnie Sewell *marketing professional, writer*
Pfeuffer, Dale Robert *secondary school social studies educator*

Macdill AFB
†Cofer, Jonathan H. *career officer*

Madeira Beach
Medins, Gunars *surgeon*

Madison
McCauley, Barbara Lynne *language educator*
Shaw, Kathleen Bentley *violist*
†Shaw, Roderick Kirkpatrick, III, *dentist*

Maitland
Bailey, Michael Keith *lawyer*
Blackburn, John Oliver *economist, consultant*
Leli, Dano Anthony *neuropsychologist, educator*
Lovelace, Dorothy Louise *volunteer*
Mansson, Joan *librarian, consultant*
Plane, Donald Ray *management science educator*
†Rajtar, Steven Allen *lawyer*
Stephens, Patricia Ann *marketing professional*
†Trees, Philip Hugh *lawyer*
Vallee, Judith Delaney *environmentalist, writer, fundraiser*
Von Hilsheimer, George Edwin, III, *neuropsychologist*

Manalapan
†Gatewood, Robert Payne *financial planning executive, retired*
Phipard, Nancy Midwood *retired special education educator, poet*

Marathon
Giffen, Lois Key *artist, psychosynthesis counselor*
†Vail, Elizabeth Forbus *volunteer*
Wiecha, Joseph Augustine *linguist, educator*

Marco Island
†Arnold, James Leonard *lawyer*
Blackwell, John Wesley *securities industry executive, consultant*
Cooper, Thomas Astley *banking executive*
Guerrant, David Edward *retired food company executive*
Hollenbeck, Karen Fern *foundation consultant*
Krause, Charles Joseph *otolaryngologist*
Lovely, Erna Susan *retired primary school educator*
Meyer, Jon Howard *utility executive, consultant*
Pettersen, Kjell Will *stockbroker, consultant*
†Sinoradzki, Felicia Teresa *journalist*
†Sundberg, Ruth Dorothy *physician, educator*
Traher, William George *automotive model maker, retired*
Wheeler, Warren G(age), Jr., *retired publishing executive*

Margate
Franks, Allen P. *research institute executive, educator*
Ory, Steven Jay *physician, educator*
†Valdes, Ramon F. *electrical engineer, consultant, math educator*

Marianna
Ledbetter, Eugene Floyd, Jr., *vocational education coordinator*

Mary Esther
McTyeire, Robert Adams *sound company executive*

Melbourne
Babich, Michael Wayne *chemistry educator, educational administrator*
Baylis, William Thomas *systems engineering specialist, writer*
Burckhalter, Joseph Harold *chemistry educator*
Bush, Norman *research and development executive*
Cacciatore, S. Sammy *lawyer*
Cacciatore, Sammy Michel *lawyer*
Cahill, Gerard Albin *university educator*
Catanese, Anthony James *academic administrator*
Ciubotaru, Alexandru Aurelian *electronics engineer*
Conneen, Mari M. *artist*
Cosentino, Paul John *civil engineering educator*

†Dean, Michael J. *lobbyist, consultant*
†Dixon, Richard Dean *lawyer, educator*
Eberle, Terry R. *editor, newspaper executive*
†Elder, Stewart Taylor *dentist, retired naval officer*
Fiore, Carmen Anthony *writer*
Glindeman, Henry Peter, Jr., *real estate developer*
Gougelman, Paul Reina *lawyer*
Helmstetter, Charles Edward *microbiologist*
Hodges, Carroll Broadus *retired army officer*
Hollingsworth, Abner Thomas *university dean*
Hughes, Ann Nolen *psychotherapist*
Hughes, Edwin Lawson *retired information technology executive*
Jenkins, Marshall *internet consultant, entrepreneur*
Jones, Elaine Hancock *humanities educator*
Kaner, Cem *lawyer, computer software consultant, educator*
Kreines, Joseph Melvin *conductor*
Krieger, Robert Edward *publisher*
Lakshmikantham, Vangipuram *mathematics educator*
Laposata, Joseph Samuel *army officer*
Lederer, William Julius *author*
MacDonald, Michael Joseph *physician, administrator*
†Maloratsky, Leo G. *electrical engineer*
McCay, Thurman Dwayne *university official*
Michalski, Thomas Joseph *city planner, developer*
Miner, Lynne Shirley *nurse midwife, educator*
Nelson, Gordon Leigh *chemist, educator*
Pocoski, David John *cardiologist*
Regis, Nina *librarian, educator*
Roub, Bryan R(oger) *financial executive*
†Russell, John Masters *aerospace engineer, educator*
†Scheuerer, Diane Thomspon *home economics educator*
Shaikh, Muzaffar Abid *management science educator*
Simokaitis, Frank Joseph *air force officer, lawyer*
†Stack, Charles Rickman *lawyer*
Stark, Norman *secondary school educator*
Stone, Elaine Murray *author, composer, television producer*
Storrs, Eleanor Emerett *research institute consultant*
Tepperman, Barbara-Dawn A. *clinical psychologist, marriage/family therapist*
Thursfield, Fred Falconer, II, *foundation administrator*
Trachtman, Jerry H. *lawyer*
Trotter, Shirley Ann *retired computer specialist*
Weaver, Lynn Edward *academic administrator, consultant, editor*

Melbourne Beach
Belefant, Arthur *engineer*
Harris, Jack Howard, II, *consulting firm executive*
Scanlon, Charles Francis *retired army officer, defense consultant, writer, publisher*

Melrose
Harley, Ruth *artist, educator*

Merritt Island
Anderson, Mary Helen Steed *volunteer*
Babcock, Hope Smith *counselor, educator, program designer*
Dean, Dorsey Edward *retired engineer*
†Deardoff, R. Bruce *automotive executive*
†Galeano, Sharon J. *institutional advancement director*
Johnson, Clarence Traylor, Jr., *state judge*
McClanahan, Leland *university director*
Smith, David Edward *business executive, aerospace engineer, aerospace scientist*
Thomas, Albert W *investment company executive, financial analyst*
Thomas, James Arthur *retired government official, electrical engineer*
Thompson, Hugh Lee *academic administrator*
Walter, George Anthony *elementary education educator*

Miami
Abraira, Carlos *endocrinologst, physician*
Abril, Marcia (Ela I. Cardinas) *writer*
Adams, William Carryl *public relations educator*
†Akar, Virginia Maya *lawyer*
Allen, Charles Norman *television, film and video producer*
Allington, Gloria Jean Ham *medical education administrator*
Alschuler, Al *freelance/self-employed writer, marketing professional*
Alvarez, Raul Alberto *internist*
Amber, Laurie Kaufman *lawyer*
Amos, Betty Giles *restaurant company executive, accountant*
†Anderson, Douglas Richard *ophthalmologist, educator, scientist, researcher*
†Anderson, Terence James *law educator*
Angones, Georgina Alfonsin *educational association administrator*
Anscher, Bernard *manufacturing executive, investor, management consultant*
Arango, Jorge Sanin *architect*
†Arison, Micky *cruise line company executive, sports team executive*
Armstrong, Floyd Daniel *pediatric psychologist*
Arteaga, Harold Augustine *lawyer*
Astigarraga, Jose I(gnacio) *lawyer*
Averch, Harvey Allan *economist, educator, academic administrator*
Bachmeyer, Steven Allan *secondary education educator*
†Baena, Scott Louis *lawyer*
Baker, Thomas Eugene *law educator*
Balás, Irene Barbara *artist*
Bandstra, Ted E. *federal judge*
Bannard, Walter Darby *artist, art critic*
Barkett, Rosemary *circuit judge*
Barry, Dave *columnist, author*
Barthel, William Frederick, Jr., *engineer, electronics company executive*
Batcheller, Joe Ann *entrepreneur*
†Batson, Dawn Kirsten *music educator, cultural consultant*
Baumberger, Charles Henry *lawyer*
Beasley, Joseph Wayne *lawyer*
Beck, Morris *allergist*
Becker, Isidore A. *business executive*
Beckham, Walter Hull, Jr., *lawyer, educator*
†Beers, Mayra E. *academic administrator*
†Bejarano, Pablo A. *physician, consultant, medical educator*
Bennett, Olga Salowich *civic worker, graphic arts researcher, consultant*
Berman, Bruce Judson *lawyer*
Berman, Mona S. *actress, playwright, theatrical director and producer*
†Betancourt, Conchita *music educator*
Bieley, Peggy M. *economist*
Birsh, Arthur Thomas *publishing executive*
Bishopric, Karl *investment banker, real estate executive, advertising executive*
Black, Creed Carter *newspaper executive*
Black, Roy *lawyer*
Blanco, Josefa Joan-Juana (Jossie Blanco) *social services administrator*
Blanco, Luciano-Nilo *physicist*
Block, Norman Louis *physician, medical educator*
†Blum, Bradley D. *food service executive*
Blumberg, Edward Robert *lawyer*
Boccagna, David Louis *finance company executive*
Bolooki, Hooshang *cardiac surgeon*
Borkan, William Noah *biomedical electronics company executive*
Bouri, Michael *civil servant*
†Bravo, Irene Maria *psychologist, educator*
Bregman, Michael Evan *urban planner*
Brenner, Esther Hannah *elementary school educator*
†Brondello, Sandy *professional basketball player*
Bronis, Stephen Jay *lawyer*
Brooten, Dorothy *nursing educator, former dean*
Brotherson, Mary Lou Nelson *education educator*
Brown, Stephen Thomas *judge*
Brownell, Edwin Rowland *banker, civil engineer, land surveyor*
†Buchwald, Peter Sandor *research scientist*
Buehler, Martin *hotel executive*
†Burke, George William, III, *surgery educator*
Burnett, Henry *lawyer*
†Burns, M. Anthony *transportation services company executive*
†Burrows, Suzetta Cecile *medical librarian*
Burton, Richard Jay *lawyer*
Butterworth, Robert A. *dean, former state attorney general*
Camner, Howard *author, poet*
Capraro, Franz *accountant*
Cardenas, Alberto R. *lawyer*
Carnesoltas, Ana-Maria *lawyer*
Carter, Harriet Vanessa *marketing professional, aide*
Cassel, John Michael *plastic surgeon*
Castro, Feinberg Rosa *education educator*
Cekauskas, Cynthia Danute *social worker*
Chabrow, Penn Benjamin *lawyer*
Chakko, Simon C. *cardiologist, educator*
Chambers, Elenora Strasel *artist*
Chang-Mota, Roberto *electrical engineer*
†Chaplin, Harvey *wine and liquor wholesale executive*
Chapman, Alvah Herman, Jr., *newspaper executive*
†Chapple, Michael Joseph *marketing professional, security firm executive*
Chen, Shu-Ching *computer science educator*
Cherry, Andrew Lawrence, Jr., *social work educator, researcher*
Chisholm, Martha Maria *dietitian*
†Ciancio, Gaetano *transplant surgeon, urologist*
Civantos, Francisco *pathologist, educator*
Clark, Ira C. *hospital association administrator, educator*
Clarke, Mercer Kaye *lawyer*
Clarkson, John G. *academic administrator, ophthalmologist*
†Coffey, Kendall Brindley *lawyer*
Cohen, Jeffrey Michael *lawyer*
Cole, Todd Godwin *management consultant transportation*
Collins, Susan Ford *leadership consultant*
Colwin, Arthur Lentz *biologist, educator*
†Connor, Terence Gregory *lawyer*
†Coro, Edys *music educator*
†Cortes, Carol Solis *school system administrator*
Cosgrove, John Francis *lawyer, state legislator*
Coton, Carlos David *finance manager*
Cristol, A. Jay *federal judge*
Cubas, Jose M(anuel) *advertising agency executive*
Cullom, William Otis *trade association executive*
†Culmer, Leome Frances *volunteer*
†Culmo, Elisabeth M. *lawyer*
Curtis, Karen Haynes *lawyer*
Cutler, Robert Brian *medical educator, researcher*
Dahlburg, John-Thor Theodore *newspaper correspondent*
Dann, Oliver Townsend *psychoanalyst, psychiatrist, educator*
Daub, S. Spencer
†David, Christopher Mark *lawyer*
Davis, Edward Bertrand *retired federal judge, lawyer*
†Davis, Richard Edmund *facial plastic surgeon*
Day, Kathleen Patricia *financial planner*
de la Guardia, Mario Francisco *electrical engineer*
de Leon, Lidia Maria *magazine editor*
Dellapa, Gary J. *aviation consultant*
†Diaz, Alan *photojournalist*
†Diaz, Benito Humberto *lawyer*
Diaz, Manuel A. *mayor*
Dickason, John Hamilton *retired foundation executive*
Dienstag, Cynthia Jill *lawyer*
Dimitriou, Dolores Ennis *computer consultant*
Dorion, Robert Charles *entrepreneur, investor*
Dorn, Gordon Joseph *artist, art educator*
Duany, Andres *architectural firm executive*
†Duchowny, Michael S. *physician, educator*
Durkin, Diane L. *nurse*
†Duvivier, Jean-Paul *investment banker, educator*
Eaton, Joel Douglas *lawyer*
Edelcup, Norman Scott *management and financial consultant*
Eftekhari, Nasser *physiatrist*
Ehrlich, Morton *international finance executive*
Eisdorfer, Carl *psychiatrist, health care executive*
Elliot, Cameron Robert *lawyer*
†Engen, John Scott *academic administrator, consultant*
Engle, Mary Allen English *physician*
Escalera, Karen Weiner *marketing professional*
Evans, Thomas William *lawyer*
Farcus, Joseph Jay *architect, interior designer*
Feinsmith, Paul Lowell *lawyer*
Feito, Jose *architect*
†Ferrari, Leonardo *small business owner*
†Ferré, Maurice A. *entrepreneur*
Ferrell, Milton Morgan, Jr., *lawyer*
Fichtner, Margaria *journalist*
Fiedler, Jay *football player*
†Fiedler, Tom *editor-in-chief*
Field, Julia Allen *activist, strategist, poet*
Finley, Gordon Ellis *psychology educator*
†Fischl, Margaret A. *education educator, researcher*
Fishman, Lewis Warren *lawyer, educator*
Fleisher, Betty *artist, educator*
Fontes, J. Mario F., Jr., *lawyer*
Foote, Edward Thaddeus, II, *university president, lawyer*
Forgione, Dana Anthony *healthcare accounting educator*
Foster, Kathryn Warner *newspaper editor*
Freeman, Gill Sherryl *judge*
†Freire, Jose A. *physicist, writer*
Freshwater, Michael Felix *plastic surgeon, educator*
Friedman, Richard Nathan *lawyer*
Friedman, Ronald Michael *judge*
Frigo, James Peter Paul *industrial hardware company executive*
Frost, Philip *pharmaceutical executive, dermatologist*
Fry, David Donald *civil engineer, consultant*
Furst, Alex Julian *thoracic and cardiovascular surgeon*
Gabor, Frank *insurance company executive*
Ganz, William Israel *radiology educator, medical director, researcher*
Garrett, Richard G. *lawyer*
†Garvin, Glenn *journalist, writer*
Geis, Tarja Pelto *educational coordinator, consultant, counselor, teacher, professor*
†Gelb, George Edward *lawyer*
Gelman, Barry *pediatrician, educator*
George, Stephen Carl *reinsurance executive, educator, medical and life consultant, expert witness, expert witness*
Getz, Morton Ernest *medical facility director, gastroenterologist*
Giller, Norman Myer *banker, architect, author*
Gindy, Benjamin Lee *insurance company executive*
Ginsberg, Myron David *neurologist*
†Gitlitz, Stuart Hal *lawyer*
Gittens, Angela *airport executive*
Glickman, Fred Elliott *lawyer*
†Glinn, Franklyn Barry *lawyer*
Glogower, Michael Howard *public housing senior functional specialist*
Godofsky, Lawrence *lawyer*
Goin-Harding, Cecilia Margaret *poet*
Goldberg, Lee Dresden *endocrinologist, medical educator*
†Golden, Donald Alan *lawyer*
†Goldstein, Burton Jack *psychiatrist*
Gomez, Nancy *engineer, architect*
Goodwin, W. Jarrard *otolaryngologist, educator*
Gragg, Karl Lawrence *lawyer*
Graham, Donald Lynn *federal judge*
†Gray, Frances Boone *minister*
Greenberg, Stewart Gary *lawyer*
Greenleaf, Walter Franklin *lawyer*
Greer, Alan Graham *lawyer*
Grist, John *retired government official, engineering consultant*
Grossman, Robert Louis *lawyer*
Haar, Ana Maria Fernández *advertising and public relations executive*
Hackman, John Clement *neuropharmacology educator, neurophysiologist*
Hajek, Robert J., Sr., *lawyer, real estate broker, commodities broker, nursing home owner*
Halberg, F. David *principal*
†Hall, Adam Stuart *lawyer*
Hall, Andrew Clifford *lawyer*
Hall, Miles Lewis, Jr., *lawyer*
Halsey, Douglas Martin *lawyer*
Hampton, John Lewis *retired newspaper editor*
Hampton, Mark Garrison *architect*
Hardy, Michael C. *performing arts administrator*
Hartz, Steven Edward Marshall *lawyer, educator*
Hauser, Helen Ann *lawyer, consultant*
Hector, Louis Julius *lawyer*
Heggen, Arthur William *insurance company executive*
Herbits, Stephen Edward *strategic consultant*
Heros, Roberto Cosme *neurosurgeon*
Heuer, Robert Maynard, II, *opera company executive*
Hickey, John Heyward (Jack Hickey) *lawyer*
Highsmith, Shelby *federal judge*
Higley, Bruce Wadsworth *orthodontist*
Hirsch, Milton *lawyer*
†Hirschberg, Joseph Gustav *educator, physicist*
Hoffman, Larry J. *lawyer*
Hollander, Frank *lawyer*
Houlihan, Gerald John *lawyer*
Howell, Ralph Rodney *pediatrician, educator, geneticist*
Hudson, Robert Franklin, Jr., *lawyer*
Humphries, Joan Ropes *psychologist, educator*
Hunter, Leland Clair, Jr., *management consultant*
Huysman, Arlene Weiss *psychologist, educator, writer*
Ibarguen, Alberto *newspaper executive*
†Ibler, Gerold *finance company executive, consultant*
Imperato, Joseph John *lawyer, composer*
†Irvin, George Lee, III, *surgeon*
Jacobson, Bernard *lawyer*
Jacobson, Claire E. *music therapist*
†Javier-Dejneka, Amelia Luisa *accountant*
†Johnson, Channey *elementary school educator*
†Johnson, Thomas Edward *plastic and reconstructive surgeon*
Johnson-Cousin, Danielle *French literature and cultural studies educator*
Johnston, Philip Connelly *lawyer*
†Jones, Janice Cox *elementary education educator, writer*
Jones, William Kinzy *materials engineering educator*
†Jones-Koch, Francena *school counselor, educator*
Jones-Wills, Eunice Stephanie *mental health nurse, researcher*
Kaiser, Gerard A. *senior vice president*
Kanet, Roger Edward *political science educator*
Kaplan, Betsy Hess *school board member*
Karl, Robert Harry *cardiologist*
Karlan, Sandy Ellen *judge*
Katz, Lawrence Sheldon *lawyer*
†Khan, Danyal Mushtaq *pediatric cardiologist*
King, James Lawrence *federal judge*
†King, Joseph *finance educator, consultant*
Kislak, Jean Hart *art director*
Kitner, Jon David *art educator*
Klock, Joseph Peter, Jr., *lawyer*
†Koncsol, Stephen Wayne *psychologist, educator*
Kooima, Linda Kay *neonatal and pediatrics nurse*
Korchin, Judith Miriam *lawyer*
†Kowalska, Maria Teresa *research scientist, educator*
Krissel, Susan Hinkle *transportation company executive*
Kritzer, Glenn Bruce *lawyer*
Kuczynski, Pedro-Pablo *investor*
†Kuker, Alan Michael *lawyer*
Kurzban, Ira Jay *lawyer*
Kwiat, David Mark *educator, actor*
Laje, Zilia L. *writer, publisher, translator*
Lampen, Richard Jay *lawyer, investment banker*
Lancaster, Kenneth G. *lawyer*
Landy, Burton Aaron *lawyer*
Lasseter, Kenneth Carlyle *pharmacologist*
Lavin, David *accountant, educator*
Lawrence, David, Jr., *journalist, early childhood development advocate*
†Lazenby, Robert Alfred *lawyer*
†Lebwohl, Nathan Howard *orthopedist, surgeon*
Lee, J. Patrick *academic administrator*
Lee, Nellie Greenberg *social worker, educator, counselor*
Lemberg, Louis *cardiologist, educator*
Leslie, Richard McLaughlin *lawyer, educator*
†Letona-Holloway, Maria E. *music educator*
Levine, Robert Jeffrey *lawyer*
Lew, Salvador *radio station executive*
Lewis, John Milton *cable television company executive*
Leyva, Luis Pablo, Jr., *obstetrician/gynecologist*
†Li, Qi *research scientist, consultant*
†Lifshitz, Felice *historian, educator*
†Ling, Jian *research scientist, consultant*
†Linn, Richard John Kuei-hsiung *engineering educator, researcher, engineering educator, consultant*
Lipcon, Charles Roy *lawyer*
†Lipoff, Norman Harold *lawyer*
†Llopiz, Jorge Luis *language educator*
Long, Maxine Master *lawyer*
†Lorenzo, Guadalupe *language educator, department chairman*
Louis, Paul Adolph *lawyer*
†Lugauer, Steven L. *management consultant*
†Luque-Escalona, Roberto Sabas *writer*
Madurga, Gonzalo F. *artistic director, actor, singer*
Maher, Stephen Trivett *lawyer, educator*
†Maidique, Modesto Alex *academic administrator*
Malinin, Theodore *medical educator, researcher*
†Maniatty, Philip Ward *lawyer*
Marcus, Stanley *federal judge*
Mares-Guia, Marcos Luiz *biochemist, consultant*
†Marin, Ana Maria *lawyer*
Martínez, Luís Osvaldo *radiologist, educator*
Martinez, Walter Baldomero *architect*
Matthews, Douglas Eugene *lawyer, educator, consultant*
Maulion, Richard Peter *psychiatrist, physician, neurolinguist*
McCabe, Robert Howard *college president*
McCain, David B. *lawyer*
McKenna, Peter Dennis *lawyer*
Mc Kenzie, John Maxwell *physician*
McKeon, John Aloysius (Jack McKeon) *professional baseball manager*
McLaughlin, Gwenn Elizabeth *pediatrician, educator*
†Meadors, Marynell *former professional basketball coach, sports team executive*
†Medina, Luis Santiago *radiologist, researcher*
Mehta, Eileen Rose *lawyer*
†Mendez, Luis Eduardo *medical educator, researcher*
Mendieta, Raquelín Maria de la Concepción *artist*
†Mendoza, Enid Duany *lawyer*
†Mendoza De Arce, Daniel Leonel *retired humanities educator*
Miguez-Burbano, Maria-Jose *medical immunologist*

Milgrim, Franklin Marshall *merchant*
Millard, Max *pathologist*
Miller, Gene Edward *newspaper reporter and editor*
†Miller, James M. *lawyer*
Miller, Raymond Vincent, Jr., *lawyer*
Miller, Stuart A. *real estate executive, lawyer*
†Miller Udell, Bronwyn *lawyer*
†Milstein, Richard Craig *lawyer*
Mintz, Daniel Harvey *endocrinologist, educator, academic administrator*
†Mitchell, Virginia Ann *investment company executive*
†Miyazaki, Anthony D. *adult education educator, consultant*
Mizel, Mark Stuart *orthopedic surgeon*
Mooers, Christopher Northrup Kennard *physical oceanographer, educator*
†Moran, Kate *sculptor, photographer*
Morgan, Dahlia *museum director*
Morgan, Marabel *author*
Morrison, Glenn *neurosurgeon*
Morton, Richard *lawyer, financial consultant*
†Mourning, Alonzo *professional basketball player*
Mudd, John Philip *lawyer*
Muench, Karl Hugo *clinical geneticist*
Muir, Helen *journalist, author*
Mullins, Edward M. *lawyer*
†Munoz, Oscar *cardiologist*
Murai, Rene Vicente *lawyer*
Murphy, Timothy James *lawyer*
Mustelier, Alina Olga *travel consultant, music educator*
†Myrberg, Arthur August, Jr., *marine biological sciences educator*
Nachwalter, Michael *lawyer*
Nadeau, Joseph Eugene *health care management consultant, information systems consultant*
†Nadji, Mehrdad *pathologist, educator*
†Nakashima, Tadayoshi *retired biochemist, researcher*
Nelson, Florence G. *retired secondary school educator*
Nestor Castellano, Brenda Diana *real estate company executive*
Neu, Charles Eric *historian, educator*
Neuman, Susan Catherine *public relations and marketing consultant*
Newlin, Kimrey Dayton *international trade consultant, political consultant, personal computer analyst*
Newman, Terrie Lynne *advertising and marketing executive*
†Newton, Terry Fernando *health information specialist, writer*
†Nishida, Seigo *surgeon, educator*
Nissen, Bruce Allen *labor studies educator*
Nixon, David Patrick *public relations executive*
†Northup, Lesley Armstrong *religious studies educator, priest*
Nouri, Keyvan *dermatologic surgeon*
Nuernberg, William R(ichard) *lawyer*
Nunez-Lawton, Miguel G. *international finance specialist*
Obolensky, Georges *retired humanities educator*
O'Connor, Kathleen Mary *lawyer*
O'Meara, Vicki A. *lawyer*
Ortiz, Loida A. *communications executive*
Osinski, Martin Henry *healthcare consultant*
Osman, Edith Gabriella *lawyer*
Ostlund, H. Gote *atmospheric and marine scientist, educator*
Pacin, Michael P. *internist, allergist*
Page, Larry Keith *neurosurgeon, educator*
†Palahach, Michael *lawyer*
†Palmberg, Paul Frederic *ophthalmologist, educator*
Paresky, Linda K. *travel company executive, educator*
Parnes, Edmund Ira *oral and maxillofacial surgeon, educator*
Parrish, Richard Kenneth, II, *medical educator*
†Patrouch, Joseph Francis *education educator*
Patterson, Rickey Lee *clergyman*
Payne, R.W., Jr., *lawyer*
Pefkaros, Kyriacos C. *internist, cardiologist*
†Peltz, Robert Dwight *lawyer*
Pena, Guillermo Enrique *lawyer*
†Penelas, Alex *mayor*
†Perez-Stable, Carlos *research scientist*
Pham, Si Mai *cardiothoracic surgeon, medical educator*
†Pietrocarlo, Nick *artist, consultant*
Pinder, Renee Monique *diplomat*
Podhurst, Aaron Samuel *lawyer*
Polen-Dorn, Linda Frances *communications executive*
Pomeranz, Felix *accounting educator*
Pope, John Edwin, III, *newspaper sports editor, columnist*
Porter, Charles King *advertising executive*
Porter, Wayne Randolph *dermatologist*
Poston, Rebekah Jane *lawyer*
Potocky-Tripodi, Miriam *social worker, educator*
Potter, James Douglas *pharmacology educator*
Pratt, John Patrick *lawyer*
Pruna, Laura Maria *lawyer*
†Przybylski-Pol, Alexander *biotechnologist*
Puliafito, Carmen Anthony *ophthalmologist, healthcare executive*
Quencer, Robert Moore *neuroradiologist, researcher*
Quentel, Albert Drew *lawyer*
Quirantes, Albert M. *lawyer*
Raez, Luis Estuardo *physician*
Raffel, Leroy B. *real estate development company executive*
Raines, Jeff *biomedical scientist, medical research director*
†Razdan, Sanjay *urologist*
Reed, Alfred *composer, conductor*
†Regev, Arie *gastroenterologist, researcher, hepatologist*
Reisman, Terry Milton *gynecologist*
†Richman, Gerald F. *lawyer*
Riley, Patrick James *professional basketball coach*
Risi, Louis James, Jr., *business executive*
Roberts, Jonathan S. *interventional cardiologist*
†Robinson, Thomas Adair *law educator, consultant*
†Rock, Howard B. *humanities educator*
†Roman, Ronald Peter *lawyer*
Ronzetti, Thomas A. Tucker *lawyer, law educator*
†Rosen, Michael James *lawyer*
Rosenbaum, Allan *public administration educator, academic administrator, international governance advisor*
Rosenberg, Mark B. *political science educator, university official*
Rosinek, Jeffrey *judge*
Roth, Michael Stewart *obstetrician-gynecologist*
Rothman, David Bill *lawyer*
†Rothstein, Ronald *professional basketball coach*
Ruffner, Charles Louis *lawyer*
†Ruggiero, Guido *historian, educator*
Russell, Elbert Winslow *neuropsychologist*
Russell, James Webster, Jr., *newspaper editor, columnist*
Sacher, Barton Stuart *lawyer*
Salazar-Carrillo, Jorge *economics educator*
Salinas, Baruj *artist, architect*
Salvaneschi, Luigi *real estate and development executive, business educator*
†Samlut, Carlos *accountant*
†Samole, Myron Michael *lawyer, management consultant*
Sanchez, Fausto H. *advertising agency executive*
Sanchez, Javier Alberto *industrial engineer*
Sanchez de Leon, Roberto J. *physician, educator, writer*
San Pedro, Ofelia *transportation services executive, energy planner*
Santoro, Thomas Mead *lawyer*
Sargent, Joanne Elaine *lawyer*
†Sari, Nazmi *economist, healthcare educator*
Savage, James Francis *editor*
†Scarborough, Jack William *business education administrator*
Schachner, Lawrence Alan *pediatric dermatologist*
Scheinberg, Peritz *neurologist*
Schiff, Eugene Roger *medical educator, hepatologist*
†Schiffrin, Michael Edward *lawyer*
Schuette, Charles A. *lawyer*
Schwade, James Gary *radiation oncologist*
†Schwartz, Bruce S. *lawyer*
Schwartz, Gerald *public relations and fundraising agency executive*
†Scully, Robert Edmund *management educator, consultant*
†Secada, Jon *musician*
Segal, Simon *real estate executive, finance company executive*
†Seitz, Patricia Ann *judge*
Sequeira, Rafael Francis *cardiologist, medical educator*
Sharpstein, Richard Alan *lawyer*
†Sherman, Beatrice Ettinger *business executive*
Shevin, Robert Lewis
Shusterman, Nathan *underwriter, financial consultant*
Siegel, Paul *judge*
Silber, Norman Jules *lawyer*
Simmons, Sherwin Palmer *lawyer*
Skolnick, S. Harold *lawyer*
Smith, Stanley Bertram *clinical pathologist, allergist, immunologist, anatomic pathologist*
Stansell, Leland Edwin, Jr., *lawyer, mediator, educator*
Stein, Allan Mark *lawyer*
†Steinberg, Marty *lawyer*
Stephan, Egon, Sr., *cinematographer, film equipment company executive*
†Stieglitz, Albert Blackwell *lawyer*
Stiehm, Judith Hicks *university official, political science educator*
Stokes, Paul Mason *lawyer*
Stolzenberg, Lisa Ann *education educator*
†Strickland, Rodney *professional basketball player*
Strinko, Thomas Edward *medical services administrator*
†Strudler, Robert Jacob *real estate development executive*
Struhl, Theodore Roosevelt *surgeon*
†Stuever, Fred Ray *lawyer*
Sugarbaker, Everett Van Dyke *surgical oncologist*
†Sussmane, Jeffrey Brett *pediatrician*
†Swienton, Gregory T. *transportation company executive*
Taylor, Joe, Jr., *writer, consultant*
†Teicher, Morton Irving *social worker, anthropologist, educator*
Tejada, Francisco *physician, educator*
†Telischi, Fred *otolaryngologist, researcher*
Temple, Jack Donald, Jr., *physician, medical educator*
†Thomas, Lowell Richard *music educator*
Thompson, Allen Joseph *construction executive, civil engineer*
Thornburg, Frederick Fletcher *diversified business executive, lawyer*
Thornton, John William, Sr., *lawyer*
Todd, Betty Clare *organization executive*
Torres, Milton John *industrial engineering educator*
Touby, Kathleen Anita *lawyer*
†Treyz, Joseph Henry *librarian*
Tucker, Gail Susan *biology science educator*
Tzakis, Andreas Gerasimos *surgeon, educator*
Ural, Oktay *civil engineering educator*
VanBrode, Derrick Brent, IV, *trade association administrator*
Van Wyck, George Richard *insurance company executive*
Vento, M. Thérèse *lawyer*
†Vielot, Alain J. *elementary school educator*
†Vilasuso, Francisco X. *anesthesiologist*
Walton, Rodney Earl *lawyer*
Warren, Emily P. *retired secondary and adult school educator*
Wasson, Roy D. *lawyer*
Wax, William Edward *photojournalist*
Weeks, Marta Joan *retired priest*
Weiner, Lawrence *lawyer*
Weinger, Steven Murray *lawyer*
Weinstein, Alan Edward *lawyer*
Weinstein, Andrew H. *lawyer*
Weiser, Ralph Raphael *business executive*
Weiser, Sherwood Manuel *hotel and corporation executive, lawyer*
†Welbaum, R(ome) Earl *lawyer*
†Wenski, Thomas Gerard *bishop*
West, Macdonald *real estate executive*
Wheeler, Steve Dereal *neurologist*
†Whisenand, James Dudley *lawyer*
Whitehead, John *poet*
Whittington, Robert Wallace *corporate professional*
Williams, Eric Joseph *transportation executive*
†Williams, Patrick Anthony *elementary school educator, consultant*
Wilson, Thomas Strong, Jr., (Tam Wilson) *judge*
Wiseheart, Malcolm Boyd, Jr., *lawyer*
Woessner, Jacob Frederick, Jr., *biochemistry educator*
Wolfenson, Azi U. *electrical, mechanical and industrial engineer, consultant*
Wolff, Grace Susan *pediatrician*
Wolfson, Aaron Howard *radiation oncologist, educator*
Worth, James Gallagher *engineer, chemist*
Wright, Pamela Jean *administrator*
Wright, Robert Thomas, Jr., *lawyer*
Yaklich, Richard E. *music educator*
†Zamora, Antonio Rafael *lawyer*
Zanakis, Steve H. *management science/information systems educator*

Miami Beach

Arbuz, Joseph Robert *lawyer*
Blassingame, Ronald Jay *social worker*
Brodie, Ronald *lawyer, author*
Gardiner, Pamela Nan *performing arts company executive*
Gibb, Robin *vocalist, songwriter*
Gitlow, Abraham Leo *retired university dean*
Hair, Gilbert Martin *foundation administrator*
Lamas, Gervasio Antonio *cardiologist, educator*
Lazović, Gavrilo *internist*
Lehrman, Irving *rabbi*
Mandri, Daniel Francisco *psychiatrist*
†Martinotti, Massimo *advertising executive*
Milne, Edward Lawrence *biomedical engineer*
Nash, Seymour Cy *surgeon, urologist*
Sharlach, Jeffrey *public relations executive*
Shula, Don Francis *former professional football coach, team executive*
Zukernick, Harry *lawyer*

Miami Gardens

Ersek, Gregory Joseph Mark *lawyer, business administrator*

Miami Lakes

Dominik, Jack Edward *lawyer*
Zwigard, Bruce Albert *brokerage house executive*

Miami Shores

Diener, Betty Jane *finance educator*
†Favalora, John Clement *bishop*
†Mowad, Louis Francis *musician, educator*

Micco

Christoph, Frances *painter*

Middleburg

King, Leo *journalist*

Milton

†Arnold, Margaret Morelock *music specialist, educator, performer*
Bassett, Chuck *English educator*
Coston, Brenda Maria Bone *language arts educator*
Jose, Shibu *agriculture educator, researcher*
Losee, Michael Patrick *music director*
Mack, Susan Prescott *practical nursing educator*
McKinney, George Harris, Jr., *training systems analyst*
Melvin, Hiram Joseph *religious organization administrator, minister*

Miramar

Besteni, Barbara Amnerys *video producer, editor, director*
Bruckenstein, Joel P. *investment company executive, financial planner*
Catalano, Carl Philip *small business owner*
González Tricoche, Cynthia Marie *human resources specialist*
†Stephens, Sallie L. *retired assistant principal, commissioner*
Walsh, Thomas Francis, Jr., *producer, writer, director*

Miramar Beach

†Sayre, George Edward *retired lawyer*

Montverde

Carlo-Melendez, Arnaldo *mathematics educator*

Mount Dora

Anderson, Chester Grant *English educator*
†Crone, Eugene N. *addictions counselor, retired educator*
Foote, Nathan Maxted *retired physical science educator*
Kirton, Jennifer Myers *artist*
Moretto, Jane Ann *nurse, public health officer, consultant*
Pahman, David A. *principal*
Scharfenberg, Margaret Ellan *retired elementary educator*
Shyers, Larry Edward *mental health counselor, educator*

Mulberry

Baumann, Arthur Nicholas *chemist, consultant*
Bowman, Hazel Lois *retired English language educator*

Naples

Anderson, John Thomas *lawyer*
Baldwin, Ralph Belknap *retired manufacturing company executive, astronomer*
Barkley, Marlene A. Nyhuis *nursing educator*
Berger, Charles Martin *lawn and garden company executive*
Berning, Randall Karl *lawyer, consultant, educator, publisher*
Berry, Donald Lee *accountant*
Blevins, Charles Russell *publishing executive*
Blumenthal, Ronnie *lawyer*
Breitenstein, David E. *newswriter*
Brooks, Joae Graham *psychiatrist*
Brown, Alan Marshall, Jr., *art dealer, curator, art appraiser*
Brown, Cindy Lynn *family nurse practitioner, critical care nurse*
Bruce, Jackson Martin, Jr., *lawyer*
Buckley, Frederick Jean *lawyer*
Budd, David Glenn *lawyer*
Burdick, Robert W. *newspaper editor*
Butler, Frederick George *retired drug company executive*
Carneiro, Ronaldo Dos Santos *surgeon*
Censits, Richard John *retired business executive*
Cimino, Richard Dennis *lawyer*
Clapp, Roger Howland *retired publishing executive*
Clark, William James *retired insurance company executive*
Cobb, Brian Eric *broadcasting executive*
Cohen, Mark George *retired cardiologist*
†Cook, Robin *author*
Craighead, Rodkey *banker*
Crehan, Joseph Edward *lawyer*
Dacey, George Clement *retired laboratory administrator, consultant*
Delano, Victor *retired naval officer*
†Demko, Cathy *artist, art educator*
Dill, John Francis *retired publishing company executive*
Dorio, Martin Matthew, Jr., *real estate company executive, investor*
Doub, William Offutt *lawyer*
Doyle, Joseph Thomas *preventive health physician*
Doyle, Robert Eugene, Jr., *lawyer*
Dykstra, David Allen *corporate executive*
†Edwards, Jennifer J. *county official*
Eldridge, David Carlton *art appraiser*
Elliott, Edward *investment executive, financial planner*
Ericson, Roger Delwin *lawyer, forest resource company executive*
Finger, Iris Dale Abrams *elementary school educator*
Franco, Anthony M. *public relations executive*
Frantzen, Henry Arthur *retired investment company executive*
Frazer, John Howard *tennis association executive*
Fultz, Robert Edward *lawyer*
Gade, Marvin Francis *retired paper company executive*
Gehring, David Austin *physician, cardiologist, administrator*
†Gifford, Nancy (Mumtaz) *artist, poet*
Gilman, John Richard, Jr., *retired management consultant, sculptor*
Griffin, Linda Louise *English language and speech educator*
Grove, William Johnson *physician, surgery educator*
Gulda, Edward James *business acquisitions executive*
Hainsworth, Melody May *information professional, researcher*
Hall, Beverly Barton *librarian*
Handy, Charles Brooks *accountant, educator*
Hauserman, Jacquita Knight *management consultant*
Hooper, John Allen *retired banker*
†Irvin, Robert Julian *lawyer*
Johnson, James Robert *ceramic engineer, educator*
Johnson, Kenneth Oscar *oil company executive*
Johnson, Walter L. *transportation company executive*
Johnson, Zane Quentin *retired petroleum company executive*
Kinder, Suzanne Fonay Wemple *historian, educator*
Kirby, Charles William, Jr., *dancer, choreographer*
Kleinrock, Virginia Barry *public relations executive*
Kley, John Arthur *banker*
Kozitka, Richard Eugene *retired consumer products company executive*
Laidig, William Rupert *retired paper company executive*
Larson, Wilfred Joseph *chemical company executive*
LaRusso, Anthony Carl *company executive, educator*
Leitner, Alfred *mathematical physicist, educator, educational film producer*
Leverenz, Humboldt Walter *retired chemical research engineer*
Lewis, Gordon Gilmer *golf course architect*
Lickhalter, Merlin Eugene *architect*
Llewellyn, Leonard Frank *real estate broker, investment company executive*
Lynn, Larry (Verne Lauriston Lynn) *engineering executive*
Madigan, Joseph Edward *financial executive, consultant, director*
Marcuvitz, Nathan *electrophysics educator*
Marino, William Francis *telecommunications industry executive, consultant*

Marshall, Charles *communications company executive*
McCaffrey, Judith Elizabeth *lawyer*
McCarthy, Joseph Harold *consultant, former retail food company executive*
McDonald, Jinx *interior designer*
†McDonnell, Michael R. N. *lawyer*
McSwiney, Charles Ronald *lawyer*
Mehaffey, John Allen *marketing, newspaper management and advertising executive*
†Miller, Donald *art critic, writer*
Moore, Mechlin Dongan *communications executive, marketing consultant*
Muir, John Douglass *physician*
Mutz, Oscar Ulysses *manufacturing and distribution executive*
Myers, Robert Jay *retired aerospace company executive*
Nelson, John Charles *retired educator*
Noe, Samuel VanArsdale, Jr., *retired urban planning educator*
Norton, Elizabeth Wychgel *lawyer*
Oliver, Robert Bruce *retired investment company executive*
Ordway, John Danton *retired pension administrator, lawyer, accountant*
Penniman, Nicholas Griffith, IV, *retired newspaper publisher*
Petersen, David L. *lawyer*
Post, Barbara Joan *elementary school educator*
Presley, Brian *investment company executive*
Putzell, Edwin Joseph, Jr., *lawyer, mayor*
Randall, Neil Warren *gastroenterologist*
Rehak, James Richard *orthodontist*
Rigor, Bradley Glenn *lawyer*
Rowe, Herbert Joseph *retired trade association executive*
Rowe, Jack Field *retired electric utility executive*
Salt, Alfred Lewis *priest*
Savitzky, Evelyn Robbins *information specialist, librarian*
Schauer, Wilbert Edward, Jr., *lawyer, manufacturing company executive*
Seavey, Christopher Gordon *psychotherapist, addiction counselor*
Sekowski, Cynthia Jean *corporate executive, contact lens specialist*
Sharpe, Robert Francis *equipment manufacturing company executive*
Shields, Bruce Maclean *management consultant*
Sims, William Ronald *advertising executive*
Slaff, Allan Paul *naval officer, university administrator, educator, entrepeneur*
Slayton, John Arthur *electric motor manufacturing executive*
Smith, Numa Lamar, Jr., *lawyer*
Sowman, Harold Gene *ceramic engineer, researcher*
†Spanton, William Floyd *lawyer, consultant*
Stastny, John Anton *real estate executive*
†Steinhouse, Carl Lewis *lawyer*
Stevens, William Kenneth *lawyer*
Strauss, Jerome Manfred *lawyer, banker*
Suziedelis, Vytautas A. *engineering corporation executive*
Taillon, James Howard *investment advisor*
Taishoff, Lawrence Bruce *publishing company executive*
Tanner, Robert Hugh *engineer, consultant*
Temple, Donald *retired allergist and dermatologist*
Thampi, Mohan Varghese *environmental health and civil engineer*
Thomas, Gary Lynn *financial executive*
Vanderslice, Thomas Aquinas *electronics executive*
von Arx, Dolph William *food products executive*
Wade, William Allen *trust company-private bank executive*
Waetjen, Daniel G. *bank executive*
†Wallace, Edward L. *biomedical researcher, consultant*
Werder, Horst Heinrich *lawyer*
†Westman, Carl Edward *lawyer*
Wheeling, Robert Franklin *computer consultant*
White, Roy Bernard *theater executive*
White, Warren Wurtele *retired retailing executive*
Whitley, Arthur Francis *retired international manufacturing company executive, engineer, lawyer*
Wiegenstein, John Gerald *physician*
Williams, Edson Poe *retired automotive company executive*
Williams, George Earnest *engineer, retired business executive*
Wroble, Lisa Ann *writer, educator*
York, Tina *painter*

Navarre
Starratt, Patricia Elizabeth *writer, actress, composer, pianist*

Neptune Beach
Forrest, Allen Wright *tax and financial services firm executive, accountant, financial planner*

New Port Richey
Assini, Vincent Paul *financial executive*
Bell, Sandra Cheever *artist*
Charters, Karen Ann Elliott *critical care nurse, health facility administrator*
Dormeyer, LaVon *school counselor*
Focht, Theodore Harold *lawyer, educator*
†Grillo, Robert S. *private investigator, protective services official*
Hanahan, James Lake *retired insurance executive*
Hauber, Frederick August *ophthalmologist*
Hlad, Gregory Michael *psychometrist, institutional test administrator, career assessment and testing manager*
Lake, Victor Hugo *former manufacturing company executive*
Maysilles, Daniel Bruce *pharmaceutical services executive*
Oosten, Roger Lester *medical manufacturing executive*
Sebring, Marjorie Marie Allison *former home furnishings company executive*
Wolf, Marilyn *volunteer*

New Smyrna Beach
Claridge, Richard *structural engineer*
Satterlee, Peter Hamilton *communications executive, military officer*
Skove, Thomas Malcolm *retired manufacturing company financial executive*
Zink, Joan Wilson *writer, poet, composer*

Newberry
Thornton, J. Ronald *technology consultant*

Niceville
Culver, Dan Louis *federal agency administrator*
†Hinze, Vicki Kay *writer, educator*
Litke, Donald Paul *business executive, retired military officer*
Rasmussen, Robert Dee *retired real estate appraiser*

Nocatee
Turnbull, David John (Chief Piercing Eyes-Penn) *cultural association executive*

Nokomis
Albano, Anthony William *retired career officer, secondary school educator*
Beck, George William *retired industrial engineer*
Brisbin, Sterling G. *engineering executive, consultant*
Hawley, Phillip Eugene *investment banker*
Lockledge, Jack E. *retired principal*
Meyerhoff, Jack Fulton *financial executive*
Novak, Robert Louis *civil engineer, pavement management consultant*
Robinson, Mary Catherine *artist*

North Fort Myers
Fishkind, Lawrence *marketing consultant*
Gray, Carlos Gibson *restaurateur, agricultural products supplier, entertainer, producer*

North Miami
Dellagloria, John Castle *city attorney, educator*
Gordon, Jack David *foundation administrator, real estate company officer*
Kopenhaver, Lillian Lodge *journalism educator*
Markson, Daniel Ben *real estate developer, consultant, syndicator*
Pierre-louis, Rosaire *elementary school educator, educator*
Roslow, Sydney *marketing educator*
Tate, Stanley G. *diversified business executive, expert witness*

North Miami Beach
†Benjamin, Yukhanan *physician*
†Katzman, Chaim *finance company executive*
Roif, Henry Irving *aeronautical engineer, electronic engineer*
Slewett, Robert David *lawyer*
Zipkin, Sheldon Lee *lawyer, educator*

North Palm Beach
Ackerman, Paul Adam *pharmacist*
Coyle, Dennis Patrick *lawyer*
Crawford, Roberta *association administrator*
Daniels, Bruce Joel *lawyer*
Edwards, William James *broadcasting executive*
Fierer, Joshua Allan *pathology educator*
Frevert, James Wilmot *financial planner, investment advisor*
Hay, Lewis, III, *utilities company executive*
†Hayman, Richard Warren Joseph *conductor*
Hushing, William Collins *retired corporate executive*
Jaffe, Melvin *securities company executive*
Lavine, Alan *columnist, writer*
Lynch, William Walker *banker*
Shaw, Stephen Ragsdale *trust investment executive*
Siegendorf, Arden M. *judge*
Sooy, William Ray *electrical engineer, systems analyst*
Spencer, Susan Namm *management consultant*
Stauder, Michael H. *lawyer*
Stein, Mark Rodger *allergist*
Woodard, Wallace William, III, *quality advocate*
Xanthopoulos, Philip, Sr., *brokerage house executive*

North Port
Coe, Laurie Lynne Barker *photojournalist, artist*
de Silva, John Arthur F. *pharmaceutical executive*
Galterio, Louis *healthcare information executive*
Hill, Wallace Harry *sports television consultant*
Seiler, Charlotte Woody *retired educator*

Oakland
Purrone, Scott *physician assistant*

Oakland Park
Gannon, Marc Jay *optometrist*
Krauser, Janice *special education educator*
Rosenthal, Susan Barbara *retired librarian*

Ocala
Altenburger, Karl Marion *allergist, immunologist*
†Belmontez, Deborah Lynn Groves *poet, editor*
Blakeman, Carol Ann *medical/surgical nursing educator*
Booth, Jane Schuele *real estate company executive, real estate broker*
†Boston, Bruce David *writer, book designer*
Fontaine, Laura Ann *social worker*
Fredericks, William John *chemistry educator*
Frow, Richard G. *retired librarian*
Gatison, Karen Ann *private school educator*
Gresham, Jack Warren *poet*
†Hatch, John D. *lawyer*
Kelly, Edward John, V, *counselor*
Kinney, Thomas J. *adult education educator*
Kofink, Wayne Alan *minister*
Michelson, Edward Harlan *retired medical educator*
Ovrebo, Judith *retired physical education educator*
Renda, Rosa A. *special education educator*
Roberts, Mary Belle *clinical social worker*
†Satterfield, Sarah Watkins *music educator*
Simon, Margaret B(allif) *elementary school educator, writer*
Sostilio, Robert Francis *office equipment marketing consultant*
Spivey, Stephen Dale *lawyer*
Stickeler, Carl Ann Louise *professional parliamentarian*
Stock, Stephen Michael *broadcast journalist*
Stone, Ira Michael *internist, cardiologist*
Sundstrom, Harold Walter *public relations executive*
Toral, Miguel A. *customer service administrator, actor*
†Vazquez, Debra Allen *literature educator*
†Westbrook, Rebecca Vollmer *secondary school educator*
Zink, David Daniel *retired English educator, writer*

Ocean Ridge
Bates, Edward Brill *retired insurance company executive*
Grabner, George John *manufacturing executive*
Mueller, Gerry *realtor, investor, former internet executive*

Ocklawaha
Silagi, Barbara Weibler *corporate administrator*

Ocoee
Davis, Elena Denise *accountant*

Odessa
Cobb, Terri Reamer (Ceci Cobb) *film and video producer*

Okeechobee
Bishop, Sid Glenwood *union official*
Egolf, James Edward *history educator, secondary school educator*
Mercer, Frances deCourcy *artist, educator*
Selmi, William, Jr., *lawyer*
Tolbert, Danny Lee *music producer, songwriter*

Oldsmar
Brunner, George Matthew *management consultant, former business executive*
Caronis, George John *insurance executive*
Craft Davis, Audrey Ellen *writer, educator*
Hirschman, Sherman Joseph *lawyer, accountant, educator*
MacLeod, Donald Martin *corporate professional*
Rogers, James Virgil, Jr., *retired radiologist and educator*
†Smith, Nicole A. *development coordinator, not-for-profit fundraiser, realtor*
Thompson, Mack Eugene *history educator*

Opa Locka
Beckett, Joshua Patrick *baseball player*
Castillo, Luis Antonio Donato *professional baseball player*
Harley, Rafael Emanuel *secondary school educator*
†Kotsay, Mark Steven *baseball player*
Lee, Derrek Leon *baseball player*
Light, Alfred Robert *lawyer, political scientist, educator*
†Perez, Tony *former baseball player*
†Wilson, Isabel Gomez *elementary school educator, consultant*

Orange City
Schaeffer, Barbara Hamilton *retired rental leasing company executive, writer*

Orange Park
Bartholomew, John Niles *retired church administrator*
Fetchero, John Anthony, Jr., *otorhinolaryngologist*
Hunt, J(ulian) Courtenay *artist*
Miller, Martin Eugene *school system consultant, negotiator, lobbyist*
Rice, Ronald James *hospital administrator*
Tracanna, Kim *elementary and secondary physical education educator*
Walsh, Gregory Sheehan *optical systems professional*
Walsh, James Anthony (Tony Walsh) *theater and film educator*

Orlando
†Abbott, Charles Warren *lawyer*
Abdel-Aty, Mohamed A. *engineering educator*
Ady, Laurence Irvin *academic administrator*
Ahlers, Glen-Peter, Sr., *law library director, educator, consultant*
Allison, Anne Marie *retired librarian*
Andrew, Brian J. *information technology company executive*
Armacost, Robert Leo *management educator, former coast guard officer*
Arman Gelenbe, Deniz *concert pianist*
Baggott, Brenda Jane Lamb *elementary educator*
Baker, Peter Mitchell *laser scientist, educator, science administrator*
Bauer, Maria Casanova *computer engineer*
Bevc, Frank Peter *electrical engineer*
Blackford, Robert Newton *lawyer, director*
Blackwell, Bruce Beuford *lawyer*
Blue, Joseph Edward *physicist*
Blum, Richard Arthur *writer, media educator*
†Bond, William L. *career officer*
†Boyd, Kenneth Andrew *music educator*
Boyles, William Archer *lawyer*
†Bredin, Brenda Ann *communications educator*
Brock, Barry James *health services administrator, educator, consultant*
Brownlee, Thomas Marshall *manufacturing executive*
Bundy, David John *civilian military employee*
†Caldero-Fiqueroa, Ana Jhanilca *language educator*
†Capouano, Albert D. *lawyer*
Carson, Thomas P. *pediatric cardiologist*
Cawthon, Frank H. *retired construction company executive*
Chong, Stephen Chu Ling *lawyer*
Christiansen, Patrick T. *lawyer*
Clinton, Stephen Michael *academic administrator*
Colbourn, Trevor *retired university president, historian*
Connolly, Joseph Francis, II, *educational executive, government consultant*
Conti, Louis Thomas Moore *lawyer*
Crawford, Patricia Ann *education educator*
†Cunningham, James Owen *lawyer*
Danielyan, Arthur A. *mathematician, researcher*
Davidson, Richard Dodge *lawyer*
Davis, H. Alan *retired airline captain, consultant*
Davis, Marvin Arnold *manufacturing company executive*
Dean, Gary Neal *artist, architect*
deBeaubien, Hugo H. *lawyer*
Deli, Steven Frank *business investment and development executive*
Dempsey, Bernard Hayden, Jr., *lawyer*
Denton, Carol Forsberg *retired training systems designer*
Deo, Narsingh *computer scientist, educator*
Dovel-Cash, Michelle *engineer*
†Dubey, Vinod Shanker *microbiologist, biochemist, researcher*
Duda, Richard Frank *architect, engineering executive*
Dunn, William Bruna, III, *journalist*
Eagan, William Leon *lawyer*
Ellens, J(ay) Harold *philosopher, educator, psychotherapist, pastor*
Feliciano, José *entertainer*
†Figner, William James *instructional systems designer, consultant*
Fildes, Richard James *lawyer*
Fottler, Myron David *health services educator*
Fournier, Donald Joseph, Jr., *mechanical engineer, consultant, educator*
†Franklin, Timothy A. *editor-in-chief, editor*
†Frey, Louis, Jr., *lawyer, federal and state government official*
†Geis, John P. *military career officer*
Glazebrook, James Grinstead *judge*
Gold, I. Randall *lawyer*
Gray, Anthony Rollin *retired finance company executive*
Griffin, Harmon Terrell *lawyer*
Guerriero, David John *physician*
Guzman, Marie Elvira *school guidance counselor*
†Ha, Yonggang *optical engineer*
Han, Deguang *mathematician, educator*
Handley, Leon Hunter *lawyer*
Harris, Gordon H. *lawyer*
Hartley, Carl William, Jr., *lawyer*
Haxton, David *filmmaker, photographer*
Healy, Jane Elizabeth *newspaper editor*
Hendry, Robert Ryon *lawyer*
Henry, William Oscar Eugene *lawyer*
†Hill, Brian Donovan *lawyer*
Hill, Grant *professional basketball player*
Hille, Robert John *lawyer, trust officer*
†Hitt, John Charles *academic administrator*
Hodel, Mary Anne *library director*
Hoff, Theodore Francis *neurological surgeon*
Houser, Ruth G. *financial executive*
†Hubbard, Susan Mary *writer, English educator*
Hurt, Jennings Laverne, III, *lawyer*
†Ihnat, Michael Anthony *administrative assistant*
Ioppolo, Frank S., Jr., *lawyer*
Jacinto, George Anthony *social worker, counselor, educator, consultant*
†Janzen, Lee *professional golfer*
Johns, Elizabeth Jane Hobbs *educational administrator*
Johnson, Shannon *professional basketball player*
Jontz, Jeffry Robert *lawyer*
†Kantor, Hal Halperin *lawyer*
Kehoe, Terrence Edward *lawyer*
Kellison, Stephen George *actuarial consultant*
†Landaeta, Rafael Ernesto *industrial engineer, researcher*
Lanier, Drew Noble *political science educator*
†Lee, Joe R. *food service executive*
Leonhardt, Frederick Wayne *lawyer*
Lisetti, Christine Laetitia *computer scientist, educator*
Llewellyn, Ralph Alvin *physics educator*
Lopez Cruz, Humberto J. *foreign language educator*
†Lubet, Marc Leslie *lawyer*
†Magnino, Marissa Estiva *internist, pediatrician*
Marinescu, Dan Cristian *computer sciences educator, consultant*
Marsh, Ella Jean *pediatrician*
Marsh, Malcolm Roy, Jr., *electronics engineer*
Mausser, Albert *municipal official*
Metz, Larry Edward *lawyer*
Mock, Frank Mackenzie *lawyer*
Moore, Wistar *cardiovascular surgeon*
Morgan, Mary Ann *lawyer*
Morgan, Robert Miles *paramedic, educator*
Morgan, Shirley Ann *information systems executive*
Moriarty, Michael Eugene *retired humanities educator*
Morrisey, Marena Grant *art museum administrator*
†Motes, Carl Dalton *lawyer*
†Mujat, Mircea *optics scientist*
†Murrah, Ann Ralls Freeman *historical association executive*
†Murrell, Robert George *lawyer*
Nadeau, Robert Bertrand, Jr., *lawyer*
Nants, Bruce Arlington *lawyer*
†Neff, A. Guy *lawyer*
Neiman, Norman *aerospace business and marketing executive*

Norris, Franklin Gray *thoracic and cardiovascular surgeon*
O'Farrell, Mark Theodore *religious organization administrator*
Okun, Neil Jeffrey *vitreoretinal surgeon*
Pauley, Bruce Frederick *history educator*
Pearlman, Louis Jay *aviation and entertainment company executive*
†Pet-Armacost, Julia Johanna Agricola *engineering educator, academic administrator*
Peterson, David Eugene *lawyer*
†Phanstiel, Otto *chemistry educator, consultant*
Pierce, Jerry Earl *business executive*
†Pierce, John Gerald (Jerry Pierce) *lawyer*
Raffa, Jean Benedict *author, educator*
Rattman, William John *electronics and electro-optic engineer*
Reed, John Alton *lawyer*
†Renk, Kimberly Dawn *social sciences educator*
Rivera, Richard Edwin *restaurant chain executive*
Rivers, Glenn Anton (Doc Rivers) *professional basketball coach, former basketball player*
Ruffier, Joan Dial *small business owner, accountant*
Russ, James Matthias *lawyer*
Salzman, Gary Scott *lawyer*
Schulte, Alfons Friedrich *physicist, educator*
Schultz, Victoria L. *entertainer, music teacher*
Scott, Kathy Lynn *peri-operative nurse*
†Sharp, Christina Krieger *nursing educator, researcher*
Sheaffer, William Jay *lawyer*
Shirek, John Richard *retired savings and loan executive*
Sims, Roger W. *lawyer*
Skambis, Christopher Charles, Jr., *lawyer*
Smetheram, Herbert Edwin *management consultant*
†Smisek, James J. *music educator*
Smyth, Joseph Vincent *manufacturing company executive*
Snively, Stephen Wayne *lawyer*
Spivey, William Franklin, Jr., *investment banker*
Spoonhour, James Michael *lawyer*
†Stegeman, George I. *physicist, educator*
†Steward, Sherry *information technology executive, educator*
Subin, Eli Harold *lawyer*
†Swann, Richard Rockwell *lawyer, banker*
Taitt, Earl Paul *psychiatrist, army officer*
Thorpe, Janet Claire *judge*
Ting, Robert Yen-ying *physicist*
Van den Berg, Egerton *airport executive*
†Vanryckeghem, Martine *speech pathology/audiology services professional, educator*
Walker, Deborah Lynne *nurse practitioner*
Walters, Linda Jane *marine biologist, educator, researcher*
Waltz, Kathleen M. *publishing executive*
†Warfield, Scott *music educator, writer*
Warren, Dean Stuart *artist*
Watson, Barry Lee *real estate and mortgage broker, investor, contractor, builder, developer*
†Weiss, Christopher John *lawyer*
Wells, Natalie Clarke *anesthesiologist*
Whitehouse, Gary *industrial engineer, educator*
Whitworth, Hall Baker *forest products company executive*
†Whyte, Ann Marie *finance educator*
†Williamson, Michael George *lawyer*
Wilson, William Berry *lawyer*
Witty, John Barber *health care executive*
Wu, Thomas Xinzhang *engineering educator, researcher*
Yates, Leighton Delevan, Jr., *lawyer*
Yesawich, Peter Charles *advertising executive*
†Yonetani, Ayako *music educator, entertainer*
Young, George Cressler *federal judge*
†Zhang, Ying *statistician, researcher*

Ormond Beach

Boyle, Susan Jean Higle *social studies educator*
Burke, Marguerite Jodi Larcombe *writer, executive services professional*
Burt, Wallace Joseph, Jr., *insurance company executive*
Burton, Alan Harvey *city official*
Cromartie, Robert Samuel, III, *thoracic surgeon*
†Cunsolo, Ronald S. *historian, educator*
Franchini, Roxanne *bank executive*
Geary, James Martin *writer, communications executive*
†Hodges, Elizabeth Swanson *educational consultant, tutor*
Hodkinson, Sydney Phillip *composer, educator*
Kanfer, Julian Norman *biochemist, educator*
Phillips, Marti *editor*
Rubin, Mark Stephen *ophthalmic surgeon*
Stogner, William Louis *pharmaceutical company executive*
Truitt, Richard byron *landscape architect*
Wendelstedt, Harry Hunter, Jr., *umpire*

Osprey

Boldt, Heinz *aerospace engineer*
Cochran, David MacDuffie *management consultant*
Gross, James Dehnert *pathologist*
Gross, Marilyn Agnes *artist, business owner, speech audiologist*
Halladay, Laurie Ann *public relations consultant, former franchise executive*
Harrington, Nancy O'Connor *volunteer*
Hirons, William Beacom *retired chemical company executive*
Holec, Anita Kathryn Van Tassel *civic worker*
Petrik, Gerd *pharmaceutical executive*
Weathermon, Sidney Earl *elementary school educator*

Oviedo

Brethauer, William Russell, Jr., *claim investigator*
Drummer, Donald Raymond *financial services executive*
Hyslop, Gary Lee *retired librarian*
MacKenzie, Charles Sherrard *academic administrator*
Millstein, Herbert Sydney *management consultant*
Parker, Harry Lee *retired army officer, counselor*
Reynolds, Samuel D., Jr., *metallurgical engineer, consultant*

Pace

Stoudenmire, William Ward *minister*

Palatka

Baldwin, Allen Adail *lawyer, writer*
†Embree, Mary Evelyn *retired secondary school educator*
Ginn, John Arthur, Jr., *insurance agent*
Ouyang, Ying *environmental scientist, educator*

Palm Bay

Bigda, Rudolph A. *business and financial consultant*
Boley, Andrea Gail *secondary school educator*
Colman, Charles Kingsbury *academic administrator, criminologist*
Galin, Tad, Sr., *home business owner*
Hanna, Emma Harmon *architectural designer, business owner, official*
Herro, John Joseph *software specialist*
Howard, Marilyn Hoey *lawyer*
Jones, Mary Ann *geriatrics nurse*
Kelley, Patricia *marketing representative*
Schaaf, Martha Eckert *author, poet, library director, musician, composer, educator, lecturer*
Seifer, Ronald Leslie *psychologist*
†Zerick, A. Lura *writer*

Palm Beach

Adler, Frederick Richard *lawyer, financier*
Amling, Frederick *economist, educator, investment advisor*
Bagby, Joseph Rigsby *financial investor*
Bagby, Martha L. Green *real estate holding company executive, writer, publishing executive*
Barrett, Robert James, III, *investment banker*
Black, Leonard Julius *retail store consultant*
Canary, Nancy Halliday *lawyer*
Coudert, Dale Hokin *real estate executive, marketing consultant*
Crawford, Sandra Kay *lawyer*
†Cummings, William Roger *international tax consultant, property management executive*
Devins, Robert Sylvester *retired lawyer*
Dillard, Rodney Jefferson *real estate executive*
Donnell, John Randolph *retired petroleum executive*
†Elson, Suzanne Goodman *community activist*
Fitilis, Theodore Nicholas *portfolio manager, financial analyst, retired*
Flanagan, Joseph Patrick *advertising executive*
Floyd, Raymond Loran *professional golfer*
Fredericks, Lillian Elizabeth *anesthesiologist*
Gaudieri, Alexander V. J. *museum director*
Gilbertson, Bernice Charlotte *artist*
Graubard, Seymour *lawyer*
Gundlach, Heinz Ludwig *investment banker, lawyer*
Habicht, Frank Henry *retired industrial executive*
Harper, Mary Sadler *financial advisor*
Hastings, Lawrence Vaeth *lawyer, physician, educator*
Hope, Margaret Lauten *civic worker*
Johnson, Theodore Mebane *investment executive*
Karp, Richard M. *advertising and communication executive*
Klotsche, Charles Martin *real estate development company executive, photographer, writer, financial columnist*
Krois, Audrey *artist*
Lee, Robert Earl *retired physician*
†Levine, Audrey Pearlstein *foundation administrator*
Levine, Laurence Brandt *investment banker*
Mandel, Carola Panerai (Mrs. Leon Mandel) *foundation trustee*
McCarter, Thomas Nesbitt, III, *investment counseling company executive*
Monath, Norman *publishing company executive*
†Ness, Evaline (Mrs. Arnold A. Bayard) *illustrator, writer*
Pryor, Hubert *editor, writer*
Rauch, George Washington *lawyer, director*
Rinker, Ruby Stewart *foundation administrator*
†Robb, Babette *retired elementary school educator*
Rukeyser, M.S., Jr., *television consultant, writer*
Rumbough, Stanley Maddox, Jr., *industrialist*
Seggev, Meir *radiologist, educator*
Simon, Harold *radiologist*
Whiteside, Patricia Lee *fine art antique and personal property appraiser*
Winkler, Joseph Conrad *former recreational products manufacturing executive*
Wirtz, Willem Kindler *garden and lighting designer, public relations consultant*

Palm Beach Gardens

Auerbach, Paul Ira *lawyer*
†Awtrey, Jim L. *sports association executive*
†Blum, Irving Ronald *lawyer*
Bonifazi, Stephen *chemist*
†Bragdon, Clifford Richardson *city planner, educator*
Colussy, Dan Alfred *aviation executive*
†Couples, Frederick Steven *professional golfer*
Dedo, Douglas Donald *physician*
Druck, Kalman Breschel *public relations counselor*
†Duval, David Robert *professional golfer*
Falk, Bernard Henry *trade association executive*
Ginsberg, Stanley Arthur *retired urologist, consultant*
Giordano, Andrew Anthony *retired naval officer*
Harnett, Joseph Durham *oil company executive*
†Henninger, Brian Hatfield *professional golfer*
Holloway, Edward Olin *human services manager*
Horton, Edward Carl *retired military officer, public administrator*
Howard, Melvin *financial executive*
Keppler, William Edmund *multinational company executive*
Kleinberg, Lawrence H. *investor, consultant*
†Kline, Adrienne Marie *news producer*
†Leonard, Justin (Justin Charles Garret Leonard) *professional golfer*
Levitt, George *retired chemist*
†Love, Davis Milton, III, *professional golfer*
†Maggert, Jeffrey Allan *professional golfer*
†Marciano, Rico *health and fitness professional*
McCall, Duke Kimbrough *clergyman*
Mendelson, Richard Donald *former communications company executive*
Mergler, H. Kent *investment counselor*
†Mickelson, Phil(ip Alfred) *professional golfer*
†Miller, John Laurence *professional golfer*
†O'Meara, Mark *professional golfer*
Orr, Joseph Alexander *educational administrator*
Pumphrey, Gerald Robert *lawyer*
Rigby, Paul Crispin *artist, cartoonist*
Samuels, Fern Jacqueline *artist, educator*
†Scott, Alan Fulton, Jr., *lawyer*
Seaman, William Bernard *physician, radiology educator*
†Seidman, Jennifer L. *lawyer*
Skinner, Margaret Sheppard *pathologist*
†Stankowski, Paul Francis *professional golfer*
Staub, W. Arthur *health care products executive*
†Strange, Curtis Northrop *professional golfer*
Telepas, George Peter *retired lawyer*
Van Allen, Veronica Elaine *marketing and public relations professional*
†Verplank, Scott Rachal *professional golfer*
†Watson, Thomas Sturges *professional golfer*
†Westwood, Lee *professional golfer*
†Woods, Tiger (Eldrick Woods) *professional golfer*

Palm City

Boss, Manley Leon *plant physiologist*
Conklin, George Melville *retired food products executive*
Derrickson, William Borden *manufacturing executive*
Henry, David Howe, II, *retired diplomat*
Mc Hale, John Joseph *baseball club executive*
Sloan, Richard *artist*
Taylor Dye, Judy Angie *engineer, consultant*
†Whichello, Carol *political scientist, educator, writer*
Wishart, Ronald Sinclair *retired chemical company executive*

Palm Coast

Barnes, Judith Ann *real estate executive*
Brumback, Gary Bruce *industrial and organizational psychologist*
Bullard, Ervin Trowbridge *horticulturist*
Cook, Gloria Houston *civic leader*
Dickson, David Watson Daly *retired college president*
Duncan, Donald William *lawyer*
Farrell, Joseph Christopher *retired mining executive, services executive*
Franco, Annemarie Woletz *editor*
Owens, Garland Chester *accounting educator*
Patz, Edward Frank *retired lawyer*

Palm Harbor

Angier, Carol C. *volunteer*
†Baker, Gary Hugh *lawyer*
Barker, Larry Lee *communications educator, educator*
Bennett, John Joseph *professional services company executive*
†Bradley, Richard *chemist, consultant*
Dunbar, David Wesley *bank executive*
Fischer, John Jules *clergy member, theology educator, writer*
Giavis, Theodore Demetrios *commercial illustrator, artist*
Grace, John Eugene *business forms company executive*
Johnson, Randall Clyde *mortgage banker*
Katzen-Guthrie, Joy *performance artist, engineering services executive*
Kessler-Hodgson, Lee Gwendolyn *actress, corporate executive*
†Krawczynski, Tony Edward *music educator*
Morgan, Albert George Leonard *retired airline pilot, writer*
Padberg, Daniel Ivan *agricultural economics educator, researcher*
Rezanka, Thomas W. *lawyer*
†Rivelli, Susan Veronica *nurse*
Summers-Powell, Alan *lawyer*
Warfield, John Nelson *retired engineering educator, consultant*
Williams, Thomas Arthur *biomedical computing consultant, psychiatrist*

Palmetto

Angulo, Charles Bonin *foreign service officer, lawyer*
Carter, Elizabeth Wackerman *retired mental health nurse*
Dielman, Ray Walter *radiologic scientist, natural hygienist, medical herbalist*
Patton, Ray Baker *financial consultant, real estate broker*
Roehl, Nancy Leary *marketing professional, educator*
Turlo, George Jerzy *architect, city planner, artist*

Panama City

Adams, Logan G. *small business owner*
Allan, Sher L. *lawyer, mediator*
†Cox, Ron Dean *non-commissioned officer, educator, psychologist*
D'Arcy, Gerald Paul *engineering executive, consultant*
Dewey, Craig Douglas *operations executive*
Gould, Gerald G. *electrical engineer*
Griffin, Donald Scott *physician assistant*
Navon, Robert *real estate investor, former book publisher*
Nelson, Edith Ellen *dietitian*
†Priest, Adam Taft *civil engineer*
Rackers, Thomas William *physicist, researcher*
Reedy-Dewey, Madeline Anne *retired occupational therapist*
Robbins, Dorothy Ann *librarian*
Roberts, Paul Craig, III, *economics educator, author, columnist*
Schafer, John Stephen *poet*
Shugart, Cecil Glenn *retired physics educator*
Smith, Larry Glenn *retired state judge*

Panama City Beach

Anderson, Ruth Nathan *syndicated columnist, TV news host, writer, recording artist, lyricist*
Fejer, T. William *pianist, composer, architect, furniture designer*

Parkland

Brancaleone, Salvatore Joseph *nutritionist, consultant*
Landman, Deborah Tracy *real estate company executive, fitness trainer, small business owner*
†Masanoff, Michael David *lawyer*

Parrish

Corey, Kay Janis *business owner, designer, nurse*
Wood, Rev. Dr. Benton *retired editor, priest*

Pass A Grille Beach

Garnett, Stanley Iredale, II, *lawyer, utility company executive*

Patrick AFB

†Beauregard, Adam *aerospace engineer*

Paxton

Kearns, John William (Bill Kearns) *electronics inventor and executive*

Pembroke Pines

†Blanco, Jana M. *assistant principal*
DeBiagi, Anna Lillian *retired educator*
†Eisenstein, Sam *pediatric dentist*
Embergher, Mary Louise *elementary educator*
Ferris, Rita Bernadette *social worker*
Motes, Joseph Mark *cruise and convention promotion company executive*
Patel, Manish M. *physiatrist*
Robinson, Howard Neil *plastic surgeon*
Sobong, Loreto Calibo *nursing researcher*
Vayda, Rose K. *community volunteer*

Penney Farms

†Muilenburg, John Powell *minister*

Pensacola

Arnold, Barry Raynor *philosophy educator, medical ethicist, minister, counselor*
Bowden, Jesse Earle *newspaper editor, author, cartoonist, journalism educator*
Bozeman, Frank Carmack *lawyer*
Brooks, Joseph Franklin *real estate executive*
†Broxton, Randall *education educator, researcher*
Bullock, Ellis Way, Jr., *architect*
†Bumgardner, Kathryn H. *retired librarian*
Burke-Fanning, Madeleine *artist*
Canady, Alexa Irene *pediatric neurosurgeon*
Carper, William Barclay *management educator*
†Chhoeu, Austin H. *surgeon*
Cox, Amie C. *publisher*
Davis, Wesley D. *psychologist, educator*
DeMaria, Michael Brant *psychologist*
Desposito, Martha Sheats *artist, educator*
Diaz, Judy L. *language educator*
†Diggs, Yonna Darlene *civilian military employee*
Dillard, Robert Perkins *pediatrician, educator*
Echsner, Stephen Herre *lawyer*
Furlong, George Morgan, Jr., *museum foundation consultant, retired naval officer*
Gaines, Robert Pendleton *retired lawyer*
Geeker, Nicholas Peter *lawyer, judge*
George, Katie *lawyer*
Gill, Becky Lorette *retired psychiatrist*
†Gonçalves, Pitagoras L. *music educator*
Hutto, Earl *retired congressman*
Jespersen, Robert Randolph *legal consultant*
Kernstock, Elwyn Nicholas *political science educator, author*
Killian, Lewis Martin *sociology educator*
Larson, Kurt Paul *fire chief*
Leach, Luann Marie *elementary school educator*
Levin, Fredric Gerson *lawyer*
Loesch, Mabel Lorraine *social worker*
Long, H. Owen *retired economics educator, fiction writer*
Maddock, Lawrence Hill *retired language educator*
Maki, Hope Marie *artist, sculptor, illustrator, poet, educator*
Maygarden, Jerry Louis *health care foundation executive*
Mazzeo, Daniel Patrick *aerospace engineer, aviation consultant*
McGovern, James Richard *historian*
Moulton, Wilbur Wright, Jr., *lawyer*
†Mountcastle, William Wallace, Jr., *philosophy and religion educator*
Olsen, Richard Galen *biomedical engineer, consultant*
†Philen, Robert Carleton *anthropologist, educator*
Porter, Henry Olin *neurologist*
Raisler, Mary E. *nurse*
†Ricard, John H. *bishop, educator*
Ricketson, George Manning, III, *retired surgeon*
Rubardt, Peter Craig *conductor, educator*
Shimmin, Margaret Ann *women's health nurse*
†Sims, Pam *writer, minister*
Sisk, Rebecca Benefield *retired secondary school educator, small business owner*
Sjolander, Richard James *marketing and economics educator*
Soloway, Daniel Mark *lawyer*
†Stecchi, Nathan John *music educator*

Steinhoff, Raymond O(akley) *consulting geologist*
Taggart, Linda Diane *women's health nurse*
Telle, Lewis Donald *surgeon*
†Temme, Leonard A. *research scientist*
†Valdez, Michael R. *physician*
Van Atta, Cheri Marie *massage therapist*
Vuksta, Michael Joseph *surgeon*
Windham, John Franklin *lawyer, educator*
†Woodward, David Luther *lawyer, consultant*
Woolf, Kenneth Howard *architect*

Pineland
Donlon, Josephine A. *diagnostic and evaluation counseling therapist, educator*
Donlon, William James *retired lawyer*

Pinellas Park
†Benedict, Gail Cleveland *music educator*
Cramer, Kenneth Lee *protective services official, consultant*
Frantzis, Theodosios George *periodontist*
Hall, Charles Allen *aerospace and energy consultant*
†Mente, Ronald F. *consulting company executive*
Tower, Alton G., Jr., *pharmacist*
West, Wallace Marion *cultural organization administrator*

Placida
Wood, Yvonne McMurray *retired nursing educator*

Plant City
Buchman, Kenneth William *lawyer*
Feola, Ralph Leonard *insurance agent*
Henry, J. Myrle *pharmacist*
†Oom, Rita K. *small business owner, consultant*
Sparkman, Steven Leonard *lawyer*

Plantation
Ballantyne, Maree Anne Canine *artist*
Bosted, Dorothy Stack *public relations executive*
Burnett, Barbara Diane *social worker*
Carmichael, Robert William *medical group administrator*
Chou, Chung-Kwang *bio-engineer*
Crespi, Ted *lawyer*
Devol, George Charles, Jr., *manufacturing executive*
Gay, John Marion *federal agency administrator, organization-personnel analyst*
Gonshak, Isabelle Lee *nurse, civic worker*
†Levine, Tara Elise *physician*
Michael, Diann Dee *psychologist, educator*
Morris, James Bruce *internist*
Nickelson, Kim René *internist*
Patterson, Janice Pauline *community and geriatrics health nurse*
Patterson, Michael Milton *neuropsychologist, educator*
Sperry, Martin Jay *lawyer*
Stone, Marc J. *lawyer*
†Weiss, David I. *land developer, business executive, lawyer*
†Wick, Mitchell A. *physician*
Young, William Benjamin *retired special education educator*

Pompano Beach
Adams, Nancy Ann *retired school system administrator*
Bethel, Marilyn Joyce *librarian*
Bliznakov, Emile George *biomedical research scientist*
Bookbinder, Robert Max *superintendent of schools*
Bowsher, Dennis James *internist, cardiologist, pharmacologist*
Brands, Robert Franciscus *business executive*
Calatchi, Ralph Franklin *investment banker, writer*
Calevas, Harry Powell *management consultant*
Corsello, Lily Joann *minister, counselor, educator*
Donnelly, Michael Joseph *management consultant*
Eger, Joseph *conductor, music director*
Fritsch, Billy Dale, Jr., *construction company executive*
†Gill, Robert Jerome *education educator*
Goldberg, Lois D. *health facility administrator, disability analyst*
Hasenauer, Judith Anne *lawyer*
Johnson, Dorothy Curfman *elementary education educator*
Kaskinen, Barbara Kay *author, composer, songwriter, musician, music educator*
Kester, Stewart Randolph *banker*
Kory, Marianne Greene *lawyer*
Meloy, Sybil Piskur *retired lawyer*
Pigott, Melissa Ann *social psychologist*
Rifenburgh, Richard Philip *investment company executive*
Roen, Sheldon R. *publisher, psychologist*
Saunders, James Dalton *lawyer*
Schwartz, Joseph *retired container company executive*
†Searle, Bernard G. *pharmacologist, dental educator*
†Service, John Gregory *law educator*
Shulmister, M(orris) Ross *lawyer*
Sichewski, Vernon Roger *physician*
Szilassy, Sandor *retired lawyer, library director, educator*

Ponte Vedra Beach
Agassi, Andre Kirk *professional tennis player*
Berry, Clare Gebert *real estate broker*
de Selding, Edward Bertrand *retired banker*
†Faxon, Brad *professional golfer*
Finchem, Tim *sports association executive*
Fiorentino, Thomas Martin *transportation executive, lawyer*
Friedmann, Elizabeth Carroll *writer, editor*
Gold, Keith Dean *advertising and design executive*

Green, Norman Kenneth *retired oil industry executive, former naval officer*
Hamilton, William Berry, Jr., *retired shipping company executive*
Hartzell, Karl Drew *retired university dean, historian*
Horty, John Francis *lawyer*
Keeler, Ross Vincent *securities company executive*
Kuhn, Bowie K. *lawyer, former professional baseball commissioner, consultant*
Langford, Dean Ted *lighting and precision materials company executive*
Leek, Jay Wilbur *management consultant*
Linnen, Thomas Francis *international strategic management consulting firm executive*
MacKowski, John Joseph *retired insurance company executive*
Moore, David Graham *sociologist, educator*
Nadler, Sigmond Harold *physician, surgeon*
O'Brien, Raymond Vincent, Jr., *banker*
Patterson, Oscar, III, *university program administrator*
Pavin, Corey Allen *professional golfer*
Ramsey, William Dale, Jr., *marketing and technology consultant*
ReMine, William Hervey, Jr., *surgeon*
Roland, Melissa Montgomery *accountant*
Slayton, Gus *foundation administrator*
†Sluman, Jeff (Jeffrey George Sluman) *professional golfer*
Spence, Richard Dee *former railroad executive*
Stricker, Steve *golfer*
Triplett, Kirk Allen *golfer*
†Tyler, Diane Lazzelle *elementary school educator*
†Wadkins, Lanny *professional golfer*
†Washington, MaliVai *professional tennis player*
Watson, John Lawrence, III, *former trade association executive*
Wood, Quentin Eugene *oil company executive*
Wu, Hsiu Kwang *economist, educator*

Port Charlotte
Al-Khatib, Tareq *surgeon*
Donovan, William Alan *retired librarian*
Gendzwill, Joyce Annette *retired health officer*
Hill, Richard Earl *academic administrator*
†Holt, Barbara Lynn *school nurse practitioner*
Kok, Hans Gebhard *consulting engineer*
Leslie, John *artist, designer, fine art photographer, sculptor*
Levin, Allen Jay *lawyer*
McMullen, G. Arthur *physician, cardiologist*
Peterson, Elaine Grace *retired technology director*
Reynolds, Helen Elizabeth *management services consultant*
Von Holden, Martin Harvey *psychologist*
Wall, Edward Millard *environmental consulting executive*
Whittaker, Douglas Kirkland *school system administrator*
Winters, Stanley B. *history educator, writer, civic activist*

Port Orange
Mehta, Ravi Ravinder Singh *international trade finance consultant, banking trainer and researcher, trade specialist*
Millar, Gordon Halstead *mechanical engineer, agricultural machinery manufacturing executive*

Port Richey
†Fry, Ronald Sylvan *music educator, director*

Port Saint Lucie
Augelli, John Pat *geographer, educator , writer, consulant, rancher*
Beatrice, Ruth Hadfield *hypnotherapist, retired educator, financial administrator*
Guglielmino, Lucy Margaret Madsen *education educator, researcher, consultant*
†Guglielmino, Paul Joseph *educator*
Hogan, Roxanne Arnold *nursing consultant, risk management consultant, educator*
Holloman, Marilyn Leona Davis *nurse non profit administrator, health products executive*
Jackson, George Mark *writer, photographer*
Keeley, Ethel S. *workforce development trainer*
Lambert, George Robert *lawyer, realtor*
Sommers, Robert Thomas *editor, publisher, author*
Verfaillie, Roland Bruce *mental health professional*
†Weber, Alban *association executive, lawyer*

Punta Gorda
Beasom, Nancy Ann *occupational therapist, consultant*
Beever, James William, III, *biologist*
Clinton, Mariann Hancock *educational association administrator*
Goodman, Donald C. *university administrator*
Haswell, Carleton Radley *banker*
Hughes, Spencer Edward, Jr., *retired financial executive, consultant*
Klarik, Bela William James Clark *retired school system administrator*
Koll, Richard Leroy *retired chemical company executive*
McDaniel, Norwood Allan *insurance broker*
Miles, Frank Charles *retired newspaper executive*
O'Donnell, Mary Murphy *retired medical/surgical nurse*
Smith, Charles Edwin *computer science educator*
Smith-Mooney, Marilyn Patricia *city government official, management consultant and facilitator*
Spaulding, Mar *retired special education educator, therapist*

Ramrod Key
Clark, John Russell *marine biologist*

Reddick
Corwin, Joyce Elizabeth Stedman *construction company executive*

Redington Beach
Alpert, Barry Mark *insurance company and banking executive*

Riverview
Cyril, Todd Alexander *military officer*
Morshed, Md Moqbul *civil and environmental engineer*
Till, Beatriz Maria *international business consultant, translator*

Riviera Beach
†Feller, Thomas Richard, Jr., *music educator*
Totten, Gloria Jean (Dolly Totten) *real estate executive, financial consultant*

Rockledge
Deitch, D. Gregory *meteorologist*
Sutton, Betty Sheriff *elementary education educator*

Roseland
Canterbury-Counts, W. Douglas *psychologist*

Royal Palm Beach
Perez, Jorge Luis *retired manufacturing executive*
Zucker, Leonard Charles *trucking executive, rabbi*

Ruskin
Briscoe, Anne M. *retired scientist, educator*
LaComb-Williams, Linda Lou *community health nurse*
Smith, Calvin Douglas *music educator, musician*

Safety Harbor
Banks, Allan Richard *artist, art historian, researcher*
Banks, Holly Hope *artist*
Dohnal, William Edward *retired steel company executive, consultant, accountant*
†Kaplan, Kerry Joseph *internist, cardiologist*
†Patterson, Sylvia K. *elementary school educator, writer*

Saint Augustine
Adams, William Roger *historian, consultant*
Ansbacher, Sidney Franklyn *lawyer*
Bishop, Claire DeArment *small business owner, former librarian*
Borchardt, Duke *federal labor relations professional*
Bourne, John David *retired city finance executive*
Connaway, Robert Wallace *artist, computer programmer*
†DeLaughter, Thomas Glenn *finance educator, consultant, academic administrator*
Flemister, Launcelot Johnson *physiologist, educator*
Henderson, Hazel *writer, lecturer*
Hibbard, Walter Rollo, Jr., *retired engineering educator*
Keys, Leslee Frances *historic preservation planner*
†Lando, Joseph P., Jr., (Louis Lento) *at-risk educator, writer, retired executive*
Lund, Frederick Henry *aerospace and electrical engineer*
Matzke, Frank J. *architect, consultant*
McCarty, Doran Chester *religious organization administrator*
Nolan, David Joseph *author, historian*
Nolan, Joseph Thomas *journalism educator, communications consultant*
Oliver, Elizabeth Kimball *writer, historian*
Poole, Sharon Alexandra *lawyer*
Preysz, Louis Robert Fonss, III, *management consultant, educator*
Proctor, William Lee *college chancellor*
Quirke, Lillian Mary *retired art educator*
Rice, David Preston *minister, educator*
Sullivan, Mary Jean *elementary school educator*
Wiles, Marilyn McCall *communications consultant*
Wilkes, Delano Angus *architect*
Witty, Robert Wilkes *insurance services company executive*

Saint Cloud
Everett, Woodrow Wilson *electrical engineer, educator*
Potts, Carol Jean Fox *geriatrics nurse, quality assurance coordinator*

Saint Leo
†Bowden, Randall Glen *marketing and business development administrator*

Saint Lucie West
Hambel, Henry Peter *clinical hypnotherapist, forensic security consultant, educator*

Saint Petersburg
Allshouse, Merle Frederick *educational organization administrator*
Alvarez, Wilson Eduardo *baseball player*
Armacost, Peter Hayden *academic administrator*
Baker, Victoria Jean *anthropology educator*
Barnes, Andrew Earl *newspaper executive*
Battaglia, Anthony Sylvester *lawyer*
Battaglia, Brian Peter *lawyer*
Beaman, Ann Thomson *volunteer*
Belich, John Patrick, Sr., *journalist*
Benbow, Charles Clarence *retired writer, critic*
Bercu, Barry Bernard *pediatric endocrinologist*
†Bernstein, Howard Mark *lawyer*
Betzer, Susan Elizabeth Beers *family physician, geriatrician*
Blankstein, Mary Freeman *violinist*
†Boydstun, Charles Bryant, Jr., *lawyer*
Bryant, Timothy Clark *investment brokerage executive*

†Buchan, Russell Paul *publisher, gas company executive, entrepreneur*
Burnette, Charles Galyon *protective services official*
Byrd, Isaac Burlin *fishery biologist, fisheries administrator*
Carlson, Jeannie Ann *writer*
Carrere, Charles Scott *law educator, judge*
Carroll, Charles Michael *music educator*
Chipman, Marion Walter *retired judge*
Christiano, Melissa *artist, educator*
Collins, Carl Russell, Jr., *industrial engineer*
Collins, Paul Steven *vascular surgeon*
Connelly, David O'Brien *art museum administrator, journalist*
Conover, Dorothy Nancy Lever *medical practice administrator, nurse*
Corty, Andrew P. *publishing executive*
DeLorenzo, David Joseph *retired public relations executive*
†Despanza-Sprenger, Lynette Charlie *small business owner*
Dimas, Marilyn J. *health resources executive*
†Dunlap, Karen F. Brown *academic administrator*
Edwards, Fred L., Jr., *writer consultant*
Emerson, William Allen *retired investment company executive*
Engel, John Jacob *communications executive*
Escarraz, Enrique, III, *lawyer*
Favre, Gregory *publishing executive*
Fleming, William Sloan *energy executive, computer company executive*
Fraser, John Wayne *insurance executive, consultant, underwriter*
Freeburg, Richard Gorman *financial derivatives company executive*
Freeman, Corinne *financial services, former mayor*
Georges, Richard Martin *lawyer, educator*
Glass, Roy Leonard *lawyer*
Godbold, Francis Stanley *investment banker, securities firm executive*
†Gooden, Dwight Eugene *professional baseball player*
Grastorf, Jean Elizabeth Hancock *artist, educator*
†Gregg, Kathy Kay *school system administrator*
Gross, Geoffrey Fries *systems engineer*
Grube, Karl Bertram *judge*
Haiman, Robert James *newspaper editor, journalism educator, media consultant*
Hansel, Paul George *physicist, consultant*
†Hargrave, Victoria Elizabeth *librarian*
Harrell, Roy G., Jr., *lawyer*
†Hersh, Ellen E. *poet*
Hooker, Robert Wright *journalist*
†Hsu, Tsong Han *chemist, researcher*
Hua, Shiping *political science educator*
Huang, Ben (Haibin Huang) *chemical engineer, researcher*
Hudkins, John W. *lawyer*
Hurley, John Kenneth *real estate and merchant banking executive*
Hussain, Basit *computer engineer, writer*
Jacob, Bruce Robert *law educator*
Jarrard, Marilyn Mae *nursing consultant, nursing researcher*
Jaworski, Dolores Daley *advanced nurse practitioner*
Jenkins, Robert Norman *reporter, editor*
Johnson, Pam *former newspaper editor, communications educator*
Kaiser, Greg Christopher *pediatric gastroenterologist*
†Keane, Michael J. *lawyer*
Keller, Natasha Matrina Leonidow *nursing administrator*
Kent, Allen *library and information sciences educator*
Kiefner, John Robert, Jr., *lawyer, educator*
Kubiet, Leo Lawrence *newspaper advertising and marketing executive*
Kuttler, Carl Martin, Jr., *academic administrator*
†Lacson, Atilano G. *pathologist*
Lang, Joseph Hagedorn *lawyer*
Leach, Jane Riley *fundraiser*
Leavell, William A. *publisher, editor*
Linhart, Joseph Wayland *retired cardiologist, educational administrator*
†Main, Timothy L. *electronics executive*
†Mancuso, Vincent *artist, art educator*
Mann, Sam Henry, Jr., *lawyer*
†McArdle, Barbara Virginia *elementary school educator*
McCluskey, Charles James, Jr., *physician assistant*
†McEwen, Aila Erman *small business owner*
†McGriff, Fred (Frederick Stanley McGriff) *baseball player*
Metzger, Kathleen Ann *computer systems specialist*
Meyer, Robert Allen *human resource management educator*
Meyers, Allan D. *archaeologist*
Mills, William Harold, Jr., *construction company executive*
Moody, Lizabeth Ann *law educator*
Mueller, O. Thomas *molecular geneticist, pediatrics educator*
Mussett, Richard Earl *city official*
Naimoli, Vincent Joseph *diversified operating and holding company executive*
Naughton, James Martin *journalist*
†Nunn, Margaret Baker *owner boutique*
Patterson, Eugene Corbett *retired editor, publisher*
Petty, Marty *publishing executive*
Piscani, Kathleen Folkerts *clinical psychiatric nurse*
Pittman, Robert Turner *retired newspaper editor*
Putnam, J. Stephen *financial executive*
Ratzlaff, Donna Cheryl *social worker*
†Reilly, Thomas *museum exhibit designer, artist, writer*
Reilly, Tracy Lynn *English educator*
Roney, Paul H(itch) *federal judge*
Root, Allen William *pediatrician, educator*

Rosenblum, Martin Jerome ophthalmologist
Ross, Howard Philip lawyer
Rummel, Harold Edwin real estate development and retail sales executive
Runde, Craig Eric academic director
Rydstrom, Carlton Lionel chemist, chemicals consultant
Schmidt, Paul Joseph physician, educator
†Schrader, Daryl Lynn mathematician, educator
Scott, Kathryn Fenderson lawyer
Scott, Lee Hansen retired holding company executive
†Sebastien, Anya Celita academic administrator, consultant
†Sembler, Mel company executive, ambassador
Simpson, Lisa Ann government agency administrator, physician
Siska, Mary Noreen nursing administrator
Smith, Sarah Jeanne gerontologist
Smyth, Walter G. real estate broker
Southworth, William Dixon retired education educator
Spence, Philip William manufacturing executive, consultant
Stark, Brandy B. news correspondent, educator, artist
Stedman, R VanGorden artist, art historian radio and television personality
Stewart, Sheila Kay anthropologist, archaeologist
Styve, Orloff Wendall, Jr., electrical engineer
†Swygert, Michael I(rven) legal educator
†Tabakovic, Dragan electrical engineer, researcher
Tash, Paul Clifford editor, publishing executive
Thompson, Dayle Ann management and accounting systems consultant
Vaughn, Gregory Lamont professional baseball player
Wadley, W(illiam) Thomas lawyer
Walker, Brigitte Maria translator, linguistic consultant
Walker, Francis Roach rehabilitation consultant
Wasserman, Susan Valesky accountant, artist, yoga instructor
†Weaver, F. Louise Beazley curator, director
Wedding, Charles Randolph architect
†Wein, Stephen Joshua lawyer
White, June Miller mathematics educator, education consultant
Williams, Larry Ross surgeon
†Williams, Minnie Caldwell retired educator
Wilson, Paul baseball player
Witt, Jeffrey R. cardiologist
Wright, Fred W., Jr., writer
Yanev, George P mathematician, educator

Saint Petersburg Beach
†Gagan, James Ephriam lawyer
Hurley, Frank Thomas, Jr., realtor

Sanford
Dickison, Alexander Kane physical science educator
Easton, Susan Shearer organizational development consultant, educator
†Linsley, Laurie Strickland information specialist/librarian
Octaviani, Hector pediatrician
Oostwouder, Peter Henry family physician
Scott, Mellouise Jacqueline educational media specialist

Sanibel
Ball, Armand Baer former association executive, consultant
Brodbeck, William Jan marketing consultant, speaker
Crown, David Allan criminologist, educator
Davie, Joseph Myrten physician, pathology and immunology educator, science administrator
Hasselman, Richard B. retired transportation company executive
Keogh, Mary Cudahy artist
†LaCombe, David M. emergency medical services educator, consultant
Ray, Charles Albert photojournalist
Sappenfield, Charles Madison architect, educator
Sheldon, Nancy Way environmental management consultant
Simontacchi, Carol Nadine nutritionist, writer

Santa Rosa Beach
Rees, Lane Charles industrial relations consultant

Sarasota
Allen, George Howard publishing management consultant
Altabe, Joan Augusta Berg artist, writer, art and architecture critic
Arreola, John Bradley
Atwell, Robert Herron higher education executive
Bailey, Robert Elliott financial executive
Balliett, John William entrepreneur, real estate executive
Bausch, James John foundation executive
Beck, Robert Alfred hotel administration educator
Benedick, James Michael psychotherapist
†Benowitz, June Melby historian, educator
Berkoff, Charles Edward pharmaceutical executive
Berman, Lewis Paul financial executive
Best, Jerry Lavon insurance consultant
Blomgren, Bruce Holmes real estate developer, marina developer, consultant
Bonn, Theodore Hertz computer scientist, consultant
Bowers, Charles Richard surgeon
Brandhorst, Wesley Theodore retired information scientist
Brassard, Virginia educator
Bushey, Alan Scott retired insurance holding company executive
Byron, E. Lee real estate broker
Campbell, Michael Harry psychologist, academic administrator
Carr, Patricia Ann community health nurse
†Carstens, Charlene B. composer, music educator
Cavanagh, Denis physician, educator
Ceo, Barbara Ann speech-language pathologist, educator
Christ-Janer, Arland Frederick college president
Christopher, William Garth lawyer
Clark, Eugenie zoologist, educator
Clarke, Garvey Elliott lawyer
Cleland, Sherrill college president
Close, Michael John lawyer
Colina, Ramon Enrique gastroenterologist
Conetta, Tami Foley lawyer
Cooper, William Ewing, Jr., retired army officer
Coufoudakis, Van political science educator
Cramer, Stanley Howard psychology educator, author
Cummings, Martin Marc medical educator, physician, scientific administrator
Dearden, Robert James pharmacist
De Gennaro, Richard retired library director, library advisor
Deutsch, Sid bioengineer, educator
Dobosz, Mark Joseph fundraiser
Doenecke, Justus Drew history educator
Drake, Diana Ashley financial planner
Dryce, H. David accountant, consultant
Ehrlich, Bernard Herbert lawyer, association executive
Eichholz, Alexander A. physiology researcher, consultant
Eller, Warren Bernson retired insurance company executive
Elmendorf-Landgraf, Mary Lindsay retired anthropologist
El Shahawy, Mahfouz internist, cardiologist, educator
Feldhusen, Hazel Jeanette elementary education educator
Fendrick, Alan Burton retired advertising executive
Fetterman, James Charles lawyer
†Foreman, Michael Loren lawyer
Garland, Richard Roger lawyer
Gauch, Eugene William, Jr., retired air force officer
Gidel, Robert Hugh real estate investor
Giordano, David Alfred retired internist, gastroenterologist
Gittelson, Bernard public relations consultant, author, lecturer
Gladding, Nicholas C. lawyer
Gordon, Sanford Daniel economics educator
Graham, Douglass of Montrose museum curator, banker, artist, poet
Greenfield, Robert Kauffman retired lawyer
Gustafson, Karin Elisabeth foundation executive
Hackl, Alphons J. publisher
Hamberg, Daniel economist, educator
Harris, Judith Ann White health occupations vocational educator, nurse
Harvey, Donald Phillips retired naval officer
Heiser, Rolland Valentine former army officer, foundation executive
Heitler, George lawyer
Hennemeyer, Robert Thomas diplomat
Herb, F(rank) Steven lawyer
Hilt, Thomas Harry minister
Hoffman, Oscar Allen retired forest products company executive
Honner Sutherland, B. Joan advertising executive
Huff, Russell Joseph public relations and publishing executive
Hughes, Allen music critic
Hull, J(ames) Richard retired lawyer, business executive
Hummel, Dana D. Mallett librarian
Iverson, Robert Louis, Jr., internist, physician
Jackel, Lawrence publishing company executive
Jacobson, Jeanne McKee humanities educator, writer
Jarzen, David MacArthur research scientist
Jelks, Mary Larson retired pediatrician
Johnson, Leland "Lee" Harry social services administrator
†Jones, George Steven civil engineer
Jones, Sally Daviess Pickrell writer
Jones, Tracey Kirk, Jr., minister, educator
Kelly, John Love public relations executive
Kendig, Calvin Fridy, Jr., financial consultant, electrical engineer, consultant
Kerker, Milton chemistry educator
Kimbrough, Robert Averyt lawyer
Krate, Nat artist
Krumholz, Richard A. physician
Landis, Edgar David business consultant
Larsen, Lawrence Bernard, Jr., priest, pastoral psychotherapist
Lee, Ann McKeighan curriculum specialist
Lee, Nancy Ranck management consultant
Lengyel, Alfonz art history, archeology and museology educator
Lewis, Brian Kreglow computer consultant
Long, Robert Radcliffe fluid mechanics educator
†Lowman, Margaret D. botanist
Magenheim, Mark Joseph physician, epidemiologist, educator
Mahadevan, Kumar marine laboratory director, researcher
Marino, Eugene Louis publishing company executive
Marks, Charles surgeon, educator
Masters, John Christopher psychologist, educator, writer
Mattran, Donald Albert management consultant, educator
McCollum, John Morris tenor
McFarlin, Diane Hooten publisher
†McLain, John Howard retired military officer
Melançon, Joseph Herman artist, educator
Metzger, Sidney retired communications engineer
Meyer, B. Fred small business executive, home designer and builder, product designer
†Michejda, Oskar civil engineer, structural engineer, consultant
Middleton, Norman Graham social worker, psychotherapist
Miles, Arthur J. financial planner, consultant
Miranda, Carlos Sa food products company executive
Mitchell, John Noyes, Jr., retired electrical engineer
†Mizer, Joyce Taylor music educator
Morris, Gordon James financial company executive, consultant
Morrow, William Earl retired government official
Mullane, John Francis pharmaceutical company executive
Myerson, Albert Leon physical chemist
Neeley, Delmar George mediator, pastoral counselor
North, Marjorie Mary columnist
O'Malley, Thomas Anthony gastroenterologist, internist
Partoyan, Garo Arakel lawyer
Paru, Marden David fundraising executive
Pender, Michael Roger engineering consultant
Phillips, Elvin Willis lawyer
Phillips, Howard William investment banker
Pierce, Richard Harry oceanographer
Pike, Nancy M. librarian
Pillot, Gene Merrill retired school system administrator
Plunket, Dolores art and archaeology educator
Proffitt, Waldo, Jr., newspaper editor
Raimi, Burton Louis lawyer
Ramsier, Paul composer, psychotherapist
Reagan, Larry Gay college vice president
†Reichert, Robert Joseph real estate appraiser
Retzer, Mary Elizabeth Helm retired librarian
Rilla, Donald Robert retired social services administrator
Rinker, H. Bruce ecologist
Roberts, Don E. accountant
Robinson, Bruce Eugene physician, educator, researcher
Rosenkoetter, Gerald Edwin engineering and construction company executive
Ross, Gerald Fred engineering executive, researcher
Rossi, William Matthew lawyer
Roth, James Frank manufacturing company executive, chemist
†Ruva, Christine Lorraine psychologist, educator
Scheitlin, Constance Joy real estate broker, accountant
Schlegel, John Frederick management consultant, speaker, trainer
†Schwartz, Francis music educator, composer
Seibert, Russell Jacob botanist, research associate
Serrie, Gretchen Ihde retired symphony executive director
Serrie, Hendrick retired anthropology and international business educator
Shulman, Arthur communications executive
Simon, Joseph Patrick food services executive
Slocum, Donald Hillman product development executive
†Snyder, Lee Daniel historian, educator
Snyder, Wesley Warren interior space planner and designer
Spencer, Lonabelle (Kappie Spencer) political agency administrator, lobbyist
Stevens, Elisabeth Goss (Mrs. Robert Schleussner Jr.) writer, journalist, graphic artist
Stevens, Leonard Berry educational consultant
Stickler, Daniel Lee health care management consultant
†Straight, Elsie Hosking retired art librarian, sculptor
Stumm, Brian J. mechanical engineer, researcher
Sturtevant, Ruthann Patterson anatomy educator
Summonte, Joseph F., Jr., lawyer
Taplin, Winn Lowell historian, retired senior intelligence operations officer
Thompson, Annie Figueroa academic director, educator
Tucci, Steven Michael health facility administrator, physician, recording industry executive
Venit, William Bennett electrical products company executive, consultant
Wadsworth, Dyer Seymour retired lawyer
Wagner von Igelgrund, Wenceslas Joseph law educator
Weeks, Albert Loren author, educator, journalist
West, Bob pharmaceutical company executive
Wetenhall, John museum director
Wetstone, Janet Meyerson designer, journalist
Williams, Julia Rebecca Keys secondary school educator
Wilson, Kenneth Jay writer
Winterhalter, Dolores August (Dee Winterhalter) art educator
†Wolfe, Richard Barry Michael retired lawyer
Yonker, Richard Aaron rheumatologist
Zavon, Mitchell Ralph occupational medicine physician
Zentner, Arnold Stuart psychiatrist

Satellite Beach
Clark, John F. aerospace research and engineering educator
†Covault, Craig editor
Koenig, Harold Paul management consultant, ecologist, evangelist, writer
Nunnally, Stephens Watson civil engineer
Osmundsen, Barbara Ann sculptor
Van Arsdall, Robert Armes engineer, retired air force officer

Sebastian
Eddy, Elsbeth Marie retired government official, statistician
Mauke, Leah Rachel retired counselor
Mauke, Otto Russell retired college president
Pieper, Patricia Rita artist, photographer

Sebring
DeWitt, Carol A. publishing executive, writer
Ibrahim, George W. physician, health facility administrator
Maire, Barbara Jean volunteer
†McCollum, James Fountain lawyer
Sherrick, Daniel Noah real estate broker
Trombley, Michael Jerome lawyer
Weimer, Peter Dwight retired mediator, lawyer, corporate executive

Seffner
†Seaman, Jeffrey executive

Seminole
Riedling, Ann Marlow education educator
Wilson, Marc Burt engineer
†Wolf, Elizabeth Ann writer, storyteller, visual arts

Shalimar
Chesser, David Michael lawyer
Sublette, Julia Wright music educator, performer, adjudicator

Silver Springs
Parks, Sherri Lou ballet dancer, thoroughbred handler

South Florida
Hoffman, Randy Michael automotive executive

South Miami
Bauman, Sandra Spiegel nurse practitioner, mental health counselor
†Keedy, Christian David lawyer
Skolnik, Phyllis dermatologist

Sparr
Tovi, Murray futurist, research scientist

Spring Hill
Burnim, Kalman Aaron theatre educator emeritus
Finney, Roy Pelham, Jr., urologist, surgeon, inventor
Hopkins, Thomas Charles behavior specialist
Martin, Gary J. retired business executive, mayor
Mericle, Suzanne Eleanor retired secondary school educator
Rojas, Victor Hugo Macedo retired vocational education educator
†Thompson, Connie Ann nurse
Vanderburg, Paul Stacey insurance executive, consultant
Wood, Shelton Eugene college educator, consultant, minister

Steinhatchee
Grubbs, Elven Judson retired newspaper publisher

Stuart
Ankrom, Charles Franklin golf course architect, consultant
†Ballinger, Richard L. orchestra director
Cocoves, Anita Petzold psychotherapist
Dimbath, Merle F. economic consultant, business educator
Donohue, Edith M. human resources specialist, educator
Hutchinson, Janet Lois historical society administrator
Jaffe, Jeff Hugh retired food products executive
Laska, Paul Robert protective services official, writer, educator
Leibson, Irving retired industrial executive
Logan, Henry Vincent transportation executive, consultant
Maldonado, Carlos Manuel surgeon
McKenna, Sidney F. retired technical company executive
McManus, F. Shields lawyer
Merrill, Vincent Nichols retired landscape architect
Robinson, Michael Hill retired zoological park director, biologist
Taudien, Edward Paul retired construction executive
Woodward, Isabel Avila educational writer, foreign language educator

Summerfield
McNulty, Carrell Stewart, Jr., retired manufacturing company executive, architect
Shahmiri, Anis Ahmad internist

Summerland Key
†Dallas, Joseph Anthony, Jr., music educator
Muth, John Fraser economics educator

Sun City Center
Crow, Harold Eugene physician, family medicine educator
Edwards, Paul Beverly retired science and engineering educator
Freeman, Myra Jessie retired farm owner, writer
Fuller, Samuel Ashby retired lawyer, mining company executive
Gummere, Walter Cooper educator, consultant
Hall, John Fry psychologist, educator
Jeffries, Robert Joseph retired engineer, educator, business executive
†L'Ecuyer, Eleanor Creed lawyer, retired career officer
Leonard, William Norris economist, educator
McGrath, John Francis utility executive
Rubin, Robert Jay toxicologist
Stanton, Vivian Brennan (Mrs. Ernest Stanton) retired educator
Ward, Jacqueline Ann Beas nurse, healthcare administrator

Sunny Isles Beach
Brunetto, Frank electrical engineer

Sunrise
Bainton, Donald J. *diversified manufacturing company executive*
Delgado, Orlando *import company executive*
Keenan, Mike *professional hockey team coach*
Kolker, Sondra G. *fund raising, special events executive*
†Larionov, Igor *hockey player*
Mason, Sherilyn Sue *artist*
Ozolinsh, Sandis *hockey player*
Sorensen, Allan Chresten *service company executive*
Thompson, Yaakov *rabbi*
Torrey, William Arthur *professional hockey team executive*
Worrell, Peter *professional hockey player*

Tallahassee
†AbdelRazig, Yassir A. *engineering educator*
Anderson, John Roy *grouting engineer*
Anstead, Harry Lee *state supreme court justice*
Ashler, Philip Frederic *international trade and development advisor*
Aurell, John Karl *lawyer*
Bagley, James Robert *freelance writer*
†Bailey, Theresa L. *director, consultant*
Bartlett, Richard Adams *American historian, educator*
Benson, Bruce Lowell *economics educator*
Bird, Mark Douglas *magnet designer, engineering researcher*
Bishop, Barney Tipton, III, *political commentator, analyst, lobbyist, consultant*
Bowden, Bobby *university athletic coach*
Boyd, Joseph Arthur, Jr., *lawyer*
Bridger, Carolyn Ann *pianist, music educator*
Buford, Barbara Fest *retired state agency employee*
Burkman, Ernest, Jr., *education educator*
Burnette, Ada M. Puryear *educational administrator*
Bush, John Ellis (Jeb Bush) *governor*
†Butler, Robert Olen *writer, educator*
†Byrd, Johnnie, Jr., *state legislator*
†Campbell, Frances Harvell *foundation administrator*
Canterbery, E. Ray *economics educator*
Carson, Leonard Allen *lawyer*
Caspar, Donald L.D. *biophysics and structural biology educator*
Choppin, Gregory Robert *chemistry educator*
Cobbe, James Hamilton *economics educator*
Cockrell, Wilburn Allen *archaeologist*
Coloney, Wayne Herndon *civil engineer*
†Conaway, Charles William *information scientist, educator*
†Conners, Patricia A. *lawyer*
Conti, Lisa Ann *epidemiologist, veterinarian*
Crew, Andrew Jackson *retired secondary school educator, band director*
†Crist, Charles (Charlie Crist) *state attorney general*
Cronin, Jerome Joseph, Jr., *marketing educator, consultant*
Cummings, Frederic Alan *lawyer*
Curtin, Lawrence N. *lawyer*
Dadisman, Joseph Carrol *newspaper executive*
D'Alemberte, Talbot (Sandy D'Alemberte) *academic administrator, lawyer*
Davis, Bertram Hylton *retired English educator*
Davis, Larry Michael *air force officer, healthcare manager, consultant*
Davis, William Howard *lawyer*
Deal, Charles Raymond *anesthesiologist*
Deeb, Larry Charles *pediatric endocrinologist, epidemiologist*
DeFoor, J. Allison, II, *lawyer*
De Forest, Sherwood Searle *agricultural engineer, agribusiness services executive*
Dillon, Millicent Gerson *writer*
Dorn, Charles Meeker *art education educator*
Downie, Robert Collins, II, *lawyer*
Drayton, Carey M. *police administrator*
†Edwards, Leigh Holladay *literature educator*
Eggebraaten, Gary Bruce *software engineer, consultant*
Elder, Joan Elizabeth *music educator, consultant*
Ericsson, Karl Anders *cognitive psychologist, educator, researcher*
†Ervin, Charles Phifer, Jr., *retired military officer, education educator*
Ervin, Robert Marvin *lawyer*
†Fiore, Carole Diane *public library consultant for youth services*
†Fiorito, Jack Thomas *education educator*
Fonvielle, Charles David *lawyer*
France, Belinda Takach *lawyer, business owner*
†Friedman, Max Paul *education educator*
Gabor, Jeffrey Alan *insurance and financial services executive*
Gary, Thomas *lawyer*
†Gievers, Karen A. *lawyer*
Gilmer, Robert *mathematics educator*
†Gleeson, Thomas Alexander *retired meteorologist*
Golden, Leon *classicist, educator*
Gomory, Tomi *educator*
Grant, Sydney R. *education educator, consultant*
Griffith, Elwin Jabez *lawyer, university administrator*
Grimes, Stephen Henry *retired state supreme court justice*
Gunter, William Dawson, Jr., (Bill Gunter) *insurance company executive, consultant*
Guy, Mary Ellen Johnston *political science educator*
†Hadden, Sally *historian, educator*
Hall, Houghton Alexander *electrical engineer, city official*
Halpern, Paul G. *history educator*
Hamilton, J. Leonard *collegiate basketball coach, former professional basketball coach*
Hammer, Marion Price *association executive*
Han, Ke *materials scientist, metallurgy consultant*
Harper, George Mills *English language educator*
Harrison, Thomas James *electrical engineer, educator*
Harsanyi, Janice *soprano, educator*
†Hernandez, Jose Yolando Balagtas *physician, surgeon*
Herndon, Roy Clifford *physicist*
Herskovitz, S(am) Marc *lawyer*
Hetrick, Charles Brady *county official*
Hicken, Russell Bradford *art dealer, appraiser*
Holcomb, Lyle Donald, Jr., *retired lawyer*
Holcombe, Randall Gregory *economics educator*
†Hood, Glenda E. *state agency administrator*
Huang, Dongzhou *civil engineer, researcher, engineering educator*
Humphrey, Louise Ireland *civic worker, equestrienne*
Hunt, John Edwin *insurance company executive, consultant*
Hunt, Mary Alice *library science educator*
†Isaac, Larry W. *sociologist, educator*
†Islam, A.K.M. Anwarul *civil engineer, consultant*
Jennings, Toni *lieutenant governor*
Johnson, Benjamin F., VI, *economist, consultant*
Johnson, Margaret Anderson *writer, publishing executive, plantation owner*
†Jordan, Tracey Alys *librarian*
Keister, Beverly Jane *accountant*
Kemper, Kirby Wayne *physics educator*
†Kerns, David Vincent *lawyer*
†King, James E. "Jim", Jr., *state legislator, personnel executive, consultant*
†Kohout, Ladislav Jan *computer science educator*
Kromhout, Robert Andrew *educator*
Laird, Doris Anne Marley *humanities educator, musician*
Laird, William Everette, Jr., *economics educator, administrator*
†Larson, Sharon D. *lawyer, human resources specialist*
Laughlin, William Eugene *retired electric power industry executive*
Leavell, Michael Ray *computer programmer, analyst*
†Leushuis, Reinier *language educator*
Lick, Dale Wesley *educational leadership educator*
Lisenby, Dorrece Edenfield *realtor*
Long, Michael Christian *forester*
Loper, David Eric *geophysics educator, mathematics educator*
Losh, Susan Carol *education educator, researcher*
Macesich, George *econmomics professor*
Maguire, Charlotte Edwards *retired physician*
Mandelkern, Leo *biophysics and chemistry educator*
Mang, Douglas Arthur *lawyer*
Manley, Walter Wilson, II, *lawyer, business educator*
Manousakis, Efstratios *physicist, educator*
Marshall, Alan George *chemistry and biochemistry educator*
Marshall, Marilyn Josephine *lawyer*
Mason, Marilyn Gell *library administrator, writer, consultant*
Mason, Robert McSpadden *technology management educator, consultant*
†Masterson, Stephen Michael *lawyer*
McBride, Donna Jannean *publisher*
McCord, Guyte Pierce, Jr., *retired judge*
McGregory, Jerrilyn *English educator*
†McHugh, William F. *legal educator*
Mele, Alfred R. *philosophy educator*
Miller, Gregory R. *lawyer*
†Miller, Morris Henry *lawyer*
Milligan, Robert Frank *state agency administrator*
Mills, Belen Collantes *early childhood education educator*
Minnick, Bruce Alexander *lawyer*
Molinari, Joseph Francis *oculist*
Moore, Kurt Richard *anthropologist, fundraiser, investor*
Morgan, Constance Louise *real estate executive*
Morgan, Lucy Ware *journalist*
Morgan, Robert Marion *educational research educator*
Morgante, John-Paul *human resources specialist*
Morphonios, Dean B. *lawyer*
Mortham, Sandra Barringer *former state official*
Moulton, Grace Charbonnet *physics educator*
Muchovej, James John *botanist, plant pathologist, educator*
†Nalley, James H., II, *music educator, musician*
Nam, Charles Benjamin *demographer, sociologist, educator*
Navon, Ionel Michael *mathematics educator*
Nichols, Eugene Douglas *mathematics educator*
†Oseroff, Andrew Bell *assistant dean*
Palladino-Craig, Allys *museum director*
Pariente, Barbara J. *state supreme court justice*
Penson, Edward Martin *management consulting company executive*
Perry-Camp, Jane *music educator, pianist*
Pettijohn, Fred Phillips *retired newspaper executive, consultant*
Pfeffer, Richard Lawrence *meteorology and geophysics educator*
Phipps, Benjamin Kimball, II, *lawyer*
†Picart, Caroline Joan (Kay) Santos *philosopher, language educator*
†Pierce, Michael Jack *education specialist*
†Plendl, Hans S. *retired physicist, editor*
Prusty, Rabin *environmental engineer*
Reid, Robert C. *lawyer*
Rice, Nancy Marie *nursing consultant*
Rikvold, Per Arne *physics researcher and educator*
Riley, Kenneth Jerome *athletic director*
†Roady, Elston Edward (Steve) *political scientist, educator*
Robbins, Jane Borsch *library science educator, information science educator*
Roberts, Rodney Glen *electrical engineering educator*
Robson, Donald *physics educator*
Saha, Bidhan Chandra *physicist, educator*
Sanchez, Robert Francis *journalist*
Sapp, Lauren B. *librarian, educator*
Schlenoff, Zeina Tamer *language educator, literary critic*
Schrieffer, John Robert *physics educator, science administrator*
Schroeder, Edwin Maher *law educator*
Serow, William John *economics educator*
†Shamsham, Fadi Michel *cardiologist*
Sheffield, Frank Elwyn *lawyer*
Slevin, Patrick Jeremiah *media relations consultant*
†Sliger, Bernard Francis *academic administrator, economist, educator*
Smith, James Cloudis *secretary of state, former state attorney general*
†Smith, Nevin *company executive*
Soliman, Karam Farah Attia *pharmacy educator*
†Sprowls, Paul Alan *lawyer*
Standley-Burt, Nancy Vilma *psychologist, educator, retired*
†Stebleton, Michelle Marie *music educator, musician*
†Stinson, Donna Holshouser *lawyer*
Streem, James Kenneth *musician, educator*
†Struhs, David B. *state agency administrator*
Summers, Frank William *retired librarian*
†Teague, James Calvin, Jr., *finance educator*
Teson, Fernando Roberto *law educator, consultant*
Thagard, Norman E. *astronaut, physician, engineer, educator*
Thiele, Herbert William Albert *lawyer*
Thomas, James Bert, Jr., *government official*
Thompson, Gregory Lee *social sciences educator*
Thompson, Jean Tanner *retired librarian*
Tookes, James Nelson *real estate investment company executive*
Tourtet, Christiane Andrée *writer, human rights activist, photojournalist, reporter*
Turnbull, Marjorie Reitz *foundation executive, former state legislator*
Varn, Wilfred Claude *lawyer*
†Wahl, Horst Dieter *physicist, researcher, educator*
Webster, Peter David *judge*
Wekezer, Jerzy Wladyslaw *civil engineering educator*
Wells, Charles Talley *state supreme court justice*
Whitney, Enoch Jonathan *lawyer*
†Wright, Thomas G. *music educator, musician*
Zachert, Martha Jane *retired librarian*
Zaiser, Kent Ames *lawyer*
Zou, Xiaolei *meteorologist, educator*

Tallevast
Celorie, Dennis Jay *not-for-profit executive*

Tamarac
Auletta, Joan Miglorisi *construction company executive, mortgage and insurance broker*
Fischler, Shirley Balter *retired lawyer*
Gould, Bernard Howard *insurance agent*
Krause, John L. *optometrist*
Page, Earl Michael *management specialist*

Tampa
†Abizaid, John P. *career officer*
†Adams, Lowell P. *assistant principal, music educator*
Adkins, Edward Cleland *lawyer*
Afield, Walter Edward *psychiatrist, service executive*
Aguinaldo, Jorge Tansingco *chemical engineer, water treatment specialist*
†Aitken, Thomas Dean *lawyer*
†Albritton, Arthur Dallas *lawyer*
Aldrich, David Alan *accountant, consultant*
Alexander, William Olin *finance company executive*
Allen, Tammy D. *psychologist*
Alley, John-Edward *lawyer*
†Alpert, Jonathan Louis *lawyer*
Alstott, Michael Joseph (Mike Alstott) *professional football player*
Anton, David *lawyer*
Anton, John Peter *philosopher, educator*
Ault, Jeffrey Michael *investment banker, commodities trader*
†Ayoub, Ashraf S. *engineering educator*
Barkin, Marvin E. *lawyer*
Barness, Lewis Abraham *physician*
†Barrow, Frederica Harrison *education educator, social worker*
†Barton, Bernard Alan, Jr., *lawyer*
Battle, Jean Allen *writer, educator*
Baynes, Thomas Edward, Jr., *judge, lawyer, educator*
†Beach, Kevin Scott *marine biologist, educator*
Bear, Marca Marie *business educator, management consultant*
Becatti, Lance Norman *financial consultant*
Bedford, Robert Forrest *anesthesiologist*
Belsole, Robert John *surgeon*
†Berarducci, Adrienne *nursing educator, researcher*
Berkowitz, Herbert Mattis *lawyer*
Blacklidge, Raymond Mark *lawyer*
Blue, James Monroe *lawyer*
Bondi, Joseph Charles, Jr., *education educator, consultant*
Boutros, Linda Nelene Wiley *medical/surgical nurse*
†Bowen, Paul Henry, Jr., *lawyer*
Bowen, Thomas Edwin *cardiothoracic surgeon, retired army officer*
Bradish, Warren Allen *internal auditor, operations analyst, management consultant*
†Brady, Kathleen Deming *psychologist, occupational therapist, educator*
Branch, William Terrell *urologist, educator*
Brantley, Stephen Grant *pathologist*
†Brewer, Priscilla Joan *historian, educator*
Brookes, Carolyn *early childhood education educator*
Brooks, Derrick Dewan *football player*
Brown, Troy Anderson, Jr., *retired electrical distributing company executive*
Buell, Mark Paul *lawyer*
Bukantz, Samuel Charles *physician, educator*
Butler, Paul Bascomb, Jr., *lawyer*
Campbell, Richard Bruce *lawyer*
Cardoso, Anthony Antonio *artist, educator*
Carnahan, Robert Paul *civil engineer, educator, researcher, consultant*
†Centeno, Grisselle *industrial engineer*
Christy, Jeff *football player*
Clark, Michael Earl *psychologist*
Clendinen, Cynthia A.A. *healthcare professional, compliance specialist*
Collins, Gwendolyn Beth *health administrator*
Corcoran, Clement Timothy, III, *lawyer*
Couturier, Gordon Wayne *computer information systems educator, consultant*
†Culpepper, Mary Kay *publishing executive*
Cunningham, Anthony Willard *lawyer*
Currey, Cecil Barr *history educator*
Dail, Joseph Garner, Jr., *judge*
Daugherty, Robert Melvin, Jr., *dean, medical educator*
Davis, Blondell Gilliam *business manager, evangelist, artist, author, poet*
Davis, Helen Gordon *former state senator*
Davis, Kirk Stuart *lawyer*
Davis, Richard Earl *lawyer*
DeSalvo, Joseph Salvatore *economics educator, researcher*
DeVane, Mindy Klein *financial planner*
DeVaney, Donna Brookes *lawyer*
†Dickson, Tim F. *music educator*
Dion, Charles J. *statistician*
Doliner, Nathaniel Lee *lawyer*
Donelan, Peter Andrew *dermatologist*
Donovan, Brian Joseph *lawyer*
†Dudley, Rick *professional hockey coach*
†Dwornik, Julian Jonathan *anatomist, researcher*
Ebel, Theron Arthur *physician*
Edberg, Judith Florence *music educator*
Eichberg, Rodolfo David *physician, educator*
Ellwanger, Thomas John *lawyer*
†Emerton, Robert Walter, III, *lawyer*
Ernst, Roger *international studies educator, consultant*
Evangelista, Allan *podiatrist, medical researcher*
Fabri, Peter J. *surgeon, educator*
†Fantauzzi, Anthony Joseph, III, *lawyer*
†Feegel, John Richard *pathologist*
Ferree, Patricia Ann *case management specialist and trainer*
Figueroa, Tomas *internist*
Flom, Edward Leonard *retired steel company executive*
Fraley, F. Ronald *lawyer*
Freedman, Sandra Warshaw *former mayor*
Freeman, Thomas Benedict *neurosurgery educator*
Frias, Jaime Luis *pediatrician, educator*
Friedlander, Edward Jay *journalist, educator*
†Fuller, Diana Lynn *lawyer*
Furland, Loren P. *civil and environmental engineer*
Gambone, Victor, Jr., *internist, geriatrician*
Gardner, J. Stephen *lawyer*
Genter, John Robert *grocery industry executive*
Germroth, Peter *biologist, educator*
Gilbert, Leonard Harold *lawyer*
†Gilbert, Richard Allen *lawyer*
Gilbert Barness, Enid *medical educator*
Gilbert-Barness, Enid F. *pathologist, pathology and pediatrics educator*
†Gill, Thomas Grandon *information technology executive, educator*
Givens, Paul Ronald *former university chancellor*
Givens, Stann William *lawyer*
Glenn, Paul M. *federal judge*
Gordon, Jeffrey (Jack Gordon) *lawyer*
Grammig, Robert James *lawyer*
Greenfield, George B. *radiologist*
Greenhalgh, Terry Lamont *marketing executive*
†Gruden, Jon *professional football coach*
Haas, Robert Lance *surgeon, consultant*
Habal, Mutaz Billah *plastic surgeon*
Hanford, Grail Stevenson *writer*
Hankenson, E(dward) Craig, Jr., *performing arts executive*
Hankins, Phillip R. *music educator*
†Hankinson, Tim *soccer coach*
Hardy, Paul Duane *lawyer*
Harkness, Mary Lou *librarian*
Harlow, Carol Jean *prospect researcher*
Harriman, Malcolm Bruce *investment advisor, financial consultant*
Hartmann, William Herman *pathologist, educator*
†Hayes, James Donald *pharmaceutical research scientist*
Hegarty, Thomas Joseph *academic administrator, history educator*
Heide, Kathleen Margaret *criminology educator, psychotherapist*
Henard, Elizabeth Ann *controller*
Henning, Rudolf Ernst *electrical engineer, educator, consultant*
Hernandez, Gilberto Juan *accountant, auditor, management consultant*
†Hevner, Alan Raymond *educator, consultant*
Heyck, Joseph Giraud, Jr., *lawyer*
Hickman, Hugh V. *science educator, researcher*
Highsmith, Jasper Habersham *sales executive*
Hoffman, Mitchel Scott *gynecologic oncologist, educator*
Holfelder, Lawrence Andrew *pediatrician, allergist*
Holmes, Dwight Ellis *architect*
Howey, John Richard *architect, writer*
Humphries, J. Bob *lawyer*
Huneycutt, Alice Ruth *lawyer*
Hunter, Larry Lee *retired electrical engineer*
Hyatt, Kenneth E(rnest) *diversified manufacturing executive*
Ismail, Mourad El-Houssieny *mathematician, educator, researcher*

Beall, Kenneth Sutter, Jr., *lawyer*
Beasley, James W., Jr., *lawyer*
Bergmann, Arthur M. *writer, former county official, former newspaperman*
Bernhardt, Marcia Brenda *mental health counselor*
†Bezerra, Márcio *musician, educator*
Bohn, Barbara Ann *retired laboratory director*
Brody, Carol Z. *artist, educator*
Brumback, Clarence Landen *physician*
Capasso, Robert *financial executive*
†Carres, Louis George *lawyer*
Chen, Zhikang (Ken Chen) *remote sensing scientist*
Chopin, L. Frank *lawyer*
Chopin, Susan Gardiner *lawyer*
Conrad, Bette Anne Kester *lawyer, writer, minister*
†Coppock, Mark Stephen *not-for-profit fundraiser*
Corts, Paul Richard *college president*
Damico, Paul Anthony *lawyer, educator*
D'Angelo, Andrew William *retired civil engineer*
Darter, Jeffrey Allen *data processing professional*
†Davidsson, Robert Iver *librarian*
Davis, Paul B. *mechanical engineer, civil engineer, retired*
Davis, Shirley Harriet *social worker, editor*
De Mastry, John A. *engineer*
Dunkum, Betty Lee *lawyer*
Dye, Thomas Roy *political science educator*
†Dytrych, Denise Distel *lawyer*
Eager, William Earl *information systems corporation executive*
Eppley, Roland Raymond, Jr., *retired financial services executive*
Escalante, Juan *performing company executive*
Eyler, Bonnie *lawyer*
Finley, Chandler R. *lawyer*
Flaxman, Fred *broadcast executive*
†Fowler, Steven Lane *compliance officer*
Gildan, Phillip Clarke *lawyer*
Glinski, Helen Elizabeth *operating room nurse*
†Gold, Bela *economist, educator*
†Grogan, Robert Harris *lawyer*
Gronlund, Robert B. *art collector, fund raising consultant*
Hale, Marie Stoner *artistic director*
Henry, Rene Arthur *author, consultant*
†Henry, Thornton Montagu *lawyer*
Herrick, John Dennis *financial consultant, former law firm executive, retired food products executive*
Hill, Thomas William, Jr., *lawyer, educator*
Hoch, Rand *lawyer, mediator*
Howard, Jean Catherine Hart *photojournalist, educator*
Iqbal, Tariq *physics educator, researcher*
Jenkins, Ruben Lee *retired chemical company executive, lawyer*
Jividen, James Carl *educational administrator*
Johnson, Martin Allen *publisher*
Kapnick, S. Jason *oncologist*
Khouri, George George *ophthalmologist*
Kiely, Dan Ray *telecommunications and banking consultant*
Koffler, Warren William *lawyer*
Kornspan, Susan Felischner *lawyer*
Lacey, John William Charles *management consultant*
Lampert, Michael Allen *lawyer*
†Lane, Matthew Jay *lawyer*
†Lappin, Bob *music director, conductor*
Layman, David Michael *lawyer*
Lichtstein, Daniel M. *medical educator*
Livingstone, John Leslie *accountant, management consultant, business economist, educator*
Longhofer, Gordan Allen *art educator, performance artist*
Lozito, Gilda Lelia *artist, painter*
Lutey, Joyce Louise *real estate broker*
†Marshall-Beasley, Elizabeth *landscape architect*
McCluskey, Neil Gerard *gerontologist, educator, literary agent*
Mendelow, Gary N. *physician, emergency consultant*
†Mims, Lloyd Lee *dean, conductor, vocalist*
Montgomery, Robert Morel, Jr., *lawyer*
Moore, George Crawford Jackson *lawyer*
Mrachek, Lorin Louis *lawyer*
Nelms, Lewis Caldwell *minister*
Newmark, Emanuel *ophthalmologist*
Nolan, Richard Thomas *clergyman, educator*
Norton, William Alan *lawyer*
Orlovsky, Donald Albert *lawyer*
Passy, Charles *arts critic*
Penalta, C. Richard *prosecutor*
†Phillips, Kenneth Wayne *music educator*
Pottash, A. Carter *psychiatrist, hospital executive*
Rafaidus, David Martin *health and human services planner*
†Rander, JoAnn Corpaci *musician, music educator*
Reid, Justus Webb *lawyer*
†Roberts, George Preston, Jr., (Rusty Roberts) *lawyer*
Robertson, Sara Stewart *private investor, entrepreneur*
Robinson, Raymond Edwin *musician, music educator, writer*
†Roderick, Robert Lee *aerospace executive*
Ronan, William John *management consultant*
Rosenberg, Leslie Karen *media buyer*
Ross, Edward Joseph *architect*
Ryskamp, Kenneth Lee *federal judge*
Sears, Edward Milner, Jr., *newspaper editor*
Sklar, William Paul *lawyer, educator*
Smith, Betsy Keiser *telecommunications company executive*
Smith, David Shiverick *lawyer, former ambassador*
Snyder, Gary Michael *music educator*
†Solomon, Louis B. *planned giving professional, professional association executive*
Spillias, Kenneth George *lawyer*
†Stambaugh, Reginald Jack *ophthalmologist*

Stauderman, Bruce Ford *writer, advertising executive*
Stern, Harold Peter *business executive*
Tabernilla, Armando Alejandro *lawyer*
Terwillegar, Jane Cusack *librarian, educator*
Thomashow, Steven Roy *military officer, intelligence officer*
Turner, Robert Alexander, Jr., *rheumatologist, consultant*
†Uzan, Bernard *artistic director*
†VanArman, Peggy Ellen Gilbert *biology educator*
Vecellio, Leo Arthur, Jr., *construction company executive*
Weitzman, Linda Sue *lawyer*
Westman, Steven Ronald *rabbi*
Whitfield, Graham Frank *orthopedic surgeon*
Wisnicki, Jeffrey Leonard *plastic surgeon*
Witt, Gerhardt Meyer *hydrogeologist*
Wroble, Arthur Gerard *judge*
Zeller, Ronald John *lawyer*

Weston

Barnes, William Douglas *advertising executive*
Boyer, Gene T. *management consultant*
Deleuze, Margarita *artist*
Holtzman, Gary Yale *retired administrative and financial executive*
Kniskern, Joseph Warren *lawyer*
Malave, Andres *pharmacologist, educator*
McAuliffe, John Anthony *hand surgeon*
Napp, Gudrun F. *artist*
Staneart, Larry William *technology company marketing executive*
†Tuchman, Roberto Fabian *neurologist*
Weiss, Eric Glenn *physician*

Wewahitchka

Stryker, Terence Wayne *secondary school educator*

Wimauma

Palmer, Louis Thomas *pathologist*

Windermere

Russell, Robert Leonard *professional association executive*

Winter Garden

Gillet, Pamela Kipping *special education educator*

Winter Haven

Burns, Arthur Lee *architect*
Bybee, Charles Forrest *writer, poet*
Cassell, Robert Holland *internist, oncologist*
†Clyne, Rosemarie Blackstone *technical services librarian*
Cody, Mark Edward *small business owner, martial arts instructor*
Dyal, Lucius Mahlon, Jr., *lawyer*
Goodman, Karen Lacerte *financial services executive*
Honer, Richard Joseph *surgeon*
Johnson, Gordon Selby *consulting electrical engineer*
Lindsey, Jane Willann *minister*
O'Connor, R. D. *retired health care executive*
Peck, Maryly VanLeer *retired academic administrator, chemical engineer*
Porter, Howard Leonard, III, *health and education policy consultant*
Radocha, Richard Francis *plastic surgeon*
Small, Norman Morton *speech and humanities educator, theatre producer, director*
Warner, Nelson Alfred *dermatologist*
†Zhou, Li *mathematician, educator*

Winter Park

Acierno, Louis Joseph *medical educator, researcher*
†Ackert, T(errence) W(illiam) *lawyer*
†Alon, Ilan *international business educator*
Benedict, Dorothy Jones *genealogist, researcher*
Boguslawski, Alexander Prus *Russian studies educator, artist, Internet designer*
Bornstein, Rita *academic administrator*
†Builder, J. Lindsay, Jr., *lawyer*
Bush, Christine Gay *dental hygienist*
†Casey, Roger Neal *English language educator, director, actor, academic administrator*
Douglas, Kathleen Mary Harrigan *retired psychotherapist, educator*
Fluno, John Arthur *entomologist, consultant*
†Galperin, Bella L. *management consultant, educator*
†Godbold, Gene Hamilton *lawyer*
Granberry, Edwin Phillips, Jr., *safety engineer, consultant*
Hadley, Ralph Vincent, III, *lawyer*
Heinle, Richard Alan *lawyer*
Holland, Robert Debnam, Sr., *investment company executive*
Jernigan, Donald *hospital administrator*
Johnson, Kraig Nelson *lawyer, mediator*
Jones, Joseph Wayne *business executive, entrepreneur*
Kerr, James Wilson *engineer*
Kincaid, Rodney Lyle *construction company executive*
Kindlund, Newton Carlton *retail executive*
Kost, Wayne L. *business executive*
Kraft, Kenneth Houston, Jr., *insurance agency executive*
Markland, Barbara Carolyn *sales and leasing professional*
Mason, Aimee Hunnicutt Romberger *retired philosophy and humanities educator*
Matulich, Serge *accounting educator, author*
McKean, Thomas Wayne *dentist, retired naval officer*
Mésavage, Ruth Matilde *language educator*
Mishra, Chandra S. *finance educator, consultant*
Olsson, Nils William *former association executive*
Pearson, R. Scott *investment advisor, editor*
Pineless, Hal Steven *neurologist*
Powers, Ronald George *management consultant*

Rogers, Rutherford David *librarian*
Seymour, Thaddeus *English educator*
†Sinclair, Gail D. *education educator*
Spake, Ned Bernarr *energy company executive*
Strawn, Frances Freeland *real estate executive*
Swan, Richard Gordon *retired mathematics educator*
Wagner, Lynn Edward *lawyer*
Werner, Thomas Lee *hospital administrator*
Wilson, Robley Conant, Jr., *English educator, editor, author*
Wisler, Willard Eugene *retired health care management executive*

Winter Springs

Bevc, Carol-Lynn Anne *accountant*
†McKinney, Frank *music educator*
San Miguel, Manuel *painter, historian, composer, poet, art collector*

Yalaha

Searcy, Dorothy James *missionary*

Zellwood

†Duffy, Thomas Patrick *retired poet*

Zephyrhills

Ayres, Jayne Lynn Ankrum *community health nurse*
†Barron, Ilona Eleanor *reading educator, consultant*
Finnerty, Nancy Wells *family physician*
Martindale, Carla Joy *retired librarian*

GEORGIA

Adel

Darby, Marianne Talley *elementary school educator*

Albany

Carter-Wommack, Barbara *retired educator*
†Ellis, Mark E. *school librarian*
Forsyth, Rosalyn Moye *middle school educator*
†Gates, Roberta Pecoraro *nursing educator*
†Hill, Kenderson *career systems development executive, city councilman*
Marbury, Ritchey McGuire, III, *engineering executive, surveyor*
Mayher, William Edgar, III, *neurosurgeon*
†Michaels, Anne E. *psychologist, educator*
†Moorhead, William David, III, *lawyer, corporate executive*
†Revills, Isaiah *minister*
†Shields, Portia Holmes *academic administrator*
Stallworth, Charles Derotha, Jr., *psychologist*
Stanley-Chavis, Sandra Ornecia *special education educator, consultant*

Alpharetta

Adams, Rex M. *telecommunications executive*
Balows, Albert *microbiologist, educator*
Baugh, Charles H. *music educator, actor*
Bolton, Robin Jean *artist, painter*
Boynton, Frederick George *lawyer*
Brands, James Edwin *medical products executive*
Bridgers, John David *retired pediatrician*
Charania, Barkat *real estate consultant*
Chatlen, Stanley Lee *logistics executive*
Christy, Robert Allen *investment advisor*
Derr, Bruce Woods *information technology executive*
Desai, Hiren D. *software engineer*
Esher, Brian Richard *chief executive officer*
Fowler, Vivian Delores *insurance company executive*
Greene, Melinda Jean *retail maintenance analyst*
Harris, James Herman *pathologist, neuropathologist, consultant, educator*
Horton, Rosalyn *underwriter*
Hung, William Mo-Wei *chemist*
Kurtz, Robert Arthur *finance company executive*
McBride, Vickie Darlene *geriatrics nurse*
†McCullar, Michael D. *pastor*
Miller, Robert Allen *software engineer, consultant*
Minner, Thomas O. *marketing executive*
Mock, Melinda Smith *orthopedic nurse specialist, consultant*
Petersen-Frey, Roland *manufacturing executive*
Puckett, Elsbeth Camille
Rettig, Terry *veterinarian, wildlife consultant*
Salay, Cindy Rolston *systems engineer, registered nurse*
Thomas, Robert L. *retired manufacturing company executive*
Troop, Paul Melvin *public relations executive, journalist*
Watts, William David *corporate executive, business owner*
Weitz, John Jerome, Jr., *city planner*
White, Carl Edward, Jr., *pharmaceutical administrator*

Americus

Capitan, William Harry *university president emeritus*
Fuller, Millard Dean *charitable organization executive, lawyer*
Gonzalez, George G. *priest, pastor*
Isaacs, Harold *history educator*
Stanford, Henry King *college president*
†Tietjen, Mildred Campbell *librarian, college official*

Andersonville

Boyles, Frederick Holdren *historian*

Appling

Jones, Nancy Steed *small business owner*

Ashburn

†Swygert, Leslie Ann *epidemiologist, consultant*

Athens

Adams, Michael Fred *university president, political communications specialist*

Agee, Warren Kendall *journalism educator*
Agosin, Moises Kankolsky *zoology educator*
Albersheim, Peter *biology educator*
Alberts, James Joseph *scientist, researcher*
Algeo, John Thomas *retired educator, association executive*
Allsbrook, Ogden Olmstead, Jr., *retired economics educator*
Amstutz, Margaret *academic administrator*
Andrews, Grover Jene *adult education educator, administrator*
Atwater, Mary Monroe *science educator*
Avise, John Charles *geneticist, educator*
†Ayers, Benjamin C. *finance educator*
†Baggett, Rebecca Gaye *academic advisor, poet*
Baile, Clifton A. *biologist, researcher*
†Balashov, Yuri V. *philosophy educator*
†Bargmann, Rolf Erwin *computer scientist, educator*
Barrow, John J. *lawyer*
Beaird, James Ralph *law educator, dean*
Bertsch, Gary Kenneth *political scientist, educator*
Black, Clanton Candler, Jr., *biochemistry educator, researcher*
†Boehmer, Robert G. *academic administrator, educator*
Brown, Jane Martin Thornton *educational administrator*
†Cantarella, Jason H. *mathematician, educator*
Carlson, Ronald Lee *lawyer, educator*
†Carroll, Archie Benjamin, III, *management educator*
†Chaffin, Verner Franklin *lawyer, educator*
Chu, Chung Kwang *medicinal chemistry educator*
Clements, Robert Donald *sculptor*
Clute, Robert Eugene *political and social science educator*
Cole, David Akinola *educational administrator, educator*
Coley, Linda Marie *retired secondary school educator*
Corey, Stephen Dale *magazine editor, poet, educator*
Crepaz, Markus Michael Leopold *political scientist, educator*
†Crowell, Allen *music educator*
Crowley, John Francis, III, *university dean*
Dagley, John C. *psychologist*
†Dashiell, Frank Stephen, IV, *writer*
David, Martha Lena Huffaker *educator*
Davis, Claude-Leonard *lawyer, university official*
DeZurko, Edward Robert *retired art educator*
Dishman, Rodney King *physical education educator*
Donovan, James M. *librarian, anthropologist*
Dorfman, Jeffrey H. *economist, educator*
Dunn, Delmer Delano *political science educator*
†Eberhart, William Coile *apparel repair specialist, writer*
Ellington, Charles Ronald *lawyer, educator*
Erwin, Goodloe Y. *physician, land company executive*
Feldman, Edmund Burke *art critic*
†Fincher, Cameron Lane *psychology educator*
Fink, Conrad Charles *journalism educator, communications consultant*
Freer, Coburn *English language educator*
Garbin, Albeno Patrick *sociology educator*
Giles, Norman Henry *educator, geneticist*
Golembiewski, Robert Thomas *educator, management consultant*
†Gómez-Martinez, José Luis *Spanish language professional, researcher*
†Heald, Paul Justin *law educator, writer*
Hellerstein, Nina Salant *French literature and language educator*
Hellerstein, Walter *lawyer*
Henderson, Alma *educator*
Herbert, James Arthur *artist, filmmaker*
Hermanowicz, Joseph Craig *sociologist, educator*
Herrman, Margaret Susan *university official, sociologist*
Holder, Howard Randolph, Sr., *broadcasting company executive*
Houser, Ronald Edward *lawyer, mediator*
Huszagh, Fredrick Wickett *lawyer, educator, information management company executive*
Johnson, Michael Kenneth *chemistry educator*
†Jones, Jimmy Wayne, Jr., *historian, educator*
Kamerschen, David Roy *economist, educator*
Kaufman, Glen Frank *art educator, artist*
Kim, Seock-Ho *educator*
†Krasnostchekova, Elena Alexander *language educator*
Kretzschmar, William Addison, Jr., *English language educator*
†Kurtz, Paul Michael *law educator*
Larson, Edward John *law educator, lawyer, historian*
Lee, Margaret Kendig *music educator*
†Loux, Nicholas Thomas *chemist, researcher*
Lynch, James Walter *mathematician, educator*
Mamatey, Victor Samuel *history educator*
†Manoguerra, Paul Andrew *curator*
Marlar, John Thomas *environmental engineer*
Masters, Orlan Vincent Wade *gynecologist*
†Mauricio, Rodney *ecological geneticist, educator*
McGregor, James Harvey Spence *comparative literature educator*
McKnight, Reginald *English educator*
McNulty, Thomas L. *sociology educator*
Melton, Wayne Charles *real estate executive*
Meyer, Gail Barry *retired real estate broker*
†Meyers, Joseph Michael *biologist, researcher*
Miller, Herbert Elmer *accountant*
Miller, Ronald Baxter *English language educator, author*
Mixon, Deborah Lynn Burton *elementary school educator*
Moore, Margaret Bear *American literature educator*
Moore, Rayburn Sabatzky *American literature educator*

Morrison, Darrel Gene landscape architecture educator
Mullins, W. Stan artist, cultural ambassador
Nelson, Stuart Owen agricultural engineer, researcher, educator
Nichols, William Curtis psychologist, family therapist, consultant
Olsen, Richard James artist, educator
O'Toole, Laurence Joseph political science educator, researcher
Paul, William Dewitt, Jr., artist, educator, photographer, videographer, museum director
Payne, William Jackson microbiologist, educator
Pelletier, S. William chemistry educator
Plummer, Gayther L(ynn) ecologist, climatologist, researcher
Posey, Loran Michael pharmacist, editor
Potter, William Gray, Jr., library director
†Prasse, Keith W. dean
Puckett, Elizabeth Ann law librarian, law educator
†Ritter, Hope Thomas, Jr., cell biologist, educator
Rosen, Sidney psychologist
Rowland, Lucy Minogue librarian
Sachs, Margaret V. law educator
Schaefer, Henry Frederick, III, chemistry educator
Smagorinsky, Peter education educator
†Sophianopoulos, Judy Ann environmental scientist
†Spears, Louise Elizabeth minister, secondary school educator
†Spence, Sarah comparatist educator
Staub, August William drama educator, theatrical producer, director
†Stipe, Michael musician
Tesser, Abraham social psychologist
Thomas, Howard Lamar chef, consultant, writer
Tollner, Ernest William agricultural engineering educator, agricultural radiology consultant
Turner, Steven Cornell agricultural economics educator
Tyler, David Earl veterinary medical educator
West, Marsha elementary school educator
Williams, Philip Lee writer
Wraga, William Gerard educator
Yamaguchi, Yukio chemistry research scientist
Yarvis, Jeffrey Scott military officer, social worker
Yen, William Mao-Shung physicist, consultant
Zhang, Qing mathematics educator

Atlanta

Aaberg, Thomas Marshall, Sr.,
†Aaron, Hank (Henry L. Aaron) professional baseball team executive
Abdel-Khalik, Said Ibrahim nuclear and mechanical engineering educator
†Abernathy, Thomas Edwards, IV, lawyer
Abrams, Harold Eugene lawyer
Ackerman, Arlene Alice accountant, business consultant, artist, writer
Ackerman, F. Duane telecommunication industry executive
Affronti, John Paul medical educator
Agrawal, Pradeep Kumar chemical engineer, educator
†Aiken, Verndy Fred economist
Albert, Ross Alan lawyer
†Aldridge, John lawyer
Alexander, Cecil Abraham college official, architect, consultant
Alexander, Constance Joy (Connie Alexander) stone sculptor
†Alexander, Kent B. lawyer
Alexander, Miles Jordan lawyer
Alexander, Robert Wayne medical educator
Allen, Robert Charles pathologist
Allison, Stuart Anthony chemistry educator, researcher
Ambrose, Samuel Sheridan, Jr., urologist, educator
Ames, William Francis mathematician, educator
Amin, Mahul B. physician, researcher, educator, consultant
Anderson, Al H., Jr., communications executive
†Anderson, Barbara Allen
†Anderson, Lynda A geriatrician, behavioral scientist
†Anderson, Peter Joseph lawyer
†Andrews, Charles wholesale distribution executive
†Anstrom, Decker broadcast executive
†Appeadu, Charles Edward finance educator, researcher
Aral, Mustafa Mehmet civil engineer educator
Arani, Ardy A. professional sports marketing executive, lawyer
Armanios, Erian Abdelmessih aerospace engineer, educator
†Arnold, Jeffrey Internet company executive
Ashley, John Bryan software executive, management consultant
†Atkinson, A. Kelley insurance company executive
†Attridge, Richard Byron lawyer
Austin, Judy Essary scriptwriter
†Ayhan, Hayriye educator
Babcock, Peter Heartz professional sports executive
Bacon, Louis Albert retired consulting civil engineer
Bahl, Roy Winford economist, educator, consultant
Bainbridge, Frederick Freeman, III, architect
Baird, Mariann Saunorus critical care clinical nurse specialist, administrator
Baker, Edward L., Jr., physician, science facility executive
Baker, Lauren Alexis psychology educator, aerial performer
Baker, Thurbert E. state attorney general
Baldwin, Daniel Flanagan mechanical engineer, researcher, educator
†Bales, Virginia Shankle health administrator
†Balloun, James S. service company executive
Banerjee, Sujit environmental scientist, educator
Bankoff, Joseph R. lawyer
Banks, Bettie Sheppard psychologist
†Banks, Linda T. legal assistant, massage therapist
Barker, Clayton Robert, III, lawyer
Barker, William Daniel hospital administrator
Barkoff, Rupert Mitchell lawyer
Barksdale, Richard Dillon civil engineer, educator
Barnett, Crawford Fannin, Jr., internist, educator, cardiologist, travel medicine specialist
†Bassett, Peter Q. lawyer
Bates, Beverly Bailey lawyer
Batson, Richard Neal lawyer
Baum, Stanley M. lawyer
†Bayor, Ronald Howard history educator
Beasley, Ernest William , Jr., endocrinologist
Beaton, Rebecca Andrea psychotherapist
†Beckham, Walter Hull, III, lawyer
Behrens, William Blade television program syndication executive
†Beik, William H. education educator, writer
†Bekkers, John food products company executive
Bell, Griffin B. lawyer, former attorney general
Bellamy, Walter retired basketball player
Bellanca, Joseph Paul engineering construction executive
Benario, Herbert William classicist, educator
†Bendelius, Arthur George engineering firm executive
Benham, Robert state supreme court justice
Benitez, Jorge Antonio microbiology educator
Bennett, Dick advertising executive
Bennett, Jay D. lawyer
†Benzi, Michele mathematics educator, researcher, consultant
Beres, Mary Elizabeth management educator, organizational consultant
Berga, Sarah Lee women's health physician, educator
Berkelhamer, Jay Ellis pediatrician
Bernhardt, Jay Michael health communications researcher, educator
†Betty, Charles Garry communications executive
Bevington, Paula Lawton museum administrator
Bevins, Karl Alten retired engineer, musician, educator
Bibb, Daniel Roland antique painting restorer and conservator
Billington, Barry E. lawyer
Binder, Sue federal agency administrator
Birch, Stanley Francis, Jr., federal judge
Bird, Wendell Raleigh lawyer
Birdsong, Alta Marie volunteer
†Bisbee, David George lawyer
Bisher, James Furman journalist, author
†Black, Carolyn Morris microbiologist, educator, science administrator
Black, Kenneth, Jr., retired insurance executive and educator, author
Blackburn, William Stanley lawyer
Blackstock, Jerry B. lawyer
†Blank, A(ndrew) Russell lawyer
Blasini-Alcivar, Lydia M. health education specialist, consultant
Block, Peter Carl internist, cardiologist
Bloodworth, A(lbert) W(illiam) Franklin lawyer
Blumenthal, Anna Catherine English educator
†Bolch, Carl Edward, Jr., petroleum company executive, lawyer
Bonds, John Wilfred, Jr., lawyer
Bondurant, Emmet Jopling, II, lawyer
Booth, Gordon Dean, Jr., lawyer
Bosah, Francis N. molecular biochemist, educator
†Bowers, Michael Joseph former state attorney general
Bowman, Douglas business educator
†Bradley, Phillip Alden lawyer
Bradshaw, Rod Eric personnel consultant
Bramlett, Jeffrey Owen lawyer
†Branch, Thomas Broughton, III, lawyer
Branch, William Thomas, Jr., medical educator
Brandenburg, David Saul gastroenterologist, educator
Bratton, James Henry, Jr., lawyer
†Bremner, James Douglas psychiatrist, researcher, education educator
Bright, David Forbes academic administrator, classics and comparative literature educator
Broadnax, Walter D. public policy educator
†Brody, Harold Joseph dermatologist
Brown, Courtney political science educator, research institute administrator
Brown, John Robert lawyer
Brown, Lorene B(yron) library educator, educational administrator
Brown, Sarah M. artist, gallery owner, educator, publisher
Brown-Olmstead, Amanda public relations executive
†Bruckman, Amy Susan computer scientist, educator
†Bruner, Michael Lane communications educator
Bull, Frank James architect
†Burns, Thomas Samuel history educator
Byrne, Granville Bland, III, lawyer
Cadenhead, Alfred Paul lawyer
Calhoun, Scott Douglas lawyer
Calvert, Matthew James lawyer
Campbell, Charles Edward lawyer
Campbell, Colin McLeod journalist
†Cantalupo, Claudio neuroscientist, researcher
Capron, John M. lawyer
Carey, Gerald John, Jr., retired research institute director emeritus, former air force officer
Cargill, Robert Mason lawyer
Carley, George H. judge
Carnes, Julie Elizabeth judge
†Carpenter, David Allan lawyer
†Carson, Christopher Leonard lawyer
Carter, Jimmy (James Earl Carter Jr.) 39th President of the United States
Casarella, William Joseph physician
Caseman, Austin Bert civil engineering educator
Cavallini, Donna Francesca law librarian
Cavin, Kristine Smith lawyer
Chafee, Ingrid Roberta Hoover Coleman French language educator
Chaffin, Tom writer
Chalker, Ronald Franklin lawyer, educator
Chambers, Anne Cox newspaper executive, former diplomat
Chambers, Robert William financial company executive
Chandler, Robert Charles healthcare consultant
†Chandra, Vinay entrepreneur
†Chang, Leng Kar interior designer
Chapman, Hugh McMaster banker
Charles, Cory Anne television guest booking director
Chartier, Kirk Lee Freund business services executive
Chasen, Sylvan Herbert computer applications consultant, investment advisor
Chernoff, Yury Olegovich biologist, educator
†Chiang, Tze I. economist, researcher, economist, consultant
Chilivis, Nickolas Peter lawyer
Chilton, Horace Thomas pipeline company executive
Chisholm, Tommy lawyer, utility company executive
Chow, Rey literature educator
†Christiansen, Bryan marketing professional, consultant
Churchill, Joseph Lacy lawyer
Circeo, Louis Joseph, Jr., research scientist, civil engineer
Clarke, Thomas Hal lawyer
Clifton, David Samuel , Jr., research executive, economist
†Clough, Gerald Wayne academic administrator
Coady, William Francis information technology executive, consultant
†Cobb, Charles Kenche lawyer, real estate broker
Coble, William Carroll computer engineer
Cohen, Ezra Harry lawyer
Cohen, George Leon lawyer
Cohen, N. Jerold lawyer
Cohen, Stanley Allen pediatric gastroenterologist
†Cohn, Bob public relations executive
Cole, Thomas Winston, Jr., chancellor, college president, chemist
Coleman, David Michael religious organization executive
†Coleman, Terry Lewis state legislator
Collier, Diana Gordon publishing executive
Collins, Donnell Jawan lawyer
Collins, Steven M. lawyer
Compans, Richard W. microbiology educator
Comstock, Robert Donald, Jr., real estate executive
Connelly, Terrence John, Sr., television and cable station executive
Cook, Don Lloyd marketing educator, lawyer, consultant
Cooper, Gerald Rice clinical pathologist
Cooper, Jerome Maurice architect
Cooper, Lawrence Allen lawyer
Cooper, Thomas Luther retired printing company executive
†Cooper, William Lewis research librarian, lawyer, consultant
Cordero, Jose Fernando pediatrician, federal agency administrator
Corr, James Vanis furniture manufacturing executive, investor, lawyer, accountant
Correa-Villaseñor, Adolfo epidemiologist, physician
Correll, Alston Dayton, Jr., (Pete Correll) forest products company executive
†Corriher, Shirley food writer
Cox, Bobby (Robert Joe Cox) professional baseball manager
Cox, Cathy state official
Cox, Lynetta Frances neonatal nurse practitioner
†Coxe, Tench Charles lawyer
Craig, Anna Maynard financial educator, consultant
Cramer, Howard Ross geologist, environmental consultant
Crimmins, Timothy James history educator
†Crist, Stephen Alan music educator
Croft, Terrence Lee lawyer
Cupp, Robert Erhard land use planner, golf course architect
Curran, Christopher economics educator
†Curran, James W. epidemiologist, educator, academic administrator
Curtis, Philip Kerry real estate developer, real estate company executive
Cutshaw, Kenneth Andrew lawyer
Daft, Douglas N. food products executive
†Dahlberg, Alfred William electric company executive
†Dalia, Thomas A. architectural firm executive
Damken, John August computer systems engineer
D'Andrea, Frances Mary special education educator
Danielson, Gilbert Lawrence consumer products company executive
†Danner, Dean Jay geneticist
Darden, Claibourne Henry, Jr., marketing research professional
Darsey, James Francis communication educator, author
†Datz, Kimberly Malaika health facility administrator, consultant
Davidson, Denise Zara historian, educator
Davies, Caleb, IV, lawyer
Davis, E(dward) Marcus lawyer
Davis, Frank Tradewell, Jr., lawyer
†Davis, Jay M. wholesale distribution executive
†Davis, Jean Lerche writer
Davis, Lawrence William radiation oncologist
Davis, Michael medical educator
Davis, Sterling Evan television executive
Dawood, Mohamed Yusoff obstetrician, gynecologist
Deane, Richard Hunter, Jr., lawyer, former federal judge
Decosta, Benjamin airport executive
Dees, Lafon Carabo brokerage house executive
†Denmark, Darron B. compliance specialist
Dennison, Stanley Scott retired forest products company executive, consultant
Denny, Richard Alden, Jr., retired lawyer
Despriet, John G. lawyer
†Devine, Owen John biostatician, public health service officer, researcher
Dial, Carmen Miranda financial counselor, evangelist
Dickinson, Robert Earl atmospheric scientist, educator
Diedrich, Richard Joseph architect
Dietz, Arthur Townsend investment counseling company executive
Dion, Jacques Edgar physician, neuroradiologist
Dobbs, C. Edward lawyer, educator
Dobes, William Lamar, Jr., dermatologist, educator
†Dobranski, Stephen Bitonti literature educator
Dobson, Bridget McColl Hursley television executive and writer
Dodson, Daniel, Jr., advertising executive
Dodson, Daniel, Sr., advertising executive
Domingo, Esther music educator
†Dongoski, Craig R. art educator
†Donoghue, John Francis archbishop
†Dowda, William F. internist
Dowling, Roderick Anthony investment banker
†Downs, William Murray political scientist, educator, researcher
Doyle, Michael Anthony lawyer
Drake, Miriam Anna librarian, educator, writer
Drake, Stanley Joseph association executive
Driver, Walter W., Jr., lawyer
Drucker, Michael Stuart lawyer
DuBose, Mary communication and media professional, educator
Duffey, Lee communications company executive
Duffey, William Simon, Jr., lawyer
†Duques, Ric information services executive
Durrett, James Frazer, Jr., retired lawyer
Dutt, Kamla medical educator
Dysart, Benjamin Clay, III, consultant, conservationist, engineer
Dzvonik, Michael D. advertising executive
†Earles, Kathi Amille pediatrician
Eckert, Charles Alan chemical engineering educator
Eckl, William Wray lawyer
†Edge, J(ulian) Dexter, Jr., lawyer
Edmondson, James Larry federal judge
Edwards, Stephen Allen lawyer
Egan, Michael Joseph retired lawyer, state legislator
†Ehrlich, Jeffrey data processing company executive
†Eisen, Arri biologist, educator
Ellingwood, Bruce Russell structural engineering researcher, educator
Ellis, Elmo Israel broadcast executive, consultant, columnist
Ellison, Earl Otto computer scientist
Emerson, James Larry beverage company executive
Endicott, John Edgar international relations educator
Epstein, David Gustav lawyer
Eskew, Michael L. package distribution company executive
Eubanks, Omer Lafayette data communications consultant, systems engineer
Evans, Dorinda art history educator
†Everett, G. Steven music educator
†Falconer, Etta Zuber mahtematics educator
Farhi, Diane C. pathologist and researcher
Farmer, Mary Bauder artist
Farnham, Clayton Henson lawyer
Feldman, Joel Martin magistrate judge
Fellows, Henry David, Jr., lawyer
Felton, Jule Wimberly, Jr., lawyer
Fermanis, Ernest George urologic surgeon
Ferris, James Leonard academic administrator
Ferriss, Abbott Lamoyne sociology educator emeritus
†Fine, Laura I language educator
Finkelstein, David Ritz physicist, educator, consultant
†Finley, Michael Valton foundation executive
Fitzgerald, John Edmund civil engineering educator
Flagg Davis, Vivian Annette librarian, researcher, public policy consultant
Flanigan, Robert Daniel, Jr., academic administrator
†Flannery, James William performing arts educator
Fleming, Julian Denver, Jr., lawyer
Fleming, Sidney Howell psychiatrist, educator
Fletcher, Andy marketing professional
Fletcher, Norman S. state supreme court justice
Foley, James David computer science educator, consultant
Forbes, Theodore McCoy, Jr., arbitrator, mediator, retired lawyer
Foreman, Edward Rawson retired lawyer
Forrestal, Robert Patrick banker, lawyer
Fote, Charles T. computer company executive
Fouché, Helen Strother editorial design executive
Fowler, Bruce Andrew toxicologist, researcher
Fox, Mary Frank sociology educator and researcher
Fox, Ronald Forrest physics educator
Fox-Genovese, Elizabeth Ann Teresa humanities educator, educator
†Franch, Harold August nephrologist, researcher
Franklin, Charles Scothern lawyer
Franklin, Shirley Clarke mayor
Freedman, Louis Martin dentist
Frenzel, James Charles lawyer
Frost, Norman Cooper retired telephone company executive
Fuller, S(heri) Marce energy executive
Fuqua, John Brooks retired consumer products and services company executive
†Furnad, V. Robert (Bob Furnad) television news executive

†Galloway, Thomas D. *dean*
Gambrell, David Henry *lawyer*
Ganaway, George Kenneth *psychiatrist, psychoanalyst*
Gannon, Mark Stephen *lawyer*
Ganz, Charles David *lawyer*
Ganzarain, Ramon Cajiao *psychoanalyst*
†Garard, Charles Justus, Jr., *language educator, writer*
Garibaldi, Ryan Skip *mathematician, educator*
Garland, LaRetta Matthews *nursing educator*
Garrow, David Jeffries *historian, author*
Gayles, Joseph Nathan, Jr., *administrator, fund raising consultant*
Geigerman, Clarice Furchgott *writer, consultant*
†Geil, Mark D. *education educator*
†Genberg, Ira *lawyer*
Gentry, David Raymond *textile engineer*
Gerberding, Julie Louise *federal agency administrator*
†Gibson, Michael *artist*
Giddens, Don Peyton *engineering educator, researcher*
Gimmestad, Gary Gene *physicist, researcher*
Girth, Marjorie Louisa *lawyer, educator*
Glaser, Arthur Henry *lawyer, mediator*
Glover, John Trapnell *real estate executive*
Godwin, John Thomas *pathologist, nuclear medicine specialist*
Goldfarb, Eric Daniel *information technology executive, computer industry analyst*
Goldstein, Elliott *lawyer, director*
Gonzalez, Emilio Bustamante *rheumatologist, educator*
Gonzalez-Pita, J. Alberto *lawyer*
Goodman, Seymour Evan *computer science and international studies educator, researcher, consultant*
Goodwin, George Evans *public relations executive*
Gordon, Frank Jeffrey *medical educator*
†Gorman, Susan E. *toxicologist, consultant*
Grady, Kevin E. *lawyer*
Grant, Walter Matthews *lawyer, corporate executive*
Gray, Phenessa Antoinette *not-for-profit developer*
Green, Holcombe Tucker, Jr., *investment executive*
Greene, Warren *advertising executive*
Gregory, Mel Hyatt, Jr., *retired insurance company executive*
Griffin, Clayton Houstoun *retired power company engineer, lecturer*
Gross, Stephen Randolph *accountant*
†Groton, James Purnell *lawyer, arbitrator*
Grove, Denise Whitlock *accounting and financial professional*
†Grummer-Strawn, Laurence M. *public health service officer, researcher*
Guberman, Sidney *painter, writer*
Gude, Albert Valdemar *retired anesthesiologist*
Guest, Rita Carson *interior designer*
Gundersen, Mary Lisa Kranitzky *finance company executive*
Gyamfi, Phyllis *research scientist, researcher*
Haas, George Aaron *lawyer*
Hakes, Jay Edward *federal agency administrator*
Hale, Jack K. *mathematics educator, research center administrator*
†Hallen, Barry *philosopher, educator*
†Halloran, M. Elizabeth *statistician, educator*
Halwig, Nancy Diane *banker*
Hanna, Frank Joseph, Jr., *credit company executive*
Hanson, Avarita Laurel *lawyer*
Hanson, Victor Arthur *surgeon*
Hardcastle, Kenneth Irvin *crystallographer, researcher*
Hardegree, Gloria Jean Fore *health services administrator*
Harkey, Robert Shelton *lawyer*
Harmer, Don Stutler *physicist, educator, nuclear engineer*
Harness, William Walter *lawyer*
Harris, Eon Nigel *dean, rheumatologist, internist*
Harris, Sidney Eugene *dean, management educator*
Harrison, Clifford *chef, small business owner*
Harrison, George Brooks *research engineer, retired career officer*
Hartle, Robert Wyman *retired foreign language and literature educator*
Hartley, Bob *professional hockey coach*
†Hasson, James Keith, Jr., *lawyer, law educator*
Hatcher, Charles Ross, Jr., *surgeon, health facility administrator*
Hawks, Barrett Kingsbury *lawyer*
Haynes, Ralph Lewis *internist, pulmonary diseases, consultant*
Hays, William Grady, Jr., *corporate financial and bank consultant*
He, Hongyu *mathematician, educator*
Heady, Eugene Joseph *lawyer*
Heatley, Dany *hockey player*
Hendricks, Nathan VanMeter, III, *lawyer*
Henry, Ronald James Whyte *university official*
Henwood, William Scott *lawyer*
Hess, Dennis William *chemical engineering educator*
Hill, Donald Dee *management consultant, lecturer, writer*
Hinchey, John William *lawyer*
Hines, Preston Harris *state supreme court justice*
Hodges, Dewey Harper *aerospace engineer, educator*
Hoff, Gerhardt Michael *lawyer, insurance company executive*
Hoffman, Fred L. *human resources professional*
Hoffman, Michael William *lawyer, accountant*
Hogan, John Donald *retired college dean, finance educator*
Hogan, William Jephtha, Jr., *financial consultant*
Holladay, Carl R. *New Testament educator*
Hollis, Timothy Martin *bank executive*
Holmes, Robert Alexander *state legislator*
Honaman, J. Craig *health facility administrator*
Hopkins, John David *lawyer*
†Houry, Debra *emergency physician, educator*
House, Donald Lee, Sr., *software executive, private investor, management consultant*
Howard, Harry Clay *lawyer*
†Howard, Pierre *former state official*
Howell, Arthur *lawyer*
†Hsu, Vincent P *epidemiologist*
Hudspeth, Gregg William *landscape architect*
†Huff, Danny W. *paper products executive*
Huff, Sara Davis *nursing manager*
Hug, Carl Casimir, Jr., *anesthesiology and pharmacology, educator*
Hughes, James Mitchell *epidemiologist*
Hull, Frank Mays *federal judge*
Humann, L. Phillip *bank executive*
†Humphrey, Stephen M. *paperboard company executive*
Hunstein, Carol *state supreme court justice*
Hunter, Forrest Walker *lawyer*
†Hunter, Howard Owen *academic administrator, law educator*
†Huo, Xiaoming *mathematician, educator*
†Hutchens, Wayne Goode *anesthesiologist*
Iacobucci, Guillermo Arturo *chemist*
†Ide, Roy William, III, *lawyer*
Ignatonis, Sandra Carole Autry *special education educator*
†Isaac, Yvonne Renee *construction company executive*
Isaf, Fred Thomas *lawyer*
Israili, Zafar Hasan *scientist, clinical pharmacologist, educator*
Ivey, Michael Wayne *mortgage broker*
Izard, John *lawyer*
Jackson, Geraldine *entrepreneur*
†Jackson, Lawrence P. *education educator*
Jackson, Richard Joseph *epidemiologist, public health physician, educator*
Jaffe, Harold W. *federal agency administrator*
Janney, Donald Wayne *lawyer*
†Jarvis, William Robert *epidemiologist, educator*
Jeffery, Geoffrey Marron *medical parasitologist*
†Jeffries, McChesney Hill, Jr., *lawyer*
Jenkins, Albert Felton, Jr., *lawyer*
Jiang, Baoming *scientist*
Johnson, Carl Frederick *marriage and family therapist*
Johnson, Jeff *marketing professional*
Johnson, Roger Warren *chemical engineer*
Johnson, Ronald Carl *chemistry educator*
†Johnson, W. Thomas, Jr., *media executive*
Johnston, Summerfield K., Jr., *food products executive*
Jones, Andruw Rudolf *professional baseball player*
Jones, Evan Wier *lawyer*
Jones, Frank Cater *retired lawyer*
†Jones, Glower Whitehead *lawyer*
Jones, J. Kenley *journalist*
Jones, Larry Wayne "Chipper", Jr., *baseball player*
Jones, Sherman J. *academic administrator, management educator, investment executive*
Jowers, Ronnie Lee *university health sciences center executive*
†Judovitz, Dalia *language educator*
Jurkiewicz, Maurice John *surgeon, educator*
Kahn, Bernd *radiochemist, educator*
†Kallin, Britta *language educator*
Kaplan, Richard N. *broadcast executive, cable*
Karp, Herbert Rubin *neurologist, educator*
Katz, Joel Abraham *lawyer, music consultant*
Kaufman, Mark David *lawyer*
Kaul, Pushkar Nath
Keil, Mark *information systems researcher*
Keiller, James Bruce *college dean, clergyman*
Kell, Michael Jon *physician, researcher*
Kellermann, Arthur L. *medical educator*
†Kelley, James Francis *lawyer*
†Kelley, Jeffrey Wendell *lawyer*
Kelly, Carol White *company executive*
Kelly, James P. *delivery service executive*
Kelly, William Watkins *educational association executive*
†Kennedy, James C. *publishing and media executive*
Kennedy, Robert *international affairs educator*
Keough, Donald Raymond *investment company executive, director*
Kessler, Richard Paul, Jr., *lawyer*
†Khuri, Fadlo Raja *oncologist, educator*
Killingsworth, Vernon Scott *technology lawyer*
Killorin, Robert Ware *lawyer*
Kimani, Grace Alexandra *internist*
Kimball, Curtis Rollin *financial analyst*
†King, Coretta Scott (Mrs. Martin Luther King Jr.) *educational association administrator, lecturer, writer, concert singer*
†King, Dexter Scott *foundation administrator*
King, K(imberly) N(elson) *computer science educator*
King, Linda Orr *museum director, consultant*
Kingsbury, Michael Bryant *organist, retired elementary and secondary education educator*
Kinkopf, Neil Joesph *law educator*
†Kintzel, Roger *publishing executive*
Kinzer, William Luther *lawyer*
†Kirby, Peter Cornelius *lawyer, policy analyst*
Kitchens, Joyce Ellen *lawyer*
Kitchens, William H. *lawyer*
Klamon, Lawrence Paine *lawyer*
†Klein, Luella Voogd *obstetrics-gynecology educator*
Kline, Lowry F. *food products executive, lawyer*
Kloer, Philip Baldwin *popular culture critic*
Knapp, Charles Boynton *economist, educator, university president*
Kneisel, Edmund M. *lawyer*
Knowles, Marjorie Fine *lawyer, educator, dean*
†Kochengin, Sergey Alexandrovich *information technology consultant*
Kokko, Juha Pekka *physician, educator*
†Kolbe, Lloyd Joseph *health facility administrator*
†Kopelman, Harry Arvin *physician*
Koplan, Andrew Bennet *lawyer*
Koplan, Jeffrey Powell *physician*
Koros, William John *chemical engineering educator*
Kovalchuk, Ilya *hockey player*
Kozlov, Vyacheslav *hockey player*
Kravitch, Phyllis A. *federal judge*
Kringelis, Kurt *portfolio manager*
Kruger, Lon *coach*
†Ku, David Nelson *medical educator*
Kuhn, Brent *advertising executive*
Kuntz, Marion Lucile Leathers *classicist, historian, educator*
L'Abate, Luciano *psychologist*
Lackland, Theodore Howard *lawyer*
Lamon, Harry Vincent, Jr., *lawyer, director*
Landau, Michael B. *law educator, musician, writer*
Landon, James Henry *lawyer*
Laney, James Thomas *former ambassador, educator*
Lanier, George H. *lawyer*
Lawley, Thomas J. *dean, medical educator*
Lawson, A(bram) Venable *retired librarian*
Leach, James Glover *lawyer*
Lee, Hamilton H. *education educator*
†Lee, William Clement, III, *lawyer*
Lehfeldt, Martin Christopher *nonprofit association executive*
Lehrer, Robert Nathaniel *retired educator, executive, consultant*
Leibel, Steven K. *lawyer*
Leonard, David Morse *lawyer*
Lester, Charles Turner, Jr., *lawyer*
Letton, Alva Hamblin *surgeon, educator*
†Levy, Bertram Louis *lawyer*
Levy, Daniel *economics educator*
Levy, Rich *advertising executive*
Lewcock, Ronald Bentley *architect, educator*
Liebmann, Seymour W. *construction consultant*
Lin, Ming-Chang *physical chemistry educator, researcher*
Linder, Harvey Ronald *lawyer, arbitrator, mediator*
Linkous, William Joseph, Jr., *lawyer*
Lipman, John Crawford *endovascular surgeon*
Lipshutz, Robert Jerome *lawyer, former government official*
Liss, Matthew M. *lawyer*
†Littrell, Jill *social sciences educator*
Lnenicka, Wade Sheridan *purchasing official, councilman*
Lobb, William Atkinson *financial services executive*
†Loewy, Robert Gustav *aeronautical engineering executive, engineering educator*
Long, Leland Timothy *geophysicist educator, seismologist*
†Longhi, Patrick George *lawyer, educator*
Longobardi, Pamela Scott Dodgen *artist, educator*
†Lore, Stephen Melvin *lawyer*
Louard, Rita Jean *endocrinologist, educator*
Loven, Andrew Witherspoon *environmental engineering company executive*
Lovewell, Marjorie Klingensmith *secondary school educator*
Lower, Robert Cassel *lawyer, educator*
Lubin, Michael Frederick *physician, educator*
Lubker, John William, II, *manufacturing executive, civil engineer*
Lui, Victor King Shing *pediatrician*
Luker, Ralph Edlin *history educator*
Lybarger, Jeffrey Allen *epidemiology research administrator*
Maddux, Gregory (Gregory Alan Maddux) *professional baseball player*
Mahan, James S. *communications company executive*
†Maines, James Allen *lawyer*
Majesté, Richard Michael *pathologist*
Majmudar, Bhagirath *medical educator*
Malhotra, Naresh Kumar *management educator*
†Mallena, Sirish *chemist, researcher*
Malone, James Hiram *graphic artist, painter, writer*
Mandel, Jack Sheldon *epidemiologist, educator*
Manley, David Bott, III, *lawyer*
Manley, Frank *retired English language educator, writer*
†Manning, Clarence Bond *lawyer*
Mantella, Tino J. *medical association administrator*
Marcus, Bernard *retired retail executive*
†Marder, Elissa *psychologist, educator*
†Marianes, William Byron *lawyer*
Marks, James S. *public health service administrator*
Marshall, John Treutlen *lawyer, educator*
Marshall, Thomas Oliver, Jr., *lawyer*
Martin, David Edward *health sciences educator*
Martinez, Ricardo *research and development company executive*
Marvin, Charles Arthur *law educator*
Massey, Charles Knox, Jr., *advertising agency executive*
Massey, Walter Eugene *physicist, science foundation administrator*
Matsuura, John Henry *surgeon*
†Mattox, Douglas E. *otolaryngologist*
Mays, Jill Duncan *social services administrator, counselor*
†McAfee, Cheryl *architect*
McAlpin, Kirk Martin *lawyer*
†McCallum, John Arthur *foundation executive*
McCloud, Robert Olmsted, Jr., *lawyer*
McDavid, Sara June *librarian*
McDowell, David Lynn *mechanical engineering educator*
McFall, John *artistic director*
†McGill, John Gardner *lawyer*
McGowan, John Edward, Jr., *clinical epidemiology educator, microbiologist, infectious diseases specialist*
McGuinn, Michael Edward, III, *retired army officer*
†McKenzie, Kay Branch *public relations executive*
†McKissick, Todd Gaillard *real estate company executive*
†McKnight, Terrance Thales *music educator*
McLean, James Albert *artist, educator*
McMahon, Donald Aylward *investor, corporate director*
McNabb, Dianne Leigh *investment banker, accountant*
McNeill, Thomas Ray *lawyer*
†McQueen, David Vincent *research scientist*
McQueen, Sandra Marilyn *educator, consultant*
†McRaney, James Thomas *choral music educator*
McTier, Charles Harvey *foundation administrator*
McVey, Walter Lewis *lawyer, educator*
Mecke, William Moyn *public affairs consultant*
Meindl, James Donald *electrical engineering educator, administrator*
Merdek, Andrew Austin *publishing/media executive, lawyer*
Meredith, Thomas C. *academic administrator*
Meyer, Ellen L. *academic administrator*
†Meyer, Richard W. *school librarian*
†Meyer, William Lorne *lawyer*
Mickens, Ronald Elbert *applied mathematician, physics educator*
Miller, Daniel Lee *surgeon*
Miller, Janise Luevenia Monica *lawyer*
Millikan, James Rolens *cleaning service executive, musician, composer, fitness consultant*
Minneman, Kenneth Paul *pharmacology educator*
Mitchell, Stephen Milton *manufacturing executive*
Mobley, John Homer, II, *lawyer*
†Moderow, Joseph Robert *lawyer, package distribution company executive*
Moeling, Walter Goos, IV, *lawyer*
Monitz, Theodore Allan *cardiologist*
Moore, Philip Nicholas *author*
Moore, Thelma Wyatt *judge*
Morgan, Anne Hutchinson *medical association administrator, consultant*
Moss, Dan, Jr., *stockbroker*
Msezane, Alfred Zakele *physics educator*
Mull, Gale W. *lawyer*
Muller, William Manning *corporate lawyer*
Mullin, Leo Francis *airline executive*
†Murphy, Ana Alvarez *obstetrician, gynecologist*
Murphy, James Jeffrey *electronics executive*
Murphy, Richard Patrick *lawyer*
Muth, Richard Ferris *economics educator*
Myers, Johnnie Dumas *law educator*
†Myrick, Cecilia Jane *education educator, consultant*
Nardelli, Robert L. *consumer home products executive*
Neil, Robert F. *broadcast executive*
Neitzel, George Paul *engineer, educator*
Nemeroff, Charles Barnet *neurobiology and psychiatry educator*
Nemhauser, George L. *industrial, systems engineer, operations research educator*
Nentwich, Michael Andreas Erhart *educator, consultant*
Nerem, Robert Michael *engineering educator, consultant*
Nesin, Barbara *artist, art educator*
†Neuenschwander, Roger *architectural firm executive*
†Neumann, Mary Louise Spink *anthropologist, researcher*
†Nielsen, Tjai Michael *psychologist, consultant, researcher*
Norwood, Samuel Wilkins, III, *financial consultant*
†Nunn, Samuel (Sam Nunn) *former senator, lawyer*
†Oakley, Mary Ann Bryant *lawyer*
O'Brien, Mark Stephen *pediatric neurosurgeon*
O'Haren, Thomas Joseph *financial services executive*
O'Kelley, William Clark *federal judge*
O'Kon, James Alexander *engineering company executive*
†Olansky, Sidney *retired dermatologist*
Oliker, Vladimir *mathematician, educator*
†Oliver, Thomas *hotel executive*
Ordover, Abraham Philip *lawyer, mediator*
Orenstein, Walter Albert *health facility administrator*
Ortiz, Jay Richard Gentry *lawyer*
Ossewaarde, Anne Winkler *real estate developer*
Ostergard, Paul Michael *not-for-profit executive*
Ottley, John K., Jr., *entrepreneur*
Owen, Robert Hubert *lawyer, former real estate broker*
Owen, Steven Keith *utility executive*
Oyesiku, Nelson Mobolanle *neurosurgeon, neuroscientist*
†Palmer, James I. *government agency administrator*
Paquin, Jeffrey Dean *lawyer*
Paredes, James Anthony *anthropologist, educator*
†Parker, Wilmer, III, *lawyer, educator*
†Parrish, Carl E. *artist, educator*
Parsons, Leonard Jon *marketing educator, consultant*
Patrick, Deval Laurdine *lawyer*
Patterson, James Hardy *entertainer, conductor, musician, educator, arranger, composer*
†Patterson, William Robert *retired lawyer*
Patton, Carl Vernon *academic administrator, educator*
†Patton, Laurie Louise *religious studies educator, writer*
Payne, Maxwell Carr, Jr., *retired psychology educator*
Peacock, George Rowatt *retired life insurance company executive*
Peacock, Lamar Batts *retired physician*
†Pearce, Bradley Dixon *neuroscientist, pharmacologist*
Pederson, Linda Lue *epidemiologist, researcher*
Pence, Ira Wilson, Jr., *material handling research executive, engineer*

†Perdue, George (Sonny Perdue) *governor, state legislator*
Persons, W. Ray *lawyer, educator*
Phillips, Barry *lawyer*
Piassick, Joel Bernard *lawyer*
Pickering, Larry Kenneth *pediatrician, researcher*
Pike, Larry Samuel *lawyer*
Pilcher, James Brownie *lawyer*
†Pillay, Allan *microbiologist*
Piper, Samuel O'Dell *engineer*
Pless, Laurance Davidson *lawyer*
†Poe, H. Sadler *lawyer*
Polk, James Ray *journalist*
†Pollard, Zane F. *ophthalmologist*
Porter, Alan Leslie *industrial and systems engineering educator*
†Powell, Douglas Richard *lawyer*
Prater, Robert Stanley, Jr., *broker*
Pratt, Harry Davis *retired entomologist*
Press, Christopher E. *health facility administrator*
Price, Edward Warren *aerospace engineer, educator*
Prilutsky, Boris Isaakovich *biophysicist*
Prince, David Cannon *lawyer*
Prince, Larry L. *automotive parts and supplies company executive*
Pryor, Shepherd Green, III, *lawyer*
Przybilla, Carrie Ellen *art curator*
Pucci, Mark Leonard *public relations professional*
Pulgram, William Leopold *architect, space designer*
Purcell, Ann Rushing *state legislator, office manager medical business*
†Puszkar, Norbert *classicist, educator*
Quatrano, Anne *chef, restaurant owner*
Raby, Kenneth Alan *lawyer, retired army officer*
Raines, Tim D. *real estate corporation executive*
†Rajan, Anandhi *lawyer*
Ramsey, Ira Clayton *retired pipeline company executive*
Raney, Jean Puckett *art gallery director, artist*
Raper, Charles Albert *retired management consultant*
†Raskin, Daniel Ellis *lawyer*
Rattray, James Bailey *lawyer*
Reda, James Francis *business consultant*
Reed, Glen Alfred *lawyer*
Reed, James Whitfield *physician, educator*
†Reese, Cynthia Dene *psychologist, educator, quality assurance professional, risk management consultant*
Reith, Carl Joseph *apparel industry executive*
Rekau, Richard Robert *architect*
†Remar, Robert Boyle *lawyer*
Remington, Thomas Frederick *political science educator*
Rhodes, Damian *hockey player*
Rhodes, Thomas Willard *lawyer*
Rich, Robert Regier *immunology educator, physician*
Richards, Jacqueline *artist, curator*
Richey, Russell E. *university dean*
Ridley, Clarence Haverty *lawyer*
Rincón-Mora, Gabriel Alfonso *electrical engineer, educator*
†Rink, Christopher Lee *information technology consultant, photographer*
†Robbins, James O. *communications executive*
Robelot, Jane *anchor*
Roberts, Bradley Edward *finance company executive*
Roberts, Edward Graham *librarian*
Roberts, Thomasene Blount *entrepreneur*
Robertson, Sandra Dee (Graen) *tax director*
†Robinson, Willie Edward *lawyer*
Robison, Carolyn Love *retired librarian*
Robison, Richard Eugene *architect*
Rodenbeck, Sven Erich *environmental engineer*
†Rodríguez, Rocío *artist*
Rogers, Brenda Gayle *educational administrator, educator, consultant*
Rogers, C. B. *lawyer*
Rojas, Carlos *Spanish literature educator*
Rosenfeld, Arnold Solomon *retired newspaper editor*
Roth, Teresa Ann *broadcast executive*
Rothbaum, Barbara Olasov *psychologist, educator*
Rouhani, Shahrokh *civil engineering/environmental consultant, educator*
Rouse, Terrie Suzitte *performing arts association administrator, museum director, consultant*
Rouse, William Bradford *systems engineering executive, researcher, educator*
Rubin, Paul Harold *economist*
Rucker, Kenneth Lamar *law enforcement officer, educator, military officer*
Rudie, Alan William *pulp and paper research and development educator*
†Rumsey, D(avid) Lake, Jr., *lawyer*
†Ryan, Charles E., Jr., *electrical engineer, researcher*
Ryan, J. Bruce *healthcare management consulting executive*
†Sack, Kevin *news correspondent*
Sacks, Michael Alan *educational consultant, educator*
Salant, Richard Frank *mechanical engineer, educator*
Salmon, Marla E. *nursing educator, dean*
Salo, Ann Sexton Distler *lawyer*
Salomone, Jeffrey Paul *surgeon, educator*
†Sansone, Victor *broadcast executive*
Savell, Edward Lupo *lawyer*
Schafer, Ronald William *electrical engineering educator*
Schaumann, Caroline *language educator*
†Schenbeck, Lawrence *musicologist*
Schreiber, Barbara *artist*
Schroder, Jack Spalding, Jr., *lawyer*
Schroeder, Eric Peter *lawyer*
†Schuerholz, John Boland, Jr., *professional baseball executive*

Schulte, Jeffrey Lewis *lawyer*
Schwartz, Sandy *publishing executive*
Scovil, Roger Morris *international business consultant*
Sears, Leah J. *state supreme court justice*
Seffrin, John Reese *health science association administrator, educator*
Semaan, Salaam J. *healthcare researcher*
Sessions, George Purd *physician*
Seto, William Roderick *public accounting company executive*
†Shafey, Omar *health facility administrator*
Shapiro, George Howard *retired lawyer*
Shaunnessy, George Daniel *medical company executive*
Sherman, Roger Talbot *surgeon, educator*
Sheth, Jagdish Nanchand *business administration educator*
Shore, Steven L. *pediatrician*
†Shur, Barry David *cell biologist, researcher*
Sibley, Horace Holden *lawyer*
Sibley, James Malcolm *retired lawyer*
Sills, Eric Scott *infertility surgeon, reproductive endocrinologist*
Simitses, George John *retired engineering educator, consultant*
Simpson, Allan Boyd *real estate company executive*
Skillrud, Harold Clayton *minister, retired bishop*
Sloan, Mary Jean *retired media specialist*
Smith, Alexander Wyly, Jr., *lawyer*
Smith, Jeffrey Michael *lawyer*
†Smith, Markham H. *architectural firm executive*
Smith, Robert Boulware, III, *vascular surgeon, educator*
Smith, Sidney Oslin, Jr., *lawyer*
†Smith, Walton Napier *lawyer*
†Smoltz, John Andrew *professional baseball player*
Smyre, Calvin *political organization executive, state legislator*
Snarey, John Robert *psychologist, researcher, educator*
Snelling, George Arthur *banker*
†Snyder, Robert Lyman *materials scientist, educator*
Soderberg, Bo S. *marketing executive*
†Sola, Augusto *pediatrician, educator*
Sommerfeld, Jude Thomas *chemical engineer, educator*
Spalten, David Elliot *lawyer*
†Spangler, Dennis Lee *physician*
Spano, Robert *conductor*
Spiegel, John William *banker*
Spillett, Roxanne *social services administrator*
Spitznagel, John Keith *microbiologist, immunologist, physician*
Stacey, Weston Monroe, Jr., *nuclear engineer, educator, physicist*
Stallings, Ronald Denis *lawyer*
Stancell, Arnold Francis *chemical engineering educator, retired oil executive*
Stanley, Ronnie L., Jr., *theology educator, college dean, clergyman*
Starr, Terrell *state senator*
Steg, Leo *research and development executive*
Steinhaus, John Edward *physician, medical educator*
Stephan, Paula Elizabeth *economics educator, university official*
Stephenson, Mason Williams *lawyer*
Stewart, Barbara Dunbar *insurance consultant*
Stewart, Michael McFadden *professional speaker*
Stillwagon, Gary Bouldin *radiation oncologist*
Stimpert, Michael Alan *agricultural products company executive*
Stine, J(ames) Larry *lawyer*
†Stojiljkovic, Igor *microbiologist, researcher*
†Stokes, James Sewell *lawyer*
Stormont, Richard Mansfield *hotel executive*
Strauss, Robert David *lawyer*
Streeb, Gordon Lee *diplomat, economist*
Strekowski, Lucjan *chemistry educator*
†Strikas, Raymond Algimantas *medical epidemiologist*
†Stringer, George Clarke *real estate company executive, construction management advisor*
Su, Kendall Ling-Chiao *engineering educator*
Subramanian, Mani *communications educator, consultant*
Sullivan, Terrance Charles *lawyer*
Summerlin, Glenn Wood *retired advertising executive*
Sweeney, Neal James *lawyer*
†Swicegood, Stephen *architect*
Swift, Frank Meador *lawyer*
Tait, C(olumbus) Downing, Jr., *physician, medical educator*
†Tanenbaum, Allan Jay *lawyer*
Tanner, W(alter) Rhett *lawyer*
Taylor, George Kimbrough, Jr., *lawyer*
Taylor, Mark *lieutenant governor*
Taylor, Richard Bertrom *accountant*
Taylor, Roger Dale *lawyer*
Teepen, Thomas Henry *newspaper editor, journalist*
Teja, Amyn Sadrudin *chemical engineering educator, consultant*
Tentzeris, Emmanouil Manos *engineering educator, researcher*
Thacker, Stephen Brady *medical association administrator, epidemiologist*
Thaxton, Mary Lynwood *librarian, researcher*
†Thomas, James Joseph, II, *lawyer*
Thompson, Hugh P. *state supreme court justice*
Thompson, Wallace Reeves, III, *physical education educator*
Thorp, Benjamin A., III, *paper manufacturing company executive*
†Thrower, Randolph William *lawyer*
Thuesen, Gerald Jorgen *industrial engineer, educator*
Thursby, Jerry Gilbert *economics educator, consultant*
Thursby, Marie Currie *economics educator*
Tilley, Tana Marie *pharamaceutical executive, registered nurse*

Tillman, Mary Norman *urban affairs consultant*
Tissue, Mike *medical educator, respiratory therapist*
Tkaczuk, Nancy Anne *cardiovascular services administrator*
Toledo, Andrew Anthony *obstetrician, gynecologist*
Tomaszewski, Richard Paul *market representation executive*
Toner, Michael F. *journalist*
Traynelis, Stephen Francis *neuroscientist, educator*
Tullis, Bill *sound recording engineer, music producer*
Ueng, Charles En-Shiuh *engineering educator, consultant*
†Unger, Roberta *architect*
Vachon, Reginald Irenee *mechanical engineer*
Valk, Henry Snowden *physicist, educator*
Van Assendelft, Onno Willem *hematologist*
Varner, Chilton Davis *lawyer*
Vaughn, Michael S. *criminal justice educator*
Veal, Rex R. *lawyer*
Verrill, F. Glenn *advertising executive*
Vigtel, Gudmund *museum director emeritus*
Villwock, Kenneth James *procurement executive*
Wagner, James Warren *academic administrator, engineering educator*
Wakefield, Stephen Alan *lawyer*
Wald, Michael Leonard *economist*
Walden, Philip Michael *recording company executive, publishing company executive*
Walker, Betsy Ellen *consulting and systems integration company executive*
Walker, Carolyn Smith *college services administrator, counselor*
Walker, Thomas H. *federal agency administrator*
Wallace, Gladys Baldwin *librarian*
Wallace, Julia Diane *newspaper editor*
Walsh, W. Terence *lawyer*
Walton, Carole Lorraine *clinical social worker*
Wang, Richard Y. *emergency physician, osteopath*
Ward, Horace Taliaferro *federal judge*
†Waters, Lou *anchorman, correspondent*
Watts, Anthony Lee *bank executive*
Weatherly, Alvis Morrison, Jr., *retired association developer*
Weathersby, James Roy *lawyer*
†Webb, J. David *lawyer*
Weber, Gerald Richard *legal association administrator, educator*
Weed, Roger Oren *rehabilitation services professional, educator*
Weintraub, William Seth *epidemiologist*
Weiss, Jay M(ichael) *psychologist, educator*
Wellon, Robert G. *lawyer*
Wenger, Nanette Kass *cardiology educator, cardiologist, researcher*
Westerhoff, John Henry, III, *clergyman, theologian, educator*
White, Ortrude B. *architect*
White, Ronald Leon *financial management consultant*
†Whitley, Deborah Marie *social worker, educator*
Whitman, Homer William, Jr., *retired investment counseling company executive*
Whitmer, William Eward *retired accountant*
Whitt, Richard Ernest *reporter*
Whittington, Frederick Brown, Jr., *business administration educator*
Wieland, John *real estate executive*
Wilding, Diane *marketing, financial and information systems executive*
Willett, Chris Godwin *securities company executive, consultant*
Williams, James Bryan *banker*
Williams, Joel Cash *lawyer*
Williams, John Young *merchant banker*
Williams, Loraine Plant *civic worker*
Williams, Neil, Jr., *lawyer*
Williams, Ralph Watson, Jr., *retired securities company executive*
Williamson, James Robert, Jr., *lawyer*
Willis, Isaac *dermatologist, educator*
Wilmer, Mary Charles *artist*
Wilson, James Hargrove, Jr., *lawyer*
Winchester, Jesse Gregory *commercial real estate company executive*
Winer, Ward Otis *mechanical engineer, educator*
Winkler, Allen Warren *lawyer, educator*
Wolbrink, James Francis *real estate investor*
Wong, Ching-Ping *chemist, materials scientist, engineer, educator*
†Wood, L. Lin, Jr., *lawyer*
Woodruff, Bradley Allen *epidemiologist*
Worley, David *lawyer*
Wright, Daniel *wine specialist, consultant*
†Wright, Frederick Lewis, II, *lawyer*
Wright, Peter Meldrim *lawyer*
†Wulkan, Mark Lewis *pediatrician, surgeon*
Wussler, Robert Joseph *broadcasting executive, media consultant*
Xi, Hongkang *medical sciences researcher*
Yancey, Asa Greenwood, Sr., *physician*
Yancey, Carolyn Dunbar *educational policy maker*
Yates, Ella Gaines *library consultant*
Young, Michael Anthony *lawyer*
†Young, Robert George *lawyer*
†Yu, Jianjun *electrical engineer, researcher*
Yu-Lee, Reginald Tomas *consultant executive*
Zabka, Sven Paul *lawyer*
Zhang, Zhuomin *mechanical engineering educator*
†Zhao, Yichuan *education educator*
†Zhong, Hua *medical educator, researcher*
Zink, Charles Talbott *lawyer*
Zumpe, Doris *ethologist, researcher, educator*

Auburn
Hutchinson, Leslie Julian *preventive medicine physician*

Augusta
Baker, Carleton Harold *physiology educator*
Barfield, W. Leon *federal judge*

Barnes, Vernon Anthony *research scientist*
†Bieberich, Erhard *biologist*
Bloodworth, William Andrew, Jr., *academic administrator*
Bowen, Dudley Hollingsworth, Jr., *federal judge*
Bradberry, Edward *opera company executive*
Chandler, Arthur Bleakley *pathologist, educator*
Cheng, Wu C. *retired patent examiner*
Christensen, David William *mathematician, engineer*
Cooney, William J. *lawyer*
Craig, Cynthia Mae *mathematics educator*
Cundey, Paul Edward, Jr., *cardiologist*
†Davis, Catherine Lucy *psychologist, medical researcher*
†Dickert, Neal Workman *lawyer*
Dolen, William Kennedy *allergist, immunologist, pediatrician, educator*
†Dukes, Michael *consumer products company executive*
Feldman, Elaine Bossak *medical nutritionist, educator*
Floyd, Rosalyn Wright *pianist, accompanist, educator*
Gambrell, Richard Donald, Jr., *endocrinologist, educator*
Gillespie, Edward Malcolm *hospital administrator*
Given, Kenna Sidney *surgeon, educator*
Grier, Leamon Forest *social services administrator*
†Griswold, Sara Y. *language educator*
Guill, Margaret Frank *pediatrics educator, medical researcher*
Gujral, Jaspal Singh *physician, internist*
†Hand, Maryanne Kelly *artist, educator*
†Hess, David Charles *neurologist, educator*
†Horuzsko, Anatolij *medical research scientist*
Imig, John David *medical educator*
†Jackson, Rosa M. *educator*
Krauss, Jonathan Seth *pathologist*
Kuhn, Walter F. *emergency medicine physician*
Kutlar, Ferdane *genetics educator, researcher*
Lee, Lansing Burrows, Jr., *lawyer, corporate executive*
Lewis, Shirley Ann Redd *college president*
Luxenberg, Malcolm Neuwahl *ophthalmologist, educator, retired*
MacLeod, James L. *minister, finance company executive, art gallery owner*
Manganiello, Louis Otto Joseph *retired neurosurgeon*
Mansberger, Arlie Roland, Jr., *surgeon*
†McDaniel, George M. *pediatrician*
†Miller, Alfred Montague *lawyer*
Mode, Donald G. *urologist, medical director*
Nesbit, Robert Raymond, Jr., *surgeon*
Ottinger, Mary Louise *podiatrist*
Ownby, Dennis Randall *pediatrician, educator, allergist, researcher*
†Pallas, Christopher William *cardiologist*
Parrish, Robert Alton *retired pediatric surgeon, educator*
Potter, Brad J. *dean, researcher, educator*
Prisant, L(ouis) Michael *cardiologist*
Pryor, Carol Graham *obstetrician, gynecologist*
Puryear, Joan Copeland *academic administrator*
Rippert, Eric Theodore *oral and maxillofacial surgeon*
Rivner, Michael Harvey *neurologist*
Rogers, Michael Bruce *orthodontist*
Rosen, James Mahlon *artist, art historian, educator*
Rowland, Arthur Ray *librarian*
Ryan, James Walter *physician, medical researcher*
Sansbury, Barbara Ann Pettigrew *nursing administrator*
Shrout, Michael Kirby *dental educator, researcher*
Smith, Randolph Relihan *plastic surgeon*
Stark, Nancy Lynn *critical care nurse*
Stern, David M. *dean, educator*
Talledo, Oscar Eduardo *medical educator*
Tedesco, Francis Joseph *university administrator*
Tikare, Satyanarayana K. *retired internist*
Tucker, Jessie L., III, *health facility administrator, educator*
†Watkins, Ralph Craig *social sciences educator*
†Wheale, Duncan Douglas *lawyer*
Whittemore, Ronald Paul *hospital administrator, retired army officer, nursing educator*
Wilde, James Alfred *pediatrician, educator*
Woodhurst, Robert Stanford, Jr., *architect*
Woods, Gerald Wayne *lawyer*
Wray, Betty Beasley *allergist, immunologist, pediatrician*
Yu, Robert Kuan-jen *biochemistry educator*

Austell
Halwig, J. Michael *allergist*
†Orr, Zellie *entrepreneur, educator, writer, researcher*
Vance, Sandra Johnson *secondary school educator*

Bainbridge
King, Steven C. *real estate agent, retired research scientist*
†Lucas, Tammi Michelle *music educator*

Baldwin
Smith, John Andrew *veterinarian*

Ball Ground
Tucker, Robert Dennard *health care products executive*

Barnesville
†Adams, Cynthia Ann *librarian, media specialist, writing instructor*
†Anderson, Nancy Dixon *librarian*
Barnard, John Phillip *technology educator*
†Horn, Jason G. *English educator*
Terry, Pamela Mays *psychology educator*

Baxley
Reddy, Yenamala Ramachandra *metal processing executive*

Bishop
Bower, Douglas William *pastoral counselor, psychotherapist, clergyman*

Blue Ridge
Walker, Sarah Harriet *English educator, administrator*

Bonaire
Rustin, Varie Beatrice *community volunteer*

Bowden
†Sulzer, Alexander Jackson *retired research microbiologist, educator*

Brunswick
Brubaker, Robert Paul *food products executive*
†Cody, Sara Elizabeth *librarian*
Herndon, Alice Patterson Latham *public health nurse*
Hopwood, Vicki Jeane *medical center official*
Iannicelli, Joseph *chemical company executive, consultant*
†McLemore, Gilbert Carmichael, Jr., *lawyer*
Mihal, Sandra Powell *systems analyst*
Mitchell, Dorothy Harvey *healthcare administrator*
Perniciaro, Charles Vincent *dermatologist, educator, entrepreneur*
†Spencer, Shirley Ann *secondary school educator, speech educator, literature educator*

Buchanan
Rainey, Terry Lee *music educator, director*

Buford
Byrd, Larry Donald *behavioral pharmacologist*
†Garwood, Robert Ashley, Jr., *systems engineer*
†Napolitano, Mary Elizabeth *nuclear engineer*
Stubbs, Thomas Hubert *company executive*

Byron
Morton, Eric *liberal arts educator*

Calhoun
Edgmon, Gary Martin *orthodontist*
†Lorberbaum, Jeffrey S. *textiles executive*
Parman, Debra Lanette *physical therapist*

Canton
Forsh, Frederick Douglas *music educator*
Hasty, William Grady, Jr., *lawyer*
Lokey, Linda H. *music educator*
Sperin, Amelia Harrison *medical/surgical nurse, obstetrics/gynecological nurse*

Carrollton
Aanstoos, Christopher Michael *psychology educator*
Alexander, Mary Gerette Blaydes *child therapist*
Bakos, Daniel Frank *music educator, organist, composer*
Beard, Charles Edward *library director, consultant*
†Boumenir, Amin *mathematician, educator*
Brewer, A. Bruce *university administrator*
Butler, Jody Talley *gifted education educator*
†Cao, Li *social studies educator, educator*
Clark, Janet Eileen *political scientist, educator*
Ferling, John E. *history educator*
Goodson, Carol Faye *librarian*
Morgan, Harry New *education educator*
Purk, Janice Kay *sociology and gerontology educator*
Sethna, Beheruz Nariman *university president, marketing, management educator*
†Steely, Melvin T. *language educator, educator*
Stone, Sandra Smith *sociologist, researcher*
†Thorn, Stuart Wallace *marketing and financial executive*
Tisinger, David Harvey *lawyer*

Cartersville
Benham, Lelia *small business owner, social and political activist*
Harris, Joe Frank *former governor*

Cave Spring
Boehm, John Charles *music educator*

Centerville
Deane, Karen Peklo *retail executive*

Chatsworth
Witherow, Jimmie David *secondary school educator*

Clayton
Martinez, Susan Barbara *human rights advocate, journalist*
Ritter, Guy Franklin *structural engineer*

Cleveland
Barrett, David Eugene *judge*
†Edwards, John Carver *retired archivist*
Inge, Walter Herndon *writer*
Lewis, Richard, Sr., *securities broker, consultant*
Raznoff, Beverly Shultz *education educator*

Cochran
†Ayres, Brenda Ann *literature educator*
Halaska, Thomas Edward *academic administrator, director, engineer*
Ricks, John Addison, Jr., *history educator*

College Park
Atkinson, Bruce Earl *clinical psychologist, christian counselor*
Fahy, Nancy Lee *food products marketing executive*
Ferguson, Wendell *private school educator*
†Payne, Harry Charles *historian, educator*
Stokes, Arch *lawyer, writer*
West-Hill, Gwendolyn *poet, educator, artist, evangelist*

Colquitt
San Jose, Angel Molina *surgeon*

Columbus
Abrahamson, William Gene *retired school counselor*
Amos, Daniel Paul *insurance company executive*
Anthony, Richard E. *bank executive*
Averill, Ellen Corbett *secondary education science educator, administrator*
Bailey, Herta Luise *real estate broker*
†Boothby, Lisa Anne *pharmacist, drug information specialist*
Bowman, Donald Campbell *accountant*
Brinkley, Jack Thomas *lawyer, former congressman*
Campbell, Edward Wilson (Ned Campbell) *theater director, actor*
Chan, Philip *dermatologist, retired army officer*
Cloninger, Kriss, III, *insurance company executive*
†Cobos, Patricio *music educator*
†Conklin, Jeffrey T. *director*
†Cummins, James Donald *retired electrical engineer*
Diaz-Verson, Salvador, Jr., *investment advisor*
Downie, Richard Duncan *military officer, government agency administrator*
Edmondson, Michael Herman *secondary school educator*
†Gibbons, Dona Alden Coe *electrical engineer*
Gore, James Arnold *biology educator, aquatic ecologist, hydrologist*
Harp, John Anderson *lawyer*
†Heard, William T. *automotive executive*
Holcombe, Alfred Robert, Jr., *museum curator*
Johnson, Walter Frank, Jr., *lawyer*
Kerr, Allen Stewart *retired psychologist*
Laney, John Thomas, III, *federal judge*
†Leebern, Donald M., Jr., *distilled beverage executive*
McFarland, Samuel P., Jr., *psychologist*
McGlamry, Max Reginald *lawyer*
Montgomery, Anna Frances *elementary school educator*
Murray, James J. *textiles executive*
Newton, Gwendolyn Stewart *elementary school educator*
†Nix, Jeffrey Alan *photographer*
Page, William Marion *lawyer*
†Patrick, James Duvall, Jr., *lawyer*
Poydasheff, Robert Stephen *lawyer*
Riggsby, Dutchie Sellers *education educator*
Riggsby, Ernest Duward *science educator, educational development executive*
Ripple, Rochelle Poyourow *educational administrator, educator*
Short, Shenita *writer*
Simpson, Minnie Peach *interior designer*
Sweeney, Robert David *communications engineer*
†Tidd, Joyce Carter *etiquette educator*
Yancey, James D. *bank executive*
Zuiderveen, Jeffrey Alan *biology educator, toxicology consultant, aquatic toxicologist*

Conley
Marcus, James Elbert *manufacturing company executive*

Conyers
Bouchillon, John Ray *education coordinator*
Closs, James William *retired non-commissioned officer, financial analyst, educator*
Griffey, Karen Rose *special education educator*
Houchard, Michael Harlow *retired organization executive*
Kelly, John Hubert *diplomat, business executive*
†Snapp, William Dorsey *lawyer*
Spearman, Maxie Ann *financial analyst, administrator*
Telnack, Methodius Richard *priest, monk, craftsman*
Waters, Roger Allen *music educator*

Cordele
†Christy, Gary Christopher *lawyer*
Helms, Bobby Gillespie *music educator, consultant*
Jordan, Randall Warren *optometrist*

Covington
Harris, Earl Douglas *state agency administrator*

Cumming
Benson, Betty Jones *retired school system administrator*
Copen, Melvyn Robert *management educator, university administrator*
Drew, Paul S. *entrepreneur*
French, James Thomas *real estate broker*
†Muirhead, Brent *secondary school educator*
†Pruitt-Streetman, Shirley Irene *small business owner*
Willadsen, Michael Chris *marketing professional, sales executive*

Cuthbert
Hinds, Glester Samuel *financial consultant*

Dacula
Daniel, Raymond *economist*
Murphree, Harold T. *retired minister*

Dahlonega
Boggan, Jeffrey Scott *college administrator*
Broman, John Michael *music educator*
Edmondson, Joanne Holt *counselor, educator*
Friedman, Barry David *political scientist, educator*
Hansford, Nathaniel *academic administrator, lawyer*
†Miller, Carol Ann *physical therapist, educator*
Newman, Thomas Daniel *minister, school administrator*
Pandres, Dave, Jr., *science educator, researcher*
Pippert, John Marvin *sociology educator*
†Wiedmann, Sally Nelson *philosophy educator*

Dallas
Schafer, Sandra Lee *geriatric nurse practitioner, educator*

Dalton
†Bouckaert, Carl M. *manufacturing executive*
Bundros, Thomas Anthony *utilities executive*
Evans, Thomas Passmore *business and product licensing consultant*
Forsee, Joe Brown *library director*
Frerichs, Joy Roberta *elementary education educator*
Hutcheson, John Ambrose, Jr., *history educator*
†Jones-Glaze, Barbara Ann *library media specialist*
Mathews, Marsha Anderson *English educator, poet, minister*
†McKay, William Paul *oncologist, health facility administrator*
Pritchett, Deborah Kaye *artist*
†Saul, Julian *retail executive*
Winter, Larry Eugene *accountant*

Danielsville
Bond, Joan *retired elementary school educator*

Darien
Davis, Ann Richardson *artist, sculptor, book dealer, writer*

Dawsonville
Jorgensen, Alfred H. *retired data processing executive*

Decatur
Anderson, Jonpatrick Schuyler *financial consultant, therapist, archivist*
Bain, James Arthur *pharmacologist, educator*
†Baker, Herman Dupree *lawyer*
Baker, Stephen Monroe *school system administrator*
†Beran, Michael James *research psychologist, primatologist*
Bleser, Katherine Alice *artist*
Bockwitz, Cynthia Lee *psychologist, psychology and women's studies educator*
Brown, William Virgil *internal medicine educator*
Cartman, Shirley Eleise *retired music educator*
Cavallaro, Joseph John *retired microbiologist*
Cooper, James Russell *retired law educator*
Cravey, Pamela J. *librarian*
Dade, Joann *critical care nurse, small business owner*
Davis, Laura Ann *executive coach, trainer, facilitator*
Denny, Dallas *psychological examiner*
Dillingham, William Byron *literature educator, author*
Downs, Jon Franklin *drama educator, director, writer*
Gann, Joyce Ann *obstetrician-gynecologist*
Gary, Julia Thomas *retired minister*
Gay, Robert Derril *public agency director*
Gueller, Samuel *civil and environmental engineer*
Guest, Abbi Taylor *lawyer, judge, educator*
Hagood, Susan Stewart Hahn *clinical dietitian*
Hagood, Thomas Richard, Jr., *minister, publisher*
Hale, Cynthia Lynette *religious organization administrator*
Hamilton, Frank Strawn *jazz musician, folksinger, composer and arranger, educator*
Hawkins, Janice Edith *medical/surgical clinical nurse specialist*
Heller, John Gaylord *orthopaedic surgery educator*
Henderson, Ralph Hale *physician*
Hinman, Alan Richard *public health administrator, epidemiologist*
Holtzman, Mary *engineering company executive*
†Keyes, Gwendolyn Rebecca *lawyer, educator*
Knight, Walker Leigh *editor, publisher, clergyman*
†Lucius, Randall H. *psychologist*
Matthews, Frank *retired pathologist*
Mc Intosh, James Eugene, Jr., *interior designer*
Morris, Robert Renly *minister, clinical pastoral education supervisor*
Morrison, Margaret L. *artist, educator, consultant*
Murphy, Deborah Jane *lawyer*
Murray, Raymond Lee *retired clothing designer, writer*
Myers, Clark Everett *retired business administration educator*
Rausher, David Benjamin *internist, gastroenterologist*
†Rimland, David *epidemiologist, researcher*
Rosenberg, Mark L. *health agency administrator*
Ross, Valdor Wendell *operating room nurse*
Shaw, Jeanne Osborne *editor, poet*
Tan, Li-Zhe *engineering educator, researcher*
Udoff, Eric Joel *diagnostic radiologist*
Veach, Daniel Lee *editor*
†Wilbur, Roger *education educator, poet*

Demorest
Vance, Cynthia Lynn *psychology educator*

Doraville
†Ambrose, Andrew M. *humanities educator*
Gerstein, Joe Willie *lawyer*
Wempner, Gerald Arthur *engineering educator*

Douglas
Newland, Hillary Reid *pathologist*
Pugh, Joye Jeffries *educational administrator*
Sims, Rebecca Littleton *lawyer*

Douglasville
Campbell, Bruce Henry *chemist*
Eddy, Julia Veronica *educator*
†Hall, Mary Hugh *retired secondary school educator*
Jackson, Cynthia Williford *special education educator*
Paterson, Paul Charles *retired private investigator, security consultant*
Wilson, Keith Mark *health services administrator*

Dublin
Alexander, Judith Elaine *psychologist*
Claxton, Harriett Maroy Jones *retired language educator*
Doster, Daniel Harris *retired counselor, minister*
Fatum, Delores Ruth *school counselor*
Folsom, Roger Lee *healthcare administrator*
Greene, Jule Blounte *lawyer*
†Nellis, Noel *thoracic surgeon, educator*
Watt, Dwight, Jr., (Arthur Dwight Watt Jr.) *computer programming and microcomputer specialist*

Duluth
Bell, Tonya Lynn *auditor*
†Brasher, Earlene D. *music educator, church organist*
Bridges, Alan Lynn *physicist, computer scientist, systems software engineer*
Brody, Aaron Leo *food and packaging consultant*
Burns, Carroll Dean *insurance company executive*
Colwell, Gene Thomas *engineering educator*
Denney, Laura Falin *insurance company executive*
†Gereben, Istvan Bela *retired oceanographer, retired acoustical engineer*
Hillstead, Richard Averill *product development executive*
Holutiak-Hallick, Stephen Peter, Jr., *retired army officer, businessman, educator*
Johnston, William David *biotechnology executive*
Kramer, Edward E. *screenwriter, editor*
Laubscher, Robert James *consumer products company executive*
Luger, Donald R. *engineering company executive*
Manley, Lance Filson *data processing consultant*
†McClung, Samuel Brenton *music educator, consultant*
Pickett, Christa Langford *elementary school counselor*
Reed, Ralph Eugene, Jr., *political party official*
Sloan, Donnie Robert, Jr., *lawyer*
Street, David Hargett *investment company executive*
Watkins, Sydney Lynn *sales executive*
Weldon, Thomas David *medical products manufacturer*

Dunwoody
Callison, James W. *former lawyer, consultant, airline executive*
Chacholiades, Miltiades *economics educator*
Clark, Faye Louise *drama and speech educator*
Duvall, Marjorie L. *English and foreign language educator*
La Motte, Louis Cossitt, Jr., *medical scientist, consultant*
†Maddox, Jerry Aven *Retired Catalog Management Executive*

East Point
Bridgewater, Herbert Jeremiah, Jr., *radio host*
†Fields, Warren C. *music educator, minister*
Harris, Carlos Ortez *elementary school educator*
Johnson, Hardwick Smith, Jr., *school psychologist*
Rogers, Rhonwyn Voncelle *therapist, psychology educator*
†Warren, Barbara Denise *special education educator*

Eastman
†Wiggins, James L. *lawyer*

Ellenwood
†Bauman, Mark Keith *historian, educator*
Pack, Bobigene *minister, writer*

Evans
Allard, David Henry *judge*
Fournier, Joseph Andre Alphonse *nurse, social worker, psychotherapist*
Large, Mary Mitchell Westall *volunteer*
Perry, Sarah Teresa Anderson (Teri Perry) *nursing administrator*
Welsh, Michael Louis *business executive*
Zachert, Virginia *psychologist, educator*

Fairburn
Bobo, Genelle Tant (Nell Bobo) *retired office administrator*

Fayetteville
Adams, Michael Keith *retired military officer*
†Brown, L(arry) Eddie *tax practitioner, business accountant, real estate broker, financial planner*
Cokuslu, Lynda Elizabeth McCord *medical assistant*
†Fox, Patrick Joseph *lawyer*
Hannum, David Lawrence *business consultant, training specialist, educator*
Harris, Glenda Stange *medical language specialist, proofreader, writer*
†Hood, Barbara W. *musician, educator*
†Neal, Joan Burkes *librarian*
Turnipseed, Barnwell Rhett, III, *journalist, public relations consultant*

Flovilla
†Lamb, Deryle Jean *preservationist*

Flowery Branch
Blank, Arthur M. *professional sports team executive, retired home and lumber retail chain executive*

Congdon, Jon Harvey *music educator*
Dunn, Warrick *football player*
Monroe, Melrose *retired banker*
†Reeves, Daniel Edward *professional football coach*
Vick, Michael *football player*

Folkston
Crumbley, Esther Helen Kendrick *realtor, former councilwoman, retired secondary education educator*
Knowles, Julie Nall *secondary school educator*

Forest Park
†Fisher, George Alexander, Jr., *lieutenant general United States Army*
†Grace-Crum, Phyllis Venetia *military officer*
†Riggs, John M. *army officer*

Fort Benning
Glushko, Gail Marie *physician, military officer*
Livingston, Joyce Torbic *civilian military employee*

Fort Gordon
†Griffin, Robert F. *military career officer*

Fort Mcpherson
Crowder, Henry Alvin *military officer*
†Edwards, Warren Chappelle *military career officer*
†Hendrix, John Walter *lieutenant general United States Army*
Piacentini, Nicholas A., Jr., *military officer*
Williamson, Kenneth N. *civilian military employee*
Yingling, John A. *military officer*

Fort Valley
Archer, Lloyd Daniel *communications educator*
Chandras, Kananur V. *psychology educator*
†Stripling, Allen James *music educator*
Swartwout, Joseph Rodolph *obstetrics and gynecology educator, administrator*

Fortson
Schmitt, Ralph George *manufacturing company executive*

Franklin
Lipham, William Patrick *principal, educator*

Franklin Springs
†Bobic, Michael P. *political scientist, educator*
†Pettyjohn, Emma Kennedy *fine arts educator*

Gainesville
Burd, John Stephen *academic administrator, music educator*
Clary, Ronald Gordon *insurance agency executive*
Davis, Connie Waters *public relations and marketing executive*
Fish-Lacey, Helen Therese *educator, author*
Gilliam, Steven Philip, Sr., *lawyer*
Givogre, John Lee *pain medicine specialist, anesthesiologist*
Hester, Francis Bartow, III, (Frank Hester) *lawyer*
Jones, William Benjamin, Jr., *electrical engineering educator*
Leet, Richard Hale *oil company executive*
Lorence, James J. *historian, educator*
McCord, Gloria Dawn Harmon *music educator, choral director, organist*
Pilgrim, James Rollins *retail furniture company executive*
†Reed, Gina Fulton *mathematics educator*
†Rivera, Cindy L. *social services administrator, medical/surgical nurse*
†Santander, Andrew Michael *music educator, researcher*
Schuder, Raymond Francis *lawyer*
Strickland, William Bradley *English educator*
Turner, John Sidney, Jr., *retired otolaryngologist, educator*
Vaughn, Betty Jean *obstetrician/gynecologist*

Grayson
Mitchell, Laura Anne Gilbert *family nurse practitioner*
Nease, Judith Allgood *marriage and family therapist*

Greensboro
Watts, Ronald Lester *retired military officer*

Griffin
Doyle, Michael Patrick *microbiologist, educator, director*
Duncan, Ronny Rush *agriculturist, turf researcher, consultant*
Marshall, Allen Wright, III, *communications executive, financial consultant*
Shuman, Larry Myers *soil chemist*

Hamilton
Byrd, Gary Ellis *lawyer*
Chewning, Martha Frances MacMillan *lawyer*

Hampton
Williams, Owen Brian *music educator*

Hazlehurst
Wilkes, E.M., III, *judge*

Hephzibah
Golphin, Elouise *writer, educator*

Hiawassee
Bayless, Carolyn Cotton *nurse*

High Shoals
Bracewell, Gaynor Lee *hydro electric plant owner, developer*

Hinesville
Baer, William Harold *business executive*
Turner, Dwayne Curtis *lawyer*
Wise, Carl Stamps *accounting educator*

Homer
Rylee, Gloria Genelle *educator*

Hoschton
Campbell, Leslie Caine (Caine Campbell) *writer, historian*

Hull
Melton, Charles Estel *retired physicist, educator*

Jasper
Marger, Edwin *lawyer*
Sutter, Jean *sculptor*
Webster, Robert McNaught *physician, researcher*

Jekyll Island
Bentley, James Luther *former journalist*
Jones, William Randolph *history educator*
McKinley, Douglas Webster (Webb McKinley) *consultant*

Jesup
Li, Jian *chemical engineer, educator*

Jonesboro
Colburn, Donald Eugene *protective services official*
Dame, Laureen Eva *nursing administrator, educator*
Dawson, Lewis Edward *minister, retired military officer*
Finley, Sarah Maude Merritt *social worker*
Galvin, John Rogers *educator, retired army officer*
Preble, Darrell Wayne *systems analyst*
Ziegler, Robert Oliver *retired music and special education educator*

Kathleen
Uzzell-Baggett, Karon Lynette *career officer*

Kennesaw
Adams, Dean (Lewis Adams) *theater director*
Barnett, Benjamin Lewis, Jr., *retired physician, educator*
†Doke, David Reed *music educator, musician*
Frank, Mary Lou Bryant *psychologist, educator*
†Graham, Dorothy H. *education educator*
Hetrick, Joan Willette *critical care nurse, administrator*
Karcher, Barbara Correnti *sociologist, educator*
Kruger, Harry *retired conductor, retired music educator*
†La Rosa, Agatino *geographer, educator*
†Li, Chien-pin *political scientist, educator*
Munoz, Steven Michael *physician associate*
†Raines, Susan Summers *mediator, educator*
Robinson, Kenneth Charles *management educator*
Shock, David Robert *political science educator*
†Siegel, Betty Lentz *university president*
Tuttle, Marshall *musician, educator*
Vandewalker, David W. *music educator*
Whittingham, Harry Edward, Jr., *retired banker*

Kingsland
†Ossick, John Joseph, Jr., *lawyer*

La Fayette
Hendrix, Bonnie Elizabeth Luellen *retired elementary school educator*
Lim, Esteban, Jr., *medical facility administrator, physician*
Muerth, Cherie Anne *social worker*

Lagrange
†Anderson, Toni P. *music educator, vocalist*
Ault, Ethyl Lorita *special education educator, consultant*
†Cook, John Granger *religious studies educator, philosopher, educator*
Copeland, Robert Bodine *internist, cardiologist*
Davidson, Joeline Dillard *laboratory services administrator*
†Greene, Annie Lucille *artist, retired art educator*
Gresham, James Thomas *foundation executive*
†Hawkins, Frances Pam *finance educator*
Hudson, Charles Daugherty *insurance executive*
Rhodes, Eddie, Jr., *medical technologist, phlebotomy technician, educator*
Turner, Fred Lamar *accountant, lawyer*
West, John Thomas *retired surgeon*
Wilkes, George Gardner, Jr., *landscape architect*

Lavonia
†Masterson Raines, Judith Amanda *marketing executive*

Lawrenceville
Allen, Julian Myrick, Jr., *industrial engineer*
Carter, Dale William *psychologist*
†Crain, Mary Ann *elementary school educator*
†Dickerson, Claudia Thompson *psychologist*
Elleby, Gail *management consultant*
Elsey, James Kevin *vascular surgeon, educator*
Fetner, Robert Henry *radiation biologist*
Gericke, Paul William *minister, educator*
Henson, Gene Ethridge *retired legal administrator*
Hobbs, Robert Ellice, Jr., *artist*
Parr, Sandra Hardy *small business owner*
Reeves, Gene *judge*
Reuter, Helen Hyde *psychologist*
Wall, Clarence Vinson *state legislator*

Leesburg
†Myers, David Wayne *legal assistant*

Lilburn
Cline, Sandra Williamson *retired elementary school educator*
Neumann, Thomas William *archaeologist*

Wagner, Douglas Alan *secondary school educator*

Lithonia
Baxter, Gene Francis *chemical researcher, consultant*
Haller, Hal Martin, Jr., *library director*
Wilson, Veta Emily *community health nurse*

Lizella
Jones, Seaborn Gustavus *poet*

Locust Grove
Bomar, Robert Linton *assistant principal*
Smith, Al Jackson, Jr., *environmental engineer, lawyer*

Loganville
Spurgeon, Barbara *music educator*
Wald, Marlena Malmstedt *health science librarian*

Lookout Mountain
Dreger, D. C. *academic administrator*

Lovejoy
Onukwuli, Francis Osita *computer scientist, secondary education educator*

Lyons
Frey, Bob Henry *psychotherapist, sociologist, educator, poet, canon lawyer*

Mableton
Armour, Christopher E. *physician*
Boyle, Robert Daniel *information technology executive*
Rowe, Bonnie Gordon *music company executive*

Macon
Adkison, Linda Russell *geneticist, consultant*
Aldridge, Melvin Dayne *engineering educator*
Anderson, Robert Lanier, III, *judge*
Andrews, Charles Haynes *economics educator*
Bagley, Cathy Lorraine *obstetrician, gynecologist*
†Bell, Andrew C. *music educator*
†Brown, Stephen Phillip *judge*
Carson, Juanita Elaine *biologist, educator*
Cole, John Prince *lawyer, university official*
Craig, Kern William *political science educator*
†Davis, Anita Yvonne *small business owner, writer*
†Dodson, Carr Glover *lawyer, director*
Drysdale, Joyce A *substance abuse counselor*
Dunwody, Eugene Cox *architect*
Ennis, Edgar William, Jr., *lawyer*
Etheridge, John Green *retired pathologist*
Franklin, Roosevelt *minister*
†Godsey, R(aleigh) Kirby *university president*
†Hash, Robert Bruce *medical educator*
Hershner, Robert Franklin, Jr., *judge*
†Hester, D. Micah *education educator*
Holliday, Peter Osborne, Jr., *dentist*
Huffman, Joan Brewer *history educator*
Hunnicutt, Victoria Anne Wilson *educator*
Hutto, Richard Jay *lawyer*
Jobe, Ann Connor *dean, educator*
Jones, John Ellis *real estate broker*
Keating, Thomas Patrick *health care administrator, educator*
Lewis, Sandra Combs *research psychologist, writer*
McFarland, Terry Lynn *construction company executive*
Mines, Richard Oliver, Jr., *civil and environmental engineer*
Murdoch, Bernard Constantine *psychology educator*
Owens, Wilbur Dawson, Jr., *federal judge*
Parrish, Carmelita B. *retired secondary school educator*
Phillips, J(ohn) Taylor *judge*
Robinson, Joe Sam *neurosurgeon, educator*
Robinson, W. Lee *lawyer*
Savage, Randall Ernest *journalist*
Scarbary, Otis Lee *lawyer*
Scheetz, Allison Paige *medical educator*
Skelton, William Douglas *physician*
†Snow, Cubbedge, Jr., *lawyer*
Staton, Cecil Pope, Jr., *religious and academic publisher, educator*
Steeples, Douglas Wayne *retired university dean, consultant, researcher*
Volpe, Erminio Peter *biologist, educator*
Walton, DeWitt Talmage, Jr., *dentist*
Weaver, Jacquelyn Kunkel Ivey *artist, educator*
†Williams, Carol Kennedy *college administrator*
Young, Henry E. *tissue engineering medical educator*
†Young-Zook, Monica M. *language educator*

Madison
Aldridge, John Watson *English language educator, author*
DuBose, Charles Wilson *lawyer*
Short, Betsy Ann *elementary education educator*

Manchester
Ellison, Betty D. *retired elementary educator*

Marietta
Ahlstrom, Michael Joseph *lawyer*
Ballard, Judy Thomas *real estate broker*
Bankers, James *military officer*
Bentley, Fred Douglas, Sr., *lawyer*
Berryhill, Henry Lee, Jr., *geologist, researcher*
Biehle, Karen Jean *pharmacist*
Billingsley, Judith Ann Seavey *oncology nurse*
Bruce, Thomas Allen *financial consultant*
†Chastain, Mark Alan *dermatologist, otolaryngologist, educator*
Clay, Charles Commander (Chuck Clay) *lawyer, state senator*
Cline, Robert Thomas *retired land developer*
Devigne, Karen Cooke *retired amateur athletics executive*

Dobrzyn, Janet Elaine *quality management professional*
Drake, Alison Brooks *physiatrist*
Dudley, Gary Edward *clinical psychologist*
Dunwoody, Kenneth Reed *magazine and book editor*
Edwards, Charles Mundy, III, *financial consultant*
Garrett, Joseph Edward *aerospace engineer*
Guentner, Gail Marie *software engineer*
Hagood, Murl Felton *surgeon*
Hays, Robert William *communications consultant, educator, writer*
Houston, Dorothy Middleton *elementary education educator*
†Howell, Roger Eugene *music educator, musician*
Ingram, George Conley *lawyer, judge*
Ivey, William Hamilton *communications consultant*
†Kearney, Colleen Ann *occupational therapist*
†Kendall, Susan Gardes *librarian*
Kiger, Ronald Lee *contract negotiator*
Laframboise, Joan Carol *middle school educator*
Lahtinen, Silja Liisa *artist*
Lee, Raymond William, III, *institutional stockbroker*
Leonard, Steven K. *orchestra director, educator*
Lewis, William Headley, Jr., *manufacturing company executive*
†Lurie, Jeanne Flora *lawyer*
†McGahan, Martin J. *health products executive*
McManus, Constance *lawyer*
Meyer, Roger Albert *surgeon*
Miles, Thomas Caswell *aerospace engineer*
†Morisco, Jerid Simon *music educator, conductor*
Opre, Thomas Edward *magazine editor, film company executive, corporate travel company executive*
Orr, John Traylor, Jr., *lawyer*
Petit, Parker Holmes *health care corporation executive*
Poor, Andrew Ford *music educator*
Pou, Linda G. *interior designer, architectural designer*
Rainey, Kenneth Tyler *English language educator*
Ranu, Harcharan Singh *biomedical scientist, administrator, orthopaedic biomechanics educator*
Rivers, Alma Faye *secondary education educator*
Rogers, Gail Elizabeth *library director*
Rossbacher, Lisa Ann *university president, geology educator, writer*
Rutherfoord, Rebecca Hudson *computer science educator*
Sanner, George Elwood *electrical engineer*
Segerhammar, Sharon K. *special education administrator*
†Shapiro, Abra Blair *real estate company executive*
Sherrington, Paul William *marketing communications executive*
Short-Mayfield, Patricia Ahlene *business owner*
Simmons, Stephen Gregory *accountant*
Sink, John Davis *scientist, clergy member*
Smith, Baker Armstrong *management executive, lawyer*
Smith, George Thornewell *retired state supreme court justice*
†Spain, Sheryl Scarbrough *school counselor, educator*
Spann, George William *management consultant*
Swanson, William Fredin, III, *manufacturing executive*
Tatnall, Peter Coolidge *civil engineer*
Wassel, Thomas Shelly *engineering executive*
†Watson, Michael Jeffrey *information technology manager*
Wells, Palmer Donald *performing arts executive*
Wheatley, Joseph Kevin *physician, urologist*
†Wheelock, Argil J. *urologist, medical company executive*
†Willoughby, Eric Alan *music educator*
†Wimberly, Linda Roberts *music educator, artist*
Yonkosky, Reena Ann *emergency physician*

Martinez
Colborn, Gene Louis *anatomy educator, researcher*
Nesbitt, Robert Edward Lee, Jr., *physician, educator, scientific researcher, writer, poet*

Mc Rae
Brown, Mary Cathleen *retired executive secretary, poet*

Mcdonough
Amarasinghe, Amarasinghe A.W. *psychiatrist, consultant*
Crumbley, R. Alex *lawyer*

Meansville
Hankins, Patricia L. *ceramic artist, educator*

Metter
Abbott, Nell Suttles *writer, poet*
Doremus, Ogden *lawyer*
Farmer, DeWayne Mark *director, photographer*
Guido, Michael Anthony *evangelist*

Milledgeville
†Bradley, Wayne Bernard *lawyer*
Buice, Bonnie Carl *lawyer, priest*
†Campbell, Scott Kenneth *management educator*
†DeVries, David John *mathematician, educator*
Engerrand, Doris Dieskow *business educator*
Friman, Alice Ruth *poet, English educator*
Gentry, Marshall Bruce *English educator*
Isaac, Walter Lon *psychology educator*
McGinnis, Michael Boyd *chemistry educator*
Peterson, Dave Leonard *psychologist*
Velimirovich, Boris *urologist*
Williamson, John Thomas, Sr., *minerals company executive*

Mineral Bluff
†Smiley, Ralph Neil (Ralph Smylea) *cook*

Moultrie
McCall, John Clark, Jr., *interior designer*
McLendon, Richard Charles *music educator*
Vereen, William Jerome *uniform manufacturing company executive*

Mount Berry
†Bissonnette, Victor L. *education educator*
†Davis, John Edward *music educator, musician*
Dhir, Krishna Swaroop *business administration educator*
Mew, Thomas Joseph, III, (Tommy Mew) *artist, educator*

Mount Vernon
†Eernisse, Glenn P. *music educator*
†Smith, David Robert *higher education administrator, minister, writer*
Williamson, C. Dean *university official*

Mountain City
Kennedy, Robinette *anthropologist, researcher*

Murrayville
Morris, Donald G. *engineering company executive*

Newnan
Barron, Lindsey Hand *real estate broker*
Barron, Thomas Willis *real estate broker*
Burns, Matthew Lynwood *surgeon*
Drake, W. Homer, Jr., *federal judge*
Franklin, Bruce Walter *lawyer*
McBroom, Thomas William, Sr., *aviation consultant*
Moore, Marianna Gay *law librarian, consultant*

Norcross
Adams, Kenneth Francis *automobile maufacturing company executive*
Bennett, Catherine June *information technology executive, educator, consultant*
Braden, Victoria Jane *small business owner*
Cramer, James Perry *management consultant, architectural firm executive, educator*
Dibb, David Walter *research association administrator*
Feeney, Michael Thomas *civil engineer*
†Goodling, Lauri Bohanan *documentation specialist*
Granger, Philip Richard *minister*
Hahn, Stanley Robert, Jr., *lawyer, financial executive*
Harrison, Gordon Ray *engineering executive, consultant, research scientist*
Hunter, Douglas Lee *ministry executive, former elevator executive*
Irons, Isie Iona *retired nursing administrator*
†Massey, Lewis *finance company executive*
†McDonald, James *science foundation executive*
†Miller, Tonya Alicia *training and development specialist, management consultant*
Moore, Christopher Barry *industrial engineer*
Nardelli-Olkowska, Krystyna Maria *ophthalmologist, educator*
Rubright, James Alfred *paperboard and packaging company executive*
Smith, David Carr *organic chemist*
Steckerl, Shally A. *executive recruiter*
Storey, Bobby Eugene, Jr., *electrical engineer, engineering consultant*
Wagner, Robert Earl *retired agronomist*
Wolkow, Alan Edward *chiropractic physician*
†Yeboah, George Kwame *medical researcher, public health service officer*

Oakwood
Jondahl, Terri Elise *importing and distribution company executive*
Martin, Johnny Benjamin *accountant*
Smith, David Claiborne *construction company executive*

Ocilla
†Pujadas, Thomas Edward *lawyer*

Oxford
Cody, William Bermond *political science educator*
McNeill, Mary Kathryn Morgan *librarian*
Sitton, Claude Fox *newspaper editor*
Stamps, George Moreland *communications consultant, facsimile pioneer*

Patterson
Cunningham, Raymond Carol, Jr., *elementary school educator*

Peachtree City
Arnold, Andrew Allen *management consultant*
Barnes, Marylou Riddleberger *retired academic administrator, educator*
Barrell, Dawn Holman *marketing specialist*
Clark, James Kermit, Jr., *real estate executive*
Crutchfield, Carolyn Ann *physical therapy educator*
Ebneter, Stewart Dwight *utility industry management consultant*
Eichelberger, Charles Bell *retired career officer*
†Green, Franklin Pasco *music educator*
Liang, Yue *engineer*
Marsh, Carole *author, photographer, publisher*
Moulder, Wilton Arlyn *financial management consultant*
Pulin, Carol *fine arts organization administrator*
Roobol, Norman Richard *industrial coatings consultant, educator*
Snyder, Franklin Farison *hydrologic engineering consultant*
Yeosock, John John *army officer*

Pine Lake
†Lawson Sylvester, Gloria Jean *mortgage planner*

Pine Mountain
Bishop, Michael *writer*
Callaway, Howard Hollis *business executive*

Powder Springs
Hodges, Mitchell *computer executive*

Quitman
Baum, Joseph Herman *retired biomedical educator*
McElroy, Annie Laurie *nursing educator, administrator*

Reidsville
†Saad, Fathy Zaki *medical association administrator, physician*

Richmond Hill
Byrnes, Thomas Raymond, Jr., *osteopath*

Ringgold
Hayes Gladson, Laura Joanna *psychologist*

Riverdale
Awachie, Peter Ifeacho Anazoba *chemistry educator, research chemist*
Lambert, Ethel Gibson Clark *secondary school educator*
Minter, Jimmie Ruth *accountant*
Waters, John W. *minister, educator*

Robins AFB
Batbie, John J., Jr., *military officer*
Head, William Pace *historian, educator*
Hedden, Kenneth Forsythe *chemical engineer*
Manley, Nancy Jane *environmental engineer*
Whaley, Wallace W. *military officer*

Robins Afb
†Haines, Dennis G. *military officer*

Rockmart
Hardin, Sherrie Ann Asfoury *commercial photographer*
Holley, Tammy Dannette Fennell *critical care nurse*

Rome
†Bell, Allen D. *art director, writer*
Brinson, Robert Maddox *lawyer*
†Carper, N. Gordon *historian, educator*
Granrose, Cherlyn Sue *psychology educator, researcher*
Janowski, Thaddeus Marian *architect*
†Jeffrey, Therber Kent *music educator*
Johnson, Alberta Clark *psychology educator*
Kines, Joan Elaine *human services administrator, consultant*
Lewis, Wayne Walton *industrial engineer*
Massing, Virginia Reeves *surgical nurse and administrator*
†McCrory, Aldous Desmond *lawyer*
Murphy, Harold Loyd *federal judge*
Potts, Glenda Rue *music educator*
Sellers, Jimmie *construction executive*
†Sheeley, Steven M. *academic administrator, minister, education educator*
Stephens, Michael Thoryne *librarian*
Sumner, Melanie *writer, educator*
†Tapia, Martha Luisa *mathematics educator*
†Wingo, Willie Bruce *secondary school educator*

Roopville
†Huckeba, Emily Causey *retired elementary school educator*

Roswell
Baker, Anita Diane *lawyer*
Birmingham, Richard Gregory *lawyer*
Boley, Dennis Lynn *construction company executive*
†Broome, Barry Dean *lawyer, estate and financial planning consultant*
Burgess, John Frank *management consultant, former utility executive, former army officer*
Christopher, Lin *artist*
Diercks, Chester William, Jr., *capital goods manufacturing company executive*
Dolan, Dennis Joseph *airline pilot, lawyer*
Eckert, Michael Joseph *television executive, media specialist*
England, John Melvin *lawyer, clergyman*
Forbes, John Ripley *museum executive, educator, naturalist*
Hill, I. Kathryn *medical certification, licensing and education consultant*
Hoskinson, Carol Rowe *middle school educator*
Huntley, William Thomas, III, *investor, consultant*
Johnson, Shirley Elaine *management consultant*
Jordan, DuPree, Jr., *management consultant, educator, journalist, publisher, business executive*
Klein, John Jacob *retired economist*
Lawler-Johnson, Dian L. *singer, instructor of voice, vocal technician*
McCloud, Melody Theresa *obstetrician-gynecologist, surgeon*
Mimms, Thomas Bowman, Jr., *lawyer*
Peterson, Donald Robert *magazine editor, vintage automobile consultant*
Roland, Raymond William *lawyer, mediator, arbitrator*
Siepi, Cesare *opera singer*
Strong-Tidman, Virginia Adele *marketing and advertising executive*
Teets, Charles Edward *international business consultant, lawyer*

Saint Marys
Hall, Lois Bremer *retired educator, volunteer*
†Smith, Charles Courtland, Jr., *lawyer, state legislator*

Saint Simons
Bell, Ronald Mack *university foundation administrator, consultant*
Cedel, Melinda Irene *music educator, violinist*
Donahoo, William Patrick *science administrator, consultant, science administrator, educator*
Douglas, William Ernest *retired government official*
Dressner, Paul Robert *outside sales and customer service representative*
Riedeburg, Theodore *management consultant, consultant*
Spivey, Ted Ray *English educator*
Sullivan, Barbara Boyle *management consultant*
Webb, Lamar Thaxter *architect*

Saint Simons Island
Mathis, Luster Doyle *college administrator, political scientist*
Thau, William Albert, Jr., *lawyer*

Sautee Nacoochee
Hill, Ronald Guy, Sr., *non-profit organization consultant*
Richardson, James Sommerfield *real estate company executive*

Savannah
Aja-Herrera, Marie *fashion designer, educator*
Aquadro, Jeana Lauren *graphic designer, educator*
Baker, Brinda Elizabeth Garrison *infectious disease nurse*
†Ball, Ardella Patricia *library media educator*
Beals, L(oren) Alan *association executive*
Belles, Martin Russel *manufacturing engineer*
Billet, Donald Franklin *civil engineer, consultant*
†Boland, John Kevin *bishop*
Bowman, Catherine McKenzie *lawyer*
Boylston, Scott Thomas *graphic design educator*
Brandner, Christine Marie *art administrator, artist*
Briggs, Niwana Page *editor, writer*
Brown, Carlton E. *college president*
Buxton, Barry Miller *museum director, historical author, educator*
Cartledge, Raymond Eugene *retired paper company executive*
Clemmons, John B. *bank executive, director, mathematician, educator*
Coffey, Thomas Francis, Jr., *writer*
Cooper, Lynda Shepard *music educator*
De Agostino, Sergio *engineering educator*
Dickerson, Lon Richard *library administrator*
Dickey, David Herschel *lawyer, accountant*
DiClaudio, Janet Alberta *health information administrator*
Dodge, William Douglas *insurance company consultant*
Dunham, Byron S. *writer*
Eaves, George Newton *lecturer, consultant, research administrator*
Edeawo, Gale Sky *publishing company executive, writer*
Fell, Cheryl Cookmeyer *artist, art educator*
†Flynn, Laura D *foundation administrator, consultant, educator*
Foley, Marilyn Lorna *artist*
†Forbes, Morton Gerald *lawyer*
†Friedman, Julian Richard *lawyer*
Gannam, Michael Joseph *lawyer*
Gilbert, John B. *retired electric and power company official*
Gillespie, Daniel Curtis, Sr., *retired non-profit company executive, consultant*
Granger, Harvey, Jr., *retired manufacturing company executive*
Greenberg, Philip B. *symphony orchestra conductor and music director*
Ham, O(scar) Emerson, Jr., *neurologist*
Hoskins, William John *obstetrician, gynecologist, educator*
Hsu, Ming-Yu *engineering educator*
Jackel, Stephanie Deck *publisher, editor, publishing executive*
John, Selena Latricia *systems analyst*
†Johnson, Eric B. *state legislator*
Krahl, Enzo *retired surgeon*
Leighton, Richard Frederick *retired dean*
Lindqvist, Gunnar Jan *management consultant, international trade consultant*
Moore, William Theodore, Jr., *judge*
Nawrocki, H(enry) Franz *propulsion technology scientist*
Otter, John Martin, III, *television advertising consultant, retired*
Painter, Paul Wain, Jr., *lawyer*
Palanca, Terilyn *software industry analyst*
Peer, George Joseph *metals company executive*
†Polite, Evelyn C. *retired middle school educator, counselor, evangelist*
†Presley, Susan Franklin *secondary school educator, department chairman*
†Ramsay, Linda *architect*
Rawson, William Robert *lawyer, retired manufacturing company executive*
†Rowan, Paula S. *academic administrator*
†Salamone, Joseph Anthony *mechanical engineer*
Sanders, James Grady *biogeochemist*
Schafer, Thomas Wilson *advertising agency executive*
Sheehy, Barry Maurice *management consultant*
Simmonds, Jimmie Neil *theatre educator*
Simonaitis, Richard Ambrose *chemist*
†Spitalnick, Benjamin David *pediatrician*
Spitz, Seymour James, Jr., *retired fragrance company executive*
Sprague, William Wallace, Jr., *retired food company executive*
Standbridge, Peter Thomas *retired insurance company executive*
Stillwell, Walter Brooks, III, *lawyer*
Taggart, Helen M. *adult education educator, nurse*
Taylor, Roslyn Donny *family physician*
Thomas, Dwight Rembert *writer*
†Thomson, Audrey Shire *volunteer*
Walter, Paul Hermann Lawrence *chemistry educator*
Weaver, Crystal Dawn *interior design educator*
Webb, James Calvin *minister*
Windom, Herbert Lynn *oceanographer, environmental scientist*
Wirth, Fremont Philip, Jr., *neurosurgeon, educator*
†Zhang, Weihua *education educator*
Zoller, Michael *otolaryngologist, head and neck surgeon, educator*

Scottdale
Borochoff, Ida Sloan *artist*

Sea Island
LaWare, John Patrick *retired banker, federal official*
Mc Swiney, James Wilmer *retired pulp and paper manufacturing company executive*
Revoile, Charles Patrick *lawyer*

Senoia
Bradley, Sally Sue *registered nurse*

Sky Valley
Wilkinson, Albert Mims, Jr., *lawyer*

Smyrna
Atkins, William Austin, Sr., (Bill Atkins) *former state legislator*
Bean, Susan Montgomery *secondary education educator*
Buck, Lee Albert *retired insurance company executive, evangelist*
Huttenbach, Dirk Erik *psychiatrist*
†Michelson, Robert C. *engineering educator, researcher*
Moore, Linda Kathleen *personnel agency executive*
Passantino, Richard J. *architect*
Rife, Elizabeth *musician, music educator*
Seigler, Michael Edward *lawyer, librarian*

Snellville
Cleland, Max *former senator*
Dhara, Venkata Ramana *physician, educator*
Giallanza, Charles Philip *lawyer*
Keyes, David Taylor *telecommunications company administrator*

Social Circle
O'Connor, Patricia Eryl *telecommunications consultant*
Penland, John Thomas *retired import and export and development companies executive*

Statesboro
Bacon, Martha Brantley *small business owner*
Beasley, John Julius *child and family development educator*
Bryan, Carolyn J. *music educator, saxophonist*
Duke-Whitaker, Lois *government and public relations educator, consultant, educator, researcher*
Gilbert, Armida Jennings *American literature educator*
†Glover, Sheena *academic administrator*
†Harbour, James William *theater educator*
Henry, Nicholas Llewellyn *public administration educator*
†Humphrey, Patricia Buslee *statistician, researcher*
Mitchell, Wilfrid Bede *librarian*
Mobley, Cleon Marion, Jr., (Chip Mobley) *physics educator, real estate developer*
Murkison, Eugene Cox *business educator*
Pearsall, Thomas Armstrong *educator*
†Pino, Nathan Willett *criminologist, educator, sociologist*
Rodell, Paul Arthur *history educator*
Stone, Ralph Kenny *lawyer*
†Suazo-Jaque, Jorge Washington *foreign language educator*
Whitaker, Mical Rozier *theater director, educator*
†Williamson, Matthew Allen *anatomist, educator, physiologist, anthropologist*
Wood, George Ambos *city manager*
†Wu, Yan *engineering educator*

Stockbridge
Curtis, Joycelyn *social worker*
Friedman, Robert Barry *physician*
Grimes, Richard Allen *economics educator*
Hughes, Woodrow Milton *real estate broker*
Sharpe, Terry Lynn *dermatologist*
Sprayberry, Roslyn Raye *retired secondary school educator*

Stone Mountain
†Adair, James Robert Jr., Jr., *religious studies educator*
Bundy, Jane Bowden *artist, educator*
†Burklin, Frederick O. *minister, educator*
Dees, Julian Worth *retired academic/research administrator*
Gotlieb, Edward Marvin *pediatrician*
Havick, John J. *political science educator*
†Le, Chi-Dinh *law educator, writer*
Lori-Gene, *artist, educator*
†Malone, Embry *property manager, advocate*
Minter, Kendall Arthur *lawyer*
Reichert, Leo Edmund, Jr., *biochemist, endocrinologist*
†Render, Nelson Leon *music educator, musician*
†Roth, Edie Cowan *psychologist*

Summerville
Spivey, Suzan Brooks Nisbet *association administrator, medical technologist*

Suwanee
Anderson, Jamal Sharif *professional football player*
†Frey, Glenn *songwriter, vocalist, guitarist*
Gerson, Martin Lyons *secondary school educator*
Shih, John Yozen *osteopathic physician*
Stevenson, Michael E. *metallurgical engineer*
Swanson, David H(enry) *consultant, retired economist, educator*
Trice, Mary Sue Williams *guidance counselor*

Swainsboro
†Cadle, Jerry Neal *lawyer*
†Edenfield, Cynthia Smith *education educator*
Hundley, Frederick Eugene, Jr., *music educator, consultant*

Sylvania
Jenkins, Michael Grady *judge*
Martin, Charles Wade *pastor*

Sylvester
Bean, Craig Baylor *music educator*

Tallapoosa
Ramsey, Paul Randall *band director*

Thomaston
Beohm, Richard Thomas *safety engineering consultant*
Brewton, Samuel Alton, Jr., *urologist*
†Brown, June Dyson *elementary education educator, administrator*
Harris, David Frederick *pathologist*
Pitts, Charles Carey *music educator*

Thomasville
Flowers, Langdon Strong *foods company executive*
†Mc Mullian, Amos Ryals *food company executive*
Stepanek, David Leslie *financial services company executive*

Tifton
†Burton, Glenn Willard *geneticist*
Dorminey, Henry Clayton, Jr., *allergist*
†Fitzgerald, Anthony Patrick *criminal justice educator*

Tiger
Corry, Robert Emmett *lawyer*

Toccoa
Maypole, John Floyd *real estate holding company executive*

Toccoa Falls
Alford, Paul Legare *college and religious foundation administrator*
†Allison Jr., Norman E. *anthropologist, educator*
Gardner, Donna Rae (Diehl) *education educator*
Stufft, William David *music educator*

Townsend
Hicks, Harold Eugene *chemical engineer*
Hicks, Virginia Hobson *bookstore owner, educator*

Tucker
Armstrong, Edwin Alan *lawyer*
Brown, William Michael *scientist, consultant, writer, editor, lawyer*
McNair, Nimrod, Jr., *foundation executive, consultant*
Osborne, Thomas Eugene *oral and maxillofacial surgeon*
Roberts, Thomas Heym *city and regional planner, consultant*
Stewart, Connie Ward *academic administrator*
Wheeler, Edd Dudley *lawyer*

Tybee Island
Pearce, Mallory *artist, educator, ecologist*
Smith, Elizabeth Mackey *financial consultant*

Union Point
Miller, Bryant Davis *healthcare administrator*

Valdosta
†Aronson-Friedman, Amy Ilene *education educator*
Bailey, Hugh Coleman *university president*
Bright, Joseph Converse *lawyer*
Campbell, J(ohn) Jette *corporate finance executive*
Cork, Robert Lander *lawyer*
Dodd, Roger J. *lawyer*
Edwards, Edith Martha *lawyer*
†Farwell, Doug George *music educator*
Greer, Mack Varnedoe *retired physician*
Halter, H(enry) James, Jr., (Diamond Jim Halter) *retail executive*
Koehler, Wallace *library and information scientist, educator, library and information scientist, researcher*
Krotseng, Marsha Van Dyke *higher education administrator*
†Montgomery, Denise Lynne *librarian, researcher*
Moss, Kirk D. *music educator*
Robertson, Dale Wayne *minister*
Sinnott, John Patrick *lawyer, educator*
Steinberg, Teresa Sherwood *paralegal, legal administrator*
Von Taaffe-Rossmann, Cosima T. *physician, writer, inventor*

Vidalia
Fortner, Billie Jean *small business owner*

Waleska
Naylor, Susan Embry *music educator*
†Robertson, Eddie B. *education educator*

Warm Springs
Stefenelli, George Edward *physician*

Warner Robins
Beck, Rhonda Joann *paramedic, educator, writer*
Cleary, Cathleen Ann *psychiatrist*
DePriest, C(harles) David *engineering executive, retired military officer*
†Klein, William Brent *surgeon*
Nugteren, Cornelius *air force officer*
Owens, Helen Dawn *elementary school educator, reading consultant*

Washington
†Dukes, Patrick Ryan *secondary school educator*
Mansfield, Norman Connie *bookkeeper*

Watkinsville
Johnson, Norman James *physician, lawyer, medicolegical consultant*
Wright, Robert Joseph *lawyer*

Waverly Hall
Merritt, Martin David *counselor, tennis professional, educator, musician*

West Point
Andrews, Gerald Bruce, Sr., *retired textile executive*
Barnwell, Madge Owen *volunteer*
Glover, Clifford Clarke *retired construction company executive*
†Hart, Brenda Rebecca *retired gifted and talented educator*

Winder
Souther, Joseph Carroll *family practice physician*

Winterville
Anderson, David Prewitt *retired university dean*

Woodland
Carter, James *mayor, educator, tax consultant, real estate agent*

Woodstock
Austin, John David *retired financial executive*
Baumann, Sara Margaret Culbreth *retired elementary school educator*
Collins, David Browning *religious institution administrator*
Smith, Jeanne Hawkins *critical care nurse*
†Soh-Harbin, Julie *music educator*

Zebulon
Bizzell Yarbrough, Cindy Lee *school counselor*
Watson, Forrest Albert, Jr., *lawyer, bank executive*

HAWAII

Aiea
†Kokame, Gregg Takashi *medical educator, researcher*
Uyehara, Harry Yoshimi *library educator*

Camp H M Smith
Hailston, Earl B. *career officer*
Hollingsworth, Bobby G. *career officer*

Ewa Beach
Chock, Alvin Keali'i *retired botanist*
Kea, Jonathan Guy *instrumental music educator*
Lewis, Mary Jane *film producer, director, scriptwriter*

Hanalei
Bunyan, S. Wyanne *arbitrator, mediator, realtor*
Schaller, Matthew Fite *architect*

Hawaii National Park
Camp, Richard J. *ecologist, statistician, researcher*
Swanson, Donald Alan *geologist*

Hickam AFB
Polk, Steven R. *military officer*

Hilo
Dixon, Paul William *psychology educator*
Follett, Peter Arnold *entomologist, researcher*
Gersting, Judith Lee *computer scientist, educator, computer scientist, researcher*
†Jarvi, Susan I. *research scientist, educator*
Kinney, Jeanne Kawelolani *English studies educator, writer*
Ko, Wen-hsiung *plant pathology educator*
Larson, Mary Bea *elementary education educator*
Lu, Christopher Dah-Cheng *nutritionist, educator, university dean*
Merk, Elizabeth Thole *investment company executive*
O'Brien, Sally K. *secondary school educator, consultant*
Skorikov, Vladimir B *researcher, educator*
Tseng, Rose *academic administrator*
Ushijima, John Takeji *state legislator, lawyer*
VanderVoort, Debra Jean *counseling psychology educator, school psychologist*

Holualoa
Scarr, Sandra Wood *psychology educator, researcher*
Stoddard, Sandol *freelance/self-employed writer*

Honaunau
Schultz-Ross, Roy Andrew *forensic psychiatrist, educator, writer*

Honolulu
Abe, Gregg Koyei *music educator*
Acoba, Simeon Rivera, Jr., *state supreme court justice, educator*
Adams, Jo-Ann Marie *lawyer*
Adams, Nancy R. *nurse, military officer*
Adaniya, Kevin Seisho *lawyer*
Adcock, Betty-Lee *real estate company executive, real estate broker*
†Aduja, Melodie Williams *state senator*
Ahmed, Iqbal *psychiatrist, consultant*
†Aiona, James R., Jr., *lieutenant governor*
Akinaka, Asa Masayoshi *lawyer*
Andrasick, James Stephen *diversified company executive*
†Arakaki, Dennis A. *state representative*
Archer, Richard Joseph *lawyer*
Aung-Thwin, Michael Arthur *history educator*
Baker, Helen Doyle Peil *realtor*
Bauman, Kay A. *physician*
†Belknap, Jodi Parry *graphic designer, writer, business owner*
Bender, Byron Wilbur *linguistics educator*
†Bennett, Mark J. *state attorney general*
Betts, Barbara Stoke *artist, educator*
Bitterman, Morton Edward *psychologist, educator*
Black, Cobey *journalist, corporate executive*
Blanchard, Robert J. *neuroscientist*
Bloede, Victor Carl *lawyer, academic executive*
Boas, Frank *retired lawyer*
Bogart, Louise Berry *education educator*
Bossert, Philip Joseph *information systems executive*
Botsai, Elmer Eugene *architect, architecture educator, retired dean*
Bourgoin, David L. *lawyer, real estate broker, trade broker, educator, video/television producer*
Brady, Stephen R.P.K. *physician*
Brantley, Lee Reed *chemistry educator*
Brislin, Richard Walter *psychology educator*
†Bronster, Margery S *state attorney general*
†Bukoski, Kika G. *state representative*
Bunda, Robert *state legislator*
Bunn, Robert Burgess *lawyer*
Cadman, Edwin Clarence *dean, health facility administrator, medical educator*
†Caldwell, Kirk *state representative*
Callies, David Lee *lawyer, educator*
Campbell, Naomi Sylvia *lawyer*
Carson, Ellen Godbey *lawyer*
Carson, Hampton Lawrence *geneticist, educator*
Case, James Hebard *lawyer*
Cassiday, Benjamin Buckles, III, *lawyer*
Chang, Rodney Eiu Joon *artist, dentist*
Char, Vernon Fook Leong *lawyer*
Chee, Percival Hon Yin *ophthalmologist*
Chen, Wai-Fah *civil engineering educator*
Chen, Yi-Leng *meteorologist, educator*
Ching, Baron Kwai Fong *internist*
Chiu, Margaret Chi Yuan Liu *retired real estate broker*
Cho, Lee-Jay *social scientist, demographer*
Chock, Clifford Yet-Chong *family practice physician*
Choy, Herbert Young Cho *federal judge*
Chung, Richard S. *health facility administrator*
†Chung, Steven Kamsein *lawyer*
†Chun Oakland, Suzanne Nyuk Jun *state legislator*
Clifton, Richard Randall *judge*
†Coates, Bradley Allen *lawyer*
†Coimbra, Carlos F.M. *mechanical engineering educator, fluid dynamicist*
Cox, Richard Horton *civil engineering executive*
Crowell, David Harrison *retired biomedical researcher, consultant*
Crumpton, Charles Whitmarsh *lawyer*
Dang, Marvin S. C. *lawyer*
Davis, Stephen Edward Folwell *banker*
Deaver, Phillip Lester *lawyer*
Devaney, Donald Everett *law enforcement official*
Devenot, David Charles *human resource executive*
Devens, Paul *lawyer*
Dobelle, Evan Samuel *academic administrator*
Dockham-Leong, Sondra Marguerite *social worker*
†Dodd, William Horace *lawyer*
Doi, Dorothy Mitsue Yano *educator, consultant*
Dougherty, Raleigh Gordon *manufacturer representative*
†Duffy, James Earl, Jr., *lawyer*
Dyen, Isidore *linguistic scientist, educator*
Edmunds, John Sanford *lawyer*
Edwards, John Wesley, Jr., *urologist*
Ekern, Paul C. *retired meteorologist*
†English, J. Kalani *state senator*
†Espero, William (Willie C.) *state senator*
Fasi, Frank Francis *state legislator*
†Faust, Anne Sonia *lawyer*
†Finney, Ben Rudolph *anthropologist, educator*
Finney, John Edgar, III, *food products executive*
Fischer, Joel *social work educator*
Fitz-Patrick, David *endocrinologist, educator*
Flannelly, Kevin J. *psychologist, research analyst*
Flannelly, Laura T. *mental health nurse, nursing educator, researcher*
Fong, Bernard W.D. *physician, educator*
Fong, Hiram Leong *former senator*
†Fox, Galen W. *state representative*
Fujita, James Hiroshi *history educator*
†Fujiyama, Wallace Sachio *lawyer*
Fukumoto, Leslie Satsuki *lawyer*
†Fukunaga, Carol A. *state legislator, lawyer*
Fukushima, Barbara Naomi *financial advisor*
Fullmer, Daniel Warren *former psychologist, educator*
Furuyama, Renee Harue *association executive*
Gandy, Hortense M. *retired endocrinologist*
Gay, E(mil) Laurence *lawyer*
Gee, Chuck Yim *dean*
†Geil, Wilma Jean *librarian*
Gelber, Don Jeffrey *lawyer*
George, Peter T. *orthodontist, consultant*
†Geshell, Richard Steven *lawyer*
Gillmor, Helen *federal judge*
Godbey, Robert Carson *lawyer*
Goldstein, Sir Norman *dermatologist*
†Gonsalves, Margaret Leboy *elementary school educator*
Goodhue, William Walter, Jr., *forensic pathologist, military officer, educator*
Graf, Edward Dutton *grouting consultant*
Graham, Donald Houston, Jr., *real estate developer*
Grande, Thomas Robert *lawyer*
Guthrie, Edgar King *artist*
Hack, Randolph C. *advocate, educator, counselor*
Haig, David M. *property and investment manager*
Haight, Warren Gazzam *investor*
†Hale, Helene H. *state representative*
Hale, Nathan Robert *architect*
Halloran, Richard Colby *writer, former research executive, former news correspondent, columnist, editor*
Hamada, Duane Takumi *architect*
Hamada, Harold Seichi *civil engineer, educator*
†Hanabusa, Colleen *state legislator, lawyer*
Harris, Jeremy *mayor*
†Hartley, Michael J. *online travel executive*
Hatfield, Elaine Catherine *psychology educator*
Hawke, Bernard Ray *planetary scientist*
†Hay-Roe, Victor *plastic surgeon*
Hays, Ronald Jackson *career officer*
†Hazlett, Mark A. *lawyer*
Heen, Walter Meheula *retired judge, former political party executive*
Heller, Ronald Ian *lawyer*
†Hemmings, Fred *state senator*
Herbig, George Howard *astronomer, educator*
Hey, Richard Noble *marine geophysicist*
Hipp, Kenneth Byron *lawyer*
Hirai, Craig Kazuo *lawyer*
Hirono, Mazie Keiko *lieutenant governor*
†Hite, Robert Griffith *lawyer*
Ho, Reginald Chi Shing *medical educator*
Ho, Stuart Tse Kong *health facility administrator*
Hoffmann, Kathryn Ann *humanities educator*
†Hogue, Bob *state senator*
Hook, Ralph Clifford, Jr., *business educator*
Hughes, Robert Harrison *former agricultural products executive*
Ichinose, Susan M. *lawyer*
†Ige, David Y. *state legislator*
†Ihara, Les, Jr., *state legislator*
Ihrig, Judson La Moure *chemist*
Iijima, Chris K. *law educator*
Ingersoll, Richard King *lawyer*
†Inouye, Lorraine R. *state legislator*
†Ishihara, Bryan K. *operations research analyst*
†Ishii, Clyde Hideo *plastic surgeon*
Ishikawa-Fullmer, Janet Satomi *psychologist, educator*
†Ito, Ken *state representative*
Iwai, Wilfred Kiyoshi *lawyer*
Jellinek, Roger *editor*
Jensen, Craig Martin *chemistry educator*
Johnson, Lawrence M. *retired bank executive*
Jordan, Amos Azariah, Jr., *foreign affairs educator, retired army officer*
Kadohiro, Jane K. *educator, nurse, diabetes consultant*
†Kahikina, Michael Puamamo *social services administrator, state legislator*
Kaiser-Botsai, Sharon Kay *early childhood educator*
Kam, Thomas Kwock Yung *accountant educator*
Kamemoto, Fred Isamu *retired zoologist*
†Kane, Joelle K.K.S. *lawyer*
Kane, Micah *political party official*
Kane, Thomas Jay, III, *orthopaedic surgeon, educator*
Kanehiro, Kenneth Kenji *insurance educator, risk analyst, consultant*
Kanenaka, Rebecca Yae *microbiologist*
†Kanno, Brian M. *state legislator, volunteer worker*
Kashiwa, Russell H. *communication executive*
Katayama, Robert Nobuichi *lawyer*
Katz, Alan Roy *public health educator*
Kawachika, James Akio *lawyer*
†Kawakami, Bertha C. *state representative*
†Kawamoto, Calvin Kazuo *state legislator*
Keil, Klaus *geology educator, consultant*
Keir, Gerald Janes *banker*
Keith, Kent Marsteller *YMCA leader, academic administrator, corporate executive, government official, lawyer, author*
Kelley, Richard Roy *hotel executive*
Kennedy, Faye *retired social worker, author*
Kennedy, Reneau Charlene Ufford *forensic psychologist, consultant*
Keogh, Richard John *firearms and explosives consultant*
Khan, Mohammad Asad *geophysicist, educator, former energy minister and senator of Pakistan*
†Kim, Donna Mercado *state senator*
King, Arthur R., Jr., *education educator, researcher*
†Klink, Paul Leo *business executive*
Klobe, Tom *art gallery director*
Kohloss, Frederick Henry *retired consulting engineer*
Koide, Frank Takayuki *electrical engineering educator*
†Kokubun, Russell S. *state senator*
†Kozok, Uli *language educator*
Kubo, Kimberly Annette *entrepreneur*
†Kudo, Emiko Iwashita *former state official*
Kumar, Raj *psychologist, hypnotherapist*
†Kuniyuki, Ken Takaharu *lawyer*
Kupchak, Kenneth Roy *lawyer*
Kwok, Reginald Yin-Wang *urban planning and development educator, architect*
Lacey, Roberta Balaam *emergency room nurse, pediatrics nurse*
La Croix, Sumner Jonathan *economics educator*
†Lacy, John R. *lawyer*
Laney, Leroy Olan *economist, banker, educator*
Langhans, Edward Allen *drama and theater educator*
Lau, Charles Kwok-Chiu *architect, architectural firm executive*
Lau, Eugene Wing Iu *lawyer*
Lau, H. Lorrin *obstetrician/gynecologist, inventor*
Lee, Candie Ching Wah *retail executive*
†Lee, Marilyn B. *state representative*
Lee, Pali Jae (Polly Jae Stead Lee) *retired librarian, writer*
†Lee, Patricia Y. *lawyer*
Lee, Yeu-Tsu Margaret *surgeon, educator*
†Leong, Bertha F.K. *state representative*
Leung, PingSun *agricultural economist*

Levinson, Steven Henry *state supreme court justice*
Leyden, Michael Joseph, II, (Lei Jie Ming) *international business executive, educator, author*
Li, PingAn *neurobiologist, educator*
Lighter, Eric Aaron *real estate and law enforcement software developer, consultant*
Lilly, Michael Alexander *lawyer, writer*
Lindes, Dorothyann Marlene *physician*
Lingle, Linda *governor*
Linman, James William *retired physician, educator*
Liu, Alfred Jitfu *otolaryngologist*
Liu, Roger Kim Sing *accountant*
Lombardi, Dennis M. *lawyer*
Lowell, Virginia Lee *librarian*
Lum, Jean Loui Jin *nursing educator*
Ma, Alan Wai-Chuen *lawyer*
Mader, Charles Lavern *chemist*
†Magaoay, Michael Y. *state representative*
Mandel, Morton *molecular biologist*
Mark, Shelley Muin *economist, educator, government official*
†Marks, Michael J. *lawyer, corporate executive*
Marrack, Alexander Case *lawyer*
†Marsella, Anthony Joseph *psychologist, educator*
Masters, Elaine *educator, writer*
Mau-Shimizu, Patricia Ann *lawyer*
McCarthy, Laurence James *physician, pathologist*
McShane, Rosemary *lawyer*
†Menor, Ron *state legislator*
Merrifield, Donald Paul *hispanic ministries coordinator*
Metz, James Robert *mathematician, educator*
Midkiff, Robert Richards *financial and trust company executive, consultant*
†Migimoto, Fumiyo Kodani *retired secondary education educator*
Miller, Clifford Joel *lawyer*
Miller, Richard Sherwin *law educator*
†Mindo, Romeo *labor union administrator*
Miyamoto, Craig Toyoki *public relations executive*
Miyasaki, Shuichi *lawyer*
†Miyawaki, Edison Hiroyuki *health care executive, physician*
Moon, Ronald T. Y. *state supreme court chief justice*
Moore, Ernest Carroll, III, *lawyer*
Moreno-Cabral, Carlos Eduardo *cardiac surgeon*
Moroney, Michael John *lawyer*
Morrison, Charles E. *think-tank executive*
†Morse, Jack Craig *lawyer*
Mortimer, Kenneth P. *retired academic administrator*
†Moses, Mark S. *state representative*
Moulin, Jane Ann Freeman *ethnomusicology educator, researcher*
Murray, Kevin Dennis *surgeon*
Nakamura, Ross Hideo *educator, band director, musician*
Nakata, Gary Kenji *lawyer*
Nakayama, Paula Aiko *state supreme court justice*
Nelson, Marita Lee *anatomist, educator*
Neubauer, Deane *academic administrator*
†Ng, Blythe Yuri Monzen *elementary school counselor*
Ng, Wing Chiu *accountant, educator, application developer, lawyer, educator, advocate*
Nigg, Claudio Renato *science educator*
Nishimura, Pete Hideo *oral surgeon*
†Noji, Deborah Teruko *not-for-profit fundraiser*
Nordyke, Eleanor Cole *population researcher, public health nurse*
Ogawa, Dennis Masaaki *American studies educator*
Ogburn, Hugh Bell *chemical engineer, consultant*
Ogburn, Nancy Wrenn *civic volunteer*
Oishi, Stephen Masato *physician*
†Okinaga, Carrie Kiyono *lawyer*
Okinaga, Lawrence Shoji *lawyer*
†Okuma-Sepe, Cheryl *lawyer*
Oldenburg, Ronald Troy *lawyer*
O'Neill, Charles Kelly *marketing executive, former advertising agency executive*
O'Neill, Ralph James *lawyer*
†Ontai, Guy Po'olanui *state representative*
†Ota, Katsuhiro Justin *language educator*
Pacific, Joseph Nicholas, Jr., *educator*
Paige, Glenn Durland *political scientist, educator*
Palia, Aspy Phiroze *marketing educator, researcher, consultant*
†Papali'i, Aumua Mata'itusi Simanu *language educator*
Parma, Florence Virginia *magazine editor*
†Parsa, Fereydoun Don *plastic surgeon*
Perkins, Frank Overton *university official, marine scientist*
Peterson, Barbara Ann Bennett *history educator, television personality*
Pfeiffer, Robert John *business executive*
Pickens, Alexander Legrand *retired education educator*
Pickens, Frances Jenkins *jewelry/metal artist, art educator*
†Plum, William J. *lawyer*
Polansky, Patricia Ann *librarian*
†Portnoy, Jeffrey Steven *lawyer*
Potts, Dennis Walker *lawyer*
Quinn, William Francis *lawyer, director*
Raleigh, Cecil Baring *geophysicist*
Rapson, Richard L. *history educator*
†Reber, David James *lawyer*
Rehg, Kenneth Lee *linguistics educator*
Reinke, Stefan Michael *lawyer*
Rexner, Romulus *publishing executive*
Riggs, Fred Warren *political science educator*
Roberson, Kelley Cleve *health care administrator*
Robinson, Robert Blacque *foundation administrator*
Rohrer, Reed Beaver *lawyer*

†Rolls, John Marland, Jr., *lawyer*
Rosendal, Hans Erik *meteorologist*
Sagawa, Yoneo *horticulturist, educator*
Saiki, Patricia (Mrs. Stanley Mitsuo Saiki) *former federal agency administrator, former congresswoman*
Sato, Glenn Kenji *lawyer*
Saxena, Narendra K. *marine research educator*
Say, Calvin *state legislator*
Schatz, Irwin Jacob *cardiologist, educator*
Scheerer, Ernest William *dentist*
Schimmelfennig, Ladona Beth *special education educator, management analysis and compliance specialist*
Schnack, Harold Clifford *retired lawyer*
Schneider, Thomas Richard *hospital administrator*
†Schweizer, Niklaus R. *German educator*
Seidensticker, Edward George *Japanese language and literature educator*
Sekine, Deborah Keiko *systems analyst, programmer*
†Shankar, Subramanian *writer, educator*
Sharma, Santosh Devraj *obstetrician/gynecologist, educator*
†Shaw, Abelina Madrid *state official*
Shay, Roshani Cari *political science educator*
†Sia, Calvin Chia Jung *pediatrician*
Simon, Gary B. *health care manager, investor*
Simonds, John Edward *retired newspaper editor*
†Slom, Samuel M. *state legislator*
Smales, Fred Benson *corporate executive*
Smith, Barbara Barnard *music educator*
Solidum, James *finance and insurance executive*
Song, Cathy *author, poet*
Sparks, Robert William *retired publishing executive*
†Spencer, James H. *social sciences educator, consultant*
Stacey, Richard Wayne *lawyer*
Stamper, Ewa Szumotalska *psychologist*
†Steinemann, Namji Kim *social studies educator*
Stephan, John Jason *historian, educator*
Sterrett, James Melville *accountant, business consultant*
Stevens, Stephen Edward *psychiatrist*
Sugiki, Shigemi *ophthalmologist, educator*
Suh, Dae-Sook *political science educator*
Sumida, Kevin P.H. *lawyer*
Suzuki, Norman Hitoshi *lawyer*
Swanson, Richard William *retired statistician*
†Takanishi, Jr., Danny M. *medical educator, department chairman*
Takumi, Roy Mitsuo *state legislator*
†Taniguchi, Brian T. *state senator*
Tanoue, Donna A. *bank executive, former federal agency administrator*
Tatibouet, Andre Stephan *condominium and resort management firm executive*
Taylor, Carroll Stribling *lawyer*
Tehranian, Majid *political economy and communications educator*
Teramura, Alan Hiroshi *science educator*
†Thielen, Cynthia Henry *lawyer, state legislator*
Tseng, George Shihchi *anesthesiologist*
Tsukayama, Derrick Kawika *police sergeant, consultant*
Turbin, Richard *lawyer*
Uhl, Philip Edward *artist, photographer, cinematographer*
Umebayashi, Clyde Satoru *lawyer*
Usui, Leslie Raymond *retired clothing executive*
†Van Dyke, Jon Markham Markham *law educator*
Varley, Herbert Paul *Japanese language and cultural history educator*
Vidal, Alejandro Legaspi (Andy Vidal) *architect*
Vogel, Carl-Wilhelm Ernst *biomedical scientist, clinical pathologist*
Wageman, Virginia Farley *editor, writer*
†Wallach, Stephen Joseph *cardiologist*
Walsh, Janice Maureen *counselor, educator*
Wang, Jaw-Kai *bioengineering educator*
Weingand, Darlene Erna *librarian educator, consultant*
Wesselkamper, Sue *academic administrator*
White, Emmet, Jr., *retirement community administrator*
White, Gary Richard *electrical engineer, plant operator*
Willes, Mark Hinckley *media industry executive*
Williams, Carl Harwell *utilities executive*
†Wills-Toro, Luis Alberto *physicist, mathematician*
Wilson, Charles Robert *port captain, harbor master*
Wilson, William James *healthcare executive*
Witeck, John Joseph *labor union representative, educator*
Wolfe, Suzanne L. *artist, art educator*
Wolff, Herbert Eric *banker, former army officer*
Wong, Alfred Mun Kong *lawyer*
Wong, Henry Li-Nan *bank executive, economist*
Wong, James Thomas *lawyer*
Woo, Vernon Ying-Tsai *lawyer, real estate developer, judge*
Wright, Chatt Grandison *academic administrator*
Xie, Shang-Ping *environmental studies educator*
Yamato, Kei C. *international business consultant*
Yang, David Chie-Hwa *business administration educator*
Yang, Guobin *sociologist, sinologist*
Yeh, Raymond Wei-Hwa *architect, educator*
Zinin, Pavel V. *physicist*

Kahului
Adachi, Athan Ken *civil engineer*
Shaw, Virginia Ruth *clinical psychologist*
†Tolliver, Dorothy *librarian*
Yamamoto, Irwin Toraki *editor, publisher investment newsletter*

Kailua
†Amos, Wally *entrepreneur*
Bone, Robert William *writer*
Lundquist, Dana Richard *healthcare executive*
Saavedra Garcia, Katherine Andrews *health group executive director*

Sullivan, Karen Lau *real estate company executive, campaign consultant, federal commissioner*
Webb, Charles Robert *lawyer, police officer*
Westerdahl, John Brian *nutritionist, health educator*
Young, Jacqueline Eurn Hai *former state legislator, consultant*

Kailua Kona
†Birtcher, Baron R. *writer, real estate broker*
†Breier, Morton A. *philosopher*
Clewett, Kenneth Vaughn *college official*
Diama, Benjamin *retired educator, artist, composer, writer*
Luizzi, Ronald *wholesale distribution executive*
Spitze, Glenys Smith *retired educator*
Wohl, Armand Jeffrey *cardiologist*
Zola, Michael S. *lawyer*

Kalaheo
Cox, Paul Alan *ethnobotanist, educator*

Kamuela
Mc Dermott, John Francis, Jr., *psychiatrist, physician*
Morgan, Andrew Lane *urologist, educator*

Kaneohe
Donahoe, Peter Aloysius *lawyer*
Fisette, Scott Michael *landscape and golf course architect*
Hanson, Richard Edwin *civil engineer*
†Huber, Thomas P. *lawyer*
Jackson, Jane W. *interior designer*
†Ko, Seung Kyun *educator, consultant*
Lange-Otsuka, Patricia Ann *nursing educator*
McGlaughlin, Thomas Howard *publisher, retired naval officer, marine surveyor*
Nagtalon-Miller, Helen Rosete *humanities educator*
Pimper, Elizabeth Marie *naval officer*
Shulman, Corinne Edwards Lewis *mediator*
Vincent, Thomas James *retired manufacturing company executive*

Kaneohe Bay
†Bogdan, Wojciech *military officer*

Kaneoke
Tokuno, Kenneth Alan *college administrator, poet*

Kapaa
duPont, Nicole *artist*
Outcalt, David Lewis *academic administrator, mathematician, educator, consultant, musician*

Kapaau
Jankowski, Theodore Andrew *artist*
McFee, Richard *electrical engineer, physicist*
Ralston, Joanne Smoot *public relations counseling firm executive*

Kapolei
†Dudley, Doris S. *music educator, small business owner*
†Sakamoto, Norman Lloyd *state legislator, civil engineer*
Wong, Edwina A. Lee *real estate broker*
†Zabanal, Eduardo Olegario *lawyer*

Kawaihae
Place, Virgil Alan *physician, pharmaceutical researcher*

Keaau
Repp, Andrew Scott *secondary school educator*

Kihei
Borchers, Robert Reece *physicist and administrator*
Burns, Richard Gordon *retired lawyer, writer, consultant*
Chin, Barbara *massage therapist*
Corell, Marcella Anne *community worker, retired educator*
Galesi, Deborah Lee *fine artist*
Numata, Nobuo *software company executive, consultant, engineer*
†Palusky, Alice *missionary, educator*
Wright, Thomas Parker *application developer*

Kilauea
McDowell, Edward R. H. *chemical engineer*
Polli, Robert Paul *lawyer*

Koloa
Cobb, Rowena Noelani Blake *real estate broker*
Donohugh, Donald Lee *physician*

Kula
Maloney, Michael Patrick *lawyer, mediator, arbitrator*
Richardson, Robert Allen *retired lawyer, educator*
Rohlfing, Frederick William *lawyer, political consultant, retired judge*

Kurtistown
Charon, Kenneth Arnold, Jr., *artist*

Laie
†Bradshaw, James R. *business educator*
James, Mark Olov *education educator*
Shumway, Eric *academic administrator*

Lanai City
Black, Anderson Duane *writer, business consultant*
Keenan-Abilay, Georgia Ann *service representative*

Laupahoehoe
Kroll, Sandra L. *retired healthcare facility administrator*

Lihue
Culliney, John James *radiologist, educator*
†Merritt, Hiroko *linguist, educator*
Stevens, Robert David *librarian, educator*

Makawao
Tanner, Barbara Ann *pediatrics nurse*

Mililani
Gardner, Sheryl Paige *gynecologist*
Magee, Donald Edward *retired national park service administrator*
Okita, George Torao *pharmacologist educator*
Olsen, Harris Leland *writer, novelist, educator, retired real estate and international business executive, diplomat*

Mountain View
Peterson, Gerald Joseph *aerospace executive, consultant*

Ocean View
Baglow, David Richard *marine facility administrator*

Pahoa
Lewis, Jack (Cecil Paul Lewis) *publishing executive, editor*

Paia
Richman, Joel Eser *lawyer, mediator, arbitrator*

Papaikou
Buyers, John William Amerman *agribusiness and specialty foods company executive*

Pearl City
†Conner, John Wallace *humanities educator*
Matsuoka, Eric Takao *mathematics educator*
Scott, David Irvin *minister*
Sue, Alan Kwai Keong *dentist*

Princeville
Forth, Kevin Bernard *beverage distributing industry consultant*

Puunene
Tocho, Lee Frank *mechanical engineer*

Tripler Army Medical Center
Cordts, Paul Roger *surgeon*
Garshnek, Victoria *physiologist, research educator*
Uyehara, Catherine Fay Takako (Catherine Yamauchi) *physiologist, educator, pharmacologist*

Wahiawa
Camery, John William *computer engineer*
Hazenfield, Hugh Norman *surgeon*
Kiyota, Heide Pauline *clinical psychologist*

Waialua
Singlehurst, Dona Geisenheyner *horse farm owner*

Waianae
Hiapo, Patricia Kamaka *lay worker*

Waikoloa
Calvert, Delbert William *energy executive*
Copman, Louis *radiologist*
Lyon, Henry Clarence *artist*
Morris, Victor Franklin, Jr., *retired meteorology educator*

Wailuku
Baker, Rosalyn Hester *state senator*
Kinaka, William Tatsuo *lawyer*
Yoshida, Lisa M.T. *accountant*

Waipahu
Chang, Walter Tuck, Sr., *drafting and AutoCAD educator, real estate agent, national defense instructor*
Look, Pauwilo *creative media developer, architecture marketer*

IDAHO

Bellevue
Pearson, Robert Greenlees *writing services company executive*

Blackfoot
Peterson, Grant Mark *obstetrician, gynecologist*

Boise
Andrus, Cecil Dale *academic administrator*
Appleton, Steven R. *electronics executive*
Bai, Bin *physicist, researcher*
Beaumont, Pamela Jo *marketing professional*
Black, Pete *retired state legislator, educator*
Blackwell, David C. *foundation administrator*
Blonshine, Sheena Kay *medical, surgical nurse*
Bolles, Charles Avery *librarian*
Boren, Robert Reed *communication educator*
Boyce, Carolyn *political organization administrator*
Burke, Cameron S. *legal administration*
†Charan, Nirmal B. *pulmonologist, educator*
Cleary, Edward William *retired diversified forest products company executive*
†Clump, Michael A. *psychologist, educator*
Cory, Wallace Newell *retired civil engineer*
Craig, Kara Lynn *children's home administrator*
Derr, Allen R. *lawyer*
Eismann, Daniel T. *state supreme court justice*
Ellis-Vant, Karen McGee *elementary and special education educator, consultant*
†Erickson, Robert Stanley *lawyer*
Ewing, Jack *communications executive*
Fiedler, John Amberg *marketing scientist*
Foster, S. Thomas, Jr., *quality management educator, consultant, writer*

ILLINOIS

Johnson, Margaret H. *welding company executive*
Lampinen, John A. *newspaper editor*
Lewin, Pearl Goldman *psychologist*
Lewin, Seymour Zalman *chemistry educator, consultant*
Li, Norman N. *chemicals executive*
†Lim, Cheryl Cheon-Ae *music educator*
Nerlinger, John William *retired trade association administrator*
Placek-Zimmerman, Ellyn Clare *school system administrator, educator, consultant*
Ray, Douglas Kent *newspaper executive*
Smith, Norman Obed *physical chemist, educator*
Telleen, Judy *counselor*
Tongue, William Walter *economics and business consultant, educator emeritus*
Tucker, Bowen Hayward *lawyer*

Augusta
Seydel, Robert Emory *mathematician, educator*

Aurora
Belcher, La Jeune *automotive executive*
Buffum, William Erwin *social worker, educator*
Camic, David Edward *lawyer*
Christiansen, Raymond Stephan *librarian, educator*
Dreyer, John Edward *lawyer*
Etheredge, Forest DeRoyce *former state senator, former university administrator*
Goebel, Edwin M. *microbiology educator, school administrator*
Halfvarson, Lucille Robertson *music educator*
Halloran, Kathleen L. *financial executive, accountant*
Hegarty, Carol Irene *painter, writer*
Hoefle, Ronald Anthony *civil engineer*
Holinger, Richard *secondary school educator, writer*
Hopp, Nancy Smith *marketing executive*
Koopman, Richard Nelson *engineer, consultant*
Lee, Robert Hugh *management executive*
†McCarthy, Mary Elizabeth (Beth) Constance *conductor, educator, music educator*
McCleary, Scott Fitzgerald *lawyer*
Settles, William Frederick *secondary and university educator, administrator*
Shevchenko, Sergey Markovich *organic chemist*
Stephens, Steve Arnold *real estate broker*
Strassberg, Barbara Ann *sociology educator, researcher*
Witanowski, Michael Frank *surgeon*

Bannockburn
Cohn, Arnold Keith *orthopedic surgeon*
†Daube, Lorrie O. *sales executive*

Barrington
Bash, Philip Edwin *publishing executive*
Chung, Joseph Sang-hoon *economics educator*
Dykla, K.H.S. Edward George *retired social services administrator*
Fowler, Susan Michele *real estate broker, entrepreneur*
Furst, Warren Arthur *retired holding company executive*
Hetzel, William Gelal *executive search consultant*
Lee, William Marshall *lawyer*
Leon, Edward *investor*
Mathis, Jack David *advertising executive, consultant*
Murphy, Robert *executive recruiter*
Porter, Stuart Williams *investment company executive*
Roland, Regina E. *elementary school educator*
Ross, Frank Howard, III, *management consultant*
Schaefer, Mary Ann *health facility administrator, consultant*
Stephens, Norval Blair, Jr., *marketing consultant*
Sweet, Charles Wheeler *retired executive recruiter*
Wyatt, James Frank, Jr., *lawyer*
Wynn, Thomas Joseph *judge, educator*

Barrington Hills
Perry, I. Chet *petroleum company executive*
Wood, Andrée Robitaille *archaeologist, researcher*

Bartlett
Lawrence, Madalena Joan Vignocchi *accountant*
Robinson, Jack Fay *clergyman*
Robinson, Lois Hart *retired public relations executive*

Bartonville
Lewis, Georgia Eileen *counselor, school counselor*

Batavia
Balbekov, Valeri I. *physicist, researcher*
Bardeen, William Allan *research physicist*
Brown, Gerald Curtis *retired army officer, engineering executive*
Chrisman, Bruce Lowell *physicist, administrator*
Fischler, Mark Steven *physicist*
Jonckheere, Alan Mathew *physicist*
Lach, Joseph Theodore *physicist*
Mann, Phillip Lynn *data processing company executive*
Quigg, Chris *physicist*
Raja, Rajendran *physicist*
†Tollestrup, Alvin Virgil *physicist*
†Yeh, Gong Ping (G.P.) *physicist*

Belleville
Bauman, John Duane *lawyer*
Boyle, Richard Edward *lawyer*
†Connors, Jimmy (James Scott Connors) *former professional tennis player*
Ferguson, John Marshall *retired federal judge*
†Gossage, Roza *lawyer, educator*
†Gregory, Wilton D. *bishop*
Hedges, Patrick Armand *information technology and communications and computer systems security specialist*

Heiligenstein, Christian Enric *lawyer*
Hess, Frederick J. *lawyer*
†Holbrook, Thomas Aldredge *state legislator*
Kramer, Andrew Joseph *clergyman*
Mathis, Patrick Bischof *lawyer*
Megahy, Diane Alaire *physician*
Neville, James Edward *lawyer*
†Parham, James Robert *lawyer*
Richmond, Richard Thomas *journalist*
Ripplinger, George Raymond, Jr., *lawyer*
Studer, Louis *priest, religious organization administrator*
Thien-Stasko, Vicki Lynn *civil engineer technician*
Tinoco, Patricia Ann *elementary education educator*
Ulven, Matthew Eric *family practice physician, educator*
Wittenbrink, Boniface Leo *priest*
Yarrington, George A. *retired public relations executive, advertising executive, writer*

Bellwood
Miller, Denyce Karlina *tax specialist*

Belvidere
Luhman, William Simon *community development administrator*

Bensenville
†Brekke, Stewart Ernest *retired chemistry and physics educator*
Kolkey, Eric Samuel *customer service representative*
Leach, Donald Paul *small business owner*
Matera, Richard Ernest *retired minister*
Mendelsohn, Zehavah Whitney *data processing executive*

Benton
Foreman, James Louis *retired judge*
Gilbert, J. Phil *federal judge*
Khan, Saeed Ahmad *internist, cardiologist*

Berwyn
Forst, Edmund Charles, Jr., *communications educator, administrator, consultant*
†Galinsky, Dennis Lee *radiation oncologist, educator*
Gordon, Dolores Joan *retired emergency medical technician*
Hudik, Martin Francis *hospital administrator, educator, consultant, writer*
Levin, Michael David *musician, educator*
Parker, Alan John *veterinary neurologist, educator, researcher*

Bethalto
†Sabaj, Nancy J. *secondary school educator*

Bloomingdale
Flaherty, John Joseph *quality assurance company executive*
Taylor, Carmen Kaye *apparel company executive*

Bloomington
†Brady, William E. *state legislator*
Bragg, Michael Ellis *lawyer, insurance company executive*
†Brakebill, Tina Stewart *historian, writer*
Bridges, Roger Dean *historical agency administrator*
Brown, Jared *theater director, educator, writer*
Casey-Beich, Micheal Louanna *theater director, artist*
Curry, Alan Chester *insurance company executive*
Daily, Jean A. *marketing executive, spokesperson*
Dick, Philip Wiens *county official*
Dietz, William Ronald *management executive*
Eckols, Thomas Aud *lawyer, educator*
Efaw, David Scott *surgeon*
Friedman, Joan M. *accounting educator*
†Fritzsche, Sonja Rae *humanities educator*
Gregor, Marlene Pierce *primary education educator, elementary science consultant*
†He, Tian-Xiao *mathematician, educator*
†Hining, Michael Lynn *music educator, conductor*
Hunt, Roger Schermerhorn *healthcare administrator*
Johnson, Earle Bertrand *insurance executive*
Joslin, Roger Scott *insurance company executive*
Kelly, Timothy William *lawyer*
Kistner, Richard Warren *university administrator*
Koos, Greg *museum director*
Laurenti, Joseph Luciano *language educator, writer*
†McHugh, Donald P. *lawyer*
Merwin, Davis Underwood *newspaper executive*
Milligan, Michael Lee *dentist*
Passetti, Lora Linda *alcohol/drug abuse services professional, researcher*
Rust, Edward Barry, Jr., *insurance company executive, lawyer*
†Setchell, Charles Marshall *music educator, consultant*
†Shekoury, Raymond N. *mathematics educator*
Skillrud, David Mark *pulmonologist, sleep specialist*
Switzer, Jon Rex *architect*
Trefzger, Richard Charles *surgeon*
Vayo, David Joseph *composer, music educator*
Walsh, William Joseph *business educator, labor arbitrator*
Ward, Jon David *insurance company executive*
White, Marilea *school social worker*
Wozniak, Debra Gail *lawyer*

Blue Island
Yager, Vincent Cook *bank executive*

Bolingbrook
Caddy, Edmund H.H., Jr., *architect*
Malicay, Manuel Alaban *physician*
Price, Theodora Hadzisteliou *individual, child and family therapist*

Relwani, Nirmal Murlidhar (Nick Relwani) *mechanical engineer*

Bourbonnais
†Ball, Karen Michele *music educator, musician, composer*
Engels, Patricia Louise *lawyer*
Wilkey, Elmira Smith *illustrator, artist, publisher, author, educator*

Braidwood
Steinacher, Ronald *music educator*

Bridgeview
Parmer, Dan Gerald *veterinarian*

Broadview
Christopher, Alexander George *transportation company executive*
Miczuga, Mark Norbert *dairy official*
Pang, Joshua Keun-Uk *trade company executive*

Brookfield
Dornhecker, Sandra Lee *human resources executive, consultant*
Rabb, George Bernard *zoologist, conservationist*

Buffalo
Coss, John Edward *retired archivist*

Buffalo Grove
Dimond, Robert Edward *publisher*
Johnson, Craig Theodore *portfolio manager*
Leonetti, Michael Edward *financial planner*
†Rivtis, Arkady *science educator, consultant*
Samors, Neal *marketing executive*
Yacktman, Donald Arthur *financial executive, investment counselor*

Burbank
Juodvalks, Egle (Egle Juodvalké) *writer*

Burlington
Nesseth, Jeffrey David *music educator*

Burr Ridge
Bottom, Dale Coyle *management consultant*
Brennan, James Joseph *lawyer, banking and financial services executive*
Clarke, Philip Ream, Jr., *retired investment banker*
Jones, Shirley Joyce *small business owner, fashion designer*
Rosenberg, Robert Brinkmann *technology organization executive*
Zaccone, Suzanne Maria *sales executive*

Cahokia
Healy, Steven Michael *accountant, city official*

Calumet City
†De Loera, David F. *religious studies educator*
Kovach, Joseph William *management consultant, psychologist, educator*
†Scullion, Annette Murphy *lawyer, educator*
Scullion, Kevin Peter *lawyer*

Cambridge
Nicholson, Tom Cotton *school district administrator*

Carbondale
Ammon, Harry *history educator*
Bauner, Ruth Elizabeth *library administrator, reference librarian*
†Benford, Robert Dee *sociology educator, editor*
†Bost, Mike *state legislator*
Burr, Brooks Milo *zoology educator*
Chavasse, Philippe *foreign languages educator*
Clemons, John Robert *lawyer*
Cole, Brad *mayor*
Covington, Patricia Ann *university administrator*
Dick, Steven Joseph *researcher, educator*
Dixon, Billy Gene *academic administrator, educator*
†Eaton, William Edward *education educator*
Gilbert, Glenn Gordon *linguistics educator*
Hahn, Lewis Edwin *philosopher, retired educator*
†Hahn, Robert Alan *philosophy educator*
†Hammond, Charles E *education educator*
Henneberger, Walter Carl *retired physicist*
†Hill, Jonathan David *anthropology researcher, educator, editor*
Humphreys, Kendra Sue *adult education educator*
Johnson, Elmer Hubert *sociologist, researcher in criminology*
Jugenheimer, Donald Wayne *advertising and communications educator, university administrator*
†Karau, Steven James *social psychologist, researcher*
Kawewe, Saliwe Moyo *social work educator, researcher*
Klubek, Brian Paul *science educator, researcher*
†Lanigan, Richard Leo, Jr., *humanities educator, writer, editor*
†Lawson, Richard Alan *literature educator, photographer*
†Lee, Mark Richard *lawyer, educator*
Mathur, Ike *finance educator*
Matthews, Elizabeth Woodfin *law librarian, law educator*
Mead, John Stanley *university administrator*
Melcher, Arlyn John *management educator*
Melone, Albert P. *political science educator, writer, researcher, consultant*
Mihalopulos, Gus, Jr., *accountant*
Mohanty, Manoj K. *mineral engineer, educator*
Molino, Michael Robert *English educator*
†Mugdadi, Abdel-Razzaq *mathematician, educator*
†Neuman, Edward George *mathematician, educator*
Nicklow, John William *civil engineer, educator*
†Paul, Souren *engineer, researcher*
†Poshard, Glenn W. *former congressman*

Schroeder, William Arthur *law educator*
Simon, Paul *former senator, educator, writer*
Snyder, Carolyn Ann *education educator, librarian*
†Townsend, Gregory Williams *music educator*
Trescott, Kathleen Marie *cultural association administrator*
Trescott, Paul Barton *educator*
†Wesley, Howard Barry *lawyer*
Whitlock, John Joseph *museum director*
†Wiesen, S. Jonathan *historian, educator*
†Xiao, Mingqing *mathematician, educator*

Carlinville
Bellm, Joan *civic worker*
Pride, Miriam R. *college president*

Carlyle
Kottmeyer, Martin S. *farmer, writer*

Carol Stream
Franzen, Janice Marguerite Gosnell *magazine editor*
Gale, Neil Jan *Internet company executive, computer scientist, consultant*
Myra, Harold Lawrence *publisher*
O'Dell, Lynn Marie Luegge (Mrs. Norman D. O'Dell) *librarian*
Schmerold, Wilfried Lothar *dermatologist*
Taylor, Kenneth Nathaniel *publishing executive, writer*

Carrollton
Strickland, Hugh Alfred *lawyer*

Carterville
†Bryant-Sala, Karen *music educator*
Lake, Tracy Marie Grace *accountant*
†Montaño, Edgar J. *language educator*
†Payne, Deborah Hindman *dean*

Carthage
Erbes, John Robert *engineering executive*
Glidden, John Redmond *lawyer*
†Ward, Roger Allen *music educator, musician*

Cary
Blevins, Steven W. *chiropractor*
Kruper, John Gerald (Jack Kruper) *sales and marketing executive*
McNulty, Diane Rose *library director*

Caseyville
Dayton, Jean *elementary school principal*
†Stanford, Diana L. *librarian*

Catlin
Asaad, Kolleen Joyce *special education educator*

Centralia
†Normansell, Steven M. *English language educator*

Champaign
†Adawi, Omar *mathematician, educator, physicist, educator*
Ahadi, Stephan Ahad *psychologist, psychometrician*
†Allen, David Joseph *music educator*
Anthony, Kathryn Harriet *architecture educator*
Arnould, Richard Julius *economist, educator, consultant*
Baker, Jack Sherman *architect, designer, educator*
Baroody, Arthur James *mathematician, educator*
Batzli, George Oliver *ecology educator*
†Boyle, Francis Anthony *law educator*
Brighton, Gerald David *accounting educator*
Brueckner, Jan Keith *economics educator*
Buschbach, Thomas Charles *geologist, consultant*
Cammack, Trank Emerson *retired university dean*
†Cantor, Nancy *academic administrator*
Cartwright, Keros *hydrogeologist, researcher*
Creamer, Bruce Cunningham *retired safety educator, property manager*
Cribbet, John Edward *law educator, former university chancellor*
Davis, James Henry *retired psychology educator*
Davisson, Melvin Thomas *consulting engineer*
Diener, Edward Francis *psychologist, researcher*
Douglas, George Halsey *writer, educator*
Due, John Fitzgerald *economist, educator emeritus*
Dulany, Donelson Edwin, Jr., *psychology educator*
Dulany, Elizabeth Gjelsness *university press administrator*
Eriksen, Charles Walter *psychologist, educator*
Espeseth, Robert D. *park and recreation planning educator*
Farmer, Helen Sweeney *psychology educator*
Farmer, James Alexander, Jr., *retired education educator*
Ferber, Marianne Abeles *economics educator*
Fredrickson, L(awrence) Thomas *composer*
Freedman, Philip *physician, educator*
Gold, Paul Ernest *psychology educator, behavioral neuroscience educator*
Grinols, Earl Leroy, III, *economist, educator*
Gross, David Lee *geologist*
†Gunsalus, Carolyn Kristina *law educator, consultant*
Guttenberg, Albert Ziskind *planning educator*
Hager, Lowell Paul *biochemistry educator*
Harden, Richard Russell *lawyer*
Hays, Robert Glenn *journalism educator*
Herzog, Beverly Leah *hydrogeologist*
Hopkins, Lewis Dean *planner, educator*
Hu, Yifan *computational mathematician*
Humphreys, Lloyd Girton *research psychologist, educator*
Hwang, Hue-Hwa *geochemist*
Ikenberry, Stanley Oliver *education educator, former university president*

Jackson, Billy Morrow *artist, retired art educator*
Jacobsen, Magdalena Gretchen *former mediator, former federal agency executive*
Kindt, John Warren *lawyer, educator, consultant*
Koenker, Diane P. *history educator*
Korst, Helmut Hans *mechanical engineer, educator*
Kotoske, Roger Allen *artist, educator*
Krause, Harry Dieter *law educator*
Kroner, Fred L. *journalist*
Krug, Edward Charles *environmental scientist*
Levin, Geoffrey Arthur *botanist*
†Loeb, Jane Rupley *university administrator, educator*
†Luo, Xiaowei *sociologist, educator*
Maggs, Peter Blount *lawyer, educator*
Mamer, Stuart Mies *lawyer*
Mc Cord, John Harrison *lawyer, educator*
McCulloh, Judith Marie *editor*
McGlathery, James Melville *foreign language educator*
Meyer, August Christopher, Jr., *broadcasting company executive, lawyer*
Meyer, David Douglas *lawyer, educator*
Michael, Steven Craig *business educator*
Mies, John Charles *internet industry executive*
Miller, Harold Arthur *lawyer*
Moore, Jerry Jay *sales executive, retired archaeologist*
Novak, Robert J. *science educator*
Nowak, John E. *law educator*
O'Neill, John Joseph *speech educator*
Osborne, Margery Diane *education educator*
†Ousterhout, Robert G. *architecture educator*
Panno, Samuel Vincent *geochemist*
†Pegg, Edward T. *webmaster, mathematician, consultant*
Perry, Kenneth Wilbur *accounting educator*
Philipp, Walter Viktor *mathematician, educator*
Ratner, Lorman Alfred *history educator*
Rawles, Edward Hugh *lawyer*
Rayward, Warden Boyd *librarian, educator*
Ridlen, Samuel Franklin *agriculture educator*
Riley, Robert Bartlett *landscape architect*
Risken, Jared Cleveland *physician*
†Ruan, Lian Jin *library director*
Sanderson, Glen Charles *science director*
Schiro-Geist, Chrisann *rehabilitation counselor*
†Schmidt, Jeffrey Brian *finance educator*
Schoenfeld, Hanns-Martin Walter *accounting educator*
Schowalter, William Raymond *college dean, educator*
†Scott, Anna Marie Porter Wall *sociology educator*
Selby, Robert Irwin
Seppala, Juha Ilmari *economist, educator*
Slichter, Charles Pence *physicist, educator*
Smith, Ralph Alexander *cultural and educational policy educator*
Sohn, Chang Wook *energy systems researcher, educator*
Spence, Clark Christian *history educator*
†Spice, Dennis Dean *venture capitalist, consultant*
Spodek, Bernard *early childhood educator*
Sprenkle, Case Middleton *economist, educator*
Stout, Glenn Emanuel *retired science administrator*
Thomas, Jo *journalist*
Triandis, Harry Charalambos *psychology educator*
Turquette, Atwell Rufus *logician*
Turquette, Frances Bond *editor*
Veasey, Byron Keith *information systems consultant*
Ward, James Gordon *education administration educator*
Watson, Jessica Lewis *writer*
Watts, Robert Allan *publisher, lawyer*
Wheeler, Richard Paul *English educator, dean*
Wicks, Eugene Claude *college president, art educator*
Wills, Bart Francis *insurance company executive*
†Winkel, Richard J., Jr., *state legislator*
Winstanley, Derek *water resource executive*
Wolfram, Stephen *physicist, computer company executive*
Yates, Ronald Eugene *newspaper editor, journalist, educator, author*

Charleston
Bagwell, Kim Diane *accountant*
Canivez, Gary Lynn *psychologist, educator*
Cooper, George Kile *business educator*
Drake, Anne Kelly *social worker, educator*
Gano, Kenneth Redman, Jr., *lawyer*
†Gordon, Yevgeniy I. *mathematician, educator*
Havey, J. Michael *psychologist, educator*
Hedges, Edith Rittenhouse *nutrition and family and consumer sciences educator*
Ignazito, Madeline Dorothy *music educator, composer*
Irwin, Bonnie D. *English language educator, researcher*
Johnson, Sarah Lynn (Lewis) *librarian, editor*
Jones, George Hilton *retired history educator, writer*
Moler, Donald Lewis *educational psychology educator*
†NeSmith, Richard A. *education educator, consultant*
Rives, Stanley Gene *university president emeritus*
Rossi, Richard Robert *music educator, conductor, performer, composer*
†Shirley, Michael Hathorn *historian, educator*
Surles, Carol D. *academic administrator*
Thornburgh, Daniel Eston *retired university administrator, journalism educator*

Chatham
Chew, Keith Elvin *healthcare services administrator*
†Post, Alan Richard *lawyer*
Powell, Carol Sue *pediatric special education educator, nursing consultant*

Chester
Felthous, Alan Robert *psychiatrist*
Welge, Donald Edward *food manufacturing executive*

Chicago
Abcarian, Herand *surgeon, educator*
Abelson, Herbert Traub *pediatrician, educator*
Abramowicz, Jacques Sylvain *obstetrician, perinatologist, educator*
Abrams, Lee Norman *lawyer*
Abrohams, Janice Elaine *social work supervisor*
Abt, Ralph Edwin *lawyer*
Acker, Ann *lawyer*
Acker, Frederick George *lawyer*
Ackerman, David Paul *lawyer*
†Adams, Rosemary Kathleen *publishing executive*
†Adducci, James Dominick *lawyer*
Adelman, Pamela Bernice Kozoll *education educator*
Adelman, Stanley Joseph *lawyer*
Adelman, Steven Herbert *lawyer*
Adler, Solomon Stanley *internist, oncologist, hematologist*
†Adomavicius, Jonas *gastroenterologist, writer*
Agema, Gerald Walton *publishing executive*
†Agoos, Jeff *professional soccer player*
Aiello, Susan *artist, illustrator, educator*
†Akers, Michelle Anne *soccer player*
Akos, Francis *violinist, conductor*
Alcantara, Anita Luisa *human resources consultant*
al-Chalabi, Suhail Abdul-Jabbar *transportation executive*
Alesia, James H(enry) *judge*
Alexander, Ian Robert *lawyer*
Aliber, Robert Z. *economist, educator*
Allampallam, Krishnan *biotechnology consultant*
Allen, Belle *management consulting firm executive, communications company executive*
Allen, Danielle *political scientist, educator*
Allen, Julie Michelle *secondary education educator*
Allen, Richard Blose *legal editor, lawyer*
Allen, Ronald Jay *law educator*
Allen, Thomas Draper *lawyer*
Almeida, Richard Joseph *finance company administrator*
Almen, Lowell Gordon *church official*
Alou, Moises *professional baseball player*
Alperin, Jonathan Lazare *mathematician, educator*
†Althage, C. Jill *librarian*
Altman, Edith G. *sculptor*
Altman, Louis *lawyer, author, educator*
†Amarasekare, Priyanga *education educator*
†Amend, James Michael *lawyer*
Amstadter, Laurence *retired architect*
Andersen, Burton Robert *physician, educator*
Anderson, J. Trent *lawyer*
Anderson, Jon Stephen *newswriter*
Anderson, Karl Stephen *editor*
Anderson, Kimball Richard *lawyer*
Anderson, Paul Stewart *lawyer*
†Anderson, Philip Vernon *retired pastor*
†Anderson, William Cornelius, III, *lawyer*
Andreoli, Kathleen Gainor *dean, nurse*
Angst, Gerald L. *lawyer*
Anthony, Michael Francis *lawyer*
Antonio, Douglas John *lawyer*
Anvaripour, M. A. *lawyer*
Appel, Nina Schick *law educator, dean*
†Archer, James G. *lawyer*
†Arena, Bruce *professional soccer coach*
Armstrong, Edwin Richard *lawyer, publisher, editor*
Aronson, Howard Isaac *linguist, educator*
Aronson, Virginia L. *lawyer*
Arpino, Gerald Peter *performing company executive*
Artest, Ron *professional basketball player*
Ash, J. Marshall *mathematician, educator*
Ashman, Martin C. *federal judge*
Aspen, Marvin Edward *federal judge*
Athas, Gus James *lawyer*
Aubin, Barbara Jean *artist*
Auerbach, Marshall Jay *lawyer*
Avery, Robert Dean *lawyer*
Ayman, Iraj *educational consultant*
Babcock, Lyndon Ross, Jr., *environmental engineer, educator*
Bacevicius, John Anthony, V, (John Bace) *research executive*
Backer, Carl Lewis *pediatric cardiac surgeon, educator*
Badel, Julie *lawyer*
Baer, John Richard Frederick *lawyer*
Bailey, Robert, Jr., *advertising executive*
Bailey, Robert Short *lawyer*
Baird, Douglas Gordon *law educator, dean*
Bajek, Frank Michael *retired army officer, financial consultant*
Baker, Bruce Jay *lawyer*
†Baker, Dusty (Johnnie B. Baker Jr.) *professional baseball team manager*
Baker, James Edward Sproul *retired lawyer*
Baker, Pamela *lawyer*
Bakwin, Edward Morris *banker*
Balasa, Florin *software engineer, mathematician*
Balasi, Mark Geoffrey *architect*
Baldwin, DeWitt Clair, Jr., *physician, educator*
Baldwin, Shaun McParland *lawyer*
Balk, Robert A. *medical educator*
Balzekas, Stanley, Jr., *museum director*
†Bandes, Susan Anne *lawyer*
Banerjee, Prashant *industrial engineering educator*
Baniak, Sheila Mary *accountant, educator*
Banoff, Sheldon Irwin *lawyer*
Banta, Don Arthur *retired lawyer*
†Barack, Peter Joseph *lawyer, educator*
Barber, Edward Bruce *medical products executive*
Barbour, Claude Marie *minister, educator*
†Bardgett, John E. *lawyer*
Bariff, Martin Louis *information systems educator, consultant*
Barker, Walter Lee *thoracic surgeon*
Barker, William Thomas *lawyer*
Barkin, Robert Lyn *pharmacologist, pharmacist*
Barney, Carol Ross *architect*
Baron, Richard L. *health services administrator*
Barr, John Robert *retired lawyer*
Barr, Sanford Lee *dentist*
†Barrett, Roger Watson *lawyer*
Barriger, John Walker, IV, *transportation executive*
†Barron, Harold Sheldon *lawyer*
Barron, Howard Robert *lawyer*
†Barrows, Michael John *endodontist, educator*
Barry, Richard A. *public relations executive*
†Bartel, Barbara M. *educator*
Bartholomay, William C. *insurance brokerage company executive, professional baseball team executive*
Barton, John Joseph *obstetrician, gynecologist, educator, researcher*
Bartter, Brit Jeffrey *investment banker*
Baruch, Hurd *lawyer*
Bashwiner, Steven Lacelle *lawyer*
†Batra, Inder P. *physics educator, researcher*
Bauer, William Joseph *federal judge*
Baugher, Peter V. *lawyer*
Baum, Bernard Helmut *sociologist, educator*
†Bauman, Jerry L. *pharmacy researcher, educator*
Baumann, Gerhard Paul *endocrinologist, educator*
Baumhart, Raymond Charles *Roman Catholic church administrator*
Baylor, Don Edward *former professional baseball manager*
Beattie, Ted Arthur *zoological gardens and aquarium administrator*
†Beatty, William Glenn *lawyer*
†Beck, Philip S. *lawyer*
Beck, Robert N. *nuclear medicine educator*
Becker, Gary Stanley *economist, educator*
Becker, Michael Allen *physician, educator*
Becker, Robert Allen *data processing executive*
Beckers, Jacques Maurice *astrophysicist*
Beedle, Dennis Dean *psychiatrist, educator*
Beem, Jack Darrel *lawyer*
Beemster, Joseph Robert *risk management consultant*
Beer, John R. *poet, educator*
Beigl, William *physician, hypnotist, acupuncturist, consultant*
Beitler, Stephen *private equity and venture capital executive*
Bell, Carl Compton *psychiatrist, researcher*
†Bell, Dean Phillip *dean*
Bell, Kevin J. *zoological park administrator*
Bellah, Kenneth David *lawyer*
Bellantoni, Maureen Blanchfield *manufacturing and retail executive*
†Bellows, Laurel Gordon *lawyer*
Belluschi, Anthony C. *architect*
†Ben-Arie, Jezekiel *electrical engineer, computer scientist, educator*
Benditzson, David Jerome *physician, educator*
Benedict, Kennette Mari *foundation executive, researcher*
Bennett, Robert William *law educator*
Bensinger, Peter Benjamin *consulting firm executive*
Benson, Irene M. *nurse*
Benson, Sara Elizabeth *real estate broker, real estate appraiser*
Benzon, Honorio Tabal *anesthesiologist*
Berardino, Joseph Francis *accounting company executive*
Berendi, Erlinda Bayaua *physician surgeon*
Berens, Mark Harry *lawyer*
Berenzweig, Jack Charles *lawyer*
Berger, Robert Michael *lawyer*
Berghoff, Paul Henry *lawyer*
Bergonia, Raymond David *venture capitalist*
Bergstrom, Betty Howard *consulting executive, foundation administrator*
†Berkhout, Bjorn Haldane *composer, music educator*
Berman, Arthur Leonard *retired state senator*
Berman, Cheryl R. *advertising company executive*
†Berman, Joel David *mathematics educator*
Bernardini, Charles *lawyer, former alderman*
Bernatowicz, Frank Allen *management consultant, expert witness*
Berner, Robert Lee, Jr., *lawyer*
†Bernick, David M. *lawyer*
Berning, Larry D. *lawyer*
†Bernstein, Charles Bernard *lawyer*
Berolzheimer, Karl *lawyer*
†Berry, Richard Morgan *lawyer*
Berry, Richard Stephen *chemist*
Betts, Henry Brognard *physician, health facility administrator, educator*
Betts, Richard Russell *science educator*
Betz, Hans Dieter *theology educator*
Beugen, Joan Beth *communications company executive*
Beutel, Ernest William *thoracic surgeon*
Bevans, Stephen Bennett *priest, educator*
Bevington, David Martin *English literature educator*
Bey, Lee *municipal official*
†Bezkorovainy, Anatoly *medical educator, biochemist*
Bidwell, Charles Edward *sociologist, educator*
Biebel, Paul Philip, Jr., *lawyer*
†Bienen, Leigh Buchanan *lawyer*
Bienias, Julia Louise *medical researcher, statistician*
Bierig, Jack R. *lawyer, educator*
Biggs, Robert Dale *Near Eastern studies educator*
Billingsley, William Patrice *mathematician, educator*
Bindenagel, James Dale *foundation executive*
†Birchenall, Javier Arturo *economist, researcher*
Bishop, Mary Oltman *retired advertising executive*
Bitner, John Howard *lawyer*
Bixby, Frank Lyman *lawyer*
†Black, Henry Richard *internist*
Black, Robert Durward *ecumenical television producer*
†Blair, Edward McCormick *investment banker*
Blankenship, Edward G. *architect*
Blatt, Richard Lee *lawyer*
†Blecic, Deborah Diana *school librarian, educator*
Block, Neal Jay *lawyer*
Block, Philip Dee, III, *investment counselor*
Block, Richard L. *sociologist, criminologist, educator*
†Bloom, Christopher Arthur *lawyer*
Blount, Michael Eugene *lawyer*
†Blumberg, Avrom Aaron *physical chemistry educator*
Blume, Paul Chiappe *lawyer*
Blumenthal, Carlene Margaret *vocational-technical school and language arts educator*
Blumenthal, Joan H. *executive recruiter*
Bobbitt, Ronald Albert *lawyer*
Boddie, Arthur Walker, Jr., *surgeon, cancer researcher*
Bodenstein, Ira *lawyer*
Bodi, Sonia Ellen *library director, educator*
Boehnen, Daniel A. *lawyer*
Boggs, Joseph Dodridge *pediatric pathologist, educator*
Bohn, Charlotte Galitz *retired real estate executive*
†Boies, Wilber H. *lawyer*
†Bolger, David P. *insurance company executive*
Bona, Jerry Lloyd *mathematician, educator*
†Bonjack, Stephanie *music librarian*
Bonow, Robert Ogden *medical educator*
Boocock, Stephen William *lawyer*
†Boodell, Thomas Joseph, Jr., *lawyer*
Booth, Wayne Clayson *English literature and rhetoric educator, author*
Bordage, Georges *physician, medical education educator*
Borenstine, Alvin Jerome *search company executive*
Borysewicz, Mary Louise *editor*
Boshes, Louis D. *physician, scientist, educator, historian, author*
Bourdon, Cathleen Jane *professional society administrator*
Bouson, J. Brooks *English educator*
Bouton, Marshall Melvin *academic administrator*
Bowe, William J(ohn) *lawyer*
†Bowen, Stephen Stewart *lawyer*
Bowman, Barbara Taylor *early childhood educator*
Bowman, James Edward *physician, educator*
†Bowman, Phillip Boynton *lawyer*
Boyer, John William *history educator, dean*
Bracken, Kathleen Ann *nurse*
†Bradley, Bob *professional soccer coach*
Brady, Geraldine *mathematician, educator*
Brake, Cecil Clifford *retired diversified manufacturing executive*
Bramnik, Robert Paul *lawyer*
Brandman, James Franklin *internist, oncologist*
Brandt, Gene Stuart *fundraising consultant*
Brandt, William Arthur, Jr., *consulting executive*
Bransfield, James Joseph *surgeon*
Bratcher, Juanita *journalist*
†Brauer, Sasha Gerritson *church musician, music educator*
†Braun, Frederick B. *lawyer*
Breen, Neil Thomas *publishing executive*
Brendler, Charles Burgess *urologist, educator*
Bresnahan, Arthur Stephen *lawyer*
Breyer, Norman Nathan *metallurgical engineering educator, consultant*
Brezina, David Charles *lawyer, educator*
Brice, Roger Thomas *lawyer*
Bridgman, Thomas Francis *retired lawyer*
Brinkman, John Anthony *historian, educator*
Bristo, Marca *human services administrator*
†Brittain, Max Gordon, Jr., *lawyer*
Brizzolara, Charles Anthony *lawyer, director*
Brodsky, William J. *options exchange executive*
Brooker, Thomas Kimball *oil company executive*
Brown, Alan Crawford *lawyer*
Brown, Charles Eric *health facility administrator, biochemist*
Brown, Donald James, Jr., *lawyer*
Brown, Gregory K. *lawyer*
Brown, Joan Phillips (Abena Joan Brown) *foundation administrator*
Brown, Richard Holbrook *library director, historian, researcher*
Brown, Steven Spencer *lawyer*
Brown, Teion O'Dell *engineering executive*
Browning, Don Spencer *religious educator*
Brumback, Charles Tiedtke *retired newspaper executive*
Brummel, Mark Joseph *magazine editor*
†Bryan, John Henry *food and consumer products company executive*
Bryant, James *pathologist*
Buckley, Joseph Paul, III, *polygraph specialist*
Bucklo, Elaine Edwards *United States district court judge*
†Bucksbaum, Matthew *real estate investment trust company executive*
Bueche, Wendell Francis *agricultural products company executive*
Buehler, Evelyn Judy *poet*
Buehrle, Mark *baseball player*
Bugielski, Robert Joseph *state legislator*
Bulger, Brian Wegg *lawyer*
†Bumbaugh, David Edward *religious studies educator, minister*
Bunn, William Bernice, III, *physician, lawyer, epidemiologist*
Burack, Elmer Howard *management educator*
†Burck, Joseph Russell *medical educator, consultant, minister*
Burd, Laurence I. *obstetrician-gynecologist*
Burdelik, Thomas L. *lawyer*
Burgdoerfer, Jerry *lawyer*
†Burke, Daniel J. *state legislator*

Burke, John Michael *lawyer*
Burke, Thomas Joseph, Jr., *lawyer*
†Burkhardt, Edward Arnold *railway executive*
†Burns, Terrence Michael *lawyer*
Busey, Roxane C. *lawyer*
Bussman, Donald Herbert *lawyer*
†Butler, Colette M. *minister*
†Butta, Deena Celeste *librarian*
Buxbaum, Alexandra *photographer*
Byekwaso, Serapio *statistician, researcher*
Bynoe, Peter Charles Bernard *real estate developer, lawyer*
†Byun, Michael *plastic surgeon*
Cacioppo, John Terrance *psychology educator, researcher*
†Cafferty, Pastora San Juan *public policy educator*
Cain, Louis Perkins, III, *economist, educator*
Calenoff, Leonid *radiologist*
Callaway, Karen A(lice) *journalist*
Calvin, James Eldon, Jr., *cardiologist, educator, researcher*
Cameron, Catherine Isabella *community volunteer*
Camper, John Jacob *speech writer*
†Campos-Pons, Maria Magdalena *artist*
†Capparelli, Ralph C. *state legislator*
Cappo, Joseph C. *journalist, writer*
Carlin, Dennis J. *lawyer*
†Carlson, LeRoy Theodore, Jr., *telecommunications industry executive*
Carlson, Richard Gregory *accountant*
Carlson, Walter Carl *lawyer*
Carlton, Dennis William *economics educator*
Carnes, Bruce Alfred *gerontologist, researcher*
Caro, William Allan *physician, educator*
Carren, Jeffrey P. *lawyer*
Carroll, William Kenneth *law educator, psychologist, theologian*
Carter, Tyrone *writer*
Cartwright, Bill *professional basketball coach*
Carvajal, Arthur Gonzalez *editor, lawyer*
Cary, Arlene D. *retired hotel company sales executive*
Casazza, Martha Ellen *developmental education educator*
Cass, Robert Michael *lawyer, consultant*
Cassel, Douglass Watts, Jr., *lawyer, educator, journalist*
Castillo, Mario Enrique *artist, educator*
Castorino, Sue *communications executive*
Catalona, William *surgeon, urologist, educator, researcher*
†Catchpole, Hubert Ralph *physiologist*
Chacko, Samuel *association official*
Chakrabarty, Ananda Mohan *microbiologist*
Chaleff, Carl Thomas *brokerage house executive*
Chambers, Donald Arthur *biochemistry and molecular medicine educator*
Chambers, Richard Leon *retired Turkish language and civilization educator*
Chan, Lawrence Siu-Yung *dermatologist, educator*
Chandler, Kent, Jr., *lawyer*
Chappell, Kathleen Diane *fundraising executive*
Chappidi, Prasad V. *neurologist*
Charles, Allan G. *physician, educator*
Chatterton, Robert Treat, Jr., *reproductive endocrinology educator*
†Chaudhary, Kamran *internist*
Cheely, Daniel Joseph *lawyer*
Chefitz, Joel Gerald *lawyer*
†Chemers, Robert Marc *lawyer*
†Chen, Chin-Tu *medical physics educator*
Cheng, Paul Hung-Chiao *civil engineer*
Cherney, James Alan *lawyer*
†Cherry, Daniel Ronald *lawyer*
Cherry, Robert Steven, III, *municipal administrator*
Chertok, Daniel Lvovich *mathematician, researcher*
†Chester, Mark Vincent *lawyer*
Chestnut, John William *lawyer*
Chiles, Stephen Michael *lawyer*
Chipparoni, Guy *communications company executive*
Choldin, Marianna Tax *librarian, educator*
†Chong, Pang Hyon *pharmacist, consultant*
†Chorengel, Bernd *international hotel corporation executive*
Christianson, Stanley David *corporate executive*
Chriszt, Dennis Francis *priest*
Chromizky, William Rudolph *accountant*
Chung, Paul Myungha *mechanical engineer, educator*
Cicero, Frank, Jr., *lawyer*
Claiborne, William *journalist*
Clarke, Jay A. *art historian, curator*
Clarke, Richard Stewart *security company executive*
Clayton, Robert Norman *chemist, educator*
Clemens, Richard Glenn *lawyer*
Clevenger, Penelope *international business consultant*
†Clifford, Robert A. *lawyer*
Clinton, Edward Xavier *lawyer*
Cloonan, James Brian *investment executive*
Closen, Michael Lee *law educator*
Coase, Ronald Harry *economist, educator*
Coe, Fredric L. *physician, educator, researcher*
†Coffey, Susanna Jean *artist, educator*
Cohen, Ira *legislative staff member*
Cohen, Melanie Rovner *lawyer*
Cohen, Melvin R. *physician, educator*
†Cohen, Stephen Bruce *lawyer*
Cohen, Ted *philosophy educator*
Cohler, Bertram Joseph *social sciences educator, clinical psychologist*
Coleman, Roy Everett *secondary education educator, computer programmer*
†Colker, David *trade association administrator*
†Collen, John *lawyer*
Collen, Sheldon Orrin *lawyer*
Collens, Lewis Morton *university president, legal educator*
†Colley, Karen J. *medical educator, medical researcher*
Conidi, Daniel Joseph *private investigation agency executive*
Conklin, Thomas William *lawyer*
Conlon, Patrick C. *family nurse practitioner, pediatric nurse practitioner*
Connelly, Mary Jo *lawyer*
Connors, Dorsey *television and radio commentator, newspaper columnist*
†Conte, Lou *artistic director, choreographer*
Conway, James Joseph *radiologist, educator*
Conway, Michael Maurice *lawyer*
Cook, Richard Borreson *architect*
Cooke, Michael *editor-in-chief*
†Cooley, John Wayne *lawyer*
Cooper, Charles Gilbert *toiletries and cosmetics company executive*
Cooper, Wylola *retired special education educator*
Copeland, Edward Jerome *lawyer*
†Corwin, Sherman Phillip *lawyer*
†Costa, Erminio *pharmacologist, cell biology educator*
†Costello, John William *lawyer*
Costin, J(oseph) Laurence, Jr., *information services executive*
†Cotter, Daniel A. *diversified company executive*
Coulson, William Roy *lawyer*
†Cousins, William, Jr., *retired judge*
Covalt, Robert Byron *chemicals executive*
Cox, Allan James *management consultant*
Cox, Clifford Ernest *information systems consulting executive, former school administrator*
Coy, Patricia Ann *special education director, consultant*
Craine, Thomas Knowlton *non-profit administrator*
Crane, Barbara Bachmann *photographer, educator*
Crane, Mark *lawyer*
Craven, George W. *lawyer*
Crawford, Dewey Byers *lawyer*
Crawford, Jean Andre *clinical therapist*
Cremin, Susan Elizabeth *lawyer*
Crisham, Thomas Michael *lawyer*
Crockett, George Ephriam *secondary education educator*
Cronin, James Watson *physicist, educator*
Cropsey, Joseph *political science educator*
Cross, Robert Clark *journalist*
Crossan, John Robert *lawyer*
Crown, James Schine *investment executive*
Crown, Lester *manufacturing company executive*
Cruthird, Robert Lee *sociology educator*
Csar, Michael F. *lawyer*
Cudahy, Richard D. *judge*
Cugell, David Wolf *medical educator*
Cullen, Charles Thomas *historian, librarian*
†Cullerton, John James *state senator, lawyer*
Culverwell, Rosemary Jean *principal, elementary education educator*
Cunningham, Robert James *lawyer*
Cunningham, Thomas Justin *lawyer*
†Curran, Raymond M. *paper-based packaging company executive*
†Curry, Raymond Howard *physician*
Curtis, Arthur William *otolaryngologist*
Curwen, Randall William *journalist, editor*
Cusack, John Thomas *lawyer*
Custer, Charles Francis *lawyer*
Daley, Richard Michael *mayor*
†Daley, Susan Jean *lawyer*
Daley, Vincent Raymond, Jr., *real estate company executive, consultant*
Daly, Patrick F. *real estate executive, architect*
†Dan, Bernard W. *trade association administrator*
Dancewicz, John Edward *investment banker*
D'Andrea, Deborah Dawn *nursing consultant, critical care nurse*
Daniels, John Draper *lawyer*
Darby, Edwin Wheeler *retired newspaper financial columnist*
Darchun, Lino Auksutis *real estate professional*
Dardai, Shahid Moinuddin *computer science educator*
Darr, Milton Freeman, Jr., *banker*
Darvodelsky, Alexander *structural engineer*
Davis, Concelor Dominguez *marriage and family therapist*
Davis, Danny K. *congressman*
Davis, Katherine Helene *vocalist, educator*
Davis, Muller *lawyer*
Davis, Scott Jonathan *lawyer*
†Davis, William L. *publishing company executive*
Davison, Richard *physician, educator*
Daze, Eric *professional hockey player*
De, Devasmita *research aquarist*
De Armas, Frederick Alfred *foreign language educator*
Debus, Allen George *history educator*
†Decker, John Francis *lawyer, educator*
Decker, Richard Knore *lawyer*
†DeCoursey, Thomas Eric *physiologist, educator*
Dee, Ivan Richard *book publisher*
Degroot, Leslie Jacob *medical educator*
Deitrick, William Edgar *lawyer*
†DeLeo, James A. *state legislator*
Deli, Anne Tynion *marketing executive*
Deliford, Mylah Eagan *mathematics educator*
Delp, Wilbur Charles, Jr., *lawyer*
Dembowski, Peter Florian *foreign language educator*
DeMiles, Edward *agent*
DeMoss, Jon W. *insurance company executive, lawyer*
Dempsey, Mary A. *library commissioner, lawyer*
Denlow, Morton *federal magistrate judge*
Deorio, Anthony Joseph *surgeon*
†deRegnier, Raye-Ann Odegaard *physician, researcher*
Derlacki, Eugene L(ubin) *otolaryngologist, physician*
Desjardins, Claude *physiologist, dean*
†Desombre, Nancy Cox *academic administrator, consultant*
D'Esposito, Julian C., Jr., *lawyer*
Despres, Leon Mathis *lawyer, former city official*
Deutsch, Thomas Alan *ophthalmologist, educator*
†DeVries, James Howard *lawyer*
DeWolfe, John Chauncey, Jr., *lawyer*
†De Yoe, David P. *lawyer*
Diamond, Seymour *physician*
Diamond, Shari Seidman *law and psychology educator, researcher*
Dickerson, Martha Ann *health facility administrator*
Dickman, Martin J. *federal agency administrator*
Diefenbach, Viron Leroy *dental, public health educator, university dean*
Di Eugenio, Barbara *computer science educator*
†Dillard, Kirk Whitfield *state legislator, lawyer*
†Dinkes, William *lawyer*
Di Prima, Stephanie Marie *educational administrator*
Ditkowsky, Kenneth K. *lawyer*
Dix, Rollin C(umming) *mechanical engineering educator, consultant*
†Dixon, Stewart Strawn *lawyer, consultant*
Dobrev, Stanislav *finance educator, researcher*
Dobrick, Jo-Anne *retail executive, environmentalist, consultant*
Dobyns, William B. *human geneticist, pediatrician, neurologist*
Docksey, John Ross *lawyer*
Dockterman, Michael *lawyer*
Doetsch, Virginia Lamb *former advertising executive, writer*
Doherty, Brian Gerard *alderman*
Dolan, Thomas Christopher *professional society administrator*
Dold, Robert Bruce *journalist*
†Domanskis, Alexander Rimas *lawyer*
†Dombrow, Anthony Eric *lawyer*
Doniger, Wendy *history of religions educator*
Donlevy, John Dearden *lawyer*
Donnell, Harold Eugene, Jr., *professional society administrator*
Donnelley, James Russell *printing company executive*
Donner, Ted A. *lawyer*
Donohoe, Jerome Francis *lawyer*
†Donohue, Craig S. *trade association administrator*
Dowling, Doris Anderson *business owner, educator, consultant*
Downing, Robert Allan *lawyer*
Doyle, John Robert *lawyer*
Drantz, Veronica Ellen *science educator and consultant*
Drechney, Michaelene *secondary education educator*
Drezner, Daniel William *political scientist, educator*
Driskell, Claude Evans *college director, educator, dentist*
Drumke, Michael William *lawyer*
Drymalski, Raymond Hibner *lawyer, banker*
†Dubbs, John William, III, *lawyer*
DuCanto, Joseph Nunzio *lawyer, educator*
Duell, Daniel Paul *artistic director, choreographer, lecturer*
†Duffy, Terrence A. *brokerage house executive*
Dunaif, Andrea Elizabeth *endocrinologist*
Duncan, John Patrick Cavanaugh *lawyer*
Dundzila, Rudra Vilius *language educator, minister*
Dunea, George *nephrologist, educator*
Dunlap, Patricia Pearl *elementary school educator*
Dunn, Christopher Joseph *telecommunications industry executive*
Dunn, Edwin Rydell *lawyer*
Dupont, Todd F. *mathematics and computer science educator*
Durchslag, Stephen P. *lawyer*
Dust, Margaret Cecile *psychology educator*
†Dutterer, Dennis Alton *lawyer*
Dwyer, Dennis D. *information technology executive*
Dykstra, Paul Hopkins *lawyer*
Early, Bert Hylton *lawyer, consultant*
Easterbrook, Frank Hoover *federal judge*
Eaton, John C. *composer, educator*
Echols, M(ary) Evelyn *travel consultant*
Edelman, Alvin *lawyer*
Edelman, Daniel Joseph *public relations executive*
Edelstein, Teri J. *art history educator, art administrator*
Egan, Kevin James *lawyer*
Eggert, Russell Raymond *lawyer*
†Eglit, Howard Charles *educator, lawyer, arbitrator*
Eimer, Nathan Philip *lawyer*
Einoder, Camille Elizabeth *retired secondary education educator*
†Eiser, Arnold Robert *internist, bioethicist, nephrologist*
Ekdahl, Jon Nels *lawyer, association executive*
Elden, Gary Michael *lawyer*
Ellison, Jeffrey Alan *educator*
Ellwood, Scott *lawyer*
Elshtain, Jean Bethke *social and political ethics educator*
Elson, Alex *lawyer, educator, arbitrator*
Elson, Miriam *social work educator*
†Emerson, Carter Whitney *lawyer*
†Emmanuel, Rahm *former federal official, investment banker*
†Emmons Jr., Charles N. *music educator*
Enenbach, Mark Henry *community action agency executive, educator*
English, Henry L. *not-for-profit association executive*
English, John Dwight *lawyer*
†Enquist, Philip *architectural firm executive*
Epstein, David M. *publishing executive*
Epstein, Raymond *engineering and architectural executive*
Epstein, Sidney *architect, engineer*
Erber, Thomas *physics educator*
Erdös, Ervin George *pharmacology and biochemistry educator*
Erens, Jay Allan *lawyer*
Erlebacher, Albert *history educator*
Ernest, J. Terry *ocular physiologist, educator*
Espat, N. Joseph *surgeon*
Esrick, Jerald Paul *lawyer*
Eubanks-Pope, Sharon G. *real estate company executive, entrepreneur*
Evans, Thelma Jean Mathis *internist*
Even, Francis Alphonse *lawyer*
Evens, Martha Walton *computer science educator*
Fabian, Susan Jean *language educator*
Fahey, Hallie Joan Miller *lawyer*
Fahn, Jay *commercial bank executive, consultant, art dealer*
Fahnestock, Jean Howe *retired civil engineer*
Fair, Hudson Randolph *recording company executive*
Fairchild, Thomas E. *federal judge*
Falkof, Melvin Milton *retired food products company executive*
†Falls, Robert Arthur *artistic director*
Farber, Bernard John *lawyer*
†Farber, Walter T. *assyriologist, educator*
†Farhadi, Ashkan *physician, researcher*
†Fawcett, Joy Lynn *soccer player*
Fazio, Peter Victor, Jr., *lawyer*
†Feagley, Michael Rowe *lawyer*
Feder, Martin Elliott *biology researcher and educator*
Feder, Robert *television and radio columnist*
†Feigenholtz, Sara *state legislator*
†Feinberg, Gary H. *lawyer, retail company executive*
Feinstein, Fred Ira *lawyer*
†Feldman, Scott Milton *lawyer*
Fellows, Jerry Kenneth *lawyer*
Felsenthal, Steven Altus *lawyer, educator*
Fennessy, John James *radiologist, educator*
Ferencz, Robert Arnold *lawyer*
Ferguson, Margaret Geneva *writer, publisher, real estate broker*
†Fernandez, James *anthropology educator*
Ferrini, James Thomas *lawyer*
Fetridge, Clark Worthington *business executive*
Field, Karen Ann (Karen Ann Schaffner) *real estate broker*
Field, Marshall *business executive*
Field, Robert Edward *lawyer*
†Fifield, Sean C. *lawyer*
Fina, Paul Joseph *lawyer*
Finke, Robert Forge *lawyer*
†Fintel, Dan James *cardiologist*
Fischbach, Charles Peter *railway executive consultant, lawyer, arbitrator, mediator*
Fish, Stanley Eugene *university dean, English educator*
Fisher, Eugene *marketing professional*
Fisher, Lawrence Edgar *market research executive, anthropologist*
Fisher, Lester Emil *zoo administrator*
†Fishman, Robert Michael *lawyer*
Fitch, Frank Wesley *pathologist educator, immunologist, educator, administrator*
Fitch, Morgan Lewis, Jr., *intellectual property lawyer*
Fitzgerald, Robert Maurice *financial executive*
Fitzgerald, Thomas Robert *judge*
Fitzpatrick, Christine Morris *legal administrator, former television executive*
†FitzSimons, Dennis Joseph *broadcasting executive*
†Fizdale, Richard *advertising agency executive*
†Flannery, John Francis *lawyer*
Flaum, Joel Martin *judge*
Flaxman, Kenneth N. *lawyer*
†Fleming, Richard H. *finance executive*
Fleury, Theoren *hockey player*
Flock, Jeffrey Charles *news bureau chief*
Florine, Jane L. *musicology educator*
Flynn, John J. *museum curator*
Foerster, James Fredrick *urban planning educator, university administrator*
Fogel, Henry *orchestra administrator*
Fogel, Robert William *economist, educator, historian*
Forbes, John Edward *financial consultant*
†Ford, Barbara Jean *library studies educator*
†Ford, Diane *lawyer*
†Forehand, Joseph W. *finance company executive*
Formeller, Daniel Richard *lawyer*
Fort, Jeffrey C. *lawyer*
Fortuna, William Frank *architectural engineer, architect*
Foster, James Reuben *travel company executive*
Foudree, Bruce William *lawyer*
†Foudy, Julia Maurine *soccer player*
Fowler, George Selton, Jr., *architect*
Fox, David Wayne *banker*
†Fox, Kathy Pinkstaff *lawyer*
Fox, Paul T. *lawyer*
Fragen, Robert Joseph *physician, anesthesiologist*
Franch, Richard Thomas *lawyer*
Francuch, Paul Charles *broadcast journalist*
†Franczek, James Clement, Jr., *lawyer*
†Franke, Richard James *arts advocate, former investment banker*
Frankel, Bernard *advertising executive*
Franklin, Richard Mark *lawyer*
†Franks, Jack Darrow *lawyer*
Frazen, Mitchell Hale *lawyer*
Frazier, Anthany Vincent Earl *addictions, small business, and technology specialist*
Frazin, Rhona Sondra *non-profit executive*
Frederiksen, Marilynn C. *physician*
†Freeborn, Michael D. *lawyer*
Freed, Karl Frederick *chemistry educator*
†Freehling, Paul Edward *lawyer*
Freehling, Stanley Maxwell *investment banker*
Freeman, Lee Allen, Jr., *lawyer*
Freeman, Leslie Gordon *anthropologist, educator*
Freeman, Louis S. *lawyer*
†Freeman, Richard Lyons *lawyer*
Freeman, Susan Tax *anthropologist, educator, culinary historian*
†Freerksen, Gregory Nathan *lawyer*

Kelly, Arthur Lloyd *management and investment company executive*
Kelly, Charles Arthur *lawyer*
Kelly, Curtis Hartt *retired publishing executive*
†Kelly, James Paul *neurologist*
Kelly, Maura Anne *reporter*
Kenas-Heller, Jane Hamilton *musician*
Kennedy, Eugene Cullen *psychology educator, writer*
Kennedy, Lawrence Allan *mechanical engineering educator*
†Kenney, Estelle Koval *artist, educator*
Kenney, Frank Deming *lawyer*
Kerbis, Gertrude Lempp *architect*
Keryczynskyj, Leo Ihor *county official, educator, lawyer*
†Keshavarzian, Ali *gastroenterologist, educator*
†Kessler, John Allen *physician, biomedical researcher*
Keys, Arlander *federal judge*
Kiefer, John Harold *chemical engineering educator*
Kikoler, Stephen Philip *lawyer*
Kim, Mi Ja *dean, academic administrator*
Kim, Michael Charles *lawyer*
†Kincaid, Richard D. *bank executive*
King, Andre Richardson *architectural graphic designer*
King, Sharon Louise *lawyer*
Kins, Juris *lawyer*
Kinslow, Monica M. *forensic scientist*
Kipper, Barbara Levy *corporate executive*
Kipperman, Lawrence I. *lawyer*
Kirkegaard, R. Lawrence *architectural acoustician*
Kirkland, John Leonard *lawyer*
Kirkpatrick, Anne Saunders *systems analyst*
†Kirkpatrick, John Everett *lawyer*
Kirsch, Jeffrey Scott *securities executive*
Kirschner, Barbara Starrels *pediatric gastroenterologist*
Kirsner, Joseph Barnett *physician, educator*
Kisor, Henry Du Bois *newspaper editor, critic, columnist, writer*
Kissel, Richard John *lawyer*
Kite, Steven B. *lawyer*
Kittle, Charles Frederick *surgeon*
†Klatt, Wayne Roy *editor, writer*
Klaviter, Helen Lothrop *magazine editor*
Klebba, Raymond Allen *property manager*
†Kleczek, David A. *lawyer*
Kleiman, Kelly (Ruth B. Kleiman) *journalist, lawyer*
Klein, Robert Marshall *lawyer*
Kleinpell-Nowell, Ruth *nursing educator and researcher, medical writer*
Klenk, James Andrew *lawyer*
Kleppa, Ole J. *chemistry educator*
Klimley, Nancy Lee *volunteer*
Klopack, Kenneth Barthon *art educator, artist*
†Knappenberger, Paul Henry, Jr., *science museum director*
Kneen, John W. *venture capitalist*
Knight, Christopher Nichols *lawyer*
Knowles, Thomas William *business educator, consultant*
†Kobler, John F. *priest, researcher*
Kobs, James Fred *direct marketing consultant*
Kocka, Frank Edward *microbiologist*
†Koernig, Stephen K. *marketing professional, educator*
Kohn, Shalom L. *lawyer*
Kohn, William Irwin *lawyer*
Kolb, Gwin Jackson *language professional, educator*
Kolek, Robert Edward *lawyer*
Kolkey, Gilda *artist*
Kolmin, Kenneth Guy *lawyer*
Konerko, Paul *baseball player*
Kopec, John William *research scientist*
Kopf, David Heath *economic consultant*
Koppe, William Paul *deputy sheriff*
Koppes, Steven Nelson *science writer, editor*
Kopytko, Edwin Edward *nursing administrator*
Kordylewski, Leszek *cell biologist, forensic scientist*
Kosinski, Richard Andrew *public relations executive*
†Kotulak, Ronald *newspaper science writer*
Kouvel, James Spyros *physicist, educator*
Kowalski, Thaddeus Lawrence *retired judge*
Kowal-Vern, Areta *pathology and pediatrics educator*
Kozak, John W. *lawyer*
Kravitt, Jason Harris Paperno *lawyer*
†Krawczyk, Eva *information systems analyst, educator*
Krawetz, Arthur Altshuler *chemist, science administrator*
Kriss, Robert J. *lawyer*
Krivkovich, Peter George *advertising executive*
Kroll, Barry Lewis *lawyer*
Krueger, Bonnie Lee *editor, writer*
†Krueger, Herbert William *lawyer*
Kubida, Judith Ann *museum administrator*
†Kubistal, Patricia Bernice *educational consultant*
Kuczmarski, Susan Smith *management consulting company executive*
Kuczwara, Thomas Paul *postal inspector, lawyer*
Kuhlman, Richard Sherwin *lawyer*
Kuhn, Ryan Anthony *information industry investment banker*
Kullberg, Duane Reuben *accounting firm executive*
Kunkle, William Joseph *lawyer*
Kupcinet, Irv *columnist*
Kurtich, John William *architect, film-maker, educator*
†Kushner, Robert F *physician*
†Kuzel, Timothy Michael *hematologist, oncologist, consultant*
Kwembe, Tor Anthony *mathematical educator, researcher*
Lach, Alma Elizabeth *food and cooking writer, consultant*
†Ladd, Jeffrey Raymond *lawyer*
†Lagarde, Christine *lawyer*

Laidlaw, Andrew R. *lawyer*
Lambert, Kirsten Schnoor *public relations executive, writer*
†Lamont, Elizabeth Bernier *physician, educator*
Lamont, Owen Austin *economist*
†Landan, Henry Sinclair *business consultant*
Landes, William M. *law educator*
Landow-Esser, Janine Marise *lawyer*
Landsberg, Jill Warren *lawyer, educator, arbitrator*
Landsberg, Lewis *dean, endocrinologist, medical researcher*
†Landsman, Stephen A. *lawyer*
Lane, Kenneth Edwin *retired advertising agency executive*
†Lane, Ronald Alan *lawyer*
Laner, Richard Warren *lawyer*
Lang, Gordon, Jr., *retired lawyer*
Langman, Craig Bradford *nephrologist*
Lapidus, Dennis *real estate developer*
Lapin, Andrew William *lawyer*
Lara-Valle, Julio *medical educator, physician*
Larson, Allan Louis *political scientist, educator, lay church worker*
Larson, Nancy Celeste *computer systems manager*
Lathon, Sheraine *clergyman*
Latimer, Kenneth Alan *lawyer*
Laumann, Edward Otto *sociology educator*
Lauth, William Brian *emergency physician, internist, educator*
†Lavin, Maud Katherine *writer, art educator*
†Lazar, Ludmila *concert pianist, music educator, pedagogue*
†Leckey, Andrew A. *financial columnist*
Lee, Raphael Carl *plastic surgeon, biomedical engineer*
Leff, Alan Richard *medical educator, researcher*
Lefkow, Michael Francis *lawyer*
Lehman, Dennis Dale *chemistry educator*
Leighton, George Neves *retired federal judge*
Leinenweber, Harry D. *federal judge*
Lelyveld, Steven *pediatric emergency physician*
Lenehan, Michael Daniel *editor, writer*
Lenhardt, Benjamin F., Jr., *investment management executive*
Lerner, Alexander Robert *association executive*
Lerner, Barbara *public policy consultant, researcher, writer*
Levenfeld, Milton Arthur *lawyer*
Leventhal, Bennett Lee *psychiatry and pediatrics educator, administrator*
Levi, John G. *lawyer*
Levin, Arnold Murray *social worker, psychotherapist*
Levin, Charles Edward *lawyer*
Levin, Jack S. *lawyer*
Levine, Donald Nathan *sociologist, educator*
†Levine, Keith F. *marketing executive*
Levinson, Dennis Joel *internist, rheumatologist, educator*
†Levy, David Henry *lawyer*
Levy, Donald Harris *chemistry educator*
Lewis, Charles A. *investment company executive*
Lewis, Evelyn *management consultant*
Lewis, Michael Ray *encyclopedia editor*
†Lewis, Russell Lamar *historian, museum administrator*
Leyhane, Francis John, III, *lawyer*
Liao, Shutsung *biochemist, oncologist*
Lichtor, Terry *neurosurgeon, neuro-oncologist*
†Lidaka, Maris V. *lawyer*
Liebenow, Franklin Eastburn, Jr., *English literature educator*
†Lieberman, Richard Elliot *lawyer*
Liebovich, Samuel David *retired steel executive*
†Lilly, Kristine Marie *soccer player*
Lin, James Chih-I *biomedical and electrical engineer, educator*
Lindberg, Richard Carl *editor, author, historian*
Linden, Henry Robert *chemical engineer, researcher*
†Lindquist, Susan Lee *biology and microbiology educator*
Ling, Kathryn Wrolstad *health association administrator*
Linklater, William Joseph *lawyer*
Lipinski, Ann Marie *newspaper editor*
Lipman, Laurie S. *psychiatrist*
Lippe, Melvin Karl *lawyer*
Lippman, Jessica G. *clinical psychologist, educator*
Lipson, Charles Henry *political scientist, educator*
Lipton, Lois Jean *lawyer*
†Lipton, Richard M. *lawyer*
Litch, C(hristopher) Scott *dental association executive, lawyer*
Litwin, Burton Howard *lawyer*
Liu, Ben-chieh *economist*
†Liu, Derong *engineering educator, electrical/computer engineer*
†Lloyd, Robert Allen *lawyer*
Lochbihler, Frederick Vincent *lawyer*
Lockwood, Frank James *manufacturing company executive*
Lockwood, Gary Lee *lawyer*
Loesch, Katharine Taylor (Mrs. John George Loesch) *communication and theatre educator*
Logan, David Samuel *investment banker*
†Loney, Mary Rose *airport administrator*
Longworth, Richard Cole *journalist*
Looman, James R. *lawyer*
Lorch, Kenneth F. *lawyer*
†Lorentzen, John Carol *lawyer*
Lorenz, Hugo Albert *retired insurance executive, consultant*
Lorenz, Katherine Mary *banker*
Lorie, James Hirsch *business administration educator*
†Lotocky, Innocent Hilarius *bishop*
Lowry, James Hamilton *management consultant*
Lubin, Donald G. *lawyer*
Lucas, Robert Emerson, Jr., *economist, educator*
†Luhrmann, Tanya Marie *anthropology educator, writer*
Lundergan, Barbara Keough *lawyer*

†Luscombe, George A. II *lawyer*
Lutter, Paul Allen *lawyer*
†Lycardi, Joan C. *small business owner, artist*
Lyerla, Bradford Peter *lawyer*
Lynch, John James *lawyer*
Lynch, John Peter *lawyer*
MacCarthy, Terence Francis *lawyer*
Macdonald, Robert Loughlin *neurosurgeon, educator*
MacDougal, Gary Edward *corporate director, foundation trustee*
Mack, Alan Wayne *interior designer*
Mack, Jim *advertising executive*
Mack, John Melvin *lawyer*
†MacMillan, Shannon Ann *soccer player*
Maczulski, Margaret Louise *event marketing professional, meeting manager*
Madansky, Albert *statistics educator*
Madara, James Lee *dean, epitheliologist, pathologist, educator*
Madigan, John William *publishing executive*
†Madigan, Lisa *state attorney general*
Madsen, Dorothy Louise (Meg Madsen) *writer*
Magoon, Patrick M. *healthcare executive*
Maher, David Willard *lawyer*
†Maher, Francesca Marciniak *lawyer, air transportation executive*
Mahowald, Anthony Peter *geneticist, developmental biologist, educator*
Makinen, Marvin William *biophysicist, educator*
Malinowski, Arthur Anthony *lawyer, labor arbitrator*
Malkin, Cary Jay *lawyer*
Malkinson, Frederick David *dermatologist, educator*
Mallory, Robert Mark *controller, finance executive*
†Mancoff, Neal Alan *lawyer*
Mandel, Reid Alan *lawyer*
Mandler, Thomas Yale *lawyer*
Manelli, Donald Dean *screenwriter, film producer*
†Maniotis, Andrew James *cell biologist, researcher*
Manning, Sylvia *English studies educator*
Mansfield, Karen Lee *lawyer*
Manzo, Edward David *patent lawyer*
Marciniak, Christina Maria *physician*
Marcus, Joseph *child psychiatrist*
†Margolin, Stephen M. *lawyer*
Marick, Michael Miron *lawyer*
†Markey, Howard Thomas *retired law educator, former federal judge*
Marshall, Cody *bishop*
Marshall, John David *lawyer*
Martin, Alan Joseph *lawyer*
Martin, Arthur Mead *lawyer*
Martin, Dennis Dale *religious studies educator*
Martin, Gary Joseph *medical educator*
Marwedel, Warren John *lawyer*
Mason, Gregory Wesley, Jr., *secondary education educator*
Mason, Richard J. *lawyer*
†Mason, William *general director of opera company*
Massad, Malek George *surgeon, researcher*
Massura, Eileen Kathleen *family therapist*
Matasar, Ann B. *former dean, business and political science educator*
Mateles, Richard Isaac *biotechnologist*
Matesky, Elisabeth Anne *international solo violinist, educator, composer, arranger*
Matthei, Edward Hodge *architect*
Mattson, Stephen Joseph *lawyer*
†Matushek, Edward J., III, *lawyer*
Maves, Michael Donald *medical association executive*
May, Aviva Rabinowitz *music educator, linguist, musician*
May, J. Peter *mathematics educator*
†Mayer, Beatrice Cummings *civic worker*
Mayer, Frank D., Jr., *lawyer*
Mayer, Raymond Richard *business administration educator*
McCaleb, Malcolm, Jr., *lawyer*
McCallister, Richard Anthony *business consulting company executive*
Mc Carter, John Wilbur, Jr., *museum executive*
Mc Caskey, Raymond F. *insurance company executive*
†McCausland, Thomas James, Jr., *brokerage house executive*
McClintock, Martha K. *biologist, educator*
McClure, James Julius, Jr., *lawyer, former city official*
McCombs, Mark James *lawyer*
McConnell, E. Hoy, II, *advertising/public policy executive*
McCracken, Thomas James, Jr., *lawyer*
McCrohon, Craig *lawyer*
McCue, Judith W. *lawyer*
McCullough, Richard Lawrence *advertising agency executive*
McCurry, Margaret Irene *architect, interior and furniture designer, educator*
McDaniel, Charles-Gene *journalism educator, writer*
McDermott, John H(enry) *lawyer*
McDermott, Mary Ann *nursing educator*
McDermott, Raymond, Jr., *physician*
McDermott, Robert B. *lawyer*
McDonald, Anne Leggett *mathematics educator*
McDonald, Larry William *neuropathologist educator*
McDonald, Theresa Beatrice Pierce (Mrs. Ollie McDonald) *church official, minister*
†McDonald, Thomas Alexander *lawyer*
McDonald, William Brice *educational association administrator*
†McDonnell, David Croft *diversified financial services company executive*
McDonough, John Michael *lawyer*
McDowell, Orlando *secondary education educator*
†McErlean, Charles Flavian, Jr., *lawyer*
†McGahey, John Patrick *lawyer*
McGinn, Bernard John *religious educator*

†McGonegle, Timothy Joseph *lawyer*
McGrail, Jeane Kathryn *artist, educator, poet, curator*
McKay, Neil *banker*
McKee, Keith Earl *manufacturing technology executive*
McKenzie, Robert Ernest *lawyer*
†McLaren, Richard Wellington, Jr., *lawyer*
McLaughlin, T. Mark *lawyer*
McLawhon, Ronald William *pathology educator, biochemist*
McLees, John Alan *lawyer*
†McMahon, Thomas Michael *lawyer*
McManus, James Laughlin *writer, educator*
†McMenamin, John Robert *lawyer*
McMillan, C. Steven *consumer packaged goods company executive*
McNally, Andrew, IV, *publishing executive, director*
McNeill, G. David *psycholinguist, educator*
McPherson, Michael Steven *former academic administrator, economist*
McQuillen, James Francis *electronics executive*
McVisk, William Kilburn *lawyer*
McWhirter, Bruce J. *retired lawyer*
Mecklenburg, Gary Alan *hospital executive*
†Medvin, Harvey Norman *diversified financial services company executive, treasurer*
Mehlman, David Joel *physician, cardiologist, medical educator*
Mehlman, Mark Franklin *lawyer*
Melamed, Leo *global consulting firm executive*
Melton, David Reuben *lawyer*
Meltzer, Bernard David *law educator*
Meltzer, David Owen *internist, educator, economist*
Meltzer, Robert Craig *lawyer, educator*
Meltzer, Sharon Bittenson *English language and humanities educator*
Menendez, Marcelino Eulogio (Marc Menendez) *marketing professional*
Mercer, Ron *professional basketball player*
†Merk, Bradley Robert *orthopedic surgeon*
Merwin, Peter Matthew *secondary school educator, writer*
Metz, Adam S. *real estate executive*
Metz, Charles Edgar *radiology educator*
Metzger, Boyd Ernest *endocrinologist, educator*
Meyer, John Albert *lawyer*
Meyer, Paul Reims, Jr., *orthopedic surgeon*
†Miceli, William Cyril, Sr., *director*
Michaels, Richard Edward *lawyer*
Michalak, Edward Francis *lawyer*
Michod, Charles Louis, Jr., *lawyer*
Migala, Lucyna J. *journalist, arts administrator, radio station executive*
Mikesell, Marvin Wray *geography educator*
Mikva, Abner Joseph *lawyer, retired federal judge*
†Milad, Magdy Peter *physician*
†Milbrett, Tiffeny Carleen *professional soccer player*
Miller, Albert J. *cardiologist, internist*
Miller, Edward Boone *lawyer*
Miller, Heidi G. *diversified financial company executive*
Miller, Irving Franklin *chemical engineering educator, biomedical engineering educator, academic administrator*
Miller, John Leed *lawyer*
Miller, Oscar *economics educator*
Miller, Paul J. *lawyer*
†Miller, Ronald Stuart *lawyer*
Miller, Stephen Ralph *lawyer*
Millichap, Joseph Gordon *neurologist, educator*
†Millichap, Paul Anthony *lawyer*
Millner, Robert B. *lawyer*
Mindes, Gayle Dean *education educator*
Miner, Thomas Hawley *international entrepreneur*
Minichello, Dennis *lawyer*
Minkowycz, W. J. *mechanical engineering educator*
Minneste, Viktor, Jr., *retired electrical company executive*
†Minogue, John P. *academic administrator, priest, educator*
Minow, Josephine Baskin *civic volunteer*
Minow, Newton Norman *lawyer, educator*
Mintzer, David *physics educator*
Mirkin, Bernard Leo *clinical pharmacologist, pediatrician*
Mirza, Leona Lousin *educator*
Mitchell, Lee Mark *communications executive, investment fund manager, lawyer*
†Moen, Ronald S. *medical association administrator*
Moffatt, Joyce Anne *performing arts executive*
†Mohammadian, Abolfazl *civil engineer, educator*
Mokhlesi, Babak *critical care physician*
†Molaro, Robert S *state legislator, lawyer*
Molins, Marcel J. *lawyer*
Mollet, Chris John *lawyer*
Molo, Steven Francis *lawyer*
Monaghan, M. Patricia *educator, writer, poet*
Mondschean, Thomas Smith *economics educator*
†Mone, Peter John *lawyer*
Montgomery, William Adam *lawyer*
Moore, Joseph Arthur *alderman, lawyer*
Moore, Patrick J. *paper company executive*
Moore, Vernon John, Jr., *pediatrician, lawyer, medical consultant*
Moran, James Byron *federal judge*
Moretti, Robert James *psychologist, educator*
Morewitz, Stephen John *behavioral scientist, consultant, educator*
Morisato, Susan Cay *actuary*
Morris, Naomi Carolyn Minner *medical educator, administrator, researcher, consultant*
Morris, Norval *criminologist, educator*
Morrison, Portia Owen *lawyer*
Morris-Rogers, Cheryl-Ann *daycare provider, director, educator*
Morrissey, George Michael *judge*
†Morrow, John E. *lawyer*
†Morrow, Monica *medical educator*

†Schnaper, H. William *pediatrician, educator*
Schneider, Dan W. *lawyer, consultant*
†Schneider, Robert Jerome *lawyer*
Schneider, Wesley Clair *marketing communications company executive*
Schneidman, Barbara Sue *psychiatrist*
Schoonhoven, Ray James *retired lawyer*
Schornack, John James *accountant*
Schoumacher, Bruce Herbert *lawyer*
Schreck, Robert A., Jr., *lawyer*
†Schriver, John T., III, *lawyer*
Schroeder, Douglas Fredrick *architect*
Schubert, William Henry *curriculum studies educator*
Schug, Kenneth Robert *chemistry educator*
Schuh, Anna Marie *human resources professional*
†Schulman, Jerry Allen *lawyer*
Schulman, Sidney *neurologist, educator*
Schulte, David Michael *investment banker*
Schulte, Stephen Charles *lawyer*
Schultz, Paul Neal *electronic publishing executive*
Schulz, Keith Donald *corporate lawyer, writer*
†Schuman, William Paul *lawyer*
Schupp, Anastasia Luka *retired lawyer*
†Schur, Gerald *lawyer*
Schwab, James Charles *urban planner*
†Schwab, Stephen Wayne *lawyer*
Schwan, David Paul *radio personality, radio producer, writer*
Schwartz, Alan Gifford *sport company executive*
Schwartz, Donald Lee *lawyer*
Schwartz, John Norman *human services administrator*
†Schwartz, Stuart Randall *lawyer*
Schwarzkopf, Gloria A. *education educator, psychotherapist*
†Schwoy, Laurie Annette *soccer player*
Sciarra, John J. *physician, educator*
Sclove, Stanley Louis *statistics educator*
Scogland, William Lee *lawyer*
Scommegna, Antonio *physician, educator*
†Scott, Nancy L. *health facility administrator, consultant*
Scott, Stephen Brinsley *theater producer*
Scott, Stuart L. *real estate company executive*
Scribner, Margaret Ellen *educational consultant, consultant*
†Scrimshaw, Susan Crosby *dean*
†Scudder, Theodore Townsend, III, *lawyer*
Scully, John Edward, Jr., *banker*
†Scurry, Briana Collette *soccer player*
Seals, Theodore Hollis *public relations executive*
Seaman, Irving, Jr., *banker*
Sebring, Penny Bender *education educator, researcher*
Sedelmaier, John Josef *filmmaker*
Seebert, Kathleen Anne *international sales and marketing executive*
Seeler, Ruth Andrea *pediatrician, educator*
Seiden, Lewis S. *neuroscientist*
Sen, Ashish Kumar *government administrator, urban planner, educator, statistician*
†Senderowitz, Stephen Jay *lawyer*
Senior, Richard John Lane *textile rental service executive*
†Sennet, Charles Joseph *lawyer*
†Sequeira, Winston *medical educator, researcher*
Serritella, James Anthony *lawyer*
Serritella, William David *lawyer*
Serwer, Alan Michael *lawyer*
Sfikas, Peter Michael *lawyer, educator*
Shafer, Eric Christopher *minister*
Shahidehpour, Mohammad *dean, academic administrator, engineering educator*
†Shaman, Jeffrey M. *law educator*
Shannon, Iris Reed *health consultant*
†Shapiro, Charles Michael *physician, consultant*
Shapiro, Harold David *lawyer, educator*
Shapiro, Nicholas John *real estate executive*
Shapiro, Richard Alan *surgeon*
Shapiro, Stephen Michael *lawyer*
Shapo, Marshall Schambelan *lawyer, educator*
Shaughnessy, Edward Louis *Chinese language educator*
Shaver, Joan Louise Fowler *adult education educator*
†Sheagren, John Newcomb *physician, educator*
Shedlock, James *library director, consultant*
Shen, Virginia Shiang-lan *Spanish and Chinese language educator*
†Sheppard, Berton Scott *lawyer*
†Sherman, Ian Matthew *lawyer*
†Shevell, Steven King *psychology educator*
Shields, Thomas Charles *lawyer*
Shields, Thomas William *surgeon, educator*
Shindler, Donald A. *lawyer*
Shirbroun, Richard Elmer *veterinarian, cattleman*
Shoenberger, Allen Edward *law educator*
Shott, Susan *medical biostatistician, educator*
Shurtz, Steven Park *lawyer*
Siegel, Howard Jerome *lawyer*
Siegler, Mark *internist, educator*
Sigler, Hollis *artist, educator, author*
Sigmon, Joyce Elizabeth *professional society administrator*
Silberman, Alan Harvey *lawyer*
Silesky, Barry T. *writer, educator*
Silets, Harvey Marvin *lawyer*
Sills, Thomas W. *physical science educator*
Silverman, Morton Mayer *psychiatrist, educator*
†Silverstein, Harry *theater director, music educator*
†Silverstein, Jonathan Charles *surgeon, researcher*
Simon, Bernece Kern *social work educator*
Simon, John Bern *lawyer*
Simon, Mordecai *religious association administrator, clergyman*
Simon, Seymour *lawyer, former state supreme court justice*
Simons, Helen *school psychologist, psychotherapist, educator*
Simovic, Laszlo *architect*
Simpson, Dick Weldon *political science educator*
Singer, Deborah Louise *medical products company executive*
Singer, Emel *staffing industry executive*
†Singleton, Gregory Holmes *historian, educator*
Sinha, Raj P. *education educator, researcher*
Sippey, Roger Boyd *corporate executive*
Siske, Roger Charles *lawyer*
Sive, Rebecca Anne *public affairs company executive*
†Sjogren, Bengt B *corporate financial executive*
Skala, Gary Dennis *management consultant*
Skiba, Aurelia Ellen *private school educator*
†Skinner, Thomas V. *government agency administrator*
Sklarsky, Charles B. *lawyer*
Skoien, Gary *real estate company executive*
Skolnick, Sherman Herbert *media host/producer, researcher, court reformer*
Sladen, Bernard Jacob *psychologist*
Slansky, Jerry William *investment company executive*
Slavin, Konstantin Vladimirovich *neurosurgeon*
†Sljivic-Simsic, Biljana B. *Slavic and Baltic languages educator*
Sloan, James Park *novelist, biographer, educator*
†Slutzky, Lorence Harley *lawyer*
Smalley, Penny Judith *healthcare technology consultant*
Smart, Allen Rich, II, *lawyer*
†Smedinghoff, Thomas J. *lawyer*
Smith, Adrian Devaun *architect*
Smith, Arthur B., Jr., *lawyer*
Smith, Craig Malcolm *architect, consultant*
†Smith, Daniel Scott *history educator, historian*
Smith, Earl Charles *nephrologist, educator*
Smith, Gordon Howell *lawyer*
Smith, Harry Buchanan, Jr., *graphic designer, painter, photographer, writer*
†Smith, Herman Eugene *retired lawyer*
Smith, James Barry *lawyer*
Smith, Kent Ernest *non-profit organization executive*
Smith, Marcia Jean *accountant, tax specialist, financial consultant*
Smith, Raymond Thomas *anthropology educator*
Smith, Ronald Charles *lawyer, educator*
Smith, Sam *columnist, author*
Smith, Scott Clybourn *media company executive*
Smith, Stan Vladimir *economist, financial service company executive*
Smith, Tefft Weldon *lawyer*
Smith, Terry Lynn *information scientist*
Snider, Lawrence K. *lawyer*
Snodgrass, Klyne Ryland *seminary educator*
Snyder, Edward Adams *dean, economics educator*
Snyder, Graydon F. *religion educator*
†Snyderman, Perry James *lawyer*
†Sobrero, Kathryn Michele *soccer player*
Sochen, June *history educator*
Socol, Michael Lee *obstetrician, gynecologist, educator*
Solaro, Ross John *physiologist, biophysicist*
Solovy, Jerold Sherwin *lawyer*
Sonderby, Susan Pierson *federal judge*
Sorensen, Leif Boge *physician, retired educator*
Sorgel, Sylvia *financial services executive*
Sosa, Samuel (Sammy Sosa) *professional baseball player*
Spain, Richard Colby *lawyer*
Sparberg, Marshall Stuart *gastroenterologist, educator*
Spargo, Benjamin H. *educator, renal pathologist*
Spearman, David Leroy *elementary education educator, administrator*
Spector, David M. *lawyer*
Spellmire, George W. *lawyer*
Spergel, Irving Abraham *social worker, researcher*
Sproger, Charles Edmund *retired lawyer*
Sprowl, Charles Riggs *lawyer*
Squires, John Henry *judge*
Stack, Paul Francis *lawyer*
Stack, Stephen S. *manufacturing company executive*
†Staley, Charles Ralls *lawyer*
Standberry, Herman Lee *school system administrator, educational consultant*
†Stanhaus, James Steven *lawyer*
†Stark, Henry *technology educator*
Starkman, Gary Lee *lawyer*
†Stassen, John Henry *lawyer*
†Stavins, Richard Lee *lawyer*
Stead, James Joseph, Jr., *securities company executive*
Stearns, Neele Edward, Jr., *investment executive*
Stein, Howard *economics educator*
Steinberg, Morton M. *lawyer*
Steiner, Donald Frederick *biochemist, physician, educator*
Steinfeld, Manfred *furniture manufacturing executive*
Steinman, Joan Ellen *law educator*
Stepke, Russ *investment banker, lawyer*
Stern, Carl William, Jr., *management consultant*
Stern, Richard Gustave *writer, educator*
Sternstein, Allan J. *lawyer*
Stevenson, Adlai Ewing, III, *lawyer, former senator*
†Stiegel, Michael A. *lawyer*
Stigler, Stephen Mack *statistician, educator*
Stillman, Nina Gidden *lawyer*
†Stirling, D. Leslie *corporate financial executive*
Stirling, James Paulman *investment banker*
Stith, Mary Beth (Rae) *marketing professional for graphic design*
Stocking, George Ward, Jr., *anthropology educator*
Stoller, Patricia Sypher *structural engineer, engineering executive*
Stolzenberg, Ross Mark *sociology educator*
†Stone, Alan *container company executive*
Stone, Geoffrey Richard *law educator, lawyer*
Stone, James Howard *management consultant*
†Stonehouse, Kimber J. *music educator, artist*
Storb, Ursula Beate *molecular genetics and cell biology educator*
Stotler, Edith Ann *retired grain company executive, financial planner*
†Stovall, Patricia *elementary school educator, writer*
Stover, Leon (Eugene Stover) *anthropology educator, writer, critic*
Straus, Francis Howe *pathologist, educator*
Straus, Lorna Puttkammer *biology educator*
†Streff, William Albert, Jr., *lawyer*
Strobeck, Charles LeRoy *real estate executive*
†Strobel, Pamela B. *energy executive*
†Strom, Michael A. *lawyer*
Strong, Dorothy Swearengen *educational administrator*
Stroscio, Michael Anthony *physicist, educator*
Strubel, Ella Doyle *advertising and public relations executive*
Struggles, John Edward *management consultant*
†Sulkin, Howard Allen *college president*
Sullivan, Barry *lawyer*
Sullivan, Bernard James *accountant*
Sullivan, Marcia Waite *lawyer*
Sullivan, Peggy (Peggy Anne Sullivan) *librarian, consultant*
Sullivan, Thomas Patrick *lawyer*
†Sumners, Pamela Lauren *lawyer*
Sussman, Arthur Melvin *law educator, foundation administrator*
Swanson, Don Richard *university dean*
Sweeney, James Raymond *lawyer*
Sweeney, John Adrian *clinical psychologist*
Swerdlow, Martin Abraham *physician, pathologist, educator*
Swibel, Steven Warren *lawyer*
Swift, Edward Foster, III, *investment banker*
Sykes, Alan O'Neil *lawyer, educator*
Szarek, Gene *religious studies educator*
†Szerlag, Chester Theodore *oncologist, consultant, academic administrator*
Tabin, Julius *patent lawyer, physicist*
Tachauer, Allan Dinu *internist*
Talbot, Pamela *public relations executive*
†Tallchief, Maria *ballerina*
Tangora, Martin Charles *mathematician, educator*
Tanner, Helen Hornbeck *historian, consultant*
†Tápanes-Inojosa, Adriana *language educator*
Taraszkiewicz, Waldemar *physician*
Tarnow, Fredric Herman *science educator*
Tarun, Robert Walter *lawyer*
Tatar, Arnold Marshall *internal medicine physician, educator*
†Tatom, John Anthony *economist*
Taub, Richard Paul *social sciences educator*
†Taylor, Collette *public relations executive*
Telfer, Margaret Clare *internist, hematologist, oncologist*
Telser, Lester Greenspan *educator, economist*
Telser, Sylvia Ruth *retired family life educator, social worker*
Tenenbaum, J. Samuel *lawyer*
†Terkel, Studs (Louis Terkel) *writer, interviewer*
†Termondt, M. James *foundation administrator*
Tessing, Louise Scire *graphic designer*
Tetzlaff, Theodore R. *lawyer*
Thaden, Edward Carl *history educator*
Thall, Robert *photographer, educator*
Theis, William Harold *lawyer, educator*
Theobald, Edward Robert *lawyer*
Theobald, Thomas Charles *banker*
Thies, Richard Brian *lawyer*
Thomas, Frank Edward *professional baseball player*
Thomas, Frederick Bradley *lawyer*
Thomas, Joseph Erumappettical *psychologist*
Thomas, Leona Marlene *health information educator*
Thomas, Richard Lee *banker*
Thomas, Stephen Paul *lawyer*
†Thompson, David F. *lawyer*
Thompson, James Robert, Jr., *lawyer, former governor*
Thompson, Jayne Carr *public relations and communications executive, lawyer*
†Thompson, John H. *social science executive*
Thompson, Kenneth Roy *management educator*
†Thompson, Michael *lawyer*
Thompson, Steven *zoological park administrator*
Thomson, George Ronald *lawyer, educator*
†Thurner, Arthur W. *historian, educator*
Tigerman, Stanley *architect, educator*
Tilton, Glenn F. *air transportation executive*
Tinaglia, Michael Lee *lawyer*
†Tinerella, Vincent P. *librarian, protective services official*
Tobin, Craig Daniel *lawyer*
Tobin, Thomas F. *lawyer*
Tomaino, Joseph Carmine *former retail executive, former postal inspector*
Tomar, Russell Herman *pathologist, educator, researcher*
†Toohey, James Kevin *lawyer*
Toriani, Denise Maria *legal administrator*
Totlis, Gust John *retired title insurance company executive*
Towers, Kenneth Dale *journalism educator*
†Towson, Thomas D. *securities trader*
Trafimow, Jordan Herman *orthopedist*
Trapp, James McCreery *lawyer*
Travis, Dempsey Jerome *author, real estate executive and developer*
Trenary, Michael *chemist, educator*
†Treston, Sherry S. *lawyer*
Trienens, Howard Joseph *lawyer*
Trierweiler, Robert Louis *rehabilitation counselor*
Tripp, Marian Barlow Loofe *retired public relations company executive*
Trost, Eileen Bannon *lawyer*
Trumpener, Katie *literature educator*
Truran, James Wellington, Jr., *astrophysicist, educator*
Tryban, Esther Elizabeth *lawyer*
Tuchman, Nancy Crandall *biology educator, aquatic ecology researcher*
†Tukes, Jamu Wayne *educator*
Tuman, Kenneth James *anesthesiologist, educator*
Turner, Bernice Cooper *social worker*
Turner, Michael Stanley *astrophysics educator*
†Turow, Scott F. *lawyer, writer*
Tyner, Howard A. *publishing executive, newspaper editor, journalist*
†Tyree, James C. *insurance company executive*
Tyson, Kirk W. M. *management consultant*
Tyson, Terri Lynn *television programming producer, consultant*
Underwood, Robert Leigh *venture capitalist*
Ungaretti, Richard Anthony *lawyer*
Upshaw, Harry Stephan *psychology educator*
†Vaisrub, Naomi Miriam Rose *statistician*
Valentine, Valerie *volunteer*
Valerio, Joseph Mastro *architectural firm executive, educator*
Valle, Rafael F. *obstetrician-gynecologist*
Valvassori, Galdino E. *physician*
Vandame, Jean-Marie Richard *management consultant*
Van Demark, Ruth Elaine *lawyer*
Van Den Hende, Fred J(oseph) *human resources executive*
VanderBeke, Patricia K. *architect*
Vander Wilt, Carl Eugene *banker*
Van Pelt, Robert Irving *firefighter*
Van Tine, Matthew Eric *lawyer*
Varchetta, Felix R. *advertising executive*
Varwig, David Lee *merchant banker*
†Vaughn, Michael *education educator*
Vazquez, Richard Michael *surgeon*
Velisaris, Chris Nicholas *corporate financial executive*
Venson, Lily Pagratis *journalist, lecturer*
Ventrelli, Anita Marie *lawyer*
†Venturini, Tisha Lea *professional soccer player*
Verschoor, Curtis Carl *business educator, consultant*
Vertreace-Doody, Martha Modena *English educator, poet*
†Veverka, Donald John *lawyer*
Vigen, Kathryn L. Voss *nursing administrator, educator*
†Vincent, Jim *performing company executive*
Vinci, John Nicholas *architect, educator*
Virasch, Rij Lee *surgeon*
Vitale, Gerald Lee *financial services executive*
Vogelzang, Jeanne Marie *professional association executive, lawyer*
Vojcanin, Sava Alexander *lawyer*
Von Mandel, Michael Jacques *lawyer*
von Rhein, John Richard *music critic, editor*
Von Roenn, Kelvin Alexander *neurosurgeon*
Vrablik, Edward Robert *import/export company executive*
Vree, Roger Allen *lawyer*
Vyn, Kathleen A. *small business owner*
Wade, Edwin Lee *author, lawyer*
Wade, Nigel *former editor in chief*
Wagner, Rose Mary *librarian*
Wahlen, Edwin Alfred *lawyer*
Walberg, Herbert John *psychologist, educator, consultant*
Wallingford, Anne *writer, editor, project developer*
†Walsh, Matthew M. *investment company executive*
Walter, Charles Sebastian *Roman Catholic priest*
Walton, Carmelita Noreen *retired nurse*
†Walton, Robert Lee, Jr., *plastic surgeon*
Wander, Herbert Stanton *lawyer*
Wang, Albert James *violinist, educator*
Wang, Yaoyu *electrical engineer*
Wanke, Ronald Lee *lawyer*
Wasan, Darsh Tilakchand *university official, chemical engineer educator*
Wasiolek, Edward *literary critic, language and literature educator*
Wastawy, Sohair F. *library dean, consultant*
Waxler, Beverly Jean *anesthesiologist, physician*
Wayman, David Anthony *state agency administrator*
Weaver, Donna Rae *company executive*
Weaver, Timothy Allan *lawyer*
Weber, Hanno *architect*
Webster, David Macpherson *lawyer*
Webster, James Randolph, Jr., *physician*
Weese, Benjamin Horace *architect*
†Wehrmacher, William Henry *physiology educator, clinical cardiologist*
†Weigel, Thomas J. *pediatrician, cardiologist*
†Weigle, Maurice S. *lawyer*
Weil, Roman Lee *accounting educator*
Weinberg, David B. *investor*
Weinberg, Lila Shaffer *writer, editor*
Weiner, Gerald Arne *stockbroker*
Weinkopf, Friedrich J. *lawyer*
Weintraub, Joseph Barton *publishing executive*
Weissman, Michael Lewis *lawyer*
Weitzman, Robert Harold *investment company executive*
Weldon-Linne, C. Michael *pathologist, microbiologist*
Weldon-Linne, Madeleine Marie *lawyer*
Wellington, Robert Hall *manufacturing company executive*
Westcott, Robert Frederick *consultant*
Wexler, Richard Lewis *lawyer*
†Whalen, Sarah Eve *soccer player*
Whalen, Wayne W. *lawyer*
Wham, David Buffington *secondary school educator*
Whelan, Winifred Olwyn *theology studies educator*
White, Linda Diane *lawyer*
Whitesides, Lawson Ewing, Jr., *investment management executive*
Whitington, Peter Frank *pediatrics educator, pediatric hepatologist*
Wied, George Ludwig *physician*
Wier, Patricia Ann *publishing executive, consultant*
Wiggins, Charles Henry, Jr., *lawyer*
Wilbur, Andrew Clayton *radiologist, educator*
Wilcox, Mark Dean *lawyer*

Wildman, Max Edward *lawyer, director*
Will, Jon Nicholson *small business owner, financial consultant*
Wille, Lois Jean *retired newspaper editor*
Williams, Ann Claire *federal judge*
Williams, Edward Joseph *banker*
Williams, Mark H. *marketing communications executive*
Williams, Philip Copelain *obstetrician, gynecologist*
Williams, Richard Lucas, III, *electronics company executive, lawyer*
Williamson, Thomas Michael *pastor, civil servant*
Willoughby, William Franklin, II, *physician, researcher*
Wilmouth, Robert K. *commodities executive*
Wilson, Clarence Sylvester, Jr., *lawyer, educator*
†Wilson, Cleo Francine *entertainment company executive*
Wilson, Gahan *cartoonist, author*
†Wilson, George Edward *religious organization administrator, minister*
Wilson, Roger Goodwin *lawyer*
Winfrey, Oprah *television talk show host, actress, producer*
†Winninghoff, Albert C. M. *advertising company executive*
Winston, Roland *physicist, educator*
Winter, Jane *medical educator*
Wirszup, Izaak *mathematician, educator*
Wirtz, William Wadsworth *real estate executive, professional sports team executive*
Wise, William Jerrard *lawyer*
Wissler, Robert William *physician, cardiovascular pathologist, educator*
Witcoff, Sheldon William *lawyer*
Witrod, Sister Mary Rosalita *nursing home administrator*
Witt, Alan Michael *lawyer, accountant*
Witt, Thomas Roy *surgeon*
†Wittenberg, Jon Albert *accountant*
Wolf, Charles Benno *lawyer*
Wolf, Linda S. *advertising executive*
Wolfe, Sheila A. *journalist*
Wong, Thomas Tang Yum *engineering educator*
Wood, James Nowell *museum director and executive*
Wood Prince, William Norman *investments and real estate professional*
Woods, Robert Archer *investment counsel*
Wooldridge, Patrice Marie *marketing professional, martial arts and meditation educator*
Workman, Robert Peter *artist, cartoonist*
Wright, Helen Kennedy *retired professional association administrator, publisher, editor, librarian*
Wright, Judith Margaret *law librarian, educator, dean*
Wright, Richard W. *lawyer, law educator*
Wyant, Carol Shumaker *not for profit management consultant*
†Wyslotsky, Ihor *engineering company executive*
Wyszynski, Richard Chester *musician, writer, conductor, educator*
Yale, Seymour Hershel *dental radiologist, educator, university dean, gerontologist*
Yamakawa, Allan Hitoshi *academic administrator*
†Yanoff, Jerome C. *writer, educator*
Yao, Tito Go *pediatrician*
†Yau, Stephen Shing-Toung *mathematician, educator*
Yeldandi, Veerainder Antiah *engineer, consultant*
Yogev, Ram *pediatrician, educator*
York, Donald Gilbert *astronomy educator, researcher*
Yoshida, Hiroyuki *mathematician, computer scientist, educator, medical science educator*
Yost, Emery Joseph *music industry producer, educator*
†Youm, Yoosik *education educator*
Young, Lauren Sue Jones *education educator*
Young, Nancy Melinda *otolaryngologist*
Young, Scott Thomas *business management educator*
Youngman, Owen Ralph *newspaper executive*
Yu, Anthony C. *religion and literature educator*
Zabel, Sheldon Alter *lawyer, law educator*
Zagar, Robert John *psychologist, researcher*
Zajicek, Jeronym *music educator*
Zander Schrage, Maryanne Elizabeth *physician assistant*
Zeid, Paula Klein *metals broker*
Zeid, Philip L. *metal recycling executive*
Zelepukin, Valeri *hockey player*
Zellner, Arnold *economics and statistics educator*
Zemm, Sandra Phyllis *lawyer*
Zenner, Sheldon Toby *lawyer*
Zgoda, Lawrence *artist*
Zimmerman, Martin E. *financial executive*
Zimmermann, Polly Gerber *emergency nurse*
†Zolno, Mark S. *lawyer*
Zonka, Constance Zipprodt *public relations executive, marketing professional*
Zorko, Mark A. *financial executive*
Zsigmond, Elemer Kalman *anesthesiologist*
Zucaro, Aldo Charles *insurance company executive*

Chicago Heights
Cifelli, John Louis *lawyer*
Croarkin, Donald J. *librarian*
†Kavis, George *engineer, photographer*
†Reed, Scott C. *music educator, writer*

Cicero
Van Cura, Joyce Bennett *librarian*

Clarendon Hills
Moritz, Donald Brooks *mechanical engineer, consultant*

Coal City
Major, Mary Jo *dance school artistic director*
†O'Brien, Mary Kathleen *state representative, lawyer*

Collinsville
Barnum, Mel Bloyce *company executive*
Freeman, David Ralph *lawyer*
†Hoffman, Jay C. *state legislator*
†Sabbert, Anne Ward *vision therapist, consultant*
†Tognarelli, Richard Lee *lawyer*

Country Club Hills
McClelland, Helen *music educator*
Scherer, George Robert *secondary education educator*

Crestwood
Cowie, Norman Edwin *credit manager*
†Rita, Robert *state representative*

Crete
†Cosme, Luke George *retired structural engineer*
Langer, Steven *human resources management consultant and industrial psychologist*
†Teykl, James Stephen *lawyer*

Crystal Lake
Althoff, J(ames) L. *construction company executive*
Anderson, Lyle Arthur *retired manufacturing company executive*
Bishop, James Francis *lawyer*
†Booth, David Layton *retired chemicals executive*
Chamberlain, Charles James *railroad labor union executive*
Christensen, Kenneth Ashley *composer, tenor, music educator*
Dabkowski, John *electrical engineering executive*
Davidson, Shirley Jean *elementary and secondary educator*
Dy, Deana Lim *allergist*
Franz, William Mansur *lawyer*
Halperin, Richard George *information technology executive*
Keller, William Francis *publishing consultant*
Salvesen, B. Forbes *artist*
Shank, William O. *lawyer*
Thoms, Jeannine Aumond *lawyer*

Danville
Craig, Hurshel Eugene *agronomist*
Garman, Rita B. *judge*
†Hubbard, Fred Leonhardt *lawyer*
Konsis, Kenneth Frank *forester, educator*
Prabhudesai, Mukund M. *pathology educator, laboratory director, researcher, administrator*
†Young, William Allen *lawyer*

Darien
Friedrich, Charles William *corporate executive*
Gardner, Howard Garry *pediatrician, educator*
Hanson, Martin Philip *mechanical engineer, farmer*
Klassek, Christine Paulette *behavioral scientist*
Kulkarni, Bidy *reproductive endocrinologist, biomedical researcher, consultant*
Russell, John Fintan *theology educator, editor*

DeKalb
†Bentley, John R. *language educator*
†Clymer, Kenton James *history educator*
Davidson, Kenneth Lawrence *lawyer, educator*
†Ewell, John Albert, III, *mathematician, educator*
†Frisch, Morton Jerome *political scientist, educator*
†Goldenberg, William Bruce *music educator, musician*
†Luo, Wei *social sciences educator*
†Rode, Denise Lynn *education educator, director*
†Shimizu, Hidetada *psychologist, educator*
†Slotsve, George Aaron *economist, educator, consultant*
Stahl, Norman A. *educator*

Decatur
Andreas, G(lenn) Allen, Jr., *agricultural company executive*
Blake, William Henry *credit and public relations consultant*
Borei, Karin Elisabet *librarian*
Bradshaw, Billy Dean *retired retail executive*
Braun, William Joseph *life insurance underwriter*
Decker, Charles Richard *investment executive*
Dunn, John Francis *lawyer, state representative*
Erlanson, Deborah McFarlin *state program administrator*
Garman, Stephen Louis *city manager*
Graf, Karl Rockwell *nuclear engineer*
Koucky, John Richard *metallurgical engineer, manufacturing executive*
Litchfield, Jean Anne *nurse*
Madding, Claudia *agricultural products executive*
†Mittal, Sushil *religious studies educator*
†Munoz, Joseph Mark *education educator, consultant*
†Rinchiuso, Diana Lynn *academic administrator*
Schmalz, Douglas J. *agricultural company executive*
Smith, David James *corporate lawyer*
Staley, Henry Mueller *manufacturing company executive*
Womeldorff, Porter John *utilities executive*

Deer Park
Buchanan, Richard Kent *electronics company executive*
Vanderpoel, James Robert *lawyer*

Deerfield
Bagley, Thomas Steven *private equity investor*
Becker, Gerald Arthur *publisher*
Bernauer, David W. *retail company executive*
Birmingham, William Joseph *lawyer*
Boyd, Joseph Don *financial services executive*
Dawson, Suzanne Stockus *lawyer*
Eastham, Dennis Michael *advertising executive*
Fry, Roy H(enry) *librarian, educator*
Gater, Chris *advertising executive*
†Gillette, Deborah Jean *music educator*
Graham, William B. *pharmaceutical company executive*
Guttman, Arnold R. *chemist, educator*
Halpin, Mary Elizabeth *psychologist*
Heiman, Marvin Stewart *finance company executive*
Howell, George Bedell *equity investing and managing executive*
Huff, Gayle Compton *advertising and marketing executive*
†Jordan, John W., II, *holding company executive*
†Kaplan, Alan Michael *lawyer*
Kraemer, Harry M. Jansen, Jr., *medical products executive*
†Lane, William Edward *lawyer, inventor*
Larsen, David Leonard *retired religion educator*
Lifschultz, Phillip *financial and tax consultant, accountant, lawyer*
†Lunde, Jonathan M. *religious studies educator*
†Marsh, Miles L. *paper company executive*
†Mason, Earl Leonard *retired food products executive*
Meyer, Mara Ellice *special education consultant, principal*
†Oettinger, Julian Alan *lawyer, pharmacy company executive*
Priest, Robert J. *intercultural educator*
Saida, Toyoyasu *chemical and biochemical engineer*
Sanner, John Harper *retired pharmacologist*
Scheiber, Stephen Carl *psychiatrist*
Schnabel, Eckhard Johannes *theologian, educator*
Scott, Theodore R. *lawyer*
Serwy, Robert Anthony *accountant*
Strubel, Richard Perry *company executive*
Vollen, Robert Jay *lawyer*
Zywicki, Robert Albert *electrical distribution company executive*

Dekalb
Azad, Abul Kashem Mohammod *engineer*
Baker, William *British literature educator*
Banovetz, James M. *public administration educator, consultant*
†Bickner, Bruce *food products executive*
Bowers, Jerome David, II, *history educator, consultant*
Bukonda, Ngoyi K. Zacharie *health care management educator*
Byrum, Linda Kluber *artist*
Folgate, Cynthia A. *social services administrator*
Hanna, Nessim *marketing educator*
Healey, Robert William *school system administrator*
James, Marilyn Shaw *secondary education educator, social service worker*
Kimball, Clyde William *physicist, educator*
King, Kenneth Paul *science educator*
Kong, Lingju *mathematician, educator*
Merritt, Helen Henry *retired art educator, ceramic sculptor, art historian*
Monat, William Robert *university official*
†Plue, Cynthia *education educator*
Reddy, Krishna P. *pathologist, laboratory director*
Rembusch, Joseph John *psychologist, management consulting company executive*
Rossing, Thomas D. *physics educator*
Schneider, Daniel Max *law educator*
†Self, Robert Thomas *humanities educator*
Skeels, Jack William *economics educator, consultant*
Sons, Linda Ruth *mathematician, educator*
Stoia, Dennis Vasile *industrial management educator*
Tió, Adrian Ricardo *artist, art educator*
Troyer, Alvah Forrest *agriculture executive, plant breeder*
Tucker, Watson Billopp *lawyer*
†Vande Creek, Drew Evan *historian, educator*
Vary, Patricia Susan *biologist, educator, retired geneticist*
Witmer, John Harper, Jr., *lawyer*
Wolfgram, Kenneth Charles *agricultural engineer*
Zar, Jerrold H(oward) *biologist, statistician*

Des Plaines
Banach, Art John *graphic artist*
Brodl, Raymond Frank *lawyer, former lumber company executive*
Carroll, Barry Joseph *manufacturing and real estate executive*
Clapper, Marie Anne *magazine publisher*
Coburn, James LeRoy *educational administrator*
Cronin, Kathleen Anne *executive search consultant*
Decker, William Alexander *editor*
†Frank, James S. *automotive executive*
†Gahan, Brian C *petroleum engineer, researcher*
†Galperin, Leonid Boris *petroleum engineer, chemical engineer, researcher*
†Gochnauer, Richard Wallis *consumer products company executive*
Henrikson, Arthur Allen *political cartoonist, educator*
Henrikson, Lois Elizabeth *photojournalist*
Koford, Stuart Keith *electronics executive*
Koller, Marita Ann *accountant*
Kotelman, Laura Mary *lawyer*
Lyu, Seung Won *metallurgical engineer, environmental scientist*
Miraglio, Angela Maria *dietitian*
Pannke, Peggy *long term care insurance agency executive*
Quellmalz, Frederick *foundation executive, editor*
Quintanilla, Antonio Paulet *retired physician, educator*
†Santisteban, Joseph Henry *personnel director*
Womack, Doug C. *labor union representative*

Dixon
†Behrendt, Richard Louis *academic administrator*
Hertel, William John *music educator*
Huber, Marianne Jeanne *art dealer, appraiser*

Downers Grove
Beres, Michael John *plant engineer*
Bielefeldt, Catherine C. *sales executive*
Clement, Paul Platts, Jr., *performance technologist, educator*
Feeney, Don Joseph, Jr., *psychologist*
†Feinstein, Robert Norman *retired biochemist*
Hasen-Sinz, Susan Katherine *state agency administrator, actress*
Jacklin, William Thomas *retired county official, educator*
Kuppuswami, Narmadha *physician, educator*
LaRocca, Patricia Darlene McAleer *middle school mathematics educator*
†Mason, Peter Ian *lawyer*
McGarr, Frank James *retired federal judge, dispute resolution consultant*
†Myers, Daniel N. *lawyer, association executive*
Nichols, Karen *academic administrator*
Punt, Leonard Cornelis *educational services company executive*
†Purcell, Joann *secondary school educator*
Saricks, Joyce Goering *librarian*
Shen, Sin-Yan *physicist, conductor, acoustics specialist, music director*
Siedlecki, Nancy Therese *lawyer, funeral director*
Smith, James C. *entrepreneur*
Soder-Alderfer, Kay Christie *counseling administrator*
†Soenen, Michael J. *flower company executive*
Thomas, Daniel J. *health services executive*
Ward, Jonathan P. *service company executive*

Dundee
Ghrist, John Russell *audio/visual technician*
Ulakovich, Ronald Stephen *real estate developer*
Weck, Kristin Willa *bank executive*

Dunlap
Reinsma, Harold Lawrence *design consultant, engineer*
St John, Ronald *retired strategic planning professional, writer, educator*

Dupo
Gallamore, Betty Lou *nurse*

East Alton
Boger, Gena Cecile *school psychologist*
Clark, Mark Jeffrey *paralegal, researcher*
†Davis, Steve *state legislator*
†Delaney, John Martin, Jr., *lawyer*

East Dundee
Simons, Gail S. *artist, educator, librarian*

East Moline
Burns, John Richard *chiropractor, educator*
†Jacobs, Denny *state legislator*
Polios, Nancy Louise *secondary school educator*
Silliman, Richard George *retired lawyer, retired farm machinery company executive*

East Peoria
†Chapman, Edgar Leon *literature educator*
Curtright, Toby Arthur *music educator*

East Saint Louis
†Clayborne, James F., Jr., *state legislator*
†Dunham, Katherine *choreographer, dancer, anthropologist*
†Harrison, Patricia Ann *educational association administrator*
Wright, Katie Harper *educational administrator, journalist*
†Younge, Wyvetter Hoover *state legislator*

Edwardsville
Adkerson, Donya Lynn *clinical counselor*
Browne, Dallas *anthropology educator*
†Butki, Brian David *psychologist, educator*
Carlson, Jon Gordon *lawyer*
Crowder, Barbara Lynn *judge*
Dietrich, Suzanne Claire *instructional designer, communications consultant*
Ferguson, Eva Dreikurs *psychologist, educator, researcher, author*
Gorman, James Edward *lawyer*
†Gu, Keqin *mechanical engineering educator*
Hampton, Phillip Jewel *artist, educator*
Hunsaker, Richard Kendall *lawyer*
Lin, Steven An-Yhi *economics educator, consultant*
Malone, Robert Roy *artist, art educator*
May, Mary Louise *elementary education educator*
Morreale, Patricia Anderson *computer scientist, educator*
Rikli, Donald Carl *lawyer*
†Sachtleben, Holly Rae *director*
†Schultz, Norbert J. *retired music educator*
†Schum, Randolph Edgar *lawyer*
Svoboda, Donna Lee *neonatal nurse*
†Ware, Robert Bruce *philosopher, educator*
Wentz, Charles Alvin, Jr., *environmentalist, chemical engineer*

Effingham
Bonutti, Boris Paul *medical company executive*
Bower, Glen Landis *lawyer*
†Hartke, Charles A. *state legislator*
Heth, Diana Sue *therapist*
Kabbes, Douglas John *physician*
Kessler, Lynne Marie *secondary education educator*
Pickett, Steven Harold

Elburn
Hansen, H. Jack *management consultant*
Willey, James Lee *dentist*

Elgin
†Akemann, David R. *lawyer*
Beyer, Karen Haynes *social worker*
Carbary, Jonathan Leigh *lawyer*
Dodohara, Jean Noton *music educator*
Duffy, John Lewis *retired Latin, English and reading educator*
Freeman, Corwin Stuart, Jr., *financial planner, investment advisor, consultant*
Jakle, Kenneth Richard *broadcasting executive*
†Juergensmeyer, John Eli *lawyer*
Kelly, Matthew Edward *association executive, retired*
Mason, Stephen Olin *nonprofit association administrator*
Moltz, Martin Paul *lawyer*
†Roberts, Elaine J. *academic administrator*
Roeser, Ronald O. *lawyer, consultant*
Rogers, Carleton Carson, Jr., *trade show and convention executive*
Turnquist, Jerry L. *teacher, journalist*
Zack, Daniel Gerard *library director*

Elk Grove Village
Bandel, David Brian *accountant*
Couto, James Robert *medical association director*
Edmiston, Cheryl Lee *educator, clergywoman*
Edwards, E. Stephen *medical association administrator*
†Field, Larry *paper company executive*
Herrerias, Carla Trevette *epidemiologist, health policy analyst*
Jan, Chwu-Ching Hwang *environmental chemistry consultant*
Meyer, Raymond Joseph *former college basketball coach*
Moser, Richard Peter *neurosurgeon*
Nadig, Gerald George *manufacturing executive*
Roberts, Verna Dean *music educator*
Stein, David Timothy *minister*
Teesdale, Randall Lee *consumer products company executive*
†Yeates, Donovan B. *education educator, researcher*

Elmhurst
†Bahariev, Dimitar B. *plant pathologist*
Banich, Francis Edward *surgeon*
Begando, Joseph Sheridan *retired university chancellor, educator*
Betinis, Emanuel James *physics and mathematics educator*
†Biggins, Robert A. *state legislator*
Blain, Charlotte Marie *internist, educator*
Burton, Darrell Irvin *engineering executive*
Choyke, Phyllis May Ford (Mrs. Arthur Davis Choyke Jr.) *management executive, editor, poet*
†Cronin, Dan *state legislator*
†Duchossois, Craig *manufacturing executive, heavy*
†Duchossois, Richard Louis *manufacturing executive, racetrack executive*
Eck, Bernard John *engineer*
Fry, Evelyn Leona *clinical social worker*
Hillman, Carole Dorothy *education educator, educator*
Parker, James John *engineering and marketing manager*
Schultz, Evelyn Ecale *artist*
Simmons, Bonnie Anderson *management information systems educator, accountant*
Weber, John Pitman *artist, educator*
Webster, Douglas Peter *emergency physician*

Elmwood Park
Spina, Anthony Ferdinand *lawyer*

Eureka
†Harrod, Daniel Mark *lawyer*
Hearne, George Archer *academic administrator*
†McCoy, Virginia Ruth *librarian*

Evanston
Abnee, A. Victor *trade association executive*
†Abrahamson, David Stephen Rodler *journalism educator, writer, management consultant*
Achenbach, Jan Drewes *engineering educator, scientist*
Allred, Albert Louis *chemistry educator*
Aronson, Judith *clinical social worker*
Arrington, Michael Browne *foundation administrator*
Atkin, Lawrence Ronald *computer software engineer*
Bazant, Zdenek Pavel *structural and materials engineering educator, scientist, consultant*
Bellow, Alexandra *mathematician, educator*
Belytschko, Ted *civil and mechanical engineering educator*
Bienen, Henry Samuel *political science educator, university executive*
Birge, John Roberts *university administrator*
Bishop, David Fulton *library administrator*
Bjorncrantz, Leslie Benton *librarian*
Blair, Virginia Ann *public relations executive*
Bloomer, William David *radiation oncologist, educator*
Bobco, William David, Jr., *consulting engineering company executive*
Borcover, Alfred Seymour *journalist*
Boye, Roger Carl *academic administrator, journalism educator, writer*
Braeutigam, Ronald Ray *economics educator*
Brazelton, William Thomas *chemical engineering educator*
Buck, Tom *journalist*
†Butchko, Harriett Hays *food products executive, physician*
†Canes-Wrone, Brandice *political scientist, educator*
Carr, Stephen Howard *materials engineer, educator*
Cates, Jo Ann *library administrator, writer*
Chen, Gui-Qiang *mathematician, educator, researcher*
Cheng, Herbert Su-Yuen *mechanical engineering educator*
†Chernev, Alexander *marketing educator, researcher*
Christian, Richard Carlton *university dean, former advertising agency executive*
Conger, William Frame *artist, educator*
Crawford, James Weldon *psychiatrist, educator, administrator*
Crawford, Susan *library director, educator, author*
†Creamer, Robert Allan *lawyer*
Dallos, Peter John *neurobiologist, educator*
Daskin, Mark Stephen *civil engineering educator*
Davis, Stephen Howard *applied mathematics educator*
Dean, Dennis Richard *language educator*
Deming, Thomas Edward *publishing company executive*
Devinatz, Allen *mathematician, mathematics educator*
DeWolfe, Ruthanne K.S. *lawyer, psychologist, accountant*
Downing, Joan Forman *editor, writer*
Dranove, David *business educator, consultant, economist*
Dreier, David Louis *editor, writer*
Eberley, Helen-Kay *opera singer, classical record company executive, poet*
Enroth-Cugell, Christina Alma Elisabeth *neurophysiologist, educator*
Felknor, Bruce Lester *editorial consultant, writer*
Fessler, Raymond R. *metallurgical engineering consultant*
Fine, Gary Alan *sociology educator*
Fine, Morris Eugene *materials engineer, educator*
Fisher, Andrew Taylor *computer software developer*
Fitzgerald, Mary Joan *music educator*
Fourer, Robert Harold *industrial engineering educator, consultant*
Frey, Donald Nelson *industrial engineer, educator, retired manufacturing executive*
Friedman, Hans Adolf *architect*
†Froula, Christine *English literature educator*
†Fu, Lei *materials scientist, research scientist*
Gaiha, Vishnu Das *cardiologist*
Galvin, Kathleen Malone *communication educator*
Gasper, George, Jr., *mathematics educator*
Gejman, Pablo Victor *physician, scientist*
Genkin, Gennady *physicist*
Gibbons, William Reginald, Jr., *poet, novelist, translator, editor*
Gladden, Robert Wiley *corporate executive*
Golbus, Joseph *rheumatologist*
Goldstick, Thomas Karl *biomedical engineering educator*
Gordon, Julie Peyton *foundation administrator*
Gordon, Robert James *economics educator*
Gore, Richard Michael *radiologist*
†Gulati, Ranjay *finance educator*
Haddad, Abraham Herzl *electrical engineering educator, researcher*
Hannan, Bradley *educational publishing consultant and executive*
†Heitsch, James Lawrence *mathematician, educator*
Hemke, Frederick L. *music educator, university administrator*
Hirshfield, Pearl *artist*
†Hunter, Albert Dale *sociology educator, poet*
Hurter, Arthur Patrick *economist, educator*
Ibers, James Arthur *chemist, educator*
Ionescu Tulcea, Cassius *research mathematician, educator*
Irons, William George *anthropology educator*
Jacobs, Donald P. *dean emeritus, banking and finance educator*
Jacobs, Norman Joseph *publishing company executive*
Jerome, Joseph Walter *mathematics educator*
Jiang, Wenxin *statistician, researcher*
Jones, Dorothy Vincent *diplomatic historian*
Jones, Robert Russell *magazine editor*
Kalai, Ehud *decision sciences educator, researcher in economics and decision sciences*
†Kalantzis, George *historian, educator*
Karlins, M(artin) William *composer, educator*
Keer, Leon Morris *engineering educator*
Keith, Thomas Warren, Jr., *marketing executive*
Khandekar, Janardan Dinkar *oncologist, educator*
Kinzie, Mary *poet, educator*
Klein, Nancy Hess *interior designer*
Kliphardt, Raymond A. *engineering educator*
†Koenigsberg, Judy Z. Nulman *clinical psychologist*
Krizek, Raymond John *civil engineering educator, consultant*
Kuenster, John Joseph *editor*
Kujala, Walfrid Eugene *musician, educator*
Lafont, Cristina *educator*
Lambert, Joseph Buckley *chemistry educator*
Langsley, Donald Gene *psychiatrist, medical board executive*
Langsley, Pauline Royal *psychiatrist*
Larson, Roy *journalist, publisher*
Lewis, Dan Albert *education educator*
Lewis, Frederick D. *science educator*
†Li, Zhifeng *industrial engineer, researcher*
Liu, Wing Kam *mechanical engineering educator*
Lloyd-Still, John Dashwood *pediatrician, educator*
Locker, Gershon Yehuda *oncologist, educator*
Macsai, John *architect*
†Margoliash, Emanuel *biochemist, educator*
†Mason, Thomas Oliver *materials science and engineering educator, researcher*
Matkowsky, Bernard Judah *applied mathematician, educator*
Matzkin, Rosa Liliana *economics educator*
McCarron, John Francis *editor*
McCarthy, Thomas Anthony *philosophy educator*
McCleary, Elliott Harold *magazine editor*
McCoy, Marilyn *university official*
McDonough, Bridget Ann *music theatre company director*
Menke, Allen Carl *industrial corporation executive*
Meshii, Masahiro *materials science educator*
Mills, Edwin Smith *economics educator*
Moore, C. Bradley *chemistry educator*
Morrison, John Horton *lawyer*
Mortensen, Dale Thomas *economics educator*
Moskos, Charles C. *sociology educator*
Murphy, Gordon John *electrical engineer, educator*
Musa, Samuel Albert *university executive*
Mustoe, Thomas Anthony *physician, plastic surgeon*
†Neuschel, Robert Percy *management consultant, educator*
Nicholson, Eleanor Ann *educator*
Novales, Ronald Richards *zoologist, educator*
Oakes, Robert James *physics educator*
Okal, Emile Andre *geophysicist, educator*
Olmstead, William Edward *mathematics educator*
Olson, Gregory Bruce *materials science and engineering educator, academic director*
Ottino, Julio Mario *chemical engineering educator, scientist*
Otwell, Ralph Maurice *retired newspaper editor*
†Paden, William D. *French literature educator*
Patankar, Neelesh Ashok *mechanical engineer, educator*
Patashinski, Alexander Z. *physicist, materials science consultant*
Peck, Abraham *editor, writer, educator, magazine consultant*
Peters, Gordon Benes *retired musician*
†Peterson, Lance Robert *physician*
Plaut, Eric Alfred *retired psychiatrist, educator*
Pople, Sir John Anthony *chemistry educator*
Prasad, Pottumarthi Vara *health facility administrator*
Prince, Thomas Richard *accountant, educator*
Rasco, Kay Frances *antique dealer*
Reilly, Francis X. *lawyer, consultant*
Reiter, Stanley *economist, educator*
†Rosic, George Steve *lawyer*
Rounds, George R. *executive coach, organization consultant*
Rubenstein, Albert Harold *industrial engineering and management sciences educator*
†Rubin, Jill M. *director*
Ruggero, Mario Alfredo *physiologist, educator*
Sachtler, Wolfgang Max Hugo *chemistry educator*
Sahakian, Alan Varteres *electrical engineer, educator*
Salem, Richard Allen *mediator*
Salzman, Arthur George *architect*
†Savin, Tatiana *mathematician, researcher*
Schluter, Robert Arvel *physicist*
Scholten, Menno Nico *mortgage banker*
Schulte, Bruce John *lawyer*
Schwartz, Neena Betty *endocrinologist, educator*
Schwartz, Theodore B. *physician, educator*
Scott, Walter Dill *management educator*
Seaman, Jerome Francis *actuary*
Seidman, David N(athaniel) *materials science and engineering educator*
Senn, Peter Richard *economist, consultant*
Shah, Surendra Poonamchand *engineering educator, researcher*
Shanas, Ethel *sociology educator*
Sheridan, James Edward *history educator*
Shriver, Duward Felix *chemistry educator, researcher, consultant*
Silverman, Richard Bruce *chemist, biochemist, educator*
†Silvestre, Stephanie *language educator*
†Skoulakis, Georgios *finance educator*
Smith, Spencer Bailey *engineering and business educator*
Sobel, Alan *electrical engineer, physicist*
Spears, Kenneth George *chemistry educator*
Spier, Kathryn Elizabeth *economist, educator*
Sprang, Milton LeRoy *obstetrician, gynecologist, educator*
Stern, Louis William *marketing educator, consultant*
Stumpf, David Allen *pediatric neurologist*
Summers, Renee Ann *clinical social worker*
Sundquist, Eric John *American studies educator*
†Sweet, Jerry James *clinical psychologist*
Taam, Ronald Everett *physics and astronomy educator*
Taflove, Allen *electrical engineer, educator, researcher, consultant*
Takahashi, Joseph S. *neuroscientist, educator*
Tanner, Martin Abba *statistics and human oncology educator*
Tarnoff, Eileen Feldman *social worker*
Thrash, Patricia Ann *educational association administrator*
Tornabene, Russell C. *communications executive*
Traisman, Howard Sevin *pediatrician*
Twaddell, Sophia Hantzes *communications executive*
Van Ness, James Edward *electrical engineering educator*
Ver Steeg, Clarence Lester *historian, educator*
Vick, Nicholas A. *neurologist*
†Vladem, Steven Allen *writer, motivational speaker*
†Wachs, Alan L *quality assurance engineer*
Walter, Robert Irving *chemistry educator, chemist*
Weber, Arnold Robert *academic administrator*
Weertman, Johannes *materials science educator*
Weertman, Julia Randall *materials science and engineering educator*
Wefler, Wilson Daniel *publisher, management consultant*
†Weisbrod, Burton Allen *economist, educator*
Well, Irwin *language educator*
Wener, Maureen G. *association executive*
Wessels, Bruce W. *materials scientist, educator*
Wilhelm, Frank Leo *publisher, writer*
Wills, Garry *journalist, educator*
Wine-Banks, Jill Susan *lawyer*
Witwer, Samuel Weiler, Jr., *lawyer*
†Worster, Carol Lynn *librarian*
Wright, John *classics educator*
Wu, Tai Te *biological sciences and engineering educator*
Yoder, John Clifford *producer, consultant*
Zeman, Gregory Oswald *physician*
Zimmerman, Mary *performing arts educator*
Ziomek, Jonathan S. *journalist, educator*

Evergreen Park
Bayrakdar, Ammar Adnan *endocrinologist*
Hong, Kuhn *nuclear medicine physician*

Fairfield
Thomason, Nola Faye *critical care-emergency supervisor*

Fairview Heights
Wu, Yunying *engineer, researcher*

Flossmoor
Crum, James Francis *waste recycling company executive*
Day, Gregory Lynn *music educator*
Gevers, Marcia Bonita *lawyer, lecturer, mediator, consultant*
Herring, Marsha Kathline *health services marketing administrator*
Lis, Edward Francis *pediatrician, consultant*
Pierce, Shelby Crawford *management and oil industry consultant*
Santos, Andrew J., III, *priest*

Forest Park
Mack, William Joseph *psychotherapist, rehabilitation specialist*
Thomas, Alan *candy company executive*

Fox Lake
Vida, Diane *high school administrator*

Fox River Grove
Abboud, Alfred Robert *banker, consultant, investor*

Frankfort
Burhoe, Brian Walter *automotive service executive*
Feeney, Kelly Lynn *management consultant*

Franklin Park
†Dean, Howard M., Jr., *food company executive*
Duncanson, Donald George *retired encyclopedia editor*
Simpson, Michael *metals service center executive*

Freeport
†Alldredge, William T. *metal products executive*
Baumgartner, Reuben Albert *retired school administrator*
†Eden, Robert Elwood *lawyer*
†Galli, Joseph, Jr., *consumer products company executive*
Pascoe, E(dward) Rudy *insurance sales executive*
Weaver, Michael Glenn *pharmacist*
Wise, Sarajane Goers *community education nurse*

Fulton
Bomgarden, Stanley Ralph *minister*

Galena
Alexander, Barbara Leah Shapiro *clinical social worker*
Crandall, John Lynn *insurance consultant, retired insurance company executive*
Hermann, Paul David *retired association executive*
Jackman, Levon Merchant O'Day *artist*
Schwerdtfeger, Carl Richard *real estate executive*

Galesburg
Bailey, Stephen *history educator*
Conway, Lowava Denise *data processing administrator*
Gupta, Madan Lal *cardiologist*
Hane, Mikiso *history educator*
Haywood, Bruce *retired academic administrator*
†Hellenga, Robert R. *language educator, writer*
Kowalski, Richard Sheldon *hospital administrator*
Mathew, James *cardiologist*
McCurry, James Patrick *philosophy and literature educator, poet, artist*
†Metz, Robin O. *writer, educator, poet*
†Polay, Bruce *music director, music educator*
Strauch, Carl Edward *physician*
Sunderland, Jacklyn Giles *former alumni affairs director*
Taylor Swisher, Debora Dianne *home health nurse*
†Tourlentes, Thomas Theodore *psychiatrist*

Galva
Heck, Melody Ann *library director*

Geneseo
Crisp, Sandra Sue *procurement analyst*

Geneva
Carella, J(oseph) Dino *printing company executive*
Gallagher, Kent Grey *theater arts educator*
Kallstrom, Charles Clark *dentist*
Klenke, Deborah Ann *band director, choral director, department chairman*
†Landmeier, Allen Lee *lawyer*
Lazzara, Dennis Joseph *orthodontist*
Mishina, Mizuho *artist*
Montgomery, Joel Robert *communications executive, consultant*
Pershing, Robert George *telecommunications company executive*

Ewing, Raymond Peyton *educator, author, management consultant*
Feng, Paul Yen-Hsiung *lawyer, chemist*
Hayes, M. M.M. *publishing executive*
McKittrick, William Wood *lawyer*
Milnikel, Robert Saxon *lawyer*
Steingraber, Frederick George *management consultant*
†Weaver, Clifford Lee *retired lawyer, winery owner*

Kewanee
Golby, James L. *school system administrator*
Lotspeich, Ellin Sue *elementary education educator*

Kildeer
Muffoletto, Mary Lu *retired school program director, consultant, editor*

Kinsman
†Kotamarthi, V. Rao *meteorologist*

Kirkland
†Olson-McGee, Pat M. *guidance counselor*

La Grange
Jaffe-Notier, Peter Andrew *secondary education educator*
Kerr, Alexander Duncan, Jr., *lawyer*
†Lyons, Eileen *state legislator*
Mahoney, Donna Marie *psychotherapist*
Mehlenbacher, Dohn Harlow *civil engineer, consultant*

La Grange Park
Brown, Helen Sauer *fund raising executive*
Butler, Margaret Kampschaefer *retired computer scientist*
Calhamer, Allan Brian *retired postal worker*

La Salle
†McClintock, Thomas Lee *lawyer*
Vickrey, Robert Fischer *publishing executive, broadcast executive*

Lafox
Seils, William George *lawyer*

Lake Barrington
Joslin, Robert Scott *pharmaceutical company executive*
Morris, Ralph William *chronopharmacologist*
†Worrell, Sharyn Dianne *retired flight attendant*

Lake Bluff
Braendle, Donald Harold *geneticist, researcher*
Burns, Kenneth Jones, Jr., *lawyer, consultant*
Fryburger, Vernon Ray, Jr., *advertising and marketing educator*
Griem, John Michael *management consultant*
†Kennedy, John Foran *retired lawyer*
Kyncl, John Jaroslav *pharmacologist*
Schreiber, George Richard *association executive, writer*
Sweetser, Marie-Odile Gauny *retired foreign language educator*
Vander Voort, George Frederic *metallurgist*

Lake Forest
†Beiriger, Eugene Edward *historian, educator, dean*
Bradley, Kim Alexandra *sales and marketing specialist*
†Brewer, Paul Huie *advertising executive, artist, portrait painter*
†Buckley, George W. *sporting goods executive*
Carter, Donald Patton *advertising executive*
Chandler, Christopher Mark (Chris Chandler) *professional football player*
Chieger, Kathryn Jean *recreation company executive*
†Covington, George Morse *lawyer*
Crawford, Robert W., Jr., *furniture rental company executive*
Crovetti, Aldo Joseph *retired chemist, consultant*
Damico, Joseph F. *medical company executive*
Davidson, Richard Alan *data communications company executive*
Emerson, William Harry *lawyer, retired, oil company executive*
Feinberg, Jeffrey Enoch *educator, author*
Ferrari, Michael Richard, Jr., *university administrator*
Fetridge, Bonnie-Jean Clark (Mrs. William Harrison Fetridge) *civic volunteer*
Francois, William Armand *lawyer*
†Frissora, Mark P. *automotive parts manufacturing company executive*
Fromm, Henry Gordon *retired manufacturing and marketing executive*
Galatz, Henry Francis *lawyer*
†George, David Sanderson *Spanish language educator, writer*
Goldstein, Marsha Feder *tour company executive*
Hamilton, Peter Bannerman *business executive, lawyer*
Hammar, Lester Everett *health care manufacturing executive, retired*
Hampton, Daniel Oliver *professional football player*
Herron, Orley R. *college president*
†Hodgson, Thomas Richard *retired healthcare company executive*
Hotchkiss, Eugene, III, *retired academic administrator*
Imperato, Joseph Philip *radiation oncologist, educator*
Jauron, Dick *professional football coach*
Johnson, Richard Darrell *management consultant*
Jones, Gordon Kempton *dentist*
Jones, Philip Newton *physician, medical educator*
Kelly, Daniel John *physician*
Kenly, Granger Farwell *marketing consultant, college official*

†Keyser, Richard Lee *distribution company executive*
Lambert, John Boyd *chemical engineer, consultant*
†Larson, Peter N. *company executive*
†Le Mahieu, Dan Lloyd *historian, educator*
Levy, Nelson Louis *physician, scientist, corporate executive*
McCaskey, Michael B. *professional football team executive*
McCormack, Robert Cornelius *investment banker*
Mitchell, Richard Charles *human resources specialist*
Mohr, Roger John *advertising agency executive*
Morell, William Nelson, Jr., *foreign trade association executive, government agency administrator*
†Muldoon, James Peter, Jr., *government agency administrator*
†Niemann, William Lovekamp *lawyer*
O'Mara, Thomas Patrick *manufacturing company executive*
Palmer, Ann Therese Darin *lawyer*
Pawl, Ronald Phillip *neurosurgery educator*
Rahe, Maribeth Sembach *bank executive*
Rand, Kathy Sue *public relations executive*
†Reyes, M. Judy *food products distribution executive*
Romans, Donald Bishop *corporate executive*
Ross, Robert Evan *bank executive*
Salter, Edwin Carroll *retired physician*
Schulze, Franz, Jr., *critic, educator*
Sherman, Jeffrey Wayne *physician, clinical researcher*
Sikorovsky, Eugene Frank *retired lawyer*
†Stecko, Paul T. *packaging company executive*
Stewart, Kordell *professional football player*
Swanton, Virginia Lee *writer, publisher, bookseller*
Taylor, Barbara Ann Olin *writer, educational consultant*
†Van Ella, Kathleen E. *fine art consultant*
Wasson, Jeffrey *music educator*
Weston, Arthur Walter *chemist, scientific and business executive*
Weston, Dawn Thompson *artist, researcher*
Wilbur, Richard Sloan *physician, executive*
Young, Ronald Faris *commodity trader*

Lake In The Hills
Kay, Dennis Matthew *retired publishing company official*

Lake Villa
Anderson, Milton Andrew *chemical executive*
Watson, Robert Edward *librarian, information specialist*

Lake Zurich
Dixon, John Fulton *village manager*
†Holdhusen, J. David *music educator*
Krolopp, Rudolph William *retired industrial designer, consultant*
Schultz, Carl Herbert *real estate management and development company executive*
†Scott, John Joseph *lawyer*
Teeters, Joseph Lee *mathematician, consultant*

Lanark
Abbott, David Henry *manufacturing company executive*
Etter, David Pearson *poet, editor*

Lansing
Ansary, Hanson Jaber *transportation and telecommunications executive*
Hill, Philip *retired lawyer*
Kaplan, Huette Myra *business educator, training consultant*
McKeown, Mary Elizabeth *educational administrator*

Lawrenceville
Dooley, David Inskeep *artist, educator*

Lemont
†Anitescu, Mihai *computer scientist, mathematician*
Colbert, Marvin Jay *retired internist, educator*
†Deen, James Robert *nuclear engineer*
Urban, Patricia A. *former elementary school educator*
Williams, Jack Marvin *research chemist*
†Zapol, Peter *research scientist*

Lewistown
Shank, Glenna Kaye *medical and surgical nurse, nursing educator*

Libertyville
Baske, C. Alan *manufacturing company executive*
Beach, Robert Mark *biologist*
Burrows, Brian William *research and development manufacturing executive*
DeSanto, James John *lawyer*
Devine, Barbara Armstrong *risk manager*
†Fato, Gildo E. *lawyer, chemical engineer*
Gallopoulos, Nicholas Efstratios *chemical engineer*
†Jenniges, Nathaniel John *marketing professional*
Rallo, Douglas *lawyer*
†Ritson, Scott Campbell *real estate management and development consultant*
Schroeder, W(illiam) Widick *religion educator*
Shen, Xiaohui *application developer, researcher*
True, Raymond Stephen *writer, editor, analyst, consultant*
Trzyna, Chris *physical education educator*

Lincoln
†Schilling, Anthony Ronald *academic administrator*
Wilson, Robert Allen *religion educator*

Lincolnshire
Aldrich, Susan Miller *entrepreneur*

Bartlett, Robert William *lawyer*
†Ben-Shir, Rya Helen *medical librarian*
Dobrin, Sheldon L. *architect*
†Gifford, Dale L. *human resources executive*
Hays, Thomas Chandler *holding company executive*
Hebda, Lawrence John *data processing executive, consultant*
†Knopik, Robert *retail executive, consultant*
Nehring, Lisa Marie *secondary school educator*
Para, Gerard Albert *lawyer, real estate broker, consultant*
Schauble, John Eugene *physical education educator*
Simes, Stephen Mark *pharmaceutical products executive*
Taub, Amy F. *dermatologist*
†Wesley, Norman H. *metal products executive*

Lincolnwood
Carroll, Howard William *lawyer, retired state senator*
Donovan, John Vincent *consulting company executive*
†Epstein, Ben Irving *management consultant*
Grant, Paul Bernard *industrial relations educator, arbitrator*
Greenblatt, Deana Charlene *elementary education educator*
Kagan, Andrew Besdin *lawyer, educator*
Lebedow, Aaron Louis *consulting company executive*
Lewitz, Amy Mae *clinical nurse specialist, geriatrics psychiatry nurse*
Rokach, Abraham Jacob *structural engineering and computer software consultant*
Stern, Adrienne Ehrlich *interior designer*
Zaremski, Miles Jay *lawyer*

Lisle
Bradna, Joanne Justice *manufacturer's representative*
Butt, Edward Thomas, Jr., *lawyer*
Davis, Gregory Thomas *marine surveyor*
Huffman, Louise Tolle *middle school educator*
†Joung, John J. *chemical engineer, researcher*
Krehbiel, Frederick August, II, *electronics company executive*
†Lorenz, Matthias E. *priest, consultant*
Mehaffey, Scott Alan *landscape architect*
Skweres, Thomas W. *advertising executive, writer*
Smith, Jared Russell William *research executive, research scientist, consultant, poet*
Sohl, Raymond, Jr., *video company executive*
Staab, Thomas Eugene *chemist*
†Tenkasi, Ramkrishnan V. *finance educator, researcher*
Vitson, Robyn Stanko *piano teacher, singer, pianist*
Ware, George Henry *botanist*

Litchfield
Deaton, Beverly Jean *nursing administrator, educator*
Jackson, David Alonzo *retired newspaper editor*
Talley, Hayward Leroy *communications executive*

Lombard
Ahlstrom, Ronald Gustin *artist*
Bachop, William Earl, Jr., *retired anatomist, zoologist*
†Devany, Donald Joseph, II, *music educator*
†Goodman, Elliott I(rvin) *retired lawyer*
Holgers-Awana, Rita Marie *electrodiagnosis specialist*
Hudson, Samuel Campbell, Jr., *art educator, artist, sculptor, portraitist*
Kasprow, Barbara Anne *biomedical scientist, writer*
McCoy, Jeanie Shearer *analytical chemist, consultant*
O'Shea, Patrick Joseph *lawyer, electrical engineer*
Velardo, Joseph Thomas *molecular biology and endocrinology educator*
†Yeager, Phillip Charles *transportation company executive*

Long Grove
Ausman, Robert K. *surgeon, research executive*
Dajani, Esam Zapher *pharmacologist*
Liuzzi, Robert C. *chemical company executive*
Obert, Paul Richard *lawyer, manufacturing company executive*
Othman, Talat Mohamad *financial consultant, investment banker*
Van Der Bosch, Susan Hartnett *real estate broker*

Loves Park
Gloyd, Lawrence Eugene *retired diversified manufacturing company executive*
†Schlub, Teresa Rae *minister*

Macomb
Anderson, Richard Vernon *ecology educator, researcher*
†Andreev, Fedor *mathematician, educator*
Barclay, Martha Jane *science educator, research scientist*
Bauerly, Ronald John *marketing educator*
Dexter, Donald Harvey *surgeon, educator*
Hallwas, John Edward *English language educator*
Hopper, Stephen Rodger *hospital administrator*
Julstrom, Rosa Drake *music educator*
Kyllonen Rose, Julie Frances *college program administrator*
†Morelli, Mario Frank *philosophy educator*
†Myers, Richard P. *state legislator*
Na'Allah, Abdul-Rasheed *writer, educator*
North, Teresa Lynn *student services administrator*
Radosh, Mary *sociology educator*
Ribbens, Eric *plant ecologist, educator*

†Romig, James *composer, educator*
†Spencer, Donald Spurgeon *historian, academic administrator*
Tang, Shengming *sociology educator*
Walzer, Norman Charles *economics educator*
Witthuhn, Burton Orrin *retired university official*

Madison
Purdes, Alice Marie *retired adult education educator*

Mahomet
Bosworth, Douglas LeRoy *international company executive, educator*
Kennedy, Cheryl Lynn *museum director*
Sundy, George Joseph, Jr., *retired engineering executive*
Thompson, Margaret M. *physical education educator*

Manhattan
Cramer, Brian Starkweather *electrical engineer*

Manteno
Balgeman, Richard Vernon *radiology administrator, alcoholism counselor*
†Conrad, David L *music educator*

Maple Park
†Callaghan, Barney *secondary school educator*
Nickels, John L. *retired state supreme court justice*

Mapleton
Hayes, Debra Troxell *family nurse practitioner*

Marengo
Franks, Herbert Hoover *lawyer*
Mrkvicka, Edward Francis, Jr., *financial writer, publisher, consultant*
Van Horn, John Henry *secondary school educator*

Marion
†Aikman, Elflora Anna *senior citizens center administrator*
Coil, Carolyn Chandler *educational consultant*
Glasco, Sue Alice *retired educator*
Munas, Falies A. *psychiatric physician*
†Pearce, Lucinda Jane *management consultant*
Schaede, Richard Edwin *family practice physician*
Yeager, Twynette *antiques and gift shop owner, retired educator*

Markham
Burkes-Rawlins, Sarah *nutritional elementary school educator, counselor*
Peacock, Marilyn Claire *primary education educator*

Marshall
†Freeman, Charles E. *writer, musician*
Mitchell, George Trice *physician*

Maryville
Stark, Patricia Ann *psychologist*

Matteson
van der Hoek, Sherry A. *counselor*

Mattoon
Finley, Gary Roger *financial company executive*
Horsley, Jack Everett *lawyer, writer*
Maris, Charles Robert *surgeon, otolaryngologist*
Phipps, John Randolph *retired army officer*

Maywood
Anderson, Douglas Edwin *neurosurgeon*
†Berman, James H. *pediatrician, gastroenterologist, educator*
†Bermes, Edward William, Jr., *biochemist, educator*
Bova, Davide *radiologist*
†Brukbaker, Linda *obstetrician, gynecologist*
Canning, John Rafton *urologist*
Celesia, Gastone Guglielmo *neurologist, neurophysiologist, researcher*
Cera, Lee Marie *veterinarian*
Dado, Diane Valentina *pediatric plastic and reconstructive surgeon*
Eidem, Benjamin Walter *cardiologist*
Ellington, Mildred L. *librarian*
†Emami, Bahman *oncologist, educator, radiologist*
Freeark, Robert James *surgeon, educator, administrator*
Hanin, Israel *pharmacologist, educator*
Hindle, Paula Alice *nursing administrator*
Joehl, Raymond Joseph *surgeon, educator*
Libka, Robert John *educational director, consultant*
Light, Terry Richard *orthopedic hand surgeon*
†McClatchey, Kenneth D. *pathology educator*
Mittendorf, Robert *physician, epidemiologist*
Newman, Barry Marc *pediatric surgeon*
Scanlon, Patrick Joseph *cardiologist, educator*
Schultz, Richard Michael *biochemistry educator, researcher*
Slogoff, Stephen *dean, anesthesiologist, educator*
Stiff, Patrick Joseph *internist, hematologist, oncologist, educator*
Vigneswaran, Wickii Thambiah *cardiothoracic surgeon, educator*
Wilber, David James *cardiologist*

Mc Gaw Park
†Mujais, Salim *nephrologist*

McHenry
Chisu, Ioan *artist*

Mchenry
Duel, Ward Calvin *retired health care consultant*
Koehl, Camille Joan *accountant*

Melrose Park
Bernick, Carol Lavin *corporate executive*
Cernugel, William John *consumer products and special retail executive*
Douglas, Kenneth Jay *food products executive*
Hillert, Richard Walter *composer, educator, author*
Lavin, Bernice E. *cosmetics executive*
Umans, Alvin Robert *manufacturing company executive*
Wechter, Clari Ann *paint manufacturing company executive*

Metamora
†Degenhart, Anne Elizabeth *music educator*

Milford
†Beall, Pamela Honn *therapist, radio talks-show host, writer*

Mokena
Sangmeister, George Edward *lawyer, consultant, former congressman*

Moline
Arnell, Richard Anthony *radiologist*
Becherer, Hans Walter *retired agricultural equipment executive*
Cleaver, William Lehn *lawyer*
Curry, Kathleen Bridget *retired librarian*
Harrington, Roy Edwards *agricultural engineer, author*
Johnson, Mary Lou *lay worker, educator*
Lane, Robert W. *farm equipment manufacturing executive*
Larson, Richard James *computer network systems executive*
†LeBlanc, Bruce David *sociologist*
Malicki, Gregg Hillard *agricultural equipment manufacturing executive*
Meredith, Lynnette Ann Logan *accountant*
Middleton, Marc Stephen *corporate insurance risk manager*
Mitchell, Lucille Anne *retired elementary school educator*
Morgan, Rebecca Susan *psychologist*
Morrison, Deborah Jean *lawyer*
Parise, Marc Robert *banker*
†Schwiebert, Mark William *lawyer, mayor*
Varela, Fernando *anesthesiologist*
Williamsen, Dannye Sue *personal development educator, health facility administrator*

Momence
†Holland, Leslie Ann *special education educator*

Monmouth
Moore, Richard Alan *optometrist*
White, Perry D. *music educator*

Monticello
†Gucker, Douglas *agronomist, consultant*
Tracy, William Francis, II, *lawyer*

Mooseheart
†Ross, Donald Hugh *fraternal organization executive*

Morris
†Fabian, Karen *publishing executive, small business owner*
Hayton, Bernard Quentin, Jr., *library media specialist*
†Rooks, John Newton *lawyer*

Morrison
Galbreath, Joseph C. *pharmacist*

Morton
Corey, Judith Ann *retired educator*
Grisham, George Robert *mathematics educator*

Morton Grove
Blanchard, James Arthur *engineer, computer systems specialist, marketing professional*
Ernst, Chester Nelson *manufacturing company executive*
Farber, Isadore E. *psychologist, educator*
†Labunski, Alma Joel *nursing educator*
McKenna, Andrew James *paper distribution and printing company executive, baseball club executive*
Vega, Steve *poet*

Mount Carmel
Fornoff, Frank J(unior) *retired chemistry educator, consultant*

Mount Carroll
Rogers, Ward Junior *retired industrial designer*

Mount Prospect
Epstein, Stephen Roger *financial executive*
Gerlitz, Curtis Neal *business executive*
McCully, William Craig *library administrator*
Mirsky, Howard *social services administrator, pharmacist*
Nedza, Sandra Louise *manufacturing executive*
O'Connor, Nan G. *social worker*
Pulsifer, Edgar Darling *leasing service and sales executive*
†Rueggeberg, Erna M. *nursing consultant, nursing administrator, researcher*
Scott, Norman Laurence *engineering consultant*
Thulin, Adelaide Ann *design company executive, interior designer*

Mount Sterling
†Tracy, Patrick F. *food products executive*

Mount Vernon
Hall, Sharon Gay *retired language educator, artist*
Harvey, Morris Lane *lawyer*
†Jones, John O. *state legislator*
Nicholson, Gerald Lee *airport administrator*
Withers, W. Russell, Jr., *broadcast executive*

Mount Zion
Burns, B. Thomas *broadcasting executive*

Mundelein
Carr, Bonnie Jean *professional ice skater*
Kottayil, Santosh George *pharmaceutical development executive*
McLeskey, Charles Hamilton *anesthesiologist, educator, pharmaceutical executive*
Meehan, Jean Marie Ross *human resources, occupational health and safety management consultant*
Strauss, Jeffrey Lewis *healthcare executive*

Murphysboro
Barrette, Linda Jones *dean*
Hall, James Robert *secondary education educator*
McCann, Maurice Joseph *lawyer*
Young, Linda Diane *speech pathology/audiology services professional*

Naperville
Arzoumanidis, Gregory G. *chemist*
Bleck, Phyllis Claire *surgeon, musician*
†Briseno, Kathleen *education educator*
Burchfield, Bruce Allen *entrepreneur*
Burken, Ruth Marie *utility company executive*
Chengalvarayan, Rathinavelu *engineering researcher*
Cowlishaw, Mary Lou *government educator*
†Curry, David Gordon *engineer, consultant*
Desch, Theodore Edward *retired health insurance company executive, lawyer*
Dhar, Promila *researcher*
Fawell, Harris W. *lawyer, former congressman*
Fenech, Joseph Charles *lawyer*
Finzer, Carolyn Lauing *artist, speaker*
†Fleming, Norman Patrick *information scientist*
Fritz, Roger Jay *management consultant*
Fuhrer, Larry *management consultant, management educator, finance company executive*
†Gannon, Jeffrey P. *trucking/relocation services executive*
†Gems, Gerald Robert *physical education educator*
Grimley, Jeffrey Michael *dentist*
†Harvard, Rita Grace *real estate agent, volunteer*
Heuer, Michael Alexander *dean, endodontist educator*
†Hilt, Meredith Dykstra *foundation administrator*
Huey, George Irving, Jr., *software consultant*
Kaduk, James Albert *crystallographer*
Katai, Andrew Andras *chemical company executive*
Kelley, Karl Neal *psychology educator*
Koch, William Joseph *public relations executive*
Koeppe, Eugene Charles, Jr., *electrical engineer*
Kotynek, George Roy *mechanical engineer, educator, marketing executive*
L'Allier, James Joseph *educational multimedia company executive, instructional designer*
Landwehr, Arthur John *minister*
Larson, Mark Edward, Jr., *lawyer, educator, financial advisor*
Levy, Steven B. *lawyer*
Martin, Joan Ellen *secondary education educator*
McCaul, Joseph Patrick *chemical engineer*
Modery, Richard Gillman *marketing and sales executive*
Nortell, Bruce *lawyer*
Penisten, Gary Dean *entrepreneur*
Rosenmann, Daniel *physicist, educator*
Rosenthal, Edward Leonard *secondary school educator*
Schaack, Philip Anthony *retired beverage company executive*
Schwab, Paul Josiah *psychiatrist, educator*
Sellers, Gregory Jude *physicist*
Shaw, Michael Allan *lawyer, mail order company executive*
Sherren, Anne Terry *chemistry educator*
Spiotta, Raymond Herman *editor*
†Staley, Charles Walter, Jr., *secondary school educator*
Tan, Li-Su Lin *accountant, insurance executive, investment consultant*
Tibble, Douglas Clair *lawyer*
Vanagas, Rimantas Andrius (Ray Vanagas) *entrepreneur*
Vora, Manu Kishandas *chemical engineer, quality consultant*
†Wake, Richard W. *food products executive*
†Wake, Thomas G. *food products executive*
Wallace, Guy William *management consultant*
Wilde, Harold Richard *college president*

Neoga
Davis, Sharon Gail *nursing assistant*

New Baden
Blue, Myrna Kay *retired music educator*

New Lenox
†Carlson, Tammi Clair *music educator, musician*

Niles
Beton, John Allen *communications company executive*
Grace, John Joseph *retired priest*
Kaden, Bruce Richard *hematologist, oncologist*
Kessell, Charles Arthur *music educator, musician*
Weisbach, Lou *advertising executive*

Normal
†Alstrum, James Joseph *education educator*
Bender, Paul Edward *lawyer*
†Besserman, Perle S. *writer, educator*
Bjorklund, Diane Louise *sociology educator*
†Brown, Lauren Evans *zoologist, researcher, zoologist, educator*
†De Santis, Christopher Charles *education educator, writer*
†Devinatz, Victor Gary *industrial relations educator*
Fry, Terry L. *retired English educator*
Hesse, Douglas Dean *English educator*
†Hickrod, George Alan Karnes Wallis *educational administration educator*
Lessoff, Alan H. *history educator*
Liechty, Daniel *social worker, educator*
Lord, Timothy Charles *philosophy educator*
Luginbuhl, Benjamin Ryan *music educator*
Matsler, Franklin Giles *retired education educator*
Mau, Benjamin *artist*
Miller, Wilma Hildruth *education educator*
†Morenus, Carlyn G. *music educator*
Parette, Howard P. *school system administrator, special education educator*
Parry, Sally Ellen *academic administrator, English educator*
Parton, Thomas Albert *speech-language pathologist*
Presley, John Woodrow *academic administrator*
Presmeg, Norma Christine *mathematics educator, researcher*
Rochelle, Victor Cleanthus *lawyer*
Shields, John Charles *American studies and African American studies and literature educator*
Skibo, James M. *anthropologist, educator*
Smith, Robert Lee *agriculturalist*
Spears, Larry Jonell *lawyer*
†Steele, Stephen K. *music educator*
Sutherland, Robert Donald *writer*
†Temple, Mark Allen *adult education educator, consultant*
Throckmorton, Peter Eugene *retired organic chemist, consultant*
Vanden Eynden, Charles Lawrence *mathematician, educator*
†Wortham, Anne Estelle *education educator*

North Aurora
Butcher, Ann Patrice *elementary school educator*
Hoover, Lola Mae *retired communications company executive*
Kuhl, Christopher Fanelli *music educator*

North Chicago
Albach, Richard Allen *microbiology educator*
Barsano, Charles Paul *medical educator, dean*
Bush, Eugene Nyle *pharmacologist, research scientist*
Chedid, Antonio *pathologist, educator, researcher*
Dayton, Nick A. *pharmaceutical executive*
de Lasa, José M. *lawyer*
Gall, Eric Papineau *physician, educator*
Hawkins, Richard Albert *medical educator, administrator*
†Katdare, Ashok V. *science administrator*
Kemp, Robert Grant *biochemist, educator*
Kim, Yoon Berm *immunologist, educator*
Kovacek, Duane Michael *secondary school educator*
†Ku, Yi-Yin *organic chemist*
Loga, Sanda *physicist, educator*
Nair, Velayudhan *pharmacologist, medical educator*
Rogers, Eugene Jack *medical educator*
Rudy, David Robert *physician, educator*
Sarma, P. S. Balasubramania *medical educator*
Schneider, Arthur Sanford *physician, educator*
Sierles, Frederick Stephen *psychiatrist, educator*
†Sladek, Celia Davis *neuroscientist, educator*
†Suskind, Robert M. *pediatrician, educator*
Wiesner, Dallas Charles *immunologist, researcher*

North Riverside
Perkins, William H., Jr., *finance company executive*
Sedlak, S(hirley) A(gnes) *freelance writer, novelist*

Northbrook
†Abbey, G(eorge) Marshall *lawyer, former health care company executive, general counsel*
Adler, Robert *electronics engineer*
Afterman, Allan B. *accountant, educator, researcher, consultant*
Beljan, John Richard *university administrator, medical educator*
Betz, Ronald Philip *pharmacist*
Boettcher, Robert Walter *civil engineer*
Bohlender, Hugh Darrow *lawyer*
Brandeisky, Kathleen Sexton *social worker, consultant*
Clarey, John Robert *executive search consultant*
Clark, David Keith *lawyer, real estate developer*
Colburn, David Dunton *investment manager*
Colton, Frank Benjamin *retired chemist*
Cruikshank, John W., III, *life insurance underwriter*
Cucco, Ulisse P. *obstetrician, gynecologist*
Dilling, Kirkpatrick Wallwick *lawyer*
Di Spigno, Guy Joseph *international management consultant, industrial psychologist*
†Dordek, Alan Eugene *marketing executive*
Edelson, Ira J. *venture banker, trade finance executive*
Ehrmann, Susanna *foreign language educator, writer, photographer*
Eman Delmar, Evelyn (Evelyn Eman Delmar) *communications executive*
Feibel, Frederick Arthur *financial consultant*
†Fox, Michael Edward *lawyer*
Ghosh, Satyendra Kumar *structural engineer, educator*
Gratalo, John, Jr., *mortgage banker, business owner*
Green, David *manufacturing company executive*
†Hale, Danny Lyman *financial executive*
Hicks, Judith Eileen *nursing administrator*
Hindo, Walid Afram *radiology educator, researcher*
Hirsch, Lawrence Leonard *physician, retired educator*
Irons, Spencer Ernest *lawyer*
Jaeger, Robert Joseph *medical supplies professional*
Kahn, Sandra S. *psychotherapist*
Kaiserman, David Norman *music educator*
Keehn, Silas *retired bank executive*
†Kessler, Harold Allan *epidemiologist, hospital administrator*
King, Robert Charles *biologist, educator*
Lapin, Harvey I. *lawyer*
Leikin, Mitchell *retired judge*
Lever, Alvin *health science association administrator*
Levy, Arnold S(tuart) *real estate company executive*
Liddy, Edward M. *insurance company executive*
Mandel, Karyl Lynn *accountant*
Marshall, Irl Houston, Jr., *franchise consultant*
McGinn, Mary J. *lawyer, insurance company executive*
Meyer, Carl James *music educator*
Morris, Marilyn Ann *social worker*
Moser, Larry Edward *marketing professional*
Newman, Lawrence William *financial executive*
†Noeth, Carolyn Frances *speech and language pathologist*
Pesmen, Sandra (Mrs. Harold William Pesmen) *editor*
Rosemarin, Carey Stephen *lawyer*
Ross, Debra Benita *jewelry designer, marketing executive*
Rotchford, Patricia Kathleen *lawyer, mediator*
Saunders, Kenneth D. *insurance company executive, consultant, arbitrator*
Sayatovic, Wayne Peter *manufacturing company executive*
Schmidt, Arthur Irwin *steel fabricating company executive*
Sernett, Richard Patrick *lawyer*
†Siegal, Judy A. *social services administrator*
†Singer, Norman Sol *food products executive, inventor*
Slattery, James Joseph (Joe Slattery) *actor*
Snader, Jack Ross *publishing company executive*
Stamper, James M. *retired English language educator*
Stewart, Charles Leslie *lawyer*
†Storhoff, James Justin *scientist*
Sudbrink, Jane Marie *sales and marketing executive*
Wajer, Ronald Edward *management consultant*
Wallace, Harry Leland *lawyer*
Williams, David Allan *dentist, educator*

Northfield
Bruns, Nicolaus, Jr., *retired agricultural chemicals company executive, lawyer*
Carlin, Donald Walter *retired food products executive, consultant*
Giza, David Alan *lawyer*
Glass, Henry Peter *industrial designer, interior architect, educator*
Hadley, Stanton Thomas *international manufacturing and marketing company executive, lawyer*
Heise, Marilyn Beardsley *public relations company executive*
Hotze, Charles Wayne *publisher, printer*
Kleinman, Burton Howard *real estate investor*
Knight, James Atwood *manufacturing executive*
Lubawski, James Lawrence *health care consultant*
Mathieson, Michael Raymond *controller*
Pratt, Murray Lester *collaborative commerce specialist*
Quaal, Ward Louis *broadcast executive*
Sawers, Peter Ritchie *management consultant, educator, retired*
Schneider-Criezis, Susan Marie *architect*
Shabica, Charles Wright *geologist, earth science educator*
Shillestad, John Gardner *financial services company executive*
Smeds, Edward William *retired food company executive*
†Sneed, Paula Ann *food products executive*
Stepan, Frank Quinn *chemical company executive*

Northlake
Haack, Richard Wilson *retired police officer*

Novubrook
Fredman, Susan Miriam *interior designer*

O Fallon
Bjerkaas, Carlton Lee *technology services company executive*
†Gilroy, Joseph M. *civil engineer*
Herrington, James Patrick *secondary education educator*
Voellger, Gary A. *business consulting executive, retired air force officer*

Oak Brook
Baar, John Greenfield, II, *school educator*
Baillie-David, Sonja Kirsteen *controller*
Baker, Robert J(ohn) *hospital administrator*
†Barnes, Karen Kay *lawyer*
†Barnholt, Brandon K. *gas station/convenience store executive*
Bennett, Margaret Airola *lawyer*
Biedron, Theodore John *newspaper advertising executive*
Bower, Barbara Jean *nurse*
Camp, Jeffery Mark *Web specialist, military officer*
†Cantalupo, Jim *food products executive*
Christian, Joseph Ralph *physician*
Congalton, Susan Tichenor *lawyer*
Degerstrom, James Marvin *retired engineering executive*
DeLorey, John Alfred *printing company executive*
Ding, Jianchi *embryologist, researcher*
Dmowski, W. Paul *obstetrician, gynecologist, educator, endocrinologist, researcher*
Duerinck, Louis T. *retired railroad executive, attorney*
Fichter, David Harry *conservationist, environmentalist*

Garrigan, William Henry, III, *firefighter, paramedic*
Greenberg, Jack M. *food products executive*
Higgens, William John, III, (Trey Higgens) *sales executive*
†Hodnik, David F. *retail company executive*
Iles, Eileen Marie *bank executive*
John, Richard C. *enterprise development organization executive*
Koufis, John Theodore *accountant*
La Petina, Gary Michael *lawyer*
Loughead, Jeffrey Lee *physician*
Marchetti, Marilyn H. *lawyer*
†Marcus, Carol A. *information technology manager*
†Miller, Ralph William, Jr., *lawyer*
Mlsna, Kathryn Kimura *lawyer*
Muschler, Audrey Lorraine *insurance broker*
Nelson, Robert Eddinger *management and development consultant*
O'Brien, Walter Joseph, II, *lawyer*
Oldfield, E. Lawrence *lawyer*
†Quinlan, Michael Robert *fast food franchise company executive*
†Ras, Robert A. *lawyer*
Rathi, Manohar Lal *pediatrician, neonatologist*
Schultz, Karen Rose *clinical social worker, author, publisher, speaker*
Turner, Fred L. *fast food company executive*

Oak Forest
Jashel, Larry Steven (L. Steven Rose) *entrepreneur, media consultant*
Kogut, Kenneth Joseph *consulting engineer*
Lee, David Chang *physician*
†Narko, Medard Martin *lawyer*

Oak Lawn
Byrnes, Michael Francis *podiatrist*
Cain, Thomas Robert *interventional radiologist*
Casey, James B. *librarian*
De Bustros, Andrée Chiniara *physician*
Jachna, Joseph David *photographer, educator*
Jandes, Kenneth Michael *superintendent of schools*
Laird, Jean Elouise Rydeski (Mrs. Jack E. Laird) *author, adult education educator*
Lehman, George Morgan *food sales executive*
Tucker, Berry Kenneth *lawyer*
Wright, Steven Randall *minister*

Oak Park
Adelman, William John *university labor and industrial relations educator*
Andre, L. Aumund *management consultant*
Baldwin, Allan Oliver *information scientist, higher education executive*
Burke, Thomas John *communications executive*
Cannon, Patrick Francis *public relations executive*
Cary, William Sterling *retired church executive*
Clark, John Peter, III, *engineering consultant*
Devereux, Timothy Edward *advertising executive*
Dong, Hanmin *forest products executive*
Fanta, Paul Edward *chemist, educator*
Gambro, John M. *priest, secondary school educator*
Gerson, Gary Stanford *rabbi*
Heitzman, Frank Edward *architect*
Jones, Rebecca Alvina Patronis *nurse*
Kinzie, Raymond Wyant *banker, lawyer*
†Leitch, Stuart *music educator, musician*
Matsuda, Takayoshi *surgeon, educator, biomedical researcher*
Pearson, Gayle Marlene *writer, editor*
Pinsky, Ellen Dodge *reading and language educator, education educator*
Rossiter, Charles Melvin *poet*
Rossof, Arthur Harold *internal medicine educator*
Schubert, Blake H. *lawyer, investor*
Sengpiehl, Paul Marvin *lawyer, former state official*
Thomas, Malayilmelathethil *minister, English language educator*
Varchmin, Thomas Edward *environmental health administrator*
Venerable, Shirley Marie *gifted education educator*

Oakbrook Terrace
Becker, Robert Jerome *allergist, health care consultant*
Berry, Lynn Marina *healthcare researcher*
Cason, Marilynn Jean *technological institute official, lawyer*
Catalano, Gerald *accountant*
†Hegenderfer, Jonita Susan *public relations executive*
Hicks, James Thomas *lawyer, physician*
Keller, Dennis James *management educator*
LaForte, George Francis, Jr., *lawyer*
Levine, Norman M. *academic administrator*
Samet, Dean Henry *safety engineer*
Weiland, Mark Bradley *corporate lawyer*
Willis, Douglas Alan *lawyer*

Olney
Boyer, A(deline) Nadine *guidance counselor*

Olympia Fields
Kasimos, John Nicholas *pathologist*
Menees, John Robert *mechanical engineer*
Sandlin, Dorothy *artist*
Sprinkel, Beryl Wayne *economist, consultant*

Onarga
Wilken, Caroline Doane *critical care, emergency, recovery room, and medical/surgical nurse*

Oregon
Hayes, Randy Alan *family therapist*
Haynes, Gary Allen *photographer, journalist, newspaper editor*

Orion
Magee, Elizabeth Sherrard *civic organization volunteer*

Orland Park
Ahmed, Shafiq *surgeon*
Antia, Kersey H. *industrial and clinical psychologist, consultant*
Capstaff, Genevieve MacKeeby *humanities educator*
English, Floyd Leroy *telecommunications company executive*
Gittelman, Marc Jeffrey *manufacturing and financial executive*
Herbert, Victor James *foundation administrator*
Kahn, Jan Edward *manufacturing company executive*
Mockus, Joseph Frank *electrical engineer*
Nasilowski, Paul *geriatrician*
Natvig, Connie Bea *clinical psychologist*

Oswego
May, Frank Brendan, Jr., *lawyer*
Weilert, Ronald Lee *data processing executive*

Ottawa
Benning, Joseph Raymond *principal*
Thornton, Edmund B. *philanthropist*

Palatine
Bender, Virginia Best *computer scientist, educator*
Butler, John Musgrave *financial consultant, consultant*
†Cannon, Benjamin Winton *lawyer, business executive*
Carranza, Cesar Augusto *surgeon*
†Cesario, Robert Charles *franchise executive, consultant*
Fortunato, Nancy *artist*
Hellyer, Timothy Michael *protective services officer*
Herriges, Greg C. *literature educator, writer*
Hershenhorn, Robert Gene *bank executive*
†Hildebrandt, Sharrie L. *legal technology educator, paralegal*
Hull, Elizabeth Anne *retired English language educator*
Keres, Karen Lynne *English language educator*
Kieft, Gerald Nelson *mechanical engineer*
Matsushima, Akira Paul *international company executive*
Medin, Lowell Ansgard *management executive*
Miletto, David Gregory *artist*
Murphy, Colleen Frances *marketing professional, public relations executive*
†Nordlof, Ragnar William *writer*
Pohl, Frederik *freelance/self-employed writer*
Ramunno, Thomas Paul *management consultant*
Ross, Mary Ann *principal*
Sharpee, Rhoda Anderson *social worker*
Spinner, Lee Louis *accountant*
Victor, Michael Gary *lawyer, physician*
Walker, Sally Y. *educational association administrator*
†Wardell, John Watson *lawyer*
†Zamarin, Ronald George *lawyer*

Palos Heights
Breems, Bradley G. *sociologist, educator*
Lysen, Lucinda Katherine *nutrition support nurse, dietitian*
Taylor, Joseph Henry *lawyer*

Palos Hills
Healy, Judith Ann *school social worker*
Porter, Joyce Klowden *theatre educator and director*
Vasiliauskas, Edmund *chemistry educator*

Palos Park
Maxwell, Dorothea Bost Andrews *civic worker*
Nelson, Lawrence Evan *business consultant*

Pana
Evans, Marsha Jo Anne *nursing administrator*
Waddington, Irma Joann *music teacher*

Paris
Anders, Larry Ermel Fagg *mechanical engineer*
Bell, Allen Andrew, Jr., *lawyer*
†Gill, Joseph F. *music educator*
Sisson, Marilyn Sue *writer*

Park Forest
Billig, Etel Jewel *theater director, actress*
Cribbs, Maureen Ann *artist, educator*
Goodrich, John Bernard *lawyer, consultant*
Orr, Marcia *child development researcher, child care consultant*
Williams, Jack Raymond *civil engineer*

Park Ridge
†Albert, Elizabeth Franz (Mrs. Henry B. Albert) *investor, artist, conservationist*
Bales, Edward Wagner *consultant, former manufacturing executive*
Barnett, Patrick Shawn *music educator*
Bitran, Jacob David *internist*
†Boe, Gerard Patrick *health science association administrator, educator*
Campbell, Bruce Crichton *hospital administrator*
Carr, Gilbert Randle *retired railroad executive*
Charewicz, David Michael *photographer*
†Devience, Alex, Jr., *law educator*
Dickieson, Richard Mark *travel company executive*
†Eubank, Edward J. *music educator*
Ewald, Robert Frederick *insurance association executive*
†Franklin, Randy Wayne *lawyer*
Fried, Walter *hematologist, educator*
†Greenspahn, Bruce Robert *cardiologist*
Hegarty, Mary Frances *lawyer*
Herting, Robert Leslie *pharmaceutical executive*
Kenney, John Patrick *dentist*
LaRue, Paul Hubert *retired lawyer*
Mahaffey, John Christopher *association executive*
Mangun, Clarke Wilson, Jr., *public health physician, consultant*

Markuson, Richard K. *pharmaceutical association executive*
†Nagel, Karen Annette Elizabeth *lawyer, editor*
Naker, Mary Leslie *legal firm executive*
Orlow, Daniel John *photographer*
†Roig, Charles *architect*
Russell, William Steven *finance executive*
Samuels, Brian Louis *oncologist, researcher*
Schmidt, Wayne Walter *law association executive*
Sersen, Howard Harry *retired interior designer, cabinetry consultant*
Weber, Philip Joseph *retired manufacturing company executive*
Weinberg, Milton, Jr., *cardiovascular and thoracic surgeon*
White, John Vincent *surgeon, consultant*
†Williams, Sandra Lynn *management consultant*
Yordan, Edgardo Luis *gynecologist*
†Zimmermann, John Joseph *lawyer*

Paw Paw
Heim, Alberta Jane *publishing executive, writer*

Paxton
Kirk, Colleen Jean *retired conductor, educator*

Pekin
Dancey, Charles Lohman *newspaper executive*
†Grewell, Johanne H. Fairs *librarian, consultant*
Schurter, Richard Allen *secondary school history educator*

Peoria
Allen, Lyle Wallace *lawyer*
Bertschy, Timothy L. *lawyer*
Brewer, Cheryl Ann *obstetrician and gynecologist, educator*
Brill de Ramírez, Susan Berry *English educator*
Buchko, Aaron Anthony *management educator*
Bussone, Frank Joseph *bank executive, television broadcaster*
Chamberlain, Joseph Miles *astronomer, educator*
Chenevert, Donald James, Jr., *lawyer*
Coletta, Ralph John *retired lawyer*
Cunningham, Raymond Leo *retired research chemist*
Curtis, R. Craig *political science educator*
†Diaz, Maria E. *director*
Disberger, Dennis Jay *manufacturing executive*
DuBois, Mark Benjamin *former utilities executive, educator*
Duncan, Royal Robert *publisher*
†Elias, John Samuel *lawyer*
†Fanta, George Frederick *chemist, researcher*
Ferrari, Gary John *lawyer*
Goitein, Bernard Joel *management educator, researcher*
Gross, Thomas Lester *obstetrician-gynecologist, researcher*
Harkrader, Alan Dale, Jr., *photojournalist*
Heiple, James Dee *retired state supreme court justice*
Hellhake-Hall, Gerri Ann *critical care nurse, cardiology nurse*
Higgs, David Lawrence *lawyer*
Jibben, Laura Ann *state agency administrator*
Kelly, Grace Dentino *secondary education educator*
Kroehler, Ralph S. *association executive*
Kroll, Dennis Edwards *industrial engineering educator*
Laible-White, Sherry Lynne *welfare reform administrator*
Lanzino, Giuseppe *physician*
†Leitch, David R. *state legislator*
McCollum, Jean Hubble *medical assistant*
McConnell, John Thomas *newspaper executive, publisher*
McMullen, David Wayne *education educator*
†McPheeters, F. Lynn *manufacturing executive*
Meriden, Terry *physician*
Michael, Jonathan Edward *insurance company executive*
Mihm, Michael Martin *federal judge*
Murphy, Sharon Margaret *educator*
Nelson, Lisa Louise *artist*
Nielsen, Eloise Wilma Soule *elementary education educator*
Nielsen, Harald Christian *retired chemist, researcher*
O'Brien, Daniel Robert *lawyer*
Parsons, Donald James *retired bishop*
†Parsons, Richard Hugo *lawyer*
Patel, Gavish N. *surgeon, educator*
Pollak, Raymond *general and transplant surgeon*
Price Boday, Mary Kathryn *choreographer, small business owner, educator*
Prusak, Maximilian Michael *lawyer*
Quanstrom, Roy Fred *non-profit organization executive*
†Reith, Maarten Edward A. *neurochemist*
Saeed, Sy Atezaz *psychiatrist, physician*
Saha, Badal Chandra *biochemist*
Saxon, Randall Lee *pastor, author, educator*
†Sinn, David Randall *lawyer*
Strodel, Robert Carl *lawyer*
†Swain, W. Timothy *lawyer*
Tietjen, Suzanne Davenport *critical care nurse*
†Traicoff, Sandra M. *lawyer*
†Twitty, Susan Kay *music educator*
Vaughan, David John *corporate financial executive*
Walker, Philip Chamberlain, II, *health care executive*
Wessler, Peter *music educator*
Winget, Walter Winfield *lawyer*

Peoria Heights
Bergia, Roger Merle *school system administrator*

Percy
Rice, Charles Dale *labor relations specialist, writer*

Peru
Carus, Milton Blouke *publisher children's periodicals*

Kurtz, James Eugene *freelance writer, minister*
†McKean, Benedict Bernard *priest*

Philo
Wood, Susanne Griffiths *environmental chemist, microbiologist*

Pinckneyville
Cawvey, Clarence Eugene *retired physician*
Johnson, Don Edwin *lawyer*

Plainfield
Chakrabarti, Subrata Kumar *marine research engineer*
Cook, Bruce Lawrence *research analyst*
Diercks, Eileen Kay *educational media coordinator, elementary school educator*
Schinderle, Robert Frank *retired hospital administrator*
Vandevender, Deborah Ann *critical care nurse*

Plano
Krieghbaum, Douglas Matthew *music educator*

Pontiac
Glennon, Charles Edward *retired judge, lawyer*

Port Byron
†Reece, Matthew Lynn *music educator*

Prospect Heights
Aldinger, William F., III, *diversified financial services company executive*
Anderson, Hugh George *bishop*
Byrne, Michael Joseph *manufacturing executive*
Clark, Donald Robert *retired insurance company executive*
Leopold, Mark F. *lawyer*
Lynch, William Thomas, Jr., *advertising agency executive*
Robinson, Martin (Marty Robinson) *television and radio broadcaster, media consultant*

Quincy
Adams, Beejay (Meredith Elisabeth Jane Adams) *sales executive*
†Bohn, Donna May *music educator*
Fecht, Lorene *surgical nurse*
Franklin, Diana Jeanne *chiropractor*
Mallory, Troy L. *accountant*
Moritz, Betty Ann *retired editor*
Points, Roy Wilson *municipal official*
†Rapp, James Anthony *lawyer, author*
†Sutherland, James William *urologist*
Taylor, Judith Caroline *entrepreneur*
†Tenhouse, Art *state representative, farmer*
Tyer, Travis Earl *library consultant*
Walters, Tom Frederick *manufacturing company official*

Rantoul
Holmes, Lois Rehder *composer, piano and voice educator*
Wolters, Paul Henry *music educator, musician*

Richton Park
Nevins, Patrick Fredrick *librarian*
†Pierce, Mary E. *retired educator, public relations consultant*

River Forest
Batlivala, Robert Bomi D. *oil company executive, economics educator*
Bush, Gail *library educator, school librarian*
Coe, Donald Kirk *retired university official*
Hamper, Robert Joseph *marketing executive*
Li, Tze-chung *lawyer, educator*
Marcello, Frank F. *lawyer, educator, writer*
McDonald, Glena June *school counselor*
O'Meara, Thomas Franklin *priest, educator*
Prendergast, Carole Lisak *musician, educator*
Sloan, Jeanette Pasin *artist*
Wirsching, Charles Philipp, Jr., *retired brokerage house executive, private investor*

River Grove
Gardner, Sandi B. *biology educator*
Hillert, Gloria Bonnin *anatomist, educator*
†LaGon, Cynthia Bostic *librarian*
Stein, Thomas Henry *social science educator*
†Traut, Christopher D. *educational materials distribution executive*

Riverdale
Hoekwater, James Warren *treasurer*
Kruszynski, Timothy Edward *retired corrections officer, poet*

Riverside
Chmell, Samuel Jay *orthopedic surgeon*
Dengler, Robert Anthony *professional association executive, educator*
Kubiczky, Stephen Ralph *lawyer*
Marty, Martin Emil *religion educator, editor*
Pollitt, Raymond Daniel John *writer, consultant*

Riverwoods
Del Tiempo, Sandra Kay *sales executive*
Douglas, Bruce Lee *oral and maxillofacial surgeon, public health educator, gerontology and workplace health consultant*
Ford, Michael W. *lawyer*

Rochester
Petterchak, Janice A. *researcher, writer*

Rock Falls
Julifs, Sandra Jean *community action agency executive*

Rock Island
Adams, Stewart Lee *special education educator*
Anderson, Richard Charles *geology educator*
Banas, John Stanley *obstetrician, gynecologist*
Cheney, Thomas Ward *retired insurance company executive*
Dziadyk, Bohdan *botany and ecology educator*

†Griffin-Brown, Dianna Lynn *entrepreneur, educator*
Horstmann, James Douglas *college official*
Kowalczyk, Paul Alan *civil engineer*
Lardner, Henry Petersen (Peter Lardner) *insurance company executive*
Sundelius, Harold W. *geology educator*
Tredway, Thomas *college president*
VanDerGinst, Dennis Allen *lawyer*
Wallace, Franklin Sherwood *lawyer, director*

Rockford
Albert, Janyce Louise *human resources specialist, retired business educator, banker, consultant, human resources specialist*
Anderson, Max Elliot *television and film production company executive*
Apgar, Jean E. *artist, consultant*
Argraves, Hugh Oliver *poet, artist, playwright*
Baptist, Errol Christopher *pediatrician, educator*
Baxter, Jeffrey Q. *graphic artist, sculptor*
Bippus, David Paul *manufacturing company executive*
Borling, John Lorin *military officer*
Cadigan, Elise *social worker*
Carlson, Allan Constantine *historian*
Casagranda, Robert Charles *industrial engineer*
Clodius, Robert LeRoy *economist, educator*
Doran, Thomas George *bishop*
Duck, Vaughn Michael *software company executive*
Eliason, Jon Tate *electrical engineer*
†Fleming, Thomas J. *editor, publishing executive*
Frakes, James Terry *physician, gastroenterologist, educator*
Fredrickson, Robert Alan *lawyer*
Gaylord, Edson I. *manufacturing company executive*
†GeRue, Gerald G. *management consultant*
Hanson, Murray *minister*
Hart-Nolan, Elsie Faye *elementary education educator*
Heerens, Robert Edward *physician*
Heinke, Warren E. *social services administrator*
Hendershott Love, Arles June *television community relations director*
Henley, Eric *physician, educator*
†Heuer, Beth Lee *music educator, composer*
Hornby, Robert Ray *mechanical engineer*
Horst, Bruce Everett *manufacturing company executive*
Hoshaw, Lloyd *retired historian, educator*
Howard, John Addison *former college president, institute executive*
Jacobi, Fredrick Thomas *newspaper publisher*
Johnson, Elizabeth Ericson *retired educator*
Johnson, Thomas Stuart *lawyer*
Kelleghan, Kevin Michael *writer, trainer*
†Knight, William D., Jr., *lawyer*
†Lafever, Francis J. *retired sales executive*
Larsen, Steven *orchestra conductor*
Mahlburg, Norine Elizabeth *retired nurse*
Masters, Arlene Elizabeth *singer*
Mateer, Don M. *lawyer*
Maysent, Harold Wayne *hospital administrator*
McClelland, Patricia G. *minister*
Mc Nelly, Frederick Wright, Jr., *psychologist*
O'Donnell, William David *retired construction firm executive*
†Olson, Lynne Diane *music educator*
Pape, Sheri *music director, educator, artist*
Petru, Suzanne Mitton *health care finance executive*
Pribbenow, Paul C. *higher education administrator, consultant*
Reinhard, Philip G. *federal judge*
Reno, Roger *lawyer*
Rifkin, Gary D. *physician, educator*
Robinson, Donald Peter *musician, retired electrical engineer*
Salafsky, Bernard *pharmacologist, educator*
Schauer, Jeffrey Edward *surgeon*
Shepler, John Edward *engineering executive*
†Sherman, Deborah Lynn
Steele, Carl Lavern *academic administrator*
Steurer, Jeffrey M *music educator*
Traci, Kathleen Frances *library media specialist*
Tregay, Susan Webb *artist, educator*
Walhout, Justine Simon *chemistry educator*
Wallem, Paul Sigurd *financial planner*
Ward, Douglas Andrew *Spanish and special education educator*
Weissbard, David Raymond *minister*
Yu, Fu-Li *biochemistry educator, cancer researcher*

Rockton
Gregoire, Eugene Harold *music educator*
Pennell, Danny Joe *social worker*

Rolling Meadows
†Bassi, Suzanne Howard *volunteer*
Cain, R. Wayne *sales, finance and leasing company executive*
†Cash, Alan Sherwin *electronics assembly specialist*
Eckel, James J. *flight test engineer*
Giese, Robert James *minister*
Roti, Thomas David *judge*
Strongin, Bonnie Lynn *English language educator*
Sullivan, Michael D. *lawyer*
Theis, Steven Thomas *public health service officer*

Romeoville
Delabre, Kevin Michael *religious organization executive*
†Hassert, Brent *state legislator*
Vander Vliet, Valerie Jeanne *biology educator*

Roscoe
Jacobs, Richard Dearborn *consulting engineering company executive*
†Panagopoulos, Janie Lynn *writer*
Sears, Donna Mae *designer, illustrator*

Roselle
Bassitt, Janet Louise *lawyer*
Marshall, James Andrew *civil engineer, real estate developer*
†Waite, Darvin Danny *accountant*

Rosemont
Ames, Sandra Patience *sales executive*
Good, William Allen *professional society executive*
Isenberg, Howard Lee *manufacturing company executive*
Meinert, John Raymond *investment banker, clothing manufacturing and retailing executive*
Rosenthal, Lawrence Edward *association executive*
Small, Richard Donald *travel company executive*

Round Lake
†Abdullah, Bashar Y. *pharmacist, researcher*
†Dalzell, Kimberly Kay *nutritionist*

Round Lake Beach
Brown, Jeffrey Don *musician*

Saint Anne
Holtzman, Michael *alcohol abuse professional*

Saint Charles
†Abts, Gwyneth Hartmann *dietitian*
Babel, Rayonia Alleen *retired librarian, educator*
†Benjamin, Lawrence *food service executive*
Frank, Ruby Merinda *employment agency executive*
Griffin, Sheila MB *strategic marketing excutive*
Kull, James Arthur *music educator*
†LaHood, Julie Ann *small business owner*
Liska, Margaret Naylor *retired small business owner*
Osowiec, Darlene Ann *clinical psychologist, educator, consultant*
Schaufenbuel, Bradley John *computer consultant, writer*
Stone, John McWilliams, Jr., *electronics executive*
†Stovall, April Leanne *music educator*

Saint Francisville
Harezi, Ilonka Jo *medical technology research executive*

Saint Jacob
Carter, Dennis R. *music educator, band director, musician*

Sauget
Baltz, Richard Arthur *chemical engineer*

Savoy
Sinclair, James Burton *retired plant pathology educator, consultant*

Scales Mound
Lieberman, Archie *photographer, writer*

Schaumburg
Adrianopoli, Barbara Catherine *librarian*
Aitken, Rosemary Theresa *financial planner, consultant*
Balasa, Mark Edward *investment consultant*
Burroughs, Susan Marie *industrial and organizational psychologist, educator*
De Lerno, Manuel Joseph *electrical engineer*
†Devonshire, David W. *financial executive*
Eickelmann, Nancy Sue *research scientist*
Fiore, Colleen Mary *meeting manager*
Frano, Andrew Joseph *lawyer, civil engineer*
Galvin, Christopher B. *electronics company executive*
†Galvin, Robert W. *electronics executive*
Gyorfi, Julius Steven *electrical engineer, researcher*
Hambley, Douglas Frederick *geological and environmental engineer*
Hill, Raymond Joseph *packaging company executive*
Hlousek, Joyce B(ernadette) *school system administrator*
Koenig, Leo John *family practice physician*
†Lawson, A. Peter *lawyer*
Little, Bruce Washington *professional society administrator*
Otis, James, Jr., *architect*
†Sikora, Sheryl L. *application developer*
Stabej, Rudolph John *computer consultant*
Tipps, Gregory Paul *music educator*
Tompson, Marian Leonard *professional society administrator*
Westlund, Maribeth *secondary school educator*
†Wojcik, Kathleen Louise *state representative*

Schiller Park
Congalton, Christopher William *lawyer*

Sherman
Boyd, Marvin G. *electrical engineer*

Shorewood
Lombardo, David Albert *actor, writer, speaker, aviation educator*
Petrella, Mary Therese *community health and women's health nurse*

Silvis
Bobb, Harold Daniel *chiropractor, consultant*
Rhee, Yang Ho *radiologist*

Skokie
†Bauer, Michael *lawyer*
Bell, Rosonald Renae *toxicologist*
Breckel, Alvina Hefeli *librarian*
Corley, William Gene *engineering research executive*
DeGutis, Dorothea Lynn *psychiatrist*
†Denkewalter, Kim Richard *lawyer*
Fan, Tai-Shen Liu *dietitian*
Gershon, William I. *marketing and communications executive, writer, voiceover actor*
†Ginn, Martin E. *writer, consultant*
Gleason, John Patrick, Jr., *trade association executive*
Gopman, Howard Z. *lawyer*
†Gotkin, Michael Stanley *lawyer, director*
†Gupta, Vishal K *pharmaceutical scientist*
†Hamer, Martin *retired chemist*
Hedien, Wayne Evans *retired insurance company executive*
†Hirsch, Lois Celeste *retired librarian*
Hoopis, Harry Peter *insurance executive, entrepreneur*
Horwitz, Irwin Daniel *otolaryngologist, educator*
Kahn, Bert L. *lawyer*
†Lang, Louis I. *state legislator, lawyer*
Langguth, Margaret Witty *health facility administrator*
Levy, Mark Hirsch *internist, medical educator, researcher*
McCarthy, Michael Shawn *health care company executive, lawyer*
Plotnick, Paul William *lawyer*
†Sachs, Irving Joseph *lawyer, accountant, pension consultant*
Schwarz, Eitan Daniel *psychiatrist*
Seeder, Richard Owen *infosystems specialist*
Siegal, Burton Lee *product designer, consultant, inventor*
Siegal, Rita Goran *engineering company executive*
Van Gelder, Marc Christiaan *retail executive*
Weidmann, K. Timothy *not-for-profit fundraiser, writer*
Whalen, Patricia Therese *marketing and public relations educator, consultant*
Yogev, Sara *psychologist*

Smithfield
Corsaw, Ardith *geriatrics nurse, administrator*

Smithton
Hostetler, Elsie J. *musician, music educator*

South Barrington
Kissane, Sharon Florence *writer, consultant, educator*

South Holland
Bell, Jason Cameron *lawyer*
Bourgeois, Marilyn Ann *piano educator, pianist*
Fota, Frank George *artist*
Larsen, Mary Ann Indovina *counselor, educator*
Perry, Joseph N. *bishop*
†Wolf, Wayne Lowell *criminal justice educator, researcher*

Spring Grove
York, Karen Kay *accountant, farmer*

Springfield
Bannister, Dan Wesley *historian, retired*
Bartolo, Donna Marie *health association executive, retired nurse*
†Beaubien, Mark H., Jr., *state representative*
Beckwith, Peter Hess *bishop*
Bell, John Perry *minister, religious organization administrator*
Bergschneider, David Philip *legal administrator*
†Black, William B. *state legislator*
Blackman, Jeanne A. *community program manager*
Blagojevich, Rod R. *governor, former congressman*
†Boland, Michael Joseph *state legislator*
†Bomke, Larry K. *state legislator*
†Bradley, Richard T. *state representative*
†Brady, Daniel P. *state representative*
Bretz, William Franklin *retired elementary and secondary education educator*
Brown, Vandella *librarian*
Campbell, Kathleen Charlotte Murphey *audiology educator, administrator, researcher*
†Chen, Eden Hsien-chang *engineering consultant*
Clark, Thomas Allen *planning and evaluation consultant*
†Collins, Annazette R. *state representative*
†Collins, Jacqueline Y *state senator*
†Crotty, M. Maggie *state senator*
Cullen, Mark Kenneth *lawyer*
†Cultra, Shane *state representative*
Currie, Barbara Flynn *state legislator*
Daniels, Lee Albert *state legislator*
Darby, Karen Sue *legal education administrator*
†Daugherty, Phyllis Lyn *secondary school educator*
†Davis, George Cullom *historian*
†Davis, Monique D. (Deon Davis) *state legislator*
†Del Valle, Miguel *state legislator*
†Demuzio, Vince Thomas *state legislator*
Dodge, Edward John *retired insurance executive*
Dorsey, J. Kevin *dean*
†Dunn, Joe *state representative*
†Eddy, Roger L. *state representative*
Ellis, Michael Eugene *documentary film producer, writer, director, marketing executive*
Evans, Charles H. *federal judge*
Feldman, Howard William *lawyer*
†Flowers, Mary E. *state legislator*
†Forby, Gary F. *state representative*
Ford, Terry Lynn *protective services official*
Frank, Stuart *cardiologist*
†Fritchey, John A. *state representative*
Gallina, Charles Onofrio *nuclear scientist*
Gamble, Douglas Irvin *state official, educator*
†Garrett, Susan *state senator*
†Geo-Karis, Adeline Jay *state legislator*
Girard, G. Tanner *state environmental officer*
†Graham, Donald R. *epidemiologist*
†Granberg, Kurt *state legislator, lawyer*
Hahin, Christopher *metallurgical engineer, corrosion engineer*
†Haine, William R. *state senator*
Hallmark, Donald Parker *museum director, lecturer*
†Halvorson, Debbie DeFrancesco *state legislator*
†Hamos, Julie E. *state representative*
†Hannig, Gary L. *state representative*
Herriford, Robert Levi, Sr., *army officer*
Holland, John Madison *retired family practice physician*
†Howard, Constance A. *state representative*
Immke, Keith Henry *lawyer*
Jacobson, Doranne *photographer*
†Jakobsson, Naomi D. *state representative*
†Jefferson, Charles E. *state representative*
†Jones, Lovana S. *state legislator*
†Jones, Wendell E. *state legislator*
†Kelly, Robin L. *state representative*
Kerr, Gary Enrico *lawyer, educator*
†Kosel, Renée *state representative*
†Krause, Carolyn H. *state legislator, lawyer*
Kuhn, Kathleen Jo *accountant*
†Kurtz, Rosemary *state representative*
†Lauzen, Christopher J. *state legislator*
†Lightford, Kimberly A. *state legislator*
†Link, Terry *state legislator*
†Londrigan, James Thomas *lawyer*
†Luechtefeld, David *state legislator*
†Lyons, Joseph M. *state representative*
Madigan, Michael Joseph *state legislator*
Malany, Le Grand Lynn *lawyer, engineer, bank executive*
Marcy-Geyston, Stephanie Vivian *interior designer*
†Martinez, Iris *state senator*
†Mathewson, Mark Stuart *lawyer, editor*
†Mathias, Sidney H. *state representative*
†McCarthy, Kevin A. *state representative*
†McKeon, Larry J. *state representative*
Mc Millan, R(obert) Bruce *museum executive, anthropologist*
†Meeks, James T. *state senator*
Mikell, Frank Leonard *cardiologist*
Miller, Benjamin K. *retired state supreme court justice*
†Miller, David E. *state representative*
Mills, Richard Henry *federal judge*
†Mitchell, Gerald Lee *state legislator*
Mogerman, Susan *state agency administrator*
†Mool, Deanna S. *lawyer*
Mooney, Christopher Zimmer *political science educator*
Morse, Saul Julian *lawyer*
†Mulligan, Rosemary Elizabeth *legislator*
†Munoz, Antonio *state legislator*
Munyer, Edward A. *zoologist, museum administrator*
Myers, Phillip Ward *otolaryngologist*
†Nekritz, Elaine *state representative*
†Obama, Barack A. *state legislator*
†Pankau, Carole *state legislator*
†Parke, Terry Richard *state legislator*
†Patton, Mary Knox *mathematician, educator*
†Peterson, William E. *state legislator*
†Petka, Ed (Edward F.) *state legislator*
Phillips, John Robert *political scientist, educator*
†Pihos, Sandra M *state representative*
Poorman, Robert Lewis *education consultant, former college president*
Porter, William L. *retired electrical engineer*
†Radogno, Christine *state legislator*
†Ramirez-Campbell, Christine M. *art council administrator*
†Rauschenberger, Steven J. *state legislator*
Reed, Robert Phillip *lawyer*
†Reents, Ray Edward *banking and stock consultant*
†Reichensperger, Joel David *neuroscientist*
†Reitz, Dan *state representative*
Reyman, Jonathan Eric *archaeologist, anthropologist, researcher*
†Righter, Dale A. *state senator*
Rogers, James Allan *music director, hymnologist, author, editor*
Rominger, M. Kyle *lawyer*
†Ronen, Carol *state legislator*
Rowe, Max L. *lawyer, corporate executive, management and political consultant, writer, judge*
†Rutherford, Dan *state legislator*
Ryan, Daniel Leo *bishop*
†Sacia, Jim *state representative*
†Saviano, Angelo *state legislator*
Schmidt, Mark James *state public health official*
†Schoenberg, Jeffrey M. *state legislator*
Schrader, Andrew Robert *music educator*
Schroeder, Joyce Katherine *state agency administrator, research analyst*
†Shadid, George P. *state legislator*
Shim, Sang Koo *state mental health official*
†Sieben, Todd *state legislator*
†Silverstein, Ira I. *state legislator*
†Slone, Ricca C *state representative*
†Smith, Michael Kent *state legislator*
†Stephens, Ronald Earl *state legislator*
Stone, Stephen Paul *dermatologist*
Stroh, Raymond Eugene *retired personnel executive*
†Sullivan, Dave *state legislator*
Sumner, David Spurgeon *surgery educator*
Swartz, Conrad Melton *psychiatrist*
†Syverson, Dave *state legislator*
Temple, Wayne Calhoun *historian, writer*
Travis, Lawrence Allan *accountant*
†Trotter, Donne E. *state legislator, hospital administrator*
†Turner, Arthur L. *state legislator*
Unanue, Enrique Jorge *architect*
Van Meter, Abram DeBois *lawyer, retired banker*
†Walsh, Lawrence M. *state legislator*
†Washington, Eddie *state representative*
Wehrle, Leroy Snyder *economist, educator*
Weinhoeft, John Joseph *data processing executive*
†Welch, Patrick *state legislator*
Whitaker, Victoria Manuela Katz *publisher, public relations executive, educator, consultant*
White, Jesse *state official*
†Wirsing, David A. *state legislator*
Wood, Harlington, Jr., *federal judge*
Woodson, Gayle Ellen *otolaryngologist*

†Woolard, Larry *state legislator*
Yaffe, Stuart Allen *physician*
†Yarbrough, Karen A. *state representative*
Zaricznyj, Basilius *orthopedic surgeon*
Zook, Elvin Glenn *plastic surgeon, educator*

Steger
Carpenter, Kenneth Russell *international trading executive*

Sterling
Donahue, Shirley Ohnstad *elementary education educator*
Moran, Joan Jensen *physical education and health educator*

Stoy
Rhoten, Kenneth D. *writer*

Sugar Grove
Burch, Susan Ann *human resource developer, educator*
†Debartolo, Hansel Marion, Jr., *otorhinolaryngology surgeon*
†Ziman, Stephen Michael *protective services official, educator, criminal justice educator*

Sullivan
Holder, Lonnie Edward *engineering administrator, design engineer*

Swansea
Chambers, Jerry Ray *school system administrator*

Sycamore
†Burzynski, James Bradley *state legislator*
Dennis, Peter Ray *environmental corporate executive*
Fanning, Gary Lee *anesthesiologist*
†Goodman, Kenneth Alan *secondary school educator*
Johnson, Yvonne Amalia *elementary education educator, science consultant*
Smith, Peter Thomas *lawyer*
Stone, Van Courtright *professional society administrator*
Vance Siebrasse, Kathy Ann *legislative staff member*
Young, Arthur Price *librarian, educator*

Table Grove
†Reller, Kristi Jo *secondary school educator*
Thomson, Helen Louise *artist*

Taylor Ridge
†Potthast, David Raymond *retired military officer, secondary school educator*

Taylorville
Austin, Daniel William *lawyer*

Techny
Vanderstappen, Harrie Albert *Far Eastern art educator*

Tinley Park
Baker, Betty Louise *retired secondary education educator*
Chin, Davis *lawyer*
Daniels, Kurt R. *speech and language pathologist*
German, Frank William *broadcaster*
Haley, David Alan *healthcare executive*
Keenan, Robert Arthur *bank executive, consultant*
Kenny, Mary Alice *lawyer, law librarian*
Leeson, Janet Caroline Tollefson *cake specialties company executive*
Mulquin, Kimberly Ann *nurse*
Taylor, Marva Jean Shipman Foulks *social worker*
†West, David Wayne *mechanical engineer*

Toledo
Prather, William C., III, *lawyer, writer*

Tunnel Hill
Webb, O. Glenn *retired farm supplies company executive*

Union
Perlick, Richard Allan *steel company executive*

University Park
†Hakala, Reino William *mathematician, educator*
Keys, Paul Ross *university provost/academic affairs official*
Leftwich, Robert Eugene *oncological and adult nursing educator*
McMaster, Michele *communications educator*
†Patton, June Odessa *writer, consultant, educator, researcher*

Urbana
Addy, Alva Leroy *mechanical engineer*
Aldridge, Alfred Owen *English language educator*
†Allain, Jean Paul *research scientist*
Antonsen, Elmer Harold *Germanic languages and linguistics educator*
Arnstein, Walter Leonard *historian, educator*
Axford, Roy Arthur *nuclear engineering educator*
Baer, Werner *economist, educator*
Baker, David Hiram *nutritionist, nutrition educator*
Balbach, Stanley Byron *lawyer*
Banwart, Wayne Lee *agronomy, environmental science educator*
Basar, Tamer *electrical engineering educator*
Baym, Nina *English educator*
Beak, Peter Andrew *chemistry educator*
Benekohal, Rahim Farahnak *civil engineering educator, researcher, consultant*
Bennett, Scott Boyce *retired librarian*
Bergeron, Clifton George *ceramic engineer, educator*
Bérubé, Michael *literature educator*
Bial, Raymond Steven *author, photographer*
Birnbaum, Howard Kent *materials science educator*
Blahut, Richard Edward *electrical and computer engineering educator*
†Bobyshev, Dmitry V. *poet, education educator*
†Bodmer, Paul Herbert *professional society administrator*
†Bombardelli, Fabián Alejandro *hydraulic engineer, researcher*
Brichford, Maynard Jay *archivist*
Bruner, Edward M. *anthropology educator*
Buetow, Dennis Edward *physiologist, educator*
Burger, Ambrose William *agronomy educator*
Burkholder, Donald Lyman *mathematician, educator*
Carmen, Ira Harris *political scientist, educator*
Carringer, Robert *English language and film educator*
Carroll, Robert Wayne *mathematics educator*
†Carter, Nicholas Carter *education educator*
Chao, Bei Tse *mechanical engineering educator*
Chato, John Clark *mechanical and bioengineering educator*
Chow, Poo *wood technologist, scientist*
Christians, Clifford Glenn *communications educator*
Clark, Jimmy Howard *nutrition educator*
Coleman, James J. *electrical engineer, educator*
Coleman, Paul Dare *electrical engineering educator*
Conry, Thomas Francis *mechanical engineering educator, consultant*
Crang, Richard Francis Earl *plant and cell biologist, research center administrator*
Crofts, Antony Richard *biochemistry and biophysics educator*
Cronan, Jr., John Emerson *microbiologist*
Cuno, Kenneth M. *historian, educator*
Cusano, Cristino *mechanical engineer, educator*
Daniel, David Edwin *civil engineer, educator*
Dash, Leon DeCosta, Jr., *journalist*
†Davis, Ollie Watts *musician, educator*
Dick, William Allen *engineering educator*
†Dikanov, Sergei A. *physicist, researcher*
Di Virgilio, Nicholas *voice music educator*
Doob, Joseph Leo *mathematician, educator*
Dovring, Karin Elsa Ingeborg *writer, poet, playwright, communication analyst*
†Due, Jean Margaret *agricultural economist, educator*
Dziuk, Philip John *animal scientist educator*
Eden, James Gary *electrical engineer, educator, physicist, researcher*
†Edgar, Jim *former governor*
Ehlen, Timothy John *music educator, musician*
†Ehrlich, Gert *science educator, researcher*
Feng, Albert *science educator, researcher*
Fitz-Gerald, Roger Miller *lawyer*
†Fitzpatrick, Krystal L. *protective services official*
Forbes, Richard Mather *biochemistry educator*
Fossum, Robert Merle *mathematician, educator*
Frazzetta, Thomas Henry *evolutionary biologist, functional morphologist, educator*
Friedman, Stanley *insect physiologist, educator*
Fujiwara, Mitsuko *chemist, researcher, chemist, educator*
Gabriel, Michael *psychology educator*
Gaddy, Oscar Lee *electrical engineering educator*
Garrigus, Upson Stanley *animal science and international agriculture educator*
†Ge, Pinghua *research scientist*
†Georgiadis, John G. *mechanical engineer, educator*
Gibb, Matthew DeWolfe *physician*
Giertz, J. Fred *economics educator*
Giles, Eugene *anthropology educator*
Ginsberg, Donald Maurice *physicist, educator*
Glick, Karen Lynne *college administrator*
†Goldman, Dara Ellen *education educator*
Goldwasser, Edwin Leo *physicist*
Goodman, David G. *Japanese, comparative literature educator, writer*
Gove, Samuel Kimball *political science educator*
Govindjee, *biophysics, biochemistry, and biology educator*
Gray, John Walker *mathematician, educator*
Greene, Laura Helen *physicist*
Greenough, William Tallant *psychobiologist, educator*
Gruebele, Martin *chemistry, physics, and biophysics educator*
Guibbory, Achsah *English educator, writer*
Haile, H. G. *German language and literature educator*
Hall, William Joel *civil engineer, educator*
Han, Jiawei *computer scientist, educator*
Hannon, Bruce Michael *engineer, educator*
Hanratty, Thomas Joseph *chemical engineer, educator*
Hansen, Kathryn Gertrude *editor, former state official*
Haziyu, Wallace Muleya *secondary school educator*
Heath, James Edward *physiology educator, retired*
Hedlund, Barbara Smith *musician, educator, music publisher*
Hedlund, Ronald *baritone*
Heichel, Gary Harold *crop sciences educator*
Hendrick, George *retired English language educator*
Hess, Karl *electrical and computer engineering educator*
Hill, Lowell Dean *agricultural marketing educator*
†Hitchins, Keith Arnold *historian, educator*
Hoeft, Robert Gene *agriculture educator*
Hoffmeister, Donald Frederick *zoologist, educator*
Holonyak, Nick, Jr., *electrical engineering educator*
Holt, Donald A. *agronomist, consultant, retired academic administrator*
Hoxie, Frederick Eugene *history educator*
Huang, Thomas Shi-Tao *electrical engineering educator, researcher*
Hymowitz, Theodore *plant geneticist, educator*
Iben, Icko, Jr., *astrophysicist, educator*
Ikenberry, Judith Life *social and charitable organization volunteer, writer*
Jacobson, Howard *classics educator*
Jockusch, Carl Groos, Jr., *mathematics educator*
Jonas, Jiri *chemist, educator*
Jones, Benjamin Angus, Jr., *retired agricultural engineering educator, administrator*
Joseph, Lura Ellen *librarian, geologist*
Kaufman, Jerome Benzion *neurosurgeon*
†Kelleher, Neil L. *chemist, educator*
Kieffer, Susan Werner *geologist, educator, real estate developer, consultant*
†Kim, Chin-Woo *linguist, educator*
Kirkpatrick, R(obert) James *geology educator*
Klein, Miles Vincent *physics educator*
Knight, Frank Bardsley *mathematics educator*
Kolodziej, Edward Albert *political scientist, educator*
Kotynek, Jan George *surgeon*
Krock, Curtis Josselyn *pulmonologist*
Kumar, Panganamala Ramana *electrical and computer engineering educator*
Kushner, Mark Jay *physics and engineering educator*
Larson, Carl Shipley *engineering educator, consultant*
Lasersohn, Peter Nathan *linguist, educator*
Lauterbur, Paul C(hristian) *chemistry educator*
Lazarus, Betty Ross *retired civic activist*
Lazarus, David *physicist, educator*
†Leggett, Anthony J. *education educator*
Lieberman, Laurence *poet, educator*
Livingstone, Carol *academic administrator*
Love, Joseph L. *history educator, former cultural studies center administrator*
Makri, Nancy *chemistry educator*
Mapother, Dillon Edward *physicist, university official*
May, Walter Grant *chemical engineer, educator*
Mayes, Paul Eugene *engineering educator, technical consultant*
McColley, Robert McNair *history educator*
McConkie, George Wilson *educational psychology educator*
Mc Glamery, Marshal Dean *crop scientist, weed science educator*
McKay, John Patrick *history educator*
Meyer, Richard Charles *microbiologist, educator*
Miley, George Hunter *nuclear and electrical engineering educator*
Miller, Robert Earl *engineer, educator*
Mortensen, Peter Leslie *English language educator*
Nanney, David Ledbetter *genetics educator*
Nelson, Ralph Alfred *physician*
Nettl, Bruno *anthropology and musicology educator*
Newman, John Kevin *classics educator*
O'Brien, Nancy Patricia *librarian, educator*
Odintsov, Boris Mikhailovich *physicist, researcher*
†Oehlers, Paul A. *composer, music educator*
Oliphant, Uretz John *physician, surgeon*
O'Morchoe, Charles Christopher Creagh *anatomical sciences educator, science administrator*
†Pahre, Robert *social sciences educator*
Pearlstein, Arne Jacob *engineer, educator*
Phinney, Leslie Mary *mechanical engineering educator*
Picchietti, Daniel Leigh *neurologist*
Rao, Nannapaneni Narayana *electrical engineer*
Rebeiz, Constantin A. *plant physiology educator, laboratory director*
Replinger, John Gordon *architect, retired educator*
Resek, Robert William *economist*
Rich, Robert F. *law and political science educator*
Ridgway, Marcella Davies *veterinarian*
Robinson, Arthur Richard *civil engineer, educator*
Robinson, Derek Scott *mathematician, educator*
Roley, Jeff W. *foundation representative*
Rotzoll, Kim Brewer *advertising and communications educator*
Rowland, Theodore Justin *physicist, educator*
Salamon, Myron Ben *physicist, educator, dean*
Satterthwaite, Cameron B. *physics educator*
Sauer, Peter William *electrical engineering educator*
†Scheeline, Alexander *chemistry educator*
†Schleis, Thomas Henry *music educator, organist*
†Schmidt, Diane Carol *librarian*
Schmidt, Stephen Christopher *agricultural economist, educator*
Schupp, Paul Eugene *mathematician, educator*
Seigler, David Stanley *botanist, chemist, educator*
Shtohryn, Dmytro Michael *librarian, educator*
Siedler, Arthur James *nutrition and food science educator*
Simon, Jack Aaron *geologist, former state official*
†Snoeyink, Vernon L. *civil engineer, educator*
Snyder, Lewis Emil *astrophysicist, educator*
Solberg, Winton Udell *history educator*
†Sousa, Ronald Wayne *foreign language educator*
Spence, Mary Lee *historian, educator*
Stallmeyer, James Edward *engineer, educator*
†Stukel, James Joseph *academic administrator, mechanical engineering educator*
Sturtevant, William T. *fundraising executive, consultant*
Sullivan, John Matthew *mathematician, educator*
Suslick, Kenneth Sanders *chemistry educator*
Swenson, George Warner, Jr., *electronics engineer, radio astronomer, educator*
Switzer, Robert Lee *biochemistry educator*
†Sydnor, Synthia *kinesiology educator*
Talbot, Emile Joseph *French language educator*
†Thies, Richard Leon *lawyer, director*
†Ting, Mingfang *geophysicist, educator*
Tondeur, Philippe Maurcie *mathematician, educator*
†Tsitsaros, Christos *composer, musician*
†Uchtmann, Donald Louis *lawyer, law educator*
†Von Gunden, Heidi *music educator*
Voss, Edward William, Jr., *immunologist, educator*
Waldbauer, Gilbert Peter *entomologist, educator*
Walker, William Hamilton *civil engineering educator*
Watson, Paula D. *library administrator*
Watts, Emily Stipes *English language educator*
†Webber, Carl Maddra *lawyer*
†Webbink, Ronald Frederick *astrophysicist, educator*
Weidner, Robert Wright *musician, music educator, musicologist*
Wert, Charles Allen *metallurgical and mining engineering educator*
†Whiteley, H. E. *dean*
Whitt, Gregory Sidney *evolution educator*
Williams, Martha Ethelyn *information science educator*
Wirt, Frederick Marshall *retired political scientist, educator*
Wolfe, Ralph Stoner *microbiology educator*
†Wong, Martin D.F. *computer scientist, educator*
Woodard, Beth Stuckey *librarian, educator*
Yoerger, Roger Raymond *agricultural engineer, educator*
Yu, George Tzuchiao *political science educator*

Urbana-Champaign
Jarrell, Wesley Michael *environmental scientist, educator*

Vernon Hills
Cho, Yong Hyo *public administrator, educator*
Claassen, W(alter) Marshall *employment company executive*
Curns, Eileen Bohan *counselor, author, speaker*
†Edwardson, John Albert *security firm executive*
†Halitsky, Steve *application developer, researcher*
†Krasny, Michael P. *computer company executive*
†Lee, Jungok Paik *music educator*
Michalik, John James *legal educational association executive*
Powers, Anthony Richard, Jr., *educational sales professional*
†Ryg, Kathleen Schultz *municipal government official*

Villa Park
Antonelli, Joseph K. *musician, educator*
Smith, Barbara Ann *gifted education coordinator*
Tang, George Chickchee *investment company executive*

Warrenville
Belchak, Frank Robert *computer technologist*
†Benson, Valerie A. *artist, writer*
Gordon, Robert M. *lawyer*
Johnson, Douglas Wells *lawyer*
Lannert, Robert Cornelius *manufacturing company executive*
Lennes, Gregory *manufacturing and financing company executive*
†Ustian, Daniel C. *trucking executive*

Washington
Blumenshine, Mahlon *banker*
Hallinan, John Cornelius *mechanical engineering consultant*
Miller, Jennifer Renee *music educator, composer, writer*
Stine, Robert Howard *retired pediatrician, allergist*

Washington Park
Krause, Richard John (RJ) *elementary school educator, coach*

Waterloo
Coffee, Richard Jerome, II, *lawyer*
Poschel, James Edward *mental health services administrator, psychotherapist*

Wauconda
Kramer, Pamela Kostenko *librarian*

Waukegan
Bairstow, Richard Raymond *retired lawyer*
Brady, Terrence Joseph *judge*
†Cherry, Peter Ballard *electrical products corporation executive*
Drapalik, Betty R. *volunteer, artist, educator*
Hall, Albert L. *retired lawyer*
†Hartman, Marshall J. *lawyer*
†Henrick, Michael Francis *lawyer*
Leibowitz, David Perry *lawyer*
Marks, Martha Alford *writer*
Martis, Leo *healthcare researcher*
Srinivasa, Venkataramaniah *engineer*

Waverly
Stahr, Ellen Marie *secondary school educator*

Wayne
Brunken, Gerald Walter, Sr., *manufacturing company executive*

Wayne City
†Blank, Stanley Bruce *secondary school educator*

West Brooklyn
Mays, K. J. *writer, musician*

West Chicago
Paulissen, James Peter *retired physician, county official*

West Dundee
Woltz, Kenneth Allen *consulting executive*

West Frankfort
Thompson, Bobby Gene *physician*

Westchester
Calder, Robert Austin *preventive medicine physician, administrator*
Castellano, Christine Marie *lawyer*
Crois, John Henry *local government official*
Faulkner, Robert Lloyd *advertising executive, graphic designer*
Lass, Nancy Anne *physician*
Masterson, John Patrick *retired English language educator*
Matuga, Edward Anthony *lawyer*
Morefield, Michael Thomas *financial executive*
†Pavelka, Elaine Blanche *mathematics educator*
Shaffer, Susan E. *nutrition specialist*
Webb, Emily *retired plant morphologist*

Western Springs
Carroll, Aileen *retired librarian*
Frommelt, Jeffrey James *management consulting firm executive*
Hanson, Heidi Elizabeth *lawyer*
Mudd, Anne Chestney *mediator, law educator, real estate broker*
Preston, William Leon *family practice*
Reggio, Vito Anthony *management consultant*
Rhoads, Paul Kelly *lawyer*
Shannon, Peter Michael, Jr., *lawyer*
Walsh, Robert Joseph *psychotherapist*
†Young, Robert Bruce *lawyer*

Westmont
†Bellock, Patricia Rigney *state legislator*
Hansen, Donald Marty *journalist, retired accountant*
†Kelley, Brian P. *transportation executive*
Moor, Roy Edward *finance educator*
†Nyien, Patricia *music educator*
†Warner, H. Ty *manufacturing executive*

Westville
Hammer, John Henry, II, *hospital administrator*

Wheaton
Allen, Henry Lee *sociology educator, consultant*
Astrup, Jens Leo *retired civil engineer*
Back, Robert Wyatt *investment executive, pharmaceutical company executive consultant*
Blair, Rosemary Kasul *social work educator*
Bogdonoff, Maurice Lambert *physician*
Boudreau, Beverly Ann *health care professional*
Brackett, Robert Clark *business valuation specialist*
†Bullock, C. Hassell *religious studies educator, minister*
†Buswell, James Oliver, III, *retired education educator, retired academic administrator*
Cunningham, William Francis *lawyer*
Didzerekis, Paul Patrick *lawyer*
Diersen, David John *financial consultant*
†Dudgeon, Thomas Carl *judge*
†Field, Harold Gregory *lawyer*
Gill, Kenneth Duane *minister, missiologist*
Hamilton, Robert Appleby, Jr., *insurance company executive*
Harper, Joannalee O. *dietician*
Harris, E(leanor) Lynn(e) *religious studies educator, literature educator, minister, writer*
Holman, James Lewis *financial and management consultant*
Horn, Daniel Paul *music educator, concert pianist*
Leston, Patrick John *judge*
Long, Charles Franklin *retired corporate communications executive*
Lowrie, Pamela Burt *educator, artist*
McCartney, Charles Price *retired obstetrician-gynecologist*
Mellott, Robert Vernon *retired advertising executive*
Miller, Lynn Breckenfelder *health and physical education educator*
†Mirabile, Thomas Keith *lawyer*
Nieves, Alvaro Lezcano *sociology educator*
Oesterle, Carolyn Scherer *pediatric ophthalmologist*
Pape, Patricia Ann *social worker, consultant*
Pappas, Barbara Estelle *Biblical studies educator, author*
Pollock, Bradley Neil *lawyer*
Potter, Janice Baber *retired school superintendent, educator*
†Roskam, Peter James *state legislator, lawyer*
Stein, Lawrence A. *lawyer*
Taylor, Mark Douglas *publishing executive*
Thompson, Bert Allen *retired librarian*
Tucker, Beverly Sowers *information specialist*
Votaw, John Frederick *educational foundation executive, educator*

Wheeling
Ebeling, Arthur William *mechanical engineer*
†Janich, Daniel Nicholas *lawyer*
Keats, Glenn Arthur *manufacturing company executive*
Kuennen, Thomas Gerard *journalist*
Kulinsky, Lois *lawyer*
Long, Sarah Ann *librarian*
Mc Clarren, Robert Royce *librarian*
Meehan, Tamiye Marcia *library director*
Ochsner, Othon Henry, II, *importer, restaurant critic*
Rogers, Richard F. *construction company executive, architect, engineer*
Schulman, Alan Michael *small business owner*
Sheeley, Harriet Spiegel *social worker*

Willowbrook
Burrows, Donald Albert *artist, painter, photographer, dean*
Foley, Joseph Lawrence *sales executive*
Mathisen-Reid, Rhoda Sharon *international communications consultant*
McCormack, Emily Anna *writer, book reviewer*
Walton, Stanley Anthony, III, *lawyer*

Wilmette
Albright, Townsend Shaul *investment banker, government benefits consultant*
Atkinson, Jeff John Frederick *law educator, lawyer, writer*
†Beck, Ralph *financial consultant*
Bowman, George Arthur, Jr.,
Brill, Marlene Targ *writer*
Brink, Marion Francis *trade association administrator*
Browder, William Bayard *corporation executive, lawyer*
Butz, Bradley Mitchell *music educator*
Coughlan, Gary Patrick *pharmaceutical company executive*
Delaplane, Sister Marjorie Marie *music educator*
Egloff, Fred Robert *manufacturers representative, writer, historian*
Ellis, Helene Rita *social worker*
Erickson, James Clifford, III, *anesthesiologist, educator*
Frick, Robert Hathaway *retired lawyer*
Fries, Robert Francis *historian, educator*
†Geller, William Alan *criminal justice researcher, police and public safety consultant*
Gilbert, Howard Earl *lawyer*
Griffith, James D. *retired lawyer*
†Griffiths, Robert Pennell *banker*
Hansen, Andrew Marius *retired library association executive*
Hier, Daniel Barnet *neurologist*
†Jampole, Michael *music educator, composer*
Klotz, Irving Myron *chemist, educator*
†Liberman, Jon C. *business development executive*
Lieberman, Eugene *lawyer*
†Mantrala, Murali K. *education educator, researcher, marketing professional*
†McClure, Julie Anne *literature educator*
Mc Nitt, Willard Charles *business executive*
Merrier, Helen *actress, writer*
Miller, Frederick Staten *retired music educator, academic administrator*
†Montgomery Tobias, Karen Twerdahl *music educator*
Muhlenbruch, Carl W. *civil engineer*
Pearlman, Jerry Kent *electronics company executive*
Rhoad, Richard Arthur *secondary school educator, writer*
Rocek, Jan *chemist, educator*
Ryan, Mike *investment advisor, consultant*
Sagarin, James Leon *rabbi, author, editor, publisher*
Schloss, Nathan *retired economist*
Stockman, Robert Harold *religious organization administrator, educator*
Wadden, Richard Albert *environmental engineer, educator, science administrator, consultant*
Walker, Ronald Edward *psychologist, educator*
Williams, Emory *former retail company executive, banker*
Wishner, Maynard Ira *retired finance company executive, lawyer*

Winfield
†Wiener, Pauline K. *psychiatrist*
Young, Quentin Hayse *family counselor*

Winnetka
Bundy, Blakely Fetridge *early childhood educator, advocate*
†Burke, John Edward *communications editor*
Burt, Robert Norcross *retired diversified manufacturing company executive*
Carrow, Leon Albert *physician*
Crowe, Robert William *lawyer, mediator*
Davis, Britton Anthony *retired lawyer*
†Fawcett, Dwight Winter *retired lawyer*
Fenton, Clifton Lucien *investment banker*
Fink, Eloise Bradley *educator, writer, editor*
Gavin, James John, Jr., *diversified company executive*
Greenblatt, Ray Harris *lawyer*
Hales, Daniel B. *lawyer*
Hartman, Robert S. *retired paper company executive*
Hausfeld, James Frank *executive director*
Hermann, Edward Robert *health engineer, educator, writer, consultant, hygieologist*
Huggins, Charlotte Susan Harrison *secondary school educator, author, travel specialist*
Kahn, Paul Frederick *executive search company executive*
Kennedy, George Danner *chemical company executive*
Klapperich, Frank Lawrence, Jr., *investment banker*
Krucks, William Norman *lawyer*
Krueger, Deborah A. Blake *school psychologist, consultant*
†Kucharski, Thomas Edward *secondary school educator*
Mathers, Thomas Nesbit *financial consultant*
Peck, Annette Biemond *retired social worker, writer*
Person, Paula (Mrs. P. Barry Person) *social skills organization executive, entrepreneur*
Piper, Robert Johnston *architect, urban planner*
Plowden, David *photographer*
†Puth, John Wells *consulting company executive*
Rossi, Ennio C. *physician, educator*
Rubnitz, Myron Ethan *pathologist, educator*
Ryan, Robert Jeffers *lawyer*
Schechter, Gail Helene *social services administrator, educator*
Schlossman, John Isaac *architect*
Schwartz, Daniel Joel *education administrator*
Sick, William Norman, Jr., *venture capital company executive*
Sutter, William Paul *lawyer*
Thomas, John Thieme *management consultant*
Toll, Daniel Roger *corporate executive, civic leader*
Weber, John Bertram *architect*
Weldon, Theodore Tefft, Jr., *manufacturing executive*

Winthrop Harbor
Getz, James Edward *legal association administrator*

Wood Dale
Sorensen, Jimmy Louis *management consultant*

Woodridge
Erickson, Diane Quinn *lawyer, artist, small business owner*
Puthenpurakal, Joseph Mathew *information technology executive*
Stall, Alan David *packaging company executive*

Woodstock
Ackley, Robert O. *lawyer*
Andel, Mark *communications specialist, educator*
Levandowski, Barbara Sue *educational administrator*

Worth
Ammeraal, Robert Neal *biochemist*

Yorkville
McEachern, Joan *medical association administrator*

Zion
Baule, Steven Michael *principal*
†Birdsall, Timothy Carroll *naturopathic physician*
Day, Mary Ann *medical/surgical nurse*

INDIANA

Albany
Patrick, Alan K. *artist*
†White, William Richard *manufacturing engineer, consultant*

Alexandria
Irwin, Gerald Port *physician*

Anderson
Carrell, Terry Eugene *manufacturing company executive*
Conrad, Harold August *retired religious pension board executive*
Day, Sandy J. *painter, writer*
King, Charles Ross *physician*
Kufeldt, George *biblical educator*
Neidert, David Lynn *administrator*
Nicholson, Robert Arthur *college president*
Pleninger, Susan Elaine *women's health and pediatrics nurse*
Smith, Kato Del *architect*
Whitaker, Audie Dale *hospital laboratory medical technologist*
†Williams, Paul Allan, Jr., *psychiatric social worker, educator*
Woodruff, Randall Lee *lawyer*

Angola
†Jones, Donald Paul *communications educator, consultant*
†Meeks, Kenneth W. *civil engineer, educator*
†Zimmerman, James Allen *historian, educator*

Atlanta
Poindexter, Beverly Kay *media and communications professional*

Attica
Harrison, Joseph William *state legislator*

Auburn
Kempf, Jane Elmira *marketing executive*

Avon
Shartle, Stanley Musgrave *consulting engineer, land surveyor*

Bedford
Hunter, Harlen Charles *orthopedic surgeon*

Beech Grove
Brown, Richard Lawrence *lawyer*
Byrkett, Gary Lee *hospital engineer*
Clapper, George Raymond *retired accountant, computer consultant*

Berne
Habegger, Cynthia A. *medical/surgical nurse*

Beverly Shores
Collins, Moira Ann *graphics and communications company executive, calligrapher*
Fammerée, Richard Arthur Noel *poet, composer, performing artist*

Bloomington
†Agranoff, Robert *political scientist, educator*
Alex-Assensoh, Yvette Marie *political scientist*
Aman, Alfred Charles, Jr., *law educator*
Anderson, Judith Helena *English language educator*
Arnove, Robert Frederick *education educator*
Assensoh, Akwasi Bretuo *historian, educator*
Austin, Joan Kessner *mental health nurse*
Baldner, Karen A. *artist, art educator*
Barnes, A. James *academic dean*
Bartleson, Amy Aileen *psychotherapist*
Baye, Michael Roy *economics educator*
†Becker, Robert Allen *economist, educator*
Belth, Joseph Morton *retired business educator*
Bernhardt-Kabisch, Ernest Karl-Heinz *English and comparative literature educator*
†Biss, Paul Martin *music educator*
Bornholdt, Laura Anna *university administrator*
Brinkman, Paul Del(bert) *foundation executive, university administrator*
†Bronstein, Lyudmila M. *chemist*
†Brown, A. Peter *music educator, researcher*
Brown, Keith *musician, educator*
Buelow, George John *musicologist, educator*
Caldwell, Lynton Keith *social scientist, educator*
Calinescu, Adriana Gabriela *museum curator, art historian*
Cate, Fred Harrison *law educator, lawyer*
†Chafel, Judith Ann *educator*
†Chaitin, Gilbert D. *humanities educator, researcher*
†Cheskidov, Alexey P. *mathematics educator*
Chitwood, Julius Richard *retired librarian*
Choksy, Jamsheed Kairshasp *historian, religious scholar, language professional, humanities educator*
Clevenger, Sarah *botanist, computer consultant*
Cohen, William Benjamin *historian, educator*
Connally, Sandra Jane Oppy *retired art educator, artist*
Conrad, Geoffrey Wentworth *archaeologist, educator*
†Cookman, Claude *journalist, educator*
Davidson, Ernest Roy *chemist, educator*
DeHayes, Daniel Wesley *management executive, educator*
Dilts, Jon Paul *law educator*
Dinsmoor, James Arthur *psychology educator*
Dunn, Jon Michael *informatics educator, dean*
Easton, Susan Dawn *biochemist, educator*
†Edgerton, William B. *foreign language educator*
Edmondson, Frank Kelley *retired astronomer*
†Eisenberg, Paul David *philosophy educator*
†Estell, David B. *psychologist, educator*
Estes, William Kaye *psychologist, educator*
†Fernhaber, Stephanie Ann *grant administrator*
Franklin, Frederick Russell *retired legal association executive*
Gealt, Adelheid Maria *museum director*
Gest, Howard *microbiologist, educator*
†Gieryn, Thomas Fredrick *sociologist, educator*
Glass, Robert L. *software engineering educator*
†Glazier, James Alexander *biophysicist, researcher*
Gordon, Paul John *management educator*
Grimmond, C. Susan B. *atmospheric scientist, educator*
†Grodner, Geoffrey Mitchell *lawyer*
Guth, Sherman Leon (S. Lee Guth) *psychologist, educator*
Hammel, Harold Theodore *physiology and biophysics educator, researcher*
†Hanks, Lawrence Julius, Sr., *management consultant, researcher*
Hanson, Karen *philosopher, educator*
Hattin, Donald Edward *geologist, educator*
Heiser, Charles Bixler, Jr., *botany educator*
Hendry, Archibald Wagstaff *physics educator*
Henson, Jane Elizabeth *information management professional, adult educati*
Herbert, Adam William, Jr., *academic administrator, educator*
†Hinds, Leonard Dale *education educator, research scientist*
Hites, Ronald Atlee *environmental science educator, chemist*
Hogan, Jeremy Robert *photojournalist*
Huffman, John Curtis *chemist*
Hustad, Thomas Pegg *marketing educator*
†Ikranagara, Kay *educational association administrator, educator*
Jacobi, Peter Paul *journalism educator, author*
†Johnson, Kevin LaMont *educator*
Johnson, Owen Verne *historian, educator*
Johnson, Sidney Malcolm *foreign language educator*
†Johnson-D'Alessio, Anna Maria *writer*
Juergens, George Ivar *history educator*
Kibbey, Hal Stephen *science writer*
Klotman, Robert Howard *music educator*
Knudsen, Laura Georgia *linguist*
Lee, Don Yoon *publisher, academic researcher and writer*
Legler, April Arington *librarian, educator*
Letsinger, Robert Lewis *chemistry educator*
Like, Lance D. *lawyer*
†Lloyd, Rosemary *language educator*
MacKay, David B.
†Mallor, Andrew C. *lawyer*
Mann, David O'Brien *venture capitalist, military officer*
Mann, Robert David *lawyer*
Markman, Ronald *artist, educator*
Martins, Heitor Miranda *foreign language educator*
Mathiesen, Thomas James *musicology educator*
Matthews, Leland Ray *obstetrician-gynecologist*
McCluskey, John Asberry, Jr., *literature educator, writer*
McRobbie, Michael Alexander *computer scientist, researcher, academic administrator*
Mehlinger, Howard Dean *education educator*
Mickel, Emanuel John *foreign language educator*
Mikesell, John L. *economics educator*
Mitchell, Bert Breon *literary translator*
Mobley, Tony Allen *foundation executive, former university dean, recreation educator*
Moore, Ward Wilfred *medical educator*
Moran, Emilio Federico *anthropology and ecology educator*
Mostafa, Javed *information scientist, educator*
†Nagendra, Harini *ecologist, researcher*
Nolan, Val, Jr., *biologist, lawyer*
†Nordloh, David Joseph *English language educator*
O'Hearn, Robert Raymond *stage designer*
Ostrom, Vincent A(lfred) *political science educator*
Oswalt, Aria Lucinda *real estate broker*
Patrick, John Joseph *social sciences educator*
Patterson, James Milton *marketing specialist, educator*
Peebles, Christopher Spalding *anthropologist, dean, academic administrator*
Peters, Dennis Gail *chemist*
Phillips, Harvey *musician, soloist, music educator, arts consultant*
Pletcher, David Mitchell *history educator*
Pollock, Robert Elwood *nuclear scientist*

Pratt, Stephen W. *music educator, conductor*
Prosser, Franklin Pierce *computer scientist*
Purdom, Paul Walton, Jr., *computer scientist*
Puri, Madan Lal *mathematics educator*
Putnam, Frank William *biochemistry and immunology educator*
Ransel, David Lorimer *history educator*
Rebec, George Vincent *neuroscience researcher, educator, administrator*
Rink, Lawrence Donald *cardiologist*
Risinger, C. Frederick *social studies educator*
Rosenberg, Samuel Nathan *French and Italian language educator*
Rudolph, Lavere Christian *library director*
Ruesink, Albert William *biologist, plant sciences educator*
Ryan, John William *academic administrator*
†St. John, Edward P. *social sciences educator*
Saunders, W(arren) Phillip, Jr., *economics educator, consultant, author*
Schaich, William L. *physics educator*
Schurz, Scott Clark *journalist, publisher*
†Schwartzkopf, Michael L. *music educator, conductor*
†Senchuk, Dennis M. *philosopher, educator*
Shreve, Gene Russell *law educator*
Sinor, Denis *Orientalist, educator*
Smith, Carl Bernard *education educator*
Smith, Frederick Robert, Jr., *social studies educator, educator*
Smith, Ronald Thomas *environmental scientist*
†Spera, Dominic Gregorio *music educator, writer*
†Sprouse, Rex A. *education educator*
Spulber, Nicolas *economics educator emeritus*
†Stephens, Jay Martin *business owner*
†Stines, Betty Irene *artist*
Strickholm, Peter William *composer, environmentalist*
Stryker, Sheldon *sociologist, educator*
Studwell, William Emmett *librarian, writer*
Svetlova, Marina *ballerina, choreographer, educator*
Tackitt, Sylvan Wright *lawyer*
Thom, James Alexander *novelist*
Timberlake, William David *psychology educator*
Torabi, Mohammad R. *healthcare educator*
†Toth, Nicholas Patrick *anthropologist, educator, archaeologist*
Valdman, Albert *language and linguistics educator*
von Furstenberg, George Michael *economics educator, researcher*
Walling, Donovan Robert *educational book editor*
Weaver, David Hugh *journalism educator, communications researcher*
Webb, Charles Haizlip, Jr., *retired university dean*
Weinberg, Eugene David *microbiologist, educator*
†Wells, Kimberly K. *not-for-profit organization executive*
Wentworth, Jack Roberts *business educator, consultant*
Wicker, Elmus Rogers *economics educator*
Wittlich, Gary Eugene *music theory educator, college administrator*
†Zeani-Rossilemeni, Virginia *music educator, soprano*

Bluffton
Elliott, Barbara Jean *librarian*
Pitts, Neal Chase *rheumatologist*

Boonville
Aylsworth, Robert Reed *lawyer*
Campbell, Edward Adolph *judge, electrical engineer*
†Neff, Mark Edward *lawyer*

Brazil
Blackwell, Dale Bascom *physicist*

Brownsburg
Diasio, Richard Leonard *power transmission executive, sports facility executive, race car manufacturer executive*
Riggs, Anna Claire *metals company executive*

Brownstown
Robertson, Joseph Edmond *grain processing company executive*
Robertson, Richard Robert *grain milling executive*

Burlington
†Roussakis, Dorothy Ferguson *artist*

Butler
Longardner, Craig Theodor *manufacturing executive*

Carmel
Ashcraft, Nancy Olson *mining engineer*
†Branstutter, Joseph Wayne *research scientist*
Brooks, Patricia Scott *principal*
Bruess, Charles Edward *lawyer*
Caraher, Michael Edward *systems analyst*
Eden, Barbara Janiece *commercial and residential interior designer*
Fadely, James Philip *educator, writer*
Haddad, Freddie Duke, Jr., *hospital development administrator*
Husman, Catherine Bigot *retired insurance company executive, actuary*
Kalwara, Joseph John *engineer*
Kellison, Donna Louise George *accountant, educator*
Mahoney, Margaret Ellis *administrative assistant*
McLaughlin, Harry Roll *architect*
†Pescovitz, Ora H. *education educator*
†Rand, Leon *academic administrator*
Rychlak, Joseph Frank *psychology educator, theoretician*
†Scott, Judson Richard *arborist, consultant*
†Shea, William J. *insurance company executive*
Shoup, Charles Samuel, Jr., *chemicals and materials executive*
Stein, Richard Paul *lawyer*
†Sukapdjo, Wilma Irene *language educator*
Swartz, Paul Frederick *clergyman*
Thomas, John David *musician, composer, arranger, graphic designer, recording engineer, producer*
Van Tassel, Charles Jackson *physician, urologist*
Walsh, John Charles *metallurgical company executive*
Wendt, Gary Carl *finance company executive*
Wilson, Randolph Preston *lawyer, businessman*

Celestine
†Stout, Robert M. *manufacturing executive*

Centerville
Wendeln, Darlene Doris *English language educator*

Chesterfield
Fry, Meredith Warren *civil engineer, consultant*

Chesterton
Brown, Gene W. *steel company executive*
Crewe, Albert Victor *physicist, artist, business executive*
Hayduk, John Matthew *English and journalism educator*
Martino, Robert Salvatore *orthopedic surgeon*
Petrakis, Harry Mark *author*
Wiemann, Marion Russell, Jr., (Baron of Camster) *biologist*

Churubusco
Morgan, Gretna Faye *retired automotive executive*

Cicero
Lay, Andrew Sean *secondary school educator, elementary school educator*

Columbia City
†Scank, Janet Marie *librarian*

Columbus
Able, Warren Walter *natural resource company executive, physician*
Abts, Henry William *banker*
Arthur, Jewell Kathleen *dental hygienist*
†Binkley, John Frey, Jr., *financial consultant, writer*
†Brunner, Ellen Margaret *not-for-profit fundraiser*
Carter, Pamela Lynn *former state attorney general*
Crump, Francis Jefferson, III, *lawyer*
†Duan, Xin-Ran *mechanical engineer, educator*
Engelking, Ellen Melinda *pattern company executive, real estate broker, manufacturing company*
Garton, Robert Dean *state legislator*
†Groves, Richard Thomas, III, *conductor, minister*
Hackett, John Thomas *retired economist*
Harrison, Patrick Woods *lawyer*
†Henderson, James Alan *former engine company executive*
Hercamp, Richard Dean *chemical engineer*
Hicks, Gregory Steven *marketing professional*
Kinsey, Helen Joan *physician*
Loughrey, F. Joseph *manufacturing executive*
Matthews, Drexel Gene *quality control executive*
Miller, Joseph Irwin *automotive manufacturing company executive*
Miller, William Irwin *finance company executive*
Nash, John Arthur *bank executive*
†Perkins Senn, Karon Elaine *lawyer*
†Richardson, Dan Earl *power cylinder engineer*
Robbins, Mary Ann *secondary school educator*
Shannon, Carolyn Jean *interior designer*
Spector, Judith Ann *English educator*
Szczurek, Thomas Eugene *business executive*
Tucker, Thomas Randall *public relations executive*
Williams, Robert Joseph *behavioral health services executive, psychologist*
†Zaharako, Lew Daleure *lawyer*

Corydon
Kelty, Paul David *physician, educator*
Speth, Camille *engineer*
†Walker, James Harper *retired security firm executive, writer*

Crane
Waggoner, Susan Marie *electronics engineer*

Crawfordsville
Barnes, James John *history educator*
Everett, Cheryl Ann *music educator, pianist*
Fisher, A. James *theater educator, director, actor*
Ford, Andrew Thomas *academic administrator*
Herzog, Tobey Church *English educator*
Servies, Richard L. *retired secondary education educator, mathematician*
Spurgeon, Nannette SuAnn (Susie Spurgeon) *special education educator*

Crown Point
Ceroke, Clarence John *engineer, consultant*
Harder, Heather Anne *education educator*
Kristevski, Alex C. *clinical psychologist*
Palmeri, Sharon Elizabeth *freelance writer, community educator*
Scheub, Richard Herman *photographer*

Danville
Baldwin, Jeffrey Kenton *lawyer, educator*

Decatur
Spady, Margaret Vidya *lawyer, nurse*

Demotte
Huff, John David *church administrator*

Depauw
Baggett, Alice Diane *critical care nurse*

East Chicago
Bhattacharya, Debanshu *metallurgical engineer*
Fortenberry, Delores B. *dean*
Platis, Mary Lou *media specialist*
Psaltis, Helen *medical and surgical nurse*
Riddle, Jared Matthew *English educator, actor*

Elberfeld
Bernhardt, Richard C. *secondary school educator, band director*

Elkhart
Bryan, Norman E. *dentist*
Cerny, Ronald Neal *business executive*
Corson, Thomas Harold *manufacturing company executive*
Drexler, Rudy Matthew, Jr., *professional law enforcement dog trainer*
Eddy, Darlene Mathis *poet, educator*
Free, Helen Mae *chemist, consultant*
Gassere, Eugene Arthur *lawyer, business executive*
Harrington, Lori Lynn *social services administrator*
Holtz, Glenn Edward *band instrument manufacturing executive*
Kloska, Ronald Frank *manufacturing company executive*
Lankford, Neill Stacy *urologist*
Leader, Christopher Robert *manufacturing executive*
Mathias, Margaret Grossman *manufacturing company executive, leasing company executive*
Mischke, Frederick Charles *manufacturing company executive*
Niederer, William Glenn *music educator*
Treckelo, Richard M. *lawyer*
Wicks, Charles Carter *lawyer*
Williams, Pauline M. *psychiatric-mental and community health nurse*

Evansville
Baugh, Jerry Phelps *lawyer*
Berger, Charles Lee *lawyer*
Blesch, K(athy) Suzann *small business owner*
Bodkin, Robert Thomas *lawyer*
Brenneman, James Alden *biology educator*
Brill, Alan Richard *entrepreneur*
†Brown, William Fredrick *art educator*
Capshaw, Tommie Dean *judge*
Clouse, John Daniel *lawyer*
Dean, K. Matthew *elementary school educator*
Drebushenko, David William *philosophy educator*
Early, Judith K. *social services director*
Ellis, Joe Mike *reclamation scientist*
Elpers, Kathleen Margaret *social work educator*
Faw, Melvin Lee *retired physician*
Flowers, Glen Dale *minister*
Frary, Charles O., III, (Chuck Frary) *venture capitalist*
Fritz, Edward Lane *dentist*
Gaither, John Francis *accountant, consultant*
Green, Robert Frederick *physician, photographer*
†Gruenwald, Mark Edward *mathematics educator*
Harrison, Joseph Heavrin *lawyer*
†Hayes, Philip Harold *lawyer*
†Heathcotte, Barry W. *mechanical engineer, consultant*
Heimburger, Irvin LeRoy *retired surgeon*
Hoy, George Philip *clergyman, county official*
Huff, Sheila Lindsey *secondary education educator, coach*
Jennings, Stephen Grant *academic administrator*
†Kimberling, Clark Hershall *mathematics educator, small business owner*
Koch, Robert Louis, II, *manufacturing company executive, mechanical engineer*
†Lasser, Bradley D. *academic administrator*
Matheson, Gordon Keith *neuroanatomist, educator, neuroendocrinologist*
Matthews, C(harles) David *real estate appraiser, consultant*
McGinness, James D. *chemist*
McGuire, Brian Lyle *educator, consultant*
Miller, Daniel Raymond *prosecutor*
Milner, Wesley Tyre *political science educator*
Moers, Joyce Ann *bookkeeper, day camp administrator*
Muehlbauer, James Herman *manufacturing executive*
Penkava, Robert Ray *radiologist, educator*
Roth, Carolyn Louise *art educator*
Sartore, J. Christopher *family practice physician*
Savia, Alfred *conductor*
†Stamps, Douglas *mechanical engineer, educator*
Streetman, John William, III, *museum official*
†Tannenbaum, Karen Jean *library services supervisor*
Tonso, William Rae *retired sociology educator, freelance writer*
Wallace, Keith M. *lawyer*
Wilson, Gregory Scott *kinesiology educator, coach*
Worman, Sylvia Easler *artist*
Zion, Roger Herschel *consulting firm executive, former congressman*

Fishers
Baach, Michael L. *internist*
Behner, Elton Dale *dentist*
†Bigatti, Silvia Marcela *science educator*
Chojnacki, Paul Ervin *pharmacist, pharmaceutical company official*
Christenson, Le Roy Howard *religious organization administrator, consultant*
Gatto, Louis Constantine *educational association administrator*

Fort Branch
Hillenbrand, Gary F. *chemist, educator*

Fort Wayne
Andorfer, Donald Joseph *university president*
Barksdale, Jacqueline Yvonne *elementary school educator*
Beineke, Lowell Wayne *mathematics educator*
Bingi, Prasad *management and marketing educator, consultant*
Bunkowske, Eugene Walter *religious studies educator*
Burns, Thagrus Asher *manufacturing company executive, former life insurance company executive*
†Cain, Tim J. *lawyer*
Carter, George Edward *education educator*
Cast, Anita Hursh *small business owner*
Coffman, Matthew Thomas *marketing executive, land use planner*
Cole, Kenneth Duane *architect*
Collins, Linda Lou Powell *manager of contracts*
Cosbey, Roger B. *federal magistrate judge*
Cummings, William Robert, Jr., *business executive*
†Cummins, Kathleen K. *retired elementary school educator*
Curtis, Douglas Homer *small business owner*
Dunsire, P(eter) Kenneth *insurance company executive*
Eastlund, Marvin Eugene *physician*
Essig, Erhardt Herbert *English educator*
Fink, Thomas Michael *lawyer*
Fischer, Bernd Jurgen *history educator*
Fox, Linda Chodosh *Spanish language educator*
Frost, Helen Marie *writer*
Gaff, Alan Dale *writer*
Gehring, Ronald Kent *lawyer*
Green, Lisa R. *journalist*
Grogg, Terrie Lynn *factory assembler*
†Gutreuter, Jill Stallings *financial consultant, financial planner*
Hamrick, Linda L. *educator*
Hannigan, John Dennis *logistics engineer*
Harwood, Virginia Ann *retired nursing educator*
Heger, James Joseph *internist, cardiologist*
Helmke, Paul (Walter Paul Helmke Jr.) *mayor, lawyer*
†Hickey, M. Gail *education educator*
Hirschy, Gordon Harold *real estate broker, auctioneer*
Kauffman, Kent David *law educator*
Kennedy, Elizabeth *health facility administrator*
Klugman, Stephan Craig *newspaper editor*
Kmety-Stevenson, Carmen Ramona *physicist*
Krull, Jeffrey Robert *library director*
†Kutsenok, Victor Y. *mathematician, educator, mathematician, researcher*
Lawson, Jack Wayne *lawyer*
Lebamoff, Ivan Argire *lawyer*
Lee, Shuishih Sage *pathologist*
Lee, Timothy Earl *international agency executive, paralegal*
Lee, William Charles *judge*
Lewton, Diane Kay *nurse practitioner*
Lyons, Jerry Lee *mechanical engineer*
†Mann, David William *minister*
Marine, Clyde Lockwood *agricultural business consultant*
Mather, George Ross *clergy member*
McMurray, Stephen D. *nephrologist*
†Molfenter, David P. *former electronics executive*
†Mueller, Carla Lynn *nursing educator*
Neuman, Paula Anne Young *cultural organization administrator*
†Owen, Dave A. *finance executive*
Oxley, Ann *television executive*
Pellegrene, Thomas James, Jr., *editor, researcher*
Pittelko, Roger Dean *clergyman, religious educator*
†Pope, Mark Andrew *lawyer, university administrator*
†Rhoad, Richard E. *healthcare executive*
Richardson, Joseph Hill *physician, medical educator*
Ridderheim, Mary Margaret *psychotherapist*
†Rifkin, Leonard *metals company executive*
†Rolland, Ian McKenzie *insurance executive, retired*
Sack, James McDonald, Jr., *radio and television producer, marketing executive*
Sandeson, William Seymour *cartoonist*
†Scaer, David Paul *religious studies educator, minister, dean*
Scheetz, Sister Mary JoEllen *English language educator*
Schweickart, Jim *advertising executive, broadcast consultant*
Shaffer, Paul E. *retired banker*
†Sharp, William Edward *engineering executive, researcher*
Shoaff, Thomas Mitchell *lawyer*
Skufca, Sherry Lee *newspaper editor*
Skup, David Alan *insurance company executive*
Stebbins, Vrina Grimes *retired elementary school educator, counselor*
Steiner, Paul Andrew *retired insurance executive*
Stevenson, Kenneth Lee *chemist, educator*
Streeter, Robert Davenport *electrical engineer, consultant*
Taritas, Karen Joyce *customer service administrator*
Vachon, Marilyn Ann *retired insurance company executive*
Weatherford, George Edward *civil engineer*
Werling, Donn Paul *environmental educator*
Young, Randy William *lawyer*

Fowler
Weist, William Bernard *lawyer*

Francesville
†Wilson, Kathy Kay *foundation executive*

Frankfort
Appleton, Alan B. *lawyer*
Borland, Kathryn Kilby *author*
†Burrows, John (Jack) Newton *music educator*
Stonehill, Lloyd Herschel *gas company executive, mechanical engineer*

Franklin
Bender, Larry Wayne *vocational educator*
Hamner, Lance Dalton *prosecutor*
Janis, F. Timothy *technology company executive*

†Hunt, Robert G. *construction company executive*
Husted, Ralph Waldo *former utility executive*
Inui, Thomas Spencer *physician, educator*
Irsay, James Steven *professional football team owner*
Irwin, Glenn Ward, Jr., *medical educator, physician, university official*
Israelov, Rhoda *financial planner, writer, entrepreneur*
Jackson, Valerie Pascuzzi *radiologist, educator*
Jacobson, Marc Peter *art educator, educator*
James, Edgerrin *football player*
†James, Sunil *aerospace engineer*
Jegen, Lawrence A., III, *law educator*
†Jewett, John Rhodes *real estate executive*
Johnson, David Allen *singer, songwriter, investment advisor, minister*
Johnson, Gerald, III, *cardiovascular physiologist, researcher*
Johnson, James P. *religious organization executive*
†Johnson, Michael *former international athlete*
Johnston, Cyrus Conrad, Jr., *medical educator*
Johnston, Joanne Spitznagel *lawyer, writing consultant*
Johnstone, Robert Philip *lawyer*
Johnting, Wendell *law librarian*
†Jones, Marion *track and field athlete*
Justice, Brady Richmond, Jr., *medical services executive*
†Kahlenbeck, Howard, Jr., *lawyer*
†Kappes, Philip Spangler *lawyer*
†Kashani, Hamid Reza *lawyer, computer consultant*
Kaufman, Barton Lowell *financial services company executive*
Kautzman, John Fredrick *lawyer*
Kaye, Gordon Israel *pathologist, anatomist, educator*
Kemper, James Dee *lawyer*
†Kendall, Rebecca O. *lawyer, pharmaceutical company executive*
Kenley, Luke *state legislator*
†Kennedy, Russell Edward *academic administrator*
Kerr, William Andrew *lawyer, educator*
King, J. Bradley *lawyer*
King, Kay Sue *investment company executive*
Kirk, Carol *lawyer*
Kirkham, James Alvin *manufacturing executive*
Kirkpatrick, Robert Hugh *communications executive*
Kittle, Jim, Jr., *state representative, political party administrator*
Klaper, Martin Jay *lawyer*
Kleiman, David Harold *lawyer*
Knauer, James A. *lawyer*
Knebel, Donald Earl *lawyer*
Knoebel, Suzanne Buckner *cardiologist, medical educator*
Koch, Edna Mae *lawyer, nurse*
Koeller, Robert Marion *lawyer, director*
Kovacik, Karen Marie *university educator*
Krasean, Thomas Karl *historian*
Krauss, John Landers *public policy, urban affairs consultant, mediator, arbitrator*
Krueger, Betty Jane *telecommunications company executive*
†La Crosse, James *retail executive*
Lacy, Andre Balz *industrial executive*
Lahiri, Debomoy Kumar *molecular neurobiologist, educator*
Landis, Larry Seabrook *state agency administrator*
†Lantzer, Jason Scott *historian, educator*
Larsen, Glen Albert, Jr., *finance educator*
†Laube, Lois Ruth *librarian*
Lee, Stephen W. *lawyer*
Lemberger, Louis *pharmacologist, physician*
†Lewis, Brian *Olympic athlete*
†Liu, Ben Shaw-Ching *marketing professional, educator*
Livers, Catherine McGhee *writer*
Lofton, Thomas Milton *lawyer*
Long, Clarence William *accountant*
Long, William Allan *retired forest products company executive*
†Loveday, William John *hospital administrator*
Lovejoy, Kim Brian *English educator*
Lowe, Louis Robert, Jr., *lawyer*
†Lowe, Mary Katherine *technology company executive, writer*
Luerssen, Thomas George *pediatric neurosurgeon, educator*
Lumeng, Lawrence *physician, educator*
Lyst, John Henry *former newspaper editor*
Lytle, L(arry) Ben *insurance company executive, lawyer*
MacDonald, Gary Bruce *communications executive*
MacDougall, John Duncan *surgeon*
Madura, James Anthony *surgical educator*
Mahomed, Yousuf *physician, cardiothoracic surgeon*
†Maine, Michael Roland *lawyer*
Manders, Karl Lee *neurosurgeon*
Manning, Peyton *professional football player*
Marsh, Michael Lawrence *track and field athlete*
Marshall, Carolyn Ann M. *church official, executive*
Mason, David Stewart *political science educator*
Mason, Thomas Alexander *historian, educator, author*
Maxwell, Florence Hinshaw *civic worker*
May, Linda *delivery business owner*
McCarthy, Harold Charles *retired insurance company executive*
McCarthy, Kevin Bart *lawyer*
†McCarthy, Leo Joseph *pathologist*
McDonell, Edwin Douglas *information systems executive, consultant, writer*
Mc Farland, H. Richard *food company executive*
McKeand, Patrick Joseph *newspaper publisher, educator*
†McKeon, Thomas Joseph *lawyer*
McKinney, Dennis Keith *lawyer*
McKinney, E. Kirk, Jr., *retired insurance company executive*
McKinney, Larry J. *federal judge*
McLaughlin, Sherry *association administrator*
McTurnan, Lee Bowes *lawyer*
†Merrill, William H., Jr., *lawyer, corporate professional*
Metz, Anthony J., III, *federal judge*
Metzner, Barbara Stone *university counselor*
Meyer, William Michael *mortgage banking executive*
†Miles-Clark, Jearl *olympic athlete, track and field*
Miller, David Anthony *lawyer*
Miller, David W. *lawyer*
Miller, Reginald Wayne *professional basketball player*
Mirsky, Arthur *geologist, educator*
Miyamoto, Richard Takashi *otolaryngologist*
Moelhman, Amy Jo *social worker*
Moffatt, Michael Alan *lawyer*
Molitoris, Bruce Albert *nephrologist, educator*
†Moore, Gregory Powell *emergency physician, consultant*
Mouser, Robert Winston *physician*
Mullen, Thomas Edgar *real estate consultant*
Murray, Michael Dennis *pharmacist*
†Namjoshi, Madhav *economist, educator*
Namyslowski, Jan *physician, interventional radiologist*
Nancrede, Sarah Elizabeth (Sally Nancrede) *reporter*
Nass, Connie Kay *state auditor*
†Neff, Robert Matthew *lawyer, financial services executive*
Ney, Michael Vincent *university administrator*
Noble, Douglas Ross *museum administrator*
Nolan, Alan Tucker *retired lawyer, labor arbitrator, writer*
†Nolan-Williams, Margaret Colleen *writer, craftsman*
Norins, Arthur Leonard *physician, educator*
Norman, LaLander Stadig *insurance company executive*
Norwalk, Kelli Curran *retail executive, entrepreneur*
†Nyhart, Eldon Howard *employee benefits consultant, lawyer*
Ochs, Sidney *neurophysiology educator*
†Oldham, Phyllis Virginia Kidd *retired librarian*
†Osgood, Robert Lincoln *education educator*
Padgett, Gregory Lee *lawyer*
Page, Curtis Matthewson *minister*
Palmer, Robert P. *professional association executive*
Pande, Prakash Narain *cardiologist, educator, consultant*
Paul, Stephen Howard *lawyer*
Peebles, Julian T. *health education administrator*
Pennamped, Bruce Michael *lawyer*
Pesut, Daniel J. *nursing educator*
†Petersen, James L. *lawyer*
Peterson, Bart *mayor*
†Peterson, Erling Winston *religion educator*
†Pettigrew, Antonio *Olympic athlete*
†Planeaux, Christopher Sean *financial analyst, educator*
Plater, William Marmaduke *English language educator, academic administrator*
Poel, Robert Walter *air force officer, physician*
Pratt, George Byington, III, *pediatric radiologist*
Pugh, Daniel Wilbert *theatre educator, costume designer*
Pyle, R. Michael *wholesale distribution executive, educator*
Quiring, Patti Lee *human resource consulting company executive*
†Ramos, Jose A. *engineering educator*
Rati, Robert Dean *data processing executive*
Rebein, Robert Brian *English studies educator, writer*
Reese, Jason Ruskin *lawyer*
Reese, Martha Grace *minister, lawyer*
Render, John Clifford *lawyer*
Rescorla, Frederick John *pediatric surgeon, educator*
Reynolds, Robert Hugh *lawyer*
†Reynolds, William Carl *law editor*
Rhoades, Rodney Allen *physiologist, educator*
Riegsecker, Marvin Dean *pharmacist, state senator*
Risdon, Michael Paul *manufacturing executive*
Ritz, Stephen Mark *lawyer*
†Roberts, Patricia Susan *lawyer*
Roberts, Wilbur Eugene *dental educator, research scientist, wine importer*
Roberts, William Everett *lawyer*
Robertson, Jean Ellis *art critic, art history educator*
Rogers, Robert Ernest *medical educator*
Ruben, Gary A. *marketing and communications consultant*
Rucker, Robert D. *state supreme court justice*
Russell, David Williams *lawyer*
Russell, Frank Eli *retired newspaper publishing executive*
†Rusthoven, Peter James *lawyer*
Rutledge, Joanne *artist, consultant*
Ryder, Henry C(lay) *lawyer*
Ryder, Kenneth William *pathologist, educator*
†Ryerson, Dennis *editor*
†Sachs, Stephen Mark *political scientist, consultant*
Salentine, Thomas James *pharmaceutical company executive*
Santini, Gino *marketing professional*
Santos, Richard J. *association administrator*
Scaletta, Phillip Ralph, III, *lawyer*
Schadow, Gunther *medical information scientist*
†Schamberger, Marcus S. *pediatric cardiologist*
Schilling, Emily Born *editor, association executive*
Schlegel, Donald Max *retired surgeon*
Schlegel, Fred Eugene *lawyer*
Schmetzer, Alan David *psychiatrist*
Scholer, Sue Wyant *state legislator*
Schreckengast, William Owen *lawyer*
†Schwarz, James Harold *lawyer*
Scism, Daniel Reed *lawyer*
Selby, Ronald Jay *electrical engineer*
Seneff, Smiley Howard *business owner*
SerVaas, Beurt Richard *corporate executive*
†SerVaas, Cory *health sciences association administrator*
†Shadley, Sue Ann *lawyer*
Shaffer, Alfred Garfield (Terry Shaffer) *service organization executive*
Shepard, Randall Terry *state supreme court chief justice*
Sherman, John Judson *public relations executive, writer*
†Shi, Lizheng *health economist*
Shideler, Shirley Ann Williams *lawyer*
Shields, V. Sue *federal magistrate judge*
Shula, Robert Joseph *lawyer*
Simon, Herbert *professional basketball team executive*
Simon, Melvin *real estate developer, professional basketball executive*
Slaymaker, Gene Arthur *public relations executive*
†Small, Joyce Graham *psychiatrist, educator*
Smiley, Wynn Ray *nonprofit corporation executive*
Smith, Carson Clay *business executive*
Smith, Donald Archie *religion business executive, consultant*
Smith, Donald Eugene *healthcare facility management administrator owner*
Smith, James Warren *pathologist, microbiologist, parasitologist*
Smith, K. Clay *machinery transport company executive*
Sokolov, Richard Saul *real estate company executive*
Solomon, Marilyn Kay *educator, consultant*
†Sowers, Jodi Louise *music educator*
†Sparks, Donald Eugene *interscholastic activities association executive*
Spechler, Martin Charles *economist*
Speth, Gerald Lennus *education and business consultant*
Standish, Samuel Miles *oral pathologist, college dean*
Stayton, Thomas George *lawyer*
Steger, Evan Evans, III, *retired lawyer*
Stein, Carole Ruth *social services administrator, researcher*
Stern, Phyllis Noerager *nursing educator*
Stewart, Paul Arthur *pharmaceutical company executive*
Stieff, John Joseph *legislative lawyer, educator*
Stone, Cynthia Lawson *nursing educator*
Stookey, George Kenneth *retired director, retired dental educator*
Storm, Janet S. *psychiatric social worker*
†Strain, James Arthur *lawyer*
Strycker, Steve Lynn *accountant*
†Subramanian, Usha *medical researcher, educator, clinician*
Surawicz, Borys *physician, educator*
Sutherland, Donald Gray *retired lawyer*
Sutton, Gregory Paul *obstetrician, gynecologist*
Suzuki, Hidetaro *violinist*
Sweezy, John William *political party official*
†Tabler, Susan Beidler *lawyer*
Talesnick, Stanley *lawyer*
†Tandy, Kisha Renee *curator*
Taurel, Sidney *pharmaceutical executive*
†Taylor, Angelo *Olympic athlete*
Taylor, Jay Gordon *lawyer*
Thomas, Jerry Arthur *soil scientist*
Tisdale, James Edward *pharmacy educator, pharmacotherapy researcher*
Tobias, Randall Lee *retired pharmaceutical company executive*
Todd, Zane Grey *retired utilities executive*
†Torrence, Gwen *Olympic athlete*
Torres, Judith *lab administrator*
Towne, Edgar Arthur *theologian, educator*
Townsend, Earl C., Jr., *lawyer, writer*
†Tracy, Paul Anthony *race car driver*
Tuchman, Steven Leslie *lawyer, consul*
Turner, Barbara A. *former dance company executive*
Usher, Phyllis Land *state official*
Vandivier, Blair Robert *lawyer*
†Vasser, Jimmy *professional race car driver*
Venzago, Mario *conductor*
Vereen, Robert Charles *retired trade association executive*
Villars, Jill Annette *webmaster*
Vlach, Jeffrey Allen *environmental specialist*
†Walker, Ross Paul *lawyer*
Wallace, Edna Marie *paralegal*
Walther, Joseph Edward *health facility administrator, retired physician*
Wampler, Lloyd Charles *retired lawyer*
Wampler, Robert Joseph *lawyer*
†Wang, Ouhong *statistician, researcher*
Ware, J(oe) Anthony *cardiologist*
Warren, Bradford Lloyd *lawyer*
Watkins, Harold Robert *minister*
Watkins, Sherry Lynne *elementary school educator*
Waymire, Bonnie Gladine *nursing administrator*
Weber, George *oncology and pharmacology researcher, educator*
Weinberger, Myron Hilmar *medical educator*
Wellnitz, Craig Otto *lawyer, English language educator*
Whale, Arthur Richard *retired lawyer*
†Wheeler, Daniel Scott *management executive, editor*
White, James Patrick *law educator*
†Wilkinson, Laura *Olympic athlete*
†Williams, Bernard *Olympic athlete*
Williams, Gregory Keith *accountant*
Wilson, Fred M., II, *ophthalmologist, educator*
Winemiller, James D. *accountant*
Winters, Peter Lee *dermatologist*
Wishard, Gordon Davis *lawyer*
Wolfe, Elaine Claire Daughetee *junior high school educator*
Wolsiffer, Patricia Rae *retired insurance company executive*
Wong, David T. *biochemist, researcher*
Wood, William Jerome *lawyer*
Woodring, DeWayne Stanley *religious organization administrator*
Woody, John Frederick *retired secondary education educator*
Woolling, Kenneth Rau *vascular internist*
Wright, David Burton *retired newspaper publishing company executive*
Yates, Robin Corriene *freelance writer*
Yee, Robert Donald *ophthalmologist*
Yerkeson, Douglas Alan *lawyer*
†Yip-Schneider, Michele Terrell *researcher*
†Yosha, Louis Buddy *lawyer*
Young, Philip Howard *library director*
Young, Richard D. *state legislator*
Yovits, Marshall Clinton *computer and information science educator, university dean*
Yune, Heun Yung *radiologist, educator*
Zapapas, James Richard *pharmaceutical company executive*
Zheng, Qi-Huang *chemist, educator*
Zipes, Douglas Peter *cardiologist, researcher*
Zurick, John *consultant, former dance company director*

Jasper

Aronoff, Donald Matthew *mental health facility administrator*
Brenner, Raymond Anthony *priest*
Newman, Leonard Jay *retail jewel merchant, gemologist*

Jeffersonville

Hoehn, Elmer Louis *lawyer, state and federal agency administrator, educator, consultant*
†McMichael, Jeane Casey *real estate company executive, educator*
Reisert, Charles Edward, Jr., *real estate executive*
Walburn, John Clifford *mental health services professional*

Kendallville

†Hooker, Joseph David *writer, minister*

Kingsport

Herron, Charles Kyle *music educator*

Knox

Weiss, Randall A. *television and radio producer, supermarket executive*

Kokomo

Bayliff, Edgar W. *lawyer*
Bukowski, Eugene Raymond *electrical engineer*
†Cameron, Ann M. *language educator*
†Charlot Jr, Joseph Leonce *preventive medicine physician*
Coppock, Janet Elaine *mental health nurse*
MacKay, Gail *librarian*
Maugans, John Conrad *lawyer*
Miller, Robert Frank *retired electronics engineer, educator*
Nierste, Joseph Paul *software engineer*
†Pati, Niranjan *finance educator*
Person, Ruth Janssen *academic administrator*
Ranney, Sandra Kay *artist, humanities educator*
Ray, Tuhin *computer engineer*
Roales, Robert R. *natural science educator*
Stein, Eleanor Bankoff *judge*
Wilson, Paul Wayne *retired real estate developer*
†Wysong, Earl Edward *sociologist, educator*

Kouts

Miller, Sarabeth *secondary education educator*

La Porte

†Drayton, V. Michael *lawyer, educator*
Morris, Leigh Edward *retired hospital executive officer*
Thordarson, Smari *diagnostic radiologist*

LaPorte

Johnson, Bruce Ross *elementary education educator*

Lafayette

Achgill, Ralph Kenneth *retired research scientist*
†Ash, Stephen R. *nephrologist*
Benton, Anthony Stuart *lawyer*
Brewster, James Henry *retired chemistry educator*
Brown, Herbert Charles *chemistry educator*
Buckles, Judith Ann *dental educator, program administrator*
Bumbleburg, Joseph Theodore *lawyer*
†Caldwell, Barrett Scott *industrial engineering educator*
Carneiro, Mervyn Joseph *mechanical engineer*
de Branges de Bourcia, Louis *mathematics educator*
Drazin, Michael Peter *mathematician, researcher*
Dure, Robert Samuel *music educator*
Dzhafarov, Ehtibar N. *mathematical psychologist*
Etzel, James Edward *environmental engineering educator*
Feuer, Henry *retired chemist*
Finch, Robert Jonathan *communications engineering consultant*
Fox, Robert William *mechanical engineering educator*
Frey, Harley Harrison, Jr., *anesthesiologist*
Fritch, John William *library and information scientist, educator*
Geddes, LaNelle Evelyn *nurse, physiologist*
Geddes, Leslie Alexander *bioengineer, physiologist, educator*
Gerde, Carlyle Noyes (Cy Gerde) *lawyer*
Gustafson, Winthrop Adolph *aeronautical and astronautical engineering educator*
Hall, Dorothy Susan *nurse, educator*
Hardin, Lowell Stewart *retired economics educator*
Harris, Donald Wayne *research scientist*

†Hart, Russell Holiday *retired lawyer*
Helmuth, Ned D. *certified financial planner*
Kanne, Michael Stephen *federal judge*
Layden, Charles Max *lawyer*
Layden, Lynn McVey *lawyer*
Liley, Peter Edward *retired mechanical engineering educator*
Lindenlaub, John Charles *electrical engineer, educator*
Loeffler, Frank Joseph *physicist, educator*
†Lusk, Jayson L. *education educator, researcher*
Maickel, Roger Philip *pharmacologist, educator*
McBride, Angela Barron *nursing educator*
McCormick, Teresa D. *accountant*
McKowen, Dorothy Keeton *educator, librarian, consultant*
McPherson, Richard Clark *surgeon*
Meyer, Brud Richard *retired pharmaceutical company executive*
Miller, Jolene K. *healthcare educator*
Miller, Larry Joe *evangelist*
Mobley, Emily Ruth *library dean, educator*
Ott, Karl Otto *nuclear engineer, consultant*
†Pennell, Stephen Richard *lawyer*
Porile, Norbert Thomas *chemistry educator*
Poulos, James Thomas *endocrinologist, educator*
Ransom, Victor Harvey *engineering educator*
Renzetti, Phyllis Jean *retired technical editor*
Revankar, Shripad T. *nuclear engineering educator*
Rosen, Arthur David *neurobiology educator*
†Scaletta, Helen Marguerite *volunteer*
Schönemann, Peter Hans *psychology educator*
Schweickert, Richard Justus *psychologist, educator*
Shook, James Creighton *real estate executive*
Troutner, Joanne Johnson *school technology administrator, educator, administrator, consultant*
VanHandel, Ralph Anthony *retired librarian*
Wagner, Lindley Heath *physician, medical educator*
Whistler, Roy Lester *chemist, educator, industrialist*

Lagrange
Brown, George E. *judge, educator*
Glick, Cynthia Susan *lawyer*

Lanesville
Cleveland, Peggy Rose Richey *cytotechnologist*

Lawrenceburg
Dautel, Charles Shreve *retired mining company executive*
Edwards, Marie D. *social services administrator*
Ewan, William Kenneth *lawyer*

Leavenworth
Kreisle, William Eckman *civil engineer, surveyor, research cartographer, writer*

Lebanon
Donaldson, John Weber *lawyer*

Liberty
Pringle, Lewis Gordon *marketing professional, educator*

Lincoln City
Blessinger, Timothy Louis *secondary school educator*

Logansport
Brewer, Robert Allen *physician*
Hall, James Alan *obstetrician-gynecologist*
Thacker, Jerry Lynn *school administrator*

Loogootee
Burcham, Eva Helen (Pat Burcham) *retired electronics technician*

Madison
†Helms, Rebecca J. *finance educator*
Rawson, Harve E. *psychologist, writer*
Snodgrass, Robert Eugene *psychiatrist*
Stoner, David A. *elementary school educator, consultant*
Tatera, James Frank *chemist, process analysis specialist*

Marion
†Boivin, Michael J. *psychologist, educator, psychologist, researcher*
Brannon, Ronald Roy *retired minister*
Clemons, Kay K. *librarian*
†DeMichael, Mark Joseph *physical education educator, baseball coach*
Fisher, Pierre James, Jr., *physician*
Lau, Patrick Hing-Leung *radiologist, educator*
†Lennox, Stephen John *theology studies educator, writer*
McIntyre, Robert Walter *church official*
Shepler, Debra Lynn *artist, secondary education educator*
†Walker, Corean Jones *evangelist*

Martinsville
Cupka, Nancy Irvine *artist, educator*
James, Timothy Dale *music educator*
†Smith, Peg L. *foundation administrator*

Merrillville
Brenman, Stephen Morris *lawyer*
Cristea Salberg, Richard Litz *neurologist, health facility administrator*
Doumanian, Heratch Ohannes *radiology*
Gioia, Daniel August *lawyer*
Hoffman, Robert Joseph *artist, art educator*
Manous, Peter J. *lawyer*
Neale, Gary Lee *utilities executive*
Nguyen, Thach Ngoc *cardiologist*
†Protho, Jessie *educator*
†Reitmeister, Noel William *certified financial planner, investment and insurance professional, author, columnist, television host and producer, educator*
Yu, Peter Legaspi *rehabilitation physician*

Michigan City
Brown, Arnold *physical therapy consultant*
†Glossinger, Donald Leo *library director*
Manny, Carter Hugh, Jr., *architect, foundation administrator*
Mothkur, Sridhar Rao *radiologist*
Pecze, David Emery *marketing professional*
Sherman, Thomas Webster, Jr., *environmental company executive*

Middlebury
Bowen, Derek Tyrone *music educator*
Guequierre, John Phillip *manufacturing company executive*

Milltown
Chapman, Sue Turner *artist*

Mishawaka
Altman, Arnold David *business executive*
Bays, June Marie *counselor, social worker*
Braunsdorf, James Allen *physics educator*
Erdel, Sally Elizabeth *nurse*
†Kapson, Jordan *automotive executive*
Ponko, William Reuben *architect*
Rubenstein, Pamela Silver
Silver, Neil Marvin *manufacturing executive*
Troyer, LeRoy Seth *architect*

Monroeville
Ray, Annette D. *business executive*
Sorgen, Elizabeth Ann *retired educator*

Monrovia
Bennett, James Edward *retired plastic surgeon, educator*

Monticello
†Guy, John Martin *lawyer*

Morgantown
Callon, Margaret Joann *writer, minister*
Siddiq, Patricia Kay *artist*

Mount Vernon
Bach, Steve Crawford *lawyer*
Baier, Elizabeth Domsic *lawyer*
Moll, Joseph Eugene *chemical engineer, chemical company executive*
Sabnis, Ram Wasudeo *research chemist*

Muncie
†Ali, Mir Masoom *statistician, educator*
Alves, Abel A. *writer*
Amschler, Denise H. *health science educator*
Anderson, Stefan Stolen *banker*
†Atherton, Leonard James Archibald *musician, conductor*
†Bakken, Douglas Adair *foundation executive*
Barber, Earl Eugene *consulting firm executive*
Bell, Stephen Scott (Steve Bell) *journalist, educator*
Bogg, Richard Allan *sociologist, educator*
Brownell, Blaine Allison *university administrator, history educator*
Cheng, Chu Yuan *economics educator*
Dennis, Ralph Emerson, Jr., *lawyer*
†Emert, John Wesley *mathematician, musician*
Felsenstein, Frank Arjeh *educator*
Fisher, John Wesley *manufacturing company executive*
Grill, Richard Louis *music educator*
Harris, Joseph McAllister *retired chemist*
Hayashi, Tetsumaro *retired literature educator, writer, editor*
Hendrix, Jon Richard *biology educator*
Henzlik, Raymond Eugene *zoophysiologist, educator*
Hoffman, Mary Catherine *retired nurse, anesthetist*
Holt, Gerald Wayne *retired counseling administrator*
Hozeski, Bruce William *English language and literature educator*
Ingelhart, Louis Edward *journalism educator, retired*
Jarvis, David Alan *engineer*
Joyaux, Alain Georges *art museum director*
Kelly, Eric Damian *lawyer, educator*
†Kitchens, Frederick Lynton, III, *education educator, researcher*
Kuratko, Donald F. *entrepreneur, educator, consultant*
Larson Mattern, Julia A. *music educator, musician*
Linson, Robert Edward *university administrator emeritus*
Massé, Mark Henry *journalism educator*
McColley, Ruth Ann *music teacher, band director*
McDowell, Lucy Jane *allergist, immunologist, pediatrician*
McIntosh, David M. *former congressman*
Mertens, Thomas Robert *biology educator*
Meyer, Fred Albert, Jr., *political science educator*
Norris, Tracy Hopkins *retired public relations executive*
Palmer, Robert Christopher *music educator, musician*
†Reed, Samuel Lee *lawyer*
Roch, Lewis Marshall, II, *ophthalmic surgeon, medical entrepreneur*
Schaefer, Patricia *librarian*
†Scheib, John W. *music educator, conductor*
Seidel, Lizbeth J. *pianist, educator*
Seymour, Richard Deming *technology educator*
Shoemaker, Helen E. Martin Achor *civic worker*
Sinclair, Brian Robert *psychologist, architect, educator*
†Smith, Gregory Butler *lawyer*
Smith, Van P. *holding company executive*
Stewart, Rita Joan *academic administrator*
†Sursa, Charles David *banker*
Swartz, B(enjamin) K(insell), Jr., *archaeologist, educator*
Swetnam, Ruth E. Danglade *curriculum director*
Terrell, Pamela Sue *pharmacist*
Volk, Christian J. *microbiologist, research scientist*
Whitaker, Sandra Sue *soprano, educator*
Wiedmer, Terry Lynn *educational administration educator, consultant*
Wise, Charles Davidson *science educator*
Yeamans, George Thomas *librarian, educator*
Zemtsov, Alexander *dermatology and biochemistry educator, inventor*
Zhong, Mei *music educator*

Munster
Amber, Douglas George *lawyer*
Corsiglia, Robert Joseph *electrical construction company executive*
Dompke, Norbert Frank *retired photography studio executive*
Fies, James David *elementary education educator*
Jano, Ghassan *oncologist, hematologist*
Luerssen, Frank Wonson *retired steel company executive*
Neff, Bonita Dostal *communication development facilitator*
Pillarella, Deborah Ann *fitness program manager, elementary education educator, consultant*
Platis, Chris Steven *educator*
Potempa, Philip Matthew *entertainment journalist, columnist, communications educator*
Shields, Robert Francis *stockbroker*
Singh, Manmohan *orthopedic surgeon, educator*
†Woods, William George *music educator*

Nappanee
Borger, Michael Hinton Ivers *osteopathic physician, educator*
Miller, Philip William *sales executive*

Nashville
Brown, Peggy Ann *artist*
Kriner, Sally Gladys Pearl *artist*
Rogers, Frank Andrew *restaurant and hotel executive*
Tracy, James Leon *artist*

New Albany
Chowhan, Naveed Mahfooz *oncologist*
Rhodes, Betty Fleming *rehabilitation services professional, nurse*
Riehl, Jane Ellen *education educator*

New Castle
†Stone, Joy Lynne *internist*

New Harmony
†Rice, David Lee *university president emeritus*

New Haven
Frantz, Dean Leslie *psychotherapist*

Newburgh
†Belleau, Leisa A. *English educator*
Byrne, Jeffrey Edward *pharmacology researcher, educator, consultant*
†Dewey, Dennis James *lawyer*
Tierney, Gordon Paul *real estate broker, genealogist*

Noblesville
Almquist, Donald John *retired electronics company executive*
†Bill, Daniel Joseph *executive planning consultant*
†Emswiller, Julie L. *not-for-profit developer*
Hart, Stuart Newton *psychologist, educator*
Monical, Robert Duane *consulting structural engineer*
Morrison, Joseph Young *transportation consultant*
Tank, Rod Gaillard *orthopaedic physical therapist*
Wilson, Norman Glenn *church administrator, writer*

North Manchester
†McFadden, Renée Fancher *education educator*
†Stan, Jeffrey Scott *physical education educator, soccer coach*
Switzer, Jo Young *academic administrator, dean*

Notre Dame
Arnold, Peri Ethan *political scientist*
Bartell, Ernest *economist, educator, priest*
Bass, Steven Craig *computer science educator*
†Bederman, Gail *education educator, historian*
Blantz, Thomas Edward *Roman Catholic priest, educator*
†Burns, Peter Carman *geologist, educator*
Chipman, Daniel Myron *chemist, researcher, educator*
†Cholak, Peter *mathematics educator*
Conlon, Edward J. *management educator*
Crosson, Frederick James *former university dean, humanities educator*
De Santis, Vincent Paul *historian, educator*
Despres, Leo Arthur *sociology and anthropology educator, academic administrator*
Doody, Margaret Anne *English language educator*
Dowty, Alan Kent *political scientist, educator*
†Dubreil, Sebastien *language educator*
Fallon, Stephen Michael *humanities educator*
†Faybusovich, Leonid *mathematician, educator*
Francis, Michael Jackson *educational administrator*
Ghilarducci, M. Teresa *economist, educator*
Goulet, Denis André *development ethicist, writer*
Gunn, Alan *law educator*
Hayes, Stephen Matthew *librarian*
Helquist, Paul M. *chemistry educator, researcher*
Huang, Roger Dominic *finance educator*
Huber, Paul William *biochemistry educator, researcher*
Hyder, Anthony K. *academic administrator, science educator*
Incropera, Frank Paul *mechanical engineering educator*
Jensen, Richard Jorg *biology educator*
†Jerez-Farran, Carlos *language educator*
Jerger, Edward William *mechanical engineer, university dean*
Klene, Mary Jean *nun, English educator*
Kogge, Peter Michael *computer scientist, educator*
Lafield, Karen Woodrow *science educator, demographer*
Lanzinger, Klaus *language educator*
Mainwaring, Scott Patterson *political scientist, educator*
Malloy, Edward Aloysius *academic administrator*
†Mark, Nelson C. *economist*
Matthias, John Edward *English literature educator*
McElroy, Jerome Lathrop *economics educator*
McInerny, Ralph Matthew *philosophy educator, writer*
McMullin, Ernan Vincent *philosophy educator*
Meisel, Dan *chemist*
Michel, Anthony Nikolaus *electrical engineering educator, researcher*
Mirowski, Philip Edward *economics educator*
Mobashery, Shahriar *chemist*
Moevs, Christian Robert *literature educator*
Moore, Kenneth E. *anthropologist, educator, writer*
†Moss, Lenny *philosopher, scientist*
Mueller, Thomas James *engineering educator, researcher*
Mukasyan, Alexander Sergeevich *scientist*
O'Meara, Onorato Timothy *academic administrator, mathematician*
Pollak, Barth *mathematics educator*
Pollard, Morris *microbiologist, educator*
Quinn, Philip Lawrence *philosophy educator*
Reilly, Frank Kelly *business educator*
†Renaud, John E. *engineering educator, aerospace engineer, mechanical engineer*
Rosenberg, Charles Michael *art historian, educator*
Scheidt, W. Robert *chemistry educator, researcher*
Schmitz, Roger Anthony *chemical engineer, educator, academic administrator*
Schuler, Robert Hugo *chemist, educator*
Sent, Esther-Mirjam *economics educator*
Shannon, William Norman, III, *marketing and international business educator, food service executive*
Shephard, William Danks *physicist, educator*
†Shin, Hojung *education educator*
Sommese, Andrew John *mathematics educator*
Stoll, Wilhelm *mathematics educator*
Stroik, Duncan Gregory *architect, architectural design educator*
Swartz, Thomas R. *economist, educator*
Tomasula, Steven Anthony *literature educator, writer*
Tripathi, Gorakh Nath Ram *physical chemist*
Trozzolo, Anthony Marion *chemistry educator*
Valenzuela, Julio Samuel *sociologist, educator*
Varma, Arvind *chemical engineering educator, researcher*
Vecchio, Robert Peter *business management educator*
Weigert, Andrew Joseph *sociology educator*
†Welch, Michael R. *sociologist, educator*
Williams, Oliver Franklin *priest, educator*
Wong, Warren James *mathematics educator*

Oakland City
Schafer, Patricia Day *physical education educator*

Ogden Dunes
Gasser, Wilbert, Jr., (Wilbert Warner Gasser Jr.) *retired banker*

Pendleton
Corby, Francis Michael, Jr., *financial executive*
Kischuk, Richard Karl *insurance company executive*

Peru
Davidson, John Robert *dentist*
Einselen, Kenneth Lee *civil engineer*
McMinn, William Lowell, Jr., *engineer*

Plainfield
Bryant, John Howard *writer*
Lucas, Georgetta Marie Snell *retired educator, artist*

Plymouth
Jurkiewicz, Margaret Joy Gommel *secondary education educator*
Stiver, James Frederick *pharmacist, health physicist, administrator, scientist*

Portage
Michael, John William *prosthetist orthotist*
Popp, Joseph Bruce *manufacturing executive*

Portland
Downing, Barbara Kay *school system administrator*

Poseyville
Joos, Steven Lee *sports editor*

Purdue University
Rutledge, Charles Ozwin *pharmacologist, educator*
†Vitter, Jeffrey Scott *academic administrator, computer science educator, researcher*

Rensselaer
†Slaby, Frank *financial executive*

Richmond
Bordo, Guy Victor *conductor*
Farber, Evan Ira *librarian*
Kennedy, Barbara Ellen Perry *art therapist*
Kirk, Thomas Garrett, Jr., *librarian*
Robinson, Dixie Faye *educator*
Veramallay, Ashton Isardatt *economist, educator*

Ridgeville
Church, Jay Kay *psychologist, educator*

Rochester
Willard, Shirley Ann Ogle *museum director, editor, historian*

Rockport
Davis, Karen Sue *hospital nursing supervisor*

Rockville
Swaim, John Franklin *physician, health care executive*

Rosemont
†Reyes, J. Christopher *food products distribution executive*

Royal Center
†Blume, Craig Lee *music educator*

Rushville
Moore, Helen Elizabeth *reporter*

Saint Meinrad
Daly, Simeon *retired librarian*

Salem
Karkut, Richard Theodore *clinical psychologist*

Sandborn
Gregg, John Richard *lawyer*
Hartsburg, Judith Catherine *small business owner*

Santa Claus
Edwards, James Dallas, III, *consulting company executive*

Schererville
Castor, Christina Pelayo *critical care nurse*
Hendricks, Stanley Marshall, II, *executive recruiter, consultant*
Jarrett, Alexis *insurance agent, lawyer*
Opacich, Milan *protective services official, musician*
Seward, John Edward, Jr., *insurance company executive*

Scottsburg
Dockery-Schillig, Linda *writer*
Kho, Eusebio *surgeon*

Sellersburg
†MacEva, Carol Ann *accountant*

Seymour
Anderson, David E. *writer, musicologist*
Benter Brock, Teresa Ann *health facility administrator*
Lake, Nancy Jean *nursing educator, operating room nurse*
Norrell, Mary Patricia *nursing educator*
Pardieck, Roger Lee *lawyer*

Shelbyville
†Clark, Rose Sharon *elementary school educator*
Harrold, Dennis Edward *lawyer*
Lisher, James Richard *lawyer*

Shirley
Deck, Darrell (Chester Deck) *minister, historian*

Shoals
Saenz, Ruth E. *missionary*

South Bend
Agbetsiafa, Douglas Kofi *financial and management consultant*
Agostino, Michael Anthony *otolaryngologist*
Anderson, Carolyn Joyce *business development executive*
Anderson, Kenneth Paul *nephrologist, administrator*
†Bauer, Burnett Patrick *state legislator*
Beker, Bernardo Enrique *anesthesiologist*
Bella, Dantina Carmen Quartaroli *human services consultant*
Bonini, James *federal court official*
Brennen, William Elbert *management consultant*
Brueseke, Harold Edward *magistrate*
Carey, John Leo *lawyer*
Carrington, Michael Davis *criminal justice administrator, educator, consultant*
†Casey, Robert Fitzgerald *lawyer, educator*
†Cerny, William *retired education educator, musician*
Charles, Isabel *university administrator*
Cohen, Ronald S. *accountant*
†Colborn, Nancy Wootton *school librarian*
Creps, Philp Lloyd *child psychiatrist*
Ford, George Burt *lawyer*
Furlong, Patrick J. *historian, educator, university administrator*
†Green, Jerry *writer*
†Guyberson, Randy Alan *writer*
Harriman, Gerald Eugene *retired business administrator, economics educator*
Horsbrugh, Patrick *architect, educator, environologist*
†House, Harold Von *science educator, consultant*
JOnes, E. Michael *editor, writer*
†Jones, Wellington Downing, III, *banker*
Kalamaros, Philip E. *lawyer*
Knight, Ida Brown *retired elementary educator*
Lampkin, Ralph, Jr., *vocalist, nightclub consultant, producer, writer, coach*
Manion, Daniel Anthony *federal judge*
†McDonnell, G. Darlene *retired business educator*
†McGuire, Gail Marie *education educator*
Norling, Bernard *retired history educator*
Oke, Festus Erhiurhore *minister, religious organization administrator*
†Palmer, Robert Joseph *lawyer*
†Redmond, Mark Leroy *secondary school educator*
Reinke, William John *lawyer*
Ripple, Kenneth Francis *federal judge*
Rodibaugh, Robert Kurtz *retired judge*
†Scanlan, Margaret *language educator*
Schurz, Franklin Dunn, Jr., *media executive*
Seall, Stephen Albert *lawyer*
Shaffer, Thomas Lindsay *lawyer, educator*
Sharp, Allen *federal judge*
Smith, E. Berry *television and radio consultant*
Smith, Thomas Gordon *architect*
Szigeti, Michelle Marie *critical care nurse*
Torstrick, Rebecca Lee *anthropologist, educator*
van Inwagen, Peter Jan *philosophy educator*
Vasta, Edward *humanities educator*
Vogel, Nelson J., Jr., *lawyer*
Wensits, James Emrich *newspaper editor*
White, Robert Dennis *pediatrician, director*
Wilson, William Leigh *lawyer, educator*
†Winkler, Erhard M. *geologist, educator, consultant*

Spencer
†Coley, Brenda Ann *elementary education educator*
Young, Frederic Hisgin *information systems executive, data processing consultant*

Sullivan
Chavez, Mary Ann *osteopathic family physician*

Syracuse
Blakesley, Wayne Lavere, Jr., *retired production engineer*

Tell City
†Rutherford, Michael Francis *retired music educator*

Terre Haute
Aldridge, Sandra *civic volunteer*
Baker, Ronald Lee *English educator*
Bitzegaio, Harold James *retired lawyer*
†Bopp, James, Jr., *lawyer*
Brennan, Matthew Cannon *English literature educator, poet*
Carmony, Marvin Dale *linguist, educator*
Chesebro, James William *communication educator*
†Christianson, Gale Edward *historian, educator*
†Cockrell, Jan Meyer *recreation therapist*
Coleson, Richard Eugene *lawyer, minister*
Damer, Linda K. *music educator*
De Marr, Mary Jean *English language educator*
Dusanic, Donald Gabriel *parasitology educator, microbiologist*
Feinsod, Arthur Bennett *theatre arts educator*
Guthrie, Frank Albert *chemistry educator*
Hightower, Jeanne Jackson *nursing administrator*
Hulbert, Samuel Foster *college president*
Hunt, Effie Neva *former college dean, former English language educator*
Kesler, John A. *lawyer, land developer*
†Kukral, Michael Andrew *geographer, educator*
Kunkler, Arnold William *retired surgeon, educator*
Lamis, Leroy *artist, retired educator*
Landini, Richard George *university president emeritus, English educator*
Leach, Ronald George *educational administration educator*
Malooley, David Joseph *electronics and computer technology educator*
†Miller, Maurice Dean *special education educator*
†Olsen, Christopher John *education educator*
Perry, Eston Lee *real estate and equipment leasing company executive*
Pickett, William Beatty *history educator*
†Pierard, Charlene Burdett *librarian*
Roshel, John Albert, Jr., *orthodontist*
Sawyer, Thomas Harrison *health, physical education and recreation director*
Siebenmorgen, Paul *retired family physician, lay church worker*
Smith, Donald E. *banker*
Tomey, Ann Louise Marriner *nursing educator*
Van Til, William *education educator, writer*
Wheelock, Larry Arthur *retired engineer, consultant*
Williams, Joseph Claude *physician assistant*

Thorntown
†Miner, Fern Pippenger *librarian*

Tipton
Hurst, Laurenda Lee *library director, music educator*
Lewis, Richart Drake *columnist*

Trafalgar
†Montgomery, Steven Charles *psychologist, minister*

Unionville
†Lyle, Melanie S. *web developer*

Upland
Harbin, Michael Allen *religion educator, writer*
Jessup, Dwight Wiley *academic administrator, educator*
Kesler, Jay Lewis *academic administrator*
Kitterman, Joan Frances *education educator, educator*
†Parker, Richard Allan *music educator*

Valparaiso
Blaschke, Lawrence Raymond *steel manufacturing executive, energy professional*
†Bognar, Joseph Andrew *music educator, musician*
Collie, John, Jr., *insurance agent*
Conison, Jay *lawyer*
Harre, Alan Frederick *academic administrator*
†Kavanagh, Frederick Graham *Japanese language educator*
Kobak, Alfred Julian, Jr., *obstetrician, gynecologist*
Koeppen, Raymond Bradley *lawyer*
†MacGregor, Matt J. *military officer*
Morgan, David A. *art history educator*
Mundinger, Donald Charles *retired college president*
Olson, Lynn *sculptor, painter, writer*
†Persyn, Mary Geraldine *law librarian, law educator*
Peters, Howard Nevin *foreign language educator*
Poracky, Bernard Francis *radiologist*
Schlender, William Elmer *management sciences educator*
Schnabel, Robert Victor *retired academic administrator*
Steil, Valerie Gladys *interior designer*
White, Linda Sue *cardiology technician*

Vincennes
Emison, Ewing Rabb, Jr., *lawyer*
Holcomb, Michelle K. *elementary education educator*
†Jackson, Sharon Sue *music educator*
Rogers, John Headley *educator*
†Smith, Bruce Arthur *lawyer*
Spurrier, James Joseph *theater educator*

Wabash
Scales, Richard Lewis *retired sales representative*

Walkerton
Snakenberg, Sharon Ann *special education educator*

Walton
Chu, Johnson Chin Sheng *retired physician*

Warren
Pattison, Deloris Jean *retired counselor, university official*

Warsaw
Holbrook, Stephen Eugene *printing executive*
Walmer, James L. *lawyer*

Washington
Graham, David Bolden *food products executive*

West Harrison
Plaster, George Francis *Roman Catholic priest*

West Lafayette
Abhyankar, Shreeram S. *mathematics and industrial engineering educator*
†Abraham, John *mechanical engineer, engineering educator*
Adelman, Steven Allen *theoretical physical chemist, chemistry educator*
Albright, Jack Lawrence *animal science and veterinary educator*
Albright, Lyle Frederick *chemical engineering educator*
Altschaeffl, Adolph George *civil engineering educator, retired*
Amstutz, Harold Emerson *veterinarian, educator*
Amy, Jonathan Weekes *scientist, educator*
Anderson, Kristine Jo *librarian*
Andres, Ronald Paul *chemical engineer, educator*
Andrews, Theodora Anne *retired librarian, educator*
Asher, J. William *education and psychology educator*
†Bache, William B. *retired literature educator, editor, writer*
†Balakrishnan, Venkataramanan *statistician, educator*
Bannatyne, Mark William McKenzie *technical graphics educator*
Barany, James Walter *industrial engineering educator*
Barnes, Virgil Everett, II, *physics educator*
Baumgardt, Billy Ray *professional society administrator, agriculturist*
Beering, Steven Claus *academic administrator, medical educator*
Belcastro, Patrick Frank *pharmaceutical scientist*
†Bergstrom, Donald E. *medical educator*
Bertolet, Rodney Jay *philosophy educator*
Borowitz, Joseph Leo *pharmacologist, educator*
†Cassers, Daniel Lee *forester, educator*
Christian, John Edward *health science educator*
Cicirelli, Victor George *psychologist*
Clifton, Christopher W. *researcher, educator*
Cohen, Raymond *mechanical engineer, educator*
Connor, John Murray *agricultural economics educator*
Contreni, John Joseph, Jr., *humanities educator, educator*
Cooper, Arnold Cook *management educator, researcher*
Cosier, Richard A. *dean, business educator, consultant*
Cramer, William Anthony *biochemistry and biophysics researcher, educator*
Cutter, Charles Ross *historian, educator*
Delleur, Jacques William *civil engineering educator*
Diamond, Sidney *chemist, educator*
Diekman, Mark A. *animal science educator*
Drnevich, Vincent Paul *civil engineering educator*
†Duerstock, Bradley S. *neurobiologist, researcher*
†Duran, Angelica Alicia *literature educator*
Eckert, Roger E(arl) *chemical engineering educator*
Edwards, Charles Richard *entomology and pest management educator*
Evanson, Robert Verne *pharmacy educator*
Farris, Paul Leonard *agricultural economist*
Fishman, Brian S. *research analyst*
†Fosmire, Michael *librarian, educator*
Frankenberger, Jane Rossing *agricultural engineer*
Frederickson, Greg Norman *computer science educator*
Frick, Gene Armin *university administrator*
Friedlaender, Fritz Josef *electrical engineering educator*
†Frosch, Robert J. *civil engineer, educator*
Galer-Unti, Regina Ann *health educator*
Gennett, Timothy *academic administrator*
Greenkorn, Robert Albert *chemical engineering educator*
Gruen, Gerald Elmer *psychologist, educator*
Hanks, Alan R. *chemistry educator*
Harding, Bruce Alan *engineering technology educator*
†Hess, Dale Eshleman *geneticist, educator*
Horwich, George *economist, educator*
Hoxie, Robert Prynne *retired entomologist*
Hunt, Michael O'Leary *wood science and engineering educator*
Ichiyama, Dennis Yoshihide *design educator, consultant, administrator*
Jagacinski, Carolyn Mary *psychology educator*
Jischke, Martin C. *academic administrator*
Johannsen, Chris Jakob *agronomist, educator, administrator*
Johns, Janet Susan *physician*
Judd, William Robert *engineering geologist, educator*
Kadiyala, Koteswara Rao *econometrics educator*
†Kelly, Janice R. *psychologist, educator*
Kirksey, Avanelle *nutrition educator*
Knudsen, Dean DeWayne *sociology educator*
†Kovenock, Daniel J. *economist, educator*
Landgrebe, David Allen *electrical engineer*
Laskowski, Michael, Jr., *chemist, educator*
†Latch, Emily Latch *geneticist*
Lechtenberg, Victor L. *agricultural studies educator*
Lefever, Maxine Lane *music educator*
Le Master, Dennis Clyde *natural resource economics and policy educator*
Lewellen, Wilbur Garrett *management educator, consultant*
†Li, Zongzhi *engineer, researcher*
Lin, Pen-Min *electrical engineer, educator*
Lipschutz, Michael Elazar *chemistry educator, consultant, researcher*
Lofgren, Donna Lee *geneticist*
Margerum, Dale William *chemistry educator*
Markee, Katherine Madigan *librarian, educator*
Marshall, Francis Joseph *aerospace engineer*
Martin, Marshall Allen *agricultural economist*
Mason, Sally Kay Frost *biology educator, provost*
Mazumdar, Ravi Rasendra *engineering and mathematics educator*
Mc Bride, William Leon *philosopher, educator*
McFee, William Warren *soil scientist*
Mc Laughlin, John Francis *civil engineer, educator*
McMillin, David Robert *chemistry educator*
Means, Catherine Elizabeth *nurse*
†Mejias, ROBERT, Dr. J. *education educator, consultant, researcher*
†Miller, Paul Chamness *language educator*
Miyamoto, Jun *nuclear engineer*
†Mocioalca, Oana *educator*
Mork, Gordon Robert *historian, educator*
Morrison, Harry *chemistry educator, university dean*
Moskowitz, Herbert *management educator*
Nelson, Philip Edwin *food scientist, educator*
Nixon, Judith May *librarian*
Ohm, Herbert Willis *agronomy educator*
Ong, Chee-Mun *engineering educator*
Overhauser, Albert Warner *physicist*
Patrick, George Frederick *agricultural economics educator*
Peck, Garnet Edward *pharmacist, educator*
Perrucci, Robert *sociologist, educator*
Phillips, Terry LeMoine *investment advisor*
Plante, Robert Donald *management educator, university dean*
Rao, Ramachandra Adiseshappa *civil engineering educator*
†Rebar, Alan H. *dean*
Ringel, Robert Lewis *university administrator*
†Robinson, Farrel Richard *pathologist, toxicologist*
Rossmann, Michael George *biochemist, educator*
Salvendy, Gavriel *industrial engineer, educator*
Saunders, James Robert *English educator*
Scaletta, Phillip Jasper *lawyer, educator*
Schendel, Dan Eldon *management consultant, business educator*
Schneider, Steven Philip *aerodynamics educator*
Schreiber, Marvin Mandel *agronomist, educator*
Schwartz, Richard John *electrical engineering educator, researcher*
Shaw, Stanley Miner *nuclear pharmacy scientist*
Shertzer, Bruce Eldon *education educator*
†Sims-Curry, Kristy *women's college basketball coach*
Stob, Martin *physiology educator*
†Sundquist, John D. *language educator*
Swensen, Clifford Henrik, Jr., *psychologist, educator*
Taber, Margaret Ruth *electrical engineering technology educator, electrical engineer*
Tacker, Willis Arnold, Jr., *medical educator, researcher*
†Tawarmalani, Mohit *engineering educator*
Theen, Rolf Heinz-Wilhelm *political science educator*
†Thomas, Marlin Uluess *industrial engineering educator, academic administrator*
Tilton, Mark Campbell *educator*
Tomovic, Mileta Milos *mechanical engineer, educator*
Viskanta, Raymond *mechanical engineering educator*
Wankat, Phillip Charles *chemical engineering educator*

Watlington, Sarah Jane *community volunteer, retired military officer*
Watts, Michael Wayne *economist*
Wegener, Duane T. *social psychology educator*
Weidenaar, Dennis Jay *economics educator*
Weinstein, Michael Alan *political science educator*
White, Joe Lloyd *soil scientist, educator*
Williams, Theodore Joseph *engineering educator*
Woodman, Harold David *historian, educator*
Yao, Bin *mechanical engineering educator*
Yih, Yuehwern *engineering educator*

Westville
Henning, Teresa Beth *English educator*

Whiting
†Finnegan, Eugene G. *religious studies educator*

Winamac
Ligocki, Gordon Michael *artist, educator*

Winona Lake
†Ashman, Charles H. *retired minister*
Davis, John James *religion educator*
†Dilling, Richard A. *mathematician, educator*
†Henry, Ronald O. *academic administrator*
Julien, Thomas Theodore *religious denomination administrator*
Plaster, David Roy *college executive*

Winslow
McKinney, Shannon J. *retired secondary school educator*

Zionsville
†Bradley, Charles Harvey *lawyer*

IOWA

Adel
Hougham, Norman Russell *financial services company executive*

Ainsworth
Sellars, Arlene Judy *gerontology nurse*

Akron
Hultgren, Dennis Eugene *farmer, management consultant*

Albia
†Pabst, Alfred Mark *lawyer*

Algona
Andreasen, James Hallis *retired state supreme court judge*
Lipps, Thomas W. *lawyer*

Altoona
Berkenes, Joyce Marie Poore *social worker*

Amana
Carroll, Charles A. *manufacturing executive*

Ames
Ahmann, John Stanley *psychologist, educator*
Anderson, Lloyd Lee *animal science educator*
Anderson, Robert Morris, Jr., *electrical engineer*
Armstrong, Daniel Wayne *chemist, educator*
†Avalos, Hector Ignacio *language educator*
Barnes, Richard George *physicist, educator*
†Barton, Thomas Jackson *chemistry educator*
Basart, John Philip *electrical engineering and remote sensing researcher*
†Baum, Robert M. *religious studies educator, researcher*
Baumann, Edward Robert *environmental engineering educator*
Beran, George Wesley *veterinary microbiology educator*
Berger, P(hilip) Jeffrey *animal science educator, quantitative geneticist*
Bhattacharya, Joydeep *economics educator*
Biner, Bulent Suleyman *materials scientist, educator*
Black, James Robert *industrial engineer*
Bonomi, Ferne Gater *public relations executive*
†Bovinette, James Thomas *musician, educator*
Bowen, George Hamilton, Jr., *astrophysicist, educator*
Brown, Robert Grover *engineering educator*
Buchele, Wesley Fisher *retired agricultural engineering educator*
Bullen, Daniel Bernard *mechanical engineering educator*
Caldwell, Wallace Caughey *physicist, engineer*
Campbell, Jessie Katherine *mathematician, educator*
Cleasby, John LeRoy *civil engineer, educator*
Clem, John Richard *physicist, educator*
Colvin, Thomas Stuart *agricultural engineer, farmer*
Courteau, Joanna *foreign language educator*
Crabtree, Beverly June *retired college dean*
Cravens, Hamilton *history educator*
Dahiya, Rajbir Singh *mathematics educator, researcher*
David, Herbert Aron *statistician, educator*
Ebbers, Larry Harold *education educator*
†Fennelly, William *basketball coach*
Fleming, Jon Lee *gastroenterologist*
†Forrest, Paula Sue *musician, music educator*
Fox, Karl August *economist, eco-behavioral scientist*
Fritz, James Sherwood *chemist, educator*
Fuller, Wayne Arthur *statistics educator*
Geoffroy, Gregory L. *academic administrator, educator*
Ghoshal, Nani Gopal *veterinarian, educator*
Gradwohl, David Mayer *anthropology educator*
Green, Detroy Edward *retired dean*
Greve, John Henry *veterinary parasitologist, educator*
Gschneidner, Karl Albert, Jr., *metallurgist, educator, editor, consultant*
Hallauer, Arnel Roy *geneticist*
Harl, Neil Eugene *economist, lawyer, educator*
Hatfield, Jerry Lee *plant physiologist, biometeorologist*
Herwig, Joan Emily *developmental education educator, researcher*
Hill, Fay Gish *librarian*
Hoffman, Mark Peter *animal scientist*
Horowitz, Jack *biochemistry educator*
Hunger, J(ohn) David *business educator*
Imsande, John David *geneticist, researcher, educator*
Isaacson, Dean Leroy *statistician*
Jacobson, Norman L. *retired agricultural educator, researcher*
Jacobson, Robert Andrew *chemistry educator*
Johnson, Howard Paul *agricultural engineering educator*
Johnson, Lawrence Alan *cereal technologist, educator, administrator*
Jones, Edwin Channing, Jr., *electrical and computer engineering educator*
Kaplan, Murray Lee *nutritionist, educator*
Karlen, Douglas Lawrence *soil scientist*
Kaufmann, Jeffrey Baer *business educator, lawyer*
Kelly, James Michael *plant and soil scientist*
Klonglan, Gerald Edward *sociology educator*
Lane, Orris John, Jr., *retired engineer*
Larsen, William Lawrence *materials science and engineering educator*
Lee, Seong-Jae *researcher*
Lieberman, Gary Mitchell *mathematics educator*
Manatt, Richard *retired education educator*
†Martin, Peter *psychology educator*
Mattila, Mary Jo Kalsem *elementary and art educator*
Meeks, Carol Jean *educator*
Mengeling, William Lloyd *retired veterinarian, virologist*
Mertins, James Walter *entomologist*
Meyer, Charles William *economics educator*
Mischke, Charles Russell *mechanical engineering educator*
†Moon, Harley William *veterinarian*
Moore, Kenneth James *agronomy educator, scientist*
Moore, Lester Leland *clergy, financial consultant*
O'Berry, Phillip Aaron *veterinarian*
Okiishi, Theodore Hisao *mechanical engineering educator*
Orazem, Peter Francis *economics educator*
Paschke, Teresa Ann *artist, educator*
†Premkumar, Prem *educator*
Quirmbach, Herman Charles *economics educator*
Richt, Juergen Albrecht *veterinarian*
Rosenberg, Ralph *former state senator, lawyer, consultant, educator, foundation administrator*
Ross, Richard Francis *veterinarian, microbiologist, educator, dean*
St. Germain, Sheryl A. *humanities educator, writer*
Sanders, Wallace Wolfred, Jr., *civil engineer*
Schuh, John Howard *higher education educator, academic administrator*
Seaton, Vaughn Allen *retired veterinary pathology educator*
Sheble, Gerald B. *engineering educator, consultant*
Smith, John Francis *materials science educator*
†Smith, Jonathan Dallas Hayden *mathematician*
Snyder, John Evan *physicist*
Somani, Arun Kumar *electrical engineer, educator*
†Stalheim, Ole Henry V. *veterinarian, educator*
†Stephenson, W. Robert *statistician*
†Sung, Shihwu *environmental engineer, educator*
Swanson, Florine Mary *foundation administrator*
†Tesfatsion, Leigh S. *economics educator, consultant*
Thiel, Patricia Ann *chemistry educator*
Thompson, Louis Milton *agronomy educator, scientist*
Topel, David Glen *agricultural studies educator*
Vaughn, Richard Clements *engineering educator*
Venkata, Subrahmanyam Saraswati *electrical engineering educator, electric energy and power researcher*
Voss, Regis Dale *agronomist, educator*
†Weber, Eric Scott *mathematician, educator*
†Wendell, Barbara Taylor *retired real estate agent*
Wheelock, Thomas David *professor chemical engineering*
†Whiteford, Michael Bonneville *anthropology educator*
Wilder, David Randolph *materials engineer, consultant*
Willham, Richard Lewis *animal science educator*
Work, George Paul *cellist*
Yeung, Edward Szeshing *chemist*
Zimmerman, Zora Devrnja *English and folklore educator, university dean*

Anita
Everhart, Robert Phillip (Bobby Williams) *entertainer, songwriter, recording artist*

Ankeny
Creswell, Dorothy Anne *computer consultant*
Houghton, Myron James *theology educator*
Kapler, Jeanne Marie *occupational therapist*
Lynn, Robert William *strategic planning consultant*
Rivers, Donald Lee *marketing professional*
†Scott, Beverly Jeanne *contractor, writer*
†Weigel, Ollie J. *dentist, former mayor*

Avoca
Hardisty, William Lee *English language educator*

Belmond
Johnson, Roger Christie *environmental engineer*

Bettendorf
Collins, Kathleen Elizabeth *pharmaceutical company official*
Hamburg, David D. *music educator*
Hanzelka, Richard Louis *education educator*
Heyderman, Arthur Jerome *engineer, civilian military employee*
Krein, David Frederick *humanities educator*
Mosby, John Singleton, Jr., *chiropractor, educator, consultant*
Nolte, Jacqueline *accountant*
Rathje, James Lee *broker*

Birmingham
Goudy, James Joseph Ralph *electronics executive, educator*

Boone
†Beckwith, F. William *food products executive*

Britt
Castillo, Leanne Marlow *artist, nurse*

Burlington
Hoth, Steven Sergey *lawyer, educator*
Lundy, Sherman Perry *secondary school educator*

Carlisle
Berning, Robert William *librarian*

Carroll
Comito, Frank Joseph *lawyer*

Cascade
Peryon, Charleen D. *education educator, consultant*

Cedar Falls
Clohesy, William Warren *philosopher, educator*
Fanelli, Michael Paul *music educator*
Floyd, Angeleita Stevens *flutist*
Gilgen, Albert Rudolph *psychologist, educator*
Hedden, Debra Gordon *music educator*
Kashef, Ali Ebrahim *industrial technology educator*
†Koob, Robert Duane *chemistry educator, educational administrator*
†Lettow, Lucille Jane *school librarian, education educator*
†Maier, Donna Jane-Ellen *history educator*
†Olsen-Dunbar, Jessica Ida *sign language educator*
†Rao, Posinasetti Nageswara *manufacturing engineering educator*
†Rawwas, Mohammed Yahya *marketing professional, educator*
Sweet, Cynthia Rae *small business owner*
Wang, Jennie *literature educator*
Wirth, David Eugene *software designer, consultant*

Cedar Rapids
Albright, Justin W. *retired lawyer*
Armitage, Thomas Edward *library director*
Arnold-Olson, Helen B. *nonprofit consultant*
Baermann, Donna Lee Roth *real estate property executive, retired insurance analyst*
Baldwin, Cynthia Ann *industrial hygienist*
Baldwin, George Koehler *retired retail executive*
Berry, Jay Robert, Jr., *English educator*
Brandt, John Edward *human services administrator*
Brooks, Debra L. *healthcare executive, neuromuscular therapist*
†Foust, LeAnne *voice educator, vocalist*
†Gray, William Oxley *retired lawyer*
Haines, Cathy Jean *middle school education educator*
Hall, Kathy L. *orchestra executive*
Hansen, David Rasmussen *federal judge*
Harms, Allan L. *patent lawyer*
Heller, Terry L(ynn) *English literature educator, writer*
Houmes, Blaine V. *emergency physician, county medical examiner*
Huber, Rita Norma *civic worker*
Hutton, Mary J. *guidance counselor*
Keller, Eliot Aaron *broadcasting executive*
Knepper, Eugene Arthur *realtor*
Lisio, Donald John *historian, educator*
Mc Manus, Edward Joseph *federal judge*
Melloy, Michael J. *federal judge*
†Nassif, Gary Tannus *singer and entertainer, art and special education educator, sculptor*
Nazette, Richard Follett *lawyer*
Nebergall, Donald Charles *rural consultant*
Norris, Albert Stanley *psychiatrist, educator*
Novetzke, Sally Johnson *former ambassador*
Patton, James Edward *school psychologist*
Pitts, Terence Randolph *museum director, consultant*
Quarton, William Barlow *broadcasting company executive*
Renter, Lois Irene Hutson *librarian*
Richardson, Robert Edward *data processing analyst*
Riley, Tom Joseph *lawyer*
Rosberg, Merilee Ann *education educator*
Smith, Cindy Thompson *special education educator*
Stephens, Ralph Renne *massage therapy educator*
Stirler, Karen Sue *special education educator, adult education educator*
Stolte, Larry Gene *marketing executive, former computer and publishing company executive*
Tiemeyer, Christian *conductor*
Toluie, Kamran *cardiologist, electrophysiologist*
Vanderpool, Ward Melvin *management and marketing consultant*
Wax, Nadine Virginia *retired banker*
Whipple, William Perry *foundation administrator*
Wiese, Daniel Edward *marketing and communications researcher*
Wilson, Robert Foster *lawyer*
Wright, Walter Edward *county official, retired army officer*
Ziese, Nancylee Hanson *social worker*

Center Junction
Antons, Pauline Marie *mathematics educator*

Chariton
†McKinley, Paul *state legislator*
Stuart, William Corwin *judge*

Charles City
Krieger, Theodore Kent *poet*
Mc Cartney, Ralph Farnham *lawyer*
McCartney, Rhoda Huxsol *farm manager*

Cherokee
Clark, Larry Dalton *civil engineer*
Simonsen, Robert Alan *marketing executive*

Clear Lake
Broshar, Robert Clare *architect*
†Peterson, Christian Carrol *farmer*

Cleghorn
Anderson, Marilyn Ruth *retired multi-media specialist*

Clinton
†Frey, A. John, Jr., *lawyer*
Vidal, Ronald Anthony *otolaryngology*
Warner, Jean Lollich *poet*
Woodman, Grey Musgrave *psychiatrist*

Clive
Miller, Kenneth Edward *sociologist, educator*
Neis, Arthur Veral *healthcare and development company executive*

Coggon
Hammer, Robert Eugene *psychologist*

Coralville
Allen, (Edwin) Lee *artist*
Lueder, Barbara Ann *school psychologist*

Corydon
Hopkins, Theodore Mark *minister, guidance counselor*

Council Bluffs
Drake, Lee J. *public administration executive, writer*
†Jennings, Dean Thomas *lawyer*
†Kurt, Johnny Thomas *music educator*
Nelson, H. H. Red *insurance company executive*
†Pechacek, Frank Warren, Jr., *lawyer*
Peterson, Richard William *retired judge, lawyer*

Davenport
Arnold, David Alan *surgeon*
Asadi, Anita Murlene *business educator*
Bannick, Janice Carol *automotive dealerships executive*
Beguhn, Sandra E. *poet, author*
Bush, Michael Kevin *lawyer*
Chowdhury, Ali Asraf *electrical engineer, researcher*
Dcamp, Charles Barton *educator, musician*
Dettmann, David Allen *lawyer*
†Driscoll, Kerry Sue *language educator*
Edgerton, Winfield Dow *retired gynecologist*
Foster, James Franklin *professional sports management executive*
†Graham, Sally Jo *information technology executive, marketing professional*
Hudson, Celeste Nutting *education educator, reading clinic administrator, consultant*
Jecklin, Lois Underwood *art corporation executive, consultant*
Juckem, Wilfred Philip *manufacturing company executive*
Kruse, Marylin Lynn *retired foreign language educator*
Lane, Gary Matthew *lawyer*
Le Grand, Clay *lawyer, former state justice*
†McAulay, Brian J. *director*
McDonald, Julie Jensen *writer, educator*
McGuire, John Francis *retired English educator, consultant*
Mitchell, Robert Carl *physicist, educator*
Pedersen, Karen Sue *electrical engineer*
Phelps, Michael Edward *publishing executive*
Preston, Ann Elizabeth *media and communication educator*
Sanborne, Lewis W. *director, English educator*
Schleicher, Donald *music director*
Shammas, Nicolas Wahib *internist, cardiologist*
Shaw, Donald Hardy *lawyer*
†Sievert, Mary Elizabeth *small business owner, retired secondary school educator*
Tsau, William Wen-Shiung *civil engineer, consultant, structural engineer*
Willett, Lance *orchestra executive*
Wilson, Frances Edna *protective services official*

De Witt
Rittmer, Elaine Heneke *retired library media specialist*

Decorah
†Christianson, John Robert *historian, educator*
Farwell, Elwin D. *minister, educational consultant*
Gray, Phyllis *educational administrator*
Nelson, Harland Stanley *retired English educator*
Wangsness, Wayne Roger *farmer*
†Williams, Lawrence H. *minister, theology studies educator*

Des Moines
Abbott, Aloris Jean *operating room nurse, administrator*
†Abel, Gregory E. *utility company executive*
Anderson, Eric Anthony *city manager*
Bamford, Carol Marie *marketing executive*
Bartschat, Klaus Richard Wilhelm *physics educator*
Beeman, David Gerard *psychologist*
Begleiter, Martin David *law educator, consultant*
Begleiter, Ronni Frankel *lawyer*

Bell, Edward Allen *pharmacy educator*
Bennett, Edward James *lawyer*
Bergman, Bruce E. *municipal official*
Blake, Darlene Evelyn *political worker, consultant, educator, author*
Blank, Myron Nathan *theater executive*
Boyle, Bruce James *publisher*
Bremer, Celeste F. *judge*
Brickman, Kenneth Alan *state lottery executive*
Brooks, Roger Kay *insurance company executive*
Brown, Loren Dennis *internist, educator*
Brown, Paul Edmondson *lawyer*
Burns, Bernard John, III, *public defender*
†Calkins, Richard M. *lawyer*
Campbell, Bruce Irving *lawyer*
Carter, James H. *judge*
Charron, Joseph L. *bishop*
†Clark, Craig Boyd *cardiologist*
Claypool, David L. *lawyer*
†Colloton, Steven M. *judge*
Conlin, Roxanne Barton *lawyer*
Corning, Joy Cole *former state official*
Cortese, Joseph Samuel, II, *lawyer*
Culver, Chester J. *state official, educator*
Davilla, Donna Elaine *school system administrator*
Deluhery, Patrick John *state legislator*
Demorest, Allan Frederick *retired psychologist*
Drake, Richard Francis *state legislator*
†Drury, David J. *insurance company executive*
Duckworth, Marvin E. *lawyer, educator*
Dukes, Vanessa Johnson *dietitian*
Edwards, John Duncan *law educator, librarian*
Edwards, Richard Alan *banker*
Eichner, Kay Marie *mental health nurse*
Ellis, Mary Louise Helgeson *retired insurance company executive, business consultant*
Elmets, Harry Barnard *retired osteopath, dermatologist*
Ely, Lawrence Orlo *retired surgeon*
Erickson, Elaine Mae *composer, poet*
Fagg, George Gardner *federal judge*
Finley, Kerry A. *lawyer*
Fisher, Thomas George *lawyer, retired media company executive*
Fisher, Thomas George, Jr., *lawyer*
Flaherty, Daniel Lee *prosecutor*
Flynn, Scott D. *lawyer*
Foxhoven, Jerry Ray *lawyer*
Frederici, C. Carleton *lawyer*
†Freeman, Denise *podiatrist, educator*
Gaines, Ruth Ann *educator*
Gartner, Michael Gay *editor, television executive, baseball executive*
Giunta, Joseph *conductor, music director*
Goodin, Julia C. *forensic pathologist, state official, educator*
†Graham, Diane E. *newspaper editor*
†Graves, Bruce *lawyer, director*
Graziano, Craig Frank *lawyer*
Grefe, Rolland Eugene *lawyer*
Griswell, J. Barry *insurance company executive*
Hall, Donald Vincent *social worker*
Hansell, Edgar Frank *lawyer*
Harris, Charles Elmer *lawyer*
Harris, K. David *senior state supreme court justice*
†Hendrickson, Gordon Olaf *archivist*
Hill, Luther Lyons, Jr., *lawyer*
Hockenberg, Harlan David *lawyer*
†Holveck, Jack *state legislator*
Hutchison, Charlotte Pancoast (Sherry Hutchison) *civic worker*
Jensen, Dick Leroy *lawyer*
†Johnson, Nancy Elizabeth *bookseller*
Kalainov, Sam Charles *insurance company executive*
Kelley, Bruce Gunn *insurance company executive, lawyer*
Kerr, William T. *publishing and broadcasting executive*
Koehn, William James *lawyer*
Kramer, Mary Elizabeth *state legislator, health services executive*
Kruidenier, David *newspaper executive*
Larson, Chuck, Jr., *state representative, political organization administrator*
Larson, Jerry Leroy *state supreme court justice*
Lavorato, Louis A. *state supreme court chief justice*
Leach, Dave Francis *editor, musician*
Lewis, Calvin Fred *architect, educator*
†Luchtel, Keith Edward *lawyer*
Lund, Doris Hibbs *retired dietitian*
†Martens, Harvey Arthur *retired government worker, academic administrator*
†Maxwell, David E. *academic executive, educator*
McDowell, Frederick Peter Woll *retired English educator*
McGiverin, Arthur A. *former state supreme court chief justice*
McGuire-Riggs, Sheila *chairman Democratic party*
Mill, Jeth *performing company executive*
Miller, Thomas J. *state attorney general*
Moulder, William H. *chief of police*
Munson, Jay Donald *statistician*
Murray, William Michael (Mike Murray) *lawyer*
Myers, Mary Kathleen *publishing executive*
Nelson, Charlotte Bowers *public administrator*
Norris, Glenn L. *lawyer*
†Nowadzky, Roger Alan *lawyer, lobbyist*
Odell, Mary Jane *former state official*
Peddicord, Roland Dale *lawyer*
Pederson, Sally *lieutenant governor*
Phipps, David Lee *lawyer*
Power, Joseph Edward *lawyer*
Pray, Ralph Rustin *internist*
Ramsden, Mary Catherine *substance abuse specialist*
†Rants, Christopher C. *state representative*
Reece, Maynard Fred *artist, author*
Richards, Riley Harry *insurance company executive*
†Rieck, Michael Quentin *educator*
Riekenberg, Warren Glenn *civil engineer*
Rodgers, Louis Dean *retired surgeon*

Rosen, Matthew Stephen *botanist, consultant*
Runge, Kay Kretschmar *library director*
Sanders, Arthur *political scientist, educator*
Schneider, William George *former life insurance company executive*
†Seitzinger, Edward Francis *lawyer*
Shors, John D. *lawyer*
Simpson, Lyle Lee *lawyer*
Sinay, Tony *economist, educator*
Smith, Diana Marie *business educator*
Smith, Neal Edward *congressman*
†Sokol, David L. *energy services provider company executive*
Song, Joseph *pathologist, educator*
Stier, Mary *publishing executive*
†Stoffregen, Philip Eugene *lawyer*
Stork, Frank James *lawyer*
Streit, Michael J. *state supreme court justice*
Szymoniak, Elaine Eisfelder *retired state senator*
Teitelbaum, Howard S. *academic administrator*
Ternus, Marsha K. *state supreme court justice*
Tipton, Sheila Kay *lawyer*
Tormey, Jerome Marshall *human services administrator*
Truck, Frederick John *artist*
Van Zante, Shirley M(ae) *magazine editor*
Vaughan, Therese Michele *insurance commissioner*
Vietor, Harold Duane *federal judge*
Vilsack, Thomas *governor*
Walters, Ross A. *federal judge*
Wattleworth, Roberta Ann *physician, medical educator*
Webb, Mary Christine *reading recovery educator, in-class reading specialist*
Wilcox, Gregory B. *lawyer*
Wilson, Sal *computer systems analyst, business executive*
Witke, David Rodney *retired newspaper editor, consultant*
Wolle, Charles Robert *federal judge*
Zagoren, Allen Jeffrey *surgeon*
†Zumbach, Steven Elmer *lawyer*

Dubuque
Arms, Gary D. *English literature educator*
Barta, James Omer *priest, psychology educator, church administrator*
Beck, Robert Raymond *priest*
Bloesch, Donald George *theologian, writer, educator*
Brimeyer, James Leon *language educator*
Burkhart, John Ernest *minister, religion educator*
Chapman, John Stephen *retired internist, medical administrator*
Churchill, Thomas John *broadcast meteorologist*
Crahan, Jack Bertsch *retired manufacturing company executive*
Ernst, Daniel Pearson *lawyer*
Hammer, David Lindley *lawyer, writer*
†Hanus, Jerome George *archbishop*
Hemmer, Paul Edward *musician, composer, broadcasting executive*
†Hughes, Brian Lee *music educator*
Jorgensen, Gerald Thomas *psychologist, educator, lawyer*
†Keller, Robert Scott *education educator*
Kolz, Beverly Anne *publishing executive*
Lisk, Alan Robert *finance educator, consultant*
McDonald, Robert Delos *manufacturing company executive*
†Nadeau, Evelyn *language educator*
Nessan, Craig Lee *minister, educator*
Perry, E. Eugene *communication educator*
Peterson, Walter Fritiof *academic administrator*
Tigges, John Thomas *writer, musician, lecturer*
Toale, Thomas Edward *school system administrator, priest*
Tully, Thomas Alois *building materials executive, consultant, educator*

Early
Myers, Kenneth L(eRoy) *secondary education educator*

Emmetsburg
Wells, Martha Johanna *elementary education educator*

Epworth
†Wozniak, John S. *dean*

Fairfield
Joshi, Prabhakar G. *educator*
Kelly, Thomas *advertising executive*
Larson, Rustin Lee *writer, educator*

Fayette
Barker, Richard Alexander *organizational psychologist*

Fonda
Tamm, Eleanor Ruth *retired accountant*

Fort Dodge
Cassady, Daniel Bennet *music educator*
Delucca, Leopoldo Eloy *otolaryngologist, head and neck surgeon*
Hanson, Richard James *art educator, artist*
Pratt, Diane Adele *talented and gifted education educator*
Smith, William G. *transportation executive*
Wolf, Robert Charles *writer, news correspondent*

Fort Madison
†Chapman, Allen D. *music educator*
Sallen, David Urban *lawyer*

Garner
†Hovda, Theodore James *lawyer*

George
Symens, Maxine Brinkert Tanner *marketing professional*

Glenwood
Campbell, William Edward *mental hospital administrator*

Greenfield
†Howe, Jay Edwin *lawyer*

Grinnell
Adelberg, Arnold Melvin *mathematics educator, researcher*
Campbell, David George *ecologist, researcher, author*
†Carl, Janet A. n *writing instructor, consultant*
†Chamberland, Marc A. *mathematician, educator*
Ferguson, Pamela Anderson *mathematics educator, educational administrator*
Irving, Donald C. *English educator*
Kaiser, Daniel Hugh *historian, educator*
Kintner, Philip L. *history educator*
McKee, Christopher Fulton *librarian, historian, educator*
Michaels, Jennifer Tonks *foreign language educator*
Mitchell, Orlan E. *clergyman, former college president*
Moyer, H. Wayne *political science educator*
Osgood, Russell King *academic administrator*
Schrift, Alan Douglas *philosophy educator*
Smith, Don Alan *educator*
Walker, Waldo Sylvester *biology educator, academic administrator*

Grundy Center
†Kliebenstein, Don *lawyer*

Harlan
†Wilson, Annette Sigrid *educator*

Hiawatha
Pate, Paul Danny *mayor*

Hopkinton
Pounds, Buzz R. *educator*

Hornick
Enstrom, Walter Gordon A. *minister*

Hudson
Mettlin, Connie Ann *social worker, educator*

Hull
De Koster, John G. *lawyer*

Humboldt
Dodgen, John N. *manufacturing executive*

Indianola
Larsen, Robert LeRoy *artistic director*
Mace, Jerilee Marie *opera company executive*
†Mapel, Patricia Jolene *farmer, consultant*
Ouderkirk, Mason James *lawyer*
Pearson, Walter Stephen *adult learning educator*
Songayllo, Raymond Thaddeus *music educator*

Iowa City
Addis, Laird Clark, Jr., *philosopher, educator, musician*
Afifi, Adel Kassim *physician*
Aikin, Judith Popovich *languages educator, academic administrator*
Albrecht, William Price *economist, educator, government official*
Alford, Steve *college basketball coach*
†Andersland, Mark Steven *electrical and computer engineering educator*
Anderson, Barrie *gynecologic oncologist*
Andreasen, Nancy Coover *psychiatrist, educator, neuroscientist*
Apicella, Michael Allen *physician, educator*
Baird, Robert Dahlen *religious educator*
Baker, Richard Graves *geology educator, palynologist*
Banker, Gilbert Stephen *industrial and physical pharmacy educator, administrator*
Barkan, Joel David *political science educator, consultant*
Bedell, George Noble *physician, educator*
Bell, Marvin Hartley *poet, English language educator*
Bentz, Dale Monroe *librarian*
Berg, Mary Jaylene *pharmacy educator, researcher*
†Bezanson, Randall Peter *law educator*
Bishara, Samir Edward *orthodontist*
Bjorndal, Arne Magne *endodontist*
Block, Robert I. *psychologist, researcher, educator*
Bonfield, Arthur Earl *lawyer, educator*
Bowlsby, Bob *athletic director*
Boyd, Willard Lee *academic administrator, educator, museum administrator, lawyer*
†Bozeman, Theodore D. *religion educator*
Brennan, Robert Lawrence *educational director, psychometrician*
Broffitt, James Drake *professor statistics and actuarial science*
Buckwalter, Joseph Addison *orthopedic surgeon, educator*
Buckwalter, Kathleen C. *academic administrator, educator*
Burns, C(harles) Patrick *hematologist-oncologist*
Burton, Donald Joseph *chemistry educator*
Butchvarov, Panayot Krustev *philosophy educator*
Butler, John Edward *biomedical sciences educator, consultant*
Campbell, Kevin Peter *physiology and biophysics educator, researcher*
Campion, Daniel Ray *editor*
†Choi, Kent Choung *surgeon, researcher*
Clifton, James Albert *physician, educator*
Collins, Daniel W. *accountant, educator*
Colloton, John William *university health care executive*
Coolidge, Archibald Cary, Jr., *English language educator, literature researcher*
Cooper, Reginald Rudyard *orthopedic surgeon, educator*
Cruden, Robert William *botany educator*
Cyphert, Stacey Todd *health facilities administrator*

Davis, Julia McBroom *college dean, speech pathology and audiology educator*
Donelson, John Everett *biochemistry educator, molecular biologist*
Downer, Robert Nelson *lawyer*
Dreher, Melanie Creagan *dean, nursing educator*
Duffy, William Edward, Jr., *retired education educator*
Dyken, Mark Eric *physician*
Eckstein, John William *physician, educator*
Erkonen, William E. *radiologist, medical educator*
Ertl, Wolfgang *German language and literature educator*
Feldt, Leonard Samuel *university educator and administrator*
Fellows, Robert Ellis *medical educator, medical scientist*
Folk, James Calvin *ophthalmologist, researcher*
Folsom, Lowell Edwin *language educator*
Forell, George Wolfgang *religion educator*
Forsythe, Robert Elliott *economics educator*
†Fuller, Kent Ralph *mathematician, educator*
Fumerton, Richard Anthony *philosopher, educator*
Galask, Rudolph Peter *obstetrician and gynecologist*
Gantz, Bruce Jay *otolaryngologist, educator*
Gelfand, Lawrence Emerson *historian, educator*
Geweke, John Frederick *economics educator*
Goldstein, Jonathan Amos *retired ancient history and classics educator*
Gray, George Trumon *test development professional*
†Green, Carin Margreta *art educator*
Green, Peter Morris *classics educator, writer, translator*
Grose, Charles Frederick *pediatrician, infectious disease specialist*
Guillory, J. Keith *pharmacist, educator*
Hammond, Harold Logan *oral and maxillofacial pathologist, educator*
Hansen, Peter Jacob *chemistry educator*
Hausler, William John, Jr., *microbiologist, educator, public health laboratory administrator*
Hawley, Ellis Wayne *historian, educator*
Hayek, John William *lawyer*
Hein, Herman August *physician*
Heistad, Donald Dean *cardiologist*
†Hell, Johannes Wilhelm *neuroscientist, researcher*
Helms, Charles Milton *medical educator, consultant*
Hettmansperger, Sue *artist, art educator*
Hines, N. William *dean, law educator, administrator*
Hobart, Thomas D. *lawyer*
Hogg, Robert Vincent, Jr., *mathematical statistician, educator*
Hudson, John Boswell *sociologist, educator*
Husted, Russell Forest *research scientist*
Huttner, Sidney Frederick *librarian*
†Johlin, Frederick Carl, Jr., *medical educator*
Johnson, Cynda Ann *physician, educator*
Johnson, Nicholas *writer, lawyer, lecturer*
Jorgensen, Palle Erik Tikob E T *mathematician, educator*
Justice, Donald Rodney *poet, educator*
Kardon, Randy H. *ophthalmologist, researcher*
Kelley, Patricia Lou *social work educator*
Kelsay, Danielle Marie Rubino *audiologist*
Kerber, Linda Kaufman *historian, educator*
Kerber, Richard E. *cardiologist*
Kessel, Richard Glen *zoology educator*
Kim, Chong Lim *political science educator*
Kinsey, Joni Louise *art history educator*
Kisker, Carl Thomas *physician, medical educator*
Koch, Donald LeRoy *retired geologist, state agency administrator*
Kottick, Edward Leon *music educator, harpsichord maker*
Kowal, Rebekah Jane *American Studies educator*
Kurtz, Sheldon Francis *lawyer, educator*
Lakshman, Venkatesh *gastroenterologist, researcher, educator*
†Landsman, Miriam Joy *social worker, educator, social worker, researcher*
Lariviere, Gene Robert *surgeon*
LeBlond, Richard Foard *internist, educator*
Linhardt, Robert John J *medicinal chemistry educator*
Loewenberg, Gerhard *political science educator*
Lonngren, Karl Erik *electrical and computer engineering educator*
†Mahoney, Larry T. *pediatrician, cardiologist*
†Mangum, Teresa Lynn *English literature educator*
Markham, Sanford Max *obstetrician-gynecologist, educator*
Marshall, Jeffrey Scott *mechanical engineer, educator*
Mason, Edward Eaton *surgeon*
Mather, Roger Frederick *music educator, writer*
†McGovern, Jennifer Anne *education educator*
Mentzer, Raymond Albert *religious history educator*
Merkel-Hess, Mary Lynne *artist*
Miller, Dwight Merrick *archivist, historian*
Montgomery, Rex *biochemist, educator*
Morriss, Frank Howard, Jr., *pediatrics educator*
Morriss, Mary Jeannette Hagan *pediatric cardiologist, educator*
†Muir, Ruth Brooks *counselor, substance abuse service coordinator*
Muller, Barbara Ann *allergist*
Myers, Virginia Anne *art educator*
†Nash, Jan R. Olive *historian, consultant*
Nathan, Peter E. *psychologist, educator*
Nelson, Herbert Leroy *psychiatrist*
Nesbitt, John Arthur *recreation service educator, recreation therapy educator*
Neumann, Roy Covert *architect*
†Noyes, Russell, Jr., *psychiatrist*
Odgaard, Anders Jacob *civil and environmental engineer, educator*

†Oetting, Thomas Andrew *medical association administrator, medical educator, educator*
Olin, William Harold *orthodontist, educator*
†Paredes, Robert Wesley *music educator*
Park, Joon Bu *biomedical engineer, researcher, educator*
Patel, Virendra Chaturbhai *mechanical engineer, educator*
†Peloso, Paul Michael *medical educator*
Percas de Ponseti, Helena *foreign language and literature educator*
Peters, John Durham *communications educator, writer*
Plapp, Bryce Vernon *biochemistry educator*
Pogue, Thomas Franklin *economics educator, consultant*
Ponseti, Ignacio Vives *orthopaedic surgery educator*
†Porter, Nancy Lefgren *reading recovery educator*
Raeburn, John Hay *English language educator*
Rao, Satish *medical educator, physician scientist*
Reynolds, David G(eorge) *retired physiologist, educator*
Richerson, Hal Bates *physician, internist, allergist, immunologist, educator*
Riesz, Peter Charles *marketing educator, consultant*
Ringen, Catherine Oleson *linguistics educator*
Robertson, Timothy Joel *statistician, educator*
Rockel, Viana Eileen *university fundraiser, consultant*
Roe, Gerald Bruce *director, writer*
†Rohrbough, Malcolm Justin *historian, educator*
Saterfiel, Thomas Horne *education researcher, administrator*
Schmidt, Julius *sculptor*
†Schulz-Stübner, Sebastian Hans Wolfgang *anesthesiologist, critical care specialist, pain specialist, psychotherapist, medical quality manager*
Scullion, Rosemarie *literature educator*
Shannon, Lyle William *sociology educator*
Siebert, Calvin D. *economist, educator*
Sivitz, William Irving *endocrinologist*
Skinstad, Anne Helene *psychologist, researcher*
Skorton, David Jan *academic administrator*
Smoker, Wendy Rue Kartinos *neuroradiologist, consultant, educator*
†Snyder, Peter M. *medical educator, medical researcher*
Solbrig, Ingeborg Hildegard *German literature educator, writer*
†Sontheimer, Richard D. *dermatology educator, researcher*
Spector, Arthur Abraham *physician, educator*
Spies, Leon Fred *lawyer*
Spriestersbach, Duane Caryl *academic administrator, speech pathology/audiology services professional, educator*
Stein, Robert A. *writer, educator*
†Stensvaag, John-Mark *legal educator, lawyer*
Strauss, John Steinert *dermatologist, educator*
Suls, Jerry M. *psychologist, educator*
Sutphin, John E. *ophthalmologist, educator*
Tallent, William Hugh *chemist, research administrator*
Tang, Jun *research scientist, educator*
Tephly, Thomas Robert *pharmacologist, toxicologist, educator*
Thompson, Basil F. *ballet master*
Thompson, Herbert Stanley *neuro-ophthalmologist*
Tomkovicz, James Joseph *law educator*
Trank, Douglas Monty *rhetoric and speech communications educator*
Van Gilder, John Corley *neurosurgeon, educator*
†Vargas, Kaaren Giselle *pediatric dentistry, molecular biologist*
Venzke, Kristina Lea *academic administrator*
Walker, Joye A. *secondary school educator*
Wallace, Robert B. *medical educator*
Wasserman, Edward Arnold *psychology educator*
Weinberger, Miles M. *physician, pediatric educator*
Weiner, George Jay *internist*
Weingeist, Thomas Alan *ophthalmology educator*
Weinstein, Stuart Leslie *orthopaedic surgeon*
Wing, Adrien Katherine *law educator*
Wunder, Charles C(ooper) *physiology and biophysics educator, gravitational biologist*
Wurster, Dale Eric *pharmacy educator*
Wurster, Dale Erwin *pharmacy educator, university dean emeritus*
Ziegler, Ekhard Erich *pediatrics educator*

Iowa Falls
Sherve-Ose, Anne *music educator*

Janesville
Jarosh, Colleen Marie *educator, mediator, consultant*

Jefferson
Said, Clifford Everett *seminar company executive, speaker, author*

Johnston
Arvidson, Robert Benjamin, Jr., *geneticist, consultant*
Berry, James Alan *plant pathologist, research scientist*
Duvick, Donald Nelson *plant breeder*
Schumacher, Larry P. *health facility administrator*
Shoafstall, Earl Fred *entrepreneur, consultant*
Thoman, Mark Edward *pediatrician*

Kalona
Skaden, Anne Marie *library director*

Kellogg
Anderson, Dale C. *state agency professional, travel consultant*

Keokuk
Hardy, Julia Irene *elementary school educator*
Hoffman, James Paul *lawyer, hypnotist*
Lowenberg, Lorraine Lynette *psychiatric and mental health nurse*

Keota
Carmichael, Richard Ardean *marketing professional*
†Greiner, Sandra *state legislator*

Knoxville
Joslyn, Wallace Danforth *retired psychologist*
Taylor, Mary Kay *medical, surgical nurse*

Lamoni
Wight, Darlene *retired speech educator, emerita educator*

Lansing
Trzil, Louis Joseph *priest*

Le Grand
Hildebrandt, Willis Harvey *artist, educator*

Le Mars
Cottrell, David Milton *sound recording engineer*
†Embree, Robert Arthur *retired psychologist, minister*
Rebstock, Theodore Lynn *chemist, educator, retired research scientist*

Leon
†Miller, Eleanora Genevieve *freelance writer, bookkeeper*

Lidderdale
Hagemann, Dolores Ann *water company official*

Madrid
Handy, Richard Lincoln *civil engineer, educator*

Marion
Prall, Barbara Jones *artist*

Marshalltown
Brennecke, Allen Eugene *lawyer*
Brooks, Patrick William *lawyer*
Cassidy, Eugene Patrick *pathologist*
Foote, Sherrill Lynne *retired manufacturing company technician*
Shawstad, Raymond Vernon *retired business owner, computer specialist*
Thomas, David Llewellyn *family practice physician*

Mason City
†Attleson, Adriana Lee *mathematics educator*
Collison, Jim *business executive*
Heiny, James Ray *lawyer*
Kuhlman, James Weldon *retired county extension education director*
†Tatkon-Coker, James Edward *cardiologist*
Winston, Harold Ronald *lawyer*

Missouri Valley
Johnson, Michael Randy *bank executive*

Monona
Johnson, Milton Lee *civil engineer*

Morning Sun
†Byers, Elizabeth *education educator*

Mount Pleasant
†Johnson, David Allen *music educator*
Scarff, Hope Dyall *photographer*

Mount Vernon
†Molleur, Joseph *religious studies educator*

Moville
Baker, Kent Alfred *broadcasting, publishing company executive*

Muscatine
Coulter, Charles Roy *lawyer*
Lande, Roger Lee *lawyer*
Nepple, James Anthony *lawyer*
Stanley, Richard Holt *consulting engineer*
Thomopulos, Gregs G. *consulting engineering company executive*

Nevada
Bilyeu, Gary Edward *government official*
Bivens, Gordon Ellsworth *economist, educator*
Countryman, Dayton Wendell *lawyer*

New Hampton
Boge, Arnold Joseph *construction executive, contractor*

New London
†Wehrle, Robert William *humanities educator*

New Sharon
Sullivan, Mary Jane *elementary school educator*

Newton
†Caldwell, Gilbert Raymond, III, *lawyer*
Jamison, Elywn Paul *secondary education educator*
Ponder, Marian Ruth *retired mathematics educator*
Ward, Dean Morris *appliance manufacturing executive*

North Liberty
Glenister, Brian Frederick *geologist, educator*

Oelwein
†Flaucher-Falck, Velma Ruth *retired special education educator*
McFarlane, Beth Lucetta Troester *former mayor*

Okoboji
Pearson, Gerald Leon *food company executive*

Orange City
Hancock, Albert Sidney, Jr., *engineering executive*
Korver, Gerry R(ozeboom) *business executive*
Scorza, Sylvio Joseph *religion educator*

Osage
Kolbet, Kevin Michael *real estate company executive*

Osceola
Reynoldson, Walter Ward *retired judge, lawyer*

Oskaloosa
Burrow, Paul Irving *secondary education educator*
Clovis, Samuel Harvey *academic administrator*
Gleason, Carol Ann *mental health nurse, educator*
Mangold, Archie Wayne II *insurance agent*
Porter, David Lindsey *history and political science educator, author*

Ottumwa
Krafka, Mary Baird *lawyer*
Lang, Janelle J. *accountant*

Pacific Junction
†Krogstad, Jack Lynn *associate dean, accounting educator*

Parkersburg
Lawler, Thomas Albert *lawyer*

Pella
Baker-Roelofs, Mina Marie *retired home economist, educator*
†Chia, Ning *history educator*
†Den Adel, Raymond Lee *classics educator*
Iverson, Thomas Edwin *retired academic administrator, mathematician, educator*
†Johnson, Mark J *computer science educator*
Muether, Charles Alexander *writer, educator*
Racheter, Donald Paul *political science educator*
Ratzlaff, Keith Alan *English educator*

Pocahontas
Poduska, Ellen Marie *writer, paralegal*

Prairie City
Buckingham, Betty Jo *library media consultant*

Sheffield
Poore-Christensen, Julie Marlene *pastor*

Sheldon
†Gifford, Carla J. *education educator*

Shenandoah
Hanna, Suzanne Louise *nurse*

Sioux Center
†Kornelis, Benjamin Douglas *education educator*
Ringerwole, Joan Mae *music educator, recitalist*

Sioux City
Andersen, Leonard Christian *former state legislator, real estate investor*
Bagley, Hughes Anderson, Sr., *retail executive, consultant*
Deeds, William Charles *university dean, executive*
Dillman, Kristin Wicker *elementary and middle school educator, musician*
Doyle, Donald Vincent *retired state senator, lawyer*
†Gerhart, Steven George *lawyer*
Giles, William Jefferson, III, *lawyer*
Hamilton, Ruth Milton Green *retired college administrator, consultant*
Hatfield, Susan Williams *school psychologist*
Huldeen, Gerald Alvin *retired music educator*
Madsen, George Frank *lawyer*
Mayne, Wiley Edward *lawyer*
O'Brien, Donald Eugene *federal judge*
Olson, Cal Wallace *editor*
Peterson, Delaine Charles *lawyer, bank executive*
†Poulson, Jeffrey Lee *lawyer*
†Rants, Carolyn Jean *college official*
†Storm, Christopher *music educator*
Waller, Ephraim Everett *retired association executive*

Sloan
Ullrich, Roxie Ann *special education educator*

Solon
de Salme, John W. *retired music educator, music association administrator*
Healey, Edward Hopkins *retired architect*

Spencer
Lemke, Alan James *environmental specialist*

Spirit Lake
Brett, George Wendell *retired geologist, philatelist*
Hedberg, Paul Clifford *broadcast executive*
van der Linden, John Edward *newspaper broker, consultant*
Wilson, Wendy Melgard *kindergarten and special education educator*

Springville
Nyquist, John Davis *retired radio manufacturing company executive*

Steamboat Rock
Taylor, Ray *state senator*

Storm Lake
Bergendoff, Robert Perry *retired civil engineer*
Franker, Stephen Grant *investment executive*
†Klavano, Ann Marie *school librarian*
McDaniel, Timothy Elton *mathematics, statistics and business educator*

Stratford
†Tollefson Conard, Margot Helena *statistician*

Sumner
†Wright, James Timothy *music educator, composer*

Tipton
Farwell, Walter Maurice *vocalist, educator*

Toddville
Hazeltine, Gerald Lester *food products executive*
Robertson, Florence Winkler *advertising and public relations agency executive*

Urbandale
Alumbaugh, JoAnn McCalla *magazine editor*

Van Horne
Arndt, James Edward *music educator, musician*

Wapello
Hicklin, Edwin Anderson *lawyer*

Washington
Hazell, Patrick James *musician, producer*

Waterloo
Hasek, Jane Ellen *academic administrator*
Haskell, Brenton Ernest *health facility administrator*
Holub, Jeanne Helen *English language educator*
Johannsen, Sonia Alicia *retired county official*
Kober, Arletta Refshauge (Mrs. Kay L. Kober) *supervisor*
Lindberg, Duane R. *bishop, historian*
Molinaro-Blonigan, Mary Robin *lawyer*
†Moore, Marilyn Ulfers *social worker*
Newcomer, James Henry *retired federal agency administrator*
Waters, Ronald W. *educator, church executive, pastor*

Waverly
Blair, Rebecca Sue *English educator, lay minister*
Fredrick, David Walter *academic administrator*
Frick, Arthur Charles *art educator*
Kampfe, Doris Elaine *storyteller, folk artist, poet*
†Langan, Patrick William *education educator, consultant*
Schroeder, Randall Lee *librarian*

West Bend
Wuebker, Colleen Marie *retired librarian*

West Branch
†Kohan, Carol E. *historical site administrator*
Mather, Mildred Eunice *retired archivist*
Walch, Timothy George *library administrator*

West Des Moines
Alberts, Marion Edward *physician*
Bobenhouse, Nellie Yates *insurance company executive*
†Branstad, Terry Edward *former governor, lawyer*
†Brown, John Lewis *lawyer*
Churchill, Steven Wayne *former state legislator, marketing professional*
Cutler, Charles Edward *lawyer*
Dooley, Donald John *retired publishing executive*
Goldsmith, Janet Jane *retired pediatric nurse practitioner*
Lynch, David William *physicist, retired educator*
Marshall, Russell Frank *consulting company executive*
†McEnroe, Michael Louis *lawyer*
McNamara, David Joseph *financial and tax planning executive*
†Pearson, Ronald Dale *retail food stores corporation executive*
Pomerantz, Marvin Alvin *business executive*
Sather, Everett Norman *accountant*
Thompson, Gerald Everett *economics educator*
Zimmerman, Jo Ann *health services and educational consultant, former lieutenant governor*

West Liberty
Woodley, Jason Lynn *music educator*

Wheatland
Knoll, August E. *retired music educator*

Williamsburg
Hogan, John Paul *consumer products company executive*

Windsor Heights
Beadel, Stephen Jay *author*

Winfield
Carty, John Wesley *lawyer*

Woodward
†Jenkins, Alice Marie *secondary school educator*

KANSAS

Abilene
Britt, Ronald leroy *retired manufacturing company executive*
†Sadowski, Vivien Lavonne *editor, publishing executive, consultant*

Americus
Grimsley, Bessie Belle Gates *retired special education educator*

Andover
Ahmad, Ayaz *economist*
Whiteside, Glenn G. *manufacturing engineer*

Anthony
Carr, Cynda Annette *elementary education educator*

Arkansas City
†Bruton, Rebecca Ann *mayor, commissioner*
†Nichols, Gregory A. *mathematician, educator*

Atchison
DeMeritt, Kelly Anne *accountant*
Homan, Thomasita *English language and literature educator*
Lane, Elizabeth Ann *genealogist, researcher*
Macierowski, Edward Michael *philosopher*
Mani, Ramaswamy *chemist, researcher*
Misceo, Giovanni Francesco *psychology educator*
O'Hare, John Michael *religious studies educator*

Atwood
Okeson, Dorothy Jeanne *educational association administrator*

Augusta
Baker, Tracy McKenzie *family practice physician*

Baxter Springs
O'Neal, Vicki Lynn *elementary education educator*
Whiteley, Henry Howard *religious studies educator, minister*

Brookville
Bohata, Emil Anton *rancher*

Burlington
Dingler, Maurice Eugene *civil engineer*

Burr Oak
Underwood, Deanna Kay *librarian*

Bushton
Cooper, Sharon Kay *school media specialist*

Caldwell
Robinson, Alice Jean McDonnell *retired drama and speech educator*

Chanute
Dillard, Dean Innes *English language educator, college official*
Froehlich, Conrad Gerald *museum director, researcher*
Vaughn, Ima Jean *minister, educator*

Chase
Stull, Evalyn Marie *artist*

Cimarron
Wiseman, susan J. *English educator*

Claflin
Burmeister, Paul Frederick *farmer*

Clay Center
Braden, James Dale *former state legislator*

Clearwater
†Taverner, Pamela Johnson *educator*

Clifton
†Taddiken, Mark *state legislator*

Coffeyville
Garner, Jim D. *state official*
Hawley, Raymond Glen *pathologist*

Colby
Baldwin, Irene S. *corporate executive, real estate investor*
Lamm, Freddie Ray *research agricultural engineer*
Ress, Richard Joseph *judge*

Coldwater
Adams, Elizabeth Herrington *banker*

Columbus
Brand, Grover Junior *retired state agricultural official*

Concordia
†Brewer, Dana *lawyer, educator*
Fowler, Wayne Lewis, Sr., *internist*

Copeland
Birney, Walter Leroy *religious administrator*

Courtland
Johnson, Dorothy Phyllis *retired counselor, art therapist*

De Soto
Silver, Joan *artist*
Strubbe, Thomas R. *insurance industry executive*

Dighton
Stanley, Ellen May *historian, consultant*

Dodge City
Clifton-Smith, Rhonda Darleen *art educator, art center administrator*
Rosel, Carol Ann *artist*
Ryan, Michael Timothy *sociology educator*
Sapp, Nancy L. *educational administrator*
†Thomas, Bill A. *minister*

Edwardsville
Morgan, Stephen R. *land surveyor*

El Dorado
Adkins, William Lloyd *state official*
Fangmann, Heather Ann *secondary educator, English*
†Mack, Valerie Lippoldt *music educator, performing arts educator, freelance/self-employed choreographer*

Emporia
†Barnett, James A. *state legislator*

Frogge, Beverly Ann *nurse, consultant*
Hashmi, Sajjad Ahmad *business educator, university dean*
Heldrich, Philip Joseph *English educator, academic administrator, writer*
Henry, Elaine Olafson *artist, educator*
†Hindi, Nitham M. *finance educator, department chairman*
Kaplan, David Marshall *psychologist, educator*
Madore, Joyce Louise *gerontology nurse*
Mallein, Darla J. *educator*
Mehring, Teresa Ann *dean, education educator*
†Meierhoff, Gayle Patrice *lawyer, accountant*
Sundberg, Marshall David *biology educator*

Enterprise
Wickman, John Edward *librarian, historian*

Eskridge
Taylor, Russell Benton *mining executive*

Eudora
Miller, David Groff *insurance agent*

Fort Leavenworth
†Berlin, Robert Harry *military studies educator*
Brown, Richard Francis *command and control systems engineer, military officer*
Oliver, Thornal Goodloe *health care executive*
Schneider, James Joseph *military theory educator, consultant*

Fort Riley
McFarren, Freddy E. *military career officer*

Fort Scott
Emery, Frank Eugene *publishing executive*
Short, Forrest Edwin *lawyer*
Weddle, Douglas Paul *family practice physician*

Frontenac
†Wilson, Donald Wallin *academic administrator, communications educator*

Galena
Heistand, Anita May *writer*

Garden City
†Loyd, Ward Eugene *lawyer, state legislator*
†Pierce, Ricklin Ray *lawyer*
†Reeve, Lee M. *farmer*
†Thomas, Gregory Hall *educator*

Gardner
Webb, William Duncan *lawyer, mediator*

Goddard
Picotte, Susan Gaynel *geriatrics nurse, nursing educator, rehabilitation nurse*

Goodland
Warren, Janet Elaine *librarian*

Great Bend
†Bealer, Richard T. *social sciences educator*
Gunn, Mary Elizabeth *retired English language educator*
Jones, Edward *pathologist*

Haven
Schlickau, George Hans *cattle breeder, professional association executive*
Schlickau, Lois Marie *farmer*

Hays
†Billinger, Wayne Michael *creative director*
†Bustos, Rudolph R. *health facility administrator*
Conger, Robert B. *music educator*
Coyne, Patrick Ivan *physiological ecologist*
†Duffy, Cheryl Hofstetter *language educator*
Gustafson, Randall Lee *city manager*
Harbin, Calvin Edward *retired educator*
Michaud, J.P. *entomologist, researcher*
Strohkirch, Carolyn Sue *communication educator*
Wagner, Paul Dean *oral and maxillofacial surgeon*
Wiese, Thomas John *biochemistry educator*
Zerr, Dean A. *legal assistant, retired nurse practitioner*

Hazelton
Winn, Anthony W. *chess player, poet, screenwriter*

Hesston
Yost, Lyle Edgar *retired farm equipment manufacturing company executive*

Highland
Casey, Brian Lee *music educator*

Hillsboro
†Miller, Douglas B. *theology studies educator*

Humboldt
Finney, Paul David *acupuncturist, Chinese herbologist, entrepreneur*

Hutchinson
Baumer, Beverly Belle *journalist*
Buzbee, Richard Edgar *retired newspaper editor*
Chalfant, William Young *lawyer, author, historian*
Crater, Timothy Andrews *internist*
Dick, Harold Latham *manufacturing executive*
Graves, Kathryn Louise *dermatologist*
Green, Thereasa Ellen *elementary education educator*
Haag, Joel Edward *architect*
Hayes, John Francis *lawyer*
†Kerr, Dave *state official, marketing professional*
O'Neal, Michael Ralph *state legislator, lawyer*
Stevens, Leota mae *retired elementary education educator*
Swearer, William Brooks *lawyer*
Wendelburg, Norma Ruth *composer, pianist, educator*

Independence
Osborn, Ralph J. *retired electrical engineer*

Inman
†Downey, Christine *state legislator*

Iola
Lynn, Emerson Elwood, Jr., *retired newspaper editor/publisher*
Strickler, Ivan K. *dairy farmer*
Toland, Clyde William *lawyer*
Toland, John Robert *lawyer*

Junction City
†Davis, Victor Allen, Jr., *executive magistrate*
Sharpe, Sharon Sue *library media services administrator*
Werts, Merrill Harmon *retired management consultant*

Kanas City
Pehlivanov, Nonko Dimitrov *gastroenterologist, researcher*

Kansas City
†Amundson, Beverly Carden *artist*
Anderson, Harrison Clarke *pathologist, educator, biomedical researcher*
Arakawa, Kasumi *physician, educator*
Atkinson, Barbara F. *dean, medical educator, academic administrator*
†Baker, Clarence Albert, Sr., *structural steel construction company executive*
Baska, James Louis *wholesale grocery company executive*
Behbehani, Abbas M. *clinical virologist, educator*
Benjamin, Janice Yukon *development executive*
Boal, Marcia Anne Riley *clinical social worker, administrator*
Campbell, Joseph Leonard *trade association executive*
Carolan, Douglas *wholesale company executive*
†Coker, John Michael *quality assurance professional*
Damjanov, Ivan *pathologist, educator*
Dunn, Marvin Irvin *physician*
Eldredge, Peggy *oncological nurse*
†Fiskin, Arthur Max, Jr., *medical educator*
Globoke, Joseph Raymond *accountant*
Godfrey, Robert Gordon *physician*
Godwin, Harold Norman *pharmacist, educator*
Greenwald, Gilbert Saul *physiologist*
†Gulliford, James B. *government agency administrator*
Hagen, Donald Floyd *university administrator, former military officer*
Heflin, Ruth Janelle *English language educator*
†Heller, Jennifer Lynn *developmental studies specialist, consultant*
Hite, Pamela Rene *emergency medicine physician*
Horseman, Barbara Ann *church musician, voice educator*
Hudson, Robert Paul *medical educator*
Jerome, Norge Winifred *nutritionist, anthropologist*
Johnson, Joy Ann *diagnostic radiologist*
Karrer, Rathe Stevens *psychophysiologist*
†Keleher, James P. *bishop*
Krantz, Kermit Edward *physician, educator*
Lawrence, Walter Thomas *plastic surgeon*
Lee, Kyo Rak *radiology educator*
Lungstrum, John W. *federal judge*
Mathews, Paul Joseph *health educator*
Mathewson, Hugh Spalding *anesthesiologist, educator*
McCallum, Richard Warwick *medical researcher, clinician, educator*
Meyers, David George *internist, cardiologist, educator*
Milligan, Donald Bruce *physician, educator*
Mohn, Melvin Paul *anatomist, educator*
†Nastri, Wayne *government agency administrator*
†Neuberger, John Stephen *preventive medicine and epidemiology educator*
Noelken, Milton Edward *biochemistry educator, researcher*
Olofson, Tom William *computer executive*
O'Neill, Thomas Tyrone *lawyer*
Pahwa, Rajesh *physician*
Penick, Elizabeth C. *psychologist*
Rawitch, Allen Barry *medical educator, academic administrator*
Rushfelt, Gerald Lloyd *magistrate judge*
Samson, Frederick Eugene, Jr., *neuroscientist, educator*
†Sanders-Hall, Patricia E. *health facility administrator*
Schloerb, Paul Richard *surgeon, educator*
Sciolaro, Charles Michael *cardiac surgeon*
Skikne, Barry S. *hematologist, educator*
†Starling, Carol King *nursing educator*
†Steineger, Chris *state legislator*
Steineger, Margaret Leisy *non-profit organization officer*
Taunton, Roma Lee *nurse educator and researcher*
Ternus, Jean Ann *nursing educator*
Twillman, Robert Keith *psychologist*
VanBebber, George Thomas *federal judge*
Varghese, George *physician, educator*
Voogt, James Leonard *medical educator*
Vratil, Kathryn Hoefer *federal judge*
†Warne, Alan M. *adult education educator, consultant*
Waxman, David *physician, university consultant*
Waxse, David John *judge*
†Whitehead, Fred *historian, educator, editor*
Williams, Shirley J. *daycare provider, educator, writer*
Ziegler, Dewey Kiper *neurologist, educator*

Kingman
†Hada, Jerrianne *librarian*

Lakin
Helms, Michael L. *priest*

Lansing
Kuk, Michael Louis *protective services official*

Larned
Cerullo, Rudy Michael, II, *psychology, theology educator, minister*
Davis, Mary Elizabeth *speech pathologist, educator, counselor*
†Linderer, Steve *historic site executive*
Zook, Martha Frances Harris *retired nursing administrator*

Lawrence
Ahl, Sally Webb *religious studies educator*
Alexander, John Thorndike *historian, educator*
Ammar, Raymond George *physicist, educator*
Angino, Ernest Edward *retired geology and engineering educator*
Antonio, Robert John *sociology educator*
Armitage, Kenneth Barclay *biology educator, ecologist*
Barnett, William Arnold *economics educator*
†Baron, Frank *language educator*
Beedles, William LeRoy *finance educator, financial consultant*
Benjamin, Bezaleel Solomon *architecture and architectural engineering educator*
Berry, James Lee *retired educator*
Bovee, Eugene Cleveland *protozoologist, emeritus educator*
Bowman, Laird Price *retired foundation administrator*
Brady, Lawrence Lee *geologist*
Briscoe, Mary Beck *federal judge*
†Brooks, Karl Boyd *historian*
†Buck, Henry William, Jr., *obstetrician-gynecologist*
Burke, Paul E., Jr., *governmental relations consultant*
Byers, George William *retired entomology educator*
Canda, Edward R. *social work educator*
†Capps, Jason Scott *education educator, researcher*
Casad, Robert Clair *legal educator*
Casagrande, Peter Joseph *humanities and English educator*
†Castle, Joyce M *mezzo soprano*
Clement, Richard Wolcott *librarian, educator*
Clowes, Edith W. *language educator, consultant, literature educator, consultant*
Conard, John Joseph *financial official*
†Corbeill, Anthony *classicist, educator*
Crowe, William Joseph *librarian*
Darwin, David *civil engineering educator, researcher, consultant*
†Daugherty, James Franklin *music educator*
Dean, Bartholomew Crispin *anthropology educator*
Debicki, Andrew Peter *foreign language educator*
†Dick, Ernst S. *retired German language educator*
Dickinson, William Boyd, Jr., *editorial consultant*
Dooley, Patrick John *graphic designer, design educator*
Dreschhoff, Gisela Auguste Marie *physicist, educator*
Duerksen, George Louis *music educator, music therapist*
Eldredge, Charles Child, III, *art history educator*
Enos, Paul *geologist, educator*
†Finger, Michael Steven *psychologist, educator, statistician, consultant*
Frederickson, Horace George *former college president, public administration educator*
Fredrickson, Karen Loraine *librarian*
Gerhard, Lee Clarence *geologist, educator*
Grabow, Stephen Harris *architecture educator*
Green, Don Wesley *chemical and petroleum engineering educator*
Greenberg, Marc Leland *education educator*
Grzymala-Busse, Jerzy Witold *engineering educator*
Gunn, James E. *English language educator*
Hale, Richard Lee *magazine editor*
Harmony, Marlin Dale *chemistry educator*
Haugh, Dan Anthony *mechanical engineer*
Heller, Francis H(oward) *law and political science educator emeritus*
†Hemenway, Robert E. *academic administrator, language educator*
Hermes, Marjory Ruth *machine embroidery and arts educator*
Hilding, Jerel Lee *music and dance educator, former dancer*
Himmelberg, Charles John, III, *mathematics educator, researcher*
†Johnson, Ellen Schultz *retired music librarian, researcher*
†Johnson, Wallace Stephen, Jr., *Asian languages educator*
Johnston, Richard Fourness *biologist, educator*
†Karcz, Andrzej *literature educator*
Karlin, Calvin Joseph *lawyer*
†Knittel, Janna Marie *literature educator*
†Kuznesof, Elizabeth Anne *history educator*
Landgrebe, John Allan *chemistry educator*
Lawler, Jennifer L. *writer, martial arts instructor*
†Levin, Murray Scott *law educator, arbitrator, mediator*
Li, Chu-Tsing *art history educator*
Lichtwardt, Robert William *mycologist*
Locke, Carl Edwin, Jr., *academic administrator, engineering educator*
†Luchies, Carl W *engineering educator, researcher*
Mackenzie, Kenneth Donald *management consultant, educator*
†Majure, Janet *writer, editor*
McCabe, Steven Lee *structural engineer*
Mc Coin, John Mack *social worker*
Merriam, Daniel F(rancis) *geologist*
Michener, Charles Duncan *entomologist, educator, researcher*
Miller, Don Robert *surgeon, educator*

Mitscher, Lester Allen *chemist, educator*
Moore, Richard Kerr *electrical engineering educator*
Muirhead, Vincent Uriel *retired aerospace engineer*
Multon, Karen Diane *psychologist, educator*
†Nam, Yoonmi *artist, art educator*
Nordling, Bernard Erick *lawyer*
Norris, Andrea Spaulding *art museum director*
†Parker, Stephen Jan *Slavic language and literature educator*
Pasco, Allan Humphrey *literature educator*
Penny, Paul Baldwin *landscape artist, artist*
Pickett, Calder Marcus *retired journalism educator*
Pozdro, John Walter *music educator, composer*
Price, Griffith Baley *mathematician, educator*
Quinn, Dennis B. *English language and literature educator*
Reeves, Patricia Houts (Trish Reeves) *English and humanities educator*
Romzek, Barbara S(ue) *public administration educator*
†Rosenbloom, Joshua Levi *economist, educator*
Roskam, Jan *aerospace engineer*
Rowland, James Richard *electrical engineering educator*
Rury, John Leslie *education educator*
Saul, Norman Eugene *history educator*
†Sax, Benjamin *literature educator*
Schoeck, Richard J(oseph) *English and humanities scholar, poet*
Searles, Lynn Marie *nurse*
Shaffer, Harry George *economics educator*
Shankel, Delbert Merrill *microbiology and biology educator*
Shimomura, Roger Y. *artist, educator*
Siemsen, Susan Anne *physician assistant*
Simons, Dolph Collins, Jr., *newspaper publisher*
Six, Fred N. *retired state supreme court justice*
Smith, Glee Sidney, Jr., *lawyer*
†Snyder, Charles Richard *psychologist, educator*
Tsubaki, Andrew Takahisa *theater director, educator*
†Tsutsui, William Minoru *historian, educator*
Turnbull, Ann Patterson *special educator, consultant, research director*
Turnbull, H. Rutherford, III, *law educator, lawyer*
Tuttle, William McCullough, Jr., *history educator*
†Van Vleck, Fred Scott *mathematician, educator, researcher*
Vossoughi, Shapour *chemical and petroleum engineering educator*
Wallace, Victor Lew *computer science educator*
Wiechert, Allen LeRoy *educational planning consultant, architect*
Winter, Winton Allen, Jr., *lawyer, state senator*
Woelfel, James Warren *philosophy and humanities educator*
Woodward, Frederick Miller *publisher*
Worth, George John *English literature educator*

Leavenworth
Arneson, George Stephen *manufacturing company executive, management consultant*
Buselt, Clara Irene *religious organization administrator*
Heim, Dixie Sharp *family practice nurse practitioner*
Novak, Michael Paul *English language educator*
Poulose, Kuttikatt Paul *neurologist*

Leawood
Bohm, Jack Nelson *retired lawyer*
Byrum-Sutton, Judith Miriam *accountant*
Gregory, Lewis Dean *trust company executive*
Johnston, Jocelyn Stanwell *paralegal*
†Joslin, Janine Elizabeth *preservation consultant*
Karmeier, Delbert Fred *consulting engineer, realtor*
Kordash, Dorothy Mae *artist*
Puppe, Gerald Clarence *trade association executive*
Tonkens, Rebecca Annette *maternal/women's health nurse*
White, Shanon Kathleen *accountant, consultant*

Lebanon
Colwell, John Edwin *retired aerospace scientist*

Lenexa
Ascher, James John *pharmaceutical executive*
Gressel, Gary Lee *computer scientist*
Pierson, John Theodore, Jr., *manufacturer*
Ramsey, John Talton *sales executive*

Lewis
Cross, David Rusk *farmer, livestock raiser*

Liberal
Wilkerson, Rita Lynn *special education educator, consultant*

Lincoln
†Crangle, Robert D. *lawyer, management consultant, entrepreneur, manufacturing executive*
Marshall, Susan *lawyer*

Manhattan
†Amtoft, Torben *adult education educator, researcher*
Babcock, Michael Ward *economics educator*
Ball, Louis Alvin *insurance company executive*
Barnett, Mark A. *psychology educator*
Chavez, Andrew *writer, poet*
Coffman, James Richard *academic administrator, veterinarian*
†Crowe, Linda K. *speech pathology/audiology services professional, educator*
Durkee, William Robert *retired physician*
Erickson, Howard Hugh *veterinarian, physiology educator*
Featherstone, Allen Merril *economics educator*
Foerster, Bernd *architecture educator*
Gillispie, Harold Leon *minister*
Glasscock, Kenton *state legislator*
Hamscher, Albert Nelson *history educator*
†Haub, Mark D. *exercise physiologist*
Higgins, James Jacob *statistics educator*
Higham, Robin *historian, editor, publisher*
Hoyt, Kenneth Boyd *educational psychology educator*
Jackson, William Lawrence (Larry Jackson) *radio station executive*
Jiang, Hongxing *physics educator, researcher*
Johnson, William Howard *agricultural engineer, educator*
Kaufman, Donald Wayne *research ecologist*
Kirkham, M. B. *plant physiologist, educator*
†Koodali, Ranjit Thazhathaveetil *chemist, researcher*
Kremer, Eugene R. *architecture educator*
Lee, E(ugene) Stanley *engineer, mathematician, educator*
†Lei, Shuting *adult education educator*
Lin, Zongzhu *mathematician, educator*
Littrell, David A. *music educator, conductor*
†Machor, James Lawrence *language educator*
Mengel, David Bruce *agronomy and soil science educator*
Middendorf, Gerad D. *sociology educator*
Morrison, Lisa Ann *psychiatric nurse practitioner*
Mortenson, Kristin Oppenheim *violinist*
Moss, Larry W. *nursing administrator, quality management consultant*
Muir, William Lloyd, III, *academic administrator*
Nafziger, Estel Wayne *economics educator*
Oehme, Frederick Wolfgang *medical researcher and educator*
†Pei, Zj *engineer, educator, researcher*
Phares, E. Jerry *psychology educator*
Posler, Gerry Lynn *agronomist, educator*
†Richardson, Ralph C. *dean*
Richter, William Louis *social sciences educator*
Russell, Eugene Robert, Sr., *engineering educator, administrator*
†Schumm, Walter Richard *family researcher, educator*
Seaton, Edward Lee *editor, publishing executive*
Setser, Donald Wayne *chemistry educator*
†Shanklin, Carol Williams *academic administrator, researcher*
Sheu, Chwen *finance educator*
Simons, Gale Gene *nuclear and electrical engineer, educator*
Stolzer, Leo William *bank executive*
†Stoney, BeEtta Lorranine *education educator*
Streeter, John Willis *information systems manager*
Suleiman, Michael Wadie *humanities educator*
Swanson, Diane L. *finance educator, researcher*
Thomas, Lloyd Brewster *economics educator*
Walker Schlageck, Kathrine L. *museum educational administrator, educator*
Wallis, Robert Ray *psychologist*
White, Neva Lois *librarian, consultant*

Mankato
Wiest, Donald Edwin *secondary education educator*

Marion
Meyer, Bill *newspaper publisher, editor*

Marysville
Herman, J. Clayton *retired adult education educator*

McPherson
†Midgley, Bryan Duaine *behavioral science educator*

Mcpherson
Grauer, Douglas Dale *civil engineer*
Hull, Robert Glenn *retired financial administrator*
†Selack, Laurene E. *music educator*

Meade
Brannan, Cleo Estella *retired elementary education educator*

Mission
Alexander, Anne A. *sales consultant*
Bonci, Andrew S. *chiropractor*
Scheel, Mark Wesley *writer, retired library and information specialist*

Mulvane
George, Donald Richard *retired principal*

Neosho Falls
Bader, Robert Smith *biology, zoology educator and researcher*

Newton
Dyck, George *psychiatry educator*
Morford, Marie Arlene *insurance company executive*
Walker, Richard Bruce *judge*

Nickerson
Kirschner, Rod *secondary education educator*

North Newton
Ediger, Marlow *education educator*
Quiring, Frank Stanley *chemist, educator*
Snider, Marie Anna *syndicated columnist*

Offerle
Herrmann, Lorena Joyce *retired music educator*

Olathe
Dennis, Patricia Lyon *adult education educator*
†Dunn, Dwayne Earle *music educator*
Epp, Garrett Wayne *music educator*
†Hackler, Ruth Ann *retired educator*
Haskin, J. Michael *lawyer*
†High, William Fray *lawyer*
Hurn, Raymond Walter *minister, religious order administrator*
Jones, Robert Lyle *emergency medical services leader, financial planner, educator*
Kamberg, Mary-Lane *writer, journalist*
Kopac, Andrew Joseph *automotive executive*
Leben, Steve *judge*
Norton, Jay Lewis *lawyer, recording company executive*
O'Connor, Kay F. *state legislator*
Scott, Robert Gene *lawyer*
Smith, Katheryn Jeanette *music educator*
Sternberg, David Edward *psychiatrist*
Stevens, Diana Lynn *elementary education educator*
Tast, Marci *business analyst*
Wilcox, Laird Maurice *researcher, writer, carpenter*

Osage City
Wooge, Daniel Lee *music educator*

Osawatomie
Jimenez, Bettie Eileen *retired small business owner*

Ottawa
Brady, Gordon Leonard, Jr., *economist*
Hoge, Medora Davidson *dance educator*
Howe, William Hugh *artist*
Tyler, Priscilla *retired English language and education educator*

Overbrook
Dale, Kenneth Ray *computer executive*

Overland Park
Abele, Robert Christopher *lawyer*
Asner, Marie A. *classical musician*
Ayers, Jeffrey David *lawyer*
†Barnett, James Monroe *lawyer*
†Benjamin, Peggy-Ann Biel *artist*
Branham, Melanie J. *lawyer*
Bronaugh, Deanne Rae *home health care administrator, consultant*
Burger, Henry G. *vocabulary scientist, anthropologist, publisher*
Callahan, Michael Thomas *lawyer, writer, arbitrator, construction executive, consultant*
Cassidy, John Lemont *retired engineering executive*
†Coatney, Sharon Ann *librarian, editor*
Conrad, William Merrill *architect*
Devlin, James Richard *lawyer*
De Vries, Robert John *investment banker*
Dockhorn, Robert John *physician, educator*
†Dodd, James B. *internet executive*
Douglas, Shirley Lorene *small business owner, councilwoman*
Finley, Jennifer Ellen *physical medicine and rehabilitation physician*
FitzGerald, Thomas Joe *psychologist*
†Forsee, Gary D. *telecommunications industry executive*
Goodale, Sean Douglas *healthcare administrator, consultant*
Guckenheimer, Daniel Paul *financial advisor*
Keplinger, Bruce (Donald Keplinger) *lawyer*
Klamann, John Michael *lawyer*
Krauss, Carl F. *lawyer*
†Kuppuswamy, Carthy *network engineer*
†Lamb, Gordon Howard *music educator*
Landry, Mark Edward *podiatrist, researcher*
Leonard, Markus Dayle *software systems engineer*
Lucas, James Raymond *business executive, leadership consultant, author, speaker*
†Martin, William F. *retired transportation executive*
McChesney, Samuel Parker, III, *real estate executive*
Miller, Mark William *investment advisor, writer*
Molz, Philip Jack *management consultant*
Ofverstedt, Margaret Elise *music educator, library and information scientist*
Ostby, Frederick Paul, Jr., *meteorologist, retired government official , science administrator*
†Pretzel, Mark William *musician*
Ruperd, Theresa *music educator*
†Ruse, Steven Douglas *lawyer*
Sampson, William Roth *lawyer*
Sawkar, Laxmidas Anant *retired internist, oncologist*
Schultz, Richard Dale *national athletic organization executive*
Smith, Daniel Lynn *lawyer*
Smith, Jill Galbreath *lawyer*
Spaeth, Nicholas John *lawyer, former state attorney general*
†Steinkamp, Robert Theodore *lawyer*
Surbaugh, Dolores Sayas *accounting and professional development educator*
Tubbs, David Eugene *mechanical engineer, marketing professional*
Voeller, John George *engineer*
Vogel, Arthur Anton *clergyman*
Voska, Kathryn Caples *consultant, facilitator*
Whelan, Richard J. *retired academic administrator*
†Willard, James Robert *retired lawyer*
Woods, Richard Dale *lawyer*
Yates, Dan Charles *insurance company official*
Zinke, Michael Duane *finance and accountancy manager*

Paola
†Norland, Richard Strand *mechanical engineer*
Peters, Aaron Sheldon *monk, priest*

Parsons
Lomas, Lyle Wayne *agricultural research administrator, educator*

Pittsburg
Beer, Pamela Jill Porr *writer, retired vocational school educator*
Behlar, Patricia Ann *political science educator*
†Berger, Reena *musician, music educator*
Darling, John Rothburn, Jr., *business educator*
Foresman, James Buckey *geologist, geochemist, industrial hygienist*
Franklin, John Thomas Ikeda *English educator*
Lee, Earl Wayne *library science educator*
Meats, Stephen Earl *English educator, editor, writer*
Nettels, George Edward, Jr., *retired mining executive*
†Runyan, Charles Kent *education educator*
†Short, Timothy Allen *lawyer*
Sullivan, William John *osteopath*

Pomona
Gentry, Alberta Elizabeth *elementary education educator*

Prairie Village
Breidenbach, Monica Eileen *educator, career counselor*
Lyon, Joanne B. *psychologist*
Sharp, Rex Arthur *lawyer*
Stanton, Roger D. *lawyer*
Trussell, Donna Laura *writer*

Pratt
Loomis, Howard Krey *banker*
†Stull, Gordon Bruce *lawyer*
Westerhaus, Catherine K. *social worker*

Rossville
†Budden, Frederick Richard *music educator*

Saint John
Robinson, Alexander Jacob *clinical psychologist*
Wibright, Eddy Ann *secondary education educator*

Saint Marys
Byers, Walter *athletic association executive*
†Dobbins, Freda J. *librarian*

Salina
Allen, Milton D. *music educator*
†Brungardt, Pete *state legislator*
Cosco, John Anthony *health care executive, educator, consultant, author*
Douglass, Mary Clement *curator, small business owner*
Dubuc-Schindler, Deborah Jo *special education educator*
†Fitzsimons, George Kinsey *bishop*
Hansen, Donna Lauren *court reporting educator*
Horst, Deena Louise *state legislator*
†Neustrom, Patrik William *lawyer*
Owens, William Dean *lawyer*
Ryan, Stephen Collister *funeral director*
†Sigai, A. Gary *engineer*

Shawnee
Beck, Jeff L. *music educator*
Chaffee, Paul David *city official*
Hudson, Tajquah Jaye *managed health care executive*
Lehmkuhl, Margie Mae *occupational health nurse*
Smokorowski, Peter *retired artist*
†Wilson, Eugene Rolland *foundation executive*

Shawnee Mission
†Adkins, David Jay *lawyer*
Badgerow, John Nicholas *lawyer*
Bartlett, Roger Danforth *engineering executive*
Bell, Deloris Wiley *physician*
Bond, Richard Lee *lawyer, state senator*
Braude, Michael *retired commodity exchange executive*
Breen, Katherine Anne *speech and language pathologist*
Esrey, William Todd *telecommunications company executive*
Fairchild, Robert Charles *pediatrician*
Flora, Jairus Dale, Jr., *statistician*
Gaar, Marilyn Audrey Wiegraffe *political scientist, educator, property manager*
Gaar, Norman Edward *lawyer, former state senator*
Gamet, Donald Max *appliance company executive*
Gastl, Eugene Francis *lawyer*
Gensheimer, Cynthia Francis *economics educator*
Goetz, Kenneth Lee *cardiovascular physiologist, research consultant, writer*
Green, John Lafayette, Jr., *education executive*
Hanson, Patti Lynn *human resources specialist*
Hartzler, Geoffrey Oliver *retired cardiologist*
Helder, Jan Pleasant, Jr., *lawyer*
Henley, Douglas E. *medical association administrator*
Hoffman, Alfred John *retired mutual fund executive*
†Johntz, John Hoffman, Jr., *lawyer*
Jones, George Humphrey *retired healthcare executive, hospital facilities and communications consultant*
Mandl, Herbert Jay *rabbi*
Martin, Donna Lee *publishing company executive, retired*
McEachen, Richard Edward *banker, lawyer*
Mealman, Glenn *corporate marketing executive*
Meiners, Phyllis Bloom *publishing executive, writer, not-for-profit developer*
Miller, Stanford *retired reinsurance executive, lawyer*
†Moeller, Laura Lee *former retail executive, library consultant*
Mooney, Justin David *motel executive, consultant*
Nulton, William Clements *retired lawyer*
Picciano, R.J. *renal technician*
Price, James Gordon *physician, educator*
Putman, Dale Cornelius *management consultant, lawyer*
Robinson, Mary Lu *retired accountant, artist*
Sader, Carol Hope *former state legislator*

Shalinsky, Joseph George *pharmacist, pharmaceutical executive*
Smith, Edwin Dudley *lawyer*
Snyder, Willard Breidenthal *lawyer*
Sparks, Billy Schley *lawyer*
Starrett, Frederick Kent *lawyer*
†Talley, Douglas Eric *music educator*
Thomas, Christopher Yancey, III, *surgeon, educator*

South Hutchinson
Armstrong, Larry Don *activist, association administrator*

Sterling
Beechan, Curtis Michael *science educator*
Kendall, Charles Terry *librarian*

Stilwell
Ledgin, Norman Michael *writer*
Roeseler, Wolfgang Guenther Joachim *city planner*

Sublette
Swinney, Carol Joyce *secondary education educator*

Syracuse
Gale, Robert Harrison, Jr., *lawyer*

Tonganoxie
Torneden, Connie Jean *bank officer*

Topeka
Allegrucci, Donald Lee *state supreme court justice*
†Allen, Barbara *state legislator*
Averill, Thomas Fox *writer, educator*
†Barbieri-Lightner, Patricia *state representative*
Barnett, Mary Lorene *real estate manager*
†Barone, James L. *state legislator*
Barton, Janice Sweeny *chemistry educator*
Berry, Michael Wayne *civil engineer*
†Brownlee, Karin S. *state legislator*
Bunten, William Daniel *retired banker*
†Bunten, William Wallace *state senator*
†Burroughs, Tom L. *state representative*
†Campbell, Larry L. *state representative*
Cann, Steven J. *political science educator*
†Carlin, Sydney *state representative*
†Carter, Eric *state representative*
Charlwood, Kevin Edward *mathematician, educator*
†Clark, Stan W. *state legislator*
Concannon, James M. *law educator, university dean*
Cox, Joseph Lawrence *judge*
†Craft, Barbara J. *state representative*
†Crow, Marti *state representative*
Crow, Sam Alfred *judge*
†Dahl, Donald L. *state representative*
†Dan, Johnson *state representative*
Davis, Robert Edward *state supreme court justice*
†Dillmore, Nile *state representative*
Dimmitt, Lawrence Andrew *retired lawyer, law educator*
†Dreher, Stanley E., Jr., *state representative*
Elrod, Linda Diane Henry *lawyer, educator*
†Faber, John M. *state representative*
†Flaharty, Geraldine *state representative*
Frahm, Sheila *association executive, former government official, academic administrator*
Franklin, Benjamin Barnum *dinner club executive*
Fyler, Carl John *dentist*
†Gatewood, Doug *state representative*
Glasscock, Joyce H. *state official*
Goetz, Roger Melvin *minister*
†Gordon, Lana G. *state representative*
†Grant, Robert *state representative*
Greene, Jane *health educator*
Hamilton, John Richard *lawyer*
†Haney, Thomas Dwight *lawyer, educator*
Hedrick, Lois Jean *retired investment company executive, state official*
Hejtmanek, Danton Charles *lawyer*
†Hill, Don *state representative*
†Horttor, Donald J. *lawyer*
Huaman-Mejia, Antonio *pathologist*
Jackson, David D. *state legislator*
†Jenkins, Lynn M. *state legislator*
Jennings, Nancy Ann *retired elementary education educator*
†Johnson, Duane Fadinand *librarian*
Karst, Gary Gene *retired architect*
Keefer, J(ames) Michael *lawyer*
†Kline, Phillip D. *state attorney general*
†Krehbiel, Carl *state representative*
†Kuether, Annie *state representative*
Lacoursiere, Roy Barnaby *psychiatrist*
Larson, Edward *state supreme court justice*
†Light, Bill *state representative*
†Long-Mast, Peggy *state representative*
MacDonald, Pamelyn Marie *psychology educator*
Mara, John Lawrence *retired veterinarian, consultant*
Marquardt, Christel Elisabeth *judge*
†McCreary, Bill *state representative*
McFarland, Kay Eleanor *state supreme court chief justice*
Menninger, William Walter *psychiatrist*
†Merrick, Raymond F. *state representative*
†Moore, John Edly *lieutenant governor*
†Morris, Stephen R. *state legislator*
Mutti, Albert Frederick *minister*
†Nason, Barry Mark *systems engineer, mathematician, educator*
Navone, Edward William *artist, educator*
†Newton, Dean *state representative*
Nichols, Rocky *state representative, non-profit consultant*
†Ochs, Robert Duane *lawyer*
†Owens, Thomas C. *state representative*
†Patterson, Doug *state representative*
Peters, Barb Waterman *artist, educator*
Plummer, Mary Elizabeth *cosmetologist*
†Reardon, William J. *state representative*
†Rehorn, Rick *state representative*
†Reitz, Roger *state representative*
Reser, Elizabeth May (Betty Reser) *bookkeeper*
Reymond, Patricia Ann *social worker*
Rivers, Julie Elaine *concert pianist, composer, recording industry executive*
Rogers, Richard Dean *federal judge*
Roy, William Robert *physician, lawyer, former congressman*
†Sabatini, Frank Carmine *lawyer, bank executive*
Saville, Pat *state senate official*
Schmidt, Derek *state legislator*
†Schodorf, Jean *state legislator*
†Schroer, Gene Eldon *lawyer*
†Schultz, LeAnne *violinist, performer, music educator*
†Schwartz, Sharon J. *state representative*
†Sebelius, Kathleen Gilligan *governor*
Sheffel, Irving Eugene *psychiatric institution executive*
†Showalter, Judy *state representative*
Sipes, Karen Kay *newspaper editor*
Slemmons, Robert Sheldon *architect*
Smith, Loran Bradford *educator*
†Snyder, Brock Robert *lawyer*
Spencer, William Edwin *telephone company executive, engineer*
Spohn, Herbert Emil *psychologist*
†Storm, Suzanne *state representative*
Stroud, Herschel Leon *retired dentist*
Stroud, Jacqueline Lucille *medical supply company executive*
Sutherland, John Bennett *chemical engineer*
†Tafanelli, Lee *state representative*
†Teichman, Ruth *state senator*
†Thornburgh, Ron E. *secretary of state*
†Thull, Tom *state representative*
Uhler, William Grant, IV, *transportation executive*
Varner, Charleen LaVerne McClanahan (Mrs. Robert B. Varner) *nutritionist, educator, administrator, dietitian*
Varner, Robert Bernard *counselor, educator*
†Ward, Jim *state representative*
†Williams, Daniel A. *state representative*
†Wilson, R. J. *state representative*
†Winn, Valdenia C. *state representative*
Wright, James C. *lawyer*
†Zaharopoulos, Thimios *media specialist, educator*
Zientara, Suzannah Dockstader *insurance agent*

Towanda
†Corbin, David R. *state legislator*

Ulysses
†Hathaway, Gary Ray *lawyer*

Valley Center
Bryan, Paul Edward *pharmacist*

Wamego
Lang, John Ernest *lawyer*

Wellington
Ferguson, William McDonald *rancher, writer, banker, retired lawyer, former state official*
Montgomery, Robert Louis *retired chemical engineer*
Willis, Robert Addison *dentist*

Westwood
Hart, Paul Vincent, Jr., *emergency and family medicine physician, inventor*
†Trevino, Lee Buck *professional golfer*

Wheaton
Willis, Joan Ellen *nurse*

Wichita
Acker, Andrew French, III, *mathematics educator, researcher*
Alexander, David Robert *astronomer, educator*
Andrew, Kenneth L. *research physicist, physics educator*
Ayres, Ted Dean *lawyer, academic counsel*
Badger, Ronald Kay *lawyer*
Baumann, Paul Arthur *radiation oncologist*
Bennett-Kastor, Tina Lynne *linguist, educator*
Berman, Mitchell A. *orchestra executive*
Berner Harris, Cynthia Kay *librarian*
Betenbaugh, Helen Reckenzaun *Episcopal priest, disabilities activist*
Brown, Wesley Ernest *federal judge*
Burket, George Edward, Jr., *retired family physician*
Cadman, Wilson Kennedy *retired utility company executive*
Chopra, Dharam Vir *statistician, educator*
†Coombs, Eugene G. *lawyer*
Cowdery, Robert Douglas *consulting geologist*
Cummings, Richard J. *retired otologist*
Depew, Spencer Long *lawyer*
Dietz, David William *structural engineer*
Docking, Thomas Robert *lawyer, former state lieutenant governor*
†Donovan, Leslie D., Sr., *state legislator*
Dorr, Stephanie Tilden *psychotherapist*
†D'Souza, Francis *chemistry educator*
Eby, Martin Keller, Jr., *construction company executive*
Ericson, David Frank *political scientist, educator*
Etter, Gregg Wayne, Sr., *police officer, educator*
†Fear, Judith A. *music educator, director*
†Foote, Richard Van *lawyer*
French, James Edward *surgeon*
Gorecki, John Paul *neurosurgeon, educator*
Guthrie, Diana Fern *nursing educator*
Guthrie, Richard Alan *physician*
†Guy, James Matheus *lawyer, realtor*
Hatteberg, Larry Merle *photojournalist*
Herr, Peter Helmut Friederich *sales executive*
Hicks, M. Elizabeth (Liz Hicks) *pharmacist*
Huber, Tonya *teacher educator, writer*
†Hund, Edward Joseph *lawyer*
Huntley, Diane E. *dental hygiene educator*
Jennison, Robin L. *former state legislator, lobbyist*
Jesseph, Linda *process analyst*
Johnson, C. Nicholas *dance company executive*
Johnson, George Taylor *training and manufacturing executive*
Johnson, Guy Charles *music educator, musician*
†Johnson, Kevin Blaine *lawyer, educator*
Kahn, Melvin A. *political science educator*
Kellerman, Rick Dean *physician, academic administrator*
†Kellogg, Darrell Dean *lawyer*
Kennedy, Joseph Winston *lawyer*
Kice, John Edward *engineer, consultant, engineer, educator*
Kinch, E. L. Lee *lawyer*
Kindrick, Robert LeRoy *academic administrator, dean, English educator*
†Knight, Robert G. *mayor, investment banker*
Koch, Charles de Ganahl *business executive*
Korf, Clifford Dean *physician assistant*
Lerman, Kenneth Barry *marketing professional, consultant*
Lowrey, Annie Tsunee *retired cultural organization administrator*
†Mau, Wei-Cheng Joseph *education educator*
†McCrary, Larry Dale *minister, religious studies educator*
McKee, George Moffitt, Jr., *civil engineer, consultant*
McKenzie, Harry James *cardiothoracic surgeon, surgical researcher*
Menefee, Frederick Lewis *advertising executive*
†Meyer, Russell William, Jr., *aircraft company executive*
Mitchell, Linda Marlene *education educator*
Moore, Peggy Sue *corporation executive*
Myers, John Moore *fraternal organization administrator*
†Nienke, Steven A. *construction company executive*
†Oxley, Dwight K(ahala) *pathologist*
Palmer, Ada Margaret *systems analyst, consultant*
Park, Chan Hyung *cell biologist, physician*
Peare, Dan C. *lawyer*
Platt, George Milo *university administrator*
Pottorff, Jo Ann *state legislator*
Randels, Ed L. *lawyer*
†Ratner, Payne Harry, Jr., *lawyer*
Riegle, Robert M. *art dealer, retired architect*
Rogers, Rita Doris Luck *family nurse practitioner*
Rueb, Sheree A. *social services administrator*
Schneegurt, Mark Allen *microbiologist, researcher*
†Schuster, James Edward *aircraft manufacturing executive*
†Seneviratne, Waruna Prasanna *research scientist*
Sewell, Andrew *music director*
Sherwood, Joan Karolyn Sargent *retired career counselor*
Shue, Shyh-Pyng Jack *aerospace engineer, electrical engineer, researcher, consultant*
Siginer, Dennis A. *mechanical engineering educator, university dean*
Sorensen, Harvey R. *lawyer*
Steele, Thomas Lee *lawyer*
Stephenson, Richard Ismert *lawyer*
Sullivan, Mitzi *accountant*
Thompson, Lee (Morris Thompson) *lawyer*
Timmerman, Dora Mae *community volunteer, art advocate*
Van Arendonk, Susan Carole *elementary school educator*
†Van Fleet, G. Nelson *financial executive*
Van Milligen, James M. *health care administrator*
Varner, Sterling Verl *retired oil company executive*
Wilhelm, William Jean *civil engineering educator*
Winkler, Dana John *lawyer*
Wolff, James August August *finance educator, researcher*
†Woolf, Amy Kaspar *librarian, storyteller*
†Woolf, John Paul *lawyer*
Zimmerman, Melva Jean *writer, retired media specialist, educator*

Winfield
Andreas, Warren Dale *lawyer*
Dolsen, David Horton *mortician*
Gray, Ina Turner *fraternal organization administrator*
Hartzell, John Mason *poet, service technician*
Krusor, Mark William *lawyer*
Laws, Carolyn Marie Roderick *medical/surgical nurse, pediatrics nurse*
Schul, Bill Dean *psychological administrator, author*

KENTUCKY

Albany
†Smith, Eugenia Sewell *funeral home executive*
†Tallent, Brenda Colene *social worker, psychotherapist*

Ashland
Barber, Phillip Robert, III, *communications executive*
Carter, David Edward *communications executive, director*
Roth, Oliver Ralph *radiologist*
St. Clair, Philip Roland *humanities educator, poet*
†Tepper, Scott M. *mining executive*
Weaver, Carlton Davis *retired oil industry executive*
†Yancey, Robert Earl, Jr., *retired oil company executive*

Baughman
†Jackson, Donnie Ray *electrical engineer, researcher*

Bellevue
Carpenter, Woodrow Wilson *enamel company executive, ceramic engineer*
Lemlich, Robert *chemical engineer, educator*

Berea
Krug, John Carleton (Tony Krug) *college administrator, library consultant*
Lamb, Irene Hendricks *medical researcher*
Turner, Charles Robert, Jr., *music educator*

Boston
†Rosenbaum, Stanley Ned *theology educator*

Bowling Green
Ahmed, S. Basheer *research company executive, educator*
†Atwell, Nedra Wheeler *education educator, consultant*
Blair, John Paul *academic administrator*
Buono, Frank Louis *orthopedic surgeon*
Cangemi, Joseph Peter *psychologist, consultant, educator*
Cooper, Davis A. *city official*
Cravens, Raymond Lewis *retired political science educator*
†Garrison, Geneva *retired administrative assistant*
†Gipson, Jim *wholesale distribution executive*
Holland, John Ben *clothing manufacturing company executive*
Huddleston, Joseph Russell *judge*
Minton, John Dean *historian, educator*
†Parker, William Jerry *lawyer*
Pierce, Verlon Lane *pharmacist, small business owner*
†Rabold, Charlene Franklin *librarian*
Rahim, M. Afzalur *management educator, editor*
Rudloff, William Joseph *lawyer*
Slocum, Donald Warren *chemist*
Sparks, David Thomas *lawyer*
Stewart, Harold Sanford *real estate investment and supply executive*
Survant, Joe *English language educator, poet*
Wassom, John Clark *economics educator*
Wells, Jerry Wayne *police official*
Wilcher, Larry K. *lawyer*

Calvert City
Butler, Sheila Morris *occupational health nurse*

Campbellsburg
Mitchell, Mary Ann Carrico *poet*

Campbellsville
Burch, John Russell, Jr., *library director*
†Chowning, John E. *political scientist, educator, minister*
Conner, Jeanette Jones *elementary school educator*
†Gaddis, John Robert *music educator*
†Imes, Daniel Alan *music educator*
†McArthur, Lisa R. *music educator*
†Roberts, M. Wesley *musician, educator*
Skaggs, Karen Gayle *elementary school educator*

Caneyville
†Embry, C B, Jr., *state representative*

Carlisle
Wolf, John Howell *retired publisher*

Central City
McMurray, Jamie *race car driver*

Clinton
Clark, Linda Wilson *educational administrator*

Columbia
Brown, Billy Charlie *secondary school educator*

Corbin
Doby, John Thomas *social psychologist*
Mahan, Shirley Jean *nursing educator*

Corinth
Wilson, Genevieve Adkins *artist*

Covington
Bates, Patti Jean *protection services official*
Berg, Lorine McComis *retired guidance counselor*
†Brothers, John Alfred *retired oil company executive*
Bush, Sister Mary Kathleen *social worker*
†Davidson, David Edgar *lawyer*
Fleischer-Rieveschl, Ellen Lee *real estate agent*
Giesbrecht, Martin Gerhard *retired economics educator, clarinetist*
†Hughes, William Anthony *retired bishop*
†Kerr, Thomas Robert *lawyer*
Littleton, Nan Elizabeth Feldkamp *psychologist, educator*
McQueen, Regenia *writer*
†O'Brien, James J. *manufacturing executive*
Quin, Joseph Marvin *oil company executive*
†Stepner, Donald Leon *lawyer*
Tenkotte, Paul Allen *history and international studies educator*
Wolnitzek, Stephen Dale *lawyer*

Crescent Springs
Chellgren, Paul Wilbur *industrial company executive*

Crestview Hills
Cory, Edward William, Jr., *underwriting executive*
Harper, Kenneth Franklin *retired state legislator, real estate broker*

Crestwood
Ray, Ronald Dudley *lawyer*
Roy, Elmon Harold *minister*
†Snow, Edwin Fawcett *management consultant*

Cynthiana
Bandurski, Bruce Lord *retired ecological and environmental scientist*

Harpel, Gerald Robert *obstetrician and gynecologist*

Danville
Breeze, William Hancock *college administrator*
Crouch, Betty Louise *real estate broker*
Kennan, Elizabeth Topham *former university president and history educator*
†Morris, Alvin Leonard *retired dentist, educational administrator*
†Roush, John A *academic administrator*

Eddyville
Cooley-Parker, Sheila Leanne *psychologist, consultant, educator*

Edgewood
Martin, Kevin Douglas *surgeon*
Rue, Nelson B. *hospital administrator*

Ekron
†Hamilton, Amelia Wentz (Amy Wentz) *elementary school educator*

Elizabethtown
Cantrell, Douglas Eugene *history educator, author*
Cooper, William S. *state supreme court justice*
†Hill, Camille Crunelle *music educator*
†Paparinov, Rafael Raytchev
Phelps, Dennis Lane *minister, educator, author*
Rahman, Rafiq Ur *oncologist, educator*

Elkton
Manthey, Frank Anthony *physician, director*

Elsmere
†Miller, Jackie Dean, I, *genealogist, historian*

Erlanger
Cuneo, Dennis Clifford *automotive company executive*

Flemingsburg
Story, Joseph C. *economist, consultant*

Florence
Frohlich, Anthony William *lawyer, master commissioner*
Gorman, Gayla Marlene Osborne *consumer affairs executive*
Lawson, Harry Wilbur *chemist, consultant, writer*
Monohan, Edward Sheehan, IV, *lawyer*
Redding, Rogers Walker *physics educator, university official*

Fort Campbell
†Clark, Robert T. *career officer*
Ruth, Bryce Clinton, Jr., *lawyer*

Fort Knox
†Gaddis, Evan R. *army officer*
Nagorski, Leonard Edward *radiologist*

Fort Mitchell
Euskirchen, George John *business administration and economics educator*
Weiskittel, Ralph Joseph *real estate broker*

Fort Thomas
Gultekin, Ebru Kadriye *pediatrician*
Hill, Esther Dianne *business education educator*
Whalen, Paul Lewellin *lawyer, educator, mediator*

Fort Wright
Sullivan, Connie Castleberry *artist, photographer*

Fountain Run
Shanks, Gerald Robert *retired insurance company executive*

Frankfort
†Adams, John W. *state representative*
†Arnold, Adrian King *state representative*
†Barrows, Joseph Howard *state representative*
†Bather, Paul *state representative*
†Belcher, Carolyn R. *state representative*
Brown, John Y., III, *state official*
†Burch, Thomas Joseph *state representative*
Carroll, Julian Morton *lawyer, former governor*
Chadwick, Robert *lawyer, judge*
Chandler, Albert Benjamin, III, *state attorney general*
†Cherry, Mike E. *state legislator*
†Clark, Lawrence D. *state representative*
†Comer, James R., Jr., *state representative*
†Congleton, Conley Cole, III, *lawyer*
†Cornett, Howard *state representative*
†Crimm, Ronald E. *state representative*
Cross, Alvin Miller (Al Cross) *political columnist, writer*
†Damron, Robert R. *state representative*
†DeWeese, Bob M. *state representative*
†Draud, Jon E. *state representative*
Dringenburg, Duane Clinton *health services executive*
†Embry, Michael Dale *writer, editor*
†Feeley, Timothy E. *state representative*
Fleming, Juanita Wilson *nursing education, university official*
Fletcher, Winona Lee *theater educator emeritus*
†Ford, Danny R. *state representative*
Gillig, John Stephenson *lawyer*
†Graham, Derrick W. *state representative, educator*
†Gray, J. R. *state representative*
†Griffith, Patricia Barnes *music educator, pianist*
Hatchett, Edward Bryan, Jr., *state auditor, lawyer*
†Haydon, Joseph A. (Jodie) *state representative*
Henry, Stephen Lewis *lieutenant governor, orthopedic surgeon, educator*
Hestand, Joel Dwight *minister, evangelist*
Johnson, Jerry D. *legislative staff member*

Johnstone, Martin E. *state supreme court justice*
Lambert, Joseph Earl *state supreme court chief justice*
†Liler, Charles L. *state representative*
†Marcotte, Paul Henry *state representative*
†McKee, Thomas M. *state representative*
†Miller, Carl Theodore *lawyer*
†Nunn, Stephen R. *state representative*
Palmore, Carol M. *state official*
Palmore, John Stanley, Jr., *retired lawyer*
Patton, Nicki *former political organization executive*
Patton, Paul E. *governor*
†Pullin, Tanya *state representative*
Richards, Jody *state legislator, journalism educator, small business owner*
Ryan, Perry T. *assistant attorney general, author*
†Shabazz, David Lorenzo *vocational school educator*
Sonego, Ian G. *assistant attorney general*
†Stein, Kathy W. *state representative*
†Tapp, Gary L. *state senator*
Taylor, Livingston Vernon *retired newspaper reporter*
Underwood, John Thomas, IV, *trade association executive, lobbyist*
†Wayne, Jim *state representative*
†Williams, David Lewis *state senator*
Williams, Ellen C. *political party official*
Williamson, Deborah McKibben *social services administrator, educator*
Wintersheimer, Donald Carl *state supreme court justice*

Frankfurt
†Miller, Charles W. *state representative*

Franklin
Clark, James Benton *railroad industry consultant, former executive*
Herndon, Wallace Eugene, Jr., *human resources manager*

Georgetown
Allison, James Claybrooke, II, *broadcasting executive*
†Caza, Brian Patrick *political scientist, educator*
†Chi, Keon Soo *editor, educator, researcher*
Klotter, James C. *historian, educator*
†Sato, Shigetaka *Japanese language educator*
White, Mary Ann *bank executive*

Glasgow
†Baker, Walter Arnold *lawyer*
Duvo, Mechelle Louise *oil company executive, consultant*
Gardner, Woodford Lloyd, Jr., *lawyer*
†Mortimer, Beverly Jo *medical/surgical nurse, director*
Wyatt, Elnoria *real estate broker*

Goshen
Dahl, Marilyn Gail *psychotherapist, nurse*
Strode, William Hall, III, *photojournalist, publisher*

Grayson
†Golightly, John Wesley *music educator*

Greenup
Stuart, Jessica Jane *writer, poet*

Greenville
Walters, Sue Fox *business executive, accountant*
†Yonts, Larry Brent *lawyer*

Hardin
Morrow, Bruce William *educational administrator, business executive, consultant, author*

Harlan
Ford, Mark L. *lawyer*
Greene, James S., III, *school administrator*

Harrods Creek
Keeney, Steven Harris *lawyer*

Hartford
Brown, Russell Jay *nurse*

Henderson
Esser, James Mark *cardiovascular and interventional radiologist*
Logan, John A., III, *hospital administrator*
Wayne, Bill Tom *secondary school educator, coach*

Hickory
†Murphy, George Ray *music educator*

Highland Heights
†Burkholder, Jo Ellen *anthropologist, educator*
†Dieffenbach, Charles Maxwell *emeritus law educator, lawyer*
Donnelly, Sharlotte K. B. Neely *anthropology educator, author*
†Forman, Sandra H. *theater educator*
†Kurk, Katherine Chenault *education educator*
Rini, Alice Gertrude *law educator, lawyer, nursing educator*
†Vitz, Robert Carl *historian, educator*

Hopkinsville
†Adams, James G., Jr., *judge, lawyer*
Estes, Scott Elliott *music educator*
Knob, Steven Edward *band director, composer*
Neville, Thomas Lee *food service company executive*

Independence
Hopgood, James F. *anthropologist, educator*

Inez
Duncan, Robert Michael *banker, lawyer, Republican national committeeman*

Kings Mountain
Gill, Allen (Dale Gill) *environmental management service*

La Grange
Morgan, Mary Dan *librarian*

Lancaster
Arnold, Cecil Benjamin *former small business owner*
Hatton, Brenda Shirley (Linda Wellington) *writer, poet, songwriter, nurse*
Sea, Sherry Lynn *poet*
Vandiviere, H. Mac *medical educator*

Lebanon
Higdon, Frederick Alonzo *lawyer, accountant*
†Higdon, Jimmy *state representative*

Lexington
Abu Kwaik, Yousef A. *microbiologist, educator, research scientist*
Anderson, James Wingo *physician*
Assael, Leon A. *dean, educator*
Avant, Robert Frank *physician, educator*
Bagby, Glen Stovall *lawyer*
Baker, Merl *engineering educator*
Barnhart, Charles Elmer *animal sciences educator*
Basconi, Pamela Bray *lawyer*
Baumann, Robert Jay *child neurology educator*
Beshear, Steven Lynn *lawyer*
†Boucher, Larry Gene *sports association commissioner*
Boyer, Lillian Buckley *artist, educator*
Braun, Janet Larson *nurse*
†Breathitt, Edward Thompson, Jr., *lawyer, railroad executive, former governor*
Brock, Louis Milton, Jr., *engineering educator, researcher*
Brown, William Randall *geology educator*
Bryson, Arthur Joseph *lawyer*
Burki, Nausherwan *pulmonologist*
Calvert, C(lyde) Emmett *former state agency administrator*
Caroland, William Bourne *structural engineer*
†Chan, Lois Mai *library and information science educator*
Chance, Kenneth Bernard *endodontist, educator, university official*
Charley, Nancy Jean *communications professional*
Chen, Zhi *electrical engineering educator*
†Chowdhury, Dipak K. *pharmaceutical executive, researcher*
Clawson, David Kay *orthopedic surgeon*
Coffman, Edward McKenzie *history educator*
Coffman, Jennifer Burcham *federal judge*
Cole, Henry Philip *educational psychology educator*
Cox, Walter Clay Jr. *lawyer, real estate broker*
Crouch, Dianne Kay *secondary school guidance counselor*
†Curlander, Paul Joseph *computer company executive*
Curtz, Chauncey S.R. *lawyer, real estate company executive*
Davey, Diane Davis *pathologist, educator*
DeLong, Lance Eric *physics educator, researcher*
DeLuca, Patrick Phillip *pharmaceutical scientist, educator, administrator*
Donohew, Robert Lewis, Sr., *communications educator*
Drake, Vaughn Paris, Jr., *electrical engineer, retired telephone company executive*
Ecabert, Peter Leo *lawyer, accountant*
Ehmann, Nancy Gallagher *civic worker*
†Elliott, Robert Lloyd *lawyer*
Ettensohn, Frank Robert *geologist, educator*
Farrar, Donna Beatrice *hospital official*
Ferguson, James Edward, II, *obstetrician, gynecologist, maternal-fetal medicine specialist*
Fink, Joseph Leslie, III, *law educator*
Forester, Karl S. *chief district court judge*
Fried, Andrew Michael *radiologist, educator*
Friedell, Gilbert Hugo *pathologist, hospital administrator, educator, cancer center director*
Frye, Wilbur Wayne *retired soil science educator, researcher, administrator*
Fryman, Virgil Thomas, Jr., *lawyer*
Gable, Robert Elledy *real estate investment company executive*
Gallagher, Eugene Bennett *sociologist, medical educator*
†Garmer, William Robert *lawyer*
Gilliam, M(elvin) Randolph *retired urologist, educator*
Glenn, James Francis *urologist, educator*
Goldman, Alvin Lee *lawyer, educator, arbitrator*
Goldman, Elisabeth Paris *lawyer*
Goodman, Norman Loyal *microbiologist, educator*
Hagen, Michael Dale *family physician educator*
Hall, Harry H. *agricultural economics educator*
Halley, Samuel Hampton, III, *architect, architectural firm executive*
†Hamilton, C. Todd *lobbyist*
Hamilton-Kemp, Thomas Rogers *organic chemist, educator*
Haney, Donald Clay *geologist*
Hasan, Saiyid Zafar *social work educator*
†Hedlund, Richard Paul *historian, educator, retired historian*
Henry, Kevin Gudgel *lawyer*
Hickey, John King *lawyer, career officer*
Hochstrasser, Donald Lee *cultural anthropologist, community health and public administrator*
Holcomb, Sara Nees *museum director, artist*
†Hollis, Jessica Lexie *literature educator*
Holsinger, James Wilson, Jr., *physician*
†Hopper, Kevin R. *biologist*
Hultman, Charles William *economics educator*
Humphries, Asa Alan, Jr., *biologist, educator, dean*
Hurley, Janet Lee *university health service administrator*

†Irtz, Frederick G., II, *lawyer*
†Jackson, Carney Brand *veterinarian*
Johnson, Jane Penelope *freelance/self-employed writer*
Johnson, Lizabeth Lettie *small business owner, insurance agent*
Johnson, Paul Brett *writer, illustrator*
Kang, Bann C. *immunologist*
Kant, Laurence Harold *religion historian*
Kaplan, Martin P. *allergist, immunologist, pediatrician*
Keeling, Larry Dale *journalist*
Keller, James *state supreme court justice*
Kelly, Timothy Michael *newspaper publisher*
Kelso, Lynn A. *acute care nurse practitioner*
Kern, Bernard Donald *retired educator, physicist*
Kissling, Fred Ralph, Jr., *publishing executive, insurance agency executive*
Klapper, Andrew *computer scientist, educator*
†Lester, Roy David *lawyer*
Leukefeld, Carl George *researcher, educator*
†Levy, Charlotte Lois *law librarian, educator, consultant, lawyer*
Lewis, Robert Kay, Jr., *fundraising executive*
Lewis, Thomas Proctor *law educator*
Lindle, Jane Clark *educator*
†Lodder, Robert A. *science educator*
Lodder, Robert Andrew *chemistry and pharmaceutics educator*
Logan, Joyce Polley *education educator*
Love, Harold Gibson *agricultural economics educator*
†Lutz, Martha Victoria Rosett *entomologist*
Male, Alan Thomas *engineering educator, association executive*
Mason, Ellsworth Goodwin *librarian*
Masterton, Lucinda Cronin *lawyer*
Mayer, Lloyd Dewald *allergist, immunologist, physician, medical educator*
McDonough, James Michael *engineer, educator*
†McKinstry, Taft Avent *lawyer*
Mentzer, Robert Melvin, Jr., *surgeon*
Michael, Douglas Charles *law educator*
Millard, James Kemper *marketing executive*
Miller, Harry B(enjamin) *lawyer*
Miller, Jill Thompson *sales support*
Miller, Pamela Gundersen *mayor*
Mitchell, George Ernest, Jr., *animal scientist, educator*
Newberry, James Henry, Jr., *lawyer*
†Noar, Seth Michael *communications researcher*
†Nugent, Christopher Donald *history educator*
†Penn, Lynn Sharon *materials scientist, educator*
Poh, Churn K. *chemical engineer, researcher*
Poundstone, John Walker *preventive medicine physician*
Rangnekar, Vivek Mangesh *molecular biologist, researcher*
†Robinson, Thomas Christopher *academic administrator, educator*
Rogers, Tina Karen Profitt *administrative assistant, writer*
Romanowitz, Byron Foster *architect, engineer*
Rowland, Randall G. *urologist*
Sandoval, Arturo Alonzo *art educator, artist*
Savage, William Earl *savings and loan executive, religious educator*
†Sekulic, Dusan P. *science educator, researcher*
Sexton, Robert Fenimore *educational organization executive*
Shawcross, John Thomas *English educator*
Sineath, Timothy Wayne *library educator, university dean*
Snowden, Ruth O'Dell Gillespie *artist*
Steele, Earl Larsen *electrical engineering educator*
Steensland, Ronald Paul *librarian*
Stempel, John Dallas *international studies educator*
†Stevens, Gary *retired jockey*
Stilwell, William Earle, III, *psychology educator, retired military officer*
Stone, Dan N. *accounting educator*
Stone, Martha Jane *musician*
Straus, Robert *behavioral sciences educator*
Taylor, Paul Franklin *college dean*
Thelin, John Robert *academic administrator, education educator, historian*
Timoney, Peter Joseph *veterinarian, virologist, educator, consultant*
Turley, Robert Joe *lawyer*
†Underwood, Richard Harvey *law educator*
†Van Meter, Woodford Spears *ophthalmologist, surgeon*
Varellas, Sandra Motte *judge*
Villaran, Yuri *physician, medical educator*
Vimont, Richard Elgin *lawyer*
Von Unrug, Thomas Paul *physician, lab administrator*
Walize, Reuben Thompson, III, *health research administrator*
Warth, Robert Douglas *history educator*
Wasilkowski, Grzegorz W. *computer scientist*
†Weitzel, William David *psychiatrist*
†Wekstein, David Robert *physiology educator, researcher*
Wethington, Charles T., Jr., *academic administrator*
†Whayne, Thomas French, Jr., *cardiologist, educator*
Whitmer, Leslie Gay *federal official*
Wildasin, David E(arl) *economics educator*
Wilson, Emery Allen *university dean, obstetrician-gynecologist, educator*
Wolff, L. Thomas *medical director*
†Woodring, John Howell *radiologist*
Worell, Judith P. *psychologist, educator*
Young, Paul Ray *medical board executive, physician*
†Young, Sandra Cooper *retired librarian*
Zack, George J. *conductor, music director*
Zentall, Thomas R. *psychologist, educator*

Liberty
Wright, Rodney H. *architect*

London
Giles, William Elmer *retired newspaper editor*

Jensen, Thomas Lee *lawyer*
Keller, John Warren *lawyer*
Siler, Eugene Edward, Jr., *federal judge*

Louisa
Cataldi, Patricia Lee *surgeon*

Louisville
Adams, Robert Waugh *state agency administrator, economics educator*
Ament, Mark Steven *lawyer*
Amin, Mohammad *urology educator*
Anderson, Linda Jean *critical care and psychiatric nurse practitioner*
Andrews, Billy Franklin *pediatrician, educator*
Appleberry, James Bruce *higher education consultant*
Ardery, Philip Pendleton *lawyer*
†Atz, Sarah J. *music educator*
Austin, Erle Harris *pediatric cardiac surgeon*
Ballantine, John Tilden *lawyer*
†Bardenwerper, William Burr *lawyer*
†Barnett, Joyce Lyndel *freelance/self-employed writer*
Barr, James Houston, III, *lawyer*
Becker, Gail Roselyn *museum director*
Belanger, William Joseph *chemist, polymer applications consultant*
Benfield, Ann Kolb *lawyer*
Bentley, James Robert *association curator, historian, genealogist*
Berger, Barbara Paull *social worker, marriage and family therapist*
Blaine, Steven Robert *lawyer*
†Bloem, James H. *managed health care executive*
Bloemer, Gary Fred *orthopedic surgeon, educator*
Boggs, Danny Julian *judge*
Brantley, William Albert *information architect, consultant*
Bratton, Ida Frank *retired secondary school educator*
Brugioni, David Michael *graphic designer, illustrator, artist*
Buckaway, William Allen, Jr., *lawyer*
Cai, Lu *biomedical scientist*
Callen, Jeffrey Phillip *dermatologist, educator*
†Chan, Ying Kit *artist, educator*
Chauvin, Leonard Stanley, Jr., *lawyer*
Chien, Sufan *surgeon, educator*
Christopher, Ray Louis *pilot, journalist, author*
Clark, John Hallett, III, *consulting engineering executive*
Clayton, M. Courtland *engineering, manufacturing sourcing and health wellness and internet technology consultant*
Coalter, Milton J., Jr., *library director, educator*
Cohen, Edwin Louis *lawyer*
Cohn, David V(alor) *biochemist, educator*
Columbus, Shanna S. *advertising executive*
Conner, Stewart Edmund *lawyer*
Cook, Christine L. *endocrinologist, gynecologist, educator*
Cook, Larry Norman *pediatrician, neonatologist, educator*
Cornelius, Wayne Anderson *electrical and computer engineering consultant*
Corwin, Hal Michael *neurologist*
Cowan, Frederic Joseph *lawyer*
Crum, Denny (Denzel Edwin Crum) *retired collegiate basketball coach*
†Cutler, Irwin Herbert *lawyer*
Dale, Judy Ries *religious organization administrator, consultant*
Dalton, Jennifer Faye *accountant*
Danzl, Daniel Frank *emergency physician*
Davidson, Gordon Byron *lawyer*
Deering, Ronald Franklin *librarian, minister*
†DeLong, James Clifford *air transportation executive*
DeMunbrun-Harmon, Donne O'Donnell *retired family physician*
†DeVitis, Joseph L. *education educator*
Doane, Christopher Philip *music educator*
Doran, Vincent Francis *economic development executive*
Dudley, George Ellsworth *lawyer*
†Duffy, Martin Patrick *lawyer*
Dugger, Richard Charles *music educator*
†Eades, Ronald Wayne *law educator*
Early, Jack Jones *foundation executive*
†Early, Stephen Barry *lawyer*
Edgell, Stephen Edward *psychology educator, statistical consultant*
Edward, David Andrew *environmental engineer*
Elin, Ronald John *pathologist, educator*
†Ely, Hiram, III, *lawyer*
†Ethridge, Larry Clayton *lawyer*
Fallat, Mary Elizabeth *pediatric surgeon*
Faller, Rhoda *lawyer*
Farman, Allan George *radiologist, oral pathologist, educator*
Fenton, Thomas Conner *lawyer*
Ferguson, Jo McCown *lawyer*
Ferré, John Patrick *communications educator*
Fiedler, Hans Karl *network analyst, consultant*
Ford, Gordon Buell, Jr., *literature educator, writer*
Foster, Teresa E. *choral director, piano teacher*
Fowler, Michael Ross *law and politics educator*
Fuchs, Olivia Anne Morris *lawyer*
Fullenlove, Carmen Millay (Kit Fullenlove) *public relations executive*
Galandiuk, Susan *colon and rectal surgeon, educator*
Gall, Stanley Adolph *physician, immunology researcher*
Ganoe, Bob (robot) *model, actor*
Garcia, Rafael Jorge *retired chemical engineer*
Garfinkel, Herbert *political science educator, university official*
Garver, David L. *psychiatrist*
Gilman, Sheldon Glenn *lawyer*
Gist, William Claude, Jr., *retired dentist*
†Glenn, Furman Eugene *industrial chemist*
†Gorman, Chris *lawyer*
Gott, Marjorie Eda Crosby *conservationist, former educator*
Gowin, Richard Bryan *lawyer*
Greaver, Joanne Hutchins *mathematics educator, author*
Green, Catherine C. *foreign language educator*
Gregg, Gary L., II, *political science educator*
Griffin, Larry Paul *obstetrician-gynecologist, educator*
Guethlein, William O. *lawyer*
Guillaume, Raymond Kendrick *banker*
Haddaway, James David *retired insurance company official*
Haddy, Richard Ian *family physician, educator*
†Hale, Roger W. *utilities company executive*
Hall, Jill Watkins *communications educator*
Hallenberg, Robert Lewis *lawyer*
Hanley, Thomas Richard *engineering educator*
Harrell, Frank William *family physician*
Hayes, William Meredith *pilot, retired career officer*
Haynes, Douglas Martin *physician, educator*
Heiden, Charles Kenneth *retired military officer*
†Hernandez, John E. *musician, music educator*
Hinson, Grady Maurice *music educator*
Hoffer, Debra Humes *educational association administrator*
Holmes, Gary Lee *medical/surgical nurse*
Holt, Homer Anthony, Jr., *urologist, educator*
Hopson, Edwin Sharp *lawyer*
Hoye, Robert Earl *systems science educator*
Huber, Lisa Ann Mari Brones *public relations executive*
Ivory, Bennie *editor*
Jacobs, Amelia Carol *orthodontist*
James, Virginia Lynn *contracts executive*
†Jewell, Franklin P. *lawyer*
†Johnson, Adria Elaine *financial analyst, accountant*
†Jones, David Allen *health facility executive*
Kaplan, Henry Jerrold *ophthalmologist, educator*
Kaplan, Joel A. *dean*
Karageorge, Thomas George *lawyer*
Kearney, Anna Rose *history educator*
†Kee, Brenda Eltrine *music educator, concert pianist*
Kelly, Thomas Cajetan *archbishop*
King, Tim *orchestra executive*
Klotter, John Charles *retired legal educator*
†Kmetz, Donald R. *retired academic administrator*
†Knox, Michael John *academic administrator*
Kuntz, Edward Lawrence *health care executive*
Kutz, Joseph Edward *hand surgeon, educator*
Landau, Herman *newspaperman retired*
†Lanier, Philip M. *lawyer*
La Rocca, Renato Vincenzo *medical oncologist, clinical researcher*
Lavelle, Charles Joseph *lawyer*
Lay, Norvie Lee *law educator*
Lei, Zhenmin *endocrinologist, reproductive biologist, researcher*
Lilly, Charles G. *protective services official, consultant*
†Littleway, Lorna *theater producer, theater educator, theater director*
†Lominadze, David *physiologist, researcher*
Longuet, Gregory Arthur *automation engineer, consultant*
Lumley, Thomas Dewey *travel professional, real estate investor*
Lunsford, W. Bruce *health facility administrator, health and medical products executive*
Lyndrup, Peggy B. *lawyer*
Maggiolo, Allison Joseph *lawyer*
Manassah, Edward E. *publishing executive*
Manly, Samuel *lawyer*
Martin, Boyce Ficklen, Jr., *federal judge*
Martin, Janice Lynn *special education educator*
Mather, Elizabeth Vivian *healthcare executive*
†Matuschka, Paul R. *pharmacist*
McCallister, Michael B. *managed health care executive*
McCormick, Steven Thomas *insurance company executive*
†McKim, Ruth Ann *financial planner*
McKinney, Owen Michael *retired security executive, consultant*
†McWane, Mark Paul *technology consultant*
†Meeks, Reginald Kline *city alderman*
Mellen, Francis Joseph, Jr., *lawyer*
Meyer, Peter Bert *economist, urban policy educator*
Min, Hokey *business educator*
Mitchell, Charlie Henry *music educator, performer, church musician*
Mohler, Richard Albert, Jr., *academic administrator, theologian*
Moon, Stephen Douglas *architectural firm executive*
Morgan-White, Stephanie Lynn *lawyer*
Morrin, Peter Patrick *museum director*
Mosier, Jo Ann *mathematics educator*
Mountz, Wade *retired health service management executive*
Mowery, Ward Franklin *retired music educator*
Naslund, Alan Joseph *communications educator*
Newby, Elizabeth Ann *elementary education educator*
Niles, Judith F. *librarian*
Noble, Stephen Lloyd *information scientist*
†Northern, Richard *lawyer*
Novak, David C. *restaurant company executive*
†Oglesby, Joseph Woodson (Mike English) *writer, publishing executive*
Oliphant, Naomi Joyce *music educator, performer*
Osborn, John Simcoe, Jr., *lawyer*
Palmer, Larry Isaac *lawyer, educator*
Parker, Joseph Corbin, Jr., *pathologist, educator*
Parkins, Frederick Milton *dental educator, university dean*
†Partin, C. Fred *lawyer*
Peden, Katherine Graham *industrial consultant*
Pedley, Lawrence Lindsay *lawyer*
Pelfrey, D. Patton *lawyer*
Pereira, Edgard Luiz *physician*
Pettyjohn, Shirley Ellis *lawyer, real estate executive*
Pitino, Richard *collegiate basketball coach, former professional basketball coach*
Polk, Hiram Carey, Jr., *surgeon, educator*
Porter, Henry Homes, Jr., *investor*
Power, David M. *advertising executive*
Power, Michael L. *advertising executive*
Prough, Russell Allen *biochemistry educator, university official*
Raff, Martin Jay *internist, infectious diseases educator, lawyer*
Rao, Ch. V. *endocrinologist, educator*
Rapp, Christian Ferree *retired textile home furnishings company executive*
Reed, David Benson *bishop*
Reed, John Squires, II, *lawyer*
Richardson, James David *surgeon*
†Robinson, Dennis Shea *music educator*
Ronald, Peter *utility executive*
Rose, Charles Alexander *lawyer*
Rose, Judy Hardin *nursing administrator*
Rosky, Theodore Samuel *insurance company executive*
Rothstein, Mark Alan *health law and bioethics educator*
Royer, Robert Lewis *retired utility company executive*
Runyon, Keith Leslie *lawyer, newspaper editor*
†Ryan-Kessler, Michael Lewis *secondary school educator*
Saunders, Robert Samuel *venture capital executive*
Scheu, Lynn McLaughlin *scientific publication editor*
Schneider, Jayne Bangs *school librarian*
Schwab, John Joseph *psychiatrist, educator*
Scott, Ralph Mason *physician, radiation oncology educator*
Segal, Uriel *music director*
Shaikun, Michael Gary *lawyer*
Shaver, Karen *performing company executive, educator, design educator*
Sherman, Mildred Mozelle *music educator, singer, actress, opera director*
Siewert, Robin Noelle *planning engineer*
†Silverthorn, Robert Sterner, Jr., *lawyer*
Skees, William Leonard, Jr., *lawyer*
Smith, Donald Ray *magazine dealer*
Smith, Robert F., Jr., *civil engineer*
Smith, R(obert) Michael *lawyer*
Spratt, John Stricklin *surgeon, educator, researcher*
†Stanton, M(orris) Duncan *psychologist, researcher, dean*
Street, William May *beverage company executive*
Sutton, John Schuhmann, Jr., *retired purchasing consultant*
Swain, Donald Christie *retired university president, history educator*
Syed, Ibrahim Bijli *medical educator and physicist, author, philosopher, theologist, public speaker, writer*
Talbott, Ben Johnson, Jr., *lawyer*
†Tanguay, Peter Eugene *child and adolescent psychiatry educator*
†Tannon, Jay Middleton *lawyer*
Tasman, Allan *psychiatry educator*
Taylor, G. Don *industrial engineering educator*
Taylor, Kenneth Grant *chemistry educator*
Taylor, Robert Lewis *management educator*
Theiss, Gena Lee *genealogist, researcher*
†Thongboonkerd, Visith *nephrologist, researcher*
Titzl, Mary Trueheart *social work educator, consultant*
Tofteland, Curt L. *producer, director*
Towles, Donald Blackburn *retired publishing executive*
Tran, Long Trieu *industrial engineer*
Tully, Carol Thorpe *social work educator, administrator*
Valenti, Michael A. *lawyer*
Vincenti, Michael Baxter *lawyer*
†Vish, Donald H. *lawyer*
Vogel, Werner Paul *retired machine company executive*
Waddell, William Joseph *pharmacologist, toxicologist*
†Wagner, James Miller *funeral director*
†Wagoner, Ruth R *education coach*
†Walker, Kandi *communications educator*
†Wang, Chung-Hsiao *industrial engineer*
Watts-Wilson, Denise *secondary school educator*
Weakley-Jones, Barbara Ann *forensic pathologist, educator*
Welsh, Sir Alfred John *lawyer, international advisor*
Wesley, Stephen Burton *training professional*
Whitelaw, Christine Cappelle *pediatrician, educator*
Whittington, Denise Lynn *music educator*
Williams, John N. *dean*
Wren, Harold Gwyn *arbitrator, lawyer, legal educator*
Wright, Jesse Hartzell *psychiatrist, educator*
Zechman, David Mark *health system executive, educator*
†Ziegler, Charles Edward *political science educator, department chairman*
Zimmerman, Gideon K. *minister*
Zimmerman, Thom Jay *ophthalmologist, educator*

Madisonville
†Kemp, Ann *retired librarian*
Kington, Barry Clark *investor, consultant*
May, Richard Warren *writer, consultant, inventor*
Stulc, Jaroslav Peter *surgeon, educator*
Vander Ploeg, Scott David *literature educator, writer*
Veazey, Doris Anne *state agency administrator, retired*

Marion
†Tedrick, Lucy Nell *minister*

Masonic Home
Schweichler, Mary Ellen *childhood education educator, consultant*

Mayfield
Viles, Henry *pathologist*

Middleburg
†Kleffman, Ken *small business owner, rancher*

Middlesboro
Money, Max Lee *family nurse practitioner*

Midway
†Smialek, William *musicologist*

Morehead
Besant, Larry Xon *librarian, administrator, consultant*
Chatham, Richard Douglas *mathematics educator*
†Detweiler, Greg Jeffrey *music educator*
†Flanagan, Gary Lee *librarian*
Mann, James Darwin *mathematics educator*
Miller, Green Russell *economist, educator*

Mount Olivet
Dorton, Truda Lou *medical, surgical and geriatrics nurse*

Mount Sterling
Kukulinsky, Nancy Elaine *health care consultant*

Munfordville
Lang, George Edward *lawyer*

Murray
Bernard, Tracey Marie *ergonomics educator, industrial engineer*
Boston, Betty Lee *investment company executive, financial consultant, financial planner*
Buckingham, David Cowan *judge*
Dycus, Mark *music educator*
†Fister, Katherine Renee *mathematician, educator*
Johnson, Dennis L. *conductor, music educator*
Keller, Randal Joseph *toxicology educator*
†Leslie, Tracy Fortson *music educator*
Milkman, Martin Irving *economics educator*
†Russell, Mary Ann *secondary school educator*
Steffa, John Amon *music educator, composer*
†Waag, C. Michael *foreign language educator*
Wilkins, Margaret Nell Stamper *music educator, musician*

Newport
Clinkenbeard, James Howard *principal*
Siverd, Robert Joseph *lawyer*
Trauth, David E. *dairy company executive*
Wehr, William James *judge*

Nicholasville
†Burton, Malinda Daugherty *school librarian*

Owensboro
Bennett, Edith Lillian *lay church worker, radio personality*
†Eaton, Clara Barbour *retired librarian*
Ford, Steven Milton *insurance agent*
Johnston, Barry Algene *housing loan administrator*
McRaith, John Jeremiah *bishop*
Miller, James Monroe *lawyer*
Oberst, Charlotte L. *physical therapist, nurse*
Roberts, Brian Wayne *middle school educator, minister*
West, William Robert *history educator*

Paducah
Graves, John William *state supreme court justice*
King, W. David *magistrate judge*
Starkey, Russell Bruce, Jr., *energy executive*
Stice, Dwayne Lee *broadcasting company executive*
Treece, Randy Lionel *lawyer*
Wurth, Susan Winsett *clinical nurse specialist*

Paintsville
Massengale, Roger Lee *lawyer*

Paris
Steffer, Robert Wesley *clergyman*
Stiles, Martha Bennett *writer*

Park Hills
Holmes, Lu Ann *interior designer, sales representative*

Pewee Valley
Gill, George Norman *newspaper publishing company executive*

Pikevill
Smith, Roger Keith *investment executive*

Pikeville
Cade, Nancy Jean *history and political science educator*
Justice, Phillip Howard *marketing professional*

Pineville
Lawson, Susan Coleman *lawyer*
Whittaker, Bill Douglas *minister*

Prestonsburg
†Mc Aninch, Robert Danford *philosophy and government affairs educator*
Pridham, Thomas Grenville *retired research microbiologist*
Stumbo, Janet Lynn *state supreme court justice*

Prospect
Aberson, Leslie Donald *lawyer*
Donahoo, Leonard E. *retired engineer*
Katsianis, John Nick *financial executive*
Kehlbeck, Joseph H. *software developer and consultant*

Radcliff
Flores, George H. *obstetrician and gynecologist*

Richmond
†Blanchard, Paul *academic administrator, educator*
Branson, Branley Allan *biology educator*
†Crosby, Richard Allen *music educator*
Engle, Fred Allen, Jr., *economics educator, author*
Inman, Larry Joe *basketball coach*
King, Amy Cathryne Patterson *retired, mathematics educator, researcher*
Myers, Marshall Dean *English educator*
Newby, Earl Fernando *educator*
†Pappas, Marjorie L. *library studies educator*
Schwendeman, Kenneth David *government official, consultant*
Springate, Karen Spears *artist*
†Weldon, C. Michael *lawyer*
Whitt, Marcus Calvin *marketing and public relations executive*

Rineyville
Jackson, Charles Wayne *food products executive, former telecommunications industry executive*

Robards
Birkhead, Thomas Larry *minister*

Rousseau
Bach, Betty Jean *health services educator*

Russell Springs
Ackerman, Anthony Wayne *secondary school educator, band director*

Russellville
Arshad, Abrar Mehmood *physician*
†Desai, Maulik Bharat *emergency physician*
Harper, Shirley Fay *nutritionist, educator, consultant, lecturer*

Shelbyville
†Hedrick, William David *secondary school educator, musician, educator*

Shepherdsville
Givhan, Thomas Bartram *lawyer*
Pike, Burlyn *retired bank director, lawyer*

Somerset
†Angevine, Roger Lee *mathematician, educator*
†Prather, John Gideon *lawyer*
Prather, John Gideon, Jr., *lawyer*

Southgate
Glenn, Jerry Hosmer, Jr., *retired language educator*

Sturgis
Thornsberry, Willis Lee, Jr., *chemist*

Summer Shade
Smith, Ruby Lucille *retired librarian*

Union
Hochstrasser, John Michael *environmental engineer, industrial hygienist*

Vanceburg
Phillips, Susan Diane *secondary school educator*

Vancleve
†Murphree, Quincy Carl *physicist, educator*

Versailles
Stober, William John, II, *economics educator*

West Paducah
†Dowell, Jennifer Ann *mechanical engineer*

Whitesburg
†Garimella, Satya V. *cardiologist*

Whitley City
Stephens, Robert Ernest *retired educator*

Wickliffe
Gray, Carol Hickson *chemical engineer*
Shadoan, William Lewis *judge*

Williamsburg
Fish, Thomas Edward *English language and literature educator*
†Smoak, Jeff C., Jr., *music educator*
†Trickett, Paula J. *assistant principal*

Wilmore
†Bell, Vicki P. *music educator, organist*
Hunter, George Gill, III, *religious studies educator*
†Kinlaw, Dennis Franklin *clergyman, society executive*
†Lee, Duk-Hyung *mathematician, educator*
Pohl, Gunther Erich *retired library administrator*
Rader, Paul Alexander *minister, religious organization administrator*
Snyder, Howard Albert *educator, author*
†Stratford, Linda Harper *humanities educator*

Winchester
Book, John Kenneth (Kenny Book) *retail store owner*
†Cantrell, Georgia Ann *realtor*
Hall, Bennett Freeman *minister*
Studebaker, John Milton *utilities engineer, consultant, educator*

LOUISIANA

Abbeville
†Cao, (Francis) Khang Van *small business owner, poet*
Hebert, Margaret Burns *social worker*

Alexandria
Bolton, Robert Harvey *banker*
Bradford, Louise Mathilde *social services administrator*
†Burns, Ronald C. *music educator*
Butler, Robert Moore, Jr., *podiatrist*
DeWitt, Charles W. *state legislator*
†Foster, Sally *interior designer*
Gist, Howard Battle, Jr., *lawyer*
†Hanley, Henry Gorman *cardiologist*
Jeffress, Charles H. *retired art educator*
Jones, Syble Thornhill *dietitian*
†Little, F. A., Jr., *judge*
†Marivani, Syrous *education educator*
Morris, Rebecca Ann Brittain *accountant*
Myers, Charles Lawrence *anesthesiologist*
O'Connor, Daniel Patrick *priest*
Richmond, Angie Anna Alice Murray *government official*
Saunders, Wesley Hugh *librarian*
Slipman, Ronald (Samuel Slipman) *hospital administrator*
Smith, Joe Dorsey, Jr., *retired newspaper executive*
Sneed, Ellouise Bruce *nursing educator emeritus*
†Thevenot, Maude Travis *retired home economist*
Thomason, Teresa *musician, educator*
Vandersypen, Rita DeBona *guidance counselor, academic administrator*
Wesse, David Joseph *higher education administrator, consultant*

Arcadia
Cummings, Kenneth Ila *coroner, medical examiner*

Arnaudville
Matas, Myra Dorothea *interior architect, designer, consultant*

Baker
†Cross, James Edward *electrical engineering educator*
Roberson, Patt Foster *mass communications educator*

Baton Rouge
Anderson, Lawrence Robert, Jr., *lawyer*
Arceneaux, William *historian, educator, association official*
Arman, Ara *civil engineering educator*
Avent, Raymond Richard, Jr., *civil engineering educator*
Beard, Thomas Rex *economics educator*
Bedeian, Arthur George *business educator*
Bengtson, Richard Lee *agricultural engineer, educator*
Bensman, Stephen J. *school librarian, researcher*
†Bernard, J. M., Jr., *manufacturing executive*
†Bernhard, James M., Jr., *engineering executive*
Besch, Everett Dickman *veterinarian, university dean and educator emeritus*
†Bingham, Elizabeth Elliott *librarian*
Blackman, John Calhoun, IV, *lawyer*
Blanco, Kathleen Babineaux *lieutenant governor*
Bohlinger, Lewis Hall *state government official*
Boren, James Edgar *lawyer*
Bray, George August *physician, scientist, educator*
Brister, Pat *political party executive*
Burns, Paul Yoder *forester, educator*
Byrd, Warren Edgar, II, *lawyer*
Caffey, H(orace) Rouse *university official, agricultural consultant*
†Callicoatte, Troy D. *loss control consultant*
Carlson, Orville James (Skip Carlson) *accountant, financial planner*
Chapman, Russell Leonard *botany educator*
Chen, Peter Pin-Shan *electrical engineering, computer science and internet/web educator, data processing executive*
Cherry, William Ashley *surgeon, state health officer*
Cole, Luther Francis *former state supreme court associate justice*
Conerly, Evelyn Nettles *educational consultant*
Constant, William David *chemical engineer, educator*
Cooper, William James, Jr., *history educator*
Cramer, Gail Latimer *economist*
Crumbley, Donald Larry *accounting educator, writer, consultant*
Crusemann, F(rederick) Ross *advertising agency official*
Culbert, David Holbrook *history educator, writer, editor*
Daniel, Ross Preston, III, *economist, educator*
Dasbach, Oliver T. *mathematician, educator*
†Decuir, Winston G., Sr., *lawyer*
†de Queiroz, Marcio S. *engineering educator*
Desmond, John Jacob *retired architect*
DeVille, Donald Charles *accountant*
DiBenedetto, Robert Lawrence *retired obstetrician, gynecologist, insurance company executive*
Doty, Gresdna Ann *theatre historian, educator*
Dunlap, Wallace Hart *pediatrician*
East, Charles E., Jr., *advertising and public relations executive*
Fenet, Robert Wickliffe *lawyer*
Finan, John Joseph *hospital administrator*
Finney, Clifton Donald *publishing executive*
Foster, M. J., Jr., (Mike Foster) *governor*
†Freedman, Carl Howard *education educator*
Gammon, Malcolm Ernest, Sr., *surveying and engineering executive*
†Garretson, Judith Anne *education educator*
Gettys, Thomas Wigington *medical researcher*
†Giger, Andreas *education educator*
Gilmore, Clarence Percy *writer, magazine editor*
Gonzalez, Gabriela Ines *physics educator*
†Groves, Michael G. *dean*
Guo, Dong-Sheng *physicist*
†Guy, Matthew Wayne *education educator, writer*
Hainkel, John J., Jr., *state senator*
Hamilton, John Maxwell *university dean, writer*
Hansel, William *biology educator*
Hardy, John Edward *English language educator, author*
Harrelson, Clyde Lee *retired secondary school educator*
Hayward, Olga Loretta Hines (Mrs. Samuel Ellsworth Hayward) *retired librarian*
Head, Jonathan Frederick *cell biologist*
†Helms, Jack Elwin, Jr., *mechanical engineer, educator*
†Henninger, Katherine *English educator*
†Hymel, L(ezin) J(oseph) *lawyer, former prosecutor*
Ieyoub, Richard Phillip *state attorney general*
Jaques, Thomas Francis *librarian*
Jeffers, Ben *political organization executive*
Jenkins, Louis (Woody) *television executive, state legislator*
Johnson, Joseph Clayton, Jr., *lawyer*
Jones, Mary Elizabeth *school counselor*
Kaiser, Mark John *research scientist, science educator*
Kelly, Mary Joan *librarian*
Khonsari, Michael M. *mechanical engineering educator*
Kidd, James Marion, III, *allergist, immunologist, naturalist, educator*
Kimball, Dorothy Jean *foundation executive*
†King, Roy Michael *music educator*
Kisner, Wendell Howard, Jr., *plastic surgeon*
Koehler, Robert Brien *priest*
Landry, Frances Leggio *lawyer*
Lane, Margaret Beynon Taylor *librarian*
Lee, Jean Clarisse *editor, writer*
Leonard, Paul Haralson *retired lawyer*
Le Vine, Jerome Edward *retired ophthalmologist*
†Litton, Nancy Joan *education educator*
Liuzzo, Joseph Anthony *food science educator*
Loveland, Anne Carol *history educator*
Lusk, Glenna Rae Knight (Mrs. Edwin Bruce Lusk) *librarian*
Lusted, Dona Sanders *music educator, consultant, organist*
Madden, David *author*
†Marchand, Suzanne Lynn *education educator*
Mathews, Sharon Walker *artistic director, secondary school educator*
Maxcy, Spencer John *education educator*
Mc Cameron, Fritz Allen *retired university administrator*
McCoy, Wesley Lawrence *musician, conductor, educator*
McDaniel, Barry Lynn *educational association administrator*
Mc Glynn, Sean Patrick *physical chemist, educator*
McKeithen, Walter Fox *secretary of state*
Mohr, Jeffrey Michael *real estate and insurance executive*
Moody, Gene Byron *engineering executive, small business owner, minister*
Mueller, Lisel *writer, poet*
Murai, Norimoto *plant molecular biologist, educator*
Norem, Richard Frederick, Sr., *musician, music educator*
O'Connell, Robert Francis *physics educator*
Olney, James *English language educator*
†Owen, Sue Ann *poet*
Oxley, James Grieve *mathematics educator*
Parker, John Victor *federal judge*
Parks, James William, II, *public facilities executive, lawyer*
Patrick, William Hardy, Jr., *wetland biogeochemist, educator, laboratory director*
Patterson, Charles Darold *librarian, educator*
Perkins, Huel Davis *academic administrator*
Phillabaum, Leslie Ervin *publisher*
Pike, Ralph Webster *chemical engineer, educator, university administrator*
†Pitombeira, Liduino *composer, educator*
†Podlaha-Murphy, Elizabeth Josephine *chemical engineer, educator*
Polozola, Frank Joseph *federal judge*
Prestage, James Jordan *university chancellor*
Pugh, George Willard *law educator*
Puyau, Francis Albert *retired physician, radiology educator*
†Pyle, Susan H. *legal association official*
†Ramirez, Arnulfo Gonzalez *language educator, linguist*
Reible, Danny David *environmental chemical engineer, educator*
Reich, Robert Sigmund *landscape architect*
Ricapito, Joseph Virgil (Giuseppe Ricapito) *Spanish, Italian and comparative literature educator*
Richards, Marta Alison *lawyer*
Riedlinger, Stephen C. *federal judge*
Riopelle, Arthur Jean *psychologist*
†Rubin, Michael Harry *lawyer, educator*
Sanders, Mary Elizabeth *author, historian*
Sasek, Gloria Burns *English language and literature educator*
Schroeder, Leila Obier *retired law educator*
Schroeder, Rolf Robert *retired chemical engineer*
Scollard, David Michael *research pathologist*
Scronce, Gary Wayne *engineer*
Sen Gupta, Barun Kumar *geology educator, researcher*
Sinclair, Glenn Bruce *mechanical engineering educator, researcher*
†Skillman, Ernest Edward, Jr., *real estate sales and management executive*
Slaybaugh, Janet Louise *social worker*
†Smith, David Jeddie *American literature educator*
†Smith, Michael *college president*
†Smith, Richard James *retired music educator*
Stockbauer, Roger Lewis *physicist, educator*
†Stracener, Carol Elizabeth *lawyer*
Taylor, John McKowen *lawyer*
Thomas, Jeffrey Cone *financial executive, consultant*
Tipton, Kenneth Warren *agricultural administrator, researcher*
Traynham, James Gibson *chemist, educator*
Tumay, Mehmet Taner *geotechnical consultant, educator, research administrator*
†Turner, Bert S. *construction executive*
Unglesby, Lewis O. *lawyer*
Vaeth, Agatha Min-Chun Fang *clinical nurse, nursing administrator, consultant*
Valsaraj, Kalliat Thazhathuveetil *chemical engineering educator*
Van Lopik, Jack Richard *geologist, educator*
Voyiadjis, George Zino *civil engineer, educator*
Walsh, Milton O'Neal *lawyer*
Wheeler, Otis Bullard *retired English educator and university official*
Wild, Dirk Jonathan *accountant*
Willett, Anna Hart *composer, painter*
Witcher, Robert Campbell, Sr., *bishop*
Wittenbrink, Jeffrey Scott *lawyer*
Yarbrough, Martha Cornelia *music educator*
†Younger, Ann Elizabeth *literature educator*
†Zibilich, Louise Anna *television news producer*

Benton
Hudson, Marguerite W. *secondary school educator*

Bogalusa
Gallaspy, Dixie *interior designer, innkeeper*
Henke, Shauna Nicole *police dispatcher, small business owner*
Hussain, Hamid *physician*
†Wood, Helen Chamblee *accountant*

Bossier City
Bond, William Jennings, Jr., *retired air force officer, scholar, educator*
Fry, Randy Dale *emergency medical technician, paramedic*
Holt, Edwin Joseph *psychology educator*
Lim, Diana Magpayo *internist*
Wheelahan, Timothy Michael *physical therapist*
Winham, George Keith *retired mental health nurse*

Bunkie
McKay, Dan Boies, Jr., *lawyer*

Calhoun
Robbins, Marion LeRon *agricultural research/extension executive*

Carencro
Ford, Deborah Hardy *nursing administrator*

Cecilia
†Girouard, Tina *artist, curator*

Chalmette
Brown, Courtney Allison *social worker*
Williamson, Ramona Diane *special education educator*

Chauvin
Sammarco, Paul William *ecologist, researcher*

Cheneyville
†Ewin, Gordon Overton *retired lawyer, farmer*

Choudrant
Ford, John Charles *artist*

Columbia
†McGee, Bruce D. *evangelist*

Covington
Blossman, Alfred Rhody, Jr., *banker*
Burton, Barbara Able *psychotherapist*
†Looney, James Holland *lawyer*
Maurin, James E. *real estate executive*
Napier, William James, Jr., *marine oil and gas construction consultant*
Paddison, David Robert *lawyer*
Rice, Winston Edward *lawyer*
Rohrbough, Elsa Claire Hartman *artist*
Thornton, Lucie Elizabeth *lawyer*
Vercellotti, John Raymond *research chemist*

Crowley
Foreman, Alfred G. *theologian, philosopher*

Cut Off
Adams, Laura Ann *critical care nurse*
†Cheramie, Carlton Joseph *lawyer, business consultant*

Denham Springs
May, Kenneth Nathaniel *food industry consultant*

Deridder
Magee, Thomas Eston, Jr., *minister*

Destrehan
Bishop, David Nolan *electrical engineer*
†Toups, Byron Joseph *musician, educator*

Donaldsonville
Watson, Stanley Ellis *clergyman, small business owner*

Dubach
Straughan, William Thomas *engineering educator*

Elm Grove
Livingston, John H. *retired engineer, retired military officer*

Ethel
Anders, Jane Virginia *genealogist*

Eunice
Al-Dujaili, Jameel Sadeq *microbiology educator, researcher*
Attole, Mary Bertha *writer*

Franklin
Domingue, Michael W. *community developer*
Fairchild, Phyllis Elaine *school counselor*
McClelland, James Ray *lawyer*
Trosclair, Kattina T. *graphics designer*

Geismar
†Comeaux, Erick J. *chemical engineer*

Gonzales
McGarr, Charles Taylor *accountant*
Noonan, Robert Harry *art and music educator*
Young, David Nelson *media and communications consultant*

Grambling
Favors, Steve Alexander *academic administrator*
†Hawthorne, Leroy, Jr., *humanities educator, musician*
†Ogunyemi, Olatunde Adegbayi *design educator, technology administrator*
Porter, Douglas Taylor *retired athletic administrator*
Porter, Wilma Jean *educational consultant*
†Robinson, Eddie Gay *college football coach*
†Simpson, Arthur Earl *music educator, assistant principal*
†Stentiford, Barry Maxfield *education educator, military officer*
Warner, Neari Francois *university president*

Gramercy
Deroche, Kathleen Samrow *elementary educator, mathematics consultant*

Gretna
Long, Daniel A. *ophthalmologist*
†Weekley, Judy Liddington *special education educator*

Hammond
†Bornier, Evelyne M *language educator*
Broussard, Francis Peter *English educator*
†Cannon, G. Alan *mathematician, educator*
Couret, Keiron Leigh *performing arts presenter*
Durand, Charles Eric *psychologist, educator*
†Haschak, Paul G. *librarian, writer*
Hemberger, Glen James *university band director, music educator*
†Johansen, David Alan *musician, educator*
†Kulkin, Heidi Sharon *education educator*
LaFargue, Melba Faye Fulmer *financial manager, real estate consultant*
Nauman, Ann Keith *education educator, department chairman*
Parish, Richard Lee *engineer, consultant*
Parker, Clea Edward *retired university president*
Richardson, Thaddeus Maurice *funeral director*
Ross, Kenneth L. *lawyer*
Thorburn, James Alexander *retired humanities educator*
†van der Jagt, Johan *special education educator*

Harvey
Pete, Eric E. *claims representative, writer*

Homer
Guenther, Gordon P. *mechanical engineer*

Houma
Babin, Regina-Champagne *artist, educator, consultant*
Bridges, Gerald Jackson *social worker*
Eschete, Mary Louise *internist*
Ferguson, Thomas Glen *internist*
Rhodes, Gene Paul *small business owner*

Iowa
Kuykendall, Richard G. *music educator*
Leonard, Linda Faye *secondary education educator*

Jackson
Payne, Mary Alice McGill *behavior management healthcare quality consultant*

Jefferson
Conino, Joseph Aloysius *lawyer*

Jennings
Golden, Willie Malcome, Jr., *band director, music educator*
Miller, Ruth Loyd *lawyer, author*

Jonesboro
Arrington, James Henry *journalist*

Keithville
Duraczynski, Donna Moore *retired accountant*

Kenner
deMonsabert, Winston Russel *chemist, consultant*
Fouchi, Dana Ray *physician*
Hallila, Bruce Allan *welding engineer*
Kuebler, David Wayne *insurance company executive, private investigator*
McShan, Clyde Griffin, II, *financial executive*
Regan, Siri Lisa Lambourne *gifted education educator*
Scherich, Edward Baptiste *retired diversified company executive*
Siebel, Mathias Paul *mechanical engineer, consultant*
Valvo, Barbara-Ann *lawyer, surgeon*
Williams, Roy *airport terminal executive*

Kinder
Arnold, Rinee' Stephen *petroleum engineer*

La Place
Cicet, Donald James *lawyer*
Fiffie Proctor, JoAnn *media and technology specialist*

Lacombe
Mangus, Carl William *technical safety and standards consultant, engineer*

Lafayette
†Angers, Winston Thomas *lawyer*
Authement, Ray P. *college president*
Barry, Mildred Castille *artist*
Breaux, Paul Joseph *lawyer, pharmacist*
†Cain, Judith Sharp *mathematics consultant*
Carstens, Jane Ellen *retired library science educator*
Ceballos, Jacqui Michot *feminist activist, organizer, administrator*
Christov, Christo Ivanov *mathematician, educator*
†Clark, Bradd Evans *dean, mathematician, educator*
Cloutier, Monique Legendre *lawyer*
Davidson, James Joseph, III, *lawyer*
Davis, William Eugene *judge*
Dickie, Shirley Dalme *vocational rehabilitation counselor and consultant*
Domingue, Emery *consulting engineering company executive, retired*
Ducrest, Willis Francis *retired music educator*
Duhe, John Malcolm, Jr., *federal judge*
Dur, Philip Francis *political scientist, educator, retired foreign service officer*
Durio, William Henry *lawyer*
Falcon, Chuck Tilton *psychologist, writer*
Fang, Cheng-Shen *chemical engineering educator*
Fontenot, Lyn *interior designer*
†Foster, David Smith *mediator, arbitrator, private adjudicator*
Gaubert, Ronald Joseph *gas and oil industry executive, management consultant, real estate broker*
Gilcrease, Jack Christopher *library science educator*
Goforth, William H. *lawyer*
†Hongthong, Siriporn *mathematician, educator*
Jolissaint, Stephen Lacy *pathologist*
Judice, Marc Wayne *lawyer*
†Laudun, John *literature educator*
MacNair, Wilmer Everett *sociologist, educator, minister*
Mallet, Alexis, Jr., *construction company executive*
Mansfield, James Norman, III, *lawyer*
Marshak, Alan Howard *electrical engineer, educator*
Misra, Devesh K. *engineering educator*
Morgan, Glenn L. *lawyer*
Myers, Stephen Hawley *lawyer*
O'Donnell, Edward Joseph *bishop, former editor*
†Owen, Dolores Bullock *librarian, research consultant*
Petry, Ruth Vidrine *principal*
Raffel, Burton Nathan *retired educator, poet, writer, translator*
Rickey, Horace B., Jr., *retired engineer*
Rieck, William Albert *secondary school educator and administrator, professor*
Rolfes, Leonard Joseph *pediatrician*
Saloom, Kaliste Joseph, Jr., *lawyer, retired judge*
Salters, Richard Stewart *engineering company executive*
†Sibille, Mark Stephen *mechanical design engineer*
Sides, Larry Eugene *advertising executive*
Skinner, Michael David *lawyer, political organization administrator*
Springer, Leonard *musician, educator*
Stephan, Mark Tyler *radiologist*
Stuart, Walter Bynum, III, *banker*
†Turner, I. Bruce *archivist*
Wyatt, Charles H. *cardiovascular surgeon*
†Young, Reginald (Reggie) S. *writer, educator*
Zuschlag, Richard Emery *small business owner*

Lake Charles
Beam, James Carroll (Jim Beam) *retired newspaper editor*
Campbell, Carol Sue *sociology, social work, psychology, and criminal justice educator*
Clement, Richard Joseph *obstetrician-gynecologist*
Dentler, Anne Lillian *artist*
Drez, David Jacob, Jr., *orthopedic surgeon, educator*
Fields-Gold, Anita *retired dean*
†Gates, Keith R. *music educator*
Gunderson, Clark Alan *orthopedic surgeon*
†Hebert, Robert D. *academic administrator*
Hinton, Juliana Guillory *biologist, educator*
Leder, Sandra Juanita *retired elementary school educator*
Levingston, Ernest Lee *engineering company executive*
Middleton, George, Jr., *clinical child psychologist*
Mocklin, Kevin Etienne *physician, medical educator*
Mount, Willie Landry *state legislator*
†Nieset, James Robert *lawyer*
Parkerson, Hardy Martell *lawyer*
Premeaux, Shane Richard *marketing educator*
Roy, Donald *artist, poet*
Sanchez, Walter Marshall *lawyer*
Shaddock, William Edward, Jr., *lawyer*
Stacey, Truman *journalist, consultant*
Trimble, James T., Jr., *federal judge*
Veron, J. Michael *lawyer, writer*
†Weeber, Stan C. *sociologist, educator*

Leesville
†Davis, Gene H. *music educator*
Gutman, Lucy Toni *school social worker, educator, counselor*
Norman, Paralee Frances *English language educator, researcher*
Smith, Simeon Christie, III, *lawyer, judge*
Smith, Simeon Christie, IV, *lawyer*
Wimberly, Beadie Reneau (Leigh Wimberly) *financial services executive*

Longville
Royer, Linda Bates *medical case manager*

Mandeville
Christian, John Catlett, Jr., *lawyer*
†Colomb, Marjorie Monroe *investor, volunteer*
Cressy, David Sarrat *lawyer*
Franke, Kathleen Eleanor *medical social worker*
†Huie, Roland Eugene, Jr., *director, music educator*
Lanclos, Ritchie Paul *petroleum engineer*
Landry, Joseph L., Jr., *retired affirmative action specialist*
Olivier, Jason (Jason Thomas Olivier) *lawyer*
Pittman, Jacquelyn *retired mental health nurse, nursing educator*
Treuting, Edna Gannon *retired nursing administrator*

Many
Byles, Robert Valmore *manufacturing company executive*
Dutton, Frank Elroy *data processing executive, writer*

Marksville
Riddle, Charles Addison, III, *district attorney, former state legislator*
Smith, Thomas Sullivan *humanities educator*
Spruill, Kerry Lyndon *judge*

Marrero
Blanchard, Bruce Roy *principal, minister*
Kenyon, Robert Wayne *career officer*
†Kushner, Frederick Gary *cardiologist, medical educator*
†Leftwich, Owen B. *ophthalmologist*

Merryville
†Joslin, Joe Edward, Jr., *secondary school educator*

Metairie
Album, Jerald Lewis *lawyer*
Ales, Beverly Gloria Rushing *artist*
†Andersson, Billie Venturatos *school learning specialist*
†Arthur, Jett Clinton *retired chemist*
Brooks, Aaron Lafette *football player*
Chambers, Thomas Edward *college president, psychologist*
Crosby, Deborah Berry *artist*
Derbes, Albert Joseph, III, *lawyer, accountant*
†Dinwiddie, Bruce Wayland *lawyer*
Doody, Barbara Pettett *computer specialist*
Doody, Louis Clarence, Jr., *accountant*
Dugan, Fortune Anthony *cardiologist, consultant*
Edisen, Clayton Byron *physician*
Evans, Carol Rockwell *nursing administrator*
†Evans, Pat Terrell *financial consultant*
Falco, Maria Josephine *political scientist, academic administrator*
Ford, Robert David *lawyer*
Friedman, Lynn Joseph *counselor*
Gauthier, Celeste Anne *lawyer*
Gereighty, Andrea Saunders *polling company executive, poet*
Grau, Shirley Ann (Mrs. James Kern Feibleman) *writer*
Grimm, John Lloyd *business executive, marketing strategist*
Hardy, Ashton Richard *lawyer*
Hartman, James Austin *retired geologist*
Haslett, Jim *professional football coach*
Haygood, John Warren *retired lawyer*
Horkowitz, Sylvester Peter *chemist*
Horton, Shearon Smith *piano educator*
Killeen, Edward Joseph *actor, designer*
Lake, Wesley Wayne, Jr., *internist, allergist, educator*
McAllister, Deuce *football player*
†Morcos, Ann Conti *Internet company executive, writer*
Nicoladis, Michael F. *engineering company executive*
Nuzum, Robert Weston *lawyer*
Ochsner, Seymour Fiske *radiologist, editor*
Reed, Jake *football player*
Rietschel, Robert Louis *dermatologist*
†St. John, Bridgette Alayne *secondary school educator*
Schwartz, Charles, Jr., *federal judge*
†Shikhris, Alexandra K. *music educator*
Weaver, Marshall Gueringer *lawyer*
Westerman, Albert Barry *marine surveyor and consultant*
Wood, Jonathan Stuart *economist, educator*

Minden
†Johnson, James McDade *lawyer*

Monroe
Cooksey, John Charles *former congressman, ophthalmic surgeon*
Curry, Robert Lee, III, *lawyer*
Fouts, Elizabeth Browne *psychologist, metals company executive*
Fouts, James Fremont *mining company executive*
Guy, William Achilles, Jr., (Rod Guy Jr.) *urban planner, economic development consultant*
†Harvey, Gordon Earl *historian, educator, writer*
†Long, Derle Ray *education educator*
McClanahan, Patsy Hitt *women's health nurse practitioner*
Sartor, Daniel Ryan, Jr., *lawyer*
Smith, Donald Raymond *librarian*
†Wall, Katharine (Adelle) *librarian*
Williamson, Stanley G. *management consultant, educator*
Zander, Arlen Ray *retired physics educator*

Morgan City
†Ramsey, Robert Scott, Jr., *lawyer*

Natchitoches
Egan, Shirley Anne *retired nursing educator*
Keller, Nadya Clark *retired biochemistry educator, researcher*
Smith, Jeffrey Robert *historian, educator*
†Thompson, J. Mark *music educator*
Wells, Carol McConnell *genealogist, retired archivist*
Wolfe, George Cropper *retired private school educator, artist, writer*

New Iberia
Grubbs, Conway E. *marine company executive*
Henton, Willis Ryan *retired bishop*

New Orleans
†Abaunza, Donald Richard *lawyer*
†Abbott, Hirschel Theron, Jr., *lawyer*
Abbott, Lawrence E. *lawyer*
†Acomb, Robert Bailey, Jr., *lawyer, educator*
Agrawal, Krishna Chandra *pharmacology educator*
Allen, Gary Curtiss *geology educator*
Alsobrook, Henry Bernis, Jr., *lawyer*
Amoss, W. James, Jr., *shipping company executive*
Amoss, Walter James (Jim), III, *editor*
Andrews, E. Wyllys *archaeologist, educator*
Angeles, Louis Dean *conductor*
†Angelico, Dennis Michael *lawyer*
Arshad, M. Kaleem *psychiatrist*
†Ates, J. Robert *lawyer*
†Autin, Nancy Pellerin *secondary school educator*
Babst, James A. *lawyer*
Bachmann, Richard Arthur *oil company executive*
Bacot, Marie *management consultant, researcher*
Bailey, Barry Stone *sculptor, educator*
Bald, Ronald James *military officer*
Balée, William L. *anthropology educator*
Barden, Janice Kindler *personnel company executive*
Barham, Mack Elwin *lawyer, educator*
Barnett, William Michael *lawyer*
†Baroni, Barry Joseph *law educator, mediator, arbitrator*
Barry, Francis Julian, Jr., *lawyer*
Barton, Fredrick Preston *English language educator, administrator*
Baudoin, Larry Anthony *academic administrator*
†Bayer, Thora Ilin *professor*
Beahm, Franklin D. *lawyer*
Beard, Elizabeth Letitia *physiologist, educator*
Beck, David Edward *surgeon*
Beck, William Harold, Jr., *lawyer*
Beer, Peter Hill *federal judge*
Bell, Bryan *real estate and oil investment executive, educator*
Belsom, John Anton (Jack Belsom) *writer, researcher*
Benerito, Ruth Rogan (Mrs. Frank H. Benerito) *chemist*
Benjamin, Adelaide Wisdom *community volunteer and activist, retired lawyer*
Benjamin, Edward Bernard, Jr., *lawyer*
Berenson, Gerald Sanders *physician*
†Berkett, Marian Mayer *lawyer*
Bertoniere, Noelie Rita *research chemist*
Best, Susan Marie *artist, educator*
Bhattacharyya, Ashim Kumar *pathology and physiology educator, researcher*
Bieck, Robert Barton, Jr., *lawyer*
Birtel, Frank Thomas *mathematician, philosopher, educator*
Boh, Robert Henry *civil engineer, construction company executive*
Bookhardt, Fred Barringer, Jr., *architect*
†Bordes, Jane S. *lawyer*
Boudreaux, Kenneth Justin *economics and finance educator, consultant*
Brazda, Frederick Wicks *pathologist, educator*
Brazier, Mary Margaret *psychology educator, researcher*
Bricker, Harvey Miller *anthropology educator*
Bricker, Victoria Reifler *anthropology educator*
Bronfin, Fred *lawyer*
Brown, Jerry A. *federal bankruptcy judge*
†Brumfield, William Craft *Slavic studies educator*
Bullard, Edgar John, III, *museum director*
Butcher, Bruce Cameron *lawyer*
Butler, Peter Joseph *lawyer*
Calogero, Pascal Frank, Jr., *judge*
Campeau, Richard John, Jr., *internal medicine and radiology educator*
Carey, Michael Emmett *neurosurgeon, educator*
Carter, James Clarence *university administrator*
Casellas, Joachim *art gallery executive*
Cefalu, Charles A. *medical educator*
†Chan, Albert W. *cardiologist*
Cheatwood, Roy Clifton *lawyer*
Childress, Steven Alan *law educator*
Claverie, Philip deVilliers *lawyer*
Clement, Edith Brown *federal judge*
Cody, Wilmer St. Clair *retired educational administrator, educational policy consultant*
Cohn, Isidore, Jr., *surgeon, educator*
Coleman, James Julian *lawyer*
Coleman, James Julian, Jr., *lawyer, industrialist, real estate executive*
Collins, Harry David *forensic specialist, mechanical engineer, nuclear engineer, claims consultant*
Collins, Richard Wayne *English literature educator*
Combe, John Clifford, Jr., *lawyer*
Connolly, Edward S. *neurological surgeon*
Cook, Victor Joseph, Jr., *marketing educator, consultant*
Corey, Orlin Russell *publisher, editor*
Correro, Anthony James, III, *lawyer*
Corrigan, James John, Jr., *pediatrician, dean*
Cospolich, James Donald *electrical engineering executive, consultant*
Cowen, Scott S. *academic administrator*
†Cramer, Cheryl Quave Wilson *not-for-profit developer, consultant*
Crumley, David Oliver *publisher, author, foundation executive*
Crumley, Martha Ann *company executive*
Crusto, Mitchell Ferdinand *lawyer, educator, consultant*
†Culbertson, Richard Allen *healthcare educator, health system director*
Curry, Dale Blair *journalist*
Dahlberg, Carl Fredrick, Jr., *entrepreneur*
Daniels, Robert Sanford *psychiatrist, administrator*
†Danner, William Bekurs *lawyer*

Saint Rose
Lennox, Edward Newman *holding company executive*

Schriever
Shaffer, Margaret Minor *retired library director*

Scott
Bergeron, Wilton Lee *physician*
Richard, Zachary *singer, songwriter, poet*

Shreveport
Albores-Saavedra, Jorge *pathologist, educator*
†Allen, Marguerite E. *legal association administrator*
†Andress, Will K. *music educator, conductor*
Arceneaux, M(artin) Thomas *lawyer*
Beaird, Charles T. *former publishing executive*
†Bellew, James William, Jr., *physical therapist, educator*
†Bogue, Ernest Grady *academic administrator, educator*
Bradley, Ronald James *neuroscientist*
†Brandl, Mary-Katherine *mathematics educator*
†Brannon, Guy Emilio *physician*
Bryant, J(ames) Bruce *lawyer*
Carmody, Arthur Roderick, Jr., *lawyer, director*
†Chastain, Merritt Banning, Jr., *lawyer*
Clark, James E. *lawyer*
Colón, Carlos Wildo *librarian*
†Conley, Dayspring Linder *retired music educator*
Conrad, Steven Allen *critical care and emergency physician, biomedical engineer, educator*
Cox, John Thomas, Jr., *lawyer*
Dhanireddy, Ramasubbareddy *neonatologist, researcher*
Driscoll, Barbara Hampton *special education educator*
†Feelisch, Martin *research scientist, consultant*
Fisher, Jacob Alexander Shultz *retired clergyman*
Fort, Arthur Tomlinson, III, *physician, educator*
Fort, Juliana Melody *psychiatrist*
Forte, Stephen Forrest *interior designer*
†Fowler, Marjorie Ellen Rees *pathologist*
Freeman, Arthur Merrimon, III, *psychiatry educator, dean*
Friend, William Benedict *bishop*
Gallagher, Patrick Timothy *emergency physician*
Ganley, James Powell *ophthalmologist, educator*
†German, Jeffrey Allen *physician*
Ghafourifar, Pedram *pharmacologist*
Goodman, Sylvia Klumok *volunteer*
Goorley, John Theodore *consulting chemist*
Green, Rachael Paulette *librarian*
Griffith, Robert Charles *allergist, educator, planter*
Haas, Lester Carl *retired architect*
Halliburton, John Robert *lawyer*
Harbuck, Edwin Charles *insurance agent*
Hardtner, Quintin Theodore, III, *lawyer*
†Hart, Michael Vincent *writer*
Heacock, Donald Dee *social worker*
Hetherwick, Gilbert Lewis *lawyer*
Hughes, Mary Sorrows *artist*
Hummel, Kay Jean *physical therapist*
James, Newell E. *music educator, musician*
Jamison, Richard Melvin *virologist, educator*
Joiner, Gary Dillard *cartographer, history educator, author*
Jones, Kenneth B., Jr., *surgeon*
Joshua, Percy *English educator*
Knight, Diane *special education educator*
Kolomytkin, Oleg *biophysicist, consultant*
Lazarus, Allan Matthew *retired newspaper editor*
Lenard, Lloyd Edgar *financial consultant*
Levine, Steven Neil *endocrinologist*
Li, Benjamin Dunlop *surgeon, researcher*
†Lin, Binshan *management educator*
Lloyd, Cecil Rhodes *pediatric dentist*
London, Steve Norman *obstetrician-gynecologist, educator*
Magness, Nan Jean *social services professional*
Mancini, Mary Catherine *cardiothoracic surgeon, researcher*
McDonald, John Clifton *surgeon*
Misra, Raghunath Prasad *physician, educator*
Morehead, Deborah Elizabeth Betts *gifted and talented educator, music educator*
Nichols, Carolyn Faye *scriptwriter*
O'Neal, Barron Johns *surgeon*
Payne, Roy Steven *judge*
Pederson, William David *political scientist, educator*
Pelton, James Rodger *librarian*
Perlman, Jerald Lee *lawyer*
Politz, Nyle Anthony *lawyer*
Ramey, Cecil Edward, Jr., *lawyer*
Robinson, Edna Earle *real estate company executive*
Robinson, Garry Lewin *television news executive*
St. Aubyn, Ronald Anthony *pediatrics nurse*
Shelby, James Stanford *cardiovascular surgeon*
Shemwell, Mary Anne *adapted physical education specialist*
Shemwell, Robert H. *federal judge*
Simons, Dennis *performing company executive*
Smith, Brian David *lawyer, educator*
Smith, Harriet Gwendolyn Gurley *secondary school educator, writer*
Staats, Thomas Elwyn *neuropsychologist*
Stagg, Tom *federal judge*
Stewart, Carl E. *federal judge*
†Sutton, Hal Evan *professional golfer*
Thomas, Bessie *primary education educator*
Van Savage, John G. *pediatric urologic and reconstructive surgeon*
†Watts, Jessica Milan *director*
†Webb, Donald Arthur *minister*
Whitlock, Laura Alice *research scientist*
Williams, Patsy Ruth *poet, freelance/self-employed writer*
Wolf, Robert Edward *physician, educator*
†Wood, Julienne Louise *school librarian, historian*
Woodman, Walter James *lawyer*
Wray, Geraldine Smitherman (Jerry Wray) *artist*

Wright, Marie Beulah Battey *retired advertising executive*
Zadeck, Donald Julian *oil and gas exploration company executive*

Slidell
Breeding, J. Ernest, Jr., (Sunny Breeding) *physicist, travel consultant, photographer, web master, webmaster*
Cotton, Joseph L *music educator*
Dearing, Reinhard Josef *city official*
Fishman, Louis *physicist, educator*
Hendricks, Donald Duane *retired school librarian*
†Jacob, Susan Marie *nurse*
†Laurent, Lynn Margaret *nurse*
McBurney, Elizabeth Innes *physician, educator*
Muller, Robert Joseph *gynecologist*
†Neale, Zahidi Sahaj *artist, educator*
Reinike, Irma *writer, fine artist, poet, lyricist*
Sanders, Georgia Elizabeth *secondary school educator*
Shamis, Edward Anthony, Jr., *lawyer*
Singletary, Alvin D. *lawyer*
Stroud, Robert Arlen *medical equipment company executive*
†Taylor, Rebecca Anne *librarian*
Tewell, Joseph Robert, Jr., *electrical engineer*
White, Elmer *physicist, researcher*

Springfield
Annable, Charles Roy *pathologist*
Carron, Ronald Joseph *electric power industry professional*

Springhill
Morgan, Larry Ronald *minister*

Thibodaux
Basham, Kay *music teacher*
Clement, Leslie Joseph, Jr., *lawyer*
Davis, Albert Joseph *languages and literature educator, novelist, poet*
Delahaye, Alfred Newton *retired journalism educator*
Fairchild, Joseph Virgil, Jr., *accounting educator*
Hulbert, Stephen Thompson *academic administrator*
Robichaux, John Wayne *art educator, writer*

Tioga
Brandow, Stephen Jon *priest*
Tenney, Tom Fred *bishop*

Vivian
Collier, Samuel Melvin *aerospace engineer*

West Monroe
Howard, Alton Johnathan *publishing company executive*
White, Coralie Heard *music educator*

Westlake
†Yarbrough, Frances Carole *music educator*

Westwego
Brehm, Loretta Persohn *secondary art educator, librarian, consultant*

Winnfield
Jones, Susie Mathis *social worker*
†Simmons, Kermit Mixon *lawyer*

MAINE

Allagash
Hafford, Faye O'Leary *writer*

Andover
Ellis, George Hathaway *retired banker and utility company executive*
Kaltsos, Angelo John *electronics executive, educator, photographer*

Auburn
†Abbott, Charles Henry *lawyer*
Bastow, Richard Frederick *civil engineer, educator, surveyor*
Clifford, Robert William *state supreme court justice*
McCann, Dervilla Mairin *physician, consultant*
Umpierre, Luz María *women studies educator, foreign language educator*

Augusta
Baldacci, John Elias *governor, former congressman*
Bennett, Richard A. *state senator*
Calkins, Susan W. *state supreme court justice*
Cheng, Hsueh Ching *physician*
Crate, Stephen Church *vocational rehabilitation specialist, consultant, author, politician*
Daggett, Beverly Clark *state legislator*
Dana, Howard H., Jr., *state supreme court justice*
Ehrenkrantz, David *medical researcher, researcher*
Gervais, Paul Nelson *foundation administrator, psychotherapist, public relations executive, author*
Gwadosky, Dan A. *secretary of state*
Huffman, Durward Roy *college system official, electrical engineer*
Jacobson, James Lamma, Jr., *data processing company executive*
†Jenkins, Pamela Lynn *music educator*
Ketterer, Andrew *state commissioner, former state attorney general*
Kilkelly, Marjorie Lee *state legislator, community development official*
Lyons, Charles M. *academic administrator*
Martin, John Lewis *state legislator*
Nickerson, John Mitchell *political science educator*
†Norman, Melora Ranney *library director, educator*

Phillips, Gwethalyn *political organization administrator*
Phillips, Joseph Robert *museum director*
†Raths, Barbara *political organization worker*
Roberts, Donald Albert *advertising, public relations, marketing and media consultant*
Rowe, G. Steven *state attorney general*
Wake, Robert Alan *lawyer*
Weil, Gordon Lee *energy executive, publishing executive*

Bangor
Albrecht, Ronald Lewis *financial services executive*
Ballesteros, Paula Mitchell *nurse*
Beaupain, Elaine Shapiro *psychiatric social worker*
Bennett, Rondi Kim Albrecht *financial services executive*
Bostwick, George Wallace *family practice physician, geriatrician*
Bullock, William Clapp, Jr., *banker*
†Coffman, Michael S. *international organization official*
Foster, Walter Herbert, Jr., *real estate company executive*
Gilbert, Charles E., III, *lawyer*
Gould, Edward Ward *lawyer*
Hsu, Yu Kao *aerospace scientist, mathematician, educator*
†King, Stephen Edwin *novelist, screenwriter, director*
Knight, Fred Barrows *forester, entomologist, educator*
Long, John Michael *neuroradiologist*
MacTaggart, Terrence Joseph *professor, former university chancellor*
McKinnon, Carolyn Ann *child care center director*
Moreau, James William *stuntman*
Moulton, Paul Rush *ophthalmologist*
Rea, Ann W. *librarian*
Rosen, Clifford James *internist*
Segal, Harvey Mordecai *physician*
Shubert, Dennis L. *neurosurgeon, medical administrator*
†Trobisch, David J. *religious studies educator*
Ward, Debora Elliott *psychologist*
†Warren, Richard Jordan *newspaper publisher*
Westphal, Joseph W. *academic administrator*

Bar Harbor
Carpenter, William Morton *English educator, writer*
Krevans, Julius Richard *university administrator, physician*
Leiter, Edward Henry *cell biologist*
Paigen, Kenneth *geneticist, science administrator*
Shultz, Leonard Donald *research scientist*
Swazey, Judith Pound *academic administrator, sociomedical science educator*
†Todd, Sean Kevin *science educator*
Woods, Bryant Prentice *national park ranger*

Bar Mills
Buchanan, Bruce *functional metal artist, photographer*

Bass Harbor
Ervin, Spencer *lawyer*

Bath
Dillon, Francis Richard *retired air force officer*
Field, Joseph Hooper *judge*
Simone, Gail Elisabeth *manufacturing administrator*
Stoudt, Howard Webster *biological anthropologist, human factors specialist, consultant*
†Watson, Thomas Riley *lawyer, state legislator*

Belfast
Coller, Robert Burton *music educator, musician*
Griffith, Patricia King *journalist*
Kennedy, Ronald Craig *anesthesiologist*
Porter, Bernard Harden *consulting physicist, author, publisher*

Belgrade Lakes
Kany, Judy C(asperson) *health policy analyst, former state senator*

Bethel
Farrar, Susan Clement *choreographer, performing company executive, writer*

Biddeford
Crockett, Ann Hemenway *psychotherapist*
Featherman, Sandra *university president, political science educator*
Ford, Charles Willard *health science educator*
Kimball, Judith Giencke *occupational therapist, educator*
†Riley, Pamela Janerico *artist*
†Rothermel, Dan *humanities educator*
Shannon, Stephen Curtis *dean, occupational health physician*

Blue Hill
Evans, Howard Morgan *acupuncturist, zero balancer*
Taylor, Robert Larry *author, freelance writer*

Blue Hill Falls
Stookey, Noel Paul *folksinger, composer*

Boothbay Harbor
Cavanaugh, Tom Richard *artist, antiques dealer, retired art educator*

Bremen
Wilson, Linda Smith *academic administrator*

Brewer
Ebitz, Elizabeth Kelly *lawyer*

Bridgton
Dunbar, Shirley Eugenia-Doris *small business owner, author, lecturer*

Bristol
Sabin, William Albert *writer*

Brooklin
Meserve, Mollie Ann *publisher*
Schmidt, Klaus Dieter *management consultant, university administrator, marketing and management educator*
Schmidt, Lynda Wheelwright *psychotherapist*

Brooksville
Sutherland, Malcolm Read, Jr., *clergyman, educator*

Brownfield
Kloskowski, Vincent John, Jr., *educational consultant, writer, educator*

Brunswick
†Antolini, Anthony Frederick *music educator, editor*
Ault, James Mase *bishop*
Crandall, Elizabeth Walbert *home economics educator*
Fiori, Michael J. *pharmacist*
Fitzgerald, John Michael *economist, educator*
Fuchs, Alfred Herman Herman *psychologist, educator*
Geoghegan, William Davidson *religion educator, minister*
Greason, Arthur LeRoy, Jr., *retired university administrator*
Guay, David Adalbert *biology educator*
Heiser, Nancy E. *freelance/self-employed writer, coach*
Hodge, James Lee *German language educator*
King, Angus S., Jr., *former governor*
Lamothe, Arthur J. *lawyer*
Martin, Harold Clark *humanities educator*
Morgan, Richard Ernest *political scientist, educator*
Nagle, Jeffrey Karl *chemist, educator*
Owen, H. Martyn *lawyer*
Pfeiffer, Sophia Douglass *state legislator, lawyer*
Riley, Matilda White (Mrs. John W. Riley Jr.) *sociologist*
Rosser, Richard Franklin *higher education consultant*
Schwartz, Elliott Shelling *composer, author, music educator*
Tucker, Allen Brown, Jr., *computer science educator*
†Yarbrough, Jean Mary *political science educator*

Bucksport
Ives, Edward Dawson *folklore educator*
Williams, Christine Hewes *elementary education educator*

Camden
Cagle, William Rea *librarian*
Daly, Daniel Anthony *artist, illustrator*
Dyer, Barbara F. *retired accountant, writer*
Fisher, Craig Becker *film and television executive*
Jenks, Glenn Arnold *musician, educator*
Moran, Elizabeth Ames *library director*
Russo, Richard *writer*
Smith, J(ames) Brian *education specialist and researcher, writer*
Thomas, Karin Ronnefeldt *interior designer*

Canton
Parsons, Lorraine Leighton *nurse, child care professional*

Cape Elizabeth
Cotter, Joseph Francis *retired hotel and bank executive*
Dalbeck, Richard Bruce *insurance executive*
Simonds, Stephen Paige *former state legislator*

Caribou
Bosse, Denise Frances *educational administrator, education educator*
Davis, Norman M. *poet, writer*
Swanson, Shirley June *emergency room nurse, travel nurse, adult education educator*

Castine
Berleant, Arnold *philosopher*
Davis, Peter Frank *filmmaker, author*
Hall, David *sound archivist, writer*
Hoople, Sally Crosby *retired humanities and communications educator*
Mancuso, Leni *artist, poet, educator*
Wiswall, Frank Lawrence, Jr., *lawyer, educator*

Center Lovell
Adams, Herbert Ryan *mediation consultant, retired clergyman, educator, publishing executive*

Cumberland Center
Brewster, Linda Jean *family nurse practitioner*
Taylor, Joseph B. *former state legislator*
Thomas, Charles Carroll *retired investment management executive*

Cumberland Foreside
Dill, William Rankin *college president*

Cushing
Magee, A. Alan *artist*

Damariscotta
Blake, Bud (Julian Watson) *cartoonist*
Fuller, Melvin Stuart *botany educator*
Swanson, Karin *hospital administrator, consultant*

Deer Isle
Smith, Gardner Watkins *physician*

Dixmont
Cummings, James William *poet*

Dover Foxcroft
†Poland, Arnold Livermore *music educator*
†Young-Coombs, Esther Elizabeth (Betsey Eveleth, Betsey L. Eveleth) *poet*

Dresden
Turco, Lewis Putnam *English educator*

East Blue Hill
†Weinberg, Holly Bartlett *music educator*

East Boothbay
Eldred, Kenneth McKechnie *acoustical consultant*
Peters, Andrea Jean *artist*

East Millinocket
Michaud, Michael Herman *congressman*

East Vassalboro
LaFleur, Kenneth Gordon *retired minister*

Eastport
Kennedy, Robert Spayde *electrical engineering educator*

Edgecomb
Carlson, Suzanne Olive *architect*
†Wait, Eleanor (Lea) Sally *writer*

Eliot
Lawrence, Mark W. *former state legislator, lawyer*

Ellsworth
Becker, Ray Everett *management consultant*
Eaton, Candace Johnson *program director*

Falmouth
Cabot, Lewis Pickering *manufacturing company executive, art consultant*
†Curran, Richard Emery, Jr., *lawyer*
Kendrick, Peter Murray *communications executive, investor*
McCoy, Carol P. *psychologist, training executive*
Pierce, Philip Sargent *clinical psychologist*
Rohsenow, Warren Max *retired mechanical engineer, educator*
Singer, Richard Bunker *physician, medical risk consultant*
Sommer, Robert Georg *dermatologist*

Farmington
Holman, Joseph Frederick *retired lawyer*
Kalikow, Theodora June *university president*
Melcher, James Patrick *political scientist, educator*

Fort Fairfield
Shapiro, Joan Isabelle *laboratory administrator, nurse*

Freeport
†Gorman, Leon A. *mail order company executive*
†Nass, Meryl J. *physician, writer, research scientist*
Sidar, Thomas Wilson *retail executive*

Friendship
Owen, Wadsworth *oceanographer, consultant*

Gardiner
Gosline, Norman Abbot *real estate appraiser, consultant*

Georgetown
Chapin, Maryan Fox *civic worker*
Ludgin, Donald Hugh *editor*

Gorham
Bearce, Jeana Dale *artist, educator*
Fall, Marijane Eaton *counselor educator*

Gray
Nickerson, Bruce Donald *medical services administrator*

Greenville
Pepin, John Nelson *materials research and design engineer*

Hallowell
MacLean, Neil V. *forensic psychologist*

Hampden
Karlson, Donna Mae *clinical social worker*

Hancock
Silvestro, Clement Mario *museum director, historian*

Harpswell
Bird, Henry Lonsdale *biologist, priest*

Hartland
†Gard, Trudy May *pre-school educator, writer*
Larochelle, Richard C. *tanning company executive*

Hollis Center
Kaake, Norman Bradford *quality assurance professional*

Houlton
†Sylvester, Torrey Alden *lawyer*

Islesboro
Maes, John Leopold *theologian, psychologist, educator*
Rogers, William Raymond *college president emeritus, psychology educator*

Jonesport
Komp, Richard Joseph *solar scientist*

Kennebunk
Damon, Edmund Holcombe *retired plastics company executive*
Escalet, Frank Diaz *art gallery owner, artist, educator*
Sholl, John Gurney, III, *physician*

Kennebunkport
Entorf, Richard Carl *retired management consultant*
Featherman, Bernard *steel company executive*
Mulvihill, James Edward *periodontist, educator*
Ray, Virginia H. S. *columnist, writer*

Kingfield
†Collins, H(erschel) Douglas *retired physician*

Kittery
Clark, Sandra Ann *clinical social worker*
McNally, James Henry *physicist, defense consultant*
†Neilson, Hope Brinser *librarian*

Kittery Point
Howells, William White *anthropology educator*

Lewiston
†Decker, Craig J. *German educator, translator, researcher*
Dennison, Gerard Francis *economic analyst*
Hansen, Elaine T. *academic administrator*
†Harward, Donald West *retired academic administrator*
Kessler, Mark Allen *political scientist, educator*
Le, Phuoc Hong *internist, consultant*
Murray, Michael Peter *economist, educator*
Payne, Jean L. *writer*

Limerick
Stewart, Harold T. *social worker, consultant*

Lincoln
Kneeland, Douglas Eugene *retired newspaper editor*

Lincolnville
Swanson, Harry Frederick *artist*
Williams, Robert Luther *city planning consultant*

Little Deer Isle
Mills, David Harlow *psychologist, association executive*

Lubec
Hayes, Ernest M. *podiatrist*
Hudson, Miles *retired special education educator*

Machiasport
Norton, Clifford M., Jr., *minister*

Manchester
Clark, Beth *minister*
Moody, Stanley Alton *entrepreneur, financial consultant*

Medway
Klein, Kathryn Ann *social worker*

Milbridge
Enslin, Theodore Vernon *poet*

Monmouth
Greenham, David *theater administrator*

Mount Desert
Crawford, Richard Bradway *biologist, biochemist, educator*
Singleton, Francis Seth *international educator*

New Gloucester
†Jaccaci, August Thayer, Jr., *architect, educator*

New Harbor
Lyford, Cabot *sculptor*
†Woolf-Wade, Sarah Jane *retired elementary school educator, writer*

New Vineyard
Smith, Frederick Orville, II, *wood products manufacturer, retired naval officer*

Newburgh
Berardelli, Catherine Marie *women's health nurse, nurse educator*

Newcastle
Waterman, Charles Albert *actor, director, retired sales executive*

Nobleboro
Birkett, James Davis *management consultant*
Fisher, Allan Campbell *retired railway executive*
Fisher, Ellen Roop *retired librarian, educator*

North Haven
White, Jerry T. *academic administrator*

North Yarmouth
Fecteau, Rosemary Louise *educational administrator, educator, consultant*
Kuhrt, Sharon Lee *nursing administrator*

Oakland
Asmussen, J. Donna *retired educational administrator, researcher, artist*
Rhein, Kevin Douglas *music educator*

Ogunquit
Carpenter, George Robert *artist*
West, Norman Ellsworth *artist*

Old Orchard Beach
Fowler, Daniel L.T. *legal services executive*

Old Town
Alex, Joanne DeFilipp *educator Montesorri school*

Orono
Barkan, Steven Edward *sociology educator*
Borns, Harold William, Jr., *geologist, educator*
Boyle, Kevin John *economics educator, consultant*
†Bradley, David Michael *mathematician, educator*
Chute, Harold LeRoy *veterinary pathologist, former chemical company executive*
Cohn, Steven Frederick *sociology educator, consultant*
Devino, William Stanley *economist, educator*
Ellis, William Grenville, Jr., *marine biologist, educator*
†Estler, Suzanne E. *education educator*
Goldstone, Sanford *psychology educator*
Hatlen, Burton Norval *English educator*
†Hess, Charles T. *education educator*
Hoff, Peter Sloat *academic administrator*
MacDonald, Elizabeth Helen *bassoonist, educator*
†MacDougall, Pauleena Mary *education educator, researcher*
Mahon, John Francis *management policy educator*
Martindale, Colin Eugene *psychology educator, author*
Munson, Henry Lee, Jr., *anthropologist, educator*
Norton, Stephen Allen *geological sciences educator*
Rauch, Charles Frederick, Jr., *retired university official and business educator*
†Rice, Edward Perry *secondary school educator*
†Risberg, Erica Lynn *archivist, film producer*
Rogers, Deborah Dee *English language educator*
†See, Scott William *history educator*
Segal, Howard Paul *history educator*
†Teisl, Mario F. *economics educator, researcher*
Weiss, Robert Jerome *psychiatrist, educator*
Wiersma, G. Bruce *dean, forest resources educator*

Orrington
Snyder, Arnold Lee, Jr., *retired air force officer, research director*

Orrs Island
Nelson, Robert Louis *lawyer*

Palermo
Anderson, Alfred Oliver *mathematician, consultant*
Robbins, Marjorie Jean Gilmartin *elementary education educator*

Pemaquid
Howell, Jeanette Helen *retired cultural organization administrator*

Perry
Breckinridge, Michael Frederick *pharmacist*

Pittsfield
†Eliopoulos, Barbara J. *health facility administrator, medical/surgical nurse*

Port Clyde
Duarte, Patricia M. *real estate and insurance broker*

Portland
Alexander, Donald G. *state supreme court justice*
Anderson, Stephen Mills *investment broker*
Becker, Seymour *hazardous materials and wastes specialist*
Bohan, Thomas Lynch *physicist, lawyer*
†Boyle, John Edward Whiteford *cultural organization administrator*
Boyson, Michael Andrew *investment consultant*
Bradford, Carl O. *judge*
Braithwaite, Karl Royden *dean*
Bucci, Thomas Vincent *music educator, pianist, composer*
Buckley, Paul Richard *insurance executive*
Burgess, Meredith Nancy Strang *advertising agency executive*
Candage, Howard Everett *insurance management consultant, agent, broker*
Carter, Gene *judge*
Chow, Amy *gymnast, Olympic athlete*
Clark, David Eugene *surgeon*
Clark, Gordon Hostetter, Jr., *physician*
Coffin, Frank Morey *judge*
Coggeshall, Bruce Amsden *lawyer*
†Courtney, Ann M. *lawyer*
Culley, Peter William *lawyer*
Donaldson, Leigh *writer, editor*
†Farrington, Hugh G. *wholesale food and retail drug company executive*
Fenton, Clarence Asa *healthcare facility administrator*
Firestone, Deborah Ilene *publishing executive*
Frank, William Fielding *computer systems design executive, consultant*
†Friedrich, Craig William *lawyer*
Gerry, Joseph John *bishop*
Gilmore, Roger *college consultant*
Glassman, Caroline Duby *state supreme court justice*
Graffam, Ward Irving *lawyer*
†Groom, Robert Craig *perfusionist*
Hansel, Gregory Paul *lawyer*
†Harte, Christopher McCutcheon *investment manager*
†Harvey, Charles Albert, Jr., *lawyer*
Henshaw, Nathaniel Venable *venture capitalist*
Hornby, David Brock *federal judge*
Hotelling, David Rawson *endocrinologist, educator*
Hunt, David Evans *lawyer*
Ingalls, Everett Palmer, III, *lawyer*
Kaplan, David K. *emergency physician, educator*
†Keenan, James Francis *lawyer*

Konkel, Harry Wagner *civic volunteer, retired career officer*
Lancaster, Ralph Ivan, Jr., *lawyer*
LeBlanc, Richard Philip *lawyer*
Lehman, Kenneth William *lawyer*
Lipez, Kermit V. *federal judge, former state supreme court justice*
Louden, Robert Burton *philosopher, educator*
†Martin, Joel Clark *lawyer*
Massaua, John Roger *retail executive*
McHold, Sharon Lawrence *lawyer, mediator*
McKusick, Vincent Lee *former state supreme court chief justice, lawyer, arbitrator, mediator*
Miller, Buffy *dancer*
Morgan, Robin Evonne *poet, author, journalist, activist, editor*
†Neagle, Christopher Scott *lawyer*
Neavoll, George Franklin *writer*
†O'Brien, John Matthew *psychologist, educator*
†O'Leary, John *ambassador*
Pattenaude, Richard Louis *university administrator*
†Powers, Ross *Olympic athlete*
Rogers, Richard Mead *food service executive*
Rundlett, Ellsworth Turner, III, *lawyer*
†Russell, Robert Jackson *music educator, conductor*
Schwanauer, Francis *philosopher, educator*
Smith, Robert Pease, Jr., *physician*
Smith, William Charles *lawyer*
Stauffer, Eric P. *lawyer*
Wathen, Daniel Everett *former state supreme court chief justice*
Watts, Helen Caswell *civil engineer*
Weir, Anne *writer*
Whedon, Ralph Gibbs *manufacturing executive*
White, Jeffrey Munroe *lawyer*
Whiting, Stephen Clyde *lawyer*
Zarr, Melvyn *lawyer, law educator*

Presque Isle
Barrett, Paul J. *pharmacist*
†Cunningham, Shawn Petrice *TV anchor*
Knopp, Michael A. *chemist, educator*

Princeton
Newman, Frederick J. *writer*

Rangeley
Gallant, Roy Arthur *writer, education educator*

Raymond
Coughlan, Patrick Campbell *lawyer, mediator*

Readfield
Fontes, Ronald Hogue *writer*

Rockland
Collins, Samuel W., Jr., *judge*
Thivierge, Bethany *biomedical technical writer, editor*
Ziegelaar, Bob W. *transportation executive*

Rockport
Goodwin, Doris Helen Kearns *history educator, writer*
†Hinrichs, Stephen Ernest *education educator, consultant*
Merrill, Mary Lee *professional society administrator*

Sanford
Allan, Jonathan David *autograph dealer, pop culture historian*
Collins, Thomas Michael *surgeon*
Will, Jerrie Ann *psychologist*

Scarborough
Connolly, Elaine Alexander Paterson *nurse*
Devlin, John Tobey *physician, educator*
†Durham, Dona Anita *special education educator*
†Hayden, Lisa C. *interpreter, translator, language educator, writer*
Raisbeck, Gordon *systems engineer, consultant*
Sadik, Marvin Sherwood *art consultant, former museum director*
Shire, Donald Thomas *retired air products and chemicals executive, lawyer*
†Shulman, Richard *musician, composer, recording industry executive*
Warg, Pauline *artist, educator*

Seal Cove
Young, David Michael *biochemistry and molecular biology educator, physician*

Seal Harbor
Forbes, Peter *architect*

Sebago Lake
Murray, Wallace Shordon *publisher, educator*

Sedgwick
Becker, Robert Clarence *retired clergyman*
Donnell, William Ray *small business owner, communications executive*
Schroth, Thomas Nolan *editor*

Sidney
Tietenberg, Thomas *economist, department chairman*

Skowhegan
†Ross, James Owen *education educator, researcher*

South Bristol
Wells, Arthur Stanton *retired manufacturing company executive*

South Paris
Martin, Charles Seymour *middle school educator*

South Portland
Cotton, Joyce E. Doherty *mental health nurse*
Fetteroll, Eugene Carl, Jr., *human resources professional*

Harris, Penny Smith fundraising consultant
Martin, Joseph Robert corporate financial executive
Wheeler, Hewitt Brownell surgeon, educator

Spruce Head
Bird, Mary Alice fund raising consultant

Starks
Medeiros, M. Joyce community health educator

Stoneham
Meka, Gail Jean chemist, consultant

Stratton
Gray, R(obert) J(ames), Jr., printmaker, editor

Sumner
Rudd, David William management consultant, engineer, consultant

Sunset
Knowlton, Leslie Brooks journalist

Surry
Kilgore, John Edward, Jr., former petroleum company executive
Pickett, Betty Horenstein psychologist
Sopkin, George cellist, music educator

Tenants Harbor
Bates, John Cecil, Jr., lawyer
Quint-Rose, Marylin Iris artist

Topsham
Arnold, Charles Burle, Jr., psychiatrist, writer

Trevett
Bettinson, Brenda artist, educator
Mathias, Cordula art dealer

Union
Perrin, Arnold Strong writer, editor

Vassalboro
Schad, Vicki Jean Reynolds piano teacher

Veazie
Kennedy, Robert Alan educational administrator

Waterford
Stockwell, William F. fundraiser, management consultant

Waterville
Adams, WilliaM D. academic administrator
Bassett, Charles Walker English language educator
Bhatnagar, Hemendra Narain otolaryngologist
Cook, Susan Farwell associate director planned giving
†Desrosiers, Muriel C. music educator, retired nursing consultant
Fleming, James Rodger science historian, educator
Gemery, Henry Albert economics educator
Gilkes, Cheryl Louise Townsend sociologist, educator, minister
Laurence, Robert Lionel chemical engineering educator
†Moroni, Mario humanities educator
Roisman, Hanna Maslovski classics educator
Tormollan, Gary Gordon health facility administrator, physical therapist

Wells
Carleton, Joseph George, Jr., lawyer, state legislator
Hanrahan, Joyce Yancey educational consultant, antiquarian bookseller
Hero, Barbara Ferrell visual and sound artist, writer
†Lahar, Cindy J. psychologist, educator

West Baldwin
Simmonds, Rae Nichols musician, composer, educator

West Southport
Barker, Walter William, Jr., artist, waiter

Westbrook
†Hammond, Jeremy Marshall engineer, educator
Lee, Shepard automobile dealership owner
Parks, George Richard librarian

Whitefield
Marden, Kenneth Allen advertising executive

Windham
Mulvey, Mary Crowley retired adult education director, gerontologist, senior citizen association administrator

Wiscasset
Plante, Paul Joseph metallurgical engineer

Yarmouth
Bischoff, David Canby retired university dean
Grover, Mark Donald computer scientist
Hart, Loring Edward academic administrator
Haynes, Peter Lancaster retired utility executive
Mansmann, Paris Taylor medical educator

York
Berlew, Frank Kingston lawyer
Hallam, Beverly (Beverly Linney) artist
Lauter, M. David family physician
Lyman, William Welles, Jr., retired architect
†Redfield, Sarah Erlick law educator
Smart, Mary-Leigh Call (Mrs. J. Scott Smart) civic worker

York Beach
Foerster, Richard Alfons editor, poet

York Harbor
Rust, Libby Karen fundraising and public relations counsel

MARYLAND

Aberdeen
de Rosset, William S. physicist

Aberdeen Proving Ground
†Berry, Patrick Lowell chemical engineer
Carrieri, Arthur Helmut physicist, researcher
Cozby, Richard Scott electronics engineer, military officer
†Doesburg, John C. military career officer
Evans, Edward Spencer, Jr., entomologist
Gibson, Annemarie writer, editor
Gupta, Aaron Das mechanical engineer
†Howard, Stephen L. chemical engineer
Miziolek, Andrzej Wladyslaw research physicist
Sliney, David Hammond medical physicist
Smith, John Richard analytical chemist
Sommer, Valerie Kulis occupational health nurse
Steger, Ralph James chemist
Stuebing, Edward Willis research scientist
Tobin, Aileen Webb educational administrator

Abingdon
Wolf, Martin Eugene lawyer, educator

Accokeek
Beddow, Richard Harold judge

Adamstown
Church, Martha Eleanor retired academic administrator, scholar
Munson, John Christian acoustician
Tidball, Charles Stanley computer scientist, educator

Adelphi
Brandt, Howard Edward physicist
Chang, Sam Shifeng meteorologist
Gaunaurd, Guillermo C. physicist, engineer, researcher
Heeger, Gerald Arthur university president
Kendrick, Kerry military officer
Kirwan, William English, II, mathematics educator, university official, academic administrator
†Mait, Joseph N. electrical engineer, educator
†Smith, Doran Dakota physicist
Sutherland, Alan Roy business educator
Torrieri, Don Joseph electronics engineer, mathematician, researcher
Whalin, Robert W. physicist

Annapolis
Alderdice, Cynthia Lou artist
Ames, Steven Reede financial planner
Anderson, William Carl association executive, environmental engineer, consultant
†Aumann, R. Karl state official, lawyer
Battaglia, Lynne Ann judge
†Beckman, John literature educator, novelist
Behrens, James William physicist, administrator, author
Bontoyan, Warren Roberts chemist, state laboratories administrator
†Branand, Claire Diane advertising executive, writer
†Brann, Eva Toni Helene educator
Brendle, Gary Allen, Sr., landscape architect
Brunk, William Edward astronomer
Burns, B. Darren lawyer
†Busch, Michael state legislator
Cann, Nancy Timanus retail yacht sales executive
Carman, Anne management consultant
Casey, Edward Dennis newspaper editor
Castleyoung, Brenda social worker, mental health nurse
Cathell, Dale Roberts judge
Chambers, Ronald D. book publishing executive
Clotworthy, John Harris oceanographic consultant
Conwell, John Fredrick lawyer
Cooper, Sherod Monroe, Jr., retired English literature educator
Core, Mary Carolyn W. Parsons health facility administrator
Coulter, James Bennett state official
†Crawford, Carol Gloria mathematician, educator
Crosby, Ralph Wolf communications executive
†Dembrow, Dana Lee lawyer
DiAiso, Robert Joseph civil engineer
DiPentima, Renato Anthony systems executive
†Duckett, Warren Bird, Jr., lawyer
Duncan, Charles Tignor lawyer
Ehrlich, Robert L., Jr., governor, former congressman
Eldridge, John Cole judge
Ellis, George Fitzallen, Jr., retired energy services company executive
Essandoh, Louis Kofi cardiologist
Evans, William Davidson, Jr., lawyer
Finerty, Martin Joseph, Jr., military officer, researcher, association management executive
Frantzich, Stephen Edward political science educator
Fry, Virginia Milne artist, poet
Gavian, Peter Wood investment banker
Gurr, Ted Robert political science educator, author
Halpern, Joseph Alan physician
Hammer, Jacob Myer physicist, consultant
Holston, A. Frank retired broadcaster, communications educator
Hoyer, Leon William physician, educator
Hyde, Lawrence Henry, Jr., industrial company executive
†Jacobs, Linda Joan educator
Jansson, John Phillip architect, consultant
Jefferson, Ralph Harvey international affairs consultant
Johnson, Bruce engineering educator
†Jones, Sylvanus Benson adjudicator, consultant, lawyer
†Kane, John political organization administrator
Katz, Douglas Jeffrey retired naval officer, consultant
Kelley, Delores Goodwin state legislator
†Klein, Robert Dale lawyer
Konkowski, Deborah Ann mathematics educator
Kozlowski, Ronald Stephan librarian
Kushner, Jack retired physician executive
Levitan, Laurence lawyer, former state senator
Libber, Samuel Mogul pediatrician
Lillard, John Franklin, III, lawyer
Love, Mary Ann E. state legislator
Lucas, George Ramsdell, Jr., philosophy educator
Lucas, Steven Mitchell lawyer
Madden, Martin Gerard former state legislator
Marienthal, George telecommunications company executive
McGuirk, Ronald Charles retired banker, economic advisor
Meima, Ralph Chester, Jr., retired diplomat, corporate executive
Menes, Pauline H. state legislator
†Michaelson, Benjamin, Jr., lawyer, director
Miller, John Grider writer
Miller, Richards Thorn naval architect, engineer
Miller, Thomas V. Mike, Jr., state legislator
Moellering, John Henry aviation maintenance company executive
Mumford, Willard Royal engineering educator, educational consultant
Nelson, Charles Arthur publisher, author
Otte, Lynda Ellen neonatal nurse
Palmer, Timothy Trow safety and health consultant
Papenfuse, Edward Carl, Jr., archivist, state official
Perkins, Roger Allan lawyer
Prout, George Russell, Jr., medical educator, urologist
Rogers, David Freeman aerospace engineering educator
Rogers, Wayne L. political organization administrator
Ross, Thomas Hugh business consultant, retired military officer
Ruben, Ida Gass state senator
†Ruth, John Nicholas lawyer, insurance company executive
Schleicher, Nora Elizabeth banker, treasurer, accountant
Smith, Robert Myron investment company executive
Stahl, David Edward trade association administrator, retired
†Steele, Michael lieutenant governor
Stern, Margaret Bassett retired special education educator, author
†Strother, Thomas W. military officer, educator
Swan, William Irving nutritionist
Teitelbaum, Leonard H. state legislator
Thoms, Josephine Bowers artist, illustrator
Trescott, Sara Lou water resources engineer
Trost, Carlisle Albert Herman retired naval officer
Tuttle, Kenneth Lewis engineering educator, consultant
Van De Mark, Brian historian, educator
Walman, A. Terry physician, lawyer
Welch, Robert Bond ophthalmologist, educator
Werking, Richard Hume librarian, historian, academic administrator
Whitford, Dennis James naval officer, meteorologist, oceanographer
Wilkes, Joseph Allen architect
Wolf, Alfred A. physicist, educator
†Wright, David Lawrence realtor, real estate broker
†Yee, Cordell D.K. cartographer, educator
Zhu, Jian Zhong computational engineer

Arbutus
Maloney, Charles Wayne gunsmith

Arnold
Brandimore, Wadie Miller retired pediatrics nurse
France, Mary Pearre rehabilitation nurse, consultant
Harris, Roger Clark psychiatrist, consultant
†Irwin, Jennifer Vogel education educator
Kellogg-Smith, Peter sculptor, educator
Kolb, Joyce Diana artist, educator
Rosen, Susan A. C. English language educator
Smith, Robert Gillen retired political science consultant
Williams, James Arthur retired army officer, information systems company executive
Yarrow, C. W. fund raiser

Ashton
Lundsager, Christian Bent retired mechanical engineer, consultant
Tabler, Shirley May retired librarian, artist
Whelan, Roger Michael lawyer, educator

Baldwin
Decker, James Ludlow management consultant

Baltimore
Abel, Francis Lee physiology educator
Achinstein, Peter Jacob philosopher, educator
Adams, Harold Lynn architect
Adkinson, N. Franklin, Jr., clinical immunologist
†Aisenstark, Avery lawyer, educator
†Alberg, Anthony J. epidemiologist
Albert, Ira Bernard social sciences educator
Albuquerque, Edson Xavier pharmacology educator
Allan, Janet D. dean
Allen, Norma Ann librarian, educator
Allen, Ronald John astrophysics educator, researcher
Alonso, Diane Lindwarm cognitive psychologist
Alpern, Linda Lee Wevodau health agency administrator
†Anderson, Brady Kevin professional baseball player
†Anderson, Gary Dean architect, planner, educator
†Anderson, Gerard Fenton economist, university program administrator
Angelos, Peter G. professional sports team executive, lawyer
Antokol-Meckler, Shirley humanities educator
Aranovich, Gregory chemical engineering educator, researcher
Archibald, James Kenway lawyer
Arnick, John Stephen lawyer, legislator
Arsham, Hossein operations research analyst
Baker, R. Robinson surgeon
Baker, Susan P. public health educator
Baker, Timothy Danforth physician, educator
Baker, William Parr lawyer
Baldwin, Henry Furlong banker
Baldwin, John Wesley history educator
Baramki, Theodore Atallah gynecologist, reproductive endocrinologist
†Barnes, Kathleen Carole medical educator
Barnhart, Jo Anne B. federal agency administrator
Barnhill, Gregory Hurd investment banker
Barnow, Burt S. economist
Bartlett, James Wilson, III, lawyer
Bartlett, John Gill infectious disease physician
Bass, Scott Arthur community psychologist, gerontologist, educator
Baumgartner, William Anthony cardiac surgeon
Bausell, R. Barker, Jr., research methodology educator
Bayless, Theodore M(orris) gastroenterologist, educator, researcher
Beasley, Robert Scott financial executive
Behm, Mark Edward university administrator, consultant
Beilenson, Peter Lowell public health official
Bell, Robert M. state supreme court justice
Bellack, Alan Scott clinical psychologist
†Belle, Albert Jojuan professional baseball player
†Benitez, Robert Michael medical educator, cardiologist
Berger, Bruce Warren physician, urologist
Berger, Daniel retired newswriter
Bergey, Gregory Kent neurology educator, neuroscientist
Berlage, Jan Ingham lawyer
Bero, Joseph Martin manufacturing engineer
Bever, Christopher Theodore, Jr., neurologist
†Bhardwaj, Anish neuroscientist, medical educator
Bigelow, George E. psychology and pharmacology scientist
†Birt, Robert Earl philosophy educator, writer
†Biser-Rohrbaugh, Ann K. physician assistant
Black, Walter Evan, Jr., federal judge
Blakeslee, Wesley Daniel lawyer, consultant
Blanton, Edward Lee, Jr., lawyer
†Block, James A. hospital administrator, pediatrician
Boardman, John Michael mathematician, educator
†Bogen, David Skillen law educator
Bohr, Vilhelm Alfred laboratory chief
Bolger, Doreen museum director
Bowen, Lowell Reed lawyer
Bowman, Donald Eugene investment counselor
Braddy, Vanessa F. civil engineer
Bradley, Wanda Louise librarian
Bradshaw, Cynthia Helene educational administrator
Brady, Joseph Vincent behavioral biologist, educator
Breazeale, Helene arts administrator, educator
Bredar, James Kelleher judge
Brem, Henry neurosurgeon, educator, researcher
Brewer, Nevada Nancy elementary education educator
Brewster, Gerry Leiper educator, lawyer
Brieger, Gert Henry medical historian, educator
Bright, Margaret sociologist
†Brodie, Angela M. biomedical researcher, educator
Brodie, M. J. (Jay Brodie) architect, city planner, government executive
Brody, Eugene Bloor psychiatrist, educator
Brody, William Ralph academic administrator, radiologist, educator
Broening, Walter Stephens, Jr., journalist, history educator
Brown, Donald David biology educator
Brown, John Eugene social science educator, minister
†Browne, Lovetie W. special education educator, small business owner
Bruner, William Gwathmey, III, lawyer
†Brushart, Thomas Marshall hand surgeon, neuroscience researcher
Brusilow, Saul pediatrics researcher
Buccino, Daniel L. psychotherapist, consultant
Bucher, Richard David sociology educator
Burch, Francis Boucher, Jr., lawyer
Busch-Vishniac, Ilene Joy mechanical engineering educator, researcher
Buser, Carolyn Elizabeth correctional education administrator
Byron, William James author, management educator, researcher, former university president
Cacossa, Anthony Alexander Romance languages educator
Cain, Marcena Jean Beesley retail executive
†Califano, III, Joseph physician
Campbell, Jacquelyn C. community health nurse
†Campe, Rüdiger humanities educator
Carbine, James Edmond lawyer
Carducci, Michael Anthony oncologist, educator
Carey, Anthony Morris lawyer
Carper, Gertrude Esther artist, marina owner
†Carrier, France medical educator
†Carroll, Christopher Dixon economics educator
Carson, Benjamin Solomon neurosurgeon

Moos, H. Warren *physicist, astronomer, educator, administrator*
†Moran, John Gregory *musician*
†Morford, Thomas *administrator*
Morrel, William Griffin, Jr., *banker*
Morris, David Michael *insurance executive, lawyer*
Morton, William Alexander, Jr., *insurance agency executive*
Moser, Hugo Wolfgang *physician*
Moser, M(artin) Peter *lawyer*
Moses, Gloria *nurse*
Motz, Diana Gribbon *federal judge*
Motz, John Frederick *federal judge*
Mower, Morton Maimon *cardiologist*
Mulligan, Michael Eugene *physician, radiologist*
†Murphy, Frances Louise, II, *retired newspaper publisher*
Murphy, Shaun Edward *bank executive*
Myslinski, Norbert Raymond *medical educator*
†Nahabedian, Maurice Y. *plastic surgeon*
Napolitano, Lena Marie *surgeon, educator*
†Narvaez, Bernice Williams *software developer, consultant*
Nathanson, Harvey Charles *electrical engineer*
Nichols, Edith Rothman *publications director, editor*
Nickon, Alex *chemist, educator*
Niemeyer, Paul Victor *federal judge*
Noar, Mark David *internist, gastroenterologist, therapeutic endoscopist, consultant, inventor*
†Noga, Stephen Joseph *oncologist, researcher*
Norman, Colin Arthur *astrophysics educator*
Norman, Philip Sidney *physician*
†Norris, Karen W. *grants specialist*
Northrop, Edward Skottowe *federal judge*
†Oldach, David *epidemiologist, researcher*
O'Malley, Martin Joseph *mayor, former councilman, lawyer*
†O'Melia, Charles Richard
†Onyemaechi, Pauline *lawyer*
Orman, Leonard Arnold *lawyer*
†Owsley, Thomas L. *oil industry executive*
Palley, Howard A. *social worker, educator*
Palmer, Denise *publishing executive*
Palumbo, Francis Xavier Bernard *pharmacy educator*
Pappas, George Frank *lawyer*
†Park, Adrian E. *surgeon*
Park, Mary Woodfill *information consultant*
Parsons, Ivy *artist, sculptor, educator*
Pass, Carolyn Joan *dermatologist*
Passano, E. Magruder, Jr., *strategic planning consultant*
Patnode, Gerald Rufus *marketing professional*
Patz, Arnall *ophthalmologist*
Peake, Charles Franklin *economist, educator*
Peirce, Carol Marshall *English educator*
Pelizzo, Riccardo *political scientist*
†Peralta, Ligia *pediatrician*
Perman, Jay Allan *pediatrician, educator*
†Permutt, Solbert *physiologist, physician*
Peterson, Ronald R. *health service administrator*
Pierce, Nathaniel Field *medical researcher, educator*
†Pincus, Fred Leonard *sociology educator*
Pinkard, Anne Merrick *foundation administrator*
Plant, Albin MacDonough *lawyer*
Platt, Austin P. *retired science educator*
Plummer, Risque Wilson *retired lawyer*
†Poindexter, Christian Herndon *utility company executive*
†Pointer, Michelle Phillips *counselor, educator, consultant*
Pokempner, Joseph Kres *lawyer*
Pollak, Joanne E. *lawyer*
†Pollak, Lisa *columnist*
Pollak, Mark *lawyer*
Pollard, Shirley *employment training director, community services administrator, consultant*
Posner, Gary Herbert *chemist, educator*
Potra, Florian Alexander *mathematics educator*
Powell, Roger Norman *lawyer*
†Pretl, Michael Albert *lawyer*
†Price, Larry C. *photojournalist*
Proctor, Donald Frederick *otolaryngology educator, physician*
†Pronovost, Peter J. *anesthesiology educator, health facility administrator*
Pruce, Rhoda Posner *social worker*
†Puglisi, Mary Joanna *psychologist*
Quarles, William Daniel, Jr., *judge*
Quinn, Michael Desmond *diversified financial services executive*
Radding, Andrew *lawyer*
Radin, Beryl Avis *public administration and policy educator*
†Rafferty, William Bernard *lawyer*
Ranney, Richard Raymond *dental educator, researcher*
Ranum, Orest Allen *historian, educator*
Rasera, Robert L. *physics educator*
Rauschenberg, Dale Eugene *music educator*
Rayson, Glendon Ennes *internist, preventive medicine specialist, writer*
Reeder, Oliver Howard *paint products manufacturing executive*
Reinhart, Walter Josef *educator*
Rennels, Marshall Leigh *neuroanatomist, biomedical scientist, educator*
Reno, Russell Ronald, Jr., *lawyer*
†Rettberg, Charles Clayland, Jr., *lawyer*
Reynolds, William Leroy *lawyer, educator*
Rheinstein, Peter Howard *healthcare company executive, consultant, physician, lawyer*
†Richardson, Earl Stanford *university president*
Richburg, Shirley *business owner, operator*
Ridgeway, Dominic Charles *advocate*
Riepe, James Sellers *investment company executive*
Roberts, Randolph Wilson *health and science educator*
Robinson, Zelig *lawyer*
†Roby, Mary Lorraine *special education educator*
Rodowsky, Lawrence Francis *retired state judge*
Roland, Donald Edward *advertising executive*
†Rolland, Donald F. *printing company executive*
†Roller, Matthew Benedict *classics educator*
†Rose, George David *biophysics educator*
Rose, Hugh *retired economics educator*
Rose, Noel Richard *immunologist, microbiologist, educator*
Roseman, Saul *biochemist, educator*
Rosen, Michael Howard *real estate executive*
Rosen, Wendy Workman *arts management and publishing executive*
†Rosenberg, Edwin Harold *systems analyst*
†Rosenstein, Beryl Joel *physician*
Rosenthal, William J. *lawyer*
Ross, Richard Starr *medical school dean emeritus, cardiologist*
Roth, George Stanley *biochemist, researcher, physiologist*
Roupe, James Paul *accountant*
Rousuck, J. Wynn *theater critic*
Rubin, Haya Rahel *physician, researcher*
†Russell, Thomas Edgie, III, *lawyer, construction materials company executive*
Russell-Wood, Anthony John R. *history educator*
Saba, Walter Pedro *health education communications executive*
†Sachs, Murray B. *audiologist, educator*
Safer, Daniel J. *psychiatrist*
Safran, Linda Jacqueline *fundraiser*
Salamon, Lester Milton *political science educator*
Sallese, Paula Marie *critical care, resuscitation nurse*
Samet, Jonathan Michael *epidemiologist, educator*
Santamaria, Barbara Matheny *retired nurse practitioner*
Sarles, Richard M. *medical educator*
Sattler, Stephen Charles *writer, editor, communications consultant*
Saudek, Christopher D. *medical association administrator, medical educator*
Sawyer, David Jonathan *educator*
†Scales, Robert H., Jr., *retired army officer*
Schaefer, Robert Wayne *banker*
Scheeler, Charles *construction company executive*
Schilling, Franklin Charles, Jr., *retail management professional*
Schneewind, Elizabeth Hughes *social worker*
Schneewind, Jerome Borges *philosophy educator*
Schochor, Jonathan *lawyer, educator*
Schoenrich, Edyth Hull *internal and preventive medicine physician*
Schreter, Carol Ann *social worker, gerontologist, writer*
Schuster, Marvin Meier *retired physician, educator*
Schwinn, Steven David *lawyer, mediator*
Scott, Frederick Isadore, Jr., *editor, business executive*
Scriggins, Larry Palmer *lawyer, director*
Semiatin, Charles Paul *computer science consultant*
Seydoux, Geraldine *molecular biologist*
Sfekas, Stephen James *lawyer, educator*
Shaeffer, Charles Wayne *investment counselor*
Shamoo, Adil Elias *biochemist, biophysicist, educator*
†Shannonhouse, Royal Graham, III, *lawyer, educator*
Shaper, Christopher Thorne *sales executive*
Shapiro, Harry Dean *lawyer*
Sherman, Alan Theodore *computer science educator*
Shi, Leiyu *educator, researcher*
Shiffman, Bernard *mathematician, educator*
Short, Alexander Campbell *lawyer*
†Short, John Rennie *geographer, educator*
Shuldiner, Alan Rodney *physician, endocrinologist, educator*
Silberg, Carol Ann Schwartz *cultural organization administrator, educator*
Silbergeld, Ellen Kovner *environmental epidemiologist, researcher, toxicologist*
Silverberg, Steven George *pathologist, educator*
Silverstein, Arthur Matthew *ophthalmic immunologist, educator, historian*
Silverstone, Harris J. *chemistry educator*
Simmons, Howard L. *education educator*
Sinnott, Jan Marie Dynda *psychologist*
Sirithara, Ramanather *cardiologist*
Skinner, Daniel Thomas *language educator*
Slavney, Phillip Richard *psychiatrist*
Smalkin, Frederic N. *federal judge*
Smith, Stephen Ross *endocrinologist*
†Snitker, Soren *biomedical researcher, educator, physician*
Snyder, Mark Allen *lawyer*
Snyder, Solomon Halbert *psychiatrist, pharmacologist*
†Soeken, Karen Lynne *research methods educator, researcher*
Sommer, Alfred *medical educator, scientist, ophthalmologist*
Speed, Leslie Bokee *lawyer*
Staats, Peter S. *pain medicine physician, surgeon*
Stacey, James Henry *writer, columnist*
Stalfort, John Arthur *lawyer*
Stanley, Julian Cecil, Jr., *psychology educator*
Stanley, Steven Mitchell *paleobiologist, educator*
Starfield, Barbara Helen *pediatrician, educator*
Steele, George Peabody *retired marine transportation executive*
Stein, Bernard Alvin *business consultant*
Steiner, Robert Frank *biochemist*
†Steinwachs, Donald Michael *public health educator*
Sterne, Joseph Robert Livingston *newspaper editor, educator*
Stewart, C(ornelius) Van Leuven *lawyer*
†Stiller, Shale David *lawyer, educator*
†Strachan, Nell B. *lawyer*
†Strickland, Marshall Hayward *bishop*
Strull, Gene *technology consultant, retired electrical manufacturing company executive*
†Sturman, Philip *lawyer*
†Sugg, Diana K. *reporter*
Sugiyama, Toku Mary *retired school administrator*
Sullam, Brian Eliot *journalist*
Summers, Thomas Carey *lawyer*
†Sun, Chen-Chih J. *pathologist, educator*
Suskind, Sigmund Richard *microbiology educator*
Sykes, Melvin Julius *lawyer*
†Takacs, Laszlo *adult education educator, physicist*
Takacs, Wendy Emery *economics educator*
Talalay, Paul *pharmacologist, physician*
Talbot, Donald Roy *consulting services executive*
Tamargo, Rafael J. *neurological surgeon, educator*
†Tapper, Leona (Leela) Siff *artist*
Taylor, Carl Ernest *physician, educator*
†Temirkanov, Yuri *music director*
Terborg-Penn, Rosalyn Marian *historian, educator*
Thakor, Nitish Vyomesh *biomedical engineering educator*
Tocco, Elaine Kay *insurance policy specialist*
Toomey, Sister Stephana *liturgical designer architectural space, nun*
Tringali, Joseph *financial planner, accountant*
†Trotter, Richard *law educator, arbitrator*
Trpis, Milan *vector biologist, scientist, educator*
Tso, Mark On-man *ophthalmologist*
Ts'o, Paul On-Pong *biophysical chemist, educator*
†Tsoukias, Nikolaos *chemical engineer, biomedical engineer, researcher*
Tyler, Anne (Mrs. Taghi M. Modarressi) *author*
Udebiuwa, Oparaugo Ihentuge *psychiatrist*
Udvarhelyi, George Bela *neurosurgery educator emeritus, cultural affairs administrator*
†Uehlinger, Gerard Paul *lawyer*
Uhl, Scott Mark *state agency administrator*
†Ushry, Roselyn *minister*
Van Riper, Robert Austin *writer, retired public relations executive*
†Vemuganti, Ramakrishan R. *business educator*
Vinores, Stanley Anthony *ophthalmology educator*
Vogelstein, Bert *oncology educator*
†Wagner, Henry Nicholas, Jr., *physician*
Wahl, Richard Leo *radiologist, educator, nuclear medicine researcher*
Walker, Irving Edward *lawyer*
Walker, Mack *historian, educator*
Walker, Wilbur Gordon *physician, educator*
Wallach, Edward Eliot *physician, educator*
Waller, Michael E. *publishing executive*
Walser, Mackenzie *physician, educator*
Wang, Hong *engineer, researcher*
†Washington, Strother Lee, Jr., *mechanical engineer, design engineer*
Wasserman, Richard Leo *lawyer*
Waterbury, Larry *physician, educator*
Weber, Nancy Walker *charitable trust administrator*
Weisfeldt, Myron Lee *physician, educator*
Weiss, James Lloyd *cardiology educator*
Welker, James Anthony *physician*
Westerhout, Gart *retired astronomer*
Wharam, Moody DeWitt, Jr., *physician, medical educator*
Whitman, Marland Hamilton, Jr., *lawyer*
Wieler, Scott Alan *investment banker*
Wierman, John Charles *mathematician, educator*
Willis, John T. *former secretary of state*
Wilson, Donald Edward *dean, medical educator, physician*
Wilson, Thomas Matthew, III, *lawyer*
Winn, James Julius, Jr., *lawyer*
Wions, Steven Paul *small business owner*
Wolf, Cyd Beth *lawyer, entrepreneur*
Wolfe, John Thomas *quality assurance professional*
Wolman, M. Gordon *geography educator*
Woodward, Theodore Englar *medical educator, internist*
Wu, Albert W. *medical educator*
Yen, Michael C. *physician*
Yossif, George *psychiatrist*
Young, Barbara *psychiatrist, psychoanalyst, psychiatry educator, photographer*
Young, Hobart Peyton *economist, mathematician, educator*
Zacur, Howard Ardlen *reproductive endocrinologist*
Zaiman, Joel Hirsh *rabbi*
†Zangen, Abraham *neuroscience researcher, consultant*
Zaruba, Allen Scott Harmon *sculptor, educator*
Zenilman, Jonathan Mark *medical educator*
Ziff, Larzer *English language educator*
Zinkham, W. Robert *lawyer*
Zizic, Thomas Michael *physician, educator*

Barnesville
Pearcy, Susan Beth Due *artist, printmaker*

Bel Air
Cash, LaVerne (Cynthia Cash) *physicist*
†Downes, Lilli M. *sociologist, social psychologist*
Faunce, William Dale *clinical psychologist, researcher, consultant*
Haupt, Sheri Lynn *pharmacist*
Kramer, Keith Allan *music educator, composer*
†Larsen, Kevin Wayne *education educator*
Lu, David John *historian, writer*
Miller, Max Dunham, Jr., *lawyer*
Nye, Daniel William *retired elementary school educator*
O'Bryon, James Fredrick *defense executive*
Osborne, Lisette Kirstie *neonatal nurse practitioner, nursing administrator*
Phillips, Bernice Cecile Golden *retired vocational education educator*
Powers, Doris Hurt *retired engineering company executive*
Rowe, Henry Theodore, Jr., (Ted Rowe) *writer, editor*
Stuempfle, Arthur Karl *physical scientist*
†Terrill, Clarence R. *criminal justice educator*
Thompson, Sandra Fay *psychiatrist*
Wilson, Christian Burhenn *lawyer*

Bel Alton
†Quesada-Embid, Mary Regina Chamberlain *library media specialist*

Beltsville
Adams, Jean Ruth *entomologist, researcher*
Andre, Pamela Q. J. *library director*
Baligar, Virupax C. *research soil scientist*
Bloch, Bobbie Ann *nurse, educator*
Chitwood, David Joseph *zoologist, researcher*
Hackett, Kevin James *insect pathologist*
Johnson, Phyllis Elaine *chemist, researcher*
Levin, Gilbert Victor *health information, services and products*
Loeb, Marcia Joan *retired research psychologist*
Miller, Ted Robert *policy analyst*
Quirk, Frank Joseph *management consulting company executive*
†Ritz, David M. *photographic retail company executive*
Schneider, Edwin Kahn *research scientist*
Sickles, Carlton Ralph *employee benefit consultant*
Tso, Tien Chioh *federal agency official, plant physiologist*
Vigil, Eugene Leon *federal agency administrator, cell biologist, retired*

Berlin
†Auxer, Cathy Joan *elementary school educator*
Passwater, Richard Albert *biochemist, author*

Berwyn Heights
Kirchknopf, Matthew Bela *research laboratory manager*

Bethesda
Abrams, Stanley David *lawyer*
Ackerman, Michael J. *government executive*
Adler, Henry Joseph *research scientist*
Ahmad, Imad Aldean *astronomer, educator, consultant*
Alexander, Duane Frederick *pediatrician, research administrator*
Altschul, Stephen Frank *mathematician*
Apud, Jose Antonio *psychiatrist, psychopharmacologist, educator*
Arons, Bernard S. *psychiatrist, educator, health services director*
Atkinson, Arthur John, Jr., *pharmacologist, educator*
Atwell, Constance Woodruff *health services executive, researcher*
Augustine, Norman Ralph *organization executive, educator*
Axelrod, Julius *pharmacologist, researcher*
Azaryan, Anahit Vazgenovna *biochemist, researcher*
Backus, Robert Coburn *biophysical chemist*
Baird, Bruce Allen *lawyer*
Baird, Charles Fitz *retired mining and metals company executive*
†Ballman, B. George *lawyer*
Balsam, Marion Joyce *retired naval officer, pediatrician*
Banik, Sambhu Nath *psychologist*
Barrett, J. Carl *cancer researcher, molecular biologist*
Battey, James F., Jr., *federal agency administrator*
Bauersfeld, Carl Frederick *lawyer*
Beatty, Richard Scrivener *retired lawyer*
†Belyakov, Igor M. *immunologist, researcher*
Bennink, Jack Richard *microbiologist, researcher*
Benson, Elizabeth Polk *art specialist*
Berger, Robert Lewis *retired biophysicist, researcher*
†Berrigan, David *epidemiologist*
Biddle, Albert George Wilkinson, III, (Jack Biddle) *venture capitalist*
Billingsley, Frank S. *gynecologist, obstetrician, educator*
Borgaonkar, Digamber Shankarrao *cytogeneticist, educator*
Bowsher, Charles Arthur *retired government official, business executive*
Bradley, Damon Frederic *headmaster*
Brady, Roscoe Owen *neurogeneticist, educator*
Bregman, Jacob Israel *environmental consulting company executive*
Brodine, Charles Edward *physician*
Brown, Dudley Earl, Jr., *psychiatrist, educator, health executive, former federal agency administrator, former naval officer*
Brunell, Philip Alfred *physician, educator*
Buccino, Alphonse *university dean emeritus, consultant*
Burdeshaw, William Brooksbank *engineering executive*
†Burg, Maurice Benjamin *physiologist, internist*
Burkhalter, Susan Shively *music educator, organist*
Burton, Charles Henning *lawyer*
Calvert, Gordon Lee *retired legal association executive*
Candotti, Fabio *geneticist*
Carney, William Patrick *medical educator*
†Caruccio, Lorraine G. *research scientist*
Castelli, Alexander Gerard *accountant*
Chan, Wai-Yee *geneticist, educator*
†Chanock, Robert Merritt *pediatrician*
Charney, Dennis S. *psychiatrist*
Chartrand, Robert Lee *information scientist*
Chase, Thomas Newell *neurologist, researcher, educator*
Chen, Philip S., Jr., *government official*
Chin, James Ying *corporate executive*
Chronister, Gregory Michael *newspaper editor*
Clapper, James R., Jr., *government agency administrator*
†Clark, A. James *real estate company executive*
†Cleary, Robert Edward *government and public affairs educator*
Cleary, Timothy Finbar *professional society administrator*

Sams, James Farid *real estate development company executive*
†SanGiovanni, John Paul *ophthalmic epidemiologist*
Sanoff, Alvin Paul *education consultant, writer*
Sarnoff, Lili-Charlotte (Lolo Sarnoff) *artist, executive*
Saul, B. Francis, II, *bank executive, director*
Saunders, Charles Baskerville, Jr., *retired association executive*
Saville, Thorndike, Jr., *coastal engineer*
Sazima, Henry John *retired oral and maxillofacial surgery educator*
Schaeffer, Charles Perry *newswriter, editor*
†Schiff, Stanley D. *diplomat, consultant*
Schifter, Richard *lawyer*
†Schimel, Richard E. *lawyer*
Schmidt, Raymond Paul *naval career officer, historian, government official*
†Schneider, Julie Ann *geneticist*
Schoem, Alan Howard *lawyer*
Schooler, Carmi *psychologist, sociologist, researcher*
Schulman, Jacque-Lynne Amann *information scientist*
Schwarz, Louis Jay *financial advisor*
Sevin-Rodgers, Imogene *occupational and environmental health sciences consultant*
Sewell, Rodney Milton *biologist*
†Shapeero, Lorraine G. *physician, educator*
Shellow, Robert *management service company executive, consultant*
Shevach, Ethan Menahem *immunologist*
Shulman, Lawrence Edward *biomedical research administrator, rheumatologist*
Sieving, Paul A. *federal agency administrator*
Silver, David *lawyer*
Singer, Dinah *federal agency administrator, immunologist, researcher*
Sizemore, R. Tom, III, *military officer, hospital administrator*
Skirboll, Lana R. *federal health policy director*
Skolnik, Jonathan *economist*
Smith, Dale Cary *medical historian, educator*
Smith, Kent Ashton *scientific and technical information executive*
Smoller, Bruce Melvyn *psychiatrist*
Snitch, Thomas Harold *science educator, consultant*
Sober, Sidney *retired diplomat, educator*
Soffer, Lowell Charles *financial executive*
Sokoloff, Louis *physiologist, neurochemist*
Solomon, Robert *economist*
Southwick, Paul *retired public relations executive*
Spector, Eleanor Ruth *corporation executive*
Spector, Melbourne Louis *retired foreign service officer*
Spiegel, Allen *federal agency administrator*
†Spong, Catherine Yvonne *obstetrician, gynecologist, researcher*
Sprott, Richard Lawrence *foundation administrator, researcher*
Stadtman, Earl Reece *biochemist, researcher*
Stearman, William Lloyd *military association executive, author*
Stern, Kate Macomber *writer, educator*
Sternberg, Esther May *neuroendocrinologist, immunologist, rheumatologist*
Stoddard, Philip Hendrick *foreign affairs analyst, writer*
Stone, Jeremy Judah *public interest activist*
Straus, Stephen Ezra *biomedical researcher*
Striner, Herbert Edward *economics educator*
Sturtz, Donald Lee *physician, educator, naval officer*
Sumberg, Theodore A. *retired economist*
†Sunderland, Trey *medical researcher, geriatrician*
†Swartz, Gordon *management consultant*
Tabak, Lawrence *federal agency administrator*
Tabor, Herbert *biochemist*
Tanenbaum, Jill Nancy *graphic designer*
†Tanenbaum, Richard Hugh *lawyer*
Tape, Gerald Frederick *former association executive*
Taylor, Lindsay David, Jr., *health care executive*
Taylor, William Jesse, Jr., *international studies educator, research corporation president*
Terragno, Paul James *information industry executive*
Theerman, Paul Harold *historian, archivist*
Tilley, Carolyn Bittner *technical information specialist*
Timenes, Nicolai *policy analyst*
Timmer, Charles Peter *agricultural and development economist*
Toomey, Thomas Murray *lawyer*
Tracy, Thomas Miles *international health organization official*
Trus, Benes Louis *structural chemist*
Ungerleider, Leslie G. *neuroscientist*
Ursano, Robert Joseph *psychiatrist*
Van Cott, Harold Porter *human factors professional*
van der Linden, Frank Morris *historian*
Vaughan, Martha *biochemist, educator*
Vest, George Southall *retired diplomat*
Viehe, Richard B. *medical association administrator*
†Villavicencio, J. Leonel *surgeon, educator*
†Vitiello, Benedetto *psychiatrist, researcher*
Wagner, Cynthia Gail *editor, writer*
Waldmann, Thomas Alexander *medical research scientist, physician*
Walsh, Trudy Catherine *journalist*
Wang, Chin-Hua *rehabilitation service professional*
†Wang, Dai-Yuan *cardiologist*
†Wardinski, Bruce David *hotel chain executive*
Wayne, Alan S. *pediatric oncologist, educator*
Webster, Henry de Forest *neuroscientist*
Wechsler, Andrew Robert *international economic consultant*
Wedgwood, Josiah Francis *pediatrician, immunologist, science administrator*
Weinberger, Alan David *lawyer, corporate executive*
Weinberger, Daniel R. *psychiatrist, neurologist*
Weinstein, Allen *educator, historian, non-profit administrator*
Wente, Van Arthur *consultant, retired government official*
Western, Karl August *physician, epidemiologist*
†Wexler, Philip *toxicologist*
Whaley, Storm Hammond *retired government official, consultant*
Wheeler, Beverly B. *cardiology and cardiothoracic nurse specialist*
Wiese, Wolfgang Lothar *physicist, researcher*
Willoughby, Anne *health facility administrator, researcher, educator*
Wishart, Leonard Plumer, III, *army officer*
Witkop, Bernhard *chemist*
†Wolman, Sandra R. *health science association administrator, pathologist, geneticist*
†Wool, Jennifer S. *marketing professional*
Work, Henry Harcus *physician, educator*
Worth, Melvin H. *surgeon, educator*
Wurtz, Robert Henry *neuroscientist*
Yamada, Kenneth Manao *cell biologist*
Yang, Key Paik *librarian, archivist*
Youker, Robert Bliss *economist, consultant*
Young, Ina Weinstein *association administrator*
Zerhouni, Elias Adam *Federal Agency Administrator, Med educator*
†Zheng, Gang *mathematician, statistician, researcher*
Zierdt, Charles Henry *microbiologist*
Zimble, James Allen *naval officer, physician*
Zoon, Kathryn Christine *biochemist*

Betterton
Kohl, Benjamin Gibbs *historian, educator*

Boonsboro
Butler, Naomi Witmer *librarian, educator*
Zeleny, Ann Douglas *sculptor*

Bowie
Conahan, Frank C. *retired government executive, educator*
†Dawodu, Segun Toyin *sports medicine physician, physiatrist*
Francois, Francis Bernard *retired association executive, lawyer, transportation consultant*
†Gottlieb, Sylma R. *music educator, performing arts educator*
McCarthy, Kevin John *lawyer*
Miller, M. Sammye *history educator*
Newhouse, Quentin, Jr., *social psychologist, educator, researcher*
Nwokeafor, Cosmas Uchenna *communications educator*
†Parr-Corretjer, Polly *singer, music educator*
Rupp, Monica Cecilia *nursing administrator*
Silva, Lawrence Kehinde *physical education educator*
Speller-Brown, Barbara Jean *pediatric nurse practitioner*
Sterling, Richard Leroy *English and foreign language educator*
Stone, Edward Harris, II, *landscape architect*
Towle, Laird Charles *book publisher*
Vidal, Pedro Jose *foreign language educator*
Winegardner, Karen Elizabeth *management consultant*
Yager, Joseph Arthur, Jr., *economist*

Boyds
Kammer, Raymond Gerard, Jr., *government official*
†Love, Dana Francis Ignatius *telecommunications industry executive*

Bozman
Peterson, H(arry) William *chemicals executive, consultant*
Wyatt, Wilson Watkins, Jr., *management and public relations executive, writer*

Brandywine
Jaffe, Morris Edward *insurance executive*

Brookeville
Johns, Warren LeRoi *lawyer*
Rowe, Joseph Charles *elementary school educator, principal*

Brooklandville
Brandt, Gregory Alan *secondary school educator*
Miller, Paul George *computer company executive*

Burkittsville
Aughenbaugh, Deborah Ann *mayor, retired educator*

Burtonsville
Covington, Marlow Stanley *retired lawyer*
Hudson, McKinley *army officer, retired zoo deputy director*
Kammeyer, Sonia Margaretha *real estate agent*
Mitchell, Keith Christopher *software engineer*
Peck, Carol Faulkner *poet, educator, writer, publishing executive*

Butler
Hardie, Thomas Gary *journalist, editor, business executive*

Cabin John
†Bergfors, Constance Marie *artist, educator*
†Capo, Rafael V. *lawyer*
Oertel, Goetz Kuno Heinrich *physicist, professional science administrator*
Shropshire, Walter, Jr., *biophysicist emeritus, pastor*
Townsend, John William, Jr., *physicist, retired federal aerospace agency executive*

California
Avram, Henriette Davidson *librarian, government official*
Barnes, Stuart Robert *physician assistant*
Jessup, Edwin Harley, III, *aerospace engineering executive*

Cambridge
Ames, George Robert, Jr., *judge*
Jenkins, Robert Rowe *lawyer*
Koch-Eilers, Evamaria Wysk *oceanographer, researcher*
Miller, Robert Edvin *environmental education specialist, researcher, industrial hygienist*
Spahr, Elizabeth *business executive*

Camp Springs
Le Comte, Douglas Munzer *meteorologist*
Wagner, Andrew James *meteorologist, elder, educator*
Weinreb, Michael Philip *physicist*

Catonsville
Forgionne, Guisseppi Antonio *information scientis, educator*
Loerke, William Carl *art history educator*
†Smith, F. Louise *elementary school educator*
Woolley, Alma Schelle *nursing educator*
Wynn, John Charles *clergyman, retired religion educator*
Zumbrun, Alvin John Thomas *law and criminology educator*

Centreville
Amos, James Lysle *photographer*
Comfort, Paul William *county administrator, lawyer, writer*

Charlotte Hall
Brown, Ira Hugo *psychologist, educator*

Chesapeake Beach
Felter, Brian Albert *sales executive*

Chesapeake City
Schweizer, Edward Sowers *insurance agency owner*

Chester
Dabich, Eli, Jr., *insurance company executive*

Chestertown
Clarke, Garry Evans *composer, educator, musician, administrator*
Docksteader, Karen Kemp *marketing professional*
†Littlefield, Lauren Montenegro *psychologist, educator*
McCall, Davy Henderson *economics educator, consultant*
Mowell, George Mitchell *lawyer*
Schreiber, Harry, Jr., *management consultant*
†Scott, Joanne *artist, painter*
Scout, Terrence Houser *business educator*
Wendel, Richard Frederick *economist, educator, consultant*
†Wharton, Keith Alan *music educator, musician*

Cheverly
LaRoche, Gérard Laurent *adult education educator, writer*
Miller, Mark Karl *journalist*
Wilkes, Deborah Ann *neonatal intensive care nurse*

Chevy Chase
Adler, James Barron *publishing executive*
Albright, Raymond Jacob *government official*
Alexander, Arthur Jacob *economist*
Allison, Adrienne Amelia *voluntary organization administrator*
Alpert, Seymour *anesthesiologist, educator*
Armbrister, Trevor *journalist, author*
Ashe, Aaron Matthew *sales professional*
†Atkinson, Janet E. *lawyer*
Auerbach, Seymour *architect*
Bacon, Donald Conrad *author, editor*
†Bargmann, Cornelia *anatomist, educator, biochemist, educator, biophysicist, educator*
Baruch, Jordan Jay *management consultant, consultant*
Bissinger, Frederick Lewis *retired manufacturing executive, consultant*
Blaunstein, Phyllis Reid *communications and marketing executive*
Broide, Mace Irwin *retired public affairs consultant*
Bruder, George Frederick *lawyer*
Bruno, Harold Robinson, Jr., *retired journalist, writer*
Bush, Frederick Morris *federal official*
Cech, Thomas Robert *chemistry and biochemistry educator*
Charen, Solomon *psychologist*
Chase, Nicholas Joseph *lawyer, educator*
Cheng, David Keun *engineering educator*
Choppin, Purnell Whittington *research administrator, virology researcher, educator*
†Clemmer, Dan Orr *librarian*
†Cline, Ruth Eleanor Harwood *translator*
Cody, Peter Malcolm *economist, development, management consultant*
Cooley, William Crockett *mechanical engineer, retired educator*
Cron, Theodore Oscar *writer, editor, educator*
Cushen, Walter Edward *contractor, consultant*
Duvall, Bernice Bettum *artist, exhibit coordinator, jewelry designer*
Emery, Robert Firestone *economist, educator*
Ewing, Frank Marion *lumber company executive, industrial land developer*
Farrell, Joseph Michael *steamship company executive*
Feldman, Bruce Allen *otolaryngologist*
Fern, Alan Maxwell *art historian, retired museum director*
Freeman, Harry Louis *investment executive*
Froomkin, Joseph *economic consultant*
Gaines, Michael Johnston *parole commissioner*
Gildenhorn, Joseph Bernard *lawyer, businessman, former diplomat*
†Goldman, Janis Meresman *lawyer, law firm executive*
Greene, Edward Allen *retired public affairs executive*
Greenspoon, Irma Naiman *business executive*
Hamill, John Richard, Jr., *physician*
Hani, Antoine George *psychiatrist, psychoanalyst*
Harlan, William Robert, Jr., *physician, educator, researcher*
Harr, Karl Gottlieb, Jr., *retired lawyer*
†Hersh, Stephen Peter *psychiatrist, psycho-oncologist, educator*
Hirschhorn, Joel Stephen *engineer*
Hudson, Anthony Webster *retired federal agency administrator, minister*
Hudson, Ralph P. *physicist*
Hunt, Frederick Talley Drum, Jr., *association executive*
Jones, Philip Howard *broadcast journalist*
Ketcham, Orman Weston *lawyer, former judge*
Kingsley, Nathan *journalist, consultant, educator*
Klain, Ronald Alan *lawyer*
Kriegsman, Alan M. *retired critic*
Kullen, Shirley Robinowitz *psychiatric epidemiologist, consultant*
Lebow, Irwin Leon *communications engineering consultant*
†Lee, Edward Brooke, Jr., *real estate executive, fund raiser*
Lewis, Gwendolyn Lorita *sociologist, policy analyst*
Lewis, Jon Roderick *political advisor*
Linowes, David Francis *political economist, educator, corporate executive*
Lukens, Alan Wood *retired ambassador and foreign service officer*
Mackall, Laidler Bowie *lawyer*
Mathis, Laurelle Sheedy *academic administrator, volunteer*
Meltzer, Rae *social worker*
Meyerson, Christopher Cortlandt *lawyer*
Michaelis, Michael *management and technical consultant*
Mielke, James Edward *geochemist*
Miller, Franklin G. *bioethicist*
Morgan, Elizabeth *plastic surgeon*
†Murphy, Brian Charles *lawyer*
Norwood, Bernard *economist*
Norwood, Janet Lippe *economist*
Opper, Barbara Negri *financial economist*
Ostar, Allan William *academic administrator, higher education consultant*
Oudens, Gerald Francis *architect, architectural firm executive*
Pilkerton, Arthur Raymond, Jr., *surgeon, educator*
Pines, Maya *writer, editor*
Pitofsky, Robert *federal agency administrator, law educator*
Pogue, John Marshall *physician, editor, researcher*
Pogue, Mary Ellen E. (Mrs. L(loyd) Welch Pogue) *youth and community worker*
Posnick, Jeffrey Craig *plastic surgeon*
Promisel, Nathan E. *materials scientist, metallurgical engineer*
Ragland, Robert Allen *lawyer*
Rockwell, Theodore *nuclear engineer*
Romansky, Monroe James *physician, educator*
Rose, John Charles *physician, educator*
Sampas, Dorothy Myers *retired government official*
†Sanz, Luis E. *gynecologist, educator*
Sapin, Burton Malcolm *political science educator, foreign policy analyst*
†Schwartzman, Robin Berman *lawyer*
Shipler, David Karr *journalist, correspondent, author*
Shogan, Robert *news correspondent*
Short, Steve Eugene *engineer*
Silver, George Albert *physician, educator*
Sinclair, Rolf Malcolm *retired physicist*
Smith, Peter Leonard *diversified financial services company executive*
Tacket, Hall Sanford *retired internist*
Teitel, Simon *economist, educator*
Toth, Robert Charles *retired polling consultant, journalist, writer*
Towsner, Cynthia Merle *educator, administrator*
Toy, Charles David *lawyer*
Van Akkeren, Lorraine Sue *research assistant*
Weiss, Harlan Lee *lawyer*
Williams, Charles Laval, Jr., *physician, international organization official*
Wolf, Michele Sue *poet, writer, editor*
Wright, Frank *artist, educator*
Wright, Helen Patton *professional society administrator*
Zurkowski, Paul George *publisher*

Chillum
Malbon, Louise *registered, nurse, hypnotherapist writer, publisher*

Claiborne
Guinness, Kenelm L. *civil engineer*

Clarksburg
Gellineau, Antonio Cortes *system software specialist*
Gonano, J. Roland *technology research and development manager*

Clarksville
Hung, Mei-Jong Chow *social worker*
Peirce, James Walter *secondary school educator, historian, educator*

Clinton
Cruz, Wilhelmina Mangahas *critical care physician, educator*
Dandy, Roscoe Greer *clinical psychotherapist, educator, public health analyst*
Hill, Keith Maurice *editor*
†Whittington, Ralph Edward *curator, librarian*

Cockeysville
Barnes, Peter retired lawyer
Fleischmann, Gisela Ebert retired psychiatrist
Hager, Louise Alger retired chaplain
Peirce, Brooke English language educator

Cockeysville Hunt Valley
Barr, Irwin Robert retired aeronautical engineer
Connor, Geoffrey Warren wine merchant, wine writer
Dans, Peter Emanuel medical educator
Donaho, John Albert consultant
Edgett, William Maloy lawyer, labor arbitrator
Elkin, Lois Shanman business systems company executive
Futcher, Palmer Howard physician, educator
Rallo, James Gilbert management company executive
Shepard, George Leo sales and marketing executive, consultant
Somerville, Warren Thomas, II, management consultant
Spinella, J(oseph) John casualty insurance company executive, consultant
Whitehurst, William Wilfred, Jr., management consultant

College Park
Aggour, Mohamed Sherif civil engineer, educator
Amershek, Kathleen education educator
Anderson, John David, Jr., aerospace engineer
Anderson, Randi Laine occupational therapist
Anisimov, Mikhail A. physicist, educator, research scientist
Antman, Stuart Sheldon mathematician, educator
Ayyub, Bilal M. civil engineering educator, researcher, executive
Barbe, David Franklin electrical engineer, educator
Beasley, Maurine Hoffman journalism educator, historian
Benedick, Richard Elliot diplomat
Berlinski, Edward Gerard writing educator, writer
Brown, Richard Harvey sociology, cultural studies and communications scholar, educator
†Brush, Stephen George history of science educator
Chavas, Jean-Paul economist, educator
Churchville, Lida Holland librarian
Coffey, Timothy physicist
Cooper, Chester Lawrence research administrator
DeFries, Ruth S. earth system scientist, researcher
†De Lorenzo, William E. foreign language educator
DeSilva, Alan W. physics educator, researcher
†Destler, William W. academic administrator
Diener, Theodor Otto plant pathologist, researcher
Dieter, George Elwood, Jr., university official
†Dopp, Bonnie Jo musicologist, school librarian
Dusold, Laurence Richard chemist, computer specialist
Edgeman, Rick Lee statistics educator, consultant
Elkin, Stephen Lloyd political science educator
†Ernstein, Julie H. archaeologist, educator, researcher
†Fagan, William F. ecologist
Fanning, Delvin Seymour soil science educator
Feinstein, Frederick Lee lawyer
Fenselau, Catherine Clarke chemistry educator
Fisher, Michael Ellis mathematical physicist, chemist
Frank, Howard systems company executive , dean, educator
†Freidlin, Mark Iosif mathematician, educator
Fu, Michael C. management science educator
†Gannon, Martin John finance educator
Gaylin, Ned L. psychology educator
Gluckstern, Robert Leonard physics educator
†Gobbel, Luther Russell lawyer
Gomery, Douglas communications educator, writer
Goode, B. Erich sociologist, educator, retired criminologist
Gordon, Lawrence Allan accounting educator
Granatstein, Victor Lawrence electrical engineer, educator
Griem, Hans Rudolf physicist, educator
Griffin, James Joseph physics educator
†Grillakis, Manoussos mathematician, educator
Grim, Samuel Oram chemistry educator
Grunig, James Elmer communications educator, researcher, public relations consultant
Gupta, Ashwani Kumar mechanical engineering educator
Hallett, Judith Peller classical studies educator
†Helms, Janet Elteser psychology educator, consultant, researcher
Helz, George Rudolph chemistry educator, research center director
Hey, Nancy Henson educational administrator
†Isaacs, Neil D. literature educator
†Izaurralde, Roberto César science educator, researcher
Jeffery, William Richard developmental biology educator, researcher
Johnson, Haynes Bonner author, journalist, television commentator
Just, Richard Eugene agricultural and resource economics educator consultant
Katz, Ronald Alan dermatologist
Kundu, Mukul Ranjan physics and astronomy educator
Langenberg, Donald Newton retired academic administrator, physicist
†Lea-Cox, John Derek plant physiologist
Levine, William Silver electrical engineering educator
Levinson, Jerrold humanities educator
Li, Zhanqing meteorologist, educator
Lichtenberg, Erik Russell economics educator
†Lin, Hung C. electrical engineer educator
Lowell, Howard Parsons archivist, federal agency administrator
Lubkin, Gloria Becker physicist
Lucas, Henry Cameron, Jr., information systems educator, writer, consultant
Lyon, Andrew Bennet economics educator
†MacDonald-Wilson, Kim Lorraine psychiatric rehabilitation counselor
Maddulapalli, Kumar Anil information scientist
†Maksimovic, Vojislav finance educator
Marcus, Steven Irl electrical engineering educator
Marshall, Monty Glenn political research scientist, consultant
Martin, L(eslie) John retired journalism educator and dean
†McCray, William Patrick historian, writer
Mc Donald, Frank Bethune physicist
McIlrath, Thomas physicist, educator
McNaughton, Kenneth John publisher
Miller, Raymond Edward computer science educator
Miller, Raymond Jarvis agronomy educator
Minker, Jack computer scientist, educator
Misner, Charles William physics educator
Modarres, Mohammad education educator
Moore, John Hays chemistry educator
Morris, Joseph Anthony health science association administrator
Moses, Claire Goldberg history and womens studies educator
Mote, Clayton Daniel, Jr., university president, mechanical engineer, educator
Murphy, Thomas James physicist, educator
Neal, Edward Garrison lawyer
Nembhard, Jessica Gitt Gordon economist
Nerlove, Marc Leon economics educator
Newcomb, Robert Wayne electrical engineer educator
†Noll, Franklin Clemens historian
Nusinovich, Gregory Semeon physicist, researcher
Olson, Charles Eric economist
Olson, Keith Waldemar history educator
Olver, Frank William John research mathematician
Oster, Rose Marie Gunhild foreign language professional, educator
Panagariya, Arvind economics educator
Pasch, Alan philosopher, educator
†Pavela, Gary Michael legal educator, administrator
Piper, Don Courtney political science educator
Presser, Harriet Betty sociology educator
Presser, Stanley sociology educator
Qi, Jianwei mechanical engineer, researcher
Quester, George Herman political science educator
†Quintero-Herencia, Juan Carlos language educator, writer
Rabin, Herbert physicist, university official
Raghavan, Srinivasa Ramamurthy chemical engineer, educator
†Ramsey, S. Robert education educator
Rao, Jaganmohan Boppana Lakshimi electrical engineer
Rasmusson, Eugene Martin meteorology researcher
Redish, Edward Frederick physicist, educator
Resnik, Harvey Lewis Paul psychiatrist
Rivers, William Patrick language policy researcher, consultant
†Rosen, Steven lawyer
Rosenberg, Norman Jack agricultural meteorologist, educator
Rosenfeld, Azriel computer science educator, consultant
Rowland, Leslie S. historian, educator
Sacks, Charles Bernard physician, educator
Schelling, Thomas Crombie economist, educator
Schneider, Benjamin psychology educator
Schwab, Susan Carroll dean
Schwedler, Jillian Marie political science educator
Segal, David Robert sociology educator
†Severn, Stephen Edwin literature educator
Shneiderman, Ben Abraham computer science educator, writer
Sigall, Harold Fred psychology educator
Silverman, Joseph chemistry educator, scientist
Sims, Henry P., Jr., management educator
Skuja, Andris physics educator
Sorenson, Georgia Lynn Jones political scientist, educator
Souza, Gilvan Castro operations and management educator
Spear, Richard Edmund art history educator
Stark, Francis C(io), Jr., horticulturist, educator
Stewart, Teresa Elizabeth elementary school educator
Stith, James Herman physics educator
Stover, Carl Frederick foundation executive
Struna, Nancy L. social historian and American studies educator
Stumpff, Robert Thomas academic administrator
Sundaresan, P. Ramnathan research chemist, consultant
Swistak, Piotr Tomasz mathematician, sociologist
Szymanski, Edna Mora dean
Tamboli, Prabhakar agriculturist, educator
Taylor, Leonard Stuart engineering educator, consultant
Terchek, Ronald John political science educator
Tismaneanu, Vladimir political science educator, researcher
Toll, John Sampson university president, physics educator
Tseng, Chung-Li engineering educator
Unsell, Lloyd Neal, Jr., association executive
Vanderveen, John E. federal agency administrator, emeritus scientist
Walters, William Ben chemistry educator
Wasserman, Paul library and information science educator
Weart, Spencer Richard historian
Weil, Raymond Richard soil scientist
Weiner, Ronald Martin microbiology and cell biology educator, research scientist
White, Marilyn Domas information science educator
Whittemore, Edward Reed, II, poet, retired educator
Winik, Jay B. writer, political scientist, consultant
Winton, Calhoun literature educator
Yaney, George history educator
Yorke, James Alan chaos mathematician
Younger, Deirdre Ann pharmacist
Zantek, Paul Francis management scientist, educator
Zelkowitz, Marvin Victor computer science educator
Zen, E-an research geologist, educator
Zhang, Da-lin D. meteorologist, educator

Colora
Borland, Raymond M. researcher

Columbia
Abel, Florence Catherine Harris social worker
Ager, David Scott landscape architect
Arnold, Karen L. writer, consultant
Bailey, John Martin retired transportation planner, educator
Bareis, Donna Lynn biochemist, pharmacologist
Beckenstein, Myron journalist
Bell, James Edward psychologist, educator
†Brown, Ronald music educator
Bruley, Duane Frederick academic administrator, consultant, engineer
Cargo, William Ira retired ambassador
Chaiklin, Harris retired social work educator
Closson, Walter Franklin child support prosecutor
Crivelli, Kenneth John physical therapist, athletic trainer
†Das, Naresh Chandra research scientist
Davis, Benjamin George theologian, educator
Davis, Janet Marie Gorden secondary education educator
Doi, Yutaka electrical engineer
Du Toit, Cornelis Frederik electronic engineer
Ernest, Michael Vance, Sr., research chemist
Fisher, Dale John chemist, instrumentation and medical diagnostic device investigator
Fox, Barry Howard software engineer
†Fritz, Steven L physicist
Go, Howard Tiang management consulting firm executive, educator
Gottfeld, Gunther Max retired urban mass transit official, consultant
Gregorie, Corazon Arzalem operations supervisor
Gruhl, Andrea Morris librarian
Gull, Hazel Joy (Connie Gull) retired nursing administrator
Harrison, Elza Stanley medical association executive
Hartman, Lee Ann Walraff educator
Hilderbrandt, Donald Franklin, II, urban designer, landscape architect, artist
†Hyde, Rebecca Medwin financial consultant
Hyman, Lawrence Robert psychiatrist
Jones-Wilson, Faustine Clarisse education educator emeritus
Keeton, Morris Teuton research scholar
Khare, Mohan chemist, researcher
Khurana, Ramesh Kumar neurologist
Klein, Sami Weiner librarian
Kurlander, Honey Wachtel artist, educator
Kurlander, Neale accounting and law educator, lawyer
Lenz, Lois Martin Elser psychiatric and mental health nurse
Lorton, Lewis researcher, computer executive, dentist
Madison, Anne Conway public relations and marketing professional
Margolis, Vivienne O. psychotherapist, educator
Marshall, Linda Murphy linguist, government official
†Maseritz, Guy B. lawyer
May, John Raymond clinical psychologist
McCuan, William Patrick real estate company executive
†Miller, James L. food products executive
Millspaugh, Martin Laurence real estate developer, urban development consultant
Morice, William Daniel business and tax counselor
Moulton, Paul Douglas (Pete Moulton) information technology consultant
Nie, Guojun research scientist
†Purcell, James Nelson, Jr., international organization administrator
Rey, Alix Charles psychiatrist
Rogers, Thomas Francis foundation administrator
Rovelstad, Gordon H. dentist, researcher
Scates, Alice Yeomans former government official, consultant
†Siegel, David Burton lawyer
Singerman, Phillip A. corporate executive
Spicknall, Joan music educator
Strain, Lucille Bewton education educator, researcher
Straja, Sorin Radu chemical engineer, mathematician, computer programmer
Ulman, Louis Jay lawyer
†Van Buiten, Robert D. aerospace engineer
Walrath, Michelle Taylor accountant
Weems, Helen Rachel piano teacher, accompanist
Whiting, Albert Nathaniel former university chancellor

Crisfield
Ryan, Jerome Francis artist

Crofton
Andrysiak, Frank Louis videographer
Boland, Gerald Lee health facility financial executive
Doherty, Daniel Joseph, III, lawyer
Fischer, Steven Thomas writer, producer, director
Hendrixson, Lewis Holston retired federal agency administrator
Kniffen, Donald Avery astrophysicist, educator, researcher
Laurenson, Robert Mark mechanical engineer
Parsley, Robert Charles minister
Ross, E(dwin) Clarke association executive, educator
Shah, Natwarlal Bhogilal physician
†Tyler, Craig Alan weather satellites engineer

Crownsville
Hanna, James Curtis state official
Irish, Leon Eugene lawyer, educator, non-profit organization executive
Selvin, Beatrice retired anesthesiologist

Cumberland
Bernstein, Louis civil engineer
Heckert, Paul Charles sociologist, educator
Shreve, Jack English and Spanish language educator
Wolford, Nancy Lou medical and surgical nurse

Damascus
Nelligan, William David professional association executive
Ventola, Dean Samuel architect, architectural company executive

Darnestown
Cohen, Sanford Irwin physician, educator
Gottlieb, Julius Judah podiatrist
Hoffer, James Brian physicist, consultant
†Lightner, Gene Cleek investment banker

Davidsonville
Blaxall, Martha Ossoff economist

Dayton
Fischell, Robert Ellentuch physicist

Denton
Doster, Rose Eleanor Wilhelm artist
Jensen, Christian Edward family practice physician

Derwood
Blank, Leta Sondra health and long term care insurance specialist
Kusterer, Thomas project administrator
†Vaughn, Steven D. veterinary administrator
Wong, Richard Lee lawyer

District Heights
†Boswell, Vivian Nicholson protective services official

Easton
Brodt, Burton Pardee retired chemical engineer, writer, researcher
Bronson, John Orville, Jr., retired librarian
Danner, David Bigelow pathologist
Eutsey, Dwayne Eugene writer, editor
Fredrick, Susan Walker tax company manager
Higgins, Michael Edward finance executive
Ikenberry, Henry Cephas, Jr., lawyer
Maffitt, James Strawbridge lawyer
Peterson, James Kenneth manufacturing company executive
Potter, Blair Burns editor
Snow, James Byron, Jr., physician, research administrator
†U'Ren, Marie Rita travel company executive, pre-school educator
Whitten, Nancy Bimmerman clinical social worker, marriage therapist

Edgewater
Hammer, Jane Amelia Ross advocate
Kushlan, James A. biologist, research administrator, author, educator
†Masson Brinsley, Margaret W. university official, historian
Staines, Charles L. entomologist, researcher

Eldersburg
Spohn, William Gideon, Jr., mathematician, musician

Elk Mills
Dorsman, Jerry addictions therapist, writer

Elkridge
†Matthews, Lois Marr musician, music educator
Morgan, Gary Lorin biophysicist, inventor, researcher
Szilagyi, Sherry Ann psychotherapist, lawyer

Elkton
Chen, Oliver Tsung-Yu chemical engineer, researcher
Howe, Patricia Moore adult education educator
Jasinski-Caldwell, Mary L. company executive
Scherf, Christopher N. trade association administrator
†Scott, Doris Petersen lawyer
Weibley, Grayce L. retired writer
Xu, Ping chemist

Ellicott City
Benjamin, Thomas Edward music educator, composer, conductor
Bers, Eric Lawrence civil engineer
Chen, Hong Yu pediatrician
Clive, Craig N. compensation executive
Gleaves, Leon Rogers marketing and sales executive
Huey, J(oseph) Wistar, III, import/export executive
†Kushnir, Andrei artist, consultant
Melaro, Constance Loraine pianist, organist, instructor
Pairo, Preston Abercrombie, Jr., lawyer

Perry, Nancy Trotter *former telecommunications company executive*
Stough, Liza Boyle *government official*
†Tinsley, Perin Delano *tax specialist, real estate agent*
Tucci, Albert William *retired human resources executive, consultant*
Veasel, Walter *minister, educator*
†Wann, Michael Stephen *music educator*
Webster, Sharon B. *economist*
White, Robert, Jr McKay *musician, consultant, musician, educator*
Woodcock, Cynthia Hardin *program development strategic planning*

Emmitsburg
†Johnson, Curtis Dean *historian, educator*
Paulison, R. David *federal agency administrator*
Zarnowski, C(hester) Frank *economics educator*

Fallston
Lewis, Howard Franklin *chiropractor*

Finksburg
Konigsberg, Robert Lee *electrical engineer*

Forest Hill
Klein, Shirley Snyderman *retail executive*
McIntosh, L(orne) William *marketing executive*

Fort Detrick
Maher, Cornelius Creedon, III, *neurologist, toxicologist, army officer*

Fort George G Meade
Black, William B., Jr., *government agency administrator*
†Hayden, Michael V. *career officer, federal agency administrator*
Schmitt, Robert Lee *computer scientist*

Fort Washington
Alexander, Gary R. *lawyer, state legislator, lobbyist*
Bradley, Melvin LeRoy *communications company executive*
Cameron, Rita Giovannetti *writer, publisher*
Caveny, Leonard Hugh *mechanical engineer, aerospace scientist, consultant*
Coffey, Matthew B. *trade association executive*
Cross, Rita Faye *librarian, early childhood educator, writer*
Diercks, Elizabeth Gorman *elementary education educator*
Isom, Virginia Annette Veazey *retired nursing educator*
McCafferty, James Arthur *sociologist*
Miller, John Richard *interior designer*
Omoike, Isaac Irabor *chemist, publishing executive, writer*
Smoot, Burgess Howard *federal official*
Wilcox, Richard Hoag *information scientist*

Frederick
Anderson, Arthur Osmund *pathologist, immunologist, army officer*
†Baker, Joanne Evelyn *retired government official*
Boyd, Ann Lewis *biology educator*
Boyle, Lisa C. *marketing and communications executive*
Bryan, John Leland *retired engineering educator*
Byron, Beverly Butcher *former congresswoman*
Cable, Dana Gerard *psychologist*
Delaplaine, George Birely, Jr., *newspaper editor, cable television executive*
†Devineni, Mohan *pharmacist*
Garver, Robert Vernon *research physicist*
Hanna, Michael George, Jr., *immunologist, pharmaceutical executive*
Hein, David *humanities educator*
Hoff, Charles Worthington, III, *banker*
Hogan, Ilona Modly *lawyer*
†Holl, David Russell *construction executive*
†Hughes, David Robert *gaming company executive*
Keefe, Arthur Thomas, III, *non-profit fund raising executive*
Knisely, Ralph Franklin *retired microbiologist*
†Kozlov, Serguei V. *medical researcher, consultant*
Lebherz, Ann Weisburger *writer, researcher, retired writer*
Lester, Noel K. *music educator, concert pianist*
†Malone, Robert Wallace *surgeon*
†McKewen Amato, Mary Patricia *musician*
†Monhollon, Rusty *historian, educator*
Narula, Ram Gopal *engineer*
Nayyar, Mohinder Lal *mechanical engineer*
Orzechowski, Alice Louise *accountant*
Pearson, Jennie Sue *retired government administrator*
Rossio, Jeffrey L. *biologist, educator*
Shull, Michael Slade *lecturer, writer, researcher*
Sica, John *lawyer*
Swanson, Norma Frances *federal agency administrator*
Vincoli, Jeffrey Wayne *safety and environmental engineering executive*
Whelihan, Alan Stuart *real estate developer, automotive executive*
Wickizer, Stephen Wesley *pharmacist*

Friendship
Clagett, Diana Wharton Sinkler *museum docent*

Frostburg
Allen, Philip Mark *arts and humanities educator, dean, writer*
†Childs, William Parker *education educator*
Clulee, Nicholas Harkins *history educator*
Root, Edward Lakin *education educator, university administrator*
†Sigerstad, Thomas Daniel *psychologist, educator*
†Williams, Pamela S. *librarian*

Fulton
Hamlin, George L. *writer*

Gaithersburg
Adams, James Michael *nuclear physicist*
Aiuto, Russell *science education consultant*
Barker, Peter Eugene *biologist, researcher*
Baum, Howard Richard *research scientist*
Bement, Arden Lee, Jr., *engineering educator*
†Bendersky, Leonid A. *metallurgist, researcher*
Boddiger, George Cyrus *insurance corporate executive, consultant*
†Boisvert, Ronald Fernand *computer scientist*
Bugg, Carol Donayre *interior designer*
Cahn, John Werner *metallurgist, educator*
Caplin, Jerrold Leon *health physicist*
Carasso, Alfred Sam *mathematician*
Carey, John Edward *information services executive*
Caswell, Randall Smith *physicist*
Celotta, Robert James *physicist*
Chang, Ren Fang *physicist, researcher*
Colle, Ronald *research chemist*
Cookson, Alan Howard *electrical engineer, researcher*
Delgado, Dwighd D(ubied) *company executive*
Dermody, William Christian *biomedical consultant*
DiMarzio, Edmund Armand *physicist*
Dowd, Carolyn Lay *social worker*
Ferrell, Charles Madison *retired nuclear engineer, health physicist*
Flickinger, Harry Harner *organization and business executive, management consultant*
French, Judson Cull *government official*
Frome, David Herman *dentist*
Gilsinn, David Edmund *mathematician, researcher*
Gorin, Barney Franklin *spacecraft systems, propulsion and robotics engineer*
†Grotenhuis, Marshall *retired nuclear engineer*
Hamer, Walter Jay *chemical consultant, science writer*
Hancock, Diane Kerr *research chemist*
Harman, George Gibson *physicist, consultant*
Hegyeli, Ruth Ingeborg Elisabeth Johnsson *pathologist, government official*
Hertz, Harry Steven *government official*
†Hesterberg, Larry Allen *aerospace engineer*
Hoferek, Mary Judith *information systems specialist, educator*
Hsu, Stephen Ming *materials scientist, chemical engineer*
Hubbell, John Howard *radiation physicist*
Irvine, Helen Isabel Becraft *interior designer*
Isbister, James David *pharmaceutical business executive*
Jacox, Marilyn Esther *chemist*
Jahanmir, Said *materials scientist, mechanical engineer*
Jevtic, Milomir *artist, sculptor*
Johnson, Betty Marie *retired nursing educator*
Johnson, George H. *financial services company executive*
Johnson, Virgil Evans, Jr., *research scientist*
Karam, Lisa Robert *research chemist*
Kemmerer, Sharon Jean *computer systems analyst*
†Kinch, Michael S. *cancer researcher*
†Landel, Michel *food service and management company executive*
†Leader, Shelah Gilbert *research scientist*
Levine, Robert Sidney *chemical engineer, consultant*
Liau, Gene *medical educator*
†Lynn, Jeffrey Whidden *research physicist, educator*
Marin, Cynthia Myers (Cheryl Marin) *systems engineer*
McDowell, Donna Schultz *lawyer, educator*
McLaughlin, William Lowndes *physicist, researcher*
†Mummaneni, Padmaja *research scientist, educator*
Peele, Roger *hospital administrator*
Phillips, William Daniel *physicist*
Pierce, Daniel Thornton *physicist*
Presser, Cary *research engineer*
Quraishi, Mohammed Sayeed *retired health scientist, administrator*
Reynolds, Frank Miller *retired government administrator*
Rosenblatt, Joan Raup *mathematical statistician*
Ross, Sherman *psychologist, educator*
Ruckman, Mark Warren *physicist*
Rupert, Hoover (Lynn Hoover Rupert) *minister, writer*
Ruth, James Perry *financial planning executive*
Sengers, Johanna M. H. Levelt *thermophysicist*
Sherer, Samuel Ayers *lawyer, urban planning consultant*
Shyam-Sunder, Sivaraj *structural engineer, researcher*
Stever, Horton Guyford *aerospace scientist and engineer, educator, consultant*
Taketomi, Susamu *physicist, researcher*
Taylor, Barry Norman *physicist*
Tenney, Lisa Christine Gray *healthcare administrator*
Tesk, John Aloysius *materials scientist*
Ulbrecht, Jaromir Josef *chemical engineer*
Wang, Francis Wei-Yu *biomedical materials scientist, researcher*
Watson, Royce Andrew *retired federal official*
†Werner, Samuel Alfred *physics and astronomy educator*
Wicklein, John Frederick *journalist, educator*
Wiederhorn, Sheldon Martin *materials scientist engineer*
Wohl, Ronald H. *management consultant, writing and editorial expert*
Wright, Richard Newport, III, *retired civil engineer*
Wu, Yung C. *retired chemist*
Zhang, Nien Fan *statistician*

Galena
†Hunsperger, Elizabeth Jane *art and design consultant, educator*

Gambrills
Messner, Howard Myron *professional association executive*
†White, Elizabeth G. *music educator*

Garrett Park
Baldwin, Calvin Benham, Jr., *retired medical research administrator*
Franklin, Benjamin A. *editor, reporter*
Kornberg, Warren Stanley *science journalist*
Lincicome, David Richard *biomedical and animal scientist*
McDowell, Eugene Charles *systems analyst, bioethicist*
Melville, Robert Seaman *chemist*
†Stites, M(ary) Elizabeth *educator*

Germantown
Bu, Rulei *artist, educator*
Foulke, Judith Diane *health physicist*
Gong, Yu *molecular biologist*
Harris, William Norman *music educator*
Hartley, James R. *musician, writer*
Hill-Fessenden, Anne Lynn *multi-faceted food and beverage consultant*
Iqbal, Zafar *biochemist, neurochemist*
Laufer, Allan Henry *chemist*
†McDougle, Loella *educational consultant*
Norcross, Marvin Augustus *veterinarian, retired government agency official*
Schlaikjer, Stephen Allan *foreign service officer*
Searles, Thomas Daniel *society administrator*
Smith, Ann Hess *guidance counselor*
Taylor, Douglas Howard *translator*
Varma, Matesh N. *materials scientist, director*
Wade, Suzanne *project manager*
Weiner, Claire Muriel *freelance writer*

Gibson Island
Forster, William Hull *aerospace executive*

Glen Arm
Harris, Benjamin Louis *chemical engineer, consultant*
Jackson, Theodore Marshall *retired oil company executive*
Larrabee, Martin Glover *biophysics educator*
Lotz, George Michael *retired computer graphics executive, graphic designer, photographer*

Glen Burnie
†Hepburn, Jeanette C. *home health nurse*
Wityk, Joseph John *radiologist*
Zabetakis, Thomas John *federal agency administrator*

Glen Echo
Stevenson, A. Brockie *retired artist*

Glencoe
Weeks, Anne Macleod *English language eductor, education director*

Glenn Dale
Helfers, Eric C. *financial analyst*
Pierson, Kenneth Lantz *motor carrier safety consultant*

Glyndon
Renbaum, Barry Jeffrey *lawyer*

Grasonville
Andrews, Archie Moulton *government official*

Greenbelt
Auerbach, Bob Shipley *librarian*
Augustyn, Frederick John, Jr., *librarian*
Beach, Linda Marie *total quality management professional*
Billingsley, Lance W. *lawyer*
Brugger, George Albert *lawyer*
Bryant, Paul T. *electronics engineering manager*
†Cohen, Steven Charles *geophysicist*
Comiso, Josefino Cacas *research scientist*
Cooper, Robert Shanklin *engineering executive, former government official*
Dantzler, Andrew Alan *science administrator*
†Eplee, Robert Eugene *geophysicist*
Ferrara, Jeffrey Francis *electronics engineer*
Fixsen, Dale J. *physicist*
†Fontaine, Kathleen Sturey *human resources specialist*
Greenwald, Andrew Eric *lawyer*
†Healey, John Joseph *engineering executive, civil engineer*
Hendley, Coit Taylor, III, *chemistry educator*
Hogensen, Margaret Hiner *librarian, consultant*
Hollis, Jan Michael *astrophysicist, scientific computer analyst*
Jackley, Michael Dano *lawyer*
Jascourt, Hugh D. *lawyer, arbitrator, mediator*
Kolasinski, John Richard *electrical engineer*
Ku, Jentung *mechanical and aerospace engineer*
Levitt, Gerald Steven *engineering services executive*
Maran, Stephen Paul *astronomer*
Mather, John Cromwell *astrophysicist*
Messitte, Peter Jo *judge*
†Middleton, Elizabeth McPhee *research scientist*
Miller, Alwin Vermar *educational advisor, consultant*
Moore, Virginia Bradley *librarian*
Moskalenko, Igor Vladimirovich *physicist, astrophysicist*
Mumma, Michael Jon *physicist, researcher*
Obamogie, Mercy A. *physician*
Ormes, Jonathan Fairfield *astrophysicist, science administrator, researcher*
Parkinson, Claire L. *climatologist*
†Shirron, Peter John *physicist*
Simpson, Joanne Malkus *meteorologist*
Stehman, Betty Kohls *financial and management consultant*
Steiner, Mark David *systems engineer*
Stief, Louis John *chemist*
†Suid, Lawrence H. *historian, writer*
†Tao, Wei-Kuo *meteorologist, researcher*

Thomas, Lindsey Kay, Jr., *research ecology biologist, educator, consultant*
Tilton, James Charles *computer engineer*
Vranish, John Michael *electrical engineer, researcher*
Wiscombe, Warren Jackman *research scientist*
Wood, H(oward) John, III, *astrophysicist, astronomer*

Gunpowder
Stevens, Jill Winifred *project expediter*

Hagerstown
Baer, John Metz *entrepreneur*
Berkson, Jacob Benjamin *lawyer, author, conservationist*
Blickenstaff, Danny Jay *retired civilian military employee*
Coffen, Richard Wayne *minister, editor*
Coles, Robert Nelson, Sr., *religious organization administrator*
Cost, Francis Howard, Jr., *physician*
†Domenico, Anthony Wayne *music educator*
†Evanson, Paul John *utilities executive*
†Gilbert, Howard William, Jr., *lawyer*
Harrison, Lois Smith *hospital executive, educator*
Jacques, Joseph Howard *human resources professional*
Noia, Alan James *utility company executive*
Perry, Cinda *music educator*
†Sanders, Korby Moss *music educator*
Spruill, Howard Vernon *former academic administrator, minister*
Strauss, Albert John, Jr., *pediatrician*
†Ward, Spring Tina *history and political science educator*
Warner, Charles David, III, *academic administrator*

Hampstead
†Merryman, Walter Spencer *protective services official*

Hanover
Alger, James Arthur *computer consultant*
†Chiarella, Donald Joseph Gray *information systems specialist, educator*
Classen, Henry Ward *lawyer, educator*
Rochdi, Myriam *pharmacist, researcher*
Schmidt, Sandra Jean *secondary school educator*

Havre De Grace
Huang, Yung-Hui *chemical engineer*
Jay, Peter Augustus *writer, farmer*
Russell, William Alexander, Jr., *environmental scientist*

Hereford
Flemmer, David Duane *clinical psychologist*

Highland
Varga, Deborah Trigg *music educator, entertainment company owner*

Hollywood
Powledge, Fred Arlius *freelance writer*
Shah, Nayan *internist*

Hughesville
Hilwig, Joseph Michael *electric company director*
Tudor, Thomas Rae *electric power industry executive*

Hunt Valley
Carney, Stephen Patrick *insurance company executive*
†Collier, Stephen N *educational consultant*
Igusa, Jun-Ichi *mathematician, educator*
Kinstlinger, Jack *engineering executive, consultant*
Plaks, Albert I. *electrical engineer, educator*

Huntingtown
Faust, William Roscoe *physicist*

Hyattsville
†Asongu, Januarius Jingwa *information technology executive*
Bender, Howard Jeffrey *software engineering consultant*
Bloomfield, Maxwell Herron, III, *history and law educator*
†Brett, Kate M. *epidemiologist, researcher*
Dukes, Rebecca Weathers (Becky Dukes) *musician, singer, songwriter*
Embody, Daniel Robert *biometrician*
Freedman, Morris *English language educator*
Golden, Marita *English language educator, foundation executive*
†Gonzalez, Joe Fred, Jr., *mathematical statistician, educator*
Kirk, James Allen *mechanical engineering educator*
Levy, David Lawrence *lawyer, legal association administrator, advocate*
†Matty, Robert Jay *lawyer*
McClain, George Nelson *economist, lawyer*
Pierce, Melvin Andrew *engineer*
Raines, Charlotte Austine Butler *artist, poet*
Rodgers, Mary Columbro *English educator, academic administrator, writer*
Rose, Deborah *epidemiologist*
Rummel, Edgar Ferrand *retired lawyer*
†Shimizu, Iris M. *statistician, consultant*
Sondik, Edward J. *health science administrator*
Spiegel, Robert Alan *lawyer*

Indian Head
Latimer, Paul Jerry *non-destructive testing engineer*
†Price, Teresa Annette *elementary school educator*

Jefferson
Dybell, Elizabeth Anne Sledden *clinical psychologist*

Ward, Susan Annette *music teacher*

Jessup
Fox, Dawne Marie *safety scientist*

Joppa
Bates, Charles Benjamin *elementary school administrator*
Kott, Beverly Parat *financial counselor, community activist*
Morgenstern, Hans George *consulting engineer*

Kennedyville
Schiff, Gary Stuart *academic administrator, educator, consultant*

Kensington
Aborn, Murray *social scientist, researcher*
Blum, Robert Allan *psychiatrist*
Choi, Young Soo *pharmacologist, toxicologist*
Cotlove, Elaine Wolf *psychiatrist, psychoanalyst*
Dauster, William Gary *lawyer, economist*
Dugua, Pierre-Yves *journalist*
Frederikse, Yolanda Rossi *painter, printmaker, art educator*
Gerra, Martin J(erome), Jr., *economist, educator*
†Groner, Isaac Nathan *lawyer*
Hayunga, Mary Ann *women's health nurse*
Holloway, William Jimmerson *retired educator*
Hum, Vance York *technology consulting executive*
Jackson, William David *research executive*
Lisle, Martha Oglesby *retired mathematics educator*
Mathias, Joseph Marshall *lawyer, judge*
Mirkin, Gabe Baron *allergist, pediatrician, medical writer, educator, radio personality, talk show host*
Murray, Thomas James *financial planner, publisher*
†Palacios, Gonzalo T. *education educator*
Rather, Lucia Porcher Johnson *library administrator*
Ricketts, Marijane Gnegy *poet*
Rosenthal, Alan Sayre *government official*
Suraci, Charles Xavier, Jr., *retired federal agency administrator, aerospace education consultant*
Szára, Stephen István *pharmacologist, consultant*

La Plata
Bivens, Kenneth Edward *physician assistant*
†Bryant, Maria Isabel *social sciences educator*
Fisher, Gail Feimster *government official*
Genz, Patricia Ann *English language and literature educator*

Landover
†Maduka, Chikezie *journalist*

Lanham
Criscimagna, Ned Henry *reliability engineer*
Degnan, John James, III, *physicist*
Fields, Stuart Howard *labor relations specialist*
Godwin, Mary Jo *editor, librarian consultant*
†Hardin, David Jesse *application developer*
†Kumako, Kuami Mawunyo *agricultural scientist*
Lyons, James Edward *publishing executive*
Pendley, Rex Dale *systems engineer*

Lanham Seabrook
Barnes, Margaret Anderson *business consultant*
Cook, Linda Kay *critical care nurse*
Corrothers, Helen Gladys *criminal justice official*
Gokulanathan, Karakat Sankaran *pediatrician, educator*
†Hill, Ben *broadcast executive*
Littlefield, Roy Everett, III, *association executive, legal educator*
†Moore, Erica *band director*
Pleasant-Jackson, Tonya *therapist, consultant*
Reupke, William Albert *engineer*

Largo
Mahaffey, Redge Allan *movie producer, director, writer, actor, scientist*
Wootten, Patricia Eileen *adult education educator*

Laurel
Babin, Steven Michael *atmospheric scientist, researcher*
Berkenblit, Scott Ira *orthopaedic surgeon*
Bowman, Bruce Alan *civil engineer*
Chrismer, Ronald Michael *federal agency administrator*
Cornett, Richard Orin *research educator, consultant*
Coursey, Sharon Martin *adult education educator, consultant*
Dallman, Paul Jerald *engineer, writer*
†Darrell, Charles G. *engineer*
Dorsey, John Wesley, Jr., *university administrator, economist*
Eaton, Alvin Ralph *aeronautical and systems engineer, research and development administrator*
Guo, Yanping *physicist*
Highman, Barbara *dermatologist*
Kossiakoff, Alexander *chemist, researcher*
Landis, Donna Marie *nursing administrator, women's health nurse*
Logsdon, Roslyn *artist, educator*
Lombardo, Joseph Samuel *acoustical engineer*
Lui, Anthony Tat Yin *physicist*
Maurer, Richard Hornsby *physicist*
†Mulich, Terrence Joseph, Jr., *aerospace engineer*
Peri, Joseph Silvio Julius *physicist, mathematician*
Rorie, Conrad Jonathan *scientist, naval officer*
Sathyamoorthy, Venugopal *research biologist*
Westhaver, Lawrence Albert *electronics engineer, consultant*

Leominster
†Markham, John Thomas *social worker, educator*

Leonardtown
Carney, Daniel L. *program and financial management consultant*
Lacer, Alfred Antonio *lawyer, educator*
Rudigier, Roberta Lynn *librarian*
Smalley, Robert Manning *government official*

Lexington Park
Donely, George Anthony Thomas, III, *economist, consultant*
†Jackameit, Kevin Charles *information scientist*
Morgan, Dennis Alan *retired federal official*
Sprague, Edward Auchincloss *retired association executive, economist*

Libertytown
Lindblad, Richard Arthur *retired health services administrator, drug abuse epidemiologist*

Linthicum
Banuk, Ron Edward (Ron Banuk) *mechanical engineer*
†Burns, Michael William *lawyer former state legislator*

Linthicum Heights
Skillman, William Alfred *consulting engineering executive*
†Stein, David Eric *physicist, defense analyst*
Tietz, Dietmar Juergen *computer Web engineer, scientist*

Lusby
Eshelman, Ralph Ellsworth *maritime historian, vertebrate paleontologist, cultural resource consultant*
Hutchins, Edith Elizabeth *accountant*
Ladd, Culver Sprogle *secondary education educator*

Lutherville
Chait, Andrea Melinda *school psychologist*
Eisenberg, Joseph Martin *psychologist, consultant*
Elma, Bayani Borja *physician*
Frank, Dana Hunt *internist, educator*
Freeland, Charles *lawyer, accountant*
Kissel, William Thorn, Jr., *sculptor*
Lowe, Gerald Scott *baseball organization executive*
Mc Kenney, Walter Gibbs, Jr., *lawyer, publishing company executive*
Morison, Warwick Lindsay *dermatologist, educator, consultant*
Moses, Howard *neurologist*
Moyer, Bernadette Ann *writer, publisher, business owner*
Proctor, Leonard Ray *otolaryngologist, educator*

Lutherville Timonium
Bevis, Robert E. *retired oil company executive*
Booth, Penelope Partridge *educator, school principal, author*
Brustein, Abram Isaac *insurance company executive*
Cedrone, Louis Robert, Jr., *critic*
Dembo, Donald Howard *cardiologist, medical administrator, educator*
†Giro, Jorge Antonio *language educator, educator*
Gray, Dahli *accounting educator and administrator*
Klasons, Ilona *accountant, consultant*
Kolker, Roger Russell *insurance executive*
Miller, John E. *retired cardiovascular surgeon*
Muuss, Rolf Eduard *retired psychologist, author*
Park, Lee Crandall *psychiatrist*
Pierpont, Ross Z. *former surgeon*
Sackett, Joyce Wilhelmina *hospitality coordinator*
Sagerholm, James Alvin *retired naval officer*
Sternberger, Ludwig Amadeus *neurologist, educator*

Madison
Hoffman, Alicia Coro *retired federal executive*
Hoffman, Kenneth Myron *mathematician, educator*

Marion Station
†Handy, Mary Thomas *retired elementary school educator*

Marriottsville
Strange, Donald Ernest *health care company executive*

Marydel
LaBarge, Christopher W. *priest*
Neil, Fred Applestein *public relations executive*

Mc Henry
Kelly, Robert William *economist*

Mcdaniel
Roth, Lisa Mae *writer*

Mechanicsville
Henderson, Madeline Mary (Berry Henderson) *chemist, researcher, consultant*
Rands, Robert Lawrence *archaeologist*

Middletown
Young, Wayne Stevens *military officer, human resources administrator*

Millersville
Schulmeyer, G(eorge) Gordon *information systems executive, consultant*
Vlavianos, John G. *retired federal agency administrator*

Millington
Kingsbury, Robert Coburn *physician, consultant*

Mitchellville
Akridge, Paul Bai *business consultant*
Ball, Robert M(yers) *social security, welfare and health policy specialist, writer, lecturer*
Blasier, Cole *political scientist, educator*
Brubaker, Lauren Edgar *minister, educator*
Chilman, Catherine Earles Street *social welfare educator, author*
Embree, Ainslie Thomas *history educator*
Heald, Morrell *humanities educator, educator*
Henle, Peter *retired economic consultant, arbitrator*
Marsh, Caryl Amsterdam *museum exhibitions curator, psychologist, advisor*

Monkton
Mountcastle, Vernon Benjamin *neurophysiologist*

Monrovia
McCurdy, John Dennis *biochemist, toxicologist*

Montgomery Village
Avedisian, Archie Harry *community organization executive*
Bingham, Raymond Joseph *neonatal/perinatal nurse practitioner*
Hewitt, Emmett Clyde, III, *software acquisition executive*
Kushner, Lawrence Maurice *physical chemist, consultant*
Murray, Peter *metallurgist, manufacturing company executive*
Robinson, Henry Ward *meteorologist*

Morningside
McClain, Edward Fifer, Jr., *retired physicist*

Mount Airy
Collins, Henry James, III, *insurance company executive*
†Scott, Leighton Reeves *marketing professional*
Wagner, Doris Walkling *volunteer, director*

Myersville
Patrick, Georgia O'Brien Lakaytis *communications executive*

New Market
Gabriel, Eberhard John *lawyer*

North Bethesda
Anderson, Owen Raymond *scientific and educational organization executive*
Chilcote, Samuel Day, Jr., *trade association administrator*
Rogul, June Audrey *fundraising executive, government relations specialist*
Shapiro, Maurice Mandel *nuclear astrophysicist*
Sherman, Deane Murray *culture organization administrator*
Sontag, James Mitchell *cancer researcher*
Szabo, Daniel *government official*

North Potomac
Geller, Ronald Gene *biomedical researcher, consultant*
†Keane, James Ignatius *lawyer, consultant*
Lehman, Leonard *retired lawyer, consultant*
Lide, David Reynolds *handbook and database editor*
Pergantis, Constantine George *lighting contractor*
Rehr, Paula Bernice Beldock *writer*

Oakland
Cavarocchi, Nicholas Guy *public relations executive*
McClintock Fost, Donna *social worker*

Ocean City
Corun, Ronald Lewis *asphalt refining executive*
O'Hanlon, Richard Thomas *counseling educator*

Ocean Pines
Crawford, Norman Crane, Jr., *academic administrator, consultant*
Mahr, Aaron Lee *retired government executive*

Odenton
†Aho, Brien *photojournalist*
Evans, William Lee *biologist, educator*
Mucha, John Frank *information systems professional*
Reich, Merrill Drury *intelligence consultant, writer*

Olney
†Baker, Carl Gwin *research administrator*
Delmar, Eugene Anthony *architect*
Michael, Jerrold Mark *public health specialist, former university dean, educator*
†Sodetz, Carol Jean *aquatic fitness educator*
Weller, Jane Kathleen *emergency nurse*
Westerman, Rosemary Matzzie *nurse, administrator*

Owings
Oring, Stuart August *visual information specialist, publisher, writer, photographer, researcher*
Parrett, Sherman O. *lawyer*

Owings Mills
Barton, Dawn Kanani *elementary school educator*
Berg, Barbara Kirsner *health education specialist*
Berman, Wulfred *pediatrician*
Billick, Brian *professional football coach*
Coates, Ben Terrence *professional football player*
Disharoon, Leslie Benjamin *retired insurance executive*
Granat, Richard Stuart *lawyer, educator*
Heck, Albert Frank *retired neurologist*
Holdridge, Barbara *book publisher*
Morris, Bosher Blyth *poet*
Nes, David Gulick *retired diplomat*
†Newsome, Ozzie *manager professional athletics*
Perkins, Tammy Jean *title coordinator*
†Reihl, Donna L. *director*
Ryan, Judith W. *geriatrics consultant, adult nurse practitioner, educator, researcher*
Sanner, George Bradley *bank executive*
Smith, Katrina Diane *writer*
Tapp, Mamie Pearl *educational association administration*
Vijayakumar, Rajagopal *filter industry executive*
Whittle, Joseph F., Jr., *engineering executive, consultant*

Oxford
Radcliffe, George Grove *retired life insurance company executive*
Shepard, William Seth *government official, diplomat, writer*
Zachai, Dohrn Dorian *artist*

Oxon Hill
†Fields, Richard Lawrence *lawyer, consultant*
†Scott, Frances Fisher Markoe *retired secondary school educator*

Parkton
Cummins, Paul Zach, II, *insurance company executive*
Fitzgerald, Edwin Roger *physicist, educator*

Parkville
Hill, Milton King, Jr., *retired lawyer*
Jensen, Arthur Seigfried *consulting engineering physicist*
Munson, Paul Lewis *pharmacologist*

Pasadena
Asti, Alison Louise *lawyer*
Dubke, Marie E. *business educator*
Young, Russell Dawson *physics consultant*

Patuxent River
Adams, Richard Eugene *aerospace engineer, project manager*
Dyer, Joseph Wendell *career officer*
Fitzhugh, David Michael *lawyer*
Frazier, William Edward *materials engineer*
Kennedy, David L. *social worker, military officer*
Tipton, Thomas Wesley *retired aerospace engineer*

Perry Point
Miller, Alan Gilmore *psychiatrist*
Yackley, Luke Eugene *nursing educator*

Phoenix
Harclerode, Howard Charles, II, (Skip Harclerode) *chemical engineer*

Pocomoke
Hickman, John Norwood *marketing professional*

Pocomoke City
†Porter, James Harry, Jr., *lawyer*

Port Deposit
Burch, G. David *sculptor*

Port Republic
Karol, Eugene Michael *school system administrator*
Sugarman, Jule Meyer *children's services consultant, former public administrator*

Port Tobacco
†Smith, Sheila Robertson *laboratory technician*

Potomac
Anfinsen, Libby Esther Shulman *social worker, clinical administrator*
Au, Mary Lee *school system administrator*
Brashear, Jerry Paul *management consultant*
Bremenstuhl, David P. *elementary school educator*
Brewer, Nathan Ronald *veterinarian, consultant*
Broderick, John Caruthers *retired librarian, educator*
Brown, Earle Palmer *advertising agency executive*
Casella, Russell Carl *physicist*
Christian, John Kenton *organization executive, publisher, writer, marketing consultant*
Cotton, William Robert *retired dentist*
Crowson, Henry Lawrence *mathematician, educator*
Cutler, Robert Sumner *engineering educator*
Dyer, Rosemary *musician*
Epstein, Mark Robert *electronics manufacturing executive*
Feldman, Myer *lawyer*
Fink, Daniel Julien *management consultant*
Foley, Joseph Patrick *public relations executive*
Foord, Robert LaVerne *intelligence executive, consultant*
Fox, Arthur Joseph, Jr., *editor*
Frey, James McKnight *government official*
Frieder, Gideon *computer science and engineering educator*
Gelatt, James Prentice *nonprofit management consultant*
Hall, William Darlington *lawyer*
Heller, Peggy Osna *psychotherapist, poetry therapist*
Johnson, Anne Hale *educational association administrator, director*
Johnson, W. Taylor *physician*
Jones, Sidney Lewis *economist, researcher, educator*
Karnow, Stanley *journalist, writer*
Karson, Emile *international business executive*
Keil, Marilyn Martin *artist*
Kernan, Barbara Desind *senior government executive*
Kessler, Ronald *author*
†Khachaturian, Zaven Setrak *neuroscientist*
Kirkendall, Thomas D. *aerospace engineer, materials scientist*
†Kling, William *economist, retired foreign service officer*

Kuykendall, Crystal Arlene *educational consultant, lawyer*
Lawrence, Robert Edward *electrical engineer*
Leva, Neil Irwin *psychotherapist, hypnotherapist*
Leva, Susan Mary *social worker*
Marincola, Elizabeth Mark *scientific society executive*
Martinez, Miguel Eduardo *development bank executive*
Medin, A. Louis *computer company executive*
Medin, Julia Adele *mathematics educator, researcher*
Meyer, Lawrence George *lawyer*
Mullenbach, Linda Herman *lawyer*
Murow, Christine *music educator*
Noonan, Patrick Francis *conservation executive*
Oh, John Kie-Chiang *political science educator, university official*
Orski, C. Kenneth *consulting company executive, lawyer, publisher*
Owen, Harrison Hollingsworth *management consultant*
Parker, Ellis Jackson, III, *lawyer, broadcaster*
Pastan, Linda Olenik *poet*
Patel, Vinod Motibhai *accountant*
Peter, Phillips Smith *lawyer*
Peters, Frank Albert *retired chemical engineer*
Powell, Robert Dominick *lawyer*
†Redding, Robert Ellsworth *lawyer*
Rehns, Marsha Lee *magazine editor, writer*
Reichley, A. James *political scientist*
Rhode, Alfred Shimon *business consultant, finance educator*
Roesser, Jean Wolberg *state official*
Rosenberg, Jacob Joseph *orthodontist*
Rosenberg, Sarah Zacher *institute arts administration executive, humanities administration consultant*
Rotberg, Iris Comens *social scientist*
Ryan, Frank Thomas *tire company executive*
Schleckser, James Henry *engineering executive, sales executive*
Schonholtz, Joan Sondra Hirsch *banker, civic worker*
Shapiro, Richard Gerald *retired department store executive, consultant*
†Shirvinski, Adam John *management consultant*
Sundick, Sherry Small *author, journalist, poet*
Troffkin, Howard Julian *lawyer, diversified company executive*
Vadus, Gloria A. *scientific document examiner*
Walker, Charls Edward *economist, consultant*
Wang, An-Ming *composer*
Wartofsky, William Victor *writer, consultant*
Waugaman, Richard Merle *psychiatrist, psychoanalyst, educator*
Weiss, Michael David *mathematician, mathematical economist*
Williams, Peter MacLellan *nuclear engineer*
Wolman, Eric *health care consultant*
Wonnacott, Paul *economics educator*
†Young, Lih Ying H. *economist, consultant*

Potomac Falls
Mc Mullen, Thomas Henry *retired air force officer*

Prince Frederick
Judge, Charles A. *physician, statistician*
Karol, Victoria Diane *educational administrator*
†Reynolds, Christopher John *lawyer*

Princess Anne
Acquah, Sarah Nipah *agricultural educator*
†Gupta, Gian Chand *environmental scientist*
Joshi, Jagmohan *agronomist, consultant*
McKinney, Frances Hathaway *university program administrator*

Quantico
Scott, David Winfield *artist, museum consultant*

Queenstown
Carr, Richard William *federal program manager*
Corn, Morton *environmental engineer, educator*

Randallstown
Hatch, Sally Ruth *foundation administrator, writer, consultant*

Reisterstown
Bart, Polly Turner *real estate developer*
Clews, William Vincent *writer*
Daley, Peter Edmund *business and human resources company executive*
†Goethe, Elizabeth Hogue *music educator*
Tannenbaum, Harvey *defense technology consultant*
Tirone, Barbara Jean *health insurance administrator*

Riva
Barto, Bradley Edward *small business owner, educator*

Riverdale
Bernard, Cathy S. *management corporation executive*
Gonzalez Arias, Victor Hugo *management executive*
Guetzkow, Daniel *technology company entrepreneur*
Kumar, Shailendra *urologist, educator*
†Williams, Lisa Monique *information technology executive*

Rock Hall
Lang, Lillian Owen *retired accountant*

Rockville
Aamodt, Roger Louis *federal agency administrator*
Armstrong, Kenneth *lawyer*
†Ashby, Florence Helen *mathematics educator*
Avery, Bruce Edward *lawyer*
†Baine, William Brennan *public health service officer, internist*

Barkley, Brian Evan *lawyer, political consultant*
Barr, Solomon Efrem *allergist, educator*
Barron, Myra Hymovich *lawyer*
Basinger, William Daniel *computer programmer*
Bayne, Kathryn Ann Louise *veterinarian*
Beer, Janusz Zygmunt *radiation and photo biologist, scientist*
Benz, Daniel Arthur *animal scientist*
Berryman, Richard Byron *lawyer*
Birns, Mark Theodore *physician*
†Brewer-Pecson, Dorothy Wynne *environmentalist*
Brown, David Harry *speech educator*
Brown, Martin Howard *physician*
Buchanan, John Donald *retired health physicist, radiochemist*
Burdick, William MacDonald *biomedical engineer*
Burt, Marvin Roger *financial advisor, investment manager*
Bush, Donna *forensic toxicologist*
Cain, Karen Mirinda *musician, educator*
Cantelon, Philip Louis *historian*
Carmona, Richard *surgeon general*
Chaney, Bradford William *educational research consultant*
†Chang, Ya-Ting *pianist, music educator, educator*
Cheston, Sheila Carol *lawyer*
Chiacchierini, Richard Philip *healthcare consultant*
Chiogioji, Melvin Hiroaki *former government official, entrepreneur*
†Chohayeb, Aida A. *dentist, educator*
†Chretien, Paul Bernard *oncologist, medical researcher*
Clancy, Carolyn *science foundation director, researcher, educator*
Clark, H. Westley *health facility administrator*
Cohen-Mansfield, Jiska *psychologist, educator, researcher*
Cooperman, Susan *educator*
Corley, Rose Ann McAfee *government official*
†Correa, Galo A. *construction executive*
Covington, Sharon Nickel *social worker, psychotherapist*
Cowan, William Maxwell *neurobiologist*
Crawford, Lester Mills , Jr., *veterinarian*
Cromwell, James Julian *lawyer*
Curie, Charles G. *federal agency administrator*
Daisley, William Prescott *lawyer*
Davies-Venn, Christian *environmental engineer*
De Jong, David Samuel *lawyer, educator*
Doyle, Thomas Edward *lawyer, educator*
Duke, Elizabeth M. *health facility administrator*
†DuPont, Robert Louis *psychiatrist, physician*
†Durr, Kenneth D. *historian*
Edinger, Stanley Evan *clinical chemist*
Edwards, Bert Tvedt *accountant*
Edwards, Leisl Marie Baum *interior designer*
Epps, Leon Anthony *government official*
Epstein, Jay Stuart *federal regulator*
†Ermolaeva, Maria D. *bioinformatician, researcher*
Ewing, Blair Gordon *federal official*
Farahani, Mahnaz *chemist, scientist*
Feigal, David W., Jr., *health science association administrator*
Feingold, S. Norman *psychologist*
Finlayson, John Sylvester *biochemist*
Fratantoni, Joseph Charles *medical researcher, hematologist, biotechnology executive*
Frazier, Walter Ronald *real estate investment company executive*
Freedman, Marc Allan *investment advisory executive*
Frye, Roland Mushat, Jr., *lawyer*
Fthenakis, Emanuel John *diversified aerospace company executive*
Furman, Robert Ralph *real estate developer*
†Futrovsky, Cheryl Jean *foundation administrator, performing company executive*
Georgiev, Goshko Atanasov *agrometeorologist, researcher*
Gluckstein, Fritz Paul *veterinarian, biomedical information specialist*
Gonzalez-Licea, Augustin *pathologist, public health service officer*
†Gordon, Michael Robert *lawyer, state legislator*
Graham, Robert *medical association executive*
Greenberg, Jerrold Selig *health education educator*
Gulya, Aina Julianna *neurotologist, surgeon, educator*
†Gutman, Steven Ifor *pathologist*
Hanes, Donald Keith *cooperative communications executive*
Haudenschild, Christian Charles *pathologist, educator*
Henderson, Harriet *librarian*
Henricson, Beth Ellen *microbiologist*
Hewlett, Richard Greening *historian*
Hill, Tabitha Kimberly *science educator*
†Hisada, Michie *physician, epidemiologist*
Hoar, William Patrick *editor, author*
Howard, Lee Milton *international health consultant*
Hsia, David *health services researcher, administrator*
Hubert, Barbara Boeklen *pharmaceutical company executive*
Jacques, Joseph William *investment advisor*
Jamieson, Graham A. *biochemist, organization official*
†Jarugula, Venkateswar Rao *medical researcher*
Johnson, Emery Allen *physician*
Juliana, James Nicholas *ordnance company executive*
†Junod, Suzanne White *historian, consultant*
Kacuba, Alice Marie *nurse*
Kadish, Richard L. *lawyer*
Kafka, Marian Stern *neuroscientist*
Kalton, Graham *survey statistician*
Kamerow, Martin Laurence *accountant*
Kamerow, Norman Warren *business owner, financial services executive*
†Kaplan, Lawrence Samuel *historian, educator*
Karp, Ronald Alvin *lawyer*

Katz, Steven Martin *lawyer, accountant*
Kelsey, Frances Oldham (Mrs. Fremont Ellis Kelsey) *government official*
Kerxton, Alan Smith *lawyer*
Kessel, John Philip *lawyer*
†Kinnane, Adrian *historian*
Kline, Raymond Adam *professional organization executive*
Kohlmeier, Louis Martin, Jr., *newspaper reporter*
Kruger, Jerome *materials science educator, consultant*
Kurkul, Wenyi Wang *musician, educator, administrator*
Kurzman, Harold Philip *transportation economist, consultant*
Landon, John Campbell *research and development company executive*
Landry, Robert Joseph *physicist*
Langley, Roger Richard *editor*
Leach, Lynnetta Jane *social worker, consultant*
Lewis, Benjamin Pershing, Jr., *pharmacist, public health service officer*
Littman, Burt A. *obstetrician-gynecologist*
Lloyd, Douglas Seward *physician, public health educator*
Long, Cedric William *health research executive*
Luxemburg, Jack Alan *rabbi*
MacArthur, Diana Taylor *advanced technology executive*
MacGregor, James Thomas *toxicologist*
Manasse, Henri Richard, Jr., *association executive*
Manderscheid, Ronald William *federal program administrator*
Marcuccio, Phyllis Rose *retired association executive, editor*
†Marroum, Patrick John *government agency administrator*
Masters, Gary Everett *librarian, educator*
McClellan, Mark B. *federal agency administrator*
†McCormick, Kathleen Ann Krym *geriatrics nurse, information scientist, federal agency administrator*
McDonald, Capers Walter *biomedical engineer, corporate executive*
McGaffigan, Edward, Jr., *federal agency administrator*
McGinnis, Thomas J. *governmemt agency administrator, pharmacist*
McQuain, Jeffrey Hunter *writer, editor, word historian*
Megan, Thomas Ignatius *retired judge*
†Mehrabi, Shah M. *economist, educator*
Menendez, Adolfo *engineering company executive*
Mertz, Walter *retired government research executive*
Meyer, F. Weller *bank executive*
Michael, Robert Roy *lawyer*
Middleton, Wanda Karen Lee *songwriter, poet, minister*
Miller, Claire Ellen *children's writer, editor, educator*
Miller, Kenneth Michael *electronics executive, director*
†Mofenson, Lynne Meryl *pediatrician*
†Mohan, Aparna Krishna *epidemiologist, physician*
Molitor, Graham Thomas Tate *lawyer*
Morella, Constance Albanese *former congressman*
Morgan, William Bruce *naval architect*
Moritsugu, Kenneth Paul *physician, government official*
Moul, Judd Wendell *urologist, surgeon*
Nevin, Joseph Francis *computer systems engineer*
Niewiaroski, Trudi Osmers (Gertrude Niewiaroski) *social studies educator*
O'Donnell, Duck Hee *cellist, music teacher*
O'Donnell, James Francis *retired health science administrator*
Parham, Deborah *health facility administrator*
Patrick, Philip Howard *lawyer*
Pennello, Gene Anthony *statistician*
Petrick, Patricia A. *physician, educator*
Petzold, Carol Stoker *state legislator*
Peyser, Hedy Jeanette *social worker*
Pfanz, Harry Willcox *historian*
Porter, John Robert, Jr., *space technology company executive, geochemist*
Pospisil, George Curtis *human research educator*
Proffitt, John Richard *business executive, educator*
Przygodzki, Ronald Mieczyslaw *pathologist, researcher*
†Rachanow, Gerald Marvin *lawyer, pharmacist*
Rankin, Rachel Ann *retired media specialist*
Rao, Potarazu Krishna *environmental consultant*
Rasmussen, Caren Nancy *hospital executive*
Reddy, Thikkavarapu Ramachandra *electrical engineer*
Rimer, Barbara K. *health facility administrator, educator*
Roberts, Christopher Chalmers *lawyer*
Robinowitz, Max *pathologist, consultant*
Rodriguez, William Julio *physician*
Rosen, Saul Woolf *research scientist, health facility administrator*
Sacchet, Edward Michael *foreign service officer*
Sansalone, William Robert *biochemistry educator, researcher*
Schindler, Albert Isadore *physicist, educator*
Scully, Martha Seebach *speech and language pathologist*
Seagle, Edgar Franklin *environmental engineer, consultant*
Senior, John Robert *internist, gastroenterologist, hepatologist, consultant*
Shah, Vinod Purushottam *research scientist*
Shekar, Sam *health facility administrator*
Sherman, Linda Ann *infectious disease physician, pathologist, researcher*
†Shojaei, Amir Hossein *pharmaceutical scientist*
Shuren, Jeffrey Eliot *behavioral neurologist, lawyer*

†Skurkovich, Simon *medical scientist*
†Smith, David Robinson *lawyer*
Smith, Mark Alan *management consultant*
Smith, Shelagh Alison *public health educator*
Soderberg, William Charles *philosophy educator*
Sorensen, John Noble *mechanical and nuclear engineer*
Souto, Carlos Dias *engineer*
Spahr, Frederick Thomas *association executive*
Sparks, David Stanley *university administrator*
Standing, Kimberly Anna *educational researcher*
Stansfield, Charles W. *educational administrator*
Stigi, John Francis *federal agency administrator*
Stonesifer, John DeWitt *priest, educator*
Sumberg, Alfred Donald *professional association executive*
Sundlof, Stephen Frederick *veterinary administrator*
Tabor, Edward *physician, researcher*
Talwar, Pankaj *physician*
Temple, Robert *physician, federal agency administrator*
†Thompson, James Lee *lawyer*
Thompson, Susan Diane *physician*
Titus, Roger Warren *lawyer*
Tomar, Richard Thomas *lawyer*
†Tracy, LaRee Ann *statistician, medical researcher*
Tripp, Frederick Gerald *investment advisor*
Trujillo, Michael H. *administrator*
Uppoor, Rajendra *pharmaceutical scientist, pharmacist, educator, researcher, private pilot*
Van Grack, Steven *lawyer*
Varricchio, Frederick Elia *pathologist, biochemist*
Veech, Richard Lewis *medical researcher, physician*
Venter, J. Craig *science foundation director*
†Vermeulen, Roel *research scientist*
Vincent, Michael Paul *plastic surgeon*
Wall, Janet E. *assessment, testing, evaluation, and career development professional*
Wallach, Harold Charles *health policy and health services research administrator, educator*
Wallenmeyer, William Anton *retired physicist*
Wang, Chung Shan *physicist*
Ward, Neil Anthony *corporate communications specialist*
†Watson, Jerome Roland *marketing professional, researcher*
Weinel, Pamela Jean *nurse administrator*
Wilson, James J. *public administration consultant*
Woodcock, Janet *federal official*
Woodhouse, Kathryn Andersen *counselor, educator*
Yang, Liqiu *physicist*
Yao, John Sen *physician*
†Yu, Mei-ying Wong *chemist, researcher*
Zaphiriou, George Aristotle *lawyer, educator*

Royal Oak
Israel, Lesley Lowe *political scientist, consultant*

Ruxton
Lewis, Alexander Ingersoll, III, *lawyer*
†Sheldon, Louise Roberts *writer*

Sabillasville
McCulloch, Anna Mary Knott *pharmacy technician*

Saint Inigoes
Dorsey, William Walter *aerospace engineer, engineering executive*
Masters, George Windsor, Jr., *electrical engineer, educator*

Saint Marys City
Clifton, Lucille Thelma *author*
†Hooper, Michael Wayne *music educator, director*
Karlin, Wayne *writer*
Krondorfer, Björn *religious studies educator*
Stabile, Donald Robert *economics educator, academic administrator*
Stover, Lois T. *education educator, department chairman*

Saint Michaels
Berlin, Donald Robert *rabbi*
Brown, Omer Forrest, II, *lawyer*
Feisel, Lyle Dean *retired dean, electrical engineer, educator*
Ferraro, Linda Ann *veterinarian*
Jones, Raymond Edward, Jr., *brewing executive*
Peck, Charles Edward *retired construction and mortgage executive*
Young, Donald Roy *pharmacist*

Salisbury
†Adams, Stephen Bernard *finance educator, consultant*
†Barzilai, Harel *education educator*
Booker, Betty Mae *poet*
Buchness, Michael Patrick *cardiothoracic surgeon*
Clarke, Wm. A. Lee, III, *lawyer*
Cugler, Carol Marie Miller *retired mental health services professional*
†Ennels, Edward Charles *mathematician, educator*
House, Charletta *librarian*
†Jennings, Louis Brown *retired humanities educator*
†Jiménez, Carmen Julia *language educator*
†Kleiman, Gary Howard *broadcast, advertising and cellular communications consultant*
Madden, Heather Ann *aluminum company executive*
†Miller, Timothy Singley *historian, educator, language educator*
Moultrie, Fred *geneticist, researcher*
Mulligan, Joseph Francis *physicist, science historian, educator*
Newton, Darrell Mottley *communication educator*
Nutter, David George *urban planner*

GEOGRAPHICAL INDEX 5927 MARYLAND

Oldland, Kevin Bradley *architect*
†Parente, Ronaldo *business educator, consultant*
†Perdue, James A. *food products executive*
Rotariu, George Julian *retired physical chemist, consultant*
Tasker, John Baker *veterinary medical educator, college dean*
Woolford, Dornell Larmont *academic administrator*
Wu, Ying *economics educator, researcher*

Sandy Spring
Kanarowski, Stanley Martin *chemist, chemical engineer, government official*

Severn
Nobles, Danny Gene *army officer*

Severna Park
Allison, John Langsdale *naval architect, marine engineer*
†Chatelaine, Kenneth Leo *education educator, psychoanalyst*
Daly, Charles Arthur *health services administrator*
Davis, Clayton *writer, pilot, photographer*
Davis, John Adams, Jr., *electrical engineer, roboticist, corporate research executive*
Ebersberger, Arthur Darryl *insurance company executive, consultant*
Elliott, Kati Marie *communications company official*
Hall, Marcia Joy *non-profit organization administrator*
Hopkins, Edith Rose *artist*
†Humphreys Troy, Patricia *communications executive*
Lesikar, James Daniel, II, *physicist, engineer*
Lilly, John Richard, II, *lawyer*
Moore, John Leo, Jr., *journalist, writer, editor*
Schick, Edgar Brehob *German literature educator*
Simonds, Valerie Deverse *prehospital educator*
Wilmot, Elizabeth C. *business owner*
Windsor, Patricia (Katonah Summertree, Perrin Winters) *author, educator, lecturer*

Shady Side
†Devine, Donald J. *management and political consultant*
Nadolski, Stephanie Lucille *artist, designer*

Showell
Grech, Christopher Alan *lawyer, consultant*

Silver Spring
Adams, Diane Loretta *physician*
Ahmad, Mirza Muzaffar *economic advisor*
Alexander, Herbert E. *political scientist*
†Altschul, B J *public relations counselor*
Alvarez, Aida *former federal agency administrator*
†Anderson, Richard McDonald *hydrologist, engineer*
†Anderson, Sherri L. *medical educator*
Ascher, Bernard *economist*
Aukamp, Ann Walkley North *social worker, consultant, small business owner*
Barkin, Robert Allan *graphic designer, newspaper executive, consultant*
Beach, Bert Beverly *clergyman*
Beard, Lillian B. McLean *physician, consultant*
Bennett, Carol(ine) Elise *retired reporter, retired actress*
Blankenheimer, Bernard *economics consultant*
†Boeringer, James Leslie *music educator*
Bonner, Bester Davis *school system administrator*
Borkovec, Vera Z. *Russian studies educator*
Boykin, Nancy Merritt *academic administrator*
Brandt, Carl David *research virologist*
Briese, Michael W. *writer*
Brog, David *consultant, former air force officer*
Burcroff, Richard Tomkinson, II, *economist*
Burke, Margaret Ann *computer and communications company specialist*
Calinger, Ronald Steve *historian*
†Camphor, James Winky, Jr., *educational administrator*
Carson, Steven Lee *newspaper publisher*
†Cathey, Mary Ellen Jackson *religious studies educator*
†Chery, Reginald *minister*
Coates, Robert Jay *retired electronic scientist, consultant*
Cole, Wayne Stanley *historian, educator*
Coles, Anna Louise Bailey *retired university official, nurse*
Compton, Mary Beatrice Brown (Mrs. Ralph Theodore Compton) *public relations executive, writer*
†Conger, Virginia Day *music educator, educator*
Craig, Paul Max, Jr., *retired lawyer*
Cruze, Kenneth *retired surgeon*
Cunningham, Keith Allen *corporate executive, accountant, lawyer, engineer*
Cunningham, Keith Allen, II, *computer services company executive*
†Doherty, William Thomas, Jr., *historian, retired educator*
†Ehrenkranz, Gil *lawyer*
Ehrlich, Charles David *physicist*
Eig, Blair Mitchell *pediatrician*
†Eiserer, Leonard Albert Carl *publishing executive*
Erk, Frank Chris *biologist, educator*
Fanelli, Joseph James *retired public affairs executive, consultant*
Fields, Daisy Bresley *human resources specialist, writer*
Flug, Janice *librarian*
Fockler, Herbert Hill *foundation executive*
Foster, Victor Lynn *translator*
Fromberg, Jean Stern *school system administrator*
†Fryauff, David J. *military officer, research scientist, microbiologist*
Gabi, Mark *engineering and management educator, consultant, researcher*
Gaydos, Joel Carl *physician*
Germain, Regina *lawyer*
Gilbert, Charles Richard Alsop *physician, medical educator*
Glickman, Albert Seymour *psychologist, educator*
Gold, George Myron *lawyer, editor, writer, consultant*
†Gold, Karen F. *operations research specialist, educator*
Goott, Daniel *government official, consultant*
†Gordon, Joy *music educator*
Gray, Allan P. *chemist, health and environmental consultant*
Grossberg, David Burton *cardiologist*
†Grosso, Stacia Strouss *foundation administrator*
Grubbs, Donald Shaw, Jr., *retired actuary*
†Halvorsen, Harald Wayne *electronics engineer*
Hannan, Myles *lawyer, banker*
Hayman, Harry *association executive, electrical engineer*
Heppner, Donald Gray, Jr., *immunology research physician, army officer*
Herbers, Tod Arthur *publisher*
Hermach, Francis Lewis *consulting engineer*
Hermanson Ogilvie, Judith *foundation executive*
Hetzel, Alice M. *statistician, researcher*
Hoch, Peggy Marie *computer scientist*
Hsueh, Chun-tu *political scientist, historian, foundation executive*
Hubbell, Katherine Jean *retired marketing professional*
Hunt, Mary Elizabeth *religious studies educator*
Jackson, Mary Jane McHale Flickinger *principal*
Jacobs, George *broadcast engineering consulting company executive*
Jaskot, John Joseph *retired insurance company executive*
Kaiser, Hans Elmar *pathology educator, researcher*
Kant, Gloria Jean *retired neuroscientist, researcher*
Katz, Jonathan L. *lawyer*
†Katz, Pearl *anthropoligist, public health analyst*
Kelly, John Joseph, Jr., *government executive*
Kenner, Mary Ellen *marketing and communications executive*
Kevess-Cohen, Ruth M. *internist, geriatrician*
Kline, Jerry Robert *government official, ecologist*
Kolodny, Debra Ruth *labor management and non-profit consultant*
Korth, Thomas A. *musician, educator*
Kramer, Gerson Balfour *lawyer*
†Kurata, Phillip Cedomir *journalist*
Latson, Richard Charles *retired audio-visual specialist*
†Laughlin, Naomi Myers *realtor*
Lederer, Max Donald, Jr., *lawyer*
Ledley, Christian Salvesen *retired social worker*
†Ledsinger, Charles A. *hotel executive*
Lett, Cynthia Ellen Wein *speaker, trainer, coach*
Levy, William Joel *endocrinologist*
†Lindler, Luther Edgar *microbiologist, researcher*
Lizanich-Aro, Suzanne *health care consultant*
Maas, Joe (Melvin Joseph Maas) *retired federal agency administrator*
Mahoney, James R. *federal agency administrator*
Mallory, Joan Matey *music educator, composer*
Markey, Paul Victor *videographer, videotape editor, production manager*
Marvin, John George *clergyman, church organization executive*
Mashin, Jacqueline Ann Cook *medical sciences administrator, nursing administrator*
McCann, Michael F. *industrial hygienist*
†McCray, Lora *real estate developer*
McGinn, Cherie M. *secondary education educator*
†Mohr, Christina *retired economist*
Mok, Carson Kwok-Chi *structural engineer*
Mooney, James Hugh *newspaper editor*
Moreno, Donna Marie *communications executive*
Neuhäuser, Mary Helen *artist, writer, playwright*
Neumann, Alfred John *music director*
Nevans, Laurel S. *rehabilitation counselor*
Nieves, Josephine *federal agency administrator*
Null, Elisabeth Higgins *librarian, writer*
Oberst, Richard B. *military officer, hospital administrator*
O'Connell, Mary Ita *psychotherapist*
Ognibene, Peter John *writer*
†Okigbo, Franklin C. *engineering company executive*
O'Meara, Noel P. *priest, religious organization administrator*
Oswald, Rudolph A. *economist*
†Park, Sangkyun *economist*
†Paulsen, Jan *clergyman, church administrator*
Peiperl, Adam *kinetic sculptor, photographer*
Perlmutter, Jerome Herbert *communications specialist*
Raphael, Coleman *business consultant*
Rayburn, Carole Ann (Mary Aida Rayburn) *psychologist, researcher, writer, consultant*
Rivera-Sinclair, Elsa *psychologist, consultant, researcher*
Roshwald, Mordecai Marceli *educator, writer*
Roth, Harriet Steinhorn *educator, public speaker*
Russo, Anthony Sebastian *telecommunications industry executive*
Sammet, Jean E. *computer scientist*
Saunders, George Wendell *management consultant, retired government official*
Scheer, Milton David *chemical physicist*
Schick, Irvin Henry *academic administrator, educator*
Scipio, L(ouis) Albert, II, *former aerospace science engineering educator, architect, military historian*
Secular, Sidney *writer, weather forecaster, actor, model, voiceover specialist, fundraiser, small business and mailorder marketing consultant*
Shaddinger, Dawn Elizabeth *medical researcher*
Shalowitz, Erwin Emmanuel *civil engineer*
Shih-Carducci, Joan Chia-mo *cooking educator, biochemist, medical technologist, author*
Sirken, Monroe Gilbert *statistician*
Smedley, Lawrence Thomas *retired organization executive*
Smith, A(rletta) Renee *agent*
†Smith, Paul Hubert *retired historian*
Speights, Michael David *newsletter editor*
†Stanic, Inja *music educator*
Telesetsky, Walter *government official*
Thompson, George Ralph *church administrator*
Vernon, Weston, III, (Wes Vernon) *broadcaster, writer, actor*
Waldmann, Katharine Spreng *public health physician*
Waldrop, Francis Neil *physician*
Wang, Kung-Lee *economics consultant*
Ware, Thaddeus Van *government official*
Weinstock, Alan Robert *internist*
Weiss, Leonard *mathematician, consultant*
Weissenborn, Anne Adkins *lawyer*
Welcome, Linda Paar *interior designer*
Whalen, John Philip *retired educational administrator, clergyman, lawyer*
†Wheeler, Anne Marie *lawyer*
White, Edmund William *chemical engineer*
White, Robert McKinley, Jr., *oncologist, federal agency administrator*
Whitmore, Frank Clifford, Jr., *geologist*
Whitten, Leslie Hunter, Jr., *author, newspaper reporter, poet*
Williams, James Thomas *physician, educator*
Williams, Paul *retired federal agency administrator*
Wilson, William Stanley *oceanographer*
Winston, Michael Russell *foundation executive, historian*
Woolard, Connie Ward *artist, retired art gallery manager*
Wooster, Martin Morse *author, editor*
†Yang, Jing-Shyang *structural engineer*
Yanowitz, Edward Stanley *allergist, educator*
†Yanushevsky, Rafael Tovie *electromechanical engineer, scientist, consultant, educator*
Yasher, Michael *retired accountant*
Youla, Sandra Lynn *land use planner, consultant*
Young, Jay Alfred *chemical safety and health consultant, writer, editor*
Zakheim, Barbara Jane *development professional*

Simpsonville
Altschuler, Bruce Robert *research dentist*
Bluher, Gregory *computer scientist, mathematician*

Solomons
Dorsey, James Francis, Jr., *naval officer*
†Heil, Kathleen Ann *librarian*

Sparks
Riley, Sarah Anne *information scientist*
Smith, Rodney Russell *operations executive*

Sparks Glencoe
†Swackhamer, Gene L. *bank executive*

Springdale
†Rucker, Michelle Renee *human resources specialist*

Stevenson
Hendler, Nelson Howard *physician, medical clinic director*
Hyman, Mary Bloom *science education programs coordinator*
Manning, Kevin James *academic administrator*
North, Percy *art historian, educator*

Street
Spangler, Ronald Leroy *retired television executive, aircraft executive, automobile collector*

Sudlersville
Covington, Donald Kingsley, Jr., *plywood sales executive*

Suitland
†Brooks, Richard C. *electrical engineer, federal government executive*
Cheng, Jian-Yu *mechanical engineer, researcher, application developer*
Doe, Patricia Louise *information technology executive*
Rao, Desiraju Bhavanarayana *meteorologist, oceanographer, educator*
Scofield, Roderick Arthur *meteorologist, researcher, educator*
Speier, Peter Michael *mathematics educator*
Vandiver, Pamela Bowren *research scientist*

Swanton
Cummins, Delmer Duane *academic administrator, historian*

Sykesville
Born, Roscoe Conklin *writer*
Crist, Gertrude H. *civic worker*
Leizear, Charles William *retired information services executive*
O'Connor, William Thomas *retired surgeon*
†Smith, George Allen, III, *music educator*
Vreeland, Russell Glenn *accountant, consultant*

Takoma Park
Dunn, John Benjamin *lawyer*
Giron, Robert LeRoy *English educator, writer*
Lancaster, Alden *educational and management consultant*
Lott, Alfred Davis *assistant city manager*
Munzer, Alfred *internist*
Richie, Robert Douglas *not-for-profit executive*
Stephenson, Patricia Ann *public health researcher, educator*
Strasser, Susan *historian, researcher, writer*
Urciolo, John Raphael, II, *real estate developer, real estate and finance educator*
von Hake, Margaret Joan *librarian*
†Walton, Charles W. *library director*

Taneytown
Morrow, Lee *communications executive*

Temple Hills
Day, Mary Jane Thomas *cartographer*
Smith, Irving *gerontologist*
Strauss, Simon Wolf *chemist, materials scientist*

Timonium
Fitzpatrick, Vincent de Paul, Jr., *retired gynecologist*
Forrester, Alfred Whitfield *psychiatrist, educator*

Towson
Baker, Jean Harvey *history educator*
†Baltzley, Patricia Creel *secondary mathematics educator*
Boucher, Laurence James *educator, chemist*
Campion, Renée *lawyer*
Caret, Robert Laurent *academic administrator*
Carney, Bradford George Yost *lawyer, educator*
†Coughlin, James Patrick *mathematician, educator*
Ferrer, Roberto O. *surgeon*
†Hirschmann, Edwin A. *historian, educator*
Hoch, David Allen *athletic director*
Huang, Joseph Chen-Huan *civil engineer*
Lazar, Jonathan Kumin *computer scientist, educator*
†Lund, Mark Fifield *secondary school educator*
Lutz, Randall Matthew *lawyer*
†Maher Arcodia, Patricia *lawyer*
McGrain, John William, Jr., *county government official*
Mc Indoe, Darrell Winfred *retired nuclear medicine physician*
McManus, Walter Leonard *investment executive*
Miller, Herbert H. *lawyer*
Mordes, Marvin *neurologist*
†Morrow, Thomas Campbell *lawyer*
†Pineo, Ronn *historian, educator*
Proctor, Kenneth Donald *lawyer*
†Propst, M. Teresa Carson *historian*
Putzel, Constance Kellner *lawyer*
Romero, Patricia Watkins *historian, educator, researcher*
†Roome, Dorothy Maud *media specialist, educator*
Serpick, Arthur Allen *health facility administrator, physician*
Shah, Shirish Kalyanbhai *computer science, chemistry and environmental science educator*
Sheredos, Carol Ann *rehabilitation clinical specialist*
Shirley, Lawrence Hoyt *mathematician, educator*
†Shriver, Pamela H. *retired professional tennis player, sports analyst*
Silverman, Linda L. *elementary educator*
Spodak, Michael Kenneth *forensic psychiatrist*
Tull, Willis Clayton, Jr., *librarian*
Young, William Sherban *investment broker*
Zimmerman, Jay James *mathematics educator*

Towson,
†Evangeliou, Christos C. *researcher, educator*

Tracys Landing
Smith, Elbert Benjamin *historian, educator*

Trappe
Anderson, Andrew Herbert *retired army officer*
Blades, G(ene) Granville *accountant*

Union Bridge
Hannah, Judy Challenger *private education tutor*

University Park
Walker, J. Samuel *historian*

Upper Marlboro
Bowles, Liza K. *construction executive*
†Brennan, William Collins, Jr., *lawyer*
Buffenbarger, R. Thomas *labor union administrator*
Chasanow, Howard Stuart *retired judge, mediator*
Freeman, Ernest Robert *engineering executive*
†Krauser, Sherrie L. *judge*
†Morrison, Anne Deinlein *law librarian*
†Rough, Marianne Christina *librarian, educator*
†Salter, Carol A. *not-for-profit executive*
Symlar, Jesse Lee *executive*
†Vaughan, James Joseph Michael *lawyer*
Wallace, Sean Daniel *lawyer, judge*

Waldorf
†Bolden, Melvin Wilberforce, Jr., *lawyer*
Gregan, John Patrick *finance executive, small business owner*
Stokely, Mary Curry *marketing specialist*
Wiggins, Stephen Edward *physician, medical association administrator*

Walkersville
Huiberts, Pieter J. *development chemist*

Washington
†Bevan, William Charles *systems analyst*

Washington Grove
†Reynolds, Thomas D. *psychiatrist*

West Bethesda
†Scully, Roger Tehan, II, *lawyer*
Sevik, Maurice *acoustical engineer, researcher*
Spurling, Everett Gordon, Jr., *architect, construction specifications consultant*
Su, Jen-Houne Hannsen *mechanical engineer*
Vogelgesang, Sandra Louise *business executive, writer*

West River
Bower, Catherine Downes *communications, management consultant*
Howl, Joanne Healey *veterinarian, writer*
Pratt, Katherine Merrick *environmental consulting company executive*

Westminster

Coley, Joan Develin *education educator*
Dulany, William Bevard *lawyer*
†Dundes, Lauren *education educator*
†Hargraves, Orin Knight *lexicographer*
Lippy, Karen Dorothy Fethe *nurse psychotherapist*
†Medina, Janet Gail *school psychologist, educator*
Preston, Charles Michael *lawyer*
Rosenthal, Michael Ross *academic administrator, consultant*
Staples, Lyle Newton *lawyer*
Wheatley, Charles Henry, III, *education and technology company executive, lawyer*
Yingling, Jacob Matthias *independent investor*

Westover

Carter, Carolyn Marie *social work executive*

Wheaton

Johnson, Laurence F(leming) *lawyer*
†Kaliner, Michael Aron *physician, researcher*
Kirchman, Eric Hans *lawyer*
Ma, Qingli *environmental hydrologist*
White, Martha Vetter *allergy and immunology physician, researcher*

White Hall

Buhite, Thomas Jesse, Sr., *employee benefits consultant*
Radigan, Frank Xavier *pharmaceutical company executive*

Williamsport

Hessler, Douglas Scott *screenwriter*

Woodbine

Nuss, Barbara Gough *artist*

Woodstock

Price, John Roy, Jr., *financial executive*
Wells, Christine Valerie *music educator*

Wye Mills

†Schisler, Amy MacWilliams *school librarian, graphics designer*
Schnaitman, William Kenneth *finance company executive*
Woods, Willie G. *dean, English language and education educator*

MASSACHUSETTS

Acton

Brody, Leslie Gary *social worker, sociologist*
Conoby, Joseph Francis *chemist*
†Coughlin, Cornelius Edward *accounting company executive*
Evans, Robert, Jr., *economics educator*
Hamel, Elizabeth Cecil *volunteer, educator*
Hicks, Walter Joseph *electrical engineer*
Kittross, John Michael *retired communications educator*
McCadden, Joseph A. *lawyer*
†Neale, John Jorgensen *research and development manager*
Smith, Raoul Normand *computer science educator*
Tuttle, David Bauman *electrical engineer*

Agawam

Kantor, Simon William *chemistry educator*
Potts, Harold Francis, Jr., *elevator company executive*
Schilling-Nordal, Geraldine Ann *retired secondary school educator*
†Sylvester, John Andrew *social studies educator*

Allston

Becton, Henry Prentiss, Jr., *broadcasting company executive*
†Burton, Gary *musician*
Mills, Daniel Quinn *business educator, consultant, author*
†Swift, Matthew Sloane *writer*

Amesbury

Bahre, Jeannette *English language and literature educator, education educator, librarian, educational consultant and tutor*
Bartnicki, Karen Jo *social services administrator*
Dowd, Frances Connelly *retired librarian*
Labaree, Benjamin Woods *history educator*
Parker, William H., III, *federal official*
Paster, Barrie *family practice physician*
Swartz, Mark Lee *lawyer*

Amherst

Abbott, Douglas Eugene *engineering educator*
Alfange, Dean, Jr., *political science educator*
Anderson, Ronald Trent *artist, educator*
Archer, Ronald Dean *chemist, educator*
Averill, James Reed *psychology educator*
Baker, Lynne Rudder *philosophy educator*
Bauschinger, Sigrid Elisabeth *German literature educator, researcher*
Benson, Lucy Wilson *political and diplomatic consultant*
Bentley, Richard Norcross *regional planner, writer, educator*
Berger, Seymour Maurice *social psychologist*
Bernstein, Herbert Joseph *physicist, consultant, educator*
†Bezucha, Robert Joseph *history educator*
†Blass, Elliott M. *psychologist, educator*
Brandon, Liane *filmmaker, educator*
Bridegam, Willis Edward, Jr., *librarian*
Byron, Frederick William, Jr., *physicist, educator, university vice chancellor*
†Clark, Carol Canda *art historian, educator*
†Cohen, Alvin P. *language educator*
†Cole, John Wallace *retired anthropologist, researcher, educator, consultant*
Cornish, Geoffrey St. John *golf course architect*

Dabrowski, Thaddeus E. *art educator, art consultant, painter*
David, Donald J. *chemist, researcher*
Demerath, Nicholas Jay, III, *sociology educator*
Feshbach, Oriole Farb *artist*
Fink, Richard David *chemist, educator*
Fleischman, Paul Robert *psychiatrist, writer*
Franks, Lewis E. *electrical and computer engineering educator, researcher*
Gettier, Edmund Lee, III, *philosophy educator*
Gibson, Walker *retired English language educator, poet, writer*
†Goldstein, Joseph Irwin *materials scientist, educator*
Grant, Daniel Howard *author*
Greene, Theodore Phinney *historian, educator*
†Haas, Peter M. *political science educator*
Hallock, Robert Bruce *physics educator*
Halpern, Joel Martin *anthropologist, photographer*
†Hayes, David Ryan *mathematics educator*
Hendricks, James Powell *artist*
Howland, Richard Moulton *retired lawyer*
†Immerman, Neil *academic administrator, computer scientist*
Katsh, M. Ethan *law educator*
†Kimball, Justin *photographer, educator*
Kinney, Arthur Frederick *literary history educator, writer, editor*
Klare, Michael Thomas *social science educator, program director*
†Komer, Matthew W. *athletic director*
Koren, Israel *electrical and computer engineering educator*
Krishnamurty, Sundar *mechanical engineer*
Larson, Joseph Stanley *environmentalist, educator, researcher*
Liebling, Jerome *photographer, educator*
Lombardi, John V. *university administrator, historian*
MacKnight, Carol Bernier *educational administrator*
MacKnight, William John *chemist, educator*
Manz, Charles C. *management educator*
Margulis, Lynn (Lynn Alexander) *biologist, educator*
†Marx, Anthony W. *academic administrator*
Mauldon, Margaret *translator*
May, Ernest Dewey *university administrator, musician, executive*
Mazor, Lester Jay *law educator*
Mc Donagh, Edward Charles *sociologist, university administrator*
Mills, Patricia Jagentowicz *political philosophy educator, writer*
Misra, Joya *sociology and public policy educator*
Nash, William Arthur *civil engineer, educator*
Oates, Stephen Baery *history educator*
†Oppenheim, Felix E. *political science educator*
Palmer, John Derry *physiology educator*
Palser, Barbara F. *botany researcher, retired educator*
Parkhurst, Charles *retired museum director, art historian*
Partee, Barbara Hall *linguist, educator*
Peterson, Gerald Alvin *physics educator*
Plaček, Roman *cellist, music educator*
Prince, Gregory Smith, Jr., *academic administrator*
Rabin, Monroe Stephen Zane *physicist*
Rager, John Ewing, III, *computer science educator*
Ratner, James Henry *dermatologist*
Roberts, Chris *strategy and finance educator, researcher*
†Rojas Joo, Juan Armando *language educator, poet*
Romer, Robert Horton *physicist, educator*
Rossi, Alice S. *sociology educator, author*
Sandweiss, Martha A. *author, American studies and history educator*
Schaubert, Daniel Harold *electrical engineering educator*
Scott, David Knight *physicist, university administrator*
†Sinha, Manisha *historian, educator*
Stein, Richard Stephen *chemistry educator*
Strickland, Bonnie Ruth *psychologist, educator*
Swift, Calvin Thomas *electrical and computer engineering educator*
†Taubman, Jane Andelman *Russian literature educator*
Taubman, William Chase *political science educator*
Tawa, Wako *foreign language educator*
Tenenbaum, Jeffrey Mark *academic librarian*
†Terpenny, Janis P. *engineering educator, researcher*
Trahan, Elizabeth Welt *retired comparative literature educator*
Velleman, Daniel Jon *mathematics educator*
Vogl, Otto *polymer science and engineering educator*
†Webley, Wilmore Christopher *microbiologist, researcher*
Whitbourne, Susan Krauss *psychology educator*
†Wideman, John Edgar *English literature educator, novelist*
Wier, Dara *poet, English language educator*
Wilcox, Bruce Gordon *publisher*
Wills, David Wood *minister, educator*
Wolff, Robert Paul *philosophy educator*
Woodbury, Richard Benjamin *anthropologist, educator*
Wyman, David Sword *historian, educator*
Yarde, Richard Foster *art educator*
Zimmermann, Robert A. *molecular biologist, educator*

Andover

Arce, Pedro L. *economic development executive, banker*
Bloom, David Lewis *radiologist*
Brophy, Susan Dorothy *adapted physical education educator*
Feinberg, Linda Sones *social worker, artist, writer*

Hasegawa, Tomohiro *marketing manager*
Jakes, William Chester *electrical engineer*
†Lang, Corbin F. *mathematician, educator*
†McDaniel, Paul R. *law educator, lawyer*
†Murray, Sabina *writer*
†Rotundo, E. Anthony *historian, educator*
Strohmeier, Gregg Robert *research scientist*
†Wetherell, David S. *communications executive*
Whidden, Robert Lee, Jr., *healthcare consultant*
Wise, Kelly *private school educator, photographer, critic*

Arlington

Berkoben, John Perri *physician*
Birk, Lee (Carl Lee Birk) *psychiatrist, educator*
†Bowen, Steven Holmes *lawyer*
†Carvotta, Crystal Champaigne *nursing administrator, consultant*
Casey, Ellen Patricia *obstetric and gynecological nurse*
Feinleib, Sidney *technology company business executive*
Fulmer, Vincent Anthony *retired college president*
†Lala, Jaynarayan Hotchand *computer engineer*
Leonardos, Gregory *chemist, odor consultant, educator*
Nahigian, Russell Ara *mathematician*
Thomas, Patricia Joanne *journalist, writer*
Van Orman, Jeanne *planning consultant*
Vaughn, Thomas Joseph *earth science educator, administrator*
Winfield, Cynthia Lees *middle school educator*

Ashburnham

†Von Deck, Joseph Francis *secondary school educator, researcher*

Ashfield

Gabriel, Peter Paul *educator*
Pepyne, Edward Walter *lawyer, psychologist, former educator*

Ashland

Iarussi, David Maurice *firefighter, farmer*
Pettinella, Nicholas Anthony *financial executive*

Attleboro

Bischoff, Marilyn Brett *clinical social worker, personal life coach*
Hammerle, Fredric Joseph *technical manufacturing executive*
Rounds, Hollis A. *secondary school educator*
†Sogge, Dale R. *automotive sensor engineer*
Stahl, Robert Alan *manufacturing executive, consultant*
Tuniewicz, Mark Anthony *political activist, corporate credit executive*

Attleboro Falls

†Kulwicki, Bernard Michael *ceramics engineer, researcher*

Auburn

Bachelder, Robert Stephen *minister*
Berg, G. Vivian *artist*

Auburndale

Bernard, Michael Mark *lawyer, city planning consultant*
†Doran, Kathleen Brewer *dean, consultant*
Fowler, Frederick Victor, Jr., *import company executive*
Kibrick, Anne *retired nursing educator and university dean*
Lindgren, Charlotte Holt *English language educator*
Tuchman, Maurice Simon *library director*
Vaccaro, Joseph Pascal *retired marketing educator, marketing consultant*
Winslow, Donald James *retired English educator, archivist*

Ayer

Anthony, Sylvia *social welfare organization executive*
Bloom, Edwin John, Jr., *retired human resources consultant*
Desper, Clyde Richard *retired polymer scientist*
Holmes, Jean Louise *real estate investor, Holocaust scholar, educator*
†Palis, Michael Richard *mechanical engineer, systems engineer*

Babson Park

Goldstein, Michael Aaron *finance educator*
Jones, Kent Albert *economist, educator*

Barnstable

Cataldo, Louis *retired protective services official*
†Mycock, Frederick Charles *lawyer*
†Perry, Blair Lane *lawyer*

Barre

Sullivan, James Edward *poet*

Bedford

†An, Hong *engineer*
Boghani, Ashok Balvantrai *entrepreneur*
†Carey, Kathleen *economist*
Daltas, Arthur John *management consultant, software services manager*
Eagles, Eugene, III, *orthodontist*
Fante, Ronald Louis *engineering scientist*
Goodman, William Beehler *editor, literary agent*
Griffin, Donald R(edfield) *zoology educator*
Jelalian, Albert V. *electrical engineer*
Kampits, Eva *accrediting association administrator, educator*
Klyosov, Anatole Alex *biochemist, researcher*
Labudovic, Marko *research scientist, consultant*
Lackoff, Martin Robert *engineer, physical scientist, researcher*
Letts, Lindsay Gordon *pharmacologist, educator*
Mahler, Philip Henry *mathematics educator*
Nason, Leonard Yoshimoto *lawyer, writer, publisher*

†Paglierani, Ronald Joseph *lawyer*
Payne, Harry Morse, Jr., *architect*
Shaw, Samuel Ervine, II, *retired insurance company executive, consultant*
Taylor, Cora Hodge *social worker*
Volicer, Ladislav *physician, educator*
Wacker-Brawley, Margaret *communications executive*
Wasson, Lila Elizabeth *educational consultant*
Webber, Howard Rodney *computer company executive*
Winter, David Louis *systems engineer, human factors scientist, retired*
Zhang, Yanwu *electrical engineer*

Belchertown

Burstein, Michael Clifford *management consultant*
Lester, Julius B. *author*
Marsh, Brian Richard *management executive, playwright, educator, clergyman*

Belmont

Benes, Francine M. *neuroscientist, psychiatrist*
Binder, Sheldon Carl *surgeon*
Bingham, George Walter Chandler *retired sales executive*
Cavarnos, Constantine Peter *philosopher, writer*
Coyle, Joseph Thomas *psychiatrist*
de Marneffe, Francis *psychiatrist, hospital administrator*
Dober, Richard Patrick *campus and facility planner, writer*
Dohanian, Diran Kavork *art historian, educator*
Durgin, Frank Herman, II, *aeronautical engineer*
Feldstein, Kathleen Foley *economist, consultant*
Fuller, Stephen Herbert *business administration educator*
†Gabrieli, Anna *voice educator*
Greer, Gordon Bruce *retired lawyer, writer*
Hanfling, Sue Carol (Suki Hanfling) *social worker*
Haralampu, George Stelios *electric power engineer, former engineering executive electric utility company*
Heyman, Gene Morris *research psychologist, educator*
Hilt, Mary Louise *artist*
Junger, Miguel Chapero *acoustics researcher*
†Kargman, Marie Witkin *marriage counselor, consultant*
†Ke, Yong *medical educator, researcher*
Killgore, William Dale (Scott), Jr., *neuropsychologist*
Klein, Martin Samuel *management consulting executive*
Kyomen, Helen H. *psychiatrist*
Levendusky, Philip George *psychologist, education administrator*
Magidson, Jay *statistician*
†McEvoy, Frances Jane Coman *writer, editor*
Merrill, Edward Wilson *chemical engineering educator*
Moore, Richard Thomas *writer, poet*
Neumeyer, John Leopold *research company administrator, chemistry educator*
Onesti, Silvio Joseph *psychiatrist*
Ottenstein, Donald *psychiatrist*
Pope, Harrison Graham, Jr., *psychiatrist, educator*
Rand, Peter *writer, editor, educator*
Reynolds, William Francis *mathematics educator*
Rich, Sharon Lee *financial planner*
Ronningstam, Elsa Frideborg *psychologist, educator*
†Rowe, Richard R. *on-line information and management services company executive*
Sifneos, Peter Emanuel *psychiatrist, educator*
Simpson, Russell Avington *retired law firm administrator*
Vuckovic, Alexander *psychiatrist*
†Zhang, Kehong *neuropharmacologist, educator*
†Zito, Frank R. *lawyer, accountant*

Berkley

Mills, Carol Andrews *mental health administrator*
Murtagh, Michael Paul *psychologist*

Berlin

Lohr, Harold Russell *retired bishop*

Beverly

Arnold, Gordon B. *social science educator*
Barger, Richard Wilson *hotel executive*
Chitre, Sharadchandra Raghunandan *physician*
†Daya, Jackie *publishing company executive*
DeVore, Dale Paul *scientific research organization executive*
Eastman, W. Dean *secondary school educator*
Hart, Claire-Marie *educator*
Ledbetter, John Stewart *urologist*
Lennox, Jo Stewart *college relations and external affairs director*
Manheim, Michael Philip *photographer*
McMahon, Joyce Arlene *public relations professional*
McReynolds, Larry Austin *molecular biologist*
Murray, Mary *educational consultant*
Roberts, Richard John *molecular biologist, consultant, research director*
†Rose, Peter Henry *nuclear physicist*
Roy, Robert William *artist, educator*
Smith, Derek Armand *information technology executive*
Smith, Merelyn Elizabeth *elementary and middle school educator*

Billerica

Furlong, Patrick David *educator, researcher*
Guivens, Norman Roy, Jr., *mathematician, engineer*
Kardauskas, Michael John *materials scientist, consultant*
Kinsman, Robert Preston *biomedical plastics engineer*
Kolb, Charles Eugene *research and development company executive*

†García-Cardeña, Guillermo *cell biologist, researcher*
Garciaparra, Nomar (Anthony Nomar Garciaparra) *professional baseball player*
Gargiulo, Andrea W. *lawyer*
Gargiulo, Antonio Rosario *reproductive endocrinologist, researcher, clinician*
Garrett, Gerald R. *sociology educator, criminologist, consultant*
Gaudreau, Russell A., Jr., *lawyer, educator*
†Gaughan, Denise Marie *epidemiologist*
Geggel, Robert Leslie *pediatric cardiologist*
Geismer, Alan Stearn, Jr., *lawyer*
Gelb, Richard Mark *lawyer*
Gelfand, Jeffrey Alan *physician, educator*
†Ghabbour, Elham A. *research scientist, educator*
Gibran, Kahlil *sculptor*
Gibson, Barry Joseph *magazine editor*
†Gibson, Cathy *administrative assistant*
Gifford, Charles Kilvert *banker*
Gifford, Nelson Sage *financial company executive*
Gilbert, Arthur Charles *aerospace engineer, consulting engineer*
Gilchrest, Barbara Ann *dermatologist*
Gill, Thomas James, IV, *orthopedic surgeon*
Gillick, Muriel Ruth *physician*
Gilman, Richard H. *newspaper publishing executive*
Gilmore, Maurice Eugene *mathematics educator*
†Gilmore, Thomas David *biologist*
Gimbrone, Michael Anthony, Jr., *research scientist, pathologist, educator*
Giso, Frank, III, *lawyer*
Glass, Renée *educational health foundation executive*
Gleason, Jean Berko *psychology educator*
†Glessner, John Jacob, III, *lawyer*
Glimcher, Melvin Jacob *orthopedic surgeon*
Glod, Carol Ann *nursing educator*
Glosband, Daniel Martin *lawyer*
Godine, David Richard *publishing company executive*
Godleski, John Joseph *pathologist*
Golan, David Eric *biophysicist, pharmacologist, hematologist, medical educator*
Goldberg, Irving Hyman *molecular pharmacology and biochemistry educator*
†Goldberg, Marcia B. *medical educator*
Golder, Herbert Alan *classics educator*
Goldhaber, Paul *dental educator*
Goldman, Eric Scot *lawyer*
Gonson, S. Donald *lawyer*
Goodman, Louis Allan *lawyer*
Goody, Joan Edelman *architect*
Gora, JoAnn M. *university chancellor*
Gossels, Claus Peter Rolf *lawyer*
Gottlieb, Leonard Solomon *pathology educator*
Goumnerova, Liliana Christova *physician, neurosurgeon, educator*
Gozonsky, Edwin O. O. *investment broker*
Graceffa, John Philip *lawyer*
Graham, John Joseph *lawyer, economics educator*
†Granoff, Barry *mathematician, educator*
†Grant, Barbara Hurwitz *educator*
Greaney, John M. *state supreme court justice*
†Green, James R. *historian, educator, historian, researcher*
Greenberger, Norton Jerald *physician*
Greenblatt, David J. *pharmacologist, educator*
Greene, Robert Allan *former university administrator*
Greer, Allen Curtis, II, *lawyer, investment management executive*
Greiner, Jack Volker *ophthalmologist, physician, surgeon, scientist*
Grimes, Heilan Yvette *publishing executive*
Griswold, Jonathan DeWitt *pediatric anesthesiologist, pharmacology educator*
Grundfast, Kenneth Martin *otolaryngologist*
†Guenther, William H. *management consultant*
Guertin, Robert Powell *physics educator, university dean*
Haddad, Ernest Mudarri *lawyer*
Hagan, David *musician, educator*
Hailey, Hans Ronald *lawyer*
Hale, Martin de Mora *investor*
†Hall, David *law educator, dean, law educator, department chairman*
Hall, Henry Lyon, Jr., *lawyer*
Halström, Frederic Norman *lawyer*
Hamann, Charles Martin *lawyer*
†Hamblin, Michael R. *biomedical researcher, educator*
Hamel, Louis H., Jr., *lawyer*
Hammond, Norman David Curle *archaeology educator, researcher*
†Hansen, Morten T. *management educator*
Harden, Patricia Keegan *financial aid officer*
Harkness, John Cheesman *architect*
Harlow, Edward E., Jr., *oncologist*
Harrington, John Michael, Jr., *lawyer*
†Harris, Andrew Michael *director*
Harris, Roy Jay, Jr., *editor, business journalist*
†Harris, Virginia Sydness *religious studies educator*
†Harvey, Mark Sumner *composer, minister, educator, musician*
Hawkey, G. Michael *lawyer, real estate investor and developer*
Hawley, Anne *museum director*
Hay, Elizabeth Dexter *embryology researcher, educator*
Hayes, Andrew Wallace, II, *consumer products company executive*
Hayes, Robert Francis *lawyer*
Hayes, Robert Herrick *technology management educator*
Hayes, Samuel Linton, III, *business educator*
†Hayward, Elizabeth *lawyer, artist*
†Healey, Kerry Murphy *lieutenant governor*
Healy, Gerald Burke *otolaryngologist*
Hedley-Whyte, E(lizabeth) Tessa *neuropathologist*
Hedley-Whyte, John *anesthesiologist, educator*
Hedlund, Ronald David *academic administrator, researcher, educator*
Heigham, James Crichton *lawyer*
Hemenway, David *public health educator*
†Hemnes, Thomas Michael Sheridan *lawyer*
†Henderson, Jeffrey J. *dean, educator*
Henry, DeWitt Pawling, II, *creative writing educator, writer, arts administrator*
Henry, John W. *professional sports team executive*
Herndon, James Henry *orthopedic surgeon, educator*
Hernon, Peter *library science educator*
Hiatt, Howard H. *physician*
Hickey, Elizabeth Louise *advertising agency executive*
Hieken, Charles *lawyer*
†Higgins, Harriet Pratt *investment advisor*
†Hill, Nicholas Snowden *physician, researcher, educator*
Hillenbrand, Shea Matthew *baseball player*
Hillery, Thomas Hungiville *journalist, financial consultant*
Hillman, William Chernick *federal bankruptcy judge, educator*
Hintikka, Jaakko *philosopher, educator*
Ho, Kalon Kl *internist, researcher*
Hobbs, Nedda Marie *pediatrician*
Hoffer, David Paul *investment banker, lawyer*
Hoffman, Andrew John *environmental management educator*
Hoffman, David Alan *lawyer*
Hoffman, Stanley Marc *editor, composer*
Hofmann, Stefan Georg *psychologist, researcher*
Holland, James R. *real estate corporation executive*
Honig, Stephen Michael *lawyer*
Horne, Ralph Albert *environmental chemist*
Hoskins, William Keller *pharmaceutical executive, mediator/arbitrator, lawyer*
Hostetter, Amos Barr, Jr., *cable television executive*
†Howard, Gregory Charles *lawyer*
Howlett, D(onald) Roger *art gallery executive, art historian*
Howley, Peter Maxwell *pathology educator*
Hrones, Stephen Baylis *lawyer, educator*
†Huang, Vivian Wenhuey Chen *lawyer*
Hubel, David Hunter *physiologist, science educator*
Hudson, Bradford Taylor *management educator*
†Hunsaker, Andetta Rotilla *physician, medical educator*
†Hunsaker, Roderick Cason *lawyer, insurance company executive*
Hunter, David George *physician, researcher*
Hunter, Durant Adams *executive search company executive*
†Hunter, Floyd Dore *lawyer*
Hurd, J. Nicholas *executive recruiting consultant, former banker*
Hutter, Adolph Matthew, Jr., *cardiologist, educator*
Huvos, Andrew *internist, cardiologist, educator*
Ireland, Roderick L. *state supreme court justice*
Ives, J. Atwood *financial executive*
Jabre, Anthony *neurosurgeon, educator*
Jabre, Joe F. *neurologist, electromyographer*
Jackson, Patience Kenney *grants adminstrator, library consultant*
Janne d'Othee, Bertrand M. *radiologist, researcher*
Jellinek, Michael Steven *psychiatrist, pediatrician*
Jennings, Jon Paul *nonprofit foundation executive*
Jochum, Veronica *pianist*
Johansen, Erling *retired dental educator and dean*
†Johnson, Abigail *investment company executive*
Johnson, Edward Crosby, III, *financial company executive*
Johnson, Michael Lewis *psychiatrist*
Johnston, Richard Alan *lawyer*
Johnstone, C. Bruce *investment company executive*
Jonas, Richard Andrew *medical educator*
Jonas, Stephen P. *investment company executive*
Jones, Robert Emmet *French language educator, novelist*
Jordan, Alexander Joseph, Jr., *lawyer*
Joseph, J. Jonathan *interior designer*
Joyce-Brady, Martin Francis *medical educator, physician, researcher*
Judson, Arnold Sidney *management consultant*
Jupiter, Jesse Bernard *orthopedic surgeon*
Kafker, Frank A. *historian, educator*
Kahn, Carl Ronald *research laboratory administrator*
Kaler, Robert Joseph *lawyer*
Kane, Robert Alan *radiologist, researcher*
Kanin, Dennis Roy *lawyer*
Kaplan, Marshall Myles *medical educator, researcher, gastroenterologist*
Kaplan, Robert Samuel *educator*
Kaplan, Steven F. *business management executive*
Karasik, David *anatomist, educator, genetic epidemiologist*
Kasper, Dennis Lee *health facility administrator, educator*
†Kassirer, Jerome Paul *medical educator, editor-in-chief*
Kassler, Haskell A. *lawyer*
Katz, Steven Theodore *religious studies educator*
Katzmann, Gary Stephen *lawyer*
Kavanaugh, James Francis, Jr., *lawyer*
Kaye, Kenneth Marc *physician, educator, scientist*
Kazemi, Homayoun *physician, medical educator*
Keating, Michael Burns *lawyer, educator*
Keeton, Robert Ernest *federal judge*
Kehoe, William Francis *lawyer*
Keller, Stanley *lawyer*
Kelley, Kevin H. *insurance company executive*
Kelly, Edmund Francis *insurance company executive*
†Kelly, Francis J., III, *global marketing company president and COO*
Kennedy, Eugene Patrick *biochemist, educator*
†Kennedy, Joseph Patrick, II, *utilities executive, former congressman*
Kenner, Carol J. *federal bankruptcy judge*
Kenney, Raymond Joseph, Jr., *lawyer*
†Kenny, David *internet professional services executive*
Kerr, William Robert *economist, consultant*
Kessler, Diane Cooksey *religious organization administrator, minister*
†Kidder, George Howell *lawyer*
Kiefer, Matthew J. *lawyer*
Kieff, Elliott Dan *medical educator*
Kikel, Rudy John *editor, writer*
Kilts, James M. *consumer products company executive*
Kimball, George Edward, III, *sports columnist*
Kindregan, Charles Peter *law educator*
King, William Bruce *retired lawyer*
Kirchick, William Dean *lawyer*
Kirk, Paul Grattan, Jr., *lawyer, administrator*
Kirkpatrick, Edward Thomson *college administrator, mechanical engineer*
Kitz, Richard John *anesthesiologist, educator*
Klafter, Craig Evan *university administrator, legal historian*
Klarfeld, Jonathan Michael *journalism educator*
Kleiner, Fred Scott *art historian, archaeologist, educator, editor*
Klema, Donald David *architect*
Klingenstein, R. James *physician*
Klotz, Charles Rodger *shipping company and investment company executive*
Knight, Norman *philanthropist, former broadcast executive*
Koch, Magaly *geologist, researcher*
†Kocher, Mininder Singh *pediaric orthopaedic surgeon, epidemiologist*
Komaroff, Anthony Leader *physician*
†Kominis, Katherine Elizabeth *librarian*
Kon, Mark Andrew *mathematics educator*
Kopaczynski, Germain *priest*
Kopelman, Leonard *lawyer*
Korff, Y. A. *grand rabbi*
Korn, Joseph Howard *physician, educator*
Kornberg, Sir Hans Leo *biochemist, educator*
†Koutoujian, Peter John *lawyer*
Kowal, Ruth Elizabeth *library administrator*
†Krainc, Dimitri *medical educator, researcher*
Krakoff, Robert Leonard *publishing executive*
Krane, Stephen Martin *physician, educator*
Krasnow, Jordan Philip *lawyer*
†Kravitz, Edward Arthur *neuroscientist*
Kressel, Herbert Yehude *medical educator*
Krolewski, Bozena K. *molecular biologist, researcher, cell biologist*
†Kruch, Aleksandr *retired gynecologist, educator*
†Kruskal, Jonathan Bruce *radiologist, research scientist*
Kulig, John Walter *pediatrician, educator*
†Kupper, Thomas S. *dermatologist, educator*
Kutchin, Edward David *lawyer*
Kuttner, Robert Louis *editor, columnist*
†Kwan, Paul W. *science educator*
†Lahav, Pnina *law educator*
†Lane, Harlan *science educator, researcher*
Langer, Robert Martin *retired chemical engineering company executive, consultant*
Larkin, Michael John *newspaper editor, journalist*
†Larsen, Ulla Margrethe *demographer educator, consultant*
Lasker, Morris E. *judge*
Last, Michael P. *lawyer*
Laursen, Richard Allan *chemistry educator*
Laussen, Peter Charles *pediatric cardiac anesthesiologist, intensive care physician*
†Lawner, Ron *advertising executive*
Lawrence, Merloyd Ludington *editor*
Lawrence, Paul Roger *retired organizational behavior educator*
†Lawson, Thomas Elsworth *advertising agency executive*
Lazarus, Shelly *advertising executive*
†Lazerow, Jama *historian, educator*
Leaman, J. Richard, Jr., *paper company executive*
LeBoff, Meryl Susan *physician, medical educator*
Lee, David Stoddart *retired investment counselor*
Lee, Donald Young (Don Lee) *publishing executive, editor, writer*
Lee, I-Min *epidemiologist*
Leeman, Susan Epstein *neuroscientist, educator*
Leff, Deborah *government executive*
†Leffert, James Steven *psychologist*
Lehar, Steven M. *research scientist*
†Leibensperger, Edward Paul *lawyer*
Leland, Timothy *retired newspaper executive*
†Lembo, Vincent Joseph *lawyer*
Le Quesne, Philip William *chemistry educator, researcher*
Lesser, Laurence *musician, educator*
†Levine, Deborah *radiologist*
Levinsky, Norman George *physician, educator*
Levitin, Lev Berovich *research scientist, educator*
Levy, Stephen Raymond *high technology company executive*
Lewis, Kim *microbiologist*
Lewis, Scott P. *lawyer*
Licata, Arthur Frank *lawyer*
Lindley, James Daniel *lawyer*
Lindsay, Reginald Carl *judge*
Linfante, Italo *physician, medical educator*
Little, Grady *professional athletics manager*
Little, John Bertram *physician, radiobiology educator, researcher*
Livingston, David Morse *biomedical scientist, physician, internist*
Lockhart, Keith Alan *conductor, musician, teacher*
Loder, John Mark *lawyer*
Lodge, George C(abot) *business administration educator*
Loeser, Hans Ferdinand *lawyer*
Lo Gerfo, Frank William *surgeon*
Looney, William Francis, Jr., *lawyer*
Loria, Martin A. *lawyer*
Loring, Arthur *lawyer, diversified financial services company executive*
Loscalzo, Joseph *cardiologist, biochemist*
Lovejoy, George Montgomery, Jr., *real estate company executive*
Lovell, Francis Joseph *investment company executive*
†Lowell, Richard Lee *music educator, musician*
Lowry, Bates *art historian, museum director*
Lowry, Lois (Lois Hammersberg) *writer*
Lukey, Joan A. *lawyer*
Lundgren, Richard John *real estate executive, city planner, preservationist*
Luongo, C. Paul *public relations executive*
†Luptak, Ivan *physician, researcher*
Lyman, Henry *retired publisher, marine fisheries consultant*
Lynch, Sandra Lea *federal judge*
Lyons, David Barry *philosophy and law educator*
Lyons, Nance *lawyer*
Lyons, Paul Vincent *lawyer*
Macauley, William Francis *lawyer*
Maciora, Joseph Gerard Vincent *reference librarian*
†MacLean, Alex Stokes *aerial photographer*
Maher, Timothy John *pharmacologist, educator*
†Maki, Dean Michael *economist*
†Makrigiorgos, Gerassimos Mike *oncologist*
Malenka, Bertram Julian *physicist, educator*
†Malley, Robert John *holding company executive, lawyer*
Malt, Ronald Bradford *lawyer*
Mankin, Henry Jay *physician, educator*
Mannick, John Anthony *surgeon*
Manning, Peter Kirby *sociologist educator*
Manning, Robert Joseph *editor*
Manning, William Frederick *wire service photographer*
Mansfield, Christopher Charles *insurance company legal executive*
Manson, JoAnn Elisabeth *endocrinologist*
Margolis, Bernard Allen *library administrator*
Marion, Donald William *neurosurgeon*
Markoff, Gary David *investment executive*
Marks, Stephen Paul *law, international affairs and public health educator, international official*
Marshall, James Peter *accountant, educator*
Marshall, Margaret Hilary *state supreme court chief justice*
Marshall, Martin Vivan *business administration educator, business consultant*
Martin, Cathie Jo *political scientist, educator*
Martin, Joseph Boyd *neurologist, educator*
Martin, Stanley A. *lawyer*
Martinez, Pedro Jaime *professional baseball player*
Martuza, Robert L. *neurosurgeon*
Mason, Charles Ellis, III, *magazine editor*
Mason, Emanuel Joel *psychology educator*
Mason, Herbert Warren, Jr., *religion and history educator, author*
Masud, Robert *lawyer*
†Matarazzo, James M. *dean, educator*
Mathews-Roth, Micheline Mary *medicine educator, clinical researcher*
Matzka, Michael Alan *lawyer*
Mayers, David *political science and history educator*
McArthur, John Hector *business educator*
†McAuliffe, Rosemary *lawyer*
McCloskey, Laura Ann *medical educator*
McClung, William Alexander *foundation administrator, educator*
McCormick, Marie Clare *pediatrician, educator*
McCourt, Joyce Elise *lawyer*
†McCraw, Thomas Kincaid *business history educator, editor, author*
McCullen, Joseph T., Jr., *venture capitalist*
McDaniel, Joyce L. *artist, educator*
McDougal, William Scott *urology educator*
McFarlan, Franklin Warren *business administration educator*
†McGovern, Patrick J. *communications executive*
†McGuire, Thomas G. *economist, educator, mental health services professional, researcher*
McIntyre, Mildred Jean *clinical psychologist, writer, neuroscientist*
McKain, Joshua Van Kirk *library director*
McKittrick, Neil Vincent *lawyer*
†McKnight, Christopher James *science educator*
†McMahon, Thomas John *lawyer, educator*
McNamee, Linda Rose *broadcast executive*
†McPhee, Jonathan *music director, conductor, composer, interim artistic coordinator*
Meenan, Robert Francis *rheumatologist, researcher, academician*
Menino, Thomas M. *mayor*
†Menoyo, Eric Felix *lawyer*
Menzies, Ian Stuart *newspaper editor*
†Mercer, Richard James *lawyer*
Merk, Frederick Bannister *biomedical educator, medical researcher*
†Merrill, Stephen *lawyer, consultant, former governor*
Merton, Robert C. *economist, educator*
Meserve, William George *lawyer*
Messerle, Judith Rose *medical librarian, public relations director*
Metcalfe, Murray Robert *venture capitalist*
Meyer, Jack Edward *radiologist, educator*
†Meyer, Michael Broeker *lawyer, consultant*
Meyerson, Matthew *pathologist, educator, researcher*
Miaoulis, Ioannis Nikolaos *mechanical engineer, educator*
Michels, William Charles *management consultant*
Mihm, Martin Charles, Jr., *pathologist, educator*
Mikels, Richard Eliot *lawyer*

Weber, Georg Franz *immunologist, cancer researcher*
Weber, Larry *public relations executive*
Weeks, Clifford Myers *musician, educational administrator*
†Weinberg, Arnold N. *physician, educator*
Weiner, Stephen Mark *lawyer*
Weinstein, Milton Charles *health policy educator*
Weinstein, Robert *hematologist, researcher*
Weiss, Earle Burton *physician*
Weiss, Scott Tillman *internist, research epidemiologist, educator*
Weitzel, John Patterson *lawyer*
Wellington, Carol Strong *law librarian*
Wendorf, Richard Harold *library director, scholar*
Wermuth, Paul Charles *retired English educator*
Westling, Jon *university administrator*
†Wexler, Barbara Lynne *lawyer*
Weygand, Bob A. *former congressman*
Wheeler, W(illiam) Scott *composer, conductor, music educator*
White, Barry Bennett *lawyer*
†White, George Edward *pedodontist, educator*
White, Jan Tuttle (Mrs. Benjamin Winthrop White) *information technology executive*
Whitlock, John L. *lawyer*
Whitters, James Payton, III, *lawyer, university administrator*
Whitworth, William A. *magazine editor*
Widmann, John Andrew *account administrator, musician*
Wiegner, Allen Walter *biomedical engineering educator, researcher*
Wiesel, Elie *writer, educator*
†Wiesner, David *illustrator, children's writer*
Wild, Victor Allyn *lawyer, educator*
Willard, Richard Kennon *lawyer*
†Willey, Ronald J. *chemical engineer, educator*
Williams, James Francis *professional baseball manager*
Williams, Mary Margaret *nurse administrator*
Williams, Rhys *minister*
Wilson, Elaine Louise *academic administrator*
†Wilson, Paul Dennis *lawyer*
Wilson, Peter Wyman *internist, cardiovascular metabolic epidemiologist*
Wilson, Scott Numo *psychiatrist*
Winkelman, James Warren *hospital administrator, pathology educator*
†Winn, Joseph Lampher *financial officer*
Wiseman, James Richard *classicist, archaeologist, educator*
Woerner, Frederick Frank *international relations educator*
Wolf, David *lawyer*
Wolf, Gary Herbert *architect*
Wolf, Philip Alan *neurologist*
†Wolfson, Jeffrey Steven *lawyer*
Woodard, Paul Esty *librarian emeritus, nurse*
Woodard, Jr., Fredrick James *music educator, musician*
†Woodburn, Ralph Robert, Jr., *lawyer*
Woodlock, Douglas Preston *judge*
Woods, Cathi L. *human services administrator*
Worthley, Harold Field *minister, educator*
Wu, Guofa Felix *computer company executive*
Wu, Tung *curator, art historian, art educator, artist*
†Wyszynski, Diego Federico *epidemiologist, educator*
†Xiao, Zhi-Xiong Jim *science educator, educator*
†Xu, Xiping *adult education educator, director*
Yang, Sue *artist*
†Yarborough, Nellie Constance *principal, minister*
Yeager, Peter Cleary *sociologist, educator*
Yoffie, David B. *educator*
Young, David William *management educator*
Young, Laura *dance educator, choreographer*
Young, Lucy H.Y. *physician, retina surgeon*
Young, Raymond Henry *lawyer*
Young, William Glover *federal judge*
†Yuan, Junying *medical educator, researcher*
†Zack, Arnold Marshall *lawyer, mediator, arbitrator*
Zaleznik, Abraham *psychoanalyst, management specialist, educator*
†Zambrano, Eduardo Vicente *pathologist, researcher*
Zander, Benjamin *conductor, educator*
†Zandrow, Leonard Florian *lawyer*
Zapol, Warren Myron *anesthesiologist*
Zarins, Bertram *orthopaedic surgeon*
Zelen, Marvin *statistics educator*
Zelnick, Carl Robert Robert *writer, educator*
Zervas, Nicholas Themistocles *neurosurgeon*
†Zhu, Guorong *management consultant, researcher*
Zinner, Michael Jeffrey *surgeon, educator*
Zobel, Rya Weickert *federal judge*

Bourne
Fantozzi, Peggy Ryone *geologist, environmental planner*

Boxboro
Berry, Robert John *architect*
Evdokimoff, Merrily Weber *nursing administrator, community health nurse*

Boxford
Siegert, Barbara (Barbara Marie Siegert) *health care administrator*
Yates, John Robert, Jr., *engineer, educator*

Boylston
Hanshaw, James Barry *physician, educator*
Healy, Patrick James *civil engineer*
Larson, Roland Elmer *health care executive*

Braintree
Riccio, Frank Joseph *lawyer, educator*
Salloway, Josephine Plovnick *psychologist, marriage and family therapist, mental health counselor, psychology educator, college counselor*

Brewster
Hillis-Dineen, Madalyn *marketing professional, astrologer, writer*
Hughes, Libby *writer*
†Kanis, Mersh Lubel *special education educator, writer*

Bridgewater
Heffernan, Peter John *state official*
Hurley, Mike (John Mathias Geretschlaeger) *English language educator*
Nelson, Marian Emma *education educator*
Nicholeris, Carol Angela *music educator, composer, conductor*
Thompson, Andrew Ernest *secondary school educator*
Tinsley, Adrian *college president*
Witherell, Nancy Louise *education educator*

Brighton
Garber, Paul William *lawyer*
†Ratto, Eugene Joseph *lawyer, commercial arbitrator and mediator, real estate broker, consultant*
Valianti, Deborah L. *playwright*

Brimfield
Curtis, William Edgar *conductor, composer*

Brockton
Anderson, Ernest Robert, Jr., *pharmacist*
†Belinsky, Ilene Beth *lawyer*
Carlson, Desiree Anice *pathologist*
Clark, Carleton Earl *tax consultant*
Compton, William Thomas *real estate investor*
Irving, Robert Churchill *retired quality assurance professional, manufacturing company executive*
Lightford, Melvin *minister*
Moore, Mary Johnson *nurse*
O'Brien, John Steininger *clinical psychologist*
O'Farrell, Timothy James *psychologist, educator*
Park, Byiung Jun *textile engineer*
Sherman, Beverly Robin *medical, surgical, pediatric, and maternity nurse*
Sullivan, Brendan Paul *state official, communications educator*

Brookfield
Anderson, Theodore Robert *physicist*
Couture, Ronald David *art administrator, design consultant*

Brookline
Alarcon, Rogelio Alfonso *physician, researcher*
Barron, Ros *artist*
Basilico, Frederick Calvin *cardiologist*
Belenky, Alexander Solomonovich *mathematician, consultant, researcher*
Bergel, Ernest Walter *psychiatrist, educator*
Boudreau, Francis Helier *obstetrician-gynecologist*
Buchin, Jacqueline Chase *clinical psychologist*
†Cottle, Thomas Joseph *sociologist*
Creasey, David Edward *physician, psychiatrist, educator*
Cromwell, Adelaide M. *sociology educator*
Eden, Murray *electrical engineer, emeritus educator*
Ellis, Sharon Henderson *arbitrator, mediator*
Epstein, Alvin *actor, director, singer, mime*
Erick, Miriam Anna *dietitian, medical writer*
Finkelstein, Norman Henry *librarian*
Frankel, Ernst Gabriel *shipping and aviation business executive, educator*
Gewirtz, Mindy L. *organizational and human relations consultant*
Golden, Herbert Hershel *retired Romance languages educator*
Goldenberg, Stephen Bernard *lawyer*
Gurian, Bennett Sheppe *psychiatrist*
Jacobson, Murray M. *chemical engineer*
Jakab, Irene *psychiatrist*
Jordan, Ruth Ann *physician*
Kanin, Doris May *political scientist, consultant*
Kawada, Janet Hansen *artist, educator*
Kay, Reed *artist, educator*
Kliman, Sylvia May Stern *film executive, editor, realtor*
†Kroll, Mark *music educator*
†Lown, Bernard *cardiologist, educator*
†McCracken, Natalie Jacobson *editor, writer*
Michopoulos, Aristotle V. *humanities educator, researcher*
†Neumann, Deborah Brochi *not-for-profit fundraiser*
Perkins, James R. *manufacturing engineering educator, researcher*
Reedy, Harry Lee *financial services executive*
†Rizzi, Marguerite Claire *music educator*
Rosner, Anthony Leopold *research director, biochemist*
Ruthchild, Rochelle Goldberg *education educator*
†Samra, Nicholas James *bishop*
Sarfaty, Suzanne *internist and educator*
Schiller, Sophie *artist, graphic designer*
Schwartz, Bernard *physician*
†Shrier, Lydia Anne *physician*
†Skeete, Helen Watkins *minister, counselor*
Storin, Matthew Victor *retired newspaper editor*
†Swirnoff, Lois *artist, color theorist*
Tuchman, Avraham *physicist, researcher*
Tyler, H. Richard *physician, educator*
Walter, Eugene Victor *writer*
Wertsman, Vladimir Filip *librarian, information specialist, author, translator*

Burlington
Barrett, David M. *urologist*
Bright, Willard Mead *manufacturing company executive*
Coffin, George Jarvis, III, *advertising executive*
DeCrosta, Susan Elyse *graphic designer*
†Entrup, Michael Harry *anesthesiologist*
†Foxlin, Eric Michael *entrepreneur, researcher*
Freidberg, Stephen Roy *neurosurgeon*
Hall, John Reginald, II, *electronics company executive, retired army officer*
Harding, Wayne Michael *sociologist, researcher*
†Khettry, Urmila *pathologist*
Kim, Nam-Deuk *electrical engineer, researcher*
McWade, Jessica Christy *marketing professional*
Moschella, Samuel L. *dermatology educator*
†Nesto, Richard William *cardiologist, researcher*
Oberfield, Richard Alan *oncologist*
Perloff, James Edward *writer, songwriter, publisher*
Reagan, Stevan Ray *cable company executive*
Reuter, Karen L. *physician, radiologist*
Schoetz, David John, Jr., *colon and rectal surgeon, educator*
Sproull, Robert Fletcher *research and development company executive*
Wilson, Daniel Donald *engineering executive*

Buzzards Bay
Daley, Michael Edward *financial consultant*

Byfield
Kozol, Jonathan *writer*
Yesair, David Wayne *biochemist*

Cambridge
Abernathy, Frederick Henry *mechanical engineering educator*
Abt, Clark C. *social scientist, executive, engineer, publisher, educator*
Ackerman, James Sloss *fine arts educator*
†Adams, Ruth-Anne *chef*
†Aitken, Ellen Bradshaw *religious studies educator*
Alberty, Robert Arnold *chemistry educator*
Alcalay, Albert S. *artist, design educator*
Alevizos, Susan Bamberger *lawyer, santouri player, author*
Alevizos, Theodore G. *lawyer, singer, author*
Alt, James Edward *political science educator*
Altman, Micah *social scientist, researcher*
†An, Shuwang *chemist, researcher*
Anderson, Stanford Owen *architect, architectural historian, educator*
Anderson, William Henry *psychobiologist, educator*
Appley, Mortimer Herbert *psychologist, university president emeritus*
†Arkani-Hamed, Nima *physicist*
Arkhipova, Irina R. *biologist*
Aronson, Michael Andrew *editor*
Aspinall, Mara Glickman *marketing and general management professional*
Auld, David Stuart *biochemist, educator*
Avakian, Laura Ann *academic administrator*
†Axelrod, Emily H. *urban planner*
Badian, Ernst *history educator*
Bailyn, Bernard *historian, educator*
†Bailyn, Lotte *psychology and management educator*
†Baird, George *architecture educator*
Bakanowsky, Louis Joseph *visual arts educator, architect, artist*
Bane, Bernard Maurice *publishing company executive*
Barger, James Edwin *physicist*
Barnes, Edward Larrabee *architect*
Barnett, David Philip *horticulturist*
Baron, Judson Richard *aerospace educator*
Bartee, Thomas Creson *computer scientist, educator*
Bator, Francis Michel *economist, educator*
Battin, Richard Horace *astronautical engineer*
Baumgartner, Mary Anne Sgarlat *academic administrator, entrepreneur*
Beckwith, Jonathan Roger *geneticist*
Beér, János Miklós *engineering educator*
Beers, Deborah Yardley *musician*
Belfort, David Ernst *lawyer*
Ben-Akiva, Moshe Emanuel *civil engineering educator*
†Benedict, Manson *chemical engineer, educator*
Beranek, Leo Leroy *acoustical consultant*
Bercaw, Roy *freelance/self-employed writer*
†Berger, Harvey James *pharmaceutical company executive, physician, educator*
Bernays, Anne Fleischman *writer, educator*
Berndt, Ernst Rudolf *economist, educator*
Biagioli, Mario *history of science educator*
Biemann, Klaus *chemistry educator*
Bizzi, Emilio *neurophysiologist, educator*
Blackmer, Donald Laurence Morton *political scientist*
†Blair, Ann *historian*
†Blake, Patricia *writer*
Bloch, Herbert *classicist, medievalist, historian, educator*
Bloom, Kathryn Ruth *public relations executive*
†Bloomfield, Steven B. *think-tank executive*
Blout, Elkan Rogers *biological chemistry educator, university dean*
Boger, Kenneth Snead *lawyer*
Bogorad, Lawrence *biologist, educator*
Bok, Derek *law educator, former university president*
Bolster, Arthur Stanley, Jr., *history educator*
Bonina, Mary *poet*
Boorstein, Beverly Weinger *judge*
Borjas, George J(esus) *economics educator*
Botkin, James W. *leadership and life coach*
Bourneuf, Henri Joseph, Jr., *librarian*
Bove, Victor Michael, Jr., *media arts and sciences educator, researcher*
Bradt, Hale Van Dorn *physicist, x-ray astronomer, educator*
Branscomb, Lewis McAdory *physicist, researcher*
Bras, Rafael Luis *engineering educator*
Breda, John Alexander *physician, musician*
Brenner, Howard *chemical engineering educator*
Brooks, Harvey *physics educator*
Brown, Edgar Cary *retired economics educator*
Brown, Lloyd David *association executive, management educator*
Brown, Robert Arthur *chemical engineering educator*
Bruce, James Donald *academic administrator*
Bruck, Phoebe Ann Mason *landscape architect*
Brusch, John Lynch *physician, educator, hospital administrator*
Brustein, Robert Sanford *English language educator, theatre director, author*
Brynjolfsson, Erik *management educator, researcher*
†Buchwald, Jed Zachary *environmental health researcher, science history educator*
Burchfiel, Burrell Clark *geology educator*
Burns, Virginia *social worker*
Campbell, John Young *economics educator*
Campbell, Robert *architect, writer*
Canizares, Claude Roger *astrophysicist, educator*
Carmichael, Alexander Douglas *engineering educator*
Caves, Richard Earl *economist, educator*
Cazden, Courtney B(orden) *education educator*
Ceyer, Sylvia T. *chemistry educator*
Champion, Hale (Charles Hale Champion) *political science educator, former public official*
Chandler, Fay Martin *artist*
†Chang, Lan Samantha *writer, educator*
Chapin, Richard *arbitrator*
Chen, Sow-Hsin *nuclear engineering educator, researcher*
Chernoff, Herman *statistics educator*
†Chin, Wayman *musician, educator*
Chomsky, (Avram) Noam (Avram Chomsky) *linguistics and philosophy educator*
Clark, George Whipple *physics educator*
Clausen, Wendell Vernon *classics educator*
Clay, Phillip L. *academic administrator*
Cleary, David Michael *composer, critic, library assistant*
†Clement McKinley, Sandi *performing arts association administrator, not-for-profit fundraiser*
Clifford, Richard John *religious studies educator*
Clifton, Anne Rutenber *psychotherapist, educator*
†Coglianese, Cary *lawyer, educator*
Cohen, Morris *engineering educator*
Cohen, Robert Edward *chemical engineering educator, consultant*
Cohn, Daniel Ross *physicist*
Cole, Heather Ellen *librarian*
Coleman, Sidney Richard *physicist, educator*
Coles, Robert *child psychiatrist, educator, author*
Colton, Clark Kenneth *chemical engineering educator*
Condry, Ian *humanities educator*
Conley, Tom Clark *literature educator*
†Connick, Harry, Jr., *jazz musician, actor, singer*
Connors, Frank Joseph *lawyer*
Cooper, Mary Campbell *information services executive*
Cooper, Richard Newell *economist, educator*
Corey, Elias James *chemistry educator*
†Costantino, Henry Raymond *chemical engineer, researcher*
Covert, Eugene Edzards *aerospace engineer, physics educator*
Cox, Archibald *lawyer, educator*
Crandall, Stephen Harry *engineering educator*
Crawford, Linda Sibery *lawyer, educator*
Cross, Frank Moore, Jr., *foreign language educator*
†Cuomo, Andrew *former federal agency administrator*
Dalgarno, Alexander *astronomy educator*
Dame, Thomas Michael *radio astronomer*
Das, Lama Surya *theology studies educator*
Davis, Paul Robert *investment manager, portfolio manager*
de Marneffe, Barbara Rowe *historic preservationist*
de Neufville, Richard Lawrence *engineering educator*
Dennis, Jack Bonnell *computer scientist, educator*
Dershowitz, Alan Morton *lawyer, educator*
Deshpandé, Rohit *business educator*
†Deutch, John M. *former federal agency administrator, chemistry educator*
de Varon, Lorna Cooke *choral conductor*
Dewey, Clarence Forbes, Jr., *engineering educator*
DiBerardinis, Louis Joseph *health and safety professional, industrial hygiene engineer, consultant, educator*
†DiGiustini, Antonetta Anna *educational association administrator, educator*
†Diop, Samba *language educator*
Dominguez, Jorge Ignacio *government educator*
Donahue, John David *public official, educator*
Dowling, John Elliott *biology educator*
†Downey, Richard Ralph *lawyer, accountant, management consultant*
Drago-Severson, Eleanor Elizabeth E. *developmental psychologist, educator, researcher*
Drake, Elisabeth Mertz *chemical engineer, consultant*
Duckett, Joan *law librarian*
Dudley, Richard Mansfield *mathematician, educator*
Duffy, Robert Aloysius *aeronautical engineer*
Dugundji, John *aeronautical engineer*
Dunlop, John Thomas *economics educator, former secretary of labor*
Durham, Bradley Paul *financial publisher*
Dyck, Arthur James *ethicist, educator*
Dyck, Martin *literary theorist, German literature theorist, mathematics historian*
†Dynarski, Susan Marie *social studies educator*
Eagar, Thomas Waddy *metallurgist, educator*
Eagleson, Peter Sturges *civil engineer, environmental engineer, educator*
Eckaus, Richard Samuel *economist, educator*
Edgerly, William Skelton *banker*
Edington, Mark David Wheeler *clergyman, educational administrator*
Effron, Seth Alan *editor, journalist*
Ehntholt, Daniel James *chemist*

Rubin, Donald Bruce *statistician, educator, research company executive*
Rubin, Lawrence Gilbert *physicist, laboratory manager*
Ruggie, John Gerard *political science educator, diplomat*
Ruina, Jack Philip *electrical engineer, educator*
Russell, George Allen *composer, theoritician, author, conductor*
Russell, Kenneth Calvin *metallurgical engineer, educator*
Russell, Mason Webster *healthcare economist, educator*
Ryan, Pauline Jen *biomedical company executive*
Sagar, Ambuj D. *environmental and technology policy professional*
Salzmann, George Stephen *biochemist, priest*
Samuelson, Paul Anthony *economist, educator*
Sander, Frank Ernest Arnold *law educator*
Sapolsky, Harvey Morton *political scientist, educator*
Satterfield, Charles Nelson *chemical engineer, educator*
Scharlack, Ronald Stuart *medical device company executive*
Schauer, Frederick Franklin *law educator*
†Schechter, Paul *physicist, educator*
Schild, Rudolph Ernst *astronomer, educator*
Schmalensee, Richard Lee *dean, economist, former government official, educator*
Schneider, Franz *psychology researcher*
Schrock, Richard Royce *chemistry educator*
Schuessler Fiorenza, Elisabeth *theology educator*
Seidel, Samuel Learned Richard Cartun *governmental researcher*
Sevcenko, Ihor *history and literature educator*
Seyferth, Dietmar *chemist, educator*
Shapiro, Irwin Ira *physicist, educator*
Sharp, Phillip Allen *biologist, educator*
Shinagel, Michael *English literature educator*
Shine, Daniel Joseph, Jr., *management consultant*
Shore, Miles Frederick *psychiatrist, educator*
Silbey, Robert James *chemistry educator, researcher, consultant*
Simon, Eckehard (Peter) *foreign language educator*
Simons, Thomas W., Jr., *educator*
Sims, Ezra *composer*
Singer, Irving *philosophy educator*
Singer, Isadore Manuel *mathematician, educator*
Skolnikoff, Eugene B. *political science educator*
Slive, Seymour *museum director, fine arts educator*
Slosburg-Ackerman, Jill Rose *artist, educator*
Smith, Henry Ignatius *engineering educator*
Smith, Kenneth Alan *chemical engineer, educator*
Smith, Merritt Roe *history educator*
†Smith, Susie Irene *histotechnologist, cytometrist*
Sollors, Werner *English language, literature and American studies educator*
Solomon, Arthur Kaskel *biophysics educator*
Solow, Robert Merton *economist, educator*
Spaepen, Frans August *applied physics researcher, educator*
Spunt, Shepard Armin *real estate executive, management and financial consultant*
Staelin, David Hudson *electrical engineering educator, consultant*
Stanley, Richard P. *mathematics educator*
Stark, Antony Albert *astronomer*
Stauffer, John William *cultural historian*
Steiner, Henry Jacob *law and human rights educator*
Steinfeld, Jeffrey Irwin *chemistry educator, consultant, writer*
Sterbenz, James Philip Guenther *computer network scientist*
Stevens, Kenneth Noble *electrical engineer, educator*
Stoddard, Roger Eliot *librarian*
Stone, Alan Abraham *law and psychiatry educator, psychiatrist*
Strandberg, Malcom Woodrow Pershing *physicist*
Strang, William Gilbert *mathematician, educator*
Suh, Nam Pyo *mechanical engineering educator*
Suleiman, Susan Rubin *romance literature educator, writer*
Summers, Lawrence *former government official, academic administrator*
Susskind, Lawrence Elliott *urban and environmental planner, educator, public dispute mediator*
Szabo, Albert *architect, educator*
Ta, Tai Van *lawyer, researcher*
Tannenbaum, Steven Robert *toxicologist, chemist*
Tarrant, R(ichard) J(ohn) *classicist, educator*
Temin, Peter *economist, educator*
Termeer, Henricus Adrianus *biotechnology company executive*
Thaddeus, Patrick *physicist, educator*
Thernstrom, Stephan *historian, educator*
Thiemann, Ronald Frank *dean, religion educator*
Thompson, Dennis Frank *political science and ethics educator, consultant*
Thompson, Robert L., Jr., *pharmaceutical executive, lawyer*
†Thompson, Samuel G. *artist*
Thompson, William Irwin *educational consultant, writer*
Thornton, Wayne Allen *naval officer, engineer, political scientist*
Ting, Samuel Chao Chung *physicist, educator*
Tinkham, Michael *physicist, educator*
Todreas, Neil Emmanuel *nuclear engineering educator*
Tonegawa, Susumu *biology educator*
Toomer, Cynthia Yvonne *information systems administrator*
Toomre, Alar *applied mathematician, theoretical astronomer*
Torriani-Gorini, Annamaria *microbiologist, educator*
Triantafyllou, Michael Stefanos *ocean engineering educator*
Trilling, Leon *aeronautical engineering educator*
Troxel, Donald Eugene *electrical engineering educator*
Tsoi, Edward Tze Ming *architect, interior designer, urban planner*
Tu, Wei-Ming *historian, philosopher, writer*
Tucker, Louis Leonard *retired historical society administrator*
Tyler, Elizabeth Cowley *writer, painter*
Ulrich, Laurel Thatcher *historian, educator*
Ungar, Eric Edward *mechanical engineer*
Urbanowski, Frank *publishing company executive*
†Vadhan, Salil Pravin *computer scientist, educator*
Vagts, Detlev Frederick *lawyer, educator*
Valiant, Leslie Gabriel *computer scientist, educator*
Vander Velde, Wallace Earl *aeronautical and astronautical educator*
Vanger, Milton Isadore *history educator*
van Houtum, Diana Chang *real estate executive and developer*
Vendler, Helen Hennessy *literature educator, poetry critic*
Verba, Sidney *political scientist, educator*
Verdine, Gregory Lawrence *chemist, educator*
Vessot, Robert Frederick Charles *physicist, researcher*
†Vest, Charles Marstiller *academic administrator*
Vicens, Guillermo Juan *engineering executive*
Vigier, François Claude Denis *city planning educator*
Villa-Komaroff, Lydia *molecular biologist, educator, university official*
Vincent, James Louis *biotechnology company executive*
Viscusi, W(illiam) G. Kip *economics educator*
Vogel, Ezra F. *sociology educator*
Vogt, Evon Zartman, Jr., *anthropologist, writer*
von Hippel, Eric Arthur *innovation educator*
von Mehren, Arthur Taylor *lawyer, educator*
Wacker, Warren Ernest Clyde *physician, educator*
†Ware, Susan W. *historian*
†Warren, Alvin Clifford, Jr., *lawyer*
Watson, Rubie *museum director*
Waugh, John Stewart *chemist, educator*
†Weill, Peter D. *research scientist*
Weinberg, Robert Allan *biochemist, educator*
†Weiner, Charles *historian, educator*
Weitzman, Arthur Joshua *English educator*
Westerlund, Elaine M. *psychologist, educator*
Westfall, David *lawyer, educator*
Westheimer, Frank Henry *chemist, educator*
Wexler, Donald *psychiatrist, educator*
Whipple, Fred Lawrence *astronomer*
White, Alan Frederick *academic administrator*
White, David Calvin *electrical engineer, energy educator, consultant*
White, John P *federal agency administrator*
Whitesides, George McClelland *chemistry educator*
Whitlock, Charles Preston *former university dean*
Whitman, Robert Van Duyne *civil engineer, educator*
Widnall, Sheila Evans *aeronautical educator, former secretary of the airforce, former university official*
Wilcox, Maud *editor*
Williams, James Henry, Jr., *mechanical engineer, educator, consultant*
Williams, Preston Noah *theology educator*
Willie, Charles Vert *sociology educator*
Wilson, Edward Osborne *biologist, educator, writer*
Wilson, Robert Woodrow *radio astronomer*
Wilson, William Julius *sociologist, educator*
Winkler, Gunther *biotechnology executive, drug development expert*
†Wise, Virginia Jo *law educator, librarian*
†Wodiczko, Krzysztof *artist, architect, educator*
†Wogan, Gerald Norman *toxicology educator*
Wolff, Christoph Johannes *music historian, educator*
Wood, John Armstead *planetary scientist, geological sciences educator*
Wood, Richard Robinson *real estate executive*
Worth, Douglas Grey *poet, songwriter, saxophonist*
Wuensch, Bernhardt John *ceramic engineering educator*
†Wurtman, Judith Joy *research scientist*
Wurtman, Richard Jay *physician, educator, inventor*
†Xiao, Yang *philosopher, educator*
†Xie, Xiaoliang Sunney *chemist, educator*
Yannas, Ioannis Vassilios *polymer scientist, educator*
†Yau, Shing-Tung *mathematics educator*
Yergin, Daniel Howard *writer, consultant*
†Yip, Winnie *health economics educator*
Yogman, Michael William *pediatrician*
†Young, Vernon Robert *nutrition, biochemistry educator*
Zeckhauser, Richard Jay *economist, educator*
Zeidenstein, George *population educator*
†Zenowitz, Allan Ralph *government official*
Zhang, Hui *research political scientist*
Zinberg, Dorothy Shore *science policy educator*
Ziolkowski, Jan Michael *medievalist educator*
†Zoll, Mary *writer, writer, educator*

Canton
†Bentas, Lily Haseotes *retail executive*
Bihldorff, John Pearson *hospital director*
†Fireman, Paul B. *footwear and apparel company executive*
Fuchs, Lawrence Howard *government official, educator*
Kurzman, Stephen Alan *accountant, educator*
†Masiello, Thomas Philip, Jr., *lawyer, risk manager*
Palihnich, Nicholas Joseph, Jr., *retail executive*
Parker, Virginia Marie *English language educator*
Rankin, James *financial services company executive*
Sawtelle, Carl S. *psychiatric social worker*

Carlisle
Drew, Philip Garfield *consultant engineering company executive*
Fohl, Timothy *consulting and investment company executive*
Hensleigh, Howard Edgar *lawyer*

Carver
Neubauer, Richard A. *library science educator, consultant*

Centerville
Anderson, Gerald Edwin *utilities executive*
Boulay, Marc Norman *civil engineer, engineering executive*
Kiernan, Owen Burns *educational consultant*
Rieber, Jesse Alvin *psychotherapist*
Scherer, Harold Nicholas, Jr., *electric utility company executive, engineer*
†Shapiro, Harvey *journalist, writer, lyricist*

Charlestown
Brown, Robert Horatio *physician, neuromuscular research scientist*
Cheng, Leo Ling *biophysicist, researcher*
Isselbacher, Kurt Julius *physician*
†Jenike, Michael Andrew *psychiatrist, educator*
Lamont-Havers, Ronald William *physician, research administrator*
Lasko, Natasha B. *psychologist*
Leaf, Alexander *physician, educator*
Moskowitz, Michael Arthur *neuroscientist, neurologist*
†Norris, Philip John *medical educator*
†Potts, John Thomas, Jr., *physician, educator*
†Puglielli, Luigi *research scientist*
†Settleman, Jeffrey *medical researcher, medical educator*
Zamecnik, Paul Charles *oncologist, medical research scientist*

Chatham
Bohman, Raynard Frederick, Jr., *transportation consultant, professional association administrator*
Escalante, Judson Robert *business consultant*
McDonell, Horace George, Jr., *instrument company executive*
Patten, Nicholas Frederick *artist*
Popkin, Alice Brandeis *lawyer*
†Weidman, Charles Ray *lawyer*

Chelmsford
Barlas, Julie Sandall *computer scientist, former librarian*
Elwell, Barbara Lois Dow *community organizer*
Fulks, Robert Grady *computer executive*
Furumoto, Horace Wataru *medical products company executive*
Grossman, Debra A. *lawyer, real estate manager, radio talk show host*
Kirkpatrick, Francis H(ubbard) *biophysicist, intellectual property practitioner, consultant*
Lerer, Neal M. *lawyer*
Sintros, James Lee *management consultant, foundation executive*

Chelsea
†Barclay, Peter Roy *minister, counselor*
Dunn, Norman Samuel *plastics and textiles company executive*
Jenkins, Alexander, III, *business executive*
†Kaneb, Gary R. *oil industry executive*
†Kaneb, John A. *corporate executive*

Chesterfield
†Schiffman, Lawrence H. *adult education educator*

Chestnut Hill
Ablon, Steven Luria *psychoanalyst*
Addis, Deborah Jane *management consultant, editor*
Altbach, Philip *director, educator*
Ayas, Karen *management consultant, educator*
Bando, Patricia Alice *director*
Barry, Joan *clinical researcher*
Barth, John Robert *English educator, priest*
Bartunek, Jean Marie *management consultant, educator*
Batchelder, Samuel Lawrence, Jr., *retired corporate lawyer*
Baum, Christopher Frederick *economics educator, consultant*
Baum, Jules Leonard *ophthalmologist, educator*
Blanchette, Oliva *philosophy educator*
†Bloom, Jonathan M. *humanities educator, writer*
Boskin, Claire *psychotherapist*
Bresnahan, James Francis *retired medical educator*
†Burgess, Ann Wolbert *nursing educator*
Carfora, John Michael *economics educator, academic administrator*
†Casey, Amy L. *communications educator, film producer*
†Chyten, Edwin Richard *lawyer*
Dahlben, Salin Abraham *neuropsychiatrist*
Flax, Martin Howard *pathologist, retired educator*
Fourkas, John T. *chemistry educator*
Franklin, Morton Jerome *emergency physician*
†Gaiser, Ted Joseph *academic administrator, minister*
Hachey, Thomas Eugene *British and Irish history educator, consultant*
Hawkins, Joellen Margaret Beck *nursing educator*
Helmick, Raymond Glen *priest, educator*
†Kaminer, Michael Seth *dermatologist*
Kosasky, Harold Jack *fertility researcher*
Leahy, William P. *academic administrator, historian, educator*
Mc Innes, William Charles *priest, academic administrator*
Monan, James Donald *university chancellor*
Newman, Morton B. *psychoanalyst, psychiatrist*
O'Block, Robert Paul *management consultant*
Reed, James Eldin *consultant, publisher, historian*
Schatkin, Margaret Amy *theology educator*
Segelman, Allyn Evan *dentist, researcher, insurance executive*
Shrayer, Maxim D. *writer, educator*
Siegel, Richard Allen *economist*
Smith, David Horton *social sciences educator*
Stanbury, John Bruton *physician, educator*
†Taylor, E. Dennis *English language educator, editor*
†Teich, Jonathan Marc *emergency medicine physician, internist*
Thier, Samuel Osiah *physician, educator*
Ting, Yu-chen *science educator, researcher*
†Torbert, William Rockwell *finance educator, researcher*
Valette, Jean Paul *writer*
Valette, Rebecca Marianne *Romance languages educator*
†Vessey, Judith Ann *nursing educator*
Williamson, John Butler *sociology educator*
Wolfe, Alan *political science educator, writer*
Woodside, Arch G. *marketing educator, researcher*
Yavarkovsky, Jerome Harold *library director*

Chicopee
Chelte, Judith Segzdowicz *secondary education educator*
Costanzo, Nanci Joy *art educator*
Czerwiec, Irene Theresa *gifted education educator*
Dame, Catherine Elaine *acupuncturist*
Pace, Eston A. *systems administrator*

Chilmark
Geyer, Harold Carl *artist, writer*
Low, Joseph *artist*

Cohasset
Dickstein, Harvey Leonard *pharmaceutical company executive*
Rabstejnek, George John *photomics executive*
Replogle, David Robert *publishing company executive*

Concord
Andrews, Joseph Lyon, Jr., *medical educator, writer, practiconer*
Bander, Edward Julius *law librarian emeritus, lawyer*
Boger, William Pierce, III, *ophthalmologist*
Brentani, Patricia Brodie *social worker*
Codere, Helen Frances *anthropologist, educator, university dean*
Collis, David John *management educator*
Davidson, Frank Paul *macroengineer, lawyer*
Domar, Carola Rosenthal *social worker*
Eberle, William Denman *international management consultant*
†Farber, Kenneth Lawrence Meyers *management consultant*
Ghosh, Partha S. *management consultant*
Glovsky, Susan G. L. *lawyer*
Gomberg, Sydelle *dancer educator*
Huxley, Hugh Esmor *molecular biologist, educator*
Ihara, Michio *sculptor*
Lilien, Elliot Stephen *secondary education educator*
MacNichol, Edward Ford, Jr., *biophysicist, educator, consultant*
†Nolin, John Charles *product specialist, engineering consultant*
†Perry, Edward Needham *lawyer*
Rarich, Anne Lippitt *management and organizational development consultant*
Rathore, Naeem Gul *retired United Nations official*
Schiller, Pieter Jon *venture capital executive*
Smith, Eric Parkman *retired railroad executive*
Smith, Peter Walker *finance executive*
Two Feathers, Morwen *event coordinating company executive*
Villers, Philippe *mechanical engineer*
Weiss, James Michael *financial analyst, portfolio manager*
White, James Barr *lawyer, real estate investor, consultant*
Wickfield, Eric Nelson *investment company executive*
Woll, Harry J. *electrical engineer*

Cotuit
Ballou, Kenneth Walter *retired business executive, university dean*
Miller, Robert Charles *retired physicist*
Thibideau, Regina *retail executive, social worker*

Cummington
Smith, William Jay *author*
Wilbur, Richard Purdy *writer, educator*

Dalton
Fumento, Rocco *retired English and film educator*

Danvers
Bilow, Howard L. *health care company executive*
Clark, Sharon Jackson *private school administrator*
Dolan, John Ralph *retired corporation executive*
Keenholtz, Steven Laurence *physician*
Kocur, Sean Edward *toxicologist*
†Shenai, Deodatta Vinayak *chemical engineer*
Waite, Charles Morrison *food company executive*
Wilkes, Brent Ames *management consultant*

Dartmouth
Connors, Robert Leo *city official*
Frothingham, Thomas Eliot *pediatrician*
Leclair, Susan Jean *hematologist, clinical laboratory scientist, educator*

Marlow, James Elliott *English language educator*
Mikolajczak, Boleslaw *computer science educator, researcher, consultant*
†Notaros, Branislav M *electrical engineer, educator*
Wang, Shouhong *business educator*

Dedham
†Balsamo, Salvatore Anthony *technical and temporary employment companies executive*
DiCamillo, Gary Thomas *manufacturing executive*
†Donahue, Michael Christopher *lawyer*
Firth, Everett Joseph *timpanist*
Ghosh, Asish *control engineer*
Janson, Barbara Jean *publisher*
Magner, Jerome Allen *entertainment company executive*
Meridan, Paula M. *interior design executive*
Redstone, Sumner Murray *entertainment company executive, lawyer*
Winder, Alvin Eliot *public health educator, clinical psychologist*

Dennis
Loveland, Donald William *retired computer science educator*
Weilbacher, William Manning *advertising and marketing consultant*

Dennis Port
Singer, Myer R(ichard) *lawyer*

Dighton
Buote, Rosemarie Boschen *retired special education educator*

Dorchester
†Baron, Martin *editor*
†Berg, John Conrad *political science educator*
†Boles, John P. *bishop*
Brelis, Matthew Dean Burns *journalist*
Goodman, Ellen Holtz *journalist*
Johnson, Crystal Elaine *psychologist, community activist, poet, writer, educator*
Lee, June Warren *dentist*
Smith, Survilla Marie *social services administrator, artist, poet*
†Weaver, Mark Franklin *social worker, pastor*
Worgaftik, Susan Carol *social worker*

Dover
Aldrich, Frank Nathan *banker*
Bonis, Laszlo Joseph *business executive, scientist*
Edwards, Carl Norman *lawyer*
Kim, Ducksoo *radiologist, inventor and educator*
Kovaly, John Joseph *consulting engineering executive, educator*
Mehta, Narinder Kumar *marketing executive*
Olsen, David Leslie *author, consultant*
Walker, Laurence Gordon *technology company executive*

Dracut
Brousseau, Catherine Dalton *retired school health services director*

Dudley
Boote, Alfred Shepard *marketing researcher, educator*

Duxbury
Albritton, William Hoyle *training and consulting executive, lecturer, writer*
Safe, Kenneth Shaw, Jr., *fiduciary firm executive*
Thrasher, Dianne Elizabeth *mathematics educator, computer consultant*
Wangler, William Clarence *retired insurance company executive*
Zachmann, William Francis *computer and communications industry market research company executive*

East Boston
†Coy, Craig P. *airport terminal executive*
Patinkin, Terry Allan *physician*

East Bridgewater
Farrell, Sharon Elaine *retired real estate broker*
Heywood, Anne *artist, educator, author*

East Dennis
Ely, David (David E. Lilienthal Jr.) *writer*
†Sheedy, John Thomas (Jack) *writer*

East Falmouth
Forte, Margaret Layman *mathematics educator*
Forte, Wesley Elbert *former insurance company executive, lawyer*
Otis, Richard Dickinson *pathologist*
Selman, Jan Collins *artist*

East Longmeadow
Skutnik, Bolesh J. *optics scientist, lay worker, lawyer*

East Orleans
Burkert, Robert Randall *artist*
Romey, William Dowden *geologist, educator*
Thomsen, Charles Hakon *real estate company executive*

East Sandwich
Clarendon, John Marsden *counselor, youth program director*

Eastham
McLaughlin, Richard Warren *retired insurance company executive*
Pratt, Elizabeth Hayes *artist, art educator*
Souther, Jean Lorraine *accounting and management educator, accountant*
†Tierney, Eugene Francis *lawyer*

Easthampton
Perkins, Homer Guy *manufacturing company executive*

Easton
Chichetto, James William *editor, educator*
Spicer, Kevin Paul *history educator, priest*

Edgartown
Rosenfeld, Walter David, Jr., *architect, writer*

Essex
Lane, Evelyn Procter Conant *computer operator*

Fairhaven
Goes, Kathleen Ann *secondary education educator, choral director*
Hotchkiss, Henry Washington *real estate broker and financial consultant*
Lopes, Myra Amelia *writer*
Merolla, Michele Edward *chiropractor, broadcaster*
Rose, Anita Carroll *retired educator*
Young, Bryan Alan *musician, educator*

Fall River
†Bessette, Heidi Dee *adult nurse practitioner*
Correia, Robert *state legislator*
Dion, Marc Munroe *newspaper columnist*
Frost, Carol A. *clinical social worker, consultant*
†Gordan, Cynthia Lee *lawyer, textile company executive*
Guillemette, Mark Edgar *textile technologist*
Lynds, Lucinda *music educator*
McDonald, John Barry, Jr., *lawyer*
Powers, Alan William *literature educator*
Washburn, Stewart Putnam *management consultant*

Falmouth
†Adelman, William J., Jr., *biophysicist*
Funkhouser, John Jeremiah *urologist*
Goody, Richard Mead *geophysicist*
Heisler, Kenneth Avery *surgeon*
Litschgi, Richard John *computer manufacturing company executive*
Milkman, Marianne Friedenthal *retired city planner*
Milkman, Roger Dawson *genetics educator, molecular evolution researcher*
Nolan, Edmund Francis *management consultant*
Pearce, Jack Bodell *marine biologist, educator*
Preston, Mark I. *retired investment company executive*
Sato, Kazuyoshi *pathologist*

Fitchburg
Aclin, Jean Anne *cancer registrar*
†Caniato, Michele *music educator, composer, conductor*
DiPace, Steven B. *lawyer*
Jareckie, Stephen Barlow *museum curator*
†Kemp, Deborah K. *secondary school educator*
†Kim, Kwahng Soo *finance educator*
Mara, Vincent Joseph *college president*
Niemi, Beatrice Neal *social services professional*
Railsback, David Phillips *former state official, lawyer*
Spero, Joshua Benjamin *political scientist, educator*

Florence
Park, Beverly Goodman *lawyer*
†Platt, Rutherford Hayes *lawyer, educator, geographer, consultant*

Forestdale
Bissell, Phil (Charles P. Bissell) *cartoonist*

Foxboro
Belichick, Bill *professional football coach*
Brady, Tom *football player*
Bush, Raymond T. *accountant, corporate professional*
Devenis, Keistutis Peter *civil engineer, consultant*
†Edwards, Robert *professional football player*
†Harkes, John *professional soccer player*
Hershman, Judith *advertising executive*
Imbault, James Joseph *manufacturing company executive*
Karelitz, Richard Alan *financial executive, lawyer*
Kaul, Alan Franklin *healthcare consultant, pharmacist*
Kraft, Robert K. *professional sports team executive*
Ryskamp, Carroll Joseph *retired chemical engineer*

Framingham
Austin, Sandra Ikenberry *nurse educator, consultant*
†Beckwitt, Richard David *biology educator, researcher*
Bogard, Carole Christine *lyric soprano*
Capobianco, Anthony G. *physician*
Casselman, Frederick Lee *computer artist*
Chiraseveenuprapund, Pat *internist, endocrinologist*
Crossley, Frank Alphonso *former metallurgical engineer*
†Curry, Thomas Francis *lawyer*
Dawicki, Doloretta Diane *analytical chemist, research biochemist, educator*
Deutsch, Marshall E(manuel) *medical products company executive, inventor*
Donovan, R. Michael *management consultant*
English, Edmond *retail company executive*
†Eykman, Christoph W. *language educator*
Feldman, Susan Eleanor *technology analyst*
Goldman, Ralph Frederick *research physiologist, educator*
Gould, Rodney Elliott *lawyer, university dean, educator*
Harrington, Joseph Francis *educational company executive, history educator*
Heng, Gerald C. W. *lawyer*
†Herrick, Stewart Thurston *lawyer*
Hillman, Carol Barbara *communications executive, consultant*
Horn, Bernard *English language educator, writer, translator*
†Jiang, Canwen *genetic scientist, researcher*
†Kannel, William B. *cardiologist, epidemiologist*
†Kenealy, Patrick *publishing company executive*
Kriegsman, Edward Michael *lawyer*
Lavin, Philip Todd *biostatistician executive*
LeDuc, Karen Lorain Leacu *elementary and middle school education educator*
Lindsay, Leslie *packaging engineer*
Mabrouk, Sarah Lou *mathematician, educator*
McCarthy, Desmond Fergus *English literature educator*
Meltzer, Jay H. *lawyer, retail company executive*
Merlini, Sandra Ann *library assistant, writer*
Munro, Meredith Vance *lawyer*
Oleskiewicz, Francis Stanley *retired insurance executive*
Ostrow, Robert *publishing executive*
†Rikleen, Lauren Stiller *lawyer*
Sargent, Ronald L. *retail office and business products executive*
Silverman, Harold Irving *pharmaceutical executive*
Sleeper, Thomas F. *journalist, consultant, insurance investigator*
Vermette, Raymond Edward *clinical laboratories administrator*
West, Doe *bioethicist, social justice activist, researcher*
Willinger, Rhonda Zwern *optometrist*
Winston, Eileen Lynn *rheumatologist*
Wulf, Sharon Ann *management consultant*
Wulf, Stanley Arthur *engineering executive*
Yonda, Alfred William *mathematician*

Franklin
Ferguson, Dennis Edward *music educator, musician*
Maril, David C. *editor*
Rafal, Keith W.L. *physician*
Roxin, Emilio Oscar *mathematics educator*
Shastry, Shambhu Kadhambiny *scientist, engineering executive, consultant*
Tsivinsky, Vladimir George *systems engineer*

Gardner
Cosentino, Patricia Byrne *English educator, poet*
Du Buske, Lawrence M. *immunologist, allergist, rheumatologist*
Hawke, Robert Douglas *retired state legislator*
Koller, John Dryden *media educator, scriptwriter*
Marceau, Judith Marie *retired elementary school educator*
†Sans, Henri Louis, Jr., *lawyer*

Gloucester
Anscombe, Roderick John *psychiatrist, educator*
†Baxter, Larry K. *electrical engineer, consultant*
Birchfield, John Kermit, Jr., *lawyer*
Collins, Pat Lowery *writer, artist, educator*
Fioravanti, Nancy Eleanor *retired banker*
Hausman, William Ray *fund raising and management consultant*
Knupp, Ralph *information technology executive*
Lanzkron, Rolf Wolfgang *manufacturing executive*
Littlefield, Paul Damon *retired management consultant*
†Mammola, Dominic *advertising executive*
McCarl, Henry Newton *economics and geology consultant, venture capitalist*
Means, Elizabeth Rose Thayer *financial consultant, writer, lawyer*
Perry, Sarah Hollis *artist*
Sallah, Majeed (Jim Sallah) *real estate developer*
Scanlan, Esther Meader *psychiatric social worker*
Socolow, Arthur Abraham *geologist*
Swigart, Joan B. *artist, art consultant*
Weller, Anthony *writer, musician*
White, Harold Jack *pathologist*

Great Barrington
Berryhill, Mary Finley *emergency nurse*
Curtin, Phyllis *music educator, former dean, operatic singer*
Drew, Bernard Alger *writer*
Drohan, Margo Angela *pediatric nurse practitioner*
†Hannoum, Abdelmajid *historian, educator, anthropologist, researcher*
Lewis, Karen Marie *writer, human services professional*
†Thalheimer, Anne N. *residence director*
Witt, Susan Carreer *environmental educator, society administrator*
Yanoff, Arthur Samuel *artist, art therapist*

Green Harbor
Gaffey, Virginia Anne *retired nurse anesthetist*

Greenfield
Blanker, Alan Harlow *lawyer*
Curtiss, Carol Perry *health care consultant*
Damon, Steven William *music educator*
Davis, Allen Jeffrey *academic administrator*
Hutcheson, Thomas Worthington *trade association official*
†Nix, Michael Charles *musician, educator*
Robinson, John Alan *logic and computer science educator*
Ruiz, Lillian *English language educator*
Sternberg, Harriet Elaine *psychiatric social worker*

Groton
Clark, Susan Frances *theater educator*
Huguenin, Nancy Hoffman *behavioral psychologist*
Munson, Lawrence Shipley *management consultant*
Searle, Andrew Barton *fund raising consultant*

Groveland
deNapoli, Paul Frederick *investment manager*
Sims, Andrew Harley, Jr., *engineering executive, public administrator*

Hadley
Abel, Robert Halsall *writer*
Goldwater, Walter Eugene *psychiatrist, musician*
McGee, Donna Louise *artist, educator*
Zion, Ellen C. *small business owner*

Hanover
Ahern, F. Daniel, Jr., *state agency administrator, management consultant*

Hanscom AFB
Harms, John Kevin *lawyer*
†Kenne, Leslie F. *military officer*
Lemieux, Joseph Anthony, Jr., *electrical engineer, computer engineer*
Mailloux, Robert Joseph *physicist*
Schmitt, Stephen Richard *electronics engineer*

Hanson
Norris, John Anthony *health products executive, lawyer, educator*

Harvard
Marolda, Anthony Joseph *management consulting company executive*

Harwich
Geberth, Frances White *painter*
Piro, Anthony John *radiologist*
Steward, Aleta Joanna *digital artist*

Harwich Port
Smith, Ralph Wesley, Jr., *retired federal judge*
Staszesky, Francis Myron *independent energy consultant*

Hatfield
Yolen, Jane *author*

Haverhill
Bigelow, Peter *electronics executive*
Cox, William Donald, Jr., *lawyer*
DeSchuytner, Edward Alphonse *biochemist, educator*
Heineman, William A. *political scientist, educator*
Kelley, David Brian *community college dean, educator, consultant*
Korinow, Ira Lee *rabbi*
Liguori, Paul Anthony *physician*
MacMillan, Francis Philip *physician*
Morris, Robert *reinsurance analyst*
Rosenbloom, Carl F. *pediatrician*
Rubinstein, Nancy G. *social worker, consultant*
Walker, Robert Ross *social worker*

Haydenville
Connolly, John Matthew *philosophy educator, administrator*
Shallcross, Doris Jane *creative behavioral educator*

Hingham
Calnan, Arthur Francis *ophthalmologist*
Harbert, Susan Randall *administrator*
Llewellyn, John Schofield, Jr., *former food company executive*

Holbrook
Crandlemere, Robert Wayne *engineering executive*
Noyes, Walter Omar *writer, tree surgeon*

Holden
Ciance, Karin Lori (Ohs) *medical/surgical nurse*
Jareckie, Gretchen Kinsman Fillmore *retired English language educator*
Price, Robert DeMille *lawyer*

Holland
†McGrory, Mary Kathleen *retired college president*

Holliston
Prosser, Robert Arthur *retired research scientist*

Holyoke
Dearborn, Maureen Markt *speech and language clinician*
Ferriter, Maurice Joseph *lawyer*
Gan, Deqiang *engineer*
Radner, Sidney Hollis *retired rug company executive*

Hopkinton
Berthiaume, Wayne Henry *electrical engineer*
Black, David Lionel *computer scientist*
Haller, William Paul *analytical chemist, robotics and automation specialist*
†Ruettgers, Michael Cadet *electronics executive*
Sen, Asok C. *research scientist*
Tucci, Joseph M. *computer software and services executive*

Housatonic
Charpentier, Gail Wigutow *private school executive director*

Hudson
Champine, George A. *computer scientist*
Chen, I-Yu *computer software executive*
†Osoff, Jeffrey Arlin *media executive*

Hull
Anderson, Timothy Christopher *educational association administrator*
†Tanzi, Rudolph Emile *neuroscientist*

Humarock
Murphy, Ann Marguerite *artist*

Hyannis
Chiotellis, Philip Nicos *cardiologist*
†Horn, Everett Byron, Jr., *retired lawyer*
Makkay, Albert *broadcast executive*
Makkay, Maureen Ann *broadcast executive*
Nicholson, Ellen Ellis *clinical social worker*
Segersten, Robert Hagy *lawyer, investment banker*

Hyde Park
Harris, Emily Louise *special education educator*

Ipswich
Barth, Elmer Ernest *wire and cable company executive*
†Brooks, Sam *publishing executive*
Bryant, Edward Curtis *college admissions consultant*
Dyer, Victor Eugene, II, *library administrator*
Getchell, Charles Willard, Jr., *lawyer, publisher*
Jennings, Frederic Beach, Jr., *economist, saltwater flyfishing guide*
Munro, Donald William, Jr., *non-profit organization executive*
Phillips, Christopher Hallowell *retired diplomat*
Wilson, Doris H. *volunteer*

Jamaica Plain
†Howland, Llewellyn, III, *publishing executive, writer*
Kent, Jeanne Yvonne *artist, poet*
Lynch, Bridget *artist*
†Parris, Thomas Martin *research scientist, consultant*
Pierce, Chester Middlebrook *retired psychiatrist, educator*
Shapiro, Ascher Herman *mechanical engineer, educator, consultant*
Snider, Gordon Lloyd *physician*
Zahn, Carl Frederick *museum publications director, designer, photographer*

Lakeville
Barry, Marilyn White *retired special education educator, dean*

Lancaster
Poduska, John William, Sr., *computer company executive*
Richter, Henry Andrew *electrical engineer*

Lawrence
Walker, Gail Flanagan *pediatrics nurse, women's health nurse, nursing administrator*

Leeds
Deane, James Garner *magazine editor, conservationist*

Leicester
Rogers, Randall Lloyd *mechanical engineer*

Lenox
Coffin, Louis Fussell, Jr., *mechanical engineer*
Gela, George *electrical engineering researcher*
Kochta, Ruth Martha *artist*
Lewis, Marianne H. *psychiatric nurse practitioner*
Newton, Frank George *bank executive*
Pirani, Conrad Levi *pathologist, educator*

Leominster
Cucchiara, Sandra Chiavaras *special education educator*
Ford, John Stephen *treasurer*
Lambert, Lyn Dee *library media specialist, law librarian*
Landry, Francis Roderick *medical librarian*
Lyons, Beryl Barton Anfindsen *sales professional*

Lexington
Aldrich, Nancy Cook *engineer, administrator*
Aronin, Lewis Richard *metallurgical engineer*
†Bahcall, Safi R. *pharmaceutical executive*
Bailey, Fred Coolidge *retired engineering consulting company executive*
Baron, Sheldon *research and development company executive*
Bernardi, John Lawrence, Jr., *economic historian, educator, consultant*
Berstein, Irving Aaron *biotechnology and medical technology executive*
Betts, Kathleen Vanetta *human resources executive*
†Beusch, John Ulrich *engineer, researcher*
Brick, Donald Bernard *software company executive*
Brookner, Eli *electrical engineer*
Buchanan, John Machlin *biochemistry educator*
Burkett, Bradford Charles *lawyer*
Burnham, Daniel Patrick *aerospace transportation executive*
Burwen, Barbara R. *painter*
Bussgang, Julian Jakub *electronics engineer*
Cardwell, Guy Adams *retired language educator*
Cho, John Yungdo Nagamichi *atmospheric research scientist*
Colby, George Vincent, Jr., *electrical engineer, consultant*
Collins, Allan Meakin *cognitive scientist, psychologist, educator*
Davis, Barbara M(ae) *librarian*
Densmore, Ann *speech pathology/audiology services professional, audiologist, writer*
Dietrich, Melinda *visual arts administrator*
Dionne, Gerald Francis *research physicist, educator, consultant*
Drouilhet, Paul Raymond, Jr., *science laboratory director, electrical engineer*
Dulchinos, Peter *lawyer*
†Elanayar, Sunil K. *research and development engineer*
Fillios, Louis Charles *retired science educator*
France-Litchfield, Ruth A. *reading and early literacy specialist*
Fray, Lionel Louis *management consultant*
Freed, Charles *engineering consultant, researcher*
Freitag, Wolfgang Martin *librarian, educator*
Frey, John Ward *landscape architect*
Frieden, Bernard Joel *urban studies educator*
Garing, Ione Davis *civic worker, club woman*
Gibbs, Martin *biologist, educator*
Glaser, Peter Edward *mechanical engineer, consultant*
†Goglia, Richard A. *corporate financial executive*
Gutheim, Allen Herman *economist*
Haldeman, Charles Waldo, III, *aeronautical engineer*
Halloran, Katherine Hess *physician, consultant*
†Harris, John D., II, *electronics executive*
Hines, Edward Francis, Jr., *lawyer*
Horowitz, Morris A. *retired economics educator*
Hurd, Philip Justin *executive search consultant*
Jaffe, Howard Lawrence *rabbi*
Jordan, Judith Victoria *clinical psychologist, educator*
†Kapples, John W. *electronics executive*
Keicher, William Eugene *electrical engineer*
†Kelly, Kevin A. *mathematician, educator*
Kennedy, X. J. (Joseph Kennedy) *writer*
Kerr, Thomas Henderson, III, *electrical engineer, researcher*
Kilson, Marion *college dean*
Klein, Lawrence Allen *accounting educator*
†Lacson, Eduardo K., Jr., *nephrologist*
†Lafrey, Raymond Richard *electrical engineer*
†Lenzen, Glenn Howard, Jr., *lawyer*
Li, Tongchuan *pharmacologist, researcher*
Linkov, Igor *conservationist, consultant*
†Lyons, W. Gregory *electrical engineer, researcher*
Martinez, David R. *electrical engineer, science educator*
McAleer, John Joseph *English literature educator*
McFarland, Philip James *educator, writer*
McGirr, David William John *pharmaceutical executive*
Melngailis, Ivars *solid state researcher*
Morrow, Walter Edwin, Jr., *electrical engineer, university laboratory administrator*
Nash, Leonard Kollender *chemistry educator*
Noether, Emiliana Pasca *historian, educator*
†O'Connell, Brian Morgan *music educator*
Ott, John Harlow *museum administrator*
Otten, Jeffrey *former hospital administrator*
Pang, Samuel Chow-Ern *reproductive endocrinologist, gynecologist-obstetrician*
Papanek, Gustav Fritz *economist, educator*
Paul, Norman Leo *psychiatrist, educator*
†Peden, Keith J. *human resources specialist*
Peet, Norton Paul *science administrator*
Perez, Carol Anne *rehabilitation services professional, consultant*
†Piano, Phyllis J. *communications executive*
†Pliner, Edward S. *corporate financial executive*
Preve, Roberta Jean *librarian, researcher*
†Rhoads, Rebecca R. *electronics executive*
†Ronchi, Donald M. *psychologist, educator*
†Roos, Albert Q. *secondary school educator*
Ryerson, Richard Alan *historian, editor*
Shapiro, Marian Kaplun *psychologist*
†Shelton, Gregory S. *electronics executive*
Silverman, Sam Mendel *physicist, lawyer*
Smith, Robert Louis *construction company executive*
Smith, Steven Thomas *signal processing engineer*
Stephens, Jay B. *lawyer, manufacturing executive*
Sussman, Martin Victor *chemical engineering educator, inventor, consultant*
†Swanson, William Henry *equipment manufacturing company executive*
Taft, S. Tucker *computer scientist*
Trainor, Bernard Edmund *retired military officer*
von Braun, Curt *aerospace engineer*
Vose, Morton, II, (Seth Morton Vose II) *art dealer, art appraiser, historian*
†Wang, Chi Hua *chemist, education educator*
Washburn, Barbara Polk *cartographer, researcher, explorer*
White, Gary Francis *investigation professional*
Williamson, Richard Cardinal *physicist*
Wolpert, Etta *artist, poet*

Lexington
Steiner, John William *retired biophysicist*

Lincoln
Barrett, Beatrice Helene *psychologist*
Brandt, John Henry *physician*
Capasso, Nicholas John *curator, art historian, public art expert*
Donald, David Herbert *author, history educator*
Giles, Allen *pianist, composer, music educator*
Gnichtel, William Van Orden *lawyer*
Green, David Henry *manufacturing company executive*
Holberton, Philip Vaughan *entrepreneur, educator, professional speaker*
Kane, Melissa L. *fundraiser*
†Kerrebrock, Jack Leo *aeronautics and astronautics engineering educator*
Kulka, J(ohannes) Peter *retired physician, pathologist*
Kusik, Charles Lembit *chemical engineer*
Langton, Jane Gillson *writer, illustrator*
LeGates, John Crews Boulton *information scientist*
Nenneman, Richard Arthur *retired publishing executive*
Payne, Roger Searle *zoology researcher and administrator, conservationist*
Schwartz, Edward Arthur *lawyer*

Littleton
Crandall Hollick, Julian Bernard Hugh *radio producer*
Crory, Mary *town official*
Engel, Charlene Stant *artist, art historian*
Kulas, Frederick John *computer company executive*
Lau, Joanna T. *information technology executive*

Longmeadow
Atamian, Charles *oncologist, surgeon*
Cobbs, Russell L(ewis) *English language educator*
Griffin, John Francis *cardiologist*
Katz, Barbara S. *special education educator*
Keady, George Cregan, Jr., *judge*
Leary, Carol Ann *academic administrator*
Lemnios, Andrew Zachery *aerospace engineer, educator, researcher*
Lo Bello, Joseph David *bank executive*
Louargand, Marc Andrew *real estate executive, financial consultant*
Miller-Sanborn, Nancy Janet *insurance agent*
Quinn, Andrew Peter, Jr., *lawyer, insurance executive retired*
Skelton, Don Richard

Lowell
†Aste, Mario Andrea *foreign language educator*
Baskin, Frank Ellis *social worker, educator*
†Berkowitz, William R. *psychologist, writer, consultant*
Coleman, Robert Marshall *biology educator*
†Cook, Charles Addison *lawyer*
Curtis, James Theodore *lawyer*
Donoghue, Eileen M. *former mayor*
Dubner, Daniel William *pediatrician*
Galizzi, Monica *economics educator*
Goodwin, Susan Ann *academic administrator*
Hayes, Donald Paul, Jr., *elementary and secondary education educator*
Kannenberg, Lloyd Chambers *physicist, educator*
†Karr, Ronald Dale *librarian, historian*
†Kazmer, David Owen *engineering educator*
Kegel, Gunter Heinrich Reinhard *physics educator, researcher*
†Kuhn, Sarah *educator, consultant*
Kunzendorf, Robert Godfrey *psychologist, educator, researcher*
LeBaron, John Francis *education educator*
Liu, Fenghai *engineer*
†Lloyd, Gerald Joseph *music educator*
Martin, William Francis, Jr., *lawyer*
†McAfee, Noelle Claire *education educator*
Natsios, Nicholas Andrew *retired foreign service officer*
Petakov, Dragan Svetozar *internist, educator*
Pike, Jonathan Hamilton *writer*
Sullivan, Anne Dorothy Hevner *artist*
Teague, Bernice Rita *accountant*
Trounstine, Jean Rollman *humanities educator, writer*
Wakim, Fahd George *physicist, educator*
Wegman, David Howe *health science educator, consultant*

Ludlow
Mondry, Paul Michael *lawyer*
Roberge, Lawrence Francis *neuroscientist, biotechnology consultant, writer, bioethicist, educator*
Tetherly, Jonathan Collieson *chaplain, educator*

Lunenburg
Schnakenberg, Lori Ann *secondary school educator*
Tallman, Susan Porri *library director*

Lynn
Astuccio, Sheila Margaret *educational administrator*
Chow, Humphrey Wai *mechanical engineer*
D'Entremont, Edward Joseph *infosystems engineer, educator*
Donovan, Elaine F. *social worker*
Kiley, Thomas Francis *civil engineer, lawyer*
McManus, Patrick J. *mayor, lawyer, accountant*
Ryder, Edward Francis *secondary education educator*

Lynnfield
†Hodgkins, Douglas Wendell *music educator*
Kerrigan, Nancy *professional figure skater, former Olympic athlete*
McGivney, John Joseph *lawyer*
McLaughlin, John J., Jr., *lawyer*
Solomon, Jerry Lawrence *sports marketing executive, educator*
Yaremchuk, Michael John *plastic surgeon*

Malden
†Finn, Marvin Ruven *lawyer*
Guild, Richard Samuel *trade association management company executive*
Jiang, Yong Ping *research scientist*
†Kemp, Loretta Christine *human services administrator*
Marques, Paul Joseph *secondary school educator, consultant*
Murphy, Mary Agnes (Meg Murphy) *adult education coordinator, artist*
Pirzada, Farouk Ahmad *cardiologist, educator*

Manchester
Arntsen, Arnt Peter *engineer, consultant*
Shepley, Hugh *architect*
†Wolfe, Robert Shenker *retired lawyer*

Mansfield
Jellows, Tracy Patrick *software engineer*

Marblehead
Cohen, Merrill *chemist*
Heins, Esther *botanical artist, painter*
Kennedy, Elizabeth Mae *musician*
Lundregan, William Joseph *lawyer*
Nilsson, Edward Olof *architect*
Page, George Alfred, Jr., *lawyer*
Phillips, Peter Lawrence *communications executive*
Quigley, Stephen Howard *executive editor*
Snow, George Bartlett *city official, accountant*
Tamaren, Michele Carol *special education educator*
Thompson, Michael Laurie *food manufacturing executive*

Marion
†Latham, Christopher Robert *alumni and development director*
McPartland, Patricia Ann *health educator and administrator*
Worley, Robert William, Jr., *retired lawyer*

Marlborough
Aclin, Keith Andrew *technical service executive, educator*
Bennett, C. Leonard *consulting engineer*
Birstein, Seymour Joseph *aerospace company executive*
Brower, David Charles *transportation executive*
†Carter, James W. *electronics executive*
Hunt, Philip Charles *engineer, consultant*

Marshfield
Arapoff, John Richard *artist*

Marshfield Hills
Krause, Dorothy Simpson *fine artist*

Marstons Mills
Martin, David Standish *education educator*
Martin, Susan Katherine *librarian*
Martin, Vincent George *management consultant*

Mashpee
Detschel, Frederick William *management consultant*
Payne, Paula Marie *minister*
Searle, William Ross *academic administrator, artist, educator*
Stein, Seymour *electronics scientist*

Mattapoisett
Andersen, Laird Bryce *retired university administrator*
Bertram, Christine G. *artist, painter/graphic designer*
Rosenfield, M(anuel) C(harles) *retired history educator, retired coastguard officer*

Maynard
Holway, Ellen Twombly Hay *primary education educator*

Medfield
Herbeck, Dale Alan *educator*
McQuillen, Jeremiah Joseph *distribution executive*
Phillips, Marion Grumman *writer, civic worker*
Woolston-Catlin, Marian *psychiatrist*

Medford
Anderson, Thomas Jefferson, Jr., *composer, educator*
Astill, Kenneth Norman *mechanical engineering educator*
Bacow, Lawrence Seldon *academic administrator, environmental educator*
Bedau, Hugo Adam *philosophy educator*
Berman, David *lawyer, poet*
Boisjoly, Russell Paul *international consultant*
Bosworth, Stephen Warren *ambassador*
Cavallaro, Mary Caroline *retired physics educator*
Chaisson, Eric Joseph *astrophysicist, science administrator, educator*
Chaturvedi, Pravin R. *pharmaceutical executive*
†Ch'en, Li-li *writer, Chinese language, literature and comparative literature educator*
Comeau, Lorene Anita Emerson *real estate developer*
Conklin, John Evan *sociology educator*
Cowen, Lenore Jennifer *mathematician, educator, computer scientist*
DeBold, Joseph Francis *psychology educator*
Elkind, David *psychology educator*
Fyler, John Morgan *English language educator*
Gardner, Geoffrey *writer, English educator*
Gittleman, Sol *university official, humanities educator*
Goldberg, Pamela Winer *finance educator, director*
Goodwin, Neva R. *economist*
Greif, Robert *mechanical engineering educator*
Gunther, Leon *physicist, educator*
Hernandez, Mark Alan *Latin American/Latino literary and cultural studies educator*
Howell, Alvin Harold *engineer, company executive, educator*
Jacob, Robert Joseph Kassel *computer scientist, educator*
†Kaul, Anton *mathematician, educator*
Kreifeldt, John Gene *mechanical engineering educator*
Laurent, Pierre-Henri *history educator*
Logan, Bernard J. *obstetrician*
†Lundquist, Eric *editor-in-chief*
Marcopoulos, George John *history educator*
Mc Carthy, Kathryn A. *physicist*
Miczek, Klaus Alexander *psychology educator*
Monsma, James Edwin *retired consulting company executive*
Nelson, Frederick Carl *mechanical engineering educator*
O'Connell, Brian *community organizer, public administrator, writer, educator*
O'Leary, David Michael *priest, educator*
Roth, Sallyann *social worker*
Salacuse, Jeswald William *lawyer, educator*
Schneps, Jack *physics educator*
†Seymour, Sloan *publishing executive*
Thacker, Vasant Mukund *obstetrician, gynecologist*
Ueda, Reed Takashi *historian, educator*
Uhlir, Arthur, Jr., *electrical engineer, university administrator*
White, Barbara Ehrlich *art history educator*
†Wilson, Jonathan Michael *language educator, writer*

Medway
†Arthur, Wallace *physicist, educator*
Civitella, Corine Antoinette *retired health facility administrator*
Hoag, David Garratt *aerospace engineer*
Saenger, Bruce Walter *consulting firm executive*

Melrose
Brown, Ronald Osborne *telecommunications and computer systems consultant*
Desforges, Jane Fay *medical educator, physician*
Henken, Bernard Samuel *clinical psychologist, speech pathologist*
McLennan, Bernice Claire *human resources professional*

Methuen
DiFruscia, Anthony R. *lawyer, real estate executive*
Jean, Patricia Anne *medical center administrator*
Mason, Phillip Howard *aircraft company executive, retired army officer*
McNaughton, William John *retired bishop*
Shetty, Santosh Kumar *physician*
Simoes, Ronald Alan *mortgage company executive*
Stanley, Malchan Craig *school system administrator, psychologist*

Middleboro
Cacciatore, Sharen Wendy *educational administrator*
Green, Michael Jeffrey *retired psychologist, consultant, administrator*
Washburn, Stewart Alexander *management consultant*

Middleborough
Lodi, Edward *writer, publisher*
†Maddigan, Bill *entrepreneur*

Middleton
Daniels, William Albert *food products executive*

Milford
Carson, Charles Henry *microwave engineer*
Cocchiarella, John Peter *pediatrician*
Correia, Alberto Abrantes *management executive*

Mill River
Jaffe, Katharine Weisman *retired librarian*

Milton
Cooperstein, Paul Andrew *lawyer, management consultant*
Corcoran, Robert Joseph *fund raising executive*
Desmond, Patricia Lorraine *psychotherapist, writer, publisher*
Frazier, Marie Dunn *speech educator, public relations and human resources specialist*
†Jespersen, John Kresten *librarian*
Randall, Lilian Maria Charlotte *museum curator*
Warren, John Coolidge *private school administrator, history educator*
Wengler, Marguerite Marie *educational therapist*

Milton Village
†Canton, Mamie Ruth *humanities educator*

Monson
De Santis, Sylvia *library director*
Krach, Mitchell Peter *retired financial services executive*

Montague
Kohler, Heinz *economics educator*

Monterey
Frye-Moquin, Marsha Marie *social worker*

Monument Beach
Sullivan, Philip G. *retired obstetrician-gynecologist*

Nantucket
Carr, James Revell *museum executive, curator*
Giddings, Lucille Cassell *nurse*
Kales, Paul Albert *engineering educator, cartoonist*
Lethbridge, Francis Donald *retired architect*
Lobl, Herbert Max *lawyer, writer*
Louderback, Peter Darragh *accountant, consultant*
Mercer, Richard Joseph *retired advertising executive, freelance writer*
Pollard, Margaret Louise *association administrator*
Rorem, Ned *composer, author*
Salomon, Lucy *psychiatrist, educator*
Sangree, Walter Hinchman *social anthropologist, educator*
Willis, Sidney Frank *artist, educator*

Natick
Abele, John E. *medical products executive*
Banderet, Louis Eugene *psychologist*
Bensel, Carolyn Kirkbride *psychologist*
Bower, Kathleen Anne *nurse consultant*
†Evans, John Clifford *statistician*
Geller, Esther (Bailey Geller) *artist*
Gottlieb, Michael Norman *internist, educator, health facility administrator*
Grassia, Thomas Charles *lawyer, writer*
Haden, Billy Harper *research biochemist*
Johnson, Richard Frederick *psychologist, researcher, educator*
Kennedy, Dallas Clarence, II, *physicist, educator, writer*
Lebowitz, Charlotte Meyersohn *social worker*
†Lewis, Stephanie L. *language educator*
†Mangual, Jesus A. *army officer*
Miller, George David *retired military officer, retired not-for-profit developer*
Nicholas, Peter M. *medical products executive*
O'Bannon, Jacqueline Michele *geriatrics and mental health nurse*
Perkins, Deborah Anne *interior designer*
Rendell, Kenneth William *rare and historical documents dealer, consultant*
Sahatjian, Ronald Alexander *science foundation executive*
Schott, John William *psychiatrist*
†Wedge, Michael T. *wholesale distribution executive*
Weisberg, Bruce Steven *bank executive*
†Zarkin, Herbert J. *retail company executive*

Needham
Bottiglia, William Filbert *humanities educator*
Boulding, Elise Marie *sociologist, educator*
Carr, Iris Constantine *artist, writer*
Cogswell, John Heyland *retired telecommunications executive, financial consultant*
Cohen, Lewis Cobrain *security products firm executive*
Criscenti, Joseph Thomas *retired history educator*
Davis, Sidney L. *journalist*
DerMarderosian, Diran Robert *rug cleaning company executive*
Di Domenica, Robert Anthony *musician, composer*
Donahue, Arthur Thomas *television producer*
Glaser, Daniel *sociologist, educator*
Grasso, James Anthony *public relations executive, educator*
Greenway, Hugh Davids Scott *journalist*
Holt, Stephen S. *astrophysicist*
Ingram, George *business executive*
†Kardon, Brian *music company executive*
Mills, Elizabeth Ann *retired librarian*
Rafferty, James Paul *telecommunications executive*
Rodman, Sumner *insurance company executive*
Ryan, Una Scully *health sciences professional, medical educator*
Safran, Edward Myron *financial consultant, banking executive*
Walworth, Arthur *author*
†Wang, Samuel James *information technology executive*
Weller, Thomas Huckle *physician, former educator*
Zambone, Alana Maria *special education educator, consultant*

Needham Heights
†Hubbell, John Platt *pediatrician, educator*

New Bedford
Anderson, James Linwood *pharmaceutical sales official*
Benoit, Richard Armand *retired police chief, lawyer*
Buff, Eugene *geneticist, researcher*
Bullard, John Kilburn *educational association administrator*
Cordeiro, Elizabeth Dalein *law enforcement training educator*
†Harrison, John, III, *music educator*
Kellaway, Richard Allen *minister, art association administrator, coordinator*
Murray, Robert Fox *lawyer*
Shapiro, Gilbert Lawrence *orthopedist*
Soares, Carl Lionel *quality control engineer, metrologist*
Speser, Phyllis Leah *social scientist, consultant*

New Town
Capestro, Susan *musician, educator, composer*
Carton, Lonnie Caming *educational psychologist*

Newbury
Ablow, Keith Russell *psychiatrist, journalist, author*
Hamond, Karen Marie Koch *secondary education educator*

Newburyport
†Lazarus, Penny Cyd *music educator*
Lessard, Arnold Fred *international business executive*
MacWilliams, Kenneth Edward *investment banker*

Newton
Adler, Jill S. *psychiatric social worker, psychotherapist*
Almozlino, Avraham *neurologist*
Aronow, Saul *radiological physicist, consultant*
Baron, Charles Hillel *lawyer, educator*
Bassuk, Ellen Linda *psychiatrist*
Bavicchi, John Alexander *music educator*
Benedict, Mary-Anne *nursing educator, consultant*
Blacher, Richard Stanley *psychiatrist*
Brilliant, Barbara *television host, producer, columnist, consultant, journalist, communications and media consultant, musician*
Buff, Gayle Helene *financial advisor*
Caplan, Hubert Irwin *medical educator*
Chalfen, Judith Resnick *community activist*
Chan, Jennie M. *retired music educator*
Chubb, Stephen Darrow *medical corporation executive*
Clarkson, Cheryl Lee *healthcare executive*
†Concannon, Thomas Bernard, Jr., *lawyer*
Coquillette, Daniel Robert *lawyer, educator*
Dunlap, William Crawford *physicist*
Frankenheim, Samuel *retired lawyer*
†Gerrity, J(ames) Frank, II, *building materials company executive*
Glazer, Donald Wayne *lawyer, business executive, educator*
Harrington, John Leo *former baseball company executive*
Havens, Candace Jean *planning consultant*
Heyn, Arno Harry Albert *retired chemistry educator*
Holbik, Karel *economics educator*
Huber, Richard Gregory *lawyer, educator*
Hume, Ellen Hunsberger *media analyst, journalist*
†Isaacson, Keith Bryan *gynecologist, medical researcher*
Isselbacher, Rhoda Solin *lawyer*
Jeanloz, Roger William *biochemist, educator*
Julian, Raymond Charles *financial planner, investment company executive*
Kosowsky, David I. *retired biotechnical company executive*
†Lane, Newton Alexander *retired lawyer*
†Li, Fan *pianist, music educator*
Lichtin, Norman Nahum *chemistry educator*
Lisman, Susan R. *anesthesiologist, educator*
Lueders, Carl L. *finance executive*
Marshall, Robert Lewis *musicologist, educator*
Messing, Arnold Philip *lawyer*
Metzer, Patricia Ann *lawyer*
Micklitsch, Christine Nocchi *health care administrator*
Monaco, Anthony Peter *surgery educator, medical institute administrator*
Monahan, Marie Terry *lawyer*
Nahigian, Robert John *real estate development broker*
Oles, Paul Stevenson (Steve Oles) *architect, perspectivist, educator*
Penezina, Oksana P. *biochemist*
Peterson, Osler Leopold *lawyer*
Porter, Jack Nusan *writer, sociologist, educator, political activist*
Saffran, Kalman *entrepreneur, venture capitalist*
Sasahara, Arthur Asao *cardiologist, educator, researcher*
Scheffler, Israel *philosopher, educator*
Stern, Edward Mayer *lawyer, educator*
Sullivan, Francis Alfred *priest, educator*
Svrluga, Richard Charles *entrepreneur*
Tannenwald, Leslie Keiter *rabbi, justice of peace, educational administrator, chaplain*
Teig, Marlowe Gilman *investment banker*
Temkin, Robert Harvey *accountant*
Tuscher, Vincent James *author*
Waggener, Thomas Barrow *research bioengineer*
Walker, Paul Howard *retired lawyer*
Ward, William Weaver *retired electrical engineer*

Newton Center
Adams, F. Gerard *economist, educator*
†Cousineau, Madeleine *sociologist, educator*
Mark, Melvin *consulting mechanical engineer, educator*
Parker, Jacqueline Yvonne *lawyer, educator*
Pill, Cynthia Joan *social worker*
Schuller, Gunther Alexander *composer*
Snyder, John Gorvers *lawyer*
†Soifer, Aviam *law educator, dean*

Newton Centre
Dagi, Linda Rabinowitz *pediatric ophthalmologist*
Kaneko, Sylvia Yelton *clinical social worker, educator*
Williamson, Susan *mathematician, educator*

Newton Highlands
Fanger, Mark *psychologist, psychotherapist, consultant*
Swain, Roger Bartlett *editor, writer, television host*

Newton Upper Falls
Hauser, Harry Raymond *lawyer*
Kaufmann, Andrew Stone *music journalist*
Pytka, Stephen Milton *office equipment executive*

Newtonville
Polonsky, Arthur *artist, educator*
Seller, Wendy *artist*
Zimmardi, James Anthony *musician, music educator, record producer*

Norfolk
Beard, Carol Elaine *art educator*

North Adams
†Howe, Candace Jo-Lynn *writer*
Sabot, Richard Henry *economics educator, researcher, investor, entrepreneur*
Thurston, Donald Allen *broadcasting executive*

North Andover
Bialla, Rowley *lawyer*
Coleman, Daniel Eugene *physician*
†Hull, Thomas Clinton *mathmatics educator*
Jannini, Ralph Humbert, III, *electronics executive*
Longsworth, Ellen Louise *art historian, consultant*
Martin, Curtis Harmon *political science educator*
Niccolini, Drew George *gastroenterologist*
Patel, Mahendra Rambhai *electronics executive*
Scully, Stephen J. *plastic surgeon*
†Shenai-Khatkhate, Deodatta Vinayak *chemical researcher*
Spring, Gary Stephen *civil engineer, educator, consultant*
Walters, Donald Benjamin, Jr., *civil engineer*
Wessler, Stanford *physician, educator*

North Attleboro
Russo, Steven P. *television producer, actor*
†Shareef, Nazeer Hussain *mechanical engineer*
Zani, Frederick Caesar *retired corporate consultant*

North Attleborough
Cote, Louise Roseanne *creative director, designer*

North Billerica
Carpenter, Elizabeth Jane *communications executive*
Chu, Jeffrey Chuan *business executive, consultant*
†Mellon, Timothy *transportation executive*

North Chatham
O'Brien, Robert Emmet *insurance company executive*
Wilson, E. B. *business executive, consultant, writer*

North Chelmsford
Aramini, Michael Joseph *software engineer*
Erkkila-Ricker, Barbara Howell *writer, photographer*

North Dartmouth
Barrow, Clyde Wayne *political scientist, educator*
Dowd, John Peter *physics educator*
†Hegedus, Stephen John *mathematician, educator, researcher*
†Lamoureux, Ann Margaret *music educator*
Law, Frederick Masom *engineering educator, structural engineering firm executive*
Linggood, Rita M. *radiation oncologist*
Magrass, Yale Robert *sociology educator, writer*
†Noel, Barbara Hughes McMurtry *retired music educator*
Sauro, Joseph Pio *physics educator*
Sitarz, Paula Gaj *writer*
†Twomey, John Humphrey, Jr., *language educator*
Werly, John McIntyre *historian, educator, retired*
†Xing, Liudong *researcher, educator*
Yoken, Mel B(arton) *French language educator, writer*

North Dighton
Cserr, Robert *psychiatrist, physician, hospital administrator*
Silvia, David Alan *insurance broker*

North Eastham
DeMuth, Vivienne Blake McCandless *artist, illustrator*
Hallowell, Burton Crosby *economist, educator*

North Easton
Bestgen, William Henry, Jr., *financial planner*
Bundy, Annalee Marshall *library director*
†Keogh, Martin Jay *dancer, educator*
Wolf-Devine, Celia Curtis *philosophy educator*

North Grafton
Schwartz, Anthony *veterinary surgeon, educator*
†Singh, Inderpal *research scientist, veterinarian*
Stokowski, Leonard James *artist*

North Oxford
Carney, Roger Francis Xavier *retired army officer*

North Reading
Day, Ronald Elwin *consulting executive*

North Waltham
†Liu-Constant, Brian *educational consultant, educator*

Northampton
†Bartók-Baratta, Edward *poet, artist*
Bloomberg, Sanford *psychiatrist*
Boutelle, Ann Edwards *poet, educator*
Bowman, John Stewart *writer, editor*
†Christ, Carol Tecla *academic administrator*
Derr, Thomas Sieger *religion educator*
Diehl, Timothy Jerel *social services administrator*
Donfried, Karl Paul *minister, theology educator*
Elkins, Stanley Maurice *historian, educator*
Ellis, Frank Hale *English literature educator*
Fleck, George Morrison *chemistry educator*
Garvey, Richard Conrad *journalist*
Gounaridou, Kiki *higher education educator*
Hastings, Wilmot Reed *lawyer, writer*
Horowitz, Shel *writer, marketing consultant*
Kaplan, James Lamport *writer, editor, publisher*
Kotker, Zane Hickcox *writer*
†Lavigne, Robert A. *writer*
Lehmann, Phyllis Williams *archaeologist, educator*
Levy, Ralph Jacob, Jr., *retired theater educator*
Miles, Harry Lehman *lawyer, educator*
Morgan, Emma *poet, essayist, educator*
Naegele, Philipp Otto *violinist, violist, music educator*
Payne, Marilyn Ann *physical therapist*
Piccinino, Rocco Michael *librarian*
Rayevsky, Robert *illustrator*
Rose, Peter Isaac *sociologist, writer*
Rupp, Sheron Adeline *photographer, educator*
Skarda, Patricia Lyn *English literature educator*
Smith, Malcolm Barry Estes *philosophy educator, lawyer*
†Snedeker, James Peter *music educator*
Thomas, Margot Eva *lawyer*
†Vaget, Hans Rudolf *language professional, educator*
†Vincent, Thomas Philip *lawyer*
von Klemperer, Klemens *historian, educator*
Wheelock, Donald F. *music educator, composer*
†Zimbalist, Andrew S. *economist, educator*

Northborough
Fulmer, Hugh Scott *physician, educator*
Jeas, William C. *aerospace engineering executive, consultant*

Norton
Dahl, Curtis *English literature educator*
Marshall, Dale Rogers *college president, political scientist, educator*

Norwell
Brett, Jan Churchill *illustrator, author*
Case, David Knowlton *management consultant*
Markham, Charles Rinklin *financial executive, tax accountant*
Mullare, T(homas) Kenwood, Jr., *lawyer*
Rolnik, Zachary Jacob *publishing company executive*

Norwood
Berliner, Allen Irwin *dermatologist*

Carpenter, Pamela Prisco *bank officer, foreign language educator*
De Noto, Thomas J. *chemical engineer*
Florian, Agustin Max *thoracic and cardiovascular surgeon*
Luiselli, James Kenneth *psychologist*
Pence, Robert Dudley *biomedical research administrator, hospital administrator*
†Reilley, Margaret Randall *secondary school educator*
Sheingold, Daniel H. *electrical engineer*

Oak Bluffs
†Lamb, Robert *industrial executive*
Rose, Kathleen Nolan *health facility administrator*

Oakham
Poirier, Helen Virginia Leonard *elementary education educator*

Onset
Barrs, James Thomas *linguistics educator*

Orleans
Avery, William Hinckley *physicist, chemist*
Baird, Julian Thompson, Jr., *art dealer*
Bast, James Louis *retired trade association executive*
Marquand, Jean MacMurtry *educational administrator*
Putnam, Allan Ray *association executive*
Rappaport, Margaret M.W.E. *psychologist, physician, author, pilot, consultant*
York, Elizabeth Jane *innkeeper*

Osterville
El-Fayoumy, J. P. Quinn *writer, poet, teacher*
McCarthy, Albert Henry *executive recruiter, consultant*
Schwarztrauber, Sayre Archie *former naval officer, maritime consultant*
Silk, Alvin John *business educator, management consultant*
Weber, Adelheid Lisa *former nurse, chemist*
Williams, Ann Meagher *retired hospital administrator*

Oxford
Holbrook, Jay Mack *publishing company executive*
Moshegov, Nikolay *engineer*
Schur, Walter Robert *physician*

Palmer
Dupuis, Robert Simeon *sales executive*

Peabody
Arons, Irving J. *technology consultant, writer*
Baures, Mary Margaret *clinical psychotherapist, author*
Bierman, George William *technical consulting executive, food technologist*
Finch, Rogers Burton *association management consultant*
Goldberg, Harold Seymour *electrical engineer, educator*
†Gordon, Bernard M. *computer company executive*
Lipman, Richard Paul *pediatrician*
Marshall, Laurence Paul *social services administrator*
Peters, Leo Francis *environmental engineer*
Rodman, Elise *physician*
Simmons, Jon L. *music educator*

Pembroke
Egan, Denise *home health nurse*

Petersham
Chivian, Eric Seth *psychiatrist, environmental scientist, educator*

Pittsfield
Bahlman, Dudley Rhodes *journalist*
Doyle, Anthony Peter *lawyer*
Fanelli, Robert D. *surgeon*
Feigenbaum, Armand Vallin *systems engineer, systems equipment executive*
†Glazer, Michael L. *consumer products company executive*
Keator, David P. G. *stockbroker, financial consultant*
Malkani, Prakash *medical educator, neuroradiologist*
Rabinowitz, Wendy *artist, art therapist*
Rich, Philip Dewey *publishing executive*
Shammas, Nazih Kheirallah *environmental engineering educator, consultant*
Wenner, Gene Charles *arts management executive*
Wheelock, Kenneth Steven *chemist*

Plainfield
Nash, June Caprice *anthropology educator*
Reynolds, Frank Everett *religious studies educator*

Plymouth
Gregory, Dick *comedian, civil rights activist*
Joseph, Rodney Randy *artist, arts society executive*
Paul, Carol Ann *retired academic administrator, biology educator*
Pieters, Richard Sawyer, Jr., *radiation oncologist, educator*
Wiederhold, Pieter Rijk *instrument company executive*

Plympton
O'Connell, Philip Edward *retired retail business owner*
Smith, Robert Rutherford *university dean, communication educator*

Pocasset
Terkelsen, Kenneth G. *psychiatrist, hospital administrator*

†Wynn, Thomas Joseph *lawyer*

Prides Crossing
†Fish, Richard VanCortlandt, Jr., *music educator*

Provincetown
Black, Constance Jane *artist*
Dickson, Vivian Franco *biomedical research consultant*
Hutchinson, Peter Arthur *artist*
Oliver, Mary *poet*
Wolfman, Brunetta Reid *education educator*

Quincy
Adams, Ronald G. *middle school educator*
Baker, Charles D. *health insurance company executive*
Britt, Margaret Mary *finance educator*
†Bunting, Carolyn Anne *writer*
Chung, Cynthia Norton *communications specialist*
Colgan, Sumner *manufacturing engineer, chemical engineer*
Hall, John Raymond, Jr., *fire protection executive*
Hayes, Mary Dianne Wixted *lawyer*
†Holway, David *association administrator*
Kelley, James Francis *civil engineer*
Levin, Robert Joseph *retail grocery chain store executive*
Lippincott, Joseph P. *photojournalist, educator*
Luo, Hong Yuan *biomedical scientist, educator*
McClung, J(ames) David *corporate executive, lawyer, academic administrator*
Moran, James Joseph, Jr., *insurance executive*
Motejunas, Gerald William *lawyer*
Roma, John Richard *civil engineer, executive*
Short, Janet Marie *principal*
Somers, Susan Eileen *business educator*
Spangler, Arthur Stephenson, Jr., *psychologist*
Wilson, Blenda Jacqueline *foundation administrator*
Wise, Carol Lewis *occupational therapist*
Young, Richard William *corporate director*
Yung, Babington Chun-kuen *radiologist*

Randolph
Cammarata, Richard John *financial advisor*
†Huntington, Robert Howard *business management executive*
Johnson, Laurence Michael *lawyer*
Manos, Sarantos John *physics educator*
Michaud, Charles A. *library director, writer*
Morrissey, Edmond Joseph *classical philologist*
Whitaker, Arthur Luther *retired minister, psychologist*

Raynham
Kaplan, Kenneth Barry *psychologist*

Reading
Burbank, Nelson Stone *investment banker*
†Frey, Joanne Alice Tupper *art educator*
†Hambartsoumian, Eduard *obstetrician, researcher, embryologist*
Melconian, Jerry Ohanes *engineering executive*
†Nordstrand, Nathalie Elizabeth Johnson *artist*
Terilli, Joseph Anthony *secondary education educator*

Rehoboth
Rose, Daniel Asa *writer, editor*

Revere
Ferrante, Olivia Ann *retired educator, consultant*
Paananen, Victor Niles *English educator*
Recupero-Faiella, Anna Antonietta *poet*

Rockland
Blethen, Sandra Lee *pediatric endocrinologist*
†LaFerney, Michael C. *mental health nurse, counselor*

Rockport
Bakrow, William John *college president emeritus*
Gavelis, Jonas Rimvydas *dentist, educator*
Harries, James Theodore *psychologist*
Johnson, Janet Lou *real estate company executive, writer*
Reardon, Bea *social worker*
Salinger, Warren *writer*
Walen, Harry Leonard *historian, lecturer, author*
Wiberg, Lars Erik *occupational compatibility consultant*

Roslindale
Driscoll, Kathleen J. *writer*

Roxbury
Benzan, John Patrick *lawyer*
Berman, Marlene Oscar *neuropsychologist, educator*
†Hamilton, James Arthur *biomedical researcher, biophysics educator*
Peters, Alan *anatomy educator*
Resnick, Oscar *neuroscientist*
Simons, Elizabeth R(eiman) *biochemist, educator*

Salem
Brown, Walter Redvers John *physicist*
†Carroll, Gregory Joseph *education educator*
Goss, Laurence Edward, Jr., *geographer, educator*
Griffin, Thomas McLean *retired lawyer*
Haskell, James Thompson *cultural organization administrator*
Higgins, Gina O'Connell *psychologist, writer*
Hudson, Christopher Giles *social worker, educator*
†Levy, Richard J. *political scientist, educator*
Marks, Scott Charles *lawyer*
McLaughlin, Michael Angelo *mortgage consultant, author*
Melby, John B. *composer, educator*
Moran, Philip David *lawyer*
Must, Dennis Patrick *writer, editor*
Prokopy, John Alfred *government consultant*

Reich, Michael Ira *obstetrician/gynecologist*
†Shachok, Mary Ellen *lawyer*
Wasserman, Stephen Alan *lawyer*
†Witt, Carol A. *lawyer*

Salisbury
Berggren, Dick *editor*
Camacho, Henry Francis *accountant*

Sandwich
Porter, John Stephen *retired television executive*

Saugus
Austill, Allen *dean emeritus*
Maillet, Martin Joseph, Sr., *retired police captain*

Scituate
†Ekstrom, John Edward *mathematician, educator*
Keating, Margaret Mary *entrepreneur, business consultant*
Peters, John Adam *retired pathologist*
Spangler, Stanley Eugene *international relations educator*

Seekonk
Backes, Joan *artist, educator*

Sharon
Kahn, Marilyn Zeldin *artist, art educator*
Reilley, Dennen *research agency administrator, educator*
Roberson, Kip Michael *library director, librarian*
Zhang, Ying Hua *research scientist*

Sheffield
Baritz, Loren *history educator*
Russell, Hilary Francis *secondary education educator*
Schmehl Morley, Susan Linda *fine arts educator, artist*
Velmans, Loet Abraham *retired public relations executive*
Young, Susan Babson *retired library director*

Shelburne Falls
Bagg, Robert Ely *poet, educator, translator*
Collard, Roberta R. *emeritus educator, researcher*

Sherborn
Anderson, James Everett *economics educator*
Cushing, Steven *linguist, educator, writer, researcher, consultant*
Hancock, William Frank, Jr., *management consultant*
Kennedy, Chester Ralph, Jr., *former state official, art director*
Pickhardt, Carl Emile, Jr., *artist*

Shrewsbury
†Baguisi, Alexander *embryologist*
Chang, Isabelle C. *librarian, educator, writer*
†Charney, Evan *pediatrician, educator*
De Rosa, Eolo *otolaryngologist*
Falter, Robert Gary *nursing home administrator, educator*
†Fondurulia, Julie A. *computer scientist*
Garabedian, Charles, Jr., *mathematician, educator*
†Kapelner, David Israel *lawyer, educator*
†Lucas, Sandra J. *psychologist*
Magee, Bernard Dale *obstetrician, gynecologist*
†McCluskey, James Francis *music educator*
Nixon, Eugene Ray *chemist, educator*
Onorato, Nicholas Louis *retired program director, economist*

Shutesbury
Creed, Robert Payson, Sr., *retired literature educator*

Siasconset
†Albani, Thomas J. *investor*
Emerson, Alice Frey *political scientist, educator emerita*

Silver Spring
†Kaplan, Arkady *optical engineer, researcher*

Somerset
†Bower, John *retired fluid mechanics engineer, commissioner*
Fletcher, Dorothy *community health and primary home care nurse*
†Girard, Jonathan Richard *conductor*
†Manchester, Steven Herbert *writer, educator*
Schaefer, Ira Marc *music educator, musician*

Somerville
Allen, Carole Newman *pediatrician*
Auspitz, Josiah Lee *writer, consultant*
†Bykanov, Alexander N. *research scientist*
†Franklin, David *small business owner, researcher*
†Fujiwara, Chris *writer*
Halevi, Marcus *photographer*
Leverich, Kathleen *writer*
Meagher, Robert Francis *international economic law consultant*
Neville, Emily Tam Lin *writer, educator*
Yu, Shan *artist*

South Boston
Adams, Rita Fuerst *management and fundraising consultant*
Clancy, Richard Francis *priest*
Nalbandian, E. Carolyn *social worker*

South Dartmouth
Greene, William Caswell *investment company executive*
LaPorte, Adrienne Aroxie *nursing administrator*
†Lincoln, Rosamond Hadley *modern painter, photographer*
Mellberg, Leonard Evert *physicist*
Ward, Richard Joseph *university dean, educator, author*

South Deerfield
Waluk, Stanley Peter *corporate engineering official*

South Dennis
Stiefvater, Pamela Jean *chiropractor*

South Egremont
†Parker, June *artist, educator*

South Hadley
Berek, Peter *English educator*
Bledzki, Leszek Andrzej *limnologist, researcher*
Burns, Michael Thornton *historian, educator, farmer*
Campbell, Mary Kathryn *chemistry educator*
Colino, Richard Ralph *communications consultant*
Creighton, Joanne Vanish *academic administrator*
Farnham, Anthony Edward *English language educator*
Johnson, Richard August *English language educator*
Kaltenbach, Jane Couffer *zoology educator*
Leal, Joseph Rogers *chemist*
Mazzocco, Angelo *language educator, cultural historian, linguist*
Shaw, Robert Burns *poet, educator*
†Townsley, Eleanor Rose *sociologist, educator*
Viereck, Peter *poet, historian, educator*
†Wartenberg, Thomas Eliot *social sciences educator, writer*

South Hamilton
Campbell, Diana Butt *lawyer*
†Ciampa, Roy Emilius *religious studies educator*
Kroeger, Catherine C. *writer, editor, educator*

South Harwich
Finn, Nita Ann *social worker*
Rigg, Charles Andrew *pediatrician*

South Natick
Cantor, Pamela Corliss *psychologist*

South Orleans
Goldman, Elliott Stanley *writer*
†Wherry, Edward John, Jr., *lawyer*

South Wellfleet
Bargellini, Pier Luigi *electrical engineer*
Blau, Monte *retired radiology educator*

South Weymouth
Edwards, Eleanor Mattiasich *singer, voice educator*
Young, Michael Chung-En *allergist, immunologist, pediatrician*

South Yarmouth
Towns, Donald Lionel *engineering executive*

Southampton
Slater, Jess Everett *artist*

Southborough
Dews, P(eter) B(ooth) *medical scientist, educator*
Madras, Bertha Kalifon *neuroscientist, educator, consultant*

Southbridge
Anderson, Ross Barrett *healthcare environmental services manager*
Mangion, Richard Michael *health care executive*
Rutanen, Roy Stewart *producer, television personality*

Southfield
†Mathews, Rita White *retired research scientist, educator*
Melvin, Ronald McKnight *retired museum director*

Spencer
Goldman, Ethan Harris *finance executive*

Springfield
Agonafer, Mulugeta Gabriel *political scientist, educator*
Albano, Michael J. *mayor*
Bock, Robert Leroy *law educator*
†Bonemery, Anne M. *language educator*
Burke, Michael Henry *lawyer*
Burkman, Ronald Thomas, Jr., *physician administrator, medical educator*
†Burstein, Merwyn Jerome *lawyer*
Caprio, Anthony S. *academic administrator*
Carvalho, Joseph, III, *museum and library executive*
Cleland, Thomas Edward, Jr., *secondary school educator*
Coe, Nicholas P.W. *surgeon*
†Cook, Kathryn Anne *secondary school educator*
Courniotes, Harry James *academic administrator*
Crampton, Rebekah Jean *judge, educator*
†D'Amour, Donald H. *supermarket chain executive*
Dibble, Francis Daniel, Jr., *lawyer*
Engebretson, Douglas Kenneth *architect, interior designer*
Ervin, Billy Maxwell *management consultant*
†Evans, Elizabeth E. *physical therapist, educator*
Faerber, Kent William *foundation administrator, consultant*
Farkas, Paul Stephen *gastroenterologist*
†Fein, Sherman Edward *lawyer, psychologist*
Fialky, Gary Lewis *lawyer*
Frankel, Kenneth Mark *thoracic surgeon*
Freedman, Frank Harlan *federal judge*
Frey, Mary Elizabeth *artist*
Friedmann, Paul *surgeon, educator*
Gallup, John Gardiner *retired paper company executive*
Gelinas, Robert Albert *lawyer*
†Geryk, Laura A. *language educator*

Goldstein, Anne Brenda *law educator*
Gonzalez De Leon, Fernando *historian, educator*
Gross, Donalyn Ann *counselor*
Habermehl, Lawrence LeRoy *philosophy educator*
Johnson, Robert Allison *life insurance company executive*
Kirkwood, John Robert *neuroradiologist*
Kottamasu, Mohan Rao (K.V.R. Mohan Rao) *physician*
Liptzin, Benjamin *psychiatrist*
Lynn, Morton Daniel *orthopedist*
Maidman, Stephen Paul *lawyer*
†Mariani, Marita C. *secondary school educator*
McCarthy, Charles Francis, Jr., *lawyer*
McGee, William Tobin *intensive care physician*
†Miles, Judith Ellen *lawyer, educator*
Miller, J(ohn) Wesley, III, *lawyer*
Miller, Leroy Paul, Jr., *secondary English educator*
Mish, Frederick Crittenden *editor*
Muhlberger, Richard Charles *former museum administrator, writer, educator*
Napolitan, Joseph *political consultant*
Neiman, Kenneth Paul *judge*
Nicolai, Paul Peter *lawyer*
O'Connell, Robert John *diversified financial services company executive*
Oldershaw, Louis Frederick *lawyer*
Parthasarathy, Gautham *chemical engineer, researcher*
Petrone, William Francis *physician, microbiologist, corporate executive*
Ponsor, Michael Adrian *federal judge*
Porter, Burton Frederick *philosophy educator, writer, dean*
Saia, Diane Plevock DiPiero *nutritionist, educator, legal association administrator*
Santopietro, Albert Robert *lawyer*
†Schmutte, Gregory Thomas *dean, consultant*
†Sheils, James Bernard *lawyer*
†Sloan, David James *sonographer*
Smist, Julianne Marie *chemist, educator*
Stack, May Elizabeth *library director*
Starr, David *newspaper editor, publisher*
Steingrub, Jay Stanley *critical care physician, educator*
†Stevens, Joyce Ann *writer, publisher, educator*
Susse, Sandra Slone *lawyer*
Utley, F. Knowlton *library director, educator*
†Vincensi, Avis A. *sales executive, medical educator*
Weiss, Ronald Phillip *lawyer*
†Zenor, Jean Ellen *language educator*

Sterling
Garafalo, Lynne Mary *audiologist, speech and language pathologist*

Stockbridge
Fitzpatrick, Jane *entrepreneur*
MacDonald, Sharon Ethel *dancer, choreographer, administrator*
Shapiro, Edward Robert *psychiatrist, administrator educator psychoanalyst*
Silverstein, Joseph Harry *conductor, musician*

Stoneham
Eaton, Amos Jorge *management consultant*
Igou, Raymond Alvin, Jr., *orthopedic surgeon*
Mc Donald, Andrew Jewett *securities firm executive*

Stoughton
Adamson, Stephen Charles *retired sales professional*
Gabovitch, Steven Alan *lawyer, accountant*
George, Arthur Charles *lawyer*
Hall, Roger Lee *musicologist, educator, composer*
Schepps, Victoria Hayward *lawyer*

Stow
Clayton, John *retired engineering executive and consultant*
Langenwalter, Gary Allan *manufacturing and management consulting company executive*
Shrader, William Whitney *radar consulting scientist*

Sturbridge
Belforte, David Arthur *business executive*

Sudbury
Aronson, David *artist, retired art educator*
Buono, Anthony Francis *business educator*
†Cheema, Zafarullah K. *management consultant*
Deutsch, Judith *clergywoman*
Fowler, Charles Albert *electronics engineer*
Henderson, Ernest, III, *health care executive*
Hillery, Mary Jane Larato *columnist, producer, television host, reserve army officer*
Kamen, Robert Irwin *research company executive*
McCree, Paul William, Jr., *systems design and engineering company executive*
Meltzer, Donald Richard *treasurer*
Nyman, Georgianna Beatrice *painter*
Richards, James Carlton *microbiologist, business executive*
†Thompson, Mary Lou *elementary school educator*
Woldman, Evelyn Jandorf *computer information specialist, educator*

Sunderland
Kamys, Walter *artist, educator*

Swampscott
Brenner, Lawrence *medical librarian, consultant*
Kaufman, William Morris *engineer consultant*
Smith, Carl Dean, Jr., *marriage and family therapist*

Swansea
Caswell, Sally Ellen *artist, art educator*

Hjerpe, Edward Alfred, III, *finance and banking executive*
Holmes, Henry *literary agent, book publicist, writer and editor*
†Ireland, Linda Ann *internist*

Taunton
Anderson, Peter D. *pharmacist, forensic scientist*
Bornstein, Myer Sidney *obstetrician, gynecologist*
Lopes, Maria Fernandina *commissioner*
McMullen, John Henry, Jr., *manufacturing company executive, educator*
Ricciardi, Louis Michael *brokerage house executive*
Schwartz, Alan Marshall *radiologist*

Tewksbury
Black, Richard Bruce *business executive, consultant*
DeAngelis, Michele F. *school system administrator*
†DeMoulas, Telemachus A. *retail grocery company executive*
Herlihy-Chevalier, Barbara Doyle *mental health nurse*
†Smith, Daniel L. *electronics executive*

Tiverton
†Brock, Dawn Marie *counselor*

Townsend
Smith, Denise Groleau *data processing professional*
Thorpe, Samuel Stanley, Jr., *artist*

Truro
Fader, Daniel Nelson *English language educator*
Friedman, Edward David *lawyer, arbitrator*
Kelley, Maryellen R. *economist, management consultant*
Woolley, Catherine (Jane Thayer) *writer*

Turners Falls
†Finley-Morin, Kimberley K. *educator*

Tyngsboro
Dascomb, Audrey Lynn *dance educator*
Lee, Joan Roberta *elementary education educator*

Vineyard Haven
Hoffman, Michael Linsay *economist*
Jacobs, Gretchen Huntley *psychiatrist*
Knowles, Christopher Allan *healthcare executive*

Waban
Christian, John Thomas *civil engineer*
Rogoff, Jerome Howard *psychiatrist, psychoanalyst, forensic expert*
Rossolimo, Alexander Nicholas *management consultant, business executive, corporate director*
Tofias, Allan *accountant*

Wakefield
†Brady, Patrick *advertising executive*
†Coffman, Dallas Whitney *financial consultant*
†Courtenay, Lisa A. *paralegal, foundation administrator*
†Crate, Darrell *political organization administrator*
Fioravanti, Jeff *artist*
Inman, Jean A. *political party official*
Kelley, John Henry *electronics company executive*
Lucas, Robert Frank *lawyer*
Menard, Joan M. *state legislator*
†Prabhala, Rao H. *pharmaceutical executive*

Walpole
Allman, Mark C. *engineer, physicist*
Coleman, John Joseph *telephone company executive*
Cotter, Douglas Adrian *healthcare executive*

Waltham
Ackerman, Robert Wallace *venture management company executive*
Adamian, Gregory Harry *academic administrator*
Arena, Albert A. *museum director*
Arrom, Silvia Marina *history educator*
Barnes-Brown, Peter Newton *lawyer*
†Bernstein, Melvin *provost*
Bernstein, Stanley Joseph *manufacturing executive*
†Bleicher, Paul Alan *health facility administrator*
Boykan, Martin *composer, music educator*
Brown, Edgar Henry, Jr., *mathematician, educator*
Buchholz, William James *communications executive, educator*
Cecchetti, Stephen Giovanni *economics educator*
†Chasalow, Eric David *composer, educator*
Colcord, Herbert Nathaniel, III, (Skip Colcord) *corporate communications executive*
Cox, Howard Ellis, Jr., *venture capitalist*
†Davis, Robert J. *internet company executive*
†Dekkers, Marijn *electronics executive*
Delaney, Mary Anne *retired theology studies educator*
De Rosier, David John *biophysicist, educator*
Deser, Stanley *physicist, educator*
†Dickie, Robert Benjamin *lawyer, consultant, educator*
Domar, Alice Diane *psychologist, educator*
Ederle, Douglas Richard *investment adviser*
Elfers, William *retired investment company director*
Epstein, Irving Robert *chemistry educator*
Fiore, Nicholas Francis *special components and materials company executive*
Fleming, Samuel Crozier, Jr., *healthcare executive*
Flesch, William B. *English educator*
Floyd, John Taylor *electronics executive*
Flynn, Patricia Marie *economics educator*

Foxman, Bruce Mayer *chemist, educator*
Galinat, Walton Clarence *research scientist*
Goodheart, Eugene *English language educator*
Gray-Nix, Elizabeth Whitwell *occupational therapist*
Gumpertz, Werner Herbert *structural engineering company executive*
Hahn, Bessie King *library administrator, lecturer*
Hale, Jane Alison *French and comparative literature educator*
†Harianawala, Abizer I. *pharmacologist, researcher*
Hoffman, W. Michael *philosophy educator, administrator*
Jackendoff, Ray Saul *linguistics educator*
Jones, Clark Powell, Jr., *financial services executive*
Kasputys, Joseph Edward *corporate executive, economist*
†Katchen, Aaron L *historian*
Lackner, James Robert *aerospace medicine educator*
Leach, Robert Ellis *physician, educator*
Lees, Marjorie Berman *biochemist, neuroscientist*
Liljestrand, James Stratton *physician administrator, internist*
†Liu, Huamin Patrick *communications engineer, researcher*
Mangano, Salvatore Nicholas *surgeon*
McClary, Loretta Mary *accountant*
McCulloch, Rachel *economics researcher, educator*
Mc Menimen, Kathleen Brennan *secondary education educator*
Mohanroy, Pradeep *physician*
†Morgan, Claudia Ann *social scientist*
Nelson, Arthur Hunt *real estate management development company executive*
Notkin, Leonard Sheldon *architect*
O'Connell, Jeanne *financial planner, insurance broker*
O'Donnell, Teresa Hohol *application developer, electrical engineer*
O'Hagen, Nicole McCauley *marketing professional*
Padmanabhan, Cape S. *geriatrician*
Petsko, Gregory Anthony *chemistry and biochemistry scientist educator*
†Pocock, J. Michael *consumer products company executive*
†Putney, Clifford Wallace *historian, educator*
Reinharz, Jehuda *academic administrator, history educator*
Reis, Arthur Henry, Jr., *university administrator*
Reisman, Bernard *theology educator*
†Saler, Benson *retired anthropologist*
Sarna, Jonathan Daniel *history educator*
Schwartz, Joseph Hersh *surgeon, educator*
Schwartz, Steven Mark *marketing executive*
†Schwarz, Gerald Walter *adult education educator*
Sekuler, Robert William *psychologist, educator*
†Shepard, Donald Sloane *public policy research educator*
Shonkoff, Jack P. *dean, educator*
†Slifka, Alfred A. *oil corporation executive*
Smith, Allen Leonard *physician*
Spoon, Alan Gary *venture capital company executive*
Staves, Susan *English educator*
Syron, Richard Francis *financial executive, economist*
Thamhain, Hans Jurgen *information technology manager, researcher*
Thomas, Janet Marie *economics educator*
Unger, Rhoda Kesler *psychology educator*
Workman, Jerome James, Jr., *chemist*
Wyner, Yehudi *composer, pianist, conductor, educator*

Ware
Zwemke, Katharine Priscilla *dietitian, diabetes educator*

Wareham
Gustafson, Deborah Lee *educational administrator, educator*

Washington
Sacco, Rudolph Augustine *retired judge*

Watertown
Amsler, Karen Marie *medical technologist, scientist*
Berk, Harold *dentist, consultant, educator*
†Boland, Elizabeth *social services company financial executive*
Cooper, Marc Lawrence *food products company executive*
Dawson, Stuart Owen *landscape architect, urban designer*
Fairbanks, Jonathan Leo *museum curator*
†Fein, Michael R. *historian, educator*
Goldstein, Arthur Louis *water purification company executive*
Kaloosdian, Robert Aram *lawyer*
†Karaian, Norma Maksoodian *lawyer*
Kupferman, David Cobb *painter*
Langstaff, John Meredith *musician*
Lin, Juchui Ray (Ju-Chui Lin) *polymer scientist*
Linden, Lynette Lois *bioelectrical engineer*
Mason, Linda Anne *daycare administrator*
†Pirolli, John Paul *poet, writer, construction executive*
Regan, Thomas Joseph *priest, educator*
Rivers, Wilga Marie *foreign language educator*
†Stoddard, Anne Maher *biostatistician, researcher, educator*
True, Edward Keene *architectural engineer*

Wayland
†Anderson, Monica Luffman *school librarian, educator, real estate broker*
Blair, John *consultant*
Brynjolfsson, Ari *nuclear physicist*
Budner, Ruth Stern *social worker*

Caristo-Verrill, Janet Rose *international management consultant*
Chodosh, Sanford *pulmonologist*
Clark, Melville, Jr., *physicist, electrical engineer*
Dergalis, George *artist, educator*
Gleason III, Charles Richard *dental industry executive, business management consultant*
Harrington, Kay Lorraine *executive secretary*
Huff, William Braid *retired publishing company executive*
Humphrey, Diana Young *fund raiser*
Huygens, Remmert William *architect*
Norris, Melvin *lawyer*
Stanvick, David J. *information scientist*
Wald, Fritz Veit *solar energy corporation executive*

Wellesley
Anderson, David Langley *management consultant*
Arnold, Peter Gordon *communications consultant*
Auerbach, Jerold S. *university educator*
Baum, Laura *educator*
Bauman, Margaret Estelle Lang *pediatric neurologist*
Birnbaum, Nathan Simcha *dentist*
Bishop, Robert Lyle *economist, educator*
Caso, Adolph *publishing company executive*
Celli, Bartolome Romulo *internist*
Charpie, Robert Alan *physicist, researcher*
Copplestone, David Wesley *artist, business owner*
Costley, Bill (Bill Costley) *poet, writer*
Coyne, Mary Downey *biologist, endocrinologist, educator*
Crane, Bonnie Loyd *art gallery owner, director, author*
Eilts, Hermann Frederick *international relations educator, former diplomat*
Flynn, Megan Alice *librarian*
Fontaine, Eudore Joseph, Jr., *artist, art historian*
Gailius, Gilbert Keistutis *manufacturing company executive*
Giddon, Donald B(ernard) *psychologist, educator*
Giroux, Eugene Xavier *lawyer*
Goglia, Charles A., Jr., *lawyer*
†Heartt, Charlotte Beebe *university official*
Henderson, Mary Louise *civic worker*
†Hobbs, Edward Craig *religious studies educator*
Jacobs, Ruth Harriet *poet, playwright, sociologist, gerontologist*
Krieg, Arthur M. *pharmaceutical company executive, internist*
Landaw, Stephen Arthur *physician, educator*
Lefkowitz, Mary Rosenthal *Greek literature educator*
†Lloyd-Jones, Sir (Peter) Hugh (Jefferd) *Greek scholar*
Mailer-Howat, Patrick Lindsay Macalpine *investment banker*
Martin, Tony *humanities educator*
Marx, Peter A. *lawyer*
Merguerian, Arshag *architect*
Miller, Linda B. *political scientist*
†Mistacco, Vicki E. *foreign language educator*
Mitchell, Donald Wayne *management consultant, investment manager, lawyer, writer*
Montague, Joel Gedney *public health officer*
Morant, Ricardo Bernardino *psychology educator*
Murray, Joseph Edward *retired plastic surgeon*
Myers, Arthur B. *journalist, author*
Paarlberg, Robert L. *political science educator*
Palmerio, Elvira Castano *art gallery director, art historian*
Pierce, Donald Shelton *retired orthopedic surgeon, educator*
Ragone, David Vincent *former university president*
Rollins, Judith Ann *sociologist, educator, researcher, writer*
Sexton, John Joseph *oral and maxillofacial surgeon, educator*
Silberman, Robert A. S. *lawyer*
Small, Parker Adams, III, *investment banker*
Stettner, Edward A. *political science educator*
Tagge, Anne *writer, not-for-profit organization administrator*
Tierney, Thomas J. *business management consultant*
Trubow, Marshall David *obstetrician-gynecologist*
Tucker, John Avery *retired academic administrator, electrical engineer*
Twitchell, Thomas Evans *neurologist, educator*
Walsh, Diana Chapman *academic administrator, sociologist, educator*
Weil, Thomas Alexander *electronics engineer, retired*
†Yun, Elise Hae-Ryung *music educator*

Wellesley Hills
†Coco, Samuel Barbin *venture consultant*
†Kurzweil, Raymond C. *computer scientist, entrepreneur*
Marcus, William Michael *rubber and vinyl products manufacturing company executive*
McAlpine, Frederick Sennett *anesthesiologist*
Nicodemus, Christopher Farley *biotechnology educator, physician, researcher*

Wellesloy
Maxwell, J. B. *financial consultant, marketing professional, consultant*

Wellfleet
Coughlin, Joan Hopkins *artist, educator*
Limpitlaw, John Donald *retired publishing executive, clergyman*
Mc Feely, William Shield *historian, writer*
Piercy, Marge *poet, novelist, essayist*

Wenham
†Beauregard, John *school librarian, consultant*
Herrmann, Robert Lawrence *biochemist, educator*

West Barnstable
†Tollefsen, Astrid *not-for-profit fundraiser*

West Boylston
†Benestad, Kelly Ann *secondary school educator*

West Bridgewater
Wyner, Justin L. *laminating company executive*

West Brookfield
Higgins, Brian Alton *art gallery owner, pastel artist*

West Chatham
Rhinesmith, Stephen Headley *management consultant*
Rowley, Glenn Harry *lawyer*

West Falmouth
Bass, Norman Herbert *physician, scientist, university and hospital administrator, health care executive*
Carlson, David Bret *lawyer*
Holz, George G., IV, *medical educator, research scientist*
King, Richard Hood *newspaper executive*
Vaccaro, Ralph Francis *marine biologist*

West Hyannisport
Devine, Nancy *postmaster*
Gingold, George Norman *insurance company executive, lawyer*

West Newbury
Dooley, Ann Elizabeth *freelance writers cooperative executive, editor*
Taylor, Bruce Stevenson *architect, planner*

West Newton
†Angiolillo, Paul F. *retired language educator*
Cox, Donald C. *economics educator*
†Logan, Georgiana Marie *psychotherapist*
Stahl, Marilyn Brown *interior designer*

West Roxbury
Aguilera, Elsa Judith *physiatrist*
Cohen, Carolyn Alta *health educator*
Ellenbogen, George *poet, educator*
McCully, Kilmer Serjus *pathologist*
Rogers, Brenda Ann *community health clinical specialist*
Seltzer, Richard Warren, Jr., *writer, editor, consultant*
†Thatte, Hemant Sadashiv *surgeon, researcher*

West Springfield
Ballard, Mildred Louise *retired adult nurse practitioner*
Desai, Veena Balvantrai *obstetrician and gynecologist, educator*
Ely, John P. *lawyer*
Morris, Michael G. *utilities executive*

West Yarmouth
Crist, Bainbridge *volunteer*

Westborough
Antalek, Eileen Elizabeth *educational consultant*
Appelbaum, Kenneth Lloyd *psychiatrist*
Bok, Joan Toland *utility executive*
Burdick, George Harold *investment company executive*
Gionfriddo, Maurice Paul *aeronautical engineer, research and development manager*
Gordon, Betty L. *health services administrator*
Higano, Norio *retired internist*
Horwitz, Eleanor Catherine *information and education official*
Lampi, Rauno Andrew *food and science engineer*
Mehta, Jatin Vinodrai *biomedical engineer*
Nichols, Guy Warren *retired institute executive, utilities executive*
Schrager, Mindy Rae *software company professional*
Staffier, Pamela Moorman *psychologist*
Tobias, Lester Lee *psychological consultant*
Trubko, Sergey Vladimir *optical designer, scientist*

Westfield
Buckmore, Alvah Clarence, Jr., *computer scientist, ballistician*
Dunphy, Maureen Milbier *educator*
Gardner, Thomas Neville *communications educator*

Westford
Endyke, Debra Joan *data communications marketing professional*
†Fennelly, Paul F. *chemist*
†Geary, Marie Josephine *art association administrator*
Haramundanis, Katherine Leonora *information scientist, writer, astronomer*
Salah, Joseph Elias *research scientist, educator*
Selesky, Donald Bryant *software developer*
Weston, Joan Spencer *editorial and production director, communications executive*
Wing, Carol *marketing professional, writer*

Weston
Alcock, George Lewis, Jr., (Peter Alcock) *investor, business strategist*
Barry, William Anthony *priest, writer*
†Bateman, Thomas Robert *lawyer*
Berwick, Robert Cregar *computer science educator*
Daly, Charles Ulick *foundation executive*
Draskoczy, Paul R. *psychiatrist*
Fine, Sally Solfisburg *artist, educator*
Fleming, Nancy McAdam *landscape designer*
†Freeman, Florence Eleanor *lawyer*
Higgins, Sister Therese *English educator, former college president*
Katz, William Emanuel *chemical engineer*
Kendall, Julius *consulting engineer*
Kim, Young Ho *orthodontist*
Kraft, Gerald *economist*
Lashman, L. Edward *arbitrator, mediator, consultant*
Lin, Alice Lee Lan *physicist, researcher, educator*
Marshall, Jean McElroy *physiologist*
†Oates, Mary Josephine *historian, educator*
Oelgeschlager, Guenther Karl *publisher*
Sanzone, Donna S. *publishing executive*
Schloemann, Ernst Fritz (Rudolf August) *physicist, engineer*
Schwartz, Edward Lester *retired lawyer*
Stambaugh, Armstrong A., Jr., *restaurant and hotel executive*
Tenney, Sarah G. *music educator*
Thomas, Roger Meriwether *lawyer*
Valente, Louis Patrick (Dan Valente) *business and financial executive*
Vetterling, Mary-Anne *Spanish language and literature educator*
Wang, Chia Ping *physicist, educator*
Wells, Lionelle Dudley *psychiatrist, educator*
Wood, Jeremy Scott *architect, urban designer*

Westport
Gormley, Robert John *publishing executive*
Nichols, C. Walter, III, *retired trust company executive*
Norcross, Alvin Watt *retired personnel administrator, consultant*

Westport Point
Bennett, Bruce Anthony *civil engineer*
Fanning, William Henry, Jr., *computer specialist*

Westwood
Bier, Louis Henry Gustav *minister*
Borgman, George Allan *journalist*
Daley, Charles Mike *consumer products company executive*
Donahue, Charles Lee, Jr., *health network executive*
Foster, Arthur Rowe *mechanical engineering educator*
Gillette, Hyde *retired investment banker*
Kushner, Jeffrey L. *manufacturing company executive*
Old, Bruce Scott *chemical and metallurgical engineer*
Plimpton, Calvin Hastings *physician, university president*
Provost, Lura Swift *civic volunteer*
Riley, Henry Charles *banker*
Smith, Denis Joseph *mathematics educator*

Whitinsville
†O'Connell, Roberta M. *realtor*

Whitman
Anderson, Beth Ellen *English literature and composition educator*

Wilbraham
Dailey, Franklyn Edward, Jr., *electronic image technology company executive, analyst, consultant*
Woloshchuk, Candace Dixon *secondary school educator, artist, consultant*

Williamstown
Blair, Phyllis E. *artist, sculptor, illustrator*
Bleezarde, Thomas Warren *retired magazine editor*
Bolton, Roger Edwin *economist, educator*
†Brown, Michael F. *anthropologist, educator*
Bruton, Henry Jackson *educator, economist*
Chandler, John Wesley *educational consultant*
Conforti, Michael Peter *museum director, art historian*
Conklin, Susan Joan *psychotherapist, educator, corporate staff developer, TV talk show host*
Cramer, Phebe *psychologist*
Dalzell, Robert Fenton, Jr., *historian, educator*
Dew, Charles Burgess *historian, educator*
Driscoll, Genevieve Bosson (Jeanne Bosson Driscoll) *management and organization development consultant*
Erickson, Peter Brown *librarian, scholar, writer*
Eusden, John Dykstra *theology educator, minister*
Fuller, Renee Nuni *psychologist, educational publisher*
Fuqua, Charles John *retired classics educator*
Glück, Louise Elisabeth *poet, educator*
†Goldstein, Darra Jane *language educator, editor*
Graver, Lawrence Stanley *English language professional*
Kassin, Saul *psychology educator*
King, Anthony Gabriel *museum administrator*
Markgraf, J(ohn) Hodge *chemist, educator*
McGill, Robert Ernest, III, *retired manufacturing company executive*
†Meyers, Peter Alexander *humanities educator, researcher*
†Nolan, James Lawry, Jr., *sociologist*
Oakley, Francis Christopher *history educator, former college president*
Park, David Allen *physicist, educator*
Pasachoff, Jay Myron *astronomer, educator*
Rudolph, Frederick *history educator*
†Schapiro, Morton Owen *university administrator*
Scull, Christina *writer*
Shainman, Irwin *music educator, musician*
Sheahan, John Bernard *economist, educator*
Solomon, Paul Robert *neuropsychologist, educator*
Sprague, John Louis *management consultant*
Stamelman, Richard Howard *French and humanities educator*
Stevens, Lauren Rogers *writer, environmentalist*
Stuebner, Erwin August, Jr., *internist*
Varese, Federico *political science educator*
Wobus, Reinhard Arthur *geologist, educator*

Wilmington
Akhavan, Farhad *electrical engineer*
Buckley, Robert Paul *aerospace company executive*
Eldada, Louay A. *fiber optic engineer*
Hayes, Carol Jeanne *physical education educator*

Winchendon
Scanio, Charles John Vincent *chemist, consultant*

Winchester
†Baratta, Edmond John *radiochemist, radiation safety officer*
Beck, William Samson *hematologist, educator, biochemist, writer*
Bigelow, Robert P. *lawyer, arbitrator, mediator, journalist*
Blackham, Ann Rosemary (Mrs. J. W. Blackham) *realtor*
Brennan, Francis Patrick *banker*
Dalton, Robert Edgar *mathematician, computer scientist*
†Ericson, William B. *orthopedic hand surgeon*
Ferrara, Lee *graphic designer, artists, art educator*
Ferrera, Arthur Rocco *food distribution company executive*
Hansen, Robert Joseph *civil engineer*
Harrison, Bettina Hall *retired biology educator*
Irving, Gitte Nielsen *secondary education educator*
Jabre, Eddy-Marco *architect*
Jackson, Francis Joseph *research and development company executive*
Kleinschmidt, Carol C. (Carol C. Fieleke) *pianist, educator*
Koppel, Lowell B. *chemical engineer*
Milburn, Richard Henry *physics educator*
Neuman, Robert Sterling *art educator, artist*
Ockerbloom, Richard C. *newspaper executive*
Reno, John F. *foundation administrator*
Totosy de Zepetnek, Steven *editor, educator*

Winthrop
Brown, Alan Anthony *marketing executive*
Brown, Patricia Irene *retired law librarian, lawyer*
Caggiano, Ernest Christopher *funeral director*
Lee, James Richard *ophthalmologist, educator*
Lutze, Ruth Louise *retired textbook editor, public relations executive*
Vettel, Niki Marcia (Monica Marcia Scher) *broadcasting executive*

Woburn
Basile, Leon Edmund *writer, editor*
†Conway, James Bernard *hospital administrator, consultant*
Crowley, Dean Timothy *occupational therapist*
Cummings, William Stanley *real estate company executive*
†Freeman, Jeanne Marie *music educator, writer*
Gelb, Arthur *electrical and systems engineering executive*
Goela, Jitendra Singh *researcher, consultant*
†Kuelthau, Paul Stauffer *lawyer*
†Loftus, Jeannine *graphics designer*
†Lovins, Nelson Preston *lawyer*
Mehra, Raman Kumar *aerospace and defense technology executive, automation and control engineering researcher*
Minkoff, Kenneth Mark *psychiatrist*
Murray, Philip Edmund, Jr., *lawyer*
†Offermann, Peter *financial executive*
Paul, Lois *public relations company executive*
Razdan, Raj Kumar *chemicals executive*
Tijmann, Willem Bert *civil engineer, consultant*
Tramonte, Michael Robert *education educator*
†Vogeli, Bernhard *research scientist*

Woods Hole
Berggren, William Alfred *geologist, research micropaleontologist, educator*
Cohen, Seymour Stanley *biochemist, educator*
Colinvaux, Paul A. *research scientist, writer*
Farrington, John William *academic administrator, dean, research scientist*
†Fenwick, Judith L. *oceanographer, researcher*
Gagosian, Robert B. *chemist, educator*
Houghton, Richard Arnold *research ecologist*
Inoué, Shinya *microscopy and cell biology scientist, educator*
Jin, Di *economist*
Laster, Leonard *physician, consultant, author*
Loewenstein, Werner Randolph *physiologist, biophysicist, educator*
Payne, Richard Earl *physical oceanographer*
Raskin, Fred Charles *transportation and utility holding company executive*
Steele, John Hyslop *marine scientist, oceanographic institute administrator*
Uchupi, Elazar *geologist, researcher*
Von Herzen, Richard Pierre *research scientist, consultant*
Woodwell, George Masters *ecology research director, lecturer*

Worcester
†Angelini, Michael P. *insurance company executive*
Appelbaum, Paul Stuart *psychiatrist, educator*
Bagshaw, Joseph Charles *molecular biologist, educator*
Baldiga, Joseph Hilding *lawyer*
Balko, George Anthony, III, *lawyer, educator*
Bassett, John E. *academic administrator, English educator*
Beaulieu, Peter Raymond *priest*
Bernhard, Jeffrey David *dermatologist, editor, educator*
†Bernstein, William Elliott *lawyer*
Billias, George Athan *history educator*
Bojar, Robert Michael *cardiothoracic surgeon*
Bowen, Alice Frances *school system administrator*
Brooks, John Edward *college president emeritus*
†Brunell-Joiner, Karlea *academic administrator, educator*
Bunuan, Josefina Santiago *early childhood education educator, graduate program coordinator*
Camougis, George *health, safety and environmental consultant*
Candib, Murray A. *business executive, retail management consultant*
Capriole, Sister Carmen Maria *geriatric nurse*
Cashman, Suzanne Boyer *health services administrator, educator*
Catto, Bonnie A. *classicist, educator*
Chaison, Gary N. *labor relations educator, researcher*
†Clark, William Anthony *religious studies educator*
Clarke, Edward Nielsen *engineering science educator*
Clifford, Jay *artist*
Covino, Paul Francis Xavier *religious executive, college chaplain, consultant*
Cowan, Fairman Chaffee *lawyer*
†Daly, Jennifer *physician*
Davidson, Lee David *insurance executive*
†Dershwitz, Mark *anesthesiologist, researcher*
Donnelly, James Corcoran, Jr., *lawyer*
Drachman, David Alexander *neurologist*
Dunlap, Ellen S. *library administrator*
Dyer-Cole, Pauline *school psychologist, educator*
Engle, Linda Jane *molecular biologist*
Felper, David Michael *lawyer*
†Fisher, William Henry *sociologist, researcher, educator*
Fragala, Guy Andrew *safety engineer, educator*
†Gandhi, Pritesh *medical educator*
Gorton, Nathaniel M. *federal judge*
Goss, Thomas Pixton *orthopaedic surgeon*
Grad, Bonnie Lee *art historian, educator*
Greenberg, Nathan *accountant*
†Hagar, Richard Joseph *music educator, musician*
Hand, Paul Desautels, Sr., *social work educator*
Hansen, Peter Holger *history educator, historian*
†Harnois, Marion C. *toxicologist, consultant*
He, Jiang *medical scientist*
Heman, Robert Jerome, Jr., *printing company executive, association executive*
Herman, Barbara Rose *interior decorator*
Hunt, John David *retired banker*
Hunter, Richard Edward *retired physician*
Johnson, Nancy Ann *education educator, educator*
Joshi, Harihar S. *medical laboratory executive*
Katz, Robert Nathan *ceramic engineer, educator*
Kennedy, Linda Mann *neuroscience educator, researcher*
†Klooster, Willem Wubbo *historian*
Kom, Ambroise *literature educator*
Kotzen, Marshall Jason *mathematics educator*
Lamothe, Donat Romeo *music educator*
Langevin, Edgar Louis *retired humanities educator*
Lanza, Robert Paul *medical scientist*
Lazare, Aaron *dean, psychiatrist*
Leach, Michael William *research pathologist*
Leppo, Jeffrey Allen *cardiologist*
Licho, Robert *physician, medical educator*
†Litofsky, N. Scott *physician, educator*
Loew, Franklin Martin *college president, biologist, consultant*
†Longcope, Christopher *physician, endocrinology educator*
Lougee, David Louis *lawyer*
Ludlum, David Blodgett *pharmacologist, educator*
Lurie, Konstantin Anatoly *mathematician, educator*
Malone, Joseph James *mathematics educator, researcher*
Marconi, Peter Paul, Jr., *financial analyst*
†Mardilovich, Ivan P *education educator*
Mathisen, Howard *psychologist, minister*
McCorison, Marcus Allen *librarian, cultural organization administrator*
McDowell, David Jamison *clinical psychologist*
McFarland, Michael C. *academic administrator*
†McGinn, John Richard *composer, educator*
Mendenhall, Harlan Vincent *research surgeon*
Moschos, Demitrios Mina *lawyer*
Moschos, Michael Christos *lawyer*
Murray, Timothy P. *mayor*
Nelson, John Martin *corporate executive*
Nompleggi, Dominic J. *gastroenterologist, medical educator*
Och, Mohamad Rachid *psychiatrist, consultant*
O'Toole, John Munster *humanities educator*
Palmer, John Anthony, III, *secondary education educator*
Parrish, Edward Alton, Jr., *electrical and computer engineering educator, academic administrator*
Parsons, Edwin Spencer *clergyman, educator*
Pavlik, James William *chemistry educator*
Radzicki, Michael Joseph *economist*
Reilly, Daniel Patrick *bishop*
Rencis, Joseph John *engineering educator, mechanical and civil engineer*
†Rifkah, Eve *performing company executive*
Rong, Yiming *manufacturing engineering educator*
Ross, Robert Jon Sanford *sociology educator*
†Saha, Deepak *metallurgist, researcher*
Scanlon, Peter Joseph *priest*
†Selin, Lisa K. *physician*
Silver, Marvin S. *lawyer*
Smith, Thomas William *neuropathologist*
Smyrnios, Nicholas A. *physician, educator*
Snyder, L. Michael *hospital administrator*
Spencer, Harry Irving, Jr., *retired banker*
Stempsey, William Edward *medical philosopher*
Stoff, Jeffrey S. *physician, educator*
Storey, Harry Stephens *lawyer*
Thomas, Ward John *political science educator*
†Tonkonogy, Joseph Moses *physician, neuropsychiatrist, researcher*
†Toomey, Sister Cathleen *academic administrator*
Turner, Billie Lee, II, *geography educator*
Uhl, Christopher Martin *lawyer*
Upshur, Carole Christofk *psychologist, educator*
Vaughan, Alden True *history educator*
Vick, Susan *playwright, educator, director, actress*

Kuhl, David Edmund *physician, nuclear medicine educator*

†Kuzon, William M., Jr., *plastic surgeon, muscle physiologist*

La Du, Bert Nichols, Jr., *pharmacology educator, physician*

†La Fountain-Stokes, Lawrence M *education educator*

†Langa, Kenneth M. *physician*

Leabo, Dick A. *retired statistics educator*

†Learned, David Walter *anesthesiologist*

Leith, Emmett Norman

Lempert, Richard Owen *lawyer, educator*

Leong, Sue *retired community health and pediatrics nurse*

Lewis, Donald John *mathematics educator*

Lewis, Robert Enzer *lexicographer, educator*

Lichter, Paul Richard *ophthalmology educator*

Lin, Mei-Ying *librarian*

†Linderman, Gerald Floyd *retired historian*

Lindner, Rudi Paul *historian, educator*

Lindsay, June Campbell McKee *communications executive*

†Ling, Song *research scientist*

Longone, Daniel Thomas *chemistry educator emeritus*

Lozoff, Betsy *pediatrician*

Lucy, Dlorah Rae *medical/surgical nurse*

†Ludwig, Martha *biochemist, educator*

Lyons, Harvey Isaac *mechanical engineering educator*

†Ma, Bing *research scientist*

†MacDonald, Michael Patrick *humanities educator*

Mackie-Mason, Jeffrey King *economics and information technology educator*

†MacKinnon, Catharine Alice *lawyer, law educator, legal scholar, writer*

Mangouni, Norman *publishing executive*

Manis, Melvin *psychologist, educator*

Margolis, Philip Marcus *psychiatrist, educator*

Markovits, Andrei Steven *political science educator*

Martel, William *radiologist, educator*

Martin, Claude Raymond, Jr., *marketing consultant, educator*

Martin, William Russell *nuclear engineering educator*

Mártonyi, Csaba Lászlo *ophthalmic photographer, imager*

†Matjias, Christian *music educator, musician*

Matthews, Rowena Green *biological chemistry educator*

Maxwell, Donald Robert *pharmacologist*

Mazumder, Jyotirmoy *mechanical and materials engineering educator*

Mazzeo, Anthony R. *chemist*

†McClamroch, N. Harris *aerospace engineering educator, consultant, researcher*

Mc Cracken, Paul Winston *retired economist, business educator*

McGinn, Terence James *business consultant, minister*

McKeachie, Wilbert James *psychologist, educator*

McPherson, Michael Robert *information scientist, university director*

Meezan, William Alan *social work educator, consultant*

†Mehta, Rajendra H *cardiologist, researcher*

†Meier, Gustav *conductor*

Meitzler, Allen Henry *electrical engineering educator, automotive scientist*

Mersereau, John, Jr., *Slavic languages and literatures educator*

Meyer, John Frederick *engineering and computer science educator, researcher, consultant*

Michalowski, Radoslaw Lucas *civil engineer, educator*

Millard, Herbert Dean *dentist*

Mitchell, Edward John *economist, retired educator*

Mizruchi, Mark Sheldon *sociology and business administration educator*

Modell, Stephen Mark *medical researcher, educator*

Moholy-Nagy, Hattula *archaeologist*

†Moje, Elizabeth Birr *education educator*

Montie, James Edward *urologist, oncologist*

Monto, Arnold Simon *epidemiology educator*

Moore, Thomas Edwin *biology educator, museum director*

†Moran, John Vincent *geneticist, molecular biologist, researcher*

Morgenstern, Lewis B. *medical educator*

Morley, George William *gynecologist*

†Morrison, Sean Joseph *medical researcher*

Mowbray, Carol Beatrice (Thiessen) *social worker, educator, mental health services professional, researcher*

†Mueggler, Erik *anthropologist, educator*

Munro, Donald Jacques *philosopher, educator*

Muraski, Anthony Augustus *lawyer*

†Musch, David C. *epidemiologist*

†Naeem, Tahira Bryant *librarian*

Neal, Homer Alfred *physics educator, researcher, university administrator*

Neidhardt, Frederick Carl *microbiologist, educator*

†Nelson, Jason Craig *company executive*

Niehoff, Leonard Marvin *lawyer*

Nikoui, Hossein Reza *quality assurance professional*

Nisbett, Richard Eugene *psychology educator*

Nordman, Christer Eric *chemistry educator*

Nriagu, Jerome Okon *environmental geochemist*

†O'Brien, Darlene Anne *lawyer*

Oliver, Marguerite Bertoni *food service executive*

Oliver, William John *pediatrician, educator*

Olynyk, Patricia *artist, educator*

Omenn, Gilbert Stanley *academic administrator, physician*

†Oral, Elif Arioglu *endocrinologist, researcher*

Orlin, Louis Lawrence *literature and history educator*

Orringer, Mark Burton *surgeon, educator*

Pan, Jwo *engineering educator*

Park, Euisu *research scientist*

Parker, Walter Gee *pediatrician*

Parkinson, William Charles *physicist, educator*

Parsons, Jeffrey Robinson *anthropologist, educator*

Pasyk, Krystyna Anna *dermatologist*

Paul, Ara Garo *university dean*

Pedley, John Griffiths *archaeologist, educator*

Pehlke, Robert Donald *materials and metallurgical engineering educator*

Penske, Roger S. *manufacturing and transportation executive*

Pepe, Steven Douglas *federal magistrate judge*

Perkins, Barbara M. *English educator, editor*

Perkins, Bradford *history educator*

Perkins, George *educator, writer*

†Perlin, Marc *engineering educator*

†Perrotta, Kevin Francis *writer, editor-in-chief*

Peterson, Julie Ann *media relations executive, consultant*

Petrick, Ernest Nicholas *mechanical engineer, researcher*

Petty, Elizabeth Marie *geneticist*

†Petty, Howard Raymond *cell biology educator*

†Phifer, Kenneth W. *minister*

Pierce, Roy *political science educator*

Pitt, Bertram *cardiologist, educator, consultant*

Pollack, Henry Nathan *geophysics educator*

Pollock, Stephen Michael *operations research engineer, educator, consultant*

Porretta, Louis Paul *education educator*

Porter, John Wilson *education executive*

Potter, David Stone *Greek and Latin educator*

Powsner, Edward Raphael *physician*

Price, Richard Henry *psychologist, educator*

†Prins, Johanna *literature educator*

Pulgram, Ernst *linguist, philologist, Romance and classical linguistics educator, writer*

†Quintyn, Conrad Bezekiah *anthropologist, educator*

Radock, Michael *foundation executive*

†Raffel, David M. *medical physicist*

Railton, Peter Albert *philosophy educator*

†Ramírez-Betances, Beatriz Eugenia *student activist*

†Ransom, Richard Frederick *biochemist*

†Rathcke, Beverly Jean *biologist, educator*

Reed, John Wesley *lawyer, educator*

Richardson, Rudy James *toxicology and neurosciences educator*

Robertson, David Wayne *pharmaceutical executive*

Robertson, Richard Earl *physical chemist, educator*

Roe, Byron Paul *physics educator*

Rogers, Bryan Leigh *artist, art educator*

Romani, John Henry *health administration educator*

Root, William Lucas *electrical engineering educator*

Rosenthal, Amnon *pediatric cardiologist*

†Roubidoux, Marilyn A. *radiologist*

Rounds, William C. *educator*

Roush, William R. *chemistry educator*

†Rowley, Larry Lee *research scientist, educator*

Rumman, Wadi (Saliba Rumman) *civil engineer, consultant*

Rupp, Ralph Russell *audiologist, educator, author*

Russell, James William *neurologist, neuroscientist, electrophysiologist*

Ryan, Marianne Elizabeth *lawyer*

Saitou, Kazuhiro *engineering educator*

†Samons, Sandra Lea *psychotherapist*

†Sanda, Martin George *urologist*

†Saper, Joel R. *neurologist, educator*

†Sarabandi, Kamal *science administrator*

Sasaki, Joseph Donald *optometrist*

Saxonhouse, Gary Roger *economics educator, consultant*

Scavarda, Donald Robert *composer, artist*

Schacht, Jochen Heinrich *biochemistry educator*

†Scheffel, Kenneth Paul *archivist*

Schneider, Carl Edward *law educator*

Schottenfeld, David *epidemiologist, educator*

Schwank, Johannes Walter *chemical engineering educator*

Schweitzer, Pamela Bifano *psychiatric and mental health nurse practitioner*

Scott, Norman Ross *electrical engineering educator*

Sears, JoAnn Marie *academic librarian*

Senior, Thomas Bryan A. *electrical engineering educator, researcher, consultant*

Serwer, Gerald Arthur *medical educator*

Shapiro, Brahm *nuclear medicine physician, endocrinologist*

Shapiro, Matthew David *economist, educator*

Shappirio, David Gordon *biologist, educator*

Sheldon, Ingrid Kristina *former mayor of Ann Arbor, bookkeeper*

Sheon, Amy Ruth *biomedical researcher*

Siedel, George John, III, *law educator*

†Simpson, Robert Urquhart *medical educator, researcher*

Singer, Eleanor *sociologist, editor*

Singer, J. David *political science educator*

Sloat, Barbara Furin *cell biologist, educator*

Smith, David John, Jr., *plastic surgeon*

Smith, Donald Cameron *physician, educator*

Smith, Sidonie *literature educator*

Solomon, David Eugene *engineering company executive*

Sovani, Sandeep Dinkar *mechanical engineer, educator, researcher*

Sprandel, Dennis Steuart *management consulting company executive*

Stafford, Frank P. *economist, educator*

Stafford, Frank Peter, Jr., *economics educator, consultant*

Steel, Duncan Gregory *physics educator*

Steiner, Peter Otto *economics educator, dean*

Stoermer, Eugene Filmore *biologist, educator*

Stoltenberg, Scott Frank *research scientist*

Stolz, Benjamin Armond *foreign language educator*

Strang, Ruth Hancock *pediatric educator, pediatric cardiologist, priest*

Stross, Jeoffrey Knight *physician, educator*

Sullivan, Thomas Patrick *academic administrator*

†Sun, Kai *materials scientist, research scientist*

Surovell, Edward David *real estate company executive*

Tai, Chen-To *electrical engineering educator*

Tandon, Rajiv *psychiatrist, educator*

Terrell, Jeffrey E. *otolaryngologist, researcher, educator*

Thompson, Norman Winslow *surgeon, educator*

Thornton, Arland *sociologist, educator*

Tinkle, Theresa L. *language educator*

Todd, Robert Franklin, III, *oncologist, educator*

Trautmann, Thomas Roger *history and anthropology educator*

†Tyler, Ilene Rogers *architect*

van der Pluijm, Bernardus Adrianus (Ben van der Pluijm) *geologist, educator*

Van der Voo, Rob *geophysicist*

†van Golen, Kenneth Louis *medical researcher*

Veltman, Martinus J.G. *retired physics educator*

Vining, Joseph (George Joseph Vining) *law educator*

Ward, Peter Allan *pathologist, educator*

Ware, Richard Anderson *foundation executive*

Warner, Robert Mark *university dean, archivist, historian*

†Warsi, M. Jahangeer *language educator, researcher*

Weatherbee, Ellen Gene Elliott *botanist, educator*

Weg, John Gerard *physician*

Wellman, Henry M. *psychology educator*

Wharton, John James, Jr., *research physicist*

White, B. Joseph *dean, business educator*

White, James Boyd *law educator*

Whitehouse, Frank, Jr., *microbiologist, educator*

Whitman, Marina Von Neumann *economist, educator*

Widmayer, Warren J. *lawyer*

Wiggins, Roger C. *internist, educator, researcher*

Wilde, Alan Conrad *mathematician*

Williams, John Andrew *physiology educator, consultant*

Williams, Melvin Donald *anthropologist, educator*

Willmarth, William Walter *aerospace engineering educator*

Wilson, Richard Christian *engineering firm executive*

Winbury, Martin Maurice *pharmaceutical executive, educator*

†Withey, Jeffrey Howard *molecular biologist, researcher*

†Wojtys, Edward M. *orthopedic surgeon, sports medicine physician*

Woronoff, Israel *former psychology educator*

Xie, Jingping *microbiologist, pediatrician*

Yagle, Andrew Emil *engineering educator*

Ye, Cang *electrical engineer*

Young, Edwin Harold *chemical and metallurgical engineering educator*

Yu, Mei-yu *medical researcher*

Zarley, Karlta Rae *Healing Touch practitioner, nurse consultant*

Zhang, Youxue *geology educator*

Zucker, Robert A(lpert) *psychologist*

†Zurier, Rebecca *art history educator*

Armada

Kummerow, Arnold A. *superintendent of schools*

Athens

Kilgore, Marchon June *transportation company executive, genealogist*

Auburn Hills

Bahman, Mujibur *engineer*

Brown, Lawrence Harvey (Larry Brown) *professional basketball coach*

Davidson, William M. *diversified company executive, professional basketball executive*

De Martin, Colleen Dianne *college official, interior designer, consultant*

Drexler, Mary Sanford *financial executive*

Etefia, Florence Victoria *school psychologist*

Farrar, Stephen Prescott *glass products manufacturing executive*

†Fluharty, David Arthur *automotive executive, statistician, consultant*

Gerson, Ralph Joseph *corporate executive*

Hoffman, Frederick William *automotive executive*

†Huss, Allan Michael *lawyer*

Mandiberg, David Michael *sculptor*

Mukundan, Gopalan *technology specialist*

Neumann, Charles Henry *mathematician, educator*

Nusholtz, Guy Samuel *executive consultant*

O'Brien, William J., III, *lawyer*

†Palmer, Wendy *basketball player*

Schumacher, Ann *artist, educator*

Trebing, David Martin *automotive executive*

Weiler, Scott Michael *machine tool manufacturing company executive*

Williams, Calvin *librarian, consultant*

Augusta

Barr, William Robert *industrial engineer, consultant*

Bad Axe

Sullivan, James Gerald *business owner, postal letter carrier*

Battle Creek

Andert, Jeffrey Norman *clinical psychologist*

Baldwin, Susan Olin *community service administrator*

Davis, Laura Arlene *retired foundation administrator*

Fisher, David Russel *government executive*

†Gates, Jeffrey Ralph *research scientist, epidemiologist*

Gutierrez, Carlos M. *grocery manufacturing company executive*

Hazel, James R. C., Jr., *small business owner, volunteer*

†Langbo, Arnold Gordon *food company executive*

Lincoln, Margaret *library media specialist*

Matthews, Wyhomme S. *retired music educator, college administrator*

Milligan, Glenn Edward *poet*

Myer, Donna Gail *writer, health researcher*

Van Almen, Karen *art educator*

Wendt, Linda M. *educational association administrator*

Bay City

Bosco, Jay William *optometrist*

†Deskin, William C. *healthcare educator*

Greve, Guy Robert *lawyer*

Nicholson, William Noel *clinical neuropsychologist*

Van Dyke, Clifford Craig *retired banker*

Zuraw, Kathleen Ann *special education and physical education educator*

Bear Lake

Richard, Timothy C. *journalist, editor*

Beaver Island

Thompson, Sarah Ellen *grants consultant*

Bellaire

Cowles, Walter Curtis *naval architect*

Keller, Theodore G., Jr., *investment property owner and manager*

Belleville

Meyer, Thomas J. *mathematics educator*

†Wilson, David James *chemistry researcher, educator*

Bellevue

Hamel, Louis Reginald *systems analysis consultant*

Belmont

Delnick, Martha Joyce *retired elementary education educator*

Benton Harbor

Alsbro, Donald Edgar *health educator*

Atwood, Harold Ashley *retired historian*

Hopp, Daniel Frederick *manufacturing company executive, lawyer*

Whitwam, David Ray *appliance manufacturing company executive*

Benzonia

Acker, Nathaniel Hull *retired educational administrator*

Berkley

Hauser, Andrew Max *cardiologist*

Berrien Springs

Lesher, William Richard *retired academic administrator*

†Lundgren, Dennis D. *intermediate school educator*

†Moskala, Jiri *religious studies educator*

Beulah

Auch, Walter Edward *securities company executive*

Edwards, Wallace Winfield *retired automotive company executive*

Beverly Hills

Hertzberg, David Gordon *retired lawyer*

Tolias, Linda Puroff *music educator*

Big Rapids

Haneline, Douglas Latham *literature educator*

Hardy, Victoria Elizabeth *management educator*

†Kantar, Andrew K. *literature educator*

Karafa, Joseph A. *psychology educator, consultant*

Mathison, Ian William *chemistry educator, academic dean*

Mehler, Barry Alan *humanities educator, journalist, consultant*

†Roy, Donald H. *political scientist, educator*

†Siddikov, Bakhodirzhon *mathematician, educator*

Slaymaker, Adrianne Lee E. *accountant, educator*

Sterling, Phillip Duncan *English educator*

†Tymes, Nathaniel, Jr., *statistician, educator*

Bingham Farms

Banas, C(hristine) Leslie *lawyer*

Burstein, Richard Joel *lawyer*

Farhy, Rodolfo David *internist, cardiologist*

Giles, Conrad Leslie *ophthalmic surgeon*

Goren, Steven Eliot *lawyer*

Gratch, Serge *mechanical engineering educator*

†Katz, Sidney Franklin *obstetrician, gynecologist*

Lebow, Michael Jeffrey *lawyer*

Birmingham

Ashleigh, Caroline *art and antiques appraiser*

Berman, Laura *journalist, writer*

Edwards, Michael Gerard *physician*

Elsman, James Leonard, Jr., *lawyer*

Foxen, Richard William *manufacturing company executive*

Harms, Steven Alan *lawyer*

Helppie, Charles Everett, III, *financial consultant*

Kaufman, Ira Gladstone *judge*

Kienbaum, Thomas Gerd *lawyer*

McCuen, John Joachim *business executive, columnist and lecturer*

Nicholson, Robert D. *manufacturing executive*

Podolsky, Arnold Mark *lawyer, physician*

Robinson, Marietta S. *lawyer*

Schaefer, John Frederick *lawyer, educator*

Smith, George Wolfram *physicist, educator*

Sweeney, Thomas Frederick *lawyer*

†Thorpe, Norman Ralph *lawyer, automobile company executive, retired air force officer*
VanDeusen, Bruce Dudley *company executive*
Wells, Steven Wayne *lawyer*
Zacharski, Dennis Edward *lawyer*

Bloomfield Hills
Abel Horowitz, Michelle Susan *advertising executive*
Adams, Charles Francis *advertising and real estate executive*
Allen, Maurice Bartelle, Jr., *architect*
Baker, Robert Edward *lawyer, retired financial corporation executive*
Belavek, Debra Louise *school psychologist*
Berline, James H. *advertising executive, public relations executive*
Berlow, Robert Alan *lawyer*
Birkerts, Gunnar *architect*
†Birnkrant, Sherwin Maurice *lawyer*
Bithell, Thomas Charles *human resources and insurance consultant*
†Breiner, Sander James *psychiatry educator, psychoanalyst*
Brodhead, William McNulty *lawyer, former congressman*
Brown, Jack Wyman *architect*
Burnett, Patricia Hill *portrait artist, author, sculptor, lecturer*
Charla, Leonard Francis *lawyer*
Clippert, Charles Frederick *lawyer*
Colladay, Robert S. *trust company executive, consultant*
Cranmer, Thomas William *lawyer*
Cuffe, Stafford Sigesmund *engineering company executive, consultant*
Cunningham, Gary H. *lawyer*
Dawson, Stephen Everette *lawyer*
Deron, Edward Michael *lawyer*
†Ebert, Douglas Edmund *corporate financial executive*
Fauver, John William *mayor, retired business executive*
Frey, Stuart Macklin *automobile manufacturing company executive*
Gabriel, Martin George *engineering consultant*
Gold, Edward David *lawyer*
Googasian, George Ara *lawyer*
Gornbein, Henry Seidel *lawyer*
Gotthelf, Beth *lawyer*
Graff, Robert Alan *computer consultant*
Greenwood, Frank *information scientist, educator*
Hagenlocker, Edward E. *retired automobile company executive*
Haidostian, Alice Berberian *concert pianist, civic volunteer and fundraiser*
Hitchcock, Lillian Dorothy Staw *educator, actress, artist*
James, William Ramsay *cable television executive*
Janover, Robert H. *lawyer*
Jones, John Paul *probation officer, psychologist*
Kasischke, Louis Walter *lawyer*
Kaufman, Jerome Seymour *retired ophthalmologist*
Kirk, John MacGregor *lawyer*
Klein, Coleman Eugene *lawyer*
Klosinski, Deanna Dupree *medical educator, consultant*
†Kollins, Michael Jerome *automotive engineer, historian, writer*
Kyes, Helen G. (Mrs. Rogers M. Kyes) *volunteer*
†Lamping, William Jay *lawyer*
Lapadot, Sonee Spinner *retired automobile manufacturing company official*
Ledwidge, Patrick Joseph *lawyer*
Leonard, Michael A. *retired automotive executive*
†Levin, Carolyn Bible *volunteer*
LoPrete, James Hugh *lawyer*
Martin, J(oseph) Patrick *lawyer*
Mathog, Robert Henry *otolaryngologist, educator*
Maxwell, Jack Erwin *manufacturing company executive*
McCuen, John Francis, Jr., *lawyer*
McDonald, Patrick Allen *lawyer, arbitrator, educator*
†McGarry, Alexander Banting *lawyer*
†McQueen, Patrick M. *bank executive*
Meyer, George Herbert *lawyer*
†Miller, Eugene Albert *retired bank executive*
Morganroth, Fred *lawyer*
Mucha, John, III, *lawyer*
Nern, Christopher Carl *lawyer*
Norris, John Hart *lawyer, director*
Nuss, Shirley Ann *computer coordinator, educator*
†O'Brien, Mark J. *real estate/residential construction executive*
Pappas, Edward Harvey *lawyer*
Poth, Stefan Michael *retired sales financing company executive*
Prasad, Niru *physician, television personality*
Putchakayala, Hari Babu *engineering company executive*
Rader, Ralph Terrance *lawyer*
Robinson, Jack Albert *retail drug stores executive*
Rom, Martin (Melvyn Rom) *investor*
Rosenzweig, Norman *psychiatry educator administrator*
Roy, Ranjit Kumar *mechanical engineer*
Sandy, William Haskell *training and communication systems executive*
Simon, Evelyn *lawyer*
Snyder, George Edward *lawyer*
Solomon, Mark Raymond *lawyer, educator*
Sommerfeld, David William *lawyer, educator*
Stewart, Michael B. *lawyer, mechanical and aerospace engineer*
Stivender, Donald Lewis *mechanical engineering consultant*
Stunz, John Henry, Jr., *retired physician*
Sugrue, Dennis Patrick *clinical psychologist*
Swift, Jonathan *educator, television host, tenor*
Syme, Daniel Bailey *rabbi, institution executive*
†Tallerico, Thomas Joseph *lawyer*
Thompson, Richard Thomas *academic administrator*
Van Dine, Harold Forster, Jr., *architect, artist*
Victor, Richard Steven *lawyer*
Weil, John William *technology management consultant*
Wermuth, Mary Louella *secondary school educator*
Williams, J. Bryan *lawyer*
Williams, Walter Joseph *lawyer*
Yamin, Joseph Francis *lawyer, counselor*

Bloomfield Township
Brown, Lynette Ralya *journalist, publicist*

Brighton
Crabtree, John David *manufacturing company executive*
Rice, Gary D. *software engineer, consultant*

Brooklyn
Freeman, Fred Wesley *forester, educator*
Vischer, Harold Harry *manufacturing company executive*

Buchanan
Falkenstein, Karin Edith *elementary school principal*
Riches, Kenneth William *nuclear regulatory engineering manager*
Stromswold, Dorothy *retired secondary educator, book reviewer*

Buckley
†Gingerich, Martin Ellsworth *literature educator*

Burt
Wolverton, Thomas Frank *automotive company supervisor*

Burton
Meissner, Suzanne Banks *pastoral associate*

Cadillac
Walker, Dale Maxwell *city official*
Whitmer, Gretchen Sue *secondary school educator*
Whitmer, Walter Glenn *band director*

Camden
Falls, Kathleene Joyce *photographer*

Canton
†Caraballo, Dimas J. *music educator*
Cattani, Luis Carlos *manufacturing engineer*
Lee, Kamee Angela *financial analyst*

Capac
Wagner, Dorothy Marie *retired senior creative designer, artist*

Caro
Galloway, Gladys *artist*

Cass City
Althaver, Lambert Ewing *manufacturing company executive*

Cedar
Kunkel, Dorothy Ann *music educator*

Cedarville
Pittman, Philip McMillan *historian*

Center Line
Litch, John Michael *lawyer*

Central Lake
Hocking, Marian Ruth *women's health nurse*

Charlevoix
Knutson, Roger M. *writer, retired science educator*
Telgenhof, Allen Ray *lawyer*

Charlotte
Herrick, Kathleen Magara *social worker*
Young, Everett J. *management consultant, agricultural economist*

Chelsea
Kendall, Kay Lynn *interior designer, consultant*
Paulsen, Serenus Glen *architect, educator*
Sawyer, Charles Henry *art educator, art museum director emeritus*
†Yarows, Steven Allen *internist*

Chesterfield
Burnett, Gary Main *social work administrator, crisis counselor*
Wilson-Pleiness, Christine Joyce *writer, poet, columnist, real estate investor*

Clarkston
†Bullard, Rockwood Wilde, III, *lawyer*
†Chapman, Clifford Kenneth *music educator*
Keough, James Gillman, Jr., *minister*
Mousseau, Doris Naomi Barton *retired elementary school principal*
†Snow, Sandra Inez *mortgage company executive*
Windeknecht, Margaret Brake *artist*
Wydra, Frank Thomas *healthcare executive*
Ylvisaker, John Richard *real estate developer, consultant*

Clifford
Staples, Lynne Livingston Mills *retired psychologist, educator, consultant*

Clinton
Anderson, Denice Anna *editor*

Clinton Township
Brown, Ronald Delano *endocrinologist*
Crawford, Betty Elizabeth *English and computer science educator*
Fontanive, Lynn Marie *special education administrator*
Ho, Robert En Ming *neurosurgeon, educator*
Stone, Beverly Ann *retired counselor*
Syropoulos, Mike *retired school system director*

Clio
McCabe, Donald James *educational research director*

Coldwater
Fisher, Estelle Maude *retired artist*

Commerce Township
Boynton, Irvin Parker *retired educational administrator*

Corunna
Sodman, Charles Edward *probation/parole agent, educator, writer*

Davison
Tauscher, John Walter *retired pediatrician, emeritus educator*
Weamer, Alan Philip *family practice physician*

Dearborn
Ahmed, Saleem *management consultant, educator*
Atkin, Rupert Lloyd *retired engineer*
Ball, James Charles *biochemist, researcher, herpetologist*
†Barnhart, Mary C. *health facility administrator*
†Barton, Robert H., III, *automotive executive*
Bautz, Jeffrey Emerson *mechanical engineer, educator, researcher*
†Beauford, Sandra *registered nurse, data processing executive*
Bixby, Harold Glenn *manufacturing company executive*
Brown, James Ward *mathematician, educator, author*
Bugli, Neville Jimmy *mechanical engineer*
Cairns, James Robert *mechanical engineering educator*
Cape, James Odies E. *fashion designer*
Chen, Weigang *applied mechanics scientist, research engineer*
Coburn, Ronald Murray *ophthalmic surgeon, researcher*
†Crosbie, Gary Mark *research scientist, artist*
†D'Alessio, Gina Maria *music educator*
Demorest, Mark Stuart *lawyer*
Dziuba, Henry Frank *retired university official*
Dzuiblinski, Gerard Arthur *theatre educator, artistic director*
Fair, Jean Everhard *retired education educator*
Ford, William Clay, Jr., *automotive executive*
Ford, William Clay *automotive company executive, professional sports team executive*
Fordyce, James George *physician*
†Fryling, Victor J. *energy company executive*
Gu, Jianmin *mechanical engineer, researcher*
Hess, Margaret Johnston *religious writer, educator*
Hogan, Brian Joseph *editor*
Ibbotson, Patricia Ann *nurse, author*
†Irick, Brett D *manufacturing engineer*
Jie, Min *mechanical engineering educator, researcher*
Kahn, Mark Leo *arbitrator, educator*
Kendall, Laurel Ann *geotechnical engineer*
Kershner, Rodger A. *corporate lawyer*
Lee, Hei Wai *finance educator, researcher*
Li, Guosong *mechanical engineering educator*
Libertiny, Susan Fryc *mechanical engineer*
†Lin, Paul kuang-Hsien *assemblyman, educator*
Linnansalo, Vera *engineer*
Little, Daniel Eastman *philosophy educator, university program director*
Little, Robert Eugene *mechanical engineering educator, materials behavior researcher, consultant*
Lundy, J(oseph) Edward *retired automobile company executive*
†McMillan, Liana *language educator*
Mohan Iyengar, Raj *automotive executive, researcher*
Olson, Richard Gottlieb *nuclear engineer*
Orlowska-Warren, Lenore Alexandria *art educator, fiber artist*
Papazian, Dennis Richard *history educator, political commentator*
†Pestillo, Peter John *automotive executive, lawyer*
†Raghava, Ram Singh *polymer scientist*
Rintamaki, John M. *automotive executive*
Sarkisian, Edward Gregory *dentist*
†Skramstad, Harold Kenneth, Jr., *museum administrator, consultant*
Tallio, Kevin Verne *engineering supervisor*
Taub, Robert Allan *lawyer*
Van Kirk, Donald John *forensic specialist, consultant, engineering executive, consultant, writer*
Wagner, Harvey Arthur *nuclear engineer, consultant*
†Wagner, Terrance Carl *automotive executive*
Wang, Dexin *research engineer*
Webb, Thomas J. *utilities executive*
Whipple, Kenneth *utilities executive*
Yang, Guangbin *engineer*

Dearborn Heights
Donoian, George *education executive*
Hatem, Ghaleb Fayez *ophthalmologist, hospital administrator*

Decatur
Kinney, Gregory Hoppes *lawyer*

Deckerville
Jarmolowicz, C. Renee *artist, art educator*

Detroit
Abel, Ernest Lawrence *education educator*
Abella Dominicis, Esteban Martin *hematologist, oncologist, pediatrician*
Aboulafia, Elie David *vascular surgeon*
Abramson, Hanley Norman *pharmacy educator*
Abt, Jeffrey *art and art history educator, artist, writer*
†Adams, James Charles *lawyer*
Alexander, Sheldon *psychology educator*
Alpert, Daniel *television executive*
Amirikia, Hassan *obstetrician, gynecologist*
†Anderson, Moses B. *bishop*
Anderson, Thomas Caryl *financial and administrative systems professional*
Andreoff, Christopher Andon *lawyer*
†Aronson, Ronald *humanities educator, writer*
Arrington, Harold M. *obstetrician*
Ashenfelter, David Louis *reporter*
Ashley, Lois A. *retired university reference librarian*
Babar, Raza Ali *industrial engineer, utility consultant, futurist, management educator, marketing strategist, author, publisher*
Babb, Ralph W., Jr., *banker*
Babcock, Charles Witten, Jr., *lawyer*
†Bahrainwala, Abdul Husein *allergist, immunologist*
Balon, Richard *psychiatrist, educator*
†Barr, Charles Joseph Gore *lawyer*
Barrett, Nancy Smith *university administrator*
Batcha, George *retired mechanical and nuclear engineer*
Beal, Graham William John *museum director*
†Bell, Sue Ellen *research analyst, administrator, nursing educator*
Bell Wilson, Carlotta A. *state official, consultant*
†Benninger, Michael Stephen *otolaryngologist*
Berke, Amy Turner *health science association administrator*
Berri, Mohamad Hussein *electrical and computer engineer, educator, researcher*
Bhalla, Deepak Kumar *cell biologist, toxicologist, educator*
Blomquist, David Wels *journalist*
Bock, Brooks Frederick *emergency physician*
†Boinpally, Ramesh Rao *research scientist, pharmacist, educator*
Bonior, David Edward *congressman*
†Booth, Betty Jean *daycare administrator, poet*
Bowen, David R. *science and technology educator, consultant*
Bowman, William Scott (Scotty Bowman) *professional hockey coach*
Boyea, Earl Alfred *bishop*
Brady, Edmund Matthew, Jr., *lawyer*
Brand, George Edward, Jr., *lawyer*
†Braunschweig, Karl David *education educator, performing arts educator, humanities educator*
Brill, Lesley *literature and film studies educator*
Brooks, Beth Ann *physician*
Brunk, Thomas Walter *art historian*
Brustad, Orin Daniel *lawyer*
Budny, James Charles *federal agency administrator*
†Buttigieg, Joseph J. *banking executive*
Calarco, N. Joseph *theater educator*
Callahan, J(ohn) William (Bill Callahan) *judge*
Candler, James Nall, Jr., *lawyer*
Cantoni, Louis Joseph *psychologist, poet, sculptor*
Catchings, Yvonne Parks *artist, educator*
Cavanagh, Gerald Francis *business educator*
Charfoos, Lawrence Selig *lawyer*
Chelios, Christos K. *hockey player*
Childress-Brown, Nazarene *small business owner, writer*
Christian, Terry Clifton *lawyer*
Coffey, C(harles) Edward *physician*
Cohan, Leon Sumner *lawyer, retired electric company executive*
Cohen, Norton Jacob *lawyer*
Cohen, Sanford Ned *pediatrics educator, academic administrator*
Colby, Joy Hakanson *critic*
Collier, James Warren *lawyer*
Connellan, William Wesley *higher education educator*
Connor, Laurence Davis *lawyer, director*
Corbitt, Eumiller Mattie *education educator, special education educator*
Corrigan, Maura Denise *judge*
Cothorn, John Arthur *lawyer*
†Dale, Shirley Marie *protective services official*
Darlow, Julia Donovan *lawyer*
Darr, Alan Phipps *curator, historian*
Dauch, Richard E. *automobile manufacturing company executive*
Day, Burnis C. *artist, educator*
†Deason, Herold McClure *lawyer*
Devaney, Dennis Martin *lawyer, educator*
Devellano, James Charles *professional hockey manager, baseball executive*
†Dhar, Josephine Patricia *medical educator*
Diaz, Fernando Gustavo *neurosurgeon*
†Di Chiera, David *general director of opera company*
Dickerson, Brian *columnist*
†DiFeo, Samuel X. *automotive executive*
Dister, John E. *religious organization administrator*
Dixson, J. B. *communications executive*
Dombrowski, Mitchell Paul *physician, inventor, researcher*
Dong, Zhong *biomedical scientist*
Draper, James Wilson *lawyer*
Drescher, Dennis George *biochemist, researcher*
†Duensing, Dorothy Jean *music educator, vocalist*
Duggan, Patrick James *federal judge*
Dunn, William Bradley *lawyer*
Dwyer, John M. *mathematician, statistician, computer scientist*
Earley, Anthony Francis, Jr., *utilities company executive, lawyer*
†Ebenezer, Jazlin V. *adult education educator*
Edelstein, Tilden Gerald *university official, history educator*
†Edison, Jonathan E. *assistant principal, motivational speaker*

Edmunds, Nancy Garlock *federal judge*
Edwards, Brian Francis Peregrine *science educator*
Edwards, Paul Andrew *vitreo-retinal surgeon, ophthalmologist*
†Ehrinpreis, Murray Norman *gastroenterologist, educator*
Eliason, James Frederick *hematology and oncology researcher*
Elkus, Robert Michael *general surgeon*
†Enam, Syed Ather *neurosurgeon, researcher*
Engelhardt, Regina *cosmetologist, artist, small business owner*
†Entenman, John Alfred *lawyer*
†Everingham, James Theodore *lawyer*
†Faison, W. Mack *lawyer*
†Fastiggi, Robert L. *religious studies educator*
Fedorov, Sergei *hockey player*
Feikens, John *federal judge*
Fellrath, Richard Frederic *lawyer*
†Felt, Julia Kay *lawyer*
Ferguson, Tamara *clinical sociologist*
Field, Judith Judy *librarian*
Finkenbine, Roy Eugene *history educator*
Fleming, George Robert *psychologist*
†Foreman, Kelly Marie *anthropologist, music educator*
Frade, Peter Daniel *chemist, educator, administrator*
Francis, Edward D. *architect*
Friedman, Bernard Alvin *federal judge*
Fromm, David *surgeon*
†Fromm, Frederick Andrew, Jr., *lawyer*
Fu, Gongkang *civil engineering educator*
Gaines, Jeffrey Thomas *architect, urban planner*
Gardin, Julius Markus *cardiologist, educator*
Garner, Phil *former professional baseball manager*
Garriott, Lois Jean *clinical social worker, educator*
Gibbs, Mary L. *writer, writers' services provider*
Glotta, Ronald Delon *lawyer*
Goodman, Allen Charles *economist, educator*
†Gottschalk, Thomas A. *lawyer*
†Green, Charles Adam *retired education educator, psychologist*
Greenwood, Harriet Lois *environmental banker, researcher*
†Grusin, Richard Arthur *literature educator, writer*
Gulley, James Clarence, Jr., *television producer, marketing specialist, internet consultant*
Gunasekera, Thilak Wijenayaka *mathematician, educator*
†Gunderson, Michael Arthur *lawyer*
Gupta, Suraj Narayan *physicist, educator*
Gushee, Richard Bordley *lawyer*
†Guthikonda, Murali *neurosurgeon*
†Haase, Donald Paul *German language, literature and culture educator*
Hampton, Verne Churchill, II, *lawyer*
†Harbour, Nancy Caine *lawyer*
Harden, Daniel Alexander, Jr., *chemical engineer*
†Harris, Patricia Skalny *lawyer*
†Henry, William Lockwood *former food products executive, brewery executive*
Heppner, Gloria Hill *medical science administrator, educator*
Higginson, Bobby *professional baseball player*
†Hock, Lisabeth Marie *language educator*
†Holland, Ken *sports team executive*
Holness, Gordon Victor Rix *engineering executive, mechanical engineer*
Hood, Antoinette Foote *dermatologist*
†Hudson, Alan Paul *microbiologist, educator, research scientist*
Hull, Brett A. *hockey player*
Hurley, Harry James, Jr., *dermatologist, educator*
Hutton, Carole Leigh *newspaper editor*
Ilitch, Marian *professional hockey team executive, food service executive*
Ilitch, Michael *professional hockey team executive*
Jacobs, John Patrick *lawyer*
†Jacox, Ada Kathryn *nurse, educator*
†Jammalamadaka, Papa Rao *molecular biologist*
†Jampel, Robert Steven *ophthalmologist, educator*
Jenkins-Anderson, Barbara Jeanne *pathologist, educator*
Johnson, Carl Randolph *chemist, educator*
Johnson, Cynthia L(e) M(ae) *lawyer*
Johnson, Lester Larue, Jr., *artist, educator*
†Johnson, Steven Carl *educational consultant*
†Joiner, Michael Charles *radation biologist, researcher*
Jones, Bruce Allen *pathologist*
Jones, James Allen *secondary education educator*
Jordan, Napoleon Bonaparte *educational consultant*
Kahalas, Harvey *business educator*
Kalman, Andrew *manufacturing company executive*
Kang, Emil J. *orchestra executive*
Kantrowitz, Adrian *surgeon, educator*
Kantrowitz, Jean *health products executive*
†Kato, Ikuko *epidemiologist*
Keith, Damon Jerome *federal judge*
Kelleher, Timothy John *publishing company executive*
Kelley, Mark Albert *physician, educator, health care executive*
†Kerin, Nicholas Zeev *cardiologist, researcher*
Kessler, William Henry *architect*
†Ketterer, Mark William *psychologist, research scientist*
†Kilpatrick, Kwame *mayor*
Kirschner, Stanley *chemist*
Kithier, Karel *pathologist, educator*
Kline, Kenneth Alan *mechanical engineering educator*
Kline, Ronald Alvin *vascular surgeon, educator*
Klurfeld, David Michael *nutritionist, pathologist*
Kobernick, Sidney D. *pathologist, educator*
Komives, Paul J. *federal judge*
Krawetz, Stephen Andrew *molecular medicine and genetics scientist*
†Krempasky, Frances M. *librarian*
Krouse, Helene June *nursing educator*
†Krsul, John Aloysius, Jr., *lawyer*
Krull, Edward Alexander *dermatologist*
Kuehn, George E. *lawyer, former beverage company executive*
Kummler, Ralph H. *chemical engineer, educator, dean*
†Labadie, Dwight Daniel *lawyer*
Lamborn, LeRoy Leslie *law educator*
Lawrence, John Kidder *lawyer*
†Lawson, Noel Seymore *pathologist, consultant*
Lerner, Stephen Alexander *microbiologist, physician, educator*
Leuchtman, Stephen Nathan *lawyer*
Levin, Charles Leonard *state supreme court justice*
Levy, Edward Charles, Jr., *manufacturing company executive*
Lewand, F. Thomas *lawyer*
Lewis, Dave *professional hockey team coach*
Li, Xiaoming *pediatrics educator, psychologist*
Lidstrom, Niklas *professional hockey player*
Lim, Henry Wan-Peng *physician*
†Lisak, Robert Philip *physician, researcher, educator*
Lockman, Stuart M. *lawyer*
Longhofer, Ronald Stephen *lawyer*
Lupulescu, Aurel Peter *medical educator, researcher, physician*
†MacDonald, Douglas Andrew *psychologist, educator*
Madgett, Naomi Long *poet, editor, publisher, educator*
Mahmood, Asim *neurosurgeon*
†Maida, Adam Joseph Cardinal *archbishop*
Maiese, Kenneth *neurologist, neuroscientist*
Mamat, Frank Trustick *lawyer*
Marotti, Arthur Francis *language educator*
Marsh, Harold Michael *anesthesiologist*
Marx, Thomas George *economist*
†Mattingly, Raymond R *pharmacologist, educator*
Maurer, David Leo *lawyer*
McArthur, Steven Francis *psychologist, educator*
McCarty, Darren *professional hockey player*
McCracken, Caron Francis *computer company executive, consultant*
McCracken, Ina *business executive*
Mc Gehee, H(arry) Coleman, Jr., *bishop*
†McGinnity, John G. *physician assistant, medical educator*
McKim, Samuel John, III, *lawyer*
McWhorter, Sharon Louise *business executive, inventor, consultant*
Mengel, Christopher Emile *lawyer, educator*
Meriwether, Heath J. *newspaper publisher*
Mika, Joseph John *library school director, educator, consultant*
†Millender, Beatrice Pennie *magistrate judge*
Miller, George DeWitt, Jr., *lawyer*
Miller, Orlando Jack *physician, educator*
Mitseff, Carl *lawyer*
Moghissi, Kamran S. *obstetrician, gynecologist, educator*
Moldenhauer, Judith A. *graphic design educator*
Morrison, Gary Ray *instructional technology educator, researcher*
Moss, Leslie Otha *protective services official*
†Motlagh, Cyrus K. *law educator*
Muller, Herman Joseph *historian, educator*
Myers, Rodman Nathaniel *lawyer*
Nadeau, Steven C. *lawyer*
Neithercut, Mark Edward *foundation executive*
Nemeth, Patricia Marie *lawyer*
Newton, Kenneth Kurt *physician, educator, administrator*
Nix, Robert Royal, II, *lawyer*
Noland, Mariam Charl *foundation executive*
Norris, Megan Pinney *lawyer*
Novak, Raymond Francis *environmental health/toxicology research institute director, pharmacology educator*
†O'Connell, John Bernard, Jr., *medical educator, chairman department of medicine*
Oliver, John Preston *chemistry educator, academic administrator*
O'Meara, John Corbett *federal judge*
Orton, Colin George *medical physicist*
†Palmer, Keturah *association administrator*
Parker, Ross Gail *lawyer*
Parrish, Maurice Drue *museum executive*
Peck, Elsie Holmes *curator, art historian, archaeologist*
Peck, William Henry *museum curator, art historian, archaeologist, author, lecturer*
Penn, Maggie Scott *school counselor, mental health therapist, small business owner*
Perry, Burton Lars *retired pediatrician*
Peters, John Douglas *lawyer, artist*
Peters, William P. *oncologist, science administrator, educator*
Petersen, Steve Alan *orthopaedic surgeon*
Pettapiece, Bob (Mervyn Arthur Pettapiece) *education educator*
Phillips, Eduardo *surgeon, educator*
Phillis, John Whitfield *physiologist, educator*
Pietrofesa, John Joseph *education educator*
Ponder, Dan *public relations executive*
Poremba, David Lee *librarian, writer*
Porter, Arthur T. *oncologist, educator, medical administrator*
Prasad, Ananda Shiva *medical educator*
Putatunda, Susil Kumar *metallurgy educator*
†Rahman, Km Wahidur *research scientist*
†Rajarethinam, Rajaprabhakaran *psychiatrist, educator, researcher*
Rajlich, Vaclav Thomas *computer science educator, researcher, consultant*
†Rakolta, John, Sr., *construction company executive*
Rasmussen, Douglas John *lawyer*
Redman, Barbara Klug *nursing educator*
Richardson, Ralph Herman *lawyer*
Robinson, Lester W. *airport executive*
Robitaille, Luc *hockey player*
Rogers, Hon Paulletto *researcher, writer*
Rogers, Richard Lee *educator*
†Rohm, Benita Jill *lawyer*
Rohr, Richard David *lawyer*
Rosen, Gerald Ellis *federal judge*
Rosenau, Pete *public relations executive*
Rozof, Phyllis Claire *lawyer*
Ryan, James Leo *federal judge*
Ryder, James Lee *missionary, community-based agency official*
Salter, Linda Lee *security officer*
Saxton, William Marvin *lawyer*
Scholler, Thomas Peter *lawyer, accountant*
Schreiber, Bertram Manuel *mathematics educator*
Schwartz, Alan E. *lawyer, director*
†Schweitzer, Peter *advertising agency executive*
Schwing, Mark David *artist*
Scott, John Edward Smith *lawyer*
Sedler, Robert Allen *law educator*
Segel, Mark Calvin *diagnostic radiologist*
Semanik, Anthony James *instructional technology supervisor*
Semple, Lloyd Ashby *lawyer*
Shaevsky, Mark *lawyer*
Shanahan, Brendan Frederick *hockey player*
Shannon, Margaret Anne *lawyer*
Shapiro, Michael Bruce *lawyer*
Shields, Anthony Frank *oncologist, hematologist*
†Shulman, Margaret Alex Rabinovich *lawyer, musician*
Shwayder, Tor Adam *dermatologist, pediatrician, musician*
Silverman, Mark *publisher*
Silverman, Norman Alan *cardiac surgeon*
Simon, Michael Richard *allergist, immunologist, internist*
Sims-McCallum, Rosalyn Patrice *pharmacist*
Sloan, Andrew Edward *neurosurgeon*
Slovis, Thomas Laurence *radiologist*
Small, Melvin *history educator*
Smiecinski-Salkowski, Alicia *genetic counselor*
†Smith, James Albert *lawyer*
Smith, John Francis, Jr., *automobile company executive*
Smith, Wilbur Lazar *radiologist, educator*
Smyntek, John Eugene, Jr., *editor*
Sokol, Robert James *obstetrician, gynecologist, educator*
†Soltanian-Zadeh, Hamid *research scientist, educator*
Spansky, Robert Alan *computer systems analyst, retired*
Sparrow, Herbert George, III, *lawyer, educator*
Spearman-Leach, Anthony Maurice Paul *public policy, communications, marketing and advertising executive*
†Spencer, William Thomas *lawyer*
†Spiller, Alan Clark *director, consultant*
Spyers-Duran, Peter *librarian, educator*
Stack, Steven John, Jr., *criminal justice educator*
Steinman, H. Robert *dean*
†Stern, Myles Steven *information technology educator, consultant*
†Stivale, Charles Joseph *French language and literature educator*
†Sullivan, Thomas Michael *lawyer*
Svoboda, Mary Beth *health physicist, environmental science educator*
Talpos, Gary B. *surgeon*
†Tarnacki, Duane L. *lawyer*
Taylor, Anna Diggs *judge*
Teagan, John Gerard *newspaper executive*
Teranes, Paul S. *county judge, mediator*
Thelen, Bruce Cyril *lawyer*
†Thomas, Russell Joseph, Jr., *lawyer*
Thoms, David Moore *lawyer*
Thurber, Peter Palms *lawyer*
†Tickner, Ellen Mindy *lawyer*
Timm, Roger K. *lawyer*
†Tobi, Martin *gastroenterologist, researcher*
Tolia, Vasundhara K. *pediatric gastroenterologist, educator*
Torpey, Scott Raymond *lawyer*
†Tran, Alison Ha *pharmacist, educator*
†Trapp, Daniel John *priest*
Treadwell, Marjorie Clarke *medical educator*
Trim, Donald Roy *consulting engineer*
Trix, Frances *linguistic anthropologist, consultant*
Tse, Harley Y. *immunologist, educator*
Valade, Alan Michael *lawyer*
Vander Heide, Richard Stuart *pathologist, educator, research scientist*
†Van Dyke, Daniel L. *geneticist*
Vigneron, Allen Henry *theology educator, rector, auxiliary bishop*
Volz, William Harry *law educator, administrator*
Voudoukis, Ignatios John *internist, cardiologist*
†Wadlington, Lorna Jackie Jones *school system administrator*
Wagoner, G. Richard, Jr., *automotive company executive*
Waldmeir, Peter Nielsen *journalist*
†Ward, George Edward *lawyer, law educator*
Washington, Lantz H. *small business owner*
Webb, Bobbie James *insurance broker*
Werba, Gabriel *public relations consultant*
†Wheater, Michelle Kurpakus *biologist, educator*
†White, Joseph B. *reporter*
Whitehouse, Fred Waite *endocrinologist, researcher*
Whitmer, Richard E. *insurance company executive*
Wiener, Joseph *pathologist*
Wise, John Augustus *lawyer, director*
Wittlinger, Timothy David *lawyer*
Woods, George Edward *judge*
†Wyrick, Jermaine Albert *lawyer*
Yin, Fang-Fang *medical physicist, educator*
†Yzerman, Steve *hockey player*
†Zalman, Marvin *law educator*
Zoubareff, Kathy Olga *administrative assistant*

Detroit
†Oliver, Jerry Alton *protective services official*

Dexter
†Hanamey, Rosemary T. *nursing educator*
Millman, Jode Susan *lawyer, writer*
Zazove, Philip *family practice physician*

Dowagiac
Gourley, Everett Haynie *educator*
Mulder, Patricia Marie *education educator*
Ott, C(larence) H(enry) *citizen ambassador, accounting educator*
†Sweet, Margaret Ellen *writer*

Duluth
Bower, John Richard Fenn *archaeologist, educator*

Durand
Cook, Bernadine Fern *book publisher, writer*

Eagle Harbor
Dawson, John Frederick *retired architect*

East Lansing
Abeles, Norman *psychologist, educator*
Abolins, Maris Arvids *physics researcher and educator*
Abramson, Paul Robert *political scientist, educator*
Allen, Bruce Templeton *economics educator*
Allen, William Barclay *political scientist, consultant, writer*
Andersland, Orlando Baldwin *civil engineering educator*
Anderson, David Daniel *retired humanities educator, writer, editor*
Anderton, James Franklin, IV, *real estate development executive*
Austin, Sam M. *physics educator*
Baillie, Richard Thomas *economist, educator*
Bandes, Susan Jane *museum director, educator*
Barlowe, Raleigh *economist, educator*
Bassett, Debra Lyn *lawyer, educator*
Beckmeyer, Henry Ernest *anesthesiologist, medical educator, pain management specialist*
Benenson, Walter *nuclear physics educator*
Bitensky, Susan Helen *law educator*
Blosser, Henry Gabriel *physicist*
Brody, Theodore Meyer *pharmacologist, educator*
Bromley, Stephen C. *zoology educator*
Brophy, Jere Edward *education educator, researcher*
Bukovac, Martin John *horticulturist, educator*
Burnett, Jean Bullard (Mrs. James R. Burnett) *biochemist, educator*
Busch, Lawrence Michael *sociologist, researcher*
Buskirk, Daniel D. *animal scientist, educator*
Byerrum, Richard Uglow *college dean*
Case, Eldon Darrel *materials science educator*
Chapin, Richard Earl *retired librarian*
Chen, Kun-Mu *electrical engineering educator*
†Crewe, Nancy Moe *psychologist and educator*
Cross, Aureal Theophilus *geology and botany educator*
Cutts, Charles Eugene *civil engineering educator*
Davis, Glenn Craig *psychiatrist*
Dennis, Frank George, Jr., *retired horticulture educator*
Dewhurst, Charles Kurt *museum director, cultural administrator, curator, folklorist, English language educator*
†Diedrich, William Frank *management consultant, speech professional*
D'Itri, Frank Michael *environmental research chemist*
Dow, Steven Benjamin *social studies educator*
Draper, Penny Kaye Pekrul *music educator, piano technician*
Dugan, LeRoy *chemist, educator*
Dye, James Louis *chemistry educator*
Ebell, Mark Herbert *physician, researcher*
†Fanizza, Michael Anthony *art educator*
Fernandez, Ramona Esther *adult education educator*
Finifter, Ada Weintraub *political scientist, educator*
Fisher, Alan Washburn *historian, educator*
Foss, John Frank *mechanical engineering educator*
Freedman, Eric *journalist, educator, writer*
Fromm, Paul Oliver *physiology educator*
Gass, Gertrude Zemon *psychologist, researcher*
Gelbke, Claus-Konrad *nuclear physics educator*
Gerhardt, Philipp *microbiologist, educator*
†Gift, David Ayres *academic administrator*
Goodman, Erik David *engineering educator*
Gottschalk, Alexander *radiologist, diagnostic radiology educator*
Greenberg, Bradley Sander *communications educator*
Hackel, Emanuel *science educator*
Harrison, Jeremy Thomas *dean, law educator*
Harrison, Michael Jay *physicist, educator*
Hilbert, Virginia Lois *computer consultant and training executive*
Honhart, Frederick Lewis, III, *academic director*
Ilgen, Daniel Richard *psychology educator*
†Izzo, Thomas *college basketball coach*
†Jackson-Elmoore, Cynthia *dean, educator*
Johnson, Clark Cumings *lawyer, educator*
Johnson, John Irwin, Jr., *neuroscientist*
Joseph, Raymond *lawyer*
Kalof, Linda Henry *sociologist, educator*
Kende, Hans Janos *plant physiology educator*
†King, Lonnie J. *dean*
Kirk, Edgar Lee *musician, educator*
Koo, Anthony Ying Chang *economist, educator*
Kreinin, Mordecha Eliahu *economics educator*
Krishnan, Ranjani *finance educator*
Kumar, Ashir *pediatrician, medical educator*
Ladenson, Mark Lawrence *economist, educator*
†La Ferle, Carrie *advertising executive, educator*
Lashbrooke, Elvin Carroll, Jr., *law educator, consultant*
Lenski, Richard Eimer *evolutionary biologist, educator*
Li, Tien-Yien *mathematics educator*
Liedholm, Carl Edward *economics educator*
Lloyd, John Raymond *mechanical engineering educator*

Whittaker, Jeanne Evans *former newspaper columnist*
Wilkinson, Warren Scripps *manufacturing company executive*

Grosse Pointe Farms
Allen, Lee Harrison *industrial consultant, wholesale company executive*
Axe, John Randolph *lawyer, financial executive*
Brucker, Wilber Marion *retired lawyer*
Christian, Edward Kieren *broadcasting station executive*
Couzens, Linda Lee Anderson *oncology nurse*
Dunlap, Connie Sue Zimmerman *real estate professional*
Kerns, Gertrude Yvonne *psychologist*
†Lada, Warren S. *communications executive*
Obolensky, Marilyn Wall (Mrs. Serge Obolensky) *metals company executive*
Surdam, Robert McClellan *retired banker*
†Thibodeau, Virginia Durbin *artist*
Valk, Robert Earl *corporate executive*
Weingart, Robert Paul *financial consultant*

Grosse Pointe Park
Blevins, William Edward *management consultant*
Centner, Charles William *lawyer, educator*
Elsila, David August *editor*
Harmon, Phyllis Darnell *mortgage banker*
Knapp, Mildred Florence *retired social worker*
Krebs, William Hoyt *company executive, industrial hygienist*
McIntyre, Anita Grace Jordan *lawyer*
Mogk, John Edward *law educator, association executive, consultant*
Pankin, Jayson Darryl *entrepreneur, biotechnologist, venture capitalist, e-mail system developer*

Grosse Pointe Shores
Caldwell, John Thomas, Jr., *communications executive*
LaHood, Mary Anne *real estate investor*

Grosse Pointe Woods
Cusmano, J. Joyce *public relations executive*
McWhirter, Glenna Suzanne (Nickie McWhirter) *retired newspaper columnist*
Pytell, Robert Henry *retired lawyer, former judge*
Sul, Yi Chul *neurologist*

Gwinn
Lasich, Vivian Esther Layne *secondary education educator*

Hamtramck
†Kaczmarek, Carla *lawyer*

Hancock
Puotinen, Arthur Edwin *college president, clergyman*
†Smith, Stephen Alan *secondary school educator*

Harbor Springs
Cappel, Constance *educational consultant, writer*
Ketcham, Warren Andrew *psychologist, educator*
Smith, Wayne Richard *lawyer*
Turner, Lester Nathan *lawyer, international trade consultant*

Harper Woods
Havrilcsak, Gregory Michael *history educator*

Harrison Township
McGregor, Theodore Anthony *chemical company executive*

Harrisville
Welch, James E. *artist*

Hartland
Ellis, Robert William *materials engineer, consultant*

Haslett
Hollenshead, Robert Earl *retired judge*
Hotaling, Robert Bachman *community planner, educator*
Warrington, Willard Glade *former university official*

Hastings
Adrounie, V. Harry *public health administrator, scientist, educator, environmentalist*
Jones, Kensinger *advertising executive*
Wright, Stephen Nathan *religious organization administrator*

Hickory Corners
Bristol, Norman *lawyer, arbitrator, former food company executive*
Lauff, George Howard *biologist*

Highland
Brown, Ray Kent *biochemist, physician, educator*
Bullard, Willis Clare, Jr., *lawyer*

Hillsdale
†Baron, Lee Ann *chemist, educator*
†Flaskerud-Rathmell, Susan Marie *musician, music educator*
†Grassl, Wolfgang *adult education educator*
Kline, Faith Elizabeth *college official*
†Knecht, Melissa *music educator, musician*
Wolfram, Gary Lee *economics educator, consultant*

Holland
Claar, Victor Vyron *economics educator*
Cook, James Ivan *clergyman, religion educator*
Franken, Darrell *counselor, writer, publisher*
†Haworth, Gerrard Wendell *office furniture manufacturing company executive*
Holmes, Jack Edward *political science educator*
Huttar, Charles Adolph *retired language educator*
Inghram, Mark Gordon *physicist, educator*
†Krasa, Robert *manufacturing executive*
Mc Gurk, James Henry *consultant company executive*
Mills, Charles Anthony *engineering company executive*
Murphy, Max Ray *lawyer*
Nieuwsma, Milton John *writer, journalist*
Nyenhuis, Jacob Eugene *college official*
Pannapacker, William Albert, III, *humanities educator*
Schieringa, Paul Kenneth *special education educator, entertainer*
Stynes, Stanley Kenneth *retired chemical engineer, educator*
†Swierenga, Robert *humanities educator, researcher*
Van Noord, Diane C. *artist, educator*
Van Voorst, Robert E. *theology educator, minister*
Van Wylen, Gordon John *former college president*
†Waltz, Jon Richard *lawyer, educator, author*
Williams, Donald Howard *chemist, educator, chemist, consultant*
Zuidema, George Dale *surgeon, educator*

Holly
Magnuson, Valerie *poet, artist, export consultant*
Stolpin, William Roger *artist, printmaker, retired engineer*

Holt
Garrison, Charles Eugene *retired automotive executive*
Henning, Sandra Jean *social worker*
Smith, Betty W. *librarian*
Wiltse, Richard Allan *association executive*

Houghton
Crittenden, John Charles *civil and environmental engineering educator*
Heckel, Richard Wayne *metallurgical engineering educator*
Huang, Eugene Yuching *civil engineer, educator*
Pelc, Karol Ignacy *engineering and technology management educator, researcher*
Tompkins, Curtis Johnston *academic administrator*
Utt, Glenn S., Jr., *motel investor, former biotech and pharmaceutical industry company executive*
White, Calvin Lamont *engineer*
Whitt, Laurie Anne *philosophy educator*

Houghton Lake
Marra, Samuel Patrick *retired pharmacist, small business owner*

Howell
†Cotton, Larry *ranching executive*
Heinel, Robert Steven *social services administrator*
Metz, Patricia Anne *school social worker*
†Parker, Robert Ernser *lawyer*
Rohrabacher, Janet Hammond *geneologist, archivist*
Wagoner, William Douglas *public administrator, urban/regional planner*
Watkins, Curtis Winthrop *artist*
Yanga, Ismael Duran *surgeon*

Huntington Woods
Gutmann, Joseph *art history educator*
Kirschner, Esther Green *social worker*
†Maxwell, Brenda J. *lawyer*

Inkster
†Bullock, Steven Carl *lawyer*

Interlochen
Masterson, Wendy Lynn *choreographer, dance educator, arts administrator*
Tacke, Eleanor *archivist*

Irons
Getty, Gerald Winkler *lawyer*

Ironwood
†Hopkins, Larry Michael *mathematics and computer science educator*

Ishpeming
Fitzgerald, Robert Hannon, Jr., *orthopedic surgeon*

Jackson
Brunner, James Edwin *lawyer*
Feldmann, Judith Gail *language professional, educator*
†Firestone, Richard Bartlett *lawyer*
Jacobs, Wendell Early, Jr., *lawyer*
Kelly, Robert Vincent, Jr., *metal company executive*
Kleiner, Elaine Laura *English literature educator*
Klingel, Patti Jean *health facility administrator*
Popp, Nathaniel *archbishop*
Silva Potts, Margarita *counseling administrator*
Straayer, Carole Kathleen *retired elementary education educator*
Trap, Jennifer Josephine *special education administrator*

Jenison
Kruse, Pamela Jean *lawyer*

Jerome
Dillon, Merton Lynn *historian, educator*

Johannesburg
Kropf, Richard William *priest, theologian*

Kalamazoo
†Aduroja, Amos Oladipo *healthcare educator, consultant*
Ahmad, Shah Mahmood *chemical engineer, consultant*
Angelo, Jim *construction company executive*
Badra, Robert George *theology studies educator, humanities educator*
Bailey, Judith Irene *university official, consultant*
Bauckham, John Henry *lawyer*
Bennett, Arlie Joyce *clinical social worker emeritus*
Blickle, Peter *German language and literature educator, novelist*
Breisach, Ernst A. *historian, educator*
†Brown, John Wilford *health products executive*
†Buchanan, Lewis Victor *research scientist*
Burns, James W. *education educator*
Bus, Roger Jay *lawyer*
Butler, Charles Francis *cardiac surgeon*
Carlson, Andrew Raymond *archivist*
Carver, Joan Willson *publishing executive, artist*
Carver, Norman Francis, Jr., *architect, photographer*
Chateauneuf, John Edward *chemistry educator, researcher*
Chou, Kuo-Chen *biophysical chemist*
†Cinabro, Robert Henry *lawyer*
Cody, Frank Joseph *secondary school educator*
Curry, John Patrick *insurance company executive, management consultant*
†DeChano, Lisa M *geographer, educator*
†Dietz, Thomas Anthony *curator, educator*
Dinculescu, Antonie *chemical engineer, scientist*
†Dirette, Diane Kay *occupational therapist, educator*
Duchamp, David James *retired pharmaceutical company executive, consultant*
Durham, Sidney Down *lawyer*
Dybek, Stuart *English educator, writer*
Edmondson, Keith Henry *retired chemical company executive*
Engelmann, Paul Victor *plastics engineering educator*
Enslen, Pamela Chapman *lawyer*
Enslen, Richard Alan *federal judge*
Fischell, Tim Alexander *cardiologist*
Fisher, George *gerontological educator*
Fredericks, Sharon Kay *nurse's aide*
†Freeberg, Edward Ronald *lawyer*
†Gershon, Richard A. *commmunications educator*
Gladstone, William Sheldon, Jr., *radiologist*
Gordon, Alice Jeannette Irwin *secondary and elementary education educator*
Gordon, Edgar George *retired lawyer*
Greenfield, John Charles *bio-organic chemist*
Grotzinger, Laurel Ann *librarian, educator*
Haenicke, Diether Hans *academic administrator emeritus, educator*
Hamilton, Diane Bronkema *nursing educator*
Hatch, Hazen van den Berg *lawyer*
Hilberry, Conrad Arthur *humanities educator, poet*
Hilboldt, James Sonnemann *lawyer, investment advisor*
Hoffman, Penelope Joan (Penny Hoffman) *adult nurse practitioner, administrator*
Hubbard, William Neill, Jr., *pharmaceutical company executive*
Hudson, Roy Davage *retired pharmaceutical company executive*
Jamison, Frank Raymond *independent video producer, retired communications educator*
Jones, Eugene Gordon *pharmaceutical company executive*
Jones, James Fleming, Jr., *academic administrator, Roman language and literature educator*
Jones, Leander Corbin *educator, media specialist*
Jones, Randall Marvin *chemist*
Kujawski, Daniel *science educator*
†Kupstas, Corrine Lynn *environmental director, chemical engineer*
Lander, Joyce Ann *nursing educator, medical/surgical nurse*
Lavery, J. Patrick *perinatologist*
†Law, Linda *physical education educator*
Lawrence, William Joseph, Jr., *retired corporate executive*
Lawson, Gary D. *audiology educator*
†Lewis, James Eldon, Jr., *education educator*
Light, Christopher Upjohn *writer, computer musician, photographer*
†Litynski, Daniel Mitchell *engineering educator, retired military officer*
Lowery, Joanne *writer, editor*
†Lubben, Craig Henry *lawyer*
Mangalaramanan, Sathya Prasad *mechanical engineer, researcher*
†Markin, David Robert *motor company executive*
Marshall, Vincent de Paul *industrial microbiologist, researcher*
Maurer, Edward Lance *chiropractor, radiologist*
Mc Allister, Lester Belden *economics educator*
Mingus, Matthew Scott *public administration educator*
Moe, James Burton *pharmaceutical company executive*
Norris, Richard Patrick *museum director, history educator*
†Nye, Jeffrey Scott *pharmaceutical executive, researcher*
Ortiz-Button, Olga *social worker*
†Ott, Jennifer Hubbell *education educator*
†Palmitessa, James R. *historian, educator*
Pérez-Stable, Maria Adelaida *librarian*
Perricone, Charles *former state legislator*
Petersen, Anne C.(Cheryl) *foundation administrator, educator*
†Pikcunas, Charles Richard *lawyer*
†Price, Kim Denise *counselor*
Ransford, Sherry *secondary education educator*
Ruoff, Cynthia Osowiec *foreign language educator*
†Saber, Alan A. *surgeon*
†Sampath, Arun *chemical engineer, consultant*
Scholfield, Arlene R. *social worker*
Selzer, Kenneth A. *neurologist, editor*
Sichel, Werner *economics educator*
†Spradling, Robert Ledford *music educator, conductor*
Stufflebeam, Daniel LeRoy *education educator*
Targowski, Andrew Stanislaw *computer information educator, consultant*
Taylor, Duncan Paul *research neuropharmacologist*
†Teagarden, Dirk Lowell *research scientist*
†VandenBussche, Heather Lynne *pharmacist*
Voshel, Elizabeth Harbeck *social worker, educator*
Walker, Kay S. *geropsychiatric nurse*
Weintraub, Jacob Michael *pediatrician*
Wijnberg, Marion Holley *social work educator*
Wilson, James Rodney *air equipment company executive*
†Yang, Li *computer scientist, educator*
Yoshida, Takashi *historian, researcher*

Kaleva
Lenz, Jeanne Ann *security professional*

Kalkaska
Batsakis, John George *pathology educator*

Keego Harbor
†Gee, Sharon Lynn *funeral director, educator*

Kentwood
Kelly, William Garrett *judge*
Yovich, Daniel John *educator*

Lake Angelus
Kresge, Bruce Anderson *retired physician*

Lake Ann
Kumjian, John Charles *musician, educator*

Lake Orion
Brewer, Judith Anne *special education educator, consultant*
†Leonard, Jacquelyn Ann *retired elementary school educator*

Lansing
†Arends, Herman Joseph *insurance company executive*
Baker, Frederick Milton, Jr., *lawyer*
Ballbach, Philip Thornton *political consultant, investor*
Barcia, James A. *state senator, former congressman*
Barnes, Carla Leddy *social worker, developmental psychologist*
Behrens, Ellen Elizabeth Cox *writer, counselor, educator*
Brennan, Thomas Emmett *lawyer*
Brewer, Mark Courtland *lawyer*
Brown, Nancy Field *editor*
Butcher, Amanda Kay *retired university administrator*
†Cannon, Patrick D. *federal offical, broadcaster*
Cavanagh, Michael Francis *state supreme court justice*
†Cherry, John D., Jr., *lieutenant governor*
Christian, Sandra Svec *retired state official*
†Cox, Mike *state attorney general*
Feight, Theodore J. *financial planner*
†Fiechtner, Justus John *rheumatologist, consultant*
Fink, Joseph Allen *lawyer*
Fitzgerald, John Warner *law educator*
Foster, Joe C., Jr., *lawyer*
Fox, Hugh Bernard, Jr., *writer, archaeologist*
Frisosky, Rosarita Marie *volunteer nurse*
Gallagher, Byron Patrick, Jr., *lawyer*
†Geckil, Ilhan Kubilay *economist, consultant*
†Glicksman, Elliot Boris *educator, lawyer*
Graham, Lester Lynn *radio journalist*
Granholm, Jennifer Mulhern *governor*
Harrison, Michael Gregory *judge*
Hills, Rusty *state official*
Johnson, Rick *state official*
†Johnson, Veronica Ann Wilkerson *information and government services director*
Kelley, Frank Joseph *lawyer, former state attorney general*
†Kissling, Paul Joseph *academic administrator, religious studies educator, minister*
Kluge, Len H. *director, actor, theater educator*
Kronzek, Charles Michael *lawyer*
Linder, Iris Kay *lawyer*
Lobenherz, William Ernest *container company/association executive, lawyer*
Loftus, Kay Douglas Colgan *social worker*
Marazita, Eleanor Marie Harmon *retired secondary education educator*
McKeague, David William *judge*
McKeague, Nancy Palmer *trade association executive*
Neiberg, Alan David *physician*
†Nsofor, Leslie Monagolum *food scientist, researcher*
Owens, Donald Stanley *judge*
Piveronus, Peter John, Jr., *education educator*
Porter, Karen Collins *non-profit administrator*
Posthumus, Richard Earl *former lieutenant governor, farmer*
Prout, Carolyn Ann *controller, personnel administrator*
Rogers, Mike *congressman*
Rooney, John Philip *law educator*
Sauer, Harold John *physician, educator*
Schott, Cheryl Suzanne *health educator*
Sharif, M. Alan *interventional cardiologist*
Shirtum, Earl Edward *retired civil engineer*
Sikkema, Kenneth R. *state legislator*
†Sinas, George Thomas *lawyer*
Spence, Howard Tee Devon *judge, arbitrator, lawyer, consultant, insurance executive, government official*
Stackable, Frederick Lawrence *lawyer*
†Stowers, Mark David *chemicals executive*
†Straus, Kathleen Nagler *education administrator, consultant*
†Styka, Ronald Joseph *lawyer*
Suhrheinrich, Richard Fred *federal judge*
Taylor, Clifford Woodworth *state supreme court justice*
Tucker, John Andrews *association executive*

GEOGRAPHICAL INDEX 5947 MICHIGAN

Vincent, Frederick Michael, Sr., *neurologist, educator*
Warren, Joseph Addison, III, *law and history educator*
Winder, Richard Earnest *legal foundation administrator, writer, consultant*

Lapeer
Parrish, Patrick Michael *music educator*
Spray, Pauline Etha Mellish *retired elementary educator, writer*
†Thomas, Robert Weston *lawyer*

Laurium
Pippenger, John Junior *fluid power engineer*

Lawrence
Fudge, Mary Ann *vocational school educator*

Lawton
Bowman, Jerry Wayne *artist, research scientist*

Leland
Hamelin, Paul Robert *pharmacist, pharmaceutical executive, consultant*
Small, Hamish *chemist*
Soutas-Little, Robert William *mechanical engineer, educator*

Lincoln Park
†Kissel, Kevin Karl *freelance/self-employed writer*
Russell, Harriet Shaw *social worker*
Zelenak, Edward Michael *lawyer, musician*

Linden
Tomaszewski, Kathleen Bernadette *social worker, educator*

Livonia
Borin, Jeffrey Nathan *real estate developer*
Chowdhury, Subir *business executive, author, researcher*
†Custer, Gerald Stockton *conductor*
†Fried, William C. *lawyer*
Gepford, Barbara Beebe *retired nutrition educator*
Gepford, William George *minister*
Guerriero, Carol Marie *librarian*
Haggard, Joan Claire *church musician, piano instructor, accompanist, adjudicator*
Hemminger, Allen Edward *retired insurance consultant*
†Hinsch, James Erwin *retired chemical engineer*
Hoffman, Barry Paul *lawyer*
Holtzman, Roberta Lee *French and Spanish language educator*
Levitt, Leon *business administration educator*
Maibach, Ben C., Jr., *service executive*
Schwartz, Randy Ken *mathematics educator*
Stamelos, Electra Georgia *artist*
Uicker, Joseph Bernard *retired engineering company executive*
Valerio, Michael Anthony *financial executive*
Woods, Edythe B. *psychology educator*

Lowell
Gerard, Donald Gordon *physician*
Jenkins, Debra Reid *artist*

Ludington
Denner, Melvin Walter *retired life sciences educator*
Puffer, Richard Judson *retired college chancellor*

Mackinac Island
Mc Cabe, John Charles, III, *writer*

Macomb
DeGiusti, Dominic Lawrence *medical science educator, academic administrator*
Farmakis, George Leonard *education educator*

Madison Heights
†Bertin, Leonard Gerard *graphics designer, artist*
Janke, Kenneth *investment consultant*
Kafarski, Mitchell I. *chemical processing company executive*
Koshy, Vettithara Cherian *chemistry educator, technical director and formulator*
Woodruff, Jane *sales executive*
Xia, Jiding *chemical engineering educator*

Mancelona
Whelan, Joseph L. *neurologist*

Manistee
Behring, Daniel William *educational and business professional, consultant*
Cooper, Kenneth Edward *artist, art educator*
Trussell, Charles Tait *columnist*

Maple City
Duff, James George *retired financial services executive*
Morris, Donald Arthur Adams *college president*
Ryant, Charles Joseph, Jr., *environment executive*

Marion
†Jager, Mark Alan *publishing executive, writer*

Marquette
†Brozzo, Shirley A. *language educator*
Burt, John Harris *bishop*
Camerius, James Walter *marketing educator, corporate researcher*
Carnahan, George Richard *business educator, consultant*
Chen, Cathleen *physician*
Curtis, Mark Allen *engineering educator, author, consultant*
Earle, Mary Margaret *marketing executive*
†Henderson, Roberta Marie *librarian, educator*
†Mahmood, Tallat *oncologist*
Manning, Robert Hendrick *media consultant*
Pesola, William Ernest *restaurant management executive*
Riipi, Linda Ruth *biology educator*
Saville, Kathleen Jo *instructional technologist*
Swaine, Howard Ralph *economist, educator, consultant*

Marshall
Davis, Henry Arnold *automotive company executive*
Garypie, Rudolph Renwick *library director*

Mason
†Dart, Kenneth *food container manufacturing executive*
Midgley, John W. *civil engineer, consultant*
Thayer, Bruce Allen *automotive executive, artist*
Toekes, Barna *chemical engineer, polymer consultant*
†Yoakam, Lynn Kelly *harpist, educator*

Mears
Binder, L. James *magazine editor, retired, journalist*

Melvindale
Saenz, Gilbert *computer programmer and analyst, poet*

Midland
†Adams, Thomas Walton *corrections official*
Barker, Nancy Lepard *university official*
Battle, Leonard Carroll *lawyer*
Black, Jacinth Baublitz *clinical social worker*
Bus, James Stanley *toxicologist*
Carson, Gordon Bloom *retired engineering executive*
Chao, Marshall *chemist*
Clarkson, William Morris *children's pastor*
Davidson, John Hunter *agriculturist*
Dorman, Linneaus Cuthbert *retired chemist*
Dreyfuss, Patricia *retired chemist, researcher*
†Gootee, Jane Marie *lawyer*
Hampton, Leroy *retired chemical company executive*
†Hazleton, Richard A. *chemicals executive*
Huntress, Betty Ann *retired small business owner, retired elementary school educator*
Leng, Douglas Ellis *chemical engineer, scientist*
Leng, Marguerite Lambert
†Lile, James Michael *pharmacist, educator*
Maneri, Remo R. *management consultant*
McCarty, Roger Leland *chemical company official*
Meister, Bernard John *chemical engineer*
Messing, Carol Sue *communications educator*
Nowak, Robert Michael *chemist*
Parker, Michael D. *chemicals executive*
Robbins, Lanny Arnold *chemical engineer*
Schmidt, William C. *chemical company executive*
Servinski, Sarah Jane (Sarah Jeroue) *language arts educator*
Snyder, Robert Lee *anesthesiologist*
So, Ying-Hung *chemistry researcher*
Stavropoulos, William S. *chemical executive*

Milan
Patton, Lisa Darlene *urban planner*

Milford
Oliveri, Eugene Alfred *gastroenterologist*

Monroe
Brodie, Catherine Anne *music educator*
Carlen, Sister Claudia *librarian, consultant*
†Carmody, Jennifer Lynn *librarian*
Lipford, Rocque Edward *lawyer, corporate executive*
Nowitzke, Gary Earl *investment company executive*
Nuechterlain, James Howard *music educator*

Montague
Hillman, Douglas Woodruff *retired judge*

Mount Clemens
†Farrell, John Brendan *lawyer*
Kolakowski, Diana Jean *county commissioner*
Robinson, Earl, Jr., *marketing and economic research executive, transportation executive, business educator, retired air force officer*

Mount Morris
Wooley, Geraldine Hamilton *writer, poet*

Mount Pleasant
Apter, Ronnie Susan *English educator, translator*
Born, James E. *art educator, sculptor*
Browne, William P. *political science educator*
Carlson, Charles Evans *university official*
Dietrich, Richard Vincent *geologist, educator*
Dunbar, Gary Leo *psychology educator*
Fornari, Marco *physicist*
Kirchner, Richard Jay *retired physical education educator*
†Kulawik, Krzysztof Andrzej *language educator*
Lee, Carl *statistician, educator*
Lenker, Susan S. *mathematician, educator, consultant*
Lynch, John Joseph *lawyer*
Novitski, Charles Edward *biology educator*
Orlik, Christina Bear *music educator*
Petrick, Michael Joseph *journalism educator*
Smallwood, Carol *librarian, writer*
Steffel, Susan Elizabeth *English language and literature educator*
Traines, Rose Wunderbaum *sculptor, educator*

Muskegon
†Blystone, John B. *manufacturing executive*
Briggs, John Mancel, III, *lawyer*
†Briggs-Erickson, Carol Ann *librarian*
Cirona, Jane Callahan *investment company executive*
DeLong, Donald R. *accountant*
Fauri, Eric Joseph *lawyer*
Gundy-Reed, Frances Darnell *marketing executive*
Jamieson, T. John *writer, English language educator*
Kara, Paul Mark *corporate executive*
†McKendry, John H., Jr., *lawyer, educator*
†McKitrick, James Thomas *retired retail executive*
Nehra, Gerald Peter *lawyer*
Roy, Paul Emile, Jr., *county official*
Sciba, JoAnn *social worker*
Swartz, Wilma Jeanne *music educator*
Van Leuven, Robert Joseph *lawyer*

Nashville
Pash, Teresa A. *piano teacher, performer*

Naubinway
Beaudoin, Robert Lawrence *small business owner*
Smith, Richard Ernest *retired insurance company executive*

Negaunee
Friggens, Thomas George *state official, historian*

New Buffalo
Stevens, William J. *lawyer*

New Haven
Shaw, Charles Rusanda *retired government investigator*

Niles
Gibbs, Denis Laurel *radiologist*
Hamburg, Roger Phillip *retired political science and public affairs educator*
Kim, Choong-Man Joseph *radiologist*
Stone, Donald P. *lawyer*

North Branch
Stevenson, James Laraway *communications engineer, consulting*

North Muskegon
Heyen, Beatrice J. *psychotherapist*

Northport
Schultz, Richard Carlton *plastic surgeon*
Scripps, Douglas Jerry *music educator, conductor, director*
Thomas, Philip Stanley *economist, educator*

Northville
Abbasi, Tariq Afzal *psychiatrist, educator*
Bohm, Henry Victor *physicist*
Clemens, Michael Terrence *furniture manufacturing representative*
Curley, Juanita Dale *pilot, writer*
Davis, Lawrence Edward *church official*
Hansen, Jean Marie *math and computer educator*
Hariri, V. M. *arbitrator, mediator, lawyer, educator*
Leavitt, Martin Jack *lawyer*

Novi
Abramowitz, Harriet C. *social worker*
Barr, David John *retired art educator*
Bricker, Gerald Wayne *marketing executive*
Chow, Chi-Ming *retired mathematics educator*
Crane, Patricia Sue *probation services administrator, social worker*
Gurnack, Dean Hilton *artist*
Kinsey, Charles John *industrial auctioneer, consultant, cattle breeder, farmer*
Maniscalco, Joseph *artist, educator*
Ragatzki, Paul A. *internist, administrator, educator*
Sobczak, Judy Marie *clinical psychologist*

Oak Park
Kaplan, Randy Kaye *podiatrist*
Novick, Marvin *investment company executive, former automotive supplier executive, accountant*
Piper, Annette Cleone *social services administrator, researcher*
Smith, Nelson David *artist educator*

Okemos
Barton, Judith Marie *lawyer, lobbyist*
Belyea, Karlene Boyes *professional association executive*
Berkman, Claire Fleet *psychologist*
†Brenneise, Harvey Ray *library director*
Dowley, Joel Edward *manufacturing executive, lawyer*
Giacoletto, Lawrence Joseph *electronics engineering educator, researcher, consultant*
Grimshaw, David Norman *physician, educator*
Hutchinson, Craig Lewis *internist*
King, John Arthur *zoologist, educator*
Klunzinger, Thomas Edward *writer, actor, director*
Luecke, Eleanor Virginia Rohrbacher *civic volunteer*
Montgomery, James Huey *state government administrator, consultant*
Ristow, George Edward *neurologist, educator*
Schneider, Karen Bush *lawyer, educator*
Solo, Robert Alexander *economist, educator*
Tuttle, Mary Celia Putnam *social worker, retired*

Olivet
Hubbel, Michael Robert *insurance company executive, educator*
†Humphrey, Roger Gavin *music educator*

Orchard Lake
Lichtwardt, Harry Edward *physician, surgeon*
Rauwerdink, William Jay *accountant*

Oshtemo
Arnold, Nancy Kay *writer*

Owosso
Bentley, Margaret Ann *librarian*
Uptigrove, Kenneth R. *library administrator*

Pentwater
†Noffke, Frank Edward *educational planner, writer, educator*

Petersburg
Hicks, George William *mechanical engineer, automotive engineer*

Petoskey
Deery, Hugh Gunner, II, *physician*
†Meengs, William Lloyd *cardiologist*
Switzer, Carolyn Joan *artist, educator*
Vernon, Doris Schaller *retired writer*
Winter, Kenneth Michael *newspaper editor, publisher*

Pigeon
†Maust, Joseph J. *agricultural products supplier*

Pinckney
Davis, Robert Leach *retired government official, consultant*
Duquet, Suzanne Frances *special education educator*
McNamara, Ann Dowd *medical technologist*

Pleasant Ridge
Krabbenhoft, Kenneth Lester *radiologist, educator*
Rizzo, Donald Charles *biology educator*
Sneed, Marie Eleanor Wilkey *retired secondary education educator*

Plymouth
Berry, Charlene Helen *librarian, musician*
Champa, John Joseph *telecommunications engineer, consultant*
deBear, Richard Stephen *library planning consultant*
Heitman, Susan Marie *artist*
Koroi, Mark Michael *lawyer*
Lou, Zheng (David) *technical specialist*
†Moore-Viculin, Charlotte Anne *artist, musician*
Morgan, Donald Crane *lawyer*
Stewart, Katherine Hewitt *advanced practice nurse*
Vlcek, Donald Joseph, Jr., *food distribution company executive, consultant, business author, executive coach*
Winzenreid, James Ernest *lawyer, entrepreneur*
Zilincik, Jerome Matthew *financial analyst*

Pontiac
Andrews, Steven Nicholas *judge*
†Brychtova, Jaroslava *sculptor*
Cohassey, John Fredrick *writer*
Decker, Peter William *academic administrator*
Hampton, Philip Michael *consulting engineering company executive*
Howard, Desmond Kevin *professional football player*
Jack, Dixie Lynn *software consultant, social worker*
Love, Sharon Irene *elementary education educator*
Mahone, Barbara Jean *automotive company executive*
Mitchell, Sheryl Lynn *analyst, educator*
Pierson, William George *lawyer*
†Sanders, Barry *retired football player*
Silbergleit, Allen *surgeon, researcher, medical educator*
Stryker, James William *automotive executive, former military officer*

Port Austin
Davis, Frederick Athie *management executive*

Port Huron
Hoffacker, Charles Edward *minister, writer*
Keyes, Allen E. *retired judge*
Miller, Theresa L. *library director*
Moss, Carl Arthur *psychologist*
Rowark, Maureen *fine arts photographer*
Wu, Harry Pao-Tung *retired librarian*

Port Sanilac
Birdsall, Arthur Anthony *chemical executive*

Portage
Chodos, Dale David Jerome *physician, consumer advocate*
†Dasgupta, Rathindra *metallurgical engineer*
†Dobler, Janis Dolores *small business owner*
Elliott, George Algimon *pathologist, toxicologist, veterinarian*
Lee, Edward L. *retired bishop*
Maury, Nancy Jane (Nancy Jane Gooch) *realtor, mortgage company executive*
Merrow, Douglas Alan *lawyer*
Seely, Robert Eugene *management consultant*
Zhang, Charles C. *financial planner*

Portland
Rainey, Derek Rexton *educator, sculptor*
Rich, Joseph John *accountant*

Powers
Kleikamp, Beverly *poet, writer, publisher*

Prescott
†Brandau, Christie Pearson *librarian*

Presque Isle
Kinney, Mark Baldwin *educator*

Rapid City
Overbeck, Gene Edward *retired airline executive, lawyer*
Ring, Ronald Herman *lawyer*

Redford
Aubertin, Madeline Katherine *retired nursing educator, medical/surgical nurse, mental health services professional*
Karpinski, Huberta Elaine *library trustee*

Reed City
Devendorf, Louise Marie *promoter, writer*

Republic
Wixtrom, Donald Joseph *translator*

Richmond
Wood, Virginia Ann *educator*
†Yaek, Megan Anne *language educator*

Riverdale
Kirby, Kent Bruce *artist, educator*

Riverview
Thompson, LaVerne Elizabeth Thomas *college official*

Rochester
†Chapman, Sara Eleanor *French historian*
†Gallagher, Edward Arthur *retired academic administrator, real estate developer*
Giordano, Joseph, Jr., *financial planner, investment consulting firm executive*
Gouldey, Glenn Charles *manufacturing company executive*
†Kubicek, Paul J. *political scientist, educator*
Kutlich, Anna *writer*
Lindemann, Charles Benard *cell biologist, researcher*
†Lu, Lunjin *science educator*
Nesbary, Dale K. *social sciences educator*
Ovshinsky, Stanford Robert *physicist, inventor, energy executive, information company executive*
Packard, Sandra Podolin *education educator, consultant*
Rossio, Richard Dominic *automobile company executive*
†Russi, Gary D. *academic administrator*
†Yang, Lianxiang *optical engineer, educator*

Rochester Hills
Badalament, Robert Anthony *urologic oncologist*
Bartunek, James Scott *psychiatrist*
Diehl, Richard Paul *lawyer*
Fritzsche, Hellmut *physics educator*
Meldrum, Richard James *electrical engineer*
Mills, Helene Audrey *education educator*
Minton, Henry Lee *psychology educator*
Pfister, Karl Anton *industrial company executive*
Romero, Josefino Tabernilla *nurse anesthetist*
Shah, Jayprakash Balvantrai *civil engineer*
†Stevenson, Gregory Matthew *religious studies educator*
Szetela, Rebecca E. Coombe *engineer*
†Thoma, August John *music educator*
Unakar, Nalin Jayantilal *biological sciences educator*

Rockford
Knape, Herbert Fritz *business executive*
Pappas, William John *principal, educator*
Teliczan, Casimir Joseph *secondary school educator*

Romulus
Yussouff, Mohammed *retired physicist, educator*

Roscommon
†Carton, Gary L. *performing arts association administrator*
Gagnier, Joseph C. *artist*
Mainprize, Donald Charles *minister, writer*

Rose Township
†Fleming, Kathryn Alice *automotive executive*

Royal Oak
Akmakjian, Alan Paul *English language, literature and creative writing educator*
Al-Sarraf, Muhyi *internist, oncologist*
Andrzejak, Michael Richard *insurance agent*
Bernstein, Jay *pathologist, researcher, educator*
Bohy, Ric *magazine editor, consultant, broadcast commentator*
Comstock, Christine Holaday *obstetrician, gynecologist, radiologist, educator*
Cook, Noel Robert *manufacturing company executive*
Corwin, Vera-Anne Versfelt *small business owner, consultant*
Dworkin, Howard Jerry *nuclear medicine physician, educator*
Franklin, Barry Allan *health facility administrator, physiologist*
Kagan, Ron *zoological park administrator*
LaBan, Myron Miles *physician, administrator*
Malik, Ghaus Muhammad *neurosurgeon*
†Maurus, Marc Allen *writer, publisher*
McCarroll, Kathleen Ann *radiologist, educator*
Pricer, Wayne Francis *counseling consultant*
Proctor, Conrad Arnold *physician*
Ryan, Jack *physician, retired hospital corporation executive*
Shetty, Sugandh Dasu *urological surgeon, researcher*
Smith, John William Hugh *civil engineer*
Stanalajczo, Greg Charles *computer and technology company executive*

Saginaw
Chaffee, Paul Charles *newspaper editor*
Cline, Thomas William *real estate leasing company executive, management consultant*
Evans, Harold Edward *banker*
Ferlinz, Jack *cardiologist, medical educator*
Gaffney, Karen Elizabeth *clinical social worker*
†Gallagher, Edward John, II, *lawyer*
Houshiar, Bobbie Kay *language arts educator*
†Jackson, Darnell *judge*
Killingbeck, Janice Lynelle (Mrs. Victor Lee Killingbeck) *journalist*
†Leppert-Largent, Anna M. *church musician*
Manning, John Warren, III, *retired surgeon, medical educator*
Martin, Walter *retired lawyer*
Mastromarco, Victor Joseph, Jr., *lawyer*
McGraw, Patrick John *judge*
Mielke, Susan Kay *mental health nurse*
Ondish, Andrea *museum educator*
Othersen-Khalifa, Cheryl Lee *insurance agent, realtor*
Scharffe, William Granville *academic administrator, educator*
Shackelford, Martin Robert *social worker*
Sudhoff, Virginia Rae *retired elementary education educator*
Wierzbicki, Jacek Gabriel *physicist, researcher*
Zanot, Craig Allen *lawyer*

Saint Clair
Kocan, Ronald Robert *secondary school educator*

Saint Clair Shores
Danielson, Gary R. *lawyer*
Elliott, Luke Alexander *family practice physician*
Field, Stephen Ira *dermatologist, educator*
Glancy, Alfred Robinson, III, *retired public utility company executive*
Hausner, John Herman *judge*
Kavadas-Pappas, Iphigenia Katherine *preschool administrator, educator, consultant*
Neal-Vittiglio, Cynthia Karen *clinical psychologist*
Ryan, Harold Martin *judge*
Shine, Neal James *journalism educator, former newspaper editor, publisher*
Smith, Frank Earl *retired association executive*
†Valetti, Leota May *artist*
Woodford, Arthur MacKinnon *library director, historian*

Saint Joseph
Akber, Syed Farooq *medical physicist*
King, George Raleigh *retired manufacturing executive*
Maley, Wayne Allen *engineering consultant*
Shirkey, William Dan *writer*
Wallace, Jon Robert *mortgage company executive, marketing professional*

Saint Louis
Novak, Joseph Anthony *law librarian*

Salem
Riddering, Donald Lee *retired language educator, historian*

Saline
Cornell, Richard Garth *biostatistics educator*
Hansen, Janice Elizabeth *psychologist*
Low, Louise Anderson *consulting company executive*

Sanford
Wilmot, Thomas Ray *medical entomologist, educator*

Saranac
†Herbrucks, Stephen *food products executive*

Saugatuck
Blair, John Raymond *educational psychology educator*

Sault Sainte Marie
†Fields, Polly Stevens *educator, writer, researcher*
Johnson, Gary Robert *political scientist*

Schoolcraft
†Foley, John Francis *retired judge, lawyer*

Sears
†McCullough, Willard G. *retired biochemist*

Shelby Township
Fillbrook, Thomas George *telephone company executive*
Heremans, Joseph Pierre *physicist*
Jacovides, Linos Jacovou *electrical engineer, researcher*
Nagy, Louis Leonard *engineering executive, researcher*

Shepherd
Herman, Mark Norman *translator*

Sidney
Rice, Sharon Jean *secondary school educator*

Sodus
†Handy, Virginia Mae *writer*

South Bend
†Demmon, Terri Lynn *educational consultant, educator*

South Branch
Savard, Christine Elizabeth *music educator*

South Haven
LaRocque, Linda Lou *interior designer, educator, playwright*
Nequist, John Leonard *retired food company executive*
†Stone, Jeannine Gail *retired writer, retired poet*
Waxman, Sheldon Robert *lawyer*

Southfield
Abbatt, Candyce Ewing *lawyer*
Adelman, Martin Jerome *law educator*
Amladi, Prasad Ganesh *management consulting executive, health care consultant, researcher*
Antone, Nahil Peter *lawyer, civil engineer*
Barnett, Marilyn *advertising agency executive*
Ben, Manuel *chemist*
Bennett, Helen *social worker*
†Bindschadler, David E. *mathematician, department chairman, application developer*
Birdsong, Emil Ardell *clinical psychologist*
Bledsoe, Laurita *small business owner, publisher*
Boyce, Daniel Hobbs *financial planning company executive*
Caponigro, Jeffrey Ralph *public relations counselor*
Chambers, Charles MacKay *university president*
Cocozzoli, Gary Richard *library director*
Dawson, Dennis Ray *lawyer, manufacturing company executive*
Denes, Michel Janet *physical therapist, rehabilitation consultant*
Fennell, Christine Elizabeth *healthcare system executive*
†Fieger, Geoffrey Nels *lawyer*
Findlay, Annette Marie *information systems executive*
Forrest, Robert Edwin *lawyer*
Gleichman, John Alan *safety and loss control executive*
Gordon, Arnold Mark *lawyer*
Graves, Ray Reynolds *retired judge*
Gregory, Karl Dwight *economist, educator, consultant*
Hammel, Ernest Martin *medical educator, academic administrator*
Hanisko, John-Cyril Patrick *electronics engineer, physicist*
Hartman-Abramson, Ilene *adult education educator*
Hotelling, Harold *law and economics educator*
Howard, Michael Joseph *communications executive, real estate developer*
Ibrahim, Ibrahim N. *bishop*
Jacobs, John E. *lawyer*
†Johnson, David (David Makenna) *writer*
†Kalter, Alan *advertising agency executive*
Kaplow, Robert David *lawyer*
Koch, Albert Acheson *management consultant*
Lee, James Edward, Jr., *educational consultant*
†Leib, Jeffrey M. *lawyer*
†Maibach, Ben C., III, *construction company executive*
Malviya, Vinay Kumar *obstetrician-gynecologist*
Martin, Marcella Edric *retired community health nurse*
McClow, Roger James *labor lawyer*
McKeen, Alexander C. *retired engineering executive, foundation administrator*
†Miller, Sheldon Lee *lawyer*
Morganroth, Mayer *lawyer*
†Naini, Mansoor Ghazinour *cardiologist*
Newman, Steven E. *neurologist*
O'Hara, John Paul, III, *orthopaedic surgeon*
Perez-Cruet, Mick Jorge *neurological surgeon, educator*
Ponitz, John Allan *lawyer*
Portnoy, Lynn Ann *fashion retailer*
Primo, Joan Erwina *retail and real estate consulting business owner*
Ragan, Stephen C. *academic administrator*
Ritchie, Alexander Buchan *lawyer*
Rossiter, Robert E. *interior auto parts manufacturing executive*
Satovsky, Abraham *lawyer*
Sedler, Rozanne Friedlander *social worker, educator*
Selis, Stuart L. *financial consultant, underwriter*
Shields, Robert Emmet *merchant banker, lawyer*
Shpiece, Michael Ronald *lawyer, educator*
Silber, Albert J. *lawyer*
Spitzer, A. Robert *physician, electrical engineer*
Sullivan, Robert Emmet, Jr., *lawyer*
Thimotheose, Kadakampallil George *psychologist*
Thomas, Judy Janet *reporter, health services professional*
Thurswell, Gerald Elliott *lawyer*
Toll, Sheldon Samuel *lawyer*
†Turner, Donald Allen *retired lawyer*
Wagner, Bruce Stanley *marketing professional*
Wagner, Muriel Ginsberg *nutrition therapist*
Weiner, Karen Colby (Karen Lynn Colby) *psychologist, lawyer*
Willingham, Edward Bacon, Jr., *ecumenical minister, administrator*
†Wisne, Lawrence A. *metal products executive*
Zobl, Eldred Gregory *cardiologist*
†Zubroff, Leonard Saul *surgeon*

Southgate
Kohn, Julieanne *travel agent*
Torok, Margaret Louise *insurance company executive*

Sparta
Bomhof, Robyn *artist, educator*
†Miller, Barbara Jean *health facility administrator*

Spring Arbor
Buratovich, Michael Anthony *geneticist*
Thompson, Stanley B. *church administrator*

Spring Lake
†Bussard, Janice Wingeier *retired educator, inventor*

Standish
Lamson, Evonne Viola *therapist, health care administrator, consultant, pastor, Christian educator*

Stanton
Winchell, George William *curriculum and technology educator*

Sterling Heights
Bajor, James Henry *musician, jazz pianist*
Burke, Thomas Joseph *civil engineer*
Campbell, Terence Warren *forensic psychologist*
Hammond-Kominsky, Cynthia Cecelia *optometrist*
Rosenfeld, Martin Jerome *healthcare executive, educator*

Sturgis
Hair, Robert Eugene *editor, writer, historian*
Reiff, James Stanley *osteopathic physician, addictions, psychiatric, surgeon*

Suttons Bay
Whitney, William Chowning *retired banker, financial consultant*

Swartz Creek
Russell, Charles Harry *music educator, restaurant manager*

Taylor
Downham, Thomas Fletcher *dermatologist*
†Drutchas, Geoffrey Gilbert *minister, historian, writer*
Leekley, John Robert *lawyer*
Manoogian, Richard Alexander *manufacturing company executive*
†Rosowski, Robert Bernard *manufacturing company executive*

Tecumseh
Herrick, Todd W. *manufacturing company executive*

Three Rivers
Boyer, Nicodemus Elijah *chemist, consultant*
Warnock, William Reid *lawyer*

Traverse City
Buehler, Thomas Lee *lawyer, educator*
Clous, James M. *electrical equipment company executive, engineer*
†Faulmann, Roger R. *music educator*
Hornberger, Lee *lawyer*
Keilitz, Gene Martin *retired association administrator*
†Parsons, John Thoren *corporate executive, inventor*
†Press, James Gordon *humanities educator*
Prusick, Vincent Roger *orthopaedic surgeon*
Quandt, Joseph Edward *lawyer, educator*
Supanich, Barbara Ann *family practice physician*
Taylor, Donald Arthur *marketing educator*
†Tobin, Patrick John *dermatologist*
VanderKolk, Mary DeDecker *nursing educator*
Weaver, Elizabeth A. *state supreme court justice*
Zimmerman, Paul Albert *retired college president, minister*

Trenton
Beebe, Grace Ann *retired special education educator*
Go, Benedict Anthony *internist*
†Tang, Cyrus *investment company executive*
Wukovits, John Francis *secondary school educator, writer*

Troy
Acton, David L(awrence) *automobile company executive*
Adderley, Terence E. *corporate executive*
Alber, Phillip George *lawyer*
Alterman, Irwin Michael *lawyer*
Arking, Lucille Musser *nurse, epidemiologist, nursing administrator*
†Barton, Stanley L. *ophthalmologist, consultant*
Battenberg, J. T., III, *automotive company executive*
Branigan, Thomas Patrick *lawyer*
Brody, Jay Howard *lawyer*
Buschmann, Siegfried *manufacturing executive*
Cantor, Bernard Jack *lawyer*
Corace, Joseph Russell *automotive executive*
Dawes, Alan S. *automotive company executive*
†Day, Julian C. *retail executive*
Dillon, Joseph Francis *lawyer*
Gelder, John William *lawyer*
Golusin, Millard R. *obstetrician and gynecologist*
Haron, David Lawrence *lawyer*
Harrison, Christine Delane *company executive*
Haryadi, Satish Govindaram *structural engineer, researcher*
†Hill, Richard A. *advertising executive*
Hintzen, Erich Heinz *lawyer*
Hunter, Lorie Ann *women's health nurse*
Janak, Peter Harold *automotive company executive*
Kruse, John Alphonse *lawyer*
†Lorencz, Mary *media relations administrator*
Maierle, Bette Jean *director nursery school*
Marshall, John Elbert, III, *foundation executive*
Martin, Raymond Bruce *plumbing equipment manufacturing company executive*
May, Alan Alfred *lawyer*
†McGlynn, Joseph Michael *lawyer*
Misra, Dwijen Cristobal *surgeon*
Moore, Oliver Semon, III, *publishing executive, consultant*
Morgan, Michael Vincent *lawyer*
Nolte, Henry R., Jr., *lawyer, former automobile company executive*
Okun, Maury *dance company executive*
Pulkkinen, Jyrki Tuomo Juhani *structural engineer*
Rappleye, Richard Kent *financial executive, consultant, educator*
†Reed, Derryl L. *marketing director*
Schafer, Sharon Marie *anesthesiologist*
†Schmidt, Michael Francis *lawyer*
Serafyn, Alexander Jaroslav *retired automotive executive*
Sharf, Stephan *automotive company executive*
Sloan, Hugh Walter, Jr., *automotive executive*
Strome, Stephen *distribution company executive*
Taber, Frances Kathryn *geriatrics nurse, administrator*
Thurber, John Alexander *lawyer*
†Webster, Robert Byron *lawyer*
Wittbrodt, Frederick Joseph, Jr., *automotive designer*
Yost, Larry D. *automotive executive*
†Zetu, Dan *statistician, educator*

Union Pier
Howland, Bette *writer*

University Center
†Dykhuizen, C. Jeffrey *child development psychologist, educator*

GEOGRAPHICAL INDEX 5949 MINNESOTA

Gilbertson, Eric Raymond *academic administrator, lawyer*
Hall, David McKenzie *business and management educator*
Hill, Alan Gordon *sociologist, educator*
Hoerneman, Calvin A., Jr., *economics educator*
Jezierski, John Vincent *historian, educator*
Pelzer, Charles Francis *human molecular geneticist, biologist, educator, research scientist*

Utica
Miller, Aileen Etta Martha *medical association administrator, nutritionist*

Wakefield
†Kendall, Gregory R. *art educator*

Walled Lake
Connelly, Thomas Joseph *lawyer*
Gillespie, J. Martin *sales and distribution company executive*
Kaldobsky, Phoebus Reeveman *retired transportation engineer, retired management consultant*
Peal, Christopher John *educational administrator*
Seglund, Bruce Richard *lawyer*
†Williams, Sam B. *engineering executive*

Warren
Bley, Ann *program analyst, business manager*
Cheng, Yang-Tse *research scientist, materials scientist, physicist*
Cutter, Jeffrey S. *secondary education educator, music educator*
Deak, Charles Karol *chemist*
†Dunker, Alan Melvin *physical chemist, researcher*
Herbst, Jan Francis *physicist, researcher*
Hopp, Anthony James *advertising agency executive*
Johnson, Leonard Gustave *research mathematician, consultant*
Lett, Philip W. *defense consultant*
†Li, Jingshan *electrical engineer, researcher*
Miko, Mary V. *personnel director, manufacturing executive*
Nefske, Donald Joseph *engineer*
†Papasavva, Stella *research engineer*
Quay, Gregory Harrison *retired secondary school educator*
Rottman, Michael *physician*
Schock, Martin Irving *oncologist*
Wisz, Joseph A., Jr., *management consultant*
Woehrlen, Arthur Edward, Jr., *dentist*
†Xia, George Z. *statistician, educator*
†Yang, Jihui *research scientist*
Zadoorian, Michael Craig *writer*

Washington
Chatterley, James Philip *retired automotive development engineer*
Gothard, Donald Lee *retired auto company executive*

Waterford
Anderson, Francile Mary *secondary education educator*
Houston, E. James, Jr., *bank officer, consultant*
Laing, James Thomas *retired not-for-profit developer*
Land, Robert Donald *business consultant*

Wayne
Carpenter, Arthur Lloyd *education educator*
Cobbs, Alfred Leon *German language educator*

Wellston
Spain, Frederick William *secondary school educator, writer*

West Bloomfield
Barr, Martin *health care and higher education administrator*
Bess, Judith Grewell *retired computer services executive, educator*
Brin, David *writer, astronomer*
†Considine, John Joseph *advertising executive*
Darke, Richard Francis *lawyer*
†Gelman, Sandor M. *lawyer*
Gullen, Christopher Roy *lawyer*
Harwood, Julius J. *metallurgist, educator*
Hepner, Michael Jules *allergist*
Jones, Lewis Arnold, Jr., *physician, radiologist, consultant*
Joseph, Ramon Rafael *physician, educator*
Lewis, Harold Allen *childcare company executive*
Mamut, Mary Catherine *retired entrepreneur*
Meyers, Gerald Carl *educator, author, expert witness, consultant*
Miller, Nancy Ellen *computer consultant*
Myers, Kenneth Ellis *hospital administrator*
Robbins, Norman Nelson *lawyer*
Sarwer-Foner, Gerald Jacob *physician, educator*
Sawyer, Howard Jerome *physician*
Schechter, Steven Hart *neurologist*
Seidman, Michael David *surgeon, educator*
Simpson, Robert Lee *university official, biology educator*
†Stern, Guy *German language and literature educator, writer*
Tobin, Bruce Howard *lawyer*
Williamson, Marilyn Lammert *English educator, university administrator*

Westland
Coates, Dianne Kay *social worker*
Mullinix, Barbara Jean *special services director*

White Cloud
De Haan-Puls, Joyce Elaine *sales account representative, educator*

White Lake
Clyburn, Luther Linn *real estate broker, appraiser, ship captain*

Whitehall
Sirotko, Theodore Francis *priest, retired military officer*

Williamsburg
Harlan, John Marshall *construction company executive*

Williamston
Johnson, Tom Milroy *academic dean, medical educator, physician*

Wixom
Sugiyama, Toru Tom *automotive executive*

Woodhaven
Kim, Hyo Sook *anesthesiologist*

Wyandotte
Aguirre, Antonio Azanes, Jr., *physician*
Aslam, Syed *chemist, research*
Dunn, Gloria Jean *artist*

Ypsilanti
Barnes, James Milton *physics and astronomy educator*
Barr, John Monte *lawyer*
Bishop, J. Joe *social studies educator*
Boone, Morell Douglas *information and communications technology educator*
Brown-Chappell, Betty L. *social worker, educator*
†Cassar, George Harris *historian, educator*
Caswell, Herbert Hall, Jr., *retired biology educator*
Cere, Ronald Carl *languages educator, consultant, researcher*
†Chamberlain, Kathleen Patricia *humanities educator, writer*
†Coykendall, Abby Lynn *literature educator*
Evans, Gary Lee *communications educator and consultant*
Farah, Badie Naiem *computer information systems educator, consultant*
Friedman, Monroe *psychologist, educator*
Gaertner, Kenneth C. *poet, educator*
†Gordon, Anitra *librarian*
Griffin, Carolyn Leigh *English educator, genealogist*
Gwaltney, Thomas Marion *education educator, writer*
Hafter, Daryl M. *educator*
Hildebrandt, H(enry) M(ark) *pediatrician*
Janardan, Konanur Gundappasetty *mathematics and statistics educator*
†Kiesbye, Stefan *writer, educator*
†Lottie, Adrian Jerome *public policy educator, consultant*
O'Connor, Bernard Joseph *priest*
Rainville, Alice Johannah *dietitian*
Robbins, Jerry Hal *educational administration educator*
†Stevens, Lizbeth Jane *special education educator, researcher*
†Thomas, Laurence W. *language educator*
Tucker, William Daniel *English educator*
Warner, Jo F. *mathematics educator*
Weinstein, Jay A. *social science educator, researcher*

Zeeland
LaGrand, Kenneth *technology products company executive*
Mast, Mae Jerene *nurse*

MINNESOTA

Ada
Sillerud, Arlen Roger *retired educator*

Aitkin
Morton, Craig Richard *real estate investor*
Prickett, Gordon Odin *mining, mineral and energy engineer*

Albert Lea
Rechtzigel, Sue Marie (Suzanne Rechtzigel) *child care center executive*
Schwab, Grace S. *state legislator*
Sturtz, William Rosenberg *retired judge*

Alexandria
Hultstrand, Donald Maynard *bishop*

Anoka
†Erickson, Phillip Arthur *lawyer, corporate executive*
Hicken, Jeffrey Price *lawyer*
Sliefert, Paula Rhea *manufacturing company executive*
Ward, Bart James *investment executive*

Apple Valley
Becker, Bruce Warren *music educator*
Brown, Francis William *chemist, consultant*
Kettle, Sally Anne *consulting company executive, educator*
Knutson, David Lee *state legislator, lawyer*

Appleton
Wilson, Orpha Hildred *writer*

Austin
Alcorn, Wallace Arthur *minister, writer*
Budd, Jim *communications manager*
Holman, Ralph Theodore *biochemistry and nutrition educator*
†Johnson, Joel W. *food products executive*
Morgan, Robert Ashton *minister, ethics and world religions educator*
Rioux, Pierre August *psychiatrist*
Schmid, Harald Heinrich Otto *biochemistry educator, academic director*
Schneider, Mahlon C. *lawyer*

Bagley
Ragan, Stephen T. *music educator*

Bayport
Bernick, Alan E. *lawyer, accountant*
†Garofalo, Donald R. *window manufacturing executive*

Bemidji
Bradley, Terrance Lee *retired music educator*
Bridston, Paul Joseph *strategic consultant*
Forseth, William J. *retired education educator*
Kief, Paul Allan *lawyer*
Logan, P. Bradley *music educator, church musician*
Martinson, Ida Marie *nursing educator, nurse, physiologist*
†Rogers, Patricia Louise *education educator, consultant*
†Wettstein, Shannon Leigh *music educator*
Woodke, Robert Allen *lawyer*

Benson
Wilcox, Donald Alan *lawyer*

Biwabik
Anderson, Davin Charles *business representative, labor consultant*

Bloomington
Allen, Mary Louise Hook *secondary education educator*
†Bekrenev, Anatoliy *physicist*
Boedigheimer, Robert David *lawyer*
Broeker, John Milton *lawyer*
Brokke, Catherine Juliet *mission executive*
†Carpel, Emmett Franklin *ophthalmologist, consultant*
Grinnell, Joseph Fox *lawyer*
†Jensen, Richard Allen *mathematician, educator*
Johnson, Leslie Carole *editor, publisher*
McDill, Thomas Allison *minister*
Miller, Kevin Robert *employee benefit consultant*
Neff, Fred Leonard *lawyer*
Nichols, Donna Mardell *nurse anesthetist*
†Norris, William C. *retired computer systems executive*
Pust, Ladislav *physicist, researcher*
Smith, Henry Charles, III, *symphony orchestra conductor*
Taylor, Susan S. *communications executive*

Blue Earth
Ellingsen, Michael O. *music educator, theater educator*

Brainerd
McTernan, Ann Cibuzar *adult nurse practitioner*
†Russell, Maxine *poet, writer*
Samuelson, Donald B. *former state legislator*
Wannamaker, Mary Ruth *music educator*

Brooklyn Park
†Okigwe, JaJa A. *marketing professional, consultant*

Buffalo
Kiernan, Thomas Edward *lawyer*

Burnsville
Hight, Tim Everett *company executive, consultant*
Lai, Juey Hong *chemical engineer*
Lakin, James Dennis *allergist, immunologist, director*
Ringquist, Lynn Anne *micrographics company executive*

Caledonia
Eppelheimer, Linda Louise *software educator*

Cambridge
Lahr, John William *optometrist*

Canby
Larson, Gary Arthur *farmer, financial consultant*

Champlin
†Lyons, Steven Gerard *music educator*

Chanhassen
†Martin, Brett Stephan *editor, writer*
Peterson, Steven A. *lawyer*
Prince, (Prince Rogers Nelson) *musician, actor*
Severson, Roger Allan *bank executive*
Thorson, John Martin, Jr., *electrical engineer, consultant*

Chaska
†Burke, Steven Francis *organization executive*
Casselman, Barry *political correspondent, nonprofit administrator, author*
Cohen, Cheryl Diane Durda *communications executive*
Kwak, Seung-Keon *research scientist*
†Spargo, Carolyn Marie *language educator, music educator*

Chatfield
†Opat, Matthew John *lawyer*

Chisago City
Miller, Robert Carl *retired library director*

Chisholm
Peterson, Marjorie *former mayor*

Circle Pines
†Barott, Pat Robert *broadcast technician*
Davis, Richard Carlton *rehabilitation services administrator*

Cloquet
Ellison, David Charles *special education educator*

Coleraine
Iwasaki, Iwao *engineering educator*

Collegeville
Haile, Getatchew *retired archivist, educator*
Joyce, Robert E. *philosopher, educator*
Raverty, Thomas Donald (Aaron Raverty) *anthropologist, monk*
†Rolfson, Helen C. *theology studies educator, translator*
Tegeder, Vincent George *historian, educator, archivist*
†Wolfe, Regina Wentzel *religious studies educator*

Coon Rapids
Bordner, Patricia Anne *insurance agent, writer*
Carlson, Linda Marie *language arts educator, consultant*

Cottage Grove
Glazebrook, Rita Susan *nursing educator*
Hudnut, Robert Kilborne *clergyman, author*

Crookston
†Balke, Victor H. *bishop*
Houske, Sister Virginia *music educator, organist*
Ring, K(arin) Elisabeth *physician assistant, registered nurse*
Shol, Kim Durand *accountant, computer programmer*

Crosslake
Beaupre, Elaine Marcia Kenow *retired chamber of commerce executive*
†Larson, Paul Michael *city planner*

Crystal
Reske, Steven David *lawyer, writer*

Cushing
Perfetti, Robert Nickolas *educational consultant*

Dayton
†Ostroot, Kathleen Ann *editor, writer, adult nurse practitioner*

Detroit Lakes
†Eginton, Charles Theodore *surgeon, educator*
Johansson, John Thomas *retired science educator*

Duluth
Aufderheide, Arthur Carl *pathologist*
Bailey, Charles William *management consultant, researcher*
Bowman, Roger Manwaring *real estate executive*
Burns, Richard Ramsey *lawyer*
Chee, Cheng-Khee *artist, educator*
Dillon, Herb Lester *critical care and emergency room nurse*
Eckman, Matthew Jay *physiatrist, educator*
Eisenberg, Richard Martin *pharmacology educator*
Engebretson, Andrew *lawyer*
Feroz, Ehsan Habib *accounting educator, researcher, writer*
Fetzer, James Henry *philosopher, educator*
Fields, Allen *artistic director*
Gallinger, Lois Mae *medical technologist*
Hanson, Curtis James *music educator, composer*
Hartley, Alan Haselton *lexicographer, stevedoring administrator*
Hazel, Stewart Jerome *physician*
Heaney, Gerald William *federal judge*
Heller, Lois Jane *physiologist, educator, researcher*
Hoffman, Richard George *psychologist*
Johnson, Arthur Gilbert *microbiology educator*
Latto, Lewis M. *broadcasting company executive*
Madich, Bernadine Marie Hoff *savings and loan executive*
McKee, David Charles *physician, neurologist*
Nelson, Dennis Lee *finance educator*
Nys, John Nikki *lawyer*
Ojard, Bruce Allen *photographer, educator*
†Osborn, Vincent Owen *music educator, musician*
Pearce, Donald Joslin *retired librarian*
Rapp, George Robert (Rip Rapp) *geology and archeology educator*
Salmela, David Daniel *architect*
Schroeder, Fred Erich Harald *humanities educator*
Sebastian, James Albert *obstetrician, gynecologist, educator*
Stender, Bruce William *business executive*
Stevenson, Jean Myers *education educator*
Stoddard, Patricia Florence Coulter *retired psychologist*
Tezla, Albert *English educator*
Thibodeau, Thomas Raymond *lawyer*
†Vasquez, Ramon Francisco *music educator*
Whiteman, Richard Frank *architect*
Whitmyer, Robert Wayne *soil scientist, consultant, researcher*
Whitney, Gwin Richard *brick distribution company executive*
Zhdankin, Viktor Vladimirovich *chemistry educator*
Ziegler, Rick *dean, science educator*

Eagan
Clemens, T. Pat *manufacturing company executive*
Miller, Alan M. *editor, educator, writer*
Todd, John Joseph *lawyer*

Eden Prairie
Anderson, Bradbury H. *retail executive*
Arthur, Lindsay Grier *retired judge, author, editor*
Carlson, Kenneth George *data processing executive*
Cohen, Robert *medical device manufacturing and marketing executive*
Culpepper, Daunte *football player*
De Bono, Luella Elizabeth *music educator*
DeMann, Michael Marcus *psychologist*

Emison, James Wade *petroleum company executive*
†Green, Dennis *professional football coach*
Henningsen, Peter, Jr., *diversified industry executive*
Higgins, Robert Arthur *electrical engineer, educator, consultant*
Knotek, Robert Frank *management consultant, educator*
†Knous, Pamela K. *wholesale distribution executive*
McCombs, Billy Joe (Red McCombs) *professional football team executive*
Moss, Randy *professional football player*
Nilles, John Michael *lawyer*
†Noddle, Jeffrey *retail and food distribution executive*
Petersen, Maureen Jeanette Miller *management information consultant, former nurse*
Schulze, Richard M. *retail electronics company executive*
†Verdoorn, Sid *food service executive*
Vincelli, Patrick Thomas *human resources specialist*
†Wiehoff, John P. *trucking executive*

Edina
Ashley, James Patrick *lawyer*
Bisping, Bruce Henry *photojournalist*
†Brooks, William James, III, *lawyer*
Brown, Charles Eugene *retired electronics company executive*
Brown, Laurence David *retired bishop*
Burbank, John Thorn *cleaning industry executive*
Burdick, Lou Brum *public relations executive*
Burk, Robert S. *lawyer*
Christensen, Nadia Margaret *writer, translator, editor, educator*
Clifford, Christine Karen *speech professional, writer*
DiGiovanni, Larry Joseph *human resources executive, small business owner*
Dubes, Michael John *retired insurance company executive*
Emmerich, Karol Denise *foundation executive, daylily hybridizer, former retail executive*
Froemming, Herbert Dean *retired retail executive*
Frys, Russell N. *obstetrician-gynecologist*
Gottesman, Irving Isadore *psychology educator*
Hollinbeck, Ethel Lindell *sculptor*
Jones-Gromacki, Lisa Dawn *health facility administrator*
Justman, Richard Allen *pediatrician*
Meyer, Warren George *vocational educator*
Polsfuss, Craig Lyle *executive coach and leadership specialist, psychologist, social worker*
Prince, Robb Lincoln *manufacturing company executive*
Putnam, Frederick Warren, Jr., *bishop*
†Rosenblum, Ava F. *sociologist, educator*
Sampson, John Eugene *consulting company executive*
Sandy, Lewis Gordon *physician, healthcare executive*
Schroeder, Albert John *retired pediatrician*
Schwarzrock, Shirley Pratt *writer, lecturer, educator*
Shadley, Robert D. *retired army officer*
Steinberg, Michael *music critic, educator*
Stryk, Robert Anthony *retired software engineer*
Tagatz, George Elmo *retired obstetrician, gynecologist, educator*
Taylor, Scott Maxfield *educator*
Wilder, Walter Llewellyn *allergist, immunologist, pediatrician*

Elk River
Goss, Cynthia Lee *tax specialist*
McClure, Alvin Bruce *technical consultant*
Sandusky, Christine Ann *English language educator*

Ely
Swenson, L. Anne *publisher*

Elysian
Thayer, Edna Louise *medical facility administrator, nurse*

Erskine
Moe, Roger Deane *former state legislator, secondary education educator*

Excelsior
Beeler, Donald Daryl *retired retail executive*
Bilka, Paul Joseph *retired physician*
Carlson, Roger Allan *retired manufacturing executive, accountant*
Fenske, Jerald Allan *minister*
Henke, Janice Carine *educational software developer and marketer*
Parker, Robert Chauncey Humphrey *clergyman, publishing executive, psychic*

Fairmont
†Fowler, Chuck *former state legislator*
†Rosen, Thomas J. *food and agricultural products executive*

Farmington
Wurdeman, Lew Edward *internet consultant*

Fergus Falls
Bigwood, Robert William *lawyer*
†Lundeen, David F. *lawyer*
MacFarlane, John Charles *utility company executive*
Overgaard, Robert Milton *retired religious organization administrator*

Finlayson
†Luoma, Judy *ranching executive*

Forest Lake
Marchese, Ronald Thomas *ancient history and archaeology educator*

Fort Ripley
Scott, Ivan Carl *historian, educator*

Frazee
Haugen, Troy Marlin *music educator*
Ulmer, James Howard *potter*

Fridley
Larson, Marilyn J. *retired elementary music educator*
Savelkoul, Donald Charles *retired lawyer*
Vlodaver, Zeev A. *cardiologist*

Glencoe
Beneke, Millie Stong *civic worker, author*

Glenwood
Olson, Nancy Ann *artist, educator*

Golden Valley
Leppik, Margaret White *municipal official*
Nager, Elizabeth Eileen *clinical social worker*
Savitt, Steven Lee *computer scientist*

Goodridge
†Hanson, Norma Lee *farmer*

Grand Marais
Kreitlow, Burton William *retired adult education educator*
Napadensky, Hyla Sarane *engineering consultant*

Grand Rapids
Crane, Faye *small business owner*
Jensen, Michael Wayne *writer*

Hackensack
†Marquart, Petra A. *training consultant*

Hallock
Hane, Jeffrey W. *lawyer*
Malm, Roger Charles *lawyer*

Harmony
Webster, Jeffrey Leon *graphic designer*

Hastings
Avent, Sharon L. Hoffman *manufacturing company executive*
Blackie, Spencer David *physical therapist, administrator*

Hibbing
Baldwin, Jan Linse *family practice physician*
Freeman, Linda Marie *consultant and technical writing company executive*

Hopkins
†Hoard, Heidi Marie *lawyer*
Hunter, Donald Forrest *lawyer*
Young, Margaret Labash *librarian, information consultant, editor*
Zins, Martha Lee *elementary education educator, media specialist*

Hugo
†Flannery, James Patrick *lawyer*

Hutchinson
†Pasche, Steven Frederick *secondary school educator, football coach*
Yira, Markus Clarence *lawyer*

Inver Grove Heights
Johnson, John D. *grain company executive*
Koenig, Robert August *clergyman, educator*
†Vogel, Steven Norman *music educator*
Wetli, Peggy Marie *performing company executive*

Jackson
McConnell, Timothy Irvin *voice educator, gymnastics coach*

Kenyon
Jacobson, Lloyd Eldred *retired dentist*
Peterson, Franklin Delano *lawyer*

Lake Elmo
Schultz, Clarence John *minister*
Tomljanovich, Esther M. *state supreme court justice*
Vivona, Daniel Nicholas *chemist*

Lakeland
Helstedt, Gladys Mardell *vocational education educator*

Lakeville
Anderson, Erik W.L. *web designer*
Setterholm, Jeffrey Miles *systems engineer*

Lauderdale
Resch, Joseph Anthony *neurologist*

Le Sueur
†Yang, Mengyan *research scientist*

Litchfield
†Huselid, Boyd Lynn *secondary school educator*

Little Canada
†Hardman, James Charles *lawyer, motor carrier executive*

Long Lake
Hofkin, Ann Ginsburgh *photographer, poet*
Lowthian, Petrena *academic administrator*

Madelia
Lucek, Donald Walter *surgeon*

Madison
Husby, Donald Evans *engineering company executive*

Mahtomedi
Brainerd, Richard Charles *human resources executive, consultant, educator*
†Pontious, Robert Wayne *music educator*

Mankato
Descy, Don Edmond *library media technology educator, writer, editor*
Dumke, Melvin Philip *dentist*
Friend, Donald Agar *geographer, geomorphologist, educator*
Gage, Fred Kelton *lawyer*
Hopkins, Layne Victor *computer science educator*
Huot, Rachel Irene *biomedical educator, research scientist, physician*
Hustoles, Mary Jo *elementary education educator*
Janavaras, Basil John *business educator, consultant*
†Janc, John J. *language educator*
†Larsson, Donald Foss *literature educator*
Manahan, James Hinchon *lawyer*
Nickerson, James Findley *retired educator*
Nickerson, Ronald George *recreation and parks educator*
Orvick, George Myron *church denomination executive, minister*
†Purscell, Keith William *minister*
Ries, Charles William *lawyer*
†Schreier, Bradley *finance company executive*
†Shellum, Renee Elise *audiologist, education educator*
Slocum, Fred *political scientist, educator*
Taylor, Glen A. *printing, direct mail and technology company executive, professional sports team executive*

Maple Grove
†Alexander, Donald L. *theologian, educator, minister*
Manthei, Robin Dickey *project coordinator*
McCally, John Frank *healthcare executive, writer*
Prins, LaVonne Kay *programmer analyst*
Shmidov, Anna *music educator, piano teacher*

Maple Lake
Haack, John Scott *special education educator, historian*

Mapleton
†Ek, Jon Merrill *music educator*
John, Hugo Herman *natural resources educator*

Maplewood
Beck, Bruce Lennart *lawyer*
†Veal, Ruffin, III, *information technology executive, county official*

Marcell
Aldrich, Richard John *agronomist, educator*

Marine On Saint Croix
Gavin, Robert Michael, Jr., *education consultant*
†Hoke, George Peabody *lawyer*

Marshall
Danahar, David C. *academic administrator, historian, educator*
†Pippin, M. Lenny *food products executive*
†Schwan, Alfred *food products executive*

Melrose
Hammarsten, James Francis *internist, educator*
Larson, Michael Len *newspaper editor, hospital administrator*

Mendota Heights
Frechette, Peter Loren *dental products executive*

Milaca
Wig, Robert Curtis *retired music educator, conductor*

Minneapolis
Aanerud, Melvin Bernard *state agency administrator*
Abi-Ghanem, Georges Victor *engineer, scientist*
Ackerman, Eugene *biophysics educator*
Ackerman, F. Kenneth, Jr., *health facility administrator*
Adams, John Stephen *geography educator*
Adlis, Susan Annette *biostatistician*
†Agler, Brian *professional basketball coach*
Agyenkwah, Kennedy Seth *communications executive*
Alton, Ann Leslie *judge, lawyer, educator*
Amdahl, Douglas Kenneth *retired state supreme court justice*
Anderson, Alan Marshall *lawyer*
Anderson, Eric Scott *lawyer*
Anderson, John Edward *mechanical engineering educator*
Anderson, Ron *advertising executive*
†Anderson, Tim *airport terminal executive*
Aris, Rutherford *applied mathematician, educator*
†Arnold, Douglas Norman *mathematician*
Asp, William George *librarian*
Atwood, John Brian *dean*
Avella, Joseph Ralph *university executive*
†Bachman, Ralph Walter *lawyer*
Bae, Seongtae *electrical engineer*
Baker, John Stevenson (Michael Dyregrov) *writer*
Bakken, Earl Elmer *electrical engineer, bioengineering company executive*
Bancroft, Ann E. *polar explorer*
Barnard, Allen Donald *lawyer*
Barnhill, Howard Eugene *insurance company executive*
Bashiri, Iraj *Central Asian studies educator*
†Battle, Willa Lee Grant *clergywoman, educational administrator*
Bednar, R. Craig *magazine and book publisher*
Benson, Donald Erick *holding company executive*
Berens, William Joseph *lawyer*
Berg, Stanton Oneal *firearms and ballistics consultant*
Berg, Thomas Kenneth *lawyer*
Bergerson, David Raymond *lawyer*
Berryman, Robert Glen *accounting educator, consultant*
Billups, Chauncey *professional basketball player*
Bingham, Christopher *statistics educator*
Bix, Brian *law educator*
Blackburn, Henry Webster, Jr., *retired physician*
Bodas, Margie Ruth *lawyer*
Boelter, Philip Floyd *real estate company officer, mortgage company executive*
Bolan, Richard Stuart *urban planner, educator, researcher*
†Bonneville, Katherine Ann *human resources specialist, consultant*
Borger, John Philip *lawyer*
Bormaster, Lisa Kay *publisher*
Boubelik, Henry Fredrick, Jr., *retired travel company executive*
Bouchard, Thomas Joseph, Jr., *psychology educator, researcher*
Boudreau, Robert James *nuclear medicine physician, researcher*
Bowie, Norman Ernest *university official, educator*
Brasket, Curt Justin *systems analyst, chess player*
Breimayer, Joseph Frederick *patent lawyer*
Bress, Michael E. *retired lawyer*
Brink, Charles Patrick *lawyer*
Brink, David Ryrie *lawyer*
Bromelkamp, David John *investment officer*
†Brooks, William Fern, Jr., *lawyer*
†Brosky, Mary Elizabeth *dental educator, dentist*
Brown, David Mitchell *physician, educator, dean*
Browne, Donald Roger *speech communication educator*
Bruner, Philip Lane *lawyer*
Brunetti, Wayne H. *utility company executive*
†Brunetti, Wayne Henry *utilities executive*
†Buchwald, Henry *surgeon, educator, researcher*
Budd, Elaine *social worker*
Buggey, Lesley JoAnne *education educator, consultant*
Buratti, Dennis P. *lawyer*
Burchell, Howard Bertram *retired physician, educator*
Burns, Robert Arthur *lawyer*
Burton, Charles Victor *physician, surgeon, inventor*
Busdicker, Gordon G. *retired lawyer*
†Bushara, Khalafalla O *neurologist*
Campbell, James Robert *retired bank executive*
Campbell, Karlyn Kohrs *speech and communication educator*
Carlson, Arne Helge *former governor*
Carlson, Thomas David *lawyer*
†Cerra, Frank Bernard *dean*
†Chamberlain, James Robert *lawyer*
Chandy, Rajesh K. *business educator*
Chavers, Blanche Marie *pediatrician, educator, researcher*
Chester, Priscilla (Perci Chester) *artist, educator*
Chipman, John Somerset *economist, educator*
Christensen, Robert Paul *lawyer*
Christiansen, Jay David *lawyer*
Clary, Bradley G. *lawyer, educator*
Clayton, Thomas Swoverland *English educator*
Clemence, Roger Davidson *landscape architect, educator*
†Cline, Richard Ryan *education educator*
†Coetzee, Johannes Christiaan *orthopedic surgeon*
Cohen, Earl Harding *lawyer*
Cohn, Jay N. *cardiologist, educator*
Cole, Phillip Allen *lawyer*
†Collins, Arthur D., Jr., *medical products executive*
Comstock, Rebecca Ann *lawyer*
†Conn, Gordon Brainard, Jr., *lawyer*
†Cooper, William Allen *banking executive*
Cope, Lewis *journalist*
†Cornelissen, Germaine *physicist, educator*
Corwin, Gregg Marlowe *lawyer*
Coskran, Kathleen Anne *principal*
†Coult, Nicholas Ashton *mathematician, educator*
Countryman, James Nelson *English language educator*
Courtney, Eugene Whitmal *computer company executive*
Cowles, John, Jr., *publisher, women's sports promoter*
Craig, James Lynn *physician*
Crosby, Jacqueline Garton *newspaper editor, journalist*
Crosby, Thomas Manville, Jr., *lawyer*
Cussler, Edward Lansing, Jr., *chemical engineer, educator*
Dahl, Gerald LuVern *psychotherapist, educator*
Dale, John Sorensen *investment company executive, portfolio manager*
D'Aquila, Barbara Jean *lawyer*
†d'Audiffret, Alexandre Christophe *surgeon, researcher, medical educator*
Davis, Howard Ted *engineering educator*
Davis, Michael J. *judge*
Devgun, Dharminder Singh *lawyer*
Dietzen, Christopher J. *lawyer*
DiGangi, Frank Edward *academic administrator*
Dillon, Helen Kaye *obstetrics staff nurse*
Doepke, Katherine Louise Guldberg *retired music educator*
†Domino, Constance Mae *genetics researcher*
†Doroschak, John Z. *dentist, consultant*
Doty, David Singleton *federal judge*
†Drucker, Christine Marie *lawyer*
Duncan, Richard Alan *lawyer*
†Dunlap, William DeWayne, Jr., *advertising agency executive*
Durdahl, Carol Lavaun *psychiatric nurse*
Dworkin, Martin *microbiologist, educator*
Dykstra, Dennis Dale *physiatrist*
Dyrud, Amos Oliver *minister, educator*
Ebeling, Brian Terry *family physician*
Eck, George Gregory *lawyer*

GEOGRAPHICAL INDEX 5951 MINNESOTA

Eckberg, E. Daniel *secondary education educator*
Eckland, Jeff Howard *lawyer*
Eickhoff, John R. (Jack Eickhoff) *business executive*
Eisenberg, Jay Lynn *marketing research professional*
†Eisenberg, Jonathan Lee *lawyer*
Eitingon, Daniel Benjamin *insurance company executive, consultant*
Elm, Dawn Rae *business educator*
†Engebretson, Mark Jerome *science educator, researcher*
Erhart, John Joseph *lawyer*
Erickson, Gerald Meyer *classical studies educator*
†Erickson, Ronald A. *retail executive*
Erickson, W(alter) Bruce *business and economics educator, entrepreneur*
Erstad, Leon Robert *lawyer*
Eyberg, Donald Theodore, Jr., *architect*
Farah, Caesar Elie *Middle Eastern and Islamic studies educator*
Faricy, John Hartnett, Jr., *lawyer*
Faricy, Richard Thomas *architect*
†Fauth, John J. *venture capitalist*
Fawcett, Marie Ann Formanek (Mrs. Roscoe Kent Fawcett) *civic leader*
†Feldman, Nancy Jane *health organization executive*
Felker, William H. (B. C. Stuvinski) *filmmaker, videomaker*
Fergus, Patricia Marguerita *English language educator emeritus, writer, editor*
Fetler, Paul *retired composer*
Fiedler, Robert Max *management consultant*
Findorff, Robert Lewis *retired air filtration equipment company executive*
Fine, Bob *lawyer, real estate developer*
†Fine, Pam *newspaper editor*
Fine, William Irwin *real estate developer*
Finzen, Bruce Arthur *lawyer*
Firchow, Evelyn Scherabon *German language and literature educator, writer*
Firchow, Peter Edgerly *language professional, educator, author*
Fisch, Robert Otto *medical educator*
Flanagan, Barbara *journalist*
Fleezanis, Jorja Kay *violinist, educator*
Fletcher, Edward Abraham *engineering educator*
Flom, Gerald Trossen *lawyer*
†Forneris, Jeanne M. *lawyer*
Forrest, Bradley Albert *lawyer*
Frank, Kerry Dean *psychology educator, consultant*
†Franz, Marion J. *dietician, consultant*
Freeman, Todd Ira *lawyer*
Freese, Richard Bradley *health care executive*
French, John Dwyer *lawyer*
†Friederichs, Norman Paul *lawyer*
Gage, Edwin C., III, (Skip Gage) *travel and marketing services executive*
Gagnon, Craig William *lawyer*
Gajl-Peczalska, Kazimiera J. *retired surgical pathologist, pathology educator*
Galambos, Theodore Victor *civil engineer, educator*
Gallagher, Gerald Raphael *venture capitalist*
†Gardebring, Sandra S. *academic administrator*
Gardenhire, Ronald Clyde *professional athletics manager*
Garfield, Joan Barbara *statistics educator*
Garnett, Kevin *professional basketball player*
Garon, Philip Stephen *lawyer*
Garton, Thomas William *lawyer*
Genia, James Michael *lawyer*
George, William Wallace *manufacturing company executive*
Gerberich, Susan Goodwin *epidemiologist, educator*
Gerdner, Linda Ann *nursing researcher, educator*
Gill, Richard Lawrence *lawyer*
Gockel, John Raymond *construction executive*
Goldberg, Luella Gross *corporation executive*
†Goldberger, Robert D. *food products company executive*
Goldman, Allen Marshall *physics educator*
Goldner, John Darrol *retired pharmacist*
Goldstein, Richard Jay *mechanical engineer, educator*
Goodman, Elizabeth Ann *lawyer*
Gordon, Corey Lee *lawyer*
†Gordon, John Bennett *lawyer*
Gorham, Eville *ecologist, biogeochemist*
Gorlin, Robert James *medical educator, educator*
Gottschalk, Stephen Elmer *lawyer*
Graham, William Franklin (William Franklin Graham) *evangelist*
Grant, David James William *pharmacy educator*
Greener, Ralph Bertram *lawyer*
Greenfield, Lee *state legislator*
Griffith, G. Larry *lawyer*
†Griffith, Sima Lynn *investment banker, consultant*
Grundhofer, Jerry A. *bank executive*
Grundhofer, John F. *banking executive*
Gudeman, Stephen Frederick *anthropology educator*
Gudmundson, Barbara Rohrke *ecologist*
†Guillaume, Germaine Cornelissen *chronobiologist, researcher*
Gullickson, Glenn, Jr., *physician, educator*
Gulliver, John Stephen *civil engineering educator, consultant*
†Guo, Meiwen *structural engineer*
Haase, Ashley Thomson *microbiology educator, researcher*
†Hackley, David Kenneth *lawyer*
Hagglund, Clarance Edward *lawyer, publishing company owner*
Hagstrom, Richard Michael *lawyer*
Hale, Roger Loucks *manufacturing company executive*
Halley, James Woods *physics educator*
Hallman, Gary L. *photographer, educator*
Halvorson, George Charles *health care insurance company executive*
Hamel, William John *church administrator, minister*
Hamermesh, Morton *physicist, educator*
Hamiel, Jeff *airport executive*
†Hand, Mary Jane *artist*
Hanson, Arthur Stuart *physician, consultant*
Hanson, Bruce Eugene *lawyer*
Hanson, Kent Bryan *lawyer*
Harper, Donald Victor *retired transportation and logistics educator*
†Harper, Patricia Nelsen *psychiatrist*
Harp-Jirschele, Mary *communications executive*
†Hart, Buster Clarence *lawyer*
Hauch, Valerie Catherine *historian, educator*
†Hays, Thomas S. *medical educator, medical researcher*
Hayward, Edward Joseph *lawyer*
†Heffelfinger, Thomas Backer *lawyer*
Heiberg, Robert Alan *lawyer*
Hendrixson, Peter S. *lawyer*
Henson, Robert Frank *lawyer*
Herbison, Priscilla Joan *public policy and law educator, consultant*
Herzog, Charles A. *cardiologist, researcher*
Hill, Gary D. *journalist*
Hillstrom, Thomas Peter *engineering executive*
Hippee, William H., Jr., *lawyer*
†Hirsch, Gordon *British literature educator*
Hobbins, Robert Leo *lawyer*
Hoch, Gary W. *lawyer*
Hoffmann, Thomas Russell *business management educator*
Hogenkamp, Henricus Petrus Cornelis *biochemistry researcher, biochemistry educator*
Holen, Norman Dean *art educator, artist*
Holmes, Thomas J. *economist, educator*
Holt, Robert Theodore *political scientist, dean, educator*
Hom, David Brian *surgeon*
Homolka, Daniel Michael *lawyer*
†Horsager, Kent *brokerage house executive*
†Houe, Poul *education educator*
Howland, Joan Sidney *law librarian, law educator*
Huang, Victor Tsangmin *food scientist, researcher*
†Humar, Abhinav *transplant surgeon, clinical researcher*
Hunsberger, Roger Moore *web site design company executive, writer, lumber company executive, musician*
†Hurwicz, Leonid *economist, educator*
†Hutchens, Michael D. *lawyer*
Idiyatullin, Djaudat Shavkatovich *research associate*
Innmon, Arlene Katherine (Tara Innmon) *artist, dancer, writer, storyteller, minister, healer*
†Isakovic, Abdel *physicist, researcher*
†Jackson, Donna Cardamone *music educator*
Jackson, Renee Leone *lawyer*
Jacob, Bernard Michel *architect*
Jacobs, Irwin Lawrence *diversified corporate executive*
†Jahn, Gary Robert *foreign language educator*
Jarboe, Mark Alan *lawyer*
Jarpe, Geoffrey Pellas *lawyer*
Jensch, Charles Campbell *lawyer*
Jensen, Steven Richard *radiologist, consultant*
Johnson, Badri Nahvi *sociology educator, real estate business owner*
†Johnson, David Chester *university chancellor, sociology educator*
Johnson, David Wolcott *psychologist, educator*
†Johnson, Dennis Robert *lawyer*
Johnson, Donald Clay *librarian, curator*
Johnson, Gary L. *publishing executive*
Johnson, Gary M. *lawyer*
Johnson, John Warren *retired association executive*
Johnson, Lola Norine *retired advertising and public relations executive, educator*
Johnson, Margaret Ann (Peggy) *library administrator*
Johnson, Robert Glenn *geology and geophysics educator*
Johnson, Walter Kline *civil engineer*
†Jones, B. Todd *lawyer, former prosecutor*
Jones, Will(iam) (William Arnold Jones) *writer, former newspaper columnist*
Jorgensen, Daniel Fred *academic executive*
Joseph, Burton M. *retired grain merchant*
Joseph, Daniel Donald *aeronautical engineer, educator*
†Kaess, John Philip *music educator, choir director*
†Kaiser, Daniel Robert *research scientist*
Kalman, Marc *radio station executive*
†Kamrath, Alan Dale *lawyer*
Kane, Robert Lewis *public health educator*
†Kapelac, Samuel James *writer, sales executive*
Kaplan, Sheldon *lawyer, director*
†Kashtan, Clifford Elliot *physician*
Keets, John David, Jr., *insurance company executive*
Keller, Kenneth Harrison *engineering educator, science policy analyst*
Kelly, A. David *lawyer*
Kelly, Tom (Jay Thomas Kelly) *retired professional sports team manager*
Kennedy, B(yrl) J(ames) *medicine and oncology educator*
Keppel, William James *lawyer, educator, writer*
Keyes, Jeffrey J. *lawyer*
Kilbourn, William Douglas, Jr., *law educator*
King, Lyndel Irene Saunders *art museum director*
Kinney, Earl Robert *mutual funds company executive*
Kirtley, Jane Elizabeth *law educator*
Klaas, Paul Barry *lawyer*
†Klein, William David *lawyer*
Klemp, Harold *minister, writer*
Kletschka, Harold Dale *cardiovascular surgeon, biomedical company executive*
Knoke, David Harmon *sociology educator*
Kohlstedt, Sally Gregory *history educator*
Koneck, John Michael *lawyer*
Konieczny, Sharon Louise *insurance agency executive*
Korotkin, Fred *writer, philatelist*
Koutsky, Dean Roger *advertising executive*
†Kralewski, John Edward *health service research educator*
†Kramer, Joel Roy *journalist, newspaper executive*
Kraus, Leslie Jay *lawyer*
Krause, Timothy Gilbert *web site manager*
Kreiser, Frank David *real estate executive*
Kroll, Paul Benedict *insurance consultant*
Kruse, Paul Walters, Jr., *physicist, consultant*
Kudrle, Robert Thomas *economist, educator*
Kuhi, Leonard Vello *astronomer, university administrator*
†Kuhn, Virginia R. *lawyer*
Kukla, Edward Richard *rare books & special collections librarian*
Kulacki, Francis Alfred *engineer, educator*
Kump, Warren Lee *retired diagnostic radiologist*
†Kuyath, Richard Norman *lawyer*
Kvalseth, Tarald Oddvar *mechanical engineer, educator*
Laing, Karel Ann *magazine publishing executive*
Lake, John Richard *gastroenterologist*
Lamb, Deborah Kathleen *music educator, vocal, choral consultant, fiber artist*
Lambert, Robert Frank *electrical engineer, consultant*
Lange, Katherine J. *writer*
Larkin, Eugene David *artist, educator*
LaValleur, June *obstetrician/gynecologist*
Lawton, Matt *professional baseball player*
Lazar, Raymond Michael *lawyer, educator*
†Lazarevic, Aleksandar *research scientist*
Lebedoff, David M. *lawyer, writer*
Lebedoff, Jonathan Galanter *federal judge*
Lee, Hon Cheung *physiology educator*
†Lehman, Tom (Thomas Edward Lehman) *professional golfer*
Lehmann, Ernest Karl *consulting company executive, geologist*
Lentz, Richard David *psychiatrist, educator*
Leon, Arthur Sol *research cardiologist, exercise physiologist*
Leonard, Brian Francis *lawyer*
Leppik, Ilo E. *neurologist, educator*
Lerner, Harry Jonas *publishing company executive*
†LeSage, Mark Gerard *pharmacologist, psychologist*
Levine, Howard Marvin *obstetrician, gynecologist*
Levitt, Seymour Herbert *physician, radiology educator*
Lewis, Stephen Richmond, Jr., *economist, educator, academic administrator*
†Lindau, Philip *commodities trader*
Lindell, Edward Albert *former college president, religious organization administrator*
Lipovetsky, Stan (Stanislav Lipovetsky) *statistician, mathematician*
Litman, Theodor James *medical educator*
Loken, James Burton *federal judge*
Long, James Jay *lawyer*
Lougee, Wendy Pradt *library director*
Lucas, Margaret Exner *housing developer*
Luepker, Russell Vincent *epidemiology educator*
Luzhansky, Dmitry M. *chemical engineer, researcher*
†Mabry, Celia Elaine Hales *librarian*
MacMillan, Peter Alan *lawyer*
†MacMillan, Whitney *food products and import/export company executive*
Magee, Paul Terry *geneticist and molecular biologist, educator*
Magnuson, Roger James *lawyer*
†Malmquist, Carl Phillip *psychiatrist*
Mammel, Russell Norman *retired food distribution company executive*
†Mandel, Sheldon Lloyd *dermatologist, educator*
†Mangen, David Joseph *statistician, researcher*
†Manning, William Henry *lawyer*
Markus, Lawrence *retired mathematics educator*
Marling, Karal Ann *art history and social sciences educator, curator*
Marshak, Marvin Lloyd *physicist, educator*
Marshall, Siri Swenson *corporate lawyer*
Martens, Leslie Vernon *dentistry educator, consultant*
Martin, Frederick Kane *portfolio manager, investor*
†Martin, Jaye Louise *lawyer*
Martin, Phillip Hammond *lawyer*
Martin, Roger Bond *landscape architect, educator*
†Martin-Estudillo, Luis *editor, researcher*
Martinson, Bradley James *lawyer*
†Mathews, Kathleen Ann *social worker, psychotherapist*
†Mathy, Robin Michelle *writer*
Matson, Wesley Jennings *educational administrator*
Matthews, James Shadley *lawyer*
†Mayerle, Thomas Michael *lawyer*
McCall, Brian Patrick *industrial relations educator*
†McConnell, Scott Rushton *educational psychology educator*
†McCune, Thomas *construction executive contractor*
McGuire, Tim *editor*
McGuire, Timothy James *lawyer, editor*
†McGunnigle, George Francis *judge*
McNeil, Mark Sanford *lawyer*
McQuarrie, Donald Gray *surgeon, educator*
Meador, Ron *newspaper editor, writer*
Meese, Robert Allen *architect*
Meininger, Eric Thomas *pediatrician, internist*
Meller, Robert Louis, Jr., *lawyer*
Mellum, Gale Robert *lawyer*
†Mellum, Wendy *lawyer*
Meshbesher, Ronald I. *lawyer*
†Micek, Ernest S. *former food products executive*
Mickelson, Stacey *state legislator*
Miller, Michael Thomas *lawyer*
Miller, Willard, Jr., *mathematician, educator*
Miller, William Alvin *clergyman, author, lecturer*
Miner, Valerie J. *literature educator, writer*
Minish, Robert Arthur *lawyer*
†Mohanty, Sunil K. *finance educator, researcher*
Mohring, Herbert *economics educator*
†Moller, Andrew K. *finance company executive*
Mondale, Joan Adams *wife of former Vice President of United States*
†Monson, Dan *college basketball coach*
Montgomery, Ann D. *federal judge, educator*
Montgomery, Henry Irving *financial planner*
Moraczewski, Robert Leo *publisher*
Morrison, Clinton *banker*
Morrison, John M. *hospital administrator, bank executive*
†Mouser, Les *advertising executive*
†Moyer, Keith J. *publishing executive*
Murphy, Diana E. *federal judge*
Murphy, Edrie Lee *laboratory administrator*
Murphy, Joseph Edward, Jr., *broadcast executive*
Musacchio, Laura R. *planning and design educator*
Najarian, John Sarkis *surgeon, educator*
Nanne, Louis Vincent *professional hockey team executive*
Nash, Elizabeth Hamilton *music and theater educator, vocalist, writer*
Nelson, Gary Michael *lawyer*
Nelson, Marilyn C. *hotel executive, food service executive, travel services executive, marketing professional*
Nelson, Richard Arthur *lawyer*
†Nelson, Steven Craig *lawyer*
Nemo, Anthony James *lawyer*
†Newhall, David Gillette *lawyer*
Nicholas, S. Scott *allergist*
Nightingale, Edmund Joseph *clinical psychologist, educator*
Noel, Franklin Linwood *judge*
Norberg, Arthur Lawrence, Jr., *historian, physicist educator*
†Nordaune, Roselyn Jean *lawyer*
Nortwen, Patricia Harman *music educator*
†Novak, Leslie Howard *lawyer*
Nuttall, Frank Quentin *physician, researcher*
Nyrop, Donald William *airline executive*
O'Connor, Patrick J. *family physician, researcher*
Ogata, Katsuhiko *engineering educator*
O'Keefe, Thomas Michael *academic administrator*
Oliver, Edward Carl *state legislator, retired investment executive*
Olson, James Richard *retired transportation company executive*
O'Neill, Brian Boru *lawyer*
Opdahl, Clark Donald *lawyer*
†Opitz, Donald L *science educator*
Oriani, Richard Anthony *metallurgical engineer, educator*
Osander, John *secondary school educator*
Ostrem, Walter Martin *librarian, educator, consultant*
Ostrom, Don *political science educator*
Palmer, Brian Eugene *lawyer*
Parsons, Charles Allan, Jr., *lawyer*
Paulu, Frances Brown *international center administrator*
Pazandak, Carol Hendrickson *liberal arts educator*
†Pentelovitch, William Zane *lawyer*
Perl, Justin Harley *lawyer*
Perlman, Lawrence *retired business executive, corporate director, consultant*
Persson, Erland Karl *electrical engineer, engineering executive*
Petersen, Douglas Arndt *financial development consultant*
Peterson, Douglas Arthur *physician*
Peterson, Phillip Keith *physician, clinical investigator*
†Peterson, William George *lawyer*
Pfender, Emil *mechanical engineering educator*
Phibbs, Clifford Matthew *surgeon, educator*
Phillips, William David *history educator*
Picconatto, Evelyn Clara *accountant*
Pillsbury, George Sturgis *investment adviser*
†Piper, Addison Lewis *securities executive*
Pluimer, Edward J. *lawyer*
†Pohlad, Carl R. *professional baseball team executive, bottling company executive*
†Pohlad, Robert C. *consumer products company executive*
Polunovsky, Vitaly Alex *cell biologist*
Polverini, Peter *dean*
Porter, Jeannette Upton *elementary education educator*
Porter, Jennifer Madeleine *producer, director*
Porter, Philip Wayland *geography educator*
Portoghese, Philip Salvatore *medicinal chemist, educator*
Potuznik, Charles Laddy *lawyer*
Pour-El, Marian Boykan *mathematician, educator*
†Prange, Michael J. *finance company executive*
Pratte, Robert John *lawyer*
Prescott, Edward C. *economist, educator*
Preuss, Roger E(mil) *artist*
Price, Joseph Michael *lawyer*
Quie, Paul Gerhardt *pediatrician, educator*
Quinlan, C. Patrick *retired diplomat, educator*
Rachie, Cyrus *retired lawyer*
Radmer, Michael John *lawyer, educator*
Rahn, Alvin Albert *former banker*
Rajkumar, Roshini Anne *reporter*
Randall, Roger David *publishing executive*
†Ransom, Lakeesha Krotonya *academic administrator*
†Rathke, Stephen Carl *lawyer*
Rauenhorst, Gerald *architectural engineer, construction and development executive*
Reichgott Junge, Ember D. *small business owner, former state senator, lawyer, writer, broadcast analyst, radio personality*
Rein, Stanley Michael *lawyer*
†Reinhart, Robert Rountree, Jr., *lawyer*

Reiss, Ira Leonard *retired sociology educator, writer*
Reister, Raymond Alex *retired lawyer*
Reuter, James William *lawyer*
†Rockenstein, Walter Harrison, II, *lawyer*
Rockwell, Winthrop Adams *lawyer*
Roe, Roger Rolland, Jr., *lawyer*
Rogers, Karen Beckstead *gifted studies educator, researcher, consultant*
Rogers, William Cecil *political science educator, consultant*
Roloff, Marvin L. *publishing executive*
Rose, Thomas Albert *artist, art educator*
Rosenbaum, James Michael *judge*
Ross, Donald, Jr., *English language educator, university administrator*
Rothenberg, Elliot Calvin *lawyer, author*
Rothenberger, David Albert *surgeon*
Rottenberg, David Allan *neurologist*
Rousseau, Eugene Ellsworth *musician, music educator, consultant*
Rubens, Sidney Michel *physicist, technical advisor*
Rubenstein, Andrea Fichman *lawyer*
†Ryan, Thomas J. *lawyer*
Rybak, R.T. *mayor*
†Sabo, Julie Ann *former state legislator*
Saeks, Allen Irving *lawyer*
Safley, James Robert *lawyer*
Sagar, Michal Bass *art educator, artist*
St. Germaine-Lattig, Charles Edwin *political writer*
Salyer, Stephen Lee *media executive*
†Sand, David Byron *lawyer*
Sanger, Stephen W. *consumer products company executive*
Sanner, Royce Norman *lawyer*
Sapiro, Guillermo *engineering educator, consultant*
Sarles, Harvey B. *humanities educator*
Saunders, Philip D. *professional basketball coach*
Savelsberg, Joachim Josef *sociologist, educator*
Sawicki, Zbigniew Peter *lawyer*
Sayles Belton, Sharon *law educator, former mayor*
Scallen, Thomas Kaine *broadcasting executive*
Schermer, Judith Kahn *lawyer*
Schlentz, Robert Joseph *biomedical, electromagnetic compatibility, regulatory, reliability and safety engineer*
Schneider, Elaine Carol *lawyer, researcher, writer*
Schnell, Robert Lee, Jr., *lawyer*
Schnobrich, Roger William *lawyer*
†Schoettle, Ferdinand P. *lawyer, educator*
Schreiner, John Christian *economics consultant, software publisher*
†Schroeder, Roger Glenn *management educator*
Schuh, G(eorge) Edward *university dean, agricultural economist*
Schultz, Louis Edwin *management consultant*
†Schutz, Ronald James *lawyer*
Schwartz, Howard Wyn *business/marketing educator, consultant*
Schwartzberg, Joseph Emanuel *geographer, educator*
Scoville, James Griffin *economics educator*
Seidel, Robert Wayne *science historian, educator*
Serrin, James Burton *mathematics educator*
Serstock, Doris Shay *retired microbiologist, educator, civic worker*
†Severinsen, Doc (Carl H. Severinsen) *conductor, musician*
Shapiro, Burton Leonard *oral pathologist, geneticist, educator*
Shaughnessy, Thomas William *retired librarian*
Sheikh, Suneel Ismail *aerospace engineer, researcher*
Shively, William Phillips *political scientist, educator*
Shnider, Bruce Jay *lawyer*
Shroyer, Thomas Jerome *lawyer*
Shulman, Yechiel *engineering educator*
Shumway, Sara Jane *cardiothoracic surgeon*
†Silver, Alan Irving *lawyer*
Silverman, Robert Joseph *lawyer*
Simon, John Ernest *psychiatrist*
Sinha, Akhouri A. *research scientist, educator*
Sippel, William Leroy *lawyer*
Sisk, Gregory Charles *lawyer, educator*
Sit, Eugene C. *investment executive*
Skare, Robert Martin *lawyer, director*
†Skovholt, Thomas Meyer *psychology educator*
Skrowaczewski, Stanislaw *conductor, composer*
Slocum, Rosemarie *physician services consultant, recruiter*
Soderquist, Ronald Bruce *minister, ministry consultant*
Sortland, Paul Allan *lawyer*
Southall, Francis Geneva *retired education educator music*
Sparrow, Ephraim Maurice *mechanical engineering scientist, educator*
Spear, Allan Henry *former state senator, historian, educator*
Spong, Douglas K. *public relations executive*
Spoor, William Howard *food company executive*
†Sroufe, Lawrence Alan *child psychologist, educator*
Staba, Emil John *pharmacognosy and medicinal chemistry educator*
Stage, Brian *hotel executive*
Stageberg, Roger V. *lawyer*
†Staley, Warren *food products company executive*
†Stang, Jamie Sue *dietician, consultant*
Steen-Hinderlie, Diane Evelyn *social worker, musician*
Steinwall, Susan Deborah *lawyer*
Stelson, Kim Adair *mechanical engineering educator*
Stenberg, Adam W. *financial advisor, investment company executive*
Stenwick, Michael William *retired internist, geriatric medicine consultant*
Stephenson, Nancy Louise *medical products company professional*
Stern, Leo G. *lawyer*
†Straughn, Robert Oscar, III, *lawyer*
Street, Erica Catherine *lawyer*
Strommen, Merton Peter *research psychologist, clergyman*
Strothman, John Henry *lawyer*
Struthers, Margo S. *lawyer*
Struyk, Robert John *lawyer*
Stuebner, James Cloyd *real estate developer, contractor*
†Sullivan, Alfred Dewitt *academic administrator*
Sullivan, Austin Padraic, Jr., *diversified food company executive*
Sullivan, Michael Patrick *food service executive*
Suryanarayanan, Raj Gopalan *researcher, consultant, educator*
Svärd, N. Trygve *electrical engineer*
Svendsbye, Lloyd August *college president, clergyman, educator*
Sveum, Richard James *allergist*
Swan, Wallace Kent *county official*
Swenson, Mark Gregory *architect*
Swiontkowski, Marc Francis *orthopedist*
†Symonds, Terri Lee *law educator*
Symosek, Peter Frank *research scientist*
Tamzarian, Armin Petrovich *physician*
Tandon, Rajiv *training company executive*
Tanick, Marshall Howard *lawyer, law educator*
Tatone, Kathy *lawyer*
Tennyson, Joseph Alan *engineering executive*
†Thaivanich, Pattana *marketing professional*
Thompson, Roby Calvin, Jr., *orthopedic surgeon, educator*
Thompson, Theodore Robert *pediatric educator*
Thorson, Steven Greg *lawyer*
Thurman, Virgil Leon *voice educator*
†Timmons, Peter John *lawyer*
Toscano, James Vincent *medical institute administration*
Tracey, Timothy Neal *technology company executive*
Tracy, James Donald *historian, educator*
†Trestman, Frank D. *distribution company executive, director*
Trucano, Michael *lawyer*
Truhlar, Donald Gene *chemist, educator*
Tufte, Brian Nelson *lawyer*
Ulrich, Robert J. *retail executive*
Ulstrom, Robert A. *pediatrician, educator*
Usacheva, Marina Nikolaevna *photochemist, researcher*
Vander Molen, Thomas Dale *lawyer*
Van Dyke, William Grant *manufacturing company executive*
†Vanska, Osmo *theater director*
Veblen, Thomas Clayton *management consultant*
Veldey, Bonnie *special education educator*
Ventres, Judith Martin *lawyer*
Verby, Jane Crawford *writer*
Vergin, Timothy Lynn *commercial real estate appraiser, broker, investor*
†Viegas, Herman Hermogio *mechanical engineer*
Wagenaar, Alexander Clarence *educator*
Wahoske, Michael James *lawyer*
Walker, Walter Willard *real estate and investments executive*
Walters, Glen Robert *banker*
†Wang, Yang *cardiology educator, researcher*
Ward, David Allen *sociology educator*
Warner, William Hamer *applied mathematician*
Watson, Dennis Wallace *microbiology educator, scientist*
Wehrwein-Hunt, Jeri Lynn *elementary education educator*
Weil, Cass Sargent *lawyer*
Weir, Edward Kenneth *cardiologist, educator*
Weiss, Gerhard Hans *German language educator*
†Werner, Lawrence H. *editor*
Whelpley, Dennis Porter *lawyer*
White, Robert James *newspaper columnist*
†Whittemore, Brian *broadcast executive*
Wickesberg, Albert Klumb *retired management educator*
Wicks, John R. *lawyer*
Wiener, Phyllis Ames *artist*
Wild, John Julian *surgeon, director medical research institute*
†Wilhelm, Gretchen *retired secondary school educator, volunteer*
Wilkinson, Jeffrey David *engineer*
Wille, Karin L. *lawyer*
Williams, David Neville *physician*
†Williams, Yolanda Yvette *music educator*
Windhorst, John William, Jr., *lawyer*
†Wittman, Randy *professional basketball coach*
Woldt, Gerald D. (Jay Woldt) *nurse anesthetist*
Wollan, Curtis Noel *theater producer, theater director*
Wood, Wellington Gibson, III, *biochemistry educator*
Wright, Frank Gardner *retired newspaper editor*
Wright, William Edward *historian, educator*
Wurtele, Christopher Angus *paint and coatings company executive*
Yost, Gerald B. *lawyer*
Younger, Judith Tess *lawyer, educator*
Yourzak, Robert Joseph *management consultant, engineer, educator*
Ysseldyke, James Edward *psychology educator, dean*
Zalk, Robert H. *lawyer*
†Zellmer-Bruhn, Mary Elizabeth *management educator*
†Zhdanov, Dmitry *information technology executive, educator, financial consultant*
Zimmermann, Robert Laurence *marketing professional*
Zoberi, Nadim *management consultant, consultant*
†Zona, Richard A. *bank executive*

Minnetonka
Anderson, Tad Stephen *landscape designer, consultant, photographer*
†Aristidou, Aristos Andrea *bioprocess company executive*
†Brunk, Sara J. *music educator*
Carpenter, Norman Roblee *retired lawyer*
Christianson, Philip D. *employee benefits executive*
Cross, Bonham E(lwood) *retired newspaper account executive*
†Erlandson, Patrick J. *medical association administrator*
Fisk, Gail Marie *music educator*
Gillies, Donald Richard *marketing and advertising consultant, educator*
Gottier, Richard Chalmers *retired computer company executive*
†Heckt, Melvin Dean *lawyer*
Humphrey, Sandra McLeod *psychologist*
Jarvis, Linda Marie *music director, music educator*
Johnson, Lennart Ingemar *materials engineering consultant*
Joseph-Kordell, Shelley M. *geriatric care administrator*
†Klapmeier, Jolie Bleeker *lawyer*
Kostka, Ronald Wayne *marketing consultant*
Kunert, Paul Charles *lawyer*
†Lubben, David J. *lawyer*
McGuire, William W. *insurance company executive*
Osterberg, Thomas Karl *construction company executive*
Robbins, Orem Olford *insurance company executive*
Rogers, James Devitt *judge*
Schmidt, Russel Alan, II, *sales executive*
Shapiro, Fred Louis *physician, educator*
Swartz, Donald Everett *television executive*
Thompson, Sally Ann *newspaper editor*
Vanstrom, Marilyn June Christensen *retired elementary education educator*
Wesselink, David Duwayne *finance company executive*
†Woo, Benson *financial executive*

Monticello
Wollan, Christine R. *clinical social worker*

Moorhead
Bense, Charles James *English educator*
Benson, John Steven *education educator*
Buckley, Joan N. *English educator*
Coomber, James Elwood *English language educator*
Dille, Roland Paul *college president*
Emmel, Bruce Henry *retired secondary education mathematics educator*
†Eyler, David Paul *music educator*
Gee, Robert LeRoy *agriculturist, dairy farmer*
Glasrud, Clarence Arthur *English educator*
Heuer, Gerald Arthur *mathematician, educator*
Holtan, Merrie Sue *communications educator*
†Houglum, Bruce Monroe *music educator*
Jacobson, Arland Dean *religion educator*
†Keup, Linda C. *management educator*
†Marquart, Steven Leonard *lawyer*
Meadows-Rogers, Robert Denton *art history educator*
Miller, Keith Lloyd *lawyer*
Noblitt, Harding Coolidge *political scientist, educator*
O'Hara, Sabine U. *academic administrator, dean, economist, educator*
Rothlisberger, Rodney John *music educator*
Ruzicka, Charles Edward *music educator, director*
Stenerson, John Gorden *lumber and building materials executive*
Strong, Judith Ann *chemist, educator*
†Totten, Gary *literature educator*
Trainor, John Felix *retired economics educator*
Treumann, William Borgen *university dean*
†Virtanen, Beth Louise *literature educator, consultant*
†Zhang, Haimeng *education educator*

Moose Lake
DeVillion, Kevin John *computer systems administrator, consultant*

Morris
†Dean, LeAnn Faye Lindquist *librarian*
Demos, Vasilikie Polytimy *sociology educator*
†Joo, Seung-Ho *political scientist, educator*
†Ng, Peh H. *education educator*

Mound
Pollock, Tony Joe *photographer*

Mounds View
†Brandt, Dean Myron *design engineer*
Calvin, Stafford Richard *academic administrator*

Nevis
Stibbe, Austin Jule *accountant*

New Brighton
Appel, William Frank *pharmacist*
Dobbert, Daniel Joseph *data analyst, researcher, educator*
Karls, Nicholas James *engineering executive*
Schwartz, Joan Lam *computer graphics consultant, writer, artist*

New Hope
Olson, Clifford Larry *management consultant, entrepreneur*

Nisswa
Marmas, James Gust *retired business educator, retired college dean*

North Oaks
Blaha, Verle Dennis *golf course executive, electrical engineer*
McDonald, Malcolm Willis *retired real estate company executive*
Woods, Robert Edward *lawyer*

North Saint Paul
O'Brien, Daniel William *lumber company executive*

Northfield
Appleyard, David Frank *mathematics and computer science educator*
Benkowski, Ann Marie *writer*
Casper, Barry Michael *physics educator*
Cederberg, James *physics educator*
Clark, Clifford Edward, Jr., *history educator*
Clark, William Hartley *political science educator*
Crouter, Richard Earl *religion educator*
Davis, Douglas Donald *physical education educator, coach*
†Dobrow, Robert Paul *statistician, educator*
†Fick, Herbert J. *chemist, consultant*
Flaten, Robert Arnold *former ambassador*
Hangen, William J. *retired business executive*
Henrickson, Eiler Leonard *retired geologist, educator*
Hong, Howard Vincent *library administrator, philosophy educator, editor, translator*
Iseminger, Gary Hudson *philosophy educator*
Levin, Burton *diplomat*
Mason, Perry Carter *philosophy educator*
McKinsey, Elizabeth *humanities educator, consultant*
†Oden, Robert A., Jr., *academic administrator*
Rand, Sidney Anders *retired college administrator*
Soule, George Alan *literature educator, writer*
Sovik, Edward Anders *architect, consultant*
Steen, Lynn Arthur *mathematician, educator*
Swanson, Stephen Olney *minister, retired English educator*
Wilkie, Nancy Clausen *classics and archaeology educator*
Yandell, Cathy Marleen *foreign language educator*

Oakdale
Be Vier, William A. *religious studies educator*
Maekawa, Koji Ogura *technology company administrator*
Tran, Nang Tri *electrical engineer, physicist*

Olivia
Cosgriff, James Arthur *physician*

Ortonville
Schrom, Elizabeth Ann *educator*

Ottertail
Anderson, Bob *state legislator, business executive*

Owatonna
†Aune, Debra Bjurquist *lawyer*
Larson, Diane LaVerne Kusler *principal*

Palisade
Kilde, Sandra Jean *nurse anesthetist, educator, consultant*

Pequot Lakes
Gray, Allen (Ernest Bungaard) *radio executive*
Weaver, Arthur Lawrence *retired rheumatologist*

Pipestone
Appeldorn, Claudia J. *nursing administrator, editor*
Scott, William Paul *lawyer*

Plymouth
Bonne, Ulrich *chemical physicist*
Chadwick, John Edwin *financial consultant*
†Friswold, Fred Ravndal *manufacturing executive*
†Hauser, Elloyd *finance company executive*
Kahler, Herbert Frederick *diversified business executive*
†Kodali, Dharma Rao *research scientist*
Losasso, Thomas James *anesthesiologist*
Park, Gyoungwon *electrical engineer, research scientist*
Peterson, Donn Neal *forensic engineer*
Prem, Konald Arthur *physician, educator*
†Saville, Derric James *lawyer*
Werden, David Ray *music educator*

Preston
Hokenson, David Leonard *secondary school educator*

Princeton
Buntrock, Robert Edward *information consultant, organic chemist*

Prior Lake
Toren, Brian Keith *futures, multimedia, management consultant*
Tufte, Obert Norman *retired research executive*

Proctor
Scheibe, Margaret Helen *elementary school educator, librarian*

Red Wing
†Fritz, Henry Eugene *historian, educator*

Remer
†Anderson, Carl Joseph *artist, educator*
McNulty-Majors, Susan Rose *special education administrator*

Richfield
Reilly, Jill Marlene *school system administrator*
Thompson, Steve Allan *writer*

Robbinsdale
Anderson, Scott Robbins *hospital administrator*

Rochester
†Ackerman, Michael John *medical educator*
Archibald, Reginald Mac Gregor *physician, chemist, educator*
Bajzer, Željko *scientist, educator*
Bartholomew, Lloyd Gibson *physician*
Bastron, James Arthur *retired neurologist*
Beahrs, Oliver Howard *surgeon, educator*
†Beckman, Thomas J. *physician*

†Berry, Daniel John *orthopedist, surgeon*
Bhattacharyya, Kalyan Kumar *scientist, biomedical engineer*
Bowie, E(dward) J(ohn) Walter *hematologist, researcher*
†Cable, David George *cardiologist, surgeon*
Canan, Elizabeth Levy *health facility administrator*
Canan, Thomas Michael *lawyer*
†Charboneau, Joseph William *radiologist, medical educator*
†Charlton, Michael R *physician, researcher*
†Cherry, Kenneth Jerome, Jr., *surgeon*
Chute, Christopher Gregory *medical educator*
Cofield, Robert Hahn *orthopedic surgeon, educator*
Croghan, Gary Alan *cancer research scientist, physician*
Czaja, Albert Joseph *physician, educator*
Danielson, Gordon Kenneth, Jr., *cardiovascular surgeon, educator*
DeRemee, Richard Arthur *physician, educator, researcher*
Deschamps, Claude *thoracic surgeon*
†Douglas, William W. *physician, consultant*
Douglass, Bruce E. *physician*
Downing, Lawrence DeWitt *lawyer*
Dyck, Peter James *neurologist, researcher, educator*
Edwards, William Dean *pathologist*
Engel, Andrew George *neurologist*
Erspamer, Peter Roy *humanities educator, writer*
Feldt, Robert Hewitt *pediatric cardiologist, educator*
†Fervenza, Fernando C. *nephrologist, educator*
Flaaten, Ruby Cheryl *nurse manager*
Foote, Robert Leonard *oncologist, educator, researcher*
Frestedt, Joy Louise *science administrator*
Fye, W. Bruce, III, *cardiologist*
†Geda, Yonas Endale *neuropsychiatrist, researcher*
Gersh, Bernard J. *cardiologist, researcher, educator*
Gertz, Morie Abraham *physician*
Gervais, Sister Generose *hospital consultant*
Gharib, Hossein *medical educator*
Gibson, Lawrence Edward *dermatologist*
†Gloviczki, Peter *surgeon*
Gomez, Manuel Rodriguez *physician*
Gorman, Colum Alphonsus *retired endocrinologist*
Gracey, Douglas Robert *physician, physiologist, educator*
Grosset, Jessica Ariane *computer analyst*
†Guo, ZengKui *research scientist*
Haddy, Francis John *physician, educator*
†Harris, Peter C. *molecular biologist, educator*
Hodgson, Jane Elizabeth *obstetrician and gynecologist, consultant*
Homan, J. Michael *library administrator*
Huffine, Coy Lee *retired chemical engineer, consultant*
Hunder, Gene Gerald *physician, educator*
Jacobsen, Van Paul *lawyer*
Jaffe, Allan S. *cardiologist, educator*
†Jankowski, Christopher James *anesthesiologist, educator*
Johnson, Charles Daniel *radiologist*
†Kauffman, Kreg Arlen *lawyer*
Key, Jack Dayton *librarian*
Kinney, Carolyn *executive secretary*
†Kummeth, Patricia Joan *nursing educator*
Kyle, Robert Arthur *medical educator, oncologist*
Lanier, William Lovel, Jr., *anesthesiologist, educator*
†Lantz, William Charles *lawyer*
Larson, Bruce Robert *lawyer, educator*
†Leung, Nelson *physician*
Liebow, Mark *physician*
Lofgren, Anne Elizabeth *musician, educator*
Lofgren, Karl Adolph *surgeon, educator*
†Loftus, Jr., Edward Vincent *gastroenterologist, writer*
Lucas, Alexander Ralph *child psychiatrist, educator, writer*
Luthra, Harvinder S. *rheumatologist, researcher*
Mackenzie, Ronald Alexander *anesthesiologist*
Maher, L. James, III, *molecular biologist*
Malek, Reza Said *urological surgeon*
Malkasian, George Durand, Jr., *physician, educator*
†Malouf, Joseph F. *cardiologist*
Mayr, James Jerome *fertilizer company executive*
Michenfelder, John Donahue *anesthesiology educator*
Midthun, David Eric *physician, consultant*
Moder, Kevin G. *rheumatologist, consultant*
Mrazek, David Allen *pediatric psychiatrist*
Neel, Harry Bryan, III, *surgeon, scientist, educator*
Nelson, Audrey May *physician*
Nevling, Harry Reed *human resources consultant*
Nienow, Beth Marie *librarian*
O'Hare, Daniel John *electrical engineer*
Ohno, Kinji *neurologist, educator*
Orwoll, Gregg S. K. *lawyer*
†Packer, Douglas L. *cardiologist*
Pairolero, Peter Charles *surgeon*
Petersen, Bret T. *gastroenterologist*
Phillips, Sidney Frederick *gastroenterologist, educator*
†Pisansky, Thomas Michael *physician*
Pittelkow, Mark Robert *physician, dermatology educator, researcher*
Podratz, Karl C. *gynecologic surgeon, oncologist, educator*
Puga, Francisco Javier *cardiac surgeon*
Reitemeier, Richard Joseph *physician*
Rhodes, Deborah Jane *internist*
†Riggs, Jeanette Templeton *civic worker*
Robbins, Thomas Landau *humanities researcher*
†Rogers, Roy Steele, III, *dermatology educator, dean*
Rosen, Charles Burke *surgeon*
Rosenow, Edward Carl, III, *medical educator*
Ryu, Jay H. *physician, educator, researcher*
Scott, John Paul *medical educator*
Segura, Joseph Weston *urologist, educator*
†Shampo, Marc Anthony *medical editor, writer, retired*
Shepherd, John Thompson *physiologist*
Sherman, Thomas Francis *education educator*
Siekert, Robert George *neurologist*
†Sim, Franklin H. *orthopedic surgery educator*
Somsen, Henry Northrop *retired lawyer*
Sprung, Juraj *anesthesiologist, educator*
Stegall, Mark D. *surgeon, medical educator*
†Stelck, Mickie Joann *technologist*
Stewart, Karen Meyer *pediatrics nurse, nursing manager*
†Stickler, Gunnar Brynolf *pediatrician*
Swanson, Jerry William *neurologist, educator*
Symmonds, Richard Earl *gynecologist*
Tarvestad, Anthony M. *psychiatrist*
Taylor, Jeffrey Lee *political science educator, author*
Thompson, Rodney Lee *infectious diseases specialist*
Verbout, James Paul *recreational therapist*
Vetter, Richard James *health physicist*
Ward, Louis Emmerson *retired physician*
Wass, C(harles) Thomas *anesthesiologist*
Weinshilboum, Richard M. *pharmacologist, educator, biomedical researcher*
Wells, Lloyd Allan *psychiatrist, educator*
Whisnant, Jack Page *neurologist*
Wiebers, David Owen *physician*
Williams, Arthur Ross *health service and public administrator*
Windebank, Anthony J. *dean*
Wood, Michael B. *chief executive officer, president*
Wood, Michael Bruce *orthopaedic surgeon, researcher, educator*
Woods, John Elmer *plastic surgeon*
Woog, John J. *plastic surgeon*

Rosemount
Aadland, Thomas Vernon *minister*
Dick, Herbert James *music educator*
†Tesch, Tamara Dianne *lawyer*
Trygestad, JoAnn Carol *secondary education educator*
†Wise, Mark Edward *aircraft maintenance technician, musician*

Roseville
Gross, Alan Gerald *rhetoric educator*
Hughes, Jerome Michael *education foundation executive*
Kane, George Francis *systems analyst*
Marten, Gordon Cornelius *research agronomist, educator, federal agency administrator*
McMillan, Mary Bigelow *retired minister, volunteer*
Ucko, Franz *research scientist, consultant, writer*

Rushford
Schober, Myron Jerome *newspaper editor and publisher*
Stras, Penny Lynn *director*

Saginaw
Stauber, Marilyn Jean *retired secondary and elementary school*

Saint Charles
Van Norman, Willis Roger *computer systems researcher*

Saint Cloud
Braun, Janice Larson *language arts educator*
Frank, Stephen Ira *political science educator*
Gainey, Kathryn O'Reilly *art education educator*
Hofsommer, Donovan Lowell *history educator*
Hughes, Kevin John *lawyer*
Korde, Umesh Arvind *ocean engineer, researcher, educator*
†Leppman, Elizabeth Jane *geographer, educator*
McIntyre, Vicky Joyce *business owner*
Nierengarten, Roger Joseph *judge*
Olagunju, Amos Omotayo *computer science educator, consultant*
Olson, Barbara Ford *physician*
Porter, Laurinda Wright *communications educator, consultant*
Prout, Robert Stephen *higher education consultant, law enforcement consultant*
Reha, Rose Krivisky *retired business educator*
Rysavy, Richard Ludwig *physician*
Saigo, Roy Hirofumi *academic administrator*
Seifert, Luke Michael *lawyer*
Tripp, Luke Samuel *educator*
†Ward, Edward Anthony *economist, educator*
Wertz, John Alan *retired secondary school educator*

Saint James
Jones, Patricia Louise *elementary counselor*

Saint Joseph
Kirick, Daniel John *agronomist*
Olheiser, Mary David *lawyer, educator*
Rowland, Howard Ray *mass communications educator*

Saint Louis Park
†Croll, Jillian Kathleen *dietician, researcher*
Nightingale, Tracy Irene *lawyer*
Schlutter, Lois Cochrane *psychologist*
†Seaburg, Jean *lawyer*
Wikman, Michael Raymond *advertising executive*

Saint Paul
Adusumalli, Prasad (Venkata) *software engineer, engineering executive*
Aggergaard, Steven Paul *journalist, educator, musician*
Allison, John Robert *lawyer*
Alsop, Donald Douglas *federal judge*
Altenberger, Andrzej Ryszard *physical chemist, chemistry educator*
†Alvi, Shahid Anwar *sociology educator*
Amidon, Paul Charles *publishing executive*
Anderson, Gordon Louis *foundation administrator*
Anderson, Gregory Shane *insurance executive*
Anderson, Paul Holden *state supreme court justice*
Anderson, Richard H. *air transportation executive*
Archer, Joan M. *trade association administrator*
Awsumb, Robert Ardin *lawyer*
Axelrod, Leonard *court administrator*
†Bachmann, Michele *state legislator*
†Baker, Lawrence Alan *environmental engineer, researcher*
Barker-Nunn, Jeanne Beverly *English educator*
Barnwell, Franklin Hershel *zoology educator*
†Bastian, Gary Warren *judge*
Baukol, Ronald Oliver *company executive*
Bender, Jeff Blaine *epidemiologist, veterinarian*
Bengston, David Neil *economist, educator*
†Bila, Thomas A. *not-for-profit fundraiser*
†Black, Bert *state administrator, lawyer*
Bly, Carol McLean *writer, educator*
Boehnen, David Leo *lawyer*
Bombardir, Brad *hockey player*
Boyle, Bradley Charles *civil engineer*
Bree, Marlin Duane *publisher, author*
Brudvig, Glenn Lowell *retired library director*
Bruener, James William *fundraiser*
Brushaber, George Karl *college-theological seminary president, minister*
†Burgstahler, Robert *manufacturing executive*
Burkart, Jeffrey Edward *communications educator*
†Calkins, Mark R. *tenor, educator*
†Caneday, Ardel Bruce *religious studies educator, writer*
Carruthers, Philip Charles *lawyer, public official*
Cassidy, Edward Q. *lawyer*
Cavert, Henry Mead *physician, retired educator*
Chaudhary, Satveer *state senator*
†Checchi, Alfred A. *airline company executive*
Cheng, H(wei) H(sien) *soil scientist, agronomic and environmental science educator*
Clark, Ronald Dean *retired newspaper editor*
†Clemenson, David Lee *philosopher, educator*
Close, Elizabeth Scheu *retired architect*
†Cobb, Elizabeth H. *lawyer*
Coppock, Bruce *orchestra executive*
†Costanzi, Marianne *retired music teacher*
Dahl, Reynold Paul *applied economics educator*
†Dahlberg, Eric Ross *music educator*
Daly, Joseph Leo *law educator*
D'Aurora, James Joseph *psychologist, consultant*
Davies, Russ *quality assurance professional*
Davis, Joy Lee *English language educator*
Davis, Margaret Bryan *paleoecology researcher, educator*
Dee, Scott Allen *veterinarian, researcher*
Degnan, John Michael *lawyer*
DeSimone, Livio Diego *retired diversified manufacturing company executive*
Dickel, Michael Huf *higher education administrator, writer*
Diesch, Stanley La Verne *veterinarian, educator*
†Dietz, Charlton Henry *lawyer*
Dresbach, David Philip *financial consultant, educator*
Duckstad, Jon Robert *lawyer, educator*
Dykstra, Robert *retired education educator*
Edwards, Jesse Efrem *physician, educator*
Eibensteiner, Ron *political organization administrator, venture capitalist*
Eidman, Vernon Roy *agricultural economist, educator*
Ek, Alan Ryan *forester, educator*
Engle, Donald Edward *retired railway executive, lawyer*
Esposito, Bonnie Lou *marketing professional*
Failinger, Marie Anita *law educator, editor*
Feeney, Daniel Arthur *veterinary radiologist*
Feinberg, David Erwin *publishing company executive*
†Fisk, Martin H. *lawyer*
†Flynn, Harry Joseph *bishop*
†Franey, Billie Nolan *political activist*
Gabrick, Robert William *secondary education educator*
Galvin, Michael John, Jr., *lawyer*
Garretson, Donald Everett *retired manufacturing company executive*
Geis, Jerome Arthur *lawyer, legal educator*
†Geisser, Seymour *statistics educator*
Gherty, John E. *food products and agricultural products company executive*
Gilgun, Jane Frances *social work educator*
Ginthner, Delores Ann *interior designer, educator*
Glancy, Helen Diane *literature educator*
Graham, Charles John *university educator, former university president*
†Griffin, Michael Scott *communications educator, writer*
†Haemig, Mary Jane *religious studies educator*
Hall, Beverly Joy *police officer*
Hanley, Mary Ann *music educator, pianist, writer*
†Hansen, Eric Peter *lawyer*
Hansen, Robyn L. *lawyer*
Harris, Duchess *social sciences educator*
Harris, Ruth Jensen *lawyer*
Hatch, Mike *state attorney general*
†Hennessey, Michael Peter *mechanical engineer, educator*
†Henning, Angela E. *controller*
Heyman, William Herbert *financial services executive*
Hill, James Stanley *computer consulting company executive*
Hollister, Clifton David *social work educator*
Holter, Arlen Rolf *cardiothoracic surgeon*
Hopper, David Henry *religion educator*
Hubbard, Stanley Stub *broadcast executive*
Huber, Sister Alberta *college president*
Indritz, Mary Eloise Stoikes *pharmacy researcher*
Jaberg, Eugene Carl *theology educator, administrator*
Jacobs, Stephen Louis *lawyer*
†Jaranson, James M. *psychiatrist, public health service officer*
Jasthi, Siva Rama Krishna *software professional, consultant*
Jensen, James Robert *dentist, educator*
Jessup, Paul Frederick *financial economist, educator*
Johnson, James Erling *insurance executive*
Johnson, Kenneth Harvey *veterinary pathologist*
Johnson, Paul Oren *lawyer*
†Johnston, Manley Roderick *research and development company executive, chemist*
Jones, C. Paul *lawyer, educator*
Joyce, Michael Daniel *personal resource management therapist and consultant, neurolearning therapist*
Kane, Lucile M. *retired archivist, historian*
Kane, Stanley Phillip *insurance company executive*
Karasov, Phyllis *lawyer*
Keillor, Garrison Edward *writer, radio host*
Kiffmeyer, Mary *state official*
Kilbourne, Barbara Jean *health and housing executive*
Kirwin, Kenneth Francis *law educator*
Kiscaden, Sheila M. *state legislator*
†Klausner, Jeffrey *dean*
Kling, William Hugh *broadcasting executive*
†Knapp, John Anthony *lawyer*
Knudson, Mark Bradley *medical corporation executive, venture capitalist*
†Kolarov, Nickolai Atanassov *musician, educator*
Kommedahl, Thor *plant pathology educator*
Kurtz, Harold Paul *foundation executive*
Kyle, Richard House *federal judge*
Lambert, LeClair Grier *writer, lecturer, consultant, state government public information administrator*
Lamon, Richard Paul *emergency physician, family practice physician*
Lampert, Leonard Franklin *mechanical engineer*
Lange, Richard Alan *music educator*
Larkin, John Edward, Jr., *orthopedic surgeon*
Larson, David Allen *law educator*
Lay, Donald Pomeroy *federal judge*
Lebedoff, Randy Miller *lawyer*
Lehr, Lewis Wylie *diversified manufacturing company executive*
Leighton, Robert Joseph *lawyer*
Lemaire, Jacques *professional hockey coach*
Leonard, Kurt John *plant pathologist, retired university program director*
†LeVander, Bernhard Wilhelm *retired lawyer*
LeVander, Harold Powrie, Jr., *lawyer*
Mabry, Paul Davis *psychobiologist, educator, researcher*
Maclin, Alan Hall *lawyer*
Magnuson, Roy William *secondary school educator*
Malecki, Edward Stanley, Jr., *political science educator*
Mason, John Milton (Jack Mason) *judge*
Mather, Richard Burroughs *retired Chinese language and literature educator*
Matteson, Clarice Chris *artist, educator*
McChesney, Margaret Lee *clinical social worker*
McDougal, Stuart Yeatman *comparative literature educator, author*
McKinnell, Robert Gilmore *retired zoology, genetics and cell biology educator*
†McNeely, John J. *lawyer*
McNerney, W. James *manufacturing executive*
McNiel, Elizabeth Ann *veterinarian, educator*
†Mesce, Karen Anne *neurobiologist, educator*
†Meyer, Theodore James *lawyer*
Michael, Alfred Frederick, Jr., *physician, medical educator*
Miller, Richard Lynn *pharmaceutical scientist*
Minge, David *former congressman, lawyer, law educator*
†Molnau, Carol *lieutenant governor*
Monson, Dianne Lynn *literacy educator*
Mullin, James Albert *executive*
Munson, Robert Dean *agronomist, soil scientist, consultant*
Myren, David James *aeronautical engineer*
Nam, Sehyun *polymer engineer*
Nash, Nicholas David *retailing executive*
Newman, Raymond Melvin *biologist, educator*
Newmark, Richard Alan *chemist*
Nice, Pamela Michele *theater director, educator, film director, educator*
†Nielsen, Suzanne Ruth *literature educator, writer*
Noonan, James C. *lawyer, mediator, arbitrator*
†O'Leary, Daniel Brian *lawyer, educator*
Oliver, Marlys Mae *retired editor, writer*
†Orzolek, Douglas C *music educator*
Pampusch, Anita Marie *foundation administrator*
Partington, Michael David *pediatric neurosurgeon*
†Pawlenty, Tim *governor*
Perry, James Alfred *environmental scientist, consultant, science educator, director*
Phillips, Ronald Lewis *plant geneticist, educator*
Pinn, Anthony Bernard *educator*
Pomeroy, Benjamin Sherwood *veterinary medicine educator*
Prager, Stephen *chemistry educator*
Radcliffe, Edward Bruce *entomologist*
Raup, Philip Martin *retired agricultural economics educator*
Rebane, John T. *lawyer*
Renner, Robert George *federal judge*
Robertson, Jerry Earl *retired manufacturing company executive*
†Rosenberg, Brian C *academic administrator*
Rosenblatt, Paul Conrad *family educator*
Rossmann, Jack Eugene *psychology educator*
†Rothman, Mitchell Lewis *lawyer, educator*
Rothmeier, Steven George *merchant banker, investment manager*
Roy, Robert Russell *toxicologist*
Rudelius, William *marketing educator*
Ruttan, Vernon Wesley *agricultural economist*

Sadowski, Richard J. *former publishing executive*
†Sarazin, Mary Eileen *lawyer*
†Sawyer, Timothy Kenneth *music educator*
Schultz, David A. *political science educator, editor, writer, lawyer*
†Schuman, Allan L. *chemical company executive*
Schwartz, A(lbert) Truman *chemistry educator*
Seagren, Alice *state legislator*
†Senkler, Robert *insurance company executive*
Seymour, McNeil Vernam *lawyer*
†Sheahan, Michael John *lawyer*
†Sheshukov, Aleksey Y. *hydrologist, researcher*
†Shmulsky, Rubin *forester, educator*
Siefken, Mark W. *small business owner*
Skillingstad, Constance Yvonne *social services administrator, educator*
Smith, Mary Hill *volunteer*
†Spencer, David James *lawyer*
Stewart, James Brewer *historian, writer, college administrator*
Stringer, Edward Charles *judge, lawyer*
Stromberg, Bert E. *veterinary medicine educator*
Stroud, Rhoda M. *elementary education educator*
Sviggum, Steven Arthur *farmer, state representative*
Swaiman, Kenneth Fred *pediatric neurologist, educator*
Swenson, Tami Charlotte *research analyst*
Thompson, Mary Eileen *chemistry educator*
Titus, Jack L. *pathologist, educator*
†Tollefson, Lee *architect*
†Tourek, Steven Charles *lawyer*
Trojack, John Edward *lawyer*
Tylevich, Alexander V. *sculptor, architect, educator*
Victor, Lorraine Carol *critical care nurse*
†Vreyens, John Robert *agricultural products executive, educator*
Wagner, Mary Margaret *library and information science educator*
Walton, Matt Savage *retired geologist, educator*
†Webster, Steven Craig *engineer*
Wehrwein, Austin Carl *newspaper reporter, editor, writer*
†Weiner, Carl Dorian *historian*
†Wendler, M. Cecilia *nursing educator*
Wendt, Hans W. *life scientist*
Westermeyer, Joseph John *psychiatrist*
†White, William Thomas *curator, historian, educator*
Willis, Bruce Donald *judge*
Wilson, Michael John *biologist, educator*
Winthrop, Sherman *lawyer*
†Woutat, Paul Gustav *lawyer*
Wright, Michelle Maria *English language educator*
Yin, Kewen Karen *chemical engineer, educator*
†You, Yali *music educator*
†Yucel, Edgar Kent *lawyer, consultant*
Zander, Janet Adele *psychiatrist*
Zimmerman, Larry John *anthropologist, educator*

Saint Peter
†Crnkovic, Denis *language educator*
Haeuser, Michael John *library administrator*
Leitch, Richard *political science educator*
McKay, John Robert *concert painist*
Mc Rostie, Clair Neil *economics educator*
Mosbo, John Alvin *dean*
Nelsen, William Cameron *educational association administrator, retired academic administrator*
Turnbull, Charles Vincent *retired real estate broker*

Sartell
Dominik, John Julius *retired advertising company executive*
Van Nostrand, Catharine Marie Herr *retired personnel director*

Sauk Rapids
Newman, Donald John *marketing executive*

Savage
Bean, Glen Atherton *entrepreneur*
Loutzenhiser, Carolyn Ann *retired elementary education educator*
Luth, James Curtis *systems consultant*

Shakopee
Gertis, Neill Allan *writer*
Gouin, Warner Peter *information technology specialist*
Qiu, Peihua *statistician, educator, statistician, researcher*

Shoreview
Liu, Benjamin Young-hwai *engineering educator*
Nolting, Earl *retired academic administrator*

Sleepy Eye
Ruddy, James Vincent, Jr., *tax advocate*

South Saint Paul
Fairhurst, Charles *civil and mining engineering educator*
†Metzen, James P. *state legislator, banker*
†Pugh, Thomas Wilfred *lawyer*

St Paul
Dayton, Charles Kelly *lawyer*
Hulbert, Linda Ann *academic librarian*
†Norton, John William *lawyer, mediator*
†Ta, Minh Tuan *lobbyist, consultant*

Staples
†Iverson, Jeffrey G. *music educator, director*

Stillwater
Cardozo, Richard Nunez *marketing, entrepreneurship and business educator*
Delaney, John Charles *pharmaceutical company executive*
Horsch, Lawrence Leonard *venture capitalist, corporate revitalization executive*
†Huelsmann, Thomas J. *retired music educator*
†Hutchinson, Michael Clark *lawyer*
Rescigno, Aldo *pharmacokinetics educator*

Thief River Falls
Reeves, Bruce *social worker*

Two Harbors
McMillion, John Macon *retired newspaper publisher*

Ulen
Harmon, Kay Yvonne *elementary education educator*

Vadnais Heights
†Martinez, Kathryn Marie *music educator*
Polakiewicz, Leonard Anthony *foreign language and literature educator*

Virginia
Knabe, George William, Jr., *pathologist, educator*

Waite Park
Bauer, Edward Alphonse *electrical contractor*

Walker
Collins, Thomas William *caterer, consultant*

Warba
Currie, Earl James *transportation executive*

Waseca
Barr, Leslie Glen *family practice physician*
Capriglione, Ralph Raymond *geologist, educator*
Frederick, Edward Charles *university official*
Strand, Melvin LeRoy *English educator*

Waubun
Christensen, Marvin Nelson *venture capitalist*

Wayzata
†Alton, Howard Robert, Jr., *lawyer, real estate and food company executive*
Blodgett, Frank Caleb *retired food company executive*
Emison, Jane Bale Larson *interior designer*
Furda, Ivan *chemist, consultant*
Johnson, Eugene Laurence *lawyer*
Johnson, Sankey Anton *manufacturing company executive*
Luthringshauser, Daniel Rene *manufacturing company executive*
Muschenheim, Frederick *retired pathologist*
Reutiman, Robert William, Jr., *lawyer*
Rich, Willis Frank, Jr., *banker*
Schoen, Charles Judd *service executive*
Swanson, Donald Frederick *retired food company executive*
Waldera, Wayne Eugene *crisis management specialist*
Wyard, Vicki Shaw *investment and insurance company executive*

Welch
Solymossy, Joseph Martin *nuclear engineer*

West Saint Paul
Cento, William Francis *retired newspaper editor*
†Kassulke, Paul Robert *secondary school educator*
†Sittard, Herman Joseph *public relations executive, editor, retired*

Wheaton
†Lanter, Martin Luther *music educator*

White Bear Lake
Holmen, Reynold Algott Emanuel *chemist*
Rogers, Megan Elizabeth *mental health therapist*

Willmar
Vander Aarde, Stanley Bernard *retired otolaryngologist*

Windom
†Blackstad, Mildred Mae *retired music educator*

Winona
Borman, John *trial lawyer, arbitrator, mediator*
Boseker, Barbara Jean *education educator*
Brosnahan, Roger Paul *lawyer*
Bures, Frank Adolph *journalist, writer*
†Draayer, Suzanne Rhodes *music educator, writer*
Haas, James Wayne *accountant*
Holm, Joy Alice *psychology educator, goldsmith, artist, art educator*
Krueger, Darrell William *academic administrator*
Nasstrom, Roy Richard *retired education educator, consultant*
†Ni, Ting *historian, educator*
O'Shea, Patrick Michael *conductor, music educator*
†Pascual, Felino Garcia *mathematician, educator*
†Ramsdell, Bruced D *music educator*
Sullivan, Kathryn Ann *librarian, educator*
Wilson, Lisa Marie *English educator*

Woodbury
Benforado, David M. *environmental engineer*
Exe, David Allen *electrical engineer*
Fraher, Elaine Adel *retired music educator*
Luther, William P. *former congressman*
Woodruff, Ellen Louise *chaplain*

Worthington
Aby, Robert Davis *physician*
Meyer, Helen Bernadine *financial services company executive*

Zumbrota
Post, Diana Constance *retired librarian*

MISSISSIPPI

Aberdeen
Davidson, Glen Harris *federal judge*
Houston, David Winston *federal judge*

Ackerman
Coleman, Frances McLean *secondary school educator*

Alcorn
†Hawkins, Sidney Taylor *mathematician, educator*

Alcorn State
Bristow, Clinton, Jr., *academic administrator*
†Conner, Deondra *education educator*
†Felder-Wright, Pamela Theresa Evans *education educator*
†Iheanacho, Vitalis A *education educator, researcher*
Sizemore, Robert Carlen *immunologist, educator*
Yu, May Huang *librarian, educator*

Amory
Brannon, Pat *poet*
Bryan, Wendell Hobdy, II, (Hob Bryan) *state senator*

Batesville
Cook, William Leslie, Jr., *lawyer*
Neal, Joseph Lee *vocational school educator*

Bay Saint Louis
Bernstein, Joseph *lawyer*
Hurlburt, Harley Ernest *ocean modeling and prediction scientist*
†Latham, Terry L. *social services administrator*
Lewando, Alfred Gerard, Jr., *oceanographer*
†Liu, Cheng-Chien *oceanographer, researcher*
†Rahman, Shamim A. *engineering executive*
Rondeau, Clement Robert *petroleum geologist*
Woodward, Ralph Lee, Jr., *historian, educator*

Belden
Whitehead, Zelma Kay *special education educator*

Biloxi
Brown, Sheba Ann *elementary education educator*
Cox, Albert Harrington, Jr., *economist*
Crumbaugh, James Charles *psychologist*
Culberson, Gary Michael *hotel manager*
†Dornan, Donald C., Jr., *lawyer*
Erickson, Georganne Morris *nursing administrator, nursing educator, psychiatric-mental health consultant*
Gentry, Nancy O'Pry *medical/surgical nurse*
Holman, Charles Milligan *urologist*
Howze, Joseph Lawson Edward *retired bishop*
Manners, Pamela Jeanne *middle school educator*
McCaughan, Della Marie *retired science educator*
O'Barr, Bobby Gene, Sr., *lawyer*
Roper, John Marlin, Sr., *federal magistrate judge*
Senter, Lyonel Thomas, Jr., *federal judge*
Zocchi, Louis Joseph *product designer, game company executive*

Brandon
Baltz, Richard Jay *health care company executive*
Guthrie, Michael Steele *magnetic circuit design engineer*
Jones, Helene Rasberry *nursing educator*
McCreery, James Allan *retired business services company executive*
Okojie, Felix A. *research administrator*
Parker, Rhonda Walker *nurse, administrator*

Braxton
†Skiffer-Robinson, Danielle K. *guidance counselor*

Brookhaven
Ledet, Henry Joseph *librarian*

Byhalia
†Tackett, Maresa D. *medical technician*

Calhoun City
Macon, Myra Faye *retired library director*

Carriere
Stanton, Sylvia Doucet *artist, art gallery owner*
Woodmansee, Glenn Edward *employee relations executive*

Centreville
Nelson, Janie Rish *hospital executive*

Clarksdale
Burnham, Van Robinson, Jr., *general practice physician*
†Connell, Edward Peacock, Sr., *lawyer*
Johnson, P. H. *federal agency administrator*
Magdovitz, Lawrence Maynard *real estate executive, lawyer*
†Schmidt, John Frederick, III, *government agency administrator, consultant*
Walters, William Lee *accountant*

Cleveland
Alexander, William Brooks *lawyer, former state senator*
†Pettway, Keith *music educator*
Spencer, William Christopher *English educator*
Taylor, Donna Buescher *marriage and family therapist*

Clinton
Bigelow, Martha Mitchell *retired historian*
Durham, Carol Elise *musician, educator*
Hensley, John Clark *religious organization administrator, minister*
Mather, Bryant *consultant*
†Montgomery, Keith Norris, Sr., *insurance executive, state legislator*
†Roberts, Bert C., Jr., *telecommunications company executive*
Sclater, James Stanley *music educator, composer, musician*
Sidgmore, John W. *telecommunications executive*
Whitlock, Betty *secondary education educator*
†Young, Craig S. *music educator, conductor*

Columbus
†Burger, Michael *humanities educator*
Dunkelberg, Kendall Alan *literature educator, poet*
Holt, Robert Ezel *data processing executive*
Labensky, Sarah Ross *culinary educator*
†Limbert, Claudia A. *academic administrator, writer*
†Nawrocki, Susan Jean *librarian*
†Tousley, Rebecca Perkins *retired librarian*
Wheeley, Nancy Janine *librarian*

Corinth
Gray, Janet D. *piano teacher, organist*

Courtland
Lindgren, Carl Edwin *educational consultant, antiquarian, historian*

Crystal Springs
†Bates, Lura Wheeler *retired trade association executive*

Diamondhead
Brinsmade, Akbar Fairchild *chemical engineering consultant*
Reddien, Charles Henry, II, *lawyer, corporate executive, consultant*

Drew
†Morris, DeVoyce Campbell *school system administrator*

Fayette
La Salle, Arthur Edward *historic foundation executive*

Florence
Anding, Robert Eugene *retired religion educator, minister*

Forest
Park, James Wallace *economics educator*

Fulton
Myers, Jeffery Mark *music educator, musician*

Gautier
Baggett, James Lamar *anatomy, physiology and microbiology educator*
Egerton, Charles Pickford *anatomy and physiology educator*

Glen
†Wigginton, Lisa Benderman *elementary school educator*

Gloster
Davis, Cynthia D'Ascenzo *lawyer*

Goodman
Jones, Rita Ann *retired speech, theater educator*

Greenville
Keating, Bern *writer, journalist*
Martin, Andrew Ayers *lawyer, physician, educator*

Greenwood
Deaton, Charles Milton *lawyer*
Jones, Carolyn Ellis *publisher, retired employment agency and business service company owner*

Grenada
Dugan, Cindy *music educator, organist*
Hill, Clyde Vernon, Jr., *prosecutor*
Thomas, Ouida Power *music educator*

Gulfport
Allen, Harry Roger *lawyer*
†Bosarge, Rick Anthony *health facility administrator*
Desmond, Susan Fahey *lawyer*
Dickerson, Monar Steve *city official*
Fooladi, Mike M. *physician, educator*
Gex, Lucien Marion, III, (Beau Gex) *legislative staff member*
Mc Call, Jerry Chalmers *retired government official*
†Owen, Joe Sam *lawyer*
Russell, Dan M., Jr., *federal judge*
Swetman, Glenn Robert *English language educator, poet*
Thatcher, George Robert *banker, columnist, author*

Hattiesburg
Adelman, Michael Schwartz *lawyer*
Barron, Jonathan *language educator*
Bedenbaugh, Angela Lea Owen *chemistry educator, researcher*
†Boatner, Jerra *legal assistant*
Burrus, John N(ewell) *sociology educator*
Chain, Bobby Lee *electrical contractor, former mayor*
Davis, Charles Raymond *political scientist, educator*
De Chiaro, John Paul *music educator*
Duhon, David Lester *business educator, management consultant*
Gunther, William David *university administrator, economics educator*
Hickman, Ronald Lee *media broker, broadcast executive*
Lucas, Aubrey Keith *retired university president*
McRaney, Joan Katherine *artist*

Noonkester, James Ralph *retired college president*
†O'Brien, Warren Gregory *historian, educator, writer*
†Polk, Noel Earl *English educator*
Saucier Lundy, Karen *nursing educator*
†Scarborough, William Kauffman *historian, educator*
†Schweinle, Amy *psychologist, educator*
†Slade, Barbie Evette Delk *special education educator*
Thames, Shelby Freland *science educator, academic administrator*
Treybig, Joel Andrew *musician, educator*
Urban, Marek W. *chemistry, polymers and coatings educator*
†Vail, Kathryn G *music educator*
Waltman, Jerold Lloyd *political scientist, educator*
Wood, Forrest E., Jr., *philosophy and religion educator*
†Wooton, John Andrew *music educator*

Hazlehurst
Blakeney, Margaret Elizabeth Fleming *counselor, educator*

Hernando
Brown, William A. *lawyer, mediator, arbitrator*

Holly Springs
Beckley, David Lenard *academic administrator*

Holly Springs,
†Frederick, Richard John *education educator*

Indianola
Matthews, David *clergyman*

Itta Bena
†Ahanonu, Chukwuma Smart *education educator*
Goldman, Lawrence *music educator*
Hudspeth, Harvey Gresham *history educator*
Newsome, Moses *social work educator*
†Wax, Benjamin *physical education educator, consultant*

Iuka
†Barnes, Betty Jean *educational administrator*

Jackson
Anglin, Linda McCluney *retired elementary school educator*
Barksdale, Rhesa Hawkins *federal judge*
Beck, Crafton *music director*
Black, D(eWitt) Carl(isle), Jr., *lawyer*
Bloom, Sherman *retired pathologist, educator*
Bobo, Len Davis *musician, educator*
Brooks, Jean Evelyn *social work educator*
Buckner-Brown, Joyce *allied health instructor*
Burch, Donald Victor *lawyer*
Burns, Robert, Jr., *architect, freelance writer, artist*
†Burrow, William Hollis, II, *dermatologist*
Campbell, G. Douglas *medical educator*
Chatham, Lloyd Reeve *lawyer*
†Clark, David Wright *lawyer*
Clark, Eric C. *state official*
†Cole, Ricky *political organization worker*
Collins, Deloris Williams *secondary school educator*
Corbett, James John *neurologist, neuroophthalmologist*
Corlew, John Gordon *lawyer*
Cruse, Julius Major, Jr., *pathologist, educator*
†Currie, Edward Jones, Jr., *lawyer*
Currier, Robert David *neurologist*
Curtis, Verna Polk *reading educator*
Das, Suman Kumar *plastic surgeon, researcher*
Deschamp, Clyde *emergency medical technician*
Diaz, Oliver E., Jr., *state supreme court justice*
Dickson, Betsy G. *social worker*
Duncan, Jennings Ligon, III, *minister*
Easley, Charles D., Jr., *state supreme court justice*
†Edds, Stephen Charles *lawyer*
Eicher, Donald E., III, *lawyer*
Evans, Owen Beverly *neurologist*
Ford, Timothy Alan *state representative*
Freeland, Alan Edward *orthopedic surgery educator, physician*
†Fuller, Phillip Roland *finance educator*
†Goodman, William Flournoy, III, *lawyer*
Gordon, Granville Hollis *church official*
†Grant, Bettye *writer*
Grant, Russell Porter, Jr., *lawyer, petroleum land man*
Graves, James E. *state supreme court justice, educator*
Gray, Duncan Montgomery, Jr., *retired bishop*
†Hafter, Jerome Charles *lawyer*
Hammond, Frank Jefferson, III, *lawyer*
Harisdangkul, Valee *physician*
†Harkins, Patrick Nicholas, III, *lawyer*
Harmon, George Marion *academic administrator*
†Hauberg, Robert Engelbrecht, Jr., *lawyer*
Hegwood, Barbara H.
Henderson, Julian Crowder *retired pathologist*
Henegan, John C(lark) *lawyer*
Herring, James H. *political organization administrator, lawyer*
Hewes, George Poindexter, III, *lawyer*
Hosemann, C. Delbert, Jr., *lawyer*
Houston, Gerry Ann *oncologist*
Howard, William Percy *physician*
Howell, Joel Walter, III, *lawyer*
Hughes, Byron William *lawyer, oil exploration company executive*
Hupp, James R. *academic administrator*
†Iraki, Waithaka Njuguna *educator, journalist*
Johnson, Mark Wayne *lawyer*
†Johnson, Ronald E. *grocery company executive*
Jolly, E. Grady *federal judge*
†Julian, Michael *grocery company executive*
Keary, David *artistic director*
Kemp, Stephen Frederick *physician*
Kermode, John Cotterill *pharmacology educator, researcher*
Kliesch, William Frank *retired physician*
†Lampton, Leslie B., Sr., *oil industry executive*
Langford, James Jerry *lawyer*
Larsen, Samuel Harry *minister, educator*
Lee, Tom Stewart *judge*
†Leonard, Pamela Dian *architect, artist*
Lewis, Robert Edwin, Jr., *pathology immunology educator, researcher*
Little, Travis Lane *state senator, motel management executive*
Malloy, James Matthew *health management executive, healthcare consultant*
†Marks, Michael *association administrator*
Martinez, Eduardo Vidal *lawyer*
†Mawson, Anthony Richard *epidemiologis, public health educator*
McDaniel, Larry Scott *microbiology and surgery educator*
McKnight, William Edwin *minister*
†McLemore-Wheeler, Linda M. *literature educator*
McLeod, Stephen Glenn *education educator, language educator*
McRae, Charles R. (Chuck McCrae) *state supreme court justice*
McWilliams Morse, Anne Washburn *retired journalist, writer*
Minocha, Anil *physician, educator, researcher*
Moak, Elizabeth *performing pianist*
Moize, Jerry Dee *lawyer, government official*
Moll, George William *pediatrician, educator*
Molpus, Dick H. *management company executive*
Moore, Mike *state attorney general*
Mosley, Jessie Bryant *retired science educator*
†Munera, Pedro Antonio *child and adolescent psychiatrist*
Musgrove, David Ronald *governor*
Neglen, Nils Peter *surgeon*
†O'Mara, James Wright *lawyer*
Pittman, Edwin Lloyd *state supreme court chief justice*
Poole, Galen Vincent *surgeon, educator, researcher*
Ray, H. M. *lawyer*
Read, Dale Gilbert *endocrinologist, educator*
Redmon, Cynthia Ann *poet, songwriter*
†Rhodes, Linda L. *medical transcriptionist, medical assistant*
Risley, Rod Alan *education association executive*
†Rivlin, Michel E. *gynecologist*
Roberts, Kristie *researcher*
Rogers, Oscar Allan, Jr., *college president*
Ross, Ian Beaudoin *neurosurgeon, educator*
Sawyer, Donald E. *physician, urologist*
Scafidel, Jim R. *freelance/self-employed writer*
†Scanlon, Pat H. *lawyer*
Shinn, Clinton Wesley *lawyer*
†Shirley, Aaron *pediatrician*
Smith, Edgar Eugene *biochemist, university administrator*
Smith, James W., Jr., *state supreme court justice*
Smith, Sharman Bridges *former state librarian*
Sneed, Raphael Corcoran *physiatrist, pediatrician*
Somekawa, Mina C. *pianist, educator*
Stovall, Jerry (Coleman Stovall) *insurance company executive*
Suess, James Francis *retired psychiatry educator*
Sugg, Robert Perkins *former state supreme court justice*
†Sullivan, Bettye Yarborough *foundation administrator*
Tchounwou, Paul Bernard *environmental health specialist, toxicologist, educator*
Thigpen, James Tate *physician, oncology educator*
Thornton, Larry Lee *psychotherapist, author, educator, minister*
†Travis, Jay A., III, *lawyer*
Tuck, Amy *lieutenant governor*
Walcott, Dexter Winn *allergist*
†Walker, John Leonard *lawyer*
West, Carol Catherine *law educator*
Williams, Thomas Kennon *retired surgeon*
†Wilson, L(eonard) H(enry) *lawyer*
Wilson, William Roberts, Jr., (Bob Wilson) *lawyer, apparel executive*
Winter, William Forrest *former governor, lawyer*
Wise, Robert Powell *lawyer*
Wolfe, Mildred Nungester *artist*
Yates, Steven Bradley *publisher*
†Zisman, Stuart *healthcare educator, social worker, counselor*

Keesler AFB
Locker, Dan Lewis *career officer*
†Pelak, Andrew J., Jr., *military officer*

Kiln
†Thissell, Charles William *lawyer*

Kosciusko
Shoemaker, William C. *journalist*

Lauderdale
Van Doren, Henrietta Lambert *nurse, anesthetist*

Laurel
Giles, Mamye Ruth *genealogy consultant, music voice educator*
Lacey, Peeler Grayson *diagnostic radiologist*
Lindstrom, Eric Everett *ophthalmologist*
Stringer, Lorrie Steen *pianist, educator*

Leland
Ayres, Mary Jo *professional speaker, writer, composer*

Liberty
†Stratton, Richard Howard *publishing executive*

Long Beach
Easton, Jill Johanna *state official*
Kanagy, Steven Albert *foundation administrator*
Miller, James Edward *computer scientist, educator*
†Smith, James Patterson *humanities educator, consultant*
White, Edith Roberta Shoemake *elementary school educator*
Williams, James Orrin *university administrator, educator*

Lorman
Ezekwe, Michael Obi *animal science educator*
Hylander, Walter Raymond, Jr., *retired civil engineer*
Panicker, Girish Kumar *agricultural scientist, consultant*

Madison
Dean, Jack Pearce *retired insurance company executive*
Hiatt, Jane Crater *arts agency administrator*
Obert, Keith David *lawyer*
Saenz, Rebecca Buchanan *family physician*

Magnolia
Coney, Elaine Marie *English and foreign languages educator*

Mccomb
Starrett, Keith *lawyer*

Meadville
Ikerd, Shirley Temple *financial planner*

Meridian
Church, George Millord *retired real estate company executive*
Cook, Donald Eugene *retired orthopedist*
Miller, Cliff *engineer*
Phillips, Patricia Jeanne *retired school system administrator*
†Primeaux, Lawrence *lawyer*
†Rackley, Emmerll *psychiatric nurse practitioner*
†Rosenbaum, Ike Alfred *foundation administrator*
Thomas, Kenneth Eugene *auditor*

Minter City
Mitchell, Patsy Malier *religious school founder and administrator*

Mississippi State
Aktosun, Tuncay *mathematical physics educator*
†Bentley, Gregory W. *literature educator*
Bumgardner, Joel David *biomedical engineer, educator*
Chrisman, James Joseph *management educator*
Cliett, Charles Buren *aeronautical engineer, educator, academic administrator*
Clynch, Edward John *political science educator, researcher*
Crudden, Adele Louise *social work research educator*
†Dobson, Edward Tauscher *mathematician*
Hughes, Patricia Newman *academic administrator*
Jenkins, Johnie Norton *research geneticist, research administrator*
Mabry, Donald Joseph *university administrator, history educator*
Martin, Edward Curtis, Jr., *landscape architect, educator*
†Qian, Chuanxi *mathematics educator*
Rabideau, Peter Wayne *university dean, chemistry educator*
Reddy, Kambham Raja *plant physiology educator*
Rent, Clyda Stokes *academic administrator*
†Taylor, Clayborne Dudley *engineering educator*
Truax, Dennis Dale *civil engineer, educator, consultant*
Vance, David A. *information systems educator*
Wall, Diane Eve *political science educator*
†Watson, Thomas Steuart *psychologist, educator*
Wiltrout, Ann Elizabeth *foreign language educator*

Moss Point
†Barnes, Anthony Clarke *music educator*

Natchez
Bramlette, David C., III, *federal judge*
Branyan, Cheryl Munyer *museum administrator, consultant*
Dunnell, Robert Chester *archaeologist, educator*
Marion, Ann *school psychologist, educator*
†McLemore, Joan Meadows *librarian, consultant*
Profice, Rosena Mayberry *elementary school educator*

Noxapater
Sumner, Margaret Elizabeth *elementary school educator*

Ocean Springs
Ales, Michael Raymond *engineering educator*
Austin, Claude Lidell *retired surgeon*
Baughn, Mary Alice Jackson *journalist*
†Denham, Earl Lamar *lawyer*
Furlow, William Lawrence *manufacturing and financial consultant*
Lee, Kathleen Mary *administration and nursing executive*
Lorenz, Ronald Theodore *manufacturing executive*
Luckey, Alwyn Hall *lawyer*
Odom, Patricia Ann (Patt Odom) *artist, educator*
Shaw, Joyce M. *librarian*

Olive Branch
†Carnall, George Hursey, II, *lawyer, business executive*
Douglas, Kenneth Dale *artist*
†Farr, Walter Evans *chemist, chemical engineer*
Harmon Brown, Valarie Jean *hospital laboratory director, information systems executive*

Oxford
Costner, Charles Lynn *retired civil engineer*
Duke, Stephen Oscar *physiologist, researcher, educator*
Hoar, Jere Richmond *journalism educator, writer*
Horton, Thomas Edward, Jr., *mechanical engineering educator*
Lewis, Ronald Wayne *lawyer*
†Mills, Michael Paul *judge*
Moorhead, Sylvester Andrew *education educator retired*
Rayburn, S. T. *lawyer*
†Rego, Cesar *science educator, researcher*
Roberts, Michael Dean *psychologist*
Walton, Gerald Wayne *retired university official*

Pascagoula
Dur, Philip Alphonse *defense aerospace executive, retired naval officer*
Horowitz, Michael Dory *cardiothoracic surgeon*
Hunter, John Leslie *lawyer*
McKee, Ronald Gene *vocational education educator*
Meredith, William Robert, Sr., *physician, educator*
Smith, Donald Vaughan *artist, educator*
†Smith, Janet *librarian*

Pass Christian
Clark, John Walter, Jr., *shipping company executive*
Henrion, Rosemary P. *mental health professional*
McCardell, James Elton *retired naval officer*

Perkinston
Mellinger, Barry Lee *community college president, vocational educator*

Picayune
Lowrie, Allen *geologist, oceanographer*

Raleigh
Price, Tommye Jo Ensminger *community health nurse*

Raymond
†Bee, Anna Cowden *dance educator*
†Ingwerson, John C. *music educator*
Moss, Jack Gibson *lawyer*

Ridgeland
Boackle, K F. *lawyer, writer, real estate broker*
Long, Roger Leonard *artist*
O'Neill, Paul John *retired psychology educator*

Ruleville
Cosue, Lamberto Gutierrez, III, *internist*

Senatobia
†Ungurait, John Bentley *music educator, consultant*

Southaven
†Taylor, Ronald Louis *lawyer*
†White, Marguerite *writer*

Starkville
Carley, Charles Team, Jr., *mechanical engineer*
†Cheathem, Mark R. *historian, educator*
Dampier, Caryn *self-defense instructor*
Ford, Robert MacDonald, III, *architect, educator*
George, Ernest Thornton, III, *financial consultant*
Gregg, Billy Ray *seed industry executive, consultant*
Jacob, Paul Bernard, Jr., *electrical engineering educator*
†Light, George Evans *humanities educator*
Martin, Theodore Krinn *former university administrator (deceased)*
Thomas, Garnett Jett *accountant*
Yoste, Charles Todd *lawyer*

Stennis Space Center
†Chin-Bing, Stanley Arthur *physicist, educator*
Fleischer, Peter *research geologist, oceanographer, educator*
Jacobs, Gregg Arthur *oceanographer, researcher*
Kamenkovich, Vladimir Moiseevich *oceanographer, educator*

Stoneville
†Hamel, Paul Bernard *ornithologist, researcher*
Ranney, Carleton David *plant pathology researcher, administrator*
Wilson, Alphus Dan *plant pathologist, researcher*

Sumrall
Downey, James Cecil *retired music and humanities educator*
Hudson, Mary Kay *executive*

Sunflower
Powell, Anice Carpenter *retired librarian*

Taylorsville
Windham, Velma Lee Ainsworth *writer, poet*

Tougaloo
†Whittington, Felicia Trenise *social services administrator, educator*

Tupelo
Bush, Fred Marshall, Jr., *lawyer*
†Clayton, Claude F., Jr., *lawyer*
Nash, Henry Warren *marketing educator*
Patterson, Aubrey Burns, Jr., *banker*
Ramage, Martis Donald, Jr., *banker*
Witty, Thomas Ezekiel, III, *psychologist, researcher*
Wooldridge, Thomas Dean *nephrologist*
Zurawski, Jeanette *rehabilitation services professional*

University
†Bougnol, Marie-Laure *finance educator*
Breazeale, Mack Alfred *physics educator*

Chen, Wei-Yin *chemical engineering educator, researcher*
†Cheng, Alexander Hung-Darh *engineering educator, consultant*
Flesher, Dale Lee *accounting educator, dean*
†Galef, David Adam *British literature educator, writer*
Gardner, William Lansing, III, *business educator*
†Guidice, Rebecca Monette *strategic management educator*
Hall, J(ames) R(obert) *English educator*
Howorth, David Bishop *lawyer*
Jordan, Winthrop Donaldson *historian, educator*
Keiser, Edmund Davis, Jr., *biologist, educator*
†Khayat, Robert Conrad *academic administrator*
Kiger, Joseph Charles *history educator*
Landon, Michael de Laval *historian, educator*
†López, Alfred J. *literature educator, writer*
Martin, Jeanette St. Clair *adult education educator*
Roach, David Giles *information technology executive*
Smith, Allie Maitland *engineering educator*
†Steel, David Warren *music history educator*
Wang, Sam Shu-Yi *hydraulic and mechanical engineer, educator*

Vaiden
Murphy, Ben Carroll *engineering company executive*

Vicksburg
Hopson, William Briggs, Jr., *surgeon*
Keulegan, Emma Pauline *special education educator*
McRae, John Leonidas *civil engineer, consultant*

Waveland
Briggs, Leslie Ray *retired mechanical engineer*

Wesson
Pickering, Garry Marlon *state official*

West Point
†Turner, Bennie L. *state legislator, lawyer*

Whitfield
Desai, Kirtida D. *medical educator*

Yazoo City
Brown, Marion Lipscomb, Jr., *publisher, photographer, writer, retired chemical company executive*
Hawthorne, Minnie *elementary school educator*

MISSOURI

Albany
Noble, Cheryl A. *library director*

Arcadia
†Davis, Jo *nurse, aromatherapist, writer, professional speaker, small business owner*

Arnold
Freukes, Patricia E. *pediatrics nurse, nursing supervisor*
McCredie, Joann Mary Rezny (Jo McCredie) *artist*
†Medart, Mike *manufacturing executive*

Arrow Rock
Bollinger, Michael *artistic director*

Ash Grove
Johnson, Iver Christian *valuation company executive*

Aurora
Goodman, N. Jane *small business owner, legal analyst*
Jay, Jerry Leon, Sr., *retired publishing executive, industrial engineer*

Ava
Murray, Delbert Milton *manufacturing engineer*

Ballwin
Ackerson, Charles Stanley *minister, social worker*
Arantes, José Carlos *industrial engineer, educator*
†Banton, Stephen Chandler *lawyer*
Bond, Dennis Earl *auditor*
Cornell, William Daniel *mechanical engineer*
Haller, Karen Sue *writer*
Pallozola, Christine *non-profit administrator*
†Rothermich, Gayla *music educator, director*
Sabacky, Jerome (Jerry Sabacky) *retired research chemist*
†Schneider, Ches *writer, educator*
Sidoti, Daniel R. *food technologist*

Belton
Blim, Richard Don *retired pediatrician*
Brown, Doris Jane *nursing aide*
Fox, Kevin Christopher *marketing professional*
†Shodean, Lisa Diane *military officer*

Benton
†Heckemeyer, Anthony Joseph *circuit court judge*

Berkeley
Campbell, Anita Joyce *computer company executive*

Bloomfield
Ferrell, Paul Cleveland *writer*

Blue Eye
Anderson, Ruth G. *retired education educator, educational consultant*

Blue Springs
Heller, John L., II, *construction executive*
McElroy, Michelle Marie *physician*

Reed, Tony Norman *aviation company executive*
Sauer, Richard John *retired non-profit executive*
Shover, Joan *retired secondary school educator*
Snyder, James Robert *protective services official, educator*

Bolivar
Brown, Autry *psychology educator, clergyman*
DeWeese, Eldonna Rose *librarian, editor*
†Harrison, Carol L. *music educator*
Hood, Michael Lee *psychologist, clinical researcher, educator*
Hooper, William Loyd *music educator, university administrator*
Rice, Cindy G. *estate planning associate*
Ryneveld, Edna Lynn Copeland *small business owner, healthcare educator*
†Thaller, Gregg P. *music educator*

Boonville
Omer, Robert Wendell *hospital administrator*

Bourbon
Heitsch, Leona Mason *artist, writer*

Bowling Green
Bruce, Judith Esther *retired music educator, elementary education educator*

Branson
Bradley, Leon Charles *musician, educator, consultant*
Coscia, Robert Lingua *surgeon, educator*
Ford, Jean Elizabeth *former English language educator*
Vinton, Bobby (Stanley Robert Vinton) *entertainer*

Branson West
Peterson, Sharon Lynn Craig *medical care manager, cost containment specialist*

Brentwood
†O'Neill, Kathryn J. *librarian, educator*

Bridgeton
Asma, Lawrence Francis *priest*
Brauer, Stephen Franklin *diplomat, manufacturing company executive*
Delaney, Robert Vernon *logistics and transportation executive*
Faulk, Marshall William *professional football player*
Hemming, Bruce Clark *microbiologist*
Kenison, Raymond Robert *fraternal organization administrator, director*

Brookfield
Sutton, Joyce Elaine *medical records director*

Bucklin
Payne, Flora Fern *real estate broker*

Butler
Baxter, Myrtle Mae (Bobbi Baxter) *artist*

Camdenton
Decker, Malcolm Doyle *insurance agent*
Hosman, Sharon *elementary education educator*

Cameron
Rose-Heim, William Bentley *minister, mediator, business owner, entrepreneur*

Canton
Ellis, James Ira *network technician*
Glover, Albert Downing *retired veterinarian*
Howe, Sandra Jo *library director*
Janney, DellAnn *accountant, educator*

Cape Girardeau
Baltz, Douglas Matthew *artist*
Blanton, Lewis M. *federal judge*
†Eom, Sean Bock *education educator, researcher*
Hathaway, Ruth Ann *chemist*
Haugland, Jerry Lee *accounting educator*
Hoffman, Steven James *historian, educator*
Lee, David Y.S. *neurologist*
Lowes, Albert Charles *lawyer*
McMahan, Gale Ann Scivally *education educator*
McManaman, Kenneth Charles *lawyer*
Miles, Donald Orval *clinical microbiologist*
Mohd Zain, A(hmad) Zaidy *counselor, educator*
†O'Loughlin, John Patrick *lawyer*
Smallwood, Glenn Walter, Jr., *utility marketing management executive*
Smith, Katherine Ellinger *artist, art educator*

Carthage
†Jett, Ernest Carroll
Weissenberger, Harry George *lawyer*

Caruthersville
Puangsuvan, Somporn *surgeon, consultant*

Cassville
†Melton, Emory Leon *lawyer, state legislator, publisher*
Sheats, Rachel Gay *computer and reading educator, videographer*

Centralia
Everhart, James Gray *retired manufacturing executive*

Charleston
Cassell, Lucille Richardson *small business owner*
Wallhausen, Mildred Carolyn *publisher*

Chesterfield
Armstrong, Theodore Morelock *financial executive*
Baumann, Carol Kay *clinical nurse specialist*
Biebel, Curt Fred, Jr., *dentist*
Carpenter, Will Dockery *chemical company executive*

Coffin, Richard Keith *lawyer*
Cooper, Kenneth Carlton *training consultant*
Cox, Glenda Jewell *retired elementary school educator*
Denneen, John Paul *lawyer*
†Doshi, Parul D. *research scientist*
Driscoll, Charles Francis *financial services company executive, investment adviser*
Falk, Barbara Marie *psychologist*
Finley, Marlynn Holt *elementary educator consultant*
Flores, Jhonson Eder *anesthesiologist*
Fowler, Marti *fine arts consultant*
Frawley, Thomas Francis *retired physician*
Fujiwara, Hideji *chemist, researcher*
Gill, Suzanne *software book publisher*
Graham, Donald James *food technologist*
†Henderson, William J. *association executive*
†Hier, Marshall David *lawyer*
Higgins, Edward Aloysius *retired newspaper editor*
Hunter, Buddy D. *holding company executive*
Jordan, Thomas E. *retired academic researcher*
King, William Terry *retired manufacturing company executive*
Kurz, James Eckhardt *retired chemist*
Landram, Christina Louella *librarian*
Logue, Jean Evelyn *music educator, educator*
Mak, Sioe Tho *retired engineer*
Malvern, Donald *retired aircraft manufacturing company executive*
Matros, Larisa Grigoryevna *medical philosophy researcher, writer*
McLain, Donald J. *educational consultant*
Metzler, Paul Raymond *electrical engineer, consultant*
Morley, Harry Thomas, Jr., *real estate executive*
Morse, Stacey Ann *art studio owner*
Pollihan, Thomas Henry *lawyer*
Rathore, Anurag Singh *chemical engineer*
Ross, Richard Lee *retired lawyer*
Selfridge, George Dever *retired dentist, retired naval officer*
Shepperd, Susan Abbott *special education educator*
†Stalnaker, Tim *lawyer*
Webster, Ronald D. *communications company executive*
Williams, Luther Steward *research scientist*
Willis, Frank Edward *retired air force officer*
†Wohl, Martin H. *retired chemical engineer, business executive*

Clayton
Ball, Kenneth Leon *manufacturing company executive, organizational development consultant*
Davenport, Dennis Lynn *protective services official*
Fluhr, Steven Solomon *lawyer*
Huddleston, Charles B. *surgeon, educator*
Kemper, David Woods, II, *banker*
Komen, Leonard *lawyer*
Mohrman, Henry J(oe), Jr., *lawyer, investment manager*
†Novelly, Paul Anthony *petrochemical and refining company executive*
†Radloff, Stuart Jay *lawyer*
Schwartz, Theodore Frank *lawyer*
†Tremayne, Eric Flory *lawyer*
Vecchiotti, Robert Anthony *management and organizational consultant*

Clinton
Boarman, Marjorie Ruth *prevention specialist, manufacturing company executive*
Kelsay, David Roland *chemist*
Wentz, Wendell Franklin *columnist, writer*

Columbia
†Abbitt, Robbyn Jo Forry *geographic information systems specialist*
Aggarwal, Kul *internist, cardiologist, educator*
Alexander, Martha Sue *retired librarian*
Alexander, Thomas Benjamin *history educator*
Allen, William Cecil *physician, educator*
Almony, Robert Allen, Jr., *librarian, businessman*
Anderson, Donald Kennedy, Jr., *English educator*
Anderson, Ralph Robert *endocrinology educator*
†Arnet, William Francis *lawyer*
†Ballard, Bruce W. *philosophy educator, religious studies educator*
Bank, Barbara J. *sociology educator*
Barrett, James Thomas *immunologist, educator*
Basu, Asit Prakas *statistician*
Bauman, John E., Jr., *chemistry educator*
†Beaujean, A. Alexander *researcher*
Beem, John Kelly *mathematician, educator*
Benson, Jerry Kenneth *sociologist*
Biddle, Bruce Jesse *social psychologist, educator*
Bien, Joseph Julius *philosophy educator*
Blevins, Dale Glenn *agronomy educator*
†Bothwell, Marcella Roper *pediatrician, educator, otolaryngologist*
†Braddock, Stephen Robert *pediatrician, educator*
Brinegar, Elizabeth Anne *critical care nurse, educator*
Brown, Olen Ray *medical microbiology and toxicology expert witness, researcher, educator, consultant, writer*
Bunn, Ronald Freeze *lawyer, academic administrator*
†Casazza, Peter George *mathematician, educator*
Chambers, Glenn Darrell *wildlife photographer, artist*
Colwill, Jack Marshall *physician, educator, dean*
Crepeau, Dewey Lee *lawyer, educator*
Cunningham, Milamari Antoinella *anesthesiologist*
David, John Dewood *biology educator*
Davis, James O(thello) *physiology educator*
Decker, Wayne Leroy *meteorologist, educator*
†Dhand, Rajiv *physician*
†Duan, Dongsheng *education educator, researcher*
Eastman, Harold Dwight *retired social studies educator, journalist*

Eaton, Gary David *physician*
Eggers, George William Nordholtz, Jr., *anesthesiologist, educator*
Ethington, Raymond Lindsay *geology educator, researcher*
Ezashi, Toshihiko *molecular biologist*
Finkelstein, Richard Alan *retired microbiology educator, consultant*
Frey, Jeffery Paul *internist, geriatrician*
Frisby, James Curtis *agricultural engineering educator*
Geary, David Cyril *psychology educator*
Geiger, Mark Watson *management educator*
George, Melvin Douglas *retired university president*
†Good, Glenn Edward *psychologist, educator*
Goodrich, James William *historian, association executive*
†Gopalakrishna, Srinath *finance educator*
†Gubrium, Jaber F. *sociology educator*
Gysbers, Norman Charles *education educator*
Harter, Philip J. *lawyer, educator*
Helvey, William Charles, Jr., *communications specialist*
Hensley, Elizabeth Catherine *nutritionist, educator*
Ho, Dominic KC *electrical engineering educator*
Hook, Martin Lawrence *music educator, director*
†Horner, Stephen VanDyke *finance educator*
Ignoffo, Carlo Michael *insect pathologist-virologist*
James, Elizabeth Joan Plogsted *pediatrician, educator*
†Johnson, E. Diane *librarian*
Justice, George Lewis *language educator*
†Keyvan, Shahla *nuclear engineer, educator*
Khojasteh, Ali *medical oncologist, hematologist*
Kierscht, Marcia Selland *academic administrator, psychologist*
Klachko, David Max *physician, educator*
†Klein, Cerry Martin *operations research and industrial engineering educator, consultant*
König, Peter *pediatrician, educator*
†Kvanvig, Jonathan L. *philosophy educator*
†Lambert, Michael Canute *psychologist, educator*
Lazzaro-Weis, Carol Marie *foreign languages educator*
Leong, Lampo (Lanbo Liang) *artist, educator*
Lo, Clarence Y. H. *sociology educator, writer*
Longo, Daniel Robert *health services researcher, medical educator*
Loory, Stuart Hugh *journalist*
Looser, Devoney Kay *English language educator*
LoPiccolo, Joseph *psychologist, educator, author*
Losanoff, Julian Emil *surgeon, educator*
†Loy, Timothy *pathologist*
Lubensky, Earl Henry *diplomat, anthropologist*
Mays, William Gay, II, *lawyer, real estate developer*
McDermott, Dennis Michael *trade association executive*
†McKinnon, James Richard *management consultant*
†Mehr, David Ralph *geriatrician, researcher*
Middleton, James Allen *music educator*
Miller, Paul Ausborn *adult education educator*
Mitchell, Roger Lowry *retired agronomy educator*
Moore, Mitchell Jay *lawyer, law educator*
Morehouse, Lawrence Glen *veterinarian, educator*
Mullen, Edward John, Jr., *Spanish language educator*
Munson, Richard Howard *horticulturist*
Nelson, C. Jerry *agronomy educator*
Nikolai, Loren Alfred *accounting educator, writer*
Nolph, Georgia Bower *physician*
Northway, Wanda I. *real estate company executive*
O'Connor, John Thomas *civil engineering educator*
Oro, John James *neurosurgeon*
Overby, Osmund Rudolf *art historian, educator*
Pacheco, Manuel Trinidad *academic administrator*
Parmeley, Jerry Paul *software support analyst*
Parrigin, Elizabeth Ellington *lawyer*
Payne, Thomas L. *university official*
†Perkoff, Gerald Thomas *physician, educator*
Peth, Howard Allen *lawyer, educator*
Phillips, Walter Ray *lawyer, educator*
Poehlmann, Carl John *agronomist, researcher*
Pringle, Oran Allan *mechanical and aerospace engineering educator*
Puckett, C. Lin *plastic surgeon, educator*
Ratti, Ronald Andrew *economics educator*
†Roberts, R. Michael *animal scientist, biochemist, educator*
Robins, Betty Dashew *antiques and arts dealer*
Rowlett, Ralph Morgan *archaeologist, educator*
Salter, Christopher Lord *geography educator*
Sanders, Keith Page *journalism educator*
Schrader, Keith William *mathematician*
Schuder, John Claude *biomedical engineer*
Schwabe, John Bennett, II, *lawyer*
Schwartz, Richard Brenton *English language educator, university dean, writer*
Sevier, Jacob Thomas *music educator*
Shang, Yi *computer scientist, educator*
†Shende, Rajesh V. *chemical engineer, materials scientist, researcher*
Silver, Donald *surgeon, educator*
Stack, Frank Huntington *painter, retired educator*
Stewart, Bobby Gene *laboratory director*
Stockglausner, William George *accountant*
Strickland, Arvarh Eunice *history educator*
Sun, Albert Yung-Kwang *biochemistry and neurochemistry educator*
Sun, Ron *computer scientist, cognitive scientist*
†Swan, Shanna Helen *epidemiologist, researcher*
Tarnove, Lorraine *medical association executive*
Timberlake, Charles Edward *history educator*
Tofle, Ruth Brent *design educator, researcher, educator*

†Turley, J. William *lawyer*
Tzou, Robert Da *engineering educator*
Vallentyne, Peter Lloyd *philosophy educator*
Vogt, Albert Ralph *forester, educator, program director*
Wagner, William Burdette *business educator*
Waidelich, Donald Long *electrical engineer, consultant*
†Wallace, Richard Lee *chancellor*
Wallach, Barbara Price *classicist, educator*
†Weems, Robert Everett, Jr., *historian, educator*
Weisman, Gary Andrew *biochemist*
Weiss, James Moses Aaron *psychiatrist, educator*
Welliver, Warren Dee *lawyer, retired state supreme court justice*
Welshons, Wade Vincent *biomedical sciences educator*
Westbrook, James Edwin *lawyer, educator*
White, Harry Houston *neurologist*
Whitman, Dale Alan *lawyer, law educator*
Winfield, Betty Houchin *communications educator*
Witten, David Melvin *radiology educator*
Wixom, Robert Llewellyn *biochemistry educator*
†Wu, Bin *industrial engineering, professor*
Yanders, Armon Frederick *biological sciences educator, research administrator*
Yarwood, Dean Lesley *political science educator*
Yasuda, Hirotsugu Koge *chemical engineering professor*
Youmans, William Barton *physiologist*
Zguta, Russell *history educator*

Concordia
Bockelman, Melvin F. *retired computer scientist, writer*

Creve Coeur
Bockserman, Robert Julian *chemist*
Kemper, Christina *small business owner, respiratory therapist, elementary educator*
Luzio, Timothy Joseph *protective services official*
Wasserman, Stephen Miles *communications director*

Crystal City
†Lourwood, David Lee, Jr., *pharmacotherapist, educator*
Sita, Michael John *pharmacist, educator*

Cuba
Lange, C. William *lawyer, educator*
Pascoe, Percy Willard *newspaper publisher*
Work, Bruce Van Syoc *business consultant*

Defiance
LeMaster, Sherry Renee *fundraising administrator, foundation administrator, consultant*

Des Peres
Sadlo, Kenneth Louis *poet, writer*

Dexter
Owens, Debra Ann *chiropractor*

Dittmer
Miller, Bertin *priest, social administrator*

Dixon
†Jackson, David Williams *music educator*

Doniphan
McCann, Lawrence Alton *music educator*

Earth City
Anderhalter, Oliver Frank *educational organization executive*
Buselmeier, Bernard Joseph *insurance company executive*
Frontiere, Georgia *professional football team executive*

Eureka
Lindsey, Susan Lyndaker *zoologist*
Sexton, Owen James *vertebrate ecology educator, conservationist*
Zimmers, Vivian Eleanor *development and administrative consultant*

Excelsior Springs
Mitchell, Earl Wesley *clergyman*

Farmington
Lees, William Glenwood *finance executive, retail executive*
Massie, Maureen Teresa *elementary school educator*

Fayette
Burres, Carla Anne *medical technologist*
Davis, H(umphrey) Denny *publisher*
†Enochs, M. Rebecca *science educator*
Hirsch, Michael Lee *mayor*
Inman, Marianne Elizabeth *college administrator*
Keeling, Joe Keith *religion educator, college official and dean*
McIntosh, William David *mathematics educator emeritus*

Fenton
Baer, Robert J. *transportation company executive*
†Maritz, W. Stephen *marketing professional, service executive*
†McClure, Richard P. *transportation executive*
Stolar, Henry Samuel *lawyer*

Ferguson
Bruns, Billy Lee *electrical engineer, consultant*
Chubb, Charles Ray *physicist, researcher*
Fieldhammer, Eugene Louis *civil engineer*
†Pescarino, Richard Angelo *mathematician, educator*

Florissant
Ashhurst, Anna Wayne *foreign language educator*

Boyle, Patrick Otto *lawyer*
Carman, Robert Eugene *secondary school educator*
Luebke, Martin Frederick *retired curator*
Owen, Robert Frederick *internist, rheumatologist*
Reese, Alferd George *retired army civilian logistics specialist*
Schutzius, Mary Jane *volunteer activist*
Stevens, Robert Edward *engineering company executive*
Stormer, John Anthony *minister emeritus, author, publisher*
Tanphaichitr, Kongsak *rheumatologist, allergist, immunologist, internist*
Tomazi, George Donald *retired electrical engineer*
Ziemer, John Robert *software engineer*

Fort Leonard Wood
†Flowers, Robert B. *military career officer*
†Ryder, Donald J. *military career officer*

Fortuna
Ramer, James LeRoy *civil engineer*

Four Seasons
Bivins, Susan Steinbach *systems engineer*

Franklin
Becker, Barbara Ann Stulac (Bobbie Becker) *small business owner*

Fredericktown
Raksakulthai, Vinai *obstetrician, gynecologist*
†Sudmeyer, Alice Jean *artist, poet*

Fulton
Backer, William Earnest *food products executive*
Jefferson, Kurt Wayne *political science educator*
Lamkin, Fletcher M., Jr., *academic administrator*

Gallatin
Wilsted, Joy *elementary education educator, reading specialist, parenting consultant*

Golden City
Howard, Joanne Frances *marketing executive, funeral director, extended care coordinator*

Grain Valley
†Love, Gary Duane *financial consultant*

Granby
Haase, Dixie Carol *retired manufacturing worker, writer*

Grandin
Wallace, Louise Margaret *nurse*

Grandview
Daugherty, Tonda Lou *special education educator*
Justesen, Don Robert *psychologist*

Gravois Mills
Dunn, Floyd Emryl *psychiatrist, neurologist, consultant*

Gray Summit
Desloge, Christopher Davis, Sr., *real estate and merchant banking executive*

Greenwood
Dickinson, Lois Jean Berwanger *adult nurse practitioner, nurse staff officer*
Klaus, Suzanne Lynne *horticulturist, production specialist*
†Zeller, Marilynn Kay *retired librarian*

Half Way
Graves, Jerrell Loren *demographic studies researcher*

Hannibal
†Andresen, Julie Ann Dothager *librarian*
Carty, Raymond Wesley *academic administrator*
Coleman, Gloria Jean *chemical manufacturing company professional*
Dugger, Tommy Ray *academic administrator*
Reinhard, James Richard *retired judge*
Welch, Joseph Daniel *lawyer*

Harrisonville
James, Mary Lee *human resources specialist, retired*

Hartsburg
Flink, Jane Duncan *columnist*

Hazelwood
Burleski, Joseph Anthony, Jr., *information technology executive*
Rose, Joseph Hugh *clergyman*
Urshan, Nathaniel Andrew *minister, church administrator*

Herculaneum
Jackson, Kirk Allan *music educator, director*

Hermann
Mahoney, Catherine Ann *artist, educator*
Puchta, Randolph E. *lawyer*

Higginsville
Rhodes, Robert Charles *cable company executive, consultant*

Highlandville
Pruter, Karl Hugo *bishop*

Hillsboro
Adkins, Gregory D. *higher education administrator*
Howald, John William *lawyer*
†Meyers, Beverly Anne *mathematician, educator*
Stinson, Stanley Thomas *project manager*

Holden
Martin, Laurabelle *real estate and farm land owner and manager*

Hollister
Herron, Gayle Ann *forensic psychologist, mental health consultant, psychotherapist, health facility administrator, columnist*

Holts Summit
Melton, June Marie *nursing educator*

Hunt Valley
Guthrie, Phillip Patrick *division production manager*

Hurley
Feazell, Johnny Ray *physicians assistant*

Imperial
McGraw, Bryan Kelly *military officer*
Usher, Mary Margaret *special education educator*

Independence
Booz, Gretchen Arlene *marketing executive*
Bryan, Kay Marie *minister*
Burnett, Crystal Blythe *marketing professional*
Cady, Elwyn Loomis, Jr., *medico legal consultant, educator*
Dorshow-Gordon, Ellen *epidemiologist*
Evans, Margaret Ann *human resources administrator, business owner*
Farrington, Buford Lee *lawyer*
Francis, Mary Frances Van Dyke *real estate executive, editor*
Grover, Robert Lavern *retired auto worker*
†Henley, Patricia Joan *principal*
Johnson, Niel Melvin *archivist, historian*
Lashley, Curtis Dale *lawyer*
Lindgren, A(lan) Bruce *church administrator*
Mallinson, Sarah Jane *volunteer civic activities*
Marlow, Lydia Lou *elementary education educator*
Marsh, Gary W. *interior designer*
Peake, Candice K. Loper *data processing professional*
Potts, Barbara Joyce *retired historical society executive*
†Rice, Guy Garner *lawyer*
Smith, R(onald) Scott *lawyer*
Sturges, Sidney James *pharmacist, educator, investment and development company executive*
Tyree, Alan Dean *clergyman*
†Wagner, Linda S. *small business owner*
Watkins, Susan Gail *lawyer*

Innsbrook
Ruwwe, William Otto *retired automotive engineer*

Ironton
Sebastian, Phylis Sue (Ingram) *real estate broker, art appraiser*

Jackson
Waldron, Kenneth Lynn *lawyer*

Jefferson City
Bartlett, Alex *lawyer*
Beatty, Grover Douglas *stockbroker*
†Benson, Joseph Fred *journalist, legal historian*
Benton, W. Duane *judge*
Blackmar, Charles Blakey *state supreme court justice*
Blunt, Matt *secretary of state*
Chang, Yi-Shih Joshua *health researcher*
Covington, Ann K. *former state supreme court justice*
Deutsch, James Bernard *lawyer*
Dey, Charlotte Jane *retired community health nurse*
Easley, Glenn Edward *lawyer*
Forbis, Bryan Lester *state agency administrator*
Giroir, Louis Eric *toxicologist*
Gonder, Sharon *special education educator*
Greene, Thomasina Talley *concert pianist, educator*
Henson, David B. *university administrator*
Holden, Bob *governor*
†Keitel, Joyce Gillilan *English educator, director*
†Kinder, Peter D. *state legislator*
King, Robert Henry *minister, church denomination executive, former educator*
Knox, William Arthur *judge*
Mahfood, Stephen Michael *governmental agency executive*
Martin, Cathleen A. *lawyer*
Maxwell, Joe Edwin *lieutenant governor*
Nixon, Jeremiah W. (Jay Nixon) *state attorney general*
Novotney, Donald Francis *superintendent of schools*
Parker, Sara Ann *librarian, consultant*
Price, William Ray, Jr., *state supreme court judge*
Pritchett, Michael Eugene Cook *lawyer*
Reidinger, Russell Frederick, Jr., *fish and wildlife scientist*
†Ridenhour, Cory Todd *association executive, consultant, accountant*
†Riner, James William *lawyer*
Scheve, May E. *state legislator, political organization worker*
Stith, Laura Denvir *state supreme court justice*
Teitelman, Richard B. *state supreme court justice*
Tettlebaum, Harvey M. *lawyer*
Wagner, Ann *political organization executive*
Westfall, Morris *state legislator*
White, Ronnie L. *state supreme court justice*
Winegar, Anthony C. *health care worker*
Wolff, Michael A. *state supreme court judge*

Jennings
Robards, Bourne Rogers *elementary education educator*

Joplin
Allman, Margaret Ann Lowrance *counseling administrator*
Butler, Paul Thurman *retired religious studies educator*
†Cassens, Patrick *mathematician, educator*
Crumpacker, Rex K. *anesthesiologist*
Daus, Arthur Steven *neurological surgeon*
Habermann, James Herbert *retired pathologist*
Huffman, Patricia Nell *entrepreneur*
†Karmanova, Tatiana Victorovna *language educator*
†Kyle, Nicholas Scott *art educator, artist*
Laas, Virginia Jeans *historian, educator*
†Mahn, Timothy W. *music educator*
Massa, Richard Wayne *retired communications educator*
McReynolds, Allen, Jr., *retired investment company executive*
Merriam, Allen Hayes *speech communication educator*
Minor, Ronald Ray *minister*
River, George Lambert *hematologist, oncologist*
Scott, Robert Haywood, Jr., *lawyer*
Singleton, Marvin Ayers *state legislator, otolaryngologist*
Wilson, Aaron Martin *religious studies educator, college executive*

Kansas City
Abdou, Nabih I. *physician, educator*
Acheson, Allen Morrow *retired engineering executive*
Adams, Charles Geoffrey *minister, educator*
Adams, James Robert *medical organization sales professional*
Andersen, Jerry Rae *music educator*
Anderson, Christopher James *lawyer*
Anderson, James Keith *retired magazine editor*
Baisden, Eleanor Marguerite *retired airline compensation executive, consultant*
Baker, John Russell *utilities executive*
Baker, Robert Thomas *interior designer*
Baker, Ronald Phillip *service company executive*
Barnes, Kay *mayor*
Bartlett, Paul Dana, Jr., *agribusiness executive*
Bartunek, Robert R(ichard), Jr., *lawyer*
Bates, William Hubert *lawyer*
Batiuk, Thomas Martin *cartoonist*
†Beck, William G. *lawyer*
Becker, Thomas Bain *lawyer*
Beckerman, Dale Lee *lawyer*
Beckett, Theodore Charles *lawyer*
†Begleiter, Michael L. *genetic counselor*
Beihl, Frederick *lawyer*
Bell, Stephanie *economics educator*
Belzer, Ellen J. *editor, negotiations and communications consultant*
Benner, Richard Edward, Jr., *community service volunteer, investor*
Benson, Mary Etta *English educator*
Bentley, Jeffrey *performing company executive*
Berkley, Eugene Bertram (Bert Berkley) *envelope company executive*
†Berkowitz, Lawrence M. *lawyer*
Bevan, Robert Lewis *lawyer*
†Blackwood, George Dean, Jr., *lawyer*
Blanchaert, Remy Henry, Jr., *oral and maxillofacial surgeon*
Bloch, Henry Wollman *tax preparation company executive*
Boggs, James Dotson *lawyer*
Bolender, Todd *choreographer*
Bové-DeWald, Marylou Goodman *university director, educator*
Bowman, Pasco Middleton, II, *judge*
Boysen, Melicent Pearl *finance company executive*
†Bradbury, Daniel Joseph *library administrator*
Bradshaw, Jean Paul, II, *lawyer*
Brake, Timothy L. *lawyer*
†Brett, George Howard *baseball executive, former professional baseball player*
Brisbane, Arthur Seward *newspaper publisher*
Brous, Thomas Richard *lawyer*
Buford, Ronetta Marie *music educator*
Bugher, Robert Dean *professional society administrator*
Burk, Norman *retired oral surgeon*
Busby, Marjean (Marjean Busby) *retired journalist*
Butler, Alice Claire *rehabilitation nurse*
Butler, Merlin Gene *physician, medical geneticist, educator*
Canfield, Robert Cleo *lawyer*
Caulfield, Joan *director, educator*
Cheng, Kuang Lu *chemist, educator*
Ching, Wai Yim *physics educator, researcher*
†Churchman, Michael Steele Bright *educational consultant, educator*
Clarke, Milton Charles *lawyer*
†Clegg, Karen Kohler *lawyer*
Cobb, Kenneth Alan *lawyer*
Colaianni, Louis Edward *voice educator*
†Cooper, Corinne *communications consultant, lawyer*
Courson, Marna B.P. *public relations executive*
Coveney, Raymond Martin, Jr., *educator*
Cowden, John William *lawyer*
Crawford, Howard Allen *lawyer*
Crist, William Gary *artist, retired educator*
Cross, William Dennis *lawyer*
Cunningham, Paul George *minister*
Das, Dilip Kumar *chemical engineer*
Davis, F(rancis) Keith *civil engineer*
Davis, James Robert *cartoonist*
Davis, John Charles *lawyer*
Davis, Mary Bronaugh *music educator*
Davis, Richard Francis *city government official*
†Dawson, Elizabeth Ann *marketing professional*
Deacy, Thomas Edward, Jr., *lawyer*
†Delaney, Michael Francis *lawyer*
De Lurgio, Stephen Anthony *management educator*
DeParle, Nancy-Ann Min *former federal agency administrator, lawyer*

Dibble, Cameron Shawn *music educator, concert pianist*
Diehl, James Harvey *church administrator*
†Dietrich, William Gale *lawyer, real estate developer, consultant*
Dillingham, John Allen *marketing professional*
Dimond, Edmunds Grey *medical educator*
Diuguid, Lewis Walter *newspaper executive, columnist*
Dixon, George David *radiologist*
Dolson, Edward M. *lawyer*
Donovan, Ann Burcham *medical office administrator*
Doyle, Wendell E. *retired band director, educator*
Drees, Betty *dean, educator*
†Dunn, Terrence P. *manufacturing executive*
Durig, James Robert *chemistry educator*
Eddy, Charles Alan *chiropractor*
Eddy, William Bahret *psychology educator, university dean*
Egan, Charles Joseph, Jr., *lawyer, greeting card company executive*
Eldridge, Truman Kermit, Jr., *lawyer*
†Ellies, Debra L *biologist*
†English, Mark Gregory *lawyer*
†English, R(obert) Bradford *marshal*
†Ernst, Mark A. *diversified financial services company executive*
Eubanks, Eugene Emerson *education educator, consultant*
Fecht, Daniel R. *psychologist, actor*
Fershee, Susan Joyce *lawyer*
†Fiorella, Russell Michael *pathologist*
Foster, Mark Stephen *lawyer*
Frantze, David Wayne *lawyer*
†Freilich, Robert H. *lawyer, educator*
Friedlander, Edward Robert *pathologist*
Frisbie, Charles *lawyer*
Gaines, Robert Darryl *lawyer, food services executive*
Gaitan, Fernando J., Jr., *federal judge*
Galloway, Margaret Elinor *social worker*
†Gansler, Robert *professional soccer coach*
Gardner, Brian E. *lawyer*
Gibson, John Robert *federal judge*
†Gilmore, Webb Reilly *lawyer*
†Gist, Richard Michael *research scientist*
Godfrey, William Ashley *ophthalmologist*
Gonzalez, Tony *football player*
Gorman, Gerald Warner *lawyer*
Graham, Charles *research psychologist*
Graham, Harold Steven *lawyer*
Gray, Helen Theresa Gott *religion editor*
Green, Frank Earl *civil engineer*
Green, Jerry Howard *investment banker*
Green, Robert K. *energy executive*
Green, Trent Jason *football player*
Grossman, Jerome Barnett *retired service firm executive*
†Gusewelle, Anne Elizabeth *lawyer*
Gusewelle, Charles Wesley *journalist, writer, documentary maker*
Hagan, John Charles, III, *ophthalmologist*
Hagsten, Ib *animal scientist, livestock consultant*
†Hall, Donald Joyce, Sr., *greeting card company executive*
†Hall, Donald Joyce, Jr., *consumer products company executive*
Hamilton, Richard Alfred *university administrator, marketing educator*
Han, Yijie *information technology educator*
Handley, Gerald Matthew *lawyer, educator*
Hanover, R(aymond) Scott *tennis management professional*
Harris, Roxanna Marie *emergency room nurse*
Hasan, Syed Eqbal *environmental geologist, educator*
Healy, Michael Patrick *lawyer*
†Hebenstreit, James Bryant *agricultural products executive, bank and venture capital executive*
Hebenstreit, Jean Estill Stark *religion educator, practitioner*
Heisey, Raymond K. *civil engineer*
Herman, Robert Stephen *lawyer*
Hernandez, Roberto *professional baseball player*
Heymach, George John, III, *physician, educator, health facility administrator, consultant*
†Hill, Stephen L., Jr., *lawyer, former prosecutor*
Hindman, Larrie C. *lawyer*
Hoffman, Gloria Levy *communications executive*
Hoffmann, Donald *architectural historian*
Holmes, Priest *football player*
†Howes, Brian Thomas *lawyer*
Hubbell, Ernest *lawyer*
Hunt, Lamar *professional football team executive*
Hunzicker, Warren John *research consultant, physician, cardiologist*
Huston, Kent Allen *rheumatologist*
†Hutson, Betty Switzer *art educator, artist*
†Jennings, Michael C. *engineer, designer, psychologist, consultant*
Johnson, Leonard James *lawyer*
Johnson, Mark Eugene *lawyer*
Johnson, Richard Dean *pharmaceutical consultant, educator*
Johnson, Sondra Lea *accountant*
†Johnston, John Steven *lawyer*
Jonas, Harry S. *medical education consultant*
Jones, Charles Calhoun *estate and business planning consultant*
Joyce, Michael Patrick *lawyer*
Juarez, Martin *priest*
†Kafoure, Michael D. *food products executive*
Kaplan, Harvey L. *lawyer*
†Kemper, Jonathan McBride *banker*
Kilroy, John Muir *lawyer*
Kilroy, William Terrence *lawyer*
King, Richard Allen *lawyer*
Kitchin, John Joseph *lawyer*
Kloth, Carolyn *meteorologist*
Knight, John Allan *clergyman, philosophy and religion educator*
Koelling, Thomas Winsor *lawyer*
Kovac, F. Peter *advertising executive*
Krause, Heather Dawn *data processing executive*
Kuhn, Whitey *advertising executive*

Langworthy, Robert Burton *lawyer*
Latshaw, John *entrepreneur, director*
Latza, Beverly Ann *accountant*
Laue, Brant Mitchell *lawyer*
Laughrey, Nanette Kay *judge, federal*
LeBeau, Bryan Frank *history educator, author, academic administrator*
†Levine, Bernard Benton *lawyer*
Lindsey, David Hosford *lawyer*
Lock, Robert Joseph *accountant*
Loeb, Jeffrey T. *English language educator*
Lofland, Gary Kenneth *cardiac surgeon*
Lolli, Don R(ay) *lawyer*
Lombardi, Cornelius Ennis, Jr., *lawyer*
Londré, Felicia Mae Hardison *theater educator*
Long, Edwin Tutt *surgeon*
Lott, Peter F. *chemist*
Lotuaco, Luisa Go *pathologist*
Lotven, Howard Lee *lawyer*
Louis, William Joseph (Jonn Garvie Monks) *theater educator, actor, director, artist, poet*
Lubin, Bernard *psychologist, educator*
†Lyon, Bob *state legislator*
Manimtim, Winston Mendoza *pediatrician, neonatologist*
Manson, Anne *music director*
Martin-Bowen, Lindsey *freelance writer*
Mast, Kande White *artist*
Matheny, Edward Taylor, Jr., *lawyer*
Mazza, Biagio *religious studies educator*
McCollum, Clifford Glenn *college dean emeritus*
McCoy, Frederick John *retired plastic surgeon*
Mc Gee, Joseph John, Jr., *former insurance company executive*
McGregor, Douglas Hugh *pathologist, educator*
McKenna, George LaVerne *art museum curator*
McKinney, Janet Kay *law librarian*
McKinsey, David Stephen *infectious diseases specialist*
McManus, James William *lawyer*
Mc Meel, John Paul *newspaper syndicate and publishing executive*
McPhee, Mark Steven *medical educator, physician, gastroenterologist*
McSweeney, William Lincoln, Jr., *retired publishing executive*
Mebust, Winston Keith *surgeon, educator*
†Menning, Melissa Christine *mathematics educator*
†Meola, Tony *professional soccer player, actor*
†Miller, George Spencer *lawyer*
Miller, William Charles *theological librarian, educator*
Milton, Chad Earl *lawyer*
Minnick, David Michael *lawyer*
Molteni, Agostino *pathology educator*
Moore, Dorsey Jerome *dentistry educator, maxillofacial prosthetist*
Moore, Stephen James *lawyer*
Mordy, James Calvin *lawyer*
Morgison, F. Edward *investment broker*
Muser, Tony *former manager professional athletics*
Mustard, Mary Carolyn *financial executive*
†Nagle, Jean Susan Karabacz *sociologist, psychologist*
Newsom, James Thomas *lawyer*
Noe, James Kirby *computer consultant*
Norton, John Hise *lawyer*
O'Bannon, Deborah Jean *civil engineering educator*
Öhman, Mikael *management consultant*
Oliphant, Patrick *cartoonist*
†O'Shields, Charlie *marketing professional*
Paden, John Bruce *community resource executive*
Palmer, Cruise *newspaper editor*
Palmer, Dennis Dale *lawyer*
Parcell, John Cleo *music educator*
Parizek, Eldon Joseph *geologist, educator, dean*
Parker, Dennis Gene *former sheriff, martial arts instructor*
Parrette, Leslie Jackson *lawyer*
Pelofsky, Joel *lawyer*
Pemberton, Bradley Powell *lawyer*
Pena, Antonio Francisco (Tony Pena) *professional athletics coach*
Peters, Ralph Irwin, Jr., *biology educator, researcher*
†Petersen, Robert R. *brokerage house executive*
Petosa, Jason Joseph *publisher*
Piepho, Robert Walter *pharmacy educator, researcher*
Plax, Karen Ann *lawyer*
Popper, Robert *law educator, former dean*
Poston, Walker Seward, II, *medical educator, researcher*
Potter, George William, Jr., *mining executive*
Price, Charles H., II, *former ambassador*
Price, James Tucker *lawyer*
†Proctor, George Edwin, Jr., *lawyer*
Pruitt, Stephen Wallace *finance educator*
†Rada, David Charles *dermatologist*
†Reardon, Michael Edward *lawyer*
Redmond, Christopher John *lawyer*
†Reichard, Larry A. *biologist, educator*
†Reinschmidt, Laura Pilioglos *choreographer, educator*
Rich, Ruthanne *musician, educator*
Roaf, William Layton *professional football player*
Robertson, Kenneth Carl *music educator*
Robertson, Leon H. *management consultant, educator*
†Rodman, Leonard C. *civil and communication engineering executive*
Roosa, Jan Bertorotta *clinical psychologist*
Rost, William Joseph *chemist*
Roth, Lawrence Frederick, Jr., (Larry Roth) *writer*
Rowden, A(lphro) J(ohn) *minister*
Rowland, Landon Hill *diversified holding company executive*
Rozell, Joseph Gerard *accountant*
Sachs, Howard F(rederic) *federal judge*
Sader, Neil Steven *lawyer*
†Sagduyu, Kemal *psychiatrist, educator, researcher*

Sands, Darry Gene *lawyer*
Satterlee, Terry Jean *lawyer*
Sauer, Brian *molecular geneticist, researcher*
Sauer, Gordon Chenoweth *retired dermatologist, educator*
Scarritt, Richard Winn *lawyer*
†Schaeffer, Ronald Lee *theatre production manager*
†Schuchman, Philip Melchor *education educator*
Scott, Deborah Emont *curator*
†Sears, Kelley Dean *lawyer*
Seigfreid, James Thomas *lawyer*
Seligson, Theodore H. *architect, interior designer, art consultant*
Setzler, Edward Allan *lawyer*
†Shapiro, Alvin Dale *lawyer*
Shaw, Gary Yale *otolaryngologist*
Shaw, John W. *lawyer*
Shaw, Richard David *marketing and management educator*
†Shaw, Willie G. *adult education educator*
Shay, David Eugene *lawyer*
Sheldon, Ted Preston *library dean*
†Sherman, Joseph Allen, Jr., *lawyer*
Shughart, Donald Louis *lawyer*
Shutz, Byron Christopher *real estate executive*
Sizemore, William Christian *retired academic administrator, county official*
Slaughter, Rochelle Denise *elementary school educator*
†Smith, Christopher D. *administrative assistant*
Smith, Louis *sports association administrator*
†Solberg, Elizabeth Transou *public relations executive*
†Spady, Michael Benjamin *entrepreneur*
Spalty, Edward Robert *lawyer*
Sparks, Stephen Stone *lawyer*
Spencer, Richard Henry *lawyer*
Steffens, John Howard *cytotechnologist*
Stein, Allison *media specialist*
Stevens, James Hervey, Jr., *retired financial advisor*
†Stowers, James W., III, *data processing executive*
Stroup, Kala Mays *educational alliance administrator, former state higher education commissioner*
†Sullivan, Charles A. *food products executive*
Suter, Carol J. *non-profit organization executive, lawyer*
Svadlenak, Jean Hayden *museum consultant*
Sweeney, Mike *professional baseball player*
Switzer, Samuel Thomas *non-profit administrator*
†Taff, Earl Wayne *lawyer*
Tammeus, William David *journalist, columnist*
Taylor, Marilyn Levere *management consultant, educator*
Terry, Robert Brooks *food products executive, lawyer*
Thompson, Catherine Rush *physical therapist, educator*
Thornton, Thomas Noel *publishing executive*
Todd, Stephen Max *lawyer*
Toll, Perry Mark *lawyer, educator*
Truitt, Kenneth Ray *owner*
Truog, William Edward, III, *pediatrician, educator, researcher*
Tunley, Naomi Louise *retired nurse administrator*
Tyler, John Edward, III, *lawyer*
Ulrich, Robert Gene *judge*
Valliere, Roland Edward *performing company executive*
Van Buren, Abigail (Jeanne Phillips) *columnist, lecturer*
†Vando, Gloria *poet, publishing executive*
Van Dyke, Thomas Wesley *lawyer*
Van Dyne, Michele Miley *information engineer*
Van Way, Charles Ward, III, *surgery educator*
Vering, John Albert *lawyer*
Vermeil, Dick *professional football coach*
Viani, James Laurence *lawyer*
Wade, Robert Glenn *engineering executive*
Warakomski, Alphonse Walter Joseph, Jr., *sales executive, marketing professional*
Weirich, Robert Wayne *musician, educator*
Werner, Betty Jean *music educator*
White, Jerusha Lynn *lawyer*
Whitener, William Garnett *dancer, choreographer*
†Whittaker, Judith Ann Cameron *lawyer*
Widmar, Russell C. *airport executive*
†Wilder, Terry L. *religious studies educator*
Wilkins, Arthur Norman *retired college administrator*
Wilkinson, Ralph Russell *biochemistry educator, toxicologist*
Williams, Randy G. *community relations executive, communication professional*
Willsie, Sandra K. *dean, physician, medical educator*
Willy, Thomas Ralph *lawyer*
Wirken, James Charles *lawyer*
Woodson, Stephen William *collection agency executive*
Worrall, Judith Rae *health and welfare plan consultant*
Wright, Scott Olin *federal judge*
Wrobel, Jerzy Michal *physicist, educator*
Wrobley, Ralph Gene *lawyer*
†Wynkoop, Mary Ann *American studies educator*
Wyrsch, James Robert *lawyer, educator, author*
Youmans, Joyce M. *curator, researcher*
Zieman, Mark *newspaper editor*

Kearney
Shrimpton, James Robert *controller*
Waltz, James Richard *physician*

Keytesville
Wheeler, James Julian *lawyer*

Kingsville
†Stimac, John Anthony *small business owner, poet, cartoonist*

Kirbyville
†McPhillen, Beverly Louise *registered nurse*

Kirksville
Davis, Adam Brooke *English educator*
†Dixon, Barbara Bruinekool *provost*
Engber, Cheryl Ann *language educator, linguist*
Festa, Roger Reginald *chemist, educator*
French, Michael Francis *non-profit education agency administrator*
†Grow-Maienza, Janice *education educator*
†Hanley, Mark Young *historian, educator, researcher*
Koutstaal, Cornelis W. *university administrator*
Maglio, Christopher John *psychologist, educator*
Nnadozie, Emmanuel *economist, educator*
Osborn, Gerald Guy *dean, psychiatrist, educator*
Peterson, Donald Fred *physiologist, educator*
Presley, Paula Lumpkin *editor*
†Reschly, Steven Dale *historian, educator*
Shumake, James Martin *emergency medicine physician*

Kirkwood
†Hoglen, Jewel Pamela *retired secondary school educator*
Holsen, James Noble, Jr., *retired chemical engineer*
Mosby, Robert J. *psychologist*
Pittman, Shepard Clifton *secondary principal*
Wood, Floyd Edward, Jr., *pharmacist, consultant*

Laddonia
Scheffler, Lewis Francis *pastor, educator, research scientist*

Lake Lotawana
†Heineman, Paul Lowe *consulting civil engineer*
Zobrist, Benedict Karl *library director, historian*

Lake Ozark
DeShazo, Marjorie White *occupational therapist*

Lake Saint Louis
Callahan, Robert John, Jr., *lawyer, arbitrator*
Dommermuth, William Peter *marketing consultant, educator*

Lamar
Geddie, Rowland Hill, III, *lawyer*

Lambert Airport
Griggs, Leonard LeRoy, Jr., *airport executive*

Lebanon
Beavers, Roy Lackey *retired utility executive, essayist, activist*
Caplinger, Patricia Ellen *family nurse practitioner*
Louderback, Kevin Wayne *business owner*

Lees Summit
Aduddle, Larry Steven *marketing and sales executive, consultant*
Carter, William Gerald *non-profit corporation executive*
Demetreon, Daiboune Elayne *minister*
Duke, Ellen Kay *planned giving administrator*
Ferguson, Julie Ann *physical education educator*
Foudree, Charles M. *retired financial executive*
†Hardy-Parcell, Cathy Kay *music educator, department chairman*
Henley, Joseph Oliver *manufacturing company executive*
Hubbard, Harold Mead *environmental scientist, consultant*
Jones, Miles James A. *pathologist, consultant*
Korschot, Benjamin Calvin *investment executive*
†Linder, Beverly L. *educator*
†Lord, Heaven *theology studies educator, consultant, minister*
†Parker, Deborah A *language educator, translator*
Rethemeyer, Robert John *social studies educator*
Smith, Dwyane *university administrator*
Walsh, Thomas Joseph *lawyer*

Lewistown
Terpening, Virginia Ann *artist*

Liberty
Armstrong, Susan J. *academic administrator*
Harriman, Richard Lee *performing arts administrator, educator*
Samuel, Robert Thompson *optometrist*
Sayles, Cathy A. *lawyer*
Tanner, Jimmie Eugene *retired dean*
Warnex, Paul David *music educator*

Linn Creek
Waldon, Marja Parker *mental health nurse*

Louisiana
Bubenik, Oldrich Venceslas *surgeon, oncologist*

Manchester
Forsman, Alpheus Edwin *lawyer*

Maplewood
Schmidt, Skip Francis *writer*

Marshall
Huff, Jane Van Dyke *secondary education educator*
†Lines, Kevin Lee *music educator*
Peterson, William Allen *lawyer*
Roberts, David Lowell *journalist, educator*
Sayer, Ronald J. *composer, educator*
†Wildt, Katherine Ann *literature educator*

Marshfield
Gloe, Donna *systems change manager*

Maryland Heights
Chinn, Rex Arlyn *chemist*
Cooper, Richard Alan *lawyer*
Goldfarb, Marvin Al *retired civil engineer*
Marcus, John *wholesale distribution executive*

Ramanuja, Teralandur Krishnaswamy *retired structural engineer*
Stevens, Julie Ann *lawyer*
Toan, Barrett A. *health products executive*

Maryville
Gorman, Karen Machmer *optometric physician*
†Hubbard, Dean Leon *university president*
Kharadia, Virabhai Chelabhai *economist, educator, researcher*
Kramer, Ernest Joachim *music educator, composer*
†Murphy, Kathryn Louise *librarian, educator*
Primm, David John *middle school educator*
†Sadek, Jawad *mathematics educator*
Schultz, Patricia Bowers *vocal music educator, performer*

Mexico
Hagan, Ann P. *lawyer*
Rice, Marvin Elwood *dentist*
†Tillman, Charles Herbert, Jr., *cardiologist*

Mound City
Reiter, David G. *music educator, musician*

Mountain Grove
Nava, Jean Anthes *writer, farmer*

Naylor
Seratt, Rodger Calvin *manufacturing executive*

Neosho
Gartner, Jessie Lee *family nurse practitioner*
Weber, Margaret Laura Jane *retired accountant*

Nevada
Campbell, Catherine Ellen *French language educator*
Goldberger, Stephen Henry *otolaryngologist*
Wassenberg, Evelyn M. *medical and surgical nurse, nursing educator*

Nixa
Kreider, Jim *farmer, former state legislator*

North Kansas City
Conner, Leonard Wayne *association administrator, layworker*
Hellman, Richard *endocrinologist*
Stout, Edward Irvin *medical manufacturing company executive*

O Fallon
Brungard, Daniel V. *small business owner, city official*
Raeuchle, John Steven *software engineer*
Wood, Leslie Ann *retail administrator*

Oak Grove
Davis, Jo *naturopath, hypnotherapist*

Olivette
Hollingsworth, Gary Mayes *sales executive, marketing professional*

Osage Beach
Orr, Rita Hope *artist*

Osborn
Findley, Delpha Yoder *retired public health nurse*

Overland
Clark, Maxine *retail executive*

Ozark
†Thornton, Andrew John *minister*

Parkville
Jacobs, Carl Eugene *printing company official*
Pettes, Robert Carlton *artist*
Schultis, Gail Ann *library director*

Peculiar
†Turley, William Homer *music educator*

Perryville
Shelby, Charles Francis *priest, not-for-profit fundraiser*

Pierce City
Hays, Otis Earl, Jr., *writer*

Pilot Grove
Chesnutt, Florence Walker Andrews *artist*

Plato
Wood, Joetta Kay *special education educator*

Platte City
Kalin, D(orothy) Jean *artist, educator*

Pleasant Valley
Nelson, Freda Nell Hein *librarian*

Point Lookout
†Hardin, Garry Joe, II, *music educator*

Poplar Bluff
Black, Ronnie Delane *religious organization administrator, mayor*
Carr, Charles Louis *retired religious organization administrator*
Duncan, Leland Ray *retired mission administrator*
Henson, Elizabeth K. *accountant*
†Rivetti, Andrew Francis *Spanish educator*
Young, William Webb *military officer, poet*

Portageville
Dial, Marshall Reece *library director*

Queen City
Wilson, Roger Byron *former governor, school administrator*

Raymore
Mehl, Donald Edward *retired marketing professional*
Miller, William Lee, Jr., *minister*

Raytown
†Coppenbarger, Cecelia Marie *special education educator*
Rice, Durwin Dan *artist, art dealer*
Smith, Robert Francis *psychologist, consultant*

Reeds Spring
†Childers, L. Doyle *state legislator*

Richmond
Seward, Nancy H. *retired band director, composer*

Richmond Heights
Chandler, James Barton *international education consultant*

Rocheport
Basye, Charles Benjamin *engineering educator*

Rock Port
Mulvania, Walter Lowell *lawyer*

Rockaway Beach
Alkire, Betty Jo *artist, commercial real estate broker, marketing consultant*

Rolla
Adawi, Ibrahim Hasan *physics educator*
Alexander, Ralph William, Jr., *physics educator*
†Bagnall, Lindsay Lomax *human resources specialist*
†Barr, David John *civil, geological engineering educator*
Belarbi, Abdeldjelil *civil engineering educator, researcher*
Chen, Genda *engineering educator*
†Christensen, Lawrence O. *historian, educator*
Crosbie, Alfred Linden *mechanical engineering educator*
Dagli, Cihan Hayreddin *engineering educator*
DuBroff, Richard Edward *electrical engineer, educator*
Finaish, Fathi Ali *aeronautical engineering educator*
Grayson, Robert Larry *mining engineering educator, mining executive*
Gregg, Jay Mason *geology educator*
Grimm, Louis John *mathematician, educator*
Hickle, William Earl *lawyer, judge*
Le, Vy K. *mathematician, educator*
Lehnhoff, Terry Franklin *mechanical engineering*
Leighly, Hollis Philip, Jr., *metallurgical engineering educator, researcher*
Madria, Sanjay *computer scientist, educator*
Malone, Edward Allen *English educator*
Mc Farland, Robert Harold *physicist, educator*
†Mendoza, Cesar *civil engineer, educator, civil engineer, researcher*
Mishra, Rajiv Sharan *metallurgical engineer, educator*
Oboh-Ikuenobe, Francisca Emiede *geologist, educator, researcher*
†Padhi, Radhakant *engineer*
Prakash, Shamsher *retired civil engineering educator, consultant*
Saperstein, Lee Waldo *mining engineering educator*
Sarangapani, Jagannathan *embedded systems and networking engineer, educator*
Sauer, Harry John, Jr., *mechanical engineering educator, university administrator*
Sotiriou-Leventis, Chariklia *chemist, educator, researcher*
†Steelman, Sarah *state legislator*
Stewart, James Andrew *librarian*
†Suzuki, Toshio *research scientist*
Thomas, Gary L. *academic administrator*
†Thomas, William Herman, Jr., *lawyer*
†Trueblood, Max Blair *physicist, educator*
†Wagner, Harold Willis, Jr., *civil engineer, educator*
Wan, Kai-tak *education educator*
Warner, Don Lee *dean emeritus*
Yu, Wei-Wen *retired engineering educator*
Zobrist, George Winston *computer scientist, educator*

Saint Ann
Gardner, Carla Deneen *social worker*
†Jamison, Darlene *geriatrics nurse*
Johnson, Harold Gene *lawyer*

Saint Charles
Burns, Betty X. *music educator*
Castro, Jan Garden *writer, arts consultant, educator*
Dorsey, Mary Elizabeth *lawyer*
Dorsey, Richard Peter, III, *lawyer, former state legislator*
Drucker, Barry Jules *environmental health specialist*
Gross, Charles Robert *bank executive, state senator*
Karll, Jo Ann *state administrative law judge, lawyer*
Kelly, James Joseph *printing company executive*
Martin, Edward Brian *electrical engineer*
Newcomb, Carolyn Jeanne *special education educator*
Nickisch, Willard Wayne *funeral director*
Pring, Robert Bradford *financial consultant*
Pundmann, Ed John, Jr., *automotive company executive*
Radke, Rodney Owen *agricultural research executive, consultant*
†Reed, Warlene Patricia *retired librarian*
Ritter, Robert Thornton *lawyer*
†Segelhorst, Cindy Marie *early childhood educator*
Wang, William Weiqi *physician*

Saint Clair
Gullet, Leon Estle *retired cartographer*

Saint James
Stevens, Helen Jean *retired music educator*

Saint Joseph
Boor, Myron Vernon *psychologist, educator*
Brown, Jean Gayle *social worker*
Chelline, Warren Herman *English educator, clergy member*
Chilcote, Gary M. *museum director, reporter*
Comerford, John Leo *college official*
Davis, Lance Barrow *lawyer, municipal judge*
†Dyer, Gary Alden *dermatologist*
Glise, Anthony LeRoy *musician, composer, writer*
Hamzaee, Reza Gholi *economics educator*
Howe, Dean Otis, Jr., *curator, consultant*
Kranitz, Theodore Mitchell *lawyer*
Laderoute, Charles David *engineer, economist, consultant*
Rachow, Sharon Dianne *realtor*
Schneider, Julia *library director*
Taylor, Michael Leslie *lawyer*

Saint Louis
Abelov, Stephen Lawrence *uniform clothing company executive, consultant*
†Acharya, Jayant Narahari *neurologist, educator*
Adams, Albert Willie, Jr., *lubrication company executive*
Adams, W. Randolph , Jr., *management consultant*
Agarwal, Ramesh Kumar *aeronautical scientist, researcher, educator*
Agrawal, Harish Chandra *neurobiologist, researcher, educator*
Albert, Stewart Gary *medical educator, internist, endocrinologist*
Alessi, Mary Jean *family life educator*
Allen, Garland Edward *biology educator, science historian*
Alpers, David Hershel *physician, educator*
Amini, Amir Arsham *biomedical engineering researcher, educator*
Antonacci, Anthony Eugene *engineer*
Appleton, R. O., Jr., *lawyer*
Arnold, Fred English *lawyer*
Arnold, John Fox *lawyer*
Arthur, Charles Gemmell, IV, *accountant*
Ashworth, Ronald Broughton *health facility executive, accountant*
Atwood, Hollye Stolz *lawyer*
Aylward, Ronald Lee *lawyer*
Babington, Charles Martin, III, *lawyer*
Bachmann, John William *securities firm executive*
Bacon, Bruce Raymond *physician*
Badalamenti, Anthony *financial planner*
Baernstein, Albert, II, *mathematician, educator*
Baldwin, Edwin Steedman *lawyer*
Ballinger, Walter Francis *surgeon, educator*
Bang, Mary Jo *poet*
Banks, Eric Kendall *lawyer*
Barken, Bernard Allen *lawyer*
Barksdale, Clarence Caulfield *banker*
Barmann, Lawrence Francis *history educator, retired*
Barnes, Harper Henderson *movie critic, editor, writer*
Bascom, C. Perry *retired foundation administrator*
†Bassoppo-Moyo, Sheila *elementary school educator*
†Bateman, Sharon Louise *public relations executive*
Baum, Gordon Lee *lawyer, non-profit organization administrator*
Baum, M(ary) Carolyn *occupational therapist*
Beare, Gene Kerwin *electric company executive*
Beck, Lois Grant *anthropologist, educator, author*
Becker, David Mandel *law educator, author, consultant*
Behrens, Brian Charles *lawyer, associate*
Bell, Laura Jeane *retired nurse*
Bender, Carl Martin *physics educator, consultant*
Benson, Jim *finance company executive*
Berendt, Robert Tryon *lawyer*
Berg, Leonard *retired neurologist, educator, researcher*
Berger, John Torrey, Jr., *lawyer*
Berkel, Edwin Martin *fire marshal*
Berland, David I. *psychiatrist, educator*
Berliant, Marcus Craig *economist*
Bernstein, Donald Chester *brokerage company executive, lawyer*
Beuc, Rudolph, Jr., *architect, real estate broker*
Bextermiller Metzger, Theresa Marie *architect, computer engineer*
Bickel, Floyd Gilbert, III, *investment counselor*
†Biondi, Lawrence *university administrator, priest*
Birman, Victor Mark *mechanical and aerospace engineering educator, academic administrator*
Bitar, Saad R. *internist*
Black, Kevin John *psychiatrist*
Blanke, Richard Brian *lawyer*
Blasi, Gerald J. *humanities educator, lawyer*
Blood, Milton Ray *association executive*
†Blumenthal, Herman Theodore *physician, educator*
Bock, Edward John *retired chemical manufacturing company executive*
Boddie, Don O'Mar *recording company executive, producer, recording artist*
Boggs, Beth Clemens *lawyer*
Boothby, William Munger *mathematics educator*
Borders, John Gillespie *psychotherapist, former corporate executive*
Bourne, Carol Elizabeth Mulligan *biology educator, phycologist*
†Boyer, Patricia Grace *education educator*
Bradley, Marilynne Gail *advertising executive, advertising educator*
Brady, Jules Malachi *philosopher, educator, priest*
Branham, Gregory Harris *facial plastic surgeon*
Brasunas, Anton de Sales *retired metallurgical engineering educator*
Brauer, Camilla Thompson (Kimmy Thompson Brauer) *civic leader*
Breece, Robert William, Jr., *lawyer*
Brickey, Kathleen Fitzgerald *law educator*
Brickey, Kristin Lynn *healthcare marketing professional*
Brickler, John Weise *lawyer*
Bridgewater, Bernard Adolphus, Jr., *retired footwear company executive, consultant*
Briggs, Cynthia Anne *educational administrator, clinical psychologist*
Briggs, William Benajah *aeronautical engineer*
†Brink, David Scott *clinical pathologist, educator*
Brockhaus, Robert Herold, Sr., *business educator, consultant*
Brodeur, Armand Edward *pediatric radiologist*
Broeg, Bob (Robert William Broeg) *writer*
Browde, Anatole *electronics company executive, consultant*
Browman, David L(udvig) *archaeologist*
Brown, JoBeth Goode *food products executive, lawyer*
Brown, Paul Sherman *lawyer*
Brownlee, Robert Hammel *lawyer*
Bruce, Isaac Isidore *football player*
Brungs, Robert Anthony *theology educator, institute director*
Bruning, Anthony Steven *lawyer*
Bryan, Henry C(lark), Jr., *retired lawyer*
Bryan, Jean Marie Wehmueller *nurse*
Bryant, Ruth Alyne *banker*
Bubash, Patricia Jane *special education educator*
Buckley, Eugene Kenyon *lawyer*
Burch, Stephen Kenneth *financial services company executive, real estate investor*
†Burger, Joan M. *judge*
Burgess, James Harland *physics educator, researcher*
Burke, James Donald *museum administrator*
Burke, Thomas Michael *lawyer*
Burkholder, Mark Alan *historian, educator*
Burton, Earl Gillespie, III, *lawyer*
Busch, August Adolphus, III, *brewery executive*
Byrnes, Christopher Ian *academic dean, researcher*
Cabbabe, Edmond Bechir *plastic and hand surgeon*
Cain, James Nelson *arts school and concert administrator*
Cairns, Donald Fredrick *engineering educator, management consultant*
Campbell, Cheryl Ann *social worker*
†Careklas, John Orestes *secondary school educator*
†Carius, Jeffrey Rapp *lawyer*
†Carlin, Seth A. *music educator, musician*
Carlson, Arthur Eugene *accounting educator*
Carlson, Mary Susan *lawyer*
Carp, Larry *lawyer*
Carr, Gary Thomas *lawyer*
Carvalho, John Joseph, IV, *molecular geneticist, philosopher of science*
Castro, Mario *medical educator, health facility administrator*
Cawns, Albert Edward *computer systems consultant*
Chakraborty, Uday Kumar *computer scientist, educator*
Chaplin, Hugh, Jr., *physician, educator*
Chignoli, C(elso) William *health care center administrator*
Choi, Dennis W. *pharmaceutical executive, neurologist, educator*
Chole, Richard Arthur *otolaryngologist, educator*
Cima, Cheryl Ann *medical/surgical nurse*
Clear, John Michael *lawyer*
Cloninger, Claude Robert *psychiatric researcher, educator, genetic epidemiologist*
Cohen, Millard Stuart *diversified manufacturing company executive*
†Colson, Kirby Lewis *music educator*
†Compton, William F. *air transportation executive*
†Condoor, Sridhar S. *information technology educator*
Conran, Joseph Palmer *lawyer*
†Constantino, John Nicholas *medical educator, researcher*
Cook, Cynthia Ann Loveland *health and mental health educator*
Corbett, Suzanne Elaine *food writer, marketing executive, food historian*
Cornfeld, Dave Louis *lawyer*
Costigan, Edward John *investment banker*
Cox, Jerome Rockhold, Jr., *electrical engineer*
Cramer, Michael William *insurance executive*
Crider, Robert Agustine *international financier, law enforcement official*
Critchfield, Scott A. *investment broker*
Croat, Thomas Bernard *botanical curator*
Cross, Dewitte Talmadge, III, *physician, neuroradiologist*
†Crowe, Robert Alan *lawyer*
Cryer, Philip Eugene *medical educator, scientist, endocrinologist*
Cullen, James D. *lawyer*
Cuoco, Lorin (Jean) *editor, writer*
Curran, Donald James *artist, illustrator*
Curran, Michael Walter *management scientist*
Curtiss, Roy, III, *biology educator*
DaCorte, Allan Francis *priest, financial consultant and advisor*
Danforth, William Henry *retired academic administrator, physician*
David, Lynn Allen *banking executive*
Davis, Irvin *advertising, public relations, broadcast executive*
Demitra, Pavol *hockey player*
†Deng, Fan *research scientist*
†Devers, Gail *track and field athlete*
Dewald, Paul Adolph *psychiatrist, educator*
DeWoskin, Alan Ellis *lawyer*
Di Bisceglie, Laureen Gail *pianist, educator*
Dill, Charles Anthony *manufacturing and computer company executive*

Dodge, Philip Rogers *physician, educator*
Dodson, W(illiam) Edwin *child neurology educator*
Dohr, John Michael, Jr., *banker*
Domahidy, Mary Rodgers *public policy educator*
Domjan, Laszlo Karoly *newspaper editor*
Donald, Arnold W. *company executive*
Dorwart, Donald Bruce *lawyer*
†Dougherty, Alfred Franklin, Jr., *lawyer*
Dougherty, Charles Hamilton *pediatrician*
Dowd, Edward L., Jr., *lawyer, former prosecutor*
Dreifke, Gerald Edmond *electrical engineering educator*
Drucker, Mark Lewis *public administration educator, consultant*
†Duchek, Michael Gerard *mechanical engineer*
Dudukovic, Milorad P. *chemical engineering educator, consultant*
Duesenberg, Richard William *lawyer*
Duhme, Carol McCarthy *civic worker*
Duhme, H(erman) Richard, Jr., *sculptor, educator*
Dunivent, John Thomas *artist, educator*
†Dykewicz, Mark Steven *physician*
Edison, Bernard Alan *retired retail apparel company executive*
Edmonds, James Patrick (Jim Edmonds) *professional baseball player*
Egger, Terrance C.Z. *publishing executive*
Ehrlich, Ava *television executive*
Eichhorn, Arthur David *music director*
Elbert, Charles Steiner *lawyer*
Elkins, Ken Joe *retired broadcasting executive*
Elliott, Howard, Jr., *lawyer, gas distribution company executive*
Elliott, Susan Spoehrer *information technology executive*
†Ellis, Dorsey Daniel, Jr., *lawyer, educator*
Engelhardt, Irl F. *coal company executive*
Engelhardt, Thomas Alexander *editorial cartoonist*
Entessar, Tahmineh *political scientist, educator*
Epstein, Lee Joan *political science educator*
†Erbs, Thomas J. *lawyer, arbitrator*
Erlinger, James H., III, *lawyer*
†Erwin, James Walter *lawyer*
†Essman, Alyn V. *photographic studios company executive*
†Evans, Johnnie P. *retired elementary school educator*
Evans, Lawrence E. *lawyer, educator*
Evens, Ronald Gene *radiologist, medical center administrator*
Ezenwa, Josephine Nwabuoku *social worker*
Falk, William James *lawyer*
Farr, David N. *electronics executive*
Favors, Adolphus C., Jr., *internist*
Feder, Gary Harold *lawyer*
Felix, David *retired economics educator, consultant*
Feman, Stephen S. *ophthalmologist*
Ferguson, Gary Warren *retired public relations executive*
†Ferkol, Thomas William *medical educator, pediatrician*
Filippine, Edward Louis *federal judge*
Fitch, Coy Dean *physician, educator*
Fitch, Rachel Farr *health policy analyst*
Fletcher, James Warren *physician*
Florin, Cynthia *psychiatrist*
Floyd, Walter Leo *lawyer*
Flye, M. Wayne *surgeon, immunologist, educator, writer*
Fogle, James Lee *lawyer*
Foley, Deborah Ann *civil engineer*
Folz, Carol Ann *financial analyst*
Fondaw, Ronald Edward *artist, educator*
Fonseca, Peter *surgeon*
Fosher, Donald Hobart *marketing professional, inventor*
†Foy, Betsy D. *counseling administrator, educator*
Freese, Raymond William *mathematics educator*
French, Douglas Dewitt *medical facility administrator*
Friedberg, Michael A. *healthcare executive*
Frieden, Carl *biochemist, educator*
Friedlander, Michael Wulf *physicist, educator*
Gacem, Debra Ann *critical care nurse*
Gaertner, Gary M., Sr., *judge*
Gass, William H. *writer, educator*
Gauen, Patrick Emil *newspaper correspondent*
Gay, William Arthur, Jr., *thoracic surgeon*
†Ge, Jisheng *pharmaceutical researcher*
Geary, Daniel Patrick *postal service worker*
Geltman, Edward Mark *cardiologist, educator*
George, Thomas Frederick *academic administrator*
Gerard, Jules Bernard *law educator*
Gianoulakis, John Louis *lawyer*
†Gilchrist, Donna Ann *librarian*
Gilhousen, Brent James *lawyer*
†Gilligan, Sandra Kaye *private school director*
Gillis, John Lamb, Jr., *lawyer*
Godiner, Donald Leonard *lawyer*
Goebel, Joel Alan *otolaryngologist*
Goebel, John J. *lawyer, director*
Gokel, George William *organic chemist, educator*
Goldberg, Anne Carol *physician, educator*
Goldberg, Norman Albert *music publisher, writer*
Goldenhersh, Robert Stanley *lawyer*
Goldstein, Julius Lester *biomedical engineer, consultant*
Goldstein, Steven *lawyer*
Goodenberger, Daniel Marvin *medical educator*
†Goodenough, Ursula Wiltshire *cell biologist, researcher, educator*
Goodman, Harold S. *lawyer*
Gould, Phillip Louis *civil engineering educator, consultant*
Gowen, Leo Francis *artist*
Graff, George Stephen *aerospace company executive*
Graham, John Dalby *public relations executive*
Graham, Robert Clare, III, *lawyer*
†Grant, Hugh *biotechnology company executive*
†Grant, Michele Byrd *secondary school educator*
Gray, Charles Elmer *lawyer, rancher, investor*
†Grebel, Lawrence Bovard *lawyer*
Green, Dennis Joseph *lawyer*
Green, Joyce *book publishing company executive*
Green, Maurice *molecular biologist, virologist, educator*
Greenbaum, Stuart I. *economist, educator*
Greenley, Beverly Jane *lawyer, educator*
Griffing, George Thomas *medical educator, endocrinologist*
Grossberg, George Thomas *psychiatrist, educator*
Grubb, Robert L., Jr., *neurosurgeon*
Gruenberg, Gladys Walleman *economics educator, arbitrator*
†Guenther, Charles John *librarian, writer*
Guerri, William Grant *lawyer*
†Gunn, Michael Peter *lawyer*
Gupta, Surendra Kumar *chemical firm executive*
Gutsche, Henry William *retired scientist, writer*
Haar, Robert Theodore *lawyer*
Haberstroh, Richard David *insurance agent*
Haley, Johnetta Randolph *musician, educator, university official*
Hall, Mary Taussig *professional volunteer*
Hall, William Kearney *retired dermatologist*
Hamilton, Jean Constance *judge*
Handel, Peter H. *physics educator*
Handelman, Alice Samuels *public relations professional, writer*
Hanley, Thomas Patrick *obstetrician-gynecologist*
Hansen, Charles *lawyer*
Hansman, Robert G. *art educator, artist*
Hanson, Lee Craig *physician*
Harmon, Clarence *former mayor, law educator*
Harris, Whitney Robson *lawyer, educator, military officer, philanthropist*
Haskins, James Leslie *mathematics educator*
Hawkins, Pamela Leigh Huffman *biochemist*
Hawkins, Peggy Anne *veterinarian*
Hays, Howard H. (Tim Hays) *editor, publisher*
†Hays, Ruth *lawyer*
Heck, Debra Upchurch *information technology, procurement professional*
Heiken, Jay Paul *physician*
Heiser, Walter Charles *librarian, priest, educator*
Hendricks, Flora Ann *small business owner, social worker, special education educator*
Herbert, Kevin Barry John *classics educator*
Herzfeld-Kimbrough, Ciby *mental health educator*
†Hiles, Bradley Stephen *lawyer*
Hilgert, Raymond Lewis *management and industrial relations educator, consultant, arbitrator*
†Hinshaw, Juanita *electric distributor executive*
Hirsch, Arthur (Buzz Hirsch) *film producer, educator*
Hirsch, Raymond Robert *chemical company executive, lawyer*
Hoessle, Charles Herman *zoo director*
Hogan, Michael Ray *life science executive*
Holland, Mark Robert *research scientist*
Holman, C. Ray *medical products executive*
Holmes, Nancy Elizabeth *pediatrician*
Holt, Glen Edward *library administrator*
†Hoock, Edward Thomas, III, *electrician, scoreboard operator*
Horwitz, William J. *treasurer*
†Hovsepian, David Minas *radiologist*
†Hruz, Paul W *pediatrician, endocrinologist, research scientist*
Hsu, Chung Yi *neurologist*
Huck, Elizabeth Louise *radiologist*
†Hulsebosch, Daniel Joseph *historian, educator*
Hundelt, Craig Thomas *realtor, engineering executive*
Hunt, Jeffrey Brian *lawyer*
Hunter, Earle Leslie, III, *retired professional association executive*
Huynh, Quang Khai *biochemist*
Hylton, John Baker *music educator, university administrator*
Inkley, John James, Jr., *lawyer*
†Irwin, Hale S. *professional golfer*
†Isik, Ugur *neurologist*
Israel, Martin Henry *astrophysicist, educator, academic administrator*
Isselhard, Donald Edward *dentist*
Izuchukwu, John Ifeanyichukwu *industrial engineer, mechanical engineer*
Jacks, Sidney *engineer*
Jacobi, Jan de Greeff *school administrator*
James, William W. *financial consultant*
†Jaudes, Richard Edward *lawyer*
Johnson, E. Perry *lawyer*
†Johnson, William Ashton *retired lawyer*
Johnston, Marilyn Frances-Meyers *physician, medical educator*
Joyner, Dee Ann *bank official*
†Joyner Kersee, Jacqueline *former track and field athlete*
Junker, James A. *radiologist*
Kaestner, John Thomas *beverage company executive*
Kahn, Eugene S. *department store chain executive*
†Kaiboriboon, Kitti *neurologist*
†Kalyanaraman, Ramki *education educator, researcher*
Kaminski, Donald Leon *medical educator, surgeon, gastrointestinal physiologist*
†Karoll, Brad R. *psychotherapist, researcher*
†Keating, Michael Joseph *lawyer*
†Keeling, Robert E. *secondary school educator*
Keffler, Karl Joseph *investment company executive, lawyer*
†Keith, Andrea L. *marketing professional*
Keller, Juan Dane *lawyer*
Kennelly, Sister Karen Margaret *retired academic administrator, church administrator, nun*
Keyes, Marion Alvah, IV, *manufacturing company executive*
Khoury, George Gilbert *printing company executive, baseball association executive*
Killenberg, George Andrew *newspaper consultant, former newspaper editor*
Kimmey, James Richard, Jr., *foundation administrator*
Kinsella, Ralph Aloysius, Jr., *physician*
Kipnis, David Morris *physician, educator*
Kling, Merle *political scientist, university official*
Klobasa, John Anthony *lawyer*
Knight, Charles Field *electrical equipment manufacturing company executive*
†Knowles, William S. *retired chemist*
Koehler, Colleen M. *accountant*
Koehler, Harry George *real estate executive*
Koff, Robert Hess *academic administrator*
†Kohn, Alan Charles *lawyer*
Kohnen, Carol Ann *librarian*
Kolker, Allan Erwin *ophthalmologist*
Kolker, Scott Lee *lawyer*
Kortenhof, Joseph Michael *lawyer, educator*
Kouchoukos, Nicholas Thomas *surgeon*
Kramer, Donald Burton *lawyer*
Krebs, Carol Marie *architect, psychiatric therapist*
Krukowski, Lucian *philosophy educator, artist*
Kuhlmann, Fred Mark *lawyer, business executive*
Lackey, Kayle Diann *elementary education educator*
Lagunoff, David *physician, educator*
†Lala, Deepak S *research scientist*
Lamming, John Harold *lawyer*
Lane, Frank Joseph, Jr., *lawyer*
Lang, Danny Robert *planning consultant*
Langness, David Gordon *manufacturing executive*
La Russa, Tony, Jr., (Anthony La Russa Jr.) *professional baseball manager*
†Lasala, John M. *cardiologist, medical educator*
Laskowski, Leonard Francis, Jr., *microbiologist*
Laster, Atlas, Jr., *psychologist*
Lauenstein, Ann Gail *librarian*
Laurie, William *sports team executive*
Lause, Michael Francis *lawyer*
†Le, Thong T. *surgeon*
Lebowitz, Albert *lawyer, writer*
Lents, Peggy Iglauer *marketing executive*
†Leonard, Eugene Albert *banker*
Leonard, Judith Price *educational advisor*
Leontsinis, George John *lawyer*
Leritz, Daniel Raymond *pharmaceutical company executive, consultant*
Leven, Charles Louis *economics educator*
Le Vine, Victor Theodore *political science educator*
†Ley, Timothy James *hematologist, molecular biologist*
†Li, Ping *pharmacologist, educator, researcher*
Lieberman, Edward Jay *lawyer*
Liggett, Hiram Shaw, Jr., *retired diversified industry financial executive*
Limbaugh, Stephen Nathaniel *federal judge*
Lindsey, Linda Lee *sociology educator*
Lock, Albert Larry, Jr., *financial services company executive*
†Loeb, Virgil, Jr., *oncologist, hematologist*
†Losos, Joseph *investment advisor*
Lovelace, Eldridge Hirst *retired landscape architect, city planner*
Lovin, Keith Harold *academic administrator, philosophy educator*
Lowenhaupt, Charles Abraham *lawyer*
Lowther, Thomas Edward *lawyer*
Lubbock, James Edward *retired writer, photographer, publicity consultant*
Luberda, George Joseph *lawyer, educator*
Lucchesi, Lionel Louis *lawyer*
Lucy, Robert Meredith *lawyer*
Ludbrook, Philip Albert *cardiologist, clinical researcher, educator*
Luebbert, Karen Merritt *academic administrator*
Luecke, Kenn Robert *software engineer*
Lutz, John Thomas *author*
Macdonald, Hugh John *music educator, writer*
Macias, Edward S. *chemistry educator, university official and dean*
MacInnis, Al *professional hockey player*
Madden, Thomas F. *medieval history eductor, author*
Mahan, David James *retired university official*
Mahsman, David Lawrence *religious publications editor*
Majerus, Philip Warren *physician*
Mandelstamm, Jerome Robert *lawyer*
Mangelsdorf, Thomas Kelly *psychiatrist, consultant*
Manne, Deborah Sue *oncology nurse, consultant, dental hygienist*
Mantovani, John F. *pediatric neurologist*
Marking, T(heodore) Joseph, Jr., *transportation and urban planner*
Marks, Murry Aaron *lawyer*
Marshall, Garland Ross *biochemist, biophysicist, medical educator*
Martens Balke, Patricia Frances *adult education educator*
†Martin, Carla A. *lawyer, veterinarian*
Martin, Kevin John *nephrologist, educator*
Martin, Wade Hampton, III, *physician, scientist*
Martínez-Solís, Luis Fernando *journalist, writer, historian*
Martz, Mike *professional football coach*
Masinelli, Anthony Dean *journalist, writer*
†Massey, Raymond Lee *lawyer*
Maupin, Stephanie Zeller *educator, consultant*
Maurer, Frederic George, III, *banker*
McCarter, Charles Chase *lawyer*
McCarter, James Philip *biotechnology company executive, researcher*
McClain, Curtis Keith, Jr., *religious studies educator, minister*
McDaniel, James Edwin *lawyer*
McDonald, Brenda Denise *librarian*
McDonnell, Sanford Noyes *aircraft company executive*
†McGinnis, W. Patrick *diversified company executive*
†McGlothlin, Erin Heather *education educator*
McGuinness, Barbara Sue *food products executive*
†McGwire, Mark David *professional baseball player*
McKelvey, James Morgan *chemical engineering educator*
McKenna, William John *textile products executive*
McKinnis, Michael B. *lawyer*
†McMahon, Judith Wantland *psychologist, educator*
McMahon, Robert M. *physician, lawyer*
McMillian, Theodore *federal judge*
Mc Namee, Maurice Basil *English language educator*
Medler, Mary Ann L. *federal judge*
Meehan, John Justin *lawyer*
Meisel, George Vincent *lawyer*
Meissner, Edwin Benjamin, Jr., *retired real estate broker*
Melman, Joy *civic volunteer*
†Mendel, Mark J. *venture capitalist*
Mendelson, David Frey *retired neurology educator*
Merrell, James Lee *religious editor, clergyman*
Merrill, Charles Eugene *lawyer*
Metcalfe, Walter Lee, Jr., *lawyer*
Meyer, John Strauch, Jr., *lawyer*
Meyersick, Sharon Kay *nurse, insurance administrator*
Michaelides, Constantine Evangelos *architect, educator*
†Michener, John Athol *lawyer*
Michenfelder, Albert A. *lawyer*
Middelkamp, John Neal *pediatrician, educator*
†Miller, Dwight Whittemore *lawyer*
Miller, Gary J. *political economist*
Miller, James Gegan *research scientist, physics educator*
†Mitchell, Louise Tyndall *special education educator*
Mohan, John J. *lawyer*
Molloff, Florence Jeanine *speech and language therapist*
Monroe, Thomas Edward *industrial corporation executive*
Monteleone, Patricia *dean*
†Montgomery, Alice Elizabeth *vocalist, speech pathologist*
Mooradian, Arshag Dertad *internist, educator*
Moore, McPherson Dorsett *lawyer*
Moore, Patricia Kay *investor, public relations director*
Morales-Galarreta, Julio *psychiatrist, child psychoanalyst*
Morley, John Edward *physician*
†Morris, John Carl *neurologist, educator, researcher*
†Mueller, Charles William *electric utility executive*
Mullens, William Reese *retired insurance company executive*
Mulligan, Michael Dennis *lawyer*
Munkel, Wayne Irvin *social worker*
Murphy, George Earl *psychiatrist, educator*
Murray, Robert Wallace *chemistry educator*
Myerson, Robert J. *radiation oncologist, educator*
Naumann, Joseph F. *bishop*
Needham, Carol Ann *lawyer, educator*
Neely, John Gail *otolaryngologist*
†Nelson, Ronald Erwin *not-for-profit fundraiser*
Neville, James Morton *retired lawyer, consumer products executive*
Newman, Andrew Edison *restaurant executive*
Newman, Charles A. *lawyer*
Newman, Joan Meskiel *lawyer*
†Nickolai, Beatrice Rose *education educator*
Noce, David D. *federal magistrate judge*
Noel, Edwin Lawrence *lawyer*
North, Carol Sue *psychiatrist, educator*
North, Douglass Cecil *economist, educator*
†Novik, Steve *finance company executive*
O'Connell, Daniel Craig *psychology educator*
O'Donnell, Mark Joseph *accountant*
Ohmer, Steven Russell *judge*
†O'Keefe, Martin D. *priest, theology studies educator*
O'Keefe, Michael Daniel *lawyer*
†Olney, John William *psychiatry educator*
Olsen, Tava Maryanne Lennon *industrial and operations engineering educator*
Olson, Robert Grant *lawyer*
O'Malley, Thomas D. *petroleum industry executive*
O'Neill, Eugene Milton *mergers and acquisitions consultant*
O'Neill, Sheila *principal*
Orton, George Frederick *aerospace engineer*
Osborn, John David *credit union executive*
Osborn, Mark Eliot *dentist*
Ottinger, Maurice Armand *software engineer, educator*
Owens, William Don *anesthesiology educator*
Ozawa, Martha Naoko *social work educator*
Pace, Orlando Lamar *football player*
Palans, Lloyd Alex *lawyer*
Pan, Yi *neurologist*
†Patterson, Miles Lawrence *psychology educator*
†Paule, Donald Wayne *lawyer*
Payne, Meredith Jorstad *physician*
Payuk, Edward William *elementary education educator*
Peck, William Arno *physician, educator, university official and dean*
Peper, Christian Baird *lawyer*
Perez, Carlos A. *radiation oncologist, educator*
Perkins, Norris Lynwood, III, (Terry Perkins) *columnist and writer*
Perotti, Rose Norma *lawyer*
Perry, Lewis Curtis *historian, educator*
Peters, David Allen *mechanical engineering educator, consultant*
Peters, Robert James, Sr., *management consultant*
†Phoenix, G. Keith *lawyer*

Pickle, Robert Douglas *lawyer, footwear industry executive*
Picus, Joel *medical educator*
Pleban, Sarah Shelledy *lawyer*
Poellot, Luther *minister*
†Polgar, Michael F. *sociology educator, researcher*
Pollack, Joe *retired newspaper critic and columnist, writer*
Pollack, Seymour Victor *computer science educator*
Poole, William *bank executive*
Pope, Mark L. *counseling psychologist, educator*
Pope, Robert E(ugene) *fraternal organization administrator*
†Porter, Paul Robert *foundation administrator*
Poscover, Maury B. *lawyer*
Posgay, Betty Marie *medical equipment company executive, artist*
Post, Stephen Lightner *psychiatrist, psychoanalyst, educator*
†Powers, William John *neurologist*
Premachandra, Bhartur Narasimhaiengar *endocrinology educator, researcher*
Prensky, Arthur Lawrence *pediatric neurologist, educator*
Pruellage, John Kenneth *lawyer*
Purdy, James Aaron *medical physics educator*
Purkerson, Mabel Louise *physician, physiologist, educator*
Quenneville, Joel *professional hockey coach*
Quenon, Robert Hagerty *retired mining consultant and holding company executive*
†Rabbitt, Daniel Thomas, Jr., *lawyer*
Rabun, John S. *forensic psychiatrist*
Radentz, Michael Grey *recording engineer, producer, composer, musician*
Radford, Diane Mary *surgeon, surgical oncologist*
Ramming, Michael Alexander *retired school system administrator*
Randolph, Jennings, Jr., (Jay Randolph) *sportscaster*
Rao, Dabeeru C. *epidemiologist, educator*
Rasche, Robert Harold *banker, retired economics educator*
Reck, Carleen Joan *social welfare administrator*
Recklein, Linda Sue *library administrator*
Rednam, Krishna Rao Venkata *ophthalmologist*
Reeg, Kurtis Bradford *lawyer*
Regnell, Barbara Caramella *retired media educator*
Reh, Thomas Edward *radiologist, educator*
Reid, Lorene Frances *middle school educator*
†Reilly, Catherine Herbert *librarian, educator*
Reynolds, Robert A., Jr., *electric distributor executive*
Rice, Canice Timothy, Jr., *lawyer*
†Rice, Charles Marcus, II, *lawyer*
Rice, Patricia Jane *journalist*
Richardson, Thomas Hampton *design consulting engineer*
Ricks, David Artel *business educator, editor*
Riddle, Veryl Lee *lawyer*
†Riew, K. Daniel *cervical spine surgeon*
Riner, Ronald Nathan *cardiologist, business consultant*
Ritter, Robert Forcier *lawyer*
Ritterskamp, Douglas Dolvin *lawyer*
Robins, Lee Nelken *medical educator*
Robins, Marjorie McCarthy (Mrs. George Kenneth Robins) *civic worker*
Rodriguez, José Luis *biochemist*
Rogers, John Russell *manufacturing company executive, engineer*
Rolen, Scott Bruce *baseball player*
†Ronen, David *logistics and operations management educator, consultant*
†Rose, Albert Schoenburg *lawyer, educator*
Rosen, Fred *travel company executive*
†Rosenblum, Barry Norton *physician*
Rosenzweig, Saul *psychologist, educator, administrator*
Ross, Monte *electrical engineer, researcher*
†Rowland, Douglas John *research scientist*
Royal, Henry Duval *nuclear medicine physician*
Royce, Robert Killian *retired physician*
Rubenstein, Jerome Max *lawyer*
†Rudd, Susan *retail executive*
Ruland, Richard Eugene *English and American literature educator, critic, literary historian*
Ruth, David Allen *accountant*
†Ryall, Jo-Ellyn M. *psychiatrist*
Sableman, Lynn *educator*
Sago, Janis Lynn *photography educator*
Sale, Llewellyn, III, *lawyer*
Sale, Merritt *classicist, comparatist, educator*
†Saleem, Kadharbatcha S *neurobiologist, research scientist*
Salisbury, Robert Holt *political science educator*
†Salsich, Gretchen B. *medical researcher, physical therapy educator*
Sandbach, Charlie Bernard *accountant*
Sant, John Talbot *lawyer*
†Scheffing, Dianne Elizabeth *special education educator*
Scheffing, Donald George *county government administrator*
Schiller, Britt-Marie Christina *philosophy educator*
†Schilling, James Stanford *physicist, educator*
Schindler, Laura Ann *piano teacher, accompanist*
Schlafly, Phyllis Stewart *writer*
Schlesinger, Milton J. *virology educator, researcher*
Schmid, Frank Andreas *economist*
Schmidt, Robert Charles, Jr., *finance executive*
†Schmitt, David E. *health facility administrator, music therapist*
†Schnuck, Craig D. *grocery store company executive*
†Schnuck, Scott C. *grocery store executive*
Schoene, Kathleen Snyder *lawyer*
Schoenhard, William Charles, Jr., *health care executive*
Schonfeld, Gustav *medical educator, researcher, administrator*

Schramm, Paul Howard *lawyer*
Schreiber, James Ralph *obstetrician, researcher*
Schwartz, Alan Leigh *pediatrician, educator*
Schwarz, Egon *humanities and German language educator, writer, literary critic*
Searls, Eileen Haughey *retired lawyer, librarian, educator*
Sehorn, Jason *football player*
Seibert, Earl Henry, Jr., (Si Seibert) *diversified financial services company executive*
Seiler, James Elmer *judge*
Seligman, Joel *dean*
Sestric, Anthony James *lawyer*
Shalowitz, Howard A. *lawyer*
Shanahan, Michael Francis *manufacturing executive, former hockey team executive*
Shapiro, Larry J. *pediatrician, scientist, educator*
†Shapiro, Robert B. *former food products manufacturing executive*
Shea, Daniel Bartholomew, Jr., *English language educator, actor*
Shepperd, Thomas Eugene *accountant*
Sherby, Kathleen Reilly *lawyer*
Shrauner, Barbara Wayne Abraham *electrical engineer, educator*
†Shreckhise, Robert Lynn *minister, theology studies educator*
Sibbald, John Ristow *management consultant*
Siegel, Barry Alan *nuclear radiologist*
†Siegel, Cordell *lawyer*
Silverman, Victoria Lillian *not-for-profit fundraiser*
Singh, Inderjit *nephrologist, internist, medical educator*
Slavin, Raymond Granam *allergist, immunologist*
Slay, Francis G. *mayor*
Smith, Arthur Lee *lawyer*
Smith, Gladys Ann *counselor, military medic*
Smith, Morton Edward *ophthalmology educator, dean*
Smith, Ozzie (Osborne Earl Smith) *retired professional baseball player*
Smith, Richard Jay *anthropologist, orthodontist, educator*
Smith, Stacey Lee *psychiatrist*
Sneeringer, Stephen Geddes *lawyer*
Sobol, Lawrence Raymond *lawyer*
Soeteber, Ellen *journalist, newspaper editor*
Soper, Nathaniel Jolas *surgeon*
Sorensen, Keld *biochemist*
Spector, Gershon Jerry *physician, educator, researcher*
Spielman, Barry E *electrical engineer, educator, department chairman*
Stanton, Frank Lawrence, Jr., *graphic designer, illustrator, educator*
Stearley, Robert Jay *retired packaging company executive*
Stencer, Mark Joseph *healthcare administrator, consultant*
Stenson, William Frederick *gastroenterologist*
†Stewart, Allan Forbes *lawyer*
Stewart, John Harger *music educator*
†Stiritz, William P. *food company executive*
Stoecker, David Thomas *banker*
†Stokes, Patrick T. *brewery company executive*
Storandt, Martha *psychologist*
Stork, Donald Arthur *advertising executive*
Stratton, Sharon Elizabeth Spahn *mental and women's health nurse, nurse supervisor*
Stretch, John Joseph *social work educator, management and evaluation consultant*
Strevey, Tracy Elmer, Jr., *army officer, surgeon, physician executive*
Strunk, Robert Charles *physician*
Stumpf, Earlwayne Schwarze *actor, advertising executive*
†Sugg, Reed Waller *lawyer*
Suhre, Walter Anthony, Jr., *retired lawyer and brewery executive*
Sullentrup, Michael Gerard *fracture mechanics engineer, consultant*
Sullivan, Edward Lawrence *lawyer*
†Supanvanij, Janikan *finance educator*
Suter, Albert Edward *manufacturing company executive*
Sutera, Salvatore Philip *mechanical engineering educator*
Sutter, Jane Elizabeth *science educator, writer, conservationist*
Switzer, Frederick Michael, III, *lawyer, arbitrator, mediator*
Szabo, Barna Aladar *mechanical engineering educator, mining engineer*
Talent, James M. *senator, former congressman, lawyer*
Taylor, Andrew C. *rental and leasing company executive*
†Taylor, Jack C. *rental and leasing company executive*
Teasdale, Kenneth Fulbright *lawyer*
Teitelbaum, Steven Lazarus *pathology educator*
Templeton, Alan Robert *biology educator*
Ternberg, Jessie Lamoin *neurological surgeon*
Thalden, Barry R. *architect*
Thomas, Pamela Adrienne *special education educator*
Thompson, Rodney Marlin *computer consultant*
Thompson, Vetta Lynn Sanders *psychologist, educator*
Thompson, William Charles *civil engineer*
Tiefenbrunn, Alan James *medical educator*
Tierney, Catherine Marie *librarian*
Tierney, Michael Edward *lawyer*
Tkachuk, Keith *hockey player*
†Trevathan, Edwin *pediatric neurologist, educator*
Trout, Keith William *electrical engineer*
†Turcotte, John Arthur, Jr., *lawyer*
Tutt, Louise Thompson *lawyer*
Tyler, William Howard, Jr., *advertising executive, educator*
Tyree, Donald Andrew *financial educator*
Ulett, George Andrew *psychiatrist*
Ullian, Joseph Silbert *philosophy educator*
Upbin, Hal Jay *consumer products executive*
van den Berg, Sara Jane *English educator*
Vandiver, Donna *public relations executive*

Van Luven, William Robert *management consultant*
Vedeniapin, Andrei B. *psychiatrist, researcher*
†Vijayan, Anitha *medical educator*
Virgo, John Michael *economist, researcher, educator*
Virgo, Katherine Sue *health services researcher*
Virtel, James John *lawyer*
†Vogel, Carl E. *telecommunications industry executive*
†Voss, K. Dirk *social sciences educator, researcher*
Walentik, Corinne Anne *pediatrician*
†Walker, George Herbert, III, *investment banking company executive, lawyer*
Walker, Robert Mowbray *physicist, educator*
†Wall, Catherine Wynne *lawyer*
Walsh, Joseph Leo, III, *lawyer*
Walsh, Thomas Charles *lawyer*
Ward, Sylvia A. *reading educator*
†Ward-Brown, Denise *sculptor, educator*
Warner, Susan *federal agency administrator*
Wassell, Loren W. *public affairs professional, writer*
Waterbury, Jackson DeWitt *retired marketing executive*
Waters, Richard *retired publishing company executive*
Watkins, Hortense Catherine *middle school educator*
Watson, Patty Jo *anthropology educator*
Watson, Richard Allan *philosophy educator, writer*
Watters, Richard Donald *lawyer*
Wayne, Jane O(xenhandler) *poet, writing educator*
Weaver, Charles Lyndell, Jr., *institutional and manufacturing facilities administrator, management and marketing systems consultant*
Webb Anderson, JoAnn Marie *lawyer, community advocate*
†Weber, Gloria Richie *retired minister, retired state legislator*
†Weck, Margaret A. *science educator, educator*
Wedner, H. James *physician, researcher*
Weidenbaum, Murray Lew *economist, educator*
Weight, Doug *professional hockey player*
Weisenfeld, Robert Beller *chemist, researcher*
Weiss, Charles Andrew *lawyer*
Weiss, Robert Francis *former academic administrator, religious organization administrator, consultant*
Weixlmann, Joseph Norman, Jr., *English educator, provost*
Welch, David William *lawyer*
Welch, Michael John *chemistry educator, researcher*
Welch, Patrick James *economics educator, author, consultant*
Weldon, Virginia V. *retired corporate executive, physician*
Wellman, Carl Pierce *philosophy educator*
Werner, Burton Kready *insurance company executive*
White, Neil H. *pediatric endocrinologist*
Whyte, Michael Peter *medicine, pediatrics and genetics educator, research director*
Wiggins, Dewayne Lee *financial executive*
Wildhaber, Michael Rene *accountant*
Wiley, Gregory Robert *publisher*
Wilke, LeRoy *church administrator*
Will, Robert John *lawyer*
†Williams, Nellie James Batt *secondary education educator*
Williams, Theodore Joseph, Jr., *lawyer*
†Williamson, Marilyn *retired secondary school educator*
Wilson, Edward Nathan *mathematician, educator*
Wilson, Margaret Bush *lawyer*
Wiltenburg, Robert Edward *university dean*
Winn, Hung Nguyen *obstetrician, gynecologist, maternal-fetal medicine physician*
Winter, David Ferdinand *electrical engineering educator, consultant*
Winter, Richard Lawrence *financial and health care company executive*
Winter, William Earl *retired beverage company executive*
Wippold, Franz Joseph, II, *medical educator*
†Withers, W. Wayne *lawyer*
Witherspoon, William *investment economist*
Witt, Michael John *history educator, priest*
Wolf, Jonathon Edward *music educator*
Woodruff, Bruce Emery *lawyer*
†Wright, Diane *procurement manager*
Wright, Gary Kennedy *educational administrator*
Wrighton, Mark Stephen *chemistry educator*
Wyrwich, Kathleen W. *health research educator*
†Yeckel, Anita T. *state legislator*
Young, Marvin Oscar *lawyer*
Young, Paul Andrew *anatomist*
Zaidi, Riaz Haider *aircraft engineer, consultant*
Zardini, Elsa Matilde *botanist, educator*
Zhu, Xin Liang *molecular biologist, researcher*
Zucchero, Frederic Joseph *medical director*
Zurheide, Charles Henry *consulting electrical engineer*
Zwikelmaier, Kurt E. *pharmaceutical executive*

Saint Peters

Gilman, Patricia Ann *artist, educator*
Huckshold, Wayne William *elementary education educator*

Salem

†Hall, Glenn Allen *lawyer, state representative*
Jessen, Chris Michael *music educator*
Sheriff, Kenneth Wayne *social services administrator*

Sedalia

Berry, Jean Stanfield *artist, retired art educator*
Gardner, R. Scott *lawyer*
Hazen, Elizabeth Frances *retired special education educator*
Miller, Toni M. Andrews *critical care nurse, educator*

Sibley

Morrow, Elizabeth Hostetter *sculptress, museum administrator, farmer, educator*

Sikeston

Tesseneer-Street, Susan *photographer, artist, writer*

Springfield

Allcorn, Terry Alan *principal, educator*
Arneson, James Herman *lawyer*
Aull, Elizabeth Berryman *real estate development executive*
†Baird, Robert Dean *mission director*
Baurichter, John Daniel *osteopath*
Baxter-Smith, Gregory John *lawyer*
Berger, Jerry Allen *museum director*
Boardman-Fite, Linda Irene *speaker, management consultant*
Boland, Beverly Joyce *music educator*
Brady, Steven L. *civil engineer, consultant*
Budzinsky, Armin Alexander *investment banker*
Burgess, Ruth Lenora Vassar *speech and language educator*
†Burling, William John *literature educator*
Busch, Annie *library director*
Carlson, Thomas Joseph *real estate developer, lawyer, mayor*
Champion, Norma Jean *communications educator, state legislator*
Crites, Richard Don *lawyer*
†Denton, D. Keith *management educator*
Easley, June Ellen Price *genealogist*
Echols, Carol Avery *music educator*
FitzGerald, Kevin Michael *lawyer, mediator*
†Fritts, Josephine Ann *education educator*
†Gardner, Steven *health insurance specialist*
Geter, Rodney Keith *plastic surgeon*
†Giglio, James Nicholas *humanities educator, writer*
Gillming, Kenneth *church administrator*
Glazier, Robert Carl *publishing executive*
Good, Stephen Hanscom *academic administrator*
Groce, Steven Fred *lawyer*
Gruhn, Robert Stephen *retired parole officer*
Hackett, Earl Randolph *neurologist*
†Haltom, Michael Fred *religious studies educator, military officer*
Hansen, John Paul *retired metallurgical engineer*
Harris, Ralph William *religious journalist*
Hawkins, Kevin Andrew *music educator*
Hedrick, Peggy Shepherd *lawyer*
†Henry, Jack Allen, Jr., *music educator*
†Hess, John *education educator, counselor*
Holstein, John Charles *former state supreme court judge*
Hulston, John Kenton *lawyer, director*
Imhoff, Richard James *trust company executive, financial planner*
Jura, James J. *electric utility executive*
Keiser, John Howard *academic administrator*
Kincaid, Paul Kent *public relations professional*
†Knotts, Tami Leigh *finance educator*
Liu, Yuan Hsiung *drafting and design educator*
Lowther, Gerald Halbert *lawyer*
Maples, Jimmie Kay *mechanical engineer*
Mathis, Alicia *biologist*
McCartney, N. L. *investment banker*
†McClellan, Norma D. *music educator*
†McCurry, Bruce *lawyer*
McDonald, William Henry *lawyer*
McGinnis, M. Sean *lawyer*
Montgomery, Linda Stroupe *county official*
Morris, Ann Haseltine Jones *social welfare administrator*
Morris, Gregory W *music educator*
Moulder, T. Earline *musician*
O'Block, Robert *entrepreneur, publishing executive*
Ownby, Jerry Steve *landscape architect, educator*
†Parsons, James *music educator*
†Powell, William Don *lawyer*
Quebbeman, Robert C. *conductor, educator*
Quinn, Rodney David *neurologist*
Roberts, Patrick Kent *lawyer*
Robertson, Ruth Ann *systems analyst, engineer*
†Rutherford, Ken Robin *political scientist, educator*
†Scroggins, Wesley Allen *finance educator, researcher*
†Sherwood, Devon Fredrick *lawyer*
†Shirley, George William *retired music educator, farmer*
Spicer, Holt Vandercook *retired speech and theater educator*
Starnes, James Wright *lawyer*
Steffen, Alan Leslie *entomologist*
Stone, Allan David *economics educator*
Stratmann, Henry George *cardiologist*
†Thomassen, Roger Clifford *music educator*
Thompson, Clifton C. *retired chemistry educator, university administrator*
Thompson, Wade S. *artist, art and design educator, administrator*
Toste, Anthony Paim *chemistry educator, researcher*
Trask, Thomas Edward *religious organization administrator*
Van Cleave, William Robert *international relations educator*
Wang, Guangmiao *business executive, consultant*
White, John Lee *theology studies educator*
Witherspoon, John Thomas *water resources consultant*

St Louis

Betsinger, Peggy Ann *retired oncological nurse*

St. Louis

†Novak, Camille *small business owner, consultant*

Stella

Yeagley, Joan Howerton *writer*

Stockton

†Hammons, Brian Kent *lawyer, business executive*

Stover
Reynolds, Sallie Blackburn *artist, civic volunteer*

Sturgeon
Fashing, Edward Michael *ranch owner, physical sciences educator*

Sullivan
Penn, Ronald Hulen *manufacturing executive*

Sweet Springs
Long, Helen Halter *writer, educator*

Tecumseh
Davis, Michael Chase *retired aerospace industry executive, retired military officer*

Theodosia
Johnson, Larry Robert *education educator*

Town And Country
Kaegel, Ray Martin *real estate and insurance broker*
Lachenicht-Berkeley, Angela Marie *marketing professional*
Levin, Marvin Edgar *physician*

Trenton
†Ensminger, John Jay *writer, poet, minister, counselor*
Myntti, Jon Nicholas *software engineer*
Pushkarsky, Louis Paul *retired mathematics educator*

Troy
Beck, James David *lawyer*

Union
Schmelz, Brenda Lea *legal assistant*

Unity Village
Boehm, Toni Georgene *seminary dean, nurse*

University City
McVey, Francis Daniel *mechanical engineer, software developer, educator*

Urbana
†Frey, Lucille Pauline *social studies educator, consultant*

Vandalia
Berry, Rebecca Diane *artist, art educator*

Verona
Youngberg, Charlotte Anne *education specialist, clergywoman*

Viburnum
West, Roberta Bertha *writer*

Villa Ridge
Kling, S(tephen) Lee *banker*

Walker
Martin, Phillip Dwight *bank consulting company executive, mayor*

Warrensburg
Collins, John W. *nurse practitioner, lecturer*
†Foley, William Edward *historian, educator, retired historian*
Horine, John William *aviation educator*
†Jones, Robert Claude *editor*
†Jurkowski, Odin Lech *medical librarian, educator*
Limback, E(dna) Rebecca *vocational education educator*
†Myers, Michelle E. *education educator, consultant*
Robbins, Dorothy Ann *foreign language educator*

Warrenton
Dapron, Elmer Joseph, Jr., *communications executive*

Washington
De Pew, David Philip *advertising executive, consultant, lecturer*

Waynesville
Learmann, Judith Marilyn *secondary school educator*

Webb City
James, Kathryn A. *secondary education educator*
Nichols, Robert Leighton *civil engineer*
Rose, Terri Kaye *obstetrical gynecological nurse practitioner, forensic exam nurse*

Webster Groves
Becker, Rex Louis *architect*
Carr, Margaret *educator*
Gergeceff-Cooper, Lorraine *artist, consultant*
Osver, Arthur *artist*

Wentzville
†de la Torre, Roger Anibal *surgeon*
†Duncan, Aaron W. *media specialist, minister*
†Garrett, Dwayne Everett *veterinary clinic executive*
†Mason, Bryan *music educator*

West Plains
Dunlap, David Houston *judge*
Fugate, Charles Royce, Sr., *civil engineer*
Wilcoxson, Roy Dell *plant pathology educator and researcher*

Weston
Murdock, Phelps Dubois, Jr., *marketing consultant, strategic planner*

Wheeling
Roe, Mary Ann *postmaster*

Whitewater
Sahlfeld Bunger, Kimberly Katherine *speech language pathologist*

Willow Springs
Hinds, C. Robert (Bob) *retired writer*

Windyville
Blosser, Pamela Elizabeth *metaphysics educator, counselor, minister*
Clark, Laurel Jan *adult education educator, author, editor, minister, counselor*
Condron, Barbara O'Guinn *metaphysics educator, school administrator, publisher*
Condron, Daniel Ralph *academic administrator, metaphysics educator*
Pearson, Dana Bart *librarian*

MONTANA

Alzada
Ericsson, Ronald James *applied biology executive*

Belgrade
Aveson, Martha Caralyn *pharmaceutical company executive*

Big Sky
Ryan, Raymond D. *retired steel company executive, insurance and marketing firm executive*

Bigfork
†Keenan, Bob *state legislator*
Shennum, Robert Herman *retired telephone company executive*

Billings
Aldrich, Richard Kingsley *lawyer*
Barnea, Uri N. *music director, conductor, composer, violinist*
†Baugh, Gary Todd *lawyer*
Beiswanger, Gary Lee *lawyer*
Chen, Yenn-Kunn Oliver *mathematician, educator*
Cochran, William Michael *librarian*
Cromley, Brent Reed *lawyer, state senator*
DeRosier, Arthur Henry, Jr., *historian*
Deschner, Jane Waggoner *photo artist, public relations consultant*
England, John David *neurologist, educator*
Fagg, Russell *judge, lawyer*
Gardiner, Steve E. *secondary school educator, writer*
Gerlach, Thurlo Thompson *electrical engineer*
†Gilluly, Mary Seana *not-for-profit executive*
Glenn, Guy Charles *pathologist*
Glenn, Lucia Howarth *retired mental health services professional*
†Guha, Sujata *education educator*
†Gulick, Walter Brooks *philosopher, educator*
Haughey, James McCrea *lawyer, artist*
†Jensen, Theodore W. *language educator*
†Jones, James Leonard *lawyer*
Larsen, Richard Lee *former mayor and city manager, business, municipal and labor relations consultant, arbitrator*
Letz, Eileen Korber *retired community health nurse*
Malee, Thomas Michael *lawyer*
Martinez, Bonnie Yvonne *retired social services worker*
†Mitchell, Laura Ann *lawyer*
Nance, Robert Lewis *oil company executive*
Rich, Joseph David *psychiatrist*
Sample, Joseph Scanlon *foundation executive*
Sites, James Philip *lawyer, consultant*
Snell, Alma Hogan *artist*
Stanfill, Patricia Mae *accountant*
Thomas, Sidney R. *federal judge*
Toole, Bruce Ryan *retired lawyer*
Towe, Thomas Edward *lawyer*

Bonner
†Smith, Annick *writer, producer*

Bozeman
Aig, Dennis Ira *writer, film producer*
Barrett, Louis C. *mathematician, educator*
Billau, Robin Louise *engineering and consulting executive*
Cokelet, Giles Roy *biomedical engineering educator*
Conover, Richard Corrill *lawyer*
†Creel, Scott *adult education educator, researcher*
Davis, Nicholas Homans Clark *finance company executive*
DeHaas, John Neff, Jr., *retired architecture educator*
†Drobizhev, Mikhail Anatolievich *physicist*
Duffié, Mary Katharine *anthropologist, researcher, educator*
Frohnmayer, John Edward *lawyer, legal scholar, ethicist, writer*
Gamble, Geoffrey *academic administrator*
Gibson, David Frederic *foundation executive, engineering educator*
†Goodrich, John M. *conservation ecologist*
Gray, Philip Howard *former psychologist, writer*
†Harris, Christopher Kirk *lawyer*
Horner, John Robert *paleontologist, researcher*
†Large, David Clay *education educator, writer*
Meister, Alice Marie *librarian*
Nehrir, M. Hashem *electrical engineer, educator*
Nelson, Steven Dwayne *lawyer*
Patten, Duncan Theunissen *ecologist educator*
†Pernarowski, Mark *mathematician, educator*
Sanks, Robert Leland *environmental engineer, emeritus educator*
Selyem, Bruce Jade *freelance/self-employed photographer*
†Sobek, Durward Kenneth, II, *engineering educator*
Stanislao, Joseph *consulting engineer, educator*
Todd, Kenneth S., Jr., *parasitologist, educator*
Vick, Jeffrey Harrison *music educator, musician*
†Wiltsie, Gordon H. *photographer*
Wylie, Paul Richter, Jr., *lawyer*

Butte
Bishop, Robert Charles *architect, metals and minerals company executive*
Burke, John James *utility executive*
Jensen, Roger Christian *industrial engineer*
Krueger, Kurt Donn *district court judge*
McCarthy, Bernard Francis *lawyer*
Mc Elwain, Joseph Arthur *retired power company executive*
†Nikoli-Tirkas, Bojana *aerospace engineer, researcher*
Reardon, Stephen James, Jr., *retired English speech educator*
Sherrill, Barbara Ann Buker *elementary school educator*

Cameron
Van Doren, Emerson Barclay *mediator*

Clancy
Ekanger, Laurie *retired state official, contractor*

Columbia Falls
Chisholm, Dean D. *lawyer*
Spade, George Lawrence (George Shenker) *scientist*

Crow Agency
Pease-Pretty On Top, Janine B. *community college administrator*

Darby
†Haugen, Margaret Ellen *daycare administrator*

Dayton
Catalfomo, Philip *retired university dean*
Volborth, Alexis von *geochemist, geological engineering educator*

Dillon
Sethi, A. S. (Jim Sethi) *business educator*

Fairfield
Graf, Ervin Donald *municipal official*

Florence
Egley, Thomas Arthur *computer services executive, accountant*

Forsyth
†Heser, Cheryl J. *library director*

Glendive
†Shields, Lisa A. *music educator*

Great Falls
Becker, Julia Margaret *artist, educator*
†Blewett, Alexander, III, *lawyer*
Christiaens, Chris (Bernard Francis Christiaens) *financial analyst, state legislator*
Davidson, David Scott *architect*
Dietrich, Dennis Ward *neurologist*
Doherty, Steve *lawyer, former state legislator*
Gallagher, Sherry E. *artist*
George, Michael Joseph *lawyer*
†Gray, Orville *lawyer*
†Hartelius, Channing Julius *lawyer*
Hodge, Glenn Roy *retired postmaster*
Johnson, Gordon James *artistic director, conductor*
Knowles, Randall Gene *financial planner*
Ledesma-Nicholson, Charmaine *psychotherapist*
Paulson-Ehrhardt, Patricia Helen *sales executive*
Schmidt, Rita *retired library media specialist*
†Semenza, Dirk A. *metal fabrication executive*
Sletten, John Robert *construction company executive*
Speer, John Elmer *paralegal, reporter, counselor*
Stevens, George Alexander *real estate broker*
Walker, Leland Jasper *civil engineer*

Hamilton
Hadlow, William *retired veterinarian, pathologist*
Langton, Jeffrey H. *judge*
Soden, Ruth M. *geriatrics nurse, educator*

Hardin
MacClean, Walter Lee *dentist*

Harlem
Brekke, Alan Lee *industrial engineer*

Havre
Clouse, Vickie Rae *biologist, paleontologist, educator*
Coffman, Barbara LeAnn *environmentalist*
Gallus, Charles Joseph *retired journalist*
Lanier, William Joseph *college program director*
Moog, Mary Ann Pimley *lawyer*

Helena
Beck, Tom *state legislator, rancher*
Brown, Jan Whitney *small business owner*
Brown, Robert J. (Bob Brown) *state official*
Clarkson, Robert Noel *commercial photographer, magician*
Cleary, Shirley Jean *artist, illustrator*
Cooney, Mike *former secretary of state*
Cotter, Patricia O'Brien *state supreme court justice*
Craig, Mary Lauri *accountant*
Crofts, Richard A. *academic administrator*
Fitzpatrick, Lois Ann *library administrator*
Gersovitz, Jeremy *lawyer*
†Grant, John Halloran *lawyer*
Gray, Karla Marie *state supreme court chief justice*
Hart, John William *theology and ecology educator*
†Holmes, Robert M. *minister, counselor, educator*
Johnson, David Sellie *civil engineer*
Jones, Charles Irving *bishop*
†Kilgore, Tulasi *artist, art educator*
Leaphart, W. William *state supreme court justice*
†Lowney, Jeremiah *sociologist, educator, priest*
Manuel, Vivian *public relations executive*
Mazurek, Joseph P. *lawyer, former state legislator*
McGee, Dan(iel) W. *state legislator*
McGrath, Mike *attorney general, lawyer*
Meadows, Judith Adams *law librarian, educator*
Mercer, John A. *former state legislator*
Miller, Ken *state legislator*
Nelson, James C *state supreme court justice*
Ohs, Karl *lieutenant governor*
Porter, Jeanne Smith *civic worker*
Ream, Bob *political organization administrator*
Regnier, James *state supreme court justice*
Rice, Jim *state supreme court justice*
†Schlesinger, Deborah Lee *librarian*
Seiler, Karen Peake *organizational psychologist*
Strege, Karen *library director*
Strickler, Jeffrey Harold *pediatrician*
Warren, Christopher Charles *electronics executive*

Hot Springs
Erickson, James Gardner *retired artist, cartoonist*

Kalispell
†Cowan, George D. *literature educator*
Freiberg, Robert Jerry *laser physicist, engineer, technology administrator, consultant*
Gallagher, Tonya Marie *family support specialist*
Klang, Mary Margaret *secondary school educator*
Nardi, Stephen J. *lawyer*
†Vickers, Lee Louise *minister*
von Krenner, Walther G. *artist, writer, art consultant and appraiser*
Winkel, R. Dennis *family practice physician*

Livingston
Beland, Charlet Sue *secondary school educator*
Jovick, Robert L. *lawyer*
Wright, Richard Kirk *physicist, materials researcher, consultant*

Malta
†Engebretson, Erik John *music educator, director*

Martinsdale
Rostad, Lee B. *rancher, writer*

Miles City
†Sleight, Garth Hessen *language educator, dean*

Missoula
Amundson, Eva Donalda *civic worker*
†Beckwith, John Bruce *pediatric pathologist*
Bowman, Jean Louise *lawyer, civic worker*
Brown, Perry Joe *university dean*
Brown, Robert Munro *museum director*
Brumit, Lawrence Edward, III, *oil field service company executive*
Chirinos, Eduardo *writer, educator*
†DeGraw, Joseph Irving, Jr., *chemist, consultant*
Dennison, George Marshel *academic administrator*
†Drake, Richard Regis *historian, educator*
Earls, Joy R. Shulman *professional society administrator*
Fawcett, Don Wayne *retired anatomist*
George, Alexander Andrew *lawyer*
Gillett, Gary Lee *music educator*
Grieves, Forest Leslie *political science educator*
Haines, John Meade *poet, translator, writer*
Kemmis, Daniel Orra *cultural organization administrator, author*
Kittredge, William Alfred *humanities educator*
Knowles, William Leroy (Bill Knowles) *television news producer, journalism educator*
†Kuhn, Thomas B *education educator*
†Langner, Heiko Walter *soil scientist, chemist*
Liston, Albert Morris *investor, administrator, educator*
Lopach, James Joseph *political science educator*
†Molloy, Donald William *lawyer*
Morales, Julio K. *lawyer*
Osterheld, R(obert) Keith *chemistry educator*
Power, Thomas Michael *economist, educator*
Reynolds, William Arthur *retired physician, educator*
Rice, Steven Dale *electronics educator*
Robertson, Gregory Howard *civil engineer*
Rowland, Paul McDonald *education educator*
Sampson, Ruth Louise *endocrinologist*
Scamman, Frederick L. *retired tool and die maker*
Swick, Herbert Morris *medical educator, humanist, neurologist*
Trask-Tyrell, Nancy *management company executive*
Vannatta, Shane Anthony *lawyer*
†Vogelsberg, Ross Timm *education educator, researcher*
Washington, Dennis *construction executive*
Wigfied-Phillip, Ruth Genivea *genealogist, author, researcher*
Williams, Pat *former congressman*
†Wilson, Jane A. *mathematician, educator*
Yee, Albert Hoy *writer, retired psychologist, educator*

Monarch
†Baker, David Warren *earth scientist*

Polson
Marchi, Jon *former investment brokerage executive, cattle rancher, exporter, venture capitalist*
Stanford, Jack Arthur *biological station administrator*
Turnage, Jean Allen *retired state supreme court chief justice*

Pony
Anderson, Richard Ernest *agribusiness development consultant, rancher*

Poplar
Gabrielson, Shirley Gail *nurse*

Red Lodge
Kauffman, Marvin Earl *geoscience consultant*

Ronan
Grainey, Philip J. *lawyer*

Saint Regis
Arney, James Douglas *forestry biometrics consultant*

Sheridan
Hendrickson, Roman Michael *physician*

Sidney
Beagle, John Gordon *real estate broker*

Stevensville
Derrick, William Dennis *retired physical plant administrator, consultant*

Terry
Bruno, Peter Jackson *pastor, counselor, consultant*

Townsend
Lefever, Hollis K. *family practice*

Troy
Sherman, Signe Lidfeldt *portfolio manager, former research chemist*

Utica
Stevenson, Sarah Schoales *rancher, business owner*

Victor
Stewart, JoAnne *director*

Whitefish
DeFranco, Boniface Ferdinand Leonard (Buddy DeFranco) *clarinetist, bandleader*
Hemp, Ralph Clyde *retired reinsurance company executive, consultant, arbitrator, umpire*
James, Marion Ray *magazine founder, editor*

Whitehall
Bernard, Donald Ray *law educator, international business counselor*

NEBRASKA

Alliance
Haefele, Edwin Theodore *political theorist, consultant*
Riemenschneider, Albert Louis *retired engineering educator*

Amelia
Jellico, Nancy Rose *painter, sculptor*

Atkinson
Sutherland, John Campbell *pathologist, educator*

Auburn
Winegardner, Rose Mary *special education educator*

Barneston
March, Darlene J. *secondary school educator, news correspondent*

Beatrice
†Riedesel, Laureen Falk *library director*

Beaver City
†Hall, Jay De *finance educator, consultant*

Bellevue
Hoell, Kathy *disability rights advocate*
Kayne, Jon Barry *industrial psychologist*
Muller, John Bartlett *university president*
†Schroeder, Van Ace *lawyer*
Woods, Michael Patrick *obstetrician, educator*
Wydeven, Joseph Jude *university dean, educator*

Blair
Christopherson, Myrvin Frederick *college president*

Boys Town
Lynch, Thomas Joseph *museum and historic house manager*

Chadron
†Hinesley, Gail Ann *social sciences educator*
Lecher, Belvadine (Belvadine Reeves) *museum curator*

Clay Center
Hahn, George LeRoy *agricultural engineer, biometeorologist*

Columbus
Micek, Isabelle *music educator*
Schumacher, Paul Maynard *lawyer*

Crawford
Buecker, Thomas Robert *museum curator*

Crete
Hoback, Ronald Dean *retired engineer*
†Monson, Larry Lee *music educator*
Panec, William Joseph *lawyer*

Crofton
Bogner, Darlene Ruth *retired social worker*

Curtis
Khamouna, Mo *communications associate, consultant*

Dakota City
Rodriguez, Manuel Alvarez *pathologist*

Doniphan
Alcorn, Donald J. *secondary school educator, band and choral director*

Eagle
Krutz, Jonathan Lawrence *non-profit association administrator*

Fremont
Dunklau, Rupert Louis *personal investments consultant*
Keasling, Gerald Frank *obstetrician-gynecologist, educator*
Line, William Gunderson *lawyer*
Roesch, Robert Eugene *dentist*
Winans, Anna Jane *dietitian*

Friend
De Bevoise, Lee Raymond *editor, writer*

Fulerton
†Brugman, Jacquelyn Joy *physician assistant*

Funk
Sjogren, Donald Ernest *farmer*

Gering
Weihing, John Lawson *plant pathologist, state senator*
Zach, Debra Jean *social worker*

Grand Island
Abernethy, Irene Margaret *civic worker, retired county official*
†Ahlschwede, Earl David *lawyer*
Buettner, Anne Yu Ramona Wing-mui *psychologist*
†Cuypers, Charles James *lawyer*
Etheridge, Margaret Dwyer *medical center director*
Hesterman, Phillip Karl *music educator*
Howard, John Kenneth *secondary school educator*
Mc Namara, Lawrence J. *bishop*
Piccolo, Gerard Anthony *lawyer*
†Weseman, Vicki Lynne *elementary school educator*
Zichek, Melvin Eddie *retired clergyman, educator*
Zichek, Shannon Elaine *retired secondary school educator*

Gretna
Druliner, Marcia Marie *education educator*

Harrison
Coffee, Virginia Claire *civic worker, former mayor*
Knudson, Ruthann *environmental consultant*

Hastings
Bush, Marjorie Evelynn Tower-Tooker *educator, media specialist, librarian*
Creigh, Thomas, Jr., *utility executive*
Dungan, John Russell, Jr., (Titular Viscount, Dungan of Clare, Hereditary PRince of ERmoy and Arra) *anesthesiologist, health facility administrator*
Freed, Donald Callen *vocal and choral musician, educator*
McCarthy, David Bruce *minister*
†Nelson, Ricky Eugene *financial executive*
Wigert, Lee Roy *psychology educator*

Hayes Center
Fornoff, Ann Lynette *secondary school educator*

Hildreth
Jelkin, John Lamoine *lawyer*

Holdrege
Hendrickson, Bruce Carl *life insurance company executive*
Klein, Michael Clarence *lawyer*

Indianapolis
†Morway, David S. *sports team executive*

Indianola
Troester, Dennis Lee *physical education educator*

Kearney
Buckner, Nathan Andrew *music educator, musician*
†Fendt, Gene J. *poet, philosopher, educator*
Fredrickson, Scott Alfred *instructional technology educator, consultant*
Harrold, Francis Bernard, Jr., *anthropology educator*
†Johnston, Gladys Styles *university official*
†Schnoor, Neal Henry *music educator*
†Svoboda, Aaron Michael *music educator*
Voigt, Steven Russell *lawyer*
Wittman, Connie Susan *oncology clinical nurse specialist*
Wubbels, Gene Gerald *chemistry educator*

Kimball
Listopadzki, Dariusz Jaroslaw *internist*

Lincoln
Adams, Charles Henry *retired animal scientist, educator*
Alexis, Carl Odman *lawyer, earth scientist*
†Ambrosius, Lloyd Eugene *historian, educator*
Angle, John Charles *retired life insurance company executive*
Atwood, Raymond Percival, Jr., *lawyer*
Auld, James S. *educational psychologist*
†Ayoub, Roula G. *artist*
Bahar, Ezekiel *electrical engineering educator*
Bancroft, Webb Ernest *lawyer*
†Barnes, Paul Edwin *concert pianist, music educator*
Beam, Clarence Arlen *judge*
Beermann, Allen J. *former state official*
Blake, William George *lawyer*
†Bodvarsson, Orn Bodvar *economist, educator*
Botts, Jack Chester *journalist*
Boyle, Anne C. *state commissioner*
Bradley, Richard Edwin *retired college president*
Brakke, Myron Kendall *retired research chemist, educator*
Brohman, Mark Allen *lawyer, biologist*
Bromm, Curt *state legislator*
Brownson, E. Ramona Lidstone Brady *retired secretary*
†Bruning, Jon Cumberland *state attorney general*
†Bruskewitz, Fabian W. *bishop*
Burnham, Stephen John *civil engineer*
Colleran, Kevin *lawyer*
Collier, Nathan Morris *musician, music educator*
Connolly, William M. *state supreme court justice*
†Cunningham, Douglas D. *state legislator*
Deegan, Mary Jo *sociology educator*
De Silva, Handunnetti Sakuntala V. *physicist*
Digman, Lester Aloysius *management educator*
Dixon, Wheeler Winston *film and video studies educator, writer*
Donovan, Gregory Stearn *human services administrator*
Dyer, William Earl, Jr., *retired newspaper editor*
Eckersley, Richard Hilton *graphics designer, educator*
Edison, Allen Ray *electrical engineer, educator*
Edwards, Donald Mervin *biological systems engineering educator, university dean, emeritus*
†Epp, Dianne Naomi *secondary educator*
†Erdman, Philip *state legislator, farmer*
†Exon, J(ohn) James *former senator*
Fisher, Calvin David *food manufacturing company executive*
†Foley, Mike *state legislator*
Freidline, Charles *science educator*
†Frobom, LeAnn Larson *lawyer*
Gale, John A. *secretary of state*
Gard, Joseph Robert *cardiologist*
†Gardner, Martin Ralph *law educator*
Genoways, Hugh Howard *systematic biologist, educator*
Gerrard, John M. *state supreme court justice*
Gitelson, Anatoly Avraam *engineering educator*
Grew, Priscilla Croswell *university official, geology educator*
Guthery, John M. *lawyer*
Hanway, Donald Grant *retired agronomist, educator*
†Harnsberger, Richard Stephen *law educator*
†Harris, Bernard *statistician, mathematician, educator*
Hasselbalch, Marilyn Jean *state official*
Hastings, William Charles *retired state supreme court chief justice*
Heineman, David *lieutenant governor*
Hendrickson, Kent Herman *university administrator*
Hendry, John *state supreme court justice*
Hermance, Lyle Herbert *retired college official*
Hewitt, James Watt *retired lawyer*
Hill, Ronald Clair *anesthesiologist*
Hoffman, Glenn Jerrald *retired agricultural and biological engineering educator, consultant*
Janzow, Walter Theophilus *retired college administrator*
Johanns, Michael O. *governor*
Johnson, Douglas Blaikie *lawyer*
Johnson, Marvin Richard Alois *architect, consultant*
†Johnson, Warren Charles *retired lawyer*
Johnson, William W. *dental educator*
Jones, Lee Bennett *chemist, educator, university official*
Kaplan, Sanford Sandy *geologist*
†Keeler, Kathleen Howard *biological sciences educator, ecologist*
Knoll, Robert Edwin *English educator*
Knox, Arthur Lloyd *investor*
Kopf, Richard G. *federal judge*
Kramer, David J. *state representative, lawyer*
Kristensen, Douglas Allan *former state legislator*
Lagerstrom, Thomas Jay *engineering executive*
Landis, David Morrison *state legislator*
Lee, Sang M. *management educator*
Leinieks, Valdis *classicist, educator*
Leiter, Richard Allen *law librarian, law educator*
†Li, Weixing *research scientist, educator*
Lichty, Warren Dewey, Jr., *lawyer*
Lienemann, Delmar Arthur, Sr., *accountant, real estate developer*
Luebke, Frederick Carl *retired humanities educator*
Lundstrom, Gilbert Gene *banker, lawyer*
Lyons, William Harry *law educator*
MacPhee, Craig Robert *economist, educator*
Magorian, James *writer, poet*
Massengale, Martin Andrew *agronomist, university president*
†Maxwell, Chip *state legislator*
McClain, Richard Douglas *lawyer*
McCormack, Michael *state supreme court justice*
McCutcheon, Allan Lee *sociology educator*
Michels, Dale E. *physician*
Milligan, Cynthia Hardin *university dean, lawyer*
†Mohebbi, Esmail *industrial engineer*
Montag, John Joseph, II, *librarian*
Morrow, Andrew Nesbit *interior designer, business owner*
Mulvaney, Mary Jean *physical education educator, department chairman*
Mutunayagam, N. Brito *architecture and planning educator*
†Naugle, Ronald Clinton *history educator*
Nelson, Darrell Wayne *university administrator, scientist*
†Nelson, Sara June *victim advocate*
Novoa, Yanira *diplomat*
Ogle, Robbin Sue *criminal justice educator*
†Olney, Alexander Ian *English educator*
Ottoson, Howard Warren *agricultural economist, former university administrator*
†Owens, John C. *academic administrator*
Parker, Keith Dwight *sociology educator*
Peterson, Wallace Carroll, Sr., *economics educator*
Piester, David L(ee) *magistrate judge*
Ramamurthy, Byravamurthy *computer engineer, educator*
Rawley, Ann Keyser *small business owner, picture framer*
Rawley, James Albert *history educator*
Reinhardt, John W. *dean, educator, researcher, consultant*
†Rembolt, James Earl *lawyer*
Revesz, Peter Z. *computer science educator*
Riefler, Roger Frank *economics educator*
†Robak, Jennie *state legislator*
Rogge, Kathleen Ruth *domestic engineer, art educator, nurse*
Rohren, Brenda Marie Anderson *therapist, educator*
Rosenow, John Edward *foundation executive*
Rowe, David Winfield *lawyer*
Sander, Donald Henry *soil scientist, researcher*
Sawyer, Robert McLaran *history educator*
Schimek, DiAnna Ruth Rebman *state legislator*
Smith, Lewis *academic administrator, educator*
†Smith, Richard Wendell *lawyer*
Splinter, William Eldon *agricultural engineering educator*
†Spreitzer, Robert Joseph *biochemist, educator*
Stange, James Henry *architect*
†Steffan, Judy Mae *medical/surgical nurse*
Steffen/Heikes, Maxine Lynn *small business owner*
†Stensaas, Starla A. *education educator, artist*
Steward, Weldon Cecil *architecture educator, architect, consultant*
Stoddard, Robert H. *geography educator*
Stover, John Ford *railroad historian, educator*
Stuart, James *banker, broadcaster*
Stuhr, Elaine Ruth *state legislator*
Tavlin, Michael John *manufacturing executive*
Taylor, Stephen Lloyd *food toxicologist, educator, food scientist*
Texel, Timothy J. *state agency director*
†Thrasher, Louis Michael *lawyer*
Tinstman, Dale Clinton *food products company consultant*
†Trainin, Guy *education educator*
Treves, Samuel Blain *geologist, educator*
Urbom, Warren Keith *federal judge*
†Van Etten, James *plant pathologist, educator*
Vestal, Lowell Alan *real estate manager*
Wagner, Rod *library director*
Wiersbe, Warren Wendell *clergyman, author, lecturer*
Wilson, Charles Stephen *cardiologist, educator*
Woollam, John Arthur *electrical engineering educator*
Wright, John F. *judge*
Yoder, Bruce Alan *chemist*
Young, Dale Lee *banker*
Zink, Walter Earl, II, *lawyer*

Lyons
Rose, Dwight Dean *music educator*

Madison
Wozniak, Richard Michael, Sr., *retired city and regional planner*

Newman Grove
†Anderson, Joyce Lorraine *nurse aid*

Norfolk
†Domina, David Alan *lawyer*
Hibl, Veronica Katherine *physician assistant*
Huse, Eugene Franklin *newspaper publisher*
Mortensen-Say, Marlys *school system administrator*
Timmer, Margaret Louise (Peg Timmer) *educator*
Wehrer, Charles Siecke *business and education educator*

North Platte
†Baumann, Larry R(oger) *lawyer*
Boerner, Sheila Gertrude *secondary education educator*
Hawks, James Wade *county highway superintendent, county surveyor*
Mueller, Wayne Dennis *music educator*
†Wohler, Ruth *education educator*

Offutt A F B
Gooch, Stanford Rondall *Air Force Operations research analyst*
†Hinson, Robert C. *career officer*
Johnson, Daniel E. *university educator, dean*
Mies, Richard W. *career officer*

Ogallala
Bourque, Richard Michael *foundation administrator*
Rausch, Paul Matthew *financial executive*

Omaha
Achelpohl, Steven Edward *lawyer, political organization administrator*
Allen, Robert Francis *economist, educator*
†Ansingkar, Kamlesh G. *health facility administrator, otolaryngologist*
Badeer, Henry Sarkis *physiology educator*
†Balaji, K.C. *urologist, researcher*
Baldwin, Jeffrey Nathan *pharmacy educator*
Baltaro, Richard J. *pathologist, medical educator*
†Bandi, Nagesh *research scientist*
Barker, Rex J. *music educator*
Barkmeier, Wayne W. *academic administrator*
Barmettler, Joseph John *lawyer*
Barrett, Frank Joseph *lawyer, former insurance company executive*
†Bartle, John R. *social sciences educator*
Batchelder, Anne Stuart *retired publisher, political party official*

Ben-Yaacov, Gideon *computer systems designer*
Bergt, Gregory Paul *chemist, consultant*
Brailey, Susan Louise *quality analyst, educator*
Brennan, Stephen James *physical education educator, consultant*
Brick, Shirley Jean *rehabilitation nurse*
†Brock, Stephen L. *supervisor international languages, consultant*
Brown, Bob Oliver *retired manufacturing company executive*
†Brown, Sandra Dean *counselor*
Brownrigg, John Clinton *lawyer*
Brumback, Roger Alan *neuropathologist, researcher*
Buffett, Susan Thompson *investment company executive*
Buffett, Warren Edward *entrepreneur*
Burke, Thomas Raymond *lawyer*
Burkholder, Roger Glenn *artist, author*
Burris, Janice Elaine *educational administrator*
Caggiano, Joseph *advertising executive*
Caporale, D. Nick *lawyer*
Carson, Steven Douglas *science educator, biomedical researcher*
Casale, Thomas Bruce *medical educator*
Chan, Wing-Chung *pathologist, educator*
Cheloha, John Anthony *city lobbyist, lawyer*
†Clark, Terry Dee *political scientist, educator*
Cleary, Pamela Ann *symphony executive*
Coccia, Peter F. *physician, pediatric hematologist and oncologist*
Cohen, Samuel Monroe *physician, pathologist, researcher*
Conces, Rory Joseph *philosophy educator*
Cross, W. Thomas *investment company executive*
Cruz, Abelardo Mer Nilo *physician, geriatrician, internist, rheumatologist, medical educator*
†Curtiss, Elden F. *bishop*
Daub, Hal *former mayor, former congressman*
Davidson, Richard K. *railroad company executive*
†Destache, Christopher J. *education educator, researcher*
†Dilly, Barbara Jane *anthropologist, educator*
Dolan, James Vincent *lawyer*
†Durham, Charles William *civil engineer, director*
Eggers, James Wesley *executive search consultant*
Ellsworth, John David *lawyer*
Erickson, James Paul *retired financial service company executive*
Fahey, Mike *mayor*
†Faith, Marshall E. *grain company executive*
Fayad, Pierre B. *neurologist*
Fleming, William Hare *surgeon*
Frank, Julie Ann *lawyer*
Frazier, Chet June *advertising agency executive*
Frey, Donald Ray *medical educator, administrator*
†Fuller, Diana Clare *lawyer*
Fusaro, Ramon Michael *dermatologist, researcher*
†Fyfe, Doris Mae *elementary school educator*
Gallagher, Paula Marie *real estate appraiser*
†Gao, Xiuhua *medical researcher*
Gendelman, Howard Eliot *biomedical researcher, physician*
Gleason, James Mullaney *lawyer, insurance executive*
†Gottschalk, John E. *newspaper publishing executive*
Grant, John Thomas *retired state supreme court justice*
Graves, Maureen Ann *self esteem and spirituality consultant*
Hamann, Deryl Frederick *lawyer, bank executive*
Hansen, Marilyn Schooley *interior designer*
Harmless, J. William *theologian, educator*
Harned, Roger Kent *radiology educator*
Hartman, Herbert Arthur, Jr., *oncologist*
Haselwood, Eldon LaVerne *retired education educator*
†Hawks, Howard L. *energy executive*
Hellbusch, Leslie Carl *neurosurgeon*
Hill, John Wallace *special education educator*
Ho, David Kim Hong *educator*
Hodgson, Paul Edmund *surgeon, department chairman*
Horning, Ross Charles, Jr., *historian, educator*
Howard, Walter Burke *chemical engineer*
Humlicek, Evelyn Clarice *volunteer, retired nursing educator*
†Huurman, Walter William *pediatric orthopaedic surgeon, educator*
Imray, Thomas John *radiologist, educator*
†Jacobsen, Jon Anthony *bank officer, lawyer*
Jenkins, Melvin Lemuel *lawyer*
Jensen, Sam *lawyer*
Jetter, Arthur Carl, Jr., *insurance company executive*
†Jiang, Hong *information scientist*
Johnson, Christine Ann *nurse*
Johnson, James David *concert pianist, organist, educator*
†Johnson, Lerlean Newsome *sociologist*
Juel, Twila Eileen *elementary education educator*
Justice, Bob Joe *corporate development executive*
Kelly, James Francis, Jr., *retired radiologist*
Kessinger, Margaret Anne *medical educator*
King, Larry *editor*
Kobayashi, Roger Hideo *allergy and immunology educator*
†Koperski, Nanci Carol *health care administrator, women's health nurse*
Korbitz, Bernard Carl *retired oncologist, hematologist, educator, consultant*
Kostecki, Martin Paul *industrial engineer*
Koszewski, Bohdan Julius *retired internist, medical educator*
Kotan, Richard Marvin *engineer*
†Kozlik, Michael David *lawyer*
Krecklow, Douglas Earl *secondary education educator, coach*
†Kreifels, Frank Anthony *lawyer, corporate executive*

Krutter, Forrest Nathan *lawyer*
†LaPuzza, Paul James *lawyer*
Lechowicz, Lisa Marie *insurance executive*
Lee, Dennis Patrick *lawyer, judge*
Leininger, Madeleine Monica *nursing educator, anthropologist, theorist, editor, writer*
Lietzen, John Hervy *human resources executive, health agency volunteer*
†Linville, Randal L. *agricultural company executive*
Lipschultz, Jeremy Harris *communication educator*
†Lockridge, Oksana *biochemist, educator, researcher*
Lynch, Benjamin Leo *oral surgeon educator*
Lynch, Thomas Gerald *surgeon, educator*
†Maher, Susan N. *language educator*
Malone, Patrick Michael *pharmacist, educator*
Mangrum, Richard Collin *law educator*
Mardis, Hal Kennedy *urological surgeon, educator, researcher*
Maurer, Harold Maurice *pediatrician*
†McCusker, Thomas J. *corporate lawyer, insurance company executive*
Miller, Larry Thomas *accountant*
†Miller, Roger James *lawyer*
Minter, Gregory Byron *lawyer, educator*
†Moeller, James Charles *writer*
Mohiuddin, Syed Maqdoom *cardiologist, educator*
Monaghan, Thomas Justin *former prosecutor*
Moore, Scott *former state official*
Moylan, James Harold *lawyer*
†Mu, Keli *occupational therapist, researcher, educator*
†Mukherjee, Sandeep *gastroenterologist, educator*
†Nawaz, Zafar *biology educator, researcher*
Neal, Bonnie Jean *real estate agent*
Neibel, Oliver Joseph, Jr., *retired medical services executive*
Newton, John Milton *academic administrator, psychology educator*
†Nielsen, Fredrick Henry *historian, educator*
Niemann, Nicholas Kent *lawyer*
Nizami, Iftikhar Riaz *research scientist*
North, Terry Claire *clinical psychologist*
†Norton, Neil S. *anatomist, researcher*
O'Brien, Richard L(ee) *medical educator, academic administrator, physician, cell biologist*
†O'Connor, Robert Edward, Jr., *lawyer*
†O'Hara, Michael James *law educator, researcher*
Patrick, Erline M. *federal agency administrator*
Pearson, Paul Hammond *physician*
Penke, Cynthia Marie *critical care nurse*
Pirsch, Carol McBride *county official, former state senator, community relations manager*
Pollak, Oliver Burt *lawyer, educator*
Polsky, Donald Perry *architect*
Quigley, Herbert Joseph, Jr., *pathologist, educator*
Ramaprasad, Subbaraya *medical educator*
†Recker, Robert R. *medical educator, internist*
Reddy, Ramakrishna L. *physician, pathologist, consultant*
Ress, Patricia Colleen *author, freelance writer*
Riley, William Jay *federal judge*
Roffman, Blaine Yale *pathologist*
Rohde, Bruce C. *food company executive, lawyer*
Roskens, Ronald William *international business consultant*
†Ross, Larry *education educator, researcher*
Rossbach, Philip Edward *civil engineer*
Runge, Patrick Richard *lawyer*
Russell, Martin John *minister*
Ryan, Mark Anthony *architect*
Saker, James Robert *music educator*
†Sattar, S. Pirzada *psychiatrist, educator, psychiatrist, researcher*
Schlegel, John P. *academic administrator*
Schlessinger, Bernard S. *retired university dean*
†Schrempp, Warren C. *lawyer*
Schropp, Tobin *lawyer*
†Schulz, Merryellen Towey *education educator*
†Scott, Walter, Jr., *construction company executive*
Seng, Jeffrey Frazier *artist, poet*
Shanahan, Thomas M. *judge*
Sharma, Manoj *health educator, research physician*
Shaw, James T. *librarian*
Sigerson, Charles Willard, Jr., *insurance agency executive*
Skau, Michael W. *English educator*
Skoog, Donald Paul *retired physician, educator*
Smith, Philip W. *epidemiologist*
Soh, Lip-Khoon (Kenneth Soh) *music educator, musician*
Sokolof, Phil *industrialist, consumer advocate*
Sooriyaarachchi, Gamini Sarathchandra *oncologist, hematologist, educator, researcher*
†Stanley, Terry Lynn *marketing professional*
Stenberg, Donald B. *lawyer*
†Stinson, Kenneth E. *construction company executive*
Strawhecker, Paul Joseph *fundraising consultant*
Strevey, Guy Donald *insurance company executive*
Strom, Lyle Elmer *judge*
Sturgeon, John Ashley *insurance company executive*
†Temple, Eloise *school system administrator*
Thies, Margaret Diane *nurse*
Truhlsen, Stanley Marshall *retired physician, educator*
Tunnicliff, David George *civil engineer*
†Tyrance, Geraldine Vaughan *music educator*
von Bernuth, Carl W. *lawyer, diversified corporation executive*
Vosburg, Bruce David *lawyer*
Ward, Vernon Graves *internist*
Watt, Dean Day *retired biochemistry educator*
Weekly, John William *insurance company executive*
Wilhelmi, Cynthia Joy *information technology professional, consultant*
Yampolsky, Victor *conductor*

Yontz, Timothy Gene *music educator*
Zaiman, K(oichi) Robert *dentist*
Zepf, Thomas Herman *physics educator, researcher*
Zuerlein, Damian Joseph *priest*

Oneill
Hedren, Paul Leslie *national park administrator, historian*

Papillion
Dvorak, Allen Dale *radiologist*
James, Geneva Behrens *secondary school educator*
Miller, Drew *financial management company executive*
Mueller, Suzanne *secondary school educator*
Rees, Patricia Glines *occupational health nurse, consultant, educator*
†Rice, John Edward *lawyer*

Pierce
Thieben, Barbara Esther *accountant, tax professional*

Scottsbluff
Baltensperger, David Dwight *education educator, researcher*
DiBacco, T(had) Jay *financial services planner, career reserve officer*
Hippe, Anne Elaine *nursing educator*
Jensen, Christopher Douglas *civil engineer*
Kabalin, John Nicholas *urologist*
Olson, Ernestine Lee *nurse*
†Schnell, Judy Kay *biology educator, division chair*
Shoemaker, Troy *hazardous materials response team coordinator, firefighter*

Seward
†Blersch, Jeffrey Neal *music educator, composer*
Etzold, Herman Albert *clergyman, theology educator*
†Kuhn, William Frank *music educator*
Vrana, Verlon Kenneth *retired professional society administrator, conservationist*

South Sioux City
Dailey, Michael Patrick *music educator*
†Wagner, R. Eugene *music educator*

Stuart
Larabee, Brenda J. *secondary education educator*

Wayne
Nelson, Jeryl L. *financial consultant, educator, portfolio manager*

Wilcox
Ziebarth, Lisa Marie *medical/surgical nurse*

Winside
†Reese, James William *writer, editor*

York
Baker, John I., III, *communications educator*
Givens, Randal Jack *communications educator*
Roush, Clark Alan *music educator, conductor*
Wilson, Gary Paul *music educator*

NEVADA

Boulder City
Fisher, Paul Cary *writing supplies company executive*
Huntoon, Peter Wesley *geoscience consultant*
Omelianowich, Janet Anne *accountant*
†Schultheis, Adam John *music educator, consultant*
Wyman, Richard Vaughn *engineering educator, exploration company executive*

Carson City
†Amodei, Mark E. *state legislator, lawyer*
†Ayers, Janice R. *social service administrator*
Ayres, Janice Ruth *social services administrator*
†Bugli, David *conductor, arranger, composer*
Burns, Dan W. *manufacturing company executive*
Crawford, John Edward *geologist, scientist*
Empey, Gene F. *real estate executive*
Evangelatos, Gregory Gerasimos *city planner*
Guinn, Kenny C. *governor*
Heller, Dean *state official*
Hughes, Robert Merrill *control system engineer*
Hull, Dennis Jacques *counselor*
Hunt, Lorraine T. *lieutenant governor*
Jones, Sara Sue Fisher *librarian*
Klippert, Richard Hobdell, Jr., *engineering executive*
†Krivan, Howard Calvin *microbiologist*
Loftis, Rebecca Hope *psychologist*
Marangi, Vito Anthony, Sr., *claim administrator*
Maupin, A. William *state supreme court justice*
O'Connell, Mary Ann *state legislator, business owner*
Reid, Belmont Mervyn *brokerage house executive*
Rocha, Guy Louis *archivist, historian*
Rose, Robert E(dgar) *state supreme court justice*
Ross, Donald Henry *lawyer*
†Sandoval, Brian *state attorney general*
†Sins, Denise M. *art educator*
Van Valkenburgh, Holly Viola *librarian, consultant*
Wadman, William Wood, III, *educational director, technical research executive, consulting company executive*

Cold Springs
†Turner VanLydegraf, Claudia Beth *writer, researcher*

Dayton
Clements, Linda L. *materials engineer, educator, journalist*

East Ely
Alderman, Minnis Amelia *psychologist, educator, small business owner*

Elko
Alleman, Kurt G. *optometrist*
†Ballew, Kathy I. *controller*
Lovell, Walter Benjamin *secondary education educator, radio broadcaster*
Puccinelli, Andrew James *lawyer*

Ely
Daniels, Frank Emmett *mathematician, educator*

Fallon
Dwyer, Doris Dawn *adult education educator*
Isidoro, Edith Annette *horticulturist*
†Venturacci, Toni Marie *artist, substitute educator*

Fernley
Weniger-Phelps, Nancy Ann *media specialist, photographer*

Gardnerville
†Smith, Roderick Joel *behavioral consultant, researcher, educator*

Genoa
Goode, John Martin *manufacturing company executive*

Glenbrook
Goldsmith, Harry Sawyer *surgeon, educator*

Hawthorne
†Pierce, Mildred Louise *librarian*

Henderson
Arumugam, Sivakumar *gastroenterologist*
Bruno, Cathy Eileen *educator, management consultant, former state official*
Chairsell, Christine *academic administrator*
Cohan, George Sheldon *advertising and public relations executive*
Creech, Wilbur Lyman *retired career officer*
Derner, Carol A. *retired librarian*
Devin, Richard *casino gaming host*
DeVol, Luana *dramatic soprano, consultant, arts administrator*
Freyd, William Pattinson *fund raising executive, consultant*
Gibson, James B. *mayor*
Hara-Isa, Nancy Jeanne *graphic designer, county official*
†Henkelman, Wallace James *critical care nurse, educator*
Holloway, Robert Wester *radiochemist*
Kelley, Michael John *newspaper editor*
Klink, Karin Elizabeth *medical communications company executive, writer*
Laurich, Lawrence Alvin *company executive*
McKinney, Sally Vitkus *state official*
Moon, David A. *manufacturing executive*
Moore, Richard *former academic administrator, educator*
†Perkins, Richard D(ale) *police official, state legislator*
Riske, William Kenneth *producer, cultural services consultant*
Roll, Irwin Clifford (Win Roll) *advertising, marketing and publishing executive*
Roth, Jeffrey Joseph *plastic surgeon*
†Sigman, Kevin Andrew *director*
Stanton, Benjamin R. *investment company executive*
Thomas, James Patrick *special education educator*
Trimble, Thomas James *retired utility company executive, lawyer*
Trivelpiece, Alvin William *physicist, educator, consultant*
Van Noy, Terry Willard *health care executive*
†Wennerstrom, Arthur John *aeronautical engineer*
Wills, Robert Hamilton *retired newspaper executive*
Wood, Benjamin Carroll, Jr., *senior loss prevention consultant*

Hendersonville
Niemeyer, Erin Janice *pharmaceutical sales consultant, journalist, editor*

Incline Village
Bixby, Robert Eugene *computer, mathematics educator*
Diederich, J(ohn) William *internet publisher*
Ealy, Cynthia Pike *artist, realtor*
Johnston, Bernard Fox *foundation executive, writer*
Jones, Robert Alonzo *economist*
Merdinger, Charles John *civil engineer, naval officer, academic administrator*
Mitton, Michael Anthony *environmental technology company executive*
†O'Connor, Thomas Patrick *screenwriter*
Strack, Harold Arthur *retired electronics company executive, retired air force officer, planner, analyst, author, musician*
Tedford, Jack Nowlan, III, *construction executive, small business owner*
Thompson, David Alfred *industrial engineer*
Timinsky, Dale *academic administrator*
Yount, George Stuart *paper company executive*

Lake Tahoe
†Sprague, Billy Michael *aerospace transportation executive*

Las Vegas
Adams, Charles Lynford *English language educator*
Adan, John *consulting interventional cardiologist*
Adashek, Joseph Abraham *obstetrician-gynecologist, educator*
Albanese, Thomas *food industry executive, consultant*

Whiting, Wallace Burton, II, *chemical engineer, educator*
Zager, Bernard Solomon *physician, consultant*

Silver City
Bloyd, Stephen Roy *environmental manager, educator, consultant*

Sparks
Bonham, Harold Florian *research geologist, consultant*
Holder, Harold Douglas, Sr., *investor, brokerage house executive, hotel executive*
Kramer, Gordon Edward *manufacturing executive*
Lagasse, Bruce Kenneth *retired structural engineer*
†McKenzie, Jr., Wesley Melvin *music educator, composer*
†Sage, Larry Guy *lawyer*
Salls, Jennifer Jo *secondary school educator, consultant*
†Tran, Can Ngoc *educator, researcher*

Sun Valley
Mumm, Christopher Eric *lawyer, county government official*

Winnemucca
†Bateman, Eric *literature educator*
Hesse, Martha O. *natural gas company executive*

Yerington
Burrowes, Robert Arthur *transportation consultant, travel-tour operator*
Dini, Joseph Edward, Jr., *state legislator*
Price, Thomas Munro *computer consultant*
Scatena, Lorraine Borba *rancher, women's rights advocate*

Zephyr Cove
Amico, Charles William *management consultant*
Barnett, Arthur Lyn *land use and environmental planner*
Hudzinski, Leonard Gerard *social sciences educator, researcher*

NEW HAMPSHIRE

Alstead
Holloway, Robert Charles *orchestrator, arranger, composer*

Alton Bay
Scott, Susan Shattuck *secondary education educator*

Amherst
Atwater, Verne Stafford *finance educator*
Buff, Margaret Anne *psychiatric nurse practitioner*
Perkins, David *English language educator*

Atkinson
Hess, David Graham *engineering administrator*

Barrington
Harris, Marie *writer*

Bartlett
Chandler, Gene G. *state legislator*

Bath
†Page, Patti (Clara Ann Fowler) *vocalist*

Bedford
Alderman, Walter Arthur, Jr., *computer company and corporate rescue executive*
Collins, Diana Josephine *psychologist*
Demers, Nancy Kae *nursing educator*
Hall, Pamela S. *environmental consulting firm executive*
Seidman, Alan *educational administrator*
Steadman, David Rosslyn Ayton *business executive, corporate director*
Twarjan, Colleen Ann *dental hygienist*
†Werner, R. Robert, Jr., *healthcare policy analyst, political organization manager*

Bennington
Verney, Richard Greville *paper company executive*
Willis, Barbara Florence *artist*

Berlin
Doherty, Katherine Mann *librarian, writer*

Bow
Emery, Paul Emile *psychiatrist*
Sytek, Donna P. *former state legislator*

Bradford
Lettvin, Theodore *concert pianist*

Brentwood
†Bunker, Dusty *writer*
Micklos, Janet M. *state agency administrator, human services director*

Broad Brook
Johnston, Robert Everett *information management executive*

Campton
Scrimshaw, Nevin Stewart *physician, nutrition and health educator*

Canaan
†Taussig, Margaret C. *artist*

Center Harbor
Shaw, Robert William, Jr., *management consultant, venture capitalist*
Smith, Paul Thomas *financial services company executive*
Smith, William Hulse *forestry and environmental studies educator*

Center Ossipee
Sargent, Douglas Robert *air force officer, engineer*

Center Sandwich
Booty, John Everitt *emeritus educator*
Folch-Pi, Willa Babcock *romance language educator*
MacDougall, Ruth Doan *writer*

Claremont
Evensen, Edward Arthur *elementary school educator*

Colebrook
Killam, David E. *retired music educator*

Concord
Arnold, Thomas Ivan, Jr., *state legislator*
Arnstein, Paul Michael *nurse practitioner, pain specialist, educator*
Bagan, Merwyn *neurological surgeon*
Benson, Craig Robert *governor*
Brock, David Allen *state supreme court chief justice*
Broderick, John T., Jr., *state supreme court justice*
Brown, Tom Christian *newspaper publisher*
Brunelle, Robert L. *retired state education director*
Caswell, William Stephen, Jr., *civil engineer*
Chamberlain, Douglas Reginald *lawyer*
Church, Gail Graham *television producer, consultant*
Colby, Virginia Little *retired elementary school educator*
Cote, David Edward *state legislator*
Day, Russell Clover *state agency administrator*
de Nesnera, Alexander Peter *psychiatrist*
DiClerico, Joseph Anthony, Jr., *federal judge*
Duggan, James E., Jr., *state supreme court justice*
Dunlap, Patricia C. *state legislator*
†Eaton, Thomas *state legislator*
Eaton, Thomas R. *state legislator, retired funeral director*
Fahey, Patricia Anne *editor*
Feder, Robert Elliot *psychiatrist*
Freeman, Rose Brodeur *retired nursing educator*
Gardner, William Michael *state official*
Garvey, John Burwell *lawyer*
Hager, Elizabeth Sears *state legislator, social services organization administrator*
†Harrison, Keith Michaele *law educator*
Hartman, Sally P. *toxicologist*
Hollingworth, Beverly A. *state legislator*
†Howard, Jeffrey R. *judge*
Lohmann, Keith Henry *police department official, consultant*
MacKay, James Robert *psychiatric social worker, mayor, educator*
Mahon, Thomas James *management consultant*
McAuliffe, Steven James *federal judge*
McDonald, Joseph F., III, *lawyer*
McLaughlin, Philip T. *lawyer, former state attorney general*
Mevers, Frank Clement *state archivist, historian*
Muirhead, James Russell *federal judge*
Nadeau, Joseph P. *state supreme court justice*
Pignatelli, Debora Becker *state legislator*
†Potter, Fred Leon *lawyer, insurance company executive, consultant*
†Rapp, Elaine *paralegal*
Rath, Thomas David *lawyer, former state attorney general*
Richardson, Barbara Hull *state legislator, social worker*
Richardson, Gary Burleigh *lawyer*
Rines, Robert Harvey *lawyer, inventor, educator, composer*
Roberts, George Bernard, Jr., *management and government relations consultant, former state legislator*
Schwartz, Jonathan Ralph *psychiatrist*
†Smith, Gregory Hayes *lawyer*
Speltz, Michael John *land protection specialist*
Taylor, Stephen H. *state commissioner*
Topham, Lee Evans *lawyer*
White, Jeffrey George *healthcare consultant*
Winterling, Ann *artist*
York, Michael Charest *librarian*

Cornish
Atkinson, James Blakely *writer, editor*

Cornish Flat
Erdrich, Louise (Karen Erdrich) *fiction writer, poet*

Danville
Girotti, Robert Bernard *medical and surgical nurse*

Deering
Hunter, Beatrice Trum *editor*
Spitzer, Morton Edward *management consultant*

Derry
Holmes, Richard Dale *history consultant*
Katsakiores, George Nicholas *state legislator, retired restauranteur*
†Sapareto, Frank Vincent, II, *investment advisor, state legislator*

Dover
Appel, Carole Stein *writer, political organizer*
Bergerson, Nancy Dahl *life and health underwriter, paralegal*
Catalfo, Alfred, Jr., (Alfio Catalfo) *lawyer*
Charos, Evangelos Nikolaou *economics educator*
Mitchell, William Clark *printmaker, graphic artist*
Nelson, Michael Underhill *association executive*
Parks, Joe Benjamin *entrepreneur, former state legislator*
Pelletier, Arthur Joseph *state legislator, educator*
Pelletier, Marsha Lynn *secondary school educator, poet*
Wentworth, William Edgar *retired journalist*
Winkler, Peter Alexander *plastic surgeon*

Dublin
†Carlton, Michael *magazine editor*
Hale, Judson Drake, Sr., *editor, writer*

Durham
Appel, Kenneth I. *mathematician, educator*
†Berona, David A. *computer systems librarian, educator*
†Boy, Angelo V. *psychology educator*
DeMitchell, Todd Allan *education educator, educator*
DeVries, Willem *philosophy educator*
Ford, Daniel (Daniel Francis Ford) *writer*
†Garcia De La Rasilla, Carmen *language educator*
Golinski, Jan Victor *history of science educator*
Greenberg, Arthur *dean, chemist*
†Gumprecht, Blake *geographer*
Hapgood, Robert Derry *English educator*
Hart, Ann Weaver *educational administration educator*
†Kempster, William Geoffrey *conductor, music educator*
Kendall-Tackett, Kathleen Ann *researcher, health psychologist*
Lanier, Douglas Mercer *English language and literature educator*
†Linden, Blanche Marie Gemrose *history educator*
Marshall, Grover Edwin *retired French and Italian language educator*
Miller, Joseph Morton *internist*
Palmer, Stuart Hunter *sociology educator*
Pistole, Thomas Gordon *microbiology educator, researcher*
†Scharff, Robert Caesar *social sciences educator, writer, humanities educator*
Selig, Todd Irving *municipal official*
Shigo, Alex Lloyd *biologist, educator, publishing executive*
Simic, Charles *English language educator, poet*
Sivaprasad, Kondagunta N. *electrical engineering educator*
†Sugerman, Deborah Ann *education educator, consultant*
Tischler, Herbert *geologist, educator*
Wheeler, Douglas Lanphier *history educator, writer*
Wheeler, Katherine Wells *retired state legislator*
Woodward, Robert Simpson, IV, *economics educator*

East Sullivan
Hoffman, John Ernest, Jr., *retired lawyer*

Enfield
Gamache, Kathleen Smith *retired psychotherapist*
Gamache, Richard Donald *retired business development executive*

Etna
Copenhaver, Marion Lamson *former state legislator*
Ferm, Vergil Harkness *anatomist, embryologist*
Judson, J. Richard *retired art educator, historian*
Rous, Stephen Norman *urologist, educator*

Exeter
Beeson, Paul Bruce *physician*
†Cole, Donald Barnard *education educator*
DeMitchell, Terri Ann *law educator*
Donahue, Michael Joseph *lawyer*
Ganley, Albert C. *retired private school educator, writer*
Harmon, Richard Wingate *management consultant*
Ingram, Lionel Rowan, Jr., *manangement consultant*
Knowles, Harvard Vaughan *literature educator*
Richardson, Artemas P(artridge) *retired landscape architect*
Singer, Karl Lawrence *physician, health facility administrator*
Thomas, Jacquelyn May *librarian*
Vogelman, Lawrence Allen *law educator, lawyer*

Farmington
†Panek, William Dominick *systems engineer executive*

Fitzwilliam
Schott, John Robert *international consultant, educator*

Francestown
Foster, Margery Somers *economics educator*
Risk, Robert Terence *printer, publisher*

Franconia
Schaffer, David Edwin *retired management systems executive*

Freedom
Keith, Barry Harold *environmental scientist*
Kucera, Henry *linguistics educator*
Lummus, Carol Travers *artist, printmaker*
Stolz, Alan Jay *youth camp executive*

Gilmanton
Osler, Howard Lloyd *retired controller*

Goffstown
Gillmore, Robert *landscape designer, author, editor, publisher*
Martel, Eva Leona *accountant*
Wajenberg, Arnold Sherman *retired librarian, educator*

Gorham
Cote, Thomas Jacques *lawyer*

Grantham
Anderson, Paul Nathaniel, III, (Trip Anderson) *visual communications consultant*
Crane, Robert Kendall *engineering educator, researcher, consultant*
Feldman, Roger Bruce *government official*
Figley, Melvin Morgan *radiologist, physician, educator*
Goss, Richard Henry *lawyer*
Grimley, Robert Thomas *chemistry educator*
Knights, Edwin Munroe *pathologist*
Smith, Dudley Renwick *retired insurance company executive*

Hampstead
Abdulla, Jennifer Ann *marketing professional, consultant*
Moore, Raymond Edward *retired physician*

Hampton
Montrone, Paul Michael *scientific instruments company executive*
Morton, Donald John *librarian*
†Russell, Richard R. *chemicals executive*

Hancock
Baddour, Anne Bridge *pilot*
Pollaro, Paul Philip *artist*

Hanover
Anthony, Robert Newton *management educator emeritus*
Baldwin, John Charles *surgeon, researcher*
Baldwin, William Lee *economics educator*
Baumgartner, James Earl *mathematics educator*
Bel Bruno, Joseph James *chemistry educator*
Bien, Peter Adolph *English language educator, author*
Blanchflower, David Graham *economics educator*
Boghosian, Varujan Yegan *sculptor, educator*
Bower, Richard Stuart *economist, educator*
Brooks, H. Allen *architectural educator, author, lecturer*
Burgess, Robert Sargent *retired human services consultant*
Campbell, Colin Dearborn *economist, educator*
Chapman, Robert James *clinical psychiatrist, educator*
Clark, Robin Ervin *public health educator*
Clement, Meredith Owen *economist, educator*
Crory, Elizabeth L. *former state legislator*
†Curphey, Thomas John *chemist, researcher*
Daniell, Jere Rogers, II, *retired history educator, consultant, public lecturer*
Danos, Paul *dean, finance educator*
Demko, George Joseph *geographer*
Dmitrovsky, Ethan *dean, cancer physician, medical educator, researcher, oncologist*
Doney, Willis Frederick *philosophy educator*
†Dong, Kui *music educator, composer*
Dunlop, David Wallace *economist, educator*
†Dycus, Elizabeth Rasmussen *academic administrator*
Ehrlich, David Gordon *film director, educator*
†Endicott, Kirk Michael *anthropologist, educator*
Feng, Xiahong *geochemist, educator*
†Fiering, Steven *medical educator*
Fischel, William Alan *economics educator*
Freedman, James Oliver *former university president, lawyer*
Gardner, Peter Jaglom *lawyer, publisher*
Garthwaite, Gene Ralph *historian, educator*
Gert, Bernard *philosopher, educator*
Gilbert, John Jouett *aquatic ecologist, educator*
Graves, Robert John *industrial engineering educator*
Green, Ronald Michael *ethics and religious studies educator*
Guest, Robert Henry *state legislator, management educator*
Hall, Raymond *sociology educator*
Harvey, Nicholas D. N., Jr., *lawyer*
Haselton, Mary Michelson *retired foreign service officer, artist*
Heffernan, James Anthony Walsh *language and literature educator*
Hemphill, Margaret Ayars *priest, artist*
Hennessey, John William, Jr., *academic administrator, educator*
†Higgins, Lynn Anthony *humanities educator, writer*
Hutchinson, Charles Edgar *engineering educator*
Kleck, Robert Eldon *psychology educator*
†Koop, Charles Everett *surgeon, educator, former surgeon general*
Kritzman, Lawrence David *humanities educator*
Kurtz, Thomas Eugene *mathematics educator*
Lamperti, John Williams *mathematician, educator*
Long, Carl Ferdinand *engineering educator*
Lundquist, Weyman Ivan *lawyer*
Lyons, Gene Martin *political scientist, educator*
Mansell, Darrel Lee, Jr., *English educator*
Masters, Roger Davis *government and neurotoxicology educator*
Montgomery, David Campbell *physicist, educator*
Moss, Ben Frank, III, *art educator, painter*
Oxenhandler, Neal *language educator, writer*
†Pauwels, Koen Hendrik *finance educator*
†Perovich, Donald Kole *geophysicist*
†Petitto, Laura-Ann *social sciences educator*
†Platt, James David *psychiatrist, educator, academic administrator*
Queneau, Paul Etienne *metallurgical engineer, educator*
Quinn, James Brian *business educator*
Rawnsley, Howard Melody *physician, educator*
Riggs, Lorrin Andrews *psychologist, educator*
Rolett, Ellis Lawrence *medical educator, cardiologist*
Rueckert, Frederic *plastic, reconstructive and hand surgeon*

Russell, Robert Hilton *Romance languages and literature educator*
Rutter, Jeremy Bentham *archaeologist, educator*
Scher, Steven Paul *literature educator, educator*
Scherr, Barry Paul *foreign language educator*
Sheldon, Richard Robert *Russian language and literature educator*
Shewmaker, Kenneth Earl *history educator*
†Spencer, Thomas A. *chemist, educator*
Spiegel, Evelyn Sclufer *biology educator, researcher*
Spiegel, Melvin *retired biology educator*
Starzinger, Vincent Evans *political science educator*
†Stemkoski, Lee John *mathematician*
Stockmayer, Walter H(ugo) *chemistry educator*
Sturge, Michael Dudley *physicist, educator*
Tomlinson, George Herbert *retired industrial company research executive*
Wegner, Gary Alan *astronomer*
Welsch, Robert Louis *anthropologist, curator*
Wood, Charles Tuttle *history educator*
Wright, James Edward *academic administrator, historian, educator*
Zubkoff, Michael *medical educator*

Henniker
Braiterman, Thea Gilda *economics educator, state legislator, selectman*

Hillsboro
Pearson, William Rowland *retired nuclear engineer*

Hinsdale
†Smith, Edwin O. *real estate executive, state legislator*

Hollis
†Castner Jr., Theodore G. *education educator*
Litchfield, Barbara Mae Smith *clergywoman*
Lumbard, Eliot Howland *lawyer, educator*
Merritt, Mary Jane *community volunteer*
Merritt, Thomas Butler *lawyer*

Hooksett
Buchan, Ronald Forbes *internal and preventive medicine physician*
Clamp, Christina A. *sociology educator*
Denaco, Parker Alden *state official, lawyer, arbitrator*
Di Stefano, Julia Mary *communications educator*
Rogers, David John *lawyer*

Intervale
Baker, Mary Jane *social worker*

Jackson
Synnott, William Raymond *retired management consultant*

Jaffrey
Press, Fred *artist*
Van Ness, Patricia Wood *religious studies educator, consultant, author*

Keene
†Alvarez, Kristin Jones *geographer, educator*
Baldwin, Peter Arthur *psychologist, educator, author, minister*
Bell, Ernest Lorne, III, *retired lawyer*
Berenson, Paul Stewart *advertising agency executive*
†Crocker, Matthew Hallowell *historian, educator, writer, researcher*
Gardner, Eric Raymond *lawyer*
†Heed, Peter W. *state attorney general*
Hickey, Delina Rose *retired education educator*
Long, Mark Christopher *English educator*
Martin, Thomas Russell *music educator, musician*
Martin, Vernon Emil *librarian*
†Vincent, Charles Paul *humanities educator*

Kingston
Merrill, Lynne Bartlett *public relations executive, advertising executive*
Saunders, Janet McGee *small business owner, healthcare administrator*

Laconia
Brody, Spencer John *pediatrician*
†Martin, Willard Gordon, Jr., *lawyer*
†Mitchell, Walter Louis, III, *lawyer*

Lancaster
Pratt, Leighton Calvin *state legislator*

Lebanon
†Baker, William Arnold *lawyer*
Bernat, James Lawrence *neurologist, educator*
Boardman, Maureen Bell *community health nurse, educator*
†Carr, Charles F. *orthopedist*
Clendenning, William Edmund *dermatologist*
Cronenwett, Jack LeMoyne *vascular surgeon educator*
Emery, Virginia Olga Beattie *psychologist, researcher*
†Fillinger, Mark F. *vascular surgeon, researcher*
Fishman, Joan Roslyn *clinical information analyst*
Fromm, Hans *gastroenterologist, educator, researcher, hepatologist*
Galton, Valerie Anne *endocrinology educator*
†Gosselin, Benoit Jean *otolaryngologist, facial plastic surgeon, head and neck and reconstructive surgeon*
†Hartov, Alexander *engineering educator*
Kelley, Maurice Leslie, Jr., *gastroenterologist, educator*
Linnell, Robert Hartley *editor-in-chief*
McCollum, Robert Wayne *physician, educator*
Moore, Frederick Appel *administrator*
Munck, Allan Ulf *physiologist, educator*
Ou, Lo-Chang *physiology educator*
†Racusin, Robert Jerrold *psychiatry educator*

†Schoolwerth, Anton C. *nephrologist, educator*
Silberfarb, Peter Michael *psychiatrist, educator*
†Simons, Michael *cardiologist*
Smith, Barry David *obstetrician-gynecologist, educator*
†Stephenson, Jane Finkeldey *social worker*
Thaker, Amish A. *engineer*
Tinker, Averill Faith *special education educator*
van Leeuwen, Dirk Jacob *hepatology educator*
Varnum, James William *hospital administrator*
Waugh, Theodore Rogers *orthopedic surgeon*
†Yeager, Mark P. *anesthesiology educator, researcher*

Lee
†Merriman, Chrisann *marketing professional*
Young, James Morningstar *physician, naval officer*

Lempster
Jillette, Arthur George, Jr., *school system administrator, educator*

Lincoln
Seletz, Jules Mortimor *surgeon*

Lisbon
Trelfa, Richard Thomas *paper company executive*

Littleton
Wilmot, Clare Julia May *surgeon*

Londonderry
Jacobs, Edward Harold *psychologist*
Parten, Priscilla M. *medical and psychiatric social worker, educator*

Loudon
Moore, Beatrice *religious organization administrator*
Tomajczyk, S(tephen) F(rancis) *communications company executive, author*

Lyme
Carmichael, Donald Scott *lawyer, business executive*
Cornwell, Gibbons Gray, III, *physician, medical educator, retired*
Dwight, Donald Rathbun *newspaper publisher, corporate communications executive*
McIntyre, Oswald Ross *physician*
Swan, Henry *forester, consultant*
†Wise, Joanne Herbert *artist representative*

Manchester
Angoff, Gerald Harvey *cardiologist*
Arnold, Barbara Eileen *state legislator*
†Bersoux, Henri Robert *management executive*
†Bolduc, Diane Eileen Mary Buchholz *psychotherapist*
Bradley, James Harold *public relations consultant*
†Brown, Stanley Melvin *lawyer*
Bussiere, Emile R. *lawyer*
Carkin, Gary Bryden *performing arts educator*
Cates, Edward William *writer, publisher*
Christian, Francis Joseph *bishop*
Colby, George Vincent, III, *logistics executive*
Cusson-Cail, Kathleen *consulting company executive*
DesRochers, Gerard Camille *surgeon*
Desrosiers, Aprylle Lynn *director, consultant*
Dorwart, Brian Curtis *geotechnical engineer, consultant*
Ellerin, Thelma Ruth *psychiatric social worker*
Goodwin, Rolf Ervine *lawyer*
Groulx, Aimé René *artist, photographer*
Hower, Philip Leland *semiconductor device engineer*
Hunt, Sean Emmet *anesthesiologist*
†Hutchins, Peter Edward *lawyer*
†Kamen, Dean *biomedical engineer*
Kuehne, Dale Stanway *minister, political science educator*
Levins, John Raymond *investment advisor, management consultant, educator*
†Maloney, Simone *accountant*
McCormack, John Brendan *bishop*
†Middleton, Jack Baer *lawyer*
Monson, John Rudolph *lawyer*
Nixon, David L. *lawyer*
†Paradis, Wilfrid H. *retired historian*
†Peltonen, John Ernest *lawyer*
Perkins, Charles, III, *newspaper editor*
Poloian, Lynda Gamans *retailing educator*
Reynolds, Gregory Edward *minister*
Richards, Thomas H. *lawyer, arbitrator*
Ronalter, Chelsea Maria *artist, graphic designer*
Rubin, Jeffrey Mark *lawyer, insurance company executive*
Stinson, Wesley R. *museum director, archaeologist*
Sullivan, Kathleen N. *political organization administrator, lawyer*
Telles, Marelyn V. Taylor *psychiatric clinical nurse specialist*
†Thornton, Edward Robert, Jr., *lawyer*
Totten, Mary Anne *internist*
Unger, Gere Nathan *emergency physician, lawyer*
Zachos, Kimon Stephen *lawyer*

Marlow
Lindholm, Ulric Svante *engineering research institute executive, retired*
McCracken, Linda *librarian, commercial artist*

Meredith
Hatch, Frederick Tasker *chemicals consultant*
Heald, Bruce Day *English and music educator, historian*
Lovett, Miller Currier *management educator, clergyman*

Merrimack
Drobny, Jiri George *chemical engineer*

†Gallup, Patricia *computer company executive*
Hosker, Donald *materials research technician*
Kotelly, George Vincent *editor, writer, electrical engineer*
Malley, James Henry Michael *industrial engineer*
Wolf, Robert Farkas *systems and avionics company executive, environmental planning consultant*

Milford
Morison, John Hopkins *casting manufacturing company executive*

Mirror Lake
Culleton, James Frederick *neurologist*

Mount Sunapee
Marashio, Paul William *humanities educator*

Munsonville
Kirk, Jane Seaver *municipal government administrator*

Nashua
Auclair, Louise A. *education educator*
†Connell, Diane Jacobs *education educator*
Descoteaux, Carol J. *health facility administrator*
Egan, John Frederick *retired electronics executive*
Fallet, George *civil engineer*
Gale, Sylvia Elizabeth *child protection professional*
Gregg, Hugh *former cabinet manufacturing company executive, former governor New Hampshire*
Hanson, Arnold Philip *retired lawyer*
Hargreaves, David William *communications company executive*
Hemming, Walter William *business financial consultant*
†La Salle, Cathy *education educator*
Marie, Linda *artist, photographer*
Meagher, Robert Michael *software engineer*
Mitsakos, Charles Leonidas *education educator, consultant*
Piper, Linda Ammann *staffing services executive*
Raudonis, Valerie Christine *lawyer*
†Sabin, Mihaela *education educator*
Seidel, Carl William *business executive, consultant*
Seifer, Arnold David *systems engineer*
Siroty, William Charles *physician*
Smith, Thomas Raymond, III, *software engineer*
Woodruff, Thomas Ellis *electronics consulting executive*

New Castle
Brink, Marion Alice *retired human resources specialist*
Friese, George Ralph *retail executive*
Klotz, Louis Herman *structural engineer, educator, consultant*
Levin, Harvey Jay *financial institution design and construction specialist, developer, auctioneer*
Rauh, John David *manufacturing company executive*

New Durham
Herman, William George *municipal government executive*
Uttal, Susan *legal administrator*
†Wellman, Helen M. *administrative secretary*

New Ipswich
Stirnweis, Shannon *illustrator, painter*

New London
Baldwin, William Howard *lawyer, retired foundation executive*
Catino, Donald *physician*
†Condict, Edgar Rhodes *medical electronics, aviation instrument manufacturing and medical health care executive, inventor, mediator, pastor*
Gepfert, Alan Harry *management consultant, business educator, author*
Mc Laughlin, David Thomas *academic administrator, business executive*
Merwin, John David *retired lawyer, former governor*
†Muyskens, Judith A. *academic administrator, dean, language educator*
Plant, David William *lawyer*
Thoma, Kurt Michael *business owner*
Twombly, Jean Sawyer *musician, educator*
Vulgamore, Melvin L. *retired college president*
Zuehlke, Richard William *technical communications consultant, writer*

Newbury
Koehler, Paul Burrell *retired medical administrator*

Newmarket
Forcier-Delgadillo, Jennifer Libby *Spanish language educator*
Getchell, Sylvia Fitts *librarian*

Newport
Gayvoronsky, Ludmila *artist, educator*
Hill, Evan *retired journalism educator, writer*
Work, Michael Jay *lawyer*

North Conway
Phaneuf, Gerald John *retired pathologist*

North Hampton
August, June *artist, educator*
Dodge, Peter *retired sociology educator*
†Jones, Leroy Welwood (Wry Welwood) *mental health services professional*
†Osenton, Thomas George *publisher*
Taylor, Donald *retired manufacturing company executive*

White, Ralph Paul *automotive executive, consultant*

North Haverhill
Brown, Susan Elizabeth S. *secondary school educator*
Charpentier, Keith Lionel *school system administrator*

North Sandwich
Penrose, Charles, Jr., *professional society administrator*

Northwood
Lynne-O'Brien, Vincent *stage manager, director, actor*

Orford
Beale, Georgia Robison *historian, educator*
Karol, John J., Jr., *producer, filmmaker*
Martin, Allen *retired lawyer*

Ossipee
Bartlett, Diane Sue *clinical mental health counselor, family therapist*

Peterborough
Day, John Sidney *management sciences educator*
Duncan, George *marketing consultant*
Eppes, William David *arts/humanities supporter*
Farnham, Sherman Brett *retired electrical engineer*
Mason, Robert Marion *mathematician, musician*
McCarthy, John Robert *tax consultant, hospital consultant*
Thomas, Elizabeth Marshall *writer*
Twombly, Stephen Doane *magazine publisher*

Pike
Teschner, Douglass Paul *project administrator*

Plainfield
Brown, Judith Olans *lawyer, educator*

Plaistow
Collins, James Francis *wildlife artist*
Senter, Merilyn P(atricia) *former state legislator and freelance reporter*
Wilder, Dwight Safford *academic administrator*

Plymouth
†Bourgelais, Paul *music educator*
Brook, Carol Ann *retired guidance director, school counselor*
Deachman, Ross Varick *lawyer*
†DeCotis, Ruth Janice *career planning administrator, educator*
†Dionne, Aubrie Anne *music educator*
Drexel, Peter George *computer science educator*
†Graff, Carleen *music educator*
†McCormack, Louise Samaha *education educator*
†Reed, Laurie Jean *administrative assistant*

Portsmouth
†Abelson, Elias *lawyer*
Beckett, William Henry Miller *lawyer*
Cole-McCrea, Candace *social sciences educator*
DeGrandpre, Charles Allyson *lawyer*
Doleac, Charles Bartholomew *lawyer*
Greene, Douglas Edward *hotel executive*
†Harman, Terrie *lawyer*
Harter, Hugh Anthony *foreign language educator*
Hopkins, Jeannette Ethel *book publisher, editor*
Lambert, Eugene Louis *engineer, manufacturing executive*
McArdle, Barry Francis *dentist*
McGee, John Paul, Jr., *lawyer*
Michelsen, W(olfgang) Jost *neurosurgeon, educator, retired*
Nylander, Jane Louise *museum director*
Powers, Henry Martin, Jr., *oil industry executive*
†Shaines, Robert Arthur *lawyer*
Thornhill, Arthur H., Jr., *retired book publisher*
Tillinghast, John Avery *utilities executive*
Tober, Stephen Lloyd *lawyer*
Volk, Kenneth Hohne *lawyer*
Ward, Bonnie J. *insurance company executive*
Watson, Thomas Roger *lawyer*

Randolph
Bradley, Paula E. *former state legislator*
Bradley, William Lee *retired foundation executive, educator*

Rindge
Bussiere, Linda Rose *writer, historian*
Costa, Kelli Ann *anthropologist, educator, archaeologist*
Dangelantonio, Sarah Teresa *academic administrator, educator*
Elam, Leslie Albert *retired museum administrator*

Rochester
Albert, Carole Annette *elementary school educator*
Coviello, Robert Frank *retail executive*
Diamond, David Roger *psychologist*
Dworkin, Gary Steven *insurance company executive*
Hall, Fred William, Jr., *lawyer*
†Jones, Franklin Charles *judge*
Kramer, Sherri Marcelle *gemologist, jeweler*
†Patel, Piyush *communications executive*
Shean, Timothy Joseph *manufacturing company executive*

Rumney
Allen, Edward John Bedford *historian, retired educator*

Rye
MacRury, King *management counselor*

Salem
Bonacorsi, Gregory James *mechanical engineer*

Silverman, Cathy Alice *anthropologist, researcher*
Simmons, Marvin Gene *geophysics educator*
Smith, Laurence Roger *journal editor*
Snierson, Lynne Wendy *communications executive*

Sanbornton
Weiant, Elizabeth Abbott *retired biology educator*

Sanbornville
Berg, Warren Stanley *retired banker*

Sandown
Densen, Paul Maximillian *former health administrator, educator*

Seabrook
Ganz, Mary Keohan *lawyer*

Silver Lake
Pallone, Adrian Joseph *research scientist*
Tregenza, Norman Hughson *investment banker*

Somersworth
Furbush, Mary Chapman *clubwoman*
Gow, Linda Yvonne Carignan Cherwin *travel executive*
Tully, Hugh Michael *music educator*

Stoddard
Whitney, Richard Wheeler *artist, educator*

Stratham
Green, Catherine Cooper *artist*
Terry, Elizabeth Hays *calligrapher, needlepoint designer*

Tamworth
Colten, Harvey Radin *pediatrician, educator*

Temple
Weston, Priscilla Atwood *library director*

Tilton
Wolf, Sharon Ann *psychotherapist*

Walpole
Burns, Kenneth Lauren *filmmaker, historian*
Gooding, Judson *writer*
Hunter, Barbara Way *public relations consultant*

Warner
Bodine, John Jermain *pastor*
†Coolidge, Daniel Scott *lawyer*
Face, Wayne Bruce *small business owner*

Waterville Valley
Grimes, Howard Ray *management consultant*

Weare
White, Karen Ruth Jones *information systems executive*

West Chesterfield
Garinger, Louis Daniel *religion educator*

West Lebanon
Day, Emerson *physician*
Halperin, George Bennett *education educator, retired naval officer*
Isaacs, Robert Charles *retired lawyer*
Lawton, Jacqueline Agnes *retired communications company executive, management consultant*
†Malik, Shazia Mumtaz *education educator, researcher*
Sullivan, Charles R. *engineering educator*

Wilton
Potter, Robert Wallace, Jr., *educator*

Winchester
MacKay, Neil Duncan *plastics company executive*
Tandy, Jean Conkey *art educator*

Windham
Arndt, Janet S. *state legislator*
†Delahunty, Joseph Lawrence *state senator, business investor*
Levin, Murray Newman *retired surgeon*

Wolfeboro
Bonin, Suzanne Jean *artist*
Croteau, Jan Helling *artist*
Hutchins, Carleen Maley *acoustical engineer, consultant*
†Mertens, Edward Joseph, II, *lawyer*
†Walker, George William *lawyer*

NEW JERSEY

Aberdeen
Smith, Marvin Frederick, Jr., *chemical engineer, consultant*

Absecon
Byrne, Shaun Patrick *law enforcement mediator*

Adelphia
Carter, Harry Robert *fire protection consultant*

Allendale
Bisanzo, Mark Thomas *sales executive*
DiBlasi, Dianne Clark *editor*
†Long, Jo-Nelle Desmond *editor, consultant, historian*
Rosenblum, Edward G. *lawyer*
Ruth, Rodney *musician, music consultant, contractor, educator*

Allenhurst
Hinson, Robert William *advertising executive, consultant*

Teicher, Henry Earl *retired education educator*
†Tognoli, Era M. *performing company executive, artistic director*

Alpine
Vandersteel, William *transportation executive*

Annandale
Baugh, Lisa Saunders (Lisa Saunders Boffa) *research chemist*
Bhagat, Phiroz Maneck *mechanical engineer*
Gorbaty, Martin Leo *chemist, researcher*
Johnston, John Eric *chemist*
Konrad, Adolf Ferdinand *artist*
Matsen, John Morris *retired engineer*
Wilson, Terry Douglas *pharmaceutical manager*

Asbury
Gardner, Janette Lynn *critical care nurse, educator*
Oostdyk, Arlene Rosa *natural health educator, nurse*

Asbury Park
Avella, John Thomas *educational administrator*
†Darnell, Alan Mark *lawyer*
Myers, Dorothy Roatz *artist*
†Rosenbloom, Norma Frisch *lawyer*
Rosenthal, Robert Irwin *consultant*

Atco
Beard, Richard Burnham *engineering educator emeritus, researcher*
Blackford, Alan Ralph *music educator*
Conrad, George John *retired design engineer, planner*

Atlantic City
†Irwin, Germaine *information technology executive*
Jacobson, Carole Renee *lawyer, educator*
Jamieson, John Edward, Jr., *social services administrator, minister, bioethicist*
Knight, Edward R. *judge, lawyer, educator, psychologist*
Logan-Sutton, Floretta R. *educator*
Marks, Robert Bosler *television producer, consultant*
†Paarz, Robert Emil *lawyer*

Atlantic Highlands
†Corodemus, Steven James *state legislator, lawyer*
Hawley, Joseph B. *property management executive, educator*
†Marshall, Anthony Parr *retired lawyer*
Ramsey, Joanne Marie *financial services representative*
Royce, Paul Chadwick *medical administrator*
Tice, George A(ndrew) *photographer*

Audubon
Sconyo, Philip *engineering consultant*

Augusta
Martin, Richard L. *retired insurance executive*

Avenel
Berg, Louis Leslie *investment executive*
†Sansone, Paul J. *automotive executive*
†Segal, Barry *compnay executive*

Avon By The Sea
Bruno, Grace Angelia *accountant, retired educator*
Potter, Emma Josephine Hill *language educator*

Barnegat
†Ackerman, Donald Robert *retired surveyor, retired real estate agent*
Bronkowski, Mark John *textiles executive, real estate agent*

Barnegat Light
Gibbs, Frederick Winfield *lawyer, communications company executive*

Barrington
Guice, Stephen Wayne *lawyer*

Basking Ridge
Abeles, James David *manufacturing company executive*
Buist, Richardson *retired corporate executive, retired banker*
Collis, Sidney Robert *retired telephone company executive*
Conklin, Donald Ransford *retired pharmaceutical company executive*
Darrow, William Richard *retired pharmaceutical company executive, consultant*
†DeBois, James Adolphus *lawyer*
Drewry, Don Neal *fire protection engineer*
Fotiades, George L. *pharmaceutical executive*
Frediani, Diane Marie *graphic designer, interior designer*
Giglio, William Vito *secondary education educator*
†Horton, Thomas W. *telecommunications executive*
†Jones, William Johnson *lawyer*
Korn, William David *technology executive*
Lachenauer, Robert Alvin *retired school superintendent*
Matthews, Craig Gerard *energy company executive*
Morgan, Samuel P(ope) *physicist, applied mathematician*
Munch, Douglas Francis *pharmaceutical and health industry consultant*
†O'Carroll, Anita Louise *lawyer*
O'Connell, Robert Brendan *public relations and editorial consultant*
Peterson, Donald K. *telecommunications executive*
Probert, Edward Whitford *foundation executive, volunteer*

Riesenberger, John Richard *pharmaceutical company executive*
Smith, Irmhild Wrede *public health nurse coordinator*
Tamarelli, Alan Wayne *venture captial executive*

Bay Head
†Kellogg, James Crane *lawyer*
O'Brien, Robert Brownell, Jr., *investment banker, consultant, yacht broker, opera company executive*

Bayonne
Doria, Joseph V., Jr., *state legislator*
Gorman, William David *artist, graphic artist*
Masella, Robert Thomas *political science and geography educator, funeral service*
McMahon, Eileen Marie *artist agent*
Pelosi, Marco Antonio *obstetrician and gynecologist*
Rogow, Louis Michael *oncologist, educator*
Wanko, Michael Andrew *school system administrator*
Zuckerman, Nancy Carol *learning disabilities specialist, consultant*

Bayville
Kropinack, John Frank *secondary education educator*

Beach Haven
Schreiber, Eileen Sher *artist*

Bedminster
David, Edward Emil, Jr., *electrical engineer, business executive*
†Dorman, David W. *telecommunications industry executive*
Gardner, David John *communications executive, recording engineer*
†Hart, Terry Jonathan *communications executive*
Hudacsko, Dennis Wayne
Shedden, Arthur *pharmaceutical executive, consultant*
Yannuzzi, Elaine Victoria *food and home products executive*

Belle Mead
†Brown, Elizabeth Schmeck *fashion historian*
Gladstone, Robert Albert *lawyer*
Goodnick, Paul Joel *psychiatrist*
Sarle, Charles Richard *health facility executive*

Belleville
†Asiaie, Reza *research scientist*
Berenfeld, Mark M. *chemist*
Caputo, Wayne James *surgeon, podiatrist*
Sales, Clifford M. *surgeon*

Belmar
De Santo, Donald James *psychologist, educational administrator*
Swett, Stephen Frederick, Jr., *artist, educator*

Belvidere
Walsh, John Alfred *retired social worker*

Bergenfield
Clark, Fred *legal writer, editor*
Hill, George Robert *musicologist, music bibliographer*
Janow, Lydia Frances *meeting planner*
Kupp, John C. *music educator*

Berkeley Heights
Connell, Grover *food company executive*
Geusic, Joseph Edward Edward *physicist*
Gottheimer, George Malcolm, Jr., *insurance executive, educator*
Mac Rae, Alfred Urquhart *physicist, electrical engineer*
Older, Richard Samuel *elementary school music educator*
Rabiner, Lawrence Richard *electrical engineer, educator*

Berlin
Flacco, Elaine Germano *computer programmer*
Lewis, Michael Seth *health care executive*
†Sabato, Mary Louise *mathematician, educator*

Bernardsville
Cooperman, Saul *educational administrator*
Dixon, Richard Wayne *retired communications company executive*
Dixon, Rosina Berry *physician, pharmaceutical development consultant*
Lazor, Patricia Ann *interior designer*
Robinson, Maureen Loretta *retired secondary school educator*
Salinger, Anthony Wilshire *educator, organization consultant*
Spofford, Sally (Sally Hyslop) *artist*
Stahl, Donald Charles *retired orthopedic surgeon*

Beverly
Taylor, Lyn Ann *principal*

Blackwood
Breve, Franklin Stephen *pharmacist*
Busky, Donald Frank *political science educator*
Cloyd, Thomas Earl *broadcast designer, consultant*

Blairstown
Bean, Bennett *artist*

Bloomfield
Bunin, Jeffrey Howard *management consultant*
†Conrad, Angela *humanities educator*
Conta, Richard Vincent *actuary*
Feldman, Max *insurance executive*
Lordi, Katherine Mary *lawyer*
McCulloch, George McQuillan *retired foundation executive, fundraiser*
Moese, Mark Douglas *environmental consultant*
Rivera, Ruth Ellen *special services director*

Tiger, Madeline J. *writer, educator*
Weisert, Kent Albert Frederick *lawyer*

Bloomingdale
Janow, Chris *mechanical engineer*

Bloomsbury
Rohloff, Claire Marie *interior designer, educator*
Williams, James Richard *human factors engineering psychologist*

Bogota
Condon, Francis Edward *retired chemistry educator*
Livingston, Kathryn E. *writer*
Oldenhage, Irene Dorothy *retired elementary school educator*

Boonton
Bona, Frederick Emil *public relations executive*
Bridges, Beryl Clarke *marketing executive*
Bucco, Anthony Mark *lawyer*
Massler, Howard Arnold *lawyer, corporate executive*
Walzer, James Harvey *lawyer, author*

Bordentown
Lowery, William Odell *personnel services executive*
†Malone, Joseph R. *state legislator*

Bound Brook
†Blumberg, Adele Rosenberg *volunteer*
Chandler, Marguerite Nella *real estate corporation executive*
Gould, Donald Everett *retired chemical company executive, consultant*
Shive, Richard Byron *architect*

Bradley Beach
†Parry, Ronald *massage therapist*

Brick
Alpiar, Hal *management and marketing consultant, author*
†Ciesla, Andrew R. *state legislator*
Grotto, Douglas Thomas Matthew *music educator*
Pistolakis, Nicholas Stelios *advertising executive*
Roache, Patrick Michael, Jr., *management consultant*
Sanseigne, Mary Josephine *nurse anesthetist*
Shortess, Edwin Steevin *marketing consultant*
Tivenan, Charles Patrick *lawyer*
†Wolfe, David W. *state legislator*

Bridgeport
Walters, Charles Joseph *real estate developer*

Bridgeton
†Fisher, Douglas Howard *retail executive*
Howell, James Burt, III, *retired agricultural products company sales consultant*
Williams, Jennifer Margaret *freelance artist, substitute teacher*

Bridgewater
Accardi, Joseph Ronald *accountant*
Baldwin, Dorothy Leila *secondary school educator*
Bernson, Marcella S. *psychiatrist*
†Chapel, Sunny *research scientist*
Conroy, Robert John *lawyer*
Dahling, Gerald Vernon *lawyer*
Ford, Frederic Hugh *secondary school educator*
Glesmann, Sylvia-Maria *artist*
Hirsch, Paul J. *orthopedist, surgeon, medical executive, educator, editor*
Holder, Neville Lewis *chemist*
Hulse, Robert Douglas *high technology executive*
Kennedy, James Andrew *chemical company executive*
Klinck, James William *insurance company executive*
Linett, David *lawyer*
†Lowman, Tyrone David *entrepreneur*
Maynard, Kenneth Irwin *medical educator, researcher*
Mc Cormick, Richard Patrick *history educator*
Rebmann, Nina Sophie *research scientist*
Schoppmann, Michael Joseph *lawyer*
Sethi, Shyam Sunder *management consultant*
Skidmore, James Albert, Jr., *management, computer technology and engineering services company executive*
Stein, Daniel Scott *physician, researcher*
Weingast, Marvin *laboratory executive*
Yang, Ruikang *research scientist*

Brigantine
Kickish, Margaret Elizabeth *elementary school educator*

Brookside
Fairchild, Samuel Wilson *professional services company executive, former federal agency administrator*
†Schaberg, Eric L. *music educator*

Browns Mills
Cha, Se Do *internist*
De Berardinis, Charles Anthony Joseph *physician*
DeWitt, Edward Francis *artist*
Di Nunzio, Dominick *educational administrator*
Lumia, Francis James *internist*

Budd Lake
Bauer, Jean Marie *accountant*
Davis-Kalugin, Dorinne Sue *audiologist*
Hilbert, Rita L. *librarian*
Khazen, Aleksandr Moiseyevich *physicist*
Webb, John Gibbon, III, *lawyer*

Burlington
Denbo, Alexander *retired bank executive*

Kennedy, Christopher Robin *ceramic engineer, director*
Rowlette, Henry Allen, Jr., *social worker*

Butler
Ward, Robert Allen, Jr., *advertising executive*

Caldwell
Beusse, Jacqueline A. *writer, marketing company executive*
Campbell, Sister Maura *religious studies and philosophy educator*
Castano, Gregory Joseph *lawyer*
Chatlos, William Edward *management consultant*
†Childress Orchard, Nan L. *music educator*
†Choi, Sook C. *physiologist, educator*
Mann, Robert Christopher *communications educator, television host, producer*
†Orians, Thomas Wayne *priest*
Ott, Walter Richard *academic administrator*
Palombo, Lisa *artist*
Randall, Lynn Ellen *librarian*
Stanton, George Basil, Jr., *engineering executive, chemical engineer*
†Surmatis, Joseph D. *retired chemist*
Werner, Patrice (Patricia Ann Werner) *college president*

Califon
Clarke, Frank Henderson *retired chemical company executive, scientist*
†Clipsham, Jacqueline Ann *artist*
Fouillade, Jean-Paul Eric *management consultant*
Rosen, Carol Mendes *artist*

Camden
Ances, I. G(eorge) *obstetrician, gynecologist, educator*
†Barbarese, J. T. *poet, educator*
Beck, David Paul *biochemist*
†Beck, Susan J. *school librarian*
Benson, Gordon D. *gastroenterologist, medical educator, dean*
Brotman, Stanley Seymour *federal judge*
†Bryant, Wayne Richard *state legislator*
Camishion, Rudolph Carmen *physician*
†Conant, Douglas R. *food products executive*
Farmer, James A., II, *lawyer*
Foley, Eugene Arthur *accountant, consultant*
†Furey, John J. *lawyer*
Gans, Samuel Myer *temporary employment service executive*
†Goertzel, Ted George *sociologist, educator*
Gordon, Walter Kelly *retired provost, English language educator*
Harrison, Russell Sage *political science educator, consultant*
Homan, Kenneth Lewis *auditor*
Huhn, Richard Dale *physician*
Irenas, Joseph Eron *judge, director*
†Joergensen, John P *librarian*
†Johnson, David Willis *former food products executive*
Jones, Larry Darnell *tax specialist*
Laskin, Lee B. *judge, lawyer, state senator*
Lawrence, Francis Leo *university president, language educator*
Madan, Deepak Sheelmohan *engineer*
Martin, Joseph Vinson *neurobiologist, educator*
†Maxymuk, John Michael *librarian, writer*
†Patterson, Dennis Michael *lawyer, educator*
Pomorski, Stanislaw *lawyer, educator*
†Robinson, Paul Harper *lawyer, educator*
Seidmon, E. James *urologist*
Simandle, Jerome B. *federal judge*
Stahl, Gary Edward *neonatologist*
Uhler, Walter Charles *government official, writer, reviewer*
Van Til, Jon *sociology educator*
†Verma, Vijayendra Kishore *internist, cardiologist*
Worrall, John Dennis *economics educator, consultant, writer*
Yamada, Tetsuji *health economist, educator*

Cape May
Caruso, Frank S. *pharmaceutical executive*
Fox, Matthew Ignatius *publishing company executive*
Lassner, Franz George *educator*
Turner, Almon Richard *retired art historian, educator*

Cape May Court House
†Altman, Brian David *pediatric ophthalmologist*
Cohen, Daniel Edward *writer*
Cohen, Susan Lois *writer*
Fineberg, Robert Alan *lawyer*
Pierson, Jeffrey Lynn *protective services officer*

Cape May Point
Fraser, Malcolm Cavanagh *mayor*
Jordan, Joe J. *architect*

Carneys Point
Baker, Natalie Michele *child therapist*

Carteret
†Neff, Richard B. *consumer products company executive*
†Scott, Eileen Rose *retail executive*

Cedar Grove
Anderson, Robert Raymond *artist, consultant*

Cedar Knolls
Clark, Sharon W. *employee benefits company executive*

Chatham
Bugen, David Henry *financial advisor*
Earle, Jean Buist *finance executve*
Frommer, Ann *systems analyst*
Glover, Janet Briggs *artist*
Hurley, Allyson Kingsley *dentist*
Jacobs, Andrew Robert *lawyer*
Lax, Philip *land developer, space planner*
Lenz, Henry Paul *management consultant*
Leonett, Anthony Arthur *banker*
Marconi, Dominic Anthony *retired bishop*
Meagher, James Proctor *editor*
Murphy, Joseph James *chiropractic physician*
†Sickler, Dean Ewin *decorative artist, educator*
Sundberg, Carl-Erik Wilhelm *telecommunications executive, researcher*
White, Benjamin Steven *mathematician, researcher*
Zegas, Alan Lee *lawyer*

Cherry Hill
Adler, John Herbert *lawyer, state legislator*
Agasar, Ronald Joseph *mortgage banker*
Bashkin, Lloyd Scott *marketing and management consultant*
Batterman, Steven Charles *engineering mechanics and bioengineering educator, forensic engineering and biomechanics consultant*
†Berman, Steven Eric *audiologist*
Betchen, Stephen Jay *marital, family and sex therapist*
Bond, John Walter *historian*
Brachfeld, Jonas *cardiologist, educator*
Brenner, Lynnette Mary *reading specialist, educator*
Bryan, Henry Collier *clergyman, retired secondary school educator*
Clauser, Donald Roberdeau *musician*
Copsetta, Norman George *real estate executive*
Deppa, Timothy Wayne *electrical engineer*
Feldman, Arnold H. *lawyer*
Fuentevilla, Manuel Edward *chemical engineer*
Gardner, Joel Robert *writer, historian*
Garrigle, William Aloysius *lawyer*
Goldberg, Jack *hematologist*
Gutin, Myra Gail *communications educator*
Hill, Connie Ray, Jr., *physicist*
Holfeld, Donald Rae *railroad consultant*
Israelsky, Roberta Schwartz *speech pathologist, audiologist*
Jacobson, Gerald *orthodontist*
Jozwiak, Steven Jay *lawyer*
Kuchler, Joseph Albert *surgeon*
†Liebman, Emmanuel *lawyer*
Margolis, Gerald Joseph *psychiatrist, psychoanalyst*
McCormick, Donna Lynn *social worker*
Melick, George Fleury *mechanical engineer, educator*
Moyer, Cheryl Lynn *non-profit administrator*
Myers, Daniel William, II, *lawyer*
Newell, Eric James *financial planner, tax consultant, former insurance executive*
Olearchyk, Andrew *cardiothoracic surgeon, educator*
Polansky, Steven Jay *lawyer*
Proper, Michael Charles *cardiologist, educator*
Rabil, Mitchell Joseph *lawyer*
Robinson, Mary Jo *pathologist*
Rose, Joel Alan *legal consultant*
†Roth, Kenneth David *lawyer*
Rovner, Leonard Irving *education educator*
Rudman, Solomon Kal *magazine publisher*
Schelm, Roger Leonard *information systems specialist*
Shapiro, Richard Allen *lawyer*
Spielberg, Joshua Morris *lawyer*
†Sullivan, Eileen Alison *reporter*
Tomar, William *lawyer*
Weinstein, Steven *lawyer*
Werbitt, Warren *gastroenterologist, educator*

Chester
†Di Battista, Anthony Paul *secondary school educator*
Fluker, Jay Edward *middle school visual arts educator*
Maddalena, Lucille Ann *management consultant*
Pfaffenroth, Peter Albert *lawyer*

Cinnaminson
Johnson, Victor Lawrence *banker*
Kauffmann, Robert Fredrick *software engineer*
†Lafragola, Margherita Raffaelina *pharmacist*

Clark
Farina, Mario G. *lawyer*
Kinley, David *physical therapist, acupuncturist*
Meilan, Celia *food products executive*

Clayton
Bertenshaw, William Howard, III, *radio and television producer*

Cliffside Park
Bedian, Maral Papazian *civil and geotechnical engineer*
De Pol, John *artist*
Diktas, Christos James *lawyer*
†Ginos, James Zissis *retired research chemist*
Goldstein, Howard Bernard *investment banker, advertising and marketing executive*
Klafter, George *urologist*
Pearlman, Mickey Lou *writer*
Perhacs, Marylouise Helen *musician, educator*
Pushkarev, Boris S. *research foundation director, writer*
Zucker, Howard Alan *pediatric cardiologist, intensivist, anesthesiologist, U.S. deputy assistant secretary for health*

Clifton
Anzaldi, James Anthony *mayor*
Bronkesh, Annette Cylia *public relations executive*
Burke, Bruce Lowell *consumer products company executive*
Charsky, Thomas Robert *elementary education educator*
Feinstein, Miles Roger *lawyer*
Giordano, Sandra L. *elementary school educator*
Held, George Anthony *architect*
†Kalata, Mary Ann Catherine *architect*
Klein, Hubert *accountant*
Lieb, L. Robert *lawyer*
Malamud, Alexander *lawyer, consultant*
McCoy, Linda Korteweg *library director*
Minkoff, John *applied mathematics, signal processing, and engineering educator*
†Mohammed, Sohail *lawyer, consultant*
Palma, Nicholas James *lawyer*
Pineda, Albert Anthony *obstetrician, gynecologist, educator*
Ressetar, Nancy *foreign language educator*
Stalbaum, Bernardine Ann *English language educator*
Yau, Edward Tintai *toxicologist, pharmacologist*

Clinton
†Cunningham, Gloria Sword *retired librarian*
†Moore, Alma Donst *writer, lyricist*
†Swift, Richard J. *engineering company executive*

Closter
Stein, Ellen F. *music therapist, songwriter*

Collingswood
Martin, Burchard V. *lawyer*
Mohrfeld, Richard Gentel *marketing professional*
Poacelli, Dolores *fine artist, graphic designer*

Colonia
Wiesenfeld, Bess G. *interior designer*

Colts Neck
Borisov, George P. *music educator*
†Mauro, Anthony Peter *small business owner*

Columbia
Timcenko, Lydia Teodora *biochemist, chemist*

Columbus
Lasorda-Sivieri, Helen Marie *school social worker*
Litman, Bernard *electrical engineer, consultant*

Convent Station
Tintle, Carmel Joseph *public relations executive*

Cranbury
†Bronner, William Roche *lawyer*
Campbell, Joseph John *financial services executive*
Gupta, Rajat Kumar *lawyer, accountant*
Hawver, Dennis A. *psychological consultant*
Iatesta, John Michael *lawyer*
Izrailev, Sergei *research scientist*
Kemmerer, Peter Ream *financial executive*
Palócz, István *electrical engineer, educator*
Perhach, James Lawrence *pharmaceutical company executive*
Roth, Richard C. *marketing executive*
Salles, Fernando Javier *molecular biologist, biotechnologist*
Yoseloff, Julien David *publishing company executive*
Yoseloff, Thomas *publisher*

Cranford
Bardwil, Joseph Anthony *investments consultant*
Crow, Lynne Campbell Smith *insurance company representative*
De Luca, Thomas George *lawyer*
Halleck, George Thomas *marketing professional*
Jenssen, Warren Donald *microbiologist, consultant*
†Messing, Sara Virginia Drick *lawyer*
†Mullen, Edward K. *paper company executive*
†Russell, John Joseph *English educator*
Schink, Frank Edward *electrical engineer*
†Vazquez, Felipe Miguel *educator*

Cresskill
†Cardinale, Gerald *state legislator*
Jurasek, John Paul *mathematics educator, counselor*
Smyth, Craig Hugh *fine arts educator*
Stern, Gerd Jakob *poet, retired import/export company executive*
Uehling, Gordon Alexander, Jr., *investment company executive*

Dayton
Adickes, Sandra Elaine *English language educator, writer*
Bassett, Alton Herman *health care company executive*
†Guo, Mintong *pharmaceutical scientist*

Deal
Becker, Richard Stanley *music publisher*
†Palaia, Joseph A. *state legislator*

Deepwater
Baillie, Joan M. *chemical company official, biology educator*

Delran
†Conaway, Herb(ert) C., Jr., *assemblyman*
Gilbert, Harry Ephraim, Jr., *retired hotel executive*
Parker, Michael J. *editor, writer, researcher*

Demarest
Brody, Saul Nathaniel *retired English literature educator*
Dornfest, Burton Saul *anatomy educator*
Ruderman, Warren *chemist*

Denville
Breed, Ria *anthropologist*
†Bucco, Anthony R. *state legislator*
Dudrow, Peter Warren *human resources executive, consultant*
Fisher, Sharon Mary *musician*
Husar, Walter Gene *neurologist, neuroscientist, educator*
Minter, Jerry Burnett *electronic component company executive, engineer*
Tartaglia, Richard V. *priest*
Tilak, Avinash G. *industrial engineer, management consultant*
†Veech, Lynda Anne *musician, educator*

Deptford
Kelly, Barbara Sue *psychologist*

Dover
Byrnes, Robert William *secondary school educator*
Freedman, Pamela Gottesman *gastroenterologist*
Kassell, Paula Sally *editor, publisher*
Seadler, Stephen Edward *social scientist*

Dumont
Chiandusse, Richard Stephen *music educator*
†Raffa, Stanley William *engineer*
Sadock, Karen *editor, writer*

Dunellen
Richmond, Ernest Leon *research engineer, consultant*

East Brunswick
Applebaum, Charles *lawyer*
Arno, Joseph Peter *physician, cosmetic surgeon*
†Avendano, Gary Fidel *cardiologist, internist*
Dombrowski, Anne Wesseling *retired microbiologist, researcher*
Einhorn, Carl Murray *psychologist*
Goldberg, Bertram J. *social agency administrator*
Hurst, Gregory Squire *director, producer, investment executive*
Liebowitz, Larry Arnold *chemical engineer*
Maman, Arie *endocrinologist*
Meningall, Evelyn L. *educational media specialist*
Miller, Andrew David *physician*
Ollwerther, William Raymond *newspaper editor*
†Savio, Frances Margaret Cammarotta *music educator*
Todd, Edward Francis, Jr., *risk management consultant, insurance broker*
Wagman, Gerald Howard *retired biochemist*
†Weiss, Robert Edward *urologist, educator*
Yahya, Muhammad Javaid *financial consultant, economist*
Yttrehus, Rolv Berger *composer, educator*
Zinkin, Lewis David *physician*

East Hanover
Bess, Alan L. *pharmaceutical executive, physician*
Cohen, Lori *computer software developer*
Dodsworth, Roy W. *pharmaceutical company executive*
Edelson, Edward Harold *research chemist*
Foley, James Edward *scientist, pharmaceutical company executive*
†Georgieva, Anna Vladimirova *mathematician*
†Iovel, Alla *music educator, writer, pianist*
Judge, Rajinder *psychiatrist*
Kayser, Kenneth Wayne *lawyer*
Kent, Bruce Jonathan *pharmaceutical executive*
Knight, Frank James *pharmaceutical marketing professional*
Marks, Peter Wayne *hematologist, oncologist, educator*
†Martelet, Francois R. *pharmaceutical executive*
Nemecek, Georgina Marie *molecular pharmacologist*
O'Byrne, Elizabeth Milikin *pharmacologist, researcher, endocrinologist*
Tamburro, Peter James, Jr., *secondary school educator*
†Wu, Johnny *internist*

East Orange
Caldwell, Toni Lucille
†Chandan, Kamlesh C. *information technology executive, researcher*
Corbitt, Ann Marie *municipal official*
Fielo, Muriel Bryant *interior designer*
†Ilogienboh, Caroline O. *protective services official, publishing executive*
Jones-Gregory, Patricia *secondary art educator*
Loebner, Hugh Gene *manufacturing company executive*
Masucci, Nicholas J. *engineering company executive*
Oderman, Stuart Douglas *pianist, composer, playwright*
Teetsell, Janice Marie Newman *business owner, lawyer*
Vasey, James Anthony *psychotherapist, consultant*
Wedeen, Richard Peter *physician*
Wolff, Derish Michael *economist, company executive*

East Rutherford
Brodeur, Martin *hockey player*
Burns, Pat *professional hockey coach*
Collins, Kerry *football player*
Fassel, Jim *professional football coach*
Glassell, Claes *health products executive*
†Holyfield, Evander *professional boxer*
Kempner, Michael W. *public relations executive*
Kidd, Jason *professional basketball player*
†Kluge, John Werner *broadcasting and advertising executive*
†Lamoriello, Louis Anthony *professional hockey team executive*
Mack, James A. *health products executive*
Mara, Wellington T. *professional football team executive*
†Moorer, Michael *professional boxer*
Scott, Byron Alton *professional basketball coach, former professional basketball player*
Shalyt, Eugene *chemical researcher*
Stevens, Scott *professional hockey player*
Strahan, Michael *football player*
†Whitaker, Pernell (Sweet Pea Whitaker) *professional boxer*

East Windsor
†Adams, Stephen M. *publishing company executive*

†Orenstein, Fran M. *director, writer*

Eastampton Township
Bowker, Nancy Anne *writer, bookseller*

Eatontown
DeGiglio, Michael A. *food products executive*
†Manzo-Goral, Carmen M. *critical care nurse*
O'Hare-VanMeerbeke, Anne Marie *dietitian*
Priesand, Sally Jane *rabbi*
Rapka, James Richard *electronics engineer*
†Rasmussen, Mark William *restaurant owner and chef*
Sager, Lawrence Cooper *psychologist*

Edgewater
Karol, Cecilia *psychiatrist, psychoanalyst*
Virelli, Louis James, Jr., *lawyer*

Edison
Agarwal, Kishan C. *physician*
Alexander, John Charles *pharmaceutical company executive, physician*
Andreasen, Charles Peter *retired electronics executive*
Arakawa, Paeter Stanhope *artist, educator*
Barcun, Gail E. *forensic economics executive*
Barcun, Seymour *economics educator*
†Barnes, Peter J., Jr., *assemblyman*
†Behr, Omri M. *lawyer*
†Buono, Barbara *state legislator*
Cangemi, Michael Paul *accountant, financial executive, writer*
Chakrapani, J(ayatheertha) *information technologist*
†Currie, Robert *communications executive*
D'Agostino, Matthew Paul *bakery executive*
Di Pasquale, Emanuel Paul *poet, English language and literature educator*
Dogra, Vijay Kumar *physician*
Doherty, Patricia Ann *computer systems analyst*
Fink, Edward Murray *lawyer, educator*
†Francis, Peter T. *gas industry executive, oil industry executive*
Haberman, Louise Shelly *consulting company executive*
Hecht, William David *accountant*
Hunter, Michael *publishing executive*
†Islam, Naushad S. *pharmacist, government agency administrator*
Kumar, Krishan *management consultant company executive*
†Kushinsky, Jeanne Alice *SAT tutor*
†Lee, Willy Weisheng *chemist, researcher*
Maeroff, Gene I. *academic administrator, journalist*
Mahadeshwar, Sanjay Sakharam *marine consultant*
Menoutis, James Vassillios *research scientist*
†Miniere, Michael Anthony *mathematician, educator*
Nessel, Edward Harry *swimming coach*
O'Brien, John Graham *lawyer*
Papamitsakis, Nikolaos I.H. *neurologist*
Robinson, Donald Warren *educator, artist*
†Roskoski, John *religious studies educator, coach*
†Vercammen, Kenneth Albert *lawyer, prosecutor*
Wexler, Annette Frances *writer*
Wolfthal, Michael Edward *director*

Egg Harbor Township
†Blee, Francis J. *state legislator, chiropractor*
Lashman, Shelley Bortin *retired judge*
Li, Huasheng *scientist*
Sykes, Paula Marie *school counselor*

Elizabeth
Arnold, Kristin Anne *chemist*
Berger, Harold Richard *physician*
Bollwage, J. Christian *mayor*
Budanitsky, Sander *lawyer*
Cinberg, James Zubow *otolaryngologist, educator*
†Cohen, Neil M. *state legislator*
†Daley, Todd Maurice *mathematician, educator*
Gellert, George Geza *food importing company executive*
Kabak, Douglas Thomas *lawyer*
†Lesniak, Raymond J. *state legislator*
Lisa, Janis P. *finance manager, auditor*
Lucco, James Perry *writer*
Lunt, Alan Nicholas *psychiatric rehabilitation counselor*
Millman, Arthur Edward *internist, cardiologist, educator*
Mogensen, Charles Ray, Jr., *food service administrator*
Rosenstein, Neil *surgeon, genealogical researcher*
Sananman, Michael Lawrence *neurologist*
†Suliga, Joseph *state legislator*
Wilchins, Sidney A. *gynecologist*

Elmwood Park
DeCondo, Anthony Paul, Sr., *elementary school educator*
Mangano, Louis *lawyer*
Mitschele, Michael Douglas *concrete and aggregate company executive*
Semeraro, Michael Archangel, Jr., *civil engineer*

Emerson
Cheslik, Francis Edward *management consultant*
†Gariolo, Richard *psychotherapist*
Hannon, Patricia Ann *library director*
Pavloski, Veronica Theresa *corporate communications specialist*
†Rooney, John Edward *state legislator, electrical company executive*

Englewood
Anuszkiewicz, Richard Joseph *artist*
Boyajian, Levon Zakar *psychiatrist, administrator*
Butler, David George *obstetrician, gynecologist*
Chandrankunnel, Mathew Michael *priest, educator*
†Chiorazzi, Mary Lorraine *psychiatrist*
Deresiewicz, Herbert *mechanical engineering educator*
Fay, Toni Georgette *communications executive*
†Gelber, Linda Cecile *lawyer, banker*
Glass, Janet Levine *primary and secondary education educator*
Hantgan, George *social services administrator*
Hoexter, Corinne Rosenfelder Katz *author, editor*
Koch, Randall Glory *hospital administrator*
†Milstein, Edward Philip *lawyer*
Neis, Arnold Hayward *pharmaceutical company executive*
Ostberg, Henry Dean *corporate executive*
Rosenbaum, David Herbert *neurologist*
Saliba, Philip E. *archbishop*
Salzer, Linda Parsons *clinical social worker*
Schmidt, Ronald Hans *architect*
Schwartz, Howard Alan *periodontist*
Strauss, Raymond Bernard *otolaryngologist*
†Svezia, Vera Tisheff *concert pianist*
Valenti, Paula Anne (Pelak) *art educator, assistant principal*
†Volk, Austin N. *insurance company executive*
Wuhl, Charles Michael *psychiatrist*
Zwilich, Ellen Taaffe *composer*

Englewood Cliffs
Books, Roberta Paula *real estate finance executive*
Dash, Barry Harold *pharmaceutical company executive*
Farrell, Patricia Ann *psychologist, educator, writer*
Haltiwanger, Robert Sidney, Jr., *book publishing executive*
Heller, Hanes Ayres *lawyer*
Lipsitz, Lawrence Irwin *publishing executive*
Masi, John Roger *lawyer*
†Saible, Stephanie Irene *magazine editor*
†Shoemate, Charles R. *former food company executive*
†Vane, Dena *magazine editor-in-chief*
Wernick, Edward Raymond *computer company executive*
Yu, Fei *internist*

Essex Fells
Thummel, Rosa *artist*
Yu, Yi-Yuan *mechanical engineering educator*

Ewing
Brunda, Daniel Donald *retired aerospace engineer, consultant, inventor*
Cole, Robert Carlton *English and journalism educator*
D'Antonio, Cynthia Maria *sales and marketing executive*
Hamm, Claire Rose *development information services administrator*
McCarty, John Albert *advertising and marketing educator, consultant*
†Meola, Marc *school librarian*
Robboy, Howard Alan *sociologist, educator*
Sanders, Philip F., Jr., *artist, computer art educator*
Steen, John *health policy company executive, consultant*
†Turner, Shirley Kersey *state legislator*

Fair Haven
Di Turi, Christopher *dentist, maxillofacial prosthodontist, educator, researcher*
McKissock, David Lee *retired manufacturing company executive*
Wyndrum, Ralph William, Jr., *communications executive consultant*

Fair Lawn
Aitchison, Suann *elementary school educator*
Delloff, Stefan T. *lawyer*
Kourkoumelis, Nick *financial analyst, consultant, finance educator*
Mazel, Joseph Lucas *publishing executive, consultant*
Shain-Alvaro, Judith Carol *physician assistant*
Wall, Mark Emanuel *banker, engineer, consultant*
Wallace, Mary Monahan *elementary and secondary schools educator*

Fairfield
Buchalter, Martin *pharmaceutical medical device company executive*
Byer, Theodore Scott *accountant*
†Connell, William Terrence *lawyer, judge*
de Smet, Lorraine May *artist*
Govic, Rudolf *structural engineer*
Purcell, Fenton Peter *engineering consultant*

Fairview
Anton, Harvey *textile company executive*
Park, Chung *painter, educator, computer software developer*

Fanwood
Berger, Ivan Bennett *magazine editor, writer*
Butler, William Langdon *manufacturers representative*
†Mitzner, Michael Jay *lawyer*
Whitaker, Joel *publisher, editor, elected public official*

Far Hills
Bruett, Karen Diesl *sales and fundraising consultant*
Corash, Richard *lawyer*
†Fay, David B. *sports association executive*
Hambleton, George Blow Elliott *retired management consultant*
McCall, David Warren *retired chemistry research director, consultant*

Farmingdale
Edwards, Ann Concetta *human resources director*
Kalnins, Andis Imants *civil engineer*
Schluter, Peter Mueller *electronics company executive*

Flanders
Huang, Jacob Chen-ya *physician, city official*

Flemington
Jaffe, Evan *rabbi*
Kettler, Carl Frederick *airline executive*
Lance, Leonard *state legislator*
†Lenagh, Thomas Hugh *lawyer, financial advisor*
Michels, Kevin Howard *lawyer*
Miller, Louis H. *lawyer*
Nielsen, Lynn Carol *lawyer, educational consultant*
Rushton, Alan R. *physician, medical historian*
Salamon, Renay *real estate broker*
Thomas, Anne Moreau *former newspaper owner*
Verniero, Peter G. *state supreme court justice*
Wiedl-Kramer, Sheila Colleen *biologist*
†Wolfson, William Steven *lawyer*

Florham Park
Atkins, Richard Bart *film, television producer*
Bossen, Wendell John *retired financial consultant*
Brodkin, Adele Ruth Meyer *psychologist*
Chase, Eric Lewis *lawyer*
†Fischer, Pamela Shadel *public relations executive*
Goguen, Healfdene Hrothgar *computer scientist, consultant*
Hardin, William Downer *retired lawyer*
Kandravy, John *lawyer*
†Kim, Hong Kook *electrical engineer, researcher*
Laulicht, Murray Jack *lawyer*
LeVine, Walter Daniel *lawyer, accountant*
Marshall, William Jeffrey *journalist, author*
Mersel, Larry *architect*
Naimark, George Modell *marketing and management consultant*
†Negi, Devendra S. *communications services company administrator*
Nittoly, Paul Gerard *lawyer*
O'Connell, Daniel F. *lawyer*
O'Keefe, Robert James *retired banker*
Pantel, Glenn Steven *lawyer*
Pollack, Jordan Ellis *pharmaceutical company executive*
Rabinovich, Michael *computer scientist*
Reid, Charles Adams, III, *lawyer*
Shor, Peter W. *mathematician, researcher*
Sinnett, William McNair *finance researcher*
Sperber, Martin *pharmaceutical company executive, pharmacist*
Weisberg, Lynne Willing *psychiatrist, consultant*

Fords
Blond, Stuart Richard *newsletter editor*

Forked River
†Connors, Christopher J. *state legislator*
†Moran, Jeffrey W., Jr., *state legislator*
Novak, Dennis E. *family practice physician*

Fort Lee
Adler, Earl *insurance executive*
Altomara, Rita Ecke *library director, writer*
Amara, Lucine *opera and concert singer*
Baiul, Oksana *clothing designer, former figure skater*
Bolster, William Lawrence *broadcast executive*
Cheng, David Hong *mechanical engineering educator*
Chessler, Richard Kenneth *gastroenterologist, endoscopist*
Cohn, Scott *television news correspondent*
Cox, Melvin Monroe *lawyer*
Dobrzynski, Judith Helen *journalist, commentator*
Fischel, Daniel Norman *publishing consultant*
Fisher, Andrew, IV, *newswriter, television producer*
Goldfischer, Jerome D. *cardiologist*
Houston, Whitney *vocalist, recording artist*
Kiriakopoulos, George Constantine *dentist*
Kofman, Mikhail *economist, engineering executive*
Li, Tien-Shun *obstetrician, gynecologist, educator*
Lippman, William Jennings *investment company executive*
Nemser, Robert Solomon *visual communications consultant, art director, creative director, designer, writer, educator*
Schiessler, Robert Walter *retired chemical and oil company executive*
†Schirmer, Helga *retired chiropractor*
Screpetis, Dennis *retired nuclear engineer, consultant*
Seitel, Fraser Paul *public relations executive*
Stuart, Carole *publishing executive*
Stuart, Lyle *publishing company executive*
Sugarman, Alan William *educational consultant, national speaker*
†Thomopoulos, Michael *music educator*

Fort Monmouth
Anderson, Bergie Wayne *human factors psychologist*
Flanigan, Richard Joseph *retired career officer, company executive*
Kosinski, John August *electrical engineer, civilian military employee*
Leciston, David John *computer scientist*
Mandelbaum, David Michael *electrical engineer*
Perlman, Barry Stuart *electrical engineering executive, researcher*
Schwering, Felix Karl *electronics engineer, researcher*
†Su, Wei *electrical engineer*
Thornton, Clarence Gould *electronics engineering executive*
Tobias, John Michael *electronics engineer*

Franklin
†Littell, Robert E. *state legislator*

Franklin Lakes
Baker, Cornelia Draves *artist*
Baker, Philip Douglas *consultant, retired investment banker*
Castellini, Clateo *retired medical technology company executive*
Friedman, Martin Burton *chemical company executive*
Ginsberg, Barry Howard *physician, researcher*
Hector, Bruce John *lawyer*
Ludwig, Edward J. *medical technology company executive*
†Mohtashemi, Paymon *physician assistant*
Williams, Edward David *consulting executive*

Franklin Park
†Jones, Frank A., Jr., *psychiatrist, educator*
Perry, Arthur William *plastic surgeon, educator*

Freehold
Bennett, John O. *state legislator*
†Cheng, Grace Zheng-Ying *music educator*
†Christ, Duane Marland *computer systems engineer*
†Farragher, Clare M. *state legislator*
Fisher, Clarkson Sherman, Jr., *judge*
Foster, Eric Harold, Jr., *retail executive*
†Greenstein, Gary *periodontist, dental educator*
Jawidzik, Edward Mark *priest*
Kwon, Joon Taek *retired chemistry researcher*
Lijoi, Peter Bruno *lawyer*
Medley, Alex Roy *executive minister*
Newman, James Michael *judge, lawyer*
Pofsky, Norma Louise *interior designer, behavioral consultant*
Schwartz, Perry Lester *information systems engineer, consultant*
Stirrat, William Albert *electronics engineer*
Vernick, Jeffrey Francis *county official*
Wilson, Nancy Jeanne *laboratory consultant, medical technologist*

Frenchtown
Fogelson, Brian David *educational administrator*
†Heck, Ronald Marshall *chemical engineer*

Garfield
Herpst, Robert Dix *lawyer, optics and materials technology executive*
Kobylarz, Joseph Douglas *secondary education educator*
Nickles, I. MacArthur *librarian*

Garwood
†Callahan, Billy T. *writer, secondary school educator*
Maher, Gary Laurence *lawyer*

Gillette
Nathanson, Linda Sue *publisher, author, technical writer*
Pfafflin, Sheila Murphy *psychologist*

Gladstone
Caspersen, Finn Michael Westby *diversified financial services company executive*
Close, Donald Pembroke *management consultant*
†Standish, Robert C. *professional sports team executive*

Glassboro
†Coulombe, Joseph Louis *literature educator*
D'Augustine, Robert *university administrator, lawyer*
Davis, Ronald P. *secondary school administrator*
Dusseau, Ralph Alan *civil and environmental engineering educator*
Gephardt, Donald Louis *university official*
Hausman, Carl Dane *writer, journalism and media educator*
Holdcraft, Janet Rulon *academic administrator*
James, Herman Delano *college administrator*
†Kadlowec, Jennifer *engineering educator*
Margolis, Jeffrey Allen *program specialist*
Robinette, Joseph Allen *theater educator, playwright*
†Walpole, MaryBeth *education educator*
†Wang, Q. Edward *history educator*

Glen Ridge
Agnew, Peter Tomlin *employee benefit consultant*
Coddington, Anne Lillian *retired English literature educator*
McGovern, Thomas Aquinas *retired utility executive*
Pendley, Donald Lee *association executive*
Rubin, Roberta Gail *pathologist*
Zbar, Lloyd Irwin Stanley *otolaryngologist, educator*

Glen Rock
Britcher, E. Drew *lawyer*
†D'Angelo, Thomas J. *not-for-profit developer, financial consultant*
Markey, Brian Michael *lawyer*
Mc Elrath, Richard Elsworth *retired insurance company executive*
Sirower, Bonnie Fox *fundraising executive*

Gloucester City
Klein, Steven George *osteopathic physician*
†Roberts, Joseph J. *former state legislator*

Green Brook
Balsamello, Melissa (Marley) *educator*
Bohanan, David John *management consultant*
†Bokhari, Sabahat *cardiologist*
Elias, Donald Francis *environmental consultant*
Hertzberg, Henry *retired radiologist*
Spoeri, Randall Keith *healthcare company executive*

Green Village
Castenschiold, René *engineering company executive, author, consultant*

Greenwich
Lane, Mark *lawyer, educator, writer*

Guttenberg
Wright, Jane Cooke *physician, educator, consultant*

Hackensack
†Abdelrazek, Rawan *economist*
Ahearn, James *newspaper columnist*
†Baer, Byron M. *state legislator*
Borg, Malcolm Austin *publishing executive*
Caminiti, Donald Angelo *lawyer*
Carra, Andrew Joseph *advertising executive*
Cicchelli, Joseph Vincent *principal*
Cipollone, Anthony Dominic *judge, educator*
Croland, Barry I. *lawyer*
Curtis, Robert Kern *lawyer, physics educator*
D'Alessandro, Dianne Marie *public defender*
De Groote, Robert David *general and vascular surgeon*
Donahoe, Maureen Alice *accounting consultant*
Duus, Gordon Cochran *lawyer*
Fatemi, Saeid *language educator, writer, researcher*
Fede, Andrew Thomas *lawyer, educator*
Ferguson, John Patrick *medical center executive*
Gerlanc, Glenn Marc *lawyer*
Gingras, Paul Joseph *real estate management company executive*
Greenberg, Steven Morey *lawyer*
Gross, Peter Alan *epidemiologist, researcher*
Haines, Kathleen Ann *physician, educator*
Heilborn, George Heinz *investor*
†Horan, John Donohoe *lawyer*
Kestin, Howard H. *judge*
†Kiel, Paul Edward *lawyer*
Margulies, James Howard *editorial cartoonist*
†Masullo, Alfredo Salvatore *dermatologist*
Mullin, Patrick Allen *lawyer*
Parisi, Cheryl Lynn *elementary school educator*
Pollinger, William Joshua *lawyer*
†Robinson, Sandra Ann *lawyer*
Rosenbloom, Donald Theodore *orthodontist, sleep disorders specialist*
†Schwartz, Mildred Anne *retired sociologist*
Shapiro, Sylvia *psychotherapist*
Sperber, Steven Jay *internist*
Stein, Gary S. *retired judge, lawyer*
Steinbach, Harold I. *lawyer*
†Strull, James Richard *lawyer*
Vort, Robert A. *lawyer*
†Xagoraris, Andreas Ector *pediatric anesthesiologist*
Zimmerman, Marlin U., Jr., *chemical engineer*

Hackettstown
†Bratten, William P. *music educator*
Fremon, Richard C. *retired infosystems specialist*
†Gregg, Guy R. *state legislator*
†Grigsby, Byron Lee *dean*
†Kobert, Joel A. *lawyer*
Mulligan, Elinor Patterson *lawyer*
†Ripmaster, Terence M. *historian, educator*
Shayner, John Anthony *English language educator, university official*
Van Campen, Stephen Bernard *executive recruiter, consultant*
Wiedemann, Charles Louis *dentist*

Haddon Heights
Cipparone, Rocco C., Jr., *lawyer*
Gwiazda, Stanley John *retired university dean*
†Weinberg, Ruthmarie Louise *special education educator, researcher*

Haddonfield
Andres, Kenneth G., Jr., *lawyer*
Bauer, Raymond Gale *sales professional*
Capelli, John Placido *nephrologist, educator*
Chiulli, E. Antoinette *lawyer*
Eklund, Thor Ignatius *aeronautical engineer, consultant*
Ewan, David E. *lawyer*
Fuoco, Philip Stephen *lawyer*
†Graziano, Ronald Anthony *lawyer*
†Halscheid, Therese Anne *poet*
Heuisler, Charles William *lawyer*
Iavicoli, Mario Anthony *lawyer*
Mitchell, Matthew Kyle *lawyer*
Newell, Russell Anderson *financial planner*
Podgorski, Miriam Coder *volunteer*
Siskin, Edward Joseph *engineering and construction company executive*
†Smith, Carol J. *legal secretary, medical transcriptionist*

Hainesport
Sylk, Leonard Allen *housing company executive, real estate developer*

Haledon
†Finkelstein, Ronald *assistant principal, director*

Hamburg
Kane, James Patrick *superintendent of schools*

Hamilton
Barclay, Robert, Jr., *chemist*
Gideon, Richard Walter *broadcasting management consultant*
Grace, Michael Judd *immunologist*
Haushalter, Harry *lawyer*
†Inverso, Peter A. *state legislator*
Kane, Michael Joel *physician*
Nashif, Taysir N. *researcher*
Pucciatti, Sandra Milstein *opera company director*
Reid-Merritt, Patricia Ann *social worker, educator, author, performing artist*

Hamilton Square
Bloor, W(illiam) Spencer *electrical engineer, consultant*
†Ridolfi, Dorothy Porter Boulden *nurse*

Hammonton
Senf, Mary *secretary, artist, writer, poet*
Woolson, Charles E., Jr., *lawyer*

Hampton
Yates, Michael Francis *management consultant*

Harmony
Van Rensselaer, Miles *artist, sculptor*

Harrington Park
Salmon, Margaret Belais *nutritionist, dietitian*

Hasbrouck Heights
Perham, Roy Gates, III, *industrial psychologist*
Walsh, Virginia *artist, educator*
Watrel, Warren George *pharmaceutical company executive*

Haworth
Albrecht, William Kenneth *lawyer*
Biesel, David Barrie *publishing executive*
Biesel, Diane Jane *editor, publishing executive*
Mango, Christina Rose *psychiatric art therapist*
Posner, Roy Edward *retired finance executive*
Strum, Brian J. *real estate executive*

Hawthorne
†Girgenti, John Alexander *state legislator*
Schlachman, Edwin *retired state agency administrator*

Hazlet
Fisher, David Bruce *land development executive*
†Shea, James Bryan *writer*
Wunsch, Anna Catherine Mary O'Brien Horton *artist, consultant*

Helmetta
†Gabay, Eleonora V. *mechanical engineer, educator*

Hewitt
Mollenkott, Virginia Ramey *English literature and language educator, author, guest lecturer*
Selwyn, Donald *engineering administrator, researcher, inventor, educator*

Highland Lakes
Ludwig, Gregory Brian *editor, writer*

Highland Park
Brudner, Harvey Jerome *physicist*
Chamberlin-Davis, Ann Elizabeth *artist, writer*
Cheiten, Marvin Harold *playwright, manufacturing executive*
Coughlin, Caroline Mary *library consultant, educator*
Feigenbaum, Abraham Samuel *nutritional biochemist*
†Feuerwerker, Elie *secondary school educator*
Grady, Joyce (Marian Joyce Grady) *psychotherapist, consultant*
Kolodzei, Natalia A. *art foundation administrator, art historian, curator*
Like, Russel C. *economist, consultant, writer*
Marin-Garcia, Jose *researcher, cardiologist*
Smith, Neil *geography educator*

Highlands
Dann, Emily *mathematics educator*
Hansen, Christian Andreas, Jr., *plastics and chemical company executive*
†Lofstrom, Arlene Katherine *primary school educator*
Psuty, Norbert Phillip *marine sciences educator*

Hightstown
Bramwell, Katharine Hone Emmet *civic worker*
Howard, Barbara Sue Mesner *artist*
Hull, Gretchen Gaebelein *lay worker, writer, lecturer*
Johnson, Ernest Frederick *chemical engineer, educator*
Johnson, Walter Curtis *electrical engineering educator*
Martin, David George *historian, Latin educator, author*
Shoemaker, Frank Crawford *physicist, educator*
Wham, George Sims *retired publishing executive*

Hillsborough
Ames, Marc L. *lawyer*
Gulko, Edward *health care executive, consultant*
Kenyhercz, Thomas Michael *pharmaceutical company executive*
Orkin, Neil S. *management consultant, speaker*
Smagorinsky, Joseph *meteorologist*
Wang, Xiang *cardiologist, researcher*
Weinman, Steven Alan *emergency nurse, researcher, writer, educator, consultant*
Yuster-Freeman, Leigh Carol *broadcasting executive*

Hillsdale
Hodinar, Michael *lawyer, publishing company executive*
Kohan, Lois Rae *community health nurse*

Hillside
†Liu, Rong (Ron) *pharmaceutical executive, researcher*

Ho Ho Kus
Bryan, Thomas Lynn *lawyer, educator*
Ciannella, Joeen Moore *museum director*
Deupree, Marvin Mattox *accountant, business consultant*
†Somerwitz, Herbert Saul *lawyer*
Van Slooten, Ronald Henry Joseph *dentist*

Hoboken
Abel, Robert Berger *science administrator*
Aronovich, Ilya *small business owner*
Attygalle, Athula Buddhagosha *chemist, researcher*
Babko-Malyi, Sergei Vladimirovitch *process engineer, researcher*
Berzinski, Patrick Anthony *media consultant*
Boesch, Francis Theodore *electrical engineer, educator*
Breuer, Ronald Karl, Sr., *investment banking executive*
Bruno, Michael Stephen *ocean engineering educator, researcher*
Fassoulis, Satiris Galahad *communications company executive*
Fernandez, Fernando Lawrence *aeronautical engineer, research company executive*
Frankenthal, Danielle *painter, sculptor*
Griskey, Richard George *chemical engineering educator*
†Hultin, Jerry MacArthur *dean, lawyer*
Kalyon, Dilhan M(ehmet) *chemical engineering educator*
†Kenny, Bernard F. *state legislator, lawyer*
Leggiere, Philip Guy *publicist, writer, consultant*
†Lenci, Marco *mathematician, educator*
†Li, Hongbin *electrical engineer*
†Mankin, Robert Stephen *financial executive*
Moeller, Joseph John, Jr., *university official*
Panikov, Nicolai Sergeyevich *microbiologist, researcher*
Paradise, Paul Richard *writer, editor*
Raveché, Harold Joseph *university administrator, physical chemist*
Rose, Roslyn *artist*
Savitsky, Daniel *engineer, educator*
Schmidt, George *physicist, educator*
Schultz, Kenneth Carl *antiques dealer*
Sisto, Fernando *mechanical engineering educator*
Sommers, George R. *lawyer*
Tang, Hansong *computational fluid dynamics researcher*
†Tardiff, Jill Alexandria *marketing professional, consultant*
Ubell, Robert Neil *editor, publisher, educator, consultant*
Widdicombe, Richard Palmer *librarian*
Woodward, Holly Lowell *educator, writer*
Yevick, George Johannus *scientist*

Holmdel
Boyd, Gary Delane *electro-optical engineer, researcher*
†Curtis, Thomas H. *physicist*
Gordon, James Power *optics scientist*
Hudson, Wendy Joy *software manager*
Kaminow, Ivan Paul *physicist*
Lang, Howard Lawrence *electrical engineer*
Mollenauer, Linn Frederick *physicist*
Mondal, Kalyan *engineering executive*
Papadias, Constantinos Basil *electrical engineer*
Polinsky, Joseph Thomas *recruiting and training consultant*
Ross, Ian Munro *electrical engineer*
Samra, Said Abou *plastic surgeon*
Slovik, Sandra Lee *retired art educator*
Smith, Sibley Judson, Jr., *historic site administrator, educator*
Suhr, J. Nicholas *lawyer*
Sullivan, Timothy Patrick *telecommunications company executive*
†Valenzuela, Reinaldo A. *communications engineer, researcher*
Vitullo, Anthony Joseph *communications executive*
Yu, Charles X. *optical engineer, researcher*
Zhang, Xuemei *reliability scientist*

Hopatcong
Oken, Robert *neuroscientist, researcher, consultant*
Reese, Harry Edwin, Jr., *electronics executive*

Hope
McDonald, John Joseph *electronics executive*

Hopewell
†Baeckler, Virginia Van Wynen *librarian*
VanMarcke, Erik Hector *civil engineer, educator*

Irvington
Alston, Goldie Venessa *early childhood educator*
Paden, Harry *municipal official*
†Stanley, Craig A. *state legislator*

Iselin
Beardsley, Jacob Edward *retired computer software company executive*
Dornbusch, Arthur A., II, *lawyer*
Goodman, Barry S. *lawyer*
Holcombe, Thomas Charles *technology executive*
†Perry, Barry W. *manufacturing executive*
Smith, Orin Robert *chemical company executive*
Walker, Linda Lee *lawyer*

Island Heights
Noble, William Parker *writer, educator*

Jackson
†Arminas, Scott Arnold *chemist, poet, writer*
Carney, Rita J. *educational administrator*
†Dancer, Ronald S. *assemblyman*
Gasparro, Madeline *banker*
Hunter, Lynn *sales executive, writer, elementary school educator*
Leveson, Irving Frederick *economist*
†McCormick, Harold J. *music educator*
Rickabaugh, Vicki *horse farm owner, dressage instructor*
Turner, Pamela *psychologist*
Wagner, Edward Kurt *publishing company executive*
Washington, William Nicolai *government official*
Wedderman, Wayne Allan *elementary school educator*

Jersey City
Adlershteyn, Leon *naval architect, engineer, educator, researcher*
Alliton, Vaughn *brokerage executive*
†Amadeo, Natial Salvatore *lawyer*
Ascolese, Michael J. *corporate communications executive*
Ashley, Willard Walden C., Sr., *minister*
Barney, Christine J. *artist*
Brandes, Joel R. *consultant, publisher, writer*
†Bruso, Arthur *artist*
Burns, Hugh L. *priest, writer*
Catalano, James Anthony *social worker, consultant*
Conner, Ruth (Edone) *not-for-profit developer*
Coreil, Raymond Clyde *English educator*
D'Alessandro, Daniel Anthony *lawyer, educator*
Dupey, Michele Mary *communications specialist*
Ezrati, Milton Joseph *investment manager, economist, writer*
Farrior, Evan Bell *special education educator, writer*
Frisch, Harry David *lawyer, consultant, investment company executive*
Goldberg, Arthur Abba *merchant banker, financial advisor*
Guarini, Frank Joseph *lawyer, real estate developer*
Gurevich, Grigory *visual artist, educator, mime*
Hordon, Harris Eugene *economics educator*
Hozer, Leszek *materials scientist, engineer*
Jennings, Sister Vivien *English language educator*
†Katz, Colleen *publisher*
Klyatis, Lev Matusovich *test engineer*
†Kohan, Fereydoon *nuclear medicine physician*
Koster, Emlyn Howard *geologist, educator*
Levine, Richard James *publishing executive*
Luza, Radomir Vojtech, Jr., *poet, actor, comedian*
Mak, Ken Ping *brokerage executive*
McFadden, Rosemary Theresa *lawyer, financial services executive*
Miller, Adele Engelbrecht *educational administrator*
†Milton, Barbara Ella, II, *psychotherapist*
Nakhla, Atif Mounir *scientist, biochemist*
Nevins, Arthur Gerard, Jr., *lawyer*
Nicoll, Daniel Jules *internist, insurance company executive*
Ortenzi, Regina (Gina Rae Ortenzi) *home fashion products designer, educator*
Patterson, Grace Limerick *library director*
†Pietrini, Andrew Gabriel *automotive aftermarket executive*
Poiani, Eileen Louise *mathematics educator, college administrator, higher education planner*
Pratt, Minnie Bruce *writer, educator*
†Quigley, Joan Marie *state legislator*
Raffelson, Michael *financial executive*
Ranieri, Joseph John *English language educator*
Russell, Helen Ross *environmental consultant, author*
Russo, Gregory Thomas *lawyer*
Schundler, Bret Davis *former mayor*
Shaik, Fatima *college official, writer*
Shulman, Yale *urologist*
Shusterman, Neil Howard *internist, nephrologist*
Signorile, Vincent Anthony *lawyer*
Singer, Howard Jack *biology educator*
Solomon, Mack Busch *retired newspaper editor*
Stertz, Stephen Allen *historian, educator*
Stinchcomb, Albert Monroe *producer, designer/realtor*
Tang, C. Mark *investment advisor, investment banker, venture capitalist, writer*
Vogel, Nadine Orsoff *finacial services marketing executive*
†Wind, Jack Jay *lawyer*

Kearny
Brady, Lawrence Peter *lawyer*
John, Ricky *state official*
Perricci, Jeffrey Michael *dentist*
Shin, John Joongsung *mechanical nuclear engineer, consultant*

Keasbey
Hari, Kenneth Stephen *painter, sculptor, writer*

Kendall Park
Berger, Richard Stanton *dermatologist*
Fisch, Joseph *lawyer*
Hershenov, Bernard Zion *electronics research and development company executive*

Kenilworth
†Abreu, Paula Cristina *statistician, researcher*
Baroudy, Bahige Mourad *biochemist, researcher*
†Duffy, Ruth Anne *pharmacologist*
Evans, Charlie Anderson *chemist*
Fargey, Michael Andrew *special education educator*
Gen, Martin *corporate executive*
Hassan, Fred *pharmaceutical executive*
Hoffman, John Fletcher *lawyer*
†Korfmacher, Walter Averill *chemist, researcher*
Pramanik, Birendra Nath *research executive*
Scott, Mary Celine *pharmacologist*
Staudinger, Heribert Wolfgang *pulmonologist*
†Yang, Tsong-Toh (T.T.) *pharmacist, researcher*

Keyport
Colmant, Andrew Robert *lawyer*
Gilmartin, Clara T. *volunteer*

Kinnelon
Haller, Charles Edward *engineering consultant*
Klaas, Nicholas Paul *management and technical consultant*
Preston, Andrew Joseph *pharmacist, drug company executive*
Richardson, Joseph Blancet *retired science educator, educational consultant*

Kirkwood Voorhees
Kahn, Marc Leslie *orthopedic surgeon*
Mansukhani, Sunder Hashmatrai *pathology educator*

Lafayette
†Tanis, Jody A. *medical researcher, fire warden*

Lake Hopatcong
Tomlinson, Gerald Arthur *writer, publisher, editor*

Lakewood
Biasini, Virginia *social worker*
Brod, Morton Shelvin *oral surgeon*
Forbes, Gordon Maxwell *sports journalist, commentator*
Houle, Joseph E. *mathematics educator*
Karol, Frederick John *industrial chemist*
†Levine, Stephen M. *psychologist, educator*
Levovitz, Pesach Zechariah *rabbi*
Wechsler, Harold Herbert *surgeon*
Williams, Barbara Anne *college president emerita*
Witman, Edward Paul *philosophy educator*
Woodman, G. Roger *management consultant*

Lambertville
Beyea, Jan Edgar *physicist*
Goodyear, John L. *artist, educator*
Mackey, Philip English *non-profit organization consultant*

Landing
Wolahan, Caryle Goldsack *nursing educator*

Laurel Springs
Cleveland, Susan Elizabeth *library administrator, researcher*
Roma, Aida Clara *artist*

Lavallette
Tesoriero, Philip James *human resource consultant*

Lawrenceville
Adams, Christine Hanson *advertising executive*
Bailey, Lloyd Robert Scott *publishing company executive, editor, historian*
Brill, Michael Henry *physicist, vision scientist, editor*
Coleman, Wade Hampton, III, *management consultant, mechanical engineer, former banker*
Cox, Teri P. *public relations executive*
Daoust, Donald Roger *pharmaceutical and toiletries company executive, microbiologist*
Enegess, David Norman *chemical engineer*
†Frantz, Charles Frederick *music educator*
Galloway, Bonnie J. *investor, sociologist*
Grannatt, Milton Henderson, III, *economist*
Hunt, Wayne Robert, Sr., *state government official*
Iorio, Dominick Anthony *philosophy educator, dean*
Leonard, Patricia Louise *education educator, consultant*
†Lorenzet, Steven Joseph *management educator, consultant*
Naar, Harry I. *fine arts educator, artist*
Newlin, George Christian *writer*
Plaut, Thomas F.A. *psychologist*
Pohlhaus, John Ernest *international marketing executive, consultant*
Pouleur, Hubert Gustave *cardiologist, consultant*
Rosenthal, Albert Lester *dermatologist, educator*
†Rozanski, Mordechai *academic administrator*
Sheats, John Eugene *chemistry educator*
Stehle, Edward Raymond *secondary education educator, school system administrator*
Stroh, Guy Weston *philosophy educator*
Tharney, Leonard John *education educator, consultant*
†Vaccaro, Kimberly Ann Chandler *performing arts educator, consultant, writer*
Yeager, Arthur Leonard *health company executive*

Lebanon
Barto, Susan Carol *writer*
DeBevoise, Francine (Franke DeBevoise) *artist*
Frascella, Daniel William, Jr., *scientist*
Hakes, Thomas Brion *manufacturing company executive, physician*
Johnstone, Irvine Blakeley, III, *lawyer*
O'Neill, Elizabeth Sterling *trade association administrator*

Leonardo
Bianchi, Hollis Dolce *writer, artist*

Leonia
Deutsch, Nina *musician, vocalist*
†Dondysh, Victoria *pianist*
Greenwald, Martin *publishing company executive*
†Kurtz, Anthony David *physicist*
Pinsdorf, Marion Kathryn *business executive, educator, author*
Silverman, Lawrence Ira *music educator, musician*
†Victoria, Dondysh L. *piano educator*
Wilson, Marcia Sandmeyer *artist*

Liberty Corner
†Apruzzese, Vincent John *lawyer*
†Cipriano, Michael Rocco *information technology consultant*
Feldman, Elda Beylerian *lawyer*
Ganz, Felix *marketing professional*
McDermott, Frank Xavier *lawyer, lobbyist*
†Thompson, T. Jay *lawyer*

Lincoln Park
Byrnes, Jo Ann *professional relations administrator*
Sichuk, George *entrepreneur, theoretical biologist*

Lincroft
Benham, Helen *music educator*
Botti, Olenio T. *retired transporation executive, writer*
Heirman, Donald Nestor *training engineering company executive, consultant*
Tessem, Steven E. *energy executive*

Linden
Ball, William Lee (Atley Fall) *sportswriter*
Bedrick, Bernice *retired science educator, consultant*
Covino, Charles Peter *chemicals executive*
Littman, David Bernard *lawyer*

Lindenwold
Jackson, Yocontalie Ann *entertainment company executive*
Kish, Elissa Anne *educational administrator, consultant*

Linwood
Cohen, Diana Louise *psychology, educator, psychotherapist, consultant*
Moss, Andrea *fundraiser, community service volunteer*
Sutman, Francis Xavier *university dean*

Little Egg Harbor Township
Dinges, Richard Allen *entrepreneur*

Little Falls
Armellino, Michael Ralph *retired asset management executive*
Birnberg, Jack *financial executive*
Blanton, Lawton Walter *retired dean*
Draper, Daniel Clay *retired lawyer*
Glasser, Lynn Schreiber *publisher*
Glasser, Stephen Andrew *publishing executive, lawyer*
Viil, Heino *retired engineer*

Little Ferry
†Navarro-Steinel, Catherine A. *municipal official*

Little Silver
Brennan, William Joseph *manufacturing company executive*
Morrison, James Frederick *management consultant*
Redden, Harral Arthur, Jr., *broker*
Schmidt, Daniel Edward, IV, *lawyer, commercial arbitrator*
Turbidy, John Berry *investor, management consultant*

Livingston
Adelsberg, Harvey *hospital administrator*
Burns, Edward Charles *infosystems specialist*
Candido, A. Michael *contracting company executive, real estate manager*
Conde, Miguel A. *hematologist, oncologist*
Daman, Ernest Ludwig *mechanical engineer*
DeGhetto, Kenneth Anselm *engineering executive, construction executive*
Duberstein, Joel Lawrence *internist, pulmonologist, educator*
Fernandes, John *physician*
Fisher, Hyman Wendell *physician*
Friedman, Merton Hirsch *retired psychologist, educator*
Goldstein, Steven Howard *podiatrist*
†Green, Richard *research scientist, consultant*
Greenberg, Aaron Rosmarin *public relations executive*
Guerra, Mary Louise *human resources executive*
Klein, Peter Martin *lawyer, retired transportation company executive*
Krieger, Abbott Joel *neurosurgeon*
Levine, Harry Bruce *stockbroker*
Marlow, Ian Michael *real estate company executive*
†Piscopo, Phil *wholesale distribution executive*
Rickert, Robert Richard *pathologist, educator*
Rinsky, Joel Charles *lawyer*
Rokosz, Gregory Joseph *emergency medicine physician, lawyer, educator*
Rommer, James Andrew *physician*
Rosenberg, Paul I. *lawyer*
Saffer, Amy Beth *foreign language educator*
Samojlik, Eugeniusz *medical educator, clinical researcher*
Sethi, Deepak *leadership development/marketing executive*
Sikora, Barbara Jean *library director*
Simon, Sheryl Joy *writer, astrologer*
†Sukoneck, Ira David *lawyer*
Templeton, Hilda B. *psychiatrist, educator*
†Tillis, Alan Casal *orthopaedic surgeon*
Vlad, Luigina Doroti *endocrinologist*

Locust
Freeman, David Forgan *retired foundation executive*

Lodi
†Arella, Ann Marietta *music educator, vocalist*
†Armington, Thomas C. *mathematician, educator*
†Guillory, Ann Verrett *psychologist, educator*
†Heck, Rose *state legislator*
Karetzky, Stephen *library director, educator, researcher*

Long Branch
Fisher, Margaret Catharine *pediatrician, epidemiologist, educator*
Goldberg, Daniel Berney *eye surgeon*
Hecht, Patricia Layton *elementary school educator, writer, consultant*
Lagowski, Barbara Jean *writer, book editor*
Pachman, Frederic Charles *library director*
Palmisano, Elsalyn *library director, consultant, archivist*
Poch, Herbert Edward *retired pediatrician, educator*
Rassas, Beverly *educator, consultant*
Shagan, Bernard Pellman *endocrinologist, educator*
Stamaty, Clara Gee Kastner *artist*
†Zinterhofer, Louis *pathologist*
Zukaukas, Charles Lawrence *surgeon*

Long Valley
Collins, Kathleen *writer*
†Landis, Daniel Scott *music educator*

Lumberton
Brown, Hershel M. *retired newspaper publisher*
Friedberg, Thomas Harold *insurance company executive*
Losse, Catherine Ann *pediatric nurse, critical care nurse, educator, clinical nurse specialist, family nurse practitioner*

Lyndhurst
Benschip, Gary John *manufacturing company executive*
Brzezanski, Jay Marian *financial executive*
Bunda, Stephen Myron *political advisor, counselor, lawyer, classical philosopher*
†Fallon, Francis E(dward) *lawyer, corporation executive*
†McNamara, Patrick James *lawyer*
Sieger, Charles *librarian*

Madison
†Ariarajah, S. Wesley *educator, former clergyman, church administrator*
Armstrong, Richard William *bank executive, management consultant*
Byrd, Stephen Fred *human resource consultant*
Calligan, William Dennis *retired life insurance company executive*
†Carter, Ashley Hale *physicist, educator*
Chang, Darwin Ray *civil engineer*
Demain, Arnold Lester *microbiologist, educator*
Denholtz, Elaine Grudin *literature educator, writer*
Edwards, Lillie Johnson *history educator*
Ellenbogen, Leon *nutritionist, pharmaceutical company executive*
Essner, Robert Alan *pharmaceutical executive*
†Farias, Joseph G. *priest, consultant*
Foy, Martin Thomas, Jr., *pharmacist*
Goodman, Michael B(arry) *communications educator*
†Guigon, John V. *corporate lawyer*
Johnson, William Joseph *investment manager*
†Leavell, John Perry, Jr., *historian, educator*
†McGrath, Joseph Patrick *lawyer*
Mertz, Francis James *university president*
Monte, Bonnie J. *performing company executive, director, educator*
O'Brien, Mary Devon *communications executive, consultant*
Parker, Henry Griffith, III, *insurance executive*
Perriman, Wendy Karen *poet, educator*
Reader, Jonathan Whittier *sociology educator, consultant*
Siegel, George Henry *international business development consultant*
†Silvestri, Michael Anthony *music educator*
Stafford, John Rogers *pharmaceutical and household products company executive*
Van Cleef, Jabez Lindsay *marketing professional*
Van Wyk, Christopher John *computer science educator*
Weiner, Lowell B. *corporate communications executive*
Yrigoyen, Charles, Jr., *church denomination executive*

Mahwah
Eisner, Susan Pamela *communications executive, management consultant, educator*
Frundt, Henry John *sociologist, educator*
Geiling, Louise Elizabeth *elementary school educator, secondary school educator*
Gerstein, David Brown *hardware manufacturing company executive, professional basketball team executive*
Grgin, Joseph Michael *environmental engineer*
†Johnson, Roger *science educator*
King, Lis Sonder *writer*
Padovano, Anthony Thomas *theologian, educator*
†Rakotobe-Joel, Thierry *engineering educator, researcher*
Wagner, Susan Jane *sales and marketing consulting company executive*
Yeh, Lun-Shu Ray *electrochemist*

Manahawkin
Logan, Ralph Andre *physicist*

Manalapan
Barratt, Donna Lee *elementary school educator*
Kelter, Richard John *physician*
†Reisman, Joan Ann *executive secretary*
†Saretzky, Gary D. *archivist*
Stone, Fred Michael *lawyer*

Manasquan
Abate, John E. *electrical and electronic engineer, communications consultant*
Branco, James Joseph *estate planner*
Pond, Thomas Alexander *physics educator, university official*
Sbarbaro, Robert Arthur *banker*

Mantua
†Holt, Robert Donald *columnist, auditor*

Maple Shade
Abidi, S. Manzoor *neurologist*
Bryant, Walter *secondary school educator*
Gordon, Paul *retired dentist, artist*

Maplewood
Hamburger, Mary Ann *medical management consultant*
†Joel, Amos Edward, Jr., *telecommunications consultant*
Johnson, Dewey, Jr., *retired biochemist*
Lally, Michael David *writer, actor*
Laramee, Elaine R. *magazine editor*
Rabadeau, Mary Frances *protective services official*
Safian, Gail Robyn *public relations executive*
Shuttleworth, Anne Margaret *psychiatrist*
Slepian, David *mathematician, communications engineer*
Tatyrek, Alfred Frank *consultant, materials and environmental engineer, analytical and research chemist*
Zoss, Abraham Oscar *chemical company executive*

Margate City
Karsten, Philip *air traffic control automation system designer*
Rose, Jodi *opera company founder and artistic director*
Stoolman, Herbert Leonard *public relations executive*
Videll, Jared Steven *cardiologist*

Marlboro
†Francisco, Deborah Antosh *educational administrative professional*
Kayafas, Stephanie Ann *special education educator, consultant, supervisor, actress*
Miller, Duane King *health and beauty care company executive*

Marlton
Benjamin, Leni Bernice *elementary education educator*
Brown-Buchanan, Deborah Ann *financial consultant*
Cheney, Daniel Lavern *retired magazine publisher*
Cheney, Eleanora Louise *retired secondary education educator*
Clemens, David Allen *minister*
Cullen, Mary Lynne *artist*
Farnath, Dorothy Whitmyer *recruitment company executive*
Farwell, Nancy Larraine *public relations executive*
Gorenberg, Charles Lloyd *financial services executive*
Gottfried, Benjamin Frank *retired manufacturing executive*
Kahn, Sigmund Benham *retired internist and dean*
Klein, Anne Sceia *public relations executive*
Klein, Gerhart Leopold *public relations executive*
Letizia, Dorothy *nursing educator*
Lindholm, Lori Ann *naval officer*
McCullen, Michael John *retired advertising executive*
Samek, Edward Lasker *service company executive*
Shapiro, Ellen Goldberg *music educator*
Sidelsky, Patricia Loney *science educator*

Marmora
Graves, Thomas Browning *investment banker*
Ingaglio, Diego Augustus *dentist*

Martinsville
†Raby, John Cornelius *secondary school educator*
Squire, Laurie Rubin *media consultant*
Weiss, Allan Joseph *transport company executive, lawyer*

Matawan
Amato, Vincent Vito *business executive*
†Campbell, Earl Duncan *computer consultant*
Katz, Irwin *marketing executive*
Liggett, Twila Marie Christensen *academic administrator, public television executive*
Rivera-Dominguez, Alberto *mathematics educator, mechanical engineer*
Swett-Brasefield, Susan *chemical engineer*
†Thompson, Samuel Donald *assemblyman*

Mays Landing
Benner, Richard Byron *philosophy educator*
Connor, Wilda *government health agency administrator*
†Gormley, William L. *state legislator*
Seigel, Andrew Mark *music educator, consultant*

Mc Afee
Fogel, Richard *lawyer, educator*

Medford
Brown, Annie Marie Vedel *real estate broker*
Burgess, Samuel Bullock *pathologist, consultant*
Dunn, Roy J. *landscape architect*
Henderson, Rita Elizabeth *literary agent, journalist*
Hogan, Thomas Harlan *publisher*
Kapfer, Miriam Bierbaum *technical documentation and training specialist*
Keele, Lyndon Alan *electronics executive*
Klugman, Peter Jay *psychologist, consultant*
Mayer, Joyce Harris *artist*
Murphy, David Thomas *secondary school educator*
†Saltus, Phyllis Borzelliere *music educator*

Mendham
Dombrowski, Robert Theodore *materials scientist and information architect*
Haldopoulos, Martha A. *psychologist*
Hesselink, Ann Patrice *financial executive, lawyer*
Kirby, Allan Price, Jr., *investment company executive*
Lunt, Harry Edward *metallurgist, consultant*
Pierson, Robert David *investor*
Posunko, Barbara *retired elementary education educator*
Posunko, Linda Mary *retired elementary education educator*
Rosensaft, Lester Jay *management consultant, lawyer, consultant*
Tramutola, Joseph Louis *lawyer, educator*

Mercerville
Wentz, Debra Linowitz *professional association executive*

Metuchen
Adlerman, Kimberly Marie *illustrator, writer, graphics designer*

†Arbeiter, Joan *artist, educator*
Eugene, John *lawyer*
Frizell, David J. *lawyer*
Macarin-Mara, Lynn *psychotherapist, consultant*
Madden, John Francis *fundraising executive*
Orr, Robert Andrew *management consultant*
Rodriguez-Laguna, Asela *Spanish language and literature educator*
Slobodien, Howard David *surgeon, educator*
Smyth, David *editor*

Middletown
†Azzolina, Joseph *state legislator, grocery executive*
Bishop, Gordon Bruce *journalist*
Braddom, Randall Lee *physician, medical educator*
Cooley, Sidney Elizabeth Ann *engineer*
†Friedman, Richard Lloyd *lawyer*
Granstrom, Marvin Leroy *civil and sanitary engineering educator*
Heng, Siang Gek *communications executive*
Hernon, Richard Francis *civil engineer*
†Iannone, Patrick Paul *optics scientist, researcher*
Jaros, Robert James *information technology executive*
Klincewicz, John Gregory *deacon, mathematician*
†Kogan, Yaakov *mathematician, researcher*
Lundgren, Carl William, Jr., *physicist*
Luo, Wei *electronics engineer*
Meyler, William Anthony *financial executive*
†Noel, Eric *electrical engineer*
O'Neill, Eugene Francis *retired communications engineer*
Orost, Joseph Martin *computer scientist*
Shields, Patricia Lynn *educational broker, consultant*

Midland Park
†Russo, David C. *state legislator*
Varallo, D. Vincent *educator*

Millburn
Diamond, Richard S. *lawyer*
Erenburg, Steven Alan *communications executive*
Grosman, Alan M. *lawyer*
Heistein, Robert Kenneth *obstetrician and gynecologist*
Kern, Arthur Stephen *physician*
Kuttner, Bernard A. *retired judge*
Sostowski, Richard Mark *physician, forensic psychiatrist, psychoanalyst*
Wilkinson, Clifford Steven *civil engineer*

Millington
Glockmann, Walter Friedrich *physicist, consultant*

Milltown
†Haws, Robert John *lawyer*
Sacharow, Beverly *gerontologist*
Sacharow, Stanley *chemist, consultant, writer*

Millville
†Bunting, John L. *counseling administrator, insurance agent*
Caldwell, Linda E. *critical care nurse*

Mine Hill
Nadeau, Michael Joseph *staff assistant*
Robertiello, Gina Marie *criminal justice educator*

Monmouth Beach
Herbert, LeRoy James *retired accounting firm executive*

Monmouth Junction
Lancaster, Barbara Mae *management consulting company executive*
Lawton, Deborah Simmons *library director, educational media specialist*
†Lien, Ting-Ting *music educator*
Prestbo, John Andrew *newspaper editor, journalist, author*

Monroe
†Greenstein, Linda R. *assemblywoman*

Monroe Township
Avery, James Stephen *oil company executive*
Cushman, Helen Merle Baker *retired management consultant*
de la Bandera, Elna Marie *interpreter, translator*
Liebson, Milt *sculptor, educator, author*
Meshowski, Frank Robert *business consultant*
Miller, Isadore *television executive, consultant*
Reichek, Morton Arthur *retired magazine editor, writer*
Rosenthal, Louis Aaron *electrical engineer*
Wallach, Jacques Burton *pathologist, educator*
Wolfe, Deborah Cannon Partridge *government education consultant, educator, clergy*
Zeigen, Spencer Steven *architect, consultant*

Montclair
Barnard, Kurt *retail trend/consumer spending forecaster, publisher*
Beerman, Miriam *artist, educator*
†Bolden, Theodore Edward *dentist, consultant, dental educator*
Brown, Geraldine Reed *lawyer, consulting executive*
†Brown, Ronald Wellington *lawyer, educator, consultant, business executive, entrepreneur*
Campbell, Stewart Fred *foundation executive*
Cannon, David Price *video executive, advertising consultant*
Cass, Mary Louise *librarian*
Chinard, Francis Pierre *physiologist, physician, consultant*
Clech, Jean Paul Marie *mechanical engineer*
Cole, Susan A. *university president, English language educator*
Conrad, David Williams *lawyer*
Delgado, Ramon Louis *educator, author, director, playwright, lyricist*
Eager, George Sidney, Jr., *electrical engineer, business executive*
Ewers, Paul Joseph *priest*
Fannin, Caroline Mather *library administrator*
George, Nashwa E. *accountant, educator*
Gill, Nia H. *state legislator*
Gollob, Herman Cohen *retired publishing company, editor*
Gregory, Maughn Rollins *education educator*
Gutman, Richard Martin *lawyer*
Harvey, Richard Dudley *marketing consultant*
Jacoby, Tamar *journalist, author*
†Ju, Semmy *educational administrator*
Kaiser, Richard Alan *surgeon*
Kowalski, Stephen Wesley *retired chemistry educator*
Lang, William Charles *financial executive*
Leggett, Paul Arthur *minister*
Luftglass, Murray Arnold *corporate financial executive*
Mason, Lucile Gertrude *fundraiser, consultant*
McConnell, Lorelei Catherine *retired library director*
O'Malley, Eileen (Eileen Ann O'Malley) *medical/surgical nurse*
Phillips, Ann Y. *art advisor*
Pransky, Joan E. *lawyer, community organizer*
†Rights, Edith Marie Anderson *retired librarian*
Seligman, Lynn *literary agent*
Walker, George Theophilus, Jr., *composer, pianist, music educator*
Ward, Roger Coursen *lawyer*
†Wasko, James W *music educator*
Weischadle, David Emmanuel *education educator*

Montvale
Corrado, Fred *food company executive*
De Caro, Barbara Ann Mary *health and physical education educator*
Dowden, Mark Vincent *editor, publishing company executive*
Fontana, John Arthur *employee benefits specialist*
Litchfield, John Edward *chemist*
Mantell, Keith C. *chemical engineer*
Politi, Beth Kukkonen *publishing services company executive*
Showalter, David Scott *accounting executive*

Montville
Buzak, Edward Joseph *lawyer*
Coleman, Earl Maxwell *publishing company executive*
Klapper, Byron D. *financial company executive*
Leeson, Lewis Joseph *research pharmacist, scientist*
Teubner, Ferdinand Cary, Jr., *retired publishing company executive*
Willis, Carl Raeburn, Jr., *pharmaceutical executive*

Moorestown
Apperson, Jack Alfonso *retired army officer, business executive*
Atilgan, Timur Faik *structural engineer*
Carson, William Charles *sales and marketing executive*
Cervantes, Luis Augusto *neurosurgeon*
Delano-Condax, Kate (Kate Delano-Condax Decker) *marketing and public relations executive*
Kearney, John Francis, III, *lawyer*
Lipscomb, Thomas Heber, Jr., *retired civil engineer*
Slemmer, Carl Weber, Jr., *retired lawyer*
Springer, Douglas Hyde *retired food company executive, lawyer*

Morganville
Kellner, Millicent H. *social worker, researcher*
Lechtanski, Cheryl Lee *chiropractor*
Sternfeld, Marc Howard *finance educator*
West, Earle Huddleston *communications company professional*

Morris Plains
Capellos, Chris Spiridon *chemist*
Chamorro, Juan Pablo *financial analyst, business development executive*
†DeCroce, Alex *state legislator*
Elias, Salwa Emil Ghabrial *allergist, immunologist, pediatrician*
Falci, Dennis Michael *sales executive, pharmaceutical executive*
Fielding, Stuart *psychopharmacologist*
Gulfo, Adele Madelyn *pharmaceutical marketing executive*
Inez, Donna Lee *hospital administrator*
†Martin, Robert J. *state legislator*
O'Neill, Robert Edward *business journal editor*
Otani, Mike *optical company executive*
Slaby, Louis Richard *civil and mechanical engineer*
Spong, John Shelby *retired bishop*

Morristown
Aspero, Benedict Vincent *lawyer*
†Barba, Julius William *lawyer*
Bartkus, Robert Edward *lawyer*
Berkley, Peter Lee *lawyer*
Bernstein, Jan Lenore *lawyer*
Bockian, James Bernard *computer systems executive, writer*
Bromberg, Myron James *lawyer*
†Bryant, George McEwan *lawyer*
Cameron, Nicholas Allen *diversified corporation executive*
†Capezza, Michelle *lawyer*
†Carroll, Michael Patrick *assemblyman*
Chevinsky, Aaron Harry *surgeon*
Clark, Grant Lawrence *corporate lawyer*
Cote, David M. *diversified technology and manufacturing company executive*
Cregan, Frank Robert *financial executive, consultant*
Cucco, Judith Elene *international marketing professional*
De Rosa, William Thomas *internist, hematologist, oncologist*
DiSerio, Frank Joseph *pharmaceutical company executive, consultant*
Doyle, David Perrie *lawyer*
†Edwards, Peter S. *executive management/computer consulting*
Finkel, Marion Judith *physician, pharmaceutical company administrator*
Fishman, Richard Glenn *lawyer, accountant*
Fletcher, Michael S. *lawyer*
Flynn, Marie Cosgrove *portfolio manager, corporate financial executive*
Fredericks, Robert Joseph *language company executive*
Garrett, Mark William *research engineer*
Geppert, John Gustave, Jr., *lawyer*
Gillen, James Robert *lawyer, insurance company executive*
Golecki, Ilan *physicist, researcher, educator*
Hafer, Frederick Douglass *utility executive*
Hansbury, Stephan Charles *judge*
Haselmann, John Philip *management consultant*
Herman, Robert Lewis *cork company executive*
Hernandez, Marissa *physicist*
Herzberg, Peter Jay *lawyer*
Hittinger, William Charles *electronics company executive*
Huck, John Lloyd *pharmaceutical company executive*
Huettner, Richard Alfred *lawyer*
Humick, Thomas Charles Campbell *lawyer*
Hyland, William Francis *lawyer*
Kagan, Val Alexander *engineer, researcher, educator*
Kearns, William Michael, Jr., *investment banker*
Kirby, Fred Morgan, II, *corporation executive*
Korf, Gene Robert *lawyer*
Kreindler, Peter Michael *lawyer*
Largman, Theodore *consultant*
LaVecchia, Jaynee *state supreme court justice*
Lieberman, Lester Zane *engineering company executive*
MacKinnis, Ann Phelps *municipal government and land use management executive*
McConnell, John Howard *personnel management consultant, writer*
†McMahon, Kevin J. *telecommunications industry executive*
Miller, Steven H. *museum director*
Moore, Milo Anderson *banker*
Morrissey, Michael Joseph *investment banker*
Munson, William Leslie *insurance company executive*
Murthy, Andiappan K.S. *technology manager*
Musa, John Davis *computer and infosystems executive, software reliability engineering researcher and expert, independent consultant, educator*
Nadaskay, Raymond *architect*
O'Grady, Dennis Joseph *lawyer*
Olcott, John Whiting *aviation executive*
Parr, Grant Van Siclen *surgeon*
†Pavlovich, John Stephen *civil engineer*
†Pokelwaldt, Robert N. *former manufacturing company executive*
Pollock, Stewart Glasson *lawyer, former state supreme court justice*
Prince, Leah Fanchon *art educator and research institute administrator*
Rainal, Attilio Joseph *retired electronics engineer, researcher*
Raziq, Yaqub *telecommunications engineer*
Reiley, T. Phillip *consultant*
Rose, Robert Gordon *lawyer*
Rosenthal, Meyer L(ouis) *lawyer*
Rusch, George Michael *toxicology and risk assessment director*
Scott, Richard Thomas Thomas, Jr., *reproductive endocrinologist*
Sherman, Sandra Brown *lawyer*
Sincoskie, W. David *computer engineer*
Speer, John Kirby *judge*
Stanton, Patrick Michael *lawyer*
†Stranghoener, Larry W. *manufacturing company executive*
†Weisman, Steven Martin *pharmacologist, consultant*
Whitmer, Frederick Lee *lawyer*
Williams, Joseph Dalton *pharmaceutical company executive*

Mount Arlington
Cohen, Irving David *science administrator*

Mount Freedom
Allen, B. Marc *managed care executive*

Mount Holly
†Basmajian, Thomas Stephen *actor, performing arts association administrator*
†Mancini, Lois Jean *elementary education educator*
Mintz, Jeffry Alan *lawyer, mediator, consultant*

Mount Laurel
†Bark, Martha W. *state legislator*
Batory, Ronald Louis *rail transportation executive*
†Bodine, Francis L. *state legislator*
Buchan, Alan Bradley *rail transportation executive, consultant*
†Chatzidakis, Larry *assemblyman*
Hayken, Gerald Dreux *orthopedic surgeon*
†Huttner, Louise Ann *mathematician, educator*
Laubach, Roger Alvin *accountant*
Li, Pearl Nei-Chien Chu *technology company executive*
Mann, Louis Eugene *financial planner*
Panichi-Egberts, Michele A. *healthcare facility manager*
Rabbe, David Ellsworth *oil company executive*
†Ruggiano, Cheryl Anna *minister, insurance agent*
Torres, Robert Alvin *dancer, singer, actor, sign language interpreter*

Mountain Lakes
Cook, Charles Francis *insurance executive*
Daniel, Royal Thomas, III, *lawyer, engineer, accountant*
†Loomis, Rebecca C. *psychology educator*
O'Gara, Barbara Ann *soap company executive*

Mountainside
Helander, Robert Charles *lawyer*
Horner, Shirley Jaye *columnist, writing and publishing consultant*
Lingle, Kathleen McCall *human resources specialist, consultant, marketing executive, entrepreneur*
Lipton, Bronna Jane *marketing communications executive*
†Nielsen, Gwyn English *writer, illustrator, publishing executive*
Slabe, James F. *business executive*
Vice, Susan F. *medicinal chemist*
Weigele, Richard Sayre *police officer*
†Weiseman, Jac Burton *lawyer*

Murray Hill
†D'Amelio, Frank Anthony *communications company executive*
†Divakaran, Ajay *electrical engineer, research and development company executive*
Garfias, Luis Francisco *chemical engineering researcher*
Kozhevnikov, Michael Boris *physicist, researcher*
Morgan, Dennis Raymond *electrical engineer*
†Ritchie, Dennis M. *software engineer*
Weiss, Alan Arthur *mathematician, researcher*

Neptune
Aguiar, Adam Martin *chemist, educator*
†Breen, Stephen P. *editorial cartoonist*
Collins, Robert T. *publisher*
†Harran, Susan R. *small business owner, writer*
Hersh, Steven Lance *clinical hypnotherapist, hypnocounselor, author*
Karlan, Andrew Warren (Drew Karlan) *pharmaceutical company executive*
Mann, William Joseph, Jr., *gynecologic oncologist*
Manuel, Sandra Lorraine *minister*
Rice, Stephen Gary *medical educator, sports medicine physician*
Ventura, Anthony Paul *artist, fine art educator*
Weber, Charles Alfred, II, *internist, rheumatologist*
Zurick, Jack *electrical engineer, consultant*

Neptune City
Axelrod, Glen Scott *publishing company executive, pet product company executive*

Neshanic Station
Muckenhoupt, Benjamin *retired mathematics educator*

New Brunswick
Aisner, Joseph *oncologist, physician*
Alexander, Robert Jackson *economist, educator*
Allender, Eric Warren *computer science educator*
Andrews, Clinton James *public affairs educator*
Aronoff, Myron Joel *anthropologist, educator, political scientist, educator*
Awan, Ahmad Noor *civil engineer*
Bachmann, Gloria Ann *physician, educator*
†Bahri, Abbas *mathematician, educator*
†Bahun, Sanja *literature educator, researcher*
Becker, Ronald Leonard *archivist*
†Bell, Rudolph *historian, educator*
Bertino, Joseph Rocco *physician, educator*
†Biribauer, Richard Frank *lawyer*
Bowden, Henry Warner *religion educator*
Brilliant, Eleanor Luria *social work educator*
Burke, James Edward *consumer products company executive*
Cate, Phillip Dennis *art museum director emeritus*
Chambers, John Whiteclay, II, *history educator*
Chandler, James John *surgeon, educator*
Day, Peter Rodney *geneticist, educator*
Day-Salvatore, Debra Lynn *medical geneticist*
†Doorley, John *marketing professional, educator*
Dougherty, Neil Joseph *physical education educator, safety consultant*
Durnin, Richard Gerry *education educator*
Dutta, Manoranjan *economics educator*
Ehrenfeld, David William *biology educator, writer*
Ettinger, Lawrence Jay *pediatric hematologist and oncologist, educator*
Figueira, Thomas John *classics educator*
Fine, Roger Seth *pharmaceutical executive, lawyer*
†Fishbein, Leslie Ellen *humanities educator*
Fisher, Hans *nutritional biochemistry educator*
Franks, Robert D. (Bob Franks) *former congressman*
Funk, Cyril Reed, Jr., *agronomist, educator*
Garner, Charles William *educational administration educator, consultant*
Gillette, William *historian, educator*
Glasser, Paul Harold *sociologist, educator, social worker, university administrator*
Glickman, Norman Jay *economist, urban policy analyst*
Gocke, David Joseph *immunology educator, physician, medical scientist*
Goffen, Rona *art educator, educator*
Gottlieb, Alice Bendix *medical educator*
Graham, Alan Morrison *surgeon*
Grassle, Judith Payne *marine biology educator*
Greenberg, Michael Richard *urban studies and community health educator*
Greenwald, Alfred Emanuel *retired cosmetic surgeon*
Griffin, Gary Arthur *technological products executive*
†Grimes, Julia Patrice *physician, researcher*
Grob, Gerald N. *historian, educator*
Gussin, Robert Zalmon *retired healthcare company executive*

Haines, William Joseph *pharmaceutical company executive*
Hartman, Mary S. *historian, educator*
†Heisen, JoAnn Heffernan *health care company executive*
Henry, Paula Louise (Paula Louise Henry Coover) *academic administrator*
Horowitz, Irving Louis *publisher, educator*
†Idler, Ellen Louise *education educator*
†Jagerman, David Lewis *mathematician*
Jaluria, Yogesh *mechanical engineering educator*
Jenkins, Alyce Mitchem *secondary school educator, writer*
†Jenkins, Reese V. *historian, educator*
Johnson, James Turner *theology studies educator*
Kansfield, Norman J. *seminary president*
Kantor, Paul *information scientist, educator*
Katz, James E. *communications educator*
†Kaufman, Kenneth Roland *psychiatrist, educator*
Kelley, Donald Reed *historian*
Killingsworth, Mark R. *economics educator, consultant*
†Kruskal, Martin David *mathematical physicist, astrophysicist*
Kubey, Robert William *media educator, developmental psychologist, television analyst and researcher*
Kulikowski, Casimir Alexander *computer science and engineering educator*
Lachance, Paul Albert *food science educator, clergyman*
Larsen, Ralph S(tanley) *retired pharmaceutical company executive*
Lears, Thomas Jackson *history educator*
Ledgin, Stephanie P. *music journalist, educator*
Lenehan, James T. *pharmaceutical executive*
†Lepore, Frederick Everett *neurologist, educator*
Levine, George Lewis *English language educator, literature critic*
†Lewis, Michael *pediatrician, educator*
Liao, Mei-June *biopharmaceutical company executive*
Louis, Barbara R. *psychologist, educator, consultant*
†Lowry, Stephen F. *surgeon, educator*
Makhija, Mohan *nuclear medicine physician*
Mandelbaum, David Ezra *pediatric neurologist*
Maramorosch, Karl *virologist, educator*
Marder, Tod A. *art historian, educator*
McCormick, Richard Levis *academic administrator*
McGuire, John Lawrence *pharmaceuticals executive*
†Mears, David R. *education educator, consultant*
Mechanic, David *social sciences educator*
Midlarsky, Manus Issachar *political scientist, educator*
Miller, Arthur Harold *lawyer*
Mills, Dorothy Allen *investor*
Mills, George Marshall *insurance consultant*
Miskiewicz, Susanne Piatek *educational administrator*
Momah, Ethel Chukwuekwe *women's health nurse*
Mondschein, Lawrence Geoffrey *medical products executive*
Montville, Thomas Joseph *food microbiologist, educator*
Moreyra, Abel E. *physician, medical educator*
Nelson, Jack Lee *education educator*
†Niessen, James Phineas *librarian, historian*
†Nixon, Kenneth Elmer *academic administrator*
†Nordstrom, Karl Fredrik *geographer, educator*
Nosher, John Louis *radiologist*
Nosko, Michael Gerrik *neurosurgeon, educator*
O'Neill, William Lawrence *history educator*
†Onwuchekova, Michael O. *accountant, educator*
Ortiz, Raphael Montañez *performance artist, educator*
Ostriker, Alicia Suskin *poet*
Pallone, Nathaniel John *psychologist, educator*
Pandey, Ramesh Chandra *chemist, executive*
Paz, Harold Louis *dean, medical educator, internist*
Pinals, Robert Stanton *physician*
Pitchumoni, Capecomorin Sankar *gastroenterologist, educator*
Pramer, David *microbiologist, educator, research administrator*
Raska, Karel Frantisek Julian, Jr., *pathologist, virologist, educator*
Reed, James Wesley *social historian, educator*
Reock, Ernest C., Jr., *retired government services educator, academic director*
†Rockoff, Hugh Touff *economist, educator*
Rona, Peter Arnold *oceanographer, researcher, educator*
Rosen, Robert Thomas *analytical and food chemist*
Rosenberg, Norman *surgeon, educator*
Rosenberg, Seymour *psychologist, educator*
Russell, Louise Bennett *economist, educator*
Sage, Jacob I. *neurologist, educator*
Saidi, Parvin *hematologist, medical educator*
Saracevic, Tefko *information science educator*
Sarode, Satyeswara Krishnappa *physician*
Scanlon, Jane Cronin *mathematics educator*
Schaer, Teresa McKinley *internist, geriatrician*
Scott, David Rodick *lawyer, legal educator*
Scully, John Thomas *obstetrician, gynecologist, educator*
Seibold, James Richard *physician, researcher*
Sewell, Robert George *librarian*
†Shapiro, Warren *anthropologist, educator*
†Shirtz, Joseph Frank *lawyer, consultant*
†Sigal, Leonard H. *physician*
Smith, Bonnie Gene *historian, educator*
Smith, Fredric Charles *electrical engineer, consultant*
Stich, Stephen Peter *philosophy educator*
Strauss, Ulrich Paul *chemist, educator*
Strawderman, William E. *statistics educator*
Strickland, Dorothy *education educator*
Swanson, Norman Rasmus *social sciences educator*
†Swee, David Ethan *physician*

Taliaferro, James Hubert, Jr., *communications educator*
Tanner, Daniel *curriculum theory educator*
Tedrow, John Charles Fremont *soils educator*
Tiger, Lionel *social scientist, anthropology consultant*
Toby, Jackson *sociologist, educator*
Trelstad, Robert Laurence *pathology educator, cell biologist*
Tripolitis, Antonia *religion, classics and comparative literature educator*
Tu, Ching-I *humanities educator, researcher*
Turock, Betty Jane *library and information science educator*
Upton, Arthur Canfield *experimental pathologist, educator*
Vayda, Andrew P. *human ecology and anthropology educator*
Wang, Yanxin *research scientist*
†Weibel, Charles Alexander *mathematician*
Weinstein, Melvin Phillip *physician educator*
Weldon, William C. *pharmaceutical executive*
Weng, George Jueng-Cious *engineering educator*
Wilson, Donald Malcolm *publishing executive*
Wilson, Robert Nathan *health care company executive*
†Yorke, Marianne *lawyer, real estate executive*
Zatlin, Phyllis *Spanish language educator, translator*

New Milford
Filardi, Eldonna Marie *music educator, accompanist*
†Rosato, Melissa Anne *educator*

New Monmouth
Santos, Sharon Lee *parochial school educator*

New Providence
Bair, Harvey Edward *polymer scientist*
Barnes, Sandra Henley *publishing company executive*
Bernstein, Nadia J. *lawyer*
Chatterji, Debajyoti *retired manufacturing company executive, educator*
Chen, Yudong *engineer, researcher*
Cho, Alfred Yi *electrical engineer*
Chobot, John Charles *lawyer*
†Cooper, Carol Diane *publishing company executive*
Cooper, R. John, III, *lawyer*
Doescher, William Frederick *communications executive*
Esser, Joseph Allen *editor*
Fitzgerald, Kathleen M. *communications company executive*
Freund, Roland Wilhelm *mathematician*
Helfand, Eugene *chemist*
†Hollister, Dean *publishing company executive*
Hurley, Lawrence Joseph *lawyer*
Kelleher, James Raymond *health care corporation executive*
Lanzerotti, Louis John *physicist*
Laskowski, Edward John *chemist*
Longfield, William Herman *health care company executive*
†Maxeiner, James Randolph *lawyer*
McCaffrey, Robert Henry, Jr., *retired manufacturing company executive*
McCarthy, G. Daniel *lawyer*
Ogawa, Seiji *research scientist, biophysicist*
†Rivo, Shirley Winthrope *artist*
Roth, Robert Howard *psychologist*
Russo, Patricia F. *communications executive*
†SanGiovanni, Mary Elizabeth *writer, freelance manager*
Savari, Serap Ayse *electrical engineer, researcher*
Sivco, Deborah Lee *research materials scientist*
Smith, George Artell *chemical engineer*
White, Alice Elizabeth *physicist, researcher*
Wilderotter, Peter Thomas *non-profit executive*
†Yaghubian, Arman Rugo *industrial engineer*

New Vernon
Dugan, John Leslie, Jr., *foundation executive*
Kushen, Allan Stanford *retired lawyer*
McCormack, John Joseph, Jr., *insurance executive*

Newark
Ackerman, Harold A. *federal judge*
Adler, Freda Schaffer (Mrs. G. O. W. Mueller) *criminologist, educator*
Alito, Samuel Anthony, Jr., *federal judge*
Apuzzio, Joseph J. *obstetrician-gynecologist*
Arabie, Phipps *marketing educator, researcher*
Aregood, Richard Lloyd *editor*
Armenante, Piero M. *chemical engineering educator*
†Arrigo, Cindy Jo *biochemist, researcher*
Askin, Frank *law educator*
†Autin, Diana Marie Therese Katherine *lawyer, educator*
Baer, Susan M. *airport executive*
Baker, Herman *medical educator, author*
Baker, Stephen R. *physician*
†Barannyk, Lyudmyla Leonidivna *mathematician, educator, researcher*
Bar-Ness, Yeheskel *electrical engineer, educator*
Barry, Maryanne Trump *federal judge*
Bergen, Stanley Silvers, Jr., *retired university president, physician*
Bielory, Leonard *allergist, immunologist, medical school administrator*
Bissell, John W. *federal judge*
Bizub, Johanna Catherine *law librarian*
Blackmore, Denis Louis *mathematics educator, researcher*
Boyd, Kanisha *nurse manager*
Brenner, John Finn *lawyer*
†Brescher, John B., Jr., *lawyer*
Cahn, Jeffrey Barton *lawyer*
†Caraballo, Wilfredo *assemblyman*
Carpinelli, John Dominick *computer engineering educator*
Carroll, John Douglas *mathematical and statistical psychologist*

Chen, Chunguang *cardiologist*
Cheng, Mei-Fang *psychobiology educator, neuroethology researcher*
Cherniack, Neil Stanley *physician, medical educator*
Clymer, Brian William *diversified financial services company executive, former state official*
†Cohen, Carol I. *lawyer*
Cohen, Stanley *pathologist, educator*
Contractor, Farok *business and management educator*
Cook, Stuart Donald *physician, educator*
Costenbader, Charles Michael *lawyer*
Creenan, Katherine Heras *lawyer*
Cummis, Clive Sanford *lawyer*
Cunningham-Stevens, Vandetta Antoinette *practical nurse, poet*
Curley, Augustine James Francis *priest, educator*
Darr, Walter Robert *financial analyst*
D'Astolfo, Frank Joseph *graphic designer, educator*
Davis, Yvonne D. *county official*
Day, Edward Francis, Jr., *lawyer*
Debevoise, Dickinson Richards *federal judge*
Dee, Francis X. *lawyer*
Defeis, Elizabeth Frances *law educator, lawyer*
Del Tufo, Robert J. *lawyer, former US attorney, former state attorney general*
Dennery, Linda *newspaper publishing executive*
Deutsch, Stuart Lewis *law educator*
Dhawan, Atam Prakash *engineering educator, dean*
Diner, Steven Jay *history educator*
Docarmo, Jerry Soares *academic administrator*
Donahoo, James Saunders *cardiothoracic surgeon*
Einzig, Stanley *pediatric cardiologist, researcher*
Eittreim, Richard MacNutt *lawyer*
†Eljabiri, Osama M. *education educator, director*
English, Nicholas Conover *lawyer*
Evans, Hugh E. *pediatrician, educator*
Everett, Richard G. *newspaper editor*
Feldman, Cecile Arlene *dentist*
Fenster, Saul K. *university president emeritus*
Ferguson, Yale Hicks *political science educator*
Ferland, E. James *electric power industry executive*
Flagg, E(loise) Alma Williams *educational administrator*
Fox, Jeanne Marie *lawyer*
Fox, Sandra Gail *insurance marketing executive*
Franklin, H. Bruce *language educator, writer*
Freilich, Irvin Mayer *lawyer*
Friedland, Bernard *engineer, educator*
Fu, Shoucheng Joseph *biomedicine educator*
Fuentes, Julio M. *federal judge*
Garde, John Charles *lawyer*
Garth, Leonard I. *judge*
Givens, Theartis Tina Mansfield *primary school educator*
Goldman, Glenn *architecture educator, architect*
†Goldman, Lois M. *transportation planner*
Gopalakrishnan, Shanthi *technology educator*
Greenaway, Joseph Anthony, Jr., *judge*
Greenberg, Stephen Michael *lawyer, business executive*
†Hadas, Rachel *poet, educator*
Hamarman, Stephanie *psychiatrist, educator*
Hanesian, Deran *chemical engineer, chemistry and environmental science educator, consultant*
Haring, Eugene Miller *lawyer*
Harrison, Roslyn Siman *lawyer*
Haycock, Christine Elizabeth *retired medical educator, health educator*
Herman, Steven Douglas *cardiothoracic surgeon, educator*
†Hill, Richard Warren *lawyer*
Hiltz, Starr Roxanne *sociologist, educator, computer scientist, writer, lecturer, consultant*
Hobson, Robert Wayne, II, *surgeon*
Hollander, Toby Edward *education educator*
Howard, M(oses) William, Jr., *minister*
Hrycak, Peter *mechanical engineer, educator*
Hudson-Zonn, Eliza *nurse, psychologist*
Iffy, Leslie *medical educator*
Jackson, Nancy Lee *geography educator*
James, Sharpe *mayor, state legislator*
Joffe, Russell T. *dean*
Johnson, Evelyn *minister, educator*
Kamalakar, Peri *pediatrician*
Kantor, Mel Lewis *dental educator, researcher*
†Kappraff, Jay Marvin *mathematics educator*
Karp, Donald Mathew *lawyer, banker*
Khera, Raj Pal *civil and environmental engineering educator*
Kimmelman, Burt Joseph *English language and literature educator*
Klein, Kenneth Michael *pathologist*
Knee, Stephen H. *lawyer*
Kott, David Russell *lawyer*
Kuller, Jonathan Mark *lawyer*
†Lama, Paul J. *surgeon, educator*
Lazar, Lynn *art association administrator, actress*
Lechner, Alfred James, Jr., *judge*
Ledeen, Robert Wagner *neurochemist, educator*
Leevy, Carroll Moton *medical educator, hepatology researcher*
Levine, Benjamin *lawyer*
Liftin, John M. *lawyer*
Liftin, John Matthew *lawyer*
Little, Alan Brian *obstetrician, gynecologist, educator*
Lowenkron, Ruth *lawyer*
†Macal, Zdenek *conductor*
Marino, William J. *insurance executive*
†Martin, Henry John *music educator, composer*
Martin, James Hanley *deputy state attorney general*
Martini, William J. *former congressman, state commissioner, judge*
Materna, Thomas Walter *ophthalmologist*
McElwee, Bernard *management educator*
†McGuire, William B(enedict) *lawyer*
McKinney, John Adams, Jr., *lawyer*

McNeil, Rodney Malcolm *poet, writer*
†Medvin, Alan York *lawyer*
Miller, Richard Allan *lawyer*
Mitra, Somenath Sam *environmental scientist, educator*
Miura, Robert Mitsuru *mathematician, researcher, educator*
Monty, Gloria *former television producer, film executive*
Morris-Yamba, Trish *educational and social service association director*
†Munoz, Eric *surgeon*
Muscato, Andrew *lawyer*
†Nakayama, Marvin K. *computer scientist, educator*
Nash, Alicia *computer programmer, physicist*
Nehring, Wendy Marie *pediatrics nurse*
Neuer, Philip David *lawyer, real estate consultant*
Newhouse, Mark William *publishing executive*
O'Connor Quinn, Deirdre *lawyer*
Pagán, Gilberto, Jr., *clinical psychologist*
Passantino, Benjamin Arthur *business/marketing executive*
Paul, James Caverly Newlin *law educator, retired dean*
†Payne, William D. *assemblyman*
Pfeffer, Edward Israel *educational administrator*
Pignataro, Louis James *engineering educator*
†Pletcher, Beth *medical geneticist*
Pollock, Jeffrey M. *lawyer*
Qiu, Zeyuan *researcher, educator*
†Rainey, Matt *photographer*
Rak, Lorraine Karen *lawyer*
†Raveson, Louis Sheppard *lawyer, educator*
Reich, Laurence *lawyer*
Reichman, Lee Brodersohn *physician*
Reilly, William Thomas *lawyer*
Reynolds, Valrae *museum curator*
†Rice, Ronald L. *state legislator*
Robertson, William Withers *lawyer*
Rosato, Anthony Dominick *mechanical engineer, educator*
Ryan, Arthur Frederick *insurance company executive*
†Ryan, Lisa Kathleen *education educator, consultant*
†Scally, John Joseph, Jr., *lawyer*
Schachter, Hindy Lauer *public management educator*
†Schachter, Paul *lawyer*
†Schleifer, Steven J *psychiatrist, educator*
Schoonmaker, L. Craig *political organization executive*
Schwartz, Robert Allen *dermatologist, educator*
Schweizer, Karl Wolfgang *historian, author*
Seiglie, Carlos *finance educator*
Serota, Scott *medical association administrator*
Sher, Richard B. *historian, educator*
†Shi, Yun Qing *electrical engineer*
†Shih, Frank Yeong-Chyang *computer scientist, researcher*
†Shishkin, Dimitri Victor *mechanical engineer, consultant*
Siegal, Joel Davis *lawyer*
Silipigni, Alfredo *opera conductor*
Simmons, Peter *law and urban planning educator*
Slavitt, Ben J. *lawyer*
Spillers, William Russell *civil engineering educator*
Spruch, Grace Marmor *physics educator*
Stevenson, Joanne Sabol *older adults care provider, educator, researcher*
Storrer, William Allin *consultant*
Thomas, Andrew Philip *physiologist*
Tischman, Michael Bernard *lawyer*
†Tucker, Donald *assemblyman*
Vajtay, Stephen Michael, Jr., *lawyer*
Valyo, Judy Ann *dean*
Varzegar, Minoo *English educator, reading specialist*
†Vatner, Stephen F. *physiologist, researcher, research scientist*
Wachenfeld, William Thomas *lawyer, foundation executive*
Waelde, Lawrence Richard *chemist*
†Wayne, Robert Andrew *lawyer*
Weiss, Gerson *physician, educator*
Weiss, Stanley H. *physician, epidemiologist, researcher, education educator, consultant, oncologist*
Willse, James Patrick *newspaper editor*
Wyer, James Ingersoll *lawyer*
Zarbin, Marco Attilio *ophthalmologist, surgeon, educator*
Ziavras, Sotirios George *computer and electrical engineer, educator*
Zuckerman, Herbert Lawrence *lawyer*

Newfield
Dreher, Jr., Frank H. *retired optician*
Hartman, Jeffrey Edward *pastor*

Newfoundland
Van Winkle, Edgar Walling *retired electrical engineer, computer consultant*

Newton
Clymer, Jerry Alan *educational administrator*
Colizza, Wayne Anthony *orthopaedic surgeon*
Cox, William Martin *lawyer, educator*
Johnson, Roland Eric *internist*
Koerber, Joan C. *retired educator*
MacMurren, Margaret Patricia *secondary education educator, consultant*
†McHose, Alison Littell *assemblywoman*
Peters, Kurt James *obstetrician, gynecologist*
Worman, Linda Kay *nursing administrator*

North Arlington
Batshaw, Marilyn Seidner *education administrator*
Benedetto, Lorraine Ann *computer scientist*
Borowski, Jennifer Lucile *corporate administrator*

GEOGRAPHICAL INDEX 5975 NEW JERSEY

North Bergen
Kim, Kun-Kil *emergency medicine physician*
Latzko, William J. *management consultant*
Micale, Joseph Nicholas *internist*
Mongelli, Thomas Guy *broadcast executive, radio personality*
Pohan, Armand *transportation executive, professional hockey club executive, lawyer*
†Schumacher, Barret *motion picture propman, writer*
†Slatner, Thomas Allen *bookseller*

North Brunswick
Bern, Ronald Lawrence *consulting company executive*
Burtnick, Ronald *software consultant, educator*
Campbell, Robert Emmett *retired health care products company executive, medical association administrator*
†Cirillo, Vincent J. *medical historian, consultant*
†Ghosh, Alok *pharmaceutical executive*
Kahrmann, Linda Irene *child care supervisor*
Mahajan, Sanjiv Rai *entrepreneur*
Shapiro, Marsha N. *social worker*
Spears, Marcia Hopp *nursing educator, health facility administrator*

North Caldwell
Stevens, William Dollard *consulting mechanical engineer*

North Haledon
Dougherty, June Eileen *librarian*
McGill, Kenneth, Jr., *mental health services professional*
Onove, Daniel James *elementary educator*

North Plainfield
Dowling, Joan E. *lawyer*
Stillwagon, Wesley William *corporate professional*
Stroppel, Betty MacNair *artist, educator*
Thomas, Lewis *physicist, researcher*
Weinberger, George Ian *dermatologist*

Northvale
Aronson, Jason *publisher*
Barna, Richard Allen *lighting company executive, broadcasting executive*
Di Mino, André Anthony *manufacturing executive, consultant*
Heslin, Cathleen Jane *artist, designer, entrepreneur*
†Kota, Venkata Rangaiah *research scientist, researcher*
Mittleberg, Eric Michael *pharmaceutical executive*

Norwood
Barbini, Richard John *chemical engineer, marketing manager*

Nutley
Andreula-Ortiz, Jo-Ellen *pharmaceutical company administrator, cosmetologist*
Bonagura, Diane Susan *global study manager*
Bukovec, Joseph Aloysius *special education educator*
Dennin, Robert Aloysius, Jr., *pharmaceutical research scientist*
English, Robert Joseph *electronic corporation executive*
Gudema, Norman H. *civil engineer*
Henning, Neil Scott *financial consultant*
†Hung, Frank Chien-Hsin *chemist, researcher*
Kong, Norman *chemist*
Liu, Chao-Min *biochemist, biotechnologist, researcher*
Mallard, Stephen Anthony *retired utility company executive*
Mostillo, Ralph *medical association administrator*
Romanoski, Barbara Ann *neonatology nurse*
Tropiano, JoAnn Alma *librarian, library director*

Oakhurst
Averbach, David Joel *surgeon*
Defino, Joseph Francis *lawyer*
Fasthuber-Grande, Traudy *financial services company executive*

Oakland
Butterfield, Charles Edward, Jr., *educational consultant*
Dressel, Margaret Jane *artist, art educator*
Goldenberg, Eva J. *lawyer*
†Guller, Irving Bernard *forensic, clinical psychologist, consultant*
Maccario, Maurice Malcolm *oral and maxillofacial surgeon, consultant*
Weiner, Marc V. *health services facility executive*

Oaklyn
Johnson, Mark Kevin *operating room nurse*

Ocean
Reich, Bernard *retired telecommunications engineer*
Weisberg, Adam Jon *lawyer*

Ocean City
Boardman, Harold Frederick, Jr., *lawyer, retired corporate executive*
Hughes, William John *former congressman, diplomat*
McLaughlin, Marcellus H. Mark, III, *writer, historian, activist*
Szczepaniak, Jane Camille *childbirth educator*
†Weir, William Thomas *retired engineering educator*

Ocean Grove
Anderson, James Frederick *clergyman*
Gabriel, Edwin Zenith *consulting engineer*

Oceanport
†D'Amico, John, Jr., *judge*

Meibauer, Amery Filippone *special education educator*

Old Bridge
Brennan, George Gerard *pediatrician*
Downs, Thomas Edward, IV, *lawyer*

Old Tappan
†Ebersole, Curt *music educator*
Gaffin, Joan Valerie *secondary school educator*

Oldwick
Griggs, Stephen Layng *management consultant*
Kellogg, C. Burton, II, *financial analyst*
Sinfelt, John Henry *chemist*
Snyder, Arthur *publishing executive*
Svoboda, Joanne Dzitko *artist, educator*
†Van Doren, Shaun Clark *chemist*

Oradell
†Bassis, Aileen *artist*
Blakeslee, Edward Eaton *lawyer, insurance executive*
†Mavroudis, John M. *lawyer*
Nesoff, Robert (Bob) *newspaper publisher*
Roe, W. Barton *engineering executive*
Struck, Norma Johansen *artist*
Tong, Hing *mathematician, educator*

Orange
Khanna, Yash Kumar *family practice physician, pediatrician*

Paramus
†Agresta, Anthony John *academic administrator, educational consultant, language educator*
†Ahearn, Matthew J. *assemblyman*
Balter, Leslie Marvin *business communications educator*
De La Cruz, Carolina *pharmacist*
Eyler, John H., Jr., *retail toy and game company executive*
Fader, Seymour Jeremiah *management and engineering consulting company executive*
Fader, Shirley Sloan *writer*
Fakharzadeh, Frederick F. *surgeon*
†Gilbert, Stephen Alan *lawyer, organization executive*
†Goldstein, Michael *retail executive*
Gordon, Scott (Harry Scott Buehlmeier) *entertainer, actor*
†Hendel, Elisa Beth *special education educator, writer*
Hibler, Robert Bennett *construction executive*
Hochstein, Martin Alan *endocrinologist*
Kovatis, Paul Evans *orthopedic surgeon, researcher, consultant*
Lenk, Richard William, Jr., *history educator*
Levy, Joseph *lawyer*
Liva, Edward Louis *eye surgeon*
Maclin, Ernest *biomedical diagnostics company executive*
†Mahoney, Joseph Francis *historian, educator*
†Perkins-Munn, Tiffany Sabrena *psychologist, researcher*
Rosenstein, Roger G. *hand surgeon*
Weinstock, George David *financial services company executive*
Younie, William John *special education educator, researcher*

Park Ridge
Ablin, Richard Joel *immunologist, educator*
Olson, Frank Albert *car rental company executive*

Parlin
Flick, Ferdinand Herman *surgeon, prevention medicine physician*
Fuks, Boris Borisovich *immunologist, researcher*

Parsippany
Azzarone, Carol Ann *marketing executive*
Belmonte, Steven Joseph *hotel chain executive*
Deones, Jack E. *corporate executive*
†Ferguson, Thomas George *retired healthcare advertising agency executive*
Ferris-Waks, Arlene Susan *compliance officer*
Fleisher, Seymour *manufacturing company executive*
†Gannon, Peter M. *healthcare executive*
Gray, Neil Harold *healthcare marketing executive*
Kallmann, Stanley Walter *lawyer*
Leviss, Stephen R. *gynecologist*
Marscher, William Donnelly *engineering company executive*
Mazur, Leonard L. *pharmaceutical company executive*
Meyer, Kevin Michael *communication executive*
Pedescleaux-Muckle, Gail *business analyst, writer*
Peyser, Irving Gerald *surgeon*
Prague, Ronald Jay *lawyer*
Rappaport, Alan Fred *clinical psychologist*
Visocki, Nancy Gayle *information services consultant*
Wechter, Ira Martin *tax specialist, financial planner*

Passaic
Haddad, Jamil Raouf *physician*
Lindholm, Clifford Falstrom, II, *engineering executive, mayor*
Mussano, Theodore Anthony *court services supervisor*

Paterson
Daniels, Cheryl Lynn *pediatrics nurse, case manager*
Deffaa, Chip *jazz critic*
Papageorgis, Jack *small business owner*
Paulhus, Thomas A. *educator*
†Pou, Nellie *assemblywoman*
†Steele, Alfred E. *assemblyman*
Stewart, Peter J. *general surgery, trauma and critical care physician*

Waitts, James Robert *marketing professional*

Paulsboro
Colacot, Thomas J. *chemicals executive, researcher*
†Langley, Michael Lee *chemist*

Peapack
Eddey, Gary Erwin *physician, administrator, educator*
Rost, Peter *pharmaceutical company executive*
Rothwell, Timothy Gordon *pharmaceutical company executive*
Walsh, Philip Cornelius *retired mining executive*

Pennington
Bertone, Thomas Lee *management consultant*
Calvo, Roque John *professional society administrator*
DeMontigney, James Morgan *health services administrator*
Donnelly, Gerard Kevin *marketing and retail executive*
Gorrin, Eugene *lawyer*
Kaschak, David James *accountant*
Kelly, Quentin Thorn *water company executive, inventor, writer*
Kozlowski, Thomas Joseph, Jr., *lawyer, trust company executive*
Mitchell, Janet Aldrich *fund raising executive, reference materials publisher*

Penns Grove
†Dion, Susan Frances *historian, poet, writer*
Graham, Albert Darlington, Jr., *educational administrator*

Pennsauken
Alday, Paul Stackhouse, Jr., *retired mechanical engineer*
Curry, Emma Beatrice *secondary education and college educator*
Sygnecki, Christina *sales executive*

Perth Amboy
Kress, Sidney C. *pathologist*
Richardson-Melech, Joyce Suzanne *music educator, singer*

Phillipsburg
Borah, Kripanath *pharmacist*
Drago, Joseph Rosario *urologist, educator*
Kim, Ih Chin *pediatrician*
Richards, Jay Claude *commercial photographer, news service executive, historian*
Rosenthal, Marvin Bernard *pediatrician, educator*
Souders, Nicole Elizabeth *oncological nurse, researcher*

Picataway
†Pardo, Janette M. *multimedia editor, archivist, librarian*

Pine Brook
Schwiederek, William Neil *engineering executive*

Piscataway
Alderfer, Clayton Paul *organizational consultant, educator, writer, administrator*
†Alexe, Gabriela *research scientist*
†Balaguru, Perumalsamy *civil engineering educator*
Benaroya, Haym *aerospace engineer, educator, researcher*
Boucher, Thomas Owen *engineering educator, researcher*
Cargill, Ursula Bardot *university official*
Champe, Pamela Chambers *biochemistry educator, writer*
†Chen, Jian *engineer*
Cherniss, Cary *psychologist, educator*
†Chin, Khew-Voon *medical educator*
Choe, Yun Hwang *chemist, educator*
Cohen, Morrel Herman *physicist, biologist, educator*
Colaizzi, John Louis *college dean*
Conney, Allan Howard *pharmacologist, researcher*
Coppola, Sarah Jane *special education educator*
D'Aloia, G(iambattista) Peter *corporate executive*
Denhardt, David Tilton *molecular and cell biology educator*
Dill, Ellis Harold *university dean*
Ebright, Richard High *molecular biologist*
Egger, M. David *neurobiology educator*
Elsayed, Elsayed Abdelrazik *industrial engineer, educator*
†Epstein, Yakov M *education educator, psychologist*
†Etter, Zana Claire *media library director*
Flanagan, James Loton *electrical engineer, researcher, engineering educator*
Fogiel, Max *publishing executive*
Freeman, Herbert *computer engineering educator*
Frenkiel, Richard Henry *retired systems engineer, consultant*
Gaffar, Abdul *research scientist, administrator*
Goldman, Alan Stuart *chemistry educator*
Guo, Qizhong *engineering educator, researcher, consultant*
Hsiao, Michael S. *electrical engineer, educator*
†Hudson, Judith Anne *developmental psychologist, researcher*
Idol, James Daniel, Jr., *chemist, educator, inventor, consultant*
Julesz, Bela *experimental psychologist, educator, electrical engineer*
Kelly, Robert Emmett *telecommunications company administrator*
Kenney, Mary R. *software engineer*
†Kiddie, Thomas James *application developer, educator*
†Kilianski, Stephen *psychologist, educator*
†Kim, Edward *medical association administrator*
Kissin, Yury Viktor *chemist, geochemist*

Kivetz, Michael Adam *artist, sculptor*
Klein, Michael Tully *university dean, chemical engineer, consultant*
†Kotliar, B. Gabriel *physics educator*
†Langrana, Noshir A. *mechanical engineer, educator, research scientist*
Leath, Paul Larry *physicist, educator, former university official*
Lebowitz, Joel Louis *mathematical physicist, educator*
Lepowsky, James *mathematician, educator*
Lindenfeld, Peter *physics educator*
Mammone, Richard James *engineering educator*
Manowitz, Paul *biochemist, researcher, educator*
Menza, Matthew A. *psychiatrist*
Mitchell, James Kenneth *geography educator*
Osofsky, Barbara Langer *mathematician, educator*
†Pae, Kook Dong *education educator*
Peterson, Donald Robert *psychologist, educator, university administrator*
Polefka, Thomas Gregory *biochemist*
Poses, Frederic M. *engineering company executive*
Rhoads, George Grant *medical epidemiologist*
Robbins, Allen Bishop *physics educator*
Robinson, David Alton *climatologist, geography educator*
Rosalsky, Barbara Ellen *artist, home health aide*
†Rothkopf, Michael H. *science educator, researcher*
†Sahota, Amrik *medical researcher, educator, lab administrator*
Sass, Louis Arnorsson *psychology educator*
Scher, Karen Maria *illustrator, multimedia specialist, systems engineer*
Schwebel, Milton *psychologist, educator*
†Seiden, David *anatomist, educational association administrator*
Shatkin, Aaron Jeffrey *biochemistry educator*
Sit, Ping-Fai *research scientist*
Smith, Bob *lawyer, state senator, educator*
Snitzer, Elias *physicist*
Stein, Arlene J. *sociology educator, writer*
Suh, Dong-Churl *pharmaceutical economics educator*
Taft, Earl Jay *mathematics educator*
†van Frankenhuijsen, Machiel *science educator*
Wagner-Westbrook, Bonnie Joan *management professional*
Wang, Tsuey Tang *science educator, venture capitalist*
Waxman, Chaim I. *sociology educator, researcher*
Welkowitz, Walter *biomedical engineer, educator*
†West, Mark Otto *psychology educator*
White, Helene R. *sociologist, educator*
Witz, Gisela *scientist, educator*
Wu, Tsong-Ho *operations researcher*
Yacowitz, Harold *biochemist, nutritionist*
Zhang, Li *engineer, researcher*
†Zhao, Dandan *molecular biologist, biomedical researcher*
Zhao, Jian Hui *electrical and computer engineering educator*

Pitman
Carpenter, Hoyle Dameron *music educator emeritus*
Cloues, Edward Blanchard, II, *lawyer*
Lamey, Mary Cocove *elementary guidance counselor*
Lloyd, David Dilsworth Talbott *emeritus educator*

Pittstown
Bell, Frank Joseph, III, *architect*

Plainfield
Allen, Stuart (Stuart Allen Sup) *film and television company executive*
Frost, David *former biology educator, medical editor, consultant*
Green, Gerald B. *state legislator*
Holdorf, Harry Hulbert *health services administrator*
Johnson, Lonnie L., Jr., *information specialist*
Keyko, George John *electronics company executive*
Lin, Janet C. *physician*
Montford, Claudian Hammond *retired gifted and talented education educator*
†Reeder, Hubert *elementary school educator*
Thomas, William Joseph *secondary school educator, administrator*

Plainsboro
Devine, Hugh James, Jr., *marketing executive, consultant*
†Dezii, Christopher Michael *medical researcher, organ transplant nurse*
Gould, Susan Eileen *social worker, elementary school educator*
McGeady, Kathleen Birmingham *grant administrator*
Schreyer, William Allen *retired investment firm executive*
Sorensen, Henrik Vittrup *electrical engineering educator*
Spiegel, Phyllis *public relations consultant, journalist*
Yam, Aileen Lynette *programmer*

Pleasantville
Andes, Derien Romaric *retired purchasing specialist*
Applewhite, Kim *music company executive, educator*
†Etim, Terris *geriatrics nurse*
London, Charlotte Isabella *secondary education educator, reading specialist*

Point Pleasant
†Albano, Pasquale Charles *management educator, management and organization development consultant*
Berkman, Samuel *materials scientist*

Marjanczyk, Joseph Anicetus *priest*
Perdunn, Richard Francis *management consultant*

Point Pleasant Beach
Herr, Philip Michael *lawyer, accountant*
†Motley, John Paul *psychiatrist, consultant*

Pomona
Bukowski, Elaine Louise *physical therapist, educator*
Colijn, Geert Jan *academic administrator, political scientist*
Comfort, Priscilla Maria *retired college official, human resources professional*
Constantelos, Demetrios John *priest, educator*
†Dagavarian-Bonar, Debra Aghavni *college administrator, consultant*
Heck, Jonathan F. *athletic trainer, photographer*
†Iyer, Renganathan Ganesan *mathematician*
Jahangir, Z(ulfiquar) M(uhammed) G(olam) Sarwar *molecular biologist, educator*
Kirk, James Barrett, III, *humanities educator, language educator*
Mench, Fred Charles *classics educator*
†Paul, Edward *chemistry educator*
Sharon, Yitzhak Yaakov *physicist, educator*

Pompton Lakes
Kubas, Christine *retired law enforcement officer*
McHugh, Robert Ernest (Bob McHugh) *pianist, composer*

Pompton Plains
Ludemann, Cathie Jane *lawyer*
Scroggs, Robin Jerome *theology educator*
Shrem, Charles Joseph *metals corporation executive*

Port Elizabeth
Ficcaglia, Leslie M. *psychologist, portrait artist*

Port Murray
Kunzler, John Eugene *physicist*

Port Norris
Canzonier, Walter Jude *shellfish aquaculturist*

Princeton
Aarsleff, Hans *linguistics educator*
Abrams, Jeffrey Stuart *sports medicine physician, surgeon*
Ackourey, Peter Paul *lawyer*
Adler, Stephen Louis *physicist*
Alford, Duncan Earl *lawyer*
Allen, Diogenes *clergyman, philosophy educator*
†Allen, Stanley T. *architect, dean, educator*
Altmann, Stuart Allen *biologist, educator*
Anderson, Ellis Bernard *retired lawyer, pharmaceutical company executive*
Armstrong, Richard Stoll *minister, educator, writer, poet*
Artzt, Alice Josephine *classical guitarist, writer*
†Arunasalam, Vickramasingam (Willie) *retired physicist*
Atkins, Thomas Herman *lawyer*
†Bahcall, John Norris *astrophysicist*
Ballou, Janice Donelon *research director*
Barlow, Walter Greenwood *public opinion analyst, management consultant*
Bartolini, Robert Alfred *electrical engineer, researcher*
Basáñez, Miguel Ebergenyi *opinion pollster, political science educator*
†Bassler, Bonnie *molecular biologist*
Beidler, Marsha Wolf *lawyer*
Belshaw, George Phelps Mellick *bishop*
Benarde, Anita Estelle *artist*
Benesch, Katherine *lawyer*
Bergman, Edward Jonathan *lawyer, educator*
Bergman, Richard Isaac *health information company executive*
†Bergman, Victoria Besterman *small business owner, consultant*
†Berinsky, Adam Jeremiah *political scientist, educator*
Bermann, Sandra Lekas *English language educator*
†Bhide, Rajeev S. *medical researcher*
Billington, David Perkins *civil engineering educator*
Bishop, James Francis *executive search consulting company executive*
Blackman, Sue Anne Batey *economics researcher*
Blair, David William *mechanical engineer*
Bogan, Elizabeth Chapin *economist, educator*
Bogucki, Peter Ignatius *archaeologist*
Bonini, William Emory *geophysics educator*
Boretz, Naomi Messinger *artist, educator*
Bowersock, Glen Warren *historian, educator*
Bradford, David Frantz *economist*
Brinkman, William Frank *physicist, research executive*
Broad, Barbara Prentice *retired real estate agent*
Brombert, Victor Henri *literature educator, author*
Brown, Leon Carl *history educator*
Bunnell, Peter Curtis *photography and art educator, museum curator*
Buttenheim, Edgar Marion *publishing executive*
†Carone, Gabriela Roxana *philosophy educator, dancer*
Carver, David Harold *physician, educator*
Cavanaugh, James Henry *medical corporate executive, former government official*
Chaikin, Mary Carrie *psychology librarian*
Chamberlin, John Stephen *investor, former cosmetics company executive*
†Chando, Theodore John *research scientist*
Chazelle, Bernard *computer science educator*
Cheadle, Louise *concert pianist, educator*
Chow, Gregory Chi-Chong *economist, educator*
Christman, Edward Arthur *physicist*
Clay, Lucius Dubignon, III, *surgeon, educator*
Cleary, Lynda Woods *financial advisor, consultant*
Coffey, Joseph Irving *international affairs educator*
Coffin, David Robbins *art historian, educator*
Cohen, Isaac Louis (Ike Cohen) *small business owner*
Cook, Michael Allan *social sciences educator*
Cooke, R(ichard) Caswell, Jr., *architect*
Cooper, Joel *psychology educator*
Cooper, John Madison *philosophy educator*
Cooper, Michael R. *dean*
Corngold, Stanley Alan *German and comparative literature educator, writer*
Crawford, Franklin David *publishing company executive*
Crespi, Irving *public opinion and market research consultant*
Cryer, Dennis Robert *pharmaceutical company executive, researcher*
Cullen, Daniel Edward *management consultant*
Curschmann, Michael Johann Hendrik *German language and literature educator*
Curtiss, Howard Crosby, Jr., *mechanical engineer, educator*
Darnton, Robert Choate *history educator*
Davidson, Ronald Crosby *physicist, educator*
Davies, Robert Abel, III, *consumer products company executive*
Debenedetti, Pablo Gaston *chemical engineering educator*
Deligne, Pierre René *mathematician*
De Lung, Jane Solberger *independent sector executive*
Deneen, Patrick John *political scientist, educator*
†Diller, Elizabeth E. *artist, educator*
Doig, Jameson Wallace *political science educator*
Dovey, Brian Hugh *health care products company executive, venture capitalist*
†Doyle, Michael W. *federal official*
Drakeman, Donald Lee *biotechnology company executive, lawyer*
Duquette, David Joseph, Jr., *lawyer, investor*
†Durdanovic, Igor *researcher*
†Durst, Robert Joseph, II, *lawyer*
Dyson, Freeman John *physicist, educator*
Ekstrom, Ruth Burt *psychologist*
Elliott-Moskwa, Elaine Sally *psychologist, researcher*
Enquist, Lynn William *molecular biologist*
Ermolaev, Herman Sergei *Slavic languages educator*
Farley, Edward Raymond, Jr., *mining and manufacturing company executive*
Fernholz, Erhard Robert *investment executive*
File, Joseph *research physics engineer*
Finn, Frances Mary *biochemistry researcher*
Fisch, Nathaniel Joseph *physicist*
Fitch, Val Logsdon *physics educator*
Fleetwood, Rex Allen *insurance company executive*
Florey, Klaus Georg *chemist, pharmaceutical consultant*
Ford, Jeremiah, III, *architect*
Fox, Mary Ann Williams *librarian*
Franze, Anthony James *pharmacist, lawyer*
Freeman, Bruce George *fundraising consultant*
Freeman, Marjorie Kler *interior designer*
Fried, Eleanor Reingold *psychologist, educator*
Fusillo, Thomas Victor *environmental engineer*
†Gallo, Ruben *Latin American literature educator, art critic*
Galloway, Patricia Denese *civil engineer*
Ganoe, Charles Stratford *banker, consultant*
†Gaudi, Bernard Scott *astronomer, researcher*
Gear, Charles William *computer scientist*
Geertz, Clifford James *anthropology educator*
George, Mary Wiedenbeck *reference librarian, educator*
George, Robert Peter *political philosopher, lawyer*
George, Thomas *artist*
Gillespie, Thomas William *theological seminary administrator, religion educator*
Gillham, John Kinsey *chemical engineering educator*
Gillispie, Charles Coulston *history of science educator*
Gilpin, Robert George, Jr., *political science educator*
Glassman, Irvin *mechanical and aeronautical engineering educator, consultant*
Glucksberg, Sam *psychology educator*
Goheen, Robert Francis *classicist, educator, former ambassador*
Goldblatt, Barry Lance *manufacturing executive*
Goldfarb, Irene Dale *retired financial planner*
Gordenker, Leon *political sciences educator*
Gould, James L. *biology educator*
Grabar, Oleg *retired art educator*
Grafton, Anthony Thomas *history educator*
Graves, Michael *architect, educator*
Greenman, Jane Friedlieb *lawyer, human resources specialist*
Greenstein, Fred Irwin *political science educator*
Gregg, John Malcolm Hall *pharmaceutical executive*
†Griffith, Ruth Marie *religious studies educator*
Griffiths, Phillip A. *mathematician, academic administrator*
Grigger, Jane Elizabeth *earth science educator, photographer*
Grisham, Larry Richard *physicist, consultant*
Gross, Charles Gordon *psychology educator, neuroscientist*
Grossman, Allen Neil *lawyer*
Groves, John Taylor, III, *chemist, educator*
†Gu, Henry Hongsheng *pharmacist, researcher*
Gund, Gordon *venture capitalist, professional sports team executive*
Gunning, Robert Clifford *mathematician, educator*
Gutmann, Amy *political science and philosophy educator, academic administrator*
Haberman, Shelby Joel *statistician, educator*
Habicht, Christian Herbert *history educator*
Hamburger, Jeffrey Allen *financial planner*
Harford, James Joseph *writer*
Harman, Gilbert Helms *philosophy educator*
Harvey, Norman Ronald *retired finance company executive*
Hawryluk, Richard Janusz *physicist*
Haynes, William Forby, Jr., *retired internist, cardiologist, educator*
Hendrickson, Robert Frederick *pharmaceutical company executive*
Hill, James Scott *lawyer*
Hill, Kenneth Wayne *physicist*
Hillier, James *technology management executive, researcher*
Hillier, J(ames) Robert *architect*
Hirschman, Albert Otto *political economist, educator*
Hitz, Frederick Porter *public and international affairs educator*
Hochschwender, Karl Albert *international trade and government relations consultant*
Hollander, Lawrence Jay *marketing executive*
Hollander, Robert B., Jr., *Romance languages educator*
Hopfield, John Joseph *biophysicist, educator*
Hough, Robert Alan *civil engineer*
Howarth, William (Louis Howarth) *education educator, writer*
Hulse, Russell Alan *physicist*
Hut, Piet *astrophysics educator*
Hynes, Samuel *English language educator, author*
Itzkowitz, Norman *history educator*
Jackson, Roy *chemical engineering educator*
Jacobs, William Paul *botanist, educator*
Jenkins, Edward Beynon *research astronomer*
Jenson, Pauline Alvino *retired speech and hearing educator*
Johnson-Laird, Philip Nicholas *psychologist*
Johnston, Robert Fowler *venture capitalist*
Jordan, William Chester *history educator*
†Ju, Yiguang *engineering educator*
†Kahneman, Daniel *psychology educator*
Kalafut, Michael Francis *civil engineer*
Kassof, Allen H. *foundation administrator*
Kateb, George Anthony *political science educator*
Katz, Stanley Nider *law history educator*
Katzenbach, Nicholas deBelleville *lawyer*
†Katzman-Teller, Sharon M. *writer*
Kauzmann, Walter Joseph *chemistry educator*
†Kawarsky, Jay A. *music educator, conductor, composer*
Kehrt, Allan William *architectural firm executive*
Kelble, William Francis *information services editor*
Kenen, Peter Bain *economist, educator*
Kenyon, Regan Clair *educational research executive*
†Khanna, Ashish *pharmacist*
Khawaja, Xavier *biochemical pharmacologist*
†Khutoryansky, Naum M. *mathematician, educator*
King, Alfred Meehan *financial executive*
†Kirstein, Philip Lawrence *lawyer, investment company executive*
Knoepflmacher, Ulrich Camillus *literature educator, educator*
Kohn, Joseph John *mathematician, educator*
†Krishnan, Mahesh *research scientist*
Krulewicz, Rita Gloria *special education educator*
Kuebler, Christopher Allen *pharmaceutical executive*
Kuenne, Robert Eugene *economics educator*
Kyin, Saw William *chemist, consultant*
Langlands, Robert Phelan *mathematician, educator*
Lavizzo-Mourey, Risa Juanita *academic administrator, medical association administrator*
Lechner, Bernard Joseph *consulting electrical engineer*
Lee, Ruby Bei-Loh *multimedia and computer systems architect*
Levin, Simon Asher *mathematician, ecologist, educator*
Levy, Kenneth *music educator*
†Lewandowski, Jerome L. *physicist*
Lewin, Ross Allen *lawyer*
Lewis, Bernard *Near Eastern studies educator*
Lieb, Elliott Hershel *physicist, mathematician, educator*
Lincoln, Anna *company executive, foreign languages educator*
Lippincott, Walter Heulings, Jr., *publishing executive*
Lipschutz-Yevick, Miriam Amalie *mathematician*
Liu, Bede *electrical engineering educator*
Lo, Arthur Wu-nien *electrical engineering educator*
Logue, Judith Felton *psychoanalyst, educator, professional coach*
Long, Frank Wesley, Jr., *chemist*
Lucas, Lorraine J. *regulatory affairs professional, clinical research scientist, epidemiologist consultant*
Lustig, Graham *artistic director*
MacPherson, Robert Duncan *mathematician, educator*
Makadok, Stanley *management consultant*
Malkiel, Burton Gordon *economist, educator*
Malkiel, Nancy Weiss *dean, historian, educator*
Manabe, Syukuro *climatologist*
Manning, Winton Howard *psychologist, educational administrator*
†Mariman, Devin R. *librarian, music educator, conductor*
Marks, John Henry *Near Eastern studies educator*
†Marshall, Carol Joyce *clinical project director*
Maskin, Eric Stark *economics educator*
Matlock, Jack Foust, Jr., *diplomat*
Matray-Devoti, Judith *medical information manager, consultant*
McClelland, Richard Lee *dentist*
McClure, Donald Stuart *physical chemist, educator*
McCullough, John Price *retired oil company executive*
McGinnis, James Michael *physician*
Mc Pherson, James Munro *history educator*
Meade, Dale Michael *experimental physicist*
Merrill, Leland Gilbert, Jr., *retired environmental science educator*
Metzger, Bruce Manning *clergyman, educator*
Mihram, George Arthur *mathematician*
Miles, Richard Bryant *mechanical and aerospace engineering educator*
Miller, George Armitage *psychologist, educator*
Miller, Patrick Dwight, Jr., *religion educator, minister*
Mills, Bradford *merchant banker*
Miner, Earl Roy *literature educator, educator*
Minton, Dwight Church *manufacturing company executive*
†Mollica, Joseph A. *pharmaceutical executive*
Moote, A. Lloyd *history educator*
Morris, Mac Glenn *advertising bureau executive*
Morrison, Toni (Chloe Anthony Morrison) *novelist*
Moynahan, Julian Lane *English language educator, author*
Muldoon, Paul *creative writing educator, poet*
Narayanan, Vadake K. *management educator, consultant*
Nash, John Forbes, Jr., *research mathematician*
Nehamas, Alexander *philosophy educator*
†Nichols, Karen *architect*
Nied, Thomas H. *media company executive*
†Notterman, Daniel A. *pediatrician, educator, scientist*
Oberg, Barbara Bowen *historian, educator, scholarly writer*
O'Donnell, Laurence Gerard *editorial consultant, former managing editor The Wall Street Journal*
Olson, Dennis Thorald *religion educator*
Ondetti, Miguel Angel *chemist, consultant*
O'Neill, Harry William *survey research company executive*
Oppenheimer, Michael *physicist*
Oppenheimer, Stephen Michael *neurologist, administrator*
Orphanides, Nora Charlotte *ballet educator*
Orrill, Robert Thomas *foundation executive, former history educator*
Ostriker, Jeremiah Paul *astrophysicist*
Paret, Peter *historian*
Parry, Scott Brink *psychologist*
Petrin, Jurij *pharmaceutical company executive*
Picco, Steven Joseph *lawyer*
Plaks, Livia Basch *foundation executive*
Plevy, Arthur L. *lawyer*
Poor, Harold Vincent *electrical engineering educator*
Potasek, Mary Joyce *physicist, researcher*
Rabb, Theodore K. *historian, educator*
Ramaprasad, Kackadasam Raghavachar *physical chemist*
Reinhardt, Uwe Ernst *economist, educator*
†Rigolot, François *French literature educator, literary critic*
Robertson, David Allan, Jr., *English educator*
Rodgers, Daniel Tracy *history educator*
Rogula, James Leroy *consumer products company executive*
†Rose, Edith Sprung *retired lawyer*
Rosen, Arye *microwave, optoelectronics and medicine researcher*
Rosenthal, Howard Lewis *political science educator*
†Rowley, Clarence W. *engineering educator*
Royce, Barrie Saunders Hart *physicist, educator*
Royds, Robert Bruce *physician*
Rozman, Gilbert Friedell *sociologist, educator*
Russel, William Bailey *engineering educator*
Rutherford, Paul Harding *physicist*
†Sabb, Annmarie Louise *chemist, researcher*
Sandman, Peter M. *risk communication consultant, speaker*
Sandoval, Amada *education program director*
Sapoff, Meyer *electronics component manufacturer*
Scasta, David Lynn *forensic psychiatrist*
Schafer, Carl Walter *investment executive*
Scheinkman, José Alexandre *economics educator*
Schofield, Robert E(dwin) *history educator, academic administrator*
Schorske, Carl Emil *historian, educator*
Seawright, James L., Jr., *sculptor, educator*
Seman, Charles Jacob *research meteorologist*
Semrod, T. Joseph *banker*
†Seymour, Paul Douglas *mathematician, educator*
Shapiro, Harold Tafler *former academic administrator, economist*
Shaub, Marvin Howard *management consultant*
Shear, Ione Mylonas *archaeologist*
Shear, Theodore Leslie, Jr., *archaeologist, educator*
†Shimer, Robert J. *economist, educator*
Shimizu, Yoshiaki *art historian, educator*
Silbergeld, Jerome Leslie *art historian, educator*
†Silverman, Jane Aresty *not-for-profit organizational consultant*
Simmons, Warren Hathaway, Jr., *retired retail executive*
Sims, Watson Shadrack *research executive, journalist*
†Sinharay, Sandip *statistician, researcher*
Smith, Arthur John Stewart *physicist, educator*
Some, Steven Edward *lobbyist, public affairs consultant*
Spence, Donald Pond *psychologist, psychoanalyst*
Spiro, Thomas George *chemistry educator*
†Srolovitz, David J. *materials scientist*
†Starr, Paul Elliot *sociologist, writer, editor, educator*
Steinberg, Malcolm Saul *biologist, educator*
Stengel, Robert Frank *engineering and applied science educator*
Stern, Gail Frieda *historical association director*
Sterzer, Fred *research physicist*
Stevens, Allan Woodard *electrical engineer*

Rhett, Haskell Emery Smith *educator*
Schirber, Annamarie Riddering *speech and language pathologist, educator*
Shah, Hash N. *plastics technologist, researcher*
Tenenbaum, Bernard Hirsh *entrepreneur, educator*
Wheelock, Keith Ward *retired consulting company executive, educator*

Smithville
Bergeron, Robert Francis, Jr., (Terry Bergeron) *software engineer*

Somers Point
Baylinson, Christopher Michael *lawyer*
Berenato, Anthony Francis *financial executive*
†Hagerthey, Gwendolyn Irene *retired music educator*
Miller, W. Denise Saunders *community health nurse*
Seitman, David Todd *anesthesiologist*

Somerset
Aronson, Louis Vincent, II, *manufacturing executive*
Austad, Vigdis *computer software company executive*
Bardoliwalla, Dinshaw Framroze *chemical executive*
Becker, Phyllis *systems analyst*
†Brahms, William Bernard *librarian, writer*
Brophy, Joseph Thomas *information company executive*
Chaudhary, Bharat Indu *chemical engineer*
†Chivukula, Upendra J. *assemblyman, electrical engineer*
Dahbany, Avivah *psychologist, educator*
De Salva, Salvatore Joseph *retired pharmacologist, toxicologist*
DiMeglio, Nicolas Joseph *real estate broker, small business owner*
Green, Jeffrey C. *lawyer*
Gruchacz, Craig M. *financial executive*
Ilogu, Noel Obiajulu *physician*
†James, Anthony F. *social worker*
Jones, Andrew William *pharmaceutical executive*
†Lau, John Tze *computers and communications executive*
Lawrence, Barbara *not-for-profit development consultant*
†Lee, Thai Theresa *information technology executive*
Lichtig, Leo Kenneth *health economist*
Miller, Phyllis Kaden *communications administrator*
Murray, Bertram George, Jr., *biology educator*
Patel, Tarun R. *pharmaceutical scientist*
Peng, Xiaoyuan *optical engineer*
Soaries, DeForest B., Jr., *former state official*
Trivedi, Harsh Mahendra *technical associate, educator, writer*
Young, James Earl *ceramics educator, educational administrator*

Somerville
†Andjelic, Sasa *engineer, polymer scientist*
†Bateman, Christopher (Kip Bateman) *state legislator*
†Biondi, Peter J. *assemblyman*
Cohen, Walter Stanley *accountant, financial consultant*
D'Alessio, Jacqueline Ann *English educator*
Dammel, Ralph Rainer *chemist, researcher*
Dobrinsky, Susan Elizabeth *human resources director*
Dunbar, Holly Jean *communications and public relations executive*
†Fesq, Jacqueline *education educator*
Fleischman, Joseph Jacob *lawyer*
Fox, Alissa Benimoff *dermatologist*
Fox, James Allen *allergist, immunologist, pediatrician*
†Fuerst, Steven Bernard *lawyer*
Gross, Carol Ann *lawyer*
†Hutcheon, Peter David *lawyer*
†Kavanaugh, Walter J. *state legislator*
Laskey, James Howard *lawyer*
†Lieberman, Marvin Samuel *lawyer*
McCracken, Anthony Vekony, Sr., *land use planner, environmental scientist*
Minus, Edward Richelieu *English language educator, writer*
†O'Brian, Harold Samuel *lawyer*
†Schroeck, Peter J. *language educator*
Yurasko, Frank Noel *judge*

South Amboy
†Burkard, Thomas Robert *publishing executive, writer*
†McDonnell, William John *lawyer*
Moskal, Anthony John *former dean, professor, management and education consultant*

South Bound Brook
Simpson-Steeber, Marybeth *educator*
Weir, Sonja Ann *artist*

South Hackensack
Belinfante, Geoffrey Warren *television producer*
Cohen, Brett I. *health products executive*
Jacobs, George Braun *neurosurgeon*
Stier, Roger Edwin *chemist, researcher*

South Orange
Amar, A. D. *finance educator, management consultant*
Bao, Xue-Ming *librarian, educator*
†Carpentier, Martha C. *English educator*
Collins, John W., Jr., *retired military officer, technologist, educator*
Delo, Ellen Sanderson *lawyer*
DeVaris, Panayotis Eric *architect*
†Deyrup, Marta Mestrovic *school librarian, writer*
Fleming, Edward J. *priest, educator*
†Friedman, Susan R. *foundation administrator, consultant*
†Frizzell, Lawrence Edward *religious studies educator, priest*
Gokcekus, Omer *education educator*
Gruenwald, Renee *special education educator*
†Hackett, Mims, Jr., *state legislator*
Hanbury, Kevin M. *dean, priest*
Hansell, Phyllis Shanley *nursing educator, administrator, researcher, consultant*
Hecht, Marion B. *mental health counselor, mental health therapist*
†Hu, Shouping *education educator*
Kluger, Richard *author, editor*
Lapinski, Frances Constance *internet product and marketing management*
Long, Philip Lee *information systems executive*
Marbach, Joseph R. *political scientist, educator*
Nussbaum Drill, Sheila *gallery director and owner*
Schectman, Stephen Barry *pharmaceuticals company executive*
Sheeran, Robert *academic administrator*
Steig, Donald Barry *management consultant*
Steiner, Gloria Litwin *psychologist*
Stringile, Marie Elizabeth *educational administrator*
Terry, Myra *administration administrator*
Thonet, John A. *environmental planning and engineering consultant*
Williams, Veronica Ann *marketing and business consultant*
Willis, Meredith Sue *writer, educator*

South Plainfield
Burke, Jacqueline Yvonne *telecommunications executive*
Choi, Soon Chae *orthopaedic surgeon*
Chu, Sung Nee George *materials scientist*
Coulter, Barbara Clare *information services company executive*
†Gopalakrishnan, Suresh *computer engineer*
Hunsinger, Doyle J. *electronics executive*
Ju, William David *pharmaceutical executive*
Kennedy, John William *engineering company executive*
Pappas, Michael *financial services company executive*
Schlossman, Mitchell Lloyd *cosmetics and chemical specialties executive*
Sipski, Mary Leonide *physician, healthcare administrator*

South River
Fontaine, Bernard Leo, Jr., *small business owner*

Southampton
Callaway, Ben Anderson *journalist*
Knortz, Walter Robert *accountant, former insurance company executive*

Sparta
Alberto, Pamela Louise *oral and maxillofacial surgeon, educator*
Guida, Pat *information broker, literature chemist*
McMeen, Elmer Ellsworth, III, *retired lawyer, guitarist*
Purrenhage, Charles Bruce *writer, editor*
Rosser, Alvin Raymon *artist*
Scianna, Irene F. *film company executive, photography executive*
Spence, Robert Leroy *publishing executive*
Truran, William Richard *electrical engineer*

Spring Lake
Bonhag, Thomas Edward *insurance company executive, financial consultant, financial planner*
D'Luhy, John James *investment banker*
Ernst, John Louis *management consultant*
Harrigan, John Thomas, Jr., *physician, obstetrician-gynecologist*
McEntee, Robert Edward *management consultant*
McGreal, Joseph A., Jr., *publishing company executive*
O'Connor, Francis X. *financial executive*
Talarico, Rudolph Dominic *retired urologist*
Wrege, Charles Deck *management educator*

Springfield
Baker, Alden *artist*
Barlow, Mara Lise *public relations executive*
DeVone, Denise *artist, educator*
Gottlieb, Helen *social worker, legal immigration consultant*
Grayson Kurzweil, Bette Rita *lawyer*
Kerner, Michael Bernard *gastroenterologist*
Marino, Natalie Marie *artist*
Mytelka, Arnold Krieger *lawyer*
Panish, Morton B. *retired physical chemist*
Perilstein, Fred Michael *electrical engineer, consultant*
Shilling, A. Gary *economic consultant, investment advisor*
Vercesi, Haydée Margarita Chacha *biomedical scientist*
Weisse, Allen Barry *educator, cardiologist, author, historian*
Wosnitzer, Morey *urologist*
†Yudes, James Peyton *lawyer*

Stanhope
Ferrara, Dominick John, IV, *music educator*

Stanton
Clayton, Raymond Arthur *purchasing executive*
Kille, John William, Jr., *toxicology and biomedical product consultant*

Stewartsville
Busch, Beverly Gail *English language educator, literature educator, instructional resource center administrator*

Stirling
Walsh, Peter Joseph *physics educator*

Stockholm
dePaolo, Ronald Francis *editor, writer*

Stockton
Leeds, Valerie Ann *curator, art historian, writer*
Mahon, Robert *photographer*
†Ritter, Paul M. *writer*
†Schoenherr, John (Carl) *artist, illustrator*
Taylor, Rosemary *artist*

Stone Harbor
Finore Hurd, Diane *marketing executive, publisher*
Koss, Rosabel Steinhauer *retired health and physical education educator*
Taylor, Robert Lee *lawyer, former judge*

Stratford
Gallagher, R. Michael *academic administrator*
†Giacabetti, Thomas *musician, educator*
†McAbee, Gary N. *osteopath, lawyer*
Scali, Victor Joseph *emergency medicine physician*

Succasunna
Romance, Mary C. *library director*

Summit
Auerbach, Andrew B *polymer engineer, chemist*
Bostwick, Randell A. *retired retail food company executive*
Buchanan, Andrew Simpson *writer*
Burbank, Robinson Derry *crystallographer*
Caming, H. W. William *lawyer, consultant*
Carniol, Paul J. *plastic and reconstructive surgeon, otolaryngologist*
†Clynes, Carolann Elizabeth *realtor*
†Cooper, John Weeks *lawyer*
Diamond, Wendi T. *physician*
Fuess, Billings Sibley, Jr., *advertising executive*
Fukui, Hatsuaki *electrical engineer, art historian*
Gerathy, E. Carroll *former insurance executive, real estate developer*
Hall, Pamela Elizabeth *psychologist*
Hickman, J. Kenneth *accounting company executive*
†Katz, Michael Albert *lawyer*
Keith, Garnett Lee, Jr., *investment executive*
Kenyon, Edward Tipton *lawyer*
Lewis, Donald Emerson *banker*
Lindars, Laurence Edward *retired health care products executive*
Macioce, Frank Michael *lawyer, financial services company executive*
Malhotra, Harish K. *psychiatrist, educator*
Malhotra, Mahamaya *psychiatrist*
Malin, Robert Abernethy *investment management executive*
May, Ernest Max *charitable organization official*
McGuire, Catherine Frances *elementary education educator*
Mele, Gregg Charles *lawyer*
Mitchell, Peter William *addictions counselor*
Mueller, Paul Henry *retired banker*
Pace, Leonard *retired management consultant*
Pawelec, William John *retired electronics company executive*
†Pfaltz, Hugo Menzel, Jr., *lawyer*
Phillips, James Charles *physicist, educator*
Pollak, Henry Otto *retired utility research executive, educator*
Rosensweig, Ronald Ellis *scientist consultant*
Rossey, Paul William *school superintendent, university president*
Rousseau, Irene Victoria *artist, sculptor*
†Saffer, Judith Mack *lawyer*
Sheris, Steven Jay *physician*
Starks, Florence Elizabeth *retired special education educator*
Vandenberg, Joka Maria *physicist, researcher*
Weinstein, Stephen Brant *communications executive, researcher, writer*
Woller, James Alan *lawyer*
Young, Diane Caroline *pharmaceutical executive*
Zachary, Louis George *chemical company consultant*

Sussex
MacMurren, Harold Henry, Jr., *psychologist, lawyer*

Swedesboro
Lovell, Theodore *electrical engineer, consultant*

Teaneck
Alperin, Richard Martin *clinical social worker, psychoanalyst*
Browne, Robert Span *economist, researcher*
Brudner, Helen Gross *social sciences educator*
Bullough, John Frank *organist, music educator*
Cassimatis, Peter John *economics educator*
Connola, Donald Pascal, Jr., *management consultant*
Czin, Felicia Tedeschi *Italian language and literature educator, small business owner*
Dewey, Ralph Jay *school system administrator*
Dowd, Janice Lee *foreign language educator*
Ehrenfeld, Phyllis Rhoda *editor, playwright, book reviewer*
Ehrlich, Ira Robert *mechanical engineering consultant*
Erlich Penchuk, Sara *social worker, psychotherapist*
Fajans, Jack *physics educator*
Feinberg, Robert S. *plastics company executive, marketing professional*
Fjordbotten, Alf Lee *language educator*
Gibbs, Margaret Smith *psycholgy educator*
Goldman, Eric A. *film company executive*
Gordon, Lois G. *English language educator*
Graham, Aaron Richard *school superintendent*
Hollman, Barbara Carol *psychoanalyst, psychotherapist, consultant*
Indick, Janet *sculptor, educational administrator*
Ladenheim, Jules Calvin *neurosurgeon*
Lehmann, Esther Strauss *investment company executive*
†Lewis, Karen Ann *director*
Mahoney, Maureen E. *retired secondary education educator*
Meno, John Peter *chorepiscopus*
Mirza, Muhammad Zubair *product development company executive, researcher, engineering consultant, inventor*
Nagy, Christa Fiedler *biochemist*
Pfeffer, Robert *chemical engineer, academic administrator, educator*
Pischl, Adolph John *school administrator*
Rojas Wahl, Roy Uwe *research scientist*
Rudy, Willis *historian*
Scotti, Dennis Joseph *educator, researcher, consultant*
Smith, Susan Elizabeth *guidance director*
†Sommer, Mark *humanities educator*
Sweeney, Eugene William *dermatologist*
Walker, Lucy Doris *secondary school educator, writer*
Wallmann, Jeffrey Miner *author*
Weinberg, Loretta *state legislator*
Westin, Alan Furman *political science educator*
Woerner, Alfred Ira *medical device manufacturer, educator*
Zwass, Vladimir *information systems educator*

Tenafly
Altman, Kenneth A(lan) *gastroenterologist, educator*
Badr, Gamal Moursi *legal consultant*
Blank, Marion Sue *psychologist, educator*
Brown, Shirley Ann *speech-language pathologist*
Gibbons, Robert Philip *management consultant, director*
Grieco, Michael Henry *allergy and infectious diseases physician*
Koons, Irvin Louis *design and marketing executive, graphic artist, consultant*
Levy, Norman Jay *investment banker, financial consultant*
Schoenberg, Coco *sculptor*
†Spike, Michele Kahn *lawyer*
Vaughan, Samuel Snell *editor, author, publisher*

Teterboro
Adams, James Mills *retired chemicals executive*
Contois, John Henry *clinical chemist, researcher*
Freeman, Kenneth W. *laboratory executive*
Gambino, S(alvatore) Raymond *medical laboratory executive, educator*
Schwartz, Joyce Gensberg *pathologist*

Three Bridges
Lawrence, Gerald Graham *management consultant*

Tinton Falls
Butler, Nancy Taylor *gender equity specialist, program director*
Eiselt, Michael Herbert *optics scientist*
†Robinson, Bruce Thomas *systems engineer, mathematics educator*
Tague, Charles Francis *retired engineering, construction and real estate development company executive*
†Westerman, H. Robert *systems analyst*

Titusville
Bhattacharjya, Ashoke Sanjoy *economist, researcher*
Cooper, Paul *retired mechanical engineer, research director*
†Klim, Christopher *editor, publishing executive, writer*
Klincewicz, Stephen Louis *preventive medicine physician*

Toms River
Berman, Michael Barry *lawyer*
Boisseau, Jerry Philip *financial services company executive*
Bosley, Karen Lee *English and journalism educator*
Boyd, Roger Allen *investment consultant*
Chopyk, Dan Bohdan *language educator, poet*
Coratti, John Edward *judicial clerk*
Donaldson, Marcia Jean *lay worker*
Fanuele, Michael Anthony *retired electronics engineer, research engineer*
Hines, Patricia *social worker, educator*
Kanarkowski, Edward Joseph *data processing company executive*
Kudryasheva, Alexandra A. *microbiologist, radiobiologist, biotechnologist, educator*
Leone, Judith Gibson *educational media specialist, video production company executive*
Leone, Stephan Robert *lawyer*
Luzky, Leonard *law enforcement official, national guard officer, educator*
Matteo, Christine E. *librarian*
Moffet, Jane Humes *retired school principal*
Okusanya, Olubukanla Tejumola *ecologist*
Rupert, Wayne Richard *protective services official*
†Schockaert, Barbara Ann *marketing professional*
Silvers, Lawrence Wynn *surgeon*
Unger, Howard Albert *artist, photographer, educator*

Totowa
Wesp, Wendy Louise *vocalist, songwriter*

Towaco
Gasperini, Elizabeth Carmela (Lisa Gasperini) *marketing consultant, graphic designer*
Huang, Pingsheng *marketing professional, consultant*
Stern, Richard Henry *advertising executive*

Trenton
†Allen, Diane Betzendahl *state legislator*
Anderson, Bruce James *electrical engineer, consultant*
Barclay, Warren M. *human resources specialist, researcher*
Ben-Asher, Daniel Lawrence *legislative researcher, writer*
Brearley, Candice *fashion designer*
Caldwell, Wesley Stuart, III, *lawyer, lobbyist*

Castro, Ida L. *state official, former federal official*
†Charles, Joseph, Jr., *state legislator*
Chavooshian, Marge *artist, educator*
Christopherson, Elizabeth Good *broadcast executive*
†Codey, Richard J. *state legislator*
†Coleman, Bonnie Watson *assemblywoman*
Collins, Jack *retired state legislator*
†Connors, Leonard T. *state legislator*
Cooper, Mary Little *federal judge, former banking commissioner*
Cowen, Robert E. *federal judge*
Cruz, Nelson Xavier *healthcare executive*
Deltuvia, John Joseph, Jr., *systems and procedural analyst*
Dimasi, Linda Grace *epidemiologist*
Doherty, Robert Christopher *lawyer*
Farmer, John J. *state commissioner, former state attorney general*
Fordyce, Theresa Rose *mental health nurse*
Frost, Barry Warren *lawyer*
†Galahad, Alexander *writer*
†Geist, George F. *state legislator*
George, Emery Edward *foreign language and studies educator, writer*
Gindin, William Howard *judge*
Greenberg, Morton Ira *federal judge*
Gupta, Rajendra Prasad *physician*
†Gusciora, Reed *assemblyman*
†Harvey, Peter C. *state attorney general*
Hughes, John J. *federal judge, educator*
†Isele, William Paul *lawyer*
Iszard, Calvin Oscar, Jr., *television production executive, public relations manager, former county freeholder*
Jones, Dale Edwin *public defender*
Joseph, Edith Hoffman *retired editor*
Kelman, Marybeth *health care consultant, health policy analyst*
Kirschner, Philip *lawyer*
Kulkosky, Chris James *social worker*
Kyrillos, Joseph M. *state legislator, political organization worker*
†Leipzig, Melvin *art educator*
Lerner, Carol Menzel *social worker*
Levin, Susan Bass *lawyer*
†Lockhart, Tina Marie *librarian*
Long, Virginia *state supreme court justice*
Martin, Linda Ann *geriatrics nurse, educator*
McGowan, Joan Yuhas *development researcher*
McGreevey, James E. *governor*
Metzger, John Mackay *lawyer*
Miller, Velvet G. *healthcare administrator*
Mintz, Herman *adult education educator*
Mroz, Richard S. *lawyer*
Nayerahmadi, Habib *psychologist*
†Obed, Leonora Rita Villegas *writer*
Old, Hughes Oliphant *research theologian, clergyman*
Parsa, Bahman *nuclear chemist*
Paul, Sindy Michelle *preventive medicine physician*
Pirog, James Michael *writer*
Poritz, Deborah T. *state supreme court chief justice, former attorney general*
Pruitt, George Albert *college president*
Rastafari, Yusuf Benyhmn *writer, educator*
Roshon, George Kenneth *manufacturing company executive*
Roy, Herbert Clarence *research scientist*
Russell, Joyce Anne Rogers *librarian*
†Sacco, Nicholas J. *state legislator*
†Singer, Robert W. *state legislator*
Smallwood, Robert Albian, Jr., *secondary education educator*
Sporn, Aaron Adolph *physician, educator*
Sterns, Joel Henry *lawyer*
Taboada, Javier Gustavo *neurologist*
†Taitsman, James P. *orthopedic surgeon*
Thatsneyakul, Yaovares *physician, consultant*
†Thomas, Regena L. *secretary of state*
Thompson, Anne Elise *federal judge*
Thurber, John Peter *academic administrator, lawyer*
Tolan, Robert Warren *pediatric infectious disease specialist*
Troyanovich, Stephen John *educational program director, poet*
Tucci, Mark A. *state agency administrator*
†Vandervalk, Charlotte *state legislator*
†Wallace, John E. *judge*
†Watson-Coleman, Bonnie *state legislator*
Weinberg, Martin Herbert *retired psychiatrist*
Zanna, Martin Thomas *physician*
Zazzali, James R. *state supreme court associate justice*

Turnersville
DePace, Nicholas Louis *physician*
Matheussen, John J. *state legislator*

Union
Bottitta, Joseph Anthony *lawyer*
†Cryan, Joseph P. *assemblyman*
Darden, Barbara S. *library director*
Darden, Joseph Samuel, Jr., *health educator*
David, Ivo *artist, poet, real estate broker*
Donovan, Craig Poulenez *public administration educator*
†Emanouilidis, Emanuel V. *computer scientist, educator*
Franklin, William George *manufacturing executive*
Greenstein, Richard Henry *lawyer*
†Jacobs-Carey, Sheila L. *immunologist*
Kaplan, Doris Weiler *social worker*
Kim, Youn-Suk Ernest *economist, educator*
Korbman, Meyer Hyman *rabbi, public school administrator*
Korn, Neal Mark *painter, art educator*
Lederman, Susan Sturc *public administration educator*
Lersch, Arthur David *director, educator*
Lewandowski, Andrew Anthony *utilities executive, consultant*
Manz, August Frederick *welding technology and safety consultant*
Nesoff, Irwin *social work educator, management consultant*
Newman, Stephen Alexander *chemical engineer, thermodynamicist*
Pasvolsky, Richard Lloyd *parks, recreation, and environment educator*
Rosenberg, A. Irving *lawyer*
Rosenthal, Judith Wolder *biological sciences educator*
Samer, Bill Fred Carl *illustrator, writer, cartoonist*
Sigmon, Scott B. *psychologist*
Silverman, Mitchell S. *endocrinologist/diabetologist*
Thomas, Ralph H. *manufacturing executive*
†Valentine, John Vartan *physical education and health educator*
White, Robert Leslie Gordon, Jr., *aerospace company executive*
Williams, Carol Jorgensen *social work educator*
Zois, Constantine Nicholas Athanasios *meteorology educator*

Union City
Bull, Inez Stewart *special education, gifted music educator, coloratura soprano, pianist, editor, author, curator*
Erbe, Gary Thomas *artist*
†Fraguela, Rafael J. *assemblyman*
Makar, Nadia Eissa *secondary education educator, educational administrator*
Rondon, Edania Cecilia *lawyer*
Sheehy, Janice Ann *education technology coordinator*
†Stier, Edwin H. *lawyer*
Younan, Joseph *bishop*

Upper Montclair
†Adarkar, Aditya *humanities educator*
Bergen, Christopher Brooke *opera company administrator, translator, editor*
Blooston, Roselee *cultural organization administrator, writer*
Bluestein, Sanfurd G. *radiologist*
Narrett, Carla Marie *university administrator*
Stock, Norman *librarian*
Thiruvathukal, John V. *science educator, consultant, writer*
†Valdez del Alamo, Elizabeth *art historian, educator*
Ververs, Beverly Joan *career development administrator*

Upper Saddle River
Cappitella, Mauro John *architect*
Hurwitz, Mark Henry *sales executive*
Marron, Darlene Lorraine *real estate development executive, financial and marketing consultant*
Oolie, Sam *manufacturing and investment company executive*
Wallace, William, III, *engineering executive*

Vauxhall
Ross, Mark Samuel *lawyer, educator, funeral director, writer*

Ventnor
†Larky, Arthur Irving *electrical engineer, educator, computer engineer, consultant*

Ventnor City
Bolton, Kenneth Albert *management consultant*
Mason, James Henry, IV, *retired surgeon*
Robbins, Hulda Dornblatt *artist, printmaker*
Zuckerman, Stuart *psychiatrist, forensic examiner, educator*

Vernon
Farrand, George Nixon, Jr., *marketing professional*
Megna, Steve Allan *secondary school educator*

Verona
Aronow, Edward *psychologist, educator*
Ayaso, Manuel *artist*
Brightman, Robert Lloyd *importer, textile company executive, consultant*
Greenwald, Robert *public relations executive*
Hock, Frederick Wyeth *lawyer*
Monacelli, Jeffrey Paul *elementary education educator*

Vincentown
Trainor, Lillian (Midge Trainor) *elections official, campaign consultant*

Vineland
†Asselta, Nicholas *state legislator*
†Bracken, Thomas *bank executive*
†Clinton, Lawrence Paul *psychiatrist*
Middleton, Denise *restaurant owner, real estate agent, educator*
O'Neill, Joseph Dean *lawyer*
Popp, Charlotte Louise *health development center administrator, nurse*
Vivarelli, Daniel George, Sr., *special education and learning disabilities educator, consultant*

Voorhees
Carter, Catherine Louise *retired elementary and middle school educator*
†Piermatti, Jack *dentist*
Reichman, Joseph Harry *plastic surgeon*
†Suflas, Steven William *lawyer*

Waldwick
Greenberg, Rita Moffett *special education educator, consultant*
Lynch, Carol *director special services, psychologist*
Samuelson, Billie Margaret *artist*

Wall
Monaco, Robert Anthony *radiologist*
Nucciarone, A. Patrick *lawyer*
O'Neill, James Paul *psychiatrist*

Wallington
Kisciras, Ross Peter *chemical engineer, plant manager*

Warren
Bernstein, Eric Martin *lawyer*
Blass, Walter Paul *consultant, management educator*
Chubb, Percy, III, *insurance company executive*
Coleman, James H., Jr., *former state supreme court justice*
DiFrancesco, Donald T. *lawyer*
DiPietro, Ralph Anthony *marketing and management consultant, educator*
Ellerbusch, Fred *environmental engineer*
†Finnegan, John D. *insurance company executive*
Gargano, Francine Ann *lawyer*
Hartman, David G. *actuary*
Hennings, Dorothy Grant (Mrs. George Hennings) *education educator*
Jackson, John Wyant *medical products executive*
Jacobson, Gary Steven *lawyer*
Kozberg, Donna Walters *rehabilitation administration executive*
Kozberg, Ronald Paul *health and human services administrator*
Kraus, Steven Gary *lawyer*
Maull, George Marriner *music director, conductor*
O'Hare, Dean Raymond *insurance company executive, director*

Washington
De Sanctis, Vincent *college president*
†Myers, Connie *assemblywoman*

Washington Township
Bilz, Laurie S. *nursing educator*

Watchung
Cohen, Melvin Irwin *retired communications systems and technology executive*
Grey, Ruthann E. *communications specialist, management consultant*
Michaelis, Paul Charles *engineering physicist executive*
Miller, John Ronald *minister*
Tornqvist, Erik Gustav Markus *chemical engineer, research scientist*

Wayne
Boronico, Jess Stephen *management science educator, academic dean*
Bowles, Suzanne Geissler *history educator*
Brandes, Joseph *historian, educator*
Bronstein, Jagoda Ewa *pediatrician*
Cetrulo, Jerry *artist, sculptor*
Chludzinski, Christopher James *information systems professional, consultant*
Donald, Robert Graham *human resources executive*
Einreinhofer, Nancy Anne *art gallery director*
Garcia, Ofelia *dean*
Gollance, Robert Barnett *ophthalmologist*
†Heyman, Samuel J. *building materials manufacturing company executive*
Jeffrey, Robert George, Jr., *industrial company executive*
†Kardan, Mahmoud *chemist, educator*
Katz, Leandro *artist, filmmaker*
Keen, M. Whitney *ink manufacturing company executive*
Khoury, Hani *surgeon, educator*
†Kresky, Jeffrey *music educator, writer, composer*
Lelyveld, David Simon *university administrator, historian*
Li, Fuan *marketing educator, researcher*
Maldonado, Raul Robert *writer, poet, playwright, actor*
Mammola, George Charles *business executive*
Meeldijk, Victor Anthony *engineering professional*
†Oriji, Gibson K. *medical educator, medical researcher*
Principe, Michael Luis *political science educator*
Rogoff, Paula Drimmer *English and foreign language educator*
Rosen, Robert Charles *English language educator*
Salny, Abbie Feinstein *psychologist*
Schmidt, Barnet Michael *communications and electronic engineer*
Sgroi, Donald Angelo *obstetrician, gynecologist*
Sheffield, Carole Jean *political science educator*
Siepser, Stuart Lewis *cardiologist, internist*
Sprayberry, Phillip Kent *public relations executive, educator, performing arts association administrator*
Stein, Robert Alan *electronics company executive*

Weehawken
Hobson, Burton Harold *publishing company executive*
†Metallo, Frances Rosebell *mathematics educator*

Wenonah
Mishik, Anthony Neal *pediatrician*

West Caldwell
Bentley, Alfred Young, Jr., *information technology and education consultant*
Dixon, Jo-Ann Conte *management consultant*
Giblin, Thomas Patrick *labor union administrator, political organization administrator*
Page, Frederick West *business consultant*
Piel, Emil J. *retired science and engineering educator*
Reboli, John Anthony *publishing executive*
Schiff, Robert *healthcare consulting company executive*

West End
Tesser, Dorothy *artist*

West Long Branch
Bass, Mary Lee *education educator, administrator*
Gaffney, Paul Golden, II, *academic administrator, military officer*
†Guarnieri, Giulia *literature educator*
Lutz, Francis Charles *university dean, civil engineering educator*
†McCaffrey, Jane Carol *addiction recovery counselor, medical/surgical nurse, consultant*
†Sarsar, Saliba *academic administrator*
Tripold, David Michael *music educator*
Ward, Kelly *social worker, educator*
Weeks, Daniel James *writer, educator, musician*

West Milford
Both, Robert Allen *recording engineer, record producer*
Colflesh, Gertrude Patterson (Trudy P. Colflesh) *counselor*
Job, Amy Grace *librarian, educator*
Stelpstra, William John *minister*

West New York
Abbadessa, Constance Immaculata *music educator, vocal artist*
Kelly, Lucie Stirm Young *nursing educator*
Rosenberg, Raymond David *special education educator, consultant*
Sires, Albio *legislative staff member, business owner*
Steinberg, Louis Marshall *dentist, researcher*

West Orange
Bornstein, Lester Milton *retired medical center executive*
Brodkin, Roger Harrison *dermatologist, educator*
Casella, Anthony John *cardiologist*
Chiaravalloti, Nancy Donofrio *neuropsychologist*
De Lisa, Joel Alan *rehabilitation physician, rehabilitation research executive*
Eisenberg, R. Neal *restoration company executive*
Gordon, Harrison J. *lawyer*
Guthrie, William Anthony *minister*
Hill, George James *physician, educator*
Jordan, Leo John *lawyer*
Katz, Alix Martha *respiratory care practitioner*
Katz, Jeffrey Ivan *urologist*
†Ko, Chia-Wen *biostatistician, researcher*
Kyle, Corinne Silverman *management consultant*
Langsner, Alan Michael *pediatric cardiologist*
Panagides, John *pharmacologist*
Petrokubi, Marilyn *film company executive, researcher, producer*
Pollara, Joanne *learning disabilities educator consultant*
Richmond, Harold Nicholas *lawyer*
Rinsky, Judith Sue Lynn *foundation administrator, educator consultant*
†Roseff, Scott *reproductive endocrinologist*
Samson, David *lawyer*
†Sharon, Jay H. *systems analyst*
Spira, Robert Sidney *gastroenterologist*
Weiner, Mervyn *retired mergers and acquisitions executive*
Zimmerman, David Carl *controller, corporate financial executive*

West Paterson
†Pataki, Andrew *bishop*
Seiffer, Neil Mark *photographer*

West Trenton
†Tessler, Steven *ecologist, data processing executive*

Westfield
Bartok, William *environmental technologies consultant*
Blum, Richard H. *obstetrician-gynecologist, educator*
Bobis, Daniel Harold *lawyer*
Brown, Shirley Mark *retired science administrator*
†Dughi, Louis John, Jr., *lawyer*
Feret, Adam Edward, Jr., *dentist*
Gajewski, Ferdinand John *music educator, musician, musicologist*
Gutterman, Alan J. *lawyer*
Hrycak, Michael Paul *lawyer*
†Hull, Kathleen Ann *humanities educator*
Jacobey, John Arthur, III, *surgeon, educator*
Jannotti, Gene Patrick *business consultant, telecommunications professional*
Mazzarese, Michael Louis *executive coach, consultant*
McDevitt, Brian Peter *history educator, educational consultant*
McLean, Vincent Ronald *former manufacturing company financial executive*
Roll, Marilyn Rita Brownlie *social worker*
Schlosberg, Theodore K. *music educator*
Simon, Martin Stanley *commodity marketing company executive, economist*
Specht, Gordon Dean *retired petroleum executive*
†Stewart, Robert Campbell *lawyer*

Westmont
Lario, Frank M., Jr., *lawyer, judge*
Martin, Burchard Samuel *lawyer*
†Stiefel, Bernard M. *psychotherapist*

Westville
Doughty, A. Glenn *minister*

Westwood
Badalamenti, Anthony Francis *mathematician, researcher*
Fabrikant, Craig Steven *psychologist*
McGuirl, Robert Joseph *lawyer*
Vandeburgt, Hendrik Jozef *designer*
Wright, Norman Albert, Jr., *middle school educator*

Wharton
Krosser, Howard S. *aerospace company executive*

Whippany
Bi, Qi *telecommunications industry executive*
Golden, John F. *packaging company executive*
Meola, Janice Grace *lawyer*
Petitto, Barbara Buschell *artist*
†Price, Deborah Kantor *educational association administrator*
Rajkumar, Ajay *computer scientist, consultant*
Xu, Hao *electrical engineer*

Whitehouse Station
Anstice, David W. *pharmaceutical executive*
Bell, Paul R. *pharmaceutical executive*
Clark, Richard T. *pharmaceutical executive*
Fiscus, Philip Wayne *underwriter*
Frazier, Kenneth C. *pharmaceutical executive*
Gilmartin, Raymond V. *pharmaceutical company executive*
Kelley, Bernard J. *pharmaceutical executive*
Lewent, Judy Carol *pharmaceutical executive*
Mahmoud, Adel A. *infectious diseases, tropical medicine physician, pharmaceutical executive*
Yarno, Wendy *pharmaceutical executive*

Whiting
†Kelsey, George E. *language educator*
Maloney, James Michael *retired writer, editor, retired language educator*
Parker, John Osmyn *management consultant*
Willis, Ben *writer, artist*

Wildwood
†Cafiero, James S. *state legislator, lawyer*

Willingboro
Denslow, Deborah Pierson *primary education educator*
Green, Riva Lee *social worker, minister*
Greene, Natalie Constance *protective services official*
Ingerman, Peter Zilahy *systems analyst, consultant*
Tarver, Margaret Leggett *lawyer, forensic scientist*

Woodbine
†White, Robert Jeffrey *psychologist*

Woodbridge
Ayub, Yacub *financial consultant*
†Babineau, Anne Serzan *lawyer*
†Barcan, Stephen Emanuel *lawyer*
Buchsbaum, Peter A. *lawyer*
DeMatteo, Gloria Jean *financial counselor*
†Friscia, Arline M. *assemblywoman*
Galkin, Samuel Bernard *orthodontist*
Golden, Daniel Lewis *lawyer*
Goldenberg, Steven Saul *lawyer*
Harris, Brett Rosenberg *lawyer*
Hoberman, Stuart A. *lawyer*
Lepelstat, Martin L. *lawyer*
Morris, David *retired electrical engineer*
†Myerson, Paul Andrew *software company executive, management consultant*
Paugh, Nancy Adele *elementary and secondary education educator*
†Qiu, Li-Hui *music educator, actress*
Schaff, Michael Frederick *lawyer*
Scolamiero, Peter *retired artist*
†Sterling, Harold G. *lawyer, real estate developer, bank executive*
†Vitale, Joseph F. *state legislator*

Woodbury
Adler, Lewis Gerard *lawyer*
Banks, Theresa Ann *retired elementary education educator*
Celano, Peter J., Jr., *lawyer*
†Nace, Donald M. *retired chemist*
O'Bryant, Cathy *retired social worker, evangelist*
Stambaugh, John Edgar *oncologist, hematologist, pharmacologist, educator*
Szgalsky, Helen A. *pediatric nurse practitioner, school nurse*

Woodcliff Lake
Bablin, Mark Edward *security administrator, mortgage consultant*
Clemen, John Douglas *lawyer*
Henkel, Herbert Ludwig *manufacturing executive*
Jacobs, Charles Nathan *editor, writer*
Kallet, Harriet Feldman *real estate broker*
Morrione, Melchior S. *management consultant, accountant*
Nachtigal, Patricia *lawyer*
Perrella, James Elbert *former manufacturing company executive*
Phillips, John C. *lawyer*
†Pollack, Jane Susan *lawyer*

Woodstown
†Rader, Jeanann Rose *secondary school educator*
Tatnall, Ann Weslager *reading educator*

Wrightstown
Drechsel, Edward Russell, Jr., *retired utility company executive*

Wyckoff
Bauer, Theodore James *physician*
Brown, James Joseph *manufacturing company executive*
Cropper, Susan Peggy *veterinarian*
Lavery, Daniel P. *management consultant*
Marcus, Linda Susan *dermatologist*
†McNamara, Henry P. *state legislator*
Spizziri, John Anthony *lawyer*
Stahl, Alice Slater *retired psychiatrist*

Yardville
Zweig, Steven Frederick *statistician*
†Dicpinigaitis, Paul Anthony *orthopaedic surgeon*

NEW MEXICO

Alamogordo
Green, Francis William *investment consultant, former missile scientist*
Lee, Joli Fay Eaton *elementary education educator*
Lindley, Norman Dale *physician*
McFadin, Helen Lozetta *retired elementary education educator*

Albuquerque
Abraham, Karen A. *university administrator*
Alfidi, Ralph Joseph *radiologist, educator*
†Allen, Hubert A., Jr., *publishing executive, writer, statistician, consultant*
Anaya, Rudolfo *educator, writer*
Anderson, Lawrence Keith *electrical engineer, consultant*
Antreasian, Garo Zareh *artist, lithographer, art educator*
Aurbach, Robert Michael *lawyer, consultant, photographer*
Ausherman, Larry Price *lawyer*
†Bailey, Robert A. *child/adolescent psychatrist*
Baker, Arnold Barry *economist*
Baker, Chester Bird *agricultural economics educator*
†Bardacke, Paul Gregory *lawyer, former attorney general*
Barry, Steve *sculptor, educator*
Basso, Keith Hamilton *cultural anthropologist, linguist, educator*
Beach, Arthur O'Neal *lawyer*
†Bear, David George
Beckel, Charles Leroy *physicist, educator*
†Belinsky, Steven Alan *health science association administrator*
Bell, Stoughton *computer scientist, mathematician, educator*
Berman, Stanley Zissman *allergist, immunologist, internist, educator*
†Betts, Dorothy Anne *elementary school educator*
Black, Bruce D. *judge*
†Block, Steven D. *music educator, composer*
Bock, Philip Karl *retired humanities educator, playwright*
Borden, Thomas Allen *urologist, educator*
Boshier, Maureen Louise *health facilities administrator*
Bova, Vincent Arthur, Jr., *lawyer, consultant, photographer*
Bradshaw, Elaine A. *pediatrician*
†Brodeur, Helen Antionette *elementary school educator*
Brooks, Alan *publications editor, writer*
†Burrows, Kathy S. *health facility administrator*
Byrne, Raymond Harry *electrical engineer*
†Caldera, Louis Edward *academic administrator, former federal official*
Capaldi, Larry Sylvestro *business educator*
Caplan, Edwin Harvey *university dean, accounting educator*
Cargo, David Francis *lawyer*
Caruso, Mark John *lawyer*
Chavez, Martin Joseph *lawyer, mayor*
Chen, Jinn-Kuen *mechanical engineer*
†Cheng, Yung Sung *research scientist*
Christensen, Ronald *statistician, educator*
Chronister, Richard Davis *physicist*
Clark, Teresa Watkins *psychotherapist, clinical counselor*
Cobb, John Candler *medical educator*
Colbert, Kathryn Hendon *lawyer*
Coleman, Barbara McReynolds *artist*
Constantineau, Constance Juliette *retired banker*
Conway, John E. *federal judge*
Cook, Marcella Kay *retired theater educator*
Cooper, Steven Mark *law educator, writer*
Culpepper, Mabel Claire *artist*
Dal Santo, Diane *writer, retired judge*
Danley, J. Mark *biologist, educator, actor*
D'Anza, Lawrence Martin *management consultant*
Danziger, Jerry *broadcasting executive*
Davidge, K. Genevieve *clinical social worker*
†Davis, Betty Bourbonia *real estate investment executive*
Davis, Jon L. *logistics consultant*
De Jong, Constance A. *artist*
Dendahl, John *political organization administrator*
DePalo, William Anthony, Jr., *Latin American studies educator*
†de Riós, María Estela *engineering company executive*
Deuble, John L., Jr., *environmental science and engineering services consultant*
DeWitt, Mary Therese *forensic anthropologist, archaeologist*
Dorato, Peter *electrical and computer engineering educator*
Dorr, Roderick A. *lawyer*
Dunn, Dennis Steven *artist, illustrator*
Durant, Penny Lynne Raife *writer, speaker, educator*
Edwards, Louise Wiseman *career counselor, educator*
Eichel, Paul Herman *electrical engineer*
†Eichenberg, Peter Thompson *state agency administrator*
†Eldredge, Jonathan DeForest *medical librarian, educator*
Eliseev, Petr Georgievich *physicist, researcher*
Ellen, Jane *composer, music educator, researcher*
Evans, Bill (James William Evans) *dancer, choreographer, educator, arts administrator*
Farmer, Terry D(wayne) *lawyer*
Feinberg, Elen Amy *artist, educator*
Feldman, Miriam Bernice *social worker*
Fisher, Don Carlton *toxicologist*
Fitzgerald, James Paul *lawyer*
Flournoy, John Charles, Sr., *civilian military employee, retired military officer*
Foster, Margaret Anne *volunteer worker*
Franchini, Gene Edward *state supreme court justice*
Freeman, Patricia Elizabeth *library and education specialist*
Friberg, George Joseph *electronics company executive*
Friedman, Herbert Sheldon *urologist*
Fuller, Anne Elizabeth Havens *English language and literature educator, consultant*
†Gallegos, Aileen Arroyo *financial consultant*
Gander, John Edward *biochemistry educator*
Garcia, F. Chris *academic administrator, political science educator, public opinion researcher*
†Gardner, Lenann McGookey *management consultant*
Garland, James Wilson, Jr., *retired physics educator*
Gatlin, Karen Christensen *English language educator, retired*
Giammo, Salvatore Joseph *public relations executive*
Giller, Edward Bonfoy *retired government official, retired air force officer*
†Gober, James Richard *writer, cartographer*
Godfrey, Richard George *real estate appraiser, consultant*
Gordon, Larry Jean *education educator*
†Gorham, Ramsay L. *state legislator, political organization administrator*
Gorman, Robert Dennis *lawyer*
Graff, Pat Stuever *secondary education educator*
Green, Mae Maera *artist*
Gregory, George Ann *writer, Native American educator*
Gross, William Allen *mechanical engineer*
Guerrant, Mary Thorington *music educator*
†Gunn, Carolyn Jean *retired elementary school educator*
†Gunn, Gordon McKay, III, *retired investment banker, retired entrepreneur*
†Gupchup, Gireesh Vijay *pharmacist, educator*
Gutierrez, Sidney M. *federal agency administrator*
Hadas, Elizabeth Chamberlayne *editor*
Haddad, Edward Raouf *civil engineer, consultant*
Haddad, Reem Mariam Edward *physician*
Haight, Cathy *artist*
Hall, Jerome William *research engineering educator*
Haltom, B(illy) Reid *lawyer*
Hancock, Don Ray *researcher*
Hansen, Curtis LeRoy *federal judge*
Harbert, Kenneth Ray *health care educator , physician*
Harris, Fred R. *political scientist, educator, retired senator*
Harrison, Charles Wagner, Jr., *applied physicist*
Hart, Frederick Michael *law educator*
Hartz, Harris L. *federal judge*
†Hauhart, Robert Charles *lawyer, educator*
Hayo, George Edward *management consultant*
Heady, Ferrel *retired political science educator*
Heffron, Warren A. *medical educator, physician*
Henderson, Rogene Faulkner *toxicologist, researcher*
†Herrera, Gilbert Victor *engineering executive*
Hovel, Esther Harrison *art educator*
Hsi, David Ching Heng *plant pathologist and geneticist, educator*
Hulsbos, Cornie Leonard *civil engineering educator*
Hutton, Paul Andrew *history educator, writer*
†Huzurbazar, Aparna V. *statistician*
Ihde, Mary Katherine *retired mathematics educator*
Ingham, Kenneth LeRoy, III, *systems programmer, consultant*
Jagnow, David Henry *petroleum geologist*
Jaramillo, Mari-Luci *retired federal agency administrator*
Johnson, Ralph Theodore, Jr., *physicist*
†Jones, Rondall Eugene *lab administrator*
Jordan, Keith M *band director, musician*
Kaehele, Bettie Louise *accountant*
Keating, David *photographer*
Keep, Marcus Floyd *neurosurgeon*
Keleher, Michael Lawrence *lawyer*
†Kerlin, Max L. *academic administrator*
King, Lowell Restell *pediatric urologist*
Kinney, Carol Naus Roberts *real estate broker*
Knospe, William Herbert *medical educator*
Koch, Jamie *political party official*
Korman, Nathaniel Irving *research and development company executive*
Krostag, Diane Theresa Michaels *clinical informatics analyst*
Lang, Thompson Hughes *publishing company executive*
Lattman, Laurence Harold *retired academic administrator*
Leach, Richard Maxwell, Jr., (Max Leach Jr.) *corporate professional*
Lee, David Oi *engineer*
Lee, Roland Robert *radiologist, educator*
Leeper, Ramon Joe *physicist*
Lewis, Linda Kathryn *librarian*
Lind, Levi Robert *classics educator, writer*
Linver, Michael Norman *radiologist*
Liss, Norman Richard *insurance executive*
Loftfield, Robert Berner *biochemistry educator*
Logan, Richard *radiologist*
Long, Stephen Carrel Mike *lawyer*
Lopez, Floyd William *lawyer*
†Lopez, Martin, III, *lawyer*
†Loss, Lynne Franklin *artist, volunteer*
Lowrance, Muriel Edwards *program specialist*
Lucchetti, Lynn L. *career officer*
Malone, Henry Charles *writer, rare book dealer*
Manzitto, Arthur Sebastian *nursing and hospital administrator*
†Mapel, Douglas Wayne *epidemiologist, educator, health facility administrator*
†Martin, John Paul (Larry R. Fisher) *writer*
†Masefield, Oliver Leslie Peter *aerospace transportation executive, aerospace engineer*
Mateju, Joseph Frank *hospital administrator*
Mauderly, Joe Lloyd *pulmonary toxicologist*
May, Philip Alan *sociology educator*
†Melton, Robert Earl *lawyer*
Messersmith, Lanny Dee *lawyer*
Miera, Lucille Catherine Miera *artist, retired educator*
Miller, Mickey Lester *retired school administrator*
†Milloy, John Arthur *structural engineer*
Moise, Steven Kahn *lawyer, rancher, merchant banker*
Moneim, Moheb S. *orthopaedic surgeon, educator*
Montoya, Patricia T. *federal agency administrator*
Moody, Patricia Ann *psychiatric nurse, artist, small business owner*
Moore, Todd Allen *poet*
Mora, Federico *neurosurgeon*
Moskos, Harry *writer, former newspaper editor*
Moulds, William J. *retired aeronautical engineer*
Mueller, Diane Mayne *lawyer*
Muggenburg, Bruce Al *veterinary physiologist*
Multhaup, Merrel Keyes *artist*
Myers, Carol McClary *retired sales administrator, editor*
Navarro, Janyte Janine *real estate executive*
Nelson, Mary Carroll *artist, writer*
Neville, Bruce David *librarian*
Nevin, Jean Shaw *artist*
Ofte, Donald *retired environmental executive, consultant*
Omer, George Elbert, Jr., *orthopaedic surgeon, educator*
Oppedahl, Phillip Edward *computer company executive*
Orman, John Leo *software engineer, writer*
Ortiz, Kathleen Lucille *travel consultant*
Papyrin, Anatolii Nikiforovich *physicist, researcher*
Parker, James Aubrey *federal judge*
†Pasternacki, Linda Lea *critical care nurse*
Payne, Lucy Ann Salsbury *law librarian, educator, lawyer*
Peck, Ralph Brazelton *civil engineering educator, consultant*
Peña, Juan José *interpreter*
Peterson, Gwen Entz *artist*
Phillips, Larry Duane *gemologist, appraiser*
Plough, Charles Tobias, Jr., *retired electronics engineering executive*
Pryor, Richard J. *physicist, researcher*
†Raish, Carol Brooks *anthropologist, archaeologist*
Ramo, Roberta Cooper *lawyer*
Rand, Ruth A. *science and computer educator*
Rayburn, William Frazier *obstetrician, gynecologist, educator*
†Renschler, Clifford L. *chemist*
Reuter, Robert Carl, Jr., *retired engineering scientist*
Rhetts, Paul Fisher *publishing executive*
Rice, Linda Angel *music educator*
Richter, Harvena *retired english literature and creative writing teacher, writer*
Rivera, Rhonda Rae *lawyer, labor artibrator*
†Robb, John Donald, Jr., *lawyer*
Roberts, Dennis William *association executive*
†Roberts, Randal William *lawyer*
Roehl, Jerrald J. *lawyer*
†Romero, Richard M. *state legislator, educator*
Roth, Paul B. *dean, emergency medicine physician*
†Rush, Eric Palmer *civil engineer*
Rutherford, Thomas Truxtun, II, *county commissioner, former state senator*
Saland, Linda Carol *anatomy educator, neuroscience researcher*
Sanchez, Raymond G. *former state legislator*
Santhanam, Balu *engineering educator*
Schacht, Catherine Ann *classical violinist, pianist, mezzo-soprano*
Schuler, Alison Kay *lawyer*
Schwerin, Karl Henry *anthropology educator, researcher*
†Seiser, Virginia *librarian*
†Sena, Kathleen F. *academic administrator*
Sisk, Daniel Arthur *lawyer*
Slade, Lynn *lawyer*
Slesnick, Natasha *psychologist, researcher*
Smith, Anthony Younger *urologist, surgeon*
Smith, Edgar Benton *dermatologist*
Smyer, Myrna Ruth *drama educator*
Snell, Patricia Poldervaart *librarian, consultant*
Solomon, Arthur Charles *pharmacist*
Stahl, Jack Leland *real estate company executive*
Stambaugh, Harriett McCardell (Harriett Wynn McCardell) *social worker*
†Steider, Doris *artist*
†Steinbach, Falko *musician, music educator*
†Stetson, Catherine Baker *lawyer, lobbyist*
Storrs, Bruce Bryson *pediatric neurosurgeon*
Straus, Lawrence Guy *anthropology educator, editor-in-chief*
Stuart, Cynthia Morgan *university administrator*
Stuart, David Edward *anthropologist, writer, educator*
Summers, William Koopmans *neuropsychiatrist, researcher*
†Szasz, Ferenc M. *historian, educator*
†Taylor, Douglas John *materials scientist, researcher, materials engineer*
†Thornton, J. Duke *lawyer*
†Tinnin, Robert Priest, Jr., *lawyer*
Torres, Barbara Wood *technical services professional*
Travelstead, Chester Coleman *former educational administrator*
Turner, Robert Stanley *orthopaedic surgeon, bioethicist*
Uhlenhuth, Eberhard Henry *psychiatrist, educator*
†Valdez, Dianna Marie *language educator, consultant*
Van Why, Rebecca Rivera *retired guidance counselor*
†Varma, Roli *public administration educator*
Vianco, Paul Thomas *metallurgist*

Wainio, Mark Ernest *insurance company consultant*
Waitzkin, Howard Bruce *internist, sociologist, educator*
Walz, Kent *publishing executive*
Ward, Katherine Marie *retired school system administrator*
Warren, Thomas Lynn *mechanical engineer*
Waxman, Alan Garlett *obstetrician/gynecologist, educator*
†Weagel, Deborah Fillerup *composer*
Weh, Allen Edward *aviation executive*
Weissman, Suzanne Heisler *analytical chemist*
Wellborn, Charles Ivey *science and technology business consultant*
†Westwood, Albert Ronald Clifton *materials scientist, researcher*
White, Robert Rankin *writer, historian, hydrologist*
Wilkinson, Frances Catherine *librarian, educator*
Williams, Marion Lester *government official*
Winslow, Walter William *psychiatrist, educator*
Witkin, Joel-Peter *photographer, poet*
Wong, Phillip Allen *osteopathic physician*
Wood, Carolyn Jane *educational leadership educator*
Word, Terry Mullins *lawyer*
Wynne, Louis *psychologist*
Zink, Lee Berkey *retired academic administrator, economist, educator*

Alto
Thrasher, Jack Dwayne *toxicologist, researcher, consultant*
Zeitelhack, Gloria Jeanne *artist*

Artesia
Horner, Elaine Evelyn *secondary education educator*

Bayard
Lopez, Linda Carol *social sciences educator*
†Richard, Mark R. *architect*

Belen
Chicago, Judy *artist*
Perry, Charles *photo-illustrator, writer, researcher*
Smith, Helen Elizabeth *retired career officer*
Toliver, Lee *mechanical engineer*

Bernalillo
Pritchard, Betty Jean *retired art educator*

Bosque Farms
Kelly, Brian Matthew *industrial hygienist*

Capitan
Reimann, Bernhard Erwin Ferdinand *retired biologist*

Carlsbad
Byers, Matthew T(odd) *lawyer, educator*
Hayes, Robert Bruce *radiological engineer*
Paviet-Hartmann, Patricia *chemist, researcher*
Regan, Muriel *librarian*
Speed, Lynn Elizabeth *nurse practitioner*
Xiong, Yongliang *geochemist*

Carrizozo
Mack, James Willard *artist, educator*

Cedar Crest
Rypka, Eugene Weston *microbiologist*
Sheppard, Jack W. *retired career officer*

Cerrillos
Briggs, Barbara Jean Holmes *real estate developer*
Harnack, Barbara Wood *artist, sculptor*
Lutz, Raymond Price *retired industrial engineer, educator*

Chama
McElhaney, James Willson *lawyer, educator, author, trial consultant*

Cloudcroft
Hadfield, Michael James *electrical engineer*

Clovis
Skarda, Lynell Griffith *lawyer, banker*

Corrales
Adams, James Frederick *psychologist, educational administrator*
Eaton, Pauline *artist, educator*
Eisenstadt, Pauline Doreen Bauman *investment company executive, state legislator*
Sageser, Kendall Wayne *mineral exploration executive*

Deming
Becker-Klicker, Margaret Chan *library director*
De Mott, Marianne *educator, artist, craftsperson, space designer*
Rogers, Alice Louise *retired bank executive, writer, researcher*
Sherman, Frederick Hood *lawyer*
Stanley, Margaret Dureta Sexton *retired speech therapist*
White, Don William *rancher, minister*

Edgewood
Hamilton, Jerald *musician*
†Villagomez, Deborah Lynn *medical/surgical nurse, horse breeder*

El Prado
Young, Jon Nathan *archeologist*

Elephant Butte
Anton, Carol J. *small business owner, writer*

Embudo
Rogers, Benjamin Talbot *former consulting engineer, solar energy consultant*

Estancia
Swenka, Arthur John *retired food products executive*

Farmington
Caldwell, John Winston, III, *petroleum engineer*
Doig, Beverly Irene *retired systems specialist*
Graham, Warren Kirkland *dentist*
Gurley, Curtis Raymond *lawyer*
Lewis, Homer Dick *retired nuclear engineer*
Macaluso, Frank Augustus *oil company executive, banker*
Marquez, Mark Lynn *education educator*
Moeller, Floyd Douglas *lawyer*
Morgan, Jack M. *lawyer*
Peters, Evelyn Joan *artist*
Seiferle, Rebecca Ann *poet, editor, publisher*
Smith, Mark Edward *music educator*
†Strother, Robin Dale *lawyer*
†Thompson, Joseph T., Jr., *health facility administrator*
†Titus, Victor Allen *lawyer*
†Tully, Richard T. C. *lawyer, petroleum landman*

Galisteo
Lippard, Lucy Rowland *writer, lecturer*

Gallup
Cattaneo, Jacquelyn Annette Kammerer *artist, educator*
Fuhs, Terry Lynn *emergency room nurse, educator*
Martinez, Marcella *language educator*
Mouttet, Jane Elizabeth *librarian*
†Noe, Sally Woodworth (Sara Noe) *educator, local history researcher*
Sarath, Carol Ann *library/media coordinator*
Smarandache, Florentin *mathematics researcher, writer*
Zongolowicz, Helen Michaeline *education and psychology educator*

Hobbs
Dill, Gary A. *academic administrator*
Ebler, Marilyn Ann *graphic designer, educator*
Garey, Donald Lee *pipeline and oil company executive*
Garey, Patricia Martin *artist*
†Landers, Billy N., Jr., *medical and surgical nurse, administrator*
Reagan, Gary Don *state legislator, lawyer*
Ritchie, Fran A. *interior designer, small business owner*
Stout, Lowell *lawyer*

Holloman AFB
†Minto, David W. *aeronautical engineer*

Jemez Springs
Lawrence, Marjorie Diane Long *computer company executive, consultant*

Kirtland Afb
Alejandro, Steven B. *physicist*
Baum, Carl Edward *electromagnetic theorist*
Degnan, James Henry *physicist*
†Gideon, Francis C., Jr., *career officer*
†Huybrechts, Steven Marc *space system technologist*
Paxton, Alan Hugh *physicist*
Tritten, James John *national security educator*

Las Cruces
Adaime, Hamed Nazin *counselor*
Adams, J. Mack *computer science educator*
Bell, M. Joy Miller *financial planner, real estate broker*
†Blair, Robert Groberg *psychiatrist, educator*
Bloom, John Porter *historian, editor, administrator, archivist*
Bosland, Paul William *agriculture educator*
Bustamante, Donald D. *information systems administrator, consultant*
Cochrun, John Wesley *financial consultant*
Coker, Cheryl Ann *kinesiologist*
Conroy, William B. *retired university administrator*
Constantini, Louis O. *financial consultant, stockbroker*
†Cooch, F. Graham *ecologist, educator, ecologist, researcher*
Dasenbrock, Reed Way *literature educator*
Egginton, Everett *educational administrator*
Flores, William Vincent *Latin American studies educator*
Ford, Clarence Quentin *mechanical engineer, educator*
Gale, Thomas Martin *university dean*
†Giordano, Thomas H. *chemist, educator*
Heger, Herbert Krueger *education educator*
Herman, George *speech educator*
†Holechek, Jerry *agricultural studies educator*
†Jay, William Walton *lawyer*
Kilmer, Neal Harold *software engineer*
Libbin, James David *agricultural economics educator*
Lindley, Jearl Ray *lawyer*
Lutz, William Lan *lawyer*
Mata, Josefina *health education coordinator, educator*
McElyea, Ulysses, Jr., *veterinarian*
Medoff, Mark Howard *playwright, screenwriter, novelist*
Meltzer, Richard Stuart *cardiologist*
Merrick, Beverly Georgianne *journalism, communications educator*
Nelson-Humphries, Tessa *writer, educator*
Peterson, Robin Tucker *marketing educator*
Richardson, Albert Edward *chemistry educator, consultant, researcher*
Roscoe, Stanley Nelson *psychologist, aeronautical engineer*
Rosile, GraceAnn *business management educator*
†Salas, Loretta *education educator, researcher*
Sandenaw, Thomas Arthur, Jr., *lawyer*
Schemnitz, Sanford David *wildlife biology educator*
Snare, Carl Lawrence, Jr., *retired accountant, financial planner*
Talamantes, Roberto *developmental pediatrician*
Tonn, Robert James *retired entomologist*
Trafimow, David A. *psychology educator*
Wang, Joseph *scientist, educator*
Ward, James D. *government educator, writer*
Welsh, Mary McAnaw *family mediator, educator*
Wilson, Keith Charles *retired English educator, poet, short story writer*
Winfree, Latham Thomas *law educator*

Las Vegas
Riley, Carroll Lavern *anthropology educator*
Simpson, Dorothy Audrey *retired speech educator*
Tyrone, Greg L. *secondary school educator*

Los Alamos
Baskes, Michael I. *materials engineer*
Beck, Charles Milburn, II, *analytical chemist*
Becker, Stephen A. *physicist, designer*
Brown, Lowell Severt *physicist, educator*
Browne, John Charles *physics researcher, former national research laboratory executive*
Butko, Vladimir Yuryevich *physicist, researcher*
Canavan, Gregory H. *science educator*
Caramana, Edward J. *physicist*
Chomko, Stephen Alexander *archaeologist*
†Clausen, Bjørn *materials scientist, researcher*
Cucchiara, Alfred Louis *health physicist*
†Duan, Yixiang *research scientist, chemist*
Dudziak, Donald John *nuclear engineer, educator*
Durkee, Joe W(orthington), Jr., *nuclear engineer*
Edeskuty, Frederick James *engineer, consultant*
Engelhardt, Albert George *physicist*
Gibson, Benjamin Franklin *physicist*
†Gonzales, Stephanie *state official*
Gregg, Charles Thornton *research company executive*
Grilly, Edward Rogers *physicist*
Hansen, Glen Arthur *scientist, researcher*
Herr, Bruce *lawyer*
Höchbauer, Tobias Franz Wolfgang *physicist, researcher*
Jackson, James F. *nuclear engineer, educator*
Johnson, Mikkel Borlaug *physicist*
Judd, O'Dean P. *physicist*
Keepin, George Robert, Jr., *physicist*
King, Jerry Wayne *research chemist*
Kloepper, David Alan *retired management consultant*
Kubas, Gregory Joseph *research chemist*
Livesay, Valorie Ann *security program analyst*
Lu, Ningping *environmental chemist*
†Lyman, John L. *chemist, researcher*
Makaruk, Hanna Ewa *theoretical physicist*
†Maloy, Stuart *materials scientist, engineer*
Masse, William Bruce *archaeologist*
†Masunov, Artem *theoretical chemist, researcher*
McDonald, Thomas Edwin, Jr., *electrical engineer*
Mead, William Charles *physicist*
Mendius, Patricia Dodd Winter *editor, educator, writer*
†Michael, Martin Nieto *theoretical physicist*
Michaudon, André Francisque *physicist*
Mihalas, Dimitri Manuel *astrophysicist, educator*
Mitchell, Terence Edward *materials scientist*
Morales, Reynaldo *physicist*
Morel, Jim E. *nuclear engineer, researcher*
Nix, James Rayford *nuclear physicist, consultant*
Nunz, Gregory Joseph *aerospace engineer, program manager, educator, entrepreneur*
Orndoff, Elizabeth Carlson *retired junior college librarian, educator*
Peratt, Anthony Lee *electrical engineer, physicist*
Petrini, Fabrizio *computer science researcher*
†Popa-Simil, Liviu I. *nuclear engineer, researcher*
Press, William Henry *astrophysicist, computer scientist*
†Redmond, Bill *former congressman, minister*
Rosen, Louis *physicist*
Sayre, Edward Charles *librarian*
Seidel, Tammy Sue *secondary education educator*
Selden, Robert Wentworth *physicist, science advisor*
Sharp, David Howland *physicist*
Sicilian, James Michael *research engineer*
Sickafus, Kurt Edward *materials scientist, researcher*
Silver, Gary L. *chemist*
Smith, Fredrica Emrich *rheumatologist, internist*
Smith, James Lawrence *research physicist*
Snell, Charles Murrell *physicist, astrophysicist*
Stoddard, Stephen Davidson *ceramic engineer, former state senator*
Terrell, James (Nelson James Terrell) *physicist*
Thompson, Lois Jean Heidke Ore *psychologist*
Van Tuyle, Gregory Jay *nuclear engineer*
†Venhaus, Thomas J. *physicist*
†Vesselinov, Velimir Valentinov *hydrogeologist, researcher*
Wahl, Arthur Charles *retired chemistry educator*
Wallace, Jeannette Owens *state legislator*
Wallace, Terry Charles, Sr., *retired technical administrator, researcher*
†Wallstrom, Timothy C. *physicist*
Wienke, Bruce R. *physicist, consultant*
Williams, Joel Mann *polymer material scientist*
†Wilson, William Bradley *nuclear engineer*
WoldeGabriel, Giday *research geologist*
†Zhang, Dongxiao *research scientist*

Los Lunas
†Robinson, Mary Reid *mathematics educator*
Seiler, Fritz Arnold *physicist*

Lovington
Stuart, Lillian Mary *writer*
Trujillo, Anna *food company administrator, city official*

Mesilla
Lewis, Delano Eugene *ambassador, former broadcast executive*

Mesilla Park
Gibson, Dianna R. *financial consultant*

Milan
Kanesta, Nellie Rose *chemical dependency counselor*

Montezuma
Geier, Philip Otto, III, *academic administrator*

Mora
†Hanks, Eugene Ralph *land developer, rancher, forester, retired military officer, investor*

Moriarty
Haver, Jurgen F. *marketing consultant*
†Moonwalker, Tu *minister, counselor*

Mountainair
†Woodruff, Joan Leslie *occupational therapist, counselor*

Nageezi
Moore, Roger Albert, Jr., *archaeologist*

Nogal
Hume, Patsy Diseker *politician*

Paterson
Rothstadt, Garry Sigmund *judge*

Pinos Altos
Rogers, Linda Lee *artist*

Placitas
Dunmire, William Werden *writer, photographer, naturalist*
†Golleher, George *food company executive*
Hidy, George Martel *chemical engineer, executive*
Long, Timothy Scott *chemist, consultant*
Pirkl, James Joseph *industrial designer, educator, writer*
Reade, Lewis Pollock *business executive, retired diplomat, engineer*
Schoen, Stevan Jay *lawyer*
Smith, Richard Bowen *retired national park superintendent*
†Spencer, Donald Clifton *writer, publishing executive*

Portales
Dal Porto, Mark Daniel *music educator*
Goodwin, Martin Brune *radiologist*
Jones, Darynda Dean *interpreter, educator*
†Miller, Bettie Gene *librarian, educator*
Morris, Donald *tax specialist*
Overton, Edwin Dean *campus minister, educator*
Romo, José León *library consultant*
Williamson, Jack (John Stewart) *writer*
†Wozencraft-Ornellas, (Betty) Jean *singer, music educator*

Questa
Sharkey, Richard David *architectural artisan, inventor, musician*

Ranchos De Taos
Marx, Nicki Diane *sculptor, painter*

Raton
Carroll, William *publishing company executive*
Charriez, Blanca Noelia *social worker*

Rio Rancho
†Belovarski, Boris V. (Morris Bolivar) *writer, producer*
Delahanty, Carlos Anthony *industrial engineer*
Goss, Jerome Eldon *cardiologist*
†Huff, Jay *music educator*
Isenberg, Abraham Charles *shoe manufacturing company executive*
Ives, John Milton *retired engineer*
Jenkins, James Sherwood, Jr., *pharmacologist*
†Kasirajan, Karthikeshwar *surgeon, researcher*
†Qualley, Charles Albert *art educator*
†Schulz, Robert *music educator, musician*
Sei, Ibrahim *process engineer*
Stevens, Roger Templeton *writer*
Weber, Alois Hughes *principal*

Rodeo
Scholes, Robert Thornton *physician, research administrator*

Roswell
Anderson, Donald Bernard *oil company executive*
Anderson, Sally Midgette *social services administrator, linguist*
Avery, Keith Willette *artist, educator*
Baldock, Bobby Ray *judge*
Bassett, John Walden, Jr., *lawyer*
†Cahill, Laurence Roy, Jr., *customer service administrator*
Franzoni, Delaina Day *special education educator, department chairman*
Hedin, Edna Jenks *musician, educator*
Johnston, Mary Ellen *retired nursing educator*
Kelly, J. Michael *petroleum consultant*
Kraft, Richard Lee *lawyer*
Lee, Mike *music educator*
†Munroe, Shirley Ann *retired hospital association executive, health care consultant*
Olson, Richard Earl *lawyer, state legislator*
Robinson, Mark Leighton *oil company executive, petroleum geologist, horse farm owner*
†Tabrez, Shams S.M. *gastroenterologist*
†Watson, Marilyn Fern *writer, artist*
Wiggins, Kim Douglas *artist, art dealer*

Ruidoso
Ayers, Kathy Venita Moore *librarian*

Brown, Arlene Meredith *family practice physician, educator*
†Dutton, Dominic Edward *lawyer*

Ruidoso Downs
Templeton, Ann *artist, educator*

Sandia Park
Greenwell, Ronald Everett *communications executive*
Pinkus, Oscar *mechanical engineer, writer*
Weitz, Jeanne Stewart *artist, educator*
Wilczynski, Janusz S. *packaging technology executive, retired physicist*
Woodfin, Martha *interior designer*

Santa Cruz
Miller, Michael *literary arts and history researcher, consultant, writer*

Santa Fe
†Aarons, Stephen D. *lawyer*
Abeles, Richard Alan *lawyer*
Allen, John Polk *environmental scientist*
Amtmann, Hans Henry *aeronautical engineer, naval architect*
Anderson, Darrell Edward *psychologist, educator*
Ballard, Louis Wayne *composer*
Bauer, Betsy (Elizabeth Bauer) *artist*
Bergé, Carol *writer*
Berne, Stanley *author*
Bienvenu, John Charles *lawyer*
Bradley, Walter D. *lieutenant governor, real estate broker*
Brandt, Richard Paul *communications and entertainment company executive*
†Brannen, Jeffrey Richard *lawyer*
Burke, Lawrence J. *editor-in-chief*
Burton, John Paul (Jack Burton) *lawyer*
Candelaria, Nash *writer*
†Caplan, Jessica Marie *small business owner, artist*
Carpenter, Richard Norris *retired lawyer*
Casey, Patrick Anthony *lawyer*
Charles, Cheryl *non-profit and business executive*
Clinard, Marshall Barron *sociologist, educator*
Clyde, Larry Forbes *banker*
Coffield, Conrad Eugene *lawyer*
†Cohen, Adam J. *plastic surgeon*
Colvin, Greta Wilmoth *entrepreneur*
Cowan, George Arthur *chemist, bank executive, director*
Cunningham, David Fratt *lawyer*
Davidson, James Madison, III, *retired engineer, technical manager*
Davis, Shelby Moore Cullom *investment executive, consultant*
Denish, Diane D. *lieutenant governor*
Dirks, Lee Edward *newspaper executive*
Dodds, Robert James, III, *lawyer*
Dreisbach, John Gustave *investment banker*
Enyeart, James L. *museum director*
Farber, Steven Glenn *lawyer*
Feist-Fite, Bernadette *international health education consultant*
Ferguson, Glenn Walker *lecturer, author*
Fisher, Philip Chapin *physicist*
Fisher, Robert Alan *laser physicist*
†Gaddes, Richard *performing arts administrator*
†Garber, Bruce Samuel *lawyer*
Gaustad, Edwin Scott *historian, educator*
Gell-Mann, Murray *theoretical physicist, educator*
George, W. Peyton *lawyer*
Gildzen, Alex *writer*
Gilmour, Edward Ellis *retired psychiatrist*
Giovanielli, Damon Vincent *physicist, consulting company executive*
Glotzbach, George Linus *retired insurance executive*
Goldstein, Morton Hill *surgeon, educator*
†Goorley, John Timothy *nuclear engineer*
Greer, George Rushton *psychiatrist*
Groseclose, Everett Harrison *retired editor*
Guthrie, Catherine S. (Catherine S. Nicholson-Guthrie) *research scientist*
Hanson, Linda N. *academic administrator, educator*
Harcourt, Robert Neff *educational administrator, journalist, genealogist*
Harding, Marie *ecological executive, artist*
†Harroun, Dorothy Summer *painter, educator*
Herdman, Susan *art educator, artist*
Hickey, John Miller *lawyer*
Hoffmann, Louis Gerhard *immunologist, educator*
Hudson, Noel *artist*
Icerman, Larry *advanced technology business consultant, research and development administrator*
Johnson, Reverdy *lawyer*
Jones, Walter Harrison *chemist, educator*
Jurkat, Martin Peter *mathematician, statistician, management educator*
Justice, Jack Burton *retired lawyer, writer*
Kellner, Richard George *mathematician, computer scientist*
Kelly, Paul Joseph, Jr., *judge*
†Kelly, Ruth *state agency administrator*
Kennedy, Roger George *museum director, park service executive*
Kiefer, Helen Chilton *emergency and trauma physician, neurologist*
Kiley, Leo Austin *retired military officer, nuclear energy industry executive*
Kingman, Elizabeth Yelm *anthropologist*
Kingsley, Judith *artist*
Knapp, Edward Alan *retired government agency administrator, scientist*
Kotin, Paul *pathologist*
Lamb, Elizabeth Searle *freelance writer, poet*
Lehmberg, Stanford Eugene *historian, educator*
Leibowitz, Jack Richard *physicist, educator*
Leon, Bruno *architect, architecture educator*
Lichtenberg, Margaret Klee *publishing company executive*
†Lippincott, Janet *artist, art educator*
†Loftin, Thelma Tee *writer*
Lujan, Ben *state representative*
Lukac, George Joseph *not-for-profit fundraiser*
†Lynn, John Eric *nuclear physics research consultant*
Madrid, Patricia A. *state attorney general*
Maehl, William Henry *historian, university administrator, educational consultant*
Maes, Petra Jimenez *state supreme court justice*
Malone, Roxanne Enyeart *artist, educator*
†Mason, Allen Smith *atmospheric chemist*
McClaugherty, Joe L. *lawyer, educator*
†McIntosh, Kathleen Ann *music educator*
Melnick, Alice Jean (AJ Melnick) *counselor*
Mercer, James Lee *management consultant*
Merrin, Seymour *computer marketing company executive*
Miller, Dwight Richard *professional hair care industry executive, cosmetologist, consultant*
Miller, Edmund Kenneth *retired electrical engineer, educator*
†Mills, Thomas C.H. *lawyer*
Minzner, Pamela Burgy *state supreme court justice*
Moll, Deborah Adelaide *lawyer*
Montgomery, Michael Davis *physics/astrophysics company executive, consultant , real estate company executive*
Myers, R. David *library director, dean*
Noble, Merrill Emmett *retired psychology educator, psychologist*
Noland, Charles Donald *lawyer, educator*
Noyes, Stanley Tinning *writer, educator, arts administrator*
Odell, John H. *construction executive*
Orduno, Robert Daniel *artist, painter, sculptor*
Peat, Randall Dean *defense analysis company executive, retired air force officer*
Perkins, Linda Gillespie *real estate executive*
Perroni, Carol *artist, painter*
†Pesic, Peter *liberal arts educator, writer, pianist*
Phipps, Claude Raymond *research scientist*
Pickrell, Thomas Richard *retired oil company executive*
Pulitzer, Roslyn Kitty *social worker, psychotherapist*
Racuya-Robbins, Ann Elizabeth *artist*
Randolph, Somers *sculptor*
†Richardson, William Blaine *governor*
Robinson, Richard Gary *management consultant, accountant*
Romanowski, Thomas Andrew *physics educator*
Rubenstein, Bernard *orchestra conductor*
Sakara, Marilyn Judith *social worker*
†Salas Stone, Susan *artist, poet, web site designer*
Sandoval, Isabelle Medina *education educator*
Saurman, Andrew (Skip Saurman) *state agency executive*
†Sayre, William O. *geologist, educator*
Schaafsma, Polly Dix *archaeologist, researcher*
Schiller, William Richard *surgeon*
†Schuyler, Robert Len *investment company executive*
Schwarz, Michael *lawyer*
Serna, Patricio *state supreme court justice*
Shubart, Dorothy Louise Tepfer *artist, educator*
Silverman, Sherri Lynn *artist, educator*
Singer, Katie Ellen *writer, medical educator*
†Singleton, Sarah Michael *lawyer*
Smith, Philip Meek *science policy consultant, writer*
†Stalker, James Raghi *meteorologist, environmental services administrator*
Stieber, Tamar *journalist*
Sumner, Gordon, Jr., *retired military officer*
Swartz, William John *retired transportation resources company executive*
Tarn, Nathaniel *poet, translator, educator*
Taylor, Beverly Lacy *stringed instrument restorer, classical guitarist*
Vigil-Giron, Rebecca *state official*
†Villela, Khristaan David *art educator*
Wagner, Robert Philip *geneticist, educator*
Wakashige, Benjamin Taka *librarian*
Watkins, Stephen Edward *accountant, newspaper executive*
Weckesser, Susan Oneacre *lawyer*
†Wertheim, Jerry *lawyer*
†Whalen, William J. *retired physiologist*
White, David Hywel *physics educator*
Whitten, David George *chemistry educator*
Williams, Ralph Chester, Jr., *physician, educator*
Williams, Stephen *anthropologist, educator*
†Wilson, Laura Eleanor *landscape architect, sculptor*
Wilson, Thomas *museum director*
†Wolford, Richard Howard *lawyer*
Zlatoff-Mirsky, Everett Igor *violinist*
Zorie, Stephanie Marie *lawyer*

Santa Teresa
Pinzon, Brian William *inventor, consultant*
Rogash, Joseph Alan *meteorologist, educator*

Seneca
Monroe, Kendyl Kurth *retired lawyer*

Shiprock
†Atcitty, Fannie L. *elementary school educator, education educator*
†Austin-Garrison, Martha A. *education educator, researcher*
Billy, Bahe *soil scientist, educator*
Hill, Melodie Anne *director*

Silver City
Cox, Robert Gene *management consultant*
Foy, Thomas Paul *lawyer, retired state legislator, retired banker*
Fryxell, David Allen *publishing executive*
Hamlin, Don Auer *financial executive*
Hodges, Norman *retired district judge*
McCray, Dorothy Westaby *artist, printmaker, educator*
Moses-Foley, Judith Ann *elementary school educator*
Snedeker, John Haggner *university president*

Smith Lake
Hansen, Harold B., Jr., *principal*

Socorro
Bond, Robert Harold *electrical engineering educator*
Broadhead, Ronald Frigon *petroleum geologist, geology educator*
†Phillips, Fred Melville *hydrology educator*
†Smith, Leslie Clark *lawyer*

Springer
Dear, John *priest*

Sunspot
Keil, Stephen Lesley *astrophysicist*

Taos
Bell, Larry Stuart *artist*
Berkeley, Seamus Osborne *artist*
†Boles, David LaVelle *lawyer*
Garcia, Christine *academic administrator, educator, researcher*
†Harmon, Barbara Sayre *artist*
Lipscomb, Anna Rose Feeny *entrepreneur, arts organizer, fundraiser*
Martin, Agnes *artist*
Price, Brenda Chloè *artist, entrepreneur*
†Tisdale, Shelby Jo-Anne *museum director, consultant*
Witt, David L. *curator, writer*

Tesuque
Bundy, Wayne M. *retired geologist, consultant*
Novak, Joe *artist*

Tijeras
Ellison, Luther Frederick *oil company executive*
Keyler, Robert Gordon *material handling company executive*
Sholtis, Joseph Arnold, Jr., *business owner, nuclear and aerospace engineer, consultant*

Truchas
Breuer, Mala Klee *artist*

Truth Or Consequences
Rush, Domenica Marie *health facilities administrator*

Tyrone
Wilson, Johnnie Lou *social work educator, retired*

Vadito
Patten, Christine Taylor *artist, writer*

Valdez
†Jacobs, Roland William *psychiatrist*

White Sands Missile Range
Arthur, Paul Keith *electronic engineer*

NEW YORK

Accord
Rivera, Beatriz *writer, educator*

Adams Center
Hood, Thomas Gregory *minister*

Afton
Schwartz, Aubrey Earl *artist, educator*

Akron
Allen, Sue Fay *music educator, conductor*

Albany
Able, Kenneth Paul *biology educator*
Aceto, Vincent John *librarian, educator*
Alba, Richard Denis *sociologist, educator*
Alessi, Robert Joseph *lawyer, pharmacist, real estate developer*
Alexander, C(lark) Everts *accountant*
Ambros, Robert Andrew *pathologist, educator, writer*
†Amilcar, Dafney *academic administrator*
Arseneau, James Charles *physician*
Balsam, Richard Fredric *cardiologist*
†Barker-Benfield, Graham John *historian*
Barsamian, J(ohn) Albert *lawyer, judge, educator, criminologist, arbitrator*
Batt, H. William *political scientist*
†Becker, Wendy S. *educator*
Bellizzi, John J. *law enforcement association administrator, educator, pharmacist*
Bennett, Edward Virdell, Jr., *surgeon*
Berman, Carol *commissioner*
Berman, Jeffrey *language educator*
Black, Robert Charles *author, lawyer*
Blount, Stanley Freeman *marketing educator*
Borys, Theodor James *state agency data center administrator*
Bowen, Mary Lu *ecumenical administrator*
Bradley, Edward James *state official, computer programmer and analyst*
Bradley, Wesley Holmes *physician*
Branigan, Helen Marie *educational consultant, academic administrator*
†Bruno, Joseph L. *state legislator, senate majority leader*
Buran, David Runyon *fundraiser*
Burger, Harold Alan *virologist*
†Burian, Jarka Marsano *performing arts educator*
Canestrari, Ronald *state legislator*
Catalano, Robert Anthony *ophthalmologist, physician, hospital administrator, writer*
†Chretien, Margaret Cecilia *public administrator*
Christakis, Michael N. *academic administrator*
Clarey, Donald Alexander *government affairs consultant*
Clark, David Albert *pediatrician, consultant*
Cole, John Adam *insurance executive*
Colombí-Monguió, Alicia de *foreign language educator, poet*
Conway de Macario, Everly *immunologist, molecular biologist*
Cornell, Ralph Lawrence, Jr., *publishing executive*
†Craigue, Leslie J. *systems analyst*
Croce, Alan J. *government agency executive*
Cross, Robert Francis *commissioner*
Cruz, José Edgardo *political science educator*
†Curry, Robert Richard *health facility administrator*
†Dal Col, Richard Herbert *cardiothoracic surgeon*
Daniels, Randy A. *secretary of state*
Davis, Paul Joseph *endocrinologist*
DeFelice, Eugene Anthony *physician, medical educator, author, consultant, magician*
D'Elia, Christopher Francis *marine biologist, educator*
DeNuzzo, Rinaldo Vincent *pharmacy educator*
Doherty, Glen Patrick *lawyer*
Donohue, Mary *lieutenant governor*
Donovan, Robert Alan *English educator*
Doyle, Joseph Theobald *physician, educator*
Duncan, Jeffrey Burt *computer systems engineer*
Eadon, George A. *scientist, administrator, educator*
†Engel, David Anthony *lawyer*
Fadeley, Eleanor Adeline *secondary education educator*
Fakundiny, Robert Harry *geologist, educator, consultant*
Fanuele, Frank John *engineering executive*
Fayo, Anthony Thomas *research scientist*
†Fein, Scott Norris *lawyer*
Fernandez, Hermes A., III, *lawyer*
Ferrara, Donna *state legislator*
Forrest, George Philip *physician*
Fortune, Anne E. *social worker, educator*
Galivan, John Henry *biochemist, educator, public health officer, research administrator*
†Gilliam, Marsha Sampson *state agency administrator*
Glazer, Joseph A. *medical association administrator*
Gosdeck, Thomas Joseph *lawyer*
†Gosende, Robert Rosalino *academic administrator*
Graffeo, Victoria A. *state appeals court judge*
†Griffiths, Gareth *humanities educator, department chairman, theater critic, writer*
Hancox, David R(obert) *audit administrator, educator*
Hanna, John, Jr., *lawyer, educator, arbitrator, mediator*
Happ, Harvey Heinz *electrical engineer, educator*
†Hassan, Stephanie Anitra *writing educator, consultant*
Herman, Robert S. *former state official, economist, educator*
Herrick, Kristine Ford *graphic design educator*
Heshmat, Hooshang *manufacturing executive*
Hilton, Joseph D. *state agency administrator*
Hobart, Thomas Yale, Jr., *union president*
Hoffman, Nancy E. *lawyer*
Hoffmeister, Jana Marie *cardiologist*
Hong, Chia-Swee *research scientist*
Howard, Lyn Jennifer *medical educator*
†Howell, Robert Charles *philosopher, educator*
Hsia, Franklin Wen-Hai *computer programmer, systems analyst, consultant*
†Iyer, Seema *chemist*
Jackson, Kenneth William *research scientist, educator*
Joyce, William George, Jr., *transportation executive*
Kadamus, James Alexander *educational administrator*
Katz, William A. *library science educator*
Kaye, Judith Smith *state court chief justice*
†Kecskes, Istvan *linguist, educator*
Kekes, John *philosopher, educator*
Kennedy, Debbie A. *plastic surgeon*
Kennedy, William Joseph *novelist, educator*
Kiang, Walter T. *environmentalist, state official*
Kim, Jai Soo *physics educator*
Klaas, Ottmar *software engineer*
Knee, Michael J. *science librarian, consultant*
Koff, Howard Michael *lawyer*
†Kornstein, Michael Allen *lawyer*
Lane, Nancy Lucille *mental health and critical care nurse*
Langer, Judith Ann *literacy educator*
Lansing, Mark Daniel *lawyer*
Lawton, Nancy *artist*
Lefkowitz, Jerome *lawyer*
Leichman, Kenneth William *investment executive*
Lepow, Martha Lipson *pediatric educator*
Ley, Ronald *psychologist, educator*
†Lnenicka, Gregory Allen *biologist, educator*
Lobosco, Anna Frances *state program development specialist*
Loneck, Barry Martin *social work researcher, educator*
Long, David Russell *academic program director*
Lovely, Thomas John *neurosurgeon, educator*
Lustenader, Barbara Diane *human resources specialist*
Macario, Alberto Juan Lorenzo *physician*
MacColl, Robert *research scientist, biomedical educator*
MacDonald, Carolyn Ann *physicist, educator*
MacDowell, Richard T. *surgeon, educator*
Martland, T(homas) R(odolphe) *philosophy educator*
Meader, John Daniel *judge*
Meho, Lokman I. *library and information scientist, educator*
†Merbler, Candace Anne *librarian*
Miesing, Paul *university educator, consultant, researcher*
Mignacca, Rita M. *American literature educator*
†Mills, Richard P. *school system administrator*
Miner, Roger Jeffrey *judge*
Mishler, Mark Sean *lawyer*
Mizejewski, Gerald Jude *research scientist*

Mlock, Mary *employee benefits professional*
Mohler, Edwin Eugene *orthopedic surgeon*
Mongin, Alexander Anatolievich *neuroscientist, educator*
Moore, Gwen Lova *social sciences educator*
†Morga Bellizzi, Celeste *editor*
Morris, Margretta Elizabeth *conservationist*
Mueller, I. Lynn *strategic planning and communications consultant*
Murray, Neil Vincent *computer science educator*
Nathan, Richard P(erle) *political scientist, educator*
Naumann, Hans J. *manufacturing company executive*
Nesler, Mitchell Scott *psychology researcher*
Novello, Antonia Coello *state health commissioner, former surgeon general*
Olmsted, Ruth Martin *educator*
Ortloff, George Christian, Sr., (Chris Ortloff) *journalist, state legislator*
Pasquariello, Julius Anthony *pharmacist*
Pataki, George E. *governor*
Paulson, Peter John *librarian, publishing company executive*
Philip, George Michael *pension fund administrator*
Poe, Suzy Crowbar *publisher, author*
Powers, John Kieran *lawyer*
Pozner, Louis-Jack *lawyer*
Provorny, Frederick Alan *lawyer, educator*
Quackenbush, Roger E. *retired secondary school educator*
†Read, Susan Phillips *judge*
Reaulo, Arthur Robert *mental health specialist, advocate*
Reese, William Lewis *philosophy educator*
Refai, Shahid *history educator*
†Regal, Evan Charles *lawyer*
Reid, William James *social work educator*
†Rieder, Conly LeRoy *cell biologist, consultant*
Robbins, Cornelius (Cornelius Van Vorse) *educational administration educator*
Robinson, John Bowers, Jr., *bank holding company executive*
Rogers, James Thomas *trade association executive*
Rosenfeld, Harry Morris *editor*
Rosenkrantz, Daniel J. *computer science educator*
†Rosenthal, Irene L. *education educator, consultant*
Roy, Rob J. *biomedical engineer, anesthesiologist*
Ruggeri, Robert Edward *lawyer*
Ruzow, Daniel Arthur *lawyer*
Salins, Peter D. *academic administrator*
Saridis, Panayota Dimarogona *civil engineer*
Sattinger, Michael Jack *economics educator, researcher*
Sbuttoni, Michael James *orthodontist, building contractor*
†Schalit, Robert Edward *advertising executive*
†Schell, Lawrence M. *education educator, biologist*
Schneider, Allan Stanford *biochemistry, neuroscience and pharmacology educator, biomedical research scientist*
Schneider, Duane Bernard *English literature educator*
Scott, William Proctor, III, *lawyer*
Selchick, Jeffrey Mark *arbitrator, judge*
Shankman, Gary Charles *art educator*
†Shanock, Linda *education educator*
†Sherman, Sandra Lynn *auditor*
Shields, Robert Michael *state agency administrator*
Shubert, Joseph Francis *librarian*
Sills, Stephen Joel *ophthalmologist*
Smith, Michael Ernest *archaeologist, educator*
Spencer, Keith G. *construction executive*
Spitzer, Eliot *state attorney general*
†Spivack, Simon Daniel *physician, scientist, educator*
†Staley, Harry Charles *retired literature educator, poet*
Standish, John Spencer *textile manufacturing company executive*
Stanton, Victoria Mead *lawyer*
†Stenson, Brian T. *academic administrator*
Stevens, Roy W. *microbiologist, researcher*
Stewart, Margaret McBride *biology educator, researcher*
Swartz, Donald Percy *physician*
Teevan, Richard Collier *psychology educator*
Tepper, Clifford *allergist, immunologist, educator*
Thompson, Frank Joseph *political science educator*
Thornton, Maurice *retired academic administrator*
Timmins, Patrick Farrell, III, *gynecologic oncologist*
Toren, Mark *state official, econometrician*
Travers, W. Lawrence *healthcare executive*
Treadwell, Alexander F. *former state official, political party chairman & leader*
†Treadwell, Sandy *legislative staff member, political organization administrator*
Veille, Jean-Claude *maternal-fetal medicine physician, educator*
Verdile, Vincent Paul *dean, emergency physician*
Volker, Dale Martin *state legislator, lawyer*
von Schack, Wesley W. *energy services company executive*
Welch, Janet Martin *librarian*
Willis, John Patrick *chemist*
Wilson, Brian Eugene *computer scientist*
Wittner, Lawrence Stephen *history educator*
Yalcintas, M. Güven *medical physicist*
Zaccari, Steven Joseph *secondary school educator*
Zimmerman, Joseph Francis *political scientist, educator*

Albertson
Brown, James Russell, III, *librarian*

Alfred
Boehlert, Carl Joseph *materials scientist, educator*
Brown, June Evelyn *librarian, documentalist*
Coll, Edward Girard, Jr., *university president*
Greil, Arthur Lawrence *sociology educator*
Higby, Wayne (Donald Higby) *artist, educator*
†Huberman, Ariana *language educator*
Pian, Carlson Chao-Ping *mechanical engineering educator, researcher*
Pye, Lenwood David *materials science educator, researcher, consultant*
Spriggs, Richard Moore *ceramic engineer, research center administrator*
Tolhurst, Fiona Catherine *English language educator*
Torpey, Robin Lee *information scientist, educator*
Wang, Xingwu *physics educator*

Alfred Station
Condrate, Robert Adam, Sr., *spectroscopy educator*

Altamont
†Armstrong, Agnes Rose Fingerlin *musicologist*
Frinta, Mojmir Svatopluk *art history educator*

Amagansett
Fleetwood, M. Freile *psychiatrist, educator*
Frankl, Jeanne Silver *association executive, lawyer*
Frankl, Kenneth Richard *retired lawyer*

Amenia
Hale, Nathan Cabot *sculptor, artist, poet*
Wetmore, William Thomson *writer, small business owner*

Amherst
Anisman, Martin Jay *academic administrator*
Aurbach, Herbert Alexander *sociology educator*
Bobinski, Mary Form *library director*
Braun, Kazimierz Pawel *theatrical director, writer, educator*
Clark, Donald Malin *professional association executive*
Cohen, Herman Nathan *private investigator*
†Edsberg, Laura E. *research scientist, consultant*
Granger, Carl V. *physician, educator*
†Hu, Yun Hang *chemical engineer*
Ismail, Abu Zafar Mohamed *physics educator, researcher, consultant*
Jen, Frank Chifeng *finance and management educator*
†Jin, Jin Yan *science educator*
Jones, E. Thomas *lawyer*
Kurtz, Paul *philosopher, author, educator, publisher*
†Kutsin, Leonid *engineering educator, researcher*
†Lawvere, Francis William *mathematician, educator*
Murray, William Michael *lawyer*
Nickell, Joe Herman *paranormal expert*
Pachan, Mary Jude Kathryn Dorothy *guidance counselor*
Paul, Laurence Johnson *retired journalist*
Roehmholdt, John Michael *urologist, educator*
Wiesenberg, Jacqueline Leonardi *lecturer*

Amityville
Brennan, Patrick Thomas *meteorology company executive, meteorologist*
Imbert, Richard Conrad *insurance company executive, real estate developer*
†Palumbo, Anthony *education educator*
Rubin, Michele S. *radiologist*
Sodaro, Edward Richard *psychiatrist*
Studer, Patricia S. *psychologist*
Upadhyay, Yogendra Nath *physician, educator*
Wright, Nannie Bell *retired secondary school educator*

Ancramdale
Weinstein, Joyce *artist*

Andover
†Hutter, Robert Grant *lawyer*

Angola
Green, Gerard Leo *priest, educator*

Annandale
†Cutler, Robert W. *biologist, educator*

Annandale On Hudson
Achebe, Chinua *writer, humanities educator*
Botstein, Leon *academic administrator, conductor, historian*
†Darrow, Emily M. *public relations executive, writer*
Ferguson, John Barclay *biology educator*
Gibbs, Christopher Howard *musicologist, educator*
Manea, Norman *writer, educator*
Papadimitriou, Dimitri Basil *economist, college administrator*
Sourian, Peter *writer, English educator*
Thomas, Sarah Rebecca *computer science educator*

Appleton
Singer, Thomas Kenyon *international business consultant, orchardist*

Ardsley
†Bogaty, Lewis *writer, publisher, lawyer, educator*
†Glauberman, Melvin L. *lawyer*
Jacobs, Sheldon *investment advisor*
Mohl, Allan S. *social worker*
Sokolow, Isobel Folb *sculptor*

Ardsley On Hudson
Lisle, Laurie *author*
Stein, Milton Michael *lawyer*

Arkville
Downing, Darlene L. *non-for-profit organization executive*

Armonk
Bolduc, Ernest Joseph *association management consultant, not-for-profit developer, consultant*
Dajnowicz, Jan *software and hardware designer, researcher*
†Dunton, Gary C. *insurance company executive*
Engel, Joel Stanley *telecommunications executive*
Gerstner, Louis Vincent, Jr., *computer company executive*
Grove, David Lawrence *economist, director*
Harreld, James Bruce *information technology executive*
Herz, Michael B. *accountant, management consultant*
Levy, Kenneth James *advertising executive*
Mellors, Robert Charles *physician, scientist, educator*
Moskowitz, Stuart Stanley *lawyer*
†Moss, Eric Harold *lawyer*
Quinn, James W. *lawyer*
Scotto, Renata *soprano*
Sydney, Doris S. *sports touring company executive, interior designer*
†Tantillo Elton, Nina *artist, graphics designer, educator*
Wolff, Kurt Jakob *lawyer, director*

Astonia
Carroll, David Joseph *stage manager*

Astoria
Matheson, Linda *retired clinical social worker*
Sarkissian, Naver Agop *pathologist*

Athens
Lew, Roger Alan *manufacturing company executive*

Atlantic Beach
Lore, Martin Maxwell *lawyer*

Auburn
Chamberlain, Michael Allen *marketing professional, consultant*
†Correll, Janet Moore *music educator*
Long, Michael Howard *urban planner, landscape architect*
Speck, David Dean *ophthalmologist*
Trapani, Janet Leigh *physical therapist*

Aurora
Leybold-Taylor, Karla Jolene *college official*
Shilepsky, Arnold Charles *mathematics educator, computer consultant*

Ava
Hicks, Phyllis Ann *retired medical, surgical nurse*

Averill Park
†Blostein, Michael David *music educator*
Costello, Amelia Fusco *educator*
Haines, Walter Wells *retired economics educator*
†Nevai, Lucia *writer*
Traver, Robert William, Sr., *management consultant, author, lecturer, engineer*

Babylon
Brackett, Ronald E. *investment company executive, lawyer*
Collis, Charles *aircraft company executive*
Epstein, Jeffrey Mark *neurosurgeon*
Garvey, Jane Roberts *lawyer*
Haley, Priscilla Jane *artist, printmaker*
Hennelly, Edmund Paul *lawyer, oil company executive*
Kroll, Brian Walter Thomas *music educator*
Schwarz, Barbara Ruth Ballou *elementary school educator*

Bainbridge
Compton, John Robinson *retired rake company executive*
Goerlich, Shirley Alice Boyce *publishing executive, educator, media consultant*

Baldwin
Abram, Blanche Schwartz *music educator, pianist*
Franz, Darren M. *writer*
Preis, Carl Otto *company executive, mechanical engineer*
†Zeitlin, Joan *federal agency administrator*
Zuckerman, Jackie Lynn *social worker*

Baldwin Place
Kurian, George Thomas *publisher*

Baldwinsville
Hansen, Beverly Anne *environmental policy educator*

Ballston Lake
Cotter, William Donald *former state commissioner, former newspaper editor*
Fiedler, Harold Joseph *electrical engineer, consultant*
McCann, Chris (Christian David McCann) *software engineer, educator*
Silverman, Gerald Bernard *journalist*

Ballston Spa
Barba, Harry *author, educator, publisher*
Brown, Ifigenia Theodore *lawyer*
†Cameron Jr, Edward John *engineer*
Knight, Jane Miller *nurse midwife, retired air force officer*
Westbrook, Jack Hall *metallurgist, consultant*

Bangall
Swanson, David Heath *agricultural company executive*

Batavia
†Belongia, Christine Giese *education educator, director*
Grieger, Donald L. *artist*
Small, Bruce Michael *health facility administrator*
Steiner, Stuart *college president*

Bath
Ward, Kenneth G. *agricultural products executive*

Bay Shore
Goldstein, Leonard Barry *dentist, educator*
†Kirsch, Scott Douglas *family practice physician*
Pinsker, Tillene Giller *retired special education administrator*
Sampino, Anthony F. *physician, obstetrician and gynecologist*
Sampino, Michele *physician assistant*
Shreve, Sue Ann Gardner *retired health products company administrator*
Williams, Tonda *entrepreneur, consultant*

Bayport
†Hurst, Matthew Thomas *music educator*
Mohanty, Christine Ann *retired language educator, actress*

Bayside
Ausubel, Hillel *librarian*
Bernstein, Barry S. *lawyer*
Cohen, Daniel *psychologist, educator*
Cortes, Engracio Padilla *oncologist*
†Du Mont, Allen André *pyschotherapist, educator*
Gavencak, John Richard *pediatrician, allergist*
Goldes, Jordan *legislative staff member, press secretary*
Madden, Joseph Daniel *trade association executive*
Roth, Joshua S. *obstetrician/gynecologist, educator*
†Sabani Leguizamón, Laura Silvia *literature educator, writer*
Skemer, Arnold Marius *writer*
Stoyan, Hortensia Rodríguez-Sánchez *library administrator*
†Weber, Christa D. *writer*
Yin, Henry Chih-Peng *educator*
Zinn, William *violinist, composer, business executive*

Bayville
Arenberg, Irving Kaufman Karchmer *fund manager, strategist*

Beacon
Mc Keown, William Taylor *magazine editor, author*
Stokes, Catherine Ann *elementary education educator*

Bear Mountain
Smith, Andrew Josef *historian, publishing executive, naturalist, writer*

Bearsville
Ruellan, Andree *artist*
Whitman, Karen *artist*

Beaver Dams
BetzJitomir, Susan Marie *financial consultant, lawyer, educator*

Bedford
Atkins, Ronald Raymond *lawyer*
Bowman, James Kinsey *publishing company executive, rare book specialist*
Chase, Chevy (Cornelius Crane Chase) *comedian, actor, author*
Chia, Pei-Yuan *banking executive*
D'Angelo, Gonda *retired social worker*
Hughart, Thomas Arthur *minister*
Husted, William Armstrong *sales executive*
Margolin, Carl M. *psychotherapist*
Philip, Peter Van Ness *former trust company executive*
Sarbin, Hershel Benjamin *management consultant, business publisher, lawyer*
Sha, Richard T. *computer company executive*
†Tischler, Gary Lowell *psychiatrist, educator*
Tognino, John Nicholas *financial services executive*

Bedford Corners
Singer, Craig *entrepreneur, investor, consultant*

Bedford Hills
Jensen-Carter, Philip Scott *photographer, photographer*
Waller, Wilhelmine Kirby (Mrs. Thomas Mercer Waller) *civic worker, organization official*

Beechhurst
Wingate, Constance Blandy *librarian*

Belle Harbor
Goldsmith, Cathy Ellen *retired special education educator*

Bellerose
Bearak, Corey B(ecker) *lawyer*

Bellmore
Andrews, Charles Rolland *library administrator*
Bregman, Steven Howard *library director*
Evers, Gene *writer*
Harris, Ira Stephen *secondary education educator, administrator*

Bellport
Graskemper, Joseph Peter *dentist*
†Hendrie, Elaine *public relations executive*
Moeller, Mary Ella *retired home economist, educator, radio commentator*
Regalmuto, Nancy Marie *small business owner, psychic consultant, therapist*

Schultheis, Edwin Milford *dean, business educator*
Straus, Oscar S., II, *foundation executive*
Sutton-Straus, Joan M. *journalist*
Townsend, Terry *publishing executive*

Bergen
Woodworth, Beth Elaine *business owner*

Berne
†Skiff, Colleen Fraser *art educator, art gallery director, recreational therapist*

Bethpage
Conti, James Joseph *chemical engineer, educator*
De Santis, Mark *osteopathic physician*
Dolan, Charles Francis *media, entertainment company executive*
†Dolan, James *communications executive*
Janczak, Andrew Anthony *executive*
Kessler, Richard J. *psychiatrist*
Lemle, Robert Spencer *lawyer*
Mahony, Sheila Anne *cable television executive*
Marrone, Daniel Scott *business, production and quality management educator*
Martin, Darryl James *audio-visual specialist*
†McEnroe, Kate *broadcast executive*
Schneider, Adam Jason *neurologist, neurophysiologist*
†Whiteside, James Brooks *mechanics engineer, researcher*

Big Flats
Keck, Donald Bruce *physicist*
Orsillo, James Edward *computer systems engineer, company executive*
Van Etten, Elwyn Robert *retired marketing specialist*

Binghamton
Anderson, Warren Mattice *lawyer*
Axtell, Clayton Morgan, Jr., *lawyer*
Beach, Beth *elementary educator*
Bearsch, Lee Palmer *architect, city planner*
Beck, Matthias *mathematician, educator*
Beck, Stephanie G. *lawyer*
Best, Robert Mulvane *insurance company executive*
Bethje, Robert *retired general surgeon*
†Biggers, Jonathan Edward *music educator, consultant*
Bochnovich, John Andrew *small business owner*
Carrigg, James A. *retired utility company executive*
Chivers, James Leeds *lawyer*
Clark, Clifford Dale *university president*
Coates, Donald Robert *geology educator, scientist*
Cornacchio, Joseph Vincent *engineering educator, computer researcher, consultant*
DeFleur, Lois B. *university president, sociology educator*
Eisch, John Joseph *chemist, educator, writer, consultant*
Florance, Douglas Allan *wholesale distributor*
Gaddis Rose, Marilyn *literature educator, translator*
Gates, Gregory Ansel *lawyer*
†Gates, Leslie Carlisle *sociology educator*
Geer, James Francis *mathematics educator*
Gerhart, Eugene Clifton *lawyer*
†Gilroy, Eileen M. *speech pathology/audiology services professional, educator*
Gouldin, David Millen *lawyer*
†Hames-Garcia, Michael R. *English language educator*
Henderson, Daniel Joseph *economist*
Hilton, Peter John *mathematician, educator*
Holder, Kathleen *elementary education educator*
†Horowitz, Michael M. *university educator*
Hudak, Michael John *environmentalist, writer, photographer*
Isaacson, Robert Lee *psychology educator, researcher*
James, Gary Douglas *biological anthropologist, educator, researcher*
Klir, George Jiri *systems science educator*
Kramer, Philip Joseph *lawyer*
Levis, Donald James *psychologist, educator*
Marella, Philip Daniel *broadcasting company executive*
Meador, John Milward, Jr., *university dean*
Michael, Sandra Dale *medical educator, medical researcher*
Nelson, Charles A. *physicist, educator*
Peckham, Eugene Eliot *surogate judge, lawyer*
Polachek, Solomon William *economist, educator*
Price, Paul Marnell *lawyer*
Regenbogen, Adam *judge*
†Reitz, Margaret Anne *musician, educator*
Rosko, Keith Allan *art educator, illustrator*
†Rowe, Steven L. *mental health nurse*
†Sadik, Omowunmi A. *electrochemist, educator*
Sklar, Kathryn Kish *historian, educator*
Stein, George Henry *historian, educator, administrator*
Swain, Mary Ann Price *university official*
Terriquez-Kasey, Laura Marie *emergency nurse*
†Thompson, Carlton Frederick *lawyer*
Wecker, William A. *preventive medicine physician, neuropsychiatrist*
†Weissman, Ann Paley *art educator, artist, consultant*
Whittingham, M(ichael) Stanley *chemist*
Yammarino, Francis Joseph *management educator, consultant*
Zaslavsky, Thomas *mathematics educator*
Zhang, Zhongfei *computer science educator, researcher, consultant*
†Ziemski, Connie Marie *social studies educator*

Blauvelt
Gillespie, John Fagan *mining executive*

Bluff Point
Fitch, Linda Bauman *educator*

Bohemia
Baglio, Vincent Paul *engineering executive*
Hausman, Howard *electronics executive*
Leddy, John Joseph, Jr., *music educator*
Maccarone, Frances Mary *publishing executive*
Manley, Gertrude Ella *librarian, media specialist*
Ortiz, Germaine Laura De Feo *secondary education educator, counselor*
Rogé, Ronald William *financial planner, investment management executive*
†Talbot, Sandra Ann *medical-surgical nurse*

Bolton Landing
Crosby, John Griffith *investment banker*

Boston
Connors, Linda Marie *community health nurse*

Brainard
Isaksen, Robert L. *retired bishop*
†Johnsen, May Ann *artist, sculptor, graver*

Breesport
Peckham, Joyce Weitz *foundation administrator, former secondary education educator*

Brentwood
Manning, Randolph H. *academic administrator*
Oshypko, John *artist, set designer*

Brewster
Bates, Barbara J. Neuner *retired municipal official*
Blyakhman, Yefim Moisei *chemist, researcher*
Killackey, Dorothy Helen *real estate professional, former educator*
Nadel, Norman Allen *civil engineer*
Simon, Andrew L. *educational publishing executive*

Briarcliff Manor
†Atwood, Donna Elaine *financial manager, retired*
Bingham, J. Peter *electronics research executive*
Driver, Sharon Humphreys *marketing executive*
Goldschmidt, Robert Alphonse *financial executive*
Hopkins, Lee Bennett *writer, educator*
Kennell, Richard Wayne *recording artist, business manager*
Leiser, Burton Myron *philosophy and law educator*
Lew, Leslie *artist*
McIlvaine, Betsy *librarian*
Pousada, Lidia *physician*
Read, John Conyers *non-profit management*
Shum, Henry *finance company executive*
Weiser, David Joseph *psychiatrist*

Briarwood
Benedict, Joseph Harold, Jr., *academic administrator, management consultant*
Takacs, Michael Joseph *educator*

Bridgehampton
Coy, Christopher James *architect*
Cummings, Richard M. *law educator, consultant, writer*
Goff, Kimberly (Kimberly Knollenberg) *art dealer, painter, writer*
McMenamin, Joan Stitt *headmistress*
Phillips, Warren Henry *publishing executive*
Smith, Christine Chew *artist, educator*

Bridgeport
Sheldon, Thomas Donald *academic administrator*

Brightwaters
Kavanagh, Eileen J. *librarian*
North, E(dward) Lee *author, former aerospace company professional*

Brockport
Bucholz, Arden *historian, educator*
Campbell, Jill Frost *university official*
Flanagan, Timothy James *criminal justice educator, university official*
Gemmett, Robert J. *university dean, English language educator*
Halquist, Shawn A. *music educator*
Heyen, William H. *literature educator, poet*
Hickerson, Dianne *artist, former educator*
†Keiser, John Dougherty *business educator*
Leslie, William Bruce *history educator*
Michaels, John G. *mathematics educator*
†Owen, Karen Ann *historian, educator*
†Rich, George Merritt *retired elementary school educator*
Stier, William Frederick, Jr., *academic administrator, educator*

Bronx
Adams, Alice *sculptor*
Adinolfi, Marion Darlyne *research scientist*
Ahmose, Nefertari A. *journalism educator*
†Albrecht, Roberta J. *writer*
Alfrey, Larry Robert *physician assistant*
†Alicea, Yvette *special education educator*
Aronowitz, Julian *management consultant*
Balka, Sigmund Ronell *lawyer*
†Basu, Parantap *economist, educator*
Bauman, Laurie Julia *sociologist, researcher*
Behnken, William Joseph *art educator, artist*
Bella, Jonathan Noriega *cardiologist*
Bennett, Michael Vander Laan *neuroscience educator*
†Berman, Wesley R. *minister, retired social worker*
Bhalodkar, Narendra Chandrakant *cardiologist*
†Bigal, Marcelo E *physician*
Billett, Henny Heisler *hematologist*
Bingham, June *writer, playwright*
Blaufox, Morton Donald *physician, educator, specialist in hypertension*
†Boctor, Fouad Nassif *pathologist, researcher*
Bowers, Francis Robert *literature educator*
Brickner, Alice *painter, illustrator*
†Brosius, Scott David *professional baseball player*
Buckley, Peter John *psychiatrist*
Bullaro, Grace Russo *literature, film and foreign language educator, speaker, book reviewer*
†Burgio, Michael *medical researcher*
Burton, Leslie Anne *psychologist*
Buschke, Herman *neurologist*
Butler, Jill Lauren Kraft *internist, educator*
Cammarata, Joan Frances *Spanish language and literature educator*
†Canavan, Francis *priest, educator*
Capodilupo, Jeanne Hatton *public relations executive*
Castora, Joseph Charles *history educator*
Chang, Mabel Li *economist, educator*
Clary, Roy *hospital administration executive*
†Clemens, Roger *professional baseball player*
Coady, Joseph William *history educator, researcher*
Cohen, Herbert Jesse *physician, educator*
Cohen, Jacob Marc *physician*
†Cone, David Brian *professional baseball player*
Conway, William Gaylord *zoologist, zoo director, conservationist*
†Corey, Elizabeth B. *poet*
Cornfield, Melvin *lawyer, university institute director*
Coupey, Susan McGuire *pediatrician, educator*
Cubeñas, José Antonio *social worker, consultant*
†Currie, Joseph Aloysius *campus ministry director, theology studies educator*
Das, Ashoke Kumar *internist, consultant*
Dauber, Leonard Gene *oncologist, medical educator*
De Blasio, Maria P. *physician*
De La Cancela, Victor *psychologist*
Delprete, Piero Giuseppe *botanist, curator, educator*
Dimler, G(eorge) Richard *German language educator, editor*
Doddi, Seshagiri Rao *psychiatrist*
Downs, Peter Campbell *small business owner*
Dulles, Avery *cardinal, theologian*
Dutcher, Janice Jean Phillips *oncologist*
Eder, Howard Abram *physician, education educator*
Elenko, Stuart S. *historian, educator*
Elkins, Alfred David *insurance company administrator*
Engoron, Arthur Fredericks *judge*
Farley, Rosemary Carroll *mathematics and computer science educator*
†Ferraro, Marie *dental hygienist*
Fidock, David Armand *microbiology educator*
Fishman, Charles Lawrence *internist*
Fishman, Joshua Aaron *sociolinguist, educator*
†Fitting, Melvin Chris *computer scientist, educator*
Fleischer, Norman Samuel *endocrinology administrator, medical educator*
Font, Cecilio Rafael *biology educator, physician*
Foreman, Spencer *pulmonary specialist, hospital executive*
Freeman, Leonard Murray *radiologist, nuclear medicine physician, educator*
†Fulop, Milford *physician*
Gang, Vanessa Noble *health facility administrator, researcher, nursing consultant*
George, Deinabo Dabibi *writer, computer specialist, educator*
Gerst, Paul Howard *physician*
Gevirtz, Clifford Mark *anesthesiologist*
Gillman, Arthur Emanuel *psychiatrist*
Goldman, Israel David *hematologist, oncologist*
Goldstein, Robert David *plastic surgeon, educator*
González, Diana M. *language educator*
Gonzalez, Rose A-Navarro *artist*
Gordon, Garet Mark *cardiologist*
Goudarzi, Behnam Malek *physician*
Greenberg, Arline Francine *artist, photographer*
Greenwald, Edward Samuel *physician*
Gucalp, Rasim Ahmet *oncologist*
Gupta, Sanjeev *physician, researcher*
Hallett, Charles Arthur, Jr., *English and humanities educator*
Hamerman, David Jay *gerontologist, educator*
Hauser, Bernice Worman *director*
Heagarty, Margaret Caroline *pediatric physician*
†Heath, Cedric Alexander *nurse, health services administrator, real estate agent, insurance agent, financial analyst*
Hennessy, Thomas Christopher *clergyman, educator, retired university dean*
Hilfstein, Erna *science historian, educator*
Himmelberg, Robert Franklin *historian, educator*
Hirano, Asao *neuropathologist*
Hodgson, W(alter) John (Barry Hodgson) *surgeon*
Hooker, Olivia J. *psychologist, educator*
Howard, Harrison Sabin *literature educator*
Hudson, Frederick Bernard *management consultant*
Humphry, James, III, *librarian, publishing executive*
Hunt, George William *priest, magazine editor*
Hurwitz, Ted H. *sports conference administrator*
Iezza, Anita Kay *physician assistant*
Jaffé, Ernst Richard *medical educator and administrator*
Janis, Michel *pathology educator*
Jankowski, Jeffery J. *developmental psychology educator*
†Jeter, Derek Sanderson *professional baseball player*
†Johnson, Anne Bradstreet *research physician, educator*
Juszczyk, James Joseph *artist*
Kahn, Thomas *medical educator*
†Karkanias, George B. *neurologist, educator*
Karwa, Gattu Lal *urologist*
Kassoy, Hortense (Honey Kassoy) *artist, sculptor, painter, printmaker*
Kelly, Mary Susan *psychologist, educator*
†Kelly, Roberto Conrado (Bobby Kelly) *professional baseball player*
Kennedy, David J. *lawyer*
Kennedy, Gary J. *psychiatrist*
Kheel, Ann Sunstein *civic worker*
†Khrapunov, Sergei *biophysicist*
Kirmse, Sister Anne-Marie Rose *nun, educator, researcher*
Kitt, Olga *artist*
Koranyi, Adam *mathematics educator*
Kornfeld, Robert Jonathan *playwright, photographer*
Koss, Leopold G. *physician, pathologist, educator*
Kostelny, Albert Joseph, Jr., *lawyer*
Kramer, Eleanor *retired real estate broker, tax practitioner, financial consultant*
Kravath, Alan Wolfe *education evaluator*
Kuhn, Leslie Alvin *cardiologist*
Lane, Gilbert Manuel *retired educational administrator*
Lerner, Laurence M. *college administrator*
Lieber, Charles Saul *physician, educator*
†Lienert, Christoph *physical education educator*
Lomke, Evander *publishing executive*
†Lyons, Maxine Evadney *small business owner, poet*
Macklin, Ruth *bioethics educator*
Margid, Leonard *lawyer*
†Martin, Amy Marie *English educator, researcher*
Marún, Gioconda *Spanish language educator*
Massaro, Dominic Robert *judge, public official, writer*
McShane, Joseph Michael *priest, theology studies educator*
Mobasher, Maher Attia *academic administrator*
Motte, Sister Mary Margaret *missionary*
Mukherjee, Asit Baran *geneticist, educator*
†Murillo, Emilio *filmmaker, writer, poet*
Murthy, Vadiraja Venkatesa *biochemist, researcher, educator*
Myers, Jr., George Joseph Stephen *historical archaeologist, researcher*
Nagler, Arnold Leon *pathologist, scientist, educator*
Nathanson, Melvyn Bernard *university provost, mathematician*
Navran, Leslie *retired clinical psychologist*
†Nofer, David Clark *education educator, researcher*
Ofodile, Ferdinand *plastic surgeon*
Okpalanma, Chika *psychiatrist*
Osborne, Claudina Rosetta *financial analyst*
Ostrow, Rona Lynn *librarian, educator*
Padnos, Mark *library administrator, literary translator*
Parker, Everett Carlton *clergyman*
Payson, Martin Saul *secondary school educator, mathematician*
Pompa Pillai, Donna Ann *social worker, educator, psychotherapist*
Porter, Spence *playwright*
Posada, Jorge Rafael *baseball player*
Procidano, Mary Elizabeth *psychologist, educator*
Purpura, Dominick P. *dean, neuroscientist*
†Pycior, Julie Leininger *historian*
Ravikumar, Thanjavur Subramaniam *surgical oncologist*
Regan, Richard Joseph *education educator, writer*
Reichert, Marlene Joy *secondary school educator, writer*
Reynolds, Benedict Michael *surgeon*
Reynolds, Joseph Patrick *chemical engineering educator, consultant*
†Reznik, Sandra E. *physician, consultant*
†Rivera, Mariano *baseball player*
Robinson, John Gwilym *conservationist*
†Rodriguez Carro, Ibis L. *language educator*
Romney, Seymour Leonard *physician, educator*
Rose, Israel Harold *mathematics educator*
Rothstein, Anne Louise *education educator, college official*
Ruben, Robert Joel *physician, educator*
Rubinstein, Arye *pediatrician, microbiologist, educator, immunologist, educator*
Ruffing, Janet Kathryn *spirituality educator*
Ryan, James Daniel *history educator*
Sable, Robert Allen *gastroenterologist*
Saenger, Elizabeth Baird *elementary school educator, writer*
Safyer, Steven M. *chief medical officer*
Samuels, Leslie Eugene *marketing and management consultant*
San Agustin, Mutya *pediatrician*
Scanlan, Thomas Joseph *college president, educator*
Schaller, George Beals *zoologist*
Scharff, Matthew Daniel *immunologist, cell biologist, educator*
Schaumburg, Herbert Howard *neurology educator*
Scheuer, James *physician, educator, researcher*
Schwam, Marvin Albert *graphic design company executive*
Schwartz, Steven *corporate executive*
Sedacca, Angelo Anthony *protective services official, educator*
Seltzer, William *statistician, social researcher, former international organization director*
Shafritz, David Andrew *physician, research scientist*
Shamos, Morris Herbert *physicist educator*
Shapiro, Nella Irene *surgeon*
Sherman, Judith Dorothy *producer, recording company owner, recording engineer*
Shinnar, Shlomo *child neurologist, educator*
Shirani, Jamshid *internist, cardiologist, researcher*
Siddons, Sarah Mae *chemist*
Siegel, Robert Errol *internist, pulmonologist, educator*
Simon, Sidney *osteopathic physician, educator*
Skurdenis, Juliann Veronica *librarian, educator, writer, editor*
Smith-Alnimer, Marie Margaret Cella *mental health nurse*
Sohler, Nancy Lynn *epidemiologist*

Mook, Sarah *retired chemist*
Moore, Anne Frances *arts administrator, consultant, educator, art appraiser*
Moore, Jane Ross *librarian, educator*
Moorman, Joyce Solomon *music educator*
†Moosazadeh, Kioomars *medical educator, researcher*
Morales, Jose *psychotherapist, writer*
Morawetz, Herbert *chemistry educator*
Morgan, Mary Louise Fitzsimmons *fund raising executive, lobbyist*
Morris, Mark William *choreographer*
†Moylan, Donna Jean *artist*
Mulvihill, Maureen Esther *writer, educator, scholar*
Murillo-Rohde, Ildaura Maria *marriage and family therapist, consultant, educator, dean*
†Nadel, Monroe Stanley
†Nadler, Nona Jean *social worker*
Nakanishi, Yuko Julie *engineering educator, consultant*
Neaderland, Louise Odes *artist, educator, professional society executive*
†Neu, Jim A *playwright*
Newbauer, John Arthur *editor*
Niesen, James Louis *theater director*
Norstrand, Iris Fletcher *psychiatrist, neurologist, educator*
Nuccio, Paul Vincent *lawyer*
Nye, William Roger *psychologist*
O'Connor, Sister George Aquin (Margaret M. O'Connor) *academic administrator, sociology educator*
Oley, Nancy H. *psychobiologist, educator*
Onken, George Marcellus *retired lawyer*
†O'Rourke, John Francis *sales executive*
†Ortega, Maria A. *security firm executive, educator*
Ortiz, Mary Theresa *biomedical engineer, educator*
Ortner, Everett Howard *magazine editor, writer*
Otterness, Tom *artist*
Oussani, James John *stapling company executive*
†Padmore Lewis, Sandra Patricia *accountant*
†Paliogiannis, Fotios Constantine *mathematician, educator*
Palm, Marion *educator*
†Pannizzo, Frank J. *general counsel*
Paris Cammer, Barbara Elaine *geriatrician*
Parker, Barbara L. *educator*
Parlamis, Michael Frank *civil engineer, construction company executive*
Pasciuto, Joseph Doria *priest*
Patan, Sybill Petra *research scientist*
Pavlakis, Steven George *medical educator, physician*
Pearce, Eli M. *chemistry educator, administrator*
Pearlstein, Seymour *artist*
Peker, Elya Abel *artist*
Pennisten, John William *computer scientist, linguist, actuary*
Periut, Richard *internist, pulmonologist, intensivist*
Pertschuk, Louis Philip *pathologist, consultant*
Peters, Mercedes *psychoanalyst*
Phillips, Gretchen *social worker*
Phillips, William Charles *T'ai Chi instructor*
†Pike, Roberta E. *librarian, educator*
Pine, Bessie Miriam *social worker, editor, columnist*
Pitou, David Walker *consulting firm executive*
Pitynski, Andrzej Piotr *sculptor*
Plotz, Charles Mindell *physician, educator*
Pohorelsky, Viktor Vaclav *federal magistrate judge*
†Ponnambalam, Ananthasekar *pediatrician, gastroenterologist*
†Prescod, Roy A. *musician, educator*
Price, Ely *dermatologist*
Purdy, James *writer*
†Quamina, Joyce *management consultant*
Quick, Walter Curtis *music company executive*
Quinones, Jose Ramon, Jr., *obstetrician-gynecologist, educator*
Radice, Beatrice Rosemarie *family nurse practitioner*
†Rakhmanchik, Emmanuil *gastroenterologist, educator*
Ramaswamy, Prema *pediatrician, cardiologist*
Raskind, Leo Joseph *law educator*
†Rauschenbusch, Stephanie *artist, educator, poet*
†Ravitz, Leonard J., Jr., *physician, scientist, consultant*
Reale, Anthony *pension investment consultant*
†Reich, Edward Stuart *lawyer*
Reich, Nathaniel Edwin *physician, poet, artist, educator*
Reichbach, Gustin Lewis *state supreme court justice*
Reichel, Walter Emil *advertising executive*
Reinisch, June Machover *psychologist, educator*
Reisler, Helen Barbara *public relations and publicity consultant*
Reminick, Marshal Scott *intensivist, pulmonologist*
Renek, Nava *writer, educator*
Reyes, Francisco I. *reproductive endocrinologist, researcher*
Reynolds, Nancy Remick *editor, writer*
†Rezkalla, Laurence *internist*
Rice, John Thomas *architecture educator*
Richmond, Eero *composer, music librarian*
Rigo, Sandra Luisa *literature educator*
Roche, John Edward *educator, human resources consultant*
Rokhvarger, Anatoly Efim *materials science and ceramic technology scientist*
†Roth, Pamela Susan *lawyer*
Rothenberg, Mira Kowarski *clinical psychologist and psychotherapist*
†Rubenstein, Allen Ira *lawyer*
Rutsky, Lester *retired textiles executive, writer*
Ryan, Leonard Eames *judge*
Safian, Harriet Sara *social worker*
Salwen, Martin J. *pathologist, educator*
Salzman, Eric *composer, writer*
†Samuel, Carren C. *hospital administrator*
Sanford, David Boyer *writer, editor*
Sarutto, Anne MArie Rita *research scientist*
Savits, Barry Sorrel *surgeon*
Sawyer, Philip Nicholas *surgeon, educator, health science facility administrator*
Schaefer, Marilyn Louise *artist, writer, educator*
Schiffman, Gerald *microbiologist, educator*
Schindelheim, Franklin David *special education guidance counselor*
Schlemowitz, Joel *film studies educator, film director*
Schneider, Adele Goldberg *librarian, educator*
Schwarz, Richard Howard *obstetrician, gynecologist, educator*
Schweikert, Edgar Oskar *dentist*
Sciabarra, Chris Matthew *political scientist*
Scult, Mel *Judaic studies educator, researcher*
Seetharaman, Mysore Lakshminarayana *internist*
†Segelnick, Stuart Lawrence *periodontist*
Shalita, Alan Remi *dermatologist*
Sharify, Nasser *educator, author, librarian*
Shaw, Kendall (George Shaw) *artist, educator*
Shaw, Leonard Glazer *electrical engineering educator, consultant*
†Shcherbakova, Estella *chemist, mathematician, educator*
Shechter, Laura Judith *artist*
Shelov, Steven Patrick *pediatrician, educator*
†Shulman, Abraham *otolaryngology educator, hospital administrator*
Sifton, Charles Proctor *federal judge*
Silverstein, Louis *art director, designer, editor*
Skrobela, Katherine Creelman *music producer*
Skyler, Marc Norman *biology educator*
†Smith, Bernadine M. *television producer, director, writer*
Smith, John W(esley), Jr., *data processing executive, consultant*
Smith, Peter Russell *physician*
Sobin, Allan J. *neurologist*
Solan, Lawrence Michael *lawyer*
Solomon, Martin M. *judge*
Solomon, Nathan Andrew *clinical psychologist*
Somers, Marion *gerontologist, family counselor*
Spector, Robert Donald *language professional, educator*
Spiegel, Allen D. *medical educator, consultant*
Spitalewitz, Samuel *nephrologist*
†Steinberg, Jerome Leonard *lawyer*
Stellman, Jeanne Mager *public health educator*
Stepherson, Brian Edward *psychological social worker, artist, writer*
Steptoe, Javaka *writer, illustrator*
Stone, Dianne St. Christine *legal aid society executive*
Strauss, Dorothy Brandfon *marital, family, and sex therapist*
Stuckey, James P. *real estate company executive*
Sun, Wei Yue *internist*
†Svetvilas, Chanika *museum program coordinator*
Sweet, Marc Steven *financial executive*
Swirsky, Judith Perlman *arts administrator, consultant, writer*
Szenberg, Michael *economics educator, editor, consultant*
Tamir, Theodor *electrophysics researcher, educator*
Thomson, David *dancer, vocalist*
Tiedge, Henri *neuroscientist, educator, researcher*
Torz, Richard J. *economics and finance educator*
Trager, David G. *federal judge*
Tronolone, Tracey Ann *social worker*
†Tsismenakis, Georgia *lawyer, tax accountant*
Twersky, Jonathan *lawyer*
van de Kamp, Alexandra P. *writer, educator, poet, editor*
Varma, Ranbir *economics educator*
†Vashist, Sudhir *pediatrician*
Vassalle, Mario *physiologist*
Vidal, Maureen Eris *theater educator, actress*
Viswanathan, Ramaswamy *physician, educator*
Von Essen, Thomas *protective services official*
Von Gizycki, Alkistis Romanoff *research scientist, educator, scholar, writer*
von Rydingsvard, Ursula Karoliszyn *sculptor*
Wachewski, Robert Thomas *health facility administrator*
Wagman, Richard Jay *internist, educator*
Walker, Joy *visual artist*
Walsh, George William *publishing company executive, editor, author*
Wapner, Myrna *retired principal*
†Wasserman, Aaron O. *biologist, educator*
Weill, Georges Gustave *mathematics educator*
Weiner, Anthony David *congressman*
Weinstein, Jack Bertrand *federal judge*
Weinstein, Marie Pastore *psychologist*
Weinstock, Judith *obstetrician/gynecologist*
Weston, I. Donald *architect*
Wexler, Joan G. *dean, law educator*
Wiener, Hesh (Harold Frederic Wiener) *publisher, editor, consultant*
Wilkes, David Ross *therapist*
Wilson, Arthur Theodore *education consultant*
Wilson, Robert Warne *philanthropist, investor*
Wolf, Edward Lincoln *physics educator*
Wolfe, Allan *physicist*
Wolfe, Ethyle Renee (Mrs. Coleman Hamilton Benedict) *college administrator*
Wolin, Doris Diamond *psychologist*
Wolintz, Arthur Harry *physician, neuro-ophthalmologist*
†Woodham, Joseph Ed *artist, art educator*
Woolley, Margaret Anne (Margot Woolley) *architect*
Yamada, Takeshi *artist, language and cultural consultant, educator, writer*
Yogeswaran, Pararajasingam *physician*
Zabriskie, Sherry LaFollette *filmmaker, author, actress*
Zakanitch, Robert Rahway *artist*
Zaman, Mohammad Hamiduz *physician*
Zelin, Jerome *retired retail executive*
Zhang, Robert *painter*
Zinnes, Alice Fich *artist, educator*
Zisser, Martin Shepherd *fur apparel manufacturer, investor and trader*
Zuk, Judith *botanic garden administrator*
Zukowski, Barbara Wanda *clinical social work psychotherapist*
†Zweig, Janet *artist, sculptor*

Brooktondale
Eberhard, Anatol *retired chemistry educator*

Brookville
Berresford, Geoffrey Case *mathematics educator*
†Kusukawa, Akira *demographer, educator*

Buffalo
Ackerman, Philip Charles *utilities executive, lawyer*
Albert, Michael Salvatore *pathologist, medical laboratory executive*
†Amato, Rosalie *educator*
Amborski, Leonard Edward *chemist*
Ambrus, Clara Maria *physician*
Ambrus, Julian L. *physician, medical educator*
Anbar, Michael *biophysics educator*
Anderson, John Thomas *librarian, historian*
Anderson, Wayne Arthur *electrical engineering educator*
Anderson, Wayne Keith *dean, educator*
Baier, Robert Edward *chemist, educator*
Bailey, Thomas Charles *lawyer*
†Bandyopadhyay, Arindam *endocrinologist*
†Barber, Janice Ann *lawyer*
Bardos, Thomas Joseph *chemist, educator*
Barney, Thomas McNamee *lawyer*
Baumler, Robert Albert *cardiologist*
Bayles, Jennifer Lucene *museum program director, educator*
†Belanger, Paul *director*
Berezney, Ronald *molecular biologist*
Bernardino, Michael E. *academic administrator, physician, educator*
Blane, Howard Thomas *research institute administrator*
Bobinski, George Sylvan *librarian, educator*
Boot, John C.G. *economist, educator*
Boyar, Benjamin *music educator*
†Brock, David George *lawyer*
Brody, Harold *neuroanatomist, gerontologist*
Bross, Irwin Dudley Jackson *biostatistician*
Brown, Jerrold Stanley *lawyer*
Brydges, Thomas Eugene *lawyer*
Bucki, Carl Leo *judge*
†Buddie, Amy M. *psychologist, researcher*
Butler, Arthur D. *retired economics educator*
Butsch, John Lord *surgeon, educator*
Cantrick, Robert Birdsall *music educator, academic administrator*
Capaldi, Elizabeth Ann Deutsch *psychological sciences educator*
Carlson, Bruce William *diversified holding company executive*
†Cathey, Patrice Antoinette *secondary school educator, director*
Clarkson, Elisabeth Ann Hudnut *volunteer*
Coburn, Lewis Alan *mathematics educator*
Cohen, Michael E. *physician*
†Coles, Robert Traynham *architect*
Coppens, Philip *chemist*
Cozzi, Ronald Lee *antiquarian book seller, rare book appraiser*
Creeley, Robert White *author, English educator*
Cryan, Richard James, Jr., *academic administrator*
†Cummings, K. Michael *research scientist*
Day, Donald Sheldon *lawyer*
Deck, Judith Z. *adult nurse practitioner*
Delaney, Tim *sociologist, educator*
De La Pedraja, René Andrés *history educator*
†De Marie, Anthony Joseph *lawyer*
Demmy, Todd Lyle *surgeon*
Dennis, Carl *poet*
Deppe, Paul Richard *electrical engineer, engineering test pilot*
†Dickson, Stanley *speech pathology/audiology services professional, educator*
Doyno, Victor Anthony *literature educator*
†Drinnan, Alan John *oral pathologist*
Dryjski, Maciej Lukasz *vascular surgeon, educator*
Duax, William Leo *biological researcher*
†Egginton, William Everett *humanities educator*
†Egilmez, Nejat K. *science educator*
Ehrlich, Isaac *economist, educator, economist, department chairman*
Elardo, Robert Anthony *secondary school educator, financial analyst*
Elfvin, John Thomas *federal judge*
Enhorning, Goran *obstetrician, gynecologist, educator*
Feldman, Irving *poet*
Feuerstein, Alan Ricky *lawyer*
†Fine, Robert Paul *lawyer*
Fisher, Cheryl Smith *lawyer*
Flood, James Duncan *music educator*
Floss, Frederick George *economics and finance educator, consultant*
Flynn, William Joseph, Jr., *surgeon*
Foschio, Leslie George *judge*
Frandina, Philip Frank *civil engineer, consultant*
Franz, Laurence W(erner) *economics educator, college official*
Freedman, Maryann Saccomando *lawyer*
Friedman, Irwin *medical and pharmaceutical educator*
Friedman, Scott Edward *lawyer, author, business consultant*
Fryer, Appleton *publisher, sales executive, lecturer, diplomat*
Fuda, Siri Narayan K.K. (Elaine T. Barber) *educator, clergy, writer*
Gallagher, Shaun Andrew *philosophy educator, writer*
Gardner, Arnold Burton *lawyer*
Gardner, Sue Shaffer *lawyer*
Garver, Newton *philosophy educator*
†Genco, Robert Joseph *immunologist, periodontist, educator, scientist*
Giambra, Joel Anthony *county executive*
Glanville, Robert Edward *lawyer*
†Goldberg, Neil A. *lawyer*
Goldhaber, Gerald Martin *communication educator, author, consultant*
Goldstein, Brian Alan *lawyer, physician*
Goldstein, Bruce A. *lawyer*
Goldstein, Marion Zucker *psychiatrist-clincian, educator, researcher*
Goodberry, Diane Jean (Diane Oberkircher) *mathematics educator, tax accountant*
Goralski, Donald John *public relations executive, counselor*
†Gorman, Gerald Patrick *lawyer*
Gort, Michael *economics educator*
Graham, Saxon (Lloyd Graham) *epidemiology educator*
Grasser, George Robert *lawyer, real estate consultant*
Greene, Robert Michael *lawyer*
†Greenspon, Burton Edward *lawyer*
Greiner, William Robert *university administrator, educator, lawyer*
Gress, Edward J(ules) *educator, consultant*
†Griswold, Kim *physician, researcher*
Gruen, David Henry *financial executive, consultant*
Haarmeyer, David Alan *computer programmer/analyst, educator*
†Hahn, Theresa *epidemiologist, researcher*
Halavais, Alexander Michael Campbell *information scientist, educator*
Halbreich, Uriel Morav *psychiatrist, educator*
Halpern, Ralph Lawrence *lawyer*
Halpert, Leonard Walter *retired editor*
Halt, James George *advertising executive, graphic designer*
Hare, Peter Hewitt *philosophy educator*
Hasek, Dominik *hockey player*
Hauptman, Herbert Aaron *mathematician, educator, researcher*
Hayes, J. Michael *lawyer*
He, Xin *computer scientist, educator*
Headrick, Thomas Edward *lawyer, educator*
Heilman, Pamela Davis *lawyer*
Herdlein, Richard Joseph, III, *college official and dean, educator*
Herdzik, Arthur Alan *lawyer*
Hetzner, Donald Raymund *social studies educator, forensic social scientist*
Ho, Alex Wing-keung *statistician*
Hoffman, Faith Louise *social worker*
†Hohn, David *physician*
†Holm, Bruce Allen *academic administrator, researcher*
†Holmes, James M. *social studies educator, educator*
†Houseknecht, Stephen *artist, educator*
Howard, Muriel A. *academic administrator*
Hrycik, Pauline Emily *educator*
†Hu, Ke *medicinal chemist, pharmacologist*
Huard, James Gerald *mathematician, educator*
Hudson, Raymond Anthony *physician*
†Hughes, Timothy F. *mechanical engineer, consultant*
Hurwitz, Mark S. *political scientist, educator, lawyer*
Iggers, Georg Gerson *history educator*
Irwin, Robert James Armstrong *investment company executive*
†Jackson, Bruce *cultural studies educator, writer, photographer*
†Jacobs, Charles P. *lawyer*
†Jacobs, Jeremy M. *diversified holding company executive, hockey team owner*
Jain, Piyare Lal *physics educator*
Jasen, Matthew Joseph *lawyer, state justice*
†Jusko, William Joseph *pharmaceutical scientist, educator*
Karwan, Mark Henry *engineering educator, dean*
Kaye, David L. *psychiatrist*
Kazmierczak, Elzbieta Teresa *graphic designer, illustrator, educator, semiotician*
Kelly, Jim (James Edward Kelly) *former professional football player*
Kipping, Hans F. *dermatologist, educator*
†Kirby, Amy Elizabeth *microbiologist, researcher*
Kordinak, Irma L. *piano teacher, musician*
†Kotaska, Gary F. *lawyer*
Kristoff, Karl W. *lawyer*
†Krzyzanski, Wojciech *pharmacokineticist, consultant, mathematician*
Kurlan, Marvin Zeft *surgeon, educator*
LaHood, Marvin John *English educator*
Lamb, Charles Moody *political scientist, educator*
Landi, Dale Michael *industrial engineer, academic administrator*
Layton, Rodney Eugene *financial executive, newspaper executive*
Lee, Genevieve Bruggeman *publishing company executive*
Levine, George Richard *English language educator*
†Levite, Laurence A. *communications executive*
Levy, Kenneth Jay *psychology educator, academic administrator*
Lifeso, Robert Murray *surgeon*
†Lippes, Jack *gynecologist, obstetrician, research scientist*
Littlewood, Douglas Burden *business brokerage executive*
†Lockwood, Alan H. *neurologist, researcher*
Manning, Kenneth Alan *lawyer*
†Masiello, Anthony M. (Tony Masiello) *mayor*
†Matsui, Sei-ichi *geneticist*
McElvein, Thomas Irving, Jr., *lawyer*
McGuire, William Dennis *health facility administrator*
†McKibbin, William Alex *artist*
Meredith, Dale Dean *civil engineering educator*
Merini, Rafika *foreign language, cultures and literatures educator*
Merowitz, Morton J. *writer, translator*
†Metzger, Erika Alma *education educator*
Metzger, Ernest Hugh *aerospace engineer, scientist*

Milgrom, Felix *immunologist, educator*
Miller, Charles Louis, II, *consultant*
Milligan, John Drane *historian, educator*
Mindell, Eugene Robert *surgeon, educator*
Mirand, Edwin Albert *medical scientist*
Mucci, Gary Louis *lawyer*
Murphy, Dennis Patrick *hotel business entrepreneur*
Naughton, John Patrick *cardiologist, educator*
Naylon, Betsy Zimmermann *artist*
Newman, Stephen Michael *lawyer*
†Nichita, Constantin Camil *industrial engineer, researcher*
Nolan, James Paul *medical educator, scientist*
Nowak, Carol Ann *city official*
O'Donnell, Denise Ellen *lawyer*
Odza, Randall M. *lawyer*
O'Loughlin, Sandra S. *lawyer*
Oppenheimer, Randolph Carl *lawyer*
Ortman, Harold Rodebaugh *retired prosthodontist*
†Otterbein, Keith F. *anthropologist, educator*
Overton, Nicole Yolanda *program analyst*
Pajak, David Joseph *lawyer, consultant*
†Parker, Catherine B. *artist, art educator*
†Parker, Michelle *lawyer*
Patel, Mulchand Shambhubhai *biochemist, researcher*
Paterson, Tony Ralph *sculptor, educator*
Payne, Frances Anne *literature educator, researcher*
Pearson, Paul David *lawyer, mediator*
Pegels, C. Carl *management science and systems educator*
Penniman, W. David *information scientist, educator, consultant*
Peradotto, John Joseph *classics educator, editor*
Perry, J. Warren *health sciences educator, administrator*
†Peterson, Lorna Ingrid *library educator*
Piver, M. Steven *gynecologic oncologist*
Priore, Roger L. *biostatistics educator, consultant*
†Rachlin, Lauren David *lawyer*
Rashba, Emmanuel Iosif *physicist, educator*
Regan, Peter Francis, III, *physician, psychiatry educator*
Reinhorn, Andrei M. *civil structural engineering educator, consultant*
Reismann, Herbert *engineer, educator*
Reitan, Paul Hartman *geologist, educator*
†Rich, Robert E., Jr., *food products company executive*
Richard, Norman Bernard *allergist*
Riepe, Dale Maurice *philosopher, writer, illustrator, educator, Asian art dealer*
Robinson, David Clinton *reporter*
†Robinson, Zan Dale *language educator, writer*
Rogovin, Milton *documentary photographer, retired optometrist*
Rosan, Robert Carl *retired physician*
†Ross, Gary Earl *writing educator*
Ruckenstein, Eli *chemical engineering educator*
†Ruff, Lindy *professional hockey coach*
Runfola, Ross Thomas *lawyer, educator, writer, journalist, poet*
St. Pierre, Cheryl Ann *retired art educator*
Salisbury, Eugene W. *lawyer, justice*
†Sankoh, Joseph S. *political scientist, educator*
Satan, Miroslav *hockey player*
Schentag, Jerome John *pharmacy educator*
Schmidli, Keith William *vocational education administrator, educator, researcher*
Schobert, Melody A. *counseling educator*
†Schoenborn, Daniel Leonard *lawyer*
†Schreck, Robert J. *lawyer*
Schroeder, Harold Kenneth, Jr., *U.S. magistrate judge*
Schultz, Douglas George *art museum director*
†Segalla, Thomas Francis *lawyer*
Seitz, Mary Lee *mathematics educator*
Seller, Robert Herman *cardiologist, family physician*
Seller, Steven Mark *pharmacist*
Shapiro, Stuart Charles *computer scientist, educator*
Shaw, David Tai-Ko *electrical and computer engineering educator, university administrator*
Shedd, Donald Pomroy *surgeon*
Shelton, Peter Arthur *retired civil engineer*
†Sherris, David Allan *surgeon, medical researcher, educator*
Sherwood, Arthur Morley *lawyer*
Shick, Richard Arlon *finance educator*
Siedlecki, Peter Anthony *English language and literature educator*
Silver, Kathleen Frances *rehabilitation counselor*
Simonson, Patricia Lou Hoffman *director health, fitness and recreation programs, grants writer*
Simpson, George True *surgeon, educator*
Singletary, James, Jr., *school board administrator*
Skretny, William Marion *federal judge*
Smith, Barry *philosophy educator, researcher*
Smukall, Carl Franklin *accountant*
Spengler, Paul Albert *grants and foundation administrator*
Starks, Fred William *chemical company executive*
Steeb, Rosemarie Christina *accountant, consultant*
Still, Ivan Henry *research scientist*
Stoll, Howard Lester, Jr., *dermatologist*
†Stoss, Frederick Warren *librarian, educator*
†Sullivan, Margaret M. *editor*
†Sun, Qi-Hong *cell biologist, immunologist*
†Swart, Michael *lawyer*
Szanyi, Kevin Andrew *lawyer*
†Tanous, James Joseph *lawyer*
Tedlock, Barbara Helen *anthropologist, educator, academic administrator*
†Tenne, Dirk *research scientist*
Tomasi, Thomas B. *cell biologist, administrator*
Toohey, Philip S. *lawyer*
Torre, Joseph John *endocrinologist*
Treanor, Charles Edward *scientist*
Trevisan, Maurizio *epidemiologist*

Triggle, David John *university dean, consultant*
Tritsch, George Leopold *biochemist, educator, retired biomedical researcher*
Trotter, Herman Eager, Jr., (Herman Trotter) *retired music critic*
†Twagilimana, Aimable *English educator, writer*
Urban, Henry Zeller *newspaperman*
Vitagliano, Kathleen Alyce Fuller *secondary education educator*
Vladutiu, Adrian O. *physician, educator*
Vogel, Michael N. *journalist, writer, historian*
Wang, Jui Hsin *biochemistry educator*
Weber, Thomas William *chemical engineering educator*
Weisstein, Naomi *neuroscientist, psychology educator, writer*
Weller, Sol William *chemical engineering educator*
†Welliver, Robert Charles *physician, researcher*
Wen, Sihai *research engineer, materials scientist*
Wieczorek, William Frederick *medical researcher*
Wiesenberg, Russel John *statistician*
Wilbur, Barbara Marie *elementary education educator*
†Williams, Lillian Serece *educator*
Wilmers, Robert George *banker*
Wisbaum, Wayne David *lawyer*
Wolck, Wolfgang Hans-Joachim *linguist, educator*
Wozniak, Richard Anthony *computer engineer*
Wright, John Robert *pathologist, educator*
†Yang, Li (Luke) Hua *medical educator, researcher*
†Younis, Tallal Hussein *internist, oncologist*
Zawicki, Joseph Leo *science educator*
†Zhang, Jie *education educator, researcher*
Zhitnik, Alexei *hockey player*

Burke
Crippen, Juanita Witherell *elementary education educator*

Burnt Hills
DeVries, Robert Charles *scientist, researcher, consultant*

Buskirk
Johanson, Patricia Maureen *artist, architect, park designer*

Cairo
Heck, Karl Thomas *community development planner*
†Ludwig, Laura Lonshein *poet*

Callicoon
Kurtz, Joel *construction company executive*

Cambridge
Eissenberg, David Martin *retired engineering executive*
Kriss, Gary W(ayne) *Episcopal priest*

Camillus
†Alvaro, Anthony Joseph *music educator*
Davis, Lynn Harry *secondary education educator*
Endieveri, Anthony Frank *lawyer*
Kearns, Sharon Elaine Johnson *retired benefits specialist*

Campbell Hall
Austin, Danforth Whitley *newspaper executive*
Greenly, Colin *artist*
Ottaway, James Haller, Jr., *newspaper publisher*

Canaan
Belknap, Michael H. P. *real estate developer*
Grant Bruce, Darlene Camille *lawyer*
Knebel, Constance *potter, ceramist*
Pennell, William Brooke *lawyer*
Rothenberg, Albert *psychiatrist, educator*
Walker, William Bond *painter, retired librarian*

Canandaigua
Barden, George V. *county official, watershed specialist*
†Handa, Y. Paul *research scientist, engineering executive*
Hansen, Widmer Case *retired weapons systems engineer, analyst*
Love, Robert Lyman *educational consulting company executive*
Lowther, Frank Eugene *research physicist*
Malinowski, Patricia A. *community college educator*
Wormer, Thomas Andrew *surgeon*

Candor
†Trinidad, William J. *pastor*

Canton
Goldberg, Rita Maria *foreign language educator*
O'Connor, Daniel William *retired religious studies and classical languages educator*
Perry, Richard John *anthropology educator*
Phelps, Wayne Howe *educational administrator*
Pollard, Fred Don *finance company executive, director*
†Shuman, James C. *education educator*
Thompson, Jean Alling *librarian*
†Thornton, Thomas *anthropologist, educator*
†Weiner, Bruce Ira *humanities educator*

Cape Vincent
Stiefel, Linda Shields *lawyer*

Carle Place
Seiden, Steven Jay *lawyer*

Carmel
Calegari, Maria *ballerina*
Grossman, Victor G. *lawyer*
Laporte, Cloyd, Jr., *lawyer, retired manufacturing executive*
Lowe, E(dwin) Nobles *lawyer*
Motola, Jay A. *urologist*

Shen, Chia Theng *former steamship company executive, religious institute official*

Carthage
Ebbels, Bruce Jeffery *physician, health facility administrator*

Castleton On Hudson
Kienzle, John Fred *history educator*
Lanford, Oscar Erasmus, Jr., *retired university vice chancellor*

Cato
†Sheckler, Ross David *engineering executive*

Catskill
†Green, Barbara R. *artist*
Green, Francis Eugene *artist, educator*
Lalor, Daniel Kevin *judge*
Tompkins, Sharon Lee *primary education educator*

Cazenovia
Carlson, William Clifford *retired defense company executive, retired naval officer*
Pavese, Jacqueline Marie *librarian*
Shattuck, George Clement *retired lawyer*

Cedarhurst
Cohen, David B. *optical company executive*
Cohen, Harris L. *diagnostic radiologist, consultant*
Cohen, Philip Herman *accountant*
†Klein, Irwin Grant *lawyer*
Lipsky, Linda Ethel *business executive*
Solymosy, Hattie May *writer, publisher, storyteller, educator*
Taubenfeld, Harry Samuel *lawyer*
Van Raalte, Polly Ann *reading and writing specialist, photojournalist*

Center Moriches
Miller-Roseman, Linda Sarah *critical care, emergency room nurse*

Centereach
Chassman, Karen Moss *educational administrator*

Centerport
Fischel, Edward Elliot *physician, educator*
McQueeney, Henry Martin, Sr., *publisher*
Rogers, Ailene Kane *retired secondary school educator*
Stevens, Martin Brian *publisher*
Trotta, Ric Charles *aerospace company executive, consultant*

Central Islip
Bernstein, Stan *federal bankruptcy judge*
Boyle, E. Thomas *federal magistrate judge*
Cyganowski, Melanie L. *bankruptcy judge*
Eisenberg, Dorothy *federal judge*
Griffith, Philip Arthur *elementary school educator*
Hendee, Susan Sykes *culinary and technology educator, consultant*
McCrain, Michael William *accountant, financial advisor*
McGowan, Harold *real estate developer, investor, scientist, author, philanthropist*
Platt, Thomas Collier, Jr., *federal judge*
Rodriguez, Teresa Ida *elementary education educator, educational consultant*
Seybert, Joanna *federal judge*
Spatt, Arthur Donald *federal judge*
Wiggins, Gloria *nonprofit organization administrator, television producer*

Central Square
BuMann, Sharon Ann *sculptor*

Chappaqua
Boal, Lyndall Elizabeth *social worker*
Castrataro, Barbara Ann *lawyer*
de Janosi, Peter Engel *research manager*
Deutsch, Alina *electrical engineer, researcher*
French, Harold Stanley *food company executive*
George, Jean Craighead *author, illustrator*
Laun, Louis Frederick *government official*
O'Neill, Robert Charles *inventor, consultant*
Pollet, Susan L. *lawyer*
Pomerene, James Herbert *retired computer engineer*
Ujifusa, Grant Masashi *editor*
Weinberger, Robert *analytical chemist*
Whittingham, Charles Arthur *publisher, library administrator*

Chateaugay
Holt, Peter Robert Bacon *geophysicist*
Kanzler, Kathleen Patricia *kennel owner*

Chatham
Fiorillo, John A(nthony) *health care executive*
Squier, Rita Ann Holmberg *graphic designer*

Chautauqua
Mackenzie, John Anderson Ross *historian, educator*
Yurth, Helene Louise *librarian*

Cheektowaga
Keem, Michael Dennis *veterinarian*
†Landahl, Steven A. *small business owner, writer*
Mruk, Eugene Robert *retired marketing professional, urban planner*
Richmond, Allen Martin *speech pathologist, educator*
Woldman, Sherman *pediatrician*

Cherry Valley
Dallemagne-Cookson, Elise Camille *writer*
Humes, Graham *investment banker*
Sapinsky, Joseph Charles *magazine executive, photographer*

Chester
Amelar, Richard Daniel *urologist, andrologist*
Karen, Linda Tricarico *interior designer*
Mackerodt, Fred *public relations specialist*

Chestnut Ridge
Burns, Richard Owen *lawyer*
Day, Stacey Biswas *physician, educator*
Huntoon, Robert Brian *chemist, food industry consultant*

Chittenango
Baum, Peter Alan *lawyer*
Cassell, William Walter *retired accounting operations consultant*

Churchville
Balch, Glenn McClain, Jr., *academic administrator, minister, writer*
†Ciarvella, David R. *music educator, plastics company executive*
Clarke, Stephan Paul *retired language educator, retired writer*
†Mead, Kevin R. *secondary school educator*
†Sovocool, Mary Anne Elizabeth Cranston *educator*

Clarence
Greatbatch, Wilson *biomedical engineer*
Hubler, Julius *artist*
Shaner, Bronwyn Marian *elementary education educator*
Trinkus, Laima Mary *special education educator*
†Xing, Weibing *research scientist*

Claverack
Barrett, William Gary *advertising and marketing executive*

Clayton
Schmidt, Karl M., Jr., *political science educator*

Clifton Park
Blais, Bernard Raymond *ophthalmologist, occupational health physician, educator*
Buhac, Ivo *gastroenterologist*
DeLong, Lawrence Albert *former legislative official*
Healy, Joseph Robert *lawyer*
Hilts, Earl T. *lawyer, government official, educator*
Mathur, Devesh *chemical engineer, researcher*
Miller, Robert Carl *real estate developer*
Monguió, Luis *Spanish language educator*
Murphy, Mary Patricia *elementary education educator*
Orsini, Paul Vincent *music educator*
†Peduto, Eloise Anne *special education educator*
Scher, Robert Sander *instrument design company executive*

Clifton Springs
DeRuyter, Marilyn *real estate broker*

Climax
Adler, Lee *artist, educator, marketing executive*

Clinton
Anthony, Donald Charles *librarian, educator*
Bahlke, George Wilbon *English language educator*
Behrens, John (Jack) *editor, writer, columnist, educator*
Couper, Richard Watrous *foundation executive, educator*
Havens, Pamela Ann *college official*
McKee, Francis John *medical association consultant, lawyer*
Pagani, Albert Louis *aerospace system engineer*
Raybeck, Douglas *anthropologist, educator*
Ring, James Walter *physics educator*
†Stevens, Mitchell L. *sociologist, educator*
Wheatley, Thomas Edward *English language educator*

Clinton Corners
McDermott, Patricia Ann *nursing administrator*
Sylvester, John Edward *social worker*

Clyde
Searle, Robert Ferguson *minister*

Cobleskill
Colony, Pamela Cameron *medical researcher, educator*
Goodale, Douglas M *dean, educator*
Ingels, Jack Edward *horticulture educator*
Wilson, Lewis Lansing *insurance executive*

Cohocton
Sarfaty, Wayne Allen *insurance agent, financial planner*

Cold Spring
Miller, Timothy Earl *planning company executive*
Pugh, Emerson William *electrical engineer*
Sprague, Elmer Delos, Jr., *philosopher, art historian*

Cold Spring Harbor
†Grodzicker, Terri I. *research scientist, educator, academic administrator*
Honey, Sangeet *molecular biologist, research scientist*
MacKay, Robert Battin *museum director*
Walton, Robert Prentiss *lawyer*
Watson, James Dewey *molecular biologist, educator*

Colonie
Mallory, Doris Ann Bourgeois *social worker, counselor*

Commack
Bond, Patricia B. *camping accessories company executive*

†Braun, Robert Alan *lawyer*
Cohen, Judith W. *retired academic administrator*
Jaiswal, Dinesh Kumar *pharmaceutical scientist, educator*
Nilson, Patricia *clinical psychologist*
Ohman, Franklin Eric *ballet educator, choreographer, choreographer*
†Price, Amelia Ruth *not-for-profit foundation president, artist, small business owner*
Somer, Stanley Jerome *lawyer*
Steindler, Walter G. *retired lawyer*

Conesus
Dadrian, Vahakn Norair *sociology educator*

Congers
Commanday, Peter Martin *educator*

Conklin
Fisher, Dale Dunbar *animal scientist, dairy nutritionist*

Cooperstown
Bordley, James, IV, *surgeon*
†Fenton, William Nelson *anthropologist, anthropology educator emeritus*
Franck, Walter Alfred *rheumatologist, medical administrator, educator*
Fullington, Cynthia Janette *pediatric nurse*
Gavey, James Edward *investment company executive*
Harman, Willard Nelson *malacologist, educator*
Huntington, Robert Graham *environmental business consultant*
Noto, Glen Anthony *educator*
Peters, Theodore, Jr., *research biochemist, consultant*
Rich, Walter George *railroad transportation executive*
Steinberg, Paul *allergist, immunologist*
Tilton, Webster, Jr., *contractor*
†Yount, Robin *retired professional baseball player*

Copake
Wahlers, Linda Ann Ford *writer*

Coram
Celella, Karen Ann *music teacher, author*
Dudnikov, Vadim G. *physicist, researcher*
Fialkow, Steven *accountant*
†Gale, Diane *music educator*
Uh, David Keun *civil engineer*

Corinth
Winslow, Norma Mae *elementary education educator*

Corning
†Ahuja, Sanjay *engineer, project manager, educator*
Behm, Forrest Edwin *glass manufacturing company executive*
†Bonomo, Timothy Paul *education educator, consultant*
Buechner, Thomas Scharman *artist, retired glass manufacturing company executive, museum director*
Cicerchi, Eleanor Ann Tomb *fundraising executive*
Davis, Francis Raymond *priest*
Ecklin, Robert Luther *materials company executive*
Hauselt, Denise Ann *lawyer*
Houghton, James Richardson *glass manufacturing company executive*
Lin, Min-Chung *obstetrician, gynecologist*
Loose, John W. *sales company executive*
Miller, Roger Allen *physicist*
Neubauer, Dean Veral *statistician*
†Pindel, David Lee *biologist, educator*
Sala, Martin Andrew *biophysicist, inventor*
Spillman, Jane Shadel *curator, researcher, writer*
†Stookey, Stanley Donald *chemist*
Ughetta, William Casper *lawyer, manufacturing company executive*
†Visovsky, Nick John *research scientist*
Whitehouse, David Bryn *museum director*
Williams, Jimmie Lewis *research chemist*

Cornwall
Smerek, Gay *pharmacist*

Cornwall On Hudson
Rosenof, Theodore Dimon *historian, educator*

Corona
Jackson, Andrew Preston *library director*
Little, Frederick Anton *landscape architect, municipal administrator*

Cortland
Gauss, Karl Frederik *internist, educator, geriatrician*
Haines, Herbert H. *sociology educator*
Hartsock, John C. *communications educator and scholar*
†Taylor, Leland Baridon *lawyer*
Young, Anderson Briggs *recreation educator, administrator*

Cortlandt Manor
†Buhler, Gregory Wallace *lawyer*
Croft, Michele Izzo *graphic designer, artist*
Frischmuth, Robert Alfred *landscape planner, filmmaker*
Galella, Joseph Peter *lawyer*
Genis, Alice Singer *psychologist*
Ratnathicam, Wijayan Senthinathan *surgeon*
Rosenberg, Marilyn Rosenthal *artist, visual poet*

Coxsackie
†Moyna, John Lawrence *priest*

Cranberry Lake
Glavin, James Edward *landscape architect*

Craryville
Kaufman, Michele Beth *clinical pharmacist, educator*

Cross River
†Lang, Robert Mays, Jr., *foundation administrator, controller*
Thorn, Susan Howe *interior designer*

Croton On Hudson
Eswein, Bruce James, II, *human resources executive*
†Hoffman, Paul Shafer *lawyer*
Johann, Anne Dorothy *visual artist, painter, printmaker, graphic artist*
Katzowitz Shenfield, Lauren *philanthropic consultant, foundation executive*
Kazim, Victor *accountant*
Lewins, Steven *security analyst, investment advisor, corporate executive, diplomatic advisor*
†Plotch, Walter *management consultant, fund raising counselor*
Plummer, Samuel Craig *editor*
Rubinfien, Leo H. *photographer, filmmaker*
Straka, Laszlo Richard *publishing consultant*
Turner, David Reuben *publisher, author*
Werman, David Sanford *psychiatrist, psychoanalyst, educator*

Crugers
Walther, Zerita Esperance *paralegal*

Cutchogue
Cottrell, Thomas Sylvester *pathology educator, university dean*
Dank, Leonard Dewey *medical illustrator, audio-visual consultant*
Gibson, Pamela *business development consultant, audio director*
†Pugliese, Ralph James, Jr., *freelance/self-employed photographer*
Strimban, Robert *graphic designer*

Dansville
Vogel, John Walter *lawyer*

De Witt
Cohen, Willard *retired cardiologist, intensivist*
Pearl, Harvey *rehabilitation psychologist*

Deer Park
D'Amore, Victor *director, choreographer, dance educator*
Martone, Jeanette Rachele *artist*
†Rolla, Mario F. *lawyer*

Delhi
†Becker, Carl Frederick *judge*
†Hartmann, James M. *lawyer*
Needham, Nancy Jean *management consultant*
†Olson, Kirby *humanities educator*
Sorgen, Herbert J. *international education educator*
Van Brunt, Arthur Hoffman (Peter) *economist, educator*

Delmar
Button, Rena Pritsker *public affairs executive*
Campas, Anna Penelope *civil engineer, architect*
Cavanaugh, John Joseph, Jr., *lawyer*
Everett, James, Jr., *lawyer*
Houghton, Raymond Carl, Jr., *education educator*
Mancuso, James Carmin *psychologist, educator*
Matuszek, John Michael, Jr., *environmental scientist, educator, consultant*
†Netter, Miriam Maccoby *lawyer*
Pember, John Bartlett *social worker, educator*
Quackenbush, Cathy Elizabeth *secondary school educator*
Shen, Thomas To *environmental engineer*

Denver
Koutroulis, Aris George *artist, educator*

Depew
Koch, Ronald Peter *retired biologist*
Saleh, David John *lawyer*

Derby
Goodell, Joseph Edward *manufacturing executive*

Dewitt
Grady, Brenda Jayne *small business owner, business consultant, instructor*

Dexter
DeVito, Shawn Joseph *music educator*

Dix Hills
Blumstein, Reneé J. *research and statistical consultant*
Braun, Ludwig *educational technology consultant*
Fouladvand, Hengameh *artist*
Guram, Gurpal Singh *mathematician, educator*
Katzberg, Jane Michaels *health care administrator, consultant, educator*
Kornhauser, Kenneth Richard *funeral director, executive*
Lee, Won Jay *radiologist*
Lin, Ching-Shen *pathologist*
Mymit, Chuck W. *music educator, musician*
Pugliese, Paul Jones *cartographer*
†Ruhl, Vincent *psychotherapist, writer*
Somerville, Daphine Holmes *retired elementary education educator*
†Tucker, Robert Henry *lawyer*
†Virostko, Joan *elementary school educator, educator*

Dobbs Ferry
Anbinder, Paul *publishing company executive*
†Barnett, Richard Earl *lawyer, distributing company executive*
Briskin, Efrem *music educator*

†Culhane, Hind Rassam *psychologist, educator, film historian*
Griesar, William Howard *lawyer*
Guggenheimer, Tobias Immanuel Simon *architect*
Juettner, Diana D'Amico *lawyer, educator*
Kraetzer, Mary C. *sociologist, educator, consultant*
Kravath, Richard Elliot *retired pediatrician, educator*
Lavinder, Gale June *medical educator, physical therapist, clinician*
LeRoy, Karen Leslie *English language educator*
Maiocchi, Christine *lawyer*
†McGrath, John Joseph *law educator*
†Minorsky, Peter Vladimir *plant physiologist*
Miss, Robert Edward *fundraiser*
†Perelle, Ira B. *psychologist, educator*
Pesetsky, Bette *writer, educator*
Poian, Edward Licio *historian*
Reddy, Vijaya *emergency physician*
Sax, Boria *intellectual history studies educator, writer*
Simon, Lothar *publishing company executive*
Smith, Charles Carter, Jr., *publishing executive*
Sutton, Francis Xavier *social scientist, consultant*

Douglaston
Balbi, Kenneth Emilio *environmental specialist, researcher*
Hornick, Susan Florence Stegmuller *secondary education educator, fine arts educator, curriculum specialist, artist*
Valero, René Arnold *clergyman*
Walsh, Sean M. *lawyer, audio-video computer forensics consultant*

Dover Plains
Rand, Christopher Edward *music educator*

Dryden
Baxter, Robert Banning *insurance company executive*
Slocum, Robert Bigney *retired librarian*

Dundee
Miller, Ronald K. *real estate broker, educator*
Pfendt, Henry George *retired information systems executive, management consultant*

Dunkirk
Huels, Steven Mark *physicist, mathematician, astronomer*
Rushboldt, Raymond Jude *political science educator*
Strauser, Jeffrey Arthur *biologist, educator*
Woodbury, Robert Charles *lawyer*

East Amherst
Soong, Tsu-Teh *engineering science educator*
Watson, Stewart Charles *construction company executive*

East Aurora
†Carfagna, Vincent O. *physician*
Hawk, George Wayne *retired electronics company executive*
Hayes, Bonaventure Francis *priest*
†Sand, Seaward Alwyn *geneticist, researcher*
Speller, Kerstin G. Rinta *psychologist*
Weidemann, Julia Clark *retired principal, educator*
Woodard, Carol Jane *educational consultant*

East Berne
Smith, Margery W. *family practice physician*

East Durham
Farren, Carol Elese *facility management consultant*

East Garden City
Bákér, J. A., II, *emeritus, executive management advisor and consultant, monetary architect, financial engineer*

East Greenbush
Mucci, Patrick John *financial consultant, realtor, commercial loan broker*

East Hampton
Banks, Monica *sculptor*
Bromley, Bruce Ditmas *language educator, writer*
Damaz, Paul F. *architect*
Dello Joio, Norman *composer*
Delson, Elizabeth *artist*
Delson, Sidney Leon *architect*
Ehren, Charles Alexander, Jr., *lawyer, educator*
Garrett, Charles Geoffrey Blythe *physicist, consultant*
Goldstein, Judith Shelley *reading and learning specialist*
Harmon, Marian Sanders *writer, sculptor*
Hope, Judith H. *former political organization administrator*
Jaudon, Valerie *artist*
Karp, Harvey Lawrence *metal products manufacturing company executive*
Kinsolving, Charles McIlvaine, Jr., *marketing executive*
Mencher, Stuart Alan *sales and marketing executive*
Murbach, David Paul *horticulturist*
Petersen, Ellen Anne *artist*
Rothholz, Peter Lutz *public relations executive*
Schetlin, Eleanor M. *retired university official*
Twomey, Thomas A., Jr., *lawyer, educator*

East Islip
Cullen, Valerie Adelia *secondary education educator*
†Levy, Joel Michael *music educator*
Orsomarso, Don Frank *school system administrator*

East Meadow
Adler, Ira Jay *lawyer*
Albert, Gerald *clinical psychologist*
Bergman, Bruce J. *lawyer*
Beyer, Norma Warren *secondary education educator*
Bunshaft, Marilyn Janosy *community services specialist*
Cymbler, Murray Joel *corporate professional*
Fuchs, Jerome Herbert *management consultant*
Hinson, Gale Mitchell *social worker*
Hyman, Montague Allan *lawyer, educator*
Kalin, Karin Bea *retired secondary school educator, consultant*

East Northport
Juliano, John Louis *lawyer*
†Kehoe, Thomas J. *food products executive*
Ryesky, Kenneth H. *lawyer*
Schlam, Mark Howard *international marketing executive*

East Norwich
Rosen, Meyer Robert *chemical engineer*

East Otto
Anderson, Ursula M. *pediatrician*

East Quogue
Weiss, Elaine Landsberg *community development management official*

East Rochester
Lilly, Eugene Francis *retired publishing company executive*

East Setauket
Adler, Hilton C. *plastic surgeon*
Badalamenti, Fred Leopoldo *artist, educator*
Barcel, Ellen Nora *secondary school educator, free-lance writer, editor*
†Maffia, Christina *elementary school educator, consultant*
Malbon, Craig Curtis *pharmacology educator, university official*

East Syracuse
Besten, Jr., John Joseph *music educator*
Nivarthi, Raju Naga *anesthesiology educator*
Wiley, Richard Gordon *electrical engineer*

Eastchester
Giuliano, Robert Paul *pharmacist*
Gottschall, Edward Maurice *graphic arts company executive*

Eden
Gephart, Michele Marie *elementary education educator*
Thomas, Jimmy Lynn *financial executive*

Edmeston
†Blackman, Dorothy F. *library director*

Elba
Kauffman, William Joseph *writer, editor*

Elizabethtown
†Houseal, Brian L. *conservationist*

Elizaville
Koeppel, Harry Saul *interior designer, educator*

Elma
†Gastle, Timothy Anthony *music educator*
Markello, Jeffrey Philip *lawyer*
Virkler, Mark William *religious educator*

Elmhurst
Kekatos, Deppie-Tinny Z. *microbiologist, researcher, lab technologist*
Masci, Joseph Richard *medical educator, physician*
Matos Morales, Germán Joseph *art and antiques dealer, advocate, fundraiser*
Matsa, Loula Zacharoula *social services administrator, educator*
Monroe, Stephen A. *educational administrator, financial consultant*
†Toueg, Sam *internist*
Visco, Ferdinand Joseph *cardiologist, educator*

Elmira
Abderhalden, Robert Thomas *internist*
Bellohusen, Ronald Michael *orthodontist, educator*
Cerio, Milissa Bausch *social worker*
Graham, David Richard *orthopedic surgeon*
Gulati, Teresa Antoinette *nursing educator*
Henbest, Robert LeRoy *retired bank and insurance company executive*
Henbest, William Harrison *insurance agent*
Horton, Martha Heim *retired newspaper editor, writer*
Huffman, Patricia Joan *retired accounting coordinator*
Liebson, Herman *special education educator*
Meier, Thomas Keith *college president, English educator*
Olthof, Randy James *commissioner*
Paul, Christopher Donald *carpenter, author*
Pratt, Linda *reading educator*
†Rusinko, Lynne Marie *education administrator*
†Shephard, Robert Parrish *historian, educator*
Singletary, Caglar Juan *minister*
Stephens, Lawrence James *chemistry educator, program director*
†Stone, Kathleen Gale *law educator*
Wright, Linda Ellen *nursing educator*

Elmont
Butera, Ann Michele *consulting company executive*
Cusack, Thomas Joseph *retired banker*

Elmsford
Fachnie, H(ugh) Douglas *film manufacturing company official*

Miranda, Robert Nicholas *publishing company executive*
Mulrain, Andrea E. *talent scout*
†Neustadt, Paul *lawyer*
†Parker, James K. *corporate lawyer*
Raymond, George Marc *city planner, educator*

Endicott
DeLuca, Paul Michael *retired physician, surgeon*
Englehart, Joan Anne *consultant*
Goodwin, Charles Hugh *technology education educator*
Powers, Steven Eugene *procurement engineer*
Schwartz, Richard Frederick *electrical engineering educator*

Endwell
Albrecht, William Melvin *research chemist, consultant*
Thesier, Leslie Ann Eisen *computer programmer, mathematician*

Fairport
Carlton, Charles Merritt *linguistics educator*
Chari, Krishnan *research scientist*
Fisher, Jerid Martin *neuropsychologist*
Graham, Susette Ryan *retired English educator*
Holtzclaw, Diane Smith *elementary education educator*
Lawrynowicz, Witold J. *chemist, writer*
Reidy, Thomas Michael *financial executive*
Rowe, Howard, Jr., *composer, arranger*
†Rueckert, William Howe *literature educator, writer*
Stewart, Barbara Dean *writer, musician, educational consultant*
Talty, Lorraine Caguioa *accountant*
Wiener, David L. *secondary education educator*
Young, Thomas Paul *lawyer*

Falconer
Benke, Paul Arthur *academic administrator*
Ruhlman, Herman C(loyd), Jr., *manufacturing company executive*

Far Rockaway
Farron, Robert *physician, family practice*
Kelly, George Anthony *clergyman, author, educator*
Madhusoodanan, Subramoniam *psychiatrist, educator*
Shonek, Arlene *dietitian*
Sussman, Laureen Glicklin *junior high school educator*

Farmingdale
†Bandyopadhyay, Amitabha *engineering educator*
Blum, Melvin *chemical company executive, researcher*
Firetog, Theodore Warren *lawyer*
Fishman, Charles M. *literature educator, poet*
†Gaab, Jeffery S. *history educator*
Lieberman, Michael Jay *ophthalmologist*
Mencarelli, Victor Aristide *microbiologist*
Nolan, Peter John *physics educator*

Farmingville
Olson, Gary Robert *banker*

Fayetteville
Chevli, Renate Naren *obstetrician, gynecologist*
Dosanjh, Darshan S(ingh) *aeronautical engineer, educator*
†Gingold, Neil Marshall *lawyer*
Hadyk-Wepf, Sonia Margaret *artist, real estate manager*
Hiemstra, Roger *adult education educator, writer*
Pachter, Irwin Jacob *pharmaceutical consultant*
Pirodsky, Donald Max *psychiatrist, educator*
Stewart, William A. *medical educator, neurosurgeon*

Feura Bush
Byrne, Donn Erwin *psychologist, educator*

Fishers Island
Baue, Arthur Edward *surgeon, educator, administrator*

Fishkill
Brocks, Eric *ophthalmologist, surgeon*
Ketcham, Gale Giroux *medical group administrator*
Leopold, Martin Robin *ophthalmologist*
Stein, Paula Nancy *psychologist, educator*

Floral Park
Brancaleone Kenna, Laurie Ann *social worker*
Calodny, Alan Lee *retired pharmacist*
Chatoff, Michael Alan *lawyer*
Corbett, William John *government and public relations consultant, lawyer*
Dudek, Henry Thomas *management consultant*
Ford, Donald Herbert *retired educator, consultant*
†Friedman, S. Lila *librarian*
†Mazlen, Roger Geoffrey *physician, clinical pharmacologist, nutritionist*

Flushing
†Alomar, Roberto Velazquez *professional baseball player*
Amsterdam, David Erik *school psychologist*
Angrilli, Albert *psychology educator*
Baik-Han, Won H. *pediatrician, educator, pediatrician, consultant*
Belden, Ursula *set designer*
Bell, Derek *professional baseball player*
Bertoni, Mae *artist*
Bezrod, Norma R. *artist*
Bird, Thomas Edward *foreign language and literature educator*
†Bonk, Sharon Catherine *librarian*
Carlson, Cynthia Joanne *artist, educator*
Cathcart, Robert Stephen *mass media consultant*
Chook, Paul Howard *publishing executive*
Commoner, Barry *biologist, educator*

Cooley, Nicole Ruth *writer, educator*
Deerson, Adele Shapiro *lawyer, educator*
Dorn, Alfred *poet, retired English educator*
†Engel, Robert *chemist, educator, dean*
Erickson, Raymond *music historian, musician*
Falk, Joan Frances *public relations executive*
Farago, John Michael *law educator, hearing officer, consultant*
Fichtel, Rudolph Robert *retired association executive*
Finks, Robert Melvin *paleontologist, educator*
Flechner, Roberta Fay *graphic designer*
†Genack, Azriel Z. *physicist, educator*
Ghazarbekian, Sahak *retired civil servant, consultant*
†Giaimo, Joseph Octavius *lawyer*
†Gizis, Evangelos John *biochemist*
Glavine, Tom (Thomas Michael Glavine) *professional baseball player*
Goldberg, Robert Theodore *ophthalmologist, educator*
Goldman, Norman Lewis *chemistry educator*
Goldsmith, Howard *writer, consultant*
Goldstein, Milton *art educator, printmaker, painter*
†Gregersen, Edgar Alstrup *anthropologist, educator, linguist, writer, researcher*
Hacker, Andrew *political science educator*
Hammerman, Pat Jo *artist, educator*
Henshel, Harry Bulova *watch manufacturer*
Hirshson, Stanley Philip *history educator*
Hon, John Wingsun *physician*
†Kao, Hui-Sheng *mathematics educator*
Karbowitz, Stephen R. *physician*
Kopp, Ilya Zinovij *energy and environmental researcher*
†Kovalyov, Mikhail *researcher, educator*
Kranepool, Harry Anthony *science educator*
Krasner, Michael Alan *political science educator*
†Kroeppel, Warren *airport terminal executive*
Kuan, Jackson Hsun *gastroenterologist*
Lakah, Jacqueline Rabbat *political scientist, consultant*
†Leiter, Alois Terry (Al) *professional baseball player*
Li, Hongzhi *Falun Dafa founder, author*
Lonigan, Paul Raymond *language professional, educator*
Lorber, Daniel Louis *endocrinologist, educator*
Mendelson, Elliott *mathematician, educator*
Min, Pyong Gap *sociologist, researcher*
Nussbaum, Michel Ernest *physician*
Pahk, Sang Kee *gastroenterologist*
†Pellitteri, John Steven *psychologist, therapist, educator*
Person, Philip *biomedical consultant, biochemist, dentist*
†Piazza, Michael Joseph *professional baseball player*
Plotnik, Katya Michele *lawyer*
Psomiades, Harry John *political science educator*
Rabassa, Gregory *Romance languages educator, translator, poet*
†Raines, Judi Belle *language educator, historian*
Ranald, Margaret Loftus *English literature educator, author*
Roberts, Kathleen Joy Doty *secondary education educator*
Rusu, Sir Andrew Peter (Sir Andrew Rusu Baron Rochefort) *ambassador, lawyer*
Salgo, Michael Nicholas *civil engineer, consultant*
Sanborn, Anna Lucille *pension and insurance consultant*
Schwartz, Estar Alma *lawyer*
†Seibel, Robert Franklin *law educator*
Smaldone, Edward Michael *composer*
Smith, Charles William *social sciences educator, sociologist*
Speidel, David Harold *geology educator*
Stahl, Frank Ludwig *civil engineer*
Swell, Lila *education educator*
Tai, Emily Sohmer *history educator, writer*
Tarasko, Alexandra *nursing educator*
Taylor, Conciere Marlana *writer*
†Totakura, Satyanarayana Raju *secondary school educator*
Tytell, John *humanities educator, writer*
Unsal-Tunay, Nuran *geological engineer, researcher*
†Vaughn, Mo (Maurice Samuel Vaughn) *professional baseball player*
Yeo, Kim Eng *artist*
†Zalesne, Deborah *law educator*
Zeile, Todd Edward *professional baseball player*

Fly Creek
Dusenbery, Walter Condit *sculptor*

Forest Hills
†Acain, Angeline Ramos *publishing executive*
Addabbo, Dominic Lucian *lawyer*
Alsapiedi, Consuelo Veronica *psychoanalytic psychotherapist, consultant*
Ashvil-Bibi, Sigalit *musician, artist*
†Bertolini, Joseph Clifford *political scientist, educator*
Casson, Ira Richard *neurologist*
Dessylas, Ann Atsaves *human resources and office management executive*
Donath, Joseph *physician*
Dybman, Nick Nison (Nick China) *poet*
Eden, Alvin Noam *pediatrician, author*
Flowers, Cynthia *investment company executive*
Gebaide, Stephen Elliot *retired mathematics and computer science educator*
Glassmann, Marvin Jean *marriage and family therapist*
Gold, Roslyn *social worker, educator*
Grant, Susan Irene *lawyer*
Guthy, George Edward *retired information systems executive*
Kra, Pauline Skornicki *French language educator*
Krikun, Boris Lvovich *neurologist*
Mindin, Vladimir Yudovich *information systems specialist, chemist, educator*

Moskowitz, Arnold X. *economist, strategist, educator*
Polakoff, Abe *baritone*
Prager, Alice Heinecke *music company executive*
Reis, Don *publishing executive*
Rivers, Theodore John *paralegal, educator*
†Rosenhaus, Steven L. *composer, conductor, music educator*
Rosman, Lawrence David *endocrinologist*
Samuel, Paul *cardiologist, educator*
Sekler-Katz, Rudolfine *internist, psychiatrist*
†Tsay, Chwen Wen *artist*
Van Westering, James Francis *management consultant, educator*
Wolpert Richard, Chava *artist*

Forestburgh
Orisek, Ivan *financial executive*

Forestville
Adams, Lee Towne *lawyer*

Fort Drum
Hilferty, Bryan Carey *public relations specialist*
†Miller, Thomas G. *career officer*

Frankfort
Conigilaro, Phyllis Ann *retired elementary education educator*

Franklin Square
Cantilli, Edmund Joseph *safety engineering educator, translator, writer, consultant*
Ciuffo, Anthony Frank *small business owner*
Indiviglia, Salvatore Joseph *artist, retired naval officer*
Vanora, Jerome Patrick *lawyer*

Franklinville
Kurzdorfer, Peter John *chess educator, writer, editor*

Fredonia
Benton, Allen Haydon *biology educator*
Berkley, John L. *geology educator, meteoriticist*
Boltz, James Donald *retired human resources specialist, photographer*
Booth, Robert Alan *artist, educator*
†Brown, William Douglas *biology educator*
Collingwood, Tracy Lynn *career counselor*
†Conradi, Janet K. *art educator*
Goetz, Thomas Henry Paul *French literature educator*
Klonsky, Bruce Gary *educator*
Krohn, Franklin Bernard *marketing specialist, educator*
Litwicki, Ellen M. *history educator*
Piorkowski, James Paul *music educator, composer, guitarist*
Reiff, Daniel D. *art history educator*
†Rudge, David Thomas *music educator, conductor*

Freehold
Maltzman, Stanley *artist*

Freeport
Berg, Alan *lawyer, arbitrator*
Burkett, Lloyd A. *secondary education educator and administrator, automotive engineer*
Burstein, Stephen David *neurosurgeon*
Dimancescu, Mihai D. *neurosurgeon, researcher, educator*
Martorana, Barbara Joan *secondary education educator*
Pullman, Maynard Edward *biochemist*
Terris, Albert *metal sculptor*
†Walker, Lula Noriega *secondary administrator*

Fresh Meadows
†Castellano, Joseph P. *assistant principal*
†Cohen, Robert L. *editor*
†Duckett, Lila Wheeler *retired language educator, writer*
Greenberg, Robert Jay *law educator*
Jackson, Rhonda *telecommunications professional, poet*

Frewsburg
Burgeson, Joyce Ann *travel agency official*

Fulton
Long, Robert Emmet *author*

Garden City
Berka, Marianne Guthrie *health and physical education educator*
Campbell, James R. *transportation executive*
Caputo, Kathryn Mary *paralegal*
Carnesi, Kenneth Brian *lawyer*
Cohen, Harvey *lawyer*
Conlon, Brian Thomas *promotion executive*
Conlon, Thomas James *marketing executive*
Cook, George Valentine *lawyer, consultant*
DaSilva, Willard H. *lawyer, educator*
Deane, Leland Marc *plastic surgeon*
Demuth, Nina Lewis *engineering company executive*
†Dent, Thomas Augustine *lawyer*
DiMascio, John Philip *lawyer*
Doucette, Mary-Alyce *computer company executive*
Egan, Frank T. *writer, editor*
Ehrlich, Jerome Harry *lawyer*
Fischoff, Gary Charles *lawyer*
Fishberg, Gerard *lawyer*
Friedenberg, Gary Howard *lawyer*
Garner, Richard Keith *classicist, educator*
†Ginsberg, Eugene Stanley *lawyer, arbitrator, mediator*
Good, Larry Irwin *physician, consultant*
Gorin, Robert Murray, Jr., *history educator*
Harwood, Stanley *retired judge, lawyer*
Haskel, Jules J. *lawyer*
Healy, Margaret Mary *retail marketing executive*
Jenkins, Kenneth Vincent *literature educator, writer*
†Jones, Lawrence Tunnicliffe *lawyer*

Kaplan, Joel Stuart *lawyer*
Klainberg, Marilyn Blau *community health educator*
Lefland, Renee Rachel *internist*
Lioz, Lawrence Stephen *lawyer, accountant*
Lovely, Thomas Dixon *banker*
Madonia, Vincent V. *cardiologist, medical educator*
Mascia, Joseph Serafino *banking, economics and finance educator*
Minicucci, Richard Francis *lawyer, former hospital administrator*
†Nicklin, George Leslie, Jr., *psychoanalyst, educator, physician, author*
Ohrenstein, Roman Abraham *economics educator, economist, rabbi*
Ostrow, Michael Jay *lawyer*
Podwall, Kathryn Stanley *biology educator*
Rhein, John Hancock Willing, III, *publishing executive*
†Sawyer, James *lawyer*
†Schupbach, Arthur Christopher *lawyer*
Scollard, Patrick John *hospital executive*
Scott, Robert Allyn *academic administrator*
†Seyfried, Vincent F. *historian*
Shneidman, J. Lee *historian, educator*
Shuart, James Martin *retired academic administrator*
†Siegfried, Robert Michael *education educator*
†Snauwaert, Dale T. *education educator*
Steil, Janice M. *social psychology educator*
Tomao, Peter Joseph *lawyer*
†Wang, Ping-chan *engineering educator*
Webb, Igor Michael *academic administrator*
Wiener, Leo *physician, oncologist*

Gardiner
Fried, Marc B. *writer*
Mabee, Carleton *historian, educator*

Garrison
Callahan, Daniel John *biomedical researcher*
Murray, Thomas Henry *bioethics educator, writer*

Geneseo
Battersby, Harold Ronald *retired anthropologist, archaeologist, linguist*
Edgar, William John *philosophy educator*
†Gouvernet, Gerard Raoul *language educator*
†Haddad, Caroline N. *mathematics educator, researcher*
†Lin, Rong *computer scientist, educator*
Macko, John *lawyer, farmer*
Olczak, Paul Vincent *psychology educator*

Geneva
†Armstrong, James Francis, III, *educator*
Best, Sharon Louise Peckham *college administrator*
Brind, David Hutchison *lawyer, judge*
†Crenner, James T. *poet, communications educator*
†Curl, Layton Seth *psychologist, consultant, educator*
†D'Amico, Francine J. *political scientist, educator*
Dickson, James Edwin, II, *obstetrician, gynecologist*
Givelber, Harry Michael *pathologist*
Harkness, Mabel Gleason *retired librarian*
Lee, Steven Peyton *philosophy educator*
†Oberbrunner, John W. *music educator, musician*
Quinby, Lee *humanities educator*
†Roelofs, Wendell Lee *biochemistry educator, consultant*
†Stranahan, Patricia *dean*

Germantown
Callanan, Laura Patrice *foundation executive*
Farberman, Harold *conductor, composer*
Geistfeld, James Gordon *veterinarian*
Linney, Romulus *author, educator*
Rollins, Sonny (Theodore Rollins) *composer, musician*

Getzville
Saveth, Edward Norman *history educator*

Gilbertsville
†Greefkes, Roland Cornelis *artist*
Roos, Casper *actor*

Gilboa
Petroff, John *economics educator, software company executive*

Glen Cove
Backman, Melvin Abraham *English educator*
Burnham, Harold Arthur *pharmaceutical company executive, physician*
†Carbuto, Nicholas *music educator*
Carroll, Robert Franklin *communications company executive*
Costa, Thomas Charles *priest*
Lewis, Felice Flanery *lawyer, educator*
Makris, Constantine John *infosystems engineer*
Mills, Charles Gardner *lawyer*
Pettersen, Kevin Will *investment company executive*
Rathkopf, Daren Anthony *lawyer*
Sainer, Arthur *writer, theater educator*
Sheehy, John Paul *pediatrician*

Glen Head
Conway, David Antony *management executive, marketing professional*
Fairman, Joel Martin *broadcasting executive*
Huber, Don Lawrence *publisher*
Savinetti, Louis Gerard *lawyer*

Glen Oaks
†Kumra, Sanjiv *psychiatrist*
†Luger, Louise *photographer*
Siris, Samuel Gidding *psychiatrist*

Glen Wild
Kaszas, William Joseph *technology educator*

Glendale
Maltese, Serphin Ralph *state legislator, lawyer*

Glenham
Douglas, Fred Robert *cost engineering consultant*

Glens Falls
Baker, Carl TenEyck *lawyer*
Bartlett, Richard James *lawyer*
†Cullum, James Edward *lawyer*
†Firth, Peter Alan *lawyer*
†Lebowitz, Jack Richard *lawyer*
Lee, Woong Man *pathologist*
McMillen, Robert Stewart *lawyer*
†Meyer, Martin Arthur *lawyer*
Pearsall, Glenn Lincoln *brokerage house executive*
Pontiff, Paul E. *lawyer*
†Tucker, Bernadine *patient registrar*
Vitvitsky, Jack *physician assistant*
Wurzberger, Bezalel *psychiatrist*
Yovanoff, James *rheumatologist*

Glenville
Anderson, Roy Everett *retired electrical engineer*

Glenwood Landing
Hahn, Joan Marjorie *public relations consultant, marketing consultant*

Goshen
Lanc, John Jan *civil and geodetic engineer, land surveyor*
Roncal, Rogelio *psychiatrist*
Ward, William Francis, Jr., *real estate investment banker*

Gouverneur
Kuehl, Alexander Edward *physician, health facility administrator, medical educator, writer*
Leader, Robert John *lawyer*

Grand Central
†Freedman, Mollie Cecille *researcher*

Grand Island
Backus, Kevin Michael *minister*
Hefner, Judith Ann *priest, counselor*
Hennigar, William Grant, Jr., *dentist*
Kutlina, Mary Louise *elementary education educator*
†Mendell, Mark *architect*
Schultz, Susan Marie *special education administrator*

Grand View
Lattes, Jane Flax *museum administrator*

Great Neck
Appel, Gerald *investment advisor*
Arams, Frank Robert *electronics company executive*
Arlow, Jacob A. *psychiatrist, educator*
†Aronson, Margaret Rupp *school psychologist*
Blanda, Sandi *artist*
Blumberg, Barbara Salmanson (Mrs. Arnold G. Blumberg) *retired state housing official, housing consultant*
Breidbart, Rory Steven *endocrinologist*
Brock, William Alton *pediatric urologist*
Bungarz, William Robert *pediatrician*
Christie, George Nicholas *economist, consultant*
Cohen, Herrick Jay *physician*
†Conovitz, Myron William *physician, consultant*
Dennett, Lissy *sculptor*
Eckstein, Ruth *artist*
Elkowitz, Lloyd Kent *dental anesthesiologist, dentist, pharmacist*
Feldman, Gary Marc *nutritionist, consultant*
Fiel, Maxine Lucille *journalist, behavioral analyst, lecturer*
Fried, Belle Warshavsky *education educator*
Friedland, Louis N. *retired communications executive*
Gior, Fino (Serafino Giordano) *electrology company executive*
Goldberg, Melvin Arthur *communications executive*
Goldman, Ira Steven *gastroenterologist*
Greenwald, Marc Lehrer *colon and rectal surgeon*
Gross, Beatrice Schaap *education educator, consultant, writer*
Gross, Lillian *psychiatrist, educator*
Haber, Diane Lois *psychotherapist, clinical specialist*
Hamovitch, William *university official*
Hampton, Benjamin Bertram *brokerage house executive*
Hecht, Marie Bergenfeld *retired educator, author*
Hurwitz, Johanna (Johanna Frank) *writer, librarian*
Joskow, Jules *economic research company executive*
Kahn, David *editor, author*
Kaplan, Seymour H. *allergist, immunologist, pediatrician*
Katz, Edward Morris *banker*
Kechijian, Paul *dermatologist, educator*
Keller, Alex Jay *plastic and reconstructive surgeon*
Kimm, Michael S. *lawyer*
Kodsi, Sylvia Rose *ophthalmologist*
Lande, Ruth Harriet *photographer, language educator*
Lowenbraun, Solomon Mortimer *lawyer*
Mayer, Susan Lee *nurse, educator*
Means, Rosaline *business executive, business educator*
Minkoff, Jack *economics educator, retired*
Packer, Samuel *ophthalmologist*
Panes, Jack Samuel *publishing company executive*
Pollack, Paul Robert *airline service company executive*
Puttlitz, Donald Herbert *medical microbiologist*
†Rieff, Harriet Lillian *librarian*
Rockowitz, Noah Ezra *lawyer*
Rosenberg, Richard F. *physician, radiologist*
Rosenthal, Gladys M. *real estate appraiser*
Roth, Harvey Paul *publishing executive*
Rothbaum, David *obstetrician-gynecologist*
Rubin, Karen Beth *publishing, marketing executive*
Rutkin, Philip *chemist*
Salzman, Stanley P. *lawyer*
Schussheim, Joan Lana *mathematics educator*
Seidler, Doris *artist*
Shons, Alan Rance *plastic surgeon, surgical oncologist, educator*
Simon, Arthur *pharmacologist, research laboratory executive*
Stancati, Richard Emanuel *cleaning company and restaurant executive*
†Sterling, Lorraine *volunteer*
Strauss, Richard Jay *surgeon*
Tepper, Robert Eric *physician*
Turofsky, Charles Sheldon *landscape architect*
Wachsman, Harvey Frederick *lawyer, neurosurgeon*
Weinstock, Gary Alan *internist, allergist*
Wershals, Paul Leonard *lawyer*
Wimpfheimer, Steven *lawyer*
Wolff, Edward *physician*
Zeiger, David *poet, retired English educator*
Zeiger, Lila L. *creative writing educator, poet, fiction writer*

Great River
Hayman, Martin Arthur *psychiatrist, educator*

Greenfield Center
Conant, Robert Scott *harpsichordist, music educator*
Dittner, Deborah Marie *nurse practitioner in family health*

Greenlawn
Bachman, Henry Lee *electrical engineer, engineering executive*
†Starost, Diane Joan *music educator*
Stevens, John Richard *architectural historian*

Greenport
Cowley, Joseph Gilbert *writer*
Loomis, Earl Alfred, Jr., *psychiatrist*
†Monsell, Thomas Oliver *secondary English educator, writer*
Richland, Lisa *library director*
Watts, Harold Wesley *economist, educator*

Greenvale
†Brier, Robert M *Egyptologist, educator, documentary presenter*
Cordaro, Matthew Charles *energy and utility executive, educator*
Dircks, Phyllis Toal *English language educator*
Halper, Emanuel B(arry) *real estate lawyer, developer, consultant, author*
†Maillet, Lucienne *educator*
Megay-Nespoli, Karen Patricia *elementary school educator*
†Pall, David B. *manufacturing company executive, chemist*
Senft, Mason George *musician*
Shenker, Joseph *academic administrator*
Smiraglia, Richard Paul *library and information science educator*
Steinberg, David Joel *academic administrator, historian, educator*
Westermann-Cicio, Mary Louise *academic administrator, library studies educator*
Zwicker, Charles *economist, educator, accountant, consultant*

Greenwich
Fung, Paul, Jr., *cartoonist, illustrator*
Smethurst, E(dward) William, Jr., *brokerage house executive*

Greenwood
Rollins, June Elizabeth *elementary education educator*

Guilderland
Berger, Morris Isaiah *humanities educator*
Gordon, Leonard Victor *retired psychology educator*
Persico, Joseph Edward *author*
Siggins, James E. *chemist*
Steblay, Raymond William *immunopathologist, researcher*

Hamburg
Calkins, Evan *physician, educator*
Dor, Caplyn *artist*
Hargesheimer, Elbert, III, *lawyer*
Iafallo, Deborah Lynn *geriatrics nurse*
Kuhn, Merrily A. *nursing educator*
Markulis, Henryk John *career military officer*
O'Day, John Ignatius *retired computer science educator*
†Voto, James Anthony *music educator*
Witt, Dennis Ruppert *secondary school mathematics educator*

Hamilton
Belanger, Kenneth Douglas *cell and molecular biologist, educator*
Berlind, Bruce Peter *poet, educator*
Blackton, Charles S(tuart) *history educator*
Blum, Lester *educator*
Busch, Briton Cooper *historian, educator*
†Cheng, Marietta N. *conductor, educator*
Chopp, Rebecca S. *university president*
Edmonston, William Edward, Jr., *publisher, educator*
†Godwin, Joscelyn *humanities educator, writer*
Haines, Michael Robert *economist, educator*
†Jacobs, Jonathan A. *philosopher, educator*
Johnston, Michael (William Johnston) *political science educator, university administrator*
Jones, Howard Langworthy *retired educational administrator, consultant*
Karelis, Charles Howard *former academic administrator*
†Khan, Halimur R. *language educator*
Moynihan, William J. *museum executive*
Soderberg, Dale LeRoy *English language educator, drama director, producer*
Tucker, Thomas William *mathematics professor*
Van Schaack, Eric *art historian, educator*

Hampton Bays
Baker, Donald Gene *social sciences educator*
†Komoski, Paul Kenneth *community activist, educational research executive*
Yavitz, Boris *business educator, corporate director*

Hancock
DeLuca, Ronald *former advertising agency executive, consultant*
Sienko, Leonard Edward, Jr., *lawyer*

Hannacroix
Schwebler, Stephen *retired chemist*

Harpursville
Sweeney, Phillip Peter *poet*

Harrison
Coulter, Judy Marie *writer*
Hertz, Natalie Zucker *retired lawyer*
Kolbrener, Jonathan *lawyer*
Northcutt, Marie Rose *educator*
Schulz, Helmut Wilhelm *chemical engineer, environmental executive*
†Strone, Michael Jonathan *lawyer*
Wadsworth, Frank Whittemore *foundation executive, literature educator*
Wilson, William James *marketing professional*

Hartsdale
Aker, Susan K. *elementary education educator*
†Bowie, April Dene't *lawyer, arbitrator*
Chait, Maxwell Mani *physician*
Goodman, Stanley Leonard *advertising executive*
Greenawalt, Peggy Freed Tomarkin *advertising executive*
Katz, David *gastroenterologist, educator*
Katz, John *investment banker*
Kroll, Arthur Herbert *educator, consultant*
Martin, Daniel Richard *pharmaceutical company executive*
McMann, Edith Brozak *performance artist, visual artist*

Hastings On Hudson
Barolini, Helen *writer, translator, educator*
Considine, Russel A. *publisher, real estate consultant*
Cooney, Patrick Louis *writer*
Cooper, Doris Jean *market research executive*
D'Antoni, Philip *producer*
Del Colle, Paul Lawrence *communications administrator, educator*
Goldstein, Eleanor *artist, social worker*
Happel, Dorothy *violinist, concertmaster*
Landau, Peter Edward *editor*
Reich, Herb *editor*
Schorr-Lesnick, Beth *gastroenterologist, internist*
Sharpe, Robert Kent *writer, director, producer, photographer*
Stillman, Jeanne Betsock *public health administrator, consultant*
Thornlow, Carolyn *law firm administrator, consultant*
Weinstein, Edward Michael *architect, consultant*
Wolfe, Stanley *composer, educator*

Hauppauge
Buckley, Robert Matthew *electrical engineer*
Kurtz, Joel Barry *finance executive*
Shalam, John Joseph *car stereo and cellular telephone company executive*
†Tublisky, Marcy *association administrator*

Haverstraw
Hoppenthaler, John Gunther *writer, educator*
Motin, Revell Judith *retired data processing executive*

Hawthorne
†Banikazemi, Mohammad *computer scientist, researcher*
†Cantor, Arnold *labor relations official*
Chen, Shyh-Kwei *computer scientist, researcher*
†Chojnicki, Eric Walter Theodore *molecular geneticist*
†Dan, Asit *computer scientist, research scientist*
Darzynkiewicz, Zbigniew D. *research scientist*
Jacobs, Jeffrey Lee *lawyer, education network company executive*
Kiamie, Don Albert Najeeb *accountant*
†Nandedkar, Sanjeev Dattatraya *medical researcher, educator*
Panitz, Lawrence *physician*
Scheffler, Eckart Arthur *publisher*
Traub, Richard Kenneth *lawyer*

Hemlock
Doty, Dale Vance *educator, psychotherapist, hypnotherapist*

Hempstead
Ades, Janet *social worker*
Ancrum, Cheryl Denise *dentist*
Beasley, Aaron Bruce *football player*
Berliner, Herman Albert *university provost and officer, economics educator*
Block, Jules Richard *retired psychologist, educator, university official*
Chapman, Ronald Thomas *musician, educator*
Charnov, Bruce Hirschl *management educator, chaplain, rabbi*
Chrebet, Wayne *professional football player*
Comer, Debra Ruth *management educator*
†Couser, G(riffith) Thomas *literature educator*
†Diamond, David Arthur *law educator*
Edwards, Herman *professional football coach*
†Evans, Joel Raymond *marketing educator*
Freeman, MaryAnn *poet, songwriter*
Freese, Melanie Louise *librarian, professor, assistant dean*
Furey, James Michael *lawyer*
Gold, Ruth Forman *education educator*
Goldstein, Stanley Philip *engineering educator*
Graffeo, Mary Thérèse *music educator, performer*
†Greenwell, Raymond N. *mathematician, educator, writer*
Hastings, Harold Morris *science educator*
Hettrick, William Eugene *music educator*
Johnson, Robert Wood, IV, *sports team executive*
Krauze, Tadeusz Karol *sociologist, educator*
Kruh, Louis *advertising executive, lawyer*
†Lazarus, Harold *management educator*
Lee, Keun Sok *business educator, consultant*
Levinthal, Charles Frederick *psychologist, psychology educator, writer*
Mahon, Malachy Thomas, Sr., *lawyer, educator*
Martin, Curtis *professional football player*
Masheck, Joseph Daniel *art critic, educator*
McLaren, Joseph *Black literature educator*
Nelson, Vivienne E. *artist, office manager*
Parola, Frederick Edson, Jr., *state official*
Pell, Arthur Robert *human resources specialist, consultant, author*
Resnick, Alan Neal *law educator, lawyer*
Sonfield, Matthew Charles *business administration educator, writer*
†Stauber, Michael C. *physicist, consultant*
Testaverde, Vincent Frank (Vinny Testaverde) *professional football player*
Wattel, Harold Louis *economics educator*
Wondolowski Gerstein, Christine Rita *academic librarian*
Yashin, Alexei *hockey player*
Yoo, Boonghee *marketing educator, researcher*
†Zapata, Miguel-Angel *language educator, writer*

Henrietta
Byfield, Bert A. *conservative humanitarian novelist*

Hensonville
Newman, Oscar *architect, city planner, sculptor*

Herkimer
Martin, Lorraine B. *humanities educator*

Hewlett
Cirker, Blanche *retired publishing executive*
Cohen, David Leon *physician*
Haralick, Robert Martin *electrical engineering educator*
Salamon, Michael Jacob *psychologist, health care and psychology educator, media consultant*
Wolff, Eleanor Blunk *actress*

Hicksville
Giuffré, John Joseph *lawyer*
Horowitz, Barry Allan *music company executive*
Moshoyannis, Phillip Demetri Alexander *educator*
Mund, Lorraine G. *English studies educator, writer*
Notaro, Anthony *software engineer*
O'Connor, Ann Ruth *information systems educator*
Stein, Melvin A. *accountant*
Tucci, Gerald Frank *manufacturing company executive*
Yen, Henry Chin-Yuan *computer systems programmer, software engineer, consulting company executive*

High Falls
Cook, Ferris *writer, illustrator*

Highland Mills
Gazzaniga, Antonette J. *secondary school educator*

Hillsdale
Lunde, Asbjorn Rudolph *lawyer*
Parmet, Herbert Samuel *historian, writer*
Richards, Joseph Edward *artist*

Himrod
Preska, Margaret Louise Robinson *education historian, administrator*

Holbrook
Watkins, Linda Theresa *educational researcher*

Holland
Loockerman, William Delmer *educational administrator, retired*

Hollis
Greenblatt, Fred Harold *data processing consultant*
Singh, Harbachan *solicitor, barrister*
Stephens, B. Consuela *minister, consultant*

Holtsville
Braff, Howard *brokerage house executive, financial analyst, solar energy consultant*
Katz, Joseph *research and development executive*
†Laureano, Mari *tax specialist, writer*

Homer
Bull, Beverly Jane *piano and voice educator*
Gustafson, John Alfred *biology educator*
MacNeill, John Sears, Jr., *civil engineer*

Honeoye
Blackmer, Sally *secondary education educator*
Stone, Alan John *manufacturing company executive, real estate executive*

Honeoye Falls
Hillabrandt, Larry Lee *service industry executive*

VanAuken, Alan Bradley *management consultant*

Hoosick Falls
Dodge, Cleveland Earl, Jr., *manufacturing executive, director*

Hopewell Junction
Ebersole, Patricia Sue *advertising executive, design educator*
Gluschenkov, Oleg *electrical engineer*
Kirihata, Toshiaki *VLSI design engineer, researcher*
†Mione, Anna J. *music educator, writer*
†Park, Byeongju *engineer*
†Sikka, Kamal K. *engineering executive*

Hornell
Pulos, William Whitaker *lawyer*

Horseheads
Josbeno, Larry Joseph *physics educator*
†Peters, Linda S. *musician, music educator*
Shabanowitz, Harry *electronics engineer, educator*

Houghton
Brautigam, David Clyde *lawyer, judge*
Chamberlain, Daniel Robert *college president*
Luckey, Robert Reuel Raphael *retired academic administrator*

Howard Beach
Iorio, John Emil *retired education educator*
Krein, Catherine Cecilia *broadcast and journalism educator*
Miller, Theresa Valentini *social worker, psychotherapist*
Watnick, Rochelle *principal*

Howes Cave
†Becker, Mary Druke *anthropologist, researcher*

Hudson
Agata, Burton C. *law educator, lawyer*
Artschwager, Richard Ernst *artist*
Davis, Deborah Lynn *lawyer*
Hanvik, Jan Michael *arts promoter, writer*
Howard, Andrew Baker *lawyer*
†Lyons, Rosemary *language educator*
Miner, Jacqueline *political consultant*
Mustapha, Tamton *gastroenterologist*
Vile, Sandra Jane *leadership training educator*

Hudson Falls
Leary, Daniel *artist*

Huletts Landing
Kapusinski, Albert Thomas *economist, educator*

Hunter
Khanzadian, Vahan *tenor*

Huntington
Alsop, Reese Fell *medical educator*
Bregman, Davis *physician, pain management specialist*
Brettschneider, Rita Roberta Fischman *lawyer*
Chmelev, Vsevolod *engineer, consultant*
Christiansen, Donald David *electrical engineer, editor, publishing consultant*
Connor, Joseph Robert *editor*
D'Addario, Alice Marie *school administrator*
Dircks, Richard Joseph *English language educator, writer*
Ferares, Kenneth *automobile executive*
Fritz, Melvin M. *physician*
German, June Resnick *lawyer*
Glickstein, Howard Alan *law educator*
Goldstein, Ilene Joy *allergist, immunologist*
Hochberg, Ronald Mark *lawyer*
Israel, Steve *congressman*
Jackson, Richard Montgomery *former airline executive*
†Jordan, Daniel Patrick, Jr., *law librarian*
Joseph, Richard Saul *cardiologist, educator*
LaTourrette, James Thomas *retired electrophysics, electrical engineering and computer science educator*
Levinthal, Beth Ellen (Kuby Levinthal) *museum administrator, educator*
Levitan, Katherine D. *lawyer*
Liput, Andrew Lawrence *lawyer, educator*
Maglione, Lili *fine artist, art consultant*
Massa, James *priest, theology studies educator*
Morris, Jeffrey Brandon *law educator*
Munson, Nancy K. *lawyer*
†Petersen, Patricia J. *real estate company executive*
Robinson, Kenneth Patrick *lawyer, electronics company executive*
Salcedo-Dovi, Hector Eduardo *anatomist, educator, surgeon*
†Sforza, Alfred Vincent *dentist, educator, writer*
Slutsky, Leonard Alan *finance executive, consultant*
Tar, Laszlo *artist*
Tucker, William P. *lawyer, writer*
Twardowicz, Stanley Jan *artist, photographer*
Weinberg, Marc Alan *cardiologist*
Zingale, Robert G. *surgeon*

Huntington Station
Agosta, Vito *mechanical and aerospace engineering educator*
Boxwill, Helen Ann *primary and secondary education educator*
Devlin, Jean Theresa *educator, storyteller*
Williams, Una Joyce *psychiatric social worker*

Hurley
LaRusso, Joseph *retired musician*
Opdahl, Viola Elizabeth *secondary education educator*
Petruski, Jennifer Andrea *speech and language pathologist*
Smith, Lewis Motter, Jr., *retired advertising and direct marketing executive*

Hyde Park
Eastwood, D(ana) Alan *author, publisher, consultant*
Hunt, Mark Alan *museum director*
Rider, Kathleen Mary *dietitian*

Ilion
Gay, Douglas MacKenzie *pharmacologist*

Interlaken
Bleiler, Everett Franklin *writer, publishing company executive*

Inwood
Soffer, Grace Florey *retired elementary school educator, artist*

Ionia
Paddock, Paula J. *geriatrics nurse*

Irvington
Bonomi, John Gurnee *retired lawyer*
Carey, Edward John *utility executive*
Devons, Samuel *educator, physicist*
Ebenstein, Judith Ann *psychiatrist, educator*
Elbaum, Marek *electro-optical sciences executive, researcher*
Rainer, Renata Urbach *artist, photographer, lecturer, educator*
Trent, Bertram James *real estate executive*

Islandia
Buckley, Terrence Patrick *lawyer*
†Gorman, Marcy *health care administrator*
†Kumar, Sanjay *computer company executive*
Pruzansky, Joshua Murdock *lawyer*

Islip
†Romeo, Anthony M., III, *music educator*
Tameling, Gary William *sales executive*

Ithaca
Abrams, Meyer Howard *English language educator*
†Aiosa, Vincent Nestor *music educator*
Alexander, Martin *environmental toxicologist, consultant*
Arquit, Nora Harris *retired music educator, writer*
Ascher, Robert *anthropologist, educator, archaeologist, educator, film producer*
Ashcroft, Neil William *physics educator, researcher*
†Assie-Lumumba, N'Dri T. *Africana studies educator*
Bailey, Lee Worth *philosophy and religion educator*
Ballantyne, Joseph M. *science educator, program administrator, researcher*
Barcelo, John James, III, *law educator*
Bardaglio, Peter Winthrop *humanities educator*
Barney, John Charles *lawyer*
Basefsky, Stuart Mark *law librarian, library and information scientist, journalist*
Bassett, William Akers *geologist, educator, retired*
Bauer, Simon Harvey *chemistry educator*
Bauman, Dale Elton *nutritional biochemistry educator*
Ben Daniel, David Jacob *entrepreneurship educator, consultant*
Beneria, Lourdes *economist, educator*
Bensel, Richard Franklin *political science educator*
Benson, Frances Goldsmith *publishing executive*
Berger, Toby *electrical engineer, educator*
Berkelman, Karl *physics educator*
Berry, Michelle Courtney *communication executive, performance artist*
Bethe, Hans Albrecht *physicist, educator*
Blackler, Antonie William Charles *biologist*
†Borden, David *composer, educator*
Bourne, Russell *publisher, author*
†Brazell, Karen Woodard *Japanese literature educator*
Briggs, Vernon Mason, Jr., *economics educator*
Burns, Joseph Arthur *planetary science educator*
Carlin, Herbert J. *electrical engineering educator, researcher*
Carpenter, Barry Keith *chemistry educator, researcher*
Chapman, Lewis Duane *economist*
Chiang, Huai Chang *entomologist, educator*
Colby-Hall, Alice Mary *Romance studies educator*
Conway, Richard Walter *computer scientist, educator*
Cornish, Elizabeth Turverey *stockbroker*
Crittenden, James Arthur *physicist*
Culler, Jonathan Dwight *English language educator*
Darlington, Richard Benjamin *psychology educator*
Davies, Peter John *plant physiology educator, researcher*
†Dear, Peter Robert *historian, educator*
De Boer, Pieter Cornelis Tobias *mechanical and aerospace engineering educator*
Dick, Richard Irwin *environmental engineer, educator*
Dietert, Rodney Reynolds *immunology and toxicology educator*
Dyckman, Thomas Richard *accountant, educator*
Dynkin, Eugene B. *mathematics educator*
Earle, Clifford John, Jr., *mathematician*
Earle, Elizabeth Deutsch *biology educator*
Easley, David *economics educator*
Eastman, Lester Fuess *electrical engineer, educator*
Eddy, Donald Davis *English language educator*
Ehrenberg, Ronald Gordon *economist, educator*
Eisner, Thomas *biologist, educator*
Elber, Ron *computer science educator*
Fakundiny, Lydia *English language educator*
Fay, Robert Clinton *chemist, educator*
Feinstein, Rosalind Deborah *social worker*
Fick, Gary Warren *agronomy educator, forage crops researcher*
Finch, C. Herbert *retired archivist, library administrator, historian*
†Finn, Robert Kaul *retired biochemical engineering educator*
Firebaugh, Francille Maloch *university official*
Fireside, Harvey Francis *political scientist, educator*
Fitchen, Douglas Beach *physicist, educator*
†Flanagan, Eanna Eamonn *physicist*
Foote, Robert Hutchinson *animal physiology educator*
Forker, Olan Dean *agricultural economics educator*
Fox, Francis Henry *retired veterinarian*
Freed, Jack Herschel *chemist, educator*
Garrison, Elizabeth Jane *artist*
Ghiorse, William Cushing *microbiology educator, editor*
Gillett, James Warren *ecotoxicology educator*
†Ginsparg, Paul *physicist*
†Gockley, Daniel L. *academic administrator*
Gold, Michael Evan *law educator*
Gold, Thomas *astronomer, educator*
Goldsmith, Paul Felix *physics and astronomy educator*
Gouldin, Frederick Caskey *mechanical and aerospace engineering professor*
Grainger, Mary Maxon *civic volunteer*
Green, Edward Thomas, Jr., *education educator*
Grippi, Salvatore William *artist*
Groos, Arthur Bernhard, Jr., *German literature and music educator*
Grunes, David Leon *research soil scientist, educator, editor*
Haas, Jere Douglas *nutritional sciences educator, researcher*
Habicht, Jean Pierre *healthcare educator, nutritionist*
Hairston, Nelson George, Jr., *ecologist, educator*
Hajek, Ann Elizabeth *insect pathologist*
Halpern, Bruce Peter *academic administrator, researcher, educator*
Hammond, Jane Laura *retired law librarian, lawyer*
Hardy, Jane Elizabeth *communications educator*
Harriott, Peter *chemical engineering educator*
Harris, Robert Lee, Jr., *history educator*
Hart, Edward Walter *physicist*
Hartmanis, Juris *computer scientist, educator*
Hay, George Alan *law and economics educator*
†Heckathorn, Douglas D. *sociologist, educator, epidemiologist*
Hedlund, James H. *traffic safety consultant*
Hess, George Paul *biochemist, educator*
Hoffmann, Roald *chemist, educator*
Hohendahl, Peter Uwe *German language and literature educator*
†Hojnowski, Jules Austin *entrepreneur*
Holcomb, Donald Frank *physicist, academic administrator*
Hopcroft, John Edward *computer scientist*
†Hotchkiss, Joseph Henry *toxicologist, educator*
†Hower, Edward *writer, journalist, educator*
Husa, Karel *composer, conductor, educator*
Hutcheson, Richard Ervin *philosophy educator, academic administrator*
Isard, Walter *economics educator*
Jagendorf, André Tridon *plant physiologist*
Jarrow, Robert Alan *economics and finance educator, consultant*
Kahn, Alfred Edward *economist, educator, government official*
Kallfelz, Francis A. *veterinary medicine educator*
Kammen, Carol Koyen *historian, educator*
Kammen, Michael *historian, educator*
Kendler, Bernhard *editor*
Kennedy, Kenneth Adrian Raine *biological anthropologist, forensic anthropologist*
Kennedy, Wilbert Keith, Sr., *agronomy educator, retired university official*
Kingsbury, John Merriam *botanist, educator*
Kinoshita, Toichiro *physicist*
Korf, Richard Paul *mycology educator*
Koschmann, J. Victor *history educator, academic program director*
Kramer, John Paul *entomologist, educator*
†Krivoshein, Arcadius V. *research scientist*
Kronik, John William *Romance studies educator*
LaCapra, Dominick Charles *historian, educator*
LaDue, Eddy Lorain *economist, educator*
LaFeber, Walter Frederick *history educator, author*
Law, Gordon Theodore, Jr., *library director*
Lee, David Morris *physics educator*
Lehman, Jeffrey Sean *college president, educator*
Leibovich, Sidney *engineering educator*
Leicht, Susan Dale *occupational therapist*
Lengemann, Frederick William *physiology educator, scientist*
Lepage, Gerard Peter *physics educator*
Lesser, William Henri *marketing educator*
Liboff, Richard Lawrence *physicist, educator*
Linke, Simpson *electrical engineering educator*
Loucks, Daniel Peter *environmental systems engineer*
†Lovelace, Richard Van Evera *education educator, research scientist*
Lowi, Theodore J(ay) *political science educator*
Lumley, John Leask *physicist, educator*
Lurie, Alison *writer*
Lyons, Thomas Patrick *economics educator*
Macey, Jonathan R. *law educator*
Mackin, Jeanne Ann *writer, educator*
Mai, William Frederick *plant nematologist, educator*
Martin, Peter William *lawyer, educator*
Maxwell, William Laughlin *retired industrial engineering educator*
McCarroll, Earl *educator, director*
McCartney, Elaina *space mission planner*
McConkey, James Rodney *English educator, writer*
McCue, Arthur Harry *artist, educator*
McGuire, William *civil engineer, educator*
McLafferty, Fred Warren *chemist, educator*
†McMillin, Scott *language educator*
McMurry, John Edward *chemistry educator*
Meinwald, Jerrold *chemist, educator*
Merle, H. Etienne *restauranteur*
Mermin, N. David *physicist, educator, writer*
Meyburg, Arnim Hans *transportation engineer, educator, consultant*
Michael, M. Todd *university educator*
Mikus, Eleanore Ann *artist*
Morgenstern, Matthew *computer scientist*
Mortlock, Robert Paul *microbiologist, educator*
Mueller, Betty Jeanne *social work educator*
†Nasrallah, June *plant pathologist, department chairman*
Nerode, Anil *mathematician, educator*
Nesheim, Malden C. *academic administrator, nutrition educator*
Nichols, Margaret Foster *librarian*
Norton, Mary Beth *history educator, writer*
Novak, Joseph Donald *science educator, knowledge studies specialist*
Oliver, Jack Ertle *geophysicist, educator*
†Olpadwala, Porus *architecture educator, dean*
O'Rourke, Thomas Denis *civil engineer, educator*
Pagliarulo, Michael Anthony *physical therapy educator*
Park, Roy Hampton, Jr., *advertising executive*
†Park, Young-Hoon *marketing educator*
Pelto, Gretel H. *nutritional anthropologist, educator*
Perry, Margaret *librarian, writer*
Phelan, Richard Magruder *mechanical engineer*
Pimentel, David *ecologist, educator*
Pinstrup-Andersen, Per *educational administrator*
Poleskie, Stephen Francis *artist, retired educator, writer*
Poppensiek, George Charles *veterinary scientist, educator*
Porte, Joel Miles *English educator*
†Radice, Mark A. *musicologist*
Radzinowicz, Mary Ann *language educator*
Rasmussen, Kathleen Maher *nutritional sciences educator*
Rawlings, Hunter Ripley, III, *academic administrator, classicist*
Renwick, J. Alan *chemist, ecologist*
Resnick, Minna *artist, educator*
Rhodes, Frank Harold Trevor *university president emeritus, geologist*
Richardson, Robert Coleman *physics educator, researcher*
Rinaldo, Peter Merritt *publishing executive*
Roberts, E. F. *lawyer, educator*
Robinson, Franklin Westcott *museum director, art historian*
Rodríguez, Ferdinand *chemical engineer, educator*
Rosen, Bernard Carl *sociologist, social psychologist, educator*
Rossi, Faust F. *lawyer, educator*
Salpeter, Edwin Ernest *physical sciences educator*
†Santiago-Irizarry, Vilma Iris *anthropologist, educator, lawyer*
Sass, Stephen Louis *education educator*
Scheraga, Harold Abraham *physical chemistry educator*
Schlafer, Donald Hughes *veterinary pathologist*
Schroeder, Caroline Theresa *humanities educator*
Schwartz, Donald Franklin *communication scientist*
Schwarz, Daniel Roger *English and American literature educator*
Scott, Norman Roy *academic administrator, agricultural engineering educator*
Seeley, John George *horticulture educator*
Seibert, Mary Lee *college official*
†Seraji-Bozorgzad, Nasrine *architecture educator*
Shaw, Harry Edmund *English educator*
Shell, Karl *economist*
Shore, Richard Arnold *mathematics educator*
Shuler, Michael Louis *biochemical engineering educator, consultant*
Siegel, Rachel Josefowitz *writer, social worker*
Silbey, Joel Henry *history educator*
Sims, William Riley *design and facility management educator, consultant, architect*
Slate, Floyd Owen *chemist, materials scientist, civil engineer, educator, researcher*
Smilgies, Detlef-Matthias Friedrich *physicist*
†Smith, Donald F. *dean*
Smith, Robert John *anthropology educator*
Smith, Robert Samuel *banker, former agricultural finance educator*
Squier, Jack Leslie *sculptor, educator*
Stedinger, Jery Russell *civil and environmental engineer, researcher*
Strassberg, Marilyn *social worker*
Streett, William Bernard *retired university dean, engineering educator*
Stycos, Joseph Mayone *retired demographer, educator*
†Summers, Robert Samuel *lawyer, author, educator*
Swieringa, Robert Jay *dean, accountant, educator*
†Taimina, Daina *mathematician, educator*
Terzian, Yervant *astronomy and astrophysics educator*
†Teukolsky, Saul *physicist, educator*
Thomas, J. Earl *retired physicist*
Thorbecke, Erik *economics educator*
Thoron, Gray *lawyer, educator*
†Todd, Michael Jeremy *mathematician, educator, researcher*
Tomek, William Goodrich *agricultural economist*
Trotter, Leslie Earl *operations research educator, consultant*
Van Houtte, Raymond A. *financial executive*
Walcott, Charles *neurobiology and behavior educator*
Waldman, Michael *economist, educator*
Wang, Kuo-King *manufacturing engineer, educator*

Wasserman, Robert Harold *biology educator*
Wavle, Elizabeth Margaret *college official*
Weinstein, Leonard Harlan *institute program director, educator*
Welch, Ross Maynard *plant physiologist, researcher, educator*
Whitaker, Susanne Kanis *veterinary medical librarian*
†Wiedmann, Martin *microbiologist, educator, environmental scientist, veterinarian*
Yale-Loehr, Stephen William *lawyer, editor*
York, James Wesley, Jr., *theoretical physicist, educator*
Zall, Robert Rouben *food scientist, educator*

Jackson Heights
Chang, Lydia Liang-Hwa *social worker, educator*
†Dacey, Paul *artist*
Fischbarg, Zulema F. *pediatrician, educator*
†Gall, Lenore Rosalie *educational administrator*
†Goldblum, A. Paul *lawyer*
Michaelson, Herbert Bernard *technical communications consultant*
Morrow, Nana Kwasi Scott Douglas *choreographer, writer, filmmaker, educator*
Olmsted, Robert Amson *civil engineer*
Parascos, Edward Themistocles *engineering consultant*
Stevenson, Amanda (Sandy Stevens) *librettist, composer, document examiner*

Jamaica
Ahmed, Jimmie *health facility administrator*
Angione, Howard Francis *lawyer, editor*
†Biafora, Frank A. *sociologist, educator, dean*
Brockway, Laurie Sue *editor, journalist, author, minister*
Brown, Kenneth Lloyd *lawyer*
Cade, Walter, III, *artist, musician, singer, actor*
Capellan, Angel *small business executive*
Chropufka, Mark A. *information management specialist, poet*
Clark, Charles Michael Andres *economics educator*
Clauss, Wayne Francis *court clerk*
Cline, Janice Claire *education educator*
Cocchiarelli, Maria *artist, educator*
Cush, John Patrick *priest, theology studies educator*
Davis-Jerome, Eileen George *principal, educational consultant*
De La Paz, Lucia *social worker, consultant*
Delener, Nejdet *college dean, marketing and international business educator*
Divale, William T.
†Drobnicki, John Arthur *librarian, educator*
Ekbatani, Glayol *English as second language educator, program director, writer*
Faust, Naomi Flowe *education educator, poet*
Fay, Thomas A. *philosopher, educator*
Feldman, Arlene Butler *aviation industry executive*
†Flake, Floyd Harold *former congressman*
Flanagan, Patrick Sean Liam *priest*
Garner, Steven C. *emergency physician*
Gati, William Eugene *architect, designer and planner*
George, Marie Ivanka *humanities educator*
†Gesualdi, Louis J. *social sciences educator*
Gitner, Fred Jay *library administrator*
Goldenshteyn, Vladimir Lev *civil engineer*
†Graser, Alfred J. *airport terminal executive, director*
Grayshaw, James Raymond *judge*
Greenberg, Jacob *biochemist, educator, consultant*
Grünwald, Hans Wolfgang *internist, hematologist, oncologist*
Gutierrez, Franklin Abel *Spanish language-Latin America literature educator*
Hall, Michael *disability processing specialist*
Harmond, Richard Peter *historian, educator*
Harrington, Donald James *university president*
Jawin, Ann Juliano *human resource specialist*
Jones, Cynthia Teresa Clarke *artist*
†Kabir, Mohammed Anowarul *pharmacologist*
Keys, Martha McDougle *educational administrator*
Kinkley, Jeffrey C. *historian*
Lee, Joseph *musician, educator*
Lees, Francis *economics educator*
†Leet-Brodwin, Leonora *literature educator, writer*
Lengyel, István *chemist, educator*
Lyons, Patrick Joseph *management educator*
Machalow, Robert Allen *librarian*
Mangru, Basdeo *secondary education educator*
Mc Kinnon, Clinton Dan *aerospace transportation executive*
†Millán, Madeline *language educator, translator*
Morrill, Joyce Marie *social worker, educator*
Moser, Martin *retired music educator*
†Nedwek, Brian *director, consultant*
Parmet, Robert David *history educator*
†Primeaux, Patrick *priest, religious studies educator*
Reid, Michelle Marie Brady *government official*
†Retzel, Frank *music educator, composer*
Sciame, Joseph *university administrator*
†Seliga, Charles G. *airport administrator*
†Shapiro, Irving *lawyer*
†Skirde, Edward George *academic administrator, consultant*
Sun, Siao Fang *chemistry educator*
Tedesco, Anne Cavolo *music educator, concert pianist*
Tschinkel, Andrew Joseph, Jr., *law librarian*
†Vindollo-Gálan, Leonidez *architect, consultant*
Waisman, Warner *retired pharmacist*
†Washington, William Thomas *technical manager, educator*
Wetherington, Roger Vincent *journalism educator, newspaper copy editor*
Wintergerst, Ann Charlotte *language educator*

Jamesport
Cardinale, Philip John *lawyer, educator*

Jamestown
Beckstrom, Charles G. *lawyer*
Elofson, Nancy Meyer *retired office equipment company executive*
Idzik, Martin Francis *lawyer*
Leising, David Michael *industrial engineer*
Leising, Mary Kathleen *manufacturing executive*
†O'Brian, Jonathan D. *recreation director, social sciences educator, language educator, educator*
Reale, Sara Jane *museum education director*
Roman, Antonio Regino *cardiologist, internist*
Thompson, Birgit Dolores *civic worker, writer*
Victor, Jeffrey Spencer *retired sociology educator*
Walker, Timothy Craig *transportation executive*
Wellman, Barclay Ormes *furniture company executive*

Jamesville
DeCrow, Karen *lawyer, author, lecturer*

Jamiaca
†Kemeny, M. Margaret *oncologist, hospital administrator, surgeon*

Jefferson Valley
Huyghe, Patrick Antoine *writer, editor*

Jeffersonville
Craft, Douglas Durwood *artist*
Harms, Elizabeth Louise *artist*
†Hoering, Helen G. *elementary educator*

Jericho
Astuto, Philip Louis *retired Spanish educator*
Axinn, Donald Everett *real estate investor and developer, poet, writer*
Blau, Harvey Ronald *lawyer*
Corso, Frank Mitchell *lawyer*
†Fitteron, John Joseph *gas industry executive, real estate company executive*
Hecht, Donald Stuart *lawyer*
Kurtzberg, Howard *lawyer*
Rehbock, Richard Alexander *lawyer*
Rosen, Robert Arnold *management company executive, real estate investor*
Schatkin, Andrew James *lawyer*
Schell, Norman Barnett *physician, consultant*
Seidman, Glenn Elliott *sales and marketing professional*
†Semel, Martin Ira *lawyer*
Shinners, Stanley Marvin *electrical engineer*
Spatafore, Anthony R. *financial executive*
†Tafaghodi, Hamid *civil engineer*

Johnsburg
McKibben, Bill *writer*

Johnson City
Bernardo, Aldo Sisto *retired foreign language educator*
†Goddard, Bryan Lance *physician, director*
Kopuz, Kasim *educator, consultant*

Johnstown
Prestopnik, Richard John *electronics and computer educator*

Jordanville
Durham, Jeanette Randall *artist, educator*

Katonah
Baker, John Milnes *architect*
Bashkow, Theodore Robert *electrical engineering consultant, former educator*
Brownlee, Delphine *actress, musician*
Fry, John *magazine editor*
Grunebaum, Ernest Michael *investment banker*
Levine, Pamela Gail *business owner*
†Marx, Eve *writer, journalist*
Simpson, William Kelly *curator, Egyptologist, educator*
Wenglowski, Gary Martin *economist*

Keene Valley
Lanyon, Wesley Edwin *retired museum curator, ornithologist*

Keeseville
Turetsky, Aaron *lawyer*

Kendall
Rak, Linda Marie *elementary education educator, consultant*

Kenmore
Elibol, Tarik *gastroenterologist, educator*
Kenny, John Edward *computer analyst*

Keuka Park
†Sorenson, E. Richard *anthropologist*

Kew Gardens
†Adler, David Neil *lawyer*
Aldea, Patricia *architect*
†Chipkin, Frederick *textile designer, consultant*
Ford, Bernadette K. *lawyer*
Klein-Scheer, Cathy Ann *social worker*
Nizin, Leslie Stephen *lawyer*
Reichel, Aaron Israel *lawyer, rabbi, editor*
Schnakenberg, Donald G. *financial administrator*
†Sparrow, Robert E. *lawyer*

Kiamesha Lake
†Cash, Jeffrey Marc *commercial artist, photographer*

Kinderhook
†West, Patricia *historian, consultant*

Kings Park
Greene, Robert William *journalism educator, media consultant*

Kings Point
Billy, George John *library director*

†Greenwald, Richard Alan *history educator*
Maclean, Walter Marcus *engineering educator, retired*
†Mazek, Warren F(elix) *academic administrator, economics educator*

Kingston
†Abrams, Bruce D *music educator*
Bradley, Vincent Gerard *judge*
Dalbo, Joanne *social worker, writing teacher, secondary educator, poet*
Dennison, Robert Abel, III, *civil engineer*
Ellison, Patricia Lee *lawyer*
†Harrington, Gerard, III, *marketing and communications executive, business consultant*
Jagoda, Robert Eugene *writer, retired communications executive*
Johnson, Marie-Louise Tully *dermatologist, educator*
Matturro, Peter John *social worker*
McGuire, Thomas Peter *show boat captain, secondary school educator*
Shaffer, Sheila Weekes *mathematics educator*
Tsirpanlis, Constantine N. *theology, philosophy, classics and history educator*

Krumville
Nagi, Catherine Raseh *retired educational administrator, financial planner*
†Schuckman, Nancy Lee *retired principal*

Lagrangeville
Liccione, Alexander Anthony *artist*

Lake George
Hayes, Norman Robert, Jr., *lawyer*

Lake Katrine
Shaut, Robert William *music educator, composer*

Lake Luzerne
Goldstein, Manfred *retired consultant*

Lake Peekskill
Wisniewski, Mark Steven *writer, editor*

Lake Placid
†Bakken, Jill *Olympic athlete*
†Gale, Tristan *Olympic athlete*
†Grimmette, Mark *Olympic athlete*
Lussi, Caroline Frances Draper *resort executive*
†Martin, Brian *Olympic athlete*
Reiss, Paul Jacob *college president*
Rossi, Ronald Aldo *sports association administrator, Olympic athlete*

Lake Ronkonkoma
Delaney, Robert Patrick *librarian, writer*
Spahr, Clinton S., Jr., *retired elementary education educator*

Lake Success
Gould, Arthur Paul *investment banker*
Milman, Perry Jay *physician, gastroenterologist*
Rickin, Sheila Anne *personnel professional*

Lake Sucess
†Epstein, Joel Donald *lawyer*

Lakewood
Anderson, Raymond Quintus *diversified company executive*
Brown, Melvin Henry *retired chemical engineer*
Howlett, Howard Thomas, Jr., *automotive sales consultant*

Lancaster
Batt, Ronald Elmer *gynecologist, scientist, historian*
†Gainey, Ernest J., III, *internet security specialist*
Kappan, Sandra Jean *elementary education educator*
Neumaier, Gerhard John *environment consulting company executive*
Scott, Harley Earle *publisher, historian*
Walsh, J(ohn) B(ronson) *lawyer*

Lansing
Dalman, Gisli Conrad *electrical engineering educator*
Gage, George H(enry) *retired high technology company executive*

Larchmont
Berridge, George Bradford *retired lawyer*
Bloom, Lee Hurley *lawyer, public affairs consultant, retired household products manufacturing executive*
Davis, Wendell, Jr., *lawyer*
Gaffney, Mark William *lawyer*
Greenwald, Carol Schiro *professional services marketing research executive*
Guttenplan, Joseph B. *biochemist, educator*
Hinerfeld, Ruth G. *civic organization executive*
Kaufmann, Henry Mark *mortgage banker*
Levi, James Harry *real estate executive, investment banker*
McSherry, William John, Jr., *lawyer, consultant*
†Moody, Kathryn Currier *small business owner*
Pelton, Russell Gilbert *retired lawyer*
Plumez, Jean Paul *advertising agency executive, consultant*
Quigley, Martin Schofield *publishing company executive, educator*
Rainier, Robert Paul *publisher, consultant*
Rockland, Lawrence Howard *psychiatrist, educator*
Siegel, Nathaniel Harold *sociology educator*
Steinberg, Lois Saxelby *marketing executive*
Swire, Edith Wypler *music educator, musician, violist, violinist*
†Ungar, Lawrence Beryl *lawyer*
White, Thomas Edward *lawyer*
Wielgus, Charles Joseph *information services company executive*

Latham
Brearton, James Joseph *lawyer*
Caruso, Aileen Smith *managed care consultant*
Condon, Joseph Dennis *broadcasting executive*
Conway, Robert George, Jr., *lawyer*
Hardies, Michael John *medical educator, internist*
†Irwin, Heather May *writer, interior designer*
LeRoy, Beth Seperack *jazz musician, piano teacher*
Lvovsky, Yuri *physicist, applied superconductivity engineer*
McGoldrick, William Patrick *educational consultant*
Piedmont, Richard Stuart *lawyer*
Schwartz, Robert William *management consultant*
Stallman, Donald Lee *corporate executive*

Laurelton
Goodman, Robert Merrill *United Nations executive, artist*

Laurens
Spoor, John Edward *physician*

Lawrence
Goldstein, Irwin Melvin *lawyer*
†Press, Marlyn Rothman *special education educator*

Levittown
†Elliott, Franklyn *psychologist*
Form, Fredric Allan *accountant*
Juszczak, Nicholas Mauro *psychology educator*
Levine, Alan Jay *physician*
Montero, Carlos F. *orthopedic surgeon*
†Romano, Joseph Scott *music educator*
Schettino, Maria Carmen *preschool educator*
Stalter, Richard B. *biology educator, researcher*

Lewiston
Askins, Nancy Ellen Paulsen *training and organizational development professional*
Dexter, Theodore Henry *chemist*
LoTempio, Julia Matild *retired accountant*
Newlin, Lyman Wilbur *bookseller, consultant*
Presutti, Robert Michael *secondary education educator*
Shimer, Alice Marie *retired educator*
Simonson, Lee J. *small business owner*
Waters, William Ernest *microelectronics executive*
†Zhou, Zongqing *hospitality and tourism educator*

Liberty
†Green, Harold Martin *social science writer*

Lido Beach
†Shear, Richard Gary *education administrator*

Lindenhurst
Conklin, Richard Allan *management consultant*
Farrell Logan, Vivian *actress*
Hamilton, Daniel Stephen *clergyman*
Hungerford, Gary A. *insurance executive, columnist, author, editor*
Lazarek, John Willliam *music educator, musician*
Sanna, Catherine Lee *special education educator*

Little Falls
Feeney, Mary Katherine O'Shea *retired public health nurse*

Little Neck
Hettrick, Jane Schatkin *music educator, classical musician*
Overton, Rosilyn Gay Hoffman *financial services executive*

Liverpool
Allen, David Charles *computer science educator*
Coggiola, Jill Angela *musician, educator*
Egan, Marsha Christine *school psychologist*
Harris, Dana Bound *software company executive*
Morabito, Bruno Paul *machinery manufacturing executive*
Naum, Christopher John *fire protection management and industrial safety specialist, training consultant, educator*
Shubsda, Stanley Richard *retired computer engineer*
Williams, John Alan *secondary education educator, coach*

Lockport
Brodsky, Felice Adrienne *lawyer*
Carr, Edward Albert, Jr., *medical educator, physician*
Cull, John Joseph *novelist, playwright*
March, Cathleen Case *education educator*
Penney, Charles Rand *lawyer, civic worker, world traveler*
Pregmon, Stephen Kenneth *music educator, musician*
Salen, Wayne Louis *risk management consultant*
Schultz, Gerald Alfred (Jerry Schultz) *chemical company executive*
†Steinagle, Martin Gene *contractor, paralegal, poet, writer*

Locust Valley
†Bentel, Carol Rusche *architect*
Bentel, Frederick Richard *architect, educator*
Chapman, Judith Coste *charitable institution volunteer administrator*
DeRegibus, William *artist*
Huron, Robert Lawrence *photojournalist*
Mathews, Walter Michael *educational consultant*
McGee, Dorothy Horton *writer, historian*
†Peek, William DeWitt, Jr., *music educator*
Schor, Joseph Martin *pharmaceutical executive, biochemist*
Zulch, Joan Carolyn *retired medical publishing company executive*

Long Beach
Bernstein, Lester *editorial consultant*
Caplan, Judith Shulamith Langer-Surnamer *genealogist, poet, researcher, editor, educator*
Levine, Samuel Milton *lawyer, retired judge, mediator, arbitrator*
Robbins, Jeffrey Howard *media consultant, research writer, educator*
Shechtman, Harry *retired judge, law educator*
Solomon, Robert H. *lawyer*
Thompson, Dorothy Barnard *elementary school educator*

Long Eddy
Hoiby, Lee *composer, concert pianist*

Long Island City
Alimaras, Gus *lawyer*
Barbanel, Sidney William *engineering consulting firm executive*
Barrett, Martin Jay *financial executive*
Corry, James Michael *insurance executive, educator*
Craig, Elizabeth Coyne *marketing executive*
Della-Giustina, Jo-Ann Subotin *lawyer*
DiGiovanni, Eleanor Elma *scaffold installation company executive*
Donneson, Seena Sand *artist*
†Falk, Charles H. (Harry Falk) *brokerage house executive*
Healy, John Joseph *financial analyst, economist*
Henick, Nita Halpern *retired social worker*
Kolm, Ron *author, editor*
Mathers, Allen Stanley *judge, arbitrator, consultant*
Munro, Roxie Jean *artist, educator, illustrator, writer*
†Popian, Lucia *artist*
Roselli, John Antimo *finance company executive*
Rosenstein, Ira H. *radio producer, poet, writer*
Rothenhaus, Robert Charles *mathematics educator*
Sadao, Shoji *architect*
Schoenberg, David Arthur *business educator*
Theodoru, Stefan Gheorghe *civil engineer, writer*
Wanderman, Susan Mae *lawyer*
Yin, Kenneth Joseph *language educator*

Loudonville
Bronner, Kevin Michael *financial analyst, researcher*
Burstein, Sharon Ann *corporate communications specialist, designer*
Fiore, Peter Amadeus *English educator, clergy*
Haverly, Douglas Lindsay *librarian, historian*
†LaRow, Edward J. *biologist, educator*
Toal, James Francis *academic administrator*

Lowville
Becker, Robert Otto *orthopedic surgery educator*
Herrman, John Clinton *surgeon*

Lynbrook
Kassimatis, Loretta Eileen *clinical social worker*
Korth, Jay Thomas *lawyer*
†Marino, William Vito *accountant, educator*
O'Malley, Edward Joseph, Jr., *financial services administrator*

Macedon
McGee, Dennis Emmett *research technologist*

Mahopac
Fliss, Albert Edward, Jr., *molecular biologist*
Gonzalez-Tornero, Sergio *artist*
Sequeira, Manuel Alexandre, Jr., *lawyer*

Malone
Grue, Thomas Andrew *lawyer*

Malverne
†Alesse, Judith *special education educator*
Benigno, Thomas Daniel *lawyer*
Freund, Richard L. *communications company executive, consultant, lawyer*
Gavalás, Alexander Beary *artist*
Knight, John Francis *retired insurance company executive*
Pollio, Ralph Thomas *editor, writer, magazine publishing consultant*

Mamaroneck
Carty, Mary Ellen *psychologist*
Coleman, Marshall Donald *psychiatrist, psychoanalyst*
†Feigin, Nancy J. *guidance counselor*
Gorup, Gregory James *marketing executive*
Halpern, Abraham Leon *psychiatrist*
Hoffert, Paul Washington *surgeon*
Holz, Harold A. *chemical and plastics manufacturing company executive*
Mazzola, Claude Joseph *physicist, small business owner*
Mizrahi, Abraham Mordechay *retired cosmetics and health care company executive, physician*
Pugh, Grace Huntley *artist*
Rosenthal, Elizabeth Robbins *physician*
†Scheidlinger, Saul *psychologist*
Topol, Robert Martin *retired financial services executive*

Manchester
†Gillis, Joan *legal administrative assistant*

Manhasset
Benewitz, Maurice Charles *labor arbitrator, educator*
Bernstein, David *gastroenterologist*
Bialer, Martin George *geneticist*
Boal, Bernard Harvey *cardiologist, educator, author*
Bradley, Thomas Paul *internist*
Brand, Oscar *folksinger, writer, educator*
Callaway, David James Edward *physicist, protein chemist, bioinformaticist, expedition mountaineer*
Calvin, Donald Lee *business executive, stock exchange consultant*
Catchi, (Catherine Oeland Childs) *artist*
Cavaliere, Terri Angela *neonatal nurse practitioner*
Chiorazzi, Nicholas *immunologist educator*
†D'Olimpio, James Thomas *oncologist*
Feinberg, Joseph *plastic surgeon*
†Fisch, Gene S. *psychologist, researcher, statistician*
Foerst, John George, Jr., *retired fundraising executive*
Fountain, Karen Schueler *physician*
†Friedenberg, Mike *publishing executive*
Gardner, Robert *financial services executive*
Gastwirth, Stuart Lawrence *lawyer*
Gauthier, Bernard Gustave *pediatric nephrologist, educator*
Goldberg, Leslie Philip *ophthalmologist*
†Hoffman, Amy *publishing executive*
Keen, Constantine *retired manufacturing company executive*
Kingsley, Peter Bernard *physics researcher*
Krumholz, Burton Alan *obstetrician-gynecologist, educator*
Lala, Dominick Joseph *manufacturing company executive*
†Lankevich, George J. *history, writer*
Margulies, Paul *internist, endocrinologist, educator*
Milhorat, Thomas Herrick *neurosurgeon*
Pam, Eleanor *behavorial sciences educator*
†Pitti, Donald Robert *financial services consultant*
†Robeson, William *medical physicist, radiation safety officer*
Rush, Stephen C. *radiation oncologist*
Scherr, Lawrence *physician, educator*
Schiller, Arthur A. *architect, educator*
Seftel, Donna Selene *architect*
Spetsieris, Phoebe George *physicist, scientific software engineer, researcher*
Temares, Lee Barnett *rare book dealer, book appraiser*
Vizard, Michael *periodical editor*
Wachtler, Sol *law educator, retired judge, arbitration corporation executive, writer*
Wadler, Gary I. *physician, consultant*
Wallace, Richard *editor, writer*
Wang, Ping *biomedical investigator*
Wecksell, Alan *radiologist*

Manhattan
†Khalil, Mounir A. *librarian, educator*

Manlius
Brophy, Mary O'Reilly *environmental scientist*
Gibson, Judith W. *clinical therapist*
Gray, Judith A. *retired school librarian, educator*
Harriff, Suzanna Elizabeth (Bahner) *advertising consultant*
Jefferies, Michael John *retired electrical engineer*
†Koch, Catherine Ann *music educator, musician*
Martonosi, Anthony Nicholas *biochemistry educator, researcher*
Mathewson, George Atterbury *lawyer*
Prior, John Thompson *pathology educator*
Vasile, Gennaro James *health care executive*
Zlomek, Elizabeth A. *customer service/business processes specialist*

Manorville
Esp, Barbara Ann Lorraine *educational researcher, educator*

Marcellus
Baker, Bruce Roy *retired art educator, artist*
Moser, David John *management consultant*

Marcy
Rishel, Kenn Charles *school superintendent*

Maryland
Miller, J(ames) Robert *chemistry educator*

Maspeth
Heppa, Douglas Van *computer specialist*
Merjan, Stanley *civil engineer, inventor*

Massapequa
Arbiter, Andrew Richard *accountant*
Batt, Alyse Schwartz *technical officer*
Bogorad, Barbara Ellen *psychologist*
Colbourn, Frank Edwin *communications educator*
Kappenberg, Marilyn Kascius *library director*
Kurtz, Judith Marsha *elementary education educator*
Margulies, Andrew Michael *chiropractor*
McCann, Susan Lynn *elementary education educator*
Mondschein, Robert H. *surgeon*
Odol, Marilyn Elaine *accountant*
†Turk, Elizabeth Ann *music educator*
Van Gorder, John Frederic *lawyer*

Massapequa Park
Blair, Carol *social worker, therapist*

Massena
†Edwards, Keith B. *airport administrator*
†O'Connor, John Lawrence, III, *writer*
Schroll, Edwin John *retired secondary educator, stage director*

Mastic Beach
Merolla, Michael B. *secondary school music educator*
Pagano, Alicia I. *education educator*

Mechanicville
Rhodes, Alan Charles *minister*

Medford
Brower, Robert Charles *rehabilitation counselor, small business owner*
Haig, Monica Elaine Nachajski *special education educator*
Snyder, Mark Jeffrey *financial consultant, actuary*
Tafuri, William *sculptor*

Melville
Atkins, William Allen *academic administrator*
†Blechschmidt, Edward Allan *data processing executive*
Bongiorno, Joseph John, Jr., *electrical engineering educator*
Bultan, Aykut *communications systems engineer*
†Cahn, Richard Caleb *lawyer*
Carter, Sylvia *journalist*
Clinard, Joseph Hiram, Jr., *securities company executive*
Copperman, Stuart Morton *pediatrician, educator*
Crowe, Kenneth Charles *writer*
Damadian, Raymond Vahan *biophysicist*
D'Angelo-Mayer, Ida *lawyer*
Davidson, Justin *music critic*
Doering, Charles Henry *research scientist, educator, editor, publisher*
Dooley, James C. *newspaper editor, director of photography*
Fine, Barry Kenneth *lawyer*
Goldstein, Mindy Sue *biologist*
Hall, Charlotte Hauch *newspaper editor*
Hildebrand, John Frederick *newspaper columnist*
Jansen, Raymond A., Jr., *newspaper publishing executive*
Johns, Michael Douglas *health care corporate executive, former federal official, writer, former federal government offical*
Kaufman, Stephen P. *former electronics company executive, business educator*
Kissinger, Walter Bernhard *retired automotive test and service equipment manufacturing executive*
Klatell, Robert Edward *lawyer, electronics company executive*
Krenek, Debby *newspaper editor*
Krusos, Denis Angelo *communications company executive*
Lane, Arthur Alan *lawyer*
Lieberman, Carol *healthcare marketing communications consultant*
Marro, Anthony James *newspaper editor*
McMillan, Robert Ralph *lawyer*
†Mitchell, William Edmund *electronics executive*
Moran, Paul James *journalist, columnist*
Newman, Samuel *retired trust company executive*
Pelle, Edward Gerard *biochemist*
Ponzi Kay, Marylou *human resources specialist*
Provenzano, Dominic *information specialist*
Richards, Carol Ann Rubright *editor, columnist*
†Saul, Stephanie *journalist*
†Schneider, Howard Stewart *newspaper editor, educator*
Schoenfeld, Michael P. *lawyer*
Scire, Frank Jackson *retired radar scientist*
Scricco, Francis M. *electronics company executive*
Sobol, Elise Schwarcz *music educator*
Sullivan, Kenneth W. *engineer*
Taub, Jesse J. *electrical engineering researcher*
Weiner, Alan E. *accountant, lawyer*

Merrick
Auteri, Rose Mary Patti *school system administrator*
Baron, Theodore *public relations executive*
Cariola, Robert Joseph *artist*
Cherry, Harold *insurance company executive*
Garfinkel, Lawrence Saul *academic administrator, educator, television producer*
Gutnik, Zhanna *physician, gastroenterology consultant*
Kaplan, Steven Mark *accountant*
Poppel, Seth Raphael *entrepreneur*
Sardo, Sanford *music educator*
Wanderman, Miriam *library studies educator*

Mexico
Sade, Donald Stone *anthropology educator*

Middle Island
†Andrews, Gaylen *measurable response public relations expert*
Linick, Andrew S. *direct marketing expert*
Sanfilippo, Stephen Nicholas *educator*

Middle Village
Kolatch, Alfred Jacob *publisher*
Rowan, John Patrick *city official*
Walter, John Frederick *historical researcher, genealogist*

Middletown
Bedell, Barbara Lee *journalist*
Broslovsky, Lewis *physician*
Freifeld, Gerald Sherman *neurosurgeon*
Fucci, Joseph Leonard *architect, librarian, editor*
Kossar, Ronald Steven *lawyer*
McCord, Jean Ellen *secondary art educator, coach*
Moore, Virginia Lee Smith *elementary education educator*
Radeboldt-Daly, Karen Elaine *medical nurse*
Schwartz, Robert Marc *psychology educator*

Millbrook
Cole, Jonathan Jay *aquatic scientist, researcher*
Flexner, Josephine Moncure *musician, educator*
Flexner, Kurt Fisher *economist, educator*
Hall, Penelope Coker *writer, magazine editor*
Jones, Clive Gareth *ecologist, researcher*
Likens, Gene Elden *biology and ecology educator, administrator*
†Lindsley, James Elliott *minister, writer*
Turndorf, Jamie *psychotherapist*

Miller Place
Leedom, E. Paul *banker*
Sanger, Eileen *artist*

Millerton
Hastings, Donald Francis *actor, writer*

Millwood
Durst, Carol Goldsmith *educator*

Mineola
†Albicocco, Santa *lawyer, county official*
†Aloia, John F. *endocrinologist, academic administrator*
Bartlett, Clifford Adams, Jr., *lawyer*
Bartol, Ernest Thomas *lawyer*
Bogen, Mark Alan *accountant*
†Cohen, Stanley Dale *lawyer*
Cunha, Burke A. *physician*
Daniels, John Hill *lawyer*
Fowler, David Thomas *lawyer*
Gibson, William Shepard *insurance company executive*
Gomolin, Irving Harold *medical educator*
Hammer, Deborah Marie *librarian, paralegal*
Hines, George Lawrence *surgeon*
Klein, Arnold Spencer *lawyer*
Kunken, Kenneth James *lawyer*
Lelyveld, Gail Annick *actress*
Levin, A. Thomas *lawyer*
Lizardos, Evans John *mechanical engineer*
Lynn, Robert Patrick, Jr., *lawyer*
Marino, Ronald Vincent *pediatrician, educator*
McGonigle, James Gregory *financial consultant*
Meyer, Bernard Stern *lawyer, former judge*
Miller, Loring Erik *insurance agent, broker*
Millman, Bruce Russell *lawyer*
Monaghan, Peter Gerard *lawyer*
Newman, Malcolm *mechanical and civil engineering consultant*
Nogee, Jeffrey Laurence *lawyer*
Paterson, Basil Alexander *lawyer*
Pogrebin, Bertrand B. *lawyer*
Rubine, Robert Samuel *lawyer*
Sandback, William Arthur *lawyer*
†Santemma, Jon Noel *lawyer*
Saulle, Nunzio *physiatrist*
Schaffer, David Irving *lawyer*
†Shaheen Alesi, Barbara *lawyer*
Smolev, Terence Elliot *lawyer, educator*
†Spizz, Harvey Warren *lawyer*
Tankoos, Sandra Maxine *court reporting services executive*
†Tannenbaum, Bernard *lawyer*
†Weinstock, Benjamin *lawyer*
†Zeldis, Steven Martin *cardiologist*

Mitchell Field
Reddy, Gerard Anthony *corporate training executive*

Mohegan Lake
Charney, Lena London *property manager, poet*
Ettinger, Jayne Gold *physical education educator*
Harris-Jones, Yvonne *national trainer, human resources consultant*
Hastings, John Jacob *writer, lyricist, consultant, activist*
Paik, John Kee *structural engineer*
Stokes, Ron *lawyer*

Monroe
†Centeno-Dainty, Sonia Margarita *artist*
†Charka, Satya Narayana *language educator, dance director*
Gocek, Matilda Arkenbout (Mrs. John A. Gocek) *librarian*

Monsey
Erickson, Barbara Martha *historian, writer, florist*
Schaefer, Rhoda Pesner *elementary school educator*
Schore, Robert *social worker, educator, consultant*

Montauk
Butler, Thomas William *retired health and social services administrator*
Kahn, Richard Dreyfus *lawyer*
Lavenas, Suzanne *writer, editor, consultant*

Montgomery
Sharpe-Arrant, Kathleen Diane *accountant, small business owner*

Monticello
Lauterstein, Joseph *cardiologist*
Sorensen, Alan John *county official*
Vamvaketis, Carole *health services administrator*

Montrose
Matthias, George Frank *retired educator*
Reber, Raymond Andrew *retired chemical engineer*

Moravia
†Dienhoffer, Margaret Quigley *historian, educator*
Kennedy, Samuel Van Dyke, III, *journalist, educator*

Morrisville
Coppola, Joseph Angelo *computer professional, educator*
Weiler, Angela M. *librarian, writer*

Mount Kisco
Appelbaum, Judith Pilpel *editor, consultant, educator*
Curran, Maurice Francis *lawyer*
Geissinger-Robertson, Ruth Fabry *retired obstetrician, gynecologist*
Goodhue, Mary Brier *lawyer, former state senator*
Green, Paul Eliot, Jr., *optical communications consultant*
Harris, Isaac Ron *lawyer*
†Icahn, Carl C. *arbitrator, options specialist, corporation executive*

Keesee, Patricia Hartford *volunteer*
Kornhaber, Eugene *psychiatrist*
Laster, Richard *biotechnology executive, consultant*
Mann, Richard O. *public relations consulting company executive*
Matusow, Naomi C. *state legislator*
Michael, Creighton *artist, educator*
Mooney, Robert Michael *ophthalmologist*
Novak, Gregory *marketing professional*
Schneider, Robert Jay *oncologist*
Schwarz, Wolfgang *psychologist*
Stein, Mitchell Brian *physician*
Stillman, Michael Allen *dermatologist*
Wolfson, Robert Allen *physician*

Mount Marion
Berg, Miriam Rosemary *association executive*
Steiner, Raymond John *art critic, editor*

Mount Sinai
Feinberg, Sheldon Norman *pediatrician, educator*
†Gillin, Donna Lynn *lawyer*

Mount Vernon
Cammarosano, Joseph Raphael *economist, educator*
Chagula, Paul Machiya *technology company executive, trade consultant*
Coombes, David Harrison *health facility administrator*
†Davison, Irwin Stuart *lawyer*
Giammartino, Frank Arnold *chiropractor*
Kaufman, Alan *internist, allergist*
†Lemos, Arthur *retired music educator*
Martin, R Keith *business and information systems educator, consultant*
Moore, W. Darin *minister*
Rossini, Joseph *contracting and development corporate executive*
Zucker, Arnold Harris *psychiatrist*

Mountainville
Johns, Margaret Bush *neuroendocrinologist, painter, researcher, educator*
Pachner, Joan Helen *art historian, curator*

Munnsville
Carruth, Hayden *poet*

Nanuet
Miney, Maureen Elizabeth *middle school educator*
†Spielman, Lisa Anne *psychologist, researcher, statistician, consultant*

Napanoch
†Kooistra, Andrew J. *painter, sculptor*

Naples
Beal, Myron Clarence *osteopathic physician*
Gelder, Donald Clifford Barnard *artist*

Narrowsburg
†Jones, Thomas Peter *priest*
†Krause, Gloria Rose *music educator*

Nassau
Moldoff, William Morris *retired lawyer*

Neponsit
†Nicastri, Ann G. *science educator*
Re, Edward Domenic *law educator, retired federal judge*

Nesconset
Cerini, Kenneth Russell *accountant*

New
†Goines, Victor Louis *music educator*

New Baltimore
Buono, Kathleen Ann Cleary *nursing specialist*

New City
Abel, Steven L. *lawyer, mediator*
Esser, Aristide Henri *psychiatrist*
Fenster, Robert David *lawyer*
Frawley-O'Dea, Mary Gail *clinical psychologist, psychoanalyst, educator*
Giambalvo, Vincent *management consultant*
Goldstein, Stanley Irving *podiatric surgeon, pharmacist*
Harari, Zaraleya Kurzweil *psychologist, psychotherapist*
Marcus, Robert Bruce *lawyer*
Savitz, Martin Harold *neurosurgeon*
Spalding, Mary Branch *psychologist, psychotherapist*
Teplitzky, Philip Herman *information technology executive*
Wechman, Robert Joseph *economist, educator*

New Hampton
Jeyamitra, Devaraj *physician*
†Sinnard, Elaine Janice *painter, sculptor*

New Hartford
Benzo-Bonacci, Rosemary Anne *health facility administrator*
Chapin, Mary Q. *television personality, arbitrator, mediator, writer, performing artist*
Dardano, Anthony Nicholas *obstetrician and gynecologist*
Eidelhoch, Lester Philip *physician, educator, surgeon*
McKennan, John T. *lawyer*
Shieh, Wei T. *senior hardware design engineer*

New Hyde Park
Bonagura, Vincent R. *pediatrician, educator, researcher*
Citron, Marc Laurence *oncologist, researcher*
Cohen, Bradley *neurologist*
Cooper, Milton *real estate investment trust executive*
DeLuca, James Patrick *graphic arts and advertising educator, consultant*
†Eberhard, Barbara Anne *rheumatologist, researcher*
Francischine, Janice Marie *pediatrics nurse*
Gelber, Philip Michael *cardiologist*
Grassi, Louis C. *accountant*
Hainline, Brian *neurologist*
Hinerfeld, Norman Martin *manufacturing company executive*
†Huebscher, Herbert *electrical engineer, educator*
Hyman, Abraham *electrical engineer*
Isenberg, Henry David *microbiology educator*
Jensen, Richard Currie *lawyer*
Kamler, Kenneth Mark *microsurgeon*
Klein, Bernard *clinical chemist*
†Klein, George *manufacturing company executive, microcomputer system and engineering consultant*
†Lanzkowsky, Philip *physician*
Lehrer, Stanley *magazine publisher, editorial director, corporate executive, museum exhibitor*
Lih-Brody, Lisa *gastroenterologist*
Lipton, Jeffrey M. *physician*
†Madhok, Ashish Brij *pediatrician, cardiologist*
Mealie, Carl A. *physician, educator*
Moldwin, Robert *physician, urologist*
Offner, Eric Delmonte *lawyer*
†Palestro, Christopher J. *physician*
Prisco, Douglas Louis *physician*
†Rai, Kanti Roop *hematologist, oncologist, medical educator*
Richards, Bernard *investment company executive*
Romano, Angela *pediatric cardiologist*
Rose, Elihu Isaac *lawyer*
Seltzer, Vicki Lynn *obstetrician, gynecologist*
Shah, Manoj Rameshchandra *psychiatrist*
Speiser, Phyllis Witzel *endocrinologist, educator*

New Kingston
St. George, Joyce *conflict and crisis management educator, writer*

New Lebanon
Baker, James Barnes *architect*

New Paltz
Azank, Roberto *artist*
†Chikwendu, Sunday C. *engineering educator, mathematician, educator*
Edwards, Peter *educator, writer*
Emanuel-Smith, Robin Lesley *special education educator*
Fakler, Mary Edith *English educator*
Flanagan Kelly, Anne Marie *academic administrator*
González, Julio Jorge *electrical engineering educator*
†Goodell, Kathy Susan *artist, educator*
Harris, Kristine *historian, educator*
Hathaway, Richard Dean *retired language educator*
Hauptman, Laurence Marc *history educator*
Ho, Hon Hing *biology educator*
Irvine, Rose Loretta Abernethy *retired communications educator, consultant*
Izadi, Baback A. *engineering educator*
Lavallee, David Kenneth *chemistry educator, researcher*
Li, Keqin *computer scientist, educator*
†Neuman, Joel H. *psychologist, educator*
Nyquist, Thomas Eugene *consulting business executive*
Pine, Patricia Palmer *aging services administrator*
Robinson, Anthony Christopher *novelist, educator*
†Schempf, Ruthanne *music educator, musician*
Schnell, George Adam *geographer, educator*
†Shine, James C. *language educator, lawyer*
Smiley, Albert Keith *economist, resort executive*
Smith, Kathleen Tener *bank executive*
Young, Marjorie Ann *librarian*

New Rochelle
Aronow, Ina Gloria Brody *journalist*
Beardsley, Robert Eugene *microbiologist, educator*
Berlage, Gai Ingham *sociologist, educator*
Black, Page Morton *civic worker*
Blotner, Norman David *lawyer, real estate broker, corporate executive*
Branch, William Blackwell *playwright, producer*
Breindel, David Saul *psychiatrist*
Cleary, James C. *audio-visual producer*
Cohen, Saul Bernard *former college president, geographer*
Conte, Susan *secondary school counselor*
Donahue, Richard James *secondary school educator*
†Ferencz, Benjamin Berell *lawyer*
Fitch, Nancy Elizabeth *historian, educator*
Gable, Carol Brignoli *health economics researcher*
Gallagher, John Francis *education educator*
Giges, Burton *psychiatrist, educator, consultant*
Gitler, Bernard *cardiologist and critical care specialist*
Glassman, George Morton *dermatologist*
†Goldstein, Laurence Evan *journalist*
Golub, Sharon Bramson *psychologist, educator*
Grimes, Tresmaine Judith Rubain *psychology educator*
Gunning, Francis Patrick *lawyer, insurance association executive*
Harkavy, Oscar *writer, consultant*
Hayes, Arthur Hull, Jr., *physician, clinical pharmacology educator, medical school dean, business executive, consultant*
Herman, William Charles *lawyer*
Hoxter, Allegra Branson *radio news and freelance writer*
Kleinman, Andrew Young *plastic surgeon*
†Kraman, Cynthia *language educator*
Levin, Henry Stuart *ophthalmologist*
Lin, Joseph Pen-Tze *retired neuroradiologist*
Lobach, Katherine S. *pediatrician, educator*
Lurie, Alvin David *lawyer*
Margolin, Harold *metallurgical educator*
Menzies, Henry Hardinge *architect*
Miller, Rita *personnel consultant, diecasting company executive*
Morello, Robert Frank *ophthalmologist*
Perry-Böttinger, Lynne Valencia *interventional cardiologist*
†Reddington, Mary Jane *retired secondary school educator*
Rothstein, Ann Laurel *clinical social worker, consultant*
Rovinsky, Joseph Judah *obstetrician, gynecologist*
Saperstein, David *novelist, screenwriter, film director*
Sarro, Michael Thomas *not-for-profit fundraiser*
Schleifer, James Thomas *history educator*
†Schwartz, Peri *artist*
Schwarz, Ralph Jacques *retired engineering educator*
Shookster, Linda Anne *rheumatologist*
Slotnick, Mortimer H. *artist*
Stevens, Roger Ross *lawyer*
Sweeny, Stephen Jude *academic administrator*
†Tassone, Gelsomina (Gessie Tassone) *metal processing executive*
Wolf, Robert Irwin *psychoanalyst, art therapist, art therapy educator, sculptor, photographer*
Wolstein, Arthur *podiatrist*

New Windsor
Antony, Ajit Ivan *urologist*
Gilman, Benjamin Arthur *former congressman, lawyer*
Hammond, Judith Anne *family nurse practitioner*
Mandel, Joel Emanuel *orthopedist*
Quintans, Alfredo Sison, Jr., *thoracic and cardiovascular surgeon*

New York
Abdelnour, Ziad Khalil *international investment banker, financier, venture capitalist, lobbyist*
Abdulezer, Susan Beth *communications educator*
†Abelle, Patsy Caples *lawyer*
Abelson, Alan *columnist*
Abernathy, James Logan *public relations executive*
Abish, Cecile *artist*
Abish, Walter *writer*
Aborn, Richard Mark *organization executive, lawyer*
Abrahamsen, Abel *wholesale and retail import company executive*
Abrams, Robert *lawyer, former state attorney general*
Abramson, Edward J. *magazine publisher*
†Abramson, Jill *newspaper publishing executive*
Abramson, Sara Jane *radiologist, educator*
Abramson, Stephanie W. *advertising executive, lawyer*
Abulhasan, Mohammad Abdulla *ambassador*
Acampora, Ralph Joseph *brokerage firm executive*
Achenbaum, Alvin Allen *marketing and management consultant*
†Aching, Gerard *language educator*
Ackerman, Valerie B. *sports association executive*
Acrivos, Andreas *chemical engineering educator*
†Adair, Wendell Hinton, Jr., *lawyer*
†Adams, Daniel Nelson *lawyer*
Adams, Dennis Paul *artist*
Adams, Edward Thomas (Eddie Adams) *photographer*
Adams, George Bell *lawyer*
Adams, Jeffrey Alan *web producer, writer*
Adams, John Brett *investment banker, company executive*
†Adams, John Coolidge *composer, conductor*
†Adams, Robert Brereton *lawyer*
†Adams, Scott *cartoonist*
Addison, Herbert John *consulting editor*
Adler, Edward I. *media and entertainment company executive*
Adler, Karl Paul *medical educator, academic administrator*
Adler, Margot Susanna *journalist, radio producer*
Adler, Richard *composer, lyricist*
Adri, (Adri Steckling Coen) *fashion designer*
†Adubato, Richard Adam (Richie Adubato) *professional basketball coach*
Affleck, Ben *actor*
Agard, Emma Estornel *psychotherapist*
Aghassi, William J. *mechanical engineer, consultant*
Agisim, Philip *advertising and marketing company executive*
†Aguilar Zinser, Adolfo Miguel *diplomat*
Aguilera, Christina *vocalist*
†Agwu, Nkechi Madonna *mathematics educator*
Ahmad, Jameel *civil engineer, researcher, educator*
†Ahrens, Lynn *lyricist*
Ahrens, Thomas H. *production company executive*
Aidinoff, M(erton) Bernard *retired lawyer*
†Aiello, Stephen *public relations executive*
Aigrain, Jacques A. *banker*
†Ailes, Roger Eugene *television producer, consultant*
†Aitken, Doug *artist*
Ajhar, Marsha G. *lawyer*
†Akfirat, Gokhan Lut *neurologist*
Aksen, Gerald *arbitrator, lawyer, educator*
Alafouzo, Antonia *marketing and business strategy professional*
Albano, David Warren *financial executive, strategic business analyst*
Albee, Edward Franklin *author, playwright*
Albee, Gloria *playwright*
Albert, Garett J. *lawyer*
Albertson, Christiern Gunnar (Chris Albertson) *broadcaster, music critic, writer*
†Albrecht, Chris *broadcast executive*
†Alcott, Mark Howard *lawyer*
Alden, Steven Michael *lawyer*
Alderson, Marjorie Jean *healthcare administrator, nurse*
Alderson, Philip Otis *radiologist, educator*
Alenikoff, Frances *choreographer, performer, writer, dancer, artist*
Alessandroni, Venan Joseph *lawyer*
Alexander, Jane *actress, former federal agency administrator, producer, author, theater educator*
Alexander, Roy *public relations executive, editor, author*
Alfano, Michael Charles *dental school dean*
†Alfonso, Vincent C *psychology educator*
Allen, Alice *communications and marketing executive*
Allen, Betty (Mrs. Ritten Edward Lee III) *mezzo-soprano*
Allen, Claxton Edmonds, III, *investment banker*
†Allen, Jeffrey C. *pediatric neurologist*
Allen, Leon Arthur, Jr., *lawyer*
†Allen, Oliver E. *writer*
†Allen, Peter Lewis *editor, educator*
Allentuck, Marcia Epstein *English language and art history educator*
†Allison, Herbert Monroe, Jr., *investment firm executive*
Allison, Michael David *space scientist, astronomy educator*
Allmendinger, Paul Florin *retired engineering association executive*
Allner, Walter Heinz *designer, painter, art director*
Almeyda, Elizabeth Ann *plastic surgeon*
†Alonso, Daniel R. *medical educator*
Alpert, Mark Zachary *performing arts executive*
Alpert, Warren *oil company executive, philanthropist*
Alpert, William Harold (Bill Alpert) *artist, painter*
Alschuler, Steven *public relations executive, communications consultant, writer, political consultant*
†Alt, Carol A. *actress, model, entrepreneur*
Alter, Eleanor Breitel *lawyer*
Alter, Jonathan Hammerman *journalist*
Altfest, Karen Caplan *diversified financial services company executive, director*
Altfest, Lewis Jay *financial and investment advisor*
Althausen, Jack Henry *computer company executive*
Altieri, Peter Louis *lawyer*
Altman, Lawrence Kimball *physician, journalist*
Altman, Robert B. *film director, writer, producer*
Altman, Roy Peter *pediatric surgeon*
†Alvarado-Juárez, Francisco *visual artist*
†Alzamora, Carlos *ambassador*
Amdur, Martin Bennett *lawyer*
Amelan, Bjorn G. *choreographer*
Ames, Richard Pollard *physician, educator, lecturer*
†Ames, Roger *recording industry executive*
Amhowitz, Harris J. *lawyer, educator*
Amitin, Mark Hall *cultural organization administrator, educator, writer, actor, director*
Amols, Howard Ira *medical physicist*
Amster, Linda Evelyn *newspaper executive, consultant*
Amsterdam, Anthony Guy *law educator*
Amsterdam, Mark Lemle *lawyer*
Anagnost, Dino *artistic director*
†Ananiashvili, Nina *ballerina*
Anastasi, William Joseph *artist*
Anchlia, Than Mal *wholesale distribution executive*
Anderegg, Julius Fidelis *diplomat, consul general*
Andersen, K(ent) Tucker *investment executive*
Andersen, Marianne Singer *clinical psychologist*
Andersen, Richard Esten *lawyer*
Andersen, Susan Marie *educator, researcher, clinician, policy advisor*
Anderson, Arthur Allan *management consultant*
Anderson, David Poole *sportswriter*
†Anderson, Dennis *computer scientist information technology educator*
Anderson, Fred Richard *minister, writer*
Anderson, Jack Warren *dance critic, poet*
Anderson, Maxwell L. *museum director*
Anderson, O(rvil) Roger *biology educator, marine biology and protozoology researcher*
Anderson, Richard Theodore *association executive, urban planner*
Anderson, Robert Woodruff *playwright, novelist, screenwriter*
†Anderson, Ross S. *architectural firm executive*
Anderson, Theodore Wellington *portfolio strategist*
Anderson, Walter Herman *magazine publisher*
Andolsen, Alan Anthony *management consultant*
†Andrade, Andres *vocalist, educator*
Andre, Carl *sculptor*
Andre, Michael (Kenneth Andre) *editor, publisher, writer*
Andreassi, John Lawrence *psychologist, educator*
†Andreasson, Kim J. *writer, consultant*
Andreopoulos, George John *history educator, lawyer, political science educator*
Andresen, Malcolm *lawyer*
Andrews, Gordon Clark *lawyer*
Andrus, Roger Douglas *lawyer*
Angelo, Larian *economist*
†Angrist, Burton Morris *retired physician, educator*
Annan, Kofi A. *international organization official*
Annenberg, Norman *lawyer*
Anspach, Ernst *economist, lawyer*
Antell, Darrick Eugene *plastic surgeon, educator*
Anthoine, Robert *lawyer, educator*
Anthony, William Graham *artist*
Antonakos, Stephen *sculptor*
Antonuccio, Joseph Albert *management consultant*

Blinken, Robert James *manufacturing and communications company executive*
Blitzer, Andrew *otolaryngologist, educator*
Blitzer, Judi Rappoport *retired bank executive, consultant*
Blobel, Günter *cell biologist, educator*
†Bloch, Peter *editor*
Block, Francesca Lia *writer*
Block, Ned *philosopher, educator*
Block, William Kenneth *lawyer*
Bloodworth, Sandra Gail *artist, arts administrator*
Bloomberg, Michael Rubens *mayor*
Bloomgarden, Karenne Jo *elementary special education educator, company president*
Bloomgarden, Kathy Finn *public relations executive*
Bluestone, Andrew Lavoott *lawyer*
Bluh, Bonnie *writer, playwright, performer*
Blum, Gerald Myron *psychiatrist*
Blumberg, Gerald *lawyer*
Blume, Judy *author*
Blume, Lawrence Dayton *lawyer*
Blumkin, Linda Ruth *lawyer*
Blyth, Jeffrey *journalist*
Boardman, Seymour *artist*
†Bobrow, Richard S. *diversified financial services company executive*
Bock, Walter Joseph *zoology educator*
Bockstein, Herbert *lawyer*
Boddie, Reginald Alonzo *lawyer*
Bodley, Harley Ryan, Jr., *editor, writer, broadcaster*
Bodovitz, James Philip *lawyer*
Boehner, Leonard Bruce *lawyer*
Bogart, Leo *sociologist*
Bogdonoff, Morton David *physician, educator*
†Boggio, Miriam Altagracia *lawyer*
Boice, Craig Kendall *management consultant*
Boisson, Jacques Louis *diplomat, ambassador*
Boley, Bruno Adrian *engineering educator*
Bollinger, Lee Carroll *academic administrator, law educator*
Bolotowsky, Andrew Ilyitch *flutist, composer*
Bonazzi, Elaine Claire *mezzo-soprano*
Bonfante, Larissa *classics educator*
Bonnett, Thomas W. *political scientist, writer*
Boodey, Cecil Webster, Jr., *political science educator*
Boorstein, Laurence *economist, educator*
Booth, Barbara Ribman *civic worker*
Booth, Edgar Hirsch *lawyer*
Booth, Mitchell B. *lawyer*
Boothby, Willard Sands, III, *bank executive*
†Borchard, William Marshall *lawyer*
Borders, William Alexander *journalist*
Bordiga, Lord Benno *art dealer*
Borelli, Francis J(oseph) (Frank Borelli) *insurance brokerage and consulting firm financial executive*
†Borenstein, Eugene Reed *lawyer*
Borer, Jeffrey Stephen *cardiologist*
Borgatta, Isabel Case *sculptor*
†Borhi, Carol *data processing executive, finance company executive*
Borisoff, Richard Stuart *lawyer*
†Bornstein, Steven M. *broadcast executive*
Boros, Jerome S. *lawyer*
Borowitz, Sidney *retired physics educator*
Borree, Yvonne *dancer*
Borrelli, John Francis *architect*
Borsody, Robert Peter *lawyer*
†Borstein, Leon Baer *lawyer*
Boskey, Adele Ludin *biochemistry educator, researcher*
Bosses, Stevan J. *lawyer*
†Bostock, Roy Jackson *advertising agency executive*
†Boston, Gretha *vocalist, actress*
Bothmer, Dietrich Felix von *museum curator, archaeologist*
Botkin, Daniel Benjamin *biologist, environmental scientist, writer*
Boudreau, A. Allan *historian, writer, educator*
†Boufford, Jo Ivey *health and human services administrator*
Boulet-Gercourt, Philippe *journalist*
Bouloukos, Theodore, II, *writer, editor, actor*
†Bourgeois, Louise *sculptor*
†Bousquet-Chavanne, Patrick *cosmetics executive*
Boutis, Tom *artist, painter, print maker*
Bove, John Louis *chemistry and environmental engineering educator, researcher*
Bowden, Sally Ann *choreographer, teacher, dancer*
Bowden, William P., Jr., *lawyer, banker*
Bowen, William Gordon *economist, educator, foundation administrator*
Bowers, Patricia Eleanor Fritz *economist*
Bowles, Erskine *White House staff member*
Bowles, Newton Rowell *United Nations executive*
†Bowman, Carl Byron *music educator, composer*
†Boxer, Jason T. *title company executive*
Boxer, Leonard *lawyer*
Boxill, Edith Hillman *music therapist, educator, writer*
†Boyd, Frances Armstrong *language educator, writer*
Boyd, Michael Alan *investment company executive, lawyer*
Boynton, James Stephen *lawyer*
†Boziwick, George E. *music librarian, composer, curator*
†Bradbury, Ray Douglas
Braden, Martha Brooke *concert pianist, educator*
Bradford, Barbara Taylor *writer, journalist, novelist*
Bradford, Robert Ernest *motion picture producer, financier*
Bradley, Courtney Jene *researcher*
Bradley, E. Michael *lawyer*
Bradley, Edward R. *news correspondent*
Bradley, Lisa M. *artist*
Bradsell, Kenneth Raymond *minister*
Bradshaw, Dove *artist*
Bradsher, Neal Clifton *investment company executive*
†Bradstock, John *advertising executive*
Brady, Adelaide Burks *public relations agency executive, giftware catalog executive*
†Brady, Mark A. *cinematographer, photographer*
Braham, Randolph Lewis *political science educator*
Braid, Frederick Donald *lawyer*
Brams, Steven John *political scientist, educator, game theorist*
†Branch, Taylor *writer*
Brand, Irving *lawyer*
Brandeis, Barry *corporate executive*
†Braslow, Dean Gerald *lawyer*
Braudy, Susan Orr *writer*
Braun, Jeffrey Louis *lawyer*
Brauner, David A. *lawyer*
Brause, Barry David *infectious diseases physician*
Braverman, Robert Jay *international consultant, public policy educator*
Brax, Ghazi Fouad *editor, writer*
Braxton, Toni *popular musician*
Brazinsky, Irv(ing) *chemical engineering educator*
Brecker, Jeffrey Ross *lawyer, educator*
Brecker, Michael *saxophonist*
Breger, William N. *architect, educator*
Breglio, John F. *lawyer*
Breinin, Bartley James *lawyer*
Breinin, Goodwin M. *physician*
Brendel, Alfred *concert pianist*
Brennan, Henry Higginson *architect*
Brenner, Beth Fuchs *publishing executive*
†Brenner, Douglas *editor*
Brenner, Michael Edward *executive search and coaching consultant*
Bresani, Federico Fernando *business executive*
Breslow, Esther May Greenberg *biochemistry educator, researcher*
Breslow, Ronald Charles *chemist*
Bressler, Bernard *lawyer*
Bressler, Richard J. *communications company executive*
†Brestle, Dan *cosmetics executive*
Brett, Nancy Heléne *artist*
Bretton-Granatoor, Gary Martin *rabbi*
Brewer, Karen *librarian*
Brewer, William Dane *lawyer*
Brewster, Robert Gene *concert singer, educator*
†Brilliant, Andrew Prince *lawyer*
Brilliant, Richard *art history educator*
Brindle, Lewis Carver *administrator,fundraiser, consultant*
Bring, Murray H. *retired lawyer*
Brinkley, Alan David *historian*
†Brinson, Monica E. *pharmaceutical sales representative*
Briskman, Robert David *engineering executive*
Brisman, Ronald *clinical neurosurgeon*
Bristol, Barbara Kammer *foundation administrator*
Bristow, Cynthia Lynn *immunologist*
Brittenham, Raymond Lee *investment company executive*
†Britz, Robert G. *stock exchange executive*
Britz Lotti, Diane Edward *investment company executive*
Broadwater, Douglas Dwight *lawyer*
†Brock, Charles Lawrence *lawyer, business executive*
†Brock-Broido, Lucie *poet, educator*
Broder, Douglas Fisher *lawyer*
Brodsky, Beverly *artist*
Brodsky, David Michael *lawyer*
Brodsky, Samuel *lawyer*
Brody, Alan Jeffrey *investment company executive*
Brody, Eugene David *investment company executive*
Brody, Jacqueline *editor*
Brody, Jane Ellen *journalist, researcher*
†Brohn, William David *conductor, orchestrator*
Brokaw, Thomas John *television broadcast executive, correspondent*
Bromberger, Allen Richard *legal association administrator*
Brome, Thomas Reed *lawyer*
Bronfman, Edgar Miles *beverage company executive*
Bronstein, Richard J. *lawyer*
Brook, Judith Suzanne *psychiatry and psychology researcher and educator*
Brooks, Anita Helen *public relations executive*
Brooks, Gary *management consultant*
Brooks, Jerome Bernard *English and Afro-American literature educator*
Brooks, Lorimer Page *patent lawyer*
Brooks, Peter Stuyvesant *real estate consultant*
Brooks, Timothy H. *media executive*
Brooks-Gunn, Jeanne *psychologist*
†Brossman, Mark Edward *lawyer*
Brothers, Joyce Diane *television personality, psychologist*
Broude, Richard Frederick *lawyer, educator*
Browar, Lisa Muriel *librarian*
Browdy, Joseph Eugene *lawyer*
Brown, Alice Dalton *artist*
Brown, Andreas Le *book store and art gallery executive*
Brown, Arnold *management consultant*
Brown, Arthur Edward *physician*
†Brown, Campbell *commentator*
Brown, Charles D. *lawyer*
Brown, Charlotte *artist*
Brown, Clifford Bryant *financial consultant*
†Brown, Craig *advertising agency executive*
Brown, Darrell James *publishing executive*
Brown, David *motion picture producer, writer*
Brown, David Warfield *management educator*
Brown, Edward James, Sr., *utility executive*
Brown, G(lenn) William, Jr., *bank executive*
Brown, Helen Gurley *editor, writer*
†Brown, James Sylvester, Jr., *lawyer*
Brown, Jason Walter *neurologist, educator, researcher*
Brown, Jonathan *art historian, fine arts educator*
†Brown, Joyce F. *academic administrator*
Brown, Mark Malloch *international organization official*
Brown, Meredith M. *lawyer*
Brown, Paul M. *lawyer*
Brown, Peter Megargee *lawyer, writer, lecturer*
Brown, Ralph Sawyer, Jr., *retired lawyer, business executive*
Brown, Robert Stephen, Jr., *physician*
Brown, Ronald *retired stockbroker*
Brown, Terrence Charles *art association executive, researcher, lecturer*
Brown, Tina *magazine editor*
Brown, Trisha *dancer*
Brown, Valerie Sharice *venture capitalist*
†Browne, Arthur *newspaper editor*
Browne, Jeffrey Francis *lawyer*
Browne, Malcolm Wilde *journalist*
Brownell, Patricia Jane *social worker, educator*
Brownwood, David Owen *lawyer*
Bruce, Duncan Archibald *investor, writer*
Bruce, Jeffrey Neil *neurosurgeon*
Bruder, Harold Jacob *artist, educator*
Brumer, Miriam *artist, educator*
Brumm, James Earl *lawyer, trading company executive*
Brun, Henry *publishing executive*
Brundige, Robert William, Jr., *lawyer*
Brunie, Charles Henry *investment manager*
†Brunkhurst, William Lee, Jr., *music educator*
Brush, Craig Balcombe *retired French language and computer educator*
†Brust, John Calvin Morrison *neurology educator*
Brustein, Lawrence *financial executive*
Bruzs, Boris Olgerd *retired management consultant*
Bryan, Barry Richard *lawyer*
Brzustowicz, Stanislaw Henry *clinical dentistry educator*
Buatta, Mario *interior designer*
†Buchholz, Ester Schaler Schaler *psychologist*
Buchman, M. Abraham *lawyer*
Buchwald, Don David *lawyer*
Buchwald, Naomi Reice *judge*
Buck, Louise Zierdt *psychologist*
Buckles, Robert Howard *retired investment company executive*
Buckley, Priscilla Langford *magazine editor*
Buckley, Robert John *academic research administrator*
†Buckley, Susan *lawyer*
Buckley, Virginia Laura *editor*
Buckley, William Frank, Jr., *magazine editor, writer*
Buckman, James Edward *lawyer*
Buckman, Thomas Richard *foundation executive, educator*
Bucolo, Gail Ann *biotechnologist*
Budd, Thomas Witbeck *lawyer*
†Budde, Neil Frederick *publishing company executive, editor, publisher*
Budig, Gene Arthur *former chancellor, professional sports executive*
Budnick, Ernest Joseph *music industry executive*
Buehler, Thomas *psychotherapist, expressive therapist, artist*
Bujold, Lois McMaster *writer*
Bull, David *fine art conservator*
Bull, Helen May *artist, writer*
Bulliet, Richard Williams *history educator, novelist*
Bulow, George Mitchell *entrepreneur*
†Bungey, Michael *advertising executive*
Bunts, Frank Emory *artist*
Burak, H(oward) Paul *lawyer*
Burbank, Jane Richardson *language educator*
Bure, Pavel *hockey player*
Burger, Chester *retired management consultant*
Burgheim, Richard *magazine editor*
†Burgman, Dierdre Ann *lawyer*
Burgweger, Francis Joseph Dewes, Jr., *lawyer*
Burke, Alexander James, Jr., *publishing company executive*
Burke, David *corporate chef, executive chef*
Burke, James Joseph, Jr., *investment banker*
Burke, Michael Desmond *pathologist, educator*
Burkhardt, Ronald Robert *advertising executive*
Burns, John Joseph, Jr., *financial and insurance holding company executive*
†Burns, Red *academic administrator*
Burns, Ward *textile company executive*
Burnshaw, Stanley *writer*
†Burrows, Kenneth David *lawyer*
Burrows, Michael Donald *lawyer*
Burrows, William E. *journalist, educator, writer*
Bursky, Herman Aaron *lawyer*
Burson, Harold *public relations executive, director*
†Burstein, Neil Alan *lawyer*
Burton, John Campbell *university dean, educator, consultant*
Burton, Peggy *advertising and marketing executive*
†Bushnell, George Edward, III, *lawyer*
Butler, Jonathan Putnam *architect*
Butler, Robert Neil *gerontologist, psychiatrist, writer, educator*
Butler, Samuel Coles *lawyer, director*
Butler, Vincent Paul, Jr., *physician, educator*
Butler, William Joseph *lawyer, educator*
†Butt, Sameer *filmmaker, writer*
Buttenwieser, Lawrence Benjamin *lawyer*
Butterklee, Neil Howard *lawyer*
Butterman, Jay Ronald *lawyer*
Buttner, Jean Bernhard *diversified financial services company executive*
Button, Richard Totten *television and stage producer, former figure skating champion*
Buttrick, Harold *architect*
Butts, Hugh Florenz *physician, psychiatrist, psychoanalyst*
Buxton, Douglas Francisco *ophthalmologist, educator*
†Bye, Michael Robert *pulmonologist, educator*
Byer, Diana *performing arts company executive*
Bylinsky, Gene Michael *magazine editor*
Byrd, Eva Wilson *communications executive*
†Byrnes, Richard James *lawyer*
Byron, Eric Howard *sculptor, museum researcher and administrator*
Bystryn, Jean-Claude *dermatologist, educator*
Cabalquinto, Luis Carrazcal *freelance writer*
†Cable, Paul Andrew *lawyer*
Caceres, Aileen *physician*
†Caesar, Godfrey Wrensford *biologist, educator*
Cage, Jack Hays *executive search consultant*
Caginalp, Aydin S. *lawyer*
Cahill, Kevin Michael *physician, educator*
Cahn, Steven Mark *philosopher, educator*
Cajori, Charles Florian *artist, educator*
Calabrese, Rosalie Sue *arts management consultant, writer*
Calame, Byron Edward *journalist*
Calder, Clive *music company executive*
Caldwell, Zoe *actress, director*
Calhoun, Craig Jackson *social scientist, educator*
Calisher, Hortense (Mrs. Curtis Harnack) *writer*
Call, Neil Judson *corporate executive*
Callo, Joseph Francis *writer*
Cameron, Nina Rao *lawyer, government official*
Camilleri, Louis C. *consumer goods company executive*
†Cammarata, Angelo *surgical oncologist*
†Cammisa, Rebecca *filmmaker, photographer*
Campagnolo, Ann-Casey *retail executive*
Campbell, David James *hospital administrator*
Campbell, George, Jr., *physicist, administrator*
Campbell, Magda *child psychiatrist, researcher, educator*
Campbell, Robert David *minerals and metals executive*
Campbell, Ronald Neil *retired magazine designer*
Cancro, Robert *psychiatrist, educator*
Canes, Brian Dennis *retirement benefits systems specialist*
Cannell, John Redferne *lawyer*
Cannistraro, Nicholas, Jr., *newspaper executive*
Canoni, John David *lawyer*
†Cantor, Louis *lawyer*
†Cantor, Melvyn Leon *retired lawyer*
Cantor, Richard Ira *physician, corporate health executive*
Cantrell, Lana *actress, singer, lawyer*
Capalbo, Carmen *theater director and producer*
Caplan, Ronald Mervyn *gynecologist, obstetrician*
Caples, Richard James *dance company executive, lawyer*
Capolarello, Joe R. *photojournalist*
†Capozzi, Lou *public relations executive*
Cappiello, Angela *meeting and marketing manager*
Capriati, Jennifer Maria *professional tennis player*
Caputo, David Armand *university president, political scientist educator*
Caputo, Lucio *trade company executive*
Caputo, Philip Joseph *author, journalist*
Caputo, Thomas Anthony *obstetrician, gynecologist*
Caraley, Demetrios James *political scientist, educator, writer*
†Card, Orson Scott (Byron Walley) *writer*
†Carden, Constance *law educator, lawyer*
Cardile, Paul Julius *fine arts dealer*
Cardozo, Benjamin Mordecai *lawyer*
Caress, Robert Seymour *personnel consultant*
Carey, Alida Livingston *political scientist, writer, reporter*
Carey, Francis James *investment banker*
†Carey, Thomas Hilton *advertising agency executive*
Carey, William Polk *investment banker*
Carhuapoma, Juan Ricardo *critical care neurologist, researcher*
Carling, Francis *lawyer, mediator*
†Carlisle, Kitty *actress*
†Carlson, Donna *art association administrator, director*
Carlson, Marvin Albert *theater educator*
Carlson, Mitchell Lans *international technical advisor*
Carlson, P(atricia) M(cElroy) *writer*
Carlson, Theodore Joshua *lawyer, retired utility company executive*
Carman, Gregory Wright *federal judge*
Carmi, Giora *illustrator*
Carneiro, Robert Leonard *museum curator, anthropologist*
Carney, Michael *orchestra leader*
Caro, Robert Allan *author*
Caroff, Phyllis M. *social work educator*
Carpenter, James Michael *curator*
†Carpenter, Mary Chapin *singer, songwriter*
Carpenter, Michael *financial services executive*
Carr, Claudia *art gallery director, owner, artist*
Carr, Gladys Justin *publishing company executive, consultant, editor, writer*
Carr, Ronald Edward *ophthalmologist, educator*
Carroll, David Paul *social welfare administrator*
Carroll, Linda Marie *vocologist*
Carter, Carolyn Houchin *advertising agency executive*
†Carter, E. Graydon *editor-in-chief*
Carter, Edward Graydon *editor*
Carter, Elliott Cook, Jr., *composer*
Carter, James Hal, Jr., *lawyer*
Carter, John Mack *publishing company executive*
Carter, Zachary W. *lawyer*
Carthay, R. Jon *hand model, actor*
Caruana, Joan *educator, psychotherapist, nurse*
†Carucci, John A. *physician*
Carver, John H. *medical science organization administrator*
†Carvette, Anthony M. *construction executive*
Casals-Ariet, Jordi *physician*
Case, Hadley *oil company executive*
Case, Stephen M. *media and entertainment company executive*
Casella, Margaret Mary *artist, photographer*
Casey, Karen Anne *banker*

Dales, Samuel microbiologist, virologist, educator
Dallas, William Moffit, Jr., lawyer
Dallen, Russell Morris, Jr., investment company executive, lawyer, publishing company executive
Dalton, Dennis Gilmore political science educator
Daly, Cheryl broadcast executive
Daly, George Garman college dean, educator
Daly, John Neal investment company executive
Damashek, Philip Michael lawyer
†D'Amato, Alfonse M. lawyer, former senator
d'Amboise, Jacques Joseph former dancer, choreographer, educator, director
†Damianakos, Phaedra Vasiliki secondary school educator
Dana, F(rank) Mitchell theatrical lighting designer
Danaher, Frank Erwin transportation technologist
Dandashi, S. Alexander operations research scientist, consultant, corporate & government advisor
Dane, Maxwell former advertising executive
D'Angelo, Ernest Eustachio brokerage house executive
D'Angelo, Joseph Francis publishing company executive
†Dangue Rewaka, Denis diplomat
Daniel, Charles Timothy transportation engineer, consultant
Daniel, David Ronald management consultant
†Daniel, Samuel J. hospital administrator, medical educator
Daniel, Samuel Michael social worker, psychotherapist
†Daniels, J. Yolande architectural firm executive, educator
†Danilek, Donald J. lawyer
Danitz, Marilynn Patricia choreographer, videographer
†Dankin, Peter Alfred lawyer
Dankner, Jay Warren lawyer
Dannhauser, Stephen J. lawyer
Danto, Arthur Coleman author, philosopher, art critic
Dantzker, David Roy venture capitalist
Daphnis, Nassos artist
Daraio, Robert Reid technical director
Darlington, Henry, Jr., investment broker
Darrell, Norris, Jr., lawyer
Darrow, Jill E(llen) lawyer
Darst, David Martin investment company executive, educator, writer
Das, Kalyan lawyer
Das, T. K. management educator, consultant
†Datema, Jessica Venning humanities educator
Dattner, Richard architect, educator
Dauer, Sheila A. human rights program director
Daum, Julie Hembrock executive recruiter
David, Hal lyricist
David, Reuben lawyer
David, Theoharis Lambros architect, educator
†Davidoff, Richard Sayles lawyer
Davidovsky, Mario composer
†Davidson, Anthony R. education educator, consultant
Davidson, Donald William advertising executive
Davidson, George Allan lawyer
Davidson, Marilyn artist
Davidson, Nancy Brachman artist, educator
Davidson, Robert Bruce lawyer
Davidson, Sheila Kearney lawyer
David-Weill, Michel Alexandre investment banker
Davin, James Manson investment banker
Davis, Clive Jay record company executive
Davis, Doris Rosenbaum (Dee Davis) artist, writer
Davis, Evan Anderson lawyer
Davis, George Linn banker
Davis, Jessica G. clinical geneticist, pediatrician
Davis, Karen fund executive
Davis, Kathryn Wasserman foundation executive, writer, lecturer
Davis, Kenneth Leon psychiatrist, pharmacologist, medical educator
Davis, Leonard physiatrist
Davis, Leonard violist
†Davis, Lewis architectural firm executive
Davis, Lisa Corinne artist
Davis, Michael Steven lawyer
Davis, Owen Kidder physician, reproductive endocrinologist
Davis, Richard Joel lawyer, former government official
†Davis, Richard Ralph lawyer
†Davis, Steven M. architectural firm executive
Davis, Thomas W. investment bank executive
Davison, Daniel P. retired banking executive
Dawson, Philip history educator
Day, James television executive
Dayson, Diane Harris superintendent, park ranger
Deak, Istvan historian, educator
Dean, Robert Stuart lawyer
De Angelis, Judy anchorwoman
Dearinger, David B. art historian, curator
†DeBaets, Timothy Joseph lawyer, legal educator
De Bellis, Robert Henry physician, medical educator
Debo, Vincent Joseph lawyer, manufacturing company executive
DeBow, Jay Howard Camden public relations executive
DeBow, Thomas Joseph, Jr., advertising executive
Debs, Richard A. investment banker
de Champlain, Vera Chopak artist, painter
de Duve, Christian René chemist, educator
Deem, George artist
Defendi, Vittorio medical research administrator, pathologist
De Ferrari, Gabriella curator, writer
†Deffina, Thomas Victor lawyer
†DeFord, Ruth I. music educator
deGroat, Diane illustrator, author children's books
DeGroff, Ralph Lynn, Jr., investment banker
Dehn, Francis Xavier lawyer, journalist
Dehn, James Keith financial advisor
†Dejammet, Alain diplomat
de Kenessey, Stefania Maria composer
Delaney, Pamela DeLeo foundation administrator
Delaney, Robert Vincent former gas company executive, economic development consultant
Delano, Lester Almy, Jr.,
de la Renta, Oscar fashion designer
Delbourgo, Joëlle Lily publishing executive
del Cerro, Gerardo sociologist, researcher
†Dell, Michael John lawyer
De Luca, Eva vocalist, writer, composer, entrepreneur, designer, inventor
Demar, Leon Kenneth dermatologist
de Margitay, Gedeon acquisitions and management consultant
DeMatteo, Ronald Paul surgeon
deMause, Lloyd psychohistorian
de Menil, Lois Pattison historian, philanthropist
†Demeny, Paul George demographer, researcher
†Demetrios, archbishop
Demler, Frederick Russel minerals economist, commodities broker
DeMonte, Claudia Ann artist, educator
de Montebello, Philippe Lannes museum administrator
De Natale, Andrew Peter lawyer
†Dendy, Mark choreographer
Denes, Agnes C. environmental artist
Denes, Ronni Carol academic administrator
DeNiro, Mary Lyn S. lawyer
Denker, Henry playwright, author, director
Denmark, Bernhardt manufacturing executive
Denn, Morton Mace chemical engineering educator
Dennis, Diane Joy Milam retired architect
Dennis, Donna Frances sculptor, art educator
Dennis, Everette Eugene, Jr., foundation executive, educator, writer
Denoon, David Baugh Holden economist, educator, consultant
Denson, G. Roger critic, writer, scriptwriter
Denton, Michael John research economist, energy risk expert, financial engineer, finance company executive
DeNunzio, Ralph Dwight investment banker
DeOrchis, Vincent Moore lawyer
Derman, Cyrus mathematical statistician
†Dermksian, George cardiologist
Derow, Peter Alfred publishing company executive
Dershaw, D. David radiologist
†Dershowitz, Nathan Zev lawyer
Derzaw, Richard Lawrence lawyer
†Desai, Nitin Dayalji international organization official
†de Saint Phalle, Pierre Claude lawyer
De Sear, Edward Marshall lawyer
†Desloge, Rosemary Byrne otolaryngologist, educator
Desnick, Robert John human geneticist
Despommier, Dickson Donald microbiology educator, parasitologist, researcher
des Rioux, Deena Victoria Coty computer artist, digital graphics artist
†Dessen, Stanley Benjamin lawyer, cosmetics company executive
Detjen, David Wheeler lawyer
†Deutsch, Donny advertising executive
Deutsch, Martin Bernard Joseph editor, publisher
De Vido, Alfredo Eduardo architect
De Vivo, Darryl Claude pediatric neurologist
†De Vivo, Edward Charles lawyer, consultant
Devlin, Mark A. pharmaceutical company executive
Devlin, Robert Manning insurance company executive
†DeVoe, David publishing executive
Dewhurst, David Litchfield university administrator
†DeWind, Josh social science researcher
DeWitt, Eula accountant
Dhondt, Steven Thomas development officer
Dhore, Prasanna G. mutual fund executive
†Diamant, Aviva F. lawyer
†Diamond, Ann Cynthia lawyer
†Diamond, Bernard Robin lawyer
Diamond, Harris corporate communications executive, lawyer
Diamondstone, Lawrence retired paper company executive
Diamonstein-Spielvogel, Barbaralee writer, television interviewer/ producer
DiBlasi, Gandolfo Vincent lawyer
Dichter, Barry Joel lawyer
†Dickey, Eleanor humanities educator
†Dickson, James Edward actor
†Di Corcia, Philip-Lorca artist, photographer
Didik, Frank X writer
Didion, Joan writer
Dienstag, Eleanor Foa corporate communications consultant
†Dierdorf, Daniel Lee (Dan Dierdorf) sports commentator, football analyst, former professional football player
†Dies, George A. lawyer
Dieterich, Douglas Thomas gastroenterologist, researcher
Diflo, Thomas transplant surgeon
Diggins, Peter Sheehan arts administrator
†DiLandro, Anthony Charles science educator, funeral director
Dillard, Annie writer
†Diller, Barry interactive commerce company executive
DiMaggio, Frank Louis civil engineering educator
†DiMarco, Brian J. food and beverage consultant
Di Meo, Dominick artist, sculptor, painter
†DiMichele, Donna medical educator, researcher
Dimino, Sylvia Theresa elementary and secondary educator
Dimling, John Arthur marketing executive
Dimond, Thomas investment advisory company executive
Dinerman, Miriam social work educator
†Dion, Celine musician
†DiPiazza, Samuel, Jr., marketing professional
†Disa, Joseph James plastic surgeon
Di Salvo, Nicholas Armand dental educator, orthodontist
Diskant, Gregory L. lawyer
†Disney, Anthea publishing executive
†DiSpirito, Rocco restaurant owner, chef
Dissette, Alyce Marie television multimedia and theatrical producer, non-profit foundation executive
Ditkoff, Edward Charles reproductive endocrinologist
†Di Vittorio, Salvatore music educator, composer, conductor
Dixon, Shirley Lee emergency physician
Djeddah, Richard Nissim investment banker
Djerejian, Robert Asbed architect
Dlugoff, Marc Alan lawyer
†Dlugoszewski, Lucia artistic director
Dobbs, John Barnes artist, educator
Dobelis, Miervaldis Christian systems designer
Dobell, Byron Maxwell magazine consultant
Dobrinsky, Herbert Colman university administrator
Dodd, Lois artist, art educator
Dodson, Daryl Theodore ballet administrator, arts consultant
Dodson, Helen Zrake television news producer
Doherty, Karen Ann import company executive
Doherty, Patrick William municipal official
Doherty, Thomas publisher
Dohrenwend, Bruce Philip psychiatric epidemiologist, social psychologist, educator
Dolack, Peter Charles editor, writer
Dolan, Peter Robert pharmaceutical executive
Dolan, Raymond Bernard insurance executive
Dole, Vincent Paul medical research executive, educator
Dolgen, Jonathan L. motion picture company executive
Dolgin, Martin cardiologist, educator
Dolice, Joseph Leo art publisher, exhibition director
Dombrowski, Bob artist, publisher
†Domino, Fats (Antoine Domino) pianist, singer, songwriter
Domowitz, Ian economics educator
Donald, Norman Henderson, III, lawyer
Donaldson, John Cecil, Jr., consumer products company executive
Donaldson, Stephen Reeder author
†Donegan, Cheryl artist
Donelian, Armen pianist, composer, author
Donohue, Margaret Anne retail company executive
Donovan, Maureen Driscoll lawyer
†Dooner, John Joseph, Jr., advertising executive
Dopf, Glenn William lawyer
Dorado, Marianne Gaertner lawyer
Dore, Anita Wilkes English language educator
Dorfman, Howard David pathologist, educator
Dorkey, Charles E., III, lawyer
Dorn, Sue Bricker consultant, retired hospital administrator
Dorris, George Edward historian, educator, editor, author
Dorsen, Norman lawyer, educator
Dorsett, Burt investment company executive
Dos Santos, Carlos ambassador
†Dotan, Z. medical researcher, urologist
Dotson, Robert Charles news correspondent
†Dottin, Robert P. biologist, educator
Doty, Shayne Taylor organist
Douglas, Paul Wolff retired mining executive
†Douglas, Philip Le Breton lawyer
Douglass, Robert Royal banker, lawyer
Dowd, Irene dance educator, choreographer
Dowling, Edward Thomas economics educator
Downey, John Alexander physician, educator
†Downs, Hugh Malcolm radio and television broadcaster
Doyle, Eugenie Fleri pediatric cardiologist, educator
Doyle, Joseph Anthony retired lawyer
Doyle, Paul Francis lawyer
Drake, Laura theater director, performer
Drake, Owen Burtch Winters association administrator
Drake, Paul detective agency owner
Draper, James David art museum curator
Drasner, Fred newspaper publishing executive
Drebsky, Dennis Jay lawyer
Drescher, Jack psychoanalyst, psychiatrist
Dresser, Noreen Dean O'Hara civilian army official, artist
Drexler, Joanne Lee art appraiser
Drexler, Millard S. retail executive
Driver, Martha Westcott English language educator, writer, researcher
Driver, Tom Faw theologian, writer, justice/peace advocate, photographer
†Drobis, David R. public relations company executive
Droller, Michael Jack urologist
Dropkin, Charles Edward lawyer
†Drum, Sydney Maria artist
Drury, Michael freelance writer
Drusin, Lewis Martin physician, educator
Druss, Richard George psychiatrist, educator
Duberman, Martin historian, educator
Dubin, James Michael lawyer
†Dublon, Dina bank executive
†Dubois, Michel anesthesiologist
Duch, Stephen corporate financial executive
Duchin, Peter Oelrichs musician
†Duerbeck, Heidi Barbara lawyer
†Duetsch, John Edwin lawyer
Duff, John Ewing sculptor
Duff, William Brandon lawyer
Duffy, Edmund Charles lawyer
Duffy, James Henry writer, former lawyer
†Duffy, W. Leslie lawyer
Duffy-King, Jan (John Mitchell Maver Wallace) journalist, information architect, public speaker
†DuGan, Gordon F. investment banker
†Dugan, Sean Francis Xavier lawyer
Duggan, Dennis Michael newspaper editor
Duke, Anthony Drexel sociologist, educator, philanthropist
†Duke, Robin Chandler Tippett retired public relations executive
†Dukmejian, Michael publishing executive
DuLaux, Russell Frederick lawyer
Du Mont, Nicolas psychiatrist, educator
Dundas, Philip Blair, Jr., lawyer
†Dunham, Corydon Bushell lawyer, broadcasting executive
Dunham, Wolcott Balestier, Jr., lawyer
†Dunkel, Ira pediatrician
Dunkelman, Loretta artist
Dunn, M(orris) Douglas lawyer
Dunne, Dana Philip C. management consultant
Dunne, Diane C. marketing executive
Dunne, Gerard Francis lawyer
†Dunne, John Gregory writer
Dunst, Laurence David advertising executive
Durkin, Dorothy Angela university official
†Dutoit, Charles conductor
Dwek, Cyril S. bank executive
Dworetzky, Murray physician, educator
†Dwyer, Cornelius J., Jr., lawyer
†Dwyer, Jim reporter, columnist
†Dylan, Bob (Robert Allen Zimmerman) singer, composer
Dyyon, Mario (LeRoy Frazier) artist
Eagan, Marie T. (Ria Eagan) chiropractor
Eaker, Sherry Ellen entertainment newspaper editor
Eakins, William Shannon lawyer
Earle, Victor Montagne, III, lawyer
Earls, Kevin Gerard insurance company executive
Early, William Tracy journalist
†Easum, Donald Boyd consultant, educator, former institute executive, diplomat
Eckert, Allan Wesley writer
Eckman, Fern Marja journalist
Edelbaum, Philip R. lawyer
Edelman, Isidore Samuel biochemist and medical educator
Edelman, Judith H. architect
Edelman, Paul Sterling lawyer
†Edelman, Richard Winston public relations executive
Edelson, Gilbert Seymour lawyer
Edelstein, Joan Erback physical therapy educator
Edinger, Lewis Joachim political science educator
Edlow, Kenneth Lewis securities brokerage official
†Edlund, Lena finance educator
Edmiston, Mark Morton publishing company executive
†Edmunds, Kenny (Babyface) popular musician
Edson, Andrew Stephen public relations executive
Edwards, Franklin R. economist, educator, consultant
Edwards, Harold Mortimer mathematics educator
Edwards, Linda Nasif economics educator
Edwards, Michael Aubrey writer, foundation executive
†Egielski, Richard illustrator
Ehinger, Albert Louis, Jr., securities trader
Ehlers, Kathryn Hawes (Mrs. James D. Gabler) physician
Ehrenkranz, Joel S. lawyer
Ehrlich, Susan Patricia banking executive
Eidsvold, Gary Mason physician, public health officer, medical educator
Eig, Norman investment company executive
Einach, Charles Donald advertising and publishing executive
Einhorn, David Allen lawyer
Eins, Stefan painter, conceptual artist, sculptor, arts curator
†Einstein, Steven Henry investment banker, lawyer, accountant
†Eisen, Edwin Roy lawyer
Eisenberg, Alan professional society administrator
Eisenberg, Sonja Miriam artist
Eisenhuth, John C. training professional
Eisenman, Peter David architect, educator
Eisenstadt, G. Michael diplomat, writer, educator, researcher
Eisenstein, Hester sociology educator
Eisenthal, Kenneth B. physical chemistry educator
Eisert, Edward Gaver lawyer
Eisner, Carole Swid artist
†Eisner, Richard Alan accountant
Elinson, Jack sociology educator
Elkes, Terrence Allen communications executive
Ellegard, Roy Whitney appraiser
†Elliman, Donald magazine company executive
Elliott, Eleanor Thomas foundation executive, civic leader
Elliott, John, Jr., advertising agency executive
Ellis, Albert clinical psychologist, educator, author
Ellis, Richard artist, writer
†Ellis, Scott theatrical director
Ellison, Nicholas Howell literary agent
†Ellroy, James writer
Elman, Naomi Geist artist, producer
Elsbach, Peter physician, medical educator
Elsen, Sheldon Howard lawyer
Elster, Samuel Kase college dean, medical educator, physician
Elwin, James William, Jr., lawyer
Ely, Stanley E. language educator, writer
Emerson, Andi (Mrs. Andi Emerson Weeks) sales and advertising executive
Emmerman, Michael N financial analyst
Emrich, Edmund Michael lawyer
Enders, Elizabeth McGuire artist

Gadsden, James *lawyer*
Gaertner, Stefan *human resources specialist, researcher*
†Gaffney, Elizabeth Mallory *editor, writer, literature educator, translator*
Gage, Beau *artist*
Gage, Robert Clifford *minister*
†Gaines, Boyd *actor*
Gainsburg, Roy Ellis *publishing executive*
†Galan, Leonidez Vindollo *architect*
Galant, Herbert Lewis *lawyer*
Galanter, Marc *psychiatrist, educator*
Galassi, Jonathan White *book publishing company executive*
Galazka, Jacek Michal *publishing executive*
Gale, Douglas Maxwell *economics educator*
Gallagher, Brian John *lawyer*
Gallagher, Tess (Theresa Jeanette Bond) *writer, poet*
Gallo, William Victor *cartoonist*
Gambari, Ibrahim Agboola *diplomat*
Gambee, Robert Rankin *investment banker*
Gamble, Theodore Robert, Jr., *investment banker*
Gamble, William Ardell, Jr., *interior designer, inventor*
Gamboni, Ciro Anthony *lawyer*
†Gambro, Michael S. *lawyer*
Gambs, Gerard Charles *consulting engineer*
Gammill, Lee Morgan, Jr., *retired insurance company executive*
†Gamper, Albert R., Jr., *insurance executive*
Gans, Herbert J. *sociologist, educator*
†Gans, Walter Gideon *lawyer*
Gant, Donald Ross *investment banker*
Ganz, David L. *lawyer*
Ganz, Howard Laurence *lawyer*
†Ganzi, Victor Frederick *publishing executive*
Garcia, Andy *actor*
Gardella, Francis John *mathematics educator*
Gardiner, E. Nicholas P. *executive search executive*
Gardino, Vincent Anthony *broadcasting executive*
Gardner, James Richard *pharmaceutical company executive*
Gardner, Janet Paxton *journalist, film/video producer*
Gardner, Joseph Lawrence *editor, writer*
Gardner, Ralph David *advertising executive*
Gardner, Richard Newton *diplomat, lawyer, educator*
Gardner, Stephen David *lawyer, law educator*
Garfield, Leslie Jerome *real estate executive*
Garfinkel, Barry Herbert *lawyer*
†Garfinkel, Lee *advertising agency executive*
Garfunkel, Alan J. *lawyer*
Garland, Sylvia Dillof *lawyer*
Garment, Leonard *lawyer, author*
Garner, Albert Headden *investment banker*
Garniez, Nancy Caballero *pianist, educator*
Garrett, Robert *financial advisory executive*
†Garritano, Joseph A. *information scientist*
Gartner, Alan P. *municipal official*
Garvey, Richard Anthony *lawyer*
Garvin, Andrew Paul *information company executive, author, consultant*
Gassel, Philip Michael *lawyer*
Gastil, Raymond Wesley *urban designer*
Gatje, Robert Frederick *architect*
Gatto, John Taylor *educational consultant, writer, speaker*
Gatto, Joseph Daniel *investment banker*
Gaughan, Eugene Francis *retired accountant*
Gaveras, Harry *architect*
Gay, Peter *history educator, author*
Gaydos, Mary *writer, researcher, actress*
†Gayer, Elliott *lawyer*
†Gaynor, Suzanne Marie *health care executive, researcher*
Gebbie, Kristine Moore *health science educator, health official*
Geckle, Robert Alan *manufacturing company executive*
Gediman, Helen K. *psychologist*
Geer, John Farr *retired religious organization administrator*
Gehringer, Richard George *publishing executive*
Geier, Philip Henry, Jr., *advertising executive*
Geiger, H. Jack *medical educator*
Geiser, Elizabeth Able *publishing company executive*
Geismar, Thomas H. *graphic designer*
Geissbuhler, Stephan *graphic designer*
Gelb, Bruce Stuart *city commissioner, consultant*
Gelb, Harold Seymour *industrial company executive, investor*
Gelb, Judith Anne *lawyer*
Gelb, Leslie Howard *organization president, lecturer*
Gelfand, Neal *oil company executive*
Gelfman, Peter Trustman *lawyer*
Gelfman, Robert William *lawyer*
Geller, Jeffrey Lawrence *financier*
Geller, Robert James *advertising agency executive*
Geller, Sandra R. *continuing legal education administrator*
Gellert, Michael Erwin *investment banker*
Gellhorn, Alfred *physician, educator*
†Gelman, Stephen *writer, editor*
†Geltzer, Robert Lawrence *lawyer, arbitrator, mediator, former retail executive*
Geltzer, Sheila Simon *public relations executive*
Genkins, Gabriel *physician*
Genova, Diane Melisano *lawyer*
Georgakopoulos, Anastasios *molecular biology*
Georges, Paul Gordon *artist, educator*
†Georgescu, Peter Andrew *advertising executive*
Georgopoulos, Maria *architect, artist, inventor*
Gerard, Whitney Ian *lawyer*
Gerard-Sharp, Monica Fleur *communications executive*
Gerber, Gwendolyn Loretta *psychologist, educator*
Gerber, Robert Evan *judge*
Gerberg, Judith Levine *human resource company executive*
Gerdts, William Henry *art history educator*
Gerety, Tom *academic administrator, lawyer, educator, philosopher*
Germano, William Paul *publisher*
Gero, Anthony George *securities and commodities trader*
Gershon, Bernard *broadcast executive*
Gerson, Donald Franklin *pharmaceutical executive*
Gersony, Welton Mark *physician, pediatric cardiologist, educator*
Gertler, Menard M. *physician, educator*
Gesmer, Ellen Frances *lawyer*
Getnick, Neil Victor *lawyer*
Gettner, Alan Frederick *lawyer*
†Gewirtz-Friedman, Gerry *editor*
Gharib, Susie *television newscaster*
†Giampietro, Philip Francis *clinical geneticist, pediatrics educator*
Gianaris, Nicholas Vasil *economics educator*
Giancotti, Filippo Giusto *cell and molecular biologist*
†Giannetti, Stephen P. *publishing executive*
Giardina, Elsa Grace Vonna *cardiologist, educator*
Gibaldi, Joseph *publishing executive*
†Gibbons, Robert John *lawyer*
Gibbs, Jamie *landscape architect, interior designer*
Gibbs, L(ippman) Martin *lawyer*
Giblin, James Cross *author, editor*
Giblin, Jean-Ellen Dorsey *university administrator, economics educator*
Gibson, Charles DeWolf *broadcast journalist*
Gibson, John *news anchor, correspondent*
Gibson, Ralph H(olmes) *photographer*
†Gibson, William S. *lawyer*
Giddens-Jones, Emily Jane *architectural and interior designer, consultant*
Gifford, William C. *lawyer, educator*
Giffuni, Flora B. *artist, educator*
†Gilburne, Miles R. *communications executive*
Gill, Ardian C. *actuary, photographer, writer*
Gill, E. Ann *lawyer*
Gill, Patrick David *lawyer*
Gillers, Stephen *law educator, university official*
Gillespie, George Joseph, III, *lawyer*
†Gillespie, Jane *lawyer*
Gillespie, John Thomas *university administrator*
Gilliam, Paula Hutter *transportation company executive*
Gillies, Trent Donald *television producer*
Gilmore, Jennifer A.W. *computer specialist, educator*
Giniger, Kenneth Seeman *publisher*
Ginsberg, David Lawrence *architect*
Ginsberg, Hersh Meier *rabbi, religious organization executive*
Ginsburg, Sigmund G. *management and executive search consultant*
Ginter, Valerian Alexius *urban historian, educator*
Ginzel, Andrew H. *artist*
Giordano, Bill A. *psychotherapist*
Giorlando, Jeanne A. *labor and delivery nurse*
Giorno, John *poet*
Giraldi, Robert Nicholas *film director*
Girard, Andrea Eaton *communications executive, consultant*
Girardi, Federico Pablo *surgeon, educator*
Gissler, Sigvard Gunnar, Jr., *journalist, educator, retired editor*
Gitelson, Susan Aurelia *business executive, civic leader*
Gitter, Max *lawyer*
Gittler, Wendy *artist, art historian, writer*
Giuliani, Rudolph W. *former mayor, consultant, lawyer*
Gladstone, William Louis *accountant*
Glanstein, Joel Charles *lawyer*
Glasberg, H(erbert) Mark *psychiatrist, educator*
Glasberg, Scot Bradley *plastic surgeon*
Glass, David Carter *psychology educator*
Glass, Philip *composer, musician*
Glassman, Alexander Howard *psychiatrist, researcher*
†Glassman, Paul *library director, architecture educator*
†Glassman, Steven J. *lawyer*
Glatt, Mitchell Steven *business executive*
Glekel, Jeffrey Ives *lawyer*
Glickman, Michael Richard *social studies educator*
Glickman, Robert Morris *physician, educator*
Glickstein, Steven *lawyer*
Glimcher, Arnold B. *art gallery executive*
Gluck, Andrew Lee *vocational economic analyst, counselor, philosopher*
Gluck, Carol *history educator*
Goble, Phillip E. *writer, biblical scholar, translator*
Gochberg, Thomas *real estate investor, financial executive*
Goddess, Lynn Barbara *commercial real estate broker*
Godman, Gabriel Charles *pathology educator*
Godosky, Robert E. *lawyer*
Goebel, William Horn *lawyer*
†Goele, Dhruv (Ostaro) *publisher, financial consultant*
Goelet, Robert G. *investment executive*
Goell, Abby Jane *painter, collage artist, artist*
Goerdt, Ann Renee *physical therapist, consultant*
Goertz, Augustus Frederick, III, *artist*
Goetz, Maurice Harold *lawyer*
†Goff, Betsy Kagen *lawyer*
Goff, Robert Edward *health care executive*
Goines, Leonard *music educator, consultant*
Goings, Ralph *artist*
Gold, Albert *artist*
Gold, Arnold P. *pediatric neurologist*
Gold, Jeffrey Mark *investment banker, financial adviser*
Gold, Lois Meyer *artist*
Gold, Sharon Cecile *artist, educator*
Gold, Simeon *lawyer*
†Gold, Stuart Walter *lawyer*
Gold, William Elliott *health care management consultant, educator*
Goldberg, Beverly *foundation administrator, consultant*
†Goldberg, David *lawyer, law educator*
Goldberg, Franklin H. *psychotherapist*
Goldberg, Harvey Lee *internal medicine*
Goldberg, Jay *lawyer*
Goldberg, Sidney *editor*
Goldberger, Leo *psychologist, educator*
Golde, David William *physician, educator*
Golden, Arthur F. *lawyer*
†Golden, Marc Alan *investment banker*
Golden, William Theodore *trustee, corporate director*
Goldenberg, Charles Lawrence *real estate company executive*
Goldenberg, Elizabeth Leigh *editor*
Goldfarb, Alisan Beth *surgeon, educator*
Goldfarb, David *investment banking executive*
†Goldfarb, Donald *industrial engineering educator*
Goldfrank, Lewis Robert *physician*
Goldin, Leon *artist, educator*
Goldman, Charles Norton *retired corporate lawyer*
†Goldman, Fatima *social services administrator*
Goldman, Lawrence Saul *lawyer*
Goldman, Marvin Gerald *lawyer*
Goldman, Peter Louis *writer*
Goldmark, Peter Francis *banker*
Goldrich, Stanley Gilbert *optometrist*
Goldschmidt, Charles *advertising agency executive*
Goldsmith, Barbara *writer, historian, journalist*
Goldsmith, Caroline L. *arts executive*
Goldsmith, Clifford Henry *former tobacco company executive*
†Goldsmith, Gary L. *advertising executive*
Goldsmith, Lee Selig *lawyer, physician*
Goldsmith, Merwin *actor, theater director*
Goldsmith, Michael Allen *oncologist, educator*
Goldsmith, Robert Lewis *youth association magazine executive*
Goldsmith, Stanley Joseph *nuclear medicine physician, educator*
Goldstein, Alvin *lawyer*
Goldstein, Charles Arthur *lawyer*
†Goldstein, Eugene E. *lawyer*
Goldstein, Gary Sanford *executive recruiter*
Goldstein, Henry *philanthropic institutions consultant*
Goldstein, Howard Sheldon *lawyer*
Goldstein, Howard Warren *lawyer*
Goldstein, Kenneth B. *lawyer*
†Goldstein, M. Robert *lawyer, judge*
Goldstein, Marc *microsurgeon, urology and reproductive medicine educator, administrator*
Goldstein, Matthew *academic administrator*
Goldstein, Michael Lewis *investment strategist*
Goldstein, Norm *editor, writer*
Goldstein, Richard A. *consumer products company executive*
†Goldstein, Sandra Cara *lawyer*
Goldstein, Stuart Zane *public affairs executive*
†Goldstone, Steven F. *consumer products company executive*
Golick, Toby *law educator, legal services administrator*
†Golomb, David Bela *lawyer*
Golomb, Frederick Martin *surgeon, educator*
†Golon, Maryanne *photojournalist*
Gomez, Francis Dean *corporate executive, former foreign service officer*
†Gomory, Ralph Edward *mathematician, manufacturing company executive, foundation executive*
†Gondolesi, Gabriel Eduardo *transplant surgeon*
†Gong, Su *computer engineer*
Gonzalez, Eugene Robert *investment banker*
Goodale, James Campbell *lawyer, media executive, television producer/host*
Goodfriend, Herbert Jay *lawyer*
Goodhartz, Gerald *law librarian*
Goodman, Gary A. *lawyer*
Goodman, George Jerome Waldo (Adam Smith) *author, television journalist, editor*
Goodman, Roger Mark *television director*
Goodman, Roy Matz *corporate president, chief executive officer, former state senator*
Goodridge, Allan D. *lawyer*
Goodstein, Les *newspaper publishing executive*
†Goodwillie, Eugene William, Jr., *lawyer*
Goodwin, Todd *banker*
†Goott, Alan F(ranklin) *lawyer*
†Goozner, Merrill *journalist*
Gordevitch, Igor *publishing company executive*
Gordon, Alan Lee *psychiatrist*
Gordon, David *playwright, director, choreographer*
†Gordon, Douglas *artist*
Gordon, Evan L. *lawyer*
Gordon, Mark *actor, theater director, theater educator*
Gordon, Mary Catherine *writer*
Gordon, Michael Mackin *lawyer*
†Gorelick, Steven Michael *academic administrator, writer*
Goss, Mary E. Weber *sociology educator*
†Gossage, Wayne *library director, management consultant, entrepreneur, executive recruiter*
Gossett, Robert Francis, Jr., *merchant banker*
†Gotschlich, Emil Claus *physician*
Gottesman, A(rthur) Edward *lawyer*
Gottesman, David Sanford *investment executive*
Gotthoffer, Lance *lawyer*
Gottlieb, Jerrold Howard *advertising executive*
Gottlieb, Paul *publishing company executive*
Gottlieb, Paul Mitchel *lawyer*
Gotto, Antonio Marion, Jr., *internist, educator*
Gotts, Ilene Knable *lawyer*
Gottschalk, Alfred *retired college chancellor, museum executive*
Gould, Harry Edward, Jr., *paper company executive*
Goulden, Joseph Chesley *author*
Goulianos, Konstantin *physics educator*
Gourevitch, Jacqueline *artist*
Gowens, Walter, II, *financial and business services executive*
†Grabé, Christopher K. *architectural firm executive*
Grabois, Neil Robert *foundation administrator, former college president*
Grad, Frank Paul *law educator, lawyer*
Grader, Patricia Alison Lande *editor*
Grader, Scott Paul *lawyer*
Graf, Peter Gustav *accountant, lawyer*
Graff, George Leonard *lawyer*
Grafton, Sue *novelist*
†Graham, Philip L., Jr., *lawyer*
Gramm, William Philip (Phil Gramm) *former senator, economist*
Grandizio, Lenore *social worker*
†Granik, Russell T. *sports association executive*
Granoff, Gary Charles *lawyer, investment company executive*
Granstein, Richard David *dermatologist*
Grant, Alfred David *orthopaedic surgeon, educator*
Grant, Cynthia D. *writer*
Grant, Sonia Vivienne *secondary school educator*
Grant, Stephen Allen *lawyer*
Grassi, Joseph F. *lawyer, mediator, arbitrator*
Grau, Marcy Beinish *real estate broker, former investment banker*
†Graves, Gail Marvel *language educator*
Graves, Thomas Vincent *sculptor*
Gray, George *mural painter*
Gray, James L. *investment company executive*
†Graziano, John Michael *music educator*
Grebow, Edward *media company executive*
Grecich, Daryl George *marketing communications executive*
Greco, Albert Nicholas *communications educator, educator*
Greeley, Sean McGovern *sales executive*
Green, Alvin *lawyer, consultant*
Green, Barbara Strawn *psychotherapist*
Green, Dan *publishing company executive*
Green, George Joseph *publishing executive*
Green, Jack Peter *retired pharmacology educator, medical scientist*
Green, Lloyd M. *lawyer*
Green, Maurice Richard *neuropsychiatrist*
Green, Robert S. *lawyer*
Greenawalt, Robert Kent *lawyer, law educator*
Greenawalt, William Sloan *lawyer*
†Greenbaum, Fred *historian, educator*
Greenbaum, Jeffrey Alan *lawyer*
Greenbaum, Maurice Coleman *lawyer*
†Greenbaum, Sheldon Marc *lawyer*
Greenberg, Daniel Herbert *lawyer*
Greenberg, Daniel Lawrence *lawyer*
Greenberg, Gary Howard *lawyer*
†Greenberg, Henry Morton *physician, educator*
Greenberg, Ira George *lawyer*
Greenberg, Jack *lawyer, law educator*
Greenberg, Jeffrey W. *professional services company executive*
Greenberg, Maurice Raymond *insurance company executive*
Greenberger, Howard Leroy *lawyer, educator*
Green-Dorsey, Jean Audrey *information technology executive*
Greene, Adele S. *management consultant*
Greene, Bernard Harold *lawyer*
Greene, Elizabeth Ivory *real estate company official*
Greene, Frank Edward Wade *writer, philanthropy adviser*
Greene, Ira S. *lawyer*
Greene, Kay C. *psychologist, author*
†Greene, Nathanael Wade *environmental scientist*
Greene, Richard H. *journalist, multimedia producer*
Greenfield, Gordon Kraus *software company executive*
Greenfield, Jeff (Henry Jeff Greenfield) *news analyst*
Greenfield, Seymour Stephen *mechanical engineer*
Greengard, Paul *neuroscientist*
†Greenhill, Robert Foster *investment banker*
Greenland, Leo *advertising executive*
Greenleaf, Eric Andrew *marketing educator, researcher*
Greenman, Frederick F., Jr., *lawyer*
†Greenspon, Robert Alan *lawyer*
Greenstein, Abraham Jacob *mortgage company executive, accountant*
Greenwald, Sheila Ellen *writer, illustrator*
Greenwood, Ted Ronald Ivan *foundation administrator*
†Greeven, Rainer *lawyer*
Grefrath, Peter Alan *marketing communications executive*
Gregorian, Vartan *foundation administrator*
Gregory, Coleman George *lawyer*
†Greifeld, Robert A. *corporate financial executive*
Greilsheimer, James Gans *lawyer*
Greilsheimer, William Henry *lawyer*
†Greiner, Stephen W. *lawyer*
Grenquist, Peter Carl *consultant*
Grew, Robert Ralph *lawyer*
Griefen, John Adams *artist, educator*
Griesa, Thomas Poole *federal judge*
†Griffel, L. Michael *music educator, researcher*
†Griffin, Adele *writer*
Griffith, Alan Richard *banker*
Griffith, Clark Dexter *risk management professional*
Griffith, Nicola *writer*
Griffiths, Sylvia Preston *physician, educator*
Grigsby, Henry Jefferson *editor*
Grimaldi, Nicholas Lawrence *fundraising executive*
†Grimes, Suzanne *publishing executive*
†Grisham, John *writer*
Griswold, Frank Tracy, III, *bishop*
Groberg, James Jay *information sciences company executive*
Groh, Jennifer Calfa *law librarian*

House, Karen Elliott company executive, former editor, reporter
Housepian, Edgar Minas neurosurgery educator
†Houston, Allan Wade professional basketball player
Hoving, Thomas museum and cultural affairs consultant, author
Howard, David educational administrator
Howard, Nathan Southard investment banker, lawyer
Howat, John Keith retired museum executive
Howe, Florence English educator, writer, publisher
Howe, Richard Rives lawyer
Howell, William Page real estate company executive
Hoxter, Curtis Joseph international economic adviser, public relations and public affairs counselor
†Hricik, Lorraine E. bank executive
Hritz, George F. lawyer
Hruska, Alan J. lawyer
Hu, Dan-Ning ophthalmologist
Huang, Limin chemist, researcher
†Huck, L. Francis lawyer
Hudes, Nana Brenda marketing professional
Hudson, Richard McLain, Jr., journalist, researcher
Hudspeth, Albert James biomedical researcher, educator
Hudspeth, Stephen Mason lawyer
†Huey, John Wesley, Jr., editor
Hughes, Kevin Peter lawyer
Hugo, Norman Eliot plastic surgeon, medical educator
Huhs, John I. international lawyer
Hulbert, Richard Woodward lawyer
Hull, Cathy artist, illustrator
Hull, Philip Glasgow lawyer
Hultberg, John artist
Humphreys, Josephine novelist
†Hunsinger, Peter publishing executive
Hunter-Bone, Maureen Claire magazine editor
Hunter-Stiebel, Penelope art historian
Huppauf, Bernd Rudiger educator
Hupper, John Roscoe lawyer
†Hurd, Ruth publishing executive
Hurley, Cheryl Joyce book publishing executive
Hurley, Dean C. bank executive, lawyer
Hurlin, Dan actor, theater director
Hurlock, James Bickford retired lawyer
†Hurst, Robert Jay securities company executive
Hutchings, Peter Lounsbery retird insurance company executive, director
†Hutchins, Traver publishing executive
†Hutchinson, Lynda Ronette (Billie Holiday Jr., Princess of Jazz, Munchie) vocalist, musician, comedian
Hutton, Ernest Watson, Jr., urban designer, city planner
Huxtable, Ada Louise architecture critic
Hwang, David Henry playwright, screenwriter
†Hwu, Wen-Jen physician, oncologist, educator
Hyde, David Rowley lawyer
Hyman, Bruce Malcolm ophthalmologist
Hyman, Jerome Elliot lawyer
Hyman, Morton Peter shipping company executive
Hyman, Seymour capital and product development company executive
†Hynes, Patricia Mary lawyer
Iannuzzi, John Nicholas lawyer, author, educator
†Ichikawa, Akiko artist, editor
†Ienner, Don music company executive
Iglauer, Edith writer, reporter
Ilacqua, Rosario Salvatore securities analyst
Ilchman, Alice Stone foundation administrator, former college president, former government official
Ilchman, Warren Frederick university administrator, foundation director, educator
Ilson, Bernard public relations executive
Imparato, Anthony Michael vascular surgeon, medical educator, researcher
Imperato, Joseph Edward otolaryngologist
Imperato-McGinley, Julianne Leonore endocrinologist, educator
†Imus, Don radio host
†Inabnet, William Barlow, III, surgeon
Incandela, Gerald Jean-Marie artist
Indursky, Arthur lawyer
Ingolfsson, Thorsteinn diplomat
Ingram, Douglas Howard psychoanalyst
Ingram, Samuel William, Jr., lawyer
Innis, Roy Emile Alfredo organization executive
Insardi, Nina Elizabeth benefits administrator
Insel, Michael S. lawyer
Intilli, Sharon Marie television director, small business owner
Intriligator, Marc Steven lawyer
Ireland, Patrick artist
Irie, Philip Shinazo physician, scientist
Isaacs, Richard B. investigative and protective services professional
†Isaacs, Robert conductor, director
Isaacson, Allen Ira lawyer
Isaacson, Melvin Stuart library director
Isay, David Avram writer, radio producer
Isay, Richard Alexander psychiatrist
Iselin, John Jay foundation president
Iseman, Joseph Seeman lawyer
Isenberg, Steven Lawrence retired publishing executive
Isogai, Masaharu international business consultant, former women's apparel executive
Isquith, Fred Taylor lawyer
Issler, Harry lawyer
Itzkoff, Norman Jay lawyer
Ivanick, Carol W. Trencher lawyer
Ivanovitch, Michael S. economist
Ivory, James Francis film director
Ivy, Robert Adams, Jr., architect, editor-in-chief
Iwamoto, Ralph Shigeto artist
†Izzo, Francesco musicologist
†Jabbur, Ramzi J. management consultant
Jablonsky, Stephen music educator, composer, artist, writer
Jacker, Corinne Litvin playwright, writer
Jackson, Anne (Anne Jackson Wallach) actress
†Jackson, James Lewis Perdue, II, entertainment company executive
Jackson, Kenneth Terry historian, administrator
Jackson, Reggie (Reginald Martinez Jackson) former professional baseball player
Jackson, Thomas Gene lawyer
†Jacob, Marvin Eugene lawyer
†Jacobowitz, Glenn Robert vascular surgeon
Jacobowitz, Harold Saul lawyer
Jacobs, Arnold Stephen lawyer
Jacobs, David Richard endocrinologist
Jacobs, Dennis federal judge
Jacobs, Harry Allan, Jr., investment firm executive
Jacobs, Jim actor, playwright, composer, lyricist
Jacobs, Paul lawyer
†Jacobs, Randall Scott David lawyer
Jacobs, Robert Alan lawyer
Jacobs, Thomas Price internal medicine educator
Jacobsen, Theodore H. (Ted H. Jacobsen) labor union administrator, secondary school educator
Jacobson, Jeffrey E. lawyer, consultant
Jacobson, Jerold Dennis lawyer
Jacobson, Lawrence Seymour television executive producer
Jacoby, Jacob consumer psychology educator
Jacoby, Robert Harold management consulting executive
Jacqueney, Stephanie A(lice) lawyer
Jacquette, Yvonne Helene artist
Jafar, Jafar Jewad neurosurgeon, educator
Jaffe, Alan Steven lawyer
Jaffe, Israeli Arron internist, rheumatologist, educator
Jaffe, Mark M. lawyer
Jaglom, Andre Richard lawyer
Jakes, John author
James, Robert Gregory investment company executive
†Jamison, Jayne magazine publisher
Jamison, Judith dancer
Janiak, Anthony Richard, Jr., investment banker
Janjigian, Vahan equity research director, editor
Janklow, Morton Lloyd lawyer, literary agent
Janney, Stuart Symington, III, investment company executive
†Janowitz, James Arnold lawyer
Janssen, Peter Anton magazine editor and publisher
†Jarblum, William lawyer
Jarecki, Henry George physician, financial executive
Jaroff, Leon Morton magazine editor
Jarvik, Robert K. biomedical research scientist
Jasper, Seymour lawyer
Jasperse, John performing company executive
Jasso, Guillermina sociologist, educator
Jassy, Everett Lewis lawyer
†Jauvtis, Robert Lloyd lawyer
Javitt, Norman B. medical educator, researcher
†Jay, Harvey H. dermatologist, educator, researcher
Jefferson, Kristin Marie museum director
†Jefferson, Margo L. journalist
Jeffries, David Hamilton investment banker
†Jelinek, Josef Emil dermatologist
Jelinek, Vera university director
Jellinek, George broadcast executive, writer, music educator
Jenkins, Anthony Charles correspondent
Jenkins, Kevin Gerard lawyer
Jenkins, Paul artist
Jenkins, Zeretha Lenore publishing executive
Jennings, Peter Charles television anchorman
Jensen, Dennis Mark marketing executive
Jepson, Hans Godfrey investment company executive, director
Jerins, Edgar artist, painter
†Jerome, John James lawyer
Jervis, Robert political science educator
†Jetter, Frances S. illustrator, educator, artist
†Jewel, (Jewel Kilcher) folk singer, songwriter
Jeydel, Richard K. lawyer
Jeynes, Mary Kay college dean
Jhabvala, Ruth Prawer writer
Jiha, Jacques economist
Jinnett, Robert Jefferson lawyer
Joachim, Brigitta Golden writer, advertising agency executive, media consultant
Jock, Paul F., II, lawyer
†Joel, Richard Marc academic administrator, law educator, dean
Joffe, Robert David lawyer
Johnsen, Niels Winchester ocean shipping company executive
Johnson, Clarke Courtney financial consultant, educator
Johnson, Evan Kenneth physical therapist, educator
Johnson, Harmer Frederik art appraiser
Johnson, Horton Anton pathologist
Johnson, J. Chester financial executive, poet
Johnson, Jeffrey Grant research scientist, psychology educator
†Johnson, Jeh Charles lawyer
†Johnson, John H. publisher, consumer products executive
Johnson, John William, Jr., executive recruiter
Johnson, Johnnie Dean investor relations consultant
†Johnson, Larry Demetric professional basketball player
Johnson, Thomas Stephen banker
†Johnston, Diane Miller librarian
Johnston, Ruth D. film studies, English literature, and women's studies educator
Jonas, Gilbert public relations and fund raising executive
Jonas, Ruth Haber psychologist
Jonas, Saran neurologist, educator
Jones, Abbott C. investment banking executive
†Jones, Christopher advertising company executive
Jones, Diana Wynne writer
Jones, Douglas Wiley lawyer
Jones, Gwenyth Ellen publishing information systems/technology executive
Jones, Kristin Andrea artist
Jones, Laurie Lynn magazine editor
Jones, Thomas E. bank executive
†Jones, Tom publishing executive
Jong, Erica Mann writer, poet
†Joo, Michael artist, educator
†Jordan, Frank J. lawyer
Jordan, Vernon Eulion, Jr., lawyer, former association official
Jorjani, Maryam psychotherapist
†Josell, Jessica (Jessica Wechsler) public relations executive
Joseph, Gregory Paul lawyer
Joseph, Leonard lawyer
Joseph, Mario Alexis lawyer
Joseph, Michael Sarkies accountant
†Joseph, Wendy Evans architect
Josephs, Ray public relations and advertising executive, writer, international relations consultant
Josephson, Diana Hayward not-for-profit company executive
Josephson, Marvin talent and literary agency executive
Josephson, William Howard lawyer
Juceam, Robert E. lawyer
†Juchem, Elmar musicologist, music educator, consultant
†Judge, Jerry business executive
†Juliber, Lois manufacturing executive
Jung, Andrea cosmetics executive
†Jung, Beverley C. accountant, advocate
Jung, Doris dramatic soprano
Jungman, Jonathan Wayne accountant
†Junkerman, William Joseph retired lawyer
Juran, Sylvia Louise editor
Jurka, Edith Mila psychiatrist, researcher
Jurmain, Suzanne Tripp freelance writer and editor
Just, Gemma Rivoli retired advertising executive
†Kabak, Bernard Joshua lawyer
Kaden, Lewis B. law educator, lawyer
†Kaess, Ken advertising executive
†Kafin, Robert Joseph lawyer
Kagan, Ilse Echt research librarian, village historian
Kaggen, Lois Sheila non-profit organization executive
Kahan, Marlene professional association executive
Kahane, Jeffrey conductor, pianist
Kahn, Alan Edwin lawyer
Kahn, Alfred Joseph social worker and policy scholar, educator
†Kahn, Alfred Robert toy manufacturing company executive
Kahn, Anthony F. lawyer
†Kahn, Jason S. investment banker, consultant
Kahn, Martin L. physician, educator
Kahn, Nancy Valerie publishing and entertainment executive, consultant
Kahn, Norman pharmacology and dentistry educator
Kahn, Wolf artist
†Kail, Kenneth Stoner lawyer
†Kailas, Leo George lawyer
Kainen, Anna writer
Kaiser, Suzanne Billo investment banker
Kaiser, Walter English language educator
Kaish, Luise Clayborn sculptor, former educator
Kaish, Morton artist, educator
Kaku, Michio theoretical nuclear physicist, educator
†Kalajian-Lagani, Donna publishing executive
Kalayjian, Anie psychotherapist, nurse, educator, consultant
†Kalech, Marc newspaper editor
†Kalich, Richard Barry writer
Kalikow, Peter Stephen real estate developer, former newspaper owner, publisher
†Kalikow, Richard R. lawyer
Kalish, Arthur lawyer
Kalish, Myron lawyer
Kallir, Jane Katherine art gallery director, author
†Kalman, Bernadette neurologist, researcher
†Kalow, David Arthur lawyer
Kalsner, Stanley pharmacologist, physiologist, educator
Kamali, Norma fashion designer
Kamerman, Sheila Brody educator, social worker
Kamin, Sherwin lawyer
Kamlot, Robert performing arts executive
Kampel, Donne academic administrator, educator
Kan, Diana Artemis Mann Shu painter, art educator, writer
Kandel, Denise Bystryn sociologist
Kandel, Eric Richard neuroscience educator
Kandel, William Lloyd lawyer, mediator, arbitrator, educator, writer
†Kane, Alice Theresa lawyer
†Kane, Marilyn real estate company executive
Kane, Siegrun Dinklage lawyer
†Kang, Eliot advertising executive
Kann, Peter Robert journalist, newspaper publishing executive
Kanof, Norman B. dermatologist
Kantor, Frederick William physicist
Kapelman, Barbara Ann physician, educator
Kaplan, Carl Eliot lawyer
†Kaplan, Jerry magazine publisher
Kaplan, Lawrence Jay economist, educator
Kaplan, Lewis A. judge
Kaplan, Madeline legal administrator
†Kaplan, Mark Norman lawyer
Kaplan, Susan lawyer
Kaplan, Theodore Norman insurance company executive
†Kaplen, Michael V. lawyer
†Kapoor, Neera optometrist
Kappagoda, Samantha economist, editor
Kappas, Attallah physician, medical scientist
Karalekas, George Steven advertising agency executive, political consultant
Karan, Donna (Donna Faske) fashion designer
Karan, Paul Richard lawyer
Karasu, T(oksoz) Byram psychiatry educator
Karatz, William Warren lawyer
Karchin, Louis Samuel composer, educator
†Kardon, Dennis artist,, educator
Kardon, Janet museum director, curator, educator
Kardon, Robert mortgage company executive
Karl, Kurt Erskine economist
†Karlgaard, Rich publishing executive
Karlin, Muriel Schlosberg information technology manager, consultant
Karls, John Spencer lawyer, accountant
Karmali, Rashida Alimahomed lawyer
†Karmazin, Mel broadcast executive
Karmel, Philip Elias lawyer
Karp, Martin Everett management consultant
Karpel, Craig S. journalist, editor
†Karpen, Marian Joan financial executive
†Karsch, Stephen E. lawyer
Karsen, Sonja Petra retired American-Hispanic literature educator
Kartiganer, Joseph retired lawyer
Kasakove, Susan interior designer
Kashmeri, Sarwar Aghajani internet publishing company executive
Kasinec, Edward Joseph library administrator
Kasinitz, Philip sociologist, educator
Kaskell, Peter Howard association executive, lawyer
Kaslick, Ralph Sidney dentist, educator
Kassebaum, John Philip lawyer
Kassel, Catherine M. community, maternal, and women's health nurse, consultant
Kassel, Virginia Weltmer television producer, writer
Kastan, David Scott university educator, writer
Katen, Karen L. pharmaceutical company executive
Kates, Brian C. newspaper editor
Katsh, Salem Michael lawyer
Katsoris, Constantine Nicholas lawyer, consultant
†Katsos, Barbara Helene lawyer
†Katsoyannis, Panayotis George biochemist, educator
†Katti, Shriniwas K. retired statistician, consultant
Katz, Abraham retired foreign service officer
Katz, Alex artist
Katz, Cheryl Ann human services manager, social worker
Katz, Jane swimming educator
Katz, Jerome Charles lawyer
Katz, Jose cardiologist, theoretical physicist, educator
Katz, Lois Anne internist, nephrologist
Katz, Marcia public relations company executive
Katz, Ronald Scott lawyer
†Katz, Stuart Z. lawyer
Katz, Thomas J. chemistry educator
Katz, Vincent Isaac writer
Katzmann, Robert Allen judge
Kauffmann, Stanley Jules author
Kaufman, Arthur Stephen lawyer
Kaufman, Bel author, educator
†Kaufman, Lawrence Jesse computer engineer
Kaufman, Robert Max lawyer, director
†Kaufman, Stephen Edward lawyer
†Kaufman, Victor A. entertainment executive, former film company executive
Kaufmann, Mark Steiner banker
†Kaur, Harminder language educator
Kauth, Benjamin podiatry consultant
Kavaler, Thomas J. lawyer
Kavaler-Adler, Susan clinical psychologist
Kavalerchik, Boris Yakovlevich information technology developer, researcher
†Kavan, Jan UN General Assembly official, former Czech Republic government official
Kavesh, Robert A. economist, educator
Kavoukjian, Michael Edward lawyer
Kawano, Arnold Hubert lawyer
†Kaye, Richard Paul lawyer
Kaye, Stephen Rackow lawyer
Kaye, Walter financial executive
†Kayse, Kathleen publishing executive
Kazemi, Farhad political scientist, educator
Kean, Hamilton Fish lawyer
Kearse, Amalya Lyle federal judge
Keech, Pamela artist, curator
†Keefer, Elizabeth J. general counsel
Keenan, John Fontaine judge
Keenan, Michael Edgar marketing professional
Keene, Donald writer, translator, language educator
†Keene, Lonnie Stuart lawyer
Kegeles, Lawrence Steven psychiatrist, researcher
Kehoe, John P. investor relations and corporate development consultant
Kehret, Peg writer
Keller, Bill editor
†Kelley, Robin D. G. education educator, writer
Kellner, George securities executive
†Kellogg, Paul general & artistic director opera company
†Kelly, Christina editor
†Kelly, James deputy managing editor
Kelly, Patrick Joseph neurosurgeon, educator
Kelly, Peter CEO, president
Kelly, Stephen Euless ophthalmologist
Kelly, Thomas Jesse, Jr., molecular biologist
Kelly, Thomas Michael lawyer
Kelly, William Michael investment executive
Kelmachter, Leslie Debra lawyer
Kelman, Edward Michael lawyer
Kelmenson, Leo-Arthur advertising executive
Kempa, Gerald manufacturing company executive
Kempf, Donald G., Jr., lawyer
†Kendall, Laurel Margarite curator, anthropologist, educator

Lee, In-Young *lawyer*
Lee, Jerome G. *lawyer*
Lee, Leslie Enders *artist*
Lee, Paul Lawrence *lawyer*
Lee, Sally A. *editor-in-chief*
Lee, Tay Bong *surgeon, otolaryngologist*
†Leebron, David Wayne *dean, law educator*
†Leeman, Cavin P. *psychiatrist*
Lees, Alfred William *writer, former magazine editor*
Leet, Mildred Robbins *corporate executive, consultant*
Leetch, Brian Joseph *hockey player*
Leff, Ilene J(afnel) *management consultant, corporate and government executive*
Leff, Sandra H. *gallery director, consultant*
Lefferts, Gillet, Jr., *architect*
Lefkowitz, Howard N. *lawyer*
Lefkowitz, Joel M. *psychologist, educator*
†LeGrady, George *photographer, educator*
Legrand, Michel Jean *composer*
Lehman, Edward William *sociology educator, researcher*
Lehman, Orin *retired state official*
Lehmann-Haupt, Christopher Charles Herbert *book reviewer*
†Lehmkuhl, Lynn *publishing executive*
Lehrer, Ruth Jeannette *social work supervisor*
Leibowitz, Herbert Akiba *English language educator, author*
Leichter, Franz S. *federal agency administrator*
Leichtling, Michael Alfred *lawyer*
†Leifer, Edgar *physician, medical educator*
Leighton, Lawrence Ward *investment banker*
Leinwand, Freda *photographer*
Leinwand, Harris Donald *lawyer*
Leisure, Peter Keeton *federal judge*
Leitman, Barry Steven *radiologist, educator*
†Leive, Cindi *editor-in-chief*
†Leland, Jack *cosmetics executive*
Leland, Richard G(uy) *lawyer*
Lelyveld, Joseph Salem *writer, retired newspaper editor, correspondent*
†Lemann, Nicholas B. *journalist, writer*
†Lemblé, Patrick *chef*
Lencek, Rado Ludovik *Slavic languages educator*
L'Engle, Madeleine (Mrs. Hugh Franklin) *writer*
Lentner, Howard Henry *political scientist*
†Leonard, Arthur Sherman *law educator, journalist*
Leonard, Edwin Deane *lawyer*
†Leonard, Elmore John *novelist, screenwriter*
†Leonard, Richard Davis *minister*
†Leonard, Zoe *artist*
†Leonardi, Peter M. *marketing professional*
†LePage, William *composer*
Leppard, Raymond John *conductor, harpsichordist*
Lerangis, Peter D. *writer*
Leritz, Lawrence R. *choreographer, singer, actor, dancer, producer*
Lerner, Frederic Howard *finance executive, educator*
Lerner, Martin *museum curator*
Lerner, Max Kasner *lawyer*
Lesch, Michael Oscar *lawyer*
†Lesk, Ann Berger *lawyer*
†Leslee, Ray *composer*
Leslie, John Webster, Jr., (Jack Leslie) *communications company executive*
Leslie, Seymour Marvin *communications executive, director*
Lesman, Michael Steven *lawyer*
Lessing, Brian Reid *actuary*
†Letterman, David *television personality, producer, comedian, writer*
Leubert, Alfred Otto Paul *international business consultant, investor*
Levai, Pierre Alexandre *art gallery executive*
Leval, Pierre Nelson *federal judge*
Levander, Andrew Joshua *lawyer*
Levandowsky, Michael *marine biologist*
Leven, Ann Ruth *financial planner, consultant*
Levi, Louise Landes *poet, translator, musician*
Levie, Joseph Henry *lawyer, banker*
Levin, Alan M. *television journalist*
Levin, Ezra Gurion *lawyer*
†Levin, Ira *author, playwright*
Levin, Martin P. *publishing executive, lawyer*
Levin, Michael Joseph *lawyer*
†Levin, Michael Stuart *steel company executive*
Levin, Roger Michael *lawyer*
Levine, Alan *lawyer*
Levine, David *artist*
†Levine, Ellen R. *magazine editor*
Levine, James *conductor, pianist, artistic director*
Levine, Lawrence Steven *lawyer*
Levine, Louis *museum director, archaeologist*
Levine, Melvin Charles *lawyer*
Levine, Naomi Bronheim *academic administrator*
Levine, Robert Jay *lawyer*
Levine, Ronald Jay *lawyer*
Levinson, Harlan Shaw *investment banker*
Levinson, Robert Alan *textiles executive*
Levinson, Warren Mitchell *broadcast journalist*
Levit, Mark Sheldon *advertising executive*
Levitan, David M(aurice) *lawyer, educator*
Levitan, James A. *lawyer*
Levitan, Max Fishel *geneticist, anatomy educator*
Levitan, Stephan J. *psychiatrist*
Levitt, Harry *speech and hearing scientist*
Levitz, Paul Elliot *publishing executive*
Levoy, Myron *author*
Levy, Alan Joseph *editor, journalist, writer*
Levy, Albert *family physician*
†Levy, Clifford J. *reporter*
†Levy, Gerald Dun *nonprofit organization administrator*
†Levy, Kenneth Michael *lawyer*
Levy, Mark Allan *lawyer*

Levy, Matthew Degen *investment banking technology and operations company executive, consumer products business development and planning executive, management consultant*
†Levy, Matthys Paul *structural engineer*
Levy, Stanley Herbert *lawyer*
Lew, Jacob *public administration educator*
Lewis, Alfred Baker *psychiatrist*
Lewis, Donna Cunningham *banker, communications consultant*
†Lewis, Frank B. *lawyer*
Lewis, Jonathan Joseph *surgical oncologist, molecular biologist, educator*
†Lewis, Loida Nicolas *food products holding company executive*
Lewis, Richard A. *educational association administrator, writer*
Lewis, Richard Warren *advertising agency executive*
†Lewis, Russell T. *publishing executive*
Lewis, Sherman Richard, Jr., *investment banker*
Lewis, W. Walker *strategic and financial advisory company executive*
LeWitt, Sol *artist*
Lewy, Robert Max *physician*
Lewyn, Ann Salfeld *retired English as a second language educator*
Lewyn, Thomas Mark *lawyer*
Li, Qin *television anchor, reporter, director, producer*
†Li, Yingchen *diversified financial services company executive, consultant*
Libby, John Kelway *financial services company executive*
†Libeskind, Daniel *architect*
Libin, Paul *theatre executive, producer*
LiBretto, John Charles *television director*
Lichtblau, John H. *economist*
Lieberman, James S. *physiatrist, neurologist*
Lieberman, Seymour *biochemist, educator*
Liebermann, Lowell *composer, pianist, conductor*
Liebman, Theodore *architect*
Lifland, William Thomas *lawyer*
Lifton, Robert Kenneth *diversified companies executive*
Lighter, Jeremiah B. *book designer, artist, illustrator, educator*
Lighter, Lawrence *lawyer*
Lilien, Mark Ira *executive*
†Limbaugh, Rush Hudson *radio and talk show host*
Lin, Maria C. H. *lawyer*
Lin, Pi-Tang *physician*
†Linares, Carlos *language educator, consultant*
Linburn, Michael Richard *investment company executive*
Lindenbaum, Samuel Harvey *lawyer*
Linder, Bertram Norman *foundation administrator, horse-breeder, actor*
Lindquist, Richard James *portfolio manager*
Lindros, Eric Bryan *hockey player*
Lindsay, George Peter *lawyer*
Lingelbach, Albert Lane *lawyer*
Lingeman, Richard Roberts *editor, writer*
†Linker, Arthur S. *lawyer*
Linsenmeyer, John Michael *lawyer*
Linz, Werner Mark *international publishing executive*
Lipan, Howard Kenneth *information and technology consultant*
Lipin, Joan Carol *healthcare executive, consultant*
Lipkin, Martin *physician, scientist*
Lipman, Ira Ackerman *security service company executive*
Lipper, Kenneth *investment banker, author, producer*
Lipscomb, Thomas Heber, III, *media executive*
Lipsey, Robert Edward *economist, educator*
Lipsky, Burton G. *lawyer*
Lipsky, Pat *artist*
Lipson, Charles Barry *finance company executive*
Lipton, Audrey King *lawyer, career management consultant*
Lipton, Charles *public relations executive*
Lipton, Charles Jules *lawyer*
Lipton, Joan Elaine *advertising executive*
Lipton, Lester *ophthalmologist, entrepreneur*
Lipton, Martin *lawyer*
Lipton, Robert Steven *lawyer*
Lisman, Richard D. *ophthalmic plastic surgeon*
Liss, Norman *lawyer*
Little, Nancy Jane *art school director*
Little, Robert David *library science educator*
Liu, Charles *astrophysicist*
Liu, Si-kwang *veterinary pathologist*
†Livshiz, Boris *software engineer*
Llinás, Rodolfo Riascos *medical educator, researcher*
Lloyd, Jean *early childhood educator*
†Lo, Shaw-Hwa *statistician, educator*
Lobo, Rogerio A. *obstetrician and gynecologist*
Lockshin, Michael Dan *rheumatologist*
Lockwood, Helshi *advertising executive*
Lodge, Henry Sears *physician*
†Lodge, Kirsten *language educator*
Loeb, John Langeloth, Jr., *investment counselor*
†Loeb, John Nichols *physician, educator*
Loeb, Larry Morris *communications company executive*
Loeb, Marshall Robert *journalist*
Loeb, Peter Kenneth *money manager*
Loengard, John Borg *photographer, editor*
Loengard, Richard Otto, Jr., *lawyer*
Logan, Don *publishing executive*
†Logan, Douglas George *sports commissioner*
Logan, J. Murray *investment manager*
†Logan, Kenneth Richard *lawyer*
Logan, Thaddeus Sumner, III, *architect*
Lombardo, Peter Charles *dermatologist*
London, Herbert Ira *humanities educator, institute executive*
London, Ira D. *lawyer*
†London, Martin *lawyer*
†Londorenko, Oksana G. *computer engineer*
Loney, Glenn Meredith *drama educator*

†Long, David L. *former magazine publisher*
Long, Donna Elaine *fundraising executive*
Longstreth, Bevis *lawyer*
Loo, Marcus Hsieu-Hong *urologist, physician, educator*
Loomis, Robert Duane *publishing company executive, author*
Lopchinsky, Richard Alan *surgeon, educator*
Lopez, Kathryn Jean *editor, reporter*
Lopez, Pedro Felipe *social worker, educator, playwright, writer*
Lopez-Cobos, Jesus *conductor*
Loprest, Frank James, Jr., *lawyer*
Lorber, Barbara Heyman *communications executive*
Lorch, Ernest Henry *lawyer*
Lorch, Maristella De Panizza *medieval and Renaissance scholar, writer*
Lord, Barbara Joanni *lawyer*
Lord, M. G. *writer*
Lord, Marvin *apparel company executive*
Lord, Richard Dennis *photographer*
Lord, Robert Wilder *retired editor and writer*
Loring, John Robbins *artist, writer*
Loscalzo, Anthony Joseph *lawyer*
LoSchiavo, Linda Bosco *library director*
Loss, Margaret Ruth *lawyer*
Lotas, Judith Patton *advertising executive*
Lotwin, Stanford Gerald *lawyer*
†Lou, Liza *artist*
Loudon, Dorothy *actress*
†Louganis, Greg E. *Olympic athlete, researcher, actor*
†Love, Robert *editor*
Lovell, Whitfield *artist*
Low, Anthony *English language educator*
Low, Richard H. *broadcasting executive, producer*
†Lowe, John Anthony *lawyer*
Lowell, Stanley Edgar *accountant*
Lowenfeld, Andreas Frank *law educator, arbitrator*
Lowenfels, Fred M. *lawyer*
Lowenfels, Lewis David *lawyer*
Lowenstein, Louis *legal educator*
Lowry, Glenn David *art museum director*
Lowy, George Theodore *lawyer*
Lubell, Michael Stephen *physicist, researcher, physics educator*
Lubetski, Edith Esther *librarian*
Lubkin, Virginia Leila *ophthalmologist*
Lublin, Fred D. *neurologist, researcher*
Lublin, Joann Sandra *journalist*
Lubovitch, Lar *dancer, choreographer*
Lubow, Nathan Myron *accountant*
Lucander, Henry *investment banker*
Lucas, James E(vans) *operatic director*
Lucci, Susan *actress*
Luce, Charles Franklin *former utilities executive, lawyer*
Luce, Henry, III, *foundation administrator*
Lucht, John Charles *management consultant, executive recruiter, writer*
Luckman, Sharon Gersten *arts administrator*
Luers, Wendy Wilson Woods *non-profit foundation executive*
Luers, William Henry *foundation administrator, former art museum administrator*
Luke, Douglas Sigler *business executive*
†Luke, John Anderson, Jr., *paper, packaging and chemical company executive*
Luks, Allan Barry *executive director*
†Luloff, Philip *medical doctor, psychiatrist, educator*
Lunardini, Christine Anne *writer, historian, school administrator*
Lundberg, George David, II, *medical editor in chief, pathologist*
†Lundgren, Terry J. *retail executive*
Lunding, Christopher Hanna *lawyer*
Lundy, Marilynn Frances *designer, consultant*
Luntz, Maurice Harold *ophthalmologist*
Lupert, Leslie Allan *lawyer*
Lupkin, Stanley Neil *lawyer*
Luria, Mary Mercer *lawyer*
Lurie, Ranan Raymond *political cartoonist, political analyst, artist, lecturer*
Lust, Herbert Cohnfeldt, II, *finance executive*
†Lustenberger, Louis Charles, Jr., *lawyer*
Lustgarten, Celia Sophie *freelance consultant, writer*
Lustig, David Carl, III, *lawyer*
Lutringer, Richard Emil *lawyer*
Lutzker, Elliot Howard *lawyer*
Lynch, Gerald Weldon *academic administrator, psychologist*
†Lynch, Luke Daniel, Jr., *lawyer*
Lynn, Judith *opera singer, artist, voice teacher*
Lynn, Theodore Stanley *lawyer*
†Lynne, Michael *film company executive*
†Lynton, Harold Stephen *lawyer*
Lyon, Carl Francis, Jr., *lawyer*
†Lyons, John Matthew *telecommunications executive, broadcasting executive*
Lyons, Nick *publishing executive*
†Lytle, Ellen Wendy *artist*
Ma, Yo-Yo *cellist*
Maas, Werner Karl *microbiology educator*
†Maazel, Lorin *conductor, composer, violinist*
Mabilangan, Felipe Hugo, Jr., *Philippine diplomat*
Mabrey, Vicki *news correspondent, anchor*
MacAfee, Norman *writer, translator*
Macan, William Alexander, IV, *lawyer*
†Macbeath, Keith S. *business strategist*
Macchiarola, Frank Joseph *academic administrator, educator*
Macdonald, R. Fulton Smith *venture developer, business educator*
MacDonald, Ronald Francis *financial services company executive*
Macer-Story, Eugenia Ann *writer, artist*
MacGowan, Sandra Firelli *publishing executive, publishing educator*
Mack, Dennis Wayne *lawyer*
†Mack, Phyllis Green *retired librarian*
Mackauf, Stephen Henry *lawyer*

MacKay, Malcolm *executive search consultant*
Macken, Daniel Loos *physician, educator*
Mackenzie, Charles Rudd *lawyer*
Mackey, Patricia Elaine *university librarian*
†Mackie, Robert Gordon *costume and fashion designer*
Mackler, Tina *artist*
MacLachlan, Patricia *author*
MacLean, Babcock *lawyer*
†MacNamara, Brian Scott *veterinarian, law educator*
MacRae, Cameron Farquhar, III, *lawyer*
Macri, Theodore William *book publisher*
Macris, Michael *lawyer*
Macris, Nicholas Theodore *allergist*
†Mactas, Mark V. *diversified financial services company executive*
Macurdy, John Edward *basso*
Macy, Steven C. *real estate investor*
Madden, John Patrick *lawyer*
Madden, Michael Daniel *finance company executive*
Madsen, Loren Wakefield *sculptor*
Madsen, Stephen Stewart *lawyer*
Maertin, James Lee *accountant*
Magee-Egan, Pauline Cecilia *psychology and management educator*
Mager, Ezra Pascal *investment management company executive*
Magliato, Henry J. *orthopedic surgeon*
Mahler, Richard Joseph *internist*
Mahon, Arthur J. *lawyer*
Mahoney, Margaret Ellerbe *foundation executive*
Maidman, Richard Harvey Mortimer *lawyer*
†Mailer, Norman *author*
Main, Patricia Englander *investor*
†Makari, George Jack *psychiatrist*
†Makovsky, Kenneth Dale *public relations executive*
Malamed, Seymour H. *motion picture company executive*
Maldonado-Bear, Rita Marinita *economist, educator*
Malefakis, Edward E. *history educator*
Malernee, James Kent, Jr., *financial consultant*
Malgieri, Nick *chef, author, educator*
Malin, Irving *English literature educator, literary critic*
Malkin, Barry *film editor, consultant*
Malkin, Michael M. *lawyer*
Malkin, Peter Laurence *lawyer, real estate investor*
Malkin, Stanley Lee *neurologist*
Mamet, David Alan *playwright, director, essayist*
Mamlok, Ursula *composer, educator*
†Manahan, Anna *actress*
Manassah, Jamal Tewfek *electrical engineer, educator, management consultant*
†Mandabach, Caryn *television producer*
Mandel, Irwin Daniel *dentist*
Mandelbaum, Harold Neil *accountant*
Mandelker, Lawrence Arthur *lawyer*
Mandelstam, Charles Lawrence *lawyer*
Mandracchia, Violet Ann Palermo *psychotherapist, educator*
Maneker, Morton M. *lawyer*
Maneker, Roberta S(ue) *public relations executive*
Maney, Michael Mason *lawyer*
Mangan, Mona *association executive, lawyer*
Manger, William Muir *internist, educator*
Manges, James Horace *investment banker*
†Manglano-Ovalle, Inigo *artist, sculptor*
Mann, Anthony *minister, dean*
Mann, Frank Bert *visual artist, painter*
†Mann, Maria *photojournalist, director*
Mann, Pamela A. *lawyer*
†Manning, Dennis J. *insurance company executive*
Manoff, Richard Kalman *advertising executive, public health consultant, author*
Mansi, Joseph Anneillo *public relations company executive*
Mansouri, Lotfollah (Lotfi Mansouri) *retired general director of opera company*
Mantel, Allan David *lawyer*
Mantle, Raymond Allan *lawyer*
Manton, Edwin Alfred Grenville *insurance company executive*
Manuell, Lynn Marie *booking agent, singer, actress*
Mapes, Glynn Dempsey *newspaper editor*
Maraynes, Allan Lawrence *filmmaker, television producer*
†Marcellino, Stephen Michael *lawyer*
Marchi, Lorraine June *social services administrator*
Marcosson, Thomas I. *service company executive*
Marcus, Eric Peter *lawyer*
Marcus, Eric Robert *psychiatrist*
Marcus, Gwen Ellen *sculptor*
Marcus, Maria Lenhoff *lawyer, law educator*
†Marcus, Norman Jay *physician, educator*
Marcusa, Fred Haye *lawyer*
Marcuse, Adrian Gregory *academic administrator*
Marden, Brice *artist*
Marder, John G. *real estate investor, marketing consultant, corporate director, bison rancher*
Marder, Michael Zachary *dentist, researcher, educator*
†Mardin, Arif *music industry executive, musician*
†Marello, Matthew *artist*
Margalith, Helen Margaret *retired librarian*
Margolin, Jean Spielberg *artist*
Margolis, David I(srael) *industrial manufacturing executive*
Margolis, Mark Neal *actor*
Margulis, Alexander Rafailo *physician, educator*
†Mariani, Michael Matthew *lawyer*
Marin, Deborah B. *psychiatrist, educator*
Marincola, John *classics educator*
Marinoff, Elaine *artist*
Mariotti, Steve J. *entrepreneur, financial educator, president and founder NFTE*
Mark, Laurence Peter *anesthesiology educator*

Mark, Reuben *consumer products company executive*
†Markard, Marlene Maria *lawyer*
†Markowitz, Gerald E. *historian, educator*
†Markowitz, Martin H. *physician*
Marks, Frances *obstetrician-gynecologist, educator*
Marks, Jon Owen *physician*
Marks, Lillian Shapiro *secretarial studies educator, author*
Marks, Paul Alan *oncologist, cell biologist, educator*
Marks, Robert *music director, composer, educator*
Marks, Theodore Lee *lawyer*
Markson, David M. *writer*
Marlas, James Constantine *holding company executive*
Marlin, John Tepper *economist, writer, consultant*
Marlin, Richard *lawyer*
†Marpillero, Sandro *architectural firm executive*
Marrero, Victor *lawyer, judge*
Marrone, Stephen Richard *critical care nurse, educator*
Marshak, Hilary Wallach *psychotherapist, owner, small business owner*
Marshall, Alton Garwood *real estate counselor*
Marshall, John Richard *opera director*
Marshall, Michael Borden *marketing executive*
†Marshall, Robert *film director, television director, theater director, choreographer*
Marshall, Sheila Hermes *lawyer*
Marshall, Thomas Carlisle *applied physics educator*
Marshella, Thomas Joseph *financial analyst*
Marston, Robert Andrew *public relations executive*
Martin, Elliot Edwards *theatrical producer*
Martin, George J., Jr., *lawyer*
Martin, Judith Sylvia *journalist, author*
Martin, Linda Gaye *demographer, economist*
Martin, Malcolm Elliot *lawyer*
Martin, Mary Anne *art gallery owner*
Martin, Michael Townsend *racing horse stable executive, sports marketing executive*
Martin, Paul Ross *editor*
Martini, Richard K. *theatrical producer*
Martino, Cheryl Derby *insurance company secretary*
†Martins, Peter *ballet master, choreographer, dancer*
Martone, Patricia Ann *lawyer*
Marty, Alvin Leonard *economist, educator*
Marx, Herbert Lewis, Jr., *arbitrator*
Maryschuk, Olga Yaroslava *artist, executive assistant*
†Marzorati, Gerald *editor*
†Marzulli, John Anthony, Jr., *lawyer*
Masey, Jack *exhibition designer*
†Masi, Jane Virginia *marketing and sales consultant*
Masin, Michael Terry *lawyer*
Maslow, Will *lawyer, association executive*
Mason, Bobbie Ann *novelist, short story writer*
Massel, Elihu Saul *lawyer*
Massey, Andrew John *conductor, composer*
Masters, Jon Joseph *corporate governance consultant, management consultant*
Masterson, James Francis *psychiatrist*
Materna, Joseph Anthony *lawyer*
Mathers, William Harris *lawyer*
Mathews, Jack Wayne *journalist, film critic*
Mathews, Michael Stone *investment banker*
†Mathews, Norman *playwright, composer*
†Mathias, Thelma *sculptor, video artist, curator*
Mathisen, Harold Clifford *portfolio management executive*
Matseoane, Carol *social worker*
†Matsui, Connie L. *youth organization executive*
Matteson, William Bleecker *lawyer*
Matthews, Norman Stuart *department store executive*
Mattila, Daniel E. *priest, social worker*
†Mattli, Walter *political scientist, educator*
Mattson, Francis Oscar *retired librarian and rare books curator*
Mattson, Marlin Roy Albin *health facility administrator, psychiatry educator*
Matus, Wayne Charles *lawyer*
Matzner, Chester Michael *writer*
Maughan, Sir Deryck *bank executive*
Maulsby, Allen Farish *lawyer*
†Maurrasse, David J. *educator, consultant*
Maxfield, Guy Budd *lawyer, educator*
Maxwell, Anders John *investment banker*
Maxwell, Kenneth Robert *historian*
May, Gita *language and literature educator*
May, William Frederick *manufacturing executive*
Mayer, Carl Joseph *prosecutor, lawyer*
Mayer, Eve Orlans *retired public relations and marketing consultant, writer*
Mayer, Rosemary *artist*
Mayer, Stephan Anthony *neurologist*
Mayer, William Emilio *investor*
Mayerson, Philip *classics educator*
Mayerson, Sandra Elaine *lawyer*
Maynard, John Rogers *English educator*
Maynard, Virginia Madden *charitable organization executive*
Maysilles, Elizabeth *speech communication professional, educator*
Maysles, Albert H. *filmmaker*
Mazzola, Anthony Thomas *editor, art consultant, designer, writer*
Mazzola, John William *former performing arts center executive, consultant*
Mazzucelli, Colette Grace Celia *author, multimedia educator*
†McCaffrey, Carlyn Sundberg *lawyer*
†McCarrick, Edward R. *magazine publisher*
†McCarthy, Cormac *writer*
McCarthy, Patrick *magazine publishing executive*
McCarthy, Robert Emmett *lawyer*
McCartin, Thomas Joseph *advertising executive*
McCarty, Maclyn *medical scientist*
McCarty, V.K. *publisher, chaplain, librarian*
McCaslin, Teresa Eve *human resources executive*
McCleary, Benjamin Ward *investment banker*
McClelland, Shearwood, Jr., *orthopaedic surgeon*
McClimon, Timothy John *lawyer*
McClintock, Robert Oliver *history and education educator*
†McConnico, John *photojournalist*
McCormack, Howard Michael *lawyer*
McCormack, Thomas Joseph *playwright, retired publishing company executive*
†McCormick, Donald E. *librarian, archivist*
McCormick, Hugh Thomas *lawyer*
McCormick, Pamela Ann *artist, sculptor*
McCormick, Steven A. *pathologist*
†McCourt, Frank (Francis McCourt) *writer*
McCrary, Eugenia Lester (Mrs. Dennis Daughtry McCrary) *civic worker, writer*
McCredie, James Robert *fine arts educator*
McCrie, Robert Delbert *editor, publisher, educator*
Mc Crory, Wallace Willard *pediatrician, educator*
Mc Cullough, J. Lee *industrial psychologist*
McCutchen, William Walter, Jr., *management educator*
McDarrah, Fred William *photographer, editor, writer, photography reviewer*
†McDavid, William Henry *lawyer*
McDermott, Alice *writer*
†McDermott, Robert J. *lawyer*
†McDonald, Audra Ann *actress*
Mcdonald, Gregory Christopher *author*
†McDonald, Stephen Douglas *banker*
McDonald, Thomas Paul *controller*
McDonell, Neil Edwin *lawyer*
McDonell, Robert Terry *magazine editor, novelist*
†McDonell, Terry *editor*
†McDowell, David Michael *psychiatrist, researcher, psychiatrist, educator*
McFadden, Mary Josephine *fashion industry executive*
McFadden, Robert Dennis *reporter*
McFeely, William Drake *publishing company executive*
McGanney, Thomas *lawyer*
McGarry, John Patrick, Jr., *retired advertising agency executive*
McGarvey, Mary Hewitt *writer*
McGeady, Sister Mary Rose *religious organization administrator, psychologist*
†McGhee, Herschey *public relations executive, writer, poet*
†McGill, Jay *magazine publisher*
Mc Gillicuddy, John Francis *retired banker*
McGlynn, William Charles *brokerage house executive*
McGoldrick, John Lewis *lawyer*
McGonagle, Duncan Francis *mental health nurse, substance abuse counselor*
†McGonigle, Thomas *writer, humanities educator*
McGowan, Richard Stephen *lawyer*
Mc Gowin, William Edward *artist*
McGrath, Christopher Thomas *lawyer*
McGrath, Eugene R. *utility company executive*
McGrath, Judith *broadcast executive*
McGrath, Thomas J. *lawyer, writer, film producer*
McGraw, Harold Whittlesey, Jr., *publishing executive*
†McGraw, Harold Whittlesey, III, (Terry McGraw) *information company executive*
McHugh, Caril Eisenstein Dreyfuss *art dealer, gallery director, consultant*
Mc Inerney, Denis *lawyer*
McIntosh, DeCourcy Eyre *independent scholar and writer*
†McKay, Geoff *private equity investor*
McKay, Kenneth Gardiner *physicist, electronics company executive*
†McKeever, Katherine *model agency executive*
†McKelvey, Andrew J. *advertising executive*
McKenna, George Norton *government educator*
McKenna, William Michael *advertising executive*
McKenzie, Kevin Patrick *artistic director*
McKenzie, Mary Beth *artist*
McKinley-Haas, Mary *artist*
McKinnell, Henry A. *pharmaceutical company executive*
McKinnon, Floyd Wingfield *textile executive*
McLachlan, Sarah *composer, musician*
McLaughlin, Joseph Michael *federal judge, law educator*
†McLaughlin, Joseph Thomas *lawyer*
†McLean, David Lyle *lawyer*
†McLendon, Sally *linguist, educator, anthropologist*
†McMillan, L. Londell *lawyer*
McMillan, Marilyn Ayres *information systems scientist, university official*
McMullan, William Patrick, III, *investment banker*
Mc Murtry, James Gilmer, III, *neurosurgeon*
†McMurtry, Larry Jeff *author*
McNally, John Joseph *retired lawyer*
†McNally, Terrence *playwright*
McNamara, J(ohn) Donald *retired lawyer, business executive*
McNamara, Mary E. *nonprofit executive, asset manager, minister*
McNelis, Edward Joseph *chemistry educator*
†McPherson, David *music company executive*
McPherson, James Lowell *writer*
†McPherson, Mary Patterson *charitable foundation executive*
McQuown, Judith Hershkowitz *author, financial advisor*
McSloy, Steven Paul *lawyer*
Meachin, David James Percy *investment banker*
Mead, Lawrence Myers, III, *political science educator*
Meade, Marion *author*
Meadow, Lynne (Carolyn Meadow) *theatrical producer and director*
†Meadows, Denis John *writer, director*
†Megibow, Alec J. *radiologist, educator*
Mehlman, Lon Douglas *information technology specialist, investment banker, venture capitalist*
†Mehta, A. Sonny *publishing company executive*
Mei, Dolores Marie *research administrator*
Meigher, S. Christopher, III, *communications and media executive, publisher*
Meisel, Martin *English and comparative literature educator*
Meisel, Perry *English educator*
Meiselas, Susan Clay *photographer*
Meister, Robert Allen *lawyer*
Meister, Ronald William *lawyer*
Mellins, Robert B. *pediatrician, educator*
Mellins, Thomas Harrison *architectural historian*
Melloan, George Richard *editor, columnist, writer*
Melnick, Ralph *library director, secondary school educator,*
Melone, Joseph James *retired insurance company executive*
Meltzer, Daniel B. *playwright, educator, writer*
†Meltzer, Harold *performing company executive, composer*
Meltzer, Milton *author*
†Meltzer, Roger *lawyer*
Melvin, Russell Johnston *magazine publishing consultant*
Menand, Louis *literature educator*
Menche, David Solomon *orthopaedic surgeon*
Mencher, Melvin *journalist, retired educator*
Mendell, Oliver M. *banking executive*
Mendelsohn, Naomi *biomedical pharmaceutical consultant*
†Mendelsohn, Susan Lynn *psychologist, researcher*
Mendelson, Haim *artist, educator, art gallery director*
Menschel, Robert Benjamin *investment banker*
Mentz, Barbara Antonello *lawyer*
Mentz, Lawrence *lawyer*
Menza, Claudia Marcella *literary agent*
†Mercado-Valdes, Frank *broadcast executive*
Merchant, Ismail Noormohamed *film producer, film director*
Mercorella, Anthony J. *lawyer, former state supreme court justice*
†Merkin, David *reference librarian*
Meron, Theodor *judge, law educator, researcher*
Merow, John *lawyer*
Merrifield, Robert Bruce *biochemist, educator*
Merrill, George Vanderneth *lawyer, investment executive*
Merrill, Thomas Wendell *lawyer, educator*
Merris, Donna Rose *lawyer*
Merriss, Philip Ramsay, Jr., *banker*
Merritt, Jean *consulting firm executive*
Mertens, Joan R. *museum curator, art historian*
Mesnikoff, Alvin Murray *psychiatry educator*
Messer, Thomas Maria *museum director*
Messier, Mark Douglas *hockey player*
Messner, Thomas G. *advertising executive, copywriter*
Mestres, Ricardo Angelo, Jr., *lawyer*
Metz, Emmanuel Michael *investment company executive, lawyer*
Metz, Robert Roy *publisher, editor*
†Metzger, Barry *lawyer*
Meunier, Monique *dancer*
Mew, Calvin Marshall *advertising executive*
†Meyer, Edgar *musician, composer*
Meyer, Edward Henry *advertising agency executive*
Meyer, Fred Josef *financial executive*
Meyer, Karl Ernest *journalist*
†Meyer, Mark Alan *lawyer*
Meyer, Pearl *executive compensation consultant*
Meyer, Pucci *newspaper editor*
Meyer, Sheldon *publisher*
Meyer-Bahlburg, Heino F.L. *psychologist, educator*
Meyerhoff, Erich *librarian, administrator*
Meyers, John Allen *magazine publisher*
Meyers, Paul Andrew *physician, educator*
†Meyers, Philip M. *physician*
Miano, Louis Stephen *arts advisor*
Michael, Douglas John (Wm. Seebring) *playwright, cartoonist*
†Michaels, Alan Richard *sports commentator*
Michaels, Lorne *television writer, producer*
Michaelson, Arthur M. *lawyer*
Michels, Robert *psychiatrist, educator*
Michelsen, Christopher Bruce Hermann *surgeon*
Michelson, Gertrude Geraldine *retired retail company executive*
Michenfelder, Joseph Francis *public relations executive*
†Michielli, Frank V. *architectural firm executive*
Michigan, Alan *lawyer*
Middendorf, John Harlan *English literature educator*
Middlebrook, Diane Wood *English language educator, writer*
Middleton, David *physicist, applied mathematician, educator*
Mikita, Joseph Karl *broadcasting executive*
Milbank, Jeremiah *foundation executive*
Mildvan, Donna *infectious diseases physician*
†Milford, Nancy Winston *writer, English educator*
Milgrim, Roger Michael *lawyer*
Miller, Alan *software executive, management specialist*
Miller, Andrew Kenneth *management consultant*
†Miller, Anthony G. *advertising executive*
Miller, Arthur Madden *lawyer, investment banker*
Miller, Barbara Kenton *retired librarian*
Miller, Bebe *choreographer*
Miller, Caroline *editor-in-chief*
Miller, Charles Hampton *lawyer*
Miller, Corbin Russell *investment company executive*
Miller, Darcy M. *publishing executive*
Miller, Edward Daniel *financial services executive*
†Miller, Erika *on-air business news reporter*
Miller, Ernest Charles *management consultant*
Miller, Harry Brill *scenic designer, actor, director, acting instructor, lyricist, interior designer*
Miller, Harvey R. *lawyer, bankruptcy reorganization specialist*
Miller, Harvey S. Shipley *foundation trustee, private investor*
Miller, Jill Lee *lawyer*
Miller, Joan Leff *artist*
Miller, John R. *accountant*
Miller, Joseph Anthony *healthcare executive, psychotherapist*
Miller, Lisa Friedman *psychology educator*
Miller, Michael Jeffrey *editor, columnist*
Miller, Morgan Lincoln *textile manufacturing company executive*
Miller, Nancy K. *literature educator*
Miller, Neil Stuart *advertising executive*
Miller, Paul S(amuel) *lawyer*
Miller, Peggy A(nn) *lawyer*
Miller, Richard Kidwell *artist, actor, educator*
Miller, Richard McDermott *sculptor*
Miller, Richard Steven *lawyer*
Miller, Robert *advertising executive*
Miller, Sanford Marvin *anesthesiology educator*
Miller, Steven Scott *lawyer*
Miller, Walter James *English and humanities educator, writer*
†Miller, William Harlowe, Jr., *lawyer*
Miller, William Jacob *public relations executive*
Millett, Kate (Katherine Murray Millett) *political activist, sculptor, artist, writer*
†Milliken, Frances J. *finance educator*
†Mills, Barry *academic administrator, lawyer*
Mills, Linda Gayle *social work and law educator*
Millstein, Ira M. *lawyer, lecturer*
Milmed, Paul Kussy *lawyer*
Milonas, Minos *artist, designer, poet*
Minarik, Else Holmelund (Bigart Minarik) *author*
Mincer, Jacob *economics educator*
Minick, Michael *publishing executive*
Minicucci, Robert A. *business executive*
Mininberg, David T. *pediatric urology surgeon, educator*
Minkel, Herbert Philip, Jr., *lawyer*
Minkowitz, Martin *lawyer, former state government official*
Minotti, Diana Lynn *art appraiser, consultant*
Mintz, Norman Nelson *investment banker, educator*
Mintz, Samuel Isaiah *English language educator, writer*
Mintz, Shlomo *conductor, violist, violinist*
Mintz, Walter *investment company executive*
Mironovich, Alex *publisher*
†Mirsky, Sonya Wohl *librarian, curator*
Mishne, Judith Marks *social work educator, psychotherapist*
†Mital, Seema *cardiologist, pediatrician, physician*
†Mitchell, Arthur *dancer, choreographer, educator*
Mitnick, Hal *rheumatologist*
Mitterand, Henri C. *education educator, writer*
Mittl, Rainer N. *ophthalmologist*
†Mittman, Lawrence *lawyer*
Mock, Eric V. *lawyer*
Mockler, Robert Joseph *management educator*
Modlin, Howard S. *lawyer*
Moerdler, Charles Gerard *lawyer*
Mohr, Jay Preston *neurologist, educator*
†Mold, David F. *performing arts educator, director*
†Moldow, Susan *publishing executive*
†Molho, Emanuel *publisher*
†Moline, Jacqueline *occupational physician*
Molleur, Denis Richard *lawyer*
Moloney, Thomas Joseph *lawyer*
Molz, Redmond Kathleen *public administration educator*
Mombaerts, Peter *biology educator*
Monahan, Courtney Wilson *lawyer*
Mondlin, Marvin *retail executive, antiquarian book dealer*
Monk, Meredith Jane *artistic director, composer, choreographer, filmmaker, director*
Montellaro, Randell *lawyer*
†Montgomerie, Bruce Mitchell *lawyer*
Mooney, Richard Emerson *writer*
†Moonves, Leslie *television company executive*
Moore, Ann S. *magazine executive*
Moore, Anne *physician*
Moore, Charles Hewes, Jr., *industrial and engineered products executive*
†Moore, David J. *media company executive*
Moore, Donald Francis *lawyer*
Moore, Honor *writer, educator*
Moore, John Joseph *lawyer*
Moore, John Kenneth *curator*
Moore, Michael Watson *musician, educator*
†Moore, Thomas Andrew *medical communications company executive*
Moore, Thomas Ronald (Lord Bridestowe) *lawyer*
†Mora, Raimundo *academic administrator, educator*
†Moran, Juliette M. *retired chemicals executive*
Moran, Martin Joseph *fundraising company executive*
†Morano, Kevin R. *mining company executive*
Morath, Max Edward *entertainer, composer, writer*
Morawetz, Cathleen Synge *mathematician*
Morehouse, Ward *human rights organization executive, publisher*
†Morehouse, Ward, III, *theater critic, playwright*
Moreira, Marcio Martins *advertising executive*
Moreno, Barry *historian, writer*
Morfopoulos, V. *metallurgical engineer, materials engineer*
Morgan, Arlene Notoro *university administrator*
Morgan, Frank Edward, II, *lawyer*
Morgan, Frederick *poet, editor*
Morgan, Jacqui *illustrator, painter, educator, writer*
†Morgan, Mary E. *publishing executive*

Morganstern, Gerald H. *lawyer*
Morgenson, Gretchen C. *reporter*
Morgenthau, Robert Morris *prosecutor*
Mori, Mariko *artist*
†Morial, Marc Haydel *former mayor, association executive*
Moroz, Pavel Emanuel *research scientist*
Morphy, James Calvin *lawyer*
Morreale, Joseph Constantino *higher education administrator, public administration educator, economic and financial consultant*
†Morris, David *publishing executive*
†Morris, Douglas Peter *recording company executive*
Morris, Edward William, Jr., *lawyer*
Morris, Eugene Jerome *retired lawyer*
†Morris, Francis Edward *lawyer*
Morris, John *composer, conductor, arranger*
Morris, Stephen Burritt *marketing information executive*
Morris, William Charles *investor*
Morrison, Patricia Kennealy *author*
Morrissey, Dolores Josephine *investment executive*
Morse, Carl Robert *writer, editor*
Morse, Edward Lewis *petroleum industry executive*
Morse, Robert Parker *investment company executive*
Morse, Stephen Scott *virologist, immunologist, epidemiologist*
†Mortimer, Ann O. *executive secretary*
†Morton, Joëlle *musician, editor*
Mosenson, Steven Harris *lawyer*
†Moses, Jeffrey Warren *cardiologist, educator*
Moskin, John Robert *editor, writer*
Moskin, Morton *lawyer, director*
†Moskowitz, Harry *pediatrics educator*
†Moskowitz, Martin A. *mathematician, educator*
†Mosley, Walter *writer*
†Moss, Adam Wender *editor*
Moss, Charles *advertising agency executive*
Moss, Melvin Lionel *anatomist, educator*
Mossavar-Rahmani, Bijan *oil and gas company executive*
†Mosse, Peter John Charles *financial services executive*
Moss-Salentijn, Letty (Aleida Moss-Salentijn) *anatomist, educator*
Most, Jack Lawrence *lawyer, consultant*
Motley, Constance Baker (Mrs. Joel Wilson Motley) *federal judge, former city official*
Mottola, Thomas *entertainment company executive*
Motzer, Robert John *oncologist, educator*
Mow, Van C. *engineering educator, researcher*
†Moy, Richard L. *virologist*
Moyer, David S. *executive search consultant*
†Moyers, Bill D. *journalist*
Moyers, Judith Davidson *television producer*
Moylan, Steve *publishing executive*
Moyne, John Abel *computer scientist, linguist, educator*
†Mtui, Estomih Phillip *medical educator*
Muccia, Joseph William *lawyer*
Muchnick, Richard Stuart *ophthalmologist, educator*
Mueller, Shirley Anne *lawyer, real estate broker*
†Mulhern, Patrick J. *lawyer, banker*
Mullaney, Thomas Joseph *lawyer*
†Mullarkey, Maureen *artist, critic*
Mullen, Peter P. *lawyer*
Muller, Charlotte Feldman *economist, educator*
Muller, Frank *mediator, arbitrator*
Muller, Jennifer *choreographer, dancer*
Mulligan, David Keith *consulting company executive, securities arbitrator*
Mulligan, Jeremiah T. *lawyer*
Mulligan, Timothy Hayden *public relations executive, writer*
Mullman, Michael S. *lawyer*
Mulvihill, William J. *former health science association administrator*
Mundell, Robert Alexander *economist, educator*
Mundheim, Robert Harry *law educator*
Munhall, Edgar *retired curator, art history educator*
Munro, Alice *author*
Munroe, George Barber *retired mining and manufacturing company executive*
Munzer, Stephen Ira *lawyer*
Muradian, Vazgen *musician, composer*
Murase, Jiro *lawyer*
†Murdoch, Lachlan Keith *publishing executive*
Murdoch, (Keith) Rupert *publisher*
Murdock, Robert Mead *curator*
†Murphy, Ann Pleshette *magazine editor-in-chief*
Murphy, Arthur William *lawyer, educator*
Murphy, Austin de la Salle *economist, educator, banker*
†Murphy, Donald B. *investment company executive*
†Murphy, Donna *actress*
Murphy, Elva Glenn *executive assistant*
Murphy, Helen *recording industry executive*
Murphy, James Edward *public relations and marketing executive*
Murphy, John Arthur *tobacco, food and brewing company executive*
Murphy, John B. *investment advisor*
Murphy, John Joseph, Jr., *investment company executive*
Murphy, Mark Joseph *enterprise sales executive*
Murphy, Patrice Ann (Pat Murphy) *writer*
Murphy, Ramon Jeremiah Castroviejo *physician, pediatrician*
Murphy, Richard William *retired foreign service officer, Middle East specialist, consultant*
Murphy, Rosemary *actress*
Murray, Richard Maximilian *insurance executive*
Musgrave, R. Kenton *federal judge*
Muskin, Victor Philip *lawyer*
Myerberg, Marcia *investment banker*
Myers, Gerald E. *humanities educator*
Nabi, Stanley Andrew *investment executive*
Nachman, Ralph Louis *physician, educator*
Nadelberg, Eric Paul *brokerage house executive*
Nadelson, Eileen Nora *lawyer*
Nadiri, M. Ishaq *economics educator, researcher, lecturer, consultant*
†Nadler-Hurvich, Hedda Carol *public relations executive*
Naegle, Madeline Anne *mental health nurse, educator*
Naftalis, Gary Philip *lawyer, educator*
Nagler, Harris M. *urologic surgeon*
Nagler, Stewart Gordon *insurance company executive*
Nagourney, Herbert *publishing company executive*
Nahas, Gabriel Georges *pharmacologist, educator, writer*
Naidich, Thomas Paul *neuroradiologist, educator*
†Naini, Ali *molecular genetisist, research scientist*
†Naka, Yoshifumi *surgeon, researcher*
Nakamura, James I. *economics educator*
Nakanishi, Koji *chemistry educator, research institute administrator*
Nance, Allan Taylor *retired lawyer*
Nash, Edward L. *advertising agency executive*
Nash, Paul LeNoir *lawyer*
†Nash, Stanley Louis *literature educator, religious studies educator*
†Nasr, George Elias *electrical engineer, consultant, computer engineer, educator*
Nassau, Michael Jay *lawyer*
†Natarajan, Mangai *criminal justice educator*
Nathan, Frederic Solis *lawyer*
Nathan, Paul S. *editor, writer*
†Nathanielsz, Peter William *physiologist*
Natori, Josie Cruz *apparel executive*
Navasky, Victor Saul *magazine editor, publisher*
Navratil, Gerald Anton *physicist, educator*
Nazem, Fereydoun F. *venture capitalist*
Necarsulmer, Henry *investment banker*
Nederlander, James Morton *theater executive*
Needham, George Austin *investment banker*
Neewoor, Anund Priyay *ambassador*
Neff, Thomas Joseph *executive search firm executive*
Negoita, Constantin Virgil *computer scientist, educator*
Negroponte, John Dimitri *ambassador*
†Neidell, Martin H. *lawyer*
Neiman, LeRoy *artist*
Nelson, Barbara Anne *judge*
Nelson, Edwin Stafford *actor, educator*
Nelson, Iris Dorothy *retired guidance and rehabilitation counselor*
Nelson, Louis *design and planning consultant*
Nelson, Merlin Edward *international business consultant, company director*
†Nelson, Richard *writer*
†Nelson, Stanley *film director, writer, film producer*
†Nelson, Wayne K. *advertising executive*
Nemec, Vernita Ellen (Vernita N'cognita) *artist, curator*
Nemser, Earl Harold *lawyer*
Netzer, Dick *economics educator*
Neubauer, Peter Bela *psychoanalyst*
Neuberg, Hans W. *internist, educator*
Neugeboren, Jay *author*
†Neuner, Robert *lawyer*
Neuspiel, Daniel Robert *pediatrician, epidemiologist*
Neuwirth, Alan James *lawyer*
Neuwirth, Gloria S. *lawyer*
Neuwirth, Robert Samuel *obstetrician, gynecologist*
Neveloff, Jay A. *lawyer*
Newbold, Herbert Leon, Jr., *psychiatrist, writer*
Newbold, John Lowe *banker, financial consultant*
†Newcomb, Jonathan *publishing executive*
Newell, Norman Dennis *paleontologist, geologist, museum curator, educator*
Newhouse, Nancy Riley *newspaper editor*
Newman, Arnold *photographer*
Newman, Craig Alan *lawyer*
†Newman, Frank Neil *retired bank executive*
Newman, Fredric Samuel *lawyer, business executive*
Newman, Geraldine Anne *advertising executive, inventor*
Newman, Howard Neal *lawyer, educator*
Newman, Joyce A. *obstetrician/gynecologist*
†Newman, Lawrence *lawyer, educator*
Newman, Lawrence Walker *lawyer*
Newman, Robert Gabriel *physician*
Ng, Helen M. *financier, civil engineer*
Nguyen, Dung Dang *physician*
Niccolini, Dianora *photographer*
Nicholas, James A. *surgeon, consultant, educator*
Nicholls, Richard H. *lawyer*
Nichols, Carol D. *real estate professional*
Nichols, Edie Diane *executive recruiter*
Nichols, Jeffrey Norman *geriatrician*
Nicholson, Shelia Elaine *senior print production manager*
†Nickoloff, Edward Lee *radiology physicist*
Nicol, Dominik *writer, photographer*
†Nicoll, Edward J. *internet financial company executive*
†Nieman, John Francis *advertising executive*
Niemiec, David Wallace *investment management executive*
Niles, Barbara Elliott *psychoanalyst*
Niles, Thomas Michael Tolliver *business association executive*
Nimer, Stephen *physician, leukemia researcher*
Nimetz, Gloria Lorch *real estate broker, photographer*
Nimkin, Bernard William *retired lawyer*
Nirenberg, Louis *mathematician, educator*
†Nisce, Lourdes *radiologist*
Nisenholtz, Martin Abram *telecommunications executive, educator*
Nixon, Agnes Eckhardt *television writer, producer*
Nixon, Daniel Walker *oncologist, researcher*
Noda, Takayo *artist*
Nolan, Christopher Aloysius, III, *real estate developer, architect*
Nolan, William Joseph, III, *banker*
Nonna, John Michael *lawyer*
†Norden, William Benjamin *lawyer*
Norell, Mark Allen *paleontology educator*
Norfolk, William Ray *lawyer*
Noris, Peter Dana *financial services executive*
Norman, Stephen Peckham *financial services company executive*
Norris, Floyd Hamilton *financial journalist*
North, Charles Laurence *poet, educator*
North, Steven Edward *lawyer, educator*
Norwick, Braham *textile specialist, consultant, columnist*
Notarbartolo, Albert *artist*
Novick, Nelson Lee *dermatologist, internist, writer, consultant, dermatological surgeon*
Novikoff, Harold Stephen *lawyer*
Novitz, Charles Richard *television executive*
Novogrod, Nancy Gerstein *editor*
Nugent, Nelle *theater, film and television producer*
Nurnberg, Charles Gordon *publishing company marketing executive*
Nurse, Sir Paul M. *academic administrator*
Nusbacher, Gloria Weinberg *lawyer*
Nussbaum, Jeffrey Joseph *musician*
Nuzum, John M., Jr., *banker*
Nyren, Neil Sebastian *publisher, editor*
Nyweide, Jeffrey O. *management and business executive*
Oates, Joyce Carol *author*
†Obaid, Thoraya Ahmed *international organization official*
O'Beil, Hedy *artist*
Oberly, Kathryn Anne *lawyer*
Oberman, Michael Stewart *lawyer*
Obernauer, Marne, Jr., *business executive*
Obernauer, Marne *corporate executive*
Obolensky, Ivan *investment banker, foundation consultant, writer, publisher*
O'Brien, Catherine Louise *museum administrator*
O'Brien, Conan *writer, performer, talk show host*
O'Brien, Geoffrey Paul *editor, writer*
O'Brien, Patricia Grace *psychiatric nurse, clinician and administrator*
†O'Brien, Tim *writer*
Obuck, John Francis *artist*
Ochoa, Manuel, Jr., *oncologist*
Ochs, Carol Rebecca *theologian, philosophy and religion educator*
O'Connell, Carmela Digristina *appraisal executive, consultant*
†O'Connor, Kevin *computer programing executive*
†O'Connor, Rory *pharmaceutical company executive, medical director*
O'Connor, William Matthew *lawyer*
O'Dea, Dennis Michael *lawyer*
Odenweller, Robert Paul *philatelist, association executive, retired airline pilot*
O'Doherty, Brian *writer, filmmaker*
†Odoner, Ellen J. *lawyer*
O'Donnell, Daniel J. *lawyer*
O'Donnell, John Logan *retired lawyer*
†O'Dwyer, Brian *lawyer, educator*
Oechler, Henry John, Jr., *lawyer*
Oettgen, Herbert Friedrich *physician*
Offit, Morris Wolf *investment advisory executive*
Offit, Sidney *writer, educator*
†Ofri, Danielle *physician*
Ogden, Alfred *lawyer*
Ogden, Peggy A. *retired personnel director*
O'Grady, Beverly Troxler *investment executive, counselor*
O'Grady, John Joseph, III, *lawyer*
†O'Hara, Robert Sydney, Jr., *lawyer*
Ohira, Kazuto *theatre company executive, writer*
Ohlson, Douglas Dean *artist, educator*
O'Keefe, Vincent Thomas *clergyman, educational administrator*
Okin, Peter Michael *cardiologist*
Okrent, Daniel *writer*
Okuhara, Tetsu *artist, photographer*
Okumura, Lydia S. *painter, sculptor*
Okun, Herbert Stuart *diplomat, educator*
Okun, Melanie Anne *venture capitalist*
†Olasov, David Michael *lawyer*
†Olcott, Richard M. *architectural firm executive*
Oldenburg, Richard Erik *auction house executive*
Oldfield, Barney *entertainment executive*
†Oldham, Joe *editor*
Oler, Wesley M., IV, *executive*
Olick, Philip Stewart *lawyer*
Olinger, Carla D(ragan) *medical advertising executive*
Olinger, Chauncey Greene, Jr., *investment executive, editorial consultant*
Oliva, Lawrence Jay *former academic administrator, history educator*
Ollman, Bertell *social sciences educator*
O'Looney, Patricia Anne *medical program administrator*
Olsen, David Alexander *insurance executive*
†Olson, Peter *publishing executive*
Olson, Roberta Jeanne Marie *art historian, author, educator, curator*
Olsson, Carl Alfred *urologist, department chairman*
Oltion, Jerry *author science fiction*
O'Neal, Hank *entertainment producer, business owner*
†O'Neal, Stanley *investment company executive*
O'Neil, John Joseph *lawyer*
O'Neil Bidwell, Katharine Thomas *fine arts association executive, performing arts executive*
O'Neill, George Dorr *investment company executive*
O'Neill, June Ellenoff *economist*
†O'Neill, Thomas J. *engineering company executive*
Ono, Yoko *conceptual artist, singer, recording artist*
†Opie, Catherine *photographer*
†Oppenheim, Jeffrey Alan *lawyer*
Oppenheimer, Ben R. *research scientist*
Oppenheimer, Martin J. *lawyer*
Oppenheimer, Paul *English comparative literature educator, poet, author*
Orben, Jack Richard *investment company executive, director*
†Orce, Kenneth W. *lawyer*
Ordal, Erik Aksel *management consultant*
Ordorica, Steven Anthony *obstetrician, gynecologist, educator*
O'Reilly, Richard John *pediatrician*
Oreskes, Irwin *biochemistry educator*
Oreskes, Susan *private school educator*
Orkin, Louis Richard *physician, educator*
Orlov, Darlene *management consultant, educator*
†Ornitz, Richard Martin *lawyer, business executive*
O'Rorke, James Francis, Jr., *lawyer*
†O'Rorke, Toby P. *architect, consultant*
†Orozco, Gabriel *artist*
Ort, Paul Joseph *orthopedic surgeon, educator*
Ortman, George Earl *artist*
Orwoll, Mark Peter *magazine editor*
Osborn, Donald Robert *lawyer*
Osborn, Frederick Henry, III, *foundation executive*
Osborn, June Elaine *pediatrician, microbiologist, educator, foundation administrator*
Osborne, Mary Pope *writer*
Osborne, Michael Piers *surgeon, researcher, health facility administrator*
Osborne, Richard de Jongh *mining and metals company executive*
†Osbourne, Ozzy (John Osbourne) *vocalist*
†Osgood, Charles *news broadcaster, journalist*
Osgood, Richard Magee, Jr., *applied physics educator, electrical engineering educator, research administrator, educator*
Oshima, Michael W. *lawyer*
Oshin, Diane *publisher*
Osmont, Ghyslain Louis *accountant*
Osnos, Gilbert Charles *management consultant*
Osnos, Peter Lionel Winston *publishing executive*
†Osorio, Pepon *artist*
Oster, Martin William *oncologist, educator*
Ostling, Richard Neil *journalist, author*
Ostrager, Barry Robert *lawyer*
Ostrander, Thomas William *investment banker*
Ostrow, Joseph W. *advertising executive*
O'Sullivan, Eugene Henry *retired advertising executive, management consultant*
O'Sullivan, Thomas J. *lawyer*
Ovadiah, Janice *cultural institute executive*
Overweg, Norbert Ido Albert *physician*
Owen, Richard *federal judge*
Owen, Thomas Llewellyn *investment executive*
Oxman, David Craig *lawyer*
Oz, Mehmet Cengiz *physician, writer*
Paalz, Anthony L. *beverage company executive*
Paaswell, Robert Emil *civil engineer, educator*
Pace, Eric Dwight *journalist, writer*
Pace, Stephen Shell *artist, educator*
Pace, Wayne H. *communications executive*
Pacella, Bernard Leonardo *psychiatrist*
Pack, Leonard Brecher *lawyer*
†Packard, George Randolph *journalist, educator*
Paddock, Anthony Conaway *financial consultant*
Pados, Frank John, Jr., *investment company executive*
†Paik, Myunghee Cho *statistician, educator*
Pakter, Jean *maternal and child health consultant*
Palackal, Joseph Joseph *researcher, musician*
Palermo, Robert James *architect, consultant, inventor*
Palgon, Sheldon *physician*
†Palhan, Vikas Bavi *molecular biologist, researcher*
Palion, Peter Thaddeus *financial planner*
Palitz, Anka A. Kriser *manufacturing and distributing company executive*
Pall, Ellen Jane *writer*
Palmer, Robert Baylis *librarian*
Palmer, Wayne Lewis *television director and producer*
Palmeri, Marlaina *school executive*
†Palsho, Dorothea Coccoli *information services executive*
Pan, Cynthia X. *geriatrician, educator, researcher*
†Panagopoulos, Costas *political scientist, educator*
Pandolfi, Frances *health facility administrator*
Paneth, Donald Joseph *editor, writer*
Panken, Peter Michael *lawyer*
Pantelopoulos, Nicholas Evan *lawyer, ship's officer*
Paolucci, Robert D. *translator*
Papalia, Diane Ellen *human development educator*
Papell, Helen Gertrude *poet, retired librarian*
Papernik, Joel Ira *lawyer*
Pappas, Milton J. *venture capitalist*
Papps, Bruce William *chartered financial analyst, investment company executive*
†Paranosic, Milica *composer, educator*
Pardes, Herbert *psychiatrist, educator*
†Parent, Louise Marie *lawyer*
Parish, J. Michael *lawyer, writer*
Parisotto, Gloria *publishing executive, poet*
Park, Leslie Desmond *health organization executive*
Park, Linda Sue *writer*
Parker, Alice *composer, conductor*
Parker, Bret I. *lawyer*
Parker, Michael G(eorge) *management consultant*
Parker, Nancy Winslow *artist, writer*
Parkin, Gerard Francis Ralph *chemistry educator, researcher*
†Parks, Gordon Roger Alexander *film director, author, photographer, composer*
Parmalee, Patty Lee *writer, educator*
Parness, Ira Allen *pediatric cardiologist*
†Paro, Jeff *publisher*
†Parrott, James Alfred *city economist*
Parsons, Andrew John *management consultant*
Parsons, Estelle *actress*

†Renwick, Neil Macdonald *pathologist, researcher*
Rescigno, Richard Joseph *editor*
Resika, Paul *artist*
Resnick, Rhoda Brodowsky *psychotherapist*
†Resnicow, Norman Jakob *lawyer*
Reuben, Gloria *actress*
†Reuter, Victor E. *pathologist, educator*
Reuther, David Louis *children's book publisher, writer*
Reutter, Eberhard Edmund, Jr., *education and law educator*
Reverdin, Bernard J. *lawyer*
Reynard, Muriel Joyce *lawyer*
Reynolds, Donald Martin *art historian, foundation administrator, educator*
Reynolds, James *management consultant*
Reynolds, Warren Jay *retired publisher*
Rheins, Carl Jeffrey
Rhoads, Geraldine Emeline *editor, consultant*
Rhodes, Richard (Lee) *writer*
Rhodes, Samuel *violist, educator*
Rhodes, William Reginald *banker*
Rhodes, Yorke E(dward) *organic chemist, educator*
Rhone, Sylvia *recording industry executive*
Riazi, Kambiz *civil engineer*
Riback, Estelle Posner *art historian*
Ribalow, Meir Z. *playwright, educator*
Ribary, Urs *neuroscientist, researcher, educator*
Rice, Anne *writer*
Rice, Barbara Lynn *stage manager*
Rice, Donald Sands *lawyer, entrepreneuer*
Rice, Joseph Lee, III, *lawyer*
Rich, Adrienne *writer*
Rich, Donna Bonem *fundraising consultant*
Rich, Frank Hart *journalist, author*
Rich, R(obert) Bruce *lawyer*
Richard, Elaine *educational therapist*
†Richard, Ellen *theater executive*
Richards, David Alan *lawyer*
†Richards, Keith *musician*
Richards, Lloyd George *theatrical director, university administrator*
†Richards, Martin *theatrical producer*
Richey, Kent Ramon *lawyer*
Richman, Martin Franklin *lawyer*
Richtman, Jack *French language educator*
Rieber, Robert W. *psychology educator, linguistics educator*
Rifkind, Arleen B. *physician, researcher*
Rifkind, Robert S(inger) *lawyer*
Rigg, Dame Diana *actress*
†Riggio, Leonard *book publishing executive*
†Riggio, Stephen *book store chain executive*
Rigney, Jane *copy editor, writer*
Rigolosi, Elaine La Monica *lawyer, educator, consultant*
Rikon, Michael *lawyer*
Riley, Scott C. *lawyer*
Riley, William *corporate executive, writer, conservationist*
Rines, John Randolph *investment banker*
Ringel, Dean *lawyer*
Ringer, James Milton *lawyer*
Ringer, Jennifer *dancer*
Ringgold, Faith *artist*
Riordan, James Quentin *retired company executive*
Riss, Eric *psychologist*
Ristich, Miodrag *psychiatrist*
Ritch, Herald LaVern *finance company executive*
Ritch, Kathleen *diversified company executive*
Ritch, Robert Harry *ophthalmologist, educator*
Ritter, Ann L. *lawyer*
†Ritterband, David C. *ophthalmologist, educator*
Rivelli, William Raymond Allan *photographer*
Rivera, Chita (Conchita del Rivero) *actress, singer, dancer*
Rivera, Geraldo *television personality, journalist*
Rivera, Walter *lawyer*
Rivlin, Benjamin *political science educator*
Rizzi, Joseph Vito *banker*
Rizzo, Frank Albert *physician*
†Roach, Margaret *editor-in-chief*
Robb, Carole *artist*
Robbins, Carrie F(ishbein) *costume designer, educator*
Robbins, John Clapp *management consultant*
Roberts, Burton Bennett *lawyer, retired judge*
Roberts, Donald Munier *retired banker, trust company executive*
Roberts, Francis Stone *advertising executive*
Roberts, John *news anchor*
Roberts, John J. *accounting firm executive*
†Roberts, Kevin *advertising executive*
†Roberts, Kevin John *ideas company executive*
†Roberts, Madelyn Alpert *publishing executive*
Roberts, Sidney I. *lawyer*
†Roberts, Thomas Raymond *lawyer*
Robertson, Andrew *dancer*
†Robertson, Andrew Whitmore *historian*
Robertson, Edwin David *lawyer*
Robertson, Hugh Dunbar *biomedical researcher, consultant*
Robertson, Mark Allen *lawyer*
Robertson, William, IV, *foundation administrator*
Robinson, Barbara Paul *lawyer*
Robinson, Daniel N. *psychology and philosophy educator*
Robinson, Enders Anthony *geophysicist, educator, writer*
Robinson, Irwin Jay *lawyer*
Robinson, James D., III, *corporate executive, investor*
Robinson, James LeRoy *architect, educator, developer*
†Robinson, Janet *publishing executive*
†Robinson, Janet L. *publishing executive*
†Robinson, Jeffrey Arnold *entrepreneur*
Robinson, Joyce McPeake *administrator*
†Robinson, Kim Stanley *science fiction author*
†Robinson, Marvin Stuart *lawyer*
Robinson, Nan Senior *not-for-profit organization consultant*
Robinson, Roxana Barry *writer, art historian*
†Roby, Joe Lindell *investment banker*
†Roccosalvo, Joseph C. *psychotherapist*
Roche, Gerard Raymond *management consultant*
Rockefeller, David *banker*
Rockefeller, Laurance S. *philanthropist*
Rocklen, Kathy Hellenbrand *lawyer*
†Rockwell, William Hearne *lawyer*
†Rodman, Lawrence Bernard *lawyer*
Rodman, Leroy Eli *lawyer*
Rodriguez, Geno (Eugene Rodriguez) *artist, arts administrator*
Rodriguez, Vincent Angel *lawyer, director*
Rodriguez-Sains, Rene S. *physician, surgeon, educator*
Roeder, Robert Gayle *biochemist, educator*
†Roen, Philip Ruben *urologist, surgeon, medical educator*
Roethenmund, Otto Emil *financial and banking executive*
Rogers, James Beeland, Jr., *investment company executive*
†Rogers, Laurence Steven *lawyer*
Rogers, Mark Charles *physician, educator*
Rogers, Michael Alan *writer*
Rogers, Theodore Courtney *investment company executive*
Rogers, Theodore Otto, Jr., *lawyer*
Rogers, Thomas Sydney *communications executive*
Rogin, Gilbert Leslie *editor, author*
Roglieri, John Louis *health facility administrator*
Rogoff, Jeffrey Scott *lawyer*
Rohatyn, Felix George *ambassador*
Rohrbach, Heidi A. *lawyer*
Roland, John *newscaster*
Rolfe, Ronald Stuart *lawyer*
Rollin, Betty *writer, television journalist, lecturer*
Romans, John Niebrugge *lawyer*
Romas, Nicholas Achilles *urologist, educator*
Romney, Richard Bruce *lawyer*
Ronde, John Herman *author, translator*
Ronson, Raoul R. *publishing executive*
Ronson, Susan *administrative assistant*
Rooney, Andrew Aitken *writer, columnist*
Rooney, Paul C., Jr., *lawyer, retired*
Roos, Jane Mayo *art history educator*
Roosevelt, Ruth Barrons *international trading consultant, artist*
Roosevelt, Theodore, IV, *investment banker*
Root, Nina J. *librarian, author*
Root, William Pitt *poet, educator*
Rootenberg, Sharyn Michele *lawyer*
Rosa, Margarita *agency chief executive, lawyer*
†Rosado, Rossana *publishing executive, editor-in-chief*
Rosand, David *art history educator*
†Rose, Aaron *artist*
Rose, Charles *television journalist*
Rose, Daniel *real estate company executive, consultant*
Rose, Elihu *real estate executive*
Rose, Joanna Semel *cultural activist*
Rose, Leatrice *artist, educator*
Rose, Robert Neal *brokerage house executive*
Rosen, Nathaniel Kent *cellist*
Rosen, Richard Lewis *lawyer, real estate developer*
Rosenberg, Alan David *accountant*
Rosenberg, Alan Stewart *lawyer*
Rosenberg, Alex Jacob *art dealer, curator, fine arts appraiser, educator*
†Rosenberg, David *lawyer*
Rosenberg, Ellen Y. *religious association administrator*
Rosenberg, Gary Marc *lawyer*
†Rosenberg, Gerald Alan *lawyer*
Rosenberg, Jerome Roy *lawyer, accountant*
Rosenberg, John David *English educator, literary critic*
Rosenberg, Marc Steven *lawyer*
Rosenberg, Michael Joseph *financial executive*
†Rosenberg, Tina *international relations educator, writer*
Rosenberg, Victor I. *plastic surgeon, educator*
Rosenblatt, Arthur Isaac *architect, former museum director*
Rosenblatt, Lester *naval architect*
Rosenbloom, Daniel *investment banker, lawyer*
Rosenblum, Robert *art historian, educator*
Rosenblum, William F., Jr., *lawyer*
Rosendorff, Clive *cardiologist*
Rosenfeld, Arthur H. *lawyer, publisher*
Rosenfeld, Steven B. *lawyer*
†Rosenfield, Allan *physician*
†Rosengarten, Frank *retired communications educator, writer*
Rosensaft, Jean Bloch *university administrator*
Rosensaft, Menachem Zwi *lawyer, writer, foundation administrator, advocate*
Rosenshine, Allen Gilbert *advertising agency executive*
Rosenthal, Charles Michael *financial executive*
Rosenthal, Donna Myra *social worker*
Rosenthal, Faigi *librarian*
Rosenthal, Gert *economist*
†Rosenthal, Jacob (Jack Rosenthal) *foundation executive*
†Rosenthal, Joel Howard *think-tank executive*
Rosenthal, Milton Frederick *chemical and minerals company executive*
Rosenthal, Nan *curator, educator, author*
†Rosenwaks, Zev *obstetrician, gynecologist, educator, endocrinologist*
Rosenzweig, Charles Leonard *lawyer*
†Rosenzweig, Theodore B. *lawyer*
†Rosner, Jonathan Levi *lawyer*
†Rosow, Malcolm Bertram *lawyer*
Rosow, Stuart L. *lawyer*
Ross, Charles *artist*
†Ross, Gerald Elliott *lawyer*
Ross, Jeffrey Allan *political scientist, educator*
Ross, John T. *artist, educator*
Ross, Matthew *lawyer*
†Ross, Michael Aaron *lawyer*
Ross, Norman Alan *publisher*
Ross, Randolph Ernest *management consultant*
Ross, Thomas Bernard *communications company executive*
Rossen, Jordan *lawyer*
Rosset, Barnet Lee, Jr., *publishing executive*
Rostenberg, Leona *rare book dealer, writer*
Rostow, Charles Nicholas *lawyer, educator*
Rostropovich, Mstislav Leopoldovich *conductor, music director, musician*
†Roth, Eric M. *lawyer*
Roth, Judith Shulman *lawyer*
Roth, Kenneth *human rights advocate*
Roth, Paul Norman *lawyer*
†Roth, Philip *writer*
Roth, Richard Alan *lawyer*
Roth, Sol *rabbi*
Rothberg, Gerald *editor, publisher, editor-in-chief*
Rothberg, Glenda Fay Morris *lawyer*
Rothenberg, Jerome *author, visual arts and literary educator*
Rothenberg, Joyce Andrea (Joyce Joyce Andrea) *composer, poet, writer, singer*
Rothenberg, Michael Andrew *lawyer, not-for-profit administrator*
Rothenberg, Robert Philip *public relations counselor*
Rothfeld, Michael B. *theatrical productions executive, investor*
Rothman, Adam Alan *financial consultant*
Rothman, Bernard *lawyer*
Rothman, David J. *history and medical educator*
Rothman, Dennis Michael *lawyer*
Rothman, Henry Isaac *lawyer*
Rothschild, Amalie Randolph *filmmaker, producer, director, digital artist, photographer*
Rothstein, Gerald Alan *investment company executive*
Rothstein, Pauline Marcus *librarian, educator*
Rotter, Steven Jeffrey *company executive*
Rouse, Christopher Chapman, III, *composer, educator*
Rover, Edward Frank *lawyer*
Rovine, Arthur William *lawyer*
†Rovit, Richard Lee *neurological surgeon*
Rowe, David Lee *financial advisor*
Rowe, Elizabeth Webb *community volunteer*
Rowen, Ruth Halle *musicologist, educator*
Rowland, Esther E(delman) *retired college dean*
Rowland, Lewis Phillip *neurology educator, editor, clinical investigator*
Rozen, Jerome George, Jr., *research entomologist, museum curator and research administrator*
†Rozentsvit, Inna *neurologist*
Ruben, Lawrence *real estate developer, building company executive, lawyer*
†Rubenstein, Atoosa Behnegar *editor-in-chief*
Rubenstein, Howard Joseph *public relations executive*
Rubenstein, Joshua Seth *lawyer*
Rubenstein, Leonard *engineering company executive*
Rubin, Albert Louis *physician, educator*
Rubin, Harry Meyer *entertainment and software industry executive*
Rubin, Herbert *lawyer*
Rubin, Joel Edward *consulting company executive*
Rubin, Richard Allan *lawyer*
Rubin, Robert Samuel *investment banker*
†Rubin, Stephen Wayne *lawyer*
Rubin, Theodore Isaac *psychiatrist, writer*
Rubino, Victor Joseph *academic administrator, lawyer*
Rubinstein, Ernest *librarian, educator*
Rubinstein, Frederic Armand *lawyer*
Rubinstein, Rosalinda *allergist, medical association administrator*
Ruda, Howard *lawyer, finance company executive*
Rudel, Julius *conductor*
Rudenstine, Neil Leon *former academic administrator, educator*
†Ruder, Usha C. *pathologist*
Ruder, William *public relations executive*
Rudin, Max Allen *publishing executive*
†Rudin, Scott *film and theatre producer*
Rudoff, Sheldon *lawyer*
Ruebhausen, Oscar Melick *retired lawyer*
Ruegger, Philip T., III, *lawyer*
Ruhlmann, William James *music critic*
Rumaker, Michael *writer, English educator*
Rumschitzki, David Sheldon *chemical engineering educator*
Rupcich, Matthew William *music educator*
Rupp, George Erik *not-for-profit administrator*
Rusch, William Graham *religious organization administrator*
†Ruscha, Edward *artist*
†Rusell, Anne M *publishing executive*
Ruskin, Richard A. *obstetrician-gynecologist*
†Rusmisel, Stephen R. *lawyer*
Russell, Andrew James *government agency official, diplomat*
Russo, Thomas Anthony *lawyer*
Russotto, Paul *artist, educator*
Ruta, Thomas V. *professional sports team executive, accounting executive*
†Ryan, Brendan *advertising executive*
†Ryan, Thomas Patrick *lawyer*
Rybin, Vitalyi Olegovich *research scientist*
Rylant, Cynthia *author*
Ryman, Robert Tracy *artist*
Sabat, Robert Hartman *magazine editor*
Sabatini, David Domingo *cell biologist, biochemist*
Sabel, Bradley Kent *lawyer*
Sabino, Catherine Ann *magazine editor*
Sacerdote, Peter M. *investment banker*
Sachar, David Bernard *gastroenterologist, medical educator*
Sachar, Louis *writer prose*
Sachs, David *lawyer*
†Sachs, Jeffrey David *economist, educator*
Sachs, Samuel, II, *museum director*
Sack, Robert David *judge, educator*
†Sacks, Ira Stephen *lawyer*
Sacks, Jeffrey Howard *psychiatrist, psychoanalyst*
†Saddler, Donald Edward *choreographer, dancer*
Sadegh, Ali M. *mechanical engineering educator, researcher, consultant*
Sadock, Benjamin James *psychiatrist, educator*
Sadove, Stephen Irving *retail executive*
†Sadr, Deborah Marusi *sales executive*
Saez Guillermo, Francisco Eduardo *photographer*
Safer, Morley *journalist*
†Saffar, Jean-Marc *healthcare consultant*
Safian, Leroy Scheller *radiologist*
†Safian, Robert *managing editor*
Saft, Stuart Mark *lawyer*
†Sagan, M J *architectural firm executive*
Sager, Clifford J. *psychiatrist, educator*
Sager, Donald Jack *librarian, consultant, former publisher*
Sahid, Joseph Robert *lawyer*
Saint-Donat, Bernard Jacques *finance company executive*
St. Lifer, Jane M. *art appraiser*
Salans, Lester Barry *physician, scientist, educator*
Saleh, Mohammed *diplomat*
Salembier, Valerie Birnbaum *publishing executive*
Salemi, Joseph Salvatore *classics and humanities educator, poet, writer*
†Salerno, Frederic V. *telecommunications company executive*
Salerno-Sonnenberg, Nadja *violinist*
Salgo, Peter Lloyd *internist, writer, anesthesiologist*
Salinger, J(erome) D(avid) *author*
†Saloman, Ora Frishberg *musicologist, educator*
Salomon, Frank Ernest *classical music administrator*
†Salomon, Philippe M. *lawyer*
†Salonen, Esa-Pekka *conductor*
Salter, Kevin Thornton *lawyer*
Salter, Mary Jo *poet*
†Salup, Stephen *lawyer, educator*
Salvan, Sherwood Allen *lawyer*
Salvesen, Magda Abercromby *art historian, garden historian*
Salwen, Marie (Manya Salwen) *social worker, psychotherapist*
Salzman, Robert Jay *accountant*
Sampras, Pete *retired professional tennis player*
Samuels, Leslie B. *lawyer*
†Sanders, B. Lamar *film educator, scriptwriter*
Sanders, Richard Louis *executive editor*
Sandhu, Harvinder Singh *spinal surgeon, educator*
Sand Lee, Inger *artist*
Sandler, Irving Harry *art critic, art historian*
Sandler, Lucy Freeman *art history educator*
Sandler, Robert Michael *insurance company executive, actuary*
Sandler, Ross *law educator*
†Sandler, Susan Silverstein *dietician, nutritionist*
Sands, Harry *psychologist, health administrator, researcher*
Sandum, Howard E. *literary agent*
Sanford, Eric *lawyer*
Sanseverino, Raymond Anthony *lawyer*
Saphir, Richard Louis *pediatrician*
Sarachik, Myriam Paula Morgenstein *physics educator*
Sarandon, Susan Abigail *actress*
Sard, Susannah Ellen *non-profit executive*
Sargent, Herb *writer, television producer*
Sargent, Joseph Dudley *insurance executive*
Sargent, Pamela *writer*
Sarkar, Indra Neil *medical informatician*
Sarnelle, Joseph R. *electronic publishing specialist, magazine and newspaper editor*
Sarno, Martha Taylor *speech and language pathologist, educator*
Sarnoff, Irving *retired psychology educator, author*
Saru, George *artist*
Sasman, Irene Deak Handberg *educational publishing executive*
Sassoon, Andre Gabriel *lawyer*
Sastry, Srin *scientist, researcher, educator*
Satine, Barry Roy *lawyer*
Saufer, Isaac Aaron *lawyer*
Saul, John Woodruff, III, *writer*
Saul, Mark E. *mathematics educator, consultant*
Saunders, Mark A. *lawyer*
Saunders, Paul Christopher *lawyer*
†Saunders, Sylvia Christie *biologist, educator*
Savage, Tom *poet*
Savas, Emanuel S. *public management and public policy educator*
Savitt, Susan Schenkel *lawyer*
Savrin, Louis *lawyer*
Sawyer, Deborah Christine *information services company executive*
Sawyer, Diane (L. Diane Sawyer) *television journalist*
†Sawyer, Linda *advertising executive*
Saxena, Brij B. *endocrinologist, biochemist, educator*
Saxon, Wolfgang Erik Georg *journalist*
†Saxton, Catherine Patricia *public relations executive*
Sayre, Linda Damaris *human resources professional*
Sbaity-Kassem, Fatima Hasan *political economist, researcher*
Scaffidi, Judith Ann *academic administrator*
†Scala, James Robert *lawyer*
Scanlon, Rosemary *economist*
†Scannell, Herb *broadcast executive*
Scarborough, Charles Bishop, III, *broadcast journalist, writer*
Scarola, John Michael *dentist, educator*
Scaturro, Philip David *investment banker, university chancellor*
Scelsa, Joseph Vincent *sociologist, educator, university executive*
Sceusa, Nicholas A. *pharmacologist*
Schaab, Arnold J. *lawyer*

Singer, Barbara Helen *photographer*
Singer, Eric T. *investment banker*
Singer, Niki *media consultant*
Singleton, Donald Edward *journalist*
Sinsheimer, Warren Jack *lawyer*
Siskind, Arthur *lawyer, director*
Siskind, Donald Henry *lawyer*
Sitarz, Anneliese Lotte *pediatrics educator, physician*
Sitomer, Sheila Marie *television producer, director*
Sitruk-Ware, Régine *research organization executive, educator*
Siv, Sichan Aun *ambassador*
Sivakumaran, Kumaraswamy *civil engineer, consultant, lawyer*
Sivy, Michael *journalist*
Size, Dennis Michael *lighting and scenery designer*
Skigen, Patricia Sue *lawyer*
Skinner, Brian Allan *writer, artist*
Skinner, Kristin A. *surgical oncologist*
†Skinner, Peter Graeme *publishing executive, lawyer*
Sklar, Stanley Lawrence *judge*
Skol, Michael *anti-corruption and counter-money laundering consultant*
Skolnick, Jerome H. *law educator*
Skomorowsky, Peter P. *retired accounting company executive, lawyer*
Skupinski, Bogdan Kazimierz *artist*
Skwiersky, Paul *accountant*
†Slade, Jeffrey Christopher *lawyer*
†Sladkus, Harvey Ira *lawyer*
†Slater, Alice Joan *lawyer*
Slavin, Arlene *artist*
Slavutin, Lee Jacob *life insurance executive*
Slawsky, Donna Susan *librarian, singer*
Sleed, Joel *columnist*
Sleigh, Sylvia *artist, educator*
Sloan, Allan Herbert *journalist*
†Sloan, Nancy L. *epidemiologist*
Slomanson, Lloyd Howard *architect, musician, photographer*
Slone, Sandi *artist*
Slonem, Hunt *artist*
Slosberg, Mike *advertising executive*
Slotkin, Todd *holding company executive*
Slusser, William Peter *investment banker*
Slutsky, Lorie A.(Ann) *foundation executive*
Small, George LeRoy *geographer, educator*
Small, Jonathan Andrew *lawyer*
Smalley, David Vincent *lawyer*
Smiley, Jane Graves *author, educator*
Smith, Andrew Alfred, Jr., *urban planner*
Smith, Barry Hamilton *foundation administrator, physician*
Smith, Betty *writer, nonprofit foundation executive*
Smith, Bradley Youle *lawyer*
Smith, Corlies Morgan *publishing executive*
Smith, Dennis (Edward Smith) *author, publisher*
Smith, Edward Paul, Jr., *lawyer*
†Smith, Edwin Lloyd *lawyer*
Smith, George Bundy *state court justice*
Smith, Gordon H. *civil engineer, consultant, forensic engineer consultant*
†Smith, Harry *newscaster*
Smith, Hilary Cranwell Bowen *investment banker*
Smith, Howard I. *insurance company executive*
Smith, Joseph Phelan *film company executive*
Smith, Julia A. *internist, oncologist, educator*
†Smith, Kiki *artist*
Smith, Liz (Mary Elizabeth Smith) *newspaper columnist, broadcast journalist*
Smith, Malcolm Bernard *investment company executive*
Smith, Malcolm Sommerville *bass*
Smith, Martin Jay *advertising and marketing executive*
†Smith, Mimi *artist*
Smith, Morton Alan *lawyer*
Smith, Patrick John *editor, writer*
†Smith, Richard Mills *editor-in-chief*
†Smith, Robert Blakeman *lawyer*
Smith, Robert Everett *lawyer*
†Smith, Robert Sherlock *lawyer, educator*
Smith, Shirley *artist*
Smith, Vincent DaCosta *artist*
Smith, Vincent Milton *lawyer, designer, Feng Shui lecturer, consultant, writer*
Smith, Warren Allen *writer*
Smithson, Charles Wayne *economist, consultant*
Smits, Helen Lida *physician, administrator, educator*
Smoak, Evan L. *lawyer*
Smolinski, Edward Albert *holding company executive, lawyer, accountant, deacon*
Smotrich, David Isadore *architect*
Snow, Charles *lawyer*
Snyder, Arlen Dean *actor*
Snyder, Jack L. *international relations educator*
Snyderman, Selma Eleanore *pediatrician, educator*
Soave, Rosemary *internist*
†Sobel, Gerald *lawyer*
Sobell, Nina R. *artist*
Socarides, Charles William *psychiatrist, psychoanalyst, educator, writer*
Socol, Sheldon Eleazer *university official*
†Sodano, Salvatore F. *stock exchange executive*
Soejima, Daisuke *international trade engineer, economist*
Softness, Donald Gabriel *marketing and manufacturing executive*
Sogani, Pramod Chandra *surgeon, educator*
Sohmer, Bernard *mathematics educator, administrator*
Solecki, R. Stefan *anthropologist, educator*
†Soley, David Benjamin *composer*
Solman, Joseph *artist*
Solomon, Andrew Wallace *author*
Solomon, Deborah Antoinnette *volunteer*
Solomon, Gail Ellen *physician*
Solomon, Howard *pharmaceutical company executive*
†Solomon, Libertina *pharmacist, educator*
Solomon, Maynard Elliott *music historian, former recording company executive*
†Solomon, Stephen L. *lawyer*
Solomons, Gus, Jr., (Gustave Martinez) *choreographer, dancer, writer*
Solov, Zachary *choreographer, ballet artist*
Somers, John Arthur *insurance company executive*
Somogyi, Jennie *dancer*
Sonneman, Eve *artist*
Sontag, Susan *writer*
Sopanen, Jeri Rainer *photography director*
Sorell, Kitty Julia *public relations executive*
Sorensen, Gillian Martin *United Nations official*
Sorensen, Jane Forester *small business owner, consultant*
Soriano, Nancy Mernit *editor-in-chief*
Sorkin, David James *lawyer*
Sorkin, Laurence Truman *lawyer*
Soros, George *fund management executive*
Sorte, John Follett *investment firm executive*
Sorter, George Hans *accounting and law educator, consultant*
Soter, George Nicholas *advertising executive*
Soter, Steven *research scientist*
†Soto, Jock *dancer*
Soto, Roberto Fernando Eduardo *journalist*
Sotomayor, Sonia *judge*
Souham, Gérard *communications executive*
Soulé, Charles Raymond, Jr., *psychologist*
Southworth, Linda Jean *artist, critic, educator, poet*
†Souto, Gustavo *painter*
Sovern, Michael Ira *law educator*
Soyer, David *cellist, music educator*
Soyster, Margaret Blair *lawyer*
Spacey, Kevin *actor*
Spaide, Richard Frederick *ophthalmologist*
Spanbock, Maurice Samuel *lawyer*
†Spandorfer, Steven David *internist*
Spangler, Arnold Eugene *investment banker*
Spatt, Robert Edward *lawyer*
Spear, Harvey M. *lawyer*
Spelfogel, Evan J. *lawyer, educator*
Speller, Robert Ernest Blakefield, Jr., *choreographer*
Speller, Robert Ernest Blakefield *publishing executive*
Spence, James Robert, Jr., *television sports executive, educator*
Spencer, Frank Cole *medical educator*
†Spencer, James M. *dermatologist*
Sperakis, Nicholas George *artist*
Sperling, Allan George *lawyer*
Spero, C. Michael *lawyer*
Spero, Joan Edelman *foundation president*
Speziale, Richard Salvatore *financial executive*
Spiegel, Elwyn *advertising agency executive, creative director*
Spiegel, Herbert *psychiatrist, educator*
Spiegel, Jerrold Bruce *lawyer*
Spielvogel, Sidney Meyer *investment banker*
†Spikes, James *psychiatrist, educator*
Spillane, Dennis Kevin *lawyer*
†Spillane, Mickey (Frank Morrison Spillane) *author*
Spindler, James Andrew *not-for-profit executive*
Spira, Robert Alan *securities company executive*
†Spivack, Edith Irene *lawyer*
Spivak, Gayatri Chakravorty *humanities educator*
†Spivak, Leonard A. *lawyer*
Sprague, Peter Julian *software company executive, lecturer*
†Sprewell, Latrell Fontaine *professional basketball player*
Spriggs, David Randall *healthcare administrator, educator*
Spring, Michael *editor, writer*
Springfield, Dempsey Stewart *physician, educator*
Sprizzo, John Emilio *judge*
†Squire, Gilda N. *brand manager, publicist, writer*
Squire, Walter Charles *lawyer*
Stack, Edward William *business management and foundation executive*
Stade, George Gustav *humanities educator*
†Staffaroni, Robert J. *lawyer*
Stahl, Lesley R. *news correspondent*
Stainrook, Harry Richard *retired banker*
Stakias, G. Michael *merchant banker*
†Stamm, Charles H. *lawyer*
Stang, Arnold *actor, director, writer*
Stang, Rolf Kristian *vocalist, actor, educator, writer, advertising executive*
Stanger, Ila *writer, editor*
†Stanton, Ronald P. *export company executive*
†Starbuck, William Haynes *business management educator*
Starer, Brian Douglas *lawyer*
†Stark, Richard Alvin *lawyer*
Stark, Richard Boies *surgeon, artist*
†Stark, Robert J. *lawyer*
Stark, Robin Caryl *psychotherapist, consultant*
Starr, Steven Dawson *photographer*
†Starren, Justin Bruce *medical educator*
Stathis, Nicholas John *lawyer*
†Stead, Jerre L. *investment company executive*
Steadman, E. Thomas *gynecologist*
†Stebbings, Robert Yeo *lawyer, partner*
†Steck, Jodi *photojournalist*
Steedman, Doria Lynne Silberberg *organization executive*
Steel, Danielle Fernande *author*
Steere, William Campbell, Jr., *pharmaceutical company executive*
†Steichen, Joanna T(aub) *psychotherapist, writer*
†Steigbigel, Neal H. *medical educator*
Steiger, Paul Ernest *newspaper editor, journalist*
†Steigman, Ernest R. *lawyer*
Stein, Bernard *stockbroker*
Stein, David Fred *investment executive*
Stein, Ellen Gail *executive manager*
Stein, Elliot, Jr., *business executive*
Stein, Howard S. *banker*
Stein, Jacob *computer programmer, analyst*
Stein, Joseph *playwright*
†Stein, Marcia *not-for-profit executive*
Stein, Marvin *psychiatrist, historian*
Stein, Richard Alan *cardiologist, educator*
Stein, Stephen William *lawyer*
Steinberg, Howard Eli *lawyer, diversified financial services company executive*
Steinberg, Leo *art historian, educator*
Steinberg, Saul Phillip *holding company executive*
Steinem, Gloria *writer, editor, lecturer*
Steiner, Richard C. *semitic linguist, educator*
†Steinfeld, Allan *sports association administrator*
Steinglass, Peter Joseph *psychiatrist, educator*
Steinherz, Laurel Judith *pediatric cardiologist*
†Stelzer, Paul *cardiac surgeon, educator*
Stempleski, Susan *English language professional, writer*
Stenzel, Kurt Hodgson *physician, nephrologist, educator*
†Stephanopoulos, George Robert *reporter*
Stephens, Gary Ralph *American literature and journalism educator*
Stephenson, Alan Clements *lawyer*
Sterling, David Mark *graphic designer*
Sterling, Robert Lee, Jr., *investment company executive*
Stern, Claudio Daniel *medical educator, embryological researcher*
†Stern, David Joel *basketball association executive*
Stern, Fritz Richard *historian, educator*
†Stern, Howard Allan *radio personality, television show host*
Stern, Isaac *violinist, performing arts executive*
Stern, James Andrew *investment banker*
Stern, Leonard *physician*
Stern, Madeleine Bettina *rare books dealer, author*
Stern, Marvin *psychiatrist, educator*
†Stern, Mitchell *broadcast executive*
Stern, Peter R. *lawyer*
†Stern, Robert Arthur Morton *architect, educator, writer*
Stern, Roslyne Paige *magazine publisher*
Stern, Walter Phillips *investment executive*
Sternberg, Seymour *insurance company executive*
Sternberg, Stephen Stanley *pathologist, educator*
Sternman, Joel W. *lawyer*
Stetler, Russell Dearnley, Jr., *private investigator*
Steuer, Gary Paul *art association administrator*
Steuer, Richard Marc *lawyer*
Stevens, Art *public relations executive*
Stevens, Jerome Hebert *entrepreneur*
Stevens, Risë *performing arts company administrator*
Stever, Donald Winfred *lawyer*
Steves, Gale C. *marketing professional, writer, retired editor-in-chief, publishing executive*
Stewart, E(dward) Nicholson *investment management executive*
Stewart, Jack *artist, educator, writer*
Stewart, James Montgomery *banker*
Stewart, Richard Burleson *law educator*
Stewart, Ruth Ann *political scientist, educator*
†Steyer, Hume Richmond *lawyer*
Stiassny, Melanie L.J. *curator*
Stich, June Jeacoma *psychotherapist*
Stiefel, Ethan *dancer*
Stiefel, Leanna *economics educator, education researcher*
Stiglitz, Joseph Eugene *economist, educator*
Stiller, Matthew James *dermatologist*
Stimmel, Barry *cardiologist, internist, educator, university dean*
†Stimmel, Todd Richard *lawyer, business executive*
Stimpson, Catharine Roslyn *English language educator, writer*
Stine, Catherine Morris *artist*
Sting, (Gordon Matthew Sumner) *musician, songwriter, actor*
†Stirling, Alexandra Lucero *science administrator*
Stock, Ben *religious organization consultant*
Stocker, Jeffrey David *film acting coach*
Stocker, Michael A. *health insurance company executive*
Stoddard, George Earl *investment company financial executive*
Stolfi, Thomas Edward *advertising executive*
Stoll, Neal Richard *lawyer*
Stolper, Pinchas Aryeh *religious organization executive, rabbi*
Stoltzman, Richard Leslie *clarinetist*
Stone, Brian A. *urologist, surgeon, educator*
Stone, Caroline Fleming *artist*
Stone, David Philip *lawyer*
Stone, Merrill Brent *lawyer*
†Stone, Robert Anthony *author*
†Stoney, George Cashel *film educator*
Stoopler, Mark Benjamin *physician*
Storch, Arthur *theater director*
Stork, Gilbert *chemistry educator, investigator*
†Storm, Hannah *newscaster*
Storm, Jackie *nutritionist, health education specialist*
Störmer, Horst Ludwig *physicist*
Storrs, Immi Casagrande *sculptor*
Stotzky, Guenther *microbiologist, educator*
Stowers, Carlton Eugene *writer*
Strand, Curt Robert *hotel executive*
Strang, John *association executive*
Strasfogel, Ian *stage director,playwright*
†Stratakis, Christ *lawyer*
Stratechuk, Michael *musician, educator*
Stratigos, William Narge *computer company executive*
Straton, John Charles, Jr., *investment banker*
Stratton, Walter Love *lawyer*
Straub, Chester John *judge*
Strauss, Carol Kahn *institute executive director, editor, consultant*
Strauss, Edward Robert *carpet company executive*
Strauss, Gary Joseph *lawyer*
Strear, Joseph D. *public relations executive*
†Streicker, Richard Daniel *lawyer, record company executive*
Strickon, Harvey Alan *lawyer*
Stringer, Howard *media executive*
Stringer, Ronald E. *lawyer, educator*
†Strock, Marcus *lawyer*
Stroer, Rosemary Ann *real estate broker*
Stroke, Hinko Henry *physicist, educator*
Strom, Milton Gary *lawyer*
†Stroman, Susan *choreographer*
Stroock, Mark Edwin, II, *public relations company executive*
Strossen, Nadine *law educator, human rights activist*
†Strum, Jay Gerson *lawyer*
Struve, Guy Miller *lawyer*
Stuart, Alice Melissa *lawyer*
†Stuart, Lori Ames *public relations executive*
Stuart, Tara *international business intelligence advisor*
Stubbs, John Howell *architectural educator, preservationist*
†Stübgen, Joerg-Patrick *neurologist*
†Studin, Jan *publishing executive*
Stupin, Susan Lee *investment banker*
Sturtevant, Peter Mann, Jr., *television news executive*
Stutman, Leonard Jay *research scientist, cardiologist*
Stypulkowski, Jacek Bogdan *geotechnical engineer*
Subak-Sharpe, Gerald Emil *electrical engineer, educator*
†Subirats, Eduardo *language educator*
Sugarman, Irwin J. *lawyer*
Sugarman, Robert Gary *lawyer*
Sugihara, Kenzi *publishing executive*
Sugiyama, Kazunori *music producer*
Sulcer, Frederick Durham *advertising executive*
Sulkowicz, Kerry J. *psychiatrist, psychoanalyst, management consultant*
†Sullivan, Graeme Leslie *art educator*
Sullivan, Jim *artist*
Sullivan, Larry Edward *librarian*
Sullivan, Stephen Gene *psychiatrist, pharmacologist, administrator*
Sult, Jeffery Scot *performing company executive, playwright, director, actor*
Sultzer, Barnet Martin *microbiology and immunology researcher*
Sulzberger, Arthur Ochs, Jr., *newspaper publisher*
Sun, Jeffrey C. *legal educator*
Sun, Tung-Tien *medical science educator*
Suraci, Patrick Joseph *clinical psychologist*
Surrey, Milt *artist*
†Susman, Sally *cosmetics executive*
†Susser, Ezra Saul *psychiatry educator*
†Susskind, Emily H. *broadcast executive*
Sussman, Alexander Ralph *lawyer*
Sussman, Gerald *publishing company executive*
Sussman, Jeffrey Bruce *public relations and marketing executive*
Sussman, Leonard Richard *foundation executive*
Sutherland, Dame Joan *retired soprano*
Sutter, Laurence Brener *lawyer*
Sutton, Karen E. *administrator*
Svenson, Charles Oscar *investment banker*
Sverdlik, Samuel Simon *physiatrist, physician*
Svinkelstin, Abraham Joshua *information technology executive*
Swain, Laura Taylor *judge*
Swain, Robert *artist*
Swan, William *actor*
Swann, Brian *writer, humanities educator*
†Swardenski, Jay Gordon *lawyer*
Swartz, Burton Eugene *artist, actor, theater director, writer, educator*
Swartz, Mark Evan *archivist*
Sweed, Phyllis *publishing executive*
Sweeley, Michael Marlin *foundation executive, public relations executive*
Sweeney, Thomas Joseph, Jr., *lawyer*
Sweeting, Charles Harvard *columnist, film director*
Swenson, Tree (Holly) *poet*
Swid, Stephen Claar *business executive*
Swift, John Francis *retired health care advertising company executive*
Swing, William Lacy *ambassador*
Swire, James Bennett *lawyer*
†Sykes, John *communications company executive*
†Syler, Rene *newscaster*
Sylla, Richard Eugene *economics educator*
†Symonette, Lys *foundation executive, musician, writer*
Szabo, Elizabeth MaryAnn *lawyer*
Szymkowiak, Mary L. *non-profit organization administrator*
Tafel, Edgar *architect*
†Tagliabue, Paul John *national football league commissioner*
Tagliaferri, Lee Gene *investment banker*
†Tagliarino, Salvatore *set designer, educator*
Taha, Assad M. *surgeon*
Takamura, Jeanette Chiyoko *dean*
Talbot, Phillips *Asian affairs specialist*
Talese, Gay *writer*
†Tallackson, Jeffrey Stephen *lawyer*
Talley, Truman Macdonald *publisher*
Tallmer, Margot Sallop *psychologist, psychoanalyst, gerontologist*
Talmi, Yoav *conductor, composer*
Tamaro, George John *consulting engineer*
Tan, Amy Ruth *writer*
Tanaka, Patrice Aiko *public relations executive*
Tancredi, Laurence Richard *law and psychiatry educator, physician*
†Tanenbaum, Gerald Stephen *lawyer*
†Tanenbaum, Jeffrey L. *lawyer*
†Tang, Youmin *research scientist*
Tannenbaum, Bernice Salpeter *national religious organization executive*
Tanner, Harold *investment banker*
Tanselle, George Thomas *English language educator, foundation executive*

Weinberg, John Livingston *investment banker*
†Weinberg, Mea Arlene *dental educator, researcher, consultant*
Weinberg, SamueL *pediatric dermatologist*
Weinberg, Steven Lewis *lawyer*
Weinberger, Harold Paul *lawyer*
Weiner, Andrew Jay *lawyer*
Weiner, Earl David *lawyer*
Weiner, Lawrence Charles *artist*
Weiner, Richard *public relations executive*
Weiner, Ronald Gary *accounting firm executive*
Weiner, Stephen Arthur *lawyer*
Weingrow, Howard L. *financial executive, investor*
Weinrich, Johnathan Edward *lawyer*
Weinschel, Alan Jay *lawyer*
Weinshenker, Naomi Joyce *clinical psychiatrist, educator, researcher*
†Weinstein, Harvey *film company executive*
Weinstein, Herbert *chemical engineer, educator*
Weinstein, I. Bernard *oncologist, geneticist, research administrator*
Weinstein, Martin *aerospace manufacturing executive, materials scientist*
†Weinstein, Robert *film company executive*
Weinstein, Ruth Joseph *lawyer*
Weinstein, Sharon Schlein *corporate communications executive, educator*
Weinstein, Sidney *retired university program director*
†Weinstock, David Marc *bone marrow transplantation and infectious diseases physician, researcher*
Weinstock, Leonard *lawyer*
Weir, Peter Frank *lawyer*
Weisbrod, Carl *lawyer, public official*
Weiser, Martin Jay *lawyer*
Weisl, Edwin Louis, Jr., *foundation executive, lawyer*
Weiss, Barry *recording industry executive*
†Weiss, Donald S. *real estate developer*
Weiss, Jonathan Arthur *lawyer*
Weiss, Lawrence N. *lawyer*
†Weiss, Mark *public relations executive*
Weiss, Myrna Grace *business executive*
Weiss, Samuel Abraham *psychologist, psychoanalyst*
†Weiss, Thomas George *university administrator, consultant*
Weissman, Susan *social services professional*
Weissmann, Gerald *medical educator, researcher, writer, editor*
Weitz, John *designer, writer*
Welch, Martha Grace *physician, researcher*
Weld, Jonathan Minot *lawyer*
Welikson, Jeffrey Alan *lawyer*
†Welish, Hester *artist*
Welish, Marjorie *poet*
Wellin, Keith Sears *investment banker*
Wellington, Harry Hillel *lawyer, educator*
Wellisz, Stanislaw *economics educator*
†Wells, Andrew Norman *lawyer*
Wells, Linda Ann *editor-in-chief*
Wells, Peter Scoville *marketing executive*
Welsh, Donald Emory *publisher*
Welt, Philip Stanley *lawyer, consultant*
Wender, Ira Tensard *lawyer*
Wender, Phyllis Bellows *literary agent*
Wenegrat, Saul S. *arts administrator, art educator, consultant*
†Wenner, Jann Simon *editor, publisher*
Werfelman, William Herman, Jr., *public relations executive*
Werner, Andrew Joseph *physician, endocrinologist, musicologist*
Werner, Robert L. *lawyer, consultant*
Werschulz, Arthur Gustav *computer and information sciences educator*
Werthamer, Nathan Richard *physicist*
Wesely, Edwin Joseph *lawyer*
Wesley, John Mercer *artist*
†Wesley, Richard C. *judge*
Wesser, Yvonne *artist*
†West, Alexander Brian *pathologist*
West, Blair *investment banker, consultant*
West, Paul Noden *author, playwright*
†West, Stephen Kingsbury *lawyer, director*
Wetschler, Ed *editor*
Wexelbaum, Michael *lawyer*
†Wexler, Allan *architect, art educator*
Wharton, Danny Carroll *zoo biologist*
Wharton, Ralph Nathaniel *psychiatrist, educator*
†Wheatley, Steven Charles *educational association administrator*
Whelan, Elizabeth Ann Murphy *epidemiologist*
Whelchel, Betty Anne *lawyer*
Whitaker, Mark Theis *magazine editor*
Whitcomb, James Howard, Jr., *investment banker*
White, Harry Edward, Jr., *lawyer*
White, John Patrick *lawyer*
†White, Kate *editor-in-chief*
†White, Katherine Patricia *lawyer*
White, Keith Gordon *bank executive, artist*
White, Lawrence J. *economics educator*
White, Mary Jo *lawyer*
White, Roger L., Jr., *graphic designer, art director*
†Whitehead, Colson *writer*
†Whitehead, Edgar Douglas *urology educator*
Whitehead, John Cunningham *bank executive, diplomat, philanthropist*
†Whitehead, William J. *advertising executive*
Whiteman, Douglas E. *publisher*
Whiteside, Duncan *disability and child welfare foundation executive*
Whiting, Anthony *executive search consultant*
Whiting, Gordon James *investment banker*
Whitman, Charles S., III, *lawyer*
†Whitman, Martin J. *portfolio manager*
Whitney, Craig Richard *journalist*
Whitney, Phyllis Ayame *author*
Whittemore, Laurence Frederick *private banker*
Whoriskey, Robert Donald *lawyer*
†Wibisono, Makarim *diplomat*
Widlund, Olof Bertil *computer science educator*
Wiener, Malcolm Hewitt *foundation executive*

Wiener, Marvin S. *rabbi, editor, executive*
Wiener, Solomon *writer, consultant, former city official*
Wiesel, Torsten Nils *neurobiologist, educator*
†Wiesenthal, Robert S. *corporate financial executive*
Wigmore, Barrie Atherton *investment banker*
Wilcox, John Caven *lawyer, corporate consultant*
†Wilcox, T.J. *filmmaker*
†Wildes, Leon *lawyer, educator*
Wilds, Bonnie *author, community volunteer*
Wile, Joan *composer, lyricist, singer*
†Wilensky, Saul *lawyer*
Wilford, John Noble, Jr., *science news correspondent*
Wilhjelm, Christian *conductor, artist*
†Wilkins, Amy P. *publishing executive*
Wilkinson, John Hart *lawyer*
Willett, Roslyn Leonore *public relations executive, food service consultant, writer*
William, Daniel Charles *retired physician*
Williams, Alexander Hazard, III, *health care executive, consultant*
†Williams, Arthur Joseph *film editor*
Williams, Dave Harrell *investment executive*
Williams, Diane *writer, editor*
Williams, Harriet Clarke *retired academic administrator, artist*
Williams, Ian George *writer*
Williams, Janice Machelle *pharmaceutical executive*
Williams, Lucinda *country musician*
Williams, Milton Lawrence *judge, educator*
Williams, Montel *television talk show host*
Williams, Reba White *financial executive, writer*
†Williams, Sue *artist*
Williamson, Douglas Franklin, Jr., *lawyer*
†Williamson, Philemona *artist*
Williamson, Richard Salisbury *ambassador*
†Williamson, Walter *lawyer*
Willinger, Lowell David *lawyer*
Willis, Beverly Ann *architect*
Willis, Ellen *journalist, educator*
Willis, John Alvin *editor*
†Willis, Richard, Jr., *writer, theater producer*
Willis, Thornton Wilson *painter*
Willis, William Ervin *lawyer*
Wilner, Joshua David *literature educator*
†Wilson, August *playwright*
Wilson, James Reid, Jr., *publishing executive*
†Wilson, Marie C. *foundation administrator*
Wilson, Morrow *actor, theater producer, writer, television producer, radio producer*
Wilson, Paul Holliday, Jr., *lawyer*
†Wilson, Robert Frank *graphics designer, property manager*
Wimpfheimer, Michael Clark *lawyer*
Winawer, Sidney J. *physician, clinical investigator, educator*
Winchester, Elizabeth Young *interior designer, consultant, space planner*
Windels, Paul, Jr., *lawyer*
Windhager, Erich Ernst *physiologist, educator*
Windsor, Laurence Charles, Jr., *publishing executive, writer*
Wineberg, Ronna I. *writer, lawyer*
Winer, Jessica Daryl *artist*
†Winfield, Richard Neill *lawyer*
Wing, John Russell *lawyer*
Winger, Ralph O. *lawyer*
Winick, Myron *educator, physician*
Winkleman, John Sandler *public relations executive*
Winship, Frederick Moery *journalist*
Winslade, Thomas Edwin *lawyer*
Winter, Roger *artist*
Winterer, Philip Steele *lawyer*
Winters, Robert Wayne *medical educator, pediatrician, healthcare executive*
†Winters, Terry *artist*
Wise, Aaron Noah *lawyer*
Wise, William Alfred *writer*
†Wiseman, Michael Martin *lawyer*
†Wishingrad, Jay Marc *lawyer*
Wishnick, Marcia Margolis *pediatrician, geneticist, educator*
Wisner, Frank George *insurance company executive, former ambassador*
Wisnosky, Thomas R. *television director*
Wit, Harold Maurice *investment banker, lawyer, investor*
Witherwax, Charles Halsey *lawyer, arbitrator, mediator*
Witkin, Eric Douglas *lawyer*
Witmeyer, John Jacob, III, *lawyer*
Wittstein, Edwin Frank *stage and film production designer*
†Wixom, Max Valentine *artist*
Wixom, William David *art historian, museum administrator, educator*
Wogan, Robert *broadcasting company executive*
Wolf, Carl F.W. *physician, biomedical engineer*
†Wolf, Diane R. *law consultant*
Wolf, Gary Wickert *lawyer*
Wolf, James Anthony *insurance company executive*
Wolf, Peter Michael *investment manager, writer*
†Wolfe, George C. *theater director, producer, playwright*
Wolfe, James Ronald *lawyer*
Wolfe, Melinda Beth *human resources executive*
†Wolfe, Thomas Kennerly, Jr., *writer, journalist*
Wolff, Alexander Nikolaus *writer*
Wolff, Edward Nathan *economist, educator*
Wolff, Jesse David *lawyer*
Wolff, Richard Joseph *public relations executive, consultant, historian*
Wolff, Virginia Euwer *writer*
Wolff, William F., III, *investment banker*
Wolff, William I. *surgeon, educator*
†Wolgemuth, Debra J. *obstetrics-gynecology educator*
Wolin, James Michael *health services executive*
Wolitzer, Steven Barry *investment banker*
Wolkoff, Eugene Arnold *lawyer*
Wolnek, Stephen S. *church administrator*
Wolper, Allan *journalist, educator*

Wolson, Craig Alan *lawyer*
†Wood, David Clarence *lawyer*
Wood, Frank *actor*
Woodcock, Les *editorial director*
Woodruff, Mark Reed *magazine editor*
Woods, Sarah Karen *communications consultant*
Wood-Smith, Donald *plastic surgeon*
Worenklein, Jacob Joshua *lawyer*
Worman, Howard Jay *internist, educator*
†Worsham, Hal Glenn *marketing professional*
Wortman, Richard S. *historian, educator*
Wray, Cecil, Jr., *lawyer*
†Wren, Gayden *playwright, theater director*
Wren, John D. *advertising executive*
†Wright, Faith-dorian *artist*
Wright, Gwendolyn *art center director, writer, educator*
Wright, Joseph Robert, Jr., *corporate executive*
Wright, Margaret Taylor *marketing consultant, publisher*
Wright, Sarah Elizabeth *writer, poet*
Wriston, Walter Bigelow *retired banker*
†WuDunn, Sheryl *journalist, correspondent*
Wulf, Melvin Lawrence *lawyer*
Wunderman, Jan Darcourt *artist*
Wuorinen, Charles Peter *composer*
Wurmfeld, Sanford *artist, educator*
Wyckoff, E. Lisk, Jr., *lawyer*
†Wyeth, James Browning *artist*
Wylie, James Malcolm *educator*
Wyn-Jones, Alun (William Wyn-Jones) *software developer, mathematician*
Wyse, Lois *advertising executive, author*
Wyss, David Alen *financial service executive*
Wyzner, Eugeniusz *diplomat*
Xia, Lulin *private equity investor*
Yablon, Leonard Harold *publishing company executive*
Yaffe, James *writer*
Yagan, Neda *physician, medical educator*
Yahalom, Joachim *radiologist, educator, oncologist, researcher*
Yalen, Gary N. *retired insurance company executive*
†Yamaguchi, Masaya *musician, educator*
Yamin, Michael Geoffrey *lawyer*
Yancey, Richard Charles *investment banker*
Yao, David Da-Wei *engineering educator*
Yao, Y. Lawrence *engineering educator*
Yapijakis, Constantine *environmental engineering educator, consultant*
Yates, Marypaul *textile company executive*
†Yeager, Dennis Randall *lawyer*
Yeager, George Michael *investment counsel executive*
Yegulalp, Tuncel M. *mining engineer, educator*
Yeh, Hsu-Chong *radiology educator*
Yelenick, Mary Therese *lawyer*
Yellin, Victor Fell *composer, music educator*
Yerman, Fredric Warren *lawyer*
Yerushalmi, Yosef Hayim *historian, educator*
Yetman, Leith Eleanor *academic administrator*
Yglesias, Helen Bassine *author, educator*
Yin, Beatrice Wei-Tze *medical researcher*
Yodowitz, Edward Jay *lawyer*
†Yoffie, Erich H. *church administrator*
Yohay, Steven Jacob *healthcare company executive, consultant*
†Yoo Bowne, Helen *otolaryngologist, educator*
†Yorinks, Arthur *children's author, writer, director*
York, Alexandra *writer, lecturer*
Yoshiuchi, Ellen Haven *health educator, clinical counselor*
Young, Alice *lawyer*
Young, Estelle Irene *dermatologist, educator*
Young, Genevieve Leman *publishing executive, editor*
Young, George Haywood, III, *investment banker*
Young, Iven S. *physician*
Young, John Edward *lawyer*
Young, Michael Warren *geneticist, educator*
Young, Nicholas *physician*
Young-Mallin, Judith *writer, archivist*
Youngwood, Alfred Donald *lawyer*
Yousef, Mona Lee *psychotherapist*
Yu, Andrew *minister*
Yurchenco, Henrietta Weiss *ethnomusicologist, writer*
Yurt, Roger William *surgeon, educator*
Zacharias, Thomas Elling *real estate executive*
Zackheim, Adrian Walter *editor*
†Zagat, Nina *publishing executive*
†Zagat, Tim *publishing executive*
Zagoren, Joy Carroll *health facility director, researcher*
Zahnd, Richard H. *professional sports executive, lawyer*
Zaitzeff, Roger Michael *lawyer*
Zammit, Joseph Paul *lawyer*
Zand, Dale Ezra *business management educator*
Zane, Arnie *performing company executive, choreographer*
Zanetti, Richard Joseph *publisher*
Zann, Nicholas T. *artist*
Zarnowitz, Victor *economist, educator*
Zaslowsky, David Paul *lawyer*
Zatlin, Gabriel Stanley *physician*
Zauderer, Mark Carl *lawyer*
Zawistowski, Stephen Louis *psychologist, educator*
Zedrosser, Joseph John *lawyer*
Zeldin, Richard Packer *publisher*
Zeligson, Sheryl *lawyer*
†Zelin, Madeleine *think-tank executive*
†Zeller, Paul William *lawyer*
†Zelnick, Strauss *entertainment company executive*
Zerin, Steven David *lawyer*
Zerman, Melvyn Bernard *publishing company executive, author*
Zeuschner, Erwin Arnold *investment advisory company executive*
†Zha, Jianying *writer, educator*
†Zheng, Changguang K. *investment banker*
Zhu, Ai-Lan *opera singer*
Zhu, Zhigang *computer science educator*
†Ziegler, Henry Steinway *lawyer*

Ziegler, John Augustus, Jr., *lawyer*
Zifchak, William C. *lawyer*
Zimmerman, Kathleen Marie *artist*
Zimmerman, Sol Shea *pediatrician*
Zimmerman, William Edwin *newspaper editor, publisher, writer*
Zimmett, Mark Paul *lawyer, educator*
†Zinczenko, David *publishing executive*
Zindel, Bonnie *writer, psychotherapist*
Zinder, Norton David *genetics educator, university dean*
Zinn, Keith Marshall *ophthalmologist, educator*
Zipay, Joanne Margaret *theatre educator, director, dramaturge*
Zirin, Ronald Andrew *classics educator, psychoanalyst*
Zirinsky, Bruce R. *lawyer*
Zirkle, William Denman *investment company executive*
†Zissu, Roger L. *lawyer*
Zitrin, Arthur *physician*
Zitsman, Jeffrey Leonard *pediatric surgeon*
†Zivin, Norman H. *lawyer*
Zlowe, Florence Markowitz *artist*
Zoeller, Donald J. *lawyer*
†Zolberg, Vera Lenchner *sociology educator*
Zolotow, Charlotte Shapiro *author, editor*
Zoogman, Nicholas Jay *lawyer*
Zornow, David M. *lawyer*
Zosike, Joanie Fritz *theater director, actor*
Zoullas, Deborah Decotis *private investor, entrepreneur*
Zuck, Alfred Christian *consulting mechanical engineer*
Zucker, Howard *lawyer*
Zucker, Stefan *tenor, writer, editor, radio broadcaster*
Zucker-Franklin, Dorothea *physician, educator*
†Zuckerman, Joseph *lawyer*
†Zuckerman, Mortimer Benjamin *publisher, editor, real estate developer*
†Zuckerman, Paul Herbert *lawyer*
Zukerman, Michael *lawyer*
Zukerman, Pinchas *concert violinist, violist, conductor*
Zumoff, Barnett *endocrinologist, medical researcher*
Zwickler, Allen *investment advisor, educator*

New York Mills
Blank, William Russell *mathematics educator*

Newark
Hemmings, Madeleine Blanchet *management consultant, media consultant, not-for-profit fundraiser*
Hughes, Owen Willard *artist*
†Reid, James Edward *lawyer*
Williams, Wayne Francis *art educator, sculptor*

Newburgh
Adams, Barbara *English language educator, poet, writer*
Aruza, Albert Francis *consulting firm executive*
Fallon, Rae Mary *psychology educator, early childhood consultant*
Geiser, William Francis *education educator*
Grossman, Stanley Lawrence *surgeon*
Joyce, Mary Ann *principal*
Ochs, Richard Wayne *artist, gallery owner*
Saturnelli, Annette Miele *school system administrator*
Schwake, Torsten *chiropractor*
Severo, Richard *writer*
Weintraub, Arthur E. *health service association executive*
Zarutskie, Andrew John *town official*
†Zeisel, Laura *lawyer, educator*

Newcomb
Chatzky, Herbert *music educator*

Newport
Wilson, Eldon Ray *minister*

Newtonville
Conroy-LaCivita, Diane Catherine *city administrator*

Niagara Falls
Askins, Arthur James *accountant, finance management and auditing executive*
Berrigan, Patrick Joseph *lawyer*
Bharadwaj, Prem Datta *physics educator*
†Douglas, Frances Sonia *minister*
Gromosiak, Paul *historian, consultant, writer, science and math educator*
Holtschneider, Dennis H. *university official, priest*
Knowles, Richard Norris *chemist*
Levine, David Ethan *lawyer*
Sarpel, Suleyman Celalettin *oncologist*

Niagara University
Foote, Chandra Jeanet *teacher educator*
Johnson, Larry Clinton *college administrator*
†Kidwell Jr., Roland E. *finance educator, writer, researcher*
Northcutt, Wayne *history educator*
O'Leary, Daniel Francis *academic administrator, priest*
Osberg, Timothy Michael *psychologist, educator, researcher*
†Sze, Susan *philosopher, educator*
Whitney, Stewart Bowman *social psychology educator and program director*

Niskayuna
Biklen, Paul *retired advertising executive*
†Chupp, Raymond Edward *mechanical engineer, researcher*
†Edelheit, Lewis S. *research physicist*
Fitzroy, Nancy deLoye *engineering executive, mechanical engineer*
†Hancu, Ileana *research scientist*
Huening, Walter Carl, Jr., *retired consulting application engineer*

†Hughes, Eric Scott *music educator*
Kambour, Roger Peabody *retired polymer physical chemist, researcher*
†Kapur, Ajay *systems engineer*
Katz, Samuel *geophysics educator*
†Kebbede, Anteneh *materials scientist, researcher*
Lafferty, James Martin *retired physicist*
Mangan, John Leo *retired electrical manufacturing company executive, international trade and trade policy specialist*
Nichols, Albert Myron *retired minister*
White, Frederick Andrew *physics educator, physicist*
Wright, Theodore Paul, Jr., *political science educator*
Yamin-Garone, Mary Sultany *writer, graphic designer*

North Babylon
Tipirneni, Tirumala Rao *metallurgical engineer*

North Bangor
†Hastings, Ralph B. *music educator*

North Boston
Herbert, James Alan *writer*

North Massapequa
Felker, Gerald Lee *music educator, musician*

North Salem
Burlingame, Edward Livermore *book publisher*
Silverman, Alice Hope *interior designer*

North Syracuse
Roberts, Robert *engineering organization executive, think-tank executive*

North Tonawanda
Coleman, Kimberlee Michele *critical care nurse*
Megahed, Mohamed Salah *neurologist, educator*
Powers, Bruce Raymond *writer, English language educator, consultant*

North Woodmere
Aviles, Alice Alers *psychologist*

Northport
Allocca, John Anthony *medical research scientist*
Cheng, Edward Hsin-Yi *gastroenterologist, researcher, educator*
†De Carolis, Philip Joseph *space designer, educator*
Donenfeld, Kenneth Jay *management consultant*
†Miller, Philip John *insurance consultant*
Oi, Chieko Munnie *physician*
Reinertsen, Norman *retired aircraft systems company executive*
Weber, Ray Everett *engineering executive, consultant*
Wingerter, John Parker *artist, photographer*

Norwich
Garzione, John Edward *physical therapist*
Palahnuk, Donald Walter, Jr., *chemical engineer*
Stratton, Josephine Mabel *special education educator*

Norwood
Church, Richard Dwight *electrical engineer, scientist*

Nyack
Brecht, Warren Frederick *retired business executive*
†Cane, Barbara Haak *lawyer*
Carey, Lois J. *psychotherapist*
Cember, M. Nathan *lawyer, speaker*
Danaher, James P. *philosopher, educator*
Degenshein, Jan *architect, planner*
Flood, Diane Lucy *retired marketing professional*
Flood, H(ulda) Gay *editor, consultant*
Gaudy, Edward *landscape architect, consultant*
Hendin, David Bruce *literary agent, writer, consultant, numismatist*
Karp, Peter Simon *marketing executive*
Keil, John Mullan *advertising agency executive, artist*
†Kenote, Marie Herseth *music educator*
†Laski, John N. *finance educator*
†Lum, Tammy Kar-Hee *concert pianist, education educator*
Mann, Kenneth Walker *retired minister, psychologist*
McMahon, Donald J. *statistician, consultant*
Oursler, Fulton, Jr., *editor, writer*
Poston, Larry Allan *religious studies educator*
Ptalis, Donald L. *telecommunications company executive, entrepreneur*

Oakdale
Carnevale, Louis *civil engineer, inventor*
Cunha, Carlos Alberto *political scientist, educator*
†Fayez, Mehanni Samuel *finance educator*
†Iberti, Elissa Tatigikis *painter, costume designer, educator, independent curator*
†Jordan, Kevin David *director, educator, minister*
Lu, Yuxin *historian, linguist*
Ventimiglia, Katharine Jane Garver *education educator*

Oakfield
Mikulski, John Michael *music educator*

Oakland Gardens
†Freeley, James *labor union administrator*

Oceanside
Behr, Donald Jay *retired internist, cardiologist, educator*
Glass, Noah F. *music educator, web site designer*
†Kyler, Arlene *advertising executive*
Rosenbaum, Frances (Phran Ginsberg) *entrepreneur*

Rubin, Hanan *retired insurance company executive*

Odessa
Stillman-Myers, Joyce L. *artist, educator, writer, illustrator, consultant*

Ogdensburg
Franz, David Arthur *library director*
Krol, John Casimir *city manager, municipal planner*
†Smith, Carol Ann *academic administrator*

Olcott
Sansone, Rosemary Margaret *retired gifted and talented education educator*

Old Bethpage
Buzzelli, Dennis Kevin *mechanical engineer*

Old Chatham
†Severs, Charles A., III, *lawyer*

Old Westbury
†Al-Douri, Taha A. *architect, educator*
Barbera, Anthony Thomas *accountant, educator*
Chaudhry, Humayun Javaid *physician, medical educator, flight surgeon, writer*
Dibble, Richard Edward *academic administrator*
†Friedman, Jonathan Block *architect, educator, writer*
†Goldstein, Leslie Deborah *library director*
†Jabbour, Georgette N. *linguist, educator*
Navia, Luis E. *philosophy educator, writer*
O'Brien, Adrienne Gratia *communications educator*
Ozelli, Tunch *economics educator, consultant*
Schure, Matthew *academic administrator*
†Tiscornia, Ana Maria *artist, educator, writer*
van Wie, Paul David *secondary school educator, historian, educator*

Olean
Broughton, Barry A. *naturopathic physician*
Horn, Daniel Joseph *pharmacist*
Lewis, Fred Harvey *allergist, immunologist*
†Mazon, Margaret Fausold *language educator*
Ratanawongsa, Boonlua *ophthalmologist*
Stevens, Edward Ira *information systems educator*

Olivebridge
Osborne, Seward Russell *writer*

Oneida
Matthews, William D(oty) *lawyer, consumer products manufacturing company executive*
†Rudnick, Marvin Jack *lawyer*
Stevens, James Walter *manufacturing representative*
†Walsh, Gregory E. *protective services official*

Oneonta
†Desjarlais, Georgia Kathrine *retired military officer*
Hickey, Francis Roger *physicist, educator*
Horner, Carl Matthew *chemistry educator*
Johnson, Richard David *retired librarian*
†Kissane, Daniel *school librarian*
Lapidus, Patricia Jean *social worker*
Malhotra, Ashok Kumar *philosophy educator*
Malone, Laurence Joseph *economics educator, writer*
Merilan, Michael Preston *astrophysicist, educator, dean*
Michaelsen, Niels Henrik *painter, illustrator*
†Nishida, Mieko *educator*
†Potter, Janet L. *university librarian, administrator*
Shrader, Douglas Wall, Jr., *philosophy educator*
Travisano, Thomas Joseph *English language educator*
Wentworth, Murray Jackson *artist, educator*
Wesley, Marilyn Clarke *English language educator*

Ontario
Loomis, Norman Richard *physician*
Nevil, Linda *nursing administrator*

Orangeburg
†Citrome, Leslie Lucien *psychiatrist, educator*
†Filoramo, Dorothy Christine *academic administrator*
†Ginsberg, Stephen D *neuroscientist*
Greenberg, William Michael *psychiatrist*
Harvey, Virginia Marie *nurse, administrator*
Hsu, Donald Kung-Hsing *educator, management consultant*
Levine, Jerome *psychiatrist, educator*
†Lin, Shang Ping *statistician, researcher*
Rivet, Diana Wittmer *lawyer, developer*
Ulrich, Max Marsh *retired executive search consultant*
†Wagoner, Russell A. *music educator*
Ye, Biqing *biomedical engineer, researcher*
Yuan, Aidong (David Yuan) *cell biologist, researcher*

Orchard Park
Biggs, Edmund Logan *college administrator*
Bledsoe, Drew *professional football player*
Franklin, Murray Joseph *retired steel foundry executive*
Geiger, Loren Dennis *classical musician*
Greenwood, Audrey Gates *retired librarian*
Keenan, John Paul *management educator, consultant, psychologist*
Lee, Richard Vaille *physician, educator*
Mariani, David Frank *artist*
Moulds, Eric Shannon *professional football player*
Oliver, Dominick Michael *business educator*
†Staebell, William A. *music educator*
Sullivan, Mortimer Allen, Jr., *lawyer*
Williams, Gregg *professional football coach*

Orient
Hanson, Thor *retired health agency executive and naval officer*

Ossining
Cadge, William Fleming *gallery owner, photographer*
Daly, William Joseph *lawyer*
Dolmatch, Theodore Bieley *management consultant*
Getts, Nino *studio owner*
Gilbert, Joan Stulman *retired public relations executive*
†Hill, Nils Arvid *artist, educator*
Maloney, William James *dentist, educator*
Perlman, John Niels *retired educator, poet*
Reynolds, Calvin *management consultant, business educator*
Robinson, Karen Vajda *clinical dietitian*
Rothman, Barbara Schaeffer *special education educator*
Sri-Jayantha, Sri Muthuthamby *mechanical engineer*
Wolfe, Mary Joan *physician*

Oswego
Baitsell, Wilma Williamson *artist, educator, lecturer*
Bishop, Rand *retired humanities educator*
Fox, Michael David *retired art educator*
Gordon, Norman Botnick *psychology educator*
Greene, Stephen Craig *lawyer*
Lisk, Edward Stanley *musician, educator, conductor*
Loveridge-Sanbonmatsu, Joan Meredith *communication studies and women's studies educator, poet*
Messere, Frank *communications educator*
Moody, Florence Elizabeth *education educator, retired college dean*
Silveira, Augustine, Jr., *chemistry educator*
Smiley, Marilynn Jean *musicologist*
†Thurber, Timothy Nels *historian, educator*

Owego
†Coppens, Laura Kathryn *special education educator*
Davis, Joan *English language educator*
Feavearyear, John Edgar *aerospace systems engineer*
Kemp, Eugene Thomas *retired veterinarian*
McCann, Jean Friedrichs *artist, educator*
Zendle, Howard Mark *software development researcher*

Oyster Bay
Bernstein, Jacob *lawyer*
Gable, John Allen *historian, association executive, educator*
Hoxie, Ralph Gordon *educational administrator, author*
Mooney, James David, Jr., *aerial photographer*
Ott, Gilbert Russell, Jr., *lawyer*
Prey, Barbara Ernst *artist*
Robinson, Edward T., III, *lawyer*
Russell, Mary Wendell Vander Poel *non-profit organization executive*
Schwab, Hermann Caspar *banker*
Trevor, Bronson *economist*
Walsh, Charles Richard *retired banker*

Ozone Park
Catalfo, Betty Marie *health service executive, nutritionist*
Singh, Seopaul *security firm executive*

Painted Post
†Kirk, Connie Ann *English educator, writer*
Ogden, Anita Bushey *nursing educator*

Palisades
Cane, Mark Alan *oceanography and climate researcher*
Davis, Dorothy Salisbury *writer*
Elevitch, Morton D. *writer, editor*
†Goddard, Lisa *meteorologist*
Hayes, Dennis Edward *geophysicist, educator*
†Huang, Huei-Ping *research scientist*
Kellogg, Herbert Humphrey *metallurgist, educator*
Knowlton, Grace Farrar *sculptor, photographer, painter*
Krainin, Julian Arthur *film director, producer, writer, cinematographer*
Mason, Simon James *climatologist*
Miller, Roberta Balstad *science administrator*
Polk, Milbry Catherine *media specialist*
Porta, Siena Gillann *sculptor, educator*
Richards, Paul Granston *geophysics educator, seismologist*

Palmyra
Blazey, Mark Lee *management consultant*
Hartman, Susan Margaret *community mental health nurse*
Hill, Cynthia Maressa *ecological planner, environmental scientist*

Patchogue
Barna, Douglas Peter *collection agency executive*
†Cartier, Rudolph Henri, Jr., *lawyer, legal educator*
Dyckman, Richard Harris *cardiologist*
Esteve, Edward V. *lawyer*
†Fawcett, Bernadine L. *marriage and family counselor*
Gibbons, Edward Francis *psychobiologist*
Igneri, David Sebastian *elementary education educator, lifeguard*
†Kelly, Dorothy Ann *language educator, writer*
Marr, Robert Bruce *physicist, educator*
Orlowski, Karel Ann *elementary school educator*

Patterson
Jaffee, Kay *musician, musicologist*

Pawling
Jones, James Earl *actor*

†Light, Sybil Elizabeth *executive secretary*
Peale, Ruth Stafford (Mrs. Norman Vincent Peale) *religious leader*
Thomas, Cheryl Ann *educational administrator*
Utter, Donald L. *music educator*
Wood, Christopher L.J. *real estate executive*

Pearl River
†Almoazen, Hassan *research scientist*
Barik, Sudhakar *microbiologist, research scientist*
†Barringer, William Charles *retired chemist*
Bigelis, Ramunas *research scientist*
Bryant, Karen Worstell *financial advisor, investment company executive*
Chen, Guodong *scientist, enzymologist, biochemical engineer*
†Doedée, Marijo *chemist*
Forgacs, Joseph *mycotoxicologist*
Galante, Joseph Anthony, Jr., *computer programmer*
†Gorovits, Boris *analytical biochemist*
Karben, Ryan Scott *state legislator*
Meyer, Irwin Stephan *lawyer, accountant*
Wang, John Xiaowu *software company executive*
Yamashita, Ayako *research scientist*

Peconic
Aldcroft, George Edward *guidance counselor*

Peekskill
†Brody, Jo-Ann *artist, educator*
Harte, Andrew Dennis *transportation company executive, travel agent*
Jackson, Linda B. *social worker*
Mason, Rebecca Sussa *retired secondary education educator*

Pelham
†Borzova, Alla Aleksandra *composer, conductor*
Eaton, Richard Gillette *retired surgeon, educator*
Hearle, Douglas Geoffrey *public relations consultant*
Weiss, Stuart Lloyd *television and radio producer, tax attorney*

Penfield
†Bagale, John R. *music educator*
†Birkby, Paul Donald *library media specialist, consultant*
Perkins-Carpenter, Betty Lou *fitness company executive*
†Weerasinghe, Renu M. *quality assurance professional*

Penn Yan
Berlyn, Sheldon *art educator, artist*
Kilburn, Penelope White *retired data processing executive*
Strouse, Wayne Steven *physician*

Perry
Kelly, Michael Joseph *lawyer*

Peru
Dawson, James Clifford *environmental science educator, geologist*

Phoenix
Ackerman, Roger G. *ceramic engineer*

Piermont
Berkon, Martin *artist*
Brechtel, Unda Jurka *library director*
Dusanenko, Theodore Robert *retired educator, county official*

Pine City
†Stepulis, Vincent G. *retired music educator*

Pine Plains
Janitschek, Hans *journalist*

Pittsford
Benson, Warren Frank *composer, educator*
Bernstein, Paul *retired academic dean*
Braunsdorf, Paul Raymond *lawyer*
Coleman, Paul David *neurobiology researcher, educator*
Dobbs, Herbert Hotaling *automotive executive, consultant, engineer, scientist, retired army officer*
Faloon, William Wassell *physician, educator*
French, Henry Pierson, Jr., *historian, educator*
George, Richard Neill *retired lawyer*
Goldstein, David Arthur *biophysicist, educator*
Green, Martin Lincoln *financial analyst, consultant*
Hampson, Thomas Meredith *lawyer*
†Hartman, James Matthew *lawyer*
Herge, Henry Curtis, Jr., *consulting firm executive*
Hollingsworth, Jack Waring *mathematics and computer science educator*
†Kalnitz, Paul Richard *software developer*
Mooney, Lillian Harnett *social worker, consultant*
Saini, Vasant Durgadas *computer software company executive*
Scutt, Robert Carl *lawyer*
Snyder, Donald Edward *corporate executive*
Stonehill, Eric *lawyer*
Taub, Aaron Myron *healthcare administrator, consultant*
Ten Haken, Richard Ervin *retired educational administrator*
Thompson, Brian John *university administrator, optics educator*
Thorndike, Elizabeth *educator*
Turri, Joseph A. *lawyer*
Willett, Thomas Edward *lawyer*

Plainview
Bell, James Thomas *housing authority official*
Fein, Leona Moss *artist*
Feller, Benjamin E. *actuary*
Kelemen, John *neurologist, educator*

Krauss, Leo *urologist, educator*
Lieberman, Elliott *urologist*
McCaffrey, John Anthony *brokerage house executive*
Mensch, Alan R. *physician, educator*
Sherwood, James Webster, III, *author, limousine company owner*
Snyder, Joel Bennett *engineering executive, educator*

Plandome
Williams, Morgan Lloyd *retired investment banker*

Plattsburgh
Beach, Charles Randall *economic developer*
Bethlen, Francis R. *emeritus business and economics educator, food distribution engineering specialist*
Dossin, Ernest Joseph, III, *credit consulting company executive*
†Ransom, Christina Roxane *librarian*
†Rumney, Thomas Arthur *geographer, educator*
†Torres-Padilla, Jose Luis *English educator*
Treacy, William Joseph *electrical and environmental engineer*
Virostek, Robert Joseph *physician*

Pleasant Valley
Avakian, Helen Ross *musician, educator*
Becofsky, Arthur Luke *arts administrator, writer*
Marshall, Natalie Junemann *economics educator*
Odescalchi, Edmond Péry *international financial consultant, author*

Pleasantville
Ahrensfeld, Thomas Frederick *lawyer*
Annese, Domenico *landscape architect*
†Campriello, Christina Matthews *lawyer, librarian*
Eschweiler, Peter Quintus *planning consultant*
Hundersmarck, Lawrence F. *theology studies educator*
†Katen, Joan Alice *political scientist, educator*
Keller, Mary Beth *consumer research consultant*
Leo, Jacqueline M. *editor-in-chief, Internet company executive*
†Maceli, Anthony G *music educator*
†McEwen, Laura *publishing executive*
Nelson, K. Bonita *literary agent*
Pike, John Nazarian *optical engineering consultant*
†Reddicliffe, Steven *periodical editor-in-chief*
Reps, David Nathan *finance educator*
†Schrier, Eric *publishing executive*
†Tao, Lixin *computer scientist, computer science educator*
Urban, Joseph Jaroslav *engineer, consultant*
†Willcox, Christopher Patrick *magazine editor*

Poestenkill
Drew, George *writer, educator*

Point Lookout
Stack, Maurice Daniel *retired insurance company executive*

Pomona
DeMaio, Barbara Patricia *social worker*
Fisch, Edith L. *lawyer*
†Frelow, Robert Dean *retired school system administrator, writer*
Gletsos, Constantine *chemist*
†Gupta, Sanjeev Kumar *pharmaceutical executive, director*
Landa, George *cardiologist, internist*
Landau, Lauri Beth *accountant, tax consultant*
Zugibe, Frederick Thomas *retired pathologist*

Port Chester
Ailloni-Charas, Dan *marketing executive*
Harris, Elisabeth Tamlyn *psychiatric social worker*
Levin, Jeffrey L. *lawyer*
Marcus, Joel David *pediatrician*
Mariam, Thomas Fred *public relations executive, radio producer*
Messina, JoAnn L. *court administrator*
Oppenheimer, Suzi *state legislator*

Port Jefferson
Davidson, Cynthia Ann *writer, English language educator*
Gilmore, Arthur Warham *retired aeronautical engineer*
Hindin, Seymour *lawyer*
Hirschl, Simon *pathologist*
Strong, Robert Thomas *former mayor, middle school educator*

Port Jervis
Rifkin, Joseph S. *political and business consultant*

Port Washington
Brownstein, Martin Herbert *dermatopathologist*
Candido, Arthur Aldo *publishing and distribution company executive*
Cunnick, Gloria Helen *artist*
Feldman, Jay Newman *lawyer, telecommunications executive*
Forman, James Douglas *lawyer*
Futter, Joan Babette *former school librarian*
Gaddis, M. Francis *mechanical and marine engineer, environmental scientist*
Goh, David Shuh-Jen *psychology educator*
Goldschein, Steven M. *computer retail executive*
Hackett, John Byron *advertising agency executive, lawyer*
Jay, Frank Peter *writer, lexicographer, educator*
Johnson, Tod Stuart *market research company executive*
Jones, Farrell *retired judge*
Kossin, Sanford Marshall *illustrator*
†Leeds, Richard *computer marketing executive*
Levy, Marlene Lois *clinical social worker*
Miller, John David *manufacturing company executive*

Mittelstaedt, Arthur Howard, Jr., *educational educator*
Phelan, Arthur Joseph *financial executive*
†Sandy, Catherine Ellen *librarian*
Sonnenfeldt, Richard Wolfgang *management consultant*
Ullman, Leo Solomon *lawyer*
Williams, George Leo *historian, landmark preservationist, educator*

Potsdam
†Atesoglu, H. Sonmez *economist, educator*
Campbell, Gregory August *engineering educator, consultant*
Chin, Der-Tau *chemical engineer, educator*
Cross, John William *foreign language educator*
DeGhett, Stephanie Coyne *writer, educator*
Fendler, Janos Hugo *chemistry educator*
†Galo, Gary A. *audio-visual specialist, educator*
Gruda, Benjamin Joseph *pharmacist*
Hanson, David Justin *sociology educator, researcher*
Harder, Kelsie Brown *retired language professional, educator*
†Hebert, Marianne *librarian*
†Helenbrook, Brian Todd *education educator*
Hopke, Philip Karl *chemical engineering educator, atmospheric scientist*
Islam, Muhammad Azadul *physicist, educator, researcher*
†Komara, Edward Michael *musicologist*
Lunt, Lora G. *international education educator, language educator*
Mackay, Raymond Arthur *chemist*
Matijevic, Egon *chemistry educator*
Mochel, Myron George *mechanical engineer, educator*
Privman, Vladimir *physics educator*
†Regan, Marie Carbone *retired language educator*
†Rengaswamy, Raghunathan *chemical engineering researcher, educator*
Rudiger, Lance Wade *secondary school educator*
Serio, John N. *language educator*
Shen, Hung Tao *hydraulic engineering educator*
Stevens, Sheila Maureen *teachers union administrator*
Vaska, Lauri *chemist, retired educator*
Wickman, Peter M. *sociologist, educator*

Poughkeepsie
†Adin, Richard H(enry) *lawyer, editor, publisher*
Bartlett, Lynn Conant *English literature educator*
†Basener, Richard Francis Joseph *mathematician, application developer*
Beck, Curt Werner *chemist, educator*
†Berlin, Doris Ada *psychiatrist*
Bodack, Mark Peter *physician, medical educator*
Brakas, Jurgis (George) Hoegh *philosopher, educator*
Brakas, Nora Jachym *education educator*
†Carino, Aurora Lao *psychiatrist, hospital administrator*
Chen, Zhaoqing *electronics engineer*
Conklin, D(onald) David *academic administrator*
Daniels, Elizabeth Adams *English language educator*
Deiters, Sister Joan Adele *psychoanalyst, nun, chemistry educator*
de Leeuw, Frank *economist*
Dietz, Robert Barron *lawyer*
Doherty, John Francis *criminal justice educator*
Dolan, Thomas Joseph *judge*
Fergusson, Frances Daly *college president, educator*
Glasse, John Howell *retired philosophy and theology educator*
Griffen, Clyde Chesterman *retired history educator*
Guski, Richard Henry *software engineer*
Hadaller, David Lawrence *dean*
Handel, Bernard *accountant, actuarial and insurance consultant, lawyer*
Hansen, Karen Thornley *accountant*
Hansraj, Kenneth Karamchand *surgeon, research scientist*
Harmelink, Herman, III, *clergyman, author, educator, ecumenist*
Heller, Mary Bernita *psychotherapist*
Henley, Richard James *health facility administrator*
†Htoo, Maung S. *communications executive*
Hytier, Adrienne Doris *French language educator*
Johnson, M(aurice) Glen *political science educator*
Johnson-Lans, Shirley B. *economist, educator*
Katopis, George A. *electrical engineer*
Kelley, David Christopher *philosopher*
†Kenny, Philip William *lawyer*
Kim, David Sang Chul *publisher, evangelist, retired seminary president*
Kranis, Michael David *lawyer, judge*
Lang, William Warner *physicist*
LaRose, Keith Vernon *lawyer*
Lewis, Richard Laurence *academic administrator, digital artist*
Logue, Joseph Carl *electronics engineer, consultant*
†Mantz, Jeffrey William *anthropologist, educator*
†Moon, Seungsook *sociologist, educator*
Murthy, Kurukundi Krishna *neurosurgeon*
O'Neil, D. James *lawyer*
Opdycke, Leonard Emerson *retired elementary, secondary and college-level educator, publisher*
†Osborne, Robert Michael *music educator, vocalist*
Ostertag, Robert Louis *lawyer*
Peck, H. Daniel *literature educator, educator*
Pliskin, William Aaron *physicist*
Rhodes, Geraldine Bryan *secondary school administrator*
Rosenblatt, Albert Martin *state appeals court judge*
Shapiro, Ronald Gary *psychologist*
Sharp, Ronald Alan *English literature educator, dean, author*

Shatz, Phillip *lawyer, banker, insurance executive*
Sherman, Ethan *contractor, publisher*
†Simons, Robert Edward *mechanical engineer, consultant*
Slade, Bernard Newton *electronics company executive*
Sproat, Christine A. *judge*
Stridsberg, Albert Borden *advertising consultant, educator, editor*
Taphorn, Joseph Bernard *lawyer*
†Torres, Robin Diller *academic administrator*
Turgeon, Paul R. *computer program manager*
VanBuren, Denise Doring *corporate communications executive*
Van Norden, Bryan William *Asian studies educator*
Van Zanten, Frank Veldhuyzen *retired library system director*
Wallace, Herbert Norman *lawyer*
Willard, Nancy Margaret *writer, educator*
Wilson, Richard Edward *composer, pianist, music educator*
Wygan, Dorothy Camilla *foundation administrator*

Poughquag
LaRussa, Joseph Anthony *optical company executive*

Pound Ridge
Abramovitz, Max *architect*
Darcy, Keith Thomas *finance company executive, educator*
Ferro, Walter *artist*
Rubino, John Anthony *management and human resources consultant*
Schwebel, Renata Manasse *sculptor*

Purchase
†Andrews, David Ralph *lawyer*
Bannon, Nancy *performing arts educator*
Cohen, Alan Norman *business executive*
Dillon, John T. *paper company executive*
Ehrman, Lee *geneticist, educator*
†Enrico, Roger A. *soft drink company executive*
†Faraci, John Vincent, Jr., *paper company executive*
Fink, Judy Smolka *social worker*
Finnerty, Louise Hoppe *beverage and food company executive*
Foner, Nancy *anthropologist, educator*
Frost, Elizabeth Ann McArthur *physician*
Gedeon, Lucinda Heyel *museum director*
Gioffre, Bruno Joseph *lawyer*
Jones, James Edwards, Sr., *religion educator*
Kelly, Edmund Joseph *lawyer, investment banker*
Lacy, Bill *academic administrator, architect*
†Lyons, Gary George *lawyer*
Magaziner, Elliot Albert *musician, conductor, educator*
†McKenna, Matthew Morgan *lawyer*
†Medoff, Rafael *historian, editor*
†Mizelle, Dary John *composer, educator*
Papaleo, Louis Anthony *accountant*
Pauley, Matthew Alfred *law educator*
†Phillips, Carly *writer*
Redkey, Edwin Storer *history educator*
Reinemund, Steven S. *food products executive*
Ryan, Edward W. *economics educator*
Sacco, John Michael *accountant*
†Shields, David Brandon *historian, educator*
Shulman, Barbara *professional counselor*
†Vardin, Patricia Anne *education educator*
†Waclawski, Janine *psychologist, educator*
Wallach, Ira David *lawyer, business executive*
Wallach, Kenneth L. *paper company executive*
Waller, Gary Fredric *English language educator, administrator, poet*
Wilson, Sherri Diane *shopping center official*
Wright, David L. *food and beverage company executive*

Putnam Valley
Amram, David Werner *composer, conductor, musician*

Queens
Hobbs, Helen T.B. *librarian*
†Singh, Ronald *social sciences educator, researcher*

Queens Village
Heckman, Lucy T. *librarian*

Queensbury
Bitner, William Lawrence, III, *retired banker, educator*
Cavaluzzi, Anthony David *English studies educator*
De Pan, Harry McCarthy *retired surgeon*
Grunblatt, Hilda Ruth *translator, editor*
Mead, John Milton *banker*
Sleight, Virginia Mae *lawyer*

Quogue
Hines, William Eugene *banker*

Ransomville
DeLorenzo, David W. J. *human resources consultant*
Mayer, George Merton *retired elementary education educator*

Ravena
†Andrews, Scott Michael *music educator*
Caulfield, Patrick Francis *physician*

Red Hook
†Cranna, Christina M. *social services specialist*
†Fitzpatrick, John *poet*
Pfeiffer, Werner Bernhard *artist, educator*
Rovigo, Connie Brigitta *jewelry and fine arts retailer*

Rego Park
Cortese, Edward *marketing and public relations executive*

Iosebashvili, Alexander *research scientist, educator*
†Manton, Thomas Joseph *former congressman*
Thomas, James Edward *accountant*
Tsui, Soo Hing *educational research consultant*
Winter, Darius Gerjon *internist*

Remsenburg
Billman, Irwin Edward *publishing company executive*
Hirsch, Ann Ullman *retired academic administrator*

Rensselaer
Hull, Raymond Whitford *public relations executive*
Nack, Claire Durani *artist, author*
Perez, Ana Veronica *developmental biology researcher*
Semowich, Charles John *art historian, art dealer and appraiser, curator, artist, musician*
Stull, Scott D. *archaeologist*

Rensselaerville
Dudley, George Austin *architect, planning consultant, educator*

Rexford
Kresge, Jennifer Alison *physician assistant*
Nitecki, Joseph Zbigniew *librarian*
Schmitt, Roland Walter *retired academic administrator*

Rhinebeck
Fink, J. Theodore *planner, consulting firm executive*
Hellerman, Leo *retired computer scientist and mathematician*
McGuire, John Francis, Jr., *construction company executive*
Melley, Steven Michael *lawyer*
Rabinovich, Raquel *painter, sculptor*
Scherr, Allan Lee *computer scientist, executive, consultant*
Swift, Paul *editor*

Rhinecliff
Conklin, John Roger *retired electronics company executive*

Richmond Hill
Hamroff, Michael Scott *archives executive*

Richmondville
†Bartholomew, Debra Lee *publishing executive*

Ridge
Blume, Martin *physicist*

Ridgewood
Jones, Harold Antony *banker*
Meehan, Richard Andrew *investment banker*

Riverdale
†Bencsáth, Katalin A. *mathematician*
Chimsky, Mark Evan *publishing consultant*
Lee, Dong Hwan *business administration educator*
Mendez, Ruben Policarpio *diplomat, educator, economist*
Nolte, Claire Elaine *history educator*

Riverhead
Daughtrey, Margery L. *plant pathologist*
Kelley, Christopher Donald *lawyer*
Kent, Robert John *marine biologist*
Roland, David Leonard *retired broadcast production educator*
Thompson, Marie Angela *computer engineer, consultant*

Rochester
Adams, G. Rollie *museum executive*
Adiletta, Debra Jean Olson *business analyst consultant*
Agrawal, Govind Prasad *optics educator*
Akiyama, Toshio *cardiologist, educator, researcher*
Amy, Michaël Jacques *art historian, educator, art critic*
Angel, Allen Robert *mathematics educator, author, consultant*
†Antonova, Natalya *music educator, musician*
†Arnold, Georgianne Lee *pediatric geneticist, clinical researcher*
Atkin, Louis Phillip *recycling business executive*
†Atkins, Carl J. *conductor, educator*
Aydelotte, Myrtle Kitchell *retired nursing administrator*
Bannon, Anthony Leo *museum director*
†Basavappa, Ravi *biophysical scientist, educator*
Batabyal, Amitrajeet Amarnath *economics educator*
Baum, John *physician*
Bauman, M. Garrett *English educator*
Benitez, John Griswold *medical toxicologist*
Bennett, John Morrison *hematologist and medical oncologist*
Berg, Robert Lewis *physician, educator*
Berman, Milton *history educator*
Bidlack, Jean Marie *pharmacologist, educator, medical researcher*
Bigelow, Nicholas Pierre *physicist, educator*
†Blades-Zeller, Elizabeth L. *music educator, vocologist*
Bluhm, William Theodore *political scientist, educator*
Blyth, John E. *lawyer, educator*
Boeckman, Robert Kenneth, Jr., *chemistry educator, organic chemistry researcher*
Bonfiglio, Thomas Albert *pathologist, educator*
Bouyoucos, John Vinton *research and development company executive*
Bowen, William Henry *dental researcher, dental educator*
†Braley, Oleta Pearl *home health care provider*
Braun, Wilhelm *retired educator*

Ketchum, William Clarence *author, educator*
Lawi, David Steven *energy, oil and gas, entertainment, agriservice and thermoplastic resins industries executive, merchant banker*
Lehman, Lawrence Herbert *consulting engineering executive*
Lehman, Myra Harriet *sculptor, dental hygienist*
McDonnell, Mary Theresa *travel service executive*
Metzger, Frank *management consultant*
Nelson, Vita Joy *editor, publisher*
Newburger, Howard Martin *psychoanalyst*
Norcia, Stephen William *advertising and internet advertising executive, consultant*
Pearson, Nathan Williams *communications and investment executive*
Schmitz, Robert Allen *publishing executive, investor*
†Tisch, Laurence Alan *diversified manufacturing and service executive*
Troller, Fred *graphic designer, painter, visual consultant, educator*
Vauclair, Marguerite Renée *communications and sales promotion executive*
Vernon, Lillian *mail order company executive*
Waltz, Joseph McKendree *neurosurgeon, educator*
Wilmot, Irvin Gorsage *former hospital administrator, educator, consultant*

Rye Brook
Aquino, Joseph Mario *clinical psychologist*
Eck, Robert Joseph *lawyer*
Kuntzman, Ronald *pharmacology research executive*
†Landegger, George F. *engineering executive*
†Levy, Howard Alan *music educator*
Masson, Robert Henry *paper company executive*
†McKenna, John A., Jr., *data processing executive*
†Schorer, Marianne T. *entrepreneur, consultant*
†Sprout, Francis *artist, educator*

Sabael
Morrill-Cummins, Carolyn *social worker, consultant*

Sag Harbor
Barry, Nada Davies *retail business owner*
Blanc, Peter (William Peters Blanc) *sculptor, painter*
Brandt, Anthony Scott *free-lance writer, consultant*
Clemente, Vince *journalist, retired English educator, historian*
Cory, David H. *museum administrator, former real esate broker*
†De Cordova, Hector Armando *artist, consultant, art educator*
Epstein, Jason *publishing company executive*
Pashman, Susan Ellen *writer*
Pierce, Lawrence Warren *retired federal judge*
Walker, Lou Ann *writer*

Sagaponack
Appleman, Philip *poet, writer, educator*
Butchkes, Sydney *artist*
Cedering, Siv *poet, writer*
Eden, John *ophthalmologist*
Korman, A. Gerd *history, educator, writer*

Saint Albans
Bess, Olean *educator, counselor*

Saint Bonaventure
†Godet-Calogeras, JeanFrançois *historian, educator*
Wood, Paul William *language educator*

Saint James
Bigeleisen, Jacob *chemist, educator*
†Richards, Fran W. *social worker*
Van Dover, Karen *middle and elementary school educator, curriculum consultant, language arts specialist, lecturer*

Salamanca
Brady, Thomas Carl *lawyer*
Patel, Arun Parmanand *physician*

Salem
Haycock, Dean Allen *writer, consultant*
Nussbaum, Jay *philosophy educator, writer*

Salt Point
Lackey, Mary Michele *physician assistant*

Sanborn
Michalak, Janet Carol *reading education educator*
Schmidt-Bova, Carolyn Marie *career and technical school administrator*

Sands Point
Busner, Philip H. *retired lawyer*
Cohen, Ida Bogin (Mrs. Savin Cohen) *import and export executive*
Cullinan, Bernice E(llinger) *education educator*
Hoynes, Louis LeNoir, Jr., *lawyer*
Lear, Erwin *anesthesiologist, educator*
Tane, Susan Jaffe *retired manufacturing company executive*
Wurzel, Leonard *retired candy manufacturing company executive*

Saranac
Smith, J. Kellum, Jr., *foundation executive, lawyer*

Saranac Lake
Brown, Jonathon Andrew *healthcare executive*
Caguiat, Carlos Jose *health care administrator, Episcopal priest*
Gibbs, Charles Clarence *anesthesiologist*
Jakobe, Virginia Ellis *retired educator*
†Smiley, Stephen Todd *research scientist*

Saratoga Springs
Bouchard, Paul Eugene *artist*
Carey, Margot Beckmann *fundraiser*
Davis, John Eugene *restaurant executive, beverage company executive, disc jockey*
Dickinson, Richard Henry *accountant*
Farley, John Joseph *library science educator emeritus*
†Fenton, Michael I. *artist, educator*
Ford, Dexter *retired insurance company executive*
Garro, Barbara *artist, writer*
†Glotzbach, Philip A. *academic administrator*
Goldensohn, Barry Nathan *poet, retired language educator*
Masie, Elliott *training executive*
McKnight, Joyce Sheldon *adult educator, community organizer, mediator*
†Millhauser, Steven *writer*
Porter, David Hugh *pianist, classicist, academic administrator, liberal arts educator*
Ratzer, Mary Boyd *secondary education educator, librarian*
Riley, Dawn C. *educational philosopher, researcher*
†Rosengarten, Lewis Bart *composer, educator*
Upton, Richard Thomas *artist*
†Van Wye, Benjamin David *conductor*
Wait, Charles Valentine *banker*
Wallner, Ludwig John *principal*
†Willig, William Paul *lawyer*

Saugerties
de Mare, George *author*

Sayville
Bernstein, Neil Howard *music educator*
Edelman, Hendrik *library and information science educator*
Lippman, Sharon Rochelle *art historian, curator, art therapist, writer, artist, filmmaker*
Trahan, Janet Marie *artist, former gallery owner, art educator*
Wurtz, Margaret Johnston *artist, calligrapher*

Scarborough
Byrne, Robert Eugene *chess columnist*
Parks, Robert Henry *consulting economist, educator*
Stigall, Phyllis Graham *retired librarian*
Taylor, Nell Cochrane *non-profit association executive*
Wittcoff, Harold Aaron *chemist*

Scarsdale
Abbe, Colman *investment banker*
†Angel, Dennis *lawyer*
Bayar, Julia Beryl *interior designer*
Beuchert, Edward William *lawyer*
Blinder, Abe Lionel *management consultant*
Blitman, Howard Norton *construction company executive*
Borg, Robert Frederic *civil engineer*
Bruck Lieb Port, Lilly *retired consumer advisor, broadcaster, columnist*
Callaghan, Georgann Mary *lawyer*
Carnase, Thomas Paul *graphic designer, typographic consultant*
Celliers, Peter Joubert *public relations specialist*
Citrin, Yale *light industry executive*
Clark, Merrell Mays *management consultant*
Clehane, Diane Catherine *journalist, writer, communications executive*
Cohen, Irwin *economist*
Decaminada, Joseph Pio *retired insurance company executive*
DeFrancis, Suellen Maria *interior architect*
Dulit, Everett Paul *psychiatrist, educator*
Edis, Gloria Toby *pediatrician*
†Ellis, James Henry *lawyer, management consultant*
Fenichel, Alvin Henry *financial executive*
Fishbach, Mitchell Harvey *cardiologist*
†Florman, Samuel Charles *civil engineer*
Gerber, Roger Alan *lawyer, business consultant*
Gollin, Stuart Allen *accountant*
Goodman, Jordan Elliot *journalist*
Goodwin, Everett Carlton *minister*
Graff, Henry Franklin *historian, educator*
Heese, William John *music publishing company executive*
Hoffman, Richard M. *lawyer*
Jacobs, Theodore Joseph *psychiatrist, educator*
Johnson, Boine Theodore *instruments company executive, mayor*
Johnson, Katharyn Price (Mrs. Edward F. Johnson) *civic worker*
Johnson, William Alexander *clergyman, philosophy educator*
Kanter, Carl Irwin *retired lawyer*
Kaufman, Robert Jules *communications consultant, lawyer*
King, Robert Lucien *lawyer*
Korzenik, Sidney S. *lawyer*
†Lawyer, William Grove *conservationist*
Lieberman, Florence *clinical social worker, educator*
†Liegl, Joseph Leslie *lawyer*
Lipman, Marvin Matthew *medical educator*
Macchia, Vincent Michael *lawyer*
Machover, Wilma Simon *musician*
Moser, Marvin *physician, educator, author*
Naughton, Ann Elsie *educator*
Newman, Stacey Clarfield *artist, curator*
O'Brien, Edward Ignatius *private investor, corporation director*
O'Neill, Michael James *editor, author*
Palmer, Trevelyan Edward *physician, thoracic and cardiovascular surgeon*
Perez, Louis Anthony *radiologist*
Perko, Kenneth Albert, Jr., *lawyer, art dealer*
Pope, Leavitt Joseph *broadcast company executive*
Porosoff, Harold *chemist, research and development director*
Ries, Martin *artist, educator*
Rogalski, Lois Ann *speech and language pathologist*
Schultz, Harley *consulting company executive*
Schwartz, Kenneth Stuart *surgeon*
Shaw, Grace Goodfriend (Mrs. Herbert Franklin Shaw) *publisher, editor*
Sheehan, Larry John *lawyer*
Stamas, Stephen *not-for-profit administrator*
Toff, Ruth Bluthenthal *editor*
†Tolliver, Lisa Marie *management consultant*
Topping, Audrey Ronning *photojournalist, author*
Topping, Seymour *author, educator*
Wesely, Yolanda Thereza *retired sociologist, marketing professional, researcher*
Wolfzahn, Annabelle Forsmith *psychologist*
Young, Pamela Ruth *social worker, consultant, therapist*

Schenectady
Afifi, Alaa Youssef *cardiothoracic surgeon*
Alpher, Ralph Asher *physicist, educator*
Barber, Nicholas Carl *tax specialist, consultant, real estate executive*
Baskous, Athan A. *retired civil engineer*
Board, Joseph Breckinridge, Jr., *political scientist, educator*
DeLuke, Dean M. *oral surgeon*
Farber, Martin Stuart *rheumatologist*
Fell, Samuel Kennedy (Ken Fell) *infosystems executive*
Fischer, Michael David *civil engineer*
†Fitzner-Atchinson, Judith Ann *youth center director*
Fleischer, Robert Louis *physics educator*
Frost, Robert Edwin *chemistry educator*
†Golub, Lewis *supermarket company executive*
†Golub, Neil *supermarket chain executive*
Grace, Ellen Maria *attorney*
†Hartman, Carmen Teresa *language educator*
Hermance, Jr., Myron E. *conductor, educator*
Hull, Roger Harold *academic administrator*
Jonas, Manfred *historian, educator*
Jones, Edward Allen *engineer*
Levine, Howard Arnold *judge*
Levine, Sanford Harold *lawyer*
Lommel, James M. *information technology manager*
Luborsky, Fred Everett *research physicist*
Mancuso, J(ohn) James *librarian*
Mayes, Brian A. *toxicologist*
†McCafferty, Dennis A. *composer, musician*
Mikata, Yozo *mechanical engineer, application developer*
Morris, John Selwyn *philosophy educator, college president emeritus*
Mueller, Philip Winfield *lawyer*
Murray, Edward Rock *insurance broker*
O'Baire, Marika *community health nurse, writer*
Pearson, Timothy Alfred *newspaper circulation executive*
Philip, A. G. Davis *astronomer, editor, educator*
Ringlee, Robert James *consulting engineering executive*
Robb, Walter Lee *retired electric company executive, management company executive*
Sager, Robert Wendell *retired social work administrator*
Schenck, John Frederic *physician*
Seltzer, Joanne *poet*
†Sharlet, Robert *political science educator, researcher*
Skudder, Paul Albert *vascular surgeon*
Smith, Lowell Scott *physicist*
Solomon, Harvey Donald *engineer, educator*
†Sorum, Christina Elliott *academic administrator*
Sternlicht, Beno *research and development company executive*
†Szokody, Aniko *pianist, educator*
Taub, Eli Irwin *arbitrator, mediator, lawyer*
Weiner, Clare Frances *social worker, psychotherapist*
†Wery, Brett Lars *music educator, conductor*
Wilson, Delano Dee *consultant*
Yablon, Jay Russell *lawyer*
Zhu, Yudong *medical imaging researcher*

Schenevus
Fielder, Dorothy Scott *retired postmaster*

Schroon Lake
†Williams, Wayne M. *music educator*

Scotia
de la Rocha, Carlos A. *retired physician*
Graper, William Earl *state agency administrator*
Mosteller, Henry W. *retired electrical engineer*
†Schulman, Ruth Meryl Aronson *development director*

Scottsville
Reitz, JoAnne Bellam *health information executive*
Williams, Henry Ward, Jr., *lawyer, writer*

Sea Cliff
Martin, David S. *retired educator, administrator*
Mourashkin, Boris V. *composer, sound therapist, poet, performer, producer*
Popova, Nina *dancer, choreographer, director*

Seaford
†Kulpa, Aldona *pharmacist*
Moore, Sister Mary Francis *parochial school educator*
Schlossberg, Fred Paul *elementary education educator*
Setzler, William Edward *chemical company executive*
Spencer, Jean *executive*
Tuzil, Teresa Jordan *clinical social worker, psychotherapist*

Seagate
Levitt, Sidney Bernard *lawyer*

Selden
Lustik, Boris *pediatrician*

Selkirk
†Christoph, Peter Richard *historical editor, archivist*

Seneca Falls
Norman, Mary Marshall *educator, counselor, therapist*
Potts, Billie Luisi *non-profit administrator*

Setauket
Becker, Kenneth H. *physician*
Davenport, Deborah Morgan *obstetrician, gynecologist*
Dunaief, Leah S. *newspaper editor, publisher, writer*
Gard, Richard Abbott *religious institute executive, educator*
Irving, A. Marshall *retired marine engineer*
Levine, Sumner Norton *industrial engineer, educator, editor, author, financial consultant*
Palmedo, Philip Franklin *management consulting company executive*
Robinson, Richard M. *technical communication specialist*
Simpson, Louis Aston Marantz *English educator, author*

Setaukey
†Venkateswaran, Pramila *educator*

Shady
Malkine-Falvey, Fern Sylvie *writer, journalist, painter*

Shelter Island
Dowd, David Joseph *banker, builder*
Moran, Daniel Thomas *dentist, poet*

Shelter Island Heights
Culbertson, Janet Lynn *artist*

Sherburne
Dodd, Jack Gordon, Jr., *physicist, educator*
Dodd, Mary Ann *organist, educator*
Smith, William Edward *sales executive, telecommunications executive*

Sherrill
Campanie, Samuel John *lawyer*

Shirley
†Harper, Catherine B. *primary school educator*
Morote, Elsa-Sofia *social sciences educator, business consultant*

Shoreham
Ciborowski, Paul John *counseling psychology educator*
Spier, Peter Edward *artist, author*

Shortsville
Rosati, Sharon Wetmore *social worker*

Shushan
†Plute, Patricia Jean *retired writer*
Villet, Barbara *writer*
†Witten, Anita *artist, editor*

Sidney
Haller, Irma Tognola *secondary education educator*
Rivers Baker, Dawn *writer, publisher, consultant*

Skaneateles
†Filkins, Susan Esther *small business owner*
Huxford, J. David *retired sales representative*
Weiss, Rhett Louis *business executive, lawyer*

Sleepy Hollow
Chia, David Thien-Shing *internist, gastroenterologist*
Ferguson, Douglas Edward *financial executive*
Flynn-Connors, Elizabeth Kathryn *editor*
Hershman, Jack Ira *urologist*
Maun, Mary Ellen *computer consultant*
Mills, Nancy Ellyn *hematologist, oncologist*
Schmidt, Klaus Franz *advertising executive*

Slingerlands
Bragle, George W. *criminal justice educator*
Childs, Rhonda Louise *motivational speaker*
Jacobs, Karen Louise *medical technologist*
Lahiri, Kajal *economics educator*
Zacek, Joseph Frederick *history educator, international studies consultant, Central and East European culture and affairs specialist*

Smallwood
Golden, Elliott *judge*

Smithtown
Austerlitz, Howard *electronics engineer, writer*
Ayrovainen, Robert Michael *music educator*
†Brooks, Sondra *lawyer*
Dowis, Lenore *lawyer*
Fritzhand, Irvin Dick *psychologist*
Goodman, Richard Shalem *lawyer, orthopedic surgeon*
Hartman, Stephen Wheeler *education educator*
†Holland, Marvin Arthur *lawyer, educator*
Pelcyger, Iran *retired principal*
Rockensies, John William *mechanical engineer*
Rosen, Bruce Ira *psychiatrist, researcher, educator*
Spellman, Thomas Joseph, Jr., *lawyer*
Sporn, Stanley Robert *retired electronic company executive*
†Tucker, Victoria Lynne *education educator, consultant*
Zippin, Allen Gerald *neurosurgeon*

Snyder
Breverman, Harvey *artist*

Somers
Anderson, John Erling *chemical engineer*

Bauman, William Allen *pediatrician, educator, health systems consultant*
Bensen, Annette Wolf *graphic art company consultant*
†Cahill, John T. *consumer products company executive*
Cohn, Howard *retired magazine editor*
Elix, Douglas Thorne *computer company executive*
Faga, Anthony, Jr., *sales operations professional*
Gulick, Donna Marie *accountant*
Lane, David Oliver *retired librarian*
Lemke, Judith A. *lawyer*
†McGuire, Pamela Cottam *lawyer*
Reznick, Steven Michael *orthopedic surgeon, educator*
Rubin, Samuel Harold *physician, consultant*
Sanford, Linda S. *information technology executive*
Sayers, Ken W(illiam) *writer, consultant and public relations executive, web editor*
Terman, Lewis Madison *electrical engineer, researcher*

South Huntington
Kelly, Michael Joseph *academic administrator, consultant*

South Ozone Park
Banks, Robert Lee *publisher, author, jazz guitarist, composer, arranger*

South Richmond Hill
Scheich, John F. *lawyer*

South Salem
Ferguson, Mary Carfagno *artist*
†Knijff, Jan-Piet *musician, educator*
Rosenbaum, Harold L. *conductor, music educator*

South Setauket
Berger, H. Jean *retired physical education educator*
Friedlander, Gerhart *nuclear chemist*
Poli, Kenneth Joseph *editor, writer, photographer*
Richardson, Charles Marsh *electrical engineer, educator*
Solomon, Randall Adam *physician*

Southampton
†Atkins, Victor Kennicott, Jr., *investment banker*
Brokaw, Clifford Vail, III, *investment banker, business executive*
Brophy, James David, Jr., *humanities educator*
Culp, Michael Bronston *investor, writer, publisher*
Freeman, Elaine Lavalle *sculptor*
Graham, Howard Barrett *publishing company executive*
Kanovitz, Howard *artist, educator*
Lerner, Abram *retired museum director, artist*
Lopez, David *lawyer*
Melter, Robert Alan *mathematics educator, researcher*
Needham, James Joseph *retired financial services executive*
†Rodas, Daniel *academic administrator, finance educator*
Roth, Howard *chemist, engineer, consultant*
†Toma, Gail C. *educator*

Southold
Bachrach, Howard L. *biochemist*
Callis, Jerry Jackson *veterinarian*
Small, Bertrice W. *writer*
Wissemann-Widrig, Nancy *artist*

Sparkill
Dahl, Arlene *actress, writer, designer, cosmetic executive*
†Lauture, Denize *language educator, writer*
Myers, Adele Anna *artist, educator, nun*
Nelson, Marguerite Hansen *special education educator*
†Sewell, Stacy Kinlock *historian, educator*

Sparrow Bush
Miiller, Susan Diane *artist*
Murray, William Bruce *opera singer*

Speculator
Kelly, Paul John *priest*

Spencer
Grunberg, Slawomir *film and television producer and director, director of photography*

Spencerport
Cassin, Sandra Jane *social worker*
Jones, Alan D. *music educator*
Vizy, Kalman Nicholas *research physicist, educator*

Spencertown
Hawkins, Robert Garvin *management educator*
Lieber, Charles Donald *publisher*

Spring Valley
†Barr, Harvey Stephen *lawyer*
†Cacciola, Patrick Barry *art association administrator*
†Liberis, George Nicholas *surgeon*
Rubin, Allan B. *radiologist, consultant*
Steinberg, Milton *civilian military employee*

Stamford
Bergleitner, George Charles, Jr., *investment banker*

Stanfordville
Tetor, David R. *agriculturist, consultant*

Staten Island
†Arcia, Luis Alfredo *artist*
Auh, Yang John *librarian, educational administrator*
Behnke, Henryk Jorg *marketing and fundraising executive*
Benjamin, Gilbert Leon *career counselor*
Berman, Barbara *educational consultant*
Black, Lawrence *librarian*
Bogin, Marc B. *internist, cardiologist*
Brady, Christine Ellen *education coordinator*
Bruckstein, Alex Harry *internist, gastroenterologist, geriatrician*
†Choo, Kristin E. *journalist*
Clark, Sylvia Dolores *business educator*
Cross, Ronald *musicologist, educator*
De Luca, Anthony James *psychoanalyst, theologian*
Dobis, Joan Pauline *education administrator*
Fafian, Joseph, Jr., *management consultant*
Ferzli, George Salem *surgeon*
Fisher, Barbara Gail *writer, educator*
Foster, Paul *playwright*
Fung, Amy Shu-Fong *accountant*
†Fusco, John Anthony *lawyer*
Garzi, John Joseph *maintenance engineer*
Gavrity, John Decker *insurance company executive*
Gelbein, Jay Joel *accountant*
Grodman, Richard Stephen *internist, cardiologist*
Herman, Robert John *artist manager, producer, author, music industry advisor*
Holder, Calvin Beresford *history educator*
Howard, Davis Jonathan *lawyer, educator, writer*
Hu, Shaohua *political scientist*
Humphries, Edward Francis *lawyer*
Jarrett, Mark Paul *rheumatologist, medical administrator*
Johansen, Robert John *electrical engineer*
†Kahn, Jim *former magazine publisher*
Kennedy, Colleen Geralyn *nurse, social worker*
Klingle, Philip Anthony *law librarian*
Landron, Michel John *lawyer*
†Lawrence, Marilyn Catherine *language educator*
†Lockhart, Patricia Ann *elementary school educator*
Lombardi, Giancarlo *Italian language educator*
Lopez Del Castillo, Alfredo *anesthesiologist*
Lutkenhouse, Anne *non-profit executive*
†Margolin, Leon *physician*
Marra, Ralph Peter *lawyer*
†Matveev, Alexei V. *business educator*
Mayer, Andrew Mark *librarian, journalist*
Meltzer, Yale Leon *economist, educator*
Mercaldo, David *elementary school educator, writer*
Miller, Claire Cody *lawyer, mediator*
Miller, Wayne *actor, designer, producer, impresario*
Nelson, Carey Boone *sculptor*
Neuberger, Jerome M. *lawyer*
†Newhouse, Donald E. *newspaper publishing executive*
†Newhouse, Samuel I., Jr., *publishing executive*
†Norberg, Tilda Ann *psychotherapist*
Parente, Louise *social worker*
Pillari, Vincent Thomas *obstetrician-gynecologist, educator*
Popler, Kenneth *behavioral health services administrator, psychologist*
Popp, Lilian Mustaki *writer, educator*
Porter, Darwin Fred *writer*
†Reilly, Margaret Catherine (Madge Reilly) *secondary school educator, writer*
Reing, Alvin Barry *special education educator, psychologist*
Robison, Paula Judith *flutist*
Roig, Miguel *psychology educator*
Saha, Paul Santosh *physician*
Santiamo, Joseph Patrick *geriatrician*
Savino, Michael Anthony *surgeon*
†Schulenberg, David Louis *musician, educator*
Seeley, David Stevens *education educator*
Shiau, John Sou-Cheng *neurosurgeon*
Shullich, Robert Harlan *systems analyst*
Silverberg, Michael Barry *anesthesiologist*
Simkhovich, Semen Lasarevich *engineering educator, researcher*
†Smart, William Okrafo *education educator, educational consultant*
Spada, Dominick *pharmacist*
†Springer, Marlene *university administrator, educator*
Stathopoulos, Peter *internist*
Stearns, Stephen Jerold *history educator, writer*
Storberg, Eric Philip *financial planner*
Thomas, Charles Columbus *educator, artist*
†Uttaro, Thomas Edward *information officer, statistician*
Velinov, Milen Todorov *physician, researcher*
†Villanueva, E. Gary *internist, educator*
Vinet, George Ellsworth, Jr., *foundation administrator*
Wilson, Alice McAteer *secondary education educator*
Winter, Steven *internist, cardiologist*
Yang, Song-Yu *research biochemist*

Stillwater
†O'Connor, Abigail Elizabeth *mathematician, educator, science educator*

Stone Ridge
Terpening, Donald Lester *science educator, medical technologist*
†Vought, Hans Peter *education educator*

Stony Brook
†Akella, Umasundari Srivenkata *research scholar*
Alexander, John Macmillan, Jr., *chemistry educator*
Anderson, Michael Thomas *mathematics researcher, educator*
Andriola, Mary R. *neurologist, pediatrician*
Aronoff, Mark H. *linguistics educator, writer, consultant*
Bilfinger, Thomas Victor *surgeon, educator*
Bokuniewicz, Henry Joseph *oceanography educator*
Bonner, Francis Truesdale *chemist, educator, university dean*
Booth, George *cartoonist*
Brandwein, Ruth Ann *social welfare educator, administrator, author*
Brown, Gerald Edward *physicist, educator*
Carlson, Harold Ernest *endocrinologist, educator*
Cesa, Michael Peter *cardiologist, consultant*
†Chandran, Latha *pediatrician, educator*
Chen, Dongqing *medical image processing researcher*
Chen, JiuHua *physicist, geophysicist, educator*
Chen, John J. *biostatistician, educator*
Cochran, James Kirk *dean, oceanographer, geochemist, educator*
Cook, Jeannine Salvo *library consultant*
Davis, James Norman *neurologist, neurobiology researcher*
Dervan, John Patrick *cardiologist*
Dietrich, Dean Forbes *academic administrator*
Dolezal, Vaclav Jan *retired mathematician, educator*
Dorojevets, Mikhail *application developer, educator*
†Franco, Charles *language educator*
Fritts, Harry Washington, Jr., *physician, educator*
Gambino, Richard Joseph *materials science engineering*
Geller, Marvin Alan *meteorology educator, researcher*
Geyer, Dennis Lynn *university administrator and registrar*
Glimm, James Gilbert *mathematician, educator*
Goldberg, Homer Beryl *English language educator*
Goodman, Norman *sociologist, researcher*
Greene, William Harris *hospital administrator*
Grim, Patrick Neal *philosopher, logician, educator*
Harris, Alice Carmichael *linguist, educator*
Harvey, Christine Lynn *publishing executive*
Heyman, Richard E. *psychology educator*
Huang, Michael Bailou *librarian*
Ihde, Don *philosophy educator, university administrator*
Jasiewicz, Ronald Clarence *anesthesiologist, educator*
Jonas, Steven *public health physician, health policy analyst, writer*
†Judex, Stefan *psychologist, educator*
Jyringi, Darlene M. *gerontologist*
Kahn, Peter B. *physics educator*
Katkin, Edward Samuel *psychology educator*
Kenny, Shirley Strum *academic administrator*
Kirz, Janos *physicist*
Koppelman, Lee Edward *regional planner, educator*
Kuchner, Eugene Frederick *neurosurgeon, educator, neuroscientist*
Kuspit, Donald Burton *art historian, art critic, educator*
Kvilekval, Kara Helle Victoria *vascular surgeon*
Lane, Dorothy Spiegel *preventive medicine physician*
Laspina, Peter Joseph *computer resource educator*
Lawson, H(erbert) Blaine, Jr., *mathematician, educator*
Lennarz, William Joseph *research biologist, educator*
Levin, Richard Louis *English language educator*
Levinton, Jeffrey S. *biology educator, oceanographer*
Liang, Jerome Zhengrong *radiology educator*
†Luft, Benjamin J. *medical educator, health facility administrator*
Lurie, Abraham *social worker, educator*
Meyers, Morton Allen *physician, radiology educator*
Michelsohn, Marie-Louise *mathematician, educator*
Mignone, Mario B. *Italian studies educator*
Miller, Frederick *pathologist*
†Mirza, Humair *cardiologist, educator*
Moll, Ute Martha *pathologist, medical researcher*
Mundie, Gene E. *nursing educator*
Neuberger, Egon *economics educator*
Ohannessian, Harry Haroutune *travel agency executive*
Ojima, Iwao *chemistry educator*
Pekarsky, Melvin Hirsch *artist*
†Peterson, Deane Millar *astronomer, educator*
Pindell, Howardena Doreen *artist*
Priebe, Cedric Joseph, Jr., *pediatric surgeon*
Ricotta, John Joseph *vascular surgeon, educator*
Rifkin, Barry *dean, medical educator, researcher*
Rohlf, F. James *biometrician, educator*
Roth, Susan Austin *author, photographer*
†Sañudo-Wilhelmy, Sergio A. *adult education educator*
Schneider, Mark *political science educator*
Schoenfeld, Elinor Randi *epidemiologist*
Segal, Jeffrey A. *political scientist, educator*
†Semmel, Bernard *historian, educator*
Semyonov, Oleg G. *research scientist*
Shamash, Yacov *dean, electrical engineering educator*
Sokoloff, Leon *pathology educator*
Sreebny, Leo M. *oral biology and pathology educator*
Steigbigel, Roy Theodore *infectious disease physician and scientist, educator*
Steinberg, Amy Wishner *dermatologist*
Stolzberg, Mark Elliott *psychologist*
Stone, Elizabeth Cecilia *anthropology educator*
Swanson, Robert Lawrence *oceanographer, academic program administrator*
Tanur, Judith Mark *sociologist, educator*
Tewarson, Reginald Prabhakar *retired mathematics educator, consultant*
Travis, Martin Bice *political scientist, educator*
Tucker, Alan Curtiss *mathematics educator*
†Videb[00e6]k, Bente A. *humanities educator*
†Weisbrot, Deborah Marcia *psychiatrist*
Wurster, Charles Frederick *environmental scientist, educator*
Yang, Chen Ning *physicist*
Yang, Yuanyuan *computer science and electrical engineer, educator*
†Yildirim, Emre Alper *adult education educator*
Zemanian, Armen Humpartsoum *electrical engineer, mathematician*

Stony Point
Carter, Richard *publisher, writer*
Diederich, Michael David, Jr., *lawyer*
Ricci, Daniel Michael *protective services official*

Stuyvesant
Tripp, David Enders *numismatist, art historian, cartoonist, author*
Tripp, Susan Gerwe *museum director*

Suffern
Bhardwaj, Sushil *medical educator*
Codispoti, Andre John *allergist, immunologist*
Hawver, Carolyn Dunn *pharmaceutical production executive*
Lefkowitz, Louis Hirsch *obstetrician-gynecologist*
Lieberman, Charles *economist*
Menon, Gopinathan Kunnariath *scientist, researcher*
ommanday, Sue Nancy Shair *English language educator*
Oppenheim, Jeffrey Sable *neurosurgeon*
Raven, Luisa Antonia *nurse, psychotherapist*
Riba, Netta Eileen *retired secondary school educator*
Stack, Daniel *lawyer, financial consultant*
Sutherland, George Leslie *retired chemical company executive*

Syosset
Barry, Richard Francis *retired life insurance company executive*
Bermas, Stephen *lawyer*
Doerfler, Leo G. *audiology educator*
Heller, Al *marketing consultant, business journalist*
Irving, Jeffrey Alan *management consultant, educator, lawyer*
Kniffin, Paula Sichel *insurance sales executive*
†Lief, Eugene Paul *physicist*
Schiff, Peter Grenville *venture capitalist*
Stevens, Daniel Francis *author*
Streitman, Jeffrey Bruce *education administrator*
†Theodosius, *retired leader of the Orthodox Church in America*
Vermylen, Paul Anthony, Jr., *oil company executive*

Syracuse
Abbott, George Lindell *librarian*
Ackerman, Kenneth Edward *lawyer, educator*
†Alao, Adekola Olatunji *psychiatrist, educator*
Albino, Joseph Xavier *writer, educator, photographer*
†Alhadheri, Shabib Ali *pediatrician, cardiologist*
Alston, William Payne *philosophy educator*
†Ashutosh, Kumar *pulmonologist, educator*
Baker, Bruce Edward *orthopedic surgeon, consultant*
Baldwin, John Edwin *chemistry educator*
Barclay, H(ugh) Douglas *lawyer, former state senator*
Basta, Carlo R. *information systems specialist, consultant*
Becker, Lorne Arthur *family physician*
Bellanger, Barbara Doris Hoysak *biomedical research technologist*
Berinstein, William Paul *business executive*
Birkhead, Guthrie Sweeney, Jr., *political scientist, university dean*
†Black, Dan A. *economist*
Bloom, Max Robert *economics educator, consultant*
Bodow, Wayne R. *lawyer*
Bogart, William Harry *lawyer*
Boghosian, Paula der *computer business consultant*
Bornhurst, Robert Allan *radiologist*
Bradley, Roger William *lawyer*
Braungart, Margaret Mitchell *psychology and bioethics educator*
Braungart, Richard Gottfried *sociology and international relations educator*
Brickwedde, Richard James *lawyer*
Bubniak, Sharon Margaret *retired elementary education educator*
†Bullock, Stephen C. *lawyer*
Bunn, Timothy David *newspaper editor*
Burgess, John H. *ergonomist, consultant*
Burstein, Alan Stuart *lawyer*
Burstyn, Harold Lewis *lawyer*
Burstyn, Joan Netta *education educator*
Carlton, Carole Gassett *medical/surgical nurse*
Charters, Alexander Nathaniel *retired adult education educator*
Christian, David Michael *athletic director, parochial school educator*
Cirando, John Anthony *lawyer*
Clausen, Jerry Lee *psychiatrist*
Cohen, William Nathan *radiologist*
Conan, Robert James, Jr., *chemistry educator, consultant*
Coppola, Elaine Marie *librarian*
Costello, Thomas Joseph *bishop*
Culebras, Antonio *neurologist*
Daly, Robert W. *psychiatrist, medical educator*
†Damron, Timothy Arthur *orthopedic surgeon, researcher*
Davis, William E. *utility executive*
De Long, Jacob Edward *real estate broker*
Denise, Theodore Cullom *philosophy educator*
†DeSiato, Donna Jean *school system administrator*
De Wan-Carlson, Anna Theresa *artist*
DiLorenzo, Louis Patrick *lawyer*
Doty, Duane Harold *business educator*
Dove, Jeffrey Austin *lawyer*
Driscoll, Matthew J. *mayor, restaurant manager, real estate developer*
Drucker, Alan Steven *mechanical engineer*

Duerr, Dianne Marie *educator, sports medicine consultant*
Dunham, Philip Bigelow *biology educator, physiologist*
Eastwood, Gregory Lindsay *academic administrator*
Elms, Ben *actor, director*
Everett, Charles Roosevelt, Jr., *airport executive*
Field, Daniel *history educator*
†Fischler, Alan Bernard *communications educator*
Fiske, Jordan Jay *lawyer, retired prosecutor*
Fiske, Sandra Rappaport *psychologist, educator*
Fitzgerald, Harold Kenneth *social work educator, consultant*
Fitzpatrick, James David *lawyer*
†Fluck, Robert R., Jr., *respiratory therapy technician, educator*
Frohock, Fred Manuel *political science educator*
Furze, Edward William *fundraising consultant*
Gaal, John *lawyer*
Gartner, Joseph Charles *business systems administrator*
Geel, Christoph W. *orthopedic trauma surgeon*
Gerber, Edward F. *lawyer, educator*
†Giacchi, Judith Adair *elementary education educator*
Gilman, Karen Frenzel *legal assistant*
Gold, Joseph *medical researcher*
Grant, William Davis *medical educator, dean*
Graver, Jack Edward *mathematics educator*
Gray, Charles Augustus *banker*
Greene, Arthur M. *lawyer*
Griffith, Daniel Alva *geography educator*
†Grizanti, Anthony J. *lawyer*
Guharoy, Roy *pharmacy director, medical educator*
Hamlett, James Gordon *electronics engineer, management consultant, educator*
Hancock, Stewart F., Jr., *law educator, judge*
Hansen, Per Brinch *computer scientist, researcher*
Harrison, Frank J. *retired bishop*
Hayes, David Michael *lawyer*
†Heath, Joseph John *lawyer*
Henry, John Bernard *pathologist, university president*
Herzog, Peter Emilius *retired legal educator*
Hevern, Vincent William *psychologist, priest*
Hole, Richard Douglas *lawyer*
Hollander, Howard Robert *software engineering executive*
Honig, Arnold *physics educator, researcher*
Horst, Pamela Sue *medical educator, family physician*
†Hsu, Lifang *statistician, department chairman*
Hubbard, Peter Lawrence *lawyer*
Hurwitz, Arthur Andrew *immunologist, educator*
†Kane, Peter Bayard *physician*
†Kaplan, Eugene Alken *psychiatry educator, department chairman*
†King, Bernard T. *lawyer*
King, Marcia Jones *potter, physicist, photographer*
King, Robert Bainton *neurosurgeon, educator*
Kopp, Robert Walter *lawyer*
Kram, Richard Corey *lawyer*
Krathwohl, David Reading *education educator emeritus*
Kriesberg, Louis *sociologist, educator*
†Lambert, Gregg *literature educator*
Lang, James Patrick *priest*
LaRue, William David *television critic*
Levy, Alan Joseph *mechanical engineer, educator*
Levy, H. Richard *biochemistry educator*
Lloyd, David Thomas *writer, English educator*
Luft, Eric v.d. *librarian, educator*
MacKillop, James John *English language educator, journalist, critic*
Mandel, James A. *civil engineer, educator*
Marcoccia, Louis Gary *accountant, university administrator*
Mazur, Allan Carl *sociologist, engineer, educator*
McCurn, Neal Peters *federal judge*
Meinig, Donald William *geography educator*
†Michaels, Beverly Ann *lawyer*
Miles, Kenneth Ontario *academic program director*
†Mizruchi, Ephraim Harold *sociologist, educator*
Mondore, Patricia Anne *health facility administrative assistant, author, composer*
Monmonier, Mark *geographer, graphics educator, essayist*
†Moynihan, James M. *bishop*
Mulcahy, Kathleen Lynn *neonatal and pediatric nurse practitioner*
Muller, Ernest H. *geology educator*
Munson, Howard G. *federal judge*
†O'Connor, Michael E. *lawyer*
Ortiz, Fernando, Jr., *commissioner*
Paquette, Steven A. *lawyer*
Pardee, Otway O'Meara *computer science educator*
†Pato, Carlos Neves *psychiatrist, researcher*
†Pellow, David Matthew *lawyer*
Phillips, Larry Arthur *artist*
Phillips, Paul Everard *physician, medical educator*
Pinchuk, Nicholas Thomas *manufacturing executive*
Powell, James Matthew *history educator*
Prucha, John James *geologist, educator*
Rabuzzi, Daniel D. *medical administrator*
Ramachandran, Tarakad Subramaniam *neurologist, physician*
Ramsey, Dan Steven *consultant, business executive*
†Reeher, Grant Davis *social sciences educator, writer*
Rivette, Francis Robert *lawyer*
Robinson, Joseph Edward *geology educator, consulting petroleum geologist*
Rogers, Sherry Anne *physician*
Romeu, Jorge Luis *mathematics educator, writer*
†Rosenthal, Alan *lawyer*
†Rothman, Robert Pierson *lawyer*
†Rubin, David M. *dean, educator*
Russo, Joseph Maria *public affairs executive*
Sage, Martin Lee *chemistry educator*
Sagerman, Robert Howard *radiation oncologist*
Sargent, Robert George *engineering educator*
Sarkar, Siddhartha *pathologist*
Scheinman, Steven Jay *medical educator*
Schiess, Betty Bone *priest*
Schiess, William Arnold *health services administrator, geriatrician*
Schwartz, Richard Derecktor *sociologist, educator*
Scullin, Frederick James, Jr., *federal judge*
Serafin, John Alfred *art educator*
Shaw, Kenneth Alan *university president*
Sheehan, Michael Gerard *allergist*
Sheehe, Paul Robert *statistician, educator, biologist*
†Shires, Linda M. *English educator, writer*
†Shulman, Barry Martin *lawyer*
†Simmons, Doreen Anne *lawyer*
†Simmons, Harvey Owen, III, *lawyer*
Skoler, Celia Rebecca *art gallery director*
Skoler, Louis *architect, educator*
Smardon, Richard Clay *landscape architecture and environmental studies educator*
Smith, Kenneth Judson, Jr., *chemist, theoretician, educator*
†Sparkes, James Edward *lawyer*
Sprafkin, Robert Peter *psychologist, educator*
Stam, David Harry *librarian*
Steigerwald, Louis John, III, *corporate executive*
Sternlicht, Sanford *English and theater arts educator, writer*
†Stone, Sheldon L. *physicist, educator*
Streeten, Barbara Wiard *ophthalmologist, medical educator*
Sullivan, Michael Joachim *financial executive*
Szasz, Thomas Stephen *psychiatrist, educator, writer*
Tanner, Jane *mathematics educator*
Tatham, David Frederic *art historian, educator*
Thomas, Sidney *fine arts educator, researcher*
†Thompson, Robert James *media specialist, educator*
Traylor, Robert Arthur *lawyer*
†Turner, Christopher Edward *cell biology educator*
Vardan, Suman *medical educator*
Verrillo, Ronald Thomas *neuroscience educator, researcher*
Waddy, Patricia A. *architectural history educator*
Wadley, Susan Snow *anthropologist*
Ware, Bennie *university administrator*
†Watts, James Washington *religion educator*
†Weiskirch, Larry M *science educator*
Weiss, Volker *university administrator, educator*
†Welch, Thomas Robert *pediatrician, educator*
Wells, Peter Nathaniel *judge, lawyer*
Whaley, Ross Samuel *environmentalist, educator*
Wiggins, James Bryan *religion educator*
Williams, William Joseph *physician, educator*
Wladis, Mark Neil *lawyer*
Wolff, Catherine Elizabeth *opera company executive*
Zimmerman, Aaron Mark *lawyer*
Zimmerman, Golda *lawyer, educator*
Zito, George Vincent *sociologist, sociology educator*

Tallman
Strasser, Joel A. *public relations executive, engineer, executive producer*

Tannersville
Byrne, Patricia Curran *small business owner*
Kline, Linda *employment consultant*

Tappan
Dell, Robert Christopher *geothermal sculptor, scenic artist*
Fox, Muriel *retired public relations executive*

Tarrytown
Andreen, Aviva Louise *dentist, researcher, academic administrator, educator*
Ashburn, Anderson *magazine editor*
Bacaloglu, Radu *chemical engineer*
Bergson, Henry Paul *professional association administrator*
†Bunton, Phil *editor-in-chief*
†Cocchiarella, Antonio *physician, educator*
Evans, Yonynah Schub (Nina Evans) *child psychiatrist*
Farrell, Gregory Alan *biomedical engineer*
Ferrari, Robert Joseph *business educator, former banker*
Field, Barry Elliot *internist, gastroenterologist*
Frisch, Celia *violinist, chamber music coach, educator*
Gutheil, Irene A. *social work educator, researcher*
Hyman, Leonard Stephen *financial consultant, economist, writer*
Kane, Stanley Bruce *food products executive*
Kenney, Dion Patrick *business strategist, entrepreneur*
Kenney, John Michel *architect*
Lawry, John D. *psychologist, educator*
†LeGrice, Stephen *magazine editor*
†Mach, Joseph David *lawyer*
Marcus, Sheldon *adult education educator*
†Miringoff, Marc L. *educational administrator, educator, researcher*
Neill, Richard Robert *retired publishing company executive*
O'Brien, Anne Therese *chemist*
Safian, Keith Franklin *hospital administrator*
Singh, Brahma Nand *pharmaceutical scientist*
Stein, Sol *publisher, writer, editor in chief*
†Sullivan, Janet Nelson *dermatologist, department chairman, health facility administrator*
Vagelos, Pindaros Roy *pharmaceutical company executive*
Waletzky, Lucy R. *psychiatrist*
Weiner, Max *educational psychology educator*
Winings, Kathy *religion educator*

Thornwood
Bassett, Lawrence C *management consultant*

Ticonderoga
Howe, Edwin A(lberts), Jr., *lawyer*

Tillson
Giordano, Sondra Britchky *nursing educator, medical and surgical nurse*
Whittington-Couse, Maryellen Frances *education administrator, not-for-profit developer, consultant*

Tonawanda
Cavanaugh, David K. *clinical psychologist*
Drozdziel, Marion John *aeronautical engineer*
Glickman, Marlene *non-profit organization administrator*
Haller, Calvin John *banker*
Krucenski, Leonard Joseph *secondary education educator*
Peterson, Dorothy Lulu *artist, writer*
Rovison, John Michael, Jr., *chemical engineer*

Troy
Ahlers, Rolf Willi *philosopher, theologian*
†Arcak, Murat *engineering educator, consultant*
Athanasiou, Robert Byron *physician, psychologist*
†Beeler, Patricia *court administrator*
Belfort, Georges *chemical engineering educator, consultant*
Berg, Daniel *science and technology educator*
Bergles, Arthur Edward *mechanical engineering educator*
Block, Robert Charles *nuclear engineering and engineering physics educator*
Boyina, Ramana Prasad Venkata *civil engineering educator, researcher*
Brazil, Harold Edmund *political science educator*
†Bruce, Melody Ann *obstetrician-gynecologist*
Burch, Mary Seelye Quinn *law librarian, consultant*
Carovano, John Martin *not-for-profit administrator, conservationist*
Chi, Benjamin E. *computer network executive*
†Clause, Steven Lee *pharmacist, researcher*
†Demertzoglou, Pindaro Epaminonda *systems administrator, education educator*
Desrochers, Alan Alfred *electrical engineer*
Doremus, Robert Heward *glass and ceramics processing educator*
Duquette, David Joseph *materials science and engineering educator*
Ehrlich, Henry Lutz *biology educator*
Feeser, Larry James *civil engineering educator, researcher*
Ferris, James Peter *chemist, educator*
Finkel, Sanford Norman *lawyer*
Fitzgerald, Edward Francis *epidemiologist, educator*
Friedman, Sue Tyler *technical publications executive*
Frost, Jerome Kenneth *lawyer*
Gerhardt, Lester A. *engineering educator, dean*
Giaever, Ivar *physicist*
Gill, William Nelson *chemical engineering educator*
Glicksman, Martin Eden *materials engineering educator*
Haviland, David Sands *architectural educator, researcher, administrator*
Hsu, Cheng *decision sciences and engineering systems educator*
Isaacs, Andrea *editor, publisher, dancer, choreographer, former educator*
Jackson, Shirley Ann *academic administrator, federal agency administrator, physicist, university official*
Jahng, Jungjoo *information technology educator*
Jones, E. Stewart, Jr., *lawyer*
Jordan, Mark Henry *retired consulting civil engineer*
Kahl, William Frederick *retired college president*
Kliman, Gerald Burt *electrical engineer*
Krause, Sonja *chemistry educator*
Lahey, Richard Thomas, Jr., *nuclear engineer, fluid mechanics engineer*
Levinger, Joseph Solomon *physicist, educator*
†Linton, Jonathan D *management researcher, educator*
Littman, Howard *chemical engineer, educator*
†Lvov, Yuri Victorovich *science educator*
Marinstein, Elliott Fred *lawyer*
McDonald, John Francis Patrick *electrical engineering educator*
Medicus, Heinrich Adolf *physicist, educator*
Messac, Achille *mechanical engineer, aerospace engineer*
Nelson, John Keith *electrical engineer, educator*
Phan, Phillip Hin Choi *business educator, consultant*
Phelan, Thomas *clergyman, academic administrator, educator*
Ross, Sydney *science educator, researcher*
Rumyantsev, Sergey L. *research scientist, educator*
St. Hilaire, David William *county official, financial manager*
St. John, William Charles, Jr., *business educator, administrator*
Sanderson, Arthur Clark *engineering educator*
Saridis, George Nicholas *electrical, computers and system engineering educator, robotics and automation researcher*
Schechter, Stephen L. *political scientist*
†Shephard, Mark Scott *civil and mechanical engineering educator*
Shuey, Richard Lyman *engineering educator, consultant*
Sperber, Daniel *physicist*
Stoloff, Norman Stanley *materials engineering educator, researcher*
Szymanski, Boleslaw Karol *computer scientist, educator, entrepreneur*
Tien, James M. *engineering educator, consultant*
Wait, Samuel Charles, Jr., *academic administrator, educator*
Wang, Kegang *physicist, materials scientist*
Watson, E Bruce *science educator*
Woods, John William *electrical, computer and systems engineering educator, consultant*
Zimmie, Thomas Frank *civil engineer, educator*

Trumansburg
Kredell, Carol Ruth *artist*
Levine, John Robert *author, lecturer*

Tuckahoe
Brecher, Bernd *management consultant*
Offner, Roxane *retired social worker*
†Silk, Eleana S. *librarian*

Tupper Lake
Johnson, David Wesley *lawyer*
Welsh, Peter Corbett *museum consultant, historian*

Tuxedo Park
Domjan, Joseph *artist*
Friedman, Rodger *antiquarian bookseller, consultant*
Lippmann, Morton *environmental health science researcher*
Regan, Ellen Frances (Mrs. Walston Shepard Brown) *ophthalmologist, educator*
Steinetz, Bernard George, Jr., *endocrinologist*

Uniondale
†Arbour, Alger *professional hockey coach*
Beck, Leland S. *lawyer*
†Bennett, James Davison *lawyer*
Brustein, Martin *financial adviser*
Cassidy, David Michael *lawyer*
Eilen, Howard Scott *lawyer, mediator*
Gillin, John F. *quality engineer*
†Good, Douglas Jay *lawyer*
Gracin, Hank *lawyer*
Hamrlik, Roman *professional hockey player*
Jones, Barbara Ann *elementary education educator*
†Kessler, Lawrence W. *law educator, lawyer*
Kestenbaum, Harold Lee *lawyer*
Naylor, Natalie *history educator*
†Osgood, Chris *hockey player*
Peca, Michael *hockey player*
Pratt, George Cheney *law educator, retired federal judge*
Wang, Charles B. *professional sports team executive*

Unionville
Kemnitz, Thomas Milton *publisher*

Upton
Bond, Peter Danford *physicist*
Carsten, Arland Leon *radiobiologist, researcher, educator, consultant*
Chaudhari, Praveen *materials physicist*
Foerster, Conrad Louis *project engineer*
Fthenakis, Vasilis *chemical engineer, consultant, educator*
†Goldhaber, Maurice *physicist, researcher*
Hamilton, Leonard Derwent *physician, molecular biologist*
Harbottle, Garman *chemist*
Hendrie, Joseph Mallam *physicist, nuclear engineer, government official*
†Lin, Mow S. *chemist*
†Lindenbaum, S(eymour) J(oseph) *physicist*
Liu, Yangang *atmospheric scientist*
Lowenstein, Derek Irving *physicist*
Meinhold, Charles Boyd *health physicist*
Melucci, Richard Charles *research institute administrator*
†Petrovic, Cedomir *research scientist*
Rau, Ralph Ronald *retired physicist*
Ruggiero, Alessandro G. *physicist, researcher*
Setlow, Jane Kellock *biophysicist*
Setlow, Richard Burton *biophysicist, researcher*
†Sheehy, Brian *physicist*
Steinberg, Meyer *chemical engineer*
Sutin, Norman *chemistry educator, scientist*
Tannenbaum, Michael J(ay) *physicist*
Volkow, Nora Dolores *psychiatrist, scientist*
Wang, Gene-Jack *physician, educator, scientist*
Zarcone, Michael Joseph *experimental physicist, consultant*

Utica
Antzelevitch, Charles *research center executive*
Austin, Michael Charles *insurance company executive*
Bowers, Roger Paul *radiologist*
Boyle, William Leo, Jr., *educational consultant, retired college president*
Brennan, John Joseph *lawyer, legal administrator*
Brooks, Sarah *software developer, consultant, educator*
Cardamone, Richard J. *judge*
De Iorio, Lucille Theresa *social worker*
Donovan, Donna Mae *newspaper publisher*
†Dumaine, Robert *research scientist, educator*
Fiori-Blanchfield, Joan *artist, art historian*
Godecki, Mark Alexander *obstetrician-gynecologist*
Hurd, David Norman *federal judge*
Iodice, Arthur Alfonso *biochemist*
Labuz, Ronald Matthew *design educator*
Millet, John Bradford *retired surgeon*
Min, Balshik *pathologist*
Mortenson, Thomas Theodore *medical products executive, management consultant*
†Noviasky, John A *pharmacist*
Plumley, Danielle L. *social worker*
Schweizer, Paul Douglas *museum director*
Wagner, Frederick Reese *language professional*

Vails Gate
Fife, Betty H. *retired librarian*

Valatie
Benamati, Dennis Charles *librarian, editor, consultant*

Valhalla
†Agarwal, Yogesh Kumar *cardiologist, internist*
†Aguero-Rosenfeld, Maria E. *pathologist, microbiologist*
Aronow, Wilbert Solomon *physician, educator*
Campbell, Debra Lynn *marketing and new venture consultant*
Chung, Fung-Lung *cancer research scientist*
Cimino, Joseph Anthony *physician, educator*
Czarnecki, Anthony J. *correction administrator, educator*
Del Guercio, Louis Richard Maurice *surgeon, educator, company executive*
De Nicola, Peter Francis *photographic distributor*
†Falvo, Cathey E. *medical educator, director, pediatrician*
Frishman, William Howard *cardiology educator, cardiovascular pharmacologist, gerontologist*
Golombek, Sergio Gustavo *pediatrician, neonatologist, educator*
†Goodman, Alvin Irwin *internist, nephrologist, educator*
Hankin, Joseph Nathan *college president*
†Jayabose, Somasundaram *pediatrician*
†Kibel, Howard David *psychiatrist*
Kleinman, Wayne Alan *research scientist*
Kline, Susan Anderson *medical school official and dean, internist*
Leone, Stephen Joseph *English language educator, computer technology consultant*
Lombardi, Don Dominick *art critic, artist*
†Lowenfels, Albert Brownold *surgeon, educator*
Madden, Robert Edward *surgeon, educator*
Mallouh, Camille *urologist, medical educator*
Margoshes, Miriam Kagan *information specialist*
†Marks, Stephen J. *neurologist, educator*
McGoldrick, Kathryn Elizabeth *anesthesiologist, educator, writer*
O'Connell, Ralph Anthony *dean, psychiatrist, educator*
†Peterson, Stephen Joseph *internist*
Reed, George Elliott *surgeon, educator, dean*
Safai, Bijan *physician, investigator*
Schwartz, Joel Lawrence *oral pathology educator*
Slim, Michel S. *surgeon, educator, health facility administrator*
Stellman, Steven Dale *epidemiologist*
†Stringel, Gustavo *pediatric surgeon*
†Tiwari, Raj Kumar *medical researcher, educator*
Weinberg, Hubert *plastic surgeon*
Weisburger, John Hans *medical researcher*
Williams, Gary Murray *medical researcher, pathology educator*
Wolf, David Cary *gastroenterologist, medical educator*
Wolin, Michael Stuart *physiology educator*
Wormser, Gary Paul *epidemiologist, researcher*
Zhong, Yuanzhen *research chemist*

Valley Cottage
Baer, Adam Scott *artist*
Lazecko, David John *broadcast executive*
Shaderowfsky, Eva Maria *photographer, writer, computer communications specialist*
Tombros, Peter George *pharmaceutical company executive*

Valley Stream
Blakeman, Royal Edwin *lawyer*
Brunell, Jerry Albert *insurance executive*
Ellis, Bernice *financial planning company executive, investment advisor*
†Eng, Mamie *librarian*
Haies, Evelyn S(olomon) *fundraiser, educator, writer*
Levine, Marilyn Markovich *lawyer, arbitrator*
Rachlin, Harvey Brant *author*
†Robbins, Harvey Arnold *textile company executive*
Rodgers, John Joseph, III, *educational administration consultant, educator*
Wollman, June Rose *clothing executive*

Van Hornesville
Durham, Ormonde George, III, *manufacturing executive*

Verona
Smith, Kathy Ann *music educator*
Smith, Michael Allen *mechanical engineer*

Vestal
Cohen, Marvin A. *writer*
Grinberg, Raul *internist*
Horwitz, Bertrand Nathan *accounting and finance educator*
McGuire, John Thomas *lawyer, educator*
Piaker, Philip Martin *accountant, educator*
Ulc, Otto *political science educator*
Wagar, (Walter) Warren (Walter Wagar) *historian, educator*
Zinner, Faith Orloff *social worker, consultant, psychotherapist*

Victor
Szalapski, Robert Francis *theoretical physicist*

Waccabuc
Krefting, Robert J(ohn) *publishing company executive*

Wading River
Budd, Bernadette Smith *lawyer, newspaper executive, public relations consultant*
Marlow, Audrey Swanson *artist, designer*

Wainscott
Henderson, William Charles *editor*
Herzog, Arthur, III, *author*
Russo, Alexander Peter *artist, educator*

Walden
Gubits, David Barry *lawyer*

Wallkill
Bittner, Ronald Joseph *computer systems analyst, magician*
Chumas, Linda Grace *elementary school educator*
Koch, Edwin Ernest *artist, interior decorator*
†Strauser, Susan Parkyn (Susan Parkyn Strauser) *performing arts educator*

Wanakena
Hunter, William Schmidt *engineering executive, environmental engineer*

Wantagh
Engros, Elaine *nurse, case manager*
†Galvan, Max *humanities educator*
Glaser, David *painter, sculptor*
Kushner, Aileen *medical/surgical nurse*
Lamb, James P. *advertising executive*
Marcatante, John Joseph *educational administrator*
Smits, Edward John *museum consultant*
Young, Morris *electrical engineering consultant*
Zinder, Newton Donald *stock market analyst, consultant*

Wappingers Falls
Haynes, Paul R. *lawyer*
Hogan, Edward Robert *financial services executive*
Johnson, Jeh Vincent *architect*
Kells, Albert John *financial consultant*
McCamy, Calvin Samuel *optics scientist*
Nolan, John Thomas, Jr., *retired oil industry administrator*
Sucich, Diana Catherine *school psychologist, counselor*

Warsaw
Dy-Ang, Anita C. *pediatrician*

Warwick
†Emery, James Patrick *composer, musician*
Franck, Frederick Sigfred *artist, author, dental surgeon*
Kaminsky, Anatol *educator, writer*
Mack, Daniel Richard *furniture designer*
Simon, Dolores Daly *copy editor*

Water Mill
D'Urso, Joseph Paul *interior designer*
Hagstrom, Jack Walter Carl Kling *retired pathology educator*
Kreimer, Michael Walter *financial planner, investment company official*

Waterford
Glavin, A. Rita Chandellier (Mrs. James Henry Glavin III) *lawyer*
Glavin, James Henry, III, *lawyer*
Gold, James Paul *museum director*
Wang, Yi-Feng *polymer scientist, consultant*

Waterloo
†Schreck, Richard Thomas *accountant*

Watertown
Brett, James Clarence *retired journalism educator*
Coe, Benjamin Plaisted *retired state official*
†Deidesheimer, Annamaria *English educator*
Dimmick, Kris Douglas *civil engineer*
Evans, Lance Michael *real estate board executive*
Fredriksen, Maryellen *physician assistant*
Garvey, Jeffrey Matthew *medical librarian, educator*
Johnson, John Brayton *editor, publisher*
Marsh, Leonard Roy *lawyer*
Militello, Samuel Philip *lawyer*
Smith, Marcia Jeanne *secondary school educator*

Watervliet
Underwood, John H. *research engineer*

Watkins Glen
Argetsinger, Cameron R. *lawyer*

Webster
Chow, Tsu Sen *research scientist*
Duke, Charles Bryan *electronics executive, physicist, educator*
Laschenski, John Patrick *accountant*
McCormack, Stanley Eugene *financial consultant*
McWilliams, C. Paul, Jr., *engineering executive*
†Meyer, Robert J. *physicist*
Nicholson, Douglas Robert *accountant*
Scherer, John V. *computing and instrumentation laboratory manager*
Scherer, Marcia Joslyn *psychologist, researcher, educator*
Southard, Paul Raymond *financial executive*
Witmer, G. Robert *retired state supreme court justice*
†Zhang, Shengliang *materials scientist, physicist*

Weedsport
†English, Richard Paul *music educator*

Wellsville
†Fuller, Bruce E. *mechanical engineer*
†Jacobs, Mary Sharron *librarian*
Tezak, Edward George *mechanics educator*
Van Tyne, Arthur Morris *geologist*

West Babylon
†Connolly, Kelly Ann *secondary school educator*
†Weinreb, Michael Leonard *lawyer*

West Bloomfield
Charron, Helene Kay Shetler *retired nursing educator*

West Chazy
Cumiskey, Gerald John *radio communications technician*

West Harrison
Brazell, James Ervin *oil company executive, lawyer*
Verano, Anthony Frank *retired banker*

West Haverstraw
Cosman, Felicia *endocrinologist, educator*

West Hempstead
Conway-Gervais, Kathleen Marie *reading specialist, educational consultant*
Guggenheimer, Heinrich Walter *mathematician, educator*
†Petorak, Bryan Thomas *music educator, musician*
Tartell, Robert Morris *retired dentist*

West Hurley
Krembs, George Michael *computer and electrical engineer*
Martucci, Vincent James *composer, pianist*

West Islip
†Carpenter, Angie M. *county legislator, small business owner, editor*
Doganay, Kazim Levent *physician*
Elkowitz, Sheryl Sue *radiologist*
Keller, Joyce *television and radio host, counselor, writer*

West Kill
Dwon, Larry *retired electrical engineer, educator, consultant*

West Leyden
Kornatowski, Susan Carol *elementary education educator*

West Nyack
Oppenheim, Robert *beauty industry executive*
Pringle, Laurence Patrick *writer*

West Point
†Boettner, Daisie Dawson *military officer, mechanical engineering educator*
†Bozeman, Laura Beth *military officer, educator*
†Burk, Roger Chapman *engineering educator*
†Dorschner, Jon Peter *education educator, diplomat*
Forest, James Franzen *university administrator*
†Leamy, Michael Joseph *mechanical engineer, educator*
†Leupold, Herbert August *physicist*
Niccoli, Anne Marie *social sciences educator*
Reel, David Mark *museum curator, art historian*
†Schweitzer, Steven John *military officer*
Watson, Georgianna *librarian*
†Zinsser, Nathaniel Wadsworth *civilian military employee, director*

West Seneca
†Wirth, Sandra Lee *real estate company owner*
Wolfgang, Jerald Ira *economic development educator*

West Shokan
Mackey, Jeffrey Allen *priest*

Westbury
Barboza, Anthony *photographer, artist*
Boes, Lawrence William *lawyer*
†Ciovacco, Robert John *lawyer*
De Pauw, Gommar Albert *priest, educator*
Dwyer, Diane Marie *lawyer, judge*
Ente, Gerald *pediatrician*
Fleisig, Ross *aeronautical engineer, engineering manager*
Fogg, Joseph Graham, III, *investment banking executive*
Goldstein, Fred *accountant*
Kremin, Daniel Paul *clinical forensic psychologist*
Lelonek, David *optometrist*
†McCann, James F. *consumer products company executive*
McGrath, Edward Gerard *retired military officer, journalist*
Mondello, John Paul *financial consultant*
†Neziri, Maria G. De Lucia *elementary school educator*
Ross-Lee, Barbara *dean, educator*
Sandler, Gerald Howard *computer science educator, company executive*
Sherbell, Rhoda *artist, sculptor*
Tulchin, Stanley *banker, lecturer, author, business reorganization consultant*
Waterman, Dianne Corrine *artist, educator, writer, ministry leader*
†Whiteman, Robert Gordon *lawyer*

Westernville
Hart, Pamela Walker *artist, educator, writer*

Westhampton Beach
Flood, Angela *interior designer, artist*
Maas, Jane Brown *advertising executive*
Ozero, Brian John *chemical engineer*

Westport
Rossi, Paul Andrew *artist, mosaicist*

White Lake
Mendelsohn, Linda Joy *physician*

White Plains
Abrams, Leigh Jeffrey *manufacturing company executive*
Alin, Robert David *lawyer*
Altman, S. Morton *community center executive*
Appelbaum, Margery Freeman *artist*
Barland, Peter *rheumatologist, medical educator*
†Bavero, Ronald Joseph *lawyer, legal educator*
Beldock, Donald Travis *corporate financial executive*
Benjamin, Barbara Bloch *writer, editor*
Beran, Samuel Jonathan *plastic surgeon*
Berlin, Alan Daniel *lawyer, international energy and legal consultant*
†Berman, Henry Stephen *lawyer*
Bernard, Robert William *plastic surgeon*
Biers, Martin Henry *physician*
†Blank, Philip Bernardini *lawyer, educator*
Blass, John Paul *medical educator, physician*
Bloom, Adam I. *psychologist*
Bober, Lawrence Harold *retired banker*
Bodnar, Peter O. *lawyer*
Bushkin, Merle Jerome *investment banker*
Carey, John *lawyer, judge*
Carlucci, Joseph P. *lawyer*
Chen, Shuang *computer science professional*
Ciardullo, Robert Carl *plastic surgeon*
†Cohn, John L. *merchant banker*
Colwell, Howard Otis *advertising executive*
Conner, William Curtis *judge*
Crames, Renee Karas *management consultant*
D'Aloise, Lawrence T., Jr., *lawyer*
Danziger, Joel Bernard *lawyer*
Davenport, Lindsay *professional tennis player*
David, Miles *association and marketing executive*
DeMond, Jeffrey Stuart *cable television and telecommunications executive*
Denham, Paul *technology sales and marketing executive*
†Doernberg, Donald Lane *law educator*
Doyle, Dennis T. *lawyer*
Dvorak, Roger Gran *health facility executive*
Eckfeld, William Grover *music educator, composer, musician*
†Eisner, Alan Bradley *entrepreneur*
Ellerby, James Edward, Jr., *judge*
Erla, Karen *artist, painter, collagist, printmaker*
Feder, Robert *lawyer*
Flanigen, Edith Marie *materials scientist, consultant*
†Fleming, Robert Burke *law educator, lawyer*
Foster, John Horace *consulting environmental engineer*
†Fowlkes, Nancy Lanetta Pinkard *social worker*
Frazier, Amy *professional tennis player*
Freed, Arthur *civil engineer*
†Gambill, Jan-Michael *professional tennis player*
†Garrison-Jackson, Zina *retired tennis player*
†Gilbert, Bradley *professional tennis coach, former professional tennis player, former Olympic athlete*
Gillingham, Stephen Thomas *financial planner*
†Gimelstob, Justin *professional tennis player*
†Giuliano, Louis J. *industrial manufacturing company executive*
Gjertsen, O. Gerard *lawyer*
Greene, Leonard Michael *aerospace manufacturing executive, institute executive*
Greenspan, Leon Joseph *lawyer*
Greenspan, Michael Evan *lawyer*
Greer, Robert E. *insurance executive, retired*
†Grossman, Ann *professional tennis player*
†Guida, Toni M. *lawyer*
Haines, Daniel Webster *engineering consultant, educator*
Halpern, Philip Morgan *lawyer*
Hardin, Adlai Stevenson, Jr., *judge*
Hawkins, Mary E. *ophthalmologist*
Heimerdinger, John Frederick *association executive*
†Heo, Moonseong *statistician, researcher*
†Horowitz, Steven F. *cardiologist*
†Howse, Jennifer Louise *foundation administrator*
†Howson, Christopher Paul *medical association administrator, epidemiologist*
†Isaak, Robert Allen *international management and political economy educator, writer*
Jacobson, Sandra W. *lawyer*
Katz, Michael *pediatrician, educator*
Kaushik, Surendra Kumar *economist*
Keane, Thomas J. *lawyer*
Keegan, Warren Joseph *business educator, consultant*
Klein, Paul E. *lawyer*
Kurzman, Robert Graham *lawyer, educator*
Leung, Betty Brigid *nursing administrator*
Levere, Richard David *internist, educator*
Levine, Steven Jon *lawyer*
Longo, Ronald Anthony *lawyer*
Lukaszewski, James Edmund *communications executive*
Machover, Carl *computer graphics consultant*
†Madden, M. Stuart *lawyer*
Maffeo, Vincent Anthony *lawyer, executive*
Manville, Stewart Roebling *archivist*
Marano, Anthony Joseph *cardiologist*
Mardirossian, Jonathan *surgeon*
Martin, Thomas Rhodes *communications executive, writer*
McCarthy, John Robert *real estate firm officer*
McDowell, Fletcher Hughes *physician, educator*
†McEnroe, Patrick *former professional tennis player, sports commentator*
†McNeil, Lori Michelle *professional tennis player*
Mitchell, Robert Dale *consulting engineer*
Monteferrante, Judith Catherine *cardiologist*
Munneke, Gary Arthur *law educator, consultant*
Nastasi, Aldo A. *judge*
Newman, Barney David *medical administrator, internist*
†Osman, Betty Barshad *psychologist, author*
Palmisano, Samuel J. *information technology executive*
Parker, Barrington D., Jr., *federal judge, lawyer*
Payson, Martin F. *lawyer*
Peyton, Donald Leon *retired standards association executive*
Pfeffer, Cynthia Roberta *psychiatrist, educator*
†Pitegoff, Thomas Michael *lawyer*
Ramlo, Sara B. *computer company executive*
Rapp, Richard Tilden *economist, consultant*
Raymond, Lisa *tennis player*
Reiffel, Robert Siskind *plastic surgeon*
Rembar, James Carlson *psychologist*
†Reneberg, Richard (Richey Reneberg) *professional tennis player*

†Robinson, Nicholas Adams *lawyer, educator*
Rosenberg, Michael *lawyer*
Ross, Herbert *physician*
Rubin, Chanda *professional tennis player*
Russo, Donna Lee *social worker*
Ryan, Robert Davis *lawyer*
†Salameh, Samer Fadi *communications executive*
†Scheinkman, Alan David *lawyer, legal educator*
†Schnyder, Patty *professional tennis player*
Scott-Williams, Wendy Lee *information technology specialist*
Sedelmaier, J. J. *filmmaker*
Silverberg, Steven Mark *lawyer*
Sloan, F(rank) Blaine *law educator*
Smith, Gerard Peter *neuroscientist*
Soley, Robert Lawrence *plastic surgeon*
Stalerman, Ruth *civic volunteer, poet*
†Sternlicht, Barry Stuart *hotel executive*
Straus, Marc Joshua *internist, oncologist, educator, poet*
†Surpris, Joseph W. *research scientist*
Sussberg, Milton Joel *marketing professional*
Taft, Nathaniel Belmont *lawyer*
Tealdi, Javier Hernan *computer/network support specialist*
Teck, Katherine *musician, writer*
Topol, Robin April Levitt *lawyer*
Turer, Gary Evan *ophthalmologist*
Underweiser, Irwin Philip *mining executive, lawyer*
Wedge, Chris *animation director, studio executive*
West, Joseph King *judge*
Westerhoff, Garret Peter *environmental engineer, executive*
†Wheaton, David *professional tennis player*
Williams, Serena *professional tennis player*
Williams, Ted Vaughnell *physical education educator*
Williams, Venus *professional tennis player*
Winterton, Joseph Henry *computer software executive*
Zevon, Sanford S. *cardiologist, educator*
Zuckerman, Marc Abraham *accountant, educator*

Whitesboro
Bulman, William Patrick *data processing executive*
Campbell, Joann Cavo *social worker*
O'Hara, Cynthia O'Connor *writer, columnist, food consultant*
Voce, Joan A. Cifonelli *retired elementary school educator*

Whitestone
Brill, Steven Charles *financial advisor, lawyer*
Caputo, Daniel Vincent *psychologist*
Fischer, Eugene *medical administrator, educator*
†Rahr, Stewart *health medical products executive*

Williamsburg
†Witherspoon, Maria Bernarda Pena *bilingual educator*

Williamstown
Mixon, Kevin Anthony *music educator, composer*

Williamsville
Altman, David J *pharmacist, consultant*
Berner, Robert Frank *managerial statistics educator, administrator*
Brown, Stephen Ira *philosophy educator*
Burnett, George John *internist*
†Canfield, Cheryl Lucas *epidemiologist*
Cloudsley, Donald Hugh *library administrator*
Danni, F. Robert *town official*
Drew, Fraser Bragg Robert *language educator*
Garton, Charles *classics educator*
Hertzog, Robert William *pathologist, consultant, educator*
Jones, Robert Alfred *retired clergyman*
Krzyzan, Judy Lynn *automotive executive*
McAfee, Paul Hindman, III, *marketing professional*
Ogra, Pearay L. *physician, educator*
Reisman, Robert E. *physician, educator*
Rekate, Albert C. *physician*
Ross, Christopher T.W. *lawyer*
Sobolewski, Timothy Richard *marketing executive*
Stoeckl, Shelley Joan *marketing professional*
Truell, George Foster *management consultant*
Whitcomb, James Stuart *videographer, photographer, production company executive*

Williston Park
Segel, J. Norman *garment manufacturing company executive*

Willow
Bley, Carla Borg *jazz composer*

Windsor
Warner, Roberta Arlene *accountant, financial services executive*

Wolcott
Bartlett, Cody Blake *lawyer, educator*

Woodbury
Agresti, Miriam Monell *psychologist*
Bleicher, Sheldon Joseph *endocrinologist, medical educator*
Guttenplan, Harold Esau *retired food company executive*
Kelly, William Henry *computer company executive, mayor*
Mangia, Angelo James *lawyer*
†Rosenthal, Marilyn *school librarian, educator*

Woodhaven
Bolster, Jacqueline Neben (Mrs. John A. Bolster) *communications consultant*

Woodmere
Jeffries, Seymour Barnard *lawyer*

Kaplan, Joel Howard *psychiatrist*
Raab, Ira Jerry *lawyer, judge*
†Ronis, Gwendlyn *music educator, musician*
Seyfert, Wayne George *secondary education educator, anatomy educator*
†Winick, Bernyce Alpert *artist, photographer*

Woodside
Beeks, Delisco James (Delisco) *vocalist, actor, poet*
Fitzgerald, Karen Marie *artist, art educator*
Johnson, Davy L. *protective services official, minister, writer*
VanArsdale, Diana Cort *social worker*

Woodstock
Banks, Rela *sculptor*
Berman, Cassia *writer, educator*
†Carson, Robert S. *retired medical researcher*
Currie, Bruce *artist*
Godwin, Gail Kathleen *writer*
Hoyt, Earl Edward, Jr., *industrial designer*
Lieberman, Josefa Nina *psychologist, educator, writer*
Ober, Stuart Alan *investment consultant, book publisher*
Smith, Albert Aloysius, Jr., *electrical engineer, consultant*
van Hamel, Manette C. *artist, writer*

Wyandanch
Hodges-Robinson, Chettina M. *nursing administrator*

Yaphank
Digilio, Jr., John Thomas *health care executive, consultant*
Freund, Pepsi *artist, art educator*
†Mlinarich, John J. *secondary school educator*

Yonkers
Alessi, George Anthony *financial advisor, consultant*
Baumel, Herbert *violinist, conductor*
Baumel, Joan Patricia French *educator, writer, lecturer*
Brickman, Miriam *concert pianist*
Chumaceiro, Rolando Jose Mendez *family practice physician*
Colabella, George Michael *management, fund raising consultant*
Connors, James Patrick *lawyer*
Daman, Harlan Richard *allergist, educator*
Denver, Eileen Ann *magazine editor*
Dinanzio, Philip Joseph *city official*
Donovan, Agnes M. *nun*
Dudley, Don *broadcast journalist, communications consultant*
Godilo-Godlevsky, Eugene Alexanderson *poet*
Goon, Gilbert *software consultant*
Gunner, Murray *religious organization administrator*
Holtz, Gilbert Joseph *steel company executive*
Johansen, Robert Joseph *consulting actuary*
Josephberg, Robert Gary *ophthalmologist, consultant, retina and vitreous surgeon*
Kagan, Julia Lee *magazine editor*
†Karpatkin, Rhoda Hendrick *consumer information organization executive, lawyer*
Lawson, Beverly Elaine *nursing administrator*
Liggio, Jean Vincenza *adult education educator, artist*
Lukach, Arthur S., Jr., *manufacturing executive*
Lupiani, Donald Anthony *psychologist*
Maritime, George *writer, photographer*
Mazzella, Anthony J. *minister, psychotherapist, musician*
Mennin, Gerald Stanley *ophthalmologist*
Monegro, Francisco *psychology educator, alternative medicine consultant*
Neal, Leora Louise Haskett *social services administrator*
O'Donnell, Robert George *fine artist*
Philipps, Edward William *banker, real estate appraiser*
Pickover, Betty Abravanel *retired executive legal secretary, civic volunteer*
Roberson, Doris Jean Herold *retired social worker*
Rosch, Elliott Carl *internist*
Singer, Cecile Doris *bank executive, state legislator*
Smith, Aldo Ralston, Jr., *brokerage house executive*
†Spagnuolo, Mario *physician*
†Speirs, Greg *artist*
Stattel, Robert John *music educator, musician*
Torrese, Dante Michael *prosthodontist, educator*
Trentanelli, John Anthony *educational administrator*
Viola, Mary Jo *art history educator*
Wen, Sheree *computer company executive*
Weston, Francine Evans *secondary education educator*
Wolfson, Irwin M. *insurance company executive*

York
Coleman, David Cecil *financial executive*

Yorktown Heights
Agerwala, Tilak Krishna Mahesh *computer company executive*
Auslander, Marc Alan *computer scientist*
†Berk, George Ellis *cardiologist*
Delmoro, Ronald Anthony *elementary school principal*
Dennard, Robert Heath *engineering executive, scientist*
d'Heurle, François Max *research scientist, engineering educator*
Dimitrakopoulos, Christos Dimitrios *materials scientist*
Donovan, Andrew Joseph *financial consultant*
Fowler, Alan Bicksler *retired physicist*
Hoffman, Alan Jerome *mathematician, educator*
Hong, Se June *computer engineer*
Jones, Lauretta Marie *artist, designer, computer science researcher*

†Kang, Sung Kwon *materials scientist, researcher*
Kessler, Bernard Milton *organizational and human resources development specialist*
Keyes, Robert W. *physicist, researcher*
Lang, Norton David *physicist*
†Lei, Hui *computer scientist*
Mooney, Patricia May *physicist*
Ning, Tak Hung *physicist, microelectronic technologist*
Puri, Ruchir *operations research specialist*
Rigoutsos, Isidore *computer scientist*
Rosenblatt, Stephen Paul *marketing and sales promotion company executive*
Saon, George A. *computer scientist, researcher*
Verma, Dinesh Chandra *computer science researcher, writer*
Wade, James O'Shea *editor and writer*
Winograd, Shmuel *mathematician*
†Witt, John J. *artist*
Wu, Chai Wah *research scientist*
Wynne, James *research scientist*
Zwick, Thomas *electrical engineer*

Youngstown
Alpert, Norman *chemical company executive*
Lamb, Charles F. *educator, retired minister*
Wolfgang, Joan Winter *insurance company executive*
Mihailescu, Manuela *marketing executive*

NORTH CAROLINA

Aberdeen
Jacobson, Peter Lars *neurologist, educator*
Marcham, Timothy Victor *pharmacist*

Advance
Cochrane, Betsy Lane *state senator*
Guth, Caryl Joy *retired anesthesiologist*
Herpel, George Lloyd *marketing educator*
Walser, Sandra Teresa Johnson *rehabilitation nurse, preceptor*

Ahoskie
Weiss, Stephen Max *healthcare administrator, surgeon, educator*

Apex
Brunet, James Robert *public administration educator*
Olson, Jean Lounsbury *social worker*
Shendrikar, Arun Dhondopant *environmental scientist, chemist*

Ararat
Marsh, Joseph Virgil *real estate broker, investment advisor*

Archdale
†O'Hara, Karen Ann *mathematician, educator*

Arden
Baker, Kerry Allen *management consultant*
Seagle, J. Harold *lawyer*

Asheboro
Burton, Bernard Ottway *lawyer*
Croom, John Henry, III, *utility company executive*
†Cunningham, Laine *editor, educator, writer, consultant*
Helsabeck, Eric H. *emergency physician*
Jones, David M. *zoological park administrator*
Purvis, Mary Craven *cosmetologist*

Asheville
Astler, Vernon Benson *surgeon*
Bissette, Winston Louis, Jr., *lawyer, mayor*
Blunk, Joyce Elaine *artist, educator*
Born, Robert Heywood *consulting civil engineer*
Boyce, Emily Stewart *retired library and information science educator*
Brooker, Lena Epps *human relations diversity management consultant*
Carr, L(ewis) Charles *clinical psychologist*
†Chapman, Gary H. *artist, educator*
Chidnese, Patrick N. *retired lawyer*
Codd, Richard Trent, Jr., *computer scientist, educator*
Cogburn, Max Oliver *lawyer*
Coli, Guido John *chemical company executive*
Cragnolin, Karen Zambella *real estate developer, lawyer*
Damtoft, Walter Atkinson *editor, publishing executive, consultant*
Davis, Roy Walton, Jr., *lawyer*
De Bruhl, A. Marshall *writer, editor, publishing consultant*
Dickens, Charles Henderson *retired social scientist, consultant*
Dillard, John Robert *lawyer*
†Dobson, Carl Wilhelm *education educator*
Easterling, David Royer *climatologist*
Fobes, John Edwin *international organization official*
Frue, William Calhoun *lawyer*
Gantt, Charles David *lawyer*
Haggard, William Henry *meteorologist*
Hamilton, Jackson Douglas *lawyer*
Howell, George Washington *lawyer, consultant*
Humphreys, David Harding *plastic surgeon*
Hyde, Herbert Lee *lawyer*
Jaslow, Howard *engineer*
Johnson, John Andrew *construction executive*
Johnston, John Devereaux, Jr., *law educator, retired*
Jones-Rafferty, Brenda Anne *personal growth and development company executive*
Keleher, Michael Cassat *cabinet maker*
Kessler, Donald Joe *research scientist, physicist, consultant*
King, Joseph Bertram *architect*
Lavelle, Brian Francis David *lawyer*
Lawrence, Betty Tenn *lawyer*
Leake, Larry Bruce *lawyer*

Lowery, Douglas Lane *retired environmental engineer*
†Mack, Carole *financial consultant*
Mareth, Paul David *multimedia producer*
McKeown, Peter Philip *medical center administrator, medical educator, cardiothoracic surgeon*
Moubray, John Mitchell *engineering company executive*
Mustin, Bob *retired civil engineer, writer*
Parresol, Bernard Ross *research biometrician, statistician*
Rogers, Garry Lee *minister, medical technician*
Scully, Bonnie Diane *financial planner*
Sgro, Beverly Huston *day school administrator, educator, state official*
Sgro, Joseph Anthony *retired psychologist, educator*
Sharpe, Keith Yount *retired lawyer*
Sims, Bennett Jones *minister, educator*
†Starnes, Oscar Edwin, Jr., *lawyer*
Summey, Steven Michael *advertising company executive*
Teutsch, Monica *health services administrator*
Thornburg, Lacy Herman *federal judge*
Turcot, Marguerite Hogan *innkeeper, medical researcher*
Vander Voort, Dale Gilbert *textile company executive*
Voigt, Ellen *literature educator*
Weed, Maurice James *composer, retired music educator*
Weimer, William Arthur *computer company executive, consultant*
Wilson, Thomas Douglas, Jr., *lawyer*

Bailey
Brna, Theodore George, Jr., *physician*

Balsam
Mangham, Mack Robert *writer*

Banner Elk
Robinson, Earl James *academic administrator, information systems and statistics educator, consultant*
Tilden, Ralph Fulton *retired music educator, organist*

Battleboro
Hardy, Linda Lea Sterlock *media specialist*

Beaufort
Burgard, Ralph *cultural and education planner*
Cullman, Hugh *retired tobacco company executive*
Macartney, Norman Scarborough *retired middle school educator*
Mackenzie, James *fire protection and industrial safety executive*
Pagano, Filippo Frank *financial broker, commercial loan consultant*
†Tilghman, Carl Lewis *lawyer*

Belmont
†Baumstein, Paschal M. *priest*
Stowe, Robert Lee, III, *textile company executive*

Bethel
Speir, Betty Smith *consultant, retired foundation administrator*

Black Mountain
Cody, Hiram Sedgwick, Jr., *retired telephone company executive*
Hibbard, Carl Roger *social services administrator*
Le Van, Nolan Gerald *lawyer, consultant*
Proctor, Jesse Harris, Jr., *political science educator*

Bladenboro
Cameron, Fred E. *band director, composer*

Blowing Rock
Barnebey, Kenneth Alan *food company executive*
Littlejohn, Mark Hays *retired radiologist, artist*

Boiling Springs
Arnold, Ernest Woodrow *minister*
†Dougherty, Mark Richard *university administrator*
Vaughan, Ted Wayne *music and communications educator, musician*
White, Martin Christopher *academic administrator*

Bolivia
Brooks, Lithia Esther *finance executive*

Boone
Aluri, Rao *book publisher*
Borkowski, Francis Thomas *university chancellor*
Bowden, Elbert Victor *banking, finance and economics educator, author*
†Clark, Heather *speech pathology/audiology services professional, educator*
Cole, Susan Stockbridge *theatre educator*
Daly, Joseph Patrick *management educator, researcher*
Duke, Charles Richard *academic dean*
†Durham, Harvey Ralph *academic administrator*
Hoffman, Marvin Kenneth *political science educator*
Jones, Dan Lewis *psychologist*
Krug, Jeffrey Alan
Land, Ming Huey *college dean*
†Lugo, Emil J. *retired secondary school educator*
Morris, Robert Darrell *reading education educator*
Oelberg, Robert Nathan *landscape architect*
Parker, William Dale *management consultant, political and presidential adviser*
Pollard, William Barlow, III, *university educator*
Stahl, Ray Emerson *freelance writer, historian, researcher*

†Turner, John B. *social worker, educator, retired dean*
Usher, Charles Lindsey *social work educator, public policy analyst*
Van Wyk, Judson John *endocrinologist, pediatric educator*
Waller, Patricia Fossum *transportation executive, researcher, psychologist*
Warren, Donald William *physiology educator, dentistry educator*
†Wasik, Barbara Hanna *psychologist, educator*
Webb, James Okrum, Jr., *insurance company executive*
Weeks, M. J. *international management consultant*
Wegner, Judith Welch *law educator, former dean*
Weiss, Charles Manuel *environmental biologist*
Weiss, Shirley F. *urban and regional planner, economist, educator*
Wetzel, Robert George *botany educator*
Wheeler, Clayton Eugene, Jr., *dermatologist, educator*
White, Raymond Petrie, Jr., *dentist, educator*
Whybark, David Clay *business educator, researcher*
Wicker, Marie Peachee *civic worker*
Wilcox, Benson Reid *cardiothoracic surgeon, educator*
Williamson, Joel Rudolph *humanities educator*
Willingham, Emagene Emanuel *social worker*
Wilson, Glenn *economist, educator*
Winfield, John Buckner *rheumatologist, educator*
Wolfenden, Richard Vance *biochemistry educator*
Wright, Deil Spencer *political science educator*
†YMaisch, William Conrad *language educator*
†York, Anne Stewart *finance educator*

Charlotte
†Aliaga-Buchenau, Ana-Isabel *humanities educator*
Anderson, Gerald Leslie *financial executive*
Aycock, Hugh David *steel manufacturing company executive*
Ayscue, Edwin Osborne, Jr., *lawyer*
Barrows, Frank Clemence *editor*
Batcho, Ronald Frank *automotive company executive*
Bates, Michael *professional football player, former Olympic athlete, track and field*
†Belk, John Montgomery *retail company executive*
Bell, Don Antonio *neuroradiologist*
Bell, Paul Buckner *lawyer*
†Belthoff, Richard Charles, Jr., *lawyer*
Bernstein, Mark R. *retired lawyer*
†Blackburn, Richard Wallace *lawyer*
†Bobbitt, Warren Leslie, Sr., *director*
Bonnefoux, Jean-Pierre *artistic director, choreographer, dancer*
†Brackett, Martin Luther, Jr., *lawyer*
†Bradley, Dana Burr *education educator, consultant*
Bragg, Ellis Meredith, Jr., *lawyer*
Brandon, William Pew, Jr., *social sciences educator*
Brazeal, Donna Smith *psychologist*
Browning, Peter Crane *packaging company executive*
Brynn, Edward Paul *former ambassador*
Buchan, Jonathan Edward, Jr., *lawyer*
Buchenau, Jurgen *historian*
Buckley, Charles Robinson, III, *lawyer*
Buckner, Jennie *newspaper editor*
†Bulow, Harry Timothy *music educator*
Burke, Peggy Hudgins (Margaret Hudgins Burke) *auditor*
Burke, Steven Charles *healthcare administration executive*
†Burner, David L. *aerospace services company executive*
Butler, Carol King *advertising executive*
†Calloway, Mark T. *lawyer, former prosecutor*
Campbell, Hugh Brown, Jr., *judge*
Cannon, Robert Eugene *library director*
†Cannon, Thomas Roberts *lawyer*
Carino, Linda Susan *business consultant*
Casey, George Edward, Jr., *construction executive*
†Castro, Mary McDermott *language educator*
Chambers, Julius LeVonne *lawyer*
Chesson, Calvin White *lawyer, educator*
Cleghorn, John Michael *communications executive*
Coffey, Marilyn June *writer, educator*
Colavita, Paul Gerard *cardiologist, medical educator*
Colvard, Dean Wallace *emeritus university chancellor*
†Connette, Edward Grant, III, *lawyer*
†Cowell, Marion Aubrey, Jr., *lawyer*
Cox, Linda Smoak *real estate broker*
Crowder, Mary Thelma *obstetrician/gynecologist*
Curlin, William G. *bishop*
Curtis, Mary Cecelia *journalist*
Dagenhart, Larry Jones *lawyer*
Dai, Xingde *mathematics educator*
†DiMicco, Daniel R. *manufacturing executive*
Driscoll, John Paul *civil engineer*
†Dunn, Jackson Thomas, Jr., *lawyer, legal educator*
Durham, J(oseph) Porter, Jr., *lawyer, educator*
Edwards, Mark Brownlow *lawyer*
Eppes, Thomas Evans *advertising executive, public relations executive*
Eppley, Frances Fielden *retired secondary education educator, author*
Ervine, Timothy DuWayne *utilities executive*
†Erwin, Betty *bank executive*
Ethridge, Mark Foster, III, *writer, publisher, media consultant*
Ferebee, Stephen Scott, Jr., *architect*
Finley, Glenna *writer*
Fitzpatrick, James Ward, Jr., *engineering technology educator*
Foss, Ralph Scot *mechanical engineer*
Fox, John *professional football coach*
Freedland, Jacob Berke *dentist, endodontist*
Freeman, Sidney Lee *minister, educator*
Fretwell, Elbert K., Jr., *retired university chancellor, consultant*
Gambrell, Sarah Belk *retail executive*
Gay, William C. *philosophy educator*
Goolkasian, Paula A. *psychologist, educator*
Graham, Sylvia Angelenia *wholesale distributor, retail buyer*
Greene, Frederick Leslie *surgeon, educator*
†Gregory, Jeannette T. *publisher, writer*
Griffith, Dewey Maurice *mechanical engineer, investor*
Grigg, William Humphrey *utility executive*
Grimaldi, James Thomas *investment fund executive*
Haines, Kenneth H. *sports television broadcasting and marketing executive*
Halas, Paul Anthony, Jr., *business appraisal and valuation specialist, consultant*
Hall, James Bryan *gynecological oncologist*
Hance, James Henry, Jr., *bank executive*
Hanna, George Verner, III, *lawyer*
†Harris, Charles Marcus *lawyer*
Harver, Andrew Robert *psychology educator*
Helton, Max Edward *minister, consultant, religious organization executive*
Hill, Ruth Foell *language consultant*
†Hopper, Edward Warren *language educator*
Horn, Carl, III, *federal judge*
†Horner, Bob *broadcast executive*
Huberman, Jeffrey Allen *architect*
Hudgins, Catherine Harding *business executive*
Hutcheson, J. Sterling *allergist, immunologist, physician*
†Iley, Martha Strawn *music educator*
Irons, George Vernon, Jr., *cardiologist*
Jenkins, John Edward, Jr., *electronics executive, engineering educator*
Johnson, Jimmie *race car driver*
†Johnston, Elaine Curry *librarian*
†Jones, Amos Nathanael *journalist, violist*
Jones, James Richard *mechanical engineer*
Kallman, Kathleen Barbara *marketing and business development professional*
Kawczak, Janusz *mathematician, educator*
Keanini, Russell Guy *mechanical engineering educator, researcher*
Kincaid, Steven Randall *marketing professional*
King, L. Ellis *civil engineer, educator, consultant*
Knauth, Stephen Craig *poet*
Labardi, Jillian Gay *financial planner, insurance agent*
†Larsen, Marshall O. *corporate financial executive*
Lea, Scott Carter *retired packaging company executive*
†Lehman, Alice *bank executive*
†Levine, Howard R. *retail executive*
Lewis, Kenneth D. *bank executive*
Linker, Raymond Otho, Jr., *lawyer*
Locke, Elizabeth Hughes *foundation executive*
Long, Jim *racing team crew chief*
Loughridge, John Halsted, Jr., *lawyer*
Lowrance, Pamela Kay *medical/surgical nurse*
Lyerly, Elaine Myrick *advertising executive*
Maday, Clifford Ronald *insurance professional*
Mallinson, James A., Jr., *student health services administrator*
Martin, James Grubbs *medical executive, former governor*
May, Benjamin Tallman *securities specialist, administrator*
McBryde, Neill Gregory *lawyer*
McClure, Howard Jean, Jr., *advocate*
†McClure, M. DeVondria *lawyer*
McColl, Hugh Leon, Jr., *bank executive*
McCrory, Patrick *mayor*
McIntyre, Jane London *association administrator*
McLanahan, Charles Scott *neurosurgeon*
McNeal, Jeannette Johnson *social worker*
Means, Natrone Jermaine *professional football player*
Mendelsohn, Robert Victor *insurance company executive*
†Mercer, Evelyn Lois *retired guidance counselor*
†Metcalf, Eric Quinn *professional football player*
†Mickle, Deloris B. *credit manager, artist*
†Miller, John Randolph *lawyer*
Misiek, Dale Joseph *oral and maxillofacial surgeon*
Monge, Jay Parry *lawyer*
Montague, Edgar Burwell, III, (Monty Montague) *industrial designer*
†Moore, Bealer Gwen *transcription company executive*
Morrison, Robert Haywood *real estate developer*
Mueller, Werner Heinrich *chemical company executive*
Muhammad, Muhsin, II, *football player*
Mullen, Graham C. *federal judge*
Murray, Peter William *airline executive, educator, college administrator*
Myers, Robert Manson *English educator, author*
Myrick, Sue *congresswoman, former mayor*
Nadeau, Jerry *race car driver*
Neel, Richard Eugene *economics and business educator*
†Nelson, Thomas C. *manufacturing executive*
Newitt, John Garwood, Jr., *lawyer*
Nicholson, Henry Hale, Jr., *surgeon*
Ogirri, Dennis Arekpita *educator, political/business management consultant*
Oliver, John William Posegate *minister*
†Orsbon, Richard Anthony *lawyer*
Osborne, Richard Jay *electric utility company executive*
Owen, Kenneth Dale *orthodontist, real estate broker*
Payne, Ronald Dean *secondary school educator, music educator*
Peacock, A(lvin) Ward *textile company executive*
Penn, Philip Julian *lawyer*
†Perkins, Jim C. *automotive executive*
Phillips, Sandra Allen *retired primary school educator*
†Polking, Paul J. *lawyer*
Powell, Dannye Romine *news columnist*
Preston, James Young *lawyer*
Preyer, Norris Watson *history educator*
Price, Charles R., Jr., *advertising executive*
Priory, Richard Baldwin *electric power industry executive*
†Pruden, James Norfleet, III, *lawyer*
Pyle, Gerald Fredric *medical geographer, educator*
Ragan, Robert Allison *private investment executive, financial consultant*
†Raper, William Cranford *lawyer*
Ras, Zbigniew Wieslaw *computer science educator*
Raymond, Lawrence William *internist, pulmonary and occupational medicine physician*
Reese, Annette Evelyn *music educator*
Reeves, John Craig *religious studies educator*
†Ridder, Peter B. *publishing executive*
Rivenbark, Jan Meredith *business consultant*
Robinson, Shawna *race car driver*
Rodite, Robert R.R. *engineering scientist*
Roels, Oswald Albert *oceanographer, educator, business executive*
Ross, David Edmond *church official*
Schulz, Walter Kurt *accountant, information technology consultant*
†Sharts, Thomas *human services administrator, social sciences educator, consultant*
Siegel, Samuel *metals company executive*
†Silvia, John Edwin *economist*
Sink, Robert C. *lawyer*
Sintz, Edward Francis *librarian*
†Smith, O. Bruton *automotive company executive*
Spangler, Clemmie Dixon, Jr., *construction company executive*
Squires, James Ralph *development company executive*
Staley, Dawn *basketball player*
Starrett, Gregory *anthropologist, educator*
Stephens, Kitty Frances *academic administrator*
Stinson, Andrea Maria *professional basketball player*
Sulg, Madis *corporation executive, entrepreneur*
Taylor, David Brooke *lawyer, banker*
Thigpen, Richard Elton, Jr., *lawyer*
Thompson, G. Kennedy *bank executive*
†Thompson, Gregory Thomas *music educator, musician*
Thompson, John Albert, Jr., *dermatologist*
Thompson, Sydnor, Jr., (Charles William Sydnor Thompson Jr.) *lawyer, mediator, arbitrator*
†Turner, Kathleen J. *communications educator, consultant*
Twisdale, Harold Winfred *dentist*
Tyson, Cynthia Haldenby *academic administrator*
Ullrich, Christopher George *neuroradiologist*
Valasquez, Joseph Louis *industrial engineer*
Van Allen, William Kent *lawyer*
Van Alstyne, Vance Brownell *arbitration management consultant*
Vinroot, Richard Allen *lawyer, mayor*
Visser, Valya Elizabeth *physician*
Waggoner, William Johnson *lawyer*
Wagner, Kenneth Lynn *lawyer*
Walker, Clarence Wesley *lawyer*
Walker, Jewett Lynius *clergyman, church official*
Walls, Wesley (Charles Wesley Walls) *football player*
Webster, Murray Alexander, Jr., *sociologist, educator*
Weinke, Chris *football player*
Welch, Jeanie Maxine *librarian*
Whelpley, David B., Jr., *lawyer*
Wiggins, Nancy Bowen *real estate broker, market research consultant*
Wood, Donald Craig *retired marketing professional*
Wood, William McBrayer *lawyer*
Woodward, James Hoyt *academic administrator, engineer*
Woolard, William Leon *lawyer, electrical distributing company executive*
Wright, Wayne Kenneth *federal agency statistician*
†Yancy, Dorothy Cowser *academic administrator*
Youngs, Jennifer Ann *lawyer*
Zeller, Michael Eugene *lawyer*

Cherokee
†Hotelling, Kurt Paul *music educator, writer*
Martin, Harry Corpening *lawyer, retired state supreme court justice*

Cherry Point
Laviolette, Bruce Edward *industrial manufacturing management executive*

Cherryville
Barger, Linda Kale *choral director*
Huffstetler, Palmer Eugene *lawyer*
Mayhew, Kenneth Edwin, Jr., *transportation company executive*

Clayton
Jenkins, Elaine Parker *secondary school educator*
Silberman, H. Lee *public relations executive, editorial consultant*

Clemmons
Church, Avery Grenfell *retired anthropology educator, poet*
†Rawls, Martha Grogan (Molly Rawls) *librarian*
Taquey, Antony *accountant*

Clinton
†Faircloth, Duncan McLauchlin (Lauch Faircloth) *former senator, businessman, farmer*
Griffin, Betty Lou *not-for-profit developer, educator*
Hobbs, Jerry Dean *county manager*

Clyde
Rogers, Frances Nichols *assistant principal*

Columbus
Blate, Michael *author, lecturer*
Brooks, Jerry Claude *safety engineer, educator*
Sauvé, Carolyn Opal *writer, journalist, poet*

Concord
Biffle, Greg *race car driver*
Busch, Kurt *race car driver*
Elder, Christian *race car driver*
†Newman, Sylvia H. *language educator*
†Price, Randy S. *music educator*
Robinson, Harold Oscar *clergyman, educator*

Conover
Carmichael, Richard E. *government official, financial manager, educator*
†Jarrett, Dale *race car driver*
Sims, Janette Elizabeth Lowman *educational director*
Williams, Randolph Stuart *urban planner*

Cornelius
Giblin, Patrick David *retired banker*
Wortman, William Jerome, Jr., *obstetrician-gynecologist*

Corolla
Schrote, John Ellis *retired government executive*

Cove City
Hawkins, Elinor Dixon (Mrs. Carroll Woodard Hawkins) *retired librarian*

Cramerton
†Kim, Paul DongUk *academic administrator, religious organization administrator, minister*

Creedmoor
Cross, June Crews *retired music educator*
†Husketh, Alma Ormond *language educator*

Crumpler
Butler, Douglas John *physician*

Cullowhee
†Bardo, John William *university administrator*
Coulter, Myron Lee *retired academic administrator*
Drew, Ruby Louise *speech-language pathologist, consultant*
Farwell, Harold Frederick, Jr., *English language educator*
Jarrell, Stephen Brooks *economics educator*
†Lusky, Jason Francis *electronics engineer*
Reed, Alfred Douglas *retired academic administrator*
Willis, Ralph Houston *mathematics educator*
Wilson, LeVon Edward *law educator, lawyer*

Davidson
Cole, Richard Cargill *English language educator*
†Grosch, Laura Dudley *artist, teacher, consultant*
Jackson, Herb *artist, educator*
Jones, Arthur Edwin, Jr., *library administrator, English and American literature educator*
McMillen, Sally Gregory *history educator*
Park, Leland Madison *librarian*
Plyler, John Laney, Jr., *retired healthcare management professional*
Ramirez, Julio Jesus *neuroscientist*
Spencer, Samuel Reid, Jr., *education consultant, former university president*
Swallow, John *mathematician, educator*
†Vagt, Robert F. *academic administrator*
Williams, Robert Chadwell *history educator*

Denton
Tuttle, Bynum R., Jr., *brokerage house executive*

Dobson
Smith, Richard Jackson *elementary education educator*

Duck
Majewski, Theodore Eugene *chemist*

Dunn
Overton, Elizabeth Nicole *elementary school educator, aerobics instructor*
†Pope, Patrick Harris *lawyer, business executive*
Robison, Frederick Mason *financial executive*

Durham
†Admay, Catherine Adcock *law lecturer, researcher*
Aldrich, John Herbert *political science educator*
†Alexander, Michael Jozef *neurosurgeon, radiologist*
Althaus, David Steven *consultant*
Amaldoss, Wilfred *marketing educator*
Amos, Dennis B. *immunologist*
Anderson, William Banks, Jr., *ophthalmology educator*
Anlyan, William George *surgeon, university administrator*
Bachini, Peter P. *insurance company executive*
Bartlett, Katharine Tiffany *law educator*
Bennett, Peter Brian *researcher, hyperbaric medicine*
Bettman, James Ross *management educator*
Bevan, William *retired foundation executive*
Blazer, Dan German, II, *psychiatrist, epidemiologist*
Blum, Jacob Joseph *physiologist, educator*
Boguslavsky, George William *psychologist, educator*
Bollerslev, Tim Peter *economics educator*
Bollinger, Ralph Randal *surgeon, researcher*
Bossen, Edward Hecht *pathologist*
Bosworth, Hayden B. *health psychologist*
Bradford, William Dalton *pathologist, educator*
†Brady, David Jones *engineering educator, entrepreneur*
Braibanti, Ralph John *political scientist, educator*
Brantley, Jeffrey Garland *health science facility administrator*

Brodie, Harlow Keith Hammond *psychiatrist, educator, past university president*
Buchanan, Robert Augustus, Jr., *cardiologist*
Buckley, Rebecca Hatcher *physician, educator*
Budd, Isabelle Amelia *research economist*
Budd, Louis John *English language educator*
Burgess, Paula Lashenske *health facility administrator*
Burmeister, Edwin *economics educator*
Busse, Ewald William *psychiatrist, educator*
†Butterfield, Marian Isbey *psychiatrist, researcher*
Cady, Edwin Harrison *English language educator, author*
Canada, Mary Whitfield *retired librarian*
Carpenter, Charles Francis *lawyer*
Carrington, Paul DeWitt *lawyer, educator*
Carter, James Harvey *psychiatrist, educator*
Casey, H(orace) Craig, Jr., *electrical engineering educator*
†Cassidy, Frederick *psychiatrist*
Chafe, William Henry *history educator*
†Challa, Pratap *ophthalmologist, researcher*
Chao, James Lee *chemist, educator*
Chesnut, Donald Blair *retired chemistry educator*
Christie, George Custis *lawyer, educator, author*
Christmas, William Anthony *internist, educator*
Clark, Arthur Watts *insurance company executive*
Clay, Diskin *classical studies educator*
Cocks, Franklin Hadley *materials scientist*
Cohen, Harvey Jay *physician, educator*
Cohn, Lindsay Pamela *political scientist, researcher*
Coleman, Ralph Edward *nuclear medicine physician, educator*
Colton, Joel *historian, educator*
Colvin, O. Michael *medical director, medical educator*
Conklin, George Henry *sociologist, educator*
Cook, Philip Jackson *economist, educator*
Cooper, Charles Howard *photojournalist, newspaper publishing company executive*
Coppridge, Alton James *urological surgeon*
Cox, James D. *law educator*
Davis, Calvin De Armond *historian, educator*
Dawson, Robert Edward, Sr., *ophthalmologist*
†Demark-Wahnefried, Wendy *nutritionist, researcher*
Dorn, Louis Otto *retired minister, consultant*
Dowell, Earl Hugh *university dean, aerospace and mechanical engineering educator*
†Edwards, Christopher Levon *medical association administrator*
Efird, James Michael *theology educator*
Elliot, Jeffrey M. *political science educator, author*
Epstein, David L. *ophthalmologist, educator*
Falletta, John Matthew *pediatrician, educator*
Fassett, John D. *retired utility executive, consultant*
Feaver, Peter Douglas *political science educator, consultant, defense analyst*
†Fischer, Sibylle Maria *literature educator*
Fisher, Stewart Wayne *lawyer*
Fiske, Edward B. *editor, journalist, educational consultant*
Foreman, John William *pediatrician, educator*
†Fowler, Vance Garrison, Jr., *internist, educator*
Franklin, John Hope *historian, educator, author*
Freemark, Michael Scott *pediatric endocrinologist and educator*
Fridovich, Irwin *biochemistry educator*
Gaede, Jane Taylor *pathologist, educator*
†Gaines, Roland H. *academic administrator*
†Gavin, Henri Philippe *engineering educator, researcher*
Giannopoulou, Athina *physician, surgeon*
Gillespie, Michael Allen *social sciences educator, writer*
Gillham, Nicholas Wright *geneticist, educator*
†Gitler, Daniel *neurobiologist, researcher*
Gittler, Joseph Bertram *sociology educator*
†Glibert, John H. *research scientist*
†Goestenkors, Gail *head basketball coach*
Golding, Martin Philip *law and philosophy educator*
†Gonzalez-Stawinski, Gonzalo Vincente *surgeon, researcher*
Goshaw, Alfred T. *physicist, educator*
Gosselin, Tracy Karen *nursing administrator*
Greenberg, Gary Norman *internist, occupational medicine physician*
Greenfield, Joseph Cholmondeley, Jr., *physician, educator*
†Grocott, Hilary Peter *adult education educator*
Guilak, Farshid *biomedical engineering researcher, educator*
Gunter, Emily Diane *communications executive, marketing professional, real estate developer, author, educator*
Guseh, James Sawalla *public administration educator*
Guy, David McCutcheon *literature educator*
Hamaker, Richard Franklin *engineer*
Hammes, Gordon G. *chemistry educator*
Hammond, Charles Bessellieu *obstetrician, gynecologist, educator*
Harman, Charles Morgan *mechanical engineer*
Harmel, Merel Hilber *anesthesiologist, educator*
Harpole, David Harold, Jr., *thoracic surgeon*
Harrell, Carlton (Benjamin Carlton Harrell) *writer, retired editor*
Harris, Jerome Sylvan *pediatrician, pediatrics and biochemistry educator*
†Harris, Robert T. *internist*
Harrison, Dean Thomas *physician assistant*
Havighurst, Clark Canfield *law educator*
Hawkins, William E. N. *newspaper editor*
Hobbs, Marcus Edwin *chemistry educator*
Holder, Angela Roddey *lawyer, educator*
Holley, Irving Brinton, Jr., *historian, educator*
Holsti, Ole Rudolf *political scientist, educator*
Horowitz, Donald Leonard *lawyer, educator, researcher, political scientist, arbitrator*
Huestis, Charles Benjamin *former academic administrator*
Hurwitz, Barrie James *neurologist*
Islam, Farhad Fuad *electronics and computer research engineer*
Jaszczak, Ronald Jack *physicist, researcher, consultant*
†Jeffreys, Arcelia Taylor *education educator*
Jennings, Robert Burgess *experimental pathologist, medical educator*
Joklik, Wolfgang Karl *biochemist, virologist, educator*
Jonassaint, Jean *French and Francophone literatures educator*
Kaprielian, Victoria Susan *medical educator*
Katz, Samuel Lawrence *pediatrician, scientist*
Keene, Jack Donald *molecular genetics and microbiology educator*
Keller, Thomas Franklin *business administration educator*
Kelley, Allen Charles *economist, educator*
Keohane, Nannerl Overholser *university president, political scientist*
Keohane, Robert Owen *political scientist, educator*
Kerckhoff, Sylvia Stansbury *mayor*
†Khismatullin, Damir Borisovich *physicist, mathematician*
†Kiss, Elizabeth *philosophy educator*
Klitzman, Bruce *physiologist, plastic surgery educator, researcher*
Koepke, John Arthur *hematologist, clinical pathologist*
†Kong, David Franklin *cardiologist, educator*
Krakauer, Thomas Henry *museum director emeritus*
Krishnan, Krishnaswamy Ranga Rama R. *psychiatry educator*
†Krishnan, Ranga Rama *psychiatrist*
†Krzyzewski, Mike *university athletic coach*
Kuniholm, Bruce Robellet *university administrator*
Lack, Leon *pharmacology and biochemistry educator*
Ladd, Helen Francis *social sciences educator, researcher*
Ladd, Marcia Lee *medical equipment and supplies company executive*
Land, Kenneth Carl *sociology educator, demographer, statistician, consultant*
Lang, Stephen Norman *orthopedist, surgeon*
Lavery, John Edward *mathematician*
†Leachman, Lori Lynn *economist, educator*
Lee, Paul P. *ophthalmologist, educator, consultant, lawyer*
†Lefkowitz, Robert Joseph *physician, educator*
Lerner, Warren *historian, educator*
†Lewis, David Olin *lawyer, educator*
Lieberman, Rochelle Phyllis *relocation company executive*
Lockhead, Gregory Roger *psychology educator*
†Lutes, Christopher Charles *environmental scientist, consultant*
Mallette, Malcolm Francis *newspaper editor, educator*
Malling, Heinrich Valdemar *geneticist*
Mark, Daniel Benjamin *cardiologist*
Markert, Mary Louise *pediatrics educator*
Markham, Charles Buchanan *retired lawyer*
Martinez, Maria Dolores *pediatrician*
†Massey, Janice Munn *neurology educator*
Maxwell, Richard Callender *lawyer, educator*
McClain, Gregory David *minister*
McClain, Paula Denice *political scientist, educator*
McCrory, Michael Elliott *radiologist*
†McCusker, Paul Donald *lawyer, educator*
McMahon, John Alexander *law educator*
Merrick, Bruce Alex *research scientist*
Meyer, Horst *physics educator*
Meyers, Eric Mark *religion educator*
Michener, James Lloyd *medical educator*
Mickiewicz, Ellen Propper *political and social science educator*
Miller, David Edmond *physician*
†Mofidi, Mahyar *dental educator*
Moore, John Wilson *neurophysiologist, educator*
Mosteller, Robert P. *law educator*
Murphy, Thomas Miles *pediatrician, educator*
†Mushak, Paul *toxicologist, consultant*
†Nadadur, Srikanth S *molecular biologist*
Nakarai, Charles Frederick Toyozo *music educator, adjudicator*
Naylor, Aubrey Willard *botany educator*
†Newman, Mark Franklin *cardiologist, anesthesiologist*
Nicklas, Robert Bruce *cell biologist, educator*
Oakley, Wanda Faye *management consultant, educator*
Oates, Elizabeth Woods *physician, psychiatrist*
Oates, John Francis *classics educator*
O'Briant, Margaret Denny *retired elementary school educator*
Otterbourg, Robert Kenneth *public relations consultant, writer*
Palmore, Erdman Ballagh *gerontologist, educator*
†Pamula, Vamsee K. *electrical engineer, researcher*
†Pappas, Theodore Nick *surgeon, educator*
†Parkerson, George Robert, Jr., *physician, educator*
Pearsall, George Wilbur *materials scientist, mechanical engineer, educator, consultant*
Peele, Anne Marie *government relations administrator*
Perkins, Ronald Dee *geologist, educator*
Peterson, Max Rupert, Jr., *chemist, researcher*
Petroski, Catherine *writer, consultant*
Petroski, Henry *engineer educator, writer*
†Pfau, Thomas *literature educator*
Pinnell, Sheldon Richard *physician, medical educator, dermatologist*
Pizzo, Salvatore Vincent *pathologist*
Plonsey, Robert *electrical and biomedical engineer*
Preston, Richard Arthur *historian*
Priest, Peter H. *lawyer*
Prosnitz, Leonard R. *radiologist*
Radtke, Rodney A. *neurologist*
Raetz, Christian R. H. *biochemistry educator*
†Ravin, Carl Eric *radiologist, educator, department chairman*
Reif, John Henry *computer science educator*
Richardson, Lawrence, Jr., *Latin language educator, archeologist*
†Richardson, Lily Pendarvis *retired occupational health nurse*
Richardson, Stephen Giles *biotechnology company executive*
Robboy, Stanley J. *pathologist, educator*
Roberson, Nathan Russell *physicist, educator*
Robertson, Horace Bascomb, Jr., *retired law educator*
Roland, Alex Frederick *history educator*
Rollins, Edward Tyler, Jr., *newspaper executive*
Rose, Donald James *computer science educator*
Rose, Jed Eugene *research scientist*
Rossiter, Alexander, Jr., *news service executive, editor*
Rouse, Doris Jane *physiologist, research administrator*
Rowe, Thomas Dudley, Jr., *law educator*
Sabiston, David Coston, Jr., *surgeon, educator*
Sanford, David Hawley *philosophy educator*
Schiffman, Susan Stolte *medical psychologist, educator*
Schmalbeck, Richard Louis *university dean, lawyer*
Schmidt-Nielsen, Knut *physiologist, educator*
Schwarcz, Steven Lance *law educator, lawyer*
Scott, Anne Byrd Firor *history educator*
Sedor, Frank A. *chemist*
Serafin, Donald *plastic surgeon, educator*
Shadduck, Phillip Price *surgeon*
Shelburne, John Daniel *pathologist*
Shimm, Melvin Gerald *law educator*
Simons, Elwyn LaVerne *physical anthropologist, primatologist, paleontologist, educator*
†Smith, Effie Barnette *caregiver*
Smith, Harmon Lee, Jr., *clergyman, moral theology educator*
Smith, Peter *chemist, educator, consultant*
†Snyder, Stephen P *chemical company controller*
Snyderman, Ralph *medical educator, physician*
Soper, John Tunnicliff *obstetrician-gynecologist, educator*
†Spach, Madison Stockton *cardiologist, educator*
Squire, Alexander *management consultant*
Staddon, John Eric Rayner *psychology, zoology, neurobiology educator*
Staelin, Richard *business administration educator*
Stead, Eugene Anson, Jr., *physician*
Steffens, David Carl *geriatric psychiatrist*
†Steinmetz, David Curtis *religious studies educator*
Stewart, Philip Robert *French language educator*
Stickel, Delford LeFew *retired general surgeon*
Stiles, Gary Lester *cardiologist, molecular pharmacologist, educator*
Surwit, Richard Samuel *psychology educator*
†Takahashi, Toku *education educator, researcher*
Talley, Joseph Eugene *psychologist*
†Tcheng, James Enlou *physician*
Tedder, Thomas Fletcher *immunology educator, researcher*
†Tendler, David Andrew *internist, educator*
Thompson, James Howard *historian, library administrator*
Thompson, John Herd *history educator*
†Thompson, Sharon Andrea *lawyer*
Thompson, William Moreau *radiologist, educator*
Tiryakian, Edward Ashod *sociology educator*
†Tupler, Larry Alan *psychologist, researcher*
Utku, Senol *civil engineer, computer science educator*
Vaslef, Steven Nicholas *surgeon*
Vatavuk, William Michael *chemical engineer, author*
†Vigdor, Jacob Lawrence *economist, educator*
†Wald, Priscilla B. *language educator*
Walker, William D. *physicist, educator, researcher*
Walter, Richard Lawrence *physicist, educator*
Ward, Robert *composer, conductor, educator*
†Ware, Ruth Winchester *social worker*
Warner, David Samuel *anesthesiologist, educator*
Weiner, Richard David *psychiatrist, researcher*
Wells, Samuel Alonzo, Jr., *surgeon, educator*
†Wescott, Joseph Warren, II, *academic administrator, education educator*
†Wesseling, John F. *neuroscientist*
†Whiddon, Curtis Scott *medical physicist*
Wicker, R. David, Jr., *lawyer*
Wilkins, Robert Henry *neurosurgeon, editor*
†Williams, Frank Earl *music educator*
Williams, George Walton *English educator*
Williams, Jocelyn Jones *reading educator*
Williams, R. Sanders *dean, academic administrator, educator, researcher*
Williams, Redford Brown *medical educator*
Wilson, Blake Shaw *electrical engineer, researcher*
Wilson, Ruby Leila *nurse, educator*
Witt, Ronald G. *historian, educator*
Wohlgemuth, William K., Jr., *psychologist*
Yancy, William Samuel *pediatrician*
Yoshizumi, Terry Takatoshi *medical physicist*
†Zhirnov, Victor *physicist, researcher*

Eden
†Doss, Marion Kenneth *lawyer*
†Sanders, Barbara Fayne *artist, educator*
Williams, Sue Darden *library director*

Edenton
Flynn, Patrick *designer, programmer, consultant*
Rossman, Robert Harris *management consultant*

Efland
Weinberg, Gerhard Ludwig *history educator*

Elizabeth City
Choudhury, Abdul Latif *physics educator*
Deaton, Fae Adams *clinical social worker, counselor*
†Harrison, Thomas R. *music educator*
Lim, Tomas Q., Jr., *physician*
†Lisowski, Joseph Anthony *language educator, poet, writer*
†Manglik, Vinod Prakash *statistician, consultant, educator*
White, Leon Samuel *college administrator*
Williams, Rita Carroll *language educator, poet*

Elkin
Gillespie, James Davis *lawyer*

Elon
Bowman, Randall Hunter *reference and instruction librarian*
Troxler, Carole Watterson *historian, educator*

Elon College
Powell, William Council, Sr., *service company executive*
Tolley, Jerry Russell *university administrator*

Fairmont
Byrne, James Frederick *banker*

Fairview
Bradley, Edward William *sports foundation executive*
Eck, David Wilson *minister*
Gaffney, Thomas Edward *physician*
Rhynedance, Harold Dexter, Jr., *lawyer, consultant*

Farmville
Hardy-Braz, Steven Thomas *psychologist*

Fayetteville
†Berryhill, Maurice Judd *human services administrator*
Carwile, Billy Price *computer engineer, civilian military employee*
Chipman, Martin *neurologist, educator, retired army officer*
Conley, Raymond Leslie *English language educator*
†Cook, James Wesley *music educator*
Curtis, Marvin Vernell *music educator*
Fietsam, Robert, Jr., *physician*
Friedman, Deborah Leslie White *educational administrator*
†Hall, Phoebe Jean *theater educator*
Hurdle, Thomas Gray *retired urologist*
Jansen, Michael John *healthcare executive*
Jordan, Karla Salge *early childhood education educator*
Kendrick, Mark Cleveland *real estate executive*
Lowe, James Edward, Jr., *plastic and reconstructive surgeon*
McMillan, Bettie Barney *English language educator*
†Rand, Anthony Eden *lawyer*
Richardson, Emilie White *manufacturing company executive, investment company executive, lecturer*
Ruppe, Arthur Maxwell *lawyer*
†Shaffer, Denny Richard *small business owner*
†Skorich, John Jovan *music educator*
Townsend, William Jackson *lawyer*
Trull, Timothy Lane *financial services executive*
†Warner, James Alex *music educator*
†Watt, Katherine Ann *administrative assistant*
Watt, Willis Martin *academic administrator, communications, adult education, leadership educator*

Fearrington Village
†Boewe, Charles Ernst *historian, educator*

Flat Rock
Childress, Richard Thomas *investment company executive*
Davidson, Clayton Leslie *chemical engineer*
Demartini, Robert John *business executive, entrepreneur*

Fletcher
†Roe, Richard Steven *writer, illustrator*
†Tolbert, Gary J. *minister*

Fort Bragg
†Boykin, William G. *career officer*
†Brown, Bryan D. *career officer*
†McNeill, Dan K. *military career officer*
†Ryneska, John Joseph *military career officer*
†Swain, Jeffery Alvin *systems analyst*

Four Oaks
Jordan, Lyndon Kirkman *family practice physician*

Franklin
Earhart, Eileen Magie *retired child and family life educator*
Johnson, Herbert Alan *history and law educator, lawyer, chaplain*

Franklinton
†Elmore, Cenieth Catherine *music educator*
Moran, John Bernard *government official, retired*

Garner
Spencer, Thomas Melvin, III, *soft drink company executive*

Gastonia
Cannon, Octavia Manetta *obstetrician-gynecologist*
Eads, Ronald Preston *Christian management consultant*
Flynn, Duane James *entomologist*
Kimbrell, Willard Duke *textile company executive*
Lawson, William David, III, *retired cotton company executive*
Prince, George Edward *retired pediatrician*
Stott, Grady Bernell *lawyer*
Teem, Paul Lloyd, Jr., *bank executive*

Gibsonville
Crawford, Kathrine Nelson *special education educator*

Goldsboro
Barkley, Monika Johanna *general contracting professional*

Granite Falls
Humphreys, Kenneth King *engineer, educator, association executive*
Power, Elizabeth Henry *consultant*

Greensboro
Adewuyi, Yusuf Gbadebo *chemical engineering educator, researcher, consultant*
Aldridge, David William *biologist, educator*
†Almeida, José Agustín *romance languages educator*
Baldwin, Jason Holt *secondary school educator*
Bardolph, Richard *historian, educator*
Beahm, Roger *advertising executive*
Benson, Brian Joseph *English language educator, author*
Black, Sylvia Sloan *business educator*
Blackwell, William Ernest
Blanchet-Sadri, Francine *mathematician, educator*
†Brooks, Darrell Lemont *collections and bad debt manager*
†Brotherton, Jonathan Paul *music educator*
Brown, Hazel Fay Nixon *women's health nurse, educator, administrator*
Bullock, Frank William, Jr., *federal judge*
†Bynum, Magnolia Virginia Wright *retired secondary school educator*
Capone, Lucien, III, *lawyer*
Carlyon, Diane Claire *nurse*
Carmichael, James Vinson, Jr., *library and information science educator*
Cazel, Hugh Allen *industrial engineer, educator*
Chandler, Austin Grace *psychologist*
Chappell, Fred Davis *English language educator, poet*
Clark, Clifton Bob *physicist*
Clark, Lawrence James *minister*
Cole, Johnnetta Betsch *university president, educator*
Compton, John Carroll *accountant*
Cotter, John Burley *ophthalmologist, corneal specialist*
†Cowett, Everett R *retired agronomist*
Coyne, William P. *advertising executive*
Davis, Herbert Owen *lawyer*
Dillon, Terri L. *consulting firm executive*
Durham, Carolyn Richardson *foreign language and literature educator*
Dyakonov, Alexander J. *physical chemist, researcher*
Dziordz, Walter Michael *priest*
Felts, John Winfred, Jr., *school librarian, educator*
Floyd, Jack William *lawyer*
Flynt, Candace Lambeth *writer*
Formo, Brenda Terrell *travel company executive*
Frye, Henry E. *retired state supreme court chief justice*
Galloway, Hunter Henderson, III, *lawyer, small business owner*
†Ganji, Jagadeesh (Jay) *cardiologist*
Gdanitz, Robert J. *research scientist, educator*
Gilbert, Marie Rogers *poet*
Gill, Diane Louise *psychology educator, university official*
Gill, Evalyn Pierpoint *editor, writer, publisher*
Glover, Durant Murrell *lawyer*
Godard, Jerry Holton Caris *psychology educator, college dean*
Goldman, Bert Arthur *psychologist, educator*
Gumbiner, Kenneth Jay *lawyer*
Hall, William Edward, Jr., *insurance agency executive*
Harrington, Ellis Jackson, Jr., *lawyer*
†Hayes, Robert Banks, II, *assistant principal*
Helms-VanStone, Mary Wallace *anthropology educator*
Hensel, William Arthur *family physician*
Herman, Roger Eliot *professional speaker, consultant, futurist, writer*
Houston, Frank Matt *dermatologist*
Hunter, Bynum Merritt *lawyer*
Irvin, Helen Adcock *interior designer*
Jellicorse, John Lee *communications and theatre educator*
Johnson, Marshall Hardy *investment company executive*
Jones, Thomas Owen, Jr., *business educator, military officer*
Kiser, Mose, III, *small business owner*
Koonce, Neil Wright *lawyer*
Korb, William Brown, Jr., *manufacturing company executive*
Kornegay, Horace Robinson *trade association executive, former congressman, lawyer*
Kovacs, Beatrice *library studies educator*
Kurepa, Alexandra *mathematician, educator*
†Lloyd, Lila G. *finance educator*
†Lloyd, Robert Blackwell, Jr., *lawyer*
†McDonald, Mackey J. *apparel company executive*
McKissick-Melton, S. Charmaine *mass communications educator*
Melvin, Charles Edward, Jr., *lawyer*
Meyers, Carolyn Winstead *mechanical engineer, educator*
Middleton, Herman David, Sr., *theater educator*
Miller, Robert Louis *university dean, chemistry educator*
Moran, William Edward *academic administrator*
Murrelle, Ronald Kemp *architectural firm executive*
†Nemati, Hamid R. *management educator*
Nunn, Robert William *sentencing services official*
Oakley, Joel Neese *lawyer*
O'Brien, William John *ecology researcher*
Pai, Devdas Mizar *engineering educator*

†Penley, Virginia Long *social worker*
Penninger, Frieda Elaine *retired English language educator*
Peterson, John Edgar, Jr., *retired nursing home executive and agricultural executive, textile executive*
Prysby, Charles Lee *political science educator*
Reed, William Edward *government official, educator*
Rowan, William Boyd *parasitologist, writer*
Ruhm, Christopher John *economics educator*
†St. George, Nicholas James *lawyer, manufactured housing company executive*
Sanders, William Eugene *marketing executive*
Schell, Braxton *lawyer*
Schleunes, Karl A. *history educator*
Schnatterly, Michael Dean *priest*
Schwenn, Lee William *retired medical center executive*
Shelton, David Howard *economics educator*
Shivakumar, Kunigal Nanjundaiah *aerospace engineer, educator*
Shotwell, Sheila Murray *medical/surgical nurse*
Smith, Lanty L(loyd) *lawyer, business executive*
Soles, William Roger *insurance company executive, director*
Staab, Thomas Robert *consumer product company financial executive*
Starling, Larry Eugene *auditor*
Stevens, Elliott Walker, Jr., *allergist, pulmonologist*
Stocks, William L. *federal judge*
Styles, Teresa Jo *producer, educator*
Sullivan, Patricia A. *academic administrator*
Swan, George Steven *law educator*
Tredinnick, Laurel Christine *social worker*
Turner, James Reginald *lawyer*
Watson, Robert Winthrop *poet*
Whalen, Thomas Brian *anesthesiologist*
Williams, Irving Laurence *physics educator*
†Wright, Kieth Carter *librarian, educator*
Zopf, Paul Edward, Jr., *sociologist*

Greenville
†Babb, Joseph Dolby *physician*
Bearden, James Hudson *university official*
Eakin, Richard Ronald *academic educator, mathematics educator*
Eribo, Festus *mass communication educator, journalist*
†Ferrell, Henry Clifton, Jr., *historian, educator*
Finkelday, John Paul *retail sales executive*
†Gilham, Hanna Kaltenbrunner *writer*
Hadden, Robert Lee *librarian*
Hoffman, Donald Richard *pathologist, educator*
Howell, John McDade *retired university chancellor, political science educator*
†Huo, Shouquan *research scientist, educator*
Jackson, Bobby Rand *minister*
†Kalinowski, Joe *humanities educator, researcher*
†Kopelman, Loretta Mary *philosophy educator*
Kragel, Peter J. *academic administrator*
†Kramar, John Shaw *voice educator, vocalist*
Krpata, Steven Allen *accountant, real estate company executive*
Lee, Kenneth Stuart *neurosurgeon, educator*
Leggett, Donald Yates *academic administrator*
Leggett, Nancy Porter *university administrator*
Lehman, John Michael *experimental pathologist-virologist*
†Lewis, Nell J. *director, consultant*
Meggs, William Joel *toxicologist, internist, emergency physician, educator*
†Moll, Kevin N. *musicologist, educator*
Muse, William Van *academic administrator*
Newton, Dale Alan *pediatrician, educator*
Perkin, Ronald Murray *pediatrician, educator*
†Pofahl, Walter Emerson *surgeon*
Pories, Walter Julius *surgeon, educator*
Rose, John David *cardiologist*
Runyan, Timothy Jack *historian, educator*
†Stevens, David Boyette *law educator*
Stuart, Andrew Michael *educator*
Summers, Kyle *biologist, educator*
Thompson, Robert Joseph *university administrator, educator*
Tingelstad, Jon Bunde *retired physician*
Wallin, Leland Dean *artist, educator*
Webster, Raymond Earl *psychology educator, director, psychotherapist*
Wilkerson, William Holton *banker*

Hampstead
Solomon, Robert Douglas *pathology educator*
Unger, Stephen Allan *publishing executive, editor*
Walters, Sherwood George *management consultant, educator*

Harrisburg
Economaki, Chris Constantine (Christopher Economaki) *publisher, editor*
Edwards, Larry Cecil *management consultant*
Hendrick, Ricky *race car driver*
†Labonte, Terry *race car driver*
Sprague, Jack *race car driver*

Havelock
Lindelof, William Christian, Jr., *financial company executive*

Henderson
Williams, Ruth Russell *artist*

Hendersonville
Brittain, James Edward *science and technology educator, researcher*
Cochran, Linda Thornthwaite *psychotherapist, social worker, consultant*
Daubert, Madeline J. *accountant, educator*
Halm, James Maurice *retired chemist, poet*
Harris, James Braxton *retired humanities educator, freelance/self-employed writer*
Haynes, John Mabin *retired utilities executive*
Heil, Mary Ruth *former counselor*
Heltman, Robert Fairchild *distribution executive*
Kratz, Howard Russel *physicist, researcher*

Lind, Robert Clarence *economist, educator*
Mankoff, Albert William *cultural organization administrator, consultant, writer*
Payne, Gerald Oliver *retired elementary education educator*
†Reinhart, John Belvin *retired child and adolescent psychiatrist, educator*
Roberts, James Allen *urologist*
Saby, John Sanford *physicist, consultant*
Stepkoski, Robert John *automobile dealership executive*
†Thomas, Stephen *retired industrial engineer*
Trexler, Edgar Ray *minister, editor*

Hertford
Cole, Janice McKenzie *former prosecutor*

Hickory
Auten, George Robert, Jr., *civil engineer*
†George, Boyd Lee *consumer products company executive*
†Kiser, Daniel *music educator, musician*
Lefler, Wade Hampton, Jr., *ophthalmologist*
†Leger-Scott, Debbie *critical care nurse*
McDaniel, Michael Conway Dixon *bishop, retired theology educator*
Smith, Young Merritt, Jr., *lawyer*
Speas, Charles Stuart *human resources consultant, entrepreneur*

High Point
Bailey, William Nathan *nutritionist, consultant*
Bardelas, Jose Antonio *allergist*
Boger, Richard Edwin, Jr., *minister*
Burnette, Marie (Helen Marie Burnette) *music educator*
†Burton, Ward *professional race car driver*
Cullom, Joseph William *surgeon*
Draelos, Zoe Diana *dermatologist, consultant*
Fenn, Ormon William, Jr., *furniture company executive*
Howard, Lou Dean Graham *elementary education educator*
†Huss, Donald Edwin, Jr., *musician*
Kandt, Raymond S. *neurologist*
Marsden, Lawrence Albert *retired textile company executive*
Martinson, Jacob Christian, Jr., *academic administrator*
McAllister, Kenneth Wayne *lawyer*
McCaslin, Richard Bryan *history educator*
Min, Sung Sik *accountant*
Moore, Jeffrey A. *municipal official*
Pate, William Patrick *city manager*
†Payne-Raymond, Howard *small business owner*
Phillips, Earl Norfleet, Jr., *diplomat, financial services executive*
Schwartz, Robert Terry *industrial design executive*
Sheahan, Robert Emmett *lawyer, consultant*
Stimson, Richard Alden *writer*
Stricklin, Hut *race car driver*
Williams, Lawrence D. *surgeon*
Wimmer, Scott *race car driver*
Winn, Walter Garnett, Jr., *marketing strategist, advertising executive*

Highlands
Sheehan, Charles Vincent *investment banker*

Hillsborough
Bolduc, Jean Plumley *journalist, education activist*
Eustice, Russell Clifford *consulting company executive, academic director*
Goodwin, Craufurd David *economics educator*
Johnston, William Webb *pathologist, educator*
Richmond, Donna *speech-language pathologist*
Wallace, Andrew Grover *physician, educator, medical school dean*
Williams, Virginia Parrott *writer, company executive*

Horse Shoe
†Parish, Maryann Kelley *advertising executive*

Hubert
Howell, Nelda Kay *home economist, retired*

Hudson
Dellinger, Charles Wade *minister*

Huntersville
McLaughlin, Mike *race car driver*
†Stewart, Tony *professional race car driver*

Jacksonville
Fischer, Violeta Pèrez Cubillas *Spanish literature and linguistics educator*
Garrett, Charles Leroy, Jr., *pathologist*
Guyer, Charles Grayson, II, *psychologist*
Kimball, Lynn Jerome *historian*
†Taylor, Vaughan Edward *lawyer, educator*

Jamestown
Schmitt, William Allen *lawyer*

Jefferson
Franklin, Robert McFarland *book publisher*
Van Arnam, Mark Stephen *manufacturing executive*

Kannapolis
Thigpen, Alton Hill *motor transportation company executive*
Whitley, Walter Ralph *educator*

Kernersville
†Hile, Elizabeth Gwyn *administrative assistant, marketing professional*
Litton, Daphne Napier Rudhman *special education educator*

Kill Devil Hills
†Lautermilch, Steven J. *poet, writer, photographer, educator*

King
Shanahan, Elizabeth Anne *art educator*

Kings Mountain
Turner, Marguerite Rose Cowles *library administrator*

Kinston
Baker-Gardner, Jewelle *interior designer, business consultant*
Braswell, Edwin Maurice, Jr., *lawyer*
†Duppstadt, Andrew Earl *historic site staff member*
†Jones, Paul Lawrence *lawyer*
Petteway, Samuel Bruce *college president*
Scott, Stephen Carlos *academic administrator*
Welch, Alexis B. *nursing administrator*
Withers, Sydnor Terry, Sr., *retired dermatologist*

Kitty Hawk
Elliott, Candice K. *interior designer*
Pratt, Alice Ford *small business owner, music educator*
Sjoerdsma, Albert *research institute executive*
Tucker, Don Eugene *retired lawyer*

La Grange
†Cannon, Alice Grace *counselor*

Lake Junaluska
Garrett, William Walton *retired law educator*
Stanton, Donald Sheldon *academic administrator*
Tullis, Edward Lewis *retired bishop*

Lake Lure
Seyboldt, Caroline *interior decorator, artist*

Landis
Lynch, Samuel Curlee, Jr., (Sir Sami Lynch) *painter*

Laurel Springs
Gilbert-Strawbridge, Anne Wieland *journalist*

Laurinburg
Alexander, W. M. *philosophy educator*
Bayes, Ronald Homer *English language educator, author*
Deegan, John, Jr., *academic administrator, researcher*

Lawndale
†Williams, Robert Leonard *publishing executive, photographer*

Leasburg
Treacy, Sandra Joanne Pratt *art educator, artist*

Leland
Barnhardt, Zeb Elonzo, Jr., *lawyer*
Karch, Jacqueline *artist*

Lenoir
Flaherty, David Thomas, Jr., *lawyer*
Moore, Mary Ellen *community health, hospice nurse*

Lewisville
Desley, John Whitney *medical illustrator*

Lexington
Brammer, T. Hawk *small business owner*
†Carter, Jason Wayne *music educator*
†Harris, Ricky E. *music educator*
Younts, Patty Lou *interior design executive,inventor, researcher*

Lincolnton
Kempster, Norman Roy *journalist*

Linwood
Barnes, Melver Raymond *retired chemist*

Little Switzerland
Gross, Samson Richard *geneticist, biochemist, educator*

Lumberton
Collier, William Gayle *psychology educator, researcher*

Marion
Burgin, Charles Edward *lawyer*

Mars Hill
†Corley, Alton L. *music educator*
†Hinners, R. Gordon *language educator*
†Lamberson, Carolyn H. *music educator*
†Newton, Paul George *musician, retired librarian*

Marshall
Jatinen, Jane Ellen *social worker, educator*

Matthews
Hixson, Nathan Hanks *retired military officer*

Mebane
Langley, Ricky Lee *occupational medicine physician*

Merritt
de Vos, Peter Jon *ambassador*

Mill Spring
Saunders, Barry Wayne *state official*

Misenheimer
†Edwards, Joyce Perry *language educator*

Mocksville
Smith, Mark Eugene *architectural engineering service company executive*

Monroe
Kwetkauskie, John A. *medical technologist*
Kyle, John Emery *mission executive*

Shaw, Talbert O. *university president*
Sheng, Quan *chemist, management consultant*
Sill, Melanie *editor*
Simpson, Steven Drexell *lawyer*
Skaggs, Richard Wayne *agricultural engineering educator*
Sloan, O. Temple, Jr., *automotive equipment executive*
Small, Alden Thomas *judge*
Smith, Sherwood Hubbard, Jr., *retired electric utilities executive*
Sneed, Ronald Ernest *engineering educator emeritus*
†Speer, Kevin Paul *surgeon*
Steed, Michelle Elnora *special education educator, counselor*
Stevens, Richard Yates *state senator*
Stewart, D. Jane *nursing educator, researcher*
Stratas, Nicholas Emanuel *psychiatrist*
Stuber, Charles William *genetics educator, researcher*
Suhr, Paul Augustine *lawyer*
†Sun, Ge *research scientist, educator*
Swaisgood, Harold Everett *biochemist, educator*
Tally, Lura Self *state legislator*
†Taylor, Raymond Mason *lawyer, former government official, educator*
Thurman, Walter N. *economics educator*
Tracy, John Michael *small business owner, composer*
Trott, William Macnider *lawyer*
Turinsky, Paul Josef *nuclear engineer, educator*
†Velev, Orlin D. *chemical engineer, educator*
Vick, Aaron Conley *contractor, consultant*
Vigen, James Bruce *minister, theologian*
Wahls, Harvey Edward *civil engineer, educator*
Webster, Debbie Ann *social worker*
Wehring, Bernard William *nuclear engineering educator*
†Weir, Bruce Spencer *statistician, educator, geneticist*
†Wentworth, Thomas Ralph *ecologist*
Wetsch, Laura Johnson *lawyer*
Whangbo, Myung Hwan *chemistry educator*
Wheeler, Lawrence Jefferson *art museum director*
Whitten, Jerry Lynn *chemistry educator*
Wicker, Dennis A. *lawyer*
Willer, Edward Herman *real estate broker*
Williams, Hugh Alexander, Jr., *retired mechanical engineer, consultant*
Wilson, Donald Hurst, III, *biopharmaceutical industry executive*
Winstead, Nash Nicks *university administrator, phytopathologist*
Zeng, Zhao-Bang *geneticist, educator*

Randleman
Andretti, John *professional race car driver*

Reidsville
Hart, Richard Wesley *religious organization administrator, pastor*

Research Triangle Park
Boorman, Gary Alexis *veterinary pathologist*
Clark, Kevin Anthony *marketing executive, communications executive*
Copeland, William Chenery *biochemist*
de Serres, Frederick Joseph *genetic toxicologist*
Diosegy, Arlene Jayne *lawyer, consultant*
Dorinsky, Paul Michael *physician, researcher, educator*
†Dryga, Sergey Alexander *biotechnologist*
†East, Larry Eugene *pharmaceutical researcher, minister*
Fisher, Robert Perry *health effects scientist*
Framil, Armando Ramon *business developer*
†Freelon, Philip G. *architectural firm executive*
†Geron, Christopher Douglas *ecologist, environmental scientist, researcher*
Greene, Amy Powers *human resources specialist*
Greenwell, Arnold *associate editor, photographer*
†Hu, Chuanpu *pharmacologist*
†Hughes, Claude L. *endocrinologist*
Johnson-Payton, Lori Renee *systems engineer*
Key, Karen Letisha *pharmaceutical executive*
Krasny, Harvey Charles *pharmaceutical executive, researcher*
†Krishen, Alok *biostatistician*
†Kunka, Robert L. *pharmacist, researcher*
†Melnick, Ronald L. *toxicologist, researcher*
Miller, Robert Reese *trade association executive*
Mumford, Stephen Douglas *research scientist*
Olden, Kenneth *science administrator, researcher*
†Pouliot, George A. *physical scientist, researcher*
Qualls, Charles Wayne, Jr., *research pathologist*
†Roses, Allen David *neurologist, educator*
Sculley, Patrick David *retired army officer, science honor society director*
Selkirk, James Kirkwood *biochemist, researcher*

Richfield
Shaver, William Adam *forester*

Roanoke Rapids
†Adiga, Giridhar U. *geriatrician, pharmacologist, researcher, internist*

Robbinsville
Ginn, Ronn *architect, urban planner, general contractor*

Rock Hill
Cornick, Michael F(rederick) *accounting educator*

Rockingham
Evans, Patricia McCormick *clinical therapist*
Spencer, Walter Jesse *accountant, consultant*

Rockwell
†Daily, James William, III, *manufacturing executive*

Rocky Mount
Davis, Barbara Judy *counselor, mental health educator*
†Dickens, Alice McKnight *minister*
Hendrix, Robert A. *otolaryngologist*
Stokes, Angela Cohoon *pharmacist*
Stubbs, Will, Jr., *pharmaceutical company manager*
†Wordsworth, Jerry L. *wholesale distribution executive*
Zipf, Robert Eugene, Jr., *legal medicine consultant, pathologist*

Rougemont
Cooney, M(uriel) Sharon Taylor *medical and surgical nurse*
Nilsson, Mary Ann *music educator*

Roxboro
Broyles, Bonita Eileen *nursing educator*
Hollingsworth, Brenda Jackson *employment consultant*
†Mitchell, P. Susan *lawyer*
Olds, William Bellamy *physician*

Rutherfordton
Conley, Katherine Logan *religious studies educator*
Isbell, Robert *writer*

Salisbury
†Blanton, Mary Rutherford *lawyer, educator*
Brautigan, June Marie *artist, poet*
Crowe, John Albert, Jr., *surgeon*
†Falocco, Joe *theater educator, actor*
†Freeman, Algeania Warren *academic administrator*
Hall, Telka Mowery Elium *retired educational administrator*
†Higbee, Dale (Strohe) *musician, retired psychologist*
Hlavay, Jay Alan *financial analyst*
†Julian, Rose Rich *music educator, director*
Shalkop, Robert Leroy *retired museum director*
†Sullivan, Sharon Lee *mathematician, educator*
Terry, Roger Harold *minister, musician, composer, author, editor*
Tseng, Howard Shih Chang *business and economics educator, investment company executive*
†Vance, Andrew Anderson, Jr., *humanities educator*

Salter Path
Wiley, Albert Lee, Jr., *physician, engineer, educator*

Saluda
McCutcheon, John Tinney, Jr., *retired journalist*

Sanford
Harrington, Anthony Ross *radio announcer, educator*
Higgins, George Edward *sculptor*
Kilmartin, Joseph Francis, Jr., *business executive, consultant*
Raisig, Paul Jones, Jr., *lawyer*
York, Carolyn Pleasants Stearns *English educator*

Seymour Johnson AFB
Demark, Robin Kay *librarian*

Shelby
Edgar, Ruth R. *retired educator*
Perry, Stephen Clayton *manufacturing executive*
Rogers, Robert Hamer *small business executive*

Smithfield
Schulz, Bradley Nicholas *lawyer*
Wiggs, Shirley JoAnn *retired secondary school educator*

Southern Pines
Caliri, David Joseph *retired lawyer, insurance agent*
Haserick, John Roger *retired dermatologist*
Kaufmann, Rachel Norsworthy *educator*
Matney, Edward Eli *fretired securities company executive*
Owings, Malcolm William *retired management consultant*
Passaro, Paul Charles *business executive*
Penick, George Dial *pathologist*
Toon, Malcolm *former ambassador*
Yarborough, William Pelham *writer, lecturer, retired army officer, consultant*

Southern Shores
Kegel, William George *mining company executive*

Southport
Harrelson, Walter Joseph *minister, religion educator emeritus*
Johnston, Dennis Roy *computer systems integrator*
Richmond, Jonathan Y. *public health administration officer*

Spencer
Kiser, Glenn Augustus *retired pediatrician, investor*

Spindale
Blanton, Madge Brantley *family practice nurse practitioner*
Howard, Elizabeth Ann Blanton *courier service executive*
Trautmann, Patricia Ann *communications educator, storyteller*

Spring Hope
Hildreth, James Robert *retired air force officer*

Spruce Pine
Rensink, Jacqueline Biddix *secondary school educator*

Statesville
Evernham, Ray *race team owner*
Linnane, James Francis, Jr., *internist, gastroenterologist*
Redman, William Walter, Jr., *realtor*
Schinck, Amelie G. *mathematician, educator*
Stelzner, Paul Burke *textile company executive*
Wright, David Alan *music educator*

Stella
Quin, Louis DuBose *chemist, educator*

Stokes
Reynolds, Betty Jane *retired nursing administrator and educator*

Summerfield
Brueckmann, Robin M. *riding instructor, horse show judge*

Sunset Beach
Mattson, Clarence Russell *safety engineer*

Supply
Jacobs, Richard Alan *management consultant*
Pollard, Joseph Augustine *advertising and public relations consultant*

Swannanoa
Stuck, Roger Dean *electrical engineering educator*
Whittington, Lorin Dale *music educator*

Swansboro
Juhl, Harold Alexander *retired career officer, construction executive*

Sylva
Babel, Deborah Jean *social worker, paralegal*
Henderson, R(ichard) Winn *physician*
O'Neal, Moya Frances *management consultant*

Tabor City
Jorgensen, Ralph Gubler *lawyer, accountant*

Tarboro
Andrews, Claude Leonard *psychotherapist*
Hopkins, Grover Prevatte *lawyer*
O'Malley, Susan Marie *lawyer*

Taylorsville
Leonhardt, Debbie Ann *counselor, writer, minister*

Thomasville
†Reynolds, Mark Floyd, II, *lawyer, management and labor consultant*
Sprinkle, Robert Lee, Jr., *podiatrist*

Trenton
Dillahunty, George Robert *minister*

Trinity
†Labonte, Bobby *race car driver*

Tryon
Flynn, Kirtland, Jr., *accountant*
McDermott, Renée R(assler) *lawyer*
Mellberg, James Richard *dental research chemist*

Tuckasegee
Lominac, Harry Gene *retired theater educator, designer*

Tyner
Sams, Robin Dahl *artist*

Vass
Glassman, Edward *public relations management creativity consultant*

Vaughan
†Jordan, Paul Richard *journalist, writer*

Wake Forest
Arnold, Eric Daniell *budget analyst, security supervisor*
Buchanan, Edward A. *education educator*
†Markoch, Andrew Richard *music educator*
†Patterson, Paige *church administrator, former seminary president*

Wallace
Johnson, James Wilson *pastor*

Warrenton
Weddington, Elizabeth Gardner (Liz Gardner) *actress, editor*

Washington
Alligood, Lola Jane Lurvey *retired educator*
†Blackwell, F. Oris *environmental scientist, educator*
Hackney, James Acra, III, *industrial engineer, consultant, retired manufacturing company executive*
Heck, Henry D'Arcy *retired toxicologist, consultant*
Timour, John Arnold *retired librarian, medical bibliography and library science educator*

Waxhaw
Edwards, Irene Elizabeth (Libby Edwards) *dermatologist, educator, researcher*
Lamparter, William C. *printing and publishing consultant, digital printing and information systems specialist*

Waynesville
Carpenter, Margaret Mary *state legislator, information technology manager*
†Cole, James Yeager *foundation administrator*
Hale, Joseph Rice *church organization executive*
†Ingle, Marti Annette *protective services official, educator*
McKinney, Alexander Stuart *neurologist, retired*
Ramsey, Patricia Prusak *artist*

Weaverville
Edwards, Otis Carl, Jr., *theology educator*
Hauschild, Douglas Carey *optometrist*
Parsons, Vinson Adair *retired computer software company executive*

Welcome
Gordon, Robby *race car driver*
Green, Jeff *race car driver*
Harvick, Kevin *race car driver*
Purvis, Jeff *race car driver*
Sauter, Johnny *race car driver*
†Skinner, Mike *professional race car driver*

Weldon
Barringer, Paul Brandon, II, *lumber company executive*

West End
Lentz, Luther Eugene *graphic arts technical specialist*

West Jefferson
Merrion, Arthur Benjamin *mathematics educator, tree farmer*

Whispering Pines
Catullo, Doris Jane *sculptor*
Enlow, Donald Hugh *anatomist, educator, university dean*

Whiteville
Gilmore, Robin Harris *nursing administrator*
Godwin, Kipling Eliga *academic administrator*

Whitsett
Fennell, Richard Arthur *artist*

Wilkesboro
Boyd, Robert Giddings, Jr., *health facility administrator*
Gray, William Campbell *lawyer*
†Hellrung, Stephen Andrew *lawyer*
Thomas, David Lloyd *accountant, consultant*
Tillman, Robert L. *home improvement company executive*

Williamston
†Mobley, Jackie *elementary school educator*
Wobbleton, Judy Karen *artist, educator*

Willow Spring
Grantham, Donald James *chemical engineer, educator, author*

Wilmington
Adams, Veronica Wadewitz *musician*
Anstatt, Peter Jan *marketing services executive*
Bachman, David *neurologist, pediatric neurologist*
Baehmann, Susan Elizabeth *artist*
Baldridge, Jane L. *graphic artist, fine artist*
Bissette, Samuel Delk *astronomer, artist, financial executive*
Bolen, Eric George *biology educator*
Bomhan, Ruth Walker *social studies educator*
Bryden, William Donald, Jr., *retired manufacturing executive, retired military officer*
Cameron, Kay *conductor, music director, arranger*
†Clinton, Lottie Dry Edwards *retired state agency administrator*
Conser, Walter Hurley, Jr., *religion and philosophy educator*
De Maria, Alfred Anthony *neurologist*
†DePaolo, Rosemary *dean, academic administrator*
Dickman, Catherine Crowe *retired human services administrator*
Gillen, Howard William *neurologist, medical historian*
Graham, Otis Livingston, Jr., *history educator*
Israel, Margie Olanoff *psychotherapist*
†Jones, Lucian Cox *lawyer*
Kelley, Virginia Wiard (Judy Kelley) *dance educator*
Kesler, James L. *ophthalmologist*
†Lapaire, Pierre-Jean G. *language educator*
Lauria, Rita Marie *media and communications researcher, consultant*
†Maness, Eleanor Palmer *research analyst*
McCauley, Cleyburn Lycurgus *lawyer*
Medlock, Donald Larson *lawyer*
†Nakayama, Don K. *surgeon*
Nubel, Marianne Kunz *cultural administrator, writer, composer*
Oakley, Carolyn Cobb *library director, academic administrator*
Perko, Mike A. *health education and health promotion educator*
Puente, Antonio E. *psychologist, educator, scientist*
Roer, Robert David *physiologist, educator*
Rorison, Margaret Lippitt *reading consultant*
Scully, Kevin Slean *orthopaedist, surgeon*
Seapker, Janet Kay *museum and architectural history consultant*
Stokes, John Lemacks, II, *clergyman, retired university official*
Swain, Mary Margaret *editor, marketing consultant*
Thompson, Donald Charles *electronics company executive, former coast guard officer*
Toth, Susan Smith *investment executive*
Van Blarcom Kurowski, Anne *artist, educator*
†Veit, Richard Connolly *language educator*
Watanabe, Wade Osamu *marine biologist*
†Webster, William David *biologist, educator*
Wilkins, Lucien Sanders *gastroenterologist*
†Wiseman, Cindy R. *education educator*

Wilson
†Atkinson, Ann Lennette *mortician*
Batchelor, Ruby Stephens *retired nurse*
Kushner, Michael James *neurologist, consultant, educator*

Ladwig, Harold Allen *neurologist*
Leonard, J. Rich *federal judge, educator*
Morris, Sharon Louise Stewart *emergency medical technician, paramedic*
Setliffe, Charles David *hospital administrator*
Stewart, Burton Gloyden, Jr., *retired banker*
Wood, Gerald David *religious organization administrator*
Wyatt, Edward Avery, V, *city manager*

Wingate
†Bostic, Ronald David *music educator*
Dodd, John Robert *non-profit organization administrator*
Pitts, E. Hampton *business educator, dean*

Winston Salem
Adams, Alfred Gray *lawyer*
Adler, Michael L. *family physician, educator*
†Alexander, Charles Jackson, II, *lawyer*
Allison, John Andrew, IV, *bank executive*
Barnett, Richard Chambers *historian, educator*
Barnhill, Henry Grady, Jr., *lawyer*
†Bayram, Ersin *electrical engineer, researcher*
Beach, Franklin Darrel *minister*
Beardsley, Charles Mitchell *retired insurance company executive*
Beaty, James Arthur, Jr., *federal judge*
Bell, William Lynn *neurologist, researcher*
†Bencherif, Merouane *medical researcher, business executive*
Berrier, J. Alan *transportation executive, entrepreneur*
Bleecker, Eugene R. *internist, educator*
†Blynn, Guy Marc *lawyer*
†Borwick, Susan Harden *musicologist, educator*
Bourne, Henry Clark, Jr., *electrical engineering educator, former academic official*
†Brett, Anthony H. *lawyer*
Brown, David G. *academic administrator*
†Capitano, Nicholas *television producer*
Capps, Richard Henry *retired minister*
Carter, Henry Moore, Jr., *retired foundation executive*
Cheng, Che Ping *cardiologist, researcher, educator*
Cheng, Heng-Jie *physician scientist*
Childs, Steve Douglas *artist, portrait painter*
Chumbley, Robert Edward *performing arts association administrator*
Cieszewski, Sandra Josephine *artist, retired manufacturing company manager*
†Clarkson, Thomas Boston *comparative medicine educator*
†Comerford, Walter Thompson, Jr., *lawyer*
Cordell, A(lfred) Robert *cardiothoracic surgeon, educator*
Cramer, John Scott *retired banker*
Crowder, Lena Belle *retired special education educator*
Cullins, Margaret Carter *customer service administrator, small business owner*
Cunningham, Carol Clem *biochemistry educator, researcher*
Dahl, Tyrus Vance, Jr., *lawyer*
Davis, Linwood Layfield *lawyer*
Dawson, Paula Dayl *oncological nurse*
Dean, Richard Henry *surgeon, educator*
Dobbins, James Talmage, Jr., *analytical chemist, researcher*
Doggett, Aubrey Clayton, Jr., *real estate executive, consultant*
Donofrio, Peter Daniel *neurology educator*
Ehle, John Marsden, Jr., *writer*
Eliason, Russell Allen *judge*
Faccinto, Victor Paul *artist, gallery administrator*
Ferree, Carolyn Ruth *radiation oncologist, educator*
Foy, Herbert Miles, III, *lawyer, educator*
Gala, Candelas S. *literature educator, language educator*
Gallimore, Margaret Martin *poet*
Gallo, Vincent John *financial planner*
†Ganz, Charles *laboratory executive*
Geary, Randolph Lee *vascular surgeon, educator*
Gibson, Christina Renee *radiation therapist*
Gitter, Allan Reinhold *lawyer*
Gmeiner, William Henry *science educator*
Gordon, William Charles *college administrator*
Graham, Gloria Flippen *dermatologist*
Graybeal, Barbara *editor, writer*
Greason, Murray Crossley, Jr., *lawyer*
Gunter, Michael Donwell *lawyer*
Gunzenhauser, Gerard Ralph, Jr., *management consultant, investor*
Hage, George Campbell *social studies educator, minister, and counselor*
Hanes, Frank Borden *author, farmer, former business executive*
Hanes, Ralph Philip, Jr., *former textiles executive, arts patron, cattle farmer networker*
†Hantgan, Roy Russell *biomedical researcher, educator*
Harris, Frederick Holladay deBrosche *business educator*
Hearn, Thomas K., Jr., *university president*
Henderson, Richard Martin *retired chemical engineer*
Hendricks, J(ames) Edwin *historian, educator, consultant, author*
Henrichs, W(alter) Dean *dermatologist*
Herring, Jerone Carson *lawyer, bank executive*
Hobgood, E(arl) Wade *college chancellor*
Holton, Walter Clinton, Jr., *lawyer*
Hopkins, Judith Owen *oncologist*
†Horne, Aaron *academic administrator*
†Housman, Tamara Salam *dermatologist*
Howell, Charles Maitland *dermatologist*
†Ibdah, Jamal A. *medical educator*
Ibrahim, Mounir Labib *physician, psychiatrist*
Israel, James Ray *psychiatrist*
James, Francis Marshall, III, *anesthesiologist*
Jarrell, Iris Bonds *elementary school educator, business executive*
Jesseph, Steven Austin *risk management consultant*
Johnston, James Wesley *retired tobacco company executive*
Jorizzo, Joseph L. *dermatology educator*
Karnes, Lucia Rooney *psychologist*
Kaufman, Charlotte S. *communications executive*
†Kelly, Robert P. *banking executive*
King, Arthur Thomas *economics educator, retired air force officer*
King, Wayne Edgar *journalist, educator*
Kohut, Robert Irwin *otolaryngologist, educator*
†Kritchevsky, Stephen Bennett *epidemiologist, educator*
Laxminarayana, Dama *geneticist, researcher, educator*
Leonard, R. Michael *lawyer*
Levine, Edward A. *surgeon, educator*
†Linster, Michelle Lynn *education educator, consultant*
†Logan, David Andrew *lawyer, educator*
Ludolf, Marilyn Marie Keaton *lay worker*
Maready, William Frank *lawyer*
†Margitić, Milorad R. *language educator, researcher*
Maselli, John Anthony *food products company executive*
†Matlaga, Brian Richard *physician*
Maynard, Charles Douglas *radiologist*
†Mchugh, David Joseph *music educator, composer*
McNair, John Franklin, III, *banker*
Mecimore, Charles Douglas *retired accounting educator*
Medlin, John Grimes, Jr., *banker*
†Mendez, John *minister*
Middaugh, Jack Kendall, II, *management educator*
Mitchener, John Edward *music educator, musician*
†Mizel, Steven B. *microbiologist, educator*
Mokrasch, Lewis Carl *neurochemist, educator*
Moyer, R. Charles *finance educator, consultant*
Mueller, Margaret S. *musician, educator*
Mueller-Heubach, Eberhard *medical educator*
Oczkowicz, Edyta Katarzyna *English educator*
Osborn, Malcolm Everett *lawyer*
O'Steen, Wendall Keith *neurobiology and anatomy educator*
Ott, David James *diagnostic radiologist*
Peters, Stephen Paul *medical educator*
†Petrozza, Patricia H. *anesthesiologist*
†Pitovski, Dimitri Zivko *otolaryngologist, educator*
Pittaway, Donald Edward *endocrinology educator, gynecologist*
Podgorny, George *emergency physician*
†Porter, Leon Eugene, Jr., *lawyer*
Powers, David Murphy *consumer products company executive*
†Pubantz, Jerry James *political science educator*
Rauschenberg, Bradford Lee *museum researcher*
Rautaharju, Pentti Matti *research scientist, educator*
Ray, Michael Edwin *lawyer*
Rights, Graham Henry *retired minister*
Robinson, Edward Norwood *lawyer*
Rodgman, Alan *chemist, consultant*
†Roemer, Henry Conrad, Jr., *lawyer*
Rogers, Lee Frank *radiologist*
†Ross, Charles Thomas *lawyer*
†Ross, Thomas Warren, Sr., *judge*
Roth, Marjory Joan Jarboe *special education educator*
Runnion, Howard J., Jr., *banker*
†St. Clair, Richard W. *medical educator, researcher, health facility administrator*
Sandridge, William Pendleton, Jr., *lawyer*
Schexnider, Alvin J. *academic administrator*
Schiller, Herbert Miles *pathologist*
Schindler, Andrew J. *tobacco company executive*
Schwartz, Robert Paul *pediatric endocrinologist*
Seckar, Joel Andreas *toxicologist, chemist*
Shapere, Dudley *philosophy educator*
Somerville, Atwell Wilson, Jr., *medical editor*
Spach, Jule Christian *church executive*
Steele, Thomas McKnight *law educator*
Stein, Barry Edward *medical educator*
Sticht, J. Paul *retired food products and tobacco company executive*
Stratta, Robert J. *surgeon*
†Strayhorn, Ralph Nichols, Jr., *lawyer*
Strickland, Robert Louis *former retail company executive*
Suttles, Donald Roland *retired academic administrator, business educator*
†Tate, David Kirk *lawyer*
Thrift, Ashley Ormand *lawyer*
Thrift, Julianne Still *academic administrator*
†Toole, James Francis *medical educator*
Torti, Frank Michael *physician, healthcare administrator*
Trautwein, George William *conductor, educator*
Twiggs, Dennis Glenn *psychologist, writer*
†Uhl, Henry Stephen Magraw *internist, educator*
†Vaughn, Robert Candler, II, *lawyer*
Volz, Annabelle Wekar *learning disabilities educator, consultant*
Walker, George Kontz *law educator*
Wallace, Roanne *hosiery company executive*
Walters, Doris Lavonne *pastoral counselor, counseling services facility administrator*
Wanders, Hans Walter *banker*
Ward, Marvin Martin *retired state senator*
Wells, Dewey Wallace *lawyer*
Whaples, Robert MacDonald *economic history educator*
Whittington, Stephen Lunn *museum director*
Williams, Frances Elizabeth *retired secondary education educator*
Wilson, John Allen *neurosurgeon*
Winn, Albert Curry *clergyman*
Wolfman, Neil T. *physician*
Womble, William Fletcher *lawyer*
Yeatts, Dorothy Elizabeth Freeman *nurse, retired county official, educator*
Yeatts, Robert Patrick *ophthalmologist*
†Zagoria, Ronald Jay *radiologist, educator*
Zubov, Lynn *special education educator, researcher*

Woodland
Wilson, Lloyd Lee *organization administrator*

Wrightsville Beach
McDonald, Wylene Booth *former nurse, pharmaceutical sales professional*
Mc Ilwain, William Franklin *newspaper editor, writer*

Youngsville
†Riggs, Susan Dunnagan *music educator, musician*

Zebulon
Ruffing, Anne Elizabeth *artist*

NORTH DAKOTA

Amidon
Bergquist, Gene Alfred *farmer, rancher, county commissioner*

Ashley
Kretschmar, William Edward *state legislator, lawyer*

Beulah
Maize, Linda Lou *elementary education educator*

Bismarck
Barrett, Carole A. *American Indian studies educator*
†Baumann, Jon Paul *music educator, director*
Brudvig, Jon Larsen *history educator*
Carlisle, Ronald Dwight *nursery owner*
Christianson, James D. *real estate developer*
Clairmont, William Edward *real estate developer*
Clark, Tony *state commissioner*
Dalrymple, Jack *lieutenant governor*
†Dever, Dick *state legislator*
Dunnigan, Earl Joseph *nephrologist*
Evanson, Barbara Jean *middle school education educator*
Gilmore, Kathi *state treasurer*
Heigaard, William Steven *state senator*
Hoeven, John *governor*
Jaeger, Alvin A. (Al Jaeger) *secretary of state*
†Joersz, Fran Woodmansee *secondary education educator*
Klemin, Lawrence R. *lawyer*
Lundberg, Susan Ona *musical organization administrator*
Murry, Charles Emerson *lawyer, official*
Nelson, Keithe Eugene *state court administrator, lawyer*
Newborg, Gerald Gordon *state archives administrator*
Oldenburger, Norma Jane *medical/surgical nurse*
Ott, Doris Ann *librarian*
Sandstrom, Dale Vernon *state supreme court justice*
Sanstead, Wayne Godfrey *school system administrator*
Schwartz, Judy Ellen *cardiothoracic surgeon*
Snyder, Robert John *lawyer*
Sperry, James Edward *anthropologist, retired state official*
Stenehjem, Wayne Kevin *state attorney general, lawyer*
Thompson, Vern *political organization executive*
Tornow, L. William *musician*
Traynor, Daniel M. *state representative*
†Urlacher, Herbert *state legislator*
VandeWalle, Gerald Wayne *state supreme court chief justice*
Van Sickle, Bruce Marion *federal judge*
Wellin, Thomas *music director*

Cavalier
Trenbeath, Thomas L. *state legislator, lawyer*

Devils Lake
Tande, Teresa Lyn *secondary educator*

Dickinson
Ficek, Vince H. *lawyer*
Greenwood, Dann Edward *lawyer*
Greenwood, Mark Lawrence *lawyer*
†Herauf, William Anton *lawyer*
Kessel, Lloyd R. *nursing administrator, educator*
†Medlar, Deborah Starkey *secondary school educator*
Wald, Francis John *state legislator*

Edgeley
Schimke, Dennis J. *former state legislator*

Edinburg
Myrdal, Rosemarie Caryle *state official, former state legislator*

Edmore
Sampson, Valerie K. Morman *music educator*

Ellendale
Schlieve, Hy C. J. *school administrator*

Fargo
Amlund, Curtis Arthur *law educator*
Anderson, Gerald Dwight *history educator*
Aquila, Samuel Joseph *bishop*
Bernstein, LeRoy G. *state legislator*
Bright, Myron H. *federal judge*
Bye, Kermit Edward *federal judge, lawyer*
†Coykendall, James B. *mathematician*
Danbom, David Byers *history educator*
†Danescu, Radu Ioan *engineering educator*
Foss, Richard John *bishop*
Helweg, Otto Jennings *civil engineer, educator*
Hill, William A(lexander) *judge*
†Johansen, Robert Henny *horticulturist, geneticist*
Li, Kam Wu *mechanical engineer, educator*
†Lin, Wei *civil engineer, educator*
Magill, Frank John *federal judge*
Mathern, Tim *state legislator*
†McWilliams, Carey Scott *small business owner, writer*
Mendez, Alejandro *neurosurgeon*
Mengedoth, Donald Roy *commercial banker*
Miller, Donald R. *pharmacist, educator*
Ness, Gary Gene *accountant*
Nickel, Janet Marlene Milton *geriatrics nurse*
Peet, Howard David *English educator, writer*
Peterson, Larry Richard *history educator*
†Potti, Anil *medical educator*
Rice, Jon Richard *managed care administrator, physician*
Riley, Thomas Joseph *anthropologist, educational administrator*
Rogers, David Anthony *electrical engineer, educator, researcher*
Sanford, Glenda Levonne *educational administrator*
Schmidt, Claude Henri *retired research administrator*
Scott, David Michael *pharmacy educator*
†Shi, Zhengzhong *finance educator*
†Sondrall, Pat *music educator*
Sullivan, James Stephen *retired bishop*
†Tallman, Dennis Earl *chemistry educator, research scientist*
Tallman, Robert Hall *investment company executive*
Tharaldson, Gary Dean *hotel developer and owner*
†Unhjem, Michael Bruce *lawyer*
Varma, Amiy *civil engineer, educator*
Wallwork, William Wilson, III, *automobile executive*

Fessenden
Streibel, Bryce *state senator*

Finley
Devlin, William Russell *newspaper owner*

Glenfield
Spickler, JoAnn Dorothy *secondary education educator*

Grand Forks
†Alfonso, Peter J. *educator*
Anderson, Damon Ernest *lawyer*
Ashe, Kathy Rae *special education educator*
†Aune, Adonica Schultz *education educator, consultant*
†Bateman, Connie Rae (Hanson) *entrepreneur, finance educator*
Caldwell, Mary Ellen *English language educator*
Carlson, Edward C. *anatomy educator*
Cilz, Douglas Arthur *lawyer*
Clapp, Richard Allen *lawyer*
Clingan, Charles Edmund *historian*
Coleman, Joyce Kit *English literature educator, literary historian*
DeMers, Judy Lee *former state legislator, university dean*
†Espegard, Duaine C. *state legislator*
Ferraro, F(rancis) Richard *psychologist, educator*
Gallo, Sergio Roberto *music educator, researcher*
Gjovig, Bruce Quentin *entrepreneur coach, consultant, entrepreneur*
Glassheim, Eliot Alan *editor, state legislator*
Hand, James Stanley *lawyer*
Hardersen, Paul Scott *planetary scientist*
Jacobs, Francis Albin *biochemist, educator*
†Kupchella, Charles Edward *academic administrator, author, educator*
†Lerma, Edgar Villaneuva *nephrologist*
Moulton, Patricia L. *experimental psychologist, researcher*
Nielsen, Forrest Harold *research nutritionist*
Nordlie, Robert Conrad *biochemistry educator*
Penland, James Granville *psychologist*
†Polovitz, Michael *state legislator*
†Ransom, Michael T. *counselor*
Rolshoven, Ross William *legal investigator, artist*
Russell, Sue Ann *clinical psychologist*
†Short, Sandra Elaine *sports psychologist, educator*
Siegel, Mark Bernard *surgeon*
Skroch, Larry Eugene *railway conductor*
Sobus, Kerstin MaryLouise *physician, physical therapist*
†Tangsrud, Robert Raymond, Jr., *finance educator*
Thomasson, Kathryn Ambler *chemistry educator, biophysical researcher*
†Tyler, John Duke *psychologist, educator*
Vogel, Robert *retired lawyer, educator*
†Wenzel, Amy Elizabeth *psychologist, educator*
Werpy, Steve *music educator, conductor*
Widdel, John Earl, Jr., *lawyer*
Wilson, H. David *dean*
Wogaman, George Elsworth *insurance executive, financial consultant*

Hazen
Lorenz, Denise Eileen *physician assistant*

Jamestown
Cox, Robert Ripley, Jr., *wildlfe research biologist*
†Ottmar, Timothy Jon *lawyer, municipal judge*

Lakota
†Hoerth, Kenneth D. *music educator*

Lehr
†Erbele, Robert S. *state legislator*

Maddock
Aadland, Kathleen A. *counselor, army intelligence officer*

Mandan
Bair, Bruce B. *lawyer*
Heitkamp, Heidi *former state attorney general*
Novak, Laura J. *secondary school educator*

Paul, Jack Davis *retired state official, addictions consultant*

Mayville
Karaim, Betty June *retired librarian*

Minnewaukan
†Every, Michael A. *state legislator*

Minot
Armstrong, Phillip Dale *lawyer*
†Backes, Orlin William *lawyer*
†Ellis, Lee *social sciences educator*
Jermiason, John Lynn *elementary school educator, farmer, rancher*
Markel, Paul Dennis *psychologist, geneticist*
Morgan, Rose Marie *retired biology educator*
Shaar, H. Erik *academic administrator*

Mountain
Melsted, Marcella H. *retired administrative assistant, civic worker*

Oakes
McLean, Stephen M. *lawyer*

Pettibone
Flanders, Paula L. *director public health*

Richardton
Miller, Jean Patricia Salmon *art educator*

Stanton
Grannis, Joseph M. *power plant operator*

West Fargo
Boutiette, Vickie Lynn *educator, reading specialist*
Martin, Bradley L *legal consultant, composer*

Williston
Adducci, Joseph Edward *obstetrician, gynecologist*
Bekkedahl, Brad Douglas *dentist*
†Benson, Robert John *physical therapist, department chairman, massage therapist*
Naranja, Rogelio Darusin, Sr., *psychiatrist*
Rennerfeldt, Earl Ronald *state legislator, farmer, rancher*
Yockim, James Craig *former state senator, foundation administrator*

Zeeland
Wolf, Trudy J. Fraase *music educator, librarian*

OHIO

Ada
Baker, Kendall L. *academic administrator*
Boyadzhiev, Khristo Nonev *mathematician, educator, researcher*
Cooper, Ken Errol *retired management educator*
†Fenton, Howard Nathan, III, *lawyer, educator*
Freed, DeBow *college president*
Herr, Sharon Marie *librarian*
Keiser, Terry Dean *biologist, educator*
Streib, Victor Lee *dean*
†Veltri, Stephen Charles *lawyer, educator*

Akron
†Akhigbe, Aigbe *education educator, researcher*
Auburn, Norman Paul *university president*
†Aynes, Richard L(ee) *law educator*
Banks, Christopher Paul *political science educator, lawyer*
Barker, Harold Kenneth *former university dean*
†Barlowe Bodman, Amy *violinist, composer*
Bell, Samuel H. *federal judge, educator*
Bird, Forrest M. *retired medical inventor*
Bonsky, Jack Alan *lawyer*
†Borowiec, Andrew *art educator, photographer*
†Brouthers, Lance Eliot *finance educator*
Brown, David Rupert *engineering executive*
Burg, H. Peter *financial executive*
Buzzelli, Charlotte Grace *educator*
Carley, Michael Jabara *historian, director*
Castronovo, Thomas Paul *architect, consultant*
†Cherpas, Christopher Theodore *lawyer*
Chrisant, Rosemarie Kathryn *law library administrator*
†Chung, Benjamin T. F. *science educator*
Collier, Alice Elizabeth *retired community organization executive*
Coyne, Thomas Joseph *economist, finance educator*
Crawford, Robert John *credit company executive*
†Davis, Theresa Mary *education educator, artist*
†Dick, John Stewart, Jr., *rheologist, consultant*
Dietz, Margaret Jane *retired public information director*
Donehey, Marilyn Moss *social services executive*
†Duan, Zhong-Hui *education educator, researcher*
Eby, Ronald K. *polymer science educator, researcher*
†Emmett, John Colin *retired inventor, consultant*
Evans, Douglas McCullough *surgeon, educator*
Fatemi, Ray S. *mechanical engineer, consultant*
Fertis, Demeter George *civil engineering educator*
Fisher, James Lee *lawyer*
Flannery, Harry Audley *lawyer*
Flick, Lynette Lowry *piano teacher*
Franck, Ardath Amond *psychologist, educator*
Frank, John V. *foundation executive*
Gent, Alan Neville *physicist, educator*
Gibara, Samir G. *tire manufacturing executive*
Glinsek, Gerald John *lawyer*
Glomski, Edward Earl *electronic company executive*
Hackbirth, David William *aluminum company executive*
Haritos, George Konstantinos *engineer, educator, military officer*
Harvie, Crawford Thomas *lawyer*
Hochschwender, Herman Karl *international consultant*
Holloway, Donald Phillip *lawyer*
Hopkins, Michael Patrick *gynecologist, oncologist, surgeon*
Hundley, Larry Willis *aerospace company executive*
Isayev, Avraam Isayevich *polymer engineer, educator*
†Jana, Sadhan C *education educator, researcher*
Jasso, William Gattis *public relations executive*
Juriga, Rosemarie *social services administrator*
Kahan, Mitchell Douglas *art museum director*
Kaufman, Donald Leroy *building products executive*
Kazle, Elynmarie *producer, performing arts executive*
†Keegan, Robert J. *manufacturing executive*
Kennedy, Joseph Paul *chemist, researcher*
Knepper, George W. *history educator*
Kreek, Louis Francis, Jr., *lawyer*
Lammert, Thomas Edward *lawyer*
Lee, Brant Thomas *lawyer, federal official, educator*
Lesner, Sharon A. *audiologist, educator*
Lombardi, Frederick McKean *lawyer*
McMahon, William Edward *philosophy educator*
Millman, Irving *microbiologist, educator, retired inventor*
Milsted, Amy *biomedical educator*
Moriarty, John Timothy *writer, transportation consultant*
Mubashir, Bashar Ahmad *internist, oncologist, hematologist*
Munetz, Mark Richard *psychiatrist*
O'Brien, Gayle Ann *nurse*
Piirma, Irja *chemist, educator*
Pipes, Robert Byron *mechanical engineer, educator*
Plusquellic, Donald L. *mayor*
Powell, Robert Eugene *computer operator*
Rebenack, John Henry *retired librarian*
Richert, Paul *law educator*
†Rooney, George Willard *lawyer*
Rothmann, Bruce Franklin *pediatric surgeon*
Ruebel, Marion A. *university president*
Ruport, Scott Hendricks *lawyer*
Sancaktar, Erol *engineering educator*
Schrader, Alfred Eugene *lawyer*
Seiberling, John Frederick *former congressman, law educator, lawyer*
Seiwald, Robert J. *retired inventor*
Snider, George Runyon, Jr., *franchising company executive*
Sonnecken, Edwin Herbert *management consultant*
Spector, Michael Lew *cardiothoracic surgeon*
Spetrino, Russell John *retired utility company executive, lawyer*
†Stark, Michael Lee *lawyer*
Sterns, Harvey Leonard *psychologist, gerontologist*
Symens, Ronald Edwin *electrical engineer, consultant*
Tannenbaum, Barbara Lee *curator, art historian*
Taormina, Charles Anthony *writer, editor, artist*
Timmons, Gerald Dean *pediatric neurologist*
Tipping, Harry A. *lawyer*
Trotter, Thomas Robert *lawyer*
Tyrity, Kathy Milica *reporter, editor*
Webb, Adele Ann *nursing administrator*
West, Michael Alan *retired hospital administrator*
†Wilding, James *music educator, composer*
†Wolfe, John Leslie *lawyer*
Wortham, James Calvin *retired mathematics educator*
†Xu, Shucheng *chemistry educator, researcher*
†Yoder, Janice Dana *psychology and women's studies educator*
†Zangrando, Robert Lewis *historian educator*

Alliance
Clem, Harriet Frances *library director*
DeStefano, L. Timothy *music educator, conductor*
†Lowe, Kelly Fisher *literature educator*

Alpha
James, Francis Edward, Jr., *investment counselor*

Amelia
Hayden, John W. *real estate company executive*
Hayden, Joseph Page, Jr., *company executive*
Hensley, Kimberly Sue *counselor*
Ullman, Susan Joyce Feldman *social worker*

Amherst
†Gerstenberger, Valerie *media coordinator*

Andover
Mathay, John Preston *elementary education educator*

Antwerp
†Schmidt, John R. *music educator*

Archbold
Bergman, Jerry Rae *science educator*

Ashland
Altalib, Omar Hisham *sociologist*
†Baker, David Weston *education educator*
†deSilva, David Arthur *theology studies educator*
Ford, Lucille Garber *economist, educator*
†Goodwin, Richard Charles *performing arts association administrator, actor*
†Hawk, L. Daniel *minister, religious studies educator*
Heimann, Beverly Ann *business educator, consultant*
Kerr, Margaret Ann *elementary education educator*
Lake-Bruse, Kristy Dean *pharmacologist, toxicologist, researcher, educator*
Reidenbach, Faith E. *medical editor, writer*
Rueger, Daniel Scott *horticulture educator*
†Schmidt-Rinehart, Barbara Coe *Spanish language educator*
Shelly, Ann Converse *education educator, administrator*
†Suggs, Robert Chinello *academic administrator, educator*
Watson, JoAnn Ford *theology educator*

Ashley
Thomas, Annabel Crawford *writer*

Ashtabula
Hornbeck, Harold Douglas *psychotherapist*

Athens
†Ahrens, Kent *museum director, art historian*
Alexander, Charles Comer *history educator, writer*
Arhangel'skii, Alexander Vladimirovich *mathematician, researcher*
Baldrachi, Ryan Michael *psychologist*
†Bayless, David J. *engineer*
Bleigh, Mildred Allen *genealogist*
Bond, Zinny Sans *linguistics educator*
Borchert, Donald Marvin *philosopher, educator*
†Bridgewater, Erle Henry *lawyer*
Bruning, James Leon *academic administrator, educator*
Bugeja, Michael Joseph *educator, writer*
Chila, Anthony George *osteopathic educator*
Condee, William Faricy *theater educator, writer*
Connor, Joan Carol *literature educator*
Crowl, Samuel Renninger *former university dean, english language educator*
†Davidson, Shae Ronald *historian, researcher*
Dinos, Nicholas *engineering educator, administrator*
Dodd, Wayne D. *poet, editor*
Gall, Robert Jay *lawyer*
Glidden, Robert Burr *academic administrator, musician, educator*
Hedges, Richard Houston *lawyer, epidemiologist*
Irwin, Richard Dennis *electrical engineering educator*
†Láscar, Amado José *language educator, writer*
Lavelle, William Ambrose *lawyer, judge*
†Mantione, Meryl E. *director, education educator*
McFarland, Richard H. *engineering educator, pilot*
Metters, Thomas Waddell *sports writer*
†Morgans, Bob D. *minister*
Neiman, Gary S. *university administrator*
Ping, Charles Jackson *philosophy educator, retired university president*
Rader, William Donald *economics educator, university administrator*
Robe, Thurlow Richard *engineering educator, university dean*
Rudy, Joel S. *retired fraternal organization administrator*
Sanders, David *university press administrator*
Scott, Charles Lewis *photojournalist*
†Senteney, David L. *accountant, educator*
Stempel, Guido Hermann, III, *journalism educator*
†Stomberg, Eric W *musician*
Stump, Earl Spencer *psychologist*
†Tao, Liang *linguistics educator, researcher*
†Tymas-Jones, Raymond *dean*
Ungar, Irwin Allan *botany educator*
†Van Hook, Cheryl W. *education educator*
Vedder, Richard Kent *economics educator*
Wen, Shih-Liang *mathematics educator*
Werner, R(ichard) Budd *retired business executive*
Whealey, Lois Deimel *humanities scholar*
Whealey, Robert Howard *historian*
Xu, Li *science educator*
†Yanity, Joseph Blair, Jr., *lawyer*

Aurora
Ashworth, David J. *management consultant, power company executive*
Berry, Dean Lester *lawyer*
Herington, Leigh Ellsworth *state legislator, lawyer*
Kirchner, James William *retired electrical engineer*
Lawton, Florian Kenneth *artist, educator*
†Su, Sunyu *MRI scientist*
Toomey, William Shenberger *retired wire manufacturing company executive*

Austintown
Kope, Joseph B. *retired humanities educator, consultant*

Avon
Grmek, Dorothy Antonia *accountant*
Smolen, Cheryl Hosaka *special education educator*

Avon Lake
Mick, Deborah West Fairchild *elementary education educator*
Morton, David Ray *sales and marketing executive*
Stives, William Robert *retired pharmacist*
Zurcher, Vickie Lee *geneticist*

Bannock
†Gentile, Anthony *coal company executive*

Barberton
Buckley, Sheryl Lea *physician, anesthesiologist*
Kitto, John Buck, Jr., *mechanical engineer*
Wietzke, Donald *industrial engineer*

Barnesville
Jefferis, Paul Bruce *lawyer*

Batavia
Bower, Kenneth Francis *electrical engineer*
†Craver, Diane Sue *writer, educator*
Muskopf, Beth A. *curriculum consultant*
Nichols, Marci Lynne *gifted education coordinator, educator, consultant*
Pattison, George Edgar *lawyer*

Bath
Bowman-Dalton, Burdene Kathryn *education testing coordinator, computer consultant*
Hoffer, Alma Jeanne *nursing educator*

Bay Village
Berger, James Hank *business broker*
Hook, John Burney *investment company executive*
Kapp, C. Terrence *lawyer*
Kocar, George Frederick *artist*
Woods, Dennis Craig *school superintendent*

Beachwood
†Cozzarin, James Robert *editor, writer*
Curran, Audrey *psychologist, educator*
Feldman, Donna B. *literature educator*
†Fufuka, Natika Njeri Yaa *business executive*
Horowitz, Lee Jerald *psychologist*
Katzman, Richard A. *cardiologist, internist, consultant*
Lewis, Cherie Sue *lawyer, English language and journalism educator*
Mendel, Roberta *editor, publisher, writer*
Moskowitz, Roland Wallace *internist*
†Pinkas, Robert Paul *lawyer, venture capitalist*
Robertson, Edward Neil *dentist*
Saiakhov, Roustem Damirovich *chemist, consultant*
Weatherhead, Albert John, III, *business executive*
Wells Bradley, Charlena Renee *editor, writer*
Wilkes, Angela Biggs *mental health consultant*
Wolf, Milton Albert *economist, former ambassador, investor*
†Wolstein, Scott Alan *real estate company executive*
Youdelman, Robert Arthur *financial executive, lawyer*

Beavercreek
Bennett, Anna Dell *minister, religion educator, retired elementary school educator*
Gupta, Vijay Kumar *chemistry educator*
Richardson, Arthur Wilhelm *lawyer*
Rinta, Christine Evelyn *nurse, air force officer*
Ruh, Robert *materials scientist*

Bedford
Hodakievic, James Joseph *retired secondary education educator*

Bellefontaine
Graber, Harry Lee *internist*

Bellevue
Davenport, Thomas Herbert *small business owner*

Bellville
Hooker, James Todd *manufacturing executive*

Berea
Bonds, Georgia Anna *writer, lecturer*
Campo, Dave *professional football coach*
†Clark, Dwight Edward *sports team executive, former professional football player*
Davis, Butch *professional football coach*
Ebert, Robert Raymond *economics educator*
Keller, Tiffany Lee *business educator*
†Kennelly, Laura Ballard *writer, educator*
Little, Richard Allen *mathematics and computer science educator*
Miller, Dennis Dixon *economics educator*
Policy, Carmen A. *professional sports team executive*

Bergholz
Goddard, Sandra Kay *elementary education educator*
McElwain, Edwina Jay *retired elementary school educator*

Bexley
Beller, Stephen Mark *university administrator*
Maloney, Gerald P. *retired utilities executive*
Unverferth, Barbara Patten *small business owner*
Yashon, David *neurosurgeon, educator*

Bluffton
Dudley, Durand Stowell *librarian*
Friesen, Ronald Lee *economics educator*
Gundy, Jeffrey Gene *English educator*
†Nisly, L. Lamar *language educator*
Schattschneider, Adam James *music educator*
Sycks, David Brent *band director, musician*

Bowerston
Spencer, Dawn Joyce *librarian, educator*

Bowling Green
†Baird, James Abington *retired judge*
Ballweg, Janet C. *artist, art educator*
Berger, Bonnie G. *sport psychologist, educator*
Browne, Ray Broadus *popular culture educator*
Clark, Eloise Elizabeth *biologist, educator*
Clark, Robert King *communications educator emeritus, lecturer, consultant, actor, model*
Dobb, Linda Sue *university official, librarian*
Fung, Chi-Keung Victor *music educator, researcher*
Guion, Robert Morgan *psychologist, educator*
Hakel, Milton Daniel, Jr., *psychology educator, consultant, publisher*
Heckman, Carol A. *biology educator*
†Krane, Vikki *psychology educator*
Lavezzi, John Charles *art history educator, archaeologist*
Luescher, Andreas *architecture educator*
Lunde, Harold Irving *management educator*
†Mayberry, Alan Reed *judge*
McCaghy, Charles Henry *sociology educator*
Merriam, John Goodwin *political scientist, educator*
Neckers, Douglas Carlyle *chemistry educator*
Newman, Elsie Louise *mathematics educator*
Ocvirk, Otto George *artist*

†Scherer, Ronald Callaway *voice scientist, educator*
Singer, Carol Ann *librarian, researcher*
Skoog, William Melvin *music/voice educator*
†Sloma, Robert J. *business process consultant*
†Trantham, Gene Starr *music educator*
Varney, Glenn Herbert *management educator*
Wolcott, Nancy Bookout *music director*
Zwierlein, Ronald Edward *athletics director*

Bratenahl
DesRosiers, Anne Booke *performing arts administrator, consultant*
Jones, Trevor Owen *biomedical industry executive, management consultant*

Brecksville
†Forsyth, T. Henry *plastic researcher*
Meyer, Karin Zumwalt *pharmacist, consultant*
Pappas, Effie Vamis *English and business educator, writer, poet, artist*
†Tesmer, Nancy Ann Stutler *retired librarian*
Ventenilla, Aurora Curamen *psychiatrist*

Bridgeport
Janos, James Donald *security and safety consultant*

Broadview Heights
Jergens, Maribeth Joie *school counselor*
Sternlieb, Lawrence Jay *marketing professional, writer*

Brooklyn
Spahnie, Michelle Marie *accountant*

Brookpark
Cotton, Barbara Jean *systems analyst*

Brunswick
Kuchynski, Marie *physician*
Reed, Jane Garson *eldercare/disability consultant*
Zahs, David Karl *secondary school educator, educational administrator*

Bryan
Carrico, Virgil Norman *physician*
†Gretick, Anthony Louis *lawyer, judge*
Stevens, Muriel Kay *elementary educator*

Bucyrus
Cooper, April Helen *family nurse practitioner*
Neff, Robert Clark, Sr., *lawyer*
Solt, Robert Lee, Jr., *retired surgeon*

Burbank
Koucky, Frank Louis *geology educator, archeogeology researcher*

Burton
†Fuller, David William *music educator*

Cadiz
Hoffman, Barbara Jo *health and physical education educator, athletic director*
Thompson, Sandra Lee *library administrator*

Canfield
Beck, James Hayes *lawyer*
Hill, Thomas Allen *lawyer*
Volenik, James Edward *music educator*
†Weiss, Susan Ellen *adult nurse practitioner, educator*

Canton
Barkan, John Martin, Jr., *architect*
†Barnhart, Gene *lawyer*
Bartlette, Donald Lloyd *social worker, counselor, educator*
Bernstein, Penny L. *biologist, educator*
†Birkholz, Raymond James *metal products manufacturing company executive*
Carpenter, Noble Olds *retired bank executive*
Caswell, Linda Kay *insurance agency executive*
Davis, Richard E. *lawyer*
Elliott, Peter R. *retired athletic organization executive*
Ewing, David Charles *automobile dealership executive*
Gonzalez, Domingo *neurosurgeon*
†Herbert, David Lee *lawyer, author*
Howland, Willard J. *radiologist, educator*
Huryn, Christopher Michael *lawyer*
†Kasturiarachi, Aloysius Bathi *mathematician, educator, mathematician, researcher*
†Kilcullen, Maureen *librarian, educator*
†Klotz, Leora Nylee *retired music educator, vocalist*
Lindesmith, Dixie Lou *retired geriatrics nurse*
†Long, Howie *former pro football player*
Lyon, James Hugh *education specialist, legislative consultant*
†Mack, Tom *retired professional football player*
Mann, John Martin *minister*
Maxwell, John Alexander, Jr., *retired newspaper editor, consultant*
Mkparu, Fidelis Okechukwu *cardiologist, educator, consultant*
Mokodean, Michael John *lawyer, accountant*
†Moses, Marcia Swartz *artist*
Nadas, John Adalbert *psychiatrist, educator*
Osborne, Harry Alan *orthodontist*
Pedoto, Gerald Joseph *supplier quality analyst*
†Plakas, Leonidas Evangelos *lawyer*
Repp, Ronald Stewart *insurance company executive*
†Sandrock, Scott Paul *lawyer*
Schauer, Thomas Alfred *insurance company executive*
†Shaw, Billy *retired professional football player*
Sicard, Guillermo Rafael *dermatologist*
Stage, Richard Lee *consultant, retired utilities executive*
Starchman, Dale Edward *medical educator*
Thomas, Suzanne Ward *public relations executive, communications educator, radio personality*
†Tzangas, George John *lawyer*
Watson, Duane Frederick *religious studies educator*
Weeks, Philip *history educator*
Zantopulos, William Theodore *sales representative, small business owner*

Cedarville
Anderson, Connie *music educator*
†Dugle, Vivian Rachelle *education educator*
Firmin, Michael Wayne *psychology educator*
Hoffmann, Kenneth Michael *music educator*
Moreno-Riano, Gerson *political science educator*
Wiggins, Robert Ray *criminal justice educator*

Celina
Fanning, Ronald Heath *architect, engineer*
†Fawcett, Colleen *economist, educator*
†Lammers, Thomas Dean *lawyer, educator*
†Myers, Daniel *lawyer*

Centerburg
Reynolds, Don William *geologist*

Centerville
†Alexander, Lora Kay *writer, composer*
Baver, Roy Lane *retired protection services official, consultant*
Corbet, Donald Lee *audio and technology company executive, technical systems educator*
Geier, Sharon Lee *special education educator*
Giffen, Daniel Harris *lawyer, educator*
Kauffold, Ruth Elizabeth *clinical psychologist*

Chagrin Falls
†Blattner, Robert A. *lawyer*
Brophy, Jere Hall *manufacturing company executive*
Brown, Jeanette Grasselli *retired university official*
Calfee, William Lewis *lawyer*
Church, Irene Zaboly *personnel services company executive*
Cordes, Loverne Christian *interior designer*
Cox, Cynthia A. *art education specialist*
Fisher, Will Stratton *illumination consultant*
Freedman, Howard Joel *lawyer*
Goldfarb, Kathleen Bliss *interior designer*
Heckman, Henry Trevennen Shick *steel company executive*
Held, Lila M. *art appraiser*
Kuby, Barbara Eleanor *personnel director, management consultant*
Lange, David Charles *journalist*
Lingl, Friedrich Albert *psychiatrist*
Obert, Charles Frank *retired banker*
Rawski, Conrad H(enry) *humanities educator, medievalist*
Ross, Sally Price *artist, painter*
Stevenson, Thomas Herbert *management consultant, writer, adult education educator*
Vail, Iris Jennings *civic worker*

Chandlersville
Herron, Janet Irene *industrial manufacturing engineer*

Chardon
Dobyns, Brown McIlvaine *surgeon, educator*
Mihalik, Phyllis Ann *consulting company executive, educator, public speaker*
Reinhard, Sister Mary Marthe *educational organization administrator*
Uscheek, David Petrovich *retired chemist*

Chesterland
Aster, Ruth Marie Rhydderch *business owner*
Spitz, Arnoldt John *international trade professional, consultant*
Wood, Kenneth Anderson *artist, designer, consultant*

Chillicothe
Atwood, Joyce Charlene *curriculum and instruction administrator, consultant*
Boulger, William Charles *lawyer*
Donahue, Jeffrey David *music educator*
El-Zawahry, M. A. Moneim *epidemiologist, tropical medicine specialist*
Fruth, Beryl Rose *physician*
Johnson, Mark Alan *biochemist*
Leedy, Emily L. Foster (Mrs. William N. Leedy) *retired education educator, consultant*
Murton, William Norman, II, *telecommunications executive*
†Polans, Robert G. *writer, consultant*
Smith, Ralph Edward *psychology assistant*
Zeigler, Joseph William *surveillance company manager*

Cincinnati
†Abate, Anne Katherine *librarian, consultant, educator*
Ackermann, Russell Albert *manufacturing company executive*
†Adams, David Hardy *voice educator, concert singer*
Adams, Edmund John *lawyer*
Adams, Mendle Eugene *minister*
Adlard, Carole Rechtsteiner *health education agency executive*
Aft, Richard Nathaniel *professional society administrator, consultant*
Agrawal, Dharma Prakash *engineering educator*
Alexander, James Wesley *surgeon, educator*
Alexander, John Kurt *history educator*
Allen, Anna Marie *financial executive*
†Altaye, Mekibib *medical educator, consultant, medical researcher*
Anderson, James Milton *lawyer*
Anderson, Jerry William, Jr., *technical and business consulting executive, educator*
Anderson, Joan Balyeat *religion educator, minister*
†Anderson, Judith Ann *artist, writer*
Anderson, William Hopple *lawyer*
Angeline, Michael E. *social worker, bereavement facilitator*
Anning, Robert Doan Hopkins *brokerage company executive*
Anthony, Thomas Dale *lawyer*
Ashley, Lynn *educator, consultant, administrator*
Augsburger, James Jay *ophthalmology educator*
†Aylesworth, Julie Ann *writer, personal care industry executive*
Azizkhan, Richard George *pediatric surgeon, educator*
Backherms, Kathryn Anne *parochial school educator*
Bahlman, William Thorne, Jr., *retired lawyer*
Bahr, Donald Walter *retired chemical engineer*
†Barrett, William Martin *environmental engineer, chemical engineer, researcher*
Barton, Keith Casey *college educator*
Baughman, Robert Phillip *physician*
Beaver, Daniel Roy *history educator*
Beckwith, Barbara Jean *journalist*
Beckwith, Sandra Shank *judge*
†Bell, David Maxwell *music educator, consultant*
†Bellingham, Roger Gerry *librian, researcher, consultant*
†Bender, Daniel F. *chemist, education educator*
†Bestehorn, Ute Wiltrud *retired librarian*
Bibus, Thomas William *lawyer*
Bieliauskas, Vytautas Joseph *psychologist, educator*
Birmingham, Stephen *writer*
Bishop, George Franklin *political scientist, educator*
Black, Robert L., Jr., *retired judge*
Black, Stephen L. *lawyer*
Bleznick, Donald William *Romance languages educator*
Bluestein, Barbara Ann *librarian*
Bluestein, Paul Harold *management engineer*
Bluestein, Venus Weller *retired psychologist, educator*
Boat, Thomas Frederick *physician, educator, researcher*
Bollen, Sharon Kesterson *artist, educator*
Boothe, Leon Estel *academic administrator emeritus, consultant*
Bower, Robert Hewott *surgeon, educator, researcher*
Boyd, Deborah Ann *pediatrician*
Brestel, Mary Beth *librarian*
Bridenbaugh, Phillip Owen *anesthesiologist, physician*
Briggs, Henry Payson, Jr., *headmaster*
Briskin, Madeleine *paleo-oceanographer, paleoclimatologist, micropaleontologist*
Brod, Evelyn Fay *foreign language educator*
Brod, Stanford *graphic designer, educator*
†Broderick, Dennis John *lawyer, retail company executive*
Bromberg, Robert Sheldon *lawyer*
Brown, Dale Patrick *retired advertising executive*
Brown, Daniel *art consultant*
†Brown, Lillie Harrison *music educator*
Brown, Mike *professional sports team executive*
†Bruno, David Joseph, Jr., *chemical engineer, researcher*
†Bruvold, Kathleen Parker *lawyer*
†Buechner, Robert William *lawyer, educator*
Buncher, Charles Ralph *epidemiologist, educator*
Burke, Timothy Michael *lawyer, educator*
†Burklow, Kathleen Ann *psychologist*
Burleigh, William Robert *newspaper executive*
CaJacob, Daniel Emerson *otolaryngologist*
†Calico, Paul B. *lawyer*
Callinan, Tom *editor*
Campbell, Audrey Leigh *communications professional*
†Carlson, Jennie Peaslack *lawyer*
Carothers, Charles Omsted *retired orthopedic surgeon*
Carr, George Francis, Jr., *lawyer*
Carraher, Charles Jacob, Jr., *professional speaker*
†Carroll, James Joseph *lawyer*
Cavallo, Tito *physician*
†Cecil, Kim Maria *radiologist, educator*
Cettel, Judith Hapner *artist, secondary school educator*
†Charriez, Laston Samuel *marketing professional, director*
Chatterjee, Jayanta *architecture and planning educator*
Chatterjee, Malaya *immunologist*
Chatterjee, Sunil Kumar *cancer research scientist*
Chesley, Stanley Morris *lawyer*
Chin, Nee Oo Wong *reproductive endocrinologist*
Christensen, Paul Walter, Jr., *gear manufacturing company executive*
Christenson, Gordon A. *law educator*
Church, Jane Evelyn *executive director, counselor*
Ciani, Alfred Joseph *language professional, associate dean*
Cioffi, Michael Lawrence *lawyer*
Cissell, James Charles *lawyer*
Clay, Eric L. *federal judge*
Cobey, John Geoffrey *lawyer, consultant*
Cohen, Edward *lawyer*
Cole, Theodore John *osteopathic and naturopathic physician*
Collins, Margaret Helen *pathologist*
Conaton, Michael Joseph *financial service executive*
†Cook, Deborah L. *judge, former state supreme court justice*
Coombe, V. Anderson *retired valve manufacturing company executive*
Corwin, Melanie S. *lawyer*
†Costigan-Kerns, Louise E. *musician*
Craig, L. Clifford *lawyer*
Crew, Spencer *museum administrator*
Cudkowicz, Leon *medical educator*
†Czarnecki, Kristin E. *humanities educator*
Datta, Sukdeb *anesthesiologist, pain management specialist*
Davis, Robert Lawrence *lawyer*
†De Courten-Myers, Gabrielle Marguerite *neuropathologist*
Dehner, Joseph Julnes *lawyer*
DeLong, Deborah *lawyer*
†de Mallet Burgess, Thomas *opera director, music educator*
Dember, William Norton *retired psychologist, educator*
Derstadt, Ronald Theodore *health care administrator*
†Desmarais, Charles Joseph *museum director, writer, editor*
Di Benedetto, Ann Louise *accounting administrator*
†Diller, Edward Dietrich *lawyer*
Dillon, Corey *professional football player*
Dillon, David Brian *retail grocery executive*
Diltz, Jerry Dwaine *computer science educator, consultant*
†Dionysiou, Dionysios Demetriou *adult education educator, researcher*
Dlott, Susan Judy *judge, lawyer*
Dornette, W(illiam) Stuart *lawyer, educator*
Dougherty, Charlotte Anne *financial planner, insurance and securities representative*
†Dumas, H. Scott *mathematician*
Dunigan, Dennis Wayne *real estate executive*
Dunsker, Stewart B. *physician, neurosurgeon*
†Eaton, Janet Ruth *lawyer*
†Eckman, Mark H. *physician, educator*
Edelman, David Joel *urban planning executive*
Ehrnschwender, Arthur Robert *former utility company executive*
†Enstice, Wayne *art educator, writer*
†Erway, Lawrence Clifton, Jr., *biologist, educator*
†Estes, Stephen Arthur *dermatologist*
Etges, Frank Joseph *parasitology educator*
†Evans, James E. *lawyer*
Everett, Karen Joan *retired librarian, genealogy educator*
Everson, Jean Watkins Dolores *librarian media technical assistant, educator*
Fairobent, Douglas Kevin *computer programmer*
Faller, Susan Grogan *lawyer*
Fenoglio-Preiser, Cecilia Mettler *pathologist, educator*
Ferrell, Susan R. *lawyer*
Finan, Richard H.
Fink, Jerold Albert *lawyer*
†Finkelstein, Norman *literature educator*
†Finney, Michael Douglas *public safety consultant*
Fischer, Patricia Ann *middle school educator*
Flanagan, John Anthony *lawyer, educator*
Fleck, David E. *neuropsychologist*
Flick, Thomas Michael *mathematics educator, educational administrator*
Fowler, Noble Owen *physician, university administrator*
Francis, Marion David *consulting chemist*
Freedman, William Mark *lawyer, educator*
Freiberg, Richard Albert *orthopaedic surgeon*
Freidheim, Cyrus F., Jr., *management consultant*
Friedman, Penny *lawyer*
Fujioka-Ito, Noriko *language educator*
†Fukasawa, Kenji *medical researcher*
Fulmer, Michael Clifford *food company administrator*
Galloway, Lillian Carroll *modeling agency executive, consultant*
Gehlert, Sally Oyler *dental hygienist, consultant*
Gelfand, Janelle Ann *music critic*
Gelfand, Michael Joseph *radiology educator*
Gerber, Michael Allen *pediatrician*
Gersin, Keith Steven *surgeon*
Gerson, Myron Craig *cardiologist, researcher*
Gettler, Benjamin *lawyer, manufacturing company executive*
Gibson, John Phillips *pathologist, toxicologist*
†Gilmore, Jeffery Mandale *artist, educator, musician, communications executive*
Glendening, Everett Austin *architect*
Gluckman, Jack Louis *otolaryngologist, educator, dean*
Goetzman, Bruce Edgar *architecture educator*
Goldstein, Sidney *pharmaceutical scientist*
Goodman, Bernard *physics educator*
†Goodman, Phyllis L. *public relations executive*
Goodman, Stanley *lawyer*
Greenberg, David Bernard *chemical engineering educator*
Greenberg, Gerald Stephen *lawyer*
Greene, Roger Lewis *social studies educator*
Greengus, Samuel *academic administrator, religion educator*
Greenwalt, Tibor Jack *physician, educator*
Griffey, Ken, Jr., (George Kenneth Griffey Jr.) *professional baseball player*
†Griffin, Robert H. *career officer*
Grinshpun, Sergey A. *science educator, science administrator*
†Groetsch, Charles William *mathematics educator*
Gyuro, Paula Candice *financial planner*
Halpert, Douglas Joshua *lawyer*
Hantush, Mohamed M. *hydrologist, researcher*
Hardwick, Kevin Dale *retired protective services official*
Hardy, William Robinson *lawyer*
Harmon, Patrick *historian, sports commentator*
Harrington, Jeremy Thomas *priest, publishing executive*
Harris, Irving *lawyer*
†Harris, Jerald David *lawyer*
Harrison, Donald Carey *university official, cardiology educator*
Hawkins, Lawrence Charles *management consultant, educator*
Heaton, Charles Lloyd *dermatologist, educator*
Heimlich, Henry J. *physician, surgeon, educator*
†Heldman, James Gardner *lawyer*
†Heldman, Paul W. *lawyer, grocery store company executive*
Henderson, Stephen Paul *lawyer*
Hensgen, Herbert Thomas *medical technologist*
Hermanies, John Hans *retired lawyer*
Hersman, Fernando William (Ferd Hersman) *retired engineering executive*

Hess, Evelyn Victorine (Mrs. Michael Howett) medical educator
Hess, Marcia Wanda retired educator
Hessler, Gene Joseph museum curator, retired musician
†Heubi, James Edward pediatrician, educator
Hicks, Irle Raymond retail food chain executive
Hill, Thomas Clark lawyer
Hills, Alan performing company executive
Hodge, Bobby Lynn mechanical engineer, manufacturing executive
Hodge, Robert Joseph retail executive
Hoffheimer, Daniel Joseph lawyer
Hoffman, Joel Harvey composer, educator
Holscher, Robert F. airport terminal executive
Holschuh, John David, Jr., lawyer
Hopkins, Jeffrey P. federal judge
Horseman, Nelson Douglas molecular and cellular physiology educator
Hoyt, Lupé Ann González social services administrator
Huber, Henry B. retired music educator
Huenefeld, Thomas Ernst financial consultant, retired banker
Huggins, Bob college basketball coach
†Husseinzadeh, Nader gynecologist, oncologist
Hust, Bruce Kevin lawyer
Hutton, Edward Luke diversified public corporation executive
Irwin, Miriam Dianne Owen book publisher, writer
Isaacs, S. Ted engineering executive
Ivey, Tom Dexter cardiac surgeon
James, George Barker, II, investment executive
†Jarvi, Paavo conductor
Jensen, Elwood Vernon biochemist
†Jin, Li education educator
†Johnson, Betty Lou secondary education educator
†Johnson, James J. lawyer
Johnson, Norma Louise accountant
Johnson, Ronda Janice professional not-for-profit fundraiser
Jones, Nathaniel Raphael retired federal judge
†Kahn, Jessica Annette pediatrics educator, researcher
Kamp, Cynthia Lea elementary education educator
Kansal, Achin Suresh marketing professional, consultant
Karam, Ernest chief magistrate
Kaune, James Edward ship repair company executive, former naval officer
Kawahara, Fred Katsumi research chemist
Kelley, Cleophus O. city official
Kelley, John Joseph, Jr., lawyer
Kelley, Rebecca Crouse (Rebecca Ann Kelley) lawyer, academic administrator, not-for-profit fundraiser
Kelz, Rochelle Shelle K. academic administrator
Kennedy, Cornelia Groefsema federal judge
Kereiakes, Dean James cardiologist
Kernan, Jerome Bernard retired marketing educator, researcher
Khan, Sohaib Ahmed cancer researcher, molecular cell biology educator
Kiel, Frederick Orin lawyer
King, Margaret Ann communications educator
Kitna, Jon football player
Kitzmiller, W. John plastic, reconstructive and hand surgeon, educator
Klein, Charles Henle lithographing company executive
Klein, Donald Charles psychologist
Klein, Jerry Emanuel insurance and financial planning executive
Knapp, Judy Ann pharmacist
Knilans, Timothy Kevin pediatrician
Knipschild, Robert artist, educator
Kohl, David dean,emeritus librarian
Kollstedt, Paula Lubke communications executive, writer
Kordons, Uldis lawyer
Kowel, Stephen Thomas electrical engineer, educator
Kramer, Randolph John bank executive
†Krass, Marc Stern lawyer
Krishnan, Hema A. finance educator
Krohn, Claus Dankertsen insurance company executive
Kuhn, John Henry retired paper industry executive
Kulwin, Dwight Robert surgeon, educator
Kuntz, Charles, IV, neurological surgeon
Kunzel, Erich, Jr., conductor, arranger, educator
Kupper, Philip Lloyd chemist
Lafley, Alan G. consumer products company executive
Lajoie, Richard John, Jr., information technology executive
Laney, Sandra Eileen service company executive
Lang, Jackie Ann nursing consultant
Lange, Scott Leslie communications company executive, voice professional
Larkin, Barry Louis professional baseball player
Lawrence, James Kaufman Lebensburger lawyer
Lawson, Randall Clayton, II, financial executive
Leahy, Kevin Sean energy company strategist
LeCroix, Charles David research and development company executive, educator
Lesick, John Richard lawyer, consultant, retired lawyer
Levin, Debbe Ann lawyer
Levine, Aaron executive
Levine, Steven Alan real estate appraiser, association executive
Levinson, Joseph E. physician, emeritus educator
Levy, Ralph David theology educator
†Lewis, Gene Dale historian, educator
Leyda, James Perkins small business consultant, retired pharmaceutical company executive
Lichtin, Leon (Judah Leon Lichtin) pharmacist
Lim, Teik C. engineering educator, consultant
Lindberg, Charles David lawyer
Linder, Carl H., III, diversified financial services company executive
Lintz, Robert Carroll retired financial holding company executive
Lippincott, Jonathan Ramsay healthcare executive
Liss, Herbert Myron communications executive
Liu, Yijun engineering educator, researcher
†Lloyd, David Livingstone, Jr., lawyer
Lockhart, John Mallery management consultant
Loggie, Jennifer Mary Hildreth medical educator, physician
Lucas, Stanley Jerome retired radiologist, physician
Lucke, Robert Vito merger and acquisition executive
Luckner, Herman Richard, III, interior designer
Lugbill, Ann lawyer
†Luse, Kimberly Ann radiologic technologist, educator
Lutz, James Gurney lawyer
†Lynch, Timothy Patrick historian, educator
Macpherson, Colin R(obertson) pathologist, educator
†Madson, Philip Ward engineering executive, consultant
Maher, Terry Marina religious organization administrator
Maltz, Robert surgeon
Manley, Robert Edward lawyer, economist
Mann, David Scott lawyer
Mantel, Samuel Joseph, Jr., management educator, consultant
Markesbery, Maria Saba lawyer
†Marks, Edward G. lawyer
Martin, John Bruce chemical engineer
Martin, William J., II, academic administrator
Marx, Marjorie McCullough service organization executive
Mates, Lawrence A., II, medical company executive, consultant
Matulewicz, Patricia Ann social worker
Maxwell, Robert Wallace, II, lawyer
McAusland, Randolph M. N. arts consultant
McClain, William Andrew lawyer
McDaniels, Audrey Evelyn microbiologist
McDowell, John Eugene lawyer
†McFarlan, Rebecca Collins secondary school educator, consultant
Mc Henry, Powell lawyer
McMullin, Ruth Roney publishing executive, trustee, management fellow
McNulty, John William retired public relations executive, automobile company executive
Meal, Larie chemistry educator, researcher, consultant
Mechem, Charles Stanley, Jr., former broadcasting executive, former golf association executive
Meinert, Walter retired chemical company executive, consultant
Meisner, Gary Wayne landscape architect
†Melnyk, Lisa Jo research scientist
Meranus, Leonard Stanley lawyer
Merchant, Mylon Eugene physicist, engineer
†Meyer, Charles Mulvihill lawyer
Meyers, Karen Diane lawyer, educator, corporate officer
†Meyers, Pamela Sue lawyer
Miles, John Bill accountant, tax advisor
Miller, Catherine Ann nursing administrator
†Miller, Gail Franklin lawyer
Miller, Sari Elizabeth (Sally Derby) writer
†Monaco, John J. molecular genetics research educator
Monder, Steven I. orchestra executive
Monroe, Erin psychiatric nurse practitioner
Moore, John Edward marketing professional, freelance writer
Morgan, Victoria performing company executive, choreographer
Morgan, William Richard mechanical engineer
Morris, Margaret Elizabeth marketing professional
Morrow, Ardythe Luxion adult education educator, researcher
Mukerjee, Debdas environmental health scientist, educator
Muntz, Ernest Gordon historian, educator
Nasrallah, Henry Ata psychiatry researcher, educator
Naylor, Paul Donald lawyer
Nechemias, Stephen Murray lawyer
Nelson, David Aldrich judge
†Nelson, Frederick Dickson judge
Nelson, W. Michael, III, psychologist, educator
Neltner, Michael Martin lawyer
Nester, William Raymond, Jr., retired academic administrator and educator
Neumark, Michael Harry lawyer
Nielsen, George Lee architect
†Nippert, Alfred Kuno, Jr., lawyer
†Nordlund, James John dermatologist
Olson, Robert Wyrick lawyer
†O'Reilly, James Thomas lawyer, educator, author
†Owens, Robert Emmett, Jr., lawyer
Paavo, Jarvi conductor
Painter, Mark Philip judge
Pan, Zigang engineering educator
Pancero, Jack Blocher restaurant executive
Pancheri, Eugene Joseph chemical engineer
†Parker, Linda Bates professional development organization administrator
Parker, R. Joseph lawyer
Pender, Richard F. communications executive, consultant, theater critic
†Pepper, John Ennis, Jr., consumer products company executive
Perlman, Burton judge
Petrie, Bruce Inglis lawyer
Petty, Priscilla Hayes writer, columnist, producer
Phillips, T. Stephen lawyer
Pichler, Joseph Anton food products executive
Pilarczyk, Daniel Edward archbishop
Porter, Robert Carl, Jr., lawyer
Powley, Elizabeth Ann health facility administrator
Preiser, Wolfgang Friedrich Ernst architect, educator, consultant, researcher
Proffitt, Kevin archivist
†Ralston, James Allen lawyer
Rand, Carolyn financial executive
Randman, Barry I. real estate developer
†Randolph, Jackson Harold utility company executive
Ratliff, Thomas Asbury, Jr., retired engineer
Rebel, Jerome Ivo financial planner
Reichert, David lawyer
†Reis, Peggy D. township official
Relyea, Carl Miller retired hydrologist
Rexroth, Nancy Louise photographer
Rich, Robert Edward lawyer
Rishel, James Burton manufacturing executive, director
Robertson, Jerald Lee physicist
Rockwell, R(onald) James, Jr., laser and electro-optics consultant
Rogers, James Eugene electric and gas utility executive
†Rogers, John Marshall judge, law educator
Rogers, Millard Foster, Jr., art museum director emeritus
Rolfes, Richard James radiologist
Roomann, Hugo architect
Rorick, Marvin Horton, III, physician, neurologist
Rose, Donald McGregor retired lawyer
Roth, Roger Douglas small business owner
Rothenberg, Marc Elliot pediatrics educator
Rub, Timothy F. museum director
Rubin, Robert Samuel lawyer
Rubin, Stanley Gerald aerospace engineering educator
Ruddy, Richard M. physician
Rudney, Bernice Snider social worker, psychotherapist
Ruehlmann, Virginia Juergens foundation creativity director, writer
Ryan, Richard J. emergency medicine physician
Saal, Howard Max clinical geneticist, pediatrician, educator
Sacher, Ronald Alan hematologist
Sallquist, Gary Ardin minister, non-profit executive
†Sanford, Jimmie securities trader, investor
Scacchetti, David J. lawyer
Schaefer, Dale W. science educator
Schaefer, Frank William, III, microbiologist, researcher
Schaefer, George A., Jr., bank executive
Scheineson, Irwin Bruce insurance and investment company executive
Scherer, Anita (Anita Stock) gerontologist, marketing consultant
Schiff, James Andrew English educator
†Schmidt, James Edward medical educator, researcher
Schmidt, Leeanne artist
Schreiner, Albert William physician, educator
Schrier, Arnold historian, educator
Schuck, Thomas Robert lawyer, farmer
Schuler, Robert Leo appraiser, consultant
†Schultz, Jo El Jean research scientist, educator
Schutzius, Lucy Jean retired librarian
Scott, Ralph C. physician, educator
Scruggs, Catherine Lynn financial manager
Segal, Richard Arthur, Jr., advertising agency executive
†Seiden, Allen Mark otolaryngologist
Semon, Warren Lloyd retired computer sciences educator
Shani, Hezekiah Gyunda Pyuza thoracic and cardiovascular surgery
Shapiro, Judith social worker
Shea, Joseph William, III, lawyer
Shepherd, Elsbeth Weichsel supply chain consultant
†Sherman, Kenneth Eliot medicine educator, researcher
Shertzer, Howard Grant health educator
Shipley, Tony L(ee) software company executive
Shore, Thomas Spencer, Jr., retired lawyer
Shott, Sally Richard otolaryngologist
Silbersack, Mark Louis lawyer
Silberstein, Edward Bernard nuclear medicine educator, researcher, oncologist
Silvers, Gerald Thomas retired publishing executive
Smale, John Gray diversified industry executive
Smith, Akili professional football player
Smith, Gregory Allgire college administrator
Smith, Sheila Marie lawyer
Smith, Timothy W. musician
Smittle, Nelson Dean military analyst, artist
Sowder, Fred Allen foundation administrator, alphabet specialist
Sperelakis, Nicholas, Sr., physiology and biophysics educator, researcher
Spiegel, S. Arthur federal judge
Spinnato, Joseph Anthony, II, obstetrician
Stahl, Donna Laura surgeon
Stanton, Jeanne Frances retired lawyer
Steger, Joseph A. university president
Steinberg, Janet Eckstein journalist
Stern, Joseph Smith, Jr., former footwear manufacturing company executive
Stimson, Evelyn Marie Reinheimer chemist
Stinson, Mary Florence retired nursing educator
†Stith, John Stephen lawyer
Stolley, Alexander advertising executive
Strakowski, Stephen M. psychiatrist
Strauss, James Lester investment sales executive
Strauss, William Victor lawyer
Sturwold, Sister Rita Mary educational administrator
Succop, Paul Allan biostatistics educator, consultant
Sunagawa, Masanori physiologist, researcher
Swigert, James Mack lawyer
Tancous, Jean Jacobs chemist
†Teasley, John Ray Sanders, Jr., writer
Tenbosch, Gerald John fundraising executive
†Thatcher, Tom religious studies educator
†Thomas, Michael A. endocrinologist, gynecologist
Thompson, Morley Punshon textile company executive
Thornell, William Clyde retired physician
Tobias, Charles Harrison, Jr., lawyer
Tobias, Paul Henry lawyer
Tocco, James pianist
Toftner, Richard Orville engineering executive
Tomain, Joseph Patrick dean, law educator
†Townsend, Robert J. lawyer
Tranter, Terence Michael lawyer
†Trauth, Joseph Louis, Jr., lawyer
†Trofe, Jennifer pharmacist, educator
Trotta, Vincent John transportation executive
†Urbansky, Edward Todd research chemist
Vander Laan, Mark Alan lawyer
Varma, Rajender Singh organic chemist
Victor, William Weir retired telephone company executive, consultant
Vilter, Richard William physician, educator
Vinciguerra, Thomas Michael chemical engineer
Vogel, Cedric Wakelee lawyer
Wales, Ross Elliot lawyer
Warrick, Peter football player
†Warshaw, Gregg geriatrician, educator
Wasnak, Lynn publishing executive, writer
Wasserman, Donald Eugene human vibration and ergonomics consultant
†Watts, Barbara Gayle law academic administrator
Weeks, Steven Wiley lawyer
Weisman, Joel nuclear engineering educator, engineering consultant
Wellington, Jean Susorney librarian
Welsh, George Franklin plastic surgeon, educator, healthcare consultant
West, Clark Darwin pediatric nephrologist, educator
Weston, Phyllis Jean art gallery director
Whipple, Harry M. newspaper publishing executive
Whitaker, Glenn Virgil lawyer
Williams, Daniel Bryan obstetrician/gynecologist, educator
Wilsey, Philip Arthur computer science educator
†Wilson, Arthur Henry charitable institution executive
Wilson, James Miller, IV, cardiovascular surgeon, educator
Winkler, Henry Ralph retired academic administrator, historian
Wiot, Jerome Francis radiologist
†Wisler, David Charles aerospace engineer, educator
Witten, Louis physics educator
Wood, Robert Emerson pediatrics educator
Woodside, Frank C., III, lawyer, educator, physician
Wright, Creighton Bolter cardiovascular surgeon, educator
Wulker, Laurence Joseph portfolio manager, educator, financial planner
Wygant, Foster Laurance art educator, educator
Yee, Leslie Mitchell physician executive, educator
Zafren, Herbert Cecil librarian, educator
Zavatsky, Michael Joseph lawyer
Zealey, Sharon Janine lawyer
Zhou, Taili metallurgist
Zimmerman, James M. retail company executive
Zimpher, Nancy Lusk academic administrator
Zola, Gary Phillip rabbi, historian, religious educational administrator
Zuccarello, Mario neurosurgeon, researcher
Zucker, David I. psychologist

Cinncinati
†Leavitt, Tod John music educator, musician

Circleville
Ammer, William retired judge
†England, Richard Jay retired chemist
†Long, Jan Michael judge
†McGuire, James Kavanaugh education and history educator
Strous, Allen poet

Clayton
Stutzman, L. Lee pastor

Cleveland
Abid, Ann B. art librarian
Abrams, Sylvia Fleck religious studies educator
†Abughali, Nazha pediatrician, consultant
Adamo, Kenneth R. lawyer
†Adams, Albert T. lawyer
Adams, Gene Autry retired military officer
Adams, H. Leslie composer
†Agani, Faton Hilmi anatomist, educator
Ainsworth, Joan Horsburgh university development director
Alcox, Patrick Joseph lawyer
Altose, Murray David physician, educator
Anders, Claudia Dee occupational therapist
Anderson, David Gaskill, Jr., Spanish language educator
Andrews, Oakley V. lawyer
Andrica, John Dean management consultant
Angus, John Cotton chemical engineering educator
Anthony, Donald Barrett engineering executive
†Appling, Christopher Michael columnist, writer
Ashmus, Keith Allen lawyer
Austin, Arthur Donald, II, lawyer, educator
Awais, George Musa obstetrician, gynecologist
Bacon, Brett Kermit lawyer
Badal, Daniel Walter psychiatrist, educator
Bahniuk, Eugene mechanical engineering educator
Baker, Melvin hospital pharmacy administrator
Baker, Saul Phillip geriatrician, cardiologist, internist
Ballou, Ronald Herman management educator
Bambakidis, Peter neurologist, educator
†Baranova, Elena basketball player
Barnett, Gene Henry neurosurgeon
Bates, Walter Alan former lawyer
†Battle, Hilary Howard minister, educator

McFadden, John Volney *retired manufacturing company executive*
McHale, Vincent Edward *political science educator*
McHenry, Martin Christopher *physician, educator*
McLarty, Colin Slator *philosophy educator*
McLaughlin, Patrick Michael *lawyer*
McQuarrie, Irvine Gray *neurosurgeon, educator*
Medalie, Jack Harvey *physician*
Mehlman, Maxwell Jonathan *law educator*
Melsop, James William *architect*
Merat, Francis Lawrence *engineering educator*
†Meyer, G. Christopher *lawyer*
Miller, Arnold *retired newspaper editor*
Miller, Genevieve *retired medical historian*
Miller, John Robert *oil industry executive*
†Millisor, Kenneth Ray *lawyer*
Millstone, David Jeffrey *lawyer*
Minai, Omar Ahmad *physician*
Miyoshi, Kazuhisa *senior research scientist*
Moceanu, Dominique *retired Olympic athlete*
Molyneaux, David Glenn *newspaper travel editor*
Monihan, Mary Elizabeth *lawyer*
Montague, Drogo K. *urologist*
†Mooney, James P. *chemicals executive*
Moore, Karen Nelson *judge*
Moore, Kenneth Cameron *lawyer*
†Morgenstern, Conrad J. *lawyer*
Morgenstern-Clarren, Pat *federal judge*
†Morgenthaler, David Turner *venture capitalist*
Morris, Thomas William *symphony orchestra administrator*
Mossad, Sherif Beniameen *physician*
Myers, Eddie Earl *clinical psychologist*
Nagel, William Lee *management consultant*
†Nahat, Dennis F. *artistic director, choreographer*
†Nave, Michele Garrick *lawyer*
Neal, Bennie F. *secondary school administrator*
†Neff, Owen Calvin *lawyer*
Nelson, Richard Alan *financial executive*
†Nemcova, Eva *professional basketball player*
Neuhauser, Duncan vonBriesen *medical educator*
Newman, John M., Jr., *lawyer*
Nickerson, Gary Lee *secondary education educator*
Noetzel, Arthur Jerome *business administration educator, management consultant*
Norman, Forrest Alonzo *lawyer*
Novick, Andrew Carl *urologist*
O'Brien, Margaret Ann *obstetrics nurse, community health nurse*
†O'Donnell, Thomas Michael *former brokerage firm executive*
O'Hara, Thomas Patrick *managing editor*
Oliver, Solomon, Jr., *judge*
Ollinger, W. James *lawyer, director*
Olness, Karen Norma *pediatrics and international health educator*
Olson, Barry Gay *advertising executive, creative director*
†Olson, Sandra *aerospace engineer*
Olson, Sandra Lee *aerospace engineer, research scientist*
Osborne, Frank R. *lawyer, educator, lecturer*
†Oyama, Akira *aerospace engineer, researcher*
Pace, Stanley Dan *lawyer*
Pallam, John James *lawyer*
Papachristou, Christos A. *engineering educator*
Papay, Francis Anthony *plastic surgeon, researcher*
Parker, Patrick Streeter *manufacturing executive*
Parker, Robert Frederic *university dean emeritus*
Pascarella, Perry James *author, editor, speaker*
Pearlman, Samuel Segel *lawyer, educator*
Perkovic, Robert Branko *retired international management consultant*
†Perris, Terrence George *lawyer*
Perry, George *neuroscientist, educator*
Petina, David Anthony *industry analyst*
Pierce, Mary *professional tennis player*
Pierson, Marilyn Ehle *financial planner*
Pike, Kermit Jerome *cultural organization administrator*
†Pilla, Anthony Michael *bishop*
†Pina, Ileana *medical educator*
Podboy, Alvin Michael, Jr., *law library director, lawyer*
Pollack, Florence K.Z. *management consultant*
Pomeranz, Jerome Raphael *dermatopathologist*
†Post, Stephen Garrard *theologian, philosopher, educator*
†Povinelli, Louis A. *aeronautical engineer*
Poza, Ernesto *business consultant, educator*
Presti, Geralyn Marie *lawyer*
Preston, Robert Bruce *retired lawyer*
Pretlow, Thomas Garrett *physician, pathology educator, researcher*
†Pucko, Diane Bowles *public relations executive*
Pursell, Carroll Wirth *history educator*
Putka, Andrew Charles *lawyer*
Queen, Joyce Ellen *elementary school educator*
Quigney, Theresa Ann *special education educator*
†Quinlan, Eileen *nun, literature educator*
Raaf, John Hart *surgeon, health facility administrator, educator*
†Rafiroiu, Anca Codruta *medical educator*
Rains, M. Neal *lawyer*
Rakita, Louis *cardiologist, educator*
Ransohoff, Richard Milton *neurologist, researcher*
Rapp, Robert Neil *lawyer*
Ratcheson, Robert Allan *neurological surgeon*
†Ratnoff, Oscar Davis *physician, educator*
†Raven, Hyacinthe L. *publishing executive, editor*
Reid, James Sims, Jr., *former automobile parts manufacturer*
†Renwick, Glenn M. *insurance company executive*
Reppert, Richard Levi *lawyer*
Reshotko, Eli *aerospace engineer, educator*
Resnick, Martin I. *urologist, educator*
Roberts, James Owen *financial planning executive, consultant*
Robiner, Donald Maxwell *lawyer, former federal official*
Robinson, Alice Helene *English language educator, administrative assistant*
Robinson, Stewart Marshall *mathematician, educator*
Rogers, Charles Edwin *physical chemistry educator*
†Romaniuk, Jaroslaw Richard *social worker, neuroscientist*
Roop, James John *public relations executive*
Rose, Peter Graham *gynecologic oncologist*
Rosenbaum, Jacob I. *lawyer*
Rosenthal, Leighton A. *aviation company executive*
Rothner, Arnold David *pediatric neurologist*
Roulet, Norman Lawrence *psychiatrist, educator*
Rudy, Yoram *biomedical engineer, biophysicist, educator*
Ruf, H(arold) William, Jr., *retired lawyer, corporation executive*
Ruff, Robert Louis *neurologist, physiology researcher*
Rupert, John Edward *retired savings and loan executive, business and civic affairs consultant*
Saada, Adel Selim *civil engineer, educator*
Sabik, Joseph Andrew *psychometrist, counselor*
Salomon, Roger Blaine *English language educator*
Sande, Theodore Anton *architect, educator, foundation executive*
Sanislo, Paul Steve *lawyer*
Savinell, Robert Francis *engineering educator*
Sawyer, Raymond Terry *lawyer, consultant, theater producer*
Scarpa, Antonio *medicine educator, biomedical scientist*
†Schatz, William Bonsall *lawyer*
†Schelling, Jeffrey Robert *biomedical researcher, nephrologist*
Schiller, James Joseph *lawyer*
Schlotfeldt, Rozella May *nursing educator, educator*
Schmidt, Patricia Jean *special education educator*
Schorr, Alvin Louis *social worker, educator*
Schrott, Norman *retired clinical social worker*
Schuele, Donald Edward *physics educator*
Schultz, Jeffrey Eric *optometrist*
Schwartz, Michael Alan *physician*
Seaton, Robert Finlayson *retired finance company executive*
Seballos, Raul John *internist, medical educator*
Seikel, George R. *research engineer*
Seitz, William Henry, Jr., *surgeon*
Seles, Monica *professional tennis player*
Shakno, Robert Julian *hospital and social services administrator*
Shapiro, Fred David *lawyer*
Sharpe, Calvin William *law educator, arbitrator*
Shepard, Ivan Albert *securities and insurance broker*
†Shore, Michael Allan *lawyer, accountant*
Shuck, Jerry Mark *surgeon, educator*
†Shumaker, Roger Lee *lawyer*
Sibley, Willis Elbridge *anthropology educator, consultant*
Sicherman, Marvin Allen *lawyer*
Silas, Paul *professional basketball coach*
†Simha, Robert *chemistry educator, researcher*
†Simmons, Clinton Craig *human resources executive*
Simon, Edgar Harmon *interior designer*
Skolnik, David Erwin *financial analyst*
Skulina, Thomas Raymond *lawyer*
Slinger, Michael Jeffery *law library director*
Slobozhanin, Lev Arkadievich *fluid mechanics researcher*
†Smith, Beverly Harriett *elementary school educator*
Smith, Mieko Kotake *education educator*
Smythe Zajc, M. Catherine *not-for-profit developer, consultant*
Sogg, Wilton Sherman *lawyer*
Solomon, Randall Lee *lawyer*
Spano, Kenneth Andrew *surgeon, educator*
Sparber, Dale Paul *banker*
Spero, Keith Erwin *lawyer, educator*
Spicer, Michael William *university educator*
Spisak-Siemientkowski, Sara Louise *small business owner, apparel executive*
†Spurgeon, Roberta Kaye *lawyer*
Stange, Kurt C. *medical educator*
Stanley, Hugh Monroe, Jr., *lawyer*
Stanton-Hicks, Michael D'Arcy *anesthesiologist, pain medicine specialist, educator*
Stark, George Robert *health science association administrator*
Stavitsky, Abram Benjamin *immunologist, educator*
Steindler, Howard Allen *lawyer*
†Steinmetz, Michael Patrick *physician, neurosurgeon*
Stepien, Carol Ann *molecular geneticist, fisheries educator*
Stern, Robert C. *physician, educator*
Stevens, Thomas Charles *lawyer*
Stewart, Jack M. *management consulting firm executive*
Stoller, Eleanor Palo *sociology educator*
Stone, Harry H. *business executive*
Stovsky, Michael David *lawyer*
Stratton-Crooke, Thomas Edward *financial consultant*
Strauch, John L. *lawyer*
†Strauss, David J. *lawyer*
Striefsky, Linda A(nn) *lawyer*
Strimbu, Victor, Jr., *lawyer*
Strome, Marshall *otolaryngologist, educator*
Stuhan, Richard George *lawyer*
†Stuhldreher, George William *lawyer*
†Suarez, Jose I. *neurologist, researcher*
Sudow, Thomas Nisan *marketing services company executive, broadcaster, chamber of commerce executive*
Suri, Jasjit S. *research scientist*
Swartzbaugh, Marc L. *lawyer*
Sweeney, Emily Margaret *prosecutor*
Szaller, James Francis *lawyer*
Szarek, Stanislaw Jerzy *mathematics educator*
Taft, Seth Chase *retired lawyer*
Tavakoli, Amir *civil engineer, educator*
Taw, Dudley Joseph *sales executive, director*
Taylor, Harris C. *consultant endocrinologist, diabetologist*
Taylor, Margaret Wischmeyer *retired language educator*
Taylor, Nellie Ruby *artist, poet*
Taylor, Steve Henry *zoologist*
Teissonniere, Gerardo *musician, educator*
†Tetzlaff, John Edwin *physician*
†Thimmig, Diana M. *lawyer*
Thomas, Faye Evelyn J. *elementary and secondary school educator*
Thomas, Richard Stephen *financial executive*
Thome, Jim *professional baseball player*
†Thornton, Glenda Ann *librarian*
†Tomsich, Robert J. *heavy machinery manufacturing executive*
Toohey, Brian Frederick *lawyer*
Toomajian, William Martin *lawyer*
†Topol, Eric Jeffrey *cardiologist, physician, educator*
†Turoff, Jack Newton *lawyer*
Unger, Paul A. *packaging and international affairs specialist*
Utian, Wulf Hessel *gynecologist, endocrinologist*
Utrata, Carl Ignatius *corporate counsel, corporate executive*
†Vance, Victoria Lynne *lawyer*
van den Bogert, Antonie Johannes *biomechanics researcher, consultant*
Vickers, Mary Louise *financial analyst*
†Vieaux, Jason Brian *musician, music educator*
Vizquel, Omar Enrique *professional baseball player*
von Mehren, George M. *lawyer*
Walcott, Robert *healthcare executive, priest*
Waldeck, John Walter, Jr., *lawyer*
Wallach, Mark Irwin *lawyer*
Walsh, Richard A. *medical educator*
Wang, Fu-Zhang *medical researcher*
†Wang, Kai *cardiologist*
Waren, Allan David *computer information scientist, educator*
Warren, Russell James *investment banker, consultant*
†Washkewicz, Donald E. *manufacturing executive*
Watson, Richard Thomas *lawyer*
†Weaver, Robin Geoffrey *lawyer, educator*
Webb, James R. *finance educator, consultant*
Weber, Robert Carl *lawyer*
Webster, Leslie Tillotson, Jr., *pharmacologist, educator*
Weidenthal, Maurice David (Bud Weidenthal) *educational administrator, journalist*
Weiler, Jeffry Louis *lawyer*
Weiner, George David *medical association executive, researcher*
Weir, Dame Gillian Constance *concert organist, harpsichordist*
†Weise, Kathryn L. *pediatrician*
†Weisman, Fred *lawyer*
Weiss, Leon Alan *lawyer*
Wells, Lesley *judge*
Welser-Möst, Franz *conductor*
†Werber, Stephen Jay *lawyer, educator*
†White, Michael Reed *former mayor*
Whitney, Richard Buckner *lawyer*
Wiedemann, Herbert Pfeil *physician*
Willenbrink, Rose Ann *lawyer*
†Willey, Andrea *surgeon, researcher*
Williams, Arthur Benjamin, Jr., *bishop*
Wilson, Jack *aeronautical engineer*
Wish, Jay Barry *nephrologist, specialist*
Withers, Carl Raymond *lawyer*
†Wolfman, Alan *medical educator, researcher*
Wolinsky, Emanuel *physician, educator*
†Womack, John W. *pharmacist*
Woyczynski, Wojbor Andrzej *mathematician, educator*
Wright, Marshall *retired manufacturing executive, former diplomat*
Wykle, May L. *dean, educator, researcher*
Wyllie, Elaine *physician*
Xiong, Fuqin *electrical engineering educator*
Yetmar, Scott Andrew *accountant, educator*
Young, James Edward *lawyer*
Young, Jess Ray *retired internist*
Yue, Cheung Cho *physician*
Zambie, Allan John *lawyer*
†Zhang, Amy Yanyun *medical educator*
†Zhang, Nengli *thermophysics scientist*
Zhu, Dongming *materials scientist*
†Zigmond, Richard Eric *neuroscientist, researcher*
Zollinger, Robert Milton, Jr., *surgery educator*
Zung, Thomas Tse-Kwai *architect*

Cleveland Heights

Byramjee, Aspi Minoo *surgeon*
Collins, Sunniva Refsnes *metallurgist*
Gutfeld, Norman E. *lawyer*
Marchetti, Donna *writer, critic*
Mofflin, Lionel Hugh (Harry Mofflin) *biomedical engineer, physician*
Sandburg, Helga *author*
†Weinbaum, Batya *language educator*

Cleves

Tolzmann, Don Heinrich *curator, educator*

Columbia Station

Goll, Paulette Susan *education educator*

Columbus

†Abraham, Brian M. *research scientist*
Adams, John Marshall *lawyer*
†Adeli, Hojjat *engineer, educator, computer scientist*
Adelson, Edward *physicist, musician*
Akers, Saundra Ruth *disability rights advocate*
Alban, Roger Charles *small business consultant*
Alexander, Carl Albert *ceramic engineer, educator*
†Alexander, Rudolph *education educator*
Alger, Chadwick Fairfax *political scientist, educator*
Allen, Cameron *genealogist, law educator*
Allen, Lois Arlene Height (Mrs. James Pierpont Allen) *musician*
†Allen, Richard Lee, Jr., *lawyer*
Altan, Taylan *engineering educator, mechanical engineer, consultant*
Anderson, Carole Ann *nursing educator, academic administrator*
Anderson, Jon Mac *lawyer, educator*
†Anderson, Kerrii B. *construction company executive*
†Antony, Louise Marie *education educator*
Aring, Monika *education economist, consultant, researcher*
Armes, Walter Scott *vocational school administrator*
Arnold, Dale Robert *farm bureau association executive*
Arnold, Kevin David *psychologist, educational researcher*
Arps, David Foster *electronics engineer*
Aukland, Duncan Dayton *lawyer*
Austin, David George *dentist*
†Austria, Steve *state legislator*
Babcock, Charles Luther *classics educator*
Bachman, Sister Janice *healthcare executive*
Bailey, Cecil Dewitt *aerospace engineer, educator*
Bailey, Daniel Allen *lawyer*
†Baird, Leonard Lynn *social scientist, educator, researcher, editor*
Balthaser, James Harvey *lawyer*
Banasik, Robert Casmer *nursing home administrator, educator*
Barker, Llyle James, Jr., *management consultant, journalism educator*
Barnes, Galen R. *insurance company executive*
Barnes, Wallace Ray *retired lawyer*
†Barrett, Phillip Heston *lawyer, director*
Barry, James P(otvin) *writer, editor*
†Barsky, Constance Kay *education educator*
Barth, Rolf Frederick *pathologist, educator*
Barthelmas, Ned Kelton *investment and commercial real estate developer*
Bastoky, Bruce Michael *human resources executive*
Battersby, James Lyons, Jr., *English language educator*
†Bauldoff, Gerene S. *nursing researcher, educator*
Bechtel, Stephen E. *mechanical engineer, educator*
Beck, Paul Allen *political science educator*
Becker, Ralph Leonard *psychologist*
Beckholt, Alice *clinical nurse specialist*
Behrman, Edward Joseph *biochemistry educator*
Beja, Morris *English literature educator*
Belton, John Thomas *lawyer*
†Bennett, Robert Thomas *lawyer, professional athletics manager*
Bergstrom, Stig Magnus *geology educator*
†Berntson, Gary Glen *psychiatry, psychology and pediatrics educator*
Berry, William Lee *business administration educator*
Beversdorf, David Quentin *neurologist, researcher*
Bhushan, Bharat *mechanical engineer*
Bilderback, George Garrison, III, *alcohol/drug abuse services professional*
Billings, Charles Edgar *physician*
Bissell, Michael Gilbert *pathologist*
Blackwell, J(ohn) Kenneth *state official*
Blankenship, Dolores Moorefield *principal, music educator, retired*
Blom, Dave *healthcare industry executive*
Bloomfield, Clara Derber *oncologist, medical institute administrator*
†Bloomfield, David Solomon *lawyer, educator*
Booker, James Douglas *retired lawyer, government official*
Boudoulas, Harisios *physician, educator, researcher*
Boué, Daniel Robert *pediatric pathologist, neuropathologist, educator*
Boyd, Richard Nelson *physics educator*
†Boyle, Kevin Gerard *historian, educator*
†Bradley, Jennette *lieutenant governor*
Brandes, Marciana Watson *civic worker*
Branscomb, Lewis Capers, Jr., *librarian, educator*
Bridgman, G(eorge) Ross *lawyer*
Brinkman, Dale Thomas *lawyer*
Brodkey, Robert Stanley *chemical engineering educator*
†Brooke, John L. *history educator*
Brooks, Richard Dickinson *lawyer*
Brown, Herbert Russell *lawyer, writer*
Brown, Rowland Chauncey Widrig *information systems, strategic planning and ethics consultant*
Brubaker, Robert Loring *lawyer*
Buchenroth, Stephen Richard *lawyer*
Buchsieb, Walter Charles *orthodontist, director*
Burke, Kenneth Andrew *advertising executive*
Caldwell, Charles M. *federal judge*
Calhoun, Donald Eugene, Jr., *federal judge*
†Campanizzi, Jane *consulting company executive*
Capen, Charles Chabert *veterinary pathology educator*
Carnahan, John Anderson *lawyer*
†Carpenter, Michael H. *lawyer*
†Carr, Michele Paige *dental hygienist, educator*
Carter, Cheryl A. *endoscopy nurse*
Casey, John Frederick *lawyer*
Catalyurek, Umit Veysel *computer engineer, researcher*
Chandrasekaran, Balakrishnan *computer and information science educator*
Chappelear, Stephen Eric *lawyer*
Charles, Bertram *radio broadcasting executive*
Charles, Gerard *performing company executive, choreographer*
Chavers, Dane Carroll *lawyer*

Schuller, David Edward *cancer center administrator, otolaryngologist*
†Schumacher, Douglass William *physicist*
†Schwartz, Robert S. *lawyer*
Selby, Diane Ray Miller *fraternal organization administrator*
†Selcer, David Mark *lawyer*
Sellers, Barbara Jackson *federal judge*
Senhauser, Donald A(lbert) *pathologist, educator*
Sestina, John E. *financial planner*
†Shapiro, Charles Louis *physician*
Sharp, Paul David *institute administrator*
†Shayne, Stanley H. *lawyer*
Sherrill, Thomas Boykin, III, *retired newspaper publishing executive*
Shipley, Martha Theresa *social worker, educational and program consultant*
Siciliani, Alessandro Domenico *conductor*
Sidman, Robert John *lawyer*
Silbajoris, Frank Rimvydas *Slavic languages educator*
Sims, Richard Lee *hospital administrator*
Simson, Bevlyn *artist*
Singh, Rajendra *mechanical engineering educator*
†Sites, Richard Loren *lawyer, educator*
Smith, Ann Marie *rehabilitation nurse*
Smith, George Curtis *judge*
Smith, Philip John *industrial and systems engineering educator*
Smith, Robert Phillip *poet*
Snyder, Susan Leach *science educator, writer*
Sokolov, Howard H. *psychiatrist*
Soloway, Albert Herman *medicinal chemist*
Solso, Theodore M. *manufacturing executive*
Speck, Samuel Wallace, Jr., *state official*
Speicher, Carl Eugene *pathologist*
Sporleder, Thomas Lynn *economist, researcher*
Stansbery, David Honor *ecologist*
†Stanton, Elizabeth McCool *lawyer*
Staten, Beverly Janet *political action administrator*
Stephan, Alexander Friedrich *German language and literature educator*
Stephens, Sheryl Lynne *family practice physician*
Stephens, Thomas M(aron) *education educator*
Stern, Geoffrey *lawyer, disciplinary counsel*
Stevenson, Robert Benjamin, III, *prosthodontist, writer*
Stewart, Mac A. *educator*
Stinehart, Roger Ray *lawyer*
†Stoner, Gary David *cancer researcher*
†Stover, Stephan Wallace *lawyer, state agency administrator*
Studer, William Joseph *library educator*
†Stull, Gary Evan *secondary school educator, writer*
Sullivan, Ernest Lee *human resources director*
Sunami, John Soichi *designer*
Sweeney, Asher William *state supreme court justice*
Sweeney, Francis E. *state supreme court justice*
Taft, Bob *governor*
Taft, Sheldon Ashley *lawyer*
Taggart, Thomas Michael *lawyer*
Taiganides, E. Paul *agricultural and environmental engineer, consultant*
Tait, Robert E. *lawyer*
Tarpy, Thomas Michael *lawyer*
Taylor, Celianna Isley *information systems specialist*
Taylor, Joel Sanford *retired lawyer*
Thomas, Duke Winston *lawyer*
†Thomas, M. Carolyn *theology studies educator*
†Thompson, Linda Lezius *foundation administrator, consultant*
Tipton, Clyde Raymond, Jr., *communications and resources development consultant*
Todd, William Michael *lawyer*
Tollifson, Thomas Gerald *retired art education consultant, teacher*
Triplehorn, Charles A. *entomology educator, insects curator*
†Tripodi, Tony *social work educator, author, editor*
Tsao, Chang Yong *pediatric neurologist*
Tuckman, Bruce Wayne *educational psychologist, educator, researcher*
Turano, David A. *lawyer*
Turnbull, Robert George *philosopher, educator*
Tyack, Thomas Michael *lawyer*
Tybout, Richard Alton *economics educator*
Tzagournis, Manuel *physician, educator, university administrator*
Uotila, Urho Antti Kalevi *geodesist, educator*
Varga, Steven Carl *human resources professional*
Vassell, Gregory S. *electric utility consultant*
Vermilyea, Stanley George *prosthodontist, educator*
Viezer, Timothy Wayne *economist, investment company executive*
Vogel, Thomas Timothy *surgeon, health care consultant, lay church worker*
Volakis, John Leonidas *engineering educator*
von Recum, Andreas F. *veterinarian, bioengineer*
Vorys, Arthur Isaiah *lawyer*
Voss, Anne Coble *nutritional biochemist*
Voss, Jerrold Richard *city planner, educator, university official*
Wachtmann, Lynn R. *state legislator*
Wagner, Robert Walter *photography, cinema and communications educator, media producer, consultant*
Wali, Mohan Kishen *environmental science and natural resources educator*
†Wang, Deliang *computer scientist, educator*
†Wang, Tianshu *music educator*
Ware, Brendan John *retired electrical engineer and utility executive*
Warmbrod, Catharine Phelps *educational researcher, consultant*
Warmbrod, James Robert *agriculture educator, university administrator*
Warner, Charles Collins *lawyer*
Watson, John Allan *clergyman*
†Wee, Alvin Gerard *dental educator*
Weinhold, Virginia Beamer *interior designer*
Weisberg, Herbert Frank *political science educator*
Wexner, Leslie Herbert *retail executive*
Whipps, Edward Franklin *lawyer*
†White, Dennis L. *political organization administrator*
†White, Doug *state legislator*
Whitlatch, Elbert Earl, Jr., *engineering educator, consultant*
Wightman, Alec *lawyer*
Wigington, Ronald Lee *retired chemical information services executive*
Wilhelmy, Odin, Jr., *insurance agent*
Wilkins, John Warren *physics educator*
Willcox, Roderick Harrison *lawyer*
Willke, Thomas Aloys *university official, statistics educator*
Wiseman, Randolph Carson *lawyer*
Wojcicki, Andrew Adalbert *chemist, educator*
Wolf, J(ohn) Steven *construction executive, land developer*
Wolper, Beatrice Emens *lawyer*
Wood, Jackie Dale *physiologist, educator, researcher*
†Xie, Chunlei *applied mechanics researcher*
†Yancey-Jones, Floristine Darlene *artist, educator*
Yeazel, Keith Arthur *lawyer*
Yenkin, Bernard Kalman *coatings and resins company executive*
Yohn, David Stewart *virologist, science administrator*
Young, Thomas Beetham *writer*
Zakin, Jacques Louis *chemical engineering educator*
Zambito, John R. *executive search firm executive*
Zapp, David Edwin *infosystems specialist, investment consultant*
Zartman, David Lester *animal sciences educator, researcher*
Zhao, Fang Li *medical researcher*
Zhu, Xiankui *mechanical engineer, researcher*
Zweben, Stuart Harvey *information scientist, educator*

Columbus Grove
Thiede, Richard Wesley *retired communications educator*

Concord
†Kushalkumar, M. Baid *chemical engineer*

Conneaut
Strawbridge, Mary Elizabeth *English educator*

Continental
Dranchak, Lawrence John *retired mechanical engineer*

Copley
Cox, Hillery Lee *retired primary school educator*
Hayasi, Nisiki *physicist, applied mathematician, business executive, inventor*
Smith, Joan H. *retired women's health nurse, educator*

Cuyahoga Falls
†Barsan, Robert Blake *dentist*
Black, Ross R., II, *family physician*
Haag, Everett Keith *architect*
Hamilton, Donald Dow Webb *publisher, freelance writer*
Harr, Jeffrey Alan *secondary school educator*
Jones, John Frank *retired lawyer*
Moses, Abe Joseph *international financial consultant*
Shane, Sandra Kuli *postal service administrator*
Smith, Margaret A. (Maggie Carroll Smith) *community volunteer*

Dayton
Alexander, Roberta Sue *history educator*
Allen, Rose Letitia *special education educator*
Anderson, Charles Austin *judge*
†Atkins, Laura Jane *music educator*
Battino, Rubin *chemistry educator, retired*
Betz, Eugene William *architect*
Bienenfeld, David Gerald *physician*
Blaschak, Thomas R. *lawyer*
Bogner, Fred Karl *civil engineering educator*
Boyle, John Robert *internist*
†Bridgman, Susan R. *tax lawyer*
Burick, Lawrence T. *lawyer*
Calico, Robert A. *dean*
Cannon, Cris A. *protective services official*
Carmody, Thomas James *cardiologist*
Carson, Richard McKee *chemical engineer*
Carter, Harold Lloyd *secondary education educator*
Carver, Todd B. *corporate lawyer, law professor*
Chema, Susan Russell *lawyer*
Chen, Chenggang *research scientist*
Chung, Soon Myoung *computer scientist, educator*
Clark, William Alfred *federal judge*
Colle, Herbert A. *psychologist, educator*
Conway, Mark Allyn *lawyer*
Cowden, Roger Hugh, II, *systems engineer*
†Crosby, Lynn A. *orthopaedic surgeon, educator*
Crowe, Shelby *educational specialist, consultant*
Ctvrtnicek, Scarlett Jane *physician assistant*
Daley, Robert Emmett *retired foundation executive*
Daoud, George Jamil *hotel and motel consultant*
Darst, Betty Jane *historian, educator*
Delgado, Clara S. *English language education specialist*
Deutsch, David M. *lawyer*
†Diggs, Matthew O'Brien, Jr., *air conditioning and refrigeration manufacturing executive*
Duncan, Richard Leo *communications educator*
Dushkina, Natalia Mitkova *physicist, researcher*
Duval, Daniel Webster *manufacturing company executive*
Elliott, Daniel Whitacre *surgeon, retired educator*
Elliott, Scott Emory *reporter*
Emrick, Donald Day *chemist, consultant*
†Farmer, Linda L. *philosophy educator*
†Farquhar, Robert Nichols *lawyer*
Faruki, Charles Joseph *lawyer*
†Gaines, Elliot *communications educator*
Garcia, Oscar Nicolas *computer science educator*
Gillen, Patrick Bernard *nurse*
Gillig, Paulette Marie *psychiatry educator, researcher*
Goelz, Robert Dean *lawyer*
Goldenberg, Kim *academic administrator, internist*
Gregor, Clunie Bryan *geology educator*
Hadley, Lawrence Hamilton *economics educator*
Hadley, Robert James *lawyer*
Hamlin, Tom *sportscaster*
Harden, Oleta Elizabeth *English educator, university administrator*
Haritos, Mary J. *language educator, interpreter*
Harlan, Norman Ralph *construction executive*
Hayes, Stephen Kurtz *writer*
Heil, Michael Lloyd *military officer, academic administrator*
†Heller, Abraham *psychiatrist, educator*
Henley, Terry Lew *computer company executive*
Heyman, Ralph Edmond *lawyer*
Hitch, David Charles *pediatric surgeon*
Hoge, Franz Joseph *accounting firm executive*
Holz, Michael Harold *lawyer*
Houpis, Constantine Harry *electrical engineering educator*
Huang, Mei Qing *physics educator, researcher*
†Hurd, Mark V. *manufacturing executive*
Isaacson, Milton Stanley (Jim Isaacson) *research and development company executive, engineer*
Janning, John Louis *research scientist, consultant*
Jelus, Susan Crum *writer, editor*
Jenefsky, Jack *wholesale company executive*
Jenks, Thomas Edward *lawyer*
Johnson, C. Terry *lawyer*
†Kanet, John Joseph *management educator*
†Kay, Jerald *psychiatry educator, researcher*
Kazimierczuk, Marian Kazimierczuk *electrical engineer, educator*
Kegerreis, Robert James *management consultant, marketing educator*
Khalimsky, Efim *mathematics and computer science educator*
Kinlin, Donald James *lawyer*
Kiser, Sharon Ann *health facility professional*
Klein, Sophia H. *entrepreneur*
Klinck, Cynthia Anne *library director*
†Kloppenberg, Lisa A. *law educator*
Knapp, James Ian Keith *judge*
Koeller, Jean Martha *artist, librarian*
†Koeller, Lynn Garver *public defender*
Krebs, Leo Francis *lawyer*
Kumar, Binod *materials engineer, educator*
Ladehoff, Leo William *metal products manufacturing executive*
Lamb, Rebecca Ann *software engineer, educator*
Lashley, William Bartholomew *county official*
Lasley, Thomas J., II, *education educator*
Lee, Sung Ho *psychiatrist*
Leigh, Gloria Lorraine *retired religious studies educator*
Leung, Jackson Yi-Shun *music educator*
Lockhart, Gregory Gordon *prosecutor*
Lyman, John Leslie *emergency physician*
Macklin, Crofford Johnson, Jr., *lawyer*
Mandrell, Gene Douglas *retired management consultant*
Martin, Herbert Woodward *English educator, poet*
Matheny, Ruth Ann *editor*
Mathews, David *foundation executive*
†Mathile, Clayton Lee *pet food company executive*
McDonald, Bronce William *community activist, advocate*
McWhorter, Stanley Bruce *English educator, researcher*
Meister, Mark Jay *museum director, professional society administrator*
Merz, Michael *federal judge*
Mick, Thomas Charles *radiologist*
Mohler, Stanley Ross *physician, educator*
Monk, Susan Marie *physician, pediatrician*
†Mukhopadhyay, Sharmila Mitra *materials engineer, educator*
†Mullinix, Susan Carlock *musician, educator*
Nanagas, Maria Teresita Cruz *pediatrician, educator*
†Nauman, Joseph George *lawyer*
Nielsen, Philip Edward *physicist, research manager*
Nixon, Charles William *acoustician*
Nyberg, Lars *former electronics company executive*
Nyerges, Alexander Lee *museum director*
O'Malley, Patricia *critical care nurse*
Owens, Mark Ernest *lawyer, legal administrator*
†Pacernick, Gary B. *literature educator, poet*
Part, Howard M. *dean*
Pasupuleti, Venumadhav *business executive, consultant*
†Petrick, Joseph Anthony *small business owner, management consultant, educator*
Petzold, John Paul *judge*
Pflum, Barbara Ann *pediatric allergist*
Phillips, Chandler Allen *biomedical/human factors engineer*
Ponitz, David H. *former academic administrator*
Ponitz, Doris Humes *volunteer*
Posey, Terry Wayne *lawyer*
Pringle, Mary Beth *English language educator, writer*
†Rambo, James Edmondson *lawyer*
Randall, Vernellia *lawyer, nurse, educator*
Rapp, Gerald Duane *lawyer, manufacturing company executive*
Reading, Anthony John *business executive, accountant*
Reid, Marilyn Joanne *state legislator, lawyer*
Repperger, Daniel William *electrical engineer*
Riley, David Richard *management consultant, retired military officer*
Roberts, Brian Michael *lawyer*
Rogers, Richard Hunter *lawyer, business executive*
†Rucker, Mary L *communications educator*
Rucker, Richard S. *information systems executive*
Ruegsegger, Donald Ray, Jr., *radiological physicist, educator*
Saul, Irving Isaac *lawyer*
Schmitt, George Frederick, Jr., *materials engineer*
Schneble, Alfred William, III, *lawyer*
Siefert, David Michael *information technology executive, manufacturing executive*
Singhvi, Surendra Singh *finance and strategy consultant*
†Snively, Ann Wilson *librarian, researcher*
Soon, Boon Yi *engineer*
Staker, Robert Dale *cost analyst, computer scientist, biologist, educator*
Stefanics, Charlotte Louise *retired mental health nurse*
†Stout, Donald Everett *real estate developer, environmental preservationist*
Taronji, Jaime, Jr., *lawyer*
†Tatar, Jerome F. *business products executive*
Taylor, Elisabeth Coler *retired secondary school educator*
Thomas, Marianna *volunteer community activist, writer, speaker*
†Tian, Mei *mathematician, educator*
Tillson, John Bradford (Brad), Jr., *newspaper publisher*
Trivedi, Hitesh K. *research scientist*
Tweel, Donna Shank *lawyer*
Uphoff, James Kent *education educator*
†Vaughn, Noel Wyandt *lawyer*
Versic, Linda Joan *nurse educator, research company executive*
Vice, Roy Lee *history educator*
Wagner, Samuel, V, *secondary school English language educator, college counselor*
Walters, Jefferson Brooks *musician, retired real estate broker*
Walusis, Eric Michael *product developer, consultant*
†Wasson, Steven *music educator, piano technician*
Watts, Steven Richard *lawyer*
Weathington, Billy Christopher *analytical chemist*
Weinberg, Sylvan Lee *cardiologist, educator, author, editor*
Welly, Michael Anthony *elementary school educator*
†Wentz, Charlotte Marie *retired librarian*
Wertz, Kenneth Dean *real estate executive*
Williams, Charles Vernon, III, *education administrator*
Williams, Michael Alan *psychologist*
Williams, Walker Richard, Jr., *social services administrator*
Wilson, William Campbell McFarland *gastroenterologist*
Wyllie, Stanley Clarke *retired librarian*
Zahner, Mary Anne *art educator*
†Zhan, Qiwen *education educator, consultant*

Defiance
Fout, Larry Roy *physician*

Delaware
Arnold, Jay *retired engineering executive, educator*
†Carpenter, Lynette *language educator*
Courtice, Thomas Barr *academic administrator*
Eells, William Hastings *retired automobile company executive*
Faerber, Abigail Hobbs *physician, farm manager*
Fry, Anne Evans *zoology educator*
Hamre, Gary Leslie William *entrepreneur*
Huml, Donald Scott *manufacturing company executive*
†Iverson, Louis Robert *research ecologist*
Jamison, Roger W. *pianist, piano educator*
Lattimore, Vergel Lyronne *minister, educator, counselor*
Lewes, Ulle Erika *English educator*
Pettigrew, Carolyn Landers *theological school official, minister*
†Remlinger, Rolf *music educator, cartoonist*
Schlichting, Catherine Fletcher Nicholson *librarian, educator*

Delphos
†Stearns, David Allen *music educator*

Delta
Miller, Beverly White *past college president, education consultation*

Dover
Miller, Mary Katherine *management consultant*

Dublin
Baker, Mary Evelyn *retired librarian*
Bordelon, Carolyn Thew *elementary school educator*
†Borror, Douglas G. *construction company executive*
Brooks, Keith *retired speech communication educator*
†Clement, Henry Joseph, Jr., *diversified building products executive*
Coco, Mark Steven *lawyer*
Conrad, Marian Sue (Susan Conrad) *special education educator*
†Farrell, Clifford Michael *lawyer*
Freytag, Donald Ashe *management consultant*
†Gray, James H., Jr., *music educator*
Inzetta, Mark Stephen *lawyer*
†Kramb, Amy Lynn *environmentalist*
Lamp, Benson J. *tractor company executive*
†Lane, James Edward *retired lawyer, consultant*
Laurence, Amy Rebecca *music educator, composer*
†Ma, Hengwei *music educator*

GEOGRAPHICAL INDEX 6035 OHIO

Major, Coleman Joseph *chemical engineer*
Maloon, Jerry L. *trial lawyer, physician, medico legal consultant*
McCauley, William Albert *business executive*
†Meyer, Betty Jane *former librarian*
Miller, Charles *business management market research consultant*
Miller, Richard J. *wholesale pharmaceutical distribution company executive*
Needham, George Michael *association executive*
Rasheed, Khalid *business executive*
Sheffer, Brent Alan *lawyer*
Smith, K(ermit) Wayne *computer company executive*
Spies, Phyllis Bova *information services company executive*
Stratton, James Edward *retired construction educator*
Tenuta, Luigia *lawyer*
Walter, Robert D. *wholesale pharmaceutical distribution executive*
Wang, Andrew Hsing-Jen *information marketing executive, journalist, librarian*

East Cleveland
†Linderman, Eric Graham *librarian*
Soule, Lucile Snyder *pianist, music educator*

East Liverpool
Feldman, Marvin Herschel *financial consultant*
Gailey, Joan Dale *retired finance educator*
Swartz, Patti Capel *literature educator*

East Palestine
Patterson, Paula Jeanne *secondary education educator*
Rohrbaugh, Lisa Anne *librarian*

Eastlake
Spohn, Wayne Robert *mechanical engineer*

Eaton
Kendall, Susan Haines *library director*
Thomas, James William *lawyer*

Edgerton
Wu, Lawrence Mg Hla Myin *physician*

Elida
†Dicke, Candice Edwards *library educator*

Elmore
Huizenga, Georgiana R. *public library director, storyteller*

Elyria
Bonnell-Mihalis, Pamela Gay *library director*
Coleman, D. Christian *journalist*
Dunaevsky, Valery *mechanical engineer, researcher*
Manner, Jennifer Fouse *social worker*
Patton, Thomas James *sales and marketing executive*

Enon
Whitlock, David C. *retired military officer*

Euclid
Dallos, Joseph *general contractor, remodeler*
Keay, Charles Lloyd *elementary school educator*
Obloy, Leonard Gerard *priest*
†Powaski, Ronald E. *education educator, writer*

Euclid Ave
†Simpfendorfer, Conrad Carlos *cardiologist*

Fairborn
Byczkowski, Janusz Zbigniew *toxicologist*
Conklin, Robert Eugene *electronics engineer*
Kingston, David L. *retired physicist*
Mayer, Michael A. *lawyer, educator*
Miles, David R. *lawyer*
†Moore, Margaret Anne *retired civilian military employee*
Nowak, John Michael *retired air force officer, company executive*
Russell-Rader, Kathleen *secondary school educator*
Shevin, David A. *English literature educator*

Fairfield
Cutter, John Michael *dentist*
Goodman, Myrna Marcia *school nurse*
Gruenwald, James Howard *association executive, consultant*
Rafalowski, Raymond Victor *printing and publishing executive*
†Walsh, Thomas James *environmental engineer, consultant*

Fairlawn
Brubaker, Karen Sue *small business owner*
France, Dorothy Daniel *minister*
Kurzweil, Alan Dennis *social worker, marriage and family therapist, consultant*

Fairview Park
Bellamy, John Stark, II, *librarian*
†Flynn, Patricia M. *director, special education educator, gifted and talented educator*
Kothari, Purnima *obstetrician/gynecologist*

Findlay
†Benedict, A. Joan *music educator*
†Dattilo, Thomas A. *diversified corporation executive*
Fry, Charles George *theologian, educator*
†Hanson, David Alan *music educator*
Jetton, Girard Reuel, Jr., *lawyer, retired oil company executive*
Kentris, George Lawrence *lawyer*
Kline, James Edward *lawyer*
Norris, Neal Albert *academic administrator*
Peters, Milton Eugene *educational psychologist*
Rakestraw, Gregory Allen *lawyer*
Reamsnyder, Margaret Elizabeth *nurse*
Resseguie, James Lynn *theology educator*

Stephani, Nancy Jean *social worker, journalist*
Wilkin, Richard Edwin *clergyman, religious organization executive*
Williams, Kathy Margene *real estate broker*
Yammine, Riad Nassif *retired oil company executive*

Franklin
Foley, Harriet Elizabeth *retired school librarian*
Wilkey, Mary Huff *investor, writer, publisher*

Fredericktown
Boyd, Donald Edgar *artist, educator*

Fremont
Albrechta, Joseph Francis *lawyer*
Wethington, Norbert Anthony *medieval scholar*

Gahanna
Breen, John Wakefield *personnel services company executive*
†Douglas, James (Buster) *boxer*
Kaye, Gail Leslie *healthcare consultant, educator*
Robbins, Darryl Andrew *pediatrician*
†Sherman, Ruth Todd *government advisor, counselor, consultant*

Gainesville
†Blue, Beth-Anne *psychologist, writer*

Galion
Butterfield, James T. *small business owner*
Cobey, Ralph *industrialist*

Gallipolis
†Ferguson, A. H. *poet, medical/surgical nurse*
Niehm, Bernard Frank *mental health center administrator, retired*
Wilcox, Victoria Lynn *nurse*

Galloway
Barner, Bruce Monroe *former state agency administrator, not-for-profit company chairman*
†Ghosh, Sanjib Kumar *retired science educator, consultant*

Gambier
Leech, Charles Russell, Jr., *lawyer*
†McNair, Glenn Maurice *historian, educator*
†Nugent, S. Georgia *academic administrator*
†Shutt, Timothy Baker *humanities educator, writer*

Garfield Heights
Chamberlin, Joan Mary *school system administrator*
Demer, Margaret Elizabeth *lawyer*

Garrettsville
Diskin, Michael Edward *plastics industry executive, food service executive*

Gates Mills
Abbott, James Samuel, III, *marketing executive*
Altman, Leslie Joan *secondary school educator*
Enyedy, Gustav, Jr., *chemical engineer*
O'Malley, Mary Kay *elementary education educator*
Pace, Stanley Carter *retired aeronautical engineer*
Reitman, Robert Stanley *business consultant, nonprofit agency advisor*
Schanfarber, Richard Carl *real estate broker*
Veale, Tinkham, II, *former chemical company executive, engineer*

Geneva
†Carrel, Marianne Eileen *music educator*
Clement, Daniel Roy, IV, *accountant, assistant nurse, small business owner, tax preparation consultant*
Epstein, Sherry Stein *lawyer*

Georgetown
Conway, Dorothy Jean Williams *economist*

Germantown
Lansaw, Charles Ray *rendering industry executive*

Glendale
Strom, Kristina Chase *writer, consultant*

Granville
Bonar, Daniel Donald *mathematics educator*
Haubrich, Robert Rice *biology educator*
Kerens, Steven Robert *real estate executive*
†Knobel, Dale Thomas *history educator, university administrator*
Lisska, Anthony Joseph *humanities educator, philosopher*
Santoni, Ronald Ernest *philosophy educator*
Vogel, Steven Michael *philosopher, educator*
Woodyard, David Oliver *religious studies educator, clergy member*

Greentown
†Pipes, Randy Paul *minister, church administrator*

Greenville
Alexander, Paul Richard *illustrator*
Franz, Daniel Thomas *financial planner*

Grove City
Hosler, Elizabeth *management consultant*
Jackson, Steven Donald *English educator*
Kilman, James William *surgeon, educator*
Kimethu, Susan Wanja *computer specialist, database manager*
Lok, Silmond Ray *pharmaceutical executive*
Purdy, Dennis Gene *insurance company executive, education consultant*
†Traini, Thomas Albert *music educator*

Groveport
Reed, Roger Duane *maintenance electrician*

Hamilton
Bressler, H.J. *lawyer, judge*
Cantrell, Joseph Sires *chemistry educator*
Epp, Mary Elizabeth *technologies consultant*
Fein, Linda Ann *nurse anesthetist, consultant*
Fein, Thomas Paul *software support specialist*
Glass, Robert Edward *retired music educator*
Johnson, Pauline Benge *nurse, anesthetist*
Jones, Rick H. *arts administrator*
New, Rosetta Holbrock *home economics educator, nutrition consultant*
†Olivas, Adolf *lawyer, mayor*
†Pollack, Frederic S. *mathematician, educator*
Ridner, Melanie Marie *writer, composer*
Royer, Diana Amelia *educator*
Willke, Thomas John *family physician*
Womack, Whitney Ayn *English and American literature educator*

Harrison
Jones, Hobert W. *health physics and radiochemistry consultant*
Kocher, Juanita Fay *retired auditor*

Hartville
†Hazlett, George Alvin *minister, mediator*
†McPherson, James Willis, Jr., *retired lawyer*

Hebron
Slater, Wanda Marie Worth *property manager*

Helena
Moss, Clifton Michael *factory laborer, small business owner*

Highland Heights
Shumate, Minerva *risk management analyst*

Highland Hills
†Sender, Maryann *director*

Hilliard
†Brown, Dale *electronics executive*
Cupp, David Foster *photographer, journalist*
†Herta, Bryan *race car driver*
Price, Virginia Ashbaugh *technical service director, workers compensation c*
Relle, Attila Tibor *dentist*
Skillman, Thomas Grant *endocrinology consultant, former educator*

Hillsboro
Carson, Jean Hopkins Kessel *civic worker*
†Coss, Rocky Alan *lawyer*

Hiram
Bane, James Wallace *music educator*
Oliver, G(eorge) Benjamin *educational administrator, philosophy educator*

Holland
Conlin, Thomas *conductor*
D'Anniballe-Holdren, Priscilla Lucille *contracting company executive*
Sacksteder, Thomas Michael *corporate executive, entrepreneur, writer*

Howard
Lee, William Johnson *lawyer*

Hubbard
Trucksis, Theresa A. *retired library director*

Huber Heights
Panayirci, Sharon Lorraine *textiles executive, design engineer*

Hudson
Antonucci, Ron *librarian, editor*
Ashcroft, Richard Carter *investment company executive*
Carducci, Judith Weeks Barker *artist, former social worker*
Duchon, Roseann Marie *business owner, consultant*
Elliott, Frances Carano *lawyer, educator*
Galloway, Ethan Charles *technology development executive, former chemicals executive*
Goheen, Janet Moore *counselor, sales professional*
Kempe, Robert Aron *venture management executive*
†Pollino, Sandra Michelle *psychotherapist, educator*
Sorgi, Mercedes Prieto *psychologist*
Stec, John Zygmunt *real estate executive*
†Szefcyk, Renee Marie *financial services executive*
Wooldredge, William Dunbar *health facility administrator*

Huron
Round, Alice Faye Bruce *school psychologist*

Independence
Boyle, Kammer *estate planner, financial analyst*
Frisman, Roger Lawrence *industrial sales executive*
Meredith, Thomas Brian *healthcare consultant*
Schwallie, Daniel Phillip *legal consultant*
Van Kirk, Robert John *nursing case manager, educator*

Ironton
†Allen, Craig Adams *lawyer, director*
Collier, James Bruce *lawyer*
†Crawford, James G. *director*
Cremeans, James L. *minister*
†Curry, Estella Roberta *education educator, consultant*
†Kadim, Satyanarayana Venkata *cardiologist*

Jackson
Benson, Steven Clark *management and engineering executive*

Lewis, Richard M. *lawyer*
Moore, Jimmie Lee *accountant*

Jackson Center
Thompson, Wade Francis Bruce *manufacturing company executive*

Jefferson
Geary, Michael Philip *lawyer*
Lemire, Jerome Albert *lawyer, geologist*
Macklin, Martin Rodbell *psychiatrist*

Kent
Aro, Ants Gustaf *manufacturing executive*
†Bansal, Arvind Kumar *computer scientist, educator*
Beer, Barrett Lynn *historian*
†Biordi, Diana L. *healthcare educator, dean*
Bissler, Richard Thomas *mortician*
†Boczek, Boleslaw Adam *retired law educator*
Buttlar, Rudolph Otto *retired college dean*
†Chism, Rebecca Lynn *language educator*
Cielinski-Kessler, Audrey Ann *technical writer, publisher, small business owner*
Cooperrider, Tom S. *botanist, educator*
Dutta, Hiran Moyee *biologist, educator*
Feinberg, Richard *anthropologist, educator*
Ference-Valenta, Mary Jean *osteopath, health facility administrator*
Gaston, Paul Lee *academic administrator, language educator*
Hassler, Donald Mackey, II, *English language educator, writer*
†House-Soremekun, Bessie *political science educator*
Juvan, Dennis Paul *securities trader*
Kasten, Wendy Christina *literacy educator, writer, consultant*
Kluth, Frederick John *computer consultant, artist*
Kwong, Eva *artist, educator*
†Lilly, Erica Barditch *academic librarian*
Los, Cornelis Albertus *financial economist, portfolio risk manager, educator*
†McCormick, Edgar Lindsley *education educator, writer*
McKee, David Lannen *economics educator*
Muñoz, Willy Oscar *language educator, researcher*
Myers, R(alph) Thomas *chemist, educator*
Neal-Barnett, Angela Marie *psychology educator*
†Neiderman, Beverly Ann *literature educator*
Nome, William Andreas *lawyer*
†Odell-Scott, David Winfield *education educator*
Prioleau, Darwin E. *dance educator, choreographer*
Qi, Min *economics educator*
†Reed, Beverly Marie *mathematician, educator*
Reid, S.W. *English educator*
Remley, R. Dirk *English educator, consultant*
†Seed, Alexander John *science educator*
Sommers, David Lynn *architect*
†Springer, Barbara Hipsman *journalism educator*
†Tiene, Drew *communications educator, consultant*
Tuan, Debbie Fu-Tai *chemistry educator*
Varga, Richard Steven *mathematics educator*
Williams, Harold Roger *economist, educator*
Zornow, William Frank *historian, educator*

Kenton
Petty, Sue Wright *library director*
Tudor, John Martin *lawyer, educator*

Kettering
Collins, Jo Anne Dilworth *secondary school educator*
Denlinger, Vicki Lee *secondary school physical education educator*
Eubank, David Lynn *lawyer, consultant*
†Fox, Allan B. *literature educator*
Hoffman, Sue Ellen *elementary education educator*
Martin, Margaret Gately *elementary school educator*
†Nuzzi, Ronald James *priest, educator*
Porter, Walter Arthur *retired judge*

Kirtland
†Armstrong, William Allen *mathematician, educator, textbook writer*
†Brown, Robert Loran *music educator*
Hess, Teresa *fine arts educator*
Johnston, Stanley Howard, Jr., *rare books curator, bibliographer*
†Petrone, John R. *music educator, composer*
Ryan, William Joseph *multimedia and distance education designer, information technology executive*
Skubby, Christopher Daniel *political science educator, social sciences educator, department chairman*

Lafayette
Dellifield, Dennis L. *conductor*

Lake Milton
Healy, Joanne P. *accounting educator*

Lakeside
Mead, Millard Wilmer *retired minister*

Lakeside Marblehead
Garrow, Robert Joseph, Jr., *mathematician, educator*
Haering, Edwin Raymond *chemical engineering educator, consultant*

Lakewood
Baxter, Howard H. *retired lawyer*
Burton, Kathleen T. *mental health services professional*
Cochran, Earl Vernon *retired manufacturing company executive*
Condon, George Edward *journalist*
†Fortunato, Christopher R. *lawyer*
Hunter, Sally Irene *interior designer*

†Olson, Carol Joan *foundation administrator, consultant*
†Pecot, Mark Andre *education educator*
Sherry, Paul Henry *minister, religious organization administrator*

Lancaster
†Crandall, Margaret Elizabeth *editor*
Katlic, John Edward *management consultant*
Libert, Donald Joseph *lawyer*
Phillips, Edward John *consulting firm executive*
Sulick, Robert John *general contractor*
Varney, Richard Alan *medical center administrator*
Voss, Jack Donald *international business consultant, lawyer*
Woodward, James Kenneth *retired pharmacologist*
†Young, Paul Garlin *principal*

Lebanon
Baldwin, James Edward *lawyer, city administrator*
Coyan, Michael Lee *art and performing arts educator*
Osborne, Quinton Albert *psychiatric social worker, inspector of institutional services*

Lewis Center
Ball, Kay Atkinson *health services consultant*
Strip, Carol Ann *gifted education specialist, educator*

Lexington
†Maxwell, Mark *music educator*

Liberty Township
Conditt, Margaret Karen *research scientist, policy analyst*

Lima
Becker, Dwight Lowell *physician*
Casey, Rebecca Lynn *music educator*
Collins, William Thomas *retired pathologist*
†Grim, Brian Keith *music educator*
Helser, Marilyn A. *business educator*
Jacobs, Ann Elizabeth *lawyer*
†Lause, Sean Maxim *language educator*
Miller, Roy Raymond *optician, oculist*
Norton, Holly Louise *English literature educator*
Palmer, Arthur Eugene *retired nursing home administrator*
Pranses, Anthony Louis *retired electric company executive, organization executive*
Robenalt, John Alton *lawyer*
Roller, Duane Williamson *archaeologist, educator*

Lisbon
Dailey, Coleen Hall *magistrate, lawyer*

Little Hocking
Corbin, David P. *counselor*

Logan
Carmean, Jerry Richard *broadcast engineer*
Conner, Leland Lavon *Indian lorist*
Kernen, Will *lawyer*
Yeagley, Kathleen Lux *community health nurse, educator*

London
Hughes, Clyde Matthew *religious denomination executive*
Lloyd, John *composer, educator*

Lorain
Bado, Kenneth Steve *automotive company administrator*
Brownson, Roger James *university official, photographer*
†Comer, Brenda Warmee *educator, real estate company executive*
†Mumford, Beverly Jean *paralegal*
Trelka, Janice Margaret Nace *retired secondary school educator*
Tucker, Thomas Edward *music educator*
†Wiersma, David Charles *lawyer*

Loveland
Dalambakis, Christopher A. *sales executive*
Grimmet, Alex J. *clergyman, school administrator, elementary and secondary education educator*
Neidhart, Carol Lynn *pharmaceutical company official*
Newton, Baldwin Charles *artist, educator*
Paul, Jerome L. *mathematician, educator*

Lucasville
†Crotty, Ladonna Deane *librarian*
Reno, Ottie Wayne *former judge*

Lyndhurst
Dellas, Marie C. *retired psychology educator and consultant*
Packer, Diana *retired reference librarian*

Lyons
†Myers, John William *minister, poet, editor, publisher*

Madison
Stafford, Arthur Charles *medical association administrator*

Maineville
Cook, Janice Eleanor Nolan *retired elementary school educator*

Malta
Peyton, Sharon Anne Reed *geriatrics nurse*

Malvern
†Crum, Clarence F. *music educator, school system administrator*

Mansfield
Adair, Charles Valloyd *retired physician*
Ash, Thomas Phillip *superintendent of schools*
Bernhardt, Carol Ann *musician, educator*
Burnell, Elvin Wallace *industrial engineer, security specialist*
Capaldo, Guy *obstetrician, gynecologist*
Crittenden, Sophie Marie *communications executive*
†Dudley, Kenneth Eugene *manufacturing company executive*
†Ellis, Mark Carlton *music educator*
Gibson, David Mark *biochemist, educator*
Gorman, James Carvill *pump manufacturing company executive*
Gregory, Deirdre Dianne *secondary educator*
Gregory, Thomas Bradford *mathematics educator*
Houston, William Robert Montgomery *ophthalmic surgeon*
Hussain, Nayyer *economics educator*
Miller, Kenneth William, II, *research and development engineering executive*
†Mitchell, Sheron Lynn *music educator*
Pesec, David John *data systems executive*
Riedl, John Orth *university dean*
Shah, James M. *actuary*
Sheridan, Mark William *mechanical engineer, strategic planner*
Shook, C. David *surgeon*
Stander, Richard Ramsay, Sr., *retired civil engineer and construction engineer*
†Stretanski, Michael F. *neurologist, educator, rehabilitation services professional*
†Whitmer, Eugene Roger *minister, retired secondary school educator*
Wolf, Marcus Alan *lawyer*

Mantua
Nelson, Hedwig Potok *marketing executive*
Ray, James Allen *research consultant*

Maple Heights
Sargent, Liz Elaine (Elizabeth Sargent) *safety consulting executive*

Marietta
†Bicoy, Bret Nalani *think-tank executive*
Fields, William Albert *lawyer*
Huck, Daniel N. *lawyer, educator*
Jache, Albert William *retired chemistry educator, scientist*
Montgomery, Jerry Lynn *retired education educator*
Putnam, Robert Ervin *chemist, consultant*
Scanlan, Carla R. *researcher, educator*
Spisak, John Francis *environmental company executive*
Taylor, Michael Brooks *economist, educator*
Wilbanks, Jan Joseph *retired philosopher*
Yi, Xiaoxiong *political scientist, educator*

Marion
Badertscher, Doris Rae *elementary education educator*
Beals, Clem Kip, III, *dentist*
Fassler, Crystal G. *marketing consultant*
Rogers, Richard Michael *judge*
Rowe, Lisa Dawn *computer programmer/analyst, computer consultant*
†Sharpe, Patricia Aldrich *artist*
Slagle, James William *lawyer*

Marysville
Baik-Kromalic, Sue S. *metallurgical engineer*
Jones-Morton, Pamela *human resources specialist*

Mason
Beary, John Francis, III, *physician, scientist, pharmaceutical executive*
†Bhatia, Aneeta *cardiac anesthesiologist*
Clements, Michael Craig *health services consulting executive, retired renal dialysis technician*
Drees, Stephen Daniel *marketing professional*
Erbe, Janet Sue *medical surgical, orthopedics and pediatrics nurse*
Jackobs, Miriam Ann *dietitian*
Meyer, Joan Marie *drug researcher*
Roemer, John Alan *financial executive*
Smith, C. LeMoyne *publishing company executive*
Snyder, Barbara Royalty *pharmaceutical executive*
†Wekselman, Kathryn *pharmaceutical researcher*
Wilson, Frederic Sandford *pharmaceutical company executive*

Massillon
†Beane, Frank Llewellyn *lawyer*
Dishong, Morris William *forensic investigator, nurse*
Kidder, J. Penelope *consultant, mental health services administrator*
Netzly, Dwight H. *lawyer*
Snyder, Rachel Ann *manufacturing company specialist*

Maumee
Anderson, Richard Paul *agricultural company executive*
Konopinski, Virgil James *industrial hygienist, consultant*
Marsh, Benjamin Franklin *lawyer*
McBride, Beverly Jean *lawyer*
Nowak, Patricia Rose *advertising executive*
Tuschman, James Marshall *lawyer*
Zouhary, Kathleen Maher *lawyer*

Mayfield
Cukrowicz, Kevin Francis *information technology manager, military officer*

Mayfield Heights
Grants, Valdis *engineering manager*
Newman, Joseph Herzl *advertising consultant*

Rankin, Alfred Marshall, Jr., *business executive*
Rebolj, Joan Kaletta *training and development professional*

Mc Comb
Ewing, Mary Eileen *radiologic technologist*

Mechanicsburg
Maynard, Joan *education educator*
Saxbe, William Bart *lawyer, former government official*
Schoonover, Amy Jo *English educator, poet*

Medina
Ballard, John Stuart *retired educator, former mayor, former lawyer*
Batchelder, Alice M. *federal judge*
Calhoun, Lyla Lea *clinical social worker, consultant*
†DeMars, Judith M. *elementary educator*
Feola, David Craig *secondary school administrator*
Graham, Stanley Belding *retired secondary school educator, writer*
Hunter, Brinca Jo *education specialist*
†Ilg, Christopher Paul *secondary school educator, music educator*
Kenat, Thomas Arthur *chemical engineer, consultant*
Liauba, Danute *music educator*
Miller, Randal Howard *health science association administrator*
†Neiman, Marcus Lawrence *educational consultant*
Smith, Richey *manufacturing executive*
Sullivan, Thomas Christopher *coatings company executive*
Surso, John Michael *physician*
Williams, Paul C(hester) *consultant*

Mentor
†Benjamin, Michael Anthony *engineer*
Callsen, Christian Edward *medical device company executive*
Core, Harry Michael *psychiatric social worker, mental health therapist and administrator*
Driggs, Charles Mulford *lawyer*
Krone, Norman Bernard *commercial real estate developer, lawyer*
†McCarter, William Kent *lawyer*
Russell, Brenda Sue *critical care nurse*
Traub, Ronald Matthew *municipal administrator*

Miamisburg
Andreozzi, Louis Joseph *lawyer*
†Brewster, Charles Edward *writer, engineer*
Byrd, James Everett *lawyer*
Haigh, Peter Leslie *software company executive, consultant*
Irizarry, Francisco Armando *information systems executive, lawyer*

Middlebranch
Kalin, Nancy Jagger *interior designer*

Middleburg Heights
Hartman, Lenore Anne *physical therapist*
Maciuszko, Kathleen Lynn *librarian, educator*
McGinnis, Robert William *electronics company executive*
Molnar, Bela *school administrator*

Middlefield
†Jaite, Gail Ann *music educator*

Middletown
†Bailey, William Rufus *lawyer, corporation executive*
Ewers, James Benjamin, Jr., *director*
Gordon, Sandy Gale Combs *medical/surgical nurse, community health nurse*
Kay, Patricia Kremer *business owner*
Marine, Susan Sonchik *analytical chemist, educator*
McClain, Michael H. *writer*
Mehdizadeh, Mostafa *economics educator*
Newby, John Robert *metallurgical engineer*
Rathman, William Ernest *retired lawyer, minister*
Redding, Barbara J. *nursing administrator, occupational health nurse*
Schaefer, Patricia Ann *retired librarian*
Turpin, Richard E. *sales executive*
Wainscott, James Lawrence *accountant*
†Wheeler, Gary *art educator, academic director*

Milan
Henry, Joseph Patrick *chemical company executive*

Milford
Conover, Nellie Coburn *retail furniture company executive*
Creath, Curtis Janssen *pediatric dentist*
†Vester, John William *biochemist, retired medical educator*

Milford Center
McDonald, Alan Thomas *lawyer*

Millersburg
Yoder, Anna A. *elementary school educator*

Mineral Ridge
Czifra, Lisa Takacs *piano educator*
Yaksich, John Joseph *music educator*

Minerva
Martin, Robert Dale *lawyer*

Mogadore
Kelly, Janice Helen *elementary school educator*

Montpelier
Deckrosh, Hazen Douglas *retired state agency educator and administrator*

Moreland Hills
Hardie, James Carl *college administrator, consultant*
Tolchinsky, Paul Dean *organization design psychologist*

Mount Vernon
Bennett, Marguerite Hildreth *college administrator, mathematics educator*
Shriver, William Russell *secondary education educator*
†Tocheff, Robert Dale *music educator*
Turner, Harry Edward *lawyer*
Wells-Maxwell, Violet *writer, artist*

Munroe Falls
†Clawson, Judith Louise *middle school educator*

Napoleon
Frame, Lawrence Milven, Jr., *inventor*
Meekison, MaryFran *writer, photographer*

Nelsonville
Davis, Mary W. Allen *medical secretary*

New Albany
Duggan, Thomas Patrick *management consultant*
†Jeffries, Michael S. *apparel executive*
Rusk, Karla Marie *nurse practitioner*
Williams, James Case *metallurgist*

New Bremen
Dicke, James Frederick, II, *manufacturing company executive*
Wierwille, Marsha Louise *elementary education educator*

New Carlisle
Bowlin, Gloria Jean *artist*
Leffler, Carole Elizabeth *mental health nurse, women's health nurse*
Peters, Elizabeth Ann Hampton *retired nursing educator*

New Matamoras
Brown, Blanche Y. *secondary education educator, genealogy researcher*

New Philadelphia
Doughten, Mary Katherine (Molly Doughten) *retired secondary education educator*
Goforth, Mary Elaine Davey *secondary education educator*
Zinkon, Lana Sue *occupational health nurse*

New Washington
†Blum, Joseph R. *secondary school educator, emergency nurse practitioner*

Newark
Billy, Gerry Dee *protective services official*
Black, Boyd Carson *small business owner*
Bloomster, Brent Noel *psychologist, counselor*
†Garmon, Lance C. *psychology educator*
Gartner, Daniel Lee *computer information executive*
†Gordon, L(eland) James *lawyer*
Hite, David L. *lawyer*
Hostetter, James William *lawyer*
†Juodvalkis, Judith L. *human resources specialist*
Mantonya, John Butcher *lawyer*
McConnell, William Thompson *commercial banker*
Meyer, Christopher Richard *lawyer*
Pacht, Eric Reed *pulmonary and critical care physician*
Paul, Rochelle Carole *special education educator*
Reidy, Thomas Anthony *lawyer*
Sanders, Paul David *music educator*
†Simpson, Linda Sue *elementary educator*
†Tebben, Joseph Richard *ancient language educator*
Van Dervort, Sharyn L. *secondary education educator*

Newcomerstown
Komorowski, Anne Marie *freelance journalist, paralegal*

North Canton
Dettinger, Warren Walter *lawyer*
Di Simone, Robert Nicholas *radiologist, educator*
Jackson, David Lee *insurance company executive*
Lynham, C(harles) Richard *company executive*
Rodriguez, Irene Tobias *artist, art educator*
Seltzer, Mitchell Sherman *hotel executive*
†Vazzano, Frank Paul *historian, educator*

North Olmsted
Bluford, Guion Stewart, Jr., *engineering company executive*
Cotman, John Martin *accountant*
Dorchak, Thomas J. *lawyer*
Galysh, Robert Alan *information technology manager*
Lundin, Bruce Theodore *engineering and management consultant*
McCafferty, Owen Edward *accountant, dental-veterinary practice consultant*
Ruben, Alan Miles *law educator*
†Schuttenberg, Ernest M. *education educator*

North Ridgeville
Stewart, Arden Ruth *automotive aftermarket manufacturing executive*

North Royalton
Pamin, Diana Dolhancyk (Diana Dolhancyk) *poet*
Shimandle, Sharon Anne *nurse anesthetist*

Northfield
Cartier, Charles Ernest *alcohol and drug abuse services professional*

†Sleeman, Mary (Mrs. John Paul Sleeman) *retired librarian*

Norton
Becker, Janet Sue *musician*
Kun, Joyce Anne *secondary education educator, small business owner*

Norwalk
Fresch, Marie Beth *court reporting company executive*
Germann, Richard P(aul) *consultant, pharmaceutical company chemist, executive*
Gutowicz, Matthew Francis, Jr., *radiologist*
Holman, William Baker *surgeon, coroner*

Norwood
Tubbs, Robin Lee *secondary education educator*

Novelty
Gutierrez, Yezid *retired pathologist*

Oberlin
†Baumann, Roland M. *historian, archivist, consultant*
Brown, John Lott *educator*
Carlton, Terry Scott *chemist, educator*
Cartier, Brian Evans *association executive*
Cleeton, David Lawrence *economist, educational administrator*
Collins, Martha *English language educator, writer*
Dye, Nancy Schrom *academic administrator, historian, educator*
English, Ray *library administrator*
Greenberg, Eva Mueller *librarian*
Kruks, Sonia R. *social sciences educator, researcher*
†Lee, Kyung Sun *music educator*
†Luck, Dennis Noel *biologist, educator, researcher*
MacKay, Alfred F. *dean, philosophy educator*
MacKay, Gladys Godfrey *adult education educator*
†Pagliai, Valentina *researcher, educator*
Reinoehl, Richard Louis *artist, scholar, martial artist*
†Rejto, Peter Alan *music educator*
Rutstein, Sedmara Zakarian *piano educator, concert pianist*
Shaeffer, Ruth Gilbert *retired nonprofit corporation executive*
Simonson, Bruce Miller *geologist, educator*
†Singer, Leonard S. *chemist, research scientist, consultant*
Taylor, Gail Richardson *freelance writer, educator, civic worker, lawyer, former university official*
Taylor, Richard Wirth *political science educator*
Warner, Robert Edson *physics educator*
Weinstock, Robert *physics educator*
Zinn, Grover Alfonso, Jr., *religion educator*

Olmsted Falls
†Semple, Jane Frances *health facility administrator*

Oregon
†Byrne, Paul Adams *pediatrician, educator*
Crain, John Kip *school system administrator*

Orrville
†Hennell, Robert William, III, *secondary school educator*
Kamp, Philip *food products executive*
Warner, Patricia Ann *secondary school educator*

Orville
†Long, Elizabeth Valk *former magazine publisher*

Orwell
†Strong, Marcella Lee *music specialist, educator*

Ostrander
Smith, Rick A. *mechanical engineer, consultant*

Ottoville
Bowery, Warren E. *music educator*

Oxford
Baird, Jay Warren *historian, educator*
Barilleaux, Ryan J. *politcal science educator*
Bauer, Steven Albert *English educator, writer*
Becker, Stephen Bradbury *fraternal organization administrator*
Bergen, Doris *psychologist, educator*
Brown, Edward Maurice *retired lawyer, business executive*
DeLue, Steven Muller *political scientist, educator*
Eshbaugh, W(illiam) Hardy *botanist, educator*
†Ganev, Venelin Iordanov *political scientist, educator*
Gordon, Gilbert *chemist, educator*
Hall, Thomas Emerson *economist, educator*
Jeep, John Michael *language educator*
Macklin, Philip Alan *physics educator*
Miller, Robert James *educational association administrator*
Moore, Frank William *computer science educator, pianist*
Newell, William Henry *interdisciplinary studies educator*
†Papanikolaou, Eftychia *music educator*
Pont, John *football coach, educator*
Pratt, William Crouch, Jr., *English language educator, writer*
Rejai, Mostafa *political science educator*
Sanders, Gerald Hollie *communications educator, educator*
Sessions, Judith Ann *librarian, university library dean*
†Shannon, Vaughn Parnell *political scientist, educator*
Shriver, Phillip Raymond *academic administrator*
Snavely, William Brant *management educator and consultant*
Thompson, Bertha Boya *retired education educator, antique dealer and appraiser*
Ward, Roscoe Fredrick *engineering educator*
†Weinrich, Barbara Diane *speech pathology/audiology services professional, educator*
Wolfe, Christopher Randall *psychologist, researcher, educator*
Yamauchi, Edwin Masao *history educator*
Yang, Kewu *chemist*
Yen, David Chi-Chung *management information systems educator*
Yost, Nancy Runyon *artist, designer, art educator*

Painesville
†Aveni, Anthony Joseph *lawyer, educator*
Blyth, Ann Marie *secondary education educator*
Campbell, Margaret Susan *defender*
Davis, Barbara Snell *college educator*
Dietrich, Joseph Jacob *retired chemist, research executive*
Humphrey, George Magoffin, II, *plastic molding company executive*
Luhta, Caroline Naumann *airport manager, flight educator*
†McQuaid, Kim *historian, educator, writer*
Pyne, William Joseph *chemist*
†Sachwartz, David Allen *secondary school educator*
Smith, William Robert *utility company executive*

Parma
Bate, Brian R. *psychologist*
Hall, Clara Jean *special education educator*
†Laycock, Randolph Philip *music educator, conductor*
Lazo, John, Jr., *physician*
Saddleton, Michael John *emergency physician*
†Scheffel, Donna Jean *elementary school educator*
Shirey, Connie Mae *secondary school educator*
Tener, Carol Joan *retired secondary education educator*
Verba, Betty Lou *real estate executive, investor*

Pataskala
Caw, Thomas William *retired publisher and editor*
Honnold, Kathryn S. *real estate agent*

Patriot
Riggle, Patricia Carol *special education educator*

Pemberville
King, Laura Jane *librarian, genealogist*

Peninsula
Ludwig, Richard Joseph *small business owner*
Shaw, Doris Beaumar *film and video producer, executive recruiter, management consultant*

Pepper Pike
†Alexander-Haynes, Sandra *psychologist, educator*
Goodman, Donald Joseph *dentist*
Mc Call, Julien Lachicotte *banker*
O'Neill, Katherine Templeton *journalist, museum administrator, former nursing educator*
†Schnell, Carlton Bryce *lawyer*
†Vail, Thomas Van Husen *retired newspaper publisher and editor*

Perry
Zehler, Linda *artist*

Perrysburg
Autry, Carolyn *artist, art history educator*
Billnitzer, Bonnie Jeanne *nurse, gerontology specialist*
Celeste, Ardella Hazel *retired writer*
Elloian, Peter *artist, educator*
Khan, Amir U. *agricultural engineering consultant*
King, John Joseph *manufacturing company executive*
Kovacik, Neal Stephen *hotel and restaurant executive*
Loeffler, William Robert *quality productivity delivery specialist, engineering educator*
Murdock, Nanci C. *women's health nurse*
Weaver, Richard L., II, *writer, speaker, educator*
Williamson, John Pritchard *utility executive*

Pickerington
Blackman, Edwin Jackson *software engineer*
Callander, Kay Eileen Paisley *business owner, retired education educator, writer*
Collins, Arlene *secondary education educator*
†Parulekar, Marc Samir *music educator*
Young, Glenna Asche *elementary education educator*

Piqua
Disbrow, Michael Ray *aerospace supplier company executive*

Plain City
Kinman, Gary *company executive*

Pleasant Hill
†Kinney, Virginia Lee *librarian, educator*

Plymouth
†Hartman, Ruth Campbell *educator*

Poland
Donatelli, Daniel Dominic, Jr., *medical/surgical and oncological nurse*
†Horton, Barbara Louise *business educator*
Mike-Nard, Beverly Jean *nurse*
Murphy, Thomas Michael *civil engineer*

Pomeroy
Edwards, John David *investment executive*

Port Clinton
Bixler, Thomas L. *music educator*
Randels, David George *secondary school educator*

Portsmouth
Akhtar, Muhammad I. *neurologist, researcher*
†Burns, Eugene Hugh, Jr., *biology educator*
Crowder, Marjorie Briggs *lawyer*
Gerlach, Franklin Theodore *lawyer*
†Grimshaw, Lynn Alan *lawyer*
Horr, William Henry *retired lawyer*
†Johnson, Janice E *education educator, writer*
Murphy, Pearl Marie *medical and surgical nurse*
Turner, Elvin L. *retired educational administrator*

Powell
†Chen, Chia-En John *dentist*
Emanuelson, James Robert *retired insurance company executive*
†Lee, Robert J. Y. *marketing professional*
Spangler, Edra Mildred *clinical psychologist*

Proctorville
†Barnett, Steven R. *director, music educator*
Wiley, Jerold Wayne *environmental services executive, retired air force officer*

Randolph
Pecano, Donald Carl *automotive manufacturing executive*

Ravenna
Drugan, Cornelius Bernard *retired school administrator, retired psychologist, musician*
Felton, Robert O'Neil, II, *secondary education educator*
Giulitto, Paula Christine *lawyer*
Turcotte, Margaret Jane *retired nurse*

Reynoldsburg
Boiman, Donna Rae *artist, art academy executive*
Dailey, Fred L. *state agency administrator*
D'Onofrio, Peter Joseph *protective services official, educator*
Gunnels, Lee O. *retired finance and management educator, manufacturing/research company director, inventor*
Odor, Richard Lane *mental health administrator, psychologist*
Powell, Edward Lee *broadcasting company executive*
Serraglio, Mario *architect*
Woodward, Greta Charmaine *construction company executive, rental and investment property manager*

Richfield
Braude, Edwin Simon *manufacturing company executive*
†Fry, W. Logan *artist*
Lewis, Sylvia Davidson *foundation executive*
Pelagalli, James A. *surgeon*

Richmond
Martin, Clara Rita *elementary school educator*

Richwood
Hoffman, Scott Lee *lawyer*

Rio Grande
Shibley, Ralph Edwin, Jr., *special education and career-technical education*

Rocky River
Grady, Francis Xavier *lawyer*
Masters, Albert Townsend *mechanical engineer*
O'Brien, John Feighan *investment banker*
Riedthaler, William Allen *risk management professional*
Shively, Daniel Jerome *retired transportation executive*

Rootstown
Blacklow, Robert Stanley *internist, educator*
Brodell, Robert Thomas *internal medicine educator*
Gibson, Denise Dawn *social worker, educator*
Gilchrist, Valerie Jean *medical educator*
Jamison, James Mark *cell biologist*
Nora, Lois Margaret *medical college administrator, dean*

Roseville
Carney, Karen Rose *music educator, pianist*

Sagamore Hills
Harvuot, Cathleen Mary *elementary school educator, consultant*

Saint Clairsville
†Casebolt, James R. *psychologist, educator*
Fisher, Sandra Irene *English educator*
Hahn, David Bennett *hospital administrator, marketing professional*
Hanlon, Lodge L. *lawyer, insurance agency executive, accountant*
†Raymond, Bruce Allen *medical association administrator*
Stepputtis, Susan Lyn *management consultant, educator*
Zavacky-DeBertrand, Lynette Michele *women's health nurse*

Saint Marys
Dallura, Sal Anthony *physician*
Kemp, Barrett George *lawyer*

Salem
Barcey, Harold Edward Dean (Hal Barcey) *real estate counselor*
Bowman, Scott McMahan *lawyer*
Fehr, Kenneth Manbeck *retired computer systems company executive*
Slack, Mark Robert *lawyer*

Sandusky
Freehling, Harold George, Jr., *respiratory therapist, consultant*
†Kowalski, Anthony Albert *music educator*
Mahmood, Khalid *physician*
Sokol, Dennis Allen *hospital administrator*
Stacey, James Allen *retired judge*

Sardinia
Evans, C(aroline) Sue *educator*
Stratton, Sondra Kay *primary school educator*

Seaman
Cartaino, Carol Ann *editor*
Young, Vernon Lewis *lawyer*

Sebring
Doty, James Edward *pastor, psychologist*
Kelley-Hall, Maryon Hoyle *retired social worker*
Saffell, John Edgar *retired history educator*

Shaker Heights
Band, Jordan Clifford *lawyer*
†Barz, Patricia *lawyer*
Brachna, Gabor (Samuel) *elementary school educator*
Brucken, Lois Gilbert *volunteer*
Donnem, Roland William *retired lawyer, real estate owner, developer*
Donnem, Sarah Lund *financial analyst, non-profit and political organization consultant*
Eakin, Thomas Capper *sports promotion executive*
Ekelman, Daniel Louis *lawyer*
†Feuer, Michael *office products superstore executive*
Ludwig, L(owell) Mark *social science educator*
McKenna, Kathleen Kwasnik *artist*
Messinger, Donald Hathaway *lawyer*
Ondrey Gruber, William Michael *lawyer*
†Richardson, Robert Frank, Jr., *neurologist*
Salomon, Elizabeth Lowenstein *social worker*
Solganik, Marvin *real estate executive*
Switzer, Brian Carl *strategic information systems designer*
Trefts, Joan Landenberger *retired educator, administrator*
White, Eugene A. *retired physician, neuroradiologist*
Winter, John Alexander *realtor, real estate appraiser*
†Wohlever, Linda L. *mathematician and science educator*

Shaker Hts
†Thomas, Rebecca Lynne *librarian, writer*

Shauck
Garvick, Kenneth Ryan *broadcast engineer, announcer, educator*

Sheffield Village
Herdendorf, Charles Edward, III, *oceanographer, limnologist, consultant*

Shelby
Gilbert, Michelle Dawn *middle and secondary school educator*
Phelan, Martha Armstrong *realtor*

Shreve
Denman, Nicholas Werner *insurance executive*

Sidney
Fahrer, Franklin James *music educator*
Laurence, Michael Marshall *magazine publisher, writer*
Lawrence, Wayne Allen *publisher*
†Marlow, Meme Elizabeth *journalist*
Mintchell, Gary Alan *editor*
Seitz, James Eugene *retired college president, freelance writer*
Stevens, Robert Jay *magazine editor*

Solon
Gallo, Donald Robert *retired English educator*
Macko, David *retired bank adjustor*
Rosica, Gabriel Adam *corporate executive, engineer*
Ward, William Edward *museum exhibition designer*

Spencer
Snyder, Teresa Ann *medical/surgical nurse*

Springboro
Saxer, Richard Karl *metallurgical engineer, retired air force officer*
†Sharts, John Edwin, III, *lawyer*
Walden, James William *accountant, educator*

Springfield
Browne, William Bitner *lawyer*
†Chen, Peng-Hsin *composer, music educator*
Dominick, Charles Alva *college official*
†Faber, Trudy *music educator*
Harkins, Daniel Conger *lawyer*
Hayden, Albert A. *retired historian, educator*
Henning, William Clifford *cemetery consulting company executive*
Hobbs, Horton Holcombe, III, *biology educator*
Kinnison, William Andrew *retired university president*
Kurian, Pius *nephrologist, educator*
†Lagos, James Harry *lawyer*
Moore, Florian Howard *retired electronics engineer*
Patterson, Martha Ellen *artist, art educator*
Ryu, Kyoo-Hai Lee *physiologist*
Stelzer, Patricia Jacobs *retired secondary school educator*
†Sweet, Robert T. *humanities educator*
Weatherby, Donald Alan *telecommunications industry executive, writer*
Wilt, Valerie Rae *lawyer*

†Winteregg, Steven Lee *composer, musician, educator*
Wood, Dirk Gregory *surgeon, physician, forensic consultant*
†Woodhouse, Elizabeth C. *retired government agency administrator*

Sterling
†Stetz, Ernest James *retired building and power consultant*

Steubenville
Fitzgerald, Michael Stuart *history educator, researcher*
†Gerogedes, Kimberly *historian, educator*
Hall, Alan Craig *library director*
†Nodes, Daniel Joseph *humanities educator, researcher*
Scanlan, Michael *priest, academic administrator*
Sheldon, Gilbert Ignatius *clergyman*

Stockport
Winebrenner, William Patrick *writer*

Stoutsville
Wernick, Edith Elaine *pianist, educator*

Stow
Hessler, William Gerhard *tax consultant*
Hollis, William Frederick *information scientist*
Kase-Janowski, Kristen Marian *healthcare educator*

Streetsboro
Kearns, Warren Kenneth *business executive*

Strongsville
†Berkey, Donald Frederick *counseling administrator*
Blumer, Frederick Elwin *retired philosophy educator*
Chidsey, Ronald Grant *counseling*
†Eley, Richard Robert *science educator*
†Lamberton, Jacquelyn E. *psychotherapist*
Mills, S. Loren *product safety manager, engineer*
Myers, Jack Fredrick *artist, educator, author*
Pinkerton, Richard LaDoyt *retired management educator*
Shambaugh, Catherine Anne *elementary education educator*
†Taghizadeh, Georgeanne Marie *medical/surgical nurse, diagnostic cardiac sonagrapher*

Struthers
Sugden, Richard Lee *pastor*

Sylvania
Bergsmark, Edwin Martin *mortgage bank executive*
Burkhart, Craig Garrett *dermatologist*
†Callahan, John Joseph *lawyer*
Gleason, Alan Harold *retired economics educator*
Lock, Richard William *packaging company executive*
Ring, Herbert Everett *management executive*
Sampson, Earldine Robison *education educator*
†Sampson, Wesley Claude *auditor, software inventor*
Verhesen, Anna Maria Hubertina *social worker*
White, Alan Edward *computer company executive*

Tallmadge
Kaul, Mohan Lal *social worker, educator*
Turner, Richard L. *retired computer software engineer*

The Plains
Klare, George Roger *psychology educator*

Tiffin
Davison, Kenneth Edwin *American studies educator, genealogist*
Debbink, Thomas Mason *management educator*
Einsel, David William, Jr., *retired army officer and consultant*
Gridley, Mark Charles *psychologist*
Hillmer, Margaret Patricia *library director*
Huth, Lester Charles *lawyer*
†Kill, Sister Marietta *nun, music educator*
†Moore, Vincent D. *humanities educator, writer*
Spellerberg, Elinor M. *riding instructor*

Tipp City
†Ahmed, Gail R. *music educator*
Taylor, Robert Homer *quality assurance professional, pilot*
Tighe-Moore, Barbara Jeanne *electronics executive*

Toledo
Alexander, Kenneth Saul *pharmaceuticals educator*
†Allotta, Joseph John *lawyer*
Al-Marayati, Abid A. *political science educator*
Anspach, Robert Michael *lawyer*
Averill, Bruce Alan *chemistry educator*
Baker, Richard Southworth *lawyer*
Barrett, Michael John *anesthesiologist*
Batt, Nick *property and investment executive*
Bell, Robert *orchestra executive*
Benham, Linda Sue *civil engineer*
Billups, Norman Fredrick *college dean, pharmacist, educator*
Block, Allan James *communications executive*
Block, John Robinson *newspaper publisher*
Block, William K., Jr., *newspaper executive*
Boggs, Ralph Stuart *retired lawyer*
Braithwaite, Margaret Christine *retired elementary education educator*
Brickey, Suzanne M. *editor*
Brower, James Calvin *graphic artist, painter*
Brown, Charles Earl *lawyer*
†Brown, David T. *manufacturing executive*
Buchanan, Debra Annette *artist, jeweler*
Calcamuggio, Larry Glenn *lawyer*
Cardwell, Michael Steven *physician, lawyer*
Carson, Samuel Goodman *retired banker, company director*
Chakraborty, Joana *physiology educator, research center administrator*
Chang, Kathryn Jinmei *accountant*
Cole, Jeffrey Clark *public relations professional*
Comerota, Anthony James *vascular surgeon, biomedical researcher*
†Condon, Elizabeth M. *education educator*
Cousino, Joe Ann *sculptor*
†Cuckovic, Zeljko *education educator*
Cummings, Erwin Karl *information technology executive*
Dalrymple, Thomas Lawrence *retired lawyer*
Dane, Stephen Mark *lawyer*
Diehl, Dean R. *engineering company executive*
Doner, Gary William *lawyer*
Duling, Edward Burger *music education educator*
Eberly, William Somers *financial consultant*
Edwards, Richard Walton, Jr., *law educator*
Eichenberg, David James *artist, educator*
†Escobar, Isabel Cristina *education educator*
†Fetzer, Derek *industrial engineer, consultant*
†Finkbeiner, Carlton S. (Carty Finkbeiner) *mayor*
Flaskamp, Ruth Ehmen Staack *retired elementary education educator*
†Franco-Saenz, Roberto *physician*
†Friedman, Howard Martin *law educator*
Geisler, Nathan David *financial consultant*
†Georgiadis, Gregory Minas *orthopedist, educator*
†Girgis-Hanna, Mary Fahim *music educator*
Glaab, Charles Nelson *educator, historian*
†Goldstein, Margaret Franks *special education educator*
Goodenday, Lucy Sherman *physician, educator*
Gottlieb, Arnold Neal *lawyer*
Gutteridge, Thomas G. *academic administrator, consultant and labor arbitrator*
Hartmann, Ann W. *financial planner*
Heintz, Carolinea Cabaniss *retired home economics educator*
Hyman, Melvin *speech-language pathologist, consultant*
Ivanov, Alexander V. *biochemist, researcher*
Jackson, Reginald Sherman, Jr., *lawyer, educator*
Jan, George Pokung *political science educator*
Jauregui, Connie Lee *internist*
Jauregui, Luis Ernesto *physician, pharmacologist*
Jhunjhunwala, Jagadish S. *retired urologist*
Kastner, Michael James *dentist*
Kimmel, Sanford Richard *family physician, pediatrician, educator*
Knorr, John Christian *entertainment executive, bandleader, producer*
†Knuth, Marya Danielle *special education educator*
Koppus, Betty Jane *retired savings and loan association executive*
Krakoff, Kenneth B. *dentist, consultant*
Kunze, Ralph Carl *retired savings and loan executive*
La Rue, Carl Forman *lawyer*
Lemieux, Joseph Henry *manufacturing company executive*
Lessick, Mira Lee *nursing educator*
Lothery, Shawne Lamarr *writer, multimedia designer*
Luckner, Kleia Raubitschek *nursing administrator, lawyer, nurse midwife*
Lynn, Christopher Kenneth *internist, educator*
†Marco, Alan Paul *hospital administrator, anesthesiologist*
†Martin, Geoffrey Kimball *academic administrator, mathematician*
Martin, John Thomas *physician, author, educator*
Martin, Robert Edward *architect*
McGlauchlin, Tom *artist*
†Medhkour, Azedine *neurosurgeon, educator*
Mehelas, Thomas James *neuro-ophthalmologist, educator*
Metress, Seamus P. *anthropology educator, Irish studies researcher*
†Miroshnichenko, Anatoly S. *astronomer, researcher*
Mohler, Terence John *psychologist*
Mulrow, Patrick Joseph *medical educator*
Nordin, Phyllis Eck *sculptor, painter, consultant*
O'Connell, Maurice Daniel *lawyer*
Ormond, Paul A. *health facility executive*
†Overmyer, Janet Elaine *counselor*
Paquette, Jack Kenneth *management consultant, writer, historian*
Pham, David Lan *secondary school educator, writer*
Pletz, Thomas Gregory *lawyer*
Potter, John William *federal judge*
†Pullins, Ellen Bolman *finance educator*
Rabideau, Margaret Catherine *retired media center director*
Randolph, Brian Walter *civil engineer, educator*
Rejent, Marian Magdalen *retired pediatrician*
Romanoff, Marjorie Reinwald *retired education educator*
Romanoff, Milford Martin *building contractor*
Royhab, Ronald *journalist, newspaper editor*
†Sabra, Ponn Mahayosnand *realtor*
St. Clair, Donald David *lawyer*
†Salyers, Kathleen Marie *education educator*
Shelley, E. Dorinda *dermatologist*
Shelley, Walter Brown *physician, educator*
Smith, Robert Freeman *history educator*
Smith, Robert Nelson *former government official, anesthesiologist*
Spitzer, John Brumback *lawyer*
Stoecker, Randy Rex *sociologist, educator*
Talmage, Lance Allen *obstetrician/gynecologist, career military officer*
Toczynski, Janet Marie *oncological nurse*
†Wang, Leslie Tsun Chung *social sciences educator*
†Ward, David A. *corporate lawyer*
Webb, Thomas Irwin, Jr., *lawyer, director*
†Weikel, Malcolm Keith *healthcare company executive*
Weinblatt, Charles Samuel *university administrator, employment consultant*
†White, Kenneth James *lawyer*
Wicklund, David Wayne *lawyer*
Willey, John Douglas *retired newspaper executive*
†Witherell, Dennis Patrick *lawyer*
Wolfe, Robert Kenneth *engineering educator*
Wolff, Edwin Ray *retired construction engineer, consultant*
†Wolter, Virginia Lynn *librarian*
Zrull, Joel Peter *psychiatry educator*

Troy
Bazler, Frank Ellis *retired lawyer*
Enright, Georgann McGee *healthcare educator*
Savage, Joseph Scott *physician*
Szoke, Joseph Louis *psychologist, mental health facility administrator*
Williams, Craig Foster *osteopathic emergency physician*

Twinsburg
†Kramer, Timothy Eugene *lawyer*
Sugar, Robert Joseph *software engineer, physicist*

Uniontown
Naugle, Robert Paul *dentist*

University Heights
†Carrington, Gary *psychologist*
Casciani, Santa *Italian studies educator*
Cook, Alexander Burns *museum curator, artist, educator*
†Eslinger, Kenneth N. *social sciences educator*
Glynn, Edward *college administrator*
†Goral, Judith Ann *educator*
Seaton, Shirley Smith *academic administrator, consultant*
Starcher-Dell'Aquila, Judy Lynn *special education educator*

Upper Arlington
Williams, Cathy Lynn *nurse*

Upper Sandusky
Baker, Harrison Scott *computer consultant*
Waggy, Corrina Jeanne *insurance agent*

Urbana
Meyers, Marsha Lynn *retired social worker*

Valley View
Miller, Susan Ann *school system administrator*

Vandalia
†Korte, Genevieve L *music educator*

Vermilion
†Baughman, Walter David *parochial school educator*
Schwensen, David Edward *writer, columnist, talent coordinator*
Smith, Al, Jr., *air traffic controller, retired*
Vance, Elbridge Putnam *mathematics educator*

Vincent
Meek, Barbara Susan *elementary education educator*

WPAFB
Reston, Rocky Russell *anesthesiologist, engineer, educator*

Wadsworth
Atwood, Glenn Arthur *engineer, educator*
Brumbaugh, John A., Jr., *electrical engineer*
Mayes, Samuel William *music educator*
†McIlvaine, James Ross *lawyer*
Neumann, Jeffrey Jay *photographer, minister*
†Paul, Dennis Edward *lawyer*
Pipitone, Phyllis L. *psychologist, educator, author*
†Ross, Jane Arlene *music educator*

Walnut Creek
Lawrence, Alice Lauffer *artist, educator*

Walton Hills
†Elliott, Stanley B. *chemist, researcher*
†Thellmann, Edward L. *mayor*

Wapakoneta
Lusk, Mary Margaret *music educator*

Warren
Blaih, Salah Moustafa *chemist, pharmacist, educator*
Letson, William Normand *lawyer*
Nader, Robert Alexander *judge, lawyer*
†Palmer, Daniel Edward *philosopher*
Robbins, Robert Marvin *accountant*
Rossi, Anthony Gerald *lawyer*
Seachrist, Denise *music educator*
Swauger, Terry Allen *lawyer*
Thompson, Eric Thomas *retail executive*
VanAuker, Lana *recreational therapist, educator*
Westman, Robert Allan *management consultant*
†Woodall, W. Dallas *lawyer*
Yoke, Carl Bernard *English language educator, critic*
Zimmerman, Doris Lucile *chemist*

Warrensville Heights
Jain, Nemi Chand *chemist, coating scientist, educator*
Stephenson, Samuel Floyd, Jr., *music educator*

Washington Court House
Fichthorn, Fonda Gay *gifted and talented educator, retired principal*

Waterford
Riley, Nancy Mae *retired vocational home economics educator*

Waterville
Yeager, Robert Julius *priest, financial consultant*

Waverly
Hays, Richard Secrest *minister*
Lovett, Francis William, Jr., *adult education educator*
Manuta, David Mark *research chemist, consultant*
†McNelly, Charles Wesley *music educator*

Waynesville
†Lenney, Shawn Edward *music educator*

Wellston
Oths, Joseph Anthony *lawyer*

West Carrollton
Rabold, Barbara Ann *artist, writer, illustrator, systems analyst*

West Chester
Loughman, Barbara Evers *immunologist researcher*
Mack, Mark Philip *chemical company executive*
Mital, Anil *engineering educator*
†Pease, Stacey Lyn *music educator*
Ulrich, Jody L. *accountant*

West Farmington
Smith, Agnes Monroe *history educator*

West Jefferson
Puckett, Helen Louise *retired tax consulting company executive*

West Union
Schlueter, James William *lawyer*

Westerville
Barr, John Michael *investor, management consultant*
†Bell, Albert Leo *retired lawyer*
Bigg, Donald Michael *chemical engineer*
Clamme, Marvin Leslie *recording engineer, electronic engineer*
Dawdy, W. David *pediatrician*
DeVassie, Terry Lee *publishing executive*
Diersing, Carolyn Virginia *educational administrator*
Feck, Luke Matthew *retired utility executive*
Giannamore, David Michael *electronics engineer*
Goh, Anthony Li-Shing *marketing professional*
Husarik, Ernest Alfred *educational administrator*
Kerr, Thomas Jefferson, IV, *academic official*
Lancione, Bernard Gabe *lawyer*
Lerner, Harold Selwyn *retired apparel executive*
†Lott, Vera Naomi *artist, educator*
Macfarlane, Alastair Iain Robert *business executive*
Markham, Richard Lawrence *chemist*
McCurdy, Kurt Basquin *real estate corporation officer*
Newkirk, Peggy Rose Wills *civic volunteer*
Schultz, Arthur LeRoy *clergyman, educator*
Strapp, Naomi Ann *women's health nurse*
†Swinehart, Timothy E. *music educator*
†Topping, Elizabeth Ann *production manager, graphics designer, historian*
Van Sant, Joanne Frances *academic administrator*
Westervelt, Charles Ephraim, Jr., *lawyer*
Williams, John Michael *physical therapist, sports medicine educator*
†Young, Sheldon Mike *lawyer, author*

Westfield Center
†Blair, Robert Cary *insurance company executive*
Bock, Carolyn A. *writer, interviewer, small business owner*
Edington, Patricia Ann *social services administrator*
Spinelli, Anne Catherine *elementary education educator*

Westlake
Coeling, Harriet Van Ess *nursing educator, editor*
Connelly, John James *retired oil company technical specialist*
Donahue, Charles Bertrand, II, *lawyer*
†FitzRandolph, Casey *Olympic athlete*
Hellman, Peter Stuart *technical manufacturing executive*
Huff, Ronald Garland *mechanical engineer*
Kolick, Daniel Joseph *lawyer*
†Kuhn, Edwin P. *travel company executive*
Lahiff, Marilyn J. *nursing administrator*
†Nedorost, Susan Todd *dermatologist*
Noveske, Francis Gregory *psychiatrist*
†Ohno, Apolo Anton *Olympic athlete*
†Parra, Derek *Olympic athlete*
†Schroth, Joyce Able *social worker*
Sheehan, John Patrick *endocrinologist, educator*
Whitehouse, John Harlan, Jr., *systems software consultant, diagnostician*

Whitehouse
Boyle, Daniel Robert *musician, delivery service executive*

Wickliffe
Dunn, Horton, Jr., *organic chemist*
Fisher, Nancy DeButts *library director*
Kidder, Fred Dockstater *lawyer*
Kornbrekke, Ralph Erik *colloid chemist*
Pevec, Anthony Edward *bishop*
Scott, Christopher G. *metallurgical engineer, researcher*

Wilberforce
Anyalewechi, Patrick Okechukwu *psychology educator*
†Elali, Taan *engineering and computer science educator*
George, Larry Darnell *dean, educator*

Hargraves, William Frederick, II, *mathematics and computer science educator*
Mulhern, Jean Kay *academic library director, consultant*
Oluyitan, Emmanuel Funso *communications educator*
†Omolewu, Gabriel Adebayo *business educator, researcher*
†Venkateswaran, Anuradha *marketing educator*
Williamson, Vikki Lyn *university official, financial executive*

Willard
†Thornton, Robert Floyd *lawyer*

Willoughby
Abelt, Ralph William *bank executive*
Baker, Charles Stephen *music educator*
Carter, John Robert *physician*
†Combs, Steven Paul *orthopedic surgeon*
Corrigan, Faith *journalist, educator, historian*
†Cruikshank, David Earl *lawyer*
Grossman, Mary Margaret *elementary education educator*
Pazirandeh, Mahmood *rheumatologist, consultant*
†Primavera, Fred Joseph *music educator*
Thanos, Daniel *retired obstetrician-gynecologist*
Trennel, Lawrence William *accountant, educator*

Wilmington
Evans, Elizabeth Ann West *retired realtor*
Schutt, Walter Eugene *lawyer*
Townsend, June H. *foreign language educator*

Wintersville
George, Gary Mark *pastor, church administrator*

Wooster
August, Robert Olin *journalist*
†Basford, James Orlando *container manufacturing company executive*
Ferree, David Curtis *horticultural researcher*
†Gallagher, Jack B(urt) *composer, music educator*
†Geiser, Robert Neil *computer scientist*
Grewal, Parwinder S. *biologist, educator*
Hales, Raleigh Stanton, Jr., *mathematics educator, academic administrator*
Haught, Sharon Kay *lawyer*
Hickey, Damon Douglas *library director*
†Johnston, John Clifford, Jr., *lawyer*
Kennedy, Charles Allen *lawyer*
Kuffner, George Henry *dermatologist, educator*
Lafever, Howard Nelson *plant breeder, geneticist, educator*
Ling, Stuart James *music educator, composer*
Lun, Lapman *internist*
Marathe, Bhaskar *development engineer*
†Moore, Arthur William *retired lawyer*
†N'Diaye, Boubacar *humanities educator, researcher*
†Pierce, Pamela Bitler *mathematics educator*
Price, Ronald James *electrical products company executive*
†Saif, Linda J. *animal scientist*
Shepherd, Mary Anne *elementary education educator*
Tranovich, Mark *orthopedic surgeon*
†Woods, Susanne *educator, academic administrator*

Worthington
Albert, Robert Hamilton *lawyer*
Barbe, Betty Catherine *retired financial analyst*
Bender, Bob *advertising executive*
Bernhagen, Lillian Flickinger *retired school health consultant*
Browning, Robert Lynn *educator, clergyman*
Compton, Ralph Theodore, Jr., *electrical engineering educator*
Juhola, Michael Duane *lawyer*
Keller, Kenneth Christen *advertising executive*
Lentz, Edward Allen *consultant, retired health administrator*
Trevor, Alexander Bruen *technology consultant*
Vankeerbergen, Bernadette Chantal *educator*
Whitney, Ray *hockey player*
Winston, Janet Margaret *real estate agent, civic volunteer*
Winter, Chester Caldwell *physician, surgery educator, historian, writer*
Wu, Tien Hsing *civil engineering educator, consulting engineer*

Wright Patterson Afb
Amend, Joseph H., III,
†Babish, Charles A., IV, *aerospace engineer*
Blasch, Erik Philip *research engineer, Air Force officer*
Boff, Kenneth Richard *engineering research psychologist*
Caudill, Tom Holden *governmental policy and analysis executive*
Garscadden, Alan *physicist*
Goltz, Mark Neil *environmental engineer*
Kankey, Roland Doyle *educator*
Kelley, Joseph E. *career officer*
Maguire, Frank Edward *retired non-commissioned military officer*
†Mall, Shankar *engineering mechanics educator, researcher*
Nielsen, Paul Douglas *Air Force officer, engineering manager*
†Paul, Richard R. *military officer*
Szucs, Andrew Eric *program manager*
†Underwood, Jeffery Scott *historian, curator*
Wallace, Robert Luther, II, *engineer*

Wyoming
Cooley, William Edward *regulatory affairs manager*

Xenia
Bigelow, Daniel James *aerospace executive*
Blanton, Linda Gayle *counselor, former educator*
Chappars, Timothy Stephen *lawyer*
Coleman, Rita Kay *writer, literature educator*
Nutter, Zoe Dell Lantis *retired public relations executive*
†Wolaver, Stephen Arthur *judge, lawyer*

Yellow Springs
Cawood, Albert McLaurin (Hap Cawood) *retired newspaper editor*
Fogarty, Robert Stephen *historian, educator, editor*
Graham, Jewel Freeman *social worker, lawyer, educator*
Keyes, Ralph Jeffrey *writer*
Schulsinger, Michael Alan *data processing executive*
Spokane, Robert Bruce *biophysical chemist*
Trolander, Hardy Wilcox *engineering executive, consultant*
Von Gierke, Henning Edgar *biomedical science educator, former government official, researcher*
Webb, Paul *physician, researcher, consultant, educator*
†Wright, Harold P. *language educator*

Youngstown
Atwater, Tony *provost,dean, educator*
Ausnehmer, John Edward *lawyer*
Binning, William Charles *political scientist, educator*
Bodoh, William T. *federal judge*
Bowers, Bege K. *English educator, academic administrator*
Briach, George Gary *lawyer, consultant*
Buckley, John Joseph *obstetrician, gynecologist*
Camacci, Michael A. *commercial real estate broker, development consultant*
Carlin, Clair Myron *lawyer*
Catoline-Ackerman, Pauline Dessie *small business owner*
†Cernica, John N. *engineering educator, civil engineer, consultant*
†DeBartolo, Edward John, Jr., *professional football team owner, real estate developer*
Fok, Thomas Dso Yun *civil engineer*
†Giannini, Matthew Carlo *lawyer, educator*
Gottron, Francis Robert, III, *small business owner*
Hassell, Jean Treverton *dietetics educator*
Jeren, John Anthony, Jr., *lawyer*
Kenner, Marilyn Sferra *civil engineer*
Lacivita, Michael John *safety engineer*
Lambert, Jean Marjorie *health care executive*
Loch, John Robert *university administrator*
McClelland, Marleen Iannucci *physical therapist, educator*
Mehra, Jagdish *economics educator*
Murcko, Donald Leroy *architect*
Nadler, Myron Jay *lawyer, director*
†Newman, Christopher John *lawyer*
Pacalo, Patrick John *writer*
Rose, Ernst *dentist*
Roth, Daniel Benjamin *lawyer, business executive*
Ruffer, David Gray *museum director, former college president*
Rupeka, Robert W. *court administrator*
Schwers, Dorothy Jean *retired music educator*
Slavin, Morris *historian, educator*
†Smotzer, Thomas David *mathematician*
Sweeney, Christopher John *psychology educator, consultant*
Tyson, Edith Slosson *retired librarian, writer*
†Usip, Ebenge Etefia *economics educator*
Valenta, Janet Anne *substance abuse professional*
Walton, Ralph Gerald *psychiatrist, educator*
Yozwiak, Bernard James *retired mathematics educator and academic administrator*
Zitto, Richard Joseph *physics educator*
Zorn, Robert Lynn *education educator*

Zanesfield
Tetirick, Jack E. *retired surgeon*

Zanesville
†Brown, Eric D. *city planner, consultant, researcher*
Brown, Karen Rima *orchestra manager, Spanish language educator*
Camma, Albert John *neurosurgeon*
Fulkerson, Sue Ellen *poet*
Kopf, George Michael *retired ophthalmologist*
Micheli, Frank James *lawyer*
O'Sullivan, Christine *retired executive director social service agency, consultant*
Ray, John Walker *otolaryngologist, educator, broadcast commentator*
Ray, Susanne Gettings *counselor*
Shatz, Mark Allen *psychologist, educator*
Whitacre, Vicki Ann *medical association administrator, retired emergency physician*
Workman, James E. *retired school psychologist*

Zoar
Fernandez, Kathleen M. *cultural organization administrator*

OKLAHOMA

Ada
Anoatubby, Bill *governor of Chickawaw Nation*
Baker, Judith Ann *retired computer technician*
Daniel, Arlie Verl *speech education educator*
Davenport, Ann Adele Mayfield *retired home care agency administrator*
Dempsey, B. *artist*
Dennison, Ramona Pollan *special education educator*
†Frye, Linda Beth (Linda Beth Hisle) *elementary, secondary education educator*
Mornhinweg, Claudia Beth Jones *music educator*
Mynatt, Cecil Ferrell *psychiatrist*
Parham, Betty Ely *credit bureau executive*
Reese, Patricia Ann *retired editor, columnist*
Stafford, Donald Gene *chemistry educator*

Altus
Rebik, James Michael *otolaryngologist*
Stine, Earle John, Jr., *radiologist*
Wilcoxen, Joan Heeren *fitness company executive*

Alva
†Hill, Sharon A. *language educator*
†Marlin, Benjamin Arthur *mathematician, researcher, computer scientist, educator*
Mitchell, Allan Edwin *lawyer*
Yates, James Newton *English educator*

Antlers
Stamper, Joe Allen *lawyer*

Atoka
Gabbard, Douglas, II, (James Gabbard) *judge*

Bartlesville
†Allen, W. Wayne *retired oil industry executive*
Byfield, Rita Rae *nursing educator, family nurse practitioner*
Chambers, Imogene Klutts *school system administrator, financial consultant*
Cox, Glenn Andrew, Jr., *petroleum company executive*
Doty, Donald D. *retired banker*
Dwiggins, Claudius William, Jr., *chemist*
Eastman, Alan Dan *chemist*
Gao, Hong Wen *retired chemical engineer*
Hogan, John Paul *chemistry researcher, consultant*
Johnson, Marvin Merrill *chemical engineer, chemist*
Koch, Robert Charles *lawyer, community activist*
Lai, Young-Jou *industrial engineer*
Meier, Paul Frederick *chemist, chemical engineer*
Mihm, John Clifford *chemical engineer*
Mulva, James Joseph *oil company executive*
Norfleet, Scott Alan *software engineer*
Olsen, David K. *engineer, chemist*
Roff, Alan Lee *lawyer, consultant*
Silas, Cecil Jesse *retired petroleum company executive*
Sweem, Billy Don *minister*
†White, Joy Kathryn *claims consultant, artist*

Bethany
Arnold, Donald Smith *chemical engineer, consultant*
†Ballweg, David Brent *music educator, conductor*
†Berryman, Warren *dean*
Crabtree, John Michael *college administrator, consultant*
Engle, Richard Victor *publishing executive*
†Halpain, Sue R. *music educator, musician*
Hendrick, Howard H. *state government administrator*
Leggett, James Daniel *bishop*
Murrow, Wayne Lee *retired communications educator, dean*

Billings
†Matthiesen, Robert L. *education educator, farmer, rancher*

Blackwell
Ghormley, Luther Wayne *surgeon*

Bristow
Primeaux, Henry, III, *automotive executive, author, speaker*

Broken Arrow
Cruzan, Clarah Catherine *dietitian*
†Huckeby, Ed D. *academic administrator, composer, conductor*
†Jones, Ronald Lee *lawyer, writer*
Stewart, Murray Baker *retired lawyer*

Buffalo
Anthony, Jack Ramon *mechanical engineer, retired*

Calera
Young, James Oliver *dentist, communication company executive*

Chandler
Swanson, Robert Lee *lawyer*

Chickasha
Brown, Steven L. *art educator*

Choctaw
Howard, David L. *music educator, conductor*
Uselton, Bill W. *secondary education educator*

Chouteau
Sasser, Charles Wayne *journalist, educator, writer*

Claremore
†Burrage, Billy Michael *lawyer, retired judge*
McCall, Charles Barnard *health facility administrator, educator*
McClain, Marilyn Russell *counselor*
†Smith, David M. *music educator*
Whinery, Michael Albert *physician*

Cleveland
Anderson, Patricia Sue *writer*
Henry, Kathleen Marie *marketing executive*

Collinsville
Councilman, Richard Robert *product development engineer*

Corn
Regier, Charles E. *music educator*

Dale
Capps, Larry Lynn *school librarian*

Disney
Hamilton, Carl Hulet *retired academic administrator*

Duncan
†Rodgers, Ricardo Juan (Rick Rodgers) *lawyer*

Durant
Christy, David Hardacker *music educator, consultant*
England, Dan Benjamin *accountant*
†Flippen, J. Brooks *historian, educator*
Hooser, Helen *artist*
Ludrick, Brad Burton *science educator*
Rice, Stanley Arthur *biology educator*
†Spencer, Mark Benner *education educator*
Wright, John Ricken *chemist, educator*

Edmond
Caire, William *biologist, educator*
Charoenwongse, Chindarat *pianist, educator, school administrator*
Conner, Leslie Lynn, Jr., *lawyer*
Graves, Paul Matthew *secondary school educator, choir director*
†Hopwood, Howard Hoppy Perry *military officer*
Keckel, Peter J. *advertising executive*
Lester, Andrew William *lawyer*
Lewis, Gladys Sherman *nurse, educator*
Loman, Mary LaVerne *retired mathematics educator*
Loving, Susan Brimer *lawyer, former state official*
McCoy, William Ulysses *journalist*
Munhollon, Samuel Clifford *investment brokerage house executive*
Necco, E(dna) Joanne *school psychologist*
Powers, G. Kay *lawyer, mathematics educator*
Pydynkowsky, Joan Anne *journalist*
Smock, Donald Joe *governmental liaison, political consultant*
†Spigner, Terry E. *special education educator*
Zabel, Vivian Ellouise *secondary education educator*

El Reno
Buendia, Imelda Bernardo *clinical director, physician*
McCurdy, Gary Dean *district judge, educator*

Enid
Abdul-Jabbar, Kareem (Lewis Ferdinand Alcindor) *professional basketball coach*
Berry, Robert Bass *construction executive*
Curtis, Albert Bradley, II, *financial planner, tax specialist*
Hamilton, Lisa Dawn *secondary education educator*
Jones, Stephen *lawyer*
McCobb, Allan Paul *not-for-profit organization executive*
McNaughton, Alexander Bryant *lawyer*
†Record, Donald D. *music educator, literature educator*
Rider, John Allen, II, *business educator, paralegal*
Russell, Rhonda Cheryl *piano educator, recording artist*
Seem, Evelyn Ashcraft *music educator*
Ward, Llewellyn Orcutt, III, *oil company executive*

Eufaula
†Dawson, Cindy Marie *lawyer*

Fort Towson
Pike, Thomas Harrison *plant chemist*

Frederick
Clayton, Ann Allman *music educator, minister*

Grove
†Illgen, Joel R. *music educator*
Trippensee, Gary Alan *aerospace executive, retired*
Winters, J(ohn) Otis *retired oil industry consultant*

Guthrie
Brooks, Larry Roger *judge*
†Davis, Frank Wayne *lawyer*
†Tickle, Jona *music educator*

Guymon
Wood, Donald Euriah *lawyer*

Healdton
Lewis, Reba Jolene *secondary school educator, consultant*

Hodgen
Brower, Janice Kathleen *library technician*

Jenks
Leming, W(illiam) Vaughn *electronics engineer*
Wootan, Gerald Don *osteopathic physician, educator*

Jennings
Nixon, Arlie James *gas and oil company executive*

Jones
Jones, Jeffery Lynn *software engineer*

Kansas
Pemberton, Merri Beth Morris *educator*

Kingfisher
Baker, Thomas Edward *lawyer, accountant*
Buswell, Arthur Wilcox *physician, surgeon*

Langston
Holloway, Ernest Leon *university president*

Lawton
†Ashton, Mark Alfred *lawyer*

Cates, Dennis Lynn *education educator*
†Dishman, Bob N. *pharmacist*
Ellenbrook, Edward Charles *county official, small business owner*
Gardner, Carol Elaine *elementary school educator*
Goetz, Gary D., Sr., *writer, retired chef, restaurateur*
Hooper, Roy B. *lobbyist, consultant*
†Jurgensen, Monserrate *clinical nurse, consultant*
Klein, Scott Richard *acting and directing educator*
Mayes, Glenn *social worker*
Moore, Roy Dean *retired judge*
†Reece, Juliette M. Stolper *community health and mental health nurse*
Smiley, Frederick Melvin *education educator, consultant*
Spencer, Mark Morris *creative writing educator*
Webb, O(rville) Lynn *physician, pharmacologist, educator*

Mangum
Bronson, William Cavolt, Jr., *counselor*

Maramec
Blair, Marie Lenore *retired elementary school educator*

McAlester
Kirby, Odell *retired small business owner, retired newswriter, writer*

Mcalester
Bartheld, Robert Lyle *dentist*
Cornish, Richard Pool *lawyer*
†Smith, Jason Richard *music educator*

Miami
†Lawson, Wayne A. *voice educator, minister*

Midwest City
Bogardus, Carl Robert, Jr., *radiologist, educator*
Gonzalez, Richard Theodore *photographer*
Hamilton, Carol Jean *retired English educator, writer, storyteller*
Lesko-Bishop, Julia *editor*
†McDowell, Cassandra *multi-media specialist*
Saulmon, Sharon Ann *college librarian*
Smith, Wayne Calvin *chemical engineer, consultant*

Monkey Island
Vanatta, Chester B. *retired business executive, educator*

Moore
Lee, Myung Woo *financial secretary, accountant*

Mooreland
†Eilers (Bowers), Betty Sue *elementary school educator, writer*

Mounds
Fellows, Esther Elizabeth *musician, music educator*
Halsey, James Albert *international entertainment impresario, theatrical producer, talent manager*

Muskogee
Coburn, Tom A. *former congressman*
Diede, Nancy *nursing educator*
†Edwards, Terri Lyn Wilmoth *education educator*
†Ehlers, Deborah Layne *educator, dramaturg, director*
Frix, Paige Lane *lawyer, accountant*
Gallant, Jeffrey Andrew *lawyer*
Kent, Bartis Milton *retired physician*
Robinson, Adelbert Carl *lawyer, judge*
Slattery, Jeffrey *management educator, consultant*
Tobin, Thomas Edward, Jr., *civil engineer*
Williams, Betty Outhier *lawyer*

Mustang
Laurent, J(erry) Suzanna *technical communications specialist*
†Wood, Jean Carol *poet, lyricist*

Newcastle
Mudroch, Kimberly Ann *veterinarian*

Newkirk
Newport, L. Joan *clinical social worker, retired psychotherapist*

Noble
Watrous, Naoma Dickson *retired clinical psychologist*

Norman
Affleck, Marilyn *sociology educator*
Aligizaki, Kalliopi K. *civil engineer, educator*
Altan, M(ustafa) Cengiz *mechanical engineering educator*
Atiquzzaman, Mohammed *engineering educator*
Atkinson, Gordon *chemistry educator*
Bagajewicz, Miguel *engineering educator*
Barwick-Snell, Katherine Lane *family human relations and women's studies educator, home economics consultant*
Bell, Robert Eugene *anthropologist educator*
Berkowitz, Robert Ari *neurobiologist*
Bert, Charles Wesley *mechanical and aerospace engineer, educator*
Bethel, Joann D. *computer programmer, analyst*
Bluestein, Howard Bruce *meteorology educator*
Brown, Sidney DeVere *history educator*
Campbell, John Morgan *retired chemical engineer*
Carpenter, Charles Congden *zoologist, educator*
Carroll, Frances Laverne *librarian, educator*
†Cheng, Deping *chemist, researcher*
Cochran, Gloria Grimes *retired pediatrician*
Corr, Edwin Gharst *ambassador*
Cowan, John James *physicist, educator, astronomer, educator*
Croft, Janet Brennan *academic librarian*
†Daniel, Sean *voice educator, baritone, artist*
Dary, David Archie *journalism educator, author*
Davies-Jones, Robert Peter *meteorologist*
Day, Adrienne Carol *artist, art educator*
Deming, David *geologist, educator*
Dille, John Robert *physician*
†Doty, Ralph Edward *classics educator*
Drayton, John N. *publishing executive*
Eilts, Michael Dean *research meteorologist, manager*
†Enrico, Eugene Joseph *music educator*
Fears, Jesse Rufus *historian, educator, academic dean*
Fogel, Norman *retired chemistry educator*
Gaskins-Clark, Patricia Renae *dietitian*
†Genova, Pamela A. *French literature educator*
Gilje, Paul Arn *history educator*
†Griffith-Barbara, Martha Jayne *music educator*
Hassig, Ross *anthropologist*
Hastie, John Douglas *lawyer*
Havlicek, Joseph Paul *educator*
Henderson, Arnold Glenn *architect, educator*
Henderson, George *educational sociologist, educator*
Hengst, Herbert Randall *retired educator*
Henkle, James L. *industrial designer*
Herstand, Theodore *theatre artist, educator*
Hufnagel, Glenda Ann Lewin *human relations educator and administrator*
Hughes, Richard Gary *engineering educator*
†Hui, Dafeng *ecologist, statistician*
Hutchison, Victor Hobbs *biologist, educator*
Javellas, Ina June *social worker*
Jones, Charlotte *principal*
Kennedy, Gregory Dustin *journalist*
Kenney, Charles Dennison *political science educator*
Kessler, Edwin *meteorology educator, consultant*
†Kidwell, Clara Sue *education educator*
Kim, Changwook *computer science educator*
Kondonassis, Alexander John *economist, educator*
Koshkin-Youritzin, Victor *art educator*
Lakshmivarahan, Sivaramakrishnan *computer science educator*
Lamb, Peter James *meteorology educator, researcher, consultant*
Leitch, Vincent Barry *literary and cultural studies educator*
Lester, June *library information studies educator*
Logue, Dennis Emhardt *financial economics educator, consultant*
Lowitt, Richard *history educator*
MacFarland, Miriam Katherine (Mimi MacFarland)
Magarian, Robert Armen *medicinal chemist, researcher, educator , author, inventor*
Magrath, Jane *music educator*
Malick, Eldon Roy *music educator, musician*
Mallinson, Richard Gregory *chemical engineering educator*
Mankin, Charles John *geology educator*
†Martin, Leisa Ann *educational consultant*
†Matlick, Eldon R. *music educator*
McFall, Sara Weer *lawyer*
†Meacham, Mary *science librarian*
†Meiller, James R. *music educator*
Morton, Linda P. *journalism educator*
O'Rear, Edgar Allen, III, *chemical engineering educator*
Pappas, James Pete *university administrator*
Perkins, Edward J. *diplomat*
†Petersen, Catherine Holland *lawyer*
Pigott, John Dowling *geologist, geophysicist, geochemist, educator, consultant*
Price, Linda Rice *community development administrator*
Provine, Lorraine *retired mathematics educator*
†Ragep, F. Jamil *academic administrator, educator*
Ross, Allan Anderson *music educator, university official*
Savage, William Woodrow, Jr., *historian, consultant, social sciences educator*
Scaperlanda, María de Lourdes Ruiz *writer, journalist, author*
Shapiro, Alan Meyer *meteorology educator, researcher*
Sharp, Paul Frederick *former university president, education consultant*
Sherman, Mary Angus *public library administrator*
Shiau, Bor-Jier (Ben Shiau) *environmental scientist, researcher*
Sorey, Thomas Lester, Jr., *architect, educator*
†Striz, Alfred Gerhard *aerospace engineer, educator*
†Sweeney, Everett John *lawyer*
Tackwell, Elizabeth Miller *social worker*
Talley, Richard Bates *lawyer*
Tihanyi, Laszlo *management educator, researcher*
Trimble, Preston Albert *retired judge*
Wang, Han *developmental biologist*
Weber, Jerome Charles *education and human relations educator, former academic dean and vice-provost*
Whittier, Charles Taylor, Jr., *consulting company executive, educational, management and scientific administrator*
Wilhite, Jeffrey Mark *librarian, educator*
†Yu, Ning *linguist, educator*
Zapffe, Nina Byrom *retired elementary education educator*
Zelby, Leon Wolf *electrical engineering educator, consulting engineer*
Zelby, Rachel *realtor*

Nowata
Moore, Jeannie Marie *education educator, writer*
Osborn, Ann George *retired chemist*

Ochelata
Hitzman, Donald Oliver *microbiologist*

Okemah
DeShields, Elizabeth Peggy Bowen *artist, educator, poet*

Oklahoma City
Ackerman, Raymond Basil *advertising agency executive*
†Adair, Larry E. *state representative*
Adams, Mary Lou *piano teacher*
Adams, Warren Lynn *alcohol/drug abuse services professional, consultant*
Alaupovic, Alexandra Vrbanic *artist, educator*
Alaupovic, Petar *biochemist, educator*
Alexander, Patrick Byron *university administrator*
Allbright, Karan Elizabeth *psychologist, consultant*
Allen, Robert Dee *lawyer*
Alley, Wayne Edward *federal judge, retired army officer*
†Andrews, M. Dewayne *dean, internist, educator*
Arbuckle, Averil Dorothy (Cookie Arbuckle) *healthcare facility administrator*
Bahr, Carman Bloedow *internist*
†Baker, Doug W. *history and humanities educator*
Barth, J. Edward *lawyer, shareholder*
Beech, Johnny Gale *lawyer*
Beleu, Steve (Dan Beleu) *librarian*
†Beltran, Eusebius Joseph *archbishop*
†Beveridge, Norwood Pierson *law educator*
Binning, Gene Barton *computer company executive*
Bishop, Wanda Caroline *geriatrics nurse, medical/surgical nurse*
Blackwell, John Adrian, Jr., *computer company executive*
Blick, Kenneth Edward *clincial chemist, educator*
†Blochowiak, Mary Ann *cultural organization administrator, writer*
Blount, James Robert *military career officer*
Bohanon, Luther L. *federal judge*
Boomer, Dennis Keith *college official, clergyman*
Boston, Billie *costume designer, costume history educator*
Boston, William Clayton *lawyer*
Bowlby, Leymond Ambrose *linguist, translator*
Boyles, S. Kay *pianist, music educator*
Bradford, Dennis Doyle *real estate broker, developer*
Bradford, Reagan Howard, Jr., *ophthalmology educator*
Branch, John Curtis *biology educator, lawyer*
Brandt, Edward Newman, Jr., *physician, educator*
†Bridges, Annita Marie *lawyer*
Brooks, Gene (Leslie Gene Brooks) *cultural association administrator*
Brown, Kenneth Ray *banker*
Browne, John Robinson *banker*
Brown-Kuykendall, Donita *early childhood educator*
Bush, William Arden *federal agency administrator*
Campbell, David Gwynne *petroleum executive, geologist*
Cassel, John Elden *accountant*
Christiansen, Mark D. *lawyer*
Claflin, James Robert *pediatrician, allergist*
Clark, Gary Ray *licensing board executive*
†Clark, Robert Lloyd, Jr., *librarian*
Clayton, Lawrence Otto *minister, writer, educator, alcohol and drug counselor*
Cleary, William B. *oil industry executive*
Coates, Eleanor Smith *civic worker*
†Coats, Andrew Montgomery *lawyer, former mayor, dean*
Collins, William Edward *aeromedical administrator, researcher*
Comp, Philip Cinnamon *medical researcher*
†Corbett, Luke R. *energy executive*
Couch, James Russell, Jr., *neurology educator*
Court, Leonard *lawyer, educator*
Craig, George Dennis *economics educator, consultant*
†Crites, Carl D. *auditor*
Cummings, Sean Spencer *oil and gas industry executive*
†Cunningham, Madeleine White *microbiologist, immunologist*
Cunningham, Stanley Lloyd *lawyer*
Davenport, Gerald Bruce *lawyer*
Dean, Chrystell Fetty *women's health nurse, educator*
Decker, Michael Lynn *lawyer, judge*
Durland, Jack Raymond *retired lawyer*
Dutcher, Brandon Tyler *think tank research director, columnist*
Edmondson, William Andrew *state attorney general*
Elder, James Carl *lawyer*
England, Gary Alan *television meteorologist*
†Epperson, Kraettli Quynton *lawyer, educator*
Everett, Mark Allen *dermatologist, educator*
Fallin, Mary Copeland *lieutenant governor*
†Fenton, Elliott Clayton *lawyer*
Ferguson, Steven Edward *lawyer*
Filley, Warren Vernon *allergist, immunologist*
†Flournoy, Dayl Jean *clinical microbiologist, educator*
Ford, Charles Reed *state legislator*
Forni, Patricia Rose *dean, nursing educator*
Friedberg, Wallace *biologist, researcher*
†Fuller, G. M. *lawyer*
†Funk, Robert Allen *personnel executive*
Garrett, Kathryn Ann Byers (Kitty Garrett) *legislative clerk*
George, James Noel *hematologist, oncologist, educator*
Gilchrist, John Mark *otolaryngologist*
Gourley, James Leland *editor, publishing executive*
Gourley, Vicki Clark *publishing executive*
Greiner, Kenneth Donald, Jr., *nursing home company executive*
Grupe, Robert Charles *corporate training consultant*
†Gustafson, William Gene *oil industry executive*
Hall, James Granville, Jr., *history educator*
Halverstadt, Donald Bruce *urologist, educator*
Hamilton, Thomas Allen *independent insurance agent, securities representative*
Hampton, Carol McDonald *priest, educator, historian*
Hampton, James Wilburn *hematologist, medical oncologist*
Hanna, Terry Ross *lawyer, small business owner*
Hansen, Mark S. *food marketing and distribution company executive*
Harbour, Robert Randall *state agency administrator*
Hargrave, Rudolph *state supreme court chief justice*
†Harlan, Ross Edgar *retired utility company executive, writer, lecturer, consultant*
Harper, Robbie Jane *critical care nurse, administrator*
Harrington, Gary Burnes *retired controller*
Haywood, B(etty) J(ean) *anesthesiologist*
Heath, Paul A. *psychologist*
Hemry, Jerome Eldon *lawyer*
†Henry, C. Brad *governor*
Henry, Robert Harlan *federal judge, former attorney general*
†Hobson, Calvin J., III, *state legislator, real estate firm executive*
Hodges, Ralph B. *state supreme court justice*
Holder, Lee *human services administrator*
†Holeman, Lora White *music educator*
Holloway, William Judson, Jr., *federal judge*
Hough, Jack Van Doren *otologist*
Humphreys, Kirk *mayor*
Ille, Bernard Glenn *insurance company executive, director*
Jacocks, Mac Alexander *surgeon*
Jenkins, LeAnn *government executive*
†Jenkins, Sherry L. *state accounting manager*
Johnson, B(ruce) Connor *biochemist, educator, consultant*
Johnson, Thomas Harold *radiologist*
Jones, Charles Edwin *historian, bibliographer, chaplain*
Jones, Renee Kauerauf *health care administrator*
Jordan, Beth McAninch *artist, educator*
Kallstrom, James David *lawyer*
Kerr, Lou C. *foundation administrator*
Kinasewitz, Gary Theodore *medical educator*
Kindschuh, Jeffery Alan *civil engineer*
†King, Barbara Sue *librarian*
Kirkpatrick, John Elson *retired oil company executive, retired naval reserve officer*
Kline, David Adam *lawyer, educator, writer*
Kline, Timothy Deal *lawyer*
LaMotte, Janet Allison *retired management specialist*
Lavender, Robert Eugene *state supreme court justice*
Lee, Ellen Faith *insurance company associate*
Legg, William Jefferson *lawyer*
Leonard, Timothy Dwight *judge*
Levine, Joel *music director, conductor*
Li, Shibo *medical genetics educator*
Lo, Patrick Punchuk *physician*
Lovelace, George David, Jr., *quality engineer*
Lumpkin, Gary leonard *judge*
†Mailman, Matthew *conductor*
Margo, Robert Cravens *lawyer*
Mass, Michael D. *state legislator*
Mather, Ruth Elsie *writer*
Mather, Stephanie June *lawyer*
Matsumoto, Hiroyuki *biochemistry educator, researcher*
McClellan, Mary Ann *pediatrics nurse, educator*
†McCook, Matt *education educator*
McEwen, Irene Ruble *physical therapy educator*
McGuigan, Patrick Bruce *editor, educator*
McKenzie, Clif Allen *Indian tribe official, accountant*
McKinnis, Lee Vern *communications executive*
McLaughlin, Lisa Marie *educational administrator*
†McMillin, James Craig *lawyer*
Mikkelson, Dean Harold *geological engineer, writer*
Miles-La Grange, Vicki *judge*
Miller, Herbert Dell *petroleum engineer*
Mitrovgenis, James William, Jr., *journalist*
Moler, Edward Harold *lawyer*
Moore, Billy Don *video scriptwriter, producer*
Moore, Joanne Iweita *pharmacologist, educator*
Morgan, Catherine Marie *psychologist, writer*
Muchmore, John Stephen *endocrinologist*
Mustion, Alan Lee *pharmacist*
†Nakagawara, Van B. *optometrist, researcher*
†Nath, Swapan K. *epidemiologist*
Necco, Alexander David *lawyer, educator*
†Nelon, Robert Dale *lawyer*
Nesbitt, Charles Rudolph *lawyer, energy consultant*
†Nichols, J. Larry *energy company executive, lawyer*
Noakes, Betty LaVonne *retired elementary school educator*
Nour, Bakr M. *surgeon, health facility administrator*
Oehlert, William Herbert, Jr., *cardiologist, administrator, educator*
Opala, Marian P(eter) *state supreme court justice*
O'Steen, Randy A. *nursing administrator*
Pain, Betsy M. *lawyer*
Paliotta, Armand *lawyer*
Pardo, Gabriel *neuro-ophthalmologist, neurologist, researcher*
Paris, Wayne *social worker, researcher*
Parke, David Wilkin, II, *ophthalmologist, educator, healthcare executive*
Parmley, Jay *political organization administrator*
Parrott, Nancy Sharon *lawyer*
Paul, William George *lawyer*
Payne, Gareld Gene *vocal music educator, medical transcriptionist*
Peace, H. W., II, *oil company executive*

Perez-Cruet, Jorge *physician, psychopharmacologist, psychophysiologist, psychiatrist, educator, addictionologist, geropsychiatrist*
Pfefferbaum, Betty Jane
Philipp, Anita Marie *computer sciences educator*
Pitts, Bryan *performing company executive*
Pratt, Billy Kenton *police officer*
†Prodan, Calin Ioan *physician*
Rahhal, Donald K. *obstetrician, gynecologist*
†Rainbolt, H. E. *bank executive*
†Rathbun, Robert Christopher *pharmacy educator*
Reich, Richard Allen *energy company executive*
†Reimer, Dennis J. *career military officer*
†Ridley, Betty Ann *religous educator, church worker*
Rix, Robert Alvin, Jr., *retired neurosurgeon*
Rockett, D. Joe *lawyer, director*
Ross, William Jarboe *lawyer, director*
Rossavik, Ivar Kristian *obstetrician, gynecologist*
Roth, James Anthony *lawyer*
Rundell, Orvis Herman, Jr., *psychologist, educator*
Russell, David L. *federal judge*
†Ryan, Patrick M. *lawyer*
Savage, Susan M. *state official, former mayor*
Schroyer, Michael Kevin *critical care nurse and hospital administrator*
Schuster, E. Elaine *lawyer*
Schwabe, George Blaine, III, *lawyer*
†Scofield, Robert Hal *physician, biomedical researcher*
Sheldon, Eli Howard *minister*
Shillingburg, Herbert Thompson, Jr., *dental educator*
Shurley, Jay Talmadge *writer, retired psychiatrist, medical educator, administrator, behavioral scientist, polar explorer, genealogist*
†Sibley, William Arthur *academic administrator, physics educator, consultant*
Siewert, Edgar Allen *retired military non-commissioned officer*
Sookne, Herman Solomon (Hank Sookne) *retirement services executive*
Sorrin, Mary Louise *artist, nurse*
Spencer, Melvin Joe *hospital administrator, lawyer*
Stanley, Brian Jordan *lawyer*
Steinhorn, Irwin Harry *lawyer, educator, corporate executive*
†Stewart, Robert D., Jr., *lawyer*
Stringer, L.E. (Dean Stringer) *retired lawyer*
Summers, Hardy *state supreme court justice*
Tang, Irving Che-hong *mathematician, educator*
Taylor, Stratton *state legislator, lawyer*
Taylor-White-Grigsby, Queen Delores *minister, consultant*
TeSelle, John *retired judge*
Thadani, Udho *physician, cardiologist*
Thomas, Gary Wayne *actor*
†Thompson, David *publishing executive*
Thompson, Ralph Gordon *federal judge*
Tillinghast, Jon Dalton *public health physician*
Tompkins, Raymond Edgar *lawyer*
Towery, Curtis Kent *lawyer*
Triplett, E. Eugene *editor*
Trost, Louis Frederick, Jr., *banker, financial planner*
Troutman, George William *geologist, petroleum geological advisor*
Tucker, Phebe Mary *psychiatrist, educator*
Tuck-Richmond, Doletta Sue *prosecutor*
Turman, Martin Allan *pediatric nephrologist, educator*
Turner, Eugene Andrew *manufacturing executive*
Twyman, Nita (Venita Twyman) *music educator*
Van De Steeg, Garet Edward *chemical consultant, environmental consultant*
†Voth, Douglas W. *dean*
†Wallace, Thomas Andrew *lawyer*
Walsh, Lawrence Edward *lawyer*
Watt, Joseph Michael *state supreme court chief justice*
Weigel, Paul Henry *biochemistry educator, researcher, consultant*
West, Lee Roy *federal judge*
Whitener, Carolyn Raye *artist*
†Willey, Benjamin Tucker, Jr., *lawyer*
Williams, Richard Donald *retired wholesale food company executive*
Williamson, Marvel *dean, sexologist, nursing administrator, author, speaker*
Wilson, Julia Ann Yother *lawyer*
Wisdom, Peggy Jean *neurologist*
Wolraich, Mark Lee *pediatrician, educator*
Woods, Harry Arthur, II, *lawyer*
Woods, Pendleton *college director, author*
Worsham, Bertrand Ray *psychiatrist*
Wortham, James Mason, Sr., *gas supply company official*
Young, Stephen K. *academic administrator*
Zanoni de los Santos, Jacqueline M. *artist, curator*
†Zeaman, Christian Michael *lawyer, writer*
Zevnik-Sawatzky, Donna Dee *retired litigation coordinator*
Zhu, Hua *biochemist, researcher*
Zuhdi, Nazih *former surgeon, administrator*

Owasso
Reed, Walter George, Jr., *osteopathic physician*

Park Hill
Lindsey, James Kendall *civil engineer*

Pawhuska
Holloway, Sharon Kay Sossamon *vocational/secondary school educator*
Strahm, Samuel Edward *veterinarian*

Perry
Beers, Frederick Gordon *writer, retired corporate communications official*
Doughty, Michael Dean *insurance agent*
Gard, Michael Floyd *research engineer*

Ponca City
Collins, Walter Lloyd George *editor*
†Fraenkel, Dan *oil industry executive, researcher*
Gallagher, Gary W(ayne) *educational services executive*
Gong, Xiaoyi *engineer*
Leonard, Samuel Wallace *oil company and bank executive*
†Linder, Donald E. *retired environmental scientist, rancher*
Northcutt, Clarence Dewey *lawyer*
Raley, John W., Jr., *lawyer*
Rice, Sue Ann *dean, industrial and organizational psychologist*
Surber, Joe Robert *assistant superintendent of schools*
Tatum, Betty Joyce *secondary school educator*
Wann, Laymond Doyle *retired petroleum research scientist*

Prague
Stefansen, Peggy Ann *special education educator*

Pryor
Burdick, Larry G. *school system administrator*
Stinson, Marion Dennis *lawyer, land use planner, judge*

Purcell
Mantooth, John Albert *judge*

Ringling
†Hammons, Ella *consumer products company executive*

Sallisaw
Buckner, JoAnn *special education educator, consultant*
Crowson, Watie Dee *foundation administrator*
Mayo, James Watie (Jim Mayo) *publishing executive*

Sand Springs
†Biggoose, Charles *counselor*
Quinn, Art Jay *veterinarian, retired educator*

Sapulpa
Gardner, Dale Ray *lawyer*
†Weinstock Rad, Katheryn Louise *music educator*

Seminole
Elsener, G. Dale *lawyer*
Moran, Melvin Robert *oil industry executive*

Shawnee
Clark, Don Eugene *music educator*
†Hackett, Patricia Jo *academic administrator, dean*
Hicks, Steve L. *artist, art educator*
Hill, Bryce Dale *school administrator*
†Tyler, Jeannie E. *music educator*
Wilks, Jacquelin Holsomback *campus ministries director*
Wilks, Thomas Milton *religious studies educator, minister*
Zuhdi, Omar *secondary education educator*

Skiatook
Harwell, Kenneth E. *chemist, researcher, consultant*

Stillwater
Agnew, Theodore Lee, Jr., *historian, educator*
Bahr, Beverly Katherine *critical care nurse*
Berlin, Kenneth Darrell Darrell *chemistry educator, consultant, researcher*
Brusewitz, Gerald Henry *agricultural engineering educator, researcher*
Campbell, John Roy *animal science educator, academic administrator*
†Chung, Jong-Moon *education educator*
Confer, Anthony Wayne *veterinary pathologist, educator*
Cooper, Donald Lee *physician*
Curl, Samuel Everett *university dean, agricultural scientist*
Darcy, Robert Emmett *political scientist, educator, statistician*
†DeGroot, Timothy *finance educator*
†Dooley, Robert S. *finance educator*
Evans, Cheryl Lynn *elementary school principal*
Ewing, Sidney Alton *veterinary medical educator, parasitologist*
Fischer, LeRoy Henry *historian, educator*
Fischer, Richard Samuel *lawyer*
Foster, Gayla Catherine *musician*
†Frye, Edward Moses *law educator*
Gilliland, Stanley Eugene *dairy-food microbiology educator*
Graham, Toni *writer*
Grischkowsky, Daniel Richard *research scientist, educator*
†Gunzenhauser, Michael Gerard *mathematician, educator*
Halligan, James Edmund *university administrator, chemical engineer*
†Hendrix, Charles C. *marriage and family therapist, educator*
Hoberock, Lawrence Linden *mechanical engineer, educator*
Jadlow, Joseph Martin *economics educator*
King, Marilyn Sodowsky *music educator*
Komanduri, Ranga *engineering educator*
Langwig, John Edward *retired wood science educator*
Lanners, Thomas Martin *music educator*
Leider, Charles L. *landscape architect, planner*
†Lu, Hongbing *aerospace engineer, consultant*
Luebke, Neil Robert *philosophy educator*
†Lynch, Thomas Bernard *science educator*
Mize, Joe Henry *industrial engineer, educator*
Moomaw, Ronald Lee *economics educator*
Ndegwa, Pius Mwangi *agricultural engineer, researcher*
†Payton, Mark Edward *statistician, educator*
Poole, Richard William *economics educator*
Qu, Hailin *hospitality and tourism professional*
†Redding, Arthur Francis *language educator*
Sherman, Robert Lee, Jr., *chemist, educator*
†Sim, May *humanities educator*
†Smallwood, James Milton *historian, educator*
Smeyak, Gerald Paul *telecommunication educator*
Steindl, Frank George *economist, educator*
†te Velde, Rebecca Groom *organist, music educator, composer*
Thompson, David Russell *engineering educator, academic dean*
†Vestal, Theodore Merrill *education educator*
†Wiley, Moira Kathleen *writer, editor*
Zhang, Minquan *chemistry educator*

Tahlequah
†Diamantopoulos, John C.D. *mathematician, educator*
Edmondson, Linda Louise *optometrist*
†Grant, Kay Lallier *early childhood education educator*
†Howard, James Kenton *academic administrator, journalist*
†Roberts, James David *pastor, construction executive*
Snyder, Travis Carroll *evangelist*
Sumner, Delores Titchywy *school librarian, educator*

Texhoma
Jackson, Paul Howard *minister*

Tinker AFB
Goodman, Ernest Monroe *military officer*
†Johnson, Charles L., II, *military officer*
Livingston, Douglas Mark *lawyer*

Tonkawa
†Fiscus, Linda Kay *music educator*

Tulsa
Abrahamson, A. Craig *lawyer*
Allwein, Robert William *mechanical engineer*
Anderson, David Walter *physics educator, consultant*
Anderson, William Carl *lawyer*
Angelini, Marcello *artistic director*
Arrington, John Leslie, Jr., *lawyer*
Arrington, Rebecca Carol *occupational health nurse*
†Bailey, Garrick Alan *anthropologist, educator*
Bailey, Keith E. *petroleum pipeline company executive*
Ball, Rex Martin *urban designer, architect*
Ballard, Elizabeth Ann *lawyer*
Balman, Steven K. *lawyer*
Baukal, Charles Edward, Jr., *mechanical engineer*
Beck, Robert James *editor, energy economist, author, consultant*
Belsky, Martin Henry *law educator, lawyer*
Bender, John Henry, Jr., (Jack Bender) *editor, cartoonist*
Berlin, Steven Ritt *oil company executive*
Biolchini, Robert Fredrick *lawyer*
Bires, Dennis Eugene *legal educator*
Blais, Roger Nathaniel *physics educator*
Blenkarn, Kenneth Ardley *mechanical engineer, consultant*
Bogomilov, Boris *medical educator*
Bowles, Margo La Joy *lawyer*
†Bowman, David Wesley *lawyer*
Boyle, Lester Joseph *marketing and broadcast executive*
Braumiller, Allen Spooner *oil and gas exploration company executive, geologist*
Brett, Thomas Rutherford *federal judge*
Brewster, Clark Otto *lawyer*
Brightmire, Paul William *retired judge*
†Brooker, Timothy Douglas *social studies educator*
†Brune, Kenneth Leonard *lawyer*
Brunk, Samuel Frederick *oncologist*
Bryant, Hubert Hale *lawyer*
Buckley, Thomas Hugh *historian, educator*
Busch, Daniel Adolph *geologist, educator*
†Cadieux, Chester *gas industry executive*
Calvert, Jon Channing *family practice physician*
Candreia, Peggy Jo *financial analyst*
Cardwell, Sandra Gayle Bavido *university admissions professional*
Chandler, Ronald Jay *lawyer*
Clark, Gary Carl *lawyer*
Clark, Joseph Francis, Jr., *lawyer*
Cobbs, James Harold *engineer, consultant*
Coffey, Robert John *pediatrician*
Cook, Harold Dale *federal judge*
Cooke, Marvin Lee *sociologist, consultant, urban planner*
Cooper, Richard Casey *lawyer*
†Cottingham, Barbara J. *music educator*
Coulter, Jean Walpole *lawyer*
Cox, William Jackson *retired bishop*
Crawford, B. *lawyer*
Crouch, Gary Clinton *financial management company executive, accountant*
Davis, Annalee Ruth Conyers *clinical social worker*
†Davis, Lourie Irene Bell *computer education and information systems specialist*
Deihl, Michael Allen *federal agency administrator*
de Leon, Antonio Carmelo, Jr., *internist, cardiologist*
Dexter, Deirdre O'Neil Elizabeth *lawyer*
†Dimiceli, Vincent Edward *mathematician, educator*
†Donaldson, Robert Herschel *university administrator, educator*
Dotson, George Stephen *drilling company executive*
Draughon, Scott Wilson *lawyer, social worker, educator*
Dugger, William Mayfield *economics educator*
Duncan, Maurice Greer *accountant, consultant*
Eagan, Claire Veronica *district court judge*
†Eagleton, Edward John *lawyer*
Earlougher, Robert Charles, Sr., *petroleum engineer*
Eaton, Leonard James, Jr., *aerospace executive*
Eldridge, Richard Mark *lawyer*
Engel, David Wayne *lawyer, federal official*
†Engle, Lars *language educator*
Faingold, Eduardo Daniel *language and linguistics educator, researcher*
Farrell, John L., Jr., *lawyer, business executive*
†Ferguson, Dallas Eugene *lawyer*
†Ferraro, Jay *psychologist, consultant*
Ferrell, Howard Hulen *retired petroleum engineer*
†Finkelman, Paul *law educator*
Fisk, Francine Joan *librarian*
Fleifil, Mahmoud Mohamed *acoustics engineer, researcher*
Fleming, Ken *publishing executive*
Franken, Joy R. *exercise physiologist*
Frazier, Mary Ann *artist*
†Frey, Martin Alan *lawyer, educator*
Friedman, Mark Joel *cardiologist, educator*
Frizzell, Gregory Kent K. *judge*
Gaberino, John Anthony, Jr., *lawyer*
Gaddis, Richard William *management educator*
Geary, Barbara Ann *recital and concert pianist, music educator*
Gentry, Bern Leon, Sr., *minority consulting company executive*
Goodman, Jerry L(ynn) *judge*
Gottschalk, Sister Mary Therese *nun, hospital administrator*
Gotwals, Charles Place, Jr., *lawyer*
Gray, Karen Kay *counselor*
†Grizzle, Trevor Lloyd *religious studies educator, minister*
Haring, Robert Westing *newspaper editor*
Hatfield, Jack Kenton *lawyer, accountant*
Hawkins, Francis Glenn *banker, lawyer*
Haynie, Tony Wayne *lawyer*
Healey, David Lee *investment company executive*
Henderson, James Ronald *industrial real estate developer*
Herrold, David Henry *lawyer*
†Hess, Stanley O. *retired art educator*
Hoe, Richard March *insurance and securities consultant, writer*
Holmes, Sven Erik *federal judge, educator*
Horkey, William Richard *retired diversified oil company executive*
Horn, Myron Kay *consulting petroleum geologist, author, educator*
Howard, Gene Claude *retired lawyer, retired state senator*
†Howland, Jacob *philosopher, educator*
Huff, Rosemary Bowers *music and voice educator*
Huffman, Robert Allen, Jr., *lawyer*
†Hughes, William Earle *lawyer*
Imel, John Michael *lawyer*
Ingram, Charles Clark, Jr., *energy company executive*
Jensen, Joli *communications educator*
Johnson, Cornelius Raymond *assistant city attorney*
Joice, Nora Lee *clinical dietitian*
†Jones, Geoffrey Kyle *telecommunications industry executive*
Jones, Jenk, Jr., *editor, educator*
Jones, Jenkin Lloyd *retired newspaper publisher*
Jones, Michael Lynn *financial consultant, branch operations manager*
Jones, Robert Lawton *architect, planner, educator*
Kaiser, George B. *corporate financial executive*
Kalbfleisch, John McDowell *cardiologist, educator*
Kemp, Sarah (Sally Leech) *developmental psychologist, neuropsychologist*
Kern, Terry C. *judge*
Kihle, Donald Arthur *lawyer*
Kincaid, James Lewis *lawyer*
King, Peter Cotterill *former utilities executive*
Knaust, Clara Doss *retired elementary school educator*
Korstad, John Edward *biology educator*
Kramer, John C. *pediatrician*
Kronfeld, Edwin *natural gas company executive*
Kukura, Rita Anne *pre-school educator*
Kyle, David L. *gas industry executive*
LaFortune, Bill *mayor*
†Lang, Andrew Stuart Ian Donald *mathematician, consultant*
Lawless, Robert William *academic administrator*
Lewis, Corinne Hemeter *psychotherapist, educator*
Liebendorfer, Richard Arthur *internist*
Lindsay, Patricia Mae *physician, medical administrator*
Lorton, Robert E., Jr., *publishing executive*
Luthey, Graydon Dean, Jr., *lawyer, educator*
Major, John Keene *radio broadcasting executive*
†Malcolm, Steven J. *petroleum pipeline company executive*
Martin, Edward Thomas *cardiologist, researcher*
Matthews, Dane Dikeman *urban planner*
Matthies, Mary Constance T. *lawyer*
McAdams, Jason David *mechanical engineer*
McCullough, Robert Dale, II, *osteopath*
Miller, Gerald Cecil *immunologist, laboratory administrator, educator*
Moffett, J. Denny *lawyer*
Mojtabai, Ann Grace *author, educator*
Moore, David Arthur *composer, music educator*
Munro, Michael Donald *air transportation executive, retired military officer*
Narwold, Lewis Lammers *paper products manufacturer*
Neal, E(verett) G(ilbert) *small business owner*
Neas, John Theodore *investment company executive*
Nemec, Michael Lee *lawyer*
Nettles, John Barnwell *obstetrics and gynecology educator*
Nevinny-Stickel, Hans Boris *oncologist*
Nigh, Robert Russell, Jr., *lawyer*

Okada, Robert Dean *cardiologist*
Orlowski, D. Faith *lawyer*
Osborn, La Donna Carol *clergywoman*
Owens, Jana Jae *entertainer*
Parker, Robert Lee, Sr., *petroleum engineer, drilling company executive*
Perryman, Robert G. *surgeon*
Plunket, Daniel Clark *retired pediatrician*
Prayson, Alex Stephen *design engineering educator*
Price, Alice Lindsay *writer, artist*
†Rayborn, M. Yvonne *physician*
Raynolds, William F., II, *lawyer*
†Redfearn, Charlotte Marie *nursing administrator*
Reed, Robert A. *performing arts executive*
Repasky, Mark Edward *oil and gas company executive*
Rex, Lonnie Royce *religious organization administrator*
Ricks, Cecil Edward *architect*
Riggs, M. David *lawyer, rancher*
Roberts, Oral (Granville Oral Roberts) *clergyman*
Roger, Jerry Lee *academic administrator*
Saied, James Guy *conductor, consultant*
Sanditen, Edgar Richard *investment company executive*
Say, Burhan *physician*
†Scott, John Prosser *television program producer, management consultant*
Seymour, Stephanie Kulp *federal judge*
Sheehan, William W. *pathologist*
Slaucitajs, Andrew Paul *videographer, video producer*
Slicker, Frederick Kent *lawyer*
Smothers, William Edgar, Jr., *geophysical exploration company executive*
†Sneed, James Lynde *lawyer*
†Sotak, John Joseph *priest, educator*
†Sowell, Debra Ann Olson *mathematician, educator, academic administrator*
Sowell, Laven *retired music educator*
†Spiegelberg, Frank David *lawyer*
Stearns, Frederic William *dermatologist*
Steltzlen, Janelle Hicks *lawyer*
Stockwell, Lance *law educator*
Strecker, David Eugene *lawyer*
Taylor, Joe Clinton *judge*
Thomas, Robert Eggleston *retired corporate executive*
†Thompson, Anne *court administrator*
Trennepohl, Gary Lee *university administrator, finance educator*
Undernehr, Laura Lee *elementary education educator*
Upton, Howard B., Jr., *management writer, lawyer*
Wagner, Ann Louise *management consultant, public relations executive*
Wagner, Clarence H., Jr., *charitable organization administrator*
Watson, Eric N. *corporate executive*
Watson, John Skelly *retired surgeon*
Wiland, George William, Jr., *legislative staff member, consultant*
Williams, John Horter *civil engineer, oil, gas, telecommunications and allied products distribution company executive*
†Wolfe, Joseph Allen *finance educator, consultant*
Wood, Emily Churchill *educator, educational consultant*

Vance AFB
Sandstrom, Dirk William *air force officer, hospital administrator*

Vinita
Castor, Carol Jean *artist, teacher*
Curnutte, Mark William *lawyer*
Johnston, Oscar Black, III, *lawyer*
Lollman, Matthew Tobias *music educator*
Neer, Charles Sumner, II, *orthopedic surgeon, educator*
Wright, Jo Anne *Episcopal priest*

Warr Acres
Phillips, Richard Carey *real estate executive*

Weatherford
Albaugh, Bernard John, II, *social science researcher*
†Aspedon, Mary D. *education educator*
Pray, Walter Steven *pharmacy educator*
Vanderslice, Ronna Jean *education educator*
†Widen, Dennis Charles *music educator*
Wolgamott, Gary Dean *medical educator*

Welling
Varner, Joyce Ehrhardt *retired librarian*

Wewoka
Trimble, Vance Henry *retired newspaper editor*

Wilburton
†Pate, Thomas Lowell *manufacturing executive*

Yukon
Clonts, George Gary *packaging company executive*
Hixson, Wendell Mark *lawyer*

OREGON

Albany
Chowning, Orr-Lyda Brown *dietitian*
Haralson, Linda Jane *communications executive*
†White, Diane O'Donnell *retired librarian*
Wood, Kenneth Arthur *retired newspaper editor, writer*

Aloha
Gorea, Lucia-Iosefina *English educator, writer, poet*
†Sheykman, Bella *music educator*

Ashland
Addicott, Warren Oliver *retired geologist, educator*
Bornet, Vaughn Davis *former social science educator, research historian*
Chamberlain, Kent Clair *business owner, poet*
Chatfield, Michael *accounting educator*
Christianson, Roger Gordon *biology educator*
Friend, Sandra Ann Covert *interior designer*
Gaulke, Mary Florence *library administrator*
Grover, James Robb *chemist, editor*
Hegler, Ellen Marie *business executive, retired educator*
Kirschner, Richard Michael *naturopathic physician, speaker, writer*
†Kostka, Robert Anton *artist, educator*
Kreisman, Arthur *higher education consultant, humanities educator emeritus*
Levy, Leonard Williams *history educator, author*
Masters, Robert Edward Lee *psychotherapist, neural researcher, human potential educator, philosopher*
Meese, Celia Edwards *pharmaceutical company executive*
†Morris, Daniel Robert *language educator*
Mularz, Theodore Leonard *architect*
†Uherbelau, Judy *lawyer, state legislator*

Astoria
Foster, Michael William *librarian*
Haskell, Donald McMillan *lawyer*

Bandon
Lindquist, Louis William *artist, writer*
Millard, Esther Lound *foundation administrator, educator*

Banks
Fleming, Kathleen Gail *retired computer operations specialist*

Beatty
Nettelbeck, Fred Arthur *poet*

Beaverton
†Austin, Glenn *retired pediatrician, medical researcher*
Barnes, Keith Lee *electronics executive*
Cassidy, Richard Arthur *environmental engineer, governmental water resources specialist*
Chartier, Vernon Lee *electrical engineer*
Davis, Stanford Melvin *engineering executive, internet consultant*
Edlich, Richard French *biomedical engineering educator*
Eisner, Alvin *optics scientist*
Guers, Christian Alain *information systems specialist*
Hebert, Carol Ann *software engineer*
Kaplan, Bradley S. *corporate financial executive*
Knight, Philip H(ampson) *apparel executive*
Liu, Kevin H. *research scientist, software architect*
Mitchell, Bettie Phaenon *religious organization administrator*
Murray, Jean Rupp *communications executive, writer, speaker*
†Nikolich-Zugich, Janko *biomedical scientist, educator*
Pond, Patricia Brown *library science educator, university administrator*
Ray, Ruth Alice Yancey *retired rancher, real estate developer*
Ricks, Mary F(rances) *archaeologist, anthropologist, consultant*
†Stewart, Kirk T. *public relations executive*
Thompson, Greg Alan *computer sciences consulting executive*

Bend
Achterman, Gail Louise *lawyer*
Acosta, Cristina Pilar *artist*
Amber, Rich *manufacturing engineer*
Brundage, Bruce Howard *cardiologist*
Donohue, Stacey Lee *English language and literature educator*
Evers-Williams, Myrlie *cultural organization administrator*
Gillem, Elise (Marie) (Elise Michaels) *radio and television personality*
Gustafson, Lewis Allan *retired geologist*
Holl, Walter John *architect, interior designer*
†Irwin, Kerri Lynne *pharmacist, writer, small business owner*
Joslin, Leslie Allen *writer*
†Löffler, Daniel G. *chemical engineer, researcher*
Nelson, Douglas Michael *school system administrator, educator*
Nosler, Robert Amos *sports company executive*
Sabatella, Elizabeth Maria *clinical therapist, educator, mental health facility administrator*
Seed, Brian Bruce *music educator*
Thompson, Mari Hildenbrand *medico-legal and administrative consultant*
Wonser, Michael Dean *retired public affairs director, art history educator*

Boring
Robinson, Jeanne Louise *writer*

Brookings
Maxwell, William Stirling *retired lawyer*
Nolan, Benjamin Burke *retired civil engineer*

Burns
Christensen, Denise Danyel *real estate broker*
Peckham, Kendall I. *music educator*
†Timms, Eugene Dale *wholesale business owner, state senator*

Canby
Drummond, Gerard Kasper *lawyer, retired minerals company executive*
Flinn, Roberta Jeanne *management, computer applications consultant*

Cannon Beach
Greaver, Harry *artist*

Hellyer, Constance Anne (Connie Anne Conway) *writer, musician*
Hillestad, Charles Andrew *lawyer*
Wismer, Patricia Ann *retired secondary education educator*

Central Point
Brown, Christopher Patrick *health care administrator, educator*
Richardson, Dennis Michael *lawyer, educator*

Cheshire
Antikajian, Sarkis Serop *artist, retired pharmacist*

Chiloquin
†Harreld, Karen L. *jewelry designer, photographer*
Siemens, Richard Ernest *retired metallurgy administrator, researcher*

Clackamas
Etulain, Richard Wayne *historian, educator*
Love, Susan Denise *accountant, consultant, small business owner*
Woods, Dennis Oliver *headmaster, market and political research analyst*

Coos Bay
†McClellan, Janet Elaine *law educator*
Van Allen, Katrina Frances (Katrina Frances) *painter*

Coquille
Lounsbury, Steven Richard *lawyer*

Corvallis
Arnold, Roy Gary *academic administrator*
Bernieri, Frank John *social psychology educator*
Boedtker, Olaf A. *physicist*
Byrne, John Vincent *higher education consultant*
†Campbell, Courtney Scott *humanities educator*
Castellano, Michael Angelo *research forester*
Castle, Emery Neal *agricultural and resource economist, educator*
Chambers, Kenton Lee *botany educator*
Chau, May Ying *librarian, educator*
Clinton, Richard Lee *international relations educator*
†Conatser, Brian Keith *music educator, musician*
Dalrymple, Gary Brent *research geologist*
Davis, John Rowland *university administrator*
Dennis, John Davison *minister*
Drake, Charles Whitney *physicist*
Engelbrecht, Rudolf *electrical engineering educator*
Forbes, Leonard *engineering educator*
Frakes, Rodney Vance *plant geneticist, educator*
Frey, Bruce E. *radiation oncologist*
Hafner-Eaton, Chris *health services researcher, medical educator, policy analyst*
†Haig, Susan *ecologist, educator*
Hall, Don Alan *editor, writer*
Healey, Deborah Lynn *education administrator*
Howland, James Chase *retired engineer, consultant*
Landers, Teresa Price *librarian*
Main, Michael Dee *information developer*
McCarthy, William Robert *minister*
†McKee-Ryan, Frances M *education educator*
McKinney, William Mark *retired geology educator*
Miner, John Ronald *bioengineer*
Moore, George W(illiam) *geologist*
Morita, Richard Yukio *microbiology and oceanography educator*
Parker, Donald Fred *college dean, human resources management educator*
Parks, Harold Raymond *mathematician, educator*
†Qu, Annie *statistician, educator*
Rapier, Pascal Moran *chemical engineer, physicist*
Ray, Edward John *economics educator, administrator*
Risser, Paul Gillan *academic administrator, botanist*
Rose, Robert William, Jr., (Robin Rose) *forest regeneration scientist, educator*
Rygiewicz, Paul Thaddeus *plant ecologist*
Schlegel, Colette Sue *musician*
Seyb, Leslie Philip *chemist, researcher*
Shiue, Wen-Tsong *electrical and computer scientist, educator*
Shoemaker, Clara Brink *retired chemistry researcher*
Simoneit, Bernd Rolf Tatsuo *geochemistry educator*
Sleight, Arthur William *chemist, educator*
Steele, Robert Edwin *orthopedic surgeon*
Sun, Osbert Jianxin *ecophysiologist, researcher*
Temes, Gabor Charles *electrical engineering educator*
Tenca, Alexandre Ferreira *computer scientist, electrical engineer*
Van Holde, Kensal Edward *biochemistry educator*
Verts, Lita Jeanne *university administrator*
Wechsler, Susan Linda *research and development software manager*
Westwood, Melvin Neil *horticulturist, pomologist*
Wilkins, Caroline Hanke *consumer agency administrator, political worker*
Yeats, Robert Sheppard *geologist, educator*
Young, J. Lowell *soil chemist, biologist*
Young, Roy Alton *university administrator, educator*
Zwahlen, Fred Casper, Jr., *journalism educator*

Culver
Siebert, Diane Dolores *author, poet*

Dallas
White, Donald Harvey *physics educator emeritus*

Dayton
McKaughan, Howard Paul *linguistics educator*

†Wright, Beverly June *sales executive*

Depoe Bay
Fish, Barbara Joan *investor, small business owner*

Dillard
Gugel, M. Sue *artist*

Dundee
Olson, Donald R. *neurosurgeon, consultant*

Eagle Point
†Blanchard, Shirley Lynn *primary school educator, consultant*

Eugene
Acker, Martin Herbert *psychotherapist, educator*
Aikens, C(lyde) Melvin *anthropology educator, archaeologist, museum director*
Aldave, Barbara Bader *law educator, lawyer*
Andrews, Fred Charles *mathematics educator*
Bailey, Exine Margaret Anderson *soprano, educator*
Baker, Alton Fletcher, III, *newspaper editor, publishing executive*
Baker, Bridget Downey *newspaper executive*
Baker, Edwin Moody *retired newspaper publisher*
Bascom, Ruth F. *retired mayor*
Bassett, Carol Ann *journalism educator, writer*
Bergquist, Peter *music educator emeritus*
†Bergquist, Timothy M. *business educator, researcher*
Burris, Vallon Leon, Jr., *sociologist, educator*
Camp, Delpha Jeanne *counselor*
Castle, Grace Eleanor *legal investigator*
Chambers, Carolyn Silva *communications company executive*
Christian, Sonya *college dean*
†Christie, Leonard George, Jr., *cardiologist, public health service officer*
Clark, Chapin DeWitt *law educator*
†Collis, Dennis K. *orthopedic surgeon*
Cone, June Elizabeth *civic worker*
Crasemann, Bernd *physicist, educator*
Csonka, Paul L. *theoretical physicist, educator*
Curtis, Charles W. *mathematician, writer*
Davis, Richard Malone *economics educator*
Donnelly, Russell James *physicist, educator*
Drennan, Michael Eldon *banker*
DuPriest, Douglas Millhollen *lawyer*
Edwards, Ralph M. *librarian*
Ellis, Barton Dee *music educator*
Etter, Orval
Evans, George William *economics educator*
Flanagan, Latham, Jr., *surgeon*
†Foley, Charles Bradford *university dean, music educator*
Frank, David Anthony *educator*
Frohnmayer, David Braden *academic administrator*
Gall, Meredith Damien (Meredith Mark Damien Gall) *education educator, writer*
†Garcia-Pabon, Leonardo *Spanish literature educator, consultant*
Gillespie, Penny Hannig *business owner*
Glaspey, Terry W. *publishing executive, writer*
Goldman, Marion Sherman *sociology and religious studies educator, consultant on cults*
Green, Paul John *independent critic*
Griffith, Osbie Hayes *chemistry educator*
Gwartney, Patricia Anne *sociology educator*
Hale, Dean Edward *social services administrator*
Hamren, Nancy Van Brasch *bookkeeper*
Hibbard, Judith Hoffman *health services researcher*
Hildebrand, Carol Ilene *retired librarian*
Holzapfel, Christina Marie *biologist*
†Isenberg, James Allen *mathematics and physics researcher, educator*
Johnston, James C. *neurologist, lawyer*
Kennevan, Walter James *computer science educator*
Khang, Chulsoon *economics educator*
Kirkpatrick, Laird Clifford *law educator*
Kono, Robert Hiroshi *writer, educator*
Landrum, Frank Woolson *library/media educator*
Leeds, Elizabeth Louise *miniature collectibles executive*
Lewis, David Gene *humanities educator*
Li, David Leiwei *English and Asian American studies educator*
Lindholm, Richard Theodore *economics and finance educator*
Littman, Richard Anton *psychologist, educator*
Loescher, Richard Alvin *gastroenterologist*
Matthews, Brian W. *molecular biology educator*
Matthews, Esther Elizabeth *education educator, consultant*
Maurer, Robert Distler *retired industrial physicist*
Mazo, Robert Marc *chemistry educator, retired*
McMillan, Adell *retired educational administrator*
Mikesell, Raymond Frech *economics educator*
Miner, John Burnham *industrial relations educator, writer*
†Moseley, John Travis *university administrator, research physicist*
Mumford, William Porter, II, *retired lawyer*
Novkov, Julie Lavonne *political scientist*
†Ojo, Adegboye P. *language educator, translator*
Pascal, C(ecil) Bennett *classics educator*
Peterson, Donna Rae *gerontologist*
Pickett, Stephen Wesley *university official, lecturer and consultant*
Piele, Philip Kern *education infosystems educator*
†Pratt, Scott Lawrence *philosopher, educator*
Retallack, Gregory John *geologist, educator*
Richards, James William *electromechanical engineer*
Rimel, Linda June *writer*
Roe, Thomas Leroy Willis *pediatrician*
†Ryer, Charles Wilfred *lawyer, court administrator*

Hagenstein, William David *forester, consultant*
Hagmeier, Clarence Howard *retired anesthesiologist*
Hall, Howard Pickering *engineering and mathematics educator*
Hall, Mike Burt (Marshall B. Hall) *artist, educator*
Hammond, George Simms *chemist, consultant*
Hanna, Harry Mitchell *lawyer*
Hansen, Thomas Edward *physician, educator*
Harary, Keith *research scientist, writer, science journalist*
†Hargrove, Linda *professional basketball coach*
†Harnden, Edwin A. *lawyer*
Harrell, Gary Paul *lawyer*
†Harris, Charles David *music educator*
Hart, Jack Robert *newspaper editor*
Hart, John Edward *lawyer*
Hartman, Cherry *clinical social worker*
†Hatfield, Mark Odom *former senator*
Haynes, Richard Walter *research scientist*
Helmer, M(artha) Christie *lawyer*
Henderson, George Miller *foundation executive, former banker*
Henning, William Thomas *curator*
Hergenhan, Kenneth William *lawyer*
Hill, James Edward *insurance company executive*
Hinckley, Gregory Keith *software industry executive*
Hinkle, Charles Frederick *lawyer, clergyman, educator*
Hirshon, Robert Edward *lawyer*
Holman, Donald Reid *retired lawyer*
Holt, Mavis Murial *parents group executive*
†Homsley, Denise Louise *music educator*
†Houser, Douglas Guy *lawyer*
†Huffman, James Lloyd *law educator*
†Huggett, Monica *performing company executive*
Hunt, David G. *state representative, coalition executive*
Hurd, Paul Gemmill *lawyer*
Hutchens, Tyra Thornton *physician, educator*
Jacob, Stanley Wallace *surgeon, educator*
†Jarvis, Peter R. *lawyer*
Jarvis, Richard S. *academic administrator*
Jene, Joanne *anesthesiologist*
Jenkins, Donald John *museum administrator*
Johnson, H. Thomas *business educator*
Johnson, Mark Andrew *lawyer*
†Johnston, David Frederick *lawyer*
Johnston, Virginia Evelyn *retired editor*
†Jolles, Bernard *lawyer*
Jones, Robert Edward *federal judge*
Josephson, Richard Carl *lawyer*
Julien, Robert Michael *anesthesiologist, writer*
Katz, Vera *mayor, former college administrator, state legislator*
†Kemp, Shawn T. *professional basketball player*
Kendall, John Walker, Jr., *medical educator, researcher, university dean*
Kennedy, Jack Leland *lawyer*
Kennedy, R(obert) Evan *engineering executive, consultant, retired structural engineer*
Kester, Randall Blair *lawyer*
Khalil, Mohammad Aslam Khan *environmental science and engineering educator, physics educator*
King, Garr Michael *federal judge*
†Kinnune, William P. *forest products executive*
†Kinsella, David *education educator*
Kitzhaber, John Albert *former governor, physician, former state senator*
Klarquist, Kenneth Stevens, Jr., *lawyer*
Kleim, E. Denise *city official*
Kocaoglu, Dundar F. *engineering management educator, industrial and civil engineer*
Kohl, Steve *pediatrician, infectious disease physician*
Kohler, Peter Ogden *physician, educator, university president*
†Kohn, Art *education educator*
Kolmes, Steven Albert *biologist, educator*
†Korb, Christine Ann *music therapist, researcher, educator*
Krahmer, Donald Leroy, Jr., *lawyer*
Krenk, Christopher Joseph *human services professional*
Kristof, Ladis Kris Donabed *political scientist, writer*
Kupel, Frederick John *business executive*
Lall, B. Kent *civil engineer, educator*
Lambert, Richard William *mathematics educator*
Lang, Philip David *former state legislator, insurance company executive*
Langrock, Karl Frederick *former academic administrator*
†Lanker, Stefan *education educator*
Larson, Wanda Z. *writer, poet*
Lavigne, Peter Marshall *environmentalist, lawyer, educator*
Leavy, Edward *federal judge*
Leineweber, Peter Anthony *forest products company executive*
Leupp, Edythe Peterson *retired education educator*
†Lewis, Kenneth *shipping executive*
Lezak, Sidney Irving *lawyer, mediator*
Lilly, Elizabeth Giles *mobile park executive*
†Lilly, Susan Martin *costume designer, educator*
Lincoln, Sandra Eleanor *chemistry educator*
Linstone, Harold Adrian *management and systems science educator*
†Livingston, Louis Bayer *lawyer*
Lorenz, Nancy *artist*
†Love, Linda C. *lawyer*
Love, William Edward *lawyer*
†Lusky, John Anderson *lawyer*
MacArthur, Carol Jeanne *pediatric otolaryngology educator*
Machida, Curtis A. *research molecular neurobiologist, educator*
Maloney, Robert E., Jr., *lawyer*
Mapes, Jeffrey Robert *journalist*
†Mark, Gregory Paul *neuroscientist, educator*
Marsh, Malcolm F. *federal judge*
Martson, William Frederick, Jr., *lawyer*
Matarazzo, Harris Starr *lawyer*
Matarazzo, Joseph Dominic *psychologist, educator*
†Matarazzo, Ruth Gadbois *psychologist, educator*
†Matejuk, Agata *immunologist*
Mazzola, Michael *lighting designer*
Mc Bride, Thomas Frederick *lawyer, former university dean, government official*
McClave, Donald Silsbee *academic administrator*
McCoy, Eugene Lynn *civil engineer*
McCullough-Dieter, Carol Mae *database administrator*
McDonald, Robert Wayne *cardiac sonographer*
†McFarland, Bentson H. *physician, researcher*
McKinley, Loren Dhue *museum director*
†Menashe, Albert Alan *lawyer*
Mersereau, Susan S. *clinical psychologist*
Meyer, Paul Richard *lawyer*
Miller, William Richey, Jr., *lawyer*
Milton, Catherine Higgs *social service entrepreneur*
Mittelstaedt, Janet Rugen *music educator, composer*
Montone, Kenneth Alan *art director, creative director, consultant*
Mooney, Michael Joseph *college president*
Morgan, James Earl *librarian, administrator*
Moss, Richard Spencer *communications executive*
†Moulun, Renee *lawyer*
Mowe, Gregory Robert *lawyer*
Mozena, John Daniel *podiatrist*
Nesbit, Gary Merlin *neuroradiologist, educator*
Nguyen, Ngan-Lien Thi *internist, surgeon*
Nokes, John Richard *retired newspaper editor, writer*
Noonan, William Donald *lawyer, physician*
Norman, Douglas James *physician*
†Nunn, Robert Warne *lawyer*
O'Brien, Kathleen *lawyer*
Olson, Roger Norman *retired health service administrator*
†O'Neill, Phoebe Joan *retired lawyer*
Orloff, Chet *historian*
O'Scannlain, Diarmuid Fionntain *federal judge*
Osterud, Harold Truman *public health and preventive medicine physician, researcher*
Palmer, Earl A. *ophthalmologist, educator*
Pamplin, Robert Boisseau, Jr., *manufacturing company executive, minister, writer*
Pamplin, Robert Boisseau, Sr., *retired textile manufacturing executive*
Panner, Owen M. *federal judge*
†Parajuli, Pramod *anthropologist, researcher*
Parsons, Lisa Kay *artist, writer*
Patterson, Beverly Ann Gross *fund raising consultant, grant writer, federal grants administrator, social services administrator, poet*
Patterson, James Randolph *physician*
Patterson, Steve *professional basketball team executive*
Pearson, David Petri *chemist*
†Pentecost, Jeffrey Owen *geriatrician, consultant, physician, researcher*
Perkowski, Marek Andrzej *electrical engineering educator*
Perotto, Gregory Todd *public relations professional*
Petersen, Devi Lynne *accountant*
Pfeifer, Larry Alan *public health service coordinator*
Pham, Kinh Dinh *electrical engineer, educator, administrator*
Phillips, Jill Meta *novelist, critic, astrologer*
Pine, William Charles *foundation executive*
Pippen, Scottie *professional basketball player*
Pippi, Mikel Eugene *media specialist, director, academic administrator*
Pladel, John Gerald *psychiatric nurse practitioner, psychologist, psychotherapist*
Plonski, Halina Maria *pharmacist*
Porter, Elsa Allgood *writer, lecturer*
Potempa, Kathleen *dean, nursing educator*
Powell, Roberta A. *medical social worker*
Prendergast, William John *ophthalmologist*
†Purcell, John F. *lawyer*
Ramsby, Mark Delivan *lighting designer and consultant*
Richards, Herbert East *minister emeritus, commentator*
Richardson, Campbell *retired lawyer*
Richardson, Mark A. *otolaryngologist*
Richter, Peter Christian *lawyer*
Riddle, Earl Waldo *retired church official, small business owner*
†Rieke, Forrest Neill *lawyer*
Robertson, Joseph E., Jr., *ophthalmologist, educator*
†Robinson, Helene M. *retired music educator*
Rooks, Charles S. *foundation administrator*
Rooks, Judith Pence *midwifery, public health consultant*
†Rosen, Steven O. *lawyer*
Rosenbaum, Lois Omenn *lawyer*
†Rosenberg, Kenneth David *epidemiologist*
Roth, Phillip Joseph *retired judge*
Rowe, Sandra Mims *editor*
Rufolo, Anthony Michael *economics educator*
Rummell, Helen Mary *critical care and pediatrics nurse*
Russell, Marjorie Rose *manufacturing company executive*
Rutherford, William Drake *investment executive*
Rutsala, Vern A. *poet, English language educator, writer*
Sacks, David Harris *historian, humanities educator*
Sand, Thomas Charles *lawyer*
Savage, John William *lawyer*
Schmidt, Stanley Eugene *retired speech educator*
Schmidt, Waldemar Adrian *pathologist, educator*
†Schreiber, Martin Allan *surgeon*
Schuster, Philip Frederick, II, *lawyer, writer, law educator*
Schwartz, Martin Lerner *physician*
†Scott, John D. *pharmacologist*
†Scott, Lewis Kelly *lawyer*
†Sells, Clifford Wayne *pediatrician*
†Seymour, Steven Wayne *lawyer*
Shaff, Beverly Gerard *education administrator*
Shapiro, Yanina *psychology educator*
Shireman, Joan Foster *social work educator*
Shoemaker, Dorothy Hays *technical writer*
Shorr, Scott Alden *lawyer*
Simpson, Robert Glenn *lawyer*
†Sims, Kathleen Marie Eichner *nursing educator*
Skopil, Otto Richard, Jr., *federal judge*
†Smith, Dennis B. *neurologist, educator*
Smith, Douglas Dean *lawyer*
†Smith, Lester V., Jr., *lawyer, educator*
Smith, Russell Wesley *management and computer applications consultant, organizational development trainer*
Sokol, Larry Nides *lawyer, educator*
†Spackman, Kent Alan *pathologist, educator*
†Spencer, John Richard *lawyer, business executive*
Standring, James Douglas *real estate developer*
†Steele, William Donald *literature educator*
Steinfeld, Ray, Jr., *food products executive*
Steinman, Lisa Malinowski *English literature educator, writer*
†Stephens, Donald L., Jr., *lawyer*
Stern, Bruce L. *marketing professional, educator*
Stewart, Janice Mae *judge*
Stewart, Marlene Metzger *financial planning practitioner, insurance agent*
Stewart, Milton Roy *lawyer*
Stickel, Frederick A. *publishing executive*
Stickel, Patrick Francis *publishing executive, newspaper*
Stone, Richard James *lawyer*
Stott, Peter Walter *forest products company executive*
Strader, Timothy Richards *lawyer*
Sullivan, Donal D. *federal bankruptcy judge*
Sullivan, Edward Joseph *lawyer, educator*
Sutherland, Donald Wood *cardiologist*
Swan, Kenneth Carl *surgeon*
Swanson, Leslie Martin, Jr., *lawyer*
†Tabor, Joshua Hamilton *academic administrator*
†Talerico, Karen Amann *science educator, consultant*
†Tanzer, Jacob *retired judge*
Taylor, J(ocelyn) Mary *museum administrator, zoologist, educator*
Taylor, Robert Brown *medical educator*
†Tegtmeyer, Kenneth Bren *pediatrician, educator*
†Terry, Mark A. *ophthalmologist, surgeon*
†Thao, Yer *education educator*
Thompson, Terrie Lee *graphic designer*
†Thune, Geraldine B. *music educator*
†Tiffany, Natasha Marie *hematologist, researcher, oncologist*
Tillett, M. Patrick C. *urban designer*
Timpe, Ronald Ernest *insurance company executive*
Tolle, Susan W. *internist, educator, educational administrator*
†Tolon, Michael Oded *music educator, director*
†Tomjack, T.J. *wholesale distribution executive*
Tremaine, H. Stewart *retired lawyer*
Tufts, Robert B. *academic administrator*
Tuska, Jon *author, publisher*
Tyson, David T. *academic administrator*
Uliano, Anthony, Jr., *industrial hygienist, educator*
†Ulmer, Todd *orthopedic surgeon*
†Unger, Karen Virginia *director*
Unis, Richard L. *judge*
Urbanowski, John Richard *lighting systems company official*
Van Hoomissen, George Albert *state supreme court justice*
Van Valkenburg, Edgar Walter *lawyer*
Vaughan, Thomas James Gregory *historian, writer*
†Vernon, Jack Allen *otolaryngology educator, laboratory administrator*
†Waggoner, James Clyde *lawyer*
Walth, Brent David *journalist, writer*
Watkins, Charles Reynolds *medical equipment company executive*
Watne, Donald Arthur *accountant, educator, retired*
Weaver, Delbert Allen *lawyer*
Weber, George Richard *financial and internet marketing executive, writer*
Weeks, Wilford Frank *retired geophysics educator, glaciologist*
†Weiss, Tiffany L. *director*
†Weleber, Richard Gordon *ophthalmologist, geneticist, medical educator, researcher*
Westwood, James Nicholson *lawyer*
Whinston, Arthur Lewis *lawyer*
White, Douglas James, Jr., *lawyer*
White, Roberta Lee *financial analyst*
†Whitlow, Lillian *retired elementary school educator, poet*
†Wieden, Dan G. *advertising executive*
Wiens, Arthur Nicholai *psychology educator*
†Wiest, William Marvin *education educator, psychologist*
Williams, Sharon A. *lawyer*
Wilson, Owen Meredith, Jr., *lawyer*
†Wilson, Thomas Dale *philanthropic fundraising consultant*
Wood, Marcus Andrew *lawyer*
Workman, Norman Allan *accountant, graphic arts consultant*
Wyatt, Bill *airport executive*
Wyse, William Walker *lawyer, real estate executive*
Yamaguchi, Tadanori *electrical engineer*
Yamayee, Zia Ahmad *engineering educator, dean*
Yatvin, Joanne Ina *education educator*
Zalutsky, Morton Herman *lawyer*
†Zerbe, Kathryn Jane *psychiatrist*
Zerzan, Charles Joseph, Jr., *retired gastroenterologist*
Zimmerman, Gail Marie *medical foundation executive*

Rhododendron
Williamson, Diana Jean *nurse*

Roseburg
Comerford, Susan Marie *artist*
†Cook, Sybilla Avery *school library consultant*
Heald, Jason A. *composer, music educator*
Johnson, Doris Ann *educational administrator*
King, Lloyd JoAnn *music educator, volunteer*
Oleskowicz, Jeanette *physician*
Oliphant, Charles Romig *retired physician*
Plunkett, Marvin Wayne *data processing company executive*

Salem
Atkinson, Perry *political organization administrator*
Bailey, Henry John, III, *retired lawyer, educator*
Baker, Edwin Stuart *retired computer consultant*
Balmer, Thomas Ancil *state supreme court justice*
†Bauer, James Richard *academic administrator*
Benson, Steven Donald *sheet metal research and marketing executive, sheet metal mechanic, programmer, author*
Benton, Jack Mitchell *management consultant*
Bradbury, William Chapman, III, *state official*
Breen, Richard F., Jr., *law librarian, lawyer, educator*
Brown, Kate *state legislator*
†Butler, Alison *agricultural studies educator, researcher*
Butts, Edward Perry *civil engineer, environmental consultant*
Callahan, Marilyn Joy *social worker*
Carson, Wallace Preston, Jr., *judge*
Casey, Patricia Carolyn *retired social worker*
†Courtney, Peter C. *state legislator*
De Muniz, Paul J. *state supreme court justice*
Derfler, Eugene L. *real estate agent, former state legislator*
Dixon, Robert Gene *retired manufacturing engineering educator, retired mechanical engineering company executive*
Dmytryshyn, Basil *historian, educator*
Durham, Robert Donald, Jr., *state supreme court justice*
Edge, James Edward *health care administrator*
Erickson, Ray Charles *retired wildlife biologist*
†Feibleman, Gilbert Bruce *lawyer*
Fore, Ann *counselor, educator, country dance instructor*
Frank, Gerald Wendel *civic leader, journalist*
Gangle, Sandra Smith *arbitrator, mediator*
Gillette, P. Roger *physicist, systems engineer*
Hall, Mark Everett *editor, writer*
†Heine, Steven Robert *telecommunications industry executive, poet, writer*
Hoff, Reno R. *academic administrator*
Kenyon, Carleton Weller *librarian*
Kulongoski, Theodore Ralph *governor, former judge*
Linde, Hans Arthur *state supreme court justice*
Mannix, Kevin Leese *lawyer, political organization executive*
Marshall, Cak (Catherine Elaine Marshall) *music educator, composer*
Milbrath, Mary Merrill Lemke *quality assurance professional*
†Minnis, Karen *state representative*
Muntz, J(ohn) Richard *clergyman*
Myers, Hardy *state attorney general, lawyer*
Nafziger, James Albert Richmond *lawyer, educator*
Nicholson, Bradley James *lawyer*
Oberg, Larry Reynold *librarian*
†Pelton, M Lee *academic administrator*
Perez, Ernest R. *librarian*
Peterson, Edwin J. *retired judge, mediator, law educator*
Pierre, Joseph Horace, Jr., *commercial artist*
Riggs, R. William *judge*
†Robertson, Joseph David *lawyer*
Robertson, Marian Ella (Marian Ella Hall) *small business owner, handwriting analyst*
Roy, Matthew Lansing *lawyer*
Simmons, Mark *state representative*
Struble, George Waring *computer science educator*
Swaim, Michael E. *lawyer, former mayor*
Turnbaugh, Roy Carroll *archivist*
Zumwalt, Roger Carl *hospital administrator*

Sandy
Silvey, Murl L. *psychologist*

Seaside
Bishop, Virginia Wakeman *retired librarian and humanities educator, small business owner*

Shady Cove
Meyers, Sharon May *sales executive*

Sherwood
Forcier, Richard Charles *information technology educator, computer applications consultant*

Silverton
†Stone, Jane Buffington *artist, writer*

Sisters
Givot, Winnie *artist, educator*

Springfield
Davis, George Donald *executive land use policy consultant*
Jennison, Brian (Lester) *environmental specialist*
Lutes, Donald Henry *architect*
Pearson, John Mark *civil and structural engineer*

Summerville
Hopkins, Gerald Frank *trade association administrator*

Sunriver
Clough, Ray William, Jr., *civil engineering educator*

Bethlehem

Ackerman, Rudy Schlegel *artist, educator*
Allen, Beatrice *music educator, pianist*
Anderson, David Martin *environmental health scientist, environmental engineer*
Aronson, Jay Richard *economics educator, researcher, academic administrator*
Barnette, Curtis Handley *steel company executive, lawyer*
Barsness, Richard Webster *management educator, administrator*
Beedle, Lynn Simpson *civil engineering educator*
Beidler, Peter Grant *English educator*
Benz, Edward John, Sr., *clinical pathologist*
Bergethon, Kaare Roald *retired college president*
Bieri, Barbara Normile *systems analyst, consultant*
Chang, Chris C.N. *physician, pediatric surgeon*
Chen, John C. *chemical engineering educator*
Cole, Jack Eli *physician*
†Collette, Maria D. *librarian*
†Distler, Megan J. *economist*
Durkee, Jackson Leland *civil engineer*
Farrington, Gregory C. *university administrator*
Felix, Patricia Jean *steel company purchasing professional*
Fisher, John William *civil engineering educator*
Frankel, Barbara Brown *cultural anthropologist*
Frey, Doug R. *electrical engineering educator, consultant*
Ghosh, Bhaskar Kumar *statistics educator, researcher*
Graham, William Henry *lawyer*
Grainger, Nessa *artist*
Grenestedt, Joachim Lennart *educator*
Hartmann, Robert Elliott *manufacturing company executive, retired*
Heath, Douglas Edwin *geography educator*
Heindel, Ned Duane *chemistry educator*
†Hemphill, Meredith, Jr., *retired lawyer*
Herman, Richard Gerald *research chemist, consultant, educator*
Herrenkohl, Roy Cecil *psychology educator*
Hertzberg, Richard Warren *materials science and engineering educator, researcher*
Hobbs, James Beverly *business administration educator, writer*
Jain, Himanshu *materials science engineering educator*
Kanofsky, Alvin Sheldon *physics educator*
Karakash, John J. *engineering educator*
Lindgren, John Ralph *philosophy educator, writer*
Lloyd, Thomas Blair *research scientist, consultant*
Lyman, Charles Edson *materials scientist, educator*
Marsh, Robert Harry *chemical company executive*
McGeady, Leon Joseph *engineer, educator*
Mirro, John *engineering company executive*
Moffitt, Augustine Edward *steel company executive*
Neti, Sudhakar *mechanical engineering educator*
Orr, Sandra Jane *civic worker, pharmacist*
Ostapenko, Alexis *civil engineer, educator*
†Penny, Roger Pratt *management executive*
Pense, Alan Wiggins *metallurgical engineer, academic administrator*
†Philpotts, Alvin T. *management consultant*
Radycki, Diane Josephine *art historian*
Rivlin, Ronald Samuel *mathematics educator emeritus*
Roberts, Leonard Robert *English language educator, poet*
Roberts, Richard *mechanical engineering educator*
Rokke, Ervin Jerome *college president*
Rosenfeld, Joel Charles *surgeon*
Rushton, Brian Mandel *chemical company executive*
Scanlon, Edward Charles *clinical psychologist*
Schattschneider, Doris Jean *mathematics educator*
†Scheirer, William Kenneth *economist, consultant*
Schiesser, William E. *mathematician, researcher*
Schumacher, Susan Louise *underwriter*
Schwartz, Eli *economics educator, writer*
†Sivakumar, K. *marketing educator*
Smolansky, Bettie Moretz *sociology educator*
Smyth, Donald Morgan *chemical educator, researcher*
Soderlund, Jean R. *historian, educator, historian, researcher*
Sossiadis, Katina *artist, filmmaker*
Spillman, Robert Arnold *architect*
Spry, Donald Francis, II, *lawyer*
Steffen, Lloyd Howard *minister, religion educator*
Stella, John Anthony *investment company executive*
†Tannenbaum, Nicola B. *education educator*
Thornton, Robert James, Sr., *economics educator, author*
Traupman, Arnold Frank *ophthalmologist, educator*
Tuzla, Kemal *mechanical engineer, scientist*
Wachs, Israel Ephraim *chemical engineering educator*
Watsula, Linda Marie *social worker*
Weisman, Melody *special education guidance counselor*
†Weissler, Chava (Lenore) *religious studies educator*
Williamson, Robert Clifford *sociology educator*
Wittreich, Warren James *psychologist, consultant*
Yu, Zicheng *paleoclimatologist*

Beyer

Cornell, William Harvey *clergyman*

Biglerville

†Marks, Nora Maralea *retired secondary school educator*

Birdsboro

Mengle, Tobi Dara *mechanical engineer, consultant*
†Williamson, Hugh David *music educator*

Blairsville

McGaughran, Alan L. *family physician*

Bloomsburg

Avenia, Ronald Joseph *ophthalmologist*
Bertelsen, Dale Alan *communications educator*
Brasch, Walter Milton *journalist, educator*
†Holloway, Sybil Lymorise *psychologist, writer*
Keyser, Leslie D. *writer*
†Kozloff, Jessica S. *university president*
Liu, Hsien-Tung *dean*
†Perner, Darlene E. *special education educator, consultant, editor*
Schwartz, Susan R. *reporter*
Strine, Harry Cornelius, III, *communications educator*
Traugh, Donald George, III, *secondary education educator*
Vann, John Daniel, III, *library consultant, historian*
Yenika-Agbaw, Vivian S. *English studies educator, researcher*

Blue Bell

Brendlinger, LeRoy R. *academic administrator*
Deschaine, Barbara Ralph *retired real estate broker*
Drye, William James, Jr., *business owner*
Elliott, John Michael *lawyer*
Faden, Lee Jeffrey *technical consultant and expert referral company executive*
Giordano, Nicholas Anthony *stock exchange executive*
Halas, Cynthia Ann *business information specialist*
Harmon-Weiss, Sandra Rhoads *physician administrator*
McAdam, Will *electronics consultant*
Nichols, James Lee *advertising executive*
Rizzo, Gary Edward *academic administrator*
†Roden, Carol Looney *retired language educator*
Root, Joan Schimpf *civic worker, museum trustee*
Staplin, David Earl *civil engineer*
Swansen, Samuel Theodore *lawyer*
†Tilghman, Christopher Joseph *marketing professional*
Weinbach, Lawrence Allen *computer company executive*
Wilson, H(arold) Fred(erick) *chemist, research scientist*
Young, Charles Randall *software and marketing professional*
Zucchi, Donna Marie *financial services executive*

Boalsburg

Gettig, Martin Winthrop *retired mechanical engineer*

Boothwyn

†Reno, Alan Ferrer *music educator, musician*

Boswell

Croft, Daniel Thomas *music educator*

Boyertown

†Boyd, Craig Stephen *lawyer*
†Lahr, Wayne Roger *music educator*
Stephen, Dennis John *financial planner*
Stires, Midge *artist, painter*
Woods Coggins, Alma *artist*

Braddock

Slack, Edward Dorsey, III, *financial systems professional, consultant*

Bradford

Cox, J. Arthur *minister*
Hauser, Christopher George *lawyer*
Laroche, Roger Renan *psychiatrist*
McCabe, Nancy G. *English educator, writer*
Rice, Lester *electronics company executive*
†Slimick, John Charles *computer science educator*

Brentwood

Swanson, Fred A. *retired communications designer, councilman*

Bridgeport

Holter, John William *medical instrument manufacturing company executive*

Bridgeville

Allen, David Woodroffe *computer scientist*
Andersen, Theodore Selmer *engineering manager*
Moore, Daniel Edmund *psychologist, educator, retired educational administrator*

Bristol

Atkinson, Susan D. *producing artistic director, theatrical consultant*
†Boneparth, Peter *retail executive*
†Kimmel, Sidney *apparel company executive*
Klocek, Gary Richard *apparel company executive*
Shenefelt, Arthur B. *transportation executive, consultant*

Brockway

†Emmer, Barbara Louise *librarian, consultant*

Brodbecks

McMenamin, Helen Marie Foran *home health care, pediatric, and maternal nurse*

Brookville

Smith, Sharon Louise *lawyer, consultant*

Broomall

†Lentini, Eugene Anthony *retired physiologist, consultant*

Saunders, Sally Love *poet, educator*

Brownsville

Martin, Richard H. *principal*

Bryn Mawr

Ackoff, Russell Lincoln *systems sciences educator*
Anderson, Eric Edward *psychologist, consultant*
Bernstein, Guy Thomas *physician, urological surgeon*
Bolger, Stephen Garrett *English and American studies educator*
Braha, Thomas I. *business executive*
Carroll, Mary Colvert *corporate executive*
Cooney, Patricia Ruth *civic worker*
Crawford, Maria Luisa Buse *geology educator*
Daly, Donald Francis *consultant, retired investment counsel*
Davis, Jean Reynolds *music educator, author, poet, composer*
Dudden, Arthur Power *historian, educator*
Duska, Brenda Shay *accountant, academic financial administrator*
Fletcher, Marjorie Amos *librarian*
Francl, Michelle *chemist, educator*
Frank, Edward David, II, *history educator*
Frick, Benjamin Charles *lawyer*
Gaisser, Julia Haig *classics educator*
Giese, William Herbert *tax accountant*
Goldstine, Herman Heine *mathematician, association executive*
Goutman, Lois Clair *retired drama educator*
Graham, Thomas Hild *neurologist*
Hankin, Mitchell Robert *lawyer*
†Henry, Ronald George *lawyer, consultant*
Hoaglund, Susan Elizabeth *music educator*
Hoffman, Howard Stanley *experimental psychologist, educator*
Hung, Paul Porwen *biotechnologist, educator, consultant*
Huth, Edward Janavel *physician, editor*
†Jackson, Millard Irving, Jr., *lawyer*
†Jimenez, Carlos Spanish *language educator*
King, Willard Fahrenkamp (Mrs. Edmund Ludwig King) *Spanish language educator*
Krausz, Michael *philosopher, educator*
Lane, Barbara Miller (Barbara Miller-Lane) *humanities educator*
Lang, Mabel Louise *classics educator*
Levitt, Robert E. *gastroenterologist*
Maehl, Jane Cecilia *social worker, administrator*
Mallory, Frank Bryant *chemistry educator*
McGinnis, David Earl *urologist, educator*
Moyer, F. Stanton *financial executive, advisor*
Noone, R. Barrett *plastic surgeon*
†Opendak, Irene *academic administrator*
†Osirim, Mary Johnson *sociology educator*
Phillips, Stephen S. *lawyer*
Porter, Judith Deborah Revitch *sociologist, educator*
Price, Trevor Robert Pryce *psychiatrist, educator*
Salisbury, Helen Holland *education educator*
Smith, Nona Coates *academic administrator*
†Stahl, Roy Howard *lawyer*
Stucky, Steven (Steven Edward Stucky) *composer, conductor*
Sylvis, Robin *dental hygiene educator*
Trout, Charles Hathaway *historian, educator*
Vickers, Nancy J. *academic administrator*
Wheeler, Grace R. *retired market researcher*

Buckingham

Altier, William John *management consultant*
Hover, John Calvin, II, *banker*

Bushkill

Ellwood, Edith Muesing *free-lance writer*
Garretto, Leonard Anthony, Jr., *insurance company executive*
Mullette, Julienne Patricia *television personality and producer, astrologer, writer, health center administrator*

Butler

†Ameduri, Michael A *education educator, consultant*
Baker, Marvin Palange *cardiologist, internist*
Coleman, Arthur Robert *retired accountant*
†Day, Margaret Ann *research librarian, information specialist*
†Donaldson, Loretta Marie *retired librarian*
Hawk, Kathleen Patricia *broadcast consultant*
Klemens, Jonathan Mark *pharmacy educator, writer*
Ledden, Dennis Bruce *literature educator, writer*
Patterson, Patricia Lynne *artist, educator*
Rettig, Carolyn Faith *educator*
Rickard, Dennis Clark *sheriff, educator*

California

Langham, Norma E. *playwright, educator, poet, composer, inventor*
Schwerdt, Lisa Mary *English language educator*
Syphers, James Edgar *retired social worker*

Cambridge Springs

Learn, Richard Leland *corrections classification program manager*

Camp Hill

Anderson, Dorothy Kentner *architect*
Besch, Nancy Adams *county official*
Brandow, Theo *architect*
Brouse, John S. *medical association administrator*
Crider, Rudyard Lee *psychotherapist*
Crist, Christine Myers *consulting executive*
Custer, John Charles *investment broker*
Haidet, Keith R. *radiologist*
Johnston, Thomas McElree, Jr., *retired church administrator*
Mackin, Charles Philip, Jr., *lawyer*
McGeary, Clyde Mills *artist, educator, advisor*
Mead, James Matthew *insurance company executive*

Miller, Robert G. *drug store chain company executive*
Nowak, Jacquelyn Louise *state agency administrator, artist, realtor, consultant*
Pearsall, Gregory Howard *naval officer, real estate executive*
Rowe, Michael Duane *artist*
Swamidoss, Stephenson *pathologist, health facility administrator*
Tokuhata, George K. *retired medical educator, epidemiologist, consultant*
Yates, James Arthur *plastic surgeon*
Zook, Merlin Wayne *meteorologist, educator*

Canadensis

Lima, Jacqueline Dutton *artist, educator*

Canonsburg

Mascetta, Joseph Anthony *principal*
Mukherjee, Siddhartha *application developer*
Prado, Gerald M. *investment banker*

Carbondale

†Morcom, Gregory Lee *elementary school educator*
Niles, John Southworth, III, *counselor, farmer*
Willis, Ellen Debora *psychiatric nurse*

Carlisle

Anderson, Howard Wayne, Jr., *training company executive*
†Durden, William G. *academic administrator*
Fish, Chester Boardman, Jr., *retired editor*
Fox, Arturo Angel *Spanish language educator*
Jacobs, Norman G(abriel) *sociologist, educator*
Jones, Oliver Hastings *consulting economist*
Laws, Kenneth L. *physics educator, author*
Long, Howard Charles *physics educator emeritus*
McKinzie, James S. *librarian*
Renaud, Robert (Edwin Renaud) *college administrator*
Robinson, Ronald Michael *financial executive, financial consultant*
Shrader, Charles Reginald *historian*
†Song, Yongyi *librarian*
Strong, Sara Dougherty *psychologist, marriage and family therapist, mediator*
Talley, Carol Lee *newspaper editor*
Turo, Ron *lawyer*
†Tuttle, James Brooks, II, *education educator, researcher*

Carlisle Barracks

Metz, Steven Kent *federal agency administrator, writer*
Terrill, W(allace) Andrew *researcher, educator*

Carnegie

†Ferro, Vincent Anthony *elementary school educator, music educator*
Moretti, Edward Charles *environmental engineer, consultant*
Tenicela, Ruben Antialon *anesthesiologist*

Cashtown

Saliu, Ion *software developer, computer programmer*

Cecil

Keddie, Roland Thomas *physician, hospital administrator, lawyer*

Center Valley

Bartolacci, Paulette Marie *middle school educator, aerobics instructor*
†Dailey, Thomas F. *religious studies educator, director*
†McGorry, Susan Yacapsin *finance educator*
Smillie, Douglas James *lawyer*
†Turner, Brian Allen *sport management director, educator*
†Wisniewski, Daniel Patrick *mathematics educator*

Central City

Brown, Robert Alan *retired construction materials company executive*

Chadds Ford

Cohen, Felix Asher *lawyer*
Duff, James Henry *museum director, environmental administrator*
Gaadt, Suzanne DeMott *graphic designer*
Isakoff, Sheldon Erwin *chemical engineer*
King, M. Jean *association executive*
Martin, David Warren *management consultant*
†Milner, John D. *architectural firm executive, educator*
Moore, Bruce E. *real estate company executive*
Reddish, John Joseph *management consultant*
Swensson, Evelyn Dickenson *conductor, composer, librettist*
†Werner DeNadai, Mary *architectural firm executive*

Chalfont

†Brown, Richard Eric *electrical engineer, consultant*
†Detwiler, Christine Wendler *special education educator*

Chambersburg

Fleming, Steven Robert *minister*
Furr, Quint Eugene *marketing executive*
†Lesher, Richard Lee *association executive, retired*
Mehrmann, CraigAnn *nurse practitioner*
†Morgan, Diane Estelle *writer, educator*
Neilson, Winthrop Cunningham, III, *communications executive, financial communications consultant, photographer*
O'Connor, John Morris, III, *retired philosophy educator*
Reber, Calvin Henry *theological studies educator, minister*
Ross, Larry Michael *county economic development official*

Rumler, Robert Hoke *agricultural consultant, retired association executive*
Scarlata, Paul Anthony *oral surgeon*

Cheltenham
Kuziemski, Naomi Elizabeth *counselor, education consultant*
Weinstock, Walter Wolfe *systems engineer*

Chester
Bruce, Robert James *retired academic administrator*
Buck, Lawrence Paul *academic administrator, educator*
†Carnwath, Thomas Howlan *academic administrator*
Ciociola, Cecilia Mary *development specialist*
DiAngelo, Joseph Anthony, Jr., *finance educator, dean*
Harris, James Thomas, III, *college administrator, educator*
McCloskey, Donna Weaver *business educator*
McFarland, Ella Mae Gaines *secondary school educator, elementary school educator*
Newell, Katherine Claiborne *librarian*
Rozycki, Edward George *education educator*
Saad, Germaine H. *finance educator, researcher*
Schulman, Elliott A. *neurologist, educator, researcher*
Waldauer, Charles *economics educator*
Wepner, Shelley Beth *education educator, software developer*

Chester Springs
Dallas, Noelle Marie *financial analyst*
†Donovan, Sean William *small business owner, writer*
Scheer, R. Scott *physician*
Siegel, Richard Charles *biochemist*

Cheswick
Nair, Bala Radhakrishnan *engineer*

Cheyney
Ellis-Scruggs, Jan *theater arts educator*

Christiana
Fitzgerald, Susan Helena *elementary educator*

Clarion
†Alviani, Henry Anthony *music educator, choral conductor, voice instructor, baritone vocalist, composer*
Canaday, Doris Charlene *retired traffic representative*
Carbone, Rose Elaine *mathematics educator*
Dingle, Patricia A. *education educator, artist*
Foreman, Thomas Alexander *dentist*
Grejda, Gail Fulton *dean*
Miller, Andrea Lynn *library science educator*
†Morelli, Michael Joseph *musician, educator*
Siddiqui, Dilnawaz Ahmed *communications educator, consultant*

Clarks Summit
Alperin, Irwin Ephraim *clothing company executive*
†Bass, Suzanne *social worker*
Beemer, John Barry *lawyer*
†Eckel, Keith William *farmer*
King, Carol Brennan *dean*
Sylvester, Robert J. *academic administrator*
†Weiss, Tammy Lee *information technology manager*
Yadouga, Michelle Marianne *computer operator*

Clearfield
Krebs, Margaret Eloise *publishing executive*
†Mandell, Raymond Andrew *music educator*
Singh, Shiwendra Prasad *civil engineer*

Clifton Heights
Domingo, Orville Harold *surgeon*
Pagano, Richard Donald *physical education educator, researcher*

Clinton
Talbot, Mary Lee *minister*

Coatesville
Ainslie, George William *psychiatrist, behavioral economist*
Bell, Robert Lloyd *retired neurosurgeon*
Budeir, Mohammed Hassan *surgeon*
Burton, Mary Louise Himes *computer specialist*
Green, Norman Marston, Jr., *minister*
†Ranft Pollitt, Patricia *retired historian educator*
Smith, Patricia Anne *special education educator*
†Zarychta, William Alex *emergency physician*

Cochranton
Miller, Carl F. *secondary school educator*

Cochranville
Sazegar, Morteza *artist*

Cogan Station
Sander, Theresa Marie *nurse practitioner*

Collegeville
Barnes, Jo Anne *investment advisor*
†Dragalin, Vladimir *research statistics director*
Kun, Kenneth A. *business executive*
Maco, Teri Regan *accountant, engineer*
Malinoski, Frank Joseph *general practice physician*
Merchenthaler, Istvan Jozsef *neuroscientist, morphologist*
Richter, Richard Paul *academic administrator*
Shao, Dalei *molecular biologist, researcher*
Trott, Edward Ashley *reproductive endocrinologist*
Witman, Philip Alan *pharmaceutical researcher, epidemiologist*
Zhou, Honghui *clinical pharmacokineticist*

Columbia
Gillmore, Vicki Longenecker *health care administrator*
McTaggart, Timothy Thomas *secondary education educator*

Columbia Cross Roads
Knauss, David Eugene *music educator*

Conneaut Lake
Egyud, Ralph David, Jr., *music educator*
Starn, Barbarajean *healthcare administrator*

Conshohocken
Bramson, Robert Sherman *lawyer*
Cunningham, James Gerald, Jr., *transportation company executive*
†Gibson, Thomas Richard *automobile import company executive*
Jacoby, Richard Allen *pathologist, dermatologist*
Johnson, Waine Cecil *dermatologist*
†Lotman, Herbert *food processing executive*
Naples, Ronald James *manufacturing company executive*
Spaeth, Karl Henry *retired chemical company executive, lawyer*

Cooksburg
Meley, Robert Wayne *structural and storage tank engineer*

Coopersburg
Bednar, Charles Sokol *political scientist, educator*
Bolle, Donald Martin *retired engineering educator*
Matulevicius, Edward *engineering company executive, consultant*
Peserik, James E. *electrical, controls and computer engineer, consultant, forensics and safety engineer, fire cause and origin investigator*
Siess, Alfred Albert, Jr., *engineering executive, management consultant*

Cooperstown
Hogg, James Henry, Jr., *retired education educator*

Coraopolis
Aichbhaumik, Dibyajyoti *metallurgical engineer*
Kay, George Paul *environmental engineer*
Koepfinger, Joseph Leo *retired utilities executive*
†Marshall, David D. *electric utilities executive*
Skovira, Robert Joseph *information scientist, educator*
Stage, Ginger Rooks *psychologist*
Victor, Ronald Joseph, Jr., *banking professional*

Corsica
†Elza, Betty Ann *retired librarian*

Coudersport
Kysor, Daniel Francis *psychologist*

Cranberry Township
†Fitzpatrick, Robert *psychologist*
Hadidian, Calvin Y. *retired surgeon*
Hogberg, Carl Gustav *retired steel company executive*
Lorenz, John George *librarian, consultant*
Moore, John Francis *emergency physician*
Moyer, Christina Beth *retired elementary education educator, reading specialist*
Tiller, Olive Marie *retired church worker*
Walsh, Arthur Campbell *retired psychiatrist*

Cranberry Twp
Patten, Charles Anthony *management consultant, retired manufacturing company executive, author*

Cresson
Clark, Threese Anne *occupational therapist, disability analyst*
Grady, Janet Laura *nurse, educator*
McCool, Deborah Joyclyn *science educator*

Cuddy
Pearlman, Seth Leonard *civil engineer*

Dallas
Baltimore, Ruth Betty *social worker*
Fiegelman, Richard Paul *sales consultant, freelance writer*
Hunter, Todd Lee *secondary school music educator*
†Madras, Diane Elizabeth *education educator, physical therapist*
Moran, Michael Lee *physical therapist, gerontologist*

Danville
Albertini, Robert Elmer *medical executive, physician, consultant*
Bakri, Younes Noaman *surgeon, oncologist, gynecologist*
Bisordi, Joseph Edmund *nephrologist, medical center administrator*
Burns, J. Robert *physician*
†Chan, Yiumo *biochemist*
†Cheung, Joseph Yat-Sing *biomedical scientist, nephrologist*
Cochran, William John *physician, pediatrician, gastroenterologist, nutritionist, consultant*
Franklin, David Perdue *vascular surgeon, educator*
Lessin, Michael Edward *oral-maxillofacial surgeon*
Maier, Vincent Baines *radiation physicist*
Makary, Adel Zaki *hematologist*
†Mirza, Mohd Ayoub *internist, researcher*
Pierce, James Clarence *surgeon, educator*
Savitsky, Maureen Elizabeth *pharmacist*
Steele, Glenn Daniel, Jr., *oncologist, healthcare system executive*

Strodel, William Edward *surgeon, medical educator*

Darby
Wardell, Lindy Constance *nonprofit organization administrator*

Dauphin
Tanner, David Harold *professional roof consultant*

Dayton
Patterson, Madge Lenore *elementary education educator*

Delmont
Mock, Robert Allen *professional figure skating coach, editor*
Thompson, Paul A. *business consultant, performance improvement expert*

Denver
Milner, Charles Fremont, Jr., *manufacturing company executive*

Devon
Boehne, Edward George *banker*
Garbarino, Robert Paul *retired administrative dean, lawyer*
Porter, Roger John *medical research administrator, neurologist, pharmacologist*
Santoleri, Nicholas Peter *artist, art publishing company executive*

Dillsburg
Bowers, Glenn Lee *retired professional society administrator*
Holmes, David James *elementary school educator*
Jackson, George Lyman *retired nuclear medicine physician*
Smith, William Raymond *farmer, thoroughbred owner, breeder and trainer, retired history educator, philosophy educator*

Donora
Todd, Norma Ross *retired government official*

Douglassville
Kirkpatrick, David Warren *educational researcher, writer*

Downingtown
Bahal, Vishal *cardiologist*
†Crescenz, Valerie J. *music educator*
Hemingway, David C. *elementary school principal*
Kelly, Edward Aloysius, Jr., *physician*
Kovach, George Daniel *writer, author*
Newman, Richard August *psychiatrist, educator*
Skrajewski, Dennis John *health care executive*

Doylestown
Bolla, William Joseph *lawyer*
Brink, Frank, Jr., *biophysicist, former educator*
†Earnheart, Frank Jones *lawyer*
Elliott, Richard Howard *lawyer*
†Gauer, Linette-Jean Crete *accountant*
Ginsberg, Barry Gavrille *psychologist, consultant, trainer*
Haeussler, Charles Louis, II, *oil company executive*
Hall, Peter C. *lawyer, defender*
†Heiligman, Deborah *writer*
Karsch, Jay Harris *lawyer*
King, Robert Edward *retired pharmacy educator*
Kohlhepp, Edward John *financial planner*
Long, Ronald Alex *real estate and financial consultant, lawyer, educator*
McGarvey, Joseph F. X., Sr., *cardiologist*
†Mellon, Thomas Edward, Jr., *lawyer*
†Meyer, Diane Christine *social worker*
Mishler, John Milton (Yochanan Menashsheh ben Shaul) *natural sciences educator, administrator, artist*
†Ohrt, Joseph Glen *music educator*
†Richie, Margaret Bye *architectural historian*
Rodenbaugh, Marcia Louise *retired elementary school educator*
Rubenstein, Alan Morris *county judge*
Slade, Edwin Walter, Jr., *oral surgeon, lawyer*
Somers, Sarah Pruyn *retired elementary school educator*
†Wachtel, Howard K. *mathematician, educator*
Waite, Frances W. *librarian, professional genealogist*
Wolfinger, Audrey Jane *retired librarian*

Dresher
Michael, Dorothy Ann *nursing administrator, naval officer*

Drexel Hill
Alexander, Lloyd Chudley *author*
†Bay, Joann Reeder *financial planner*
Breslin, Elizabeth Walker *biological scientist, biomedical consultant*
Malin, Seth Arnold *surgeon, educator*
Martino, Michael Charles *entertainer, musician, actor*
McDonnell, Michael T., Jr., *lawyer*
Schiazza, Guido Domenic (Guy Schiazza) *educational association administrator*
Student, John Michael *secondary school educator*
Thompson, William David *minister, homiletics educator*

Drums
Frask, Robin Ann Kostanesky *secondary school educator*

Du Bois
Bonavita, Dennis Joseph *newspaper publisher*
Forsythe-Adamson, Velma Brown *accountant, consultant, English language educator*
Williams, Kathryn Blake *retired librarian*

Dunmore
Krogh-Jespersen, Mary-Beth *academic administrator*
†McDonald, Nancy E. *retired secondary school educator*
Pencek, Carolyn Carlson *treasurer, educator*
Sebastianelli, Mario Joseph *internist, nephrologist, health services administrator*

Dushore
Getz, Mary E. *medical/surgical nurse*

Eagles Mere
Gruver, William Rolfe *investment banker*
Sample, Frederick Palmer *former college president*

East Berlin
Greer, Robert Bruce, III, *retired orthopedic surgeon, educator*

East Earl
Jonassen, Gaylord D. *computer company executive, new products and market development*

East Springfield
Vadzemnieks, Michael Lester *plastics company executive*

East Stroudsburg
Allen, Frank Charles *writer*
Bishop, Gerald Iveson *pharmaceutical executive*
Boyd, Katherine Ann *clinical therapist*
Bunjun, Seewoonundun *economics educator*
Crackel, Theodore Joseph *historian, consultant*
Crotty, Patricia McGee *political science educator*
Dillman, Robert John *academic administrator*
Donaghay, Marie Martenis *historian, educator*
Dorian, Patrick Charles *music educator*
Jacobson, Gilbert H. *lawyer, director*
Lane, Miharu Qualkinbush *artist, educator*
Maroney, James Frederick *music educator*
Miller, Robert W. *music educator, musician*
Rosenblum, Stewart Irwin *recording industry executive*

Easton
Bader, Cal Joseph, Jr., *broadcast executive*
Brown, Robert Carroll *lawyer*
Danjczek, Michael Harvey *social service administrator*
†DeGrandis, Ronald Wayne *music educator*
Delong, Ronald *artist, educator*
Fried, Bernard *parasitologist, biology educator*
Grunberg, Robert Leon Willy *nephrologist, educator*
Hay, Samuel Arthur *theater educator, playwright*
†Holmes, Larry, Jr., *retired professional boxer*
Kincaid, John *political science educator, editor*
Molino, Mildred A. *lawyer*
Murphy, Bruce Allen *government and law educator, author*
Noel, Nicholas, III, *lawyer*
Pysher, Zane Kermit *counselor*
Rothkopf, Arthur J. *college president*
†Sanborn, Joshua A. *education educator*
Stitt, Dorothy Jewett *journalist*
Stitt, Thomas Paul, Sr., *lawyer*
Sun, Robert Zu Jei *manufacturing company executive, inventor*
Traldi, Lorenzo *mathematician, educator*
†Upton, Lee *English language educator*
Van Antwerpen, Franklin Stuart *federal judge*
Viscomi, B. Vincent *civil engineer*

Ebensburg
Ramsdell, Richard Adoniram *marine engineer*

Edinboro
Cocco, Karen Jean *school psychologist*
Cox, Clifford Laird *retired academic administrator*
†Hass, Robert Bernard *literature educator*
Jones, Jean Grace *speech educator*
Miller, G(erson) H(arry) *research institute director, mathematician, computer scientist, chemist*
Patterson, John Keith *civil engineer, consultant*
Paul, Charlotte Patricia Peggram *nursing educator*
Thomas, Paul Milton *retired science educator*
Thompson, Richard W. *retired health facility administrator*

Eighty Four
Capone, Alphonse William *retired industrial executive*
Hardy, Joseph A., Sr., *wholesale distribution executive*
†Magerko, Maggie Hardy *lumber company executive*

Elizabethtown
Brown, Dale Weaver *clergyman, theologian, educator*
†Chambers, David Lee *music educator*
†Coren, Jonathon Silow *science educator, researcher*
Gottfried, Paul Edward *humanities educator, editor*
Johnson, Clarence Ray *minister*
Kitchen, Otis Dorsey *music educator*
†Likos Ricci, Patricia Anne *art historian, artist*
Madeira, Robert Lehman *professional society administrator*
Ronning, Debra Diane *music educator*
Selcher, Wayne A. *political science educator*

Elizabethville
†McCartney, Chad Edward *music educator*
Rippon-Lovett, Dodie *social worker*
Romberger, John Albert *scientist, historian*

Elkins Park
Burnley, June Williams *secondary school educator*

Davidson, Abraham Aba *art historian, educator, photographer*
Eisman, Audrey Waldo *psychologist*
Erlebacher, Martha Mayer *artist, educator*
Glijansky, Alex *psychiatrist, psychoanalyst*
Goode, Paul *psychologist, educator, consultant*
Havir, Bryan Thomas *urban planner*
Pak, Hyung Woong *community advocate*
Prince, Morton Bronenberg *physicist*
†Romberg, Osvaldo *artist*
Schatz, Charlotte Asness *artist, educator*
Schneider, Carl William *lawyer*
Shmukler, Stanford *lawyer*
Siegel, Seymour *retired internist*
Verma, Satya Bhushan *optometrist, educator*
Yun, Daniel Duwhan *physician, foundation administrator*
Zelac, Ronald Edward *physicist*

Emmaus
†Adcock, Albert Eugene (Gene) *night vision equipment company executive*
Bowers, Klaus D(ieter) *retired electronics research development company executive*
†Bricklin, Mark Harris *magazine editor, publisher*
†Favorule, Denise *publishing executive*
†Rodale, Ardath Harter *publishing executive*
Zahradnik, Fredric Douglas *publishing executive*

Enola
Myers, Alfred Frantz *retired state education official, educator*

Ephrata
Sager, Gilbert Landis *investment company executive*
Wolbach, Albert Bogh, Jr., *family practice physician*
Young, David Samuel *minister*

Erdenheim
†Gottesman, Charles R. *music educator*
Murphy, Mary Marguerite *artist*

Erie
Adair, Evan Edward *lawyer*
Adovasio, J. M. *anthropologist, archeologist, educator*
Allshouse, Robert Harold *history educator*
†Belfiore, Phillip Joseph *education educator, researcher*
Bennett, Charles Andrew *economics educator*
Bernard, Bruce William *lawyer*
Boyes, Karl W. *state legislator*
Bracken, Charles Herbert *banker*
Brunner-Martinez, Kirstin Ellen *pediatrician, psychiatrist*
Chitester, Robert John *television producer*
Crankshaw, John Hamilton *mechanical engineer*
DeCrease, William Maurice *total quality management consultant*
Dockstader, Emmett Stanley *engineer, construction executive*
Drexler, Nora Lee *retired educator, writer, illustrator*
Duval, Albert Frank *paper company executive*
Eberlin, Richard D. *education educator*
Egan, Corrine Halperin *management consultant*
Ferretti, Silvia *dean*
Gagliano, Christine Louise *social worker*
Glinsky, Albert Vincent *composer, educator*
Gottschalk, Frank Klaus *real estate company executive*
Gruenwald, Geza *plastics consultant*
Gupta, Srabana *economist, researcher*
Haeseler, Carl William *pomology and viticulture educator*
Hagen, Thomas Bailey *business owner, former state official, retired insurance company executive*
Hauck, Barbara Jean *fund raising executive, writer, artist*
†Henry, Martin Daniel *university president*
†Janikowski, Stanley M. *retired tax specialist, advocate*
Kish, George Franklin *thoracic and cardiovascular surgeon*
†Long, Richard William *cardiothoracic surgeon*
Lund, Edwin Harrison *business accounting systems executive*
Lyon, Howard Peters *musician, educator*
Mason, Gregg Claude *orthopedic surgeon, researcher*
Mencer, Glenn Everell *federal judge*
Michaelides, Doros Nikita *internist, medical educator*
Monahan, Thomas Andrew, Jr., *accountant*
Murphy, Michael Joseph *retired bishop*
†Myers, Jeffrey Daniel *concert pianist, music educator*
Nihill, Karen Bailey *nursing home executive, nurse clinician*
Nygaard, Richard Lowell *federal judge*
Pett, Stephen Donohoe *cardiovascular surgeon*
Reitz, Mary Ellen *pathologist, health facility administrator*
Rowley, Robert Deane, Jr., *bishop*
Ryan, James Thomas *organizational consultant, business owner*
Sensor, Mary Delores *hospital official, consultant*
Steckler, Jessica Ann *continuing nursing education educator*
†Trautman, Donald W. *bishop*
Trautman, Ned Richard *music educator*
Vanco, John L. *art museum director*
†Yeager, Kathleen M. *court administrator*
Zamboldi, Richard Henry *lawyer*

Essington
†Piasecki, Frank Nicholas *aircraft corporation executive, aeronautics engineer*

Etters
Peltz, Alan Howard *manufacturing company executive*
†Steps, Barbara Jill *lawyer*

Exeter
Henderson, Robb Alan *minister*

Export
Carter, Linda Whitehead *oncology nurse, educator, consultant, researcher*

Exton
Ashton, Mark Randolph *lawyer*
Dorsey, Jeremiah Edmund *pharmaceutical company executive*
Duvivier, Jean Fernand *management consultant, consultant*
Fu, Don Hongbin *software engineer*
Hedges, Donald Walton *lawyer*
†Hidalgo, Ismael J. *pharmaceutical scientist*
Ma, Jinpeng *economics and business educator*
Mauch, Robert Carl *service industry executive, venture capitalist*
†Meegalla, Sanath *research scientist*
Molloy, Christopher John *molecular and cellular pharmacologist*
Shollenberger, Sharon Ann *secondary school educator*
Webber, Helen *artist, designer*

Fairfield
Freund, John Richard *former English educator*

Fairless Hills
Marable, Simeon-David *artist*
Rosella, John Daniel *clinical psychologist, educator*

Fairview Village
†Filippini, Christine Marie *counselor*

Fayetteville
Blewitt, George Augustine *physician, consultant*
Taylor, Margaret Uhrich *educational administrator*

Feasterville
Dickstein, Jack *chemist*

Felton
Shoemaker, Eleanor Boggs *television production company executive*

Fleetwood
Lewis, Dana Kenneth *human services/communications consultant, author*
Lindeman, Jack *retired literature educator, poet*
Maurer, Gernant Elmer *metallurgical executive, consultant*

Flourtown
Brown, Melissa M. *ophthalmologist*
Christy, John Gilray *financial company executive*
Dressler, Mark Christopher *writer*
Lambert, Joan Dorety *elementary education educator*
Lee, Adrian Iselin, Jr., *journalist*

Fogelsville
Crooker, Barbara Ann *writer, educator*

Ford City
†Skamai, Robert Walter *music educator*
Ursiak, David Allen *operations executive, consultant*

Forest City
Kameen, John Paul *newspaper publisher*

Fort Washington
Blumberg, Donald Freed *management consultant*
†Chao, Georgia *biostatistician*
Chen, Jen-Chi *polymer chemist*
Creech, Hugh John *chemist, researcher*
Elliott, Bruce Roger *secondary education educator, artist*
Manfredi, Deanna Ann *psychologist*
Moulton, Hugh Geoffrey *lawyer, retired business executive*
Nelson, Edward Blake *medical products executive*
Pappas, Charles Engelos *plastic surgeon*
Saurman, George Edwin *legislator, retired*
Visek, Albert James *semi-retired computer engineer*
Wint, Dennis Michael *museum director*
Wuchter, Richard B. *retired research scientist, real estate agent*

Forty Fort
Meeker, Robert Gardner *English language educator*
Millington, Michele *musician, business owner*
Olerta, Leslie Anne *nuclear medicine technologist*

Foxburg
Piroch, Joseph Gregory *retired internist, cardiologist*

Franklin
Moore, Mary Julia *educator*
Suk, Jin Hong *pathologist*

Frederick
Mellon, Bradley Floyd *pastor, religion educator*

Friendsville
Babb, Harold *psychologist, educator*

Gaines
Beller, Martin Leonard *retired orthopaedic surgeon*

Gettysburg
Coughenour, Kavin Luther *career officer, military historian*
Fortnum, Donald H *chemistry educator, retired*
Frassanito, William Allen *historian, consultant, writer*
Gritsch, Ruth Christine Lisa *editor*
†Haaland, Gordon Arthur *psychologist, university president*
Hallberg, Budd Jaye *management consulting firm executive*
Kile, Marcia Ann *education consultant*
Nelson-Small, Kathy Ann *foundation administrator*
Roach, James Clark *government official*
†Schneider, Katherine P. *retired elementary school educator*
†Viswanathan, Byravan *retired physician*

Gibsonia
†Benson, Stuart Wells, III, *lawyer*
Cauna, Nikolajs *physician, medical educator, scientist*
Haas, Eileen Marie *homecare advocate*
Korchnak, Lawrence C. *educational administrator, consultant, writer*

Gilbertsville
†Poste, George Henry *pharmaceutical company executive*

Girardville
Dempsey, Thomas Joseph *retired postmaster*

Gladwyne
Acton, David *lawyer*
Allen, Theresa Ohotnicky *neurobiologist, consultant*
Booth, Harold Waverly *lawyer, finance and investment company executive*
Cathcart, Harold Robert *hospital administrator*
Fenichel, Richard Lee *retired biochemist*
Geisel, Cameron Meade, Jr., *investment professional*
Gonick, Paul *retired urologist*
Kaye, Donald *physician, educator*
Patten, Lanny Ray *industrial gas industry executive*
Stick, Alyce Cushing *systems administrator, consultant*

Glen Mills
Churchill, Stuart Winston *chemical engineering educator*
Dunion, Celeste Mogab *consultant, township official*
Turner, Janet Sullivan *painter, sculptor*

Glen Riddle Lima
Newett, Edward J., Jr., *accountant*

Glen Rock
†Steger, Karl L. *music educator*

Glenmoore
Moulton, Frank Ray, Jr., *retired oil company executive*

Glenshaw
Guentner, James Francis, Jr., *art educator, artist*
Yates, Diane Greiner *librarian*

Glenside
Block, Isaac Edward *professional society administrator*
Crivelli-Kovach, Andrea *public health and nutrition consultant, educator*
†Evert, Thomas L., III, *music educator*
Frudakis, Rosalie *small business owner*
Frudakis, Zenos Antonios *sculptor, artist*
Hargens, Charles William, III, *electrical engineer, consultant*
Kalkwarf, Leonard V. *minister*
†McCartney, Dan G. *theology studies educator, musician*
Medel, Rebecca Rosalie *artist*
Mermelstein, Jules Joshua *lawyer, township commissioner*
†Powlison, David A. *writer*
Ralston, Steven Philip *portfolio manager, financial analyst*
Reiss, George Russell, Jr., *physician*
Sacks, Robert D. *educational administrator, fund raiser*

Glenwillard
Milne, Christopher McQuiston Wilmoth *photographer, journalist*

Gouldsboro
Nass, Leonard Ira *chemist, consultant*

Grantham
Eby, John Wilmer *sociology educator*
†Kreamer, Carolyn Lee *nursing educator, community health nurse*

Grantville
Sudor, Cynthia Ann *sales and marketing professional*

Greencastle
†Horst, Carolyn Diane *accountant*

Greensburg
Boyd, Robert Wright, III, *lamp company executive*
Catalano, Louis William, Jr., *neurologist*
Duck, Patricia Mary *librarian*
†Flórez-Estrada, Nancy B. *language educator*
Gounley, Dennis Joseph *lawyer*
Gribschaw, Victoria Marie *social sciences educator, department chairman*
Hager, Edward Paul *development executive*
Heubel, William Bernard *lawyer, international contract consultant*
†Highberger, Edgar *music educator*
Neff, Mary Ellen Andre *retired elementary school educator*
Ramm, Douglas Robert *psychologist*
Shafer-Kenney, Jolie E. *writer, columnist*
†Spurlock, John *social studies educator, social sciences educator*
Sumner, Christine Marie *counselor*
†Zornosa, Betty Butcher *music educator*

Greentown
Askins, Wallace Boyd *manufacturing company executive*
Forcheskie, Carl S. *former apparel company executive*

Greenville
†Hall, Mary Theresa *literature educator*
†Parmiter, Karen Lynn *education educator*
†Schrader, Eric Byron *music educator*
Stuver, Francis Edward *former railway car company executive*

Grove City
†Campbell, George Van Pelt *sociology and religion educator*
Coulter, Michael L *political scientist, educator*
Harp, Gillis John *history educator*
McBride, Milford Lawrence, Jr., *lawyer*
Sellers, Patricia Ann *home health nurse*
Smith, Gary Scott *historian, educator, clergyman*

Gwynedd
Bieber, Konrad Ferdinand *retired language educator*
LeFevre, Perry Deyo *minister, theology educator*

Gwynedd Valley
†Dern, John Andrew *language educator*
Duclow, Donald Francis *philosophy educator, researcher*
†McGarry, Lisa Coughlin *language educator*
Strasburg, William Edward *retired newspaper publisher*

Hallstead
Remakus, Bernard Leo *physician, medical journalist, author, educator*

Hamburg
Schappell, Abigail Susan *speech, language, hearing and massage therapist*

Hanover
Clark, Sandra Marie *school administrator*
Conway, Samuel Anthony *retired chiropractor*
Davis, Ruth Carol *pharmacy educator*
Howard, Thomas K. *surgeon*
Kline, Donald *food company executive*
Kuntz, Larry E., Jr., *music educator*
Thomas, Charles Edmund *anesthesiologist, health facility administrator*

Harleysville
Bell, Michael G. *trade association administrator*
Daller, Walter E., Jr., *banking executive*
Hauber, Patricia Anne *educator*
Kwortnick, Linda Marie *emergency nurse*

Harrisburg
Antoun, Annette Agnes *newspaper editor, publisher*
†Baker Knoll, Catherine *lieutenant governor*
Boswell, James Aurthur, Jr., *English language educator*
Breslin, Michael Joseph, III, *social services administrator, educator*
Brown, John Walter *vocational education supervisor*
Burcat, Joel Robin *lawyer*
Burns, Rebecca Ann *educator, librarian*
Cadieux, Roger Joseph *physician, mental health care executive*
Campbell, Carl Lester *banker*
Chambers, Clarice Lorraine *clergy, educational consultant*
Chernicoff, David Paul *osteopathic physician, educator*
†Cicconi, Christopher M. *lawyer*
Cline, Andrew Haley *lawyer*
Cooper, Jane Todd (J. C. Todd) *poet, writer, educator*
Czikowsky, Leon Lawton *legislative aide*
†Dattilo, Nicholas C. *bishop*
DeKok, David *writer, reporter*
Diehm, James Warren *lawyer, educator*
Dietz, John Raphael *consulting engineer executive*
Downey, Brian Patrick *lawyer*
Ellenbogen, Elisabeth Alice *retired accountant*
Elliott, Scott Dean *public relations executive*
Emerick, John L. *library director*
†Feinour, John Stephen *lawyer*
Fisher, D. Michael *state attorney general*
Frye, Mary Catherine *prosecutor*
†Gerlach, James William *congressman*
Gibson, Shere Capparella *foreign language educator*
†Gornish, Gerald *lawyer*
Gover, Raymond Lewis *retired newspaper executive*
†Greenleaf, Stewart John *state legislator*
†Grobman, Gary M. *writer*
Hafer, Barbara *state official*
Hafer, Joseph Page *lawyer*
Hanson, Robert DeLolle *lawyer*
Herman, Lynn Briggs *state legislator*
Howett, John Charles, Jr., *lawyer*
Jeffries, Richard Haley *physician, broadcasting company executive*
Jones, David John, III, *preventive medicine physician, medical executive*
Jubelirer, Robert C. *lieutenant governor*
Kane, Yvette *lawyer, federal judge*
Kelly, Robert Edward, Jr., *lawyer*
Khanzhina, Helen P. *English educator, translator*
Kittinger, Thomas W. *retired music educator*
Klein, Michael D. *lawyer*
Knackstedt, Mary V. *interior designer*
†Kukovich, Allen Gale *state legislator, lawyer*
Kury, Franklin Leo *lawyer*
Lee, Seung Jai *lawyer, legal administrator*
Lighty, Fredrick W. *lawyer*
Logue, James Nicholas *epidemiologist*
Long, Robert Howard, Jr., *lawyer*

Mahey, John Andrew *retired museum director*
†Margolis, David Leslie *government agency administrator*
Miller, Leslie Anne *lawyer*
Miller, Sheila *state legislator*
Moritz, Milton Edward *security consultant*
Mowery, J. Ronald *geologist, physicist, educator*
†Murren, Philip Joseph *lawyer*
Novak, Alan P. *political organization administrator*
O'Connor, Charles Edward, Jr., *state government official, lawyer*
O'Donnell, John Joseph, Jr., *optometrist*
Partin, Daniel Ray *secondary school educator*
Patrick, David Bruce *chiropractor*
†Perzel, John Michael *state legislator*
Pizzingrilli, Kim *state official*
Plawsky, Bernard Morris *retired social work administrator*
Popnik, Marlene Alita *school librarian, retired*
Potok, Julian Walter *pathologist*
Preski, Brian Joseph *lawyer*
Prioleau, Sara Nelliene *dentist*
Rambo, Sylvia H. *federal judge*
Reed, Stephen Russell *mayor*
Reigel, Timothy John *accountant*
Reiley, Robert *lawyer, educator*
Rendell, Edward Gene *governor, former mayor, lawyer*
†Rooney, Terence Joseph (T.J.) *political organization worker, state legislator*
Ross, Sheila Moore *philanthropic executive*
Rudy, Frank R. *pathologist*
Schore, Niles *lawyer*
Selkowitz, Larry Bryan *lawyer*
Sheldon, J. Michael *lawyer, educator*
†Skelly, Joseph Gordon *lawyer*
Staub, Shalom David *cultural organization administrator*
Stefanon, Anthony *lawyer*
Stwalley, Brian David *pharmacist*
Sullivan, John Cornelius, Jr., *lawyer*
Tartaglione, Christine M. *state legislator*
Teplitz, Robert Forman *lawyer*
Trautlein, Joseph J. *medical administrator*
Tyson, Gail L. *health federation administrator*
Van Zile, Philip Taylor, III, *lawyer, educator*
Warshaw, Allen Charles *lawyer*
†Wenger, Noah W. *state legislator*
†West, Eileen M. *caseworker*
West, James Joseph *lawyer*
Williams, Karl *writer, musician*
Willow, Judith Ann Loye *tax preparer*
Wissler-Thomas, Carrie *professional society administrator, artist*
Wolfe, Gary Donald *library commissioner, retired state education official*
†Zuern, David Ernest *bank executive*

Harrison City
McWilliams, Samuel Robert *secondary education educator*

Harveys Lake
Wolensky, Joan *occupational therapist, interfaith minister*

Hatboro
Carroll, Lucy Ellen *choral director, music coordinator, educator*
John, Robert McClintock *lawyer*
Quigley, Robert Charles *insurance industry consultant*

Hatfield
Jesberg, Robert Ottis, Jr., *educational consultant, science educator*
Madden, Theresa Marie *elementary education educator*
Taylor, Alan Charles *chaplain, counselor, researcher*

Haverford
Aronson, Carl Edward *pharmacology and toxicology educator*
Bowman, Frank Paul *retired humanities educator*
Brand, Charles Macy *history educator*
†Brownlow, Donald Grey *private school educator*
de Laguna, Frederica *anthropology educator emeritus, writer, publisher*
Erickson, Ralph O. *botany educator*
Goppelt, John Walter *physician, psychiatrist*
†Gross, Stanley Carl *marketing consultant*
Gruen, Jane Swan *retired educator, lecturer*
Jorden, Eleanor Harz *linguist, educator*
Kee, Howard Clark *religion educator*
Maller, Owen *clinical psychologist*
Mellink, Machteld Johanna *archaeologist, educator*
Merrill, Arthur Alexander *financial analyst*
Miller, Geraldine B. *music educator*
Northrup, Herbert Roof *economist, business executive*
Olson, Robert Edward *coal mining executive*
Rosefsky, Jonathan Benensohn *pediatrician*
Shenkin, Henry Arnold *retired neurosurgeon*
Stiller, Jennifer Anne *lawyer*
Stroud, James Stanley *retired lawyer*
†Stuard, Susan Mosher *education educator*
Talucci, Samuel James *retired chemical company executive*
Tritton, Thomas Richard *academic administrator, biologist, educator*

Havertown
Beck, Elaine Kushner *elementary and secondary school educator*
Besser, Amy Helene *lawyer*
Brinker, Thomas Michael *finance executive*
Gardner, Seth Frederick *music educator*
Koenig, Robert Emil *clergyman*
Korényi-Both, András Levente *pathologist, educator*
Smith, Phillip Thurmond *historian, educator*
Somach, S. Dennis *communications executive*
Tassone, Bruce Anthony *chemical company executive*
†Wright, Cecilia Powers *gifted and talented educator*

Hawley
Dilmore, Joseph Eric *carpenter, poet, writer*
Kanzer, Larry *small business owner, food service director*
Persche, Henry-Peter *art consultant, artist*
Vierra, Deborah *critical care, community health nurse*

Hazleton
Miller, David Emanuel *physics educator, researcher*
Pascucci, Mary Frances *pathologist*
†Pedri, Charles Raymond *lawyer*
Tseo, George Kuang Yu *geography educator*

Hellertown
Claps, Judith Barnes *educational consultant*
McCullagh, James Charles *publishing executive*

Henryville
†Dittmer, Luther Albert *publisher, educator*

Herman
Dittmer, Sylvester Stephen Wess *retired nursing administrator*

Herminie
Taylor, John Calvin *missionary, dentist*

Hermitage
Durek, Dorothy Mary *retired English language educator*
Garay, Stephen R. *secondary school educator*
Mayne, Ruth E. *medical nurse*

Hershey
Anderson, Allan Crosby *hospital executive*
Ballard, James Otis, III, *medical educator, physician*
Berlin, Cheston Milton, Jr., *pediatrician, educator*
Blouch, Timothy Craig *food company executive*
Botti, John Joseph *obstetrician-gynecologist*
Burkhart, Keith Karl *emergency medicine physician, medical toxicologist*
Caputo, Gregory Michael *physician, educator*
†Christensen, Dawn Michelle *family practice nurse practitioner, consultant*
†Collins, Christopher Michael *engineering educator*
Davis, Dwight *cardiologist, educator*
Dias, Mark Steven *neurosurgeon*
Domen, Ronald Eugene *physician*
Eyster, Mary Elaine *hematologist, educator*
†Field, John McCabe *medical educator*
Gabbay, Robert Abraham *physician, educator*
Geder, Laszlo *neurologist, educator*
Hammond, James M. *endocrinologist*
†Jones, Marshall Bush *education educator, researcher*
†Kees-Folts, Deborah *pediatrician, educator*
King, Carolyn Marie *mathematics educator*
King, Steven Harold *health physicist*
Kirch, Darrell Gene *academic administrator, dean*
Lang, Carol Max *veterinarian, educator*
Leaman, David Martin *cardiologist, educator*
Leaman, Thomas Leed *medical educator*
†Lenny, Richard Herbert *food products executive, marketing professional*
Lindenberg, Steven Phillip *counselor, consultant*
Marks, James Garfield, Jr., *dermatologist*
Marshall, Wayne Keith *anesthesiology educator*
McLoughlin, Lucille C. *physician*
Michel, Nancy Claire *physician assistant*
Moskowitz, Jay *health sciences educator*
Naeye, Richard L. *pathologist, educator*
†Naides, Stanley J. *physician, educator, researcher*
†Nickolaus, Michelle J *family practice nurse practitioner*
†Norgren, Ralph *neuroscientist*
Ouyang, Ann *physician, researcher, educator*
Ozereko-deCoen, Mary T. *therapeutic recreation specialist and therapist*
Pierce, William Schuler *cardiac surgeon*
Pincock, Garry LaMar *association administrator*
†Reese, Robert M. *corporate lawyer*
Rohner, Thomas John, Jr., *urologist*
Ruth, Edward B. *supervisor*
Severs, Walter Bruce *pharmacology educator, researcher*
†Simmons, Bryan John *lawyer*
†Sumera, Sherry A. *secondary school educator*
Tan, Tjiauw-Ling *psychiatrist, educator*
Undar, Akif
Vesell, Elliot Saul *pharmacologist, educator*
Waldhausen, John Anton *retired surgeon, editor*
Wassner, Steven Joel *pediatric nephrologist, educator*
Wilson, Philip Kevin *science and medical historian*
†Wolfe, Kenneth L. *food products manufacturing company executive*
Zelis, Robert Felix *cardiologist, educator*

Hidden Valley
Betta, Pamela Albers *community health nurse, administrator, educator*

Holland
Hosey, Sheryl Lynn Miller *educator, editor, theater director*
Umbreit, Wayne William *bacteriologist, educator*

Hollidaysburg
Bloom, Lawrence Stephen *retired clothing company executive*
†Cottle, Harold Ranson *pathologist, laboratory owner*
†Evey, Merle Kenton *lawyer*
Mariano, Ana Virginia *retired pathologist*
Savage, Patricia Werner *nonprofit health and human service agency executive*

Hollywood
Tomezsko, George Anthony *writer*

Holtwood
Liebman, Shirley Anne *analytical research scientist*

Homestead
Thompson, Bradley Scott *music educator*

Honesdale
Barbe, Walter Burke *education educator*
Clark, Christine May *editor, author*

Honey Brook
DePaul, Anthony Kenneth *lawyer*

Horsham
Best, Franklin Luther, Jr., *lawyer*
Coker, Caroline Tiffany *lawyer*
†Dariano, Joseph *publishing company executive*
†Fisher, Darryl *information services company executive*
Johnson, G. Carol *financial services executive*
Naydan, William J. *music educator*
Schopp, David L. *music educator*

Houston
†Briggs, Rich *secondary school educator*

Hughesville
Bellmore, Lawrence Robert, Jr., *financial planner*

Hulmeville
Jackson, Mary L. *health services executive*

Hummelstown
Clouse, Jerry Allan *architectural historian*
Moffett, Dawn Schulten *retired elementary education educator*

Hunker
Bromke, Cindy Rose *geriatrics, rehabilitation and home health nurse*

Huntingdon
Durnbaugh, Donald Floyd *church history educator, researcher*
Kepple, Thomas Ray, Jr., *college administrator*
Schock, William Wallace *pediatrician*
Trexler, John Peter *retired geology educator, researcher*
†Tuten, James H. *educational association administrator, educator*
†Wang, Xinli *education educator*

Huntingdon Valley
†Abend, Kenneth *electrical engineer*
Edelman, Janice *artist, educator*
Forman, Howard Irving *lawyer, former government official*
Godfrey, John Carl *medicinal chemist*
Goff, Kenneth Wade *electrical engineer*
Goldstein, Neil Warren *filmmaker*
Isard, Phillip Isaac *medical nutritionist, consultant*
Kaufman, David Joseph *lawyer*
Lefton, Harvey Bennett *gastroenterologist, educator, author*
Vollum, Robert Boone *management consultant*
West, A(rnold) Sumner *chemical engineer*

Immaculata
Hickey, Gregory J. *priest, academic administrator*

Indiana
Barbor, John Howard *lawyer*
Bell, Paul Anthony, II, *lawyer*
Bowers, Fredalene Barletta *education educator, consultant*
Cashdollar, Charles David *history educator*
Garvin, C(larence) Alexander, Jr., *economics educator*
†Horner, Ronald George *music educator, musician*
†Hunter, Herbert M. *science educator*
†Jeckavitch, David M. *music educator*
Kulis, Ellen Mae *elementary education educator*
†LaRoche, Lynda *artist, educator*
Masilela, Calvin Onias *land use planner, educator*
Mc Cauley, R. Paul *criminologist, educator*
McPherson, Donald Scott *employment relations educator, arbitrator/mediator*
Miller, Vincent Paul, Jr., *geography and regional planning educator*
Perlongo, Daniel James *composer, educator*
Pettit, Lawrence Kay *university president*
Rife, John Merle, Jr., *retired educator, pilot*
†Rodriguez, Lydia H. *language educator*
Roumm, Phyllis Evelyn Gensbigler *retired literature educator, writer*
Ruddock, Ellen Sylves *business consultant*
†Shim, Leem Seop *computer scinetist, educator, researcher*
Soule, Robert D. *safety and health educator, administrator*
Steelman, Sara Gerling *art association administrator*
Stern, T. Noel *political scientist, educator*
Thibadeau, Eugene Francis *education educator, consultant*
Tobin, Lois Moore *home economist, educator, retired*
Walker, Donald Anthony *economist, educator*

Irwin
†Biancheria, Amilcare *environmental scientist, consultant*
Brown, Donald Clyde *surgeon*
Kuhn, Howard Arthur *engineering executive, educator*
Runser, Dianne Strong *music educator, music director*

Jamison
Thorne, John Watson, III, *advertising and marketing executive*
Touhill, C. Joseph *environmental engineer*

Jeannette
LaFave, Richard *engineer, consultant*

Jenkintown
Dickstein, Joan Borteck *arbitrator, conflict management consultant*
Fisher, Joseph Saul *endocrinologist, consultant*
†Frazer, Janet Lynn *historian, educator*
Greenspan-Margolis, June E. *psychiatrist*
Lowry, Karen M. *biomedical research scientist, pharmacist*
†O'Neill, Judith Jones *insurance agent*
Reese, Francis Edward *retired chemical company executive, consultant*
Rigney, Thomas Gregory *music educator, musician*
Sadoff, Robert Leslie *psychiatrist, educator*
Schwartz, Sergiu *concert violinist, conductor, educator*
†Spergel, Philip *psychologist*

Jermyn
Crotti, Rose Marie *special education educator*

Jersey Shore
Dent, Jeffrey *music educator*
Flayhart, Martin Albert *lawyer*

Jessup
Karluk, Lori Jean *craft designer, copy editor*

Jewkintown
†Jih, Chang-Shin *education educator*

Jim Thorpe
Umbehocker, Kenneth Sheldon *priest*

Johnstown
Alcamo, Frank Paul *retired educational administrator*
Babik, Dennis Allen *social worker, consultant*
Brice, William Riley *geology educator, planetary science educator*
†Depra, Alan Jay *mechanical engineer*
†Ferencak, Michael Neill *mathematician, educator*
Glosser, William Louis *lawyer*
Green, James Matthew *anesthesiologist*
Grove, Nancy Carol *academic administrator*
Hull, Patricia Ann *nursing administrator*
Kaharick, Jerome John *lawyer*
Kaminsky, Ira Samuel *lawyer*
Keiper, Jeffrey Lynn *counselor, therapist, lawyer*
Lovingood, Rebecca Britten *elementary school educator*
McNiesh, Lawrence Melvin *radiologist*
Miloro, Protopresbter Frank *church official, religious studies educator*
Nicholas, (Richard G. Smisko) *bishop*
†Puto, Anne-Marie *reading specialist*
Samples, Jerry Wayne *military officer, educator*
Sheehan, Edward James *technical consultant, former government official*
Simmons, Elroy, Jr., *retired utility executive*
Smisko, Nicholas Richard *bishop, educator*
Smith, D. Brooks *federal judge*
Teich, Alan Harvey *psychology educator, clinical psychologist*
Van Blerkom, Dianna L. *education educator*

Jones Mills
Fish, Paul Waring *lawyer*

Kennett Square
†Bainbridge, John Seaman *retired law school administrator, law educator, lawyer*
Bell, Philip Wilkes *accounting and economics educator*
Fish, Robert H. *long term care industry executive*
Fussell, Catharine Pugh *biological researcher*
Harrington, Anne Wilson *medical librarian*
Hennes, Robert Taft *former management consultant, investment executive*
Landstrom, Elsie Hayes *retired editor*
Lippincott, Sarah Lee *astronomer, graphologist*
Martin, George (Cheney Whitney Martin) *writer*
May, Harold Edward *chemical company executive*
Partnoy, Ronald Allen *lawyer*
†Poppenga, Robert H. *veterinary toxicology educator*
†Temple, L. Peter *lawyer*
†Whitlock, Herbert Ian *systems analyst*
Whitlock, Robert H. *veterinarian, educator*
Wilson, Armin *chemist, retired*

Kimberton
Williams, Lawrence Soper *photographer*

King Of Prussia
Abbott, Henry James *electro-mechanical engineer*
Anderson, Jerry Allen *financial analyst*
†Angie, Jill Elizabeth *quality assurance professional*
Boles, Donald Michael *lawyer*
Broido, Arnold Peace *music publishing company executive*
Cannon, Lynne Marple *investment management company executive*
Clauson, Sharyn Ferne *consulting company executive, educator*
de La Morandiere, Brice *finance executive*
DeMaria, Joseph Carminus *lawyer*
Gadsden, Christopher Henry *lawyer, educator*
Gallis, Carole Campbell *secondary education educator*
Gallis, John Nicholas *retired military officer, executive leadership training consultant*
Greenberg, Lon Richard *energy company executive, lawyer*

Hawes, Nancy Elizabeth *mathematics educator*
Hegedus, L. Louis *chemical engineer, research and development executive*
Helmetag, Diana *music educator*
Katz, Arnold Martin *insurance brokerage firm executive*
†Lee, Robert *engineer*
Marcus, Stephen Cecil *former printing company executive*
McCairns, Regina Carfagno *pharmaceutical executive*
McFarland, Andrew George *analytical chemist, researcher*
Miller, Alan B. *hospital management executive*
Pownall, James Richard *electronics executive*
Schneider, Pam Horvitz *lawyer*
†Schumann, Paula M. L. *writer*
Sidor, Michael Louis *orthopedic surgeon*
Spielvogel, Lawrence George *engineer*
Swank, Annette Marie *software designer*
Szabo, Joseph Laszlo *management consultant*
Volpe, Ralph Pasquale *insurance company executive*
Webb, Richard Stephen *manufacturing executive*
†Yan, Ying *statistician, researcher*

Kingsley
McNabb, Corrine Radtke *librarian*

Kingston
Benovitz, Madge Klein *civic volunteer*
Denaro, Anthony Thomas *psychiatrist*
Friedman, Pauline Poplin *civic worker, consultant*
†Luksa, Joseph Edward *music educator*
Marko, Andrew Paul *school system administrator*
Meyer, Martin Jay *lawyer*
†Shaffer, Charles Alan *lawyer*
Van Scoy, Gary *social services administrator*
Weisberger, Barbara *artistic director, educator, choreographer*

Kinzer
Blake, Richard E. *sculptor, art educator*

Kittanning
Smits, Ronald Francis *English educator, poet*

Knox
Rupert, Elizabeth Anastasia *retired university dean*

Kulpsville
DiDomizio, Robert Anthony, Jr., *mechanical engineer*

Kutztown
Dougherty, Percy H. *geographer, educator, politician, planner*
Johnson, Nils, Jr., *minister*
†Mack, Sara Rohrbach *librarian, educator*
Messics, Mark Craig *civil engineer*
Meyer, Susan Moon *speech language pathologist, educator*
Ogden, James Russell *marketing educator, consultant, lecturer, writer*
Tumbleson, Raymond Dana *English educator*
Watrous, Robert Thomas *academic director*

La Plume
Boehm, Edward Gordon, Jr., *college administrator, educator*

Lafayette Hill
Delacato, Janice Elaine *learning consultant, educator*
Edwards, JoAnn Louise *human resources executive*
Hess, Wanda Jean *health facility administrator*
King, Diane Averbach *teacher educator*
King, Leon *financial services executive*

Lake Ariel
Casper, Marie Lenore *middle school educator*

Lake Harmony
Polansky, Larry Paul *court administrator, consultant*

Lancaster
Ashby, Richard James, Jr., *bank executive, lawyer*
Auster, Carol Jean *sociology educator*
Baylor, Scott Allen *chemistry educator*
Bentman, Julius *periodontist*
Binkley, Luther John *philosophy educator*
Brod, Roy David *ophthalmologist, educator*
Brunner, Lillian Sholtis *nurse, writer*
Buchanan, Lovell *entertainer*
Carlisle, James Patton *entrepreneur*
Drum, Alice *academic administrator, educator*
Eaby, Christian Earl *lawyer, small business owner*
Ebersole, J. Glenn, Jr., *engineering, marketing, management and public relations executive*
Ebersole, Mark Chester *emeritus college president*
Finger, Robert Roy *marketing executive*
Fisher, Sarah Young *money manager, financial adviser*
Freeman, Clarence Calvin *financial executive*
Galligan, Carolyn M.B. *artist, educator*
Glick, Garland Wayne *retired theological seminary president*
†Goodling, Kimberly Hall *language educator, consultant*
†Gray, Kathleen Ann *lawyer*
Groff, Tracey Anne *social worker*
Heil, Paul Samuel *radio program producer*
High, S. Dale *diversified company executive*
Hoffer, Roy *forensic electrical engineer, fire and explosion analyst*
Hudak, Joseph David *forensic engineer, educator, police investigator*
Jordan, Lois Wenger *foundation official*
Joseph, John *history educator*

Kane, Edward Joseph *educator*
Kelly, Robert Lynn *advertising agency executive*
Kendall, Leigh Wakefield *surgeon*
Kent, Charles Imbrie, III, *artist, former university official*
Kermes, Constantine John *artist, industrial designer*
Kirsch, Stephen Augustine *retired geology educator*
†Kneedler, Richard (Alvin Kneedler) *former academic administrator*
Liddell, W. Kirk *specialty contracting company executive*
Linton, Joy Smith *primary school educator*
†Lockhart, Michael D. *electric company executive*
Nast, Dianne Martha *lawyer*
Pyfer, John Frederick, Jr., *lawyer*
Roda, Joseph Francis *lawyer*
Rung, George W. *physician*
Rupp, Theodore Hanna *retired French language educator*
Saganich, Bonnie Sue *medical/surgical nurse*
Shaw, Charles Raymond *journalist*
Shenk, Willis Weidman *newspaper executive*
Showers, Krista Ann *accountant*
Simmons, Deidre Warner *performing company executive*
Smith, Thomas Clair *retired manufacturing company executive*
Steiner, Robert Lisle *retired language consultant*
Stephenson, Donald Grier, Jr., *government studies educator*
Stewart, Arlene Jean Golden *designer, stylist*
Taylor, Ann *human resources specialist, educator*
Teague, Peter Wesley *college president*
†Watson, Mark S. *music educator*
Whare, Wanda Snyder *lawyer*
Young, Mary Frances Braccio *educational consultant*
Zeager, Lloyd *librarian*
Zimmerman, D(onald) Patrick *lawyer*

Langhorne
Babb, Wylie Sherrill *college president*
†Barta, Daniel Stephen *music educator, composer*
Bishop, Ann Shorey *oncological nurse*
†Black, Dorothy Mary *librarian*
Boyce, Andrea Zygmunt *nurse*
FitzGerald, Dorothy Stickle *librarian*
Hillje, Barbara Brown *lawyer*
†Killough, Stephen Pinckney *lawyer, director*
†Spreat, Scott *psychologist*

Lansdale
Alpert, Marc H. *surgeon*
Elliott, Arthur Y. *microbiologist, administrator*
Fawley, John Jones *retired banker*
†Gaskins-Dainis, Ina R. *retired real estate agent*
Habecker, Sandra K. *retired nurse*
†Holloway, M(ary) Katharine *research scientist, chemist*
Sag, Jerome E. *internist*
Schwartz, Louis Winn *ophthalmologist*
Strohecker, Leon Harry, Jr., *orthodontist*
Sultanik, Jeffrey Ted *lawyer*

Lansdowne
Kyriazis, Arthur John (Athanasios Ioannis Kyriazis) *lawyer, biotechnologist*

Latrobe
Daughenbaugh, Terry Lee *steel industry executive*
Fazzi, Charles *accounting educator*
Watson, Bradley Charles Stephen *political science educator, lawyer, writer*

Lebanon
Bard, Judy Kay *librarian*
Gallaher, William Marshall *dental laboratory technician*
McMindes, Roy James *aggregate company executive*
Ondrusek, David Francis *discount store chain executive*
Paul, Herman Louis, Jr., *valve manufacturing company executive*
Synodinos, John Anthony *academic administrator*

Lederach
Hallman, H(enry) Theodore, Jr., (Ted Hallman) *artist, textile designer*

Leesport
Jackson, Eric Allen *philatelist*

Lehigh Valley
†McGonagle, John Joseph, Jr., *lawyer*

Lehman
†Felty, Wayne Lee *chemist, educator*
†Ivanov, Anatoli F. *education educator*
Williams, Thomas Alan *elementary education educator, coach*

Lemoyne
Deeg, Emil Wolfgang *manufacturing company executive, physicist*
Klein, Michael Elihu *physician*
Powell, Fredrick Charles *business executive*
Stewart, Richard Williams *lawyer*
Yenchko, Suzanne *research and development company executive*

Leola
Gehman, Terry Lee *music industry professional*
Wedel, Paul George *retired hospital administrator*

Levittown
Ferraro, Ronald Louis *health facility administrator*
Halberstein, Joseph Leonard *retired associate editor*

Henshaw, Jonathan Cook *manufacturing company executive*
†Zinke, Nancy Carol *humanities educator*

Lewisberry
Smith, Bruce I. *state legislator*

Lewisburg
Aldrich, Robert Adams *agricultural engineer, consultant*
Bannon, George *retired economics educator, department chairman*
Candland, Douglas Keith *educator*
Hetherington, Bonita Elizabeth *elementary education educator*
Jump, Chester Jackson, Jr., *clergyman, church official*
Kim, Jai Bin *civil engineering educator*
†Knight, Louise Osborn *lawyer*
Knisely, Charles William, Jr., *engineering educator, researcher, consultant*
Lowe, John Raymond, Jr., *mechanical engineer*
Neuman, Nancy Adams Mosshammer *civic leader*
Orbison, James Graham *civil engineer, educator*
†Payne, Michael David *English language educator*
†Roberts, Ruth W. *retired elementary school educator*
†Rogers, Steffen H. *academic administrator*
Rote, Nelle Fairchild Hefty *business consultant*
†Schlegel, Richard LaMar *advocate, writer*
Sojka, Gary Allan *biologist, educator, university official*
Warner-Mills, Susan *organizational and community development consultant*

Ligonier
†Lear, M. Kathleen *artist, music educator, small business owner*
Mattern, Gerry A. *engineering consultant*
Mellon, Seward Prosser *investment executive*
Pilz, Alfred Norman *manufacturing company executive*

Lincoln
†Dade, Lennell R. *humanities educator*

Lincoln University
†Babatunde, Emmanuel Debo *education educator*
†Chapp, Jeffrey A *education educator, artist*
†Getaneh, Misganaw *physicist, educator*
Nelson, Ivory Vance *academic administrator*
†Nwachuku, Levi Akalazu *social sciences and behavioral studies educator*
†Pettaway, Charles H. *music educator*
†Pettaway, Charles Henry, Jr., *musician, educator*
Racine, Linda Jean *college health nurse*
Williams, Willie, Jr., *physicist, educator*

Lititz
Haines, Ronald H. *retired bishop*
Hartz, Brian David *physical therapist, educator, small business owner*
†Kline, Richard L. *retired music educator*
Koch, Bruce R. *diplomat*
Martin, Harold Sheaffer *minister, educator*
Mershon, Charles Richard *family physician*

Lock Haven
Almes, June *retired education educator, librarian*
Arnone, Samuel Frank *music educator, consultant*
Chang, Shirley Lin (Hsiu-Chu Chang) *librarian, educator*
†Chen, Charles *music educator, musician*
Congdon, Howard Krebs *philosopher, clergyman, educator*
†Forbes, Edward John, III, *developmental psychologist, educator*
Hartline, Darrell G. *retired healthcare executive*
Ivory, Patrick J. *physician assistant*
†Moyer, Anna Blackburn *retired secondary and elementary school educator*
Snowiss, Alvin L. *lawyer*
Willis, Craig Dean *academic administrator*

Loretto
Melusky, Joseph Anthony *political science educator*
Sackin, Claire *retired social work educator*

Lower Burrell
Kinosz, Donald Lee *business process consultant*
Nordmark, Glenn Everett *civil engineer*

Lower Gwynedd
Pendleton, Robert Grubb *pharmacologist*

Lumberville
Fallon, Robert Thomas *English language educator*
Katsiff, Bruce *artist*

Lyon Station
Breidegam, DeLight Edgar, Jr., *battery company executive*

Macungie
Dwyer, John James *mechanical engineer*
Farr, Lona Mae *non-profit executive, business owner*
Moore, Joyce Kristina *financial planner, director*
Rubin, Arthur Herman *retired university official, consultant*

Malvern
†Bedford, Anne Marie *musician, educator, insurance agent*
Bedrosian, Gregory Ronald *investment banker*
Berkwits, Leland *physical medicine and rehabilitation physician*
Brahmbhatt, Sudhirkumar *chemical company executive*
Brighton, Ruth Louise *lay worker, educator*
Brock, Lynmar, Jr., *food service executive*

Cameron, John Clifford *lawyer, health science facility administrator*
†Doerr, John Maxwell *lawyer*
†Espe, Matthew J. *manufacturing executive*
Fisher, Sallie Ann *chemist*
†Forese, James John *business machine company executive*
Hendrix, Stephen C. *financial executive*
Herring, Raymond Mark *marketing professional, researcher*
†May, Judy Royer *lawyer*
Rucker, Donald W. *emergency physician, educator, consultant*
Stainback, John Philip *public/private finance and development executive*
Stuckey, Susan Jane *perioperative nurse, consultant*

Manheim
Frederick, Susan Louise *preschool educator*
†Metzger, James Edwin *band director*

Manns Choice
Braendel, Douglas Arthur *hotel executive*

Mansfield
Dettwiler, Peggy Diane *music educator*
†Donahue, Martha *librarian, educator, retired*

Maple Glen
Jacobson, Bonnie Brown *energy consulting company executive, statistician, writer, researcher*
Weaver-Stroh, Joanne Mateer *education educator, consultant*

Marietta
Jones, Shannon Shawna Marie *elementary guidance counselor*
Shumaker, Harold Dennis *lawyer*

Marion Center
Bomboy, John David *mathematics educator*

Mars
McChesney, Charles E. *retired marketing professional*
Prijatelj, Charles Anthony *music educator, musician*
†Protho, Christopher Alan *music educator*

Marshalls Creek
†Johnson, Loren Charisse *publishing executive, writer*

Martinsburg
Keith, Tammy Leah *geriatrics nurse*
Neff, Robert Wilbur *academic administrator, educator, minister*

Matamoras
Linden, Harold Arthur *interior designer, consultant*

Mc Kees Rocks
Barczynski, John Leslie *periodontist*

Mc Keesport
Kessler, Steven Fisher *lawyer*

Mc Murray
Brzustowicz, John Cinq-Mars *lawyer*
Celento, Florence M. *librarian*
Cmar, Janice Butko *home economics educator*
Diamond, Daniel Lloyd *surgeon*
Langenberg, Frederick Charles *business executive*
Mortimer, James Winslow *analytical chemist*

Meadowbrook
Baeckstrom, Marianne *actuary*

Meadville
Adams, Earl William, Jr., *economics educator*
Cable, Charles Allen *mathematician*
Cable, Mabel Elizabeth *urban planner, artist*
†Crowe, Virginia Mary *retired librarian*
Dixon, Armendia Pierce *school program administrator*
Durlesser, James Arthur *clergyman, writer, lecturer*
Gilles, Bruce Carlson *civil engineer*
Helmreich, Jonathan Ernst *history educator*
Katope, Christopher George *English language educator*
McGuigan, Charles James *rehabilitation therapist*
Shafer, Raymond Philip *lawyer, business executive*
Stewart, Anne Williams *historian, writer, researcher*

Mechanicsburg
Bitner, Jerri Lynne *information technology professional, consultant*
Clousher, Fred Eugene (Freddie Cee Clousher) *entertainment producer, booking agent, musician*
Davis, Frank Daniel *retired journalist*
Denison, Richard Eugene *retired agricultural services company executive*
Derr, William James *retired non-commissioned officer*
Gibbons, Miles Joseph, Jr., *foundation administrator*
Harper, Diane Marie *retired communications retailer*
Kinney, Linford Nelson *retired army officer*
McBeth, David Paul *fundraising consultant*
Moore, Kenneth Lee *executive*
Murphy, Stephan David *electrical engineer*
Nattress, Debra Lynn *computer systems analyst*
Ostdahl, Roger Harold *neurological surgeon*
†Shank, Lucille M. *music educator*
Stone, Thomas Richardson *management consultant*

Stouffer, Nancy Kathleen *publishing company executive*
Wagner, Tanya Suzanne Lineberry *health facility administrator*

Mechanicsville
Bye, Ranulph DeBayeux *artist, author*

Media
Allen, Anne Norgaard *social worker*
Berman, Bernard Mayer *lawyer*
Black, Robert Corl *biology educator*
Blake, David Gordon *lawyer*
Brobeck, John Raymond *physiology educator*
†Cimbala, Stephen Joseph *political science educator*
†Cole, Phyllis Blum *literature educator*
Cook, Joseph V. *physician*
Coyle, Edward J. *physical education coordinator*
†Cramp, John Franklin *lawyer*
D'Amico, Andrew J. *lawyer*
†Derby, Steven R. *foundation administrator*
DiOrio, Robert Michael *lawyer, public official*
DiRosa, Steven Joseph *primary and secondary school educator*
†Durham, James W. *lawyer*
Emerson, Sterling Jonathan *lawyer*
Ewing, Robert Clark *lawyer*
Firkser, Robert Michael *lawyer*
Garrison, Walter R. *corporate executive*
Garvin, Florence Ward *management consultant*
Ginsberg, Robert E. *philosophy educator, editor*
Gordon, Lisa Diane *psychologist*
Hemphill, James S. *investment management executive, financial advisor*
Kessler, Woodrow Bertram *family practice physician, geriatrician, educator*
Lewandowski, Theodore Charles *psychology educator*
Lipton, Robert Stephen *lawyer*
†List, Anthony Francis *lawyer*
Malloy, Michael Joseph *lawyer*
McDonnell, Leo Francis *engineer, consultant*
†McNitt, David Garver *lawyer*
†Mulligan, John Thomas *lawyer*
†Resnick, Stewart Allen *diversified company executive*
Smith, David Gilbert *political science educator*
Sorkin, Adam J. *English educator*
†Steinhardt Gutman, Bertha *artist, educator*
Strunk, Betsy Ann Whitenight *education educator*
Tomlinson, Herbert Weston *lawyer*
Turner, Letitia Rhodes *artist*
Voltz, Sterling Ernest *physical chemist, researcher*
†Wood, Richard D., Jr., *retail executive*

Melrose Park
Steinlauf, Michael Charles *historian*

Mendenhall
Frangopoulos, Zissimos A. *banker*
Lee, Virginia Diane *lay worker*
Reinert, Norbert Frederick *patent lawyer, retired chemical company executive*

Mercer
Kochems, Robert Gregory *lawyer*
Zellers, Robert Charles *materials engineer, consultant, speaker*

Mercersburg
Gift, Gerald Brenton *biology educator*
Tompkins, Christopher Robin *director, educator*

Merion Station
Camp, Kimberly N. *museum administrator, artist*
Coppa, Anthony Patrick *engineer, consultant*
Freeze, James Donald *administrator, clergyman*
Lewis, Paul Le Roy *pathology educator*
Littell, Marcia Sachs *Holocaust and genocide studies educator*
Pearcy, Lee Theron *secondary education educator, writer*
Schick, Paul K. *hematologist*
Ueland, Elizabeth Pritchard *English educator*

Mertztown
Allison, Robert Harry *school counselor*

Middletown
Culpan, Refik *finance educator*
Dodge, Clifford Howle *geologist*
Johnson, Patricia Ellen *humanities educator*
Pannebaker, James Boyd *lawyer*
†Plant, Jeremy Francis *political scientist, educator*
Richman, Irwin *history educator, author, consultant, lecturer*
Yucelt, Ugur *marketing professional, educator*

Midland
Vosler Petrella, Brenda Gayle *family nurse practitioner, educator, researcher*

Mifflinburg
Bayly, Thomas Glen *minister, publisher religious material*

Milford
Le Guin, Ursula Kroeber *writer*
Reynolds, Edwin Wilfred, Jr., *retired secondary education educator*
Rosenblum, Jeffrey Ira *consulting economist*

Milford Square
Sewell, Gloriana *piano teacher*

Mill Hall
Greenberg, Michael Richard *family practice physician*

Millersville
†Bensur, Barbara Jean *art educator, researcher*
Bookmiller, Robert James *political science educator*
Craven, Roberta Jill *educator in literature and film*
Giblin, Claire L. *artist*
Heintzelman, Carol Ann *social work educator*
Kabacinski, Stanley Joseph *health and physical education educator, consultant, speaker*
Miller, Steven Max *humanities educator*

Mohnton
Bowers, Richard Philip *manufacturing executive*
Cottrell, G. Walton *manufacturing executive*
Hart, LeRoy Banks *financial software executive*
Hildreth, Eugene A. *physician, educator*
Konnick, Dianne Cheryl *financial executive*

Monaca
Jaskiewicz, David Walter *optometrist*
Nutter, James Randall *management educator*

Monongahela
Brandon, John Mitchell *physician*
†Yovanof, Silvana *physician*

Monroeville
Baker, Faith Mero *retired elementary education educator*
Baum, Alan Stuart *lawyer*
Bowlden, Henry James *computer science consultant*
Di Gioia, Anthony Michael, Jr., *civil engineer, business executive*
Hribar, John Anthony *civil engineer, consultant*
Jacobi, William Mallett *nuclear engineer, consultant*
†Kennedy, Kathy Kay *library director*
Klink, Ron *former congressman, reporter, newscaster*
Mandel, Herbert Maurice *civil engineer*
Parker, James Roger *chemist*
Schlesser, Thomas Piper *civil engineer*
†Sehring, Hope Hutchison *library science educator*
Skolnick, Marilyn *civic worker*
Valentine, Ruthann *counseling company executive*

Mont Alto
Achampong, Francis Kofi *law educator, consultant*
Hill, Elizabeth Trezise *economics educator*
Russo, Peggy Anne *English language educator*

Montgomeryville
Potsko, Maureen Kathryn *chemical engineer*
Schmidt, William Max *management consultant, business executive*

Montoursville
Woolever, Naomi Louise *retired editor*

Moon Township
Alstadt, Lynn Jeffery *lawyer*
Bacher, Lutz *film, video and photography educator*
Giel, James Arthur, Jr., *employee benefits manager*
Hagar, Joanne Marie *physician assistant*
Rabosky, Joseph George *engineering consulting company executive*
Tannehill, Darcy Anita Bartins *academic administrator*

Morrisville
Dobin, Edward I. *lawyer*
Heefner, William Frederick *lawyer*
†Hershenson, Gerald Martin *lawyer*
Stabenau, Walter Frank *systems engineer*

Moscow
Shotko, Kurt Joseph *entrepreneur, music entertainer*

Mount Gretna
Pakola, Richard Stephen *psychiatrist*
Warshaw, Roberta Sue *lawyer, financial specialist*

Mount Joy
Lodde, Gordon Maynard *health physics consultant*

Mount Pleasant
Domit, John *surgeon*
Johnson, Michael A. *lawyer*
Juriga, Raymond Michael *dentist*
Morgan, Joyce Kaye *social worker*
Pierce, Gordon Carl *retired architect*

Mountainhome
Buttz, Charles William *outdoor advertising executive*

Mountaintop
†Pendziwiatr, William J. *music educator*

Muncy
†West, Thomas James *music educator*

Murrysville
Lain, David Cornelius *health scientist, researcher*
Maurer, Richard Michael *investment company executive*
McWhirter, James Herman *consulting engineering business executive, financial planner*

Myerstown
†Krause, Kenneth Michael *music educator*

Nanticoke
Dalmas-Brown, Carmella Jean *special education educator*
Donohue, Patricia Carol *academic administrator*

Narberth
Chait, Arnold *retired radiologist*
Comer, Nathan Lawrence *psychiatrist, educator*
Estefan, Nabil *finance and business executive*
Grenald, Raymond *architectural lighting designer*
Nathanson, Neal *virologist, epidemiologist, educator*
†Pollack, Sonya A. *artist*
†Rovner, David Patrick Ryan *lawyer*
Strom, Brian Leslie *internist, educator*

Narvon
High, Linda Oatman *author*

Nazareth
Bader, William Alan *computer engineer*
Halberstadt, Robert Bilheimer *optometrist*
Haynes, Thomas Morris *philosophy educator*
†Sanguinito, Bryan Thomas *music educator*

New Alexandria
Ackerman, Robert Lloyd *chemical engineer, environmental tree farmer*

New Britain
Herb, Samuel Martin *manufacturing company executive*

New Buffalo
Cramer, John McNaight *lawyer*

New Castle
Craig, Stephen John *urban planner*
Denniston, Marjorie McGeorge *retired elementary school educator*
Grzebieniak, John Francis *psychologist*
Kelly, Lawrence M. *lawyer*
Mangino, Matthew Thomas *lawyer*
†Mojock, David Theodore *lawyer*
Roux, Mildred Anna *retired secondary school educator*
Sands, Christine Louise *English educator*

New Cumberland
Gorman, Ida Niebauer *HMO outsourcing company executive*
Peters, Ralph Edgar *architectural and engineering executive*
†Wilson, Wanda Mae French *animal association administrator*
Yakowicz, Vincent X. *lawyer, consultant*

New Freedom
Sedlak, Valerie Frances *retired English language educator, retired academic administrator*

New Galilee
†McKim, James O., Jr., *secondary school educator*

New Holland
Fanus, Pauline Rife *librarian*
Papadakis, Emmanuel Philippos *physicist, consultant*

New Hope
Brandes, Doris *artist, art administrator, journalist*
Isbrandt, Lester Reinhardt *pharmaceutical executive*
Knight, Douglas Maitland *educational administrator, optical executive, writer*
Lee, Robert William *organic chemist*
Raabe, Gerhard Karl *epidemiologist*
Roazzi, Vincent Michael *marketing professional*
Sergey, John Michael, Jr., *investment company executive*
Thomsen, Thomas Richard *retired communications company executive*
Williamson, Frederick Beasley, III, *rubber company executive*

New Kensington
Demmler, Albert William, Jr., *retired editor, metallurgical engineer*
Jarrett, Noel *chemical engineer, researcher*
†Kalavar, Jyotsna Mirle *education educator*
†Wallace, Henry Jared, Jr., *lawyer*

New Kingstown
DiSipio, Rocco Thomas *writer*

New Oxford
Arnold, Ellen Holt *continuing care retirement community administrator*
Frock, J. Daniel *transportation executive, retired manufacturing company executive*
Rohrbaugh, Nova R *retired music educator*

New Tripoli
Hess, Darla Bakersmith *cardiologist, educator*

New Wilmington
†Magyary, Cynthia Marie *elementary school educator, music educator*
†Swerdlow, Milagros Zapata *language educator*
†Taylor, Gary B. *music educator*

Newry
LaBorde, Terrence Lee *audit consultant, negotiator*

Newtown
Brennan, Thomas John *city and state official, consultant, educator*
Buermann, Peter Bruce *psychologist, program administrator*
†Conrad, Stephen Edward *secondary school educator*
Derivan, Mary Collins *nursing consultant, oncological nurse*
Fiore, James Louis, Jr., *public accountant, educator, professional speaker, trainer consultant*
Flum, Joseph *lawyer*
Godwin, Robert Anthony *lawyer*
Kardos, Mel D. *lawyer, educator*
Keenan, Terrance *foundation executive*
Long, Harry (On-Yuen Eng) *chemist, science and technology executive, consultant*
†Nowak, Gerald C. *music educator, musician, writer*
Renninger, John Snowden *lawyer*
Richard, James Thomas *retired psychologist, educator*
Ross, Edwin William *rubber company executive*
Schroeder, Alfred Christian *electronics research engineer*
†Sheridan, John J. *musician, music educator*
Somers, Anne Ramsay *retired medical educator*
Woods, Howard James, Jr., *civil engineer*

Newtown Square
Benenson, James, Jr., *manufacturer*
Bower, Ward Alan *management consultant, lawyer*
†Crowley, James Michael *lawyer*
de Rivas, Carmela Foderaro *psychiatrist, hospital administrator*
Graf, Arnold Harold *employee benefits executive, financial planner*
Lang, Lothar A. *engineer*
Lawrence, Theodore *physician*
Lewis, James Earl *financier*
Perrone, Nicholas *mechanical engineer, business executive*
Rothermel, Rodman Schantz *manufacturing company executive*
Sacks, Susan Bendersky *mental health clinical specialist, educator*
Scholl, David Allen *former federal judge, lawyer*
Staats, Dean Roy *retired reinsurance executive*
Vela, Laurie Story *illustrator, writer, publisher, producer*

Norristown
Aman, George Matthias, III, *lawyer*
Andrews, Cheri D. *lawyer*
Becker, Michael Anthony *osteopathic family physician, educator*
Biondi, Anthony *municipal official*
Britt, Earl Thomas *lawyer*
Colcher, Robert Ely *surgeon*
Cowperthwait, Lindley Murray *lawyer*
†Dat, Manabendra Nath *civil engineer, consultant*
Gaber, Robert *psychologist*
Garabedian, Joseph Andre *physician*
Gerdes, Michelle Ann *designer*
†Gold-Bikin, Lynne Z. *lawyer*
†Gowen, Thomas Leo, Jr., *lawyer*
Gregg, John Pennypacker *lawyer*
Hunter, Patricia Phelps *physician assistant*
Kofsky, Phillip Mark *surgeon*
Milner, Kenneth Paul *lawyer*
Rees, Thomas Dynevor *lawyer*
†Reilley, Gail Goodwin *soprano, music educator, musician*
Rounick, Jack A. *lawyer, company executive*
†Sosnov, Amy W(iener) *lawyer*
Steinberg, Arthur Irwin *periodontist, educator*
Tornetta, Frank Joseph *anesthesiologist, educator, consultant*

North Huntingdon
Brazer, Barbara Roback *accountant*

North Wales
†Brady, George Charles, III, *lawyer*
Mann, Elaine Renee *marketing manager*
Napier, Thomas M. *electrical engineer*
Neu, Peter S. *music educator*
Sheares, Bradley T. *pharmaceutical executive*

Northern Cambria
Kimmel, Richard E. *music educator*

Northumberland
Wert, Barbara J. Yingling *special education consultant*

Nottingham
White, Richard Edmund *marketing executive*

Noxen
†Wood, Thomas G. *chemist, educator*

Oakdale
Gilden, Robin Elissa *elementary education educator*
Wang, Chuan-Bao *chemist, research scientist*

Oakmont
Bryce, Marguerite Maher *social worker, educator*

Oil City
Kumar, Harinath V. *urologist, surgeon*
†Sabousky, Richard Anthony *adult education educator*

Olyphant
Batzel, Edward Lee *surgeon*

Orefield
†Dimmich, Jeffrey Robert *lawyer*

Oreland
Maerker, Gerhard *food science consultant*

Orwigsburg
Garloff, Samuel John *psychiatrist*

Oxford
Hostert, Leona Teressa *research librarian*

Palmyra
Singer, William Harry *interactive multimedia architect, software engineer, expert systems designer, consultant, entrepreneur, ceramic artist*
Toney, Brian Michael *music educator*

Paoli
Denny, William Murdoch, Jr., *investment management executive*
†Glassner, Michael J. *obstetrician, gynecologist*

Gotshall, Jan Doyle *financial planner*
Griffith, Edward *lawyer*
Lanza, Ralph Andrew *internist*
†Rosenblatt, Barbara S. *educator, writer*
Scovill, Curtis Neal *physician*
Shubin, Seymour *writer*
†Yake, Sarah Louise *poet*

Paradise
Eshleman, Silas Kendrick, III, *retired psychiatrist*

Parkesburg
Procyson, Mary G. Walton *critical care nurse*
Zevtchin, J. Mark *financial executive, consultant*

Patton
†Pompa, Louise Elaine *secondary school educator*
Reed-Gates, Mary Louise *natural health professional*

Peach Glen
Carey, Dean Lavere *fruit canning company executive*

Pen Argyl
†Martocci, Lewis Nicholas, III, *writer*

Penn Valley
Newhall, John Harrison *retired non profit company executive*

Pennsburg
Shuhler, Phyllis Marie *physician*

Perkasie
Ferry, Joan Evans *school counselor*
Laincz, Betsy Ann *nurse*

Petersburg
White, Elizabeth Loczi *academic researcher, civil engineer*

Philadelphia
Aaron, Kenneth Ellyot *lawyer*
†Abernathy, Corbin Brett *music educator, theater educator*
†Abraham, Richard Paul *lawyer*
Abramowitz, Robert Leslie *lawyer*
Abreu, Bobby *professional baseball player*
Abrutyn, Elias *infectious diseases physician, administrator*
Adamany, David Walter *law and political science educator*
Adams, Arlin Marvin *lawyer, arbitrator, mediator, retired judge*
Adawi, Nadia Sharon *energy cooperative executive*
†Adler, Martin William *neuropharmacologist*
Agran, Raymond Daniel *lawyer*
Ahima, Rexford Sefah *neuroendocrinologist, internist*
Aiken, Linda Harman *nurse, sociologist, educator*
Ajzenberg-Selove, Fay *physicist, educator*
Alexander, Elmore Rosebur, III, *business educator, dean*
Alexander, William Herbert *business educator, former construction executive*
Allen, Julian Lewis *medical educator, researcher*
†Allen-Castellitto, Anita LaFrance *law educator*
†Allison, Paul David *sociologist, educator, sociologist, consultant*
Anders, Jerrold P. *lawyer*
Anderson, Christopher Jon
Anderson, Rolph Ely *finance educator*
Andrisani, Paul J. *business educator, management consultant*
Angell, M(ary) Faith *federal magistrate judge*
Anyanwu, Chukwukre *alcohol and drug abuse facility administrator*
†Appleby, David Curtis *dentist, educator*
Arce, A. Anthony *psychiatrist, educator*
Arnold, Lee *library director, archivist*
Aronstein, Martin Joseph *law educator, lawyer*
Asbury, Arthur Knight *neurologist, educator*
Ascenzi, John C. *writer, editor*
†Ashvo-Muñoz, Alira *language educator*
†Assoian, Richard Kenneth *molecular biologist, educator*
Augoustides, John George Themistocles *cardiothoracic anesthesiologist, educator*
†Austan, Frank Acosta *clinician, educator*
Austrian, Robert *physician, educator, department chairman*
Auten, David Charles *lawyer*
Aversa, Dolores Sejda *educational administrator*
Azzolina, David Sean *librarian*
Babbel, David Frederick *finance and insurance educator*
Baccini, Laurance Ellis *lawyer*
Bachman, Arthur *lawyer*
Bacon, Edmund Norwood *city planner*
Bailey, Elizabeth Ellery *economics educator*
Bajscy, Ruzena *computer engineer*
Balliet, Arthur Gerald *molecular biologist, researcher*
†Baltuch, Gordon Hirsh *neurosurgeon*
Bamberger-Herrmann, Julia Kathryn *social worker*
Banerji, Ranan Bihari *mathematics and computer science educator*
Bantel, Linda Mae *former museum curator, consultant*
Barchi, Robert Lawrence *clinical neurologist, neuroscientist, educator*
Barker, Clyde Frederick *surgeon, educator*
Barnett, Jonathan *architect, urban planner, educator*
Barnett, Samuel Treutlen *international company executive*
Barrett, James Edward, Jr., *management consultant*
Barrett, John J(ames), Jr., *lawyer*
Barsoum, Michel W. *materials engineer, educator*
Bartle, Harvey, III, *federal judge*
Bartlett, Allen Lyman, Jr., *retired bishop*
Bass, Aaron *school system administrator*
Bates, James Earl *academic administrator*
†Battis, David Gregory *lawyer*
Baum, Stanley *radiologist, educator*
Baxt, William Gordon *medical educator*
†Beam, Robert Charles *lawyer*
Bearn, Alexander Gordon *physician, retired pharmaceutical executive*
Beasley, James Edwin *lawyer*
Bechtle, Louis Charles *lawyer, retired federal judge*
†Beck, Aaron Temkin *psychiatrist, educator*
Beck, John Robert *pathologist, information scientist*
Becker, Edward Roy *judge*
Beeman, Richard Roy *historian, educator*
Beilstein, Henry Richard *microbiologist, educator*
Bennett, Amanda *editor*
Berenato, Mark Anthony *lawyer, insurance executive*
Berg, Ivar Elis, Jr., *social science educator*
Berger, David *lawyer*
Berger, Harold *lawyer, electrical engineer*
†Berger, Lawrence Howard *lawyer*
Berkley, Emily Carolan *lawyer*
Berkman, Richard Lyle *lawyer*
Bernard, John Marley *lawyer, educator*
Bershad, Jack R. *retired lawyer*
Bibbo, Marluce *physician, educator*
Biddle, Daniel R. *editor, reporter*
Bildersee, Robert Alan *lawyer*
Binder, David Franklin *lawyer, author*
Binzen, Peter Husted *columnist*
Birch, Eugenie Ladner *urban planning educator*
†Bisaccia-Hanson, Betty *marketing professional, public relations executive*
Black, Allen Decatur *lawyer*
Blavat, Jerry (Gerald Joseph Blavat) *radio and television personality, actor*
Bleshman, Michael Henry *radiologist*
Blissitt, Patricia Ann *nurse*
Blumberg, Baruch Samuel *academic research scientist*
Blume, Marshall Edward *finance educator*
Blumstein, Edward *lawyer*
Boden, Guenther *endocrinologist*
Bodine, James Forney *retired civic leader*
Bodner, Susan Rachel *marketing and communications executive*
Boggia, Eugene Stephen *lawyer*
Bogutz, Jerome Edwin *lawyer, educator*
Bonovitz, Sheldon M. *lawyer*
Booth, Anna Belle *accountant*
Borislow, Alan Jerome *hospital dental department chairman*
Boscia, Jon Andrew *insurance company executive*
Boss, Amelia Helen *law educator, lawyer*
Botwinick, Milton Edward *genealogist, researcher*
Bove, Alfred Anthony *medical educator*
Bowa, Lawrence Robert (Larry Bowa) *professional baseball manager*
†Bowers, Toni M. *literature educator*
Bowman, Marjorie Ann *family practice physician, educator*
Boyd, Larry Chester *recruitment manager*
Bracey, Cookie Frances Lee *minister*
†Bradshaw, William Elbert *lawyer*
Brady, Luther W., Jr., *physician, radiation oncology educator*
†Branche, Anna Louise *physical education educator, performing arts educator, religious studies educator*
Breitman, Joseph B. *prosthodontist, dental educator*
Bressler, Barry E. *lawyer*
Brewer-Smyth, Kathleen *nursing researcher, nursing educator*
†Brier, Bonnie Susan *lawyer*
Brighton, Carl Theodore *orthopedic surgery educator*
Brinster, Ralph Lawrence *biologist, educator*
Brittain, Willard Woodson, Jr., (Woody Brittain) *diversified financial services company executive*
Broder, Michael S. *psychologist*
Brodkin, Edward Stuart *psychiatrist, geneticist*
Broennle, A. Michael *anesthesiologist*
Brooks, John Samuel Joseph *pathologist, researcher*
Brooks, Robert Mark *civil engineer, educator*
†Brooks-Kayal, Amy R. *pediatrician, researcher, neurologist*
Brown, Betty Marie *government agency administrator*
Brown, Denise Scott *architect, urban planner*
Brown, Ronald Rea *software engineer, artist*
Brown, Stephen D. *lawyer*
Brown, William Hill, III, *lawyer*
Browne, Stanhope Stryker *lawyer*
†Broytman, Vladislav I. *hygenist*
†Brucker, Paul C. *academic administrator, physician*
Buccino, Ernest John, Jr., *lawyer*
Buckwalter, Ronald Lawrence *federal judge*
Buerkle, Jack Vincent *sociologist, educator*
Burbank, Stephen Bradner *law educator*
Burch, Francis Floyd *clergyman*
Burstein, Elias *physicist, educator*
Butz, Geneva Mae *pastor*
Byer, Harold George *civil/environmental engineer*
Cabot, Stephen Jay *lawyer*
Caldwell, John Warwick *lawyer*
Calman, Robert Frederick *mining executive*
Calvert, Jay H., Jr., *lawyer*
Camp, Donald Eugene *experimental photographer, educator*
Cannon, John, III, *lawyer*
†Capers, Gregg *secondary school educator, musician*
Capizzi, Robert Lawrence *physician*
Cappelli, Peter H. *human resources educator*
Caravasos, NiaLena *lawyer*
Carey, Arthur Bernard, Jr., *editor, writer, columnist*
Carnecchia, Baldo M., Jr., *lawyer*
Carpenter, Amy Tacy *architect*
Carpenter, Nathaniel Dennard *resident health services director*
†Carson, Timothy Joseph *lawyer*
Carter, John Swain *museum administrator, consultant*
Casey, Rita Jo Ann *nursing administrator*
†Cashmore, Anthony *biologist, educator*
Casper, Charles B. *lawyer*
†Cass, David *economist, educator*
Cassel, Christine Karen *physician*
†Chance, Britton *biophysics and physical chemistry educator emeritus*
Chapman, John Donald *research biophysicist*
†Charney, Natalie J. *behavioral health services administrator, researcher*
Chauhan, Vijay Lakshmi *English educator, writer*
Chen, Sow-Yeh *pathology educator*
Cherken, Harry Sarkis, Jr., *lawyer*
Chertoff, Michael *judge*
Cheston, George Morris *lawyer*
Childress, Scott Julius *medicinal chemist*
Chimples, George *lawyer*
†Chung, Jennifer M. *not-for-profit executive*
Clark, Christopher Michael *neurologist, educator, clinic director*
Clark, John Arthur *lawyer*
Clark, John J. *economist, educator, finance educator*
Clark, William H., Jr., *lawyer*
Clarke, John Rodney *surgeon*
†Clarke, Robert Earle (Bobby Clarke) *hockey executive*
Clarke, Sean Patrick *nursing researcher, educator*
Clarkin, John Francis *health care management executive*
†Claudio, Pier Paolo *surgeon, researcher*
Clearfield, Harris Reynold *physician*
Coché, Judith *psychologist, educator*
Cohen, David Michael *newspaper editor, journalist*
Cohen, David Walter *academic administrator, periodontist, educator*
Cohen, Ira Myron *aeronautical and mechanical engineering educator*
Cohn, Mildred *biochemist, educator*
Cole, C. Suzanne *librarian*
Coleman, Robert J. *lawyer*
Colli, Bart Joseph *lawyer*
Collings, Robert L. *lawyer*
†Collins, Lynn H. *psychologist, educator, web site designer*
Collons, Rodger Duane *decision sciences educator*
Colman, Robert Wolf *physician, medical educator, researcher*
†Colson, Rosemary *music educator*
Comisky, Hope A. *lawyer*
Condon, J. Emmett *information technology executive*
Conn, Rex Boland, Jr., *physician, educator*
†Connor, Bernadette Yvonne *retired writer*
Connor, Joseph Patrick, III, *lawyer*
Connor, Nancy L. *foundation executive*
†Conrad, Bruce Phillips *mathematics educator*
Conway, John W. *manufacturing executive*
Cooney, J(ohn) Gordon, Jr., *lawyer*
Cooper, Edward Sawyer *cardiologist, internist, educator*
Cooper, Richard Lee *newspaper editor, journalist*
Cooperman, Barry S. *educational administrator, educator, scientist*
Coraza, Mary Catherine *psychologist*
Cornelius, Jeffrey Michael *music educator*
†Corprew, Helen Barbara *mental health services professional*
Cortner, Jean Alexander *retired physician, educator*
Coss, Ronald Allen *radiation biologist, cell biologist*
Cotler, Jerome Marvin *orthopaedic surgeon*
Coulson, Zoe Elizabeth *retired consumer marketing executive*
Cowles, Roger E. *computer consultant*
Cox, Roger Frazier *lawyer*
Coyne, Charles Cole *lawyer*
Cramer, Harold *lawyer*
†Craven, Charles Warren *lawyer*
†Crissey, Harrington E., Jr., *English as second language educator*
Croce, Pat *author, fitness trainer, former sports team executive*
†Cromarty, G. Geoffrey *academic administrator*
Cross, Milton H. *lawyer*
Crumb, George Henry *composer, educator*
†Cummins, John David *economics educator, consultant*
†Cunningham, Jessie Jerome *entrepreneur*
Czech, Paul Andrew *lawyer*
Dabrowski, Doris Jane *lawyer*
Dagit, Charles Edward, Jr.,
Dalinka, Murray Kenneth *radiologist, educator*
Dalton, David Robert *chemistry educator*
Dalzell, Stewart *federal judge*
Damsgaard, Kell Marsh *lawyer*
D'Angio, Giulio John *radiologist, educator*
Darling, Pamela Ann Wood *writer, editor, speaker, religious consultant*
Dasgupta, Indranil *physician, educator*
†Davatzikos, Ph.D., Christos *research scientist, educator*
Davidson, Rhonda Elizabeth *preschool educator*
Davidson, Stuart West *lawyer*
Davis, Alan Jay *lawyer*
Davis, Allen Freeman *history educator, author*
†Davis, C. VanLeer, III, *lawyer*
Davis, Howard Jeffrey *lawyer*
Davis, Raymond, Jr., *physical chemistry researcher*
Dean-Zubritsky, Cynthia Marian *psychologist, researcher*
DeBunda, Salvatore Michael *lawyer*
de Cani, John Stapley *statistician, educator*
Deforest, Adamadia *pediatric virologist*
de Francesco, John Kenneth *foreign language educator*
†DeFusco Ochal, Mary Theresa *lawyer*
DeHoratius, Raphael Joseph *rheumatologist*
†De Kok, Daniel John *music educator*
DeLong, David G. *architect, urban planner, educator*
Del Raso, Joseph Vincent *lawyer*
Devlin, John Gerard *lawyer, author*
d'Harnoncourt, Anne *museum director, executive*
Diaz, Nelson *lawyer*
Di Benedetto, C. Anthony *marketing educator*
DiBerardino, Marie Antoinette *developmental biologist, educator*
Dichter, Mark S. *lawyer*
Diebold, Francis X. *economist, educator*
†Di Falco, Gerard A. *visual artist*
Dilks, Park Bankert, Jr., *lawyer*
Dinoso, Vicente Pescador, Jr., *physician, educator*
DiPalma, Joseph Rupert *pharmacology educator*
Djerassi, Isaac *physician, medical researcher*
†Dobbs, Stanley *military officer, information quality engineer*
†Doherty, Roger Davidge *adult education educator, consultant*
†Donaher, Joseph G *speech pathology/audiology services professional, director*
Donaldson, Thomas *ethicist, educator*
Donner, Henry Jay *lawyer*
Donohue, James J. *lawyer*
Donohue, John Patrick *lawyer*
Doran, William Michael *lawyer*
Dorfman, John Charles *lawyer*
Dormans, John Paul *surgeon, educator*
Doty, Richard L. *medical researcher*
†Dowdall, George William *sociology educator*
Downey, Michael S. *physician, podiatrist*
Drake, Jayne Kribbs *university administrator, English educator*
Drake, William Frank, Jr., *lawyer*
†Driver, Robert Baylor, Jr., *opera company administrator*
Drosdick, John Girard *oil company executive*
Drozdis, Marie Trese *crisis intervention nurse*
Druckrey, Inge Heide *graphic designer, educator*
Dubin, Leonard *lawyer*
Dubin, Stephen Victor *lawyer*
†Duclow, Geraldine *historian, theatre and film librarian*
Duker, Nahum Johanan *pathologist, educator*
Dunkman, W(illiam) Bruce *physician, educator*
Durant, Marc *lawyer*
Dutton, P(eter) Leslie *biochemist, educator*
Dworetzky, Joseph Anthony *lawyer, city official*
†Eberwine, James *molecular biologist, educator*
Ehrlich, George Edward *rheumatologist, international pharmaceutical consultant*
Eisen, Howard Joel *physician, researcher*
Eisenberg, Burton L. *surgeon*
Eisenberg, Ted Steven *plastic and reconstructive surgeon*
Eisenstein, Toby K. *microbiology educator*
Eiswerth, Barry Neil *architect, educator*
†Elliott, Homer Lee *lawyer*
El-Sherif, Mahmoud A. *electrical engineering educator*
†Emerson, Stephen G. *hematologist, educator, oncologist*
Engheta, Nader *electrical engineering educator, researcher*
Epstein, Alan Bruce *lawyer*
Erdmann, James Bernard *educational psychologist*
Eskin, Bernard Abraham *obstetrics and gynecology educator, medical researcher*
Esser, Carl Eric *lawyer*
Esterhai, John Louis, Jr., *surgeon, medical educator*
Evan, William Martin *sociologist, educator*
Everett, Carl Bell *lawyer*
†Ewald, William Bragg, III, *law educator, philosopher, educator*
Exler, Samuel *retired advertising executive, writer*
Fader, Henry Conrad *lawyer*
Fagin, Claire Mintzer *nursing educator, administrator*
Fala, Herman C. *lawyer*
Falkie, Thomas Victor *mining engineer, mining executive*
Faraghan, George Telford *photographer*
†Farley, Barbara L. *lawyer*
Farley, Joseph Michael *human relations executive, editor, publisher*
Farren, Ann Louise *chemist, information scientist, educator*
Feinsmith, Norman *cardiovascular disease physician*
Feirson, Steven B. *lawyer*
Feldman, Arthur M. *cardiologist*
Feldman, Michael Saul *cardiologist, educator*
Fenik, Victor Borisovich *neurobiologist, researcher*
Feninger, Claude *industry management services company executive*
Fernandez, Happy Craven (Gladys Fernandez) *academic administrator*
Fernandez, Mike *healthcare company executive*
†Fernholz, Luisa Turrin *statistician, educator*
Ferniany, Isaac William *health system administrator*
†Ferrari, Victor Alfred *cardiologist*
Fickler, Arlene *lawyer*
Fiebach, H. Robert *lawyer*
Fiel, Stanley Bruce *internist, pulmonogist, educator, researcher*
Fielding, Allen Fred *oral and maxillofacial surgeon, educator*
†Fine, Lawrence B. *lawyer*
Fine, Miriam Brown *artist, educator, poet, writer*
Finkelstein, Joseph Simon *lawyer*
Finney, Graham Stanley *management consultant*
Fish, Elizabeth Ann *physical education educator*

McCarron, Jeffrey Baldwin *lawyer*
McClurken, James Bartholomew *surgeon*
McCord, Joan *sociologist, educator, rsearcher*
McCormick, Rod *sculptor, art educator*
†McGurk, Eugene David, Jr., *lawyer*
McHugh, James Joseph *lawyer*
McKee, Theodore A. *federal judge*
McKeever, John Eugene *lawyer*
†McMenamin, Richard F. *lawyer*
McNabb, Donovan *football player*
McNamara, Kevin John *academic administrator*
†McNeill, Corbin Asahel, Jr., *utility executive*
McQuiston, Robert Earl *lawyer*
Means, John Barkley *foreign language educator, association executive*
Mee, Michael F. *retired pharmaceutical executive*
Meigs, John Forsyth *lawyer*
Meleis, Afaf Ibrahim *nurse sociologist, educator, clinician, researcher*
Mellman, Leonard *real estate investor and advisor*
Messa, Joseph Louis, Jr., *lawyer*
Meyer, Marshall Warner *management and sociology educator*
Meyer, Paul William *arboretum director, horticulturist*
Meyers, Howard L. *lawyer*
Meyerson, Margy Ellin *urbanist, civic volunteer*
Meyerson, Martin *university educator, urban and regional planner*
Meyer Weisgerber, Martha Lindsey *account executive*
Michael, Henry N. *geographer, anthropologist*
Micko, Alexander S. *financial executive*
Micozzi, Marc Stephen *health executive, physician, educator*
Milbourne, Walter Robertson *lawyer*
Miller, Henry Franklin *lawyer*
Miller, Ronald Eugene *regional science educator*
Miller Calandra, Linda Marguerita *pediatric nurse practitioner*
Milone, Francis Michael *lawyer*
Mirabello, Francis Joseph *lawyer*
Mitchell, Ehrman Burkman, Jr., *architect*
Mitchell, James Edwin *architect, educator*
Miyamoto, Curtis Trent *medical educator*
Mode, Charles J. *mathematician, educator*
†Monos, Dimitrios *medical educator, researcher*
Moore, Faye L. Mitchell *financial executive*
†Moore, Robin D. *humanities educator*
Morello, Celeste Anne *historian, criminologist*
†Moreno, Michele R. *court reporter*
Morlok, Edward Karl *engineering educator, consultant*
†Morman, Edward Terry *librarian, medical historian*
†Morris, Roland *lawyer*
†Moses, Bonnie Smith *lawyer, educator*
Moss, Arthur Henshey *lawyer*
Moss, Roger William *historian, writer, administrator*
Most-Levin, Carol Lynn *physician, geriatrician*
Mostovoy, Marc Sanders *conductor, music director*
Movsas, Benjamin *radiation oncologist, researcher*
Mulford, Richard Albert *mechanical engineer, professional society administrator*
Mulholland, S. Grant *urologist*
Mullinix, Edward Wingate *lawyer*
†Mulvey, W. Michael *lawyer*
Muntean, Andrei Mihai *legislative staff member, educator*
Murdoch, Lawrence Corlies, Jr., *retired banker, economist*
Murphy, William Patrick *lawyer, editor, writer*
†Mutombo, DiKembe (Dikembe Mutombo Mpolondo Mukamba Jean Jacque Wamutombo) *professional basketball player*
Myers, Allen Richard *rheumatologist*
†Naidu, Jaideep Taragula *science educator, researcher*
†Nalle, Peter Devereux *publishing company executive*
Narangajavana, Kanthaka *mass spectrometrist*
†Nath, Amar *chemist, educator*
Neff, P. Sherrill *venture capitalist*
†Neill, Richard Alan *medical educator, director*
Neubauer, Joseph *food services company executive*
Newberg, Aaron Nelson *physician, pediatrician*
Newberg, Andrew B. *neuroscientist*
Newcomer, Clarence Charles *federal judge*
Newman, Cory Frank *clinical psychologist*
†Newman, George Henry *lawyer*
Nickels, Thom *writer, journalist*
Nigro, Russell M. *state supreme court justice*
Nimoityn, Philip *cardiologist*
Nobel, Glenn Lloyd *investment group director, arbitrator, mediator*
Nofer, George Hancock *lawyer*
Noordergraaf, Abraham *biophysics educator*
Norris, Charles Morgan *laryngologist, educator*
Nowell, Peter Carey *pathologist, educator*
†O'Brien, Charles P. *psychiatrist, educator*
O'Brien, James Jerome *construction management consultant*
O'Brien, William Jerome, II, *lawyer*
O'Connor, Joseph A., Jr., *lawyer*
Oh, Michael Young-Suk *PhD student & researcher, minister & theological seminary president*
†O'Leary, Brendan (Denis O'Leary) *political science educator, journalist*
Olenginski, Jan Anthony *surgeon*
Oliva, Terence Anthony *marketing educator*
Ominsky, Andrew Michael *lawyer*
Ominsky, Harris *lawyer*
O'Neill, Thomas Newman, Jr., *federal judge*
O'Reilly, Timothy Patrick *lawyer*
Orlovskaya, Nina *materials scientist*
Orne, Emily Carota *research psychologist*
†Orr, Nancy A. *educational psychologist*
Ossip, Michael J. *lawyer*
Oswald, Stanton S. *lawyer*

Othmer, David Artman *television and radio consultant*
Owens, Gary Mitchell *family physician*
Owens, Rochelle *poet, playwright*
Padulo, Louis *university administrator*
Paglia, Camille *writer, humanities educator*
Pagliaro, James Domenic *lawyer*
†Pahlavan, Pantea *obstetrician, gynecologist*
Palmer, Richard Ware *lawyer*
Palmer, Russell Eugene *investment executive*
Panek, Edward Stanley, Jr., *lawyer*
†Panzer, Mitchell Emanuel *lawyer*
Paone, Peter *artist*
Papadakis, Constantine N. *university executive*
†Pappas, Charles Nicholas, III, *dentist, educator*
Parry, Lance Aaron *newspaper executive*
Parry, William DeWitt *lawyer*
Pasek, Jeffrey Ivan *lawyer*
Patrick, Ruth (Mrs. Ruth Hodge Van Dusen) *limnologist, diatom taxonomist, educator*
Patton, Peter Mark *lawyer*
Pauciulo, John William *lawyer*
Paulus, Ronald Alan *health executive, physician*
Pawlowski, Nicholas Alexander *pediatrician, allergist*
Payne, Deborah Anne *medical company officer*
Peasnall, Brian Lee *archaeologist, educator*
Peck, Robert McCracken *naturalist, science historian, writer*
Peck, Susan Nell *pediatric nurse*
†Peiss, Kathy L. *historian, educator*
Pepe, Frank A. *cell and developmental biology educator*
Perkins, George Holmes *architectural educator, architect*
Permut, Stephen Robert *physician, lawyer*
†Perry, David *lawyer, insurance executive, real estate consultant*
Perry, Robert Palese *molecular biologist, educator*
Peters, Edward Murray *history educator*
Pew, Robert Anderson *retired real estate and equipment leasing corporation officer*
Phelps, Charlotte DeMonte *retired economics educator*
Phillips, Fred Ronald *insurance company executive*
Piccolo, Joseph Anthony *hospital administrator*
†Pillai, K. G. Jan *law educator, lawyer*
†Pilvin, Barbara Jeanne *librarian*
†Pinola, Richard J. *management consultant*
†Piola, Erika G. *archivist*
Pipes, Daniel *writer*
Platsoucas, Chris Dimitrios *immunologist*
Plumer, Alvin H. (Bud) *realtor*
Pollack, Michael *lawyer*
Pollak, Louis Heilprin *judge, educator*
Ponte-Castañeda, Pedro *mechanical engineering educator*
Popovics, Sandor *civil engineer, educator, researcher*
Porrata-Doria, Rafael Alfonso *law educator*
Porter, Gerald Joseph *mathematician, educator*
Posner, Edward Martin *lawyer*
†Potamkin, Robert *automotive executive*
Potsic, William Paul *physician, educator*
Potter, Alice Catherine *clinical laboratory scientist*
Poul, Franklin *lawyer*
Powell, Walter Hecht *labor arbitrator*
Powers, Michael Roland *educator, insurance consultant*
†Poythress, Vern Sheridan *religion educator, minister*
Presseisen, Barbara Zemboch *retired educational director, researcher*
Presser, Janice *business executive*
Presser, Stefan *lawyer, educator*
Preston, Samuel Hulse *demographer*
†Prewitt, David Edward *lawyer*
Price, Robert Stanley *lawyer*
Primeau, Keith *hockey player*
Promislo, Daniel *lawyer*
Pugliese, Maria Alessandra *psychiatrist*
Putney, Paul William *lawyer*
Pyeritz, Reed Edwin *medical geneticist, educator, research director*
Quann, Joan Louise *French language educator, real estate broker*
Quinn, John Albert *chemical engineering educator*
Rabinowitz, Howard K. *physician, educator*
Rabinowitz, Samuel Nathan *lawyer*
Rachofsky, David J. *lawyer*
Rackow, Julian Paul *lawyer*
Raff, Daniel Martin Gorodetsky *economist, economic and business historian, educator*
Rainone, Michael Carmine *lawyer*
Rainville, Christina *lawyer*
Ramsey, Natalie D. *lawyer*
†Randall, Peter *plastic surgeon*
Rastogi, Anil Kumar *medical device manufacturer, executive*
†Ratcliffe, Sarah Jane *biostatistician*
Rauch, John Keiser, Jr., *architect*
Ray, Evelyn Lucille *arts facilitator, small meetings planner*
Raymond, Fred Douglas, III, *lawyer*
†Real, Frank Joseph, Jr., *lawyer, accountant*
†Reath, Henry (Thompson) *lawyer*
Reed, Lowell A., Jr., *federal judge*
Reed, Sally Gardner *cultural organization administrator*
Regan, Robert Charles *English language educator*
Reich, Abraham Charles *lawyer*
Reid, Andy *professional football coach*
Reid, Mary Wallace *retired secondary education educator*
Reimer, Charles Wilson *curator, consultant*
Reinecke, Robert Dale *ophthalmologist*
Reintzel, Warren Andrew *trust company executive*
Reisman, Jason Eric *lawyer*
Reiss, John Barlow *lawyer*
Reiter, Joseph Henry *lawyer, retired judge*
Reitz, Curtis Randall *lawyer, educator*

Rendell, Marjorie O. *federal judge*
Rescorla, Robert Arthur *psychology educator*
Resnick, Stephanie *lawyer*
Retz, William Andrew *retired naval officer*
Rhoads, Nancy Glenn *lawyer*
Rhodes, Alice Graham *lawyer*
Rickels, Karl *psychiatrist, physician, educator*
†Rickels, Michael Roehrhoff *physician*
†Rigali, Justin F. *archbishop*
Rima, Ingrid Hahne *economics educator*
†Rimm, Robert *writer, educator*
Ritchie, Wallace Parks, Jr., *retired surgeon, educator*
Roberts, Brian L. *communications executive*
Roberts, Carl Geoffrey *lawyer*
Roberts, Ralph Joel *telecommunications, cable broadcast executive*
Robreno, Eduardo C. *federal judge*
†Robson, Roy Raymond *historian, educator*
Rodin, Judith Seitz *academic administrator, psychology educator*
Roebuck, James Randolph, Jr., *state legislator*
Roenick, Jeremy *hockey player*
Rogers, Fred Baker *medical educator*
Rollins, James Calvin *baseball player*
Romer, Daniel *university official, psychologist, educator*
Root, Stanley William, Jr., *lawyer, retired*
Rorer, John Whiteley *publisher, consultant*
Rorke, Lucy Balian *neuropathologist*
†Rosen, Philip *retired writer*
Rosen, Rhoda *obstetrician, gynecologist*
Rosenberg, Robert Allen *psychologist, educator, optometrist*
Rosenbleeth, Richard M. *lawyer*
Rosenbloom, Bert *marketing educator, consultant, writer*
Rosenbloom, Joel *molecular biologist, educator*
Rosenbloom, Sanford M. *lawyer*
Rosenstein, James Alfred *lawyer, mediator, negotiation facilitator*
†Rosenthal, Edward Charles *management science educator*
Ross, Daniel R. *lawyer*
Ross, Darrin *composer*
Ross, Leonard Lester *anatomist, educator*
†Ross, Murray Louis *lawyer, business executive*
†Rost, Gregory Stuart *academic administrator*
Roth, Marilyn Dorothy *information scientist*
Rothrock, Robert William *physician assistant*
Rowan, Richard Lamar *business management educator*
Rubenstein, Arthur Harold *medical school official, physician*
Rubin, Emanuel *pathologist, educator*
Rubin, Stephen Curtis *gynecologic oncologist, educator*
Rudczynski, Andrew B. *academic administrator, medical researcher*
†Rudley, Lloyd Dave *psychiatrist*
Rueter, Thomas James *federal judge*
Rufe, Cynthia Marie *judge*
Rumpf, John Louis *civil engineer, consultant*
Russo, Irma Haydee Alvarez de *pathologist*
Rutman, Robert Jesse *bioscience researcher*
Rybczynski, Witold Marian *architect, educator, writer*
Ryken, Philip Graham *minister, theologian, writer*
Rykwert, Joseph *architecture and art history educator*
Sabloff, Jeremy Arac *archaeologist*
Saiz, Leonor *physicist, researcher*
Saline, Carol Sue *journalist*
Salzberg, Brian Matthew *neuroscience and physiology educator*
Samuel, Ralph David *lawyer*
Samway, Patrick H. *secondary education educator*
Sands, Roberta G. *social work educator*
Sanger, Joseph William *cell biologist*
Santomero, Anthony M. *bank executive, public policymaker*
Sanyour, Michael Louis, Jr., *diversified financial services company executive*
†Sartorius, Peter S. *lawyer*
Satinsky, Barnett *lawyer*
†Saul, April *photographer*
Saul, Ralph Southey *financial service executive*
Saunders, James C. *neuroscientist, educator*
Savage, Michael Paul *medicine educator, interventional cardiologist*
Savage, Timothy Joseph *judge*
Savitz, Samuel J. *actuarial consulting firm executive*
Savoie, James Anthony *university official*
†Sawallisch, Wolfgang *conductor*
Sayed, M. Gary *healthcare administrator, educator, scientist*
Saylor, Peter M. *architect*
Scaglione, Louis, III, *music educator, conductor*
Scandura, Joseph Michael *cognitive scientist, software engineer*
Scanlin, Thomas F. *pediatrician, researcher*
Scedrov, Andre *mathematics and computer science researcher, educator*
Schaff, Barbara Walley *artist*
Schaub, Harry Carl *lawyer*
†Schaubroeck, John Michael *education educator, academic administrator*
†Scheele, Dorothy R. *secondary school educator*
Scheib, Garry L. *hospital administrator*
Scher, Howard Dennis *lawyer*
Schidlow, Daniel *pediatrician, medical association administrator*
Schiffman, Harold Fosdick *Asian language educator*
Schimmer, Barry Michael *rheumatologist*
Schless, Guy Lacy *endocrinologist*
Schneider, Richard Graham *lawyer*
Schoener, George Francis, Jr., *lawyer*
Schorling, William Harrison *lawyer*
Schotland, Donald Lewis *retired medical educator, neurologist*
Schultz, Jane Schwartz *health research administrator*

Schumacher, H(arry) Ralph *internist, rheumatologist, medical educator, researcher*
Schuyler, Robert L. *anthropologist, archaeologist*
Schwan, Herman Paul *electrical engineering and physical science educator, research scientist*
Schwartz, Arthur *social worker*
Schwartz, Arthur Gerald *microbiology educator*
Schwartz, Gordon Francis *surgeon, educator*
Schwartz, Robert M. *lawyer*
Schweiker, Mark S. *former governor*
Scirica, Anthony Joseph *federal judge*
Scogno, Stacie Joy *financial services company executive*
Sebold, Russell Perry, III, *Romance languages educator, writer*
Segal, Bernard Louis *physician, educator*
Segal, Robert Martin *lawyer*
†Seider, Warren D. *engineering educator*
Selles, Robert Hendrikus *actuary, consultant*
†Seneca, Michael Joseph *historian*
†Sewell, Catherine Angela *obstetrician, gynecologist*
Shakespeare, Edward Oram, III, *retired secondary school educator*
Shapiro, Paula *retired maternal/women's health nurse*
Shapiro, Raymond L. *lawyer*
Shapiro, Sandor Solomon *hematologist*
Shatz, Stephen Sidney *mathematician, educator*
Sheils, Denis Francis *lawyer*
Sherman, Lawrence William *criminologist*
Shestack, Jerome Joseph *lawyer*
Shiekman, Laurence Zeid *lawyer*
Shils, Edward B. *management educator, lawyer, arbitrator and mediator*
Shoemaker, Innis Howe *art museum curator*
†Shore, Eric Eugene *internist, consultant, lawyer*
†Shuman, Robert Z. *architect*
Sibolski, Elizabeth Hawley *higher education administrator*
Siddiqui, Shahram Mohammad *lawyer*
Siderer, Jack Philip *engineering executive*
Siegel, Bernard Louis *lawyer*
Sigmond, Richard Brian *lawyer*
Silberberg, Donald H. *neurologist*
Silberman, Edward Kenneth *physician, educator*
Silvers, Willys Kent *geneticist*
Simkanich, John Joseph *lawyer, engineer*
Simpson, Carol Louise *investment company executive*
Slap, Joseph William *psychiatrist*
Slaughter-Defoe, Diana Tresa *education educator*
†Slipman, Curtis W. *rehabilitation medicine physician*
†Sloane, Richard *lawyer*
Sloviter, Dolores Korman *federal judge*
Smith, David Stuart *anesthesiology educator, physician*
†Smith, John Francis, III, *lawyer*
Smith, Lloyd *musician*
Smith, Woollcott *statistician, educator*
Snider, Edward Malcolm *professional hockey club executive*
Soffer, Martin Harvey *environmentalist, city planner*
Sohn, Catherine Angell *pharmaceutical executive, pharmacist*
Solano, Carl Anthony *lawyer*
Solmssen, Peter *academic administrator*
Solomon, Phyllis Linda *social work educator, researcher*
†Sonnenfeld, Marc Jay *lawyer*
†Sorokin, Sharon L. *lawyer*
Soslow, Arnold *quality consultant*
Souders, Beryl V. *medical/surgical and rehabilitation-detox nurse*
Sovie, Margaret Doe *nursing administrator, educator, clinician, researcher*
Sox, Harold Carleton, Jr., *physician, educator, editor*
Spaeth, Edmund Benjamin, Jr., *retired lawyer, retired law educator, former judge*
Spaeth, George Link *physician, ophthalmology educator, writer, educator*
Spandorfer, Merle Sue *artist, educator, author*
†Spector, Martin Wolf *lawyer, business executive*
Speyer, Debra Gail *lawyer*
Spolan, Harmon Samuel *lawyer*
Stalberg, Zachary *newspaper editor*
Stallman, Robert *concert flutist, recording artist, editor, arranger*
Staloff, Arnold Fred *financial executive*
Stambaugh, Robert F. *finance educator*
†Steinberg, Janet DeBerry *optometrist, educator, researcher*
†Steinberg, Jonathan *historian*
Steinberg, Marvin Edward *orthopaedic surgeon, educator*
Steinberg, Robert Philip *lawyer*
Steinhardt, Nancy Shatzman *art historian, educator*
Stern, Joan Naomi *lawyer*
Stevens, Mark Alan *lawyer, environmental engineer*
Stevens, Rosemary A. *medicine and public health historian*
Stevenson, Josiah, IV, *cultural arts administrator*
Stewart, Marvin Lewis *human resources professional*
Stewart, Robert Forrest, Jr., *lawyer*
Stinnett, James LeBaron *psychiatrist*
Strasbaugh, Wayne Ralph *lawyer*
Strauss, Jerome Frank, III, *physician, educator*
Strazzella, James Anthony *law educator, lawyer*
Strickler, Matthew M. *lawyer*
†Stroebel, John Stephen *lawyer*
Stunkard, Albert James *psychiatrist, educator*
Stuntebeck, Clinton A. *lawyer*
Subak, John Thomas *lawyer*
Sudak, Howard Stanley *physician, psychiatry educator*
†Sulyk, Stephen *retired archbishop*
Summers, Anita Arrow *public policy and management educator*
Summers, Clyde Wilson *law educator*
Summers, Robert *economics educator*

Sun, Hun H. *electrical engineering and biomedical engineering educator*
Swan, Ralph Edward *education educator*
Szewczyk, Samuel Hideyo *financial economist, educator*
†Szyld, Daniel Benjamin *mathematician, educator*
Takashima, Shiro *biophysics educator*
Talerman, Aleksander *pathologist, educator*
†Tasman, William Samuel *ophthalmologist, medical association executive*
Tate, Loretta Clara *health educator*
Taylor, Susan C. *dermatologist*
Tegenu, Mesfin *health services administrator, consultant*
Temin, Michael Lehman *lawyer*
Terry, John Joseph *transportation investor*
Terzian, Karnig Yervant *civil engineer*
Thoman, Charles James *chemistry educator*
Thomas, Lowell Shumway, Jr., *lawyer*
Thomson, Keith Stewart *biologist, author*
Tiger, Ira Paul *lawyer*
Tokar, Bette Lewis *economics educator*
Tom, Lawrence Wah-Chan *pediatric otolaryngologist*
Tomiyasu, Kiyo *consulting engineer*
Torg, Joseph Steven *orthopaedic surgeon, educator*
Toto, Mary *elementary and secondary education educator*
Tourtellotte, Charles Dee *physician, educator*
Tractenberg, Craig R. *lawyer*
Tran, John Kim-Son Tan *chemical senses executive, research administrator*
Truant, Allan L. *medical educator, research scientist, health science association administrator*
†Tuan, Kailin *management consultant, educator*
Tucker, Cynthia Delores Nottage (Mrs. William M. Tucker) *political party official, former state official*
†Tunkel, Allan Robert *infectious diseases physician, internist, educator*
Turner, Evan Hopkins *retired art museum director*
Tyler, Donald Charles *anesthesiologist*
Tyng, Anne Griswold *architect*
Unger, Michael *physician, researcher, educator*
†Vaccaro, Alexander R. *orthopedist*
Vaira, Peter Francis *lawyer*
Van Arsdalen, Keith Norman *urologist*
†Vanbiesbrouck, John *hockey player*
Van Decker, William Arthur *cardiologist*
Van der Spiegel, Jan *engineering educator*
Van De Walle, Etienne *demographer*
Van Dongen, Hans Philemon Anna *research scientist, educator*
Van Horn, Keith *professional basketball player*
Varlotta, Laurie *pediatrician, pediatric pulmonologist*
Veit, Kenneth *dean, educator*
Venturi, Robert *architect*
Vitek, Vaclav *materials scientist*
†Vitez, Michael *reporter*
†Voluck, Jeffrey M. *lawyer*
†Vredenburgh, Judy *youth organization executive*
Wachman, Marvin *former university president and chancellor*
Wadden, Thomas Anthony *psychologist, educator*
Wales, Walter D. *physicist, educator*
Walinsky, Paul *cardiology educator*
Walker, Allen Lyon *logistics analyst*
Walker, Manuel Lorenzo *physician*
Wallace, Anthony Francis Clarke *anthropologist, educator*
†Wallace, Emily Mitchell *writer, editor, educator*
Wallace, Rasheed *professional basketball player, marketing professional*
†Walsh, Peter Newton *physician, researcher*
Wang, Yen *nuclear medicine physician, radiologist*
Warner, Frank Wilson, III, *mathematics educator*
Warner, Theodore Kugler, Jr., *lawyer*
Warnick, Patricia Ann *healthcare consultant, nurse ethicist*
Watson, Bernard Charles *educator, foundation administrator*
Webber, John Bentley *orthopedic surgeon*
Webber, Ross Arkell *management educator*
Weidner, C. Ken, II, *management and business ethics educator, consultant*
Weigley, Russell Frank *history educator*
Weil, Jeffrey George *lawyer*
Wein, Alan Jerome *urologist, educator, researcher*
Weiner, Charles R. *federal judge*
Weiss, Mary Alice *insurance economics educator*
Welch, Patrick *health insurance company executive*
Weller, Elizabeth Boghossian *child and adolescent psychiatrist*
†Welsh, Donald S. *government agency administrator*
Wengert, Timothy *church history educator, clergyman*
Wert, Robert Clifton *lawyer*
Werth, Victoria Patricia *dermatologist, educator*
Whinston, Stephen Alan *lawyer*
Whitaker, Linton Andin *plastic surgeon*
Whiteside, William Anthony, Jr., *retired lawyer*
†Whitman, Jules Isidoré *lawyer*
Wickstrom, Eric *biophysical chemist, educator*
†Wiener, Ronald Martin *lawyer*
Wiglesworth, Michael Bland *advertising executive*
Wild, Richard P. *lawyer*
Wilde, Norman Taylor, Jr., *investment banking company executive*
Wilensky, Robert L. *cardiologist, educator*
Wiley, Catherine Anne *literature educator*
Wilkinson, Signe *cartoonist*
Willet, E(verett) Crosby *artist*
Williams, James Boughton *artist, art educator*
Williams, Sankey Vaughan *health services researcher, internist*
Winey, Karen I. *engineering educator, researcher*
Winfrey, Marion Lee *retired television critic*
Wing, Kennard Thompson *educational organization official*
Winkler, Gail Caskey *design historian, writer, educator*
Winkler, Sheldon *dentist, educator*
Wittels, Barnaby Caesar *lawyer, writer*
Wivel, Nelson Auburn *physician, medical researcher, educator*
Wolf, Gregory H. *insurance company executive*
Wolf, Robert B. *lawyer*
Wolfe, J. Matthew *lawyer*
Wolff, Deborah H(orowitz) *lawyer*
Wolitarsky, James William *securities industry executive*
†Woodside, Lisa Nicole *humanities educator*
Woosnam, Richard Edward *venture capitalist, lawyer*
†Wright, Barbara Clare *business librarian*
Wright, Minturn Tatum, III, *lawyer*
Wrobleski, Jeanne Pauline *lawyer*
†Wroblewski, Krzysztof *chemist, educator*
Xiao, Ying *medical physicist, researcher, educator*
Yanoff, Myron *ophthalmologist*
Yaros, Constance Greenberg *painter, sculptor*
†Yoh, Harold L., III, *company executive*
Yohn, William H(endricks), Jr., *federal judge*
Young, Andrew Brodbeck *lawyer*
Young, Donald Stirling *clinical pathology educator*
Young, Robert Crabill *medical researcher, science facility administrator, internist*
Yunginger, John W. *allergist*
Zaller, Robert Michael *history educator*
Zheng, Robert Zhiwei *educational technology educator*
Ziegler, Donald Robert *accountant*
Zietz, Stanley *mathematics educator*
Zimmer, Janie Louise *mathematics educator, administrator*
Zorowitz, Richard David *physiatrics educator*
Zucker, William *retired business educator*

Philipsburg
Genesi, Susan Petrovich *educator, consultant*
†Warg, Ilse-Rose *language educator*

Phoenixville
Brundage, Russell Archibald *retired data processing executive*
†Harkin, Ann Winifred *elementary school educator, psychotherapist*
Koenig, Michael Edward Davison *information science educator*
Lukacs, John Adalbert *historian, retired educator*
Rippel, Harry Conrad *mechanical engineer, consultant*

Pipersville
Erickson, Edward Leonard *biotechnology company executive, administrator*
McNutt, Richard Hunt *manufacturing company executive*
Sigety, Charles Edward *lawyer, family business consultant*

Pitcairn
Rose, Robert Didier *neurophysiologist*

Pittsburgh
Aaron, Marcus, II, *lawyer*
Adebimpe, Victor Rotimi *psychiatrist*
Aderson, Sanford M. *lawyer*
Adibi, Siamak A. *medical researcher*
Alexander, Andrew James *investment banker*
Allen, Thomas E. *obstetrician, gynecologist*
Alper, Cuneyt M. *pediatric otolaryngologist*
Andrews, George Reid *historian, educator*
Anthony, Edward Mason *linguistics educator*
Apone, Carl Anthony *journalist*
Arnett, Ronald Charles *communication educator*
Aronson, Mark Berne *retired attorney, consumer advocate*
Artz, Frederick James *diversified manufacturing company executive*
Artz, John Curtis *lawyer*
†Balach, Claudia Ann *director*
Balada, Leonardo *composer, educator*
Balas, Egon *applied mathematician, educator*
Baldauf, Kent Edward *lawyer*
Baldwin, Carla Suzann *psychologist*
†Bandix, George C. *dean, chemist, educator*
Barasch, Shirley Ruth *musician, educator*
Barazzone, Esther Lynn *academic administrator, educator*
Bardyguine, Patricia Wilde *ballerina, ballet theatre executive*
†Barrett, Karen Moore *lawyer*
Barry, Herbert, III, *psychologist, educator*
Bartley, Burnett Graham, Jr., *oil company and manufacturing executive*
Bashore, George Willis *retired bishop*
Basinski, Anthony Joseph *lawyer*
Bauccio, Lisa Valentine *obstetric nurse, high-risk perinatal nurse*
Becherer, Richard John *architecture educator*
Becker, George *labor union administrator*
Belda, Alain J. P. *metal products executive*
Bell, Lori Jo *crisis counselor, psychiatric nurse*
Bellinger, Mark Frederick *urology educator*
Bender, Charles Christian *retail home center executive*
Benson, Jeryl Disanti *occupational therapist*
Berenato, Agnus McGlade *women's basketball coach*
Bergmann, Carl Adolf *chemical engineer, researcher*
Bernt, Benno Anthony *business executive, entrepreneur and investor*
Berry, Guy Curtis *polymer science educator, researcher*
Bettis, Jerome Abram *professional football player*
†Bianco, Anthony *music educator*
Bickel, Minnette Duffy *artist*
Biondi, Manfred Anthony *physicist, educator*
Bleier, Carol Stein *writer, researcher*
Bleier, Michael E. *lawyer*
Blenko, Walter John, Jr., *lawyer*
Bloom, William Millard *furnace design engineer*
Blumstein, Alfred *urban and public affairs educator*
Bly, James Charles, Jr., *financial services executive*
Bobrow, Davis Bernard *public policy educator*
†Bocea, Marian *mathematician*
Bonessa, Dennis R. *lawyer*
Bonner, Shirley Harrold *business communications educator*
†Borovetz, Harvey Selwyn *biomedical engineer, educator*
Boswell, William Paret *lawyer*
Bothner-By, Aksel Arnold *chemist, horseman*
Bouldin, Chapman Whitfield, Jr., *educator, consultant*
Boyce, Doreen Elizabeth *lecturer, civic development foundation executive*
Braun, Thomas W. *academic administrator*
Brauner, Ronald Allan *religion educator*
Breault, Theodore E(dward) *lawyer*
Brennen, Carole J. *researcher in human services*
Brignano, Russell Carl *English educator, research specialist*
†Brockmann, Stephen Matthew *education educator*
Brown, David Ronald *lawyer*
Brown, Ronald James *lawyer, consultant*
Brustein, William Irving *sociology educator*
Buchanan, Gloria Jean *sales executive*
Buchanan, James Junkin *classics educator*
Burger, Herbert Francis *advertising agency executive*
Burgess, David Lowry *artist*
†Burgess, John Paul *minister, religion educator*
Burnham, Donald Clemens *manufacturing company executive*
†Busquets, Miguel Antonio *ophthalmologist*
Candris, Laura A. *lawyer*
Carbo, Toni (Toni Carbo Bearman) *information scientist, educator*
Cardenes, Andres Jorge *violinist, music educator*
Caritis, Steve Nick *obstetrician, gynecologist, educator*
Carney, Ann Vincent *retired secondary education educator*
Carr, Walter James, Jr., *research physicist, consultant*
Casasent, David Paul *electrical engineering educator, data processing executive*
†Cassaro, James P. *musicologist*
Cassidy, William Arthur *geology and planetary science educator*
Casturo, Don James *venture capitalist*
†Cendes, Zoltan Joseph *electrical engineer, educator*
Chaban, Lawrence Richard *lawyer*
Charap, Stanley Harvey *electrical engineering educator*
Charochak, Dale Michael *airport executive*
Chase, Norma *lawyer*
Cheever, George Martin *lawyer*
Cheever, Meg *non-profit organization administrator*
Chelemer, Harold *engineering educator, consultant*
Chengappa, Roy K. N. *psychiatrist, educator*
Chipman, Debra Decker *paralegal*
Chiu, Chao-Lin *civil engineer*
Choyke, Wolfgang Justus *physicist*
Chrysanthis, Panos Kypros *computer science educator, researcher*
†Chute, Alan Dale *lawyer*
Cicero, J. Deborah *management consultant*
Clack, Jerry *classics educator*
†Classon, Rolf Allan *pharmaceutical company executive*
†Claussen, Dane Sherman *newspaper consultant, journalism educator*
Cohen, Bernard Leonard *physicist, educator*
Cohen, Henry C. *lawyer*
Cohen, Jacqueline *university researcher, sociology educator*
Cohen, Robert (Robert Avram Cohen) *lawyer*
Cohill, Maurice Blanchard, Jr., *federal judge*
Cohon, Jared L. *academic administrator*
Colen, Frederick Haas *lawyer*
Collins, Rose Ann *minister*
Coltman, John Wesley *physicist*
†Colville, Robert E. *judge*
Coney, Aims C., Jr., *lawyer, labor-management negotiator*
Conlon, Raymond Joseph *lawyer*
Connors, Eugene Kenneth *lawyer, educator*
†Constantine, Kevin *professional hockey coach*
Constantino-Bana, Rose Eva *nursing educator, researcher, lawyer*
Conti, Joy Flowers *judge*
Conti, Ronald Samuel *electronics engineer, fire prevention engineer*
Contractor, Farhad M. *diagnostic radiologist, educator*
Cooper, Thomas Louis *lawyer*
Cooper, William Marion *physician*
Corbett, Thomas Wingett, Jr., *lawyer*
†Corcoran, Thomas A. *metals and mining company executive*
Cornuejols, Gerard Pierre *operations research educator*
Cosetti, Joseph Louis *federal judge*
Costel, Daniel Eugene *financial analyst*
Courtsal, Donald Preston *manufacturing company executive, financial consultant*
Cowan, Barton Zalman *lawyer*
Cowher, Bill *professional football coach*
†Craig, Fiona Elizabeth *pathologist*
Crawford, Robin Yvette *county caseworker*
†Crayne, Larry Randolph *lawyer*
Cruz, Robyn Flaum *research scientist, clinician*
Cullen, Wanda Jane *writer, financial consultant*
Curran, Dennis Patrick *chemist, educator*
Curry, Nancy Ellen *educator, psychoanalyst, psychologist*
Cutler, John Charles *physician, educator*
Dameshek, H(arold) Lee *physician*
Daniel, Robert Michael *lawyer*
Daniels, James R. *poet, English language educator*
Dannenberg, Roger Berry *computer scientist*
Davenport, Ronald Ross, Jr., *lawyer*
†Davidson, George A., Jr., *retired utility company executive*
†Davis, Diane J. *director, educator*
Davis, Lewis U., Jr., *lawyer*
Davis, Otto Anderson *economics educator*
Dawes, Robyn Mason *psychology educator*
Dawson, Mary Ruth *curator, educator*
Deerfield, David Wiley, II, *chemist*
DeForest, Walter Pattison, III, *lawyer*
deGroat, William Chesney *pharmacology educator*
Dekay, Michael L. *decision science educator*
DeKosky, Steven Trent *neurologist*
Demmler, John Henry *retired lawyer*
Dempsey, Jacqueline Lee *special education director*
Dempsey, Jerry Edward *retired service company executive*
†Desai, Niranjan A. *chemical engineer*
Detre, Thomas *psychiatrist, educator*
DeWalt, Bill *museum director*
Diamond, Gustave *federal judge*
†Dick, David E. *construction company executive*
Dieter, Richard Charles *marketing and management professional*
Di Medio, Gregory Lawrence *writer, information systems specialist*
Dinman, Bertram David *retired metal products executive, health educator*
Dixit, Balwant Narayan *pharmacology and toxicology educator*
Doft, Bernard Harvey *ophthalmologist*
Donahoe, David Lawrence *state and city official*
Donahue, John Francis *investment company executive*
Donnelly, Thomas Joseph *lawyer, director*
Doreian, Patrick *sociologist, educator*
Doria, Cataldo *transplant surgeon*
Dormish, Jeffrey Frank *chemist*
Doty, Robert Walter *lawyer*
Dougherty, Charles John *university administrator, philosophy and medical ethics educator*
Drabiska, Frank John *priest, parochial school educator*
Drennan, Robert D. *archeology educator, researcher*
Drescher, Seymour *history educator, writer*
Druzdzel, Marek Jozef *researcher and educator*
Dubaniewicz, Thomas H., Jr., *electrical engineer, bioengineer*
Duncan, George Thomas *statistician, educator*
Dybeck, Alfred Charles *labor arbitrator*
Eaton, Joseph W. *sociology educator*
Eckert, Jean Patricia *elementary education educator*
Edelman, Harry Rollings, III, *engineering and construction company executive*
Edmonds, Mary Patricia *biological sciences educator*
Ehrenwerth, David Harry *lawyer*
Ehrlich, Garth David *molecular biologist*
Einhorn, Jerzy *internist, endocrinologist, consultant*
Emmerich, Werner Sigmund *physicist, educator*
Evans, Bruce Dwight *lawyer*
†Fabrega, Horacio, Jr., *psychiatry and anthropology educator*
†Faigen, Anne Gussin *secondary school educator, writer*
Fararo, Thomas John *sociologist, educator*
†Feindel, Janet Madelle *performing arts educator*
Feingold, David Sidney *microbiology educator*
†Feldstein, Jay Harris *lawyer*
Feller, Robert Livingston *chemist, art conservation scientist*
Fetkovich, John G. *physics educator*
Fienberg, Stephen Elliott *statistician*
Finegold, David Neal *medical educator*
†Fink, Bruce *psychoanalyst, educator*
Fireman, Philip *pediatrician, allergist, immunologist, medical association executive*
Fischhoff, Baruch *psychologist, educator*
Fisher, Bernard *surgeon, educator*
Fisher, Edwin R. *pathologist*
Fisher, Henry *investment banker*
Fisher, James Aiken *industrial marketing consultant*
Fitzgerald, Judith Klaswick *federal judge*
Flaherty, John Paul, Jr., *judge*
†Flanagan, Joanna Scarlata *lawyer*
Flatley, Lawrence Edward *lawyer*
Fletcher, Ronald Darling *microbiologist educator*
Flinn, Michael James *lawyer*
Fontes, Paulo A. *surgeon, educator*
†Ford, Amanda Melody *director*
Fort, James Tomlinson *lawyer*
Foucart Vincenti, Valerie *retired art educator*
Frank, Alan I W *manufacturing company executive*
Frank, Ellen *medical educator, psychiatrist, psychologist, researcher*
†Frank, Frederick Newman *lawyer*
Frank, Ronald William *lawyer, financier*
Franklin, Kenneth Ronald *franchise company executive, consultant*
Frezza, Ermenegildo Eldo *physician, surgeon*
Friday, Gilbert Anthony, Jr., *pediatrician*
Friede, Samuel A(rnold) *health care executive*
†Froehlich, Fritz Edgar *communications educator, telecommunications scientist*
Gale, Robert Lee *retired American literature educator and critic*
†Galey, R. Kent *oral surgeon*
†Galletta, Dennis F. *business administration educator, consultant*
Gal-Or, Esther *educator*
Gaynor, Martin Scott *economist*
Geeseman, Robert George *lawyer*
Genge, William Harrison *advertising executive, writer*

George, John Anthony *health corporation executive*
†Gerard, Leo W. *trade association administrator*
Gerjuoy, Edward *physicist, lawyer*
Germanowski, Janet *women's health and medical surgical nurse, educator, researcher*
†Giannoukakis, Nick *educator*
Giles, Brian Stephen *baseball player*
Giliberti, Michael Richard *financial planner*
Gindroz, Raymond L. *architect*
Ginsburg, Mark Barry *comparative sociology of education educator*
Goertzen, Irma *hospital executive*
Gold, Harold Arthur *lawyer*
Goldberg, Mark Joel *lawyer*
Goldschmidt, Yadin Y *science educator*
Goldstein, Bernard David *physician, educator*
Goldstein, David Meyer *physician*
Goldstein, Donald Maurice *historian, educator*
Goldstein, Gerald *research scientist*
Gordon, Murray Bruce *endocrinologist*
Graham, Laurie *editor, writer*
Griffin, Donald Spray *mechanical engineer, consultant*
Grossmann, Ignacio Emilio *chemical engineering educator*
Grubbs, Arlene Busse *social worker, consultant*
†Grunbaum, Adolf *philosophy educator, author*
Guinn, Kathleen Anne *human resources specialist*
†Gulley, Joan Long *banker*
Gurtin, Morton Edward *mathematics educator*
†Haley, Roy W. *finance company executive*
Hammond, Paul Young *political scientist, educator*
Haney, Edward Francis *social studies educator, educator*
Hansen, Stephen Christian *banker*
Hardesty, Lara Ann *radiology educator*
Hardie, James Hiller *lawyer*
Harper, Douglas Albert *sociologist, researcher*
Harrell, Edward Harding *newspaper executive*
Harris, Ann Birgitta Sutherland *art historian*
†Harrison, Eric Jay *construction executive, consultant*
Harrold, Ronald Thomas *research scientist*
Harth, Sidney *musician, educator*
Hartman, Ronald G. *lawyer*
†Harty, James Quinn *lawyer*
†Haunschild, Robert L. *bank executive*
Heaton, Charles Huddleston *retired church musician*
Heckler, Frederick Roger *plastic surgeon*
Heilman, Marlin Stephen *medical products executive*
Heindl, Mary Lynn *magazine editor*
Heinecke, Deborah Ann *pediatrics nurse*
Heitzenroder, David August *financial services professional, investment advisor, investment banker*
Hellman, Arthur David *law educator, consultant*
Helmrich, Joel Marc *lawyer*
Hendrickson, Chris Thompson *civil and environmental engineering educator, researcher*
†Herchenroether, Peter Young *lawyer*
Herleman, Laura Ann *nursing administrator*
Hershey, Dale *lawyer, educator*
Hershey, Nathan *lawyer, educator*
Hess, Emerson Garfield *lawyer*
Hicks, Wendell Leon *history educator, publisher, political scientist*
Hill, John Howard *lawyer*
Hillman, Henry L. *investment company executive*
†Himmelhoch, Jonathan M. *psychiatrist, educator*
†Hitt, Leo N. *lawyer, educator*
Hoburg, James Frederick *electrical engineering educator*
Hodge, Patricia Andrea *archivist, consultant*
Hodges, Margaret Moore *author, educator*
Holder, Gerald D., Jr., *dean*
Hollingsworth, Samuel Hawkins, Jr., *bassist*
Hollinshead, Earl Darnell, Jr., *lawyer*
Holzner, Burkart *sociologist, educator*
Hornak, Mark Raymond *lawyer*
Horowitz, Carole Spiegel *landscape contractor*
Horowitz, Don Roy *landscape company executive*
†Houck, Patricia Rose *statistician, researcher*
Hudachek, Susan Marie *contracts specialist; consultant*
Hull, John Daniel, IV, *lawyer*
Humphrey, Watts Sherman *technical executive, author*
Huntington, James Cantine, Jr., *equipment manufacturing company executive*
Hurnyak, Christina Kaiser *lawyer*
Hyman, Lewis Neil *investment company executive, investment advisor*
Ijiri, Yuji *accounting and economics educator*
†Inman, John Jeffrey *finance educator*
Irvine, Peter Bennington *clergyman*
Isabella, Mary Margaret *lawyer*
Ismail, Yahia Hassan *dentist, educator*
Itkin, Ivan *nuclear scientist, applied mathematician*
Jakub, Kathleen Ann *medical/surgical nurse*
Jannetta, Peter Joseph *neurosurgeon, educator*
Janosko, Rudolph E. M. *psychiatrist*
†Jansons, Mariss *orchestra conductor*
Jefferson, Joseph Murray *banker*
Jen-Jacobson, Linda *biochemist, educator*
Johnson, Barbara Elizabeth *lawyer*
Johnson, Jonas Talmadge *otolaryngologist, educator*
Johnson, Robert Alan *lawyer*
Johnson, William R. *food products company executive*
Jones, Craig Ward *lawyer*
Jordan, Angel Goni *electrical and computer engineering educator*
Josey, E(lonnie) J(Unius) *librarian, educator, former state administrator*
†Joshi, James Bikram Dhoj *information scientist, educator*
Joyner, Claude Reuben, Jr., *physician, medical educator*
Kadane, Joseph B. *statistics educator*
†Kadow, Clemens Martin Joachim *engineer, researcher*
Kalnicki, Shalom *radiologist, educator*
Kamboh, M. Ilyas *geneticist*
Kamienska-Carter, Eva Hanna *designer, artist*
†Kamlet, Mark *provost*
Karol, Meryl Helene *medical educator, researcher*
Kearns, John J., III, *lawyer*
Keefe, William Joseph *political science educator*
†Keeling, Sr., Kenneth Augustus *music educator, headmaster*
†Kemerer, Chris F. *information scientist, educator*
Kenkel, James Lawrence *economics educator*
Kenrick, Charles William *lawyer*
Ketchum, David Storey *retired fundraising executive*
Ketter, David Lee *lawyer*
Khurana, Ramesh Chander *physician, nutritionist, educator*
Kiesling, Scott Fabius *linguist, educator*
Kiger, Robert William *botanist, science historian, educator*
Kimm, Sue Young Sook *academic medical researcher*
King, Elaine A. *curator, art historian, critic*
†King, Paul Martin *lawyer*
†King, William Richard *business educator, consultant*
†Kingsbury, Lisa R. *instructional design consultant*
Kitzes, Arnold S. *retired chemical engineer, retired nuclear engineer*
†Klein-Seetharaman, Judith *biochemist*
Klett, Edwin L. *lawyer*
Kochanek, Patrick Michael *pediatrician, educator*
Koedel, Robert Craig *minister, historian, educator*
Kolmen, Samuel Norman *retired consultant*
Kondziolka, Douglas *neurosurgeon*
Korytkowksi, Mary T. *physician*
Krause, Helen Fox *physician, otolaryngologist*
Krebs, Robert Alan *lawyer*
Kriebel, Charles Hosey *management sciences educator*
Kryder, Mark Howard *computer and electrical engineering executive, educator, consultant*
Ku, Andrew *interventional neuroradiologist*
†Kuddus, Ruhul Haque *medical educator*
Kumar, Vijaya Bhagavatula *electrical engineering educator, consultant*
†Kum-Nji, Philip *pediatrician, educator*
Kumta, Prashant Nagesh *materials science educator, engineering educator, consultant*
Kupfer, David J. *psychiatry educator*
Lahey, Regis Henry *bank executive*
LaJohn, Lawrence Anthony *research scientist*
Lally-Green, Maureen Ellen *superior court judge, law educator*
†Lashay, Jill Maria *lawyer*
†Lasorda, David Michael *cardiologist*
Laughlin, David Eugene *materials science educator, metallurgical consultant*
Laughlin, Patricia *university dean*
Lauterbach, Robert Emil *steel company executive*
Lave, Judith Rice *economics educator*
LeBoeuf, Raymond Walter *manufacturing company executive*
Lee, Donald John *federal judge*
Lega, Mark *internist, pulmonologist*
Lehoczky, John Paul *statistics educator*
Lemieux, Mario *professional sports team executive, professional hockey player*
Leney, George Willard *retired consulting engineer*
Leo, Peter Andrew *newspaper columnist, writing educator*
Lerach, Richard Fleming *lawyer*
Letwin, Jeffrey William *lawyer*
Levine, Arthur Samuel *dean, physician, scientist*
Levine, David Lawrence *software engineer*
Levine, Macy Irving *physician*
Lewis, Jessica Helen (Mrs. Jack D. Myers) *physician, educator*
Lewis, Richard Allan *financial planner, business consultant*
Li, Ching-Chung *electrical engineering and computer science educator*
Li, Hanna Wu *music educator*
†Linke, Erika C. *school librarian*
Litman, Roslyn Margolis *lawyer, educator*
†Livi, Ivan David *retired educational administrator*
Lloyd, Robert Albert *retired foundation administrator*
†Loftness, Vivian Ellen *architecture educator, department chairman*
Logsdon, Marge A. *education educator*
†Lopes, Jerry *broadcast executive*
Lorensen, Frederick Hamilton *educational administrator, consultant*
†Lotze, Michael T. *immunologist*
†Lovett, Robert G. *lawyer*
Lowery, Willa Dean *obstetrician, gynecologist*
Lu, Songwei *materials scientist*
†Lucchino, Frank Joseph *lawyer, county official*
Ludwig, Karl David *psychiatrist*
Lyberatos, Andreas *physicist, researcher*
Lyjak Chorazy, Anna Julia *pediatrician, medical administrator, educator*
Lynch, Victor K. *lawyer*
†Lyncheski, John E. *lawyer*
MacBeth, Lynn Ellen *lawyer*
MacLeod, Gordon Kenneth *physician, educator*
†Magovern, James Anthony *thoracic surgeon*
Maguire, Lambert *social worker, educator*
Mahood, James Edward *lawyer*
†Maiolini, Gloria J. *nurse case manager, poet, writer*
Mann, Alfred N. *chemical engineer*
Marazita, Mary Louise *genetics researcher*
Markle, William Howard *family physician, educator*
Marra, Kacey G. *research scientist, educator*
Marshall, Meriam Doris *federal agency administrator*
†Marsico, Leonard Joseph *lawyer*
Martich, Dawna *nurse*
†Martin, Sean Elliot *literature educator, writer*
Maśka, Rudolf *retired chemist, finance executive*
Massalski, Thaddeus Bronislaw *materials scientist, educator*
Mathay, William Lewis *metal products executive*
Mathis, Terance *professional football player*
Matyjaszewski, Krzysztof *chemist, educator*
Matzke, Gary Roger *pharmacist, educator*
Maximos, Metropolitan (Maximos Demetrios Aghiorgoussis) *bishop, metropolitan*
Mazariegos, George Vincent *pediatric transplant surgeon*
McAvoy, Bruce Ronald *engineer, consultant*
†McCallum, Bennett Tarlton *economist, educator*
McCartney, Robert Charles *retired lawyer*
McClatchy, Kevin S. *professional sports team executive*
McClelland, James Lloyd *psychology educator, cognitive neuroscientist*
McCoid, Donald James *bishop*
McCullough, M. Bruce *judge*
Mc Dowell, John B. *bishop*
McDuffie, Keith A. *literature educator*
McGinley, John Regis, Jr., *lawyer*
McGough, Walter Thomas, Jr., *lawyer*
McGrath, Edward Leo *banker*
McHoes, Ann McIver *academic administrator, computer systems consultant*
McLaughlin, John Sherman *lawyer*
Mead, Nancy Rose *software engineer*
Means, Dwight Bardeen, Jr., *financial consultant, educator*
Mehta, Harshad R. *cardiologist*
Meiksin, Zvi H. *electrical engineering educator*
Meisel, Alan *law educator*
†Melnick, Michael S. *dentist, educator*
Meltzer, Allan H. *economist, educator*
†Merenstein, Joel Harvey *physician, researcher*
Meyers, Jerry Ivan *lawyer*
†Michalopoulos, George Konstantine *academic administrator*
Mickle, Marlin Homer *electrical engineer, educator*
Miller, Charles Jay *dentist*
Miller, David William *historian, educator*
Miller, David A. *lawyer*
Milnes, Arthur George *electrical engineer, educator*
Milsom, Robert Cortlandt *banker*
Mina, John Louis (Ivan Minea) *religious studies educator, archivist*
Minnigh, Joel Douglas *library director*
Missiriotis, Irene *geriatric services professional, artist*
Mitchell, Ann Margaret *nursing educator, psychiatric nurse practitioner*
Mitchell, George Charles *diplomat, international consultant, mediator, educator, writer*
Mitre, Blima Kirmayer *pathologist, educator*
†Moalli, Pamela Ann *surgeon, researcher, obstetrician, gynecologist*
†Moiseev, Igor Valentinovich *information scientist*
Mokotoff, Michael *pharmaceutical sciences educator*
Moore, Pearl B. *nursing educator*
Moore, Robert Yates *neuroscience educator*
Morrison, L. Warren *computer engineer*
†Morrow, Lisa A. *neuropsychologist, researcher*
Morse, Lewis David *microencapsulation polymer chemist, consultant*
Moura, José Manuel Fonseca *electrical engineer, educator*
Muder, Robert Richard *physician, epidemiologist*
Mulloney, Peter Black *retired steel, oil and gas executive*
†Mulsant, Benoit Henri *psychiatry educator, medical researcher*
Mulvihill, Keithley D. *lawyer*
Murdoch, David Armot *lawyer*
Murphy, Robert Francis *biology educator and researcher*
Murphy, Thomas J., Jr., *mayor*
Muto, Susan Annette *religion educator, academic administrator*
Myers, Eugene Nicholas *otolaryngologist, otolaryngology educator*
Myers, William Richard *minister, educator*
Nagle, John Frederick *physicist*
†Nanda, Ajaya Kumar *chemist, educator*
†Nasri, William Zaki *legal educator, copyright consultant*
Nastac, Laurentiu *materials and metallurgy engineer*
Nath, Raghu *management consultant, educator*
Neel, John Dodd *cemetery executive*
Neft, Suzi Terry *television producer, marketing, public relations executive, advertising executive*
Neuman, Charles P. *electrical and computer engineering educator*
Newcomer, Janet Ann *family physician*
†Noll, Walter *mathematics educator*
Nordenberg, Mark Alan *law educator, academic administrator*
Norris, James Harold *lawyer*
Novick, Ivan Jay *real estate executive*
Ober, Russell John, Jr., *lawyer*
O'Connor, Edward Gearing *lawyer*
O'Donnell, William James *engineering executive*
Ogul, Morris Samuel *political science educator, consultant*
Olson, Josephine Eva *economics educator*
Olson, Stephen M(ichael) *lawyer*
Omiros, George James *medical foundation executive*
O'Neill, Paul Henry *former government official*
†O'Reilly, Anthony John Francis *food company executive*
†Orr, Terrence S. *dancer, ballet master, artistic director*
Orsatti, Ernest Benjamin *lawyer*
Packard, Rochelle Sybil *elementary school educator*
Page, Lorne Albert *physicist, educator*
†Paradise, Jack Leon *pediatrician, educator*
†Parker, James Lee *lawyer*
Partanen, Carl Richard *biology educator*
†Paterson, David Leslie *epidemiologist*
Paul, Robert Arthur *steel company executive*
Paulston, Christina Bratt *linguistics educator*
Pautler, Stanislav *retired anesthesiologist*
Pease, Robert Barnard *civil engineer*
Peele, Pamela Bonifay *economics educator*
Peitzman, Andrew Bertram *surgeon*
†Pennell, Daniel Mark *researcher*
†Perkins, Kenneth Alan *physical education educator*
Perlman, Mark *economist, educator*
Perloff, Robert *psychologist, educator*
†Perry, John F. *lawyer*
Perry, Jon Robert *lawyer*
Petersen, Jean Snyder *association executive*
Peterson, Robert Scott *electrical engineer*
Petesch, Natalie L. Maines *English language educator, author*
Pettit, Frederick Sidney *metallurgical engineering educator, researcher*
Pfaff, Robert James *lawyer*
Phillips, Larry Edward *lawyer*
Planinsic, Raymond M. *anesthesiologist, educator*
Plazek, Donald John *materials science educator*
Plowman, Jack Wesley *lawyer*
Pohland, Frederick George *environmental engineering educator, researcher*
Pollack, David L. *lawyer*
Pollock, Bruce Godfrey *psychiatrist, educator*
Post, James Christopher *pediatric otolaryngologist, molecular geneticist*
†Post, Peter David *lawyer*
Posvar, Mildred Miller *opera singer*
Powderly, William H., III, *lawyer*
†Praytor, Kent Dwayne *career planning administrator*
Price, Fredric Victor *physician, educator, medical researcher*
Prosperi, Louis Anthony *lawyer*
†Purse, William Edward *music educator, writer*
Quimpo, Rafael Gonzales *civil engineering educator*
†Rabin, Yoed *biomedical engineer, consultant*
Rago, Ann D'Amico *university official, public relations professional*
Ramalingam, Sakkaraiappan *oncologist*
Randolph, Robert DeWitt *lawyer*
Rathke, Sheila Wells *strategic and marketing consultant*
Rault, Raymond Marcel *nephrologist*
Rawski, Evelyn Sakakida *history educator*
Reed, W. Franklin *lawyer*
†Reed, William Ferguson *corporate financial executive*
Reichblum, Audrey Rosenthal *public relations executive, publishing executive*
†Renne, Paul F. *food products executive*
Rescher, Nicholas *philosopher, educator*
Restivo, James John, Jr., *lawyer*
Reznik, Alan A. *petroleum engineering educator*
†Rial, Martha *photographer*
†Richard, Jean-Francois *education educator, consultant*
Richards, Aleta Williams *marketing and quality professional*
†Richards, Robert Byam *lawyer*
Rimer, John Thomas *foreign language educator, academic administrator, writer, translator*
Ritchey, Patrick William *lawyer*
Roche, Karen Ruth *plastic surgeon*
Rohr, James Edward *banker*
Romoff, Jeffrey Alan *health care executive*
Rooney, Daniel M. *professional football team executive*
Rosen, Richard David *lawyer*
Rosen, Robert Stephen *humanities, theatre arts, TV and English educator*
Rosenberg, Jerome Laib *chemist, educator*
Rosenberger, Bryan David *lawyer*
Ross, Eunice Latshaw *judge*
Ross, Madelyn Ann *newspaper editor*
Roth, Loren H. *psychiatrist*
Rubin, Deborah Jean *social worker*
Rubin, Robert Terry *physician, researcher, educator*
†Ruddy, Francis (Frank) Henry *nuclear physicist*
Rudzki, Robert A. *chemicals and life sciences company executive*
Ruskin, Ryan Scott *packaging company executive*
Russell, Alan James *chemical engineering and biotechnology educator*
Saito, Reisuke *pathologist, researcher*
Sanfilippo, Joseph Salvatore *physician, reproductive endocrinologist, educator*
Sarraf, Roberta Jean *planning consultant*
Sashin, Donald *pet physicist, radiological physicist, educator*
†Saunders, Martin Johnston *lawyer*
Saykiewicz-Sajkiewicz, Jan Napoleon *marketing educator*
Schäffer, Juan Jorge *mathematics educator*
Schaub, Gary John, Jr., *political scientist*
Schaub, Marilyn McNamara *religion educator*
Scheinholtz, Leonard Louis *lawyer*
Schleyer, Titus Karl Ludwig *dental educator*
Schorr-Ribera, Hilda Keren *psychologist*
Schultheiss, Emily Ekonen *management consultant, writer*
Schultz, Jerome Samson *biochemical engineer, educator*
†Schultz, Stephen Mason *musician, educator*
Schwalb, Harry *artist*
Schwendeman, Paul William *lawyer*
†Seehausen, Jobst Wilfried *energy company executive*
Segal, Frederick Leslie *lawyer*
Sekerka, Robert Floyd *physics educator, scientist*
Seligson, Mitchell A. *Latin American studies educator*
Sell, William Edward *law educator*
Sensenich, Ila Jeanne *judge*

Serene, Harry E. *surgeon*
Sessoms, Sandra Lea *hospital administrator*
†Seymour, Donald Edward *lawyer*
Shadel, William Gustav *psychologist, educator*
Shaffer, Terry George *pastor*
†Shane, Peter Milo *law educator*
Shapiro, Zalman Mordecai *chemist, consultant*
Shaw, Mary M. *computer science educator*
Sheon, Aaron *art historian, educator*
Sherry, John Sebastian *lawyer*
†Shribman, David Marks *editor*
Shu, Peter H.C. *research scientist*
Shuman, Joseph Duff *lawyer*
Shusterman, Vladimir *medical researcher*
Siker, Ephraim S. *anesthesiologist*
Silverman, Arnold Barry *lawyer*
Simaan, Marwan *electrical engineering educator*
Simmermon, James Everett *credit bureau executive*
Simmons, Richard L. *surgeon*
†Simmons, Richard P. *retired steel company executive*
Simms, Michael Arlin *poet, publishing executive*
Simonds, John Ormsbee *landscape architect*
Simpson, Daniel H. *ambassador*
†Singer, Paul Meyer *lawyer*
Skwaryk, Robert Francis *judge*
Sladack, David Robert *advertising executive*
†Slusser, Michael *theology studies educator, department chairman, priest*
Smartschan, Glenn Fred *school system administrator*
Smith, Dennis Bruce *software engineer*
†Smith, James Ignatius, III, *bar association executive*
Smrekar, Karl George, Jr., *financial planner*
†Sobehart, Helen C *academic administrator, educator*
Sokol, Stephen M. *lawyer*
Sokoloff, Terri Ann *real estate broker*
Spalding, Rita Lee *artist*
†Specter, Howard Alan *lawyer*
†Spellman, Susan V. *historian*
Sperling, Mark A. *physician, scientist*
Spohn, Janice *elementary education educator, consultant*
†Springer, Eric Winston *lawyer, director*
Stahl, Laddie L. *electrical engineer, manufacturing company executive*
†Stahlfeld, Kurt R *surgeon*
Standish, William Lloyd *judge*
Stanger, Robert Henry *psychiatrist, educator*
Starzl, Thomas Earl *physician, educator*
Steele, Cheryl A. *oncology nurse*
Stevens, William Talbert *financial services executive*
Stirewalt, John Newman *coal company executive*
Strader, James David *lawyer*
Straka, Martin *hockey player*
Strauss, Robert Philip *economics educator*
Strick, Sadie Elaine *psychologist*
Stroyd, Arthur Heister *lawyer*
Sullivan, Loretta Roseann *elementary education educator*
Sussna, Edward *economist, educator*
Sutton, William Dwight *lawyer*
Suzuki, Jon Byron *medical educator, periodontist, microbiologist*
Sweeney, Clayton Anthony *lawyer, business executive*
Swerdlow, Steven Howard *hematopathologist*
Symons, Edward Leonard, Jr., *investment adviser*
Tancin, Charlotte Ann *librarian*
Tarasi, Louis Michael, Jr., *lawyer*
Tarr, Joel Arthur *history and public policy educator*
†Taylor, Mark Chandlee *choreographer*
Thomas, W(illiam) Bruce *retired steel, oil, gas company executive*
Thompson, Thomas Martin *lawyer*
Thorne, John Reinecke *business educator, venture capitalist*
Thurman, Andrew Edward *lawyer*
Tierney, John William *chemical engineering educator*
Tobin, Robert Edwin *regional director*
Tobon, Hector *gynecologic pathologist, educator*
Toeplitz, Gideon *symphony society executive*
Toker, Franklin K. *art history educator, archaeologist, foundation executive*
Tracht, Allen Eric *electronics executive*
Trapani-Hanasewych, Marybeth Ann *speech language pathologist*
†Traugh, Daniel Howard *music educator*
Troen, Philip *physician, educator*
†Tropeck, Kevin D. *information technology manager, writer*
†Trumble, Dennis Robert *biomedical engineer*
Tully, Bernard Michael *lawyer*
†Tungate, David E. *lawyer, educator*
Turner, Harry Woodruff *lawyer*
†Ubinger, John W., Jr., *lawyer*
Udler, Rubin Yakovlevitch *linguist*
Ulrich, Lucinda Dykes *librarian*
Ulven, Mark Edward *lawyer*
†Ummer, James Walter *lawyer*
Urbach, Andrew Harley *pediatrician*
†Usher, Thomas James *steel executive, energy executive*
Vagley, Richard Thomas *plastic surgeon*
Van Dusen, Albert Clarence *university official*
Van Kirk, Thomas L. *lawyer*
Vater, Charles J. *lawyer*
Veeder, Peter Greig *lawyer*
Vogel, Victor Gerald *medical educator, researcher*
von Waldow, Arnd N. *lawyer*
Wagner, Florence Zeleznik *telecommunications executive*
Wald, Arnold *gastroenterologist*
Wald, Niel *public health educator*
Walton, James Mellon *investment company executive*
†Wang, Huamin *research scientist*
Ward, Thomas Jerome *lawyer*
†Watters, Edmond Clair *ophthalmologist, educator*
Webb, Geneá Lynetta *journalist*
Weidman, John Carl, II, *education educator, consultant*
†Weil, Andrew L. *lawyer*
Weingartner, Rudolph Herbert *philosophy educator*
Weis, Joseph Francis, Jr., *federal judge*
Welch, William Charles *neurosurgeon*
†Wenger, Sharon Louise *pediatrics educator, researcher, cytogeneticist*
Wesner, John William *engineering educator*
Westerberg, Arthur William *chemical engineering educator*
White, Robert Marshall *physicist, government official, educator*
Wilberger, James E. *neurosurgeon*
Wilde, Patricia *retired artistic director*
†Wiley, S. Donald *lawyer, food products executive*
Wilkins, Ann Thomas *classics educator*
Wilkins, David George *fine arts educator*
Wilkinson, James Allan *lawyer, healthcare executive*
Willard, Louis Charles *librarian*
Williams, Lisle Edward *civil, planning and structural engineer*
Wilson, George David *school administrator*
Wilson, Wanda Lee Davis *entertainment promotions professional, casting director*
†Wiltse, James Burdick *lawyer*
Winnie, Glenna Barbara *pediatric pulmonologist*
†Winter, Nelson Warren *lawyer*
Winter, Peter Michael *anesthesiologist, educator*
Wohleber, Lynne Farr *archivist, librarian*
†Woo, Savio Lau-Yuen *bioengineering educator*
Yang, Wen-Ching *chemical engineer*
†Yaskolko, Sergey *application developer*
Yates, John Thomas, Jr., *chemistry educator, research director*
Yoldas, Bulent Erturk *materials scientist, educator*
Yorsz, Stanley *lawyer*
Young, Eveline *social worker*
Young, Hugh David *physics educator, writer, organist*
Youngner, Julius Stuart *microbiologist, educator*
Yourison, Karola Maria *librarian services professional*
Yushmanov, Victor Evgenievich *biophysicist, researcher*
Zamboni, Beth Ann *statistician, educator*
Zanardelli, John Joseph *healthcare services executive*
Zangrilli, Albert Joseph, Jr., *lawyer*
Zdilla, Robyn Lynn *occupational therapist*
Zehel, Wendell Evans *surgeon*
†Zeolla, Kim Anne *minister*
Zhang, Yingze *molecular biologist*
Ziegler, Arthur P., Jr., *foundation executive*
Ziegler, Donald Emil *federal judge*
Zimmerman, Richard Kent *family physician, preventive medicine specialist*
†Zitelli, Basil J. *pediatrician, educator*
Zittrain, Lester Eugene *lawyer*

Pittston
Komensky, Paul Louis *music educator*

Plymouth
†Castner, Deborah A. *librarian*
Musto, Joseph John *lawyer*

Plymouth Meeting
Cooper, Jeffrey Todd *music educator*
Kranzdorf, Norman M(elvin) *lawyer, real estate executive*
Nobel, Joel J. *biomedical researcher*
Siegal, Jacob J. *management and financial consultant*

Polk
Hall, Richard Clayton *retired psychologist*

Port Royal
Wert, Jonathan Maxwell, II, *management consultant*

Portland
Hutton, William Michael *manufacturing executive*

Pottstown
Bause, David Francis *printing company professional*
Czuj, Chester Francis, Jr., *food service professional*
Hylton, Thomas James *author*
Mitchell, Eric Ehrman *photographer, stock broker*
Nash, William Lewis, III, *retired music education educator*

Pottsville
Boran, Robert Paul, Jr., *orthopedic surgeon*
Tamulonis, Frank Louis, Jr., *lawyer*
Thomas, Mark P. *conductor, educator*

Presto
Moeller, Audrey Carolyn *retired energy company executive, corporate secretary*

Punxsutawney
Dinsmore, Roberta Joan Maier *library director*
Graffius, Richard Stewart, II, *middle school educator*

Quakertown
Ambrus, Lorna *medical/surgical nurse, geriatrics nurse*
Ashcom, John M. *sales executive, general management executive*
Kulik, Beth A. *physician assistant, educator*

Quarryville
Armerding, Hudson Taylor *retired college president, consultant*
Bird, L. Raymond *investor*
Harris, Robert Laird *minister, theology educator emeritus*
Schreiner, Helen Ann *special education educator*
†Weston, Janice Leah Colmer *librarian*

Radnor
Buck, James Mahlon, Jr., *venture capital executive*
Castle, Joseph Lanktree, II, *energy company executive, consultant*
Eagleson, William Boal, Jr., *banker*
Giordano, Antonio *medical educator*
Marland, Alkis Joseph *rental company executive, computer scientist, educator, financial planner*
McCluskey, Gayla Jacque *health, safety and environmental executive*
Paier, Adolf Arthur *computer software and services company executive*
Stearns, Milton Sprague, Jr., *financial executive*
Templeton, John Marks, Jr., *retired pediatric surgeon, foundation executive*
Thompson, Pamela Padwick *public relations executive*

Rahns
Graeff, David Wayne *maintenance executive, consultant*

Reading
Bell, Frances Louise *medical technologist*
Bennett, Richard Clark *fundraising consultant*
Bilger, Dorinne Potter *musician, educator*
†Blessing, Tim H. *historian, educator*
†Boscov, Albert *retail executive*
Bowles, Patricia Mary *secondary education educator*
Brigham, Robert Allan *surgeon, educator*
Brown, Gerard Daniel *neonatologist, pediatrician*
†Bush, George Arthur *illustrator*
Cinfici, William Frank *historian*
†Creasy, Dana Eugene *communications educator*
Dersh, Rhoda E. *management consultant, business executive*
Dietrich, Bruce Leinbach *planetarium and museum administrator, astronomer, educator*
Dietrich, Renée Long *fund raising executive*
Ehlerman, Paul Michael *motorcycle and recreational batteries manufacturing company executive*
Hackenberg, Barbara Jean Collar *retired advertising and public relations executive*
Hollander, Herbert I. *consulting engineer*
Kiehne, Frank Charles, Jr., *foreign affairs adviser*
Kraras, Gust C. *hotel executive*
Lacki, Allan Vincent *industrial engineer*
†Linton, Jack Arthur *lawyer*
Lusch, Charles Jack *oncologist*
Mattern, Donald Eugene *retired association executive*
McVey, Diane Elaine *accountant*
Millar, Robert James *social science educator*
Moriarty, John Klinge *electronics engineer, consultant*
Murphy, Kevin Keith *foundation executive*
†Page, Clemson North, Jr., *lawyer*
Rochowicz, John Anthony, Jr., *mathematician, mathematics and physics educator*
Roesch, Clarence Henry *banker*
†Roland, John Wanner *lawyer*
Rothermel, Daniel Krott *lawyer, holding company executive*
†Scoboria, Francine Mary *writer*
Shultz, Lois Frances Casho *nursing supervisor*
†Snyder, Clair Allison *banker*
†Unser, Alfred, Jr., *race car driver*
Weiland, Jonathon A. *nursing and rehabilitation facility administrator*
†Wentzel, Judith Ann *librarian*
White, Thomas David, II, *academic administrator*
†Yoder, James Dale *adult education educator*
Young, Richard Robert *logistics and transportation educator*
Zug, Elizabeth E. *concert pianist, educator*

Rebersburg
Kuhns, Nancy Evelyn *minister*

Red Hill
DiMarco, Thomas William *software engineer*

Red Lion
Hartman, Charles Henry *not-for-profit developer, education educator, consultant*
Van Kouwenberg, Martha Nester *secondary education educator*

Reedsville
Garner, Douglas *music educator*

Richboro
Higginbotham, Kenneth James *financial services executive*

Richlandtown
Winters, Kay Lanning *writer*

Ridgway
Aiello, Gennaro C. *insurance company executive*
Redmount, Melvin Berr *chemical engineer, consultant*

Ridley Park
Clark, John H., Jr., *lawyer*
Walls, William Walton, Jr., *management consultant*

Roaring Spring
Smith, Larry Dennis *paper mill stores executive*

Robesonia
Fuhrman, Gwendolyn Sue *secondary school educator*

Rochester
Garlathy, Frank Bryan *minister*
Solai, Lalithkumar Kuppusamy *psychiatrist, educator*

Rosemont
Brunt, Manly Yates, Jr., *psychiatrist*

Rosemount
Berliner, Ernst *chemistry educator*

Royersford
Rhoads, Michael Dennis *sales executive*

Russellton
Curtis, Paula Annette *elementary and secondary education educator*

Rydal
Bacon, George Hughes, Jr., *retired systems analyst*
Black, Thomas Donald *retired religious organization administrator*
Boreen, Henry Isaac *computer company executive*
Fernberger, Marilyn Friedman *events organizer, consultant, civic leader*
Heebner, Albert Gilbert *economist, educator, bank executive*

Saint Davids
Baird, John Absalom, Jr., *retired college official*
Bertsch, Frederick Charles, III, *business executive*
Cary, Phillip Scott *philosphy educator*
Chang, Heewon *education educator, Electronic Journal Editor*
Denenberg, Herbert Sidney *journalist, lawyer, former state official*
Donnella, Michael Andre *lawyer, pharmaceutical company executive*
McCarthy, Justin Milton *marketing professional*
Pollard, Edward Ellsberg *banker*
Rogers, James Gardiner *accountant, educator*
Sheftel, Roger Terry *merchant banker*

Saint Marys
Quirk, Gail Elizabeth Manz *community services administrator*
†Sensor, Joseph Lloyd *music educator*
†Sorg, David Joseph *materials physicist*

Saint Peters
†Detterline, Milton E., Jr., *minister*

Saltsburg
Pidgeon, John Anderson *headmaster*

Sayre
Brittain, Nancy Hammond *accountant*
Davies, Chris Thomas *plastic and reconstructive surgeon*
Gu, Jeng Yul *radiologist*
Moody, Robert Adams *neurosurgeon*
†Smith, Robin L. *municipal official*

Schnecksville
Kiechel, Barbara Bernadette *vocational school educator*
†Schillow, Ned William *mathematics educator*

Schwenksville
De Bias, Dennis Anthony *physician*

Scottdale
†Brittain, Paul S. *editor*

Scranton
Alexander, Steven *artist, educator*
Baumann, Christopher Anthony *chemist, educator*
Blewitt, Thomas Michael *federal magistrate judge*
Borja, Marianne E. *healthcare educator*
Bourcier, Richard Joseph *French language and literature educator*
Brandreth, Elizabeth Anne *library director*
Burke, Henry Patrick *lawyer*
Cannon, J. Timothy *psychology educator, neuroscientist*
Cimini, Joseph Fedele *law educator, lawyer, former magistrate*
Clymer, Jay Phaon, III, *science educator*
Conaboy, Richard Paul *federal judge*
De Celles, Charles Edouard *theologian, educator*
Dolis, John *English educator*
Domenico, Roy Palmer *history educator*
†Dougherty, John Martin *bishop*
Eckersley, Richard Laurence *accountant*
†Farrell, Marian Louise *nursing educator*
Friedrichs, David O. *legal educator*
Giunta, Agatino John *economist, educator*
Haggerty, James Joseph *lawyer*
Harhut, Chet *judge*
†Herrema, Robert Dale *music educator*
Homer, Francis Xavier James *history educator*
Howley, James McAndrew *lawyer*
Janoski, Henry Valentine *investment advisor, former banker*
Kennedy, Lawrence William *historian*
Lemoncelli, Lorine Barbara *counselor, elementary school educator*
Lynett, William Ruddy *publishing, broadcasting company executive*
Maislin, Isidore *hospital administrator*
Nealon, William Joseph, Jr., *federal judge*
Nee, Sister Mary Coleman *college president emeritus*
O'Malley, Carlon Martin *judge*
Pang-White, Ann A. *philosophy educator, researcher*
Parente, William Joseph *political science educator*
Passon, Richard Henry *English language educator, former administrator*
†Reif, Jo Ann *art historian, educator*
Rhiew, Francis Changnam *radiologist, physician*
Sebastianelli, Carl Thomas *clinical psychologist*
Shovlin, Joseph Patrick *optometrist*

Tarutis, William John, Jr., *ecology educator, wetlands scientist*
Timlin, James Clifford *bishop*
Turock, Jane Parsick *nutritionist*
Vanaskie, Thomas Ignatius *judge*
Williams, Holly Thomas *retired business executive*
Wilson, Charles Frank *lawyer, law educator*
†Yamanouchi-Rynn, Midori *social sciences educator*
†Zaydon, Jemille Ann *English language and communications educator*

Selinsgrove
Connolly, Elma Troutman *artist, contractor, designer*
Davis, Richard Owen *lawyer*
DiCola, Theodore *music educator*
Fincke, Gary W. *writer, educator*
Kolbert, Jack *foreign language educator, French literature educator, humanities educator*
†Levinsky, Gail Beth *music educator*
Whitman, Jeffrey Paul *philosophy educator*

Sellersville
Hollander, Irwin Joel *pathologist, educator*
Rilling, David Carl *surgeon*

Sewickley
Bouchard, James Paul *steel manufacturing and planning executive*
Jehle, Michael Edward *financial executive*
†Mance, Jack Michael *retired lawyer, insurance company executive*
Munoz, Alfredo Nectario *emergency medicine physician, pediatrician*
Ostern, Wilhelm Curt *retired holding company executive*
Russell, John Robert *neurosurgeon*
Thorbecke, Willem Henry *international company executive, consultant*

Shady Grove
†Bust, Jeffry D. *manufacturing executive*
†Schoonmaker, Stephen J. *mechanical engineer*

Shamokin Dam
Matter, Harry H. *retired wholesale business executive and vice president, reflexologist*

Sharon
†Devey, Richard H. *language educator*
Dill, William Allen *lawyer*
Kosmowski, Audra Michele *lawyer*
Myers, Ronald Kosty *manufacturing executive, inventor*
Rosenblum, Harold Arthur *grocery distribution executive*

Shavertown
†Motyka, Susanne Victoria *music educator*

Shickshinny
Geffken, Meg Comstock *secondary education educator*
Luksha, Rosemary Dorothy *art educator*

Shillington
†Lidman, William G. *mechanical engineer, consultant*

Shippensburg
Bej, Emil *economics educator, researcher, journalist*
Collier, Duaine Alden *manufacturing and distribution company executive*
France, Olin Kenneth, Jr., *psychologist*
Kaluger, George *clinical psychologist, educator*
Kaluger, Meriem Fair *psychologist, educator*
Luhrs, H. Ric *toy manufacturing company executive*
Miller, Linda Lou *education administrator, communications specialist*
Stone, Susan Ridgaway *marketing educator*
Sturtz-Davis, Shirley Zampelli *artist, retired arts administrator/educator, fashion archivist*
White, David Lawrence *marketing professional*

Shippenville
†Fortis, Marie-Jose *editor*

Shiremanstown
Gould, Thomas Denton *lawyer*
Nesbit, William Terry *small business owner, consultant*

Shohola
Harding, Linda Otto *gerontological nurse, diabetes educator*
Williams, Carolyn Woodworth *retired elementary education educator, consultant*

Slatington
†Heffelfinger, Karl William *retired draftsman*

Slippery Rock
Bruya, John Robert *art educator*
Chmielewski, Jerry George *botanist, educator*
Cobb, Larry Russell *ethics educator*
Fulton, Jane *health science institution administrator*
†Hawk, Stephen L. *music educator, musician*
†Mukherjee, Pracheta *management educator, researcher, consultant*
†Skeele, David B. *theater educator, writer*
Smith, Grant Warren, II, *university administrator, physical sciences educator*
Smith, Robert Mason *academic administrator*
Wilson, Bradley Evans *philosophy educator*
Zinni, Hannah Case *foreign language educator*

Solebury
Anthonisen, George Rioch *sculptor, artist*
Cross, Robert William *lawyer, venture capital executive*
Gart, Herbert Steven *communications executive, producer*

Valentine, H. Jeffrey *legal association executive*

Somerset
Barkman, Jon Albert *lawyer*
†Kline, Eva Jane *library services administrator, educator*
Nair, Velupillai Krishnan *cardiologist*

Souderton
Hoeflich, Charles Hitschler *banker*
Lapp, James Merrill *clergyman, marriage and family therapist*
Moyer, June Faye *retired critical care nurse*

South Park
Kokowski, Palma Anna *nurse consultant*
Kuchta, Beatrice L. Esken *English educator*

South Sterling
Bancroft, Peggy *editor*

Southampton
Bendiner, Robert *writer, editor*
Levin, Lynn Ellen *poet*
Tepper, Richard Edward *infectious disease physician*

Southeastern
Amichetti, Dennis Joseph *advertising executive*
Rassbach, Herbert David *marketing executive*
Zlotolow-Stambler, Ernest *real estate executive, architectural executive*

Spring City
Blanchard, Norman Harris *retired pharmaceutical company executive*
Middleton, Dawn E. *education educator*

Spring Grove
Alcon, Sonja L. *retired medical social worker*
Butler, Raymond Archibald *cartographer*
Helberg, Shirley Adelaide Holden *artist, educator*
†Sterner, Deborah Kay *volunteer*
Todorovic, John *chemical engineer*

Spring House
Hann, William Mathis *chemist, researcher*
†Hurley, Kevin *publishing executive*
Rieck, Albert Charles *chemist*
Rosoff, William A. *lawyer, executive*
van Steenwyk, John Joseph *health care plan consultant, educator*

Spring Mills
Gillan, Garth Jackson *writer, psychotherapist, deacon, emeritus educator*

Springboro
Lillie, Marshall Sherwood *college safety and security director, educator*

Springfield
Arsht, Edwin David *physician*
†Austin, Susan Rebecca *librarian, writer, storyteller*
Carter, Frances Moore *educator, writer, foundation executive*
Maclay, Donald Merle *retired lawyer*
Reeves, Thomas A. *naturalist*
Sing, Robert Fong *physician*

State College
Aitken, Ruth Elaine Willson *educational and career/job search consultant*
Barnoff, Robert Mark *civil engineering educator*
Book, Edward R. *consultant, retired association executive*
Byrom, Fletcher Lauman *chemical manufacturing company executive*
Cannon, Frederick Scott *water engineer, educator, consultant*
Cao, Guohong *computer science educator*
Carnes, James Edward *technology executive*
Darnell, Doris Hastings *performance artist*
Day, David Vaughan *psychology educator*
Day, Lee Monroe *agriculture economics educator*
Foderaro, Anthony Harolde *nuclear engineering educator*
Garrett, Steven Lurie *physicist*
†German, Randall Michael *materials engineering educator, consultant*
Ginoza, William *former biophysics educator*
Goldschmidt, Arthur Eduard, Jr., *history educator, author*
Gordon, Richard Lewis *mineral economics educator*
Grimes, Dale Mills *physics and electrical engineering educator*
Haas, John C. *architect*
Henisch, Heinz Kurt *retired physics educator*
Henshaw, Beverly Ann Harsh *women's health nurse, consultant*
Hettche, L. Raymond *research director*
Hoffa, Harlan Edward *retired university dean, art educator*
Kowalczyk, Kim Jan *editor, writer*
Lamb, Robert Edward *retired diplomat, professional society administrator*
Loviscky, Douglas Charles *tax lawyer*
†Madjid, A. Hamid *retired science educator*
Maneval, David Richard *mineral engineering consultant*
Max, Elizabeth *educator*
McKeel, Lillian Phillips *retired education educator*
Moon, Marla Lynn *optometrist*
†Mutmansky, Jan M. *retired engineering educator, consultant*
Nollau, Lee Gordon *lawyer*
Olson, Donald Richard *mechanical engineering educator*
Petrie, Howard Lane *engineer, researcher*
Phillips, Janet Colleen *retired educational association executive, editor*
Redford, Donald Bruce *historian, archaeologist*

Remick, Forrest Jerome, Jr., *former university official*
Robinett, Betty Wallace *linguist, educator*
†Roy, Della Martin *materials science educator, researcher*
Schaie, K(laus) Warner *human development and psychology educator*
Schmalstieg, William Riegel *retired Slavic languages educator*
Schmalz, Robert Fowler *geology educator*
Shaikh, Nazrul Islam *industrial engineer, researcher*
Sibul, Leon Henry *electrical engineer*
†Sinha, Sunil K. *engineer, educator*
†Strauss, Susan Gayle *linguistics educator*
Subler, Edward Pierre *advertising executive*
Swinton, John Ralph *retired language educator, writer*
Tehie, Janice Beveridge *education educator*
Toombs, William Edgar *professor*
Wilson, Keith B. *rehabilitation educator*
Wyand, Martin Judd *economics educator, retired military officer*

Steelton
Zimmerman, Connie Ann *public administrator*

Stevens
Shenk, Lois Elaine Landis *writer*

Strasburg
Goss, Stephen D. *music educator, musician*
Lindsay, George Carroll *former museum director*
Rawleigh, Floyd Ernest, Jr., *music educator*

Stroudsburg
Kratz, Charles E., Jr., *dean*
Macmillan, Robert Francis *director university service*
Miller, Nancy A. *nursing administrator*
†Upright, Kirby Grant *lawyer*
Weitzmann, William Henry *education educator, photographer*
Wormack, Karen Elise *small business owner, poet*

Summerdale
†Zeiders, Jeffrey Alan *secondary school educator, historian, educator*

Sunbury
Carey, Scott M *music educator*
Ely, Donald J(ean) *clergyman, secondary school educator*
Fernsler, John Paul *lawyer*
Hetrick, Theodore Lewis, Jr., *emergency medicine physician*
Maue, Leta Jo *special education administrator*
Saylor, Charles Horace *lawyer, judge*
Weis, Robert Freeman *supermarket company executive*

Swarthmore
Bannister, Robert Corwin, Jr., *historian, educator, retired historian*
Bilaniuk, Oleksa Myron *physicist, educator*
†Bloom, Alfred Howard *academic administrator, educator*
Carey, William Bacon *pediatrician, educator*
Devin, Lee (Philip Lee Devin) *dramaturg, author*
Elman, Gerry Jay *lawyer*
†Freeman, James Douglas *music educator*
Frost, Jerry William *religion and history educator, library administrator*
Gelzer, David Georg *English educator, missionary*
Gilbert, Scott Frederick *biologist, educator, author*
Hollister, Robinson Gill, Jr., *economics educator*
Hopkins, Raymond Frederick *political science educator*
Hyde, Harry, Jr., *technical writer, editor, consultant*
Katz, Lauren Freidus *psychiatrist*
Kaufman, Antoinette D. *business services company executive*
Kaufman, John Robert *marketing and information management consultant*
Keith, Jennie *anthropology educator and administrator, writer*
Kelemen, Charles F. *computer science educator*
Kitao, T. Kaori *art history educator*
Krendel, Ezra Simon *systems and human factors engineering consultant*
Lacey, Hugh Matthew *philosophy educator*
†Morgan, Kathryn Lawson *historian, educator*
North, Helen Florence *classicist, educator*
Ostwald, Martin *retired classicist*
†Pagliaro, Harold Emil *English language educator*
Pasternack, Robert Francis *chemistry educator*
Pryor, Frederic L. *economist, educator*
Redden, Taylor Tilghman *musician*
Sawyers, Claire Elyce *arboretum administrator*
Ullman, Roger Roland *lawyer, realtor*

Swiftwater
†Braithwaite, Barbara J. *secondary school educator*
Woods, Walter Earl *biomedical research and development executive*

Swissvale
Skrbin, Aaron T. *assistant principal*

Tannersville
Moore, James Alfred *ski company executive, lawyer*

Tarentum
McGuire, Timothy William *economics and management educator, dean, management executive*

Taylor
Champagne, Cecile Belisle *nursing educator, maternal/child health nurse*

Temple
Stump, Richard Carl *environmental services administrator, consultant*
VonNieda, Jean Lorayne *infection control practitioner*

Thorndale
Hodess, Arthur Bart *cardiologist*

Tionesta
Martincic, John Edward *engineering executive*

Titusville
Campasino, Ellen Marie *elementary school educator*
Hall, Mary Ann *English language educator*
Mulcahy, Richard Patrick *history educator, consultant*

Tobyhanna
Lapidus, Arnold *mathematician, educator*

Topton
Knight, Cheryl DuBois *library director*

Towanda
†Singh Gaur, Raj Pal *research scientist*

Transfer
Larson, Sharon Lynn *oncological nurse*

Trevose
McEvilly, James Patrick, Jr., *lawyer*
Satz, Ronald Wayne *systems engineer, consultant*

Trout Run
McKissick, Michael Landon *transportation consultant*
Nelson, Richard Lloyd *systems engineer, consultant*

Tunkhannock
Gilmore, Haydn Lewis *English educator*
McNabb, Leonard Matthew *clinical social worker, administrator*

Tylersport
Raub, Donald Wilmer *minister, author*

Tyrone
Bonta, Marcia Myers *freelance nature writer, researcher, columnist*
Spewock, Theodosia George *principal, elementary school educator*

Uniontown
†Coldren, Ira Burdette, Jr., *lawyer*
†Davis, James Thomas *lawyer*
†Eberly, Robert Edward *foundation administrator*
Franks, William J. *judge*
†Pasqua, Michael G. *music educator, radio producer, small business owner*
Prescott, Janelle *medical and surgical nurse, emergency room nurse, psychiatric nurse*

Unionville
De Marino, Donald Nicholson *international business executive, former federal agency administrator*
Forney, Robert Clyde *retired chemical industry executive*
Martin, Helen Elizabeth *educational consultant*

University Park
Allcock, Harry R. *chemistry educator*
Andrews, George Eyre *mathematics educator*
Antle, Charles Edward *statistics educator*
Aplan, Frank Fulton *metallurgical engineering educator*
Askov, Eunice May *adult education educator*
Austin, Leonard George *mineral engineer*
Baisley, Robert William *music educator, educator*
Ballora, Mark Edward *music educator*
Barlow, Jesse Louis *computer scientist, educator*
Barnes, Hubert Lloyd *geochemistry educator*
Bazirjian, Rosann V. *dean, librarian*
†Belz, Julie Anne *language educator*
†Benkovic, Stephen James *chemist*
Blackadar, Alfred Kimball *meteorologist, educator*
Bollag, Jean-Marc *soil biochemistry educator, consultant*
Bose, Nirmal Kumar *electrical engineering, mathematics educator*
Brault, Gerard Joseph *French language educator*
Brockman, William S. *librarian*
Brown, John Lawrence, Jr., *electrical engineering educator*
†Broyles, Michael E. *music history educator, writer*
Buskirk, Elsworth Robert *physiologist, educator*
Buss, Edward George *geneticist*
Cahir, John Joseph *meteorologist, educational administrator*
Castleman, Albert Welford, Jr., *physical chemist, educator*
Chander, Subhash *educator*
Coleman, Michael Murray *polymer science educator*
Collins, John Clements *physicist, educator*
†Cook, Kim Diane *concert cellist*
†Danner, Ronald Paul *chemical engineering educator*
Davids, Norman *engineering science and mechanics educator, researcher*
†De Jong, Gordon Frederick *education educator, consultant*
Demirci, Ali *microbiological and food engineer*
Duda, John Larry *chemical engineering educator*
†Duiker, Sjoerd Willem *soil scientist, educator*
Dutton, John Altnow *meteorologist, educator*
Eaton, Nancy Ruth Linton *librarian, university dean*
Ebitz, David MacKinnon *art historian, educator*
†Edmondson, Jacqueline *education educator*
Epp, Donald James *economist, educator*

†Erickson, Rodney Allen *university executive, provost*
†Ertekin, Turgay *petroleum engineer educator, researcher, consultant*
†Eser, Semih *science educator, consultant, researcher*
Fedoroff, Nina Vsevolod *research scientist, consultant, educator*
Felson, Richard Barnet *educator*
Feng, Tse-yun *computer engineer, educator*
Firebaugh, Glenn Allen *sociology educator*
Ford, Donald Herbert *psychologist, educator*
†Fóti, Véronique M. *philosophy educator*
Fowler, H(oratio) Seymour *retired science educator*
Friedman, Robert Sidney *political science educator*
†Goulias, Konstadinos G. *director*
Grimes, Craig Alan *electrical engineering educator*
Grosholz, Emily Rolfe *philosophy educator, poet*
†Guo, Ruyan *engineering educator, researcher*
Hagen, Daniel Russell *physiologist, educator*
Halsey, Martha Taliaferro *Spanish language educator*
Hammes-Schiffer, Sharon *chemist, educator*
†Herr, Edwin Leon *educator, academic administrator*
Holl, John William *engineering educator*
Hosler, Charles Luther, Jr., *meteorologist, educator*
Howell, Benjamin Franklin, Jr., *geophysicist, educator*
†Humphrey, Craig Reed *social studies educator*
†Ibrahim, Ibrahim Awad *adult education educator*
Ivanov, Kostadin Nikolov *educator*
Jackman, Lloyd Miles *chemistry educator*
Jackson, Ronald L., II, *communications educator*
Joyce, William Leonard *librarian*
Kabel, Robert Lynn *chemical engineering educator*
†Kadir, Djelal *literature educator, writer, translator, editor*
Kasting, James Fraser *research meteorologist, physicist*
Kelley, Eugene John *retired business educator*
Klein, Philip Alexander *economist*
Knott, Kenneth *engineering educator, consultant, expert witness*
Lacy, Norris J. *literature educator*
Larson, Russell Edward *university provost emeritus, consultant agriculture research and development*
Lauchle, Gerald Clyde *acoustics educator*
Lee, Robert Dorwin *public affairs educator, administrator*
Lima, Robert *Hispanic studies and comparative literature educator*
Liu, Zi-Kui *materials science and engineering educator*
Ma, Hong *plant molecular biologist, educator*
Ma, Xiaoliang *research scientist*
†MacEwan, Bonnie *librarian*
Mahan, Gerald Dennis *physics educator, researcher*
Mayers, Stanley Penrose, Jr., *public health educator*
McCormick, Barnes Warnock *aerospace engineering educator*
McDonnell, Archie Joseph *environmental engineer*
McKeown, James Charles *accounting educator, consultant*
†McNeese, Michael D. *educator*
McPheron, Bruce Alan *entomologist*
Mentzer, John Raymond *electrical engineer, educator*
Messer, Andrea Elyse *anthropologist, archaeologist, science writer*
†Modest, Michael Fritz *mechanical engineering educator*
Muhlert, Jan Keene *art museum director*
†Murray-Kolb, Laura Elaine *nutritionist, researcher*
Muscarella, Christopher James *finance educator*
†Naydan, Michael M. *foreign language educator*
†Newsome, Lee Ann *anthropologist, educator*
Nicely, Robert Francis, Jr., *education educator, administrator*
†Nielsen, Aldon Lynn *literature educator*
Nisbet, John Stirling *electrical engineering educator*
†Park, Jonghun *science and technology educator*
Ramani, Raja Venkat *mining engineering educator*
†Rangaswamy, Arvind *marketing educator, consultant*
Ray, William Jackson *psychologist*
Rolls, Barbara Jean *nutritionist, educator, director*
†Rose, Adam Zachary *economist, educator*
Rose, Paul Lawrence *history educator*
†Rosen, Scott Lowell *researcher*
†Ross, A. Catharine *biochemist, educator*
Rotz, C. Alan *agricultural engineer, educator*
Roy, Rustum *interdisciplinary educator, materials researcher*
Ruud, Clayton Olaf *engineering educator*
Scanlon, Andrew *structural engineering educator*
Semouchkina, Elena *physicist, researcher*
Snow, Dean Richard *anthropology educator, archaeologist*
†Sokol, Paul E. *physicist, educator, physicist, researcher*
Song, Chunshan *chemist, chemical engineer, educator*
Spanier, Graham Basil *university president*
Spanier, Sandra Whipple *English language educator*
Stern, Robert Morris *gastrointestinal psychophysiology researcher, psychology educator*
Stinson, Richard Floyd *retired horticulturist, educator*
†Story, Julie Ann *English educator*
Thompson, William, Jr., *engineering educator*
†Tikalsky, Paul J. *civil engineering educator, structural engineer*
Tittmann, Bernhard Rainer *engineering science and mechanics educator*
†Trinkley, Bruce *music educator, director*
Ulmer, Jeffery Todd *sociology educator*
Vannice, M. Albert *chemical engineering educator, researcher*
†Vennam, Venkata Surya Prakash *engineering educator, researcher*
Ventura, Jose Antonio *industrial engineer, educator, researcher*
Walden, Daniel *humanities and social sciences educator*
Walker, Alan C. *anthropologist, educator*
Wang, James Ze *computer scientist, educator*
†Wanner, Adrian J. *literature educator*
†Waterhouse, William Charles *mathematics educator*
Webb, Ralph Lee *mechanical engineering educator*
Wheeler, C. Herbert *architect, consultant, educator*
†Wheeler, Stephen Michael *classicist*
White, William Blaine *geochemist, educator*
Williams, Edward Vinson *music history educator*
Winograd, Nicholas *chemist*
Witzig, Warren Frank *nuclear engineer, educator*
Wysk, Richard A. *engineering educator, researcher*
Yoder, Edgar Paul *education educator*
Yu, Fushun *physiologist, research scientist*
†Yu, Wenhua *science educator*
Zatsiorsky, Vladimir Moiseevich (Michailovich) *biomechanics educator, researcher*

Upland
†Jones, Ancil Arthur *cardiologist*

Upper Burrell
†Franco Gómez, María Angeles *language educator*

Upper Darby
†Horwitz, Seth *information technology executive*
Hudiak, David Michael *academic administrator, lawyer*
†Kahler, Nancy J. *music educator, director*
Leiby, Bruce Richard *secondary education educator, writer*
Toney, Angela M. *medical administrator and educator*

Upper Saint Clair
Anderson, Catherine M. *consulting company executive*
Van Dusen, Margaret Davis *community volunteer, consultant*

Valencia
Hill, Ellen Brockett Brown *emergency medicine nurse, geriatrics services professional*
Richards, David Christopher *small business owner, organist*

Valley Forge
Bogle, John Clifton *investment company executive*
Bovaird, Brendan Peter *lawyer*
Corchin, Mark Alan *lawyer*
Dachowski, Peter Richard *manufacturing executive*
Erb, Doretta Louise Barker *polymer scientist*
Erb, Robert Allan *physical scientist*
Guttentag, Jack Mark *economist, educator*
LaBoon, Lawrence Joseph *human resources specialist, consultant*
Miller, Betty Brown *freelance writer*
Phelizon, Jean Francois *business executive*
†Walters, Bette Jean *lawyer*
†Wright-Riggins, Aidsand F., III, *religious organization executive*

Vandergrift
Bullard, Ray Elva, Jr., *retired psychiatrist, hospital administrator*
Kulick, Richard John *computer scientist, researcher*

Verona
Bruno, Louis Vincent *special education educator*
Koch, Robert Wotring *chemical engineer*

Villanova
†Alter, Maria Pospischil *language educator*
Beck, Christine Safford *photographer, publisher, volunteer*
Beck, Robert Edward *computer scientist, educator*
Beletz, Elaine Ethel *nurse, educator*
Bergquist, James Manning *history educator*
Bersoff, Donald Neil *lawyer, psychologist*
†Caverly, Robert *adult education educator*
Clement, Barbara Koltes Sadtler *academic administrator*
Cordes, Eugene Harold *pharmacy and chemistry educator*
Cox-Klaczak, Karen Michelle *marketing educator, computer company official*
DeLaura, David Joseph *English language educator*
Dobbin, Edmund J. *university administrator*
†Durán, Jaime *language educator*
Edwards, John Ralph *retired chemist, educator*
Eigo, Francis Augustine *theology studies educator*
Fitzpatrick, M. Louise *dean, nursing educator*
Friend, Theodore Wood, III, *foundation executive, historian, writer*
Gould, Lilian *writer*
Hafkenschiel, Joseph Henry, Jr., *cardiologist, educator*
Hunt, John Mortimer, Jr., *classical studies educator*
Johannes, John Roland *political science educator, academic administrator*
Maule, James Edward *law educator, lawyer*
McLaughlin, Philip VanDoren, Jr., *mechanical engineering educator, researcher, consultant*
Mulroney, Michael *lawyer, law educator, graduate program director*
Norton, Douglas Evatt *mathematician, educator*
Olsen, Judith Johnson *reference librarian*
Phares, Alain Joseph *physicist, educator*
Ray, Eva Konig *biomedical consultant*
Redding, Richard Ellsworth *psychologist, lawyer*
Salmon, John Hearsey McMillan *historian, educator*
Savitz, Fred *education educator*
Scheffler, Barbara Jane *statistician, business executive*
Scott, Robert Montgomery *museum executive, lawyer*
Smith, Standish Harshaw *non-profit company executive*
Tomlinson, J. Richard *engineering services company executive*
Urbach, Frederick *physician, educator*
Vander Veer, Suzanne *aupair business executive*
Zearfoss, Herbert Keyser *lawyer*
Zhang, Yimin *researcher*

Volant
Moore, Janet Marie *accountant, state official*

Wallingford
Cook, Harvey Carlisle *law enforcement official*
McCarthy, Carol A. *pediatric nurse practitioner*
Medina, Harold Raymond, III, *marketing executive*
Morrison, Donald Franklin *statistician, educator*
Parker, Jennifer Ware *chemical engineer, researcher*
Peabody, William Tyler, Jr., *retired paper manufacturing company executive*
Scherer, Frederic Michael *economics educator*
Severdia, Anthony George *chemistry researcher*

Walnutport
†Fister, Michael J. *music educator*

Warminster
Ciao, Frederick J. *school system administrator, educator*
Dinkins, Tyrone Morris *music educator, conductor*
Hull, Lewis Woodruff *manufacturing company executive*
Sibley, Lewis Branch *engineering executive*
Tatnall, George Jacob *aeronautical engineer*

Warren
Bergstein, Jack Marshall *surgeon*
Crone, John Rossman *pharmacist*
†Johnson, Newkirk Lynn *not-for-profit developer*
Ristau, Mark Moody *lawyer, petroleum consultant*

Warrendale
Rumbaugh, Max Elden, Jr., *professional society administrator*
Scott, Alexander Robinson *engineering association executive*
Snyder, Linda Ann *editor*

Warrington
Miller, Lynne Marie *critical care nurse, administrator*
O'Hara, Timothy Patrick *marketing professional*
Shaw, Milton Herbert *conglomerate executive*
Ward, Hiley Henry *journalist, educator*

Washington
Allison, Jonathan *retired lawyer*
Balta, Andrew Stephen *oral and maxillofacial surgeon*
Erdner, Jon W. *small business owner, securities trader*
Forrest, Robert Gilliland *mathematics educator*
Grimm, Donald Lee *executive*
Kastelic, Robert Frank *aerospace company executive*
Lerner, William C. *lawyer*
Maloney, Patricia Diana *artist, educator*
Mc Cune, Barron Patterson *retired federal judge*
Posner, David S. *lawyer*
Richman, Stephen I. *lawyer*
Robinson, Jennifer Lynn *nursing educator*
Schwarz, Frederick A.O., Jr., *lawyer*

Washington Bord
†Snyder, John Jacob *researcher*

Washington Crossing
Clevenger, Roy Edward *credit and collections manager*
Hauf, John George *real estate broker*
†Sloca, Steven Lane *lawyer*

Wayne
Agersborg, Helmer Pareli K. *pharmaceutical company executive, researcher*
Burget, Dean Edwin, Jr., *plastic surgeon*
Carroll, Robert W. *retired business executive*
Curry, Thomas James *retired manufacturers representative*
Dixon, E. A., Jr., *lawyer*
Etris, Samuel Franklin *trade association research consultant*
Fabbri, Anne R. *art critic, curator*
Garrison, Guy Grady *librarian, educator*
Grace, Thomas Lee *health facility administrator, emergency nurse practitioner*
Guernsey, Louis Harold *retired oral and maxillofacial surgeon, educator*
Higgs, Jon Scott *computer company executive, researcher*
Howard, Harold Charles *provost, strategic planner, consultant*
†Kauffman, Joel Mervin *chemistry educator, researcher, consultant*
Krutsick, Robert Stanley *retired science center executive*
Lefevre, Thomas Vernon *retired utility company executive, lawyer*
Lief, Harold Isaiah *psychiatrist*
†Lockyer, Nigel S *physicist*
Long, Peter Avard Chipman *retired rear admiral United States Navy*
Mackey, Betty Barr *writer*
MacNeal, Edward Arthur *economic consultant*
Meltser, Thomas Avrum *corporate executive*
Mestre, Oscar Luis *financial consultant*
Parasuraman, T. V. *pharmaceutical executive*
Rabii, Patricia Berg *church administrator*
Rubley, Carole A. *state legislator*
Stevens, Willis A. *music educator*
Thelen, Edmund *research executive*
Wilson, Bruce Brighton *retired transportation executive, lawyer*
Wilson, James Lawrence *retired chemical company executive*
Yoskin, Jon William, II, *insurance company executive*
Yost, R. David *healthcare manufacturing company administrator*
Youman, Roger Jacob *editor, writer*
Zlotowski, Martin *psychologist*

Waynesboro
Benchoff, James Martin *manufacturing company executive*
Cryer, Theodore Hudson *ophthalmologist, educator*
†Kirk, Daniel Lee *retired physician, consultant*
Martin, Harold G. *engineering consultant*
Maxwell, LeRoy Stevenson *retired lawyer*

Waynesburg
†Maguire, Mildred May *chemistry educator, magnetic resonance researcher*
Visser, Richard Edgar *minister*

Wellsboro
Baker, Matthew Edward *state legislator*
Driskell, Lucile G. *artist*

Wernersville
Panuska, Joseph Allan *academic administrator*

West Aliquippa
Peya, Prudence Malava *retired elementary education educator*

West Chester
Abbott, Ann Augustine *social worker, educator*
Abernethy, Hugh C., Jr., *writer*
Benzing, Cynthia Dell *economics educator*
Blasiotti, Robert Vincent *accountant, consultant*
Bove, Patrice Magee *elementary education educator*
Branman, M. Jeffrey *investment fund company executive*
†Briggs, Douglas D. *communications executive*
Burton, John Bryan *music educator*
Dinniman, Andrew Eric *county commissioner, history educator, academic program director, international studies educator*
Dunlop, Edward Arthur *computer company executive*
Eddy, Heath Robert *urban planner*
Ewing, Joseph Neff, Jr., *retired lawyer*
Flood, Dorothy Garnett *neuroscientist*
Gadsby, Robin Edward *chemical company executive*
Gallagher, Terrence Vincent *editor*
Gougher, Ronald Lee *foreign language educator and administrator*
Green, Andrew Wilson *lawyer*
Hammonds, Jay A. *retired secondary education educator, administrator*
Handzel, Steven Jeffrey *accountant*
Hanna, Colin Arthur *county official, management and computer consultant*
Hanson, Diane Charske *management consultant*
†Hardy, Charles Ashley, III, *historian, educator, film producer*
Heaps, Marvin Dale *retired food services company executive*
†Heston, Thomas J. *education educator*
Hickman, Janet Susan *college administrator, educator*
Hipple, Walter John *English language educator*
Knuth Fischer, Cynthia Strout *environmental consultant*
Lenfest, Harold Fitz Gerald *former cable television executive, lawyer*
Mahoney, William Francis *editor/author*
Meystel, Michael A. *Internet executive*
Morgan, John David *middle school educator*
†Myrsiades, Kostas Yannis *literature educator*
Osborn, John Edward *lawyer, pharmaceutical and biotechnology industry executive, former government official, writer*
Palmer, Donald Curtis *retired interdenominational missionary society executive*
Patin Falini, Nancy Marie *dietitian*
Pennington, Robert Edgar *music educator*
Perkins, Brenda Elizabeth *veterinarian*
Swope, Charles Evans *bank president, lawyer*
Taylor, Bernard J., II, *banker*
Walls, Thomas Francis *professional services administrator*

West Conshohocken
Boenning, Henry Dorr, Jr., *investment banker*
Ceccola, Russ *game strategy guide writer*
Evans, Ellen Frasca *pharmaceutical company executive*
Hochreiter, Joseph Christian, Jr., *engineering company executive*
Mullen, Eileen Anne *human resources executive*
Newman, Sandra Schultz *state supreme court justice*
Taylor, Martha Elizabeth (Betsy Taylor) *investment company executive*
Teillon, Louis Pierre, Jr., *lawyer*

West Grove
Allman, Margo Hutz *sculptor, painter*

Allman, William Berthold *musician, engineer, consultant*
†Cornell, Suzanne *youth services executive*
Fuller, Jack Glendon, Jr., *retired plastics engineer*
Seder, Jeffrey A. *entrepreneur*

West Mifflin
†Archey, Mary Frances Elaine (Onofaro) *academic administrator, educator*
Ardash, Garin *mechanical engineer*
Aumiller, David *nuclear engineer*
Clayton, John Charles *scientist, researcher*
Kemp, Kathleen Nagy *lawyer*

West Point
Buckland, Barry Christopher *chemical engineer*
†Hartman, George David *chemist, director*
Hilleman, Maurice Ralph *virus research scientist*
Keyser, Janet Marie *pharmaceutical industry executive*
Kim, Peter Sungbai *pharmaceutical executive, educator*
†Lee, Jonghwi *chemical engineer, researcher*
†Lindsley, Craig William *physicist, researcher*
Manning, Barton Harley *neuroscientist*
†Schaffner, Carolyn Marie *research administrator, biologist*
†Shahinfar, Shahnaz *pharmaceutical executive, nephrologist*
Silber, Jeffrey Lee *physician*
Weekley, Leslie Bruce *veterinarian, pharmacologist*

West Reading
Carter, Frank Moulton *physician*

West Sunbury
Stewart, Mark Thomas *gas industry executive*

Westtown
Jackson, Katherine Church *former elementary school educator, reading educator*

Wexford
Hartwig, Thomas Leo *civil engineer, environmental engineer, sports association administrator*
Hutchinson, Barbara Winter *elementary school educator*
Micale, Frank Jude *lawyer*
Reid, Robert H. *engineering consultant*

White Haven
Velzy, Charles O. *mechanical engineer*

Whitehall
Budd, Patricia Jean *counselor*
Tufton, Janie Lee (Jane Tufton) *dental hygienist, animal rights lobbyist, activist*

Wilkes Barre
Brady, Patricia Marie *nurse*
Campbell, Sophie Ann Oriszko *manager and senior health care consultant*
Casale, Alfred Stanley *thoracic and cardiovascular surgeon*
Hayes, Wilbur Frank *retired biology educator*
†Hepp, John Henry, IV, *historian, lawyer*
†Legg, Timothy James *nursing educator*
McHale, Maureen Bernadette Kenny *controller*
Mech, Terrence Francis *library director*
Ogren, Robert Edward *biologist, educator*
Rosenn, Max *federal judge*
Roth, Eugene *lawyer*
Schiowitz, Mark F. *surgeon*
Schwartz, Roger Alan *judge*
†Stokes, Kimberly Ann *counselor*
Swanek, Susan Ann *quality assurance professional*
Ufberg, Murray *lawyer*

Wilkes-Barre
†Krawczeniuk, Joseph Volodymyr *humanities educator*
†Reboli, Denise M. *education educator*
Simon, Philip George *music educator, musician*

Williamsport
†Boone, Daniel Lee *retired music educator*
Cox, Albert Edward *retired pastor*
Ertel, Allen Edward *lawyer, former congressman*
Gouldin, Judith Ann *nuclear medicine physician*
Knecht, William L. *lawyer*
Largen, Joseph *retailer, furniture manufacturer, book wholesaler*
Lattimer, Gary Lee *physician*
McClure, James Focht, Jr., *federal judge*
McDonald, Peyton Dean *brokerage house executive*
Muir, Malcolm *federal judge*
Rauhut, John Frederick *pastor*
Rosebrough, Carol Belville *cable television company executive*
Schultz, Carole Lamb *community volunteer*
†Weaver, Kent Curtis *music educator*
Williams, Robert L. *principal*

Willow Grove
†Asplundh, Christopher B. *tree service company executive*
Chatterjee, Hem Chandra *electrical engineer*
Glassmoyer, Thomas Parvin *lawyer*
†Levin, Joshua Zev *computer scientist, consultant*
Moore, Norma Jean *real estate broker*
Schiffman, Louis F. *management consultant*
Sirota, Robert Alan *physician, nephrologist*
Suer, Marvin David *architecture, consultant*
Yuan, Joan Reynolds *community health nurse*

Windber
Ott, Clarice Jean *social worker*

Womelsdorf
Worley, Jane Ludwig *lawyer*

Woolrich
Himes, Kenneth Alan *retired marketing executive*

Wormleysburg
Cherewka, Michael *lawyer*
Grass, Alexander *retail company executive*

Wyncote
Leinweber, Bruce Kornblatt *obstetrician, gynecologist, educator*
Schaffner, Roberta Irene *retired medical, surgical nurse*

Wyndmoor
Farrell, Harold Maron, Jr., *chemist*
Fishman, Marshall Lewis *chemist*
Irwin, Peter Lloyd *biochemist, microbiologist*
Liu, Lin Shu *biomaterials scientist*
†Marmer, William N. *chemist, researcher*
Pfeffer, Philip Elliot *biophysicist*

Wynnewood
Alter, Milton *neurologist, educator*
Belinger, Harry Robert *retired business executive*
Bernfeld, Gerald E. *editor, writer, retired nursing educator*
Brady, John Paul *psychiatrist*
Brown, Michael John *publishing executive*
Buffum, Kathleen D. *artist*
Cander, Leon *retired physician*
Frankl, Razelle *management educator*
Frankl, William Stewart *cardiologist, educator*
Fugaro, Anthony Joseph *anesthesiologist*
Harrison, Donald *newspaper editor*
Keshgegian, Albert Arakel *pathologist*
†Khurana, Poonam *neonatologist*
McNally, Michael James *priest*
Meyers, Mary Ann *writer, consultant*
Phillips, Almarin *economics educator, consultant*
Prendergast, George C. *cancer biologist, researcher*
Prior, Joseph Gerard *priest, educator*
Robinson, Robert L. *former financial service company executive, lawyer*
Rosen, Gerald Harris *physicist, consultant, educator*
Rubin, Leonard Sidney *physiologist, educator, researcher*
Russell, Horace Orlando *theology studies educator*
†Sell, Christian *biomedical researcher*
Sider, Ronald J. *theology educator, author*
†Stapleton, Larrick B. *lawyer*
Waber, Harry Edward *insurance agency executive*
Wachs, Saul Philip *Jewish education educator*

Wyomissing
Beaver, Howard Oscar, Jr., *retired alloys manufacturing company executive*
Doherty, Edmond John *retired librarian*
Gebbia, Robert James *tax executive*
Kessler, Leona Hanover *interior designer*
Moll, Lloyd Henry *banker*
Pellecchia, Eve Wassall *management consultant*
Spatcher, Dianne Marie *finance executive*
Turner, David Eldridge *lawyer*
Williams-Wennell, Kathi *human resources consultant*

Yardley
Ahrens, Henry William *art educator, consultant, puppeteer*
Breitenfeld, Frederick, Jr., *retired educational consultant, former public broadcasting executive*
Brick, John *biological psychologist, educator, researcher*
Desai, Cawas Jal *business executive*
Du Bois, Paul Zinkhan *library consultant, book dealer*
Elliott, Frank Nelson *retired college president*
Finn, Marie Frances *artist*
Fraser, David William *epidemiologist*
Gilmour, D(avid) James *financial analyst, systems analyst*
Grossman, Irving Gross *retired geologist*
Hamberg, Gilbert Lee *lawyer*
Harris, Charney Anita *painter, sculptor*
Huret, Barry S. *marketing professional, consultant*
Lamonsoff, Norman Charles *psychiatrist*
Lindenbaum, Jeffry Alan *osteopathic family physician, consultant*
Minter, Philip Clayton *retired communications company executive*
Newsom, Carolyn Cardall *management consultant*
Newsom, John Harlan *family physician*
Somma, Beverly Kathleen *medical and marriage educator*
Soultoukis, Donna Zoccola *library director*
Watson, Joyce Leslie *elementary educator*
Weaver, William Clair, Jr., (Mike Weaver) *human resources development executive*
Yee, David *chemist, technology analyst*
Zulker, Charles Bates *broadcasting company executive*

York
Aarestad, James Harrison *retired educational administrator, army officer*
Bartels, Bruce Michael *health care executive*
Binder, Mildred Katherine *retired public welfare agency executive*
Chronister, Virginia Ann *school nurse, educator*
Clautice, Edward Wellmore *retired industrial engineer*
Day, Ronald Richard *retired financial executive*
†Gill, Sukhdeep *education educator, researcher*
Grossman, Robert Allen *transportation executive*
Hake, Theodore Lowell *auction house owner*
†Hershey, Dave Michael *musician, music educator*
†Hoffmeyer, William Frederick *lawyer, educator*
Horn, Russell Eugene *engineering executive, consultant*
Horn, Russell Eugene, Jr., *business executive*
Jackson, Renée Bernadette *English language educator*
Jacobs, Laura *probation/parole officer*
Keiser, Paul Harold *retired hospital administrator*
Kodadek, William F(rancis) *communication educator*
Kulbicki, Melvin Andrew *political science educator*
Laucks, Therese Elaine *commercial art instructor*
Livingston, Pamela A. *corporate image and marketing management consultant*
McMillan, Wendell Marlin *agricultural economist*
Miller, Donald Kenneth *engineering consultant*
Moul, Marlin Eugene *real estate broker*
Owens, Marilyn Mae *elementary school educator, secondary school educator*
Rebert, Jephrey Lee *transportation planner, musician*
Roetenberg, Aaron David *retail consultant*
Rosen, Raymond *health facility executive*
Russell, Stephen Speh *lawyer*
Shultz, Suzanne Marie *medical librarian*
Snyder, Jan Louise *administrative aide*
Thornton, George Whiteley *investment company executive*
White, Timothy Paul *brokerage house executive*
Wiles, William Wharton *retired federal government official*

Youngstown
Palmer, Arnold Daniel *professional golfer*

Youngwood
Duvall, Hollie Jean *music educator*

Zelienople
Efaw, Cary Ross *manufacturing executive*

RHODE ISLAND

Adamsville
Cumming, Patricia A. *writer*

Barrington
Carpenter, Charles Colcock Jones *physician, educator*
Deakin, James *writer, former newspaperman*
Graser, Bernice Erckert *elementary school principal, educational consultant, psychologist*
Mates, Susan Onthank *physician, medical educator, writer, violinist*
Mihaly, Eugene Bramer *corporate executive, consultant, writer, educator*
Paolino, Ronald Mario *clinical psychologist, consultant, psychopharmacologist, pharmacist*
Rosenbloom, Mindy Sharon *psychiatrist*
Soutter, Thomas Douglas *retired lawyer*

Block Island
Connolly, Violette M. *small business owner*
Gasner, Walter Gilbert *retired dermatologist*

Bristol
†Berman, Garrett L *education educator*
Bogus, Carl Thomas *law educator*
†Camara, Joan Ellen *dean*
Clark, Esther Frances *law educator*
Danzberger, Alexander Harris *chemical engineer, consultant*
Deekle, Peter Van *library director*
†Hendrix, John Shannon *architecture educator*
Kent, Robert Brydon *law educator*
†McMullen, Susan Taylor *librarian*

Carolina
O'Neill, Lawrence T. *artist, poet*

Central Falls
Leclerc, Leo George *guidance counselor*

Charlestown
Ungaro, Joseph Michael *newspaper publishing executive, consultant*

Chepachet
†Benetti, Lynn *music educator*
Jubinska, Patricia Ann *ballet instructor, choreographer, artist, artist*
Pentleton, Carol June *visual communications designer*

Coventry
†Schweinsburg, Jane Duberg *librarian*

Cranston
Ahlgren, Charles Stephen *educator, business and public policy consultant*
Coletti, John Anthony *lawyer, furniture and realty company executive*
Factor, Alfred *lawyer*
Ioanes, Joyce *lawyer, social worker*
Langlois, Michael A. *financial adviser, consultant*
MacGunnigle, Bruce Campbell *manufacturing company executive*
Migliori, Joseph Louis *physician*
Morrissey, Ronald James *chemical company executive, chemist*
Mruk, Charles Karzimer *agronomist*
Parravano, Amelia Elizabeth (Amy Beth Parravano) *recording industry executive*
†Simonian, John S. *lawyer*
Vavala, Domenic Anthony *medical scientist, educator, retired air force officer*
Yu, Chen *family practice physician*

Cumberland
Rossi, Joseph Anthony *film and television make-up artist, educator*

East Greenwich
Carlson, Shawn Eric *physicist*
Dence, Edward William, Jr., *lawyer, banker*
Hunter, Garrett Bell *investment banker*
Jordan, Ronald P. *pharmacist, pharmaceutical executive, consultant*
†Raykhman, Alexander M. *entrepreneur, consultant*
Schibler, John J. *health facility administrator, consultant, educator*
†Spivack, Gloria Jean *music educator*
White, Sidney Howard *English educator*

East Providence
Furtado-Lavoie, Julia *new business startup consultant, accountant*
Guggenheim, Frederick Gibson *psychiatry educator*
†Parziale, John R. *physiatrist*
Tripp, Michael Windsor *accountant*

Esmond
†Seabra, James Joseph *music educator, professional musician*

Fiskeville
Mc Feeley, John Jay *chemical engineer*

Foster
Sawyer, Mildred Clementina *retired real estate agent*

Hope Valley
Devin, Carl Eric *artist*

Jamestown
Logan, Nancy Allen *library media specialist*
Parks, Albert Lauriston *lawyer*
Todd, Thomas Abbott *architect, urban designer, city planner*
Worden, Katharine Cole *sculptor*
Wright, Harrison Morris *historian, educator*

Johnston
†Spina, Douglas John *priest, educator*

Kingston
Alexander, Lewis McElwain *geographer, educator*
†Beauregard, Raymond A. *mathematician, educator*
†Biller, Henry Burt *psychologist, educator*
Burkett, John Philip *economics educator*
Caldwell, Naomi Rachel *library media specialist, educator*
Carothers, Robert Lee *academic administrator*
Cunnigen, Donald *sociologist, educator*
Devin, Robin B. *librarian, anthropologist*
†Felner, Robert David *psychology educator, researcher, consultant*
Fuchs, Henry Carl *music educator, pianist*
Gilton, Donna Louise *library and information scientist, educator*
Goos, Roger Delmon *mycologist*
Green, Angel Yvonne *literature educator*
Harrison, Robert William *zoologist, educator*
Katzanek, Robin Jean *physical therapy educator*
†Keefe, Margaret Johnson *librarian*
Kim, Yong Choon *philosopher, theologian, educator*
†Klein, Maurice (Maury) Nickell *education educator, writer*
†Ladewig, James L. *music history educator, reseacher*
Lee, Kang-Won Wayne *engineer, educator*
MacLaine, Allan Hugh *English language educator*
†Markin, Karen Mary *research scientist, journalist*
Mazze, Edward Mark *marketing educator, consultant*
†Molloy, David Scott, Jr., *labor relations educator*
Newman, Barbara Miller *psychologist, educator*
Nixon, Scott West *oceanography science educator*
†Parang, Keykavous *chemist, educator*
†Park, Eugene *education educator, consultant*
Seifer, Marc Jeffrey *psychology educator*
Shaikh, Zahir Ahmad *toxicologist, educator*
Stark, Dennis Edwin *university official*
Sundlun, Bruce *former governor*
†Takasawa, Manabu *music educator*
Taylor, Suzanne S. *educational association administrator, educator*
Turnbaugh, William Arthur *archaeologist, educator*
Wen, Yuming *research scientist*

Lincoln
Barlow, August Ralph, Jr., *minister*
Carter, Wilfred Wilson *financial executive, controller*
Volmer, Suzanne *artist*

Little Compton
Caron, Wilfred Rene *retired lawyer*
Middendorf, J. William, II, *investment banker*

Middletown
Cooper, Michele F. *writer, editor, analyst*
Demy, Timothy James *military chaplain*
Jackson, John Edward *educator, logistician, retired naval officer*
†Ottaviano, Doris Baginski *librarian*

Narragansett
Bentley-Scheck, Grace Mary *artist*
Menihan, Cydney Afriat *nurse midwife, medical sonographer*
O'Keefe, Beverly Disbrow *state official, federal official*
Pierson, Douglas H. *special education educator*
Pilson, Michael Edward Quinton *oceanography educator*

Newport
Brown, David William *economist, educator, consultant*

Burgin, William Lyle *architect*
†Carpenter, Stanley Dean MacDonald *military officer, educator*
†Delaney, Robert Finley *columnist, political sociologist, lecturer*
Ehrlich, Stanley Leonard *acoustical engineer, consultant*
Flowers, Sandra Joan *elementary education educator*
†Grassey, Thomas Brandt *humanities educator*
Haas, William Paul *humanities educator, former college president*
Koch, Robert Michael *research scientist, consultant, educator*
†Korolenko, Kyrill V. *electrical engineer*
Lawber, Harold Ernest, Jr., *economist, educator*
Liotus, Sandra Mary *lighting designer, business owner, consultant*
Lowe, Alfred Mifflin, III, *advertising agency executive, writer*
Lynch, Robert Stephen, Jr., *electrical engineer, researcher and developer*
MacLeish, Archibald Bruce *museum administrator*
Malkovich, Mark Paul, III, *musician, artistic director, scientist, sports agent*
†Maurer, John Henry *education educator*
McConnell, David Kelso *lawyer*
Mullaney, Joann Barnes *nursing educator*
Nash, Karen Marsteller Myers *sculptor, designer, systems analyst*
†Newman, Howard H. *painter, sculptor, artist*
Rogers, Rita *artist, conservator*
Sands, Harold Winthrop *banker, financial adviser*
Scheck, Frank Foetisch *retired lawyer*
Schnare, Robert Edey, Jr., *library director, educator*
Stone, Edward Luke *private equity investor, realtor*
Tarpgaard, Peter Thorvald *naval architect*
Uhlig, Frank, Jr., *editor, writer*
Wood, Berenice Howland *educator*
Wurman, Richard Saul *architect*

North Kingstown
Andraka, Raymond Joseph *digital electronics design engineer, consultant*
Dutwin, Phyllis *writer, scholarly*
Kilguss, Elsie Schaich *artist, gallery owner*
Kullberg, Gary Walter *advertising agency executive*
Resch, Cynthia Fortes *secondary education educator*
Sharpe, Henry Dexter, Jr., *retired manufacturing company executive*

North Providence
†Bain, Marissa *social worker*
Lombardi, Valentino Dennis *lawyer*
Maciel, Patricia Ann *development professional*
Stankiewicz, Andrzej Jerzy *physician, biochemistry educator*

North Scituate
Dupree, Thomas Andrew *forester, state official*

Pawtucket
Boghossian, Joan Thompson *artist*
Bose, Kingshuk *research engineer*
†Chopra, Pradeep *physician, educator*
Crowley, James Patrick *hematologist, medical educator, immunologist*
DeWerth, Gordon Henry *management consultant*
Friedman, Joseph Harold *neurologist*
Glicksman, Arvin S(igmund) *radiation oncologist*
†Gordon, Harold P. *manufacturing executive*
Greenblatt, Samuel Harold *neurosurgeon*
Hassenfeld, Alan Geoffrey *consumer products company executive*
†Hendel, Maurice William *lawyer, consultant*
Kranseler, Lawrence Michael *lawyer*
†McGill, Kenneth R. *mayoral aide*
Metivier, Robert Emmett *retired mayor*
O'Neill, John T. *retired toy company executive*
Orson, Barbara Tuschner *actress*
Poses, Roy Maurice *physician, educator*
Tarpy, Eleanor Kathleen *social worker*
†Verrecchia, Alfred Joseph *consumer products company executive*

Peace Dale
Brennan, Noel-Anne Gerson *anthropologist, educator, writer*

Portsmouth
Becken, Bradford Albert *engineering executive*
Bergstrom, Albion Andrew *military officer, educator*
Levie, Howard S(idney) *lawyer, educator, writer*
Needham, Richard Lee *magazine editor*
Parker, Nancy Knowles (Mrs. Cortlandt Parker) *retired publishing executive*

Providence
Ajello, Edith H. *state legislator*
Algiere, Dennis Lee *state legislator*
Allio, Robert John *management consultant, educator*
Amaral, Joseph Ferreira *surgeon*
Anton, Thomas Julius *political science and public policy educator, consultant*
Aronson, Stanley Maynard *physician, educator*
Avery, Donald Hills *metallurgist, educator, ethnographer*
Baar, James A. *public relations and corporate communications executive, author, consultant, internet publisher, software developer*
Barnhill, James Orris *theater educator*
Barnum, William Milo *architect*
Beckmann, Martin Joseph *retired economics educator*
Bensmaia, Reda *French studies educator, researcher*
Berkelhammer, Robert Bruce *lawyer*
Besdine, Richard William *medical educator, scientist*
†Bewes, Timothy Richard Thomas *language educator*
Biron, Christine Anne *medical science educator, researcher*
†Blume, Jeffrey David *adult education educator, researcher*
†Blumstein, Sheila Ellen *former academic administrator, linguistics educator*
Boegehold, Alan Lindley *classics educator*
Bonin, Paul Joseph *real estate and banking executive*
†Bou, Enric *language educator*
Briant, Clyde Leonard *metallurgist, educator*
†Bristow, Lonnie Robert *physician*
Burns, Robert E. *bank executive*
Cady, Blake *surgical oncologist*
Calabresi, Paul *oncologist, educator, pharmacologist*
Campbell, Lewis B. *aerospace technology executive*
†Carcieri, Donald L. *governor*
Carlotti, Stephen Jon *lawyer*
Carpenter, Gene Blakely *crystallography and chemistry educator*
Ceriani, Peter John *medical association administrator*
†Cervone, Laureen Avery *educational consultant, researcher*
Chambers, Timothy Edward *philosopher, educator*
Chen, Qian *cell biologist, developmental biologist*
†Choquette, Paul Joseph, Jr., *construction company executive*
Church, Russell Miller *psychology educator*
†Conley, Patrick T. *lawyer*
Cooper, Leon N. *physicist, educator*
Cooper, Reid Franklin *geoscience and materials science educator*
Courage, Thomas Roberts *lawyer*
Curran, Joseph Patrick *lawyer*
Dafermos, Constantine Michael *applied mathematics educator*
Dahlberg, Albert Edward *biochemistry educator*
D'Andrea, Vincent Charles *postal clerk*
Davis, Philip J. *mathematician*
Davis, Robert Paul *physician, educator*
Deal, Joseph Maurice *academic administrator, art educator, photographer*
Demopulos, Harold William *lawyer*
Dempsey, Raymond Leo, Jr., *radio and television producer, moderator, writer*
Dickersin, Kay *researcher, educator*
†DiGiovanni, Christopher William *orthopedic surgeon, orthopedist*
Dobbins, Richard Andrew *engineering educator, researcher*
Donahue, John Edward *physician*
†Donovan, Bruce Elliot *classics educator, university dean*
Dowben, Robert Morris *physician, scientist*
Dujardin, Richard Charles *journalist*
Duncan, David Frank *community health specialist, educator*
Easton, J(ohn) Donald *neurologist, educator*
Elbaum, Charles *physicist, educator, researcher*
†Elfenbein, Gerald Jay *physician, educator*
Eltringham, Dana Kristin *writer*
Enteman, Willard Finley *philosophy educator*
Erikson, G(eorge) E(mil) (Erik Erikson) *anatomist, archivist, historian, educator, information specialist*
Ewing, John Harwood *mathematics educator*
Farmer, Susan Lawson *broadcasting executive, former secretary of state*
Farrell, Margaret Dawson *lawyer*
Feldman, Allan Maurice *economist*
Field, Noel Macdonald, Jr., *lawyer*
Fishman, Bernard Philip *museum director*
Fleming, Wendell Helms *mathematician, educator*
Fogarty, Charles Joseph *lieutenant governor*
Fogarty, Edward Michael *lawyer*
Forliti, Amy Marie *reporter*
Fornara, Charles William *historian, classicist, educator*
Freiberger, Walter Frederick *mathematics educator, actuarial science consultant, educator*
Frerichs, Ernest Sunley *religious studies educator*
Freund, Lambert Ben *engineering educator, researcher, consultant*
Furland, Joseph *engineering educator*
Furness, Peter John *lawyer*
Gaebe, Morris J. *academic administrator*
Gale, Edwin John *judge*
Gasbarro, Pasco, Jr., *lawyer*
Gerlach, Murney *administrator, educator, historian*
Gerritsen, Hendrik Jurjen *physics educator, researcher*
Gibbs, June Nesbitt *state legislator*
Gill, Mary Louise Glanville *educator of classics and philosophy*
Gleason, Abbott *history educator*
Glicksman, Maurice *engineering educator, former dean and provost*
Gnepp, Douglas Robbin *anatomic pathologist*
Goldberg, Maureen McKenna *state supreme court justice*
Goldstein, Joshua S *writer, educator*
Goldstein, Sidney *sociology educator, demographer*
Goodman, Elliot Raymond *political scientist, educator*
†Gordon-Seifert, Catherine Elizabeth *musicologist, educator*
Gorn, Elliott Jacob *historian, educator, writer*
Gottschalk, Walter Helbig *mathematician, educator*
Goulder, Caroljean Hempstead *retired psychologist, consultant*
Graziano, Catherine Elizabeth *state legislator, retired nursing educator*
Greene, Edward Forbes *chemistry educator*
Greer, David S. *university dean, physician, educator*
Grimaldi, Vince *artist*
Groden, Gerald *psychologist*
Grossman, Herschel I. *economics educator*
Hagopian, Jacob *federal judge*
Hamerly, Michael T. *librarian, historian*
Hamolsky, Milton William *physician*
Harman, Carole Moses *retired art educator, artist*
Hastings, Edwin H(amilton) *lawyer*
Hay, Susan Stahr Heller *museum curator*
Hazeltine, Barrett *electrical engineer, educator*
Head, James W., III, *geological sciences educator*
Heath, Dwight Braley *anthropologist, educator*
Hennessey, James Vincent *physician, educator*
Herz, Rachel Sarah *research psychologist*
Hesthaven, Jan Sickmann *mathematician, educator*
Heyman, Lawrence Murray *printmaker, painter*
Hitt, Mary Frances Lyster *environmentalist, deacon*
Holloway, Robert Ross *archaeologist, educator*
Houghton, Anthony *physics educator, research scientist*
Howes, Lorraine de Wet *fashion designer, educator*
†Hunt, Cheryl Ruth *librarian*
Hutchinson, Park William, Jr., *theatre educator*
Immonen, Gerald Matthew *artist*
Intrator, Orna *statistician, educator, health services researcher*
Israel, Kay Frank *communications educator*
Jackson, Benjamin Taylor *retired surgeon, educator, medical facility administrator*
Jackson, Ivor *endocrinologist, educator*
†Jenny, Carole *physician, researcher*
Johnson, Vahe Duncan *lawyer*
Jones, Ferdinand Taylor, Jr., *psychologist, educator*
Jones, Lauren Evans *lawyer*
Joukowsky, Artemis A. W. *private investor*
Kagan, Marilyn D. *retired architect*
Kane, Agnes Brezak *pathologist, educator*
Kane, Steven Michael *psychotherapist, educator*
†Kates, Robert William *geographer, educator*
Kean, John Vaughan *retired lawyer*
†Keough, Joseph Aloysios *judge*
Kersh, DeWitte Talmadge, Jr., *lawyer*
Khrushchev, Sergei Nikitich *engineering educator, educator*
Kim, Jaegwon *philosophy educator*
Kitzes, David Louis *cardiologist, educator*
Klyberg, Albert Thomas *historical society administrator*
Konstan, David *classics and comparative literature educator, researcher*
†Kosmider, Alexia M. *language educator*
Kraemer, Michael Frederick *lawyer*
Kramer, Ilse Elisabeth *rare book bibliographer*
Kushner, Harold Joseph *mathematics educator*
Lagueux, Ronald Rene *federal judge*
Lamond, Sharon Ann *health administrator*
Lanou, Robert Eugene, Jr., *physicist, educator*
Lederberg, Seymour Samuel *molecular biologist, educator*
Lemons, James Stanley *history educator*
Lesko, Leonard Henry *Egyptologist, educator, publisher*
Levin, Frank S. *physicist, educator*
Levin, Leonard Irving *newspaper editor*
Lewis, David Carleton *medical educator, university center director*
Licht, Richard A. *lawyer*
Lisi, Mary M. *federal judge*
†Liu, Jianhong *sociologist, educator*
†Lohrum, Frederick *bank executive*
Long, Beverly Glenn *retired lawyer*
Long, Nicholas Trott *lawyer*
†Lynch, Patrick C. *state attorney general*
Mandel, Peter Bevan *writer, columnist*
†Mandle, Earl Roger *design school president, former museum executive*
Marek, Kiersten L. *social worker*
Marsh, Donald Jay *medical school dean, medical educator*
Marsh, Robert Mortimer *sociologist, educator*
Mayer, Kenneth Hugh *physician*
McAndrew, Thomas Joseph *lawyer*
McCann, Gail Elizabeth *lawyer*
McElroy, Michael Robert *lawyer*
McIntyre, Jerry L. *lawyer*
†McMahon, John Joseph *lawyer*
McNeil, Paul Joseph, Jr., *employment security interviewer*
Medeiros, Matthew Francis *lawyer*
Mehlman, Edwin Stephen *endodontist*
Merlino, Anthony Frank *orthopedic surgeon*
Metrey, George David *social work educator, academic administrator*
Miller, G. Wayne *writer*
Monteiro, George *English educator, writer*
Monteiro, Lois Ann *medical science educator*
†Monti, Peter M. *medical educator, researcher*
†Mulvee, Robert Edward *bishop*
Murphy, Christine *medical facility administrator*
†Murphy, William J. *state legislator*
Nazarian, John *academic administrator, mathematics educator*
Needleman, Alan *mechanical engineering educator*
Nunes-Düby, Simone Edith *molecular biology researcher*
O'del, John Nicholas *educator*
Oh, William *physician*
Olsen, Hans Peter *lawyer*
Olyan, Saul Mitchell *religious studies educator*
†Orr, Marion *political scientist, educator*
†Ostiguy, Stephen W. *human resources specialist*
Pagliarini, John Raymond *public affairs executive*
†Papitto, Ralph Raymond *manufacturing company executive*
Perkins, Whitney Trow *political science educator emeritus*
Pieters, Carle McGetchin *geology educator, planetary scientist, researcher*
†Pine, Jeffrey Barry *lawyer, former state attorney general*
Pivin, Jeanette Eva *psychotherapist*
Plotz, Richard Douglas *pathologist*
†Prentiss, Richard Daniel *lawyer*
Pueschel, Siegfried M. *pediatrician, educator*
Putnam, Michael Courtney Jenkins *classics educator*
Raaflaub, Kurt Arnold *classics educator*
Ragosta, Vincent A.F. *judge*
Ratcliffe, J. Richard *lawyer*
Reid, Margaret Kathleen *literature educator*
Reilly, Charles James *lawyer, educator, accountant*
Resnik, David Alan *manufacturing company executive*
Richman, Marc Herbert *forensic engineer, educator*
Riordan, Cornelius *sociology educator, writer, consultant*
Robinson, William Philip, III, *lawyer*
Rohr, Donald Gerard *history educator*
Rosenberg, Alan Gene *newspaper editor*
Roussel, Normand Lucien *advertising executive*
Rueschemeyer, Marilyn Schattner *sociology educator*
Saint-Amand, Pierre Nemours *humanities educator*
Salter, Lester Herbert *lawyer*
†Salvadore, Guido Richard *lawyer*
Satterthwaite, Franklin Bache, Jr., *management educator, executive coach, author*
Savage, John Edmund *computer science educator, researcher*
Schevill, James Erwin *poet, playwright*
Schiff, Stephen Frank *urologic surgeon*
Schulz, Juergen *art history educator*
Selya, Bruce Marshall *federal judge*
†Shah, Samir Ashok *gastroenterologist, educator*
Shapiro, Raquel *school psychologist, educator, counselor*
Sherman, Deming Eliot *lawyer*
Shetty, Taranath *neurologist, educator*
Shu, Chi-Wang *mathematics educator, researcher*
†Silver, Paul Allen *lawyer*
Silverman, Joseph Hillel *mathematics educator*
Simmons, Ruth J. *academic administrator*
Siqueland, Einar *psychology educator*
Skowron, Gail *medical educator, researcher*
Smith, Philip A. *academic administrator*
Smith, Robert Ellis *lawyer, journalist*
Sosa, Ernest *philosopher, educator*
Spalter, Anne Morgan *artist*
Staples, Richard Farnsworth *lawyer*
Stein, Jerome Leon *economist, educator*
Steinbach, Meredith Lynn *novelist*
Stratt, Richard Mark *chemistry researcher, educator*
Stultz, Newell Maynard *retired political science educator*
Sutton, Howard G. *publishing executive*
Suuberg, Eric Michael *chemical engineering educator*
Symonds, Paul Southworth *mechanical engineering educator, researcher*
†Takao, Motoharu *physiologist*
Tauc, Jan *physics educator*
Taylor, Richard Henry *minister*
Terras, Victor *Slavic languages and comparative literature educator*
Thayer, Walter Raymond *internist*
†Tobin, Bentley *lawyer*
†Tracy, Thomas Francis, Jr., *pediatric surgeon, resarcher, educator*
Tramonti, John, Jr., *lawyer*
Trueblood, Alan Stubbs *former modern language educator*
Vezeridis, Michael Panagiotis *surgeon, educator*
Vogel, Paula Anne *playwright*
†Vorenberg, Michael *history educator*
Waite-Franzen, Ellen Jane *academic administrator*
Walker, Howard Ernest *lawyer*
Weiner, Jerome Harris *mechanical engineering educator*
Weisberger, Joseph Robert *retired judge*
†Weitberg, Alan Barry *physician, researcher*
†Whiting, Brian Christopher *hospitality consultant*
Widgoff, Mildred *physicist, educator*
Williams, Frank J. *judge, historian, writer*
Williams, Robert Raymond *obstetrician and gynecologist*
Wolston, Jon *psychiatrist*
Wood, Craig Breckinridge *paleobiologist, natural science educator*
Wood, Gordon Stewart *historian, educator*
Wunderlich, Alfred Leon *artist, art educator*
†Yena, John A. *academic administrator*
Younkin, Richard Ambrose *state official, air quality specialist*
Zavada, Michael Stephen *plant science educator*

Rumford
†Irons, William V. *state legislator*

Saunderstown
Donovan, Gerald Alton *retired academic administrator, former university dean*
Knauss, John Atkinson *former federal agency administrator, oceanographer, educator, former university dean*
Leavitt, Thomas Whittlesey *retired museum director, educator*

Scituate
Gorham, Bradford *lawyer*

Smithfield
Kosowski, Mary *artist, educator*
Litoff, Judy Barrett *history educator*
Morahan-Martin, Janet May *psychologist, educator*

South Kingstown
Pembrook, Richard Charles *internist, cardiologist*

Wakefield
†Boothroyd, Geoffrey *industrial and manufacturing engineering educator*
Coffin, Tristram Potter *retired English educator, writer*
Fera, Steven Raymond *internist, cardiologist, educator*
Hart, Kenneth Nelson *lawyer*
Leete, William White *artist*
Mason, Scott MacGregor *entrepreneur, inventor, consultant*
Moore, George Emerson, Jr., *geologist, educator*
†Morrison, Fred Beverly *real estate consultant*
Newman, Philip Robert *psychologist*
Phipps, Lynne Bryan *interior architect, educator, minister*
Rothschild, Donald Phillip *lawyer, arbitrator*
Wyman, James Vernon *newspaper executive*

Warwick
Baffoni, Frank Anthony *biomedical engineer, consultant, internist*
Banick, Cheryl R. *librarian*
Berube, Richard Henry *electrical engineering educator, consultant*
Charette, Sharon Juliette *library administrator*
Darlington, David Alan *government relations professional*
Galamaga, Donald Peter *health and mental health systems consultant*
Halperson, Michael Allen *publishing executive*
Hamilton, Andrew David *publishing company executive, writer*
Izzi, John *educator, author*
Jennings, Julianne *cultural organization administrator*
Knowles, Charles Timothy *lawyer, state legislator, military officer, educator*
Lac, Ming Q. *Information technology and electronics executive*
Palumbo, Edward Paul *real estate appraiser, writer*
Patchis, Pauline *handwriting expert, consultant*
†Penza, Joseph Fulvio, Jr., *lawyer*
Revens, John Cosgrove, Jr., *state legislator, lawyer*
Ribezzo, John Steven *business administration educator, accountant*
†Riffkin, Mitchell Sanford *lawyer*
†Sarkissian, Karry Rafael *translator, educator*
Worthington, Samuel Andrew *social welfare administrator*

West Greenwich
†Duggan, John David, Jr., *computer technician*

West Kingston
Haring, Howard Jack *newsletter editor*
Storm, Carlyle Bell *chemist*

West Warwick
Bottella, Tammy Ann *lawyer*
Lancellotta, John Jerry-Louis *foundation administrator*
Pollock, Bruce Gerald *lawyer*

Westerly
Bachmann, William Thompson *dermatologist*
Christy, Nicholas Pierson *physician*
Dauphinais, Richard Murray *pathologist*
Gillie, R. Bruce *internist*
Hindle, Marguerita Cecelia *textile chemist, consultant*

Wood River Junction
Carlson-Pickering, Jane *gifted education educator*

Woonsocket
Altongy, Gilbert Joseph *physician*
Eno, Paul Frederick *editor, writer*
Koutsogiane, Phillip Charles *lawyer*
†Lankowsky, Zenon P. *lawyer*
†Roszkowski, Joseph John *lawyer*
Ryan, Thomas M. *drug store chain executive*
St. Godard, Edward G. *Roman Catholic priest*
Stubbs, Donald Clark *secondary education educator*

SOUTH CAROLINA

Abbeville
Cellura, A(ngele) Raymond *psychologist*

Aiken
Alan, Matthew W. A. *lawyer*
Amabile, John Louis *lawyer*
Dickson, Paul Wesley, Jr., *physicist*
Ely, Duncan Cairnes *non profit/human services executive, civic leader*
Felkel, Charlene Campbell *family nurse practitioner, nursing educator*
Heyl, Guy Carlisle, Jr., *orthopedic surgeon*
Hootman, Harry Edward *retired nuclear engineer, consultant*
†Isaacs-Bright, Susan Virginia Kirkpatrick *research librarian, public speaker, advocate*
Li, Rao *mathematician, computer scientist*
Madory, James Richard *hospital administrator, former air force officer*
Marine, Andrew Craig *lawyer*
Murphy, Edward Thomas *engineering executive*
†Nagnur, Shreedhar M. *internist, medical researcher*
†Naifeh, Steven Woodward *writer*
Pearce, Richard Lee *lawyer*
Rudnick, Irene Krugman *lawyer, former state legislator, educator*
Salter, David Wyatt *secondary school educator*
Silton, Ronald Helmut *electrical engineer*
Smith, Gregory White *writer*
Voss, Terence J. *human factors scientist, educator*
Zirps, George Thomas *marine engineer, consultant*

Anderson
Abercrombie, Stoney Alton *family physician, educator*
†Atang, Christopher *humanities educator*
Bailey, Jake Schultz *volunteer, retired electrical engineer*
Caperton, Richard Walton *photographer, automobile repair company executive, educator, consultant*
Chipman, Dennis Clarence, Jr., *psychiatrist*
George-Lepkowski, Sue Ann *retired echocardiographic technologist*
Graham, Tony Randall *anesthesiologist*
Martin, Terrell Owen *retired university administrator*
Meador, Valerie Lane *clinical dietitian*
Pruitt, Rosanne Harkey *nursing educator, human services researcher*
†Rhoe, Wilhelmina Robinson *retired science educator*
Rich, Linvil Gene *civil engineering educator*
Sustar, T. David *religious organization administrator*
Vallo, Victor William, Jr. *military officer, music educator*
Whitaker, Evans Parker *academic administrator*
Wisler, Darla Lee *pastor*
†Woodall, Hunter Earl *physician, educator*

Andrews
Pittman, Joey Jay *music educator*

Barnwell
Miller, Elizabeth Jane *secondary education educator*
Nichols, M(arian) Theresa *radio station executive*

Beaufort
Chambers, Henry Carroll *realty broker*
Cross, Harold Dick *physician*
†Fielder, William James, III, *electrical engineer, consultant*
Flannagan, Roy Catesby, Jr., *English literature educator, editor*
Harvey, William Brantley, Jr., *lawyer, former lieutenant governor*
Horn, Lois Burley *pianist, educator*
†Moussatos, Martha Ann Tyree *librarian*
Pinkerton, Robert Bruce *mechanical engineer*
Raines, Karen Cornell *secondary education educator*
Shaw, Danny Wayne *educational consultant, musician*

Bennettsville
Kinney, William Light, Jr., *newspaper editor, publisher*

Bishopville
Cox, Janson L. *museum administrator*
†Jennings, Jacob Hill *lawyer, director*

Blackstock
King, Robert Thomas *editor, freelance writer*

Bluffton
Brown, Dallas Coverdale, Jr., *retired army officer, retired history educator*
†Cann, Sharon Lee *retired health science librarian*
Pendley, William Tyler *naval officer, international relations educator*
Reuben, Alvin Bernard *communications and entertainment executive*

Blythewood
Daniels, James Douglas *retired academic administrator*
Falcone, Anthony *mechanical engineer*

Camden
Buckley, Claude Langford *artist*
Chapman, Robert Foster *judge*
Daniels, John Hancock *agricultural products company executive*
Jacobs, Rolly Warren *judge*
†Sindler, Allan Jay *chemical engineer, sculptor, educator*

Cayce
McElveen, William Lindsay *broadcasting executive, lecturer*
Paynter, Vesta Lucas *pharmacist*
Sheldon, Jeffrey Andrew *social sciences researcher*

Central
†Holcombe, Joseph Steven *academic administrator, educator*
Jalili, Nader *mechanical engineer, educator*
Smith-Cox, Elizabeth Shelton *art educator*

Chapin
Branham, Mack Carison, Jr., *retired theological seminary educator, minister*
Freitag, Carol Wilma *state official, political scientist*
McNinch, Michel Cottingham *artist, educator*
†Mills, James H. *music educator*
Pettit, James Robert *computer programmer*

Charleston
Adelson, Gloria Ann *financial executive*
†Agrest, Emmanuil M. *mathematician, physicist, educator*
An, Yuehui Huey *orthopaedic surgeon, educator*
Appleget, Terri Lynn *elementary education educator*
Bailey, Dawn Marie *fund raising systems consultant*
†Barboza, Sandra Livingston *language educator*
Barrett, Michael Baker *historian, educator*
Basler, Thomas G. *librarian, administrator, educator*
Bell, Norman Howard *physician, endocrinologist, educator*
Bolin, Edmund Mike *electrical engineer, franchise engineering consultant*
†Bonds, John Bledsoe *musician, educator*
Bowman, C. Michael *physician*
Bowman, Daniel Oliver *psychologist*
†Bradley, Scott M. *surgeon*
Branham, C. Michael *lawyer*
Brown, Ann Catherine *investment company executive*
Brown, Carroll Smith *anesthesiologist*
Cannon, Hugh *lawyer*
Cantwell, Don *artistic director*
Carek, Donald J(ohn) *child psychiatry educator*
Carter, James Folger *obstetrician-gynecologist, educator, consultant*
Chambers, Joe Carroll *physician, consultant, educator*
Chapman, Howard Reed *city and county transportation engineer, consultant*
Chen, Mei-Qin *mathematics educator*
Cheng, Kenneth Tat-Chiu *pharmacy educator*
†Chiaramida, Salvatore *cardiologist, educator, health facility administrator*
Clawson, Harry Quintard Moore *retired business executive*
Coleman, Dorothy Zipper *retired educational administrator*
Crossley, Gary Exley *organization executive*
Daniell, Herman Burch *pharmacologist*
Delli Colli, Humbert Thomas *chemist, product development specialist*
De Wolff, Louis *management consultant*
Dobson, Richard Lawrence *dermatologist, educator*
Donehue, John Douglas *interdenominational ministries executive*
Dowell, Richard Patrick *technology company executive*
Edwards, Darrell *orchestra executive*
Farr, Charles Sims *lawyer*
Ferguson, Esther B. *philanthropist*
†Forsythe, Dennis M. *biology educator*
Franklin, Paul Deane *financial services executive, investor*
Freer, Robert Elliott, Jr., *lawyer*
†Fricano, Scott D. *counselor*
Gaillard, John Palmer, Jr., *former government official, former mayor*
Garro, Susan Ann *adult nurse practitioner*
Gay, Frances Marion Welborn *private school educator*
Geentiens, Gaston Petrus, Jr., *former construction management consultant company executive*
Goff, R. Garey *architect*
Good, Joseph Cole, Jr., *lawyer*
Greenberg, Raymond Seth *academic administrator, educator*
Grinalds, John Southy *military officer, academic administrator*
Groves, Stephen Peterson, Sr., *lawyer*
Grush, Owen Charles *psychiatry educator*
Gunn, Morey Walker, Jr., *secondary education educator, choir director, organist*
Haines, Stephen John *neurological surgeon*
Harding, Enoch, Jr., *clothing executive*
Hawkins, Falcon Black, Jr., *federal judge*
Helms, William Collier, III, *lawyer*
Henson, Kenneth Tyrone *education educator*
†Herbert, Teri Lynn *librarian*
Hines, Judith Albergotti *social worker, management consultant*
Hittner, James Bryant *psychologist, educator*
Hoffman, Brenda Joyce *gastroenterology educator*
Hollis, Bruce Warren *experimental nutritionist, industrial consultant*
Huang, Peng *statistician*
†Huang, Peng *science educator*
Hughes, Blake *retired architectural institute administrator, publisher*
†Hughston, Thomas Leslie, Jr., *lawyer*
Infinger, Gloria Altman *retired nursing administrator*
Jacobs, Walter Darnell *political scientist, educator*
†Jaffa, Ayad A. *medical educator, medical researcher*
Jaffe, Murray Sherwood *retired surgeon*
Jenrette, Joseph Malphus, III, *radiation oncologist*
Johnson, Dewey E(dward), Jr., *dentist*
Kahn, Ellis Irvin *lawyer*
Kaplan, Allen P. *physician, educator, researcher*
Key, Janice Dixon *physician, medical educator*
Killeen, Therese *therapist*
Kimmel, Herbert David *psychology educator*
Kitner, Harold *artist, educator*
†Kitner, Kathi R. *anthropologist*
Lader, Philip *lawyer, government official, diplomat, business executive, university president*
Lally, Margaret Mates *English educator, poet*
Langdale, Emory Lawrence *retired physician*
Langley, Lynne Spencer *newspaper editor, columnist*
Lavelle, Mary Lee Demetre *psychiatric nursing educator*
Leonard, Mary Eileen *retired medical technologist, educator*
Limehouse, Harry Bancroft, Jr., *real estate developer, transportation consultant*
Lovinger, Sophie Lehner *child psychologist*
Lutz, Myron Howard *obstetrician, gynecologist, surgeon, educator*
Mahoney, John Joseph *business executive, educator*
Maize, John Christopher *dermatology educator*
Margolius, Harry Stephen *pharmacologist, physician*
Maricq, Hildegard Rand *physician, researcher*
Martin, Roblee Boettcher *retired cement manufacturing executive*
Mayfield, Ronald Keith *endocrinologist, educator*
McCurdy, Layton *medical educator*
Means, Robert Taylor, Jr., *hematologist, educator*
Mohr, Lawrence Charles *physician*
Moore, William Vincent *political science educator*
Morris, Valerie Bonita *performing arts administrator*
O'Bryant-Seabrook, Marlene Loretta Linton *retired educator*
†Ogretmen, Besim *science educator, molecular biologist, researcher*
Oldham, John Michael *physician, psychiatrist, educator*
Osguthorpe, John David *otolaryngologist, educator*
Osteen, Louis *chef*
Othersen, Henry Biemann, Jr., *pediatric surgeon, physician, educator*
Patrick, Charles William, Jr., *lawyer*
Perry, Evelyn Reis *communications company executive*
Prewitt, William Chandler *finance company executive*
†Quinn, E. Moore *adult education educator, researcher, consultant*
Ray, Swapan Kumar *molecular biologist*
Reed, Stanley Foster *editor, author, publisher, lecturer*
Reuben, Adrian *clinician, researcher, medical educator*
Reves, Joseph Gerald *dean, anesthesiology educator*
Rhea, Marcia Chandler *accountant*
Robinson, Neil Cibley, Jr., *lawyer*
Roof, Betty Sams *internist*
Rustin, Rudolph Byrd, III, *surgeon, educator*
Sade, Robert Miles *physician, bioethicist, educator*
Salmon, Edward Lloyd, Jr., *bishop*
Sanders, Tence Lee Walker *elementary education educator*
†Saul, J. Philip *pediatrician, educator*
Schreadley, Richard Lee *writer, retired newspaper editor*
Schuman, Stanley Harold *epidemiologist, educator*
Sharpe, Kathryn Moye *psychologist*
Simson, Jo Anne *retired anatomy and cell biology educator, biologist, educator*
Sloan, Mark Hamilton *art gallery director, educator, author*
Smedley, Charles Vincent *sociology educator*
Spitz, Hugo Max *retired lawyer*
†Strange, Charlton Bell, III, *internal medicine educator*
Stuart, Robert Kenneth *internist, oncologist, hematologist, educator*
Suggars, Candice Louise *special education educator*
Sutusky, John Charles *higher education educator*
Tarleton, Larry Wilson *editor*
†Thomas, Emory M. *history educator*
Thompson, W(ilmer) Leigh *pharmaceutical company executive, physician, pharmacologist*
Tilley, Barbara *statistician, consultant*
†Uflacker, Renan *radiologist, researcher*
Underwood, Paul Benjamin *gynecologist, educator*
Waggoner, Robert *chef*
Waller, John Louis *anesthesiology educator*
†Warrick, Kenneth Ray *dermatologist, cosmetic surgeon*
Watts, Claudius Elmer, III, *retired military officer*
Willi, Steven Matthew *physician, educator, researcher*
Williams, Barbara Stambaugh *editor*
Wilson, Frederick Allen *medical educator, medical center administrator, gastroenterologist*
Worthington, Ward Curtis, Jr., *university dean, anatomy educator*
Young, Roger M. *judge*
†Yu, Shan Ping *neuroscientist, educator*

Chesnee
†Saunders, J. Farrell *historic site director*

Chester
†Ryan, John Joseph *physician*

Chesterfield
Shields-Cassidy, Gloria Ann *adult education educator, poet*

Clemson
Amirkhanian, Serji N. *civil engineering educator*
Bailey, Beatrice Naff *researcher and educator in English*
Beyerlein, Adolph Louis *retired chemist, educator*
Boykin, Joseph Floyd, Jr., *librarian*
†Brawley, Joel Vincent *mathematician, educator*
†Cawthon, Tony W. *social sciences educator*
Clayton, Donald Delbert *astrophysicist, nuclear physicist, educator*
Cox, Headley Morris, Jr., *lawyer, educator*
Davies, Brian Ewart *environmental sciences educator*
Denham, Bryan Errol *communications educator*
†Felder, Frankie Ottowiess *academic administrator*
Golan, Lawrence Peter *mechanical engineering educator, energy researcher*
Goodwin, James Gordon, Jr., *engineering educator, consultant, researcher*
Grady, C.P. Leslie, Jr., *engineering educator*
Grant, H. Roger *history educator*
Halfacre, Robert Gordon *ombudsman,landscape architect, horticulturist, educator*
†Harrell, William Rodney *electronics engineer*
†Hickman, James J. *research scientist, educator*
†Juang, Charng Hsein *adult education educator*
Kelly, John William, Jr., *university administrator*
†Kimmel, Robert Michael *education educator, consultant*
†Kostreva, Michael Martin *mathematics educator*
Krause, Lois Ruth Breur *chemistry educator*
Leonard, Michæl Steven *industrial engineering educator*

Melton, Gary Bentley *psychology and law educator*
Mino, Michael George *engineering executive*
Morrissey, Lee *literature educator*
Nilson, Linda Burzotta *academic administrator*
Paul, Frank Waters *mechanical engineer, educator, consultant*
Petzel, Florence Eloise *textiles educator*
Pursley, Michael Bader *electrical engineering educator, communications systems research and consulting*
†Sluss, Dorothy Louise *education educator, researcher*
Straka, Thomas James *forester, educator*
Underwood, Richard Allen *English language educator*
Vogel, Henry Elliott *retired university dean and physics educator*
Vyavahare, Narendra R. *biomedical researcher, educator*
Williamson, Robert Elmore *engineering educator*
Xu, Xiao-Bang *engineering educator*
Zumbrunnen, David Arnold *mechanical engineering and materials science educator, consultant*

Cleveland
†Balent, Andrew *composer, musician*

Clinton
Cornelson, George Henry, IV, *retired textile company executive*
Griffith, John Vincent *academic official*
†Meeks, Mary Janice *librarian*
†Stokes, James Porter, II, *music educator*

Clover
Easter, Jr., Willie *artist, writer*
Kirsh, Herb *state legislator*

Columbia
†Adams, John Hurst *bishop*
Adcock, David Filmore *radiologist, educator*
Aelion, C. Marjorie *adult education educator*
Akhavi, Shahrough *educator*
Almond, Carl Herman *surgeon, physician, educator*
Amidon, Roger Lyman *retired health administration educator*
Arvay, Nancy Joan *lawyer*
Ashley, Perry Jonathan *journalism educator*
Averyt, Gayle Owen *retired insurance executive*
Babcock, Keith Moss *lawyer*
Badders, Rebecca Susanne *military officer, educator, writer*
Baird, Davis W. *philosophy educator*
†Ballington, Don Avell *medical educator*
Barnum, William Douglas *retired communications company executive*
Baskin, C. R. *retired civil engineer, physical scientist*
†Bauer, R. Andre *lieutenant governor*
†Bell, Isaac, Jr., *music educator*
†Bellon, Michael Kenneth *director, music educator*
Bernstein, Barry Joel *lawyer*
Blanton, Hoover Clarence *lawyer*
Boggs, Jack Aaron *banker, publisher, municipal government official*
†Bowman, Ned David *medical administrator*
Breedin, Berryman Brent *journalist, public relations, historian, consultant*
Briggs, Ward Wright *classics educator*
Bristow, Thomas Cole, Jr., *social work educator*
Bristow, Walter James, Jr., *retired judge*
Brockelsby, Jeffrey Lind *investment executive*
Brooker, Jeff Zeigler *cardiologist*
Bruccoli, Matthew Joseph *English educator, publisher*
Bryan, Charles Stone *internal medicine educator*
†Bryant, Douglas E. *public health service official*
Buchanan, William Jennings *lawyer, judge*
Bueno, Otavio Augusto *philosopher, educator*
Burnett, E. C., III, *state supreme court justice*
Carpenter, Charles Elford, Jr., *lawyer*
Chernoff, Marvin *advertising executive*
Clark, David Randolph *food distributor*
Cleveland, Elbin L. *theatre design and technology educator*
Cohn, Elchanan *economics educator*
Conrad, Paul Ernest *transportation consultant*
Cooper, Robert Gordon *lawyer*
Corey, David Thomas *invertebrate zoology specialist*
†Cotty, William Frank (Bill Cotty) *lawyer, state legislator*
Courson, John Edward *state legislator, insurance company executive*
†Cross, Joseph Russell, Jr., *law librarian*
Crystal, Nathan Maxwell *law educator, consultant*
†Cuffe, Steven Paul *psychiatrist*
da Silva, Ercio Mario *physician*
Davis, Keith Eugene *psychologist, educator, consultant*
†Dawson, Katon *political organization administrator*
Day, Richard Earl *lawyer, educator*
Donald, Alexander Grant *psychiatrist, educator*
†Douglas, Samuel Osler *musician, educator*
Duffie, Virgil Whatley, Jr., *retired state agency administrator*
Duggan, Carol Cook *research director*
Duggan, Kevin *information technology professional*
Eastman, Caroline Merriam *computer science and engineering educator*
Edgar, Walter Bellingrath *historian, educator*
Edge, Ronald Dovaston *physics educator*
Edwards, James Benjamin *accountant, educator*
†Ehrhardt, Margaret Wright *retired librarian*
Elkins, Toni Marcus *artist, art association administrator*
Ettel, Zita Moak *nursing administrator, food services executive*
Farber, Emmanuel *pathology and biochemistry educator*
Faulkner, Larry R. *dean, educator, researcher, writer*
Feldman, Daniel Charles *adult education educator*
†Felix, Robert Louis *law educator*
†Fields, Harriet Gardin *counselor, educator, consultant*
Finkel, Gerald Michael *lawyer*
Flanagan, Clyde Harvey, Jr., *psychiatrist, psychoanalyst, educator*
Fowler, Linda McKeever *hospital administrator, management educator*
†Fox, Alvin None *bacteriology educator, researcher*
Fried, Morris Louis *retired humanities educator*
Friedman, Myles Ivan *education educator*
Gadala-Maria, Francis Arturo *chemical engineering educator*
Garde, Anand Madhav *materials scientist*
Gasque, Harrison (Allard Harrison Gasque) *optical supply company executive*
Geckle, George Leo, III, *retired English language educator*
Gibbes, William Holman *lawyer*
Gibbons, Joseph Harrison *engineering educator, farmer*
Ginsberg, Leon Herman *social work educator*
Gore, David Curtiss *investor*
†Graulty, Robert Thomas *engineer, consultant*
†Gray, Elizabeth Van Doren *lawyer*
Griffin, Mary Frances *retired library media consultant*
Grimball, Caroline Gordon *retail sales professional*
†Halford, Raymond Gaines *lawyer*
Hamilton, Clyde Henry *judge*
Handel, Richard Craig *lawyer*
Hansen, Harold John (Harry Hansen) *artist, educator*
†Hansen, William Frank *hydrologist*
Harpootlian, Richard Ara *lawyer*
Harvin, Charles Alexander, III, *state legislator, lawyer*
†Headrick, John David *music educator*
Heiney, Sue Porter *psychosocial oncology nurse*
Helsley, Alexia Jones *archivist*
Hollis, Charles Eugene, Jr., *savings and loan association executive*
Horger, Edgar Olin, III, *obstetrics and gynecology educator*
Howard-Hill, Trevor Howard *English language educator*
Hughes, Austin Leland *biological sciences educator*
Hultstrand, Charles John *architect*
Humphries, John O'Neal *physician, educator, university dean*
Hwang, Te-Long *neurologist, educator*
†Ingram, Jonathan Hall *music educator*
Inkley, Scott Russell, Jr., *state agency administrator*
Ivester, Joy Godshall *educational administrator*
†Jesselson, Robert *musician, educator*
Johnson, James Bek, Jr., *library director*
Jones, Donald Lee *religious studies educator*
Jones, Hartwell Kelley, Jr., *lawyer*
Kennedy, Richard McKinne, III, *anesthesiologist*
†Khushf, George Peter *bioethicist*
Kiker, Billy Frazier *economics educator*
†Kosko, George Carter *judge*
†Land, John Calhoun, III, *lawyer, state legislator*
†Leaman, Clifford Lynn *saxophone educator*
Leaphart, Ashley Regan *pharmacist*
Leatherman, Hugh Kenneth, Sr., *state legislator, business executive*
Lester, Ken Harrison *lawyer*
Lett, Mark *editor*
Leventis, George Chris *lawyer*
†Lewis, Ernest Crosby *lawyer*
Lin, Tu *endocrinologist, educator, researcher, academic administrator*
Linyard, Samuel Edward Goldsmith *retired civil engineer*
Littlefield, Daniel Curtis *historian, educator, researcher*
Logan, Sandra Jean *retired economics and business educator*
Long, Eugene Thomas, III, *philosophy educator, administrator*
Long, Robert Glendon *pediatrician*
†Lowery, John Wesley *education educator*
Luna, Gene Irving *academic administrator, education educator*
Luoma, Gary A. *accounting educator*
Mack, Francis Marion *lawyer, engineer*
Markovsky, Barry Neil *sociology educator*
Martin, Robert William *econometrician*
Matthews, Steve Allen *lawyer*
†Mazur, Marjorie Akers *retired librarian*
†McConnell, Glenn F. *state legislator, lawyer, art gallery executive*
McCullough, Ralph Clayton, II, *lawyer, educator*
†McGill, Jennifer Houser *non-profit association administrator*
McLeod, Walton James *lawyer, state legislator*
McMaster, Henry Dargan *state attorney general*
McQuillan, Barbara Glatz *paralegal*
Meriwether, James Babcock *retired English language educator*
Metropol, Harry Jack *general and thoracic surgeon*
Monahan, Thomas Paul *accountant*
Morris, John Allen, Jr., *state government administrator, educator*
Morrison, Stephen George *lawyer*
Mott, Frederick B., Jr., *publishing executive*
Murray, George William *university president*
Nagpal, Madan Lal *biochemist, educator, researcher*
Newton, Rhonwen Leonard *writer, microcomputer consultant*
Nexsen, Julian Jacobs *lawyer*
Norman, George Buford, Jr., *foreign language educator*
†Olenchak, Frank Richard *music educator, musician*
†Oswald, Billy Robertson *lawyer*
Outin, Mary Louise *business, multi-cultural history and geneology educator*
†Painter, Samuel Franklin *lawyer*
Palms, John Michael *academic administrator, physicist*
Pansegrau, Phaedra Renée *lawyer*
Paulson-Crawford, Carol *conservator, educator*
†Peck, Edward T., Jr., *historian, educator, real estate agent*
Petty, Donna Matthews *middle school educator*
Pickens, Randi Ellen *social worker*
†Pollard, William Albert *lawyer*
Powell, Donald Ashmore *clinical research psychologist*
Powell, J(ohn) Key *estate planner, consultant*
†Power, James Tracy *historian*
Pritchett, Samuel Travis *finance and insurance educator, researcher, consultant*
Profeta, Salvatore, Jr., *chemist*
Quinn, Michael William *public affairs educator*
Rabb, Gael Caution *mental health consultant*
Ramsey, Bonnie Jeanne *mental health facility administrator, psychiatrist*
Rawlinson, Helen Ann *librarian*
Reid, Claude G. *engineer, consultant*
Ringer, Keith William *state education professional, consultant*
Rippeteau, Bruce Estes *archaeologist, administrator*
Robinson, Robert Earl *chemical company executive*
Rouse, LeGrand Ariail, II, *retired lawyer, educator*
Rowland, Thomas C., Jr., *obstetrician, gynecologist*
Sanford, Marshall (Mark Sanford) *governor, former congressman*
Schwarz, Fred *lawyer, ophthalmic plastic surgeon*
Scotti, Anthony John, Jr., *historian, educator*
Secor, Donald Terry, Jr., *geologist, educator*
Shafer, John Milton *hydrologist, consultant, software developer*
Shatalov, Maxim S. *electrical engineer, researcher*
†Shearer, Ellen Marie *music educator*
†Shedd, Dennis W. *federal judge*
Sheftman, Howard Stephen *lawyer*
Sheppe, Joseph Andrew *surgeon*
Shmunes, Edward *dermatologist*
Silver, Rick *marketing professional*
Sloan, Saundra Jennings *real estate company executive*
†Smith, Mark Michael *historian, educator*
Smith, W. Thomas, Jr., *author, journalist*
†Songer, Donald Raymond *political science educator*
Sorensen, Andrew Aaron *university president*
Sproat, John Gerald *historian, educator*
Starr, Harvey *political scientist, educator*
Starrett, William *dancer, artistic director*
Still, Charles Neal *neurologist, consultant*
Strom, J. Preston, Jr., *lawyer*
Strong, Franklin Wallace, Jr., *lawyer*
†Summer, Munson *music educator*
Sumwalt, Robert Llewellyn, Jr., *retired construction company executive*
Swerling, Jack Bruce *lawyer*
†Swinton, David Holmes *academic administrator*
Synnott, Marcia Graham *history educator*
Tate, Harold Simmons, Jr., *lawyer*
Tetreault, Donald Richard *education educator*
Thompson, Charles Otis *lighting designer*
†Thornhill, Joshua Taylor, IV, *psychiatrist, academic administrator*
†Timmerman, William B. *utilities company financial executive*
Toal, Jean Hoefer *state supreme court chief justice*
†Todd, Albert Creswell, III, *lawyer*
Toombs, Kenneth Eldridge *librarian*
†Tripathi, Ramesh Chandra *ophthalmologist, researcher, educator*
Tunstall, Dorothy Fiebrich *early childhood educator*
Turk, John Cobb *architect, educator*
†Vidal, Jose *science educator*
†Voris, John Charles *pharmacy educator*
Waites, Candy Yaghjian *former state official*
Walling, Linda Lucas *librarian, educator*
Warren, Charles David *library administrator*
Watabe, Norimitsu *biology and marine science educator*
†Weidner, John Walter *chemical engineer, educator*
White, Ralph Edward *chemical engineer, educator*
Wilder, Ronald Parker *economics educator*
Wilkins, David Horton *state legislator*
Willis, Paul Allen *librarian*
Wilson, Karen Wilkerson *paralegal*
Witherspoon, Walter Pennington, Jr., *orthodontist, philanthropist*
Wood, Oliver Gillan, Jr., *economist, educator*
Wright, Harry Hercules *psychiatrist*
Yarborough, Clinton Joseph *lawyer*
Young, Robert *lawyer*
Zaepfel, Glenn P. *psychologist*
Zheng, Deyi *physician*
Zimmerman, Nancy Picciano *library science educator*

Conway
Delia, Claude William *retired physician, pathologist*
†Dozier, Etrulid Pressley *school librarian*
Henderson, James David *history educator*
Johnson-Leeson, Charleen Ann *former elementary school educator, insurance agent, insurance consultant, regional executive assistant*
Martin, Gregory Keith *lawyer, mayor*
Nale, Julia Ann *nursing educator*
†Nale, Robert D. *finance educator*
†Rauhut, Nils Christian *philosopher, educator*
Shaw, M. Beatryce *retired publishing executive, writer*
Squatriglia, Robert William *university dean, educator*
Stanley, Covia LeVance *physician, clergyman*
Suggs, Michael Edward *lawyer*
Wiseman, Dennis Gene *academic administrator*

Cowpens
†Bishop, Alan Douglas *music educator*

Darlington
Bischoff, Frederick Christopher, III, *retired accountant*
Isgett, John *auto dealership executive*

Denmark
Dolezal, Dale Francis *truck manufacturing company executive*

Dillon
Chandler, Marcia Shaw Barnard *farmer*

Due West
Carlock, John Bruce, Jr., *English educator*
Koonts, Jones Calvin *retired education educator*
Warren, John Floyd *music educator*

Easley
Cole, Lois Lorraine *retired elementary school educator*
Failing, George Edgar *editor, clergyman, educator*
McLaughlin, Bruce Duane *materials scientist*
Spearman, David Hagood *veterinarian*
Spearman, Patsy Cordle *real estate broker*

Eastover
†Jones, Shirley Green *librarian*

Edgefield
Gambrell, Olin Eric, III, *municipal official*

Edisto Island
Cannon, David C. *mechanical engineer, consultant*
Van Metre, Margaret Cheryl *artistic director, dance educator*

Elgin
Ladmer, William Edward *food product engineering executive*
Peake, Frank *middle school educator*

Florence
Baroody, Albert Joseph, Jr., *pastoral counselor*
Carter, Luther Fredrick *university president*
†Fitzkee, Thomas L. *education educator*
Havens, Timothy John *physicist*
Imbeau, Stephen Alan *allergist*
Jones, Michael Stuart *music educator*
†Kaufman, Victor Scott *historian, educator*
Rutherford, Vicky Lynn *special education educator*

Fort Jackson
†Brinsfield, John Wesley *military officer, educator*

Fort Mill
†Bowles, Crandall Close *textiles executive*
Park, John *finance, investment consultant*
Prud'homme, Albert Fredric *securities company executive, financial planner*

Gaffney
†Howie, Henry S., III, *social worker, educator*
Suttle, Helen Jayson *retired education educator*
Sweeney, Christopher Robert *music educator, researcher*
Wheeler, William Earl *general surgeon*

Gaston
†Taylor-Mcbride, Briggette *surgical technologist, writer*

Georgetown
Bowen, William Augustus *financial consultant*
McGrath, James Charles, III, *financial services company executive, lawyer, consultant*
Moore, Albert Cunningham *lawyer, insurance company executive*
Robinson, Betty Hefner *artist*
Sprinkle, Ralph Stephen *podiatrist*

Gilbert
McGill, Cathy Broome *gifted and talented education educator*

Goose Creek
Floss, Mark Thaddeus *civil engineer, computer scientist*

Graniteville
Learnard, James Michael *middle school educator, former finance company executive, special education educator*

Gray Court
†West, Jack *art dealer*

Green Pond
Ittleson, H(enry) Anthony *foundation executive*

Greenville
†Abrams, Douglas Carl *social studies educator*
Alford, Robert Wilfrid, Jr., *elementary school educator*
Algary, Ruth Wilkins *community volunteer*
Bauknight, Clarence Brock *consultant*
Bell, Robert Daniel *religious studies educator*
Bonner, Jack Wilbur, III, *psychiatrist, educator, administrator*
Boone, William Rogers *health facility administrator, educator, researcher*
Callahan, Ralph Wilson, Jr., *advertising agency executive*
Cargill, Paula Marie *social worker, gerontologist*
Christophillis, Constantine S. *lawyer*
†Coates, William Alexander *lawyer*

†Cochran, Kathy Holcombe *music educator, conductor*
Cowan, John Joseph *retired lawyer*
Crawford, William David *real estate broker, consultant*
Cureton, Claudette Hazel Chapman *biology educator*
DeLoache, William Redding *pediatrician*
Dobson, Robert Albertus, III, *lawyer, executive, volunteer*
Dreskin, Erving Arthur *pathologist, educator*
Edwards, Harry LaFoy *lawyer*
Eskew, Rhea Taliaferro *newspaper publisher*
Ferguson, Donald Littlefield *lawyer*
Fitzgerald, Eugene Francis *management consultant*
Foulke, Edwin Gerhart, Jr., *lawyer*
Gerretsen, Gilbert Wynand (Gil Gerretsen) *marketing mentor*
Goforth, Augustus Johnson, III, *physician*
Henderson, Alan Scott *humanities educator*
Hendrix, Susan Clelia Derrick *civic worker*
Hill, Grace Lucile Garrison *education educator, consultant*
Hipp, William Hayne *broadcast executive*
Horton, James Wright *retired lawyer*
†Hutson, Melvin Robert *lawyer*
†Inglis, Robert D. (Bob Inglis) *former congressman, lawyer*
†Jones, Bob, III, *academic administrator*
Kilgore, Donald Gibson, Jr., *pathologist*
Klasing, John Christoph *manufacturing executive*
†Lynch, J. Timothy *lawyer*
Manly, Sarah Letitia *retired state legislator, ophthalmic photographer, angiographer*
Mann, James Robert *former congressman*
†Massey, Raymond David *lawyer*
†Matzko, John Austin *historian*
Mauldin, John Inglis *public defender*
Maynard, George Fleming, III, *philanthropic consultant*
†McArthur, William Duncan, Jr., *English language educator*
McCune, Linda Williams *artist, educator*
McKinney, Ronald W. *lawyer*
†Myers, Daniel Thomas *educational consultant, consultant, writer*
Omidvar, Bijan *structural engineer, researcher*
Oxner, Glenn Ruckman *financial executive*
Phillips, Joseph Brantley, Jr., *lawyer*
Plumstead, William Charles *quality engineer, consultant*
Purtle, Jeffery Allan *music educator*
Riley, Richard Wilson *lawyer, federal official*
Rogers, Jon Martin *financial consultant, financial company executive*
†Shi, David E. *academic administrator, historian*
Shockley, Milton M., Jr., *real estate brokerage executive*
Simmons, David Jeffrey *real estate executive*
Smith, Philip Daniel *academic administrator, education educator*
Smythe, Thomas Ira, Jr., *finance educator, researcher*
Tchivzhel, Edvard *music director*
Tenney, William Frank *pediatrician*
Todd, John Dickerson, Jr., *retired lawyer*
Townes, Bobby Joe *travel agency executive*
Traxler, William Byrd, Jr., *federal judge*
Trevillian, Wallace Dabney *economics educator, retired dean*
Varin, Roger Robert *textile executive*
Walters, Johnnie McKeiver *lawyer*
Wang, Ming De *engineer*
Westrope, Martha Randolph *psychologist, consultant*
Whittle, Mack Ira, Jr., *banking executive*
Wilkins, William Walter *federal judge*
Wyche, Cyril Thomas *lawyer*
Wyche, Madison Baker, III, *lawyer*

Greenwood
Boxx, Rita McCord *banker*
†Collins, Julianne Shea *research scientist*
Hunton, Richard Edwin *family practice physician*
Jackson, Larry Artope *retired college president*
Moore, James E. *state supreme court justice*
Nexsen, Julian Jacobs, Jr., *lawyer*
†Self, W. M. *textile company executive*
Williams, Sylvester Emanual, III, *educator, consultant*

Greer
Gregg, Marie Byrd *retired farmer*
Taylor, Carter W. *aviation educator, consultant, lecturer*
Vaught, Richard Loren *urologist*

Hardeeville
Kadar, Karin Patricia *librarian*

Hartsville
Menius, Espie Flynn, Jr., *electrical engineer*

Hemingway
†Chandler, William Henry *lawyer*

Hilton Head Island
Adams, William Hensley *ecologist, educator*
Becker, Karl Martin *lawyer*
Berry, Loren Curtis *retired lawyer, consultant*
Birk, Robert Eugene *retired physician, educator*
Bogart, Keith Charles *retired neurologist*
Brown, Arthur Edmon, Jr., *retired army officer*
†Bruun, Per Moller *civil engineer, consultant*
Carpenter, William G. *chemist, consultant*
Cunningham, William Henry *retired food products executive*
†Donohoe, James Day *lawyer*
Duvall, Charles Patton *retired internist, oncologist*
Engelman, Karl *physician*
Estrin, Deborah Perry *human resources executive*
Field, James Bernard *internist, educator*
Finn, Chester Evans *retired lawyer*
Fleischman, Kathryn Agnes *secondary education educator*
Gruchacz, Robert S. *real estate executive*
Gui, James Edmund *architect*
Hagoort, Thomas Henry *lawyer*
Hardin, Bryan David *occupational safety and health specialist*
Harty, James D. *former manufacturing company executive*
Hewes, Robert Charles *radiologist*
Hirsch, Carl Herbert *retired manufacturing company executive*
Huckins, Harold Aaron *chemical engineer*
Humphrey, Edward William *surgeon, medical educator*
Kearney-Nunnery, Rose *nursing administrator, educator, consultant*
†Kimbell, David Lawrence *music educator*
Knox, John, Jr., *philosopher, educator*
Lauer, Clinton Dillman *automotive executive*
Lefer, Allan Mark *physiologist*
Lewis, Gene Evans *retired medical equipment company executive*
Lindner, Joseph, Jr., *physician, medical administrator*
Little, Thomas Mayer *public relations executive*
Love, Richard Emerson *retired equipment manufacturing company executive*
Male, Roy Raymond *English language educator*
McKay, John Judson, Jr., *lawyer*
McKeldin, William Evans *management consultant*
Mersereau, Hiram Stipe *wood products company consultant*
Patton, Joseph Donald, Jr., *management consultant*
Pritchard, Dalton Harold *retired electronics research engineer*
Reed, Frances Boogher *writer, actress*
Rose, William Shepard, Jr., *lawyer*
Rulis, Raymond Joseph *manufacturing company executive, consultant*
Russell, Allen Stevenson *retired aluminum company executive*
Scott, Kerrigan Davis *private investor, philanthropist*
Scovel, Mary Alice *retired music therapy educator*
†Shaheen, Jack George *communications educator*
Shea, Gerald Patrick *engineering executive*
Shepard, Steven Louis *graphic artist, painter*
Simpson, John Wistar *energy consultant, former manufacturing company executive*
Slachta, Gregory Andrew *urologist*
Smith, Paul David *electrical engineer, administrator*
Wallace, Arthur, Jr., *retired college dean*
Wesselmann, Glenn Allen *retired hospital executive*
†West, John Carl *lawyer, former ambassador, former governor*
Windman, Arnold Lewis *retired mechanical engineer*
Woodrum, Robert Lee *executive search consultant*

Hopkins
Garrett, Robin Scott *public information officer*

Inman
Fudenberg, Hugh *neuroimmunologist, educator*

Irmo
Brown, Leonard Ashleigh (Smokey), Jr., *lawyer*

Isle Of Palms
Elliott, Larry Paul *cardiac radiologist, educator*
Lorince, L(ois) Margaret *music educator*

Iva
Gentry, Margaret Burton *retired elementary school teacher*

Jenkinsville
Loignon, Gerald Arthur, Jr., *nuclear engineer*

Johns Island
Behnke, Wallace Blanchard, Jr., *consultant, engineer, retired utility executive*
Cameron, Thomas William Lane *investment company executive*
†Carter, Mary Andrews *paralegal*
Norton, Norman James *retired exploration geologist, educator*
Richbart, Carolyn Mae *mathematics educator*
Schenck, Benjamin Robinson *insurance consultant*

Johnston
†McKinney, Steven Dallas *music educator*

Kershaw
Mackey, Margaret Emmie *library media specialist*

Kiawah Island
Coyle, Martin Adolphus, Jr., *lawyer, consultant*
Neuman, Robert Henry *lawyer*
Reed, Rex Raymond *retired telephone company executive*
Warren, Russell Glen *academic administrator*
Zurio, Eugene John *pharmaceutical executive*

Ladson
Cannon, Major Tom *special education educator*

Ladys Island
Yates, Linda Snow *financial services marketing executive, real estate*

Lake Wylie
Sanford, James Kenneth *public relations executive*

Lancaster
Bundy, Charles Alan *foundation executive*
Carnes, Laura *financial analyst*
Carter, Richard Bonner *application developer*
Garris, William Ralph *criminal justice educator*
†Hassell, Darris Anthony *Spanish educator*
Wozniak, Robert *physician*

Langley
Bell, Robert Morrall *lawyer*

Laurens
Chandler, Margaret McNeill *home economist, educator*
Cooper, William Copeland *public library director*
Sheppard, Anne Thomson *retired secondary school educator*
Williams-Tims, Lillie Althea *distribution administrator, genealogist, preservationist, tax specialist*

Leesville
Covington, Tammie Warren *elementary education educator*
Crumley, James Robert, Jr., *retired clergyman*

Lexington
†Blind, Joy Bailey *women's health nurse*
†Gatch, Jerald V. *music educator*
Holland, Gene Grigsby (Scottie Holland) *artist*
†Kennedy, Sandra Elaine *small business owner*
Morris, Earle Elias, Jr., *retired state official, business executive*
Resch, Mary Louise *town agency administrator*

Little River
Ehrlich, John Gunther *writer*
Green, Beverly Jean *nurse*
Sarvis, Elaine Magann *retired assistant principal*

Marion
Inabinet, Lawrence Elliott *retired pharmacist*
Kirkpatrick, Donald Robert *secondary school educator*
Waller, John Henry, Jr., *state supreme court justice*

Mauldin
†Looper-Wilson, Leah Marie *human resources specialist, controller, interior designer*
†Martin, Sharon D. *automotive executive*
Wood, Myra Linden Frank *consultant*

Mc Cormick
Clayton, Verna Lewis *retired state legislator*
Hofer, Ingrid *artist, educator*
Zeller, Michael James *psychologist, educator*

Meggett
†Stoots, Leigh Henderson *music educator*

Moore
Parris, Michael Lynn *academic administrator*

Mount Pleasant
Abbott-Lyon, Frances Dowdle *journalist, civic worker*
Ayres, Paul Erdman *artist*
Falkowski, Edward J. *executive consultant, business coach*
Gilbert, James Eastham *academic administrator*
Hill, Larkin Payne *real estate company data processing executive*
Lupo, David Emory *computer scientist*
Macdonald, Robert Rigg, Jr., *retired museum director*
McConnell, John William, Jr., *lawyer*
Mixon, Janet Sandhoff *physical education educator*
Thordarson, William *retired hydrogeologist*

Murrells Inlet
Howard, Joan Alice *artist*
Justice, Franklin Pierce, Jr., *oil company executive*
Kelly, Gerald Wayne *chemical coatings company executive*
Schumaker, William Thomas *retired insurance company executive*
Washburn, John Lee *music educator*

Myrtle Beach
Atkinson, Harold Witherspoon *utilities consultant, real estate broker*
Breen, David Hart *lawyer*
Fowler, Marilyn S. Atlas *social worker*
Harwell, David Walker *retired state supreme court chief justice*
Nirenstein, Jack *writer*
†Rice, Hugh Thompson, Jr., *tax lawyer*

Newberry
Lander, James Albert *retired military officer, comptroller*
†O'Shea, Michael Joseph *humanities educator*
†Partridge, William Franklin, Jr., *lawyer*

North Augusta
McRee, John Browning, Jr., *physician*

North Charleston
Fei, James Robert *engineering executive, consultant*
Laddaga, Lawrence Alexander *lawyer*
Mintzer, Jacobo E. *physician, researcher*
Reilly, David Henry *university dean*
†Spitler, John Robert *music educator, musician*
Zucker, Jerry *chemical manufacturing executive*

North Myrtle Beach
Damerst, William *English and humanities educator*

Orangeburg
Andrews, Fran Wolfe *medical educator*
†Bozinovski, Stevo *computer science educator, researcher*
†Bullard-Dillard, Rebecca *biochemist, educator*
Byers, Keith Thomas *librarian, educator*
Caldwell, Rossie Juanita Brower *retired library service educator*
Champy, William, Jr., *mathematician, educator, researcher, scientist, writer, biologist, chemist, inventor, physicist*
Creekmore, Verity Veirs *media specialist*
Finney, Ernest Adolphus, Jr., *retired state supreme court chief justice*
Graule, Raymond (Siegfried) *metallurgical engineer*
Hare, Ester Rose *physician*
†Harrold, Stanley *historian, educator*
Hill, Howard Darnell *educator, university administrator*
Hong, Jae-Dong *industrial engineering educator*
Johnson, Alex Claudius *English language educator*
Kalapathy, Uruthira Pasupathy *food scientist, researcher*
Kent, Harry Ross *construction executive, lay worker*
†McIver, Barbara Basore *language educator*
Onunkwo, Emmanuel Nwafor *economics educator*
Robinson, Ruth Hubbard *retired elementary school educator*
Sims, Edward Howell *editor, publisher*
Smoak, Randolph Duncan, Jr., *surgeon*
†Vincent, Elaine Sistare *academic administrator, psychologist, educator*
†Viswanath, Guttalu Ramachandra Rao *mathematics educator, consultant, researcher*

Pacolet
Dineen, Joseph Lawrence *legal compliance professional, consultant*

Pawleys Island
Alexander, William D., III, *civil engineer, consultant, former army air force officer*
Gromults, Joseph Michael, Jr., *internist*
Grubb, William Francis Xavier *consumer software executive, marketing executive*
Hannan, Robert Emmet *business development consultant*
Hudson-Young, Jane Smither *investor*
Kay, Thomas Oliver *agricultural consultant*
Noble, Joseph Veach *fine arts administrator*
Proefrock, Carl Kenneth *academic medical administrator*
Tarbox, Gurdon Lucius, Jr., *retired museum executive*

Pendleton
Fehler, Polly Diane *neonatal nurse, educator*
†Marshall, Gerald Lee *mathematician, educator*
Spain, James Dorris, Jr., *biochemist, educator*

Pickens
†White, Leeanne J. *music educator*

Piedmont
Davis, Robert Barry *technician, religious studies educator*
Winter-Neighbors, Gwen Carole *art and special education educator, consultant*

Prosperity
Hause, Edith Collins *college administrator*
Jennings, Wirt Holman, Jr., *retired marketing executive*
Long, William McMurray *physiology educator*

Richburg
Cox, Kevin Monterey *school administrator*

Ridgeland
Gardner, James *recreational management executive*

Rock Hill
†Abdel-Aal, Hisham A *adult education educator*
†Bessinger, Raymond Carlton *dietician, educator*
Bristow, Robert O'Neil *writer, educator*
Collins, Francis Winfield *chemicals executive*
†Dickert, Lewis, Jr. H. *music educator, musician*
Hardin, James Carlisle, III, *lawyer, educator*
Herring, Mark Youngblood *librarian, university dean*
Lynch, Fran Jackie *investment advisory company executive*
†Pantuosco, Louis J., Jr., *economist, educator*
Wishert, Jo Ann Chappell *music educator, elementary and secondary education educator*

Saint Helena Island
Dunn, Adolphus William *orthopedic surgeon*

Salem
†Darnell, William Headen *chemical engineer, medical/surgical nurse, nursing educator*
Everett, C(harles) Curtis *retired lawyer*

Seneca
Clausen, Hugh Joseph *retired army officer*
Curry, Mary Earle Lowry *poet*
Fairleigh, Marlane Paxson *retired management educator*
Grant, Martha F. *social worker*
Oppenheimer, Nancy Bea *artist*
Uden, David Elliott *cardiologist, educator*

Shaw A F B
†Cameron, Hugh C. *career officer*

Simpsonville
Furrow, John Mayo *secondary school educator*
Gilstrap, Leah Ann *media specialist*
Hamilton, Martha Jean Anderson *media specialist*
Kanzler, George *journalist, critic*
†Maguire, D. E. *electronics executive*
Seaman, Duncan Campbell *civil engineer*

Spartanburg
Allen, Robert Watson *retired textile company executive*
Anderson, Frank J(ohn) *retired librarian*
Anthony, Kenneth C., Jr., *lawyer*

Bolton, Calvin *music educator*
Browning, Kathryn Whelchel *psychiatric nurse, corporate compliance officer*
Bullard, John Moore *religion educator, church musician*
Codespoti, Daniel Joseph *computer science educator*
Deku, Afrikadzata *international, French, English and Afrikan-centric Continental Afrikan scholar, researcher, publisher, writer, educator*
Dent, Frederick Baily *former mill executive, former ambassador, former secretary of commerce*
Doyle, Sharon Thomas *school system administrator*
Fields, Ricky Edward *counselor*
Glassick, Charles Etzweiler *academic foundation administrator*
Gray, Gwen Cash *real estate broker*
Gray, Nancy Ann Oliver *college administrator*
Hilton, Theodore Craig *computer scientist, Internet company executive*
Jones, William Osborne, II, *physician assistant*
Kay, Charles D. *philosophy educator*
Kuhn, Hans Heinrich *retired chemist*
†Lefebvre, John Charles *medical educator, researcher*
Leonard, Walter Raymond *retired biology educator*
Lucktenberg, Jerrie Cadek *music educator*
Mahanes, Michael Wayne *organizational development executive*
McAbee, Thomas Allen *psychologist*
McDaniel, Thomas Robb *academic administrator, educator*
McGehee, Larry Thomas *university administrator*
Milliken, Roger *textile company executive*
†Norrell, Thomas H. *minister, educator*
Parmley, Richard Turner *pediatric hematologist, oncologist*
†Pate, John Gillis, Jr., *financial consultant, accounting educator*
Reid, Alliston King *psychology educator, researcher*
Richards, Marty Grover *university foundation director*
†Robbins, Malcolm Scott *composer, education educator*
†Smith, William Douglas *lawyer*
Smithey, Pamela *consultant, organist, freelance accompanist*
Stephens, Bobby Gene *college administrator, consultant*
Stewart, James Charles, II, *insurance agent*
Valainis, Gregory Thomas *physician*
†Wallace, Robin Evan *musicologist, educator*
Wise, Steven Lanier *lawyer, clergyman*

Spring Island
Hardin, James Neal *German and comparative literature educator, publisher*

Sullivans Island
Robb, Nathaniel Heyward, Jr., *retired remote sensing company executive*
Romaine, Henry Simmons *investment consultant*

Summerville
Bukala, Phyllis *social worker*
†Capps, Phillip Lewis *music educator*
Christie, Joseph Francis *city planner*
Diamond, Michael Shawn *science and math educator, computer consultant*
Holler, Adlai Cornwell, Jr., *minister*
†O'Brien, Doris J. *librarian*
Reisman, Rosemary Moody Canfield *writer, humanities educator*
Sexton, Donald Lee *retired business administration educator*
Shakibanasab, Lauren Vorwerk *music director, educator*

Sumter
Blair, Charlie Lewis *elementary school educator*
Gagne, Armand Joseph, Jr., *business administration and computer science educator, consultant*
Justus, Adalu *writer, designer*
Kellum, Donald Arthur *military officer*
Kolb, Wade S., Jr., *lawyer*
Moore, Verna *county official*
Van Bulck, Hendrikus Eugenius *accountant*
van Bulck, Margaret West *accountant, financial planner, educator*

Surfside Beach
Edwards, George Henry *retired aeronautical engineer*
Favaro, Mary Kaye Asperheim (Mrs. Biagino Philip Favaro) *pediatrician, writer*
Turner, Gloria Townsend Burke *social services association executive*

Swansea
Inabinet, George Walker, Jr., *retired state agency administrator*

Tamassee
Martof, Mary Taylor *retired nursing educator*

Taylors
†Erwin, Joseph Arnold *political organization worker, advertising executive, creative director*
†Riddle, Thad (Tad) W., III, *music educator, webmaster*
Smith, Morton Howison *religious organization administrator, educator*
Vaughn, John Carroll *minister, educator*

Timmonsville
McDonald, Robert Irving *secondary education mathematics educator*

Townville
Wright, George Cullen *electronics company executive*

Walhalla
†Andrus, Susan Joyce *librarian*

Walterboro
†Cone, George Wallis *lawyer*
Meshach, Joseph Robert *music educator*

Wedgefield
McLaurin, Hugh McFaddin, III, *military officer, historian consultant*

West Columbia
Byars, Merlene Hutto *accountant, visual artist, writer, publisher*
Carter, Saralee Lessman *immunologist, microbiologist*
Jedziniak, Lee Peter *lawyer, educator, insurance company officer*
Klutzow, Friedrich Wilhelm *neuropathologist*
Moxon, Barbara Wischan *volunteer*

West Union
Klutz, Anthony Aloysius, Jr., *health, safety and environmental manager*

Westminster
Duncan, Gwendolyn McCurry *elementary education educator*

White Rock
Aull, James Stroud *retired bishop*

Williamston
Alewine, James William *financial executive*

Winnsboro
McCants, Clyde Taft *retired clergyman*
McMaster, Mary Rice *civic worker*

Woodruff
Childers, Bob Eugene *educational association executive*

Yemassee
Olendorf, William Carr, Jr., *small business owner*

York
Blackwell, Paul Eugene, Sr., *army officer*
Clinch, Nicholas *assistant principal*

SOUTH DAKOTA

Aberdeen
Eldredge, Robert John *social services administrator, psychologist*
Geier, Constance B. *education educator*
Hedges, Mark Stephen *clinical psychologist*
Hollingsworth, John Arthur *business educator*
†Houge, Timothy Todd *education educator*
Johnson, Edna Scott *English language educator, volunteer*
†Manhart, Grant Lee *music educator*
Markanda, Raj Kumar *mathematics educator*
†Matta, William B. *language educator*
Omland, Jacqueline Leigh-Knute *secondary school educator, small business owner*
Pesicka, Harlene Neave *mental health services professional*
Ruud, Jay Wesley *dean*
Stoia, Viorel G. *life underwriter*
Tebben, Sharon Lee *education educator*
†Wieland, William John *music educator, composer*

Black Hawk
Maicki, G. Carol *former state senator, consultant*

Brandon
Hunt, Roger *former state legislator*

Britton
Farrar, Frank Leroy *lawyer, former governor*

Brookings
Brandt, Linda Ann *social worker*
†Brown, Arnold M. *state legislator*
Burge, Steven Donald *city administrator*
†Crowe, Don Raymond *music educator, consultant*
Duffey, George Henry *physics educator*
Evans, David Allan *English educator*
†Funchion, Michael F. *historian, educator*
Gilbert, Howard Alden *economics educator*
Graper, Mary Caspers *librarian*
Iverson, John Wilfred *educator*
Landau, Elvita Ann *library director*
Lundeen, Ardelle Anne *retired economist*
Marquardt, Steve Robert *library director*
McClure-Bibby, Mary Anne *former state legislator*
Melby, Paul Elliott *electrical engineer*
Miller, Peggy Gordon Elliott *university president*
Ryder, Mary Ruth *English language educator*
Tolle, Gordon J. *political science educator*
†Williams, Elizabeth Evenson *writer*

Buffalo Gap
Pengra, Lilah *anthropologist, consultant*

Canton
Kaufman, Angela J. *music educator*
Perkinson, Robert Ronald *psychologist, consultant*

Crazy Horse
Ziolkowski, Ruth *foundation administrator, postmistress*

Dakota Dunes
†Peterson, Robert L. *meat processing executive*
Purves, Sherrill J. *retired neurologist*

Deadwood
Johns, Timothy Robert *judge*

Elk Point
Chicoine, Roland Alvin *farmer, former state legislator*

Fort Pierre
†Poches, Charles, Jr., *lawyer*

Freeman
Roussos, Stephen Bernard *minister*

Gregory
†Johnson, Charles Rick *lawyer*

Hermosa
Schirber, James Emmanuel *retired physicist*

Herreld
†Schumacher, Michelle Kelly *music educator*

Howard
Hattervig, Robin Lynn *dentist*

Huron
Clatworthy, Catherine Lynn *educational trainer, graphics designer*
Saylor, Howard Leroy, Jr., *retired surgeon*

Kadoka
Stout, Maye Alma *educator*

Keystone
Wagner, Mary Kathryn *sociology educator, former state legislator*

Kyle
Davies Silcott, Loma Geyer *freelance writer, English educator*

Lennox
Brendtro, Larry Kay *psychologist*

Madison
Talley, Daniel Alfred *economics educator*
Tunheim, Jerald Arden *academic administrator, physics educator*

Marion
†Nielson, Helen M. *music educator*

Martin
Kampfe, Nancy Lee *communications educator*

Miller
Morford, JoAnn (JoAnn Morford-Burg) *state senator, investment company executive*

Mitchell
Almjeld, Paul F. *conductor, music educator*
Widman, Paul Joseph *insurance agent*

Mobridge
Hall, Jo(sephine) Marian *newspaper editor, photographer*

Mud Butte
Ingalls, Marie Cecelie *former state legislator, retail executive*

Philip
†Grossenburg, John Anthony *minister*

Pierre
Collins-Adler, Catherine Kay *social services professional*
†Daugaard, Dennis M. *lieutenant governor*
†Diedtrich, Elmer *state legislator*
†Eichstadt, Craig Martin *lawyer*
†Frederick, Randall Davis *political organization administrator, state legislator*
Fulton, Neil *lawyer*
†Gerdes, David Alan *lawyer*
Gilbertson, David *state supreme court justice*
Johnson, Julie Marie *lawyer, lobbyist, judge*
Konenkamp, John K. *state supreme court justice*
†Long, Larry *state attorney general*
Miller, Robert Arthur *former state supreme court chief justice*
Miller, Suzanne Marie *state librarian*
Olson, Judith Mary Reedy *retired public information officer, former state senator*
Pederson, Gordon Roy *state legislator, retired military officer*
Perry, Robert Tad *educational official*
†Repsys, Andrew J. *aquatic biologist, limnologist, water quality specialist, environmental biologist*
Sabers, Richard Wayne *state supreme court justice*
†Thompson, Charles Murray *lawyer*
†Weyer, Dianne Sue *health facility administrator*
Zinter, Steven L. *state supreme court justice*

Platte
Pennington, Beverly Melcher *financial services company executive*

Rapid City
Clark, Lynda Kay *entrepreneur*
†Collins, Rey *financial analyst*
Corwin, Bert Clark *optometrist*
Eccarius, Scott *state official, eye surgeon*
Foye, Thomas Harold *lawyer*
Hagg, Rexford A. *lawyer, former state legislatorr*
Hamilton, Douglas Warren *real estate executive*
Hillard, Carole *former lieutenant governor*
Hughes, Stella Platt *sociology educator*
Hughes, William Lewis *former university official, electrical engineer*
Johnson, William Jennings *marketing consultant, entrepreneur*
Lebrun, Gene N. *lawyer*
Lien, Bruce Hawkins *minerals and oil company executive*
Olson, James Warren *lawyer*
Prodan, John *aviation executive*
Ramakrishnan, Venkataswamy *civil engineer, educator*
Rogers, Deborah S. *human biology educator, writer*
Schleusener, Richard August *college president*
Scofield, Gordon Lloyd *mechanical engineer, educator*
†Shultz, Donald Richard *lawyer*
Squillace, Paul J *hydrologist, researcher*
†Stuck, Haven Laurence *lawyer*
Sykora, Harold James *military officer*
Thatcher, Anna Marie *lawyer, law educator*
Van Nuys, Frank *historian, educator*

Rosebud
†MacKichan, Margaret Anna *artist, art educator*

Saint Lawrence
Lockner, Vera Joanne *farmer, rancher, legislator*

Selby
Akre, Donald J. *school system administrator*

Sioux Falls
Aldern, Robert Judson *architectural, liturgical and landscape artist*
Balcer, Charles Louis *college president emeritus, educator*
Bennett, Thomas *orchestra executive*
Carlson, Robert James *bishop*
Carlson Aronson, Marilyn A. *English language and education educator*
Carpenter, Paul Lynn *cardiologist*
Christensen, David Allen *manufacturing company executive*
Cowles, Ronald Eugene *church administrator*
DeGeus, Wendell Ray *photographer*
Dertien, James LeRoy *librarian*
Engen, Lee Emerson *retired savings and loan executive*
Fenton, Lawrence Jules *pediatric educator*
Flohr, Charles E. *radiologist*
Garson, Arnold Hugh *publishing executive*
Haas, Joseph Alan *court administrator, lawyer*
Hattervig, Karen Ann *lawyer*
†Hayes, Robert E. *lawyer*
†Herman, Charles Wendell *history educator*
†Hicks, Patrick *writer, educator*
†Howard, Cynthia *lawyer, county official*
Huseboe, Arthur Robert *American literature educator*
Jaqua, Richard Allen *pathologist*
Johnson, Richard Arlo *lawyer*
†Johnson, Thomas Jerald *lawyer*
Justman, Dick Joseph *public works administrator*
Kilian, Thomas Randolph *rural economic developer, consultant*
Koepsell, Pamela Ann *nursing educator*
†Luce, Michael Leigh *lawyer*
Marshall, Mark F. *lawyer*
†Masters, Lee *broadcast executive*
†McDowell, Robert James *music educator, composer*
McMillin, Joan Austin *social worker*
Mikesell, Janice Harlan *writer, poet, photographer*
Nygaard, Lance Corey *nurse, data processing consultant*
Olson, Gary Duane *history educator*
Paisley, Keith Watkins *former state senator, retired small business owner*
Peters, John Henry *artist*
Piersol, Lawrence L. *federal judge*
Reynolds, Leo Thomas *electronics company executive*
Richards, LaClaire Lissetta Jones (Mrs. George A. Richards) *social worker*
Rosenthal, Joel *manufacturing executive*
Rossing, David Robert *internist*
Rossing, William Osmund *healthcare administrator*
Severson, Glen Arthur *circuit court judge*
Smit, Paula Francine *research scientist*
Smith, Murray Thomas *transportation company executive*
Staggers, Kermit LeMoyne, II, *history and political science educator, state legislator, municipal official*
Talley, Robert Cochran *medical school dean and administrator, cardiologist*
Thompson, Harry Floyd, II, *research collections and book publications director*
Thompson, Ronelle Kay Hildebrandt *library director*
Trujillo, Angelina *endocrinologist*
VanDemark, Michelle Volin *critical care, neuroscience nurse*
Van Pelt, Frances Evelyn *management consultant*
Viste, Arlen Ellard *chemistry educator*
Vogt, Harry Bruce *physician*
Wegner, Karl Heinrich *physician, educator*
Wegner, Mary Josephine *civic volunteer, farmer*
†Wilkes, Jeffrey Blaine *real estate appraiser*
Wollman, Roger Leland *federal judge*
Zawada, Edward Thaddeus, Jr., *physician, educator*
†Zinz, David Albert *humanities educator*

Spearfish
Erickson, Richard Ames *physicist, emeritus educator*
Hood, Earl James *lawyer, state legislator*
Termes, A. Dick *artist*
Thie, Genevieve Ann Robinson *retired secondary school educator*
Wishard, Della Mae *former newspaper editor*

Vermillion
Carlson, Loren Merle *political science educator*
Clem, Alan Leland *political scientist, educator*
Dahlin, Donald C(lifford) *academic administrator*
†Davidson, John Henry *legal educator*
Gasque, Thomas James *retired English educator*
†Haddad, Emily Anne *literature educator*
†Lio, Yuhlong *mathematician, educator*
Wang, X. T. (Xiaotian Wang) *psychologist, educator*

Volga
Moldenhauer, William Calvin *soil scientist*

Volin
Aiello, Frank John *music educator*

Wagner
Szabo, Andras *internist*

Watertown
Hanson, Dorene Kay *engineering draftsman*
Niemann, Jody Marie *occupational therapist*
Witcher, Gary Royal *minister, educator*

Yankton
Crandall, Terrence Lee *counseling administrator*
Ferris, Alan Russel *psychology educator*
Foster, James Caldwell *academic dean, historian*
Heubaum, William Lincoln *retired lawyer*
†Ostergaard, David Arne *mechanical engineer*

TENNESSEE

Alamo
Finch, Evelyn Vorise *financial planner*

Alcoa
Dunlap, Bill *municipal administrator*
Lucas, Melinda Ann *pediatrician, educator*
†Lyon, Terri L. *industrial and organizational psychologist*

Antioch
Ely, Joe *singer, songwriter*
Worthington, Melvin Leroy *minister, writer*

Arnold AFB
Davis, John William *government science and engineering executive*

Athens
Brown, Sandra Lee *art association administrator, watercolorist*
†Dannel, James Micheal *voice educator*
†Higgins, Kenneth Dyke *lawyer*

Bartlett
Huffman, Delton Cleon, Jr., *pharmacy association executive*

Big Sandy
Chastain, Kenneth Duane *retired foreign language educator*
Hancock, Sandra Olivia *secondary school educator, elementary school educator*

Blaine
Bull, James C. *poet*

Bluff City
Vaughn, JoAnn Wolfe *family nurse practitioner*

Brentwood
Flanagan, Van Kent *journalist*
Goodwin, William Dean *consulting company executive*
Jordan, Robert Andrew *accountant*
LeBlanc, Larry Joseph *management educator*
Lodowski, Charles Alan *business association executive*
Martin, William Edwin *business executive, lawyer, government official*
McClary, Jim Marston *accounting executive, consultant*
Mc Creary, James Franklin *lawyer, mediator*
Orr, Frank Howard, III, *architect*
Provine, John Calhoun *retired lawyer*
Raskin, Edwin Berner *real estate executive*
Schreiber, Kurt Gilbert *lawyer*
Smith, Wayne Thomas *healthcare company executive*
Stephens, Shirley Lynne *writer, editor*
White, Michael James *healthcare facilities administrator*

Brighton
Iles, Roger Dean *business educator*

Bristol
Allerton, Jeffrey Paul *oncologist*
Anderson, Jack Oland *retired college official*
†Flannagan, William Patrick *music educator*
Gaines, John Strother *retired educator, writer, municipal official*
Hardin, Gerald Larson *city planner and community developer, educator*
Hill, Kenneth Clyde *clergyman*
Macione, Kyle Pritchett *pharmaceutical company executive, lawyer*

Broomfield
†Scott, John Atwood, Jr., *hypnoanalyst, psychologist, marriage and family therapist*

Brownsville
Kalin, Robert *retired mathematics educator*

Camden
Burchum, Jacqueline Rosenjack *family nurse practitioner*
Carter, Tamera Lynnette *clinical nurse specialist*
†Jasper, Doris J. Berry *nurse*

Chapel Hill
Christman, Luther Parmalee *retired dean, dean, consultant*

Chattanooga
Akers, Samuel Lee *lawyer*
†Banasiak, Mayme Kay Hampton *mathematician, educator*
Barker, William M. *state supreme court justice*
Bartoo, Eugene Chester *academic administrator, educator*
Bernhardt, Robert *music director, conductor*
†Bowen, Maurice Richard, Jr., *lawyer, director*
Bryan, Rosemarie Luise *lawyer*
Butler, David Alfred *music educator*
Callahan, North *author, educator*
Campbell, Paul, III, *lawyer*
Campbell, William Buford, Jr., *materials engineer, chemist, forensic consultant*
†Campbell, William O'Neal *retired physician*
Carden, Zachary Frank, Jr., *dentist*
Clapp, David Foster *library administrator*
Clark, Jeff Ray *economist*
Cofer, Joseph Broaddus *surgeon*
Cooper, Gary Allan *lawyer*
†Dawson, Gail Alesia *management educator*
Derthick, Alan Wendell *architect, architectural firm executive*
Drennon-Gala, Donney Thomas *sociologist, educational consultant, writer*
Duckworth, Jerrell James *electrical engineer*
Edgar, R(obert) Allan *federal judge*
Enriquez, Manuel Hipolito *physician*
Foster, Edwin Powell, Jr., *educator, structural engineer*
Fouquet, Anne (Judy Fuqua) *musician, music educator*
Franks, Herschel Pickens *judge*
†Gearhiser, Charles Josef *lawyer*
Gould, Mary Christa *small business owner*
Guo, Zibin *medical anthropologist*
†Haden, Benjamin *minister, retired publishing executive, broadcast executive*
Harman, William P. *religious studies educator*
Hays, Melissa Padgett *lawyer*
Helton, Thomas Oswald *lawyer*
Hensley, Marble John, Sr., *civil engineer, consultant*
Holmberg, Albert William, Jr., *retired publishing company executive*
†Holmes, Everlena McDonald *health science administrator, consultant, retired dean*
†Jessup, William Eugene *lawyer*
Johnson, Joseph Erle *mathematician*
†Kennedy, Daniel *mathematics educator*
Lutgen, Robert Raymond *newspaper editor*
Maloney, J. Patrick *minister, educator, seminary administrator*
Martin, Chester Y. *sculptor, painter*
Matherley, Steve Allen *cost accountant*
McNeill-Murray, Joan Reagin *volunteer consultant*
†Melvin, Terry Ann *physician, director*
Meyer, Roger Arnold *management consultant, writer*
Mills, Olan, II, *photography company executive*
Mohney, Nell Webb *religion educator, speaker, author*
Moore, Hugh Jacob, Jr., *lawyer*
Morgan, John Ronald *pediatric cardiologist*
†Morris, Buckner Stuart *lawyer*
Obear, Frederick Woods *academic administrator*
Parker, Christine Wright *medical director*
Piatt, Albert Earl *educator, researcher, consultant*
Powers, John Y. *federal judge*
†Proctor, John Franklin *lawyer*
Quinn, Patrick *tranportation executive*
Rabin, Alan A. *economics educator*
Ragan, Charles Oliver, Jr., *lawyer*
Ragon, Robert Ronald *clergyman*
Riggs, Claudesta Lavern *professional storyteller*
†Royer, William A. *language educator*
†Russell, Lynn Mawk *actuary*
Sachsman, David Bernard *communications educator*
†Sacks, Richard *electrical engineer*
St. Goar, Herbert *retired food corporation executive*
Scott, Mark Alden *hospital network executive*
†Secrest, Rose Marie *writer*
Steinhoff, Anthony James *European history educator*
Swanger, Daniel Anthony-Ignatius *artist*
Thow, George Bruce *surgeon*
Tracy, Carol Cousins *association executive, former educator*
†Tsai, Sin-Hsing *musician, music educator*
Vital, Patricia Best *lawyer*
Walker, Robert Kirk *lawyer*
†Ward, James Arthur, III, *educator*
Weinmann, Judy Munger *nurse*
†Wilkes, Gary S. *music educator*
†Williams, Rosemary Helen *paralegal*
†Willimon, William Parker *academic administrator*
Wilson, Richard Lee *political science educator*
†Winham, Richard Paul *radio director, English and communications educator*
Young, Sonia Winer *public relations director, educator*

Clarksville
†Baldwin, Kathryn Leigh *psychologist, educator, consultant*
Hester, Bruce Edward *library media specialist, lay worker*
Love, Michael Joseph *lawyer*
Reaves, Barry Reco *minister*
†Schutz, Gregory John *academic administrator*
†Stoddard, Peter Hawkins *education educator, consultant*

Cleveland
Breuer, William Bentley *writer*
†Garren, Sanford M. *secondary school educator*
Knight, Sandra Norton *civil engineer*
Lewis, Charlton Scott *civil engineer*
Lockhart, Madge Clements *educational organization executive*
Metallo, Thomas Joseph *international studies and political science educator*
Miles, Doris Cooper *bank executive*
†Preston, Forrest L. *health care executive*
Rhodes, Arthur Delano *benefits administrator*
Suttles, David Clyde *educator*
Taylor, William Al *church administrator*
Watson, S. Michele *school nurse*

Clinton
Birdwell, James Edwin, Jr., *retired banker*
Hutchens, Gail R. *chemist*
Seib, Billie McGhee Rushing *nursing administrator, consultant*
Tyndall, Richard Lawrence *microbiologist, researcher*

College Grove
Battle, William Robert (Bob Battle) *retired newspaper executive*

Collegedale
McKee, Ellsworth R. *food products executive*
†Moore, Robert Crumley *mathematician, educator*

Collierville
Duke, Gary James *electronics executive*
Hays, Louise Stovall *retail fashion executive*
McKinney, William Douthitt, Jr., *sales and engineering company executive*
Springfield, James Francis *retired lawyer, banker*

Columbia
Cantrell, Sharron Caulk *principal*
Curry, Beatrice Chesrown *retired English educator*
†Scheusner, Ronald L. *music educator*
Tamberrino, Frank Michael *professional association executive*

Cookeville
Acuff, John Edgar *lawyer*
Adkisson, Randall Lynn *minister*
Alfred, Suellen *English education educator*
Black, Gary William *industrial engineer*
Campana, Phillip Joseph *German language educator*
Chowdhuri, Pritindra *electrical engineer, educator*
Day, David Owen *lawyer*
Elkins, Donald Marcum *dean, agronomy educator*
Forest, Herman Silva *biology educator*
†Jackson, Mark James *engineering educator*
Kumar, Krishna *retired physics educator*
Musacchio, Marilyn Jean *nurse midwife, educator, administrator*
Peters, Ralph Martin *academic administrator*
Qualls, Steven Daniel *lawyer*
†Ramaswamy, Srini *computer science educator, software consultant*
Sissom, Leighton Esten *engineering educator, dean, consultant*
Swanson, Gale Alden *accountant, educator*
Volpe, Angelo Anthony *former university president, chemistry educator*

Cordova
Griffin, Walton W. *performing company executive*
Hamilton, David John *information technology administrator*
Lieberman, Phillip Louis *allergist, educator*
Pugh, Dorothy Gunther *artistic director*
Romanoff, Stanley M., Jr., *human resource specialist*
†Swan, Michael Robert *lawyer*

Covington
Key, Thomas Marshall *music educator*
Kinningham, Alan Goodrum *music educator, composer/arranger*

Crossville
Bell, Charles Eugene, Jr., *industrial engineer*
Drabik-Nowak, Renata Anna *internist*
Lansford, Edwin Gaines *accountant*
Lawrence, Ralph Waldo *manufacturing company executive*
Marlow, James Allen *lawyer*

Dandridge
Comer, Evan Philip *manufacturing company executive*
Martin, Earl Richard *theology educator*

Dayton
Cornelius, Richard Meredith *English language educator*
†Luther, Sigrid *music educator*

Dunlap
Nelson, Roger Theodore *surgeon*

Dyersburg
McGrail, Susan King *travel agency executive, accountant*
Scearce, Janna Luebkemann *sales professional*
Wilson, Leigh Ann *writer, educator, historian*

Eads
Dwyer, John Thomas, Jr., *educator, researcher*
Ratzlaff, David Edward *minister*

Elizabethton
Taylor, Wesley Alan *accountant, consultant*

Elkton
Newman, Sharon Lynn *elementary education educator*

Fairfield Glade
†Dixon, Fred *retired literature educator*
Pitt, Woodrow Wilson, Jr., *engineering educator, educator*

Fairview
†Hutchison, Barbara Bailey *singer, songwriter*

Fayetteville
Bone, Lawson Mitchell *songwriter, poet*
Dickey, John Harwell *lawyer*
Ralston, J. Fred, Jr., *internist*
Wolfhard, Hans Georg *research scientist*

Franklin
†Bouldin-Payor, Elizabeth Gai *educator (K-12)*
Bull, Sandy (Alexander Benjamin Bull) *musician, composer*
Daniel, Cathy Brooks *tutor, educational consultant*
Duduit, Michael *editor, university administrator*
Eddy, Mark James *healthcare industry executive*
Felch, James Walton *ophthalmologist*
Garey, Mark Edward *secondary school educator, band director*
Guthrie, Glenda Evans *academic counselor, development specialist*
Jowdy, Jeffrey William *development executive*
Miller, Dennis Edward *health medical executive*
Moessner, Harold Frederic *allergist*
Sloan, W(ilson) Keith *actuary*
†Smith, Michael W. *popular musician*
Smolenski, Lisabeth Ann *family practice physician*
Stafford, Clay *writer, film producer, director, actor, educator, public speaker*
Sybinsky, Estrella Besinga *political science educator*
Young, William Edgar *religious organization official*

Gallatin
Bradley, Nolen Eugene, Jr., *personnel executive, educator*
Ellis, Joseph Newlin *retired distribution company executive*
Flynn, John David *writer, educator*

Gatlinburg
Cave, Kent R. *national park ranger*
Flanagan, Judy *special events professional, entertainment and marketing specialist, professional public speaker*

Germantown
Allison, Beverly Gray *seminary president, evangelism educator*
Arendall, Charles Steven *management consultant, educator*
Davis, Tom Ivey, II, *management executive*
Depperschmidt, Thomas Orlando *economist, consultant*
Floyd, John David *theology educator, minister*
Hall, Johnnie Cameron *pathologist*
†Kontos, George John, Jr., *surgeon*
Nolly, Robert J. *hospital administrator, pharmaceutical science educator*
†Richards, Janet Leach *lawyer, educator*
Waddell, Phillip Dean *lawyer*
Wiatr, Jeanne Malecki *education educator, educator*

Goodlettsville
Harper, Jewel Benton *pharmacist*
†Shaffer, Donald S. *retail executive*
Tongate, Darrel Edwin *accountant*
Vatandoost, Nossi Malek *art school administrator*

Gray
Combs, Stephen Paul *pediatrician, health facility administrator*

Greenback
Weeks, Robert Andrew *materials science researcher, educator*

Greenbrier
Newell, Paul Haynes, Jr., *engineering educator, former college president*

Greeneville
Ashworth, Denise Marchant *retired landscape architect*
Bowman, Betsey Jean *social worker*
Breckenridge, Judith Watts *writer, educator*
Casteel, DiAnn Brown *principal*
†Corey, Mark *historic site director*
Ford, Sally J. *physical education educator*
Frederick, George Francis *retired manufacturing executive*
Renner, Glenn Delmar *agricultural products executive*
Smith, Myron John, Jr., *librarian, author*

Harrogate
†Daniel, Barbara Ann *realtor, advertising executive*

Henderson
†Hay, Thomas Franklin *music educator*

Hendersonville
Ambrose, Charles Stuart *sales executive*
Burt, Alvin Miller, III, *anatomist, cell biologist, educator, writer*
Clark, Alan Martin *band director*
Davis, Robert Norman *hospital administrator*
†Jantz, Cynthia Marie *librarian*
Linville, Mary Todd *family nurse practitioner*
McCaleb, Joe Wallace *lawyer*
Miller, Creighton Herbert *music educator*
†Skaggs, Ricky *country musician*

Henning
†Parker, Joann Maudie *freelance/self-employed writer, retired reporter*

Hermitage
Chambers, Curtis Allen *clergyman, church communications executive*
Fulmer, Douglas Alan *political consultant, journalist*
Quaintance, Alice Lynn *elementary school media specialist*

Hickory Valley
Weaver, Peggy (Marguerite McKinnie Weaver) *plantation owner*

Hixson
Twitty, H. R. *hospital official*

Martin, Ron *editor, superintendent of schools, consultant, minister*

McKenzie

†Hetrick, William P. *marketing professional, educator*

Memphis

Abston, Dunbar, Jr., *management executive*
†Adams, John C. *transportation executive*
Adsit, Russell Allan *landscape architect*
†Ajanaku, Amana M. *poet*
Allen, Laurie Louise *retired medical social worker*
Allen, Newton Perkins *lawyer*
†Anghelescu, Doralina Lucia *anesthesiologist*
†Anzaldo-González, Demetrio *literature educator*
Archer, Ward, Jr., *advertising executive*
Bhattacharya, Syamal Kanti *biomedical scientist, educator*
†Blake, Norman *hotel executive*
Bland, James Theodore, Jr., *lawyer*
†Bond, Beverly Greene *education educator, writer*
Booth, Linda Leigh *vocational educator, homemaker*
†Boucher, Bradley Albert *pharmacist, educator*
Brandon, Elvis Denby, Jr., *financial planner*
Brandon, Elvis Denby, III, *financial planner*
Brandon, Raymond Wilson *financial planner, securities principal*
Broadhurst, Jerome Anthony *lawyer*
Brooks, Kathleen *journalist*
Burton, Fred Clifford *visual artist, educator*
Butts, Herbert Clell *retired dentist, educator*
Cannon, Joe Louis *retired orthodontist*
Carr, Oscar Clark, III, *lawyer*
Carroll, Billy Price *artist*
Carter, Michael Allen *nursing educator*
Chafetz, Samuel David *lawyer*
†Chambliss, Prince Caesar, Jr., *lawyer*
Champion, Herman Daniel, Jr., *college dean*
Chesney, Russell Wallace *pediatrician*
†Chester, James A. *music educator*
Ching, James Michael *artistic director opera company, composer, conductor*
Chung, King-Thom *microbiologist, educator*
Clark, Ross Bert, II, *lawyer*
†Coffman, Claude T. *law educator, lawyer*
Cook, August Joseph *lawyer, accountant*
Cowan, George Sheppard Marshall, Jr., *surgeon, educator, research administrator*
Cox, Clair Edward, II, *urologist, medical educator*
Cox, Larry D. *airport executive*
Crain, Frances Utterback *retired dietitian*
Crane, Laura Jane *research chemist*
Crawford, Sheila Jane *elementary education librarian, reading consultant*
†Crews, Kristine Radomski *pharmacologist*
Crist, William Miles *dean, physician*
Czestochowski, Joseph Stephen *museum administrator*
Dagogo-Jack, Samuel E. *medical educator, physician scientist, endocrinologist*
Daniel, Coldwell, III, *economist, educator*
Daughdrill, James Harold, Jr., *academic administrator*
De Mere-Dwyer, Leona *medical illustrator*
De Saussure, Richard Laurens, Jr., *retired neurosurgery educator*
Desiderio, Dominic Morse, Jr., *chemistry and neurochemistry educator*
†Dickerson, Roland Nelson *pharmacy educator, clinical consultant*
†Diener, Andrew M. *educator*
Diggs, Walter Whitley *health science facility administrator*
†Dixon, Samuel B *retired comedian, film director, film producer*
Drescher, Judith Altman *library director*
Dunathan, Harmon Craig *college dean*
†Dunavant, William Buchanan, Jr., *textiles executive*
Dunnigan, T. Kevin *electrical and electronics manufacturing company executive*
†Edwards, Gary Thomas *historian, educator*
Elliott, Rodney Gorhman *urologist, educator*
Evans, James Mignon *architect*
Fain, John Nicholas *biochemistry educator*
Faudree, Ralph J. *academic administrator, mathematician, educator*
†Ferreira, Antonio Mario *chemist, educator*
Fields, W(ade) Thomas *dental educator*
Foote, Shelby *author*
Ford, Harold Eugene *consultant, former congressman*
Forster, Hamish *engineer*
Foster, Stephan Lyle *pharmacist, educator*
Fountain, Robert Allen *organizational management executive*
Franklin, Stanley Phillip *computer scientist, cognitive scientist, mathematician, educator*
Freeman, Bob A. *retired microbiology educator, retired dean*
Gerald, Barry *radiology educator, neuroradiologist*
Getske, Kathrine *psychiatric social worker*
Gibbons, Julia Smith *federal judge*
Gilman, Ronald Lee *judge*
†Glassman, Richard *lawyer*
Godsey, William Cole *physician*
Goldstein, Jerome Arthur *mathematics educator*
Gourley, Dick R. *college dean*
Gourley, Greta Ann Kimbrough *pharmaceutical sciences educator*
Grace, Wesley Gee, Jr., *engineer*
Graf, Alan B., Jr., *transportation executive*
†Grafton, Edna Fisher *writer*
Green, Joseph Barnet *neurologist, educator*
Haizlip, Henry Hardin, Jr., *real estate consultant, former banker*
Harris, Edward Frederick *orthodontics educator*
Harvey, Albert C. *lawyer*
Head, Willis Stanford *music educator, performer*
Heimberg, Murray *pharmacologist, biochemist, physician, educator*
Herenton, Willie W. *mayor*
Herrod, Henry Grady, III, *dean, allergist, immunologist*
†Hofmann, Polly A. *physiologist, science educator*
Holland, Nicholas V., III, *music educator*
†Holmes, Jenanne Nelson *lawyer*
Hord, Pauline Jones *primary school educator, educator*
Horn, Ralph *bank executive*
Howe, Martha Morgan *microbiologist, educator*
Huddleston, Jeffrey Lawrence *music educator*
Hughes, Walter Thompson *physician, pediatrics educator*
Hunt, James Calvin *academic administrator, physician*
Iftekharuddin, Khan M. *engineering educator, researcher*
Jackson, Thomas Francis, III, *lawyer*
†Jalenak, Peggy Eichenbaum *volunteer*
Jarvis, Daphne Eloise *laboratory administrator*
Jernigan, Howard Maxwell, Jr., *biochemistry educator, researcher*
Jolly, William Thomas *foreign language educator*
†Jones, Effie L. *social sciences educator*
Jurand, Jerry George *periodontology educator, researcher*
†Kahn, Bruce Meyer *lawyer*
Kamery, Rob Herlong *economics educator, management consultant*
Kaplan, Robert J. *dermatologist*
Karp, Harvey L. *metal products manufacturing executive*
Kaste, Sue Creviston *pediatric radiologist, researcher*
Klyman, Fred Irwin *healthcare executive*
Knight, H. Stuart *law enforcement official, consultant*
Korones, Sheldon Bernarr *physician, educator*
†Kuhn, Brian Lawrence *lawyer*
Kushma, David William *journalist*
Lait, Hayden David *lawyer*
Lane, Sheryl Leanne *music educator, organist, violinist, pianist*
Lasslo, Andrew *medicinal chemist, educator*
Lazar, Rande Harris *otolaryngologist*
Leal, Gumersindo R. *physician*
Ledbetter, Paul Mark *lawyer, writer*
†Levy, Robert Halle *apparel executive, writer*
Lew, D(ukhee) Betty *physician*
†Luo, Rensheng *structural biologist, researcher*
Lynch, Denis Patrick *dentist, educator*
Magrill, Joe Richard, Jr., *religious organization administrator, minister*
Manire, James McDonnell *lawyer*
Mann, Donald Cameron *record company executive*
Mantey, Elmer Martin *food company executive*
Martin, Daniel C. *surgeon, gynecologist, educator*
Martinez-Hernandez, Antonio *pathology educator*
†Masterson, Kenneth Rhodes *lawyer*
Matthews, Paul Aaron *lawyer*
Mauer, Alvin Marx *physician, medical educator*
McConnico, Nancy Mann *civic worker*
McCullar, Bruce Hayden *oral and maxillofacial surgeon*
†McKenzie, Steven L. *theology studies educator, writer*
McLean, Robert Alexander *lawyer*
McPherson, Larry E(ugene) *photographer, educator*
McRae, Robert Malcolm, Jr., *federal judge*
Mendel, Maurice *audiologist, educator*
†Mirvis, David Marc *health administrator, cardiologist, educator*
Moffitt, Carolyn Mullins *university official*
Monypeny, David Murray *lawyer*
Moore, Dwight Terry *lawyer*
†Moriarty, Herbert Bernard, Jr., *lawyer*
Morreim, E. Havvi *medical ethics educator*
Nienhuis, Arthur Wesley *physician, researcher*
†Noel, Randall Deane *lawyer*
†Odland, Steve *retail executive*
Papachristou, Patricia Towne *economics educator*
Parish, Barbara Shirk *writer, educator*
Patton, Charles Henry *lawyer, educator*
Pezeshki, S. Reza *educator*
Pfeffer, Lawrence Marc *cell biologist*
Piazza, Marguerite *opera singer, actress, entertainer*
Pohlmann, Marcus D. *political science educator*
Pourciau, Lester John, Jr., *retired librarian*
†Pulido, Miguel Lazaro *marketing professional*
†Quinn, Amelia Turner *writer*
†Raghow, Sharan Dhaliwal *scientist, educator*
†Raines, Jim Neal *lawyer*
Ranta, Richard Robert *university dean*
Rawlins, Donald Ray *lawyer*
Reaves, Charles Durham *investment company executive, lawyer*
Reynolds, Stephen Curtis *hospital administrator*
Rice, George Lawrence, III, (Larry Rice) *lawyer*
Riss, Murray *photographer, educator*
Rubin, Rose Mohr *economics educator*
Sanford, Susan Haspel *not-for-profit executive*
Schaefgen, Philip P. *business owner, insurance agent, real estate broker, consultant, certified public accountant*
Schelp, Richard Herbert *mathematics educator*
Schuler, Walter E. *lawyer*
Scroggs, Larry Kenneth *lawyer, state legislator*
Shea, Martin Coyle *physician*
†Sherman, Janann Margaret *history educator, writer*
Shochat, Stephen Jay *pediatric surgeon*
Shorb, Gary Seymour *hospital administrator*
Sigler, Lois Oliver *retired educator*
†Simpson, Timothy Young *music educator*
Smith, Frederick Wallace *delivery service executive*
Solomon, Solomon Sidney *endocrinologist, pharmacologist, scientist*
Soskel, Norman Terry *physician*
Sossaman, William Lynwood *lawyer*
Stagg, Louis Charles *English language and literature educator*
†Stegall, Susan Elizabeth *elementary school educator*
†Steib, James Terry *bishop*
Stokes, Henry Arthur *journalist*
Strauser, David Ross *healthcare educator*
Summitt, Robert Layman, Jr., *obstetrician, gynecologist*
†Tabachnick, Stephen Ely *English literature educator*
†Talati, Ajay Jayantilal *pediatrician, researcher*
Tate, Stonewall Shepherd *lawyer*
†Taylor, Jerry F(rancis) *lawyer*
Terry, Joseph Ray, Jr., *lawyer*
†Tipton, Nathan Glen *librarian*
Todd, Virgil Holcomb *clergyman, religion educator*
Tonkin, Ina Lynn Dyer *cardiovascular radiologist, educator*
†Troutt, William Earl *academic administrator*
Tutko, Robert Joseph *law enforcement officer, radiology administrator*
Umholtz, Clyde Allan *financial analyst*
Van Arsdale, Stephanie Kay Lorenz *cardiovascular clinical specialist, nursing educator, researcher*
Van Middlesworth, Lester *physiology, biophysics and medicine educator*
†Vargo, Timothy D. *auto part executive*
Vescovo, Diane Kirkland *federal judge*
Vest, James Murray *foreign language and literature educator*
Vetscher, Timothy John *reporter, anchor on TV news show*
†Walker, Randolph Meade *minister*
Waller, Robert Rex *ophthalmologist, educator, foundation executive*
Wallis, Carlton Lamar *librarian*
Walsh, Thomas James, Jr., *lawyer*
Webb, Kathleen Rochford *lawyer*
Werle, Robert Geary *academic administrator*
West, Christopher Eugene *military officer*
Whitesell, Dale Edward *retired association executive, natural resources consultant*
Wicks, Mona Newsome *medical/surgical nurse, educator*
†Widjanarko, Taufiq *engineering educator*
Wilcox, Harry Hammond *retired medical educator*
Williams, David Russell *retired music educator*
Williams, Edward F(oster), III, *environmental engineer*
Williams, J. Maxwell *lawyer, arbitrator and mediator*
†Williams, Jason *professional basketball player*
Williams, Russ *marketing professional*
†Winchester, Richard Lee, Jr., *lawyer*
Wingate, Robert Lee, Jr., *internist*
Winters, Darcy LaFountain *medical management company executive*
†Wise, George Urban *botanic garden administrator, horticulturist, entomologist*
Wright Carrier, J. T. *business owner*
†Yankaway, Jerel Jerome *application developer*

Milligan College

Mills, Lori Lynne *psychologist, educator*

Morristown

Bruce, Dania Gayle *interior decorator*
Culvern, Julian Brewer *retired chemist, educator*
Johnson, Evelyn Bryan *airport terminal executive*
Marz, Loren Carl *environmental engineer, chemist, meteorologist*
†Rowland, Kyla Faye *gospel songwriter*

Mount Juliet

Bauernfeind, James Charles *secondary education educator*
†Dent, Cedric Carl *musician, educator*
Garvey, Pat *vocalist, composer, actor, novelist*

Mountain Home

Lucas, R. Robert *finance engineer, corporate tax planner*

Munford

Harrington, Herbert H. *accountant*

Murfreesboro

†Bloomer, Lisa A. *mathematician, educator*
Breault, Kevin D. *sociology educator, research scientist*
Coleman, Jack Andrew, Jr., *otolaryngologist*
Conard, Rebecca Ann *historian, educator*
†Diaz-Ortiz, Oscar A. *education educator, researcher*
†Dougan, John *music educator*
Doyle, Delores Marie *retired principal*
Ford, William F. *banker*
†Heffington, Jack Grisham *lawyer, banker, insurance company executive, horse breeder*
Klein, Christopher Carnahan *economist*
Littlepage, Glenn E. *social psychology educator*
MacDougall, Preston John *chemistry educator*
Marshall, John David *retired librarian, author*
†McCash, June Hall *language educator, writer*
†McDaniel, Rhonda Louise *literature educator*
Roose-Church, Lisa Ann *reporter, secondary school educator*
Rupprecht, Nancy Ellen *historian, educator*
†Staples, Amy L.S. *historian, educator*
Walker, David Ellis, Jr., *educator, minister, consultant*
Zietz, Joachim *economics educator*

Nashville

†Adams, Kenneth Stanley, Jr., (Bud Adams) *energy company executive, football executive*
†Albright, Julia Szur *artist*
Allbritton, Cliff *personal and organizational consultant*
Allen, George Sewell *neurosurgery educator*
Allison, Fred, Jr., *physician, educator*
Anderson, Janice Linn *real estate brokerage professional, paralegal*
Andrews, Holdt *investment banker*
Auerbach, Stanley Irving *ecologist, environmental scientist, educator*
Auld, Bernie Dyson *civil engineer, consultant*
Autry, Philip Earl *music educator, musician*
Averbuch, Mark Stephen *internist*
†Bader, David Mansfield *education educator*
Baldwin, Harold Scott *pediatrician*
Barnett, Joey Victor *pharmacologist, educator, researcher*
Barrett, George Edward *lawyer*
Bart, Teddy *journalist*
Bass, James Orin *lawyer*
Basu, Prodyot Kumar *civil engineer, educator*
Bates, George William *obstetrician, gynecologist, educator, medical products executive*
Bayuzick, Robert J. *materials scientist, educator*
Beasley, John Snodgrass, II, *university administrator*
Beaty, Sandy *lobbyist, lawyer*
Beauchamp, John Jones *mathematician, educator*
Beck, Robert Beryl *real estate executive*
Belton, Robert *law educator*
Benbow, Camilla Persson *psychology educator, researcher*
Bernard, Louis Joseph *surgeon, educator*
Birch, Adolpho A., Jr., *state supreme court justice*
Bird, Caroline *author*
†Blasi, Anthony Joseph *sociology educator, writer*
Bloch, Frank Samuel *law educator*
Blumstein, James Franklin *law educator, lawyer, consultant*
†Bohn, Cynthia Jane *lawyer*
Boorman, Howard Lyon *history educator*
Bostick, Charles Dent *retired lawyer, educator*
Boutaud, Olivier Gilles *biochemistry research educator*
Boyd, Theophilus Bartholomew, III, *publishing company executive*
Bradford, James C., Jr., *brokerage house executive*
Bramlett, Paul Kent *lawyer*
Bramlett, Shirley Marie Wilhelm *interior decorator, artist*
Bredesen, Philip Norman *governor*
Brett, John Brendan, Jr., *corporate advertising and public relations executive*
Brill, Aaron Bertrand *nuclear medicine educator*
Brophy, Jeremiah Joseph *former financial company official, former army officer*
Brown, Joe Blackburn *judge*
Brown, Wendy Weinstock *nephrologist, educator*
†Bruce, William Roland *lawyer*
Buckles, Stephen Gary *economist, educator*
Burch, John Christopher, Jr., *investment banker*
Burk, Raymond Franklin, Jr., *physician, educator, researcher*
Burnett, Lonnie Sheldon *obstetrics and gynecology educator*
Byrd, Andrew Wayne *investment company executive*
Byrne, Daniel William *biostatistician, educator*
Cadzow, James Archie *engineering educator, researcher*
Carlson, Robert Marshall *hospital professional services official*
Carr, Davis Haden *lawyer*
Carroll, Frank Edward *radiologist, researcher*
Carson, Paul Eugene *insurance examiner*
†Casagrande, Vivien Alice *neuroscientist, researcher*
Cecelic, Jerone Charles *lawyer*
Chambers, Carol Tobey *elementary school educator*
Chandler, Nettie Johnson *artist*
Chaney, Sharon Henderson *secondary education educator, consultant*
†Chapman, Morris Hines *denominational executive*
†Charney, Jonathan Isa *law educator, lawyer*
Cheek, James Howe, III, *lawyer, educator*
Chenicek, Laura *artist, educator*
†Christie, William Gary *finance educator, dean*
Churchill, Larry Raymond *ethics educator*
Chytil, Frank *biochemist*
Clayton, Ellen Wright *medical educator, pediatrician*
†Cleveland, Ashley *musician*
Clinton, Mary Ellen *neurologist*
Cobb, Stephen A. *lawyer*
†Cohen, Stephen Ira *lawyer, state legislator*
Collett, Walter Lee *electrical engineer*
Collins, Joe Lena *retired educator*
Compton, John Joseph *philosophy educator*
Coney, PonJola *dean, researcher, educator*
Conkin, Paul Keith *history educator*
Conner, Lewis Homer, Jr., *lawyer*
Conway-Welch, Colleen *dean, nurse midwife*
†Cooil, Bruce Kimo *mathematical statistician, statistics educator*
Cook, Ann Jennalie *English language educator*
Cooney, Charles Hayes *lawyer*
Cornwell, Ilene Jones *writer, editor*
Cotton, Robert Bell *pediatrician, neonatologist, researcher*
†Crutchfield, William Ward *lawyer, state legislator*
Cunningham, Gunther *professional football coach*
Cunningham, Leon William *biochemist, educator*
Daane, James Dewey *banker*
Dalton, James Edgar, Jr., *health facility administrator*
Darnell, Riley Carlisle *state government official, lawyer*
Daughtrey, Martha Craig *federal judge*
Dauser, Kimberly Ann *physician assistant*
Day, John Arthur *lawyer*
Dedman, Bertram Cottingham *retired insurance company executive*
DeHart, Roy Lynch *physician, educator*
Dettbarn, Wolf-Dietrich *neurochemist, pharmacologist, educator*
Dickerson, Dennis Clark *history educator*
Dobbs, George Albert *funeral director, embalmer*

Doyal, Linda E. *clinical pharmacist*
Drowota, Frank F., III, *state supreme court chief justice*
†Du Bois, Tim *recording industry executive*
Dupont, William Dudley *biostatistician, educator*
Dykes, Archie Reece *financial services executive*
Echols, Robert L. *federal judge*
Edwards, Samuel Hollis *lawyer, urban/regional planner*
Eisen, Steven Jeffrey *lawyer*
†Elam, Lloyd Charles *psychiatrist, educator*
†Ely, James Wallace, Jr., *law educator*
Estes, Robert Lewis *ophthalmologist*
Estrin, Kari (Karen Ruth Estrin) *artist and tour manager, agent, consultant*
Evans, Franklin Bachelder *marketing educator emeritus*
Fabian, Jane *former ballet company executive*
Farmer, William H. *political organization worker, lawyer*
†Fazio, Sergio *medical educator, researcher*
Feldman, Leonard Cecil *physicist*
Fels, Rendigs *economist, educator*
†Fields, James Perry *dermatologist, dermatopathologist, allergist*
Finder, Stuart Gregg *medical ethics educator*
Fischer, Charlotte Froese *researcher, educator*
Fischer, Patrick Carl *computer scientist, retired educator*
Fisher, Jeff *professional football coach*
Fitzgerald, Edmund Bacon *electronics industry executive*
†Fleck, Bela *country musician*
Fleischer, Arthur C. *medical educator, radiologist*
Fort, Tomlinson *chemist, chemical engineering educator*
Foster, Henry Wendell *medical educator*
Freudenthal, Ernest Guenter *technology and business educator*
Frist, Thomas Fearn, Jr., *hospital management company executive*
Gabbe, Steven Glenn G. *dean, obstetrician, gynecologist, educator*
Galloway, Kenneth Franklin *engineering educator*
Gannon, John Sexton *lawyer, management consultant, arbitrator, mediator*
Gaultney, John Orton *life insurance agent, consultant*
Gee, Elwood Gordon *academic administrator*
†George, Alfred L., Jr., *medical educator, researcher*
George, Eddie *professional football player*
Giallombardo, Leslie *publishing executive*
Gillmor, John Edward *lawyer*
Girgus, Sam B. *English literature educator*
Gleaves, Edwin Sheffield *librarian*
Gore, Steven Lowell *financial consultant*
Gore, Tipper (Mary Elizabeth Gore) *wife of the former vice president of the United States*
Gove, Walter R. *sociology educator*
Graham, George J., Jr., *political scientist, educator*
Graham, Thomas Pegram, Jr., *pediatric cardiologist*
†Graves, Jo Ann *state legislator*
Green, Lisa Cannon *online editor*
†Griffin, Patti Elaine *medical educator, consultant*
Guinsburg, Philip Fried *alcohol and substance abuse counselor*
Gusky, Diane Elizabeth *state agency administrator, planner*
Hahn, George Thomas *materials engineering educator, researcher*
Hall, Douglas Scott *astronomy educator*
Hall, Richard Clyde, Jr., *retired religious educational administrator*
Hamberg, Marcelle Robert *retired urologist*
†Hancock, Terry Blackmon *psychologist, educator*
Hanselman, Richard Wilson *entrepreneur*
Hardin, Hal D. *lawyer, judge, federal official*
Hargrave, James Lee *editor, consultant*
Hargrove, Erwin Charles, Jr., *political science educator*
Harris, J(acob) George *health care company executive*
Harris, Thomas Raymond *biomedical engineer, educator*
Harrison, Clifford Joy, Jr., *banker*
Hart, Richard Banner *lawyer*
Harwell, Beth H. *political organization worker*
Hass, Joseph Monroe *automotive executive*
Hassel, Rudolph Christopher *English educator*
Havens, Murray Clark *political scientist, educator*
†Hazelip, Herbert Harold *academic administrator*
Heard, Alexander *retired educator and chancellor*
Heiser, Arnold Melvin *astronomer*
Henderson, Milton Arnold *professional society administrator*
Hercules, David Michael *chemistry educator, consultant*
Hillenmeyer, Henry Reiling, Jr., *restaurant company executive*
†Hirt, Janet Rose *law educator, law librarian*
†Hoffman, Cheri *social services administrator*
Hofstead, James Warner *laundry machinery company executive, lawyer*
Howell, John Floyd *insurance company executive*
†Hudgens, Ann Young *librarian, counselor*
†Ingram, Martha Rivers *company executive*
†Ingram, Orrin Henry, II, *transportation executive*
James, H. Neal *video, record, movie producer, director*
James, Kay Louise *management consultant, healthcare executive*
Jennings, Henry Smith, III, *cardiologist*
Jensen, Roy Andrew *pathologist*
†Johnson, Anita Rochelle *mental health specialist*
Johnson, David *medical administrator*
Johnson, Greg *professional hockey player*
Johnson, Hollis Eugene, III, *foundation executive*
Jones, Evelyn Gloria *medical technologist, educator*
Jonsson, Bjarni *mathematician, educator*
Joyner, John Wesley *psychologist, educator*
Kahan, Sheldon Jeremiah (Christopher Reed) *musician, singer*
Kaine, Paul *performing company executive*
Kearse, Jevon *football player*
Kelley, James Russell *lawyer*
†Kirshner, Howard S *neurologist, medical educator*
Kmiec, Edward Urban *bishop*
Kono, Tetsuro *biochemist, physiologist, educator*
†Krauss, Alison *country musician*
Kuhn, Paul Hubert, Jr., *investment counsel*
Land, Rebekah Ruth *marriage and family therapist*
Land, Richard Dale *minister, religious organization administrator*
†Lawless, Thomas William *lawyer*
†Lawrence, Thomas Patterson *public relations executive*
Lazar, Irving *psychologist*
†Leathers, Ramsey Barthell *lawyer*
Ledyard, Robins Heard *lawyer*
Lee, Douglas A. *music educator*
Leftwich, Russell Bryant *allergist, immunologist, consultant*
Legwand, David *hockey player*
†Letson, Ruth Stafford *librarian*
†LeVan, Martin Douglas *chemical engineering educator*
Lewis, Lynn C. *English educator, writer*
†Little, Hampton Stennis, Jr., *lawyer, educator*
Livingston, Robert A. *brewing company executive*
Longhurst, Robert Russell *retired secondary school educator*
Loper, Linda Sue *special collections librarian*
Lowell, Roland M. *lawyer*
†Luis, William *language educator*
Lukehart, Charles Martin *chemistry educator*
†Lyle, Virginia Reavis *retired archivist, genealogist*
Lynch, John Brown *plastic surgeon, educator*
†Lyon, Philip K(irkland) *lawyer*
Maier, Harold Geistweit *law educator, lawyer*
†Manning, Charles W. *university chancellor*
Manning, David Lee *financial executive*
Marney, Samuel Rowe, Jr., *physician, educator*
Martin, James Larence *dentist, educator*
Martin, Peter Robert *psychiatrist, pharmacologist*
Mason, Derrick *football player*
†May, James M. *medical educator, medical researcher*
May, Joseph Leserman (Jack May) *lawyer*
Mayden, Barbara Mendel *lawyer*
Mayhew, Aubrey *music industry executive*
McCarthy, John Aloysius *language educator, literature educator*
McCarty, Richard Charles *psychology educator, university dean*
McCowan, Otis Blakely *mathematics educator*
McDonald, Reginald Adrian *musician, educator*
McGinnis, Harrill Coleman *humanities educator*
McKeel, Sheryl Wilson *pharmacist*
McLeod, Alexander Canaday *physician*
McMurry, Idanelle Sam *educational consultant*
McNair, Steve LaTreal *professional football player*
McNeely, Mark *marketing professional, journalist*
McPhee, Scott Douglas *occupational therapist, educator*
Medwedeff, Fred Marshall *dentist*
†Meltzer, Herbert Yale *psychiatry educator*
Meredith, Owen Nichols *public relations executive, genealogist*
Merritt, Gilbert Stroud *federal judge*
†Mizell, Andrew Hooper, III, *concrete company executive*
Moore, William Grover, Jr., *management consultant, former air freight executive, former air force officer*
Morrow, Jason Drew *medical and pharmacology educator*
†Moss, Carl Michael *minister, religious studies educator*
Murray, Richard Keith *marketing executive*
Naifeh, James O. (Jimmy Naifeh) *state legislator, speaker of the house*
Neilson, Eric Grant *physician, educator, health facility administrator*
Nelson, Edward Gage *merchant banking investment company executive*
Nixon, John Trice *judge*
Oates, John Alexander, III, *medical educator*
Oates, Sherry Charlene *portraitist, artist, photographer*
O'Day, Denis Michael *ophthalmologist, educator*
O'Neill, James Anthony, Jr., *pediatric surgeon, educator*
O'Reilly, Susan Whitee *health facility administrator*
Orgebin-Crist, Marie-Claire *biology educator*
Ossoff, Robert Henry *otolaryngological surgeon*
Parker, John Randolph *pathologist, educator*
Parker, Mary Ann *lawyer*
Partain, Clarence Leon *radiologist, nuclear medicine physician, educator, administrator*
†Patterson, Robert Shepherd *lawyer*
Pearson, Sela *poet, speaker*
Penny, William Lewis *lawyer*
Person, Curtis S., Jr., *state legislator, lawyer*
Petrey, R. Claybourne, Jr., *lawyer*
†Pfanner, Helmut Franz *German language educator*
Phillips, John A(tlas), III, *geneticist, educator*
Pinson, Charles Wright *transplant surgeon, educator, hospital administrator*
†Pinter, Mike *mathematician, educator*
Policinski, Eugene Francis *newspaper editor, foundation executive, radio producer, television producer*
Porter, Andrew Calvin *academic administrator, psychologist, educator*
Porter, Ronald *artist, educator*
Propper, Michael Walles *psychiatrist, educator*
Pursell, Cleo Wilburn *church official*
Ramayya, Akunuri V. *physics educator*
Ramer, Hal Reed *academic administrator*
Rayburn, Ted Rye *newspaper editor*
Reid, Donna Joyce *small business owner*
Richmond, Samuel Bernard *management educator*
†Ricketts, Todd *researcher, educator*
Ridley, Carolyn Fludd *retired social studies educator*
Riley, Harris DeWitt, Jr., *pediatrician, medical educator*
†Rivera, Maximiano Marquez *academic administrator, writer*
†Robert, Pousman Marc *physician, hospital administrator*
Roberts, Kenneth Lewis *investor, lawyer, foundation administrator*
†Robertson, Rose Marie *cardiologist, educator*
†Robinson, Nathaniel David, Jr., *physician, consultant*
Robinson, Roscoe Ross *nephrologist, educator*
Roden, Dan Mark *clinical pharmacologist, cardiologist, medical educator*
Rogers, Barbara Jean (B.J. Rogers) *writer, editor*
Roos, Charles Edwin *physicist*
Ross, Joseph Comer *physician, educator, academic administrator*
†Rush, Stephen Kenneth *lawyer*
Russell, Clifford Springer *economics and public policy educator*
Saltsman, John B. *former political party executive, commissioner*
†Sanders, James F. *lawyer*
†Saposnik, Ira Stephen *physician, historian*
Saunders, Ted Elliott *accountant*
Schermerhorn, Kenneth *music director*
Schnelle, Karl Benjamin, Jr., *chemical engineering educator, consultant, researcher*
†Schoenfeld, Michael *academic administrator, education educator*
Schoggen, Phil H(oward) *psychologist, educator*
Schwartz, Herbert S. *surgical oncology educator*
Sergent, John S. *hospital administrator, medical educator*
†Sevin, Dieter Hermann *language and literature professional, educator*
Shack, R. Bruce *plastic surgeon*
Sharp, Katherine Street *artist, business owner*
Shaw, Carole *editor, publisher*
Shell, Owen G., Jr., *retired banker*
Sherborne, Robert *editor*
Shipley Biddy, Shelia *artist management executive*
†Shneyder, Artyom V. *science educator, researcher*
Shockley, Ann Allen *librarian, writer*
Siegfried, John *association officer*
Silberman, Enrique *physics researcher and administrator*
†Silver, Heidi Jaye *nutritionist, educator, researcher*
†Sims, Wilson *lawyer*
†Singh, Surendra P. *educator*
Sircy, Bob C., Jr., *accountant, financial executive*
Sloan, Reba Faye *dietitian, consultant*
†Smith, Agnes Eyvonda *writer*
Smith, Bradley E. *anesthesiologist*
Smith, Dani Allred *sociologist, educator*
Smith, Troy Francis *domestic violence detective*
Soderquist, Larry Dean *law educator, lawyer, consultant, writer*
Speece, Richard Eugene *civil engineer, educator*
Spengler, Dan Michael *orthopedic surgery educator, researcher, surgeon*
Stahlman, Mildred Thornton *pediatrics and pathology educator, researcher*
†Steele, Robert Michael *lawyer*
†Stevens, Amy W. *lawyer*
Stewart, David Marshall *librarian*
Stone, Lawrence Mynatt *publishing executive*
Strupp, Hans Hermann *psychologist, educator*
Sullivan, James Nelson *physician*
Summers, Paul *state attorney general*
Surowiec, Andrew Julius *biophysicist, researcher*
Sutherland, Frank *publishing executive, editor*
Swan, Patricia Brintnall *research administrator*
Swensson, Earl Simcox *architect*
Tanner, Robert Dennis *chemical engineering educator*
†TeSelle, Eugene Arthur, Jr., *religion educator*
Thomas, Hazel Beatrice *state official*
Thomas, Randall Stuart *lawyer, educator*
†Thomas, Robert Paige *lawyer*
Thompson, Dean Allan *cattleman*
Thornton, Spencer P. *ophthalmologist, educator*
†Todd, Margo *historian, educator*
Torrey, Claudia Olivia *lawyer*
Trauger, Aleta Arthur *judge*
Treible, Kirk *retired academic administrator, foundation administrator*
Trotz, Barry *professional hockey coach*
Tudor, Bynum Ellsworth, III, *lawyer*
Tuke, Robert Dudley *lawyer, educator*
Turk, Thomas Liebig *arts consultant*
†Turner, Cal, Jr., *discount stores executive*
Twain, Shania *country musician*
Ullestad, Merwin Allan *tax services executive*
Urmy, Norman B. *hospital administrator*
Valentine, Alan Darrell *symphony orchestra executive*
van Eys, Jan *retired pediatrician, educator, administrator*
Van Mol, Louis John, Jr., *public relations executive*
Van Orden, Lucas S. *psychiatrist*
Vasterling, Paul *artistic director*
Voegeli, Victor Jacque *history educator, dean*
†Voight, Michael Lee *physical education educator*
†Wadley, Fredia Stovall *state commissioner*
Wagner, Michael Grafton *investor, corporation executive, resources advisor, business consultant*
†Walkup, John Knox *lawyer*
†Warner, Tokesha L *health facility administrator*
†Wasserman, David H. *medical educator, researcher*
Waterhouse, Rachel L. *lawyer*
Weingartner, H(ans) Martin *finance educator, educator*
Wert, James Junior *materials scientist, educator*
Westfield, Fred M. *economics educator*
Wilder, John Shelton *lieutenant governor*
Williams, Marsha Rhea *computer scientist, educator, researcher, consultant*
Wilson, Carolyn Taylor *librarian*
Winstead, Elisabeth Weaver *poet, writer, English language educator*
Winstead, George Alvis *law librarian, biochemist, educator, consultant*
Wire, William Shidaker, II, *retired apparel and footwear manufacturing company executive*
Wiseman, Thomas Anderton, Jr., *federal judge*
†Woods, Larry David *lawyer, educator*
Wyatt, Joe Billy *academic administrator*
Wycheck, Frank *football player*
Yarbrough, Edward Meacham *lawyer*
Yoo, Christopher S. *law educator*
Youngblood, Elaine Michele *lawyer*
Yuspeh, Alan Ralph *lawyer, healthcare company executive*
Zibart, Michael Alan *wholesale book company executive*

Newport
Ball, Travis, Jr., *educational consultant, editor*
Bell, John Alton *lawyer, judge*
Bunnell, John Blake *lawyer*
†Campbell, Roy Timothy, Jr., *lawyer*
Gregg, Ella Mae *writer*
Porter, James Kenneth *retired judge*
Runnion, Cindie J. *elementary school educator*

Nolensville
†Lessard, Lisa Kathleen Hamlin *spiritual counselor*

Oak Ridge
†Ball, Jacqueline Snyder *librarian, educator*
Borie, Bernard Simon, Jr., *retired physicist, educator*
†Byun, Thak-Sang *research scientist, educator*
Carlsmith, Roger Snedden *chemistry and energy conservation researcher*
Clapp, Neal Keith *experimental pathologist*
Congdon, Charles C. *pathologist, researcher*
Dai, Sheng *chemist, materials scientist*
Das, Sujit *policy analyst*
Dickens, Justin Kirk *nuclear physicist*
Dixon, Warren Everett *robotics engineer*
†Fox, Janie *environmental engineer*
Gifford, Franklin Andrew, Jr., *meteorologist, consultant*
Gu, Baohua *soil scientist, chemist*
†Hartley, Dean S., III, *operations research specialist*
Hartman, Frederick Cooper *biochemist, researcher*
†Holloway, Jacqueline *county commissioner*
Horak, James Albert *materials scientist, nuclear engineer, educator*
Hu, Michael Z. *chemical engineer, educator*
Hu, Zhiyu *research scientist, educator*
Hudson, Sheila Donnette *waste management administrator*
Jang, Young-Il *research scientist, consultant*
Jones, Virginia McClurkin *retired social worker*
Klueh, Ronald Lloyd *metallurgist*
Krause, Manfred Otto *physicist*
†Kress, Thomas Sylvester *engineer, consultant*
Larson, Bennett Charles *solid state physicist, researcher*
Lee, Donald William *mechanical engineer, researcher*
†Lindberg, Steven Eric *geochemist*
Maienschein, Fred *retired physicist*
Manly, William Donald *metallurgist*
†Mei, Viung Chung (Vince G. Mei) *research scientist, mechanical engineer*
Mosko, Sigmund Weiner *electrical engineer, researcher*
†Phillips, Debra Helen *soil scientist, researcher*
Plasil, Franz *physicist*
Postma, Herman *physicist, consultant*
Poutsma, Marvin L. *chemical research administrator*
†Protopopescu, Vladimir Alexandru *research scientist, educator*
Raridon, Richard Jay *computer specialist*
†Regan-Stanton, Christa Maria *artist*
†Reid, Michael David *human resources specialist, consultant*
Rivera, Angel Luis *chemical engineer*
Rosenthal, Murray Wilford *chemical engineer, science administrator*
Slusher, Kimberly Goode *researcher*
Spray, Paul Ellsworth *retired surgeon*
Turov, Daniel *financial writer, investment executive*
†Wang, Jian-Guang *engineering physicist*
Watson, Evelyn Egner *radiation scientist*
Weinberg, Alvin Martin *physicist*
†Wilkinson, Robert Warren *lawyer*
Xu, Ying *computational biologist*
Yoo, Man Hyong *materials scientist*
Young, Jack Phillip *chemist*
Zinkle, Steven John *engineer, researcher*
Zucker, Alexander *physicist, administrator*

Oliver Springs
Davis, Sara Lea *pharmacist*
Heacker, Thelma Weaks *retired elementary school educator*

Ooltewah
Culpepper, Richard Groom *engineer*
Mixon, Valorie Johnson *physician assistant*

Paris
McNutt, Gwyn Bellamy *archivist*
Wiedemann, Ramona Diane *occupational therapist*

Parsons
†Townsend, Edwin Clay *lawyer*

Pegram
Barnes, Craig Martin *minister*

Pigeon Forge
Parton, Dolly Rebecca *singer, composer, actress*

Pinson
Bailey, James Andrew *principal*

Pleasant Hill
Hull, Charles William *retired special education educator*

Pleasant Shade
Blackburn, Bryan David *title abstractor*

Powell
Cossé, R. Paul *realty company executive*
Hyman, Roger David *lawyer*

Pulaski
Calvert, Lois Prince *health facility administrator, geriatrics nurse*

Rockvale
†Ritter, Sparkle Whitaker *lighting designer, educator*

Rockwood
Raymond, Betty Jean *critical care nurse*

Rogersville
Fairchild, Dorcas Sexton *English educator*
Skelton, Mark Albert *lawyer*

Sevierville
Koff, Shirley Irene *writer*
Waters, John B. *lawyer*

Sewanee
Camp, Thomas Edward *retired librarian*
Croom, Frederick Hailey *academic administrator, mathematician, educator*
Cunningham, Joel Luther *university president, vice-chancellor*
Dunkly, James Warren *theological librarian*
Ende, Arlyn Ruth *textile artist, arts administrator*
Hawkins, Travis Montgomery, Sr., *horticulturist, landscape consultant*
Hughes, Robert Davis, III, *theology studies educator*
†Lytle, Guy Fitch, III, *priest, educator, dean*
McGlothlin, Karen Leah *science educator*
Mohiuddin, Yasmeen Niaz *economics educator*
Patterson, William Brown *university dean, history educator*
Scarbrough, Cleve Knox, Jr., *museum director*
Warburton, Minnie *writer, artist*
Watson, Gail H. *librarian*
Williamson, Samuel Ruthven, Jr., *historian, emeritus university president*
Yeatman, Harry Clay *biologist, educator*

Seymour
Steele, Ernest Clyde *retired insurance company executive*

Shelbyville
Nelson, Clara Singleton *human resources consultant*
Russell, William Lee *surgeon*

Shiloh
†Allen, Stacy Dale *historian, parks director*

Signal Mountain
Anderson, Charles Hill *lawyer*
Cooper, Robert Elbert *state supreme court justice*
Hall, Thor *religion educator*
Howe, Lyman Harold, III, *chemist, researcher*
†Makansi, Munzer *chemical engineer, researcher*
Swann, Nat Henderson, Jr., *physician*
Swasey, Martha Gracy *school administrator*
Wakim, Judith *nursing educator*

Smithville
†Vaughn, Eulalia Cobb *retired science educator, mathematician*

Smyrna
Faules, Barbara Ruth *retired elementary education educator*
Lee, Elizabeth Mullins *automotive executive*

Sneedville
Dodson, Danita Joan *secondary school educator, consultant*

Soddy Daisy
Leitner, Paul Revere *lawyer*
McDermott, David (John) *marketing professional, artist*
Swafford, Douglas Richard *corporate credit executive*

Soddy-Daisy
†Payne, Deborah Sue *radiation technologist*

South Pittsburg
Cordell, Francis Merritt *instrument engineer, consultant*

Sparta
Langford, Jack Daniel *elementary school educator*
Mitchell, Annie-Martin *volunteer civic worker*
Young, Olivia Knowles *retired librarian*

Springfield
Nutting, Paul John *city manager*
Richter, Lisa Sherrill *lawyer*
Wilks, Larry Dean *lawyer*

Strawberry Plains
†Blanchard, Pamela Snyder *special education educator*

Talbott
†Collins, Fleda Mae *librarian*

Tazewell
Herrell, Virgil Lee *county official*

Telford
Mashburn, Donald Eugene *educator*

Townsend
Sundquist, Don *former governor, former congressman, sales corporation executive*

Trenton
Harrell, Limmie Lee, Jr., *lawyer*
†Malone, Gayle *lawyer, consultant*
McCullough, Kathryn T. Baker *social worker*

Tullahoma
Gossick, Lee Van *consultant, executive, retired air force officer*
Hill, Susan Sloan *safety engineer*
Keele, Jean A. *medical, surgical, geriatrics and home health nurse*
Smith, L. Montgomery *electrical engineering educator*

Union City
Graham, R(ichard) Newell *soft drink bottling company executive*

Waverly
†Peeler, William James *lawyer*

Waynesboro
Owen, Timothy Andrew *minister*

TEXAS

Abilene
Bailey, Fred Arthur *history educator*
Baird, Larry Don *minister, nurse*
Baughn, Cynthia J. *human services administrator*
Bentley, Clarence Edward *savings and loan executive*
Boone, Billy Warren *lawyer, judge*
Boone, Celia Trimble *lawyer*
Boyll, David Lloyd *broadcasting company executive*
Campbell, Lillie Spurgin *social worker*
Cawood, Jenny Lind *social worker, poet*
†Christopher, Mary M. *education educator, consultant*
Crymes, Mary Cooper *secondary school educator*
†Eaves, Stephen R. *music educator*
Ellis, Laura Renee *music educator*
Godsey, Martha Sue *speech-language pathologist*
Hennig, Charles William *psychology educator*
†Hernandez, Patricia B. *biologist, educator*
Marler, Charles Herbert *journalism educator, historian, consultant*
McCaleb, Gary Day *university official*
Morgan, Clyde Nathaniel *dermatologist*
Morrison, Shirley Marie *nursing educator*
Patterson, Coleman E.P. *management educator*
†Puckett, Lauren Joy *music educator*
Retzer, Kenneth Albert *mathematics educator, entrepreneur*
Richert, Harvey Miller, II, *ophthalmologist*
Robinson, Vianei Lopez *lawyer*
Rogers, Gary Steven *consultant*
†Roy, Wayne Morris *academic administrator*
Sartain, James Edward *lawyer*
†Scarbrough, Michael *music educator*
†Sickbert, Murl Julius, Jr., *music librarian, musicologist*
Specht, Alice Wilson *university libraries dean*
Springer, Lorene Hargrove *music educator*
†Stevenson-Williams, Deydra *court administrator*
Suttle, Stephen Hungate *lawyer*
†Tolosa, Gustavo Alberto *music educator*
Tucker, John Mark *librarian, educator*
†Turner, Stafford *education educator, baritone*
Wehmeyer, Donald Lee *hand surgeon*
†Westman, Lanie Jo *music educator, performing company executive, performing arts educator*
Wilson, Stanley Patterson *retired lawyer*

Addison
Anderson, Jack Roy *health care company executive*
Cohn, Linkie Seltzer *professional speaker, author*
Grote, Dick (Richard Charles Grote) *management consultant, educator, author, radio commentator*
Hranitzky, Rachel Robyn *lawyer*
Kimbler, Larry Bernard *real estate executive, accountant*
†Kneipper, Richard Keith *lawyer*
Lawson, Gary B. *lawyer*
†Lynch, Jeffrey Scott *lawyer*
†Murray, Patrick M. *oilfield service company executive*
Parr, Richard Arnold, II, *lawyer*
†Pommerening, Edwin Carlton *lawyer*
Pryor, Richard Walter *telecommunications executive, retired air force officer*
†Rogers, Richard Raymond *cosmetics company executive*
Smith, Cece *venture capitalist*

Alamo
Fellenstein, Cora Ellen Mullikin *retired credit union executive*
Pritchett, Thomas Ronald *retired metal and chemical company executive*
Reese, Norma Carol *clinical psychologist*

Aledo
Rowe, Sheryl Ann *librarian*
Worcester, Donald Emmet *history educator, writer*

Alice
Tetlie, Harold *priest*
†Thomas, Katherine Carol *educator*

Allen
Anderson, Robin Marie *secondary education educator*
Battat, Emile A. *management executive*
†Desthieux, Bertrand M. *optical engineer, editor-in-chief*
Garner, Julie Lowrey *occupational therapist*
Gilliland, Mary Margarett *healthcare consultant*
Lim, Jae Doeg *systems engineer, researcher*
Plum, Charles Walden *retired business executive and educator*
Warren, Rita Simpson *manufacturing company executive*
Williams, Bryan *university dean, medical educator*

Alpine
Kittlitz, Rudolf Gottlieb, Jr., *chemical engineer, researcher*
Morgan, Raymond Victor, Jr., *university administrator, mathematics educator*
†Nelson, Barbara *literature educator, writer*
Sechrest, Larry J. *economist, educator*
†Snyder, John Edward, Jr., *education educator*

Alvin
Crider, Allen Billy *English educator, novelist*
Johnson, Cheryl Elizabeth *writer, publisher, educator*
Roberson, Deborah Kay *secondary school educator*

Amarillo
Arnold, Winnie Jo *retired mental health nurse, nursing administrator*
Ayad, Joseph Magdy *retired psychologist*
Berry, Jacob Obadiah *not-for-profit developer, rancher*
Biggs, William Curtis *endocrinologist*
†Bohachef, Janet Mae *medical educator*
Bull, Walter Stephen *police officer*
†Busch, Mildred Moorman *music educator*
Chisum, Matthew Eual *research scientist, laboratory administrator*
Crain, Mary Tom *volunteer*
†Cross, Janis Alexander *lawyer*
DeVaughn, Michael Richard *minister, administrator*
Elkins, Lloyd Edwin, Sr., *petroleum engineer, energy consultant*
Horton, Thomas Mark *futures and options trader, commodity consultant*
Ingraham, Joseph Edwin *financial officer*
Johnson, Philip Wayne *judge*
†Kauffman, Robert Porter *gynecologist, educator*
Keaton, Lawrence Cluer *safety engineer, consultant*
Klein, Jerry Lee, Sr., *religion educator, minister*
†Laur, Noel Paul Douglas *music educator*
Laur, William Edward *retired dermatologist*
Madden, Wales Hendrix, Jr., *lawyer*
Marmaduke, John H. *retail executive*
Martin, Luan *accountant, payroll and timekeeping supervisor*
Marupudi, Sambasiva Rao *surgeon, educator*
McDougall, Gerald Duane *lawyer*
Parker, Gerald M. *osteopath, researcher*
†Parker, Lynda Michele *psychiatrist*
Pratt, Donald George *physician*
Robinson, Mary Lou *federal judge*
Simpson, Chad W. *pharmacist, educator*
Smithee, John True *lawyer, state legislator*
†Stapleton, Claudia Ann *dean*
Stubben, Dolus Jane (D. J. Stubben) *advertising executive*
Utterback, Will Hay, Jr., *retired labor union administrator, genealogist*
Von Eschen, Robert Leroy *electrical engineer, consultant*
Woods, John William *retired lawyer*

Aransas Pass
Stehn, Lorraine Strelnick *physician*

Argyle
Merritt, Joe Frank *industrial supply executive*
Pettit, John Douglas, Jr., *management educator*
Stallings, Frank, Jr., *industrial engineer, realtor*

Arlington
Adams, Phyllis Curl *nursing educator*
†Adams, Quentin Mark *neurologist*
Ahmed, M. Basheer *psychiatrist, educator*
Alvarez, Juan M. *baseball player*
Anderson, Dale Arden *aerospace engineer, educator*
†Ausbrooks, Carrie Y. Barron *education educator, researcher*
Bruton, Carole Diane *music educator*
Byas, Teresa Ann Uranga *customer service representative, interior designer*
Carey, Milburn Ernest *musician, educator*
Clark, Dayle Meritt *civil engineer*
†Cohen, Philip Gary *English language educator, dean, academic administrator*
Cole, Richard Louis *political scientist, educator*
Corduneanu, Constantin C. *mathematician, educator*
Cuntz, Manfred *astrophysicist, researcher, educator*
Damuth, John Erwin *marine geologist*
Depken, Craig A., II, *economics educator*
de Sousa, Byron N.S. *educator, physician, health and medical consultant*
Dickinson, Roger Allyn *business administration educator*
Dowdy, John Vernard, Jr., *lawyer, educator, arbitrator, mediator*
English, Marlene Cabral *management consultant*
†Everard, Noel J. *structural engineer, educator*
Farrar-Myers, Victoria Anne *political scientist*
Ferrier, Richard Brooks *architecture educator, architect*
Fouse, David Jesse *architect*
Gates, Richard Daniel *retired manufacturing company executive*
Gilbert, Susan Lynn *software engineer*
†Green, George N. *historian, educator*
Greenspan, Donald *mathematician, educator*
Guerin, Bill *professional hockey player*
Hall, Anna Christene *retired government official*
Han, Chien-Pai *statistics educator*
Harris, Vera Evelyn *human resources specialist*
Ignagni, Joseph Anthony *humanities educator, associate dean*
Imrhan, Sheik Nazir *industrial engineer, educator*
Jordan, Catheleen *social worker, educator*
†Kier, Carlos M. *rheumatologist*
Kirk, Wiley Price, Jr., *physics and electrical engineering educator*
†Kojouharov, Hristo Venelinov *mathematician, educator, mathematician, researcher*
†Lau, Irene B. *music educator*
Lewis, Frank Leroy *electrical engineer, educator, researcher*
Lingerfelt, B. Eugene, Jr., *minister*
Liu, Hanli *biomedical engineer, educator*
Mansen, Steven Robert *manufacturing company executive*
†McIntyre, Corwin L. *pharmacist*
Mc Keen, Chester M., Jr., *retired business executive*
Otto, Ludwig *publisher, educator, consultant, evangelist*
Palmeiro, Rafael Corrales *professional baseball player*
Pomerantz, Martin *chemistry educator, researcher*
Ramsey, Charles Eugene *sociologist, educator*
Reilly, Michael Atlee *financial company executive, venture capital investor*
†Rollins, Albert Williamson *civil engineer, consultant*
Rosenberry, William Kenneth *lawyer, educator*
†Ryan, Nolan *former professional baseball player*
Satterlee, Warren Sanford, II, *retail management professional*
Savage, Ruth Hudson *poet, writer, speaker*
Sawyer, Dolores *motel chain executive*
Shanmugam, Ganapathy *geologist, researcher*
†Shiakolas, Panayiotis Stavros *mechanical engineering educator, researcher*
Showalter, Buck (William Nathaniel Showalter III) *major league baseball team manager*
Simon, Hank *information science executive*
Sims-Person, LeAnn Michelle *human resources specialist*
Sky-Eagle, Melissa Jean *musician, pianist*
Smatresk, Neal Joseph *physiologist, biology educator, science education consultant*
Smith, Charles Isaac *geology educator*
Sobol, Harold *retired dean, manufacturing executive, consultant*
Sorber, Charles Arthur *academic administrator*
Stevens, Gladstone Taylor, Jr., *industrial engineer*
Swanson, Peggy Eubanks *finance educator*
†Thomas, Lois C. *organist, music educator*
Tingley, Floyd Warren *retired physician*
†Turcotte, Karen M. *music educator*
†White, Alisa *communications educator, consultant*
Wiig, Karl Martin *knowledge management expert and consultant*
†Willoughby, Sarah-Margaret C. *chemist, educator, chemical engineer, consultant*
Wright, James Edward *judge*
Zurlo, John Anthony *English educator, writer*

Athens
Geddie, Thomas Edwin *retired small business owner*

Aubrey
†Pizzamiglio, Albert Theodore (Al Pierson) *conductor*
Pizzamiglio, Nancy Alice *performing company executive*

Austin
Abbott, Greg Wayne *state attorney general, former state supreme court justice*
Abel, Robert L. *healthcare quality improvement professional*
Abraham, Jacob A. *computer engineering educator, consultant*
Adair, Dwight Rial *film director, educator*
Akins, Vaughn Edward *retired engineering company executive*
†Alanís, Javier Rolando *theologian, religious studies educator*
Alexander, Drury Blakeley *architectural educator*
Allday, Martin Lewis *lawyer*
Allison, James Purney *lawyer*
†Allison, John Robert *lawyer, educator, author*
Al-Omari, Ra'ed M. *computer engineer, consultant, computer scientist, researcher*
Alpert, Mark Ira *marketing educator*
Ancker-Johnson, Betsy *physicist, engineer, retired automotive company executive*
Anderson, David Arnold *law educator*
Anderson, Richard Michael *lawyer*
Anderson, Urton Liggett *accounting educator*
Antokoletz, Elliott Maxim *music educator*
Arkeen, Solomon Jae *forensic counselor*
†Armstrong, Lance *professional cyclist*
Armstrong, Neal Earl *civil engineering educator*
Ascher, Mark Louis *legal educator*
Ashworth, Kenneth Hayden *public affairs specialist*
Attal, Gene (Fred Eugene Attal) *hospital executive*
Aubery, Stephen Royston Edmund *film producer*

Austin, David Mayo *social work educator*
Austin, John Riley *surgeon, educator*
Auvenshine, Anna Lee Banks *school system administrator*
Ayres, Robert Moss, Jr., *retired university president*
Baade, Hans Wolfgang *legal educator, law expert*
Baker, Lee Edward *biomedical engineering educator*
Baker, Mark Bruce *lawyer, educator*
Banerjee, Sanjay Kumar *electrical engineer, director*
Banks, Virginia Anne (Ginger Banks) *association administrator*
Barbara, Paul Frank *chemistry educator*
Bard, Allen Joseph *chemist, educator*
Barkley, Roy Reid *historian, educator, editor, writer*
Barnes, Natasha Lynn *lawyer*
†Barnes, Richard Dale *college basketball coach*
Barnes, Sally Anderson *human resources consultant, organization effectiveness and employee involvement facilitator*
Barnes, Thomas Joseph *writer*
Bauer, Sydney Meade *lawyer*
Baumgartner, Robert *consultant*
Benavides, Fortunato Pedro (Pete Benavides) *federal judge*
Benedict, Anthony Wayne *lawyer*
Benesh, William Stephen *lawyer, partner*
Bengtson, Roger Dean *physicist, department chairman*
Bernard, David Kane *minister, writer, editor*
Bernstein, Robert *retired physician, state official, former army officer*
Bersuker, Isaac Borukhovich *chemistry researcher, educator*
Bhat, Chandra R. *engineering educator, consultant*
Biesele, John Julius *biologist, educator*
Billings, Harold Wayne *library director, editor*
†Bingham, Ouita Hyams *librarian*
Blodgett, Warren Terrell *public affairs educator*
Bobbitt, Philip Chase *writer, educator, public official*
†Boggiano, Michael Humberto *geneticist, small business owner*
Boggs, James Ernest *chemistry educator*
Bonjean, Charles Michael *foundation executive, sociologist, educator*
Bordie, John George *linguistics educator*
†Boretz, Avron A. *anthropologist, educator*
†Botsford, David L. *lawyer*
Box, John Harold
Bradford, Mary Pinkney *music educator*
Brannon-Peppas, Lisa *chemical engineer, researcher*
Bray, Austin Coleman, Jr., *lawyer, investor*
Breen, John Edward *civil engineer, educator*
Breunig, Robert Glass *botanical facility administrator*
Brewer, Thomas Bowman *retired university president*
Bright, Garry Michael *executive*
Brock, James Rush *chemical engineering educator*
Brockett, Oscar Gross *theatre educator*
Bronaugh, Edwin Lee *electromagnetic compatibility engineer, consultant*
†Brown, Dick Terrell *lawyer*
Brown, Norman Donald *history educator*
†Brown, Vivian Anderson *retired government agency administrator*
Buchanan, Bruce, II, *political science educator*
Burnaman, Stephen Paul *music educator*
Burnham, Walter Dean *political science educator*
Burns, Ned Hamilton *civil engineering educator*
Cannon, William Bernard *retired university educator*
Cantú, Norma V. *law educator, former federal official*
Carballo, Juan-Antonio *research scientist*
Cardozier, Virgus Ray *higher education educator*
Carleton, Don Edward *history center administrator, educator, writer*
Carlton, Donald Morrill *research, development and engineering executive*
†Carmical, Phil *editor*
Carner, William John *banker*
Casey, James Francis *management consultant*
Castaldi, Frank James *environmental engineer, consultant*
Causey, Robert Louis *philosopher, educator, consultant*
Churgin, Michael Jay *law educator, educator*
Clark, Charles T(aliferro) *retired business statistics educator*
Clark, Pat English *lawyer*
Clark, Roy Thomas, Jr., *chemistry educator, administrator*
Cleaves, Peter Shurtleff *foundation official*
Cleland, Charles Carr *psychologist, educator*
†Comas, Alice Cuprill *lawyer*
Conine, Ernest *newspaper commentator, writer*
Connolly, Carla Garcia *lawyer*
Cook, J(ohn) Rowland *lawyer*
Cooke, Carlton Lee, Jr., *mayor*
Cooper, William Wager *business educator*
Coronado, Santiago Sybert (Jim Coronado) *judge*
Corredor, Mary B. *language educator, consultant, translator*
Cortez, Hernan Glenn *lawyer*
†Coultas, Edward Owen *lawyer*
Covington, Veronica Pro *librarian, educator*
Crane, Gary Wade *mathematician, physicist*
Craparo, John S. *information technology executive*
†Crenshaw, Ben *professional golfer*
Crum, Lawrence Lee *banking educator*
†Cruz, Ted *lawyer*
Culp, Joe C(arl) *electronics executive*
†Cundiff, Edward William *marketing educator*
Cunningham, Judy Marie *lawyer*
Cunningham, William Hughes *former academic administrator, marketing educator*
Curle, Robin Lea *computer software industry executive*
Cywar, Adam Walter *management engineer*
Dabbs Riley, Jeanne Kernodle *retired public relations executive*
Danielson, Wayne Allen *journalism and computer science educator*
Davis, Donald Gordon, Jr., *librarian, educator, historian*
Davis, Donald Robert *nutritionist, researcher, consultant*
†Davis, Robert Larry *lawyer*
Deal, Ernest Linwood, Jr., *banker*
Deisler, Paul Frederick, Jr., *retired oil company executive*
Delco, Exalton A., Jr., *retired biology educator*
Dennis, Elizabeth P. *social worker, therapist, consultant*
Denny, Mary Craver *state legislator, rancher*
DeVere, Ronald *neurologist*
†Dewhurst, David *lieutenant governor*
DeWitt-Morette, Cécile *physicist*
Dirienzo, Margaret Helen *nursing administrator*
Divine, Robert Alexander *history educator*
Doenges, Rudolph Conrad *finance educator*
Doluisio, James Thomas *pharmacy educator*
Dorsch, Jeffrey Peter *journalist*
Dougal, Arwin Adelbert *electrical engineer, educator*
Dougherty, John Chrysostom, III, *retired lawyer*
Dougherty, Molly Ireland *organization executive*
Drake, Stephen Douglas *clinical psychologist, health facility administrator*
Drolla, John Casper Dodt, Jr., *lawyer*
Drongowski, Steve *advertising executive*
Drummond Borg, Lesley Margaret *clinical geneticist*
†DuBose, Gaylan Ray *elementary school educator, musician, writer*
Dukes, Katharine Lee *lawyer*
Dulles, John Watson Foster *history educator*
Duncombe, Raynor Lockwood *astronomer*
Durbin, Richard Louis, Sr., *healthcare administration consultant*
Dusansky, Richard *economist, educator*
Dyer, Cromwell Adair, Jr., *lawyer, international organization official*
Easley, Christa Birgit *nurse, researcher*
†Ehrle, William Lawrence *lawyer, association executive*
Ehrlich, Stacy Wheeler *school fundraiser, administrator*
Eldredge, Linda Gaile *psychologist*
Elequin, Cleto, Jr., *retired physician*
Ell, Travis Eugene *electronics engineer*
Ellis, Glen Edward, Jr., *insurance agent, financial planner*
Epright, Charles John *retired aerospace engineer*
Epstein, Jeremiah Fain *anthropologist, educator*
†Erengil, Mehmet Erdal *aeronautical engineer, researcher*
Ersek, Robert Allen *plastic surgeon, inventor*
Erskine, James Lorenzo *physics educator*
†Escoto, Luz *language educator*
Eskew, James Robert *otolaryngologist*
Evans, Walter Reed *retired engineering executive, consultant*
Fair, James Rutherford, Jr., *chemical engineering educator, consultant*
Farrell, Edmund James *retired English language educator, author*
Faulkner, Larry Ray *university official, chemistry educator*
Fearing, William Kelly *art educator, artist*
†Feazell, Vic *lawyer*
Firey, Walter Irving, Jr., *retired sociologist, educator*
Fisher, William Lawrence *geologist, educator*
Fisk, Doris Rosalie Scanlan *volunteer*
Fleeger, David Clark *colon and rectal surgeon*
Fletcher, Robin Mary *health care administrator*
Folk, Robert Louis *geologist, educator*
†Folkers, Karl August *chemistry educator*
†Fomel, Sergey *geophysicist*
Fonken, Gerhard Joseph *retired chemistry educator, academic administrator*
Fowler, David Wayne *architectural engineering educator*
Fox, Beth Wheeler *library director*
Franklin, G(eorge) Charles *retired academic administrator*
Franklin, Robert Drury *oil company executive, lawyer*
Freedenberg, Debra *physician, geneticist*
Freeman, Robert Schofield *musicologist, educator, pianist*
Friedman, Alan Warren *humanities educator*
†Furlong, Richard W. *structural engineer, educator*
Gagarin, Michael *literature educator*
Galinsky, Gotthard Karl *classicist, educator*
Gambrell, James Bruton, III, *lawyer, educator*
Gangstad, John Erik *lawyer*
Gardner, Joan *medical, surgical nurse*
†Garmong, Robert Allen *philosophy educator*
Garner, Harvey Louis *computer scientist, consultant, electrical engineering educator*
Garstka, John Edward *interior design educator*
Garwood, William Lockhart *judge*
Garza, Thomas Jesus *language educator*
Gates, Charles Woodley, Sr., *city official*
Gavande, Sampat Anand *agricultural engineer, soil scientist*
Gentle, Kenneth William *physicist*
George, Walter Eugene, Jr., *architect*
†Gesn, Paul Randall *social psychologist, researcher*
Gibson, George Edward, Jr., *civil engineering educator, consultant, researcher*
Gibson, Jerry Leigh *oil company executive*
Gillman, Leonard *mathematician, educator*
†Gilmson, Sophia *music educator*
†Gimble, Johnny *country musician*
Gionfriddo, Paul *healthcare executive*
Glade, William Patton, Jr., *economics educator*
†Glenn, Norval Dwight *sociologist, educator*
Gloyna, Earnest Frederick *environmental engineer, educator*
Godfrey, Cullen Michael *lawyer, academic administrator*
Golden, Edwin Harold *insurance company executive*
Golden, Kimberly Kay *critical care, flight nurse*
Goldstein, E. Ernest *lawyer, consultant*
Goldstein, Peggy R. *sculptor*
Golemon, Ronald Kinnan *lawyer*
Gomes, Norman Vincent *retired industrial engineer*
Goodenough, John Bannister *engineering educator, research physicist*
Gracy, David Bergen, II, *archivist, information science educator, writer*
Graglia, Lino Anthony *lawyer, educator*
Graham, Don Ballew *literature educator, writer*
Graham, Seldon Bain, Jr., *lawyer, engineer*
Grangaard, Daniel Robert *psychologist*
Granof, Michael H. *accounting educator*
Grant, Verne Edwin *biology educator*
Graydon, Frank Drake *retired accounting educator, university administrator*
Green, Shirley Moore *retired public affairs and communications executive*
Greene, John Joseph *lawyer*
Greenhill, Joe Robert *former chief justice state supreme court, lawyer*
Greig, Brian Strother *lawyer*
Griffin, Alan Nash *psychologist*
Griffy, Thomas Alan *physics educator*
Grimm, Clayford Thomas *architectural engineer, consultant*
†Grosenheider, Delno John *lawyer*
Guerin, John William *artist*
Gustafsson, Lars Erik Einar *writer, educator*
Haas, Joseph Marshall *petroleum consultant*
†Hackney, Clint Porter *lawyer, lobbyist*
Hagerty, Polly Martiel *financial analyst, construction executive*
Hale, Louis Dewitt *lawyer*
Hall, Beverly Adele *nursing educator*
Hamermesh, Daniel Selim *economics educator*
Hamilton, Dagmar Strandberg *lawyer, educator*
Hansen, Niles Maurice *economics educator*
Hardin, Dale Wayne *retired lawyer, federal official*
Harms, Robert Thomas *linguist, educator*
Harris, Ben M. *education educator*
Harris, Richard Lee *engineering executive, retired army officer*
Harrison, Richard Wayne *lawyer*
Hart, Roderick P. *communications educator, researcher, author*
Hatgil, Paul Peter *artist, sculptor, educator*
†Hayes, Burgain Garfield *lawyer*
Hayes, Patricia Ann *health facility administrator*
Hazel, Joseph Patrick *retired law educator*
Head, Ben Thomas *lawyer*
Hecht, Nathan Lincoln *state supreme court justice*
Helman, Stephen Jody *lawyer*
Henderson, George Ervin *lawyer*
†Henley, Paul Thomas *music educator, researcher*
Hernandez, Mack Ray *lawyer*
†Herrin, David Leslie *educator*
Herrington-Borre, Frances June *sign language school director*
Hetzler, Susan Elizabeth Savage *educational administrator*
High, Timothy Griffin *artist, educator, curator, writer*
Himmelblau, David Mautner *chemical engineer*
Hinich, Melvin Jay *government and economics educator*
Hinojosa-Smith, Roland *language educator, writer*
Hitchcock, Joanna *publisher*
Hixson, Elmer L. *retired engineering educator*
Holtzman, Joan King *musician, composer*
Holtzman, Wayne Harold *psychologist, educator*
Holz, Robert Kenneth *retired geography educator*
†Hopkins, Mitchell Shade *music educator*
†Howard, Carol Spencer *librarian, journalist*
Howard, John Loring *retired trust banker*
Howell, John Reid *mechanical engineering educator*
Huber, John Charles *information technology executive, director*
Hudspeth, Harry Lee *federal judge*
Huff, David L. *geography educator*
Hull, David George *aerospace engineering educator, researcher*
Hunter, Brother Eagan (Donald J. Hunter) *retired education educator*
Hutchins, Karen Leslie *psychotherapist*
†Ibison, Michael *physicist, researcher*
Ikard, Frank Neville, Jr., *lawyer*
Inman, Bobby Ray *educator, investor, former electronics executive*
Iscoe, Ira *psychology educator*
Ivy, John L. *medical educator, researcher*
Jackson, Eugene Bernard *librarian, educator*
Jackson, William Vernon *library science and Latin American studies educator*
Jacobson, Antone Gardner *zoology educator*
†Janes, Brandon Chaison *lawyer*
Jefferson, Wallace B. *state supreme court justice*
Jentz, Gaylord Adair *law educator*
†Jinkins, Wm. Michael *theology studies educator*
Johnson, Cheryl Ann *judge*
Johnson, Corwin Waggoner *law educator*
†Johnson, Karen Lee *lawyer*
Johnson, Lady Bird (Mrs. Claudia Alta Taylor) *wife of former President of United States*
Johnson, Sandra Lynn Terry *education consultant*
Jones, William Richard *database administrator*
Jordan, Bryce *retired university president*
Jordan-Bychkov, Terry Gilbert *geography educator*
Judson, Philip Livingston *lawyer*
Jumper, Douglas Cameron *publication coordinator, media consultant*
Kane, James Robert *financial executive*
†Kawaguchi, Meredith Ferguson *lawyer*
Keith, Timothy Zook *psychology educator*
Kendrick, David Andrew *economist, educator*
Kennan, Kent Wheeler *composer, educator*
Kerr, Stanley Munger *investigator, lawyer, educator*
†Kibler, William Westcott *French language and literature educator*
Kimberlin, Sam Owen, Jr., *financial institutions consultant*
Kimmel, Troy Max, Jr., *meteorologist*
Kirk, Lynda Pounds *biofeedback therapist, neurotherapist, counselor*
Klym, Kendall *journalist, dancer, educator, choreographer*
Knapp, Mark Lane *communication educator, consultant*
Kockelman, Kara Maria *engineering educator*
Koen, Billy Vaughn *mechanical engineering educator*
Koepsel, Wellington Wesley *electrical engineering educator*
Krishna, Hari J. *engineer*
†Kroll, John Hennig *humanities educator*
Lafferty, Joyce G. Zvonar *retired middle school educator*
Laine, Katie Myers *communications consultant, executive coach*
Lam, Simon Shin-Sing *computer science educator*
Lamb, Jamie Parker, Jr., *retired mechanical engineer, educator*
Landsberger, Sheldon *nuclear engineer, educator, radiation engineer, educator*
†Laosa, Mike *publishing executive*
Lariviere, Richard Wilfred *university administrator, educator, consultant*
Larkam, Beverley McCosham *clinical social worker, family therapist*
Larson, Kermit Dean *accounting educator*
Lary, Banning Kent *video producer, publisher*
La Salle, Peter *English educator, writer*
Lauchner, Kathryn Ann *nursing educator*
Laves, Alan Leonard *lawyer*
Laycock, Harold Douglas *law educator, writer*
†Leaverton, Mark Kane *lawyer*
Leeds, Sanford J., III, *financial executive, educator*
Lehmann-Carssow, Nancy Beth *secondary school educator, coach*
†Lehmberg, Rosemary *prosecutor*
Lemens, William Vernon, Jr., *banker, finance company executive, lawyer*
Lenoir, Gloria Cisneros *consultant, educator*
Leonhardt, Thomas Wilburn *librarian, library director*
Lewis, Nancy Louine Lambert *school counselor*
Livingston, Ann Chambliss *lawyer*
Livingston, William Samuel *university administrator, political scientist*
Lochridge, Lloyd Pampell, Jr., *lawyer*
Lockett, Landon Johnson *former linguistic educator, researcher*
Loehlin, John Clinton *psychologist, educator*
Long, Bert Louis, Jr., *artist*
Lopreato, Joseph *sociologist, writer*
Louis, William Roger *historian*
†Lucio, Eduardo Andres, Jr., *state legislator*
Luedecke, William Henry *mechanical engineer*
Lukenbill, Willis Bernard
†Maar, Rosina *medical organization executive*
MacDonald, Martha Frances *clarinetist, music educator*
Mackey, Louis Henry *philosophy educator*
Maguire, Kevin *travel management consultant*
Malcolm, Molly Beth *political party official, counselor*
†Mann, Roy Bernard *landscape architect, educator*
†Manthiram, Arumugam *materials science and engineering educator*
Mark, Hans Michael *physicist, government official*
Mark, Marion Thorpe *writing educator*
Marse, Linda Moody *music educator*
Martin, Frederick Noel *audiology educator*
Mason, Franklin Rogers *retired automotive executive*
†Matheson, Daniel Nicholas, III, *lawyer*
Mathias, Reuben Victor (Vic Mathias) *chamber of commerce executive, real estate investor*
†Matthews, Jay Arlon, Jr., *publisher, editor*
Maxwell, Arthur Eugene *oceanographer, marine geophysicist, educator*
Mayer, Susan Martin *art educator*
Mayes, Wendell Wise, Jr., *broadcasting company executive*
Mazzetti, Robert F. *real estate manager, retired orthopedic surgeon*
†McConnico, Stephen E. *lawyer*
McCullough, Frank Witcher, III, *lawyer*
McDaniel, Myra Atwell *lawyer, former state official*
Mc Donald, Stephen Lee *economics educator*
McElroy, Mary M. (Mickie McElroy) *educational writer*
McFadden, Dennis *experimental psychology educator*
Mc Ketta, John J., Jr., *chemical engineering educator*
Mc Kinney, Michael Whitney *trade association executive*
†Mear, Charles Eugene *geologist, consultant*
Meigs, Montgomery Cunningham, Jr., *retired military officer, educator*
†Meikle, Jeffrey L. *history educator, writer*
Mersky, Roy Martin *law educator, librarian*
†Meston, Cindy M(ay) *psychologist, educator*
†Meyer, Delia Perez *humanities educator*
†Meyers, Lawrence Edward *state judge*
Middleton, Christopher *Germanic languages and literature educator*
Middleton, Harry Joseph *foundation administrator*
Miller, Charles E. (Chuck Miller) *judge*
Mills, Stephen *artistic director*

Moag, Rodney Frank *language educator, country music singer*
†Montreuil, Jean-Pierre Y. *language educator*
†Mooney, John Bradford, Jr., *oceanographer, engineer, consultant*
†Moreno, David *artist*
Morrow, Sandra Kay *librarian*
Moss, Bill Ralph *lawyer*
Moss, Logan Vansen *lawyer*
Moyers, Robert Charles *systems analyst, state official, microcomputer consultant, government systems developer*
Mueller, Peggy Jean *dance educator, choreographer, rancher*
Mullen, Ron *insurance company executive*
Murphy, Michele Sandra *musician, educator*
Murthy, Vanukuri Radha Krishna *civil engineer*
†Neblett, Stewart Lawrence *lawyer*
†Neeld, Elizabeth Harper *author, retreat and workshop leader, consultant*
†Neubert, Bernard David *music educator*
Nevola, Roger *lawyer*
Nicastro, David Harlan *forensic engineer, consultant, author*
Nichols, Steven Parks *mechanical engineer, lawyer, educator*
Novak, Gordon S., Jr., *computer scientist, educator*
Nowlin, James Robertson *federal judge*
O'Connor, James T. *civil engineering educator*
Oden, John Tinsley *engineering educator, mathematician, consultant*
O'Geary, Dennis Traylor *retired contracting/engineering company executive*
†Olsen, Christopher Mark *research scientist*
O'Neill, Harriet *state supreme court justice*
Oppel, Richard Alfred *newspaper executive*
Oram, Robert W. *library administrator*
†Osborn, Joe Allen *lawyer*
Osborne, Duncan Elliott *lawyer*
†Otto, Byron Leonard *lawyer, state administrator*
Owen, Priscilla Richman *state supreme court justice*
†Pachon, Julian Enrique *research scientist, consultant*
Painter, Theophilus Shickel, Jr., *internist, allergist*
Parrino, Robert *finance educator*
Pate, Jacqueline Hail *retired data processing company executive*
Patman, Philip Franklin *lawyer*
Patterson, Donald Eugene *research scientist*
Paul, Donald Ross *chemical engineer, educator*
Payne, John Ross *rare books, archives and photographs appraisal consulting company executive, library science educator*
Payne, Tyson Elliott, Jr., *retired insurance executive*
Pearson, Jim Berry, Jr., *human resources specialist*
†Pells, Richard H. *historian, educator*
Pena, Richard *lawyer*
Peppas, Nikolaos Athanassiou *chemical and biomedical engineering educator, consultant*
Perkins, Robert Anton *judge*
Perry, Rick *governor*
Peterson, Robert Allen *marketing educator*
Phillips, Joseph Daniel *geophysicist, oceanographer*
Phillips, Thomas Royal *judge*
†Phillips, Travis R. *lawyer*
Pingree, Dianne *psychotherapist*
Pope, Andrew Jackson, Jr., (Jack Pope) *retired judge*
Porter, Jenny Lind *writer*
Posey, Daniel Earl *analytical chemist*
Probus, Michael Maurice, Jr., *lawyer*
†Ramon, Emilio *language educator*
Rasbury, Julian George *financial services company executive*
Rascoe, Paul Stephen *librarian, researcher*
Ratliff, William *former stae senator; lieutenant governor, civil engineer*
Ray, Cread L., Jr., *retired state supreme court justice*
Reavley, Thomas Morrow *federal judge*
Rector, Clark Ellsworth *advertising executive*
Reed, Lester James *biochemist, educator*
Reese, Claudia *artist*
Reese, Lymon Clifton *civil engineering educator*
Reid, Jackson Brock *psychologist, educator*
†Rentfrow, Peter J *psychologist*
Rich, John Martin *humanities educator, researcher*
Richards, Ann Willis *former governor*
†Ricker, George M. *minister, educator*
Rider, Brian Clayton *lawyer*
Rider, Katherine Loveta Thompson *clinical social worker*
Roach, James Robert *retired political science educator*
Roan, Forrest Calvin, Jr., *lawyer*
Robbins, Mary *concert pianist*
Robinson, Priscilla Jane *artist*
Robinson, Richard Allen, Jr., *human resources development trainer, consultant*
Rodden, John Gallagher *communications educator, writer*
Rogers, Lorene Lane *university president emeritus*
Rossen, William R. *engineering educator*
Rostow, Elspeth Davies *political science educator*
Rotunda, Joseph Louis *retail and service company executive*
Roueche, John Edward, II, *education educator, leadership program director*
Roueche, Suanne Davis *university administrator*
†Roy, Indrajit Ghosh *geophysicist, educator*
Royal, Darrell K. *university official, former football coach*
†Ruez, Dennis R. *geology educator*
Ruiz, Cookie *performing company executive*
†Rush, Sharron Anne *writer, nonprofit executive officer*
Rylander, Henry Grady, Jr., *mechanical engineering educator*
Sanchez, Isaac Cornelius *chemical engineer, educator*
Sandberg, Irwin Walter *electrical and computer engineering educator*
†Sarkar, Sahotra *biologist, philosophy educator*
Saunders, Jimmy Dale *aerospace engineer, physicist, naval officer*
Sawyer, Margo Lucy *artist, educator*
Schleuse, William *retired psychiatrist, psychoanalyst*
Schmandt, Jurgen A. *public affairs educator*
Schmitt, Karl Michael *retired political scientist*
Schulze, Eric William *lawyer, legal publications editor, publisher*
Schwartz, Aaron Robert *lawyer, former state legislator*
Schwartz, Leonard Jay *lawyer*
Sciance, Carroll Thomas *chemical engineer*
†Scott, Laurie P. *music educator*
Seifoullaev, Roustam Kafar *mathematician, programmer*
Seung, Thomas Kaehao *philosophy educator*
Shapiro, David L. *lawyer*
Shaw, James *information technology specialist*
Shea, Gwyn *secretary of state*
†Shiff, Richard Allen *director, art historian*
Shilling, Roy Bryant, Jr., *academic administrator*
Sims, Robert Barry *lawyer*
Smith, Alfred Goud *anthropologist, educator*
Smith, Barry Alan *hotel executive, real estate broker*
Smith, Bert Kruger *retired mental health services professional*
Smith, Daniel Montague *engineer*
Smith, Dorothy Brand *retired librarian*
Smith, Jeffrey Carlin *lawyer*
Smith, Jeffrey Chipps *art educator*
†Smith, Lawrence Shannon *lawyer*
Smith, Todd Malcolm *political consultant*
Sober, Debra Evonne *environmental services administrator*
†Sole, Carlos A. *language educator*
Sparks, Sam *federal judge*
Spielman, Barbara Helen New *editor, consultant*
Spielman, David Vernon *retired insurance, finance and publications consultant*
†Spivey, Broadus Autry *lawyer*
Staley, Thomas Fabian *language professional, academic administrator*
Steinfink, Hugo *chemical engineering educator*
Stephen, John Erle *lawyer, consultant*
Stewart, Kent Kallam *analytical biochemistry educator*
Stoll, William Hermann *real estate company executive*
Strauser, Robert Wayne *lawyer*
Streetman, Ben Garland *electrical engineering educator*
Sturdevant, Wayne Alan *executive management consultant*
Sturley, Michael F. *law educator*
Stutts, William Floyd, Jr., *lawyer, educator*
Sullivan, Jerry Stephen *electronics company executive*
Sullivan, Teresa Ann *law and sociology educator, academic administrator*
†Sun, Shuyu *mathematician, chemical engineer, petroleum engineer*
Sutherland, William Owen Sheppard *English language educator*
†Sutton, Beverly Jewell *psychiatrist*
Sutton, Harry Eldon *geneticist, educator*
Sutton, John F., Jr., *law educator, dean, lawyer*
Swartzlander, Earl Eugene, Jr., *engineering educator, former electronics company executive*
Swinney, Harry Leonard *physics educator*
Tatham, Robert Haines *geophysicist, educator*
Temple, Larry Eugene *lawyer*
†Tesar, Delbert *machine systems and robotics educator, researcher, manufacturing consultant*
†Theriot, Edward C. *museum director*
Thiessen, Delbert Duane *psychologist*
Thompson, Larry Flack *nanotechnology and semiconductor process company executive*
Thornton, Joseph Scott *research institute executive, materials scientist*
Thurston, George Butte *mechanical and biomedical engineering educator*
†Todd, Bruce M. *public affairs executive, former mayor*
Touba, Nur Ali *electrical engineering educator*
Townsend, Richard Marvin *government insurance executive, city manager, consultant*
Trafton, Laurence Munro *astronomer, researcher*
Turney, James Edward *computer scientist*
Tyler, Ronnie Curtis *historian*
Udagawa, Takeshi *physicist, educator*
Van Buren, William Benjamin, III, *retired pharmaceutical company executive*
Vande Hey, James Michael *corporate executive, former air force officer*
Vandel, Diana Geis *management consultant*
Velte, Paul Christian, IV, *lawyer*
Vykukal, Eugene Lawrence *wholesale drug company executive*
Wadlington, Warwick Paul *English language educator*
Wahlberg, Philip Lawrence *former bishop*
Walker, James Roy *microbiologist*
Walls, Carl Edward, Jr., *food service executive*
Walter, Virginia Lee *psychologist, educator*
Walton, Charles Michael *civil engineering educator*
Warner, David Cook *public affairs educator*
†Warr, Eric Mark *sociologist, educator*
Watson, Brenda Bennett *insurance company executive*
Weddington, Sarah Ragle *lawyer, educator, speaker, writer*
Weddington, Susan *political party official*
Weinberg, Louise *law educator, author*
Weintraub, Russell Jay *lawyer, educator*
Weismann, Donald Leroy *art educator, artist, filmmaker, writer*
Welch, Ashley James *engineering educator*
Wellborn, Olin Guy, III, *law educator, educator*
†Wentworth, Earl Jeffrey *lawyer, realtor, state legislator*
Werbow, Stanley Newman *language educator*
West, Glenn Edward *investment banking executive*
†West, Royce *lawyer, state legislator*
Westbrook, Jay Lawrence *law educator*
†Wester, Ruric Herschel, Jr., *lawyer*
Wheeler, John Craig *astrophysicist, writer*
Whitbread, Thomas Bacon *English educator, author*
White, Alice Virginia *college campaign program administrator*
White, John Michael *chemistry educator*
White, Tom Martin *playwright, music publisher*
Williams, Calvit Herndon *environmental chemist*
Williams, Diane Elizabeth *architectural historian, photographer*
Williams, Mary Pearl *judge*
Williamson, Hugh Jackson *statistician*
Williamson, Thomas Arnold *publishing company executive*
Willson, C. Grant *chemistry educator, engineering educator*
Winegar, Albert Lee *computer systems company executive*
†Winters, Sam *lawyer*
†Wise, Miguel David *lawyer*
Wittliff, Danny Joe *environmental engineer*
Wolf, Harold Arthur *finance educator*
†Wood, Donald F. *lawyer*
Woodson, Herbert Horace *retired electrical engineering educator*
Worden, Sue Janine *engineer, scientist*
Worthing, Carol Marie *minister*
Wurzbach, Linda *educational consultant*
†Wynn, Will *mayor*
†Yoon, SungPil *aerospace engineer, researcher*
York, Candace A. *marketing professional, writer*
Yudof, Mark George *law educator, university system chancellor*
Ziegler, Daniel Martin *chemistry educator*
†Zrno, John M. *communications executive*

Baird
Rodenberger, Charles Alvard *aerospace engineer, consultant*

Bandera
Bartley, William Call *science administrator*

Bangs
Whiteley, James Morris *retired aerospace engineer*

Bastrop
Carpenter, Delbert Stanley *educational administration educator*

Bay City
†Peden, Robert F., Jr., *retired lawyer*

Baytown
Adams-Anderson, Niki Maria *communications company executive*
Black, Sarah Joanna Bryan *secondary school educator*
†Botto, Robert Irving *analytical chemist, antique dealer*
Chavez, John Anthony *lawyer*
Kolb, Rainer *chemist*
Leiper, Robert Duncan *local government official*
†Loyka, Jeffrey J. *environmental engineer*
†Martinez, Jerry *import/export agent*
Williams, Drew Davis *surgeon*

Beaumont
Alter, Nelson Tobias *jewelry retailer and wholesaler*
Alter, Shirley Jacobs *jewelry store owner*
Bahrim, Cristian *physicist, educator*
Baker, Mary Alice *communication educator, consultant*
Bias, Dana G. *lawyer*
Black, Robert Allen *lawyer*
Brailsford, June Evelyn *musician, educator*
Brentlinger, William Brock *college dean*
Brooks, Jack Bascom *former congressman*
Burgess, Don R. *judge*
Castloo, Shirley Annette *government official, retired civilian military employee*
Chiou, Paul C.J. *statistician, educator*
Ciallella, Emil Anthony *library director, consultant*
Cobb, Howell *federal judge*
Dowell, James Dale *lawyer*
Dryden, Woodson E. *lawyer*
Ellsworth, Myrna Ruth *accountant*
Gagne, Mary *academic administrator*
Hawkins, Emma B. *humanities educator*
Hopper, Jack Rudd *chemical engineering educator*
Janak, Robert Louis *foreign language educator*
Jao, Mien *civil engineer educator*
Johnson, Leanne *lawyer*
Koehn, Enno *engineering educator, researcher*
Lord, Evelyn Marlin *mayor*
Lozano, Jose *nephrologist*
McCord, Michael David *anesthesiologist*
McKenney, Scott Alan *oncologist*
Morales, Emmitt *mechanical consultant*
Myler, Harley Ross *electrical engineer, educator*
Newton, John Wharton, III, *lawyer*
Oxford, Hubert, III, *lawyer*
†Roth, Lane *communications educator*
Scofield, Louis M., Jr., *lawyer*
Smith, Floyd Rodenback *retired utilities executive*
Tucker, Gary Wilson *nursing educator*
Ware, John David *valve and hydrant company executive*

Bedford
Champney, Raymond Joseph *advertising and marketing executive, consultant*
Farhat, Georges Antoun *anesthesiologist*
Hamstra, Christine Josephine *social worker*
Walther, Richard Ernest *psychology educator, library administrator*

Bedias
Williamson, Norma Beth *adult education educator*

Beeville
†Switzer, Linda Thrall *music educator*

Bellaire
Haywood, Theodore Joseph *physician, educator*
†Hollrah, David *lawyer*
Jacobus, Charles Joseph *lawyer, title company executive, writer*
†Lilienstern, O. Clayton *lawyer, educator*
Lundy, Anstis Burwell *artist*
Lundy, Victor Alfred *architect, educator*
†Martin, John Randolph *judge*
Mayo, Clyde Calvin *organizational psychologist, educator*
Mote, Marie Therese *reference librarian*
Pokorny, Alex Daniel *psychiatrist*
Rhodes, George Frederick, Jr., *lawyer*
†Streeter, Kevin D. *management consultant*
Teas, John Frederick *small business owner*
Wisch, David John *structural engineer*

Bellville
Neely, Robert Allen *retired ophthalmologist*

Belton
Andreason, George Edward *university administrator*
†Burrows, Jon Hanes *lawyer*
†Gary, Jonathan Mark *academic administrator*
†Guess, David Lynn *education educator*
Harrison, Benjamin Leslie *retired army officer*
Miller, Richard Joseph *lawyer*
Shoemaker, Robert Morin *retired army officer, county government official*
†Wood, Connie Garrison *music educator*

Benbrook
Margolis, Susan Ellen *psychiatric clinical nurse specialist, artist*

Bertram
Albert, Susan Wittig *writer, English educator*

Big Spring
Fryrear, Donald William *agricultural engineer, researcher*
Reddy, Gaddum Jagan Mohan *surgeon*
Wylie, Mary Ann *critical care nurse*

Blanco
Dudley, Brooke Fitzhugh *educational consultant*

Boerne
Daugherty, Linda Hagaman *private school executive*
Goode, Bobby Claude *retired secondary education educator, writer*
Mitchelhill, James Moffat *retired civil engineer*
Price, John Randolph *writer*
Richmond, James Ellis *retired restaurant company executive*
†Vaughan, Edward Gibson *lawyer*
Wittmer, James Frederick *preventive medicine physician, educator*

Bogata
†Marris, Roy O. *agriculturist, consultant*

Borger
Allen, Bessie Malvina *music educator, church organist*
Pace, Rosa White *lawyer*

Breckenridge
Jones, Karen Annette *civic volunteer*
Reaugh, O(rland) H. *oil industry executive*

Brenham
Dalrymple, Christopher Guy *chiropractor*
†Lubbock, Mildred Marcelle (Midge Lubbock) *former small business owner*
†Moorman, Richard Hal, IV, *lawyer*
Moorman, Robert Lawson *real estate appraiser and broker*
Mueller, Renee Ann *lawyer*
Pipes, Paul Ray *county commissioner*
†Plaag, Joel Fredrick *music educator, director*
Rothermel, James Douglas *retired finance educator*

Brooks AFB
Caldwell, John Alvis, Jr., *experimental psychologist*
†Patterson, John C. *clinical psychology researcher*
Polhamus, Garrett Douglas *biomedical engineer*

Brooks City Base
Balldin, Ulf Ingemar *medical researcher*
†Tanner, Gordon Owen *lawyer*

Brownfield
Denison, James Dickey *broadcasting executive*
†McNamara, Derek Michael *education educator, minister*

Brownsville
Adams, William Leigh *history educator*
†Boze, Betsy Vogel *university dean, marketing educator*
Fitzpatrick, John J. *bishop*
Fleming, Tommy Wayne *lawyer*
†Garcia, Juliet Villarreal *university administrator*
Garza, Reynaldo G. *federal judge*
†Gilbert, Marilyn del Bosque *architectural engineer*
Gómez, Carlos Guillermo *artist, educator, curator*
Imperial, Henry L. *internist*
Pena, Raymundo Joseph *bishop*

Ray, Mary Louise Ryan *lawyer*
Santa-Coloma, Bernardo *secondary school educator, counselor*
Soldan, Angelika *philosopher, political scientist, educator*
†Stone, Michael John *music educator, conductor*
†Walsh, Lawrence Adrian *lawyer, consultant*
Walss, Rodolfo J. *obstetrician-gynecologist, hypnotherapist, artist*
Weisfeld, Sheldon *lawyer*
†Yi, Taeil *mathematician, educator*
†Zdansky, Janice Cecelia *mathematician*

Brownwood
†Banks, Patricia Anne *music educator, minister*
Bell, Mary E. Beniteau *accountant*
Bell, William Woodward *lawyer*
Roby, Annie Beth Brian *librarian*
†Weeks, Patsy Ann Landry *librarian, educator*

Bryan
Anderson, Frank Gist, Jr., *ophthalmologist, educator*
Branson, Robert Earl *marketing economist*
Bryant, Keith Lynn, Jr., *history educator*
Dirks, Kenneth Ray *pathologist, medical educator, army officer*
Ezzell, Catherine *librarian*
†Guitry, Loraine Dunn *community health nurse*
Helpert-Nunez, Ruth Anne *clinical social worker, psychotherapist*
Hubert, Frank William Rene *retired university system chancellor*
Jackson, Thomas O. *real estate appraiser, urban planner*
Luepnitz, Roy Robert *psychologist, consultant, small business owner, entrepreneur*
Lusas, Edmund William *food processing research executive*
Milford, Murray Hudson *retired soil science educator*
Miller, Thomas Eugene *lawyer, writer*
Parrott, Thena Elizabeth *nurse educator*
Samson, Charles Harold, Jr., (Car Samson) *retired engineering educator, consultant*
Smith, Elouise Beard *restaurant owner*
Smith, Steven Lee *judge*
Steelman, Frank (Frank Sitley) *lawyer*
†Valdez-Flores, Ciriaco *risk management consultant*
†Van Ouwerkerk, Anita Harrison *reading educator*

Bryan
Hanks, Clay David *academic administrator*

Buchanan Dam
Miloy, Leatha Faye *university program director*

Buffalo
Standley, John Robert *city official*

Buffalo Gap
Simpson, Patricia Elaine *education educator, dean*

Bullard
Morley, William George *retired military officer, educator*

Bulverde
†Donbavand, James Joseph, Jr., *medical facility administrator*

Burkburnett
Ratliff, Janice Kay *legal administrator*

Burleson
Buford, Evelyn Claudene Shilling *retired consumer products company executive*
Just, Philip Ray *auditor*
Lisi, Lori A. (Lori Fredeking) *freelance/self-employed editor, writer*

Burnet
Burris, Darrel Gene *retired company executive*

Bushland
Unger, Paul Walter *retired soil scientist*

Calvert
Alemán, Marthanne Payne *environmental planner, consultant*

Canton
Sanders, Bobby Lee *lawyer*
White, Jeffery Howell *lawyer*

Canyon
Burton, Robert Clyde *science educator*
†Furnish, Shearle Lee *English and modern languages educator*
Hanson, Trudy L. *speech professional, educator*
Long, Russell Charles *academic administrator*
†Nix, Susan Jenkins *principal, education educator*
†Peddie, Ian A. *language educator*
Roper, Beryl Cain *writer, publisher, retired library director*
†Sheffield, Jovonna Michele *music educator*
Stewart, B(obby) A(lton) *soil scientist, educator*
†Teichmann, Sandra Gail *English educator, writer, playwright, artist*
†Thoman, Roy Edward *political scientist, educator*
Welch, Reed Lynn *political scientist, educator*
Williams, Donald Mace *newswriter, writer*

Canyon Lake
Reinhardt, Linda Kay *minister*

Carrollton
Ades, Bruce Allan *engineering executive, researcher*
Conrad, Philip Jefferson *software development engineer*
Councill, William Thomas, III, *computer engineer, consultant*
Daily, Ellen Wilmoth Matthews *technical publications specialist*
Fricke, Raymond W. *religious school administrator*
Guy, Marc Duane *assistant city manager*
Hart, Elizabeth Ann *foundation administrator*
†Heath, Jinger L. *cosmetics executive*
Henderson, William David *mechanical engineer*
†Hulbert, Paul William, Jr., *paper, lumber company executive*
Laurent, Duane Giles *memory design engineer*
Riggs, Arthur Jordy *retired lawyer*
Turner, Bruce Edward *lawyer*
Varner, Bruce H., Jr., *fire department official, educator*
Withrow, Lucille Monnot *nursing home administrator*

Carthage
†Brumley, Larry Gene *music educator*
Cooke, Walta Pippen *automobile dealership owner*

Cedar Creek
†Odiorne, James Thomas *lawyer, accountant*

Cedar Hill
Ebozue, Benson Obian *financial analyst*
Garrett, C. Lynn *researcher, business consultant*
Hickman, Traphene Parramore *library director, storyteller, library and library building consultant*
Moore, Jacquelyn *art educator, artist*
Shower, Robert Wesley *financial executive*

Cedar Park
Albin, Leslie Owens *biology educator*
Fuller, Mitchell Franklin, II, *political scientist, educator*
Lam, Pauline Poha *library director*

Center
Morris, William Lewis *mathematician*

Channelview
Wallace, Betty Jean *elementary school educator, lay minister*

Channing
Brian, Mary H. *librarian*

Chillicothe
Brock, Helen Rachel McCoy *retired mental health and community health nurse*

Christoval
Mueller, James H. *priest*

Cibolo
Newsom, Melvin Max *retired research company executive*
Smith, Harry Leroy *securities firm executive*

Cleburne
†Arnold, Sandra Ruth Kouns *photographer*
†Black, Alvin M. *application developer*
Bushor, Mark Eldon *pastor, writer, consultant*
Gates, Steven Leon *physician*
Gorman, Charlotte A. *family and consumer sciences agent*
†MacLean, John Ronald *lawyer*

Cleveland
Campbell, Selaura Joy *lawyer*
Rice, J. Andrew *management consultant, tree farmer*

Clutch City
†Rice, Glen Anthony *professional basketball player*

Coldspring
Bunch, Robert Craig *librarian*

College Station
†Adams, H. Richard *dean*
Adams, Marvin Lee *nuclear engineer, researcher*
Adkisson, Perry Lee *university system chancellor*
Armstrong, Robert Beall *physiologist, educator*
Arnold, J(ames) Barto, III, *marine archaeologist*
Arnowitt, Richard Lewis *physics educator, researcher*
Bass, George Fletcher *retired archaeology educator*
Beaver, Bonnie Veryle *veterinarian, educator*
Berg, Robert Raymond *geologist, educator*
Bierman, Leonard *management educator*
Black, Samuel Harold *microbiology and immunology educator*
Bond, Jon Roy *political science educator*
Borlaug, Norman Ernest *agricultural scientist*
†Bowen, Ray Morris *academic administrator, engineering educator*
Bridges, Charles Hubert *veterinarian, educator*
Brown, Robert Dale *wildlife science educator, department head*
Burk, James Steven *sociologist*
Button, Joe Wade *civil engineer, researcher, consultant*
Byrne, C. William, Jr., *athletics program director*
Calhoun, John C., Jr., *academic administrator*
Cannon, Garland *linguist, educator*
Carlton, Dean *lawyer*
Carlton, Paul Kendall, Jr., *physician, retired air force officer*
Christensen, Paul Norman *English educator, writer*
Christiansen, James Edward *agricultural educator*
Cocanougher, Arthur Benton *business administration educator*
Cochran, Robert Glenn *nuclear engineering educator*
†Cohen, Aaron *aerospace engineer*
†Colenda, III, Christopher Columbus *psychiatrist*
Conway, Dwight Colbur *chemistry educator*
Cotton, Frank Albert *chemist*
Dees, William Leslie *veterinary medicine educator*
†De Petro, Thomas Gerard *librarian, educator*
Dethloff, Henry Clay *historian, educator*
Drees, Bastiaan Meijer *entomologist*
†Dunlap, Thomas R. *historian, educator*
Eaton, Gordon Pryor *geologist, consultant*
Edwards, George Charles, III, *political science educator, writer*
Ehsani, Mehrdad (Mark Ehsani) *electrical engineering educator, consultant*
†Entchev, Pavlin Borissov *aerospace and mechanical engineer*
Erlandson, David Alan *education administration educator*
Ewing, Richard Edward *mathematics, chemical and petroleum engineering educator*
Fackler, John Paul, Jr., *chemistry educator*
Fitzpatrick, Paul Frederick *biochemistry educator*
Fletcher, Leroy Stevenson *mechanical engineer, educator*
Furubotn, Eirik Grundtvig *economics educator*
Gibson, Claude Louis *English educator*
Godbey, Luther David *architectural and engineering executive*
Goodman, David Wayne *research chemist, educator*
Greenhut, Melvin Leonard *economist, educator*
Gunn, Clare Alward *travel consultant, writer, retired educator*
Hall, Kenneth Richard *chemical engineering educator, consultant*
Hall, Timothy Couzens *biology educator, consultant*
Hann, Roy William, Jr., *civil engineer, educator*
Hardy, John Christopher *physicist, educator*
Harner, James Lowell *English language educator*
Hise, Richard Todd *marketing professional, educator, consultant*
Holcombe, Troy Leon *marine geologist*
Holste, James Clifton *chemical engineering educator*
Huang, Chang-Shan *landscape architect, educator*
Isdale, Charles Edwin *chemical engineer*
Kainthla, Ramesh Chand *manufacturing company executive*
Kallendorf, Craig William *English, speech and classical languages educator*
Kier, Ann Burnette *pathologist*
†Kirk, Ivan Wayne *agricultural engineer*
Knutson, Ronald Dale *economist, educator, academic administrator*
Kohel, Russell James *geneticist*
Kunze, Otto Robert *retired agricultural engineering educator*
Kuo, Way *industrial engineer, researcher*
Laane, Jaan *chemistry educator*
Lee, William John *petroleum engineering educator, consultant*
Lindner, Luther Edward *pathology educator*
†Logan, Erin Nicole *researcher*
Lowery, Lee Leon, Jr., *civil engineer*
Lu, Mi *computer engineer, educator*
Lynn, Laurence Edwin, Jr., *university administrator, educator*
Lytton, Robert Leonard *civil engineer, educator*
Machann, Clinton John *English educator*
Mannan, M. Sam *chemical engineer, educator, consultant*
Maret, Elizabeth Gardner *sociology educator*
Martin, Carol Jacquelyn *educator, artist*
Mathewson, Christopher Colville *engineering geologist, educator*
McCallum, Roderick Eugene *dean, microbiologist*
McCrady, James David *veterinarian, educator*
McIntyre, John Armin *physics educator*
McIntyre, Peter Mastin *physicist, educator*
Meier, Kenneth John *political scientist*
Mercer, Melvin Ray *electrical engineer, educator*
†Mohamed, Ahmed A. *chemist, researcher*
Monroe, Haskell Moorman, Jr., *retired university educator*
†Moroney, John Rodgers *economist, educator*
Nachman, Ronald James *research chemist*
Natowitz, Joseph B. *chemistry educator, research administrator*
†Nederman, Cary Joseph *political scientist, director*
Neill, William Harold, Jr., *biological science educator and researcher*
†Nelson, Claudia B. *literature educator, writer*
†Nobles, Maria Morgun *soil scientist, researcher*
O'Connor, Rod *chemist, consultant, inventor*
Page, Robert Henry *engineer, educator, researcher*
Painter, John Hoyt *electrical engineer*
Palen, Joseph William *chemical process research company executive*
†Paprock, Kenneth Edward *education educator, consultant*
Parlos, Alexander George *systems and control engineering educator*
Parzen, Emanuel *statistical scientist*
Patton, Alton DeWitt *electrical engineering consultant*
Prescott, John Mack *biochemist, retired university administrator*
†Priddy, Sharon *television producer*
Reddy, J. N. *mechanical engineering educator*
Reed, Raymond Deryl *architect*
Reid, Robert Osborne *oceanographer*
Reinarz, Alice G. *academic administrator*
Reinschmidt, Kenneth Frank *engineering and construction executive, educator*
Richardson, Herbert Heath *mechanical engineer, educator, institute director*
Riskowski, Gerald Lee *engineering educator*
Rosberg, David William *plant sciences educator*
Sadoski, Mark Christian *education educator*
Sampson, Herschel Wayne *anatomy educator*
Saving, Thomas Robert *economics educator, consultant*
†Schunicht, Shannon Anthony *retired army officer, politician*
Scott, Alastair Ian *chemistry educator*
Serpedin, Erchin *electrical engineering educator, researcher*
Shepley, Mardelle McCuskey *architect, educator*
Slocum, Richard Copeland (R.C. Slocum) *university athletic coach*
†Song, Joon Jin *research scientist, educator*
Sorescu, Alina *marketing professional, educator*
Steffy, John Richard *nautical archaeologist, educator*
Stewart, Robert Henry *oceanographer, educator*
Stone, Mary Elizabeth *artist*
†Thomadakis, Michael Evaggelos *computer scientist, educator, computer scientist, researcher*
Tiffany-Castiglioni, Evelyn *biomedical science educator, researcher*
Trache, Andreea Apostol *physicist*
Trache, Livius-Marian *physicist, research scientist, educator*
Turner, Nancy Delane *nutritionist, educator, researcher*
Unterberger, Betty Miller *history educator, writer*
Vandiver, Frank Everson *institute administrator, former university president, author, educator*
Vandiver, Renee Lillian Aubry *interior designer, architectural preservator*
Van Riper, Paul Pritchard *political science educator*
Wegener, Robert Paul *communications educator*
Wichern, Dean William *business educator*
Wild, James Robert *biochemistry and genetics educator*
Wilding, Lawrence Paul *retired pedology educator, soil science consultant*
Woodcock, David Geoffrey *architect, educator*
†Wu, Xiaoqiang *molecular biologist, researcher*
Wurbs, Ralph Allen *civil engineering educator, consultant*
†Yang, Lingui *language educator, researcher*
Zhao, Wei *academic administrator*
†Zheng, Qi *statistician, biomathematician*
Zhu, Jianting *hydrologist*

Colleyville
Collins, Stephen Barksdale *retired health care executive*
Dodson, George Wayne *computer company executive, consultant*
Donnelly, Barbara Schettler *retired medical technologist*
Hodgell, Murlin Ray *university dean*
Love, Ben Howard *retired organization executive*
Roth, Robert William *technology specialist*
Tigue, Virginia Beth (Ginny Tigue) *volunteer*

Comanche
Droke, Edna Faye *elementary school educator, retired*

Commerce
Avard, Stephen Lewis *finance educator*
†Chang, Fenia I-fen *music educator, pianist*
McLemore, Matthew Hunter *education educator*
Scott, Joyce Alaine *university official*
Seawell, Thomas Robert *artist, retired educator*

Conroe
†Abney, Joe L. *lawyer*
Ballard, Carrie *artist*
Bowersox, Thomas H. *lawyer*
Bruce, Rachel Mary Condon *retired nurse practitioner*
Ewing, Joseph Graham *family practice physician*
Fleming, Michael Paul *lawyer*
†Harrison, Paula Jean *music educator*
†Irvin, Charles Leslie *lawyer*
Judge, Dolores Barbara *real estate broker*
Mitchell, Robert James *petroleum company executive*
Nachman, Joseph Frank *metallurgical consultant*
Sowers, Amelia Barnet *speech and language pathologist*
Taylor, Mary Curtis Smith *musician*

Converse
Droneburg, Nancy Marie *geriatrics nurse*

Coppell
†Griffin, Jim *secondary school educator*
†Minyard, Liz *food products executive*
Owen, Cynthia Carol *sales executive*
Robinson, Charles Emanuel *systems engineer, consultant*
†Sellers, James Justin *real estate analyst, consultant*
Smothermon, Peggi Sterling *middle school educator*

Copperas Cove
Haas, Lu Ann *counselor*

Corpus Christi
Alberts, Harold *lawyer*
Allison, Joan Kelly *music educator, pianist*
Angell, Ellen *interior designer*
Appel, Truman Frank *surgeon*
Benner, Richard Walter *oil company executive, geologist, engineer*
Berkebile, Charles Alan *geology educator, hydrogeology researcher*
Bexley, James Byron *banker*
Bockhop, Clarence William *retired agricultural engineer*
Branscomb, Harvie, Jr., *lawyer*
Brennecke, Henry Martin *chemical engineer, researcher*
Cassidy, Jack *academic administrator, educator*
Chodosh, Robert Ivan *retired middle school educator, coach*
Clark, Joyce Naomi Johnson *retired nurse, counselor*
Cook, Kenneth Ray *radiologist*

Cox, William Andrew cardiovascular thoracic surgeon
Cutlip, Randall Brower retired psychologist, university president emeritus
Davis, Martin Clay lawyer, professor
DuVall, Lorraine recreation center owner
Elarba, Nagib A. mechanical engineer, consultant
†Ellison, Bobbie Dilworth retired music educator, composer
Erwin, Linda McIntosh librarian, consultant
Fancher, Rick lawyer
Finley, George Alvin, III, wholesale executive
†Foster, Bayard Everson writer
French, Dorris Towers Bryan volunteer
Furgason, Robert Roy university president, engineering educator
Gaylor, James Leroy biomedical research educator
Goode, Jane Kinney artist
Haas, Paul Raymond petroleum company executive
Harper, Sandra Stecher university administrator
Head, Hayden Wilson, Jr., judge
Jack, Janis Graham judge
Jones, Audrey Beyer dietitian
Kane, Sam meat company executive
Kylstra, Johannes Arnold physician
Laws, Gordon Derby lawyer
Lee, Jim economist, educator
Leon, Rolando Luis lawyer
Lim, Alexander Rufasta neurologist, clinical investigator, clinical neurophysiologist, educator, writer
Long, Ralph Stewart clinical psychologist
†McEndree, Phillip education educator
Miller, Carroll Gerard, Jr., (Gerry Miller) lawyer
Nadkarni, Ashok B. electrical engineer
Norman, Wyatt Thomas, III, landman, consultant
Pappas, John Douglas cardiologist
Paulson, Bernard Arthur oil company executive, consultant
Rios, Jo Marie political science educator
Schake, Lowell Martin animal science educator
Shackelford, Patricia Ann lawyer
Snouffer, Nancy Kendall English and reading educator
Sommers, Maxine Marie Bridget travel writer, author, educator, publisher
Stanford, Jane Herring management consultant and educator, author
Stetina, Pamela Eleanor nursing educator
†Stukenberg, Michael Wesley lawyer
Ullberg, Kent Jean sculptor
Vargas, Joe Flores insurance claims executive
Vaughan, Alice Felicie accountant, real estate executive, tax consultant
†Vokurka, Robert John finance educator, researcher, finance educator, consultant
Ward, Harold William Cowper oncologist, educator
†Wojcik, John Casimir music educator, director
Wood, James Allen retired lawyer
Wooster, Robert history educator

Corrigan
†Jeffrey, J. Jann artist, educator

Corsicana
Carroll, Ray Dean, Sr., veterinarian
Dyer, James Mason, Jr., investment company executive
McCally, Charles Richard construction company executive, consultant, mathematician, educator
Orsak, Charles George college district official
Roberts, Nancy Mize retired librarian, composer, pianist
Senkarik, Mikki oil painter

Crane
Crawford, Judy Carol energy services company executive

Crockett
Gibbs, James Howard broadcast executive
LaClair, Patricia Marie physical education director, paramedic

Crowley
Sizemore, Deborah Lightfoot writer, editor

Crystal Beach
Dunn, Glennis Mae retired writer, lyricist

Cypress
Burghduff, John Brian mathematics educator
Callegari, William A., Jr., lawyer, mediator
Day, Robert Michael oil company executive
Heath, Frank Bradford retired dentist
Hlozek, Carole Diane Quast business executive
†LaCroix, Jeffrey William management consultant

DFW Airport
Hinkle, Minerva Hernandez airport terminal executive

Dallas
Abney, Frederick Sherwood lawyer
Abramson, Harold Calvin federal bankruptcy judge
Acker, Rodney lawyer
†Adelman, Graham Lewis lawyer
†Ajaev, Vladimir S. mathematician, educator
Alexander, Roger Eugene oral and maxillofacial surgeon, educator
Allen, Terry Devereux urologist, educator
Alpern, Robert J. dean, medical educator
Alvey, David Lynn advertising executive, artist, curator, poet
Anderson, Barbara McComas lawyer
Anderson, E. Karl lawyer
Anglin, Michael Williams lawyer
Armour, James Lott lawyer
Arpey, Gerard J. air transportation executive
†Atkinson, Bill artistic director
Augur, Marilyn Hussman distribution executive
Austin-Thorn, Cynthia Kay religious organization administrator, poet
Baggett, Steven Ray lawyer
Baggett, W. Mike lawyer
Bailey, Calvin Dean audio engineer
Bailon, Gilbert newspaper editor
†Bair, Donna Marlene medical laboratory administrator
Baker, James Edward city planner
†Baker, James Guy health facility administrator
Barnes, Robert Vertreese, Jr., masonry contractor executive
Barr, Richard Stuart computer science and management science educator
Bartlett, Richard Chalkley business executive, writer, conservationist
Bartos, Jerry Garland corporate executive, mechanical engineer
Bashour, Fouad Anis cardiology educator
Bayne, James Elwood investor and financial consultant
†Beane, Jerry Lynn lawyer
†Beard, Kevin E. language educator
Beck, Jay M. gynecologist
†Bellavance, Maria Isabel librarian
Berbary, Maurice Shehadeh physician, military officer, hospital administrator, educator
†Bergstresser, Paul Richard dermatologist, educator
†Berry, Buford Preston lawyer
Betts, Dianne Connally economist, educator
Beuttenmuller, Rudolf William lawyer
Bick, Rodger Lee hematologist, oncologist, researcher, educator
†Bickel, John W., II, lawyer
Biegler, David W. energy executive
Biermacher, Kenneth Wayne lawyer
Birkeland, Bryan Collier lawyer
†Bishop, Gene Herbert financial corporate executive
†Blanchette, James Grady, Jr., lawyer
†Blankenbaker, Zarina adult education educator, consultant
Bleiberg, Lawrence Russell journalist
Blessen, Karen Alyce artist, writer
Bliss, Robert Harms lawyer
Blome, Dorothy Carter pediatrics nurse
†Blomquist, Preston Howard ophthalmologist
Blomqvist, Carl Gunnar cardiologist
†Blount, Charles William, III, lawyer
Blue, J(ohn) Ronald evangelical mission executive
Bockstruck, Lloyd DeWitt librarian
Bolesta, Michael Joseph orthopedic surgeon
Bonesio, Woodrow Michael lawyer
Bonte, Frederick James radiology educator, physician
†Boswell, George Marion, Jr., orthopedist, health care facility administrator
Brachman, Malcolm K. oil company executive
†Bradford, William Edward oil field equipment manufacturing company executive
Bradley, John Andrew hospital management company executive
†Braun, Susan foundation administrator
†Brewer, David Madison lawyer
Brierley, Harold M. advertising executive
Brin, Royal Henry, Jr., lawyer
†Brister, Bill H. lawyer, former bankruptcy judge
Bromberg, John E. lawyer
Bronstein, Fred orchestra executive
†Brooks, Edgar R. (Dick Brooks) utility company executive
Brooks, James Elwood geologist, educator
Brown, Benjamin A. investment advisor
Brown, E. Sherwood psychiatrist
Brown, Gloria Vasquez central banker
Brown, James Earle lawyer
Brown, Michael Stuart geneticist, educator, administrator
†Bruce, Erika Lynn lawyer
†Brucker, Mary C. nurse midwife
Bruene, Warren Benz electronic engineer
Bryant, John Wiley former congressman
Bryant, L. Gerald management consultant
Buchholz, Donald Alden stock brokerage company executive
Bucy, J. Fred, Jr., retired electronics company executive
Bumpas, Stuart Maryman lawyer
Burke, William Temple, Jr., lawyer
Burns, Sandra lawyer, educator
Burns, Scott columnist
Busbee, Kline Daniel, Jr., law educator, lawyer
Buschang, Peter Heinz dental educator
Byrd, Ellen Stoesser school nurse administrator
†Byrom, Joe Alan lawyer
Caetano, Raul psychiatrist, educator
Cahill, Michael Clark linguist
Caldwell, Thomas Howell, Jr., accountant, financial management consultant
Callahan, Rickey Don business owner
Cameron, Glenn Nilsson mortgage company executive
Campaigne, Linda Mary special education educator
Campos, Nora government official
Cantrell, Scott newspaper music critic
Caperton, Bob W. risk manager
Carl, Robert E. retired marketing company executive
Carman, George Henry retired physician
Carnes, Joseph Sydney clergyman
†Carpenter, Gordon Russell retired lawyer, banker
Carson, Virginia Hill oil and gas executive
Case, Thomas Louis lawyer
Caughfield, Lance Eric lawyer
Cavanagh, Harrison Dwight ophthalmic surgeon, medical educator
Chadbourne, John Frederick, Jr., engineering executive
†Chase, J. Scott Lawyer (corporate)
Chason, Jacob (Leon Chason) retired neuropathologist
Chawner, Lucia Martha English educator
Cheirif, Jorge Berkstein cardiologist, consultant
Chen, Zhangxin John mathematics educator
Cirilo, Amelia Medina educational consultant, supervisor
Clark, Robert Murel, Jr., lawyer
†Clary, Rebecca Kristen social services administrator
Cline, Bobby James insurance company executive
†Clossey, David F. lawyer
Cloutman, Edward Bradbury, III, lawyer
Cobb, William Dowell, Jr., lawyer
Cochran, George Calloway, III, retired bank executive, lawyer
Cochran, Kendall Pinney economics educator
Cochran, Mona Sheinfeld economics educator, consultant
Cockerham, Sidney Joe professional society administrator
Coggins, Paul Edward, Jr., lawyer
Coldwell, Philip Edward financial consultant
Cole, James S. academic administrator
Coleman, Robert Winston lawyer
Collins, Lynn M. oncology clinical nurse specialist
†Collins, Michael Homer lawyer
Collins, Robert Howard, Jr., oncologist
Coln, C. Dale pediatric surgeon, educator
Comini, Alessandra art historian, educator
†Compton, Harold F. retail executive
Conant, Allah B., Jr., lawyer
Cook, Gary Raymond university president, clergyman
†Cook, William Staton medical researcher
†Cooper, Lamar Eugene, Sr., academic administrator, minister
Copley, Edward Alvin lawyer
Countryman, Edward Francis historian, educator
Cowart, T(homas) David lawyer
Cox, Rody P(owell) medical educator, internist
Crain, John Walter historian, educator
Creel, Luther Edward, III, lawyer
†Crichton, Thomas, IV, lawyer
Crockett, Dodee Frost brokerage firm executive
Cromartie, Eric Ross lawyer
Croskell, Madelon Byrd music educator, classical vocalist
Crotty, Robert Bell lawyer
Crowley, James Worthington retired lawyer, business consultant, investor
Cruikshank, Thomas Henry energy services and engineering executive
Cummins, James Duane correspondent, media executive
Curran, G. Michael lawyer
Curry, Gregory William lawyer
Dalton, Harry Jirou, Jr., (Jerry Dalton) public relations executive
†Daly, David Michael information technology executive
Daniels, Russell Howard lawyer
Dasgupta, Udayan electrical engineer, researcher
Daves, Don Michael minister
Davis, Daisy Sidney history educator
†Davis, John F., III, travel company executive
Davis, Patricia M. educator
Davis, Rachel Lee Mostert advertising executive
Dawson, Edward Joseph merger and acquisition executive
†Dealey, Lynn Townsend artist
†Dean, David Allen lawyer
Decherd, Robert William newspaper and broadcasting executive
Dedman, Robert Henry sales executive
†Dee, Ronda poet, photographer
Dees, Tom Moore, II, internist
DelHomme, Beverly Ann lawyer
Dewey, Richard B., Jr., medical educator, administrator
Dieste, Tony marketing professional
Dillon, David Anthony journalist, lecturer
Dillon, Donald Ward management consultant
†Dir, Dave professional soccer coach
Doke, Marshall J., Jr., lawyer
Doran, Mark Richard real estate financial executive
Douglass, Frank Russell lawyer
†Dowdle, Jeff real estate broker
Dozier, David Charles, Jr., marketing public relations and advertising executive
Dufner, Edward Joseph editor
Dumerer, Lorraine JoAnne Lori social studies educator, clinician, consultant
Dutton, Diana Cheryl lawyer
Dyess, Bobby Dale lawyer
Dykeman, Alice Marie public relations executive
Dykes, Virginia Chandler occupational therapist, educator
Eads, John A. accountant
†Early, James education educator
Eberhart, Robert Clyde biomedical engineering educator, researcher
Eichenwald, Heinz Felix physician
Einspruch, Burton Cyril psychiatrist
Elkins-Elliott, Kay law educator
Ellis, Alfred Wright (Al Ellis) lawyer
†Ellis, James Alvis, Jr., lawyer
Ellis, June B. human resource consultant
Emmett, Michael physician, educator
Engles, Gregg L. food company executive
English, Que public relations executive
Ericson, Ruth Ann retired psychiatrist
†Esqueda, Octavio Javier religious studies educator
Essary, Andrew Charles philosophy educator, financial analyst
Estabrook, Ronald Winfield chemistry educator
†Estep, Robert Lloyd lawyer
†Etgen, Ann ballet educator, artistic director, choreographer
†Ethridge, Joseph Alfred manufacturing executive (heavy)
Evans, Dvorah A. organization executive, professional organizer
Evans, Roger lawyer
Everbach, Otto George lawyer
†Falk, James Nathan not-for-profit organization administrator, consultant
†Falk, Robert Hardy lawyer
Fanning, Barry Hedges lawyer
†Farrington, Jerry S. utility holding company executive
Favor, Lesli Joanna writer, researcher
Fegan, Jeffrey P. airport executive
†Feiner, Joel S. psychiatrist
Feld, Alan David lawyer
Fenner, Suzan Ellen lawyer
Fenves, Andrew Zoltan nephrologist
Fielder, Charles Robert oil industry executive
Fields-Hill, Valerie journalist
Fifield, William O. lawyer
Figari, Ernest Emil, Jr., lawyer, educator
Fisher, Richard Welton investor, ambassador
Fishman, Edward Marc lawyer
Fix, Douglas Martin electrical engineer
Flatt, Adrian Ede surgeon
†Fleckenstein, James Lawrence radiologist
Flegle, Jim L. lawyer
Flood, Joan Moore paralegal
†Flowers, Terry James headmaster
Fogwell, Ted E. obstetrician and gynecologist
Fomby, Thomas Blake economist, educator, consultant, researcher
Fontana, Robert Edward electrical engineering educator, retired air force officer
Fortado, Michael George lawyer
Foutch, Michael James actor, dancer, lighting designer, producer
France, Newell Edwin former hospital administrator, consultant
†Frank, Paula Feldman business executive
Frank, Steven Neil chemist
Frazee, Ronald Leroy lawyer
Free, Mary Moore biological and medical anthropologist
†Freiberger, Katherine Guion composer, retired piano educator
French, Joseph Jordan, Jr., lawyer
Frenkel, Eugene Phillip physician
†Freytag, Sharon Nelson lawyer
Friedberg, Errol Clive pathology educator, researcher
Friedheim, Jan V. education administrator
Friedheim, Stephen Bailey educational consultant
†Frisbie, Curtis Lynn, Jr., lawyer
Fritz, Terrence Lee investment banker, strategic consultant
†Gafford, Ronald J. construction executive
Gajewski, Ronald S. consulting and training company executive
†Galante, Joseph A. bishop
Gant, Norman Ferrell, Jr., obstetrician, gynecologist
Gantt, James Raiford thoracic surgeon
Gantz, Ann Cushing artist, educator
Garner, Bryan Andrew law educator, consultant, writer
Garner, Paul Trantham auditor
†Geiger, Richard Stuart lawyer
Gensheimer, Elizabeth Lucille software specialist
Gerberding Cowart, Greta Elaine lawyer
Gibbs, James Alanson geologist
Gibby, Mabel Enid Kunce psychologist
Gibson, John Wheat lawyer
Giesecke, Adolph Hartung anesthesiologist, educator
Gifford, Porter William retired construction materials manufacturing company executive
†Giggleman, Gene Felton academic administrator, veterinarian
Gillett, Grover author
†Gilliam, John A. lawyer
Gilman, Alfred Goodman pharmacologist, educator
†Gilmore, Jerry Carl lawyer
Girards, James Edward lawyer
Glancy, Walter John lawyer
†Glazer, Bennett J. wholesale distribution executive
Glazer, Rachelle Hoffman lawyer
Glendenning, Don Mark lawyer
Glines, Carroll Vane, Jr., magazine editor
Goel, Ajay molecular biologist, researcher
Goldmann, James Allen healthcare consultant
Goldstein, Joseph Leonard physician, medical educator, molecular genetics scientist
Goodell, Sol retired lawyer
Goodstein, Barnett Maurice lawyer
Gores, Christopher Merrel lawyer
Goss, James Walter oil company executive
Govett, Brett Christopher lawyer
†Govil, Manish Kumar customer service administrator
†Grahmann, Charles V. bishop
Grammer, John Colquitte cardiologist
Grange-Maasoumi, Lynette Danielle community health nurse, educator
Grant, Joseph Moorman finance executive
Gratton, Patrick John Francis oil company executive
Gray, James Larry international business executive
†Gray, Peter Frederick software engineer, educator
Greiner, Mary Louise lawyer, psychotherapist
Griffeth, Landis King nuclear medicine physician
Griffith, Gary Ernest public affairs executive
Grimes, David Lynn communications company executive
Gross, Gary Neil allergist, physician
Gross, Harriet P. Marcus religious studies and writing educator
Guerin, Dean Patrick executive
†Guillot, Patrick Carl lawyer, judge
Gully, Russell George lawyer
Gumbiner, Anthony Joseph investment banker, lawyer
Guthrie, M. Philip corporate financial executive
Guy, L(eona) Ruth medical educator
Gyemant, Robert Ernest diversified financial services company executive, merchant
Haayen, Richard Jan university official, insurance company executive
†Hackney, Hugh Edward lawyer

Trivedi, Madhukar H. *psychiatrist*
True, Roy Joe *lawyer*
Tsyganov, Edward N. *physicist, educator*
Tubb, James Clarence *lawyer*
Tucker, Laurey Dan *lawyer*
Turgeon, Pierre *professional hockey player*
†Turner, Jim L. *bottler manufacturing executive*
Turner, Robert Gerald *university president*
†Turner, Sara Weidner *librarian*
Turocy, Catherine *performing company executive*
Udashen, Robert Nathan *lawyer*
Uhr, Jonathan William *immunologist, educator, researcher*
Unger, Roger Harold *physician, scientist*
Valentine, Foy Dan *clergyman*
Vanderveld, John, Jr., *international business development specialist*
Veach, Robert Raymond, Jr., *lawyer*
Vetter, James George, Jr., *lawyer*
Vitetta, Ellen Shapiro *microbiologist educator, immunologist*
Vogel, Donald Stanley *gallery executive, artist*
Von Kennel, Gary Phillip *marketing company executive*
Walker, Gordon Beverley Moore, Jr., *business educator*
Walkowiak, Vincent Steven *lawyer*
†Walts, William Edward, II, *lawyer*
Washington, Karen Roberts *lawyer*
Wassenich, Linda Pilcher *retired health policy analyst, fund raiser*
Waters, Rollie O. *management consultant*
Weakley, Clare George, Jr., *insurance executive, theologian, entrepreneur*
Weinkauf, William Carl *instructional media company executive*
Wendorf, Denver Fred, Jr., *anthropology educator*
Wenrich, John William *college president*
Westfall, Constance Courtney *lawyer*
Wheeler, Edward Norwood *chemical consultant*
Wheeler, M. Cass *health science association administrator*
White, James Richard *lawyer*
White, Tom Willingham *private investor*
Whitson, James Norfleet, Jr., *retired diversified company executive*
Whitt, Robert Ampudia, III, *advertising executive, marketing professional*
Wilber, Robert Edwin *corporate executive*
Wilbur, Janis A. *financial consultant, sales professional*
Wilde, Patrick Joseph *administrator*
Wildenthal, C(laud) Kern *physician, educator*
Wiles, Charles Preston *minister*
†Wilkerson, Patricia Helen *director child development center*
Williams, Charles Edward *engineer*
Willingham, Clark Suttles *lawyer*
†Willis, Monte Shaw *research scientist*
Wilson, Catherine Cooper (Kitty Wilson) *communications executive, writer*
Wilson, Claude Raymond, Jr., *lawyer*
Wilson, Jean Donald *endocrinologist, educator*
Wilson, Jean Marie Haley *civic worker*
Wolfe, Jane *writer*
†Wood, Charles Monroe *theology educator*
Woolley, Bryan (Lowell Bryan Woolley) *author, journalist*
Wrucke-Nelson, Ann C. *elementary education educator*
Yeslow, Rosemarie *real estate professional*
Young, Barney Thornton *lawyer*
Young, Julia Anne *librarian, elementary education educator*
Zeiger, Timothy David *lawyer*
Zhou, Xin (Joseph Zhou) *pathologist, medical scientist*
Ziff, Morris *internist, rheumatologist, educator*
Zimmerman, S(amuel) Morton (Mort Zimmerman) *engineering executive*
†Zimmermann, Walter Halen *finance company executive*
Zisman, Barry Stuart *lawyer*
Zubov, Sergei *professional hockey player*
Zumwalt, Richard Dowling *flour mill executive*

Deer Park
Deutsch, Lawrence Ira *minister*
Fotsch, George Bernard, III, *chemical addiction counselor*
Sandstrum, Steve D. *engineering executive*
†Wester, R. Glen *music educator, director*

Del Rio
Garrett, James William *computer company executive*
Prather, Gerald Luther *management consultant, retired air force officer, judge*

Denison
O'Toole, Dennis P. *music educator, musician*

Denton
†Abunasser, Rima Jamil *education educator*
†Bean, Judith Mattson *academic administrator, educator*
Belfiglio, Valentine John *political science educator, pharmacist*
Bonduris, Thad Santikos *music educator*
†Boukerchi, Azzedine *adult education educator, computer scientist, researcher*
Callicott, John Baird *philosopher, educator*
Carlson, William Dwight *college president emeritus*
Chang, Yongbin *physicist*
†Chet, Guy *historian, educator*
Chilton, Bradley Stewart *law educator, educator*
Cissell, William Bernard *health studies educator*
Cobb, Jeanne Beck *education educator, researcher, consultant*
Cohen, Nicki Sandra *music educator, music therapist*
†Couturiaux, Clay James *musician*
Cox, Barbara Claire *costume designer, educator*
†Crawford, Gladys Pauline *microbiologist, educator*

Eames, Robert Newton *lawyer*
†Eustis, Lynn Eleanor *music educator, vocalist*
†Galindo, Rebeca *administrative assistant*
Gibbs, Tyson *chairman anthropology department*
†Golding, Terry David *engineering educator, researcher*
Gough, Clarence Ray *retired designer, educator*
Hurley, Alfred Francis *historian, academic administrator emeritus, retired air force officer*
Kamman, William *historian, educator*
Keating, AnaLouise *educator, author*
†Kennedy, James H. *biologist, educator*
Kesterson, David Bert *English language educator*
Latham, William Peters *composer, former educator*
Lawhon, John E., III, *lawyer, former county official*
Leung, Paul *psychologist, rehabilitation educator*
†Marshall, David Douglas *science educator*
Mathes, Dorothy Jean Holden *occupational therapist*
Mauldin, Richard Daniel *mathematics educator*
McDonald-West, Sandi MacLean *headmaster, consultant*
McKee, William Lee *economist, arbitrator, mediator*
McTee, Cindy *classical musician, educator*
Millay, Kathleen Kriner *communication disorders educator*
†Narsutis, John Keith *lawyer*
Naylor, Larry Lee *anthropologist, educator*
†Nestler, Eric M. *music educator*
†Nik, Ninfa *language educator*
Paul, Pamela Mia *concert pianist*
Pettit, Alexander Drummond *English language educator*
†Phipps, Graham H. *music educator*
Poole, Eva Duraine *librarian*
Preston, Thomas Ronald *English language educator, researcher*
Prybutok, Victor Ronald *business educator*
†Reikofski, Helen Dewey *musician, educator*
Renka, Robert Joseph *computer science educator, consultant*
Ryan, Melbagene T. *retired food and nutrition service director*
Saleh, Farida Yousry *chemistry educator*
Schumacker, Randall *educational psychologist*
Schwalm, Fritz Ekkehardt *biology educator*
Shelton, James Keith *journalism educator*
†Simpson, Carol Mann *librarian, consultant, editor*
†Smith, H. Morgan *environmental scientist, educator*
Smith, Howard Wellington *education educator, dean emeritus*
†Snapp, Elizabeth *librarian, educator*
Snapp, Harry Franklin *historian, educator*
Staples, Donald Edward *radio, film and television educator*
Swigger, Kathleen Mary *computer science educator*
Swigger, Keith *dean*
Vaughn, William Preston *historian, educator*
Ver Duin, D'Arlene K. *research scientist*
Wallace, William Hall *economic and financial consultant*
†White, Nora Lizabeth *language educator*
†Wilhite, Barbara C. *recreational therapist, educator*

Deport
Sawyer, Mary Catherine *retired hospital administrator*

Desoto
Ball, Millicent Joan (Penny Ball) *science educator, consultant*
Harrington, Betty Byrd *entrepreneur*
Tyrer-Ferraro, Polly Ann *music instructor, software developer*

Diboll
Fisher, Richard Forrest *research scientist, department chairman*

Dickinson
Bush, Robert Thomas *shipping company executive*

Dripping Springs
Ballard, Mary Melinda *financial communications and investment banking firm executive, consumer advocate*
†Guess, Aundrea Kay *accounting educator*
Nicholas, Nickie Lee *retired industrial hygienist*

Dublin
Johnson, Nancy Ruth *nurse*

Duncanville
Jenkins, Tony Dean *salesman*
Terry, Martin Michael *visual artist, art therapist*
Trotter, Ide Peebles *financial planner, investment manager*

East Bernard
Boettcher, Armin Schlick *lawyer, banker*

Edgewood
Cates, Sue Sadler *educational diagnostician*

Edinburg
†Grossman, Morley Keith *music educator*
Hannan, Mohammad A. *physicist, educator*
†Haule, James Mark *literature educator*
Helstern, Linda Lizut *language educator, poet*
Hinojosa, Federico Gustavo, Jr., *judge*
Jou, Jerwen *psychology educator*
Mahmood, Akhtar Hasan *physicist, educator, researcher*
†Martínez-López, Carmen Leonor *management consultant, educator*
†Mizener, Charlotte Lynn Pearson *music educator, musician*
Nevarez, Miguel A. *academic administrator*

Wilson, Bruce Keith *men's health nurse*
†Wu, Xiaodong *computer science educator*
†Zeng, Liang *education educator*

Edna
Schrimsher, Joanne Johnson *professional counselor*

Egypt
Wynn, John Thomas *retired college president, farming executive, economic consultant, oil and gas producer*

El Paso
Allen, Anna J. *chiropractor*
Armitage, Shelley Sue *American studies educator*
Arnett, Rita Ann *small business owner, consultant*
Bailey, Kenneth Kyle *history educator*
Bartlett, Janet Sanford (Janet Walz) *school nurse*
Beard, Jane Alida *retired accountant*
Benning, Mary Etzold *interior designer*
Briones, David *judge*
Caballero, Raymond Cesar *former mayor*
Clement-Fouts, Shirley George *educational services executive*
Conway, John Bell *health educator, university dean*
Copeland, Randolph Leigh *orthopedic surgeon*
Coronado, Irasema *political scientist, educator*
Cox, Helen Adelaide (Holly Cox) *artist, writer*
Cox, Sanford Curtis, Jr., *lawyer*
Cunningham, Monica Dixson *lawyer, city administrator*
†Dailey, Maceo Crenshaw, Jr., *humanities educator*
†Darnell, James Oral *lawyer*
Deckert, Myrna Jean *small business owner, consultant*
Deerman, Ruth Gillett *sales professional, flying instructor*
DiNardo-Ekery, Dorothy Maria *retired internist, cardiologist, educator*
Dinsmoor, Robert Davidson *lawyer, judge*
Diong, Billy Ming *energy control engineering researcher*
Dombrowski, Frank Paul, Jr., *pharmacist*
Eisner, David George *retired surgeon*
Erskine, William Crawford *academic administrator, accountant, health facility administrator*
Fahy, Michael P. *civil and environmental engineer*
†Ferrell, Robert E. *writer, educator*
Feuille, Richard Harlan *lawyer, director*
Foged, Leslie Owen *mathematician, educator*
Foley, John Donald *physician*
†Foster, Helen R. *language educator*
Fox, Ronnie Ilaine *volunteer educator, densitometry technician*
†Freeman, Mary Anna *librarian*
Fullerton, Thomas Mankin, Jr., *economist*
Gardner, Kerry Ann *librarian*
†Gijon, José Enrique *special education educator*
Gilmer, Robert William, III, *economist*
Goodman, Gertrude Amelia *civic worker*
Gordon, Erline Schecter *educational administrator*
Gordon, Norman James *lawyer*
Grieves, Robert Belanger *engineering educator*
Gupta, Tej P. *physician*
†Harlass, Frederick E. *obstetrician, gynecologist, perinatologist*
Hedrick, Wyatt Smith *pharmacist*
Heide, John Wesley *engineering executive*
Hernandez, Roberto Reyes *secondary school educator, educator*
Huchton, Paul Joseph, Jr., *pediatrician*
†Ituah, Martins O. *pharmacist*
Jesurun, Carlos Antonio *pediatrician, educator, neonatologist*
Johnson, Jerry Douglas *biology educator*
Juarez, Antonio *psychotherapist, consultant, counselor, educator*
Keller, Robert M. *real estate broker*
Kelley, Sylvia Johnson *financial services firm executive*
Korth, Charlotte Williams *furniture and interior design firm executive*
Lyle, James Arthur *real estate broker*
Marshall, Richard Treeger *lawyer*
†Martinez, Luis E. *education educator, consultant*
†McCotter, James Rawson *lawyer*
Miller, Deane Guynes *salon and cosmetic studio owner*
Mitchell, Paula Rae *nursing educator, college dean*
†Mulla, Zuber *epidemiologist*
†Müller, Gene Alan *historian, consultant*
Natalicio, Diana Siedhoff *academic administrator*
Nava, Patricia Ann *electrical engineering educator, researcher*
Olvera, Joe Enrique *alcohol/drug abuse services professional*
†Patterson, Burton Harvey *lawyer*
Patty, William Robert *educator, administrator*
Pazmiño, Patricio Augusto *physician, scientist, consultant*
Penley, Julie Anne *psychologist, educator*
Peterscheck, Walter Hermann *chemical engineer*
Potter, Wylie Shattuck *marketing professional*
Prendergast, Thomas A. *investments and management consultant*
†Rash, Alan Vance *lawyer, director*
†Riter, Stephen *university administrator, electrical engineer*
Roberts, Ernst Edward *marketing consultant*
Salewski, Ruby Marie Graf *nursing educator*
†Showery, Charles George, Jr., *financial services company executive, consultant*
Sipiora, Leonard Paul *retired museum director, art appraiser*
Small, Ray *university administrator*
Smith, Tad Randolph *lawyer*
Stanley, Duffy B. *architect, planner*

Strait, Viola Edwina Washington *librarian*
Taber, David O. *urological surgeon*
Tchoshanov, Mourat Ashirovich *mathematician, educator*
Tess, Alice Charlene *writer, retired secondary school educator*
Thering, Harlan Robert *plastic surgeon, retired army officer*
Treadwell, Hugh Wilson *publishing executive*
Villalobos, Raul *lawyer*
von Tungeln, George Robert *retired university administrator, economics consultant*
†Wardy, Joe *mayor*
Williams, Darryl Marlowe *medical educator*
Williford, Lex Akers *educator*
Wootten, John Robert *investor*
Yetter, Richard *lawyer*
†Youngman, Daryl Ray, Jr., *operations research specialist*
Zaloznik, Arlene Joyce *oncologist, retired army officer*

Eldorado
Kosub, James Albert *lawyer*

Electra
†Hayers, Paul Hugh *lawyer*

Elgin
Hallenbeck, Pomona Juanita *artist*
Shelby, Nina Claire *special education educator*

Elmendorf
Teague, Mary Elizabeth *small business owner*

Ennis
Swanson, Wallace Martin *lawyer*

Euless
Leding, Anne Dixon *artist, educator*
Mabry, Philip T. *political consultant*
Paran, Mark Lloyd *retired lawyer*
†Roark, Sheila B. *writer*
Tunnell, Clida Diane *air transportation specialist*

Fair Oaks Ranch
Dixon, Robert James *aerospace consultant, former air force officer, former aerospace company executive*

Fairview
Chapdelaine, Perry Anthony, Jr., *public health and preventive medicine physician, educator*

Farmers Branch
Armand, Susanne Marie *pharmaceutical products executive*
Walsh, Elizabeth Jameson *musician*

Farmersville
Seward, Richard Bevin *lawyer*

Farnsworth
Gramstorff, Jeanne B. *retired farmer*

Floresville
Vontur, Ruth Poth *retired elementary school educator*

Flower Mound
Cox, David Leon *telecommunications company executive*
Hunt, David Ford *lawyer*
Kolodny, Stanley Charles *oral surgeon, air force officer*
Maddocks, Robert Allen *lawyer, manufacturing company executive*
Morrish, Thomas Jay *golf course architect*
Wells, Margaret Ann *piano educator*
Zoellner, Sandra Ann *accountant*

Fort Davis
Gadberry, Vicki Lynn Himes *librarian*

Fort Hood
†Anderson, Nanci Louise *computer analyst*
†Scott, Karen Lou *systems analyst*

Fort Mc Kavett
Stokes, Charles Eugene, Jr., *wool merchant, textile executive*

Fort Sam Houston
Convertino, Victor Anthony *physiologist, educator, research scientist, civil servant*
†DeWitt, Ralph Ogden, Jr., *military career history*
†Givens, Melissa Lousie *emergency physician*
Gordon, Ella Dean *health and nurse educator, women's health and orthopedic nurse*
Hewitson, William Craig *physician, career officer*
†Kragh, John Frederick, Jr., *orthopedist, educator*
†Mangelsdorff, Arthur David *psychologist, educator*
Moloff, Alan Lawrence *military officer, physician*
Nelson, James Harold *health sciences administrator*
†Pak, Hon S. *dermatologist, researcher*
†Peake, James Benjamin *military career officer*
Robinson, Naomi Jean *educational training systems educator*
†Williams, Pat L. *military officer*

Fort Worth
†Alexander, Elizabeth Urban *education educator*
Allen, William Marion, III, *retired graphic designer, artist*
Allmand, Linda F(aith) *retired library director*
Appel, Bernard Sidney *marketing consultant, former electronic company executive*
Ard, Harold Jacob *library administrator*
Armiger, Gene Gibbon *telecommunications executive, consultant*
Auping, Michael G. *curator*
Bailey, James Stephen *scientist*
Baker, Robert Woodward *airline executive*

Voge, Victoria Mae *occupational medicine physician*

Graham
†Richie, Boyd Lynn *lawyer*

Granbury
Adams, Christopher Steve, Jr., *retired defense electronics corporation executive, former air force officer*
Almy, Earle Vaughn, Jr., (Buddy Almy) *real estate executive*
Faith, James Albert, Jr., *minister*
Garrison, Truitt B. *architect*
McCuistion, Robert Wiley *hospital administrator, management consultant, lawyer*

Grand Prairie
Amil-Barker, Jana Kay *social worker*
Benson, Carol Kay Cantrell *English and Latin educator*
†Fickling, Karl Frederick *church consultant, educator*
Loo, Maritta Louise *nurse, national guard officer*
†Puckett, Mary Alice *primary school educator, consultant*
†Ritterhouse, Kathy Lee *librarian*
Thomas, Michael S. *software engineer*

Grapevine
†Blair, Sylvia H. *computer engineer, small business owner*
Franks, Jon Michael *lawyer, mediator*
Hirsh, Cristy J. *principal*
Killebrew, James Robert *architectural engineering firm executive*
Stack, George Joseph *philosopher, writer*

Greenville
Brown, Harley Mitchell *retired computer company executive, writer*
†Siles, Fernando M. *child psychiatrist*

Groveton
Pyle, Benjamin Malrey *investor*

Hale Center
Courtney, Carolyn Ann *school librarian*
Laney, James Earl (Pete Laney) *state representative, speaker of the house, farmer*

Hallettsville
Baber, Wilbur H., Jr., *lawyer*

Harker Heights
Hughes, William Foster *career officer, surgeon, obstetrician, gynecologist*

Harlingen
Farris, Robert Gene *transportation company executive*
Johnson, Orrin Wendell *lawyer*
Klein, Garner Franklin *cardiologist, internist*
Martin, Leland Morris (Pappy Martin) *history educator*
Matz, James Richard *municipal official*
Pope, William L. *lawyer, judge*

Hartley
Cooley, Regina Kae *educational administrator*

Heath
Hargrave, Robert Warren *retired hair styling salon chain executive*
Kolodey, Fred James *lawyer*

Hempstead
Propst, Catherine Lamb *biotechnology company executive*

Henderson
†Rhoades, Eva Yvonne *retired elementary school educator*

Hermleigh
Barnes, Maggie Lue Shifflett (Mrs. Lawrence Barnes) *nurse*

Highland Village
Lawrence, William Clarence *business executive, lawyer, mediator, politician*
Richardson, K. Scott *sales executive*

Hillsboro
McClendon, Fred Vernon *real estate professional, business consultant, equine and realty appraiser, financial consultant*

Hitchcock
Shaffer, Richard Paul *business owner, retired career military officer*

Hockley
Able, Luke William *pediatric surgeon, consultant*
†Patterson, Maria Riland *medical technician, writer*

Hollywood Park
Smith, Richard Thomas *retired electrical engineer*

Hondo
†Bryant, Jannie *accountant*

Horseshoe Bay
Anderson, Kenneth Ward *investor, consultant*
Jorden, James Roy *oil company engineering executive, consultant*
Simpson, H. Richard (Dick Simpson) *retailer*
†Welch, Robert Morrow, Jr., *lawyer*

Houston
Abbey, George W. S. *space center executive*
Adams, C. Lee *marketing executive*
Adams, Daniel Clifford *music educator*
Addison, Linda Leuchter *lawyer, writer*

†Aguilar, Eugenio Alfredo, III, *plastic surgeon*
†Aguilar-Bryan, Lydia *medical educator, medical researcher*
Ahmad, Salahuddin *nuclear scientist*
†Ahn, Chul *medical educator*
†Alderman, Richard Mark *legal educator, lawyer, television and radio commentator*
Alexander, Harold Campbell *insurance consultant*
†Alexander, Leslie Lee *professional sports team executive*
Alexanian, Raymond *hematologist*
Alford, Bobby Ray *physician, educator, university official*
Allen, John Timothy *mechanical engineer*
Allen, Steven Jeffrey *anesthesiologist, educator*
Allender, John Roland *lawyer*
Altman, William Carl *health facility administrator, merger and acquisitions specialist, investment manager, consultant*
Amandes, Christopher Bruce *lawyer*
Amann, Leslie Kiefer *lawyer, educator*
†Amaon, Gary P. *lawyer*
†Amato, Paula *medical educator*
Amdur, Arthur R. *lawyer*
†Anani, Tarig *lawyer*
Anderson, Doris Ehlinger *lawyer*
Anderson, Eric Severin *lawyer*
Anderson, Helen Sharp *civic worker*
Anderson, Richard Carl *geophysical exploration company executive*
Anderson, Thomas Dunaway *retired lawyer*
Anderson, William, Jr., (William Albion Anderson Jr.) *investment banker*
Archambault, Lee Joseph *astronaut*
†Arcilla, Demetrio Ballares, Jr., *health facility administrator, rehabilitation services professional, writer, genealogist*
†Arcilla, Juanita R. *physical rehabilitation physician*
†Arens, James F. *anesthesiologist, educator*
Armentrout, Debra Catherine *neonatal nurse practitioner*
Armstrong, Greg L. *oil company executive*
Arnold, James Phillip *religious studies educator, history educator*
†Arowosafe, Muyi *education educator*
Ashby, Jeffrey S. *astronaut*
Asher, Jerry L. *retired government agency administrator*
Askew, William Earl *chemist, educator*
Assouad, Mario *internist, nephrologist*
†Atkins, Bruce Alexander *lawyer*
Atlas, Nancy Friedman *judge*
Atlas, Scott Jerome *lawyer*
Austin, Harry Guiden *engineering and construction company executive*
Ayadi, Olusegun Felix *finance educator*
Ayus, Juan Carlos *nephrologist*
Bag, Remzi *nuclear medicine physician, internist, pulmonologist, critical care physician, transplant pulmonologist*
Bagwell, Jeff (Jeffrey Robert Bagwell) *professional baseball player*
Bahl, Saroj Mehta *nutritionist, educator*
Bai, Yong *engineering executive, educator*
Bailey, Harold Randolph *surgeon*
Bair, Royden Stanley *retired architect*
†Baker, Denise R. *technical computer educator, consultant*
Baker, Michael A. *astronaut*
Baker, Stephen Denio *physics educator*
†Ballanfant, Richard Burton *lawyer*
Ballantyne, Christie Mitchell *medical educator*
Baranovich, Diana Lea *music educator*
Barcenas, Camilo Gustavo *physician*
Bargfrede, James Allen *lawyer*
Barlow, Jim B. *retired columnist*
Barnett, Donald Blake *corporate financial executive*
Barnett, Edward William *lawyer*
Barracano, Henry Ralph *retired oil company executive, consultant*
Barrere, Clem Adolph *business brokerage company executive*
Barrere, Jamie Newton *real estate executive*
Barrett, Bernard Morris, Jr., *plastic and reconstructive surgeon*
Barrett, Michael Joseph *priest*
†Barricklo, Jack Nelson *small business owner*
Barrow, Thomas Davies *oil and mining company executive*
Barry, Allan Ronald *ship pilot, corporate executive*
Bartling, Phyllis McGinness *oil company executive*
Barton, Sarah Muriel *lawyer*
Bartunek, Kenneth Steven *financial consultant*
Baskin, David Stuart *neurosurgeon, educator*
Bast, Robert Clinton, Jr., *medical researcher, medical educator*
Battin, R. Ray (Rosabell Harriet Ray) *audiologist, neuropsychologist*
Baysal, Edip *executive*
Beard, Dennis Alton *pastor*
Bech, Douglas York *lawyer, resort executive*
†Bedikian, Agop Y. *internist, oncologist, educator*
Beirne, Martin Douglas *lawyer*
†Belk, Joan Pardue *English educator*
Bellatti, Lawrence Lee *lawyer*
Bentsen, Kenneth Edward *architect*
Berg, David Howard *lawyer*
Berger, Barry Stuart *lawyer*
Bering, Edgar Andrew, III, *physicist, educator*
†Berner, Arthur Samuel *lawyer*
Bethea, Louise Huffman *allergist*
Bethune, Gordon *airline executive*
†Bezold, Louis Irving, III, *pediatrician, cardiologist*
Biggio, Craig *professional baseball player*
Bilger, Bruce R. *lawyer*
Bischoff, Susan Ann *newspaper editor*
Bishop, Calvin Thomas *landscape architect, educator*
†Bistline, F. Walter, Jr., *lawyer, photographer*
Black, David Charles *astrophysicist*

Black, Marilyn Hammer *non-profit organization executive*
Blackburn, Sadie Gwin Allen *executive*
Blackmon, Willie Edward Boney *judge, military officer*
Blackshear, A. T., Jr., *lawyer*
Bland, John Lloyd *lawyer*
Blanton, Jack Sawtelle *oil company executive*
Blasingim, Charlotte Oren DeShazor *counselor, consultant*
Bliss, Ronald Glenn *lawyer*
Block, Nelson R(ichard) *lawyer*
Bloomfield, Michael J. *astronaut*
†Blount, Darlene *small business owner, consultant*
Bluestein, Edwin A., Jr., *lawyer*
Bodey, Gerald Paul *medical educator, physician*
Bollich, Elridge Nicholas *brokerage house executive*
Bonner, Billy Edward *physics educator*
Bonneville, Richard Briggs *retired petroleum exploration and production executive*
Bookout, John Frank, Jr., *oil company executive*
Boren, William Meredith *manufacturing executive*
Bott, Simon Gregory *chemistry educator, researcher*
Bovay, Harry Elmo, Jr., *retired engineering company executive*
Bowen, William Jackson *retired gas company executive*
Bowers, Paula Jean *medical/surgical nurse*
Bowersox, Kenneth D. *astronaut*
Bowman, Jeffrey Neil *podiatrist*
Bowron, Edgar Peters *art museum curator, administrator*
Bozeman, Ross Elliot *engineering executive*
Braden, John Alan *accountant*
†Bradford, C.O. *protective services officer*
Bradie, Peter Richard *lawyer, engineer*
†Brady, Norman Conrad *lawyer, corporate executive*
Brandenstein, Daniel Charles *astronaut, retired naval officer*
Brann, Richard Roland *lawyer*
Bridges, David Manning *lawyer*
Brinkley, William R. *dean*
Brinson, Gay Creswell, Jr., *retired lawyer*
Brito, Dagobert Llanos *economics educator*
Brody, Baruch Alter *medical educator, academic center administrator*
Brooks, Philip Russell *chemistry educator, researcher*
Brotzen, Franz Richard *materials science educator*
Brown, David Hurst *lawyer, partner*
Brown, Glenda Ann Walters *ballet director*
Brown, Jack Harold Upton *physiologist, biomedical engineer, academic administrator*
Brown, Lee P. *mayor*
Brown, Lee Patrick *mayor, city official, law enforcement educator*
†Brown, William Alley *lawyer*
Bruner, Janet M. *neuropathologist*
Brunson, John Soles *lawyer, investor*
Bryan, James Lee *oil field service company executive*
†Bryan, J(ames) P(erry), Jr., *energy company executive*
Bryan, Mary Ann *interior designer*
Bryant, John Bradbury *economics educator, consultant*
Buckingham, Edwin John, III, *lawyer*
Bue, Carl Olaf, Jr., *retired federal judge*
Bui, Khoi Tien *college counselor*
†Bulmahn, T. Paul *oil and gas company executive*
Bungo, Michael William *physician, educator, science administrator*
†Burau, Keith Dean *science educator, researcher*
Burbank, Daniel C. *astronaut*
Burch, Voris Reagan *retired lawyer, mediator, arbitrator*
Burg, Brent Lawrence *lawyer*
Burgos-Sasscer, Ruth *chancellor emeritus*
Burke, Kevin Charles Antony *geologist*
Burnett, Clarence Aubrey (Rusty Burnett) *personnel services company executive*
Burnett, Susan Walk *personnel service company owner*
Bursch, Daniel W. *astronaut*
Burton, Joseph Randolph *lawyer*
Burzynski, Stanislaw Rajmund *internist*
Busby, Justin Brett *lawyer*
Buster, John Edmond *gynecologist, medical researcher*
Butel, Janet Susan *research scientist, virology educator*
Butler, Ian John *neurologist*
Butler, William Thomas *college chancellor, physician, educator*
Bux, William John *lawyer*
Buyse, Leone Karena *orchestral musician, educator*
Cabana, Robert D. *astronaut*
†Cabioglu, Neslihan *surgeon*
Caddy, Michael Douglas *lawyer*
Caldwell, Rodney Kent *lawyer*
†Callahan, Gerald William *lawyer, oil company executive*
Callender, Norma Anne *psychology educator, counselor*
Cameron, William Duncan *plastics company executive*
Camfield, William Arnett *art educator, educator*
Campbell, Bert Louis *lawyer, mediator, arbitrator*
Campbell, Carl David *oil industry executive*
†Campos, Elizabeth Balli *lawyer*
Capps, Ethan LeRoy *oil company executive*
Carabello, Blase Anthony *cardiology educator*
Caram, Dorothy Farrington *educational consultant*
Carameros, George Demitrius, Jr., *natural gas company executive*
Cardus, David *physician*
Carey, Duane Gene (Digger) *astronaut*
Carlberg, W. Charles *advertising executive*
Carr, Edward A. *lawyer*

†Carroll, James Vincent, III, *lawyer*
Carroll, Michael M. *academic dean, mechanical engineering educator*
Carstarphen, Edward Morgan, III, *lawyer*
Carter, John Boyd, Jr., *oil operator, bank executive*
Carter, John Francis, II, *lawyer*
Carter, John Loyd *lawyer*
Castañeda, James Agustín *Spanish language educator, university golf coach*
Castillo, Josephine *small business owner, educator*
†Castriotta, Richard J. *medical educator, physician*
Catlin, Francis Irving *physician*
†Caudill, William Howard *lawyer*
Cazalot, Clarence P., Jr., *oil industry executive*
Chalmers, David B. *petroleum executive*
Chance, Jane *English literature educator*
†Chancellor, Van *professional basketball coach*
Chandler, George Francis, III, *lawyer, naval architect*
Chang-Diaz, Franklin R. *astronaut*
†Chatterjee, Amitava *finance educator, consultant*
Cheatham, John Bane, Jr., *retired mechanical engineering educator*
†Chen, Jinling *science administrator*
Cheung, Kam-Fong Monit *social worker, educator*
Chiao, Paul J. *molecular biologist, educator*
†Chiappetta, Eugene Louis *science educator*
Chima, Felix O. *social work educator*
Chiou-Tan, Faye *physician, educator*
Chiquelin, David Bryan *mechanical engineer*
Chu, Paul Ching-Wu *physicist, educator*
Chu, Wei-Kan *physicist, educator*
Cizik, Robert *manufacturing company executive*
†Clanton, Thomas Oscar *orthopedic surgeon*
Clark, Geoffrey *accountant*
Clark, Ron D(ean) *cosmetologist*
Clarke, Robert Logan *lawyer*
†Clayman, Gary L. *surgeon, educator*
Clearwater, John Murray *political analyst*
Clifton, Guy L. *neurosurgeon, educator*
Cline, Vivian Melinda *lawyer*
Clore, Lawrence Hubert *lawyer*
Clyburn, Rose Mary Reed *construction materials company executive*
Cockrell, Kenneth D. *astronaut*
Coghlan, Kelly Jack *lawyer*
Cohen, Jeff *editor*
†Colborn, Jack P. *engineering company executive*
†Coleman, Francis J., Jr., *lawyer*
Condit, Linda Faulkner *economist*
Conlon, Michael William *lawyer*
†Connelly, George William *lawyer*
Conner, Cecil C., Jr., *performing company executive*
†Conrad, Charles A. *neurologist, neuro-oncologist*
Cook, B. Thomas *lawyer*
Cook, Eugene Augustus *lawyer*
Cooley, Denton Arthur *surgeon, educator*
Cooney, James Patrick *lawyer*
†Cooper, Thomas Randolph *lawyer*
†Coppola, Eileen *philosopher, educator*
Corriere, Joseph N., Jr., *urologist, educator*
Cotros, Charles H. *food products company executive*
Couch, Jesse Wadsworth *retired insurance company executive*
Couch, Robert Barnard *physician, scientist, educator*
Cox, Frank D. (Buddy Cox) *oil company executive, exploration consultant*
Cox, James Talley *lawyer*
Craig, Robert Mark, III, *lawyer, educator*
†Crain, Alan Rau, Jr., *lawyer*
†Crane, John S. *architectural firm executive*
Creamer, Timothy J. *astronaut*
Crinion, Gregory Paul *lawyer*
Crispin, Andre Arthur *international trading company executive*
†Crocker, Samuel Sackett *lawyer*
†Crowl, Rodney Keith *lawyer*
Crystal, Jonathan Andrew *executive recruiter*
Cunningham, Ronnie Walter *venture capitalist*
Cunningham, Terence Thomas, III, *hospital administrator*
†Cunningham, Tom Alan *lawyer*
Curbeam, Robert L., Jr., *astronaut*
Curl, Robert Floyd, Jr., *chemistry educator*
Currie, John Thornton (Jack Currie) *retired investment banker*
Currie, Nancy Jane *astronaut*
Curry, Alton Frank *lawyer*
Cuthbertson, Gilbert Morris *political science educator*
Cutler, John Earl *landscape architect*
D'Agostino, James Samuel, Jr., *financial executive*
Danburg, Jerome Samuel *oil company executive*
Dang, Nam Hoang *medical educator*
Darst, Mary Lou *secondary school educator*
†Davenport, Bill *sculptor*
Davidson, Chandler *sociologist, educator*
Davis, Bruce Gordon *retired principal*
Davis, Leon *oil company executive*
Davis, Martha Algenita Scott *lawyer*
Davis, Rex Lloyd *insurance company executive*
Davis, Stephen Drake *lawyer*
†Dawson, Harry (Terry) Samuel, Jr., *policy analyst/advisor, consultant*
Dean, Robert Franklin *insurance company executive*
DeBakey, Lois *science communications educator, writer, editor*
†DeBakey, Michael Ellis *cardiovascular surgeon, educator, scientist*
DeBakey, Selma *science communications educator, writer, editor, lecturer*
DeGregori, Thomas Roger *economics educator, consultant*
de Kanter, Ellen Ann *English and foreign language educator*
DeMent, James Alderson, Jr., *lawyer*
DeMoss, Harold Raymond, Jr., *federal judge*

Deter, Russell Lee, II, *obstetrical ultrasonographer*
DeVault, John Lee *oil company executive, geophysicist*
Devlin, Francis James *lawyer*
Devoy, Stephen Douglas *marine engineer*
Diaz-Arrastia, George Ravelo *lawyer*
Dice, Bruce Burton *exploration company executive*
Dienstbier, Dan *gas and oil company executive*
†Dilg, Joseph Carl *lawyer*
†Dillard, Stephen C. *lawyer*
Dillon, Jimi *protective services official*
Dimachkie, Mazen Mohammad *health care educator*
Dinkins, Carol Eggert *lawyer*
Disher, David Alan *lawyer, consultant*
Djerejian, Edward Peter *institute administrator, former diplomat*
Doi, Takao *astronaut*
†Dorey, Louis J. *gas industry executive, lawyer*
Douglas, James M. *university president*
Douglas, P C *producer, director, reporter, editor*
Downing, Margaret Mary *newspaper editor*
Drew, Katherine Fischer *history educator*
Dreyer, Alec Gilbert *independent power producer*
†Driscoll, Michael Hardee *lawyer*
Dronamraju, Krishna Rao *geneticist*
Drury, Leonard Leroy *retired oil company executive*
Drutz, Jan Edwin *pediatrics educator*
Duerr, David *civil engineer*
†Dula, Arthur McKee, III, *lawyer*
Duncan, Charles William, Jr., *investor, former government official*
Duncan, Cheryl L. *critical care and cardiac catherization nurse*
†Duncan, Dan L. *gas company executive*
Dunham, Archie Wallace *petroleum and chemical products company executive*
Dunlop, Fred Hurston *lawyer*
DuPont, Herbert Lancashire *medical educator, researcher*
Durham, Susan K. *research scientist*
Durham, William Andrew *lawyer*
Dutta, Nripendu *stress analyst, consultant*
Dworkin, Anthony Gary *sociologist, educator*
Dworsky, Clara Weiner *lawyer, former merchandise brokerage executive*
Dykes, Osborne Jefferson, III, *lawyer*
Eastin, Keith E. *lawyer*
Edens, Donald Keith *oil company executive*
Edwards, Blaine Douglass *lawyer*
Eichberger, LeRoy Carl *mechanical engineer, consultant, stress analyst*
Eiland, Gary Wayne *lawyer*
Eisner, Diana *pediatrician*
†Eknoyan, Garabed *medical educator, researcher*
Elkins, James Anderson, Jr., *banker*
Elkins, James Anderson, III, *investment professional*
†Ellis, David Dale *lawyer*
Ellis, Walter Leon *minister*
Engerrand, Kenneth G. *lawyer, law educator*
Englesmith, Tejas *actor, producer, curator*
†Ertan, Atilla *medical educator, physician, researcher, health facility administrator*
Esmaeli, BitA *ophthalmologist*
Essmyer, Michael Martin *lawyer*
Esteva, Francisco Javier *physician, researcher*
†Etkin, Laurence D. *geneticist, educator*
Eubank, J. Thomas *lawyer*
Evans, Harry Launius *pathology educator*
Ewoh, Andrew Ikeh Emmanuel *political science educator*
Fan, Leland Lane *pediatrician, educator, medical researcher*
†Fannin, Tom *architectural firm executive*
Farenthold, Frances Tarlton *lawyer*
†Farley, Jan Edwin *lawyer*
Farnsworth, T. Brooke *lawyer*
Fason, Rita Miller *lawyer*
†Fassihi, Mohammad Reza *engineering executive*
†Feig, Barry W. *surgeon, oncologist*
Feigin, Ralph David *medical school administrator, pediatrician, educator*
†Feigon, Judith Tova *ophthalmologist, surgeon, educator*
Ferguson, J. Scott *quality management coordinator*
Ferrendelli, James Anthony *neurologist, educator*
Finch, Michael Paul *lawyer*
Fincke, Edward Michael (Mike) *astronaut*
†Fiorenza, Joseph A. *bishop*
Fischer, Craig Leland *physician*
†Fischer, Norman Charles *music educator*
Fisher, Anna Lee *physician, astronaut*
Fisher, Janet Warner *secondary school educator*
Fishman, Marvin Allen *pediatrician, neurologist, educator*
Fladung, Richard Denis *lawyer*
†Flanders, Melanie G. *information architect*
Flato, William Roeder, Jr., *software development company executive*
Fleming, George Matthews *lawyer*
Florian-Lacy, Dorothy *therapist, educator*
Foale, C. Michael *astronaut*
Focht, John Arnold, Jr., *geotechnical engineer*
Foreman, Michael J. *astronaut*
Forlano, Frederick Peter *lawyer*
Fornage, Bruno Denis *radiologist, educator*
Forrester, Patrick G. *astronaut*
Fossati, Humberto Mario *electrical engineer, researcher*
Foster, Charles Crawford *lawyer, educator*
Foster, Dale Warren *political scientist, educator, management consultant, real estate broker, accountant*
Foster, Joe B. *oil company executive*
Fox, Connie Steitz *freelance writer, editor, graphic designer*
Fox, George Edward *molecular biology educator*
Frankhouser, Homer Sheldon, Jr., *engineering and construction company executive*
Freeman, John Clinton *meteorologist, oceanographer*
Freeman, Marjorie Schaefer *mathematician, educator*
Freireich, Emil J *hematologist, educator*
Frick, Stephen N. *astronaut*
Friedman, Janet Teri *mortgage company executive*
Fritsch, Derek Adrian *nurse anesthetist*
†Frost, Adaani *internist*
Frost, Charles Estes, Jr., *lawyer*
Frost, John Elliott *minerals company executive*
Fuglesong, Christer *astronaut*
Fullenweider, Donn Charles *lawyer*
Fulwiler, Robert Neal *oil company executive*
Gabbard, Glen Owens *psychiatrist, psychoanalyst*
Galvani, Christiane Mesch *English as a second language educator, translator*
Garcia-Gregory, Jorge A. *cardiologist*
Gardezi, Syed A. *medical researcher*
Gardner, Everette Shaw, Jr., *information sciences educator, consultant, author*
Garrison, David Lacey, Jr., *oil company executive*
Gates, Stephen Frye *lawyer, oil industry executive*
Gaucher, Jane Heyck *retail executive*
Gayle, Gibson, Jr., *lawyer*
Gearhart, John Wesley, III, *musician, educator*
Geer, Ronald Lamar *mechanical engineering consultant, retired oil company executive*
†Geilikman, Mikhail Boris *research scientist, educator*
Geisinger, Kurt Francis *university administrator, psychometrician*
George, Deveral D. *editor, journalist, advertising consultant*
Gerhart, Glenna Lee *pharmacist*
Getz, Lowell Vernon *financial advisor*
†Ghayour, Kaveh *aeronautical engineer*
Gibson, Everett Kay, Jr., *space scientist, geochemist*
Gibson, Rex Hilton *lawyer*
Gigli, Irma *physician, educator, academic administrator*
Gilbert, David Wallace *retired aerospace engineer*
Gilbert, Harold Stanley *retired warehousing company executive*
Gildenberg, Philip Leon *neurosurgeon*
†Gilger, Mark Alan *pediatrician, educator*
Gillette, Lynn G. *dean*
†Gillis, Malcolm (Stephen Gillis) *academic administrator, economics educator*
†Gillmore, Kathleen Cory *lawyer*
Gilmore, Vanessa D. *federal judge*
†Gilstrap, Larry Cowan *obstetrician gynecologist*
Girouard, Peggy Jo Fulcher *ballet educator*
†Gissel, L. Henry, Jr., *lawyer*
Glassell, Alfred Curry, Jr., *investor*
Glasser, Adrian *physiologist, researcher, scientist*
Glassman, Armand Barry *physician, pathologist, scientist, educator, administrator*
†Gloriod, Paul *architectural firm executive*
Glowinski, Roland *mathematics educator*
†Gockley, David (Richard David Gockley) *opera director*
Goff, Robert Burnside *retired food company executive*
Goings, Austin Nelson *sales executive*
†Goldberg, Charles Ned *lawyer*
Goldberg, William Jeffrey *accountant, financial planner*
Goldman, Nathan Carliner *lawyer, educator*
Goldman, Stanford Milton *medical educator*
Goldsmith, Billy Joe *real estate broker, rancher*
Goldstein, Margaret Ann *biologist*
Golinkin, Webster Fowler *healthcare executive, media consultant*
Goloby, George William, Jr., *environmental scientist, editor, ornithologist, aviculturist*
Golubitsky, Martin Aaron *mathematician, educator*
†Gomez, Lynne Marie *lawyer*
Goodman, Herbert Irwin *petroleum company executive*
†Goodman, Joe Read *utilities executive*
†Gorbunova, Vera *biologist*
†Gorry, G. Anthony *medical educator, educator*
Gover, Alan Shore *lawyer*
Grace, James Martin, Jr., *lawyer*
Graf, Hans *conductor*
Graham, David Yates *gastroenterologist*
Graving, Richard John *law educator*
Grayson, Charles Jackson, Jr., *research association executive*
Green, Sharon Jordan *interior decorator*
†Gries, Michael F. *industrial maintenance industry executive*
Griffith, Martha *controller*
†Grimes, Richard Michael *public health educator*
†Grossberg, Marc Elias *lawyer*
Grossett, Deborah Lou *psychologist, consultant*
Grossman, Herbert Barton *urologist, researcher*
Grossman, Robert George *physician, educator*
Gruber, Ira Dempsey *historian, educator*
†Guest, Floyd Emory, Jr., *lawyer*
Guiberteau, Milton J. *radiologist*
Guilliouma, Larry Jay, Jr., *performing arts administrator, music educator*
Gunn, Albert Edward, Jr., *internist, educator, lawyer, administrator*
Gunn, Joan Marie *health care administrator*
Gunsel, Selda *chemical engineer, researcher*
†Gunter, Joseph Clifford, III, *lawyer*
Gutheinz, Joseph Richard, Jr., *lawyer, former politician, investigative consultant, retired army officer and NASA official, educator, author*
†Gutierrez, Edith G. *freelance/self-employed music educator, composer, lyricist*
Guynn, Robert William *psychiatrist, educator*
†Ha, Chul S *radiation oncologist*
Hackerman, Norman *chemist, academic administrator*
Hadfield, Chris A. *astronaut*
Hafner, Joseph A., Jr., *food company executive*
Halbouty, Michel Thomas *geologist, petroleum engineer, petroleum operator*
Halen, Walter John *music educator, composer*
Hall, Charles Washington *lawyer*
Hall, Robert Joseph *physician, medical educator*
Halyard, Raymond James *aerospace engineer, mathematics educator*
Hamel, Lee *lawyer*
Hamilton, Carlos Robert, Jr., *internist, educator, university official*
Hamilton, Jacqueline *art consultant*
Hammond, DeAnna *educator*
Hammond, Ken *newspaper magazine editor*
Haney, Peter Michael *pediatrics educator*
Hanks, George Carol, Jr., *state judge*
Hanrahan, Lawrence Martin *healthcare consultant*
Hargrove, James Ward *financial consultant*
Harper, Alfred John, II, *lawyer*
Harrington, Bruce Michael *lawyer, investor*
Harris, Lyttleton Tazwell, IV, *property management-investment company executive*
Harris, Richard Foster, Jr., *insurance company executive*
Harris, Venita Van Caspel *retired financial planner*
Harris, Warren Wayne *lawyer*
†Hartgrove-Freile, Janice Lynn *psychologist, educator, writer*
†Hartrick, Janice Kay *lawyer*
Hartsfield, Henry Warren, Jr., *electronics executive, retired astronaut*
†Harvin, David Tarleton *lawyer*
†Haskell, Thomas Langdon *history educator*
†Hassoun, Heitham Talal *surgeon, researcher*
†Hasten, Ralph Gerald *minister, protective services official*
Hawash, Michael Andrew *lawyer*
Hawes, William Kenneth *communication educator, author*
Haymond, Paula J. *psychologist, diagnostician, hypnotherapist*
Haynie, Thomas Powell, III, *physician*
Heckler, Walter Tim *association executive*
Heilman, William Joseph *research scientist, consultant*
Heinrich, Randall Wayne *lawyer*
Heinrich, Timothy John *lawyer*
Helland, George Archibald, Jr., *management consultant, manufacturing executive, former government official*
Hellums, Jesse David *chemical engineering educator and researcher*
Hempel, John P. *mathematics educator*
†Hempfling, Linda Lee *nurse*
Henington, David Mead *library director*
Henley, Ernest Justus *chemical engineering educator, consultant*
†Henry, Louise L. *educational association administrator*
Henry, Randolph Marshall *investments executive, real estate broker*
Herndon, John Wyatt *otolaryngologist*
Herring, Linda *pianist, music educator*
Herrington, John B. *astronaut, military officer*
Herzog, Cynthia Elaine *physician, educator*
Hicks, John Bernard *retired internist*
Higginbotham, Joan E. *astronaut*
Hilkemeyer, Renilda Estella *nurse*
Hinton, Paula Weems *lawyer*
Hittner, David *federal judge*
Ho, Ching *surgeon*
Ho, Yhi-Min *university dean, economics educator*
Hoang, Hung Manh *technology advisor*
Hobaugh, Charles O. *astronaut*
Hobby, William Pettus *broadcast executive, retired*
†Hobdell, Martin Howard *dental educator, researcher*
Hoffman, Philip Guthrie *former university president*
Hoglund, Forrest Eugene *petroleum company executive, retired*
Holloway, Gordon Arthur *lawyer*
Hollyfield, John Scoggins *lawyer*
Holmes, Ann Hitchcock *journalist*
Holmes, Harry Dadisman *health facility administrator*
Holmes, Roscette Yvonne Lewis *organizational development and training consultant*
Holstead, John Burnham *retired lawyer*
Honeycutt, George Leonard *photographer, retired*
Hook, Harold Swanson *former management consulting executive*
Hope, Henry Welcker *lawyer*
Hornak, Anna Frances *library administrator*
Hortobagyi, Gabriel N. *physician*
Horvitz, Paul Michael *finance educator, educator*
Hoyt, Kenneth M. *federal judge*
Hoyt, Mont Powell *lawyer*
Hsu, Katharine Han Kuang *pediatrics educator*
Hsu, Thomas Tseng-Chuang *civil engineer, educator*
Hu, Daniel David *lawyer*
Huang, Hsien-Lu *electrical engineer*
Huang, Jaou-Chen *obstetrician-gynecologist, reproductive endocrinologist*
Huang, Shawn Shaoping *engineer*
Hubert, Jean-Luc *chemicals executive*
Huddle, Donald Leroy *economist, educator*
†Hudson, Franklin *lawyer, real estate developer*
Hudspeth, Chalmers Mac *lawyer, educator*
Huffington, Roy Michael *business executive, former ambassador*
Hughes, Lynn Nettleton *federal judge*
Hunt, Michael Allen *psychologist, educator*
†Hurd, John R. *lawyer*
Hussain, Moinuddin Syed *geologist, reservoir engineer, consultant*
Huston, John Dennis *English educator*
†Hutchinson, Janis Faye *humanities educator, researcher*
Hyman, Harold M. *history educator, consultant*
†Hynes, Thomas N. (Toby Hynes) *automotive company executive*
†Ibbott, Geoffrey Stephen *physicist*
Ifft, Lewis George, III, *company administrator*
Ingersoll, Maryann E. Patterson *health educator, holistic nurse*
†Ionascu, Ileana *mathematician, educator*
†Irvin, Michael P. *lawyer*
Irwin, John Robert *oil and gas drilling executive*
†Issa, Jean-Pierre J *education educator, medical educator*
Itaketo, Umana Thompson *systems and control engineer*
Ivanov, Lyuben Dimitrov *naval architecture researcher, educator*
Ivins, Marcia S. *astronaut*
Jackson, Donna Ann *musician, piano instructor*
Jackson, Gilchrist L. *surgeon*
Jackson, Susanne Leora *retired creative placement firm executive*
Jackson, Wanda Britton *educator*
Jankovic, Joseph *neurologist, educator, scientist*
Jansen, Donald Orville *lawyer*
Janssens, Joe Lee *controller, consultant*
Jeanneret, Paul Richard *management consultant*
Jeevarajan, Judith A. *chemist*
Jemison, Mae Carol *physician, engineer, entrepreneur, philanthropist, educator, former astronaut*
Jenkins, Jerry Wayne *musician*
Jensen, William Powell *lawyer, educator*
Jeske, Charles Matthew *lawyer*
Jett, Brent W. *astronaut, military officer*
Jewell, George Hiram *lawyer*
Jhin, Michael Kontien *health care executive*
Jhingran, Anuja *oncologist, educator*
Jimmar, D'Ann *elementary education educator, fashion merchandiser*
Johnson, Craig M. *real estate development executive*
Johnson, Olin Glynn *computer science educator*
Johnson, Richard James Vaughan *newspaper executive, retired*
Johnson, Sandra Ann *educator, counselor*
Johnson, Wayne D. *gas industry executive*
Johnston, Marguerite *journalist, author*
Jones, Dan Brigman *ophthalmologist, educator*
Jones, Edith Hollan *federal judge*
Jones, Edith Irby *physician*
Jones, Eli, III, *marketing/sales educator*
Jones, Florence M. *music educator*
Jones, Frank Griffith *lawyer*
Jordan, Charles Milton *lawyer*
Jordon, Robert Earl *physician*
Joyce, James Daniel *clergyman*
Juneja, Harinder Singh *hematologist*
Jurtshuk, Peter, Jr., *microbiologist, educator*
Justice, Blair (David Blair Justice) *psychology educator, author*
Kahan, Barry Donald *surgeon, educator*
†Kakadiaris, Ioannis *computer science educator*
†Kanellos, Nicolás *foreign language and liberal studies educator, publisher*
†Kapadia, Asha Seth *education educator, consultant*
Kaplan, Alan Leslie *gynecology educator, oncologist*
†Kaplan, Lee Landa *lawyer*
†Kaptopodis, Louis *supermarket chain executive*
Karff, Samuel Egal *rabbi*
Karger, Walter *mechanical engineer*
Kasi, Leela Peshkar *pharmaceutical chemist*
Katrana, David John *plastic and reconstructive surgeon*
Kaufman, Raymond Henry *physician*
Kay, Joel Phillip *lawyer*
Keating, Tim *chef*
Keen, Brenda Denniston *lawyer*
Keenmon, Kendall A. *geologist, consultant, writer*
†Keiter, Aaron *lawyer*
Kellaway, Peter *neurophysiologist, researcher*
Keller, Robert Bounds *marketing professional, consultant, inventor*
Kelly, Hugh Rice *retired lawyer, retired energy executive*
Kelly, Mark E. *astronaut*
†Kelly, Robert Corby *energy executive, writer*
†Kelso, R. Randall *law educator*
Kemp, Roland Connor *lawyer*
†Kendall, Frank Russell, Sr., *lawyer*
Kendrick, Robert Warren *county official*
†Kennedy, John Edward *lawyer*
Kent, Jeffrey Franklin *professional baseball player*
Kerr, Baine Perkins *oil company executive*
Ketchand, Robert Lee *lawyer*
Key, James Everett *ophthalmologist*
†Khabashesku, Valery N. *chemist, educator*
Kilrain, Susan *astronaut*
Kim, Han-Seob *pathologist*
Kim, Pyung-Soo *martial arts educator*
King, Carolyn Dineen *federal judge*
King, Harry Richard *heart surgeon*
Kinnaird, Susan Marie *special education educator*
Kinsey, James Lloyd *chemist, educator*
Kirk, John Robert, Jr., *lawyer*
Kirkland, John David *oil and gas company executive, lawyer*
Kirkland, Rebecca Trent *pediatric endocrinologist*
Kit, Saul *biochemist, educator*
Kite, Lewis Donald *pharmaceutical executive*
Klausmeyer, David Michael *scientific instruments manufacturing company executive*
Kline, Allen Haber, Jr., *lawyer*
Klotz, David Wayne *executive, civil engineer*
†Knapp, David Hebard *banker*
Knauss, Robert Lynn *international business educator, corporate executive*
Knight, Jack Vernon *medicine and microbiology educator*
Koch, Douglas Donald *ophthalmologist, educator*
Kochi, Jay Kazuo *chemist, educator*
Koenig, Rodney Curtis *lawyer, rancher*
Koerner, Jo Ellen *health facility administrator*
†Koh, Moon-Soo *urologist, researcher*

†Kolb, John E. *lawyer*
Kollaer, Jim C. *real estate executive, architect*
†Kone, Bruce C. *medical educator, nephrologist*
Konisky, Jordan *microbiology educator*
†Kono, Junichiro *adult education educator*
Kors, R. Paul *search company executive*
†Kosterev, Anatoliy A. *research scientist*
Kouri, Donald Jack *chemist, educator*
Kraft, Irvin Alan *psychiatrist*
†Krajewski, Michael *conductor*
Kramm, Deborah Ann *information technology executive*
Kratochvil, L(ouis) Glen *lawyer*
Krebs, Arno William, Jr., *lawyer*
Kregel, Kevin R. *astronaut*
Krueger, Artur W. G. *international business consultant*
†Kruse, Charles Thomas *lawyer*
†Kruse, Layne E. *lawyer*
Kuntz, Hal Goggan *petroleum exploration company executive*
†Kurz, Thomas Patrick *lawyer*
†Kurzrock, Razelle *internist, educator*
Kutka, Nicholas *nuclear medicine physician*
LaBoon, Robert Bruce *lawyer*
†Lacey, David Morgan *lawyer, school administrator*
Lachar, David *psychologist, educator*
†LaFuze, William L. *lawyer*
Lahart, Daniel Kenneth *priest, educational administrator*
Lake, James Ronald *behavioral neuroscience researcher*
Lake, Kathleen Cooper *lawyer*
Lake, Sim *federal judge*
Lamb, Sydney MacDonald *linguistics and cognitive science educator*
†Lammers, Michael Lee *aerospace engineer*
Lamont, Gene *professional baseball coach, former professional baseball team manager*
Lampl, Lee Ann *internet marketing professional*
Lane, Neal Francis *physics educator, former government official*
Langford, Roland Everett *environmental scientist, safety engineer, writer*
Lanier, Robert C. (Bob Lanier) *real estate owner, developer, former mayor*
†Lanza, Frank Leo *gastroenterologist, researcher*
Larkin, Lee Roy *retired lawyer*
Larkin, William Vincent, Jr., *company executive*
Latimer, Roy Truett *museum executive*
Latting, Jean Kantambu *social worker, educator*
†Layne, Charles Shannon *medical educator*
Leak, Jessie Aronow *anesthesiologist*
Ledford, Tanner O'Brain *music educator*
Lee, Janie C. *curator*
Lee, Robert Leyne *conglomerate advisor, consultant*
Lehrer, Kenneth Eugene *economic consultant*
Leiber, Justin *philosophy educator, writer*
Lenox, Angela Cousineau *healthcare consultant*
Lepow, Ronald S. *podiatrist*
†Lerup, Lars G. *architecture educator, college dean*
Letbetter, R. Steve *energy company executive*
†Leth, Steven A. *management consultant*
Letsou, George Vasilios *cardiothoracic surgeon*
†Levit, Max *wholesale distribution executive, food service executive*
†Levit, Milton *grocery supply company executive*
Levy, Robert Edward *management consultant*
Lewis, Edward Sheldon *chemistry educator*
Lewis, Nelda Conner *social worker, therapist*
Li, George *cardiologist*
Liang, Edison Parktak *astrophysicist, educator, researcher*
†Lickteig, Bernard Fabian *retired priest, retired parochial school educator*
Lienhard, John Henry, IV, *mechanical engineer, educator*
Ligon-Borden, Betty Lee *academic director*
Liles, Clifton Roy *software designer*
Lindemulder, Laurie *piano educator, concert pianist*
†Linden, William M. *lawyer*
Lindsey, John Horace *insurance agency executive*
Litvinov, Dmitri *advisory development engineer*
Lobo, Rebecca *professional basketball player*
†Loftis, Jack D. *newspaper editor, newspaper executive*
Lopez, David Tiburcio *lawyer, educator, arbitrator, mediator*
Lopez-Alegria, Michael Eladio *astronaut*
Louderback, Truman Eugene *environmental project manager*
Loveland, Eugene Franklin *petroleum executive*
Low, Morton David *physician, educator, policy consultant*
†Lowman, Sara Allison *library director*
Lowry, Montecue Judson *military historian*
Lu, Bao-Yuan *biochemist, researcher*
Lu, Edward Tsang *astronaut*
Lu, Hsin Huang *radiologist, educator*
Luigs, Charles Russell *retired gas and oil drilling industry executive*
Luss, Dan *chemical engineering educator*
Lutz, Gretchen Kay *English language educator*
Lynch, John Edward, Jr., *lawyer*
Lyons, Phillip Michael, Sr., *insurance accounting and real estate executive*
†Ma, Jingjing *mathematician*
Macdonald, Eleanor Josephine *epidemiology educator, cancer epidemiology consultant*
Mahadeva, Manoranjan *financial executive, accountant*
Maligas, Manuel Nick *metallurgical engineer*
Malkoff, Marc David *neurologist*
†Malley, Wendi Sheree *statistician, researcher*
†Mallia, Marianne Hagar *medical writer*
Malone Watkins, Lisa R. *accountant, scheduler*
†Mampre, Virginia Elizabeth *communications executive*
Mansell, Joyce Marilyn *special education educator*
†Marchand, Wayne *architectural firm executive*
Margotta, Maurice Howard, Jr., *management consultant*
Margrave, John Lee *chemist, educator, university administrator*
Marlow, Orval Lee, II, *lawyer*
†Maroney, James Francis, III, *lawyer*
Marrack, David *pathologist*
Marston, Edgar Jean, III, *lawyer*
Martin, James Kirby *historian, educator*
Martin, Jay Griffith *lawyer*
Martin, Kenneth Frank *insurance company executive*
Martin, Paul Edward *lawyer*
Martin, Randi Christine *psychology educator*
Martin, Raymond Anthony *neurologist, educator*
Martin, William C. *sociology educator, writer*
Marzio, Peter Cort *museum director*
Massad, Stephen Albert *lawyer*
Massin, Edward Krauss *physician*
Masters, Claude Bivin *lawyer*
Matalon, Marlene *artist*
Mathis, James Forrest *retired petroleum company executive*
Matthews, Charles Sedwick *petroleum engineering consultant, research advisor*
Matthews, Kathleen Shive *biochemistry educator*
†Mattox, Ethel Odessa *writer*
Max, Ernest *surgeon*
Mayo, Carolyn *marketing professional, public relations executive*
Mayor, Heather Donald *medical educator, molecular biologist*
†Mazas, Carlos Adalberto *psychologist, researcher*
McCleary, Beryl Nowlin *civic worker, travel agency executive*
McCleary, Henry Glen *geophysicist*
McCleskey, Jerry Michael *retired chemical company executive*
McClure, Daniel M. *lawyer*
McCollam, Marion Andrus *consulting firm executive, educator*
†McDade, Thomas Rambaut *lawyer, rancher*
McDaniel, Jarrel Dave *lawyer*
McDavid, George Eugene (Gene Mc David) *retired newspaper executive*
†McDonald, Donald C. *lawyer*
McEvoy-Jamil, Patricia Ann *English language educator*
Mc Fadden, Joseph Michael *history educator*
McFall, Donald Beury *lawyer*
Mc Ginty, John Milton *architect*
McIntire, Larry Vern *biomedical engineering educator*
McIntire, Mary *university administrator*
McKechnie, John Charles *gastroenterologist, educator*
McKim, Paul Arthur *management consultant, retired petroleum executive*
McLeod, Harry O'Neal, Jr., *petroleum engineer, consultant*
†McNamara, Kevin Richard *humanities educator*
McPherson, Alice Ruth *ophthalmologist, educator*
†McQuarrie, Claude Monroe, III, *lawyer*
Meek, Susan Bieber *lawyer, physician, mediator, consultant*
†Meeks, Dodie Messer *writer*
Mehra, Man Mohan *medical products executive, small business owner*
Mendelsohn, John *oncologist, hematologist, educator*
Mendelson, Robert Allen *polymer scientist, rheologist*
Menscher, Barnet Gary *steel company executive*
Meredith, John *non-profit executive*
Merrill, Joseph Melton *medical educator*
Meyer, John Stirling *neurologist, educator*
Michael, Charles Joseph *lawyer*
†Michaels, Kevin Richard *lawyer*
Miele, Angelo *engineering educator, researcher, consultant, author*
Milam, John Daniel *pathologist, educator*
Miles, Brian John *urologist*
Miller, Charles Rickie *thermal and fluid systems analyst, engineering manager*
Miller, Gary Evan *psychiatrist, mental health services administrator*
Miller, Geoffrey *child neurologist*
Miller, Harry Freeman *university administrator*
Miller, Janel Howell *psychologist*
Miller-Hance, Wanda C. *anesthesiologist*
Minter, David Lee *English literature educator*
Minton, Melanie Sue *neuroscience nurse*
†Mintz-Hittner, Helen Ann *physician, researcher*
Mo, Yi-Lung *structural engineering educator*
Moehlman, Michael Scott *lawyer*
Moncure, John Lewis *lawyer*
†Montague, H. Dixon *lawyer*
†Montesinos, Marlene C. *lawyer, mediator, arbitrator*
Moore, Lois Jean *health science facility administrator*
Moorhead, Gerald Lee *architect*
†Morabito, Philip A. *public relations executive*
†Moran, Maria D. *elementary school educator*
Morgan, Richard Greer *lawyer*
†Morgan, William V. *oil and gas pipeline and storage executive*
Morin, Lee Miller Emile *astronaut*
Moroney, Linda L.S. (Muffie) *lawyer, educator*
Morris, Carloss (William Morris) *lawyer, insurance company executive*
Morris, Owen Glenn *engineering corporation executive*
Morrison, Scott David *management consultant*
Mouchaty, Suzette Kay *biologist*
Mu, Yaoming *physicist, researcher*
Mulholland, Jane E. *management consultant*
Munisteri, Joseph George *construction executive*
Munk, Zev Moshe *allergist, researcher*
Munsell, Debra S. *physician assistant, educator*
Murad, Ferid *physician*
Murphy, Ewell Edward, Jr., *lawyer*
Murphy, William Alexander, Jr., *diagnostic radiologist, educator*
Myers, A. Maurice *transportation executive*
Myers, Franklin *oil industry executive*
Myers, James Clark *advertising and public relations executive*
†Nachlinger, R. Ray *marine engineer, consultant, mechanical engineer, educator*
Nacol, Mae *lawyer*
Nance, Weldon Bailey *petroleum engineer*
Nanz, Robert Hamilton *petroleum consultant*
Nations, Howard Lynn *lawyer*
Nelson, David Leon *foundation administrator, lawyer, accountant*
Nelson, David Loren *geneticist, educator*
Nelson, John Robert *theology educator, clergyman*
Nelson-Thorpe, Carlon Justine *engineering and operations executive*
†Nemphos, Speros P. *chemist, consultant*
Nesbitt, DeEtte DuPree *small business owner, investor*
†Neslage, John Edward *lawyer*
Nestvold, Elwood Olaf *oil and gas industry consultant*
Neuhaus, Philip Ross *investment banker*
Ney, Judy Larson *lawyer, sociology educator*
Nichols, Mark Edward *aerospace engineer*
Nielsen, Niels Christian, Jr., *theology educator*
Nolen, Roy Lemuel *retired lawyer*
Nora, Hope *healthcare consultant*
Nordgren, Ronald Paul *engineering educator, researcher*
Nordlander, Peter Jan Arne *physics educator, researcher*
Noriega, Carolos I. *astronaut*
†Norman, Kenneth Glen *lawyer*
†Nunnally, Knox Dillon *lawyer*
Nyberg, Donald Arvid *oil company executive*
O'Brien, Eva Fromm *lawyer*
O'Brient, David Warren *sales executive, consultant*
O'Connor, Bryan D. *astronaut*
O'Connor, Ralph Sturges *investment company executive*
O'Laughlin, Francis Michael, III, *management consultant*
Oldham, Darius Dudley *lawyer*
Oldham, J. Thomas *lawyer, educator*
Olstead, Christopher Eric *consulting executive, talent manager*
O'Neil, John *artist*
Oren, Bruce Clifford *newspaper editor, artist*
Orr, Carole *artist*
Osgood, Christopher Mykel *radio sales executive*
†Osterberg, Edward Charles, Jr., *lawyer*
Osterberg, Susan Snider *communications educator, farmer*
Ostrow, Stuart *theatrical producer, educator, writer*
Oswalt, Roy E. *baseball player*
Ouyang, Liangbiao *petroleum engineer, researcher, petroleum engineer, educator*
†Paden, Lyman R. *lawyer*
Padmanabhan, Sivakumar *physician*
Pailes, William *astronaut*
Palmer, Chris *professional football coach*
Palmer, James Edward *public relations executive*
Parazynski, Scott E. *astronaut*
Park, Cheryl Antoinette *women's health nurse, educator*
Parker, Norman Neil, Jr., *software systems analyst, mathematics educator*
Parkerson, John E. (Sandy) *art dealer*
Parsons, Edmund Morris *investment company executive*
Pasternak, Joanna Murray *humanities educator*
Pate, A. J. *financial services advisor*
Pate, Patricia Ann *women's health nurse*
Patten, Robert Lowry *English language educator*
Paul, Alida Ruth *arts and crafts educator*
Paul, Thomas Daniel *lawyer*
Paulsen, James Walter *law educator*
Pawelczyk, James A. *astronaut, educator*
Payton, Gary E. *astronaut*
Peabody, Arlene L. Howland Bayar *retired, nurse*
Peng, Liang-Chuan *mechanical engineer*
†Perkyns, Jane Elizabeth *music educator, composer, actress*
Pesikoff, Bette Schein *lawyer*
Peterkin, George Alexander, Jr., *marine transportation company executive*
Pettiette, Alison Yvonne *lawyer*
Phung, Nguyen Dinh *medical educator*
Pickering, James Henry, III, *academic administrator, educator*
†Piech, Ruth Diane *nursing administrator*
Pinson, Artie Frances *retired elementary school educator*
Pitts, Gary Benjamin *lawyer*
Plaeger, Frederick Joseph, II, *lawyer*
Plunkett, Jack William *writer, publisher*
Poats, Lillian Brown *education educator*
Pognonec, Yves Maurice *steel products executive*
Poindexter, Alan *astronaut*
Poitevent, Edward Butts, II, *lawyer*
†Pollack, Howard J. *music educator, writer*
Pontes, Marcos C. *astronaut*
†Porter, Exa Lynn *librarian*
†Porter, Thomas William, III, *lawyer*
Portman, Ronald Jay *pediatric nephrologist, researcher*
Potluri, Venkateswara Rao *medical facility administrator*
Poulos, Michael James *insurance company executive*
Powell, Alan *scientist-engineer*
Powers, Hugh William *newspaper executive*
Powers, William Edward *emergency physician, educator*
Prats, Michael *petroleum engineer, educator*
Pravel, Bernarr Roe *lawyer*
Precourt, Charles J. *astronaut, retired military officer*
Prestridge, Pamela Adair *lawyer*
Prieto, Victor Gerardo *physician*
†Pritchard, William Winther *lawyer, drilling company executive*
Prokurat, Michael *theology studies educator, minister*
Pryor, William Daniel Lee *humanities educator*
Pudwill Gorie, Dominic L. *astronaut*
Pugsley, Frank Burruss *lawyer*
Pusey, Walter Carroll, III, *geologist, consultant*
Radoff, Leonard Irving *librarian, consultant*
Raijman, Isaac *gastroenterologist, endoscopist, educator*
†Raley, John Wesley, III, *lawyer*
Ramsey, Kathleen Sommer *toxicologist*
Rao, P. Syamasundar *pediatric cardiologist*
†Rapini, Ronald Peter *dermatology educator*
Rappaport, Norman Harvey *plastic surgeon*
†Rassidakis, George Z *pathologist, researcher*
Rawson, Jim Charles *accountant, executive*
Ray, Hugh Massey, Jr., *lawyer*
Read, Michael Oscar *editor, consultant*
Reasoner, Barrett Hodges *lawyer*
Reasoner, Harry Max *lawyer*
†Redden, Joe Winston, Jr., *lawyer*
Reed, Kathlyn Louise *occupational therapist, educator*
Reid, Katherine Louise *artist, educator, author*
Reid, Robert John *architect*
Reinbolt, Donna McNulty *lawyer*
Reso, Anthony *geologist, educator, earth resources economist*
†Reynolds, John Terrence *oil industry executive*
Rhodes, Allen Franklin *engineering executive*
Ribble, Anne Hoerner *communications executive*
Ribble, John Charles *medical educator*
Rice, Emily Joy *retired secondary school and adult educator*
Richards, Leonard Martin *investment executive, consultant*
Richter, Dawn Slater *lawyer*
Riedel, Alan Ellis *retired manufacturing company executive, lawyer*
Riedi, Rudolf Hermann *mathematics researcher*
Rieke, Ronald Alfred *computer company executive*
Riesser, Gregor Hans *arbitrage investment advisor*
Riley, William John *neurologist*
†Rios de Lumbreras, Kristina Marie *language educator*
†Rives, Terry Edward *public health service officer, researcher, epidemiologist*
Robb, Geoffrey Lawrence *plastic surgeon*
Robbins, Susan Paula *social work educator*
†Roberson, Clifford Eugene *law educator, lawyer*
Roberts, Paul *chef*
Robertson, James Woolsey *lawyer*
†Rock, Douglas Lawrence *manufacturing executive*
Roff, J(ohn) Hugh, Jr., *energy company executive*
Rogers, Arthur Hamilton, III, *lawyer*
Roman, Gregg William *geneticist, researcher*
Rong, Shu *materials scientist, researcher*
Roos, Sybil Friedenthal *retired elementary school educator*
Rose, Franklin Arthur *plastic surgeon*
Rose, Robert Ernest *gas & oil drilling industry executive*
Rosenthal, Lee H. *federal judge*
Rosenthal, Morris William *pediatrician*
Rosin, Lindsay Zweig *clinical psychologist*
Ross, Jerry L. *astronaut*
Ross, Michael Wallis *public health educator*
Ross, Patti Jayne *obstetrics and gynecology educator*
†Rossler, Willis Kenneth, Jr., *petroleum company executive*
Rowland, Robert Alexander, III, *lawyer*
Rozzell, Scott Ellis *lawyer*
Rubenfeld, Sheldon *thyroidologist*
†Rubenzer, Steven James *foresnic psychologist*
Rudolph, Andrew Henry *dermatologist, educator*
Rudolph, Frederick Byron *biochemistry educator*
Ruiz, Pedro *psychiatrist*
Ruppert, Susan Donna *acute/critical care nursing educator, family and adult nurse practitioner*
†Russell, Donald Glenn *oil company executive*
Russell, John Francis *retired librarian*
†Ruvolo, Peter *molecular biologist*
Ryan, Thomas William *lawyer*
Ryan, Vince *lawyer*
Sadowski, Chester Philip, Jr., *real estate executive*
Saizan, Paula Theresa *oil company executive*
Saks, Judith-Ann *artist*
†Salam, Debera Jean *accounting company executive*
Salch, Steven Charles *lawyer, mediator, arbitrator*
Sales, James Bohus *lawyer*
Salinas, Martha F. *manufacturing executive*
†Samman, Mahmod *engineering educator, consultant*
Samo, Tobias Charles *physician*
Sanderson, Mary Louise *medical association administrator*
Sapp, Walter William *lawyer, energy company executive*
†Sargent, John *psychiatrist*
Sass, Ronald Lewis *biology and chemistry educator*
Satitpunwaycha, Pon *surgeon*
Saunders, Charles Albert *lawyer*
Saunders, William Arthur *management consultant*
Sayer, Coletta Keenan *gifted education educator*
Sazama, Kathleen *pathologist, lawyer*
Scarbrough, Sara Eunice *librarian, archivist, consultant*
Schachtel, Barbara Harriet Levin *epidemiologist, educator*
Scharold, Mary Louise *psychoanalyst, educator*
Schechter, Arthur Louis *lawyer*
Schein, Daniel *webmaster, photographer*
Schiflett, Mary Fletcher Cavender *retired health facility executive, researcher, educator*
†Schnieders, Richard J. *food products executive*
†Scholin, Margo S. *lawyer*
†Scholl, Stephen Gerrard *lawyer*
Schoolar, Joseph Clayton *psychiatrist, pharmacologist, educator*

Schultz, Stanley George physiologist, educator
†Schumacher, Diane Kosmach manufacturing executive, lawyer
Schwartz, Charles Walter lawyer
Schwartzel, Charles Boone lawyer
Schwarz, Paul Winston judge
Scott, David Warren statistics educator
Scott, John McGregor oil and gas industry executive, real estate investor
Scott, Ronald lawyer
Scuseria, Gustavo Enrique theoretical chemist
†Sdringola-Maranga, Stefano medical educator, researcher
†Seale, Robert Arthur, Jr., lawyer
Sears, David Alan medical educator
Seaton, Alberta Jones biologist, educator, consultant
†Segal, Steven E. lawyer
Segner, Edmund Peter, III, natural gas company executive
†Sellingsloh, John S. lawyer
Sercombe, William John geologist
†Shackouls, Bobby S. oil and gas industry executive
Shaddock, Carroll Sidney lawyer
Shaffer, Anita Mohrland counselor, educator
Shahjahan, Munir medical researcher
†Shan, Kesavan cardiologist, researcher
†Shannon, Joel Ingram lawyer
Sharp, Douglas Andrew secondary school educator, educator
Shead, William C. lawyer
Shearer, William Thomas pediatrician, educator
Shelley, Clyde Burton artist
†Sheppard, Ben H., Jr., lawyer
Sher, George Allen philosophy educator
†Sherman, Robert Taylor, Jr., lawyer
†Sherman, Steven I. endocrinologist, educator
Shook, Joan E. medical educator
†Shouse, August Edward lawyer
Shriver, Loren J. astronaut
†Shuart, Carey Chenoweth farmer, volunteer
Shulman, Robert Jay pediatrician, educator, nutritionist
Shurn, Peter Joseph, III, lawyer
†Sickles, Robin C. economics and statistics educator, consultant
†Siess, Charles P., Jr., manufacturing company executive
Sill, Gerald de Schrenck hotel executive
†Silva, Eugene Joseph lawyer
Simmons, Stephen Judson lawyer
Simpson, Joe Leigh obstetrics and gynecology educator
Sing, Doris Anne music educator
Sing, William Bender lawyer
Singletary, Sonja Eva surgeon, educator
Sipahioglu, Hatice Elcin diplomat, interpreter/translator
Sisson, Virginia Baker geology educator
Skolnick, Malcolm Harris biophysics researcher, educator, lawyer, mediator, biotechnology executive
Skura, Meredith Anne English educator
†Slaydon, Kathleen Amelia lawyer
Smalley, Richard Errett chemistry and physics educator, researcher
†Smith, Alison Leigh lawyer
Smith, Arthur Kittredge, Jr., academic administrator, political science educator
Smith, Claire chef
†Smith, Dan F. oil company executive
Smith, David Kingman retired oil company executive, consultant
Smith, Gordon Eugene pilot
Smith, J. Thomas mental health consultant
Smith, Jerry Edwin federal judge
†Smith, Walter John lawyer
Smythe, Cheves McCord dean, medical educator
Snowden, Bernice Rives former construction company executive
Soileau, Kerry Michael aerospace technologist, researcher
†Soliman, Sam gas, oil and chemical industry executive, investment company executive
Solymosy, Edmond Sigmond Albert international marketing executive, retired army officer
Sondock, Ruby Kless retired judge
Sonfield, Robert Leon, Jr., lawyer
Sorrels, Randall Owen lawyer
Southwell, Samuel Beall English educator
Spalding, Andrew Freeman lawyer
Spanos, Pol Dimitrios engineering educator
Spencer, Dennis D. medical educator, director
Sperber, Matthew Arnold direct marketing company executive
Spira, Melvin plastic surgeon
Springer, Wayne Gilbert computer company executive
†Stacks, Thistle N. mathematician, educator
Staine, Ross (Ross Donan Allison Staine Jr.) lawyer
Stapleton, Ronald James investment manager
Starkey, Elizabeth LaRuffa accountant
Starkschall, George medical physicist
†Stayer, Stephen A anesthesiologist
Steele, James Harlan former public health veterinarian, educator
Stephens, Carson Wade minister
†Stephens, R(obert) Gary lawyer
Stevenson, Ben artistic director
Stewart, Michael Glenn medical educator, physician
Stewart, Pamela L. lawyer
Still, Charles Henry, Sr., lawyer
Stimson, Paul Gary pathologist
†Stradley, William Jackson lawyer
Streng, William Paul lawyer, educator
Strieder, Leon F. priest, theology studies educator
Strommer, Anne Elizabeth Rivard retired librarian
Stryker, Daniel Ray adult education educator
Sturckow, Frederick W. (Rick) astronaut
Susman, Morton Lee lawyer
Susman, Stephen Daily lawyer
Suter, Jon Michael academic library director, educator
Sweeney, Jack publishing executive
Sweet, James Brooks oral and maxillofacial surgeon
Swoopes, Sheryl Denise professional basketball player
Sydow, Michael David lawyer
Szalkowski, Charles Conrad lawyer
†Tabak, Morris lawyer
Talapatra, Dipak Chandra aerospace engineer
†Talbert, Arthur Thomas music educator
Talmage, Edward Arthur anesthesiologist
Talwani, Manik geophysicist, educator
†Tamboli, Pheroze pathologist
Tani, Daniel M. astronaut
Tanner, Joseph Richard astronaut
Tarlov, Alvin Richard former philanthropic foundation administrator, physician, educator, researcher
†Tartt, Blake lawyer
Tavormina, John William lawyer
Taylor, James Sheppard communications educator
Temple, Robert Winfield chemical company executive
Templeton, Robert Earl engineering and construction company executive
Teruya, Jun hematologist, clinical pathologist
Texas, Sam Fayad small business owner, political activist
Tezduyar, Tayfun Ersin engineering educator
Thirsk, Robert Brent astronaut
Thomas, Andrew S.W. astronaut
Thomas, Donald A. astronaut
Thomas, Katherine Jane magazine and newspaper columnist
Thomas, Orville C. retired physician, consultant
Thompson, Ewa M. foreign language educator
Thompson, Tina professional basketball player
†Thurmond, Gerald Pittman lawyer
Tice, Pamela Paradis scientific editor, writer
Tilghman, Richard Granville bank executive
Timpani, Nancy Evelyn elementary school educator
Tiras, Herbert Gerald engineering executive
†Toedt, D(ell) C(harles), III, lawyer
Tong, Louis Lik-Fu information scientist
†Torre-Amione, Guillermo cardiologist, researcher
Touchy, Deborah K.P. lawyer, accountant
Tran, Qui-Phiet English educator
Trichel, Mary Lydia middle school educator
Tripp, Karen Bryant lawyer
Tryggvason, Bjarni V. astronaut
Tsai, Tom Chunghu chemical engineer
Tucker, Hillary Albert retired intelligence officer, writer
Tulloch, Brian Robert endocrinologist
Turner, Kelley Bailey non-profit consultant, volunteer program administrator
†Turner, Leland architectural firm executive
Turner, Max Allen career officer, chemical engineer
†Tyson, Carla Lea director
Untermeyer, Charles Graves (Chase Untermeyer) academic administrator
Urbina, Febe Gloria elementary school principal
Urbina, Manuel, II, legal research historian, history educator
Vacar, Richard M. airport executive
Vallbona, Carlos physician
Vallbona, Rima-Gretel Rothe foreign language educator, writer
†Vallejo, Bernardo linguist, anthropologist, consultant, administrator, writer
van Cleave, Kirstin Dean (Kit van Cleave) martial arts educator, writer, educator, publishing executive
Vanderploeg, James M. preventive medicine physician
Van Dusen, Glenn T. business executive
Van Dyke, Gene oil company executive
Van Fleet, George Allan lawyer
†Van Gundy, Jeff professional basketball coach
Vant-Hull, Lorin L. physics educator, consultant
†Van Winkle, Danny L. lawyer
Varma, Datla G.K. radiologist, researcher
Varner, David Eugene lawyer
Vaughan, Eugene H. investment company executive
Vickery, Edward Downtain lawyer
Vilas, Faith aerospace scientist
†Vipulanandan, Cumaraswamy civil engineer, educator
Vollmer, Helen public relations executive
Voss, James S. astronaut
Voss, Janice E. astronaut
Wagner, Billy baseball player
Wagner, Charlene Brook publishing consultant
Wagner, Donald Bert health care consultant
Wagner, Paul Anthony, Jr., education educator
Wakil, Salih Jawad biochemistry educator
Walbridge, Willard Eugene broadcasting executive
Walker, Charles D. astronaut
Walker, William Easton surgeon, educator, lawyer
Wall, Kenneth E., Jr., lawyer
Wall, Matthew J., Jr., surgeon, scientist
Wallis, Olney Gray lawyer
Walls, Martha Ann Williams (Mrs. B. Carmage Walls) newspaper executive
Walton, Conrad Gordon, Sr., retired architect
Walton, Dan Gibson lawyer
†Waltrip, Robert L. environmentalist
Walz, Carl E. astronaut
Wang, Chao-Cheng mathematician, engineer
Wang, Fu-kuo Albert finance educator
Wang, Xiaozhi structural engineer
Ward, David Henry (Dave Ward) television news reporter, anchorman
†Ward, Stephanie G. education educator
†Watson, Chuck energy and communications industry executive
Watson, David A. biomedical researcher, educator
Watson, John Allen lawyer
†Weathers, Barbara Hiller librarian
Webb, Jack M. lawyer
Webb, Marty Fox principal
Weber, Fredric Alan lawyer
Wei, Ying chemist
†Weiner, Sanford Alan lawyer
Weinstein, Roy physics educator, researcher
Weisgarber, Robert Lee corporate financial executive
Weisman, R(obert) Bruce physical chemist, educator
†Welch, Stanton performing company executive
†Weller, Philip Douglas lawyer
†Wells, Benjamin Gladney lawyer
Wells, Damon investment company executive
†Welsh, H. Ronald lawyer
Weng, Han-Rong neuroscientist, researcher
†Wensel, Theodore G. biochemist, educator
Westby, Timothy Scott lawyer, researcher
Wetherbee, James D. astronaut
†Wharton, Thomas H(eard), Jr., lawyer
Wheelan, R(ichelieu) E(dward) lawyer
Wheless, James Warren neurologist
Whitaker, Gilbert Riley, Jr., academic administrator, business economist
White, David Alan, Jr., manufacturing company executive
White, Nancy Elizabeth psychologist, artist
White, Ronald Joseph life and biomedical scientist, physiology educator
Whiting, Martha Countee retired secondary education educator
Wiemer, David Robert plastic surgeon
†Wiese, Larry Clevenger lawyer
†Wiesner, Mark Robert environmental engineer, educator
Wike, D. Elaine business executive
Wilcutt, Terence W. astronaut
Wilde, Carlton D. lawyer, director
Wilde, William Key lawyer
†Wiley, Michael E. oil industry executive
†Wiley, Shirley Winona Walters adult education educator, artist
†Wilfong, Hugh C., II, lawyer
†Wilhelmus, Kirk Robert ophthalmologist
Williames, Lee John university official, history educator
Williams, Curtis Chandler, III, retired chemical engineer, consultant
Williams, David R. astronaut
Williams, Edward Earl, Jr., entrepreneur, educator
Williams, Jeffrey N. astronaut
Williams, Jimy professional athletics manager
†Williams, Marjorie L. retired lawyer
Williams, Robert Henry oil company executive
Williams, Robert Lyle corporate executive, consultant
Williams, Sunita L. astronaut
Williams, Temple Weatherly, Jr., internist, educator
†Williamson, Bruce A. oil industry executive
Williamson, Peter David lawyer
Willmann, Donnie Glenn safety executive
Wilson, Carl Weldon, Jr., construction company executive, civil engineer
Wilson, Edward Converse, Jr., oil and natural gas production company executive
Wilson, Richard Harold government official
Wilson, Thomas Leon physicist, researcher
†Wilton, Donald Robert engineering educator
Windle, Pamela Evelyn surgical nurse
†Windsor, Oliver Duane business and public administration educator
†Winniford, Lee language educator
Wisecup, Barbara Jean retired medical and surgical nurse
Witmer, John Richard librarian
Wnuk, Wade Joseph manufacturing and service company executive
Wolinsky, Jerry Saul neurology educator
Wombwell, John Futrell air transportation executive
Woo, Walter computer systems consultant
†Wood, Judson Robert lawyer
Woodhouse, John Frederick food distribution company executive
Woods, Stephanie Elise computer company executive, entrepreneur
†Woodson, Michael E. humanities educator
Worthington, William Albert, III, lawyer
Woung-Chapman, Marguerite Natalie lawyer
Wray, Thomas Jefferson lawyer
Wren, Robert James aerospace engineering manager
Wright, Clark Phillips computer systems specialist
Wu, Kenneth Kun-Yu physician, scientist
Wuensche, Vernon Edgar construction company executive
Wuenschel, Peter Cyril educational association administrator, social worker
Xu, Xiaochun biologist, researcher
Yetter, R. Paul lawyer
Yiu, Fang structural engineer, researcher
Yokubaitis, Roger T. lawyer
York, James Martin judge
†Young, Amy E. obstetrician, gynecologist, educator
Young, John Watts astronaut
Yu, Aiting Tobey engineering executive
Yuen, Benson Bolden airline management consultant, software executive
Zamka, George D. astronaut
Zander, Dani S. pathologist, educator
Zarin, Jerald Lawrence pediatrician, physician executive
Zeff, Stephen Addam accounting educator
Zeigler, Ann dePender lawyer
Zhang, Chunlong environmental educator
†Zhao, Zhongshan structural engineer, researcher
Zhou, Juhua molecular biologist
Zoghbi, Huda Y. pediatric neurology and genetics educator

Humble

Brinkley, Charles Alexander geologist
†Brown, Samuel Joseph, Jr., engineer, scientist
†Gaffney, Richard Cook lawyer
Gruman, Robert Richard energy management consultant
†Pickle, George Edward lawyer
Trowbridge, John Parks physician

Hunt

Price, Donald Albert veterinarian, consultant

Huntsville

Cesario, Robert James music educator, performer
†Coffey, Joan L. humanities educator
Conwell, Halford Roger physician
Hopper, Margaret Sue academic administrator, educational diagnostician, consultant
Lea, Stanley E. artist, educator
†McInturf, William Matthew music educator
Nolan, Patrick Bates museum director
Payne, David Emer university administrator
†Peck, Leonard Warren, Jr., lawyer
†Plugge, Scott Douglas music educator, saxophonist
Raymond, Kay E(ngelmann) Spanish language educator, consultant
†Ruffin, Paul Dean English language educator
Russell, George Haw video production company executive
Smyth, Joseph Philip travel industry executive
Sower, Victor Edmund management educator
Stowe, Charles Robinson Beecher management consultant, educator, lawyer
Vick, Marie retired health science educator
Ward, Richard Hurley university dean, writer
Warner, Laverne education educator

Hurst

Benge, Raymond Doyle, Jr., astronomy educator
Bishara, Amin Tawadros management and consulting firm executive, technical services executive
Dodd, Sylvia Bliss special education educator
Dooley, Lena Rose (Nelson) writer, editor
Hurley, Linda Kay psychologist
Kotas, Robert Vincent research physician, educator
Leach, Terry Ray lawyer, judge

Industry

Huitt, Jimmie L. rancher, oil, gas, real estate investor

Ingleside

Naismith, James Pomeroy civil engineer

Ingram

Hughes, David Michael oil service company executive, rancher

Iowa Park

Harvill, Melba Sherwood retired university librarian

Irving

Adams, Charles Paul communications engineer, consultant
Aikman, Troy professional football player
Allen, Barbara Ann musician, educator, personnel contractor
Anderson, Michael Curtis computer industry analyst
†Beach, Charles Addison lawyer
Bielss, Otto William, Jr., secondary school educator
Carter, Quincy football player
Chase, Pearline adult education educator
Clark, Priscilla Alden retired elementary education educator
Coakley, Dexter football player
Conger, Sue Ann computer information systems educator
Coslet, Bruce N. professional football coach
Crowley, L. C. telecommunications company executive
Dinicola, Robert consumer products company executive
†Donehower, John W. retired paper company executive
Eudaly, Nathan H. insurance company executive
†Falk, Thomas J. paper company executive
Forson, Norman Ray controller
French, Colin Val lawyer
Fukui, George Masaaki microbiology consultant
Galloway, Joe football player
Gibson, Colvin Donald human resources specialist
Gretzinger, Ralph Edwin, III, management consultant
Halbert, David D. health management services executive
Halter, Jon Charles magazine editor, writer
Hardy, Kevin Lamont football player
Hatcher, Darien hockey player
Hendrickson, Constance Marie McRight chemist, consultant
Hicks, Allen Morley hospital administrator
†Hitchcock, Ken professional hockey coach
Holdar, Robert Martin chemist
†Humphreys, Donald D. oil company executive
†Irvin, Michael Jerome professional football player
Ismail, Raghib (Rocket Ismail) professional football player
†Jones, Jerry (Jerral Wayne Jones) professional football team executive
Kaiser, Fran Elizabeth endocrinologist, gerontologist
Kuckelman, Brian Thomas architect
Lee, Michael Wayne structural engineer, consultant
†Lites, James R. professional hockey team executive
Lockyer, Charles Warren, Jr., corporate executive
Longwell, Harry oil company executive

Lutz, Matthew Charles *oil company executive, geologist*
Martin, Stacey *accountant*
Martin, Thomas Lyle, Jr., *academic administrator*
†Matthews, Charles W. *lawyer*
McCormack, Grace Lynette *civil engineering technician*
McVay, Barbara Chaves *secondary education mathematics educator*
Meyerson, Lawrence Bernard *physician*
Milgrim, Samuel G. *television producer*
†Nottingham, Jeffrey E *energy executive*
Nugent, John Hilliard *communications executive*
Olson, Herbert Theodore *trade association executive*
Papakostas, Achilleas *telecommunications engineer, researcher*
†Parcells, Bill (Duane Charles Parcells) *professional football coach*
Pennington, William Lane *manufacturing executive*
Piqué, Fernando Rafael *international art dealer, artist*
Plaskett, Thomas George *transportation company executive, corporate director*
Potter, Robert Joseph *technical and business executive*
†Rose, Rachel *marketing professional*
Rosemann, Philipp Wolfram *philosopher, educator*
†Rutledge, Deborah Jean *secondary school educator, music educator*
Sambaluk, Nicholas Wayne *auditor, educator*
Sanders, Deion Luwynn *professional football player*
Sommerfeldt, John Robert *historian, educator*
Steele, C. William *scouting organization administrator*
†Tonelli, Mark Louis *performer, composer, music educator*
†Vamanan, Mayur *advisory consultant*
Walley, James Marvin, Jr., *engineering and real estate executive, management consultant*
†Whisennand, Cynthia Simmons *librarian*
Whitaker, Heidi Sue *accountant, auditor, information systems specialist*
Whittington, James Leland *management educator*
Wicks, William Withington *retired public relations executive*
Young, J. Warren *magazine publisher*

Jacksonville
Blaylock, James Carl *clergyman, librarian*
Brewer, Brett *lawyer*
Thrall, Gordon Fish *publishing executive*
Wonnacott, James Brian *physician*

Johnson City
†Pollock, Margaret Landau Peggy *elementary school educator*
Schneider, David Paul, Sr., *entrepreneur*

Junction
Evans, Jo Burt *communications executive, rancher*

Karnes City
Davis, Troy Arnol *reflexologist, hypnotherapist*

Katy
Gibert, Charlene West *gifted education educator*
†Golka, Anna Maria *musician, educator*
Huffaker, E. Wayne *artist*
Poland, Sydney Wade *software designer*

Kaufman
Teagle, David Bryan
Tygrett, Howard Volney, Jr., *judge, lawyer*

Keene
Beary, Shirley Lorraine *retired music educator*
†Stembridge, Allen Frederick *management educator*
†Willis, Lloyd Allan *religious studies educator*

Keller
†Flournoy, Edward Brian *financial consultant, consultant*
Patterson, Ronald R(oy) *health care systems executive*

Kelly A F B
†Bielowicz, Paul L. *career officer*
†Elliott, Carol C. *career officer*

Kemah
Cofran, George Lee *telecommunication consultant*

Kemp
Skinner, John Vernon *retail credit executive*

Kerrville
Chance, F. Earlayne *artist*
Cremer, Richard Eldon *marketing professional*
Dozier, William Everett, Jr., *newspaper editor and publisher*
Ference, L.W. *psychologist*
Frudakis, Evangelos William *sculptor*
Lawson, Carole Jean *religious educator, author, poet*
Matlock, Hudson *civil engineer, educator*
O'Shields, Richard Lee *retired natural gas company executive*
Parmley, Robert James *lawyer, consultant*
Rhodes, James Devers *psychotherapist*
Shaw, Alan Bosworth *geologist, paleontologist*
†Sparks, Don Bertrand *retired geophysicist*
Williams, William Henry, II, *publisher*
Zuber, Randolph Clark *urologist*

Kilgore
†Neal, Paul *music educator*
Rorschach, Richard Gordon *lawyer*

Killeen
†Bryan, Arthur Lee *music educator*
Campbell, Troy David *officer*
Rappaport, Claudia Diane *social worker, educator*
Roberts, Burk Austin *lawyer*
Seigman, Deborah Werst *literature educator*

Kingsville
†Beach, Regina Lee *librarian*
Cecil, David Rolf *mathematician, educator*
Hessong, Cindy Hoch *music educator*
†Li, Shuhui *engineer, educator*
Morey, Philip Stockton, Jr., *mathematics educator*
Pray, Ronald Wayne *protective services official*
Robins, James Dow *counselor*
Schreur, Barbara *computer science educator*
Wiley, Millicent Yoder *realtor, pianist, accompanist, retired secondary school educator*

Kingwood
Barkley, Bronson Lee *minister*
Bowman, Stephen Wayne *quality assurance engineer, consultant*
†Chamoun-Nicolas, Habib *business development consultant*
Delap, J. Q., Jr., *gas company executive*
†Hagen, Barbara C. *music educator*
Hawk, Phillip Michael *service corporation executive*
†Ribeiro, Frank Henry *banker, energy consultant*
Spartz, Alice Anne Lenore *retired retail executive*
Wigglesworth, David Cunningham *business and management consultant*

Kyle
Saunders, Patricia Gene *freelance writer, editor*

La Feria
Philip, Sunny Koipurathu *municipal official*

La Porte
Levi, Janice Lawan *counselor*
†Svambera, Beatrice Alice *secondary school educator*

Lackland A F B
Burghardt, Walter Francis, Jr., *veterinarian*
†Chiou, Andy C. *surgeon*
†Dremsa, Theresa Lynn *military officer, researcher*
†Dunn, William Jackson *dental educator, researcher*
†Farage, Michael N. *career officer*
†Kashyap, Vikram S. *vascular surgeon, military officer*
†Mabry, Earl W. *military officer*
†Mealey, Brian L *periodontist, military officer*

Lago Vista
Barrett, Archie Don *retired federal official, educator*
Garcia y Carrillo, Martha Xochitl *pharmacist*
Hilton, James Gorton *pharmacologist*
Hughes, James Baker, Jr., *retail executive, consultant*

Lake Creek
Smith, Shirley Ann Nabors *retired secondary school educator*

Lake Dallas
Richardson, Wanda Louise Gibson *nurse*

Lake Jackson
Elbert, James Peak *independent insurance agent, minister*
Resnick, Harvey *physician*
Tasa, Ken *college dean*

Lakehills
Spears, Diane Shields *artist, retired art academy administrator*

Lakeway
Boswell, Gary Taggart *investor, former electronics company executive*
Gans, Dennis Joseph *information technology manager, financial analyst*

Lamesa
Saleh, John *lawyer*

Lampasas
Stephens, Billie Lowell *information assurance manager*

Lancaster
†Sewell, Cameron Dee *lawyer*

Laredo
Ali, Ashraf *psychiatrist*
Black, Clifford Merwyn *academic administrator, sociologist, educator*
Engling, Ezra Samuel *Spanish and literature educator, researcher*
Fierros, Ruth Victoria *retired secondary school educator*
†Gonzalez, Rene *government executive*
†Keck, Ray Marvin, III, *academic administrator*
†Kohl, John Preston *management educator*
Mayfield, Jacqueline Rowley *business educator, department chairman*
Mendiola, Anna Maria G. *mathematics educator*
Purpura, Peter Joseph *museum curator, exhibition designer*
Watson, Helen Richter *educator, ceramic artist*
Zaffirini, Judith *state legislator, small business owner*

League City
Burns, Richard Robert *chemicals executive*
Kanuth, James Gordan *chemical engineer*

Leander
Erickson, Ralph D. *retired physical education educator, small business owner, consultant*
Johnson, Vicki Valeen *paramedic, technical advisor movie studios*

Lewisville
Ferguson, R. Neil *computer systems consultant*
Mebane, Barbara Margot *artistic director, choreographer*
Myers, Madeleine Becan *secondary school educator*
Tucker, Phyllis Anita *sales representative, guidance counselor*
Vacca, John Joseph, Jr., *television executive*
†Willmott, Peter Sherman *retail executive*

Liberty
Hughes, Paul Anthony *minister, musician, songwriter, author, publisher*
Wheat, John Nixon *lawyer*

Liberty Hill
West, Felton *retired journalist, councilman*

Lindale
Carter, Thomas Smith, Jr., *retired rail transportation executive*
Jackson, Gary Dean *lawyer*

Livingston
Gordon, Pamela Ann Wence *pianist*
Hayes, Gordon Glenn *civil engineer*
Horner, Jennie Linn *retired educational administrator, nurse*

Lockhart
McCormick, Michael Jerry *retired judge*
†Shomette, Donna M. Dixson *paralegal*

Lometa
Thompson, Mary Koleta *sculptor, non-profit organization management consultant*

Longview
Fouse, Anna Beth *education educator*
Frase, Larry Lynn *medical oncologist*
Gentry, Vernessa Diana *principal, consultant*
†Harrison, Guy Newell *lawyer*
Haymes, Jerry Lynn *entertainment industry executive*
LeTourneau, Richard Howard *retired college president*
Mann, Jack Matthewson *bottling company executive*
Martin, William Clifford, III, *judge*
McKinley, Jimmie Joe *business executive*
†Richardson, Patricia Kay *librarian*
†Roller, Robert H. *dean, finance educator*
Sonnier, David Joseph *wholesale distributing executive*
Welge, Jack Herman, Jr., *lawyer*
Winn, Walter Terris, Jr., *civil and environmental engineer*

Lorena
Maricle, Robyn LuAnn (Ford) *band director, choir director*

Los Fresnos
Martin, José Ginoris *education administrator*

Lubbock
Adamcik, Joe Alfred *retired chemistry educator, retired attorney*
Aker, Suzanne Deverse *physical movement educator*
Allison, Jane Shawver *medical school administrator, management consultant*
Angstadt, Frances Virginia *language arts and theatre arts educator*
Archer, James Elson *engineering educator*
Askins, Billy Earl *education educator, consultant*
Baiza, Mary Pesina *development management consultant*
Beck, George Preston *anesthesiologist, educator*
Blevins, Stanley Nance *minister, educator*
Bronwell, Nancy Brooker *writer*
Broselow, Linda Latt *medical office technician, aviculturist*
Buesseler, John Aure *ophthalmologist, management consultant*
Burns, John Mitchell *academic administrator*
†Chung, Ya-Li *music educator*
Conover, William Jay *statistics educator*
Crowson, James Lawrence *lawyer, financial company executive, academic administrator*
Davis, Alvin G. *company executive*
Davis, Jimmy Frank *assistant attorney general*
†Dolter, Gerald Thomas *voice educator*
Dudek, Richard Albert *engineering educator*
Everse, Johannes *biochemist, researcher*
Fontenot, Andrea Dean *communications executive*
†Gelca, Razvan *education educator*
Giesselmann, Michael *engineering educator*
Gilliam, John Charles *economist, educator*
†Good, Stephen Boyd *librarian*
Haragan, Donald Robert *university administrator, geosciences educator*
Hentges, David John *microbiology educator*
Hester, Ross Wyatt *retired business forms manufacturing executive*
†Hice, Christine Lorraine *research scientist*
Hisey, Lydia Vee *educational administrator*
Hurst, Mary Jane *English language educator*
Illner-Canizaro, Hana *physician, oral surgeon, researcher*
Jackson, Raymond Carl *cytogeneticist*
†Joshi, Atul B. *physician*
Kaye, Alan David *anesthesiologist, researcher*
Ketner, Kenneth Laine *philosopher, educator*
Kiesling, Ernst Willie *civil engineering educator*
Killian, Janice Kay Nelson *music educator, researcher*
Kristiansen, Magne *electrical engineer, educator*
†Kuethe, Allan J. *historian, educator*
Kurtzman, Neil A. *medical educator*
Laing, Malcolm Brian *geologist, consultant*
Lawson, Melanie Kay *management administrator, early childhood consultant*
Levitas, Valery *mechanics and materials educator, researcher*
Lucas, Don John *music educator*
May, Donald Robert Lee *ophthalmologist, retina and vitreous surgeon, educator, farmer*
McBeath, Don B. *health administrator*
†McKay-Wilkinson, Julie Ann *minister, marriage and family therapist*
McMillen, Robert Paul *agricultural engineer*
Mittemeyer, Bernhard Theodore *urology and surgery educator*
Montford, John Thomas *state legislator, academic administrator, lawyer*
†Nelson, Jack Odell, Jr., *lawyer*
Nelson, Toza *retired elementary school educator, church administrator*
†Neusel, Mara Dicle *mathematician, educator*
Neyland, Malcolm *priest, curator*
†Nikishin, Sergey A. *electrical engineering educator, researcher*
Nugent, Connie *elementary education educator*
†Ode, Arthur Henry, III, *music educator*
Pelley, Patricia Marie *Asian history specialist*
†Porrua, Enrique J. *adult education educator*
†Prien, Samuel David *medical educator, researcher*
Purdom, Thomas James *lawyer*
Purinton, Marjean D. *English language educator, researcher*
Reid, Ted W. (Ted Warren Reid) *ophthalmology educator*
Roberts, Evan Elijah, Jr., *structural engineer, architect*
Schiffer, Randolph Brenton *physician*
Schmidly, David J. *university president, biology educator*
†Schneider, Andreas *education educator, researcher*
Sears, Edward L. *English language educator, real estate investor*
Sears, Robert Stephen *finance educator, university dean*
Selby, John Horace *surgeon*
Shaw, Gwen Ellen Grose *social worker*
Skillern, Frank Fletcher *law educator*
Skoog, Gerald Duane *science educator*
Spallholz, Julian Ernest *biochemistry educator, consultant*
Stem, Carl Herbert *business educator*
Stuart, Frank Adell *county official*
†Syapin, Peter John *pharmacologist, research scientist*
van Appledorn, Mary Jeanne *composer, music educator, pianist*
Varma, Surendra K. *pediatrician, educator*
†Viatchenko-Karpinski, Serge *biophysicist, researcher*
Wall, Betty Jane *real estate consultant*
Warren, Donald John *retired surgeon, educator*
Way, Barbara Haight *dermatologist*
Wendt, Charles William *soil physicist, educator*
Willingham, Mary Maxine *fashion retailer*
Willingham, Welborn Kiefer *psychologist, educator*
Wolfe, Verda Nell *pension consultant, financial planner*
Wood, Richard Courtney *library director, educator*
Woolam, Gerald Lynn *surgeon*
Yoder-Wise, Patricia Snyder *educator*
Young, Teri Ann Butler *pharmacist*
Zhang, Hong-Chao *manufacturing engineer, educator*

Lufkin
Dean, Odell Joseph, Jr., *urologist, educator*
Harmon, Jacqueline Baas *librarian, infosystems specialist*
Mott, Earl *artist, poet, writer*
Perry, Lewis Charles *emergency medicine physician, osteopath*
Williams, Mary Hickman *social worker*

Luling
†Collie, Paula Renea *secondary school educator*

Mabank
Smith, Thelma Tina Harriette *gallery owner, artist*

Magnolia
Esmond, Cheri Sue *secondary school educator*
†Girard, Louis Joseph *ophthalmologist, educator*
Gray, Robert Steele *publishing executive, editor, writer*

Manor
Young, William David *computer scientist*

Mansfield
Icenhower, Della Maude *retired school librarian*
Parnell, Charles L. *speechwriter*
Siméus, Dumas M. *food products executive*

Marfa
Chambers, Johnnie Lois (Tucker Chambers) *elementary school educator, rancher*
†Edge, Daniel *education educator, artist, consultant*
McBride, Elizabeth Anne Wilmore *writer, artist*
Meyer, Ellen Adams *arts and small business development specialist*

Marshall
Magrill, Rose Mary *library director*
Shaw, Dianne Elizabeth *school administrator*
†Snowden, James W. *music educator, musician*
Sudhivoraseth, Niphon *pediatrician, allergist, immunologist*

Mason
Johnson, Rufus Winfield *lawyer*

GEOGRAPHICAL INDEX 6083 TEXAS

Maxwell
Peters, Carol Ann *secondary school educator*

Mc Camey
Farley, Gail Conley *retired librarian*

Mc Kinney
Dickinson, Richard Raymond *retired oil company executive*
†Dowdy, William Clarence, Jr., *retired lawyer*
Fairman, Jarrett Sylvester *retail company executive*
Gill, David Brian *electrical engineer, educator*
Goldstein, Lionel Alvin *personal financial and investment advisor*
Kessler, John Paul, Jr., *financial planner*
Roessler, P. Dee *lawyer, mediator, former judge, educator*
Thompson, Jeannine Lucille *community health nurse*
Williams, James Lee *financial industries executive*

McAllen
†Liu, Agnete Mei-cheng *librarian*

McKinney
†Easttom, Chuck *computer scientist, educator*
†Schottlaender, Colin *electronics executive*

Mcallen
Carrera, Victor Manuel *lawyer*
Casso, Ramiro Paul *retired family physician, college official*
Connors, Joseph Aloysius, III, *lawyer*
Gonzalez, Rolando Noel *secondary school educator, religion educator, photographer*
Hinojosa, Ricardo H. *federal judge*
Martínez, Marianela *state agency administrator*
McGee, William Howard John *librarian, administrator*
†Mills, William Michael *lawyer*
Ramirez, Mario Efrain *physician*
Robalino, Benjamin David *cardiologist*
Sands, Norman Earl *elementary school educator, composer*
†Thaddeus, Aloysius Peter, Jr., *lawyer*
Tupper, Ron *public health, policy, and management educator*
†Villarino, Mario Alberto *veterinarian, researcher*
Whisenant, B(ert) R(oy), Jr., *insurance company executive*

Meadowlakes
†Wilcox, Mary Reba *music educator*

Memphis
†Mahato, Ram Ishwar *pharmacist, educator*

Mesquite
†Ellison, John Vogelsanger *retired engineer*
†Gant, Linda Gayle *elementary school educator*
†Holt, Mildred Frances *educator*
Kessner, Micheal J. *elementary school educator*
Patrick, Pamela Ann *research consultant*
Pratt, Sharon L. *retired secondary and elementary education educator*
Sepulvado, Joseph Michael *computer information scientist*
Vaughan, Joseph Lee, Jr., *education educator, consultant*
Williamson, Barbara Jo *retired community health nurse, educator*

Mexia
Chambers, Linda Dianne Thompson *social worker*

Mico
Shockey, Thomas Edward *real estate executive, engineer*

Midland
Berner, Leo De Witte, Jr., *retired oceanographer*
Bradshaw, Troy Wayne *nurse educator*
Celia, George *composer, writer*
Corwin, James A. *radiation oncologist*
Craddick, Thomas Russell *speaker of state house of representatives*
Estes, Andrew Harper *lawyer*
Frost, Wayne N. *lawyer*
Furgeson, William Royal *federal judge*
Groce, James Freelan *financial planning specialist*
Grover, Rosalind Redfern *oil and gas company executive*
King, Mary Lou *artist, medical technologist*
Maha, Callen Dale *project manager engineer*
†Morrow, William Clarence *judge, lawyer, mediator*
Osborne, Willie Carroll *petroleum geologist, consultant*
Powers, Patricia Kennett *piano and organ educator*
Sherpa, Fran Magruder *geography educator, animal scientist, small business owner*
Sullivan, Patricia G. *maternal, child and women's health nursing educator*
Syed, Elizabeth Chance *health facility administrator, critical care nurse*
Taylor, Nicholas C. *lawyer, state agency administrator, energy executive*
Tom, James Robert *accountant*
Truitt, Robert Ralph, Jr., *lawyer*

Midlothian
Esberger, Karen Ann *school nurse*
Sibley, James Scarborough *career officer*

Mineola
Bruce, Robert Denton *lawyer*
Rosene, Ralph Walfred *consulting company executive*
Tabor, Beverly Ann *retired elementary school educator*

Mineral Wells
Braun, Gustav Milan *facial plastic surgeon, otolaryngologist*
Warfield, Gerald Alexander *composer, writer*

Mission
McClendon, Maxine Nichols *artist*

Missouri City
Chang, Jeffrey Chai *dentist, educator, researcher*
Hodges, Jot Holiver, Jr., *retired lawyer, business executive*
†Tchamengo, Mathias Ngoufi *energy executive, mathematician*

Montgomery
Falkingham, Donald Herbert *oil company executive*
Gooch, Carol Ann *psychotherapist consultant*
Kelsey, Clyde Eastman, Jr., *philosophy and psychology educator*
Smith, John Brewster *library administrator*
Steed, Theresa Jean *manufacturing company executive*
Tharp, Benjamin Carroll, Jr., *retired architect*

Moody
Judah, Frank Marvin *retired school system administrator*

Mount Pleasant
McCauley, Dan Paul *dentist*

Nacogdoches
Bommanna, Vasudeva M. *allergist, immunologist*
Brennan, Thomas George, Jr., *audiologist, speech-language pathologist*
Gaston, Edwin Willmer, Jr., *retired English language educator*
†Jacobsen, Jeffrey Richard *music educator*
Migl, Donald Raymond *therapeutic optometrist, pharmacist*
Tkacik, Michael Patrick *political science educator, lawyer*
Wagner, William Michael *academic administrator*
†Zhang, Zhizhen *chemist*

Nevada
Dillard, Ronda Lenser *software engineer*

New Braunfels
Alexander, Anna Margaret *artist, writer, educator*
Belzung, Paul Edward *engineering executive*
Benfield, Marion Wilson, Jr., *law educator*
Bryant, Dennis Michael *publisher, educator*
Griffin-Thompson, Melanie *accounting firm executive*
Krueger, Robert Charles *former ambassador, former senator, congressman*
Oestreich, Charles Henry *retired university president*
†Reimer, Bill Monroe *lawyer*
Wilson, James Lee *retired geology educator, consultant*
Zipp, Ronald Duane *judge, priest, real estate broker*

New Caney
Hayes, Ann Carson *computer services executive*

Normangee
Rector, M. Eugene *community pharmacist*

North Richland Hills
Mutz, Gregory Thomas *insurance company executive*

Odessa
Boyd, Claude Collins *educational specialist, consultant*
Brumelle, Kenneth Coy *retail store owner*
Cibley, Laurence Jay *obstetrician, gynecologist*
†Dry, Marsha G. *librarian*
Forsyth, Beverly K. *language educator, writer*
Grubbs, Donald Ray *educational director, educator, welder*
Hendrick, Benard Calvin, VII, *lawyer*
Hewitt, Timothy Martin *museum curator*
Knox, Glenda Jane *retired health and safety specialist, educator*
†McHattie, Thomas John *obstetrician, gynecologist, medical educator*
Moseley, Clifford Wayne *writer, poet*
Nickel, James Alvin *mathematician, educator, consultant*
Phillips, Barry *artist, educator*
Pokky, Eric Jon *clinical pharmacist*
Pugh, Jessie Truman *minister*
Rasor, Doris Lee *retired secondary education educator*
Toruño, Rhina M. *Literature educator, researcher, writer*

Olney
Timmons, Gordon David *economics educator*

Orange
Dugas, Louis, Jr., *lawyer*
Odom, Sarah Bernice *elementary school educator*

Ozona
†York, Sherry White *librarian*

Palestine
Sellers, Wayne Chadick *newspaper publisher, editor, retired*
Williams, Franklin Cadmus, Jr., *bibliographer*

Pampa
Alexander, Steven Ray *chemical engineer*
Cain, Donald Ezell *judge*
Cooley, Loralee Coleman *professional storyteller*
Powell, Dan Clayton *physician*

Panhandle
Sherrod, Lloyd Bruce *nutritionist*

Paris
Proctor, Richard Owen *historian, public health administrator, army officer*
Standifer, Rick M. *lawyer*

Pasadena
Blue, Monte Lynn *college president*
Burt, Billy George *oil company professional*
Cowles, Charles Eugene, Jr., *medical educator*
Fogo, Peter C. *educator, novelist, poet*
Gilley, Mickey Leroy *musician*
Gross, Cynthia Sue *petrochemicals manufacturing executive*
Hall, Georganna Mae *elementary school educator*
Harrison, Brooks Talton *law firm official*
†Holland, Peter Marc *ophthalmologist*
Kenagy, Cheri Lynn *nurse*
Martinez, Fernando V. *civil engineer*
McClay, Harvey Curtis *data processing executive*
Moon, John Henry, Sr., *banker*
Root, M. Belinda *chemist*
Shapiro, Edward Muray *dermatologist*
Smith, Oscar William *nursing home administrator*
†Stahl, Charlyn Beth *medical educator*
Stephens, Sidney Dee *chemical manufacturing company executive*
Thompson, Marian Nell *poetry, historical, non-fiction and fiction writer, educator, poet*

Pearland
Claridge, Elmond Lowell *retired engineering educator, consultant*
Hammond, Raymond William *pharmacotherapy specialist*
Shurtleff, Malcolm C. *plant pathologist, consultant, educator, extension specialist*

Pearsall
†Galloway, Gale Lee *oil and gas executive, rancher*

Penitas
Loomis, Robert Arthur *retired sales executive*

Perryton
Doerrie, Bobette *secondary education educator*

Pflugerville
Carlsen, John Richard *engineer*
Munzer, Annette Elizabeth *cultural affairs consultant*
Schroer, Jane Hastings *nurse practitioner*

Pharr
Medina, Jesse James *protective services official, educator*

Plainview
Crawford, Felix Conkling *dentist*
Lafont, William Harold *lawyer, farmer*

Plano
Bain, Travis Whitsett, II, *manufacturing and retail executive*
Benn, Douglas Frank *information technology and computer science executive*
Blachly, Jack Lee *lawyer*
Bode, Richard Albert *retired financial executive*
Carver, Rita *fundraising consultant*
Collumb, Peter John *communications company executive*
Cotter-Smith, Cathleen Marie *art educator, artist*
†Cumming, Marilee *apparel company executive*
Daley, William M. *former federal government official*
Davani, Bahman Faghaie *telecommunications engineer*
Dougherty, F(rancis) Kelly *data processing executive*
Edmonds, Albert J. *career officer*
Findley, John Sidney *dentist*
Fleming, Christina Samusson *special education educator*
†Friedlander, D. Gilbert *lawyer*
Frock, Scott Joseph *music educator*
Gallardo, Henrietta Castellanos *writer*
Grogan, Timothy James *business executive, golf professional*
Haggard, Geraldine Langford *primary school educator, adult education educator, consultant*
Hahn, Cathy Ann Clifford *sales executive*
†Heller, Jeffrey M. *data systems executive*
Hemingway, Richard William *law educator*
†Hiegel, James Edward *mechanical engineer*
James, Michael Thames *information technology executive, consultant*
Kellogg, James Warner *aerospace management consultant*
†Kuddes, Kathryn M. *fine arts director*
Levine, Harold *lawyer*
†Lotter, Charles Robert *corporate lawyer, retail company legal executive*
MacAlpine, Michelle Lewis *neuroscientist*
McWilliams, Chris Pater Elissa *elementary school educator*
Miller, Ken Leroy *religious studies educator, consultant, writer*
†Naimi-Tajdar, Reza *petroleum engineer*
Naor, Daniel *food products executive*
Neppl, Walter Joseph *retired retail store executive*
†Philips, Coby Nelson *education educator, special education educator*
Questrom, Allen I. *retail executive*
Reisner, Elena Mackay *retired educational administrator*
Rhodes, Doris Chaney *freelance/self-employed secondary school educator*
†Rochon, John Philip *cosmetics company executive*
Samford, Karen Elaine *small business owner, consultant*

Satz, Jeffrey S. *telecommunications industry executive, consultant*
Schuh, Frank Joseph *drilling engineering company executive, consultant*
Scott, Terry Lee *communications company executive*
Seals, Ryan Brown *electronics engineer*
Sexton, Karen Kay *piano teacher, singer, actress*
†Shaddock, William Charles *lawyer*
Smith, Jerralyn Renée *marketing professional, consultant*
Taylor, Paul Peak *pediatric dentist, educator*
Thompson, Joshua A. *music educator*
Wilke, Chet *real estate broker*

Point
Middleton, Ida Lavelle *dairy executive, comptroller*

Port Aransas
Beimers, George Jacob *financial executive*
Lehmann, William Leonardo *electrical engineer, educator*
Swetnam, Monte Newton *petroleum exploration executive*
Turner, Elizabeth Adams Noble (Betty Turner) *real estate company executive*
Van Baalen, Donna Gale *artist, retired pharmacist*

Port Arthur
†Munoz, Andrea Lee *human resources specialist*
Vinecour, Oneida Agnes *nurse*

Port Isabel
Pon-Salazar, Francisco Demetrio *diplomat, educator, deacon, counselor*

Port Lavaca
Boyd, Ann Fisher *office administrator*
Cummins, Michelle Marie *otolaryngologist, head and neck surgeon*

Post
Earl, Lewis Harold *economics and management consultant, lawyer*
Killian, Lawrence Harding, II, (Larry H. Killian) *sculptor*
Warren, Jennifer Elizabeth *family nurse practitioner*

Pottsboro
Hanning, Gary William *utility executive, water company executive, consultant*
Jackson, Nona Armour *writer, illustrator*
Thomas, Ann Van Wynen *law educator*

Prairie VIew
French, Laurence Armand *social science educator, psychology educator*

Prairie View
Gonzalez, Antonio *academic administrator, mortgage company executive*
Hines, Charles A. *academic administrator*
†Wyatt, Lucius Reynolds, Sr., *music educator*

Rancho Viejo
Garza, Roberto Jesus *retired education educator*

Randolph A F B
†Lamontagne, Donald A. *career officer*
†Welser, William, III, *military officer*

Ranger
Jones, Roger Walton *English language educator, writer*

Raymondville
Montgomery-Davis, Joseph *osteopathic physician*

Red Oak
Jones, Genia Kay *emergency supervising nurse, consultant*

Richardson
Anderson, John Kerby *talk show host*
Andrews, Melinda Wilson *human development researcher*
Armstrong, Robert Stevenson, Jr., *sales executive*
Austin, Ann Sheree *lawyer*
Avadhut, HitendranandaAcarya *spiritual counselor, yoga teacher*
Beron, Kurt James *economics educator*
Berry, Brian Joe Lobley *geographer, political economist, urban planner*
Bonura, Larry Samuel *writer*
Bray, Carolyn Scott *education educator*
Burke, Thomas William *executive benefits consulting company official*
Chlamtac, Imrich *computer company executive, educator*
Conkel, Robert Dale *lawyer, pension consultant*
Conrad, Flavius Leslie, Jr., *retired minister*
†Constantinescu, Tiberiu *mathematician*
DeBusk, Manuel Conrad *lawyer, business executive*
Douglas, John Paul *lawyer*
†Downey, Margie Lee Cooper *educator, writer*
Duan, Xiaodong *engineer*
Dunn, David E. *university dean*
Fahrlander, Henry William, Jr., *management consultant*
Garreans, Leonard Lansford *protective services official, criminal justice professional*
Gray, Donald Melvin *molecular and cell biology educator*
Harpham, Edward John *political science educator, dean, writer, research*
†Holmes, Jennifer Smith *political scientist, educator*
†Huesca Dorantes, Patricia *researcher*
Johnson, Francis Severin *physicist*
Jones, Malinda Thiessen *telecommunications company executive*

Kelly, Rita Mae *academic administrator, researcher*
Killam, Jill Minervini *oil and gas company executive*
†Krauss, Henry Frederick, Jr., *optometrist*
†Leaf, Murray John *anthropologist, consultant*
Lee, Jimmy Che-Yung *city planner*
Lowe, J. Allen *minister*
Madden, Marie Frances *marketing professional*
†Manton, William Inwood *geologist, educator*
Martin, Richard Kelley *lawyer*
McDaniel, Dolan Kenneth *oil exploration service company executive*
†Murphy, Priscilla Parrish *music educator*
Neely, Vicki Adele *accountant, legal assistant, poet*
Nosratinia, Aria *engineering educator, researcher*
Olson, Dennis Oliver *lawyer*
†Paranchych, David Walter *electrical engineer*
Patrick, James Nicholas, Sr., *radio, television, newspaper commentator, consultant*
Redman, Timothy Paul *English language educator, author, chess federation administrator*
†Riccio, Thomas Patrick *theater director*
Richards, Frederick Francis, Jr., *manufacturing company executive*
Rogers, Mal David, Jr., *chemical engineer*
Rutford, Robert Hoxie *geologist, educator*
†Schjerven, Robert E. *manufacturing executive*
†Scotch, Richard K. *sociologist, educator*
Senderling, Jon Townsend *journalist, public affairs specialist*
Sowers, Wesley Hoyt *lawyer, management consultant*
Sperrin, Graham Frederick *marketing professional*
Vijverberg, Wim Petrus Maria *economics educator*
White, Irene *insurance professional*
Wiesepape, Betty Holland *writing educator*
Williams, James Francis, Jr., *religious organization administrator*
Witherspoon, William Tom *company executive*
Wood, Joseph George *neurobiologist, educator*
†Wylie, Mary Lucinda *healthcare administrator*
†Zeng, Guoping *application developer, researcher, education educator*

Richmond
Barratt, Cynthia Louise *pharmaceutical company executive*
Elliott, Brady Gifford *judge*
Eversole, Sandra Joy *operating room nurse*
Johanson, Knut Arvid, Jr., *retired engineering executive*

Roanoke
Kleinkort, Joseph Alexius *physical therapist, consultant*
Steward, Jerry Wayne *air transportation executive, consultant*

Rochelle
Bull, Kenneth Winson *retired rancher*

Rockdale
Estell, Dora Lucile *retired educational administrator*

Rockport
Benningfield, Carol Ann *lawyer*
Johnson, Marilyn *retired obstetrician, gynecologist*
Minor, Joseph Edward *civil engineer, educator*
Porter, Charles Raleigh, Jr., *retired lawyer*
†Stachiw, Jaroslaw (Jerry) Drahomyr *mechanical engineer, consultant*

Rockwall
Bruce, Dana Glenn *lawyer*
Bush, Larry Don *communications company administrator*
Crooks, Patricia Kay *counselor*
Fisher, Gene Jordan *retired chemical company executive*
Griffith, James William *systems engineer, consultant*
Holt, Charles William, Jr., *lawyer, mediator*
Wallace, Mary Elaine *opera director, author*
Wiorkowski, Gabrielle Kay *database consultant*

Roscoe
†Beeks, Cheryl Elaine *elementary school educator*

Rosebud
Mey, Rindy *physician assistant*

Rosenberg
Tourtellotte, Mills Charlton *mechanical and electrical engineer*

Rosharon
Jenkins, Judith Alexander *bank consultant*

Round Mountain
McReynolds, Mary Maureen *small business owner*

Round Rock
†Anandan, Santhosh *application developer*
Dell, Michael S. *computer company executive*
Hill, David Wayne *geologist*
†Hudson, Michel Colette *consultant*
Khalid, Humayun *computer scientist, consultant*
Ledbetter, Sharon Faye Welch *retired educational consultant*
Puri, Rajendra Kumar *business and tax specialist, consultant*
Regan, James Richard, Jr., *computer company executive*
Ricklefs, Dale Lynne *library director*
Wahl, William Bryan *marketing professional, real estate officer*

Round Top
Lentz, Edwin Lamar *art historian*

Rowlett
Efrussy, Alan Maurice *urban planner*
Lyon, Robert Charles *lawyer*
Patterson, Edward Palmer *retired physical scientist*

Rusk
Cart-Rogers, Katherine Cooper *emergency nurse, nurse consultant*
†Hendrick, Zelwanda *drama and psychology educator*
†McMinn, J. B. *retired philosophy educator, composer*

Sabinal
Soos, Richard Anthony *pastor*

Saint Jo
Ashley, Raymond Weldon *writer*

Salado
Parks, Lloyd Lee *oil company executive*
Willingham, Douglas Barton *dentist*
Wilmer, Harry Aron *psychiatrist, educator*

San Angelo
Anderson, Garry Michael *diagnostic radiologist*
Butler, Michael Ward *economics educator*
Chatfield, Mary Van Abshoven *librarian*
Coe, Robert Stanford *retired management educator*
†Curtin, David *music educator*
Davison, Elizabeth Jane Linton *education educator*
Fischer, Duncan Kinnear *neurosurgeon*
Garza, Adolph Aranda *broadcast engineer, consultant*
†Kroll, Connie Rae *librarian, information services consultant*
†McLaughlin, John Mark *lawyer*
Mobley, Nancy Elizabeth *artist, art educator*
Mowrer, Robert Ranck *educator*
Rivero, Magda *counselor*
Smith, Karen B. *educational consultant*
Sutton, John Ewing *lawyer*

San Antonio
Abramson, Hyman Norman *engineering and science research executive*
Adcox, Mary Sandra *dietitian, consultant*
†Ait-Daoud, Nassima *psychiatrist, researcher*
†Allison, Stephen Philip *lawyer*
Alvey, Dennis H. *government agency administrator*
Ammann, Lillian Ann Nicholson *writer, editor, small business owner*
Anderson, Kathryn B. *psychology educator*
Armstrong, William Tucker, III, *lawyer*
Arnold, Stephen Paul *investment professional*
Atchley, Curtis Leon *mechanical engineer*
†Atherton, Flora Cameron *volunteer*
Aust, Joe Bradley *surgeon, educator*
Bachrach, Steven Maurice *chemistry educator*
Bagley, William Evan *application technology specialist*
†Bailey, Steven R. *cardiologist, researcher*
Baker, Floyd Wilmer *surgeon, retired army officer*
Barrera, Elvira Puig *counselor, therapist, educator*
Barton, James Cary *lawyer*
†Bauerle, James Ernest *oral surgeon*
†Bayern, Arthur Herbert *lawyer*
Becker, Douglas Wesley *lawyer*
Beckmann, Charles Henry *cardiologist, educator*
Behrens, Richard James *language educator*
Bellows, Thomas John *political scientist, educator*
Bennett, Sister Elsa Mary *retired secondary education educator*
Benz, George Albert *economist, consultant , retired economist educator*
Best, Thomas L. *trainer, consultant*
†Bettac, Robert Edward *lawyer*
Beverly, Zylphia Marie *mental health services professional*
Biery, Evelyn Hudson *lawyer*
†Blonkvist, Tim *architectural firm executive*
Bowden, Virginia Massey *librarian*
Brazil, John Russell *academic administrator*
Breit, William *economist, educator, writer*
†Brennan, James Patrick, Sr., *lawyer, insurance company executive*
Brewster, Olive Nesbitt *retired librarian*
Bromley, Ernest W. *communications executive*
Brooks, Franklin Ramon *psychologist, army officer*
†Bsoul, Samer A. *dentist, educator*
Budalur, Thyagarajan Subbanarayan *chemistry educator*
Bunten, Brenda Arlene *geriatrics nurse*
Burch, James Leo *science research institute executive*
Burton, Russell Rohan *aerospace scientist, researcher*
Butt, Charles Clarence *food service executive*
Cao, Weiming *mathematician, educator*
†Carroll, John Arthur *musician, educator*
Carroll, William Marion *financial services executive*
†Castorena, Maria Ancelita *writer*
Catto, Henry Edward *former government official, former ambassador*
Celmer, Virginia *psychologist*
Cepeda, Claudio *psychiatrist*
Champion, Michael Edward *physician assistant, clinical perfusionist*
Chance, Truett Lamar *retired secondary school educator*
Chiego, William J. *museum director*
Chiscano, Alfonso *surgeon*
Cisneros, Henry G. *homebuilding executive, broadcast executive, former federal official*
Clark, Robert Phillips *newspaper editor, consultant*
Clarke, Mary Elizabeth *retired career officer*
Cloud, Bruce Benjamin, Sr., *construction company executive*
Cohen, Melvin Lee *pediatrician, psychiatrist, educator*
Colyer, Kirk Klein *insurance executive, real estate investment executive*
†Condos, Barbara Seale *real estate broker, developer, investor*
†Condos, J. Alexander *mortgage company executive*
Corrigan, Helen González *retired cytologist*
Cottingham, Stephen Kent *real estate development executive, researcher, minister, educator*
Countryman, Thomas Arthur *lawyer*
Crabtree, Ben C. *neuromuscular therapy clinic director*
†Cragnolino, Gustavo Adolfo *research scientist*
Crichton, John Hayes *investment banker*
Crockett, David Anthony *political science educator*
†Croft, Harry Allen *psychiatrist*
†Currie, Donald M *medical educator*
†Dacbert-Friese, Sharyn Varhely *social worker, evangelist*
†Daniel, Marian Phillips *language educator, secondary school educator*
Davenport, Pamela Beaver *rancher*
Davis, George Edward *industrial designer*
Davis, Robert G. *insurance executive*
†Davis, Sarah Jane *health care professional*
Dean, Jack *protective services official*
†de la Garza, Luis Adolfo *lawyer*
Denny, John Bernard *biochemist, educator*
Detro, John Fitzgerald *military officer*
Di Maio, Vincent Joseph Martin *forensic pathologist*
Dowdy, Eugene Brown *music educator*
†Duggirala, Ravindranath *geneticist, researcher*
Duncan, A. Baker *investment banker*
Duncan, Sarah Baker *judge*
†Duncan, Tim *professional basketball player*
Durbin, Richard Louis, Jr., *lawyer*
†Dwyer, Mary Jo *medical librarian*
Elder, Gene Wesley *artist*
†Ellis, James D. *communications executive, corporate lawyer*
Endresen, Lisa Castro *curatorial assistant*
†Ereshefsky, Larry *psychopharmacologist educator, consultant*
Espino, David V. *geriatrician, family practice physician*
Estep, Myrna Lynne *systems analyst, philosophy educator*
Eyster, Charles Richard *lawyer, oil and gas exploration executive*
Fecher, Vincent John *priest*
Fehrenbach, T(heodore) R(eed) *author, businessman*
†Ferguson, Charles Alan *lawyer*
Ferry, Robert Jean, Jr., *pediatric endocrinologist*
†Firulli, Anthony B. *physiologist, educator*
Fischer, Marsha Leigh *civil engineer*
Fisher, Dierdre Denise *mental health nurse, administrator, educator*
†Flynn, Norma Jean *librarian*
Fonseca, Joseph Mojica, Jr., *financial analyst, educator*
Frazer, Robert Lee *landscape architect*
Freeman, Theodore Monroe *physician*
Frigerio, Charles Straith *lawyer*
Frisch, Paul Andrew *librarian*
Fuhrmann, Charles John, II, *strategic and finance consultant*
Furino, Antonio *economist, educator*
Gambitta, Richard Anthony *political science educator*
Garb, Howard Neil *clinical psychologist, educator*
Garcia, Henry Frank *supply management and project management consultant and trainer*
Gardner, Raymond Alan *webmaster, writer*
Garner, Jo Ann Starkey *retired elementary and special education educator*
Garza, Ed *mayor*
Garza, Emilio M(iller) *federal judge*
Garza, Xavier *artist, writer*
Gates, Mahlon Eugene *applied research executive, former government official, former army officer*
†Gaulin, Jean *gas industry executive*
Gilliland, Irene Lydia *nursing educator*
Gladstone, George Randall *planetary scientist*
Glueck, Sylvia Blumenfeld *writer*
Goelz, Paul Cornelius *university dean*
Goldsmith, Richard Elsinger *lawyer*
Gonzalez, Hector Hugo *nurse, educator, consultant*
Graves, Kenneth Martin *architect*
Greehey, William Eugene *energy company executive*
†Grosu, Daniel *computer scientist*
Grubb, Robert Lynn *computer system designer*
Gruenbeck, Laurie *librarian*
Guess, James David *lawyer*
Gwathmey, Joe Neil, Jr., *broadcasting executive*
†Hale, William Grant *veterinarian, educator*
Hall, Denise *special education educator*
Hall, Douglas Lee *computer science educator*
†Hamill, Frank Alexander *biologist, researcher*
Hammond, Linda *artist*
Hammond, Weldon Woolf, Jr., *hydrogeologist*
Hannah, John Robert, Sr., *accountant*
Hardberger, Phillip Duane *judge, lawyer, journalist*
Hardy, Harvey Louchard *retired lawyer*
Hatcher, Donald W. *government agency administrator*
Hedrick, John O. *transportation executive*
Heloise, *columnist, lecturer, broadcaster, author*
†Hemminghaus, Roger Roy *energy company executive, chemical engineer*
Henderson, Connie Chorlton *city planner, artist and writer*
Henderson, Dwight Franklin *dean, educator*
Henington, C. Dayle *retired economist*
Hermann, John Robert *political science educator*
†Herres, Robert Tralles *financial services executive*
Higdon, James Noel *lawyer*
Hill, William Victor, II, *retired army officer, secondary school educator*
Hirsch, Barry T. *economist, educator*
†Hogan, Donna Helen *school librarian, educator*
†Hohman, A. J., Jr., *lawyer*
†Holt, Peter M. *sports team executive*
Honore, Gerard Marcel *endocrinologist, reproductive endocrinologist*
†Hood, Sandra Dale *librarian*
†Hornsby, David McMillan *musician, music educator*
Horowitz, Rosalind *education educator, researcher*
Horton, Granville Eugene *occupational medicine physician, retired air force officer*
Huff, Robert Whitley *obstetrician, gynecologist, educator*
Irving, George Washington, III, *veterinarian, research director, small business executive*
Jackson, Earl, Jr., *medical technologist, retired*
Jacobson, Helen Gugenheim (Mrs. David Jacobson) *civic worker*
Javore, Gary William *lawyer*
†Jiménez, Leonardo *popular accordionist*
Johnson, Anne Stuckly *retired lawyer*
†Johnson, Vincent Robert *law educator, educator*
Jones, Daniel Hare *librarian, consultant*
Jones, James Richard *business administration educator*
†Jones, Oscar Calvin *minister, dean*
Jorgensen, James H. *pathologist, educator, microbiologist*
Juárez, José Roberto, Jr., *law educator*
†Junek, Heather Diane *medical/surgical nurse*
†Kaye, Celia Ilene *pediatrics educator*
Keck, Judith Marie Burke *business owner, retired career officer*
†Kelfer, Marvin Gerald (Jerry Kelfer) *lawyer*
†Kelling, George Horton *retired military officer*
Keyser-Fanick, Christine Lynn *banking executive, marketing, strategic planning, investments and insurance professional*
†King, Kandi J. *secondary school educator, consultant*
King, Ronald Baker *federal judge*
†Kittle, Joseph S. *science administrator, consultant*
Klaerner, Curtis Maurice *former oil company executive*
Kline, John William *retired air force officer, management consultant*
†Kolaparthi, VenkataSubbaRao *oncologist*
†Koppenheffer, Julie B. *lawyer*
Koster, Kim Richard *anesthesiologist*
Kozuch, Julianna Bernadette *librarian, educator*
†Krier, Joseph Roland *chamber of commerce executive, lawyer*
Labay, Eugene Benedict *lawyer*
Labenz-Hough, Marlene *dispute resolution professional*
Laurence, Dan H. *author, literary and dramatic specialist*
†Le, Dung *mathematics educator, researcher*
Ledford, Frank Finley, Jr., *surgeon, army officer*
Ledvorowski, Thomas Edmund *secondary education educator*
Leies, John Alex *theology educator, clergyman*
Leighton, Albert Chester *history educator*
Le Maistre, Charles Aubrey *internist, epidemiologist, educator*
Lenke, Joanne Marie *publishing executive*
Leon, Robert Leonard *psychiatrist, educator*
†Lien, Donald *economist, educator*
Liesenfeld, Vincent Joseph *lawyer*
†Lomeli, Ruth M. *accountant*
†Lopez, M. Edward *small business owner*
Lowe, Douglas Howard *architect*
Lussky, Warren Alfred *librarian, educator, consultant*
Lutter, Charles William, Jr., *lawyer*
Lyle, Robert Edward *chemist*
Lyles, Mark Bradley *advanced technology company executive, dentist*
Madrid, Olga Hilda Gonzalez *retired elementary education educator, association executive*
Maloney, Marynell *lawyer*
Marbut, Robert Gordon *communications, electronic security and broadcast executive, investor*
Markwell, Dick R(obert) *retired chemist*
Marlin, Arthur Edward *pediatric neurosurgeon, educator*
†Maroscher, Betty Jean *librarian*
Marsh, Nelson Leroy *military officer*
Martinez, Joe Louis, Jr., *neurobiologist, educator*
Marvin, Catherine A. *financial consultant*
Masinter, Thomas Alan *composer*
Masoro, Edward Joseph, Jr., *physiology educator*
Massaro, James C. *military officer, government agency administrator*
Massey, Patti Chryl *elementary school educator*
Masters, Bettie Sue Siler *biochemist, educator*
Mathews, Jennifer Pauline *anthropologist, educator, archaeologist*
Maxwell, Diana Kathleen *early childhood education educator*
†Mays, L(ester) Lowry *broadcast executive*
Mc Allister, Gerald Nicholas *retired bishop, clergyman*
McBee, Lucy Armijo *retired elementary education educator, administrator, singer, actress, writer*
McClane, Robert Sanford *former bank holding company executive, entrepreneur*
McComas, David John *science administrator, space physicist*
McCoy, Reagan Scott *oil company executive, lawyer*
McCuistion, Peg Orem *hospice administrator*
†McDonald, James H. *anthropologist, educator*
McFadden, Robert Stetson *hepatologist*
McFee, Arthur Storer *physician*
McGill, Henry Coleman, Jr., *pathologist, educator, researcher*
McIntosh, Dennis Keith *veterinarian, consultant*

The Woodlands
†Allison, Robert James, Jr., *oil and gas company executive*
Bala, Sriram *research scientist*
Blickwede, Donald Johnson *retired steel company executive*
Blume, Shane L. *music educator*
Crain, Richard Charles *school district music director, retired*
Desjardins, Raoul *medical association administrator, financial consultant*
Dougan, Deborah Rae *neuropsychology professional*
Glenn, Gerald Marvin *marketing, engineering and construction executive*
Hagerman, John David *lawyer*
Jack, Nancy Rayford *supplemental resource company executive, consultant*
Jones, Lincoln, III, *army officer*
Jones, Susan Chafin *management consultant*
King, Carl Edward *employee screening executive*
Lewis, Daniel Edward *information technology executive*
Logan, Mathew Kuykendall *journalist*
Machle, Edward Johnstone *theology educator, retired*
Manson, Lewis Auman *energy research executive*
Martineau, Julie Peperone *social worker*
Pistorius, Alvin William, Jr., (Bill Miller) *communications educator*
Saikowski, Ronald Alexander *consulting engineer*
Schlacks, Stephen Mark *lawyer, educator*
Sharman, Diane Lee *secondary school educator*
Sharman, Richard Lee *telecommunications executive, consultant*
Sudbury, John Dean *religious foundation executive, petroleum chemist*
Turek, Douglas D. *lawyer*
Westmoreland, Thomas Delbert, Jr., *chemist*
†Zhang, Nan *oncologist, health science association administrator*

Thorndale
Fish, Howard Math *aerospace industry executive*

Tomball
Ham, Sommy L. *publisher, writer*

Trophy Club
Caffee, Virginia Maureen *executive assistant*
Hardy, Vicki *elementary school principal*
Holley, Cyrus Helmer *management consulting service executive*

Tulia
†Irlbeck, Amber Rose *journalist, scriptwriter*

Tyler
Albertson, Christopher Adam *librarian*
Alworth, Charles Wesley *lawyer, engineer*
†Bailey, Nan Hutchins *mathematician, educator*
Blasingame, Donald Ray (Don Blasingame) *banker*
Brock, Dee Sala *television executive, educator, writer, consultant*
†Brookshire, Bruce G. *retail grocery store executive*
†Cooper, Kelli D. *music educator*
Corrada del Rio, Alvaro *bishop*
Davidson, Jack Leroy *academic administrator*
†Dunlap, Martha McKinzie *elementary school educator*
†Edwards, D. M. *retail, wholesale distribution and commercial real estate investment executive*
Ellis, Donald Lee *lawyer*
Ellis, John David *data processing executive*
Gonzalez-Byrd, M. Teresa *physician assistant*
Green, Douglas Alvin *retired library director*
Guin, Don Lester *insurance company executive*
Guthrie, Judith K. *federal judge*
Hadden, Arthur Roby *lawyer*
Hatfield, James Allen *theater arts educator, administrator*
Hyman, William Jay *internist, oncologist*
Kulkarni, Arun Digambar *computer science educator*
Lake, David Alan *investments lawyer*
Martin, William Allen *sociology educator*
†Mastern, Dean Scott *personal growth and development consultant*
McKee, Harry W. *federal judge*
Morgan, Freeman Louis, Jr., *engineer, consultant*
Neuenschwander, Pierre Fernand *medical educator*
Parker, Robert M. *federal judge*
Patterson, Donald Ross *lawyer, educator*
Pinkenburg, Ronald Joseph *ophthalmologist*
Resnik, Linda Ilene *marketing and information executive, publisher, consultant, writer*
Rogers, Cheryl Lynn *music and dance educator*
†Rumbley, Philip Lee *music educator, musician, photographer*
Smith, Howard Thompson *business executive*
Steger, William Merritt *federal judge*
Trent, Warren C. *mechanical engineer*
Waller, Wilma Ruth *retired secondary school educator and librarian*
Warner, John Andrew *foundry executive*
West, Syntha Jane Traughber *mental health services professional*

Universal City
Lamoureux, Gloria Kathleen *nurse, retired air force officer, consultant*
Parsa, Brian Bahram *surgeon, military officer*
Sargeant, Stephen T. *military officer*

Uvalde
Graham, Robert Albert *research physicist*
Ramsey, Frank Allen *veterinarian, retired army officer*

Valley View
Wallace, Donald John, III, *rancher, former pest control company executive*

Van Alstyne
Hazelton, Juanita Louise *librarian*

Vernon
Roberson, Mark Allen *physicist, educator*
Slosser, Jeffrey Eric *research entomologist*

Victoria
†Fellhauer, David E. *bishop*
Haynes, Karen Sue *academic administrator, educator*
†Lee, Yong-Gyo *accountant, educator*
Logan, Mary Calkin *development and public relations consultant*
†Nguyen, PeterMinh V. *pharmacist*
Rainey, John David *federal judge*
Stubblefield, Page Kindred *banker*

Waco
Achor, Louis Joseph Merlin *psychology and neuroscience educator*
Anandaraman, Ramanathan *retired physician*
Belew, John Seymour *academic administrator, chemist*
Brooks, Roger Leon *university president*
Bryan, John Joseph *physician*
†Cherry, David Earl *lawyer*
Cleaver, Gerald Bryan *physicist, researcher*
Collmer, Robert George *English language educator*
Colvin, Herbert, Jr., (Otis Herbert Colvin) *musician, educator*
Corley, Carol Lee *retired school nurse*
†Crook, Betty Ross *lawyer*
Davis, Charles Elliot *accounting educator*
Dewlen, Alton LeRoy (Al Dewlen) *writer*
†Donnelly, Phillip Johnathan *literature educator*
Dow, David Sontag *retired ophthalmologist*
Farison, James Blair *electrical biomedical engineer, educator*
Flanders, Henry Jackson, Jr., *religious studies educator*
†Fulmer, Phillip *university football coach*
†Garcia-Corales, Guillermo S. *language educator*
†Girouard, Tandy Denise *special education educator, psychology educator*
Hall, Donald Orell *lawyer, rancher*
Hartberg, Warren Keith *biologist, educator*
†Hassell, Clinton Alton *chemist, educator*
Henderson, Johnny *mathematician, educator*
Hillis, William Daniel *biology educator*
Hollingsworth, Martha Lynette *secondary school educator*
Hunt, Maurice Arthur *English educator, researcher*
Kagle, Joseph Louis, Jr., *artist, arts administrator, art educator*
Kramer, Denny B. *professional communication educator*
†Lee, Myeongwoo *molecular biologist, cell biologist*
Lewis, Martha Nell *Christian educator, minister, expressive arts therapist*
Lindsey, Jonathan Asmel *university official, librarian, educator*
Mackenzie, Charles Alfred *lawyer*
McKinney, Joseph Arthur *economist, educator*
Meyer, Paul James *communications company executive*
Morrison, Michael Dean *lawyer, law educator*
Odell, Patrick Lowry *mathematics educator*
Osborne, Harold Wayne *sociology educator, consultant*
Page, Jack Randall *lawyer*
Pedrotti, Leno Stephano *physics educator*
Rapoport, Bernard *life insurance company executive*
Reddy, Vemula Shanth *physician*
Reynolds, Herbert Hal *academic administrator*
Richie, Rodney Charles *critical care and pulmonary medicine physician*
Rolf, Howard Leroy *mathematician, educator*
Rose, John Thomas *finance educator, department chairman*
Sawyer, Dianne Waddell *obstetrician-gynecologist*
Scott, Richard Elton *health facility administrator*
Selke, Oscar O., Jr., *physiatrist, educator*
Sharp, Ronald Arvell *sociology educator*
Skains, Timothy Karl *electrical engineer*
Slade, Harry Warren *neurological surgeon*
Smith, Cullen *lawyer*
Solomon, Charles Francis *electronics educator*
Talbert, Charles Harold *religion educator*
Teal, Elisabeth Jane *business educator, researcher*
†Tomey, Dick *university football coach*
†Ullman, Beth Robin *vocalist, voice educator*
Villarreal, Fernando Marin *lawyer*
Walbesser, Henry Herman *computer science educator*
Ward, Bennie Franklin Leon *physics educator*
Wivagg, Daniel Edwin *biology educator, editor*

Warda
Kunze, George William *retired soil scientist*

Waring
†Leslie, Wendyl Keith *financial consultant*

Waxahachie
†Fulmer, Daniel A. *music educator, composer*
†Gallo, Tony Giovanni *musician, educator*
Johnson, Ronald Kay *retail company executive*
†Tschoepe, Thomas *retired bishop*

Weatherford
Bergman, Anne Newberry *civic leader*
Buckner-Reitman, Joyce *psychologist, educator*
Colton, James Patrick *community college administrator*
Estes, Carolyn Ann Hull *retired elementary school educator*
†Miller, Dixie Davis *elementary school educator*
Reitman, Sanford *radiologist*

Webster
Dickard-Green, Roxanne Lynn *choreographer, dance educator*
Farnam, Jafar *allergist, immunologist, pediatrician*
Kobayashi, Herbert Shin *electrical engineer*

Weimar
Rocha, Osbelia Maria Juarez *librarian, assistant principal*

Weslaco
Pomerantz, Jerald Michael *lawyer*

West
Eisma, Jose A. *physician*

West Columbia
†Walker, Phyllis LeVonne *elementary school educator*

Wharton
†George, Lila Gene Plowe Kennedy *music educator*
†Giovanoni, Stephen Francis *music educator*
Jackson, Larry C. *publishing executive*
†Medina, Debra Parker *medical/surgical nurse, consultant*
Roades, John Leslie *lawyer*
Schulze, Arthur Edward *biomedical engineer, researcher*
Walker, Douglas Baynard *science educator*

Whitehouse
Baker, Rebecca Louise *musician, music educator, consultant*
Cavanaugh, Charles Davis *computer scientist, educator*

Whitney
Williams, Margaret Lu Wertha Hiett *nurse*

Wichita Falls
Altman, William Kean *lawyer*
Bourland, D(elphus) David, Jr., *linguist, educator*
Goff, Robert William, Jr., *lawyer*
Haff, Guy Gregory *exercise science educator, researcher*
†Hoffman, Thomas Paul *realtor, educator*
Kindig, Everett William *history educator*
†Leavell, Landrum Pinson, II, *seminary administrator, clergyman, educator*
Passos, Nelson Luiz *computer science educator*
Rodriguez, Louis Joseph *academic administrator, economist, educator*
Silverman, Gary William *financial planner*
Stange, Terrence V. *education educator*
†Wesbrooks, Perry *lawyer, consultant*

Willis
Rappaport, Martin Paul *internist, nephrologist, educator*
Snider, Robert Larry *management consultant*

Willow Park
Bynumn, Jeanette Lynn *holistic health nurse*

Wimberley
Brinsmade, Lyon Louis *retired lawyer*
Ellis, John *small business owner*
Koeppe, Patsy Poduska *internist, educator*
Skaggs, Wayne Gerard *financial services company executive, retired*
Troester, Waltraud *artist, graphic designer, consultant*

Woodway
†McCorkle, William Littleton *journalism educator, writer*

Wortham
Lee, Gordon Kenneth *physician assistant*

Wylie
†Andrews, Sharon Millicent Parrish *historian, educator*

Yoakum
Kvinta, Charles J. *lawyer*
Leahy, Lawrence Marshall *health care administrator, marketing consultant*

Zephyr
Lancaster, Carroll Townes, Jr., *business executive*
†Cacayorin, Edwin D. *diagnostic and interventional neuroradiologist*

UTAH

American Fork
†Entezari-Taher, Mohammad *neurologist, researcher*
Reinhold, Allen Kurt *graphic design educator*
Zhou, Bing-Nan *chemist, educator*

Bluffdale
†Bliss, Rick Wayne *engineer*

Bountiful
Brooke, Edna Mae *retired business educator*
Burningham, Kim Richard *former state legislator*
Clement, Walter Hough *retired railroad executive*
†King, Chad Lavere *music educator*
Mangum, Garth Leroy *economist, educator*
†Peterson, Rose Ann *artist*
Rawlins, Jan *principal*

Brigham City
Bishop, Robert *former political organization administrator, secondary school educator*
Fife, Dennis Jensen *chemistry educator, air force officer*
Hepworth, John Leonard *chemist, researcher*
Krejci, Robert Henry *aerospace engineer*
Tolle, Melinda Edith *engineer, scientist*

Castle Valley
Zavada, Barbara Johanna *artist*

Cedar City
Leibovit, Arnold L. *film producer, director*
†Mills, James *language educator*
Templin, Carl Ross *college dean, educator*

Corinne
Ferry, Miles Yeoman *state legislator*

Dugway
†Benson, Morgan *energy engineer, military officer*
Eshom-Oviatt, Corina May *air transportation executive*
Phan, Richard Man *chemist*

Ephraim
Blauer, A. Clyde *microbiologist, educator, botanist*

Fort Duchesne
Cameron, Charles Henry *supervisory petroleum engineer*

Garden City
Campbell, Jane Turner *retired realtor, retired secondary school educator*

Genola
†Newcomb, Helene E *retired research scientist*

Heber City
McLean, Hugh Angus *management consultant*

Highland
Baum, Kerry Robert *retired military officer, director*

Hildale
Wall, Lloyd L. *geological engineer*

Hill Air Force Base
Bergren, Scott C. *career officer*
†Roellig, Richard H. *career officer*

Holladay
O'Halloran, Thomas Alphonsus, Jr., *physicist, educator*

Hyde Park
Wood, Dennis Allen *pathologist*

Kaysville
Ashmead, Allez Morrill *speech, hearing, and language pathologist, orofacial myologist, consultant*
Hendricks, Steven Ron *music educator*

Layton
Hendren, Debra Mae *critical care nurse*

Logan
Ahlstrom, Callis Blythe *university official*
Aust, Steven Douglas *biochemistry, biotechnology and toxicology educator*
†Beasley, LeRoy B. *mathematics educator*
Bowles, David Stanley *engineering educator, engineering consultant*
Callister, Ronda *management and human resources educator*
Clyde, Calvin Geary *civil engineer, educator*
Emert, George Henry *former academic administrator, biochemist*
Fifield, Marvin G. *psychologist, educator*
Gay, Charles W., Jr., *academic administrator*
Grover, Scott W *surgeon*
†Hall, Kermit Lance *academic administrator, historian, educator*
Hargreaves, George Henry *civil and agricultural engineer, researcher*
†Hartman, Cathy *economist, educator*
Hillyard, Lyle William *state legislator, lawyer*
Honaker, Jimmie Joe *lawyer, ecologist*
Hunsaker, Scott Leslie *gifted and talented education educator*
Kadis, Jonathan Brynn *information technology executive*
Keller, Jack *agricultural engineering educator, consultant*
McKell, Cyrus M. *retired college dean, plant physiologist*
†McNeal, Lyle Glen *science educator, rancher, consultant*
Merrill, M. David *education educator*
Rasmuson, Brent J. *photographer, graphic artist, lithographer*
Rasmussen, Harry Paul *horticulture and landscape educator*
Roberts, Donald Wilson *pathologist, consultant*
Schunk, Robert Walter *space physics research administrator*
Shaver, James Porter *education educator, university dean*
Sidwell, Robert William *virologist, educator*
†Subprasom, Kitti *civil engineer*
Wade, Kenneth Alan *physician assistant*

Manti
Petersen, Benton Lauritz *paralegal*

Mapleton
Hillyard, Ira William *pharmacologist, educator*

Midvale
Dahl, Everett E. *lawyer*
Mansell, L. Alma *state legislator*
Teerlink, J(oseph) Leland *real estate developer*

Midway
Hughes, Dean Thomas *English language educator, writer*

Oakes, Claudia *museum administrator*
Ockey, Ronald J. *lawyer*
Oliveira Aldamiz, Jose Maria *scriptwriter*
Olsen, Glenn Warren *historian, educator*
Olson, Ferron Allred *metallurgist, educator*
Osborne, Christine Megan *musician, educator*
†Osherow, Jacqueline Sue *poet, English language educator*
Owen, Amy *library director*
†Packer, Boyd K. *church official*
†Parkin, James Lamar *otolaryngologist, educator*
Parry, Robert Walter *chemistry educator*
Passey, Mark Lyman *sports association executive*
Perkins, Sherrie Lynn *pathologist, educator*
†Perry, L. Tom *religious organization administrator, merchant*
Pershing, David Walter *chemical engineering educator, researcher*
Petersen, Finn Bo *oncologist, educator*
Picard, M(eredith) Dane *geologist*
Pickering, AvaJane *specialized education facility executive*
Quinn, Eugene Frederick *foreign service officer, clergyman*
Rasmussen, Thomas Val, Jr., *lawyer, small business owner*
Renzetti, Attilio David, Jr., *physician*
Rigtrup, Kenneth *state judge, arbitrator, mediator*
†Roberts, Jack Earl *lawyer, ski resort operator, wood products company executive, real estate developer*
Roberts, William Lewis *clinical pathologist*
†Roens, Steven Thomas *music educator, dean*
†Romney-Manookin, Elaine Clive *music educator, composer*
Salisbury, Frank Boyer *plant physiologist, educator, author*
Sam, David *federal judge*
Sanchez Alvarado, Alejandro *embryologist, molecular biologist*
Sandquist, Gary Marlin *engineering educator, researcher, consultant, writer*
Schow, Terry D. *state official*
Schutz, Roberta Maria (Bobbi Schutz) *social worker*
Schwendiman, Stephen Glenn *lawyer*
Scofield, David Willson *lawyer*
†Scott, Richard G. *religious organization administrator*
Seader, Junior DeVere (Bob Seader) *chemical engineering educator*
Shea, Patrick A. *lawyer, educator*
Shelledy, James Edwin, III, *newspaper editor*
Shepherd, Karen *former congresswoman*
Shurtleff, Mark L. *state attorney general*
Sillars, Malcolm Osgood *communication educator*
Silver, Barnard Joseph Stewart *mechanical and chemical engineer, consultant, inventor*
Simmons, Rulon Andrus *internist*
Sine, Wesley Franklin *lawyer*
†Sloan, Jerry (Gerald Eugene Sloan) *professional basketball coach*
Smith, Donald E. *broadcast engineer, manager*
Smith, Eldred Gee *church leader*
†Smith, Janet Hugie *lawyer*
Sohn, Hong Yong *chemical engineer, educator, metallurgical engineer, educator*
Sorenson, Roger A. *international relations consultant*
Spurgeon, Edward Dutcher *law educator, foundation administrator*
Steiner, Richard Russell *textile & apparel company executive*
Stephens, Martin R. *state official*
Stitley, James Walter, Jr., *food manufacturing executive*
Stock, Peggy A(nn) *college president, educator*
†Straughn, Joanna Marzia *poet*
Stringfellow, Gerald B. *engineering educator*
†Teitelbaum, Lee E. *law educator, former dean*
†Thomas, David Snow *plastic surgeon*
Thompson, Neil Daniel *legal and genealogical researcher, retired lawyer*
Tsodikov, Alexander David *biostatistician, educator*
Velick, Sidney Frederick *research biochemist, educator*
†Verhaaren, Harold Carl *lawyer*
Walden, David Michael *historian, writer*
Walker, Marion Lavelle *neurosurgeon*
Walker, Olene S. *lieutenant governor*
Wallace, Matthew Walker *retired entrepreneur*
Ward, John Robert *physician, educator*
Welch, Dominic *publishing consultant*
West, Stephen Allan *lawyer*
†Williams, J. Richard *service executive, real estate executive*
Williams, Natalie *professional basketball player, restaurant executive*
†Wirthlin, Joseph B. *religious organization administrator*
Wolf, Harold Herbert *pharmacy educator*
Wood, Gregory Burton, Jr., *brokerage house executive*
†Workman, H(arley) Ross *patent lawyer*
Zhdanov, Michael Semenovich *geophysicist, educator*
Zimmer, Markus Bernhard *federal court administrator*

Sandy
†Andriano, Kirk Patrick *pharmaceutical executive*
Clark, Jeffrey Raphiel *research and development company executive*
George, Mary Gae *music educator*
Jorgensen, Leland Howard *aerospace research engineer*
Macumber, John Paul *insurance company executive*
Park, William Laird *agricultural economics educator, consultant, college associate dean*
Pierce, Ilona Lambson *educational administrator*
Sabey, J(ohn) Wayne *academic administrator, consultant*
Skidmore, Joyce Thorum *public relations and communication executive*
Smith, Willard Grant *psychologist*
York, Theodore Robert *retired consulting company executive*

South Jordan
Larson, Bryan A. *lawyer*
Rowley, Maxine Lewis *home economics and consumer educator, writer*

Spanish Fork
Ashworth, Brent Ferrin *lawyer*

Springdale
Bimstein, Phillip Kent *composer*

Springville
†Bybee, Paul Joseph *zoologist, educator*
Francis, Rell Gardner *artist, photographer, writer*

Stansbury Park
Moyer, Linda Lee *artist, educator, author*

Sundance
Grant, Raymond Thomas *arts administrator*

Taylor
Atwater, Julie Demers *critical care nurse*

Tremonton
Eakle, Arlene Haslam *genealogist*
Kerr, Kleon Harding *former state senator, educator*

Vernal
Judd, Dennis L. *lawyer*

Vineyard
†Cannon, Joseph A. *steel products company executive, political party official*

West Jordan
Shepherd, Paul H. *elementary school educator*
Wyness, Steven Charles *illustrator*

West Valley City
†Morales, Nancy Sabrina *translator, consultant*

Woods Cross
†Blackley, Cheryl Ann *freelance/self-employed music educator, musician*
†Hendriksen, Neil Evan *music educator*
Ingles, Joseph Legrand *social services administrator, political science educator*

VERMONT

Arlington
Nowicki, George Lucian *retired chemical company executive*

Barnard
Larson, John Hyde *retired utilities executive*

Barre
Adamski, Gary Matthew *language educator, real estate broker*
Black, Percy *psychology educator*
†Koch, Thomas Frederick *lawyer*
Togut, Torin Dana *lawyer*

Bellows Falls
†Massucco, Lawrence Raymond *lawyer*
Obuchowski, Michael J. *state legislator*

Belvidere Center
Lipke, Kathryn *artist, educator*

Bennington
Burkhardt, Frederick Henry *editor*
Feitlowitz, Marguerite *writer, literary translator*
Killen, Carroll Gorden *electronics company executive*
Perin, Donald Wise, Jr., *former association executive*
Rector, Liam *university program director*
†Wang, Shunzhu *humanities educator, researcher, translator*

Bondville
Ambach, Gordon Mac Kay *educational association executive*

Bradford
†Kaplow, Leonard Samuel *pathologist, educator*

Brandon
Farnsworth, Frank Albert *retired economics educator*

Brattleboro
Agallianos, Dennis Dionysios *psychiatrist*
Ames, Adelbert, III, *neurophysiologist, educator*
Beal, Donna Lee *association executive*
Brofsky, Howard *musician, music educator*
Bussino, Melinda Holden *human services administrator*
Cohen, Richard B. *grocery company executive*
Cooper, Wyn *poet, editor, songwriter*
Cramer, Janet French *social worker, marriage and family therapist*
Fantini, Alvino E. *language educator, humanities educator, consultant*
Gorman, Robert Saul *architect*
†Hawkes, Mary Newgeon *minister, educator, retired*
Kotkov, Benjamin *clinical psychologist*
McCarty, William Michael, Jr., *lawyer*
Milkey, Virginia A. *state legislator*
†Murtha, J. Garvan *federal judge*
Oakes, James L. *federal judge*
Reid, David G. *lawyer*
Smiley, Carol Anne *home health administrator, sculptor*
Stewart-Smith, David *adult education educator, historian, researcher*

Bristol
Dendler, Royce *painter, sculptor, writer*

Brookfield
†Newton, Earle Williams *editor, museum director, library and museum consultant*

Brownsville
Olderman, Gerald *retired medical device company executive*

Burlington
†Aleong, John *statistician, educator*
Allard, Judith Louise *secondary education educator*
Angell, Kenneth Anthony *bishop*
†Berkowitz, Stephen David *sociologist, educator*
Bernard, Ronald Allan *computer performance analyst*
Blackwood, Eileen Morris *lawyer*
†Bousquet, Daniel William *forester, educator*
Brandenburg, Richard George *management educator*
Brown, Kenneth Andrew *cardiologist, educator*
Carlisle, Lilian Matarose Baker (Mrs. E. Grafton Carlisle Jr.) *writer, lecturer*
Ciongoli, Alfred Kenneth *neurologist*
Clavelle, Peter *mayor*
Cooper, Sheldon Mark *medical educator, immunology researcher, rheumatologist*
Cram, Reginald Maurice *retired air force officer*
Cutler, Stephen Joel *sociologist, educator*
Daniels, Robert Vincent *history educator, former state senator*
Davis, John Herschel *surgeon, educator, retired*
Dean, Howard *former governor*
Dinitz, Jeffrey H. *mathematics educator*
Dinse, John Merrell *lawyer*
Dorwart, Roger Wilson *retired civil engineer*
†Dungy, Kathryn R. *humanities educator*
Ennis, Alana *chief of police*
†Erno, Margaret Jean *social worker, consultant*
Fillmore, Mary Dingee *management consultant*
†Flores, Yolanda *literature educator*
Fogel, Daniel Mark *administrator, English language and American literature educator, author*
†Frank, Joseph Elihu *lawyer*
Glitman, Maynard Wayne *foreign service officer*
Hall, Robert William *philosophy and religion educator*
Harrison, David Michael *finance educator, consultant*
Haugh, Larry Douglas *statistics educator*
Hearon, Shelby *writer, lecturer, educator*
Heffernan, Patricia Conner *management consultant*
†Helzer, John Earl *academic administrator, educator, psychiatrist*
Hendley, Edith Di Pasquale *physiology and neuroscience educator*
Hilberg, Raul *political science educator*
†Kindstedt, Paul Stephen *food science educator*
Krag, Martin Hans *physician, orthopaedist, educator, researcher*
Lawson, Robert Bernard *psychology educator*
†Leddy, John Thomas *lawyer*
Lidofsky, Steven David *medical educator*
Liley, Elizabeth Ellen *journalist, educator*
†Lisman, Bernard *lawyer*
Lucey, Jerold Francis *pediatrician*
†Maugans, Todd Allen *pediatric neurosurgeon*
McMahon, Dennis C. *lawyer, writer*
Mead, Philip Bartlett *healthcare administrator, obstetrician, educator*
†Miller, Elizabeth H. *lawyer, educator*
Milliard, Aline *retired social worker*
†Morrow, Emily Rubenstein *lawyer, estate planner*
Morrow, Paul Lowell *forensic pathologist*
†Moses, Peter L. *gastroenterologist, researcher*
†Murakami, Kentaro *education educator, neuroscientist*
Nyborg, Wesley Lemars *physics educator*
Outwater, John Ogden *mechanical engineering educator*
Pinder, George Francis *engineering educator, scientist*
†Rendall, Donald James, Jr., *lawyer*
Riddick, Daniel Howison *obstetrics and gynecology educator, priest*
Sampson, Samuel Franklin *sociology educator*
†Schneider, Wayne J. *music history educator, organist*
Shattuck, Gary G. *lawyer*
Sobel, Burton Elias *physician, educator*
†Stout, Neil Ralph *retired history educator*
Tampas, John P. *radiologist*
†Toner, Donald Thomas *music educator*
Tourin, Peter Tanny *computer scientist, educator*
Tranmer, Bruce Ian *neurosurgeon*
Van Raalte, Barbara G. *retired realtor*
Warshaw, Joseph Bennett *dean, pediatrician*
Waterman, Gerald Scott *psychiatrist, physician educator*
†Weed, Lawrence L. *biochemist*
†Weissgold, David Jay *ophthalmologist, educator*
Wick, Hilton Addison *lawyer*
Willis, Russell Edward *academic administrator*

Calais
Levin, Herbert *retired diplomat, retired foundation executive*

Castleton
Stafford, Robert Theodore *lawyer, former senator*

Cavendish
Shapiro, David *artist, art historian*

Charlotte
†Kiley, Daniel Urban *landscape architect, planner*
Melby, Edward Carlos, Jr., *veterinarian*
Monsarrat, Nicholas *newspaper editor, writer, educator*
Naylor, Thomas Herbert *economist, educator, consultant*
Pricer, Wilbur David *electrical engineer, educator*
Robinson, Sally Winston *artist*

Chester
Coleman, John Royston *writer*
†Holme, John Charles, Jr., *lawyer*

Colchester
†Ashline, George Lawrence *education educator*
Danielson, Ursel Rehding *psychiatrist*
†Garcia, Luis Cesareo *lawyer*
Kenney, John Peter *dean, educator*
Lawton, Lorilee Ann *fire sprinkler contractor company owner, accountant*
Salmon, Thomas Paul *lawyer, academic administrator*
Sweeny, Arthur, III, *realtor*
vanderHeyden, Marc A. *academic administrator*

Concord
Norsworthy, Elizabeth Krassovsky *lawyer*

Danby
Peel, Harris *art gallery owner, retired diplomat*

Dorset
Bamford, Joseph Charles, Jr., *gynecologist, obstetrician, educator, medical missionary, writer*
Pember, John Scott *poet*

East Calais
de Gogorza, Patricia *sculptor, educator*
Harding, John Hibbard *retired insurance company executive*

East Corinth
Freeman, Carole Cook *education educator*

East Thetford
Cummings Rockwell, Patricia Guilbault *psychiatric nurse*

East Wallingford
Graf, Marjorie Beck *sales and marketing executive*

Enosburg Falls
Svendsen, Alf *artist, art educator*

Essex Junction
Aitken, John Malcolm *engineer, educator*
Dietzel, Louise Alverta *psychologist*
Ishaq, Mousa Hanna *materials engineer*
Lampert, S. Henry *retired dentist*
Lee, Mankoo *device engineer, scientist*
Tedd, Monique Micheline *artist*
Walsh, Robert Anthony *lawyer*

Greensboro
Hill, Lewis Reuben *horticulturist, nursery owner, author*

Groton
Shields, Margaret Agnes *land surveyors association executive*

Guilford
Gregg, Michael B. *health science association administrator, epidemiologist*
†Olle, David Arthur *writer, researcher*

Hardwick
Holtz, Laurence *artisan, photographer*

Hartland Four Corners
Brady, Upton Birnie *editor, literary agent*

Hyde Park
Fitzpatrick, Philip J. *probate judge, retired lawyer*

Jacksonville
Dell, Ralph Bishop *pediatrician, researcher*
Hein, Karen Kramer *pediatrician, epidemiologist*

Jericho
Bolin, Henry Robert *retired engineer*

Johnson
Farara, Joseph Montgomery *library director*
Whitehill, Angela Elizabeth *artistic director*

Lincoln
Kompass, Edward John *consulting editor*

Lower Waterford
Burnham, Patricia White *consultant, advocate, writer, business executive*
Burnham, Robert Alan *academic administrator, educator*

Ludlow
Davis, Vera *elementary school educator*

Lyndon Center
Dame, William Page, III, *bank executive, educational administrator*

Lyndonville
Toborg, Alfred *history educator*

Manchester
Carey, James Henry *banker*
Kouwenhoven, Gerrit Wolphertsen *retired museum director*

Manchester Center
Armstrong, Jane Botsford *sculptor*
Sossi, Marie Frances *elementary education educator*

Cooper, Roger Merlin *information technology executive, federal government official, school administrator*
Coryell, Glynn Heath *financial services executive*
Costagliola, Francesco *retired government official*
Courtney, William Harrison *business executive*
Crane, Stephen Charles *professional society administrator*
Cromley, Raymond Avolon *syndicated columnist*
Cross, Dorothy Abigail *retired librarian*
Cross, Eason, Jr., *architect*
Crundwell, Duncan James *electronics executive*
Culkin, Charles Walker, Jr., *retired trade association administrator*
Curtin, Gary Lee *air force officer*
Danaher, James William *retired federal government executive*
Davis, Ruth Margaret (Mrs. Benjamin Franklin Lohr) *technology management executive*
De Barbieri, Mary Ann *nonprofit management consultant*
Del Fosse, Claude Marie *aerospace software executive*
DeLuca, Anthony J. *civilian military employee*
Dennison, Donald Lee *lawyer*
Devantier, Paul W. *communications executive, broadcaster, administrator*
†DiMuro, Bernard Joseph *lawyer*
Dubin, Martin Steven *principal*
Duffett, Benton Samuel, Jr., *lawyer*
Dunham, Frank Willard *lawyer*
Dunn, Bernard Daniel *former naval officer, consultant*
Eckhart, Myron, Jr., (Max Eckhart) *retired marine engineer*
Edgell, Karin Jane *reading specialist, special education educator*
Elkins, Dan *small business owner, educator*
Elston, Michael James *lawyer, educator*
Engler, Brian David *association executive*
Ensslin, Robert Frank, Jr., *retired association executive and military officer*
†Falk, Stanley Lawrence *historian, consultant*
Falter, Vincent Eugene *retired army officer, consultant*
Farrell, William Christopher *lobbyist*
Fedorochko, William, Jr., *retired army officer, defense policy analyst*
Fichenberg, Robert Gordon *newspaper editor, consultant*
Fisher, Donald Wayne *medical association executive*
Fitton, Harvey Nelson, Jr., *former government official, publishing consultant*
Flater, Morris Eugene *executive, lawyer*
Fleming, Douglas Riley *journalist, publisher, public affairs consultant*
Flood, Sandra Wasko *artist, educator*
Foster, Robert Francis *communications executive*
Foxwell, Elizabeth Marie *editor, writer*
Francis, Samuel Todd *columnist*
†Franklin, Jeanne F. *lawyer*
Freeman-Wilson, Karen *former attorney general, prosecutor, educational association administrator*
Frommer, Lawrence Julian *retired travel company executive*
Furash, Edward Elliott *banker, investment company executive, writer, lecturer, theater producer*
Garcia, Gillian Glenys *economist*
†Garrett, Thomas W. *career officer*
†Gatanas, Harry D. *career officer*
Georges, Peter John *lawyer*
†Gernand, Bradley Elton *library manager, archivist*
Glynn, Ernest B. *civil engineer, environmental engineer*
Goodling, William F. *former congressman*
Goodman, Sherri Wasserman *lawyer*
Goolrick, Robert Mason *lawyer*
Gormley, Dennis Michael *research scholar*
Gould, Phillip *engineer*
Graham, John H., IV, *health science association administrator*
†Gray, Dorothy Louise Allman Pollet *librarian*
Greenstein, Ruth Louise *research institute executive, lawyer*
Guerra, Gonzalo Enrique *economist*
†Gust, David R. *military career officer*
Handal, Ephrem I. (Ihsan Handal) *theology studies educator, deacon*
Hark, William Henry *medical executive, retired military officer*
Harris, David Ford *management consultant, retired government official*
Hathaway, Fred William *lawyer*
Havens, Harry Stewart *former federal assistant comptroller general, government consultant*
Hawkins, Edward J. *retired lawyer*
Helman, Gerald Bernard *government official*
Henderson, Paul Bargas, Jr., *economic development consultant*
Henton, Melissa Kaye *analyst*
Herrera, Clarita *medical association administrator*
Higgins, Mary Celeste *lawyer, researcher*
Hinkle, Wade P. *political scientist*
Hirsch, Robert Louis *energy executive*
Hobbs, Michael Edwin *broadcasting company executive*
Holcomb, Richard Dennis *lawyer*
Huckabee, Harlow Maxwell *lawyer, writer*
Huddy, Margaret *artist, writer, educator*
Hughes, Grace-Flores *business execuitve*
Hurley, John Arthur *national security advisor*
Hussey, Ward MacLean *lawyer, former government official*
Hutchison, Elizabeth Doran *social worker, educator*
Hutzelman, Martha Louise *lawyer*
Inman, Stephen Eugene *finance officer*
Ivanetich, Richard John *information technology executive*
†Jackson, Gary Lee *military analyst*
†Jackson, Nancy Morrison *architect*
James, Carol Lee *communications executive*
Jenkins, John Smith *retired academic dean, lawyer*
Johnson, Edgar McCarthy *psychologist*
Johnson, JoAnn Mardelle *federal agency administrator*
†Johnson, Marlys Marlene *elementary school educator*
Jokl, Alois Louis *electrical engineer*
Jolly, Bruce Overstreet *retired newspaper executive*
†Jordan, Carole Jean *political organization administrator*
Justesen, Benjamin Ray, II, *writer*
†Kaplan, David Jeremy *research scientist, consultant*
†Kaplan, Richard Alan *government official*
Kemble, James Richard *retired engineering services executive*
Kim, Sook Cha *artist*
Kinzler, Peter *lawyer*
Kiyonaga, John Cady *lawyer*
Kolar, Mary Jane *trade and professional association executive*
Kollander, Mel *social scientist, statistician*
Kopp, Eugene Paul *lawyer*
Kotlarchuk, Ihor O. E. *lawyer*
Krebs, Martha *physicist, federal science agency administrator*
Kroesen, Frederick James *retired army officer, consultant*
Krueger, Gerald Peter *psychologist*
Lachance, Janice Rachel *former federal agency administrator, lawyer*
Lantz, Phillip Edward *corporate executive, consultant*
Larson, Charles Robert *naval officer*
Lasser, Howard Gilbert *chemical engineer, consultant*
Lauderdale, Katherine Sue *lawyer*
Laurent, Lawrence Bell *communications executive, former journalist*
LeBlanc, James Leo *business executive, consultant*
Leestma, Robert *federal agency administrator, educator*
†Lendsey, Jacquelyn L. *foundation administrator*
Lenz, Edward Arnold *trade association executive, lawyer*
Levine, Steven Mark *lawyer*
Lewis, Lloyd Alexander *priest, educator*
Liesemer, Ronald Newell *plastics company executive*
Lundeberg, Philip Karl Boraas *curator, consultant*
Luttig, J. Michael *federal judge*
Lyons, James Aloysius, Jr., *naval officer*
Lytle, Michael Allen *criminologist, consultant*
Magazine, Alan Harrison *association executive, consultant*
Maloof, Farahe Paul *lawyer*
Mandil, I. Harry *nuclear engineer*
Mann, Seymour Zalmon *political science and public administration educator emeritus, union official*
Masterson, Kleber Sanlin, Jr., *physicist*
Mathews, Thomas Jay *reporter, columnist, writer*
†Mathias, Melvin Merle *nutrition scientist*
Matz, Deborah *federal agency administrator*
McCaffrey, Barry Richard *federal official, retired army officer*
McClure, Roger John *lawyer*
McCulloch, William Leonard *trade association administrator*
McDowell, Charles Eager *lawyer, retired military officer*
McGuire, Roger Alan *retired foreign service officer*
McMillan, Charles William *consulting company executive*
McNair, Carl Herbert, Jr., *army officer, aeronautical engineer*
McNicol, David Leon *federal official, consultant*
†Meserole, Lisa Christine *music educator*
Michael, Ann Dozier Marino *real estate broker*
Milling, Marcus Eugene, Sr., *geologist*
Montgomery, Gillespie V. (Sonny Montgomery) *former congressman*
†Moran, Donald Will *consulting company executive*
Morris, Robert Crane *management training executive*
†Morris, Warren Frederick *retired government agency executive*
Morse, Burnham Spottswood *broadcast executive*
Muir, Warren Roger *chemist, executive*
†Murray, Robert John *think-tank executive*
Murray, Russell, II, *aeronautical engineer, defense analyst, consultant*
Murtagh, William John *preservationist, educator*
Nelson, David Leonard *process management systems company executive*
Newton, Hugh C. *public relations executive*
Nodeen, Janey Price *company executive*
Noland, Royce Paul *association executive, physical therapist*
O'Brien, Patrick Michael *library administrator*
O'Connor, Thomas Edward *petroleum geologist, management consultant*
Oh, Kongdan *international policy analyst, consultant*
O'Hara, John Patrick *lawyer, accountant*
O'Leary, Brian Michael *lawyer*
Pastin, Mark Joseph *association executive*
Paturis, E(mmanuel) Michael *lawyer*
Penrose, Cynthia C. *retired health care consultant*
Perchik, Benjamin Ivan *operations research analyst*
†Pitzer, Jack Todd *purchasing agent, consultant, purchasing agent, educator*
Poehlein, Gary Wayne *retired chemical engineering educator*
Pringle, Robert Maxwell *diplomat*
Pyle, Howard *lawyer, consultant*
Rabun, John Brewton, Jr., *criminal justice agency administrator*
Radewagen, Fred *publisher, organization executive*
Rainwater, Joan Lucille Morse *investment company executive*
Ray, Terrill Wylie *physical scientist*
†Rebman, Jack Arthur *communications engineer*
Rector, John Michael *association executive, lawyer*
Reed, Leon Samuel *policy analyst, writer, photographer*
Reinl, Harry Charles *economist*
Reuss, Martin Alan *historian*
Richards, Darrie Hewitt *investment company executive*
Richman, Arleen *professional society administrator*
Rogers, Paul A'Court *management consulting executive*
Romney, Carl F. *seismologist*
Roof, Michael Kitching *demographer, researcher*
Rosenfeld, Stephen Samuel *newspaper editor*
†Rosenthal, Edward Scott *lawyer*
Saloom, Joseph A., III, *diplomat*
Schlachtmeyer, Albert Stephen *management consultant*
Schubert, Richard Francis *consultant*
Schultz, Franklin M. *retired lawyer*
Schweikart, Debora Ellen Ellen *lawyer*
Sczudlo, Walter Joseph *lawyer*
Seely, James Michael *defense consultant, retired naval officer, small business owner*
Senese, Donald Joseph *former government official, research administrator*
†Siegel, Kenneth Eric *lawyer*
Simmons, Richard De Lacey *mass media executive*
Simonds, Marie Celeste *architect*
Skoug, Kenneth Nordly, Jr., *diplomat*
Smith, Harold Allen *education administrator, researcher, educator*
Smith, Jeffrey Greenwood *industry executive, retired army officer*
†Smith, Kevin Hopkins *lawyer*
†Smith, Larry G. *career military officer*
†Smith, Robert Luther *management educator*
Snyder, James P. *audio and digital television engineer, videographer, editor*
Starr, James Edward *logistics management executive*
Stempler, Jack Leon *government and aerospace company executive*
Stevens, Alice Marie *educational consultant*
Stone, Ann E.W. *direct marketing company executive*
Straub, Peter Thornton *lawyer*
Sturtevant, Brereton *retired lawyer, former government official*
Sulick, Joseph Edward, Sr., *information technology professional*
Swift, Stephen Christopher *lawyer*
Swinburn, Charles *lawyer*
Tarpley, James Douglas *journalism educator, magazine editor*
Taylor, William Brockenbrough Newton *engineer, consultant, management consultant*
Tesler, Diane Elaine *artist*
Thomas, Carlton Eugene (Sandy Thomas) *electrical engineer, researcher*
Ticer, Patricia *state senator*
Tichenor, Charles Beckham, III, *operations research analyst*
Toulmin, Priestley *retired geologist*
Trent, Darrell M. *academic and corporate executive*
Tucker, Alvin Leroy *retired government official*
Tucker, Howard McKeldin *investment banker, consultant*
Turner, Mary Jane *educational administrator*
Van Cleve, Ruth Gill *retired lawyer, government official*
Von Drehle, Ramon Arnold *lawyer*
Vosbeck, William Frederick, Jr., *architect*
Walker, William Woodard, Jr., *management consultant, telecommunications technology*
Walkup, Charlotte Lloyd *lawyer*
Walkup, Homer Allen *lawyer, writer*
Wallace, Barbara Brooks *writer*
Ware, Thomas Earle *building consultant*
Wasko-Flood, Sandra Jean *artist, educator*
Weisberg, Leonard R. *engineering executive, researcher, retired*
Wendel, Charles Allen *lawyer*
Wesberry, James Pickett, Jr., *financial management consultant, auditor, international organization executive*
†Whelden, Craig B. *army officer*
†Whitson, Elizabeth Temple *graphics designer*
Widner, Ralph Randolph *retired civic executive*
Wieder, Bruce Terrill *lawyer, electrical engineer*
Wilcox, David Eric *electrical engineer, educational consultant*
Williams, John Edward *lawyer*
Williams, Justin W. *government official*
Winzer, P.J. *lawyer*
Wofford, Harris *former senator, national service executive*
Woolley, Mary Elizabeth *research administrator*
†Wooten, Ralph G. *career officer*
Yoder, Edwin Milton, Jr., *columnist, educator, editor, writer*
Zook, Theresa Fuetterer *gemologist, consultant*

Amelia Court House

Smith, Adeline Mercer *retired librarian*

Amherst

Campbell, Catherine Lynn *elementary school educator*
†Copp, Cindy Pierce *education educator*
Herbert, Amanda Kathryn *special education educator*

Amissville

Coutu, Charles Arthur *deacon*
Hunter, Beverly Claire *research scientist, educator*

Annandale

Abdellah, Faye Glenn *retired public health service executive*
†Armstrong, Henry Jere *judge, lawyer*
Blodgett, Todd Alan *publisher, marketing executive*
Bohen, Dolores Boylston *retired school administrator*
†Brotton, Joyce Dupras *English language educator*
Christianson, Geryld B. *government relations consultant*
Connair, Stephen Michael *financial analyst*
Geiger, Richard Bernard *engineer, retired federal agency administrator*
Gioconda, Thomas F. *management consultant, retired military officer*
Greinke, Everett Donald *corporate executive, international programs consultant*
Hagn, George Hubert *electrical engineer, researcher*
Hanrahan, Margaret Villar (Peggi Hanrahan) *oil company executive*
Hedrick, Floyd Dudley *retired government official, writer*
Henretty, Donald Bruce *history educator*
Herbst, Robert LeRoy *organization executive*
Hovis, Robert Houston, III, *lawyer*
Hudson, William L. *conductor*
Hutcheon, Wallace Schoonmaker *history educator*
Jarvis, Elbert, II, (Jay Jarvis) *employee benefits specialist*
Khim, Jay Wook *high technology systems integration executive*
Lefrak, Edward Arthur *cardiovascular and thoracic surgeon*
Matuszko, Anthony Joseph *research chemist, administrator*
Ochs, Walter J. *civil engineer, drainage adviser*
Rogers, Stephen Hitchcock *former ambassador*
Schoenberg, Mark George *government agency administrator*
Shamburek, Roland Howard *physician*
Simonian, Simon John *surgeon, scientist, educator*
Smith, Ralph *artist*
Tavallali, Morad *plastic and reconstructive surgeon*
Veney, M. Beatrice *professional counselor*
Wilhelmi, Mary Charlotte *education educator, college official*
Willner, Larry Elliott *telecommunications company executive, consultant*
Wood, John Thurston *cartographer, jazz musician*
Wunderlich, Gene Lee *economist*

Appomattox

Morris, Dorothea Louise *nurse midwife*

Arlington

Adams, Hunter (Patch Adams) *internist, health facility administrator*
Adreon, Beatrice Marie Rice *pharmacist*
Adreon, Harry Barnes *architect*
Aggrey, Orison Rudolph *former ambassador, university administrator*
Alam, Shawn *biologist*
Allard, Dean Conrad *historian, retired naval history center director*
Allen, David *systems engineer*
Allison, Graham Tillett, Jr., *federal government official*
†Alper, Joanne Fogel *lawyer*
Anderson, Dean William *educational administrator*
Angell, Wayne D. *economist, banker*
Ankudinov, Vladimir Konstantinovich *naval architect*
Anthony, Robert Armstrong *lawyer, educator*
Asbell, Fred Thomas *health industry association executive*
Askey, Thelma J. *federal agency administrator*
Atkins, Walter J. *electrical engineer*
Bakke, Dennis W. *energy company executive*
Barry, Lance Leonard *judge*
†Bawa, Raj *education educator, educator, biodefense specialist, biotechnology company executive, patent agent*
Beaty, James Thomas *retired buyer*
Beazley, Hamilton Scott *writer, educator*
Beck, Buddy *systems engineer*
Becker, Fred Reinhardt, Jr., *association executive, lawyer, retired military officer*
Behney, Clyde Joseph *health policy researcher*
Berg, Sister Marie Majella *president emerita*
Beyer, Barbara Lynn *aviation consultant*
Bianchi, Charles Paul *technical and business executive, money manager, financial consultant*
†Blanchard, David Joseph *research scientist*
Bolster, Archie Milburn *retired foreign service officer*
Bordogna, Joseph *engineer, educator*
Bosch, Brian James *retired military officer*
Boster, Davis Eugene *retired ambassador*
Bowers, Ray Landis *editor*
Boylan, Michael A. *philosophy educator, writer*
Bradburn, Norman M. *behavioral science educator*
Breckinridge, James Bernard *optical engineer*
Brenner, Edgar H. *law administrator*
Brown, Gardner Russell *engineering executive*
Brown, Robert Lyle *retired foreign affairs consultant*
†Buckley, F.H. *economist, educator*
Bune, Karen Louise *criminal justice official*
Burkhart, Jennifer Ellen *business psychologist*
Carbaugh, John Edward, Jr., *lawyer*
Carr, Kenneth Monroe *naval officer*
Cavanaugh, Margaret Anne *chemist*
Cheney, David Warren *science and technology policy analyst, executive*
Chipman, Susan Elizabeth *psychologist, researcher*
Chubb, Talbot Albert *physicist*

Cinca, Silvia (Roberta King) *writer, producer*
Clare, Kenneth Guilford *economist, consultant*
Clayton, James Edwin *journalist*
Coady, Philip James, Jr., *retired naval officer*
Coats, Warren L., Jr., *economist*
Cobble, Steven Bruce *political consultant, strategist*
Cocolis, Peter Konstantine *business development executive*
Cohen, Jay *government agency administrator*
†Cohen, Sheldon Irwin *lawyer*
Coleman, Rodney Albert *government affairs consultant*
Colwell, Rita Rossi *microbiologist, molecular biologist, federal agency administrator, medical educator*
†Costello, John *military officer*
Cosumano, Joseph *military officer, government agency administrator*
Covington, James Edwin *government agency administrator, psychologist*
Cox, Henry *research company executive, research engineer*
Cragin, Charles Langmaid *lawyer*
†Culligan, Thomas M. *electronics executive*
Cummings, John William, Jr., *logistician, systems analyst*
Czech, Brian Martin *biologist, economist*
Dalglish, Lucy Ann *lawyer, organization executive*
Danjczek, David William *manufacturing company executive*
Davis, Lynn Etheridge *political scientist, educator*
†Davis, Russell C. *career officer*
Davis, Sharon Eileen *congressional staff member*
Davis-Imhof, Nancy Louise *retired elementary school educator*
Debney, George C. *mathematical physicist*
DeFilippi, George *retired air force officer*
Dickman, Robert Laurence *physicist, researcher*
Dietrick, Kevin M. *military officer*
Dobeck, Robert Bradley *lawyer*
Dorman, Craig Emery *oceanographer, academic administrator*
Douglass, John W. *commissioner*
Downing, Diane Virginia *community health nurse*
Doyle, Gerard Francis *lawyer*
Draeger, Susanne Yarbrough *interior designer*
Drayton, William *social entrepreneur, lawyer, management consultant*
Dubin, Henry C. *civilian military employee*
Dvorak, Josef Cermin *endocrinologist*
Edmondson, William Brockway *retired foreign service officer*
Ehrman, Madeline Elizabeth *federal agency administrator*
England, Robert Stowe *writer*
Ensminger, Luther Glenn *chemist, consultant*
Eppink, Jeffrey Francis *energy and environment consultant*
Ericsson, Sally Claire *not-for-profit organization administrator*
Erwin, Frank William *personnel research and publishing executive*
Facklam, Roger Lee *engineer, physicist*
Feeley, Karen Adler *training services executive, consultant*
Ferraz, Francisco Marconi *neurological surgeon*
†Finta, Frances Mickna *secondary school educator*
Fleischman, Phil *radio news executive*
Forrester, Eugene Priest *former army officer, management marketing consultant*
Fosdick, Cora Prifold (Cora Prifold Beebe) *management consultant*
Fowler, David Lucas *corporate lawyer*
Frame, Kathleen S. *non-profit education association administrator*
†Frederick, William George DeMott *defense company executive, consultant*
French, Mary B. *educator, editor, photographer, poet and former*
Fuchs, Roland John *geography educator, university science official*
Fujito, Wayne Takeshi *international business company executive*
Gallagher, Anne Porter *business executive*
Galloway, William Jefferson *former foreign service officer*
†Gangwal, Rakesh *airline executive*
Garfinkel, Patricia Gail *speech writer, policy analyst, poet*
Garnett, Griffin Taylor *lawyer, writer*
Gault, Jeffrey Wayne *information technology executive*
Gianturco, Delio E. *management consultant, educator, author*
Gilmore, Marjorie Havens *civic worker, lawyer*
†Glazier, Jonathan Hemenway *lawyer*
Goetze, Richard B., Jr., *association administrator*
Goldberg, Lawrence Spencer *science foundation engineering administrator, physicist*
Goldman, William Scott *lawyer*
Goodman, Mark *journalist, educator*
†Goodpasture, Bruce *retired editor, publisher, social sciences educator*
Gracey, James Steele *corporate director, retired coast guard officer, consultant*
Graves, Ernest, Jr., *retired army officer, engineer*
Green, Richard Alan *lawyer*
Guirguis, Raouf Albert *health science executive*
†Gunhus, Gaylord T. *military career officer*
Gunn, Joseph Ridgeway, III, *consulting economist*
Hall, Carl William *agricultural and mechanical engineer*
Hanle, Paul Arthur *museum administrator*
Hansen, Kenneth D. *lawyer, ophthalmologist*
Hansen, Orval *lawyer, former congressman, think tank executive*
Haq, Bilal Ul *national science foundation program director, researcher*
Harper, Michael John Kennedy *obstetrics and gynecology educator*
Harrington, George Fred *aviation consultant*
Harris, William James, Jr., *research administrator, educator*
Hassett, Valerie Jane *interior designer, architect, educator*
†Hazelrigg, George Arthur, Jr., *systems engineer, educator*
Heineken, Frederick George *biochemical engineer*
Held, Joe Roger *veterinarian, epidemiologist*
Henderson, Robert Earl *mechanical engineer, educator, consultant*
Hendrickson, Daniel C. *association administrator*
Hickman, Elizabeth Podesta *retired counselor, educator*
†Hidalgo, Henry *aerospace engineer, consultant*
Hill, Donald Wain *education accreditation commission executive*
†Hollander, Rachelle D.
Holt, Pat Mayo *journalist*
Howenstine, E. Jay *housing economist*
Howlett, Clifford Theodore, Jr., (Kip Howlett) *chemicals executive*
Hunkele, Lester Martin, III, *retired federal agency administrator*
Hunter, Jody Jean *association executive, naturalist*
Hunter, J(ohn) Robert *insurance consumer advocate*
Irizarry, Estelle Diane *foreign language educator, writer, editor*
Isaacson, Jeffrey Alan *think-tank executive, physicist*
†Itoh, William H. *former ambassador*
†Jackson, Nancy Gertrude *retired federal government librarian*
†James, Daniel, III, *military officer*
Jewell, Susan Diane *wildlife biologist, writer*
Johnson, Charles Owen *retired lawyer*
Johnson, Rosemary Wrucke *personnel management specialist*
Junker, Bobby Ray *research and development executive, physicist*
Kamensky, John Michael *management consultant*
Kanter, L. Erick *public relations executive*
Kappaz, Michael H. *engineering and energy executive*
Katona, Peter Geza *biomedical engineer, educator*
†Katzen, Jay Kenneth *foundation administrator, consultant, former foreign service officer*
Kearney, Stephen Michael *corporate executive*
†Kelly, John James *lawyer*
Kem, Richard Samuel *retired army officer*
Kerns, Wilmer Lee *social science researcher*
Kim, John Chan Kyu *electrical engineer*
†Kinsey, John Allen *systems engineer, director*
Knowlton, William Allen *political and military consultant, educator*
Korman, James William *lawyer*
Kostoff, Ronald Neil *aerospace scientist*
Krauss, Michael Ian *law educator*
Krys, Sheldon Jack *retired foreign service officer, career minister*
Kuelbs, John Thomas *lawyer*
†Kumar, Srikanta Ponnathpur *electrical engineer, researcher*
Lampe, Henry Oscar *securities trader*
Lampe, Margaret Sanger *community activist*
Landry, Walter Joseph *lawyer*
Langstaff, David Hamilton *aerospace industry executive*
Langworthy, Everett Walter *association executive, natural gas exploration company executive*
Lasowski, Anne-Marie F. *federal agency administrator*
Lauriski, Dave D. *federal agency administrator*
†Lean, Judith *physicist, researcher*
Lehrer, James Charles *television journalist*
Leinen, Margaret Sandra *oceanographic researcher*
Leland, Marc Ernest *trust advisor, lawyer*
Lester, Barnett Benjamin *editor, retired foreign affairs officer*
Levinson, Lawrence Edward *lawyer, corporation executive*
†Levitt, Tod S. *entrepreneur, researcher*
Lewis, Hunter *financial advisor, publisher*
Lieberman, Robert J. *federal audit agency administrator*
Lisanby, James Walker *retired naval officer*
Litman, Richard Curtis *lawyer*
Long, Madeleine J. *mathematics and science educator*
Luchok, Joseph Alan *communications executive, consultant*
Lundeen, William Bruce *radiologist*
†Lupia, Eugene A. *military officer*
Lurie, Nicole *former health science association administrator*
†Lurry, Michael Christopher *graphics designer, writer*
MacDonald, Paul Edward *electrical engineer*
MacDougall, William Lowell *magazine editor*
MacNeil, Robert Breckenridge Ware *retired broadcast journalist, writer*
Mainwaring, Thomas Lloyd *management consultant, former motor freight company executive*
Malone, William Grady *retired lawyer*
Mastromarco, Dan Ralph *lawyer, consultant*
Mathis, Mark Jay *lawyer*
Matthews, Allan Freeman *geologist*
May, Sterling Randolph *health association executive*
†Mazzarella, David *newspaper editor*
McClure, William Earl *financial advisor*
†McCoart, Janice Greenberg *art educator*
McDermott, Francis Owen *retired lawyer*
Mc Donald, Gail Faber *musician, educator*
Mc Donald, John Warlick *diplomat, global strategist*
McGinn, Daniel G. *public relations executive*
McKee, Thomas J. *association administrator*
†McKeown, Marilyn Godlewski *coronary care nurse, public health researcher, consultant*
McKinnon, Russel Francis Daniel *professional society administrator*
†McTique, Maurice P. *director*
McWethy, John Fleetwood *journalist*
Mears, Walter Robert *journalist*
Metz, Craig Huseman *business executive*
Miller, Kenneth Gregory *retired air force officer*
Mirrielees, James Fay, III, *publishing executive*
Monroe, Carl Dean, III, *lawyer*
†Moore, Guy Will *retired public information officer, historian, writer*
Morris, John Woodland, II, *businessman, former army officer*
Morris, Roy Leslie *lawyer, electrical engineer, venture capitalist*
†Morse, Larry Eugene *botanist, conservationist*
Mossinghoff, Gerald Joseph *lawyer*
Muchow, David John *lawyer, business executive*
Myers, Elissa Matulis *publisher, association executive*
Neikirk, William Robert *journalist*
Newburger, Beth Weinstein *medical telecommunications company executive*
Nguyen-Dinh, Thanh *internist, geriatrician, acupuncturist*
Nirschl, Robert Phillip *orthopedic surgeon*
Obermayer, Herman Joseph *newspaper publisher*
Ochmanek, David Alan *defense analyst*
O'Day, Paul Thomas *trade association executive*
O'Neill, Brian *research organization administrator*
Ordway, Frederick Ira, III, *educator, consultant, researcher, writer*
†Orkis, Lambert *musician, music educator*
Page, Harry Robert *business administration educator*
Parker, Jeffrey Scott *law educator*
Paynter, Harry Alvin *retired trade association executive*
†Perry, Walter Leo *information scientist, operations research specialist*
†Pfister, Karstin Ann *human services administrator*
Pickering, Thomas Reeve *diplomat*
Plevyak, Thomas Joseph *communications executive*
†Polak, Carol Schrier *lawyer*
Politi, John J. *association administrator*
Pomeranz, Morton *lawyer, educator*
Potvin, William Tracey *management consultant*
Preeg, Ernest Henry *manufacturers alliance executive*
Price, Jack C. *association administrator*
Putnam, George W., Jr., *retired army officer*
Quinn, John Collins *publishing executive, newspaper editor*
†Racette, Nancy Kelly *development company executive, consultant*
Rahman, Muhammad Abdur *mechanical engineer*
Ramaley, Judith Aitken *former university president, endocrinologist*
Rascon, Alfred *federal agency administrator*
Reagan, Lawrence Paul, Jr., *systems engineer*
Reed, Paul Allen *artist*
Rees, Raymond F. *military officer*
Reiss, Susan Marie *editor, writer*
Reyna, Benigno G. *federal agency administrator*
Reynolds, Peter James *physicist*
Robb, Charles Spittal *former senator, former governor, lawyer, educator*
†Rockefeller, Sharon Percy *broadcast executive*
Rogers, Alan Victor *former career officer*
Rogers, James Frederick *banker, management consultant*
Rogers, Sharon J. *education consultant*
Rosenblatt, Louise Michel *emerita educator*
Rotunda, Ronald Daniel *law educator, consultant*
†Rubottom, George Milton *foundation administrator, chemist*
Salmon, William Cooper *mechanical engineer, engineering academy executive*
Samburg, A. Gene *security company executive*
Sands, Frank Melville *investment manager*
Scarborough, Robert Henry, Jr., *enterpreneur*
Schneck, Paul Bennett *computer scientist*
Schneider, Clara Garbus *dietitian, nursing consultant*
Schneider, William, Jr., *commissioner*
†Schultz, Roger C. *career officer*
†Schwartz, Lyle Howard *materials scientist, science administrator*
Seamans, Andrew Charles *editorial and public relations consultant, columnist, author*
Seedlock, Robert Francis *engineering and construction company executive*
Sewell, William George, III, *electronics engineer*
Shaker, William Haygood *marketing professional, public policy reformer*
Shannon, Thomas Alfred *retired educational association administrator emeritus*
Shine, Kenneth Irwin *cardiologist, educator*
Shortal, Terence Michael *systems company executive*
Siddayao, Corazón Morales *economist, educator, consultant*
†Siegel, David N. *air transportation executive*
Simms, Frances Bell *retired elementary education educator*
Simonson, David C. *retired newspaper association executive*
Singstock, David John *military officer*
Smith, Myron George *former government official, consultant*
Solimando, Dominic Anthony, Jr., *writer, consultant, pharmacist, educator*
Southern, Hugh *retired performing arts manager*
Stelter, Paul James *editor, freelance writer*
Stevens, Donald King *retired aeronautical engineer, consultant*
Stevens, Robert J. *former aerospace transportation executive*
Stewart, Gordon Mead *architect*
Stokes, B. R. *retired transportation consultant*
Stolgitis, William Charles *professional society executive*
Stout, Mary Webb *education program specialist*
Strelau, Renate *historical researcher, artist*
Stuart, Charles Edward *electrical engineer, oceanographer*
Sundquist, James Lloyd *retired political scientist*
Swanberg, Neil Ralph *scientist, educator*
Sweeney, Randall W. *aerospace transportation executive*
Swenson, Diane Kay *lawyer*
Tabibi, S. Esmail *pharmaceutical researcher, educator*
Taddesse, Samuel *economist, consultant*
Taggart, G. Bruce *government program executive*
Taylor, Robert William *professional society administrator*
Terzian, Grace Paine *publisher*
Thompson, Robert Lee *agricultural economist, retired nonprofit executive*
Timperlake, Edward Thomas *government agency administrator, writer*
Tolbert, Margaret Ellen Mayo *science foundation administrator*
Trask, Roger R. *historian*
Trombley, Edward Francis, III, *educational administrator*
†Tugwell, Franklin *think-tank executive*
Tyrrell, Robert Emmett, Jr., *periodical editor, writer*
Umminger, Bruce Lynn *government official, scientist, educator*
Uncapher, Mark Elson *lawyer, trade association administrator*
Verburg, Edwin Arnold *management consultant*
Walker, Robert S. *government agency administrator*
Walker, Woodrow Wilson *retired lawyer, cattle and timber farmer, real estate investor*
Watkins, Birge Swift *investment banker*
Watson, Alexander Fletcher *organization executive, former ambassador*
†Weaver, Paul A., Jr., *career officer*
Weber, Alfons *physicist*
Weidemann, Celia Jean *social scientist, international business and financial development consultant*
†Weinberg, Robert Lester *lawyer, law educator*
Weiss, Joel Alexander *environmental and manufacturing executive*
Welty, Charles Douglas *lawyer*
Whitcomb, James Hall *geophysicist, foundation administrator*
Wilcox, John Gregor *military analyst*
Wilcox, Shirley Jean Langdon *genealogist*
Wilson, Minter Lowther, Jr., *retired officers association executive*
Winter, Harvey John *retired government official*
Wolf, Stephen M. *airline executive*
Wood, Heidi *commissioner*
†Woollen, Edmund *electronics executive*
Wu, Michael Ming-Kun *software engineer*
†Yoder, James A. *oceanographer, educator*
Zanfagna, Philip Edward *government executive, urban planner*
Zirkind, Ralph *physicist, educator*
Zorthian, Barry *communications executive*

Aroda
Nisly, Loretta Lynn *medical and surgical nurse, geriatrics nurse*

Ashburn
Arrington, Lavarr *football player*
Bennett, Lawrence Herman *physicist*
Boyne, Walter James *writer, former museum director*
†Cuteri, Frank R., Jr., *automotive executive*
Davis, Stephen *football player*
†Murrell, Adrian Bryan *professional football player*
Pavsek, Daniel Allan *banker, educator*
Snyder, Daniel *professional sports team executive, communications executive*
†Spurrier, Steve *professional football coach*
Tice, Raphael Dean *army officer*
†Torrico, Saúl A. *electrical engineer, engineering educator*
Walsh, Geraldine Frances *nursing administrator*
Weyman, Steven Aloysius *military officer, retired*

Ashland
Inge, Milton Thomas *American literature and culture educator, author*
Martin, Roger Harry *college president*
†Rice, Adrian Clifford *education educator*
†Tuell, Steven Shawn *religious studies educator, minister*

Assawoman
Holley, Pamela Spencer *retired librarian*

Barboursville
Cameron, William Wesley *investment executive*

Bassett
Spilman, Robert Henkel *furniture company executive*

Basye
James, Louis Meredith *personnel executive*
†Stanley, Robert Warren *association executive*

Bedford
Ramsey, Forrest Gladstone, Jr., *retired engineering company executive*
Turpin, Richard Ben *civil engineer*

Big Island
Durham, Betty Bethea *therapist*
Durham, John I. *retired religious studies educator*

Big Stone Gap
Harris, William Stacy *physics educator*
Ogbonnaya, Chuks Alfred *entomologist, agronomist, environmentalist*

Blacksburg
Barksdale, Mary Alice *education educator*
Batra, Romesh Chander *engineering mechanics educator, researcher*
Baumgartner, Frederic Joseph *history educator*
Bliznakov, Milka Tcherneva *architect, educator*
Boardman, Gregory Dale *environmental engineer, educator*
Brown, Gary Sandy *electrical engineering educator*
Brown, Gregory Neil *university administrator, forest physiology educator*
Brozovsky, John A. *accounting educator*
Bryant, Clifton Dow *sociologist, educator*
Burkhart, Harold Eugene *forestry educator*
Connerley, Mary L. *psychologist, educator*
Cook, Samuel Robert *anthropologist, educator*
Cowles, Joe Richard *biology educator*
Davis, Carole Carrera *watercolor artist*
de Wolf, David Alter *electrical engineer, educator*
Disney, Ralph L(ynde) *retired industrial engineering educator*
Doswald, Herman Kenneth *German language educator, academic administrator*
Easterling, William Samuel *structural engineering educator*
†Eyre, Peter *dean*
Fabrycky, Wolter Joseph *engineering educator, author, industrial and systems engineer*
†Fowler, Virginia C. *literature educator*
Gablik, Suzi *art educator, writer*
Glasser, Wolfgang Gerhard *chemical engineering wood science researcher, educator*
Good, Irving John *statistics educator, mathematician, philosopher of science*
Gray, Festus Gail *electrical engineer, educator, researcher*
Graybeal, Jack Daniel *chemist, educator*
Grisso, Robert Dwight, Jr., *engineering educator*
Grover, Norman LaMotte *theologian, philosopher*
Gwazdauskas, Francis Charles *animal science educator, dairy scientist*
Hallerman, Eric Michael *geneticist, educator*
Haugh, Clarence Gene *agricultural engineering educator*
Hirt, Joan B. *education educator*
Inman, Daniel John *mechanical engineer, educator*
Jannuzi, F. Tomasson *economics educator*
Jensen, Walter Edward *lawyer, educator*
†Kabir, Firoz *wood technologist, researcher*
King, Stephen Emmett *educational administrator*
†Knox, Paul L. *architecture educator, dean*
Lee, Fred C. *electrical engineering educator*
Mandelstamm, Allan Beryle *economics educator, consultant*
Mitchell, James Kenneth *civil engineer, educator*
Moore, Laurence John *business educator*
Morgan, George Emir, III, *financial economics educator*
Nayfeh, Ali Hasan *mechanical engineering educator*
Patterson, Douglas MacLennan *finance educator*
Pearce, David Harry *biomedical engineer, consultant*
Pearson, Ronald Earl *educator, researcher*
Perumpral, John Verghese *agricultural engineer, administrator, educator*
Phadke, Arun G. *electrical engineering educator*
Porter, Duncan MacNair *editor, educator*
Randall, Clifford Wendell *civil engineer, educator*
Redican, Kerry John *health education educator*
Rodriguez-Camilloni, Humberto Leonardo *architect, historian, educator*
Sandu, Adrian *mathematician, computer scientist, educator*
†Schetz, Joseph Alfred *aerospace engineer, educator*
Shepard, Jon Max *sociologist, educator*
Smoot, Raymond D., Jr., *academic administrator*
Squires, Arthur Morton *chemical engineer, educator*
Steger, Charles William *university administrator*
Stutzman, Warren Lee *electrical engineer, educator*
Swiger, L. A. *agricultural studies educator, educator*
Täuber, Uwe Claus *physicist*
Taylor, Charles Lewis *political science educator*
Tillar, Thomas Cato, Jr., *university alumni relations administrator, consultant*
Torgersen, Paul Ernest *academic administrator, educator*
†Vikesland, Peter John *environmental engineering educator, researcher*
Walcott, Charles Eliot *political science educator*
Walker, Richard David *civil engineer, educator*
Wall, Robert Thompson *secondary school educator*
Weaver, Pamela Ann *hospitality research professional*
†Weiner, Frank H. *architect, educator*
Youngs, Robert Leland *forestry educator*

Blackstone
Allen, Jeffrey Rodgers *lawyer*

Bland
†Newberry, Elizabeth Guthrie *librarian, educator*

Blue Ridge
Elmore, Walter A. *electrical engineer, consultant*

Bluemont
Kobetz, Richard William *criminologist, consultant*

Boston
Engle, Reed Laurence *landscape architect*
Fisher, John Morris *association official, business executive, educator*

Boyce
Murray, Arthur Joseph *engineering executive, speaker*

Boyd Tavern
Darden, Donna Bernice *special education educator*

Bridgewater
†Barkley, Terrell Wayne *school librarian, museum curator*
Bittel, Muriel Albers *managing editor*
†Geisert, Wayne Frederick *educational consultant, retired administrator*
Heatwole, John Lawrence *historian, sculptor*

Bristol
Alan, Sondra Kirschner *lawyer*
Richardson, Carl Colley, Jr., *thoroughbred farm owner*

Bristow
Mac Donald, Margaret Clark *retired real estate agent*
Schrock, Simon *retail executive*

Broad Run
Kube, Harold Deming *retired financial executive*

Buena Vista
Tichenor, James Robert, III, *retired military officer*

Burgess
Burch, Michael Ira *public relations executive, former government official*
Krebs, Rockne *artist*
Towle, Leland Hill *retired government official*

Burke
†Austin, Sandra J. *small business owner*
Bermant, Gordon *psychologist, lawyer, consultant, writer*
Emery, Vicki Morris *school library media administrator*
Hipfel, Steven J. *lawyer*
†Lingo, Robert S(amuel) *lawyer*
Lynch, Charles Theodore, Sr., *materials science engineering researcher, consultant, educator*
O'Connor, Edward Cornelius *army officer*
†Papas, Christa *writer*
Pfister, Cloyd Harry *consultant, former career officer*
†Smith, Pearl Richardson *management consultant*
Ward, Barry Lee *music educator, musician*
Werfel, Sandra Diane *clinical social worker*
White, Terry Joe *writer, editor*
Wood, C(harles) Norman *former association executive, military officer*
Woodruff, C(harles) Roy *consultant, retired professional association executive*
Zelasko, Nancy Faber *research scientist educator*

Castleton
Hahn, James Maglorie *former librarian, farmer*

Catlett
Broderick, Anthony James *air transportation executive*

Chantilly
Anderson, Maynard Carlyle *national and international security executive*
Carlson, Robert Charles *financial advisor, writer*
Chrzanowski, Leye Jeannette *publisher*
†Crawford, Tommy F. *career officer*
Evans, Richard Taylor *aerospace engineer, consultant*
Gavin, Mary Ellen *consultant*
Lalley, Frank Edward *computer company executive*
Nathan, Richard Arnold *technology company executive*
Pajak, Roger F. *federal official, policy adviser, lecturer, writer*
Priem, Richard Gregory *writer, information systems executive*
Saunders, Norman Thomas *consultant*
Sroka, John Walter *trade association executive*
Sullivan, Penelope Dietz *computer software development company executive*
†Tobin, Robert G. *supermarket chain executive*
Wallace, Renee Michelle *corporate executive*
Watkins, Felix Scott *printing company executive*
Watkiss, Eric John *naval officer*
Zirkle, William Vernon *philanthropist*

Charlottesville
Abbot, William Wright *history educator*
Abraham, Henry Julian *political science educator*
†Abraham, Kenneth Samuel *law educator*
Alford, Neill Herbert, Jr., *retired law educator*
†Allen, Joseph P. *psychologist, educator*
Anderson, Robert Barber *architect*
Arnold, Albert James *foreign language educator*
Barrett, Eugene Joseph *researcher, medical educator, physician*
Battestin, Martin Carey *retired English language educator*
Bayliss, E. Virginia *psychiatrist, educator*
Bednar, Michael John *architecture educator*
Beller, George Allan *medical educator*
Berkeley, Edmund, Jr., *retired archivist, educator*
Berkeley, Francis Lewis, Jr., *retired archivist*
Biltonen, Rodney Lincoln *biochemistry and pharmacology educator*
Bishop, Ruth Ann *coloratura soprano, voice educator*
Bloomfield, Louis Aub *physicist, educator*
Bly, Charles Albert *nuclear engineer, research scientist*
Bly-Monnen, April M. *quality assurance professional*
Bonnie, Richard Jeffrey *law educator, lawyer*
†Brewer, Philip Warren *retired civil engineer*
Brill, Arthur Sylvan *biophysics educator*
Brown, Holmes *public affairs executive*
†Bruns, David Eugene *medical educator, researcher*
Bull, George Albert *retired banker*
Cannon, Jonathan Z. *lawyer, educator*
Cano-Ballesta, Juan *Spanish language educator*
Cantrell, Robert Wendell *otolaryngologist, head and neck surgeon, educator*
Carey, Robert Munson *medical educator, physician*
Casey, John Dudley *writer, English language educator*
Casteen, John Thomas, III, *university president*
Catlin, Avery *engineering and computer science educator, writer*
†Chaidarun, Sushela Songtanin *endocrinologist, researcher*
Chandler, Lawrence Bradford, Jr., *lawyer*
Chapel, Robert Clyde *stage director, theater educator*
Cherno, Melvin *humanities educator*
Chevalier, Roger Alan *astronomy educator, consultant*
Childress, James Franklin *theology and medical educator*
†Clayton, Anita Louise *psychiatrist, physician*
Cohen, Edwin Samuel *lawyer, educator*
Cohen, Helen Herz *camp owner, director*
Coleman, Jonathan Mark *writer, English language educator*
Colley, John Leonard, Jr., *educator, author, management consultant*
Conway, Brian Peter *ophthalmologist, educator*
Cook, Lynn J. *nursing educator*
†Corbett, Eugene C., Jr., *medical educator*
Craig, James William *physician, educator, university dean*
Crigler, B. Waugh *US magistrate judge*
†Crosby, Ivan Keith *cardiologist, educator*
Cushman, Stephen Bigelow *English educator, writer*
Dalton, Claudette Ellis Harloe *anesthesiologist, educator, university official*
Daniel, Leon *journalist, newspaper columnist, editor*
Davis, Edward Wilson *business administration educator*
Denommé, Robert Thomas *foreign language educator*
Detmer, Don Eugene *health management and policy researcher, medical educator, surgeon*
†Dienstag, Joshua Foa *political scientist, educator*
Dooley, Michael P. *law educator*
Dove, Rita Frances *poet, English language educator*
†Dunn, William Wyly *corporate lawyer*
Durbin, Charles G., Jr., *anesthesiologist, intensivist, educator*
Durr, Leslie Martina *nurse, psychotherapist*
†Elias, W. Jeffrey *neurosurgeon*
Ellett, John Spears, II, *retired taxation educator, accountant, lawyer*
†Elzinga, Kenneth Gerald *economics educator*
Epstein, Robert Marvin *anesthesiologist, educator*
Feigert, Frank Brook *retired political science educator, writer*
Finley, Robert Van Eaton *minister*
Flickinger, Charles John *anatomist, educator*
Foard, Susan Lee *editor*
Forbes, John Douglas *architectural and economic historian*
Frantz, Ray William, Jr., *retired librarian*
Fredrick, Laurence William *astronomer, educator*
†Frey, Jr., Sherwood Charles *education educator, consultant*
Frieden, Charles Leroy *university library administrator*
Friedman, Susan Lynn Bell *economic development professional*
Gaden, Elmer Lewis, Jr., *chemical engineering educator, retired*
Garrett, George Palmer, Jr., *creative writing and English language educator, writer*
Garrett, Reginald Hooker *biology educator, researcher*
Garson, Arthur, Jr., *dean, medical educator*
Gaskin, Felicia *biochemist, educator*
Gay, Spencer Bradley *radiologist, educator*
Gianniny, Omer Allan, Jr., *retired humanities educator*
†Gillenwater, Jay Young *urologist, educator*
Gladstone, Arthur M. *artist, author*
Goeree, Jacob Klaas *economist, educator*
Good, Richard Standish *geologist*
†Goyne, Christopher Paul *aerospace scientist, educator*
Graebner, Norman Arthur *history educator*
Greenwood, Virginia Maxine McLeod *real estate executive, broker*
†Greville, Florence Nusim *secondary school educator, mathematician*
Greyson, Charles Bruce *psychiatrist*
Grimes, Russell Newell *chemistry educator, inorganic chemist*
Grohskopf, Bernice *writer*
Groiss, Fred George *lawyer*
Gröschel, Dieter Hans Max *physician, educator*
Gunter, Bradley Hunt *capital management executive*
†Haberly, David Tristram *language educator*
Haigh, Robert William *business administration educator*
Haimes, Yacov Yosseph *systems and civil engineering educator, consultant*
Handler, Jerome Sidney *anthropology educator*
Hanft, Ruth S. Samuels (Mrs. Herbert Hanft) *health care consultant, economist*
Hawkins, Deborah Craun *community health nurse, family practice nurse practitioner*
Henderson, Stanley Dale *lawyer, educator*
Hendrickson, Jerome Orland *trade association executive, lawyer*
Henry, Laurin Luther *public affairs educator*
Hetherington, Eileen Mavis *psychologist, educator*
†Hillman, Bruce Jay *radiologist, researcher, consultant, educator*
Hine, Jonathan Trumbull, Jr., *educator, translator*
Hinnant, Clarence Henry, III, *health care executive*
Hirsch, Eric Donald, Jr., *English language educator, educational reformer*
Hodous, Robert Power *lawyer*
Hoel, Lester A. *civil engineering educator*
Hogshire, Edward Leigh *judge*
†Holmes, Carolyn Coggin *museum director*
Holt, Charles Asbury *economics educator*
Hornberger, George Milton *environmental science educator*
Howard, Arthur Ellsworth Dick *law educator*
Hudson, John Lester *chemical engineering educator*
Humphreys, Paul William *philosophy educator, consultant*
Hunt, William B. *cardiopulmonary physician*
Hymes, Dell Hathaway *anthropologist, educator*
Inigo, Rafael Madrigal *retired electrical engineering educator*
Iwasaki, Tetsuya *engineering educator*
†Jagger, Janine *epidemiologist*
Jones, Rayford Scott *surgeon, medical educator*
Jordan, Daniel Porter, Jr., *foundation administrator, history educator*
Kaiserlian, Penelope Jane *publishing company executive*
Kassell, Neal Frederic *neurosurgery educator*
Kattwinkel, John *physician, pediatrics educator*
Keats, Theodore Eliot *physician, radiology educator*
Kehoe, William Joseph *educator, researcher, writer, consultant*
†Keith, Delorese Parker *elementary school educator*
Kellermann, Kenneth Irwin *astrophysicist, scientist*
Kellogg, Robert Leland *English language educator*
†Kelly, Thaddeus Elliott *medical geneticist*
Kerr, Anthony Robert *scientist*
†Kerrigan, D. Casey *physiatrist, educator*
†Kett, Joseph Francis *historian, educator*
Kiewra, Gustave Paul *psychologist, educator*
Kitch, Edmund Wells *lawyer, educator, private investor*
†Koester, Robert James *publishing executive, educational consultant*
†Kountakis, Stilianos E *surgeon, otolaryngologist*
Kraehe, Enno Edward *history educator*
†Krushkal, Vyacheslav S. *mathematician, educator*
Krzysztofowicz, Roman *systems engineering and statistical science educator, consultant*
Kudravetz, David Waller *lawyer*
Kuhlmann-Wilsdorf, Doris *materials scientist, educator*
Landess, Fred Stone *lawyer*
Lang, Cecil Yelverton *English language educator*
Langbaum, Robert Woodrow *English language educator, author*
†Laseter, Timothy Marks *finance educator*
Lee, Jae Kyun *biomedical researcher, educator*
Leffler, Melvyn P. *history educator*
Levenson, Jacob Clavner *English language educator*
Lin, Zongli *electrical engineering educator*
Linden, Peppy G. *museum director*
Little, W(illia)m A(lfred) *foreign language educator, researcher*
Long, Charles Farrell *insurance company executive*
Loo, Beverly Jane *publishing company executive*
†Lott, Eric William *literature educator*
Lupton, Mary Hosmer *retired small business owner*
Lyder, Courtney Harvey *nursing educator, consultant*
Lyons, John David *French, Italian and comparative literature educator*
MacIlwaine, Mary Jarratt *public relations executive*
Mandell, Gerald Lee *physician, medicine educator*
Marshall, John Crook *internal medicine educator, researcher*
Martin, David Alan *law educator*
Martin, Nathaniel Frizzel Grafton *mathematician, educator*
Martin, Robert Bruce *chemistry educator*
Matson, Robert Edward *public management educator, leadership consultant*
McCrimmon, Barbara Smith *writer, librarian*
McGann, Jerome John *English language educator*
McGinnis, Charles Irving *civil engineer*
McKay, John Douglas *lawyer*
McLaren, John Edward *economics educator*
Meador, Daniel John *law educator*
Meeks, Debra *realtor*
Meem, James Lawrence, Jr., *nuclear scientist*
Megill, Allan D. *historian*
Meiburg, Charles Owen *business administration educator*
Menefee, Samuel Pyeatt *lawyer, anthropologist*
†Merrill, Richard Austin *lawyer*
Middleditch, Leigh Benjamin, Jr., *lawyer, educator*
Midelfort, Hans Christian Erik *history educator*
Mikalson, Jon Dennis *classics educator*
Miller, Margaret Alison *education educator*
Minehart, Jean Besse *tax accountant*
Monaghan, Charles *writer, editor*
Monahan, John T. *law educator, psychologist*
Moore, John Norton *lawyer, diplomat, educator*
Moreno, Zerka Toeman *psychodrama educator*
Morgan, Raymond F. *plastic surgeon*
Morton, Jeffrey Bruce *aerospace engineering educator*
Muller, William Henry, Jr., *surgeon, educator*
Musselman, Robert Metcalfe *lawyer*
Newsom, David Dunlop *foreign service officer, educator*
Nohrnberg, James Carson *English language educator*
Nolan, Stanton Peelle *surgeon, educator*
†Norment, Rachel Gobbel *artist, educator, writer*
O'Connell, Jeffrey *law educator*

Saverot, Pierre-Michel *nuclear waste management company executive*
†Schwartz, Philip *lawyer*
Scimecca, Joseph Andrew *sociologist, educator*
Scott, Robert William *mediator, lawyer, educator, consultant*
†Secrest, Meryle *writer*
Shapiro, Stephen Robert *cardiologist*
†Shea, Gerald A. *statistician, consultant*
†Silcox, Gordon Bruce *career management consultant*
Smith, Vernon Lomax *economist, researcher*
Snyder, Roger Alan *physician, neurologist*
†Soyfer, Valery Nikolayevich *geneticist, biophysicist*
Stage, Thomas Benton *psychiatrist*
Stalick, Wayne M. *chemistry educator, law firm consultant*
Stearns, Peter Nathaniel *history educator*
Steele, Howard Loucks *economic development consultant, author*
Stitt, David Tillman *judge*
†Tichy, Susan *education educator, writer*
Tobin, Paul Edward, Jr., *naval officer*
†Travis, Toni-Michelle C. *political analyst, educator*
Tringale, Anthony Rosario *insurance executive*
Truong, Long Khanh *software consultant*
Tullock, Gordon *economics educator*
Van Eeckhoudt, Marc Victor Celestin *purchasing manager*
Wagner, Richard E. *economist, educator*
Ward, George Truman *architect*
†Welles, Judith *public affairs executive*
Williams, Marcus Doyle *judge*
Williams, Thomas Rhys *anthropologist, educator*
Witek, James Eugene *retired public relations executive*
†Xing, Guang-Qian *aerospace scientist*
Yoon, Yong Joon *economist, educator*
Zimmerman, Thomas Fletcher, III, *medical educator, consultant*

Fairfax Station
Abuzaakouk, Aly Ramadan *publishing executive*
Baer, Robert Jacob *retired army officer*
†Barringer, Joan Marie *counselor, educator, artist, writer*
Bishop, Alfred Chilton, Jr., *lawyer*
Carver, George Allen, Jr., *retired lawyer*
Cary, Ann Hagan *nurse, educator, health facility administrator*
Coaker, James Whitfield *mechanical engineer*
Duff, William Grierson *electrical engineer, educator*
Graul, Faye Anne *lobbyist*
Kaminski, Paul Garrett *federal agency administrator, investment banker*
Starry, Donn Albert *former aerospace company executive, former army officer*
Taylor, Eldon Donivan *government official*
Thompson, Jonathan Sims *army officer*

Fairfield
Harrawood, Paul *civil engineering educator*

Falls Church
Akkara, Joseph Augustine *chemist, educator*
Aukofer, Frank Alexander *journalist*
†Bankson, Marjory *religious association administrator*
Barkley, Paul Haley, Jr., *architect*
Barton, Robert Leroy, Jr., *judge, educator*
Beeman, Josiah Horton *diplomat*
Benson, William Edward (Barnes) *geologist*
Benton, Nicholas Frederick *publisher*
†Beyer, Donald Sternoff, II, *state official*
Bingman, Charles Franklin *public administration executive and educator*
Bowman, Richard Frederick *banker*
Brady, Rupert Joseph *lawyer*
†Brown, Lorraine A. *literature educator*
Bruck, William *business executive*
Bucur, John Charles *neurological surgeon*
Butler, Quincy Gasque *musician*
Cain, David Lee *corporate executive*
†Cain, Eddie *army officer*
Calkins, Susannah Eby *retired economist*
Cazan, Matthew John *political science educator*
Chabraja, Nicholas D.
†Chester, Linnes Lee, Jr., *healthcare association administrator*
Christman, Bruce Lee *lawyer*
Clizbe, John Anthony *psychologist, organization administrator*
Cooper, James Nelson *medical educator*
Cooper, Jean Saralee *judge*
Copes, Marvin Lee *college president*
Cromley, Allan Wray *journalist*
Diamond, Robert Michael *lawyer*
Elderkin, Helaine Grace *lawyer*
Elliott, Virginia F. Harrison *retired anatomist, kinesiologist and educator, investment advisor, publisher, philanthropist*
Evans, Peter Yoshio *ophthalmologist, educator*
Field, David Ellis *lawyer*
Fink, Charles Augustin *behavioral systems scientist*
French, John Lawrence *university educator, researcher*
Froelich, Robin Ann *systems analyst, educator*
Geithner, Paul Herman, Jr., *retired banker*
Golden, Wilson *lawyer*
Golomb, Herbert Stanley *dermatologist*
Grabenstein, John Douglas *pharmacist, army officer*
Gray, D'Wayne *retired marine corps officer*
Green, James Wyche *sociologist, anthropologist, psychotherapist*
Hahn, Thomas Joonghi *accountant*
Halpern, Judith *social worker*
Han, Syung D. *international trade consultant, financier*
Harshfield, Neil Alan *sculptor, educator*
Hart, C(harles) W(illard), Jr., *zoologist, curator*
†Hartshorn, Roland DeWitt *lawyer*
Hauda, William Edward, II, *emergency physician*
†Hernandez, Antonio *gynecologist*
†Hill, Mack C. *career officer*
Honigberg, Carol Crossman *lawyer*
Inglefield, Joseph T., Jr., *allergist, immunologist, pediatrician*
Inzana, Barbara Ann *professional musician, educator*
Isaac, William Michael *investment firm executive, former government official*
Jennings, Thomas Parks *lawyer*
Johnson, William David *retired university administrator*
Jones, Linda R. Wolf *company executive*
Jones, Russel Cameron *civil engineer, educator*
Kaplow, Herbert Elias *journalist*
Karpick, Ronald John *pulmonologist, internist, geriatrician*
Kirk, Dennis Dean *lawyer*
Kurtzke, John Francis, Sr., *neurologist, epidemiologist*
Layman, Lawrence *naval officer*
Leighton, Frances Spatz *writer, journalist*
Lorenzo, Michael *engineer, government official, real estate broker*
†Lotz, Denton *minister, church official*
†Lynn, Edward E. *corporate executive, lawyer*
Maroni, Yves *retired economist*
May, Carol Lee *mechanical engineer*
McCorkle, Constance Marie *anthropology educator*
McCue, David J. *information systems specialist, entrepreneur*
McCullough, William Lawrence *medical readiness consultant*
†McWilliams, Edmund Francis, Jr., *foreign service officer, human rights activist*
†Meserve, Richard Andrew *lawyer*
Miller, Mary Jeannette *office management specialist*
Montanye, James Alan *economist, consultant*
Mortensen, Robert Henry *landscape architect, golf course architect*
Nashman, Alvin Eli *computer company executive*
Nulty, Mary Anne *clinical social worker*
Nunes, Morris A. *lawyer*
Orben, Robert *editor, writer*
Orkand, Donald Saul *management consultant*
Padilla, David Joseph *lawyer, diplomat*
†Parson, Stephen Richard *education educator, consultant*
Perkins, Jack Edwin *lawyer*
†Poza, Hugo Bernardo *aerospace company executive*
Purvis, Ronald Scott *financial counselor, real estate professional*
Randolph, Leonard McElroy, Jr., *career officer*
Reilly, Patrick John *nonprofit executive*
Rice, Rick Blackburn *computer programmer, systems analyst*
†Robey, Daniel Lance *lawyer*
Rosenberg, Theodore Roy *financial executive*
Schmidt, Paul Wickham *lawyer*
Scott, Hugh Patrick *physician, naval officer*
Seifert, Patricia Clark *cardiac surgery nurse, educator, consultant*
Severin, Scott Robert *veterinarian, army officer*
Shah, Syed-Waqar *science educator*
Shriner, Robert Dale *economist, management consultant*
Simpson, John Arol *retired government executive, physicist*
Spindel, William *retired chemist, consultant*
†Teodorovic, Dusan *educator*
Tether, Anthony John *aerospace executive*
Thomas, William Griffith *lawyer*
Thomsen, Samuel Borron *non-profit executive, consultant*
Todd, Shirley Ann *school system administrator*
Villarreal, Carlos Castañeda *engineering executive*
Vodra, Richard Earle *financial planner*
Wali, Sima *foundation administrator*
†Walker, William P(Scot) *writer, real estate investor*
Ward, George Frank, Jr., *ambassador*
Ward, Joe Henry, Jr., *retired lawyer*
Weiss, Armand Berl *economist, association management executive*
Whitehead, Kenneth Dean *author, translator, retired federal government official*
Wise, Thomas Nathan *psychiatrist*
Woo, Dah-Cheng *hydraulic engineer*
Wood, John Martin *lawyer*
Work, Jane Magruder *retired professional society administrator*
†Yoshimura, Yoshiko *librarian*

Farmville
Adrian, Mitchell *management consultant, educator*
Amoss, Benjamin McRae, Jr., *language educator*
Boyer, Calvin James *librarian*
Dorrill, William Franklin *political scientist, educator*
Hevener, Fillmer, Jr., *English language educator, writer, portrait artist*
†Kinzer, Charles Edward *music educator*
Moon, William Arthur, Jr., *petroleum geologist, consultant*
†Rowland, Rhonda Stockton *mathematician, educator*
Terry, Wayne Gilbert *healthcare executive, hospital administrator*

Farnham
Durham, James Michael, Sr., *marketing executive, retired army officer*

Fincastle
Cummings, Kevin Bryan *minister*

Flint Hill
Dietel, William Moore *former foundation executive*
Forbush, Sandra M. *artist, educator*
Williamson, Richard Hall *association executive*

Floyd
Clemens, Donald Faull *chemistry educator*
Cosby, John Canada *retired lay worker*

Fort Belvoir
Ainsley, James Robert *academic administrator*
†Anderson, Frank J., Jr., *career officer*
Barnholdt, Terry Joseph *chemical, industrial, and general engineer*
†Foley, David W. *career officer*
Molholm, Kurt Nelson *federal agency administrator*
†Noonan, Robert W., Jr., *career officer*
O'Reilly, Kenneth William *military officer*
Ramsey, Donna Elaine *librarian*
St. John, Adrian, II, *retired army officer*
Smith, Margherita *writer, editor*

Fort Eustis
†Smail, Laurence Mitchell *lawyer, educator*

Fort Lee
†Courter, Robert J., Jr., *air force officer*
Simmonds, Robert Maurer *education educator*
†Solomon, Billy K. *army officer*
Sterling, Keir Brooks *historian, educator*

Fort Monroe
†Abrams, John N. *army officer*

Fort Myer
Hart, Herbert Michael *military officer*

Franklin
Cobb, G. Elliott, Jr., *lawyer*
Culpepper, Jo Long *librarian*
Fleming, June Helena *retired city manager*

Franktown
Holcomb, Caramine Kellam *volunteer worker*
Johnson, Claudia Anderson *psychologist, Jungian analyst*

Fredericksburg
Adams, Cynthia Ann *nursing administrator*
Allen, Edward Lefebvre *lawyer*
Anderson, Roberta June *computer engineer*
Bailey, Amos Purnell *clergyman, syndicated columnist, author*
Billingsley, Robert Thaine *lawyer*
Brown, Harold Eugene *retired magistrate*
Crippen, Timothy Alan *sociology educator*
Dorman, John Frederick *genealogist*
Dyal, William M., Jr., *retired federal agency administrator*
Emory, Samuel Thomas *retired educator*
†Eslinger-Brown, Vanessa Pauline *humanities educator*
Farnsworth, Stephen James *political science educator, writer*
Geary, Patrick Joseph *security administrator, writer*
†Givens, Florence Rosie *author, editor, publishing executive*
Goolrick, John Cole *congressional staff member, writer, consultant*
Goss, Georgia Bulman *freelance/self-employed translator*
Hajek, Otomar *mathematician, educator*
†Hasenfus, Harold Joseph *retired mechanical engineer, naval technical director*
Hedke, Richard Alvin *retired gifted education educator*
Herndon, Cathy Campbell *artist, educator*
Hickman, Margaret Capellini *advertising executive*
Hickman, Richard Lonnie *advertising executive*
Jarnecke, Roy William *clinical psychologist*
Jenks-Davies, Kathryn Ryburn *retired daycare provider and owner, civic worker*
Kusserow, Richard Phillip *government official, business executive*
†Marler, Helen *writer, actor*
Medding, Walter Sherman *retired environmental engineer*
†Merrill, Sammy R. *language educator*
Nikolic, Jean *artist*
†Nikolić, Nikola *physics educator*
†Pitts, Angela L. *humanities educator, researcher*
Rampersad, Peggy A. Snellings *sociologist, consultant*
Schmutzhart, Berthold Josef *sculptor, educator, art and education consultant*
Scriven, Wayne Marcus *lawyer*
Speirs, Carol Lucille *nurse, naval officer*

Free Union
LeBoutillier, Megan *writer*

Front Royal
Andes, Larry Dale *minister*
†Armstrong, Hamilton Reed *sculptor, educator*
Bonzagni, Vincent Francis *lawyer, program administrator, analyst, researcher*
†Carroll, Warren Hasty *retired historian*
†Cosby, Lynwood A. *electrical engineer*
Douglas, J(ocelyn) Fielding *toxicologist, consultant*
Napier, Ronald Lewis *lawyer*
Stanley, Douglas Parnell *county planner, administrator*

Gainesville
Burke, Marjorie Tisdale *retired special education educator*
Levell, Edward, Jr., *retired aiport executive*
Steger, Edward Herman *chemist*
Tuck, Russell R., Jr., *former college president*

Galax
Kapp, John Paul *lawyer, physician, educator*

Garrisonville
Emely, Charles Harry *trade association executive, consultant*

Glasgow
Riegel, Kurt Wetherhold *environmental protection executive*

Glen Allen
Batzli, Terrence Raymond *lawyer*
Fife, William Franklin *retired drug company executive*
Hinkle, Douglas Paddock *retired languages educator*
Minor, George Gilmer, III, *drug and hospital supply company executive*
Murphey, Robert Stafford *pharmaceutical company executive*
†Settlage, Steven Paul *lawyer*
Spitzer, William John *healthcare social work administrator, educator*
†Stokely, John E. *food distribution executive*
Wright, Sylvia Hoehns *speech professional*

Gloucester
Hicks, C. Flippo *lawyer*

Great Falls
Andrews, Betty Bauserman *retired secondary school educator, property manager*
Anikeeff, Anthony Hotchkiss *lawyer*
Bachner, John Philip *business consultant*
Castro-Klaren, Sara *Latin American literature educator*
DiBona, Charles Joseph *retired trade association executive*
Garrett, Wilbur (Bill Garrett) *magazine editor*
Hesse, Richard Joseph *construction engineer*
Klimczuk, Stephen John *business executive, foundation director*
Neidich, George Arthur *lawyer*
Preston, Charles George *lawyer*
Rath, Francis Steven *lawyer*
Skeen, David Ray *systems engineer, consultant, engineering executive, educator*

Grundy
Davis, W. Jeremy *dean, law educator, lawyer*

Halifax
Greenbacker, John Everett *retired lawyer and naval officer*

Hampden Sydney
Joyner, Weyland Thomas *physicist, educator, business consultant*

Hampton
Axenson, Theresa J. *physicist*
Barnes, Myrtle Sue Snyder *editor*
Bartels, Robert Edwin *aerospace engineer*
Brauer, Harrol Andrew, Jr., *broadcasting executive*
Bridges, Roy Dubard, Jr., *federal agency administrator*
Brown, Loretta Ann Port *physician, geneticist*
†Burgess, Gary Thomas *social studies educator, consultant*
†Daniels, Cindy Lou *space agency executive*
Douglass, James Frederick *business administration educator*
Drummond, James Everman *defense technology transfer consultant, former army officer*
Edmonds, Michael Darnell *music educator, educator*
Elmustafa, Abdelmageed Ahmed *senior research scientist*
Ganzburg, Mikhail *mathematics educator, researcher*
Gatski, Thomas Bernard *research scientist*
†Harris, Carl G. *music educator*
Harvey, William Robert *university president*
Houbolt, John Cornelius *physicist*
Jin, Zhonghai *physicist*
Joshi, Suresh Meghashyam *research engineer*
Kostel, Laura Everitt *social worker*
Krueger, Ronald *aerospace engineer*
Kulp, Eileen Bodnar *social worker*
†Makagon, Andrzej Leszek *education educator*
McNider, James Small, III, *lawyer*
Meyers, James Frank *electronics engineer*
†Moser, Eugene Paul, Jr., *retired secondary school educator*
Nelson, Wallace Jay *patent attorney*
Reid, Anna Louise *nurse anesthetist*
†Robertson, Natalie Suzette *history educator, researcher*
†Satterthwaite, Janice Ursula *academic administrator*
Singleterry, Robert Clay, Jr., *aerospace technologist, physicist, NASA administrator*
Sobieski, Jaroslaw *aerospace engineer*
†Spearman, Morris Leroy *aeronautics and aerospace researcher*
Tessler, Alexander *aerospace engineer*
Tripathi, Ram Kishore *physicist, researcher*
†Verma, Arun K. *mathematician, educator*
Weiser, Erik Saul *materials research engineer, project manager*
White, Debra Saunders *technology executive*
Wiedman, Timothy Gerard *management educator*
†Yamakov, Vesselin Ivanov *aerospace scientist, researcher*

Hardyville
White, Gordon Eliot *historian*

Harrisonburg
Alotta, Robert Ignatius *historian, educator, writer*
Arthur, Thomas Hahn *theater educator, director*
Augsburger, Aaron Donald *clergyman*
Baker, George Harold, III, *physicist*
Burkholder, Owen Eugene *religious organization administrator*
Carrier, Ronald Edwin *academic administrator, director*
Culbertson, Charles Randall *historian, writer*
Francfort, Alfred John, Jr., *educator*
Geary, Robert Francis, Jr., *English educator*

Gill, Gerald Lawson *librarian*
Hedrick, Eric Todd *musician, educator*
Helmuth, Les N. *fund raising executive, non-profit consultant*
Horst, Samuel Levi *history educator, researcher, writer*
†Hyser, Raymond M. *humanities educator*
Ivory, Ming Marie *political scientist*
Larson, Kenneth Oscar *occupational therapist*
†Miller, Brian Keith *human resources specialist, educator*
Morey, Ann-Janine *English educator*
†Reid, Susan L. *conductor*
Rollman, Steven Allan *communication educator*
Rosser, John Barkley, Jr., *economics educator*
Swope, Frances Alderson *retired librarian*
Theodore, Crystal *artist, retired educator*
†Wang, Greg G. *education educator, consultant*
Wubah, Daniel Asua *microbiologist, educator, dean*

Hartwood
Brugioni, Dino Anthony *writer, lecturer, consultant*

Hayes
Casson, Richard Frederick *lawyer, travel bureau executive*

Haymarket
Crafton-Masterson, Adrienne *real estate company executive*
Doolittle, Warren T. *retired federal official*
Frank, Jacob *lawyer*
Katz, Alan Charles *toxicologist*
Phillips, Robert Benbow *financial planner*

Heathsville
Daniel, John Griffith *physician*
McKerns, Charles Joseph *lawyer*
Sisson, Jean Cralle *retired middle school educator*
†Thompson, Alice Roxana (Ann Thompson) *labor economist*
Winkel, Raymond Norman *aerospace industry consultant, avionics manufacturing executive, retired naval officer*

Herndon
Berry, Fred Clifton, Jr., *author, magazine editor, book packager*
†Boyer, Mark E *public policy expert, Internet company executive*
Burns, Patrick Owen *venture capital company executive*
†Butler, Taryn Darnella *systems analyst*
Childers, Charles *communications executive*
Crossfield, Albert Scott *aeronautical science consultant, pilot*
Douglass, Robert Joseph, Jr., *computer scientist*
†Drew, Lawrence James *geologist, statistician*
Duceman, Mark Eugene *planner*
Frazier, Paul Ignatius *marketing professional*
†Geldon, Fred Wolman *lawyer*
Glacel, Robert Allan *retired military career officer*
Goss, Kay Collett *data company executive*
Hermansen, John Christian *computational linguist*
†Hollis, Katherine Mary *information scientist, consultant*
†Jones, Reba (Becki) Pestun *elementary school educator, music educator*
Meiselman, David Israel *economics educator*
Miller, Donald Lane *publishing executive*
Montgomery, Hugh Everett, Jr., *civilian military executive*
Ras-Work, Andenet T. *software company executive*
†Rongen, Thomas *professional soccer coach*
Shevis, James Murdoch *journalist*
†Walker, Lawrence Howard, Jr., *music educator, department chairman*
White, Matthew C. *advertising executive*
Wilkin, William Edmund *lawyer*

Hillsville
Becker, Elizabeth Anne *secondary education educator*

Hmpden Sydney
†Arieti, James Alexander *classics educator, writer*

Hopewell
Vartanian, Isabel Sylvia *retired dietitian*

Hot Springs
†Deeds, Robert Creigh *lawyer, state legislator*

Huddleston
Kopp, Richard Edgar *electrical engineer*

Hudgins
Story, Martha vanBeuren *retired librarian*

Independence
Craig, James Hicklin *fine arts consultant*

Irvington
Brown, Mahlon Carl *retired social science educator*
†Ward, Richard Alvord *retired lawyer*

Ivy
Wilcox, Harvey John *lawyer*

Keswick
Fletcher, John Caldwell *bioethicist, educator*
Halfen, David *retired publishing executive*
Johansen, Eivind Herbert *special education services executive, former army officer*
Nosanow, Barbara Shissler *art association administrator*
Pochick, Francis Edward *financial consultant*
Rafajko, Robert Richard *medical research company executive*
Rowe, William Joseph *internist*

Woods, Reginald Foster *management consulting executive*

Keysville
Nipper, Patricia Diane *accounting and economics educator*

Kilmarnock
Ibañez, Alvaro *patent design company executive, artist*

King George
Agnew, Christopher Mack *minister, historian*
Lund, Rita Pollard *construction executive*
Newhall, David, III, *former government official*
Revercomb, Horace Austin, III, *judge*

Kingstowne
Hixson, Stanley G. *speech, language and computer technology educator*

Lake Ridge
Englert, Helen Wiggs *writer*
Ingrassia, Anthony Frank *human resource specialist*

Lancaster
Beane, Judith Mae *psychologist*
Rowden, William Henry *naval officer*
Spiers, Robert Franklin *music educator*
Vehse, Robert Chase *management consultant, educator*

Langley AFB
†Bigum, Randall K. *career officer*
†Perryman, Gerald F., Jr., *career officer*

Lansdowne
Fujishiro, Katakazu Kenneth *retired urban/regional planner, engineer*
Green, May Clayman *early childhood educator and administrator*
Ink, Dwight A. *government agency administrator*
Stanley, Lila Gail *political scientist, antique appraiser*

Lebanon
Compton, Carnis Eugene *lawyer*

Leesburg
†Alwani, Ahmed J. *dean, consultant*
†Fall, Dorothy Eleanor *librarian*
Jacob, Walter Charles *lawyer*
Johnson, Julia A. *writer*
Kelsey, Ronald Grant *environmental engineer*
Magraw, Richard Shannon *security consultant*
†Mahood, Ken *music educator*
Mims, William Cleveland *state legislator, lawyer*
Mitchell, Russell Harry *dermatologist*
Mokhtarzadeh, Ahmad Agha *agronomist, consultant*
†Navarro-Ramirez, Daniel *application developer*
†Price, Stephen Conwell *lawyer*
†Robertson, Ruth *artist, art gallery owner*

Leon
Han, Nong *artist, sculptor, painter*

Lexington
Adams, James Lamont *educational foundation executive*
†Ball, Gordon Victor *adult education educator, writer, editor, photographer*
†Brodie, John *music educator*
Brooke, George Mercer, Jr., *historian, educator*
Burish, Thomas Gerard *academic administrator*
†Cumming, Douglas O. *journalist, educator*
DeSilvey, Dennis Lee *cardiologist, educator, university administrator*
DeVogt, John Frederick *management science and business ethics educator, consultant*
Elmes, David Gordon *psychologist, educator*
Gaines, James Edwin, Jr., *retired librarian*
Hodges, Louis Wendell *religion educator*
Jarrard, Leonard Everett *psychologist, educator*
John, Lewis George *political science educator*
Jost, Timothy Stoltzfus *law educator*
Kirgis, Frederic Lee *law educator*
Krantz, Linda Law *librarian*
Krotoszynski, Ronald James, Jr., *law educator*
†Leach, Maurice Derby, Jr., *librarian, educator*
Lubin, Timothy Norman Thomas *humanities educator*
Luecke, Pamela *professor, former editor*
Lynn, Michael A. *historic site director*
Partlett, David F. *dean, law educator*
Paxton, Matthew White, IV, *newspaper publisher*
Phillips, Charles Franklin, Jr., *economist, educator*
Ryan, Halford Ross *speech educator*
Sessions, William Lad *philosophy educator, administrator*
Smitka, Michael John *economics educator*
Spencer, Edgar Winston *geology educator*
†Squire, James C *adult education educator, engineer, consultant*
Stuart, Dabney *poet, author, English language educator*
Sundby, Scott Edwin *law educator*
Thelin, John Robert *academic administrator, writer*
Tierney, Michael John *mathematics and computer science educator*
Tyree, Lewis, Jr., *retired compressed gas company executive, inventor, technical consultant*
†Warren, James Perrin *language educator*
Wiant, Sarah Kirsten *law library administrator, educator*
Winfrey, John Crawford *economist, educator*
Young, Bruce Kenneth *film director*
Young, Kenneth Evans *educational consultant*

Lightfoot
Morris, Robert Louis *management consultant*

Locust Grove
Grante, Jullian Irving *criminal justice consultant*

Lorton
Sun, Li-Teh *economics educator*

Louisa
Small, William Edwin, Jr., *association and recreation executive*

Luray
Burzynski, Norman Stephen *editor*

Lynchburg
Angel, James Joseph *lawyer*
Barkley, Henry Brock, Jr., *research and development engineering executive*
†Brindle, Wayne Allan *religious studies educator*
Burnette, Ralph Edwin, Jr., *judge*
†Carey, Charles William, Jr., *historian, educator*
Cooper, Alan Michael *psychiatrist*
Cornett, Robert Arnold *philosophy educator*
Cunniff, Suzanne *surgical technician*
Davenport, James Robert *retired city official, retired utility executive*
†Davidson, Frank Gassaway, III, *lawyer*
Denham, Paul Raymond *construction executive*
Duff, Ernest Arthur *political scientist, educator*
Elson, James Martin *retired historic foundation director*
Falwell, Jerry L. *minister*
†Gale, J. Darren *nuclear energy industry executive*
Groshner, Maria Star *nuclear engineer*
†Harris, Dale Hutter *judge, lecturer*
Healy, Joseph Francis, Jr., *lawyer, retired air transportation executive*
Heptinstall, Debra Lou *marketing professional*
Hudson, Walter Tiree *artist*
Husted, Stewart Winthrop *dean, marketing educator, consultant*
Johnson, Robert Bruce *historic preservationist*
†Kerr, Stephen Paul *music educator*
Kulp, James *finance company executive*
Massie, Anne Adams Robertson *artist*
McClenon, John Raymond *retired chemistry educator*
McRorie, William Edward *lawyer, retired life insurance company executive*
Moon, Norman K. *judge*
Morgan, Evan *retired chemist*
Morland, John Kenneth *sociology and anthropology educator*
Packert, G(ayla) Beth *retired lawyer*
†Partie, David John *language educator*
Quakenbush, Brian Clay *music educator*
Quillian, William Fletcher, Jr., *retired banker, former college president*
†Schewel, Rosel Hoffberger *education educator*
†Simmons, Tracy Lee *editor, writer*
Snead, George Murrell, Jr., *army officer, scientist, consultant*
Stephens, Bart Nelson *former foreign service officer*
†Terzic, Petar *mathematician, educator*
Vaughn, Susan Marie *journalist, educator*
Weimar, Robert Henry *clinical hypnotherapist*
Whittemore, Linda Genevieve *clinical psychologist*
Womack, Edgar Allen, Jr., *energy executive*

Lyndhurst
Dieter, Melvin Easterday *retired minister, educator*

Manakin Sabot
†Bayliss, John Temple *retired science educator, retired energy executive*
Bright, Craig Bartley *lawyer*
Henson, Kristin L. *veterinary pathologist*

Manassas
Adamson, Heidi Beth *English educator*
Archer, Chalmers, Jr., *retired education educator*
†Bottorff, Gerald L. *retired military officer, foundation administrator*
Cypess, Raymond Harold *bioscience organization executive*
†Cznadel, John Paul *music educator*
Foote, John Holland *lawyer*
†Gelooo, Nadim Ahmad *cardiologist*
Heishman, Ricci Lynn *information technology educator*
Isbister, Jenefir Diane Wilkinson *microbiologist, researcher, educator, consultant*
Kinsler, Bruce Whitney *air traffic controller, aerospace engineer*
Locigno, Paul Robert *public affairs executive*
Lytton, Linda Rountree *marriage and family therapist, test consultant*
†Maguire, Edward Ross *social sciences educator, consultant*
Nemfakos, Charles Panagiotis *defense industry executive*
Parrish, Frank Jennings *retired food products executive*
Storing, Paul Edward *retired foreign service officer*
Van Broekhoven, Rollin Adrian *federal judge*
Wilson, Robert Spencer *magazine editor*

Marion
Armbrister, Douglas Kenley *surgeon*
Elledge, Glenna Ellen Tuell *journalist*
Greer, Carole Kilby *reading specialist*
Grinstead, Paul Lee *materials company official*

Marshall
†Thompson, Philip Douglas *federal agency administrator, educator*

Martinsville
Frith, Douglas Kyle *retired lawyer*
Kidd Hill, Leonice Thompson *musician, writer*
Plonk, William McGuire *retired minister*
Shackleford, William Alton, Sr., *minister*
†Smith, James Randolph, Jr., *lawyer*

Mason Neck
Mc Curdy, Patrick Pierre *editor, consultant*

Mathews
Busby, Morris D. *former ambassador*

Mc Dowell
Harkleroad, Jo-Ann Decker *special education educator*

Mc Lean
Adler, Larry *marketing executive*
Alberts, Henry Celler *real estate company executive*
Alexander, Fred Calvin, Jr., *lawyer*
Andrews, Minerva Wilson *retired lawyer*
Anthony, Joan Caton *administrative judge*
Aucutt, Ronald David *lawyer*
Auerbach, Anita L. *clinical psychologist*
†Baker, Keith Leon *lawyer*
Bardack, Paul Roitman *lawyer, consultant*
Bartlett, John Wesley *consulting firm executive*
†Baumann, Martin F. *savings and loan association executive*
†Blair, Bonnie *former professional speedskater, former Olympic athlete*
Blanchard, Townsend Eugene *retired service companies executive*
Brady, Phillip Donley *lawyer*
†Brown, Frank Eugene, Jr., *lawyer*
Brown, Thomas Cartmel, Jr., *lawyer*
Bullard, Marcia *publishing executive*
Burke, Sheila P. *federal administrator*
Byrnes, William Joseph *lawyer*
Cahill, Harry Amory *diplomat, educator*
Callahan, Vincent Francis, Jr., *state legislator, publisher*
Canes, Michael Edwin *research economist*
Cannon, Mark Wilcox *government official, business executive*
Capone, Lucien, Jr., *management consultant, former naval officer*
Cardwell, Thomas Augusta, III, *research scientist, retired career officer, executive*
Carlson, Richard Warner *journalist, diplomat, federal agency administrator, broadcast executive*
Carnicero, Jorge Emilio *aeronautical engineer, business executive*
Carter, William Walton *physicist, researcher*
Casciano, John P. *executive*
Cerkevitch, Taras Joseph *psychologist, consultant*
†Chang, Michael *tennis player*
Chaplin, Stephen Michael *retired diplomat*
Chapple, Thomas Leslie *lawyer*
Chase, Emery John, Jr., *nuclear engineer, researcher*
Church, Randolph Warner, Jr., *lawyer*
Clema, Joe Kotouc *computer scientist*
Corson, J. Jay, IV, *lawyer*
Cowhill, William Joseph *retired naval officer, consultant*
Cuffe, Robin Jean *nursing educator*
†Daniels, Michael Alan *lawyer*
DeCell, Hal C. *federal agency administrator*
Dempsey, James Raymon *industrial executive*
Dewar, James McEwen *marketing, aerospace and defense executive, developing nations consultant*
Dobson, Donald Alfred *retired electrical engineer*
Doyle, Frederick Joseph *retired government research scientist*
Drew, K. *financial advisor, management consultant*
Duncan, Robert Clifton *retired government official*
†Dunn, James Edward, Jr., *corporate consultant, lawyer*
Edgar, Janelle Diane Ward *financial services executive*
Estren, Mark James *business and media consultant, TV producer, author*
Fairbank, Richard D. *diversified financial services company executive*
Feller, Mimi *newspaper publishing executive*
Filerman, Gary Lewis *health educator*
Firestone, Roger Morris *computer scientist*
Flagg, Michael James *communications and graphics company executive*
Freund, Henry Philip *physicist*
Freyer, Victoria C. *fashion and interior design executive*
Fritz, Thomas Vincent *business executive*
Frostic, Frederick Lee *strategic planning and defense policy consultant*
Gammon, James Alan *lawyer*
García-Godoy, Cristián *historian, educator*
Gardenier, John Stark *statistician, research ethicist, lecturer, writer*
Gladeck, Susan Odell *retired social worker*
Gniewek, Raymond Louis *newspaper editor*
Gregus, Linda Anna *government official*
Hale, Robert Fargo *government consultant*
Halik, Eugene Egon *engineering consultant*
Head, James Philip *lawyer*
Healy, Theresa Ann *former ambassador*
Herge, J. Curtis *lawyer*
Hicks, C. Thomas, III, *lawyer*
Hill, Jimmie Dale *retired government official*
Hjort, Howard Warren *consultant, economist*
Hoffman, Ronald Bruce *biophysicist, life scientist, consultant*
Hoffmann, Martin Richard *lawyer*
Hope, Melissa B. *radio and television correspondent*
Ingersoll, William Boley *lawyer, real estate developer*
Johnson, Omotunde Evan George *economist*
Jurgensen, Karen *newspaper editor*
†Kargbo, Ranya *educational association administrator*
Keevey, Richard Francis *government official, educator*
Kennedy, Cornelius Bryant *retired lawyer*
Kim, Jay *former congressman*
Kipniss MacDonald, Betty Ann *artist, educator*
Klopfenstein, Rex Carter *electrical engineer*
Kohli, Harinder S. *business executive, development economist*

Kolombatovic, Vadja Vadim *retired management consulting company executive*
Kondracki, Edward John *lawyer*
†Kruchko, John Gregory *lawyer*
Krugman, Stanley Liebert *science administrator, geneticist*
Landfield, James Seymour *small business owner*
Layson, William McIntyre *retired research consulting company executive*
Lazar, Dale Steven *lawyer*
Lee, Daniel Kuhn *economist*
LeSourd, Nancy Susan Oliver *lawyer, writer*
Levy, Michael Howard *environmental management professional*
Loatman, Robert Bruce *computer scientist, researcher*
Lovaas, John L. *foreign aid executive, community activist*
Mahan, Clarence *retired govenment official, writer*
Malley, Raymond Charles *retired foreign service officer, industrial executive*
Marino, Michael Frank, III, *lawyer*
†Mars, Forrest E., Jr., *candy company executive*
Mars, Jacqueline Badger *food products executive*
Mars, John Franklin *candy company executive*
Martin, Raymond S. *international health consultant*
Martin, Todd *professional tennis player*
Mathews, Linda McVeigh *newspaper editor*
McCambridge, John James *civil engineer*
McCorkindale, Douglas Hamilton *lawyer, publishing company executive*
McIlwain, Clara Evans *agricultural economist, consultant*
McInerney, James Eugene, Jr., *trade association executive*
McLean, Robert, III, *real estate company executive*
McManus, Douglas Alexander *economist*
Metters, Samuel *engineering executive*
Michalowicz, Karen Dee *secondary education educator*
Moeller, Robert Charles (Bud Moeller) *management consultant*
Mohleji, Satish Chandra *electrical engineer*
Molineaux, Charles Borromeo *lawyer, arbitrator, columnist, poet*
Molino, Thomas Michael *retired military officer*
†Moon, Craig *publishing executive*
Morris, James Malachy *lawyer*
Murphy, Thomas Patrick *lawyer*
Neel, Samuel Ellison *lawyer*
Newman, William Bernard, Jr., *government consultant*
Nobil, James Howard, Jr., *real estate investor, developer, consultant, broker*
Nothaft, Frank Emile *economist*
O'Brien, Francis Anthony *retired lawyer*
Olsen, Robert Eric *lawyer, educator, writer*
Olson, Walter Justus, Jr., *management consultant*
Olson, William Jeffrey *lawyer*
Oren, John Birdsell *retired coast guard officer*
†Parseghian, Gregory J. *savings and loan association executive*
Parshall, Gerald *journalist*
Paschall, Lee McQuerter *retired communications consultant*
Paul, Andrew Robert *defense and legislative consultant*
†Paul, Peterson T. *savings and loan association executive*
Pho, Long Ambrose Ba *business educator, consultant*
Redmond, Robert *lawyer, educator*
Reichenbach, Roy Earl *engineering executive*
Rose, Susan Porter *consultant*
Rosenbaum, David Mark *engineering executive, consultant, educator*
Rugala, Karen Francis (Karen Francis) *painter, television producer*
Russell, Theodore Emery *diplomat*
Safer, John *artist, lecturer, banker, real estate developer*
†Schar, Dwight C. *construction company executive*
Schauer, Franz Peter *civil and nuclear engineer, educator*
Schmeidler, Neal Francis *engineering executive*
Scott, Concetta Ciotti *artist, art educator*
Scribner, Sherlie Ann *educator*
Shapiro, Nelson Hirsh *lawyer*
Sherzer, Harvey Gerald *lawyer*
†Shrader, Ralph W. *management consultant*
Skantze, Pat *model, consultant*
Smith, Carey Daniel *acoustician, undersea warfare technologist*
Smith, Esther Thomas *communications executive*
Smith, Russell Jack *former intelligence official*
Smith, Thomas Eugene *investment company executive, financial consultant*
Sonnemann, Harry *electrical engineer, consultant*
Sowle, Donald Edgar *management consultant*
Sparks, Robert Ronold, Jr., *lawyer*
Spaulding, Wallace Holmes *retired federal agency professional*
Stackpole, Kerry Clifford *association executive*
Stephens, William Theodore *lawyer, business executive*
Stevens, Richard Gordon *political scientist, educator*
Stump, John Sutton *retired lawyer*
Susko, Carol Lynne *lawyer, accountant*
Tabrizi, Mehdi Fakher *obstetrician/gynecologist*
Talbot, Lee Merriam *ecologist, educator, association executive*
Talbot, Martha Hayne *conservationist, biologist*
Tansill, Frederick Joseph *lawyer*
Taylor, Priscilla Sheppard *editor*
Theon, John Speridon *meteorologist, researcher*
Topping, Eva Catafygiotu *writer, lecturer, educator*
Topping, Peter *historian, educator*
Townsend, Christopher Gordon *lawyer*
Trout, Margie Marie Mueller *civic worker*
Trout, Maurice Elmore *diplomat*
Ullmann, Owen *journalist*
Vandemark, Robert Goodyear *retired retail company executive*
Van Lare, Wendell John *lawyer*
†Wall, Barbara Wartelle *lawyer*
Wallace, Robert Bruce *surgeon, retired*
Walsh, John Breffni *aerospace consultant*
Walsh, Marie Leclerc *nurse*
†Walter, Michael Joseph *lawyer*
Watson, Jerry Carroll *advertising executive*
Weeks, Stanley Byron *foreign and defense policy consultant*
Welch, Jasper Arthur, Jr., *security company executive, consultant*
Whitehead, Clay Thomas *business executive*
Williams, Thomas Blake *natural resources consultant, educator*
Wright, William Evan *physician*
Yancik, Joseph John *government official*
Yarborough, William Glenn, Jr., *military officer, forest farmer, defense and international business executive*
Young, Loretta Ann *auditor*
Youngs, William Ellis *motion picture engineer, projectionist*

McLean

†Gallagher, Brian *editor-in-chief*
†Harry, Charles Thomas *economist*
†Johnson, Christopher Layne *computer scientist, researcher*
†Kasmeridi, Sofia *translator, researcher*
†Kitchens, Clarence Wesley, Jr., *technology administrator*
†Park, Sunwoo *engineer*
†Staats, Richard Charles *computer engineer*

Mechanicsville

Galloway, Joseph Edward, Jr., *retired highway engineer*
Gerrish, Brian Albert *theologian, educator*
†Gorman, Joseph Batterton *elementary school educator*
Henshaw, William Raleigh *retired middle school educator*
Hinkle, Barton Leslie *retired electronics company executive*
Lordi, William Michael *psychiatrist, child psychiatrist*
McEntire, Jean Reynolds *music educator*
Peterson, William Canova *architect*
†Watkins, Carol A. *special education educator*

Merrifield

Earley, Mark Lawrence *not-for-profit administrator, former state attorney general*
Earner, William Anthony, Jr., *naval officer*
†Rodriguez, Leopoldo *wholesale distribution executive*

Middleburg

Beddall, Thomas Henry *lawyer*
Coven, Robert Michael *secondary school educator, researcher, writer*
Kaplan, Jean Gaither (Norma Kaplan) *reading specialist, retired educator*
Langley, Rolland Ament, Jr., *retired engineering technology company executive*
McNichols, Gerald Robert *consulting company executive*
Parkinson, James Thomas, III, *investment consultant*
Robinson, Michael Francis *private art dealer and appraiser*
Sodolski, John *retired association administrator*
†Tucker, John Richard *mathematician, educator, writer, researcher*

Midlothian

Campbell, James Albert Barton *association executive, retired marketing executive*
Chapman, Gilbert Whipple, Jr., *publishing company executive*
†Cruse, Robert Ridgely *retired research chemist*
Crutchfield, George Thomas *journalism educator*
Friedel, Robert Oliver *physician*
†Hall, Franklin Perkins *lawyer, banker, state official*
Hanes-Stevens, LaVerne E. *minister, social services administrator*
Kellum, Betsy M. *artist, educator*
McCarney, William Christopher *music educator*
†Nelson, Margaret Rose *lawyer, legal educator*
O'Shanick, Gregory John *physician, medical association administrator*
Pearson, Gregory David *publisher, media specialist*
Perkins, Raymond Lamont *retired government official*
Shands, William Ridley, Jr., *lawyer*
Smith, Alma Davis *elementary education educator*
Sowder, Donald Dillard *pharmaceutical executive*
Stringham, Luther Winters *economist, administrator*
Tuttle, Roger Lewis *lawyer, educator*
Wadsworth, Robert David *advertising agency executive*
Wang, Buqian *materials research scientist*
†Yohe, David Edward *music educator*

Millboro

Minetree, James Lawrence, III, *retired military officer, educator*

Mineral

Donald, James Robert *federal agency official, economist, outdoors writer*
Speer, Jack Atkeson *publisher*

Moneta

Pfeuffer, Robert John *musician*
Ulmer, Walter Francis, Jr., *consultant, former army officer*
Wiatt, Carol Stultz *elementary education educator*

Monroe

†Pettus, William G. *retired nuclear scientist, research scientist*

Monterey

†Blanchard, Julia Smith *secondary school educator*
Tabatznik, Bernard *retired physician, educator*

Montross

Fountain, Robert Roy, Jr., *farmer, industrial executive, naval officer*

Mount Jackson

Sylvester, George Howard *retired air force officer*

Mount Vernon

Brownson, Anna Louise Harshman *publishing executive, editor*
Rees, James Conway, IV, *historic site administrator*
Spiegel, H. Jay *lawyer*

Naval Base

†Barton, Laura Ann *aerospace experimental psychologist, consultant, researcher*

Nellysford

McWane, Joyce Hobbs *title company executive*
†Pfaltz, Katharine *small business owner, writer*
Sims, John Rogers, Jr., *lawyer*

New Hope

Hough, Michael James *sculptor, educator*

Newport News

Abbott, Beverly Stubblefield *artist*
Banks, Charles Augustus, III, *manufacturing executive*
Behlmar, Cindy Lee *business manager, consultant, speaker*
Booker, Henry Marshall *economics educator*
†Boykin, Amy Williams *librarian*
Buranelli, Vincent John *writer*
Camp, Hazel Lee Burt *artist*
†Clarkson, Stephen Batchelder *lawyer*
†Crane, Martha Beavers *music educator*
Cuthrell, Carl Edward *lawyer, educator, clergyman*
Donaldson, Coleman duPont *aeronautical engineer, consultant, aerospace engineer, consultant*
Eastman, John Robert *educator*
Fusek, Serena Rebecca *poet*
Goldberg, Ivan Baer *real estate executive*
Goldberg, Stanley Irwin *real estate company executive*
†Harris, Charles George *research scientist, consultant*
Hatten, Robert Randolph *lawyer*
Hightower, John Brantley *arts administrator*
Hoffman, Nannette Hertz Schweig *artist, poet, educator*
Hubbard, Harvey Hart *aeroacoustician, noise control engineer, consultant*
Kamp, Arthur Joseph, Jr., *lawyer*
Keator, Margaret Whitley *legislative aide*
Krafft, Geoffrey Arthur *physicist*
†Kyte, Shannan Dyan *multimedia designer*
Laroussi, Mounir *electrical engineer*
Le Mons, Kathleen Ann *securities company executive, investment officer, portfolio manager*
Martin, Terrence Keech *lawyer, city councilor*
Mazur, Rhoda Himmel *community volunteer*
Moore, Mildred Thorpe *dietician*
Nichols, Allen Bryant *physician, cardiologist*
Noblitt, Nancy Anne *aerospace engineer*
Powell, Jouett Lynn *college dean, philosophy and religious studies educator*
Santoro, Anthony Richard *history educator*
Saunders, Bryan Leslie *lawyer*
Segall, James Arnold *lawyer*
Summerville, Richard M. *mathematician, academic administrator*
Thro, William Eugene *lawyer, university administrator*
†Trachuk, Lillian Elizabeth *music educator*
Trible, Paul Seward, Jr., *former United States senator*
Warren, Daniel Churchman *health facility administrator*

Nickelsville

Osborne, Kermit Charles, Jr., *contractor, consultant*

Nokesville

Jaynes, Robert Henry, Jr., *retired military officer*

Norfolk

†Adam, John Anthony *mathematician, educator*
Adams, David Huntington *judge*
Addis, Kay Tucker *newspaper editor*
Ahrari, M. Ehsan *political science educator, researcher, consultant*
Andrews, Mason Cooke *mayor, obstetrician, gynecologist, educator*
Andrews, William Cooke *physician*
Archer, Robert Patrick *psychologist, educator*
Baird, Edward Rouzie, Jr., *lawyer*
Barry, Richard Francis, III, *publishing executive*
Berent, Irwin Mark *writer, software executive*
†Berndt, Martin R. *career officer*
Bishop, Bruce Taylor *lawyer*
Blount, Robert Haddock *corporate executive, retired naval officer*
Bonney, Hal James, Jr., *federal judge*
Braswell, Ronald Lee *music educator, tenor*
†Broadbent, Arthur, III, *music educator*
Bucher, Katherine Toth *education educator, librarian*
Burnette, Thomas N. *career officer*
Carpenter, Dee *publishing executive*
†Cash, Dean W. *military career officer*
Clark, Morton Hutchinson *lawyer*
Clarke, J. Calvitt, Jr., *federal judge*
†Colberg-Ochs, Sheri Renee *physiologist, educator*
Combs, Charles Donald *academic administrator*
†Corrigan, James Joseph, II, *retired lawyer*
Counselman, Francis L. *emergency medicine physician, educator*
Cranford, Page Deronde *lawyer*
Crenshaw, Francis Nelson *retired lawyer*
Cutchins, Clifford Armstrong, III, *banker*
Davis, Russell Haden *consultant*
Davis, Terry Hunter, Jr., *lawyer*
DeVenny, Lillian Nickell *trophy company executive*
DiCroce, Deborah Marie *college president*
Donohue, David Patrick *engineering executive, retired navy rear admiral*
Drescher, John Webb *lawyer*
Dungan, William Joseph, Jr., *insurance broker, economics educator*
†Epplein, Lawrence Elliott *hospitality management educator*
Estes, Edward Richard, Jr., *engineering consultant, engineer, retired educator*
Evans, Rod L. *philosophy educator*
Evett, Russell Dougherty *internist, educator*
Farmer, Evan R. *academic administrator, dermatologist, researcher*
Faulconer, Robert Jamieson *pathologist, educator*
†Fletcher, Thomas D. *psychologist, researcher*
Frieden, Jane Heller *art educator*
†Glasser, Michael A. *lawyer*
Goode, David Ronald *transportation company executive*
Griffin, O. Daniel, Jr., *reporter, writer, photographer, audio engineer, videographer*
Jackson, Raymond A. *federal judge*
Jenson, Hal Brockbank *physician*
†Johnson, Thomas G., Jr., *lawyer*
Jones, Franklin Ross *education educator*
†Kasparov, Andrey R. *composer, pianist, conductor, educator*
†Kent, Susan *anthropologist, educator, anthropologist, researcher*
†Kernan, William Frank *career officer*
Klain, David Richard *naval officer*
Knight, Montgomery, Jr., *lawyer*
Koch, James Verch *academic administrator, economist*
Konetzni, Albert H., Jr., *career officer*
Kubic, Charles Richard *naval officer*
†Land, Charles Edwards *lawyer*
†Lawrence, Joe Gray, Jr., *lawyer*
Leavitt, Sheldon Joseph *civil engineer, architect, consultant*
†LeFever, Gretchen B. *clinical psychologist, educator*
Lester, Richard Garrison *radiologist, educator*
Maly, Kurt John *computer science educator*
Mark, Peter *director, conductor*
†Marr, Richard C. *military officer*
Martin, Wayne A. *clinical social worker*
†Mayo, Alex T., Jr., *lawyer*
McKee, Timothy Carlton *taxation educator*
McKinnon, Arnold Borden *retired transportation company executive*
Meslang, Susan Walker *educational administrator*
Miller, Joseph Aaron *lawyer, musician*
Miller, Tommy Eugene *federal judge*
Miller, Yvonne Bond *state legislator, educator*
Morgan, Henry Coke, Jr., *judge*
Morrison, Ashton Byrom *pathologist, medical school official*
Musgrave, Thea *composer, conductor*
†Myers, Ronald J. *music educator*
†Nixon, Patricia Saunders *music educator, performer*
Noginov, Mikhail A. *physicist, researcher, educator*
Notti, Donna Betts *special education educator*
†Oehninger, Sergio C. *endocrinologist, obstetrician, gynecologist*
Oelberg, David George *neonatologist, educator, researcher*
†Opfer, Steven Earl *education educator, researcher*
Orgel, Vivian August *beauty expert*
Parker, Richard Wilson *lawyer, rail transportation executive*
†Parsons, Rymn James *lawyer*
Pearson, John Yeardley, Jr., *lawyer*
Prince, William Taliaferro *retired federal judge*
Rashkind, Alan Brody *lawyer*
Rephan, Jack *lawyer*
Ritz, John Michael *education educator*
Rogers, Candace Marie *nursing educator*
Rohn, Reuben David *pediatric educator and administrator*
Ruehlmann, William John *communications educator*
Runte, Roseann *academic administrator*
Russell, C. Edward, Jr., *lawyer*
Rutyna, Richard Albert *history educator*
Ryan, John M. *lawyer*
†Sampson, Gayle Vernice *freelance/self-employed writer*
†Samuels, John M., Jr., *industrial engineer*
Sebren, Lucille Griggs *retired educator*
Shannon, John Sanford *lawyer, retired railway executive*
Shaw, Michael Evan *librarian*
Shumadine, Anne Ballard *financial advisor, lawyer*
Sizemore, William Howard, Jr., *journalist*
†Smith, Richard Muldrow *lawyer*
Stallings, Valerie A. *physician, state official*
†Stanley-Brown, Josephine Blanche *entrepreneur, education educator*
Steele, James Eugene *retired school system administrator*
Stepanovich, Paul *management educator*
Strait, Patricia Bellin *organizational management educator*
†Taylor Claud, Andrea *educational consultant*
†Tedrow, Lara Bryan *psychologist*

Tobias, Stephen C. *rail transportation executive*
Train, Harry Depue, II, *retired naval officer*
Valone, James Austin, Jr., *retired surgeon*
Ventker, David Neil *lawyer*
Wall, Curtiss Edwin *mathematician, educator*
†Ware, Guilford Dudley *lawyer*
Wei, Benjamin Min *engineering educator*
Wiltse, James Clark *civil engineer*
Wolcott, Hugh Dixon *obstetrics and gynecology educator*
Zahn, Richard William, Jr., *lawyer*

North
Fang, Joong *philosopher, mathematician, educator*

North Garden
Moses, Hamilton, III, *medical educator, hospital executive, management consultant*

Norton
Jessee, Roy Mark *lawyer*
Vest, Gayle Southworth *obstetrician and gynecologist*
Vest, Steven Lee *gastroenterologist, hepatologist, internist*

Oak Hill
Adler, Dale Atkins *artist*
Okay, John Louis *management consultant*
†Ritter, Elza K. *music educator*

Oakton
Brauer, Gwendolyn Gail *real estate broker*
Curry, Thomas Fortson *electronics engineer, defense industry executive*
†Cutchin, James McKenney, IV, *lawyer, engineer*
Divone, Louis Vincent *aerospace engineer, educator, federal official, author*
Drummond, Carol Cramer *voice educator, singer, artist, writer*
Duesenberg, Robert H. *retired lawyer*
Entzminger, John Nelson, Jr., *federal agency administrator, electronic engineer, researcher*
Farwell, Albert Edmond *retired government official, consultant*
Frost, S. David *retired naval officer*
†MacCracken, Thomas Gregg *musicologist*
Mosemann, Lloyd Kenneth, II, *business executive*
Pratsch, Lloyd Wilmer *government official*
Randolph, Christopher Craven *lawyer*
Rees, Clifford Harcourt, Jr., (Ted Rees) *retired association executive, retired air force officer*
†Steele, Robert David *computer company executive*
Vernava, Anthony Michael *lawyer*
Zhang, Ming *policy analyst*

Occoquan
Nemecek, Albert Duncan, Jr., *retail company executive, investment banker, management consultant*

Onley
Schonfeld, Walter Tibor *retired jewelry importer, writer*

Orange
Burke, Robert Lawrence *consultant*
Daniel, Daniele Mallison *elementary school educator*

Orlean
Kulski, Julian Eugeniusz *architect, planner, educator*

Paeonian Springs
Sloyan, Patrick Joseph *journalist*

Palmyra
Avers, Carl Dennison *computer engineer*
Brown, Nan Marie *clergywoman*
Chapin, Suzanne Phillips *retired psychologist*
Mulckhuyse, Jacob John *retired energy conservation consultant*
Sahr, Morris Gallup *financial planner*

Pearisburg
Morse, F. D., Jr., *dentist*

Penhook
Coar, Richard John *mechanical engineer, aerospace consultant*
Hahn, John William *retired insurance company executive*

Petersburg
†Abbott-Ryan, Pat *painter, writer*
Baskervill, Charles Thornton *lawyer*
Boyd, Herbert Reed, Jr., *dentist*
Brown, Jack D(elbert) *chemist, researcher*
Ende, Milton *internist*
Everitt, Alice Lubin *labor arbitrator*
Garrott, Carl Lee *foreign language educator*
Miles, Ruby Williams *secondary education educator*
Rosenstock, Louis Anthony, III, *lawyer*
Ryan, James Herbert *retired security and retail services company executive*
Spero, Morton Bertram *retired lawyer*
Stronach, Carey Elliott *physicist, educator*
Watkins, Sherry Ligon *medical facility data executive, nurse*
†White, William Earle *lawyer*
Wilson, John Robert, Jr., *pharmaceutical and chemical company executive*

Philomont
Conte, Joseph John, II, *meteorologist, management consultant*

Poquoson
Holloway, Paul Fayette *retired aerospace executive*
Parry, Thomas Herbert, Jr., *school system administrator, educational consultant*

Tai, Elizabeth Shi-Jue Lee *library director*

Portsmouth
Brennan, John William *lawyer, real estate broker*
Clare, Frank Brian *neurosurgeon, neurologist*
Eaton, James Alonza *humanities educator*
†Lavin, Barbara Hofheins *lawyer*
Mapp, Alf Johnson, Jr., *writer, historian*
Mintz, Susan Ashinoff *apparel manufacturing company executive*
Moody, Willard James, Sr., *lawyer*
Nolen, Crystal Me'Kelle *poet, educator*
O'Malley, Timothy Patrick *otolaryngologist*
†Paquette, William Arthur *historian, educator*
Porter, J. Ridgely, III, *lawyer*
Williams, Lena Harding *educational administrator*
Yarbrough, Terry Pinckney *physician*

Potomac Falls
Merna, Gerald Francis *advertising executive, retired marine officer, retired postal executive*

Prince George
Dent, Edward Eugene *manufacturing company specialist*
Farrar, Andrew Lockett *agricultural education educator*

Providence Forge
Richardson, William Winfree, III, *lawyer*

Pulaski
McCarthy, Thomas James, Jr., *lawyer*

Purcellville
Christ, Thomas Warren *electronics research and development company executive, sociologist*
Sharples, Winston Singleton *automobile importer and distributor*

Quantico
Akst, George *operations analyst, mathematician*
Cann, John Pearce, III, *educator*
Harmon, Christopher C. *international relations educator, writer*
Harrington, Jeffrey Michael *military officer*
†Howard, Patrick Gene *marine corps officer*
Mangan, Terence Joseph *federal agency professional, retired protective services official*
Sanftleben, Kurt Allen *career officer*

Radford
Camphouse, Mark David *music educator, composer, conductor*
Carter, Kimberly Ferren *nursing educator*
Davis, Richard Waters *lawyer*
†du Plessis, Eric Hollingsworth *literature educator, language educator*
James, Clarity (Carolyne Faye James) *mezzo-soprano*
Kessler, Kendall Seay Feriozi *artist*
McNeil, Ramsey English *religious studies educator*
†Phillips, David B. *music educator, composer*
Scartelli, Joseph Paul *music therapy educator, dean*
Templeton, Dennie, III, *educational administrator, consultant*
Turk, James Clinton, Jr., *lawyer*

Rapidan
Grimm, Ben Emmet *former library director and consultant*
Powers, Evelyn Mae *education educator*

Raven
Joyce, Larry Wayne *physician*

Restan
Phillippi, Elmer Joseph, Jr., *data communications consultant*

Reston
Bredehoft, Elaine Charlson *lawyer*
Brennan, Norma Jean *professional society publications director*
Brooker, Susan Gay *employment consulting firm executive*
Brown, James Robert *retired air force officer*
†Carroll, Terence Evan *professional society administrator*
Cerf, Vinton Gray *telecommunications company executive*
Chattman, Raymond Christopher *foundation executive*
Choi, Michael Kamwah *aerospace engineer, mechanical engineer, researcher*
Christian, Eliot Jordan *federal agency administrator, computer specialist*
Clapp, Stephen Caswell *journalist*
Coulter-Harris, Deborah Marcella *government analyst*
Cramond, Richard, Jr., *structural and systems engineer, diversified aerospace company executive*
Crawford, Lawrence Robert *aviation and aerospace consultant*
Davy, William Allen *account executive*
Deremer, Susan René *artist*
Donahue, Timothy M. *communications executive*
Easton, Glenn Hanson, Jr., *management and insurance consultant, federal official, naval officer*
†Evan, Bryan J. *electronics executive*
Ewell, Dena Lynette *administrative management executive*
Foster, William Anthony *management consultant, educator*
Fox, Edward A. *business executive*
Gates, James David *retired association executive, consultant*
Gorog, William Francis *corporate executive*
Groat, Charles George *geologist, science administrator*
Harmon, Robert Gerald *health company executive, educator*

Harris, Paul Lynwood *retired aerospace transportation executive*
Harvey, Aubrey Eaton, III, *industrial engineer*
Hepworth-Woolston, Connie Jo *choreographer*
Hill, Jim Tom *retired consulting firm executive*
Holthausen, Martha Anne *interior designer, painter*
Hope, Samuel Howard *accreditation organization executive*
Kader, Nancy Stowe *nurse, consultant, bioethicist*
†Kahn, Robert E. *electrical engineer*
Keefe, James Washburn *educational writer, researcher, consultant*
Kramish, Arnold *physicist, historian, author*
Kreyling, Edward George, Jr., *railroad executive*
Lanfear, Kenneth Joseph *engineering administrator, hydrologist*
Levner, Louis Jules *contract administrator*
Lowell, Bret *lawyer*
†Mahlmann, John James *music education association administrator*
Maitland, Guy Edison Clay *lawyer*
Mendelsohn, Stuart *lawyer, elected official*
Menzie, William David, II, *geologist, educator*
Miller, John Edward *army officer, technology executive, educational administrator*
Miller, Lynne Marie *environmental company executive*
Minton, Joseph Paul *retired safety organization executive*
Mitchell, Ellen Clabaugh *investment executive*
Mowbray, Robert Norman *natural resource management consultant, forest ecologist*
Naylon, Michael Edward *retired army officer*
Norris, Susan Elizabeth *social worker*
O'Brien, Morgan Edward *communications executive, lawyer*
Palumbo, James Fredrick *financial services company executive*
Payne, Roger Lee *geographer*
Peck, Dallas Lynn *retired geologist*
†Picard, Dennis J. *retired electronics company executive*
Platt, Leslie A. *lawyer*
Plum, Kenneth Ray *state legislator*
Polemitou, Olga Andrea *accountant*
Powell, Anne Elizabeth *editor*
Rau, Lee Arthur *lawyer*
Robey, Constance Rhind *marketing professional*
Salisbury, Alan Blanchard *information systems executive*
Sarreals, Sonia *data processing consultant*
Scharff, Joseph Laurent *lawyer*
Scheeler, James Arthur *architect*
Schick, Michael William *public relations executive*
Schleede, Glenn Roy *energy market and policy consultant*
Smith, Ralph Lee *author, musician*
Thayer, Edwin Cabot *musician*
Toole, John Harper *lawyer*
Van Putten, Mark *environmentalist*
Walton, Edmund Lewis, Jr., *lawyer*
Wilkinson, Edward Anderson, Jr., *retired naval officer, business executive*

Richlands
†Claytor, Katherine W. Moss *secondary education educator*
Stefanini, Mario *physician, pathologist*

Richmond
Accardo, Pasquale J. *pediatrician, educator*
Addison, David Dunham *lawyer*
Adiele, Moses Nkwachukwu *state official*
Aghdami, Farhad *lawyer*
Aigner, Emily Burke *Christian lay minister*
Aiken, Peter Haynes *systems engineer, educator*
Allen, Wilbur Coleman *lawyer*
Anderson, Frederick Jarrard *historian*
Anderson, Patricia Coulter *paralegal*
†Anutta, Lucile Jamison *lawyer*
†Archer, Kellie Jo *education educator*
Ashe, Reid *publishing executive*
Ayres, Stephen McClintock *physician, educator*
†Bagley, Philip Joseph, III, *lawyer*
†Baker, Julie Ann *language educator*
Baliles, Gerald L. *lawyer, former governor*
Balster, Robert Louis *psychopharmacologist*
Barker, Thomas Carl *retired health care administration educator, executive*
Barton, Jonathan Miller *clergyman*
Bates, Hampton Robert, Jr., *pathologist*
Beaman, Mary Anina *psychiatric nurse, educator*
Becker, Herman Eli *retired pharmacist*
Beckett, Joyce *educator, social worker*
Belcher, Dennis Irl *lawyer*
Bentley, Kia Jean *social worker, educator*
Berry, Boyd McCulloch *English educator*
Bickerstaff, Patsy Anne *judge, writer, poet*
Bing, Richard McPhail *lawyer*
Black, Robert Perry *retired banker, executive*
Blank, Florence Weiss *literacy educator, editor*
Blumberg, Michael Zangwill *allergist*
Blumberg, Peter Steven *manufacturing company executive*
Bohannan, Jay Kirby *artist*
Bohannon, Sarah Virginia *personnel professional*
†Bonfiglio, Thomas Paul *literature and linguistics educator*
Booker, Lewis Thomas *lawyer*
†Boone, David Eason *lawyer*
Boone, Elwood Bernard, Jr., *physician, urologist*
Boudinot, Frank Douglas *dean*
Brackenridge, N. Lynn *not-for-profit developer*
Braeckmans, Paul *advertising executive*
Brasfield, Evans Booker *lawyer*
†Bray, Patricia Shannon *music educator, musician, small business owner*
†Broadbent, Peter Edwin, Jr., *lawyer*
Broaddus, John Alfred, Jr., *bank executive, economist*
Brockenbrough, Henry Watkins *lawyer*
Brooks, Robert Franklin, Sr., *lawyer*
Bryan, John Stewart, III, *newspaper publisher*
Bryan, Lisa Margaret Stevenson *volunteer*

Budd, Richard Wade *university official, communications scientist, priest*
Buffenstein, Allan S. *lawyer*
Buford, Robert Pegram *lawyer*
Bunzl, Rudolph Hans *retired manufacturing executive*
Burke, John K(irkland), Jr., *lawyer*
Burner, Clara Miller *librarian*
Burrus, Robert Lewis, Jr., *lawyer*
†Burtch, Jack Willard, Jr., *lawyer*
Butler, Donald K. *lawyer*
Cafaro, Patricia L. *nurse practitioner, nurse, clinical administrator*
Campbell, Neal Franklin *music educator*
Campbell, Thomas Corwith, Jr., *economics educator*
Cantor, Irvin Victor *lawyer*
Canup, James W.C. *lawyer*
Capps, Thomas Edward *utilities company executive, lawyer*
Carlton, Buzz (Clyde Gordon Carlton Jr.) *singer, songwriter, entertainer, recording artist*
†Carr, Marcus Eugene, Jr., *internist*
Carrell, Daniel Allan *lawyer*
Carrico, Harry Lee *retired judge*
Carter, Joseph Carlyle, Jr., *lawyer*
†Casini, Jane Sloan *wholesale distribution executive*
Catlett, Richard H., Jr., *retired lawyer*
Charlesworth, Arthur Thomas *mathematics and computer science educator*
Chichester, John H. *state legislator*
Christenbury, Leila *education educator*
Ciulla, Joanne Bridgett *business ethics educator*
Clinard, Robert Noel *lawyer*
Cohn, David Stephen *lawyer*
Compton, Asbury Christian *state supreme court justice*
Compton, Olin Randall *consulting electrical engineer, researcher*
†Coogle, Constance L. *gerontology educator, researcher*
Cooper, William Edwin *university president, educator*
†Cross, John Robert *retired telecommunications industry executive, travel consultant*
†Croushore, Dean Darrell *economist*
†Curley, John J. *diversified media company executive*
Cutchins, Clifford Armstrong, IV, *lawyer*
Dabney, H. Slayton, Jr., *lawyer*
†Danilkovitch, Alla *research scientist*
David, Ronald Brian *child neurologist*
†DeCamps, Charles Michael *lawyer*
DeLorenzo, Robert John *neurologist, molecular neuroscientist*
†Dennis, Shay *social worker*
Denny, Collins, III, *lawyer*
Dessypris, Emmanuel Nicholas *hematologist-oncologist*
DeWitt, Brydon Merrill *development consultant*
Dilworth, Robert Lexow *career military officer, educator*
†Doarn, Charles R. *medical educator*
Dombalis, Constantine Nicholas *minister, writer*
Dotson, Donald L. *lawyer*
Downs, Robert Woodward, Jr., *endocrinologist, researcher*
Drain, Cecil B. *university dean, nurse anesthetist educator, retired army officer*
Dray, Mark S. *lawyer*
Dunn, Leo James *obstetrician, educator, gynecologist, educator*
Dye, David Ray *tax accountant, financial advisor*
Edmonds, Thomas Andrew *legal association administrator*
Ellis, Andrew Jackson, Jr., *lawyer*
Ellis, Anthony John *education educator*
Elmore, Edward Whitehead *lawyer*
Epperson, Wallace W., Jr., *investment banker*
Fenn, John Bennett *chemist, educator*
Fischer, Carl Robert *retired health care facility administrator*
Fisher, Edgar Jacob, Jr., *religious organization administrator*
Fletcher, Paul Edwin, III, *publishing executive, editor-in-chief*
Flippen, Edward L. *lawyer*
†Framme, Lawrence Henry, III, *political organization administrator, lawyer*
Franko, Bernard Vincent *pharmacologist, educator*
†Frazer, Susan Hume *independent scholar and consultant*
Freed, David Clark *artist*
†Freeman, George Clemon, Jr., *lawyer*
Freund, Emma Frances *medical technologist*
Gad-el-Hak, Mohamed *aerospace and mechanical engineering educator, scientist*
†Galbis-Reig, David *health facility administrator, physician, consultant, researcher*
Gandy, Gerald Larmon *rehabilitation counseling educator, psychologist, writer*
Gary, Richard David *lawyer*
Geary, David Patrick *criminal justice educator, consultant, writer*
†Gehr, Lynne Connolly *anesthesiologist*
Gilinsky, Stanley Ellis *department store executive*
†Girone, Joan Christine Cruse *realtor, former county official*
Goodpasture, Philip Henry *lawyer*
Goodykoontz, Charles Alfred *newspaper editor, retired*
†Goolsby, Allen Cunningham, III, *lawyer*
Gordon, John L., Jr., *historian, educator*
Gorr, Louis Frederick *investment consultant*
Gottwald, Floyd Dewey, Jr., *chemical company executive*
Graham, Sam Dixon *urologist*
Graves, H. Brice *retired lawyer*
†Gray, C. Michael *food products executive*
Gregory, Jean Winfrey *ecologist, educator*
Gregory, Roger Lee *federal judge*
Gwin, James Ellsworth *librarian*
Hackney, Virginia Howitz *lawyer*

Hager, John Henry *state official, former lieutenant governor*
Hall, James H(errick), Jr., *philosophy educator, writer*
Hall, Stephen Charles *lawyer*
Hamel, Dana Bertrand *academic administrator*
Hamlett, Robert Barksdale *systems engineer*
Hammel, Alice Maxine *music educator*
Hardy, Richard Earl *rehabilitation counseling educator*
Harris, Louis Selig *pharmacologist, researcher*
Harris, Ruth Hortense Coles *retired accounting educator*
Hassell, Leroy Rountree, Sr., *state supreme court chief justice*
†Heilman, E. Bruce *academic administrator*
Helwig, Arthur Woods *chemical company executive*
Hettrick, George Harrison *lawyer*
†Hicks, Douglas A. *religious studies educator, minister*
Hoffer, George E. *economist, educator*
†Holmes Martin, Norma Anne *electronic and computer consultant, web site designer, writer*
Horsley, Waller Holladay *lawyer*
Hoskie, Lorraine *consumer products representative, poet*
Howell, George Cook, III, *lawyer*
†Howell, William James *state legislator*
Hull, Rita Prizler *retired accounting educator*
Hunt, Ronald J. *academic administrator*
Huntsinger, Jerald E. *advertising executive*
†Jacobs, Harry Milburn, Jr., *advertising executive*
James, Allix Bledsoe *retired university president*
Jamgochian, Victoria *interior designer*
Jandl, Henry Anthony *architect, educator*
Joel, William Lee, II, *interior and lighting designer*
Johnson, Katherine Anne *health research administrator, lawyer*
Jones, Catesby Brooke *retired banker*
Jones, Jeanne Pitts *pre-school administrator*
Jones-Atkins, DeBorah Kaye *state official*
Kaine, Timothy M. *lieutenant governor*
Kaplowitz, Lisa Glauser *physician, educator*
Kay, Saul *retired pathologist*
Kearfott, Joseph Conrad *lawyer*
†Kellett, Janet *telecommunications industry executive, educator*
Kevorkian, Richard *artist*
Kilgore, Jerry *state attorney general*
King, Robert Leroy *business administration educator*
†King, William H., Jr., *lawyer*
Kinser, Cynthia D. *state supreme court justice*
†Kok, Lai Chow *physician, medical educator*
Lacy, Elizabeth Bermingham *state supreme court justice*
†Landin, David Craig *lawyer*
Laskin, Daniel M. *oral and maxillofacial surgeon, educator*
Lawrence, Walter, Jr., *surgeon, educator*
Ledbetter, David Oscar *lawyer*
Lee, Peter James *bishop*
Lemons, Donald W. *state supreme court justice*
Levit, Héloïse B. (Ginger Levit) *art historian, art dealer, journalist, art consultant, journalist*
Levit, Jay J(oseph) *lawyer*
Ligare, Kathleen Meredith *strategy and marketing executive*
Lilly, Arnys Clifton, Jr., *physicist*
Lingerfelt, Alan Thomas *civil engineer, real estate executive*
Linkonis, Suzanne Newbold *probation officer, counselor*
Lohuis, Ardyth June *musician, educator*
Long, Stephen Paul *anesthesiologist*
Ludden, George Clemens *engineer*
Luo, Shawn Haisheng *retail company executive*
Malone, Nicholas Sherlon *systems analyst, consultant*
Mann, Stephen Ashby *financial counselor*
†Marciano-Cabral, Francine M. *microbiology and immunology educator, protozoologist*
Mast, Rick *race car driver*
Mattauch, Robert Joseph *electrical engineering educator*
Mauck, Henry Page, Jr., *medical and pediatrics educator*
McCarthy, Charles R. *bioethicist, consultant*
McClard, Jack Edward *lawyer*
McCollough, W. Alan *electronics retail executive*
†McCollum, Rudolph C., Jr., *mayor*
McFarlane, Walter Alexander *lawyer, educator*
McGhee, Annette Booker *educator*
Merhige, Robert Reynold, Jr., *lawyer*
Merrell, Ronald Clifton *surgeon, educator*
Meyer, Brian Lee *psychologist*
†Mezzullo, Louis Albert *lawyer*
†Miles, Donna Jones *education educator*
Miles, Donna Regina *educator, researcher*
†Miller, Lewis Nelson, Jr., *banker*
Milme, Patrick Joseph *retired lawyer*
Minardi, Richard A., Jr., *lawyer*
Minor, Marian Thomas *elementary and secondary school educational consultant*
Mollen, Edward Leigh *pediatrician, allergist and clinical immunologist*
Moore, Andrew Taylor, Jr., *banker*
Moore, John Sterling, Jr., *retired minister*
Moore, Thurston Roach *lawyer*
†Moss, Tony Tyrone *mathematician*
Murdoch-Kitt, Norma Hood *clinical psychologist*
Musick, Robert Lawrence, Jr., *lawyer*
Nagle, David Edward *lawyer, columnist*
Narula, Subhash Chander *management science and statistics educator*
Neal, Gail Fallon *physical therapist, educator*
Neal, Marcus Pinson, Jr., *radiologist, medical educator*
Neifeld, James Paul *surgical oncologist*
†Neufeld, Jacob A. *pediatrician, psychiatrist*
Newsome, Heber H. *academic administrator*
O'Keeffe, Charles B. *pharmaceutical executive*
O'Neal, Robert Steven *criminologist, consultant, judge*
†Osgood, Nancy Jean *college educator, author*

Owen, Duncan Shaw, Jr., *physician, medical educator*
Owens, Arne Wesley *systems analyst*
Palen, J(oseph) John *sociology educator*
Parham, Iris Ann *gerontology educator*
Pasco, Hansell Merrill *retired lawyer*
†Patterson, Robert Hobson, Jr., *lawyer*
†Pauley, Stanley Frank *manufacturing company executive*
Payne, William Sanford *insurance company executive*
†Pearsall, John Wesley *lawyer*
Petera, Anne Pappas *state official*
Petrie, Paul Eric *interior design educator*
Phillips, James Dixon *mediator, consultant, educator*
Phillips, Thomas Edworth, Jr., *financial advisor, investment mangement consultant*
Pinckney, Charles Cotesworth *lawyer*
Poff, Richard Harding *retired state supreme court justice*
Pollard, Overton Price *state agency executive, lawyer*
Pope, Robert Dean *lawyer*
Powell, Kenneth Edward *investment banker*
Powell, Lewis Franklin, III, *lawyer*
Putney, Lacey Edward *state legislator*
Rada, Heath Kenneth *social service organization executive*
Rainey, Gordon Fryer, Jr., *lawyer*
†Raper, Mark Irvin *public relations executive*
Ravaux-Kirkpatrick, Francoise *language professional*
Reed, Austin F. *lawyer*
Reed, Christopher Robert *civil engineer*
Richardson, David Walthall *cardiologist, educator, consultant*
Riddick, Joseph Robert *health analyst, columnist*
†Riehl, Jeffrey S. *music educator*
Rigsby, Linda Flory *lawyer*
Rilling, John Robert *history educator*
Rimler, Anita A. *secretary of state*
Robinson, John Victor *lawyer*
†Robinson, Thomas Hart *lawyer, educator*
Rogers, Isabel Wood *retired theological educator*
Rolfe, Robert Martin *lawyer*
Rowe, James William, Sr., *engineer*
†Rowe, William L. S. *lawyer*
Rucker, Douglas Pendleton, Jr., *lawyer*
Rudlin, David Alan *lawyer*
†Ryland, Walter H. *lawyer*
†Safo, Martin K. *research scientist, educator*
Savedge, Anne Creery *artist, photographer*
Schaar, Susan Clarke *state legislative staff member*
Scott, George Cole, III, *investment advisor*
Scott, Sidney Buford *financial services company executive*
Seals, Margaret Louise *newspaper editor*
†Sedaghat, Hassan *mathematician, educator*
Sharer, John Daniel *lawyer*
†Sheehan, Jeremiah J. *former metal company executive*
Sheehan, Kathy Renee *quality improvement administrator*
†Shields, William Gilbert *lawyer*
Sirica, Alphonse Eugene *pathology educator*
Slater, Thomas Glascock, Jr., *lawyer*
Slaughter, Alexander Hoke *lawyer*
†Smith, Julious Perry, Jr., *lawyer*
Smith, R. Gordon *lawyer*
Smith, Ted Jay, III, *mass communications educator*
Smolla, Rodney Alan *lawyer, educator, dean*
Sneed, Jimmy *chef, restaurant owner*
Snellings, Eleanor Craig *retired economics educator*
Sobin, Rodney *technology analyst*
Solan, Stuart Miley *physician*
Spahn, Gary Joseph *lawyer*
†Sper, Jane *lawyer*
Sprinkle, William Melvin *audio-acoustical engineer, engineering administrator*
Starke, Harold E., Jr., *lawyer*
†Street, Walter Scott, III, *lawyer*
Strickland, William Jesse *lawyer*
†Su, Lianyong *research scientist*
Sugerman, Harvey Jay *surgery educator*
Talley, Charles Richmond *commercial banking executive*
Thomas, John Charles *lawyer, former state supreme court justice*
Thompson, Francis Neal *financial services consultant*
Thompson, Paul Michael *lawyer*
Thornhill, Barbara Cole *marketing executive*
Tice, Douglas Oscar, Jr., *federal bankruptcy judge*
Tiedemann, Albert William, Jr., *retired chemist*
Totten, Arthur Irving, Jr., *retired metals company executive, consultant*
†Totten, Randolph Fowler *lawyer*
Trani, Eugene Paul *university president, educator*
Treadway, Sandra Gioia *library director*
Trott, Sabert Scott, II, *marketing professional, consultant*
Troy, Anthony Francis *lawyer*
Tuck, Grayson Edwin *real estate agent, former natural gas transmission executive*
Tunner, William Sams *urological surgeon*
Turner, Elaine S. *allergist, immunologist*
Tuszynski, Daniel J., Jr., *sales, management and marketing consultant*
Urelius, Shawn Renea *lawyer*
†Urofsky, Melvin Irving *historian, educator, director*
Vaughn, Ann Marie *art educator, artist*
†Vijayaraman, Pugazhendhi *medical educator*
†Waddell, William Robert *lawyer*
Walsh, James Hamilton *lawyer*
Walsh, William Arthur, Jr., *lawyer*
Walton, G. Clifford *family practice physician*
Ward, Harry Merrill *history educator*
Ward, John Wesley *retired pharmacologist*
†Warner, Mark R. *governor*
†Warthen, Harry Justice, III, *lawyer*

Washburn, John Rosser *entrepreneur*
Watkins, Hays Thomas *retired railroad executive*
†Wellford, Hill B., Jr., *lawyer*
Wenzel, Richard Putnam *internist*
White, Hugh Vernon, Jr., *lawyer*
White, Kenneth Ray *health administration educator, consultant*
White, Morris Fred, Jr., *physicist*
Whitlock, Julie Marie *lawyer*
†Wight, Jonathan B. *economist, educator*
Wilder, L(awrence) Douglas *former governor*
Wilkinson, David Stanley *pathologist, consultant, researcher, educator, physician*
Williams, Karen Johnson *federal judge*
Williams, Richard Leroy *federal judge*
†Williamson, Thomas W., Jr., *lawyer*
Winkler, Katherine Maurine *management consultant, educator*
Winslett, Stoner *artistic director*
Wise, Christopher Murray *internist, rheumatologist*
Witt, Walter Francis, Jr., *lawyer*
Wood, Jeanne Clarke *charitable organization executive*
Wooten, Joan Hedrich *minister*
Wright, Wiley Reed, Jr., *lawyer, retired judge, mediator*

Roanoke
Barnhill, David Stan *lawyer*
Bates, Harold Martin *lawyer*
Beagle, Benjamin Stuart, Jr., *columnist*
Blaiklock, Paul Musgrave *marketing consultant*
Blanar, George J. *business development executive*
Blevins, Adrian Ellen *writer, educator*
Butler, Manley Caldwell *retired lawyer*
†Castellani, Lawrence P. *automotive company executive*
†Cirasunda, Esther Bond *librarian*
†Claytor, Katharine Draney *human resources executive*
Cole, Evelyn Marie *day care administrator*
Dagenhart, Betty Jane Mahaffey *nursing educator, administrator*
Densmore, Douglas Warren *lawyer*
Duff, Doris Eileen (Doris Shull) *critical care nurse*
Easterling, Eddie Jean *publisher*
Effel, Laura *lawyer*
†Farnham, David Alexander *lawyer*
Fishwick, John Palmer *retired lawyer, retired railroad executive*
Fitzgerald, Mary Eileen *museum program director*
Garrett, Lee (Homer Simmons Holcomb) *retired broadcaster*
Glenn, Robert Eastwood *lawyer*
Goad, Danny Harlan *mechanical engineer*
Harris, Bayard Easter *lawyer*
†Harrison, David George *lawyer*
Hartless, Keith D. *music educator*
Hudick, Andrew Michael, II, *finance executive*
Hutcheson, Jack Robert *hematologist, medical oncologist*
Hylton, Myles Talbert *lawyer*
Jennings, James Wilson, Jr., *lawyer*
Johnson, Julia Mae *literature educator, poet*
Kennedy, Stephen Smith *hematologist, oncologist, educator*
Kinzie, Brenda Asburry *counselor*
Landis, John William *engineering and construction executive, government advisor*
†Larkin, Peter S. *legislative aid*
Lemon, William Jacob *lawyer*
†Livingston, Jeffrey Charles *obstetrician, gynecologist*
MacLean, Iain Stewart *minister, educator*
†Marshall, Heman Alexander, III, *lawyer*
McKenna, John Dennis *environmental testing engineer*
Milam, Michael Ray *music educator*
Mundy, Gardner Marshall *lawyer*
Osterhaus, Greg S. *artist, graphic designer*
Reese, Joan Carol *mediator, consultant, coach*
Sandidge, June Carol *retired physical education educator*
Schlegel, Beverly Faye *private club administrator*
Sitton, Michael *musician, educator*
†Stadler, Donald Arthur *management engineer*
†Steele, Anita Martin (Margaret Anne Martin) *law librarian, legal educator*
Turk, James Clinton *federal judge*
Vermillion, Robert Lee *obstetrician, gynecologist*
Warren, William Kermit *retired media company executive*
Woodrum, Clifton A., III, *lawyer, state legislator*
Woods, Walter Ralph *retired agricultural scientist, administrator*
Zomparelli, Wendy *newspaper publisher*

Roseland
Arey, William Griffin, Jr., *former government official*
Stemmler, Edward Joseph *physician, retired association executive, retired academic dean*
Wood, Maurice *medical educator*

Rosslyn
McCarthy, Michael James *military intelligence officer*

Round Hill
Bergeman, George William *mathematics educator, software author*
Gunberg, Edwin Woodrow, Jr., *counseling psychologist, consultant, researcher*

Saint Paul
Gregory, Ann Young *editor, publisher*

Salem
Brand, Edward Cabell *retail executive*
Cartwright, Keith Allen *literature educator*
†Crowder, Rebecca Byrum *music educator, elementary school educator*

Fisher, Charles Harold *chemistry educator, researcher*
†Griffith, H(oward) Morgan *lawyer*
Koontz, Lawrence L., Jr., *state supreme court justice*
Pearson, Henry Clyde *retired judge*
Ramsey, Lloyd Brinkley *retired savings and loan executive, retired army officer*
Shaffner, Patrick Noel *retired architectural engineering executive*
Weiss, Gregory Lee *sociology educator*

Sandston
†Zhao, Wei (Wayne) *materials scientist, researcher*

Schley
McVey, Henry Hanna, III, *retired lawyer*

Sedley
Briggs, Martha Wren *publishing executive, writer*

Smithfield
Luter, Joseph Williamson, III, *meat packing and processing company executive*

South Hill
Clay, Carol Ann *family nurse practitioner*

Spotsylvania
Clower, William Dewey *retired trade association executive*
Hardy, Dorcas Ruth *business and government relations executive*
Kozloski, Lillian Terese D. *history of aerospace technology educator*
Lipscomb, Stephen Leon *retired mathematician*
Manthei, Richard Dale *retired lawyer, health care company executive*
Orsini, Eric Andrew *army official*

Springfield
Adams, William B. *author, inventor, educator, consultant , columnist, communications executive, systems architect*
Bartlow, Gene Steven *association executive, retired air force officer*
†Basham, W. Ralph *federal agency administrator*
Bentz, Edward Joseph, Jr., *energy, environment and transportation management consulting firm executive*
Bowen, Harry Ernest *management consultant*
Bruen, John Dermot *executive consultant*
Casazza, John Andrew *electrical engineer, business executive, educator*
Chappell, Milton Leroy *lawyer*
Chatelier, Paul Richard *aviation psychologist, training company officer*
Costello, Daniel Brian *lawyer, consultant*
Dake, Marcia Allene *retired nursing educator, university dean*
†Doran, Doris Jeanne *librarian*
Eastman, Donna Kelly *composer, music educator*
Edwards-LeBoeuf, Renee Camille *public relations professional, logistics engineer*
†Eley, Randall Robbi *lawyer*
Englert, Roy Theodore *lawyer*
Fedewa, Lawrence John *management consulting firm executive, entrepreneur*
Franklin, Jude Eric *electronics executive*
Galvin, Cyril Jerome, Jr., *coastal engineer*
Green, Gerald *editor, consultant*
Hillis, John David *television news executive, producer, writer*
Hunt, Robert Gayle *former government official*
Hyland, Patricia Ann (Pat Hyland) *writer*
Igo, Donald James *economist*
Insalaco-De Nigris, Anna Maria Theresa *middle school educator*
Jones, Bonnie Damschroder *government agency administrator*
Kratovil, Jane Lindley *think tank associate, developer/fundraiser*
†Kropp, Edward H. *education educator, consultant*
LaJeunesse, Raymond John, Jr., *lawyer*
Larson, Reed Eugene *foundation administrator*
Lautzenheiser, Marvin Wendell *computer software engineer*
Leake, Charles Robert *systems analyst, educator*
†Leavitt, Mary Janice Deimel *special education educator, civic worker*
Long, Clarence Dickinson, III, *lawyer*
Meikle, Philip G. *engineer, retired government agency executive*
Nelson, Kimberly Susan *not-for-profit fundraiser*
Quick, Danny Richard *computer systems engineer*
Rankin, Jacqueline Annette *communications expert, educator*
Roberts, Paul Franklin, II, *financial executive*
Schlegelmilch, Reuben Orville *electrical engineer, consultant*
Stottlemyer, David Lee *government official*
Taylor, John Darryl *computer scientist*
Thompson, Morris Mordecai *civil engineer, researcher, consultant*
†Townsend, Joachim Rudiger (Jack Townsend) *lawyer*
Watts, Helena Roselle *military analyst*
Williams, Cecilia Lee Pursel *optometrist*

Stafford
Haddock, Raymond Earl *career officer*
Kline, Denny Lee *hazardous devices and explosives consultant*
Lambert, Linda Margaret *reading specialist*
Sedlak, James William *organization administrator*
Tallent, Robert Glenn *chemical and environmental engineer, entrepreneur*
Williams, Carlisle M., Jr., *municipal official*

Stanardsville
Anns, Philip Harold *international trading executive, former pharmaceutical company executive*

GEOGRAPHICAL INDEX 6099 VIRGINIA

Keel, Alton Gold, Jr., *ambassador*

Staunton
†Arnold, Ruth Southgate *librarian*
Balsley, Philip Elwood *entertainer*
Cook, Clarence Edgar *research facility scientist*
Dixon, Corbin *retired electrical engineer, conservationist*
Grewe, Marjorie Jane *protective services official*
Hagen, Agnes Mary *adult education educator, writer*
Hammaker, Paul M. *retail executive, business educator, author*
Huffer, Melissa Wynne Clem *accountant*
Kopp, George Philip, Jr., *minister*
†Metraux, Daniel Alfred *humanities educator*
Mohn, Stephen Michael *commodity manager*
Smith, Rodney Wike *engineering executive*

Stephens City
†Amos, George *music educator, coach*
Stephenson, Richard Walter *librarian, historian, geographer*

Stephenson
Johnson, Eva Maria *retired translator*

Sterling
Baskir, Geoffrey Scott *airport planner*
Bennett, William Leo, Jr., *management consultant*
Bernal-Labrada, Emilio *writer, poet, translator*
Block, Robert Michael *endodontist, educator, researcher*
Blum, John Curtis *agricultural economist*
†Bridwell, Carolyn Elizabeth *elementary school educator*
Clegg, Roger Burton *lawyer*
Cleveland, Harlan *political scientist, public affairs executive*
Coulter, David Creswell *research engineer*
Friedheim, Jerry Warden *museum consultant*
Gilbert, Douglas Brainerd *management executive*
Heberling, Timothy Alan *information scientist*
Jaffe, Russell Merritt *pathologist, research director*
Jefferson, Sandra Traylor *choreographer, ballet coach*
Martin, Roger John *computer scientist*
Munger, Paul David *company executive, educational administrator*
Oller, William Maxwell *retired energy company executive, retired naval officer*
Piper, Thomas Samuel *minister, consultant*
Port, Arthur Tyler *retired government administrator, lawyer*
Sanfelici, Arthur H(ugo) *editor, writer*
†Thompson, David Walker *astronautics company executive*

Stuart
Coleman, Lawrence Gerald, II, *music educator*
Sadler, Elliott *race car driver*

Suffolk
Birdsong, George Yancy *manufacturing company executive*
Carroll, George Joseph *pathologist, educator*
†Glasson, Linda *hospital security and safety official, healthcare*
Hall, Wayne Michael *management consultant*
Hines, Angus Irving, Jr., *petroleum marketing executive*
Holloway, Christopher Matthew *brokerage house executive*
Hope, James Franklin *mayor, civil engineer, consultant*
Sorensen, Carl Edward *company executive*
Young, Hubert Howell, Jr., *lawyer, real estate investor and developer*

Sumerduck
McCamy, Sharon Grove *English educator*

Surry
Sprouse, Earlene Pentecost *special education educator*

Susan
Ambach, Dwight Russell *retired foreign service officer*

Sweet Briar
Green, Jonathan David *music educator, composer, conductor*
Grubbs, Judith Evans *classical studies educator*
Miller, Reuben George *economics educator*
Piepho, Lee (Edward Lee Piepho) *humanities educator*
Shea, Brent Mack *social sciences educator*
Wassell, Stephen Robert *mathematics educator, researcher*

Swoope
Avery, Robert Newell *sculptor*

Syria
†Altaffer, Lawrence F., III, *retired physician, artist*

Tazewell
Garner, June Brown *journalist*
†Mullins, Roger Wayne *lawyer*
Weeks, Ross Leonard, Jr., *museum executive*

The Plains
Gibbons, John Howard Howard (Jack Gibbons) *government official, physicist*

Toano
Carlson, David Emil *physicist, researcher*

Triangle
†Roach, Edward James *historian*

Tysons Corner
Hogue, Dale Curtis, Sr., *lawyer*

Upperville
†Powell Gebhard, Joy Lee (Bok Sin Lee) *small business owner, importer*
Smart, Edith Merrill *civic worker*
Smart, Stephen Bruce, Jr., *business and government executive*

Urbanna
†Garey, Francis Benjamin *retired merchant banker*
Salley, John Jones *university administrator, oral pathologist*

Vienna
Abbott, Gayle Elizabeth *human resources consultant and coach*
Almaguer, Frank *ambassador*
Benton, Stephen Richard *civil and mechanical engineer*
†Bhide, Manohar Gopal *nuclear scientist, educator*
Bonacquist, Harold Frank, Jr., *lawyer*
Brandel, Ralph Edward *management consultant*
Burr, Ronald Edwin *publisher*
Chamberlin, Edward Robert *career officer, educator*
Chandler, Hubert Thomas *former army officer*
Colosi, Thomas R. *educator, mediator*
Damon, Shirley Stockton *art gallery owner*
de Bearn, Gaston, XIV, *pharmaceutical company executive, consultant*
DeWitt, Charles Barbour *federal government official*
Edwards, Phillip Milton *retired import-export company executive*
Freeman, Neal Blackwell *communications corporation executive*
Gardenier, Turkan Kumbaraci *statistical company executive, researcher*
Gardner, Joel Sylvanus *tempest products company executive*
†Gavin, Donald Glenn
Gerson, Elliot Francis *foundation administrator*
Hagberg, Chris Eric *lawyer*
Hale, Thomas Morgan *professional services executive*
Higginbotham, Wendy Jacobson *political adviser, writer*
Jenkins, Robert Gordon *retired air force officer, technology executive, government executive*
Johnson, Richard Clark *lawyer*
Keiser, Bernhard Edward *engineering company executive, consulting telecommunications engineer*
Kinsolving, Sylvia Crockett *musician, educator*
Klosk, Russell Martin *human resources executive*
Kumar, Verinder *accountant, financial executive*
Lublinski, Michael *lawyer*
Maiwurm, James John *lawyer*
Marx, Gary Dean *international education consultant, association executive*
Mc Arthur, George *journalist*
McElveen, Joseph James, Jr., *journalist, author, educator, mass media executive*
Miller, Christine Marie *marketing executive, public relations executive*
Milton, Carol Lynne *artist*
Mott, Charles Davis *civil engineer*
Mujumdar, Vilas Sitaram *structural engineer, trade association administrator*
Ogrean, David William *sports executive*
Olshaker, Mark Bruce *author, film maker*
†Price, Ilene Rosenberg *lawyer*
†Quarles, Orage, III, *professional society administrator*
Razzano, Frank Charles *lawyer*
Roellig, Paul David *publishing executive*
Rogers, Raymond Jesse *retired federal railroad associate administrator*
Salah, Sagid *retired nuclear engineer*
†Schuyler, Marilynn L. *lawyer, mediator, government administrator*
Schwartz, Richard Harvey *pediatrician*
Settle, Eric Lawrence *lawyer*
Shaver, Timothy Roddy *surgeon*
Sheinbaum, Gilbert Harold *international management consultant*
Shelby, Ronald Van Dorn *information technology executive*
Spiro, Robert Harry, Jr., *foundation and business executive, educator*
Stearns, Frank Warren *lawyer*
†Stockstill, Charles James *lawyer, engineer*
†Sturm, John F. *trade association administrator*
Tennyson, Edson Leigh *transportation engineer*
Thompson, Louis Milton, Jr., *association executive, horse breeder*
Titus, Bruce Earl *lawyer*
Townsend, Irene Fogleman *accountant, tax specialist*
Urbanas, Alban William *estate planner*
Van Stavoren, William David *consultant, retired government official*
Walker, Edward Keith, Jr., *business executive, retired naval officer*
Wallman, Steven Mark Harte *financial computer services provider*
Webb, William Loyd, Jr., *army officer*
Welters, Anthony *health services executive*
Whitaker, Thomas Patrick *lawyer*
Wiesnet, Donald Richard *retired hydrologist*
Woodward, Kenneth Emerson *retired mechanical engineer*
Yamaguchi, Yuriko Fujita *artist*
Zoeller, Jack Carl *financial executive*

Virginia Beach
Alexander, William Powell *business advisor*
Allen, Elizabeth Maresca *marketing and telecommunications executive*
†Benson, Robert A. *photojournalist*
Blachman, Michael Joel *lawyer*
Buzard, David Andrew *lawyer*
Carlston, John A. *allergist*
Cehelska, Olga M. *musicologist, music therapist*
Christy, Larry Todd *publisher*
Clark, Donald H. *lawyer*
Clark, Suzanne Underwood *writer*
†Crawford-Harris, Patrice Ann *accountant, financial consultant*
Davies, George Patrick *city official*
Denyes, James Richard *industrial engineer*
Denzler, James Wyatt *pharmacist*
DiCarlo, Susanne Helen *financial analyst*
†Divaris, Michael B. *real estate development company*
Dixon, John Spencer *international executive*
Drozda, Donna Jean *artist, educator, inventor*
Eleuterius, Nancy Lea *health administrator*
Foss, William Otto *writer*
Foster, Jeanne O'Cain *poet, fine arts educator*
Frantz, Thomas Richard *lawyer*
Friedman, Andrew Mitchell *director housing and neighborhood preservation*
Gallagher, Vicki Smith *real estate agent*
Guckert, Nora Jane Gaskill *medical and surgical nurse, hospice nurse, holistic consultant*
Hajek, Francis Paul *lawyer*
†Hamilton, George Henry, Jr., *energy consultant*
†Hardy, Romayne Adams *music educator*
Harrell, Charles Lydon, Jr., *lawyer*
Harrison, William Wright
Harter, John J. *economic analyst*
Hernandez, Michael Vincent *law educator*
Hilgers, John Jack William *management and transportation consultant*
Jones, Robert Clair *middle school educator*
Kawczynski, Diane Marie *elementary and middle school educator, composer*
Keenan, Barbara Milano *judge*
Krudop, Donald W. *music educator, choral director*
Laskey, Frances M. *business executive*
Lawson, Beth Ann Reid *strategic planner*
Lliteras, Daniel Serafin *writer*
Lowe, Cameron Anderson *dentist, endodontist, educator*
Martin, Roy Butler, Jr., *museum director, retired broker*
Martin, William Raymond *retired financial manager*
McDaniel, David Henry *physician*
Morgan, Raymond Franklin *education educator*
Oberndorf, Meyera E. *mayor*
O'Brien, Robert James *financial consultant, business owner*
Panoff, Stephen Edward *music educator*
Pefley, Charles Saunders *real estate broker*
Pickett, Owen B. *lawyer, congressman*
†Prescott, David L. C., Jr., *music educator*
Price, Alan Thomas *business and estate planner*
Reece-Porter, Sharon Ann *international human rights educator*
Rigg, Richard Lee *church musician, composer, music educator*
†Ripley, Jennifer Sulouff *psychologist, educator*
Ruben, Leonard *retired art educator*
Savage, Toy Dixon, Jr., *lawyer*
Schon, Alan Wallace *lawyer, actor*
Schroff, Lois Grunwell *artist, color researcher*
Selig, William George *university official*
Seward, William W(ard), Jr., *writer, retired educator*
Short, James Ferebee *investment company executive*
Sims, Martha J. *library director*
Smith, Ruth Hodges *city clerk*
Spitzli, Donald Hawkes, Jr., *lawyer*
Spivak, Maurice Sidney *chief project management, consultant*
Stanton, Pamela Freeman *interior designer, writer*
Swope, Richard McAllister *retired lawyer*
Synan, Harold Vinson *minister, university dean*
Tarbutton, Lloyd T. *franchise consultant*
Wick, Robert Thomas *retired supermarket executive*
Wicker, Richard Fenton, Jr., *editor*
Williams, J(ohn) Rodman *theologian, educator, clergyman*
Wilson, Angela Saburn *nursing educator*
Wootten, Thomas Franklin *retired criminal justice administrator*

Wachapreague
Wilkins, Guy (Ira Wilkins) *painter, art teacher*

Wallops Island
Habeger, Steven Richard *science administrator*
†Myatt, Sue Henshaw *nursing home administrator*

Warrenton
Brimelow, Peter *journalist*
†Brooke, Edward William *lawyer, former senator*
David, Joseph Raymond, Jr., *writer, periodical editor*
Estaver, Paul Edward *writer, poet*
Fox, Raymond Graham *educational technologist*
Gullace, Marlene Frances *information engineer, systems analyst, consultant*
Howard, Blair Duncan *lawyer*
Malmgren, Harald Bernard *economist*
Rodgers, Lynne Saunders *women's health nurse*

Washington
Lynch, Reinhardt *chef, restaurant owner*
Skowronski, Frank Stanley *foreign service officer, consulting executive*

Washingtons Birthplace
†Donahue, John Joseph *park and recreation director*

Waterford
Hallberg, Parker Franklin *environmental company executive*
Harper, James Weldon, III, *finance consultant*
Harris, Caspa, Jr., *lawyer, educator, association administrator*

Waynesboro
Dillon, William Henry *retired secondary school educator*
Edwards, William Bennett *firearms industry consultant, gun dealer*

Kerby, Robert Browning *media consultant*

Weems
Merrick, Roswell Davenport *educational association administrator*

West Springfield
Sproul, Joan Heeney *elementary school educator*

White Stone
Ames, John Lewis *lawyer*
†Duer, Ellen Ann Dagon *anesthesiologist, general practitioner*
Wroth, James Melvin *retired military officer*

Williamsburg
Aaron, Bertram Donald *engineering executive, management consultant*
Ackerman, Lennis Campbell *retired management consultant*
Aldrow-Liput, Priscilla Reese *retired elementary education educator*
Armbrecht, Thomas Jeffrey Dexter *foreign language educator, writer, critic*
Axtell, James Lewis *history educator*
Ball, Donald L. *retired English language educator*
†Bell, Christine Marie *secondary educator*
Birney, Robert Charles *retired academic administrator, psychologist*
Burdette, Robert Bruce *retired lawyer*
Calver, Richard Allen *retired college dean*
Campbell, Colin Goetze *foundation president*
Cappetta, Pamela Guyler *counselor*
Cauthen, Charles Edward, Jr., *retail executive, business consultant*
Cell, Gillian Townsend *historian, educator*
Chandler, Kimberley Lynn *educational administrator*
Chappell, Miles Linwood, Jr., *art history educator*
Christison, Muriel Branham *retired art museum director emeritus, fine arts educator*
Church, Dale Walker *lawyer*
Coleman, Henry Edwin *art educator, artist*
Connell, Alastair McCrae *physician*
Crapol, Edward P. *history educator*
Cross, Dennis Wayne *academic administrator*
Davis, Richard Bradley *internal medicine, pathology educator, physician*
DeFotis, Gary Constantine *chemical physicist, educator*
†Dewhirst, John Ward *lawyer*
Dowling, John Clarkson *language educator*
Drum, Joan Marie McFarland *federal agency administrator, educator*
Dunn, Ronald Holland *civil engineer, management executive, consultant*
Dunning, Kenneth Laverne *research physicist*
Ely, Melvin Patrick *historian, writer, educator*
Esler, Anthony James *historian, novelist, educator*
Farrar, John Thruston *health facility administrator*
Flanders, Raymond Alan *dentist, governmental health agency administrator*
Geddy, Vernon Meredith, Jr., *lawyer*
Gentry, James William *retired state official*
Goodwin, Bruce Kesseli *retired geology educator, researcher*
Gordon, Baron Jack *stockbroker*
†Graham, David Browning *lawyer*
†Gray, Sarah Virginia *retired librarian*
Griffith, Melvin Eugene *entomologist, public health official*
Guastaferro, Angelo *science administrator, consultant*
Haufe, Bonnie Campbell *foundation affiliate*
Herbert, Albert Edward, Jr., *interior and industrial designer*
Herrmann, Benjamin Edward *former insurance executive*
Hoffman, Ronald *historical institute administrator, educator*
Holmes, David Lynn *religion educator*
Holstein, William Kurt *business administration educator*
Hoving, John Hannes Forester *consulting firm executive*
Jacoby, William Jerome, Jr., *internist, retired military officer*
Kottas, John Frederick *business administration educator*
Landen, Robert Geran *retired historian, educator, university administrator*
†Longo, Daniele Alexander *psychologist, researcher, consultant*
Lorenz, Hans Ernest *photographer*
Lund, Wendell Luther *retired lawyer*
Maloney, Milford Charles *retired internal medicine educator*
Marcus, Paul *law educator*
Margolin, Robert Jeremy *lawyer*
McGiffert, Michael *retired history educator, editor*
McLane, Henry Earl, Jr., *philosophy educator*
McLennan, Barbara Nancy *international tax specialist*
†Merritt, James Edward *lawyer*
Messmer, Donald Joseph *business management educator, marketing consultant*
Moorman, John A. *librarian*
†Myers, Roger Paul *writer, playwright, actor*
†Ndegwa, Stephen N. *political scientist, educator*
†Nelson, Scott Reynolds *historian*
Nettels, Elsa *English language educator*
Oakley, John Howard *humanities educator*
O'Connell, William Edward, Jr., *finance educator*
†Palmer, Jonathan Wold *education educator, academic administrator*
Price, Richard *anthropologist, author*
Reveley, Walter Taylor, III, *dean*
Roberson, Robert S. *investment company executive*
Robinson, Jay (Jay Thurston Robinson) *artist*
Rodman, Leiba *mathematician*

Sass, Arthur Harold *educational executive*
Schwartz, Miles Joseph *cardiologist*
†Shean, Glenn Daniel *psychologist, educator*
Shoosmith, John Norman *retired aerospace engineer*
†Sisk, Albert Fletcher, Jr., *retired insurance agent*
Smith, James Brown, Jr., *secondary school educator*
Smith, Roger Winston *political theorist, educator*
Smith, William Henry Preston *writer, editor, former corporate executive*
Spitzer, Cary Redford *avionics consultant, electrical engineer*
Starnes, William Herbert, Jr., *chemist, educator*
Sullivan, Timothy Jackson *law educator, academic administrator*
Tate, Thaddeus W(ilbur), Jr., (Thad Tate) *history educator, historical institute executive, historian*
Terman, C. Richard *science educator*
†Tschannen-Moran, Megan *education educator*
Voorhess, Mary Louise *pediatric endocrinologist*
Wallach, Alan *art historian, educator*
Whyte, James Primrose, Jr., *former law educator*
Williamson, Michael Allen *music educator*
Wilson, Catherine Ann *critical care nurse, educator, health policy analyst*
Yocum, Tonia Sheets *physician assistant*
Zhang, Xiaodong *computer scientist, educator, researcher*

Winchester
Bechamps, Gerald Joseph *surgeon*
Bonometti, Robert John *technology management and strategy executive*
Byrd, Harry Flood, Jr., *newspaper executive, former senator*
Creasy, Richard Alan *anesthesiologist*
Dumm, Robert Wayne *musician, educator, writer*
Engelage, James Roland *business executive*
Gaither, George Manney *marketing consultant*
Herzfeld, Garson *rabbi*
†Hofstra, Warren Raymond *historian, educator*
Holland, James Tulley *retired plastic products company executive*
Isenhower, Nelson Nolan *anesthesiologist*
Jolly, Bruce Dwight *manufacturing company executive*
Kohl, Harold *missionary, educator*
Lewis, John Gibboney *architectural historian*
Ludwig, George Harry *physicist, electrical engineer*
Meschutt, David Randolph *historian, curator*
Moore, Richard Carroll, Jr., *family physician*
Pleacher, David Henry *secondary school educator*
†Ruiz-Bernal, Gabriel *concert pianist, music educator*
Russell Jr., John Wallace *composer, educator*
†Suverkrop, Bard *vocalist, voice educator*
†Tisinger, Billy Joe *lawyer*

Wintergreen
Omohundro, William Addison *research marketing executive*

Wise
†Jansen, Kevin P. *biology educator*
Kennedy, J. Jack, Jr., *court administrator, lawyer*
†O'Quinn, Mary Darcy *psychology educator, researcher*
Smiddy, Joseph Charles *retired academic administrator*

Woodberry Forest
Campbell, Dennis Marion *educator, university administrator, theologian*

Woodbridge
Andrews, Michael William *librarian, information specialist*
†Denison, Cynthia Lee *accountant, tax specialist*
Dillaber, Philip Arthur *budget and resource analyst, economist, consultant*
Flori, Anna Marie DiBlasi *nurse anesthetist, educational administrator*
Garon, Richard Joseph, Jr., *political organization worker*
Hoefler, Eric Alexander *language educator*
Hood, Ronald Chalmers, III, *historian, writer*
Kreipke, Merrill Vincent *civil engineer, consultant*
†Messerschmidt, William Harclerode *retired army noncommissioned officer, percussionist*
Packard, Mildred Ruth *middle school educator*
Peck, Dianne Kawecki *architect*
†Phillips-LeSane, Fay M. *mental health professional*
Trussell, Charlie Ward *physicist*
Yount, Thomas David *writer, columnist*

Woodstock
Kabriel, Marcia Gail *psychotherapist*
†Maggiolo, Paulette Blanche *writer*
Walker, Charles Norman *retired insurance company executive*
Walton, Morgan Lauck, III, *lawyer*

Woodville
Mc Carthy, Eugene Joseph *writer, former senator*

Wytheville
Baird, Thomas Bryan, Jr., *retired lawyer*
McConnell, James Joseph *internist*
Starks, Charles Wiley *minister*

Yorktown
Gross, Leroy *sugar company executive*
Ivy, Richard F. *retired minister*
Osborn, James Henshaw *operations research analyst*
Ray, Charles Dean *neurosurgeon, spine surgeon, bioengineer, inventor*
Rogers, Sheila Wood *elementary and secondary school educator*
Romjue, John Lawson *historian, writer*
Wood, James Edward, Jr., *religion educator, author*

Zacata
Gardiner, William Ralph *electrical engineer, consultant*

WASHINGTON

Aberdeen
†Murrell, Gary *historian, educator*

Anacortes
†Bacani, Nicanor-Guglielmo Vila *civil and structural engineer, consultant*
Felger, Ralph William *educator, retired military officer*
Higgins, Robert (Robert Walter Higgins) *career officer, physician*
Hoffmann, Manfred Walter *consulting company executive*
Kuure, Bojan Marlena *operating room nurse*
Mc Cracken, Philip Trafton *sculptor*
Randolph, Carl Lowell *chemical company executive*

Arlington
Bullington, Gayle Rogers *writer, researcher*
Kell, Lyle Nicholas *retired minister, retired real estate broker*

Auburn
Blum, Sarah Leah *nurse psychotherapist*
Colburn, Gene Lewis *insurance and industrial consultant*
Howard, George Harmon *management consultant*
Ketchersid, Wayne Lester, Jr., *medical technologist*
Nazaire, Michel Harry *physician*
†Sata, Lindbergh Saburo *psychiatrist, educator*
†Thornton, Laird Michael *music educator, baritone*
Whitmore, Donald Clark *retired engineer*

Bainbridge Island
Bowden, William Darsie *retired interior designer*
Browning, Jesse Harrison *entrepreneur*
Burns, Shirley M. *artist, educator*
Carlson, Robert Michael *artist*
Cioc, Charles Gregory
Eber, Lorenz *aeronautical engineer, civil engineer, inventor*
Grisham, Jeannie *artist*
Marsh, Donald Reppert *holding company executive*
†Morisset, Mason Dale *lawyer*
Oechsli, Christopher George *foundation executive, business executive*
Otorowski, Christopher Lee *lawyer*
Rosner, Robert Allan *advocate*

Battle Ground
Fineran, Diana Lou *association administrator*
Hansen, James Lee *sculptor*

Belfair
Cooper, Shirley Ruth *artist, illustrator*
Hager, Robert Worth *retired aerospace company executive*

Bellevue
Andersen, James A. *retired state supreme court justice*
Arnold, Robert Lloyd *investment broker, financial advisor and planner*
Arnold, Ronald Henri *nonprofit organization executive, consultant*
Benveniste, Jacob *retired physicist*
Berkley, James Donald *clergyman*
Brockenbrough, Edwin Chamberlayne *surgeon*
Carlson, Curtis Eugene *orthodontist, periodontist*
Clark, Richard Walter *education consultant*
Clay, Orson C. *insurance company executive, director*
Cowan, Douglas Leo *lawyer*
Dickerson, Eugenie Ann (Genie Dickerson) *writer, journalist*
Edwards, Kirk Lewis *medical services company executive*
Elkins, Steven Paul *architect*
Faris, Charles Oren *civil engineer*
Gonlin, Nancy *archaeologist, educator*
Graham, John Robert, Jr., *financial executive*
Groten, Barnet *energy company executive*
Hackett, Carol Ann Hedden *physician*
Hall, Eleanor Williams *public relations executive*
Hand, Bruce George *lawyer*
Hannah, Lawrence Burlison *lawyer*
Hibbard, Richard Paul *industrial ventilation consultant, educator*
Hoag, Paul Sterling *architect*
Kiest, Alan Scott *social services administrator*
Killgore, Mark William *civil engineer*
Kocher, Cynthia *investment specialist, financial executive*
Landau, Felix *lawyer*
Lipton, Judith Eve *psychiatrist*
McCutcheon, James Edward, III, *lawyer*
†Medved, Robert Allen *lawyer*
Mosher, Charles D. *mayor, real estate manager*
Neate, Robert Edward *lawyer*
†Neuzil, Dennis R. *civil engineer*
Nowik, Dorothy Adam *medical equipment company executive*
†O'Byrne, Michael *management consultant*
O'Keefe, Kathleen Mary *state government official*
Olson, Robert William *writer, retired counselor*
Page, Roy Christopher *periodontist, scientist, educator*
Parker, Omar Sigmund, Jr., *lawyer*
Payton, Gary Dwayne *professional basketball player*
Phillips, Zaiga Alksnis *pediatrician*
Pigott, Mark C. *automotive executive*
Porad, Francine Joy *poet, painter*
Reinleitner, Katherine Mindlin *psychologist, foundation administrator*
Sebris, Robert, Jr., *lawyer*
Shurtleff, David *pediatrician, educator*
Shushkewich, Kenneth Wayne *structural engineer*
Sweeney, David Brian *lawyer*
†Tee, Virginia *lawyer*
†Tian, Hongqi *application developer, researcher*
Tyndall, Jay Mark *lawyer*
Ure Dunagan, Heather Eileen *writer*
Wang, Xing *power systems engineer*
Warren, James Ronald *retired museum director, writer, columnist*
Watson, Mathew D. *optical scientist*
Wells-Henderson, Ronald John *investment counselor*
Westergaard, George Henry *secondary education educator*
†Whatmore, George Bernard *physician, scientist, clinical neurophysiologist*
Wilson, Johnny Lee *publishing executive*
†Yarington, Barbara J. *lawyer*
†Zackey, Jonathan Thomas *lawyer*
Zhu, Jizhong *engineering educator*

Bellingham
Albrecht, Albert Pearson *electronics/systems engineer, consultant*
Anderson, David Bowen *lawyer*
Burdge, Rabel James *sociology educator*
Buri, Philip James *lawyer*
Cox, David Jackson *biochemistry educator*
†Gallay, Alan *history educator*
Haensly, Patricia Anastacia *psychology educator*
†Haggen, Donald E. *food products executive*
Hansen, Leonard Joseph *writer, journalist, editor, communications executive*
Harell, George S. *radiologist*
Howe, Warren Billings *physician*
†James, Helen Ann *plastic surgeon*
Jansen, Robert Bruce *consulting civil engineer*
Krmpotich, Frank Zvonko *fiberglass company executive, consultant*
Larner, Daniel M. *theater educator, playwright, author*
Lippman, Louis Grombacher *psychology educator*
Livesay, Thomas Andrew *museum administrator, lecturer*
Mache, Ulrich *German language educator*
Murdock, Mary-Elizabeth *history educator*
Packer, Mark Barry *lawyer, financial consultant, foundation official*
Pritchett, Russell William *lawyer, educator*
Raas, Daniel Alan *lawyer*
Ross, Steven Charles *business administration educator, consultant*
Shokeir, Marc Omar *pathologist*
Wayne, Marvin Alan *emergency medicine physician*
Whisenhunt, Donald Wayne *history educator*
Whyte, Nancy Marie *performing arts educator*
†Yusa, Michiko *language educator, researcher, philosopher*

Benton City
†Kromminga, An-Marie *special education educator*

Black Diamond
Morris, David John *mining engineer, consultant, mining executive*

Blaine
Cox, Gregory Allen *musician*
Miller, Ronald *writer, critic*

Bothell
Alvi, Khisal Ahmed *chemist*
Anders, Harley Dillon, Sr., *retired federal agency administrator*
Banks, Cherry Ann McGee *education educator*
Hawthorne, Nan Louise *Internet resources consultant, web designer, writer, editor*
†Krishnamurthy, Sandeep *writer, researcher*
†Lal, Manjari *pharmacologist, researcher*
McConnell, Sarah Stacey *film producer, French language educator*
McDonald, Michael Lee *clinic administrator, retired naval officer*
†Watts, Linda Susan *humanities educator*
Weiden, Paul Lincoln *cancer researcher, oncologist, educator*
†Wilds, Daniel O. *health products executive*
Wirt, Sherwood Eliot *minister, writer*

Bremerton
Cunningham, Gary Allen *lawyer*
Fischer, Mary E. *special education educator*
Holk, George Bertwell *accountant*
Hower, Jeanne Louise *landscape designer*
Lamberg, John David *internist*
Milander, Henry Martin *educational consultant*
Welle, Talman Jamison *music educator*

Buckley
Christensen, Doris Ann *antique dealer, researcher, writer*

Burien
Burgess, Charles Orville *history educator*

Camano Island
Clowes, Garth Anthony *electronics executive, consultant*
Hartley, Celia Love *nursing consultant, writer, retired nursing educator, nursing administrator*
Thayer, Thomas Manor, Jr., *artist*

Camas
Liem, Annie *pediatrician*

Carlsborg
Scairpon, Sharon Cecilia *retired information scientist*

Centralia
Bates, Charles Walter *lawyer, human resources executive, politician*
Buzzard, Steven Ray *lawyer*
†Fast, Linda Lee *music educator*
Gimbel, Hervey Willis *public health physician, medical administrator*
†Hansen, Bruce Lynn *retired music educator*
Kirk, Henry Port *academic administrator*
Meany, Philip Augustus *library director*
Miller, James McCalmont *pediatrician*

Chattaroy
Ezelle, Robert Eugene *diplomat*

Chehalis
Burrows, Robert Paul *optometrist*
Detrick, Donald Howard *minister*
Neal-Parker, Shirley Anita *obstetrician and gynecologist*
Nichols, James Raymond, Jr., *civil engineer*

Cheney
Bunting, David Cuyp *economics educator, consultant*
Feeney, Kendall Greer *art director, music educator*
Jordan, Stephen M. *university president*
Smith, Grant William *English language educator, civic fundraiser*
†Stearns, Susan A *education educator*
Steiner, Henry-York *English language and literature educator*

Chimacum
Hollenbeck, Dorothy Rose *principal*

Clarkston
Chinchinian, Harry *pathologist, educator*
†Knight, Brian *writer*
Torgerson, Linda Belle *music educator*

Cle Elum
Wampler, Stephen George *music educator*

Clinton
Holtby, Kenneth Fraser *retired manufacturing executive*
Jacobs, Harold Robert *mechanical engineering educator, practitioner*

Clyde Hill
Condon, Robert Edward *surgeon, educator, consultant*

College Place
†Anderson, Clarence Glen *dean*

Connell
Wells, Roger Stanley *software engineer*

Coupeville
Mayhew, Eric George *medical researcher, educator*
Thom, Richard David *retired aerospace executive*

Davenport
Harper, Rob *secondary school educator*

Des Moines
†Andrews, William F. *minister*
Ortmeyer, Carl Edward *retired demographer*
Ray, Marianne Yurasko *social services administrator*
Tuell, Jack Marvin *retired bishop*

Dupont
Pettit, Ghery St. John *electronics engineer*

Duvall
†Weiss, William Hans *small business owner*

East Sound
de Boor, Carl *mathematician*

East Wenatchee
Berkley, Robert John *retired federal agency professional*
†Marion, Sarah Kathleen *music educator*

Eastsound
Fowles, George Richard *physicist, educator*

Edmonds
Bray, Ronald Eugene *obstetrician/gynecologist*
Brinton, Richard Kirk *marketing executive*
Crone, Richard Allan *cardiologist, educator*
Crump, David Lee *lawyer*
Deering, Anne-Lise *artist, retired real estate salesperson*
Hall, Michael Wayne *lawyer, judge*
Johnson, d'Elaine Ann Herard *artist, consultant*
Kasama, Hideto Peter *international business and investment advisor*
Monroe, James Walter *retired organization executive*
Owen, John *retired newspaper editor*
Paul, Ronald Stanley *research institute executive*
Peckol, James Kenneth *consulting engineer*
Schmit, Lucien André, Jr., *structural engineer*
Terrel, Ronald Lee *civil engineer, business executive, educator*
Thyden, James Eskel *diplomat, educator, lecturer*
Yoon, Jay Myoung *oncologist, hematologist, internist*

Ellensburg
Bates, Dwight Lee *retired mechanical engineer*
Bennett, John J. *writer, publisher*
Comstock, Dale Robert *mathematics educator*
†Gray, Loretta *language educator*

McClelland, Kamilla Kuroda *news reporter, proofreader, book agent*
Miller, Allen Terry, Jr., *lawyer*
Montgomery, Anne M. *family practice physician, educator, consultant*
Myers, Sharon Diane *auditor*
O'Brien, Robert S. *state official*
Olson, Steven Stanley *social service executive*
Owen, Bradley Scott *lieutenant governor*
Randlett, Mary Willis *photographer*
Raphael, Martin George *research wildlife biologist*
Reed, Sam *secretary of state*
†Reynolds, Dennis Dean *lawyer*
Roe, Charles Barnett *lawyer*
Sanders, Richard Browning *judge*
Sesonske, Alexander *nuclear and chemical engineer*
Smith, Charles Z. *retired state supreme court justice*
Stohl, Esther A. *senior citizen advocate*
Thomas-John, Yvonne Maree *artist, interior designer*
†Vavrus, Michael J. *education educator, researcher*
Walker, Francis Joseph *lawyer*
Weese, Bruce Eric *sales executive*
Welsh, John Beresford, Jr., *retired lawyer*
Wilson, Wesley M. *retired lawyer, writer*
†Winsley, Shirley J. *state legislator, insurance agent*
Yake, William Ellsworth *environmental scientist, writer, poet*
Zimmerman, Michael Phillip *management systems specialist*
Zussy, Nancy Louise *librarian*

Onalaska
Leadbetter, Mark Renton, Jr., *orthopedic surgeon*

Otis Orchards
Coffin, Mary Ann *elementary school educator*

Palouse
Russman, Irene Karen *artist*

Port Angeles
†Barker, Barbara *registered nurse, medical researcher*
Brewer, John Charles *journalist*
Burton, Fredda Jean *writer, artist*
†Gailey, Douglas Mitchell *music educator*
Gay, Carl Lloyd *lawyer*
†Grier, George Edward *music educator, musician*
Kane, Patrick J. *high school principal*
Muller, Carolyn Bue *physical therapist, volunteer*
Muller, Willard C(hester) *writer*
Osborne, Richard Hazelet *anthropology and medical genetics educator*
Richmond, Mardell C. *family nurse practitioner*
Sonnenfeld, Joseph *geographer, researcher*

Port Ludlow
Pihl, James Melvin *electronic engineer*
†Trzaska, Joyce Anne *publishing executive*

Port Orchard
Bonsell, Thomas Allen *journalist, publisher*
Huber, Virginia Rollo *photojournalist, educator, artist*

Port Townsend
Buhler, Jill Lorie *editor, writer*
Cady, Jack Andrew *writer, educator*
Hiatt, Peter *retired librarian studies educator*
†Jamison, Margaret Ruth *psychotherapist, freelance/self-employed writer*
Jones, John Wesley *entrepreneur*
Kahn, Sy Myron *humanities educator, poet*
†Long, Karen Draut *librarian*
MacLean, Barbara Hutmacher *author, retired journalist*
Wald, Quentin Roosevelt *research aerodynamics and hydrodynamics engineer*
†Wallin, Madge Marie *retired librarian, musician*
Woolf, William Blauvelt *retired association executive*

Poulsbo
Carle, Harry Lloyd *social worker*
†MacKichan, Barry B. *computer company executive*
Meyer, Roger Jess Christian *pediatrics educator*
O'Morchoe, Patricia Jean *pathologist, educator*
Wayne, Kyra Petrovskaya *writer*

Preston
Fadden, Delmar McLean *retired electrical engineer*

Prosser
Cooper, Lynn Dale *retired minister, retired navy chaplain*
Proebsting, Edward Louis, Jr., *retired research horticulturist*

Pullman
Banas, Emil Mike *physicist, educator*
Baugh, Bradford Hamilton *occupational and environmental health advisor*
Burbick, Joan *English educator*
†Chermak, Gail D. *audiologist, educator*
Chmelir, Lynn Kay *academic librarian*
Dillman, Donald Andrew *sociologist, educator, survey methodologist*
†Franz, Eldon Henry *environmental scientist, educator, ecologist*
Funk, William Henry *retired environmental engineering educator*
Gramm, Warren Stanley *economics educator*
†Gursoy, Dogan *hospitality and tourism educator, researcher*
Henson, James Bond *veterinary pathologist*
Hipps, Kerry W(ayne) *chemistry educator, research scientist*
Hosick, Howard Lawrence *cell biology educator, academic administrator*
†Hu, Ming *pharmaceutical scientist*
†Kaag, Cynthia Stewart *library and information scientist, educator, librarian*
Kallaher, Michael Joseph *mathematics educator*
Katona, Michael George *civil engineer, educator*
Kelley, Margaret Mary *music educator, musician*
†Lewis, Norman G. *academic administrator, researcher, consultant*
Li, Haijun *mathematician, educator, mathematician, consultant*
McSweeney, Frances Kaye *psychology educator*
Munson, Charles Lee *university educator*
Nofsinger, John *finance educator, consultant*
†Ostrom, Theodore G. *mathematician*
Rawlins, V. Lane *university president*
†Robison, Linda M. *epidemiologist, medical researcher*
Rosenman, Robert Edward *economist, educator, researcher*
Ryan, Clarence Augustine, Jr., *biochemistry educator*
Samizay, Mohammad Rafi *architect, educator*
†Satterlee, James D. *chemist, educator*
Scheer, Gary Werner *electrical engineer*
Sclar, David Alexander *medical policy educator*
Shrope, Nancy Ruth *research administrator*
Stock, David Earl *mechanical engineering educator*
Swan, Susan Linda *history educator*
†Tseng, Chi-Ting *music educator*
Warner, Dennis Allan *psychology educator*
†Yasinitsky, Gregory Walter *music educator*
†Yurgel, Svetlana N. *microbiologist, researcher*
Zlatos, Christy *librarian*

Puyallup
Muchmore, Don Moncrief *retired museum, foundation, educational, financial fund raising and public opinion consulting firm administrator, banker*

Quincy
†Silk, Michael Loren *music educator*

Redmond
Allchin, Jim *information technology executive*
Arbogast, Brian *information technology executive*
Ayala, Orlando *information technology executive*
Bach, Robert J. *information technology executive*
Ballmer, Steve *software company executive*
†Barton, Richard N. *computer company executive*
Belluzzo, Rick *information technology executive*
Black, Deborah *information technology executive*
Blakeley-Perez, Jose Alfredo *software architect*
Boggs, Scott *information technology executive*
Borgs, Christian H. *mathematical physicist*
Brass, Dick *information technology executive*
Brummel, Lisa *information technology executive*
Burgman, Doug *information technology executive*
Butler, Jannette Sue *human resources professional*
Button, Tom *information technology executive*
Cabrera, Luis Felipe *software architect*
Caouette, David Paul *public relations executive*
Chayes, Jennifer Tour *mathematical physicist, educator*
Christensen, Juha *information technology executive*
Cole, David *information technology executive*
De Blasi, Camille E. *advocate, counselor*
DelBene, Kurt *information technology executive*
DeVaan, Jon *information technology executive*
Devenuti, Richard R. *information technology executive*
Dill, Richard Everett *software company development executive*
Doman, Margaret Horn *government policy and process consultant, civic official*
Egner, John David *electrical engineer*
Elliot, Gerri *information technology executive*
Emerson, Richard P. *information technology executive*
Enbysk, H. Monte *writer, editor*
English, Donald Marvin *loss control representative*
Fade, Richard *information technology executive*
Flessner, Paul *information technology executive*
Gates, Bill (William Henry Gates III) *software company executive*
George, Grant *information technology executive*
Gorin, Ralph Edgar *software engineer, consultant*
Hebert, Kathleen *information technology executive*
Judah, Norman *information technology executive*
Kaplan, Richard *information technology executive*
Kelman, Bruce Jerry *toxicologist, consultant*
Kimmich, Jon Bradford *computer science program executive*
Kinsley, Michael E. *magazine editor*
Kirilova, Svetlana Nikolova *psychologist, consultant*
Koch, Mitchell *information technology executive*
Kolomiets, Alexei *computer programmer*
Kong, Kenneth Sehkiang *software testing engineer*
Lane, James F. *software engineer*
Lappenbusch, Richard W. *software company official*
Levin, Lewis *information technology executive*
Lomet, David Bruce *computer scientist*
Moore, Lori *information technology executive*
Muglia, Bob *information technology executive*
Mundie, Craig *information technology executive*
Nadella, Satya *information technology executive*
†Neukom, William H. *lawyer*
Norman, Bill *information technology executive*
Oaks, Lucy Moberley *retired social worker*
Pacholski, Richard Francis *retired securities company executive, financial advisor, consultant*
Parthasarathy, Sanjay *information technology executive*
Pathe, Peter *information technology executive*
Poole, Will *information technology executive*
Quinn, Michael Llyn *construction executive*
Raikes, Jeff *information technology executive*
Rashid, Richard F. *information technology executive*
Rawding, Michael *information technology executive*
Rudder, Eric *information technology executive*
Sasenick, Joseph Anthony *animal health and food safety company executive*
Shaw, Kendrick Matthew *software engineer*
Short, Robert *information technology executive*
Sinneck, Michael *information technology executive*
Sinofsky, Steven *information technology executive*
Smith, Bradford Lee *information technology executive*
Sobey, Edwin J. C. *museum director, oceanographer, consultant*
Somasegar, Sivarama Kichenane *information technology executive*
Sowder, Robert Robertson *architect*
Sparks, Lindsay *information technology executive*
Stockdale, Russell *information technology executive*
Toutonghi, Michael *information technology executive*
Turnbull, Lawrence F. *retired anesthesiologist*
Valentine, Brian *information technology executive*
Vaskevitch, David *information technology executive*
Veghte, Bill *information technology executive*
Vigil, Henry P. *information technology executive*
Waldbaum, Alan G. *lawyer*
Waldman, Ben *information technology executive*
Willard, H(arrison) Robert *electrical engineer*
†Zeglis, John D. *communications company executive, lawyer*
Zhang, Zhengyou *computer scientist*
†Zhu, Min *application developer, researcher*

Renton
†Darrin, Karen Irene *medical/surgical nurse, nursing administrator*
Huck, Larry Ralph *manufacturing executive, sales consultant*
Klaff, Leslie J. *physician, research company executive*
†Majors, James Edward *electrical engineer*
St. Hilaire, Cherie Ann *pharmacist*
Swanson, Arthur Dean *lawyer*

Republic
Ferguson, Robert Bruce *minerals company executive*

Richland
Adam, William James *nuclear scientist*
Bair, William J. *retired radiation biologist*
Baker, June Frankland *poet*
†Baker, Timothy Kevin *education educator*
†Bauman, Robert Alan *humanities educator, consultant*
Bevelacqua, Joseph John *physicist, researcher*
Bratvold, Thomas Erik *physicist*
Bush, Spencer Harrison *metallurgist, consultant*
Chikalla, Thomas David *retired science facility administrator*
Cochran, James Alan *mathematics educator*
Elderkin, Charles Edwin *retired meteorologist*
†Exarhos, Gregory James *physical chemist, research scientist*
Fruchter, Jonathan Sewell *research scientist, geochemist*
Harris, Robert Vail, Jr., *research scientist, information scientist*
†Hrma, Pavel *materials scientist, educator*
Jacobsen, Gerald Bernhardt *biochemist*
Lin, Yuehe *research scientist*
Madni, Imtiaz K. *mechanical engineer*
Miller, James Vince *university president*
Moore, Emmett Burris, Jr., *physical chemist, educator*
†Mushen, Robert Linton *ophthalmologist, consultant*
Napier, Bruce Alan *physicist*
Nolan, John Edward *retired electrical corporation executive*
Norris, Kenneth Michael *lawyer*
Onishi, Yasuo *environmental researcher*
Piper, Lloyd Llewellyn, II, *engineer, government and service industry executive*
Ristow, Gail Ross *art educator, paralegal, children's rights advocate*
Roop, Joseph McLeod *economist*
Sinerius-Rupp-Bloor, Sharon Kay *sculptor*
†Sonnenfeld, David Allan *sociologist*
Stenner, Robert David *environmental and health research engineer, toxicologist*
Sundaram, Shanmugavelayutham Kamakshi *materials scientist, consultant*
Thevuthasan, Theva Suntharampillai *research scientist*
Wright, Malcolm Sturtevant *nuclear energy industry executive, retired military officer*
Xie, YuLong *geostatistician, researcher*
Zirkle, Lewis Greer *orthopedist*

Rollingbay
Morris, Donald Charles *real estate company executive*

Ronald
Kelly, Dennis Ray *sales executive*

Sammamish
†Ding, Shusen *mathematics educator*
†Marsh, B. Duane *researcher*
†Waitt, Robert Kenneth *lawyer*

Seabeck
Genuit, David Walter *podiatrist*

Seattle
Abbott, Robert Dean *education scientist*
Abdin, Maria *research service executive, publisher*
†Ackerley, Barry *professional basketball team executive, communications company executive*
†Agoff, S. Nicholas *surgical pathologist*
Aigner, B. Robert *neurologist*
†Alberg, Tom Austin *investment company executive, lawyer*
Albrecht, Richard Raymond *retired airplane manufacturing executive, lawyer*
Aldea, Gabriel S. *cardiothoracic surgeon, educator*
†Alden, Dauril *historian*
†Alsdorf, Robert Hermann *lawyer*
†Andersen, Marin (Robyn) *research scientist*
Andersen, Niels Hjorth *chemistry educator, biophysics researcher, consultant*
†Anderson, Gene S. *lawyer*
Anderson, Peter MacArthur *lawyer*
Andrew, Lucius Archibald David, III, *bank executive*
Andrews, J. David *lawyer*
Ansell, Julian S. *physician, retired urology educator*
†Aprikyan, Andranik Goorgen *molecular biologist, biomedical researcher*
Aramburu, John Richard *lawyer*
Arnold, Robert Morris *banker*
Arthur, William Lynn *environmental/political program director*
†Aspinall, Cassandra Louise *social worker, researcher*
Austin, Erik *physician, osteopath*
Austin-Seymour, Mary M. *radiation oncologist*
Awasthi, Vidya Nidhi *accounting educator*
Babb, Albert Leslie *biomedical engineer, educator*
Bagshaw, Bradley Holmes *lawyer*
Bain, William James, Jr., *architect*
Baker, Roland Jerald *educator*
Banks, James Albert *educational research director, educator*
Banse, Karl *retired oceanography educator*
Bassingthwaighte, James Bucklin *physiologist, educator, medical researcher*
Bateman, Heidi S. *lawyer*
Baum, William Alvin *astronomer, educator*
Beale, Jane Guthrie *music publisher, music educator, pianist*
Beezer, Robert Renaut *federal judge*
Beighle, Douglas Paul *aerospace industry executive, retired*
Berendt, Paul *political organization worker*
†Berger, Paul Eric *artist, photographer*
Bernard, Eddie Nolan *oceanographer*
Berni, Rosemarian Rauch *rehabilitation and oncology nurse*
Beyers, William Bjorn *geography educator*
†Bezos, Jeffrey P. *multimedia executive*
Bichsel, Hans *physicist, consultant, researcher*
Bird, Sue *professional basketball player*
Birmingham, Richard Joseph *lawyer*
Black, W. L. Rivers, III, *lawyer*
Bladen, Edwin Mark *lawyer, judge*
†Blair, M. Wayne *lawyer*
Blake-Inada, Louis Michael *cardiologist, researcher*
Blase, Nancy Gross *librarian*
Blethen, Frank A. *newspaper publisher*
Blom, Daniel Charles *lawyer, investor*
†Blomstrand, Doreen Kathryn *retired physician assistant*
†Blumenfeld, Charles Raban *lawyer*
Boardman, David *newspaper editor*
Boeder, Thomas L. *lawyer*
Boersma, P. Dee *marine biologist, educator*
Boman, Marc Allen *lawyer*
Borden, Weston Thatcher *chemistry educator*
Borgatta, Edgar F. *social psychologist, educator*
Bornstein, Paul *physician, biochemist*
Bosworth, Thomas Lawrence *architect, architecture educator*
Bottenberg, Joyce Harvey *social services executive*
Bowden, Douglas McHose *neuropsychiatric scientist, educator, research center administrator*
Bowen, Jewell Ray *chemical engineering educator*
Boylan, Merle Nelson *librarian, educator*
Brammer, Lawrence Martin *psychology educator*
Brandauer, Frederick Paul *Asian language educator*
Breslow, Norman Edward *biostatistics educator, researcher*
Bridge, Herbert Marvin *jewelry executive*
†Bridge, Jonathan Joseph *lawyer, retail executive*
Bringman, Joseph Edward *lawyer*
Brody, David *artist, educator*
Brown, Craig William *physical chemist*
Brown, Janiece Alfreida *pilot*
Brown, Robert Alan *atmospheric science educator, research scientist*
Brownstein, Barbara Lavin *geneticist, educator, university official*
Bruch, Barbara Rae *artist, educator*
Buck, Gene *graphics company executive, satirist, historian*
Buckner, Philip Franklin *newspaper publisher*
Bufano, Ralph A. *museum director*
Buhner, Jay Campbell *former professional baseball player*
Bultmann, William Arnold *historian, educator*
Burges, Stephen John *civil engineer, hydrologist*
Burke, William Thomas *law educator, lawyer*
Burns, Michael Joseph *operations and sales-marketing executive*
†Burns, Robert William *lawyer*
Burrows, Elizabeth MacDonald *religious organization executive, educator*
Butler, Keith Arnold *psychologist, software researcher*
Butler, Octavia Estelle *free-lance writer*
Calderon, Mark A. *artist, sculptor*
†Calvin, William Howard *neurophysiologist*

Campbell, Robert Hedgcock *investment banker, lawyer*
Carlsen, Russell Arthur *county official*
Carlson, Dale Arvid *university dean*
Carter, Becky Sue *neonatal/perinatal nurse practitioner, consultant*
†Casper, Corey *physician, researcher*
Catterall, William A. *pharmacology, neurobiology educator*
Cavanaugh, Michael Everett *lawyer, arbitrator, mediator*
Char, Patricia Helen *lawyer*
†Chartier, Timothy P. *mathematician, educator*
†Chatard, Peter Ralph Noel, Jr., *aesthetic plastic surgeon*
†Cheong, Jonathan Cheeyong *medical researcher*
Chilgren, D. Dianne *concert pianist, piano teacher*
Chirot, Daniel *sociology and international studies educator*
Christian, Gary Dale *chemistry educator*
Christiansen, Walter Henry *aeronautics educator*
Chung, Sung-Sook (Yoojin) *music educator*
Claflin, Arthur Cary *lawyer*
Clark, Kenneth Courtright *retired physics and geophysics educator*
Clark, Robert Newhall *electrical and aeronautical engineering educator*
Clarren, Sterling Keith *pediatrician*
Clauss, James Joseph *classics educator*
Cline, Robert Stanley *retired air freight company executive*
Clinton, Richard M. *lawyer*
Clowes, Alexander Whitehill *surgeon, educator*
Coburn, Robert Craig *philosopher, educator*
Cockburn, John F. *retired bank executive*
Coldewey, John Christopher *English literature educator*
Coleman, Debra Lynn *electrical engineer*
Collett, Robert Lee *financial company executive*
†Colquhoun, James S. *physician*
†Comfort, Robert Dennis *lawyer*
Condit, Philip Murray *aerospace executive, engineer*
Conway, Howard *geophysicist, educator*
Cornell, Kenneth Lee *lawyer*
Corning, Nicholas F. *lawyer*
Coulter, John Arthur *academic administrator*
Couser, William Griffith *medical educator, academic administrator, nephrologist*
Covington, Germaine Ward *municipal agency administrator*
Cox, Frederick Moreland *retired university dean, social worker*
Creager, Joe Scott *geology and oceanography educator*
Creim, Jerry Alan *lawyer*
Criminale, William Oliver, Jr., *applied mathematics educator*
†Cross, Bruce Michael *lawyer*
†Croston, Stephen Paul *writer, systems manager, social studies educator*
Cullen, James Douglas *banker, finance company executive*
†Cumbow, Robert Charles *lawyer, writer, educator*
Cutler, Philip Edgerton *lawyer*
Czarny, Ph.D., Frank Silvey *social problems specialist, human and organizational systems consultant*
Dailey, Michael Dennis *painter, educator*
†Dale, Beverly A. *biochemist, researcher*
Dale, David C. *physician, medical educator*
Dalton, Larry Raymond *chemistry educator, researcher, consultant*
Dalton, Thomas George *paralegal, social worker, legal consultant*
Davidson, Robert William *not-for-profit executive*
Davis, Earl James *chemical engineering educator*
Davis, John MacDougall *lawyer*
†Davison, Audrey M. *lawyer, consultant*
Dawson, Patricia Lucille *surgeon*
Day, Robert Winsor *preventive medicine physician, researcher*
De Alessi, Ross Alan *lighting designer*
Dear, Ronald Bruce *social work educator*
Dehmelt, Hans Georg *physicist, educator*
†Demorest, Steven McGregor *music educator*
†Denke, Conrad William *motion picture producer*
Denny, Brewster Castberg *retired university dean*
de Tornyay, Rheba *nurse, former university dean, educator*
†DeVore, Paul Cameron *lawyer*
†DeWitt, Dawn E. *medical educator, dean*
Diamond, Josef *lawyer*
Dillard, Marilyn Dianne *property manager*
Dimmick, Carolyn Reaber *federal judge*
Dolan, Andrew Kevin *lawyer*
Domino, Karen Barbara *anesthesiology educator*
†Donald, James *food service executive*
Donaway, Carl D. *messenger service executive*
Dorpat, Theodore Lorenz *psychoanalyst*
Dreisbach, Rodney Lewis *structures engineer, researcher*
Drumheller, Kirk *retired engineering company executive*
Duckworth, Tara Ann *insurance company executive*
Duncan, Dale A. *publishing executive*
Dunn, Erin C. *psychologist, researcher*
†Dunn, Lin *professional basketball coach*
Dunner, David Louis *medical educator*
Dworkin, Samuel Franklin *dentist, psychologist*
Easter, Scott Beyer *lawyer*
Ecklund, Ralph Earl *property manager*
†Eicher, Theo Stefan *economist*
†Eigsti, Roger Harry *retired insurance company executive*
Ellegood, Donald Russell *publishing executive*
Ellings, Richard James *political and economic research institution executive*
†Ellis, Georgiana Kehr *internist*
Ellis, James Reed *retired lawyer*
Ellison, Herbert Jay *historian, educator*
Elyn, Mark *retired opera singer, educator*
Erdmann, Joachim Christian *physicist*
Erickson, Virginia Bemmels *chemical engineer*
Eschbach, Joseph Wetherill *nephrology educator*
Eskelin, John Thurston *city planner*
Evans, Bernard William *geologist, educator*
Evans, Charles Albert *microbiology educator*
Evans, Jack R. (J. Glenn Evans) *writer, poet*
Evans, Richard Lloyd *financial services company executive*
Evans, Robert Vincent *sales and marketing executive*
Fall, Gordon Frederick Francis *family physician*
Fancher, Michael Reilly *newspaper editor, newspaper publishing executive*
†Farbanish, Thomas *sculptor*
Farrell, Anne Van Ness *foundation executive*
Farrington-Hopf, Susan Kay *plumbing and heating contractor*
Farris, Jerome *federal judge*
Farwell, George Wells *retired physicist*
†Fazakas, Art Herschel *writer, educator, editor*
Feiss, George James, III, *financial services company executive*
Feldman, Roger Lawrence *artist, educator*
Ferrer, Rafael Douglas Paul *lawyer*
†Fetterly, Mary E. *counseling administrator*
Fetters, Norman Craig, II, *banker*
Fidel, Raya *library science educator*
Fine, Arthur I. *philosopher, educator*
Fine, James Stephen *physician*
Finlayson, Bruce Alan *chemical engineering educator*
Fischer, Edmond Henri *biochemistry educator*
Fischer, Fred Walter *physicist, engineer, educator*
†Fitzpatrick, Joan Marie *law educator*
Fix, Wilbur James *department store executive*
Fletcher, Betty Binns *judge*
Floss, Heinz G. *chemistry educator, scientist*
Fluke, Lyla Schram (Mrs. John M. Fluke Sr.) *publisher*
Forbes, David Craig *musician*
†Foster, Barry Alan *cultural organization researcher, educator*
Free, Robert Alan *lawyer*
Freeman, Antoinette Rosefeldt *lawyer*
Friedman-Barone, Ronnie Eva
Fry, John Craig, Jr., *portfolio manager*
†Gardella, Carolyn M *medical researcher, director, medical educator*
Gardiner, John Jacob *leadership educator, writer, philosopher, speaker*
Gardiner, T(homas) Michael *artist*
Garfield, Leonard *museum director*
Gartz, Paul Ebner *architect, systems engineer*
Gaskill, Herbert Leo *accountant, engineer*
Gates, Theodore Allan, Jr., *database administrator*
Gault, Rosette Ford *artist, writer, composer, inventor*
Gayle, Helene D. *public health physician*
Gerberding, William Passavant *retired university president*
Gerhart, James Basil *physics educator*
†Gerrard, Keith *lawyer*
Gerstenberger, Donna Lorine *humanities educator*
Geyman, John Payne *physician, educator*
†Gibbs, Nancy Patricia *lawyer*
†Giblett, Eloise Rosalie *hematologist, educator*
Gibson, John Eric *judge*
Gilbert, Paul H. *engineering executive, consultant*
Giles, Robert Edward, Jr., *lawyer*
Gillispie, Steven Brian *systems analyst, researcher*
†Ginsberg, Phillip H(enry) *lawyer*
Gist, Marilyn Elaine *organizational behavior and human resource management educator*
Gittinger, D. Wayne *lawyer*
†Glaser, Robert *communications company executive*
†Glover, Karen E. *lawyer*
Godden, Jean W. *columnist*
†Goeltz, Thomas A. *lawyer*
Gonick, Peter B. *lawyer*
Goodlad, John Inkster *education educator, writer*
Gordon, Milton Paul *biochemist, educator*
Gores, Thomas C. *lawyer*
Gorton, Slade *attorney, former senator*
†Gospe, Sidney Maloch, Jr., *child neurologist*
Gottlieb, Daniel Seth *lawyer*
Gould, Ronald Murray *federal judge*
Gouldthorpe, Kenneth Alfred Percival *publisher, state official*
Gouterman, Martin Paul *chemistry educator*
Graham, Stephen Michael *lawyer*
Gray, Marvin Lee, Jr., *lawyer*
†Grayston, J. Thomas *medical and public health educator*
†Green, Joshua, III, *retired banker*
Greenan, Thomas J. *lawyer*
†Greenfield, Ester Frances *lawyer*
†Greggs, Elizabeth May Bushnell (Mrs. Raymond John Greggs) *retired librarian*
Grembowski, David Emil *educator, researcher*
Grinstein, Gerald *transportation executive*
Grisham, Andrew Fletcher *aerospace engineer, consultant*
Gross, Catherine Mary (Kate Gross) *writer, educator*
Gross, Edward *sociologist, educator*
Guntheroth, Warren Gaden *pediatrician, educator*
Gwinn, Mary Ann *newspaper reporter*
Halar, Eugen Marian *physiatrist, educator*
Halferty, Frank Joseph *middle school music educator*
†Halmi, Nicholas *language educator*
Halver, John Emil *nutritional biochemist*
Haman, Raymond William *lawyer*
Hampton, Shelley Lynn *hearing impaired educator*
Hands, Eric William *civil engineer, general engineer, researcher*
†Hanel, Douglas Paul *orthopedist, surgeon*
†Hannaford, Janet Kirtley *software administrative manager*
Hansen, Wayne W. *lawyer*
Harder, Virgil Eugene *business administration educator*
Harmon, Daniel Patrick *classics educator*
Harrington, LaMar *curator, museum director*
Hartwell, Leland Harrison *geneticist, educator*
Hazelton, Penny Ann *law librarian, educator*
Hazzard, William Russell *geriatrician, educator*
Heath, George Ross *oceanographer*
Hecht, Irene Margret *lawyer*
Hechter, Michael Norman *sociologist*
Heer, Nicholas Lawson *Arabist and Islamist educator*
Hegyvary, Sue Thomas *nursing school dean, editor, nursing educator*
†Heimfeld, Shelly *hematologist, researcher, immunologist, researcher*
Helgerson, Steven Dale *epidemiologist, educator*
Henderson, Maureen McGrath *medical educator*
†Henderson, Rickey Henley *professional baseball player*
Henley, Ernest Mark *physics educator, university dean emeritus*
Herman, Lloyd Eldred *curator, consultant, writer*
Hermann, Albert Joseph *oceanographer*
†Hermsen, James R. *lawyer*
Herring, Susan Weller *dental educator, oral anatomist*
Hertzberg, Abraham *aeronautical engineering educator, university research scientist*
Hille, Bertil *physiology educator*
Hills, Regina J. *journalist*
Hilpert, Edward Theodore, Jr., *lawyer*
Hinshaw, Mark Larson *architect, urban planner*
Hirschman, Charles, Jr., *sociologist, educator*
Hodge, Paul William *astronomer, educator*
Hoffman, Allan Sachs *chemical engineer, educator*
†Hohmann, John G. *neurobiologist*
Hollender, Lars Gösta *dental educator*
Holm, Vanja Adele *developmental pediatrician, educator*
Holmes, King Kennard *medical educator*
Hood, Leroy Edward *molecular biologist, educator*
Hornbein, Thomas Frederic *anesthesiologist*
†Horsey, David *editorial cartoonist*
Hough, Mark Mason *lawyer*
Huber, Vandra Lee *businesss educator, consultant*
Humphries, Edna Bevan *music educator, choir director*
†Huntsman, Lee *university provost, academic administrator*
Huston, John Charles *law educator*
Hutcheson, Mark Andrew *lawyer*
Ingalls, Robert Lynn *physicist, educator*
†Inlow, Edgar Burke *political science educator*
†Ioannov, George N. *gastroenterologist, researcher*
Isaki, Lucy Power Slyngstad *lawyer*
Ishimaru, Akira *electrical engineering educator*
Jackson, Lauren *professional basketball player*
Jacobs, Deborah L. *librarian*
Jacobson, Phillip Lee *architect, educator*
†Jaffe, Robert Stanley *lawyer*
Janes, Joseph W. *library and information science educator*
Jenkins, Speight *opera company executive, writer*
†Jennerich, Elaine *librarian*
Johnson, Bruce Edward Humble *lawyer*
†Johnson, Marcia J. *dental hygienist*
Johnson, Mildred Grace Mash *investment company executive*
Johnson, Wayne Eaton *writer, editor, former drama critic*
Johnston, Norman John *retired architecture educator*
Johnston, William Frederick *emergency services administrator*
Jonassen, James O. *architect*
Jones, Edward Louis *historian, educator*
Jones, Grant Richard *landscape architect, planner*
Jones, Samuel Leander *conductor*
Judie, Joyce Fox *tax specialist, educator*
Judson, C(harles) James (Jim Judson) *lawyer*
†Kahn, Steven Emanuel *medical educator*
Kalina, Robert Edward *opthalmologist, educator*
Kane, Alan Henry *lawyer*
Kangas, Matthew Arvid *art critic, curator*
Kaplan, Barry Martin *lawyer*
Kaplan, Laurence Scott *computer engineer*
Kapur, Kailash Chander *industrial engineering educator*
Karl, Helen Weist *pediatric anesthesia and pain management educator, researcher*
Karr, James Richard *ecologist, educator, research director*
†Katsov, Kirill *education educator, researcher*
Keegan, John E. *lawyer*
†Kelley, John F. *airline executive*
Kells, Lyman F. *research scientist*
Kennedy, Mary Virginia *diplomat*
Keyt, David *philosophy and classics educator*
Kilbane, Thomas M. *lawyer*
Killinger, Kerry Kent *bank executive*
King, Indle Gifford *industrial designer, educator*
King, Ivan Robert *astronomy educator*
Kinsey, Ronald C., Jr., *lawyer*
Kippenhan, Charles Jacob *mechanical engineer, retired educator*
Kirby, Ronald Eugene *fish and wildlife research administrator*
Klausner, Richard D. *cell biologist, researcher*
Klebanoff, Seymour Joseph *medical educator*
Klee, Victor La Rue *mathematician, educator*
Klein, Jonathan D. *finance company executive*
Klein, Otto George, III, *lawyer*
Kobayashi, Albert Satoshi *mechanical engineering educator*
Koehler, Reginald Stafford, III, *lawyer*
Kolb, Keith Robert *architect, educator*
Kolbeson, Marilyn Hopf *holistic practitioner, educator, artist, advertising executive*
Korg, Jacob *English literature educator*
Kovchegov, Yuri V. *physicist, educator*
†Kozarek, Richard Anthony *gastroenterologist, educator*
Kraft, Elaine Joy *community relations and communications official*
Kraft, George Howard *physician, educator*
†Kreager, William *architect*
Krebs, Edwin Gerhard *biochemistry educator*
Krochalis, Richard F. *municipal government official*
Krohn, Kenneth Albert *radiology educator*
Kruckeberg, Arthur Rice *botanist, educator*
Kruse, Paul Robert *retired librarian, educator*
Kuhrau, Edward W. *lawyer*
†Kumar, Subodha *information scientist, educator*
Kwiram, Alvin L. *physical chemistry educator, university official*
Lam, Arthur M. *anesthesiologist, educator*
LaPoe, Wayne Gilpin *retired business executive*
Larrabee, Wayne Fox, Jr., *facial plastic surgeon*
Larson, Eric B. *hospital administrator*
Law, Marcia Elizabeth *counselor aide*
Leale, Olivia Mason *import marketing company executive*
Lee, John Marshall *mathematics educator*
Leed, Roger Melvin *lawyer*
†Leen, David Arthur *lawyer*
Leitzell, Terry Lee *lawyer*
†Lemly, Thomas Adger *lawyer*
Levi, Margaret *humanities educator*
†Levy, Barbara Jo *lawyer, personal life coach*
Likosky, William Harris *neurologist, epidemiologist*
Lindsey, Gina Marie *airport executive*
Loeser, John David *neurosurgeon, educator*
Loftus, Thomas Daniel *lawyer*
Lord, Jere Johns *retired physics educator*
Loso, Christi Ball *television producer*
Lovett, Wendell Harper *architect, educator*
Lubatti, Henry Joseph *physicist, educator*
Lundgren, Gail M. *lawyer*
†Lundin, John W. *lawyer, urban planner*
Lynn, Anne Marie *anesthesiologist, pediatrician*
MacLachlan, Douglas Lee *marketing educator*
Maleng, Norm *prosecutor*
Malins, Donald Clive *biochemistry, researcher*
†Malkin, Michelle Lynn *lawyer*
Malone, Thomas William *lawyer*
Mankoff, David Abraham *nuclear medicine physician*
Marshall, David Stanley *lawyer*
Martin, George M. *pathologist, gerontologist, educator*
Martin, Thomas R. *medical educator, medical association administrator*
Martínez, Yolanda R. *social services administrator*
Mastroianni, Anna Catherine *law educator*
Matchett, William H(enry) *English literature educator*
†Matesky, Nancy Lee *music educator*
Matsen, Frederick Albert, III, *orthopedic educator*
†Matsueda, Ross Lawrence *sociologist, educator*
McCann, Richard Eugene *retired lawyer*
McConaughy, Bennet Alan *lawyer*
McCune, Philip Spear *lawyer*
Mc Feron, Dean Earl *mechanical engineer, educator*
McGavick, Michael S. *insurance and financial services company executive*
Mc Govern, Walter T. *federal judge*
McKay, John *lawyer*
McKay, Michael Dennis *lawyer*
McKinstry, Ronald E. *lawyer*
†McKone, Edward Francis *medical educator*
†McLaughlin, Thomas Jeffrey *lawyer*
McNab, Susan Elizabeth *human resources executive*
McNamara, Robert James *English language educator, poet*
McReynolds, Neil Lawrence *management consultant*
Medved, Michael *film critic, author, talk show host*
†Mesiwala, Ali Hakim *neurologist, surgeon*
Michael, Ernest Arthur *mathematics educator*
Mines, Michael *lawyer*
Mini, Anne Alexandra Apostolides *writer, educator*
†Mitchell, Robert Bertelson, Jr., *lawyer*
Miyata, Keijiro *culinary arts educator*
Modabber, Farrokh *immunologist*
†Moe-Lobeda, Cynthia Diane *theology studies educator*
Monsen, Elaine Ranker *nutritionist, educator, editor*
Montgomery, David Randolph *aeronautical engineer*
†Montine, Thomas Jude *neuropathologist, researcher*
Moore, Benjamin *theatrical producer*
Moore, Daniel Charles *anesthesiologist*
†Moren, Charles Verner *lawyer, judge*
Morrill, Richard Leland *geographer, educator*
†Moseley, Colin *lumber company executive*
Motulsky, Arno Gunther *geneticist, physician, educator*
Mucklestone, Peter John *lawyer*
†Mull, Robert W. *filmmaker, curator*
Murphy-Daniels, Karen Ilene *environmental, safety and health professional*
Murray, James Dickson *mathematical biology educator*
Murray, Michael Kent *lawyer*
Mussehl, Robert Clarence *lawyer*
†Nalder, Eric Christopher *investigative reporter*
Narver, John Colin *business administration educator emeritus*
Needle, Jeffrey Lowell *lawyer*
†Nelp, Wil B. *physician, medical educator*
Nelson, Allen F. *proxy solicitation company executive*
Nelson, James Alonzo *radiologist, educator*
Neppe, Vernon Michael *neuropsychiatrist, psychopharmacologist, forensic specialist, author, educator, playwright*

Newmeyer, Frederick Jaret *linguist, educator*
Nicholls, Stephen Charles *surgeon, educator*
Nickels, Greg *mayor*
Niemi, Janice *retired lawyer, former state legislator*
Nijenhuis, Albert *mathematician, educator*
Nordstrom, Blake W. *retail executive*
Northen, Helen E(sther) *retired social work educator, consultant*
Novotny, Patricia Susan *lawyer, educator*
Nutting, Maureen Murphy *historian, educator*
†Nye, Daniel Alan *lawyer, consultant*
Oehler, Richard William *lawyer*
†Oelschlager, Brant Kurt *surgeon, researcher*
Oglesby, Roger *publishing executive*
Olerud, John Garrett *professional baseball player*
Olsen, Harold Fremont *lawyer*
Olson, David John *political science educator*
Olson, James William Park *architect*
Olstad, Roger Gale *science educator*
Olver, Michael Lynn *lawyer*
O'Mahony, Timothy Kieran *writer*
O'Malley, Robert Edmund, Jr., *mathematics educator*
Oman, Henry *retired electrical engineer, engineering executive*
Orcutt, James Craig *ophthalmologist*
Orians, Gordon Howell *biology educator*
Ostrom, Katherine Elma *retired educator*
Ozaki, Nancy Junko *performance artist, performing arts educator*
Pagon, Roberta Anderson *pediatrics educator*
Palmer, Douglas S., Jr., *lawyer*
Parker, Donald Edward *aeronautics and aerospace educator*
†Parks, Gerald Thomas, Jr., *lawyer, business executive*
Parks, Patricia Jean *lawyer*
Pascal, Naomi Brenner *editor-at-large, publishing executive*
Patrick, Donald Lee *social scientist, health services researcher*
Patterson, Beverley Pamela Grace *accountant*
Paul, Thomas Frank *lawyer*
Payne, Ancil Horace *retired broadcasting executive*
Pearl, Nancy Linn *librarian*
†Perisho, Russell L. *lawyer*
Perkin, Gordon Wesley *international health executive*
†Perozo, Jaime J. *humanities educator*
Perrin, Edward Burton *health services researcher, biostatistician, public health educator*
Perthou, Alison Chandler *interior designer*
Petersdorf, Robert George *physician, medical educator, academic administrator*
Peterson, Jan Eric *lawyer*
Petrie, Gregory Steven *lawyer*
Pitts, Barbara Towle *accountant, painter*
Piven, Peter Anthony *architect, management consultant*
Pizzorno, Joseph Egidio, Jr., *business executive*
Plotnick, Robert David *educator, economic consultant*
Pocker, Yeshayau *chemistry, biochemistry educator*
Porter, Stephen Cummings *geologist, educator*
Prentke, Richard Ottesen *lawyer*
Pressly, Thomas James *history educator*
Price, John Richard *lawyer, law educator*
†Pritchard, Llewelyn G. *lawyer*
Probstfield, Jeffrey Lynn *cardiology educator, consultant*
Proctor, Richard Macfarlane *art educator, artist, writer, gallery owner*
Pyke, Ronald *mathematics educator*
Pyle, Kenneth Birger *historian, educator*
Qian, Hong *mathematician, biologist*
Rabinovitch, Benton Seymour *chemist, educator emeritus*
Ralston, Charles Philip *elementary school educator*
Ramsey, Paul Glenn *dean, internist*
†Ranganathan, Rajesh *neuroscientist, researcher*
Ratner, Buddy Dennis *bioengineer, educator*
Ravenholt, Reimert Thorolf *epidemiologist, researcher*
Ray, Charles Kendall *retired university dean*
Redman, Eric *lawyer*
Reed, Ronald Keith *oceanographer, researcher*
†Reinert, Otto *language educator*
Reinhardt, William Parker *chemical physicist, educator*
Reis, Jean Stevenson *administrative secretary*
†Riley, Stewart Patrick *lawyer*
Risse, Guenter Bernhard *physician, historian, educator*
Ritter, Daniel Benjamin *lawyer*
Rivara, Frederick Peter *pediatrician, educator*
†Riviera, Daniel John *lawyer*
Robb, Bruce *former insurance company executive*
Robb, John Wesley *religion educator*
Roche, Judith *poet, art educator*
†Roeder, Charles William *structural engineering educator*
Rojas, Eddy M. *engineering educator*
Rosen, Jon Howard *lawyer*
Rothstein, Barbara Jacobs *federal judge*
†Routt, Milton Lee (Chip) *orthopedic trauma surgeon, educator*
Rowell, Loring Bernard *medical educator, researcher*
Ruff, Lorraine Marie *technology management consultant*
Rummage, Stephen Michael *lawyer*
Russell, Francia *ballet director, educator*
Russell, Robie George *lawyer*
Rutledge, Joe *pathologist, scientist*
Ryder, Hal *theater educator, director*
Safonov, Alexandre Anatolevich *artist*
Sale, George Edgar *pathologist*
Sandahl, Bonnie Beardsley *health services executive and provider, educator*
Sander, Susan Berry *environmental planning engineering corporation executive*
†Sandler, Michael David *lawyer*
Sandman, Irvin W(illis) *lawyer*
Sandstrom, Alice Wilhelmina *accountant*
Saneto, Russell Patrick *pediatric neurologist, epileptologist, neurobiologist*
Sasaki, Tsutomu (Tom Sasaki) *real estate company executive, international trading company executive, consultant*
Sausser, Gail Dianne *lawyer*
Saxberg, Borje Osvald *management educator*
Sayre, Matt Melvin Mathias *lawyer*
Schall, Lawrence Delano *economics educator, consultant*
Schell, Paul E.S. *former mayor*
†Schenkman, Kenneth A. *physician, biomedical researcher*
Schiffrin, Milton Julius *physiologist*
†Schlosser, Ann E. *science educator*
Schmidt, Peter Gustav *shipbuilding industry executive*
Schneidler, Jon Gordon *lawyer*
Schoenfeld, Walter Edwin *manufacturing company executive*
Schultz, Howard *entrepreneur, professional basketball team owner*
Schwartz, Irwin H. *lawyer*
†Schwartz, Pepper Judith *sociologist, educator*
Scott, Brian David *lawyer*
Scott, John Carlyle *retired gynecologist, oncologist*
Scott, Samuel Joseph *art educator, artist*
Scroggie, Wayne Lee *trade and computing consultant*
Segal, Jack *mathematics educator*
Sellick, Kathleen A. *hospital administrator*
†Sharify, Shahab John *journalist*
Shepard, Thomas Hill *physician, educator*
Sherman, Daniel Adam *psychiatrist*
Silver, Michael *school superintendent*
†Simburg, Melvyn Jay *lawyer*
Simkin, Peter Anthony *internist, educator*
Singer, Sarah Beth *poet*
†Sizemore, Herman Mason, Jr., *newspaper executive*
Sleicher, Charles Albert *chemical engineer*
Smith, Douglas George *orthopaedic surgeon, educator*
†Smith, James Alexander, Jr., *lawyer*
Smith, Mara A. *small business owner, artist*
Smith, Orville Auverne *physiology educator*
Snow-Smith, Joanne Inloes *art history educator*
Soltys, John Joseph *lawyer*
Somerman, Martha J. *academic administrator*
Song, Michael *marketing educator*
Spindel, Robert Charles *electrical engineering educator*
Spitzer, Hugh D. *lawyer*
Sprague, Dale Joseph *writer*
Squires, William Randolph, III, *lawyer*
Starr, Isidore *law educator*
Startz, Richard *economist*
Staryk, Steven Sam *violinist, concertmaster, educator*
Stearns, Susan Tracey *lighting design company executive, lawyer*
†Steel, John Murray *lawyer*
Stenchever, Morton Albert *obstetrician, gynecologist*
Stephenson, Gary Van *electro-optics systems engineer*
Stern, Edward Abraham *physics educator*
†Stern, Rosella Lee *English educator, writer, director*
†Stewart, Thomas J. *wholesale distribution executive*
Stoebuck, William Brees *law educator*
†Stokke, Diane Rees *lawyer*
Stolov, Walter Charles *physician, rehabilitation educator, physiatrist*
†Stowell, Kent *ballet director*
Strahilevitz, Meir *inventor, researcher, psychiatry educator*
Stringer, William Jeremy *university official*
Strombom, Cathy Jean *transportation planner, consultant*
†Stroup, Elizabeth Faye *librarian*
Stumbles, James Rubidge Washington *multinational service company executive*
†Suciu, Dan *computer scientist, educator*
†Sullivan, Daniel Frederick *lawyer*
Sundborg, Stephen V. *academic administrator*
Sundem, Gary Lewis *accounting educator*
Sussman, Neil A. *lawyer*
Sutter, Joseph F. *aeronautical engineer, consultant, retired aircraft company executive*
Sutton, Sharon Egretta *architect, educator, artist, musician*
Swanson, August George *physician, retired association executive*
Szeto, Hung *publisher*
Talachian, Reza *filmmaker*
Tallman, Richard C. *federal judge, lawyer*
†Tausend, Fredric Cutner *lawyer, dean*
†Teitz, Carol *orthopedist, surgeon, educator*
Terrell, W(illiam) Glenn *university president emeritus*
Tesler, Lawrence Gordon *technology company executive*
Tessier, Dennis Medward *paralegal, lecturer, legal advisor, consultant, cartoonist*
†Tews, Leonard L. *retired science educator, poet*
Thomas, Edward Donnall *physician, researcher*
Thomas, Elizabeth *lawyer*
Thomas, Irv *journalist, publisher*
†Thomas, John Val *architect*
Thompson, Arlene Rita *nursing educator*
Thornton, Dean Dickson *retired airplane company executive*
Thorson, Lee A. *lawyer*
Thouless, David James *retired physicist, educator*
Tift, Mary Louise *artist*
†Tomlinson, John Randolph *lawyer*
Tousley, Russell Frederick *lawyer*
Treiger, Irwin Louis *lawyer*
Tucker, Gary Jay *physician, educator*
Tucker, Kathryn Louise *lawyer, educator*
Tukey, Harold Bradford, Jr., *horticulture educator*
†Tune, James Fulcher *lawyer*
Turecek, Frantisek *chemistry educator*
Turner, Wallace L. *reporter*
Turnovsky, Stephen John *economics educator*
†Urban, Nicole D. *biostatistician*
Utter, Fred M *science educator, researcher*
VanArsdel, Rosemary Thorstenson *English studies educator*
†Vance, Christopher *political organization worker*
van den Berghe, Pierre Louis *sociologist, anthropologist*
Van Kampen, Al *lawyer*
Van Lierop, John Henry, Jr., *music educator*
†Vitiello, Michael V. *gerontologist, educator*
†Voegtlin-Anderson, Mary Margaret *secondary school educator, music educator*
Vogel, David Seth *lawyer*
Vreeland, Victoria Lynn *lawyer*
Wagoner, David Everett *lawyer*
Wagoner, David Russell *writer, educator*
†Waldhausen, John Henry Trescher *pediatric surgeon, educator*
†Waldman, Bart Jay *lawyer*
Walker, Walter Frederick *professional basketball team executive*
Walsh, Kenneth Andrew *biochemist*
Warlum, Michael Frank *training, consulting and writing company executive*
Warren, Jared Scott *psychologist*
Washington, James Winston, Jr., *artist, sculptor*
†Wasley, Patricia A. *dean*
Wayne, Robert Jonathan *lawyer, educator*
Wechsler, Mary Heyrman *lawyer*
Weinberg, John Lee *federal judge*
Weitkamp, William George *retired nuclear physicist*
Wenk, Edward, Jr., *civil engineer, policy analyst, educator, writer*
Wesley, Virginia Anne *real estate property manager*
†Wessells, Hunter *urologist, researcher*
†West, John Garrett *political scientist, educator*
West, Richard Vincent *art museum director*
†Weston, Nathaniel Parker *historian, educator*
†Westphal, Paul *professional basketball coach*
†White, Rick *lawyer, former congressman*
White, Thomas S. *lawyer*
Whitehead, James Fred, III, *lawyer*
Whitson, Lish *lawyer*
Wilets, Lawrence *physics educator*
Williams, J. Vernon *retired lawyer*
Wilmering, Katharine Jean *social worker, clinical nurse specialist*
Wilson, Richard Randolph *lawyer*
Winn, H. Richard *surgeon*
Wood, Stuart Kee *retired engineering manager*
Woods, Nancy Fugate *dean, women's health nurse*
Wooster, Warren S(criver) *marine science educator*
Wott, John Arthur *arboretum and botanical garden executive, horticulture educator*
Wright, Eugene Allen *federal judge*
Wylie, Laurie Jean *health care executive, nurse practitioner*
†Yalowitz, Kenneth Gregg *lawyer*
Yeh, Ying Chin *electrical engineer*
Yuan, Chun *physicist, educator*
Yue, Agnes Kau-Wah *otolaryngologist*
Zabinsky, Zelda Barbara *operations researcher, industrial engineering educator*
†Zager, Richard A. *medical educator, researcher*
Ziadeh, Farhat J. *Middle Eastern studies educator*
Zilly, Thomas Samuel *federal judge*
Ziskind, Andrew A. *cardiologist, dean*
†Zumeta, William Mark *public policy educator*

Seaview
McNeil, Helen Jo Connolly *nursing educator, public health administrator*

Sedro Woolley
Hinckley, Ted C. *historian, educator, writer*
Peterson, Carol Powell *restaurant owner*

Selah
Markin, Karl Edward *obstetrician/gynecologist*

Sequim
Beaton, Roy Howard *retired nuclear industry executive*
Belson, Patricia A. *artist*
Guilmet, George Michael *cultural anthropologist, educator*
Guilmet, Glenda Jean *artist*
Huntley, James Robert *government official, international affairs scholar and consultant*
Huston, Harriette Irene Otwell (Ree Huston) *retired county official*
Jackson, Patrick Joseph *real estate company officer*
Kretschmer, Keith Hughes *investor*
Laube, Roger Gustav *retired trust officer, financial consultant*
†Lidgate, Doreen Wanda *retired librarian*
McGee, Jane Marie *retired educator*
Mc Hugh, Margaret Ann Gloe *retired psychologist*
McMahon, Terrence John *retired foreign service officer*
Meacham, Charles Harding *government official*
Pearson, Walter Howard *marine biologist, researcher*
Walker, Raymond Francis *business and financial consulting company executive*

Shoreline
Hanson, Kermit Osmond *business administration educator, university dean emeritus*
Hutton, Winfield Travis *management consultant, educator*
†Kim, Steve *music educator, musician*
Merendino, K. Alvin *surgical educator*
†Reid, Doug B. *music educator*

Silverdale
†Raum, Mary Beth *ballet educator*
Tozer, William Evans *entomologist, educator*
Walske, M(ax) Carl, Jr., *physicist*

Snohomish
Guzak, Karen Jean Wahlstrom *artist*
Meister, John Edward, Jr., *technical educator, systems administrator*
Philpott, Larry La Fayette *horn player*
Renkens, Madeline A. *lawyer*

Snoqualmie
Nelson, Walter William *computer programmer, consultant*

South Bend
Heinz, Roney Allen *civil engineering consultant*

South Hill
†Minkler, Douglas Glen *music educator*

Spanaway
Campbell, Thomas J. *chiropractor, legislator*
Loete, Steven Donald *pilot*
†Parker, Lynda Christine Rylander *secondary education educator*

Spokane
Anderson, Robert Edward *lawyer*
Baker, Danial Edwin *director, consultant, pharmacy educator*
†Baker, Sylvia Halldorson *music educator*
Beebe, James *leadership studies educator*
Bender, Betty Wion *librarian*
Brock, Randall J. *poet*
Cameron, Alex Brian *accounting educator*
Carriker, Robert Charles *history educator*
†Chamberlain, Barbara Kaye *small business owner, communications executive*
†Clements, Theodore *lawyer, law educator, dean*
Coffee, Gale Furman *musician, educator*
Cohen, Arnold Norman *gastroenterologist*
Coker, Charlotte Noel *political activist*
Connolly, K. Thomas *lawyer*
Cope, Kathleen Adelaide *critical care and parish nurse, educator*
Cowles, William Stacey *newspaper publisher*
Crosby, Glenn Arthur *chemistry educator*
†Danke, Virginia *educator, travel consultant*
†Edwards, James Robert *religious educator*
Eliassen, Jon Eric *retired utility company executive*
Ely, Gary G. *utilities company executive*
Esposito, Joseph Anthony *lawyer*
Eymann, Richard Charles *lawyer*
Falkner, James George, Sr., *foundation executive*
Fosseen, Neal Randolph *business executive, former banker, former mayor*
Fowler, Betty Janmae *dance company director, editor*
†Fowler, Walton Berry *franchise developer, educator*
Gibson, Melvin Roy *pharmacology educator*
Gilpatrick, Janet *public affairs and public relations consultant*
Givens, David Bradley *anthropologist, educator*
Gray, Alfred Orren *retired journalism educator*
Grovdahl, Steven Noel *court commissioner*
†Halvorson, Marjory *opera director*
Harbaugh, Daniel Paul *lawyer*
†Helgeson, James G. *education educator*
Hendershot, Carol Miller *physical therapist*
†Herzer, Marian Day *not-for-profit developer, educator*
Higgins, Shaun O'Leary *media executive*
Hight, Gaye Demetrice *poet*
Hosking, Neville John *educational administrator*
Imbrogno, Cynthia *magistrate judge*
Johnson, Alan M. *optometric physician*
Kafentzis, John Charles *journalist, educator*
Koegen, Roy Jerome *lawyer*
Kolsrud, Henry Gerald *dentist*
†Kovacevich, Robert Eugene *lawyer*
Kunkel, Richard Lester *public radio executive*
Lang, Melanie Sue *physician, oral and maxillofacial surgeon*
Lee, Hi Young *physician, acupuncturist*
Lee, Richard Francis James *evangelical clergyman, media consultant, lawyer*
Leighton, Jack Richard *small business owner, former educator*
†Leipham, Jay Edward *lawyer*
Lindsey, David Stewart *entrepreneur*
Matters, Clyde Burns *former college president*
McManus, Patrick Francis *educator, writer*
McWilliams, Edwin Joseph *banker*
Michaelsen, Howard Kenneth *lawyer*
Moe, Orville Leroy *racetrack executive*
†Mohrlang, Roger Lloyd *philosopher, educator*
Murphy, James Michael *retired judge, mediator, arbitrator*
†Murray, James Michael *librarian, law librarian, legal educator, lawyer*
Nandagopal, Mallur R. *engineer*
Nicolai, Eugene Ralph *public relations consultant, editor, writer*
Novak, Terry Lee *public administration educator*
Nyman, Carl John, Jr., *university dean and official*
Phillips, John Grant (Jack Phillips) *theatre director*
Polley, Harvey Lee *retired missionary, math and science educator*
Pontarolo, Michael Joseph *lawyer*
Powers, John T., Jr., *mayor*
†Powers, Mark Gregory *consultant, lawyer*
Pugh, Kyle Mitchell, Jr., *musician, retired music educator*
Richard, Gerald Lawrence *retired soil scientist*
Robinson, Herbert Henry, III, *educator, psychotherapist*
Robinson, William P. *academic administrator, consultant, speaker*

GEOGRAPHICAL INDEX 6105 WEST VIRGINIA

Russell, Byron Edward *physical therapy educator*
†Scanlon, Robert Charles *lawyer*
†Schuchart, Frederick Mark *lawyer*
Siegel, Louis Pendleton *forest products executive*
†Sines, Randy Dwain *business executive*
Spitzer, Robert J. *academic administrator*
Stackelberg, John Roderick *history educator*
Steadman, Robert Kempton *oral and maxillofacial surgeon*
Steele, Karen Dorn *journalist*
Stone, Michael David *landscape architect*
Storey, Francis Harold *business consultant, retired bank executive*
Strauch, Richard C. *music educator*
Teets, Walter Ralph *accounting educator*
Tsutakawa, Edward Masao *management consultant*
Vandervert, Larry Raymond *psychologist, educator, writer*
Van Sickle, Frederick L. *federal judge*
†Watson, William M *director*
Whaley, Robert Hamilton *judge*
Wirt, Michael James *library director*
Woodard, Alva Abe *business consultant*
Woodbury, Sara Jean *poet*

Stanwood
Finney, Linnea Ruth *tailor, writer*

Stehekin
†Spagna, Ana Maria *writer*

Sumas
Hemry, Larry Harold *former federal agency official, writer, inventor*

Sumner
Olson, Ronald Charles *aerospace executive*
Wickizer, Cindy Louise *retired elementary school educator*

Tacoma
Anderson, Lynn L. *trust company executive*
Arnold, J. Kelley *U.S. magistrate judge*
†Azarow, Kenneth S. *surgeon*
Baldassin, Michael Robert *secondary school educator*
†Barline, John *lawyer*
Barnett, Suzanne Wilson *historian, educator*
Bartlett, Norma Thyra *retired administrative assistant*
Beale, Robert Lyndon *lawyer*
Brenner, Elizabeth (Betsy Brenner) *publishing executive*
Bryan, Robert J. *federal judge*
†Carlisle, Dale L. *lawyer*
Condon, David Bruce *lawyer*
Crisman, Mary Frances Borden *librarian*
Cuevas, Eduardo Samaniego *internist*
Davis, Albert Raymond *secondary education educator*
Ebersole, Brian *former mayor*
Ernst, John Allan *clinical neuropsychologist*
Gilbert, Ben William *retired newspaper editor*
†Gorbman, Claudia L. *literature educator, researcher*
Graybill, David Wesley *chamber of commerce executive*
Habedank, Gary L. *brokerage house executive*
Harris, Robert Gaylen *art director, graphic designer, illustrator*
†Hawk, Marsha K. *health facility administrator*
†Hinkley, Nancy Emily Engstrom *foundation administrator, educator*
Holt, William E. *lawyer*
Hori, Kiyoaky *retired anesthesiologist*
Hostnik, Charles Rivoire *lawyer*
Hudson, Edward Voyle *linen supply company executive*
Hutchings, George Henry *food company executive*
Jensen, Mark Kevin *foreign language educator*
King, Gundar Julian *retired university dean*
†Kram, Peter *lawyer*
Krueger, James A. *lawyer*
Lewis, Jan Patricia *education educator*
Liddle, Alan Curtis *retired architect*
Lind, Eric Hawthorn *sales executive*
†Lowenberg, Timothy Joseph *lawyer*
Malanca, Albert Robert *lawyer, mediator*
Maloney, Patsy Loretta *nursing educator*
Maynard, Steven Harry *writer*
Miller, Judson Frederick *lawyer, former military officer*
Mowery, Gerald Eugene *publisher, writer*
Neff Balch, Betty Marie *retired nursing educator*
Peterson, Thomas Charles *minister, pastoral counselor and therapist*
Porter, Karen Ann *anthropologist, educator*
Powell, Laurel Ann *social worker*
Rahe, Richard Henry *psychiatrist, educator*
Reid, Clement Michael *composer, educator, musician*
Reigstad, Ruth Elaine *lay worker, retired physical therapy consultant*
†Rose, John Creighton *child psychiatrist*
Schauss, Alexander George *psychologist, biomedical researcher*
Sloan, Daniel Kay *electrical engineer*
†Strege, Timothy Melvin *economic consultant*
†Taylor, Peter van Voorhees *advertising and public relations consultant*
Verhey, Joseph William *psychiatrist, educator*
Vlasak, Walter Raymond *state official, human resource manager*
†Waldo, James Chandler *lawyer*
Wang, Arthur Ching-li *administrative law judge, law educator*
Wiegman, Eugene William *minister, former college administrator*
Wolf, Frederick George *environmental scientist, administrator*
†Wu, Dane Wenzhen *educator*
Zeeck, David *newspaper editor*

Toppenish
Ross, Kathleen Anne *college president*

Warren, Larry Michael *clergyman*

Tukwila
Lamb, Ronald Alfred *editor*
Talmadge, Philip Albert *former state supreme court justice, former state senator*

Tumwater
Edmondson, Frank Kelley, Jr., *lawyer, legal administrator*
†Satran, Jill Marie *policy analyst, lawyer*

University Place
Bourgaize, Robert G. *economist*
Flemming, Stanley Lalit Kumar *family practice physician, mayor, state legislator*
Pliskow, Vita Sari *anesthesiologist*
Reim, Ruthann *career and personal counselor, corporate trainer*
Seiber, Richard Allan *retired minister*

Vancouver
Benton, Donald Mark *state legislator, political organization chairman*
Cohen, Norm *chemist*
Congdon, Roger Douglass *theology educator, minister*
Craven, James Michael *economist, educator*
†Erickson, Sally Alice *social welfare administrator*
Hamby, Barbara Jean *writer, poet*
Hanbey, Teresa *healthcare executive, consultant*
Harris, Robert L(ee) *judge*
†Hobbs, Gary G *music educator*
Hulburt, Lucille Hall *artist, educator*
Iverson, Richard Matthew *earth scientist*
†McDonnell, Patrick John *city manager*
Middlewood, Martin Eugene *technical communications specialist, writer, consultant*
Ogden, Daniel Miller, Jr., *government official, educator*
Ogden, Valeria Munson *management consultant, state representative*
Oppegaard, Brett *journalist*
Perlstein, Abraham Phillip *psychiatrist, educator*
Price, Ernest Howell *retired family practice physician, administrator*
†Rama, Shelby R. *accountant, finance educator, researcher*
Scott, Gary LeRoy *photographic manufacturing executive, photographer*
Simpson, Carolyn Marie *critical care nurse*
†Smith, Linda A. *former congresswoman*
Smith, Sam Corry *retired foundation executive, consultant*
Taylor, Carson William *electrical engineer*
Tower, Sue Warncke *artist*
†Tuttle, Marcia *retired elementary school educator, music educator*
Valanis, Kirk Christian *theoretical mechanics researcher, educator*
Woodward, Jonathan Morgan *mental health specialist*

Vashon
Canavor, Frederick Charles, Jr., *lawyer*
Ingalls, Pamela Lynn *artist, educator*
Mann, Claud Prentiss, Jr., *retired television journalist*
Mantle, Peter John *aerospace executive, consultant*
Vallarta, Josefina M. *retired child neurologist*

Walla Walla
Belay, Halefom *economist, educator*
Carlsen, James Caldwell *musicologist, educator*
Cronin, Thomas Edward *academic administrator*
Gallinat, Michael Paul *fisheries biologist*
Hayner, Herman Henry *lawyer*
Krieger, William Carl *English language educator*
Mitchell, Michael Sherman *lawyer*
Oliver, Dan David *banker*
†Palmer, James F. *minister*
Perry, Louis Barnes *retired insurance company executive*
Potts, Charles Aaron *management executive, writer, publishing executive*
Yaple, Henry Mack *librarian*

Washougal
Harness, William Edward *tenor*

Wenatchee
Elfving, Don C. *horticulturist, educator*
Knecht, Ben Harrold *surgeon*
Rappé, Teri Wahl *piano educator*
Schrader, Lawrence Edwin *plant physiologist, educator*
Williams, Keith Roy *museum director*

West Richland
Ryan, Jack Lewis *chemist, researcher, consultant, educator*

White Salmon
Verry, William Robert *retired mathematics researcher*

Woodinville
Alvarez, Bryan *newsletter editor, writer*
Lanter, Sean Keith *software engineer*
Sanders, Richard Kinard *actor*

Woodland
Hansen, Walter Eugene *insurance executive*
Mairose, Paul Timothy *mechanical engineer, consultant*

Woodway
Kent, Aimee Bernice Petersen *interior designer, artist, landscape designer*

Yakima
Boyd, Lauri Louise *lawyer, judge*
Hefflinger, LeRoy Arthur *agricultural manager*
Jongeward, George Ronald *retired systems analyst*
Larson, Paul Martin *lawyer*
McDonald, Alan Angus *federal judge*
Meshke, George Lewis *drama and humanities educator*
Newland, Ruth Laura *small business owner*
Ramsey, Douglas Arthur *journalist, writer, critic, foundation executive*
Simonson, Susan Kay *hospital clinical care coordinator*
Suko, Lonny Ray *judge*

Yelm
Kelley, Richard Allen, Jr., *software engineer*

WEST VIRGINIA

Athens
Marsh, Joseph Franklin, Jr., *emeritus college president, educational consultant*
Westbrook, Gary Wayne *music educator, consultant*

Beckley
Brownlee, Sarah Hale *elementary special education educator*
†Carpenter, J.D. *academic administrator*
Dinh, Anthony Tung *internist*
†Finch, Melody Renee *nurse*
Hooper, William Dale *surgeon*
Kennedy, David Tinsley *retired lawyer, labor arbitrator*
Rehbein, Edward Andrew *minister, geologist, consultant*

Belmont
†Drane, A. D. *adult education educator*

Bethany
†Collaros, Pandel Lee *music educator*
Cooey, William Randolph *economics educator*
†Dunbar, Jeffrey Bartlett *social services administrator*
Shelek-Furbee, Katherine *social worker educator*

Bluefield
Blevins, Thomas E. *college administrator, educator*
Brown, Sheri Lynn *artist, poet, educator*
Evans, Wayne Lewis *lawyer*
Jessee, Deborah Williams *nursing administrator*
Kantor, Isaac Norris *lawyer*
Loundmon-Clay, Juanita L. *educator, academic administrator*
Patsel, E. Ralph, Jr., *retired registrar, research director*
Reid, William James *mining executive*

Bridgeport
Gainer, Earl Mark *pharmacist*

Buckhannon
Johnson, Danette Ifert *communication educator*
†McCormick, Rodger John *biologist, educator, minister*
Oiler, Dorilou Wemlinger *artist*

Bunker Hill
Marple, Thomas Franklin *columnist, reporter*

Charles Town
McDonald, Angus Wheeler *farmer*
Na, Tsung Shun (Terry Na) *Chinese studies educator, writer*

Charleston
Albright, Joseph P. *state supreme court justice*
Arrington, Carolyn Ruth *education consultant*
Bateman, Mildred Mitchell *retired psychiatrist*
Bell, Harry Fullerton, Jr., *lawyer*
Bennett, Robert Menzies *retired gas pipeline company executive*
†Berthold, Robert Vernon, Jr., *lawyer*
Bhasin, Madan Mohan *research scientist*
Boland, James Pius *surgeon, educator*
Brenneman Harrah, Sandra *lawyer*
Brewer, Lewis Gordon *judge, lawyer, educator*
†Brightbill, Janet M. *music educator*
Brookshire, Michael L. *forensic economist, economics educator*
Brown, James Knight *lawyer*
†Callaghan, Dan O. *lawyer*
†Chaney, Vincent Verlando
Chapman, John Andrew *retired chamber of commerce executive*
Chilton, Elizabeth Easley Early *newspaper executive*
Cochran, Robert Carter *surgical educator*
Cooper, Grant *composer, conductor, music educator*
Davis, Billie Johnston *school counselor*
Davis, James Hornor, III, *lawyer*
Davis, Robin Jean *state supreme court justice*
Dissen, James Hardiman *lawyer*
Douglass, Gus Ruben *state agency administrator*
Etter, Alan Yancy *legal administration executive*
Galya, Thomas Andrew *geologist*
Gardner, Edward Tytus, III, *company executive*
George, Larry Wayne *lawyer*
Gillespie, William Harry *forestry executive, geology educator*
Grimes, Richard Stuart *editor, writer*
Haden, Charles Harold, II, *federal judge*
Haught, James Albert, Jr., *journalist, newspaper editor, author*
†Heath, Mark E. *lawyer*
Hechler, Ken *former state official, former congressman, political science educator, writer*
Helfrich, Paul A. *orchestra executive*
Helmick, Walt *state legislator*
Isabella, Mark Douglas *management consultant*
Ives, Samuel Clifton *minister*
King, Robert Bruce *federal judge*
†Kiss, Robert *state legislator*
Koleske, Joseph Victor *chemical engineer, consultant*
†Kopelman, Larry Gordon *lawyer*
Lamb, Patrick John *financial consultant, state official*
†Lane, Charlotte *lawyer*
Leasor, Jane *religion and philosophy educator, musician*
Lewis, Charles Raymond, II, *traffic engineer, consultant*
†Manchin, Joe, III, *secretary of state*
Manning, Sherry Fischer *college president emeritus, business executive*
Marland, Melissa Kaye *judge*
Maroney, Thomas P. *lawyer, political party executive*
Maynard, Elliott *state supreme court justice*
McClaugherty, John Lewis *lawyer*
Mc Graw, Darrell Vivian, Jr., *state attorney general*
McGraw, Warren Randolph *state supreme court justice*
McKee, William Herman, Jr., *accountant*
†Melton, G. Kemp *former mayor*
Michael, M. Blane *federal judge*
Moore, Jeanne *retired arts educator and administrator*
†Neely, Richard *lawyer*
O'Connor, Otis Leslie *lawyer, director*
†Pfister, Alfred Karl *internist, educator*
†Price, Brian Alton *lawyer*
†Robinson, E. Glenn *lawyer*
†Rowe, Larry Linwell *lawyer*
†Schott, Michael J. *library director*
Scott, Olof Henderson, Jr., *priest*
†Slack, John Mark, III, *lawyer*
Stanley, Mary Elizabeth *judge*
Starcher, Larry Victor *state supreme court chief justice*
Sterling, Donald Eugene *civil engineer*
†Teare, John Richard, Jr., *lawyer*
Tomblin, Earl Ray *state legislator*
Victorson, Michael Bruce *lawyer*
Welch, Edwin Hugh *academic administrator*
Wilson, Robert Bryan *judge*
Wise, Robert Ellsworth, Jr., (Bob Ellsworth) *governor, former congressman*
Zak, Robert Joseph *lawyer*

Clarksburg
Coonley, Craig Joseph *internist, hematologist, oncologist*
de la Pena, Cordell Amado *pathologist*
†Leuliette, Connie Jane *secondary educator*
Sarino, Edgardo Formantes *radiologist, physician*
Walmsley, James Naylor *hydroponic farming executive*

Dunbar
†Given, Melissa Ann *elementary school educator, educational consultant*
Russell, James Alvin, Jr., *college administrator*

Elkins
Khatter, Prithipal Singh *radiologist*
Maxwell, Robert Earl *federal judge*

Fairmont
Ford, Alma Regina *union official, educator*
Fulda, Michael *space policy researcher*
Hardway, Wendell Gary *retired academic administrator*
Koppel, Donald M(aurice) *internist*
Lach, Peter *humanities educator*
O'Connor, John Edward *theater educator, director*
Richardson, Tia Maria *civil engineer, educator*
Sanford, Rhonda Lemke *English educator*
Stanton, George Patrick, Jr., *lawyer*
Stevens, Earl Patrick *minister*

Fairview
Bunner, William Keck *lawyer*

Falling Waters
Schellhaas, Linda Jean *toxicologist, consultant*

Fayetteville
†Seay-Bell, Margaretta *pastoral counselor*

Fort Gay
Napier, Michelle H. *nursing educator*

Gallipolis Ferry
Brown, Nancy Jane *human resources specialist*

Glen Jean
Beverly, Laura Elizabeth *special education educator*

Glenville
†Schmetzer, Frances Myers *secondary school educator*
Tubesing, Richard Lee *library director*

Greenville
Warner, Kenneth Wilson, Jr., *editor, association and publications executive*

Harpers Ferry
Bailey, Nancy Joyce *educator*
Boucher, Wayne Irving *policy analyst*
Cooley, Hilary Elizabeth *county official*
†Heriot, Ruthanne *librarian*
†Startzell, David N. *sports association executive*

Hedgesville
Oates, Cynthia Anne *public relations executive*

Hinton
Glaser, Robert Harvey, Sr., *retired pastor*

Huntington
†Anderson, Lorraine Pearson *dean*
Bagley, Charles Frank, III, *lawyer*
Chertow, Bruce S. *endocrinologist*
Cocke, William Marvin, Jr., *plastic surgeon, educator*
Darby, H. Darrel *podiatric surgeon*

deBarbadillo, John Joseph *metallurgist, management executive, metal products executive*
Driscoll, Henry Keane *endocrinologist, researcher*
Engle, Jeannette Cranfill *medical technologist*
Fischer, Robert Lee *engineering executive, educator*
Gould, Alan Brant *academic administrator*
Hayes, Robert Bruce *former college president, educator*
Henderson, Dan W. *psychiatric therapist, educator*
Hooper, James William *educator*
Kent, Calvin Albert *university administrator*
McGuire, James Grant *lawyer*
McKown, Charles Henry *dean*
McSorley, Danny Eugene *sales executive*
Molina, Rafael Evencio *urologist*
Morabito, Rocco Anthony *urologist*
Mufson, Maurice Albert *physician, educator*
Nerhood, Robert Clarke *obstetrician and gynecologist*
Reynolds, Marshall Truman *printing company executive*
Ritchie, Garry Harlan *television broadcast executive*
Sebert, Stephen L. *physician*
Shondel, William J. *academic administrator*
†Sypher, Blake *medical educator*
Wenzel, Loren Alvin *accounting educator*

Institute
Moore, Mark Tobin *art educator, artist, retired museum curator*
†Richards, John Dale *social worker, educator, counselor*

Inwood
Rizzetta, Carolyn Teresa *musical instrument, sound recording entrepreneur*

Kearneysville
Biggs, Alan Richard *plant pathologist, educator*
Lotze, Evie Daniel *psychodramatist*
Wilson, Charles Lindsay *research scientist*

Keyser
Falkowski, Theresa Gae *chemistry educator*

Kingwood
Moyers, Sylvia Dean *retired medical record librarian*

Lewisburg
Adelman, Michael *dean*
Ford, Richard Edmond *lawyer*
Kennedy, Leila *accounting educator*
Mazzio-Moore, Joan L. *radiology educator, physician*

Logan
Hrutkay, Lidella Wilson *lawyer, state legislator*

Mannington
Schumacher, Theresa Rose (Terry Schumacher) *singer, musician, legal assistant*

Martinsburg
Ayers, Anne Louise *small business owner, consultant, counselor*
†Day, Michael Gordon *information technology executive, educator*
Hill, Philip Bonner *lawyer*
Malin, Howard Gerald *podiatrist*
Martin, Clarence Eugene, III, *lawyer*
Wendel, Joseph Arthur *retired secondary education educator*
Wilkes, Christopher Comas *judge*

Maysel
†Paxton, James R. *minister*

Montgomery
Gourley, Frank Arnett, Jr., *engineering educator*
Sathyamoorthy, Muthukrishnan *engineering researcher, educator*

Morgantown
Albrink, Margaret Joralemon *medical educator*
Allamong, Betty D. *academic administrator*
†Bajura, Richard Albert *university administrator, engineering educator*
Bang, Ki Moon *epidemiologist, educator*
Barba, Roberta Ashburn *retired social worker, writer*
Beattie, Diana Scott *biochemistry educator*
Bell, Lewis Clay *economics educator, government administrator*
Beresford, Annette Diana *researcher*
Biddington, William Robert *university administrator, dental educator*
†Blakeman, Robyn L. *advertising executive, educator*
Blaydes, Sophia Boyatzies *English language educator*
Brazaitis, Mark Thomas *writer, English educator*
Bruner, Jeffrey Benham *foreign language educator*
Bucklew, Neil S. *educator, past university president*
Cayton, Mary Evelyn *minister*
Chen, Teh-Hsun Bean *federal agency researcher*
Chisholm, Lionel Donald John *ophthalmologist*
Cleckley, Franklin D. *law educator*
Cochrane, Robert Lowe *biologist*
Colyer, Dale Keith *agricultural economics educator*
†Conner, Patrick W. *literature educator*
D'Alessandri, Robert M. *dean*
De Vore, Paul Warren *technology educator*
Douglas, Stephen Lane *academic administrator*
Drvar, Margaret Adams *vocational education educator*
D'Souza, Gerard Eugene *economist, educator*
Ducatman, Alan Marc *physician*
Eck, Ronald Warren *civil engineer, educator*

†Emery, Sanford Emil *orthopedic surgeon*
Fisher, John Welton, II, *law educator, magistrate judge, university official*
Fleming, William Wright, Jr., *pharmacology educator*
†Fusco, Andrew G. *lawyer*
Gagliano, Frank Joseph *playwright*
Gladfelter, Wilbert Eugene *physiology educator*
Glover, Douglas Dennis *obstetrics, gynecology and pharmacology educator*
Gray, Donald Dwight *civil engineering educator*
Guthrie, Hugh Delmar *chemical engineer*
Haggett, Rosemary Romanowski *academic administrator*
Hardesty, David Carter, Jr., *university president*
Hill, Ronald Charles *surgeon, educator*
†Hilloowala, Rumy A. *retired anatomist and anthropologist*
Hogan, Mary Beth *medical educator*
Jabbour, Nabil Milad *ophthalmologist*
Kemp, Emory Leland *civil engineering educator*
Kim, Hong Nack *political science educator*
Kinsey, Donna Lee *music educator*
Levine, Ann Mebane *university administrator*
†Li, Qingdi Quentin *physician, research scientist, medical educator*
Liu, Shiyao *statistician*
Martin, James Douglas *neurologist*
McNerney, Kathleen *literature educator*
†Mei, Betty Muichi *director*
Morris, William Otis, Jr., *lawyer, educator, writer*
Nath, Joginder *genetics and biology educator, researcher*
Nellis, M. Duane *dean, geography educator*
Peterson, Sophia *international studies educator*
Pyles, Rodney Allen *archivist, county official*
Ringer, Darrell Wayne (Dan Ringer) *lawyer*
Rock, Gail Ann *obstetrical and gynecological nurse*
Seehra, Mohindar Singh *physics educator, researcher*
Shuck, L. Zane *research scientist*
Singer, Armand Edwards *foreign language educator*
Smart, Suzanne D. *social worker*
Stewart, Guy Harry *university dean emeritus, journalism educator*
Voelker, Joseph L. *neurosurgeon*
†Weisse, Martin Edward *pediatrician, educator*
Wilson, Mary Alice *violinist, music teacher*
Witt, Tom *economics researcher, educator*
†Wu, Ying *statistician, educator*

Mt. Gay
†Pierce, Calisa A. *director*

New Martinsville
†Francis, Elizabeth Romine *secondary school educator, theater director*

Nitro
Lucas, Panola *elementary education educator*

Oak Hill
Janney, Sally Baggs *civic worker*

Paden City
Ezharath, Joseph *pastor*

Parkersburg
†Bush, Roberta B. *psychotherapist, accountant*
Fahlgren, H(erbert) Smoot *advertising executive*
Gilbert, Kenneth G. *art educator*
Gunter, Norma *artistic director*
Keltner, Robert Earl *lawyer, researcher, business executive*
Meadows, Lois Annette *elementary education educator*
†Richardson, William Berkley *lawyer*
†Sperati, Carleton Angelo *retired industrial scientist*

Parsons
Burns, Robert Alan *economic developer, educator*

Princeton
Barker, Donald Dewayn *psychotherapist*
Gindin, R. Arthur *retired neurosurgeon*
Worrell, Mason Dewey

Ranson
Rudacille, Sharon Victoria *medical technologist*

Redmond
†Hylbert, Paul *construction executive*

Reedsville
Williford, Drury Fisher, Jr., *historical researcher, writer, editor*

Ronceverte
Hooper, Anne Dodge *pathologist, educator*

Saint Albans
Smith, Robert Carlisle *department administrator, welding educator*

Salem
Hensel, Robin Ann Morgan *mathematics and computer science educator*
Raad, Virginia *pianist, lecturer*

Shenandoah Junction
Showen Jr., Donald Eugene *music educator*

Shepherdstown
Daily, Larry Z. *psychology educator*
Elliott, Jean Ann *librarian emeritus*
Hresan, Sally L. *journalism educator*
Snyder, Joseph John *editor, historian, author, lecturer, consultant*
†Wilson, Rebecca Ann *English and special education educator, retired*

Shinnston
Spears, Jae *state legislator*

South Charleston
Nielsen, Kenneth Andrew *chemical engineer*
Warner, Kris *political organization administrator*

Spanishburg
Jenks, William Robert *music educator*

Summit Point
Taylor, Harold Allen, Jr., *industrial mineral-speciality metals marketing consultant*

Triadelphia
McCullough, John Phillip *management consultant, educator*

Vienna
Arthur, Margaret Ferne *nurse, insurance paramedic*
†Terry, Ralph Bruce *education educator*
Wells, Gordon Lee *science educator*

Walton
Parker, Theresa Ann Boggs *special education educator, music educator*

Washington
Pace, John Edward, III, *chemical engineer*

Webster Springs
†Moore, Alma Merle *association executive*

Weirton
Adamczyk, Edmond David *metallurgical engineer*
Diniaco, Gus G. *real estate appraiser*
†Fundis, Lois Aleta *librarian*
Wojnakowski, Mary Melissa *nurse anesthetist, researcher*

Welch
†Baker, Nadine Diane *writer*

Wellsburg
Viderman, Linda Jean *paralegal, corporate executive*

West Liberty
Forrester, James Ronald *educator*
Young, Patricia Jean Hedrick *mental health nurse, educator*

Weston
Billeter, Robert James *newspaper publisher*

Wheeling
Campbell, Clyde Del *academic administrator*
Fox, Thomas George *health science educator*
Gardill, James Clark *lawyer*
Gompers, Joseph Alan *lawyer*
Good, Laurance Frederic *medical foundation administrator*
Hogan, Susan Cox *association executive*
Hughes, Mary Elizabeth *interior designer*
†Keppel, John H. *minister*
Phillis, Marilyn Hughey *artist*
†Recht, Arthur *former state supreme court justice*
†Thurston, Bonnie Bowman *religion educator, minister*
Tucker, Gina Louise *women's health nurse*
Urval, Krishna Raj *health facility administrator, educator*
Welker, William Andrew *reading specialist*
Wilmoth, William David *lawyer*

Williamsburg
Scott, Pamela Moyers *physician assistant*

WISCONSIN

Altoona
James, Henry Thomas *former foundation executive, educator*
Powell, Christopher Robert *systems engineering and management consultant*

Antigo
Dewey, Jeff D. *music educator*

Appleton
Abitz, James H. *religious organization executive*
Amm, Sophia Jadwiga *artist, educator*
Barlow, F(rank) John *mechanical contracting company executive*
Boldt, Oscar Charles *construction company executive*
†Boncher, Austin J. *music educator, director*
Boren, Clark Henry, Jr., *general and vascular surgeon*
Chaney, William Albert *historian, educator*
†Chudacoff, Bruce Michael *lawyer*
Dintenfass, Mark *writer, English educator*
†Doeringer, Franklin M. *historian, educator*
Fisher, Robert Warren *accountant*
Froehlich, Harold Vernon *judge, former congressman*
Goldgar, Bertrand Alvin *literary historian, educator*
Goldsmith, Robin Jean *anesthesiologist*
Grayson, David S. *paper company executive*
Herscher, Susan Kay *English language educator*
Hess, Sharon Marie *computer programmer*
Lillge, Eugene Francis *state official*
†Lokensgard, Jerrold Paul *chemist, educator, organic chemist*
Lonergan, Kevin *lawyer*
Luther, Thomas William *retired physician*
Meidl, Kevin *secondary education educator*
Murray, John Daniel *lawyer*
Myers, Rex Charles *history educator, retired college dean*
Oppmann, Andrew James *newspaper editor*

Petinga, Charles Michael *transportation executive*
Rankin, Arthur David *retired paper company executive*
Richards, Susan Lynne *library director*
Schmitz, Larry W. *management consultant, computer professional*
†Siddall, Michael Sheridan *lawyer*
Spiegelberg, Harry Lester *retired paper products company executive*
Thenell, Heather Jo *lawyer*
Underhill, Robert Alan *consumer products company executive*
Warch, Richard *academic administrator*

Argyle
Daley, Ron (Ronald Eugene Daley) *playwright, poet, director, producer*

Ashland
†Small, Michele Geslin *English studies and modern languages educator*
Smith, Jane Schneberger *retired city administrator*

Aurora
†Thurlow, Stephen *music educator, department chairman*

Balsam Lake
Mattson, Carol Linnette *social services administrator*

Barron
Johnson, Eleanor Mae *education educator*

Bayfield
Wilhelm, Sister Phyllis *religious studies educator, director*

Bayside
Kaufman, Harvey Isidore *neuropsychology consultant*

Beaver Dam
Butterbrodt, John Ervin *real estate executive*
Manthe, Cora De Munck *real estate company executive*
Shturmakov, Alexander Joseph *automotive industry executive*

Beloit
†Blake, Kenneth Wayne, III, *principal, music educator*
†Blakely, Robert George *lawyer*
Burris, John Edward *academic administrator, biologist, educator*
Davis, Harry Rex *political science educator*
Gillen, Shawn P. *English language educator, writer*
Green, Harold Daniel *dentist*
Green, William *archaeologist*
†Hendricks, Kenneth *wholesale distribution executive*
Kaplan, Kenneth Franklin *manufacturing company financial executive*
Kreider, Leonard Emil *economics educator*
Melvin, Charles Alfred, III, *superintendent of schools*
Rodeman, Frederick Ernest *accountant*
Tubbs, Charles Allan *protective services official*
†Wheeler, Karla *education educator*

Berlin
McShane, Franklin John, III, *nurse anesthetist*
†Schwersenska, Sarah Elizabeth *broadcast executive*

Black Earth
†Klug, Scott Leo *former congressman*

Black River Falls
Michaels, Marion Cecelia *writer, editor, news syndicate executive*

Bowler
Bartholomaus, Brett William *small business owner*
Maas, Duane Harris *distilling company executive*

Brillion
Kjelstrup, Cheryl Ann *librarian*

Brookfield
†Bader, Ronald L. *advertising executive*
Benson, Scott Michael *lawyer*
Breu, George *accountant*
Cifaldi, Rosalie *private investigator*
Curfman, Floyd Edwin *engineering educator, retired*
Fibich, Howard Raymond *retired newspaper editor*
Hardman, Harold Francis *pharmacology educator*
Hundt, Paul Anthony *financial planner*
Kortebein, Stuart Rowland *orthopedic surgeon*
Nelson, William George, IV, *software company executive*
Saam, Robert Harry *human resources specialist, consultant*
Thomas, John *mechanical engineer, research and development*
Vitek, Richard Kenneth *scientific instrument company executive*
Wenzler, Edward William *architect*
Zander, Gaillienne Glashow *psychologist*

Burlington
†Oestmann, Mary Jane *retired senior radiation specialist*
†Roeschen, Marlene Y. *retired elementary school educator*

Cadott
Blair, David Chalmers Leslie *composer, writer*
Sanchez, Romulo Manalo *physician*

Cambridge
Vance, Leslie Edwin *information technology educator*

Cameron
†Joosten, Michael John *music educator*

Cascade
Baumann, Carol Edler *retired political science educator*

Cashton
†Johnson, David Paul *music educator*

Cedar Grove
Feider, Gary Joseph *newspaper editor*

Cedarburg
Schaefer, Gordon Emory *food products executive*
Tamsen, Christi Marie Wagner *secondary school educator, coach*

Chippewa Falls
Copeland, Christine Susan *therapist*
Hunt, Heather M. *lawyer*
Schmider, Mary Ellen Heian *American studies educator, academic administrator*

Cleveland
DeKarske, Steven Ronald *purchasing agent*

Clintonville
Simpson, Vinson Raleigh *manufacturing company executive*

Colby
Nikolay, Frank Lawrence *lawyer*

Columbus
Brinkman, Michael Owen *health care consultant, educator*

Cottage Grove
Lund, Daryl Bert *food science educator*

Cross Plains
Moretti, Jay Donald *lawyer*

Cudahy
Shen, Gangshu *metallurgist*

Darien
Miller, Malcolm Henry *manufacturing sales executive, real estate developer*

De Forest
O'Neil, J(ames) Peter *computer software designer, educator*

De Pere
Dykes, Kathryn A. *community health nurse, educator, administrator, gerontological nurse practitioner*
†Ellis, Bradford Graham *Spanish language educator, literature educator*
†Lasee, Alan J. *state legislator*
Rueden, Henry Anthony *accountant*
Tepe, Judith Mildred *vocal music teacher, choral director*

Deerfield
Pappas, David Christopher *lawyer*

Delafield
Gulgowski, Paul William *German language, social science, and history educator*
Kurth, Ronald James *university president, retired naval officer*
McClure, Thomas James *lawyer*
Walters, Ronald Ogden *mortgage banker*

Delavan
Lepke, Charma Davies *musician, educator*

Dodgeville
Dentinger, Ronald Lee *comedian, speaker, freelance writer*
Eisenberg, Lee B. *communications executive, author*

Drummond
Kingdon, Henry Shannon *retired physician, biochemist, educator, executive*

Dunbar
†Gerdt, Barry Lee *music educator*
†Habing, Brett William *music educator*

Eagle River
Kulzick, Ken Stafford *retired lawyer, travel writer*

Eau Claire
Biegel, Eileen Mae *retired hospital executive*
Brill, Donald Maxim *educator, writer, researcher*
†Brummer, James J. *adult education educator, writer*
Cecchini, Penelope Crawford *piano educator*
Clark, Mark William *dean, educator*
Davidson, John Kenneth, Sr., *sociologist, educator, researcher, writer, consultant*
Dick, Raymond Dale *psychology educator*
Frank, John LeRoy *lawyer, government executive, educator*
Heidel, Richard Mark *music educator*
Helland, Mark Duane *small business owner*
Joos, Winnie J. *home and community educator*
Juett, Samuel Joseph *administrative officer, consultant*
Keys, Anthony C. *management information systems educator*
Kirby, H(arry) Scott *priest*
Kozbial, Richard James *retired elementary education educator*
Larson, Brian Foix *architect*
Leary, Robin Janell *administrative secretary, county government official*
Lippold, Judith Rosenthal *retired occupational therapist*
Mash, Donald J. *college president*
Menard, John R., Jr., *home improvement retail executive*
†Nowlan, Robert Andrew *literature educator*
†Pace, Joel Frederic *language educator, researcher*
Patterson, Donald Lee *music educator*
†Rasmussen, Earl R *lumber company and home improvement retail executive*
†Richards, Jerry Lee *academic administrator, religious educator*
Rusch, Gerald Allen *financial representative*
Sen, Asha *English educator*
†Stark, Lisa Kay *lawyer*
Tiefel, Virginia May *librarian*
Weil, D(onald) Wallace *business administration educator*
†Whitfield, Scott Burwick *physics educator*
†Yasuda, Nobuyoshi *music educator*
†Young, Jerry Allen *music educator*

Edgerton
Douglas, Susan *data processing specialist, consultant*
Peck, David Blackman *electrical engineer*
†Porter, Donald Robert *statistician, math*

Elcho
†Hatfield, Deborah L. *lawyer*

Elkhorn
Dunn, Walter Scott, Jr., *writer, former museum director, consultant*
Herr, Richard Joseph *sculptor, educator*
O'Brien, Francis Joseph *internet company executive*
Reinke, Doris Marie *retired elementary education educator*
Sweet, Lowell Elwin *lawyer, writer*

Elm Grove
Steen Crawford, Andrea *village manager*

Evansville
Connors, William Edward *lawyer*

Fall River
†Barker, David Matthew *music educator*
Hurst, Jeffrey Paul *agricultural products executive*

Fennimore
Croft, Candace Ann *psychology educator, academic administrator*

Ferryville
Tedeschi, John Alfred *historian, librarian*

Fond Du Lac
†English, Dale Lowell *circuit court judge*
†Ingle, Sud Ranganath *management consultant*
Reed, Jeffrey Garth *organizational psychologist, educator*
Treffert, Darold Allen *psychiatrist, author, hospital director*

Fond du Lac
†Demerath, Julie Ellen *music educator*

Fort Atkinson
Anschuetz, Harold Fredric, Jr., *family physician*
Jones, Alan Porter, Jr., *food manufacturing executive*
Knox, Brian Victor *newspaper publisher and editor*
Knox, William David *publishing company executive*
Meyer, Eugene Carlton *retired editor*
†Schumacher, Mabel G. *director, consultant*

Fox Point
King, Frederic *health services management executive, educator*
Stahl, Mary Gail *elementary educator*

Franklin
Akhter, Syed H. *business educator*
†Rauschenberger, Margaret Ann *nursing educator*
Roark, Barbara Ann *librarian*
Schutte, Richard David *diversified financial services company executive*

Freedom
†Moscinski, David Joseph *educational administrator, school psychologist*

Genoa
†Parkyn, John Duwane *nuclear engineer*

Germantown
Boegel, Nick Norbert *accountant, lawyer*
Ehlinger, Ralph Jerome *lawyer*
Hargan, Charles James *retired lithographer, village official*
Reichert, Julie Anne *registered nurse, medical transcriptionist*

Glendale
Foran, David John *public relations consultant*
†Hill, John Glenwood, Jr., *university counsel, lawyer*
Schenker, Eric *university dean, economist*
Sharma, Prem S. *novelist, retired dean*

Gordon
La Liberte, Ann Gillis *graphic artist, consultant, designer, educator*

Grafton
Duback, Sally Wood *artist, educator*
Schneider, Carol Ann *staffing services company executive*
Yarger, James Gregory *chemical company executive*

Green Bay
Anthony, Lewis George *retired internist, cardiologist*
Banks, Robert J. *bishop*
†Bush, Robert G. *food service executive*
Daley, Arthur James *retired magazine publisher*
Duaime, Ginette Suzanne *poet, songwriter*
†Duncan, Sam K. *retail executive*
†Elwell, Mark W. *writer*
Favre, Brett Lorenzo *professional football player*
†Ferguson, Larry P. *food products executive*
Finesilver, Alan George *rheumatologist*
Fischer, Robert Leo *insurance agent, financial consultant*
Geisendorfer, James Vernon *religious writer, researcher*
Green, Ahman *football player*
Harlan, Robert Ernest *professional football team executive*
Kraft, Michael Eugene *political science educator*
†Kress, William F. *manufacturing company executive*
†Kuehne, Carl W. *food products executive*
†Lofgren, Christopher B. *trucking executive*
Manske, Lynn Darlene *surgical nurse*
†Meng, John C. *food service executive*
Mervilde, Michael John *clinical social worker*
Nickerson, Hardy Otto *football player*
Panchalavarapu, Poornachandra Rao *industrial engineer, consultant*
Pearson, Carol Ann *chemistry educator, science resource manager*
†Perkins, Mark L. *university chancellor*
†Schneider, Donald J. *trucking company executive*
†Schober, Thomas Leonard *lawyer*
†Shepard, W. Bruce *academic administrator*
Sherman, Michael Francis *professional football coach*
†Vesta, Richard V. *meat packing company executive*
Weidner, Edward William *university chancellor, political scientist*
Welhouse, Lucille Marie *musician, educator*

Greendale
Bull, Margaret Jane *nurse educator*
Kaiser, Ann Christine *magazine editor*

Greenfield
Helland, Sherman M. *writer*
McKillip, Patricia Claire *operatic soloist*
Nelson, Kay Ellen *speech and language pathologist*

Hales Corners
Case, Karen Ann *lawyer*
Keesler, Rachael Gay *management professional*
Kuwayama, S. Paul *physician, allergist, immunologist*
Lautz, David A. *pediatrician*
McNally, Vincent Joseph *historian, educator*
Michalski, Wacław (Żur-Żurowski Wacł Michalski) *adult education educator*
Wesener, Barbara A. *association executive*

Hartland
Burrus, Daniel Allen *research company executive, consultant*
Stamsta, Jean F. *artist*

Hayward
Peterson, Louis Robert *retired consumer products company executive*
Ueland, Sigurd, Jr., *retired lawyer*

Highland
Kreul, Carol Ann *nurse*

Hollandale
Colescott, Warrington Wickham *artist, printmaker, educator*

Holmen
Meyer, Karl William *retired university president*

Horicon
†Bohn, Monica J. *multi-media specialist, educator*
Gasner, Donn Allan *music educator*

Hudson
Dahle, Johannes Upton *retired academic administrator*
Kathan, Debra *personnel director, educator*

Hurley
Nicholls, Thomas Maurice *business owner*

Iola
Krause, Chester Lee *publishing company founder*
Mishler, Clifford Leslie *publisher*
Rosenberger, Carolyn Ann *art educator*
Van Ryzin, Robert Richard *magazine editor*

Ixonia
Peebles, Allene Kay *manufactured housing company executive*

Jackson
†Kasica, George Raymond *computer technician, consultant, emergency medical technician*

Janesville
Blazkowski, Phillip *community development and planning official*
Butters, John Patrick *educator, tour director*
Detert-Moriarty, Judith Anne *graphic artist, educator, civic activist*
Fitzgerald, James Francis *cable television executive*
Gianitsos, Anestis Nicholas *surgeon*
Roth, Sarah Eve *occupational safety professional*
Steil, George Kenneth, Sr., *lawyer*
Thomas, Margaret Ann *educational administrator, art educator*
Williams, Mary Beth *lawyer*

Jefferson
Morgan, Gaylin F. *public relations consultant*
Myers, Gary *public relations executive*

Juneau
Carpenter, David Erwin *county planner*

Kenosha
Adler, Seymour Jack *social services administrator*
†Arif, Mohammed *education educator*
Armstrong, Leona May Bottrell *retired counselor, educator*
Brown, Howard Jordan *media executive*
Campbell, F(enton) Gregory *college administrator, historian*
Clarke, Alan William *lawyer*
Crowley, James Francis *composer, educator*
Cyr, Arthur I. *political science and economics educator*
†Eigenberger, Martin E *education educator*
†Higgins, John Patrick *lawyer, mediator, educator, lobbyist*
Infusino, Achille Francis *financial and administrative support executive*
†Kaye, Dina Lynn *librarian*
†Kazell, Doris Lillian *librarian*
Kummings, Donald Dale *English educator*
Levis, Richard George *secondary school educator*
†Li, Zhaohui *science educator*
†Manion, Michael T. *finance educator*
Olsen, Jonathan Robert *political scientist*
Potente, Eugene, Jr., *interior designer*
Ramesh, Kalahasti Subrahmanyam *materials scientist*
†Richter, David Jerome *lawyer*
†Rose, Terry William *lawyer*
Rosenberg, Helen *sociology educator*
†Saucedo, Matthew Dan *college band director, counselor*
Trager, Lillian *anthropologist, educator*
Turner, Michael D. *chemical engineer*
VanDahm, Thomas Edward *economist, educator*
Wright, David Jonathan *finance educator*

Kewaunee
Allen, Gerald Campbell Forrest *management consulting company owner*

Kohler
†Kohler, Herbert Vollrath, Jr., *diversified manufacturing company executive*
†Potter, Calvin J. *retired library director*

La Crosse
Anderson, Gwyn C. *computer company executive, computer consultant*
Corser, David Hewson *pediatrician, retired*
Davy, Michael Francis *civil engineer, consultant*
Gelatt, Charles Daniel *manufacturing company executive*
†Harwood, Larry D. *education educator*
Judson, John Irving *retired English educator, poet, writer, editor*
Klos, Jerome John *lawyer, director*
Landercasper, Jeffrey *surgeon*
†Lentz, Kirby Warren *academic administrator*
Matchett, Andrew James *mathematics educator*
Medland, William James *university president*
Morehouse, Richard Edward *psychology educator*
Nix, Edmund Alfred *lawyer*
Polodna, David Lee *library director*
Rausch, Joan Mary *art historian*
Ross, Arthur J., III, *physician*
†Ross, William Henry *human resources specialist, educator*
†Rouvel, Jason C. *mathematician, educator*
Rozelle, Lee Theodore *physical chemist, researcher*
Rude, Brian David *utilities company executive*
Schorr, Timothy Brian *music educator, concert pianist*
Schumacher, Philip Gerard *fundraising executive*
Silva, Paul Douglas *reproductive endocrinologist*
Sleik, Thomas Scott *lawyer*
Smith, Martin Jay *physician, biomedical research scientist*
Thomas-Williams, Pamela Rae *publishing executive, writer*
Wallin, Susan Marie *secondary school counselor*
Webster, Stephen Burtis *physician, educator*
Zollweg, William Glen *sociology educator, researcher*

Lake Geneva
Braden, Berwyn Bartow *lawyer*
Dobray, Alan Michael *theoretical physicist, research scientist*
Liebman, Monte Harris *retired psychiatrist*
McCormack, Joanne Marie *lawyer*
Petersen, Edward Schmidt *retired physician*
Slocum, Robert Boak
Weed, Edward Reilly *marketing executive*

Lake Mills
Lazaris, Pamela Adriane *community planning and development consultant*

Land O Lakes
Jaroski-Graf, Jill Ann *biology educator, writer, dental hygienist*

Little Chute
Cornett, Paul Michael, Sr., *lawyer*

Madison
Aberle, Elton David *dean*
Abrahamson, Shirley Schlanger *state supreme court chief justice*
Adler, Julius *biochemist, biologist, educator*
Albanese, Mark Alan *medical educator*
Albert, Daniel Myron *ophthalmologist, educator*
Aldag, Ramon John *management and organization educator*
Anderson, Louis Wilmer, Jr., *physicist, educator*

Anderson, Michael Steven *lawyer*
Andreano, Ralph Louis *economist, educator*
Arenas, Andrea Teresa *academic administrator*
Askey, Richard Allen *mathematician, educator*
Bablitch, William A. *state supreme court justice*
†Bajad Sunil, Uttamrao *pharmacologist, researcher*
Balantekin, Akif Baha *physicist, educator*
Baldwin, Gordon Brewster *law educator, lawyer*
Baldwin, Janice Murphy *lawyer*
†Baldwin, Robert Edward *economics educator*
Barger, Vernon Duane *physicist, educator*
Barish, Lawrence Stephen *nonpartisan legislative staff administrator*
Barnes, Robert F *agronomist*
Barnhill, Charles Joseph, Jr., *lawyer*
Barnick, Helen *retired judicial clerk*
Barr, James, III, *telecommunications company executive*
Barry, Terence Patrick *endocrinologist, aquaculturist*
Bartell, Angela Gina Baldi *judge*
Bartell, Jeffrey Bruce *lawyer*
Bass, Paul *pharmacology educator*
Bauman, Susan Joan Mayer *mayor, lawyer*
Baylis, Thomas Arthur *political science educator*
Beachley, Norman Henry *mechanical engineer, educator*
Beck, Anatole *mathematician, educator*
Becker, David *artist, educator*
Beinert, Helmut *biochemist*
Bell-Jackson, Marianne Jeanne *elementary and secondary education educator*
†Bennett, Dick *college basketball coach*
Bennett, Kenneth Alan *retired biological anthropologist*
Bentley, Charles Raymond *geophysics educator*
Bentz, Michael Lloyd *plastic and reconstructive surgeon*
Berg, William James *French language educator, writer, translator*
Berggren-Moilanen, Bonnie Lee *education educator*
Berghahn, Klaus Leo *German and Jewish studies educator*
Berthouex, Paul Mac *civil and environmental engineer, educator*
Berven, Norman Lee *counselor, psychologist, educator*
Bespalec, Dale Anthony *clinical psychologist*
Beyer-Mears, Annette *physiologist*
Bird, Robert Byron *chemical engineering educator, author*
Bisgard, Gerald Edwin *biosciences educator, researcher*
Blanchard, Brian Wheatley *lawyer*
Blank, Robert Daniel *medical educator*
†Blankenburg, Julie J. *librarian*
Bloch, Peter Conrad *economist, educator*
Bochert, Linda H. *lawyer*
Bogue, Allan George *history educator*
Botez, Dan *physicist*
Boucher, Joseph W(illiam) *lawyer, accountant, educator, writer*
Boyer, Dennis Lee *lawyer, lobbyist, writer*
†Boyer, Paul Samuel *history educator*
Boyle, William Charles *civil engineering educator*
Braden, Betty Jane *legal association administrator*
Bradley, Ann Walsh *state supreme court justice*
Brembeck, Winston Lamont *retired speech communication educator*
Bremer, Howard Walter *lawyer, consultant*
Brennan, Patricia Flatley *nursing educator, systems engineering educator*
Brewster, Francis Anthony *lawyer*
Brock, Thomas Dale *microbiology educator*
Brock, William Allen, III, *economist, educator*
Brown, Arnold Lanehart, Jr., *pathologist, educator, university dean*
Buchholz, Ronald Lewis *architect*
Bugge, Lawrence John *lawyer, educator*
†Bühnemann, Gudrun *social studies educator*
Bumpass, Larry Lee *sociologist, educator*
Bunge, Charles Albert *library science educator*
Burgess, Richard Ray *oncology educator, molecular biology researcher, biotechnology consultant*
Burkholder, Wendell Eugene *retired entomology educator, researcher*
Burris, Robert Harza *biochemist, educator*
Busby, Edward Oliver *retired dean*
†Bush, Sargent, Jr., *English language educator*
Callen, James Donald *plasma physicist, nuclear engineer*
Carbon, Max William *nuclear engineering educator*
†Card, Claudia Falconer *philosophy educator*
Cassinelli, Joseph Patrick *astronomy educator*
†Chandler, Richard Gates *lawyer*
Chapman, Loren J. *psychology educator*
†Christensen, Marguerite Alice *librarian*
Christensen, Nikolas Ivan *geophysicist, educator*
Churchwell, Edward Bruce *astronomer, educator*
Ciplijauskaite, Birute *humanities educator*
Clay, Clarence Samuel *acoustical oceanographer*
Cleland, W(illiam) Wallace *biochemistry educator*
Code, Arthur Dodd *astrophysics educator*
Cohen, Bernard Cecil *political scientist, educator*
†Cohen, Charles Lloyd *history and religious studies educator*
Connors, Kenneth Antonio *retired chemistry educator*
Converse, James Clarence *agricultural engineering educator*
Cooper, Peggy (Mary Margaret) *artist, educator, poet, composer, choreographer*
Craddock, Campbell (John Campbell Craddock) *geologist, educator*
Cravens, Stanley H. *software development manager*
Cripps, Derek J. *dermatologist, educator*
Croake, Paul Allen *lawyer*
Crocker, Stephen L. *federal magistrate judge*
Cronin, Kevin Brian *lawyer*
Cronin, Patti Adrienne Wright *state agency administrator*
Cronon, William *history educator*
Crow, James Franklin *retired genetics educator*
Culbertson, Frances Mitchell *psychology educator*
Curry, Robert Lee *lawyer*
Curtiss, Charles Francis *chemist, educator*
Davis, Erroll Brown, Jr., *utility executive*
†De Foliart, Gene Ray *retired entomologist, researcher, educator*
Deininger, David George *judge*
De Main, John *orchestra musical director*
Denton, Frank M. *newspaper editor*
Derzon, Gordon M. *hospital administrator*
DeWerd, Larry Albert *medical physicist, educator*
Dietmeyer, Donald Leo *retired electrical engineer, educator*
Dodson, Vernon Nathan *physician, educator*
†Doran, Kenneth John *lawyer*
Dott, Robert Henry, Jr., *geologist, educator*
Downs, Donald Alexander, Jr., *political scientist, educator*
Doyle, James E(dward) *governor*
Drechsel, Robert Edward *journalism educator*
†Dubrow, Heather *English educator*
Duffie, John Atwater *chemical engineer, educator*
Dunwoody, Sharon Lee *journalism and communications educator*
†Durcan, Deborah Ann *finance company executive*
DuRose, Stanley Charles, Jr., *insurance executive*
Earl, Anthony Scully *former governor of Wisconsin, lawyer*
Easterday, Bernard Carlyle *veterinary medicine educator*
Ediger, Mark D. *chemistry educator*
Edil, Tuncer Berat *civil and environmental engineering educator*
†Ehlke, Bruce Frederic *lawyer*
Eisler, Millard Marcus *financial executive*
†El-Guebaly, Laila Ahmed *nuclear engineer*
Emmert, Gilbert Arthur *engineer, educator*
Evenson, Merle Armin *chemist, educator*
†Everard, Gerald Wilfred *lawyer, trust company executive*
Fahien, Leonard August *physician, educator*
Faillace, Walter Joseph *medical educator*
Faith, Tristan *counselor*
Farrar, Thomas C. *chemist, educator*
Farrell, Philip M. *dean, physician, educator, researcher*
Faulkner, Julia Ellen *opera singer*
Fennema, Owen Richard *food chemistry educator*
Fermanich, Mark Leon *education researcher, consultant*
Field, Henry Augustus, Jr., *lawyer*
Fitchen, Allen Nelson *publisher*
Fleischli, George Robert *lawyer*
Ford, Charles Nathaniel *otolaryngologist, educator*
Forster, Francis Michael *physician, educator*
†Foust, Charles William *judge*
Fox, Michael Vass *Hebrew educator*
Frey, Perry A. *biochemistry educator*
Frykenberg, Robert Eric *historian, educator*
Fuguitt, Glenn Victor *sociologist*
Garver, Thomas Haskell *curator, art consultant, writer*
Gavin, Mary Jane *medical and surgical nurse*
†Gern, James E. *physician, researcher*
Glassroth, Jeffrey *physican, medical educator*
Goldberger, Arthur Stanley *economics educator*
Gorski, Jack *biochemistry educator*
Graf, Truman Frederick *agricultural economist, educator*
Greaser, Marion Lewis *science educator*
Greenfield, Norman Samuel *psychologist, educator*
Greenspan, Daniel S. *molecular biologist, educator*
Grogan, Paul J. *retired engineering educator*
Gruber, John Edward *editor, railroad historian, photographer*
Guillery, Rainer Walter *anatomy educator*
Gunderson, Scott Lee *state legislator*
†Gurney, Mary Kathleen *pharmacist*
Hachten, William Andrews *journalism educator, author*
Hagedorn, Donald James *phytopathologist, educator, agricultural consultant*
Hahn, David Louis *family practice physician, educator*
Hall, David Charles *retired zoo director, veterinarian*
Haller, Archibald Orben *sociologist, educator*
Hamalainen, Pekka Kalevi *historian, educator*
Hamers, Robert J. *chemistry educator, researcher*
Hansen, W. Lee *economics educator, author*
Hanson, David James *lawyer*
Hartmann, Henrik Anton *medical educator*
Haslanger, Philip Charles *journalist*
Haughton, Victor Mellet *physician, educator*
†Hecht, Rudolph C. *physician, educator*
Hedden, Gregory Dexter *environmental science educator, consultant*
Heffernan, Nathan Stewart *retired state supreme court chief justice*
Heim, Marcy Lynn Schultz *foundation executive*
Helstad, Orrin L. *lawyer, legal educator*
Hempe, A. Henry *lawyer, state agency official*
Henderson, Arvis Burl *data processing executive, biochemist*
Henriques, Jeffrey Barlow *psychology educator, consulting statistician*
Hester, Donald Denison *economics educator*
Heymann, S. Richard *lawyer*
Hickman, James Charles *finance educator, dean*
Higby, Gregory James *historical association administrator, historian*
Hildebrand, Daniel Walter *lawyer*
Hill, Charles Graham, Jr., *chemical engineering educator*
Himpsel, Franz Josef *physicist, educator*
†Hirano, Shigeru *surgeon, researcher*
Hofeldt, John W. *lawyer*
Hokin, Lowell Edward *biochemist, educator*
Honold, Linda Kaye *political organization executive, human resources development executive*
Hopen, Herbert John *horticulture educator*
Hopson, James Warren *publishing executive*
Houghton, David Drew *meteorologist, educator*
Hoyt, James Lawrence *journalism educator, athletic administrator*
Hutchison, Jane Campbell *art history educator, researcher*
Hyde, Janet Shibley *psychologist, educator*
Iltis, Hugh Hellmut *plant taxonomist-evolutionist, educator*
Iskandar, Bermans Jamil *pediatric neurosurgeon*
†Jackson, Jerlando F.L. *education educator*
†January, Craig Taylor *cardiologist, researcher*
Javid, Manucher J. *retired neurosurgery educator*
Jeanne, Robert Lawrence *entomologist, educator*
Jefferson, James Walter *psychiatry educator*
Johnson, Jean Elaine *nursing educator*
Johnson, Maryl Rae *cardiologist*
Johnson, Millard Wallace, Jr., *mathematics and engineering educator*
†Johnson, Richard Arnold *statistics educator, consultant*
Jones, James Edward, Jr., *retired law educator*
Kaesberg, Paul Joseph *virology researcher*
Karofsky, Peter Stuart *pediatrician, medical educator*
Keesey, Richard E. *retired behavioral neuroscience educator*
Kemnitz, Joseph William *physiologist, researcher*
†Kennedy, Debora A. *lawyer*
Kettl, Donald Francis *political science educator*
Kiessling, Laura Lee *chemist, researcher*
Kim, Kyung-Sun *library and information scientist, educator*
†Klein, Marjorie Hanson *psychiatry educator*
Klein, Sheldon *computational linguist, educator*
Kleinhenz, Christopher *foreign language educator, researcher*
Klodt, Gerald Joseph *product development executive*
Knapstein, Michael *advertising executive*
Knowles, Richard Alan John *English language educator*
Korenic, Lynette Marie *librarian*
Kreuter, Gretchen V. *academic administrator*
Kuehling, Robert Warren *lawyer, accountant*
Kulcinski, Gerald LaVerne *dean*
Kutler, Stanley Ira *history and law educator, author*
Kuzuhara, Loren Wyatt *management consultant, educator*
Laessig, Ronald Harold *preventive medicine and pathology educator, state official*
La Follette, Douglas J. *secretary of state*
Lagally, Max Gunter *physics educator*
Langer, Richard J. *lawyer*
†Langer, Stanley Harold *chemical engineer, educator*
Lardy, Henry A(rnold) *biochemistry educator*
Larson, John David *insurance company executive, lawyer*
Lasseter, Robert Haygood *electrical engineering educator, consultant*
†Lautenschlager, Peggy A. *state attorney general*
Lawler, James Edward *physics educator*
†Lawton, Barbara *lieutenant governor*
Leckie, Carol Mavis *retired state government administrator*
†Lee, Mark Charles *engineer*
Lee, Peter *materials scientist*
Lemanske, Robert F., Jr., *allergist, immunologist*
Lightfoot, Edwin Niblock, Jr., *retired chemical engineering educator*
Lillesand, Thomas Martin *remote sensing educator*
Lindgren, Richard Dan *retired radiologist, healthcare administrator*
Linstroth, Tod Brian *lawyer*
Little, George Daniel *clergyman*
†Loewentsein, David *literature educator*
†Long, Theodore James *lawyer*
Long, Willis Franklin *electrical engineering educator, researcher*
Loper, Carl Richard, Jr., *metallurgical engineer, educator*
Lovell, Edward George *mechanical engineering educator*
Luening, Robert Adami *agricultural economics educator emeritus*
Lyall, Katharine C(ulbert) *academic administrator, economics educator*
Mackie, Richard H. *orchestra executive*
MacKinney, Archie Allen, Jr., *physician*
Maersch, Nancy Kay *health facility administrator*
†Magnan, Sally Sieloff *language educator*
Maher, Louis James, Jr., *geologist, educator*
Mahvi, David M. *surgeon, educator*
Maki, Dennis G. *medical educator, researcher, clinician*
Malinowski, Dennis Edmund *government consultant*
Malkus, David Starr *retired mechanics educator, applied mathematician*
†Mandrekar, Michelle Nelson *research scientist*
†Manoogian, Vartan *musician, educator*
Marrett, Cora B.
Martin, Robert David *judge, educator*
†Mau, Bob *statistician*
McNelly, John Taylor *journalist, educator*
†Mebane, David Cummins *lawyer*
Melli, Marygold Shire *law educator*
Mertens, Diane K. *secondary education educator*
Mertz, Janet Elaine *molecular biology researcher, educator, consultant*
Michaelis, Karen Lauree *law educator*
Michel, Sharon Lee *systems and information technology director*
Miernowski, Jan *foreign language educator*
Migas, Rosalie Ann *social worker*
†Miller, Frederick William *publisher, lawyer*
†Mitby, John Chester *lawyer*
†Mitchell, Julie Carol *mathematician, educator, biochemist, educator*
Morgan, Theodore *economist*
Morton, Stephen Dana *chemist, consultant*
†Mowris, Gerald William *lawyer*
Mueller, Willard Fritz *economics educator*
Mukerjee, Pasupati *chemistry educator*
Mullins, Jerome Joseph *real estate developer, consulting engineer*
†Murray, Julia Killin *art history educator*
Myers, Franklin Lewis, II, *ophthalmologist*
Narveson, Joyce Ann *public services administrator*
Nembhard, David A. *engineering educator, researcher*
Neuman, William Lawrence, Jr., *sociology educator*
Nevin, John Robert *business educator, consultant*
Newcomb, Eldon Henry *retired botany educator*
Nichols, Donald Arthur *economist, educator*
Niederhuber, John Edward *surgical oncologist and molecular immunologist, university educator and administrator*
Nisbet, Thomas K. *architect*
Nishikida, Koichi *research scientist*
†Noguera, Antonio *language educator*
Nordby, Eugene Jorgen *orthopedic surgeon*
Novotny, Donald Wayne *electrical engineering educator*
O'Brien, James Aloysius *foreign language educator*
Odden, Allan Robert *education educator*
Odom, John Yancy *human resources specialist, writer*
Ono, Ken *mathematician, educator*
†Osborn, J. Marshall *mathematician, educator*
Parter, Seymour Victor *computer science and mathematics educator*
Passman, Donald Steven *mathematician, educator*
†Peercy, Paul Stuart *laboratory director, physics researcher*
Pella, Milton Orville *retired science educator*
Perlman, Katherine Lenard (Kato Lenard) *organic chemist*
†Pernitz, Scott Gregory *lawyer*
Peters, Henry Augustus *neuropsychiatrist*
Petershack, Richard Eugene *lawyer*
Pierce, Harvey R. *insurance company executive*
Pitot, Henry Clement, III, *pathologist, educator*
Pitzner, Richard William *lawyer*
Powell, Barry Bruce *classicist, educator*
Prange, Roy Leonard, Jr., *lawyer*
Pray, Lloyd Charles *geologist, educator*
Provis, Timothy Alan *lawyer*
†Radano, Ronald Michael *musicologist, educator*
Ragatz, Thomas George *lawyer*
Rankin, Gene Raymond *lawyer*
†Raymond, Christopher Scott *mathematician, consultant*
†Reilly, Kevin P. *academic administrator*
Reizner, George Terry *medical educator*
Resnick, Daniel Karel *neurosurgeon, spinal surgeon, medical educator*
Reuschlein, Robert William *accountant, researcher*
Reynolds, Ernest West *retired physician, educator*
Reynolds, Ronald *research scientist, educator*
Rice, Joy Katharine *psychologist, educational policy studies and women's studies educator*
Rich, Daniel Hulbert *chemistry educator*
Rideout, Walter Bates *English educator*
Ring, Gerald J. *real estate developer, insurance executive*
Ris, Hans *zoologist, educator*
Risser, Fred A. *state legislator*
Roberson, Linda *lawyer*
Roberts, Leigh Milton *psychiatrist*
Robinson, Arthur Howard *geography educator*
Robinson, Stephen Michael *applied mathematician, educator*
Roessler, Carol Ann *state legislator*
Rosser, Annetta Hamilton *composer*
Rueckert, Roland Rudyard *retired virologist, educator*
Rux, Paul Philip *management consultant, educator*
Sanchez, Cheryl Pimentel *pediatrician, educator*
Saunders, Charles David *state official*
Savage, Blair deWillis *astronomer, educator*
Sazhin, Sergey Victorovich *electrochemist, researcher*
Scarborough, John Samuel *pharmacy, medicine and ancient history educator*
†Scherdin, Mary Jane Liskovec *librarian, information professional, researcher*
Scherer, Victor Richard *physicist, computer specialist, consultant, musician*
†Scheub, Harold *language educator, literature educator*
Schmid, John Henry, Jr., *lawyer*
Schmidt, Cheryl A. Zeise *family practice nurse practitioner*
Schmidt, John Richard *agricultural economics educator*
Schmidt, Martha Bubeck *educator, counselor*
Schooler, Steven James *lawyer*
Schutta, Henry Szczesny *neurologist, educator*
Selvaggi, Suzanne Marie *pathologist, educator*
†Severson, Shawn Ross *Spanish educator*
Sewell, Richard Herbert *historian, educator*
Shabaz, John C. *judge*
Shain, Irving *retired chemical company executive and university chancellor*
Sharkey, Thomas David *educator, botanist*
Sih, Charles John *pharmaceutical chemistry educator*
Sims, Terre Lynn *insurance company executive*
Singer, Marcus George *philosopher, educator*
Skiles, James Jean *electrical and computer engineering educator*
Skinner, James Lauriston *chemist, educator*
Slesinger, Doris Peyser *sociology educator*

†Smith, Michael James *industrial engineering educator*
Sobkowicz, Hanna Maria *neurology researcher*
Sondel, Paul Mark *pediatric oncologist, educator*
Sonnedecker, Glenn Allen *pharmaceutical historian, pharmaceutical educator*
Spear, Thomas Turner *history educator*
†Steingass, Susan R. *lawyer*
Stewart, Warren Earl *chemical engineer, educator*
Stites, Susan Kay *writer, human resources consultant*
Stoddard, Glenn McDonald *lawyer*
Stone, John Timothy, Jr., *writer*
†Stotsky, David M.
Strier, Karen Barbara *anthropologist, educator*
†Stump, Kurt Edward *research scientist*
†Sun, Dandan *neuroscientist, researcher*
†Sun, Hongyu *electrical engineer, researcher*
Sunde, Milton Lester *retired poultry science educator*
†Suri, Jeremi A. *education educator*
Susman, Millard *geneticist, educator*
Suttie, John Weston *biochemist*
Sykes, Diane S. *state supreme court justice*
†Symon, Keith Randolph *physics educator, consultant*
Szybalski, Waclaw *geneticist, educator*
Temkin, Harvey L. *lawyer*
†Terasawa-Grilley, Ei *medical educator*
Thiesenhusen, William Charles *agricultural economist, educator*
†Thomas, Gloria *lawyer, nurse, state program administrator*
Thomas, J. Mark *sociology educator, research fellow, minister*
Thompson, Barbara Storck *state official*
Tishler, William Henry *landscape architect, educator*
†Tomé, Wolfgang Axel *physicist, researcher, educator*
†Trier, Todd T. *neurosurgeon*
Trubetskoy, Vladimir Sergeevich *polymer chemist*
Turner, Robert Lloyd *state legislator*
Vandell, Kerry Dean *real estate and urban economics educator*
†Vanderheiden, Gregg C. *engineering educator, research scientist*
Van Ryzin, Gary James *lawyer, accountant*
Vaughan, Michael Richard *lawyer*
Vaughan, Worth Edward *chemistry educator*
†Voight, Jack C. *state official*
Vowles, Richard Beckman *literature educator*
Wagner, Burton Allan *lawyer*
Wakker, Bart P. *astronomer*
Waldo, Robert Leland *retired insurance company executive*
Walker, Duard Lee *medical educator*
Walsh, David Graves *lawyer*
Wanek, Ronald Melvin *orthodontist*
Webster, John Goodwin *biomedical engineering educator, researcher*
Weimer, David Leo *political science educator*
Weinbrot, Howard David *English educator*
Welker, Wallace Irving *neurophysiologist, educator*
Wenger, Ronald David *surgeon*
†Wengler, Michael J. *music educator*
Wertsch, Paul Anthony *family physician, medical administrator*
West, Kenneth D. *economist, educator*
Westman, Jack Conrad *child psychiatrist, educator*
Whiffen, James Douglass *surgeon, educator*
Whitney, Lori Ann *legislative staff member*
Wiesenfarth, Joseph John *retired literature educator*
Wilcox, Jon P. *state supreme court justice*
†Wiley, John D. *academic administrator*
Wilson, Franklin D. *sociology educator*
Wilson, Jacquelyn *writer*
Wolfe, Barbara L. *economics educator, researcher*
Wolman, J. Martin *retired newspaper publisher*
Wood, Tracey Ann *lawyer*
Young, Merwin Crawford *political science educator*
Young, Rebecca Mary Conrad *state legislator*
Yuill, Thomas MacKay *academic administrator, microbiology educator*
Zhu, Junyong *research scientist*
†Zhu, Xinsheng *physiologist, biochemist*
Zimmerman, Howard Elliot *chemist, educator*
Zweifel, David Alan *newspaper editor*

Malone
Tyunaitis, Patricia Ann *elementary school educator*

Manawa
Koehler, Carol Jean *nurse*

Manitowoc
Behnke, Elizabeth Doelker *community volunteer, retired nurse*
Klingeisen, Richard Herman *priest*
Schuh, Martha Schuhmann *mathematics educator*
Shimek, Rosemary Geralyn *medical/surgical nurse*
Trader, Joseph Edgar *orthopedic surgeon*

Marathon
Natzke, Paulette Ann *manufacturing executive*

Marinette
†El-Jack, Mohammed S. *urologist*

Markesan
Chamberlain, Robert Glenn *retired tool manfacturing executive*

Marshfield
Bibbo, Christopher *physician*
Gardner, Ella Haines *artist*
†Liu, Kejian *statistician*
McCarty, John Edward *medical clinic administrator*
†Myers, William Osgood *thoracic and cardiovascular surgeon*
Tak, Tahir *cardiologist, researcher*
Vidaillet, Humberto J., Jr., *physician, researcher*
Wesbrook, Frederic P. *health facility administrator, physician*
†Yale, Steven Howard *internist*

Mayville
†Schabel, Lorie Ann *pre-school educator*

Mc Farland
†Abbott, William Anthony *lawyer*
Deniston-Trochta, Grace Marie *educator, artist*

Menasha
Anderson, Kenneth Fritz *dramatic arts educator*
†Leahy, Stephen Michael *history educator*
Mahnke, Kurt Luther *psychotherapist, clergyman*
Mills, Laurel *writer*
†Peter, Gregory A. *sociology educator*
†Taheri, Abbas Ali *economist, educator*

Menomonee Falls
Bujanovich, William Matthew *marketing professional*
Chicorel, Ralph *composer, lyricist, playwright*
DeBoer, Bernice Mary *nurse*
Fisher, Robert Henri *physician*
Griswold, Paul Michael *clinical psychologist, consultant*
Hinnrichs-Dahms, Holly Beth *middle school educator*
†Hurt, Michael Carter *lawyer*
Janzen, Norine Madelyn Quinlan *medical technologist*
†Mansell, Kevin B. *retail executive*
Montgomery, R. Lawrence *department store chain executive*
Schlagel, David Mark *academic administrator*

Menomonie
†Brey, Eric Trent *hospitality and tourism educator*
Cutnaw, Mary-Frances *emeritus communications educator, writer, editor, publisher*
Eggert, James Edward *economics educator, writer*
Lueder, Dianne Carol *library director*
Schuler, Robert Jordan *English educator, writer*

Mequon
Arnholt, Philip J. *biologist, educator*
Beaudry, Diane Fay Puta *medical quality management executive*
Bell, Scott William *private school educator, principal*
Berry, William Martin *financial consultant*
Bloom, James Edward *commodity trading and financial executive*
†Burroughs, Charles Edward *lawyer*
Cheema, Mohammad Aslam *retired cardiothoracic surgeon, community leader*
Diesem, John Lawrence *business executive*
Dohmen, Frederick Hoeger *retired wholesale drug company executive*
Dohmen, Mary Holgate *retired primary school educator*
Elias, Paul S. *marketing executive*
Ellis, William Grenville *academic administrator, management consultant*
Krausen, Anthony Sharnik *plastic surgeon*
Locklair, Gary Hampton *computer science educator*
†Rapkin, Stephanie Gayle *lawyer, educator*

Merrill
Gebhardt, Suzanne Marie *insurance company executive*
Whitburn, Gerald *insurance company executive*

Middleton
Baron, Alma Fay S. *management educator*
Berman, Ronald Charles *lawyer, accountant*
†Caldwell, Michael Francis *psychologist*
Conaway, Jane Ellen *elementary education educator*
Cotherman, Audrey Mathews *management and policy consultant, administrator*
Dorner, Peter Paul *retired economist, educator*
Erichsen-Hubbard, Isabel Janice *music educator*
Lee, Leslie Warren *marketing executive, public speaker*
McDermott, Molly *lay minister*
Semmes, Sally Peterson *choreographer, educator*
†Taylor, Christopher Philip *pianist*
Taylor, Fannie Turnbull *social education and arts administration educator*

Milwaukee
†Abdoo, Richard A. *utilities company executive*
Abraham, William John, Jr., *lawyer*
Adelman, Lynn *federal judge*
†Agha, Zia *physician, researcher*
Aman, Mohammed Mohammed *dean, library and information science educator*
Arbit, Bruce *direct marketing executive, consultant*
†Ariker, Shanti Alice *lawyer*
Armstrong, Douglas Dean *journalist*
Auer, James Matthew *art critic, journalist*
Babler, Wayne E., Jr., *lawyer*
Bader, Alfred Robert *chemist*
Baker, John Edward *cardiac biochemist, educator*
†Ballman, Patricia Kling *lawyer*
Bannen, John Thomas *lawyer*
Barboi, Alexandru Cezar *neuroscientist, researcher*
Barnes, Paul McClung *lawyer*
Barth, Karl Luther *retired seminary president*
Beals, Vaughn Le Roy, Jr., *retired motorcycle manufacturing executive*
Behrendt, David Frogner *retired journalist*
Beightol, Scott Christopher *lawyer*
Beliavsky, Yuri *violinist, educator*
†Benesh, Sara C. *adult education educator*
Berkoff, Marshall Richard *lawyer*
Bernstein, Paul Steven *cardiologist*
Bibby, John Franklin *political science educator, writer*
Biehl, Michael Melvin *lawyer, author*
†Biernat, Kathy A. *instructional designer*
Biller, Geraldine Pollack *art consultant, curator*
Biller, Joel Wilson *lawyer, former foreign service officer*
Bishop, Charles Joseph *manufacturing company executive*
Blain, Peter Charles *lawyer*
Blasinski, Clare Marie *librarian*
Blau, Richard Miles (Dick Blau) *performing arts educator, photographer, film director*
†Bleustein, Jeffrey L. *automotive executive*
Bliss, Richard Jon *lawyer*
Blumberg, Sherry Helene *Jewish education educator*
Boese, Gil Karyle *cultural organization executive*
†Bolger, T(homas) Michael *lawyer*
Bratt, Herbert Sidney *lawyer*
Bremer, John M. *lawyer*
Brever, Michael Stephen *non-profit executive director, alderman*
Brideau, Leo Paul *healthcare executive*
Bruce, Peter Wayne *lawyer, insurance company executive*
Burch, Thaddeus Joseph, Jr., *physics educator, clergyman*
†Burckel, Nicholas C. *historian, educator, school librarian, dean*
Busch, John Arthur *lawyer*
Buss, Daniel Frank *environmental scientist*
Calise, William Joseph, Jr., *lawyer*
Campbell, Bruce Hegstad *otolaryngologist, educator*
Cannon, David Joseph *lawyer*
Carballo, Fernando Anthony *gastroenterologist, hepatologist*
†Carter, Charlene Ann *psychologist*
Casey, John Alexander *lawyer*
Casper, Richard Henry *lawyer*
Cassell, Samuel James *basketball player*
Chan, Carlyle Hung-lun *psychiatrist, educator*
Chandler, Edward William *communication systems engineer, electrical engineer, electrical engineering educator*
†Cheatham, Wallace McClain *music educator*
Christensen, Erik Regnar *engineering educator, researcher*
Christiansen, Keith Allan *lawyer*
Clark, James Richard *lawyer*
†Clayton, Rebecca D. *customer service administrator*
Cohen, Steven Howard *allergist, immunologist, educator*
Cohn, Lucile *psychotherapist, nurse*
Colbert, Virgis W. *food products executive*
Colbert, Virgis William *brewery company executive*
Cole, John Dewey *management consultant*
Connelly, Mark *writer, educator*
Conner, David Lee *secondary educator*
Connolly, Gerald Edward *lawyer*
†Constable, John *advertising executive*
Coogan, Frank Neil *health and social services administrator*
Cook, Wayne Evans *music educator*
Cooper, Kristine Marie *internist*
Cooper, Richard Alan *hematologist, college dean, health policy analyst*
Crocker, Ray Dean *musician, musical director*
Cutler, Richard W. *lawyer*
Cutler, Verne Clifton *engineering educator, consultant*
Daily, Frank J(erome) *lawyer*
Dale, Scott *Spanish educator*
Dallman, Robert Edward *lawyer*
†Davis, Don H., Jr., *multi-industry high-technology company executive*
Davis, Thomas William *computer company executive*
Delfs, Andreas *conductor, musical director*
†Delwiche, William Arthur *economist, researcher*
Demerdash, Nabeel Aly Omar *electrical engineer*
Dencker, Lester J. *lawyer*
Donahue, John Edward *lawyer*
Downey, John Wilham *composer, pianist, conductor, educator*
Duback, Steven Rahr *lawyer*
Dunn, Michael J. *dean*
Dye, Sharon Elizabeth Herndon *speech pathologist*
†Enk, Scott *editor, researcher, activist*
Ericson, James Donald *lawyer, insurance executive*
Ertel, Gary Arthur *accountant*
Esterly, Nancy Burton *physician*
Evans, Terence Thomas *federal judge*
Farris, Trueman Earl, Jr., *retired newspaper editor*
Feinsilver, Donald Lee *psychiatry educator*
Ferguson, Nancy L. *social worker, psychotherapist*
Fitzgerald, Kevin Gerard *lawyer*
Florsheim, Richard Steven *lawyer*
†Fluharty, George Mark *speech pathology/audiology services professional*
Foldy, Seth Leonard *public health officer, family practice physician*
Fonner, Kelly S. *educational technologist, consultant*
Foster, Richard *journalist*
Fournelle, Raymond Albert *engineering educator*
Frank, Dennis *psychotherapist, educator*
Franklin, Scott Bradley *accountant, lawyer*
Frautschi, Timothy Clark *lawyer*
Frey, James Severin *educational association executive*
Friedman, James Dennis *lawyer*
Friman, H. Richard *political science educator*
Frittitta, Peter Anthony *health maintenance organization executive*
Gaggioli, Richard Arnold *mechanical engineering educator*
†Gagliani, William Dennis *school librarian*
Gaines, Irving David *lawyer*
Galanis, John William *lawyer*
Gallagher, Richard Sidney *lawyer*
Gallop, Jane (Jane Anne Gallop) *women's studies educator, writer*
Garbaciak-Bobber, Joyce Katherine *news anchor*
Gefke, Henry Jerome *lawyer*
Gemignani, Joseph Adolph *lawyer*
Ghiardi, James Domenic *lawyer, educator*
Giese, Heiner *lawyer, real estate investor*
Gimbel, Franklyn M. *lawyer*
Glazer, Gerald Sherwin *real estate broker*
Goetsch, John Hubert *consultant and retired utility company executive*
Goldstein, Paul H(enry) *ophthalmologist, educator*
Gondek, Mary Jane (Mary Jane Suchorski) *property manager*
Gonnering, Russell Stephen *ophthalmic plastic surgeon*
†Gonzalez, Jorge Antonio *education educator*
Goodkind, Conrad George *lawyer*
Goodstein, Aaron E. *federal magistrate judge*
Graber, Richard William *lawyer, political organization worker*
Grabowski, Michael Joseph *financial executive*
Graef, Luther William *civil engineer*
Greaves, William Walter *preventive medicine physician, educator*
†Green, Edward Anthony *museum director*
Greenler, Robert George *physics educator, researcher*
Grenig, Jay Edward *law educator*
Griffith, Owen Wendell *biochemistry educator*
†Haasler, George Bruce *cardiothoracic surgeon*
Haberman, F. William *lawyer*
Habush, Robert Lee *lawyer*
Hansen, John Herbert *university administrator, accountant*
Harrington, John Timothy *retired lawyer*
Harris, Christine *dance company executive*
Harvieux, Anne Marie *psychotherapist*
Hase, David John *lawyer*
†Hatch, Michael Ward *lawyer*
Haworth, Daniel Thomas *chemistry educator*
Healy, Cletus S. J. *priest*
Heim, Kathryn Marie *psychiatric nurse, author*
Heinen, James Albin *electrical engineering educator*
Hendee, William Richard *medical physics educator, university official, radiologist*
Heo, Uk *political scientist, educator*
Hernandez, Jose *baseball player*
Herr, Sister Annette Ellen *pharmacist*
Hirsch, June Schaut *priest*
Hoefle, Paul Ryan *lawyer*
Hoffman, Nathaniel A. *lawyer*
Hoffmann, Gregg J. *journalist, author, publisher*
Holme, Thomas A. *chemistry educator, researcher*
Holz, Harry George *lawyer*
Horowitz, Alan Joel *civil engineer, educator*
†Hsieh, Jiang *research scientist*
Hudson, Katherine Mary *manufacturing company executive*
Huebner, Sister Rosemarita *nun, art educator*
Hunter, Victor Lee *marketing executive, consultant*
Hur, Su-Ryong *physician, anesthesiologist*
Huss, William Lee *computer analyst*
Huston, Kathleen Marie *library administrator*
Hutz, Reinhold Josef *physiologist, educator*
Iaquinta, Leonard Phillip *university official*
Iding, Allan Earl *lawyer*
Ignacio, Reinere John Dy *research scientist*
†Israel, Scott Michael *lawyer*
Jenkins, Clarence William, Jr., *academic administrator*
Jirovec, Mary Ann *music educator*
Joerres, Jeffrey A. *staffing company executive*
Johannes, Kay L. *insurance company executive*
†Johnson, James N. *lawyer*
Joseph, Jules K. *retired public relations executive*
Jost, Lawrence John *lawyer*
†Jung, Patrick Joseph *humanities educator*
†Kadel, Lee A. *computer engineer*
Kaiser, Martin *newspaper editor*
†Kampine, John P. *anesthesiology and physiology educator*
Karkheck, John Peter *physics educator, researcher*
Kasten, G. Frederick, Jr., *investment company executive*
†Kendall, Leon Thomas *finance and real estate educator, retired insurance company executive*
Kerr, Dorothy Marie Burmeister *marketing executive, consultant*
Kessler, Joan F. *lawyer*
Keyes, James Henry *manufacturing company executive*
Kidder, Thomas Michael *otolaryngologist*
Kircher, John Joseph *law educator*
†Knight, George B. *lawyer*
Kochar, Mahendr Singh *physician, educator, administrator, scientist, writer, consultant*
†Korabic, Edward Walter *medical educator, speech pathology/audiology services professional*
Kovnar, Edward H. *pediatric neurologist, medical educator*
Kraut, Joanne Lenora *computer programmer, analyst*
Kringel, Jerome Howard *lawyer*
Kritzer, Paul Eric *media executive, communications lawyer*
Krueger, Raymond Robert *lawyer*
Kubale, Bernard Stephen *lawyer*
Kupst, Mary Jo *psychologist, researcher*
Kurtz, Harvey A. *lawyer*
LaBudde, Roy Christian *lawyer*
Ladd, Louise Elizabeth *investments company executive*

LaMalfa, Joachim Jack *retired clinical psychologist*
Landis, Fred *mechanical engineering educator*
Larson, David Lee *surgeon*
Laubenheimer, Jeffrey John *civil engineer*
†Laughlin, Steven L. *advertising executive*
†Lea, Filomena *literature educator, writer*
Leonard, Richard Hart *journalist, educator*
Levit, William Harold, Jr., *lawyer*
Levy, Alan M. *lawyer*
Li, Jin *environmental engineer, educator*
†Lockett, Sandra Anita Johnson Bokamba *librarian*
Lopes, Davey *former professional baseball manager*
Lueders, Wayne Richard *lawyer*
MacGregor, David Lee *lawyer*
Machulak, Edward Leon *real estate, mining and advertising company executive*
MacIver, John Kenneth *lawyer*
Mahler, Stephanie Irene *retired administrative manager*
Maiman, Dennis Jay *neurosurgeon*
†Mali, Amol Dattatraya *computer scientist, educator*
Mamalakis, Markos John *economics educator*
Manning, Kenneth Paul *technologies company executive*
Mannisto, Richard Todd *music educator*
Margolis, Marvin Allen *lawyer*
Marringa, Jacques Louis *manufacturing company executive*
†Marten, James Alan *historian, educator*
Martin, Quinn William *lawyer*
Martin, Vincent Lionel *manufacturing company executive*
†Massey, Benson Talmage *gastroenterologist*
Maynard, John Ralph *lawyer*
McGaffey, Jere D. *lawyer*
McSweeney, Maurice J. (Marc McSweeney) *lawyer*
Medved, Paul Stanley *lawyer*
Meldman, Clifford Kay *lawyer*
Meldman, Robert Edward *lawyer*
Melin, Robert Arthur *lawyer*
Meyer, Jon Keith *psychiatrist, psychoanalyst, educator*
Michaels-Paque, Joan Marie *artist, educator*
Michelstetter, Stanley Hubert *lawyer*
Miller, Edward Carl William *physician*
†Misner, Paul *theology educator*
Moberg, David Oscar *sociology educator*
Moffie, H. Steven *psychiatrist*
†Morris, George L. *neurologist, educator*
Mulcahy, Robert William *lawyer*
Murphy, Josephine Mancuso *critical care nurse, adult nurse practitioner*
Muszynski, Cheryl Ann *neurosurgeon*
Namdari, Bahram *surgeon*
Nelson, Randy Scott *lawyer*
Nelson, Roy Hugh, Jr., *lawyer, mediator, arbitrator*
Norquist, John Olaf *mayor*
Novak, Joseph Anthony *physician, pathologist*
Nystrom, Paul Clifdon *business educator*
Oldham, Keith T. *surgeon*
Olivieri, José Alberto *lawyer*
Olson, Frederick Irving *retired history educator*
†O'Neill, James Martin *venture capitalist*
O'Shaughnessy, James Patrick *lawyer*
†Pagel, Paul Stanley *anesthesiologist*
Papas, George Nick *bakery company executive*
Paque, Joan Michaels *multimedia artist, author, educator*
Parker, Charles Walter, Jr., *consultant, retired equipment company executive*
†Patzke, John Charles *lawyer*
Paul, Mary *human resources professional*
Peck, Curtiss S. *organization development consultant, author, educator*
Peckerman, Bruce Martin *lawyer*
Peltin, Sherwin Carl *lawyer*
Perlman, Richard Wilfred *economist, educator*
†Pettit, Roger Lee *lawyer*
Phillips, Thomas John *lawyer*
Pindyck, Bruce Eben *lawyer, corporate executive*
†Pink, Michael *performing company executive*
†Platt, Jeb Buchanan *health facility administrator*
†Pless, Joel Loren *humanities educator*
Port, Steven Charles *cardiologist, educator*
†Porter, Terry *professional basketball coach*
Powell, Edmund William *lawyer*
†Prucha, Francis Paul *historian, priest*
†Quadracci, Thomas A. *printing company executive*
Quereshi, Mohammed Younus *psychology educator, consultant*
Radke, Dale Lee *religious organization administrator, deacon, editor, pastor*
Randall, William Seymour *leasing company executive*
Rathour, Rajendra Singh *internist*
Read, Sister Joel *academic administrator*
Reardon, Timothy P. *lawyer*
Redlin, Bruce Michael *financial consultant*
Reed, John Kennedy Emanuel *elementary school teacher*
†Reynolds, Barbara E *mathematics educator*
Rhead, William James *biochemical geneticist*
Rheams, Annie Elizabeth *education educator*
Rhoten, Juliana Theresa *retired school principal*
Richman, Stephen Erik *lawyer*
Rieselbach, Allen Newman *lawyer*
Rintelman, Donald Brian *lawyer*
Ritz, Esther Leah *civic worker, volunteer, investor*
Rivero, Albert J. *English educator*
Roberson, Reniti Renea *elementary school educator*
Robertson, Michael Swing *minister*
Roeming, Robert Frederick *foreign language educator*
Roge, Bret Alan *lawyer*
Roozen, Mary Louise *public relations executive*
Rosenblatt, Suzanne Maris *performance artist, poet, visual artist*
Rosenblum, Martin Jack *historian*
Ryan, Patrick Michael *lawyer*
Saldin, Dilano Kerzaman *physicist, educator*
Samson, Allen Lawrence *investor, bank executive*
Samson, Richard Max *theatre director, investment/real estate executive*
Sanfilippo, Jon Walter *lawyer, commissioner*
Sankovitz, James Leo *retired development director, lobbyist*
†Sayles, Ronald Lyle *computer executive*
†Schaefer, Jame *science educator*
Schmitz, Francis David *lawyer*
Schneider, Thomas Paul *non-profit agency administrator*
Schnoll, Howard Manuel *financial consultant, investment company executive*
Schnur, Robert Arnold *lawyer*
†Schrader, David M. *physicist, researcher, writer*
Schroeder, John H. *university chancellor*
Schultz, Richard Otto *ophthalmologist, educator*
Scrabeck, Jon Gilmen *dental educator*
Scrivner, Thomas William *lawyer*
Setright, Mildred Alberta *educator*
Sexson, Richmond Lockwood *baseball player*
Shaker, Reza *gastroenterologist, educator*
Shapiro, James Edward *judge*
Shapiro, Robert Donald *management advisor on strategy and acquisitions/divestitures*
†Shapiro, Robyn Sue *lawyer, educator*
Shetty, Kaup Rajmohan *endocrinologist, educator*
Shidham, Vinod Baburao *pathologist, cytopathologist, surgical pathologist*
Shiely, John Stephen *company executive, lawyer*
Shriner, Thomas L., Jr., *lawyer*
Siegel, Kristi Ellen *English educator*
Siegel, Robert Harold *English literature educator, writer*
Silverman, Franklin Harold *speech pathologist, educator*
Simoneau, Daniel Robert *accountant, watercolorist, educator, application developer*
Skipper, Walter John *lawyer*
Slavik, Donald Harlan *lawyer*
Smith, David Bruce *lawyer*
Soergel, Konrad Hermann *physician*
Solomon, Donald William *mathematics and computer science educator, consultant*
†Somers, Kristina Elizabeth *lawyer*
†Sosnovsky, George *chemist, educator*
†Sostarich, Mark Edward *lawyer*
Spore, Keith Kent *newspaper executive*
†Spransy, Celeste Bower *artist*
Stadtmueller, Joseph Peter *federal judge*
Stefaniak, Norbert John *business administration educator*
Steinmiller, John F. *professional basketball team executive*
Stephens, Marla Jean *lawyer*
Sterner, Frank Maurice *industrial executive*
Stokes, Kathleen Sarah *dermatologist, educator*
†Stowe, David F *physiologist*
Stubbe, Ray William *minister, writer*
Sturm, William Charles *lawyer*
Surridge, Stephen Zehring *lawyer, writer*
Swanson, Roy Arthur *classicist, educator*
†Tector, Alfred J. *cardiothoracic surgeon*
Telford, Gordon Laing *surgeon, educator*
Temmer, James Donald *museum director*
Terry, Leon Cass *neurologist, educator*
Terschan, Frank Robert *lawyer*
Theis, Peter George *retired classics educator*
Theoharis, Athan George *history educator*
Thrall, Arthur Alvin *artist, educator*
†Tillett, Jacquelynn *nurse midwife*
Titley, Robert L. *lawyer*
Trecek, Timothy Scott *lawyer*
Trytek, David Douglas *insurance company executive*
Uecker, Bob *actor, radio announcer, former baseball player, TV personality*
Ullman, Pierre Lioni *retired Spanish educator*
Vairavan, Kasivisvanathan *electrical engineering and computer science educator*
Valance, Marsha Jeanne *library director, story teller*
Verhaalen, Marion *music educator*
Viets, Hermann *college president, consultant*
Wackym, Phillip Ashley *surgeon, researcher, otolaryngologist*
Wagner, Marvin *general and vascular surgeon, educator*
Wake, Madeline Musante *academic administrator, nursing educator*
Waldbaum, Jane Cohn *art history educator*
Waller, Mary Bellis *psychotherapist, education educator, consultant*
Walmer, Edwin Fitch *lawyer*
Walthers, Bruce Julius *hobby industry executive*
Warltier, David Charles *anesthesiologist, medical researcher*
Warren, Richard M. *experimental psychologist, educator*
Weakland, Rembert G. *retired archbishop*
Weber, Ralph Edward *history educator*
Wei, Yehua Dennis *geography educator*
Weisner, David *illustrator*
†Wen, Haifang *transportation engineer*
Whyte, George Kenneth, Jr., *lawyer*
Widera, Georg Ernst Otto *mechanical engineering educator, consultant*
Wild, Robert Anthony *university president*
Wiley, Edwin Packard *retired lawyer*
Wilkie, Charles A. *chemistry educator*
Will, Trevor Jonathan *lawyer*
Williams, Clay Rule *lawyer*
Wilsdon, Thomas Arthur *product development engineer, administrator*
Winsten, Saul Nathan *lawyer*
Wolfe, Christopher *political science educator*
Wucherer, Ruth Marie *business owner*
Wynn, Stanford Alan *lawyer*
†Yakovlev, Vladislav *education educator, researcher*
†Yancey, Kim Bruce *dermatology researcher*
Yontz, Kenneth Fredric *medical and chemical company executive*
Young, Craig C. *sports medicine physician, educator*
Zeidler, Frank P. *former association administrator, mayor, arbitrator, mediator, fact-finder*
†Zore, Edward John *financial services executive*
Zuperku, Edward John *biomedical engineering educator*

Minocqua
Jaye, David Robert, Jr., *retired hospital administrator*
†Lund, John Richard *lawyer, director*

Monona
Brandes, Stuart Dean *historian, educator*

Monroe
Kelly, James Evans *internist*
Kittelsen, Rodney Olin *lawyer*
Wilcox, Winton Wilfred, Jr., *communications specialist, consultant*

Mosinee
Hartz, Luetta Bertha *legal secretary*
Schira, Diana Rae *lawyer*

Mukwonago
Scarvie, Walter Bernard *clergyman*

Nashotah
Munday, Robert Stevenson *priest, academic administrator*
Vincent, Norman L. *retired insurance company executive*

Neenah
Bergstrom, Dedric Waldemar *retired paper company executive*
†Orm, Sally S. *music educator, consultant*
Wang, James Hongxue *polymer scientist*

Nekoosa
†Ramirez, Mary Catherine *retired secondary school educator*

New Berlin
Bielke, Patricia Ann *psychologist*
Duszynski-Waldbillig, Cynthia *piano teacher, performer, adjudicator*
Marsh, Clare Teitgen *retired school psychologist*
Schober, Thomas Gregory *lawyer*
Winkler, Dolores Eugenia *retired health facility administrator*

New Glarus
Etter, Peter Erich *retired school district administrator*
Sippy, David Dean *dentist*

New London
Fitzgerald, Laurine Elisabeth *university dean, educator*

New Richmond
†Schwan, LeRoy Bernard *artist, retired educator*

Oak Creek
Giblin, Louis *lawyer*
Kim, Zaezeung *allergist, immunologist, educator*
Thomae, Mary Joan Pangborn *special education educator*

Oconomowoc
Conrader, Constance Ruth *artist, writer, librarian*
†Driscoll, Virgilyn Mae (Schaetzel) *retired art educator, artist, consultant*
Dupies, Donald Albert *retired civil engineer*
Kneiser, Richard John *accountant*
Luedke, Patricia Georgianne *microbiologist*
Reich, Rose Marie *retired art educator*
Schacht, Ruth Elaine *nursing educator*
Vespa, Ned Angelo *photographer*

Oconto
Watson-Boone, Rebecca A. *library and information studies researcher, educator*

Onalaska
Pertzsch, Evelyn Maria *civic worker*
Waite, Lawrence Wesley *osteopathic physician, educator*

Oregon
†Draeger, Norman Arthur *physical chemist, research and development company executive*
Latimer, James Harold *percussionist, conductor, composer, consultant, educator*
Roselle, Paul Lucas *material scientist*

Osceola
Finster, James Robert *library media specialist*

Oshkosh
Alderson, Jo Bartels *writer, poet*
Barwig, Regis Norbert James *priest*
Cooper, Janelle Lunette *neurologist, educator*
Curtis, George Warren *lawyer*
Drebus, Richard William *pharmaceutical company executive*
†Earns, Lane Robert *academic administrator, historian, educator*
Grieb, Kenneth Joseph *historian, educator*
Gruberg, Martin *political science educator*
Herzog, Barbara Jean *secondary school educator, administrator*
Hu, Li *art educator*
†Kelly, John Martin *lawyer*
Kerrigan, John E. *academic administrator*
Khan, Zillur Rahman *foundation executive*
Liu, Baodong *political scientist, consultant*
McWilliams, Robert Lindsay *music educator, musician, conductor*
Olejniczak, Bernard Charles *education educator*
Poberezny, Tom *federal agency administrator*
†Ristow, Thelma Frances *elementary educator*
Schoenrock, Tracy Allen *airline pilot, aviation consultant*
Siepmann, James Patrick *research company executive, retired physician*
Smith, Merilyn Roberta *art educator*
†Utke, Allen R(ay) *chemist, educator*
Wilde, William Richard *lawyer*
Zierdt, Alyson Kathleen *lawyer*
Zuern, Rosemary Lucile *manufacturing executive, treasurer*

Palmyra
Hammiller, Ruth Ellen *school official and psychologist*

Pepin
Seymour, Mary Frances *lawyer*

Peshtigo
†Gard, John *state legislator*

Pewaukee
†Carlson, Kathleen *not-for-profit fundraiser, writer, journalist*
Engel, John Charles *lawyer, lobbyist*
Farrow, Margaret Ann *former state official*
Jasiorkowski, Robert Lee *real estate broker, computer consultant*
Lee, Jack (Jim Sanders Beasley) *broadcast executive*
Long, Robert Eugene *banker*
†Mariano, Robert A. *retail executive*

Pine River
†Sallee, Lynn Kant *librarian*

Platteville
Dennis, Gregory James *music educator, secondary school educator*
Lindahl, Thomas Jefferson *retired university dean*
†Markee, David James *university official, education educator*
†Van Buren, David Paul *criminal justice educator*

Pleasant Prairie
Morrone, Frank *electronic manufacturing executive*
Pollocoff, Michael R. *village administrator*

Plymouth
Gentine, Lee Michael *marketing professional*
Sharon, Mark William *family practice physician*

Port Washington
Check, Melvin Anthony *lawyer*
Kettling, Virginia *health facility administrator*

Portage
Jensen, Hans William *library director*

Prescott
Kees, Mary Adele *school psychologist*

Racine
†Baldukas, Ann-Mari Peirce *dean*
†Bradley, Paul N. *special education educator*
Campbell, Edward Joseph *retired machinery company executive*
Coates, Glenn Richard *lawyer*
Crawford, Timothy Patrick *lawyer, accountant*
Du Rocher, James Howard *lawyer*
Dye, William Ellsworth *lawyer*
Gasiorkiewicz, Eugene Anthony *lawyer*
Hamberger, Larry Kevin *clinical psychologist, educator*
Isenberg, Norbert *chemist, educator*
Keehn, Richard H. *economics educator emeritus*
Klein, Gabriella Sonja *retired communications executive*
Konz, Gerald Keith *retired manufacturing company executive*
Langenegger, Armin *radiation physicist*
†MacPhail, Jessica Holman Whitehead *librarian*
Mekeel, Steven Leyon *lawyer*
†Miller, Yolanda *publisher, writer*
†Perez, William D. *chemical company executive*
†Rosso, Jean-Pierre *electronics executive*
Rudebusch, Alice Ann *lawyer*
Schoening, Ruth Irene *retired music educator, musician*
†Schoone, Adrian Paul *lawyer*
Sikora, Suzanne Marie *dentist*
Singh, Susan Marie *medical/surgical nurse*
Stephens, James Linton *mechanical engineer*
Stewart, Richard Donald *internist, educator, biographer*
†Stutt, John Barry *lawyer*
Wright, Betty Ren *children's book writer*

Redgranite
Borchardt, Betsy Olk *artist*

Reedsburg
Miotke, David Roy *music educator*

Rhinelander
Agre, James Courtland *physical medicine and rehabilitation*
†McEldowney, Todd Richard *lawyer*
Mussehl, Allan Arthur *program director*
Reese, Kirk David *lawyer*
Saari, John William, Jr., *lawyer*
Van Brunt-Bartholomew, Marcia Adele *social worker*

Rice Lake
Alho, Sister Bonnie Kathleen *pastoral associate*
Strong, Linda Louise *music educator*

Richland Center
Gollata, James Anthony *library director, educator*
Heinen, John Timothy *environmental engineer*

Ripon
Prissel, Barbara Ann *paralegal, law educator*

Steinbring, John Henry (Jack Steinbring) *archaeologist*

River Falls
Brown, Kevin James *researcher, consultant*
Hayden, Paul Allan *speech pathology educator, consultant, researcher*
Hedahl, Gorden Orlin *theatre educator, university dean*
LeCapitaine, John Edward *counseling psychology professor, researcher, writer*
†Lydecker, Ann Marie *college administrator*
†Montgomery, Karen E. *library and information scientist*
Potts, Glenn Thomas *economics educator*
Thibodeau, Gary A. *academic administrator*

River Hills
Tollaksen, Thomas William *village manager*

Salem
Hayes, Doris Ann *elementary education educator, consultant*

Saukville
Gulan, Bonnie Marion *writer, researcher*

Schofield
Adams, James William *former chemist*
Gontarz, Michael Joseph *school psychologist*

Shawano
†Heikes, Keith *science administrator*
Lyon, Thomas L. *agricultural organization administrator*
Swetlik, William Philip *orthodontist*

Sheboygan
†Abbay, Alemseged *education educator*
Cecil, Louis Anton *retired mathematics educator*
Elder, Karl Curtis *writer, educator*
Merkel, Daniel A. *dental products company executive*
†Schoemer, Jack Robert (John Robert Schoemer) *human resources specialist, director*
Strysick, Michael Otto *terrestrial ecologist, physicist, microbiologist*

Shell Lake
†Hawes, Grace Maxcy *retired archivist, researcher*

Shorewood
Lietz, Jeremy Jon *educational administrator, writer*

Soldiers Grove
Quebe, Jerry Lee *retired architect*

South Milwaukee
Kitzke, Eugene David *research and development company executive*
Knoll, Gregg A. *artist, printmaker, educator*
Thibaudeau, May Murphy *writer*

Spencer
†Herder, Paul O. *secondary school educator*

Stevens Point
†Blakeman, John Charles *political science educator*
Doherty, Patricia Anne *psychologist*
Hamlar, Portia Yvonne Trenholm *lawyer, writer, educator*
†Holland, Patricia Christine *music educator, musician*
†Huncharek, Michael Stephen *oncologist*
†Piotrowski, Cynthia Louise *not-for-profit developer*
†Teeple, Scott D. *conductor, music educator, director*
Wang, Jin *economics educator*

Stone Lake
Voss, William Charles *retired oil company executive*

Stoughton
†Wetzel, Volker Knoppke *law educator*

Sturgeon Bay
Greaves, Alison Ash *retired physician*
Korb, Joan *lawyer*
Van Duyse, Francis Donald (Fritz Van) *publisher*

Sturtevant
†Brandes, Jo Anne *lawyer*
†Johnson, Samuel Curtis *chemical company executive*
†Lawton, Gregory E. *manufacturing executive*
†Marschke, Sean M. *police commander, emergency management director*

Sun Prairie
Berkenstadt, James Allan *lawyer*
Eustice, Francis Joseph *lawyer*
Rollette, Harold Henry *insurance company executive*
Schmidt, Glenn Norbert *special education educator*
Sveum, Steven John *secondary school educator*
†Terhune, Karen Marie *mathematician, secondary school educator*

Superior
Billig, Thomas Clifford *publishing executive, marketing professional*
Bischoff, Joan *English educator*
Grittner, James Russell *artist, educator, department chair*
McKnight, Patricia Gayle *musician, artist, writer, educator*
Peterson, Charlene Marie *educational administrator*
Robek, Mary Frances *business education educator*
Rodne, Kjell John *healthcare administrator*

Sutter, Barton E. *literature educator, writer*

Sussex
Losee, John Frederick, Jr., *manufacturing executive*
†Ryan, Sandra C. *music educator, musician*
Stromberg, Gregory *printing ink company executive*

Thiensville
Dickow, James Fred *management consultant*
Hobbs, Walter Clarence *retired educator*
Roselle, William Charles *librarian*

Tomah
Hillman, Lin (Linda Lou Hillman) *nursing administrator*
Johnson, Linda Arlene *petroleum and flatbed semi-freight transporter*

Two Rivers
Heller, Mark *communications executive*

Union Grove
†Roettgen, Dale R. *essayist*

Valders
Lindholm, William Robert *elementary school educator*

Verona
Brachman, Richard John, II, *financial services consultant, banking educator*
Moynihan, Carolyn Jean *clinical social worker*

Warrens
Potter, June Anita *small business owner*

Washington Island
Raup, David Malcolm *paleontology educator*
Schweikert, Norman Carl *retired musician*

Waterford
Karraker, Louis Rendleman *retired corporate executive*

Waterloo
†Burke, Richard A. *manufacturing executive*

Watertown
Degnitz, Dorothy Elsie *retired nurse*
Henry, Helga Irmgard *liberal arts educator*
†Townsend, Rick David *music educator, writer*

Waukesha
Bohren, Michael Oscar *lawyer*
Cahill, Charles Adams, III, *psychiatrist*
†Davis, J. Mac *lawyer, state judge*
Dreyfus, Lee Sherman *international speaker*
Graham, George Andrew, Jr., *psychologist, consultant*
†Gustafson, Mardel Emma *secondary school educator, writer*
†Jastroch, Leonard Andrew *lawyer*
†Kocharian, Armen *physicist*
Larson, Russell George *magazine publisher*
Leatherberry, Anne Knox Clark *architect*
Macy, John Patrick *lawyer*
Mielke, William John *civil engineer*
†Ringhand, Ryan Randall *career planning administrator, educator*
†Satterlee, William Thomas *career planning administrator, consultant*
Trebon, Thomas *academic administrator*
Wallskog, Joyce Marie *nursing educator, psychologist*

Waupun
Wendt, Thomas Gene *finance executive*

Wausau
Ament, Richard Rand *psychologist*
Builer, Dorothy Marion *business owner*
†Dietrich, Dean Richard *lawyer*
†Drengler, William Allan John *lawyer*
†Eldred, Heather Ann *librarian*
Gau-Krueger, Susan Marie *social worker*
Gray, Robert Joseph *lawyer*
†Grischke, Alan Edward *lawyer*
†Hering, Helen Dora *controller*
†Kammer, Robert Arthur, Jr., *lawyer*
Krause, Steven Albert *writer*
Orr, San Watterson, Jr., *lawyer*
Switalski, Michael Mathew *secondary educator, lawyer*
Veninga, James Frank *humanities educator, editor, author*
Wadzinski, Mary Beth *administrative assistant*
Whitney, John Denison *English educator, writer*

Wauwatosa
†Alexander, Robert Gardner *lawyer*
Bonneson, Paul Garland *lawyer*
Bub, Alexander David *acoustical engineer*
Dupuis, Kateri Theresa *retired elementary education educator*
Franke, Brent Douglas *real estate/insurance executive*
Hollister, Winston Ned *pathologist*
Kostecke, B. William *utilities executive*
Wright, Isaac Wilson, Jr., *quality assurance professional*

Webster
Punch, William Anthony (Nicholas Punch) *priest*

West Allis
Aderman, Ralph Merl *language educator*
Fiorelli, Karen Lynn *registered nurse*

West Bend
Christianson, Marcia LaRaye *middle school educator*
Dries, Kathleen Marie *social worker*
Fraedrich, Royal Louis *magazine editor, publisher*
†Rodee-Schneider, Robin *marketing educator*

VanBrunt-Kramer, Karen *business administration educator*

Weyauwega
Hanneman, Elaine Esther *salesperson*

Whitefish Bay
Hawkins, Brett William *political science educator*
Nortman, M. Judith Haworth *geriatrics nurse*
†Pustejovsky, Susan F. *education educator*

Whitehall
Nordhagen, Hallie Huerth *nursing home administrator*

Whitewater
Arntson, Amy Ellen *artist, art educator*
†Baica, Malvina Florica *mathematician, educator*
Busse, Eileen Elaine *special education educator*
Connor, James Richard *retired foundation administrator*
†Ellenwood, Christian Kent *music educator*
Gauger, Michele Roberta *photographer, studio administrator, corporate executive*
Greenhill, H. Gaylon *retired academic administrator*
†Gwalla-Ogisi, Nomsa *education educator, consultant*
†Iyengar, Jagannathan Vijay *computer scientist, educator*
Kirst-Ashman, Karen Kay *social work educator*
†Kolb, Sharon Marie *educator, cognitive disabilities director*
Kolda, Thomas Joseph *non-profit organization executive*
Laurent, Jerome King *economics educator*
Marks, Louis Denton, Jr., *economist, educator, researcher*
Ritterbusch, Dale E. *English educator*
Zbikowski, John Michael *education educator*

Williams Bay
Hobbs, Lewis Mankin *astronomer*

Wisconsin Rapids
Drew, Richard Allen *retired electrical and instrument engineer*
Engelhardt, LeRoy A. *retired paper company executive*
Knuteson, Miles Gene *advertising executive*
Kronholm, Martha Mary *elementary education educator*
Macdonald, Andrew *entrepreneur*
Olson-Hellerud, Linda Kathryn *elementary school educator*
Pahl, Randall *principal, parochial school educator*
Parker, Arnold John *minister*
Sheker, William Clyde *dentist*

Zenda
Sills, William Henry, III, *investment banker*

WYOMING

Aladdin
Brunson, Mabel (Mabel Dipper) *researcher*

Big Horn
Schultz, Harry Pershing *chemistry researcher, retired educator*

Bondurant
Ellwood, Paul Murdock, Jr., *health policy analyst, consultant*

Buffalo
†Kirven, Timothy J. *lawyer*
Urruty, Katherine Jean *secondary school educator*

Casper
Bennion, Scott Desmond *physician*
†Benson, Kimberly Dawn *paralegal*
†Burke, Daniel Martin *lawyer*
Combs, W(illiam) Henry, III, *lawyer*
Constantino, Becky *political organization administrator*
Cottam, Keith M. *librarian, educator, administrator*
†Cowell, Jennifer M. *music educator*
Cvancara, Alan Milton *geologist, educator*
Davis, Lois Ann *computer specialist, educator*
Donley, Russell Lee, III, *former state legislator*
Durham, Harry Blaine, III, *lawyer*
†Durham, Lynda Laurene *language educator*
Gray, Jan Charles *lawyer, business owner*
Hinchey, Bruce Alan *environmental engineering company executive, state legislator*
Hjelmstad, William David *lawyer*
Keim, Michael Ray *dentist*
Lowe, Robert Stanley *lawyer*
†McCall, Donn Jay *lawyer*
†Moler, Mary *secondary school educator*
†Navarro, Christopher J. *artist*
Ptasynski, Harry *geologist, oil producer*
Reed, James Earl *protective services official*
†Reese, Thomas Frank *lawyer*
†Richardson, Bruce Alan *academic administrator*
Ryan, Linda Lee *sculptor, art educator*
Stoval, Linda *political party official*
Stroock, Thomas Frank *oil and gas company executive*
Sullivan, Michael John *ambassador, former governor*
Tempest, Rick *state representative*
True, Jean Durland *entrepreneur, oil company executive*
Unruh, Eric W. *music educator, academic administrator*
Wilkes, Shar (Joan Charlene Wilkes) *elementary education educator*
Wold, John Schiller *geologist, former congressman*

Centennial
Russin, Robert Isaiah *sculptor, educator*

Cheyenne
†Bailey, Henry Franklin, Jr., *lawyer*
Boughton, Lesley D. *library director*
Brimmer, Clarence Addison *federal judge*
Brorby, Wade *federal judge*
Carlson, Kathleen Bussart *law librarian*
†Carmichael, David H. *lawyer*
†Crank, Pat *state attorney general*
Dyekman, Gregory Chris *lawyer*
Flick, William Fredrick *surgeon*
†Freudenthal, David D. *governor*
Freudenthal, Steven Franklin *lawyer, political organization chairman*
Golden, T. Michael *state supreme court justice*
Hanes, John Grier *lawyer, state legislator*
†Hart, Joseph H. *bishop emeritus*
Hart, Kerry *college administrator, music educator*
Hill, William U. *state supreme court chief justice*
†Hoffman, Steven Arlie *musician*
Kite, Marilyn S. *state supreme court justice, lawyer*
Knight, Robert Edward *banker*
†Kunz, April Brimmer *state legislator, lawyer*
Lehman, Larry L. *state supreme court justice*
McKinley, John Clark *lawyer*
Meyer, Joseph B. *state official, former academic administrator*
Moore, Mary French (Muffy Moore) *potter, community activist*
Myers, Rolland Graham *investment counselor*
Noe, Guy *retired social services administrator*
O'Brien, Terrence Leo *federal judge*
†Palma, Jack D. *lawyer*
†Parady, Fred *state representative*
Rice, Wallace William *secondary education educator*
Richardson, Earl Wilson *elementary education educator, retired*
Rounds, Linnea Paula *library administrator*
Schliske, Rosalind Routt *journalism educator, journalist*
Schuman, Gerald Eugene *soil scientist, researcher*
Scorsine, John Magnus *lawyer*
Simons, Lynn Osborn *state agency administrator*
Southworth, Rod Brand *retired computer science educator*
Stoughton, Herbert Warren *geodetic engineer*
Thomson, Thyra Godfrey *former state official*
Voigt, Barton R. *state supreme court justice*
Weigner, Brent James *secondary education educator*
Wilson-McKee, Marie *museum director*
Woodhouse, Gay Vanderpoel *former state attorney general, lawyer*
Woodman, Lucy Rhodes *music educator*

Cody
Coe, Henry H. R. *state legislator*
Garry, James B. *historian, naturalist, storyteller, writer*
Jackson, Harry Andrew *artist*
†Johnson, Wallace Harold *lawyer*
Patrick, H. Hunter *judge*
†Price, B. Byron *historian*
†Riley, Victor J., Jr., *financial services company executive*
Shreve, Peg *retired state legislator, retired elementary school educator*
Simpson, Alan Kooi *former senator, lawyer*
Stradley, Richard Lee *lawyer*

Cowley
Henderson, James Harold *entrepreneur, business executive, financial planner*

Douglas
Twiford, Jim *former state legislator*

Dubois
Glasser, Pamela Jean *musician, music educator*

Ethete
†Tepper, Marcy Elizabeth *drug education director*

Fe Warren Afb
†Neary, Thomas H. *career officer*

Fort Laramie
†Mack, James A. *parks director*

Gillette
Jennings, Linda Sturgill *volunteer*

Glenrock
Bennington, Leslie Orville, Jr., *insurance agent*

Green River
†Albers, Dolores M. *secondary education educator*
Logan, Howard G. *retired science and technology educator*

Hanna
Turner, Lillian Erna *retired nurse*

Jackson
Begelman, Kenneth Marc *cardiovascular surgeon*
Daily, John G. *retired protective services official*
Furrer, John Rudolf *retired chemicals executive*
Gordon, Stephen Maurice *manufacturing company executive, rancher*
Herrick, Gregory Evans *technology corporation executive*
Hirschfield, Alan James *entrepreneur*
LaLonde, Robert Frederick *state senator, retired*
Law, Clarene Alta *innkeeper, state legislator*
†Mack Weed, Joni *writer*
Massy, William Francis *education educator, consultant*
Ninnemann, Thomas George *secondary education educator*

Roll-Preissler, Audrey *artist*
Schuster, Robert Parks *lawyer*
Shockey, Gary Lee *lawyer*
Spence, Gerald Leonard *lawyer, writer*

Jackson Hole
Farkas, Carol Garner *nurse, administrator*

Kelly
Harrice, Cy (Nicholas Psiharis) *commercial radio and television announcer*

Lander
†Bakke, Luanne Kaye *music educator*
Raynolds, David Robert *buffalo breeder, writer*
†Sain, Laurie C. *instructional design consultant, poet*
Tipton, Harry Basil, Jr., *state legislator, physician*

Laramie
Allen, John Logan *geographer, department chairman*
Barbier, Edward B. *economist, educator*
Bellamy, John Cary *civil engineer, meteorologist*
Boresi, Arthur Peter *writer, educator*
Chai, Winberg *political science educator*
Chatton, Barbara Ann *education educator*
Chisum, Emmett Dewain *historian, archeologist, researcher*
Crocker, Thomas Dunstan *economics educator*
Darnall, Roberta Morrow *association executive*
Dickman, Francois Moussiegt *former foreign service officer, educator*
Dubois, Philip Leon *university administrator, political science educator*
†Frost, Carol D. *geology educator*
Gill, George Wilhelm *anthropologist*
Griffin, Leah G. *art specialist*
Hansen, Matilda *former state legislator*
Hanson, Mary Louise *retired social services administrator*
Hausel, William Dan *economic geologist, martial artist, public speaker, writer, artist*
Kelley, Robert Otis *medical science educator*
Kinney, Lisa Frances *lawyer*
Konstantinov, Vassil Alexandrov *finance educator*
†Landis, Bruce Chapman *academic administrator*
Lewis, Randolph Vance *molecular biologist, researcher*
Maxfield, Peter C. *state legislator, law educator, lawyer*
McBride, Judith *elementary education educator*
McDonnel Smedts, Anna Christina *biologist*
Meyer, Edmond Gerald *energy and natural resources educator, resources scientist, entrepreneur, former chemistry educator, university administrator*
Nye, Eric William *English language and literature educator*
†Pope, John Michael *research and development company executive, researcher*
Rechard, Paul Albert *retired civil engineering company executive, consultant*
Reif, David (Frank David Reif) *artist, educator*
Renaud, Paula Marie *researcher*
Roberts, Philip John *history educator, editor*
Robertson, Raymond Eliot *research chemist*
Schmitt, Diana Mae *elementary education educator*
†Selig, Joel Louis *lawyer, educator*
Shaffer, Sherrill Lynn *economist*
Smith, Thomas Shore *lawyer*
Spears, Diana Faye *computer scientist*
Spiegelberg, Emma Jo *business education educator, academic administrator*
St Clair, James Sheldon *agricultural economics educator*
Villemez, Clarence Louis *biologist, educator*
†Weatherford, Lawrence *science educator, consultant*
Williams, Roger Lawrence *historian, educator*
Wright, Cameron Harrold Greene *electrical engineer*

Moose
Schreier, Carl Alan *writer, publisher*

Powell
Brophy, Dennis Richard *psychology and philosophy educator, administrator, clergyman*

Riverton
Bebout, Eli Daniel *oil executive*
Clark, Stanford E. *accountant*
Girard, Nettabell *lawyer*
Peck, Robert A. *newspaper publisher, state legislator*
Pickinpaugh, Richard Neal *assistant principal, educator*

Rock Springs
Arambel, Phyllis Ann *elementary education educator*
Garrison, Kathleen Marie *social worker*
†Tyler, Marvin Lee *lawyer, educator*

Saratoga
Collamer, Sonja Mae Soreide *retired veterinary facility administrator*

Sheridan
Aguirre-Batty, Mercedes *Spanish and English language and literature educator*
Batty, Hugh Kenworthy *physician*
Lonabaugh, Ellsworth Eugene *retired lawyer*
†Pilch, Margaret L. *grant consultant*
Ryan, Michael Louis *controller*
Taylor, Judith Ann *marketing and sales executive*

Story
†Bredehoeft, John Dallas *geologist*

Torrington
Hamer, Jeanne Marie Huntington *soprano, retired voice educator*

Wheatland
Bunker, John Birkbeck *cattle rancher, retired sugar company executive*
Hunkins, Raymond Breedlove *lawyer, rancher*
Jones, Eric E. *lawyer*
Whitney, Ralph Royal, Jr., *financial executive*

Wilson
Breitenbach, Mary Louise McGraw *psychologist, chemical dependency counselor*
Chrystie, Thomas Ludlow *investor*
Fritz, Jack Wayne *communications and marketing company executive*
Harrell, Samuel Macy *agribusiness executive*
Lawroski, Harry *nuclear engineer*
Sage, Andrew Gregg Curtin, II, *corporate investor, manager*

Worland
Foster, William Silas, Jr., *minister*
Sweeny, Wendy Press *lawyer*
Woods, Lawrence Milton *airline company executive*

Yellowstone National Park
Cole, Patricia Eisenbise *educational organzation executive*
Cole, Stephen E. *magistrate judge*
Whipple, Jennifer Jean *botanist*
†Bly, Carl Anthony *retired music educator*
Brown, Carroll *diplomat, association executive, consultant*
Wajda, Shirley Teresa *historian*

TERRITORIES OF THE UNITED STATES

AMERICAN SAMOA

Pago Pago
†Faalevao, Aviata Fano *attorney general, political organization worker*
†Mailo, Toetagata Albert *territory attorney general*
†Sunia, Aitofele Toese F. *lieutenant governor*
†Sunia, Muagututia Fiti *American Samoa attorney general*
Tulafono, Togiola T.A. *governor*
Weitzel, John Quinn *bishop*

FEDERATED STATES OF MICRONESIA

Chuuk
Samo, Amando *bishop*

Pohnpei
Hezel, Francis Xavier *clergy member, educator*

GUAM

Agana
Apuron, Anthony Sablan *archbishop*
Bordallo, Madeleine Mary (Mrs. Ricardo Jerome Bordallo) *congresswoman*
Espaldon, Ernesto Mercader *plastic surgeon, former senator*
George, Duane M. *editor*
†San Agustin, Joe Taitano *political organization worker*

Anigua
†Moylan, Kaleo *lieutenant governor*

Hagatna
Black, Frederick A.
†Camacho, Felix Perez *governor*
Gutierrez, Carl T. C. *former governor*
†Maraman, Katherine Ann *judge*
†Moylan, Douglas *state attorney general*
Salas, Joaquin Leon Guerrero *protective services official*
†Troutman, Charles Henry, III, *lawyer*

Mangilao
Iverson, Thomas John *economist, educator*
†Lobban, Christopher Simon *science educator*
Tsuda, Roy Toshio *marine biologist, educator*

Talofofo
Taylor, James John *academic administrator*

Tamuning
Wresch, Robert Richard *ophthalmologist, medical educator*

Yigo
Duenas, Laurent Flores *health and nursing consultant*

NORTHERN MARIANA ISLANDS

Saipan
Babauta, Juan Nekai *governor*
†Benavente, Diego T. *lieutenant governor*
†Kaufer, Connie Tenorio *retired reading specialist*
Khorram, K. David *ophthalmologist*
†Manglona, Ramona V. *state attorney general*
Soll, Herbert D. *lawyer*
†Tenorio, Pedro Pangelinan *former governor*

PUERTO RICO

Aguadilla
Gómez-Jiménez, Carlos *science educator, microbiologist, geneticist*

Angeles
Avila, Carlos Alberto *physics researcher, inventor*

Bayamon
Herrans-Perez, Laura Leticia *psychologist, educator, research consultant*
†Ocasio, Luis Alberto *mechanical engineer, consultant*
Ortiz, William *composer, music educator*
†Quinones, Areliz *counselor*
Rosa, Helen *dean*

Caparra
†Cuevas-Santiago, Nelly *collections and bad debt manager*

Carolina
†Agosto, Jose A. *psychiatrist*
†González Echevarria, Amelia L. *librarian, counselor*

Cayey
†Acevedo-Loubriel, Suzette *adult education educator*

Dorado
Spector, Michael Joseph *agribusiness executive*

Fajardo
Millan, Alvin *speech pathology/audiology services professional, educator*

Hato Rey
†Ferre, Luis A. *political organization administrator*
Ferrer, Miguel Antonio *brokerage firm and investment bank executive*
Vilches-O'Bourke, Octavio Augusto *accounting company executive*
Wirshing, Herman *protective services official*

Hormigueros
Acosta, Ursula *psychologist*

Luquillo
Pinney, Frances Bailey *art therapist, artist, consultant*

Mayaguez
Collins, Dennis Glenn *mathematics educator*
†Meléndez, Enrique *chemist, educator*
Rodriguez, Grisell *librarian, educator*
Sahai, Hardeo *medical statistics educator*

Old San Juan
Weinstein-Bacal, Stuart Allen *lawyer, educator*

Ponce
†López-Alvarez, Carmen A. *language educator*

Ramey
†Aponte, Abraham *secondary school educator*

Rio Piedras
†Prosper-Sánchez, Gloria D. *linguist, language educator*

San German
Mojica, Agnes *academic administrator*

San Juan
Acosta, Raymond Luis *federal judge*
Andreu-Garcia, Jose Antonio *territory supreme court chief justice*
Aponte Martinez, Luis Cardinal *archbishop emeritus*
Calderón, Sila M. *governor*
†Candelas, Graciela C. *biologist, educator*
Carreras, Francisco José *retired university president, foundation executive*
Casellas, Salvador E. *judge*
Castellanos, Jesus Antonio *U.S. magistrate judge*
†Cruz-Korchin, Norma I. *plastic surgeon*
†Del Toro Soto, Jaime *psychiatrist*
†Dominguez, Daniel R. *judge*
Fernandez-Martinez, Jose *physician*
Fusté, José Antonio *federal judge*
Fuster, Jaime B. *supreme court justice*
†Garcia, Marc Anthony *diplomat*
Gonzalez, Michael John *nutrition scientist, nutriologist*
Gonzalez, Roberto O. *bishop*
†Grovas, Carlos *orthopedic surgeon*
Guillermo, Figueroa *conductor*
Hernandez-Denton, Federico *supreme court justice*
†Hillyer, George V. *microbiologist, educator, medical researcher*
Irizarry-Yunque, Carlos Juan *lawyer, educator*
Joglar, Francisco *academic administrator*
Lopez, Angel R. Pagan *dean, dentist*
Lopez-Davila, Liana Esther *radiologist*
Luna Padilla, Nitza Enid *photography educator*
†Martinez-Munoz, Hector *lawyer*
Marvel, Thomas Stahl *architect*
Matheu, Federico Manuel *university chancellor*
Mercado-Ramos, Ferdinand *secretary of state*
Merly, Miriam Naveira *state supreme court justice*
Ocasio-Melendez, Marcial Enrique *history educator*
†Ortiz, Pedro P *orthopedic surgeon*
Pasnicu, Cornel *mathematician, educator*
†Pedreira, Mark Alan *education educator*
Pierluisi, Pedro R. *lawyer*
Prevor, Ruth Claire *psychologist*
Ramos, Carlos E. *law educator*
Rebollo-Lopez, Francisco *state supreme court justice*
Rivera Perez, Efrain E. *state supreme court justice*
Rivera-Urrutia, Beatriz Dalila *psychology and rehabilitation counseling educator*
Rodriguez, Agustin Antonio *surgeon*
Rodriguez, Annabelle *state attorney general*
Rodriguez Arroyo, Jesus *gynecologic oncologist*
Rodriguez-Diaz, Juan E. *lawyer*
Romero-Barceló, Carlos Antonio *former congressman, former governor of Puerto Rico, former mayor of San Juan*
Rosario-Guardiola, Reinaldo *dermatologist*
San Miguel, Lolita *artistic director*
†Santini, Jorge *mayor*
†Sepúlveda, Sandra *communications educator*
†Teleman, Silviu *mathematician, educator*

Trujillo Alto
†Matos, Brenda Enid *psychiatrist*

Vega Alta
Matos, Cruz Alfonso *environmental consultant*

VIRGIN ISLANDS

Charlotte Amalie
Barnard, Geoffrey W. *magistrate judge*
Bolt, Thomas Alvin Waldrep *lawyer*
Feuerzeig, Henry Louis *lawyer*
Stridiron, Iver Allison *attorney general*

Christiansted
Finch, Raymond Lawrence *chief judge*
Franks, William Woolery *lawyer*
James, Gerard Luz Amwur, II, *former lieutenant governor*
Resnick, Jeffrey Lance *federal magistrate judge*
†Richards, Vargrave A. *lieutenant governor*

Frederiksted
Petrait, Brother James Anthony *secondary education educator, clergy member*

Kingshill
Llanos, Luis Socorro *retired public administrator, mediator, arbitrator, public affairs consultant*

Saint Croix
King, Robert Howard *marketing professional*

Saint John
Fradley, Frederick Macdonell *retired architect*
Walker, Ronald R. *writer, editor, educator*

Saint Thomas
Clark, Jessie Dona *social worker*
O'Bryan, James A. *communications specialist, political organization administrator*
Prior, Cornelius Bernard, Jr., *utilities company executive, financial consultant*
Shapiro, Adam Marc *otolaryngologist*
Turnbull, Charles W. *governor*

St Croix
Moore, Thomas Kail *magistrate district court judge*

St Thomas
Caffee, Lorren Dale *lawyer*
†Kean, Orville *academic administrator*
Kleinfeld, Denis Alan *lawyer*
†Morse, Theodore Freeman *dean, writer*

MILITARY ADDRESSES OF THE UNITED STATES

AA

Apo
Bond, Clayton Alan *foreign affairs fellow*
†Danilovich, John J. *ambassador*
†Jett, Dennis Coleman *foreign service officer*
†Linares, Olga F. *anthropologist, researcher*

Fpo
Green, Kevin Patrick *career officer*

AE

APO
Webster, Christopher White *foreign service officer*

Apo
†Baptiste, Thomas L. *career officer*
†Begert, William J. *lieutenant general United States Air Force*
Carson, Johnnie *ambassador*
Cejas, Paul L. *diplomat, executive*
†Corley, John D. W. *military officer*
†Fowler, Wyche, Jr., *ambassador*
Frame, Nancy Davis *lawyer*
Gnehm, Edward W., Jr., *ambassador*
Kammerer, Kelly Christian *lawyer*
†Kurtzer, Daniel *ambassador*
McGowan, Gerald S. *diplomat*
†Ohman, Diana J. *government agency administrator, former state official*
Ralston, Joseph W. *career officer*
†Romero, Edward L. *diplomat, environmental engineering executive*
Schoonover, Brenda B. *ambassador*
Simpson, Sandra Kay *logistics management specialist*
†Sokolowski, Denise Georgia *librarian, university administrator, educator*
Wakefield, Marie Annette *librarian*

Fpo
Blazewick, Robert B. *lawyer, educator, military officer*
Bucheister, Patricia Louise (Patt Parrish) *author, artist*
Holmes, Michael L. *career officer*
Klosson, Michael *foreign service officer*
Neumann, Ronald Eldredge *diplomat*

AP

Apo
Benenson, Michael William *physician, epidemiologist*
Dunkle, Keith Allen *military officer*
†Dunn, Michael M. *military officer*
†Herrin, Mark Malachi *military officer*
†Hester, Paul V. *career officer*
Mangum, Ronald Scott *army officer*
Moseley, William Earl *career officer*
†Pearson, Teressa M. *military officer*
Ray, Charles Aaron *foreign service officer*
Turner, David Lowery *system safety engineer*

Fpo
Bishop, Donald Michael *foreign service officer*
Rice, James Philip *surgeon*
Stone, David M. *career officer*
Tarpeh-Doe, Linda Diane *controller*

CANADA

ALBERTA

Athabasca
McGreal, Rory Patrick *university official*

Calgary
Anderson, J.C. *oil and gas exploration company executive, rancher*
Besant, Derek Michael *artist, educator*
†Boettger, Roy Dennis *barrister, solicitor*
Campbell, Finley Alexander *geologist, consultant*
Cruess, Leigh Saunders *financial executive*
†Cumming, Thomas Alexander *stock exchange executive*
†Dumbrava, Adrian *chemical engineer, process engineer*
Faithfull, Timothy William *petroleum industry executive*
†Fuhr, Grant *hockey player*
George, Richard Lee *oil industry executive*
Glockner, Peter G. *civil and mechanical engineering educator*
Haskayne, Richard Francis *petroleum company executive*
Heidemann, Robert Albert *chemical engineering educator, researcher*
Holman, J(ohn) Leonard *retired manufacturing corporation executive*
Horton, William Russell *retired utility company executive*
Hotchkiss, Harley N. *professional hockey team owner*
Hovdestad, Wayne Roy *petroleum engineer*
Hughes, Margaret Eileen *law educator, former dean*
Hume, James Borden *corporate professional, foundation executive*
†Iverach, Robert John *lawyer*
Jones, Geoffrey Melvill *physiology research educator*
Lam, Galen Ka-Ron *electrical engineer*
Lederis, Karolis Paul (Karl Lederis) *pharmacologist, educator, researcher*
Leung, Alexander Kwok-Chu *pediatrician*
Libin, Alvin G. *business executive*
Lougheed, Peter *lawyer, former Canadian premier*
MacDonald, Alan Hugh *librarian, university administrator*
Maier, Gerald James *corporate executive*
Malik, Om Parkash *electrical engineering educator, researcher*
Manz, Calvin Kim *technology sector entrepreneur*
McCaig, Jeffrey James *transportation company executive*
McDaniel, Roderick Rogers *petroleum engineer, consultant*
McEwen, Alexander Campbell *cadastral studies educator, former Canadian government official, land administration consultant*
McKinnon, F(rancis) A(rthur) Richard *utility executive*
Milavsky, Harold Phillip *real estate executive*
Monk, Allan James *baritone*
Morgan, Gwyn *oil and gas executive*
Mossop, Grant Dilworth *geologist, researcher*
Neale, E(rnest) R(ichard) Ward *retired university official, consultant*
O'Brien, David Peter *business executive*
Pick, Michael Claude *international exploration consultant*
Pourbaix, Alexander *energy executive*
Raeburn, Andrew Harvey *performing arts association executive, record producer*
Roberts, John Peter Lee *cultural advisor, administrator, educator, writer*
Ruhe, Guenther Harry *mathematician*
Seaman, Daryl Kenneth *oil company executive*
†Shaw, Jim, Jr., *broadcast executive*
†Skulmoski, Gregory James *project management engineer*
Slater, Gary *retail executive*
Smith, Eldon *cardiologist, physiologist, educator*
Southern, Nancy C. *utilities executive*
Southern, Ronald D. *diversified corporation executive*
Stebbins, Robert Alan *sociology educator*
Sutter, Darryl John *professional hockey coach*
Swartout, Hank B. *oil and gas industry executive*
Telitchev, Igor Yevgenievich *aerospace engineering educator, researcher*
Travis, Vance Kenneth *petroleum business executive*
Turek, Roman *hockey player*
Varadarajan, Kalathoor *educator, researcher*
Wagner, Norman Ernest *corporate education executive*
Walker, Roger Geoffrey *geology educator, consultant*
Watanabe, Mamoru *former university dean, physician, researcher*
White, Terrence Harold *academic administrator, sociologist*
Yoon, Ji-Won *virology, immunology and diabetes educator, research administrator*

Calmar
Tomaszeski, Josephine Gallas *retired nursing educator*

Canmore
Janes, Robert Roy *museum executive, archaeologist, museum consultant*

Drumheller
Currie, Philip John *research paleontologist, museum curator*

Edmonton
Adams, Peter Frederick *university president, civil engineer*
Christian, Ralph Gordon *agricultural research and animal health consultant*
Cossins, Edwin Albert *biology educator, academic administrator*
Davis, Wayne Alton *computer science educator*
Fields, Anthony Lindsay Austin *health facility administrator, oncologist, educator*
Fraser, Catherine Anne *Canadian chief justice*
Freeman, Milton Malcolm Roland *anthropology educator*
Gough, Denis Ian *geophysics educator*
Gyenes, Gábor *physician, educator*
Harris, Walter Edgar *chemistry educator*
Hughes, Linda J. *newspaper publisher*
Kay, Cyril Max *biochemist, educator*
†Kennedy, John William *lawyer*
Kratochvil, Byron George *chemistry educator, researcher*
Krotki, Karol Jozef *sociology educator, demographer*
Lock, Gerald Seymour Hunter *retired mechanical engineering educator*
Mac Neil, Joseph Neil *archbishop*
Marcotte, Brian *transportation executive*
Mardon, Austin Albert *geographer, writer, researcher*
McDougall, John Roland *civil engineer*
McKenna, Patrick James *management consultant*
McMaster, Juliet Sylvia *English language educator*
Miller, Jack David R. *radiologist, physician, educator*
Morgenstern, Norbert Rubin *civil engineering educator*
Muzyka, Ray *application developer*
Offenberger, Allan Anthony *electrical engineering educator*
Otto, Fred Douglas *chemical engineering educator*
Patrick, Lynn Allen *lawyer, corporate governance and land development*
Rahfeldt, Daryl Gene *minister*
Rutter, Nathaniel Westlund *geologist, educator*
†Singleton, John Robinson *lawyer*
Stelck, Charles Richard *geology educator*
Stevenson, William Alexander *retired justice of Supreme Court of Canada*
Stollery, Robert *construction company executive*
†Tyrrell, D. Lorne J. *university dean*
Zeschuk, Greg *application developer*
Zuo, Ming Jian *industrial engineering educator*

Lethbridge
Cho, Hyun Ju *retired veterinary research scientist*
†Rand, Duncan Dawson *librarian, retired*

Red Deer
Donald, Jack C. *corporate executive*

Saint Albert
Randhawa, Bikkar Singh *psychologist, educator*

BRITISH COLUMBIA

Bamfield
Druehl, Louis Dix *biology educator*

Burnaby
Borden, John Harvey *entomologist, educator*
Brantingham, Paul Jeffrey *criminology educator*
Buitenhuis, Peter Martinus *language professional, educator*
Copes, Parzival *economist, researcher*
†Fleming, James Dougal *English educator, writer*
Kimura, Doreen *psychology educator, researcher*
Kitchen, John Martin *historian, educator*
Shen, John Jianyue *fuel cell company executive*
Switlo, Janice Georgina Alice E. *barrister, solicitor, mediator, negotiator, legal and business consultant, strategist*
Wainwright, David Stanley *intellectual property professional*
Yip, Chi Yan Toby *social worker, journalist, researcher*

Cobble Hill
Cox, Albert Reginald *academic administrator, physician, retired*

Coquitlam
Chan, Buddy Tak-Biu *investment company executive*

Duncan
Hughes, Edward John *artist*

Kelowna
Muggeridge, Derek Brian *dean, engineering consultant*

Langley
Van Brummelen, Harro Walter *education educator*

Lions Bay
Bartholomew, Gilbert Alfred *retired physicist*

New Westminster
Cogswell, Frederick William *English language educator, poet, editor, publisher*

North Vancouver
†Ellis, Sarah Elizabeth *librarian*
Gibbs, David George *retired food processing company executive*

Prince George
Kerr, Nancy Karolyn *pastor, mental health consultant*

Richmond
Plomp, Teunis (Tony Plomp) *minister*
Zeigler, Earle Frederick *physical education-kinesiology educator*

Salt Spring Island
Kandler, Joseph Rudolph *financial executive*
Raginsky, Nina *artist*

Sidney
Bigelow, Margaret Elizabeth Barr (M.E. Barr) *mycology educator*
Kendrick, William Bryce *biology educator, writer, publisher, consultant*
Mann, Cedric Robert *retired institute administrator, oceanographer*
Petrie, William *physicist, researcher*
Saddlemyer, Ann (Eleanor Saddlemyer) *educator, critic, theater historian*
van den Bergh, Sidney *astronomer*

Sooke
Howard, John Lindsay *lawyer, forest industry company executive*

Surrey
†Igali, Daniel (Daniel Igali Baraladei) *Olympic athlete*

Vancouver
Aalto, Madeleine *library director*
†Abdul-Rahim, Shareef *professional basketball player*
Aberle, David Friend *anthropologist, educator*
Baird, Patricia Ann *physician, educator*
Batts, Michael Stanley *German language educator*
Bentley, Thomas Roy *English language educator, writer, consultant, professor emeritus*
Bloom, Myer *physicist, educator*
†Bonifacho, Bratsa *artist*
Bonner, Robert William *lawyer, director*
Bowering, George Harry *writer, English literature educator*
Boyd, David William *mathematician, educator*
†Bringhurst, Robert *poet*
Brunstein, John David *biochemist, researcher*
Campbell, Bruce Alan *corporate and executive coach*
Campbell, Jack James Ramsay *microbiology educator*
Chan, Raymond *Canadian government minister*
†Chu, Allen Yum-Ching *automation company executive, systems consultant*
Clark, Colin Whitcomb *mathematics educator*
Collins, Mary *management consultant, former Canadian legislator*
Conway, John S. *history educator*
Cormier, Jean G. *communications company executive*
Crawford, Carl Benson *retired civil engineer, government research administrator*
Crawford, Marc *professional hockey coach*
Cynader, Max Sigmund *psychology, physiology, brain research educator, researcher*
de Weerdt, Mark Murray *retired judge*
Doyle, Patrick John *otolaryngologist, department chairman*
Durrant, Geoffrey Hugh *retired English language educator*
Eaves, Allen Charles Edward *hematologist, medical agency administrator*
†Eckbo, Bjorn Espen Espen *economics educator*
Erickson, Arthur Charles *architect*
Ericson, Richard Victor *sociologist, educator, law educator, academic administrator*
Feaver, George Arthur *political science educator*
Feldman, Joel Shalom *mathematician*
Finnegan, Cyril Vincent *retired university dean, zoology educator*
Frey, Gerrard Rupert (Gary Frey) *management executive, consultant*
Friedman, Sydney M. *anatomy educator, medical researcher*
Gardiner, William Douglas Haig *bank executive, director*
Gilbert, John Humphrey Victor *speech scientist, educator*
†Giles, Jack Michael *lawyer*
Grace, John Ross *chemical engineering educator*
Granirer, Edmond Ernest *mathematician, educator*
Grauer, Gay Meredith (Sherrard Grauer) *artist*
Harcourt, Michael Franklin *retired premier of Province of British Columbia, lawyer, educator*
Hardwick, David Francis *pathologist*
Hardy, Walter Newbold *physics educator, researcher*
Hastings, Paul J. *pharmaceutical executive*
Haycock, Kenneth Roy *educator, consultant, administrator*
Head, Ivan Leigh *law educator*
Hoar, William Stewart *zoologist, educator*
Holsti, Kalevi Jacque *political scientist, educator*
Jones, David Robert *zoology educator*
Jones, Lawrence Donald *economics educator*
Keevil, Norman B. *mining executive*
Kesselman, Jonathan Rhys *economics educator, public policy researcher*
†Ladner, Thomas E. *lawyer*
Langdon, Frank Corriston *political science educator, researcher*
Laponce, Jean Antoine *political scientist, educator*
Lee, Jong-Hyeon *computer and communications security researcher, mobile communications researcher*
Lindsey, Casimir Charles *zoologist, educator*
Lipsey, Richard George *economist, educator*
Lyons, Terrence Allan *merchant banking, investment company executive*
Lysyk, Kenneth Martin *judge*
Maclachlan, Gordon Alistair *biology educator, researcher*
Marchak, Maureen Patricia *anthropology and sociology educator*
Mattessich, Richard Victor (Alvarus) *business administration researcher*
McCaw, John E., Jr., *professional sports team executive*
McEachern, Allan *lawyer*
McGeer, Edith Graef *neurological science educator*
Mc Lean, Donald Millis *microbiology, pathology educator, physician*
McNeill, John Hugh *pharmaceutical sciences educator*
McWhinney, Edward Watson *Canadian government legislator*
Mizgala, Henry F. *physician, consultant, retired medical educator*
Murray, Anne *singer*
Nemetz, Peter Newman *economics researcher, policy analysis educator*
Newman, Murray Arthur *aquarium administrator*
Olsen, Inger Anna *psychologist, educator*
Overmyer, Daniel Lee *Asian studies educator*
†Owen, Stephen *member of parliament, secretary of state*
Ozier, Irving *physicist, educator*
Pacheco-Ransanz, Arsenio *Hispanic and Italian studies educator*
Paty, Donald Winston *neurologist, educator*
Penikett, Antony David John *negotiator, writer, politician*
Peterson, Leslie Raymond *barrister*
Phillips, Anthony George *neurobiology educator*
Phillips, John Edward *zoologist, educator*
Pickard, George Lawson *physics educator*
Pincock, Richard Earl *chemistry educator*
Piternick, Anne Brearley *librarian, educator*
Rennie, Paul Steven *research scientist*
Riedel, Bernard Edward *retired pharmaceutical sciences educator*
Robinson, John Lewis *geography educator*
Rothstein, Samuel *librarian, educator*
Roy, Chunilal *psychiatrist*
Russell, Richard Doncaster *geophysicist, educator, geoscientist*
Salcudean, Martha Eva *mechanical engineer, educator*
Saunders, Peter Paul *investor*
Saywell, William George Gabriel *business development and management consultant*
Segal, Gary Stephen *investment and venture capital company executive*
Shaw, Michael *biologist, educator*
Shearer, Ronald Alexander *economics educator*
Sinclair, Alastair James *geology educator*
Sion, Maurice *mathematics educator*
Slaymaker, Olav *geography educator*
Snider, Robert F. *chemistry educator, researcher*
†Sorensen, Poul Henrik Bredahl *physician, research scientist, pathologist*
Stewart, Ross *chemistry educator*
Suedfeld, Peter *psychologist, educator*
Sutter, Morley Carman *medical scientist*
Tees, Richard Chisholm *psychology educator, researcher*
Tingle, Aubrey James *pediatric immunologist, research administrator*
Unger, Richard Watson *history educator*
Vogt, Erich Wolfgang *physicist, academic administrator*
Webber, William Alexander *university administrator, physician*
Wellington, William George *entomologist, ecologist, educator*
Yaffe, Barbara Marlene *journalist*
Young, Lawrence *electrical engineering educator*

Victoria
Antoniou, Andreas *electrical engineering educator*
Batten, Alan Henry *astronomer*
Best, Melvyn Edward *geophysicist*
Cooperstock, Fred Isaac *physics educator, researcher*
D'Orbán, Paul Theodore *psychiatrist*
Finlay, James Campbell *retired museum director*
Fuller, James Chester Eedy *retired chemical company executive*
Gardom, Garde Basil *lieutenant governor of British Columbia*
†Halsey-Brandt, Greg *mayor*
Harvey, Donald *artist, educator*
Hollis, Reginald *archbishop*
Hutchings, John Barrie *astronomer, researcher*
Israel, Werner *physics educator*
Leffek, Kenneth Thomas *chemist, educator*
Lind, Niels Christian *civil engineering educator*
†MacIsaac, Ronald Francis *lawyer*
Manning, Eric *computer science and engineering educator, university dean, researcher*
Meadow, Charles *information scientist, consultant*
Morton, Donald Charles *astronomer*
Nuttall, Richard Norris *management consultant, physician*
Richards, Vincent Philip Haslewood *retired librarian*
Segger, Martin Joseph *museum director, art history educator*
Stetson, Peter Brailey *astronomer*
Turner, Robert Comrie *composer*
Turpin, David Howard *biologist, educator*

†van Veggel, Frank C.J.M. *physical-organic chemist, materials chemist*
Welch, S(tephen) Anthony *university administrator, Islamic studies and arts educator*
Wiles, David McKeen *chemist*

West Vancouver
Donaldson, Edward Mossop *research scientist, aquaculture consultant*
Rae, Barbara Joyce *former employee placement company executive*
Seyhoun, Houshang *architect*
Wynne-Edwards, Hugh Robert *geologist, educator, entrepreneur*

Westbank
Wedepohl, Leonhard Martin *electrical engineering educator*

MANITOBA

Churchill
Rouleau, Reynald *bishop*

Saint Andrews
Lang, Otto *industry executive, former Canadian cabinet minister*

Winnipeg
†Alfa, Michelle Josephine *microbiologist, educator*
Anderson, David Trevor *law educator*
Angel, Aubie *physician, academic administrator*
Asper, Leonard *communications executive*
Birtwhistle, Tara *dancer*
Burns, James William *business executive*
Chang, Johnny W. *dancer*
Cohen, Albert Diamond *retail executive*
†Cohen, Harley *civil engineer, science educator*
Corrales, Jesús *dancer*
Curtis, Charles Edward *Canadian government official*
Edwards, Clifford Henry Coad *law educator*
Eyre, Ivan *artist, educator*
Ferguson, Robert Bury *mineralogy educator*
Filmon, Gary Albert *Canadian provincial premier, civil engineer*
†Friesen, Henry George *endocrinologist, educator*
Haworth, James Chilton *pediatrics educator*
Israels, Lyonel Garry *hematologist, medical educator*
Lewis, André Leon *artistic director*
Liba, Peter Michael *Canadian provincial government official*
MacKenzie, George Allan *company executive*
Mantsch, Henry Horst *chemistry educator*
†McCallum, John Stuart *finance educator, columnist*
Morrish, Allan Henry *electrical engineering educator*
Mufti, Aftab A. *civil engineering educator*
Naimark, Arnold *medical educator, physiologist, educator*
Oberman, Sheldon Arnold *writer, educator*
Persaud, Trivedi Vidhya Nandan *anatomy educator, researcher, consultant*
Poettcker, Henry *retired academic administrator*
Reyes, Reyneris *dancer*
†Ronald, Allan Ross *internal medicine and medical microbiology educator, researcher*
Ross, Robert Thomas *neurologist, educator*
Rozumnyj, Jaroslav *literature educator, researcher*
Schacter, Brent Allan *oncologist, health facility administrator*
Schaefer, Theodore Peter *chemistry educator, retired*
Schnoor, Jeffrey Arnold *lawyer*
Smith, Ian Cormack Palmer *biophysicist*
Stalker, Jacqueline D'Aoust *academic administrator, educator*
Suzuki, Isamu *microbiology educator, researcher*
Vargas, Arionel P. *dancer*
Watchorn, William Ernest *venture capitalist*
Wreford, David Mathews *magazine editor*

NEW BRUNSWICK

Fredericton
Bray, Dale Irving *civil engineering educator*
†Grotterod, Knut *retired paper company executive*
†Hanson, Dana W. *dermatologist*
Kenyon, Gary Michael *gerontology educator, researcher*
Lewell, Peter A. *international technology executive, researcher*
Lumsden, Ian Gordon *art gallery director*
Strange, Henry Hazen *judge*

Moncton
Hanson, John Mark *ecologist, researcher*
McKenna, Frank Joseph *lawyer*

Rothesay
Fairweather, Robert Gordon Lee *lawyer*

Saint Andrews
Anderson, John Murray *operations executive, former university president*

Saint John
Condon, Thomas Joseph *university historian*
Mowatt, E. Ann *women's voluntary leader, lawyer*

Sussex
Secord, Lloyd Douglas *healthcare administrator*

Westfield
Logan, Rodman Emmason *retired jurist*

NEWFOUNDLAND

Corner Brook
Coyne, John Michael *artist, educator*
Payne, Sidney Stewart *retired archbishop*

Portugal Cove
Creates, Marlene Ruth *artist*

Saint John's
†Clark, Jack Ivor *civil engineer, researcher*
Davis, Charles Carroll *aquatic biologist, educator*
Grattan, Patricia Elizabeth *retired art gallery director*
May, Arthur W. *retired academic administrator, educator*
Meisen, Axel *chemical engineering educator, university dean*
Rochester, Michael Grant *geophysics educator*
Rowe, Allan Duncan *company executive*

St John's
Gibbons, Rex Vincent *geologist*

Torbay
Dabinett, Diana Frances *visual artist*

NOVA SCOTIA

Bedford
Birdsall, William Forest *retired librarian*
Hennigar, David John *investment broker*

Chester Basin
Parr-Johnston, Elizabeth *economy and policy consultant*

Dartmouth
Elliott, James A. *oceanographer, researcher*
Horrocks, Norman *library and information scientist, educator, editor*
Keen, Charlotte Elizabeth *marine geophysicist, researcher*
Mann, Kenneth Henry *marine ecologist*

Halifax
Carrigan, David Owen *history educator*
Casson, Alan Graham *thoracic surgeon, researcher*
Chowdhury, Dhiman *physician, consultant*
Dahn, Jeff Raymond *physics educator*
Dexter, Robert Paul *lawyer*
Dykstra Lynch, Mary Elizabeth *library and information science educator*
Fillmore, Peter Arthur *mathematician, educator*
Fowler, Charles Allison Eugene *retired architect, engineer*
Glube, Constance Rachelle *Canadian chief justice*
Gratwick, John *management consulting executive, writer, consultant*
Gray, James *English literature educator*
Hall, Brian Keith *biology educator, author, scientist*
Hiltz, Arnold Aubrey *former chemist*
†Jaeger, Leslie Gordon *university administrator*
Jones, William Ernest *chemistry educator*
Kulyk, Karen Gay *visual artist*
Langley, George Ross *medical educator*
Lenzer, Irmingard Isolde *psychology educator*
LeValliant, Debbie *information technology executive*
Mann, David *energy and services company executive*
Mingo, James William Edgar *lawyer*
Murray, Thomas John (Jock Murray) *medical humanities educator, medical researcher, neurologist*
Oldfield, Karen *transportation executive*
Ozmon, Kenneth Lawrence *retired university president, educator*
Pincock, Douglas George *electronics company executive*
Renouf, Harold Augustus *business consultant, retired*
Stairs, Denis Winfield *political science educator*
Thompson, William Grant *management executive*
Tonks, Robert Stanley *pharmacology and therapeutics educator, former university dean*
†Winham, Gilbert Rathbone *political science educator*

Kentville
Baker, George Chisholm *engineering executive, consultant*

Lawrencetown
Pottie, Roswell Francis *Canadian federal science and technology consultant*

Little Bras d'Or
LeForte, John Stewart Archibald *retreat house manager*

North Sydney
†Nickerson, Jerry Edgar Alan *business executive*

Nova Scotia
Collins, John Alfred *retired obstetrician-gynecologist, educator*
Sweet, William *educator, author, administrator*

Stellarton
Sobey, David Frank *food company executive*
Sobey, Donald Creighton Rae *real estate developer*

Tatamagouche
Roach, Margot Ruth *retired biophysicist, educator*

Timberlea
Verma, Surjit Kumar *retired school system administrator*

Victoria Beach
Fisher, James W., Jr., *management consultant*

Wallace
Boyle, Willard Sterling *physicist, researcher*

Waverley
Grady, Wayne J. *government official*

Wolfville
Bartkiw, Roman *artist*
Colville, David Alexander *artist*
Elliott, Robbins Leonard *consultant*
Ogilvie, Kelvin Kenneth *university president, chemistry educator*

ONTARIO

Ajax
Mills, Jon K. *psychologist, educator, philosopher*

Ancaster
Smith, Newman Donald *retired financial executive*

Arnprior
†Shideler, Janet L. *adult education educator*

Arva
Weldon, David Black *company director*

Aurora
Lanthier, Ronald Ross *retired manufacturing company executive*
Stronach, Belinda *retail executive*

Barry's Bay
Horoszewicz, Juliusz Stanislaw *oncologist, cancer researcher, laboratory administrator*

Belleville
Buckley, Edward Joseph *retired academic dean*

Bowmanville
Evans, Essi H. *research scientist*

Bracebridge
Evans, John David Daniel *judge*
MacKenzie, Lewis Wharton *military officer*

Brampton
Bastian, Donald Noel *retired bishop*
†Hu, Qiang *research scientist, educator, engineer*
Malhi, Gurbax Singh *legislator*
Paikeday, Thomas M. *lexicographer and linguistic consultant*
Plastina, Frank *communications executive*
†Roth, John Andrew *internet communications executive*
Savoie, Leonard Norman *transportation company executive*

Brantford
Inns, Harry Douglas Ellis *retired optometrist*

Brockville
Spalding, James Stuart *retired telecommunications company executive*

Burks Falls
Cameron, Gordon Murray *chemical engineer*

Burlington
Harris, Philip John *engineering educator*
McMulkin, Francis John *retired steel company executive*

Cambridge
Brown, Gregory Michael *psychiatrist, educator, researcher*
MacBain, William Halley *minister, theology educator, seminary chancellor*
Turnbull, Robert Scott *manufacturing company executive*
White, Joseph Charles *manufacturing and retailing company executive*

Chatham
McKeough, William Darcy *investment company executive, director*
Shakhmundes, Lev *mathematician*

Collingwood
Morley, Lawrence Whitaker *geophysicist, remote sensing consultant*

Deep River
Davies, John Arthur *physics and engineering educator, scientist*
Milton, John Charles Douglas *nuclear physicist, researcher*
Newcombe, Howard Borden *biologist, consultant*

Don Mills
Atwood, Margaret Eleanor *writer*
French, William Harold *retired newspaper editor*
Hyde, Michael Arthur *chemical company executive*

Dorchester
Fanning, William James *professional baseball team executive, radio and television broadcaster*

Downsview
Eggleton, Arthur C. *former Canadian government official, member of Parliament*
Forer, Arthur H. *biology educator, researcher, editor*
Ribner, Herbert Spencer *physicist, educator*
Thomas, Clara McCandless *retired English language educator, biographer*

Etobicoke
Aska, Warabé (Takeshi Masuda) *artist, writer*
Howe, James Tarsicius *retired insurance company executive*
McIntyre, John George Wallace *real estate development and management consultant*
Scholefield, Peter Gordon *health agency executive*

Freelton
Sonnenberg, Hardy *data processing company research and development executive, engineer*

Gloucester
Boisvert, Laurier Joseph *communications executive*
Malouin, Jean-Louis *university educator*
†Pelletier, David *Olympic athlete, ice skater*
†Salé, Jamie *Olympic athlete, ice skater*

Grampton
Dunn, Frank A. *communications executive*

Greely
Lister, Earle Edward *animal science consultant*

Guelph
Beveridge, Terrance James *microbiology educator, researcher*
Bewley, John Derek *botany researcher, educator*
Dickinson, William Trevor *hydrologist, educator*
Jorgensen, Erik *forest pathologist, educator, consultant*
Karl, Gabriel *physics educator*
Kasha, Kenneth John *agriculturist, educator*
Land, Reginald Brian *library administrator*
Oaks, B. Ann *retired plant physiologist, educator*

Halton Hills
McCoubrey, R. James *advertising and broadcast executive*

Hamilton
Bandler, John William *electrical engineering educator, consultant*
Basmajian, John Varoujan *medical scientist, educator, physician*
Bienenstock, John *physician, educator*
†Brackney, William Henry *archivist, historian*
Campbell, Colin Kydd *electrical and computer engineering educator, researcher*
Crowe, Cameron Macmillan *chemical engineering educator*
Datars, William Ross *physicist, educator*
Garland, William James *engineering physics educator*
George, Peter James *economist, educator*
Gershman, Alexei *electrical engineer, researcher*
†Ghosh, Raja *engineering educator*
Gillespie, Ronald James *chemistry educator, researcher, writer*
Hantho, Chuck *retired metal products executive*
Jonasson, Ralph George *research chemist*
Lee, Alvin A. *literary educator, scholar, author*
MacLean, David Bailey *chemistry educator, researcher*
McKay, Alexander Gordon *classics educator*
Robinson, Daniel Baruch *retired banker*
Roland, Charles Gordon *physician, medical historian, educator*
Ryan, Ellen Bouchard *psychology educator, gerontologist*
Schwarcz, Henry Philip *geologist, educator*
Shaw, Denis Martin *university dean, former geology educator*
Spenser, Ian Daniel *chemist educator*
Sprung, Donald Whitfield Loyal *physics educator*
Steiner, George *management science, operations research educator*
Telmer, Frederick Harold *steel products manufacturing executive*
Wong, Kon Max *electrical engineer educator*

Hanover
Adams, John David Vessot *manufacturing company executive*

Harrow
†Kurtz, James P. *administrative law judge*

Holland Landing
†Dempster, Barry (Edward) *writer, poet*

Kanata
Butcher, Paul *communications executive*
Smith, Don *communications executive*

Kincardine
Braswell, Paula Ann *artist*

Kingston
Akenson, Donald Harman *historian, educator*
Batchelor, Barrington de Vere *civil engineer, educator*
Campbell, L(ouis) Lorne *mathematics educator*
Dick, Susan Marie *English language educator*
Ewan, George Thomson *physicist, educator*
†Fam, Amir Z. *engineering educator, researcher*
Kaliski, Stephan Felix *economics educator*
Kaufman, Nathan *pathology educator, physician*
Leggett, William C. *biology educator, academic administrator*
Lewis, William John *aerospace engineer*
Low, James A. *physician*
Mac Kenzie, Norman Hugh *retired English educator, writer*
MacKinnon, James Gordon
McDonald, Arthur Bruce *physics educator*
Meisel, John *political scientist*
Read, Allan Alexander *minister*
Smallman, Beverley N. *biology educator*
Spencer, John Hedley *biochemistry educator*
Stewart, Alec Thompson *physicist, educator*
Szarek, Walter Anthony *chemist, educator*
Wyatt, Gerard Robert *biology educator, researcher*

Kitchener
Coles, Graham *conductor, composer*

Bohme, Diethard Kurt *chemistry educator*
Bohn, Jason *golfer*
Boland, Janet Lang *judge*
Bolley, Andrea *artist*
Bond, John Richard *astrophysicist*
Boorne, Ryan *ballet dancer*
Boultbee, John Arthur *publishing executive*
†Bradshaw, Richard James *general director of opera company*
Braithwaite, J. Lorne *real estate executive*
Bristow, David Ian *lawyer*
Broder, Irvin *physician, educator*
Brook, Adrian Gibbs *chemistry educator*
Brooks, Robert Leslie *bank executive*
Bruce, William Robert *physician, educator*
Bryant, Josephine Harriet *library executive*
Budrevics, Alexander *landscape architect*
Bugg, Jace *golfer*
Butt, William *corporate financial executive*
Carder, Paul Charles *retired advertising executive*
Carlen, Peter Louis *neuroscientist educator, science administrator*
Carr, Jack Leslie *economics educator, economic consultant*
Carrothers, Gerald Arthur Patrick *environmental and city planning educator*
†Carter, Butch *professional basketball coach, former sports team executive*
Carter, Vince *professional basketball player*
Chester, Robert Simon George *lawyer*
Cleghorn, John Edward *business executive*
Clitheroe, Eleanor *utilities executive*
Cockwell, Jack Lynn *business executive*
Colgrass, Michael Charles *composer*
Colombo, John Robert *poet, editor, writer*
Comper, Tony *banker*
Connell, Philip Francis *food industry executive*
Conway, Heather *communications executive*
Cook, Stephen Arthur *mathematics and computer science educator*
Cook-Bennett, Gail *pension fund administrator*
Cowan, Charles Gibbs *lawyer, corporate executive*
Cunningham, Gordon Ross *financial executive*
Curlook, Walter *management consultant*
Dale, Robert Gordon *business executive*
D'Alessandro, Dominic *financial executive*
Davenport, Paul *golfer*
Davis, William Grenville *lawyer, former Canadian government official*
Davison, Edward Joseph *electrical engineering educator*
Dean, Geoffrey *book publisher*
Detlefsen, Michael E. *food products executive*
Dey, Peter J. *investment company executive*
Dickens, Bernard Morris *law educator*
Dimma, William Andrew *real estate executive*
Dobson, Wendy Kathleen *economics educator*
Downing, John Henry *columnist, journalist*
Downing, Robert James *artist*
†Dryden, Ken *sports team executive*
Dryer, Douglas Poole *retired philosophy educator*
Dubin, Charles Leonard *lawyer*
Dunlop, David John *geophysics educator, researcher*
Eagles, Stuart Ernest *business executive*
Egoyan, Atom *film director*
Eisenberg, Howard Edward *physician, psychotherapist, consultant, medical educator, writer*
Eklof, Svea Christine *ballet dancer*
Elder, Richard Bruce *artist, writer*
Elkhadem, Saad Eldin Amin *foreign language and literature educator, writer, editor, publisher*
Elliott, Roy Fraser *lawyer, holding and management company executive*
Endrenyi, Janos *research engineer, educator*
Espinosa, Carlos *golfer*
Evans, John Robert *former university president, physician*
Evans, Martin G. *management educator*
Eyton, John Trevor *senator, business executive*
Farkas, Leslie Gabriel *plastic surgeon*
Farquharson, Gordon MacKay *lawyer, director*
Fatt, William R. *hospitality company executive*
Ferguson, Kingsley George *retired psychologist*
Fierheller, George Alfred *corporate director*
Fife, Edward H. *landscape architecture educator*
Finlay, Terence Edward *archbishop*
Floyd, John Earl *economics educator*
†Fox, Wayne C. *brokerage house executive, corporate financial executive*
Fraser, William Neil *government official, retired*
Freedman, Harry *composer*
Fregosi, James Louis *professional baseball team manager*
Friedlander, John Benjamin *mathematician, educator*
Fullerton, R. Donald *banker*
Fuss, Melvyn Allan *educator, researcher*
Galloway, David Alexander *publishing company executive*
Ganczarczyk, Jerzy Jozef *civil engineering educator, wastewater treatment consultant*
Geiger, John Grigsby *editor, writer, reporter*
†Godsoe, Peter Cowperthwaite *banker*
Goetschel, Willi *literary and intellectual historian, philosopher, educator*
Goh, Chan Hon *ballerina*
Goldfarb, Martin *sociologist, researcher*
†Goodenow, Robert W. *labor union administrator*
Goring, David Arthur Ingham *chemical engineering educator, scientist*
Gotlieb, Allan E. *former ambassador*
Gotlieb, Calvin Carl *computer scientist, educator*
Granatstein, Jack Lawrence *history educator*
Grayson, Albert Kirk *Near Eastern studies educator*
Greenwood, Lawrence George *banker*
Gregor, Tibor Philip *retired management consultant*
Hanna, William Brooks *literary agent*
Harris, Nicholas George *publisher*
Harris, Sydney Malcolm *retired judge*
Hayhurst, James Frederick Palmer *career and business consultant, inspirational speaker, author*
Helleiner, Gerald Karl *economics educator*
Herbst, Renate Diane *lawyer*
Herren, Michael Wayne *classical studies educator*
Hickson, Robin Julian *mining company executive*
Hirst, Peter Christopher *consulting actuary*
Hodgkinson, Greta *dancer*
Hofmann, Theo *biochemist, educator*
Holyday, Douglas Charles *city councillor*
Hon Goh, Chan *dancer*
Hore, John Edward *commodity futures educator*
Hyland, Geoffrey Fyfe *energy service company executive*
Israelievitch, Jacques H. *violinist, conductor*
Jacob, Ellis *entertainment company executive*
Janischewskyj, Wasyl *electrical engineering educator*
Jaworska, Tamara *painter, tapestry maker*
Jay, Charles Douglas *religion educator, college administrator, clergyman*
Johnson, Robert Eugene *historian, academic administrator*
Kalow, Werner *pharmacologist, toxicologist*
Kerr, David Wylie *natural resource company executive*
Khristich, Dimitri *hockey player*
Kingston, Rebecca Edith Dawson *political science educator*
Knowlton, Thomas A. *university dean, retired food products executive*
Kooluris Dobbs, Linda Kia *artist*
Kramer, Burton *graphic designer, educator*
Kresge, Alexander Jerry *chemistry educator*
Kudelka, James *choreographer, artistic director*
Kunov, Hans *biomedical and electrical engineering educator*
Kushner, Eva *academic administrator, educator, author*
Landsberg, Michele *journalist*
Lastman, Melvin D. *mayor*
Lawson, Jane Elizabeth *bank executive*
Leech, James William *investment company executive*
Lennox, R. Ian *health products executive*
Lewis, Robert *journalist, media executive*
Lewitt, Wilfred G. *health products executive*
Lindsay, Roger Alexander (Baron of Craighall) *investment executive*
Lindsay, William Kerr *surgeon*
Litherland, Albert Edward *physics educator*
Liversage, Richard Albert *cell biologist, educator*
Lowe, Robert Edward
Macdonald, Donald Stovel *corporate director*
Macdonald, Hugh Ian *university president emeritus, economist, educator*
MacDougall, Hartland Molson *corporate director, retired bank executive*
MacLaren, Roy *retired federal official*
MacLennan, David Herman *research scientist, educator*
Magford, Mary *investment company executive*
Mann, George Stanley *real estate and financial services corporation executive*
Mann, Susan *history educator*
†Marks, Ray *education educator, researcher*
Marrié, William *dancer*
Martin, Robert William *corporate director*
Martin, Roger Lloyd *educator, management consultant*
Mc Culloch, Ernest Armstrong *physician, educator*
McKenna, Marianne *architect*
McKeown, William Philip *lawyer*
McMurtry, R. Roy *chief justice*
McRae, Marion Eleanor *critical care nurse*
McWilliam, Joanne Elizabeth *retired religion educator*
Meagher, George Vincent *mechanical engineer*
Mercier, Eileen Ann *corporate financial executive*
Millgate, Jane *language professional*
Millgate, Michael (Michael Henry Millgate) *retired English educator*
Moens, Peter B. *biology researcher and educator*
Moggridge, Donald Edward *economics educator, author*
Mogilny, Alexander *professional hockey player*
Moore, Carole Irene *librarian*
Moore, Christopher Hugh *writer*
Morey, Carl Reginald *musicologist*
Morneau, Bill *financial consultant*
Mounsey, Joseph Backhouse *investment consultant*
Munk, Peter *mining executive*
Munro, John Henry Alexander *economics educator, writer*
Naldrett, Anthony James *geology educator*
Nan Yu, Xiao *dancer*
Nesbitt, Lloyd Ivan *podiatrist*
Nesbitt, Mark *management consultant*
Nolan, Owen *professional hockey player*
Norris, Geoffrey *geology educator, consultant*
Novak, David *Judaic studies educator, rabbi*
Ogilvie, Richard Ian *clinical pharmacologist*
Oliphant, Randall *financial executive*
O'Mara, John Aloysius *retired bishop*
Osler, Gordon Peter *retired utility company executive*
Ostry, Sylvia *academic administrator, economist*
†Oundjian, Peter *conductor*
Packer, Katherine Helen *retired library educator*
Packham, Marian Aitchison *biochemistry educator*
Peterson, David Robert *lawyer, former Canadian government official*
†Peterson, Robert B. *petroleum company executive*
Phillips, Robert Allan *scientist, administrator*
Plaut, Wolf Gunther *minister, author*
Polistuk, Eugene V. *electronics manufacturing services executive*
Pollock, Samuel *diversified financial services company executive*
Poprawa, Andrew *financial services executive, accountant*
Pratt, Robert Cranford *political scientist, educator*
†Price, Timothy R. *accountant*
Pritchard, Huw Owen *chemist, educator*
Quinn, Pat (John Brian Patrick Quinn) *professional sports team manager*
Rakoff, Vivian Morris *psychiatrist, writer*
Rapoport, Anatol *peace studies educator, mathematical biologist*
Rasky, Harry *producer, director, writer*
Reaney, James Crerar *dramatist, poet, educator*
Rimrott, Friedrich Paul Johannes *engineer, educator*
Rodriguez, Sonia *dancer*
Rogers, Edward Samuel *communications company executive*
Rooney, Paul George *mathematics educator*
Rose, Jeffrey Raymond *economist, educator, negotiator*
Rowe, David John *physics educator*
Runnalls, Oliver John Clyve (John Runnalls) *nuclear engineering educator*
Salama, C. Andre Tewfik *electrical engineering educator*
†San, Nguyen Duy *psychiatrist, educator*
Sandelands, Eric Alan *publisher, educator, editor*
Schramek, Tomas *ballet dancer, educator*
Schwartz, Gerald Wilfred *financial executive*
Seaquist, Ernest Raymond *astronomy educator*
Sedra, Adel Shafeek *electrical engineering educator, academic administrator*
Seiersen, Nicholas Steen *management consultant*
Semak, Michael William *photographer, educator*
Semlyen, Adam *electrical engineering educator*
†Sennah, Khaled M. *structural engineering educator, consultant*
†Sessle, Barry John *adult education educator, researcher*
Sharp, Isadore *hotel facility executive*
Shaw, Andrew R. *performing arts association administrator*
†Shearing, George Albert *pianist, composer*
Shepherd, Gordon Greeley *space physics educator, researcher*
Silk, Frederick C.Z. *financial consultant*
Sirman, Robert *performing company executive*
Skvorecky, Josef Vaclav *English literature educator, novelist*
Slaight, Gary *broadcasting executive*
Slawter, Mark *golfer*
Slemon, Gordon Richard *electrical engineering educator*
Sloan, David Edward *retired corporate executive*
Smith, Lawrence Berk *economist, educator*
Smith, Peter William Ebblewhite *electrical engineering educator, scientist, physicist*
Sole, Michael Joseph *cardiologist*
Stadelman, William Ralph *chemical institution executive*
Staines, Mavis Avril *artistic director, ballet principal*
Stavro, Steve A. *professional hockey team executive*
Stefanschi, Sergiu *dancer*
Stoicheff, Boris Peter *physicist, educator*
†Stymiest, Barbara *trade association administrator*
Sundin, Mats Johan *hockey player*
Tall, Franklin David *mathematics educator*
Taylor, Allan Richard *retired banker*
Thall, Burnett Murray *retired newspaper executive*
Thase, Gunter Hermann *marketing executive*
†Thomas, Steve *hockey player*
Thomson, Kenneth R. (Lord Thomson of Fleet) *publishing executive*
Thomson, Richard Murray *retired banker*
Till, James Edgar *medical educator, researcher*
Tilley, Shermaine Ann *investment company executive*
Tobe, Stephen Solomon *zoology educator*
Tolmie, Kenneth Donald *artist, author*
Tsubouchi, David H. *Canadian provincial official*
Tulving, Endel *psychologist, educator*
Turner, John Napier *former prime minister of Canada, legislator*
Turner, Robert Edward *psychiatrist, educator*
Van Der Wyst, Geon *dancer*
van Ginkel, Blanche Lemco *architect, educator*
Venetsanopoulos, Anastasios Nicolaos *electrical engineer, educator*
Viner, Peter *communications executive*
Volpé, Robert *endocrinologist, researcher, educator*
Webb, Anthony Allan *banker*
†Webster, Jill Rosemary *historian, educator*
†Weston, W. Galen, Sr., *diversified holdings executive*
Wevers, John William *retired Semitic languages educator*
†Whitfield, Simon *Olympic athlete*
†Willis, Kevin Alvin *professional basketball player*
Wilson, Lynton Ronald *retired telecommunications company executive*
Wilson, Michael Holcombe *investment banker, former Canadian government official*
Wilson, Thomas Arthur *economics educator*
Winter, Frederick Elliot *fine arts educator*
Wleugel, John Peter *manufacturing company executive*
Wonham, Walter Murray *electrical engineer, educator*
Yu, Xiao Nan *dancer*
Zeng, Hong *audio system architect, researcher*
Zhuo, Min *neurobiology educator*

Unionville
Gulden, Simon *lawyer, investment/real estate development executive, business and legal consultant*

Vineland Station
Errampalli, Deena *molecular plant pathologist, researcher*

Waterloo
Aczél, János Dezsö *mathematician*
Balsillie, Jim *information technology executive*
Berczi, Andrew Stephen *academic administrator, educator*
Falding, Harold Joseph *sociology educator*
Gladwell, Graham Maurice Leslie *mathematician, civil engineering educator*
Haworth, Lawrence Lindley *philosophy educator*
Hynes, Hugh Bernard Noel *biologist, educator*
Jeyakumar, Ramanujam *physicist*
Lazaridis, Mike *information technology executive*
Morgan, Alan Vivian *geologist, educator*
Nelson, J. Gordon *geography educator*
Paldus, Josef *mathematics educator*
Penlidis, Alexander *chemical engineering educator*
Smith, Rowland James *educational administrator*
Sprott, David Arthur *statistics and psychology educator*
Stewart, Max Douglas *economics educator, consultant*
Suits, Bernard Herbert *philosophy educator*
Urquhart, Tony *artist, educator*
Van Seters, John *biblical literature educator, retired*
Vlach, Jiri *electrical engineering educator, researcher*
Vogel-Sprott, Muriel Doris *psychology educator, researcher*
Warner, Barry Gregory *ecologist, educator*
Wen, Geyi *applied physics educator*
Wright, Douglas Tyndall *business executive, university executive emeritus*

Willowdale
Kerner, Fred *book publisher, writer*
Sze, Michael Ming-Chih *actuary, consultant*
†Wolfe, Rose *former academic administrator*

Windsor
Auld, Frank *psychologist, educator*
Gurvich, Victor Alexander *physicist, engineer*
Hackam, Reuben *electrical engineering educator*
†Kennedy, John Baptist *civil engineer*
La Rocque, Eugene Philippe *bishop emeritus*
Thibert, Roger Joseph *clinical chemist, educator*

PRINCE EDWARD ISLAND

Montague
Cregier, Don Mesick *historian, educator, researcher, consultant*

QUEBEC

Beaconsfield
Harder, Rolf Peter *graphic designer, painter*

Beauharnois
Lebel, Robert *bishop*

Brossard
Allen, Harold Don *mathematics educator, science writer, monetary historian*

Chelsea
Warren, Jack Hamilton *former diplomat and trade policy adviser*

Chicoutimi
Cain, Michael Haney *lawyer*
Couture, Jean Guy *bishop*

Eastman
Emond, Lionel Joseph *management consultant*

Fossambault Sur Le Lac
Maranda, Guy *retired oral maxillofacial surgeon, Canadian health facility executive, educator*

Hull
Blondin-Andrew, Ethel *Canadian government official*
Bradshaw, Claudette *federal government official, parliamentarian*
Copps, Sheila *Canadian government official*
Ebacher, Roger *archbishop*
Gagliano, Alfonso *Canadian government official*
Stewart, Jane *Canadian government minister*

Ile Perrot
Lalonde, Marc *lawyer, former Canadian government official*

Ile des Soeurs
Dagenais, Marcel Gilles *economist, educator*

Laval
†Adrian, Donna Jean *retired librarian*
Pavilanis, Vytautas *microbiology educator, physician*
Pichette, Claude *former banking executive, university rector, research executive*
Savoie, Paul-André *information technology executive*
Talbot, Pierre Joseph *microbiologist, researcher*

Leclercville
Morin, Pierre Jean *retired management consultant*

Longueil
Archambault, Louis *sculptor*

Montpellier
Poirier, Louis Joseph *neurology educator*

Montreal
Audet, Henri *retired communications executive*
Barrette, Jean *physicist, researcher*
Beardmore, Harvey Ernest *retired physician, educator*
Beauregard, Luc *public relations executive*

Becker, Herbert Lawrence *writer, accountant*
Becklake, Margaret Rigsby *physician, educator*
Bentley, Kenneth Chessar *oral and maxillofacial surgeon, educator*
Beugnot, Bernard Andre Henri *French literature educator*
Bisson, Claude *retired chief justice of Quebec*
Bissonnette, Anik *dancer*
Brecher, Irving *economics educator*
Brecher, Michael *political science educator*
Brisebois, Marcel *museum director*
Brown, Peter Gilbert *philosopher, educator, tree farmer*
Bruemmer, Fred *writer, photographer*
†Burgess, John Herbert *physician, educator*
Butler, Susan Ruth *clinical psychologist*
Caillé, André *public service company executive*
Carignan, Claude *astronomer, educator*
Carroll, Robert Lynn *biology educator, vertebrate paleontologist, museum curator*
Cedraschi, Tullio *investment management company executive*
Chang, Thomas Ming Swi *medical scientist, biotechnologist*
Charney, Melvin *artist, architect, educator*
Clermont, Yves Wilfrid *anatomy educator, researcher*
Cobbett, Stuart Hanson *lawyer*
Couture, Armand *civil engineer*
Crowston, Wallace Bruce Stewart *management educator*
Cruess, Richard Leigh *surgeon, university dean*
Cyr, J. V. Raymond *telecommunications industry executive*
Daly, Gerald *accountant*
Dansereau, Pierre *retired ecologist*
Das Gupta, Subal *physics educator, researcher*
Davidson, Colin Henry *architect, educator*
Dealy, John Michael *chemical engineer, educator*
Desmarais, Paul *holding company executive*
de Takacsy, Nicholas Benedict *physicist, educator*
Diksic, Mirko *research scientist, educator*
Dubuc, Serge *mathematics educator*
Dufour, Jean-Marie *economics researcher, educator*
Duquette, Jean-Pierre *French language and literature educator*
Eisenberg, Adi *chemist*
†Engen, D(onald) Travis *diversified telecommunications company executive*
Feindel, William Howard Howard *neurosurgeon, consultant*
Ferguson, Michael John *electronics and communications educator*
Freedman, Samuel Orkin *university official*
Freeman, Carolyn Ruth *radiation oncologist*
French, Stanley George *university dean, philosophy educator*
Gabbour, Iskandar *city and regional planning educator*
Genest, Jacques *physician, clinical scientist, administrator*
Gibbs, Sarah Preble *biologist, educator*
Gillespie, Thomas Stuart *business executive*
Girard, Francois *film director*
Gold, Alan B. *former Canadian chief justice*
Gold, Phil *immunologist, educator, researcher*
Goldbloom, Victor Charles
Goltzman, David *endocrinologist, educator, researcher*
Gouin, Serge *corporate executive*
Granger, Luc Andre *university dean, psychologist*
Gratton, Robert *diversified financial services company executive*
Guérard, Geneviève *dancer*
Guerrero, Vladimir *professional baseball player*
Gulkin, Harry *arts administrator, film producer*
Haccoun, David *electrical engineering educator*
Herling, Michael *steel company executive*
Hoffmann, Peter Conrad Werner *history educator*
Hopkins, Tom *artist*
Hutchison, Andrew Sandford *archbishop*
Ikawa-Smith, Fumiko *anthropologist, educator*
Ivanier, Paul *steel products manufacturing company executive*
Jeanniot, Michel Andre *lawyer*
Johnstone, Rose Mamelak (Mrs. Douglas Johnstone) *biochemistry educator*
Jolicoeur, Paul *molecular biologist*
Jones, Barbara Ellen *neuroscientist, educator*
Kaufman, Donna S. *lawyer*
Kinsley, William Benton *literature educator, retired*
Kramer, Michael Stuart *pediatric epidemiologist*
Krausz, Peter Thomas *artist, gallery director, educator*
†Lacombe, Jacques *conductor, music director*
Lacoste, Paul *lawyer, educator, university official*
Ladanyi, Branko *civil engineer, educator*
Lagacé, Bernard *performing company executive*
Lamarre, Bernard *engineering, contracting and manufacturing advisor*
Large, John Andrew *library and information service educator*
Laurin, Pierre *finance company executive*
Leblond, Charles Philippe *anatomy educator, researcher*
Lemire, Andre *investment company executive*
Leroy, Claude *physics educator, researcher*
Lowy, Frederick Hans *academic administrator, psychiatrist*
Maag, Urs Richard *statistics educator*
Mac Lean, Lloyd Douglas *surgeon*
Matziorinis, Kenneth N. *economist*
Melzack, Ronald *psychology educator*
Messing, Karen *occupational health researcher*
Michaud, Georges Joseph *astrophysics educator*
Milic-Emili, Joseph *physician, educator*
Milner, Brenda Atkinson Langford *neuropsychologist*
Milner, Peter Marshall *psychology educator*
Molson, Eric H. *beverage company executive*
Morin, Yves-Charles *linguistics educator, researcher*
Moser, William Oscar Jules *mathematics educator*
Mulder, David S. *cardiovascular surgeon*
Mulroney, Brian (Martin Brian Mulroney) *former prime minister of Canada*
Mysak, Lawrence Alexander *oceanographer, climatologist, mathematician, educator*
Nadeau, Bertin Felix *diversified company executive*
†Nadeau, Jacques O. *brokerage house executive*
Nadeau, Reginald Antoine *medical educator*
Nattel, Stanley *cardiologist, research scientist*
Nayar, Baldev Raj *political science educator*
Neveu, Jean *printing company executive*
Normandeau, Andre Gabriel *criminologist, educator*
Ormsby, Eric Linn *educator, researcher, writer*
Paidoussis, Michael Pandeli *mechanical engineering educator*
†Pankov, Gradimir Krunislav *ballet artistic director*
Panneton, Jacques *librarian*
Pasternac, André *cardiologist, educator*
Perlin, Arthur Saul *chemistry educator*
†Picard, Laurent A(ugustin) *retired management educator, administrator, consultant*
†Plourde, Gerard *company executive*
Podgorsak, Ervin B. *medical physicist, educator, administrator*
Popovici, Adrian *law educator*
Pound, Richard William Duncan *lawyer, accountant*
Radacovský, Mário *dancer*
Ramachandran, Venkatanarayana Deekshit *electrical engineering educator*
Raynauld, Andre *economist, educator*
Redfern, John D. *manufacturing company executive*
Robb, James Alexander *lawyer*
Robillard, Edmond *priest*
Rolland, Lucien Gilbert *paper company executive, director*
Romanov, Volodymyr Alexeevich *computer science educator, researcher*
Rothman, Melvin L. *judge*
Saint-Pierre, Guy *engineering executive*
Saumier, Andre *finance executive*
†Scraire, Jean-Claude *lawyer, investment management executive*
Scriver, Charles Robert *medical scientist, human geneticist*
Selvadurai, Antony Patrick Sinnappa *civil engineering educator, applied mathematician, consultant*
Silverthorne, Michael James *classics educator*
Sirois, Charles *communications executive*
Solomon, Samuel *biochemistry educator, administrator*
Souhami, Luis *physician, radiation oncology*
Speirs, Derek James *diversified corporation financial executive*
Stewart, Jane *psychology educator*
Suen, Ching Yee *computer scientist and educator, researcher*
Szabo, Denis *criminologist, educator*
Taras, Paul *physicist, educator*
Tavares, Tony *professional hockey and baseball leagues executive*
Tellier, Paul M. *railroad transportation executive*
Theodore, Jose *hockey player*
Thompson, John Douglas *financier*
Torrey, David Leonard *investment banker*
Tournier, Jean-Pierre *consultant company executive*
Toutant, Sylvain *retail executive*
Tremblay, Andre Gabriel *lawyer*
Trigger, Bruce Graham *anthropology educator*
Turcotte, Jean-Claude Cardinal *archbishop*
Turmel, Jean Bernard *banker*
Vaillancourt, Jean-Guy *sociology researcher and educator*
Vennat, Michel *lawyer, bank executive*
Von Gencsy, Eva *dancer, choreographer, educator*
Waller, Harold Myron *political science educator*
Webster, Norman Eric *journalist, charitable foundation administrator*
Weir, Stephen James *financial executive*
Whitehead, Michael Anthony *chemistry educator*
Wood, Dennis *communications executive*

Mount Royal
Chauvette, Claude R. *building materials company administrator*
Elie, Jean André *investment banker*
Glezos, Matthews *consumer products and services company executive*

North Hatley
Jones, Douglas Gordon *retired literature educator*

Outremont
Derderian, Hovnan *church official*
Larose, Roger *retired pharmaceutical executive, retired dean*
Letourneau, Jean-Paul *business association executive and consultant*
Levesque, Rene Jules Albert *retired physicist*

Pointe Claire
Bachynski, Morrel Paul *physicist*
Bolker, Henry Irving *retired chemist, research institute director, educator*

Pointe-Claire
Lapointe, Lucie *Canadian government official*

Quebec
Belanger, Gerard *economics educator*
Cote, Steeve D. *biologist*
LeMay, Jacques *lawyer*
L'Heureux-Dubé, Claire *judge*
Page, Michel *biochemist, researcher*
Potvin, Pierre *physiologist, educator*
Stavert, Alexander Bruce *bishop*
Tavenas, François *civil engineer, educator*
Theodorescu, Radu Amza Serban *mathematician, educator*
Tremblay, Marc Adélard *anthropologist, educator*
Trudel, Marc J. *botanist, educator*
Verge, Pierre *legal educator*
Zagolski, Francis *remote sensing expert, executive, researcher*

Rimouski
Blanchet, Bertrand *archbishop*

Rosemere
Hopper, Carol *meeting and incentive trip administrator*

Rouyn
Hamelin, Jean-Guy *bishop*

Sain -Sauveur
Hanigan, Lawrence *retired railway executive*

Saint-Adele
†Rousseau-Vermette, Mariette *artist*

Saint-Anne-Des-Lacs
Rochette, Louis *retired shipowner and shipbuilder*

Saint-Faustin-Lac-Carre
Des Marais, Pierre, II, *communications holding company executive*

Saint-Foy
Dussault, Jean H. *endocrinologist, medical educator*

Saint-Lambert
Terreault, Charles *engineer, management educator, researcher*

Saint-Laurent
†Jundi, Bilal *principal*

Saint-Urbain-de-Charlevoix
Beyer, Martin Gottfried *geologist, consultant*

Sainte-Anne-de-Bellevue
Broughton, Robert Stephen *irrigation and drainage engineering educator, consultant*
Grant, William Frederick *geneticist, educator*

Sainte-Foy
Bonnelly, Claude *library director*
LeDuy, Anh *engineering educator*
Murray, Warren James *philosophy educator*
Normand, Robert *retired lawyer*

Sherbrooke
Bourget, Edwin Robert *marine ecologist, educator*
Tremblay, André-Marie *physicist*

Sillery
Dinan, Robert Michael *lawyer*
La Rochelle, Pierre-Louis *civil engineering educator*

Sutton
†Bolduc, J. Emilien *bank executive*

Varennes
Bartnikas, Raymond *electrical engineer, educator*

Verdun
Gauthier, Serge Gaston *neurologist*
Lessard, Michel M. *finance company executive*

Westmount
Coolidge, Robert Tytus *deacon, historian, educator*
Fortier, L. Yves *barrister*

Westmount
Kalaycioglu, Serdar *space robotics engineer, manager*

SASKATCHEWAN

Regina
Barber, Lloyd Ingram *retired university president*
Bayda, Edward Dmytro *judge*
Clayton, Raymond Edward *government official*
Cleveland, Ray LeRoy *history educator*
Davis, Gordon Richard Fuerst *retired biologist, translator*
Haverstock, Lynda M. *lieutenant governor*
MacKay, Harold Hugh *lawyer*
Mollard, John Douglas *engineering and geology executive*
Phillips, Roger *retired steel company executive*
Powell, Trevor John David *archivist*
Spencer, Larry *member of parliament*
Symes, Lawrence Richard *computer science educator, university dean*
Vanderhooft, Rob *investment company executive*

Saskatoon
Babiuk, Lorne Alan *virologist, immunologist, research administrator*
Billinton, Roy *engineering educator*
Blakeney, Allan Emrys *Canadian government official, lawyer*
Bornstein, Eli *artist, sculptor*
Hirose, Akira *physics educator, researcher*
Houston, C(larence) Stuart *radiologist, educator*
Huang, Pan Ming *soil science educator*
Irvine, Vernon Bruce *accounting educator, administrator*
Ish, Daniel Russell *law educator, academic administrator*
Jacobson, Sverre Theodore *retired minister*
Kartha, Kutty Krishnan *plant pathologist*
Kennedy, Marjorie Ellen *librarian*
Khachatourians, George (Gharadaghi) *microbiologist, educator*
Knott, Douglas Ronald *college dean, agricultural sciences educator, researcher*
Martell, Keith *bank executive*
†Popkin, David Richard *obstetrician, health science administrator*
Shokeir, Mohamed Hassan Kamel *medical geneticist, educator*
†Smith, C. D. *civil engineering educator*

Calgary
†Grand-Maitre, Jean *performing company executive*

Montreal
†Labadie, Bernard *performing company executive*
†Lock, Edouard *performing company executive*
†Moss, David *conductor*

Oakville
Jelinek, John Joseph *public relations executive*

Ottawa
†Easter, Arnold Wayne *solicitor*

Quebec
Morin, Louis *government agency administrator*

Richmond
Cordoba, Mike *food service executive*

Saskatoon
Zhao, Jingang *economist, educator*

Sherbrooke
Deslongchamps, Pierre *chemistry educator*

Whale Cove
Rodnunsky, Sidney *lawyer, educator*

Winnipeg
†Hodgkins, William F. *career officer*

MEXICO

Aguascalientes
Godinez Flores, Ramon *bishop*

Chapola
Brady, Wray Grayson *mathematician, educator*

Col Centro
Gil Diaz, Francisco *minister of finance for Mexico*

Col Cordesa
†Blanco Mendoza, Herminio *Mexican government official*

Col Jardines Montana
†Carabias Lillo, Julia *government official*

Col Lomas de Chapultepec
Guajardo Touché, Ricardo *bank executive*

Colonia Cuauhtemoc
†Garza, Antonio O. *ambassador*

Cuauhtemoc
†Aleman, José Vicente Aguinaco *legal administrator*

Cuernavaca
†Bolivar Zapata, Francisco *biochemist*

Distrito Federal
de la Fuente Ramirez, Juan Ramon *Mexican government official, academic administrator*

Garza Garcia
Gustafson, Eric William *real estate investor, wildlife habitat conservationist*

Guadalajara
†Sandoval Iñiguez, Juan Cardinal *archbishop*

Guanajuato
Cardno, Donald Barry *retired personnel director*

La Noria
†Campos, Jorge *professional soccer player*

Mexico City
†Abascal Carranza, Carlos Maria *secretary of labor and social planning for Mexico*
†Barrio Terrazas, Francisco *government official of Mexico*
Bruton, John Macaulay *trade association executive, consultant*
†Burgos, Hector Hugo *trading company executive*
Cabrera-Jimenez, Jorge Alberto *scientific researcher*
†Cerisola y Weber, Pedro *secretary of communications and transportation for Mexico*
†Chavez, Julio Cesar *professional boxer*
†Creel Miranda, Santiago *secretary of the interior for Mexico*
†De La Riva, Myriam Ann *artist*
†Derbez Bautista, Luis Ernesto *secretary of foreign affairs of Mexico*
†Fox, Vicente (Vicente Fox Quesada) *President of Mexico*
Friedeberg, Pedro *painter, sculptor, designer*
†Gurria Trevino, José Angel *former Mexican government official*
Guzman-Arenas, Adolfo *computer science researcher, electronics engineer*
†Herrera Tello, Maria Teresa *secretary of agrarian reform for Mexico*
Kim, Earnest Jae-Hyun *import and export company executive*
Leon-Portilla, Miguel *historian, educator*

†Lichtinger, Victor *secretary of environment, natural resources and fisheries for Mexico*
†Macedo de la Concha, Rafael *attorney general of Mexico*
†Martens, Ernesto *air, aerospace transportation executive*
Murphy, Edward Stack *pathologist*
†Navarro, Leticia *Mexican government official*
Nicholas, Ronald Wayde *business consultant*
Olechnowicz Fridman, Elias *civil engineer*
Ortiz, Guillermo *banker*
Peimbert, Manuel *astronomer*
†Peyrot Gonzalez, Marco A. *secretary of the navy of Mexico*
Porraz, Mauricio Jimenez Labora *civil engineer, researcher*
†Rivera Carrera, Norberto Cardinal *archbishop*
Soberon Kuri, Alejandro *performing company executive*
†Tamez Guerra, Reyes S. *secretary of public education for Mexico*
Thomas, Zdeněk *retired civil engineer, researcher*
†Trevino, Guillermo Prieto *brokerage house executive*
†Usabiaga Arroyo, Javier *secretary of agriculture, livestock and rural development for Mexico*
Vargas Legaspi, Juan *manufacturing company executive*
†Vazquez Mota, Josefina *secretary of social development for Mexico*
†Vega Garcia, Gerardo Clemente R. *secretary of defense for Mexico*
†Zedillo Ponce de León, Ernesto *former president of Mexico*

Mexico DF
Ceniceros, Maciel Hector Alfonso *business systems executive, consultant*
Gonzalez-Sanchez, Enrique *economist*

Mich
di Cori, Pat Miller *painter, sculptor*

Monterrey
Amores, Jose E. *cultural director*

Morelia
Warren, J. Benedict *retired history educator*

Oaxaca de Juárez
Hallberg, Thomas Boone *education educator*

Piso
†Tellez Kuenzler, Luis *government official*

Puebla
Creuheras, Santiago *social scientist*
Powell, Benjamin Loomis *government management analyst*

Reynosa
†Asomoza, Miguel A. *researcher, educator*

San Miguel de Allende
Seator, Lynette Hubbard *freelance writer*

San Nicolas
†Suarez Rivera, Adolfo Antonio Cardinal *retired archbishop*

San Pedro Garza García
†Defiore, Perry Dennis *academic administrator, business owner*

Toluca
†Tapia Reyes, Gustavo *prosthodontist*
†Arroyo Marroquin, Románico *former federal official*
†Carrasco Altamirano, Diódoro *former federal official*
†Farell Cubillas, Arsenio *former Mexican government official*
†Limón Rojas, Miguel *former Mexican government official*
†Lorenzo Franco, José Ramón *former Mexican government official*
†Martens Rebolledo, Ernesto *secretary of energy for Mexico, glass products company executive*
†Robledo Rincón, Eduardo *former federal official*

ARGENTINA

Buenos Aires
Berardi, Jorge Enrique *economist*
Farias Bouvier, Nestor *consulting company executive*
†Green Macias, Rosario *ambassador*
Gutierrez, Lino *diplomat*
Levy, Joseph Bruno *foundation administrator, educator*
†Lopez-Murphy, Ricardo Hipolito *economist*
Mettler, Norma Evangelina *poet, research scientist*
Montes, Leopoldo Feliciano *dermatologist, educator*
†Rocha, Manuel *diplomat*

AUSTRALIA

Adelaide
Brissenden, Alan (Alan Theo Brissenden) *writer*
Choate, Ray *university librarian*

Altona
Daniel-Dreyfus, Susan B. Russe *civic worker*

Armadale
Searby, Richard Henry *academic administrator, lawyer*

Armidale
Cooksey, Ray Wagner *human resource management educator*

Bankstown
Kruckenberg, Teresa May *research engineer, consultant*

Camberwell
Peterson, Douglas Pete (Pete Peterson) *ambassador, former congressman*

Cammeray
Besley, Morrish Alexander (Tim Besley) *civil engineer*

Canberra
Gani, Joseph Mark *statistics educator, administrator, researcher*
Harris, Stuart Francis *educator, researcher*
Snooks, Graeme Donald *political economist, stratologist*
Taylor, Stuart Ross *geochemist, author*
Thayer, Carlyle Alan *educator*

Clayton
De Wilde, Craig James *music educator, researcher*

Darlinghurst
Davis, Judy *actress*

Double Bay
Peacock, Penne Korth *ambassador*

Double Bay Sydney
Guerin, Didier *magazine executive*

Hawthorn
Base, Graeme Rowland *illustrator, author*

Karrinyup
Young, Deidra Jane *educational researcher*

Killara
Lesser, Steven John *organizational development consultant*

Malanda
Cooper, William Thomas *natural history artist*

Melbourne
Batrouney, Clive M. *corporate financial executive*
Bellin, Howard *management consultant company executive*
Corden, Warner Max *economics educator*

Nedlands
Oxnard, Charles Ernest *anatomist, anthropologist, human biologist, educator*

Norfolk Island
McCullough, Colleen *author*

North Sydney
Scott, Brian Walter *management consultant*

Paddington
Keneally, Thomas Michael *author*

Parkville
Azer, Samy Aziz *gastroenterologist, medical educator*
Denton, Derek Ashworth *medical researcher, medical scientist*
Metcalf, Donald *biomedical researcher*

Perth
Dow, Simon *artistic director*
Riley, Richard Haydn *anaesthetist, researcher*

Randwick
Hall, Peter Francis *physiologist*

Redfern
Campion, Jane *director, screenwriter*

Saint Lucia
Edwards, Sir Llewellyn Roy *company executive*

Southport
Buckley, Ralf Christopher *research scientist*

Springfield
Spalvins, Janis Gunars *steamship company executive*

Sydney
Encel, Solomon *education educator, consultant*
Guthrie, James Ernest *accounting educator*
Lucas, Peter Charles *investment company executive*

Townsville, Queensland
Ho, Yik Hong *colon and rectal surgeon*

Victoria Armadale
†Neil, Sandra Eilleen Silverberg *psychologist*

AUSTRIA

OR

Portland
†Kalmar, Carlos *music director*

Graz
Prisching, Manfred *sociology educator*
Reinitzer, Sigrid Friedrun *librarian, educator*
Weisstein, Ulrich Werner *English literature educator*

Kitzbuehel
Newman, Claire Poe *private investor*

Salzburg
Angermüller, Rudolph *music foundation executive*
Sperl, Wolfgang *pediatrician*

Vienna
al-Omair, Saleh *trade association administrator*
†Arlacchi, Pino *protective services official*
Dee, James Phillip *human resources consultant*
Higgins, William Woods *painter, art educator*
†Liebscher, Klaus *stock exchange executive, banker*
Mag Walz, Günther *artist*
Matzner, Egon *economics educator*
†Sindelka, Josef *postal service and telecommunications administrator*
Steinbruckner, Bruno Friedrich *foreign language educator*
Swięcicki, Marcin *politician, economist*

THE BAHAMAS

Nassau
Crone, John Thomas, IV, *portfolio manager, financial analyst*
Dingman, Michael David *industrial company executive, international investor*
†Harrison, Johnnie Sheppard *religious organization administrator*

BAHRAIN

Manama
Sarhan, Mansoor Mohamed *library director*

BANGLADESH

Dhaka
Hossain, M. Iqbal *pediatrician, researcher*
†Thomas, Harry K., Jr., *ambassador*

Kushtia
Latifur Rahaman, Rasul Boaksh *legal profession executive*

BARBADOS

Christ Church
Waithe, Mary Rebecca *personnel director, dance instructor*

BELARUS

Minsk
Sychov, Alyaksandr *diplomat*

BELGIUM

Antwerp
Snyders, Dirk Johan *electrophysiologist, biophysicist, educator*
Wilford, William Gustaaf *investment company executive*

Brussels
Barnum, John Wallace *lawyer*
Berna, Marie-Rose *international organization executive*
Bustin, George Leo *lawyer*
Buysse, Paul Henri Maria *trading company executive*
Everard, Eric *company administrator*
Jadot, Jean Lambert Octave *clergyman*
Kempe, Frederick Schumann *newspaper editor, columnist, author*
Kerber, Frank John *diplomat*
Liebman, Howard Mark *lawyer*
Maroy, Michel *European affairs consultant*
McCullough, Ross A., Jr., *delivery service executive*
Nelson, Marcella Simonetta *artist*
Prodi, Romano *economist, educator, researcher, former prime minister of Italy*
Rossi, Pierre Marie *consultancy company executive*
Staab, Diane D. *lawyer*

Ghent
Deforce, Dieter Luciën Daniël *research scientist, educator*
Hulstaert, Frank *pharmaceutical company executive*
Vandepitte, Daniël Camille Cornelis *civil engineering educator*

Heusden
Stallaerts, Robert *librarian, researcher*

Hornu
Selvais, Philippe Leon *endocrinologist*

Leuven
Buyst, Erik Cesar *economic history educator*
Huypens, Jozef Maria Alfons *communication consultant*
Novoa de Armas, Hector *scientific researcher*

Liège
Mosora-Stan, Florentina Ioana *physics educator*

Oost-Vlaanderen
Stroobandt, Dirk Rudy *research scientist, educator*

Roeselare
Libbrecht, Gaspar Joseph *civil engineer, educator*

Shape
Gates, Sheree Hunt *counseling administrator, educator, writer*
Vergnes, Bernard *information technology executive*

BELIZE

Belize City
Brown, Sir George Noel *chief justice*

Cayo
Wulff, Roger LaVern *museum administrator*

BERMUDA

Hamilton
Johnston, Malcolm (Calum) *bank executive*
Kramer, Donald *insurance executive*

Saint George
Saadian, Javid *cultural organization administrator, consultant*

Saint Georges
Jackson, Hermoine Prestine *psychologist*

BRAZIL

70403-900
†Hrinak, Donna Jean *ambassador*

Brasília
Amorim, Celso Luiz Nunes *government official*
†Pertenece, Jose Paulo Sepulveda *legal administrator*

Rio de Janeiro
Resende, Marcelo *economist, educator*
Sales, Eugenio de Araujo Cardinal *emeritus archbishop*

Sao Paolo
†Rawl, Arthur Julian (Lord of Cursons) *retail executive, accountant, consultant, author*

Sorocaba
Martins, Nelson *physics educator*

Vitória
Lievore, Ruston *pathologist, consultant*

BULGARIA

Sofia
Exerowa, Dotchi Russeva *chemist, researcher*
†Kovachev, Lubomir Miltchev *physicist, researcher*

CAYMAN ISLANDS

Chehalis
Hughey, David Vaughn *business administration educator, educational consultant*

CHAD

N'Djamena
Goldthwait, Christopher E. *ambassador*

CHANNEL ISLANDS

Guernsey
Hunter, John Graham *investment management company executive*
Schere, Jean *researcher*

CHILE

La Reina Santiago
Beshears, Charles Daniel *insurance executive*

Santiago
Wilkey, Malcolm Richard *retired ambassador, former federal judge*

Talca
McNamee, Sister Catherine *educator*

CHINA

Bangkok
†Johnson, Darryl Norman *ambassador*

Beijing
Banister, Judith *demographer, educator*
Han, Rui *pharmacologist, educator*
Melville, Richard Allen *investment company executive*
†Prueher, Joseph W. *military officer*
Ren, Jiyu *library director*
Shu, Wenlong *environmental engineer, educator*
†Yizhong, Li *business executive*
Zhao, Ren Wei *economist, educator*

Guangzhou
Chen, Concordia Chao *mathematician*

Hong Kong
†Kee, Lee Shau *real estate developer*
Li, Ka-Shing *international entrepreneur*
Ng, Chi-Sing *pathologist, consultant*

Jinan Shandong
Fan, Xijun *education educator*

Nanjing
†Gao, Hongjun *mathematician*

Shanghai
†Chueh, Chun Fei *import/export company executive*
Jackson, Robert Keith *manufacturing company executive*
Sun, Rongqi *organic chemistry educator, researcher*
Xu, Bin *research scientist*
Yun, Liang *marine engineer, educator*

Taijichang, Beijing
Huasun, Qin *diplomat*

COLOMBIA

Cali
Keppel, Timothy Anderson *humanities educator, writer*
Rao, Idupulapati Madhusudana *plant nutritionist, plant physiologist*

COSTA RICA

San José
Arias Sanchez, Oscar *former president of Costa Rica*
Bien, Amos *ecologist*
Hoffman, Irwin *orchestra conductor*

COTE D'IVOIRE

Abidjan
Perry, Cynthia Shepard *federal agency administrator*

CROATIA

Zagreb
Solter, Miljenko *endocrinologist, educator*
Štambuk, Nikola *research scientist*

CUBA

Minamar
Lajous, Roberta *diplomat, editor*

CYPRUS

Limassol
†Christophi, Costas A *statistician, accountant*

Nicosia
Aloneftis, Andreas *financial and investment executive*

CZECH REPUBLIC

Kromeriz
Benada, Jaroslav *research scientist, consultant*

Prague
Bubeník, Jan *cancer researcher, biology educator*
Čejka, Jiří
†Gubta, Indrajit *trade association administrator*
Jech, Thomas J. *mathematics educator*
Kalkus, Stanley *librarian, administrator, consultant*
Manas, Miroslav *economics educator, researcher*
†Tu, Nguyen Van *former trade association administrator*
Turková, Helga *library director*
Zharikov, Alexander Nikolaevich *trade union federation executive*

DEMOCRATIC REPUBLIC OF CONGO

Kinshasa
†Hooks, Aubrey *ambassador*

DENMARK

Aarhus
Herborg-Nielsen, Thorkild *retired business educator*
Hjalager, Anne-Mette *management consultant*
Vastrup, Claus *economist*

Aarhus V
Smith, Nina *economics educator*

Charlottenlund
Garner, Fradley Hamilton *freelance writer, editor, narrator*

Copenhagen
Drakeman, Lisa N. *biotechnology company executive*
Elmer, Michael Bendik *legal administrator*
Holm, Erik *foundation director, political scientist, economist*
Jiménez-Beltran, Domingo *executive*
Joergensen, Per Bay *economist, insurance executive*
Koktvedgaard, Mogens *education educator*
Lage, Cristina *secretary general*
Larsen, Poul Steen *library educator*
Martin, Vivian *soprano*
†Mottelson, Ben R. *physicist*
Nielsen, Jens Evald *retired engineer*
Olgaard, Anders *economics educator*
Pethick, Christopher John *physicist*
Sestoft, Leif *endocrinologist, researcher, educator*

Frederiksberg
Jørgen, Ulm *retired computer scientist*

Gentofte
Egsmose, Ragna Kopp *cultural sociologist, researcher*

Hoersholm
Sørensen, Erik *international company executive*

Holstebro
Schaufuss, Peter *dancer, producer, choreographer, ballet director*

Lyngby
Sumer, B. Mutlu *civil engineer, educator, researcher, consultant*

Odense
Keldmann, Erik Christian Vilhelm *innovation company executive*
Lauritsen, Kaj Torben *lawyer, former association executive*

Roskilde
Poulsen, IB *mass communications educator, researcher*

Soro
Ersgaard, Ole Kristian *marketing and management consultant, business developer*

Vedbaek
Nordqvist, Erik Askbo *shipping company executive*
Svensson, Sven Eilif *civil engineer, consultant*

Vejle
Vagn-Hansen, Carsten Peter Mathias *health consultant, physician*

Århus
Mosekilde, Leif *endocrinologist, educator*

EGYPT

Cairo
Basilious, Nagi Moussa *artist, painter*
Bieber-Roberts, Peggy Eilene *communications educator, editor, journalist, researcher*
Elaraby, Nabil A. *Egyptian diplomat*
Fahmy, Ibrahim Mounir *hotel executive*
Miller, Harry George *education educator*
Morsi, Abd el Wahab *artist*
Pendleton, Mary Catherine *foreign service officer*
Sullivan, Earl Le Roy *political science educator, academic administrator*
†Welch, David C. *ambassador*
Wichman, Edna Carol *media specialist, librarian*

Damietta
†Mansour, Ahmed Hamed *educational technology educator, academic administ*

Garden City
Norris, James Arnold *federal agency administrator, consultant*

ENGLAND

Aldwych London
O'Brien, Patrick Karl *economic history educator*

Ascot
Monk, Anthony John *engineer*

Ascot Berkshire
Grubman, Wallace Karl *chemical company executive*

Askett
Irons, Jeremy John *actor*

Balcombe
Scofield, Paul *actor*

Barnston Wirral
Scragg, Thomas William *librarian, historical researcher, solicitor*

Beckenham Kent
Lader, Malcolm Harold *pharmaceutical consultant*

Bedfordshire
Gelman, Leonid Moiseevich *scientist, vibroacoustician, educator*
Montgomery, John Warwick *law educator, theologian*

Berkshire
Perry, Sir Michael (Sir Michael Sydney Perry) *industrialist*

Beverley
Edles, Gary Joel *lawyer*

Birmingham
Browne, Roger Michael *oral pathology educator, consultant*

Bournemouth
Pritchard, Colin *social work educator*

Brentford, Middlesex
Ingram, Robert A. *pharmaceuticals company executive*

Brighton
Hirst, Paul Heywood *retired education educator*
Kroto, Harold Walter *chemistry researcher, educator*

Bristol
Silver, Ian Adair *pathology educator*

Buckinghamshire
Wager, Elizabeth *writer*

Cambridge
Buckingham, Amyand David *chemistry educator*
Edwards, Sir Samuel Frederick *physicist, educator*
Hogwood, Christopher Jarvis Haley *music educator*
Huxley, Sir Andrew (Sir Andrew Fielding Huxley) *physiologist, educator*
Kermode, Frank (John Kermode) *literary critic, educator*
Kidonakis, Nikolaos *physicist*
Klug, Aaron *molecular biologist*
Merrington, Oliver J. *information scientist*
Mirrlees, Sir James Alexander *economics educator*
Rees, Martin John *astronomy educator*
Renfrew, Andrew Colin (Lord Renfrew of Kaimsthorn) *archaeologist, academic administrator*
Richard, Alison Fettes *anthropology educator*
Sanger, Frederick *retired molecular biologist*
Sen, Amartya Kumar *economist, educator*
Singh, Ajit *economist*
Steiner, George (Francis Steiner) *author, educator*

Canterbury
Holwell, Peter *management consultant*
Lynch, Edward Philip *management consultant*

Chard
Beer, John Vincent *pathologist, consultant*

Charlbury
Belkin, Boris David *violinist*

Chelmsford
Hayes, Eric James *consulting company executive*

Chiswick
Adams, Norman *artist, educator*

Coulsdon
Vijayaratnam, Kanapathipillai *civil and environmental engineer, consultant, director, educator*

Coventry
Thomas, Howard *business educator*

Croydon
Katin, Peter Roy *pianist*

Devon
Rossmiller, George Eddie *agricultural economist*

Doncaster
Warde-Norbury, William George Antony *financial executive*

Durham
Galloway, David Malcolm *retired education educator*
Miller, Susan Janet *business educator, researcher*
Moberly, Elizabeth Rosamund *archaeologist, educator*
Spooner, Frank Clyffurde *economic history educator*

Eastbourne
Baylen, Joseph Oscar *retired history educator*

Ely Cambridgeshire
March, Lionel John *architecture educator, researcher*

Falmer
Cornforth, Sir John Warcup *chemist*

Godalming
Port, Stanley Robert *civil engineer, data management engineer*

Greenwich London
de Savorgnani, Adriane Aldrich *health care administrator, nurse*

Grimsby
Burgess, John Richard *engineer*

Guildford
Bulmer, Martin *sociologist, educator*

Harmondsworth
Marshall, Lord Colin (Lord Marshall of Knightsbridge) *airline executive*

Hatfield
Payton, Roger Louis *consultant*

Hayes
Hounsfield, Godfrey Newbold *radiation scientist*

Henley-on-Thames
Ashbrook, Kate Jessie *charitable organization director*

Herefordshire
Jacobus, George Anthony Bodley (Anton Jacobus) *investment banker*

High Holborn
Russo, Anthony Joseph *public relations professional*

Hingham
Pollini, Francis *author*

Isle of Wight
Stigwood, Robert Colin *theater, movie, television and record producer*

Kent
Pecorino, Lauren Teresa *biologist*

Kent Cranbrook
Hattersley-Smith, Geoffrey Francis *retired government research scientist*

Keynsham
Obolensky, Nicholas *entrepreneur*

Kingsbridge
Durant, Graham John *medicinal chemist, drug researcher*

Leeds
Gibson, Robert Myles *neurosurgeon, consultant*
Nixon, David *dancer*
Phillips, Oliver *tropical forest ecologist*
Rastall, George Richard *music educator*

Leicester
Harijan, Ram *technology transfer researcher*
Landy, Leigh (Harry Leigh Landy) *music educator, composer*

Letchworth
Everitt-Newton, Katherine Evelyn *international management consultant*

Lincolnshire
Axcell, Douglas Norman *business consultant, minister*

Liverpool
Barr, Wally *social worker, researcher*
Reilly, Thomas *humanities educator*
Sawko, Felicjan *civil engineering educator*

London
Akin, Steven Paul *financial company executive*
Alexeev, Dmitri Konstantinovich *pianist*
Alvarez, A. (Al Alvarez) *writer*
Amis, Martin Louis *author*
Andsnes, Leif Ove *concert pianist*
Ashkenazy, Vladimir Davidovich *concert pianist, conductor*
Bate, Jennifer Lucy *musician*
Bates, Alan (Arthur Bates) *actor*
Bell, Joshua *musician*
Bergman, Mark Steven *lawyer*
†Bevan, Tim *film producer*
Binney, Robert Harry *bank executive*
†Bland, Sir Christopher (Francis Buchan Bland) *freight company executive*
Blundell, Richard William *economics educator*
†Bourne, Matthew *performing company executive, artistic director*
Brierley, Peter William *charitable foundation administrator*
†Brotherston, Lez *set designer, costumer*
†Carrow, Robert Duane *lawyer, barrister*
Chadwick, Derek James *foundation administrator*
Cleese, John Marwood *writer, comedian*
Codron, Michael Victor *theatrical producer*
Cole, Richard A. *retired lawyer*
Collins, Paul John *banker*
Conti, Tom *actor, writer, director*
Cope, Wendy *poet*
Cornelius, Peter Klaus *economist*
Dahrendorf, Lord Ralf Gustav *social scientist, educator*
Davis, Crispin *publishing company executive*
†Davis, Ian *management consulting firm executive*
Deighton, Len *author*
Desai, Anita *writer*
Dohnányi, Christoph von *musician, conductor*
Drabble, Margaret *writer*
Duncan, Lindsay Vere *actress*
†Dyson, Tim *public relations executive*
Edwards, Sylvia Ann *artist*
Elizabeth, Her Majesty , II, (Elizabeth Alexandra Mary) *Queen of United Kingdom of Great Britain and Northern Ireland, and her other Realms and Territories, head of the Commonwealth, Defender of the Faith*
Ellis, Claud M. Buddy *diversified financial services company executive*
Elson, Sarah Lee *art historian and consultant*
Ettinghausen, Thomas Andrew David *investment banker, writer*
†Eustace, Dudley Graham *diversified financial services company executive*
Fabricant, Arthur E. *lawyer, corporate executive*
†Farish, William S. *U.S. ambassador to United Kingdom*
†Fellner, Eric *film producer*
Fine, Anne *author*
Fleming, Robert *investment company executive*
Flint, Douglas J. *business executive*
Foldes, Lucien Paul *economics educator*
Fowles, John *author*
Fox, James *actor*
Funnell, Christina Mary *non-profit consultant*
†Furse, Clara *stock exchange executive*
Galloway, Janice *writer, editor*
†Gibson, William Ford *author*

Gillam, Sir Patrick *oil company executive, banker*
†Glass, Douglas B. *lawyer*
Glazer, Barry David *lawyer*
Goeltz, Richard Karl *distilled spirits and wine company executive*
Gomulka, Stanislaw *economist, educator*
Graubard, Stephen Richards *history educator, editor*
Gray, Simon James Holliday *writer, educator*
Greener, Anthony *telecommunications industry executive*
Habgood, Anthony John *corporate executive*
Haggerty, Jean Marie *journalist*
Hakim, Catherine *sociologist*
Hall, Sir Peter Geoffrey *urban and regional planning educator*
Hallissey, Michael *strategic consultant*
Hanson, Lord (Lord James Edward Hanson) *industrialist*
Harney, Kathryn Ann *opera singer*
†Harwood, Ronald *screenwriter, playwright*
Haubold, Samuel Allen *lawyer*
Hayward-Williams, Carolyn Rose *management and technology consultant*
Hazell, Robert John Davidge *policy institute director, government educator*
Hemmings, Peter William *deceased orchestra and opera administrator*
Hicks, J. Portis *lawyer*
Hill, Gregory Paul *oil company executive*
Hiller, Susan *artist*
Hoge, Warren M. *newspaper and magazine correspondent, editor*
Hornyak, Eugene Augustine *bishop*
Hudson, Manley O., Jr., *lawyer*
Hunter Blair, Pauline Clarke *author*
James, P(hyllis) D(orothy) (Baroness James of Holland Park of Southwold in County of Suffolk) *author*
†John, Elton Hercules (Reginald Kenneth Dwight) *musician*
Johnson, Newell Walter *oral pathologist, physician*
Jourdren, Marc Henri *investment banking company executive*
Junz, Helen B. *economist*
Kallakis, Achilleas Michalis S. *shipping company executive*
Keevil, Philip Clement *investment banker*
King, Mervyn Allister *economist, educator*
Kuper, Adam Jonathan *anthropologist, educator*
Lamaze, Jean-Hugues de *equity analyst executive*
Larsson, Per Olof *management consultant*
Leaf, Robert Stephen *public relations executive*
Leigh, Mike *film director*
Lessing, Doris (Doris May) *writer*
Mackerras, Sir Charles (Alan Maclaurin) *conductor*
Mackintosh, Cameron *musical theater producer*
Mandly, Charles Robert, Jr., *lawyer*
†Martines, Lauro *historian, writer*
†Masur, Kurt *conductor*
McCowen, Alec *actor*
McDonald, Joel Matthews *lawyer*
McIntyre, Norman F. *petroleum industry executive*
Melling, John Kennedy *accountant*
Mendes, Sam (Samuel Alexander Mendes) *film director, theater director*
Mendoza, Ryan *artist*
Meyer, Sir Christopher J.R. *former diplomat*
Miller, Jonathan Wolfe *theater and film director, physician*
Minton, Yvonne Fay *mezzo-soprano*
Mitchell, Geoffrey Bentley *accountant*
Moody, Ron *actor, writer*
Moon, Peter Geoffrey *investment executive*
Morris, Desmond (John) *zoologist, author, artist*
Morrison, William David *lawyer*
Mosselmans, Carel Maurits *investment banker*
Naipaul, Vidiadhar Surajprasad *author*
†Navarrete, Jorge Eduardo *ambassador*
Nelson, Elizabeth Hawkins *public association administrator*
Nelson, Walter Henry *communications consultant, author*
†Newell, Mike *film director*
Nordberg, Donald *communications executive*
Nordland, Rodney Lee *news correspondent*
Northrip, Robert Earl *lawyer*
Oliver, Diane Frances *publisher, writer*
Palin, Michael Edward *actor, screenwriter, writer*
Parry, Roger George *entrepreneur, writer*
Paton Walsh, Jill *author*
Paulus, Michael John *government official, bank executive, economist*
Pennant-Rea, Rupert Lascelles *banker, economist*
Perkin, Harold James *retired social historian, educator*
Phillips, Caryl *writer*
Phocas, George John *international lawyer, business executive*
Pietruska, Alexander Michael *investment banker*
Pinner, Stephen John *management consultant*
Pinter, Harold *playwright*
Plowright, Joan Anne *actress*
Portes, Richard David *economics educator*
Pryce, Jonathan *actor*
Quillen, Cecil Dyer, III, *lawyer*
Ralston, Anthony *computer scientist, mathematician, educator*
Ramos, Theodore Sanchez de Piña *artist, educator*
Read, Piers Paul *author*
†Rice, Sir Timothy Miles Bindon *lyricist*
Richardson, Ian William *actor*
Richardson, Miranda *actress*
Rolle, Martha Collins (Martha Traudt Collins) *lawyer*
†Rowling, J.K. *writer*
Rubin, James P. *international affairs analyst, public affairs administrator*
†Rubin, Patricia Lee *art historian*
Rutter, Michael Llewellyn *child psychiatry educator*
Saraste, Jukka-Pekka *conductor*

Sarkis, Ziad Joseph *private equity executive*
Scardino, Marjorie Morris *publishing company executive*
Scheinman, Stanley Bruce *international financial executive, lawyer*
†Seardino, Marjorie *investment company executive*
Shankar, Ravi *musician, sitar player, composer*
Sharif, Khalid *educational association administrator*
Shaw, Timothy Milton *political science educator*
Shmueli, Alfred *accountant, educator*
Sinclair, David Grant *accountant*
†Slatkin, Leonard Edward *conductor, music director, pianist*
Spillane, Mary Catherine *television producer*
Stanhope, Richard Graham *pediatric endocrinologist, consultant, pilot*
†Steele, Howard L. *psychology educator*
†Stern, Stephen Jeffrey *lawyer*
Stevens, Robert Bocking *lawyer, educator*
Taylor, John Michael *research director*
Thomas, Allen Lloyd *lawyer, private investor*
Tizard, Barbara *education and child development researcher*
Uchida, Mitsuko *pianist*
van der Wateren, Jan Floris *librarian, psychotherapist, consultant*
Vicari, Andrew *artist*
Waldegrave, Lord (Lord Waldegrave of North Hill) *financial services company executive*
Wallinger, John D(avid) A(rnold) *investment banker*
West, Christopher John (Kit West) *visual and special effects supervisor*
†Willett, Joseph T. *investment company executive*
Williams-Jones, Michael Robert *media company executive*
Winner, Michael Robert *film director, writer, producer*
Wolf, Peter Otto *civil engineer, consultant*
†Zonana, Victor *lawyer, educator*

Luton Bedfordshire
Ndikum, Philip Forsang *barrister*

Macclesfield
Graham, Dorothy Ruth *software engineering consultant*

Manchester
Briscoe, John *classical languages educator*
Wilson, Keith Dudley *retired media and music educator, consultant*

Middlesex
Walji, Jabir Mohamed *strategic consultant*

Milton Keynes
Throdahl, Mark Crandall *medical technology company executive*

North Wales
Hands, Terence David (Terry Hands) *theater and opera director*

Norwich
Aston, Peter George *music educator, composer, conductor*
Smith, Richard David *economics educator*

Oaker
Pickering, Pollyanna *artist*

Oxford
Carey, John *English language educator, literary critic*
†Da'Luz Vieira, Lorraine Christine C. *acupuncturist, researcher*
†Emsley, Sarah Louise Baxter *critic, educator*
Gowans, Sir James Learmonth *science administrator, immunologist*
Gulbrandsen, Natalie Webber *religious association administrator*
Halsey, Albert Henry *sociologist*
Heilbron, John L. *historian, educator*
Kaser, Michael Charles *economist, educator*
Ker, Ian Turnbull *priest, scholar*
May, Robert McCredie *biology educator*
Nicholls, Christine Stephanie *writer, editor*
Robinson, Mary *former U.N. high commissioner for human rights*
Vaisey, David George *librarian, archivist*

Oxfordshire
Rousseau, George Sebastian *humanities educator, historian*

Oxon
Quinlan, Michael Edward *retired civil servant*

Petts Wood
Bompas, Donald George *charitable organization executive, consultant*

Preston
Davis, Charles Harvey *neurosurgeon, consultant*

Reading
Barnes, John Gilbert Presslie *computer language designer*
Ryder, Timothy Thomas *classics educator*

Reigate
Baker, Martin William *management consultant*

Richmond
Te Kanawa, Kiri *opera and concert singer*

Richmond Surrey
Armfield, Diana Maxwell *artist, educator*

Richmond-upon-Thames
Smith, Norman Raymond *academic administrator*

Rottingdean
Matthews, John Floyd *writer, educator*

Saint Albans Herts
Thomas, Norman *education educator*

Saint Margaret's
†Attenborough, Baron Richard Samuel *actor, producer, director, goodwill ambassador*

Slough
Mobbs, Sir Gerald Nigel *property investment executive*

South Mimms
Stacey, Glyn Nigel *cell biologist*

Southampton
Brebbia, Carlos Alberto *educator, engineering consultant*
Weller, Roy Oliver *neuropathologist*

Stevenage
Follett, Kenneth Martin *author*

Stokenchurch
Barratt, Eric George *accountant*

Storrington
Osborne, Stephen J. *philatelist*

Stroud
Robinson, John Beckwith *development management consultant*

Suffolk
Mawby, Colin John *musician, composer, writer*

Surrey
†Els, Theodore Ernest *professional golfer*
†Olazabal, Jose Maria *professional golfer*
Vere Hodge, Richard Anthony *pharmaceutical executive, consultant*
Weston, Sir John (Sir Philip John Weston) *company non-executive director, retired diplomat*

Teddington
Roberts, Melville Parker *neurosurgeon, neuroanatomist, educator*

Tunbridge Wells
Howden, Frank Newton *Episcopal priest, humanities educator*
Singer, Norbert *health services professional, education consultant*

Warwick
Cowlishaw, Michael Frederic *electronic engineer*

West Sussex
Aiken, Joan (Joan Delano) *author*

Westminster
Broers, Sir Alec Nigel *engineering educator*

Whitchurch
Adams, Richard George *writer*

Wiltshire
Sherwin, James Terry *lawyer*

Windsor Berkshire
†Ekberg, Jan *retired pharmaceutical company executive*

York
Moore, Philip John *organist, artistic director, conductor, composer*
Williams, Alan Harold *economics educator*
Kingsley, James Gordon *college administrator*

ESTONIA

Tallinn
Köörna, Arno *economist, educator*

Tartu
Bichevin, Victor Vasily *research scientist*

FINLAND

Espoo
Nuckols, William Marshall *electrical goods manufacturing executive*

Helsinki
Juhani, Erma *lawyer, former stock exchange executive*
Kurvonen, Timo Lauri *research scientist*
Liewendahl, Bo Kristian *clinical pathologist, nuclear physician*
Tuomi, Tapani Mika *research scientist*

Jyväskylä
Kari, Jouko *education educator*

Tampere
Lehtinen, Seppo Ilmari *retired management consultant, educator*
Malminiemi, Kimmo Heikki *pharmaceutical company executive, researcher*
Pöntinen, Pekka Juhani *anesthesiologist, consultant*

Turku
Dunlap, Riley Eugene *sociologist*
Suotmaa, Juha Olavi *training manager, journalist, lecturer*

FRANCE

Arles
Clergue, Lucien Georges *photographer*

Avignon
De Mori, Renato *computer science educator, researcher*

Boulogne
de Tilly, Charles-Edouard *sales professional*

Carriéres s/Seine
Saunier, Bernard-Marie *civil engineer*

Chambéry
Starcher, George William *management consultant*

Collonges
Morgenstern, Sheldon Jon *symphony orchestra conductor*

Creteil
Renoux, André *physicist, educator*

Epinay Sur Orge
Naszályi, Baron Philippe Jacques *economics educator, publication director*

Fontainebleau
Ayres, Robert Underwood *environmental economics and technology educator*

Gif-sur-Yvette
Duplessy, Jean Claude *research scientist*

Guyancourt
Dubar, Claude Roger *sociologist*

Lyon
Bazin, Patrick *library director*
Brown, James Chandler *college administrator*
Naaoush, Sabah Faraj *economist, consultant*

Maine et Loire
Wilkinson, Una McCann *artist*

Maisons-Laffitte
Queffélec, Anne *pianist*

Montpellier
Herbert, Catherine Deming *English educator*

Montpon
Durca, Eric Marcel *physician for addictions*

Mulhouse
Mondadori, Cesare *neurobiologist, researcher*

Nanterre
Payri, Joel *pharmaceutical marketing executive*

Nedules
Masurel, Jean-Louis Antoine Nicolas *investment company executive*

Neuilly
Goldmark, Peter Carl, Jr., *publishing executive*

Neuilly-sur-Seine
Hewes, Thomas Francis *physician*

Noisy le Grand
Le Quéré, Jean François Marie *scientific instrumentation researcher*

Orsay
Fiszer-Szafarz, Berta (Berta Safars) *research scientist, researcher*
Friedel, Jacques *physics educator*

Pantin
Limantour, Philippe *computer science research executive, educator*

Paris
Allais, Maurice Felix *economist*
Annaud, Jean-Jacques *film director, screenwriter, producer*
Baum, Axel Helmuth *lawyer*
Bedjaoui, M. Mohammed *former judge International Court of Justice*
Boccara, Nino *physicist*
Boulez, Pierre *composer, conductor*
Charyn, Jerome *novelist*
Collomb, Bertrand Pierre *cement company executive*
Courtaud, Bernard Jean-Jacques *human resource consulting executive*
Courtois, Jean-Philippe *information technology executive*
Danon, Laurence Miriel *business executive*
Dausset, Jean *immunologist*
Dean, John Gunther *diplomat*
de Gennes, Pierre-Gilles *physicist, educator*
Dryansky, Gerald Y. *writer, editor, film producer, scriptwriter*
†Edwards, John David *university educator*
Fitoussi, Jean-Paul Samuel *economist, educator*
Garnier, Olivier Pierre *economist*
Jacob, François *biologist, educator*
Janicot, Daniel Claude Emmanuel *foundation administrator*
Jenny, Frederic Yves *economist, educator*
†Jeunet, Jean-Pierre *film director*
Jolas, Betsy *composer, educator*
Kourilsky, François Michel *research scientist*
Kurtz, Eugene Allen *composer, educator, consultant*
Lacroix, Christian Marie Marc *fashion designer*
Landers, Steven E. *lawyer*
Langley, Joseph Jeremiah *artist, poet*
Lecerf, Olivier Maurice Marie *construction company executive*
Lehn, Jean-Marie Pierre *chemistry educator*
Levee, John Harrison *artist, designer*
Levy, David Alfred *immunology educator, physician, scientist*
Lucas, Georges *physicist, researcher*
Marcus, Claude *advertising executive*
Memmi, Albert *sociologist, educator*

†Messier, Jean-Marie *corporate financial executive*
Mestrallet, Gérard *professional society administrator*
Montagnier, Luc Antoine *virologist*
Myerson, Jacob Myer *retired diplomat*
Peugeot, Patrick *insurance executive*
Raharinaivo, André Léon *research executive, educator*
Raimondi, Ruggero *opera singer*
Ramette, Vincent Alfred *legal information specialist*
Reeves, Van Kirk *lawyer*
Régnier, Marc Charles *lawyer, corporate executive*
†Reza, Yasmina *author, playwright*
Robillard, Alain Richard *civil engineer*
Rosenberg, Pierre Max *museum director*
Rouvillois, Philippe *research and development executive*
Salans, Carl Fredric *lawyer*
Serre, Jean-Pierre *mathematician, scholar*
†Tuckwell, Henry Clavering *mathematician, researcher*
Ungaro, Emanuel Matteotti *fashion designer*
†Unwin, Geoff *consulting company executive*
Williams, C(harles) K(enneth) *poet, literature and writing educator*
Yuechiming, Roger Yue Yuen Shing *mathematics educator*

Paris
Couteau, Marie-José *sociologist*

Ramatuelle
Collins, Larry *author, journalist*

Saint Ceols
Saisselin, Remy Gilbert *fine arts educator*

Suresnes
de Pouzilhac, Alain Duplessis *advertising executive*

Toulouse
Courtés, Joseph Jean-Marie *humanities educator, writer, semiotician*

Vanves
Dubs, Patrick Christian *publisher*

Vence
Polk, William Roe *historian*

Villefranche-sur-Mer
Legendre, Louis *oceanographer, educator, research scientist*

Villeneuve d'Ascq
Allain, Louis *literature educator, scientific advisor*

GEORGIA

Tbilisi
†Bibilashvili, Tamar *physicist, educator*

GERMANY

Aachen
Pischinger, Franz Felix *engineer, researcher*

Baunatal
Kahlfuss, Hans Júergen Wilhelm *retired librarian*

Berlin
Blankart, Charles Beat *economics educator*
Iannone, Dorothy *visual artist, writer*
Luehrs-Kaiser, Kai *writer, scholar, critic*
Meckseper, Friedrich *painter, printermaker*
Meyer-Tischler, Jörg Rudolf Erich *pharmaceutical company executive*
Ollenburg, Guenter Wilhelm *retired economics educator, tax consultant*
Stock, Günter *pharmaceutical company executive*
Weiss, Dieter Waldemar *economics educator, consultant*

Bielefeld
Dehmlow, Eckehard Volker *education educator, educator*

Bochum
Folkers, Cay *economics educator*
Meyers, Albert Thomas Marie *academic counsellor*

Bonn
Albach, Horst *economist*
†Coats, Daniel Ray *former senator*
Krelle, Wilhelm Ernst *emeritus economics educator*
Selten, Reinhard *retired economist, educator*

Braunschweig
Duddeck, Heinz Werner *civil engineering educator*
Fricke, Reiner *education educator*
Rass, Hans Heinrich *politics educator*

Bremen
Fahle, Manfred *ophthalmology researcher*
Wells, Raymond O'Neil, Jr., *mathematics educator, researcher*

Cologne
Erickson, Diane Sue *singer, artist, educator, moderator, music kinesiologist*
Fels, Gerhard *economist*
Hempleman, Warwick *small business owner*
Karimi-Nejad, Abbas *retired neurosurgeon, educator*

Licht, Christoph *medical professional*
Neisser, Horst *library director*
Tüllner, Horst-Ulrich *research scientist, science administrator*

Dortmund
Vogt, Hartmut *education educator*

Dresden
†Haitink, Bernard J. H. *conductor*
Schreier, Peter *tenor*

Düren
Rathert, Peter *urologist*

Düsseldorf
Joppen-Hellwig, Sandra *linguist, researcher*
Lüschen, Günther Rudolf Friedo *sociology educator*
†Schulz, Ekkehard *business executive*
†Simson, Wilhelm *company executive*

Essen
†Albrecht, Theo *business executive*

Frankfurt
Ammann, Jean-Christophe *art director*
Fozzati, Aldo *investment banker*
Glatzer, Wolfgang P. W. *sociology educator*
Hauck, Michael Georg *real estate company executive*
Michel, Hartmut *biochemist*
Neukirchen, Kajo *industry executive*
Simitis, Spiros *legal educator*

Frankfurt am Main
Tietz, Reinhard *economics educator*
von Rosen, Rüdiger *stock exchange executive*

Friedrichshafen
Duerr, Johannes Klaus *research scientist*

Garching
Fischer, Ernst Otto *chemist, educator*

Goettingen
Kucera, Gustav *economics educator*

Golm
†Krasnov, Kirill *physicist, researcher*

Greifswald
Knöppel, Hans-Armin *librarian*

Göttingen
Achtenhagen, Frank *economics educator*
Eigen, Manfred *physicist*
Sheldrick, George Michael *chemistry educator, crystallographer*
Starck, Christian Walter *jurist*

Halle
Schmoll, Hans Joachim *internal medicine, hematology, oncology educator*

Hamburg
Brogan, John Andrew, III, *capital management company executive*
Holler, Manfred Joseph *economics educator*
Lüdecke, Dieter Konrad *neurosurgeon*
Ludwig, Walther *classical and neo-Latin studies educator*
Lüst, Reimar *foundation president*
Neumeier, John *choreographer, ballet company director*

Hannover
Schnaus, Peter *musical history educator*

Heidelberg
Swanson, Barry Ernest *securities company executive*

Ilmenau
Schuller, Gerald Diedrich Thomas *electrical engineer*

Karlsruhe
†Geib, Karlmann *legal administrator*

Kiel
Clausen, Lars *social scientist*
Siebert, Horst *economics educator, institute administrator*

Koblenz
†Harbusch, Karin Maria *education educator, researcher*

Leipzig
Loh, Gerhard *librarian*
Mancke, Richard Bell *economist, educator, investor*

Luebeck
Pagels, Jürgen Heinrich *balletmaster, dance educator, dancer, choreographer, writer*

Lübeck
Arnold, Hans Richard *neurosurgeon*
Fligge, Jörg *librarian, library director*

Mannheim
Henn, Fritz Albert *psychiatrist*

Mayen
Gartz, Rolf Fritz *foundation administrator*

Muenchen
Schneider, Christian Claus *veterinarian, researcher, investment company executive*

Munich
Araiza, Francisco (José Francisco Araiza Andrade) *opera singer*
Huber, Robert *biochemist, educator*
Leskien, Hermann Adalbert *library director*

Magill, Samuel Wallace *international relations specialist*
Miller, Gerald Milton, II, *management consultant*
Reimann, Helga Luise *sociologist*
†Viermetz, Kurt F. *banker*
Whetten, Lawrence L. *international relations educator*

Münster
Spevack, Marvin *English educator*

Neu Isenburg
†Hoare-Temple, Piers Howard *building maintenance executive*

Nuremberg
Doerries, Reinhard René *modern history educator*

Obertshausen
†Albrecht, Karl *automotive and household plastic parts executive*

Otterfing
Carregal-Ferreira, Jorge *software company executive*

Regensburg
Rupprecht, Herbert Harald *pharmaceutical technologist*

Rostock
†Liddle, Brantley Thomas *research scientist*

Schleusingen-Gethles
Frank, Dieter *retired chemicals executive*

Schwerte
Rosenberg, Alex *mathematician, educator*

Siegen
Buhr, Walter Heinrich Wilhelm *economics educator*

Spraitbach
Kaffenberger, Ernst Wilhelm *engineer*

Stuttgart
Anderson, Reid Bryce *performing company executive*
Bettisch, Johann *linguist, researcher*
Cardona, Manuel *physics educator*
Geh, Hans-Peter *retired library director, consultant*
von Klitzing, Klaus *research facility administrator, physicist*

Swisttal
Terjung, Birgit *internist, researcher*

Tubingen
Stenzl, Arnulf Karl Marbod *urologist*

Tübingen
Flitner, Andreas Hermann *education educator*
Nüsslein-Volhard, Christiane *medical researcher*

U'haching
Ruge, Michael Helmuth *research scientist, consultant, mathematician*

Witten
Gaengler, Peter Wolfgang *dentist, researcher*

Wuppertal
Schubert, Guenther Erich *pathologist*
Vaitkus, Steven Anthony *sociologist, researcher, educator*

Würzburg
Hölldobler, Berthold Karl *zoologist, educator*

GREECE

Athens
Baltas, George *finance educator*
Burns, R. Nicholas *federal official*
†Hoesly, Eileen M. *academic administrator, educator*
Kalamotousakis, George John *economist, merchant banker, educator*
Koulourianos, Dimitri Theodore *economist*
Larounis, George Philip *manufacturing company executive*
Logothetis, Nickolas *management consultant, researcher, educator*
Panayiotis, Chinas *school psychologist, consultant*
Papadakis, Panagiotis Agamemnon *financier, international business executive*

Ioannina
†Theodorou, Daphne J. *radiologist*

Palia Pendeli Athens
Simeon, George Prodrom *healthcare company executive*

GRENADA

Saint George's
Helgerson, John Walter *lawyer*

GUATEMALA

Antigua
Rodgers, Frank *librarian*

Guatemala City
Harris, Randy Jay *university official, finance executive*

HONG KONG

Central Hong Kong
†Hanrahan, Paul Thaddeus *marketing executive*

Hong Kong
Choo, Yeow Ming *lawyer*
Kao, Charles Kuen *electrical engineer, educator*
Laurie, James Andrew *journalist, broadcaster*
Mak, Wing Kwong Tony *life insurance executive, training consultant*
O'Brien, Timothy James *lawyer*
Pacter, Paul Allan *accounting standards researcher*
†Randt, Clark Thorp, Jr., *ambassador, lawyer*
Scown, Michael John *lawyer*
Tse, Edmund Sze-Wing *insurance company executive*
Tsui, Lap-Chee *molecular genetics educator*

Kowloon
Burton, Barry Lawson *librarian, educator*
Cheng, Joseph Yu-shek *political scientist, educator*
Kung, Shain-dow *molecular biologist, academic administrator*
Qiu, Larry Dongxiao *economics educator*
Randall, David John *physiologist, zoologist, educator*

Pokfulam
McNaughton, William Frank *translator, educator*

Shatin
†Luo, Jessica Chaoying *actuary*
Wong, Ngai Ying *educator*

Tai Po NT
Pien, Shyh-Jye John *mechanical engineer*

Taipo
Fung, Richard Lap Chung *business executive*

Wanchai
Iwasawa, Isoo (Francis Iwasawa) *accountant, management consultant*

HUNGARY

Budapest
Bajtai, Attila *pathologist*
Evans, Myron Wyn *physicist, researcher*
Forgó, Ferenc *economics educator*
Hámori, Éva Lydia *economist*
Nagy, Imre V. *civil engineer, educator*
Pentelényi, Thomas John *neurosurgeon*
Poprády, Géza *librarian*
Rózsa, György *academy library foundation president*
Simai, Mihaly *economics and business educator*
Starosolszky, Ödön *civil engineer*
Szende, Béla *pathologist*
Tetenyi, Pal Gabor *research scientist, former national agency official*
Tóth-Orowan, Lóránt Miklós *civil engineer*

Szeged
†Nyúl, László G. *mathematician, educator, researcher*

INDIA

Baner Pune
Ohri, Sangeeta Jean Mary *social educator*

Bangalore
Nagpurwala, Quamber Husain *scientist*

Calcutta
Garai, Gautam *engineer, researcher*
Kothari, Amitav *accountant*

Fort Mumbai
Woodard, Nina Elizabeth *banker*

New Delhi
Anderson, Michael Hugh *diplomat*
Narain, Prem *agricultural scientist, educator, researcher*
Srivastava, Radhey Shyam *scientist, researcher*
†Watson, Paul *photojournalist, correspondent*

Ranchi
Srivastava, Vishnu Chandra *agronomy educator*

Shakti Vihar
Singh, Shashi Prabha *library and informations science educator*

Trivandrum
Sambasivan, Mahadeva Iyer *neurosurgeon, consultant*

INDONESIA

Jakarta
Callison, Charles Stuart *retired foreign service officer, development economist*
Colfer, Carol Jean Pierce *anthropologist, researcher*
Hsi, Edward Yang *lawyer, industrialist, medical venture capitalist, political advisor*
Slamet, Yohan Robertus *communications executive*

Jakarta Pusat
†Boyce, Ralph L. *ambassador*

IRAN

Tehran
Mardinkha, Khnania, IV, *church administrator*

IRELAND

Carlow
Cunningham, Patrick Colm *research scientist, science administrator*

County Kildare
Kabdebo, Thomas George *library director*

Donegal
Friel, Brian (Bernard Patrick Friel) *author*

Dublin
Calvani, Terry *lawyer*
Dooge, James Clement Ignatius *civil engineer, hydrologist, former senator*
Sheridan, Jim *director, screenwriter*

Galway
Hynes, Garry *theatre director*
†Mullen, Marie *actress*

Limerick
Flood, Patrick Christopher *business educator, researcher, corporate speaker*
Parnas, David Lorge *engineering educator, computer scientist*

Mullingar
Donleavy, James Patrick *writer, artist*

ISRAEL

Arad
Hollander, Samuel *economist, educator*

Ariel
Alexenberg, Mel (Mel Alexenberg Menahem) *artist, art educator*

Beer Sheva
Brosilow, Coleman Bernard *chemical engineering educator*
Hare, A(lexander) Paul *sociology educator*
Justman, Moshe *economics educator*

Givatayim
Findler, Hans Josef *retired business executive*
Kornel, Ludwig *medical educator, physician, scientist*

Haifa
Mayersdorf, Assa *neurologist*

Herzlia
Gruder, Yaron E. *foundation administrator*

Holon
Morris, David Joseph *communications systems consultant, educator*

Jerusalem
Kessler, Avraham Albert *economist, researcher*
Macarov, David *former social work educator*
Menses, Jan *artist, draftsman, etcher, lithographer, muralist*
Pantel-Bakst, Sharon S. *social worker*
Pomerantz, Sherwin Bernard *economic development consultant*
Rosenne, Meir *lawyer, government agency administrator*
Shrensky, Don Steven *accountant, consultant*

Karkur
Hillel, Daniel *soil physics and hydrology educator, researcher, consultant*

Metar
Lithwick, Norman Harvey *economics educator*

Petah Tiqwa
Rappaport, Zvi Harry *neurosurgeon*

Ra ananna
Hayon, Elie M. *chemist, educator*

Ramat-Gan
Aron, Roberto *lawyer, writer, educator*
Rier, David Alan *sociologist, educator*

Rehovot
Sachs, Leo *geneticist, educator*
Sharon, Nathan *biochemist*
Zipori-Beckenstein, Pninit *business administration educator, researcher*

Rosh-Pina
Gophen, Moshe *research scientist*

Savyon
Bushinsky, Jay (Joseph Mason) *journalist, radio/TV correspondent, columnist*

Tel Aviv
Bahiri, Simcha *economist*
Eliaz, Noam *materials engineer, researcher*
Gross, Joseph H. *lawyer, educator*
Jortner, Joshua *physical chemistry scientist, educator*

ITALY

Augusta
Bella, Giovanni *shipping agent*

Camaiore
Lavatelli, Carla *sculptor, weaver*

Florence
Cecil, Charles Harkless *artist, educator*

Frascati
Haegi, Marcel *physicist*

Genoa
Cosulich, Paolo Ulisse *shipping company executive, consultant*

Genova
Montanari, Franco *classicist, educator*

Iseo (Brescia)
Cavagna, Antonino Fortunato *management consultant*

Milan
Barbanti, Paolo *management consultant*
DeBenedetti, Carlo *entrepreneur*
De Miranda, Fabrizio
Honegger, Federico *artist*

Naples
†de Simone, Giovanni *cardiologist, educator*
Tarro, Giulio *virologist*

Padova
Shea, William Rene *historian, science philosopher, educator*

Padua
Schrefler, Bernhard Aribo *civil engineering educator*

Palermo
Mendola, Louis André Mantegna *business consultant marketing and advertising, historian*

Pesaro
Surian, Elvidio *music educator*

Pietrasanta
Marinsky, Harry *artist*
Swarz, Sahl *sculptor*

Pietrasanta Lu
Bugliani, Ann C. *international studies educator*

Pisa
Settis, Salvatore *archaeologist, art historian*

Rome
†Bartholomew, Reginald *diplomat*
Baum, William Wakefield Cardinal *archbishop emeritus*
Billy, Dennis Joseph *priest*
Chang, Hiang-Chu Ausilia *education educator, researcher*
Creagan, James Francis *diplomat, academic administrator*
Flood, Gregory Charles *human resources management specialist*
†Fulci, Francesco Paolo *diplomat*
†Gagnon, Edouard Cardinal *ecclesiastic*
Hall, Tony P. *ambassador, former congressman*
Kolvenbach, Peter Hans *priest, religious order superior*
Levi-Montalcini, Rita *neurobiologist, researcher*
McGurn, William Barrett, III, *lawyer*
†Piovani, Nicola *composer*
Scognamiglio, Carlo *economics and finance educator, Italian government senator*
Sisulu, Sheila Violet Makate *diplomat*
Skodon, Emil Mark *diplomat*
Westley, John Richard *economist*
Wilson, George Peter *international organization executive*

San Donato
Bellussi, Giuseppe Carlo *research manager*

Torino
Antonelli, Cristiano *economist, educator*

Turin
Dianzani, Mario Umberto *pathology educator*
Gros-Pietro, Gian Maria *economics educator*

Vatican City
Foley, John Patrick *archbishop*
Stafford, James Francis *cardinal*
Szoka, Edmund Casimir Cardinal *archbishop*

Venice
Pasinetti, Pier Maria *author*

Verona
Bonadonna, Riccardo C. *endocrinologist*
Pozzo, Riccardo *philosophy educator*

JAMAICA

Nassau
†Denison, Barry Reed *human rights association executive*

JAPAN

TK

Shinagawa-Ku
†Ando, Kunitake *consumer products company executive*

Abiko Chiba
Sakaguchi, Takehiro *health educator, researcher*

Amagasa ki
Hayakawa, Toru *neurosurgeon*

Bunkyo
Kobayashi, Seiei *English literature educator*

Chofu Tokyo
Sayama, Hiroki *researcher*

Choyoda-ku
†Sakoda, Futoshi *executive*

Gummaken
Okada, Ryozo *educator, clinician and researcher*

Gyoda
Shibasaki, Yoshio *chemistry educator, researcher*

Hachioji
Kojima, Takeshi *law educator, arbitrator, writer*

Higashi-Hiroshima
Suzuki, Nobutaka *chemistry educator*

Higashi-Osaka
Kazuya, Tetsuji *business educator*

Ibaraki
Kawano, Toshiaki *retired economics educator*

Ichihara
Kuma, Hisao *information systems educator*

Inagi Tokyo
Iinuma, Hiroichi *international economics and trade educator, researcher*

Izumisano Shi
Ando, Seiichi *economics, Japanese history educator*

Kanagawa
Kato, Tomiko *artist*
Yanagawa, Tsutomu *technology transfer company engineer*

Kanagawa-Ken
Fukatsu, Tanefusa *retired Chinese classics educator*

Kanagawa-ken
Hoshino, Yoshiro *industrial technology critic*

Kashiwara
Hori, Keiko *English literature educator*

Kumatori
Ohashi, Shoichi *business administration educator*

Kyoto
Ohno, Yutaka *information sciences educator*
Zikmund, Barbara Brown *minister, church history educator*

Mie
Isshiki, Masayuki *sociologist, educator, dean*

Minato-Ku Tokyo
Ishizuka, Nobuhisa *lawyer*

Minato-ku Tokyo
Scullion, Tsugiko Yamagami *non-profit organization executive*

Mitaka
Okamura, Hideki *research scientist, physicist*

Nagoya
Kajitani, Motohisa *sociology educator*
Kaneyoshi, Takahito *physicist, educator*
Kojima, Akinori *public health counselor, pathologist*
Maeda, Kenji *medical educator*
Seland, John Joseph *priest, educator*
Senda, Jun-ichi *economics educator*
Sendo, Takeshi *mechanical engineering educator, researcher, author*
†Takeyama, Eizo *company executive*
Yamori, Nobuyoshi *economist*

Nara
Kasami, Tadao *information science educator*

Okayama
Morooka, Hiroshi *neurosurgeon*
Okada, Shigeru *pathology educator*
Ubuka, Toshihiko *biochemist, educator, academic administrator*

Okazaki
Ebashi, Setsuro *scientist, educator*

Osaka
†Hibiki, Takashi *nuclear scientist, educator*
Horioka, Charles Yuji *economics educator*
Ikeda, Kazuyosi *physicist, poet*
†Ishihara, Tsuyoshi *humanities educator*
Takada, Fujio *jewelry store owner*

Ota-ku
Sano, Keiji *neurosurgeon, educator*

Saitama
Hozumi, Motoo *medical educator, researcher*

Sakai
Fujita, Sei *political economist, educator*

Sanda City Hyogo-ken
Brown, Sylvia G. *law educator*

Sapporo
Asari, Eikichi *information sciences educator, researcher*
Nakagawa, Koji *endocrinologist, educator*

Sayama-shi Saitama-Ken
Hazelrigg, Meredith Kent *education consultant*

Shimizu
Uyeda, Seiya *geophysics educator*

Shinjuku
Shimada, Haruo *physical chemistry educator*

Shizuoka
Anma, So *engineer consultant*

Tochigi
Honma, Koichi *pathologist, researcher*
Hyodo, Haruo *radiologist, educator*

Tokorozawa
Nakamura, Hiroshi *urology educator*

Tokyo
Akaike, Masami *communications technology educator*
Akutsu, Yoshihiro *communications educator*
Arai, Toshihiko *retired microbiology and immunology educator*
†Baker, Howard Henry, Jr., *ambassador, former senator, lawyer*
Brooke, James Bettner *news correspondent*
†Chang, Steve *internet security company executive*
Esaki, Leo *physicist, foundation executive, university president*
Eto, Hajime *information scientist, educator*
†Foley, Thomas Stephen *diplomat, former speaker House of Representatives*
Fujimoto, Junichiro *pathologist*
†Fukuma, Toshikatsu *investment banking executive*
Fukushima, Kiyohiko *economist*
†Gustafson, Albert Katsuaki *lawyer, engineer*
Gyohten, Toyoo *economist*
†Hakoshima, Shin-ichi *business executive*
Harada, Norio *software engineer, researcher, educator*
Hori, Yukio *engineering educator, scientific association administrator*
Iida, Shuichi *physicist, educator*
Ishii, Akira *medical parasitologist, malariologist, allergologist*
Kato, Shuichi *information engineering educator*
Kato, Yoshiki *international economics educator*
†Kondo, Masanobu *investment company executive*
Krisher, Bernard *foreign correspondent*
†Kusamichi, Masatake *investment company executive*
Lo, Fu-chen *economist, educator, ambassador*
Maki, Atsushi *economics educator*
Makihara, Minoru *diversified corporation executive*
Manz, Johannes Jakob *Swiss diplomat*
Maurer, P(aul) Reed *pharmaceutical company executive*
Miura, Akio *quality assurance management professional*
Miyazaki, Koichi *economics educator*
†Murray, Julia Kaoru (Mrs. Joseph E. Murray) *occupational therapist*
Nagata, Akira *publishing executive*
Nakajima, Hiroshi *education educator*
Nakamura, Hideo *law educator*
†Nishimura, Masao *diversified financial services company executive*
Nishiwaki, Takeo *structural engineering educator*
Nishiyama, Chiaki *economist, educator*
†Ohmura, Nobuaki *investment company executive*
Osawa, Paula Mariani *trading company executive*
†Ozawa, Seiji *conductor, music director*
Porté, Thierry Georges *investment banker*
Saba, Shoichi *manufacturing company executive*
Saito, Shuzo *electrical engineering educator*
Sakurada, Yutaka *chemist*
Sakuta, Manabu *neurologist, educator*
Sakuta, Masaaki *engineering educator, consultant*
Shirai, Shun *law educator, lawyer*
†Ueshima, Shigeji *investment company executive*
Van Ginkel, Johannes Auguste *geographer, educator*
Wakumoto, Yoshihiko *electronics company executive, grants executive*
Yamamoto, Yoshiro *former diversified financial services company executive*
†Yasutake, Shiro *investment/commodities company executive*
Yonezu, Takehiko *retired investment company executive*

Toyama
Ishii, Yoshinori *environmental science educator*

Toyota
Toyoda, Shoichiro *automobile company executive*

Tsukuba-shi
Kobayashi, Susumu *computer company executive*
Shimizu, Kazuhiko *education educator*

Wakayama
Ryuzo, Higuchi *medical educator*

Yokohama
Ito, Noboru *electric power industry executive*
Kaneko, Yoshihiro *cardiologist, researcher*
Kuroda, Yasumasa *political science educator, researcher*
Tokutani, Masao *risk management educator*

JORDAN

Amman
Jalal, Ibrahim Mohammad *pharmaceutical executive*
Johnson, Barbara Jane *music educator*

KAZAKHSTAN

Almaty
Sadykova, Vera Philippovna *librarian, educator*

KENYA

Eldoret North Rift
Elias, G.D. Onditi *radiologist, educator*

Nairobi
†Kim, Caleb Chul-Soo *theology studies educator, minister*

LATVIA

Riga
Buholte, Agnese *library director*
Malinkovskaja, Sofija Sergej *library director*
Strautins, Vilnis *flute educator, past symphony orchestra executive*

LEBANON

Beirut
†Habre, Samer S *mathematician, educator*
Khatib, Rustom Atfat *gynecologist, researcher, endocrinologist, consultant, economist*
†Nassaar, Christopher Suheil *literature educator, writer*

LITHUANIA

Vilnius
Butkevičiené, Birute *librarian*

LUXEMBOURG

Brussels
Lenz, Carl Otto *European advocate general*

Kirchberg
Leger, Philippe *legal administrator*

Luxembourg
Warner, Scott Dennis *investment banker*

MALDIVES

Male
Habeeb, Habeeba Hussain *library director*

MALTA

Valletta
†Bonello, Michael C. *economist*

MONACO

Monte Carlo
Lovett, Laurence Dow *retired real estate and steamship executive*

MONGOLIA

Ulaanbaatar
Mandel, Leslie Ann *investment advisor, business owner, author*

NEPAL

Kathmandu
†Baker, Ian Archbald *explorer, educator, writer, photographer*

NETHERLANDS

Aerdenhout
Vinken, Pierre Jacques *publishing executive*

Amsterdam
Kolko, Gabriel *historian, educator*
Liem, Edwin T.H. *lawyer*
Verkruijsse, Pieter Jozias *classicist, educator*

Anstelveen
†Reilly, Paul C. *consulting company executive*

Krimpen a/d Yssel
Houtzager, Marianne Johanna (Marian de Boyen) *writer, artist, photographer*

Leerdam
†Blom, Frans Leendert *quality assurance professional*

Leiden
Dornbush, K. Terry *former ambassador, consulting company executive, educator*

Maastricht
Van Praag, Herman Meir *psychiatrist, educator, researcher*

Nymegen
Braaksma, Johanna *educational consultant, researcher*

The Hague
Aldrich, George Hoover *judge, arbitrator*
Allison, Richard Clark *judge*
Brower, Charles Nelson *lawyer, judge*
Buergenthal, Thomas *international judge, educator*
Fleischhauer, Carl-August *judge of international court of justice*
Higgins, Dame Rosalyn *judge of international court of justice*
Jiuyong, Shi *judge*
Kooijmans, Pieter Hendrik *judge International Court of Justice*
Koroma, Abdul G. *judge of international court of justice*
†Martens, S.K. *legal administrator, retired*
Parra-Aranguren, Gonzalo *judge International Court of Justice*
Rezek, Francisco *judge, former supreme court justice, educator*
Schneider, Cynthia Perrin *ambassador, art historian, educator*
Tomka, Peter *Slovakian diplomat, lawyer, judge*
Van Wachem, Lodewijk Christiaan *petroleum company executive*

Utrecht
Packer, Corinne Angéline Agnés *human rights law consultant*
't Hooft, Gerardus *physicist, educator*

Zoetermeer
†Ritzen, Jozef Maria Mathias *economist*

NEW ZEALAND

Auckland
Cuba, Ivan *artist*

Dunedin
Dominik, William John *classicist, educator*

Palmerston North
Krone, Cheryl A. *research scientist, consultant*

Rolleston
†Ullrich, (Noel) Bruce *investment banker*

Wellington
†Paquin, Anna *actress*
von Kohorn, Baron Ralph Steven *retired investment banker, author*

Wellington
†Judd, James *conductor, music director*

Wellington South
Delahunt, Brett *pathologist*

NIGERIA

Abeokuta Ogun State
†Soyinka, Wole *writer*

Abuja
Kouyaté, Lansana *economist, international official, diplomat*

Ibadan
Grillo, Isaac Adetayo *surgery educator, consultant*

Ijebu Ode
Adedeji, Adebayo *economist, former government official*

Umuahia Abia State
Ukaegbu, David Okwukanmanihu *accountant, management consultant*

NORTHERN IRELAND

Belfast
†Corrigan-Maguire, Mairead *peace worker*

NORWAY

Kjeller
Maeland, Arnulf Julius *research scientist*

Oslo
Fitzpatrick, Whitfield Westfeldt *lawyer*
Fleischer, Carl August *law educator, consultant*
Heyerdahl, Jens P. *business executive*
Nyborg, Karine *economist, researcher*
Ong, John Doyle *ambassador, retired manufacturing executive*
Ravnan, Kari Lise *musician*

Sandvika
Kriger, Mark Phillip *management education educator, consultant, writer*

Stavanger
Farmen, Ragne Kristin Bentsen *molecular biologist, researcher*

Trondheim
Lunde, Øivind *cultural organization administrator, archaeologist*
Søvik, Nils *education educator*

OMAN

Medinat Qaboos
Craig, John Bruce *ambassador*

PAKISTAN

Islamabad
†Powell, Nancy J. *ambassador*

Lahore
Geoffrey, Iqbal (Mohammed Jawaid Iqbal Jafree) *artist, educator, lawyer*
Rai, Maqbool Ahmad *civil engineer, consultant*

PERU

Lima
Arrarte, Eduardo R. *travel agency executive*
Lee, Henry *lawyer*
Suazo, Miguel *civil engineer, consultant*

PHILIPPINES

Laguna
Schellner, Reinhard Anton *business executive*

Makati
Thompson, Willard Scott (W. Scott Thompson) *social sciences educator*

Makati City
Locsin, Enrique Lopez *company executive*

Malate
†Aluquin, Vincent Protacio Roy *pediatric cardiologist*

Manila
†Ricciardone, Francis *diplomat*
Sumida, Gerald Aquinas *lawyer*

Paranaque
Mabasa, Teresa Albar *social welfare association administrator*

Quezon City
Bunyi, Milagros Calderon *economics and marketing research executive*
Go, Josiah Lim *business executive, educator*

POLAND

Cracow
Kasper, Horst Manfred *lawyer*
Mytnik, Halina Zofia *retired librarian*
Tadeusiewicz, Ryszard *scientist, biomedical engineer, educator*

Gdańsk
Mokrzecki, Lech Marian *history of education educator*

Jelenia Gora
Dziedzic, Zuzanna *economist*

Lodz
†Laszkiewicz, Bogumil *chemist, educator*
Mortimer-Szymczak, Halina Barbara *economics educator*

Lublin
Orlowski, Ryszard *economist, educator*

Poznan
Buchowski, Michal Janusz *anthropologist*
Skrzypczak, Jozef Aleksander *education educator*

Warsaw
Abakanowicz, Magdalena *artist, sculptor*
Jagielska, Janina *retired librarian*
Koscielak, Jerzy *scientist, science administrator*
Pluta, Ryszard *neuropathologist, educator*
Rotfeld, Adam Daniel *research institute administrator, government official*

PORTUGAL

Algés
Horta, José Carlos de Oliveira Sousa *civil engineering consultant*

Armacão de Pêra
Litzenboerger, Wolfgang *software engineering executive, industrial consultant*

Coimbra
Holm, John Alexander *linguist, educator*

Funchal
Mayda, Jaro *lawyer, educator, writer, consultant*

Lisbon
Serôdio, Ilídio de Ayala *civil engineer*

QATAR

Doha
†Zednik, Jay Juraj *marine engineer*

REPUBLIC OF KOREA

An San
Lee, Dohyung *aeronautics research scientist*

Daegu
Park, Soong-Kook *internist, researcher*

Kwangju
Kim, Kyou Yung *economist, educator*
Lee, Jung-Koo *economist, educator*

Pusan
Ha, Chang Sik *polymer science educator*

Seoul
†Ahn, Choong Yong *economics educator*
Han, Oksoo *pianist, music educator*
†Hubbard, Thomas C. *ambassador*
†Hyun, Myung-Kwan *investment company executive*
Jang, Song-Hyon *management consultant*
Kim, Geun-Eun *surgeon, educator*
Park, Won Kuk *foundation administrator*

Sodaemoon-ku Seoul
Lee, Sungho H. *education educator, consultant, dean*

Suwon
Lee, Tong Hun *economics educator*

Taegu
Kim, Doohie *retired public health educator*

Taejon
Kang, Kyungin *electronics engineer, researcher*
Park, Seok-Kyun *civil engineer, educator*

ROMANIA

Iasi
Tarca, Mihai *economist, educator*

RUSSIA

Moscow
Ginzburg, Vitaly Lazarevich *physicist*
Goldanskii, Vitalii Iosifovich *chemist, physicist*
Gusev, Yeugeniy Mikhailovich *research scientist*
Khaladjan, Nikolai Nikolaevich *academic administrator*
Saltykov, Boris Georgievich *economist, politician*
Serebryany, Andrey Ninelovich *physical oceanographer, researcher*
Solzhenitsyn, Aleksandr Isayevich *writer*
Vershbow, Alexander R. *diplomat*
Zubritsky, Alexander Nickolaevich *pathologist*

Novocherkassk
Kiyanitza, Lubov Denisovna *library director*

SAINT LUCIA

Gablewoods Mall
Branch, Winston Patrick *artist*

SAUDI ARABIA

Riyadh
†Al-Saud, Alwaleed Bin Talal Bin Abdulaziz *investment company executive*
Alsubaie, Abdulaziz Mohamed *civil engineer*
†Faraidy, Abdulaziz Abdullah *national public security officer*
Ismail, Nuhad *medical educator*
Taylor, Frederick William, Jr., (Fritz Taylor) *lawyer*

SCOTLAND

Cellardyke
Roff, William Robert *history educator, writer*

Dundee
Black, Sir James (Sir James Whyte Black) *pharmacologist*
Lee, Thomas Alexander *accountant, educator*

Edinburgh
Atiyah, Sir Michael Francis *mathematician*
Fenton, Alexander *writer*
MacKenzie, Donald Angus *sociology educator*
Macneil, Ian Roderick *lawyer, educator*
Matheson, Ann *librarian, writer*
McMaster, Brian John *artistic director*
Napuk, Kerry F. *management executive*
Sinha, Brajraman Prasad *civil engineer, educator*

Fife
Scott, Adam *jurist, educator, clergyman*

Gullane
Collins, Jeffrey Hamilton *research facility administrator, electrical engineering educator*

Melrose
Russell, Thomas *retired British government official*

Nottingham
Newman, Judith Alice *education educator, educator*

Saint Andrews
Dover, Sir Kenneth James *retired Greek scholar*

Lenman, Bruce Philip *historian, educator*

Tighnabruaich
Reisinger, Ronald Busch (Baron of Inneryne, Baron of Culbin Laird of Ascog Castle, Laird of Eilean Na Beithe) *bank executive*

Turnberry
Kerr, William Revill *housing association executive*

SENEGAL

VA

Dulles
†Tall, Aliou *secondary school educator, researcher*

SERBIA AND MONTENEGRO

Novi Sad
Vuksanović, Miro *library director, writer*

SINGAPORE

Singapore
Bay, Yew Chuan *conglomerate company executive*
Frank, Ronald Edward *marketing educator*
†Liu, Thai-Ker Nil *architect, land use planner*
Olds, John Theodore *banker*
Reid, Anthony John Stanhope *historian, educator*
†Zhou, Wei *engineer, educator*
Bopry, Jeanette *education educator*

SLOVAKIA

Bratislava
Fristacky, Norbert *computer engineering educator, researcher*

SLOVENIA

Ljubljana
†Rotar, Tomaz *stock exchange executive*
Rupel, Dimitrij *diplomat*
Veselinovič, Draško *stock exchange executive*

Maribor
Strojnik, Tadej *neurosurgeon, researcher*

SOUTH AFRICA

Bellville
Tapscott, Christopher Peter *sociologist*

Cape Town
Tutu, Desmond Mpilo *archbishop emeritus*

Halfway House
Cleary, Sean Michael *executive*

Johannesburg
†Berk, Philip Woolf *journalist*
Dunn, David B. *ambassador*
Tager, Louise Arlene *high court advocate*

Parklands
Koekemoer, Carl Lodewicus *college official, business consultant*

Port Elizabeth
Botha, Maria Magdalena *education educator, researcher*

Pretoria
†Hume, Cameron R. *ambassador*

Rivonia
Machuca, Carlos R. *financial, management consultant*

Scottsville
Savage, Michael John *agrometeorologist, researcher, educator*

Waterkloof
Aiello, James Andrew *lawyer*

Yaoundé, Cameroon
Provencher-Kambour, Frances *business development advisor*

SPAIN

Adeje
Grindley, Bruce Alan *real estate agency executive*

Alcobendas
†Pumares, Luis Jose *industrial engineer*

Barcelona
de Larrocha, Alicia *concert pianist*
†Vidal, Merce *art historian, education educator*

Canary Islands
Wells, Melissa Foelsch *foreign service officer*

Castellon
Georgantzis, Nikolaos *economist*

Macharaviaya
Harvey, Robert Martin *artist*

Madrid
Albi, Emilio *economist*
†Almodovar, Pedro *filmmaker*
Delgado Barrio, Francisco Javier *president supreme court of Spain*
Feltenstein, Harry David, Jr., *chemical executive*
Frühbeck de Burgos, Rafael *conductor*
Herrero Rodriguez de Miñon, Miguel *former Spanish member of parliament, lawyer, international legal consultant*
Merino, Fernando *economist, researcher, educator*
Muniain, Javier P. *computer software company executive, theoretical physicist, researcher*
†Sanchez-Cespedes, Montserrat *molecular biologist, researcher*

Palafrugell, Girona
Carner, George *foreign service executive, economic strategist*

Pamplona
Masdeu, Jose Cruz *neurologist, medical school administrator*

Santander
†Ballesteros, Severiano *professional golfer*

Seville
Sanchez, Leonedes Monarrize Worthington (His Royal Highness Duke de Leonedes of Spain Sicily Greece) *fashion designer*

SRI LANKA

Battilacoa
Miller, Benjamin Henry *priest, human rights advocate*

Colombo
Kannangara, Vijith Julian *entrepreneur*
Spain, James William *political scientist, writer, investor*

SWEDEN

Askim
Bakhuizen, Willem Anthonie Hendrik Johannes *civil engineer*

Bjuv
Persson, Ronny Anders *accountant, historian*

Bralanda
Emilson, Henry Bertil *artist*

Bromma
Orrje, Olle *civil engineer, jazz musician, poet*

Gothenburg
Wallmark, John Torkel *scientist, educator*

Göteborg
Bornstein, Jan Martin *computer engineer*
†Johansson, Lennart Valdemar *Swedish industrialist*

Karlstad
Lindqvist, Gunilla *education educator*

Lerum
Borei, Sven Hans Emil *translator*

Lidingö
Crapon de Caprona, Count Noël François Marie *lawyer, retired United Nations official, historian*

Linköping
Brunk, Ulf Tjelvar *pathology educator, consultant*

Lund
Bauhn, Per Roald *sociology educator*
Janacek, Bedrich *organist*

Malmö
Akesson, Anders Gustav *lawyer*

Nykoping
Hakansson, Kjell Georg *business consultant*

Orno
Hallberg, Bengt O. *systems strategy director, fiber optic specialist*

Saltsjo-Duvnas
Lundgren, Nils Gustav Herman *economist*

Stockholm
Altéus, Åke *foundation administrator*
Blomström, Magnus Conrad *economics educator*
Ekman, Peter Erik *urologist, educator*
Gyll, John Sören *company executive*
Iverius, Per-Henrik *physician, biochemist, educator*
Johnson, Antonia Axson *corporate executive*
Lidman, Tomas Erik *national archivist*
Lindström, Lars Ernst Simon *education educator*
Persson, Ivar Lennart *military program director*
Peskov, Vladimir Dmitrievich *physicist, educator, consultant*
Soederstrom, Elisabeth Anna *opera singer*
Sohlman, Michael *foundation administrator*
Stachowiak, Dennis Kenneth *trading company executive*
Stare, Peter Knut Johan *human resource consultant*
Stubert, Harald Gunnar *management consultant*

Sundberg, Johan Emil Fredrik *music educator, researcher*
Wachtmeister, Count Wilhelm H. F. *diplomat*
Wanden, Stig *economist, researcher*
†Westerberg, Lars *automotive safety systems company executive*

Södertälje
Federsel, Hans-Jürgen *pharmaceutical company executive*

Uppsala
Carr, Andrew *zoologist*
Himmelstrand, J. Ulf I. *sociology educator, writer*
Tottie, Thomas J.H. *librarian*
Wörman, Anders Lars Edvard *civil engineering educator*

Österskär
Bolin, Bert Richard Johannes *atmospheric physicist, research meteorologist*

SWITZERLAND

Aarau
Rich, Georg *economist, bank executive*

Arth
Stanek, Bruno L. *software developer, author, commentator*

Basel
Arber, Werner *microbiologist*
Gehring, Walter Jakob *biology and genetics educator*
†Jetzer, Alexandre F. *pharmaceutical executive*

Bern
Gonzalez, Guillermo Enrique *diplomat*
Jauslin, Jean-Frédéric *library director*
Leavey, Thomas Edward *international organization administrator*

Brig
Guntern, Gottlieb *foundation executive, physician*

Chambesy
Javits, Eric Moses *lawyer, diplomat*

Chateau d'Oex
Berman, Joshua Mordecai *lawyer, manufacturing company executive*

Fribourg
Gurley, Franklin Louis *lawyer, military historian*

Geneva
Aaronson, Robert Jay *aviation executive*
Barenboim, Daniel *conductor, pianist*
Brown, Kent Newville *ambassador*
Capron, Alexander Morgan *lawyer, educator, philosopher*
Charpak, Georges *physicist, nuclear scientist*
Farman-Farmaian, Ghaffar *investment company executive*
Fetherston, Marianne Renee *artist, painter*
Jacquesson, Alain L. *librarian*
Maglacas, A. Mangay *nursing researcher, educator*
Marchi, Sergio Sisto *Canadian government official*
†Ogata, Sadako *United Nations official*
Pelou, Pierre Marie *librarian*
†Rossier, William *world trade organization*
Schweitzer, Theodore Gottlieb, III, *United Nations administrator*
†Sidjanski, Dusan *economist, educator*
Sommaruga, Cornelio *humanitarian services organization administrator, diplomat*
Steinberger, Jack *physicist, educator*
Twarog, Sophia Nora *economist, international civil servant*

Geneva
Jovanovic, Miroslav N. *economics educator*

Grancia
Mantegazza, Sergio *executive*

Lausanne
†Muller, Peter-Alexander *legal administration executive*

Montreux
Favre, Jacques *neurosurgeon*

Prilly
†Domeniconi, Reto *business executive*

Versoix
†Frenk, Julio Jose *secretary of health for Mexico, health systems researcher, consultant*
Mahler, Halfdan Theodor *physician, health organization executive*

Wollerau
Rohrer, Heinrich *physicist*

Zurich
Binnig, Gerd Karl *phycisist, educator*
Burkert, Walter *Greek language educator, historian*
Ernst, Richard Robert *chemist, educator*
Eschenmoser, Albert *chemist*
Gazzetta, Moreno Augusto *engineer*
Groebli, Werner Fritz *professional ice skater, realtor*
Hjelmér, Patrick *investment banker*
†Kalman, Rudolf Emil *research mathematician, system scientist*
Leite de Faria, Hernani J. *investment analyst*
Morari, Manfred *chemical engineer, educator*

Siegenthaler, Walter Ernst *internal medicine educator*
Taub, Ethan *neurosurgeon*
Wüthrich, Kurt *molecular biologist, biophysical chemist, educator*
Boutros-Ghali, Boutros *former U.N. secretary general*

TAIWAN

Kaohsiung
Chien, Yie W. *pharmaceutical science educator, university dean*
Sohigian, Diran John *humanities educator*
Wang, Gwo Jaw *orthopaedic surgery educator*

Taichung
Lu, Shih-Peng *history educator*
Ou, Yen-Chuan *urologist*
Wilson, Thomas Woodrow, III, *research scientist, consultant*
Yen, Gili *economics researcher*

Tainan
Huang, Ting-Chia *chemical engineering educator, researcher*
Lin, Jiin-Huey Chern *engineering educator*

Taipei
Chang, Parris Hsu-cheng *law-maker, political science educator, writer*
Ho, Low-Tone *physician, researcher, educator*
†Huang, Hertz *market researcher, statistician*
Lee, Yuan Tseh *chemistry educator*
Tsung, Christine Chai-yi *financial executive*

TANZANIA

Arusha
Rapp, Stephen John *international prosecutor*

Moshi
Pomfret, David B. *medical educator, internist*

THAILAND

Bangkok
Kornell, Ronald Frank *economist*
Kruck, Donna Jean *special education educator, consultant*
†Sammon, William Joseph *historian, consultant*

TUNISIA

Carthage
Sehili, Mahmoud *artist*

TURKEY

Ankara
†Edelman, Eric Steven *ambassador*
†Pearson, W. Robert *ambassador*

Atakoy
Donma, Hatice *artist*

Bilkent Ankara
Akman, Varol *computer engineer, educator*

Istanbul
Tugcu, Nejat *investment consultant, information systems expert*

Kucuk Bebek Istanbul
Ongan, Nilgün Erdal *decorator, architect, artist*

UKRAINE

Kiev
†Pascual, Carlos *ambassador*

Mariupol
Vasiljev, Alexander Valerjovich *metallurgical engineer, economist*

Truskavets
Popovych Ihor, L'vovych *physician, researcher*

UNITED ARAB EMIRATES

Abu Dhabi
Dajani, Jarir Subhi *civil engineer, consultant*

Al Ain
Carruthers, S. George *medical educator, physician*

VATICAN CITY

Citta del Vaticano
†Stafford, J. Francis Cardinal *archbishop*

Vatican City
John Paul, His Holiness Pope, II, (Karol Jozef Wojtyla) *bishop of Rome*

VENEZUELA

Caracas
†Andrade, Juan Carlos *lawyer*

Gunczler, Peter *pediatric endocrinologist*

VIETNAM

Da Lat
†Ha, Quan Manh *adult education educator*

Hanoi
†Burghardt, Raymond Francis, Jr., *ambassador*

WALES

Cardiff
†Field, Helen *soprano*

Gwynedd
Kuncheva, Ludmila Ilieva *engineering educator*

Porthmadog
Owen, Walter Shepherd *materials science and engineering educator*

WEST INDIES

Grand Cayman Island
Ronald, Pauline Carol *retired art educator*

YEMEN

Aden
†Al-Hamid, Abu-Bakr Muhsin *translator*

ZAMBIA

Nangoma
Hansen, Florence Marie Congiolosi (Mrs. James S. Hansen) *social worker*

ZIMBABWE

Harare
Salahuddin, Ahmad *civil engineer, educator*

ADDRESS UNPUBLISHED

†Aalberts, Nola Jean *social worker, administrator*
Aall, Christian Bergengren *software company executive*
Aaron, Bud *systems analyst*
Aasen, Arne *civil engineer, researcher, artist*
Aaslestad, Halvor Gunerius *college dean, retired*
Abarbanel, Judith Edna *marketing executive*
Abbe, Elfriede Martha *sculptor, graphic artist*
Abbey, Richard Lawrence *human resources specialist*
Abbott, Bob *state supreme court justice*
Abbott, Edward Leroy *finance executive*
Abbott, Linda Joy *stained glass artisan, educator, photographer*
Abbott, Rebecca Phillips *museum director, art consultant, photographer*
Abbott, Regina A. *neurodiagnostic technologist, consultant, business owner*
†Abdaladze, Merabi *physicist*
Abdelaal, Ahmed Tharwat *marketing educator, marketing professional, consultant*
Abdullaev, Yalchin *neuroscientist, physician, educator*
†Abedin, Mohammad Zainul *medical educator, researcher*
Abedin, Sultanal *research phytotaxonomist*
Abel, Elie *reporter, broadcaster, educator*
Abeles, Kim Victoria *artist*
Abeles, Sigmund M. *painter, printmaker, sculptor*
Aber, Ita *multimedia designer, conservator, historian*
†Aberlin, Betty Kay *actor*
Abernathy, Ronald Fittz *pharmacist*
Abernathy, Vicki Marie *retired nurse*
†Abernethy, Sharron Gray *language educator*
Abetti, Pier Antonio *consulting electrical engineer, technology management and entrepreneurship educator*
Abraham, Nathan Samuel *advertising agency and public relations executive, marketing professional*
Abrahams, Samuel *writer, retired lawyer*
†Abrahamson, Karen K. *theologian, editor*
Abramowitz, Morton I. *former ambassador*
†Abrams-Hakeem, Venita M. *performing arts educator, theater producer, director, performing company executive*
†Abramson, Elliott Myron *law educator, researcher*
†Abruzzo, Margaret Nicola *historian*
Absher, Donna Atkins *textile designer*
Accordino, Frank Joseph *architect*
Acerra, Michele (Mike Acerra) *engineering and construction company executive*
Achord, James Lee *gastroenterologist, educator*
Achorn, Robert Comey *retired newspaper publisher*
†Ackerman, Don Eugene *venture capital executive*
Ackerman, Jack Rossin *investment banker*
Ackerman, Melvin *investment company executive*
Ackerson, Barry James *social worker*
Aczel, Mollie Goodman *educational consultant*
Adam, John, Jr., *insurance company executive emeritus*
†Adam, Paul James *mechanical engineer*
Adams, Christine Beate Lieber *psychiatrist, educator*
Adams, Corlyn Holbrook *nursing facility administrator*
Adams, Daniel Otis *chemist*
Adams, David Gray *lawyer*
Adams, Edwin Melville *former foreign service officer, actor, author, lecturer*
Adams, Frances Grant, II, *lawyer*
Adams, Hilary Shiels *theater director*
Adams, James Blackburn *former state government official, former federal government official, lawyer*
Adams, James Thomas *surgeon*
†Adams, Jocelia *oncological nurse, educator*
Adams, Mason *actor*
Adams, Michael John *retired air force non-commissioned officer*
Adams, Renee Bledsoe *retired elementary school educator*
Adams, Robert McCormick *anthropologist, educator*
†Adams, Susan Lois *music educator*
Adams, Thomas Lynch, Jr., *lawyer*
Adams, Warren Sanford, II, *retired food company executive, lawyer*
Adams, Wilburn Clifton *communication educator*
Adams, William White *retired manufacturing company executive*
Adamson, James B. *business executive*
Adamson, Jane Nan *retired elementary school educator*
Adamson, Michael Robert *history researcher, consultant, educator*
†Adams-Passey, Suellen S. *elementary education educator*
Adato, Perry Miller *documentary producer, director, writer*
Adcroft, Patrice Gabriella *former editor*
Addo, Charles Kwame *municipal official*
Adducci, Regina Marie *medical/surgical nurse*
Addy, Frederick Seale *retired oil company executive*
Adekson, Mary Olufunmilayo *therapist, counselor educator*
Adelman, Richard Charles *gerontologist, educator*
Adkins, Thomas Samuel *library director*
Adkinson, Brian Lee *manufacturing company executive*
Adler, Alexander *former federal government health service executive*
Adler, Jonathan L. *physician*
†Adler, Posy (Roslyn) *artist, educator*
Adler, Raphael *educator emeritus, speech pathologist*
†Adler, Renata *writer*
Adler, Richard Melvin *architect, planner*
Adler, Ruth Gratt *financial planner, securities arbitrator*
Adler, Samuel Hans *retired conductor, composer*
Adolph, Kathryn Ann *passenger service employee*
Afelbil, Martin *statistician, researcher*
Aftel, Mandy *perfumer*
Agar, John Russell, Jr., *school district administrator*
Agarwal, Chhavi *pediatrician*
Agarwal, Suman Kumar *editor*
†Aggarwal, Lalit K. *company executive, educator*
†Agins, Barnett Robert *electrical engineer, educator*
†Agnew, Jennifer Marie *literature educator*
Agraz, Francisco Javier, Sr., *lawyer, public affairs representative*
Aguinsky, Richard Daniel *electrical engineer, administrator*
Agwunobi, John Oderah *pediatrician*
Ahearne, John Francis *scientific research administrator, researcher*
Ahl, Roger John *producer, writer*
Ahlers, Paul *emergency physician*
Ahlquist, Paul Gerald *molecular biology researcher, educator*
Ahmad, Moghissuddin *research chemist*
Ahmad, Syeda Sultana *physician*
Ahmed, Syed Z. *anthropologist*
Ahmer, Inam
Ahrens, Franklin Alfred *veterinary pharmacology educator*
†Ahuja, Satinder *chemist, consultant*
Aiken, Lewis Roscoe, Jr., *psychologist, educator*
Aiken, Michael Thomas *former academic administrator*
†Aikens, Martha Brunette *national park service administrator*
Aikman, Albert Edward *lawyer*
Ainsworth, Harriet Crawford *journalist, public relations consultant*
Aitchison, Anne Catherine *environmental activist, retired*
†Aitken, Robert Baker *religious studies educator, writer*
Ajax, Ernest Theodore *retired neurology educator*
Ajimal, Gurjit Singh *anesthesiologist*
Akasofu, Syun-Ichi *geophysicist, educator*
Akel, Ollie James *oil company executive*
Akiyama, Carol Lynn *motion picture industry executive*
†Aladjem, Henrietta H. *writer*
Albano, Maureen Teresa *artist*
†Albaugh, Ed *retired journalist*
Albensi, Benedict Charles *biomedical consultant, computer programmer, neuroscientist, educator, science writer, editor*
Alberger, William Relph *lawyer, government official*
Alberico, Salvatore J. *psychiatric social worker, educator, researcher*
Albers, Charles Edgar *investment manager*
Albers, Edward James, Sr., *retired secondary school educator*
Albert, Margaret Cook *communications executive*
Alberternst, Judith Ann *pension administrator*
Alberts, David *theater director, performance artist*
†Alberts, Renée Miller *substance abuse and mental health professional*
Albertson, Susan L. *retired federal government official*
Albin, Barry G. *lawyer, rabbi, energetic healer*
†Albin, Woodrow Ross *civil engineer*
Albini, Joseph Louis *retired medical educator*
Albright, Judith Anne *writer, educator*
Albright, Madeleine Korbel *former secretary of state*
Albritton, William Harold, III, *federal judge*
†Albrizio, Eileen Marie *commentator, poet*
Alcantara, Felicisima Garcia *dietitian, nutrition consultant*
Alday, Marta Perdomo *library technology consultant, media consultant, art dealer*
†Al-Delaimy, Wael *epidemiologist*
†Alderman, Annabel (Elsie Higgs Griner Jr.) *writer*
Aldredge, Theoni Vachliotis *costume designer*
Aldrich, Franklin Dalton *research physician*
Aldrich, Patricia Anne Richardson *retired magazine editor*
Aldridge, Donald O'Neal *military officer*
Aleandri, Emelise Francesca *producer, director, television personality, actress*
Alexakos, Frances Marie *counselor, business owner, psychology educator, researcher, producer, editor*
Alexander, Charles Michael M *internist*
Alexander, Doris Muriel *humanities educator, writer*
Alexander, Edward Russell *retired disease research administrator, educator*
Alexander, George L. *radiologist*
†Alexander, James H. *industrial designer*
Alexander, John Stone *retired radiologist*
Alexander, Jonathan *cardiologist, consultant*
Alexander, Marjorie Anne *artist, hand papermaker, art consultant*
†Alexander, Nancy A. *information technology manager, consultant*
Alexander, Ruth Batchelder *interior decorator, environmental activist*
Alexander, Thomas G. *chemist, researcher*
Alexandratos, Spiro Dionisios *chemistry educator, dean*
Alfano, Edward Charles, Jr., *elementary education educator*
Alfaro, Felix Benjamin *retired physician*
†Alfinito, Peter Daniel *neuroscientist*
Alfonso, Roberta Jean *emergency room nurse*
Alford, Becky Dianne *food products executive*
Alfred, Stephen Jay *retired lawyer*
†Ali, Muhammad (Cassius Marcellus Clay) *retired professional boxer*
Alig, Frank Douglas Stalnaker *retired construction company executive*
Aliga, Olivia R. *music teacher, choral director*
†Alipio, Gary Glynn *writer, consultant*
Aljian, James Donovan *investment company executive*
Alker, Hayward Rose *political scientist, educator*
Allard, Michael Alan *music educator, conductor*
Allbaugh, Joe M. *federal agency administrator*
Allbritton, Joe Lewis *diversified holding company executive*
Allen, Alfred William *chemical engineer, consultant*
†Allen, Bennie Carnel *employee relations specialist*
Allen, Bonnie Lynn *optometrist*
Allen, Charles Eugene *university administrator, agriculturist, educator*
†Allen, Dianna *language educator*
Allen, Donald Vail *investment executive, writer, concert pianist*
Allen, Edgar Burns *records management professional*
Allen, Jocleta Dalton *retired social worker, writer*
Allen, Joseph H. *retired radiologist, educator*
†Allen, Joseph T. *musician, educator*
Allen, Joyce Doyle *social worker, preschool and elementary educator*
Allen, Leatrice Delorice *psychologist*
Allen, Lew, Jr., *laboratory executive, former air force officer*
Allen, Linda Graves *real estate agent*
Allen, Marilyn Myers Pool *theater director, video producer*
Allen, Paul G. *computer company executive, professional sports team executive*
Allen, Ralph Gilmore *dramatist, producer, drama educator*
Allen, Roberta *fiction and nonfiction writer, conceptual artist, photographer*
Allen, Thomas B. *writer*
†Allen, Todd M. *immunologist, researcher*
Allen, William *lawyer*
Allen, William Sheridan *retired social sciences educator*
†Allen, Woody (Allen Stewart Konigsberg) *director, actor, writer*
Allerton, John Stephen *association executive*
†Alley, Glenda Pauline *music educator*
Allgrim, Caroline Denham *retired college official*
Alligood, Elizabeth Ann Hiers *retired special education educator*
Allinson, Carl *radiologist*
Allison, Andrew Marvin *church administrator*
Allison, Dianne J. Hall *retired insurance company official*
Allison, Donna M. (Donna Maughan) *critical care nurse*
†Allison, Glorietta Travis *vocal educator, soprano*
Allison, John McComb *retired aeronautical engineer*
Allmendinger, David Frederick, Jr., *history educator*
†Allmon, Michael W, Sr., *sales executive*
Allukian, Myron, Jr., *government administrator, public health educator, dental educator*
Allums, James A. *former cardiovascular surgeon*
Almond, Lincoln *lobbyist, former governor*
Aloff, Mindy *writer*
†Alonso-Crespo, Eduardo *composer, conductor*
Alper, Barbara Joy *anesthesiologist*
Alper, Merlin Lionel *finance company executive*
Alpern, Andrew *lawyer, architect, historian*
†Alpert, Ann Sharon *retired insurance claims examiner*
Alpher, Victor Seth *consultant, clinical psychologist*
†Al-Ramadan, Saeed Y. *veterinarian, researcher*
Altekruse, Joan Morrissey *retired preventive medicine educator*
Altenbernd, Chris W. *judge*
Altheide, Phyllis Sage *computer scientist, software engineer*
Altman, Barbara Jean Friedman *lawyer*
Altman, Irwin *psychology educator*
Altschuler, Samuel *retired electronics company executive*
Altshuler, Alan Anthony *political scientist, educator*
Altshuler, Kenneth Z. *psychiatrist, educator*
†Alvare, Charles Daguerre *television producer*
†Alvarez, Maria Auxiliadora *language educator, poet, graphics designer*
†Alvarez, René Luis *historian, educator*
Alvarez-Galloso, Roberto C. *mental health professional*
†Alvarez-Gomariz, Husayn *simulation engineer, physicist*
Alves, Kyrin Jean *association executive, educator*
Amadio, Bari Ann *metal fabrication executive, former nurse*
Amancio, Ruth Carson *safety engineer*
Amann, Charles Albert *mechanical engineer, researcher*
Amatangelo, Nicholas S. *retired financial printing and document management services exeutive*
†Amato Chiaramonte Bordonaro, Baron Carlo Camillo *ambassador, consultant*
†Amaya, Carlos C. *education educator, researcher*
†Ambard, Alberto J *prosthodontist*
Amberg, Stanley Louis *lawyer*
Ambrose, Daniel Michael *publishing executive*
Ambrosi, Sandra Elizabeth *retired nurse, educator*
Ambrosio, Deborah Ann *critical care nurse*
Ambrozic, Aloysius Cardinal (His Eminence Aloysius Cardinal Ambrozic) *cardinal*
Ames, Donald Paul *retired aerospace company executive, researcher*
Amgott, Steven Mitchell *mathematics educator*
Amiel, David *orthopaedic surgery educator*
Amis, Edward Stephen, Jr., *physician, retired naval officer*
Ammeraal, Brenda Ferne *secondary school educator*
†Amos, Linda K. *academic administrator*
Amos-Ganther, Linda *poet*
Amparado, Keith D. *communications company executive*
Amspacher, John Clair Elder *retired human services manager*
Amstutz, Daniel Gordon *international agriculture industry consultant, former grain dealer, government and intergovernment official*
Amundson, Robert A. *state supreme court justice*
Amuzegar, Jahangir *economic consultant*
Amylon, Michael David *physician, educator*
Anasazi, Maria *artist, educator*
Ancheta, Caesar Paul *software developer*
Ancoli-Israel, Sonia *psychologist, researcher*
Ancona, George Efrain *photographer, author*
†Andela, Valentine Bisangena *medical researcher*
Anderegg, Karen Klok *business executive*
Anderer, Joseph Henry *textile company executive*
Anderman, David E. *minister*
Andermann, Greg *producer, director, consultant*
Anders, Edward *chemist, educator*
Anders, George Charles *writer, journalist*
Andersen, Hans Christian *chemistry educator*
†Andersen, Kurt Byars *writer*
†Andersen, Roy Stuart *physicist*
Anderson, Alan Stewart *lawyer*
†Anderson, Amy Lee *realtor*
†Anderson, Ann *writer, actor*
Anderson, Bernard E. *economist*
Anderson, Christopher Ralston *financial consultant*
†Anderson, David *Canadian government official*
Anderson, Donna Elaine *elementary and secondary school educator*
Anderson, Dorothy Fisher *social worker, psychotherapist*
Anderson, Dyke A. *former medical association administrator*
Anderson, Edgar Ratcliffe, Jr., *career officer, hospital administrator, physician*
Anderson, Fletcher Neal *chemical executive*
Anderson, Gary William *physician*
Anderson, Geoffrey Allen *retired lawyer*
Anderson, George Kenneth *physician, foundation executive, retired air force officer*
Anderson, Geraldine Louise *medical researcher*
†Anderson, Gregory Thomas *secondary school educator, researcher, historian*
Anderson, Herschel Vincent *retired librarian*
Anderson, Iris Anita *retired secondary education educator*
Anderson, Ivan Verner, Jr., *newspaper publisher*
†Anderson, Jacqueline Annette *computer specialist*
†Anderson, James Allen *psychologist, writer*
Anderson, James George *sociologist, educator*
†Anderson, Janice M. *freelance/self-employed photojournalist*
Anderson, Jerry Lee *pianist, music educator*
Anderson, Jerry Maynard *speech educator, retired*
†Anderson, Jock Robert *adult education educator, consultant*
Anderson, John Bayard *lawyer, educator, former congressman*
Anderson, John Firth *church administrator, librarian*
Anderson, John Gaston *electrical engineer, consultant*
Anderson, Jon Eric *lawyer*

Anderson, Joseph Norman *executive consultant, former food company executive, former college president*
Anderson, Keith *retired lawyer, retired banker*
Anderson, Laurie Ann *critical care nurse*
Anderson, Lois D. *nursing administrator, mental health nurse*
Anderson, Mark Robert *data processing executive, biochemist*
Anderson, Mary Jane *public library consultant*
†Anderson, N. C. *writer, artist*
Anderson, Ned, Sr., *Apache tribal chairman*
†Anderson, Odin Waldemar *sociologist, educator*
Anderson, Philip Warren *physicist, educator*
†Anderson, PT (Paul Thomas IV) *film director*
Anderson, Rachael Keller *retired library administrator*
Anderson, Richard McLemore *internist*
Anderson, Robert Orville *oil and gas company executive*
Anderson, Ruth Lucille *interior designer, educator, artist, librarian, archivist*
†Anderson, Suellen *lawyer*
Anderson, Thomas Patrick *mechanical engineer, educator*
Anderson, Warren Lee, II, *marketing professional*
Anderson, Wayne Carl *public affairs officer, former corporate executive*
Anderson, William Robert *career naval officer*
Anderson-Harold, Beth *composer, piano teacher*
Anderson-Spivy, Alexandra *writer, editor*
Andersson, Craig Remington *retired chemical company executive*
Andersson, Per Lennart *computer engineer, consultant*
Andes, Phoebe Cabotaje *retired women's health nurse, educator*
Andrade, Edna *artist, art educator*
Andrain, Charles Franklin *political science educator*
†Andras, Oscar Sidney *oil company executive*
Andrassy, Timothy Francis *trade association executive*
Andrau, Maya Hedda *physical therapist*
Andrea, Mario Iacobucci *engineer, scientist, gemologist, appraiser*
†Andreas, David Lowell *retired banker*
Andreas, Dwayne Orville *business executive*
Andreatta, Susan L. *anthropologist*
†Andretti, Daniel *secondary school educator*
Andretti, Mario *retired race car driver*
Andrews, Adelaide *real estate company executive*
Andrews, Carol *primary education educator*
Andrews, Jean *artist, writer*
Andrews, Linda Wasmer *writer*
Andrews, Richard Vincent *physiologist, educator*
Andrews, William Frederick *manufacturing executive*
Andrey, Ladislav George *scientist*
Andringa, Michael Robert *management consultant*
Andringa, Patricia Perkins *fundraiser, consultant*
Andriole, Stephen John *information systems executive*
Andrisani, John Anthony *editor, author, golf consultant*
Angel, Armando Carlos *rheumatologist, internist*
†Angelis, Victoria Saris *restaurant manager, consultant*
Angell, Richard Bradshaw *philosophy educator*
Angelo, George *pediatric sales representative, lawyer*
Angelov, George Angel *pediatrician, anatomist, teratologist*
†Angermeier, Patricia *occupational therapist*
Angst, Karen K. *mental health nurse, hospice nurse*
Angus, Robert Carlyle, Jr., *naturopathic physician, health administrator*
Anison, George C. *retired otolaryngologist*
Ankrom, Barbara Burke *journalist*
Ansbro, John Joseph *philosopher, educator*
Ansley, Shepard Bryan *lawyer*
Anson, Wayne Melvin *social welfare administrator*
†Antar, Ghassan Youssef *research scientist*
†Antioco, John F. *entertainment company executive*
†Antliff, Robert Mark *humanities educator*
Antolin, Stanislav *patent lawyer*
Anton, Barbara *writer*
†Anton, Bryan Larry *music educator, musician*
Antonelli, Rosemary *writer*
Antoun, Mikhail *medicinal chemistry and pharmacognosy educator*
Anzai, Earl I. *former state attorney general*
Aouriri, Chedley *software engineer, computer science educator*
Apel-Brueggeman, Myrna L. *entrepreneur*
†Apfel, Meri F *not-for-profit developer*
†Apodaca, Patrick Vincent *lawyer*
Appachana, Anjana *writer, educator*
Appatov, Semyen Iosifovich *historian*
Appelbaum, Michelle Gellman *family nurse practitioner*
Appell, Louise Sophia *consulting company executive*
Appenzeller, Otto *neurologist, researcher*
Applegate, Christina *actress*
†Applegate, Edward C. *education educator, researcher, writer*
†Apps, Jerold Willard *adult education educator, writer*
Apted, Michael David *film director*
Aptekar, Sheldon I. *speech, theatre, and performing art educator*
†Araghizadeh, Farshid Yeganeh *surgeon*
Arango, Richard Steven *architect, graphic and industrial designer*
Arat, Metin *retired psychiatrist*
Arbeit, Wendy Sue *researcher, writer*
†Archangelsky, Dmitry A *application developer, researcher*
Archer, Dave *artist*
†Archer, Dennis Wayne *lawyer, former mayor*
Archer, Hugh Morris *consulting engineer, retired manufacturing executive*
Archer, Stephen Hunt *economist, educator*
Archer-Sorg, Karen S. *secondary school educator*
†Archibald, Nolan D. *household and industrial products company executive*
Arcos, Cresencio S. *ambassador*
Arcot, Prakash Kumar B *engineer, consultant*
†Ard, Kenneth Paul *music educator*
Arden, Bruce Wesley *retired computer scientist, retired engineering educator*
Arden, Sherry W. *publishing company executive*
Arditti, Fred D. *economist, educator*
Areen, Judith Carol *law educator, university dean*
Arenal, Julie (Mrs. Barry Primus) *choreographer*
Arenberg, Jonathan William *engineer*
Arenberg, Julius Theodore, Jr., *retired accounting company executive*
Arenson, Nathan *retired radiologist*
Arenstein, Walter Alan *environmental scientist*
†Arfsten, Debra J *music educator*
Argirion, Michael *editor*
†Argiris, Athanassios *oncologist, researcher*
Arian, Eyal *mathematician*
Ariens, Karla Rae *library director*
†Arkin, L. Jules *lawyer*
Arlen, Michael J. *writer*
Arlidge, John Walter *retired utility company executive*
Armacost, Mary-Linda Sorber Merriam *former academic administrator, consultant*
Armaingaud, Franck *engineer*
Armey, Richard Keith (Dick Armey) *former congressman*
Armistead, Katherine Kelly (Mrs. Thomas B. Armistead III) *interior designer, travel consultant, civic worker*
Armstrong, Anne Legendre (Mrs. Tobin Armstrong) *former ambassador, corporate director*
Armstrong, Donald *biochemistry, pathophysiology educator*
Armstrong, Edward Bradford, Jr., *oral and maxillofacial surgeon, educator*
Armstrong, F(redric) Michael *retired insurance company executive, consultant*
Armstrong, (Arthur) James (Arthur Armstrong) *educator, consultant, lecturer, writer*
Armstrong, Karen Lee *special education educator*
Armstrong, Michael David *investment banker*
Armstrong, Terry Lee *publishing executive, carpenter*
Armstrong, Thomas Newton, III, *art and garden specialist*
Armstrong-Law, Margaret *school administrator*
Arnett, Edward McCollin *chemistry educator, researcher*
†Arnheim, Louise A *marketing professional*
Arnold, Craig Anthony (Tony Arnold) *law educator*
Arnold, Deborah Ann *human services director*
Arnold, Gloria Malcolm *artist, educator*
Arnold, Henri *cartoonist*
Arnold, Jean Ann *health science facility administrator*
Arnold, Jerome Gilbert *lawyer*
Arnold, Leslie Ann *special education educator*
Arnold, P. A. *special education educator*
Arnold, Ruth Ann *elementary education educator*
Arnold, William Howard *retired nuclear fuel executive*
Arnott, Howard Joseph *biology educator, university dean*
Aron, Peter Arthur *charitable foundation executive, private investor*
Aronsky, Amy Jill *physician*
Aronson, Jan *artist, educator*
Aronson, Luann Marie *actress*
Aronson, Marc *artist*
Aronson, Norman Leonard *publishing executive, consultant*
Arp Lotter, Donna *venture capitalist, investor*
Arrathoon, Leigh Adelaide *medievalist, editor, writer, educator*
†Arrigo, Jan Elizabeth *photographer, writer*
Arrigo, Robin Jean Sempey *piano educator, accompanist*
†Arrington, Richard, Jr., *former mayor*
Arrott, Patricia Graham *artist, art instructor*
Arthur, John Morrison *retired utility executive*
Arveson, Raymond Gerhard *retired state official*
Asato, Yukio *molecular geneticist, educator*
Aschauer, Charles Joseph, Jr., *corporate director, former company executive*
†Ascher, Richard Alan *lawyer*
Aschheim, Eve Michele *artist, educator*
Ascone, Teresa Palmer *artist, educator*
Asensi, Gustavo *advertising executive, filmmaker*
†Ashby, Franklin Charles, Jr., *business executive, author*
Ashby, Norma Rae Beatty *journalist, beauty consultant*
Ashcraft, Charles Olin *business educator*
Ashe, Bernard Flemming *arbitrator, educator, lawyer*
Ashley, Renee *writer, creative writing educator, consultant*
Ashman, Alicia Koninska *civic activist*
Ashraf, Elizabeth Ann *pharmaceutical company executive*
Ashton, Betsy Finley *broadcast journalist, author, lecturer*
Ashton, Harris John *business executive*
Ashton, Thomas Walsh *investment banker*
Ashworth, Lawrence Nelson *retired bank executive*
†Aslan, Madalyn *writer, educator*
Asmar, Laila Michelle *lawyer*
Asmussen, Nils Wirenfeldt *pharmaceutical executive*
†Asner, Glen R. *historian*
Asokan, Unisa *information professional*
Asplin, Edward William *retired packaging company executive*
Assael, Alyce *artist*
Assunto, Richard Anthony *human resources specialist*
Astaire, Carol Anne Taylor *artist, educator*
Astill, Robert Michael *credit manager*
†Astin, John Alexander *musician, researcher*
†Astorga, Alicia Margarita *retired librarian*
Astriab, Steven Michael *army officer*
Ataie, Ata Jennati *oil products marketing executive*
Atal, Bishnu Saroop *retired speech research executive*
Atamian, Susan *nurse*
Atcheson, Sue Hart *business educator*
Atchison, Joseph Edward *pulp and paper industry consultant*
Atchison, Richard Calvin *trade association director*
Atchison, Rodney Raymond *retired lawyer, arbitrator*
Athanasian, Edward Aram *surgeon*
Atherton, William *actor*
Atkin, Edith *artist, poet*
Atkin, J Myron *science educator*
Atkins, Ernest Eugene *chemist, retired*
Atkins, Jeannine Catherine *writer*
Atkins, John *concert pianist, voice teacher*
†Atkins, Robert Alan *lawyer*
Atlas, David *meteorologist, research scientist*
†Attaway, Fritz Edward Edward *lawyer*
Attebery, Louie Wayne *English language educator, folklorist*
†Atterbury, Robert Rennie, III, *retired lawyer*
Attig, John Clare *secondary education educator, consultant*
Atwater, Phyllis T. *municipal administrator*
Auberjonois, René Murat *actor*
Aubrey, James Reynolds *English educator*
Audet, Paul Andre *retired newspaper executive*
August, Robert William *designer, educator*
Augustinus, Norman Theodore *inventor, writer*
Aulbach, George Louis *retired real estate company executive*
Aurilia, Christine Marie *administrative assistant*
Aurin, Robert James *entrepreneur*
Austin, Grant William *real estate appraiser*
Austin, John DeLong *judge*
Austin, Robert Clarke *naval officer*
Austin, Robert Daniel
†Austin, Robyn Michelle *development administrator, speech professional*
Autrey, Kathy W. *social worker*
Auwarter, Brian William *sculptor*
†Avant, Gayle *political science educator*
Aved, Barry *retail executive, consultant*
Avery, James Thomas, III, *lawyer, management consultant*
Avery, Pat McGrath *writer*
Avery, Stephen Neal *playwright, author*
Avian, Bob *choreographer, producer*
Avnet, Jonathan Michael *motion picture company executive, film director*
Axelson, Joseph Allen *professional athletics executive, publisher*
Axilrod, Stephen Harvey *global economic consultant, economist*
Ayala, Isaac Ben *musician*
†Azad, Gm Salam *engineer, researcher*
Azadeh, Mohammad *electrical engineer, researcher*
†Azar, Fred S. *biomedical engineer, researcher*
Azarnoff, Daniel Lester *pharmaceutical company consultant*
Azrael, Judith Anne *educator*
Baba, Marietta Lynn *business anthropologist, university administrator*
†Babailov, Igor V. *artist, educator*
Babb, Frank Edward *lawyer, executive*
Babb, James Ronald *editor, writer*
Babb, Roberta Joan *educational administrator*
Babbitt, Samuel Fisher *retired university official*
†Babcock, James William *geotechnical engineer*
Babitzke, Theresa Angeline *health facility administrator*
Babuts, Nicolae *French educator*
Baca, Jim *former mayor*
Baca, Joseph Francis *retired judge*
Bach, Jan Morris *composer, educator*
Bach, Jonathan P.G. *political scientist*
†Bach, Judit *music educator*
†Bacharach, Burt *composer, conductor*
Bacharach, Melvin Lewis *retired venture capitalist*
Bachtel, Ann Elizabeth *educational consultant, researcher, educator*
Backer, Joanne Arlene *case manager*
Bacon, Caroline Sharfman *investor relations consultant*
Bacon-Smith, Camille *educator, writer*
†Bacot, John Carter *retired banking executive*
Baddour, Raymond Frederick *chemical engineer, educator, entrepreneur*
Bade, Carl August *retired secondary education educator*
Bader, Lorraine Greenberg *textile stylist, designer, consultant*
Badgley, Theodore McBride *psychiatrist, neurologist*
Baehr, Theodore *religious organization administrator, communications executive*
Baena, Robert Bob *interior designer*
Baerg, Richard Henry *podiatrist, surgeon*
Baeza, Cheryl Anne *psychiatric social worker*
Bagby, John R. *management consultant*
Baggett, Donnis Gene *journalist, editor*
Bagley, William Thompson *lawyer*
Bagstad, Kristin Kim *pediatric nurse practitioner*
Bagwill, John Williams *retired pension fund company executive*
Bahbah, Bishara Assad *editor, business executive, philanthropist*
Bahr, Jane Marie *writer, retired English educator*
Baier, Edward John *former public health official, industrial hygiene engineer, consultant*
Baigis, Wendy Sue *probation and parole officer*
Bailar, Barbara Ann *statistician, researcher*
Bailey, Carla Lynn *nursing administrator*
Bailey, Charles-James Nice *linguistics educator*
Bailey, David Roy Shackleton *classics educator*
Bailey, Joselyn Elizabeth *physician*
†Bailey, Michael Scott *cardiovascular electrophysiologist*
Bailey, Michael Wallace *aerospace engineer*
Bailey, Rita Maria *investment advisor*
Bailey, Steven Scott *operations research analyst*
Bailey, William Waddell *writer, communications executive*
Bailey-Stein, Deena Tamara *health care administrator*
Baiman, Gail *real estate broker*
Bain, Diane Martha D'Andrea *clinical nurse specialist in critical care*
Bain, William Donald, Jr., *lawyer, chemical company executive*
Bainbridge, Dona Bardelli *international marketing executive*
Baird, Alan C. *screenwriter*
Baird, Donald Robert *retired secondary school educator*
Baird, William David *retired anesthesiologist*
Baker, Augustus L., Jr., *surgeon, retired*
Baker, C. B. *retired day care director, organizer, communicator*
Baker, Carol Ann *elementary school educator*
Baker, Daniel Neil *physicist*
Baker, Don R. *musician*
Baker, Donald *lawyer, director*
Baker, Edward Kevin *retail executive*
Baker, Edward Martin *engineering and industrial psychologist*
Baker, Eva Lee *education educator, researcher*
Baker, Henry S., Jr., *retired banker*
†Baker, Jack Thomas *design engineer, environmental scientist, consultant*
Baker, James A. *lawyer, former state supreme court justice*
Baker, Katherine June *elementary school educator, minister, artist*
Baker, Ronald James *English language educator, university administrator*
Baker, Susan Marie Victoria *writer, artist*
Baker, Suzanne Martin *artist, rancher*
Baker, William Thompson, Jr., *lawyer*
Baker, Zachary Moshe *librarian*
Bakht, Baidar *civil engineer, researcher, educator*
Bakken, Gordon Morris *law educator*
Bakkensen, John Reser *lawyer*
†Balakrishnan, P.V. (Sundar) *finance educator*
Balch, Henry H. *surgeon, educator, retired*
Baldassano, Vincent J. *artist*
Baldrige, Letitia *writer, management training consultant*
Baldwin, C. Andrea, Jr., *retired science educator*
Baldwin, Deanna Louise *dietitian*
Baldwin, George Curriden *physicist, educator*
†Baldwin, Marie Hunsucker *retired educator*
Baldwin, William Russell *optometrist, foundation executive*
Bales, Gertrude A. *retired otolaryngologist*
Bales, John Foster, III, *retired lawyer*
Bales, Susan Ford *social service spokesperson*
Balick, Kenneth D. *international business executive*
Balis, Jennifer Lynn *academic administrator, computer technology educator*
Balkcom, Carol Ann *insurance agent*
Ball, Carroll Raybourne *anatomist, medical educator, researcher*
Ball, Howard Guy *education specialist educator*
Ball, James Herington *retired lawyer*
Ball, John Robert *healthcare executive*
Ball, Lawrence *retired physical scientist*
Ball, Margie Barber *elementary school educator*
Ballaine, Jerrold Curtis *artist*
Ballard, Marion Scattergood *software development professional*
Ballas, Zuhair Khamis *physician*
†Ballhaus, William Louis *engineering executive*
Balliett, Whitney *writer, critic*
†Balog, Rita Jean *retired librarian*
Balser, Robert Edward *animation film producer, director*
Baltazzi, Evan Serge *engineering research consulting company executive*
Balter, Frances Sunstein *civic worker*
Bamberger, Gerald Francis *plastics marketing consultant*
Bamberger, Joseph Alexander *mechanical engineer, educator*
Bambrick, James Joseph *labor economist, labor relations executive*
†Bancila, Mihaela *humanities educator*
Bandeen, William Reid *retired meteorologist*
Bandopadhyaya, Amitava (Amit Bando) *economist, consultant, educator*
Bandy, Jack D. *lawyer*
Bandyopadhyay, Ram Shyamal *molecular biologist, researcher*
†Banerjee, Kalyani *science educator, researcher*
Banerjee, Kaustav *electrical and computer engineering educator*
Baney, Richard Neil *physician, internist*
Banis, Robert Joseph *pharmaceutical company executive, educator, publisher*
Banks, David Russell *former health care executive*
Banks, Deirdre Margaret *retired church organization administrator*
Bannister, Candida Cleve *data processing executive*
Bannister, Geoffrey *university president, geographer*
Bansak, Stephen A., Jr., *investment banker, financial consultant*
Bansil, Arun *research scientist*
Bantry, Bryan *entrepreneur, producer, director*
Bao, Lichun *application developer, educator*
†Baquet, Charles R., III, *former federal agency administrator, international studies educator*

Barabino, William Albert *science and technology researcher, inventor*
Barad, Jill Elikann *family products company executive*
†Baramova, Irina Antonova *investment banker*
Barbakow, Jeffrey C. *former healthcare industry executive*
Barbee, George E.L. *financial services and business executive*
Barbee, Steven George *engineer*
†Barber, Clarence Lyle *economics educator*
Barber, James Alden *navy officer, educator*
†Barber, John Joseph *minister, writer*
Barber, Marsha *company executive*
Barber, Phyllis Nelson *writer, educator*
†Barber, Richard William *publishing executive*
Barber, Theodore Francis *aircraft mechanics professional*
Barbera, Joseph *motion picture and television producer, cartoonist*
†Barbey, Adélaïde *publisher*
Barca, George Gino *winery executive, financial investor*
Barca, James Joseph *fire department administrative services executive*
Barca, Kathleen *marketing executive*
†Barch, Davis R. *neuroscientist, application developer*
Bar-Cohen, Avram *mechanical engineering educator*
Bard, Marjorie *social welfare administrator*
Bardin, Clyde Wayne *biomedical researcher*
Bare, Bruce *retired life insurance company executive*
Bare, Steven Wayne *consulting services company executive*
Barfield, Stewart Bayne *counseling therapist*
Barger, William James *management consultant, educator*
†Bargetto, Paul C. *theater director*
Barham, Charles Dewey, Jr., *electric utility executive, lawyer*
Baril, Maurice *career officer*
Barker, Hilda Jean *retired library director*
Barker, Verlyn Lloyd *retired minister, educator*
Barker, Virginia Lee *nursing educator*
Barkey, Brenda *technical writer, publications manager*
†Barkley, Charles Wade *sports broadcaster, retired professional basketball player*
Barkley, Richard Clark *ambassador*
Barlow, Jean *art educator, painter*
Barlow, John Sutton *neurophysiologist, electroencephalographer, lexicographer*
†Barlow, William Kyle *lawyer, state legislator*
Barnard, Donald Roy *medical and veterinary entomologist*
Barnes, John Allen *writer*
Barnes, Robert Vincent *retired elementary and secondary school art educator*
Barnes, Roy Eugene *former governor, lawyer*
Barnes, Samuel Henry *political scientist, educator*
Barnes, Wesley Edward *energy and environmental executive*
Barnes-Kempton, Isabel Janet *microbiology educator, college dean*
†Barnett, Allen *pharmacologist, consultant*
Barnett, Elizabeth Hale *organizational consultant*
Barnett, Margaret Edwina *nephrologist, researcher, business consultant, entrepreneur, clinical hypertension specialist*
Barnett, Mark William *former state attorney general*
Barnett, Peggy G. *music educator*
†Barnett, Randy Evan *law educator*
Barney, Austin Dunham, II, *estate planner*
†Barney, Donna Nadyne *writer*
†Barnidge, Jason *biomedical researcher*
†Barnidge, Leroy, Jr., *military officer*
†Barolini, Nicoletta E. *artist*
Baron, Barton Leonard *engineer*
Baron, Jeffrey *retired pharmacologist*
Barone, John Anthony *academic administrator emeritus*
Barr, John Baldwin *chemist, research scientist*
Barr, Kenneth L. *former mayor*
Barr, Kevin Curtis *poet, computer graphics designer*
Barr, Marlene Joy *volunteer*
Barr, Michael Charles *financial journalist*
Barrack, William Sample, Jr., *petroleum company executive*
Barraclough, Charles Arthur *retired endocrinologist, educator*
Barré, Lloyd Milton *retired religion educator, researcher, writer*
†Barreto, Bernardo *artist*
Barrett, Andrea Fuller *writer*
Barrett, Evelyn Carol *retired secondary education educator*
Barrett, Izadore *retired fisheries research administrator*
Barrett, James Emmett *retired judge*
Barrett, Janet Tidd *academic administrator*
Barrett, Jessica (Donna Ann Nipert) *psychotherapist*
Barrett, Judith Ann *salon owner*
Barrett, Katherine *writer, multimedia producer*
Barrett, Linda L. *real estate consultant*
Barrett, Lisa Marie *acupuncture physician, herbologist, hypnotherapist*
Barrett, Paulette Singer *public relations executive*
Barrett, Robert Todd *surgeon, retired*
Barrett, Thomas M. *congressman*
Barrett, William E. *former congressman*
Barrickman, Les L. *psychiatrist*
Barricks, Michael Eli *retired surgeon*
Barrington, Judith M. *writer, educator*
†Barritt, Christy *freelance/self-employed writer*
Barron, Almen L. *microbiologist, department chairman*
Barron, Bruce Albrecht *physician, educator, medical researcher*
Barron, Charles Elliott *retired electronics executive*
Barron, Peggy Pennisi *management consultant*
Barrow, Charles Herbert *investment banker*
Barrow, Lionel Ceon, Jr., *communications and marketing consultant*
Barrow, Robert Earl *retired agricultural organization administrator*
Barrow, Thomas Francis *artist, educator*
Barry, Miranda Robbins *educator, internet and television producer, writer*
†Barrymore, Drew *actress*
Barshis, Victoria R. Garnier *social worker*
†Barsky, Irene J. *graphics designer*
Barson, Ross J. *music educator, assistant principal*
Barsuk, Sidney Alan *management consultant, educator*
Bartels, Betty Jane *nurse*
Barth, David Keck *distribution industry consultant*
Barth, Frances *artist*
Bartholomew, Dennis *sculptor, fine arts company executive*
Bartle, Richard Allan *computer games designer*
Bartlett, Arthur Eugene *food service executive*
Bartlett, David *management consultant*
Bartlett, Desmond William *engineering company executive*
Bartlett, Eugene Fred *retired surgeon*
Bartlett-Powers, John David *social worker, elementary education educator*
Barto, Rebecca Lynn *business analyst*
Bartolini, Bruce Anthony *real estate executive*
Barton, Ann Elizabeth *retired financial executive*
Barton, Ellen Louise *lawyer, educator, consultant*
Barton, Glen A. *manufacturing company executive*
Barton, Joe Linus *congressman*
Barton, Leslie L. *physician*
Bartrem, Duane Harvey *retired military officer, designer, building consultant*
†Bartz, David John *lawyer*
Bartzatt, Ronald Lee *research biochemist, consultant*
Barzun, Jacques *author, literary consultant*
Bashore, Irene Saras *art association administrator*
Basinger, Karen Lynn *renal dietitian*
†Basiszta, Martin Winston *lawyer*
Basnett, Margaret G. *reading and language arts educator, consultant*
Bass, Lynda D. *retired medical/surgical nurse, retired nursing educator*
Bass, Robert Olin *retired manufacturing executive*
†Bassett, Clyde M. *music educator*
Bassett, Elizabeth Ewing (Libby Bassett) *writer, editor*
Bassett, Leslie Raymond *composer, educator*
Bassford, Lynn Foster *physicist, engineer*
Bassin, Gilbert Sheldon *manufacturing executive, engineer*
Batalden, Paul Bennett *pediatrician, health care educator*
Bateman, Robert McLellan *artist*
Bates, Charles Turner *lawyer, educator*
Batson, Raymond Milner *retired cartographer*
Battaglia, Francine *mechanical engineering educator, researcher*
Batterden, James Edward *retired business executive*
Battin, Patricia Meyer *librarian*
Battistelli, Joseph John *electronics executive*
Battle, Emery Alford, Jr., *sales executive*
Batts, Warren Leighton *retired diversified industry executive*
Batzer, John L. *systems engineer*
†Bauer, Antonie Gertrud *journalist*
Bauer, Barbara Ann *marketing consultant*
Bauer, Bernard Oswald *geography educator*
Bauer, Fred L. *judge, lawyer, accountant, arbitration*
Bauer, Henry Hermann *chemistry and science educator*
Bauer, Richard Carlton *nuclear engineer*
†Baugh, Jeremy Richard *music educator*
Baul, Mary Ann *correctional counselor*
Baum, Carol Grossman *physician*
†Baum, Roger S. *writer*
Baum, Stanley David *lawyer*
Bauman, Marilyn Adrienne *artist, educator*
Bauman, Richard Arnold *coast guard officer*
Bauman, Robert Patten *diversified company executive*
Bauman, Winfield Scott *finance educator*
Baumann-Sinacore, Patricia Lynn *nursing administrator*
Baumgartner, John H. *refining and petroleum products company executive*
Baur, Werner Heinz *mineralogist, educator*
Bavington, Bette Anne *special needs educator*
Bavota, Michael Francis (Michael Ryan) *food products executive, freelance writer*
Baxter, Cecil William, Jr., *retired college president*
†Baxter, Cindi Choate *librarian*
†Baxter, Decima Christine *hospital administrator, military officer*
Baxter, Duby Yvonne *government official*
†Baxter, Elizabeth Palm *music educator*
†Baxter, Judith Lee *academic administrator, mathematician*
Baxter, Stephen Bartow *retired history educator*
Bayack, Patricia Elaine *psychotherapist, social welfare administrator, social worker*
Bayard, Susan Shapiro *adult education educator, small business owner*
Bayer, Robert Edward *retired defense department official, consultant*
Bayless, Betsey *state official*
†Bayly, George V. *manufacturing executive*
Bayne, David Cowan *priest, legal scholar, law educator*
Bays, Mona Rae *retired librarian*
Baysinger, Stephen Michael *quality assurance professional*
Beach, David Williams *music educator, dean*
Beach, Milo C. *former art museum director*
†Beach, Nancy Ann Helen *special education educator, educator*
Beadle, John Grant *retired manufacturing company executive*
Beagrie, George Simpson *dentist, educator, dean emeritus*
Beahm, Donald Lee *political science educator*
Beal, Merrill David *conservationist, museum director*
Beal, Wanda Elnora *psychologist, writer, artist*
Beals, Nancy Farwell *former state legislator*
†Bean, Bruce Winfield *lawyer*
†Bear, Geraldine M. *nursing assistant, poet*
Bearak, Richard Lee *architect, city planner*
Beard, Audrey Lucille *artist, art educator*
Beard, Leo Roy *retired civil engineer*
Bearg, Esther Marilyn *retired school counselor, educational consultant*
Beasley, Albert Sidney *pediatrician*
Beasley, Barbara Starin *sales executive, marketing professional*
†Beasley, David Muldrow *former governor, consultant*
Beaton, Meredith *enterostomal therapy clinical nurse specialist*
Beattie, Charles Robert, III, *lawyer*
†Beattie, Donald Gilbert *lawyer*
Beattie, George Chapin *retired orthopedic surgeon*
Beatts, Anne Patricia *writer, producer*
Beatty, Frances *civic worker*
Beatty, Wilbur C. *contract management executive*
Beauzay, Victor H(ilton) *lawyer*
Beavers, Karen Marjorie *small business owner*
Becherer, Richard Joseph *science administrator, physicist*
Bechtol, Larry Owen *pastor*
Becich, Raymond Brice *healthcare consultant, mediator, trainer, educator*
Beck, Albert *manufacturing company executive*
Beck, Barbara Nell *elementary school educator*
Beck, Gustav Julius *retired pulmonologist, allergist, immunologist*
Beck, Irene Clare *educational consultant, writer*
Beck, Stuart Edwin *lawyer*
Beck, Timothy Daniel *human resources specialist, consultant*
†Becker, Bruce Alan *music educator, director*
Becker, Bruce Carl, II, *physician, educator, health facility administrator*
Becker, Charles McVey *economics and finance educator*
Becker, Elizabeth Wallace *elementary school guidance counselor*
Becker, Jon Andrew *arts and education consultant*
Becker, Lawrence Carlyle *philosopher, educator, writer*
Becker, Paul Albert *investment executive*
Becker, Walter Heinrich *vocational educator, planner*
Becker, Wendy Jeanne *music and drama educator, songwriter, singer*
Beckett, Victoria Ling *physician*
Beckjord, Eric Stephen *nuclear engineer, energy researcher*
Beckwith, Larry Edward *mechanical engineer*
Beckwith, Sidney Johnson *director special programs, curriculum administrator*
†Bedell, Elizabeth Snyder (Betty Bedell) *editor-in-chief, marketing professional*
Bednoff, Stuart Leon *obstetrician, gynecologist, educator*
Bedrij, Orest *investment banker, scientist*
Beeber, Marshall Lawrence *sales executive*
Beecher, Graciela Fernandez *language educator, writer*
Beers, R. Rand *former narcotics and law enforcement administrator*
†Beery, Barbara Faye *secondary school educator*
†Beggan, Robert M. *non-profit executive*
Beggs, William H. *microbiologist, researcher*
Begley, Ed, Jr., *actor*
Begum, Momotaz *medical researcher, consultant, educator*
Behl, Wishvender Kumar *research chemist*
Behlmer, Rudy H., Jr., *director, writer, film educator*
Behnke, Doleen *computer and environmental specialist, consultant*
Behr, Marion Ray *artist, writer, business executive*
Behr, Raymond Anthony *psychiatrist*
Behrendt, John Charles *geophysicist researcher, writer*
Behrmann, Joan Gail *newspaper editor*
Beighey, Lawrence Jerome *packaging company executive*
Beisner, Ralph Andrew *judge*
†Bejjani, Bassem A *molecular researcher*
†Belafonte, Harry (Harry George Belafonte Jr.) *singer, concert artist, actor*
Belanger, Cherry Churchill *elementary school educator*
†Belcher, Charles William *education educator*
Belco, Karen Marie *cardiology nurse*
Beldock, Myron *lawyer*
Beldon, Sanford T. *publisher*
†Belinsky, Rachel *mathematician, educator*
†Bell, Burwell Baxter, III, *general United States Army*
†Bell, Daniel Mark *music educator*
Bell, Dorothy Frances *nurse, educator*
†Bell, Elva Glenn *retired secondary school educator, retired counseling administrator, interpreter*
Bell, Haney Hardy, III, *lawyer*
Bell, Jacqueline Michelle *marketing professional, public relations executive*
Bell, Karen June *critical care nurse*
Bell, Linda Green *psychology educator, therapist*
Bell, Rebecca *psychotherapist, journalist*
Bell, Regina Jean *corporate consulting company executive*
Bell, Susan Jane *nurse*
Bell, Theodore Augustus *advertising executive*
Bellacosa, Joseph W. *retired state supreme court justice*
Bellamy, James Carl *retired insurance company executive*
Bellamy, Jennifer Wiggins *artist*
Belland, Brian Robert *language educator*
Beller, Luanne Evelyn *accountant*
Belles, Donald Arnold *pastoral therapist, mental health counselor*
Belleville, Philip Frederick *lawyer*
Bellow, Donald Grant *mechanical engineering educator*
Bellow, Saul C. *writer, educator*
Belluomini, Frank Stephen *accountant*
†Belluomini, Wendy *microprocessor design researcher*
Belmont, Larry Miller *retired public health executive*
†Beloff, Zoe *artist, educator*
Belonick, Cynthia Ann *psychiatric-mental health nurse*
†Belson, Abby Avin *writer*
Benario, Janice Martin *retired classics educator*
Benbow, Richard Addison *psychological counselor*
Bencini, Sara Haltiwanger *concert pianist*
Bender, Hy *writer*
Bender, Ross Thomas *minister*
Bender, Sheila Sue *essayist, poet, author*
Benedict, John Anthony, II, *army officer*
Benedict, Stewart H. *writer, playwright*
Benenson, Claire Berger *investment and financial planning educator, finance educator*
Benfield, John Richard *surgeon, educator*
Benford, Anne Michele (Anne Sass) *pediatric nurse practitioner, clinical nurse specialist*
Benivegna, Vito Nicholas *language educator*
Benjamin, Arlin James *physicist*
Benjamin, David Nicholas *architect, researcher*
Benjamin, Laura J. *management consultant, speech professional*
†Bennack, Frank Anthony, Jr., *publishing company executive*
Benner, Charles Henry *retired music educator*
Bennett, Carrie *retired chemical company executive*
Bennett, Cornelius *retired professional football player*
Bennett, Geraldine Eudora (Jerrie Bennett) *mental health services professional, nursing educator*
Bennett, Harriet Cook *social worker, educator*
Bennett, Jay Brett *healthcare industry executive*
Bennett, June Newton *interior designer*
Bennett, Lerone, Jr., *retired magazine editor, author*
Bennett, Peter Dunne *retired marketing educator*
Bennett, R. Dawn *social worker*
Bennett, Richard Thomas *retired manufacturing executive*
Bennett, Robert LeRoy *computer software development company executive*
Bennett, Ronald Thomas *photojournalist, government official*
Bennett, Saul *public relations agency executive*
Bennett, Steven Alan *lawyer*
Bennett, Velma Joyce (Joyce Williams) *writer, poet*
Bennett, William Ralph, Jr., *physicist, educator*
Benney, Douglas Mabley *direct marketing executive, consultant*
†Benson, Ellen Marie *elementary school educator*
Benson, Loyd *retired state legislator*
†Bentsen, Lloyd *former government official, former senator*
†Benussi, Elena *financial consultant*
Benz, Edward John, Jr., *physician, educator*
Benz, Maudy Louise *writer, educator*
Benzle, Curtis Munhall *artist, art educator*
Beracha, Barry Harris *retired food products executive*
Bercel, Nicholas Anthony *neurologist, neurophysiologist*
Bercovitch, Sacvan *English language professional, educator*
†Berenbeim, Jane Rosen *not-for-profit developer*
†Beresin, Marta Ilene *lawyer*
Berezin, Tanya *acting coach, educator, actress*
Berg, Bruce Jeffrey *psychiatrist*
Bergan, William Luke *lawyer*
Bergau, Frank Conrad *real estate, commercial and investment properties executive*
Bergelt, Philip Robert, Jr., *printer, antiques dealer*
†Bergen, Candice *actress, writer, photojournalist*
Berger, Anita Hazel *psychotherapist, adult educator, organizational consultant*
Berger, Arthur Seymour *organization executive, city official*
Berger, Deborah Kornbluth *educator, educational consultant*
Berger, Frank Stanley *management executive*
Berger, Frederick Jerome *electrical engineer, educator*
Berger, Joyce Muriel *foundation executive, author, editor*
Berger, Linda Fay *writer*
Berger, Marc Joseph *lawyer*
Berger, Miriam Roskin *creative arts therapy director, educator, therapist*
Berger, Samuel Martin *physician*
†Berger-Knorr, Lawrence *education educator, information technology manager*
Berger-Kraemer, Nancy *speech and language pathologist, artist*
Bergeron, Earleen Fournet *actress*
Bergeron, Elmo P. *chemical engineer, consultant*
Bergfield, Gene Raymond *engineering educator*
Bergin, Allen Eric *clinical psychologist, educator*
Berglund, Robin G. *child psychiatrist, former corporate executive*
Bergman, Hermas John (Jack Bergman) *retired college administrator*
Bergmann, Donald Gerald *pharmaceutical company executive*
Bergoust, Eric *Olympic athlete*

Bergquist, Sandra Lee *medical and legal consultant, nurse*
Bergsman, Kenneth Lloyd *hematologist, oncologist*
Bergstrom, Richard William Houlder, Sr., *information technology executive*
Beringer, William Ernst *mediator, arbitrator, lawyer*
Berke, Judie Kleyman *publisher, editor*
Berkhofer, Robert Frederick, Jr., *retired history educator*
†Berkley, Erma Van Meter *retired librarian*
Berkley, Gail Winnick *psychotherapist*
Berkley, Stephen Mark *computer industry entrepreneur and investor*
Berkovitz, Leonard David *mathematician, educator*
Berle, Peter Adolf Augustus *lawyer, media director*
Berley, Marc S. *foundation administrator, English educator*
†Berlin, Edward Alan *musicologist, writer, retired application developer*
Berlin, Howard Richard *investment advisory company executive*
Berlin, Meredith Rise *editor*
Berlincourt, Marjorie Alkins *government official, retired*
Berlind, Roger Stuart *stage and film producer*
Berliner, Ruth Shirley *real estate company executive*
Berlinger, Warren *actor*
Berman, Eleanore *artist*
Berman, Miriam Naomi *librarian*
Berman, Richard Angel *health and educational administrator*
Berman, Robert S. *marketing consultant*
Berman, Siegrid Visconti *interior designer*
Berman, William H. *publishing company executive*
Berman-Hammer, Susan *public relations executive*
Bermann, Nancy Stewart *artist*
Bern, Lynda Kaplan *women's health and pediatric nurse*
†Bernard, Marcelle Thomasine *physician*
Bernard, Richard Lawson *geneticist, retired*
Berner, Judith *mental health nurse*
Bernfeld, Peter Harry William *retired biochemist*
Bernhardt, Arthur Dieter *building industry executive and consultant*
Bernheimer, Martin *music critic*
Bernsen, Harold John *manufacturing executive*
†Bernstein, Bruce S. *chemist, consultant*
Bernstein, George L. *lawyer, accountant*
Bernstein, Henrietta Ruth *publishing executive, writer*
Bernstein, I. Melvin *university official and dean, materials scientist*
Bernstein, Merton Clay *law educator, lawyer, arbitrator*
Bernstein, Phyliss Louise *psychologist*
†Bernt, Joseph Philip *communications educator*
Bernthal, Harold George *healthcare company executive*
†Berquist, Angela Su *writer, philosopher*
Berra, P. Bruce *computer educator*
Berra, Robert Louis *human resources consultant*
Berran, Lawrence Charles *finance company executive*
Berresford, Susan Vail *philanthropic foundation executive*
Berrey, Robert Forrest *lawyer*
†Berridge, Mary Lloyd *photographer*
†Berry, Cynthia Joan *psychologist, consultant*
Berry, Leora Mary *school nurse*
†Berry, Mary Pat *real estate developer, consultant*
Berry, Omega Makeece *nursing assistant*
Berry, Richard Lewis *writer, magazine editor, lecturer, programmer*
Berry, Robert Vaughan *retired electrical manufacturing company executive*
Berry, Robert Worth *lawyer, educator, retired army officer*
Berry, Sharon Elaine *interior designer*
Berry, William Willis *retired utility executive*
†Berry, Winifred L. *medical technologist*
Berryhill, Georgia Gene *web designer, photographer, educator*
Bers, Abraham *electrical engineering and physics educator*
Bers, Donald Martin *physiology educator*
Bershad, Neil Jeremy *electrical engineering educator*
Bersin, Alan Douglas *lawyer, school system administrator*
Bersin, Richard Lewis *physicist, plasma process technologist*
Bersin, Ruth Hargrave *priest, social services administrator*
Bert, Clara Virginia *retired home economics educator, administrator*
Bertelsman, William Odis *federal judge*
Berthaud, Vladimir *physician*
Berthold, John William, III, *physicist*
Bertin, John Joseph *aeronautical engineer, educator, researcher*
†Bertram, Jean DeSales *writer*
Bertram, Manya M. *retired lawyer*
†Bertram, Melissa C. *agricultural research scientist*
Bertram, Susan *rehabilitation counselor*
Bertrand, Frederic Howard *retired insurance company executive*
Bertucelli, Robert Edward *accountant, educator*
Berzas, Elizabeth Ann *marketing professional, public relations executive*
†Besaw, Jennea D. *music educator, entrepreneur*
†Bescher, Eric Pascal *engineering educator, researcher*
Besing, Ray Gilbert *lawyer, writer, lecturer*
Beston, Rose Marie *retired college president*
†Bethke, Louise Virginia *music educator, writer*
Bettenhausen, Matthew Robert *lawyer*
Betti, John Anso *federal official, former automobile manufacturing company executive*
Betts, James William, Jr., *financial analyst, consultant*
Beukema, John Frederick *lawyer*
Beumer, Richard Eugene *engineer, architect, construction firm executive*
Beutler, Arthur Julius *manufacturing company executive*
Bevilacqua, Anthony Joseph Cardinal *archbishop emeritus*
Bevington, E(dmund) Milton *electrical machinery manufacturing company executive*
Bey, Joan S. *retired public information specialist, writer*
†Beyer, La Vonne Ann *special education educator*
Beyersdorf, Marguerite Mulloy *educator*
†Beyle, Thad Lewis *political science educator*
Beyman, Jonathan Eric *information officer*
†Bhanot, Karan *education educator*
Bhat, Ram J. *anesthesiologist*
†Bhatia, Rajan *engineer, physicist, researcher*
†Bianconi, Marcelo *education educator*
Bible, Geoffrey Cyril *former tobacco company executive*
Bice, Michael David *retail and wholesale executive, marketing consultant, insurance consultant*
Bick, Katherine Livingstone *neurobiologist, international liaison, consultant*
Bidwell, Roger Grafton Shelford *biologist, educator*
Biederman, Edwin Williams, Jr., *retired petroleum geologist*
Biegel, David Eli *social worker, educator*
Biegel, Jeffrey Robert *composer*
Biehl, Kathy Anne *author, lawyer*
Biemuller, Martha Lydia *retired obstetrician-gynecologist*
†Bierce, William B. *lawyer*
Bierley, Paul Edmund *aeronautical engineer, musician, author, publisher*
Bierman, Sandra *artist*
Bieron, Louise T. *physician placement executive*
Bierstedt, Peter Richard *lawyer, entertainment industry consultant*
Bierwirth, John Cocks *retired aerospace manufacturing executive*
Bigelow, Charles Cross *retired biochemist, retired university administrator*
†Biggers, Cornelia Anderson *musician*
Biggers, William Joseph *retired manufacturing company executive*
Biggs, Arthur Edward *retired chemical manufacturing company executive*
Bigham, James George *structural engineer*
Bikales, Norbert M. *chemist, science administrator*
Biklen, Stephen Clinton *retired student loan company executive*
Bilbray, Brian P. *former congressman*
Bilbray, James Hubert *former congressman, lawyer, consultant*
†Biles, Gloria C. *historian, educator*
Billauer, Barbara Pfeffer *lawyer, educator*
Billingsley, Shirley Ann *writer, poet*
Binder, Madeline Dotti *retail executive*
Bingham, Jinsie Scott *broadcast company executive*
Binienda, John J. *state legislator*
Binkley, Timothy *computer graphics educator*
†Binns, Jane Camille *humanities educator*
Bino, Marial Desolyn *librarian, educator, psychologist*
†Binsfeld, Connie Berube *former state official*
Birch, Patricia *choreographer, director*
Birchard, Catherine Suzanne Sieh *artist*
†Bird, Patricia Coleen *business owner*
Birgeneau, Robert Joseph *physicist, educator*
Birk, John R. *management consultant*
Birkmayer, Donald Tefft *retired college official*
Birman, Linda Lee *retired elementary school educator*
Birmingham, Thomas F. *lawyer, former state legislator*
Bisconti, Ann Stouffer *public opinion research company executive*
Bishop, Budd Harris *retired museum administrator, artist*
Bishop, C. Diane *state agency administrator, educator*
Bishop, Carol *oil industry executive*
Bishop, Charles Edwin *university president emeritus, economist*
†Bishop, Delores Ann *artist, educator*
Bishop, Oliver Richard *retired state official*
Bishop, Paul Leslie *civil and environmental engineering educator, environmental engineering consultant*
Bishop, Sue Marquis (Ina Sue Marquis Bishop) *dean, psychiatric and mental health nurse educator, researcher*
Bishop, William Peter *science administrator, management consultant*
Bissell, Brent John *advertising and direct marketing executive*
Bissell, James Dougal, III, *motion picture production designer*
†Bitoy, Michele Gardner *radio traffic director*
Bivens, Lynette Kupka *director*
Biziou, Peter *cinematographer*
†Bizzell, Mary Ann *counselor*
Bjerknes, Michael Leif *dancer*
Bjorndahl, David Lee *electrical engineer*
Blacher, Joan Helen *psychotherapist, educator*
Black, David *writer, educator, producer*
Black, David deLaine *retired investment consultant*
†Black, Rebecca Leree *special education educator*
†Black, Recca Marcele *educator*
Black, Ruth Idella *museum curator*
Blackbourn, David Gordon *history educator*
Blackburn, Joy Martin *librarian*
†Blacker, Harriet *public relations executive*
Blackledge, David William *retired academic administrator*
Blackson, Benjamin F(ranklin) *clinical social worker*
Blackwell, Thomas George *military police officer*
Blaine, Davis Robert *investment banker, valuation consultant executive*
Blair, Fred Edward *social services administrator*
Blair, Frederick David *interior designer*
Blair, Kathie Lynn *social services worker*
Blair, Sandra Jean *author, publisher*
Blair, Warren *artist, educator*
Blake, John Edward *retired car rental company executive*
†Blake, John Freeman *financial lawyer*
†Blake, Stanford *judge, lawyer*
†Blake Ramos, Debra Barbara *writer*
Blancato, Louis Sebastian *anesthesiologist*
Blanchard, David Lawrence *aerospace executive, real estate developer, management consultant*
Blanchard, George Samuel *retired army officer*
Blanchard, Richard Frederick *construction executive*
Bland, Eveline Mae *real estate broker, musician, music instructor*
Bland, Marybeth *volunteer, artist*
Blander, Milton *chemist*
Blank, Rebecca Margaret *economist*
Blaszczynski, Andre Boguslaw *economist, educator*
Blatt, Harold Geller *lawyer*
Blatt, Lawrence M. *pharmaceutical company executive*
Blattner, Florence Anne *retired music educator*
Blatz, Linda Jeanne *management professional*
Blau, Helen Margaret *molecular pharmacology educator*
Blauvelt, Barbara Louise *nutritionist*
Blazey, Judith Leiston *school district administrator*
Blazina, Janice Fay *transfusion medicine physician*
Blazzard, Norse Novar *lawyer*
Blecke, Arthur Edward *retired principal*
Bleveans, John *lawyer*
Blevins, Jeffrey Alexander *lawyer*
Blick, Robert Howard *economist, consultant*
Blinder, Janet *art dealer*
Blissett, William Frank *English literature educator*
Blitt, Rita Lea *artist*
Bloch, Erich *retired electrical engineer, former science foundation administrator*
Bloch, Julia Chang *educator, former ambassador, former bank executive*
Block, Dennis Jeffrey *lawyer*
Block, Dennis William *emergency physician*
Block, Emil Nathaniel, Jr., *retired air force officer*
Block, Lawrence *author*
Block, Lynne Wood *accountant*
Block, Richard Raphael *lawyer, arbitrator*
†Block, Thomas Alan *artist, educator*
Block, William *newspaper publisher*
†Blodgett, David William *preventive medicine physician*
†Blodgett, Dean Scott *product development executive*
Blodgett, Omer William *electric company design consultant*
Blood, Archer Kent *retired foreign service officer*
Blood, Peggy A. *college administrator*
†Bloodgood-Abrams, Jane Marie *artist*
Bloodworth, Gladys Leon *educator*
Bloom, Charles Joseph *lawyer*
†Bloom, Eugene Charles *gastroenterologist, educator*
Bloom, Frances Virginia *retired music educator*
Bloom, Jill Elizabeth *physician assistant*
Bloomer, Harold Franklin, Jr., *retired lawyer*
Bloomfield, David Charles *lawyer, educator, public and not-for-profit executive*
†Bloomfield, John V. *musician, educator*
Bloomquist, Kenneth Gene *music educator, university bands director*
Blossom, Beverly *choreographer, dance educator*
Blount, Benroe Wayne *physician*
Blow, George *lawyer*
Blue, China *artist*
Bluestone, Barry Alan *economics educator*
Bluitt, Karen *information technology executive*
Blum, Barbara Davis *investor*
Blum, Barbara Meddock *retired association executive*
Blum, Betty Ann *footwear company executive*
Blum, Gerald Henry *department store executive*
Blum, Samuel *retired research scientist*
Blumberg, Mark Stuart *health services researcher*
Blume, Arthur Walter, IV, *addictive behaviors researcher, therapist*
Blumenfeld, Rochelle S. Reznik *artist*
†Blumenthal, William *lawyer*
Blummer, Kathleen Ann *counselor*
Blumstein, Susan Bender *fundraiser*
Blunck, Klaire Darlene *nurse*
†Blyth, Myrna Greenstein *publishing executive, editor, author*
†Boal, Danielle K. *radiologist, educator*
Boal, Dean *retired arts center administrator, educator*
Boardman, Elizabeth Drake *naval reserve officer*
Boardman, Eunice *retired music educator*
Boatwright, Charlotte Jeanne *marketing professional, public relations executive*
Bobbitt, Juanita Crawford *international organization executive*
Bocaya, Renato Biso *pharmaceutical sales and marketing executive, entrepreneur*
†Boccardi, Louis Donald *retired news agency executive*
Bochner, Hart *actor, director*
Bock, Jerry (Jerrold Lewis) *composer*
Bockius, Ruth Bear *nursing educator*
Bockus, Kimmerle *photographer, consultant*
Bodanszky, Miklos *chemist, educator*
Bodden, Jane Ellen *retired airline reservations manager*
Boddie, Lewis Franklin *retired medical educator*
Bodensieck, Ernest Justus *mechanical engineer*
Bodey, Richard Allen *minister, educator*
Bodger, Carole *writer*
Bodine, Larry *marketing consultant*
Bodner, Bruce Ira *ophthalmologist*
Bodsworth, Fred *author, naturalist*
Boe, David Stephen *musician, educator, dean*
Boedo, Stephen *mechanical engineer, consultant*
Boesch, Diane Harriet *retired elementary education educator*
Boese, H. Lamar *surgeon*
Boesel, Milton Charles, Jr., *lawyer, business executive*
Boeshe, Barbara Louise *real estate executive*
Bogart, Carol Lynn *columnist, journalist, writer*
Bogdanowicz, Loretta Mae *artist, educator*
Bogdon, Glendon Joseph *retired orthodontist*
Boggs, Charles Harmon, Jr., *retired surgeon*
Boggs, Robert Wayne *human services administrator, consultant*
Bohannan, Paul James *anthropologist, writer, former university administrator*
†Bohland, Eugene R., Jr., *music educator*
Bohle, Robert Heyn *journalism educator*
Bohn, Marsha J. *anthropologist, researcher*
Boho, Dan L. *lawyer*
Boise, Audrey Lorraine *retired special education educator*
†Boitano, Brian *Olympic athlete*
Bok, Sissela *philosopher, writer*
Boldosser, Randy Richard *communications company executive*
Boldt, Patricia C. *social worker*
Bolek, Catherine *university research director*
Bolen, David Benjamin *ambassador, former corporation executive*
Boles, John *professional baseball coach, manager*
Boling, Eldon Avery *physician*
Bollenbacher, Herbert Kenneth *steel company official*
Bolliger, Eugene Frederick *former surgeon*
Bolsterli, Margaret Jones *English educator, farmer*
Bolstridge, Alice M. *writer, educator*
Bolt, Dawn Maria *financial coach*
Bolton, Julia Gooden *human services administrator*
†Bolton, Marie *elementary school educator, minister*
†Bombaci, Nancy Margaret *literature educator*
Bomer, Elton *former state official*
Bonanni, Victoria *writer, small business owner*
Bonassi, Jodi *artist, marketing consultant*
†Bonato, Paolo *electrical engineer, educator*
Bond, Julian *civil rights leader*
†Bond, Meredith *medical educator*
Bond, Victoria Ellen *conductor, composer*
Bondar, Richard Jay Laurent *biochemist*
Bonfils, Darcy Reyne *television producer*
Bonham, John Dwight *retired lawyer*
Bonham-Yeaman, Doria *retired law educator*
Boni, Miki *artist*
Bonn, Ethel May *psychiatrist, educator*
Bonnard, Raymond *theater director*
†Bonnell, Victoria Eileen *sociologist, educator*
Bonner, John Tyler *biology educator*
Bonner, Thomas, Jr., *English language educator*
Bonomo, Joseph Ralph *naval officer*
†Bonura, Jacqueline *special education educator*
Boobyer, Don J. *computer operator, bookkeeper*
Booher, Alice Ann *lawyer*
†Book, Kevin *information technology executive, consultant*
Booker, Nana Laurel *art gallery owner, consul*
Boone, Earle Marion *business executive*
Boone, Harold Thomas *retired lawyer*
Boone, Richard Winston, Sr., *lawyer*
Boone, Robert Raymond *former professional baseball coach*
Boone, Stephen Christopher *retired neurosurgeon*
†Booth, Robert Ward *lawyer*
Booty, Michael Richard *mathematician educator*
Boppe, Charles William *aeronautical engineering educator*
Borchardt, Donald Arthur *visual and performing arts educator*
†Borchert, Carol Ann *school librarian*
Borda, Richard Joseph *retired insurance company executive*
Bordner, Marjorie Rich *educator, civic worker*
Bordy, Bill (William James Bordy) *publisher*
Boren, Roger W. *judge*
Borenstein, Milton Conrad *lawyer, manufacturing company executive*
Borenstein, Nathaniel Solomon *computer programmer, inventor, educator*
Borg, Ruth I. *home nursing care provider*
Borges, William, III, *management consultant*
Borgstahl, Kaylene Denise *health facility administrator*
†Borish, Irvin Max
Bork, Robert Heron *lawyer, author, educator, former federal judge*
Born, Ethel Wolfe *religious writer*
Bornhorst, Kenneth Frank *electromagnetics and systems engineer*
Borntrager, John Sherwood *principal*
Borowitz, Albert Ira *lawyer, author*
Borrowdale-Cox, Deborah Elizabeth *museum curator*
Borst, Philip West *academic administrator*
Borum, Rodney Lee *financial business executive*
Bos, John Arthur *retired aircraft manufacturing executive*
†Bosco, Anthony Gerard *bishop*
†Bosco, Frederick J. *language and linguistics educator*
Bosco, Philip Michael *actor*
Bose, Anjan *electrical engineering educator, academic administrator*
Bosgraaf, Peter John *music educator*
Bosmajian, Haig Aram *speech communication educator*
Bosse, Margaret Fisher Ishler *education educator*
†Bossio, Salvatore *lawyer*
Bost, Raymond Morris *retired college president*
Bost, Thomas Glen *lawyer, educator*

GEOGRAPHICAL INDEX 6129 ADDRESS UNPUBLISHED

Bostain, Nancy S. *psychologist, educator*
Bostic, Jeff Q. *child psychiatrist*
Boston, Bruce Ormand *writer, editor, publications consultant*
†Bostrom, Robert Everett *lawyer*
Boswell, Tommie C. *retired middle school educator*
†Boswell, Wendy R. *finance educator, researcher*
Botelho, Bruce Manuel *former state attorney general, mayor*
Bothwell, John Charles *retired archbishop*
Botkin, Monty Lane *computer company executive*
Botway, Lloyd Frederick *computer scientist, consultant*
Boudreaux, John *public relations/internet specialist*
Boundy, David Eric *patent lawyer, computer engineer*
Bourguignon, Erika Eichhorn *anthropologist, educator*
†Boutelle, Steven W. *army officer*
Bouvier, Marshall Andre *lawyer*
Bova, Benjamin William *author, editor, educator*
Bovey, Terry Robinson *insurance executive*
†Bowe, Riddick Lamont *professional boxer*
Bowen, Janice *musician, music educator*
Bowen, Jean *retired librarian, consultant*
Bowen-Forbes, Jorge Courtney *artist, author, poet*
Bower, Janet Esther *writer, educator*
Bower, Jean Ramsay *lawyer, writer*
†Bower, Laurel Lee *education educator, researcher*
Bower, Shelley Ann *business management consultant*
†Bowers, Larry Donald *chemistry and pathology educator*
Bowers, Patricia Newsome *communications executive*
Bowes, Frederick, III, *publishing executive, consultant*
Bowes, Henry Edward *retired communications executive*
Bowlby, Richard Eric *retired computer systems analyst*
Bowles, Barbara Landers *investment company executive*
Bowles, L. Thompson *retired medical association administrator*
Bowlin, Michael Ray *retired oil company executive*
†Bowling, Kelly K *management consultant*
Bowman, Charles Hay *retired engineering educator, petroleum company executive*
Bowman, Fay Louise *artist*
Bowman, Larry Wayne *investigator, English and criminal justice educator*
Bowne, Shirlee Pearson *finance and housing consultant*
Boxer, Alan Lee *accountant*
Boyarsky, Terry Linda *music educator*
Boyatt, Thomas David *former ambassador*
Boyce, David Edward *transportation and regional science educator*
Boyce, Joseph Nelson *retired journalist, consultant, educator*
Boyd, Danny Douglass *financial counselor*
Boyd, Julianne Mamana *theater director, educator*
Boyd, Kenneth R. *application and web programmer, mathematician*
Boyd, Robert Carr, Jr., *fire fighter, paramedic, graduate student*
Boyd, Thomas Marshall *lawyer*
Boyd, William Harland *historian, writer*
Boyd-Brown, Lena Ernestine *history educator, education consultant*
Boyenga, Cindy A. *secondary education educator*
Boyer, Dale Kenneth *English educator*
Boyer, Herbert Wayne *retired biochemist*
Boyer, Robert Allan *business executive*
Boyes, Stephen Richard *hydrogeologic consultant*
†Boyette, Lisa Wynn *retired research scientist*
Boykin, Robert Heath *banker*
Boyle, Bryan Douglas *computer and network systems architect*
Boyle, Marylou Olsen *nursing administrator*
†Boyle, R. Emmett *metal products executive*
Boyle, Richard James *banker*
†Boyle, Tatiana Gennadievna *research scientist*
Boyles, James Kenneth *retired banker*
†Boysen, Thomas Cyril *educational association administrator*
Boyson, William Albert *retired obstetrician, gynecologist*
Brabec, Rosemary Jean *retail executive*
Brabon, David Lawrence *plastic reconstructive surgeon*
Bracco, Lorraine *actress*
Bracey, Earnest Norton *political science educator*
Brach, Paul Henry *artist*
Bracken, Peg *writer*
Brackett, Colquitt Prater, Jr., *judge, lawyer*
Bradbeer, Clive *biochemistry and microbiology educator, research scientist*
Braddock, Walter David, III, *economist*
Braden, Charles Hosea *physicist, university administrator*
Braden, Thomas Wardell *news commentator*
Bradford, Barbara Reed *lawyer*
Bradford, David Paul *psychotherapist*
Bradford, Matthew Silas *music educator*
Bradford, Peter Corey *design consultant*
Bradford, Susan Anne *broadcast journalist, writer*
Bradley, Amelia Jane *lawyer*
†Bradley, Bill *former senator*
Bradley, William Bryan *cable television regulator*
Bradshaw, John Robert Covington, III, *internet service company executive*
Bradshaw, Peter *engineering educator*
Brady, Jean Stein *retired librarian*
Brady, Sally Ryder *writer, literary agent*
Brady-Borland, Karen *retired reporter, columnist*
Brafford, William Charles *lawyer*
Bragdon, Paul Errol *educator*
Bragiel, Sue A. *social work educator, clinical practitioner*
Bragonier, John Robert *obstetrician-gynecologist*
Brain, George Bernard *university dean*
Brainard, Melissa *accountant*
Braley, Russell Norton *retired journalist, author*
Bram, Leon Leonard *publishing company executive*
Brame, Marillyn A. *hypnotherapist*
†Bramucci, Raymond L. *employment and training executive*
Branagan, James Joseph *lawyer*
Branagh, Kenneth *actor, director*
Branca, Frank Joseph *realtor, retired police officer*
Brancato, Leo John *manufacturing company executive*
Brandinger, Jay Jerome *electronics executive*
Brandl, John Edward *public affairs educator*
Brandt, Mitzi Marianne *retired educational specialist*
Brandt, Robert Frederic, III, *retired newspaper editor, journalist*
Brandt, Ronald Stirling *retired editor, researcher*
Brannick, Ellen Marie *retired management consultant*
†Brannman, Ward Scott *elementary school educator*
Bransdorfer, Stephen Christie *lawyer*
Branson, Harley Kenneth *finance executive*
†Branstetter, Cecil Dewey, Sr., *lawyer*
Brantz, George Murray *retired lawyer*
Branyan, W. David *novelist, real estate broker*
Brar, Berinder Pal Singh *engineer*
Brar, Gurdarshan Singh *soil scientist, researcher*
Brashear, William Ronald *lawyer, writer*
Brashears, Sumner *funeral director*
Bratt, Nicholas *investment management and research company executive*
Bratton, William Edward *electronics executive, management consultant*
Bratzler, Mary Kathryn *desktop publisher*
Braude, Robert Michael *retired medical library administrator*
Braudy, Dorothy McGahee *artist, educator*
†Brauer, Donna Jeanne *nursing educator, researcher*
Brauer, Rhonda Lyn *lawyer*
Brault, G. Lorain *healthcare executive*
†Braun, Artur *physicist*
†Braun, Daniel *physicist, researcher*
Braun, Jerome Irwin *lawyer*
Braun, Mary Lucile Dekle (Lucy Braun) *therapist, consultant, counselor, educator*
Braungard III, Charles W. *music educator*
Brautigan, Mark W. *emergency physician*
Brawer, Catherine Coleman *foundation executive, curator*
Brawner, Lee Basil *retired librarian, consultant*
Brawner, Nancy Jayne *social worker, psychotherapist*
Brawner, Sharon Lee *bilingual education educator, researcher*
Brazier, Don Roland *retired railroad executive*
Brdlik, Carola Emilie *retired accountant*
Breakiron, Lee Allen *astronomer*
Brearey, Susan Winfield *artist, art educator*
Breathed, Berkeley *cartoonist*
†Brechbill, Susan Reynolds *lawyer, educator*
Brecht, Sally Ann *quality assurance executive*
Bredehoft, Michael Roger *lawyer, mediator*
Bredfeldt, John Creighton *economist, financial analyst, retired air force officer*
Breed, Henry Eltinge, III, *diplomat, educator*
Breen, Janice DeYoung *health services executive, community health nurse*
Brehl, James William *lawyer*
Breitling, Julius *financial executive*
Bremner, John McColl *agronomy and biochemistry educator*
Brendsel, Leland C. *former mortgage company executive*
Brennan, Ciaran Brendan *accountant, oil industry executive*
Brennan, Donna Lesley *public relations company executive*
Brennan, Elizabeth Lane *educator, program director*
Brennan, Lawrence Edward *electronics engineer*
†Brennan, Sara Jean *retired artist*
Brennen, Stephen Alfred *international business consultant*
Brent, Rebecca Kemp *volunteer, calligrapher and textile artist*
Brent, Robert Leonard *radiology and pediatrics educator*
Brenton, Hatice *painter, graphics designer*
Breslin, Evalynne Louise Wood-Robertson *retired psychiatric nurse*
†Bresse-Rodenkirk, Robert Francis *journalist*
†Brester, Gary W. *educator*
Brettell, Richard Robson *art historian, museum consultant, educator*
Bretthauer, Erich Walter *chemist, educator*
†Brevetti, Lucy S *surgeon*
Brewer, Carey *retired academic administrator*
Brewer, Edward Cage, III, *law educator*
Brewer, Timothy Francis, III, *retired cardiologist*
Brewster, Elizabeth Winifred *English language educator, poet, novelist*
Breza, Kevin S. *wellness consultant, writer*
Brickell, Charles Hennessey, Jr., *marine engineer, retired military officer*
†Bridenbaugh, Peter Reese *industrial research executive*
Bridger, Baldwin, Jr., *electrical engineer*
Bridges, Eileen *marketing educator*
Bridges, Leonard Hal *retired history educator, writer*
Bridges, William Lloyd *radiologist*
Brigeois, Evelyne Brigitte *artist, publisher*
Briggle, Gary Lee *singer, actor, director, educator*
Briggs, James Henry, II, *engineering administrator*
Briggs, Janet Marie Louise *nurse practitioner*
Briggs, Philip *insurance company executive*
Briggs, Philip James *political science educator, author, lecturer, reviewer*
†Brigham, Henry Day, Jr., *retired lawyer*
†Brigham, Judith X. *philosophy educator*
Brightbill, David John *state legislator, lawyer*
Brill, Winston Jonas *microbiologist, educator, research director, publisher and management consultant*
Brim, Orville Gilbert, Jr., *former foundation administrator, author*
Brinberg, Herbert Raphael *publishing company executive, information management*
Brink, Richard Edward *lawyer*
Brint, Steven Gregory *sociologist, educator*
Briscoe, Clarence Conway *retired obstetrician-gynecologist*
Briscoe, Marianne Grier *development professional, educator*
Bristol, Carol *retired librarian*
Bristol, Louise Fitzgerald *educator, retired nurse*
Bristow, William Harvey, Jr., *psychiatrist*
Britt, John Roy *banker*
Britt, Rebecca Fae *communications executive*
Broadrick-Allen, Sandra Carol *retired city manager, consultant, civic worker*
Broadwater, James E. *publisher*
Broberg, Merle *retired social worker*
Brock, Eric John *urban planner, historian, consultant*
Brock, John Morgan (Juno), Jr., *composer, performer, producer*
Brock, Mary Anne *research investigator, consultant*
Broderson, Thelma Sylvia *marketing professional*
Brodhead, David Crawmer *lawyer*
Brodie, Alice Velma *health and ethics advocate*
Brodie, Theodore Hamilton *construction company executive*
Brodsky, Robert Jay *wholesale executive*
†Brody, Adrien *actor*
Brody, Jacob Jerome *art history educator*
Brody, Martin *food service company executive*
Broek, Howard Windolph *real estate executive*
Brohammer, Richard Frederic *psychiatrist*
†Bronfman, Edgar Miles, Jr., *diversified business executive, producer*
Bronkar, Eunice Dunalee *artist, art educator*
Bronner, James Russell *retired lawyer*
†Bronson, Carol E. *administrative health facility coordinator*
†Bronson, Robert Lee *engineering company inventor, retired*
†Bronzi, Philip A. *social worker, educator*
Brooke, Francis John, III, *foundation administrator*
Brooke, Ralph Ian *dental educator*
Brooker, Robert Elton, Jr., *retired manufacturing company executive*
Brookner, Anita *writer, educator*
Brooks, Andrée Aelion *journalist, educator, author*
Brooks, Babert Vincent *publisher*
†Brooks, (Troyal) Garth *country music singer*
†Brooks, Gilbert Gil *association development director*
Brooks, Kenneth N. *forestry educator*
Brooks, Lorraine Elizabeth *retired music educator*
Brooks, Mark Hunter *information technology project administrator*
Brooks, Michael Paul *urban planning educator*
Brooks Shoemaker, Virginia Lee *librarian*
†Brooks-Turner, Myra *music educator*
Broome, Burton Edward *former insurance company executive*
Broome, Oscar Whitfield, Jr., *accounting educator, administrator*
†Brosda von Kupferber, Baron Alexander Christian *investment banker*
Brosnan, Peter Lawrence *documentary filmmaker*
Brosz, Margaret Headley *pediatrics nurse*
†Broten, Robert Gary *optician, writer*
Brotman, David Joel *retired architectural firm executive, consultant*
Broude, Ronald *music publisher*
Broughton, Phillip Charles *lawyer, director*
Brouse, Virginia May (Ginny Brouse) *retired rehabilitation nurse*
†Broussard, Angela G. (Milicent Maxwell) *writer, poet, playwright*
Browder, Felix Earl *mathematician, educator*
Brown, Alice Elste *artist*
Brown, Alton Raymond *mathematician, researcher*
Brown, Anne Rhoda Wiesen *civic worker*
†Brown, April Schlea *pharmacist*
Brown, Barbara June *hospital and nursing administrator*
Brown, Barbara S. *environmental scientist*
Brown, Beulah Louise *retired elementary educator*
Brown, Billye Jean *retired nursing educator*
Brown, Britt *retired publishing company executive*
Brown, Bruce Maitland *philanthropy consultant*
Brown, Carol *artist*
Brown, Charles Dodgson *lawyer*
Brown, Crystal Jeanine *writer*
Brown, David Richard *school system administrator, minister*
Brown, Deborah A. *social worker, therapist*
Brown, Denise *poet*
†Brown, Diana L. *elementary education educator*
Brown, Donald Douglas *transportation company executive, retired air force officer, consultant*
Brown, Donald McCarty *economic development specialist*
Brown, Donald Richard *capacitor engineer*
Brown, Eli Matthew *anesthesiologist, department chairman*
Brown, Elizabeth Eleanor *retired librarian*
Brown, Geraldine *nurse, freelance writer*
Brown, Henry Bedinger Rust *financial management company executive*
Brown, J. E. (Buster Brown) *lawyer, consultant*
Brown, James Gaston *retired obstetrician, gynecologist*
†Brown, James Justin *artist*
Brown, James Nelson, Jr., *retired accountant*
†Brown, Jeannette Elizabeth *retired science educator*
†Brown, Jennifer N. *humanities educator*
Brown, Jerry Milford *medical company executive*
†Brown, Joseph W., Jr., (Jay Brown) *insurance company executive*
†Brown, Julie Katharine *social historian, photographic historian*
Brown, June Gibbs *retired government official*
Brown, Les (Lester Louis) *journalist*
Brown, Lillie McFall *elementary school principal*
Brown, Lynda Nell *nursing educator*
Brown, Marcia Joan *author, artist, photographer*
Brown, Michael *information technology executive*
Brown, Michael John *retired judge*
Brown, Michael Robert *finance specialist*
Brown, Peter Ogden *lawyer*
Brown, Rhonda Rochelle *chemist, health facility administrator, lawyer*
Brown, Richard Harris *information technology executive*
Brown, Robert Charles *retired radiologist*
Brown, Robert E. *retired transportation executive*
Brown, Robert Laidlaw *state supreme court justice*
Brown, Ronald Delano *scriptwriter, playwright, actor*
Brown, Ronald Miles *retired academic administrator*
Brown, Samuel *retired corporate executive*
Brown, Stephen Hayze, Jr., *human services caseworker*
Brown, Steven Bernard *counselor*
Brown, Suzanne Wiley *museum director*
Brown, Sylvia *public relations executive, advertising executive*
Brown, Timothy William *writer*
Brown, W. Michael *publishing company executive*
Brown-Banks, Jennifer Elaine *writer, public relations administrator*
Browne, Ann April *purchasing manager*
Browne, Diana Gayle *artist, social services*
†Browne, Frederick Douglas *physiologist, educator*
Browne, (Edmund) John Phillip *oil company executive*
Browne, Thomas Reed *neurologist, researcher, educator*
Browning, Colin Arrott *retired banker*
Browning, Vivian Berniece *land developer*
†Brownlee, June McGaugh *health facility administrator*
Brownlee, Paula Pimlott *higher education consultant, former academic administrator*
Brownrigg, Walter Grant *cartoonist, corporate executive*
Brownsberger, Mary Grace *social services administrator, consultant*
†Brown-Waite, Virginia (Ginny Brown-Waite) *congresswoman*
†Brown-Zekeri, Lolita Molanda *elementary school educator*
Brozowski, Laura Adrienne *mechanical engineer*
Brubaker, Crawford Francis, Jr., *federal agency official, aerospace consultant*
Brubaker, James Edward *mechanical engineer*
Bruce, David Lionel *retired anesthesiologist, educator*
Bruce, Debra *poet, English language educator*
†Bruce, Dickson Davies, Jr., *history educator*
Bruce, James Edmund *retired utility company executive*
†Bruce, Tammy *writer, columnist*
†Bruch, Virginia Irene Sullivan *librarian, writer*
Brugger, David John *media consultant*
Brumbaugh, John Moore *lawyer*
Brundtland, Gro Harlem *international organization executive*
Brune, Eva *fundraiser*
Brungraber, Robert J. *civil engineer, educator*
†Brunner, Kathleen Marie *humanities educator*
Bruno, Barbara Altman *social worker*
Brunson, Burlie Allen *aerospace transportation executive*
Brunt, Harry Herman, Jr., *psychiatrist*
†Brustman, Richard D. *civil engineer, consultant*
Bryan, Lawrence Dow *college president*
Bryant, Bertha Estelle *retired nurse*
Bryant, Donald Ashley *molecular biologist*
Bryant, Edward *former congressman, lawyer*
Bryant, Janice Ann *special education department administrator*
Bryant, John *author, publisher*
Bryant, Paul Thompson *English language educator*
†Bryant, Veronica Maria *hospital administrator, writer*
†Bryant, Winston *former state attorney general*
†Buccella, William Victor *lawyer*
Buccheri, Elizabeth C. *musician, educator*
Bucciero, Joseph Mario, Jr., *executive consultant*
†Buchanan, John Lynn *retired broadcast executive*
Buchanan, Scott Eugene *political science educator*
Buchanan, William H., Jr., *retired lawyer, venture capitalist*
Buchbinder, Darrell Bruce *lawyer*
Buchbinder, Sharon Bell *health care management educator*
Buchin, Jean *psychologist, educator*
Buchmann, Alan Paul *lawyer*
Buck, Earl Wayne *insurance investigator, motel owner*
†Buck, James E. *financial exchange executive*
Buck, Jane Louise *psychology educator*
Buck, John E. *sculptor, print maker, educator*

Buck, Linda Dee *executive recruiting company executive*
Buck, Robert Treat, Jr., *gallery director, former museum director, educator*
Buck, William Joseph *theatrical designer, educator*
Buckalew, Martha Harter *music educator, musician*
Buckels, Marvin Wayne *savings and loan executive*
Buckholtz, Thomas Joel *computer and telecommunications executive*
Buckler, Marilyn Lebow *school psychologist, educational consultant*
†Buckley, Edward T., Jr., *career officer*
Buckley, James Lane *retired judge*
Buckley, Michael J. *theology educator*
Buckner, Sally Beaver *English educator, writer*
Bucknum, Michael John *research scientist, crystallographer, educator*
Buckstein, Caryl Sue *writer*
Buckwalter, Roger Jerome *editor, columnist, TV interviewer*
Bucove, Arnold David *psychiatrist*
Budnick, Lawrence David *physician, medical educator*
Budoff, Penny Wise *retired physician, author, researcher*
Budzinski, James Edward *interior designer*
Buechel, William Benjamin *lawyer*
†Buehler, John Wilson *lawyer*
†Buell, Dexter *artist, sculptor*
†Bueno, Pablo Cesar *aeronautical engineer, educator*
Buffkins, Archie Lee *television executive*
Bugbee, Joan Barthelme *retired corporate communications executive*
Bugno, Walter Thomas *civil engineer*
Buhagiar, Marion *editor, author*
†Buhl, Cynthia Maureen *foreign policy educator and advocate*
Buker, Robert Hutchinson, Sr., *army officer, thoracic surgeon*
Bula, Raymond J. *agronomist*
†Bulan, Liana *dentist*
Bull, Bergen Ira *retired equipment manufacturing company executive*
Bulla, Clyde Robert *writer*
†Bullard, Judith Eve *psychologist, systems engineer*
Bullard, Sharon Welch *librarian*
Bullock, Molly *retired elementary school educator*
Bullock, Sandra *actress*
Bullock, Theodore Holmes *biologist, educator*
Bullough, Vern LeRoy *sexologist, historian, nursing educator, researcher*
Bulow, Jack Faye *retired library director*
Bumbery, Joseph Lawrence *diversified telecommunications company executive*
Bumgarner, Marlene Anne *writer, editor, educator*
Bunch, Franklin Swope *retired architect*
Bunch, Jennings Bryan, Jr., *electrical engineer*
Bundi, Renee *art director, graphic designer*
Bundy, Cheryl LaSota *non-profit executive, consultant*
Bundy, Mary Lothrop *retired clinical social worker*
Bunim, Mary-Ellis *television producer*
Bunker, Robert Joseph *national security consultant, educator*
Bunyan, Ellen Lackey Spotz *retired chemist*
Burakoff, Steven James *immunologist, educator*
Buras-Elsen, Brenda Allynn *retired public affairs executive*
Burbridge, Ann Arnold *music educator, choir director*
Burch, Hamlin Doughty, III, *retired sheet metal professional*
Burchard, John Kenneth *retired chemical engineer*
†Burchett, Michael Henry *education educator*
Burchman, Leonard *government official*
Burch-Martinez, Berkeley Alison *primary education educator*
Burden, Ordway Partridge *investment banker*
Burdett, James Richard *treasurer*
Burgdoerfer, Jerry J. *marketing and distribution executive*
Burge, John Wesley, Jr., *management consultant, consultant*
†Burger, David Mark *composer, educator, multimedia designer*
Burgess, Hayden Fern (Poka Laenni) *lawyer*
Burgess, Marjorie Laura *retired protective services official*
Burgess, Michael H. *management consultant*
Burhans, Frank Malcolm *mechanical engineer*
Burke, Grace Dora Reynolds *medical/surgical nurse*
Burke, Joseph C. *former university official*
Burkes, Lionel Seaton *science educator, writer, researcher*
†Burket, John McVey *retired dermatologist*
Burkett, Rosemary L. *artist*
Burkey, Lee Melville *lawyer*
Burki, Fred Albert *labor union official*
Burks, Brenda Rounsaville *retired music educator, city council*
Burnett, Howard Jerome *academic administrator emeritus*
Burnham, J. V. *retired sales executive*
Burnley, Kenneth Stephen *school system administrator*
Burns, Barbara Belton *investment company executive*
Burns, Bebe Lyn *journalist*
Burns, Brenda Carolyn *retired special education administrator, chemical dependence counselor*
Burns, Carol J. *architect, educator*
Burns, Denver P. *forestry research administrator*
Burns, Donald Snow *registered investment advisor, financial and business consultant*
Burns, James Milton *retired educator*
Burns, Joseph M. *economist*
Burns, Kevin Michael *editor*
Burns, Kitty *playwright*
Burns, Leslie Kaye *artist*
Burns, Marie T. *retired secondary education educator*
Burns, Richard Francis *mechanical engineer*
Burns, Robert Edgar *retired protective services official, writer*
Burnside, Orvin Charles *agronomy educator, researcher*
Burrill, Kathleen R. F. (Kathleen R. F. Griffin-Burrill) *Turkologist, educator*
Burris, Lauren Bayleran *business owner*
Burroughs, Pamela Gayle *information systems specialist*
Burrows, Edwin Gladding *retired broadcaster, writer, poet*
†Burrows, Maile Leilani *court clerk*
†Bursley-Hamilton, Susan *secondary school educator*
Burton, Al *producer, director, writer*
†Burton, Jeff *race car driver*
Burton, Lavon D. *education educator*
Burton, Raymond Charles, Jr., *retired transportation company executive*
Burton, Robert Gene *printing and publishing executive*
Burton, Sigrid *artist*
Busch, Frederick Matthew *writer, literature educator*
Busch, Joyce Ida *small business owner*
Busch, Kyle *counseling administrator*
Busch, Nancy Elizabeth *artist, educator*
Bush, Barbara Pierce *former First Lady of the United States, volunteer*
Bush, George Walker *43d President of the United States*
†Bush, Janice *principal*
Bush, Marilyn Wolin *management consultant, software engineer*
Bush, Richard Clarence, III, *think-tank associate*
Bush, Sandi Tokoa *elementary school educator*
Bush, Sarah Lillian *historian*
Bush, Yvonne *writer, counselor*
Bushnell, Prudence *diplomat, management consultant*
Bushwick, Nathaniel Lewis *translator, researcher*
Bussard, Carmen Adelaide *speech professional*
Busse, Leonard Wayne *banker, financial consultant*
Butcher, Harry William *educational administrator, educator, historian*
Butler, Jack Fairchild *semiconductors company executive*
Butler, James Robertson, Jr., *lawyer*
Butler, Orton Carmichael *earth science educator, climatologist*
Butler, Robert Thomas *retired advertising executive*
†Butler, Sheryl L. *systems engineer, consultant*
Butrimovitz, Gerald Paul *financial planner, securities analyst, investment advisor*
Butterfield, Alexander Porter *former business executive, government official*
Butterfield, Bruce Scott *publishing, communications and education executive, consultant*
Butterfield, Deborah Kay *sculptor*
Butterfield, G. K., Jr., *former state supreme court justice*
Buttrey, Donald Wayne *lawyer*
Butts, Carol Henderson *human resources specialist, consultant*
Buttz, Gabriela I *chemical engineer, artist*
Buzard, James Albert *healthcare management consultant*
Buzash, Michael D. *Romance languages educator*
Buzzelli, James Raymond *pharmaceutical company executive*
Byers, Frank Matthew *surgeon*
Byers, Steven John *health facility administrator*
†Byford, Emma *rancher*
Byington, Diane B. *social work educator*
Bynes, Frank Howard, Jr., *physician*
Bynum, Richard Cary *author, former publisher*
†Byrd, Jeffery *performance artist*
†Byrd, Joan Eda *film librarian*
Byrd, Lloyd Garland *civil engineer*
†Byrd, Lorenda Sue *nursing administrator*
Byrd, Marc Robert *designer, florist*
Byrne, Carol Cunkle *medical/surgical nurse*
Byrne, John Joseph *surgeon*
Byrne, Judy Susanne *writer, educator*
Byrne-Dempsey, Cecelia (Cecelia Dempsey) *journalist*
Cabanas, Elizabeth Ann *nutritionist, educator*
Cabell, Ben B. *retired pediatrician, naval officer*
Cabot, Hugh, III, *painter, sculptor*
Cabrera, Joao B.D. *information scientist*
Cacciatore, Ronald Keith *lawyer*
Cacciavillan, Agostino *cardinal*
Cáceres, Franklin Thomas *writer*
Cachia, Pierre Jacques *Middle East languages and culture educator, researcher*
Caffey, James Enoch *civil engineer*
Cahill, Charles L. *retired university administrator, chemistry educator*
Cai, Ting *biomedical scientist*
Caine, Raymond William, Jr., *retired public relations executive*
Cairns, Diane Patricia *motion picture executive*
Calabrese, Karen Ann *artist, educator*
Calalang, Sesinando Sebastian *retired obstetrician-gynecologist*
Calamar, Gloria *artist*
†Calcaterra, Edward Lee *construction company executive*
Calder, Iain Wilson *publishing company executive*
Calder, Robert Mac *aerospace engineer*
†Caldwell, Cicely *human resources specialist, consultant*
Caldwell, Elwood Fleming *food scientist, educator*
Caldwell, Judy Carol *advertising executive, public relations executive, consultant, writer, designer*
Caldwell, Louise Phinney *historical researcher, community volunteer*
Caldwell, William Edward *educational administration educator, arbitrator*
Caldwell-Smith, Gaetana Lee *writer*
†Caletti, Deb L. *writer*
†Calhoun (Gayle), Linda Margaret *music educator*
†Califano, Joseph Anthony, Jr., *lawyer, public health policy educator, writer*
Callahan, Daniel Joseph *surgeon, consultant*
Callahan, Sonny (H.L. Callahan) *former congressman*
Callahan, Thomas Jay *petroleum engineer, geologist, consultant*
†Callan, Jamie *writer, educator*
Callan, Richard John *elementary school educator*
Callanan, Kathleen Joan *retired electrical engineer*
Callander, Bruce Douglas *journalist, freelance writer*
Callard, Carole Crawford *librarian, educator*
Callard, David Jacobus *investment company executive*
†Callaway, Julienne Morriss *financial consultant*
Callow, Keith McLean *judge*
Callow, William Grant *retired judge*
Calmenson, Marvin *retired surgeon*
Calore, Paul *retired writer*
Calsbeek, Franklin *health promotion educator*
Caltrider, Paul Gene *pharmaceutical company executive, microbiologist*
Calvano-Smith, Rita *journalist, small business owner*
Calvert, Jack George *atmospheric chemist, educator*
Calvert, James Francis *manufacturing company executive, retired admiral*
†Calvert, Laura Cristina *private school educator*
†Calvert, Peter Deane *neuroscientist, medical educator*
Calvert, William Preston *radiologist*
†Camacho, Hector *boxer*
†Cambon, Elise Murray *music educator, musician*
Cambrice, Robert Louis *lawyer*
Cameron, Daniel Forrest *communications executive*
Cameron, J. Elliot *retired parochial educational system administrator*
Cameron, Kirk MacGregor Drummond *statistician*
Cameron, Lucille Wilson *retired dean of libraries*
Cameron, Mary Emily *pediatrics nurse, nursing researcher*
Cameron, Roy Eugene *scientist*
†Caminiti, Kenneth Gene *professional baseball player*
Cammack, Ann *librarian, secondary school educator*
Camp, Alethea Taylor *executive and organizational design consultant*
Camp, Clifton Durrett, Jr., *rancher, retired publishing executive*
Campagna, Richard Samuel *investment management executive*
Campbell, Addison James, Jr., *writer*
Campbell, Andrea S. *writer*
Campbell, Andrew William *immunotoxicology physician*
Campbell, Arthur Andrews *retired government official*
Campbell, Brian Scott *army officer*
Campbell, Byron Chesser *publishing company executive*
Campbell, Claire Patricia *nurse practitioner, educator*
Campbell, Demarest Lindsay *artist, interior designer, writer*
Campbell, Douglas *physician*
Campbell, Edward Clinton *small business owner, violin maker*
Campbell, Edward Wallace *nutritionist*
Campbell, Edwin Denton *consultant*
Campbell, Frederick Hollister *retired lawyer, historian*
Campbell, Henry Cummings *librarian*
†Campbell, James L. *military career officer*
Campbell, John M. *judge*
Campbell, John William *prosecutor*
Campbell, Josephine Anne Conrad *news service executive*
Campbell, Patton *stage designer, educator*
Campbell, Richard Alden *electronics company executive*
†Campbell, Russell Bruce *mathematics educator*
Campbell, Sarah *elementary education educator, special education specialist*
†Campbell, Sharon Milligan *mathematician, educator*
†Campbell, Stanley Clinton *retired school system administrator, retired military officer*
Campbell, Todd J. *judge*
Campbell, Tom *former congressman, dean*
Campbell, Vincent Bernard *judge, lawyer*
Campbell, William *research analyst, educator, artist*
Campello, Florencio Lennox *artist*
Camper, John Saxton *public relations and marketing executive*
Campion, Thomas Francis *lawyer*
†Canady, Charles Terrence *lawyer, former congressman*
Canarina, Opal Jean *nurse, administrator, educator, consultant, lecturer*
Candlish, Malcolm *manufacturing company executive*
Cane, David E. *chemistry educator*
Canelli, Jeanne *early childhood educator*
Canfield, Constance Dale *retired accountant, retired medical/surgical nurse*
Cannell, Elizabeth Ann May *interior designer*
Cannell, Robert Quirk *former agricultural sciences educator*
Cantone, Vic *political cartoonist*
Cantor, Norman Frank *history educator, writer*
†Cantril, Albert H(adley) *public opinion analyst*
Cao, L. Charlie *structural engineer, consultant*
†Capanoli, Brian Mario *sales executive*
Capasso, Federico *physicist*
†Cape, Francis *artist*
Capell, Cydney Lynn *editor*
Capellas, Michael D. *telecommunications industry executive*
Capice, Philip Charles *television production executive*
Caplan, Susan Robin *artist, writer, educator*
†Caplice, Noel M. *cardiologist, researcher*
Capon, Edwin Gould *church organization administrator, clergyman*
Capone, Helen Diana *retired internist*
†Capozziello, Martha M. *medical/surgical nurse*
Cappello, Eve *speaker, trainer, author*
Capps, James Leigh, II, *lawyer, reserve military career officer*
Cappuccio, Richard *language educator*
†Caputo, Joseph Anthony *retired university president*
†Carasik, Michael *writer, researcher*
Carcaterra, Lorenzo Gabriel *writer*
†Cardella, John F. *radiologist*
Cardinali, Albert John *lawyer*
Cardman, Lawrence Santo *physics educator, research administrator*
Cardone, Bonnie Jean *freelance photojournalist*
†Cardwell, Kathleen R. *music educator, pianist*
Cardwell, Nancy Lee *editor, writer*
†Caretti, Richard Louis *lawyer*
Carey, Audrey Lane *interior designer, motivational speaker, educator*
†Carey, Drew *actor*
Carey, Edward John *insurance company executive*
Carey, Eleanor Mackey *lawyer, financial consultant*
Carey, John Jesse *academic administrator, religion educator*
†Carey, Ronald *former labor union leader*
†Carl, Susan Marie *photographer, photojournalist*
Carley, Michael John *organization official, playwright, actor*
Carlile, Christopher Blake *military officer, pilot*
Carlin, Betty *educator*
†Carlin, Phyllis Eva Scott *education educator*
Carlisle-Frank, Pamela L. *researcher and writer, consultant*
Carls, Alice Catherine *history educator*
Carlsen, Mary Baird *clinical psychologist*
Carlson, Charles Edward *sportswriter*
Carlson, Deanna Lynn *social worker*
Carlson, Donald Otto *magazine publisher, editor*
Carlson, Gary R. *publishing executive*
Carlson, Gustav Gunnar *anthropology educator*
Carlson, Janet Frances *psychologist, educator*
†Carlson, Julia Gage *poet, social worker*
Carlson, Robert Codner *industrial engineering educator*
†Carlson, Roger David *psychologist, clergyman, educator*
Carlton, Doug A. *standards engineer*
Carmack, Mildred Jean *retired lawyer*
Carmack, Sharon DeBartolo *genealogist, writer*
Carman, Susan Hufert *nurse coordinator*
Carmichael, Judy Lea *record industry executive, concert jazz pianist*
Carnahan, Jean *former senator*
Carner, Charles Robert, Jr., *screenwriter, director*
Carney, Kate *actor, director, educator, playwright, storyteller*
Carpenter, Derr Alvin *landscape architect*
Carpenter, Edward Kearney *writer, editor*
Carpenter, Myron Arthur *manufacturing company executive*
†Carpenter, Rosalie T. *education educator, consultant*
Carpenter-Mason, Beverly Nadine *quality assurance professional, medical/surgical nurse*
†Carpentieri, Sarah C. *neuropsychologist, researcher, clinical psychologist*
Carr, Bessie *retired middle school educator*
Carr, Elizabeth Davis-Jackson *municipal manager*
Carr, Harold Noflet *investment corporation executive*
Carr, Larry Dean *not-for-profit company executive*
Carr, Paul Wallace *actor*
†Carrasquel-Belandria, Jose Ramon *language educator*
†Carreau, Pierre *chemical engineering educator*
Carreker, John Russell *retired agricultural engineer*
Carrell, Heather Demaris *school system administrator*
Carrillo, Elisa Anna *history educator, consultant*
†Carrington, Arese U. *medical doctor, public health consultant*
Carrol, Nora *educational/communication company executive, artist*
†Carrol, Robert Kelton *lawyer*
Carroll, Brenda Sandidge *volunteer civic worker*
Carroll, Harvey Franklin *chemistry and nutrition educator*
Carroll, Joseph J(ohn) *lawyer*
Carroll, Marie-Jean Greve *retired educator, artist*
Carroll, Marshall Elliott *architect*
Carroll, Mary Patricia *writer*
†Carroll, Philip Joseph, Jr., *engineering company executive*
Carroll, Rosemary Frances *historian, educator, lawyer*
Carruthers, Claudelle Ann *occupational and physical therapist*
†Carson, Mary Silvano *career counselor, educator*
Carson, Regina E. *healthcare administrator, geriatric specialist, pharmacist, educator*
Carstairs, Sharon *state legislator*
Carswell, Jane Triplett *retired family physician*
Carten, Francis Noel *lawyer*
Carter, Cris *retired professional football player, sportscaster*
†Carter, Danita M. *writer, securities trader*

†Clements, Michael Taylor *academic administrator, educator*
Clemetson, Charles Alan Blake *physician*
Clemmons, Evelyn Yvonne *administrative assistant*
Clemons, Julie Payne *telephone company manager*
Clerici, Paul Camilio *writer-photographer*
Clewett, Raymond Winfred *mechanical design engineer*
Cliff, Karissa *consumer researcher, recruiter*
Clifford, Maurice Cecil *physician, former college president, foundation executive*
Clifton, Russell B. *banking and mortgage lending consultant, retired mortgage company executive*
Cline, Carolyn Joan *plastic and reconstructive surgeon*
Cline, Pauline M. *educational administrator*
†Cling, B. J. *lawyer, psychologist*
Clinger, William Floyd, Jr., *retired congressman*
Clogan, Paul Maurice *English language and literature educator*
Cloonan, Patrick Michael *radio producer, writer*
†Close, Thomas James *school administrator*
Closset, Gerard Paul *forest products consultant*
Cloud, Stanley Wills *journalist, editor, writer*
Clough, Lauren C. *retired special education educator*
Clouston, Ross Neal *retired food and related products company executive*
Clow, Timothy James *lawyer*
Clymer, Wayne Kenton *bishop*
Coate, David Edward *acoustician, consultant*
Coates, Karen Jeanne *journalist, educator*
Coates, Shirley Jean *finance educator, secondary school educator*
†Cobb, Edward Ray *actor*
Cobb, John Boswell, Jr., *clergyman, educator*
Cobb, John Cecil, Jr., (Jack Cobb) *communications specialist and executive*
Cobb, Miles Alan *retired lawyer*
Cobb, Ruth *artist*
Coble, Howard *congressman, lawyer*
Coburn, D(onald) L(ee) *playwright*
†Coburn, Steven D. *musicologist, educator, musician*
Cochetti, Roger James *international communications and internet company executive*
Cochran, Carolyn *library director*
Cochran, George Moffett *retired judge*
Cochran, John P. *economics educator*
Cochran, Thad *senator*
Cochrane, Shirley Graves *writer, educator*
Cochrane, Walter E. *academic administrator, music educator, conductor*
Cockerham, Lorris G. *radiation toxicologist*
Cockrum, William Monroe, III, *investment banker, consultant, educator*
Cody, Arlene J. Clark Brattain *interior designer*
Cody, Judith *composer, writer*
†Cody, Richard A. *army officer*
Coe, Rodney Michael *medical educator*
†Coen, John Joseph *physician, oncologist*
Coenson, Barbara *marketing and sales professional*
Cofer, Deborah End *artist*
Coffee, Joseph Denis, Jr., *retired college chancellor*
Coffey, Dennis James *performance technology consultant*
Coffey, John Louis *judge*
†Coffey, Mary Margaret *pharmacist*
Coffin, Bertha Louise *telephone company executive*
Cogan, John Dennis *artist*
Cogan, Karen Elizabeth *author, educator*
Cohen, Allan Richard *broadcasting executive*
Cohen, David John *cardiothoracic surgeon*
Cohen, Eliot Dorsey *electrical engineer*
Cohen, Gail Ehrlich *lawyer, banker*
Cohen, Jerome *psychology educator, electrophysiologist*
Cohen, Larry *film director, producer, screenwriter*
Cohen, Mark Herbert *broadcasting company executive*
Cohen, Norman Girard *retired social worker*
Cohen, Philip *retired hydrogeologist*
Cohen, Roberta Jane *government executive*
Cohen, Sandon Lee *lawyer*
Cohen, Sharleen Cooper *interior designer, writer*
Cohen, Stanley *biochemistry educator*
Cohen, Stanley Alvin *land use planner*
†Cohen, William Alan *marketing educator, author, consultant*
Cohn, Avern Levin *district judge*
Cohn, Marianne Winter Miller *civic activist*
Cohn, Robin Jean *crisis management executive, author*
Coin, Sheila Regan *organization and management development consultant*
Coke, Frank Van Deren *museum director, photographer*
†Colage, Beatrice Elvira *education educator*
Colaianni, Joseph Vincent *judge*
Colangelo, James Joseph *psychotherapist*
Colbert, Margaret Matthew *artist*
Colburn, Nancy Douglas *social worker, educator*
Cole, Clifford Adair *clergyman*
Cole, Jerome Foster *research company executive*
†Cole, Merrill Grant *language educator*
Cole, Nancy Stooksberry *educational research executive*
Cole, Reginald David *water treatment executive*
Coleman, Claire Kohn *public relations executive*
Coleman, Gary William *retired elementary school educator*
Coleman, Henry James, Jr., *management educator, consultant*
Coleman, Jean Black *nurse, physician assistant*
Coleman, Joseph Dale *architect*
Coleman, Mary Sue *academic administrator*
†Coleman, Nicholas Vass *microbiologist*
Coleman, Richard William *retired lawyer*
Coleman, Robert Lee *retired lawyer*
Coleman, Ronald Lee *insurance claims executive*
Coles, H. Brent *former mayor*
Colgate, Stephen *small business owner*
Colgate-Lindberg, Catharine Pamella *educator*
Colker, Edward *artist, educator*
Collette, Frances Madelyn *retired tax consultant, lawyer*
†Colley, Caren R. *language educator*
Collier, Herman Edward, Jr., *retired college president*
Colline, Marguerite Richnavsky *maternal, women's health and pediatrics nurse*
Collins, Allen Howard *psychiatrist*
Collins, Angelo *science educator, educator*
Collins, E. Dorlee (E. Dorlee Woodyard) *business counselor*
†Collins, Eileen Marie *astronaut*
†Collins, Frank, Jr., *dentist, educator*
Collins, Frank Charles, Jr., *industrial and service quality specialist*
Collins, George William, II, *astrophysics educator, writer*
Collins, Harker *economist, manufacturing executive, publisher, marketing, financial, business and legal consultant*
Collins, J. Michael *retired public broadcasting executive*
Collins, Joan Henrietta *actress*
†Collins, Joda Lee *minister*
Collins, Kathleen Anne *artistic director*
Collins, Melissa Ann *oncological nurse*
Collins, Paul Douglas (Doug Collins) *former professional basketball coach*
Collins, Richard Andrew *pathologist, biochemist*
†Collins, Richard Stratton (Dick Collins) *retired public relations executive*
Collins, Sandra Kay *pianist, composer, music educator*
Collins, Theodore John *lawyer*
†Collins, William J. *poet, educator*
Collinson, Vivienne Ruth *education educator, researcher, consultant*
Collyer, Robert B. *trade association administrator*
Colman, Richard Thomas *retired lawyer*
Colodny, Edwin Irving *lawyer, retired air transportation executive*
Cologne, Gordon Bennett *lawyer*
Colomb, Camille Marie *anesthesiologist*
Colonnier, Marc Leopold *neuroanatomist, educator*
Colosimo, Mary Lynn Sukurs *psychology educator*
Colsky, Andrew Evan *lawyer, mediator, arbitrator*
Colton, Sterling Don *lawyer, business executive, missionary*
Coluccio, Josephine Catherine *primary and elementary school educator*
†Colvin, James Edward *freelance journalist, publicist*
Colwell, Bryan York *private investor, philanthropist*
Colwell, Joshua Edwards *astronomer, researcher*
Combest, Larry Ed *retired congressman*
Combs, Robert Kimbal *museum director*
Combs, Roy James, Jr., *analyst, researcher*
Comegys, Ethel Blanche *brokerage house administrator*
†Comisky, Ian Michael *lawyer*
Compton, Allen T. *retired state supreme court justice*
†Compton, Michael *music educator*
Compton, Norma Haynes *retired university dean, artist*
†Compton, Robert *private school educator*
Compton, W. Dale *physicist, researcher, engineer*
Conant, Steven George *psychiatrist*
Conaway, Charles C. *former retail company executive*
Condayan, John *foreign service officer, diplomat, consultant*
†Condini, Ned *translator*
Condit, Doris Elizabeth *retired historian*
Condit, Gary Adrian *former congressman*
Condon, Charles Molony *former state attorney general*
Condra, Allen Lee *lawyer, state official*
Condry, Robert Stewart *retired hospital administrator*
Cone, Dennis Allen *music educator*
Cone, Edward Toner *composer, emeritus music educator*
Cone, Frances McFadden *data processing consultant*
Conerly-Perks, Erlene Brinson *retired chemist*
Conger, Harry Milton *mining company executive*
†Conine, Gary Bainard *lawyer, educator*
Conklin, Eric Linwood *artist*
Conklin, William Frank *writer*
Conley, Sarah Ann *health facility administrator*
Conley Riedy, Mary Therese *peri-operative nurse*
†Conlon, Cynthia Kelly *lawyer, educator*
†Conn, Richard Lee *computer scientist, educator*
Connell, Carol Matheson *corporate strategist, consultant*
†Connell, Charles R. *language educator*
Connell, Evan Shelby, Jr., *writer*
Connell, George Edward *former university president, scientist*
Connell, Hugh P. *foundation executive*
Connell, Marion Fitch *retired government official, management consultant*
Connell, Shirley Hudgins *public relations professional*
Connell, William D. *lawyer*
Connelly, Elizabeth Ann *retired state legislator*
Connelly, Sharon Rudolph *lawyer*
Conner, Natalie Ann *community health nurse specialist*
†Conner, William J. *diversified financial services company executive*
Conners, Peter Hamilton *writer*
†Connor, Daniel F. *child and adolescent psychiatrist, researcher*
Connor, Joseph E. *former international organization official*
†Connors, Loren M. *composer, guitarist*
Conover, Lloyd Hillyard *retired pharmaceutical research scientist and executive*
Conover, Nancy Anderson *retired secondary school counselor*
Conrad, David Paul *business broker, retired restaurant chain executive*
Conrad, Donald Glover *insurance executive*
Conrad-England, Roberta Lee *pathologist*
Conroy, Tamara Boks *artist, special education educator, former nurse*
Consiglio, Helen *nursing educator and consultant*
Consoli, Marc-Antonio *composer*
Constantine, Michael *actor*
Conti, Indalicio Palomar *accountancy educator*
Contillo, Lawrence Joseph *financial and computer company executive*
Convery, Fredrick Richard *retired surgeon, orthopedist*
Conway, Edward Gerald, Jr., *university educational technology administrator*
Conway, Gene Farris *cardiologist*
Conway, James Valentine Patrick *forensic document examiner, former postal service executive*
Conway, Richard Ashley *environmental engineer*
Coogan, Mary Ellen *musician, educator*
†Cook, Beth Marie *writer, poet, volunteer*
Cook, Charles Wilkerson, Jr., *retired banker, former county official*
Cook, Charles William, Jr., *manufacturing executive*
Cook, Chequetta Lynn Favors *nurse*
Cook, Christopher L. *accountant*
†Cook, Donald Charles *lawyer*
Cook, Edward Joseph *college president*
Cook, Iva Dean *education educator*
†Cook, Jane Hampton *communications executive, consultant*
†Cook, Jeffrey Arthur *engineer*
Cook, Julian Abele, Jr., *federal judge*
Cook, Sister M(ary) Mercedes *educator, educational administrator*
Cook, Merrill A. *former congressman, explosives industry executive*
Cook, Michelle Westerman *special education educator*
Cook, Norma Baker *consulting company executive*
Cook, Pamela Margaret *French educator*
Cook, Petronelle Marguerite *writer*
Cook, Quentin LaMar *lawyer, healthcare executive, church leader*
Cook, Rebecca McDowell *former state official*
†Cook, S. Alan *lawyer, accountant*
Cook, Stephen Champlin *retired shipping company executive*
Cooke, Thomas Paul *education educator*
Cooke, William L. *lawyer*
Cookson, Albert Ernest *telephone and telegraph company executive*
Cooley, James William *retired executive researcher*
Coolidge, Charles H., Jr., *career officer*
Cooney, John Thomas *retired banker*
Cooney, Joseph J. *microbiologist, educator*
Coonts, Stephen Paul *novelist*
†Coop, Andrew *chemist, educator*
Coop, Frederick Robert *retired city manager*
Cooper, Austin Morris *chemist, chemical engineer, consultant, researcher*
Cooper, Charles Donald *association executive, editor, retired career officer*
Cooper, Charles Gordon *insurance consultant, former executive*
Cooper, Cynthia *retired professional basketball coach, retired professional basketball player*
Cooper, David Frederick *poet, translator*
Cooper, David Wayne *product engineer*
Cooper, Elva June *artist, writer*
Cooper, Erlyne S. *social worker*
Cooper, Eugene Bruce *speech, language pathologist, educator*
Cooper, Hal *television director*
Cooper, Hal Dean *lawyer*
Cooper, James Michael *education educator*
Cooper, James Robert, III, *computer software company executive, mobile communications consultant*
Cooper, Janis Campbell *retired public relations executive*
Cooper, John Arnold *financial analyst*
Cooper, John Byrne, Jr., *airline pilot*
Cooper, John Milton, Jr., *history educator, author*
Cooper, Josephine Smith *trade association and public relations executive*
Cooper, Kathy Stegall *school counselor*
Cooper, Kenneth Banks *business executive, former army officer*
Cooper, Norton J. (Sky Cooper) *liquor, wine and food company executive*
Cooper, Patricia Gorman *management consultant*
Cooper, Rebecca *art dealer*
Cooper, Signe Skott *retired nurse educator*
Cooper, William Thomas *retired air force officer, writer, educator*
Coover, Doris Dimock *artist*
Cope, Kenneth Wayne *chain store executive*
Copeland, Henry Jefferson, Jr., *former college president*
†Copeland, Phillips Jerome *former academic administrator, former air force officer*
Coplin, Mark David *lawyer*
Coppie, Comer Swift *retired state official*
†Coppola, Francis Ford *film director, producer, writer*
Corallo, N. Ralph *health care products design engineer*
Corbett, Gordon Leroy *minister*
Corbett, James Joseph *retired computer programmer*
Corbett, Lenora Meade *mathematician, community college educator*
Corbett, Michael Arthur, Jr., *business management consultant*
Corcoran, David *designer, artist*
†Corcoran, Philip E. *wholesale distribution executive*
†Cordell, Bobbie B. *music educator*
†Cordell, Philip Granvile *music educator, musician*
Corder, Steven Lee *non-profit organization executive*
Cordwell, Arthur George *not-for-profit fundraiser*
†Corey, Claire *artist*
Corey, Kenneth Edward *urban planning and geography educator, researcher*
Corkery, James Caldwell *retired Canadian government executive, mechanical engineer*
Corkran, Virginia B. *retired realtor*
Corle, Frederic William, II, *marketing professional*
†Corle, James Thomas *lawyer*
Corlett, Cleve Edward *government administrator*
Corlett, Edward Stanley, III, *retired lawyer*
†Cornelison, Sally J. *art historian*
Cornell, Robert Arthur *retired international government official, consultant*
Cornett, Cathy G. Turner *consulting company executive, artist*
Cornett, Gregg *newspaper publisher, newspaper editor, computer company executive*
Cornish, Richard Joseph *international affairs consultant, retired diplomat*
†Cornwell, Linda Lee *media specialist*
Cortese, Richard Anthony *computer company executive*
Cortez, Joseph Anthony *retired surgeon*
Corto, Diana Maria *lyric-coloratura, producer, educator*
Cortright, Louise Vera *retired medical technologist, small business owner*
Corvino, Ernesta *ballet dancer*
†Corvo, William Kenneth *writer*
Corwin, William *psychiatrist*
Cosby, Bill *actor, entertainer*
†Cosby, Stephanie Bennett *health services professional*
Cosenza, Arthur George *opera director*
Cosman, Francene Jen *former government official*
Cossa, Dominic Frank *baritone*
Costa-Gavras, (Constantin Gavras) *director, writer*
Costanzo, Hilda Alba *retired banker*
†Costello, Caroline *epidemiologist*
Costello, Daniel Walter *retired bank executive*
Costello, James Joseph *retired electrical manufacturing company executive*
Coté, Kathryn Marie *psychotherapist, stress management educator*
Cotrubas, Ileana *opera singer, retired lyric soprano*
Cotruvo, Joseph Alfred *environmental and public health consultant*
Cotsakos, Christos Michael *former internet financial services company executive*
Cotsonas, Nicholas John, Jr., *physician, medical educator*
Cotten, Annie Laura *psychologist, educator*
Cotter, Lawrence Raffety *management consultant*
Cotting, James Charles *manufacturing company executive*
Cottrell, Mary-Patricia Tross *bank executive*
Couch, Daniel Michael *healthcare executive*
Couch, Rex Dee *pathologist, medical executive*
Couchman, Robert George James *human services consultant*
Coughlan, Kenneth L. *lawyer*
Coughlin, Jack *printmaker, sculptor, art educator*
Coughlin, Tom *former professional football coach*
†Coughran, Jane Nora *writer, editor, researcher*
Cougill, Roscoe McDaniel *mayor, retired air force officer*
Coukis, Peter George *musician, composer*
Coullard, Chad *information systems specialist*
Coulter, Jack Benson, Jr., *financial planner*
Counsil, William Glenn *electric utility executive*
†Courtenay, William James *historian, educator*
Courtney, Edward *retired classics educator*
Courtney, Sheryl *rehabilitation nurse, consultant*
Couto, Nancy Vieira *poet, literary consultant*
Couture, Jean G. *retired surgeon, educator*
Covell, Christopher Greene *management executive*
†Coven, Alysa Louise *advertising/marketing professional*
Covi, Lino *psychiatrist, educator*
Coviello, Frank Joseph *lawyer*
Covin, Carol Louise *computer consultant*
Covington, Marsha Elaine *communications consultant*
Covino, Jennifer Kathryn *freelance/self-employed writer*
Covintree, George E. *retired anesthesiologist*
Cowan, Andrew Glenn *television writer, producer, performer*
Cowan, Robert Jenkins *radiologist, educator*
Cox, Chapman Beecher *lawyer, corporate executive*
Cox, Gary Walter *political science educator*
Cox, James Carl, Jr., *chemist, researcher, lexicographer, consultant*
Cox, John Curtis *healthcare and educational administrator*
Cox, John Francis *retired cosmetic company executive*
Cox, Joy Dean *business executive*
Cox, Marshall *lawyer*
Cox, Marvin Melvin, Jr., *finance executive, corporate officer*
Cox, Pat *artist*
Cox, Richard Garner *music educator*
Cox, Wilford Donald *retired food company executive*
Cox, William Frederick *hospital executive*
Coyle, Marie Bridget *retired microbiology educator, laboratory director*
†Coyne, William Joseph *former congressman*

Deemer, Albert Earl *social worker, director*
Deering, Fred Arthur *retired insurance company executive*
Dees, Bowen Causey *institute executive, retired*
Dees, C. Stanley *lawyer*
Deets, Dwain Aaron *retired aerospace technology executive*
†de Fee, Nicole Reneé *education educator*
†DeFelice, James L. *writer*
De Felitta, Frank Paul *producer, writer, director*
Defever, Susanna Ethel *English language educator*
Deffner, Norman Fred *dermatologist*
de Freitas, Gabriel Fernandes *surgical oncologist*
Degenhardt, Robert Allan *architectural firm executive, engineering executive*
De Gette, Diana Louise *congresswoman, lawyer*
DeGraff, Helen Marie *artist*
DeHority, Miriam A. (Miriam Newman) *artist*
Deisenhofer, Johann *biochemistry educator, researcher*
Deitz, Susan Rose *columnist*
DeJack, Jacqueline Elvadeana *artist, educator*
†DeJesus, Onofre T *chemist*
Dejewski, Deborah Elizabeth *pharmacist*
Delacampagne, Christian H. *humanities educator*
Dela Cruz, Jose Santos *retired state supreme court justice*
DeLaFuente, Charles *lawyer, educator, journalist*
Delahanty, Rebecca Ann *school system administrator*
†Delaney, Atima Chumpa *pediatrician*
Delap, Bill Jay *engineer, consultant*
de la Piedra, Jorge *orthopedic surgeon*
de Lattre, Candace Lorraine *singer, voice teacher*
†Delaty, Simone *retired language educator*
De Leonardis, Nicholas John *bank executive, financial lecturer, educator*
†del Gizzo, Suzanne *language educator*
Dell, Thomas Charles *nurse anesthetist*
Dellagnena, Gail Lynn *computer programmer analyst, consultant*
Della Rocca, Gregory John *orthopaedic surgeon*
Dellere, Diana Marie *school psychologist*
†DelliBovi, Alfred A. *bank executive*
†Delmarre, David *formulation scientist*
De Loach, Bernard Collins, Jr., *retired physicist*
Deloatch, Cheryl Allen *communications company executive*
DeLong, Janice Ayers *education educator*
De Lorenzo, Robert Allan *emergency physician*
DeLoyht-Arendt, Mary Isobel *artist*
Del Papa, Frankie Sue *former state attorney general*
†del Rosario, Anna Antonio *director*
De Lutis, Donald Conse *investment adviser, consultant*
Dely, Steven *aerospace company executive*
Demenchonok, Edward Vasilevich *philosopher, linguist, researcher, educator*
Demharter, Cheryl Ann Marie *foreign language educator, former administrator*
De Mille, Barbara Munn *writer, former English literature educator*
†DeMille, Dale Esther *medical/surgical nurse, educator*
DeMille, Nelson Richard *writer*
DeMint, James Warren *congressman, marketing professional*
†Demissie, Yemane I. *filmmaker*
DeMita, Geraldine *librarian*
Demmitt, Joyce Miller *management consultant*
Dempsey, Cedric W. *former sports association administrator*
Dempsey, David Allan *company official*
Denaro, Charles Thomas *lawyer*
Dench, Judith Olivia *actress*
Denegall, John Palmer, Jr., *construction executive*
de Neufville, Pierre *retired brokerage house executive*
Denevan, William Maxfield *geographer, prehistorian, ecologist*
†Denham, Carolyn Hunter *academic administrator, statistics educator*
Denious, Jon Parks *retired publishing executive*
Denious, Sharon Marie *retired publisher*
Denn, Cyril Joseph *financial advisor*
Dennany, Kelly *mechanical engineer, test engineer*
Dennick, Lori Ann (Loranden) *artist, model, actress*
†Denning, Karen Craft *finance educator*
†Denny, Jera Cecilia Jane Elizabeth *musician, graphics designer*
Denton, Joan Cameron *reading consultant, former educator*
†Denton, Kathryn M. *merchant banker, writer*
Denton, Medona Bonner *research chemistry educator*
Deoul, Kathleen Boardsen *publishing executive*
DePalma, Ralph George *surgeon, educator*
Derbyshire, William Wadleigh *language educator, translator*
Derchin, Michael Wayne *portfolio manager and financial analyst*
De Reineck, Marie *interior designer*
Derickson, Stanley Lewis *minister, writer*
Dermanis, Paul Raymond *architect*
De Roest, Jan Marie *mental health counselor*
DeRosa, David Francis *finance educator, trading company executive*
De Rossi, Julie Anne *music promoter, entrepreneur, freelance editor, retail consultant*
Derrickson, Denise Ann *secondary school educator, educator*
Deryuga, Vyacheslav O. *nuclear physicist, computer scientist, consultant*
†Desai, Sima S. *internist*
DeSando, John Anthony *retired humanities educator*
Desbarats, Peter Hullett *journalist, academic administrator*
DeShazer, Ruth Shomler *health facility administrator, consultant*
Desjardins, Benoit *physician, researcher*
Desjardins, Daniel Dee *poet, composer, translator and playwright*
De Sofi, Oliver Julius *data processing executive*
Despres, Patrick John *artist, art educator*
Desselle, Debra Duke *social worker*
Detert, Miriam Anne *chemical analyst*
Detweiler, David Kenneth *veterinary physiologist, educator*
Detwiler, Christina LeFevre *elementary school educator*
de Urioste, George Adolfo *software company executive*
Deutsch, Didier (Delaunoy Deutsch) *music producer, writer*
Deutsch, Herbert Arnold *music educator*
†Deutsche, Kirsten Hansen *pharmaceutical company executive*
†Deutschman, Louise Tolliver *curator*
Deutz, Natalie Rubinstein *actress, consultant*
DeVaney, Carol Susan *management consultant*
DeVaris, Jeannette Mary *psychologist*
DeVera, Gertrude Quenano *education educator*
Devereux, Richard Blyton *internal medicine educator*
†Devgun, Mohan S. *manufacturing engineer, educator, metallurgical engineer, consultant*
de Vink, Lodewijk J. R. *former consumer pharmaceutical products company executive*
De Vita, Michael Richard *obstetrician-gynecologist*
DeVita, Vincent Theodore, Jr., *oncologist*
DeVivo, Ange *former small business owner*
Devlin, Michael Coles *bass-baritone*
DeVore, Kimberly K. *business executive*
†DeVries, Linda Jane *music educator*
DeVries, Robert Allen *foundation administrator*
Dew, Joan King *freelance/self-employed writer*
Dewald, William Guenthner *economist*
†Dewey, Colin David *merchant seaman*
Dewhurst, Peter *industrial engineer, educator*
deWilde, David Michael *management consultant, former executive search consultant, financial services executive, lawyer*
Dewing, Henry Woods, Sr., *telecommunications executive*
Dex, Walter John *radiologist*
Dey, Carol Ruth *secondary education educator*
†Dharamsi, Shamez Shiraz *marketing professional, consultant*
d'Heurle, Adma Jeha *psychology educator*
Diamond, Fred I. *electronic engineer*
Diamond, Richard *retired secondary education educator*
Diamond, Robert Mach *higher education administrator*
Diamond, Stuart *business executive, educator, lawyer, consultant*
Diamond, Susan Zee *management consultant*
Dianto, Linda Christine *therapeutic activities coordinator, administrator*
Dias, Kathleen R. *foreign language educator*
†Diaz, Alphonso Vincent *aerospace executive*
Diaz, Oscar, Jr., *voice educator, music company executive*
†Diaz-Arce, Raul *professional soccer player*
†Diaz-Zubieta, Ana Maria *social worker*
DiBattiste, Carol A. *lawyer*
DiBenedetto, Emmanuele *molecular physiology, biophysicist, writer*
DiBiaggio, John A. *university president*
Dibner, David Robert *architect, writer*
†DiCaprio, Leonardo *actor*
DiCarlo, Laurette Mary *nurse*
Di Cicco, Joseph Nicholas, Jr., *chemical engineer*
Dick, James Cordell *concert pianist*
Dickau, Keith Michael (Mike Dickau) *artist, secondary school educator*
Dickens, Alycia Thompson *nurse practitioner*
Dickerman, John Melvin *lawyer*
†Dickerson, Eric Demetric *former professional football player*
†Dickerson, John Robert *retired automotive engineer*
Dickes, Robert *psychiatrist*
Dickeson, Robert Celmer *retired university president, foundation executive, political science educator*
Dickey, Jay W., Jr., *former congressman, lawyer*
Dickey, Joseph William *utility executive, engineer*
Dickey, Robert Marvin (Rick Dickey) *property manager*
Dickey, Sally Ann *retired cultural organization administrator*
Dickinson, Carol Rittgers *arts administrator, writer, executive director*
Dickinson, Donald Charles *library science educator*
Dickinson, Gail Krepps *educator*
Dickinson, Victoria Ann *visual arts administrator*
Dickinson, William Richard *retired geologist*
Dickison, Joie Lei *medical editor*
Dickman, James Bruce *photojournalist*
Dickman, James Earl *financial services executive*
Dickman, Robert S. *aerospace consultant, retired career officer*
Dickson, Eva Mae *credit manager*
Dickson, James Francis, III, *surgeon*
DiCorcia, Edward Thomas *retired oil industry executive*
Diddle, Albert W. *obstetrician, gynecologist*
Didlo, Larry L. *writer, educator*
DiDomenico, Mauro, Jr., *communication executive*
Diedrick, Geraldine Rose *retired nurse*
DiEdwardo, Mary Ann Pasda *artist, writer*
Diehl, Carol Lou *library director, retired, library consultant*
Diehl, Deborah Hilda *lawyer*
Diehl, Harry Alfred *chemist, genealogist*
Diehl, Stephen Anthony *human resources consultant*
Diehr, David Bruce *retired social service administrator*
†Diem, Richard A. *social studies educator, educational consultant*
Diemer, Emma Lou *composer, music educator*
Diener, Erwin *immunologist*
Diener, Royce *corporate director, retired healthcare services company executive*
Dietderich, Shirley (Jane Rohlfing) *interior decorator*
Dietel, James Edwin *lawyer, consultant*
Dieter, Robert Sean *physician*
Dietze, Joachim *librarian*
Diffrient, Niels *industrial designer*
DiFronzo, Michael A. *lawyer, accountant*
Di Giacomo, Fran *artist*
DiGiacomo, Jody Christopher *physician*
Di Giovanni, Anthony *retired coal mining company executive*
DiGirolamo, Glen Francis *actor*
DiIenno, Joseph Anthony *psychiatrist*
†Diipla, Joyce Katherine Marie *physician*
Dike, Margaret Hopcraft *retired education administrator*
Dill, Laddie John *artist*
Dillon, Clifford Brien *retired lawyer*
Dillon, Phillip Michael *construction company executive*
Dillon, Robert Sherwood *retired government official*
Dillon-McHugh, Cathleen Theresa *librarian, consultant, editor*
Dills, James Arlof *retired publishing company executive*
DiMatteo, Rhonda Lynn *speech-language pathologist, audiologist*
†Dimengo, Josephine *medical/surgical nurse*
Dimitry, Theodore George *retired lawyer*
Dimon, James *bank executive*
†Di Natale, Marisa Lyn *economist*
Dincecco, Jennie Elizabeth Williams *healthcare administrator, mentor, volunteer*
†Ding, Ai-Yue *conductor, music educator*
†Ding, Jinwen *biomedical researcher*
Ding, Michael S. *physical scientist*
†Dingle, Carol A. *state agency administrator, writer*
†Diniz-Piraino, Siglia Leite *cardiologist*
Dinkel, John George *automotive executive, consultant*
†Dinsmoor, Mara Jean *obstetrician-gynecologist, educator*
†Diodato, Luis Hector *physician, researcher*
Di Paolo, Maria Grazia *language educator, writer*
DiPiazza, Michael Charles *insurance company executive*
Dipko, Thomas Earl *retired minister, national church executive*
Dirks, Leslie Chant *communications and electronics company executive*
Dirvin, Gerald Vincent *retired consumer products company executive*
DiSalle, Michael Danny *secondary education educator*
Disbrow, Lynn Marie *communication educator*
Disch, Thomas M(ichael) *author*
†Disch, William Burton *psychologist, researcher*
Dishy, Bob *actor*
†Dissen, Walter Charles *lawyer*
Di Suvero, Mark *sculptor*
Ditka, Michael Keller *former professional football coach*
Dito, William Robert *pathology educator*
Dittenhafer, Brian Douglas *banker, economist*
Dittman, Duane Scott *registrar*
†Dittmann, Melissa Ann *journalist*
Ditto, Edward Wilson, III, *retired family physician*
Dix, Gary Errol *engineering executive*
Dix, Samuel Morman *industrial engineer, physical economist, appraiser*
Dixon, Ann Renee *writer*
Dixon, Denise *psychologist, educator*
Dixon, Gordon Henry *biochemist, educator*
†Dixon, John Morris, Jr., *lawyer*
Dixon, Marc Alan *numismatist, consultant, illustrator*
Dixon, Michael Wayne *designer, writer, researcher*
†Dixon, Steven Bedford *lawyer*
Dixon, William Robert *musician, composer, educator*
Dizer, John T., Jr., *engineering educator*
Djordjevic, Dimitrije *historian, educator*
Dmytryk, Eugene Thomas *retired surgeon*
Doan, Mary Frances *advertising executive*
Dobbel, Rodger Francis *interior designer*
Dobler, Donald William *retired college dean, consultant, corporate executive*
Dobriansky, Lev Eugene *economist, educator, diplomat*
†Dobrzanski, Slawomir *music educator*
Doby, Margaret Gail *interior designer*
Dockery, J. Lee *retired medical school administrator*
Dodd, Joe David *safety engineer, consultant, administrator*
Dodd, Steven Louis *systems engineer*
Dodds, Brenda Kay *nurse*
Dodds, Lawrence Donald *lawyer*
Dodds, Linda Carol *special education educator*
Doderer, Minnette Frerichs *retired state legislator*
Dodge, R(alph) Edward, Jr., *physician*
Dodson, Donald Mills *retired restaurant executive*
Dodson, Samuel Robinette, III, *investment banker*
Doebler, Bettie Anne *language educator, researcher, writer*
Doerper, John Erwin *journal editor, publishing executive*
Dogançay, Burhan C. *artist, photographer, sculptor*
Dogoloff, Lee Israel *clinical social worker, psychotherapist, consultant*
Doherty, Charles Vincent *investment counsel executive*
Doherty, Evelyn Marie *data processing consultant*
Doherty, Peter Charles *immunologist*
Doherty, Thomas Joseph *financial services industry consultant*
Dohrmann, Russell William *manufacturing company executive*
Dokurno, Anthony David *lawyer*
Dolan, Edward Francis *writer*
Dolan, John F. *lawyer*
†Dolan, Peter Brown *lawyer*
Dolan, Peter J. *corporate financial consultant*
Dolce, Julia Wagner *lawyer*
Dole, Arthur Alexander *psychology educator*
Dole, Vincent Paul, III, *food products executive*
†Dolev, Jacqueline *physician, researcher*
Dolgow, Allan Bentley *management consultant*
Dolich, Andrew Bruce *sports marketing executive*
Doll, Patricia Marie *marketing and public relations advertising consultant*
Dolman, John Phillips, Jr., (Tim Dolman) *communications company executive*
Dolph, Wilbert Emery *lawyer*
Domeracki, Frank Robert *physician*
Dominguez, Eddie *artist*
†Dominick, Kathleen Marilyn *small business owner, consultant*
Dominowski, Roger L. *psychologist, educator*
Domzella, Janet *retired library director*
Donahue, Patricia Toothaker *retired social worker, administrator*
†Donahue, Rafe Michael *statistician*
Donald, Aida DiPace *retired publishing executive*
†Donald, James E. *career officer*
Donaldson, Loraine *economics educator*
Donaldson, Myrtle Norma *music educator, musician*
Donaldson, Wilma Crankshaw *elementary education educator*
Donath, Fred Arthur *geologist, geophysicist*
Donath, Therese *artist, author*
Dondanville, John Wallace *lawyer*
Doniger, Jay *health information executive*
Donley, Deedra Ann *medical educator*
Donnally, Patricia Broderick *writer*
Donnally, Robert Andrew *lawyer*
†Donnelly, Paja Lee *nursing educator and nurse practitioner*
Donnelly-Kempf, Moira Ann *nursing administrator*
D'Onofrio, Mary Ann *medical transcription company executive*
Donohue, George L. *mechanical engineer, educator*
Donohue, Marc David *chemical engineering educator*
Donovan, Brian *freelance journalist*
Donovan, Dorothy Diane *adult nurse practitioner*
Donovan, Marie Phillips *television executive*
Donovan, Marion Conran *school social worker*
Dooley, Jo Ann Catherine *retired publishing company executive*
Dooley, Susan Margaret *writer*
Doorenbos, Judy Tucker *cardiology critical care nurse*
Doorish, John Francis *physicist, mathematician, educator*
†Doraiswamy, P. Murali *physician*
†Doraiswamy, P(udugramam) Murali *psychiatrist, educator, researcher, neuroscientist*
Doran, Charles Edward *textile manufacturing executive*
†Doren, Bonnie E. *special education educator, researcher*
Dorfman, Benjamin Fridel *physicist*
†Dorighi, Nancy S. *computer engineer*
Dorman, Patricia M. *sociologist, educator*
Dorman, Richard Frederick, Jr., *association executive, consultant*
Dorn, Natalie Reid *consultant*
Dorn, Norman Philip *management consulting firm executive*
†Dornan, Reade Whiting *literature educator, writer*
Dornette, Ralph Meredith *religious organization administrator, educator, minister*
†Dornhoffer, John Louis *neurologist*
Dornin, Catharine Quillen *music educator, concert pianist*
Dorning, John Joseph *nuclear engineering, engineering physics and applied mathematics educator*
†Dorsky, Nathaniel *filmmaker*
Dos, Serge Jacques *surgeon, physiology researcher*
Dosé, Frederick Philip, Jr., *art historian, art and antiques appraiser, consultant, liquidator*
†Dossena, Tiziano Thomas *environmental scientist*
Dotson, John Louis, Jr., *former newspaper publisher*
Doty, Philip Edward *accountant*
Doubleday, Nelson *former professional baseball team executive*
Doucette, Betty *public and community health and geriatrics nurse*
Doud, Wallace C. *retired information systems executive*
Dougherty, Floyd Wallace *design engineer*
Dougherty, Robert Anthony *retired manufacturing company executive*
Douglas, Karin Nadja *engineer*
†Douglas, Mary Younge Riley *secondary education educator*
†Douglas, Maurice LaJohn *private school educator, music educator*
†Douglas, Philip A. *writer*
Douglas, Roxanne Grace *secondary school educator*
Douglass, Betty Jean *retired executive secretary*
Douglass, Jane Dempsey *theology educator*
Douglass, Susan Daniel *retired consultant*
Doumani, George Alexander *earth and environmental scientist*
Douty, Lucy Evelyn *sales and marketing executive*

Dove, Lorraine Faye *gerontology nurse*
†Doviak, Ingrid Ellinger *elementary school educator*
Dow, Garnett McCormick *geoscientist*
Dow, Peter Anthony *advertising agency executive*
Dow, William French, III, *lawyer*
Dowben, Carla Lurie *lawyer, educator*
Dowd, Morgan Daniel *political science educator*
Dowie, Ian James *management consultant*
Dowling, Michael Paul *foundation administrator*
Dowling, Paul Dennis *bilingual special education educator*
Downen, Robert Lynn *international affairs analyst and political consultant, editor, writer*
Downes, Rackstraw *artist*
Downey, Deborah Ann *systems specialist*
Downing, M. Scott *budget systems analyst*
Downs, Amy Louise *psychologist*
Downs, Kathleen Anne *health facility administrator*
†Downs, Leslie G *music educator, musician*
Dowsett, Peter John *retired obstetrician, gynecologist*
†Dowty, Marcus Duaine *music educator*
Doyle, Gillian *actress*
Doyle, Irene Elizabeth *electronic sales executive, nurse*
Doyle, L. F. Boker *retired trust company executive*
Doyle, Patrick Lee *retired insurance company executive*
Doyle, Tom *sculptor, retired educator*
Dozier, Glenn Joseph *diversified financial services company executive*
Dozier, Gloria Anne Clifton *retired buyer*
Dozier, James Lee *former army officer*
Dozier, Nancy Kerns *retired geriatrics nurse*
Drabkin, Murray *lawyer*
Dracker, Robert Albert *physician*
Dragon, William, Jr., *footwear and apparel company executive*
Dragoumis, Paul *electric utility company executive*
Draime, Charles Douglas *poet, short story writer, playwright*
Drake, Barbara Ruth *writer*
Drake, Donald Charles *journalist, playwright*
Drake, Ervin Maurice *composer, author*
Drake, George Albert *college president, historian*
Drake, Rodman Leland *investment company executive, consultant*
†Drance, Stephen Michael *ophthalmologist, educator*
Draper, Edgar *psychiatrist*
Drasler, Gregory John *artist*
†Drayton, Joyce Renee *physician*
Draznin, Jules Nathan *educator*
Drennen, William Miller, Jr., *cultural administrator, film executive, producer, director, mineral resource executive*
Drepaul, Loris Omesh *internist, infectious diseases physician*
Dresbach, Mary Louise *state educational administrator*
Dressel, Irene Emma Ringwald *alcoholism and family therapist*
†Dresser, Mary T. *journalist*
Dressler, David Charles *retired aerospace company executive*
Drew, Elizabeth Heineman *publishing executive*
Drew, Walter Harlow *retired paper industry executive*
Drews, Jürgen *pharmaceutical researcher*
Dreyfuss, John Alan *retired health facility administrator*
Driscoll, Garrett Bates *retired telecommunications executive*
Driskill, Elita Martin *humanities educator*
Dritschilo, William *educator*
†Drost, Marianne *lawyer*
Droullard, Steven Maurice *jewelry company executive*
Drozd, Leszek Stanislaw *composer, performer*
Drucker, Peter Ferdinand *writer, consultant, educator*
†Drucker, Stephen *former magazine editor-in-chief*
Drummond, Dorothy Weitz *geography education consultant, educator, author*
†Dryman, Amy *epidemiologist*
†Dubay, Thomas E. *priest, writer*
Dubé, Ronald Norman *elementary school educator*
Dubill, Robert A. *former newspaper editor*
Dubin, Daniel Herschel Eli *physicist, educator*
Dubois, Nancy Q. *elementary school educator*
Du Boise, Kim Rees *artist, photographer, art educator*
Dubuc, Carroll Edward *lawyer*
Dubuque, Theodore Julien, Jr., *retired surgeon*
Duckworth, Paula Oliver *secondary school educator, freelance artist, writer, photographer*
†Ducoste, Joel J. *research scientist, educator*
Dudash, Karen Shreffler *community health nurse*
Dudick, Michael Joseph *retired bishop*
Dudics-Dean, Susan Elaine *interior designer*
Dudley, Craig James *retired executive recruiter*
Dudley, Elizabeth Hymer *retired security executive, community volunteer*
†Dudley, Richard George *fisheries and natural resources consultant*
Dudman, Richard Beebe *journalist*
Dudycha, Anne Elizabeth *retired special education educator*
Duecker, Robert Sheldon *retired bishop*
Duerr, Herman George *retired publishing executive*
Duff, John Bernard *college president, former city official*
Duffy, John Joseph *retired academic administrator, history educator*
Duffy, Martin Edward *management consultant, economist*
Duffy, Mary Kathleen *neonatal nurse*
Dugan, Patrick Raymond *microbiologist, university dean*
†Duhaime, Nina Lee *business research and development*
†Duhl, Olga Anna *literature educator, researcher*
Duigan, John *film director*
Duke, William Edward *public affairs executive*
Dukes, Deborah Feagans *counselor, administrator*
Dull, William Martin *retired engineering executive*
Dulles, Frederick Hendrik *lawyer*
Dumas, Sandra Lee *medical technologist, microbiologist*
Dumont, Allan Eliot *retired physician, educator*
DuMontier, Clarissa Williams *lawyer*
†Dunau, Anastasia Thannhauser *retired administrative law judge*
Dunaway, Frank Rosser, III, *emergency physician*
Dunaway, Margaret Ann (Maggie Dunaway) *retired state agency consultant*
Dunbar, Bruce Stephen *photographer, gallery administrator*
Dunbar, Maurice Victor *English language educator*
Duncan, Pope Alexander *college administrator*
Duncan, Robert Bannerman *strategy and organizations educator*
Duncombe, Patricia Warburton *retired social worker*
Dunfee, Thomas Wylie *law educator*
Dungan, Gloria Kronbeck *critical care nurse*
Dunham, Benjamin Starr *editor, art association administrator*
Dunham, Rebecca Betty Beres *school administrator*
Dunkerley, Erna Lee *musician*
†Dunkley, Larnell, Jr., *literature educator*
Dunlap, James *poet, writer*
†Dunlap, Paul Edward *secondary school educator, writer*
Dunlap, Richard Donovan *artistic director*
Dunlop, Dorothy D. *statistician*
Dunmeyer, Sarah Louise Fisher *retired health care consultant*
Dunn, Carola *writer*
†Dunn, Helen Elizabeth *retired secondary school educator*
Dunn, John Raymond, Jr., *stockbroker*
†Dunn, Marija Gavrilova *psychologist, educator*
Dunn, Neil F. *retired computer science educator*
Dunn, Patricia C. *retired social work educator*
†Dunn, Peter Colt *not-for-profit developer*
Dunn, Robert Giddings *writer, educator*
Dunn, Robert Lawrence *lawyer*
Dunn, Robert S. *writer, artist*
Dunn, Warren Howard *retired lawyer, brewery executive*
†Dunn Kelly, Ruth Emma *management consultant*
Dunsky, Menahem *retired advertising agency executive, communications consultant, painter*
†Dunst, Isabel Paula *lawyer*
Dunworth, John *retired college president*
Duplessis, Audrey Joseph *school system administrator*
Dupps, John Avery, Jr., *process machinery company executive*
Durant, John Ridgeway *retired physician, consultant*
Durbetaki, N. John *software company executive*
Durell, Jack *psychiatrist*
Durfield, Timothy Richard *legal assistant*
Durgom-Powers, Jane Ellyn *lawyer*
Durham, Thena Monts *microbiologist, researcher, management executive*
Durr, Robert Joseph *construction firm executive, mechanical engineer*
Durrani, Sajjad Haidar *retired space communications engineer*
Dusenbury, Ruth Cole *business owner*
Dutson, Thayne R. *university dean*
Duval-Carrié, Edouard *artist*
Duvall, Gene Robert *radiologist*
DuVall, Patricia Arlene *secondary education educator*
Dwan, Dennis Edwin *broadcast executive, photographer*
Dwight, Harvey Alpheus *retired small business owner*
Dwinell, Ann Jones *retired special education educator*
Dworin, Micki (Maxine Dworin) *automobile dealership executive*
Dwyer, Gerald Paul, Jr., *economist, bank executive*
Dyal, Edith Colvin *retired music educator*
†Dye, Linda Kaye *elementary school educator*
Dye, Robert Harris *retired manufacturing company executive*
Dyer, Arlene Thelma *retail company owner*
Dyer, L. Keith *film company executive*
Dyer, Natalie Mary *health products company executive, physician*
Dyer, Wayne Walter *psychologist, writer, radio and television personality*
Dyess, Joseph Dwight *commercial banker*
Dyrstad, Joanell M. *former lieutenant governor, consultant*
Dysart, Richard A. *actor*
Dyson, Allan Judge *retired librarian*
Dziewanowska, Zofia Elizabeth *neuropsychiatrist, pharmaceutical executive, researcher, educator*
†Dzindolet, Mary Teresa *psychology educator*
†Dzwik, Leigh Settlemair *director*
Eagle, Jack *commercial actor, comedian*
Eaglet, Robert Danton *electrical engineer, aerospace consultant, retired military officer*
†Eaken, Bruce Webb, Jr., *lawyer*
Earl, Boyd L. *mathematician*
Earle, Arthur Percival *textile company executive, airport executive*
Earle, Timothy Keese *anthropology educator*
†Eason, Karen E. *public health service officer, researcher*
East, Don Gaylord *computer engineer, archaeologist, writer*
East, Janette Diane *marketing consultant*
Easterbrook, Eliot Knights *chemist*
Easterling, Charles Armo *lawyer*
Easterling, William Ewart, Jr., *retired obstetrician, gynecologist*
Easterly, Susan *music and humanities educator*
Easterson, Sam *artist*
Easton, Charles Clement, Jr., *corporate executive*
Easton, Kelly Anne *writer, educator*
Easton, Michelle *foundation executive*
Eastup, Lavonda Jo *writer, poet, songwriter*
Eaton, Dorel *elementary school educator*
†Eaton, Emma Parker *special education educator*
Eaton, Joe Oscar *federal judge*
Eaton, Katherine Girton *retired library educator*
Eaton, Larry Ralph *lawyer*
Eaton, Merrill Thomas *psychiatrist, educator*
†Eaton, Shirley M. *medical/surgical nurse*
Eaves, Sandra Austra *social worker*
Ebata, Masako *artist*
Ebb, Fred *lyricist, librettist*
Ebben, Joy Marie *human factors/ergonomics psychologist*
Eberhard, Franz Valentin *association executive*
†Eberhardt, H. Alfred *retired manufacturing executive, retired mechanical engineer*
Eberhart, Ralph E. *career officer*
Eberle, Charles Edward *paper and consumer products executive*
Eberstein, Arthur *former biomedical engineering educator, researcher*
Ebert, Dorothy Elizabeth *retired county clerk*
Ebert, Viola Roth *neuropsychologist, entrepreneur*
Ebie, William D. *museum director*
Ebisuzaki, Yukiko *retired chemistry educator*
Eby, Carl Peter *English educator*
Eby, Cecil DeGrotte *English language educator, writer*
Eck, Robert Edwin *physicist*
Ecklund, Judith Louise *academic administrator*
Eckstein, Jerome *philosopher, educator*
Economou-Pease, Bessie Carasoulas *city planner, consultant*
Ecton, Donna R. *business executive*
Eddy, David Maxon *health policy and management administrator*
Eddy, Don *artist*
Eddy, Melissa Jane *small business owner*
Edel, Abraham *philosophy educator*
Edelman, Norman Herman *medical educator, university dean and official*
Edelmann, Carolyn Foote *writer, poet, editor, photographer*
Edelsberg, Sally Comins *physical therapy educator and administrator*
Edelson, Marshall *retired psychiatry educator, psychoanalyst*
Edelstein, Rosemarie (Rosemarie Hublou) *medical/surgical nurse, educator, medical and legal consultant*
Edens, Betty Joyce *reading recovery educator*
Eder, Elaine AnnMarie *lawyer*
Edgar, Thomas Flynn *chemical engineering educator*
Edgreen, Robert J. *equity company executive*
Edgren, Gretchen Grondahl *magazine editor*
Edmo, Jean Umiokalani *artist, poet*
Edmonds, Anne Carey *librarian*
Edmondson, Robert Campbell *retired hematologist, oncologist, internal medicine educator*
Edmunds, Jane Clara *communications consultant*
Edmunds, Lowell (Arthur Lowell Edmunds) *philology educator*
Edrington, Sue Ellen *critical care nurse*
Edson, Margaret *playwright*
†Edwards, Anthony *actor*
Edwards, Ardis Lavonne Quam *retired elementary education educator*
Edwards, Bruce George *retired ophthalmologist, naval officer*
Edwards, Charles *neuroscientist, educator*
†Edwards, Christine Annette *retired lawyer, securities firm executive*
Edwards, Ephraim Zeno *retired anesthesiologist*
Edwards, Geoffrey Hartley *newspaper publisher*
†Edwards, Helen Thom *physicist*
†Edwards, James Malone *lawyer*
Edwards, Jerome *lawyer*
Edwards, June Caroline *retired education educator*
Edwards, Kathleen *real estate broker, former educator*
Edwards, Larry David *internist, educator*
Edwards, Patrick Ross *former retail company executive, lawyer, management consultant*
Edwards, Priscilla Ann *paralegal, business owner*
Edwards, Richard Alan *retired lawyer*
†Edwards, Robert Hazard *retired college president*
Edwards, Ryan Hayes *baritone*
Edwards, Sharon Jane *nurse*
Edwards, Victor Henry *chemical engineer*
Edwards, William Thomas, Jr., *lawyer, consultant*
†Edwards-Mitchum, Lillian (Red the Poet) *secondary school educator, writer*
Effner, Marsha Gay *retired employee development officer*
Efros, Leonid *computer software scientist and developer*
Egan, Edward M. *cardinal*
Egan, Wesley William *former ambassador*
Egelston, Roberta Riethmiller *writer*
†Egenes, Thomas Arthur *ancient language educator*
Egerer, Karen Ann *association executive*
Eggan, Hugh Melford *retired accountant*
Eggleston, Claud Hunt, III, *company executive, venture capitalist*
Eggleston, G(eorge) Dudley *management consultant, publisher*
Eglee, Charles Hamilton *television and movie writer, producer*
Egnor, Joanne McClellan *psychology educator*
Ehrhart, William Daniel *writer, poet*
Ehrling, Sixten *orchestra conductor*
Eichel, Edward William *psychotherapist, painter*
Eichhorn, Frederick Foltz, Jr., *retired lawyer*
†Eidt, Jacob Ivan *language educator*
Eikleberry, Carol *psychologist, writer*
Eimers, Jeri Anne *retired therapist*
†Einhorn, Martin B. *physics educator*
Eisenberg, Albert Charles *senior government official*
†Eisenberg, Daniel *filmmaker*
†Eisenberg, Gary Julius *writer, musician, printmaker*
Eisenhower, John Sheldon Doud *former ambassador, author*
Eisenstat, Theodore Ellis *colon and rectal surgeon, educator*
Eisler, Robert David *engineer*
Eisner, Eleanor *social worker*
Eisner, Peter Norman *journalist, author, news agency executive*
†Eisner, Sigmund *retired English language educator*
Eissmann, Robert Fred *retired manufacturing engineer*
Eissmann, Walter James *consulting company executive*
Ekey, Carrie Rae *elementary education educator*
Eklof, Paul C. *mathematician, educator*
Elam, Fred Eldon *retired career army officer*
Elbery, Kathleen Marie *lawyer, accountant, cartoonist*
Elbin-Schell, Carol Gertrude *television promotion manager*
Elcik, Elizabeth Mabie *fashion illustrator*
Elder, Mary Louise *librarian*
Eledge, Jean Dorothy *French language educator, administrator*
Eley, Lynn W. *political science educator, former mayor*
†Elfers-Mabli, Linda M. *educational consultant, educator*
†Elfman, Jenna *actress*
Elgart, Larry Joseph *orchestra leader*
Elgart, Mervyn L. *dermatologist, educator*
Elgin, Gita *psychologist*
†Elias, Alan *physician, educator*
Elikann, Lawrence S. (Larry Elikann) *television and film director*
Eliot, Charles William John *former university president*
†Eliot, Theodore Lyman, Jr., *international consultant*
Elizondo, Hector *actor*
Elkin, Norman *urban planner*
Elkind, Mort William *business consultant*
Ellenberger, Jack Stuart *law librarian*
Ellett, Alan Sidney *real estate development company executive*
Ellig, Bruce Robert *personnel director*
Ellington, Howard Wesley *architect*
Ellington, James Willard *retired mechanical engineer*
†Elliott, Bill *race car driver*
Elliott, Brig (Chip) *network scientist*
Elliott, David LeRoy *mathematician, educator, engineering educator*
Elliott, James Ward *lawyer*
Elliott, Tommy *secondary school educator*
Elliott-Zahorik, Bonnie *nurse, administrator*
Ellis, Anne Elizabeth *fundraiser*
Ellis, Carolyn Terry *lawyer*
†Ellis, Edward R. *career officer*
Ellis, Harold Donald *auto repair company executive, consultant*
Ellis, James O., Jr., *military officer*
Ellis, John Martin *German literature educator*
†Ellis, Kem Byron *public library administrator*
Ellis, Larry R. *military officer*
Ellis, Michael David *aerospace engineer*
Ellis, Patricia Weathers *small business owner, retired electronic technician*
Ellis, Steven George *public relations/corporate communication executive*
Ellis, William Ben *environmental educator, retired utility executive*
†Elliston, Kristine *not-for-profit fundraiser*
Ellner, Paul Daniel *clinical microbiologist*
Ellstrom-Calder, Annette *research consultant*
Ellsworth, Frederick Lee *music educator*
Elmendorf, Douglas William *economist*
†Elmore, Joann Grace *medical researcher, medical educator, physician*
Else, Carolyn Joan *retired library director*
Elson, Edward Elliott *diplomat*
Elson, Hannah Friedman *biologist, researcher*
Elster, J. Robert *lawyer*
Eltringham, Thomas James Gyger *telecommunications professional*
Elverum, Gerard William, Jr., *retired electronic and diversified company executive*
†Elway, John Albert *retired professional football player*
Elwood-Akers, Virginia Edythe *retired librarian, archivist*
Ely, Laurence Driggs, III, *theoretical Christian astrologer*
Ely, Paul C., Jr., *electronics company executive*
†Elzay, Richard Paul *retired dental school administrator*
Embry, Stephen Creston *lawyer*
Emek, Sharon Helene *risk management consultant*
Emerling, Carol G(reenbaum) *consultant*
Emerson, Ann Parker *dietitian*
Emerson, Daniel Everett *retired communications company executive*
Emerson, R. Clark *priest, business administrator*
Emery, Alan Roy *museum executive*
Emma, Lynne Anne *healthcare administrator*
Emmett, Rita *professional speaker*
Emmons, Robert Duncan *diplomat*
†Emory, Lee (Whitney Eden) *writer*
†Empey, Kerry McGarr *pharmacist*
Emrich, Jeanne Ann *poet, artist*
Endicott, Jennifer Jane Reynolds *education educator*
Endicott, William F. *journalist*
Enfield, Susan Ann *secondary school educator*

Engel, Albert Joseph *retired federal judge*
Engel, Bernard Theodore *psychologist, educator*
Engel-Arieli, Susan Lee *physician*
Engelhardt, John Hugo *lawyer, banker*
Engelmann, Rudolph Herman *electronics consultant, writer*
Engels, Beatrice Ann *retired real estate company executive, poet, artist*
Engels, Lawrence Arthur *retired metals company executive*
Engels, Thomas Joseph *sales executive*
Enger, Edward Henry, Jr., *retired editor, writer*
Engibous, Thomas James *electronics company executive*
England, Douglas M. *pathologist*
†Englander, Tom *business owner*
Engle, Howard A. *retired pediatrician*
Engle, Steve Eugene *artist*
Engleman, Dennis Eugene *electrical engineer, author, photographer, musician*
Engler, John *governor*
English, Bruce Vaughan *environmental consultant*
English, Christine A. *accountant, business development manager*
†English, Gregory Bruce *lawyer*
English-Anderson, San Dei *minister*
Engstrom, Marlene M. *volunteer*
Ennest, John William *bank executive*
Eno, Amos Stewart *natural resource foundation administrator*
Enoch, Craig Trively *state supreme court justice*
Ensign, William Lloyd *architect*
Epcar, Richard Michael *actor, writer, director*
†Ephron, Nora *writer, director*
Epp, Eldon Jay *religion educator*
Epperson, Margaret Farrar *civic worker*
Epps, Charles Harry, Jr., *retired orthopaedic surgery educator*
Epps, William David *priest*
Epstein, Judith Ann *judge*
Erb, Richard Louis Lundin *resort and hotel executive*
Erbe, Yvonne Mary *music educator, marketing specialist, guidance counselor*
Erdeljac, Daniel Joseph *retired manufacturing company executive*
†Erden, Sybil Isolde *artist*
Erenberger, Timothy *writer*
Erfani, Shervin *academic administrator, engineering educator*
Erickson, Alan Eric *librarian*
Erickson, Garwood Elliott *computer consulting company executive, entrepreneur*
†Erickson, Stacy Lynn *literature educator*
Erlebacher, Arlene Cernik *retired lawyer*
Erlenborn, John Neal *lawyer, educator, former congressman*
Erlichson, Miriam *fundraiser*
Erlicht, Lewis Howard *broadcasting company executive*
Ernst, Edward Willis *retired electrical engineering educator*
Ernzen, Mary Anne *women's health nurse, clinical nurse specialist*
Ertl, Rita Mae *elementary education educator*
Ertwine, Dean R. *retired military officer*
Erwin, Elmer Louis *vintager, cement consultant*
Erwin, Judith Ann (Judith Ann Peacock) *writer, photographer, lawyer*
Erzinger, Dennis Eugene, Sr., *factory automation executive*
†Escobar, Elaine Ofelia *television producer, writer*
†Esparza, Monica *nursing administrator*
Espenlaub, Margo Linn *women's studies educator, writer, artist*
Espinosa, Horacio Dante *mechanical engineering educator, consultant*
†Espiricueta, Sylvia *counseling administrator*
†Esposito, Mark Mario *lawyer*
Esquivel, Agerico Liwag *retired research physicist*
Essa, Lisa Beth *elementary school educator*
†Essegaier, Skander *education educator, researcher*
Essig, Kathleen Susan *university official, management consultant*
Esterhammer, Angela *literary theorist, educator*
Estes, Carl Lewis, II, *lawyer*
Estes, Elaine Rose Graham *retired librarian*
†Esther, Queen *playwright, scriptwriter, actor*
Estrin, Herbert Alvin *financial consultant, entertainment company executive*
Estrin, Richard William *real estate broker, retired newspaper editor*
†Estrin, Thelma Austern *retired electrical engineer*
Esty, John Cushing, Jr., *writer, teacher, advisor to non-profit boards*
Etheridge, Diana Carol *internet business executive*
Etra, Lionel *lawyer*
Ettinger, Harry Joseph *industrial hygiene engineer , project manager*
Ettinger, Joseph Alan *lawyer*
Etzel, Ruth Ann *pediatrician, epidemiologist, educator*
Eu, March Fong *ambassador, former state official*
†Eubanks, Jessica Lynn *protective services official*
Eugster, Albrecht Konrad *veterinarian, laboratory director, emeritus*
Euster, Joanne Reed *retired librarian*
Eustis, Albert Anthony *lawyer, diversified industry corporate executive*
Evangelista, Anita Loretta *freelance writer, psychologist, nurse, publishing executive*
Evangelista, Nick Forrest *fencing master, writer, publisher*
Evanoff, George C.
Evans, Bonita Dianne *adult education educator*
Evans, Charles Wayne, II, *biologist, researcher*
Evans, Geraldine Ann *academic administrator*
†Evans, Jack *city official*
Evans, James Handel *university administrator, architect, educator*
Evans, Judith Ann Futral *artist*
Evans, Lance *psychology educator*
Evans, Rosemary Hall *civic worker*
†Evans, Teresa Rinaldi *music educator, vocalist*
Evans, Victor Miles *retired funeral home, cemetery company executive*
Evatt, Parker *former state commissioner, former state legislator*
Evdokimova, Eva *prima ballerina assoluta, choreographer, director, producer, actress*
Everdell, William *retired lawyer*
†Everett, Aubrey Leigh *musician*
Everett, Elbert Kyle *marketing executive, consultant*
†Everett, Robert Rivers *electrical engineer*
Everett, Tom *actor*
Everly, George Stotelmyer, Jr., *psychologist, psychophysiologist, educator, mathematician*
†Evert, Chris (Christine Marie Evert) *retired professional tennis player*
Eviatar, Lydia *pediatric neurologist*
†Ewald, Laura Anne *school librarian*
†Ewanchuk, Michael *retired school system administrator*
Ewen, H.I. *physicist*
Ewing, Edgar Louis *artist, educator*
Ewing, Elisabeth Anne Rooney *priest*
Ewing, James E. *priest*
Ewing, Martin S. *astronomer, electrical engineer*
Ewing, Raymond Charles *retired ambassador*
Ewing, Thomas William *former congressman, lawyer*
Ewing, Wayne Turner *coal company executive*
Eyerman, David John *software engineer*
†Eyring, Maxine Louise *small business owner, esthetician*
Faber, Michael Warren *lawyer*
†Fabian, D'Arline D. *music educator*
Fagin, David Kyle *natural resources executive*
Fahey-Cameron, Robin *artist, photographer, writer*
Fahlbeck, Douglas Alan *corporate development executive*
Fahringer, Catherine Hewson *retired savings and loan association executive*
Fahrnbruch, Dale E. *retired state supreme court justice*
Fair, Marcia Jeanne Hixson *retired educational administrator*
Fairleigh, James Parkinson *music educator*
Falconer, Marguerite Elizabeth *artist*
Faletra, Robert *technology company executive*
Falk, Marshall Allen *retired university dean, physician*
Faller, Jason *physician*
†Fallon, William J. *career officer*
†Fan, Cong *music educator*
Fan, Hung Y. *virology educator, consultant*
Fan, Qi *mechanical engineer*
Fang, Mark (Yanchu Fang) *geneticist*
Fanos, Kathleen Hilaire *osteopathic physician, podiatrist*
Fant, Clyde Edward, Jr., *religion educator*
Fanwick, Ernest *lawyer*
†Fappiano, Tara C. *lawyer*
Farah, Kimberly Sue *chemistry educator, researcher*
†Fare, Elizabeth Carol *music educator*
Fares, Michael Issam *bank executive, investor, philanthropist*
†Fargo, Thomas Boulton *career officer*
†Farid, Farid O. *mathematics educator*
Farinella, Paul James *retired arts institution executive*
Faris, James Vannoy *interventional cardiologist, cardiology educator, hospital executive*
Fariss, Bruce Lindsay *endocrinologist, educator*
Farkas, Daniel Frederick *food science and technology educator*
Farley, Barbara Suzanne *lawyer*
Farley, Benjamin Wirt *religious studies educator, writer*
Farmakides, John Basil *lawyer*
Farmer, Cornelia Griffin *lawyer, consultant, hearings official*
Farmer, Kenneth, Jr., *military officer*
Farnsworth, Elizabeth *broadcast journalist*
Faron, Fay Cheryl *private investigator, writer*
Farquhar, Robin Hugh *former university president*
Farr, Ivanne Estelle *small business owner, consultant, artist, sculptor*
Farr, Jesse F. *federal agency administrator*
Farrall, Harold John *retired accountant*
Farrar, Elaine Willardson *artist*
Farrar, Richard Bartlett, Jr., *school system administrator*
†Farrell, Edward Wagner *retired dentist, educator*
Farrell, William Edgar *sales executive, infosystems specialist, management consultant*
Farrelly, Peter John *screenwriter*
Farrington, Bertha Louise *retired nursing administrator*
Fasick, Adele Mongan *information services consultant*
Fatzinger, James A. S. *construction educator, estimator*
Faucette, Gloria Marie *accountant, educator*
†Faucette, Merilon Cooper *retired elementary educator*
Faulkner, Lewis L. *architect*
Favorite, Malaika *artist*
Fawcett, John Thomas *archivist*
Faxon, Alicia Craig *art educator, department chairman*
Fay, Conner Martindale *retired business executive*
Fay, Peter Thorp *judge*
Fayer, Steve *writer*
Fazio, Evelyn M. *publisher*
Feagles, Gerald Franklin *marketing executive*
Fearrington, Ann Peyton *writer, illustrator, newspaper reporter, portraitist*
Feathers, Gail M. Wratny *social worker*
†Feazell, Thomas Lee *lawyer, business executive*
†Fecht-Gramley, Mary E. *trauma specialist, health facility educator*
†Fecteau, Francis Roger *judge*
Feder, Adam Barry *software engineer*
Federici, William Vito *newspaper reporter*
Federing, Eric K. *congressional communications director, motion picture preservationist, educator, public policy advisor*
Fedorowicz, Jane *information systems educator*
Fehr, Gregory Paris *marketing and distribution company executive*
Fehr, Lola Mae *health organization administrator*
†Fehrenbach, Margaret Jean *dental hygienist, educator*
Fehribach, Ronald Steven *investment executive*
Feierstein, Mark Errol *retired lawyer*
Feiler, Jo Alison *artist*
Fein, Seymour Howard *pharmaceutical executive*
Feinberg, Glenda Joyce *restaurant chain executive*
Feiner, Ava Sophia *public affairs and management consultant, economist*
Feinstein, Martin *performing arts consultant, art director*
Feinstein, Robert P. *dermatologist*
Feitelson, Mark Alan *biomedical scientist, educator*
Fekete, George Otto *judge, lawyer, pharmacist*
†Feldman, David Edward *playwright*
Feldman, David Henry *psychologist, educator*
Feldman, Douglas A. *anthropologist*
Feldman, Jack L. *neurobiology educator*
Feldman, Lillian Maltz *early childhood education consultant*
Feldmann, Frank Neil *chemistry educator*
Feldstein, Joshua *educational administrator*
Felgar, Raymond E(ugene) *pathologist, medical educator*
Felhofer, Marylouise Katherine *nursing administrator*
Felicetti, Daniel A. *academic administrator, educator*
Felix, Cheryl A. *air transportation executive*
Fell, Jennifer Anne *writer*
Fella, Marie Ann *intelligence analyst, drug enforcement administration*
Feller, Robert William Andrew *baseball team public relations executive, retired baseball player*
Fellers, Rhonda Gay *lawyer*
Fellman, Gerry Louis *lawyer, arbitrator*
Fenech, Daniel Thomas *cartoonist*
†Feng, Bao Qi (Pao Chi) (Edward) *mathematician, educator*
Fennebresque, Kim Samuel *investment banker*
Fennell, Tracy Lee *music educator, composer*
Fenwick, James Henry *editor*
†Fenwick, Lynda Beck *lawyer, writer*
Ferguson, Bradford Lee *lawyer*
Ferguson, Earl Wilson *cardiologist, medical executive, telemedicine consultant*
Ferguson, Emmet Fewell, Jr., *surgeon*
Ferguson, James Clarke *mathematician, algorithmist*
Ferguson, Lewis LeRoy *retired senior correspondent*
Ferguson, Whitworth, III, *pastor*
†Ferk, Franc *information technology executive*
Fernald, Harold Allen *publishing executive*
Fernández, Alberto Antonio *security professional*
Fernandez, Mary Joe *retired professional tennis player*
Fernández-Velazquez, Juan Ramon *university chancellor*
Fero, Lester Kniffin *aerospace engineer, consultant*
Ferraro, Geraldine Anne *lawyer, former congresswoman*
Ferre, Antonio Luis *newspaper publisher*
Ferreira, Armando Thomas *sculptor, educator*
Ferreira, Jo Ann Jeanette Chanoux *time-definite transportation industry executive*
Ferreira, Linda Doreen *long term, acute care and rehabilitation nurse*
Ferrell, David Stanley *aerospace company executive*
Ferri, Ronald Domenico *artist, painter*
Ferstenfeld, Julian Erwin *internist, educator*
Fertig-Dykes, Susan Beatrice *communications executive, human resources professional, community and civil society facilitator*
Fetherston, Brian Lloyd *artist, painter, sculptor*
Fetler, Andrew *author, educator*
†Fetterly, Lynn Lawrence *real estate broker, developer*
Feuer, Marshall Zev *import/export company executive*
†Fey, Willard *global environmental researcher, educator*
Fiala, Dennison Fairchild *technical consultant*
Fibiger, John Andrew *life insurance company executive*
Fiddick, Paul William *government official, broadcasting executive*
Field, Arthur Norman *lawyer*
Field, Charles Twist *artist, retired art educator*
Field, Ellen *marketing professional*
Field, Margaret M. *retired librarian*
Field, Michael Jay *education educator*
†Field, Sally *actress*
†Fields, Cleo *state legislator*
Fields, Dan *newspaper editor*
Fields, Douglas Philip *building supply wholesale company executive*
Fields, Freddie *producer, agent*
Fields, Leo *former jewelry company executive, investor*
†Fields, Tina Rae *artist, ecopsychologist*
Fields, Velma Archie *medical/surgical nurse*
†Fiennes, Ralph Nathaniel *actor*
Fife, Jonathan Donald *higher education educator*
Figlar, Anita Wise *retired banker*
Fiks, Yevgeniy *artist, critic*
Fila, Joseph Duncan *marketing and sales executive, public relations executive, real estate broker, investor*
Filchock, Ethel *education educator, poet*
Filer, Emily Symington Harkins *retired foundation administrator, writer*
Filerman, Michael Herman *television producer*
Filler, Susan Melanie *musicologist*
Fillmore, John Dillon *artist*
Filshie, Michele Ann *editor*
†Filvaroff, Ellen H. *research scientist*
†Finder, Joseph Alan *writer*
Finder-Stone, Patricia Ann *nurse, health educator, volunteer*
†Findling, Rhonda Barbara *psychotherapist*
Finelsen, Libbi June *lawyer*
Finestone, Sheila *legislator, state official*
Finger, Harold B. *consultant*
Fingerson, Leroy Malvin *engineering executive, mechanical engineer*
†Fink, Alma *retired elementary education educator*
Fink, John Francis *retired newspaper editor, columnist, writer*
Fink, Norman Stiles *lawyer, educational administrator, fundraising consultant*
Finkelstein, David *retired cardiologist*
Finkelstein, Seymour *business consultant*
Finlay, Robert Derek *food company executive*
Finn, Daniel Kevin *economics and theology educator, former dean*
Finn, Mary Ralphe *artist*
Finnberg, Elaine Agnes *psychologist, editor*
Finnegan, Sara Anne (Sara Lycett) *publisher*
Finner, Stephen Lawrence *labor union administrator*
†Finneran, Kevin Joseph *editor*
Finnigan, Robert Emmet *retired small business owner*
Fino, Marie Georgette Keck *retired real estate broker*
†Fino, Teresa Cristina *legal secretary, business owner*
Finocchiaro, Alfonso G. *bank executive*
Fiorito, Edward Gerald *lawyer*
Fioto, George Anthony *chemist*
Firestein, Cecily Barth *artist*
†Firschein, Sylvia *librarian, elementary education educator*
First, Craig Patrick *composer, educator*
†Fischer, A(lbert) Alan *family physician*
Fischer, Angela Brown *business executive, civic volunteer*
Fischer, Clare *composer*
Fischer, David Jon *lawyer*
Fischer, David Seymour *internist, consultant*
†Fischer, Harald Maximilian *education educator, researcher*
Fischer, Linda Marie *nursing educator*
Fischer, Lucy Rose *gerontologist, researcher, artist*
Fischer, Maxim *electronics engineer*
Fischer, Michael Ludwig *environmental executive*
Fischer, Russell Leonard *public relations executive*
Fischer, William Samuel *composer, lecturer*
Fischer, Zoe Ann *real estate and property marketing company executive, consultant*
Fish, Brian R *music educator*
Fish, Janet Isobel *artist*
†Fishback, David Simon *lawyer*
Fisher, Allan Michael *government official, educator*
Fisher, Anita Jeanne (Kit Fisher) *language educator*
Fisher, Fenimore *business development consultant*
Fisher, Gordon McCrea *mathematician, educator*
Fisher, Herbert Calvin *retired surgeon*
Fisher, Linda J. *federal agency administrator*
Fisher, Lyman McArthur *retired clinical pathologist, hematologist*
†Fisher, Margaret *artist, researcher*
Fisher, Nancy *writer, producer, director*
Fisher, Peter R. *federal agency administrator*
Fisher, Robert Bruce *priest*
Fisher, Robert Charles Haru *publishing company executive, editor*
Fisher, Steven Jay *architect*
Fishman, Bernard *mechanical engineer*
†Fishman, Glenn I. *medical educator*
Fishman, Lawrence Martin *endocrinologist, educator*
Fishman, Marc Judah *physician, researcher, executive*
†Fishwick, Marshall W. *education educator*
Fisk, Ian T. *economic development consultant, publishing executive*
Fisk, Merlin Edgar *judge*
Fiss, Owen M. *law educator, educator*
Fittro, Ronald G., Jr., *healthcare executive, consultant*
Fitts, Catherine Austin *investment advisor*
Fitts, Janet Sue *emergency nurse practitioner, educator, homeschool educator, cosmetics executive, consultant*
FitzAlan-Howard, Bennett-Thomas Henry Robert *public administration and policy analyst, political theorist , theologian*
Fitz-Enz, David G. *retired military officer, television producer*
Fitzgeorge, Harold James *former oil and gas company executive*
Fitzgerald, Daniel R. *artist, consultant*
Fitzgerald, Michael Francis *journalist*
†Fitzgerald, Walter George *marketing consulting company executive*
Fitzgerald-Verbonitz, Dianne Elizabeth *healthcare executive*
Fitzmaurice, Laurence Dorset *retired bank executive*
†Fitzpatrick, Kathleen G. *education educator, accountant*
Fitzpatrick, Lorraine *accountant*
Fitzpatrick, Nancy Hecht *editor*
Fitzpatrick, Ruth Ann *education educator*
Fiume, Barbara Parenty *social worker*
Fiumefreddo, Charles A. *investment management company executive*
Fix, John Neilson *banker*
Flagg, Norman Lee *retired advertising executive*
Flanagan, Harry Paul *publishing executive*

†Flanagan, Kathleen Theresa *education educator*
†Flanary, Donald Herbert, Jr., *lawyer*
†Flaten, Alfred N. *retired food and consumer products executive*
Fleetwood, Mary Annis *education association executive*
Fleischman, Herman Israel *lawyer*
Fleisher, Gary Mitchell *employment industry and management consulting executive*
Fleishman, Philip Robert *internist*
†Fleming, Brian Anthony *musician, educator*
†Fleming, Cecil *business executive*
†Fleming, Horace Weldon, Jr., *educator, former university president*
Fleming, James Stuart, Jr., *retired pharmaceutical company manager*
Fleming, Rhonda *actress, singer, humanitarian*
Fleming, Susan F. *artist*
Flemming, David Paul *biologist*
Flick, Arnold L. *retired physician, community activist*
Flick, Carl *electrical engineer, consultant*
Flick, John Edmond *lawyer*
Flickinger, Joe Arden *telecommunications educator*
Flinner, Beatrice Jeffreys Allayaud *retired library and media sciences educator*
Flint, John E. *historian, educator*
Flint, Lou Jean *retired state agency administrator*
Flipse, John Edward *naval architect, mechanical engineer*
Flitcraft, Richard Kirby, II, *former chemical company executive*
Flood, James Tyrrell *broadcasting executive, public relations consultant*
Flood, Patrick James *political scientist, writer, retired diplomat*
Flor, Loy Lorenz *retired chemist, corrosion engineer, consultant*
†Flores, Alfinio *mathematician, educator*
Flournoy, John Craig *journalism educator*
†Floyd-Hooper, Carol Ann *musician, educator*
Fluth, John Adam *educational administrator*
Flynn, George William *chemistry educator, researcher*
†Flynn, Michael *lawyer*
Flynn, Paul Bartholomew *foundation executive*
Flynn, Peter Anthony *judge*
Flynn, Robert James *electronic commerce executive*
Fodiman, Aaron Rosen *publishing executive*
Fodrea, Carolyn Wrobel *educational researcher, publisher, consultant*
Fogel, Esther Marian (Esther Marian Roseig) *veterinary researcher*
†Fogelman, Ann Florence *nutritionist, consultant*
Fogg, Richard Lloyd *food products company executive*
Foglesong, Paul David *molecular biology and microbiology educator*
Foglia, Stephen Phillip *musician, recording industry executive*
†Foglietta, Thomas Michael *former diplomat, former congressman*
Foldi, Andrew Harry *retired singer, educator*
Foley, Gary J. *research chemical engineer, computer scientist, federal agency administrator*
†Foley, Paul E. *political scientist, educator*
Folk, Marie Gwynn *library technician*
Folker, Cathleen Ann *business educator*
Follingstad, Carol C. *psychologist, consultant, educator*
Folsom, Virginia Jean *music educator*
Foltiny, Stephen Vincent *special education educator*
Folz, Kathleen Louise *elementary education educator*
Fomon, Samuel Joseph *physician, educator*
†Fonda, Peter *actor, director, producer*
Fontana, Mario H. *nuclear engineer*
Foote, Evelyn Patricia *retired military officer*
†Foote, Horton *playwright, scriptwriter*
†Foote, William Chapin *business executive*
†Foran, Chris *poet, educator*
Forbes, Marjorie Webster *volunteer counselor*
Forbes, Michael Patrick *former congressman*
†Forbes, Thais R. *anthropologist, consultant*
†Forbush, Robert Raymond, Sr., *financial consultant, small business owner, educator*
Forcinio, Hallie Eunice *editor*
Ford, Ashley Lloyd *lawyer, retired consumer products company executive*
Ford, E(mma) Jane *public relations executive*
Ford, Ford Barney *retired government official*
†Ford, Harrison *actor*
Ford, Jerry Lee *service company executive*
Ford, Judith Ann Tudor *retired natural gas distribution company executive*
Ford, Kay Louise *innovation consulting executive*
Ford, Kenneth William *physicist*
Ford, Mark Lee *aerospace engineer, scientist*
Ford, Nancy Louise *composer, scriptwriter*
†Ford, Richard *writer*
Ford, William Francis *retired bank holding company executive*
†Fordice, Kirk (Daniel Kirkwood Fordice Jr.) *former governor, construction company executive, engineer*
†Foreman, George *former boxer, minister, boxing broadcaster*
Forest, Eva Brown *songwriter, producer, performer, publisher*
Forester, Jean Martha Brouillette *innkeeper, retired librarian, educator*
Forister, Jean Whitby *retired guidance counselor, consultant*
Forlini, Frank John, Jr., *cardiologist*
Forman, Edgar Ross *mechanical engineer*
Forney, Ronald Dean *elementary school educator, consultant, educational therapist*
†Forno, Karin Ida *physician, educator*
†Foronda, Barbara Elaine *professional organizer, writer*
Forry, John Ingram *retired lawyer*

Forry, Steven *not-for-profit fundraiser*
Forst, Marion Francis *bishop*
Forster, Clifford *lawyer*
†Forster, Donald R. *vocational school educator*
Forsyth, Ben Ralph *academic administrator, medical educator*
Forsythe, Henderson *actor*
†Fort, Denise Douglas *law educator, former state official*
†Fortgang, Charles *wholesale distribution executive*
†Fortune, Annetta *management educator, accountant*
Foshay, Maxine Valentine Shottland *civic worker, public relations executive*
Foss, Charles R. *contracting officer*
Foss, Lukas *composer, conductor, pianist*
†Fossuo Talom, Patrick *research scientist*
Foster, Charles Henry Wheelwright *former foundation officer, consultant, author*
Foster, Fredericka *artist*
Foster, Joy Via *retired library media specialist*
Foster, Judith Christine *lawyer, writer*
†Foster, Lloyd Bennett *lawyer, musician*
Foster, Mary Christine *motion picture and television executive*
Foster, Robert Lawson *retired judge, deacon*
†Foster, Sonja Marguerite *musician, educator*
Foster, Stephen Kent *banker*
Foti, Joanne Erminia *painter, textile designer, educator*
Foulke, Robert Dana *English educator, travel writer*
Fountain, Andre Ferchaud *academic program director*
Fountain, Linda Kathleen *health science association executive*
Fournier, Walter Frank *real estate executive*
†Fout, Mary Jane *librarian, educator*
Fowler, Donald Raymond *retired lawyer, educator*
Fowler, Flora Daun *retired lawyer*
Fowler, Hugh Charles *charter school consultant & developer*
Fowler, Robert Asa *diplomat, consultant, business director*
Fowler, Stephen Eugene *retired military officer, human resources executive*
†Fox, Carol Jean *librarian*
Fox, Eleanor Mae Cohen *lawyer, educator, writer*
Fox, Gretchen Hovemeyer *freelance editor, genealogical consultant*
†Fox, James R. *telecommunications technician*
Fox, Jeffrey *journalist*
Fox, Jennifer Joy *artist, educator*
Fox, Joan Phyllis *environmental engineer*
Fox, John David *educator, physicist*
†Fox, Jon D. *former congressman*
Fox, Kelly Diane *financial adviser*
Fox, Lloyd Allan *insurance company executive*
Fox, Michael Wilson *veterinarian, bioethicist, animal behaviorist*
Fox-Clarkson, Anne C. *computer company executive*
†Foy, Alexis *professional athletics coach*
Foy, Charles Daley *retired soil scientist*
†Foy, Edward Joseph *sociologist, educator, social worker*
Frackman, Noel *art critic*
Fradkin, David Milton *physicist, educator*
†Fraga, Mike A. *history educator, accountant*
Frago-Zito, Ivy Marie *accountant*
Fraidin, Stephen *lawyer*
Fralinger, Jack Bruce *surgeon*
Franciosa, Anthony (Anthony Papaleo) *actor*
Franciosa, Joseph Anthony *health care consultant*
Francis, Philip Hamilton *management consultant*
Francisco, Wayne *automotive executive*
Francke, Linda Bird *journalist*
Frank, Charles Raphael, Jr., *financial advisor*
Frank, Edgar Gerald *retired financial executive*
Frank, Edmund Paul, Jr., *accountant*
†Frank, JoAnn *photographer*
Frank, Lawrence James *library director*
Frank, Leona *artist*
†Frank, Marshall *protective services official, writer*
Frank, Stanley Donald *publishing company executive*
Franke, John Charles *retired human resources executive*
Franke, Wayne Thomas *retired government affairs director, consultant*
†Frankel, Albert J. *registrar*
Frankel, James Burton *retired lawyer*
Frankel, Jeffrey *neurologist*
Frankel, Judith Jennifer Mariasha *clinical psychologist, consultant*
Frankenberger, Bertram, Jr., *investor, consultant*
Frankish, Brian Edward *film producer, director*
Franklin, Billy Joe *international higher education specialist*
Franklin, Bonnie Selinsky *retired federal agency administrator*
†Franklin, Charles E. *manufacturing executive*
Franklin, Jon Daniel *writer, journalist, educator*
Franklin, Margery Bodansky *psychology educator, researcher*
Franklin, Mary Ann Wheeler *educator, higher education and management consultant*
Franklin, Michael Harold *arbitrator, lawyer, consultant*
Franks, Tommy Ray *retired army officer*
Frankson-Kendrick, Sarah Jane *publisher*
†Frantiska Jr., Joseph John *systems engineer, educator*
Franz, John E. *bio-organic chemist, researcher*
Franz, Judy R. *physics educator*
Franzen, Richard *writer*
Franzetti, Lillian Angelina *former automobile dealership owner*
Frappia, Linda Ann *management executive*
†Fraser, Ailana Margaret *mathematician, educator*
Fraser, Donald C. *engineering executive, educator*

Fraser, Donald MacKay *former mayor, former congressman, educator*
Fraser, Frederick Ewart *art educator*
Fraser, Russell Alfred *author, educator*
Frauenhoffer, Rose Marie *visual artist, cosmetologist*
Frawley, Michael Keith *lawyer*
†Frazier, DuEwa M. *literature educator, writer*
Frazier, Henry Bowen, III, *retired judge, government official, lawyer*
Frazier, Lois E. *business and economics educator*
Frazier, Thomas C. *protective services official*
Frear, Jon S. *pet services company executive*
Fréchette, Louise *international organization official*
Frederick, Elizabeth Eleanor Tatum *watercolor artist, retired educator*
Frederick, Robert Melvin *retired farm organization executive*
Fredericks, Joan DeLanoy *retired health science administrator*
Fredericks, Patricia Ann *real estate executive*
Fredman, Mimi Ungar Coppersmith *advertising and publishing executive*
Fred-Mensah, Ben Kwame *international development educator, consultant*
Fredrichs, Anne Marie Johnson *pediatric nurse practitioner*
Fredrickson, Sharon Wong *accountant, controller*
Freed, Evan Phillip *lawyer*
Freedman, Monroe Henry *lawyer, educator, columnist*
Freedman, Russell Bruce *author*
Freeland, Aaron Leonard *painter, printmaker*
Freeman, Arthur *veterinarian, retired association administrator*
Freeman, Charles E. *state supreme court justice*
Freeman, Glenn *political organization worker, retired non-commissioned military officer*
Freeman, Kevin David *portfolio management executive, entrepreneur*
Freeman, Maynard Lloyd *nuclear medicine physician, researcher*
Freeman, Meredith Norwin *former college president, education educator*
Freeman, Ralph Carter *investment banker, management consultant*
Freese, Barbara Tapp *nursing educator*
Freilich, Morris *anthropologist, educator*
Freilicher, Jane *artist*
†Freimark, Jeffrey Philip *corporate financial executive*
Freitag, Harlow *retired computer scientist and corporate executive*
French, Clarence Levi, Jr., *retired shipbuilding company executive*
French, Daniel J. *former prosecutor*
French, Marilyn *writer, critic*
†Freshman, Brenda Lee *psychologist, educator, psychologist, researcher*
†Freston, Thomas E. *cable television programming executive*
†Freund, Samuel J. *lawyer*
Frey, Katie Manciet *education educator*
Frey, Margo Walther *career counselor, columnist*
Fri, Robert Wheeler *retired museum director*
Friars, Eileen M. *bank executive*
Frick, Ivan Eugene *college president emeritus, education consultant*
Fricklas, Anita Alper *retired religious organization administrator*
Fricklas, Richard Leon *roofing educator, educational institute administrator*
Fricks, Ernest Eugene *management consultant*
Friday, Katherine Orwoll *artist*
Fridley, Robert Bruce *agricultural engineer, educator*
Fried, Charles *law educator*
Fried, Emanuel Joseph *actor, writer*
†Frieden, Brenda Joyce *secondary school educator*
Friedlander, Charles Douglas (Chuck Friedlander) *space consultant*
†Friedlander, James Stuart *lawyer*
Friedman, Arnold Carl *radiologist*
Friedman, Betsy Sue *artist*
Friedman, Marcia L *photographer, writer*
Friedman, Marla Lee *marketing professional*
Friedman, Martin *museum director, arts adviser*
†Friedman, Martin Philip *applied behavior sciences specialist, education educator*
Friedman, Mildred *architectural and design educator, curator, consultant*
Friedman, Paul Richard *lawyer*
Friedman, Sanford Howard *information scientist*
Friedman, Victor Allen *linguist, educator*
Friedrich, Su G. *filmmaker, educator*
Frieling, Gerald Harvey, Jr., *specialty steel company executive*
Friendly, Ed *television producer*
Fries, Raymond Sebastian *manufacturing company executive*
Frimerman, Leslie *retired financial services company executive*
Frischkorn, David Ephraim Keasbey, Jr., *investment banker*
Frisco, Louis Joseph *retired materials science company executive, electrical engineer*
Frishberg, Benjamin M. *neurologist*
Fristoe, Macalyne *speech-language pathologist, psychologist, educator, writer*
Fritcher, Earl Edwin *civil engineer, consultant*
Fritz, Ethel Mae Hendrickson *writer*
Fritz, Jan Marie *planning educator, mediator, clinical sociologist*
Fritz, Rene Eugene, Jr., *manufacturing executive*
Froberg, Brent Malcolm *classics educator*
Froehlke, Robert Frederick *financial services executive*
Frohlichstein, Alan *retinal angiographer*
Frohman, Larry Philip *neuro-ophthalmologist*
†Froiland, Kathryn Grace *nursing educator*
Fromlet, K. Hubert *banking economist*
Fromm, Joseph *retired magazine editor, foreign affairs consultant*
Frost, Ellen Louise *political economist*

Frost, Everett Lloyd *anthropologist, academic administrator*
Frost, J. Ormond *otolaryngologist, educator*
Frost, Linda Gail *clergyman, hospital chaplain*
Frost, Sterling Newell *arbitrator, mediator, management consultant*
†Fruisen, Catherine Myler (Violet LeMay) *illustrator*
Fry, Amelia Roberts *biographer, oral historian*
Fry, Hedy *member of parliament*
Fry, Malcolm Craig *retired clergyman*
Fryburger, Lawrence Bruce *lawyer, mediator, writer*
Fryer, Thomas Waitt, Jr., *writer and editor*
Frymer, Murry *writer, theater and film critic*
†Fuchs, Anne Sutherland *magazine publisher*
Fuchs, Betty Corcoran *retired fundraising consultant*
Fuchs, Joseph Louis *retired magazine publisher*
†Fuchs, Michael Joseph *television executive*
†Fuchsberg, Lawrence J. *writer, editor, performing arts association administrator, consultant*
†Fucuals, Ronald H. *conductor, director*
Fuentes, Carlos *writer, former ambassador*
Fuerstner, Fiona Margaret Anne *ballet company executive, ballet educator*
Fujitani, Martin Tomio *software engineer*
†Fukasawa, Natsuki *music educator*
Fulbright, Harriet Mayor *educational association administrator*
Fulbright-Brock, Vivian *supervisory probation officer*
Fuld, Richard Severin, Jr., *investment banking executive*
Fullenwider, Nancy Vrana *music composer, dance educator, pianist*
†Fuller, Charles H, Jr., *playwright*
Fuller, Margaret Jane *medical technologist*
Fuller, Maxine Compton *retired secondary school educator*
Fuller, Pamela Dorr *software engineer*
Fuller, Richard Kenneth *retired alcohol/drug abuse services professional*
†Fuller, Stephen W. *science educator*
Fullerton, Gail Jackson *university president emeritus*
Fullmer, Lee Wayne *retired minister*
Fulp, Errin *computer science educator*
Fulrath, Andrew Wesley *retired small business owner*
Fumagalli, Barbara Merrill *artist, printmaker*
Funck, Dennis Light *chemist, researcher*
Fung, Bing Man *chemistry educator*
Funk, Vicki Jane *librarian*
Funkhouser, Erica *writer, educator, communications educator*
Funseth, Robert Lloyd Eric Martin *international consultant, lecturer, retired senior foreign service officer, foundation administrator*
Furnas, David William *plastic surgeon, educator*
Furst, E. Kenneth *accountant*
†Furth, Karen J. *artist, art educator*
Futter, Victor *lawyer*
Gabel, Creighton *retired anthropologist, educator*
Gabel, Katherine *retired academic administrator*
Gabel, Ronald Glen *telecommunications executive*
Gaberman, Harry *retired lawyer*
Gable, Karen Elaine *health science educator*
†Gabor-Hotchkiss, Magda *research scientist, librarian*
Gabria, Joanne Bakaitis *health and education volunteer, former information processing systems equipment company executive*
Gabriel, Judith A. *bodywork therapist, educator, writer*
Gabriel, Rennie *financial counselor, author, publisher*
Gaddis, John Lewis *history educator*
Gadol, Peter Daniel *writer*
Gaertner, Donell John *retired library director*
Gaffney, Thomas *banker*
Gage, Patrick (Leonard Patrick Gage) *biotech/pharmaceutical consultant*
Gage, Tommy Wilton *retired pharmacologist, dentist, pharmacist, educator*
Gagnon, Ronald Adelard *library director*
Gahagan, Thomas Gail *obstetrician, gynecologist*
Gaiber, Lawrence Jay *financial company executive*
Gaillard, George Siday, III, *architect*
Gainer, Jeffery A. *writer, consultant*
†Gaines, Cherie Adelaide *lawyer*
†Gainey, Robert Michael *professional hockey coach, former player*
Gainor, Thomas Edward *banker*
Galan, Vincent *anesthesiologist*
Galanopoulos, Kelly *biomedical engineer*
Galante, Jane Hohfeld *pianist, music historian*
†Galbraith, Allan Lee *lawyer*
Galbraith, Nanette Elaine Gerks *forensic and management sciences company executive*
Galbraith, William Bruce *physician, educator*
Galdi-Weissman, Natalie Ann *secondary education educator*
Galison, Peter Louis *history of science educator*
Gallagher, Cynthia *artist, educator*
†Gallagher, Cynthia Polansky *writer*
Gallagher, John Paul *association administrator*
Gallagher, Lindy Allyn *banker, financial consultant*
Gallagher, Robert P. *bank executive*
Gallaher, Frederick Blake *public health specialist*
Gallert, Barbara Lynn *communications executive*
Galliher, Clarice A. Andrews *secondary education educator*
†Gallinger, Robert Arthur *retired military officer, writer*
Galloway, William Rodney *military officer*
Galt, John William *actor, writer*
Galvao, Louis Alberto *import and export corporation executive, consultant*
Galvin, Thomas John *Former information science policy educator and librarian*

Galvis y Assmus, Patricia *computer animator, educator, filmmaker*
Gamble, Desirata *artist, poet*
Gamble, E. James *lawyer, accountant*
Gamble, Mary G(race) *marketing and organizational development professional*
†Gamble, Scott L. *civil engineer*
Gambrell, Luck Flanders *corporate executive*
†Gamin, Judith *poet*
Gammon, Samuel Rhea, III, *association executive, former ambassador*
Gamroth, Arthur Paul *small business owner*
Gamsky, Neal Richard *academic administrator, psychology educator*
Gandolf, Raymond L. *media correspondent*
Gandolfo, Lucian John *minister, federal official*
Gandy, Bonnie Sergiacomi *oncological and intravenous therapy nurse*
Gangarosa, Raymond Eugene *epidemiologist, electrical engineer*
Ganske, J. Greg *former congressman, plastic surgeon*
Gantz, Carroll Melvin *industrial design consultant, consumer product designer*
†Gao, Haiyan *science educator*
Garahan, Peter Thomas *software company executive*
Garbacz, Patricia Frances *school social worker, therapist*
Garber, Victor *stage and film actor*
Garberding, Larry Gilbert *retired utilities companies executive*
Garcia, Alexander *orthopedic surgeon*
Garcia, Gus *former mayor*
†Garcia, Julia Theresa *secondary school educator*
Garcia, Marietta Kaye *elementary school educator, writer*
†Garcia, Sara Kruger *lawyer*
Garcia, Tierry Fernandez *otolaryngologist*
Garcia-Mely, Rafael *retired education educator*
Gard, Judy Richardson *artist, educator*
Gardner, Anne Lancaster *judge*
Gardner, Bruce Lynn *agricultural economist*
Gardner, Clyde Edward *healthcare executive, consultant, educator*
Gardner, David Chambers *adult education educator, psychologist, business executive, author*
Gardner, Elizabeth Ann Hunt *artist, poet, genealogist*
Gardner, Emerson N., Jr., *military officer*
Gardner, Grace Joely *author, consultant*
Gardner, Gwendolyn Smith *retail executive*
Gardner, John Howland, III, *neurologist*
Gardner, Meredith Lee *communication consultant*
Gardner, Nancy Augustine *researcher*
†Gardner, Renee Vanessa *pediatric hematologist/oncologist, researcher*
Gardner, Richard Hartwell *retired oil industry executive*
†Gardner, Rulon E. *Olympic athlete*
Gardner, Wanda Joyce *harpist, business owner, home educator*
Gardner, Wilford Robert *physicist, educator*
Garfield, Robert Edward *journalist*
Garfield-Woodbridge, Nancy *writer*
Garfinkle, Elaine Myra *writer*
Garfinkle, Robert Allen *writer, astronomer*
†Garg, Sandeep *oncologist*
Garibaldi, Marie Louise *former state supreme court justice*
Garland, Howard *mathematician, educator*
Garling, Carol Elizabeth *real estate executive and developer*
Garner, Carlene Ann *fundraising consultant*
Garner, Doris Traganza *educator*
†Garner, Jay Montgomery *former career officer*
Garnick, Jerry Jack *periodontist, educator*
Garniss, Joan Brewster *musician, educator*
†Garosshen, Paulette Sharon *writer*
Garpow, James Edward *retired financial executive*
†Garrard, John Gordon *educator*
Garrett, Marshall Lee, Jr., *anesthesiologist, educator*
Garrett, Roberta Kampschulte *nurse*
Garrett, Shirley Gene *nuclear medicine technologist*
Garriott, Owen Kay *astronaut, scientist*
Garrison, Paul Cornell *retired office products company executive*
Garrity, Thomas John *pharmaceutical executive*
Garruto, John Anthony *cosmetics executive*
Garruto, Ralph Michael *research anthropologist, educator, biologist, neuroscientist*
Gartenberg, Seymour Lee *retired recording company executive*
Gartner, Lawrence Mitchel *pediatrician, medical college educator*
Garwood, William Everett *chemist researcher*
†Gascoine-Molina, Jill Viola *actress, writer*
†Gaslow, Pam *writer, artist*
Gasper, Jo Ann *consulting firm executive*
Gasper, Ruth Eileen *real estate executive*
†Gass, Saul Irving *educator*
Gasteyer, Carlin Evans *museum administrator, museum studies educator*
Gaston, Paul E. *former professional basketball team executive*
Gat, Uri *engineer, scientist*
Gatch, Milton McCormick, Jr., *library administrator, clergyman, educator*
Gates, Martina Marie *food products company executive*
Gates, Susan Inez *magazine publisher*
Gatewood, Barbara J. *medical legal consultant, lawyer*
Gatewood, Willard Badgett, Jr., *retired historian*
Gathright, John Byron, Jr., *colon and rectal surgeon, educator*
Gaul, Stuart Crawford *lawyer*
Gaunt, Janet Lois *arbitrator, mediator*
†Gauthier, Abbie Gail *administrative assistant, writer*
Gavin, Joan Elaine *special education educator*
Gaw, James Richard *corporate executive*

Gawf, John Lee *foreign service officer*
Gay, David Edward Ryan *economist*
Gay, Pamela Diane *dance critic, historian, educator*
Gay, William Ingalls *veterinarian, health science administrator*
Gayle, Margot *preservationist, writer*
Gaylin, Willard *physician, educator*
†Gazaway, Barbara Ann *music educator, art educator*
†Ge, Xianping *computer scientist*
Geake, Raymond Robert *psychologist*
Gebauer, Phyllis Victoria Feltskog *writer, educator*
†Gedevanishvili, Shalva *materials scientist, researcher*
Gedroc, Maria *artist*
Gee, Robert Neil *law librarian*
Gee, Sharri A. *physician*
Gee, William *surgeon*
Geertz, Hildred Storey *anthropology educator*
Gegelmann, Sharon Fay *piano teacher*
Gehm, Denise Charlene *ballerina, arts administrator*
Gehring, Donald D. *education educator*
Gehrke, Karen Marie *retired accountant*
Geiger, Albert J., Jr., *radiologist, retired*
Geiger, Gordon Harold *engineer*
Geisel, Harold Walter *diplomat*
Geiselhart, Lorene Annetta *English language educator*
Geiser, Marjorie Eileen *dietitian, life coach*
Geisselmann, Friedrich *librarian*
Geissinger, Frederick Wallace *finance company executive*
Geist, Kathe Sternbach *art history, cinema and English educator, writer*
Geistfeld, Ronald Elwood *retired dental educator*
Gekas, George William *former congressman*
Gelb, Alvin Meyer *physician*
Gelboin, Harry Victor *biochemistry educator, researcher*
Gelenbe, Sami Erol *computer scientist, educator*
Gelfand, Israel Moseevich *mathematician, biologist*
Geller, Norman Harvey *music arranger, conductor*
Geller, Seymour *retired educator, researcher*
Gellinek, Christian Johann *German educator*
Gellis, Willard Leon *poet, English educator*
Gellman, Isaiah *environmental consultant*
Gelman, Larry *actor, film director*
Geloso-Barone, Rosalia A. *lawyer*
Gelpi, Armand Philippe *internist*
Gemell, Nicholas I. *retired radiologist*
Gemignani, Michael Caesar *clergyman, retired educator*
Gemming, Mary Frances *college educator, writer, astrologer*
Genaro, Donald Michael *industrial designer*
Gendell, Gerald Stanleigh *retired public affairs executive*
Genét, Barbara Ann *accountant, travel counselor*
Gengler, Sue Wong *health educator, evaluation consultant, speaker, trainer*
Gens, Ralph Samuel *electrical engineering consultant*
Gentilcore, Eileen Marie Belsito *elementary school principal*
Geoffroy, Charles Henry *retired business executive*
George, Cecelia G. *photographer, writer, artist, musician*
†George, Joey F. *computer science educator*
George, Joyce Jackson *lawyer, judge emeritus*
George, Linda Shumaker *writer, educator*
†George, Stephan (Steve) Anthony *web site designer*
†George, William Douglas, Jr., *retired consumer products company executive*
†Gera, Ralucca Mihaela *mathematician, educator*
Gerald, Michael Charles *pharmacy educator, dean*
Gerard, Gary *neurologist*
Gerard, Roy Dupuy *oil company executive, retired*
Gerbehy, Christine Petric *medical, surgical, and mental health nurse*
†Gerber, Natalie Ellen *editor*
Gere, James Monroe *civil engineering educator*
Gere, Richard *actor*
Gereau, Mary Condon *political corporate executive*
†Gerhardt, Carol Ashby *visual artist*
†Gerhardt, Fritz *ecologist, educator, researcher*
Gerlach, Douglas Eldon *financial writer, Internet developer*
†Gerloff, Gary Martin *writer*
German, Monica Ann *small business owner*
Germany, Daniel Monroe *aerospace engineer*
†Gerras, Stephen Joseph *military officer, psychologist*
Gerry, Debra Prue *psychotherapist, recording artist, writer*
Gersch, Charles Frant *lawyer*
†Gershkoff, Ira *architectural firm executive, consultant*
Gerson, Donald Jerome *computer scientist, consultant*
Gersoni-Edelman, Diane Claire *author, editor*
†Gerstein, Mark Bender *biophysicist, bioinformatician*
†Gerstman, Buddy Burt *health science educator*
†Gerstner, Jonathan Neil *religious studies educator*
Gerstner, Mary Jane *nurse*
Gertenbach, Robert Frederick *medical research organization executive, accountant, lawyer*
Gervay, Joseph Edmund *chemist, researcher, retired research scientist*
Gerwin, Leslie Ellen *lawyer, public affairs and community relations executive*
Getting, Ivan Alexander *physicist, former aerospace company executive*
Getz, Robert Lee *newspaper columnist*
Gewitz, Michael Harold *pediatrician*

Gherardi, Gherardo Joseph *pathologist*
Ghigna, Charles *poet*
Ghymn, Esther Mikyung *English educator, writer*
†Giambastiani, Edmund P., Jr., *military officer, federal agency administrator*
†Giannascoli, B. Greg *musician, entrepreneur*
†Giaquinto, Jane Schneider *finance executive*
Gibb, Roberta Louise *lawyer, artist*
Gibbs, Carroll Robert *historian, writer*
Giblett, Phylis Lee Walz *middle school educator*
Gibson, Beatrice Ann *retired systems analyst, artist*
Gibson, Milton Eugene *cardiologist*
Gibson, Orpha Ray *educator*
Gibson, Patricia *family educator*
Gibson, Scott Russell *nurse*
†Giddings, Helen *personnel management executive*
Giebel, Miriam Catherine *librarian, genealogist*
Giffin, Marjie G. *writer*
Gifford, Heidi *writer, editor*
Gifford, John Irving *retired agricultural equipment company executive*
Gil, David Georg *social policy educator*
†Gilbert, Elayne Rhoda *writer*
Gilbert, Frederick E. *development planner, Africanist, consultant*
Gilbert, Greg *former professional hockey coach*
Gilbert, Melissa *actress*
Gilbert, Rebecca J. *marketing executive*
Gilbert, Ronald Rhea *lawyer*
†Gilbert, Samuel Lawrence *publishing executive*
†Gil Casado, Pablo *Romance languages educator*
Gilchrest, Thornton Charles *retired association executive*
†Gilchrest, Yadira Vellon *computer scientist*
Gilchrist, Ellen Louise *writer*
Gilchrist, Gerald Seymour *pediatric hematologist, oncologist, educator*
†Gildart, Charles Rolland, Jr., *mechanical engineer*
†Gilden, Richard Henry *lawyer*
Giles, James Francis *financial executive*
Gilford, Dorothy Morrow *statistician, researcher*
Gilford, Leon *business executive and consultant*
Gilinsky, Victor *physicist*
Gill, Henry Herr *photojournalist*
Gill, Thomas James, III, *physician, educator*
Gill, William Robert *soil scientist*
Gillespie, Adrienne Amalia *artist, editor, researcher*
Gillespie, Gary Don *physician*
Gillespie, Gerald Ernest Paul *comparative literature educator, writer*
†Gillett, Mary Caperton *military historian*
Gillett, Patricia *family and acute care nurse practitioner, clinical nurse*
Gillett, Richard Clark, Jr., *physician, educator, health facility administrator*
Gillette, W. Michael *state supreme court justice*
Gillice, Sondra Jupin (Mrs. Gardner Russell Brown) *sales and marketing executive*
Gillin, Carol Ann *middle school educator*
Gillin, James *pharmaceutical company executive*
Gillinson, Andrew Stuart *marketing communications executive*
Gillmer, Thomas Charles *retired naval architect*
†Gilmore, Connie Sue *educator*
Gilmore, Louisa Ruth *retired nurse, retired firefighter*
Gilmour, Doug *hockey player*
Gilroy, Frank Daniel *playwright*
Gilroy, Sue Anne *state official*
†Gimbel, David Nelson *archaeologist*
Gimenez, Daniel *soil scientist, educator*
Gingold, Dennis Marc *lawyer*
Gingras, Anne Elizabeth *geriatrics, rehabilitation nurse*
Ginsberg, Ernest *lawyer, banker*
†Ginsberg, Marc David *lawyer*
†Ginsburg, Iona Horowitz *psychiatrist*
Giombetti Clue, Diane *writer*
†Giovinazzo, Vivian Curry *writer*
Gipstein, Milton Fivenson *lawyer, psychiatrist*
Girgus, Signe Linscott *interior designer*
Girling, Peter Michael *analyzer systems engineer, consultant*
Girouard, Shirley Ann *nurse, policy analyst*
Gish, Robert Franklin *English language educator, writer*
Gist, John Montfort *publishing executive, educator*
Gitner, Deanne *retired school system administrator*
Gitner, Gerald L. *air transportation executive, investment banker*
†Gittler, Steven *lawyer, law educator*
Gittman, Elizabeth *retired educator*
Giusti, Joseph Paul *retired academic administrator, consultant*
†Giusti, William Roger *lawyer*
Glacel, Barbara Pate *management consultant*
Glad, Suzanne Lockley *retired museum director*
†Gladden, Joseph Reah, II, *lawyer*
Gladden, Vivianne Cervantes *healthcare consultant, writer*
Gladstone, Carol Lynn *education educator*
Glanzer, Mona N. *lawyer, arbitrator*
Glasberg, Laurence Brian *private investor, business executive*
Glaser, Robert Joy *retired physician, foundation administrator*
Glasgow, Agnes Jackie *social welfare administrator, therapist*
†Glasgow, Karen *principal*
Glashow, Sheldon Lee *physicist, educator*
Glass, Dorothea Daniels *physiatrist, educator*
Glass, Kenneth Edward *management consultant*
Glasser, Ira Saul *civil liberties organization executive*
Glasson, Lloyd *sculptor, educator*
Glatzer, Robert Anthony *marketing and sales executive*
Glaze, Lynn Ferguson *development consultant*
Glazer, Barry Michael *anesthesiologist*
Gleach, Frederic Wright *anthropologist, educator*

†Gleason, Harriet Hall *nurse*
†Gleason, Stephen Charles *physician*
†Gleason-Jordan, Irene *pathologist*
Gleba, Beth Ann (Beth Ann Coleman) *communications executive*
Gleeson, Paul Francis *retired lawyer*
Glen, Niki *artist*
Glendening, Parris Nelson *former governor, political science educator*
Glendening, Terry Sky *psychologist*
Glennen, Robert Eugene, Jr., *retired university president*
Glesk, Ivan *physicist, educator, researcher*
Gleue, Lorine Anna *elementary education educator*
Glick, J. Leslie *bio and information technology entrepreneur*
†Glick, Ruth Burtnick *author, lecturer*
Glickman, Gladys *lawyer, writer*
†Glikin, Anton Arkadievich *architectural designer, artist*
Glismann, Clementine *elementary school educator, researcher*
†Gloman, David J. *artist*
Glosser, Jeffrey Mark *lawyer*
Glover, Douglas Herschel *writer, educator, editor*
†Glover, Eryn M. *music educator*
Glover, Lisa Marie *transportation consultant*
Glueck, Michael Wells *retired investment analyst, freelance/self-employed editor*
†Gluskin, Lisa L. *poet, editor, writer*
Gluys, Charles Byron *retired marketing management consultant*
Glynn, Carlin (Carlin Masterson) *actress*
Glynn, Peter Alexander Richard *healthcare consultant*
Gnanadesikan, Ramanathan *retired statistics educator, researcher*
Gobel, John Henry *lawyer*
Goble, Paul *author, illustrator, artist*
Godager, Jane Ann *retired social worker*
Godbee, Gary Russell *artist*
†Godbey, Ronald Lee *lawyer*
Godbey, Terry *poet, newspaper copy editor*
Goddard, Claude Philip, Jr., *lawyer*
Goddard, Thelma Taylor *critical care nurse, nursing educator*
Godinez, Magdalena *cardiology nurse*
†Godoff, Ann *book editor*
Godsey, Jeffrey Lynn *actor, educator*
Godwin, Pamela June *financial services executive*
Godwin, Ralph Lee, Jr., *real estate executive*
†Godwin, Robert Duane *language educator*
Goeble, Deborah Squires *clinical social worker*
Goehring, Maude Cope *retired business educator*
Goel, Mahesh Chand *urologist, renal transplant surgeon*
Goellner, Jack Gordon *publishing executive*
†Goen, Bob *television show host*
Goepp, Robert August *dental educator, oral pathologist*
Goerke, Glenn Allen *university administrator*
Goertz, Roger Lamar *retired education counselor*
Goetz, Angella Marie *infection control nurse, researcher*
Goetz, Clarence Edward *retired judge, retired chief magistrate judge*
Goetz, Jack Ralph *dean*
†Goetzinger, Laurel Eldredge *music educator*
Goff, Jane E. *secondary school educator*
Goffman, Thomas Edward *radiation oncologist, researcher*
Goggin, John R. *software quality engineer*
Goggins, Jean *biomedical engineer, foundation administrator*
Gold, Betty Virginia *artist*
Gold, Evan Bruce *ophthalmologist*
Gold, Judith Hammerling *psychiatrist*
Gold, Leonard Singer *librarian, translator*
Gold, Martin Elliott *lawyer, educator*
Goldberg, Alan Michael *music educator*
†Goldberg, Arthur H. *brokerage services company executive*
Goldberg, Burton David *pathologist, researcher, educator*
Goldberg, David Alan *investment banker, lawyer*
Goldberg, Gerald Jay *writer, educator*
Goldberg, Joel Henry *lawyer*
Goldberg, Lee Winicki *furniture company executive*
Goldberg, Mark Arthur *neurologist*
Goldberg, Michael Ellis *neurologist, neuroscientist*
Goldberg, Nancy G. *business owner, community volunteer*
Goldberg, Norma Lorraine *retired public welfare administrator*
Goldberg, Samuel *retired mathematician, foundation officer*
Goldberg, Victor Joel *retired data processing company executive*
†Goldberg, Whoopi (Caryn Johnson) *actress*
†Goldberger, Allen Sanford *lawyer*
Goldberger, Arthur Earl, Jr., *industrial engineer, executive*
Goldberger, Blanche Rubin *sculptor, jeweler*
Goldberger, George Stefan *finance company executive*
Goldberger, Marvin Leonard *physicist, educator*
Goldblatt, Eileen Witzman *art director, director, management consultant*
Golden, David Edward *physicist*
Golden, Gerald Samuel *retired national medical board executive*
†Golden, Harry W. *writer*
Golden, Judith Greene *artist, educator*
Goldenberg, Marvin Manus *pharmacologist, pharmaceutical developer*
Goldfarb, Helene Diane *school counselor, retired*
Goldfarb, Muriel Bernice *marketing and advertising consultant*
Goldfarb, Ruth *poet, educator*
Goldfine, Alan *obstetrician, gynecologist*
Goldin, Ian Andrew *executive*
Goldin, Marion Freedman *television news producer, reporter*

Golding, Carolyn May *former government senior executive, consultant*
Goldman, Alan Ira *investment banking executive*
Goldman, Alfred Emmanuel *marketing research consultant*
Goldman, Benjamin Allen *statistician, writer*
Goldman, Gerald Hillis *beverage distribution company executive*
Goldman, Joseph Elias *retired advertising executive*
Goldman, Mia *film editor*
Goldman, Rachel Bok *civic volunteer*
Goldner, Leonard Howard *lawyer*
Goldner, Sheldon Herbert *export-import company executive*
Goldoff, Anna Carlson *public administration educator*
Goldsmith, Aaron Clair *retired federal government executive, dean*
Goldsmith, Elsa M. *painter, graphic artist*
†Goldsmith, Jeff Charles *management consultant*
Goldspiel, Arnold Nelson *real estate executive*
Goldstein, Alfred George *retail and consumer products executive*
Goldstein, Barry Bruce *biologist, food company executive, lawyer*
Goldstein, Bernard *transportation and casino gaming company executive*
Goldstein, Debra Holly *judge*
Goldstein, Dora Benedict *pharmacologist, educator*
Goldstein, Irving Solomon *chemistry educator, consultant*
Goldstein, Laurence Alan *trade association executive*
Goldstein, Norman Ray *international trading company executive, consultant*
Goldstein, Phyllis Ann *art historian, educator*
Goldstein, Walter Carl *retired physician*
Goldstene, Paul Norton *writer, educator*
Goldston, Stephen Eugene *community psychologist, educator, consultant*
†Golemon, Patricia Lynn *education educator, writer*
Goll, Stephen E. *telecommunications executive*
Gollin, Rita Kaplan *English literature educator*
Gollings, Ruth Erickson *community health nurse*
†Goloversic, Mary Cecelia *writer*
†Golubeva, Anna *mathematician, application developer*
†Golubock, Rhona *lawyer*
†Gomis Porqueras, Pedro *economics eduator*
Gomoll, Allen Warren *cardiovascular pharmacologist*
†Gonzales, Gregory *music educator*
Gonzales, Richard Robert *counselor*
Gonzalez, Arturo Francis, Jr., *journalist*
Gonzalez, John M. *educator*
Good, Linda Lou *elementary education educator*
Good, Walter Raymond *investment executive*
Goodale, Toni Krissel *development consultant*
Goode, Janet Weiss *elementary school educator*
Goode, Stephen Hogue *publishing company executive*
Goodfellow, Robin Irene *surgeon*
Goodkin, Michael Jon *publishing company executive*
Goodman, Daniel Solomon *real estate broker, consultant*
†Goodman, Diane M. *critical care nurse, geriatrics nurse*
Goodman, Erika *dancer, actress*
Goodman, Gail Busman *small business owner*
†Goodman, Rebecca Gruver *education educator, writer*
†Goodman, Robert Lee *nursing administrator*
†Goodney, Philip Paul *surgeon, researcher*
Goodrich, Kenneth Paul *retired college dean*
Goodsell, Charles True *retired educator*
Goodson, Raymond Eugene *business educator, former automotive executive*
Goodstone, Edward Harold *retired insurance company executive*
Goodwin, Andrew Wirt, II, *radiologist*
Goodwin, Irwin *journalist, writer*
Goodwin, Phillip Hugh *hospital administrator*
Goodwin, Richard Hale *botany educator*
†Goodwyn, Betty Ruth *librarian*
Goolsby, Charles William *artist, educator*
Gora, Daniel Martin *lawyer*
†Gorbunovs, Anatolijs *engineer, construction specialist, politician*
†Gorder, Jennifer LeAnn *special education educator*
Gordimer, Nadine *author*
Gordis, David Moses *academic administrator, rabbi*
Gordis, Enoch *retired science administrator, internist*
Gordly, Avel Louise *state legislator, community activist*
Gordon, Audrey Kramen *healthcare educator*
Gordon, David Zevi *retired lawyer*
Gordon, Ezra *architect, educator*
Gordon, Marjorie *lyric coloratura soprano, opera producer, teacher*
Gordon, Peter Lowell *federal agency administrator*
†Gordon, Ruby Daniels *retired nursing educator, counselor*
Gordon, William Edwin *physicist, engineer, educator, university official*
Gordon-Love, Sharel E. *consumer products company executive, writer*
†Gore, Albert, Jr., *former Vice President of the United States*
Gorenberg, Norman Bernard *aeronautical engineer, consultant, retired*
Gorence, Patricia Josetta *judge*
†Gorenstein, Samuel *retired mathematician, educator*
Gorin, Abbye Alexander *electronics researcher*
Gorman, Joseph Tolle *automotive parts manufacturing executive*
Goron, Mara J. *social studies educator, assistant principal*
Gorske, Robert H. *retired lawyer*
Gorsline, Stephen Paul *security specialist*
Gosciewski, Robert Louis *logistician*
†Goslin, Thomas B. *career officer*
Goss, Joel Francis *writer*
Goss, Martha Clark *consulting company executive*
†Gotlieb, Lawrence Barry *lawyer*
Gottfried, Eugene Leslie *physician, educator*
†Gotthelf, Eric *astrophysicist, research scientist*
Gottlieb, Alan Merril *advertising, fundraising and broadcasting executive, writer*
Gottschalk, Charles M. *international energy consultant*
Gould, Howard Richard *retired physician*
Gould, Martha Bernice *retired librarian*
Goulet, Charles Ryan *retired insurance company executive*
Gouletas, Evangeline *investment executive*
Goulimis, Janet Theresa *human resources professional*
†Gourvitz, Elliot Howard *lawyer*
Gouse, S. William, Jr., *engineering executive, scientist*
Govan, Gladys Vernita Mosley *retired critical care and medical/surgical nurse*
Grab, Frederick Charles *lawyer*
†Graber, Samuel David *environmental and water resources engineer, consultant*
Grace, Jason Roy *advertising agency executive*
Grace, Marcia Bell *advertising executive*
Gracias, Maurice *economist*
Grady, Lee Timothy *pharmaceutical chemist*
Grady, Maureen Frances *lawyer*
Graebner, James Herbert *transportation executive*
Graessley, William Walter *retired chemical engineering educator*
Graf, Robert Arlan *retired financial services executive*
Graham, Brenda J. *nurse*
Graham, Christopher Francis *lawyer*
Graham, Claxton A. *business systems analyst*
Graham, David G. *preventive medicine physician, psychiatrist*
Graham, James Herbert *dermatologist*
Graham, Jan *former state attorney general*
Graham, John Hamilton, II, *professional athletics manager*
Graham, K(athleen) M. (K. M. Graham) *artist*
Graham, Kirsten Rae *computer scientist, educator*
Graham, Lanier *art historian, curator, cultural planner*
Graham, Norma Van Surdam *psychologist, educator*
Graham, Parker Lee, II, *information executive*
†Graham, Steven Anthony *writer*
Graham, Sylvia Swords *secondary school educator, retired*
†Graham, Warren Kenyon *counselor*
Grahn, Barbara Ascher *retired publishing executive*
Gralla, Lawrence *publishing company executive*
Gralla, Milton *publisher*
Grames-Lyra, Judith Ellen *retired artist, building plans examiner*
†Grams, Diane M. *artist, educator*
†Grams, Rodney D. *former senator, former congressman*
Grand, Cindy *foundation director*
Grandi, Attilio *engineering consultant*
Grandstrand, Ruth Helena *retired community health and gerontology nurse*
†Grange, George Robert, II, *lawyer*
†Grange, Mary Jane *writer, adult nurse practitioner*
Granger, Kay *congresswoman*
†Grann, Phyllis *former publisher, editor*
Grant, Alexander Marshall *ballet director*
†Grant, Anjali *architectural firm executive*
†Grant, Isabella Horton *retired judge*
Grant, James Colin *banker*
†Grant, Janett Ulrica *medical/surgical nurse*
Grant, Leonard Tydings *clergyman*
†Grant, Linda Hess *educator*
Grant, Merrill Theodore *producer*
Grant, Richard Earl *retired medical and legal consultant*
Grant, Sandra Lynn *family practice nurse practitioner*
†Grasserbauer, Doris *computer scientist, educator*
Grasso, Richard A. *stock exchange executive*
†Graubard, John J(oseph) *lawyer*
Graver, Mary Kathryn *medical, surgical nurse*
Graves, Lorraine Elizabeth *dancer, educator, coach*
†Graves, Michael Kenneth *nurse anesthetist*
Graves, Ruth Parker *educational executive, educator*
Graves, Sid Foster, Jr., *retired library and museum director*
Graves, Wallace Billingsley *retired university executive*
Graves, William Preston *governor*
Gray, Barbara Bronson *nurse, foundation administrator, writer, public relations executive*
Gray, Barbara May *artist*
†Gray, Clarence Jones *foreign language educator, dean emeritus*
Gray, Darlene Agnes *nurse*
Gray, David Lawrence *retired air force officer*
Gray, Deborah Mary *wine importer*
Gray, Francine du Plessix *author*
Gray, Gavin Campbell, II, *computer information engineer*
Gray, Gordon L. *communications educator*
Gray, Harry Joshua *electrical engineer, educator*
†Gray, Hazel Irene *retired special education educator, counselor, consultant*
Gray, John Leonard *retired lawyer*
Gray, Lillia Ann *lawyer*
†Gray, Lori Ann *psychologist, researcher, educator*
Gray, Mary Jane *obstetrician-gynecologist*
Gray, Richard Alexander, Jr., *retired chemical company executive*
Gray, Richard Arden *retired transportation executive*
Gray, Richard Moss *retired college president*
Gray, Roland William *pediatrician*
Gray, Thomas Stephen *journalist, writer*
Grayeski, Mary Lynn *chemist, consultant*
†Grayson, Edward Davis *lawyer, manufacturing company executive*
Greaser, Constance Udean *automotive industry executive*
Great, Don Charles *composer, music company executive*
Greaves, William Webster *chemist, patent analyst, community liaison*
Grebb, Michael D. *military officer, systems analyst*
Grebstein, Sheldon Norman *university administrator*
†Grechanik, Jeffrey *military officer*
†Greco, Christopher Jon *musician, composer, educator*
Greeley, Andrew Moran *sociologist, author*
†Greeley, Jennifer Ann *military officer, educator*
Green, Barbara *communications educator*
Green, Bennett Donald *biotechnologist*
Green, Beth Ingber *intuitive practitioner, counselor, author, composer, spiritual educator*
Green, Carol H. *lawyer, educator, journalist*
†Green, Carole L. *lawyer*
Green, Harland Norton *lawyer, accountant*
Green, Howard Alan *management consultant, educator*
Green, Laura Lorraine *foundation administrator*
Green, Linda Gail *retired international healthcare and management consultant, nurse educator*
Green, Louis Harry *retired surgeon*
Green, Nancy Loughridge *newspaper executive*
Green, Patricia Pataky *school system administrator, consultant*
Green, Richard Calvin, Jr., *electric power and gas industry executive*
†Green, Richard James *federal agency administrator, aerospace engineer*
Green, Robert Bailey *insurance executive, retired*
†Green, Thomas George *retired architect*
Green, Thornton George *software engineer*
†Green, Tracy V. *financial consultant, management consultant*
Greenberg, Albert *art director*
Greenberg, Barbara Levenson *literature educator, poet*
Greenberg, Carolyn Phyllis *anesthesiologist, educator*
Greenberg, Hinda Feige *library director*
Greenberg, Jonathan *neurosurgeon*
Greenberg, Judith Ann *real estate developer*
Greenberg, Larrie Warren *pediatrician*
Greenberg, Marvin *retired music educator*
Greenberg, Ronald David *lawyer, law educator*
Greenberg, Stephen Robert *retired pathology educator*
Greenblatt, Maurice Theodore *transportation executive*
Greenburg, Dan *author*
Greene, Alan Guyer *retired radiologist*
Greene, Alvin *service company executive, management consultant*
Greene, Donald Richard *dermatologist, educator*
Greene, Elinore Aschah *speech and drama professional, writer*
Greene, Frank Sullivan, Jr., *investment management executive*
Greene, John Colton *retired history educator*
Greene, Laurence Whitridge, Jr., *surgical educator*
Greene, Lynne Jeannette *fashion designer*
Greene, Monica Lynn Banks *recreational therapist, director*
Greene, Richard Thaddeus *bank executive*
Greenebaum, Leonard Charles *retired lawyer*
Greene Lloyd, Nancy Ellen *retired infosystems specialist, physicist*
Greenfield, James M. *retired fund raiser*
Greenfield, Linda Sue *nursing educator*
Greenfield, Sanford Raymond *architect*
Greenfield, Val Shea *ophthalmologist*
Greenhut, Deborah Schneider *management consultant*
Greenman, David Lewis *retired physiologist and toxicologist*
Greenstein, Robert *retired radiologist*
Greenwald, John Edward *newspaper and magazine writer, editor and executive, painter*
Greenway, Joan M. *dean*
Greenwood, Janet Kae Daly *psychologist, educational administrator, marketing professional*
Greer, Carl Crawford *petroleum company executive*
Greer, Germaine *author*
†Greer, K. Gordon *banker*
†Greer, Suzanne Michelle *music educator*
Greever, Margaret Quarles *retired mathematics educator*
Gregersen, Max A. *structural, earthquake and civil engineer*
Gregg, David, III, *investment banker*
Greggs, Elanora *social worker*
Gregor, Dorothy Deborah *retired librarian*
Gregory, Claire Distelhorst *television producer*
†Gregory, George G. *retired lawyer*
Gregory, James Alexander *editor, writer*
Gregory, Mary Sharon *educator*
Gregory, Myra May *religious organization administrator, educator*
Gregson, Merry Chris (Merry Smith) *artist*
Grell, Lewis Adam *retired association executive*
Grenander, Ulf *mathematics educator*
†Grenier, Laura Margiotta *medical/surgical nurse*
Grenitz, Robert *retired obstetrician-gynecologist*
†Gretes, Frances Constance *information specialist*
Gretser, George Westfall *publisher*
Greve, Sally Doane *English educator*
Grewe, John Mitchell *orthodontist, educator*
Grey, Francis Joseph *accountant, accounting company executive, educator*
Grey, Robert Dean *academic administrator, biology educator*
Gribben, Monica Anne *social scientist, researcher*
Gribble, Mary Louise *freelance/self-employed poet, writer*
Grier, Dorothy Ann Pridgen *secondary education specialist*
†Grier, Phillip Michael *lawyer, former association executive*
Griesbauer, Michele Elaine *newspaper official*
Griesé, John William, III, *astronomer, educator, mental health advocate*
†Grieser, Jeanne K. *writer*
Grieve, Pierson MacDonald *retired chemicals executive*
Griffen, Ward O., Jr., *surgeon, educator, medical board executive*
Griffie, Gayle G. *retired principal*
Griffin, Campbell Arthur, Jr., *retired lawyer*
Griffin, Carleton Hadlock *accountant, educator*
Griffin, Christopher Oakley *healthcare professional, humanities educator, entrepreneur*
Griffin, Gloria Jean *retired elementary school educator*
Griffin, James Anthony *bishop*
Griffin, John Henry *medical researcher*
Griffin, Laura Mae *retired educator*
Griffin, Linda French *artist, activist, consultant*
Griffin, Pauline M. *publishing executive*
Griffin, Robert Paul *former United States senator, state supreme court justice*
Griffith, B(ezaleel) Herold *physician, educator, plastic surgeon*
†Griffith, David A *marketing educator, consultant*
Griffith, Madlynne Veil *college administrator*
Griffith, Steven Franklin, Sr., *lawyer, real estate title insurance agent and investor*
Griffith, Tracy Cox *counselor, nurse*
Griggs, John Robert *financial and consumer credit services executive*
Grijns, Laine *investment company executive*
Grim, Ellen Townsend *artist, retired art educator*
Grim, Patricia Ann *retired banker*
†Grimes, Gary A. *music educator*
Grimes, James Gordon *geologist*
†Grimes, Katherine Elizabeth *child psychiatrist, researcher*
Grimes, Michael David *podiatrist*
Grimm, Larry Leon *psychologist*
Grindal, Mary Ann *former sales professional*
†Grindstaff, Mark Joseph *historian*
Grine, Florence May *secondary education educator*
Griner, Paul Francis *physician*
Grinnell, Helen Dunn *musicologist, arts administrator*
†Grisham, Richard Bond *lawyer, retired oilfield service company executive*
Grodsky, Jamie Anne *law educator*
Grody, Donald *actor, judge, lawyer, arbitrator*
Grody, Mark Stephen *public relations executive*
Groenier, James Scott *civil engineer*
†Groening, Matthew *writer, cartoonist*
Grolli, Frank Thomas *retired pharmacist*
Gromen, Richard John *historian, educator*
Grosbard, Ulu *director*
Groscost, Jeff *former state legislator, small business owner*
Groskopf, Aubrey Bud *motion picture television executive, lawyer*
Grosland, Emery Layton *banker*
Gross, Dorothy-Ellen *library director, dean*
Gross, Laura Ann *marketing and communications professional, acupuncturist, herbalist*
Gross, Leslie Pamela *sales executive, consultant*
Gross, Rosalie-Ethelyn *secretary*
Gross, Ruth Taubenhaus *former pediatrician*
Grossman, Cissy *curator, art historian, art exhibit designer, appraiser*
†Grossman, Janice *former magazine publishing company executive*
Grossman, Jerrold B. *pharmaceutical executive*
Grossman, Joyce Renee *pediatrician, internist*
Grossman, Marc *federal agency administrator*
Grossman, Robert James *retired architect*
Grotta, Sandra Brown *interior designer*
Grove, Myrna Jean *elementary education educator*
Grove, Richard Charles *retired power tool company executive*
Groves, Michael *banker*
Groves, Sheridon Hale *orthopedic surgeon*
Grow, Robert Theodore *economist, association executive*
Growick, Philip *advertising executive*
Gruber, Fredric Francis *financial planning and investment research executive*
Gruberg, Cy *educational administrator*
†Gruchot, Linda *secondary school educator*
Gruen, Margaret *actress*
Gruenfeld, Kevin E. *marketing professional, researcher*
Grunder, Fred Irwin *industrial hygienist, consultant*
Grundlehner, Conrad Ernest *information company executive, economic consultant*
Grutman, Jewel Humphrey *lawyer, writer*
†Gruy, Henry Jones *engineering company executive, petroleum engineer*
Gschwind, Donald *management and engineering consultant*
Guan, Shangbo G. *physician*
†Guan, Zhuang-Dan Daniel *mathematician, educator*
†Guarente, Lenny *medical geneticist, educator*
Guarno, Peter Gary *consumer products company executive*
Guay, Gordon Hay *federal agency administrator, marketing educator, consultant*
†Gubbins, Keith Edmund *chemical engineering educator*
†Guccione, Robert Charles Josep *publisher*
Gudenberg, Harry Richard *arbitrator, mediator*

Gudmundsson, Finnbogi *library administrator*
Guerra, Armando J. *corporate professional*
Guerrera, Vittorio *priest*
Guerrero, Lilia *school nurse*
Guevarra, Manuel Robinson *artist, retired military officer*
Gugel, Craig Thomas *advertising and strategic research executive*
Gugino, Carl Frank *orthodontist, educator*
Guild, Nelson Prescott *retired state education official*
Guiliano, Francis James *office products manufacturing company executive*
Guinn, Janet Martin *psychologist, consultant*
Guittar, Lee John *retired newspaper executive*
Gulbrandsen, Patricia Hughes *physician*
Gulcher, Robert Harry *aircraft company executive*
Gulko, Paul Michael *insurance executive*
†Gulledge, Irene O. *retired music educator*
Gulledge, Sandra Smith *publishing executive, film producer*
Gummel, Hermann Karl *retired physicist, laboratory administrator*
Gummere, John *insurance company executive, director*
Gumpel, Liselotte *retired language educator*
Gumpert, Gustav *public relations executive*
Gundersheimer, Werner Leonard *library director*
Gunderson, Judith Keefer *golf association executive*
Gunderson, Ted Lee *security consultant*
Gundy, Richard L. *freelance/self-employed writer*
Gunn, Janet Penelope *engineer*
Gunn, Lee Fredric *career officer*
Gunter, William Dayle, Jr., *physicist, consultant*
†Guo, Daqing *medical researcher*
Guo, Sheng Ming *retired history educator*
Guo, Xiaofeng *physicist*
Gupta, Krishan Lal *physician, medical educator*
Gurian, Mal *telecommunications executive*
Gurney, Daniel Sexton *race car manufacturing company executive, racing team executive*
†Gurnow, Michael Erwin *literature and film educator, art educator*
Gurspan, Mitchell Scott *technology architect, author*
Gurspan, Susan Judith *English as Second Language educator, consultant*
Gurwitch, Arnold Andrew *communications executive*
Gurwitz-Hall, Barbara Ann *artist*
Guskin, Alan E. *university president*
Gusman, Robert Carl *lawyer*
Gustafson, Craig Thomas *theatrical director, playwright, graphic artist*
Gustafson, Richard Alrick *university president*
Gustafson, Sandra Lynne *retired secondary school educator*
Gustavson, Mark Steven *lawyer*
Guter, James L. *music educator*
†Gutfinger, Dan Eli *cardiologist, surgeon*
Guthrie, James Uhl *retired surgeon*
Guthrie, Janet *professional race car driver*
Guthrie, Robert Val *retired psychologist and educator*
Guthrie, Wallace Nessler, Jr., *naval officer*
Gutierrez, Gerald Andrew *theatrical director*
Gutiérrez, Mary Carmen *artist*
Gutman, Richard Edward *lawyer*
Gutmann, David Leo *psychology educator*
Gutmann, Reinhart Bruno *clergyman, social worker*
Gutsch, William Anthony, Jr., *astronomer*
Gutstein, Carol Feinhandler *realtor*
Guttentag, Joseph Harris *lawyer, educator*
Guy, Eleanor Bryenton *writer*
Guymon, Gary LeRoy *civil engineering educator, consultant*
Guyton, William Lehman, Jr., *retired surgeon*
Guzik, Estelle Marion *professional society administrator*
†Guzman, Jose Javier *aeronautical engineer*
Guzzo, Glenn *former newspaper editor*
Gwinn, Robert P. *publishing executive*
†Gwyther, Robert Edwin *physician, consultant*
†Gyekenyesi, Andrew *mechanical engineer*
Gyles, Mary Francis *retired history educator*
†Gyuras, Brian Joseph *music educator*
Haag, Walter M(onroe), Jr., *philatelist*
Haak, Harold Howard *university president*
†Haar, Franklin Duane *musician, writer*
Haas, Carolyn Buhai *elementary education educator, publisher, writer, consultant*
Haas, Charlie *screenwriter*
Haas, Edward Lee *business executive, consultant*
Haas, Frederick Carl *retired paper and chemical company executive*
†Haas, Sheila Sperber *writer, consultant*
Habeck, James Roy *lawyer*
Haber, Joel Abba *lawyer*
Haber, Lynn Becker *English language educator*
Haber, Ralph Norman *psychology consultant, researcher, educator*
Haberl, Valerie Elizabeth *physical education educator, company executive*
Haberman, Charles Morris *mechanical engineer, educator*
†Habich, Elizabeth Chamberlain *librarian*
Habkirk, Sue Ann *education educator, consultant*
Hackel-Sims, Stella Bloomberg *lawyer, former government official*
†Hacker, Michelle Wendy *auditor, researcher, finance educator*
Hackett, Robert John *lawyer*
Hackett, Roger James *editor*
Hackett, Wesley Phelps, Jr., *lawyer*
Hadas, Julia Ann *social services administrator*
Haddock, Harold, Jr., *retired accounting firm executive*
Haden, Clovis Roland *university administrator, engineering educator*
Hadley, Jane Byington *psychotherapist*
Hadley, William Melvin *retired dean*
Haeberle, Rosamond Pauline *retired educator*
Haeberle, William Leroy *corporate director, business educator, entrepreneur*
Haegele, John Ernest *business executive*
†Hafner, Thomas Mark *lawyer*
Haft, Gail Klein *pediatrician*
Hagan, Joseph Henry *higher education consultant*
Hagee, Jesko Michael *naval officer*
Hagel, John, III, *management consultant*
Hagel, Raymond Charles *publishing company executive, educator*
Hagelstein, Robert Philip *publisher*
Hageman, Katherine Elizabeth *secondary school educator*
Hageman, Richard Philip, Jr., *educational administrator*
Hagemier, Herman Frederick *chemist*
Hagenbeck, Franklin Lee *military officer*
Hager, Paula Michele *critical care nurse*
Hagerman, Michael Charles *lawyer, arbitrator, mediator*
Haggerty, Robert Johns *physician, educator*
Hahn, Frank Horace *economics educator*
Hahn, Helene B. *motion picture company executive*
Hahn, Mary Downing *writer*
Hails, Robert Emmet *aerospace consultant, business executive, former air force officer*
†Hain, Patricia A. *music educator*
Haines, Lee Mark, Jr., *religious denomination administrator*
Haining, Jeane *psychologist*
Hairston, James Christopher *food service distribution executive*
Haithcock, William Dana, Jr., *physician*
Hajikano, Maki *artist*
Hajost, James E. *music educator, conductor, composer*
Hakala, Karen Louise *retired real estate administrator*
†Hake, Ralph F. *appliance manufacturing executive*
Hakim, Besim Selim *architecture and urban design educator, researcher and consultant*
Hakimoglu, Ayhan *electronics company executive*
Hakkila, Eero Arnold *retired nuclear safeguards technology chemist*
Halberstam, David *journalist, author*
Halberstam, Heini *mathematics educator*
Halbrooks, James Richmond (Ricky Halbrooks) *sheet metal mechanic*
Haldeman, Joe William *novelist*
Hale, Todd Benjamin *military officer, electrical engineer*
Hales, Charles Albert *physician, educator*
Haley, George Brock, Jr., *retired lawyer*
Haley, George W. *ambassador*
Haley, Sally Fulton *artist*
Hall, Barry G. *evolutionary biologist*
Hall, David *newspaper editor*
†Hall, Douglas Erskine *artist, educator*
Hall, Ella Taylor *clinical school psychologist*
†Hall, Floyd *retired retail executive*
Hall, Frederick Keith *chemist*
Hall, Grace Rosalie *physicist, educator, writer*
Hall, Hansel Crimiel *communications executive*
†Hall, James Evan *lawyer*
Hall, James Stanley *jazz guitarist, composer*
Hall, Jay *social psychologist*
Hall, Joan Torrens *lawyer*
Hall, John Hopkins *retired lawyer*
Hall, Keith R. *retired federal official*
†Hall, Kirstina J. *humanities educator*
Hall, Milton Reese *retired oil company executive*
Hall, Mina Elaine *geriatrics nurse*
Hall, Monty *television producer, actor*
Hall, Ralph Carr *retired lawyer, real estate consultant*
Hall, Susan Laurel *artist, educator, writer*
Hall, Wanda Jean *mental health professional, consultant*
Hall, Zach Winter *academic administrator*
Hall-Barron, Deborah *lawyer*
Halleck, Charles White *lawyer, photographer, former judge*
Haller, Robert Terrence *marketing, advertising and public relations consultant*
Hallett, William Jared *retired nuclear engineer*
Halliday, William Ross *retired physician, speleologist, writer*
Halperin, Michael Howard *writer, educator*
Halpern, Alvin Michael *retired physicist, educator, consultant*
Halpern, Peggy Louise *social welfare researcher*
Halpin, Daniel William *civil engineering educator, consultant*
Haluska, Bonnie Frati *rehabilitation nurse*
Hamada, Omar Louis *physician*
Hambidge, Douglas Walter *archbishop*
Hamblen, John Wesley *computer scientist, genealogist*
Hamblen, Lapsley Walker, Jr., *judge*
Hamburger, Brian S. *lawyer, consultant*
Hamdan, Barbara Brunet *preventive medicine physician*
Hamdy, Mostafa Kamal *microbiologist, educator*
Hamel, Louise *artist, writer, muralist*
Hamelin, Marcel *historian, educator*
Hamilton, Allan Corning *retired oil company executive*
†Hamilton, Ann Katherine *artist*
Hamilton, Judith Hall *computer company executive*
Hamilton, Kim Renee *chiropractor, educator*
Hamilton, Shirley Siekmann *arts administrator*
Hamilton, Stanley Ralph *pathologist*
Hamilton, Thomas Michael *marketing executive*
Hamilton, William Howard *laboratory executive*
Hamister, Donald Bruce *retired electronics company executive*
Hamit, Francis Granger *freelance writer*
Hamlin, Sonya B. *communications specialist*
†Hamm, Aurolyn Melba *elementary school educator, writer*
Hamm, Vernon Louis, Jr., *management and financial consultant*
Hammam, M. Shawky *electrical engineer, educator*
Hammer, Harold Harlan *oil company financial executive*
Hammer, Wade Burke *retired oral and maxillofacial surgeon, educator*
Hammerschmidt, John Paul *retired congressman, lumber company executive*
Hammett, Louise Barfield *community service volunteer, artist, historian, playwright*
Hammond, Charles Ainley *clergyman*
Hammond, Glenn Barry, Sr., *lawyer, electrical engineer*
†Hammond, John Baptiste, III, *academic administrator*
Hammond, Mary Sayer *art educator*
Hammond, Robert Lee *retired feed company executive*
†Hammond, Robie Lee *health science association administrator*
Hammond, Teena Gay *editor*
Hammondd, Charlotte Claren *writer, researcher*
Hampton, Charles Edwin *lawyer, mathematician, computer programmer*
†Hampton, Nanette Davina *private school educator, writer*
Hampton, Rex Herbert *former mining executive, director*
Hamrock, Margaret Mary *retired educator, writer*
†Han, Qiwen *research scientist*
†Han, Xianlin *education educator, consultant*
Hanan, Laura Molen *artist*
†Hanbery, Donna Eva *lawyer*
Hancock, John Coulter *telecommunications company executive*
Hand, Herbert Hensley *finance educator, writer, entrepreneur*
Handler, Harold Robert *lawyer*
Handy, Carolyn *nonfiction writer*
Handy, Edward Otis, Jr., *retired financial services executive*
†Handy, John W. *career officer*
Haneke, Dianne Myers *retired education educator*
Hanes, Darlene Marie *marketing professional*
†Haney, Marlene Carol *music educator*
Hanford, Agnes Rutledge *retired financial adviser*
Hanford, George Hyde *retired educational administrator*
Hankin, Lawrence Alan *actor*
Hankinson, Deborah G. *former state supreme court justice*
Hanks, Gary Arlin *psychology educator*
†Hanley, Jodi Ann *mathematician, educator*
Hanmer, Stephen Read, Jr., *retired government executive*
Hanna, Duke Ellsworth *neurological surgeon*
Hanna, Lee Ann *critical care nurse*
†Hannaman, Alberta Anna *artist*
Hanneman, Rodney Elton *metallurgical engineer*
Hanni, Geraldine Marie *retired therapist*
†Hannon, Gerard V. *lawyer*
†Hannon, Patricia *literature educator, writer*
†Hanrahan, Patricia Lee *healthcare educator, researcher*
Hanratty, Carin Gale *pediatric nurse practitioner*
Hansell, John Royer *retired physician*
†Hansen, Hal T. *retired investment company executive*
Hansen, Leland Joe *communications executive*
Hansen, Nick Dane *lawyer*
Hansen, Rex Cossey *mechanical engineer*
Hansen, Sally Jo *educational consultant*
†Hansen, Wells Stevenson *language educator, researcher*
Hansen-Carter, Marilyn Ray *nurse*
Hanshaw, Leann Viala *counseling administrator*
†Hanshe, John *musicologist, writer*
Hanson, Carl Malmrose *financial company executive*
Hanson, Dennis Michael *medical imaging executive*
†Hanson, J. Donald *retired diversified financial services company executive*
Hanson, Janice Crawford *artist, financial analyst*
Hanson, Jo *artist, lecturer, writer*
Hanson, John M. *civil engineering and construction educator*
Hanson, John C. *investment company executive*
†Hanson, Richard Joseph *computer scientist, consultant*
Hanson, Wendy Karen *retired chemical engineer*
Hanushek, Eric Alan *economics educator*
Hanzlik, Rayburn DeMara *lawyer*
Hapner, Mary Lou *securities trader and dealer*
Harbert, Charles Armon *medicinal chemist*
Harbus, Richard *arbitrator, mediator*
†Hard, Brian *truck leasing company executive*
Hardage, Page Taylor *elementary education educator*
Hardaway, Robert Morris, III, *retired physician, educator, retired army officer*
Harden, Patrick Alan *journalist*
Harder, Robert Clarence *state official*
Hardin, Clifford Morris *retired university chancellor, cabinet member*
Hardin, Joan Rothchild *psychologist, artist*
Hardin, Martha Love Wood *civic leader*
†Harding, Laura J. *music educator*
Harding, Major Best *former state supreme court chief justice*
Harding, Robert William *academic administrator*
Harding, Susan Kathleen *early childhood and elementary school educator, writer, poet*
Harding, Teresa J. *interior designer, property management*
Hardison, Donald Leigh *retired architect*
Hardman, Joel Griffeth *retired pharmacologist*
Hardy, Chester Alfred *engineer*
Hardy, Clarence Earl, Jr., *government, nonprofit and corporate sector executive*
Hardy, James Chester *speech pathologist, educator*
Hardy, Ralph W. F. *biochemist, biotechnology executive*
Hardy, Robert Paul *lawyer*
Hardy, Thomas Cresson *insurance company executive*
†Hare, Frances Hutcheson, Jr., *lawyer, educator*
Hare, Norma Q. *retired school administrator*
Harff, Charles Henry *lawyer, retired diversified industrial company executive*
Hargadon, Bernard Joseph, Jr., *retired consumer goods company executive*
Hargrove, Mike (Dudley Michael Hargrove) *former professional baseball team manager*
Haring, Ellen Stone (Mrs. E. S. Haring) *philosophy educator*
†Harkless, Angela *lawyer, publishing executive*
Harkness, Peter Anthony *editor, publisher*
Harkness, S. Suzan Jane *political scientist, educator*
Harlan, Kathleen Troy (Kay Harlan) *management consultant*
Harlan, Raymond Carter *retired communication executive, writer, educator*
Harlow, Elizabeth Mary *retired music educator*
Harlow, Joan Beverley *writer*
Harman, Donald Lee *nurse, educator, consultant*
Harman, Robert John *retired religious organization administrator*
Harman, Wallace Patrick *lawyer*
Harmon, Debra Mae *journalist*
Harnack, Don Steger *retired lawyer*
Harold, Tom *advertising executive*
Harp, Chadwick Allen *writer, educator*
Harper, Charles H. *columnist, reporter*
Harper, Charles Michel *food company executive*
Harper, Christine Johnson *psychiatric clinical nurse, administrator*
Harper, Conrad Kenneth *lawyer, former government official*
Harper, Harlan, Jr., *lawyer*
Harper, Henry H. *retired military officer*
Harper, James Robert *graphic designer, sculptor*
Harper, Janet Sutherlin Lane *retired educational administrator, writer*
Harper, Odena Irene *retired communications educator*
Harper, Richard Henry *film producer, director*
Harper, W(alter) Joseph *financial consultant*
†Harr, Lucy Loraine *public relations executive*
Harrell, Carolyn Hardison *nursing home administrator*
Harrell, Ina Perry *maternal/women's and medical/surgical nurse*
Harrell, Margaret Ann *writer, educator, researcher, photographer*
Harrell, Steven Jeffrey *lexicographer*
Harrigan, Anthony Hart *author*
Harriman, John Howland *retired lawyer*
Harrington, Donald Francis *lawyer*
Harrington, Jean Patrice *college president*
Harrington, John Tolan *medical educator, dean, physician*
Harris, Ann *elementary school teacher*
†Harris, Darlene *judge, lawyer, county legislator*
Harris, David Philip *crisis management executive*
Harris, Delmarie Jones *elementary education educator*
Harris, Denise Michelle *advertising account executive*
Harris, Dolores M. *academic administrator*
†Harris, Elaine K. *medical consultant*
Harris, Howard Hunter *oil company executive*
Harris, Janine Diane *lawyer*
†Harris, Jay Stephen *lawyer, producer*
Harris, Jewell Bachtler *social worker*
Harris, John H., Jr., *radiologist*
Harris, Judith Rich *writer*
Harris, Louis *public opinion analyst, columnist*
Harris, Marcelite Jordan *retired career officer*
Harris, Merle Wiener *college administrator, educator*
Harris, Morton Allen *lawyer*
Harris, Paul Smith *human resources professional*
Harris, Richard Eugene Vassau *lawyer*
Harris, Robert A. *retired music educator*
Harris, Robert Norman *advertising and communications educator*
Harris, Rogers Sanders *bishop*
Harris, Teresa Ann *retired social services executive, social worker*
Harris, Theodore Clifford *songwriter, music publisher*
Harris, Theodore Edward *mathematician, educator*
Harris, William John *retired management holding company executive, consultant*
Harrison, Alonzo *construction company executive*
Harrison, Charles Maurice *lawyer, former communications company executive*
Harrison, Earl Grant, Jr., *educational administrator*
Harrison, Harold Henry, Sr., *physician, scientist, educator*
Harrison, John Alexander *financial executive*
Harrison, John Raymond *foundation executive, retired newspaper executive*
Harrison, Moses W., II, *state supreme court chief justice*
Harrison, Saul Isaac *child psychiatrist, medical educator*
Harrison, Sue Ann McHaney *writer*
Harrison, William Burwell, Jr., *bank executive*
Harrod, Lois Marie *secondary school educator, poet*
Harrop, Daniel Smith, III, *psychiatrist*
Harrop, Diane Glaser *shop owner, mayor, writer, consultant*
Harshbarger, Richard B. *economics educator*
Harshman, Marc *writer, poet, consultant*
†Harshman, Raymond Brent *lawyer*
Hart, Arthur Alvin *historian, author*
Hart, Cecil William Joseph *otolaryngologist, surgeon*
Hart, James Warren *retired academic administrator, retired football player*
Hartgen, Vincent Andrew *museum director, educator, artist*
Harth, Erica *French language and comparative literature educator*
Hartley, Corinne *painter, sculptor, educator*

†Hillery, Susie Moore *retired elementary school educator*
Hilley, Joseph Henry *lawyer*
Hilliard, Sam Bowers *geography educator*
Hillman, Leon *electrical engineer*
†Hills, John F. *design educator*
Hilsabeck, Larry L. *education educator*
Hilsman, Roger *government educator*
Himes, Barbara Alison (Sydney Kendall) *writer*
Himes, Diane Adele *buyer, fundraiser, actress, lobbyist*
Himes, John Harter *medical researcher, educator*
Himmelfarb, Milton *editor, educator*
Hind, Harry William *pharmaceutical company executive*
Hinderliter, Richard Glenn *electrical engineer*
Hinds, Edward Dee *insurance and investment professional, financial planner*
Hiner, Elizabeth Ellen *pharmacist*
Hinerfeld, Lee Ann *veterinarian*
Hines, Andrew Hampton, Jr., *utilities executive*
Hines, Voncile *special education educator*
Hing, Barbara Lim *elementary school educator, assistant principal*
Hingle, Pat *actor*
Hinkley, Everett David, Jr., *physicist, business executive*
Hinman, Eve Caison *retired academic administrator*
Hinshaw, Edward Banks *retired broadcasting company executive*
Hinton, Karolyn Kay *retired elementary school educator*
Hinton, Norman Wayne *retired information services executive*
Hirahara, Patti *public relations executive*
Hires, William Leland *psychologist, consultant*
Hirose, Teruo Terry *surgeon, educator*
Hirsch, Horst Eberhard *business consultant*
Hirsch, Larry Joseph *retired retail executive, lawyer*
Hirschberg, Besse Bryna *social worker*
Hirschberg, Vera Hilda *writer*
†Hirsh-Pasek, Kathryn Ann *psychology educator*
Hirst, Heston Stillings *former insurance company executive*
Hitchcock, Vernon Thomas *farmer, lawyer*
Hitchcock, Walter Anson *educational consultant, retired educational administrator*
Hittle, Larry Glenn *lawyer, electrical engineer*
Hitz, Duane Everett *brokerage executive*
Ho, Chih-Ming *physicist, educator*
Ho, Chu Eu *civil engineer*
Ho, John Wing-Shing *biochemistry educator, researcher*
†Ho, Matthew R *physician*
Hoadley, John Frank *health policy analyst, educator*
†Hoar, Frederick M. *public relations executive*
Hoart, Gladys Gallagher *English language educator*
Hoch, Frederic Louis *medical educator*
Hoch, Ivo *former library director*
Hoch, Orion Lindel *corporate executive*
Hochfeld, William Sidney *construction executive, consultant*
Hochheimer, Frank Leo *brokerage executive*
Hochreiter, John Allen *computer company owner, firefighter*
Hochschild, Carroll Shepherd *computer company and medical equipment executive, educator*
Hochstein, Eric Cameron *software executive*
Hock, Morton *entertainment advertising executive*
Hockeimer, Henry Eric *business executive*
Hockings, Paul Edward *anthropologist, editor*
†Hodge, David R. *social science researcher*
Hodge, Patricia Marie Cascio *nurse practitioner in psychiatry*
Hodge, Verne Antonio *retired chief judge*
Hodgen, Maurice Denzil *management consultant, retired education educator*
Hodges, Ann *actress, singer, dancer*
Hodges, Jim *former governor*
Hodges, Sharon Green *editor, consultant, writer*
†Hodgson, Dorothy L. *social studies educator*
Hodnicak, Victoria Christine *pediatric nurse*
Hoeg, Donald Francis *chemist, consultant, former research and development executive*
Hoeprich, Paul Daniel *physician educator*
Hoffheimer, Minette Goldsmith *community service volunteer*
Hoffleit, Ellen Dorrit *astronomer*
Hoffman, Alan Craig *lawyer, consultant*
Hoffman, Daniel (Daniel Gerard Hoffman) *literature educator, poet*
Hoffman, Darnay Robert *management consultant*
Hoffman, Ira Eliot *lawyer*
Hoffman, Jerry Irwin *retired dental educator*
Hoffman, John R. *mediator, arbitrator*
Hoffman, Judy Greenblatt *preschool director*
Hoffman, Margaret May *writer*
Hoffman, Neil James *academic administrator*
Hoffman, S. David *lawyer, engineer, educator, artist*
Hoffmann, Christoph Ludwig *lawyer*
†Hoffmann, Frances Porter *librarian, development coordinator*
Hofford, James Loveday *Christian evangelist, columnist, poet*
†Hofmann, George W. *artist, educator*
Hofmann, Paul Bernard *healthcare consultant*
†Hogan, Katie J. *English educator, women's studies researcher*
†Hogan, Martha A. *academic administrator, educator*
Hogan, Neville John *mechanical engineering educator, consultant*
Hogan, Robert Henry *trust company executive, investment strategist*
Hogan, Thomas Francis *federal judge*
Hogen-Esch, Thieo E. *chemistry educator*
Hogg, Karen Sue *telecommunications and information systems executive*
Hoggard, Lara Guldmar *conductor, educator*
Hoglund, John Andrew *lawyer*
Hogness, John Rusten *physician, academic administrator*
†Hogsett, Joseph H. *political organization worker, former state official*
Hogue, James Larry *retired academic administrator, business executive*
Hoke, Sheila Wilder *retired librarian*
Holaday, Susan G. *editor*
†Holand, Pamela Krisida *professional organizer*
Holbrow, Charles Howard *physicist, educator*
Holcepl, James Robert *sales professional*
†Holcomb, Mildred Geneva Comrie *elementary education educator*
Holcomb, Rita *landscaper*
Holden, Rebecca Lynn *artist*
Holden, William Hoyt, Jr., *lawyer*
Holeman, George Robert *health physicist, consultant*
Holeman, Russell Kent *civil engineer*
Holiday, Edith Elizabeth *former presidential adviser, cabinet secretary*
Holifield, Pearl Kam (Kam Holifield, Momi Kam Holifield) *poet*
Holland, Burt S. *statistics educator, consultant*
†Holland, Charles R. *military officer*
Holland, David Thurston *former editor*
Holland, Henry Norman *marketing and management consultant*
Holland, Michael James *computer services administrator*
†Holland, Richard A. *statistician*
Holland, Robert Campbell *anatomist, educator*
Holland, Samuel Stinson *music educator, writer, musician*
Hollander, Anne *writer*
Holle, Reginald Henry *retired bishop*
Holleb, Doris B. *urban planner, economist*
Holleman, John L. *priest*
Holleman, Sandy Lee *religious organization administrator*
Hollenberg, Harvard *lawyer, writer*
Holliday, Polly Dean *actress*
Holliday, Robert Kelvin *corrections officer, retired state senator, former newspaper executive, educator*
†Hollie, Gladys Miriam *nurse*
Hollis, Janice Denise *publishing executive, minister*
Hollis, Mary Fern Caudill *nurse educator, music educator, writer*
Hollis, Robbie Smagula *marketing communications executive*
Hollister, Alan Scudder *clinical pharmacologist, internist*
†Holloran, Thomas Edward *business educator*
†Holloway, Charles Edward *language educator*
Holloway, James Lemuel, III, *foundation executive, retired naval officer*
Holloway, Kimberley Michele *freelance/self-employed writer, communications executive, language educator*
Holloway, Richard Lawrence *marriage-family therapist, college official*
Holm, Celeste *actress*
Holm, Sir Ian *actor*
Holman, Bill *composer*
Holman, Frederick John *landscape architect*
†Holman, Margaret Alice *writer*
†Holman, Sandy Lynne *writer, consultant*
Holmes, David Richard, Jr., *cardiologist*
Holmes, Francis William *plant pathologist, educator*
Holmes, Henry Allen *government official*
Holmes, Jerry Dell *retired chemist*
Holmes, Michael Gene *lawyer*
†Holmes, Paul Kinloch, III, *former prosecutor*
Holmes, Paul Luther *political scientist, educational consultant*
Holmes, Richard Albert *software engineer, consultant*
Holmes, Susan G. *educator*
Holmquist, Jeffery R. *retail executive*
Holsgrove, Gareth John *medical association administrator*
Holsinger, Adena Seguine *music educator, community volunteer*
Holt, Carolyn Marie *youth employment and training specialist, secondary school educator*
Holt, Marjorie Sewell *lawyer, retired congresswoman*
Holt, Rochelle Lynn *writer, lecturer*
Holte, Debra Leah *investment executive, financial analyst*
Holter, Patra Jo *artist, art education consultant*
Holtkamp, Susan Charlotte *elementary education educator*
Holtmeier, Robert J. *accountant*
Holton, Grace Holland *accountant*
†Holton, William *artist*
Holtzman, David H. *technologist, security and privacy expert*
Holtzman, Robert Neil Nehemiah *neurosurgeon, neurologist*
Holzer, Barbara Coursey *innkeeper, minister, writer, educator*
Holzer, Jenny *artist*
Holzman, D. Keith *management consultant, record company executive, producer, arts consultant*
Hom, Doris Soo *consultant, investment manager*
Homb, Scott Michael *rehabilitation services professional*
Honea, Joyce Clayton *critical care nurse*
Honeystein, Karl *lawyer, entertainment company executive*
Honkanen, Jari Olavi *telecommunications company executive*
Honnold, John Otis *law educator*
Honse, Robert W. *agricultural company executive*
†Hoobler, Elizabeth Dressel *anthropologist, educator*
Hood, Luann Sandra *special education educator*
Hood, William Boyd, Jr., *cardiologist, educator*
Hook, Jerry B. *pharmaceutical consultant*
Hooker, Renée Michelle *perinatal and perianesthesia nurse*
Hooper, Gerry Don *retired information systems specialist, consultant*
Hooper, Henry Olcott *retired academic administrator, physicist*
Hooper, Josh *screen actor, director, media producer, writer*
Hooper, Robert Alexander *television producer, international educator*
Hooper, Roger Fellowes *retired architect*
Hoopes, Roy Harry, Jr., *writer*
Hoopes, Townsend Walter *retired management consultant, retired federal agency administrator*
Hoops, William James *clergyman*
Hoover, John Elwood *former military officer, consultant, author, speaker on US military history*
Hope, Thomas Walker *marketing professional*
Hopkins, Cynthia *composer*
Hopkins, George Mathews Marks *retired patent lawyer, business executive*
Hopkins, Jeffrey Willard *economist, researcher*
†Hopkins, Kevin W *education educator*
Hopkins, Philip Joseph *journalist, information technology executive*
Hopkins, Robert Elliott *music educator*
†Hopping, Richard Lee *college president emeritus*
Horisberger, Don Hans *conductor, musician*
Horn, Andrew Warren *lawyer*
†Horn, Howard M. *labor union administrator, consultant*
Horn, Lee Shawn *sports analyst*
Horn, Stephen *congressman, political science educator*
Horn, Vickie Lynn *medical and surgical nurse, nursing educator*
†Hornacek, Jeffrey John *professional basketball player*
Hornak, Thomas *retired electronics company executive*
Hornback, Joseph Hope *mathematics educator*
Hornby, Kenneth Peter *office technology executive*
Hornby-Anderson, Sara Ann *metallurgical engineer, marketing professional*
Horne, Alexander Douglas *journalist*
Horner, George Marlin *retired obstetrician-gynecologist*
Horner, Matina Souretis *retired college president, corporate executive*
Hornick, Katherine Joyce Kay *artist, small business owner*
†Hornyak, Roy Robert *music educator, minister*
Horovitz, Zola Philip *pharmaceutical company executive*
†Horsman, David A. Elliott *writer, financial services executive, educator*
Horsman, Lenore Lynde (Eleanora Lynde) *soprano, educator, actress*
Horswill, C. Weir *retired obstetrician-gynecologist, photographer*
Horton, Patricia Mathews *artist, violist and violinist*
Horton, Robert Carlton *geologist*
†Horton-Stevenson, Rhonda Anna *writer, educator*
†Horton-Wright, Alma Irene *educator*
Horvath, Imre Gabor *television producer and director*
Horwitz, David Larry *pharmaceuticals company executive, researcher, educator*
Horwitz, Donald Paul *lawyer*
Horwitz, Ronald M. *business administration educator*
†Hosang, Robert Michael *research scientist*
Hosea, Julia Hiller *communications executive, paralegal*
Hosek, James Robert *economist*
Hoskins, Iffath Abbasi *obstetrician-gynecologist*
Hoskins, John Howard *urologist, educator*
Hosman, Sharon Lee *music educator*
Hosmer, Hilary Holden *computer systems educator*
†Hostetter, Elizabeth A. *music educator*
Hostettler, Stephen John *naval officer*
†Hottenstein, Erin *journalist*
Hough, Thomas Henry Michael *retired lawyer, educator*
Houghtaling, Pamela Ann *technology marketing professional, writer*
†Houghton, Diane Murley *actor, vocalist*
Houghton, Katharine *actress*
Houle, Jeffrey Robert *lawyer*
Houlihan, Patrick Thomas *museum director*
Hourani, Laurel Lockwood *epidemiologist*
†House, Ernest Robert *education educator, educational evaluator*
House, Stephen Eugene *information systems consultant*
Houseman, Ann Elizabeth Lord *educational administrator, state official*
House-Wade, Susan Patricia *writer, educator*
Houston, Gloria *author, educator, consultant*
†Houston, Stanley Dunsmore *retired public relations executive*
Houtz, Duane Talbott *hospital administrator*
Houze, Herbert George *writer*
Howard, Alex T., Jr., *federal judge*
Howard, David *ballet school administrator*
Howard, Dean Denton *electrical engineer, researcher, consultant*
Howard, Donald Searcy *banker*
†Howard, Edward Francis *lawyer*
†Howard, James Joseph, III, *utility company executive*
Howard, James Webb *investment banker, lawyer, engineer*
Howard, John Kenneth *accountant, consultant*
Howard, John Wayne *lawyer*
Howard, Joseph Harvey *retired librarian*
Howard, Michael Eliot *historian, educator*
Howard, Robert Elliott *former federal official, consultant, educator*
Howard, Robert Franklin *observatory administrator, astronomer*
Howard, Stephen Wrigley *telecommunications executive*
Howard, Tammy Williams *nurse practitioner*
Howard, Terry Thomas *obstetrician, gynecologist*
Howard-Peebles, Patricia N. *clinical cytogeneticist*
Howards, Stuart S. *urologist, educator*
†Howe, Gordon *former professional hockey player, sports association executive*
Howe, John Prentice, III, *health science center executive, physician*
Howe, Richard Cuddy *state supreme court justice*
Howe, Virginia Hoffman *nurse administrator*
Howell, Ally Windsor *lawyer, author, editor*
Howell, Connie Rae *critical care nurse*
Howell, Donald Lee *lawyer*
Howell, Joel DuBose *internist, educator*
Howell, Julius Ammons *retired plastic surgeon*
†Howell, Neil *music educator*
†Howell, Thomas Lee *composer, writer*
Howell, William Robert *retail company executive*
Howells, John Gwilym *medical scientist*
Hower, Frank Beard, Jr., *retired banker*
Howes, Sophia DuBose *writer*
Howitt, Pamela Tesler *development and philanthropy association administrator*
Hoy, Harold Joseph *marketing educator, retail executive, writer, military officer, editor, management consultant*
Hoyle, William Vinton, Jr., *lawyer*
Hoyt, Mary Finch *author, editor, media consultant, former government official*
Hricak, Hedvig *physician, radiologist*
Hsu, Patrick Kuo-Heng *retired languages educator, librarian*
Huang, Shouhua *electronics engineer*
Hubbard, Elizabeth *actress*
Hubbard, Michael James *lawyer*
Hubbard, Robert Glenn *former federal agency administrator*
Hubbard, Stevan Ralph *biophysicist, educator*
Hubbe, Henry Ernest *financial forecaster, funds manager*
Huber, Ann Cervin *nurse*
Huber, Colleen Adlene *artist*
Huber, Douglas Crawford *pathologist*
†Huber, Jeanne Leonce *development director, consultant*
†Huber, Mark *foundation administrator*
Huber, Vida Swartzentruber *nursing educator*
Hubley, Reginald Allen *publishing executive*
Huckaby, Mark Anson *paramedic, educator, emergency medical services specialist*
Huckstead, Charlotte Van Horn *retired home economist, artist*
Hudak, Thomas F(rancis) *finance company executive*
Hudson, Alan C.H. *music educator, tropical fruit farmer*
Hudson, Donald J. *retired stock exchange executive*
Hudson, Franklin Donald *diversified company executive, consultant*
†Hudson, Kate *actress*
†Hudson, Michael Darren *agricultural economics educator*
Hudson, Stanton Harold, Jr., *public relations executive, educator, academic administrator*
Hudson, William Jeffrey, Jr., *manufacturing company executive*
Hudson, William Mark *insurance company executive, owner*
Hudson, Yeager *philosophy educator, minister*
Huenemann, Rodney Karl *state administrator, executive*
Huey, Ward L(igon), Jr., *retired media executive*
Huff, Janet House *special education educator*
Huffington, Anita *sculptor*
Huffman, Carol Koster *retired elementary school educator*
Huffman, James Thomas William *oil exploration company executive*
Huffman-Klinkowitz, Julie Ann *genealogist, researcher*
Hufschmidt, Maynard Michael *resources planning educator*
Huggins, Charles Edward *obstetrician, gynecologist, educator*
Huggins, Robert Brian *nonprofit organization official*
Hughes, Ann Hightower *retired economist, international trade consultant*
†Hughes, David Henry *manufacturing company executive*
†Hughes, Edward T. *retired bishop*
Hughes, Edward Thomas *retired English educator, consultant*
†Hughes, Keith William *banking and finance company executive*
Hughes, Kenneth Martin *planner*
†Hughes, Lorraine Williams *credit counselor, housing specialist*
Hughes, Michael Patrick *artist*
Hughes, Michaela Kelly *actress, dancer*
Hughes, Sue Margaret *retired librarian*
Hughes, Thomas Parke *history educator*
Hughes, W. James *optometrist*
Hughey, Richard Kohlman *author, lawyer*
Hui, Ho-Wah *pharmaceutical scientist*
Huie, Carol P. *information systems educator*
Huie, Robert Elliott *research chemist*
Hukins-Rodrigue, Dana Ann *community health nurse*
Hull, Elaine Mangelsdorf *psychology educator*
Hull, Jane Dee *former governor, former state legislator*
Hull, Louise Knox *retired elementary educator, administrator*
Hull, Margaret Ruth *artist, educator, consultant*
Hull, McAllister Hobart, Jr., *retired university administrator*
†Hull, Ronald R. *human resources specialist*
Hulse, Dexter Curtis *manufacturing executive*
Hulsey, Rachel Martinez *secondary school educator, columnist*
†Humann, Richard *artist*
Humbach, Miriam Jane *marketing and financial professional*

Johnstone, John William, Jr., *retired chemical company executive*
Johns-Treat, Corinne V. *management consultant*
Joiner, Charles Wycliffe *judge*
Jolly, Charles Nelson *lawyer, pharmaceutical company executive*
Jones, Anita Katherine *computer scientist, educator*
Jones, Bill *former state official, rancher*
Jones, Billy Ernest *dermatology educator*
Jones, Carleton Shaw *information systems company executive, lawyer*
Jones, Carolyn Evans *writer, speaker*
Jones, Christine Massey *retired furniture company executive*
Jones, David Charles *retired air force officer, former chairman Joint Chiefs of Staff*
Jones, David Rhodes *consulting editor*
Jones, Dorothy Joanne *social services professional*
Jones, Edward Douglass, III, *economist*
Jones, Everett Bruce *retired civil engineer, hydrologist*
Jones, Gerre Lyle *marketing and public relations consultant*
†Jones, James Clyde *management consultant, researcher*
†Jones, James L., Jr., *military officer*
Jones, Jane *artist*
Jones, Joan Megan *anthropologist*
Jones, John Harding *photographer*
Jones, Kacy Douglas *accountant*
Jones, Keith Alden *lawyer*
Jones, Lawrence Neale *university dean, minister*
Jones, Leonade Diane *media publishing company executive*
†Jones, Lupe Sirena *insurance agent*
†Jones, Marie C. *language educator*
Jones, Martha Lee *social worker, consultant*
†Jones, Matthew O. *engineering educator*
Jones, Peter d'Alroy *historian, writer, retired educator*
Jones, Phyllis Gene *judge*
Jones, Richard Melvin *bank executive, former retail executive*
Jones, Richard Wallace *interior designer*
†Jones, Robert Henry *automotive distribution executive*
Jones, Roger Alan *chemistry educator, researcher, consultant*
Jones, Shirley *actress, singer*
Jones, Stephanie J. *photojournalist, artist*
Jones, Suzanne Louise *physical therapist*
Jones, Thornton Keith *research chemist*
†Jones, Tommy Lee *actor*
Jones, Walton Linton *internist, former government official*
Jones, William Augustus, Jr., *retired bishop*
Jones, William Rex *law educator*
Jones-Johnson, Gloria *sociologist, educator, consultant*
†Jong, Nancy *financial consultant*
Jordan, Anne Devereaux *writer, educator*
†Jordan, Bruce Leslie *music educator, musician*
†Jordan, Deovina Nasis *administrative nurse*
Jordan, Howard Emerson *retired engineering executive, consultant*
Jordan, James Jackson *architect*
Jordan, James Lowell *educator, writer*
Jordan, Marvin Evans, Jr., *record company executive*
Jordan, Michael Hugh *information technology executive*
Jordan, Michael Jeffrey *retired professional basketball player, former professional sports team executive, retired baseball player*
Jordan, Robert Reed *geologist, educator*
Jordan, Robert Smith *political science educator*
Jordan, Thomas Fredrick *physics educator*
Jordania, Vakhtang *conductor, educator*
Jorden, William John *writer, retired diplomat*
†Jorndt, Louis Daniel *former retail drug store chain executive*
†Jorres, Daniel *literature educator*
Joseph, Geri Mack (Geraldine Joseph) *former ambassador, educator, journalist*
Joseph, Michael Thomas *broadcast consultant*
Josephson, Kenneth Bradley *artist, retired educator*
Joshi, Pratibha C. *immunologist, researcher*
Joslin, David Bruce *bishop*
†Joy, William N. (Bill Joy) *former computer company executive*
Joyce, William Robert *textile machinery company executive*
Juberg, Richard Kent
Judge, Jean Frances *management consultant*
Judge, Rosemary Ann *oil company executive*
Jügelt, Karl-Heinz Burkhard *librarian, researcher*
Juhl, Daniel Leo *manufacturing and marketing firm executive*
†Julander, Paula Foil *health care and political consultant, state senator*
†Jump, Sharyl A. *special events coordinator*
June, Roy Ethiel *lawyer*
Jung, Doranne *public relations, marketing and advertising consultant*
Jung, Hilda Ziifle *retired physicist*
†Jung, Seong-Ook *engineer*
Jupina, Andrea Ann *executive search consultant*
Jurasek, Randall John *educational consultant*
Juricic, Davor *mechanical engineering educator*
Juskenas, Nellie K. *retired anesthesiologist*
Juskowiak, Terry Eugene *career military officer*
Just, Ward Swift *author*
Juviler, Peter Henry *political scientist, educator*
Kabat, Linda Georgette *civic leader*
Kachur, Betty Rae *elementary education educator*
Kacprowicz, Donna Marie (Donna Leonetti) *staff nurse*
†Kaculi, Xhemal T. *oil industry executive, researcher*
Kacur, Lois Marie *obstetric and pediatric nurse*
Kader, Fred J. *pediatric neurologist*
Kadota, Takashi Theodore *mathematician, electrical engineer*
†Kåge, Jonas *ballet company artistic director*
Kahan, Rochelle Liebling *lawyer, concert pianist*
Kahana, Eva Frost *sociology educator*
†Kahle, Brewster *communications executive*
Kahmann, Sarah Stuber *retired foundation administrator*
Kahn, Charles Howard *architect, educator*
Kahn, Herta Hess (Mrs. Howard Kahn) *retired securities trader*
Kahn, Irwin William *industrial engineer*
Kahn, James Steven *retired museum director*
Kahn, Laurence Michael *lawyer, business consultant*
Kahn, Susan *artist*
Kahrmann, Robert George *educational administrator*
Kailian, Aram Harry *architect, consultant*
Kaiser, Keith Allen *music educator, researcher, conductor*
Kaiser, Nina Irene *health care consultant*
Kalba, Kas *international telecommunications consultant*
Kalidindi, Surya Raju *science educator*
Kalil, Nelson *oncologist, researcher*
†Kalinina, Olga *economist*
Kaliski, Mary *psychologist*
Kalkhoff, William Webster *sociologist, educator*
Kallenberg, John Kenneth *retired librarian*
Kallgren, Edward Eugene *retired lawyer*
Kalmanson, Jennifer Dawn *systems engineer, physicist*
Kaltvedt, Larry Dean *elementary school educator*
†Kalu, Kalu Ndukwe *public administration educator, researcher, consultant*
Kam, Mitchell M.T. *business professional*
Kamen, Harry Paul *retired life insurance company executive, lawyer*
Kamin, Blair Douglass *newspaper critic*
Kamins, Theodore I. *electrical engineer*
Kaminsky, Alice Richkin *English language educator*
Kamm, Laurence Richard *television producer, director*
Kamm, Linda Heller *lawyer*
Kamman, Alan Bertram *communications consulting company executive*
Kampf, Marilyn Jeanne *medical analyst*
Kampmeier, Curt *management consultant*
Kamrin, Michael Arnold *toxicology educator*
†Kanada, Gary N. Kahaho'omalu *adult education educator*
Kane, Diane Grinkevich *architectural historian, educator, planner*
Kane, Karen Marie *public affairs consultant*
Kane, Michael Joseph *director*
Kane, Patricia Lanegran *language professional, educator*
Kane, Robert Barry *career officer*
Kane, Sydell *elementary school principal*
Kane Hittner, Marcia Susan *bank executive*
Kanin, Fay *screenwriter*
Kannenstine, Margaret Lampe *artist*
Kantor, Harvey Sherwin *retired medical educator*
†Kantor, Mary Louise *music educator*
Kanuk, Leslie Lazar *management consultant, educator*
Kao, Simon C. *radiologist, educator*
†Kapalcik, Michele Lida *therapist, guidance counselor*
Kapcsandy, Louis Endre *building construction and manufacturing executive, chemical engineering consultant*
Kapitonov, Vladimir V. *molecular biologist*
Kaplan, David L. *retired communications educator, actor, artist, sculptor*
Kaplan, Erica Lynn *typing and word processing service company executive, pianist, educator*
Kaplan, Gabriela Diana *radiologist*
Kaplan, Helene Lois *lawyer*
†Kaplan, Jerry (S. Jerrold Kaplan) *former electronics company executive*
Kaplan, Leonard Eugene *accountant*
Kaplan, Phyllis *artist, composer*
Kaplan, Richard James *producer, director, writer, educator, consultant*
Kaplan, Robert B. *linguistics educator, consultant, researcher*
†Kapner, Lewis *lawyer*
Kapnick, Richard Bradshaw *lawyer*
Kapnick, Stewart *investment banker*
†Kappner, Augusta Souza *academic administrator*
Kaprielian, Walter *advertising executive*
†Karabell, Zachary *economic analyst*
Karakey, Sherry JoAnne *real estate company executive, interior designer*
Karalekas, Anne *business executive*
Karalis, John Peter *retired computer company executive, lawyer*
Karczmar, Mieczyslaw *economist*
Karen, Joel S. *plastic surgeon*
Kari, Daven Michael *religious studies educator*
Karl, George *professional basketball coach*
Karlin, Gary Lee *insurance executive*
Karlstrom, Paul Johnson *art historian*
Karnaugh, Maurice *computer scientist, educator*
Karnofsky, Mollyne *artist, poet*
Karol, Michael Alan *editor*
Karp, Gerald Charles *biologist, educator, writer*
Karp, Rosanne *oncology and women's health nurse*
Karpinos, Robert Douglas *anesthesiologist*
Karr, Gerald Lee *agricultural economist, state senator*
Karr, Norman *communications consultant, public relations executive*
Karson, Samuel *psychologist, educator*
Karttunen, Frances Esther *retired linguist, research scientist*
Karwecki, Margaret *nurse practitioner, consultant*
Kasdan, Lawrence Edward *film director, screenwriter*
Kaser, David *retired librarian, educator, consultant*
Kashikhin, Vadim *electrical engineer, researcher*
†Kasich, John R. *former congressman*
Kasimis, Basil S. *oncologist*
Kaskowitz, Edwin *social services executive*
Kaslow, Florence Whiteman *psychologist, educator, family business consultant*
†Kaspar, Frances Wolf *music educator*
Kaspar, Victoria Ann *school administrator*
Kasper, Victor, Jr., *economics educator*
†Kasperson, Jeanne Xanthakos *librarian, editor, educator*
Kaspin, Jeffrey Marc *floor covering professional*
Kaspin, Susan Jane *child care specialist*
Kasprzak, Lucian Alexander *physicist, researcher, technical manager*
Kass, David Norman *accountant, lawyer*
Kass, Jerome Allan *writer*
Kassal, Robert James *polymer research scientist*
Kassapoglou, Christos *aeronautical engineer*
†Kassinove, Jeffrey Ian *psychologist, educator, research scientist*
Kaster, Laura A. *lawyer*
Kastner, Marc Aaron *physics educator*
Kastor, Frank Sullivan *English language educator*
†Kastrup, Dieter *diplomat*
Katchor, Ben *cartoonist, artist, writer*
Kather, Gerhard *retired federal administrator*
†Katinsky, Steven *communications company executive*
†Katz, Alexander *chemical engineering educator*
Katz, Anne Harris *biologist, educator, writer, aviator*
Katz, Harriet Marx *retired social worker*
Katz, Mira Lynn *vascular ultrasound technologist, medical educator*
Katz, Sanford Noah *lawyer, educator*
Katz, Susan Arons *language arts specialist, author, poet*
Katz, William Loren *author*
Katz, William Michael *writer*
Katzman, Merle Hershel *retired orthopaedic surgeon*
Katzper, Meyer *analyst*
Kauffman, Dagmar Elisabeth *writer, researcher*
Kauffman, Kaethe Coventon *art educator, artist, author*
†Kauffman, Tim L. *physical therapist, educator*
Kaufman, Helene *legal secretary*
Kaufman, Irving *retired engineering educator*
Kaufman, Janice Horner *foreign language educator, women's and gender studies educator*
Kaufman, Luna Amalia *musicologist*
Kaufman, Stephen Lawrence *radiologist, educator*
Kauger, Yvonne *state supreme court justice*
Kavalek, Lubomir *chess expert*
Kavanaugh, Bonnie B. *corporate communications executive*
Kavanaugh, Frank James *film producer, educator*
†Kaveripatnam, Sandesh *venture capitalist*
Kavulich, John Steven, II, *international marketing executive*
Kawano, James Conrad *investment analyst*
Kay, Sean I. *politics and government educator*
Kaye, Daniel Theodore *editor*
Kaye, Stuart Martin *lawyer*
Kayfetz, Victor Joel *writer, editor, translator*
Kaylan, Howard Lawrence *musical entertainer, screenwriter, composer*
†Kayo, Ide *research scientist*
†Kazal, Louis Anthony, Jr., *health facility administrator*
†Kazan, Alexandra Khan *photographer, web site designer*
Kazmarek, Linda Adams *secondary education educator*
Keady, Walter James *writer*
Keala, Francis Ahloy *security executive*
Keane, James R. *neurologist*
†Keane, John Michael *career officer*
Kearney, Nancy Jean *artist*
Kearns, Ellen Veronica *artist*
Kearns, James Joseph *artist*
†Kearns, Michael Shawn *career officer*
Keating, Regina G. *computer analyst consultant*
Keaty, Robert Burke *business consultant*
Kebblish, John Basil *retired coal company executive, consultant*
Keebler, Lois Marie *elementary school educator*
Keech, Elowyn Ann *interior designer*
Keegan, John Robert *lawyer, educator*
Keeler, James Leonard *food products company executive*
Keeler, William H. *archbishop*
Keeling, J(ohn) Michael *lawyer, trade association administrator*
Keenan, Anthony Lee *trucking company executive*
Keene, Mary Ellen *federal agency executive*
Keene-Burgess, Ruth Frances *military official*
†Keesling, Brian *writer*
Keffer, Charles Joseph *consultant*
Kehew, George Mansir *artist*
Kehlmann, Robert *artist, critic*
Keidel, Robert Wooler *management consultant, writer, educator*
Keil, Harold H. (Bill Keil) *writer*
Keil, M. David *retired international association executive*
Keill, Stuart Langdon *psychiatrist*
Keilty, Bryan T. *government agency administrator*
Keim, Betty Lou *actress, literary consultant*
Keiper, Marilyn Morrison *elementary education educator*
Keith, Brian Thomas *automobile executive*
†Keith, Robert William *banker*
Keithler, John William *investment executive*
Kelalis, Barbara Anna Lisa *interior design company executive*
Kelehear, Carole Marchbanks Spann *senior legal secretary*
Kell, Scott K. *lawyer*
Kell, Vette Eugene *retired lawyer*
Kellaigh, Kathleen *conservatory artistic director*
Kellam, Norma Dawn *medical, surgical nurse*
Kellar, Marie Terese *special education educator*
Kelleher, Richard Cornelius *marketing and communications executive*
Keller, Ben Robert, Jr., *gynecologist*
Keller, Nancy Joan Byers *retired education educator*
Keller, Paul *advertising agency executive*
Kellerman, Edwin *lawyer, physician*
Kellerman, Jonathan Seth *writer, pediatric psychologist*
Kelley, A. Benjamin *author, consultant*
†Kelley, Dana Lyn *social studies educator, consultant*
Kelley, Edward Allen *publisher*
Kelley, Edward Watson, Jr., *former federal agency administrator*
Kelley, Larry Dale *retired army officer*
Kelley, Mary Elizabeth (Mary LaGrone) *information technology executive*
Kelley, Patrick Alan *neurologist, educator*
Kelley, Sheila Seymour *public relations consultant*
Kelley, Wayne Plumbley, Jr., *retired federal official*
Kellgren, George Lars *manufacturing company executive*
Kellner, Mark Allen *writer*
Kellogg, David *publisher*
†Kelly, Anastasia Donovan *lawyer*
Kelly, Anthony Odrian *flooring manufacturing company executive*
Kelly, Brendan William *retired engineering executive*
Kelly, Cheryl Ann *healthcare administrator*
†Kelly, Daniel Thomas *statistician*
Kelly, Sister Dorothy Ann *Ursuline Provincial college chancellor*
Kelly, J. Peter *steel company executive*
†Kelly, Michael Joesph, II, *publishing executive*
Kelly, Nancy Folden *arts administrator*
Kelly, Susan Croce *corporate affairs professional*
Kelly-Jones, Denise Marie *critical care nurse*
†Kelsey, Donald Ross *chemist*
Kelso, John Hodgson *former government official*
Kelts, David William *elementary education educator*
†Kemble, Penn *government official*
†Kemmerer, Lisa Ann *humanities educator*
Kemmett, William Joseph *poet, educator*
Kemp, Flo *artist*
Kemp, Kenneth Omer *writer, lawyer*
Kemper, John Dustin *mechanical engineering educator*
Kempner, Maximilian Walter *law school dean, lawyer*
Kempski, Ralph Aloisius *bishop*
†Kempskie, Jeffrey T. *music educator*
Kendall, Harry Ovid *internist*
Kendall, Jacqueline A. *social worker*
Kendig, William Lamar *retired government official, accountant*
Kendrick, Budd Leroy *psychologist*
Kendrick, James Earl *business consultant*
Kendzior, Robert Joseph *marketing executive*
Kennedy, Charles *retired neuroscientist, retired medical educator*
Kennedy, Debra Joyce *marketing professional*
Kennedy, Harold Edward *lawyer*
Kennedy, Jerrie Ann Preston *public relations executive*
Kennedy, Karen Syence *advertising agency executive*
†Kennedy, Kathleen *film producer*
Kennedy, Leo Raymond *engineering executive*
†Kennedy, Linda Dale *music educator, pianist, organist*
Kennedy, Marla Catherine *psychologist*
Kennedy, Raymond Arthur *writer*
Kennedy, Thomas J. *lawyer*
Kennedy, William F. *army reserve technician*
Kennedy-Minott, Rodney *international relations educator, former ambassador*
†Kennedy-Nolle, Sharon Diane *educator*
Kennefick, Christine Marie *materials scientist*
†Kennelly, Joy A. *public relations specialist*
†Kenny, H. Sharie *music educator*
†Kent, Christopher R. *communications executive*
Kent, Denise Ann *nurse, educator, nursing administrator*
Kent, Gary Warner *film director, writer*
Kenworthy, William Eugene *judge*
Kenyon, Daphne Anne *economics educator*
Kercher, David Max *mechanical engineer*
Kern, Charles William *retired university official, chemistry educator*
Kern, Irving John *retired food company executive*
Kern, Jerome H. *lawyer*
†Kern, Paul John *army officer*
Kernan, Joseph E. *governor*
Kerner, Michael Philip *lawyer*
Kerney, Yolonda V. *music historian*
†Kernochan, Sarah M. *film director, scriptwriter, composer*
Kernodle, Robert Gary *dance and exercise ecucator*
Kerns, Brian D. *former congressman*
Kerr, Donald MacLean, Jr., *physicist*
Kerr, Forrest David *actor, writer, producer*
Kerr, Frederick Hohmann *retired health care company executive*
Kerr, Harry Davidson *emergency physician*
Kerr, Janet Spence *physiologist, pharmacologist*
†Kerrick, Donald L. *career officer*
Kerstetter, Wayne Arthur *law educator, lawyer*
Kersting, Edwin Joseph *retired university dean, veterinarian*
Kerwin, Larkin *retired physics educator*
Kerwin, Walter Thomas, Jr., *career officer, consultant*
†Keskinocak, Pinar *adult education educator*
Kessler, Roslyn Marie *financial analyst*
Kessler, Stephen James *writer, editor*
Kessler-Harris, Alice *historian, educator*

Krishnamachari, Sadagopa Iyengar mechanical engineer, consultant
Kristensen, Hans M. think-tank executive, researcher
Kristensen, Marlene early childhood education educator
Kristofferson, Karl Eric writer
†Krivai, Galina manufacturing executive
Kriz, George James former agricultural research administrator
Krizan, Kelly Joe physician, leather craftsman
Krob, Melanie Gordon writer
Krobath, Krista Ann pharmacist
Kroeger, Susan Jean accountant
Krogius, Tristan Ernst Gunnar international marketing consultant, lawyer
Krohnke, Duane W. retired lawyer
Kroll, David Lee music educator
†Kromer, Debra Gonzales researcher
†Krongard, Howard J. lawyer
Kronschnabel, Robert James retired manufacturing company executive
Krop, Stephen retired pharmacologist
Kropschot, Richard Henry retired physicist, science laboratory administrato
Krouse, Clyde Francis writer
Krown, Seymour Richard film production executive
Krueger, Eugene Rex academic program consultant
†Krueger, Karli Ann music educator
Krueger, Ralph Arthur motel and food executive
Kruger, Barbara audiologist, speech and language pathologist
Kruger, Charles Herman, Jr., mechanical engineering educator
Kruger, Mollee Coppel writer
Krulik, Barbara S. director, writer, curator
Krupansky, Blanche retired judge
Krupat, Kitty Weiss writer, educator
Krupp, James Arthur Gustave consultant
Kruse, Rosalee Evelyn accountant, auditor, executive
Kryzak, Linda Ann educational administrator
Kubiak, John Michael academic administrator
†Kubisch, Anne Christine political scientist
Kucera, Daniel William retired bishop
Kuczynski, Les Stanislaus non-profit organization administrator
Kudrow, Lisa actress
Kuehn, James Marshall newspaper editor
Kuehn, Ronald L., Jr., natural resources company executive
Kuesel, Thomas Robert civil engineer
Kuest, Kristina M. manufacturing engineer
Kufus, Martin W. security specialist
Kuhens, Brian Scott investment company executive, publishing company exexcutive
Kuhl, Ronald Webster retired marketing executive
Kuhler, Deborah Gail grief therapist, former state legislator
Kukla, Maija Meijer research scientist, educator
Kula, Katherine Sue dentist
Kulak, Daryl Wayne holistic health business educator
Kulesha, Kevin John investment banker
Kulik, Rosalyn Franta food company executive, consultant
Kull, Bryan Paul business information/technology executive
Kulstad, Guy Charles public works official
Kult, Amy Elaine marketing consultant
Kultermann, Udo architectural and art historian, educator, author
Kumao, Heidi Elizabeth artist, educator
Kumar, Kaplesh materials scientist
†Kumar, Nanda Prativadi lawyer
†Kumar, Sanjaya epidemiologist, statistician
†Kunakemakorn, Numsiri C education educator
Kundel, Harold Louis radiologist, educator
Kundla, John Albert retired coach
Kundu-Raychaudhuri, Smriti Kana biomedical scientist
Kung, Patrick Chung-Shu biotechnology executive
Kunkel, David Nelson lawyer
Kunstadter, Geraldine Sapolsky foundation executive
†Kunz, Alexandra Cavitt physician, anthropologist, researcher
†Kuo, Michelle Chen (Chou-hsia Chen) musician, educator
Kuper, Daniela F. writer, speaker
†Kuperman, Michael Aron language educator, writer
Kupferman, Meyer composer
†Kurahashi, Yuko theater educator
†Kurdi, Ramsey music educator
Kurfehs, Joseph Morris information security executive
Kurk, Mitchell physician
Kurnick, Nathaniel Bertrand retired oncologist-hematologist
Kurotsuchi, Roy Yutaka obstetrician, gynecologist
Kurtz, Dolores May civic worker
Kurtz, Myra Berman microbiologist
†Kurtzer, Benjamin Louis networking engineer
†Kurz, Alan Scott retired small business owner
Kush, Charles Andrew, III, telecommunications executive, internet entrepreneur
Kushmar, Neal accountant
Kushner, Harvey David management consultant
Kushner, Todd Roger computer scientist, software engineer
†Kushner, Tony playwright
Kushner-Cohen, Carol Ann school nurse
Kushwaha, Sudhir Singh internist, cardiologist, educator
Kuska, John Joseph, Jr., accountant, management consultant
Kusma, Kyllikki lawyer
Kussrow, Nancy Esther educational association administrator
Kustin, Kenneth chemist
Kutrzeba, Joseph S. theatrical and film producer, director
Kutscher, Ronald Earl retired federal government executive
Kutscher, Thomas Alan electrical engineer
Kutyna, Donald Joseph air force officer
Kuykendall, John Wells academic administrator, educator
Kvitko, Arkady mathematician, researcher
Kwasnick, Paul Jack retail executive
†Kydd, William former medical association administrator
Kye, Hoon Taik retired anesthesiologist, educator
Kyles-Omari, Cynthia Lee editor, career consultant
LaBarre, Carl Anthony retired government official
Labbe-Webb, Elizabeth Geralyn arts administrator, theatre artist
Labella, Janice Marie peri-operative nurse
†Labiner, Caroline architect
La Blanc, Robert Edmund consulting company executive
Labor, Earle Gene English language educator
Labrecque, Richard Joseph retired industrial executive
Labriola, Angelina Marie librarian
Lacerenza, Joseph Charles research scientist
Lacey, Aaron Michael actor, director, screenwriter, executive producer
Lacey, Cloyd Eugene retired insurance company executive
Lachcik, Nancy Lou Marshall lawyer, educator
Lackenmier, James Richard academic administrator, priest
Lackland, John lawyer
†Lacroix, Pierre professional sports team professional
†LaCroix, Sophia Marie artist
Ladd, Diane Rose actress
Ladd, James Roger international business executive and consultant
Ladd, Joseph Carroll retired insurance company executive
†Lafair, Theodore investment company executive, financial consultant
La Falce, John Joseph former congressman, lawyer
LaFemina, Gerry writing and literature educator
Lafleur, Laurette Carignan artist
Lafley, Alan Frederick retired banker
†Lague, Michael Robert biological anthropologist
Lahmann, Robert Oscar retired artist
Lai, Eric Pong Shing family physician, educator
Lai, Feng-Qi instructional designer, educator
Laidlaw, Robert Richard publishing company executive
Laird, Betty Ann writer, researcher, actress
Laisure, Thomas James artist, sculptor
Lajiness-Polosky, Danine Theresa psychiatric-mental health nurse, pediatric nurse
†Lake, James A. molecular biology educator
†Lam, Cuong Kim research scientist
Lamalie, Robert Eugene retired executive search company executive
LaMantia, Charles Robert management consulting company executive
LaMantia, Paul Christopher (W. Zombek) artist
Lamb, Sister Jane Marie bereavement counselor, nurse
Lambert, Edythe Rutherford retired language educator, civic volunteer
Lambert, Jon Kelly mechanical engineer
Lambert, Joseph Parker retired dentist
Lambert, Rebecca Fotouhi investment company executive
Lambert, Richard Bowles, Jr., festival administrator
Lambert, William Jesse, III, writer
Lambrix, Winifred Marie McFarlane retired elementary education educator
Lamdin, Lois Symons English educator
Lamel, Linda Helen professional society executive, former insurance company executive, former college president, lawyer
Lamm, Harriet A. mathematics educator
Lamont, Alice accountant, consultant
LaMotta, Connie Frances communications consultant, executive coach
La Moy, June Inez graphic designer
Lampert, Eleanor Verna retired human resources specialist
Lampson, Butler Wright computer scientist
Lamy, M(ary) Rebecca consultant, land developer, government official
Lan, Xuekui engineer
Lancaster, Jeanette (Barbara Lancaster) dean, nursing educator
Lancaster, John Howard civil engineer, consultant
Lancaster, Michael Dean artist, marketing executive
Lancaster, Sally Rhodus retired non-profit executive and consultant
Lance, Alan George former state attorney general
Land, Allan Stephen surgeon
Land, Kenneth Dean test and balance agency executive, building commission agent, energy and environmental consultant
†Landau, Susan computer scientist
Landes, George Miller biblical studies educator
Landes, William Alan publishing executive
Landgarten, Helen Barbara art psychotherapist, educator
Landi, Diane Marie graphics designer, consultant
Landis, Robert Kumler, III, investment banker, lawyer
†Landman, Eric Christopher lawyer
Landon, Robert Gray retired manufacturing company executive
Landon, William J. intelligence officer
Landovsky, Rosemary Reid figure skating school director, coach
Landsberger, Kurt scientific and medical products executive
Landsman, Richard investment company executive, finance educator
Landy, Lisa Anne lawyer
Lane, Adelaide Irene computer systems specialist, researcher
†Lane, Diane actress
Lane, John Rodger art museum director
Lane, Lilly Katherine museum staff member
Lane, Patricia Peyton nursing consultant
Lane, William W. electronics executive
Lang, Ernst Frederick radiologist
Langdale, Noah Noel, Jr., research educator, former university president
Lange, Frederick Edward, Jr., computer information systems architect
Lange, William Michael lawyer
Langeloh, Jean Kleppinger interior designer
Langenkamp, Sandra Carroll retired human services administrator
†Langer, Alois communications executive
Langer, Bernhard professional golfer
Langer, Dennis Henry pharmaceutical company executive
Langer, Edward L. trade association administrator
Langer, Ralph Ernest journalist, newspaper executive and editor
Langerak, Esley Oren retired research chemist
Langford, Laura Sue ratings analyst
Langford, Walter Martin retired greeting card and gift wrap manufacturing executive
Langham, Gail B. writer
Langley, Joellen S. music educator
Langley, Lester Danny educator
†Lang-Piaseki, Vera Jean former publishing company executive
Lansdale, H. Parker minister, historian, non-profit administrator
Lantz, Joanne Baldwin academic administrator emeritus
Lantz, Susan Ruppalt operating room nurse
Lanzillotti, Robert Franklin economist, educator
Lanzl, Christina Anna visual artist, arts coordinator
Lape, Michael John small business owner
Lape, Robert Cable broadcast journalist
LaPidus, Jules Benjamin educational association administrator
†Lapidus, Steven Richard lawyer
†Lapinsky, Joseph F. manufacturing company executive
Laporte, Leo Frederic earth sciences educator, paleontologist
Larar, Gerald N. physician, research scientist
Lardner, Cynthia Marie-Martinovich lawyer
Large, G. Gordon M. computer software company executive, retired
Largent, Steve former congressman, former professional football player
Larkin, Joan poet, English educator
Larkin, Lawrence Albert retired computer engineer
La Rocca, Isabella artist, educator
LaRocco, Elizabeth Anne management information systems professional
LaRoche, Jane Lawton emergency physician
LaRoche, Linda writer
Larr, Peter retired banker, consultant
Larrimore, Randall Walter retired wholesale company executive
†Larsdotter, Anna-Lisa retired translator, artist
Larsen, Anita Donice writer, consultant, speaker
Larson, Ada Copp artist
Larson, Carole Allis library and information scientist, educator
Larson, Charles Fred consultant
Larson, Janice Talley computer science programmer
Larson, Paul William public relations executive
Larson, Richard Smith pathologist, researcher
Larson, Robert William education educator, consultant
†Larson, Roger Keith physician, writer
Larson, Vicki Lord communication disorders educator
†Larsson, Hans Peter science educator
LaRue, Renee educator
Lashley, Lenore Clarisse lawyer
Lashner, Marilyn Auerbach communication content analyst, forensic expert
Laskey, Richard Anthony biomedical device executive
Lasky, Richard Donald psychoanalyst, educator
Lassiter, Kenneth T. photography educator, consultant
Lasswell, Anita Diane nutrition educator
†Laszlo, Pierre chemistry educator
†Latham, Chad J. management consultant
Latham, James Richard research scientist
Latham, Joseph William judge
Latham, Joyce Eileen writer/editor, poet, photojournalist
†Lathrop, Ann librarian, educator
Lathrope, Daniel John law educator
†Latif, David Ata pharmacy educator
Latimer, Margaret Petta retired nutrition and dietetics educator
Latino, Mark Vincent rapid transit executive
Latiolais, Minnie Fitzgerald nurse, hospital administrator, retired
Latorraca, Joseph Paul writer
Latta, Jean Carolyn financial analyst
†Lau, Fred H. protective services official
Lau, Roy Esme surgeon
†Lauderdale, Pat L. law educator, social scientist
Lauderdale, Vance, Jr., anesthesiologist
Laudone, Anita Helene lawyer
†Laufer, Joanna writer
Laufer, William Hervey artist, printmaker
Laufman, Harrington Butler systems programmer
Laughlin, Louis Gene economic analyst, consultant
Laupus, William Edward physician, educator
Laurenzo, Vincent Dennis industrial management company executive
†Lauryssen, Carl neurosurgeon, director
Lautenbacher, Conrad Charles, Jr., naval officer, management consultant, federal government executive
Lauterbach, Edward Charles psychiatric educator
LaVelle, Arthur anatomy educator
†Laven, Karen Julig writer, scriptwriter
Lavengood, Lawrence Gene management educator, historian
Lavidge, Robert James marketing research executive
Lavington, Michael Richard venture capital company executive
†La Vista, Jaqueline Gable air transportation executive
†Law, Bernard Francis Cardinal retired archbishop
†Law, Beth environmental protection specialist
Lawer, Betsy banker
Lawler, Thomas Comerford intelligency agency official, government agency administrator
Lawless, Michael Rhodes pediatrics educator
Lawrence, Christine physician
Lawrence, David M. health facility administrator
Lawrence, David Long radiologist
Lawrence, Glenn Robert arbitrator, mediator, lawyer
Lawrence, Margery H(ulings) marketing consultant
Lawrence, Mary Josephine (Josie Lawrence) artist, retired library official
Lawrence, Ruth writer, illustrator
Lawrence, Sally Clark academic administrator
Lawrence, Stephen Lee secondary school principal, mechanic
Lawrence-Cox, Nancy Nell retired executive secretary, artist
†Laws, Eric Laban psychologist, educator
Lawton, Jean Margaret volunteer
Laycraft, James Herbert retired judge
Layde, Peter Mark epidemiologist, preventive medicine educator
Layeghi, Gholam Reza engineer, researcher, editor
Layne, James Nathaniel vertebrate biologist
Layton, Robert lawyer
Layton, William George retired management consultant, human resources executive, export-import executive
Lazio, Rick A. former congressman, lawyer, association administrator
Lazo, Caroline Evensen writer
Le, Yvonne Diemvan chemist
†Lea, Bih-Ru computer science educator
Lea, Lorenzo Bates lawyer
Leach, Janet C. publishing executive
Leachtenauer, Jon Clark optical scientist
Leader, Joyce E. ambassador
Leak, Nancy Marie artist
Leal, José Henrique museum director, marine biologist
†Leaptrott, John accountant
Leason, Jody Jacobs newspaper columnist
Leath, Kenneth Thomas research plant pathologist, educator, agricultural consultant
Leather, Victoria Potts college librarian
†Leatherdale, Douglas West insurance company executive
Leatto, Renne director, writer
Leavitt, Maura Lynn elementary education educator
Leavitt, Victoria Seyferth marketing professional
Leavy, Herbert Theodore publisher
Leb, Arthur Stern lawyer
LeBaron, Edward Wayne, Jr., retired lawyer
LeBeau, Dick former professional football coach, retired football player
LeBeau, Lawrence R. family practice physician
Lebensohn, Jeremy sculptor
LeBlanc, Hugh Linus political science educator, consultant
LeBlanc, Leonard Joseph electronics company executive
†LeBlanc, Matt actor
LeBlond, Paul Henri oceanographer, educator
Le Cocq, Frank retired obstetrician/gynecologist
Leddy, Susan nursing educator
†Leder, Philip geneticist, educator
Lederer, Katherine Gay English language educator
Lederer, Paul Edward landscape architect
Lederer, Peter David lawyer
Lederman, Leon Max physicist, educator
Ledet, Phyllis L. educational administrator
Ledford, Brenda Kay writer
Ledford, Janet Marie Smalley real estate appraiser, consultant
Ledley, Tamara Shapiro earth system scientist, climatologist
Ledogar, Stephen J. retired diplomat
LeDoux, John Clarence retired law enforcement official
Ledwig, Donald Eugene association executive, former broadcasting executive, former naval officer
Lee, Aldora G. social psychologist
†Lee, Anne music educator
Lee, Christopher Frank Carandini actor, author, singer
Lee, Corinne Adams retired educator
†Lee, Courtney investment company executive, educator
Lee, Cynthia television producer, playwright, filmmaker
Lee, Dan M. retired state supreme court chief justice
Lee, David Sack Yee internist
Lee, Dong Hoon mathematician, educator
Lee, Douglas Ocwah medical educator
Lee, Gwendolin Kuei retired ballet educator
Lee, Harrison Hon naval architecture librarian, consultant
Lee, James Matthew Canadian politician
Lee, Jeanne Kit Yew administrative officer
Lee, Joseph William sales executive
Lee, Kwangjin engineer, researcher

Lee, Marilyn Modarelli (Irma Lee) *lawyer, retired library director*
Lee, Nancy T. *human services administrator, educator*
†Lee, Paul M., Jr., *military officer*
Lee, Pui Luen *civil engineer*
Lee, Richard Kenneth *software company executive*
Lee, Robert W(illiam) *journalist, researcher*
Lee, Susan Ann *social worker, therapist*
Lee, Thomas Tehwen *neurosurgeon*
Lee, William Franklin, III, *musician, composer*
Leedom-Ackerman, Joanne *writer, educator*
Leeds, Douglas Brecker *advertising agency executive, theatre producer*
Leeds, Nancy Brecker *sculptor, lyricist*
Leeson, Susan M. *former state supreme court judge*
Leeves, Jane *actress*
LeFevre, Edmund Arthur, Jr., *scenic designer*
Leff, Joseph Norman *yarn manufacturing company executive*
Lefferts, George *producer, writer, director*
Lefkowitz, Alan Zoel *lawyer*
Lefranc, Margaret (Margaret Schoonover) *artist, illustrator, editor, writer*
Legere, Kathy Ann *artist, poet*
Leggett, Roberta Jean (Bobbi Leggett) *retired social services administrator*
Lehman, Christopher M. *international business consultant*
Lehman, David *poet, writer, editor*
Lehman, Joan Alice *real estate executive*
Lehman, John F., Jr., *industrialist*
Lehman, Paul Robert *retired music educator*
Lehman, Todd Wilson *artist*
†Lehmann, Danica Maria *psychotherapist*
Lehmann, (A) Spencer *retired chemist, retired chemical engineer*
Lehner-Quam, Alison Lynn *library administrator*
Lehrer, Leonard *artist, educator*
Lehrer, Merrill Clark *retail sales consultant*
Lehrman, Nat *magazine editor*
†Leiber, Jerry *songwriter*
Leiber, Judith Maria *designer, manufacturer*
†Leibler, Kenneth Robert *financial service executive*
Leibowitt, Sol David *lawyer*
Leibowitz, Leonard D. *retired pediatrician*
Leidy, John William, Jr., *endocrinologist, educator*
Leigh, Vincenta M. *health administrator*
Leighton, Leslie Steven *gastroenterologist*
Leikhim, Nance *artist*
Leimas, Carol Ann *women's association consultant*
Leipzig, Arthur *photographer, educator emeritus*
†Leiva, Nicolas *artist*
Leman, Craig Billings *surgeon*
LeMarbe, Edward S. *marketing executive, engineering manager, engineer*
Lemesis, Guntis Victor *human resources specialist*
Lemisch, Jesse *history educator, writer*
Lemmon, Harry Thomas *retired state supreme court justice*
Lemmon, Marilyn Sue *retired advertising and human resources executive*
Lenhart, Gary Alan *poet*
†Lenix-Hooker, Catherine Jeanette *librarian*
Lennon, Joseph Luke *college official, priest*
Leo, Michael Charles *emergency physician, surgeon, educator*
Leonard, Carolyn Branch *publisher, editor, writer*
Leonard, Guy Meyers, Jr., *international holding company executive*
†Leonard, Sugar Ray (Ray Charles Leonard) *retired professional boxer*
Leonetti, Evangeline Phillips *retired nursing educator*
†Leonetti, John P. *otolaryngologist, surgeon, educator*
Leoni, Tea (Elizabeth Tea Pantaleoni) *actress*
Lepage, Robert *actor, director, playwright*
Lepkowski, Wil (Wilbert Charles Lepkowski) *journalist*
L'Eplattenier, Nora Sweeny Hickey *nursing educator*
LePome, Penelope Marie *rehabilitation counselor, educator*
Lepp, Gerald Peter *lawyer*
Lerner, Herbert J. *tax consultant*
Lerner, Ilya *artist*
Lerner, Vladimir Semion *computer scientist, educator*
LeRoy, G. Palmer *art dealer*
Le Shana, David Charles *retired academic administrator*
Lesher, Gloria Jean *writer*
Lesiak, Karen Ann *librarian*
Lesko, Harry Joseph *transportation company executive*
Leslie, Maureen Heelan *university director*
Lesly Stevens, Elizabeth *journalist*
Lesniewski-Laas, Marek *lawyer*
Lesser, Eve Gertrude *retired investment banker*
Lesser, Felice A. *choreographer, dancer, playwright, screenwriter, filmmaker*
†Lesser, Gerson Theodore *medical educator, researcher*
Lesser, Loryn Sari *director*
LesStrang, David Matthew *public relations executive, government affairs executive*
Lester, Alicia L. *financial analyst*
Lester, Robin Dale *educator, author, former headmaster*
†Lester, Shane Michael *information technology executive, educator*
Lester, Virginia Laudano *education administrator*
Leston, Gerd *research chemist, retired*
†Lette, Daniel Ivan *pilot*
†Leung, Mary Ann Elizabeth *chemist*
Leung, Roderick Chi-tak *architect*
Leus McFarlen, Patricia Cheryl *water chemist*
Leva, James Robert *retired electric utility company executive*
Levaux, Hugh Pierre *pharmaceutical executive, consultant*
LeVay, Simon *neuroscientist, writer, educator*
Leveille, Gilbert Antonio *food products executive*
†Leven, Linda *application developer, writer, actor, model, artist*
Levenback, Karen L. *educator, writer, editor*
Levens, Joseph David *investment company executive*
†Levenson, Anait S. *cancer researcher, consultant*
Levenson, Marc David *optics and lasers specialist, scientist, editor*
Leventhal, Ellen Iris *portfolio manager, financial services executive*
Leventhal, Nathan *performing company executive, lawyer, municipal official*
Leventhal, Ruth *retired parasitology educator, university official*
Levi, Barbara Goss *physicist, editor*
Levi, Josef Alan *artist*
Levi, Maurice David *economics educator*
Levin, Alan Scott *pathologist, allergist, immunologist, lawyer*
Levin, Judith Maria *health science association administrator, consultant*
Levin, Morton D(avid) *artist, printmaker, educator*
Levin, Peter J. *hospital administrator, public health educator*
Levin, Steven James *artist*
Levin, William Edward *lawyer*
†Levine, Alan J. *entertainment company executive*
Levine, David M. *newspaper editor*
Levine, Gail Carson *writer*
Levine, Jack *artist*
Levine, Maita Faye *mathematics educator*
Levine, Michael Elias *law educator, executive*
Levine, Michael Joseph *economic development executive*
Levinson, Herbert Sherman *civil and transportation engineer*
Levinson, Kenneth S. *lawyer, corporate executive*
Levinson, Peter Joseph *retired lawyer*
Levinson, Stephen Eliot *engineering educator, electrical engineer*
Levitas, Miriam C. Strickman *documentary filmmaker, designer, consultant intergenerational relationships*
†Levitt, Arthur, Jr., *investment company executive*
Levitt, B. Blake *medical and science writer*
Levitt, Ronald Larry *public relations consulting executive, freelance writer/journalist*
Levy, Arthur James *public relations executive, writer*
Levy, David *consultant, retired lawyer, insurance company executive*
†Levy, David B. *school librarian, education educator, researcher*
Levy, Leah Garrigan *federal official*
Levy, Leslie Ann *application developer*
Levy, Louis Edward *retired accounting firm executive*
Levy, Valery *publisher*
Lewin, Marion Ein *consultant, physician, former medical association administrator*
Lewin, Rhoda Greene *editor, historian, columnist*
Lewinger, Jean Elizabeth *pediatrics nurse, neonatal intensive care nurse*
Lewinsohn, Hilton Cecil *physician*
Lewis, Andrew Lindsay, Jr., (Drew Lewis) *former transportation and natural resources executive*
Lewis, Anthony *newspaper columnist*
Lewis, Arthur Dee *corporation executive*
Lewis, Brock *investment company executive*
†Lewis, Carl (Frederick Carlton Lewis) *Olympic track and field athlete*
Lewis, Charles Leonard *psychologist*
Lewis, Claudia Jean *marketing professional*
Lewis, Dale Kenton *retired lawyer, mediator*
Lewis, Dennis Carroll *writer, publisher, educator*
Lewis, Douglas *art historian*
Lewis, Emanuel Raymond *historian, psychologist, retired librarian*
Lewis, Floyd Wallace *former electric utility executive*
Lewis, James Lee, Jr., *actuary*
Lewis, Josephine Victoria *retired marketing executive*
Lewis, Martin Edward *shipping company executive, foreign government concessionary*
Lewis, Martin R. *paper company executive, consultant*
Lewis, Philip *educational and technical consultant*
Lewis, Rita Hoffman *plastic products manufacturing company executive*
Lewis, Robert Turner *former psychologist*
Lewis, Samuel Winfield *retired government official, former ambassador*
Lewis-Griffith, Dorothy Ellen *music educator, pianist*
Lewis Mill, Barbara Jean *school psychologist, educator*
Lewitt, Miles Martin *computer engineering company executive*
Lewitus, Marla Berman *lawyer*
Lewitzky, Bella *choreographer*
Leybourn, Carol *musician, educator*
†Leydig, Carl Frederick *lawyer*
Li, Bao Qin *mathematics educator, researcher*
†Li, Bingguang *business educator*
Li, Leslie Denise *novelist, journalist, playwright*
Li, Qing'an *scientist, researcher*
†Li, Ruowei Rosie *nutritionist, epidemiologist*
Li, Tingye *electrical engineer*
†Li, Xiaojie *statistician, consultant*
Li, Yao-En *chemical engineer*
Li, Zhen *medical researcher*
Liang, Junxiang *aeronautics and astronautics engineer, educator*
Libassi, Frank Peter *lawyer*
Libava, Jerry Ronald *franchise consultant*
Liberman, Gail Jeanne *editor*
Libertiny, Thomas Gabor *mechanical engineer, administrator, stock broker*
Lichenstein, Richard *physician, health services administrator*
Lichtenberg, Byron K. *futurist, manufacturing executive, space flight consultant, pilot*
Lichtenstein, Harvey *performing arts executive*
Lichtenstein, Natalie G. *lawyer*
Lichtenstein, Sarah Carol *lawyer*
Licke, Wallace John *lawyer*
Liddell, Jane Hawley Hawkes *civic worker*
Lidsky, Ella *retired law librarian*
Lie, Yu-Chun Donald *electrical engineer*
Liebeler, Susan Wittenberg *lawyer*
Lieberman, Anne Marie *retired financial executive*
Lieberman, Gail Forman *investment company executive*
Lieberman, Louis (Karl Lieberman) *artist*
Lieberman-Cline, Nancy *sports commentator, former professional basketball coach, former player*
Liebman, Nina R. *economic developer*
Lief, Thomas Parrish *sociologist, educator*
Lieverman, Theodore Mark *lawyer*
Liew, Fah Pow *mechanical engineer*
Liffers, William Albert *retired chemical company executive*
Lifson, Kalman Alan *retired management consultant, banking executive*
Ligenza, Andrea Angela *nurse*
†Light, April Gene *music educator*
Light, Arthur Heath *bishop*
Light, Pamela Delamaide *interior designer*
Lightburn, Faye Marie *genealogist*
Lightman, Alan Paige *writer, physicist, educator*
Lightstone, Ronald *lawyer*
Lightwood, Carol Wilson *writer*
Ligotti, Eugene Ferdinand *retired dentist*
Liljegren, Frank Sigfrid *artist, art association official*
Lilley, William, III, *information and communications business executive*
Lilly, Edward Guerrant, Jr., *retired utility company executive*
Lilly, Thomas Gerald *retired lawyer*
†Lim, Jerry Teik-Chuan *composer, music educator*
Liman, Ellen *painter, writer, arts advocate*
Lin, Henry Baohua *consultant, writer*
Lin, Linda I-li *computer consultant, trainer*
†Lin, Shinemin *math and computer educator*
†Lin, Yachen *data mining expert, business strategiest*
Linaker, David Scott *athletic trainer, educator*
†Lincoln, James Henry, Sr., *writer*
Lind, Lanette Mina *piano teacher*
Linda, Gerald *advertising and marketing executive*
Lindblom, Laurie Beth *physician*
Linde, Maxine Helen *lawyer, business executive, private investor*
†Linden, Gordon L. *music educator*
Lindenberger, Herbert Samuel *writer, literature educator*
Lindgren, William Dale *librarian*
†Lindley, Cheryl A. *artist, writer*
Lindner, Carl Henry, Jr., *sports team executive, insurance company executive*
Lindorff, Joyce Zankel *harpsichordist*
Lindquist, Michael Adrian *career military officer*
†Lindrose, Rebecca Susan *counselor*
Lindsay, James Wiley *retired agricultural company executive*
Lindsey, Dottye Jean *marketing executive*
Lindsey, Lawrence Benjamin *economist*
Lindsey, Roberta Lewise *music researcher, historian*
Lindsey, Ruth *retired education educator*
Lindstrom, Donald Fredrick, Jr., *priest, consultant*
Lines, Sandra Ramsey *forensic document examiner*
Lingle, Marilyn Felkel *freelance writer, columnist, author*
Linhares, Judith Yvonne *artist, educator*
Link, George Hamilton *retired lawyer*
Link, William Theodore *television writer, producer*
†Link-Plante, Julia A. *horticulturist, entomologist, writer*
Linn, Richard *federal judge*
Linz, Anthony James *osteopathic physician, consultant, educator*
Linz, Gerhard David *psychologist, consultant*
Linzell, Daniel Gattner *civil and structural engineer*
Lionetti, Frank Carmine *graphic design executive*
Lipinski, Tara Kristen *retired professional figure skater*
†Lipke, William Alan *music educator, musician*
Lipkin, Randie Tina *novelist*
Lipman, David *retired journalist, multimedia consultant*
Lippert, Christopher Nelson *dentist, consultant*
Lippincott, James Lippincott *biochemistry and biological sciences educator*
Lippincott, Philip Edward *retired paper products company executive*
Lippman, Dorothy *nurse practitioner*
Lipschutz, Marian Shaw *secondary education educator, writer*
Lipsey, Joseph, Jr., *water bottling company executive, retail and wholesale corporation executive*
Lipsitt, Lewis Paeff *psychology educator*
Lipsky, Stephen Edward *engineering executive, electronics engineer*
Lipsman, Richard Marc *lawyer, educator*
†Lipton, Glenn E. *orthopaedic surgeon*
Lipton, Nina Anne *healthcare executive*
†Lish, Debra Elaine *historian, educator*
Liskamm, William Hugo *architect, urban planner, educator*
Lisoni, Gail Marie Landtbom *lawyer*
†Lissakers, Karin Margareta *former federal agency administrator*
Lister, Linda Joanne *music educator, composer, vocalist*
Listgarten, Max Albert *periodontics educator*
Litman, Harry Peter *lawyer, educator*
†Little, Charlotte Louise *poet, writer*
Little, Freed Sebastian *retired petroleum equipment manufacturing company executive*
Little, Loren Everton *musician, ophthalmologist*
Little, Mildred Miller *music educator, soloist*
Littleford, William Donaldson *retired publishing executive*
†Littlejohn, Lance L. *mathematics educator*
Littler, Gene Alec *professional golfer*
Littleton, Harvey Kline *artist*
Littlewood, Thomas Benjamin *retired journalism educator*
Littman, Earl *advertising and public relations executive*
Littrell, Dennis Allen *writer*
†Litzenberger, Lesley Margaret *textiles executive*
Liu, Alan Fong-Ching *mechanical engineer*
Liu, Katherine Chang *artist, art educator*
†Liu, Kexi *music educator*
Liu, Margaret C. *music educator*
Liu, Pamela Pei-Ling *landscape architect, graphic designer*
Liu, Ralph Yieh-Min *investment management and banking executive*
Liu, Rhonda Louise *librarian*
Liu, Ruth Wang *educator, researcher*
Liu, Xiaoqing Frank *computer scientist, educator*
†Liu, Yaozen *artist*
†Liu, Yong *computer scientist, researcher*
Lively, John Pound *magazine editor, publisher*
Lively, Pierce *federal judge*
†Livengood, Stanley *music educator, conductor*
Livingston, Alan Wendell *communications executive*
Livingston, Margaret Gresham *civic leader*
Livingstone, Susan Morrisey *consultant, former federal agency administrator*
Livingstone, Trudy Dorothy Zweig *dancer, educator*
Lloyd, Michael Jeffrey *recording producer*
Lloyd, Michael L. *nursing administrator, educator*
Lo, Shui-yin *physicist*
Loach, Paul Allen *biochemist, biophysicist, educator*
Loarie, Thomas Merritt *healthcare executive*
Lobanov-Rostovsky, Oleg *management consultant*
Lobao, Linda Mary *sociologist, educator*
†Lobenhofer, Louis F. *law educator*
Lober, Lionel M. *screenwriter, producer*
Localio, Marcia Judith *medical/surgical nurse*
Lockart, Barbetta *fabric designer, textile and fine artist, jeweler, art educator*
Locke, Edwin Allen, III, *psychologist, educator, retired*
Locke, John Howard *retired lawyer*
Locke, Norton *hotel management and construction company executive*
Locke, William Henry *lawyer*
Locke Lloyd, Jennifer C. *elementary school educator, consultant*
Lockett, Tyler Charles *retired state supreme court justice*
Lockhart, Aileene Simpson *retired dance, kinesiology, physical education educator and editor*
Lockheed, Marlaine Elizabeth *sociologist, World Bank official*
Lockwood, John LeBaron *plant pathologist, educator*
Lockwood, Robert W. *management consultant*
†Lockwood, Suzanne *secondary school educator, special education educator*
Lockwood, Theodore Davidge *former academic administrator*
Loder, Victoria Kosiorek *information broker*
Lodge, Arthur Scott *mechanical engineering educator*
Löe, Harald *retired dentist, educator, researcher*
Loeb, Ronald Marvin *lawyer*
Loeffler, James Joseph *lawyer*
Loehden, Otto Louis *retired surgeon*
Loew, Brenda *publisher*
Loffredi, Deborah Lynn *music educator, actress*
Loftin, Richard Bowen *physics and computer science educator, researcher*
Loftus, Elizabeth F. *psychology educator*
Logan, Dan *investor, writer*
Logan, David Bruce *health care administrator, nurse*
Logan, Douglas Orr *magazine editor*
Logan, Earl Steven *artist*
Logan, James Kenneth *lawyer, former federal judge*
LoGiudice, Elaine A. *nursing administrator*
Loguinov, Dmitri *computer scientist, educator*
Lohman, Gordon Russell *retired manufacturing executive*
Lohmann, George Young, Jr., *neurosurgeon, hospital executive, international business executive, artist*
Lohmuller, Martin Nicholas *bishop*
Lohrer, Richard Baker *investment consultant*
Loiello, John Peter *diplomat*
Loken, Barbara *marketing educator, social psychologist*
Lokmer, Stephanie Ann *international business development consultant*
†Lomax, Elisabeth Louise *music educator*
Lombard, Karen Virginia *economist*
Lombard, Richard Spencer *lawyer*
Lonegan, Thomas Lee *retired restaurant corporation executive*
Lonergan, Thomas Francis, III, *criminal justice consultant*
Long, Alfred B. *former oil company executive, consultant*
Long, Charles Thomas *lawyer, history educator*
Long, Elaine *writer, editor*
Long, John D. *retired insurance educator*
†Long, Larry Dean *contractor*
Longaberger, Tami *home decor accessories company executive*

Longden, Claire Suzanne *retired financial planner, investment advisor*
Long-Ignaszewski, Joan *accountant*
Longini, Peter Richard *communications executive*
Longo, Salvador Eugene *biomedical engineer*
Longobardo, Anna Kazanjian *engineering executive*
Longstreet, Renee Schonfeld *television writer, producer*
Longstreet, Stephen (Chauncey Longstreet) *author, painter*
Loomie, Edward Raphael *lawyer*
Loomis, Janice Kaszczuk *artist*
Loomis, Salora Dale *psychiatrist*
Looser, Donald William *academic administrator*
Lopatka, Susana Beaird *retired nursing consultant*
Lopez, Barry Holstun *writer*
Lopez, Luz-Maria *visual artist*
†Lopez Heredia, Hubert *artist*
Lopez Lysne, Robin *counselor, writer*
Loppnow, Milo Alvin *clergyman, former church official*
Lord, Kathleen Virginia Anderson *fundraising executive, educator*
†Loredo, Elvira Nieves *researcher*
Lorelli, Michael Kevin *consumer products and services executive*
Lorenzi, Virginia *nursing administrator, pediatrics nurse, educator*
Loring, Gloria Jean *singer, actress*
Lorio, Penny Sue (P.S.) *playwright, composer*
†Lorne, Simon Michael Michael *lawyer*
Lornitzo, Frank *retired chemist*
Lortie, John William *solar research company executive*
Los, Marinus *retired agrochemical researcher*
Loschen, Earl Lee *psychiatrist, educator*
Loser, Joseph Carlton, Jr., *dean, retired judge*
†Losey, Michael Robert *retired professional society administrator*
Losi, Maxim John *medical communications executive*
Loss, John C. *architect, retired educator*
Losse, John William, Jr., *mining company executive*
Lotz, Joan Theresa *public relations company executive*
†Lou, Gang *engineer, researcher*
Loube, Samuel Dennis *physician*
Louderback, Tom *auditor*
Loughran, James Newman *philosophy educator, college administrator*
Louis-Cotton d'Englesqueville, Francois Pierre *automobile company executive*
†Louison, Deborah Finley *global public affairs consultant*
Lourenco, Ruy Valentim *physician, educator*
†Love, Margaret Marks *business owner*
Love, Nancy Lorene *communication and political strategist, educator*
Lovecchio, Joseph A. *music educator, conductor*
Lovelace, Julianne *former library director*
Lovelace, Rose Marie Sniegon *federal space agency administrator*
Lovell, Mary Ann *secondary education educator*
Lovell, Walter Carl *engineer, inventor*
LoVetri, Jeannette Louise *voice educator*
†Lovett, David M. *musician, acoustical engineer*
Lovinger, Warren Conrad *emeritus university president*
Lovisi, Gary *writer*
Low, Emmet Francis, Jr., *mathematics educator*
Low, Louise O. *civic volunteer*
†Low, Paul Charles *protective services specialist*
Lowden, John L. *retired corporate executive*
†Lowe, Denise Nola-Faye *writer, educator*
Lowe, John, III, *consulting civil engineer*
Lowenberg, Georgina Grace *retired elementary school educator*
Lowenthal, Constance *art historian, consultant*
Lowenthal, Susan *artist, designer, retired finance executive*
Lowrie, Kathryn Yanacek *special education educator*
†Lowrie, Walter Olin *management consultant*
Loy, Carl Aaron *retired structural design engineer*
Loy, Frank Ernest *retired government official*
Loy, Richard Franklin *civil engineer*
Loyd, Pamela Ann *academic administrator, educator*
†Lozano, Albert H. *education educator*
Lubell, Ellen *writer*
Lubic, Ruth Watson *health facility administrator, nurse midwife*
Lubick, Donald Cyril *lawyer*
Lubin, Steven *concert pianist, musicologist*
Lubinsky, Menachem Yechiel *communications executive*
†Lubman, Brad *conductor, composer, music educator*
Lucas, Bert Albert *pastor, social services administrator, consultant*
†Lucas, Joan Dawson *music educator*
Lucas, Nancy Broome *music educator*
†Lucas, Paul David Mark *lawyer*
Lucas, Wayne Lee *sociologist, educator*
Lucas, William Ray *aerospace consultant*
Luce, Donald Sanders *social worker*
Luce, Priscilla Mark *public relations executive*
Luchansky, Edward *obstetrician-gynecologist, educator*
Lucier, P. Jeffrey *publishing consultant*
Lucker, Jay K. *library science consultant*
Luckey, Doris Waring *civic volunteer*
Ludden, John Franklin *retired financial economist*
Ludwig, Allan Ira *photographer, artist, author*
Ludwig, Christa *mezzo-soprano*
Ludzik, Steve *former professional hockey coach*
†Luedeke, J. Barton *academic administrator*
Luedtke, Roland Alfred *retired lawyer*
Lueke, Donna Mae *yoga instructor, Reiki practitioner, instructor*
Lueptow, Lloyd Benjamin *retired sociology educator*
Luetkehoelter, Gottlieb Werner (Lee Luetkehoelter) *retired bishop, clergyman*
†Luft, Cecile E. *music educator*
Lugenbeel, Edward Elmer *publisher*
Luhn, Robert Kent *writer, magazine editor*
Lui, Eric Mun *civil engineering educator, practitioner*
Luk, Tei Lewis *financial company executive*
Lukacs, Michael Edward *electro-optics researcher*
†Lukasiewicz, Paul Manus *music educator*
Luke, David Lincoln, III, *retired paper company executive*
†Lukens, Max L. *manufacturing company executive*
Lukomsky, Vera *musicologist, pianist, music educator*
Lumb, Sandra Jayne *elementary school educator*
Lumpkin, Anne Craig *retired television and radio company executive*
Luna, Patricia Adele *marketing executive*
Lund, David Nathan *artist*
Lundgren, Cissi *painter, poet*
Lundgren, Leonard, III, *retired secondary education educator*
Lundgren, Regina Ellen (Regina Scott) *research scientist*
Lundin, Shirley Matcouff *early childhood and adult educator, consultant*
†Lundine, Lucinda R. *artist, horse rancher, interior designer*
Lundquist, James Harold *lawyer*
†Lundy, Richard Alan *physicist, consultant*
†Lungren, Daniel Edward *former state attorney general*
Lupu, Radu *pianist*
Lurensky, Robert Lee *economist, educator*
Lurie, Daphne *clinical psychologist, lecturer, educator*
Lurix, Paul Leslie, Jr., *chemist*
Lurye, Helen *artist*
Lusk, Harlan Gilbert *national park superintendent, business executive*
†Luskin, Joseph *law educator, researcher*
†Lustig, Robert Michael *lawyer*
Lusztig, Peter Alfred *university dean, educator*
Luthy, Richard Godfrey *environmental engineering educator*
Lutts, Ralph Herbert *scholar, educator, museum administrator*
†Lutzen, Sherry Lynn Blanco *art educator*
Lyding, John Frederick *retired government administrator, editor*
LyListon, William Phillip *writer, poet*
†Lyn, Jean *interior designer*
Lynch, Amanda Kathryn *writer*
Lynch, Charles Andrew *chemical industry consultant*
Lynch, Charlotte Andrews *retired communications executive*
†Lynch, Daniel C. *multimedia executive*
Lynch, Harry James *retired biologist*
Lynch, John Thomas *retired science foundation administrator, physicist*
Lynch, Laura Ellen *elementary education educator*
†Lynch, Patricia Gates *broadcasting organization executive consultant, former ambassador*
Lynch, Richard Anthony *philosopher, educator*
Lynch, Robert Berger *retired lawyer*
Lynch, Robert Emmett *mathematics educator*
Lynch, Robert Martin *lawyer, educator*
Lynch, Thomas Peter *securities executive*
†Lynch, Thomas Wimp *lawyer*
†Lynd, Phyllis *artist, educator*
Lyndall, Janice Thompson *vocational counselor*
Lyne, Dorothy-Arden *educator*
Lyngbye, Jørgen *hospital administrator, researcher*
Lynn, Bonnie Jane *music educator*
†Lynn, Enid *retired artistic director*
Lynn, Genevieve *artist*
Lynn, Naomi B. *academic administrator*
Lyon, Martha Sue *research engineer, retired military officer*
Lyon, Mary Kuehlewind *nurse*
†Lyons, Anthony Patrick *acoustician, acoustical engineer, researcher*
Lyons, John W(inship) *retired government official, chemist, consultant*
†Lyons, Julie Kathleen Hunt *writer, editor*
Lyons, Natalie Beller *family counselor*
Lyons, Patrice Ann *lawyer*
†Lypka, Gerald L. *product designer, artist*
Lyshak-Stelzer, Frances *artist*
Maas, Anthony Ernst *retired pathologist*
Maatman, Gerald Leonard *insurance company executive*
Mabee, Sandra Ivonne *timpanist, percussionist, educator, clergyman*
Mabry, Bobby Scott *lawyer*
†Macan, Edward L. *music educator*
†Macaulay, David (Alexander) *author, illustrator*
MacAvoy, Thomas Coleman *glass manufacturing executive, educator*
MacCarthy, Talbot Leland *civic volunteer*
MacCarthy, Timothy Charles *association executive*
MacCullagh, Bruce Scott *fund raiser, software designer*
Macdonald, James Kennedy, Jr., *executive search consultant*
Macdonald, Sheila de Marillac *company executive*
MacDonough, Robert Howard *consulting engineer, tax specialist, consultant*
MacDougall, Sir Donald (Sir George Donald Alastair MacDougall) *economist*
MacDougall, Ingeborg Reibling *mental health nurse*
†MacDougall, William Roderick *lawyer, county official*
Mace, Stephen Alan *investment advisor*
†MacGregor, James Grierson *retired civil engineering educator, structural engineering consultant*
†MacGregor, William Bracey *art historian, educator*
Machen, Ethel Louise Lynch *retired academic administrator*
†Machuca, Francisco Javier *electrical engineer, researcher*
†Maciejewski, Matthew Leonard *education educator, researcher*
Macioce, Marie Elizabeth (Marie Tomas) *writer*
MacIsaac, John Anthony *retired municipal official*
Mack, Charles Daniel, III, *labor union executive*
Mack, Gaye Ferris *health care educator, flower essence practitioner*
MacKenzie, Donald Murray *healthcare administrator*
Mackenzie, Linda Alice *media company executive, radio personality, writer, hypnotherapist*
†MacKenzie-Smith, Sydney (Lord Whitford) *marketing and financial executive*
MacKinnon, John Alexander *lawyer*
Mackle, Elliott *writer*
†Macklin, Leo *mechanical engineer, consultant*
†MacLane, Saunders *mathematician, educator*
MacLaury, Robert E(than) *language educator*
MacLean, Judith E. *writer, editor*
MacLennan, Beryce Winifred *psychologist*
Macleod, Angus *internist*
MacLeod, Donald William *secondary school educator*
MacLeod, Gordon C. *surgeon*
MacLeod, Normajean *writer*
MacMillan, Hoke *former state attorney general*
Macmillan, William Hooper *dean, educator*
MacMullen, Jean Alexandria Stewart *nurse, administrator*
†MacNaughton, Jeff A. *physical therapist*
MacNeill, James William *international environment consultant*
†Macomber, Patricia Lee *writer, editor*
†Macoul, Michael K. *business executive, recruiter*
MacPherson, Shirley *clinical therapist*
†Madden, John J. *lawyer*
Madden, Richard Blaine *forest products executive*
Maddin, Robert *metallurgist educator*
Madeira, Francis King Carey *conductor, educator*
Madell, Samuel H. *radiologist*
Madison, T. Jerome *business executive*
Madix, Robert James *chemical engineer, educator*
Madlang, Rodolfo Mojica *retired urologic surgeon*
Madrick, Jeffrey G. *writer, editor, economic consultant*
Madsen, H(enry) Stephen *retired lawyer*
Mady, Beatrice M. *artist*
Maeda, Koichi *pathologist*
Maehl, William Harvey *historian, educator*
Maehr, Martin Louis *psychology educator*
Maestrone, Frank Eusebio *diplomat*
Magafas-Kufta, Diania Lee *geriatric nurse consultant, administrator*
Magee, John Francis *research company executive*
Magee, Karen Strope *nurse, health facility administrator*
†Magerlein, James M. *operations research specialist*
†Maginnis, Robert P. *bishop*
Maglich, Bogdan Castle *physicist*
Magnabosco, Louis Mario *chemical engineer, researcher, consultant*
Magnano, Salvatore Paul *retired financial executive, treasurer*
Magno, Gil D. *music educator*
Magnuson, Paul Arthur *federal judge*
Magnuson, Robert Martin *retired hospital administrator*
Magoni, Despo *artist*
Magoon, Donald W. *retired business educator*
Magor, Louis Roland *conductor*
Maguire, James Harvey *physician*
Maguire, Robert Francis, III, *real estate investor*
Maguire-Zinni, Deirdre *federal community development management analyst*
Magurno, Richard Peter *lawyer*
Maharidge, Dale Dimitro *journalist, educator, writer*
†Maher, John A. *lawyer, law educator*
Maher, Lisa Krug *editor*
Maher, Patrick Joseph *retired utility company executive*
Maher, Robert Raymond, Jr., *music educator*
Mahle, Christoph Erhard *electrical engineer*
Mahmoud, Ahmed Mohamed *information technology executive*
Mahoney, Ann Dickinson *fundraiser*
†Mahoney, John *actor*
Mahoney, John L. *English literature educator*
†Mahoney, Kimberly Lynne *event and facility executive*
Mahoney, Linda Kay *mathematics educator*
Mahoney, Michael Robert Taylor *art historian, educator*
Mai, Chao Chen *engineer*
Maier, Robert Henry *real estate executive*
Main, Myrna Joan *retired mathematics educator*
Main, Robert Gail *communications educator, training consultant, television and film producer, former army officer*
Maines, Leah *writer, poet*
Maioriello, Richard Patrick *retired otolaryngologist*
Maiotti, Dennis Paul *travel company executive*
†Mair, Charles *social studies educator*
Mair, Douglas Dean *medical educator, consultant*
Maisel, Herbert *computer science educator*
Maitra, Subir Ranjan *medical educator*
Major, Patrick Webb, III, *principal*
Majors, Nelda Faye *physical therapist*
Mak, Ben Bohdan *engineer*
†Makarov, Oleg P. *physicist, educator*
Makhov, Alexander Mikhailovich *medical educator, molecular biology researcher*
Mäkitalo, Asko *engineer*
Makowski, Edgar Leonard *obstetrician and gynecologist*
Malach, Monte *physician*
Malek, Marlene Anne *healthcare advocate, foundation administrator*
Malerstein, Abraham Joseph *psychiatrist, researcher*
†Malhotra, Gouri Gupchup *research scientist*
Mali, Paul *publisher, retired management educator*
†Malin, Harold Martin, Jr., *sexologist, educator*
Maling, George Croswell, Jr., *physicist*
Malishenko, Timothy Peter *business executive*
Malit, Lee Arnall *physician*
Malizzio, Donna Marie *social worker*
Mallet, Marlys Kaye *artist*
Mallo-Garrido, Josephine Ann *advertising agency owner*
Mallory, Arthur Lee *university dean, retired state official*
Malloy, John Richard *lawyer, chemical company executive*
Malloy, Johnn Edward *media artist, writer*
†Malloy, Michael Dennis *radio personality*
Malloy, Michael Terrence *journalist, newspaper editor*
Malme, Jane Hamlett *lawyer, educator, advisor*
Malone, Richard P. *psychiatrist*
Maloney, James Henry *former congressman*
Maloney, Therese Adele *insurance company executive*
Malott, Adele Renee *editor*
Malouf-Cundy, Pamela Bonnie *film editor, video editor*
Malphurs, Roger Edward *biomedical marketing executive*
Malsack, James Thomas *retired manufacturing company executive*
Maltby, Florence Helen *library science educator*
Maltin, Freda *retired university administrator*
†Maltsev, Nikolai Elyseevich *research scientist*
Manahan, Joan Elsie *health and physical education educator*
Manakos, Froso P. *real estate executive*
Manasse, Arlynn H. *pediatric nurse practitioner*
†Mancell, Donald Wayne *music educator*
Manchester, Kenneth Edward *electronics executive, consultant*
Manchester, William *writer*
Mancini, Elaine Carol *public relations executive, marketing consultant*
†Mancusi, Roberto Francesco Costantino *vocalist, educator*
Mancuso, John Henry *retired lawyer, bank executive*
Mandell, Arlene Linda *communications educator*
Mangan, Patricia Ann Pritchett *statistician*
Manganaro, Francis Ferdinand *naval officer*
Mangapit, Conrado, Jr., *manufacturing company executive*
†Mangi, Abeel Abdullah *cardiologist, surgeon*
Mangler, Robert James *lawyer, judge*
Mangold, John Frederic *manufacturing company executive, former naval officer*
Mangold, Sylvia Plimack *artist*
Manika, John Francis *computer systems educator, computer information systems analyst*
Mankiewicz, Thomas Frank *screenwriter, director, producer*
Manley, Joan A(dele) Daniels *retired publisher*
Manley, John Hugo *computing technology executive, educator*
Manley, Judith L. *director*
Mann, Clarence Charles *real estate company official*
Mann, Daniel *religious organization worker*
Mann, Emily Betsy *writer, artistic director, theater director*
Mann, Robert Paul *retired lawyer*
Mann, Roger Ellis *business development, food service business, pool and spa and real estate executive*
Manne, Henry Girard *lawyer, educator*
Mannes, Elena Sabin *film and television producer, director*
†Manning, Chandra Miller *humanities educator*
†Manning, J. Terry *company executive*
Mannino, J(oseph) Robert *medical educator*
†Mansfield, James E. *marketing professional, consultant*
Manso, Leira A. *Latin American literature educator, poet*
Manson, David Joseph *producer, director*
Mansour, Stephen Malik *software developer, mathematician*
Manuel, Jerry *former professional sports team manager*
Manuel, Ralph Nixon *former private school executive*
Maple, Opal Lucille *school psychologist*
Mapp, Edward Charles *speech educator*
Marabella, Dawn Marie *ESL educator*
†Maraziti, Joseph James, Jr., *lawyer*
Marble, Melinda Smith *writer, editor*
†March, Jacqueline Front *retired chemist*
Marchant, JoAnn Reviczky *English language educator, actress*
Marchetti, Reesa *web manager, editor*
Marci-Mariani, Anita *designer, illustrator, fine artist, educator*
Marcinek, Margaret Ann *nursing educator*
†Marcks, Ronald Henry *lawyer, business executive*
Marcoux, Julia A. *midwife*
Marcus, Greil Gerstley *critic*
†Marcus, H. B. *writer, web site designer*
†Marcus, Kenneth Ben *lawyer*
Marcus, Lee Evan *small business owner, consultant, accountant*
Marcus, Walter F., Jr., *retired state supreme court justice*
Marcuse, Dietrich *retired physicist*
Marcy, Alvin Newell *contractor*
†Marderosian, Armena Pearl *music educator*

GEOGRAPHICAL INDEX 6149 ADDRESS UNPUBLISHED

Mardis, Richard Lyle *television producer and director, production manager*
Margolis, Benjamin Robert *lawyer, pharmacist*
Margolis, Daniel Herbert *lawyer*
Margrave, Kathy Christine *nurse anesthetist*
Mariani, Amy Cashore *lawyer*
Mariano, Raymond V. *former mayor*
Marinetti, Guido V. *biochemistry educator*
Marini, Dominic, Jr., *elementary and secondary education educator*
Marinis, Thomas Paul, Jr., *lawyer*
†Marino, Richard J. *publishing executive*
Marion, Marjorie Anne *English language educator, education consultant*
†Mariska, Bradley Clayton *composer, musicologist*
Mark, Jonathan Greenfield *political scientist, educator, writer*
Mark, Michael Laurence *retired music educator*
Marken, William Riley *magazine editor*
†Marker, David Carl *finance educator*
Marker, Marc Linthacum *lawyer, investor*
†Markey, Randolph David *marketing professional*
†Markham, Fred William, Jr., *medical educator*
†Markham, Thomas Lowell *mathematics educator*
Markle, Cheri Virginia Cummins *nurse*
Markle, Roger A(llan) *retired oil company executive*
†Marko, Marlene *psychiatrist*
Markoe, Arnold Michael *radiation oncologist*
Markovich, Patricia Helen *economist*
Markowicz, Elaine C. *writer*
Marks, Bernard Bailin *lawyer, director*
Marks, Bruce *artistic director, choreographer*
Marks, Janet Goldberg *poet, writer*
Marks, Jeffrey Alan *freelance/self-employed writer*
Marks, Leonard, Jr., *retired corporate financial executive*
†Marks, Mitchell Lee *organizational psychologist*
†Marks, Terry *artist*
Marlar, Janet Cummings *retired public relations officer*
Marlçr, Larry John *nonprofit organization administrator*
Marlow, Edward A. *former army officer*
†Marlow, Marcia Marie *secondary school educator, publishing executive*
Marlowe, Willie *artist, fine arts educator*
Marmer, Nancy *editor*
Maroney, Jane P. *former state legislator, consultant*
Maropis, Nicholas *engineering executive*
Marot, Lola *retired accountant*
Maroyka, Eric Martin *military officer, pharmacist*
Marple, Gary Andre *management consultant*
Marquardt, Sandra Mary *activist, lobbyist, researcher*
Marquis, Harriet Hill *social worker*
Marr, Carmel Carrington *retired lawyer, retired state official*
Marren, Judy Ann *paramedic*
Marrington, Bernard Harvey *retired automotive company executive*
†Marsalis, Wynton *musician*
Marsee, Susanne Irene *mezzo-soprano*
Marselis-Moore, Jadeh *emergency room nurse, alcohol/drug abuse nurse*
Marsh, Joan Knight *educational film, video and computer software company executive, publisher children's books*
Marsh, Merrilyn Delano *sculptor, painter*
Marshak, Robert Reuben *former university dean, medical educator, veterinarian*
Marshall, Carol Sydney *labor market analyst, employment counselor*
Marshall, Charles Noble *rail transportation executive*
Marshall, Donald Thomas *retired medical technician*
Marshall, George Dwire *retired supermarket chain executive*
Marshall, Gerald Francis *physicist*
Marshall, John Paul *broadcast engineer*
Marshall, Julie W. Gregovich *investor relations executive*
Marshall, Kathryn Sue *lawyer*
Marshall, Peter *actor, singer, game show host*
Marshall, Phyllis Ellinwood *health facility administrator, consultant*
Marshall, Robert Charles *computer company executive*
†Marshall, William Ross *professional society administrator*
Marsocci, Velio Arthur *engineering educator, researcher*
Martarella, Franc David *television executive, not-for-profit fundraiser*
Martens, Donald Mathias *orthodontist*
†Marti, Gerardo *minister, sociologist, educator*
†Marti, Virgil *artist*
Martin, Albert Charles *manufacturing executive, lawyer*
Martin, Connie Ruth *retired lawyer*
Martin, George J. *investment banker, financial consultant*
Martin, Ione Edwards *social worker*
Martin, James Kay *government official*
Martin, James Richard *music educator*
Martin, James Victor, Jr., *foreign service officer, writer*
Martin, James William *lawyer*
Martin, John Joseph *journalist*
Martin, John Swanson *retired educator*
Martin, John William, Jr., *retired lawyer, automotive industry executive*
Martin, Leonard Austin, II, *music educator*
Martin, Marilyn Mann *retired library media specialist*
Martin, Marta *learning disability specialist, educator*
Martin, Mary *secondary education educator*
Martin, Noel *graphic design consultant, educator*
†Martin, Preston *financial services writer*
†Martin, Raymond Edward *management consultant*
Martin, Thomas MacDonald *lawyer*
Martin, William Collier *hospital administrator*
†Martinez, Efrain *humanities educator, researcher*
Martinez, Matthew Gilbert *former congressman*
Martinez, Rey Antonio *artist, writer*
Martinez-Maldonado, Manuel *medical service administrator, physician*
Martini, Robert Edward *wholesale pharmaceutical and medical supplies company executive*
Martino, Donna Frances *newspaper sales administrator*
†Martino, Joseph F. *bishop*
Martino, Joseph Paul *research scientist, researcher*
Martino, Silvana *osteopath, medical oncologist*
Martinson, Elizabeth Ann *archaeologist*
Martone, William James *physician*
Martyl, (Mrs. Alexander Langsdorf Jr.) *artist*
Martz, Judy Helen *governor*
Martz, Lawrence Stannard *retired periodical editor*
Maruoka, Jo Ann Elizabeth *retired information systems manager*
Marvin, William Glenn, Jr., *former foreign service officer*
Marx, Anne (Mrs. Frederick E. Marx) *poet*
Marx, Gary T. *sociologist, writer*
Marzinski, Lynn Rose *oncological nurse*
Masa, George John *retired regional director*
Mascara, Frank R. *former congressman*
Mascheroni, Eleanor Earle *communications executive*
Mascola, Richard F. *former medical association administrator*
Masek, Mark Joseph *writer*
†Mashnik, Stepan G. *physicist*
Masiello, Rocco Joseph *airlines and aerospace manufacturing executive*
Masih, Tara Lynn *book editor, writer*
Masket, Edward Seymour *television executive*
†Maslanka, Sandra Karen *social worker, educator, educational consultant*
Maslansky, Carol Jeanne *toxicologist*
Mason, Dwight Newell *foreign and defense policy consultant*
Mason, Frank Henry, III, *automobile company executive, leasing company executive*
Mason, George Henry *business educator*
Mason, Johanna Hendrika Anneke *retired secondary education educator*
Mason, John Latimer *engineering executive*
Mason, John Oliver *freelance journalist, poet, community activist*
Mason, Linda *physical education educator, softball and basketball coach*
Mason, Lois E. (J. Day Mason) *painter, poet, actress, educator*
†Mason, Margaret Crather *elementary school educator*
†Mason, Matthew E. *humanities educator*
Mason, Robert Lester *engineer, small business computer consultant*
†Masquelette, Philip Edward *lawyer*
Massa, Salvatore Peter *psychologist*
†Massad, Jordan Elias *mathematician*
Massey, Robert Unruh *physician, university dean*
Massey, Stephen Charles *rare books and manuscripts appraiser, auctioneer*
Massey, Thomas Benjamin *educator*
Massey, William Walter, Jr., *sales executive*
†Massoudi, Bahram Barry *management consultant*
Massura, Edward Anthony *accountant*
Mast, Stewart Dale *retired airport manager*
†Masten, Jacqueline Gwendolyn *small business owner*
Masters, Joseph Henry *pathologist*
Masterson, Peter *actor, director*
Mastin, Wayne Alan *strategic planning consultant*
Mastrangelo, Lisa Siobhan *humanities educator*
Mastroianni, Thomas Owen *musician, music educator*
Matasovic, Marilyn Estelle *business executive*
Matayoshi, Coralie Chun *lawyer, bar association executive*
Matelic, Candace Tangorra *museum studies educator, consultant, museum director*
Matema, Zsun-nee Kimball (Annette K. Miller) *social sciences educator*
Mater, Maud *lawyer*
Matera, Frances Lorine *elementary educator*
Materia, Kathleen Patricia Ayling *nurse*
Materson, Richard Stephen *physician, educator*
Mates, Robert Edward *mechanical engineering educator*
Mathelier, Amedee C. *obstetrician-gynecologist*
Matheny, Adam Pence, Jr., *child psychologist, educator, consultant, researcher*
Matheson, Scott Milne, Jr., *dean, law educator*
Mathews, Barbara Jean *genealogist*
Mathews, Mary Beth *nursing education administrator*
Mathias, Julian Robert *investment manager*
Mathias, Mervin A. *retired surgeon*
Mathieson, Garrett Alfred *insurance brokerage executive*
Mathieu, Georges Victor Adolphe *artist*
Mathieu, Michele Suzanne *computer scientist, consultant*
Mathis, Sharon Bell *author, retired elementary educator and librarian*
Matlow, Linda M. *photographic agency executive, publishing executive*
Matsuda, Fujio *retired university president*
Matsunaka, Stanley T. *former state legislator*
Matsushita, Marimi *educator, mathematician*
Mattar, Philip *writer*
Matteo, Christopher Peter *electronics executive, researcher*
Mattern, Joanne *writer, educator*
Matthew, Lyn *sales executive, consultant, marketing professional, consultant*
Matthews, Bruce Rankin *former professional football player*
Matthews, Gail Thunberg *marketing executive*
Matthews, George Robert *retired radiologist*
†Matthews, L. White, III, *railroad executive*
Matthews, Warren Wayne *state supreme court justice*
Matthews, Wendy Schempp *psychologist, researcher*
Mattice, Howard LeRoy *retired education educator*
Mattingly, Mack Francis *former ambassador, former senator, entrepreneur*
Mattoli, Agostino Marron *international business projects advisor*
†Matuozzi, Robert Norman *historian, archivist*
Maumus, Craig W(alther) *psychiatrist, consultant*
Maunder, Addison Bruce *agronomic research company executive*
Mauney, Thomas Lee *theater designer*
Maurer, Beverly Bennett *school administrator*
Mauser, Kevin Edward *finance executive*
Mauskopf, Seymour Harold *history educator*
†Mautino, Frank J. *state legislator*
Mautz, Karl Emerson *engineering executive*
Mauzy, Michael Philip *environmental consultant, chemical engineer*
Maxaner, Catherine L. *business and political consultant*
Maxwell, James L. *non-profit management executive*
Maxwell, Jerome Eugene *corporate executive*
Maxwell, Patricia Joy *fund raising executive*
Maxwell, Raymond Roger *retired accountant*
†May, Denise Eaton *general counsel*
May, Edgar *former state legislator, nonprofit administrator*
May, Phyllis Jean *financial executive*
Maybury, Greg J. *academic administrator*
Mayer, Allan *crisis communications consultant, writer*
Mayer, Anthony John *investment company executive*
†Mayer, James Joseph *retired corporate lawyer*
†Mayer, John William *lawyer*
Mayer, Patricia Lynn Sorci *mental health nurse, educator*
Mayfield, Robert Charles *university official, geography educator*
Maynard, Natalie Ryshna *pianist, piano educator*
Mayo, C(atherine) M(ansell) *writer, editor, economist*
Mayo, Dana Walker *chemistry educator*
Mayo, John Sullivan *telecommunications company executive*
Mayo, Robert Porter *banker*
Mayoras, Donald Eugene *corporate executive, writer, consultant, educator*
Mayson, Preston B., Jr., *retired lawyer*
Mazankowski, Donald Frank *Canadian government official*
Maze-Davis, Lauri *psychiatric mental health nurse*
Mazur, Deborah Joan *assistant principal*
Mazur, Jay J. *trade union official*
Mazza, Terilyn McGovern *finance executive*
†McAdams, Donald Ray *education educator, consultant*
McAlhany, Toni Anne *lawyer*
†McArthur, John William *economist, researcher*
McBride, Jack J. *financial services executive*
McBride, Sandra Teague *psychiatric nurse*
McBride, Sharon Sue *artist*
McBride, Thomas Dwayne *management consultant*
McBurney, Margot B. *librarian*
McCabe, Thomas Edward *lawyer, business executive*
McCain, Lynne Annette *counselor*
McCalla, Sandra Ann *educational administrator*
†McCallister, Michael S. *writer*
McCallum, Scott *former governor*
McCandless, Carolyn Keller *retired human resources executive*
†McCann, Elizabeth Ireland *theater, television and motion picture producer, lawyer*
McCann, Joyce Jeannine *retired elementary education educator*
McCann, Lee I. *psychology educator*
McCann, Peter Paul *biology researcher, educator*
McCargar, Eleanor Barker *portrait painter*
McCarthy, Daniel William *management consultant*
McCarthy, J. Thomas *lawyer, educator*
McCarthy, Jean Jerome *retired physical education educator*
McCarthy, Patricia Bennett *social worker*
McCarthy, Paul Fenton *aerospace executive, former naval officer*
McCarthy, Susan Stacy *company executive*
McCarthy, Vincent Paul *lawyer*
Mc Carthy, Walter John, Jr., *retired utility executive*
McCartney, James Robert *psychiatrist*
McCarty, Thomas Joseph *publishing company executive*
McCauley, Floyce Reid *psychiatrist*
McCauley, Jane Reynolds *journalist*
McCaw, Valerie Sue *civil engineer*
McClain, Lena Alexandria *protective services official*
Mc Clellan, Catharine *anthropologist, educator*
McClellan, Larry Allen *educator, writer, minister*
McClellan, Robert Edward *civil engineer*
McClellan, Roger Orville *toxicologist*
†McClelland, George Duncan *business executive*
†McClendon, Susan K. *secondary education educator*
Mc Clendon, William Hutchinson, III, *retired lawyer*
McClintock, George Dunlap *retired lawyer*
McClinton, Donald George *retired diversified holding company executive*
McClinton, James Leroy *city administrator*
McClinton, Wendell C. *religious organization administrator*
McCloskey, J(ohn) Michael *retired association administrator*
McClure, Ann Crawford *judge, lawyer*
McClure, Evelyn Susan *historian, photographer*
McClure, Helen Playfair *writer*
†McClure, Jennifer Bonner *psychologist, researcher*
†McClurg, Patricia A. *minister*
McCluskey, Jean Ashford *nursing educator, retired*
McCobb, John Bradford, Jr., *lawyer*
Mc Collum, Ira William, Jr., (Bill Mc Collum) *former congressman*
†McColman, William Ernest *construction company executive*
McComb, Ronald Graeme *filmmaker*
McConnell, Edward Bosworth *legal organization administrator, lawyer*
McCorkle, Michael *electrical engineer*
McCormick, David Arthur *lawyer*
McCormick, Donald Bruce *retired biochemist, educator*
McCormick, Homer L., Jr., *lawyer*
McCormick, John Owen *retired comparative literature educator*
†McCormick, Kenneth L. *pediatrics educator, researcher*
McCormick, William Thomas, Jr., *electric and gas company executive*
McCown, Hale *retired judge*
McCoy, Edain *writer*
†McCoy, Gordon R. *minister*
McCoy, John Joseph *lawyer*
McCoy, Mary Ann *state official*
Mc Coy, Tidal Windham *former government official*
†McCracken, Edward R. *electronics executive*
McCready, Kenneth Frank *former electric utility executive*
McCready, Sam *theatre educator, actor, director, writer*
McCullough, David L. *urologist*
McCullough, Edward Eugene *patent agent, inventor*
McCully, Emily Arnold *illustrator, writer*
Mc Cune, John Francis, III, *retired architect*
McCurdy, Larry Wayne *automotive parts company executive*
McCurdy, Michael Charles *illustrator, author*
McCurley, Robert Lee, Jr., *lawyer, educator*
McCutchan, William M. *banker*
†McCutcheon, Russell Gene *music educator*
McDade, James Russell *management consultant*
†McDade, Joseph Michael *former congressman*
McDaniel, Charlotte *health care ethics professional*
McDaniel, John Mark *lawyer*
McDaniel, Mike *former political association executive*
McDaniel, Sue Powell *cultural organization administrator*
McDarrah, Gloria Schoffel *editor, author*
McDermott, Agnes Charlene Senape *philosophy educator*
McDermott, Kevin J. *engineering educator, consultant*
McDermott, Lucinda Mary *ecumenical minister, teacher, philosopher, poet, author, psychologist*
McDonagh, Thomas Joseph *physician*
†McDonald, Arlys Lorraine *retired librarian*
McDonald, Douglas Robert *non profit agency executive*
McDonald, Forrest *historian, educator*
McDonald, Josh William *surgical pathologist*
McDonald, Mark Douglas *electrical engineer*
McDonald, Tanny *actress*
McDonald, William Henry *financial executive*
McDonald-UmBayemake, Linda *librarian, rehabilitation counselor*
Mc Donnell, Loretta Wade *lawyer*
Mc Donough, John Richard *lawyer*
Mc Donough, Richard Doyle *retired paper company executive*
McDougal, Marie Patricia *retired educator, freelance writer and editor*
McDougall, Donald Blake *retired government official, librarian*
McDougall, Roderick Gregory *lawyer*
McDowell, Elaine *retired federal government executive, educator*
McEachran, Angus *retired editor*
McElveen-Combs, Gail Marie *middle school educator*
McElwee, Doris Ryan *psychotherapist*
McEvoy, Michael Joseph *economist*
McEwen, Bruce S. *neuroendocrinology educator*
†McEwen, James Wallace, Jr., *former publishing executive*
Mc Fadden, George Linus *retired army officer*
McFadden, Irene Frances *medical and surgical nurse, nursing educator, consultant*
McFadden, Millidene Kathleen *nurse educator*
McFadden, Peter William *retired mechanical engineering educator*
McFadden, Robbyn Kilbane *interior designer, public policy specialist*
McFall, Catherine Gardner *poet, critic, educator*
McFarlane, Donovan Anthony *writer, poet, researcher*
McFarlane, James L. *artist, educator*
McFate, Kenneth Leverne *trade association administrator*
McFate, Patricia Ann *foundation executive, scientist, educator*
Mc Fee, Thomas Stuart *retired government agency administrator*
†McGahren, Eugene Dewey, Jr., *lawyer*
McGann, Lisa B. Napoli *language educator*
McGarry, Marcia *retired community service coordinator*
†McGarry, Richard Gale *linguist, educator*
†McGarvey, Daniel Shane *composer, educator*
†McGarvie-Munn, Iain Lachlan *curator, writer, agent*
†McGaughey, Jerry Joseph *lawyer, educator*
McGaughy, Richard Wayne *nuclear engineer, consultant*
†McGee, Carrie L. *artist*
McGee, Harold Johnston *former academic administrator*
†McGee, Humphrey Glenn *architect*

McGee, Patrick Edgar *postal service clerk*
McGeever, Kathleen Marie *theater studies educator*
McGervey, Teresa Ann *technical information specialist*
McGhee, Lori Jean Vote *medical/surgical nurse*
McGill, Carol Ann Michalski *medical, surgical and psychiatric nurse, writer, poet*
†McGill, Jefferey Trent *writer, educator*
McGillivray, Donald Dean *seed company executive, agronomist*
†McGinn Miller, Janet Scrivner *elementary school educator, writer*
McGinty, Brian Donald *lawyer, author*
McGonigle, John Leo, Jr., *retired civil engineer*
McGough, Brian Edward *investment banker, lawyer*
McGough, Duane Theodore *economist, consultant, retired government official*
†McGovern, Frances *retired lawyer*
†McGovern, John Francis *former financial executive*
McGowan, Ian Duncan *retired librarian*
McGowan, Keith Richard *environmental planner*
McGowan, William Andrew *lawyer*
McGrath, Anna Fields *retired librarian*
McGrath, Eileen Marie *pediatric nurse*
McGraw, Patrick Allan *lawyer*
†McGreevy, Mary Sharron *former psychology educator*
McGuffey, Carroll Wade, Jr., *lawyer*
†McGuigan, Michael R. *sport science educator*
McGuire, John W., Sr., *advertising executive, marketing professional, author*
McGuire, Robert C. *retired federal bankruptcy judge*
McGuirk, Terrence *former broadcasting company executive*
†McGuirt, William Frederick *otolaryngologist, educator*
McGunigle, Dorothy Greene *interior designer, artist*
McHargue, Melissa Kay *school counselor, speech pathologist*
†McHugh, Sean Paul *artist, writer*
†McInerney, Gary John *lawyer*
†McIntier, Russell J. *retired writer*
McIntosh, Amy Bennett *publishing/internet company executive*
McIntosh, Carolyn Meade *retired educational administrator*
†McIntosh, Claude T. *school system administrator, financial consultant*
McIntyre, Bruce Herbert *media and marketing consultant*
McIntyre, Carol Chrisman *social services administrator*
†Mc Intyre, Vonda Neel *writer*
Mc Isaac, George Scott *retired management consultant, government official*
McKay, John M. *former state senator*
McKay, Renee *artist*
McKean, Robert Jackson, Jr., *retired lawyer*
McKee, Roger Curtis *retired federal judge*
McKeever, Jeffrey D. *computer company executive*
†McKeever, Kenneth Harrington *veterinarian, educator*
McKellen, Sir Ian *actor*
McKelway, Alexander Jeffrey *religion studies educator*
McKenna, John Francis *media executive*
McKenna, Terence Patrick *retired insurance company executive*
McKenzie, Norma DeeAnn *psychiatrist, educator*
McKeown, Lorraine Laredo *travel company executive, writer*
McKey, Thomas J. *retired lawyer*
McKinley, Ellen Bacon *priest*
McKinney, Jerry Wayne *retired journalist*
†Mc Kinney, Joseph Crescent *retired bishop*
McKnight, Patricia Marie *elementary education educator*
McKnight, Thomas Frederick *artist*
McLaren, Susan Smith *therapist, healing touch practitioner, instructor*
McLauchlan, Sylvia June *charity organization executive*
McLaughlin, Joseph *lawyer*
McLaughlin, Michael John *retired insurance company executive*
McLaughlin, Michael Rob *secondary school educator, coach*
McLaughlin, Patricia Ann *writer*
McLaughlin, William Irving *space technical manager, writer*
McLean, Craig Elliott *retired non-commissioned officer*
McLean, Hon. Walter Franklin *consultant, pastor, legislator*
McLean, Julianne Drew *concert pianist, educator*
McLean, Ryan John *sales professional*
Mc Lendon, Heath Brian *securities investment company executive*
McLendon, Melburne Dekalb *lawyer, arbitrator*
McLendon, Susan Michelle *lawyer, nurse*
†McLennan, Conor Thomas *cognitive psychologist, researcher*
McLennan, Robert Gordon *asset management company executive*
McLeod, Willis B. *academic administrator*
McLoone, Eugene P. *education educator*
McLoud, Theresa Claire *radiologist*
†McMahon, John E. *not-for-profit fundraiser*
†McMahon, Thomas Patrick *lawyer, state official*
†McManus, Gillian Coxhead *musician, writer*
McManus, James William *chemist, researcher*
McManus, Jason Donald *editor, retired*
McManus, Joseph Warn *urban planner, architect*
McManus, Richard Philip *lawyer, agricultural products company executive*
McMaster, Belle Miller *religious organization administrator*
†McMillan, Beverly C. *writer*
McMillan, Terry L. *writer, educator*

McMillen, Abbie *environmental manager*
McMillen, Elizabeth Cashin *artist*
McMinn, Virginia Ann *human resources consulting company executive*
McMorrow, Margaret Mary (Peg McMorrow) *retired educator*
†McMullen, Jennifer Anne *secondary school educator*
McMullen, Ralph Edgar *convention center administrator*
†McMurray, David McCain *German studies educator*
McNair, John William, Jr., *civil engineer*
McNair, Norma Dianne *nurse*
McNamara, Tom *scientific consulting corporation executive*
McNeal, Thomas Roy *computer software consultant*
†McNeely, Bonnie L. (K.W. Rowe Jr.) *retired internist and educator*
McNeely, Thomas Holmes *writer, educator*
McNeil, Edward Warren *real estate company executive*
†McNeill, Robert Patrick *investment counselor*
McNeil Staudenmaier, Heidi Loretta *lawyer*
†McNown, Edythe S. *music educator*
McNulty, Kathleen Anne *clinical social worker, psychotherapist, business consultant*
McPeak, Allan *career services director, educator, lawyer, consultant*
McPeters, Sharon Jenise *artist, writer*
McPhearson, Geraldine June *medical and surgical nurse*
McPhee, John Angus *writer*
Mc Pheeters, Edwin Keith *architect, educator*
McPherson, James Alan *writer, educator*
Mc Pherson, Peter *academic administrator*
Mc Quade, Lawrence Carroll *lawyer, corporate executive*
McQuarrie, Terry Scott *technical director*
McQuary, Vaughn *management company executive*
McQueen, Marjorie Marie Wynkoop *retired archivist, writer*
McQuigg, John Dolph *retired lawyer*
McQuilkin, John Robertson *religion educator, academic administrator, writer*
McShefferty, John *retired research company executive, consultant*
McSpadden, Katherine Frances *English language educator*
McSweeny, William Francis *petroleum company executive, author*
McTague, John Paul *materials scientist, educator, chemist, researcher*
McVeigh-Pettigrew, Sharon Christine *communications consultant*
McVicker, Jesse Jay *artist, educator*
McWethy, Patricia Joan *educational association administrator*
McWhorter, Diane *writer*
McWilliams, Michael *writer, publisher*
†Meacham, Margaret Marks *writer, educator*
†Mead, Elizabeth *artist*
Meade, Kenneth Albert *retired minister*
Meade, Patricia Sue *marketing professional*
Meadors, Howard Clarence, Jr., *electrical engineer*
Meaker, Marijane Agnes *author*
Meara, Anne *actress, playwright, writer*
†Measelle, Richard Leland *accountant*
Mebane, Felicia Eugenia *health policy, news media educator, researcher*
Mecham, Steven Ray *school system administrator*
†Mechanic, William M. *former television and motion picture industry executive*
Mecik, Z. Richard *communications executive*
Medavoy, Mike *motion picture company executive*
†Medina, Janie *not-for-profit fundraiser*
Medina, Kathryn Bach *book editor*
Medina, Sandra *social worker, educator*
Medley, Donald Matthias *education educator, consultant*
Mednick, Robert *accountant*
Mednicoff, David Michael *lawyer, educator*
Medrek, Joseph *computer operator*
Meek, Amy Gertrude *retired elementary education educator*
Meek, Carrie P. *former congresswoman*
Meek, Forrest Burns *retired trading company executive*
Meek, Mary Virgelia Cleveland *special education administrator, psychologist*
Meeker, Guy Bentley *banker*
Meekins, Frederick Boyd *writer*
Meffert, Roland Matthew *periodontist, educator*
Mehdizadeh, Parviz *insurance company executive*
†Mehiel, Dennis *paper and packaging company executive*
Mehne, Paul Randolph *associate dean, medical educator*
Mehring, Nancy *medical and surgical nurse, administrator*
Meier, Enge *preschool educator*
Meier, Henry George *architect*
Meilman, Edward *physician*
†Meiners, Mark Robert *geriatrics services professional, economist, educator*
Meinhardt, Vicki R. *communications executive, consultant*
Meintsma, Peter Evans *history and political science educator*
Meiring, Linda Jean *communications executive*
Meisels, Judith A. *piano instructor, pianist*
Melady, Thomas Patrick *academic administrator, ambassador, author, public policy expert, educator*
Melanson, Susan C. *herbalist*
Melczek, Dale J. *bishop*
Melhado, L. Lee *social worker, chemist*
Meli, Salvatore Andrew *lawyer*
Melillo, Joseph Vincent *producer, performing arts*
†Mell, William Eric *mathematician*

Mellema, Donald Eugene *retired radio news reporter and anchor*
Mellendorf, Patricia Jean *retired personnel professional*
Mellins, Harry Zachary *radiologist, educator*
Melman, Cynthia Sue *special education educator*
Melnick, Jodi *dancer*
†Melnikova, Vladislava Olegovna *photobiologist*
Melnyczuk, Askold *writer*
Melody, Michael Edward *publishing company executive*
Melsheimer, Mel P(owell) *venture capital and consumer products executive*
Melson, Gordon Anthony *dean*
†Melton, Augustus Allen, Jr., *retired airport executive*
Meltzer, E. Alyne *elementary school educator, social worker, volunteer*
Melville, Marguerita W. *advertising executive*
Melvin, Billy Alfred *clergyman*
Melvin, Peter Joseph *astrophysicist, educator*
Melzer, Barbara Evelyn *minister*
Menaker, Ronald Herbert *retired bank executive*
Mench, John William *retail store executive, electrical engineer*
Mende, Robert Graham *retired engineering association executive*
Mendels, Joseph *psychiatrist, educator*
Mendelson, Sol *physical science educator, consultant*
†Mendelssohn, Michéle *language educator*
Mender, Mona Siegler *writer, music educator*
Mendlin, Ronald C. *employment specialist, writer*
Mendoza, George *poet, author*
Meneeley, Edward Sterling *artist*
Menefee, Linnea-Norma *antique dealer*
Mengel, Charles Edmund *physician, medical educator*
Menke, Catherine Christine Hudson *critical care, oncological nurse, cardiology information specialist*
Menn, Julius Joel *scientist*
Meo, Roxanne Marie *critical care nurse*
Mercer, Edwin Wayne *lawyer*
Mercuri, Joan B. *museum administrator*
Mercurio, Laura Deubler *textile design company executive*
Mercurio, Renard Michael *real estate corporation executive*
Merenda, Sam John *retired radiologist*
Mereschak, Volmar A. *retired obstetrician-gynecologist*
Mergenovich, Shirley Ann *educator*
†Merino, Ana *poet*
Merkin, Donald H. *internist*
†Mermelstein, Paula *broadcasting executive*
Mero, Marjorie Anne *retired compensation specialist*
†Merrell, James Hart *history educator*
Merriam, Robert W. *engineering executive, educator*
Merrick, George Boesch *aerospace company executive*
Merrick, Patricia Ann *radiological nurse*
†Merricle, William *medical technician, poet*
Merrifield, Leroy Sorenson *law educator*
Merrill, Jean Fairbanks *writer*
Merrill, Robert *baritone*
Merring, Robert Alan *lawyer, arbitrator, mediator*
Merritt, Bruce Gordon *lawyer*
Merritt, Eleanor Lynette *artist, educator*
Merritt, John Howard *secondary school educator*
Merryfield, David W. *pharmacist*
Meryhew, Vern Arthur *engineering executive, retired*
Mesa-Lago, Carmelo *economist, educator*
Meserve, Walter Joseph *drama studies writer, publisher*
Meshel, Harry *state senator, political party official*
Meskill, Victor P. *academic administrator, educator*
Mesrobian, Arpena Sachaklian *publisher, editor, consultant*
Messens, Mark Richard *entrepreneur*
†Messick, Wiley Sanders *retired lawyer*
Messier, Pierre *lawyer, manufacturing company executive*
Messmore, David William *construction executive, former psychologist*
Metcalf, Karen *retired foundation executive*
Metcalf, William Edwards *educator, museum curator*
Mettee, Stephen Blake *publishing executive*
Metz, Steven William *small business owner*
Metz, T(heodore) John *librarian, consultant*
†Metz, Werner Adam *physicist*
†Metzenbaum, Shelley H. *public information officer*
Metzger, Jeffrey Paul *lawyer*
Metzler, Ruth Horton *genealogical educator*
Metzner, Charles Miller *federal judge*
Mewhinney, Len Everette *lawyer*
†Meyer, Andrew W. *retired publishing executive*
Meyer, Charlotte Lois *medical geriatric social worker, consultant*
Meyer, Daniel Kramer *real estate executive*
†Meyer, Donald Robert *state agency administrator, banker, lawyer*
Meyer, Frances Margaret Anthony *elementary and secondary school educator, health education specialist*
Meyer, George Wilbur *internist, health facility administrator*
Meyer, Greg Charles *psychiatrist*
Meyer, Harry Martin, Jr., *retired health science facility administrator*
Meyer, Henry Lewis, III, *banker*
Meyer, J. Theodore *lawyer*
Meyer, John Edward *nuclear engineering educator*
Meyer, Kathleen Marie *gifted education educator, writer*
Meyer, Lasker Marcel *retail executive*
Meyer, Max Earl *lawyer*

Meyer, Robert Lee *secondary education educator*
Meyer, Roberta *mediator, communication consultant*
Meyer, Ruth Krueger *museum administrator, educator, art historian*
Meyer, Sandra Palmer *financial executive*
Meyerink, Victoria Paige *film producer, actress*
Meyers, Charles Jerome *history educator*
Meyers, Kimberly Sue *physical therapist*
Meyers, Richard James *landscape architect*
†Meza, Jane L. *biostatistician, educator*
†Mezacapa, Edna S. *music educator, elementary school educator*
Miah, Abdul Malek *electrical engineer, educator*
†Mianzo, Lawrence Andrew *engineer, researcher*
†Michael, Harold Kaye (Bud Michael) *sales, marketing and operations executive*
†Michael, Mark Dixwell *lawyer*
Michalak, Craig Lance *real estate executive, consultant*
Michaud, Norma Alice Palmer *paralegal, real estate investor*
Michel, Bernard *civil engineering educator, consultant*
Michel, Clifford Lloyd *lawyer, investment executive*
Michel, Daniel John *broadcast educator, writer, photographer, artist*
Michel, Elizabeth Cheney *social reform consultant*
Michels, Dia Loren *publishing executive, writer*
Mickelson, H(erald) Fred *electric utility executive*
Micklish, Clara Jo *nurse anesthetist*
Micucci, Dana Ann *writer*
Middaugh, Robert Burton *artist*
Middleton, James Boland *retired lawyer*
Miele, Joel Arthur, Sr., *civil engineer*
Migue, Jean Luc *economics educator*
†Mihara, Thomas George *healthcare educator, researcher, military officer*
Mikel, Thomas Kelly, Jr., *laboratory administrator*
Mikiewicz, Anna Daniella *marketing and international business exporter*
Mikitka, Gerald Peter *investment banker, financial consultant*
†Mikulas, Dana Cameron *voice educator, music educator*
Mikulski, Barbara Ann *senator*
Milam, June Matthews *life insurance agent*
†Miles, Andrea Nicole *special education educator, dance instructor*
Miles, Jim *state official*
Miles, John Frederick *retired manufacturing company executive*
Miles, Ray *technology executive*
Milewski, Barbara Anne *pediatrics nurse, neonatal/perinatal nurse practitioner, critical care nurse*
Milhouse, Paul William *bishop*
Millar, Jeffery Lynn *writer*
Millar, John Donald *occupational and environmental health consultant, essayist, speaker*
Millard, Charles Phillip *manufacturing company executive*
Millard, Charles Warren, III, *museum director, writer*
Miller, Alan Jay *rare book dealer, author*
Miller, Allen Richard *retired mathematician*
Miller, Anthony Bernard *physician, medical researcher*
Miller, Arjay *retired university dean*
Miller, Arthur *playwright, author*
†Miller, Barry Irwin *law educator*
Miller, Beverly *marketing consultant*
†Miller, Beverly A(nn) *reference librarian*
Miller, Carole Ann Lyons *editor, publisher, video and marketing specialist, writer, producer*
Miller, Charles Edmond *retired library administrator*
Miller, Cheryl DeAnn *former professional basketball coach, broadcaster*
†Miller, Deanna *editor, writer*
Miller, Diane Doris *executive search consultant*
Miller, Donald LeSessne *publishing executive*
Miller, Donald Muxlow *accountant*
Miller, Ellen S. *marketing communications executive*
†Miller, Emily Elizabeth *elementary school educator, editor*
Miller, Esther Scobie Powers *appraiser, water colorist, gallery owner*
Miller, Harold Edward *retired manufacturing conglomerate executive, consultant*
Miller,.Herman Lunden *retired physicist*
Miller, Jacqueline Winslow *library director*
Miller, Jane Andrews *accountant*
Miller, Jay Alan *retired civil rights association executive*
Miller, Jerry Huber *retired university chancellor*
Miller, John Eddie *lawyer*
Miller, Judy E. *social worker, researcher*
Miller, Kenneth Roye, Jr., *executive recruiter*
Miller, Lenore Wolf Daniels *speech-language pathologist*
Miller, Lillie M. *nursing educator*
Miller, Linda Karen *retired secondary school educator, social studies educator, law educator*
†Miller, Lori *writer, humanities educator*
Miller, Marilyn Joane *retired social worker*
Miller, Marilyn Lea *library science educator*
Miller, Mary Hotchkiss *lay worker*
Miller, Norman Charles, Jr., *editor, reporter*
Miller, Patrick William *research administrator, educator*
Miller, Paul McGrath, Jr., *executive search consulting company executive*
Miller, Phillip Edward *environmental scientist*
Miller, Robert Branson, Jr., *retired newspaper publisher*
Miller, Roberta Ann *gastroenterology nurse*
Miller, Ross Hays *retired neurosurgeon*
Miller, Steven *medical administrator*
†Miller, Susan M. *science educator, researcher*

Munsey, Virdell Everard, Jr., *retired utility executive*
Munson, Ronald Alfred *retired chemist*
Munson, Virginia Aldrich *interior designer, decorator*
Munster, Andrew Michael *surgeon, educator*
†Munsterman, Ingrid Anita *assistant principal*
Muntz, Charles Edward *school system administrator*
Munzner, Robert Frederick *biomedical engineer*
Murarka, Shyam Prasad *science and engineering educator, administrator*
Murchison, David Claudius *lawyer*
Murdock, Chloe Conger *artist*
Muren, Dennis E. *visual effects director*
Murgatroyd, Eric Neal *data processing executive*
†Murillo, Marisela *English educator*
Murillo, Velda Jean *social worker, counselor*
Murnion, William Edward *philosopher*
Murphey, Sheila Ann *infectious diseases physician, educator, researcher*
Murphy, Benjamin Edward *actor*
Murphy, Daniel Ignatius *lawyer*
Murphy, Eddie *comedian, actor*
Murphy, Francis *English language educator*
Murphy, George *special effects expert*
Murphy, Gerald *retired government official, consultant*
Murphy, Jo Anne *lawyer*
Murphy, Kathleen Ann *writer*
Murphy, Kathleen Mary *former law firm executive*
Murphy, Lewis Curtis *lawyer, former mayor*
Murphy, Margaret A. *nursing educator, adult nurse practitioner*
Murphy, Marion Colucci *writer, poet*
Murphy, Robert James *language educator, consultant*
Murphy, Sandra Robison *lawyer*
Murphy, Thomas Bailey *retired state legislator*
†Murphy-Pilon, Monica *cultural organization administrator*
Murr, James Coleman *retired federal government official*
Murray, Albert Lee *writer, educator*
Murray, Allen Edward *deceased oil company executive*
Murray, David George *architect*
Murray, Dorothy Speicher *educator*
Murray, Ernest Don *artist, educator*
Murray, Florence Kerins *retired state supreme court justice*
Murray, Joseph James, Jr., *zoologist*
†Murray, Michael Paul, Jr., *conductor*
Murray, Pius Charles William *priest, librarian, educator*
Murray, Raymond Harold *physician*
Murray, Robert Gray *sculptor*
Murray, Terry (Terence Rodney Murray) *former professional hockey team coach*
Musante, Tony (Anthony Peter Musante Jr.) *actor*
Musgrave, Michael G. *musicologist, musician*
Musgrave, Story *astronaut, surgeon, pilot, physiologist, educator*
Musgrove, Kay Awalt *retired school system administrator*
†Musico, Ann J. *executive secretary, writer*
†Muskopf, Margaret Rose *educator*
Muslin, Lee *artist*
Muson, Howard Henry *writer, consultant*
Muszynska, Agnieszka (Agnes Muszynska) *mechanical engineering researcher, consultant*
Mutalipassi, Louis Richard *psychologist, educator*
†Muth, John Bernard *retired physician*
†Mutsuddi, Mousumi *research scientist*
Mydland, Gordon James *judge*
Myer, Donald Beekman *architect*
Myerowitz, P(aul) David *cardiac surgeon*
Myers, Harold Mathews *academic administrator*
Myers, Jesse Jerome *lawyer*
Myers, John Herman *investment company executive*
Myers, John Thomas *retired congressman*
Myers, Lawrence W. *neurologist*
†Myers, Mike *actor, writer, producer*
Myers, Miller Franklin *finance company executive, retail executive*
Myers, Phillip Fenton *financial services and technology company executive*
Myers, Phillip Samuel *mechanical engineering educator*
Myers, Robert T. *anesthesiologist*
Myers, Shirley Diana *art book editor*
Myerson, Alan *film and television director*
Nabers, Claude Lowrey *retired periodontist, writer*
Nabors, Robert L. *military officer*
Nabrit, Samuel Milton *retired embryologist*
Nacchio, Joseph P. *former communications executive*
Nachman, Gerald Weil *columnist, critic, author*
Nadeau, John *marketing and corporate communications consultant*
Nadel, Elliott *investment firm executive*
Nader, Suzanne Nora Beurer *elementary education educator*
Nader-Heikenfeld, Rita Maria *culinary educator, food writer*
Naeve, Milo Merle *curator, director*
Nagel, M. Constance *poet*
Nagel, Thomas *philosopher, educator*
†Nagle, Robert Owen *lawyer*
Naglieri, Eileen Sheridan *special education educator*
Nagys, Elizabeth Ann *environmental issues educator*
Nah, Fiona Fui-Hoon *information technology educator, researcher*
Nahman, Norris Stanley *electrical engineer*
Naidorf, Louis Murray *architect*
Naito, Michiro *financial analyst*
Najarian, Jack George *investment banker*
Nakamoto, Carolyn Matsue *principal*
Nakayama, Wataru *engineering educator, consultant*
Nakazawa, Paul Wesley *architect, consultant*
Nalin, David Robert *retired pharmaceutical executive*
Nalwa, Hari Singh *materials scientist, polymer chemist*
Nanay, Bence *philosopher, critic*
Nance, David W. *minister*
Nance, Sandra June Taddie *blood service administrator*
†Nanda, Seema *mathematician, educator, entrepreneur*
Nangle, John Francis *federal judge*
Napoleon, Donald Paul *retail executive*
Napoli, Mary *education educator*
Naquin, Patricia Elizabeth *employee assistance consultant*
Narayanaswamy, Onbathiveli Subrahmanyan *computer engineer, consultant*
†Narboni, Lilian *writer*
†Narcisi, Lara Suzanne *educational consultant, educator*
†Nardini, Luisa *music educator*
Narita, Hiro *cinematographer*
Nas, Tevfik Fikret *economics educator*
Nasgaard, Roald *museum curator*
Nash, Janet Rae *geriatrics nurse*
Nash, Leonard David *writer, consultant*
Nash, Mary Harriet *artist, educator*
Nash, Melvin Samuel *lawyer*
Nash, Ted Russell *musician*
Nason, Dolores Irene *computer company executive, social services administrator, eucharistic minister*
†Nasser, Jacques *sr. partner, One Equity Partners*
Natani, Kirmach *forensic psychologist*
Natcher, Stephen Darlington *lawyer, business executive*
Natello, Gregory William *cardiologist, educator*
Nation, David Arthur *retired computer scientist, sculptor*
†Natividad, Lisalinda Salas *family advocacy outreach manager*
Natkin, Robert *painter*
Natsuyama, Harriet Hatsune Kagiwada *mathematician, educator*
Naughton, John Alexander *lawyer*
Naugle, Jean Marie *legal nurse consultant*
Navickas, John *retired fluid dynamics engineer, researcher, consultant*
†Navratilova, Martina *former professional tennis player*
Nawy, Edward George *civil engineer, educator*
Neal, Margaret Sherrill *writer, editor, graphics designer, web designer*
Neal, Robert Lee, Jr., *government official*
Neal, Teresa Schreibeis *secondary education educator*
Neame, Ronald *director, producer*
Neary, Patricia Elinor *ballet director*
†Nederlander, James Laurence *theater owner, producer*
Nederveld, Ruth Elizabeth *retired real estate executive*
†Needham, Jonathan Anton *language educator, poet*
Needles, Belverd Earl, Jr., *accountant, educator*
Neel, Judy Murphy *association executive*
Neely, Marion Victoria *community volunteer*
Neff, Diane Irene *university administrator*
Neff, Donald Lloyd *news correspondent, writer*
Neff, Jack Kenneth *apparel manufacturing company executive*
†Neff, Jennifer Ellen *painter, computer graphics designer*
†Negandhi, Manoj Mahendra *technology consultant*
Nehrbass, Richard George *literature educator, writer*
Neiberger, Richard Eugene *pediatrician, nephrologist, educator*
Neitzel, Lisa Ann *newscaster, reporter*
Nell, James Leo *association administrator*
Nell, Patricia Ann *retired allergist*
†Nellas, Louis Spiro *secondary school educator*
†Neller, Todd W. *computer science educator*
†Nellums, Robert O. *retired chemical engineer*
Nelson, Ben, Jr., *retired air force officer*
Nelson, Carl Roger *retired lawyer*
†Nelson, Christopher Grant *dermatologist*
Nelson, Glen David *medical products executive, physician*
†Nelson, Helen Martha *retired library director*
†Nelson, James Lars *writer*
Nelson, Luther Sullivan *radiologist*
Nelson, Martha Jane *magazine editor*
Nelson, Mary Ellen Dickson *retired actuary*
Nelson, Murry Robert *education educator*
Nelson, Norman Daniel *government official*
Nelson, Ralph Stanley *lawyer*
†Nelson, Richard Perry *lawyer*
Nelson, Robert Arthur *civil engineer*
Nelson, Robert Charles *retired publishing executive*
Nelson, Ron *composer, conductor, educator*
Nelson, Thomas Adams *electrical engineer, transportation consultant*
Nelson, Walter Gerald *retired insurance company executive*
Nelson, William Rankin *surgeon, educator*
†Nelson-Le Gall, Sharon A. *science educator, researcher*
Nemec, David Joseph *writer, baseball historian*
Nemec, Josef *retired organic chemist, researcher*
Nemec-Kessel, Charlene *artist, educator*
Nemiroff, Maxine Celia *art educator, gallery owner, consultant*
†Nephew, Julia Anne *language educator*
†Nepstad, Sharon Erickson *sociologist, educator*
Nesbit, Phyllis Schneider *judge*
Nesbitt, Virginia *special education educator, poet*
Nesheim, Robert Olaf *retired food products executive*
Nesmelova, Irina Vladislavovna *research scientist, physicist*
Neswald, Barbara Anne *advertising executive, writer, printmaker, artist*
Netterville, George Bronson *retired minister*
Neuenschwander, Daniel Paul *music educator*
†Neugarten, Jerrold Lee *lawyer*
Neuhaus, Christian E.O.S. *writer*
Neuman, Linda Kinney *retired state supreme court justice*
Neuman, Robert Harold *communication executive*
Neumann, Forrest Karl *retired hospital administrator*
Neumark, Gertrude Fanny *materials science educator*
Neunzig, Carolyn Miller *elementary, middle and high school educator*
†Neureuther, Brian *business educator, researcher*
Neustadter, Rudolf Peter *retired engineer*
Neuwirth, Allan Charles *designer, director, screenwriter*
Nevill, William Albert *chemistry educator*
Neville, Phoebe *choreographer, dancer, educator*
†Nevins, Sheila *television programmer and producer*
New, Anne Latrobe *public relations, fund raising executive*
New, Thomas L. *public affairs, consultant*
Newbern, William David *retired state supreme court justice*
Newbery, Ilse Sofie Magdalene *German language educator*
Newborn, Jud *anthropologist, writer, curator, educator*
Newcomb, Robert Carl *retired naval officer, real estate broker*
Newcomb, Robert Douglas *optometrist, clinician, educator*
Newell, William Keith *neurobiological researcher*
Newell, William Talman, Jr., *hospital administrator*
Newhall, Edith Allerton *writer*
Newill, James Wagner *accounting executive*
Newkirk, John Burt *metallurgical engineer, administrator*
Newman, Barbara Mae *retired special education educator*
Newman, Bruce Murray *antiques dealer*
Newman, Carol L. *lawyer*
†Newman, Georgia A. *literature educator*
Newman, Jay Hartley *financial company executive*
Newman, Larry *music educator*
†Newman, Marcy Jane Knopf *literature educator, writer*
Newman, Mary Lynn Canmann *lawyer*
Newman, Muriel Kallis Steinberg *art collector*
Newman, Rachel *magazine editor*
Newman, Steven Harvey *insurance company executive, director*
Newman, Suzanne Dinkes *web site development executive*
Newman, Theodore Roosevelt, Jr., *judge*
Newman, William Guy *producer, director, consultant*
†Newport, Patrick Owen *manufacturing executive*
†Newsome, Michael Christopher *marketing professional*
†Newton, Elizabeth Purcell *counselor, consultant, author*
Newton, Roger Gerhard *educator, physicist*
†Ng, Edward W. *aerospace scientist*
†Ng, Kam Chuen *mathematician*
Ng, Woon Lam *artist, educator*
†Ngo, Thinh Dinh *mechanical engineer, educator*
Nguyen, Charles Cuong *engineering educator, researcher, dean*
Nguyen, Clifford Ham-Thiem *telecommunications engineer*
†Nguyen, Dong *computer scientist, researcher*
†Nguyen, Duy *writer*
Nguyen, Paul Dung Quoc *lawyer*
Nguyen, Phu Thien *obstetrician-gynecologist*
†Nguyen, D.O., Tuan H. *cosmetic surgeon, general surgeon*
Ni, Luqun *research scientist*
Ni, Shawn *economics educator*
Nibley, Andrew Mathews *editorial executive*
Nicholas, Henry Thompson, III, *former communications engineering executive*
Nicholas, Lawrence Bruce *advisory company executive*
Nicholas, Lynn Holman *historian, researcher, writer*
Nicholls, Richard Aurelius *obstetrician, gynecologist*
Nicholls, Robert Lee *civil engineer, educator*
Nichols, Cherie L. *songwriter, art publishing executive, artist representative*
Nichols, Iris Jean *illustrator*
Nichols, John David *insurance agent*
†Nichols, Mike *stage and film director*
†Nichols, Wendalyn R. *publishing executive*
Nicholson, June C. Daniels *retired speech pathologist*
Nicholson, Leland Ross *retired utilities company executive, energy consultant*
Nickels, Mavis Lanore *secondary education education, farmer*
†Nicklaus, Jack William *professional golfer*
Nickle, Dennis Edwin *electronics engineering consultant, church deacon*
†Nickles, Shelley Kaplan *curator, educator*
Nicols, Angela C. *software engineer, computer consultant*
Niculescu, Florin Ioan *immunology and rheumatology researcher, educator*
Nidetz, Myron Philip *health care delivery systems consultant*
†Niedermeier, Donna M. *newswriter, lyricist*
†Niederstrasser, Carlos Guillermo *aerospace engineer*
†Niedmann, Peter *composer, musician*
Niehaus, Deborah Ann *peri-anesthesia/perioperative care nurse*
Niehoff, Karl Richard Besuden *financial executive*
Nielsen, Jakob *computer interface engineer*
Nielsen, Linda Miller *city councilwoman*
Nielson, Alyce Mae *poet*
†Niemczak, Barbara Elaine *retired secondary school educator*
Niemiec, Edward Walter *professional association executive*
Nieto, Juan Manuel *emergency medicine physician*
†Nieva, Constantino S. *priest, researcher*
Nikaido, Hiroshi *microbiologist*
Nine, John Edward *pharmaceutical company executive*
Ninos, Nicholas Peter *retired career officer, physician*
Nirenberg, Marshall Warren *biochemist*
Nisbett, Dorothea Jo *retired nursing educator*
Nishimura, Joseph Yo *retired retail executive, accountant*
Nix, Martin Eugene *engineer*
†Nix, Patricia *artist*
Nixon, Marni *singer*
Nixon, Sandra L. *retired registrar*
Noah, Julia Jeanine *retired librarian*
Nobles, Laurence Hewit *retired geology educator*
Nobrega, Fred Thomas *medical society executive*
†Nocera, Joseph P. *principal*
†Nochlin-Soto, David *neuropathologist*
Nochman, Lois Wood Kivi (Mrs. Marvin Nochman) *retired educator*
Noddings, Nel *education educator, writer*
Noddings, Sarah Ellen *lawyer*
Noe, Elnora (Ellie Noe) *retired chemical company executive*
Noëldechen, Joan Marguerite *writer*
Noeth, Louise Ann *journalist*
Noffke, Jane Bunge *sculptor, writer*
Noh, Jun-yong *computer scientist, researcher*
Nolan, Patrick Joseph *screenwriter, playwright, educator*
Noland, Kenneth Clifton *artist*
Nolen, William Giles *lawyer, accountant*
Noll, Richard Dean, Jr., *psychologist, educator, historian*
Nolte, Nick *actor*
Nondorf, Janice Kathryn *special education educator*
†Noonan, Patrick Sutton *management educator*
Nora, James Jackson *physician, writer, educator*
Norbeck, Jane S. *retired nursing educator*
Nord, Eric Thomas *retired manufacturing executive*
Nordel, Patricia A Olmstead *medical/surgical, critical care, and obstetrical nurse*
Nordley, Gerald David *writer, investor*
Nordlund, Donald Elmer *manufacturing company executive*
Nordyke, Robyn Lee *primary school educator*
†Norgren, Brenda D. *secondary school educator*
Norgren, William Andrew *retired religious denomination administrator*
Norkin, Cynthia Clair *retired physical therapist*
Norman, Albert George, Jr., *lawyer*
Norman, Arlene Phyllis *principal*
Norman, Donald Arthur *cognitive scientist*
†Norman, Gregory John *professional golfer*
Norman, Matthew West *psychiatrist*
†Normand, Gilbert *government official*
Norrid, Henry Gail *osteopathic physician and surgeon, biologist, researcher, human anatomy and physiology educator*
Norris, Chuck (Carlos Ray) *actor*
Norris, Darell Forest *retired insurance company executive*
Norris, Katharine Eileen *communications professional, educator*
North, Anita *secondary education educator*
North, John Adna, Jr., *accountant, real estate appraiser*
Norton, Andre Alice *author*
Norton, Karen Ann *accountant*
Norton, Nathaniel Goodwin *marketing executive*
Norton, Robert Michael *mathematician, educator, statistician*
Norton, Wayne Anderson *public information officer, retired journalism educator, public relations specialist*
Norwood, B.J. Scott *business and management educator, Russian studies, pro bono public service*
Noshi, Mohammed Salah-Eldin *physician, consultant*
Nostrand, Howard Lee *retired humanities educator*
†Nott, Tara Lee *Olympic athlete*
Nottingham, William Jesse *retired church mission executive, minister*
Nova, Craig *writer*
Novack, Alvin John *physician*
Novack, Sandy Alissa *social worker*
Novack, Tevor D. *surgeon, consultant*
Novak, Alan Lee *retired pharmaceutical company executive*
Novak, Barbara *art history educator*
Novak, John Alfred *mechanical engineer*
†Novak, John Philip *state legislator*
†Novak, Jon *information technology executive*
Novick, Julius Lerner *theater critic, educator*
Novotny, Deborah A. *management consultant*
Nowak, Jerzy Mieczyslaw *cultural organization administrator*
Nowik, Henry Ian *marketing executive, consultant*
Nowlin, Susan Rae *social service administrator*
†Nucatola, Diane Christina *researcher*
†Nucifora, Giuseppina *molecular biologist, researcher*
Nuechterlein, Donald Edwin *political scientist, educator, writer*
Nugent, Helen Jean *history educator*
Nugent, Shane Vincent *lawyer*
Nugent, Walter Terry King *historian*
Null, James Wesley *educator*
†Nunez, Jacinto Arnaldo *music educator*
Nunez, Paul Lee *biomedical engineering educator, brain physicist*
Nunn, Charles Burgess *religious organization executive*
Nurenberg, David *retired oil company executive*

Patchett, Arthur Allan *medicinal chemist, pharmaceutical executive*
Pate, John Louis *educational consultant*
Pate, Virginia Frances *artist, educator*
†Pate Hewitt, Mellgwin *music educator*
Patel, Aneel N. *retired neuropsychiatrist*
Patel, Anil S. *biomedical engineer, researcher, medical products executive*
Paterson, Robert E. *trading stamp company executive*
Patmos, Adrian Edward *retired dean*
Patrick, Brenda Jean *educational consultant*
Patrick, Mary Kathleen *freelance/self-employed writer, food service executive*
Patrick, Michele Mary *government official*
Patrick, Thomas H. *investment company executive*
Pattanaik, Prasanta Kumar *economics educator*
Patterson, Collis Delano *secondary school educator*
Patterson, Dennis Joseph *management consultant*
Patterson, Elizabeth Johnston *former congresswoman*
Patterson, James *former mayor*
Patterson, James Willis *pathology and dermatology educator*
Patterson, Joseph Flanner, Jr., *surgeon, anesthesiologist*
Patterson, Mildred Lucas *retired teaching specialist*
Patterson, Patricia Lynn *applied mathematician, physicist, inventor*
Patterson, Richard North *novelist, writer, lawyer*
Patterson, Robert Hudson *research library consultant*
Pattillo, Manning Mason, Jr., *academic administrator*
Pattison, Jon Allen *computer scientist, consultant*
Patton, Susan Oertel *clinical social worker, educator*
†Patty, William Jordan *historian*
Pauken, Thomas Weir *venture capital executive, mediator*
Paul, Arthur *artist, graphic designer, illustrator, art and design consultant*
Paul, Eve W. *retired lawyer*
Paul, Evelyn Rose *critical care nurse*
Paul, Frank Allen *physician*
Paul, Richard Wright *lawyer*
Paul, Ron *congressman*
Paul, Vera Maxine *mathematics educator*
Paul, Yvonne C. *retired elementary educator, administrator*
†Paule, Wendelin J. *cell biologist, educator*
Pauley, Jane *television journalist*
Paulose, Anil Chiramel *financial market data/trading systems software infrastructure consultant*
Paulsen, Frank Robert *college dean emeritus*
Paulson, Kenneth Alan *journalist, lawyer, foundation executive*
Paulus, Norma Jean Petersen *lawyer*
Pauly, John Edward *anatomist, educator*
Paup, Martin Arnold *real estate and securities investor*
Paupp, Terrence Edward *research associate, educator*
Pautler, Maria Christine Sadusky *environmental scientist*
Pawlik, James David *lawyer, historian*
Paxton, Juanita Willene *retired university official*
†Payne, Kevin Joseph *professional sports team executive*
Payne, Ladell *retired college president*
Payne, Mary Libby *retired judge*
Payton, Thomas William *corporate finance consultant executive*
Pazdera, John Paul *regulatory services executive*
Pazlamatchev, Ivan Gueorguiev *artist, art restorer*
†Peabody, Gary Douglas *scriptwriter, poet, actor*
Peabody, Sylvia Rockwood *retired community health nurse, agency administrator*
†Peace, John T. *religious studies educator*
Peacock, Mary Willa *magazine editor*
†Peak, Howard W. *former mayor*
Peapples, George Alan *retired automotive executive*
Pear, Charles E., Jr., *lawyer*
Pearce, Paul Francis *retired aerospace electronics company executive*
Pearl, B. Michael *business owner*
Pearl, Laurence Dickson *retired federal government executive*
Pearlstein, Philip *artist*
Pearson, Ralph Gottfrid *chemistry educator*
Pearson, Richard Joseph *archaeologist, educator*
Pearson, Susan Winifred *dean, consultant*
Peaslee, Margaret Mae Hermanek *zoology educator*
Peattie, Lisa Redfield *urban anthropology educator*
Peay, J.H. Binford, III, *retired army officer*
Peccarelli, Anthony Marando *lawyer*
Peck, Arthur John, Jr., *diversified manufacturing executive, lawyer*
Peck, Daniel Farnum *chemical company executive*
Peck, Edwin Russell *retired real estate management executive*
Peck, Kay Chandler *resource development professional*
Peck, Paul Lachlan *minister*
Peck, Robert David *educational foundation administrator*
Peckham, Donald Eugene *retired utilities company executive*
Peckham, Ellen *artist, poet*
Pedersen, Knud George *economics educator, academic administrator*
Pedersen, Michael *research scientist*
Pedersen, Paul Bodholdt *psychologist, educator*
Pedini, Egle Damijonaitis *radiologist*
Pedini, Kenneth *radiologist*
†Pedolsky, Alan Robert *enrolled agent*
Pedretti, Michael A. *performing company executive, artistic director, festival director*
Peeler, Bob *lieutenant governor*
Peeples, Rufus Roderick, Jr., (Roddy Peeples) *farm and ranch news radio broadcaster*
Pefley, Norman Gordon *consultant*
Pegues, June Allen *social work educator*
Peiris, Suhithi Mahesica *research chemist*
Péladeau, Marius Beaudoin *art consultant, retired museum director*
Peleg, Ilan *political science educator*
Pelizzoni, Virginia Matko *writer, editor, consultant*
Pell, Claiborne *former senator*
Pelletier, Louis Conrad *surgeon, educator, health facility administrator*
Pelletier, Nancy Anne *obstetrical and gynecological nurse, educator*
Pellman, James Carl *artist*
Peltier, Eugene Joseph *civil engineer, former naval officer, business executive*
†Pelton, Walter Eugene *information technology executive, mathematician, physicist*
Pelz, Herman H. *physician*
†Peña, Federico Fabian *retired federal official*
Penachio, Anthony Joseph, Jr., *psychotherapist, hypnotherapist, behavioral therapist*
†Pence, Jean Virginia *retired real estate broker*
Pendergrass, Henry Pancoast *physician, radiology educator*
Pendleton, Barbara Jean *retired banker*
Pendleton, Gail Ruth *newspaper editor, writer, educator*
Pendleton, Joan Marie *microprocessor designer*
†Penfold, Linda Margaret *reproductive physiologist, researcher*
†Peng, Weiqun *physicist, research scientist*
Penkul, Linda Marie *poet*
Pennington, Robert Michael *marketing professional, consultant, communications educator, consultant*
Penny, Brent Anthony *career officer*
†Penrod, Marian Penuel *retired school librarian*
Pensis, Henri Bram *music educator, conductor*
Penso, Christine Arety *obstetrician-gynecologist*
†Penson, David Fredrick *urologic surgeon, researcher*
Penzer, Mark *lawyer, editor, corporate trainer, former publisher*
Peoples, John Arthur, Jr., *former university president, consultant*
Pepelea, Kimberli Rae *case manager*
Pepin, Yvonne Mary *artist, writer*
Pepper, Dorothy Mae *nurse*
Peppin, Richard Joseph *engineer*
Peppler, William Norman *aviation executive*
Percy, Lee Edward *motion picture film editor*
†Perdigó, Luisa Marina *foreign language and literature educator*
†Perdue, Franklin P. *retired poultry/agricultural products executive*
†Peregrine, Peter Neal *archaeologist, writer*
Peretti, Marilyn Gay Woerner *human services professional*
†Perez, Dianne M. *medical researcher*
Perez, Felipe Pablo *physician*
Perez, Luz Lillian *psychologist*
†Pérez-Monforti, Jessica L. *social sciences educator, researcher*
Peri, Linda Carol *librarian*
Peri, Winnie Lee Branch *educational director*
Perine, Maxine Harriet *retired reading educator*
Perinelli, Marguerite Rose *women's health nurse, educator*
Perkins, Anthony B. *editor-in-chief, writer, educator*
†Perkins, Dosite Hugh, Jr., *retired lawyer*
Perkins, James Wood *lawyer*
Perkins, Leeman Lloyd *music educator, musicologist*
†Perkins, Nancy Jane *industrial designer*
Perko, Walter Kim *pilot, computer engineer, songwriter, poet*
Perks, Micah Eve *writer, educator*
Perle, George *composer*
Perlman, Richard Brian *lawyer*
Perlov, Dadie *management consultant, consultant*
Perlstein, William James *lawyer*
Perraud, Pamela Brooks *human resources professional*
Perreca, Michael Andrew *artistic director, freelance editor, theater director*
Perrenod, Douglas Arthur *engineer, astronaut*
†Perrero, Laurel *executive secretary, writer*
Perrin, Lisa C. *fiber artist*
Perrin, Michael Warren *lawyer*
†Perritt, Henry Hardy, Jr., *law educator*
Perrot, Paul Norman *museum director*
Perry, George Williamson *lawyer*
Perry, James DeWolf *retired management consultant*
†Perry, Jane A. *service assistant*
Perry, Kenneth Walter *retired integrated oil company executive*
†Perry, Matthew *actor*
Perry, Ruth *writer*
Perry, Thomas Edmund *novelist, television screenwriter, producer*
†Perry, Victor Lynn *pediatric neurosurgeon*
Persoff, Nehemiah *actor, artist*
†Perusich, Stephen Albert *chemical engineering educator*
Peruzzo, Albert Louis *actuary, accountant*
Pesch, LeRoy Allen *physician, educator, health and hospital consultant, business executive*
Peshkin, Samuel David *lawyer*
Pesola, Gene Raymond *physician, educator*
Peszke, Michael Alfred *psychiatrist, writer*
Peter, Richard Ector *zoology educator*
Peters, Carol Ann Dudycha *counselor*
Peters, Douglas Alan *medical-legal consultant, appeals analyst*
Peters, Douglas Cameron *mining engineer, geologist*
†Peters, Linda Marie Leitch *research scientist, educator*
Peters, Mary Catherine *journalist, researcher, announcer*
Peters, Michael P. *former mayor*
Peters, Patricia L. *elementary education educator*
Peters, R. Jonathan *lawyer, manufacturing company executive*
Peters, Ralph Frew *retired investment banker*
Petersen, Arne Joaquin *chemist*
Peterson, Ann Sullivan *physician, health care consultant*
Peterson, Carl Eric *metals company executive, banker*
†Peterson, Christopher *psychologist*
Peterson, Clark C. *announcer, writer, poet, speaker*
Peterson, Howard Cooper *lawyer, accountant*
Peterson, Kevin Bruce *newspaper editor, publishing executive*
Peterson, Martha *artist*
Peterson, Robert Austin *manufacturing company executive retired*
Peterson, Sharon L. *community health nurse*
Petok, Samuel *retired manufacturing company executive*
Petoskey, Thomas W. *secondary school educator*
Petow, Joan Claudia *orthopedic nurse*
Petrequin, Harry Joseph, Jr., *foreign service officer*
Petri, Peter Alexander *economist, educator, director*
Petrie, Hugh Gilbert *philosophy of education educator*
Petrillo, Leonard Philip *retired corporate securities executive, lawyer*
Petrou, Anastasis D. *consultant, adjunct faculty*
Petryshyn, Walter Alexis *otolaryngologist*
Petterson, Margo *artist*
†Pettigrew, L. Eudora *retired academic administrator*
Pettis-Roberson, Shirley McCumber *former congresswoman*
†Pettit, Diana A. *music educator*
Pettit, Ghery DeWitt *retired veterinary medicine educator*
Pettitt, Jay S. *architect, consultant*
Petty, Cindy *music educator*
Petz, Thomas Joseph *internist*
Pevear, Roberta Charlotte *retired state legislator*
Peyser, Joseph Leonard *educator, author, translator, historical researcher*
†Peyton, John *mayor*
Pezeshki, Kambiz Andrew *metallurgical engineer*
†Pfeiffer, Ronald Frederick *neurologist, researcher*
Pfeister, Raymond Lynn *diversified financial services company executive*
Pfister, Howard Frederick Carl *retired surgeon*
Pflanze, Otto Paul *history educator*
†Pham, Lara Bach-Vien *small business owner*
Pham, Tan Diem *physician*
†Phan, Long Thanh *structural engineer, researcher*
Phelps, Gerry Charlotte *economist, minister*
Phelps, James Solomon, III, *astrodynamic engineer*
Philip, James (Pate Philip) *retired state legislator*
Philipp, Jeanne *artist*
Philippon, Marc Joseph *orthopaedic surgeon*
†Philippus, Al A. *protective services official*
Philipson, Morris *university press director*
Phillips, Charles Alan *accounting firm executive*
Phillips, Dorothy Kay *lawyer*
Phillips, Florence Tsu *lawyer, choreographer, dance educator*
Phillips, Glynda Ann *editor*
Phillips, Joy Eugenia *counselor, consultant*
Phillips, Juanita M. *maternal/women's health and neonatal nurse*
Phillips, Julia Mae *physicist*
†Phillips, Kate *writer*
Phillips, Leo Harold, Jr., *lawyer*
Phillips, Marrise Mason *clinical research coordinator*
Phillips, Ronald Edward *artist, sales executive*
Phillips, Stuart *retired composer, record producer*
Phillips, Winifred Patricia *radio producer, composer*
Phinizy, Robert Burchall *electronics company executive*
†Phogat, Sanjay Kumar *molecular virologist, researcher*
Pianko, Theodore A. *lawyer*
†Pichanick, Josephine Susan *management consultant*
†Pick, Daniel Maynard *application developer, researcher*
Pickard, John Benedict *English language educator*
†Pickard, Terry Roy *lawyer*
†Picker, John M. *literature educator*
Pickle, Linda Williams *biostatistician*
Pickrel, Paul *English educator*
Picower, Warren Michael *editor*
Pidgeon, Leslea Sharon *artist, writer*
Pielou, Evelyn C. *biologist*
Pierce, Benedict Enol *social worker*
Pierce, Charles Earl *software engineer, entrepreneur*
Pierce, David Hyde *actor*
Pierce, Hilda (Hilda Herta Harmel) *painter*
†Pierce, John Thomas *industrial hygienist, clinical toxicologist*
Pierce, Lisa Margaret *telecommunications executive, product and market development manager, lecturer*
Pierce, Marian Marie *writer, educator*
Pierce, Ponchitta Ann *TV host, producer, journalist, writer, consultant*
Pierce, Shaheeda Laura *midwife, consultant*
†Pierce, Susan Resneck *academic administrator, English language educator*
Pierik, Marilyn Anne *retired librarian, piano teacher*
Pierre, Natasha Unada *accountant*
Pierro, Richard Salvatore *electrical engineer*
Pies, Ronald E. *retired city official*
†Pietrzak, Alfred Robert *lawyer*
Pifer, Alan (Jay Parrish) *former foundation executive*
Piga, Stephen Mulry *retired lawyer*
Pi-González, Amaury Francisco *announcer, journalist*
†Pike, Mary L. *school nurse practitioner*
†Pike II, Thomas Ray *music educator, firefighter*
Pilette, Patricia Chehy *healthcare organizational management consultant*
Pilgrim, Dianne Hauserman *retired museum director*
Pilisuk, Marc *community psychology educator*
†Pimentel, Vania de Almeida *music educator*
Piniat, Shirley Zina *artist, educator*
Pinilla, Ana Rita *neuropsychologist, researcher*
†Pinilla, Miguel *industrial engineer*
†Pinkett-Smith, Jada *actress*
Pinkney, D. Timothy *investment company executive*
†Pinnock, Monica D. *realtor, minister*
Pinsker, Walter *retired allergist, immunologist*
Pinter, Gabriel George *physiology educator*
Pinto, Rosalind *retired educator, civic volunteer*
†Pipa, Anthony *foundation administrator, director*
Pipchick, Margaret Hopkins *advance practice nurse, marriage and family therapist*
Piper, Margarita Sherertz *retired school administrator*
Pippin, Linda Sue *pediatrics nurse, educator*
Pirie, Robert Burns, Jr., *defense analyst*
Pirkle, George Emory *television and film actor, director*
Pirro, Alfred Anthony, Jr., *physician*
Pisciotta, Vivian Virginia *psychotherapist*
Piskitel, Joellen Bonham *musician, educator*
Pitasi, Judy *nurse*
Pitcher, Griffith Fontaine *lawyer*
Pitcock, James Allison *retired pathologist*
Pitelka, Louis Frank *ecologist*
Pitman, LaVern Frank *retired librarian*
Pitman, Sharon Gail *middle school counselor*
Pitt, Harvey Lloyd *former federal agency administrator*
Pitts, Deborah Krueger *healthcare consultant*
Pizzuro, Salvatore Nicholas *special education educator*
Pizzuto, Emanuelina Maria *concert pianist, composer*
Plaisted, Carole Anne *elementary education educator*
Plangere, Jules Leon, Jr., *retired media company executive*
†Plank, Stephen Brandt *sociologist*
Plants, Walter Dale *retired elementary school educator, minister*
Platau, Gerard Oscar *chemist, consultant*
Platis, James George *secondary school educator*
Platti, Rita Jane *educator, draftsman, writer, inventor*
†Plaza, Eva M. *lawyer*
Plerou, Vasiliki *physicist*
Pleshette, Suzanne *actress, writer*
Pletcher, Eldon *editorial cartoonist*
Plimpton, Peggy Lucas *trustee*
Plotkin, Stanley Alan *medical virologist*
Plottel, Gloria Susanne Stone *marketing professional*
Plummer, Carol Ann *social worker*
†Plummer, Daniel John *medical researcher*
Pniakowski, Andrew Frank *structural engineer*
Poad, Flora Virginia *retired librarian and educator*
Pocock, Frederick James *environmental scientist, engineer, consultant*
Podell, Robert Mann *obstetrician-gynecologist*
Podgorski, Robert Paul *human resources executive*
Podhoretz, Norman *magazine editor, writer*
Poe, Bob *political organization worker, communications company executive*
†Poe, Donald Raymond *state legislator*
Poehner, Raymond Glenn *retired bank executive*
Pogue, Richard Welch *lawyer*
Pohorecky-Dolinsky, Larissa Alexandra *pharmacologist*
Poindexter, John Michael *language educator, writer*
Poitier, Sidney *actor, director*
Poker, Nathan *retired radiologist*
†Pokras, Sheila Frances *retired judge*
Polage, Danielle Cristi *psychology educator*
Polakoff, Murray Emanuel *university dean, economics and finance educator*
†Poldrack, Russell A. *education educator*
†Poleshuk, Alicia L. *alcohol/drug abuse services professional*
Poliakoff, Gary A. *lawyer, educator*
†Polimeno, Mark Anthony *entrepreneur, music educator*
Poling, Jerome Paul *journalist*
Polisar, Joseph Michael *protective services official*
†Polistena, Joyce Carol *art historian, educator*
Poll, Heinz *choreographer, artistic director*
Poll, Martin Harvey *film producer*
†Pollack, Fred *sales executive, writer, comedian*
Pollack, Gerald Alexander *economist, government official*
Pollard, Henry *mediator, arbitrator*
†Pollard, Stephen Randall *social sciences educator*
Pollet, Elizabeth *retired writer, educator*
†Polley, Richard Donald *microbiologist, polymer chemist*
†Polliack, Adrian A. *biomedical engineer, researcher*
Pollock, Karen Anne *computer analyst*
†Polonchak, Richard *music educator*
Polsky, Howard David *lawyer*
Pomerantz, James Robert *psychology educator, academic administrator*
Pomeroy, Kent Lytle *physical medicine and rehabilitation physician*
Pond, Phyllis Joan Ruble *state legislator, educator*
Ponder, Henry *educational association administrator*
†Ponton, Michael Kamano *engineer, educator*
Pool, John Thomas *risk management consultant*

Rayzman, Viktor Lazarevich *metallurgist, consultant*
†Raza, Asim *psychiatrist*
Rea, Ann Hadley Kuehn *retired social organization marketing administrator*
Rea, James Jason *engineer*
Read, Richard Eaton *newspaper reporter*
Reamer, Shirley Jean *minister*
Reason, J. Paul *naval officer*
Reath, George, Jr., *lawyer, mediator, arbitrator*
†Reaves, Christina Lee *writer, photographer*
Reaves, Ray Donald *civil engineer*
Rebay, Luciano *Italian literature educator, literary critic*
Reber, Cheryl Ann *consultant, social worker, trainer*
Reber, Joseph E. *lawyer*
Rebhun, Joseph *allergist, immunologist, medical educator*
Recanati, Elias Isaac *retired shipping company executive*
Rechy, John Francisco *writer*
Recine, Judy Ann *medical/surgical nurse*
Rector, William David *civil engineer*
Redburn, Amber Lynne *nurse*
†Reding, Barbara Grace *artist*
Redleaf, Diane Lynn *lawyer*
†Redlich, Fredrick Carl (Fritz) *psychiatrist, educator*
Redmond, Patricia Ann *lawyer*
Redmont, Bernard Sidney *university dean, journalism educator*
Redwine, John Newland *state legislator, physician*
Reeb, Sue Ellen *biochemist*
Reece, David Bryson *information systems administrator*
Reece, Robert Mayhall *pediatrician*
Reed, Angelica Denise *sculptor, writer, illustrator*
Reed, Diane Marie *psychologist*
Reed, James Donald *journalist, author*
†Reed, JoyLynn Hailey *communications educator, consultant*
Reed, Kit *writer*
Reed, Scott Warren *respiratory therapist, consultant*
Reed, Thomas Lee, II, *minister, social worker, educator*
Reeder, Robert Harry *retired lawyer*
Reeder, Thomas Allen *television writer*
Reedy, Edward K. *retired academic administrator*
†Rees, Michael S. *sculptor, educator*
Reese, Edward James, Jr., *computer scientist*
Reese, Hayne Waring *psychologist, educator*
†Reese, Michael *mathematics educator*
Reeves, Barbara *writer, educator*
Reeves, David Charles *secondary educator, construction executive*
Reeves, Lucy Mary *retired school educator*
Reeves, Nancy Alice *critical care nurse*
Reeves, Peggy Lois Zeigler *accountant*
Regalado, Raul L. *airport executive*
Regan, Paul Jerome, Jr., *manufacturing company executive, consultant*
Regelbrugge, Roger Rafael *steel company executive*
Regenstreif, Herbert *lawyer*
Reggie, Doris Boustany *volunteer*
Regn Fraher, Bonnie *special education educator*
†Reh, Sheila Natkins *humanities educator*
Rehm, Leo Frank *civil engineer*
Rehmus, Charles Martin *law educator, arbitrator*
Rehnquist, Janet *federal agency administrator*
Reho, James Hughes *religious studies educator*
Reich, Harvey Steven *critical care physician*
Reiche, Frank Perley *lawyer, former federal commissioner*
†Reichert, Marc G. *pharmacist*
Reichmanis, Elsa *chemist*
Reid, Geraldine Wold (Geraldine Reid Skjervold) *artist*
Reid, Harry *senator*
Reid, Janet Warner *biologist consultant*
Reid, Joan Evangeline *lawyer, stockbroker*
Reid, Joseph Browning *retired architect*
Reid, Robert Lelon *retired mechanical engineering educator, dean*
†Reid, Shelley Marie *music educator*
Reidenbaugh, Lowell Henry *retired sports editor*
Reidenberg, Joel R. *law educator*
Reidenberg, June Wilson *editor, writer*
Reider, Richard Gary *geographer, educator*
Reilly, Charles Edmund, Jr., *communications company executive*
Reilly, Edward Francis, Jr., *federal agency administrator, former state senator*
†Reilly, John C. *actor*
Reilly, Robert Joseph *counselor*
†Reimer, Marilyn Ruth *music educator*
Reina, Charles Ricca *orthopedic surgeon*
Reinertsen, Gloria May *elementary education educator*
Reinertson, James Wayne *retired pediatrician*
Reinfelds, Juris *computer engineer, educator*
Reinhardt, John Edward *former international affairs specialist*
Reinhardt, Stephen Roy *federal judge*
Reinke, Ralph Louis *retired academic administrator*
Reis, Harold F. *lawyer*
Reisch, Michael Stewart *social work educator, political organization worker*
†Reischman, Richard Alan *language educator*
†Reisman, Sara Hannah *curator, consultant*
Reiss, Alvin Herbert *writer, consultant*
†Reiss, Jerome *retired lawyer*
Reister, Ruth Alkema *lawyer, business executive*
Reitan, Daniel Kinseth *electrical and computer engineering educator*
Reiter, Glenn Mitchell *lawyer*
†Reith, Daniel I. *retired lawyer*
Reitz, Douglas John Frank *airline captain, computer consultant*
†Rell, Bianca Grace *play center administrator*
Remelius, Roger Martin *broadcasting and licensing executive*
Remer, Donald Sherwood *engineering educator, engineering economist, cost estimator, management consultant*
Reminger, Richard Thomas *lawyer, artist*
Ren, Chung-Li *engineer*
Ren, Xing Jian *physician*
†Ren, Ying *engineer*
Renard, Deborah Elaine *psychologist, counselor, educator*
Renaud, Bernadette Marie Elise *author*
Renda, Dominic Phillip *airline executive*
Rendal, Camille Lynn *artist*
Rendu, Jean-Michel Marie *mining executive*
Reno, Janet *former attorney general*
Reno, Thomas Richard *education educator*
Renouf, Anne *technology commercialization financier*
Rényi, Judith A. *foundation administrator*
Renyi, Thomas A. *bank executive*
†Repa, Scott J. *production manager*
Repik, Aleksandr Vladimirovich *molecular biologist*
Repko, Lisa *medical/surgical nurse*
†Repp, Joan Mercedes *retired librarian*
Requénez, Eunice Loida *medical, surgical, and community nurse*
Resnick, Myron J. *retired insurance company executive, lawyer*
Reuber, Grant Louis *banking insurance company executive*
Reuther, Ronald Theodore *museum director*
Revankar, Nagesh Subray *economics educator*
Reveal, Ernest Ira, III, *retired lawyer*
Revere, Virginia Lehr *clinical psychologist*
Revor, Barbara Kay *secondary school educator*
Rewcastle, Neill Barry *neuropathology educator*
†Rewoldt, Todd H. *music educator, musician*
†Reyes, María Elena *academic program director*
Reyes, Silvestre *congressman*
†Reynerson, Charles *aerospace engineer, educator*
Reynik, Robert John *materials scientist, research and education administrator*
Reynolds, Betty Ann *elementary education educator*
Reynolds, Billie Iles *financial representative and counselor, former national association executive director*
Reynolds, Clark Winton *economist, educator*
Reynolds, Elizabeth Burson *social worker*
Reynolds, Ellen Aaker *pediatric nurse practitioner*
Reynolds, Geneva B. *special education educator*
Reynolds, John Francis *insurance company executive*
Reynolds, John Hughes, IV, *retired research and development executive*
Reynolds, Karen Jeanne *musician*
Reynolds, Lewis Dayton *pastor*
Reynolds, Louise Maxine Kruse *retired school nurse*
†Reynolds, Robert (Gary) *artist, educator*
Reynolds, Wade *artist*
Reynolds, William Bradford *lawyer*
Rhea, Jerry Dwaine *director consumer lending*
Rhee, Albert *lawyer, author*
†Rheinfrank, Elizabeth Scales *playwright*
†Rheinfrank, Sally Lyman *volunteer*
†Rhoades, M. Stephen *career officer*
Rhoads, James Berton *archivist, former government official, consultant, educator*
Rhodes, Karren *public information officer*
Rhodes, Lawrence *artistic director*
Rhodes, Peter Edward *label company executive*
†Rhodes, Raymond Earl *professional sports team executive*
Rhyne, James Jennings *condensed matter physicist*
Riasanovsky, Nicholas Valentine *retired historian, educator*
†Ribaudo, Ronald Salvatore *lawyer*
Ricci, Mary Jean *community health nurse, educator*
Ricciardi, Christine Secola *international trade consultant*
Rice, Dale R. *education educator*
Rice, Gary Russell *special education educator*
†Rice, Herbert Williams, Sr., *dean*
Rice, Joseph Albert *banker*
Rice, Patricia Oppenheim Levin *special education educator, consultant*
Rice, Richard Campbell *retired state official, retired army officer*
Rice, Richard Lee *retired architect*
Rice, Roberta G. *retired surgeon*
Rice, Stuart Alan *chemist, educator*
Rice, Walter Herbert *federal judge*
Rich, Cynthia Gay *elementary education educator*
Rich, David Barry *financial executive, accountant, entertainer*
Rich, Lawrence *Spanish language educator*
Rich, Michael Joseph *lawyer*
Rich, Norman Minner *surgeon*
Richard, Edward H. *manufacturing company executive, former municipal government official*
Richard, Jack *retired internist, state agency administrator*
Richard, Susan Mathis *communications executive, screenwriter*
Richards, Carmeleete A. *computer training executive, network administrator, consultant*
Richards, David Gleyre *German language educator*
Richards, Earl Frederick *electrical engineer, educator*
†Richards, James Howard *retired music educator, piano technician*
Richards, Morris Dick *social work administrator, psychotherapist, educator*
Richards, Patricia Jones *artist, poet*
Richards, Paul Linford *physics educator, researcher*
Richards, Ruth *psychiatrist, educational psychologist*
Richards, Wesley Jon *newscaster, writer, producer*
Richards-Barnard, Sandra L. *control systems engineer, computer graphics consultant*
Richardson, Charles Clifton *biochemist, educator*
†Richardson, F. C. *academic administrator*
Richardson, Jasper Edgar *nuclear physicist*
Richardson, John Carroll *lawyer, tax legislative consultant*
Richardson, Margaret Milner *former accounting firm executive, lawyer*
†Richardson, Natasha Jane *actress*
Richardson, Robert Dale, Jr., *English language educator*
Richardson, Robert John *producer, director animation*
Richardson, Roy *management consultant*
Richardson, Thomas Andrew *business executive, educator*
Richart, Douglas Stephen *retired chemist*
Richburg, Billy Keith *healthcare manager, consultant, entrepreneur*
Riche, Wendy *television producer*
Richenburg, Robert Bartlett *artist, retired art educator*
Richeson, Hugh Anthony, Jr., *lawyer*
Richgels, Glen William *mathematics educator*
Richman, Alan *magazine editor*
Richman, Paul *semiconductor industry executive, educator*
Richman, Peter *electronics executive*
†Richman, Stephen Charles *lawyer*
Richmond, Anthony Henry *sociologist, emeritus educator*
Richmond, Julius Benjamin *retired physician, health policy educator emeritus*
Richstone, Beverly June *psychologist, writer*
Rickard, David Lawrence *fundraising consultant*
Rickard, Ruth David *retired history and political science educator*
Rickel, Annette Urso *psychology and psychiatry researcher, educator*
Rickerd, Donald Sheridan *foundation executive*
Rickert, Jonathan Bradley *retired foreign service officer*
Ricketts, Sondra Lou *librarian*
Ricklefs, Roger Ulrich *retired newspaper editor*
Ricks, Joycia Camilla *complaints manager, lawyer*
Ridder, Paul Anthony *newspaper executive*
Riddle, Mark Alan *child psychiatrist*
Riddle, Marnita Marie *medical nurse*
Riden, Michael David *nuclear engineer*
Rideout, Patricia Irene *operatic, oratorio and concert singer*
Rider, Gregory Ashford *investment company executive*
Rider, Paul Edward *physicist, educator*
Rider, Susan Marie *musician*
†Ridge, Davy-Jo Stribling *school librarian*
Ridge, Martin *historian, educator*
Ridgway, James Mastin *retired government official*
Ridgway, Rozanne LeJeanne *retired diplomat, executive*
Ridlen, Lillian May Heigle *public relations, sales and marketing executive, writer, inventor*
Ridloff, Richard *real estate investment advisor, lawyer, consultant*
Ridolfi, Patrick Murphy *music educator, tenor*
Riecken, Henry William *psychologist, research director*
Riehecky, Janet Ellen *writer*
Riehle, Robert Arthur, Jr., *medical director, surgeon*
Ries, Barbara Ellen *alcohol and drug abuse services professional*
Rieselman, Deborah Sue *editor*
Riffe, Delmar Ray *engineer*
†Riffenburgh, Robert Harry *biostatistician, researcher*
Rifkind, Richard Allen *physician*
Rifman, Eileen *music educator*
Rigdon, David Tedrick *air force officer, geneticist, director*
Riggs, Kenneth Allan *music educator*
Riggs, Michael David *writer, editor*
Riggs, Sonya Woicinski *elementary school educator*
Righter, Walter Cameron *bishop*
Riikonen, Charlene Boothe *international health administrator*
Riker, William Kay *pharmacologist, educator*
†Riklis, Meshulam *manufacturing and retail executive*
†Riles, Jesse *tax examiner, writer*
Riley, Betty Stanley *material manager*
†Riley, James Clifford *military career officer*
Riley, Robert Shean *Colonel, United States Army, retired, writer, publisher*
†Riley-Davis, Shirley Merle *advertising agency executive, marketing consultant, writer*
†Rimel, Ira Wesley *writer, U.S. Navy supply officer, real estate specialist, real estate appraiser, real estate broker*
Rimel, Rebecca Webster *foundation executive*
Rinaldi, Robert R., Jr., *artist, photographer, publisher*
Rinde, John Jacques *retired internist*
Rinder, Herbert Roy *retired electrical engineer*
Rindone, Joseph Patrick *clinical pharmacist, educator*
Rinehart, Alice Day Duffy *retired education educator*
Rinella, Barbara *book dramatist*
Ring, Nancy Gail *writer, artist*
Ring, Renee Etheline *lawyer*
Ringler, Lenore *educational psychologist, educator*
Ringo, Betty Penfold *hypnotherapist*
Rinker, Marianne Marie *rehabilitation nurse*
Rinsland, Roland DeLano *retired university official*
Ripken, Calvin Edwin, Jr., (Cal Ripken) *professional baseball player*
Ripley, Alexandra Braid *author*
Ripper, Rita Jo (Jody Ripper) *strategic planner, researcher*
Rishel, Richard Clinton *retired banker*
Risley, Todd Robert *psychologist, educator*
Riss, Robert Bailey *real estate investor*
Ritchey, Paul Andrew *accountant*
†Ritchie, Christine Seel *geriatrician, educator*
Ritchie, Steven John *foundation administrator, fundraising consultant*
Ritchings, Frances Anne *priest*
Rittel, Kathleen Ann Maurer *educator*
Ritter, Alfred Francis, Jr., *retired communications executive*
Ritter, Elise Dawn *therapist, clinical social worker, writer*
Ritter, Jack Charles *mathematician, computer graphics designer*
Ritter, Madeliene *practical nurse, surgical technologist*
Rivera, Oscar R. *lawyer, corporate executive*
Rivero, Andria *education educator*
Rivers, Kenneth Jay *retired judicial administrator, consultant*
Rivers, Lynn N. *former congresswoman*
Rivkind, Perry Abbot *federal railroad agency administrator*
Rizel, Paul Jonas *small business owner*
Rizk, Mysoon *art historian, artist, educator*
†Rizkallah, Morris Z. *translator*
Rizzi, Teresa Marie *speech and language pathologist*
†Rizzuto, Rahna Reiko *writer*
Roaden, Arliss Lloyd *retired higher education executive director, former university president*
Roark, Robert Cameron *insurance broker*
†Robbearts-Bunch, Rebecca Diane *voice educator*
Robbins, Dennis Alan *health services executive, educator*
Robbins, Jack *artist*
Robbins, Ray C. *manufacturing company executive*
Robbins, Rebecca Irwin *foundation administrator*
Roberson, James O. *foundation executive*
Robert, Cavett McNeill, Jr., *neurosurgeon*
Roberts, Alan Silverman *orthopedic surgeon*
Roberts, Albert Dee *internist*
Roberts, Bruce Dan *application developer, department chairman*
Roberts, Corinne Boggs (Cokie Roberts) *correspondent, news analyst*
Roberts, Delmar Lee *editor*
Roberts, Doris *actress*
†Roberts, George Edward *retired systems engineer*
Roberts, Judith Marie *librarian, educator*
Roberts, Margaret Harold *editor, publisher*
Roberts, Marie Dyer *retired computer systems specialist*
Roberts, Mark (Robert Ellis Scott) *actor, writer*
Roberts, Maura M. *retired secondary school educator*
†Roberts, Michael Wayne *music educator*
Roberts, Patricia Lee *education educator*
Roberts, Ray Crouse, Jr., *retired economics educator*
†Roberts, Russell L. *artist*
Roberts, Suzanne Catherine *artist*
Roberts, Thomas George *retired physicist*
Robertson, A. Haeworth *actuary, benefit consultant, foundation executive*
Robertson, Charles James *museum director emeritus*
Robertson, Jack Clark *accounting educator*
Robertson, John Archibald Law *nuclear scientist*
Robertson, Mark Wayne *investment specialist*
Robertson, Wyndham Gay *university official, journalist*
Robinette, Betty Lou *retired occupational health and infection control nurse*
Robins, Natalie *poet, writer*
Robins, Norman Alan *strategic planning consultant, former steel company executive*
Robinson, Angela Tomei *clinical laboratory technologist, laboratory manager*
Robinson, Annettmarie *entrepreneur*
†Robinson, Carol W. *librarian*
Robinson, David Bradford *scientific writer, poet*
Robinson, David Brooks *retired naval officer*
Robinson, David Zav *non-profit agency consultant*
Robinson, Gail Patricia *retired mental health counselor*
Robinson, Glenda Carole *pharmacist*
†Robinson, Harlow Loomis *language educator, historian, educator, writer*
Robinson, Hugh Granville *consulting management company executive*
Robinson, James Arthur *policy scientist*
†Robinson, Larry Clark *professional hockey coach*
Robinson, Laurie Overby *former assistant attorney general*
†Robinson, Linda Gosden *communications executive*
Robinson, Lynda Hickox *artist*
Robinson, Marguerite Stern *anthropologist, educator, consultant*
†Robinson, Mark Allen *music educator*
Robinson, Marshall Alan *economics educator, foundation executive*
Robinson, Mary Frances *retired French language educator*
Robinson, Maura *artist*
Robinson, Nancy Nowakowski *academic administrator*
Robinson, Ronald Gene *military contract negotiator, educator*
Robinson, Verna Cotten *retired librarian, property management owner*
Robinson, William Andrew *health service executive, physician*
Robison, William Christopher *management accountant*
†Robles-Cereceres, Oscar F. *adult education educator, writer*

Sager, Philip Travis research physician, cardiologist, cardiac electrophysiologist
Saha, Arun Kumar engineering educator, researcher
Saiff, Joshua M. mechanical engineer
Sailer, Ruth Luckenbill retired women's health nurse
Sainani, Ram Hariram civil engineer
Saint, Eva Marie actress
St. Clair, Thomas McBryar mining and manufacturing company executive
St. Claire, Frank Arthur lawyer
St. Cyr, John Albert, II, cardiovascular and thoracic surgeon
St. David, Eileen music educator, stage director
St. Germain, Fernand Joseph retired congressman
Saint-Girard, Christian theatre director, choreographer, actor, educator, theater producer
Saint-Jacques, Bernard linguistics educator
St. John, Bill Dean diversified equipment and services company executive
†St. John, Donald J. lawyer
St. Pierre, Joyce Bourré art educator
Saito, Robert Shunichi writer, poet
†Sajda, Paul biomedical engineer, educator
Sakai, Kiyoko artist
Sakaoka, Yasue artist, educator
Saks, Eric Maurice film producer, film director
Saks, Gene theater and film director, actor
Saks, William Joseph, Jr., osteopathic physician, educator
Sakson, Robert George artist
Salamon, Miklos Dezso Gyorgy mining engineer, educator
Salamone-Kochowicz, Jean Gloria retired banker
†Salas Sommer, Dario writer, educator
Salathe, John, Jr., manufacturing company executive
Salatino, David critical care nurse
Salatka, Charles Alexander retired archbishop
Saleeby, Eli Richard dermatologist
Saleh, Brian Behrooz aerospace executive
Salem, Susanne Frances consulting executive
Salerno, Cherie Ann (C. S. Mau) artist
Salerno, Sister Maria nursing educator, adult and gerontological nurse
Sales, Angel Rodolfo financial executive
Salgado, Lynn Enza Grant educator
Salgado, Susana Musicologist, researcher, consultant
Saliba, Jacob manufacturing executive
Saligman, Harvey retired consumer products and services company executive
Salinger, Pierre Emil George journalist
Salinger, Ruth Angier international trade company executive, environmental administrator
Saliola, Frances retired corporate administrator
†Salisbury, Fayann Annie elementary school educator
Saliterman, Richard Arlen lawyer
Salkind, Michael Jay technology administrator
Sallen, Marvin Seymour investment company executive
Sallis, James writer
Salmaggi, Guido Godfrey former diplomat, opera agent
Salovey, Peter psychology educator
Salthe, Stanley Norman retired theoretical biology educator
Salts, Nancy Lee critical care, emergency nurse
Saltzman, Barry actor
†Saltzman, Michael I. lawyer, educator, author
Saltzman, Philip television writer, producer
†Salvatore, Diane J. editor
Salvatore, Richard John cinematographer, company executive
Salvatorelli, Joseph J. engineer, consultant
Salwin, Arthur Elliott software engineer
Salzmann, Zdenek anthropology educator
Sameroff, Arnold Joshua developmental psychologist, educator, research scientist
Samper, Joseph Phillip retired photographic products company executive
Sampson, David Synnott lawyer
Sampson, Robert Neil natural resources consultant
Samson, Alvin former distributing company executive, consultant
Samuels, Barry Ivan radiologist, medical educator
Samuels, Janet Lee lawyer
Samuels, John Stockwell, III, mining company executive, financier
Samuels, Linda S. science administrator
Samuels, Marc health care consultant
Samuelson, Dennis Ray retired pathologist
Samuelson, M. Kristin music educator, vocalist
Sanabria, Sherry Zvares artist
Sanborn, Melinde Lutz genealogist, writer
Sandberg-Morgan, Barbara retired communication and women's studies educator
Sanders, Charles Franklin management and engineering consultant
Sanders, Franklin D. retired insurance company executive
Sanders, John Kenneth marketing communications executive
Sanders, Judith Brown clinical nurse specialist
Sanders, Marlene anchor, journalism educator
Sanders, Theresa Lynn writer, systems analyst, consultant
Sanders, Wayne R. paper products manufacturing executive
Sanderson, James Richard naval officer, planning and investment company consultant
Sandford, Virginia Adele motivational speaker, writer
†Sandlin, Lisa literature educator
Sandor, Gyorgy pianist
†Sandorsen, Cassiopeia public health service officer
Sandt, John Joseph psychiatrist, educator
Sandy, Stephen writer, educator
Sanfilippo, Mary Helena nun
Sanford, Geraldine Agnes retired editor, retired English language educator
Sanghoee, Sanjay investment banker
Saniga, Erwin Martin educator, painter
†Sanner, Kristin Noelle language educator
Sansbury, Olin Bennett, Jr., retired university/orchestra administrator
†Santangelo, Gaspare Charles education educator, retired principal
Santina, Dalia nutritionist, writer
†Santini, Debrah Ann artist, educator
Santini, Rosemarie writer
Santman, Leon Duane lawyer, former federal government executive
Santos, Lisa Wells critical care nurse
Santoso, Irene art director, graphics designer
†Santuzzi, Alecia Marie psychologist, educator, psychologist, researcher
Sapp, John Raymond lawyer
Sapsowitz, Sidney H. entertainment and media company executive
Saravolatz, Louis Donald epidemiologist, physician educator
†Saraya, Nusshy physician, education educator
Sardeson, Lynda Schultz nurse, parish nurse, diabetes educator
Sargent, Thomas Andrew retired political science educator
Sargent, William Winston retired anesthesiologist
Sarris, Andrew George film critic
Sarry, Christine ballerina
Saseen, Sharon Louise artist, painter, educator
Sastrowardoyo, Teresita Manejar nurse
Satinover, Jeffrey B. physicist, psychiatrist, writer
Satorius, Daniel Mark lawyer, film producer, television producer
Satterlee, George Leonard, Jr., retired civil engineer, consultant
Satterthwaite, Helen Foster retired state legislator
†Satterwhite, Marc music educator, composer
Sattler, Rolf retired plant morphologist, educator
Saucier, Gene Duane retired state legislator
Saucier, Guylaine corporate director
Sauder, Virginia Lynne Heisey paralegal
Sauerbrey, Ellen Elaine Richmond former radio talk show host
Sauerhaft, Stan public relations executive, consultant
†Sauerwein, Andrew Mark music educator
†Saul, Bradley Scott communications, advertising and entertainment executive
Saunders, Donna M. accountant
Saunders, James Harwood accountant
Saunders, Lonna Jeanne lawyer, newscaster, talk show host
†Saunders, Mari Pittman psychologist
Saute, Robert Emile drug and cosmetic consultant
Savage, Richard Mark retired systems engineer
†Savercool, Susan Elisabeth elementary school educator
†Savin, Ronald Richard chemical company executive, inventor
Savitz, Maxine Lazarus aerospace company executive
Savocchio, Joyce A. former mayor
†Savov, Jordan D. physician, researcher
Savoy, Suzanne Marie advanced practice nurse
Savrun, Ender engineering executive, researcher, engineer
Sawczuk, Ihor S. urologist
Sawyer, Dianne M. obstetrician-gynecologist
Sawyer, Thomas C. former congressman
Sawyer-Morse, Mary Kaye nutritionist, educator
Sax, Joseph Lawrence lawyer, educator
†Saxena, Vishal mechanical engineer
Say, Carlos C. physician, surgeon
Sayles, Leonard Robert management educator, consultant
Sayre, David retired physicist
Sayre, Robert Freeman English language educator
Sazawal, Vijay Kumar engineering executive
Scaffidi-Wilhelm, Gloria Angelamarie elementary education educator
Scaglione, Cecil Frank marketing executive, publisher
Scala, James health care industry consultant, writer
Scala, Marilyn Campbell literacy and inclusion consultant, writer
Scandary, E. Jane special education educator, consultant
Scanlan, John Douglas foreign service officer, former ambassador
Scanlon, Peter Redmond accountant
†Scarborough, Ann Barlow secondary school educator
Scarborough, Joe former congressman
†Scarlett, Novlin Rose public health nurse, educator
Scarwid, Diana Elizabeth actress
Scavone, Edmond retired surgeon
Sceiford, Mary Elizabeth retired public television administrator
Schabner, Dawn Freeble artist, educator
Schacht, Ronald Stuart lawyer
†Schacter, John Lawrence educational psychologist, researcher
†Schade, George August, Jr., judge
Schaechter, Moselio microbiology educator
Schaefer, C. Barry railroad executive, lawyer, investment banker
†Schaefer, Dan L. former congressman
Schaefer, Heinrich C. retired anesthesiologist
Schaefer, Robert Paul software engineer
Schaefer, William Goerman lawyer
Schaeffer, Robert Allen strategic communications consultant, educator, writer
Schafer, Edward T. former governor, real estate company executive
†Schaler, Jeffrey Alfred psychologist, educator
Schallert, William Joseph actor
Schanfield, Fannie Schwartz community volunteer
Schanstra, Carla Ross technical writer
Scharf, William artist
Scharff, Monroe Bernard investor relations consultant
Scharlemann, Robert Paul religious studies educator, clergyman
Schatz, Lillian Lee playwright, molecular biologist, educator
Schaudies, Jesse P., Jr., business executive
Schaut, Joseph William retired banker
Scheel, Nels Earl financial executive, accountant
Scheele, Paul Drake former hospital supply corporate executive
Scheetz, Raymond John, Sr., retired radiologist
Schefman, Robert Bankle artist, educator
Scheiberg, Susan L. librarian
Scheidecker, Jane management consultant, academic administrator
Scheier, Ivan Henry volunteer, writer
†Scheiner, Jac David nuclear medicine physician, radiologist
Schell, Allan Carter retired electrical engineer
Schell, Catherine Louise family practice physician
Schellenberger, Robert Earl retired management educator and department chairman
Schenck, Jack Lee retired electric utility executive
Schenkel, Susan psychologist, educator, author
Schenker, Leo retired utility company executive
Schenkkan, Robert Frederic writer, actor
Scher, Jordan Mayer physician, psychiatrist, drug abuse specialist
†Scherer, James R. research scientist
Scherrer, George M. electrical engineer
Scheuerman, Eleanor Joyce Miller medical association administrator
Schewe, Donald Bruce archivist, library director
Schexnayder, Brian Edward opera singer, voice educator
Schiaffino, S(ilvio) Stephen retired medical society executive, consultant
Schiavo, Geraldine Elizabeth (Geri Schiavo) poet, screenwriter
Schiff, Zina Leah violinist
Schiller, Gerald Alan writer
Schiller, Lawrence Julian writer, motion picture producer, director
†Schindler, Holly Suzanne freelance/self-employed writer
Schlachter, Kathleen community health administrator, director
Schlagel, Richard H. philosophy educator
†Schlegel, Dick Reeves lawyer, judge
†Schlesser, Ethan Marc music educator, musician
Schleuning, Jay James reporter
Schleuter, Scott L. music educator
†Schley, Michael Dodson lawyer
†Schlichting, Kimberly Sue psychologist, educator, health facility administrator
Schloesslin, Mark Edward software quality engineer
Schloss, Claudia Z. investment executive
Schlossman, Beryl Fern literature educator, writer
†Schlub, Robert Louis plant pathologist, educator
Schlueter, Linda Lee law educator
Schmalz, Carl Nelson, Jr., artist, educator, printmaker
Schmandt-Besserat, Denise archaeologist, educator
Schmid, Andrew Michael, Jr., advertising executive
Schmid, Lynette Sue child and adolescent psychiatrist
Schmidt, B. June education educator
Schmidt, Diane Joy photographer, author, educator
†Schmidt, Eric (Emerson) information technology executive
Schmidt, Harvey Martin economic forecaster, educator, financial consultant
Schmidt, Kathleen Marie lawyer
Schmidt, Lawrence Kennedy philosophy educator
Schmidt, Robert retired mechanics and civil engineering educator
Schmidt, Rodney Albert computer science educator, retired
Schmidt, Ruth Ann academic administrator emerita
Schmidt, Ruth A(nna) M(arie) geologist
Schmidt, Sara Marie English educator
†Schmidt, Sheila Elizabeth physician, writer
Schmidt, Sheri Lynn band director
Schmiel, David Gerhard clergyman, religious education administrator
Schmitt, Howard Stanley minister
Schmitz, Barbara art preservationist
Schmitz, Dennis Mathew English language educator
†Schmoke, Kurt L. mayor
Schmoll, Harry F., Jr., lawyer, educator
Schmults, Edward Charles lawyer, corporate and philanthropic administrator
Schmutz, Charles Reid university foundation executive
Schneck, Stuart Austin retired neurologist, educator
Schneider, Calvin physician
†Schneider, Chris Allan mathematician, educator, statistician, educator
Schneider, Edgar Rolf Gottfried retired mathematician, application developer, writer
Schneider, Jan retired obstetrics and gynecology educator
Schneider, Janet M. arts administrator, curator, painter
Schneider, Mary Louise retired elementary education educator
Schneider, Phyllis Leah writer, editor
Schneider, Rita Joyce property management company executive, real estate broker, mortgage broker
Schneider, Sharon M. systems administrator, information technologist
Schneider, Thomas Aquinas surgeon, educator, retired surgeon
Schnelle, Phillip David electrical engineer, consultant
†Schnitzer, Jay Jeffrey pediatric surgeon, educator
Schnitzlein, Harold Norman anatomy educator
Schnuda, Daniel Nasr internist, pathologist
†Schnuriger, Sarah social sciences educator, historian
Schoen, Allen Harry retired aerospace engineering executive
Schoen, Carol Bronston retired English language educator
Schoen, Howard Franklin computer programmer, analyst
Schoen, William Jack financier
Schoenberg, April Mindy nursing administrator
Schoenberger, James Edwin retired federal agency administrator
†Schoenwald, Maurice Louis retired lawyer
Schoettler, Gail Sinton former ambassador
†Schofield, Barbara Curtright retired school administrator
Scholes, Edison Earl army officer
†Schollander, Wendell, III, lawyer
Scholz, Christopher Henry geophysicist, writer
Schonberg, Alan Robert management recruiting executive
Schonholtz, George Jerome orthopaedic surgeon
Schonhorn, Harold chemist, researcher
Schooley, Robert T. medical educator
Schor, Laura Struminger historian
Schorr, Daniel Louis broadcast journalist, author, lecturer
Schoss, Maximillian surgeon
Schrader, Henry Carl retired civil engineer, consultant
Schrag, Philip Gordon law educator
Schrage, Rose educational administrator
Schram, Ronald Byard lawyer
Schramm, Alicia Larrimore writer
†Schramm, Geoffrey Saunders webmaster
Schrand, Richard Henry broadcaster, writer
Schreckinger, Sy Edward advertising executive, consultant
†Schremp, Faith Maryanne writer
Schrenko, Linda C. state agency administrator
†Schrier, Morris M. consultant
Schrier, Steven Robert television producer, director
Schroeder, Edward james lawyer
Schroeder, Gerald Frank state supreme court vice chief justice
Schropfer, David Waldron pharmaceutical executive, educator, consultant
Schubert, Barbara Schuele retired performing company executive
Schubert, Glendon political scientist, educator
†Schubert, Helen Celia public relations executive
Schuch, Cynthia Silleck nurse
Schuck, Peter Horner lawyer, educator
†Schuckman, Gregory A. academic administrator
Schueler, Gerald Joseph technical writer, systems analyst, counselor
Schuelke, John Paul religious organization administrator
Schulberg, Jay William foundation official
Schulman, Harold obstetrician, gynecologist, perinatologist
Schult, Dain Leslie broadcast executive, consultant
Schulte, Gregory Alan art educator
Schulte, Timothy J. psychologist, counselor, educator, consultant
Schulte Shields, Mary Ann finance executive
Schultz, Albert Barry engineering educator
Schultz, Dennis Bernard lawyer
Schultz, Eileen Hedy graphic designer
†Schultz, Lois Eileen librarian
Schultz, Louis William retired judge
†Schultze, Andrew W. bass-baritone, educator
Schulz, Lawrence A. lawyer
Schulz, Marianne accountant
Schulz, Michael John fire and explosion analyst, consultant
Schulz, Ralph Richard publishing consultant
Schulz, Raymond Alexander medical marketing professional, consultant
Schulz, William Frederick human rights association executive
Schumacher, Cynthia Jo retired elementary and secondary education educator
Schumacher, William Jacob retired army officer
Schunk, Mae former state official
Schur, Maxine Rose travel essayist, children's author
Schure, Alexander university chancellor
Schurgin, Robert Daniel television producer
Schurmeier, Harris McIntosh aeronautical engineer
Schuster, Elaine civil rights professional
Schuster, Robert Conrad consulting engineer
Schuth, Mary McDougle interior designer, educator
Schutt, Allan Jackson retired medical oncologist
Schutz, Donald Frank geochemist, environmental corporate executive
Schuur, Diane Joan vocalist
Schwab, Eileen Caulfield lawyer, educator
Schwaber, Evelyne Albrecht psychiatrist
Schwantes, Carlos Arnaldo history educator, consultant
Schwartz, Arthur Jay lawyer
Schwartz, Charles Phineas, Jr., financial and business consultant, lawyer
†Schwartz, Debra Ann journalist, educator
†Schwartz, Eleanor Brantley academic administrator
Schwartz, Ilene psychotherapist
Schwartz, Joan Ruth writer
Schwartz, John J. association executive, consultant
Schwartz, Lillian Feldman artist, filmmaker, art analyst, writer, nurse

†Silsby, Graham Forbes *mechanical engineer, consultant*
Silva, Omega Logan *physician*
Silver, Ann-Louise Schlesinger *psychoanalyst, psychiatrist*
Silver, Carol Ruth *lawyer*
Silver, George *metal trading and processing company executive*
Silver, Malcolm David *pathologist, educator*
Silverberg, Mark Victor *lawyer, educator*
Silverman, Ellen-Marie *speech and language pathologist*
Silverman, Ira Norton *news producer*
Silverman, Kenneth Eugene *English educator, writer*
Silvers, Ann *peri-operative nurse, educator*
Silverstein, Barbara Ann *conductor, artistic director*
Silverstein, Martin Elliot *surgeon, consultant, writer*
Silvestri, Alan Anthony *film composer*
Silvey, Anita Lynne *editor*
†Silvio, Heather *social worker*
Simaie, Joseph R. *dentist*
Simari, Nanci Joan *herbalist*
Simeral, William Goodrich *retired chemical company executive*
Simmons, Geoffrey Stuart *physician*
Simmons, Harry Dady *physician, pathologist*
Simmons, Jonathan Kimble (J.K. Simmons) *actor*
Simmons, Karen Elaine *artist*
Simmons, Marguerite Saffold *pharmaceutical sales professional*
Simmons, Raymond Hedelius *lawyer*
Simmons, Scott Martin *information specialist*
Simmons, Ted Conrad *writer*
Simms, John William *retired foreign service officer, consultant*
Simms, Maria Ester *health services administrator*
Simms, Maria Kay *writer, non-profit organization executive*
Simms, Robert D. *former state supreme court justice*
Simon, James *writer*
Simon, John Oliver *poet, educator*
Simon, Leonard Samuel *banker*
†Simon, Marsha Jean *political scientist*
Simon, Marvin Kenneth *electrical engineer, consultant*
Simon, Peter E. *publishing executive*
Simon, Robert G. *lawyer*
Simons, Lewis Martin *journalist*
†Simonsen, Gregory Mark *lawyer*
Simonson, Lee Stuart *broadcast company executive*
Simonson, Steven Neil *psychotherapist*
†Simonton, Robert Bennet *lawyer*
Simpson, Andrea Lynn *communications executive*
Simpson, Frederick James *retired research administrator*
†Simpson, Gerald D *retired research scientist, consultant, educator*
†Simpson, Hugh L *news correspondent, newswriter*
Simpson, Jack Benjamin *medical technologist, business executive*
Simpson, John Noel *healthcare administrator*
Simpson, Murray *engineer, consultant*
Sims, Elizabeth LaNeal *association executive*
Sims, Kent Otway *economist*
†Sims, Lorene Joy *music educator*
†Sims, Pauline Andrée Villarico *artist*
Sims, Robert Bell *retired professional society administrator, public affairs official, newspaper publisher*
Sims Iannelli, Kimberly *writer*
Sinai, Allen Leo *economist, educator*
Sinclair, Carole *publisher, editor, author*
Sinclair, Sara Voris *health facility administrator, nurse*
Sinclair, Virgil Lee, Jr., *judge, writer*
Sincoff, Michael Z. *human resources and marketing professional*
Singer, Beth J. *philosopher*
Singer, David Michael *marketing and public relations company executive*
Singer, Donna Lea *writer, editor, educator*
Singer, Jeffrey Michael *organic analytical chemist*
Singer, Joyce Zandra *physician*
Singer, Kurt Deutsch *news commentator, writer, publisher*
Singer, Markus Morton *retired trade association executive*
Singer, Renata *publisher, writer, editor*
Singer, S(iegfried) Fred *geophysicist, educator*
†Singer-Cohen, Karen Beth *mathematician, educator*
†Singh, Anoop K. *emergency physician, orthopedic bioengineer*
†Singhal, Rajan *engineering executive, consultant*
Singletary, Patricia Ann *minister*
Singleton, Robert Culton *graduate school administrator, Bible educator*
Singleton-Wood, Allan James *communications executive*
Siper, Cynthia Dawn *special education educator*
Siporin, Sheldon *lawyer, consultant*
†Sisemore, Claudia *educational films and videos producer, director*
Sisk, Jane Elizabeth *economist, educator*
Sisley, Emily Lucretia *retired psychologist, medical writer*
Sissel, George Allen *manufacturing executive, lawyer, engineer*
Sisto, Grace Wexler *social welfare consultant*
Sit, Hong Chan *minister*
Sitnyakovsky, Roman Emmanuil *scientist, writer, inventor, translator*
Siu, Wang-Ngai *solicitor*
Sizemore, Barbara Ann *Black studies educator*
Sjostrand, Fritiof Stig *biologist, educator*
Skaff, Joseph John *retired state agency administrator, army officer*
Skaggs, Bebe Rebecca Patten *college dean, clergywoman*
Skarda, Richard Joseph *clinical social worker*
Skeels, Stephen Glenn *civil engineer*
Skelland, Anthony Harold Peter *chemical engineering educator*
Skibell, Joseph Freer *writer, educator*
Skinner, Alastair *retired accountant*
Skinner, Knute Rumsey *poet, English educator*
Skinner, Patricia Morag *state legislator*
Skinner, Shari L. *dermatologist*
Skinner, Thomas *broadcasting and film executive*
Sklansky, David Bruce *gambling expert, writer*
†Skoda, Mary E. *mathematician, educator*
Skoglund, Elizabeth Ruth *marriage and family therapist*
†Skolnick, Lawrence *neonatologist, medical administrator*
Skolnik, Barnet David *retired lawyer*
Skotheim, Robert Allen *retired college and museum administrator*
Skov, Arlie Mason *petroleum engineer, consultant*
Skowronski, Vincent Paul *concert violinist, recording artist, executive producer, producer classical recordings*
Skrdla, W. Blake *physician, psychiatrist*
Skrocki, Edmund Stanley, II, *health fair promoter, executive*
Skromme, Lawrence H. *consulting agricultural engineer*
Skwarczyński, Henryk Adam (Henryk Skwar) *writer*
†Skylar, Alayne *television producer, writer, talent scout, talent agent*
Slade, Paul Graham *physicist*
Slagle, Jacob Winebrenner, Jr., *food products executive, real estate agent*
Slakter, Edmund Lee *psychiatrist*
†Slate, Ronald S. *music educator*
Slater, Brian (Rauen Slate) *writer*
Slater, Kristie *small business owner*
Slatkin, Daniel Nathan *pathologist*
Slaughter, Djuanique Naté *healthcare analyst, consultant*
Slaughter, Freeman Cluff *retired dentist*
Slaughter, Richard Arthur *political scientist, economist, educator*
Slavens, Thomas Paul *library science educator*
Slavit, David Hal *otolaryngologist*
Slavitt, David Walton *retired lawyer*
†Slay, Brandon *Olympic athlete*
Slaydon-Wolbert, Jeanne Miller *secondary school educator*
Slee, Vergil N. *healthcare informatics executive, physician, author*
Sleeter, John William Higgs *retired physician, health service administrator*
Slepowitz, Gary A. *pediatrician*
Sliger, Herbert Jacquemin, Jr., *lawyer*
†Slive, Steven Howard *lawyer*
†Sliwa, Krzysztof *education educator, researcher*
Sloan, Jason Gerard *aerospace engineer*
Sloane, Neil James Alexander *mathematician, researcher*
Sloat, Jane Roberts DeGraff *government official, civic worker, consultant*
Slonaker, Norman Dale *lawyer*
†Slough, Major Carl *lawyer*
Sloyan, Gerard Stephen *religious studies educator, priest*
Small, Daniel Priestley *lawyer, educator*
Smally, Donald Jay *consulting engineering executive*
†Smardz, Zofia Jadwiga *editor, writer*
†Smason, Ivan *psychologist, writer*
Smiley, Ronald Michael *communications executive*
Smith, A. Robert *editor, author*
Smith, Albert Carl *physician, scientist*
†Smith, Angela Elsie *media relations executive, interior designer*
Smith, Ann Hamill *retired religion educator*
Smith, Barbara Anne *healthcare management company consultant*
Smith, Barbara Dail *school nurse*
Smith, Barbara Jeanne *retired librarian*
†Smith, Becky J. *educational association administrator*
Smith, Betty Pauline *television producer*
†Smith, Beverly J. *foundation administrator, not-for-profit developer, minister*
Smith, Brenda Joyce *author, editor, social studies educator*
Smith, Brian *business consultant, educator*
Smith, Carole Dianne *retired lawyer, editor, writer, product developer*
Smith, Charles Haddon *geoscientist, consultant*
†Smith, Cheryl Diane *music educator*
†Smith, Clodus Ray *retired academic administrator*
Smith, Cynthia S. *writer*
Smith, D(aisy) Mullett *publisher*
†Smith, Debbie Ilee Randall *elementary school educator*
†Smith, Debra A. *insurance company medical director*
Smith, Deirdre O'Meara *lawyer*
Smith, Dwight L., III, *academic administrator*
Smith, Edward Reaugh *retired lawyer, retired funeral home executive*
Smith, Ethel Farrington *retired social worker, genealogist, writer*
Smith, Floyd Leslie *insurance company executive*
Smith, Frank Neale *materials and corrosion engineer*
Smith, Frederick Coe *retired manufacturing executive*
Smith, George Drury *publisher, editor, collagist, writer*
Smith, George Patrick, II, *lawyer, educator*
Smith, Goff *industrial equipment manufacturing executive*
Smith, Grover C(leveland) *English language educator*
Smith, Hamilton Othanel *molecular biologist, educator*
Smith, Harold Charles *private pension fund executive*
†Smith, H(arold) Lawrence *lawyer*
Smith, Hedrick Laurence *journalist, television producer, correspondent, author, lecturer*
Smith, Helen Marie *social worker, hospital administrator*
Smith, Hoke LaFollette *university president*
Smith, Hugh Elmore *retired obstetrician and gynecologist*
Smith, James A. *lawyer*
Smith, Jamesetta Delorise *author*
Smith, Jane Marilyn Davis (Jane Maxwell) *writer*
†Smith, Janice M. *poet, artist*
†Smith, Jean Kennedy *former ambassador*
Smith, Jeanette Elizabeth *lawyer*
Smith, John Joseph, Jr., *financial management executive*
Smith, John Wallace *retired surgeon, educator*
Smith, Joy Karen Turnheim *lawyer*
Smith, Joyce Ann *secondary school educator*
Smith, Karen Ann *visual artist*
Smith, Kathleen Ann *mathematics educator*
Smith, Kevin S. *civil engineer*
Smith, Lauren *interior designer, writer*
Smith, Lauren Ashley *lawyer, journalist, clergyman, physicist*
Smith, Leila Hentzen *artist*
†Smith, Leonard Glenn *artist, educator*
Smith, Leonore Rae *artist*
Smith, Linda Ann Glidewell *accountant*
Smith, Lois Arlene *actress, writer*
Smith, Loretta Mae *civilian military officer*
†Smith, Marcia K. *government agency administrator*
Smith, Margaret Taylor *volunteer*
Smith, Marjorie Aileen Matthews *museum director*
Smith, Mark Joseph *cartographer*
Smith, Martha Virginia Barnes *retired elementary school educator*
Smith, Martin Bernhard *journalist*
Smith, Martin Henry *retired pediatrician*
Smith, Martin Lane *biomedical researcher*
Smith, Mary Elizabeth *retired art historian*
†Smith, Mary Louise *real estate broker*
Smith, Marya Jean *writer*
Smith, Maura Abeln *lawyer*
Smith, Melissa Christine-Mary *flight nurse*
Smith, Michael Alan *retired insurance industry analyst*
Smith, Michael William *construction executive, consultant*
Smith, Nancy Angelynn *federal agency administrator*
†Smith, Paul Eric *writer*
Smith, Paul Vergon, Jr., *corporate executive, retired oil company executive*
Smith, Paula Marion *urology and medical/surgical nurse*
†Smith, Rachel Hudson *retired librarian*
Smith, Robert Clinton *former senator*
Smith, Robert P. *physician*
Smith, Robert Powell *former ambassador, former foundation executive*
Smith, Robert William *state official, educator*
Smith, Rodney *retired electronics executive*
Smith, Ronald Ehlbert *lawyer, educator, pastor, public speaker, writer, motivator, real estate developer*
Smith, Ronald Emory *financial executive*
†Smith, Samuel Howard *academic administrator, plant pathologist*
†Smith, Serafina Gangemi *artist, drug counselor*
Smith, Sheryl Velting *organization administrator*
Smith, Stanford Sidney *former state treasurer*
†Smith, Stuart Douglas *military officer, minister*
Smith, Stuart Lyon *psychiatrist, corporate executive*
Smith, Susan Porter *artist, environmentalist*
Smith, Sydney David *data processing executive*
Smith, Thomas Hunter *ophthalmologist, ophthalmic plastic and orbital surgeon*
Smith, Thomas Winston *cotton marketing executive, retired*
Smith, Tom *poet, educator, retired*
Smith, V. Kerry *economics educator*
Smith, Verna Mae Edom (Vme Edom Smith) *sociology educator, freelance writer, photographer*
Smith, Vestal Beecher, Sr., *physician*
Smith, Virgil Baker *retired electrical engineer*
†Smith, Walter Ernest *lawyer*
Smith, Warren Daniel *surgeon, retired*
Smith, Wendy Haimes *federal agency administrator*
Smith, Wendy L. *foundation executive*
Smith, Wilburn Jackson, Jr., *retired bank executive*
Smith-Epstein, Mary Kathleen *dancer*
Smither, Howard Elbert *musicologist, educator*
Smither-Kopperl, Margaret Lydia *research scientist*
†Smith-Hilliker, Renée Anne *executive secretary*
Smits, Kathleen Curran *artist, educator*
†Smits, Rik *retired professional basketball player*
Smock, Raymond William *historian*
Smoker, Roy Ellis *retired military officer*
Smolek, Rochelle Thérèse *interior designer*
Smouse, H(ervey) Russell *lawyer*
Smyth, Cornelius Edmonston *retired hotel executive*
Smyth, Nicholas Patrick Dillon *surgeon*
Snedden, James Douglas *retired health service management consultant*
Sneider, Joyce Pappachristou *dietitian, educator*
Snellen, Deborah Sue *training consulting company executive*
Snelling, Barbara W. *retired state legislator*
Snelling, Robert Orren, Sr., *franchising and employment executive*
Snelson, Kenneth Duane *sculptor*
Snider, L. Britt *government executive*
†Sniffen, Frances P. *artist*
Snodgrass, Lynn *small business owner, former state legislator*
Snook, Paul *real estate company executive*
Snortland, Howard Jerome *education financial consultant*
Snow, Claude Henry, Jr., *information services executive, consultant*
Snow, Joel Alan *research director*
Snow, Marina Sexton *writer*
Snowden, Lawrence Fontaine *retired aircraft company executive, retired marine corps general officer*
†Snowden, Ruth *artist, educator, legal secretary*
Snyder, Dorothy Z. *social worker*
Snyder, John Millard *travel company executive, educator*
Snyder, Marvin *neuropsychologist*
Snyder, Nathan *entrepreneur*
Snyder, Robert Carl *retired minister*
Snyder, William Brandon *linguistics educator*
Snyder, William Burton *insurance company executive*
Snyder, Ph.D., Carolyn L. Smith *medical writing director*
Sobin, Leslie Howard *pathologist, educator*
Soble, Mark Richard *lawyer*
Sobolev, Alexandre Andreevich *physicist*
†Sobrer, Josep Miquel *language educator, writer*
Sodums, Dzintars *writer*
†Softic, Tanja *artist*
Sognier, John Woodward *retired judge*
†Soifer, Jed Joshua *mathematics and science educator*
Sojka, Sandra Kay *investor, livestock conservator*
Sokal, Robert Reuven *biology educator, author*
Solano, Julio Rafael *priest, educator*
Solar, Richard Leon *banker*
†Solberg, Ronald Louis *investment adviser*
†Solberg, Thomas Allan *lawyer*
Soles, Ada Leigh *former state legislator, government advisor*
Solis-Klein, Ruth Elizabeth *foreign language educator*
Solkoff, Jerome Ira *lawyer, consultant, lecturer*
Sollars, Candis Kay *social worker, therapist*
Sollender, Joel David *management consultant, financial executive*
†Solloway, C. Robert *retired forest products company executive*
Solo, Joyce Rubenstein *volunteer*
Solomon, Beth Carol *writer*
†Solomon, Connie Scott *chief of staff*
Solomon, Eldra Pearl Brod *psychologist, educator, biologist, writer*
Solomon, Goody Love *journalist, editor*
†Solomon, Jack D. *investment banker*
Solomon, Norman *author, columnist*
Solomon, Risa Greenberg *clinical social worker, child and family therapist, former entertainment industry executive*
Solomon, Robert Charles *philosopher, educator*
†Solomon, Susan *chemist, scientist*
†Solomon-Arnold, Irene Lena *language educator*
Soloway, Jay Stephen *consulting firm executive*
Soltero-Harrington, Luis Rubén *surgeon, educator*
Somasundaran, Ponisseril *surface and colloid engineer, applied science educator*
Somers, Louis Robert *retired food company executive*
Somerville, James Middleton, III, *retired philosophy educator, writer*
Somes, Joan Marie *emergency nurse*
Sommerfeld, Marianna *retired social worker, writer*
Sommers, Paul Martin *economics educator*
Sommers, William Paul *management consultant, research and development institute executive*
Sonderegger, Theo Brown *psychology educator*
Sondheim, Stephen Joshua *composer, lyricist*
Song, Young D. *interior designer, artist*
Sonnenschein, Hugo Freund *academic administrator, economics educator*
†Sonnier, Patricia Bennett *business management educator*
†Sonsino, Rifat *retired rabbi*
Soper, James Herbert *botanist, curator*
Sopranos, Orpheus Javaras *manufacturing company executive*
Sorel, Edward *artist*
SoRelle, Ruth Doyle *medical writer, journalist*
Sorensen, Elizabeth Julia *retired cultural administrator*
Sørensen, Flemming Brandt *pathologist*
Sorensen, Sheila *state legislator*
†Sorgi, Deborah B(ernadette) *educational software company executive*
Sorley, Lewis *writer*
Sormaz, Dusan Nedeljko *industrial engineer, educator, researcher*
Sorrell, Rozlyn *singer, recording artist, actress, educator, entrepreneur*
Sorrells, Frank Douglas *retired mechanical engineer*
Sorrentino, Gilbert *English language educator, novelist, poet*
Sorter, Bruce Wilbur *federal program administrator, educator, consultant*
Sosnick, Fay Maxine *retired educator, volunteer*
Sotirhos, Michael *ambassador*
Soto-Fernandez, Liliana *education educator*
Souders, Jean Swedell *artist, educator*
Soued, Steven Michael *physician*
†Soul, Veronika *filmmaker, animator*
†Soulen, Sarah Kay *psychologist, consultant*
Sourial, Alfy Saif *surgeon*
Souter, David Hackett *United States supreme court justice*
Southerland, S. Duane *manufacturing company executive*
Southwick, Charles Henry *zoologist, educator*
Southworth, Jamie MacIntyre *retired education educator*
Souveroff, Vernon William, Jr., *business executive*
Souzdaltsev, Igor Nikolayevich *economist*

Stumpe, Warren Robert *county official, retired scientific, engineering and technical services company executive*
Stumpf, Heinrich J. *psychometrician, research consultant*
Stumpf, Mary Rita *administrator, executive director*
Stumpf, Suzanne Elizabeth *classical musician*
Sturges, John Siebrand *management consultant*
Stutz, Pearl Hewlett *retired photojournalist*
Stutzman, Sandra Louise *advanced nurse practitioner*
Styblo, Clarence John *retired surgeon*
Styler, Anda Jasamine *artist, educator*
Styne, Marlys Marshall *retired English educator*
Styron, William *writer*
†Su, Mark L. *physician*
Suarez, Michael Anthony *civil engineer, consultant*
†Subbarao, Kamesh *aeronautical engineer*
Suber, Robin Hall *former medical and surgical nurse*
Subin, Florence *retired lawyer*
Subramanian, R. Shankar *chemical engineer, educator*
Subramanian, Ravi *electrical engineer*
Suchyta, Casimir John, III, *computer analyst, researcher*
Sudanowicz, Elaine Marie *government executive*
Sudarsky, Jerry M. *industrialist*
Sugintas, Nora Maria *veterinarian, scientist, medical company executive, performing arts dancer, photographer*
Sugnet, Linda A'Brunzo *elementary education educator*
Suhr, Geraldine M. *medical/surgical nurse*
Sukopp, Karl Martin *sculptor, painter, graphic artist*
Sulc, Jean Luena (Jean L. Mestres) *lobbyist, consultant*
Sullivan, Barbara Jean *artist*
Sullivan, Charles *dean, educator, author*
Sullivan, Colleen Anne *physician, educator*
Sullivan, Daniel Joseph *theater critic*
Sullivan, Eugene John Joseph *manufacturing company executive*
Sullivan, Evelin Elisabeth *writer, educator*
Sullivan, George Edward *author*
†Sullivan, Gerald Joseph *Latin and English educator*
Sullivan, Gregory Patrick, Sr., *research engineer*
Sullivan, Harry Truman *research scientist*
Sullivan, James Lenox *clergyman*
Sullivan, John Louis, Jr., *retired search company executive*
†Sullivan, Keith Montgomery *operations research specialist*
Sullivan, Mary Rose *English language educator*
Sullivan, Nell Inklebarger *retired administrative official, counselor*
Sullivan, Nicholas G. *science educator, speleologist*
Sullivan, Paul Andrew *retired research electrical engineer*
†Sultan, Cornel *research scientist, consultant*
Sulton, Anne Thomas *lawyer, criminologist*
†Sulzbach, Deborah *law librarian*
Sulzer-Azaroff, Beth *psychology educator*
†Sumerlin, Katherine Marie *retired librarian*
Sumers, Rebecca Ann *interior designer*
Summerfield, John Robert *textile curator*
Summers, David Stewart *neurologist, consultant*
Summers, Lorraine Dey Schaeffer *retired librarian*
Summers, Richard Henry *music educator, musician*
†Summitt, Patricia Head *college basketball coach*
Sumrall, Linda *geophysicist*
†Sun, Chenghua *composer, music educator*
†Sun, Yi *optical engineer, researcher*
†Sun, Zijie *urologist, surgeon, medical educator*
†Sun, Zuo *research scientist, consultant*
Sundaram, Ramakrishnan *engineering educator*
Sundaresan, Mosur Kalyanaraman *physics educator*
Sunderman, Deborah Ann *apparel executive, fashion and business educator*
Sunderman, Duane Neuman *chemist, research institute executive*
†Sung, Myong-Hee *mathematician, researcher*
Sunward, Justin Hugo *artist, writer*
Suppes, Patrick *philosophy, statistics, psychology educator and education*
Suprun, Harry Zvi *pathologist*
Suput, Ray Radoslav *librarian*
Surles, Richard Hurlbut, Jr., *retired law librarian*
Surplus, Robert Wilbur *retired music educator*
Surratt, John Richard *lawyer*
Sussman, Barry *author, public opinion analyst and pollster, journalist*
Sussman, Howard S(ivin) *lawyer*
Sustendal, Diane *media executive*
Suter, Susan Virginia *retired social worker*
Suthaharan, Shanmugathasan *computer science educator, researcher*
Sutherland, Melanie Jan *theatre director and producer*
Suthers, Hannah Louise Bonsey *biologist*
Sutlin, Vivian *advertising executive*
Sutowski, Thor Brian *choreographer, educator*
Sutton, Dolores *actress, writer*
Sutton, James Hercules *poet, former educational association administrator*
Sutton, Julia *musicologist, dance historian*
†Sutton, Julia Zeigler *retired special education educator*
Sutton, Nigel James *aeronautical engineer, test flight officer*
†Suzuki, Bob H. *retired academic administrator*
Suzuki, Kunihiko *biomedical educator, researcher*
Svarlien, Diane Arnson *verse translator, classics educator*
†Svatek, Patrick Lawrence *aerospace engineer*
Svensson, Lars Georg *cardiovascular and thoracic surgeon*
Svikhart, Edwin Gladdin *investment banker*
Svikla, Alius Julius *pharmacist*
Svoboda, Janice June *nurse*
Svrcek, Debbie M. *English educator*
Swacker, Frank Warren *lawyer*
†Swain, Michael William *labor union administrator, protective services official*
Swain, Virginia M. *executive mentor, conflict resolution, reconciliation and peace education consultant, educator*
Swallum, Maryann *musician, music educator*
Swalm, Thomas Sterling *aerospace executive, retired military officer*
†Swan, Beth Ann *nursing administrator*
Swaner-Smoot, Paula Margetts *clinical psychologist*
Swanger, Sterling Orville *appliance manufacturing company executive*
Swann, Barbara *lawyer*
Swanner, Barbara Melson *artist*
Swanson, David Elmer *editor*
Swanson, Ralph William *aerospace executive, consultant, engineer*
Swanstrom, Thomas Evan *economist*
Swartz, Jon David *psychologist, educator*
†Swartzell, Ann Garling *librarian*
Swaters, Cherie Lynn Butler *nurse*
†Swayd, Samy *religious studies educator*
†Sweatmon, U'Nita Faye Rogers *music educator*
Swecker, John H. *secondary school educator*
Swedlow, Judith Meyer *volunteer*
Sweedler, Barry Martin *transportation safety consultant*
Sweeney, Deidre Ann *lawyer*
Sweet, Philip W. K., Jr., *former banker*
Sweet, Robert Workman *federal judge*
Sweetland, Loraine Fern *librarian, educator*
Swensen, Mary Jean Hamilton *graphic artist*
†Swenson, Douglas *management consultant*
Swett, Richard Nelson (Dick Swett) *diplomat, former congressman*
Swezey, Christopher Stephen *geologist*
Swiatek, Mary Ann *psychologist*
Swiff, Kelly *food products executive, civic volunteer, writer*
†Swift, Aubrey Earl *lawyer, petroleum engineer*
Swift, Jane Maria *former governor*
Swift, Jill Anne *industrial engineer, educator*
†Swinehart, David *music educator*
Swinson, Betty White *composer*
Swisher Harnetty, Stacey Elaine *mechanical engineer*
Swislocki, James Paul *music educator, soccer coach*
Swist, Marian Irene *emergency nurse*
Switzer, Maurice Harold *journalist*
Switzer, Toccoa *artist*
Swoap, David Bruce *government affairs consultant*
Swope, Donald Downey *retired banker*
Sydnor, Edgar Starke *lawyer*
†Sykes, Sam Jones *French educator*
Sykora, Barbara Zwach *state legislator*
Sylver, Nenan *writer, educator, psychotherapist, singer-songwriter*
Symchowicz, Samson *retired biochemist*
Synnestvedt, Kirstin *musician, educator*
Szabo, Yurika Lin *marketing executive, advertising executive*
Szantai, Linda Marie *speech and language therapist*
†Szarvas, Tibor Ferenc *mathematician, educator*
Szuch, Clyde Andrew *lawyer*
Szybicki, Edmund *executive*
Szydlowski, Ralph *retired die maker, formability consultant*
Tabor, Anna Marie *writer*
Tabor, Linda J. *educator*
Tabussi, Stephen John *banker*
Tacha, Deanell Reece *federal judge*
Tachau, Herman *structural engineer*
†Tachna, Ruth C. *retired lawyer*
Tack, Theresa Rose *women's health nurse*
†Tackett, Viti Lee *writer*
Taddei, Lois Annette Magowan *artist, decorator*
Tadlock, Anita Conner *volunteer*
Taft, Nellie Leaman *artist*
Tagiuri, Consuelo Keller *child psychiatrist, educator*
Tagliente, Josephine Marlene *artist*
Takanishi, Ruby N. *foundation administrator, researcher*
†Takesue, Renee Kimiyo *research geologist*
Talal, Marilynn Glick *poet*
Talarico, Maria Theresa *tax accountant*
Talavera, Francisco *pharmacist, writer*
†Talbot, Alfred Kenneth, Jr., *sociologist, educator*
Talbott, John *mayor*
†Talebi, Norollah *mathematics educator, researcher*
†Talent, Ronnie *publishing executive, writer*
Taliaferro, Henry Beauford, Jr., *retired lawyer*
Taliaferro-Regonini, Yvon Rochelle *accountant, consultant*
Tallett, Elizabeth Edith *biopharmaceutical company executive*
Talley, Robert Morrell *aerospace company executive*
Tallo, Diane *endocrinologist*
Talmage, David Wilson *microbiology and medical educator, physician, former university administrator*
Tambs, Lewis Arthur *diplomat, historian, educator*
Tamen, Harriet *lawyer*
†Tamimi, Maher M. *language educator*
Tamm, Mary Anne DeCamp *social services administrator*
Tan, Hui Qian *computer science and civil engineering educator*
Tanaka, J(eannie) E. *lawyer*
Tandler, Bernard *cell biology educator*
Tanenbaum, Jay Harvey *lawyer*
Tank, Gerhard Willi *obstetrician and gynecologist*
Tannenberg, Dieter E. A. *retired manufacturing company executive*
Tanner, Eric Benson *lawyer*
Tanner, Laurel Nan *education educator*
Tanner, Lynn *actress*
Tanner, Peggy *retired nurse*
Tansor, Robert Henry *investor*
Taplett, Lloyd Melvin *human resources management consultant*
Tapley, James Leroy *retired lawyer, railway corporation executive*
Taranto, Maria Antoinette *psychology researcher and educator*
Tarar, Afzal M. *management consultant*
Tarbi, William Rheinlander *secondary education educator, curriculum consultant, educational technology researcher*
Tardos, Anne *artist, writer, composer*
Taren, James Arthur *neurosurgeon, educator*
Tarjan, Robert Wegg *retired information services executive, part-time math teacher*
Tarkowski, Larry Michael *town official*
Tarnow, Malva May Wescoe *post-anesthesia care nurse*
Tarr, Curtis W. *business executive*
Tarrance, Vernon Lance, Jr., *public opinion research executive*
†Tarses, Jamie *television network executive*
Tarzian, Anita Jeanne *nurse, researcher, ethicist*
†Tashev, Kirsten *museum administrator*
†Tasker, Joseph *lawyer, educator*
†Tassin, Paul Dwayne *music educator*
Tassos, Alice Crowley *writer, linguist*
†Tate, Raymond Grant *research and consulting executive*
Tatgenhorst, Robert (Charles Tatgenhorst) *lawyer, educator*
Tatlock, Anne M. *trust company executive*
Taub, Nadine *law educator*
Tauber, Sonya Lynn *nurse*
Tauscher, Ellen O. *congresswoman*
Tavrow, Richard Lawrence *lawyer, corporate executive*
Tayler, Irene *English literature educator*
†Taylor, Billy (William Edward Taylor) *jazz musician*
Taylor, Casper R., Jr., *lobbyist, former state legislator*
Taylor, David George *retired banker*
Taylor, David Spencer *engineer*
Taylor, Edna Jane *retired employment program counselor*
†Taylor, Elizabeth Rosemond *actress*
Taylor, George Frederick *newspaper publisher, editor*
Taylor, James L. *naval officer*
Taylor, Jill Olsen *lawyer, artist*
Taylor, John Jackson (Jay Taylor) *writer, documentalist, retired foreign service officer*
Taylor, Karen Annette *mental health nurse*
Taylor, Kathleen (Christine Taylor) *physical chemist, researcher*
Taylor, Lesli Ann *pediatric surgery educator*
Taylor, Leslie George *mining executive, finance company executive*
Taylor, Lewis Jerome, Jr., *priest*
Taylor, Linda Rathbun *investment manager*
Taylor, Margaret Turner *clothing designer, architectural designer, economist, writer, planner*
Taylor, Mary Lee *retired college administrator*
†Taylor, Michelle Y. *human resources consultant*
Taylor, Murry Allan *retired forester*
Taylor, Nathalee Britton *nutritionist*
Taylor, Pamela Ann *social worker*
Taylor, Peyton Troy, Jr., *gynecologic oncologist, educator*
Taylor, Randall William *quality assurance administrator*
Taylor, Richard James *lawyer*
Taylor, Robert Morgan *electronics executive*
Taylor, Roy Lewis *botanist, educator*
Taylor, Thomas Fuller *religious society administrator*
Taylor, Velande Pingel *author, publisher*
†Taylor, Welton Ivan *microbiologist, consultant, food scientist*
Taylor, Wesley Bayard, Jr., *retired army officer*
Taylor, Wilson H. *retired diversified financial company executive*
Taylor-Brown, Cameron Ann *artist, educator, consultant*
Tazeau, Yvette Nicole *psychologist*
Teague, Frances Nicol *English language educator*
Teal, Monika Josepha *artist*
Teater, Dorothy Seath *retired county official*
Tecco, Romuald Gilbert Louis Joseph *violinist, concertmaster*
Tedesco, Paul Herbert *humanities educator*
Tedford, Charles Franklin *biophysicist*
Teeple, Fiona Diane *librarian, lawyer*
Teison, Herbert J. *editor, publisher*
Tejada, Audrey Dolar *artist, writer*
†Tejada, Roberto *poet, critic*
†Telesco, Grace A. *sociology and criminal justice educator*
†Temam, Roger M. *mathematician, educator*
Temerlin, Liener *advertising agency executive*
Temple, Joseph George, Jr., *retired pharmaceutical executive, retired chemicals executive*
Templin, Kenneth Elwood *paper company executive*
†Temsamani, Driss *marketing professional*
Tenenhaus, Mayer *plastic surgeon*
Teng, Shuye *research scientist*
†Teng, Xiaolin *education educator, researcher*
TenHoeve, Thomas *academic administrator*
Tenney, Frank Putnam *marketing executive*
†Teoli-Phelps, Brook Elaine *advocate, dance educator*
Teplow, Theodore Herzl *retired valve company executive*
Tepper, Howard *partner*
Tepper, Lloyd Barton *physician*
Terezis, Nick Louis *surgeon*
Ter Horst, Jerald Franklin *public affairs counsel*
Ter-Mikirtychev, Valerii Vartanovich *physicist, researcher*
Termini, Roseann Bridget *law educator*
Terp, Thomas Thomsen *lawyer*
Terrell, G. Irvin *lawyer*
Terris, Susan *physician, cardiologist*
†Terry, Barbara L. *human services administrator*
Terry, Clifford Lewis *journalist*
Terry, Kay Adell *marketing executive*
Terry, Richard Frank *data transcriber*
Tesarek, Dennis George *retired business consultant, writer, educator*
†Teshirogi, Jerry Takahide *aerospace engineer*
Tetelbaum, Solomon David *research engineer*
Tetley, Glen *choreographer*
Tew, E. James, Jr., *management services company executive*
†Tewfik, Diane Burak *occupational therapist, educator*
Textor, Robert Bayard *cultural anthropology writer, consultant, educator*
Thackray, Arnold Wilfrid *historian, foundation executive*
Thackston, Edward Lee *engineer, educator*
Thaler, Richard Winston, Jr., *investment banker*
Tham, Hilary *poet*
Tharp, Twyla *dancer, choreographer*
Tharpe, Frazier Eugene *journalist*
Thatcher, Gayle Marie *sales executive*
Thayer, Martha Ann *small business owner*
†Theberge, Norman Bartlett *educator, lawyer*
Theodoli-Braschi, Giovanni Angelo (Duke of Nemi, Grandee of Spain) *investment banker*
†Theoret, Julie Marie *mathematician, educator*
Theroux, Paul Edward *author*
Therrien, Anita Aurore *elementary school educator*
Therrien, Michel *former professional hockey coach*
Thiel, David Brian *physician assistant*
Thiel, Philip *design educator*
Thiele, Howard Nellis, Jr., *lawyer*
Thielen, Jean Rose *artist*
Thimm, Alfred Louis *management educator*
†Thios Jr., John Thomas *marriage and family therapist, information technology manager*
Thomajan, Robert *lawyer, management consultant*
Thoman, Henry Nixon *lawyer*
Thomas, Adrian Wesley *laboratory director*
Thomas, Betty *director, actress*
Thomas, Beverly Irene *special education educator, educational diagnostician, substance abuse counselor*
Thomas, Cherryl T. *former federal agency administrator*
Thomas, Dale *film, video and live event producer*
Thomas, Franklin Augustine *lawyer, consultant*
Thomas, Isiah Lord, III, *former professional basketball coach.*
Thomas, James Edward, Jr., *brokerage house executive*
Thomas, Joe Carroll *retired human resources director*
Thomas, Kenneth Glyndwr *mining executive*
Thomas, Larry Dee *retired corrections administrator, poet*
†Thomas, Matthew Shawn *civil engineer*
†Thomas, Meltonia Antionette *secondary school educator, music educator*
Thomas, Patricia Goodnow *journalist*
Thomas, Robert Rene *physician assistant, athletic trainer*
†Thomas, Stephen Crawford *social worker*
Thomas, Tarquin Craig *computer scientist, writer*
Thomas, Teresa Ann *microbiologist, educator*
Thomas, Tom *retired plastics company executive*
Thomas, Vickie Mueller *medical laboratory director*
Thomas, William Geraint *museum administrator*
†Thomas, William Griffith, III, *humanities educator, consultant*
†Thomas, Jr., Joseph M. *language educator*
Thomason, Harry Jack Lee, Jr., *mechanical engineer*
Thomas-Roots, Pamela M. *writer*
†Thomopoulos, Anthony D. *retired motion picture company executive*
Thompson, Alan Eric *economics educator*
Thompson, Ana Calzada *secondary education educator, mathematician*
Thompson, Barry Hammond *medical geneticist*
†Thompson, Bonita *writer*
Thompson, Craig Snover *corporate communications executive*
†Thompson, Diana Rosebud *poet, educator, history exhibit coordinator, marketing consultant, playwright, lyricist*
†Thompson, Emily *historian*
Thompson, Eugene Mayne *retired minister*
Thompson, Fred Dalton *former senator*
Thompson, Hunter Stockton *author, political analyst, journalist*
Thompson, J. Andy *bank executive*
Thompson, Jack Edward *mining company executive*
†Thompson, Jennifer B. *Olympic swimmer*
Thompson, John W. *information technology executive*
Thompson, Joyce Lurine *retired information systems specialist*
†Thompson, Kenneth *software engineer*
Thompson, Lola May *music educator, volunteer*
Thompson, Michael Alan *political cartoonist*
Thompson, Ralph Newell *former chemical corporation executive*
Thompson, Richard Lloyd *retired pastor*
Thompson, Richard Stephen *management consultant*
Thompson, Theodis *retired healthcare executive, health management consultant*
Thompson, Thomas Daniel *biology and chemistry educator*
Thomson, Alexander Bennett, Jr., *financial planner, tax and management consultant*
Thongsak, Vajeeprasee Thomas *business planning executive*
Thorn, Rosemary Kost *former librarian*

van Hengel, Maarten R. *financial executive*
†Van Himbergen, Thomas *manufacturing company executive*
van Hoften, James Dougal Adrianus *business executive, former astronaut*
†Van Hooser, Patricia Lou Scott *art educator*
Van Horn, Rebecca Ann *presentation specialist*
Van Houten, Elizabeth Ann *corporate communications executive, painter*
Van Houten, James Forester *educator, consultant, retired insurance company executive*
Vanier, Jacques *physicist*
van Itallie, Jean-Claude *playwright*
†Vankat, John Lyman *science educator, researcher*
Van Lone Trieschman, Janet Anne *graphic arts educator*
VanMeter, Vandelia L. *retired director*
Van Ness, John Ralph *university official, educator*
Van Ness, Patricia Catheline *composer, violinist*
†Van Ness, Stephen A. *systems analyst, writer*
Vannozzi, Thomas *cameraman*
Van Orden, Phyllis Jeanne *librarian, educator*
Van Riper, Kenneth Alan *astrophysicist and researcher*
van Schilfgaarde, Jan *retired agricultural engineer, government agricultural research service administrator*
Van Scotter, Richard Dale *education policy executive, writer*
Van Stone, William Webb *psychiatrist*
†Van Susteren, Greta Conway *news anchor, lawyer*
Van Tassel, Daniel Ellsworth *academic administrator, consultant, educator*
Van Tassel, James Henry *retired electronics executive*
Van Vleet, William Benjamin *retired lawyer, life insurance company executive*
Varacalli, Joseph Anthony *humanities educator, writer*
Vargo, Beth Copeland *curator*
†Varki, Ajit *medical educator*
Varner, Gary Robert *social services administrator, writer*
Varney, Suzanne Glaab *health facility administrator*
Varro, Barbara Joan *retired editor*
Vasenius, Linda Lea *librarian, consultant*
Vasholz, Lothar Alfred *retired insurance company executive*
†Vasilevski, Valeria *theater director, librettist*
Vasily, John Timothy *information systems executive, state government official*
Vasko, Peter Theodore Frederick *priest*
†Vassallo, Robert *physician, educator, research scientist*
Vaszily, Brian William *writer*
Vaughan, Gary David *history and government educator*
Vaughan, John Charles, III, *horticultural products executive*
Vaughan, Kenneth Harold *psychologist*
Vaughan, Nadine *psychologist*
†Vaughn, John *information technology manager, consultant*
Vaughn, Pamela W. *music educator*
Vaz, Katherine Anne *language educator*
Vázquez, Lourdes *poet*
†Veach, Allen Marshall *research physicist*
Veenhuis, Philip Edward *psychiatrist, educator, preventive medicine physician, administrator*
Vega, Alberto Leon *financial executive*
Vega, J. William *aerospace engineering executive, consultant*
Vejvoda, Edward *aerospace company executive*
†Velev, Miroslav N. *electrical engineer, educator*
†Velez Cruz, Virginia *poet*
†Velkley, Richard Lee *educator, journal editor*
Vellenga, Kathleen Osborne *retired state legislator*
†Velmurugan, Soundarapandian *microbiologist, researcher*
†Venkatu, Doulatabad A. *retired metallurgist*
Ventura, Jesse (James Janos) *former governor*
Vér, István László *acoustical engineer, consultant*
†Vera Negron, Sandra *literature educator, translator*
Verbov, Lev Falkovich *metallurgical engineer, writer, translator*
Verderber, Joseph Anthony *capital equipment company executive*
Verdery, David Norwood *broadcast programming executive*
Vergano, Lynn (Marilynn Bette Vergano) *artist*
†Vergara, Camilo José *photographer*
†Verma, Devesh *pharmaceutical executive, researcher*
†Verma, Geeta K. *science educator*
Vermel, Paul *conductor*
Vernon, Carl Atlee, Jr., *retired wholesale food distributor executive*
Vernon, Lawrence Gordon *librarian*
Vero, Radu *freelance medical and scientific illustrator, educator, writer, consultant*
Veronis, George *geophysicist, educator*
Verplanck, William Samuel *psychologist, educator*
Versch, Esther Marie *artist*
Verschraegen, Claire Florence *oncologist*
Veseth, Michael Aaron *economics educator*
Vesey, Mary Frances *writer, educator*
Vesper, Ethel Rose *language educator, consultant*
Vessey, John William, Jr., *army officer*
Vestal, Marilyn Anita *writer, researcher, educator*
†Veverka, Ruth Tonry *retired educator*
Vichiola, Christopher Michael *educator, writer*
Vickers, George Ross *non-profit organization executive, sociology educator*
Vickers, Mark Stephen *business educator, travel industry executive, sculptor, painter*
Vickers, Stanley *biochemical pharmacologist*

Vickery, Byrdean Eyvonne Hughes (Mrs. Charles Everett Vickery Jr.) *retired library services administrator*
Victor, Jay *retired dermatologist*
Viest, Ivan M(iroslav) *consulting structural engineer*
Viets, Elaine Frances *writer*
†Vigil, David Charles *lawyer*
Vila, Adis Maria *lawyer, academic administrator*
Vilenchik, Michael Marc *biophysicist, oncologist*
Vilk, Victor Joseph *retired radiologist*
†Villaire, Holly Hennen Hood *theater producer, director, actress, educator*
†Villanueva, Ronald *endocrinologist, educator*
Villella, Edward Joseph *ballet dancer, educator, choreographer, artistic director, performing arts administrator*
Villforth, John Carl *health physicist*
Vinar, Benjamin *lawyer*
†Vincent, Bruce Havird *oil and gas company executive*
Vincent, Charles Eagar, Jr., *sports columnist*
Vincent, Hal Wellman *marine corps officer, investor*
Vinet, Luc *physicist*
Vinson, James Spangler *academic administrator*
Viorst, Judith Stahl *author*
Viorst, Milton *writer*
Virkhaus, Taavo *symphony orchestra conductor*
Viscardi, Peter G. *risk management and environmental affairs executive*
Vita, Steven *poet*
†Vitale, David J. *former banker*
Vitale, Paul *accountant*
Vitt, David Aaron *medical manufacturing company executive*
†Viverito, Louis Samuel *state legislator*
Vlachos, Peter George *economics educator*
†Vlazny, John George *bishop*
Vo, Huu Dinh *pediatrician, educator*
Vo, Nghia Van *materials scientist, electrical engineer*
Voelker, Margaret Irene (Meg Voelker) *gerontology, medical, surgical nurse*
Voell, Richard Allen *retired private investor*
Vogel, H. Victoria *psychotherapist, trauma, post-traumatic stress disorder and addiction recovery counselor and educator, author*
Vogel, Julius *retired consulting actuary*
Vogel, William Dickerman *financial services executive*
†Vogt, Christy *music educator*
Vohs, James Arthur *health care program executive*
†Voigt, Cynthia *author*
†Voigt, Heidi M *music educator*
Voketaitis, Arnold Matthew *bass-baritone, educator*
Volcker, Paul A. *economist*
Voldman, Steven Howard *electrical engineer*
Volk, Patricia Gay *fiction writer, essayist*
Volkering, Mary Joe *special education educator*
Volkhardt, John Malcolm *food company executive*
Volkman, Alvin *physician, research scientist, educator, retired*
Vollmer, Howard Robert *artist, photographer*
Volpe, Edmond L(oris) *college president*
Volpe, Eileen Rae *retired special education educator*
von Ber, Ina *management educator, clinical psychologist*
Von Brandenstein, Patrizia *production designer*
Von Burg, Frederick E., Sr., *secondary school educator, writer*
Vonderbrink, Gerald William *retired academic administrator, property manager*
von Furstenberg, Betsy *actress, writer*
Von Gonten, Kevin Paul *priest, liturgist, theologian*
Von Herrmann, Denise Keefer *educator*
von Hoffman, Nicholas *writer, former journalist*
von Sauers, Joseph F. *lawyer*
VonSchulze-Delitzsch, Marilyn Wandling (Lady VonSchulze-Delitzsch) *artist, writer*
Vook, Frederick Ludwig *physicist, consultant*
Voorhees, James Dayton, Jr., *lawyer*
Voorhees, Kent Jay *chemist*
Voss, Omer Gerald *truck company executive*
†Vrenios, Alexander *computer software systems developer*
Vronskiy, Vadim Viktorovich *financial company executive*
Vu, Joseph Duong *financial educator*
†Vucanovich, Barbara Farrell *retired congressman*
†Wachal, Barbara Schwarz *writer, educator*
Wachbrit, Jill Barrett *accountant, tax specialist*
Wachob, Tom Webb, Jr., *retired obstetrician-gynecologist*
†Wachtel, Shirley Russak *English language educator, writer*
Wachtell, Esther *non-profit management executive, consultant*
Waddle, John Frederick *former retail chain executive*
Wade, David Stuart *surgeon*
†Wadi Ramahi, Shada Jamal *physicist, researcher*
†Wadleigh, Kevin Richard *mathematician*
Wadley, M. Richard *consumer products executive*
Wadsworth, Jacqueline Dorèt *private investor*
Wagman, Robert John *journalist, author*
Wagner, Ann Prentice *art historian*
Wagner, Arthur Ward, Jr., *lawyer*
Wagner, Diana Mae *English language educator*
Wagner, Durrett *former publisher, picture service executive*
Wagner, Ellyn S(anti) *mathematics educator*
Wagner, John Philip *safety engineering educator, science researcher*
Wagner, Julia A(nne) *retired editor*
Wagner, Leana Moree *computer executive, graphic designer, fine artist*
Wagner, Marilyn Faith *retired elementary school educator*
Wagner, Mark Anthony *videotape editor*
Wagner, Richard *athletics consultant, former baseball team executive*

†Wagner, Thomas Joseph *lawyer, insurance company executive*
Wagoner, Geraldine Vander Pol *music educator*
Wahl, Floyd Michael *geologist*
Wahlsteen, Herbert Gunnar *music publisher, writer*
Wain, Christopher Henry Fairfax Moresby *actuary, insurance and investment consultant*
Wait, Eugene Meredith *historian, writer*
†Wait, Ronald A. *state legislator*
Waite, Gerald Phillip *English language educator*
Waitley, Douglas D. *writer*
†Waitz, Michael Louis *editorial trainer*
Wakefield, Dawn Lee *communications and fundraising consultant*
Wakeman, Thomas Herbert, III, *civil engineer, regional administrator*
Walasek, Otto Frank *chemical engineer, biochemist, photographer*
Wald, Francine Joy Weintraub (Mrs. Bernard J. Wald) *physicist, academic administrator*
Wald, Mary S. *retired risk management and personal finance educator*
†Wald, Michael H. *lawyer, educator*
Walden, Joseph Lawrence *career officer*
Walder, Noeleen Gwynaeth *lawyer*
Waldon, Alton Ronald, Jr., *judge*
Walenga, Jeanine Marie *medical educator, researcher*
Walker, Craig Michael *lawyer*
Walker, Debra *artist*
Walker, Fred Elmer *broadcasting executive*
Walker, Garland Wayne *aircraft inspector*
Walker, Gordon Davies *former government official, writer, lecturer, consultant*
Walker, Helen Smith *retired real estate broker*
Walker, James Steven *osteopath, emergency physician*
Walker, John Lowell *music educator*
Walker, John Seibels *artist*
†Walker, Jordan Clyde, Sr., *lawyer, real estate executive*
Walker, Lars *writer*
Walker, Loren Haines *electrical engineer*
Walker, Mark A. *lawyer*
†Walker, Richard E., Jr., *music educator*
†Walker, Richard Henry *lawyer*
†Walker, Ronald C. *retired magazine publisher*
Walker, Roslyn Adele *museum director*
†Walker, Shonn Wayne *lawyer*
Walker-Williams, Hope Denise *administrator, business consultant*
WalkingStick, Kay *artist, art educator*
Walkowiak, Robert G. *retired obstetrician and gynecologist*
†Wall, Carolyn Raimondi *communications executive*
Wall, Frederick Theodore *retired chemistry educator*
Wall, M. Danny *financial services company executive*
Wallace, F. Blake *aerospace executive, mechanical engineer*
Wallace, Jane House *retired geologist*
Wallace, Michele *writer, educator*
Wallace, Robert Carlson *real estate investor*
Wallace, Robert Earl *geologist*
†Wallace, Stewart S. *career military officer*
Wallach-Levy, Wendee Esther *astrophotographer*
†Wallack, Rina Evelyn *lawyer*
Waller, John Henry *author*
Waller, Martha S. *retired English educator, writer*
Waller, Ray Albert *statistician*
Wallerstein, Judith Saretsky *psychologist, researcher*
Wallin, James Peter *lawyer*
Wallis, Diana Lynn *artistic director*
Wallis, John James (Jimmy Wallis) *comedian, impressionist, ventriloquist, comedy writer, Internet site designer*
Walls, Carmage Lee, Jr., *newspaper publisher/executive, consultant*
†Walls, Ray *computer science educator*
Wallschlaeger, Josephine Ingeborg *mental health nurse*
Walner, Robert Joel *lawyer*
Walser, Clarke L. *management consultant*
Walsh, Diane *pianist*
Walsh, Dolores Ann Gonczo (Lorry Walsh) *special education educator*
Walsh, Joseph Thomas *state supreme court justice*
Walsh, Juanita Marie *theatre educator, actress*
Walsh, M. Emmet *actor*
Walsh, Nan *fine artist, painter, sculptor, consultant*
Walsh, Roger N. *psychiatry, philosophy and anthropology educator*
Walsh, William Albert *management consultant, former naval officer*
Walston, Lola Inge *dietitian*
Walter, J. Jackson *consultant*
Walters, Donald Lee *education educator*
Walters-Lucy, Jean Marie *personal growth educator, consultant*
†Waltner, Beverly Ruland *artist*
Walton, Donald Cameron, Jr., *retired obstetrician, gynecologist*
Walton, Harold Vincent *former agricultural engineering educator, academic administrator*
Walton, Kami Sue *public relations executive*
†Waltrip, Darrell Lee *race car driver*
Waltz, Alan Kent *clergyman, denominational executive*
Waltz, Kenneth Neal *political science educator*
†Wambaugh, Joseph A., Jr., *author*
†Wang, Allan Xu Hui *physician*
Wang, Chen-ku *retired library director*
Wang, George K.F. *international lawyer*
Wang, Leon Ru-Liang *civil engineer, educator*
Wang, Qigui *materials engineer, researcher*
Wang, Qin *computer engineer, researcher*
Wang, Wanlong *engineer, researcher*
Wang, Wei *research scientist*
†Wang, Xi Cheng (David Wang) *mechanical engineer*

Wantland, William Charles *retired bishop, lawyer*
Warach, Marie *artist*
Ward, Albert Eugene *archaeologist, ethnohistorian, research center executive*
Ward, Anthony G. *stock, options and futures exchange consultant*
†Ward (Bailey), Daisy Dale *writer*
Ward, Jeannette Poole *retired psychologist, educator*
Ward, JoAnn Boettner *convention and tourist bureau administrator*
†Ward, Nari *sculptor*
Ward, Vicki Dawne *family nurse practitioner, rural health specialist*
Warder, Richard Currey, Jr., *dean, mechanical aerospace engineering educator*
†Wardrop, Richard M., Jr., *former steel holding company executive*
Ware, James Latané *plastic surgeon*
Wargowsky, Robin Kay *nurse*
Warheit, Peter S. *anesthesiologist*
†Waring, Belle *poet*
Waring, Mary Louise *retired social worker*
Warne, William Robert *economist*
Warner, Heidi Celeste *clinical trials consultant*
Warner, Shauna Ruth *city official*
Warner, Walter Duke *corporate executive, director*
Warnstadt, Steven H. *state legislator*
Warren, Cindy Michelle *author*
Warren, John William *professional society administrator*
†Warren, Julia Diane *musician, music educator*
Warren, Mark Edward *lawyer*
Warres, Margie Black *social work administrator emerita*
Wartluft, David Jonathan *retired librarian, minister*
†Warwick, Margaret Ann *health science facility administrator, consultant*
Washburn, Caryl Anne *occupational therapist*
Washburn, Donald Arthur *business executive, private investor*
Washburn, Dorothy A. *entrepreneur*
†Washburn, Patricia Cheyne *retired psychologist, environmentalist, conservationist*
Washington, Denzel *actor*
†Washington, Donna Janel *engineer*
Washington, Valora *non-profit administrator*
†Washington-Cretter, Brian E. *minister, sheet metal assembler, riveter*
Waskow, Joyce Ann *school administrator*
†Wasserman, Gerald Steward *psychobiology educator*
Wasserman, Helene Waltman *art dealer, artist*
Wasserman, Karen Boling *clinical psychologist, nursing consultant*
†Wasserman, Paul S. *corporate development executive*
Wasserstein, Wendy *playwright*
Wasson, James Walter *aircraft electronics manufacturing company executive*
Watanabe, Kyoichi A(loysius) *chemist, researcher, pharmacology educator*
Waterford, Gwen Antionette *poet*
Waters, Betty Lou *newspaper reporter, writer*
Waters, Donald Eugene *academic administrator*
Waters, Ed (Edward Sarsfield Waters) *screenwriter, television producer, writer*
Waters, Terrance J *architect*
Waters, William Carter, III, *retired internist, educator*
Watkins, Dean Allen *electronics executive, educator*
Watkins, James David *federal official, military officer*
Watkins, Ronda Gail *interior design company executive*
†Watkins, Wendy R. *artist*
Watkins, Wesley Wade *retired congressman*
Watkins, William David *editor, writer, consultant, mentor*
Watring, Watson Glenn *retired gynecologic oncologist, educator*
Watson, Cheryl S. *cell and molecular biology educator, researcher*
Watson, Donald Charles *cardiothoracic surgeon, educator*
Watson, George Henry, Jr., *journalist, broadcaster*
Watson, George W. *energy executive*
Watson, John Michael *lawyer*
Watson, Kathy *political organization administrator*
Watson, Marilyn Kaye *elementary education educator*
†Watson, Patricia Jane *writer, editor, sculptor*
Wattenberg, Albert *physicist, educator*
Watts, Ginny (Virginia C. Watts) *artist*
Watts, Glenn Ellis *union official*
Watts, J. C., Jr., *former congressman, retired football player*
Watts, John Ransford *university administrator*
†Watts, Karen Southall *management consultant*
Watts, Mary Ann *retired elementary education educator*
Waud, Roger Neil *economist, educator*
Wawrose, Frederick Eugene *psychiatrist*
Waxman, Ronald *computer engineer*
Waxman, Seth Paul *lawyer*
Way, Jacob Edson, III, *museum director*
Wearn, Wilson Cannon *retired media executive*
Weathersby, George Byron *business executive*
†Weaver, Agnes Jin Ai *medical/surgical nurse*
Weaver, Barbara Frances *librarian, consultant*
Weaver, Carolyn Leslie *economist, public policy researcher*
Weaver, Charles Horace *educator*
†Weaver, Franklin Thomas *retired newspaper executive*
Weaver, Howard C. *newspaper executive*
Weaver, Leah Ann *journalist, speech writer*
Weaver, William Charles *retired industrial executive*
Weaver, William Schildecker *retired electric power industry executive*

Willson, Mary Frances *ecology researcher, educator*
Willson, Parker O. *non-profit organization administrator*
†Wilmer, Archie, III, *mathematician, educator*
Wilmore, Douglas Wayne *surgeon, educator*
Wilpon, Fred *professional baseball team executive, real estate developer*
Wilson, Almon Chapman *surgeon, physician, retired naval officer*
†Wilson, Anne Judith *writer, educator*
†Wilson, Brandon Laine *writer, advertising and public relations consultant, explorer*
Wilson, C. Daniel, Jr., *library director*
Wilson, Colin Henry *writer*
Wilson, Doris Fanuzzi *learning disabilities consultant, educator*
Wilson, Dwight Liston *former military officer, investment advisor*
Wilson, Frances C. *career military officer*
Wilson, Glen Parten *professional society administrator*
Wilson, Hugh Steven *lawyer*
Wilson, Jane *artist*
Wilson, Karen Lee *museum director*
Wilson, Kenneth Geddes *physics research administrator*
Wilson, Lanford *playwright*
Wilson, Lawrence Woodrow *retired air force officer, family physician*
Wilson, Linda Ann *renal dialysis nurse*
Wilson, Lois M. *minister*
Wilson, Mary Elizabeth *geriatrics nurse*
Wilson, Matthew Frederick *former newspaper editor*
Wilson, Melissa Elizabeth *artist, educator*
Wilson, Melvin Edmond *civil engineer*
Wilson, Patricia Potter *library science and reading educator, educational and library consultant*
Wilson, Paul W., Jr., *lawyer, entrepreneur*
†Wilson, Pete *former governor*
Wilson, Ralph Cookerly, Jr., *professional football team executive*
Wilson, Rhys Thaddeus *lawyer*
Wilson, Richard George *journalism educator*
Wilson, Robert M. *business executive*
Wilson, Robin Scott *retired academic administrator, writer*
†Wilson, S. Liane *bank executive*
Wilson, Sloan *writer, educator*
Wilson, Tamra McElroy *writer*
Wilson, Virgil James, III, *lawyer*
Wilson, Walter Clinton *retired gas industry executive*
†Wilson, Warren Samuel *clergyman, bishop*
†Wilson, Zara D *speaker, consultant*
†Wilson-Stewart, Marilyn Lucille *retired human resources director*
†Wimmer, Kathryn *retired elementary school educator*
Wimpress, Gordon Duncan, Jr., *corporate consultant, foundation executive*
Winder, Robert Owen *mathematician, computer engineer, geophysicist*
†Windland, Evert *music educator*
Windom, Stephen Ralph *former leutenant governor, lawyer*
Windom, William *actor*
†Winfield, Paul Edward *actor*
Wingate, Bettye Faye *librarian, educator*
Wingham, Erma Doris *secondary education educator*
Wink, Doreen Musto *interior designer*
Winkelman, Johnny Martin *lawyer, real estate development consultant and Indian gaming consultant*
Winnowski, Thaddeus Richard (Ted Winnowski) *bank executive*
Winokur, Neil *photographer*
Winslet, Kate *actress*
†Winslow, David Allen *chaplain, retired naval officer*
Winslow, F(rancis) Dana *judge, former record company owner*
Winslow, John Franklin *lawyer*
Winslow, Julian Dallas *retired lawyer, historian, writer*
Winsor, David John *cost consultant*
Winston, Thomas George *engineering educator, consultant*
†Winter, Nancy Fitz *media and public relations executive*
Winter, Richard Samuel, Jr., *computer training company owner, writer*
†Winterbottom, Goddard Williams *retired editor*
Winterling, George Alfred *meteorologist, broadcaster*
†Winters, David Forrest *state legislator*
Winters, Sheila *family nurse practitioner*
Winterstein, James Fredrick *academic administrator*
Wintle, Rosemarie *biomedical electronics engineer*
Winton, Howard Phillip *retired optometrist*
Winwood, Stephen Lawrence *musician, composer*
Wirth, Russell D. L., Jr., *investment and merchant banker*
Wirtz, William Willard *lawyer*
Wirz, Pascal Francois *trust company executive*
Wirzba, Norman R. *philosophy educator*
†Wise, Allen F. *health care administrator*
Wise, Patricia *opera singer and educator*
Wise, Sandra Casber *lawyer*
Wise, Susan Tamsberg *management and communications consultant, speaker*
Wise, William Allen *energy company executive*
Wisehart, Arthur McKee *property management executive, lawyer*
Wisehart, Mary Ruth *retired religious organization executive*
Wiseman, Douglas Carl *education educator, department chairman, dean*
Wiseman, Jay Donald Donald *photographer, inventor, mechanical designer and contractor, land developer, writer*

Wiseman, Tamara Wynese *writer, director*
Wishnia, Kenneth J.A. *writer, translator, educator*
Wisniewski, Thomas Joseph *music educator*
Wisoff, Hugh Solomon *neurosurgeon*
Wiswall, Dorothy Roller *language educator*
Witcher, Daniel Dougherty *retired pharmaceutical company executive*
†Witkowski, Allen *aeronautical engineer*
Witt, Hugh Ernest *technology consultant*
†Witt, James Lee *business executive*
Witt, Nancy Camden *artist*
Witte, Ann Dryden *economics educator*
Witte, Arline (Lyn Witte) *author, poet*
Witte, Merlin Michael *oil company executive*
†Wittebols, James Henry *communications educator*
Wittich, John Jacob *retired academic administrator, business executive*
Wittig, Raymond Shaffer *lawyer, information technology manager, consultant*
Wittman, Allan Henry *publishing executive*
Wittmann, Dietmar H. *surgery educator*
Woelflein, Kevin Gerard *banker*
Woessner, Warren Dexter *lawyer*
Woestendiek, John, Jr., (William John Woestendiek) *newspaper reporter*
Wofford, Terry *artist*
†Wohlschlaeger, Frederick George *lawyer*
Wolaner, Robin Peggy *internet and magazine publisher*
Wold, Margaret Barth *religion educator, author*
†Wolf, Anna Madlene *music educator*
Wolf, Christine Strelow *piano teacher*
Wolf, Cynthia Tribelhorn *librarian, library educator*
Wolf, Dale Edward *state official*
Wolf, Edith Maletz *retired educator*
Wolf, Frank *business educator, consulting executive*
Wolf, Larry Louis *biology educator*
Wolf, William Martin *computer company executive, consultant*
Wolfberg, Melvin Donald *optometrist, educational administrator, consultant*
Wolfe, Gary John *wildlife conservationist and biologist*
Wolfe, Gregory Baker *international relations educator*
†Wolfe, James Michael *education educator, researcher*
Wolfe, Joan Luedders *non-profit organizations consultant*
Wolfe, Linda *writer*
Wolfe, Townsend Durant, III, *retired art museum director, curator*
Wolff, Brian Richard *metal products executive*
†Wolff, Dennis C. *farm owner*
Wolff, Henning Otto August *private public school administrator*
Wolff, Manfred Ernst *medicinal chemist, pharmaceutical company executive*
Wolff, Peter Adalbert *physicist, educator*
†Wolfgang, Hugh Edwin *application developer*
Wolfman, Ira Joel *editor, writer*
Wolfram, David Anthony *computer scientist*
Wolfson, Michael George *lawyer*
Wollert, Gerald Dale *retired food company executive, investor*
Wollman Rusoff, Jane Susan *journalist, writer*
Wolotkiewicz, Marian M. *business executive*
Woltering, Margaret Mae *retired secondary school educational consultant*
†Wolverton, Mark *writer*
†Wolverton, Susan E. Quinn *secondary school educator*
Wolverton, Terry L(ynn) *writer, consultant*
†Womack, Nora Lynn *marketing professional*
Wonders, William Clare *geography educator*
Wong, David Yue *academic administrator, physics educator*
Wong, Elaine Dang *foundation executive*
Wong, Jeffrey Yun Chung *radiation oncologist, medical researcher*
Wong, Kainam Thomas *electrical engineer*
†Wong, Kuok-Shoong Daniel *research scientist*
Wong, Liliane *architect, architecture educator*
Wong-Diaz, Francisco Raimundo *lawyer, educator*
Woo, Jonathan C. G. *chemist, portfolio manager, management consultant*
Wood, Allen John *electrical engineer, consultant*
†Wood, Anne Hillsman *writer*
Wood, Corinne *former state official*
Wood, Diane Pamela *judge*
Wood, Frances Diane *medical secretary, artist*
Wood, Joan *retired chemist*
Wood, John Arthur *nurse*
Wood, Kate *artist*
†Wood, Margo *academic administrator*
Wood, Marian Starr *publishing company executive*
Wood, Norma J. *nurse practitioner*
Wood, Robert Charles *lawyer, real estate developer*
Wood, Robert Coldwell *political scientist*
Wood, Vivian Poates *mezzo soprano, educator, writer*
Wood, William Preston *author, lawyer*
Wood, Willis Bowne, Jr., *retired utilities executive*
Woodard, Deana Safford *artist, travel consultant*
Woodbridge, John Dunning *history and church history educator*
Woodbury, Nathalie Ferris Sampson *anthropologist, editor*
Wooden, John Robert *former basketball coach*
†Woodland, N. Joseph *retired optical engineer, retired mechanical engineer*
Woodman, Jean Wilson *educator, consultant*
Woodring, Margaret Daley *architect, planner*
†Woodrow-Lafield, Karen Ann *demographer*
Woodruff, Truman O(wen) *physicist, emeritus educator*
Woodruff, Virginia *broadcast journalist, writer*
Woodrum, Patricia Ann *librarian*
†Woods, Alison *publisher*

†Woods, Cheryl *financial analyst*
Woods, Christine L. *manufacturing company executive*
Woods, David Lyndon *publishing and broadcast executive, former federal agency executive*
Woods, Harriett Ruth *retired political organization president*
Woods, Phyllis Michalik *librarian*
Woods, Sandra Kay *real estate executive*
Woodside, George Robert *computer software developer*
Woodsworth, Anne *university administrator, librarian*
Woodward, Clinton Benjamin, Jr., *civil engineering educator*
Woodward, John Russell *motion picture production executive*
Woodward, Thomas Morgan *actor*
Woodward, William Lee *retired savings bank executive*
Wooldridge, William Charles *lawyer*
Woolsey, John Munro, Jr., *retired lawyer*
Woolworth, Susan Valk *primary school educator*
Woosnam, Ian Harold *professional golfer*
Wooten, Cecil Aaron *retired religious organization administrator*
Wooten, Frank Thomas *retired research facility executive*
Workman, Kayleen Marie *special education and adult education educator*
Workman, Willard Allyn *association executive*
Worner, Theresa Marie *internist, educator*
†Worrall, John L. *criminologist*
Worrell, Cynthia Celeste *school nurse*
Worrell, Richard Vernon *orthopedic surgeon, college dean, dean*
Worth, Gary James *communications executive*
Worthen, John Edward *retired academic administrator*
Worthey, Carol *composer*
Worthington, Daniel Glen *lawyer, educator*
Wortman, William Allen *librarian*
Woskow, Catherine Rose *artist*
Wozniak, Stephen Gary *computer scientist*
Wren, Stephen Corey *mathematician, inventor*
Wright, Beth Segal *art historian, educator*
†Wright, Brian Richard *lawyer, banker*
†Wright, Brian Theodore *retired engineering executive*
†Wright, Dell *residential care and treatment facility executive,*
Wright, Donald Franklin *retired newspaper executive*
†Wright, Elizabeth Rebecca *humanities educator*
Wright, Franz Paul *poet, writer, translator*
Wright, Gladys Stone *music educator, composer, writer*
Wright, James David *sociology educator, writer*
Wright, Judith Rae *retired accountant*
Wright, Mae A. *engineering, communications and nuclear waste management specialist*
Wright, Max *information processing executive, consultant, youth leadership corporate training executive*
Wright, Nancy Means *author, educator*
Wright, Randolph Earle *retired petroleum company executive*
Wright, Robert Payton *lawyer*
Wright, William Wynn *chemist*
Wriston, Kathryn Dineen *lawyer, business executive*
Wroblowa, Halina Stefania *electrochemist*
Wruble, Bernhardt Karp *lawyer*
Wruble, Brian Frederick *private investor*
Wruck, Erich-Oskar *retired foreign language educator, administrator*
Wu, Andy Ting *research scientist*
Wu, Margaret Anne *computer scientist, educator*
†Wu, Xinglu *retired, writer*
Wulf, Janie Scott McIlwaine *gifted and talented education educator*
Wunderlich, Howard Jeffrey *lawyer*
Wunsch, Kathryn Sutherland *retired lawyer*
Wyatt, Marcia Jean *fine arts educator, administrative assistant*
Wyatt, Robert Lee, IV, *lawyer*
Wyatt, Robert Saunders *executive search consultant*
Wyatt, Susan Melinda Clough *career counselor, writer*
Wyche, Samuel D(avid) *sportscaster*
Wykoff, Beverly Young *social worker*
Wylan, Barbara *artist*
†Wyle, Noah *actor*
Wylie, Pamela Jane *writer, producer, consultant, small business owner*
Wynar, Bohdan Stephen *librarian, writer, editor*
Wynn, Karla Wray *artist, agricultural products company executive*
Wynne, Terry Lynne *career counselor, trainer, writer*
Wyrtki, Klaus *oceanography educator*
Wyshak, Lillian Worthing *lawyer*
†Xiang, Mengqing *molecular biologist*
†Xiao, Jizhong *engineering educator, researcher*
Xu, Chen-Wei *data processing executive*
†Xu, Hui *physician*
†Xu, J.M. (Jimmy) *physicist, educator, engineer*
Yack, Patrick Ashley *editor*
Yackel, James William *mathematician, academic administrator*
Yadav, Sunil *mechanical engineer*
Yadrick, Robert Martin *occupational analyst*
Yaeger, Therese Francis *management professional*
Yakich, David Eli *international sales executive*
†Yale, Melpomene Fotine *anthropologist, archaeologist, art historian, conservator, researcher*
Yamaguchi, Kristi Tsuya *ice skater*
Yamamoto, Joe *psychiatrist, educator*
Yang, Xiangzhong *research scientist, administrator, educator*
Yang, Xiaoping *engineering researcher*
†Yang, Zejiang *statistician, educator*
Yannella, Donald *educator*

Yannuzzi, Giuseppe Alberto *elementary education educator, writer*
Yao, James Tsu-Ping *retired civil engineer*
†Yao, Yongwei *mathematician, researcher*
Yarbro, Alan David *lawyer*
Yarbrough, Kathryn Davis *public health nurse*
Yarchoan, Robert *clinical immunologist, researcher*
†Yared, Gabriel *composer*
†Yarick-Cross, Doris *voice educator, soprano*
Yarington, Charles Thomas, Jr., *surgeon, administrator*
Yates, David John C. *chemist, researcher*
†Yates, Karen E. *research scientist*
†Yates, Steven A. *artist, curator*
Yates, William Tennyson, II, *educational consultant, management consultant*
Yavorsky, James Anthony *chemist, educator*
†Yde, Jacqulyn Rae *interior designer, architectural colorist*
Ye, Nan *engineer*
Yeager, Anson Anders *writer, former columnist and newspaper editor*
Yeager, Kurt Eric *research institute official*
Yeager, Mark Leonard *lawyer*
Yeh, Jung-Hua *senior mechanical engineer*
†Yen, Bing Cheng *retired civil engineer, retired engineering educator*
Yen, Duen Hsi *corporate executive, physicist*
Yen, Wen Liang *retired aerospace engineer*
Yerion, Michael Ross *civil engineer*
Yetto, John Henry *company executive*
Yglesias, Rafael Jose *novelist*
Yielding, K. Lemone *physician*
†Yielding, (Mildred) Louise *maternal/infant nurse*
†Yin, Zhiping *engineer*
Ying, Jackie *chemical engineer, educator*
Yingling, Robert Granville, Jr., *accountant*
Yitts, Rose Marie *nursery school executive*
Ynda, Mary Lou *artist, educator*
Yngve, Victor H. *linguist, researcher*
Yntema, Mary Katherine *retired mathematics educator*
Yocam, Delbert Wayne *retired software products company executive*
†Yocam, Eric Wayne *engineer*
Yodaiken, Ralph E. *pathologist, occupational medicine physician*
Yoder, Anna Mary *reading educator*
Yoder, Myron Eugene *secondary school educator*
Yoder, Randall D. *music educator*
†Yoh, Harold Lionel, Jr., *retired engineering, construction and management company executive*
Yollick, Bernard Lawrence *otolaryngologic surgeon*
Yolton, John William *philosopher, educator*
†Yomoah, Bruno Kyapuoku *language educator, consultant*
Yong, Raymond Nen-Yiu *civil engineering educator*
Yood, Harold Stanley *retired internist*
Yool, George Richard *dean*
†Yoon, Sei Seung *engineer*
†York, Robert Lee, Jr., *health facility administrator*
York, Walter Allen *cinematographer*
Yost, Paula Lynn *accountant*
†Yost, Randy *secondary school educator*
Yost, William Albert *psychology educator, hearing researcher*
Youmans, Julian Ray *neurosurgeon, educator*
Young, Andrew Jackson *civil rights leader, clergyman, former mayor, former ambassador, former congressman*
Young, C. Clifton *former state supreme court justice*
Young, Deborah (Deborah Ayling Yanowitz) *social worker, librarian*
†Young, Edwin S. W. *federal agency official*
Young, Elizabeth Bell *consultant*
Young, George R. *educator*
Young, James E. *business executive, engineer*
Young, Jay Maitland *healthcare communications consultant*
Young, Jennifer Law *photojournalist, documentary producer*
Young, Jerry Wesley *retired animal nutrition educator*
Young, John Alan *electronics company executive*
Young, John Hardin *lawyer, corporate executive*
Young, Judith Anne *animal conservationist*
†Young, Katharine Galloway *writer*
Young, Kim Ann *health facility administrator*
Young, Leo *electrical engineer*
Young, Margaret Chong *elementary education educator*
Young, Michael Kent *dean, lawyer, educator*
Young, Patrick *writer, editor*
Young, Richard Alan *association executive*
Young, Ruth Brooks *retired elementary education educator*
Young, Sean (Mary Sean Young) *actress*
Young, Sharon Laree *mathematics educator*
Young, Steve G. *former labor union administrator*
Young, Teresa Gail Hilger *adult education educator*
Young, Virgil Monroe *education educator*
Younger, Betty Nichols *social worker*
†Youngman, Paul A. *language educator*
Youngs, Diane Campfield *learning disabilities specialist, educator*
Youngstrom, Paul Clarence *anesthesiologist*
Younker, Kathleen Teuber *pianist, music educator*
Youst, David Bennett *career development educator*
Yu, David U.L. *physicist, researcher*
Yu, Fermin Tong *retired surgeon*
†Yu, Jessica *director, producer, writer, editor*
†Yu, Jun *biologist*
Yue, Alfred Shui-choh *metallurgical engineer, educator*
Yun, James Kyoon *electrical engineer*

Professional Index

AGRICULTURE

UNITED STATES

ALABAMA

Montgomery
Frazer, Stuart Harrison, III, *cotton merchant*

Tuskegee Institute
Hill, Walter A. *agricultural sciences educator, researcher*

ARIZONA

Sun City
†Coffman, Harold Emerson *retired agricultural products supplier, retail merchant*

ARKANSAS

Humphrey
Wilson, Victoria Jane Simpson *farmer, nurse*

CALIFORNIA

Berkeley
Perloff, Jeffrey Mark *agricultural and resource economics educator*

Fresno
Epperson, Robert Dale *farmer*

Modesto
†Gallo, Ernest *vintner*
†Gallo, Joseph E. *vintner*

Napa
Chiarella, Peter Ralph *vintner*

Pacific Palisades
Jennings, Marcella Grady *rancher, investor*

San Diego
†Caughlin, Stephenie Jane *organic farmer*

San Francisco
Hills, Austin Edward *vineyard executive*

San Jose
D'Arrigo, Stephen, Jr., *agricultural company executive*

COLORADO

Denver
Decker, Peter Randolph *rancher, former state official*
†Lothrop, Robert S. *agricultural studies educator*

Springfield
Wessler, Melvin Dean *farmer, rancher*

DISTRICT OF COLUMBIA

Washington
Jorgensen, Ann *farmer*
†Ribaudo, Marc Owen *agricultural economist*

FLORIDA

Gainesville
Nair, Ramachandran P.K. *agroforestry educator, researcher*

Milton
Jose, Shibu *agriculture educator, researcher*

Sun City Center
Freeman, Myra Jessie *retired farm owner, writer*

GEORGIA

Atlanta
Stimpert, Michael Alan *agricultural products company executive*
Wright, Daniel *wine specialist, consultant*

HAWAII

Waialua
Singlehurst, Dona Geisenheyner *horse farm owner*

ILLINOIS

Danville
Konsis, Kenneth Frank *forester, educator*

Jacksonville
Randall, Robert Quentin *retired nursery executive*

Northfield
Bruns, Nicolaus, Jr., *retired agricultural chemicals company executive, lawyer*

Tunnel Hill
Webb, O. Glenn *retired farm supplies company executive*

Urbana
Hill, Lowell Dean *agricultural marketing educator*

INDIANA

Hanover
Heck, Richard T. *tree farmer*

Indianapolis
Hegel, Carolyn Marie *farmer, farm bureau executive*

West Lafayette
Lechtenberg, Victor L. *agricultural studies educator*

IOWA

Akron
Hultgren, Dennis Eugene *farmer, management consultant*

Ames
Jacobson, Norman L. *retired agricultural educator, researcher*
Topel, David Glen *agricultural studies educator*

Charles City
McCartney, Rhoda Huxsol *farm manager*

Clear Lake
†Peterson, Christian Carrol *farmer*

Decorah
Wangsness, Wayne Roger *farmer*

Indianola
†Mapel, Patricia Jolene *farmer, consultant*

Mason City
Kuhlman, James Weldon *retired county extension education director*

KANSAS

Brookville
Bohata, Emil Anton *rancher*

Claflin
Burmeister, Paul Frederick *farmer*

Garden City
†Reeve, Lee M. *farmer*

Haven
Schlickau, George Hans *cattle breeder, professional association executive*
Schlickau, Lois Marie *farmer*

Iola
Strickler, Ivan K. *dairy farmer*

Lewis
Cross, David Rusk *farmer, livestock raiser*

Wellington
Ferguson, William McDonald *rancher, writer, banker, retired lawyer, former state official*

MARYLAND

Havre De Grace
Jay, Peter Augustus *writer, farmer*

Princess Anne
Acquah, Sarah Nipah *agricultural educator*

MASSACHUSETTS

Brockton
Sullivan, Brendan Paul *state official, communications educator*

MICHIGAN

Allegan
Drozd, Phyllis Ann *agricultural products supplier*

Ann Arbor
Heydon, Peter Northrup *farmer, educator, philanthropist*

Howell
†Cotton, Larry *ranching executive*

Pigeon
†Maust, Joseph J. *agricultural products supplier*

MINNESOTA

Canby
Larson, Gary Arthur *farmer, financial consultant*

Finlayson
†Luoma, Judy *ranching executive*

Goodridge
†Hanson, Norma Lee *farmer*

Minneapolis
Joseph, Burton M. *retired grain merchant*

Saint Paul
Sviggum, Steven Arthur *farmer, state representative*

MISSISSIPPI

Starkville
Gregg, Billy Ray *seed industry executive, consultant*

MISSOURI

Nixa
Kreider, Jim *farmer, former state legislator*

Sturgeon
Fashing, Edward Michael *ranch owner, physical sciences educator*

MONTANA

Martinsdale
Rostad, Lee B. *rancher, writer*

Pony
Anderson, Richard Ernest *agribusiness development consultant, rancher*

Utica
Stevenson, Sarah Schoales *rancher, business owner*

NEBRASKA

Funk
Sjogren, Donald Ernest *farmer*

NEVADA

Yerington
Scatena, Lorraine Borba *rancher, women's rights advocate*

NEW JERSEY

Jackson
Rickabaugh, Vicki *horse farm owner, dressage instructor*

NEW MEXICO

Deming
White, Don William *rancher, minister*

Las Cruces
Bosland, Paul William *agriculture educator*
†Holechek, Jerry *agricultural studies educator*

NORTH DAKOTA

Amidon
Bergquist, Gene Alfred *farmer, rancher, county commissioner*

OHIO

Columbus
Ockerman, Herbert W. *agricultural studies educator*

OREGON

Beaverton
Ray, Ruth Alice Yancey *retired rancher, real estate developer*

Medford
†Smith, Robert F. (Bob Smith) *rancher, former congressman*

Salem
†Butler, Alison *agricultural studies educator, researcher*

PENNSYLVANIA

Clarks Summit
†Eckel, Keith William *farmer*

Dillsburg
Smith, William Raymond *farmer, thoroughbred owner, breeder and trainer, retired history educator, philosophy educator*

SOUTH CAROLINA

Dillon
Chandler, Marcia Shaw Barnard *farmer*

Greer
Gregg, Marie Byrd *retired farmer*

Pawleys Island
Kay, Thomas Oliver *agricultural consultant*

SOUTH DAKOTA

Elk Point
Chicoine, Roland Alvin *farmer, former state legislator*

Saint Lawrence
Lockner, Vera Joanne *farmer, rancher, legislator*

TENNESSEE

Hickory Valley
Weaver, Peggy (Marguerite McKinnie Weaver) *plantation owner*

Nashville
Thompson, Dean Allan *cattleman*

TEXAS

Cleburne
Gorman, Charlotte A. *family and consumer sciences agent*

College Station
Christiansen, James Edward *agricultural educator*

Farnsworth
Gramstorff, Jeanne B. *retired farmer*

Houston
Lee, Robert Leyne *conglomerate advisor, consultant*
†Shuart, Carey Chenoweth *farmer, volunteer*

Industry
Huitt, Jimmie L. *rancher, oil, gas, real estate investor*

Rochelle
Bull, Kenneth Winson *retired rancher*

San Antonio
Davenport, Pamela Beaver *rancher*
Petty, Scott, Jr., *rancher*

Valley View
Wallace, Donald John, III, *rancher, former pest control company executive*

VIRGINIA

Blacksburg
Swiger, L. A. *agricultural studies educator, educator*

Bristol
Richardson, Carl Colley, Jr., *thoroughbred farm owner*

Mc Lean
McIlwain, Clara Evans *agricultural economist, consultant*

Montross
Fountain, Robert Roy, Jr., *farmer, industrial executive, naval officer*

Prince George
Farrar, Andrew Lockett *agricultural education educator*

WASHINGTON

Yakima
Hefflinger, LeRoy Arthur *agricultural manager*

WEST VIRGINIA

Charles Town
McDonald, Angus Wheeler *farmer*

WYOMING

Lander
Raynolds, David Robert *buffalo breeder, writer*

Wheatland
Bunker, John Birkbeck *cattle rancher, retired sugar company executive*

ADDRESS UNPUBLISHED

Brooks, Kenneth N. *forestry educator*
†Byford, Emma *rancher*
Camp, Clifton Durrett, Jr., *rancher, retired publishing executive*
Cannell, Robert Quirk *former agricultural sciences educator*
Erwin, Elmer Louis *vintager, cement consultant*
Hiler, Edward Allan *agricultural and engineering educator*
Hitchcock, Vernon Thomas *farmer, lawyer*
†Hudson, Michael Darren *agricultural economics educator*
Johnson, Cyrus Edwin *grain farmer, former food products executive*
Johnson, Maurice Verner, Jr., *agricultural research and development executive*
Kontny, Vincent L. *rancher, engineering executive*
Stanley, Marlyse Reed *horse breeder*

ARCHITECTURE & DESIGN

UNITED STATES

ALABAMA

Auburn
Lechner, Norbert Manfred *architect educator*
Millman, Richard George *architect, educator*

Berry
Moore, Elizabeth Ann Davis *home fashion products specialist*

Birmingham
Gilchrist, William Aaron *architect*

Madison
Vo, Hieu N. *intern architect*

Mobile
Winter, Arch Reese *retired architect*

ARIZONA

Oro Valley
McConnell, Robert Eastwood *architect, educator*

Payson
Hershberger, Robert Glen *architect, educator*

Phoenix
Elmore, James Walter *architect, retired university dean*
Ferreira, Donna Blair *interior designer*
Hawkins, Jasper Stillwell, Jr., *architect*
Schiffner, Charles Robert *architect*
Sourbrine, Richard Don, II, *architect*
Winslow, Paul David *architect*

Scottsdale
Ailloni-Charas, Miriam Clara *interior designer, consultant*
Brown, Shirley Margaret Kern (Peggy Brown) *interior designer*
†Wong, Joe Bing *retired architect*

Sonoita
Cook, William Howard *architect*

Sun City West
Dementis, Katharine Hopkins *retired interior designer*

Tucson
Breckenridge, Klindt Duncan *architect*
Nelson, Edward Humphrey *architect*
Seehausen, Richard Ferdinand *architect*
Wallach, Leslie Rothaus *architect*

ARKANSAS

Fayetteville
Jones, Euine Fay *architect, educator*

Little Rock
Burruss, Terry Gene *architect*

Truemper, John James, Jr., *retired architect*

Winslow
Burggraf, Frank Bernard, Jr., *landscape architect, retired educator*

CALIFORNIA

Atherton
Ritter, Mary L. *interior decorator*

Bakersfield
McAlister, Michael H. *architect*

Belvedere
Gale, Daniel Bailey *architect*
Hugenberg, Patricia Ellen Petrie *product designer*

Berkeley
Brocchini, Ronald Gene *architect*
Burger, Edmund Ganes *architect*
Cardwell, Kenneth Harvey *architect, educator*
Stoller, Claude *architect*

Beverly Hills
†Buchberg, Akiva *product designer, inventor, consultant*
Dillard, Suzanne *interior designer*

Bodega Bay
King, Leland W. *architect*

Burlingame
Diebel, Gary R. *architect*

Carlsbad
Harrington-Lloyd, Jeanne Leigh *interior designer*

Ceres
Abbott, Dan-San *parachute designer*

Chula Vista
Weiss-Cornwell, Amy *interior designer*

Corona Del Mar
Yeo, Ron *architect*

Coronado
Wagener, Hobart D. *retired architect*

Culver City
Sussman, Deborah Evelyn *designer, company executive*

El Cerrito
Komatsu, Shigego Richard *architect*

Encino
Rance, Quentin E. *interior designer*

Fresno
Darden, Edwin Speight, Sr., *architect*
Patnaude, William Eugene *architect*
Pings, Anthony Claude *architect*

Glendale
Stanfill, Latayne Colvett *non-fiction writer*

Huntington Beach
†Lans, Carl Gustav *architect, economist*

Irvine
Kraemer, Kenneth Leo *architect, educator, urban planner*
Olsson, Carmen *interior designer*

La Canada
Larsen, Traci Lyn *interior designer*

Laguna Niguel
Axon, Donald Carlton *architect*

Los Angeles
DeCherney, Deanna Saver *interior designer*
Dworsky, Daniel Leonard *architect, educator*
Eisenshtat, Sidney Herbert *architect*
Fickett, Edward Hale *architect, planner, arbitrator*
Kline, Lee B. *retired architect*
Krag, Olga *interior designer*
Man, Lawrence Kong *architect, entrepreneur, graphics, furniture and fashion designer*
McCullagh, Grant Gibson *architect*
Moe, Stanley Allen *architect, consultant*
Nelson, Mark Bruce *interior designer*
Neutra, Dion *architect*
†Noble, Douglas *architecture educator*
Phelps, Barton Chase *architect, educator*
†Stout, Randall *architect*
Tucker, Robert Paul *landscape architect, city planner*

Manhattan Beach
Blanton, John Arthur *architect, writer*

Marshall
Evans, Robert James *architect*

Mill Valley
D'Amico, Michael *architect, urban planner*
Whiting, Christine Light *art librarian*

Montrose
Greenlaw, Roger Lee *interior designer*

Mountain View
Kobza, Dennis Jerome *architect*

Napa
†Ianziti, Adelbert John *industrial designer*

Newport Beach
Anderson, Paul Scott *architect*
Bissell, George Arthur *architect*
Richardson, Walter John *architect*

Novato
Thompson, Peter Layard Hailey, Sr., *landscape and golf course architect, architectural firm executive*

Oakland
Matsumoto, George *architect*
†Roesling, Marjorie Inez *interior designer*

Oceanside
Eichman, Patricia *retired interior designer*

Orange
Mason, Naomi Ann *interior designer*
Shirvani, Hamid *architect, educator, author, administrator, philosopher*

Oxnard
O'Connell, Hugh Mellen, Jr., *retired architect*

Palm Springs
†Munyon, William Harry, Jr., *architect*

Pasadena
Goei, Bernard Thwan-Poo (Bert Goei) *architectural and engineering firm executive*
Thomas, Joseph Fleshman *retired architect*
Wyllie, F(rances) Rosemary (Romy Wyllie) *interior designer, educator*

Pleasant Hill
Hassid, Sami *architect, educator*

Pleasanton
Fehlberg, Robert Erick *architect*

Point Reyes Station
Temple, Lee Brett *architect, songwriter*

Redondo Beach
Shellhorn, Ruth Patricia *landscape architect*

Riverside
†Deal, Kevin Paul *furniture designer*

Sacramento
Dahlin, Dennis John *landscape architect, environmental consultant*
Lionakis, George *architect*
Ross, Terence William *architect*
Wasserman, Barry L(ee) *architect*

San Diego
†Angyal, Charles *architect*
Delawie, Homer Torrence *retired architect*
Henderson, John Drews *architect*
†Naslund, Eric *architectural firm executive*
Paderewski, Sir Clarence Joseph *architect*
Wilson, Richard Allan *landscape architect*

San Francisco
Blake, Laura *architect*
Bull, Henrik Helkand *architect*
Diwakar, Deepti *architect, dancer*
†Ellis, John *urban designer*
Fehrman, Kenneth Ray *educator, interior designer, author, researcher*
Field, John Louis *architect*
†Freed, Eric Corey *architect*
Friedrichs, Edward Charles *architect*
Kriken, John Lund *architect*
†Leddy, William *architect*
Minar, Paul G. *design consultant*
Moris, Lamberto Giuliano *architect*
Raeber, John Arthur *architect, construction consultant*
Ream, James Terrill *architect, sculptor*
†Solomon, Daniel *architectural firm executive*
Thistlethwaite, David Richard *architect*
†Torney, Anne *architectural firm executive*
Worthen, William James *architect*

San Jose
Lotten, Larry Lynn *architect*
Tanaka, Richard Koichi, Jr., *architect, planner*

San Luis Obispo
Deasy, Cornelius Michael *architect*

San Marcos
Harmon, Harry William *architect, former university administrator*

San Mateo
Castleberry, Arline Alrick *interior designer*
Sadilek, Vladimir *architect*

San Rafael
Badgley, John Roy *architect*
Clark, Charles Sutter *interior designer*

San Ramon
Jue, Susan Lynne *interior designer*

Santa Ana
†Hukel, Dennis Randall *industrial designer, translator*

Santa Barbara
Burgee, John Henry *architect*
Kruger, Kenneth Charles *architect*

Santa Monica
Eizenberg, Julie *architect*
Gehry, Frank Owen *architect*
Koning, Hendrik *architect*

Santa Rosa
Gilger, Paul Douglass *architect*
†Morris, Jack G. *architecture educator, writer*

Seal Beach
Rossi, Mario Alexander *architect*

Sonoma
Woodbridge, John Marshall *architect, urban planner*

South Pasadena
Girvigian, Raymond *architect*

Tarzana
Smith, Mark Lee *architect*

Thousand Oaks
Conant, David Arthur *architectural acoustician, educator, consultant*

Venice
Beal, Jason Eliot *architect*

Ventura
Ruebe, Bambi Lynn *interior, environmental designer*

Villa Park
Buffington, Linda Brice *interior designer*

Walnut
Muszynski, Jane *interior designer, colorist, space planner*

Westlake Village
Friedman, Collette Sweet *kitchen and interior designer*

COLORADO

Aspen
Caudill, Samuel Jefferson *architect*

Aurora
Durkop, Georgia F. *interior designer*

Boulder
Carlson, Devon McElvin *architect, educator*
Hoffman, Charles Fenno, III, *architect*

Broomfield
Williams, John James, Jr., *architect*

Centennial
†Hunt, Gerald G., Jr., *architect, real estate broker*

Denver
Abo, Ronald Kent *freelance/self-employed architect*
Anderson, John David *architect*
Brownson, Jacques Calmon *architect*
Dominick, Peter Hoyt, Jr., *architect*
Fuller, Robert Kenneth *architect, urban designer*
Havekost, Daniel John *architect*
Hynek, Frederick James *architect*
Nelson, Nevin Mary *interior designer*
Prosser, John Martin *architect, educator, urban design consultant*
Robins, Judy Roselyn *interior designer*
Shirkey, Linda Sue *interior designer, film company executive, set designer*
Steenhagen, Robert Lewis *landscape architect, consultant*
Wirkler, Norman Edward *architectural, engineering, construction management firm executive*

Englewood
Asarch, Elaine *interior designer, anthropologist*
Cowley, Gerald Dean *architect*

Fort Collins
Grandin, Temple *industrial designer, science educator*

Fort Garland
Boyer, Lester Leroy, Jr., *architecture educator, consultant*

Littleton
Shepherd, Donna Lou *interior designer*

Vail
Vosbeck, Robert Randall *architect*

CONNECTICUT

Branford
Blake, Peter Jost *architect*
Wright, Nancy Howell *interior designer*

Cheshire
Rowland, Ralph Thomas *retired architect*
Saad, Edward Theodore *architect*

Fairfield
Ingis, Gail *interior designer, educator, writer, photographer, artist*

Greenwich
Anderson, Carolyn Ruth Hunt *interior designer, realtor*
de Mar, Leoda Miller *designer*
Hershaft, Elinor *space planner, interior designer*
Marks, Charles *architect*
Matthaei, Gay Humphrey *interior designer*
Mock, Robert Claude *architect*

Hamden
Roche, Eamonn Kevin *architect*
Strong, James Alan *architect*

Hartford
Amatuli, Robert Alexander *architect*
Leibin, Harvey Bruce *architect*

Lyme
Hoyt, Charles King *architect, editor*

Monroe
Paniccia, Mario Domenic *architect*

New Canaan
Dean, Robert Bruce *architect*

Risom, Jens *furniture designer, manufacturing executive*

New Haven
Chilton, William David *architect*
Clarke, Fred W., III, *architect, architectural firm executive*
Newick, Craig David *architect*
Pelli, Cesar *architect*
Platner, Warren *architect*
Roth, Harold *architect*

New Preston Marble Dale
Myers, Robert Luther *architect, artist*

Newtown
Geckle, Katherine L. *interior designer*

Niantic
Danos, Harry John *architect, educator, artist*

Norfolk
Rallo, Harry *architect, artist*

Northford
Gregan, Edmund Robert *landscape architect*

Norwalk
Crosbie, Michael James *architect, writer, educator*

Ridgefield
†Tamsett, Susan O. *architect, artist*

Salisbury
White, Norval Crawford *architect*

Stamford
Kobrin, Jay Arthur *interior designer, fiber artist*
Papp, Laszlo George *architect*

Stonington
Stoddard, Alexandra *designer, writer, lecturer*

Trumbull
Watson, Donald Ralph *architect, artist, educator, author*

Waterbury
Bellemare, David John *architectural designer*

Westport
Ferris, Roger Patrick *architect*
Rothenberg, Abraham Joseph *architect*

Woodbury
Moeckel, Henry Theodore *architect*

DELAWARE

Newark
Stick, Thomas Howard Fitchett *corporate architect, construction litigation consultant*

DISTRICT OF COLUMBIA

Washington
Barr-Kumar, Raj *architect*
†Birnbaum, Charles A. *landscape architect*
Coffin, Beatriz de Winthuysen *landscape architect*
Coffin, Laurence Edmondston, Jr., *landscape architect, urban planner*
Cox, Warren Jacob *architect*
Fry, Louis Edwin, Jr., *architect*
Gentner, Paul LeFoe *architect, consultant*
†Goetz, Lewis J. *architect*
Greene, Thomas Hardy *architect*
Hartman, George Eitel *architect*
Hellmuth, George William *architect*
Holladay, Wilhelmina Cole *interior design and museum executive*
Jacobsen, Hugh Newell *architect*
Keyes, Arthur Hawkins, Jr., *architect*
Liebenson, Gloria Krasnow *interior design executive, freelance writer*
Murray, Christopher Charles, III, *architect*
Oehme, Wolfgang Walter *landscape architect*
†Pahnke, Robert David *architect, interior designer*
Prigmore, Kathryn Bradford Tyler *architecture educator, architect*
Ramberg, Walter Dodd *architect*
†Sarring, Kevin Lee *architect, archaeologist*
Schlesinger, B. Frank *architect, educator*
Siegel, Lloyd Harvey *architect, real estate developer, consultant*
White, George Malcolm *architect*
Yerkes, David Norton *architect*

FLORIDA

Bal Harbour
Spiegel, Siegmund *architect*

Boca Raton
Balter, Murray *interior designer*
Kephart, Larry Robert *architect*

Boynton Beach
Stubbins, Hugh A(sher), Jr., *architect*

Clearwater
Hirzel, Charles K. *retired architect*

Coral Gables
Warburton, Ralph Joseph *architect, engineer, planner, educator*

Daytona Beach
Amick, William Walker *golf course architect*
Xepapas, Anargyros *architect*

Delray Beach
Love, Marsha Lynn *interior decorator*
Rippeteau, Darrel Downing *retired architect*
Schultz, Joel Sidney *architect*

Fort Myers
†Mair, Bruce Logan *interior designer, company executive*

Gulf Breeze
French, Jere Stuart *landscape architect*

Hollywood
Harringer, Olaf Carl *architect, museum consultant*

Indian River Shores
Ahrens, William Henry *architect*

Jacksonville
Morgan, William Newton *architect, educator*
Rumpel, Peter Loyd *architect, educator, artist*

Lake Worth
Levow, Judith L(ee) Holtz (Judi Levow) *interior designer*

Largo
†Klutho, Mark Paul *landscape architect, educator*

Leesburg
Twiss, Wanda May *interior designer*

Longwood
Gasperoni, Ellen Jean Lias *interior designer*

Miami
Arango, Jorge Sanin *architect*
Duany, Andres *architectural firm executive*
Farcus, Joseph Jay *architect, interior designer*
Feito, Jose *architect*
Hampton, Mark Garrison *architect*
Martinez, Walter Baldomero *architect*

Naples
Lewis, Gordon Gilmer *golf course architect*
Lickhalter, Merlin Eugene *architect*
McDonald, Jinx *interior designer*

Orlando
Dean, Gary Neal *artist, architect*
Duda, Richard Frank *architect, engineering executive*

Ormond Beach
Truitt, Richard byron *landscape architect*

Palm Bay
Hanna, Emma Harmon *architectural designer, business owner, official*

Palm Beach
Wirtz, Willem Kindler *garden and lighting designer, public relations consultant*

Palmetto
Turlo, George Jerzy *architect, city planner, artist*

Pensacola
Bullock, Ellis Way, Jr., *architect*
Woolf, Kenneth Howard *architect*

Saint Augustine
Matzke, Frank J. *architect, consultant*
Wilkes, Delano Angus *architect*

Saint Petersburg
Wedding, Charles Randolph *architect*

Sanibel
Sappenfield, Charles Madison *architect, educator*

Sarasota
Snyder, Wesley Warren *interior space planner and designer*

Stuart
Ankrom, Charles Franklin *golf course architect, consultant*
Merrill, Vincent Nichols *retired landscape architect*

Tallahassee
Bird, Mark Douglas *magnet designer, engineering researcher*

Tampa
Holmes, Dwight Ellis *architect*
Howey, John Richard *architect, writer*
Jennewein, James Joseph *architect*

Vero Beach
Gibson, James Elliot *architect*
Lagin, Neil *landscape designer, consultant*

Wellington
Foster, Mary Kathleeen *interior designer*

West Palm Beach
†Marshall-Beasley, Elizabeth *landscape architect*
Ross, Edward Joseph *architect*

Winter Haven
Burns, Arthur Lee *architect*

GEORGIA

Alpharetta
Puckett, Elsbeth Camille

Athens
Morrison, Darrel Gene *landscape architecture educator*

Atlanta
Bainbridge, Frederick Freeman, III, *architect*
Bull, Frank James *architect*
†Chang, Leng Kar *interior designer*
Cooper, Jerome Maurice *architect*
†Dalia, Thomas A. *architectural firm executive*
Diedrich, Richard Joseph *architect*
Guest, Rita Carson *interior designer*
Hudspeth, Gregg William *landscape architect*
Lewcock, Ronald Bentley *architect, educator*
†McAfee, Cheryl *architect*
†Neuenschwander, Roger *architectural firm executive*
Pulgram, William Leopold *architect, space designer*
Rekau, Richard Robert *architect*
Robison, Richard Eugene *architect*
†Smith, Markham H. *architectural firm executive*
†Swicegood, Stephen *architect*
†Unger, Roberta *architect*
White, Ortrude B. *architect*

Augusta
Woodhurst, Robert Stanford, Jr., *architect*

Columbus
Simpson, Minnie Peach *interior designer*

Decatur
Mc Intosh, James Eugene, Jr., *interior designer*

Lagrange
Wilkes, George Gardner, Jr., *landscape architect*

Macon
Dunwody, Eugene Cox *architect*

Marietta
Pou, Linda G. *interior designer, architectural designer*

Moultrie
McCall, John Clark, Jr., *interior designer*

Rome
Janowski, Thaddeus Marian *architect*

Saint Simons
Webb, Lamar Thaxter *architect*

Savannah
†Ramsay, Linda *architect*
Weaver, Crystal Dawn *interior design educator*

Smyrna
Passantino, Richard J. *architect*

HAWAII

Hanalei
Schaller, Matthew Fite *architect*

Honolulu
Botsai, Elmer Eugene *architect, architecture educator, retired dean*
Hale, Nathan Robert *architect*
Hamada, Duane Takumi *architect*
Lau, Charles Kwok-Chiu *architect, architectural firm executive*
Song, Cathy *author, poet*
Vidal, Alejandro Legaspi (Andy Vidal) *architect*
Yeh, Raymond Wei-Hwa *architect, educator*

Kaneohe
Fisette, Scott Michael *landscape and golf course architect*
Jackson, Jane W. *interior designer*

Waipahu
Chang, Walter Tuck, Sr., *drafting and AutoCAD educator, real estate agent, national defense instructor*

IDAHO

Sun Valley
†McLaughlin, James Daniel *architect*

ILLINOIS

Bloomington
Switzer, Jon Rex *architect*

Bolingbrook
Caddy, Edmund H.H., Jr., *architect*

Champaign
Anthony, Kathryn Harriet *architecture educator*
Baker, Jack Sherman *architect, designer, educator*
Hopkins, Lewis Dean *planner, educator*
†Ousterhout, Robert G. *architecture educator*
Riley, Robert Bartlett *landscape architect*
Selby, Robert Irwin

Chicago
Amstadter, Laurence *retired architect*
Balasi, Mark Geoffrey *architect*
Barney, Carol Ross *architect*
Belluschi, Anthony C. *architect*
Blankenship, Edward G. *architect*
Cook, Richard Borreson *architect*
†Enquist, Philip *architectural firm executive*
Epstein, Sidney *architect, engineer*
Fowler, George Selton, Jr., *architect*
†Gardunio, Joseph *landscaping company executive*
†Garofalo, Douglas *architectural firm executive, educator*
Gold, Allan Harold *architect, structural engineer, educator*
Grunsfeld, Ernest Alton, III, *architect*
Hackl, Donald John *architect*

Hayes, Richard Donald *architect*
Holabird, John Augur, Jr., *retired architect*
Kerbis, Gertrude Lempp *architect*
Kirkegaard, R. Lawrence *architectural acoustician*
Kurtich, John William *architect, film-maker, educator*
Mack, Alan Wayne *interior designer*
Matthei, Edward Hodge *architect*
McCurry, Margaret Irene *architect, interior and furniture designer, educator*
Phillips, Frederick Falley *architect*
Robertson, Donna Virginia *architect, educator, dean*
Roubik, Susanne Eileen *architect*
†Rugo, Steven Alfred *architect*
Schirn, Janet Sugerman *interior designer*
Schroeder, Douglas Fredrick *architect*
Simovic, Laszlo *architect*
Smith, Adrian Devaun *architect*
Smith, Craig Malcolm *architect, consultant*
Tigerman, Stanley *architect, educator*
Valerio, Joseph Mastro *architectural firm executive, educator*
VanderBeke, Patricia K. *architect*
Vinci, John Nicholas *architect, educator*
Weber, Hanno *architect*
Weese, Benjamin Horace *architect*

Evanston
Friedman, Hans Adolf *architect*
Klein, Nancy Hess *interior designer*
Macsai, John *architect*
Salzman, Arthur George *architect*

Glenview
Bradtke, Philip Joseph *architect*

Highland Park
Dubin, Arthur Detmers *architect*
Tobin, Calvin Jay *architect*
Weinstein, Barry Alan *architect*

Hinsdale
Akins, Marilyn Parker *interior designer*
Anderson, Harry Frederick, Jr., *architect*
Unikel, Eva Taylor *interior designer*

Lake Zurich
Krolopp, Rudolph William *retired industrial designer, consultant*

Lincolnshire
Dobrin, Sheldon L. *architect*

Lincolnwood
Stern, Adrienne Ehrlich *interior designer*

Lisle
Mehaffey, Scott Alan *landscape architect*

Mount Carroll
Rogers, Ward Junior *retired industrial designer*

Mount Prospect
Thulin, Adelaide Ann *design company executive, interior designer*

Northfield
Glass, Henry Peter *industrial designer, interior architect, educator*
Schneider-Criezis, Susan Marie *architect*

Novubrook
Fredman, Susan Miriam *interior designer*

Oak Park
Heitzman, Frank Edward *architect*

Park Ridge
†Roig, Charles *architect*
Sersen, Howard Harry *retired interior designer, cabinetry consultant*

Schaumburg
Otis, James, Jr., *architect*

Skokie
Siegal, Burton Lee *product designer, consultant, inventor*

Springfield
Marcy-Geyston, Stephanie Vivian *interior designer*
Unanue, Enrique Jorge *architect*

Urbana
Replinger, John Gordon *architect, retired educator*

Winnetka
Piper, Robert Johnston *architect, urban planner*
Schlossman, John Isaac *architect*
Weber, John Bertram *architect*

INDIANA

Anderson
Smith, Kato Del *architect*

Carmel
Eden, Barbara Janiece *commercial and residential interior designer*
McLaughlin, Harry Roll *architect*

Columbus
Shannon, Carolyn Jean *interior designer*

Fort Wayne
Cole, Kenneth Duane *architect*

Indianapolis
Florestano, Dana Joseph *architect*

Michigan City
Manny, Carter Hugh, Jr., *architect, foundation administrator*

Mishawaka
Ponko, William Reuben *architect*
Troyer, LeRoy Seth *architect*

Notre Dame
Stroik, Duncan Gregory *architect, architectural design educator*

South Bend
Horsbrugh, Patrick *architect, educator, environologist*
Smith, Thomas Gordon *architect*

Valparaiso
Steil, Valerie Gladys *interior designer*

IOWA

Clear Lake
Broshar, Robert Clare *architect*

Des Moines
Lewis, Calvin Fred *architect, educator*

Iowa City
Neumann, Roy Covert *architect*

Solon
Healey, Edward Hopkins *retired architect*

KANSAS

De Soto
Silver, Joan *artist*

Hutchinson
Haag, Joel Edward *architect*

Lawrence
Grabow, Stephen Harris *architecture educator*
Penny, Paul Baldwin *landscape artist, artist*

Manhattan
Foerster, Bernd *architecture educator*
Kremer, Eugene R. *architecture educator*

Overland Park
Conrad, William Merrill *architect*

Prairie Village
Trussell, Donna Laura *writer*

Topeka
Karst, Gary Gene *retired architect*
Slemmons, Robert Sheldon *architect*

KENTUCKY

Lexington
Halley, Samuel Hampton, III, *architect, architectural firm executive*
Romanowitz, Byron Foster *architect, engineer*

Liberty
Wright, Rodney H. *architect*

Louisville
Moon, Stephen Douglas *architectural firm executive*

Park Hills
Holmes, Lu Ann *interior designer, sales representative*

LOUISIANA

Alexandria
†Foster, Sally *interior designer*

Arnaudville
Matas, Myra Dorothea *interior architect, designer, consultant*

Baton Rouge
Desmond, John Jacob *retired architect*
Reich, Robert Sigmund *landscape architect*

Bogalusa
Gallaspy, Dixie *interior designer, innkeeper*

Grambling
†Ogunyemi, Olatunde Adegbayi *design educator, technology administrator*

Lafayette
Fontenot, Lyn *interior designer*

New Orleans
Bookhardt, Fred Barringer, Jr., *architect*
†Eskew, R. Allen *architect, director*
Favrot, Henri Mortimer, Jr., *architect, real estate developer*
Filson, Ronald Coulter *architect, educator, college dean*
Frantz, Phares Albert *architect*
Latorre, Robert George *naval architecture and engineering educator*
Mathes, Edward Conrad *architect*
Meric, Rene Pierre, Jr., *shipbuilding marine construction executive*

Shreveport
Forte, Stephen Forrest *interior designer*
Haas, Lester Carl *retired architect*

MAINE

Camden
Thomas, Karin Ronnefeldt *interior designer*

Edgecomb
Carlson, Suzanne Olive *architect*

New Gloucester
†Jaccaci, August Thayer, Jr., *architect, educator*

Seal Harbor
Forbes, Peter *architect*

York
Lyman, William Welles, Jr., *retired architect*

MARYLAND

Annapolis
Brendle, Gary Allen, Sr., *landscape architect*
Jansson, John Phillip *architect, consultant*
Miller, Richards Thorn *naval architect, engineer*
Wilkes, Joseph Allen *architect*

Baltimore
Adams, Harold Lynn *architect*
†Anderson, Gary Dean *architect, planner, educator*
Brodie, M. J. (Jay Brodie) *architect, city planner, government executive*
Donkervoet, Richard Cornelius *architect*
Ford, John Gilmore *interior designer*
Miller, Jeffrey Michael *architect*
Toomey, Sister Stephana *liturgical designer, architectural space, nun*

Bethesda
Popescu, Daniel *interior designer*

Bowie
Stone, Edward Harris, II, *landscape architect*

Chevy Chase
Auerbach, Seymour *architect*
Oudens, Gerald Francis *architect, architectural firm executive*

Columbia
Ager, David Scott *landscape architect*

Damascus
Ventola, Dean Samuel *architect, architectural company executive*

Fort Washington
Miller, John Richard *interior designer*

Gaithersburg
Bugg, Carol Donayre *interior designer*
Irvine, Helen Isabel Becraft *interior designer*

Olney
Delmar, Eugene Anthony *architect*

Rockville
Edwards, Leisl Marie Baum *interior designer*
Morgan, William Bruce *naval architect*

Salisbury
Oldland, Kevin Bradley *architect*

Severna Park
Allison, John Langsdale *naval architect, marine engineer*

Silver Spring
Welcome, Linda Paar *interior designer*

West Bethesda
Spurling, Everett Gordon, Jr., *architect, construction specifications consultant*

MASSACHUSETTS

Amherst
Cornish, Geoffrey St. John *golf course architect*

Bedford
Payne, Harry Morse, Jr., *architect*

Boston
Anthony, Ethan *architect*
Costa, Daniel Lawrence *architect*
Elkus, Howard Felix *architect*
Finegold, Maurice Nathan *architect*
Flansburgh, Earl Robert *architect*
Goody, Joan Edelman *architect*
Harkness, John Cheesman *architect*
Joseph, J. Jonathan *interior designer*
Klema, Donald David *architect*
Tappé, Albert Anthony *architect*
Wolf, Gary Herbert *architect*

Boxboro
Berry, Robert John *architect*

Brookline
Walter, Eugene Victor *writer*

Cambridge
Anderson, Stanford Owen *architect, architectural historian, educator*
†Baird, George *architecture educator*
Barnes, Edward Larrabee *architect*
Bruck, Phoebe Ann Mason *landscape architect*
Campbell, Robert *architect, writer*
Green, Richard John *architect*
†Jones, Mary M. *landscape architect*
Kobus, Richard Lawrence *architect, designer, executive*
Kruger, Kenneth *architect*
†Mori, Toshiko *architecture educator*

Newman, John Nicholas *naval architect, educator*
Porter, William Lyman *architect, educator*
†Rowe, Peter Grimmond *architecture educator, researcher*
Szabo, Albert *architect, educator*
Tsoi, Edward Tze Ming *architect, interior designer, urban planner*

Concord
†Nolin, John Charles *product specialist, engineering consultant*

Dedham
Meridan, Paula M. *interior design executive*

Edgartown
Rosenfeld, Walter David, Jr., *architect, writer*

Lexington
Frey, John Ward *landscape architect*

Manchester
Shepley, Hugh *architect*

Marblehead
Nilsson, Edward Olof *architect*

Nantucket
Lethbridge, Francis Donald *retired architect*

Natick
Perkins, Deborah Anne *interior designer*

Newton
Oles, Paul Stevenson (Steve Oles) *architect, perspectivist, educator*

Springfield
Engebretson, Douglas Kenneth *architect, interior designer*

Waltham
Notkin, Leonard Sheldon *architect*

Watertown
Dawson, Stuart Owen *landscape architect, urban designer*

Wayland
Huygens, Remmert William *architect*

Wellesley
Merguerian, Arshag *architect*

West Newbury
Taylor, Bruce Stevenson *architect, planner*

West Newton
Stahl, Marilyn Brown *interior designer*

Weston
Fleming, Nancy McAdam *landscape designer*
Wood, Jeremy Scott *architect, urban designer*

Winchester
Jabre, Eddy-Marco *architect*

Worcester
Herman, Barbara Rose *interior decorator*

MICHIGAN

Ann Arbor
Beckley, Robert Mark *architect, educator*
Benford, Harry Bell *naval architect*
Flowers, Damon Bryant *architect, facility planner*
Groat, Linda Noel *architectural educator*
†Tyler, Ilene Rogers *architect*

Bellaire
Cowles, Walter Curtis *naval architect*

Bloomfield Hills
Allen, Maurice Bartelle, Jr., *architect*
Birkerts, Gunnar *architect*
Brown, Jack Wyman *architect*
Van Dine, Harold Forster, Jr., *architect, artist*

Chelsea
Kendall, Kay Lynn *interior designer, consultant*
Paulsen, Serenus Glen *architect, educator*

Detroit
Francis, Edward D. *architect*
Gaines, Jeffrey Thomas *architect, urban planner*
Kessler, William Henry *architect*

Eagle Harbor
Dawson, John Frederick *retired architect*

Farmington Hills
Reddig, Walter Eduard *architect, master cabinet maker*

Grand Rapids
Dickerson, Allen Bruce *interior designer, consultant*
West, Terence Douglas *furniture company design executive*

Kalamazoo
Carver, Norman Francis, Jr., *architect, photographer*

South Haven
LaRocque, Linda Lou *interior designer, educator, playwright*

Troy
Wittbrodt, Frederick Joseph, Jr., *automotive designer*

MINNESOTA

Duluth
Salmela, David Daniel *architect*
Whiteman, Richard Frank *architect*

Minneapolis
Clemence, Roger Davidson *landscape architect, educator*
Eyberg, Donald Theodore, Jr., *architect*
Faricy, Richard Thomas *architect*
Jacob, Bernard Michel *architect*
Martin, Roger Bond *landscape architect, educator*
Meese, Robert Allen *architect*
Musacchio, Laura R. *planning and design educator*
Swenson, Mark Gregory *architect*

Minnetonka
Anderson, Tad Stephen *landscape designer, consultant, photographer*

Northfield
Sovik, Edward Anders *architect, consultant*

Saint Paul
Close, Elizabeth Scheu *retired architect*
Ginthner, Delores Ann *interior designer, educator*
†Tollefson, Lee *architect*

Wayzata
Emison, Jane Bale Larson *interior designer*

MISSISSIPPI

Biloxi
Zocchi, Louis Joseph *product designer, game company executive*

Jackson
Burns, Robert, Jr., *architect, freelance writer, artist*
†Leonard, Pamela Dian *architect, artist*

Mississippi State
Martin, Edward Curtis, Jr., *landscape architect, educator*

Starkville
Ford, Robert MacDonald, III, *architect, educator*

MISSOURI

Columbia
Tofle, Ruth Brent *design educator, researcher, educator*

Independence
Marsh, Gary W. *interior designer*

Kansas City
Baker, Robert Thomas *interior designer*
Seligson, Theodore H. *architect, interior designer, art consultant*

Saint Louis
Beuc, Rudolph, Jr., *architect, real estate broker*
Bextermiller Metzger, Theresa Marie *architect, computer engineer*
Krebs, Carol Marie *architect, psychiatric therapist*
Lovelace, Eldridge Hirst *retired landscape architect, city planner*
Michaelides, Constantine Evangelos *architect, educator*
Thalden, Barry R. *architect*

Springfield
Liu, Yuan Hsiung *drafting and design educator*
Ownby, Jerry Steve *landscape architect, educator*

Webster Groves
Becker, Rex Louis *architect*

MONTANA

Bozeman
DeHaas, John Neff, Jr., *retired architecture educator*

Butte
Bishop, Robert Charles *architect, metals and minerals company executive*

Great Falls
Davidson, David Scott *architect*

NEBRASKA

Lincoln
Johnson, Marvin Richard Alois *architect, consultant*
Morrow, Andrew Nesbit *interior designer, business owner*
Mutunayagam, N. Brito *architecture and planning educator*
Stange, James Henry *architect*
Steward, Weldon Cecil *architecture educator, architect, consultant*

Omaha
Hansen, Marilyn Schooley *interior designer*
Polsky, Donald Perry *architect*
Ryan, Mark Anthony *architect*

PROFESSIONAL INDEX 6173 ARCHITECTURE & DESIGN

NEVADA

Las Vegas
†Serfas, Richard Thomas *architecture educator, urban planner, county official*

NEW HAMPSHIRE

Exeter
Richardson, Artemas P(artridge) *retired landscape architect*

Goffstown
Gillmore, Robert *landscape designer, author, editor, publisher*

Hanover
Brooks, H. Allen *architectural educator, author, lecturer*

NEW JERSEY

Bernardsville
Lazor, Patricia Ann *interior designer*

Bloomsbury
Rohloff, Claire Marie *interior designer, educator*

Bound Brook
Shive, Richard Byron *architect*

Cape May Point
Jordan, Joe J. *architect*

Chatham
†Sickler, Dean Ewin *decorative artist, educator*

Clifton
Held, George Anthony *architect*
†Kalata, Mary Ann Catherine *architect*

Colonia
Wiesenfeld, Bess G. *interior designer*

East Orange
Fielo, Muriel Bryant *interior designer*

Englewood
Schmidt, Ronald Hans *architect*

Florham Park
Mersel, Larry *architect*

Freehold
Pofsky, Norma Louise *interior designer, behavioral consultant*

Jersey City
Ortenzi, Regina (Gina Rae Ortenzi) *home fashion products designer, educator*

Medford
Dunn, Roy J. *landscape architect*

Monroe Township
Zeigen, Spencer Steven *architect, consultant*

Morristown
Nadaskay, Raymond *architect*

Newark
Goldman, Glenn *architecture educator, architect*

Pittstown
Bell, Frank Joseph, III, *architect*

Princeton
†Allen, Stanley T. *architect, dean, educator*
Cooke, R(ichard) Caswell, Jr., *architect*
Ford, Jeremiah, III, *architect*
Freeman, Marjorie Kler *interior designer*
Graves, Michael *architect, educator*
Hillier, J(ames) Robert *architect*
Kehrt, Allan William *architectural firm executive*
†Nichols, Karen *architect*

Sewell
Spagnuola, Francis Michael *interior designer*

South Orange
DeVaris, Panayotis Eric *architect*

Upper Saddle River
Cappitella, Mauro John *architect*

NEW MEXICO

Bayard
†Richard, Mark R. *architect*

Hobbs
Ritchie, Fran A. *interior designer, small business owner*

Placitas
Pirkl, James Joseph *industrial designer, educator, writer*

Questa
Sharkey, Richard David *architectural artisan, inventor, musician*

Sandia Park
Woodfin, Martha *interior designer*

Santa Fe
Leon, Bruno *architect, architecture educator*
†Wilson, Laura Eleanor *landscape architect, sculptor*

NEW YORK

Binghamton
Bearsch, Lee Palmer *architect, city planner*

Bridgehampton
Coy, Christopher James *architect*

Bronxville
Frost, A. Corwin *architect, consultant*

Brooklyn
Katavolos, William *architecture educator, furniture designer*
†Nadel, Monroe Stanley
Rice, John Thomas *architecture educator*
Weston, I. Donald *architect*
Woolley, Margaret Anne (Margot Woolley) *architect*

Buffalo
†Coles, Robert Traynham *architect*

Chester
Karen, Linda Tricarico *interior designer*

Corona
Little, Frederick Anton *landscape architect, municipal administrator*

Cortlandt Manor
Frischmuth, Robert Alfred *landscape planner, filmmaker*

Cranberry Lake
Glavin, James Edward *landscape architect*

Cross River
Thorn, Susan Howe *interior designer*

Dobbs Ferry
Guggenheimer, Tobias Immanuel Simon *architect*

East Hampton
Damaz, Paul F. *architect*
Delson, Sidney Leon *architect*

Elizaville
Koeppel, Harry Saul *interior designer, educator*

Grand Island
†Mendell, Mark *architect*

Great Neck
Turofsky, Charles Sheldon *landscape architect*

Greenlawn
Stevens, John Richard *architectural historian*

Hastings On Hudson
Weinstein, Edward Michael *architect, consultant*

Hensonville
Newman, Oscar *architect, city planner, sculptor*

Ithaca
†Olpadwala, Porus *architecture educator, dean*
†Seraji-Bozorgzad, Nasrine *architecture educator*
Sims, William Riley *design and facility management educator, consultant, architect*

Jamaica
Gati, William Eugene *architect, designer and planner*
†Vindollo-Gálan, Leonidez *architect, consultant*

Katonah
Baker, John Milnes *architect*

Kew Gardens
Aldea, Patricia *architect*

Locust Valley
†Bentel, Carol Rusche *architect*
Bentel, Frederick Richard *architect, educator*

Long Island City
Sadao, Shoji *architect*

Manhasset
Schiller, Arthur A. *architect, educator*
Seftel, Donna Selene *architect*

Middletown
Fucci, Joseph Leonard *architect, librarian, editor*

New Lebanon
Baker, James Barnes *architect*

New Rochelle
Menzies, Henry Hardinge *architect*

New York
†Anderson, Ross S. *architectural firm executive*
†Baird, Penny Drue *interior designer*
Beer, David Wells *architect*
†Bentel, Paul L. *architect, educator*
Bland, Frederick Aves *architect*
Borrelli, John Francis *architect*
Breger, William N. *architect, educator*
Brennan, Henry Higginson *architect*
Buatta, Mario *interior designer*
Butler, Jonathan Putnam *architect*
Buttrick, Harold *architect*
Cavaglieri, Giorgio *architect*
Chan, Lo-Yi Cheung Yuen *architect*
Charles, Michael Harrison *architectural interior designer*
Cobb, Henry Nichols *architect*
Cohn, Ian J. *architect*
Cutler, Laurence Stephan *architect, urban designer, museum founder, advertising executive, educator*
Czajka, James Vincent *architect*
†Daniels, J. Yolande *architectural firm executive, educator*
Dattner, Richard *architect, educator*
David, Theoharis Lambros *architect, educator*
†Davis, Lewis *architectural firm executive*
†Davis, Steven M. *architectural firm executive*
Dennis, Diane Joy Milam *retired architect*
De Vido, Alfredo Eduardo *architect*
Djerejian, Robert Asbed *architect*
Edelman, Judith H. *architect*
Eisenman, Peter David *architect, educator*
Franzen, Ulrich J. *architect*
Fredette, Diane Kaufman *architect*
†Freed, James Ingo *architect*
†Galan, Leonidez Vindollo *architect*
Gamble, William Ardell, Jr., *interior designer, inventor*
Gastil, Raymond Wesley *urban designer*
Gatje, Robert Frederick *architect*
Gaveras, Harry *architect*
Georgopoulos, Maria *architect, artist, inventor*
Gibbs, Jamie *landscape architect, interior designer*
Giddens-Jones, Emily Jane *architectural and interior designer, consultant*
Ginsberg, David Lawrence *architect*
†Grabé, Christopher K. *architectural firm executive*
Guise, David Earl *architect, educator*
Gunther, Margot Webster *interior design*
Gwathmey, Charles *architect*
Halpin, Anna Marie *architect, writer*
Halsband, Frances *architect*
Hariri, Gisue *architect, educator*
Hinz, Theodore Vincent *architect*
Holub, Martin *architect*
Huxtable, Ada Louise *architecture critic*
Ivy, Robert Adams, Jr., *architect, editor-in-chief*
†Joseph, Wendy Evans *architect*
Kasakove, Susan *interior designer*
Kinnear, John Kenyon, Jr., *architect*
Kliment, Robert Michael *architect*
Kliment, Stephen Alexander *architect, editor, journalist*
Kohn, A. Eugene *architect*
†Krebs, Carl F. *architectural firm executive*
Lau, Harry Hung-Kwan *acoustical and interior designer, consultant*
La Vita, Roberto *architect, art director, designer*
Lefferts, Gillet, Jr., *architect*
†Libeskind, Daniel *architect*
Liebman, Theodore *architect*
Logan, Thaddeus Sumner, III, *architect*
Lundy, Marilynn Frances *designer, consultant*
†Marpillero, Sandro *architectural firm executive*
Masey, Jack *exhibition designer*
Mellins, Thomas Harrison *architectural historian*
†Michielli, Frank V. *architectural firm executive*
Nelson, Louis *design and planning consultant*
†Olcott, Richard M. *architectural firm executive*
†O'Rorke, Toby P. *architect, consultant*
Palermo, Robert James *architect, consultant, inventor*
†Paxson, William H. *architectural firm executive*
†Pei, Ieoh Ming *architect*
Peretz, Eileen *interior designer*
Pomeroy, Lee Harris *architect*
Quennell, Nicholas *landscape architect, educator*
Robinson, James LeRoy *architect, educator, developer*
Rosenblatt, Arthur Isaac *architect, former museum director*
Rosenblatt, Lester *naval architect*
†Sagan, M J *architectural firm executive*
Schwarz, Ekkehart Richard Johannes *architect, urban designer*
Sevely, Maria *architect*
Slomanson, Lloyd Howard *architect, musician, photographer*
Smotrich, David Isadore *architect*
†Stern, Robert Arthur Morton *architect, educator, writer*
Stubbs, John Howell *architectural educator, preservationist*
Tafel, Edgar *architect*
Varney, Carleton Bates, Jr., *interior designer, columnist, educator*
†Vidler, Anthony *architecture educator, dean*
Voorsanger, Bartholomew *architect*
†Wexler, Allan *architect, art educator*
Willis, Beverly Ann *architect*
Winchester, Elizabeth Young *interior designer, consultant, space planner*

North Salem
Silverman, Alice Hope *interior designer*

Northport
†De Carolis, Philip Joseph *space designer, educator*

Nyack
Degenshein, Jan *architect, planner*
Gaudy, Edward *landscape architect, consultant*

Old Westbury
†Al-Douri, Taha A. *architect, educator*
†Friedman, Jonathan Block *architect, educator, writer*

Pleasantville
Annese, Domenico *landscape architect*

Pound Ridge
Abramovitz, Max *architect*

Rensselaerville
Dudley, George Austin *architect, planning consultant, educator*

Rye
Anderson, Allan *architectural firm executive*

Scarsdale
Bayar, Julia Beryl *interior designer*
DeFrancis, Suellen Maria *interior architect*

Syracuse
Skoler, Louis *architect, educator*
Smardon, Richard Clay *landscape architecture and environmental studies educator*

Tarrytown
Kenney, John Michel *architect*

Troy
Haviland, David Sands *architectural educator, researcher, administrator*

Utica
Labuz, Ronald Matthew *design educator*

Wappingers Falls
Johnson, Jeh Vincent *architect*

Warwick
Mack, Daniel Richard *furniture designer*

Water Mill
D'Urso, Joseph Paul *interior designer*

Westhampton Beach
Flood, Angela *interior designer, artist*

Woodstock
Hoyt, Earl Edward, Jr., *industrial designer*

NORTH CAROLINA

Asheville
King, Joseph Bertram *architect*

Boone
Oelberg, Robert Nathan *landscape architect*

Chapel Hill
Dixon, Frederick Dail *architect*
Godschalk, David Robinson *architect, urban development planner, educator*
Stipe, Robert Edwin *design educator*

Charlotte
Ferebee, Stephen Scott, Jr., *architect*
Huberman, Jeffrey Allen *architect*
Montague, Edgar Burwell, III, (Monty Montague) *industrial designer*

Greensboro
Irvin, Helen Adcock *interior designer*
Murrelle, Ronald Kemp *architectural firm executive*

High Point
Schwartz, Robert Terry *industrial design executive*

Kinston
Baker-Gardner, Jewelle *interior designer, business consultant*

Kitty Hawk
Elliott, Candice K. *interior designer*

Lake Lure
Seyboldt, Caroline *interior decorator, artist*

Lexington
Younts, Patty Lou *interior design executive,inventor, researcher*

Pisgah Forest
Albyn, Richard Keith *retired architect*

Raleigh
Clarke, Lewis James *landscape architect*
Flournoy, William Louis, Jr., *landscape architect*
Godwin, James Beckham *retired landscape architect*
†Peele, Katherine N. *architect*

Research Triangle Park
†Freelon, Philip G. *architectural firm executive*

Robbinsville
Ginn, Ronn *architect, urban planner, general contractor*

OHIO

Akron
Castronovo, Thomas Paul *architect, consultant*

Bowling Green
Luescher, Andreas *architecture educator*

Canton
Barkan, John Martin, Jr., *architect*

Celina
Fanning, Ronald Heath *architect, engineer*

Chagrin Falls
Cordes, Loverne Christian *interior designer*
Goldfarb, Kathleen Bliss *interior designer*

Cincinnati
Chatterjee, Jayanta *architecture and planning educator*
Glendening, Everett Austin *architect*
Goetzman, Bruce Edgar *architecture educator*
Luckner, Herman Richard, III, *interior designer*
Meisner, Gary Wayne *landscape architect*
Nielsen, George Lee *architect*
Preiser, Wolfgang Friedrich Ernst *architect, educator, consultant, researcher*
Roomann, Hugo *architect*

Cleveland
Behnke, William Alfred *landscape architect, planner*
†Bostwick, Robert Lewis *architect*
Bowen, Richard Lee *architect*
Gellert, Edward Bradford, III,

Gibans, James David *architect*
†Hancock, James Beaty *interior designer*
Kelly, John Terence *architect*
Little, Robert Andrews *architect, designer, painter*
Madison, Robert Prince *architect*
Melsop, James William *architect*
Sande, Theodore Anton *architect, educator, foundation executive*
Simon, Edgar Harmon *interior designer*
Zung, Thomas Tse-Kwai *architect*

Columbus
Kirk, Ballard Harry Thurston *architect*
Weinhold, Virginia Beamer *interior designer*

Cuyahoga Falls
Haag, Everett Keith *architect*

Dayton
Betz, Eugene William *architect*

Kent
Sommers, David Lynn *architect*

Lakewood
Hunter, Sally Irene *interior designer*

Middlebranch
Kalin, Nancy Jagger *interior designer*

Reynoldsburg
Serraglio, Mario *architect*

Toledo
Martin, Robert Edward *architect*

Youngstown
Murcko, Donald Leroy *architect*

OKLAHOMA

Norman
Henderson, Arnold Glenn *architect, educator*
Henkle, James L. *industrial designer*
Sorey, Thomas Lester, Jr., *architect, educator*

Stillwater
Leider, Charles L. *landscape architect, planner*

Tulsa
Ball, Rex Martin *urban designer, architect*
Jones, Robert Lawton *architect, planner, educator*
Ricks, Cecil Edward *architect*

OREGON

Ashland
Friend, Sandra Ann Covert *interior designer*
Mularz, Theodore Leonard *architect*

Bend
Holl, Walter John *architect, interior designer*

Chiloquin
†Harreld, Karen L. *jewelry designer, photographer*

Lake Oswego
Largent, Margie *retired architect*

Lorane
Plésums, Guntis *architect, retired educator*

Medford
Straus, David A. *architectural firm executive*

Otter Rock
Eaton, Leonard Kimball *retired architecture educator*

Portland
Allen, Rex Whitaker *retired architect*
Bruechert, Beverly Ann *interior design consultant, recording artist, pianist*
Hacker, Thomas Owen *architect*
Tillett, M. Patrick C. *urban designer*

Springfield
Lutes, Donald Henry *architect*

Tigard
Devlin, Jamie L. *interior designer*

Tualatin
Broome, John William *retired architect*

Welches
Merrill, William Dean *retired architect, medical facility planning consultant*

PENNSYLVANIA

Ambler
†Libby, Valencia *architecture educator, consultant*
Swansen, Donna Maloney *landscape designer, consultant*

Bethlehem
Spillman, Robert Arnold *architect*

Camp Hill
Anderson, Dorothy Kentner *architect*
Brandow, Theo *architect*

Chadds Ford
†Milner, John D. *architectural firm executive, educator*
†Werner DeNadai, Mary *architectural firm executive*

Harrisburg
Knackstedt, Mary V. *interior designer*

Matamoras
Linden, Harold Arthur *interior designer, consultant*

Mount Pleasant
Pierce, Gordon Carl *retired architect*

Narberth
Grenald, Raymond *architectural lighting designer*

New Cumberland
Peters, Ralph Edgar *architectural and engineering executive*

Philadelphia
Barnett, Jonathan *architect, urban planner, educator*
Brown, Denise Scott *architect, urban planner*
Carpenter, Amy Tacy *architect*
Dagit, Charles Edward, Jr., *architect*
DeLong, David G. *architect, urban planner, educator*
Eiswerth, Barry Neil *architect, educator*
French, Jeffrey Stuart *architect*
†Greenberger, Alan *architectural firm executive*
Hamme, David Codrington *architect*
†Harris, Samuel Y. *architect, educator*
Hayes, John Freeman *architect*
Hotes, Robert Joseph *architect*
†Ivy, Jacqueline M. *interior architect*
†Keefe, Mary *architectural firm executive*
†Kelley, Daniel *architectural firm executive*
Kise, James Nelson *architect, urban planner*
†Kolker, James Hamilton *architect*
Lawson, John Quinn *architect*
†Leatherbarrow, David *architecture department chair*
Magaziner, Henry Jonas *architect, writer*
Malkawi, Ali Mahmoud *architecture educator, researcher*
Mitchell, Ehrman Burkman, Jr., *architect*
Mitchell, James Edwin *architect, educator*
Perkins, George Holmes *architectural educator, architect*
Rauch, John Keiser, Jr., *architect*
Rybczynski, Witold Marian *architect, educator, writer*
Rykwert, Joseph *architecture and art history educator*
Saylor, Peter M. *architect*
†Shuman, Robert Z. *architect*
Tyng, Anne Griswold *architect*
Venturi, Robert *architect*
Winkler, Gail Caskey *design historian, writer, educator*

Pittsburgh
Becherer, Richard John *architecture educator*
Gindroz, Raymond L. *architect*
†Kingsbury, Lisa R. *instructional design consultant*
†Loftness, Vivian Ellen *architecture educator, department chairman*
Simonds, John Ormsbee *landscape architect*

Slatington
†Hefflefinger, Karl William *retired draftsman*

State College
Haas, John C. *architect*

University Park
Wheeler, C. Herbert *architect, consultant, educator*

Willow Grove
Suer, Marvin David *architecture, consultant*

Wyomissing
Kessler, Leona Hanover *interior designer*

RHODE ISLAND

Bristol
†Hendrix, John Shannon *architecture educator*

Jamestown
Todd, Thomas Abbott *architect, urban designer, city planner*

Newport
Burgin, William Lyle *architect*
Tarpgaard, Peter Thorvald *naval architect*
Wurman, Richard Saul *architect*

Providence
Barnum, William Milo *architect*
Kagan, Marilyn D. *retired architect*

Wakefield
Phipps, Lynne Bryan *interior architect, educator, minister*

SOUTH CAROLINA

Charleston
Goff, R. Garey *architect*

Clemson
Halfacre, Robert Gordon *ombudsman,landscape architect, horticulturist, educator*

Columbia
Hultstrand, Charles John *architect*
Turk, John Cobb *architect, educator*

Hilton Head Island
Gui, James Edmund *architect*

TENNESSEE

Brentwood
Orr, Frank Howard, III, *architect*

Chattanooga
Derthick, Alan Wendell *architect, architectural firm executive*

Greeneville
Ashworth, Denise Marchant *retired landscape architect*

Knoxville
Rabun, Josette Hensley *interior design educator*

Memphis
Adsit, Russell Allan *landscape architect*
Evans, James Mignon *architect*

Morristown
Bruce, Dania Gayle *interior decorator*

Nashville
Bramlett, Shirley Marie Wilhelm *interior decorator, artist*
Swensson, Earl Simcox *architect*

TEXAS

Arlington
Ferrier, Richard Brooks *architecture educator, architect*
Fouse, David Jesse *architect*

Austin
Alexander, Drury Blakeley *architectural educator*
Box, John Harold
Garstka, John Edward *interior design educator*
George, Walter Eugene, Jr., *architect*
†Mann, Roy Bernard *landscape architect, educator*

Bellaire
Lundy, Victor Alfred *architect, educator*

College Station
Huang, Chang-Shan *landscape architect, educator*
Reed, Raymond Deryl *architect*
Shepley, Mardelle McCuskey *architect, educator*
Vandiver, Renee Lillian Aubry *interior designer, architectural preservator*
Woodcock, David Geoffrey *architect, educator*

Corpus Christi
Angell, Ellen *interior designer*

Dallas
Kolb, Nathaniel Key, Jr., *architect*
Rees, Frank William, Jr., *architect*
Schwartz, Irving Donn *architect*
†Shipley, Dan *architect*
Skaggs, Ronald Lloyd *architect*
Stacy, Dennis William *architect*

Denton
Gough, Clarence Ray *retired designer, educator*

El Paso
Benning, Mary Etzold *interior designer*
Korth, Charlotte Williams *furniture and interior design firm executive*
Stanley, Duffy B. *architect, planner*

Flower Mound
Morrish, Thomas Jay *golf course architect*

Granbury
Garrison, Truitt B. *architect*

Houston
Bair, Royden Stanley *retired architect*
Bentsen, Kenneth Edward *architect*
Bishop, Calvin Thomas *landscape architect, educator*
Bryan, Mary Ann *interior designer*
†Crane, John S. *architectural firm executive*
Cutler, John Earl *landscape architect*
†Fannin, Tom *architectural firm executive*
†Gloriod, Paul *architectural firm executive*
Green, Sharon Jordan *interior decorator*
Ivanov, Lyuben Dimitrov *naval architecture researcher, educator*
†Lerup, Lars G. *architecture educator, college dean*
†Marchand, Wayne *architectural firm executive*
Mc Ginty, John Milton *architect*
Moorhead, Gerald Lee *architect*
Reid, Robert John *architect*
†Turner, Leland *architectural firm executive*
Walton, Conrad Gordon, Sr., *retired architect*

Irving
Kuckelman, Brian Thomas *architect*

Montgomery
Tharp, Benjamin Carroll, Jr., *retired architect*

San Antonio
†Blonkvist, Tim *architectural firm executive*
Davis, George Edward *industrial designer*
Frazer, Robert Lee *landscape architect*
Graves, Kenneth Martin *architect*
Lowe, Douglas Howard *architect*

San Marcos
Treanor, Betty McKee *interior design educator*

UTAH

Ogden
Ellis, Geoffrey Ernest *landscape architect*

Salt Lake City
Beall, Burtch W., Jr., *architect*
Brems, David Paul *architect*
Chong, Richard David *architect*
Christopher, James Walker *architect, educator*
Miller, William Charles *architect, educator*

VERMONT

Brattleboro
Gorman, Robert Saul *architect*

Charlotte
†Kiley, Daniel Urban *landscape architect, planner*

VIRGINIA

Alexandria
Cross, Eason, Jr., *architect*
†Jackson, Nancy Morrison *architect*
Simonds, Marie Celeste *architect*
Vosbeck, William Frederick, Jr., *architect*
Ware, Thomas Earle *building consultant*

Arlington
Adreon, Harry Barnes *architect*
Ankudinov, Vladimir Konstantinovich *naval architect*
Draeger, Susanne Yarbrough *interior designer*
Hassett, Valerie Jane *interior designer, architect, educator*
Stewart, Gordon Mead *architect*

Blacksburg
Bliznakov, Milka Tcherneva *architect, educator*
†Knox, Paul L. *architecture educator, dean*
Rodriguez-Camilloni, Humberto Leonardo *architect, historian, educator*
†Weiner, Frank H. *architect, educator*

Boston
Engle, Reed Laurence *landscape architect*

Charlottesville
Anderson, Robert Barber *architect*
Bednar, Michael John *architecture educator*
Root, James Benjamin *landscape architect*
Swofford, Donald Anthony *architect*

Fairfax
Ward, George Truman *architect*

Falls Church
Barkley, Paul Haley, Jr., *architect*
Mortensen, Robert Henry *landscape architect, golf course architect*

Mechanicsville
Peterson, William Canova *architect*

Orlean
Kulski, Julian Eugeniusz *architect, planner, educator*

Reston
Holthausen, Martha Anne *interior designer, painter*
Scheeler, James Arthur *architect*

Richmond
†Frazer, Susan Hume *independent scholar and consultant*
Jamgochian, Victoria *interior designer*
Jandl, Henry Anthony *architect, educator*
Joel, William Lee, II, *interior and lighting designer*
Petrie, Paul Eric *interior design educator*

Virginia Beach
Stanton, Pamela Freeman *interior designer, writer*

Williamsburg
Herbert, Albert Edward, Jr., *interior and industrial designer*

Woodbridge
Peck, Dianne Kawecki *architect*

WASHINGTON

Bainbridge Island
Bowden, William Darsie *retired interior designer*

Bellevue
Elkins, Steven Paul *architect*
Hoag, Paul Sterling *architect*

Bremerton
Hower, Jeanne Louise *landscape designer*

Kenmore
Springer, Floyd Ladean *architect*

Kirkland
Mitchell, Joseph Patrick *architect*
Steinmann, John Colburn *architect*

Mill Creek
Latta, Diana Lennox *retired interior designer*

Mount Vernon
Klein, Henry *architect*

Olympia
Bagg, Carter Davis *architect, urban planner*

Pullman
Samizay, Mohammad Rafi *architect, educator*

Redmond
Sowder, Robert Robertson *architect*

ARTS: LITERARY *See also* COMMUNICATIONS MEDIA

Kenvin, Roger Lee *writer, retired English educator*
Sloane, Beverly LeBov *writer, consultant*

Atascadero
†Locke, Virginia Otis *writer*

Belmont
†MacLennan, Amy Marie *poet*
Morris, Bruce D. *technical writer, test engineer, educator, literary historian*

Berkeley
Brooke, Tal (Robert Taliaferro) *writer*
Callenbach, Ernest *writer, editor*
Dundes, Alan *folklorist, educator*
Ellis, Ella Thorp *writer, retired educator*
Gifford, Barry Colby *writer*
Guest, Barbara *author, poet*
Meltzer, David *author, musician, educator*
Miller, Adam David *poet, publishing executive*
†Milosz, Czeslaw *poet, writer, educator*
Ratch, Jerry *writer*
Russell, Charlie L. *writer*
Scott, Peter Dale *writer, retired English language educator*
Temko, Allan Bernard *writer*

Beverly Hills
Ball, Alan *screenwriter*
Basichis, Gordon Allen *writer, scriptwriter, marketing professional, media consultant*
†Bass, Ronald *screenwriter*
Belknap, Maria Ann *writer*
†Darabont, Frank *screenwriter, director*
Eisele, Robert Henry *screenwriter, producer, playwright, educator*
Farrelly, Bobby (Robert Leo Rarrelly Jr.) *writer, producer, director*
Filosa, Gary Fairmont Randolph V., II, *columnist, theater and film producer*
Gelbart, Larry *writer, producer*
Goldman, William *writer, scriptwriter*
†Maitland-Lewis, Stephen *writer*
†Rabe, David William *playwright*
†Roth, Eric *screenwriter*
Schulian, John (Nielsen Schulian) *screenwriter, author*
†Shepard, Sam (Samuel Shepard Rogers) *playwright, actor*
†Sorkin, Aaron *scriptwriter*
Ward, David Schad *screenwriter, film director*
Williamson, Kevin *writer, producer, director*

Big Bear Lake
Brueske, Charlotte *poet, composer*

Burbank
Goldstein, Kenneth F. *entertainment executive, software publisher*

Camarillo
Alexander, John Charles *editor, writer*

Cambria
Stephens, John Richard *writer*

Capitola
Wolff, Jean Walton *writer, artist*

Carlsbad
Farrell, Warren Thomas *author*

Cayucos
Shahan, Sherry Jean *writer, educator*

Chatsworth
Dunwich, Gerina *writer, magazine editor, astrologer*

Chico
†Cooper, Erwin *writer*
Davidson, Robert G. *writer, English language educator*

Citrus Heights
†Daves, Sandra Lynn *poet, lyricist*
Knight, Kit Marie *poet, writer, movie critic*

Claremont
Riley, Judith Merkle *writer, educator*
Tilden, Wesley Roderick *writer, retired computer programmer*
†Wachtel, Albert *writer, educator*

Clovis
Shields, Allan Edwin *writer, photographer, retired educator*

Compton
Shiloh, Allen *writer, postal employee*

Concord
Albrecht, Donna G. *author*

Corona
Amato, Carol Joy *writer, anthropologist*

Coronado
Stockdale, James Bond *writer, research scholar, retired naval officer*

Corte Madera
†Gajdusek, Robert Elemer *writer, retired language educator*

Cotati
Hill, Debora Elizabeth *writer, journalist, screenwriter*

Covina
Durham, Betty Louise *poet*

Cromberg
Kolb, Ken Lloyd *writer*

Culver City
Binder, Bettye B. *author, lecturer*
†Crowe, Cameron *screenwriter, film director*

Cupertino
Zobel, Louise Purwin *author, educator, lecturer, writing consultant*

Cypress
Edmonds, Ivy Gordon *writer*

Dana Point
Walker, Doris Isaak *writer, historian, educator*

Davis
Bunch, Richard Alan *writer, educator*
Major, Clarence Lee *poet, novelist, educator, artist*

Del Mar
Morton, Frederic *author*
Smith, Robert Hamil *writer, fund raiser*

Discovery Bay
Higgins, John Ralph *writer, educator*

Duarte
O'Donnell, John Patrick *journalist, photographer*

Dublin
Ingram, Judith Elizabeth *writer, counselor*

Fairfax
Ryan, Kay Pedersen *poet*

Fontana
†Tong, Freda Madeline *writer*

Fresno
Garrison-Finderup, Ivadelle Dalton *writer, educator*
†Lanter, Lanore *writer, educator*
Levine, Philip *poet, retired educator*
Petrochilos, Elizabeth A. *writer, publisher*

Garden Valley
Price, Lew Paxton *writer, engineer, scientist*

Glendale
†Burr-Stienon, Elaine *writer, minister, private school educator*

Goleta
Crowfoot, Betsy M. *writer*
Loomis, Edward Warren *writer, educator*

Healdsburg
Erdman, Paul Emil *author*
Myers, Robert Eugene *writer, educator*

Hillsborough
Atwood, Mary Sanford *writer*

Hollywood
Melchior, Ib Jorgen *author, television and motion picture writer, director*
Powell, Leslie *poet*
Shurtleff, C. Michael *writer*

Huntington Beach
Flakes, Susan *playwright, screenwriter, director*

Irvine
Shusterman, Neal Douglas *writer, screenwriter*

Jacumba
Johnson, Crane *writer, lawyer*

Julian
Rice, Earle, Jr., (Earle Wilmont Rice Jr.) *writer*

Kensington
Littlejohn, David *writer*

La Habra
Cramer, Esther Ridgway *author, historian, retired supermarket executive*

La Jolla
Antin, David *poet, critic*
Havis, Allan Stuart *playwright, theatre educator*
Iddings, Kathleen *poet, editor, publisher, consultant*
Seslar, Patrick George *writer, artist*
Sherman, Wilson *poet*

La Mesa
Mitry, Darryl Joseph *writer, educator*

La Mirada
Stone, Leland Edward *writer*

Lafayette
James, Muriel Marshall *writer, lecturer, psychotherapist*

Laguna Beach
†Ghiselin, Brewster *author, English language educator emeritus*
Taylor, Theodore Langhans *author*

Laguna Niguel
Malott, John Raymond *writer, consultant*

Lakeside
Koski, Donna Faith *poet*

Landers
Landers, Vernette Trosper *writer, educator, association executive*

Lodi
Schulz, Laura Janet *writer, retired secretary*

Long Beach
Hansell, Susan *writer, educator*

Los Angeles
Basil, Douglas Constantine *writer, educator*
Berek, Jonathan Samuel *writer, educator, dean, surgeon, gynecologist*
Carothers, A. J. *scriptwriter*
Corwin, Norman *writer, director, producer*
Edmonson-Nelson, Gloria Jean *freelance writer*
Fisher, Jay Todd *writer, educator*
†Freedman, Deborah Colette *playwright, actor*
Good-Black, Edith Elissa (Pearl Williams) *writer*
Hethmon, Robert H. *writer, educator*
†Johnson, Carole A. *writer, artist*
Kaplan, Nadia *writer*
Lettich, Sheldon Bernard *director, screenwriter*
Maker, Janet Anne *writer, retired literature educator*
Messerli, Douglas *writer, publisher*
Noguchi, Thomas Tsunetomi *author, forensic pathologist*
Patrick, Robert *playwright*
Pleasants, Ben *writer, poet, playwright, educator*
Schulberg, Budd *author*
Shapiro, Mel *playwright, director, drama educator*
Silverman, Treva *writer, producer, consultant*
Sivertsen, Linda Joyce *writer, publishing consultant, editor*
Steel, Ronald Lewis *writer, historian, educator*
Thomas, Shirley *author, educator, business executive*
Vangelisti, Paul Louis *poet*
Weiser, Stanley *screenwriter*
Westheimer, David Kaplan *novelist*
Yoshiki-Kovinick, Marian Tsugie *author*
†Zone, Ray *writer*

Los Gatos
Dahlberg, Thomas Robert *writer, lawyer, educator, software company executive*

Mammoth Lakes
Fitzgerald, Timothy K. *writer, political organizer, non-profit administrator*

Menlo Park
Dorset, Phyllis Flanders *technical writer, editor*

Mill Valley
Owings, Alison June *writer, journalist*

Modesto
Nash, Edgar Mason *writer*
Turner-Silvia, JoAnn *writer, vocalist, actress, music producer*

Monterey
von Drachenfels, Suzanne Hamilton *writer*

Moraga
Sestanovich, Molly Brown *writer*

Napa
Leggett, John Ward *writer*

Newport Beach
Wentworth, Diana von Welanetz *author*

North Hollywood
Kuter, Kay E. *writer, actor*

Northridge
Barnard, Ian *writer, educator*

Oakland
Foley, Jack (John Wayne Harold Foley) *poet, writer, editor*
†Halpern, Mark *writer*
†Horton, David Harrison *writer, educator*
†Knox, Helene Margrethe *writer*
†Massachi, Dalya Faith *writer, non-profit administrator*
Narell, Irena *freelance writer, history educator*
Raver, Miki (Mikala) *scriptwriter, film producer*
Schacht, Henry Mevis *writer, consultant*
Silverberg, Robert *author*
†Turner, Tom *writer, editor*

Oceano
Scott, Donald Michael *writer, educator*

Oceanside
Humphrey, Phyllis A. *writer*

Orange
†Stevens, Cherita Wyman *writer, educator*

Orinda
Strong, Susan Clancey *writer, communication consultant, editor*

Pacific Palisades
McGinn, James Thomas *writer, producer*

Palm Desert
Friesz, Mary Lee *freelance/self-employed poet*
Ryan, Allyn Cauagas *writer, educator*

Palm Springs
Racina, Thom (Thomas Frank Raucina) *television writer, editor*

Palo Alto
Briskin, Mae *writer*
Love, Brenda Zejdl *writer*
†Schutt, Geoff *writer, performance artist*
Wright, Kirby Michael *writer, editor*

Palos Verdes Peninsula
Unger, Ken R. *writer*

Pasadena
Arrieta, Marcia *poet, editor, publishing executive, educator*
Brogden-Stirbl, Shona Marie *writer, researcher*
Bunting, Anne Evelyn (Eve Bunting) *author*
†Littke, Lael Jensen *author*

Penngrove
Chadwick, Cydney Marie *writer, art projects executive*

Petaluma
†Hass, Robert L. *writer, educator*
Pronzini, Bill John (William Pronzini) *writer*
†Spiegelman, Art *author, cartoonist*

Playa Del Rey
McNeill, Daniel Richard *writer*

Playa Vista
Mikesell, Richard Hugh *writer*

Rancho Mirage
Olderman, Murray *columnist, cartoonist*

Rancho Palos Verdes
†Zar, Judith L. (Mickey McBride) *writer*

Rancho Santa Fe
Byrd, Betty Rantze *writer*
Simon, William Leonard *film and television writer and producer, writer*

Red Bluff
†Peters, Michael Morgan *playwright, consultant, theater director, theater critic, educator*

Redondo Beach
Battles, Roxy Edith *novelist, consultant, educator*

Reedley
Carey, Ernestine Gilbreth (Mrs. Charles E. Carey) *writer, lecturer*

Rohnert Park
Haslam, Gerald William *writer, educator*

Rolling Hills Estates
Price, Lia Scott *writer*

Ross
Godwin, Sara *writer*

Sacramento
Gerringer, Elizabeth (The Marchioness de Roe Devon) *writer, lawyer*
Stenzel, Larry Gene *writer*
Tranum, Jean Lorraine *freelance writer*

Saint Helena
†Wiggins, Rita Cassidy *poet*

San Anselmo
Torbet, Laura *writer, artist, photographer, graphic designer*

San Diego
Boersma, June Elaine (Jalma Barrett) *writer, photographer*
†Brennan-Sparks, Jennifer Anne *writer*
Cassady, Marsh G. *writer, editor*
†Chun Fat, George *writer*
Crumpler, Hugh Allan *author*
Lederer, Richard Henry *writer, educator, columnist*
Liber, Hillary Selese Jacobs *writer, educator*
Mahdavi, Kamal B. *writer, researcher*
Prescott, Lawrence Malcolm *medical and health science writer*
Skwara, Erich Wolfgang *novelist, poet, educator, literary critic*
Stein, Eleanor Benson (Ellie Stein) *playwright, writer*
Steward, Harold David (Hal Steward) *author, journalist, retired army officer*
†Sturman, George *poet, volunteer*
†Valdez, Jose Carbajal, Jr., *poet, lyricist*
Yarber, Robert Earl *writer, retired educator*

San Francisco
Bayer, William *writer*
Carlisle, Henry C. *author*
Conboy, Roy *playwright, educator*
Cousineau, Philip Robert *writer, filmmaker*
Ferlinghetti, Lawrence *poet*
Ferris, Russell James, II, *freelance writer*
Gold, Herbert *author*
Gunn, Thom(son) (Thomson William Gunn) *poet, retired English educator*
Hiemstra, Marvin Roy *poet, humorist, literary consultant*
†Inman, Robert Anthony *writer*
Kazalia, Marie Ann *writer*
Keats, Jonathon *writer*
Morrison, Ellen M. *writer, researcher*
O'Connor, Sheila Anne *freelance writer*
Pratt, James Norwood *scholarly writer*
Sachs, Marilyn Stickle *author, lecturer, editor*
†Sterkina, Sofiya *writer*
Taylor, Kent (Paul Taylor) *poet, medical researcher*

San Jose
Bleznick, Susan Risa *writer, television producer, photographer*
Chang, Iris Shun-Ru *writer*
Loventhal, Milton *writer, playwright, lyricist*

San Leandro
Wycoff, Charles Coleman *writer, retired anesthesiologist*

San Luis Obispo
Bunge, Russell Kenneth *writer, poet, editor*

San Luis Rey
Williams, Elizabeth Yahn *writer, lecturer, lawyer*

San Marcos
Winebrenner, Susan Kay *writer, educational consultant*

San Marino
Hull, Suzanne White *writer, retired administrator*

San Rafael
Brett, Peter D. *writer*
Follett, Carolyn Brown *poet, artist*
Henry, Marie Elaine *poet*
Nelson, James Carmer, Jr., *writer, editor, advertising executive*
Turner, William Weyand *writer*

Santa Barbara
Bock, Russell Samuel *writer*
Cunningham, Julia Woolfolk *author*
Jackson, Beverley Joy Jacobson *columnist, lecturer*
Mitchell, Shawne Maureen *author*
Pochini, Judy Hay *interior designer, writer, editor*
Poynter, Dan *author, publisher, speaker*
Ramsay, William Charles *writer, composer*

Santa Clara
Simmons, Janet Bryant *writer, publisher*
Singh, Loren Chan *technical writing specialist*

Santa Cruz
Houston, James D. *writer*
Sherman, Frieda Frances *writer*

Santa Monica
Crichton, Michael (John Crichton) *author, film director*
Jones, Janet Dulin *writer, film producer*
Kronenberg, S. Allyx *poet, writer, lyricist*
Mora, Philippe *screenwriter, producer, director, painter*
†Roney, Alice Lorraine Mann *poet*
†Spataro, Janie Dempsey Watts *writer*

Seal Beach
Olechno-Huszcza, Czeslaw *retired translator and educator*

Sebastopol
Arnold, Marsha Diane *writer*
†Marler, Joan *writer, educator*

Sherman Oaks
Ellison, Harlan Jay *author, screenwriter*
†LeBlanc, Rena *writer*

Simi Valley
Hochheiser, Marilyn *author, actress*
Shawn, Eric *author, artist, film director*

Somis
Premack, Ann J. *writer*

Sonoma
Kizer, Carolyn Ashley *poet, educator*

South Pasadena
White, W. Robin *writer*

Stanford
Berger, Joseph *author, educator, counselor*
Bocock, Maclin *writer*
Conquest, (George) Robert (Acworth) *writer, historian, poet, critic, journalist*
Duncan, Debbie *writer*
Girard, René Noel *author, educator*
Wolff, Tobias (Jonathan Ansell Wolff) *writer*

Stockton
Torregian, Sotère *poet*

Studio City
Elias, Merle *writer, consultant*
Parish, James Robert *author, cinema historian*
Shavelson, Melville *writer, theatrical producer and director*
Slade, Bernard *playwright*

Sugarloaf
Black, Victoria Lynn *writer, artist*

Sun City
†LaRoe, Thomas Dean *office manager, writer*

Sun Valley
Casey, Paul Arnold *writer, composer, photographer, producer, director*

Trinidad
Green, Benjamin W. *poet*

Tustin
Poyer, Joseph John *writer, publisher*

Ukiah
†Van Dusen, Wilson M. *writer, psychologist*

Valencia
Parks, Suzan Lori *playwright*
Webb, Margot *writer*

Venice
Eliot, Alexander *author, mythologist*
Padilla, Mario René *literature educator, writer, actor*

Vernon
Kim, Ho Gill *poet*

Walnut Creek
Chu, Valentin Yuan-ling *author*

West Hollywood
Grasshoff, Alex *writer, producer, director*
Thaw, Mort *writer*

Westminster
Amalsad, Meher Dadabhoy *writer, speaker, seminar leader*

Whittier
Caro, Evelyn Inga Rouse *writer*

Wilmington
†Farabi-Nance, Khadijah *writer*

Yorba Linda
Medland, Maurice Blue *writer*

COLORADO

Aurora
As-Salaam, Jamaal (William Louis Williams Jr.) *poet, film producer, writer*

Black Hawk
Jones, Linda May *tour guide*

Boulder
Carlson, Rhonda *writer, law educator*
Hurd, Jerrie *writer*
Martinez, Jose Rafael *writer, educator, poet*
Mitchell, David Spear *writer, editor, publisher, science educator*

Canon City
Watson, Carrie Ann *writer, artist*

Cascade
Seger, Linda Sue *script consultant, lecturer, writer*

Castle Rock
Rogers, Pattiann *poet, educator, poet, writer*

Colorado Springs
Dassanowsky, Robert von *educator, producer, writer, editor*
Hicks, David Earl *writer, inventor*
Leasure, Robert Ellis *writer, photographer*
Murphy, James Rodney *playwright*
Rhodes, Daisy Chun *writer, researcher, oral historian*

Denver
Akers, Keith *writer, information technology consultant*
†Avi, (Avi Wortis) *author*
Carlson, Robert Ernest *freelance writer, architect, lecturer*
Dallas, Sandra *writer*
Ducker, Bruce *novelist, lawyer*
Howse, Cathy L. *writer, researcher, entrepreneur*
MacGregor, George Lescher, Jr., *freelance writer*
Nemiro, Beverly Mirium Anderson *author, educator*
Owen, Maureen A. *poet*
Sheldon Epstein, Vivian *author, publisher*
Vosevich, Kathi Ann *writer, editor, scholar*

Durango
Korns, Leota Elsie *writer, mountain land developer, insurance broker*

Englewood
Irwin, Mark *writer, educator*
Simendinger, Theodore John *writer, publishing executive*

Golden
Eber, Kevin *science writer*

Grand Junction
Armstrong, Linda Jean (Gene Armstrong) *writer, artist*
†Nizalowski, John Anthony *writer, educator*

Greeley
Longwell, Robert Leroy *writer*
Willis, Connie (Constance E. Willis) *author*

Ignacio
Craig, Roy Phillip *writer, educator, rancher*

Lyons
Spring, Kathleen *writer*

Peyton
Ball, Jennifer Leigh *writer, editor*

Silverton
Voorlas, Stephanie Katherine *freelance/self-employed writer, photographer*

Vail
Knight, Constance Bracken *writer, realtor, corporate executive*

Westminster
Lingle, JoLynn Fleishman *writer, educator*

Wheat Ridge
Morriss, Frank *writer, educator*

CONNECTICUT

Chester
Stark, Evelyn Brill *poet, musician*

Clinton
Adler, Peggy Ann *writer, illustrator, investigator*

Darien
Hailey, Arthur *author*

East Hampton
Tucceri, Clive Knowles *science writer and educator, consultant*

Easton
Maloney, John Joseph *writer*

Ellington
Edgar, Gregory T. *author*

Fairfield
Barone, Rose Marie Pace *writer, retired educator, entertainer*
Ladd, Louise *writer*
Rogers, Louis Jerome *writer, educator*

Greenwich
Ewald, William Bragg, Jr., *author, consultant*
Hoberman, Mary Ann *author*
Walker, Robert Martin *writer, minister*
Wallach, Magdalena Falkenberg (Carla Wallach) *writer*

Guilford
Peters, William *author, producer, director*

Hamden
Davis, Lorraine Jensen *writer, editor*

Hanover
Cheney, Glenn Alan *writer, educator*

Hartford
Hedrick, Joan Doran *writer, university educator*

Madison
Carlson, Dale Bick *writer*

New Canaan
Fredericks, Jeanne Maria Judson *literary agent*

New Haven
Alwood, Edward McQueen *writer, journalist, media specialist*
Bly, Mark John *playwright, educator*
Hayden, Dolores *author, architect, educator*
Scarf, Margaret (Maggie Scarf) *author*
†Shaumyan, Alexander *poet, education educator*

New London
†Bouchard, Jae Arlene *writer, poet, interior designer*
Espinosa, Resurreccion *playwright, theater director, writer*

New Preston Marble Dale
Biddle, Flora Miller *writer*

Niantic
Mountzoures, Harry Louis *writer*

Norwalk
Bortolot, Gary *writer, educator*

Old Greenwich
†Roca-de-Togores, Luis D. *writer*

Old Lyme
St. George, Judith Alexander *author*

Portland
Rundle, Margaret *literary arts educator*

Preston
Gibson, Margaret Ferguson *poet, educator*

Ridgefield
Riche, Robert Savery *writer*

Roxbury
Gurney, Albert Ramsdell *playwright, novelist, educator*

Salisbury
Magowan, Robin *writer*

Stamford
†Tenaglia, Douglas Joseph *advertising copywriter*

Storrs Mansfield
Rimland, Lisa Phillip *writer, composer, lyricist, artist*

Stratford
Walker, Gladys Lorraine *author*

Suffield
†Sullivan, Edmund Bertram *writer*

Waterford
Commire, Anne *playwright, writer, editor*

West Cornwall
Klaw, Spencer *writer, editor, educator*

West Hartford
Calip, Roger *writer, educator*

Westbrook
Hall, Jane Anna *writer, model, artist*

Weston
Brodax, Albert Philip *writer, film producer and director*
Diforio, Robert George *literary agent*
Kilty, Jerome Timothy *playwright, stage director, actor*

Westport
Hotchner, Aaron Edward *author*
†Mallon, Thomas *writer*

Wilton
†Nugent, Gordon Walker *writer*

DELAWARE

Hockessin
†Mertz, Anne Morris *writer, researcher, freelance journalist, teacher, lecturer*

Newark
†Snair, Roger Clifford *writer, comedian*
Yagoda, Ben James *author, English educator*

Wilmington
Michel, Sandra Seaton *writer*
Ziolkowska-Boehm, Aleksandra *writer*

DISTRICT OF COLUMBIA

Washington
Alperovitz, Gar *author, educator*
Alvarez de DeClaris, María Clemencia *writer, educator*
Angell, Lois Louise *writer, speaker, poet, comedian*
Arndt, Richard Tallmadge *writer, consultant*
Arnold, Elizabeth Brown *poet, educator*
Atlas, Liane Wiener *writer*
Barnet, Richard Jackson *author, educator*
Becker, Jerome David *writer*
Birnbaum, Norman *author, humanities educator*
†Brownstein, Elizabeth Smith *writer*
Burnham, David Bright *writer, educator*
Burns, David Mitchell *writer, musician, former diplomat*
Cavnar, Samuel Melmon *writer, publisher, activist*
Chaffee, Kevin St. Clair *writer*
Conroy, Richard Timothy *writer, retired foreign service officer*
Darr, Ann Russell *poet, educator*
Dunbar, Leslie Wallace *writer, consultant*
Freeman, Jo *writer, political consultant, lawyer*
Furgurson, Ernest Baker, Jr., (Pat Furgurson) *writer*
George, Gerald William *author, administrator*
Gioia, (Michael) Dana *poet, literary critic*
Goldberg, Kirsten Boyd *science journalist*
Gorlin, Rena Ann *writer*
Grossblatt, Norman *science editor*
Hecht, Anthony Evan *poet*
Innis, Pauline *writer, publishing company executive*
Jasper, John A. *writer, lawyer*
†King, Mary Elizabeth *writer, educator*
Kramer, Simon Paul *writer*
Lilienthal, Alfred M(orton) *author, historian, editor*
May, Stephen *writer, former government official*
Merrell, Jesse Howard *writer*
Mezey, Robert
Miller, Hope Ridings *author*
Muravchik, Joshua *writer*
Murphy, Joanne Becker *writer*
†Parker, Ché André *writer, journalist*
Parker, Richard Bordeaux *writer, educator*
Richardson, David B. *writer, journalist*
Ritchie, Elisavietta *writer, poet, educator, editor, translator*
Robb, Lynda Johnson *writer*
Shaw, Russell Burnham *author, journalist*
Smith, Stuart Seaborne *writer, government official, union official*
†Torain, Terri Lisa *writer, consultant*
Williams, Leaford Clemetson *writer, political scientist*
†Williamson, Michael *photographer*
Wouk, Herman *writer*
Yarrow, Andrew Louis *writer, journalist, educator, international relations consultant*
Zietz, Karyl Lynn Kopelman *writer, opera critic, television correspondent, producer, documentary filmmaker*

FLORIDA

Altamonte Springs
Baker, Mark Allen *author, historian, consultant, graphologist*

Babson Park
Morrison, Kenneth Douglas *author, columnist*

Belleair Beach
Fuentes, Martha Ayers *playwright*

Boca Raton
Keyes, Daniel *author*

Cape Canaveral
Hess, Terry Lee *writer, educator*

Citrus Springs
Tillery, Billy Carey *writer, poet*

Davie
Labowitz, Shoni *writer, lecturer*

Daytona Beach
Chesnut, Nondis Lorine *screenwriter, consultant, reading and language arts educator, instructor, counselor*
Mc Collister, John Charles *writer, clergyman, educator, executive producer*

Delray Beach
Frazer, Vernon *writer, musician*
Murphy, Kevin George *novelist*
Robinson, Richard Francis *writer, author, geneaologist, historian*

Eustis
Chorosinski, Eugene Conrad *writer, poet, author*

Fort Lauderdale
Heidelberg, Paul *writer*

Fort Myers
Hartman, Earl Kenneth *writer*
†Monear, Edwin Everett *writer*
Wall, Robert J. *author, researcher*

Gainesville
†Briones, Nick Alcantara *writer*
Holland, Norman Norwood *literary critic*
†Langstaff, Margaret J. *writer and editor*
Leahy, Thomas Melvin, Jr., *writer*

Leavitt, David Adam *writer, English educator*
Smith, Jo Anne *writer, retired educator*

Hallandale
†Rose, Lucille Marie *retired writer*

Highland Beach
Tolf, Robert Walter *writer*

Hollywood
Krane, Jessica (Aida Jessica Kohnop-Krane) *writer, educator*

Homosassa
Carmichael, Roberta Kay *writer*

Homosassa Springs
Burch, Annetta Jane *writer*

Jacksonville
Moses, Daniel *writer, singer*

Key West
†Lawrence, Judith M. *writer, journalist*

Lakeland
Arndt, Melvin C. *writer*

Leesburg
Thompson, Mary B. *writer, illustrator*

Longboat Key
Hazan, Marcella Maddalena *writer, educator, consultant*

Melbourne
Fiore, Carmen Anthony *writer*
Lederer, William Julius *author*
Stone, Elaine Murray *author, composer, television producer*

Miami
Abril, Marcia (Ela I. Cardinas) *writer*
Alschuler, Al *freelance/self-employed writer, marketing professional*
Camner, Howard *author, poet*
Goin-Harding, Cecilia Margaret *poet*
Laje, Zilia L. *writer, publisher, translator*
†Luque-Escalona, Roberto Sabas *writer*
Morgan, Marabel *author*
Taylor, Joe, Jr., *writer, consultant*
Whitehead, John *poet*

Naples
†Cook, Robin *author*
Wroble, Lisa Ann *writer, educator*

Navarre
Starratt, Patricia Elizabeth *writer, actress, composer, pianist*

New Smyrna Beach
Zink, Joan Wilson *writer, poet, composer*

Niceville
†Hinze, Vicki Kay *writer, educator*

Ocala
†Belmontez, Deborah Lynn Groves *poet, editor*
†Boston, Bruce David *writer, book designer*
Gresham, Jack Warren *poet*

Oldsmar
Craft Davis, Audrey Ellen *writer, educator*

Orlando
Blum, Richard Arthur *writer, media educator*
†Hubbard, Susan Mary *writer, English educator*
Raffa, Jean Benedict *author, educator*

Ormond Beach
Burke, Marguerite Jodi Larcombe *writer, executive services professional*
Geary, James Martin *writer, communications executive*

Palm Bay
Schaaf, Martha Eckert *author, poet, library director, musician, composer, educator, lecturer*
†Zerick, A. Lura *writer*

Panama City
Schafer, John Stephen *poet*

Panama City Beach
Anderson, Ruth Nathan *syndicated columnist, TV news host, writer, recording artist, lyricist*

Pensacola
†Sims, Pam *writer, minister*

Pompano Beach
Kaskinen, Barbara Kay *author, composer, songwriter, musician, music educator*

Ponte Vedra Beach
Friedmann, Elizabeth Carroll *writer, editor*

Port Saint Lucie
Jackson, George Mark *writer, photographer*

Saint Augustine
Nolan, David Joseph *author, historian*
Oliver, Elizabeth Kimball *writer, historian*

Saint Petersburg
Carlson, Jeannie Ann *writer*
Edwards, Fred L., Jr., *writer consultant*
†Hersh, Ellen E. *poet*
Wright, Fred W., Jr., *writer*

Sarasota
Jones, Sally Daviess Pickrell *writer*
Weeks, Albert Loren *author, educator, journalist*
Wilson, Kenneth Jay *writer*

Seminole
†Wolf, Elizabeth Ann *writer, storyteller, visual arts*

Stuart
Woodward, Isabel Avila *educational writer, foreign language educator*

Tallahassee
Bagley, James Robert *freelance writer*
†Butler, Robert Olen *writer, educator*
Dillon, Millicent Gerson *writer*
Johnson, Margaret Anderson *writer, publishing executive, plantation owner*
Tourtet, Christiane Andrée *writer, human rights activist, photojournalist, reporter*

Tampa
Battle, Jean Allen *writer, educator*
Hanford, Grail Stevenson *writer*
Shimberg, Elaine Fantle *writer*
Westcott, Joan Clark *poet*

The Villages
Oetjen, David L. (Jon David Douglas) *writer, film producer*

Valrico
Joyce, Veronica Delores *writer, educator*

Venice
Thomas, Terence Patrick *writer, researcher, electronics design engineer*

Vero Beach
Lamoureux, William Albert *poet*

West Palm Beach
Henry, Rene Arthur *author, consultant*

Winter Haven
Bybee, Charles Forrest *writer, poet*

Zellwood
†Duffy, Thomas Patrick *retired writer*

GEORGIA

Athens
†Dashiell, Frank Stephen, IV, *writer*
Williams, Philip Lee *writer*

Atlanta
Austin, Judy Essary *scriptwriter*
Chaffin, Tom *writer*
†Corriher, Shirley *food writer*
†Davis, Jean Lerche *writer*
Geigerman, Clarice Furchgott *writer, consultant*
Moore, Philip Nicholas *author*

Cleveland
Inge, Walter Herndon *writer*

College Park
West-Hill, Gwendolyn *poet, educator, artist, evangelist*

Columbus
Short, Shenita *writer*

Duluth
Kramer, Edward E. *screenwriter, editor*

Hephzibah
Golphin, Elouise *writer, educator*

Hoschton
Campbell, Leslie Caine (Caine Campbell) *writer, historian*

Lizella
Jones, Seaborn Gustavus *poet*

Metter
Abbott, Nell Suttles *writer, poet*

Milledgeville
Friman, Alice Ruth *poet, English educator*

Peachtree City
Marsh, Carole *author, photographer, publisher*

Pine Mountain
Bishop, Michael *writer*

Rome
Sumner, Melanie *writer, educator*

Savannah
Briggs, Niwana Page *editor, writer*
Coffey, Thomas Francis, Jr., *writer*
Dunham, Byron S. *writer*
Thomas, Dwight Rembert *writer*

Statesboro
Gilbert, Armida Jennings *American literature educator*

HAWAII

Holualoa
Stoddard, Sandol *freelance/self-employed writer*

Honolulu
Halloran, Richard Colby *writer, former research executive, former news correspondent, columnist, editor*
†Shankar, Subramanian *writer, educator*

Kailua Kona
†Birtcher, Baron R. *writer, real estate broker*

Lanai City
Black, Anderson Duane *writer, business consultant*

IDAHO

Hailey
Dolas, Evelyn Ann *poet, musician*

Lewisville
Lindstrom, Joyce E. *author*

Sandpoint
†Hoff, Benjamin Lloyd *writer, scriptwriter*

Twin Falls
Fanselow, Julie Ruth *writer*

ILLINOIS

Burbank
Juodvalks, Egle (Egle Juodvalké) *writer*

Carlyle
Kottmeyer, Martin S. *farmer, writer*

Champaign
Watson, Jessica Lewis *writer*

Chicago
Beer, John R. *poet, educator*
Buehler, Evelyn Judy *poet*
Carter, Tyrone *writer*
Ferguson, Margaret Geneva *writer, publisher, real estate broker*
Hoover, Paul *poet*
Lach, Alma Elizabeth *food and cooking writer, consultant*
†Lavin, Maud Katherine *writer, art educator*
Madsen, Dorothy Louise (Meg Madsen) *writer*
Manelli, Donald Dean *screenwriter, film producer*
McManus, James Laughlin *writer, educator*
Perlberg, Mark *poet, educator*
Schandelmeier, Cathleen Ann *playwright, poet, producer*
Silesky, Barry T. *writer, educator*
Sloan, James Park *novelist, biographer, educator*
Stern, Richard Gustave *writer, educator*
†Terkel, Studs (Louis Terkel) *writer, interviewer*
Wallingford, Anne *writer, editor, project developer*
†Yanoff, Jerome C. *writer, educator*

Evanston
Gibbons, William Reginald, Jr., *poet, novelist, translator, editor*
Kinzie, Mary *poet, educator*
†Vladem, Steven Allen *writer, motivational speaker*

Galesburg
†Metz, Robin O. *writer, educator, poet*

Highland Park
Greenblatt, Miriam *writer, editor, educator*

Lake Forest
Swanton, Virginia Lee *writer, publisher, bookseller*
Taylor, Barbara Ann Olin *writer, educational consultant*

Lanark
Etter, David Pearson *poet, editor*

Macomb
Na'Allah, Abdul-Rasheed *writer, educator*

Marengo
Mrkvicka, Edward Francis, Jr., *financial writer, publisher, consultant*

Marshall
†Freeman, Charles E. *writer, musician*

Morton Grove
Vega, Steve *poet*

Normal
†Besserman, Perle S. *writer, educator*
Sutherland, Robert Donald *writer*

North Riverside
Sedlak, S(hirley) A(gnes) *freelance writer, novelist*

Oak Lawn
Laird, Jean Elouise Rydeski (Mrs. Jack E. Laird) *author, adult education educator*

Oak Park
Pearson, Gayle Marlene *writer, editor*
Rossiter, Charles Melvin *poet*

Palatine
†Nordlof, Ragnar William *writer*
Pohl, Frederik *freelance/self-employed writer*

Paris
Sisson, Marilyn Sue *writer*

Peru
Kurtz, James Eugene *freelance writer, minister*

Riverside
Pollitt, Raymond Daniel John *writer, consultant*

Rockford
Kelleghan, Kevin Michael *writer, trainer*

Roscoe
†Panagopoulos, Janie Lynn *writer*
Sears, Donna Mae *designer, illustrator*

Skokie
†Ginn, Martin E. *writer, consultant*

South Barrington
Kissane, Sharon Florence *writer, consultant, educator*

Stoy
Rhoten, Kenneth D. *writer*

University Park
†Patton, June Odessa *writer, consultant, educator, researcher*

Urbana
Bial, Raymond Steven *author, photographer*
†Bobyshev, Dmitry V. *poet, education educator*
Dovring, Karin Elsa Ingeborg *writer, poet, playwright, communication analyst*
Lieberman, Laurence *poet, educator*

Waukegan
Marks, Martha Alford *writer*

West Brooklyn
Mays, K. J. *writer, musician*

Willowbrook
McCormack, Emily Anna *writer, book reviewer*

Wilmette
Brill, Marlene Targ *writer*

INDIANA

Beverly Shores
Fammerée, Richard Arthur Noel *poet, composer, performing artist*

Bloomington
†Johnson-D'Alessio, Anna Maria *writer*
Kibbey, Hal Stephen *science writer*
Mitchell, Bert Breon *literary translator*
Thom, James Alexander *novelist*

Chesterton
Petrakis, Harry Mark *author*

Crown Point
Palmeri, Sharon Elizabeth *freelance writer, community educator*

Elkhart
Eddy, Darlene Mathis *poet, educator*

Fort Wayne
Frost, Helen Marie *writer*
Gaff, Alan Dale *writer*

Frankfort
Borland, Kathryn Kilby *author*

French Lick
Kalla, Alec Karl *writer, rancher*

Howe
Bowerman, Ann Louise *writer, genealogist, educator*

Indianapolis
Budniakiewicz, Therese *writer*
Carter, Jared *poet*
Hoppe, David Rutledge *writer, editor*
Livers, Catherine McGhee *writer*
†Nolan-Williams, Margaret Colleen *writer, craftsman*
Yates, Robin Corriene *freelance writer*

Kendallville
†Hooker, Joseph David *writer, minister*

Morgantown
Callon, Margaret Joann *writer, minister*

Muncie
Alves, Abel A. *writer*

Notre Dame
Goulet, Denis André *development ethicist, writer*

Plainfield
Bryant, John Howard *writer*

Scottsburg
Dockery-Schillig, Linda *writer*

Seymour
Anderson, David E. *writer, musicologist*

South Bend
†Green, Jerry *writer*
†Guyberson, Randy Alan *writer*

IOWA

Charles City
Krieger, Theodore Kent *poet*

Clinton
Warner, Jean Lollich *poet*

Davenport
Beguhn, Sandra E. *poet, author*
McDonald, Julie Jensen *writer, educator*

Dubuque
Tigges, John Thomas *writer, musician, lecturer*

Fairfield
Larson, Rustin Lee *writer, educator*

Fort Dodge
Wolf, Robert Charles *writer, news correspondent*

Rockport
Salinger, Warren *writer*

Salem
Must, Dennis Patrick *writer, editor*

Shelburne Falls
Bagg, Robert Ely *poet, educator, translator*

Somerset
†Manchester, Steven Herbert *writer, educator*

Somerville
Auspitz, Josiah Lee *writer, consultant*
†Fujiwara, Chris *writer*
Leverich, Kathleen *writer*
Neville, Emily Tam Lin *writer, educator*

South Hadley
Shaw, Robert Burns *poet, educator*
Viereck, Peter *poet, historian, educator*

South Hamilton
Kroeger, Catherine C. *writer, editor, educator*

South Orleans
Goldman, Elliott Stanley *writer*

Springfield
†Stevens, Joyce Ann *writer, publisher, educator*

Truro
Woolley, Catherine (Jane Thayer) *writer*

Watertown
†Pirolli, John Paul *poet, writer, construction executive*

Wellesley
Costley, Bill (Bill Costley) *poet, writer*
Jacobs, Ruth Harriet *poet, playwright, sociologist, gerontologist*

Wellfleet
Piercy, Marge *poet, novelist, essayist*

West Newbury
Dooley, Ann Elizabeth *freelance writers cooperative executive, editor*

West Roxbury
Ellenbogen, George *poet, educator*
Seltzer, Richard Warren, Jr., *writer, editor, consultant*

Williamstown
Glück, Louise Elisabeth *poet, educator*
Scull, Christina *writer*
Stevens, Lauren Rogers *writer, environmentalist*

Woburn
Basile, Leon Edmund *writer, editor*

Worcester
Vick, Susan *playwright, educator, director, actress*

MICHIGAN

Allendale
Osborn, William Palmer *writer, English language educator*

Ann Arbor
†Perrotta, Kevin Francis *writer, editor-in-chief*

Battle Creek
Milligan, Glenn Edward *poet*
Myer, Donna Gail *writer, health researcher*

Charlevoix
Knutson, Roger M. *writer, retired science educator*

Chesterfield
Wilson-Pleiness, Christine Joyce *writer, poet, columnist, real estate investor*

Detroit
Gibbs, Mary L. *writer, writers' services provider*
Madgett, Naomi Long *poet, editor, publisher, educator*

Dowagiac
†Sweet, Margaret Ellen *writer*

East Lansing
Perrin, Robert *editorial consultant, writer*
Wakoski, Diane *poet, educator*

Farmington
†Palazzolo, Laurie A. *writer*

Farmington Hills
Wiloch, Thomas *writer, editor*

Grand Rapids
Foster, Linda Nemec *poet, educator*
Redmond, Jeffrey *author, journalist*

Holland
Nieuwsma, Milton John *writer, journalist*

Holly
Magnuson, Valerie *poet, artist, export consultant*

Kalamazoo
Light, Christopher Upjohn *writer, computer musician, photographer*
Lowery, Joanne *writer, editor*

Lansing
Behrens, Ellen Elizabeth Cox *writer, counselor, educator*
Fox, Hugh Bernard, Jr., *writer, archaeologist*

Lincoln Park
†Kissel, Kevin Karl *freelance/self-employed writer*

Mackinac Island
Mc Cabe, John Charles, III, *writer*

Mount Morris
Wooley, Geraldine Hamilton *writer, poet*

Muskegon
Jamieson, T. John *writer, English language educator*

Okemos
Klunzinger, Thomas Edward *writer, actor, director*

Oshtemo
Arnold, Nancy Kay *writer*

Pontiac
Cohassey, John Fredrick *writer*

Powers
Kleikamp, Beverly *poet, writer, publisher*

Republic
Wixtrom, Donald Joseph *translator*

Rochester
Kutlich, Anna *writer*

Saint Joseph
Shirkey, William Dan *writer*

Shepherd
Herman, Mark Norman *translator*

Sodus
†Handy, Virginia Mae *writer*

South Haven
†Stone, Jeannine Gail *retired writer, retired poet*

Southfield
†Johnson, David (David Makenna) *writer*

Union Pier
Howland, Bette *writer*

Warren
Zadoorian, Michael Craig *writer*

West Bloomfield
Brin, David *writer, astronomer*

Ypsilanti
Gaertner, Kenneth C. *poet, educator*
†Kiesbye, Stefan *writer, educator*

MINNESOTA

Appleton
Wilson, Orpha Hildred *writer*

Brainerd
†Russell, Maxine *poet, writer*

Edina
Christensen, Nadia Margaret *writer, translator, editor, educator*
Schwarzrock, Shirley Pratt *writer, lecturer, educator*

Grand Rapids
Jensen, Michael Wayne *writer*

Minneapolis
Baker, John Stevenson (Michael Dyregrov) *writer*
†Kapelac, Samuel James *writer, sales executive*
Korotkin, Fred *writer, philatelist*
Lange, Katherine J. *writer*
†Mathy, Robin Michelle *writer*
St. Germaine-Lattig, Charles Edwin *political writer*
Verby, Jane Crawford *writer*

Northfield
Benkowski, Ann Marie *writer*

Richfield
Thompson, Steve Allan *writer*

Saint Paul
Bly, Carol McLean *writer, educator*
Keillor, Garrison Edward *writer, radio host*
Lambert, LeClair Grier *writer, lecturer, consultant, state government public information administrator*

Shakopee
Gertis, Neill Allan *writer*

MISSISSIPPI

Amory
Brannon, Pat *poet*

Greenville
Keating, Bern *writer, journalist*

Jackson
†Grant, Bettye *writer*
Redmon, Cynthia Ann *poet, songwriter*
Scafidel, Jim R. *freelance/self-employed writer*

Southaven
†White, Marguerite *writer*

Taylorsville
Windham, Velma Lee Ainsworth *writer, poet*

MISSOURI

Ballwin
Haller, Karen Sue *writer*
†Schneider, Ches *writer, educator*

Bloomfield
Ferrell, Paul Cleveland *writer*

Des Peres
Sadlo, Kenneth Louis *poet, writer*

Kansas City
Martin-Bowen, Lindsey *freelance writer*
Roth, Lawrence Frederick, Jr., (Larry Roth) *writer*
†Vando, Gloria *poet, publishing executive*

Maplewood
Schmidt, Skip Francis *writer*

Mountain Grove
Nava, Jean Anthes *writer, farmer*

Pierce City
Hays, Otis Earl, Jr., *writer*

Saint Charles
Castro, Jan Garden *writer, arts consultant, educator*

Saint Louis
Bang, Mary Jo *poet*
Broeg, Bob (Robert William Broeg) *writer*
Corbett, Suzanne Elaine *food writer, marketing executive, food historian*
Gass, William H. *writer, educator*
Lubbock, James Edward *retired writer, photographer, publicity consultant*
Lutz, John Thomas *author*
Schlafly, Phyllis Stewart *writer*
Wayne, Jane O(xenhandler) *poet, writing educator*

Stella
Yeagley, Joan Howerton *writer*

Sweet Springs
Long, Helen Halter *writer, educator*

Trenton
†Ensminger, John Jay *writer, poet, minister, counselor*

Viburnum
West, Roberta Bertha *writer*

Willow Springs
Hinds, C. Robert (Bob) *retired writer*

MONTANA

Bonner
†Smith, Annick *writer, producer*

Bozeman
Aig, Dennis Ira *writer, film producer*

Missoula
Chirinos, Eduardo *writer, educator*
Haines, John Meade *poet, translator, writer*
Yee, Albert Hoy *writer, retired psychologist, educator*

NEBRASKA

Kearney
†Fendt, Gene J. *poet, philosopher, educator*

Lincoln
Magorian, James *writer, poet*

Omaha
†Moeller, James Charles *writer*
Ress, Patricia Colleen *author, freelance writer*

Winside
†Reese, James William *writer, editor*

NEVADA

Cold Springs
†Turner VanLydegraf, Claudia Beth *writer, researcher*

Incline Village
†O'Connor, Thomas Patrick *screenwriter*

Las Vegas
Ashbaugh, Nancy Gould *writer, performing arts educator*
French, Richard Edmund *writer*
†Kern, Jeffrey D *writer*
Latimer, Heather *writer*
Palmer, Lynne *writer, astrologer*

Pahrump
†Sodeman, Harold Burdick Michael, Jr., *writer, photographer*

Reno
Grady, Sean Michael *writer*
Scrimgeour, Gary James *writer, educator*

NEW HAMPSHIRE

Barrington
Harris, Marie *writer*

Brentwood
†Bunker, Dusty *writer*

Center Sandwich
MacDougall, Ruth Doan *writer*

Cornish
Atkinson, James Blakely *writer, editor*

Cornish Flat
Erdrich, Louise (Karen Erdrich) *fiction writer, poet*

Dover
Appel, Carole Stein *writer, political organizer*

Durham
Ford, Daniel (Daniel Francis Ford) *writer*

Manchester
Cates, Edward William *writer, publisher*

Peterborough
Thomas, Elizabeth Marshall *writer*

Rindge
Bussiere, Linda Rose *writer, historian*

Walpole
Gooding, Judson *writer*

NEW JERSEY

Bergenfield
Clark, Fred *legal writer, editor*

Bloomfield
Tiger, Madeline J. *writer, educator*

Bogota
Livingston, Kathryn E. *writer*

Caldwell
Beusse, Jacqueline A. *writer, marketing company executive*

Camden
†Barbarese, J. T. *poet, educator*

Cape May Court House
Cohen, Daniel Edward *writer*
Cohen, Susan Lois *writer*

Cherry Hill
Gardner, Joel Robert *writer, historian*

Cliffside Park
Pearlman, Mickey Lou *writer*

Cresskill
Stern, Gerd Jakob *poet, retired import/export company executive*

Eastampton Township
Bowker, Nancy Anne *writer, bookseller*

Edison
Wexler, Annette Frances *writer*

Elizabeth
Lucco, James Perry *writer*

Garwood
†Callahan, Billy T. *writer, secondary school educator*

Glassboro
Hausman, Carl Dane *writer, journalism and media educator*

Haddonfield
†Halscheid, Therese Anne *poet*

Hazlet
†Shea, James Bryan *writer*

Highland Park
Cheiten, Marvin Harold *playwright, manufacturing executive*

Hoboken
Paradise, Paul Richard *writer, editor*

Island Heights
Noble, William Parker *writer, educator*

Jersey City
Luza, Radomir Vojtech, Jr., *poet, actor, comedian*
Pratt, Minnie Bruce *writer, educator*

Lake Hopatcong
Tomlinson, Gerald Arthur *writer, publisher, editor*

Lawrenceville
Newlin, George Christian *writer*

Lebanon
Barto, Susan Carol *writer*

Leonardo
Bianchi, Hollis Dolce *writer, artist*

Livingston
Simon, Sheryl Joy *writer, astrologer*

Long Valley
Collins, Kathleen *writer*

Madison
Perriman, Wendy Karen *poet, educator*

Mahwah
King, Lis Sonder *writer*

Maplewood
Lally, Michael David *writer, actor*

Friedman, B(ernard) H(arper) *writer*
Gallagher, Tess (Theresa Jeanette Bond) *writer, poet*
Gaydos, Mary *writer, researcher, actress*
†Gelman, Stephen *writer, editor*
Giblin, James Cross *author, editor*
Giorno, John *poet*
Goble, Phillip E. *writer, biblical scholar, translator*
Goldman, Peter Louis *writer*
Goldsmith, Barbara *writer, historian, journalist*
Goodman, George Jerome Waldo (Adam Smith) *author, television journalist, editor*
Gordon, David *playwright, director, choreographer*
Gordon, Mary Catherine *writer*
Goulden, Joseph Chesley *author*
Grafton, Sue *novelist*
Grant, Cynthia D. *writer*
Greenwald, Sheila Ellen *writer, illustrator*
†Griffin, Adele *writer*
Griffith, Nicola *writer*
†Grisham, John *writer*
Gross, Michael Robert *writer, editor*
†Guare, John *playwright, educator*
†Haber, Leo M. *writer, editor-in-chief*
Hadley, Leila Eliott-Burton (Mrs. Henry Luce III) *writer*
Hague, William Edward *editor, author*
Hamburger, Philip (Paul) *writer*
Hannibal, Edward Leo *copywriter*
Hardwick, Elizabeth *writer*
Hazzard, Shirley *author*
Henley, Arthur *author, editor, television consultant*
Herschberger, Ruth Margaret *writer*
Hershenson, Roberta Mantell *writer, photographer*
†Hershman, Morris *writer*
Hesse, Karen (Karen Sue Hesse) *writer, educator*
Heymann, C(lemens) David *author*
Hillman, Howard Budrow *author, editor, publisher, consultant*
Hirsch, Edward Mark *poet, English language educator, foundation administrator*
Hjortsberg, William Reinhold *writer*
Hoagland, Edward *author*
Holroyd, Michael *author*
†Hoover, Thomas E. *writer*
Horosko, Marian *writer, educator*
Hotz, Robert Lee *science writer, editor*
†Huey, John Wesley, Jr., *editor*
Humphreys, Josephine *novelist*
Hwang, David Henry *playwright, screenwriter*
Iglauer, Edith *writer, reporter*
Isay, David Avram *writer, radio producer*
Jacker, Corinne Litvin *playwright, writer*
Jakes, John *author*
Jhabvala, Ruth Prawer *writer*
Joachim, Brigitta Golden *writer, advertising agency executive, media consultant*
Jones, Diana Wynne *writer*
Jong, Erica Mann *writer, poet*
Josephson, Marvin *talent and literary agency executive*
Jurmain, Suzanne Tripp *freelance writer and editor*
Kainen, Anna *writer*
†Kalich, Richard Barry *writer*
Katz, Vincent Isaac *writer*
Kauffmann, Stanley Jules *author*
Kaufman, Bel *author, educator*
Keene, Donald *writer, translator, language educator*
Kehret, Peg *writer*
Kennedy, Adrienne Lita *playwright*
Kimball, Robert Eric *author*
Kinnell, Galway *poet, translator*
Kisner, Jacob *poet, editor, publisher*
Kitt, Sandra Elaine *writer, librarian*
Klein, T(heodore) E(ibon) D(onald) *writer*
Koke, Richard Joseph *author, exhibit designer, museum curator*
†Koontz, Dean Ray *writer*
Kotlowitz, Robert *writer, editor*
Kotrich, Alexandra *writer*
†Kramer, Jane *writer*
Krantz, Judith Tarcher *novelist*
†Kress, Nancy *writer*
Kumin, Maxine Winokur *poet, writer*
Laber, Jeri Lidsky *writer, human rights activist*
Lader, Lawrence *writer*
Lapierre, Dominique *writer, historian, philanthropist*
Lauber, Patricia Grace *writer*
†le Carré, John (David John Moore Cornwell) *author*
L'Engle, Madeleine (Mrs. Hugh Franklin) *writer*
†Leonard, Elmore John *novelist, screenwriter*
Lerangis, Peter D. *writer*
Levi, Louise Landes *poet, translator, musician*
†Levin, Ira *author, playwright*
Levoy, Myron *author*
Lord, M. G. *writer*
Lunardini, Christine Anne *writer, historian, school administrator*
Lustgarten, Celia Sophie *freelance consultant, writer*
MacAfee, Norman *writer, translator*
Macer-Story, Eugenia Ann *writer, artist*
MacLachlan, Patricia *author*
†Mailer, Norman *author*
Mamet, David Alan *playwright, director, essayist*
Markson, David M. *writer*
Mason, Bobbie Ann *novelist, short story writer*
†Mathews, Norman *playwright, composer*
Matzner, Chester Michael *writer*
Mazzucelli, Colette Grace Celia *author, multimedia educator*
†McCarthy, Cormac *writer*
†McCourt, Frank (Francis McCourt) *writer*
McDermott, Alice *writer*
Mcdonald, Gregory Christopher *author*
McGarvey, Mary Hewitt *writer*
†McGonigle, Thomas *writer, humanities educator*
McIntosh, DeCourcy Eyre *independent scholar and writer*
†McMurtry, Larry Jeff *author*
†McNally, Terrence *playwright*
McPherson, James Lowell *writer*
McQuown, Judith Hershkowitz *author, financial advisor*
Meade, Marion *author*
†Meadows, Denis John *writer, director*
Meltzer, Daniel B. *playwright, educator, writer*
Meltzer, Milton *author*
Menza, Claudia Marcella *literary agent*
Michael, Douglas John (Wm. Seebring) *playwright, cartoonist*
†Milford, Nancy Winston *writer, English educator*
Minarik, Else Holmelund (Bigart Minarik) *author*
Mooney, Richard Emerson *writer*
Moore, Honor *writer, educator*
Morgan, Frederick *poet, editor*
Morrison, Patricia Kennealy *author*
Morse, Carl Robert *writer, editor*
†Mosley, Walter *writer*
Munro, Alice *author*
Murphy, Patrice Ann (Pat Murphy) *writer*
†Nelson, Richard *writer*
Neugeboren, Jay *author*
Nicol, Dominik *writer, photographer*
Nixon, Agnes Eckhardt *television writer, producer*
North, Charles Laurence *poet, educator*
Oates, Joyce Carol *author*
†O'Brien, Tim *writer*
O'Doherty, Brian *writer, filmmaker*
Offit, Sidney *writer, educator*
Okrent, Daniel *writer*
Oltion, Jerry *author science fiction*
Oppenheimer, Paul *English comparative literature educator, poet, author*
Osborne, Mary Pope *writer*
Pall, Ellen Jane *writer*
Paolucci, Robert D. *translator*
Papell, Helen Gertrude *poet, retired librarian*
Park, Linda Sue *writer*
Parmalee, Patty Lee *writer, educator*
Patchett, Ann *writer*
Paterson, Katherine Womeldorf *writer*
†Patterson, James Brendan, Jr., *writer, former advertising agency executive*
Peacock, Molly *poet, educator*
Peck, Richard Wayne *novelist*
Pérez-Rivera, Francisco (Frank Rivera) *writer*
Pezzullo, Ralph Michael *writer, playwright*
†Pierce, Tamora *writer*
Pirsig, Robert Maynard *author*
Pogrebin, Letty Cottin *writer, lecturer*
Pollack, Barbara Grace *writer*
Pool, Mary Jane *writer, lecturer*
Poole, William Daniel *writer, editor*
Price, Reynolds *novelist, poet, playwright, essayist, educator*
†Proctor, William Gilbert, Jr., *writer*
Proulx, (Edna) Annie *writer*
Ratcliff, Carter Goodrich *writer, art critic, poet*
Rathmann, Peggy *author, illustrator*
Ratner, Rochelle *writer, editor*
Ray, Brenda *writer*
†Reed, Ishmael Scott (Emmett Coleman) *writer*
Reig, June Wilson *scriptwriter, television director, television producer*
Renehan, Edward John *writer*
Rhodes, Richard (Lee) *writer*
Ribalow, Meir Z. *playwright, educator*
Rice, Anne *writer*
Rich, Adrienne *writer*
†Robinson, Kim Stanley *science fiction author*
Robinson, Roxana Barry *writer, art historian*
Rogers, Michael Alan *writer*
Rollin, Betty *writer, television journalist, lecturer*
Ronde, John Herman *author, translator*
Rooney, Andrew Aitken *writer, columnist*
Root, William Pitt *poet, educator*
†Roth, Philip *writer*
Rothenberg, Jerome *author, visual arts and literary educator*
Rothenberg, Joyce Andrea (Joyce Joyce Andrea) *composer, poet, writer, singer*
Rumaker, Michael *writer, English educator*
Rylant, Cynthia *author*
Sachar, Louis *writer prose*
Salinger, J(erome) D(avid) *author*
Salter, Mary Jo *poet*
Sandum, Howard E. *literary agent*
Sargent, Herb *writer, television producer*
Sargent, Pamela *writer*
Saul, John Woodruff, III, *writer*
Savage, Tom *poet*
Schaffner, Cynthia Van Allen *writer, curator, lecturer*
Schisgal, Murray *playwright*
Schlesinger, Arthur, Jr., (Arthur Meier Schlesinger) *writer, educator*
Schultz, Philip *poet*
Seaman, Barbara (Ann Rosner) *author*
Segal, Lore *writer*
†Sendak, Maurice Bernard *writer, illustrator*
Shaffer, Peter (Sir Peter Shaffer) *playwright*
†Shao, Wei *writer, educator*
Sheehan, Susan *writer*
Sheldon, Sidney *author, producer*
Shulevitz, Uri *author, illustrator*
Simon, Neil *playwright, television writer*
Skinner, Brian Allan *writer, artist*
Smiley, Jane Graves *author, educator*
Smith, Betty *writer, nonprofit foundation executive*
Smith, Warren Allen *writer*
Solomon, Andrew Wallace *author*
Sontag, Susan *writer*
†Spillane, Mickey (Frank Morrison Spillane) *author*
†Squire, Gilda N. *brand manager, publicist, writer*
Steel, Danielle Fernande *author*
Stein, Joseph *playwright*
Steinem, Gloria *writer, editor, lecturer*
†Stone, Robert Anthony *author*
Stowers, Carlton Eugene *writer*
Swann, Brian *writer, humanities educator*
Swenson, Tree (Holly) *poet*
Talese, Gay *writer*
Tan, Amy Ruth *writer*
Teachout, Terry *writer, critic*
Tomkins, Calvin *writer*
Toobin, Jeffrey Ross *writer, legal analyst*
Towle, Tony *poet, editor*
Trillin, Calvin *writer*
Turner, Megan Whalen *author*
†Uhry, Alfred Fox *playwright*
†Valerio, Anthony *writer*
Vaughan, David George *writer*
Vonnegut, Kurt, Jr., *writer*
Wager, Walter Herman *author, communications director*
Walker, Alice *author*
†Waller, Robert James *writer*
Ward, Geoffrey Champion *author, editor*
Wasserman, Albert *film producer, writer, director*
Watt, Douglas (Benjamin Watt) *writer, critic*
Welish, Marjorie *poet*
Wender, Phyllis Bellows *literary agent*
West, Paul Noden *author, playwright*
†Whitehead, Colson *writer*
Whitney, Phyllis Ayame *author*
Wiener, Solomon *writer, consultant, former city official*
Wilds, Bonnie *author, community volunteer*
Williams, Diane *writer, editor*
†Willis, Richard, Jr., *writer, theater producer*
†Wilson, August *playwright*
Wineberg, Ronna I. *writer, lawyer*
Wise, William Alfred *writer*
†Wolfe, Thomas Kennerly, Jr., *writer, journalist*
Wolff, Virginia Euwer *writer*
†Wren, Gayden *playwright, theater director*
Wright, Sarah Elizabeth *writer, poet*
Yaffe, James *writer*
Yglesias, Helen Bassine *author, educator*
†Yorinks, Arthur *children's author, writer, director*
York, Alexandra *writer, lecturer*
Young-Mallin, Judith *writer, archivist*
†Zha, Jianying *writer, educator*
Zindel, Bonnie *writer, psychotherapist*
Zolotow, Charlotte Shapiro *author, editor*

Newburgh
Severo, Richard *writer*

Niagara Falls
Gromosiak, Paul *historian, consultant, writer, science and math educator*

Niskayuna
Yamin-Garone, Mary Sultany *writer, graphic designer*

North Boston
Herbert, James Alan *writer*

North Tonawanda
Powers, Bruce Raymond *writer, English language educator, consultant*

Nyack
Hendin, David Bruce *literary agent, writer, consultant, numismatist*

Olivebridge
Osborne, Seward Russell *writer*

Palisades
Davis, Dorothy Salisbury *writer*
Elevitch, Morton D. *writer, editor*

Plainview
Sherwood, James Webster, III, *author, limousine company owner*

Pleasantville
Nelson, K. Bonita *literary agent*

Poestenkill
Drew, George *writer, educator*

Potsdam
DeGhett, Stephanie Coyne *writer, educator*

Poughkeepsie
Willard, Nancy Margaret *writer, educator*

Purchase
†Phillips, Carly *writer*

Queensbury
Grunblatt, Hilda Ruth *translator, editor*

Red Hook
†Fitzpatrick, John *poet*

Rochester
Glatzer, Jenna *writer*
Hines, Virginia Lee *poet, writer*
Hoch, Edward Dentinger *writer*
Nixon, David Michael *poet*
Rothberg, Abraham *author, educator, editor*

Rockaway Beach
Kostelanetz, Richard *writer, media and visual artist*

Rockville Centre
†Schwartz, Arthur *playwright, poet*

Rome
Treadway, Susan Marie *technical writer*

Rye
Hurwitz, Sol *writer, consultant*
Ketchum, William Clarence *author, educator*

Sag Harbor
Brandt, Anthony Scott *free-lance writer, consultant*
Pashman, Susan Ellen *writer*
Walker, Lou Ann *writer*

Sagaponack
Appleman, Philip *poet, writer, educator*
Cedering, Siv *poet, writer*

Salem
Haycock, Dean Allen *writer, consultant*

Saratoga Springs
Goldensohn, Barry Nathan *poet, retired language educator*
†Millhauser, Steven *writer*

Saugerties
de Mare, George *author*

Schenectady
Seltzer, Joanne *poet*

Shady
Malkine-Falvey, Fern Sylvie *writer, journalist, painter*

Shushan
†Plute, Patricia Jean *retired writer*
Villet, Barbara *writer*

Sidney
Rivers Baker, Dawn *writer, publisher, consultant*

Southold
Small, Bertrice W. *writer*

Staten Island
Fisher, Barbara Gail *writer, educator*
Foster, Paul *playwright*
Popp, Lilian Mustaki *writer, educator*
Porter, Darwin Fred *writer*

Stony Brook
Roth, Susan Austin *author, photographer*

Syosset
Stevens, Daniel Francis *author*

Syracuse
Albino, Joseph Xavier *writer, educator, photographer*
Lloyd, David Thomas *writer, English educator*

Trumansburg
Levine, John Robert *author, lecturer*

Valley Stream
Rachlin, Harvey Brant *author*

Vestal
Cohen, Marvin A. *writer*

Wainscott
Herzog, Arthur, III, *author*

West Nyack
Pringle, Laurence Patrick *writer*

White Plains
Benjamin, Barbara Bloch *writer, editor*

Whitesboro
O'Hara, Cynthia O'Connor *writer, columnist, food consultant*

Woodstock
Berman, Cassia *writer, educator*
Godwin, Gail Kathleen *writer*

Yonkers
Baumel, Joan Patricia French *educator, writer, lecturer*
Godilo-Godlevsky, Eugene Alexanderson *poet*
Maritime, George *writer, photographer*

NORTH CAROLINA

Balsam
Mangham, Mack Robert *writer*

Boone
Stahl, Ray Emerson *freelance writer, historian, researcher*

Broadway
†Carwell, Gloria Jean *writer*

Candler
†Furches, W. Ralph, Jr., *writer*

Chapel Hill
Beam, Jeffery Scott *poet, editor*
Biswas, Brian *writer*
Spencer, Elizabeth *author*
Tilly, Nancy McFadden *writer, retired educator*

Charlotte
Coffey, Marilyn June *writer, educator*
Finley, Glenna *writer*
Knauth, Stephen Craig *poet*

Columbus
Blate, Michael *author, lecturer*
Sauvé, Carolyn Opal *writer, journalist, poet*

Durham
Petroski, Catherine *writer, consultant*

Fletcher
†Roe, Richard Steven *writer, illustrator*

Greensboro
Flynt, Candace Lambeth *writer*
Gilbert, Marie Rogers *poet*
Watson, Robert Winthrop *poet*

Greenville
†Gilham, Hanna Kaltenbrunner *writer*

High Point
Stimson, Richard Alden *writer*

Hillsborough
Williams, Virginia Parrott *writer, company executive*

Kill Devil Hills
†Lautermilch, Steven J. *poet, writer, photographer, educator*

Morrisville
†Clancy, Thomas L., Jr., *novelist*

Mount Olive
Rigsbee, David E. *poet, educator*

Pittsboro
Betts, Doris June Waugh *writer, English language educator*

Raleigh
Reed, Janine Regale *English composition and language educator*

Rutherfordton
Isbell, Robert *writer*

Southern Pines
Yarborough, William Pelham *writer, lecturer, retired army officer, consultant*

Winston Salem
Ehle, John Marsden, Jr., *writer*
Gallimore, Margaret Martin *poet*
Hanes, Frank Borden *author, farmer, former business executive*

OHIO

Akron
Moriarty, John Timothy *writer, transportation consultant*
Taormina, Charles Anthony *writer, editor, artist*

Ashley
Thomas, Annabel Crawford *writer*

Athens
Dodd, Wayne D. *poet, editor*

Batavia
†Craver, Diane Sue *writer, educator*

Berea
Bonds, Georgia Anna *writer, lecturer*

Centerville
†Alexander, Lora Kay *writer, composer*

Chillicothe
†Polans, Robert G. *writer, consultant*

Cincinnati
†Aylesworth, Julie Ann *writer, personal care industry executive*
Birmingham, Stephen *writer*
Miller, Sari Elizabeth (Sally Derby) *writer*
†Teasley, John Ray Sanders, Jr., *writer*

Circleville
Strous, Allen *poet*

Cleveland
Finn, Robert *writer, lecturer, broadcaster*
Gleisser, Marcus David *writer, lawyer, journalist*
Kovel, Ralph M. *writer, antiques expert*
Kovel, Terry Horvitz (Mrs. Ralph Kovel) *writer, antiques authority*

Cleveland Heights
Marchetti, Donna *writer, critic*
Sandburg, Helga *author*

Columbus
†Hilliard, Andrea Leigh *writer*
Smith, Robert Phillip *poet*
Young, Thomas Beetham *writer*

Dayton
Hayes, Stephen Kurtz *writer*
Jelus, Susan Crum *writer, editor*

Gallipolis
†Ferguson, A. H. *poet, medical/surgical nurse*

Glendale
Strom, Kristina Chase *writer, consultant*

Hamilton
Ridner, Melanie Marie *writer, composer*

Kent
Cielinski-Kessler, Audrey Ann *technical writer, publisher, small business owner*

Middletown
McClain, Michael H. *writer*

Mount Vernon
Wells-Maxwell, Violet *writer, artist*

Napoleon
Meekison, MaryFran *writer, photographer*

North Royalton
Pamin, Diana Dolhancyk (Diana Dolhancyk) *poet*

Perrysburg
Celeste, Ardella Hazel *retired writer*
Weaver, Richard L., II, *writer, speaker, educator*

Stockport
Winebrenner, William Patrick *writer*

Toledo
Lothery, Shawne Lamarr *writer, multimedia designer*

Vermilion
Schwensen, David Edward *writer, columnist, talent coordinator*

Westfield Center
Bock, Carolyn A. *writer, interviewer, small business owner*

Xenia
Coleman, Rita Kay *writer, literature educator*

Yellow Springs
Keyes, Ralph Jeffrey *writer*

Youngstown
Pacalo, Patrick John *writer*

Zanesville
Fulkerson, Sue Ellen *poet*

OKLAHOMA

Cleveland
Anderson, Patricia Sue *writer*

Lawton
Goetz, Gary D., Sr., *writer, retired chef, restaurateur*
Spencer, Mark Morris *creative writing educator*

Mustang
†Wood, Jean Carol *poet, lyricist*

Norman
MacFarland, Miriam Katherine (Mimi MacFarland)
Scaperlanda, María de Lourdes Ruiz *writer, journalist, author*

Oklahoma City
Mather, Ruth Elsie *writer*
Shurley, Jay Talmadge *writer, retired psychiatrist, medical educator, administrator, behavioral scientist, polar explorer, genealogist*

Perry
Beers, Frederick Gordon *writer, retired corporate communications official*

Stillwater
Graham, Toni *writer*
†Wiley, Moira Kathleen *writer, editor*

Tulsa
Mojtabai, Ann Grace *author, educator*
Price, Alice Lindsay *writer, artist*

OREGON

Beatty
Nettelbeck, Fred Arthur *poet*

Bend
Joslin, Leslie Allen *writer*

Boring
Robinson, Jeanne Louise *writer*

Cannon Beach
Hellyer, Constance Anne (Connie Anne Conway) *writer, musician*

Culver
Siebert, Diane Dolores *author, poet*

Eugene
Kono, Robert Hiroshi *writer, educator*
Rimel, Linda June *writer*
Salisbury, Ralph James *poet*
Wilhelm, Kate (Katy Gertrude) *author*

Grants Pass
Stafford, Patrick Purcell *poet, writer, management consultant*

Gresham
Jamison, Warren *writer, lecturer, publisher*

Marcola
Kelso, Mary Jean *author*

Mcminnville
Kherdian, David *writer*

Medford
Jackson, Elizabeth Riddle *writer, translator, educator*

Portland
Larson, Wanda Z. *writer, poet*
Phillips, Jill Meta *novelist, critic, astrologer*
Porter, Elsa Allgood *writer, lecturer*
Rutsala, Vern A. *poet, English language educator, writer*
Shoemaker, Dorothy Hays *technical writer*
Tuska, Jon *author, publisher*

PENNSYLVANIA

Aguadilla
†Martinez-Marquez, Alberto A. *writer, educator*

Altoona
Moore, Dinty William *writer, educator*

Ardmore
Kline, George Louis *author, translator, retired philosophy and literature educator*

Bensalem
†Marcopul, Kimberly Ann *writer*

Berwyn
Krasner, William *freelance/self-employed writer*

Bloomsburg
Keyser, Leslie D. *writer*

Broomall
Saunders, Sally Love *poet, educator*

Bushkill
Ellwood, Edith Muesing *free-lance writer*

California
Langham, Norma E. *playwright, educator, poet, composer, inventor*

Chambersburg
†Morgan, Diane Estelle *writer, educator*

Douglassville
Kirkpatrick, David Warren *educational researcher, writer*

Downingtown
Kovach, George Daniel *writer, author*

Doylestown
†Heiligman, Deborah *writer*

Drexel Hill
Alexander, Lloyd Chudley *author*

East Stroudsburg
Allen, Frank Charles *writer*

Flourtown
Dressler, Mark Christopher *writer*

Fogelsville
Crooker, Barbara Ann *writer, educator*

Glenside
†Powlison, David A. *writer*

Greensburg
Shafer-Kenney, Jolie E. *writer, columnist*

Harrisburg
Cooper, Jane Todd (J. C. Todd) *poet, writer, educator*
†Grobman, Gary M. *writer*
Williams, Karl *writer, musician*

Hollywood
Tomezsko, George Anthony *writer*

Kennett Square
Martin, George (George Whitney Martin) *writer*

King Of Prussia
†Schumann, Paula M. L. *writer*

Milford
Le Guin, Ursula Kroeber *writer*

Narvon
High, Linda Oatman *author*

New Kingstown
DiSipio, Rocco Thomas *writer*

Paoli
Shubin, Seymour *writer*
†Yake, Sarah Louise *poet*

Pen Argyl
†Martocci, Lewis Nicholas, III, *writer*

Philadelphia
Ascenzi, John C. *writer, editor*
†Connor, Bernadette Yvonne *retired writer*
Fussell, Paul *author, English literature educator*
Gaillard, Theodore Lee, Jr., *writer*
Goldstein, Melissa Anne *writer*
Granato, Carol Anne *writer*
†Kinsella, Thomas *poet*
Nickels, Thom *writer, journalist*
Owens, Rochelle *poet, playwright*
Paglia, Camille *writer, humanities educator*
Pipes, Daniel *writer*
†Rimm, Robert *writer, educator*
†Rosen, Philip *retired writer*
†Wallace, Emily Mitchell *writer, editor, educator*

Pittsburgh
Bleier, Carol Stein *writer, researcher*
Cullen, Wanda Jane *writer, financial consultant*
Daniels, James R. *poet, English language educator*
Hodges, Margaret Moore *author, educator*
Simms, Michael Arlin *poet, publishing executive*

Pottstown
Hylton, Thomas James *author*

Reading
†Scoboria, Francine Mary *writer*

Richlandtown
Winters, Kay Lanning *writer*

Southampton
Bendiner, Robert *writer, editor*
Levin, Lynn Ellen *poet*

Spring Mills
Gillan, Garth Jackson *writer, psychotherapist, deacon, emeritus educator*

Stevens
Shenk, Lois Elaine Landis *writer*

Swarthmore
Hyde, Harry, Jr., *technical writer, editor, consultant*

Tyrone
Bonta, Marcia Myers *freelance nature writer, researcher, columnist*

Valley Forge
Miller, Betty Brown *freelance writer*

Villanova
Gould, Lilian *writer*

Wayne
Mackey, Betty Barr *writer*

West Chester
Abernethy, Hugh C., Jr., *writer*

West Conshohocken
Ceccola, Russ *game strategy guide writer*

Wynnewood
Meyers, Mary Ann *writer, consultant*

RHODE ISLAND

Adamsville
Cumming, Patricia A. *writer*

Barrington
Deakin, James *writer, former newspaperman*

North Kingstown
Dutwin, Phyllis *writer, scholarly*

Providence
Eltringham, Dana Kristin *writer*
Goldstein, Joshua S *writer, educator*
Mandel, Peter Bevan *writer, columnist*
Miller, G. Wayne *writer*
Schevill, James Erwin *poet, playwright*
Steinbach, Meredith Lynn *novelist*
Vogel, Paula Anne *playwright*

Warwick
†Sarkissian, Karry Rafael *translator, educator*

SOUTH CAROLINA

Aiken
†Naifeh, Steven Woodward *writer*
Smith, Gregory White *writer*

Columbia
Newton, Rhonwen Leonard *writer, microcomputer consultant*

Hilton Head Island
Reed, Frances Boogher *writer, actress*

Little River
Ehrlich, John Gunther *writer*

Myrtle Beach
Nirenstein, Jack *writer*

Rock Hill
Bristow, Robert O'Neil *writer, educator*

Seneca
Curry, Mary Earle Lowry *poet*

Summerville
Reisman, Rosemary Moody Canfield *writer, humanities educator*

Sumter
Justus, Adalu *writer, designer*

SOUTH DAKOTA

Brookings
†Williams, Elizabeth Evenson *writer*

Kyle
Davies Silcott, Loma Geyer *freelance writer, English educator*

Sioux Falls
†Hicks, Patrick *writer, educator*
Mikesell, Janice Harlan *writer, poet, photographer*

TENNESSEE

Blaine
Bull, James C. *poet*

Chattanooga
Callahan, North *author, educator*
Riggs, Claudesta Lavern *professional storyteller*
†Secrest, Rose Marie *writer*

Cleveland
Breuer, William Bentley *writer*

Dyersburg
Wilson, Leigh Ann *writer, educator, historian*

Franklin
Stafford, Clay *writer, film producer, director, actor, public speaker*

Gallatin
Flynn, John David *writer, educator*

Greeneville
Breckenridge, Judith Watts *writer, educator*

Henning
†Parker, Joann Maudie *freelance/self-employed writer, retired reporter*

Jackson
McFadden, Gloria Arlene Ruth *poet, songwriter, screenwriter*

Kingsport
Kiss, Mary Catherine Clement *writer*

Knoxville
Lammers, Laura Bea *writer, communications executive*

Loudon
†Randall, Marilyn Mae *writer*

Memphis
†Ajanaku, Amana M. *poet*
Foote, Shelby *author*
†Grafton, Edna Fisher *writer*
Parish, Barbara Shirk *writer, educator*
†Quinn, Amelia Turner *writer*

Nashville
Bird, Caroline *author*
Cornwell, Ilene Jones *writer, editor*
Pearson, Sela *poet, speaker*
†Smith, Agnes Eyvonda *writer*
Winstead, Elisabeth Weaver *poet, writer, English language educator*

Newport
Gregg, Ella Mae *writer*

Oak Ridge
Turov, Daniel *financial writer, investment executive*

Sevierville
Koff, Shirley Irene *writer*

Soddy Daisy
McDermott, David (John) *marketing professional, artist*

TEXAS

Addison
Cohn, Linkie Seltzer *professional speaker, author*

Alvin
Johnson, Cheryl Elizabeth *writer, publisher, educator*

Arlington
Savage, Ruth Hudson *poet, writer, speaker*

Austin
Barnes, Thomas Joseph *writer*
Gustafsson, Lars Erik Einar *writer, educator*
McElroy, Mary M. (Mickie McElroy) *educational writer*
†Neeld, Elizabeth Harper *author, retreat and workshop leader, consultant*
Porter, Jenny Lind *writer*
†Rush, Sharron Anne *writer, nonprofit executive officer*
White, Tom Martin *playwright, music publisher*

Bertram
Albert, Susan Wittig *writer, English educator*

Boerne
Price, John Randolph *writer*

Canyon
Roper, Beryl Cain *writer, publisher, retired library director*

Corpus Christi
†Foster, Bayard Everson *writer*
Sommers, Maxine Marie Bridget *travel writer, author, educator, publisher*

Crowley
Sizemore, Deborah Lightfoot *writer, editor*

Crystal Beach
Dunn, Glennis Mae *retired writer, lyricist*

Dallas
†Dee, Ronda *poet, photographer*
Favor, Lesli Joanna *writer, researcher*
Gillett, Grover *author*
Hougland, Mark Allyn *writer*
Murray, John William, Jr., *writer, legal investigator*
Phillips, Betty Lou (Elizabeth Louise Phillips) *author, interior designer*
Sealander, John Arthur *writer, educator*
Sundgaard, Arnold Olaf *playwright*
Wolfe, Jane *writer*

Denton
Keating, AnaLouise *educator, author*

El Paso
†Ferrell, Robert E. *writer, educator*

Euless
†Roark, Sheila B. *writer*

Fort Worth
†Cope, Ginny *poet*
de Toledo, Catherine Holt *medical writer*
†Douglas, Carole Nelson *writer*
Munday, Stephen Dale *writer, artist*
Simmons, Naomi Charlotte *poet*

Houston
Fox, Connie Steitz *freelance writer, editor, graphic designer*

†Meeks, Dodie Messer *writer*
Plunkett, Jack William *writer, publisher*

Hurst
Dooley, Lena Rose (Nelson) *writer, editor*

Lubbock
Bronwell, Nancy Brooker *writer*

Mansfield
Parnell, Charles L. *speechwriter*

Marfa
McBride, Elizabeth Anne Wilmore *writer, artist*

Odessa
Moseley, Clifford Wayne *writer, poet*

Pasadena
Thompson, Marian Nell *poetry, historical, non-fiction and fiction writer, educator, poet*

Plano
Gallardo, Henrietta Castellanos *writer*

Pottsboro
Jackson, Nona Armour *writer, illustrator*

Richardson
Bonura, Larry Samuel *writer*
Wiesepape, Betty Holland *writing educator*

Saint Jo
Ashley, Raymond Weldon *writer*

San Antonio
Ammann, Lillian Ann Nicholson *writer, editor, small business owner*
†Castorena, Maria Ancelita *writer*
Fehrenbach, T(heodore) R(eed) *author, businessman*
Glueck, Sylvia Blumenfeld *writer*
Laurence, Dan H. *author, literary and dramatic specialist*
Rogers, Frances Evelyn *author, retired educator and librarian*
Swiggett, Harold E. (Hal Swiggett) *writer, photographer*

Smithville
Clark, LaVerne Harrell *writer, photographer*

South Padre Island
Jumper, Roy Davis Linville *writer, educator*

Sulphur Springs
Behlen, Charles William *poet, consultant*

Terrell
†Whitaker, Kay *poet*

Texarkana
†Presley, James Wright *writer, environmentalist*

Texas City
Buck, Pitman August, Jr., *writer*

Waco
Dewlen, Alton LeRoy (Al Dewlen) *writer*

UTAH

Park City
Solomon, Dorothy Jeanne Allred *writer, communications executive*

Provo
†Hart, Edward LeRoy *poet, educator*

Salt Lake City
Chamberlin, Ann *novelist, playwright*
Oliveira Aldamiz, Jose Maria *scriptwriter*
†Osherow, Jacqueline Sue *poet, English language educator*
†Straughn, Joanna Marzia *poet*

VERMONT

Bennington
Feitlowitz, Marguerite *writer, literary translator*

Brattleboro
Cooper, Wyn *poet, editor, songwriter*

Burlington
Carlisle, Lilian Matarose Baker (Mrs. E. Grafton Carlisle Jr.) *writer, lecturer*
Hearon, Shelby *writer, lecturer, educator*

Chester
Coleman, John Royston *writer*

Dorset
Pember, John Scott *poet*

Guilford
†Olle, David Arthur *writer, researcher*

Marlboro
Stevenson, Laura Caroline *writer, educator*

Marshfield
†Stockwell, Samn *poet, primary school educator*

Middlebury
Bain, David Haward *writer*
MacDonald, Kenneth R., Jr., *author, artist*

Morrisville
Besser, Gretchen Rous *writer, educator*

Shaftsbury
†Sugarman, Robert Edward *retired writer*

South Royalton
Powers, Thomas Moore *writer*

Thetford
Paley, Grace *author, educator*

Wilmington
Reeve, Franklin D. *writer, literature educator*

Windsor
Anthony, Francis Polipnick (Francis Anthony Polipnick) *poet, writer*

VIRGINIA

Afton
Brown, Rita Mae *writer*

Aldie
Weaver, Kitty Dunlap *author*

Alexandria
Byrne, John Edward (JEB Byrne) *writer, retired government official*
Justesen, Benjamin Ray, II, *writer*
Wallace, Barbara Brooks *writer*

Arlington
Beazley, Hamilton Scott *writer, educator*
Cinca, Silvia (Roberta King) *writer, producer*
England, Robert Stowe *writer*
Garfinkel, Patricia Gail *speech writer, policy analyst, poet*
Solimando, Dominic Anthony, Jr., *writer, consultant, pharmacist, educator*

Ashburn
Boyne, Walter James *writer, former museum director*

Burke
†Papas, Christa *writer*
White, Terry Joe *writer, editor*

Chantilly
Priem, Richard Gregory *writer, information systems executive*

Charlottesville
Casey, John Dudley *writer, English language educator*
Dove, Rita Frances *poet, English language educator*
Grohskopf, Bernice *writer*
McCrimmon, Barbara Smith *writer, librarian*
Monaghan, Charles *writer, editor*
Viebahn, Fred *writer, journalist*

Clarksville
Worth, Lynn Harris *writer*

Clifton
Cavileer, Sharon E. *writer, public relations executive, consultant*

Fairfax
Bausch, Richard Carl *writer, educator*
†Cosing, Arthur Paul, Jr., *writer, artist*
Parrish-St. John, Florence Tucker *writer, educator, retired government official*
†Secrest, Meryle *writer*

Falls Church
Leighton, Frances Spatz *writer, journalist*
Orben, Robert *editor, writer*
†Walker, William P(Scot) *writer, real estate investor*
Whitehead, Kenneth Dean *author, translator, retired federal government official*

Fort Belvoir
Smith, Margherita *writer, editor*

Fredericksburg
†Givens, Florence Rosie *author, editor, publishing executive*
Goss, Georgia Bulman *freelance/self-employed translator*
†Marler, Helen *writer, actor*

Free Union
LeBoutillier, Megan *writer*

Hartwood
Brugioni, Dino Anthony *writer, lecturer, consultant*

Lake Ridge
Englert, Helen Wiggs *writer*

Leesburg
Johnson, Julia A. *writer*

Lexington
Stuart, Dabney *poet, author, English language educator*

Newport News
Buranelli, Vincent John *writer*
Fusek, Serena Rebecca *poet*

Norfolk
Berent, Irwin Mark *writer, software executive*
†Sampson, Gayle Vernice *freelance/self-employed writer*

Portsmouth
Mapp, Alf Johnson, Jr., *writer, historian*
Nolen, Crystal Me'Kelle *poet, educator*

Reston
Smith, Ralph Lee *author, musician*

Roanoke
Blevins, Adrian Ellen *writer, educator*

Springfield
Hyland, Patricia Ann (Pat Hyland) *writer*

Stephenson
Johnson, Eva Maria *retired translator*

Sterling
Bernal-Labrada, Emilio *writer, poet, translator*

Vienna
Olshaker, Mark Bruce *author, film maker*

Virginia Beach
Clark, Suzanne Underwood *writer*
Foss, William Otto *writer*
Foster, Jeanne O'Cain *poet, fine arts educator*
Lliteras, Daniel Serafin *writer*
Seward, William W(ard), Jr., *writer, retired educator*

Warrenton
David, Joseph Raymond, Jr., *writer, periodical editor*
Estaver, Paul Edward *writer, poet*

Williamsburg
†Myers, Roger Paul *writer, playwright, actor*
Smith, William Henry Preston *writer, editor, former corporate executive*

Woodbridge
Yount, Thomas David *writer, columnist*

Woodstock
†Maggiolo, Paulette Blanche *writer*

Woodville
Mc Carthy, Eugene Joseph *writer, former senator*

WASHINGTON

Arlington
Bullington, Gayle Rogers *writer, researcher*

Bellevue
Dickerson, Eugenie Ann (Genie Dickerson) *writer, journalist*
Olson, Robert William *writer, retired counselor*
Porad, Francine Joy *poet, painter*
Ure Dunagan, Heather Eileen *writer*

Bothell
†Krishnamurthy, Sandeep *writer, researcher*

Clarkston
†Knight, Brian *writer*

Ellensburg
Bennett, John J. *writer, publisher*

Issaquah
Cain, Coleen W. *writer, educator*

Kent
Raymond, Eugene Thomas *technical writer, consultant, retired aircraft engineer*

Kirkland
Szablya, Helen Mary *writer, language professional, lecturer*

La Conner
Robbins, Thomas Eugene *writer*

Leavenworth
†Taub, Alex A.G. *writer, educator*

Lynnwood
Bear, Gregory Dale *writer, illustrator*

Medina
Lucas, Patricia Latourette *writer*

Olympia
Mahood, James Herbert *writer*

Port Angeles
Burton, Fredda Jean *writer, artist*
Muller, Willard C(hester) *writer*

Port Townsend
Cady, Jack Andrew *writer, educator*

Poulsbo
Wayne, Kyra Petrovskaya *writer*

Redmond
Enbysk, H. Monte *writer, editor*

Richland
Baker, June Frankland *poet*

Seattle
Bottenberg, Joyce Harvey *social services executive*
Butler, Octavia Estelle *free-lance writer*
†Croston, Stephen Paul *writer, systems manager, social studies educator*
Evans, Jack R. (J. Glenn Evans) *writer, poet*
†Fazakas, Art Herschel *writer, educator, editor*
Gross, Catherine Mary (Kate Gross) *writer, educator*
Mini, Anne Alexandra Apostolides *writer, educator*
O'Mahony, Timothy Kieran *writer*
Roche, Judith *poet, art educator*
Singer, Sarah Beth *poet*
Sprague, Dale Joseph *writer*
Thomas, Irv *journalist, publisher*
Wagoner, David Russell *writer, educator*

Spokane
Brock, Randall J. *poet*
Hight, Gaye Demetrice *poet*

Ehrhart, William Daniel *writer, poet*
†Eisenberg, Gary Julius *writer, musician, printmaker*
†Emory, Lee (Whitney Eden) *writer*
Emrich, Jeanne Ann *poet, artist*
†Ephron, Nora *writer, director*
Erenberger, Timothy *writer*
Erwin, Judith Ann (Judith Ann Peacock) *writer, photographer, lawyer*
†Esther, Queen *playwright, scriptwriter, actor*
Esty, John Cushing, Jr., *writer, teacher, advisor to non-profit boards*
Evangelista, Anita Loretta *freelance writer, psychologist, nurse, publishing executive*
Farrelly, Peter John *screenwriter*
Fayer, Steve *writer*
Fearrington, Ann Peyton *writer, illustrator, newspaper reporter, portraitist*
†Feldman, David Edward *playwright*
Fell, Jennifer Anne *writer*
Fetler, Andrew *author, educator*
†Finder, Joseph Alan *writer*
Fisher, Nancy *writer, producer, director*
†Foote, Horton *playwright, scriptwriter*
†Foran, Chris *poet, educator*
†Ford, Richard *writer*
Franzen, Richard *writer*
Fraser, Russell Alfred *author, educator*
Freedman, Russell Bruce *author*
French, Marilyn *writer, critic*
Fritz, Ethel Mae Hendrickson *writer*
Fryer, Thomas Waitt, Jr., *writer and editor*
Frymer, Murry *writer, theater and film critic*
†Fuchsberg, Lawrence J. *writer, editor, performing arts association administrator, consultant*
Fuentes, Carlos *writer, former ambassador*
†Fuller, Charles H, Jr., *playwright*
Funkhouser, Erica *writer, educator, communications educator*
Gadol, Peter Daniel *writer*
Gainer, Jeffery A. *writer, consultant*
†Gallagher, Cynthia Polansky *writer*
†Gamin, Judith *poet*
Gardner, Grace Joely *author, consultant*
Garfield-Woodbridge, Nancy *writer*
Garfinkle, Elaine Myra *writer*
Garfinkle, Robert Allen *writer, astronomer*
†Garosshen, Paulette Sharon *writer*
†Gaslow, Pam *writer, artist*
Gebauer, Phyllis Victoria Feltskog *writer, educator*
Gellis, Willard Leon *poet, English educator*
George, Linda Shumaker *writer, educator*
†Gerloff, Gary Martin *writer*
Gersoni-Edelman, Diane Claire *author, editor*
Ghigna, Charles *poet*
Giffin, Marjie G. *writer*
Gifford, Heidi *writer, editor*
†Gilbert, Elayne Rhoda *writer*
Gilchrist, Ellen Louise *writer*
Gilroy, Frank Daniel *playwright*
Giombetti Clue, Diane *writer*
†Giovinazzo, Vivian Curry *writer*
†Glick, Ruth Burtnick *author, lecturer*
Glover, Douglas Herschel *writer, educator, editor*
†Gluskin, Lisa L. *poet, editor, writer*
Goble, Paul *author, illustrator, artist*
Godbey, Terry *poet, newspaper copy editor*
Goldberg, Gerald Jay *writer, educator*
†Golden, Harry W. *writer*
Goldfarb, Ruth *poet, educator*
Goldstene, Paul Norton *writer, educator*
Gordimer, Nadine *author*
Goss, Joel Francis *writer*
†Graham, Steven Anthony *writer*
†Grange, Mary Jane *writer, adult nurse practitioner*
Gray, Francine du Plessix *author*
Greenburg, Dan *author*
Greer, Germaine *author*
Gribble, Mary Louise *freelance/self-employed poet, writer*
†Grieser, Jeanne K. *writer*
†Groening, Matthew *writer, cartoonist*
Gundy, Richard L. *freelance/self-employed writer*
Guy, Eleanor Bryenton *writer*
Haas, Charlie *screenwriter*
†Haas, Sheila Sperber *writer, consultant*
Hahn, Mary Downing *writer*
Haldeman, Joe William *novelist*
Halperin, Michael Howard *writer, educator*
Hamit, Francis Granger *freelance writer*
Hammondd, Charlotte Claren *writer, researcher*
Handy, Carolyn *nonfiction writer*
Harlow, Joan Beverley *writer*
Harp, Chadwick Allen *writer, educator*
Harrell, Margaret Ann *writer, educator, researcher, photographer*
Harrigan, Anthony Hart *author*
Harris, Judith Rich *writer*
Harrison, Sue Ann McHaney *writer*
Harshman, Marc *writer, poet, consultant*
†Hartman, Bruce *writer*
Harvey, Willard Albertson, Jr., *writer, publisher*
Haskell, Molly *writer*
†Hawes, Louise E *writer, education educator*
†Haybach, Patty Jean *writer, medical/surgical nurse*
Hayes, Gail Boyer *writer, editor*
Heckelmann, Charles Newman (Charles Lawton) *author, publishing consultant*
Heller, Aimee Kim *writer*
Heller, Ruth M. *writer*
Helprin, Mark *author*
Hemphill, Paul James *author*
Henigson, Ann Pearl *freelance writer, songwriter, lyricist*
Herbert, Mary Katherine Atwell *writer*
Herman, George Adam *retired writer and educator*
Herman, Hank *writer*
Hernandez, Joel Thomas *writer*
Herrmann, John *writer, editor, journalist*
Hersh, Burton David *author*
Herson, Karen J. *writer, audio producer, freelance writer*
Herstein, Howard Joseph *author*
Heverly, John C. *writer, journalist*
†Hickey, Gerald Vincent *writer*
Hiebel, William Raymond *writer, artist, photographer, composer, retired English educator*
†Hijuelos, Oscar *novelist*
Hill, Donna Marie *writer, retired librarian*
Hillerman, Tony *writer, former journalism educator*
Himes, Barbara Alison (Sydney Kendall) *writer*
Hirschberg, Vera Hilda *writer*
Hoffman, Margaret May *writer*
Holifield, Pearl Kam (Kam Holifield, Momi Kam Holifield) *poet*
Hollander, Anne *writer*
Holloway, Kimberley Michele *freelance/self-employed writer, communications executive, language educator*
†Holman, Margaret Alice *writer*
†Holman, Sandy Lynne *writer, consultant*
Hoopes, Roy Harry, Jr., *writer*
†Horsman, David A. Elliott *writer, financial services executive, educator*
†Horton-Stevenson, Rhonda Anna *writer, educator*
House-Wade, Susan Patricia *writer, educator*
Houston, Gloria *author, educator, consultant*
Houze, Herbert George *writer*
Howes, Sophia DuBose *writer*
Hoyt, Mary Finch *author, editor, media consultant, former government official*
Hughey, Richard Kohlman *author, lawyer*
†Hunter, Evan (Ed Mc Bain) *author*
Hurtt, Frances Scott *author*
Huston, Nancy Louise *writer, educator*
Hutchinson, Robert Joseph *writer*
†Hynes, James *writer*
Imhof, Susan Anne *poet*
†Insana, Arthur Gerard *writer, director*
Irving, John Winslow *writer*
Isaacs, Susan *novelist, screenwriter*
†Isom, Kevin *writer*
Jabs, Carolyn Ruth *writer*
Jackson, Charles Ian *writer, consultant*
†Jacobs, Nova *scriptwriter, filmmaker*
Jaffee, Annette Williams *novelist*
James, Tracey Faye *screenwriter*
†Janko, James Anthony *writer, educator*
Jenks, Tom *writer*
†Jesurun, John Alberto *playwright, director*
Johnson, Mary P. *freelance writer*
Jones, Carolyn Evans *writer, speaker*
Jordan, Anne Devereaux *writer, educator*
Jorden, William John *writer, retired diplomat*
Just, Ward Swift *author*
Kanin, Fay *screenwriter*
Kass, Jerome Allan *writer*
Katz, William Loren *author*
Katz, William Michael *writer*
Kauffman, Dagmar Elisabeth *writer, researcher*
Keady, Walter James *writer*
†Keesling, Brian *writer*
Keil, Harold H. (Bill Keil) *writer*
Kellerman, Jonathan Seth *writer, pediatric psychologist*
Kellner, Mark Allen *writer*
Kemmett, William Joseph *poet, educator*
Kemp, Kenneth Omer *writer, lawyer*
Kennedy, Raymond Arthur *writer*
Kessler, Stephen James *writer, editor*
Kidder, Tracy (John Tracy Kidder) *writer*
Kimbrell, Grady Ned *writer, educator*
King, Joy Rainey *poet, retired medical secretary*
King, Larry L. *playwright, actor*
Kingston, Maxine Hong *writer, educator*
†Kiser, Brenda Hathaway *freelance/self-employed writer, editor*
Klaidman, Stephen David *writer*
Knotts, Robert Spencer (Bob Knotts) *writer, playwright*
Knowles, Jocelyn Wagner *health writer, women's health specialist*
Koch, Margaret Rau *writer, artist, historian*
Kohn, Rita *writer, playwright, journalist, educator*
Konigsburg, Elaine Lobl *writer*
Korman, Jess J. *writer*
Kotlowitz, Alex *writer, journalist*
Kremers, Carolyn Sue *writer, musician, educator*
Kristofferson, Karl Eric *writer*
Krob, Melanie Gordon *writer*
Krouse, Clyde Francis *writer*
Kruger, Mollee Coppel *writer*
Krupat, Kitty Weiss *writer, educator*
Kuper, Daniela F. *writer, speaker*
†Kushner, Tony *playwright*
Laird, Betty Ann *writer, researcher, actress*
Lambert, William Jesse, III, *writer*
Langham, Gail B. *writer*
Larkin, Joan *poet, English educator*
LaRoche, Linda *writer*
†Larsdotter, Anna-Lisa *retired translator, artist*
Larsen, Anita Donice *writer, consultant, speaker*
Latham, Joyce Eileen *writer/editor, poet, photojournalist*
Latorraca, Joseph Paul *writer*
†Laufer, Joanna *writer*
†Laven, Karen Julig *writer, scriptwriter*
Lawrence, Ruth *writer, illustrator*
Lazo, Caroline Evensen *writer*
Ledford, Brenda Kay *writer*
Leedom-Ackerman, Joanne *writer, educator*
Lehman, David *poet, writer, editor*
Lenhart, Gary Alan *poet*
Lesher, Gloria Jean *writer*
Levine, Gail Carson *writer*
Levitt, B. Blake *medical and science writer*
Lewis, Dennis Carroll *writer, publisher, educator*
Li, Leslie Denise *novelist, journalist, playwright*
Lightwood, Carol Wilson *writer*
Lin, Henry Baohua *consultant, writer*
†Lincoln, James Henry, Sr., *writer*
Lindenberger, Herbert Samuel *writer, literature educator*
Lingle, Marilyn Felkel *freelance writer, columnist, author*
Link, William Theodore *television writer, producer*
Lipkin, Randie Tina *novelist*
†Little, Charlotte Louise *poet, writer*
Littrell, Dennis Allen *writer*
Lober, Lionel M. *screenwriter, producer*
Long, Elaine *writer, editor*
Longstreet, Stephen (Chauncey Longstreet) *author, painter*
Lopez, Barry Holstun *writer*
Lorio, Penny Sue (P.S.) *playwright, composer*
Lovisi, Gary *writer*
†Lowe, Denise Nola-Faye *writer, educator*
Lubell, Ellen *writer*
Luhn, Robert Kent *writer, magazine editor*
LyListon, William Phillip *writer, poet*
Lynch, Amanda Kathryn *writer*
†Lyons, Julie Kathleen Hunt *writer, editor*
†Macaulay, David (Alexander) *author, illustrator*
Macioce, Marie Elizabeth (Marie Tomas) *writer*
Mackle, Elliott *writer*
MacLean, Judith E. *writer, editor*
MacLeod, Normajean *writer*
†Macomber, Patricia Lee *writer, editor*
Madrick, Jeffrey G. *writer, editor, economic consultant*
Maines, Leah *writer, poet*
Manchester, William *writer*
Mankiewicz, Thomas Frank *screenwriter, director, producer*
Mann, Emily Betsy *writer, artistic director, theater director*
Marble, Melinda Smith *writer, editor*
†Marcus, H. B. *writer, web site designer*
Markowicz, Elaine C. *writer*
Marks, Janet Goldberg *poet, writer*
Marks, Jeffrey Alan *freelance/self-employed writer*
Marx, Anne (Mrs. Frederick E. Marx) *poet*
Masek, Mark Joseph *writer*
Mathis, Sharon Bell *author, retired elementary educator and librarian*
Mattar, Philip *writer*
Mattern, Joanne *writer, educator*
Mayo, C(atherine) M(ansell) *writer, editor, economist*
†McCallister, Michael S. *writer*
McClure, Helen Playfair *writer*
McCoy, Edain *writer*
McFall, Catherine Gardner *poet, critic, educator*
McFarlane, Donovan Anthony *writer, poet, researcher*
†McGill, Jefferey Trent *writer, educator*
†McIntier, Russell J. *retired writer*
†Mc Intyre, Vonda Neel *writer*
McLaughlin, Patricia Ann *writer*
†McMillan, Beverly C. *writer*
McMillan, Terry L. *writer, educator*
McNeely, Thomas Holmes *writer, educator*
McPhee, John Angus *writer*
McPherson, James Alan *writer, educator*
McWhorter, Diane *writer*
McWilliams, Michael *writer, publisher*
†Meacham, Margaret Marks *writer, educator*
Meaker, Marijane Agnes *author*
Meekins, Frederick Boyd *writer*
Melnyczuk, Askold *writer*
Mender, Mona Siegler *writer, music educator*
Mendoza, George *poet, author*
†Merino, Ana *poet*
Merrill, Jean Fairbanks *writer*
Micucci, Dana Ann *writer*
Millar, Jeffery Lynn *writer*
Miller, Arthur *playwright, author*
†Miller, Lori *writer, humanities educator*
Miller, Vickie Gail *writer*
†Miller, W. Kievit *writer*
†Minard, Anne E. *writer*
Minkowitz, Donna *writer, journalist*
Mintz, Morton Abner *author, former newspaper reporter*
Mitchell, Marcia Jeanne *freelance/self-employed writer, events producer*
Mitrany, Devora *writer, editor*
Moats, Patrick Andrew *poet*
Mogel, Leonard Henry *writer*
Monts, Rodd LyDell *writer, journalist*
Moody, R. Bruce *writer, actor*
Moore, Margaret Rives *writer, financial manager*
Morang, Diane Judy *writer, television producer, business entrepreneur*
†Morocco, Joyce Marie *writer, accountant*
Morris, Dorothy Kay *writer*
†Morrison, Lillian *writer, retired librarian*
Morrison, Sarah Lyddon *author*
Morrow, Barry Nelson *screenwriter, producer*
Morse, Flo *writer*
Muehl, Lois Baker *writer, retired language educator*
Muldoon, Thomas Lyman *writer*
Murphy, Kathleen Ann *writer*
Murphy, Marion Colucci *writer, poet*
Murray, Albert Lee *writer, educator*
Muson, Howard Henry *writer, consultant*
Nagel, M. Constance *poet*
†Narboni, Lilian *writer*
Nash, Leonard David *writer, consultant*
Neal, Margaret Sherrill *writer, editor, graphics designer, web designer*
†Nelson, James Lars *writer*
Nemec, David Joseph *writer, baseball historian*
Neuhaus, Christian E.O.S. *writer*
Newhall, Edith Allerton *writer*
†Nguyen, Duy *writer*
Nielson, Alyce Mae *poet*
Noëldechen, Joan Marguerite *writer*
Nolan, Patrick Joseph *screenwriter, playwright, educator*
Nordley, Gerald David *writer, investor*
Norton, Andre Alice *author*
Nova, Craig *writer*
Nurkse, Dennis *writer, poet*
†Ober, Doris Ann *writer, editor, consultant*
O'Brien, Beatrice Marie *poet, writer*
†O'Brien-Palmer, Michelle Ann *educational writer, consultant*
O'Connor, Patrick Joseph *writer, musician, university educator*
†O'Leary, Kathleen Ann *writer*
O'Leary, Patsy Baker *writer, educator*
†Oliver, Karen Lee *writer*
†O'Neill, Susan Kramer *writer*
†Oransky, Ivan *writer, web editor*
O'Reilly, Wenda Brewster *writer, researcher*
Orkin, Jenna *writer*
Orlowsky, Pelahia Dzvinia *poet, publisher, educator*
Orrmont, Arthur *writer, editor*
Ortiz, Fernando, Jr., *scriptwriter, film researcher, stage manager*
Osborn, Patricia Ann *writer, teacher*
Osborne, Linda Barrett *writer, editor*
Owens, Betsy Kingsolver *writer*
Ozick, Cynthia *author*
†Padgett, Ron *writer*
Pakula, Dennis Paul *writer, photographer*
Pakula, Hannah *writer*
†Palmer, Charlotte Marie *writer*
†Pampellonne, Terese *playwright, writer*
†Panning, Sara J. (Sara Jordan) *writer*
Pantaleo, Jack *writer, composer, social worker, harpist*
Paolucci, Anne Attura *playwright, poet, English and comparative literature educator, educational consultant*
Parrott, Wanda Sue *writer, journalist*
Patrick, Mary Kathleen *freelance/self-employed writer, food service executive*
Patterson, Richard North *novelist, writer, lawyer*
†Peabody, Gary Douglas *scriptwriter, poet, actor*
Pelizzoni, Virginia Matko *writer, editor, consultant*
Penkul, Linda Marie *poet*
Perks, Micah Eve *writer, educator*
Perry, Ruth *writer*
Perry, Thomas Edmund *novelist, television screenwriter, producer*
†Phillips, Kate *writer*
Pierce, Marian Marie *writer, educator*
Pollet, Elizabeth *retired writer, educator*
†Pratt, Robin Lynn *writer*
Prescott, Peter Sherwin *writer*
Prescott, Richard Chambers *writer*
†Pressman, Linda Jayne *writer*
†Prince-Hughes, Dawn *writer, education educator*
Pugh, Christina Anne *poet, educator*
Pullman, Philip Nicholas *author*
Purmell, Ann *children's writer, school presenter, inspirational speaker*
Rader, Dotson Carlyle *author, journalist*
Ragans, Rosalind Dorothy *textbook author, retired art educator*
Ramsden, Karen McCoin *writer*
†Rasey, Patricia A. *writer*
Raucher, Herman *novelist, screenwriter*
Ravetch, Irving *screenwriter*
†Rawa, Mannee Jean *writer*
†Reaves, Christina Lee *writer, photographer*
Rechy, John Francisco *writer*
Reed, Kit *writer*
Reeder, Thomas Allen *television writer*
Reeves, Barbara *writer, educator*
Reiss, Alvin Herbert *writer, consultant*
Renaud, Bernadette Marie Elise *author*
†Rheinfrank, Elizabeth Scales *playwright*
Riehecky, Janet Ellen *writer*
†Rimel, Ira Wesley *writer, U.S. Navy supply officer, real estate specialist, real estate appraiser, real estate broker*
Ring, Nancy Gail *writer, artist*
Ripley, Alexandra Braid *author*
†Rizzuto, Rahna Reiko *writer*
Robins, Natalie *poet, writer*
Robinson, David Bradford *scientific writer, poet*
Rockstein, Morris *science writer, editor, consultant*
Rogers, David *playwright, novelist, actor*
Rohrbach, Peter Thomas *writer*
Romana, Kathleen *writer, artist*
Root, Phyllis Idalene *writer*
Roseman, Janet Lynn *writer, dance educator*
Rosenblatt, Roger *writer*
Rosenfeld, Albert Hyman *science and medical writer*
Rosmus, Anna Elisabeth *writer*
Royse, Brooke Sarno *editor, writer*
†Rubenfeld, Vik *writer*
Rubin, Charles Alexis *writer*
Rush, Norman *author*
Russ, Joanna *author*
Russell, Pamela Redford *writer, film documentarian*
Ruta, Suzanne *writer*
Rutkowski, Thaddeus *author*
Ruyechan, Michael James, Jr., *writer*
Ryan, Joyce Ethel *artist, author*
†Ryan, Thomas Phillip *writer, federal agency administrator*
Saito, Robert Shunichi *writer, poet*
†Salas Sommer, Dario *writer, educator*
Sallis, James *writer*
Sanders, Theresa Lynn *writer, systems analyst, consultant*
Sandy, Stephen *writer, educator*
Santini, Rosemarie *writer*
Schanstra, Carla Ross *technical writer*
Schatz, Lillian Lee *playwright, molecular biologist, educator*
Schenkkan, Robert Frederic *writer, actor*
Schiavo, Geraldine Elizabeth (Geri Schiavo) *poet, screenwriter*
Schiller, Gerald Alan *writer*
†Schindler, Holly Suzanne *freelance/self-employed writer*
Schneider, Phyllis Leah *writer, editor*
Schramm, Alicia Larrimore *writer*
†Schremp, Faith Maryanne *writer*
Schueler, Gerald Joseph *technical writer, systems analyst, counselor*
Schwartz, Joan Ruth *writer*
†Schwartz, Peter Isaac *poet*
Scott, Dorothy *writer*
Seamans, William *writer, commentator, former television and radio journalist*
Seidel, Frederick Lewis *poet*
Selby, Hubert, Jr., *writer*

PROFESSIONAL INDEX 6187 ARTS: PERFORMING

Senerchia, Dorothy Sylvia *author, urban planner*
Severin-Hansen, Jeanne Anne *poet*
Shagan, Steve *screenwriter, novelist, film producer*
Shannon, Elizabeth Joanna *writer, literary agent*
Shapiro, Harvey *poet*
Shapiro, Harvey Dean *writer*
Shattuck, Roger Whitney *author, educator*
Sheehan-Miles, Charles Edward *writer*
Shemkovitz, Greg *playwright*
Shep, Robert Lee *editor, publisher, textile book researcher*
Sher, Steven J. *writer, educator*
Sherman, Carol *poet, educator*
Sherman, Susan Jean *writer, educator, editor*
†Shermer, Michael *writer, educator, publishing executive*
Shore, Herbert *writer, poet, educator*
Shortz, Wilma Wildes *writer, Arabian horse breeder*
Shreve, Susan Richards *author, English literature educator*
†Siebert, Charles *writer*
Siegel, Mary Ann Garvin *writer*
Signori, Jacqueline M. *writer, educator*
Simmons, Ted Conrad *writer*
Simon, James *writer*
Simon, John Oliver *poet, educator*
Sims Iannelli, Kimberly *writer*
Singer, Donna Lea *writer, editor, educator*
Skibell, Joseph Freer *writer, educator*
Skinner, Knute Rumsey *poet, English educator*
Skwarczyński, Henryk Adam (Henryk Skwar) *writer*
Slater, Brian (Rauen Slate) *writer*
Smith, Brenda Joyce *author, editor, social studies educator*
Smith, Cynthia S. *writer*
Smith, Jamesetta Delorise *author*
Smith, Jane Marilyn Davis (Jane Maxwell) *writer*
†Smith, Janice M. *poet, artist*
Smith, Marya Jean *writer*
†Smith, Paul Eric *writer*
Smith, Tom *poet, educator, retired*
Snow, Marina Sexton *writer*
Sodums, Dzintars *writer*
Solomon, Beth Carol *writer*
Solomon, Norman *author, columnist*
SoRelle, Ruth Doyle *medical writer, journalist*
Sorley, Lewis *writer*
Spada, James *author, photographer, publisher*
Spinelli, Jerry *writer*
†Spire, Hazel Jean *writer*
Stano, Mary Gerardine *writer, tax accountant*
Stashower, Daniel Meyer *writer*
Steed, Kelly Renée *writer, poet*
†Stenson O'Brien, Suzanne Michele *writer*
Stepak, Asa Martin *writer, linguist*
Stern, Daniel *author, executive, educator*
Stevens, Shane *novelist*
†Stine, R(obert) L(awrence) *children's book author*
†Stone, Oliver *screenwriter, director*
Strand, Mark *poet*
Straub, Peter Francis *novelist*
Strong, Virginia Wilkerson *freelance writer, former educator*
Stroud, Patricia Tyson *writer*
Strouse, Jean *writer*
Styron, William *writer*
Sullivan, Evelin Elisabeth *writer, educator*
Sullivan, George Edward *author*
Sussman, Barry *author, public opinion analyst and pollster, journalist*
Sutton, James Hercules *poet, former educational association administrator*
Sylver, Nenan *writer, educator, psychotherapist, singer-songwriter*
Tabor, Anna Marie *writer*
†Tackett, Viti Lee *writer*
Talal, Marilynn Glick *poet*
Tassos, Alice Crowley *writer, linguist*
Taylor, John Jackson (Jay Taylor) *writer, documentalist, retired foreign service officer*
Taylor, Velande Pingel *author, publisher*
†Tejada, Roberto *poet, critic*
Tham, Hilary *poet*
Theroux, Paul Edward *author*
Thomas-Roots, Pamela M. *writer*
†Thompson, Bonita *writer*
†Thompson, Diana Rosebud *poet, educator, history exhibit coordinator, marketing consultant, playwright, lyricist*
Thompson, Hunter Stockton *author, political analyst, journalist*
Thornburg, Linda A. *writer*
Thurner, Henry *retired writer*
Tickle, Phyllis Alexander *writer, publisher*
Tobias, Sheila *writer, educator*
Trubo, Richard M. *writer*
Truman, Margaret *author*
†Tubbs, Bobbye *poet*
Tucker, Jack William Andrew *writer, film editor, producer, lecturer*
Twichell, Chase *poet*
Ubell, Earl *writer, consultant*
Ulku, Alpay Kilicarslan *poet*
†Unger, Barbara *poet, retired educator*
Updike, John Hoyer *writer*
Ursu, Anne Elizabeth *writer*
Utz, Heidi M. *writer*
Valiunas, Algis *writer, bass-baritone*
Vallicella, William F.
Van de Mark, Richard J. *retired writer, artist*
Van Duyn, Mona Jane *poet, educator*
Van Dyke, Henry Lewis *retired educator, writer*
van Itallie, Jean-Claude *playwright*
Vázquez, Lourdes *poet*
†Velez Cruz, Virginia *poet*
Vesey, Mary Frances *writer, educator*
Vestal, Marilyn Anita *writer, researcher, educator*
Viets, Elaine Frances *writer*
Viorst, Judith Stahl *author*
Viorst, Milton *writer*
Vita, Steven *poet*
†Voigt, Cynthia *author*
Volk, Patricia Gay *fiction writer, essayist*
von Hoffman, Nicholas *writer, former journalist*
†Wachal, Barbara Schwarz *writer, educator*
Waitley, Douglas D. *writer*
Walker, Lars *writer*
Wallace, Michele *writer, educator*
Waller, John Henry *author*
†Wambaugh, Joseph A., Jr., *author*
†Ward (Bailey), Daisy Dale *writer*
†Waring, Belle *poet*
Warren, Cindy Michelle *author*
Wasserstein, Wendy *playwright*
Waterford, Gwen Antionette *poet*
†Watson, Patricia Jane *writer, editor, sculptor*
Webb, David Allen *writer*
Weiner, Cherry *literary agent*
†Weiner, Jonathan David *writer*
Weis, Margaret Edith *writer, editor*
Weishaus, Joel *writer*
Weisman, John *author*
Wenzel, Lynn *writer, editor*
West, Bill *writer, artist, photographer, composer*
Whalen, Charles William, Jr., *author, business executive, educator*
Whaley, Charles E. *writer, consultant*
Whelchel, Sandra Jane *writer*
Whitaker, Marsha Jones *author, educator*
Whouley, Kate *book industry consultant, writer*
†Wilder, Dianna M. *freelance/self-employed writer, poet*
Wilder, Eleanor Marie (Nora Roberts Wilder) *writer*
Wilkinson, Claude Henry *writer, artist, English literature educator*
Will, Roland Tracy, II, *writer, editor, journalist, publisher, actor*
Willenz, June Adele *writer, public affairs executive, playwright, screenwriter, writer, columnist, scholar, speaker*
Willey, Margaret Mary *author, educator*
†Williams, Niama Leslie JoAnn *writer, educator*
†Wilson, Anne Judith *writer, educator*
†Wilson, Brandon Laine *writer, advertising and public relations consultant, explorer*
Wilson, Colin Henry *writer*
Wilson, Lanford *playwright*
Wilson, Sloan *writer, educator*
Wilson, Tamra McElroy *writer*
Witte, Arline (Lyn Witte) *author, poet*
Wolfe, Linda *writer*
†Wolverton, Mark *writer*
Wolverton, Terry L(ynn) *writer, consultant*
†Wood, Anne Hillsman *writer*
Wood, William Preston *author, lawyer*
Wright, Franz Paul *poet, writer, translator*
Wright, Nancy Means *author, educator*
Yeager, Anson Anders *writer, former columnist and newspaper editor*
Yglesias, Rafael Jose *novelist*
†Young, Katharine Galloway *writer*
Yurchak, Katherine Sasso *writer*
Zablocki, Elaine *writer*
Zagaski, Chester Anthony, Jr., *author, researcher*
Zavatto, Amy Elizabeth *freelance/self-employed writer, editor*
Zhiglevich, Eugenia *writer, actress*
Zimmerman, Robert *writer, filmmaker*
Zinn, Stacie *writer*
Ziporyn, Terra Diane *writer*

ARTS: PERFORMING

UNITED STATES

ALABAMA

Alexandria
Conaway, Charles Alan *music educator*

Auburn
Powell, William Clayton *music educator*

Birmingham
Allinder, David Randall *musician, educator*
Chapman, Wes *dancer, performing company executive*
†Cleveland, Edwin Pittman *music educator*
Dougherty, Dana Dean Lesley *television producer, educator*
Janes, Clarence Harrison, Jr., *music educator*
Westerfield, Richard *music director*
†Wienhold, Lisa J. *musician, educator*

Columbiana
Pizzitola, Patricia Gallman *music educator*

Cullman
Key, Randall Don *band director, musician*
Silvey, Tony Lee *music educator*
Taylor, Garry Lance *music educator*

Daleville
†Burkett, Trenton Shane *music educator*
†Turner, Chad Wesley *music educator*

Decatur
Cooper, John Burton *band director*

Enterprise
†Grice, Robert E., Jr., *music educator, composer*

Florence
†Woodford, Martha Haddock *retired music educator*

Homewood
†Pence, Ronald Kaylor *music educator*

Huntsville
†Carney, Horace R., Jr., *performing arts educator*
Mohan, Annette Imelda *producer, educator*
Mohan, Tungesh Nath *television and film producer, film educator*
Osterman, Eurydice V. *music educator*
Wilson, Timothy Wayne *music educator, musician*

Mobile
†Habib, Thomas Mark *musician, educator*
Talley, Beverly M. *music educator*
†Trippe, Annette Guy *music educator*

Montgomery
†Elrod, Stephen Roy *theater educator*

Muskogee
†Hearn, William Charles *music educator, music minister*

Normal
Wesley, Arthur Bernell, II, *music educator, musician*
Yates, Derrick K. *music educator, director*

Point Clear
Englund, Gage Bush *dancer, educator*

Troy
Jinright, John William *music educator*
Moffett, Thomas Delano *music educator*

Tuscaloosa
†Parsons, Laura Elizabeth *music educator, freelance/self-employed musician*
†Peles, Stephen Victor *composer*
†Spurlin, Adam Corey *music educator*

Vestavia Hills
†Coleman, Travis Brent *music educator*

Wadley
†Caldwell, Ann B. *music educator*

ALASKA

Anchorage
†Katzke, Mary Rosanne *filmmaker, scriptwriter*
†Olivares, Walter G. *music educator*
Zeiger, Maria Theresia *music educator*

Indian
Wright, Gordon Brooks *musician, conductor, educator*

Kenai
Means, Lane Lewis *entertainer*

Palmer
Kent, E(verett) Allen *performing arts administrator, theatrical producer*
Lambert, Tobias P. *music educator*

Soldotna
Petersen, Lance W. *fine arts educator*

ARIZONA

Avondale
Jaeger, Kenneth John *music educator*

Chandler
†Carpenter, Ron D. *music educator*
†Faust, Donny D. *music educator*
Simon, Diane Rose *music educator, writer, poet*
Zinman, David Joel *conductor*

Flagstaff
Gunderson, Margaret Steeble *music educator*
†Swann, Gloria S. *music educator*
†Weidenaar, Gary Alan *music educator*

Fort Huachuca
†Howdeshell, Daniel Thomas *music educator*

Fountain Hills
Tyl, Noel Jan *baritone, astrologer, writer*

Gilbert
Bennett, Kevin Ray *music educator, musician*

Glendale
Zinn, Dennis Bradley *magician, actor, comedian*

Holbrook
Eiler, Jason E *music educator*

Mesa
†Kent, Sherie Lynn *music educator*
Loose, Mary Ellen *musician*
Mason, Marshall W. *theater director, educator*
McIlray, John Frederick *organist*
McKinnon, Elizabeth Longo *musician, educator*
†Skoldberg, Phyllis Linnea *music educator, musician*

Nogales
Percious, Jacquelin Marlyn *musician, travel writer*

Oro Valley
†Hodge, Mark Louis *music educator, conductor*

Phoenix
Anderson, Gary Gene *music educator*
†Anderson, Ib *performing company executive*
†Chang, Gail Cathryn May *music educator*
Darnell, Yolanda (Yolanda Darnell) *videomaker, filmmaker, writer*
Godfrey, John William *retired music educator*
Long, Michael Alan *musician, writer*
Nijinsky, Tamara *actress, puppeteer, author, librarian, educator*
†Pittman, Timona Miller *arts adminstrator*
Thomas, Jim Gus *music educator*
Wheaton, Marilyn *music educator, pianist, organist*

Saint Johns
DuBoise, Aaron T. *music educator*

Scottsdale
Ash, Fayola Foltz *musician, music educator*
†Baack, Paula D. *music educator*
Fosgate Heggli, Julie Denise *producer*
†Kuschell, Daniel J *radio personality*
†Newman, Ursula Irene *music educator*
Peterson, John Willard *composer, music publisher*

Sedona
Griffin, Jean (Alva Jean Griffin) *entertainer*
Rhines, Marie Louise *composer, violinist*

Sierra Vista
†Boughan, Zanetta Louise *music educator*

Tempe
†Lang, Scott M. *music educator*
Lombardi, Eugene Patsy *retired orchestra conductor, violinist, educator*
Russell, Timothy Wells *music educator, researcher, conductor*
†Wytko, Joseph Rudolph *music educator*

Tucson
†Apel, Harry James *composer*
Armstrong, R(obert) Dean *entertainer*
Aurand, Charles Henry, Jr., *music educator, educator*
Birdman, Jerome Moseley *drama educator, consultant*
†Boyle, Michael Frederick *retired television producer, actor*
Coleman, Dan *composer, arranger, recording engineer, educator*
Franks, Sondra Lou *music educator, organist*
†Hayashi, Kim *music educator*
Lounsbury, James Richard *retired broadcaster, pilot, writer*
†Ostromencki, Nancy Lee *music educator*
†Rees, Jay Carlyle *music composition educator*
Seaman, Arlene Anna *retired musician, educator*
†Spillane, James (Jamie) D. *music educator*
Tentser, Alexander *music educator, conductor*
Zeffirelli, Lucia *dance instructor, music teacher, choreographer, director, dancer, actress*

Vail
†Cardieri, Alexander M. *music specialist, music educator*

Wickenburg
†Johnson, Timothy D. *music educator, composer, poet*

ARKANSAS

Conway
Shires, Brent Alan *music educator, musician*
†Showell, Jeffrey Adams *music educator, academic administrator, musician*

Fayetteville
†Caldwell, Sarah *opera producer, conductor, stage director and administrator*
Mains, Ronda M. *music educator, musician*

Forrest City
†Warren, Charlene *music educator*

Fort Smith
Husarik, Stephen *music educator*
†Walker, Rosilee *music educator*

Jonesboro
†Bartee, Neale *music educator, musician, conductor*

Little Rock
†Brack, Robert Louis *retired music educator*
Itkin, David *music director, conductor*
Munoz, Olivier *artistic director*
Raney, Miriam Day *actress*
Vickery, William *arts administrator*

Magnolia
Campbell, Robert Gordon *music educator*

CALIFORNIA

Albany
Boris, Ruthanna *dancer, choreographer, dance therapist, educator*
Ginzberg, Abigail *video producer*

Anaheim
†Hicks, Eva Fern *retired music educator*
†Vidergar, Teresa *music educator, musician*

Antioch
Adams, Liliana Osses *music performer, harpist*

Apple Valley
Beller, Gerald Stephen *professional magician, former insurance company executive*
Lavallee, Charles Phillip *music educator, musician*

Arcadia
Khoo-Zeng, May-Sze (Macy Khoo-Zeng) *music educator*
Zimmerman, Amy J. *television producer, television director*

Arroyo Grande
Mott, Robert Lewis *writer, sound effects artist*

Azusa
Durbin, Timothy Terrell *music educator*

Bakersfield
†Provencio, Roberto Enrique *music educator, music minister*

Bell
†Jackman, Hugh *actor*

Bellflower
de Thouars, Victor Ivan Charles *professional martial artist, educator*

Belvedere Tiburon
Kline, Donna S. *musician, educator*

Berkeley
†Crocker, Richard Lincoln *retired music educator*
Dresher, Paul Joseph *composer, music educator, performer*
Imbrie, Andrew Welsh *composer, educator*
Kleiman, Vivian Abbe *filmmaker*
Matsumura, Vera Yoshi *pianist*
†Ogden, Dunbar Hunt *author, theatre educator*
Stork, Susan Diana *musician, composer*

Beverly Hills
†Alexander, Jason (Jay Scott Greenspan) *actor*
†Allen, Joan *actress*
†Allen, Tim (Timothy Allen Dick) *actor, comedian*
Amiel, Jon *film director, film producer*
†Anderson, Wes *film director*
†Avary, Roger Roberts (Frank Brauner) *film director, producer, writer*
Avildsen, John Guilbert *film director*
Badham, John MacDonald *motion picture director*
Bailey, John *cinematographer*
Bancroft, Anne (Mrs. Mel Brooks) *actor, director, screenwriter*
†Banderas, Antonio *actor*
Bassett, Angela *actress*
Bates, Kathy *actress*
†Bay, Michael Benjamin *film director*
Beal, John Everett *composer, conductor*
Beatty, (Henry) Warren *actor, producer, director*
Becker, Harold *film director, producer*
Bedelia, Bonnie *actress*
Belushi, James A. *actor*
†Bening, Annette *actress*
†Berkus, James *talent agent*
Berry, Halle *actress*
†Bigelow, Kathryn *film director*
Bogdanovich, Peter *film director, writer, producer, actor*
Bonham-Carter, Helena *actress*
Boyle, Lara Flynn *actress*
Braun, Zev *motion picture and television producer*
†Bridges, Jeff *actor*
†Brillstein, Bernie J. *producer, talent manager*
†Broderick, Matthew *actor*
Brokaw, Norman Robert *talent agency executive*
Burnett, Carol *actress, comedienne, singer*
†Burnham, John Ludwig *agent*
Burns, Edward J., Jr., *actor, film director*
Carreras, José *tenor*
†Carrey, Jim *actor*
†Carter, Chris *producer, director*
Casey, Sue (Suzanne Marguerite Philips) *actress, real estate broker*
†Cattrall, Kim *actress*
†Channing, Carol *actress*
†Cheadle, Don *actor*
†Cher, (Cherilyn Sarkisian) *singer, actress*
Christensen, Hayden *actor*
Chritton, George A. *theater producer*
†Clooney, George *actor*
Close, Glenn *actress*
†Coen, Ethan *film director, writer*
†Coen, Joel *film director, writer*
Cole, Natalie Maria *singer*
Collette, Toni *actress*
†Columbus, Chris *film director, screenwriter*
Connelly, Jennifer *actress*
†Connery, Sir Sean (Thomas Connery) *actor*
†Corbett, John *actor*
Corman, Eugene Harold *motion picture producer*
Cox, Courteney *actress*
Crowe, Russell *actor*
†Cruz, Penelope *actress*
†Curtis, Jamie Lee *actress*
Dahl, John *film director*
†Daly, Tyne *actress*
Damon, Matthew Paige *actor*
†DeBont, Jan *cinematographer, director*
Demme, Jonathan *actor, director, producer, writer*
†De Niro, Robert *actor*
†Dennehy, Brian *actor*
†Depp, Johnny *actor*
†DeVito, Danny Michael *actor, director, producer*
Diaz, Cameron *actress*
Dorff, Stephen *actor*
Dotrice, Roy Louis *actor*
†Dreyfuss, Richard Stephan *actor*
†Duvall, Robert *actor*
Eastwood, Clint *actor, film director, former mayor*
†Falco, Edie *actress*
Finstad, Suzanne Elaine *writer, producer, lawyer*
Flaum, Marshall Allen *television producer, writer, director*
Fleder, Gary *film director, producer*
Foch, Nina *actress, creative consultant, educator, director*
Foley, David *television and film actor*
Foster, Lawrence *concert and opera conductor*
Fradis, Anatoly Adolf *film producer*
Gilpin, Peri *actress*
†Glover, John *actor*
Graham, Heather *actress*
†Green, Seth *actor*
Gregg, Rodman Walter *motion picture and television producer, publisher*
†Grey, Brad *producer, agent*
Griffin, Merv Edward *former entertainer, television producer, entrepreneur*
Hackman, Gene (Eugene Alden Hackman) *actor*
Hallstrom, Lasse *director*
Hamilton, Lisa Gay *actress*
Hanks, Tom *actor, producer, director*
Harmon, Angie (Angie Sehorn) *actress*
Harvey, Simon *actor, writer*
Haskell, Peter Abraham *actor*
†Hawn, Goldie *actress*
Heaton, Patricia *actress*
†Helgeland, Brian Thomas *film director, writer, producer*
Holmes, Katherine Noelle *actor*
†Hopkins, Sir Anthony (Philip) *actor*
Howard, Ron *director, actor*
†Hughes, John W. *film producer, screenwriter, film director*
†Hunt, Helen *actress*
Hurd, Gale Anne *film producer*
Hurley, Elizabeth *actress, model, producer*
†Hurt, William *actor*
†Huvane, Kevin *talent agent*
Jackson, Janet Damita *singer, dancer*
Jackson, Mick *film director, producer*
†Jackson, Peter *film director*
†Jagger, Mick (Michael Philip Jagger) *singer, musician*
Jolie, Angelina *actress*
†Jonze, Spike *film director*
Jordan, Glenn *director*
†Josephson, Nancy *talent agent*
†Judd, Ashley *actress*
†Keaton, Diane *actress*
Kidman, Nicole *actress*
†Kilmer, Val *actor*
Kingston, Alex(andra) *actress*
Knoxville, Johnny *actor*
Kozak, Harley Jane *actress*
†Kravitz, Lenny *singer, guitarist*
†Lane, Nathan (Joseph Lane) *actor*
†Lange, Jessica *actress*
†Lansbury, Angela Brigid *actress*
†LaPaglia, Anthony *actor*
†Law, Jude *actor*
†Lawrence, Martin *actor, comedian*
Lear, Norman Milton *producer, writer, director*
†Leder, Mimi *television director*
†Lee, Ang *filmmaker*
Leguizamö, John *actor*
Lehmann, Michael Stephen *film director*
†Levy, Eugene *actor, director, screenwriter*
Lewis, Juliette *actress*
†Limato, Edward Frank *talent agent*
Linkletter, Arthur Gordon *radio and television broadcaster*
Linney, Laura *actress*
Lloyd, Christopher *actor*
Lopez, Jennifer *actress, dancer, singer*
†Lourd, Bryan *talent agent*
†Lovett, Richard *talent agency executive*
†Lyne, Adrian *film director*
†Macy, William H. *actor*
Malkovich, John *actor*
Manheim, Camryn *television and film actress*
†Mann, Michael K. *producer, director, writer*
Margulies, Julianna *actress*
Martin, Kellie (Noelle) *actress*
Martinson, Constance Frye *television program hostess, producer*
Masterson, Mary Stuart *actress*
Matovich, Mitchel Joseph, Jr., *film producer, film company executive*
†McDormand, Frances *actress*
Messing, Debra *actress*
†Midler, Bette *singer, entertainer, actress*
†Moore, Demi (Demi Guynes) *actress*
Moore, Julianne (Julie Anne Smith) *actress*
†Moore, Michael *film director*
†Morissette, Alanis *musician*
†Murray, Bill *actor, writer*
†Nicita, Rick *agent*
Norton, Edward *actor*
Novak, Kim (Marilyn Novak) *actress*
†O'Connor, David *talent agent*
O'Connor, Pat *film director*
O'Donnell, Rosie *television personality, comedienne, actress*
Pacino, Al (Alfredo James Pacino) *actor, film director, film producer*
Paltrow, Gwyneth *actress*
†Pantoliano, Joe *actor*
Parker, Alan (William) (Sir Alan Parker) *film director, writer*
Parker, Sarah Jessica *actress*
Penderecki, Krzysztof *composer, conductor*
Pfeiffer, Michelle *actress*
Phillippe, Ryan *actor*
Pitt, Brad *actor*
†Polanski, Roman *film director, writer, actor*
†Pollack, Sydney *film director*
Portman, Natalie *actress*
Ptak, John *talent agent*
Reese, Della (Deloreese Patricia Early) *singer, actress*
†Reeves, Keanu *actor*
†Reiner, Rob *director, writer, actor*
Renfro, Brad *actor*
†Ricci, Christina *actress*
Riley, Jack *actor, writer*
Roberts, Julia Fiona *actress*
Rohrer, Susan Earley *film producer, writer, director*
†Rush, Geoffrey *actor*
Russell, Kurt Von Vogel *actor*
Ryan, Meg *actress, producer*
Saget, Bob *director, actor, comedian, writer*
Sandrich, Jay H. *television director*
†Scott, Ridley *film director*
†Shadyac, Thomas *film director, producer*
†Shalhoub, Tony *actor, television producer*
†Short, Martin *actor, comedian*
†Shue, Elisabeth *actress*
Shuler Donner, Lauren *film producer*
†Shyamalan, Manoj Night *film director*
†Simpson, Michael *talent agent*
Sinise, Gary *actor, director*
Skerritt, Tom *actor*
†Smith, Will *actor, rapper*
Snyder, Liza *actress*
Sommers, Stephen *film director, scriptwriter, film producer*
†Sonnenfeld, Barry *director, cinematographer*
†Sorvino, Mira *actress*
Spacek, Sissy (Mary Elizabeth Spacek) *actress*
Spielberg, Steven *motion picture director, producer*
Stefano, Joseph William *film and television producer, writer*
Stern, Sandor *film writer, director*
Stowe, Madeleine *actress*
Streep, Meryl (Mary Louise Streep) *actress*
Sutherland, Donald *actor*
Sutherland, Kiefer *actor*
†Theron, Charlize *actress*
Thompson, Larry Angelo *motion picture and TV producer, lawyer, personal manager, writer*
Travolta, John *actor*
Van Ark, Joan *actress*
Van Dyke, Dick *actor, comedian*
†Vaughn, Vince *actor*
†Verhoeven, Paul *film director*
Ward, Sela *actress*
Waters, John *film director, writer, actor*
Weaver, Sigourney (Susan Alexandra Weaver) *actress*
Weber, Jeffrey Randolph *record producer*
Weir, Peter Lindsay *film director*
Weisz, Rachel *actress*
Weitz, Bruce (Peter Weitz) *actor*
†Wiatt, James Anthony *theatrical agency executive*
†Willis, Walter Bruce *actor, singer, writer*
†Wilson, Luke *actor*
†Wilson, Owen *actor*
Winkler, Irwin *motion picture producer*
†Winningham, Mare *actress*
†Wirtschafter, David *agent*
Witherspoon, Reese (Laura Jean Witherspoon) *actress*
†Wu, Yusen (John Woo) *film director*
†Yorn, Rick *talent agent*
Zellweger, Renee *actress*
Zeta-Jones, Catherine *actress*

Brea
†Ellis, Cynthia Bueker *musician, educator*

Burbank
Bader, Diedrich *actor*
†Baker, Rick *make-up artist*
†Berman, Bruce *entertainment company executive, television producer*
†Bright, Kevin S. *producer*
Chiarelli, Robert Charles *audio engineer*
†Clapton, Eric *musician*
†Costner, Kevin *actor*
†Crane, David *producer*
†Donner, Richard *film director, producer*
†Fishburne, Laurence, III, *actor*
Franco, James *actor*
†Gibson, Mel *actor, film director, producer*
†Henley, Don *singer, drummer, songwriter*
Janney, Allison *actress*
†Kinney, Kathy *actress*
†Leno, Jay (James Douglas Muir Leno) *television personality, comedian, writer*
Levinson, Barry L. *film director*
†Meyer, Barry Michael *motion picture executive*
†Mitchell, Joni (Roberta Joan Anderson) *singer, songwriter*
Neill, Ve *make-up artist*
†Samaha, Elie *producer, film company executive, business owner*
†Schumacher, Joel *director, writer*
†Silver, Joel *film producer*
Stiles, Ryan *actor*
Wachowski, Andy *film director*
Wachowski, Larry *film director*
†Wells, John Marcum *producer, writer*
†Wonder, Stevie (Stevland Morris) *singer, musician, composer*

Calabasas
Andrews, Ralph Herrick *television producer*
Isham, Mark *composer, jazz musician*
Landau, Martin *actor*

Camarillo
Hall, Cynthia Jean *music educator, author, composer, musician*

Capitola
Peduto, Ralph *actor, author, producer*

Carmel Valley
Meckel, Peter Timothy *arts administrator, educator*

Cathedral City
Hoffman, Jetha L. *piano and vocal teacher, musician*

Chico
King, Claudia Louan *film producer, lecturer*

Claremont
†Bradley, Rochelle Elaine *music educator*

Coarsegold
Samuelson, William Allen *music educator*

Concord
†Christian, John Robert *music educator*

Corona
Hagmann, Lillian Sue *violin instructor*

Corona Del Mar
Karson, Burton Lewis *musician, educator*

Coronado
Neblett, Carol *soprano*

Costa Mesa
McEnary, John Walter *music educator*

Cotati
†Baker, Sarah E. *music educator, composer, writer*

Culver City
†Brooks, James L. *writer, director, producer*
Brooks, Mel *producer, director, writer, actor*
†Chaffin, Cean *producer*
†Coolio, (Artis Ivey Jr.) *popular musician*
Ewing, Michael Snyder *producer, film company executive*
†Guber, Peter *executive producer*
†Kaufman, Richard Stuart *conductor, music director*
Mark, Laurence Maurice *film producer*
†Marshall, Penny (C. Marshall) *director, actress*
†Tisch, Steven Elliot *TV and movie producer*
Wick, Douglas *producer*
†Ziskin, Laura *television producer, film producer*

Dana Point
Camp, Joseph Shelton, Jr., *film producer, director, writer*

Davis
Handel, Darrell Dale *composer, retired music educator*
Swift, Richard G(ene) *composer, educator*

Del Mar
Ogdon, Wilbur (Will Ogdon) *composer, music educator*

El Cerrito
Mendoza, Lydia *vocalist*

Encinitas
Litvin, Inessa Elizabeth *piano educator*

Encino
Ehrlich, Kenneth James *television producer*
Gavin, Delane Michael *television writer, producer, director*
†Ginty, Robert *actor*
†Husain, Shujaat *music educator*
Ingels, Marty *theatrical agent, television and motion picture production executive*
Medak, Peter *film director*
Pryor, Richard *actor, writer*
Shire, David Lee *composer*
Westmore, Michael George *make-up artist, writer*
Zsigmond, Vilmos *cinematographer, director*

Escondido
Ehrhart, Joseph Edward *retired television broadcast engineer*
Rockwell, Elizabeth Goode *dance company director, consultant, educator*

Folsom
†Munroe, Jeanette C. *music educator*

Fontana
†Mayse, Susan Galilee *music educator*

Fountain Valley
†de Jong-Pombo, Teresa Maria *concert pianist, educator*

Fremont
Hsu, Gloria *piano teacher*

Fresno
†Ishigaki, Miles Mitsurn *musician, educator*
†Saul, Walter Biddle, II, *music educator, composer*

Fullerton
Wiley, David Cole *producer*

Gilroy
George, Marilyn L. *music educator, musician*

Glendale
Carley, Kurt *actor*
Sherman, Eric *director, writer, educator*
Sprosty, Joseph Patrick *producer, writer, weapons specialist*

Glendora
†Prukesatonkul, Kamol *music educator*

Hermosa Beach
Lay, Alfred Alan *recording engineer, musician*
Rowland, Christopher Lee *filmmaker, educator, artist*

Hollywood
†Calva, Robert Baraquiel *music educator*
Milhous, David Matthew *film and television editor*
Roberts, Mel (Melvin Richard Kells) *retired film editor*
Salzman, David Elliot *entertainment industry executive*
Thomas, Tony *producer*

Huntington Beach
Carter, Henrietta McKee *educator*
†Typaldos, Sylvia Joyce *musician, writer*

Inglewood
Wakefield, Marie Cynthia *performing arts educator, playwright, poet*

Irvine
Davis, Clifton Duncan *actor, composer*
Puhl, Jennifer Louise *music teacher, pianist, organist*

Kaweah
Foster, Joseph Kevin, IV, *entertainer, scribe*

Kentfield
Halprin, Anna Schuman (Mrs. Lawrence Halprin) *dancer*

La Crescenta
Phillips, Mary Linda *actress*

La Habra Heights
Agajanian, Gilda *pianist*

La Jolla
Bastien, Jane Smisor *music educator*
Corrigan, Mary Kathryn *theater educator*
Hujsak, Ruth Joy *musician, educator*
†Lewis, George *music educator*
Reynolds, Roger Lee *composer, educator*

La Quinta
Holman, David Calvin *independent television and film producer and director*

Laguna Woods
McClure, Hal H.

Lake Arrowhead
Tinturin, Noëlle Compinsky *pianist, music educator*

Lakeview Terrace
Coolidge, Martha *film director*

Lancaster
Bell, Gary Lynn *owner production company, video and audio producer*

Larkspur
Earley, Edward Joseph, Jr., *studio musician, composer, copyist, trombonist*

Littleriver
Van Dyck, Wendy *dancer*

Livermore
Darter, Thomas Eugene, Jr., *composer, musician, writer*

Long Beach
Fischler, Sandy Lynn *event producer*
Hirshtal, Edith *concert pianist, educator, chamber musician*
Kelly, Chuck H. *singer, writer, trombonist*

Los Altos
Clark, Sondra *composer, musicologist, educator*
Collins, Gordon Dent *recording company executive*

Los Angeles
Aniston, Jennifer *actress*
Armistead, Thomas Boyd, III, *television and film producer*
Arpesella, Pietro *actor, writer*
†Auch Yellin, Barbara Ann *musician*
Bain, Conrad Stafford *actor*
†Ballard, Glen *composer*
Barker, Robert William *television personality*
Bell, Lee Phillip *television personality, television producer*
Bergman, Marilyn Keith *lyricist, writer*
†Berman, Richard Keith *television producer, film producer*
Biggs, Jason *actor*
Brown, Carol *make-up artist*
†Burrows, James *television and motion picture director, producer*
†Burton, Tim *film director*
Buzzi, Ruth *comedienne*
Caine, Michael *actor*
Calman, Craig David *writer, actor, director*
Cates, Gilbert *film, theater, television producer and director*
Champlin, Charles Davenport *television host, book critic, writer*
Chapman, Carolyn *broadcasting director*
†Charles, Ray (Ray Charles Robinson) *musician, singer, composer*
†Chiklis, Michael *actor*
Conley, Darlene Ann *actress*
†Cooper, Chris *actor*
Corman, Roger William *motion picture producer, director*
†Cowan, Georgianne *dancer, educator, writer*
Crockett, Donald Harold *composer, university educator*
D'Accone, Frank Anthony *music educator*
Davis, Terri Judith *television producer, writer*
Diehl, Dolores *communication arts director*
Douglas, Kirk (Issur Danielovitch) *actor, motion picture producer*
†Dr. Dre, (Andre Young) *rapper, record producer*
DuMont, James Kelton, Jr., *actor, theater producer*
Duncan, Michael Clarke *actor*
Dunst, Kirsten *actress*
Elrod, Lu *music educator, actress, author*
Eubanks, Rachel Amelia *music educator*
Ferrell, Conchata Galen *actress, acting teacher and coach*
†Fincher, David *film director, film producer*
Finneran, Katie *actress*
Fleischmann, Ernest Martin *music administrator*
†Flockhart, Calista *actress*
Foster, Jodie (Alicia Christian Foster) *actress, producer, director*
†Franz, Dennis *actor*
Franz, Elizabeth *actress*
Fritzsche, Kathleen (Dragonfire Fritzsche) *performing arts educator*
†Fung, Peter E. H. *actor, martial arts educator, apparel designer*
†Gandolfini, James *actor*
†Garrett, Brad *actor, comedian*
Goldsmith, Jerry *composer*
†Gooding, Cuba, Jr., *actor*
Gordon, Allen Barry *musician, composer*
†Gordon, Mark, II, *film producer*
Grammer, Kelsey *actor*
Greenberg, Barry Michael *talent executive*
Griffiths, Rachel *actress*
†Hancock, Herbert Jeffrey (Herbie Hancock) *composer, pianist, publisher*
Hartke, Stephen Paul *composer, educator*
Hartnett, Josh *actor*
Hiller, Arthur *motion picture director*
Hirsch, Judd *actor*
†Hoblit, Gregory *film director, television executive*
Hoffman, Dustin Lee *actor*
†Hoffman, Philip Seymour *actor*
Hu, Kelly *actress*
Ireland, Kathy *actor, apparel designer*
†Jennings, Willbur *musician, popular*
Johnson, Charles Floyd *television executive, producer*
Kaplan, Alan I. *film producer*
Keith, David *symphony orchestra conductor*
Kelley, David E. *producer, writer*
Klauss, Kenneth Karl *composer, educator*
Lansing, Sherry Lee (Heimann) *motion picture executive*
Laudicina, Salvatore Anthony *film industry executive*
Ledger, Heath *actor*
Lee, Lance *theater and film educator, writer*
†Levinsohn, Gary *producer*
Lew, Joycelyne Mae *actress*
London, Andrew Barry *film editor*
Maguire, Tobey *actor*
Main, Laurie (Laurence George Main) *actor*
Malden, Karl (Malden Sekulovich) *actor*
Malick, Terrence (David Whitney II) *film director*
Mann, Delbert *film, theater, television director and producer*
Marshall-Daniels, Meryl *telecommunications executive, lawyer, mediator*
†Mason, Andrew *film producer*
McQueen, Justice Ellis (L. Q. Jones) *actor, director*
Menefee, John William, III, *cinematographer, producer*
Merlis, George *television producer*
†Metheny, Patrick Bruce *musician*
Michelson, Sonia *music educator, author*
†Milchan, Arnon *film producer*
Moore, Ronald Bruce *visual effects producer*
Mueller, Carl Richard *theater arts educator, author*
Muldaur, Diana Charlton *actress*
Mulligan, Robert *film director, producer*
Nelligan, Kate (Patricia Colleen Nelligan) *actress*
Newhart, Bob *entertainer*
Newman, Randy *singer, songwriter, musician*
†Nicholson, Jack *actor, director, producer*
Nilles, Laila Padorr *musician, record producer*
Noble, James Wilkes *actor*
Nunez, Victor *film director, producer, writer*
O'Connell, Taaffe Cannon *actress, publishing executive*
O'Day, Anita Belle Colton *entertainer, singer*
†Ohlmeyer, Donald Winfred, Jr., *film and television producer*
Oldman, Gary *actor*
†Orbach, Jerry *actor, singer*
Peña, Elizabeth *actress*
Perry, Antoinette Krueger *pianist, instructor*
Peterson, Lowell *cinematographer*
†Pettibon, Raymond *video artist*
†Phillips-Oland, Pamela Barbara *lyricist, writer*
†Ponty, Jean-Luc *violinist, composer, producer*
†Potenza, Frank William *music educator*
†Quaid, Dennis *actor*
Quan, Denise Alane *music educator*
Rabinovitz, Jason *film and television consultant*
Richmond, Rocsan *television and video producer, director, publicist, actress, inventor, teacher*
Rickles, Donald Jay *comedian, actor*
Rosenberger, Carol *concert pianist*
Ross, Marion *actress*
Roth, Tim *actor*
Rubin, Stanley Creamer *producer*
Ruskin, Joseph Richard *actor, director*
Schmidt, Arthur *film editor*
†Schwimmer, David *actor*
†Scott, Tony *film director*
Selleck, Tom *actor*
Shatner, William *actor*
†Shay, Anthony Victor *choreographer, dance historian*
Simon, Elinor Dee *music educator*
†Smits, Jimmy *actor*
†Somrack, F. Daniel *film producer, writer*
Spelling, Aaron *film and television producer, writer, actor*
Spinotti, Dante *cinematographer*
Stark, Ray *motion picture producer*
Stevenson, Robert Murrell *music educator*
†Stokes, Sheridon Willard *musician, music educator*
Streisand, Barbra Joan *singer, actress, director*
Takei, George Hosato *actor*
†Tarantino, Quentin *film director, screenwriter*
Thornton, Billy Bob *actor, film producer*
†Trembly, Dennis Michael *musician*
Van Der Beek, James *actor*
Waits, Thomas Alan *composer, actor, singer*
†Waterston, Samuel Atkinson *actor*
†Watson, Emily *actress*
Webber, Peggy *actress, producer, director, writer*
Winters, Barbara Jo *musician*
†Wise, Robert *film producer, director*
Woessner, Frederick T. *composer, pianist*
Woyt, James Charles (Jim Woyt) *actor*
†Zemeckis, Robert L. *film director*

Los Osos
†Kreitzer, Jacalyn Bower *vocalist, voice educator*

Malibu
Almond, Paul *film director, producer, screenwriter, novelist*
Carson, Johnny *television personality*
Harris, Ed(ward Allen) *actor*
Herschensohn, Bruce *film director, writer*
Keach, Stacy, Jr., *actor, director, producer, writer, musician, composer*

Manhattan Beach
Champion, David *music educator*

Marina Del Rey
Fash, Michael William *cinematographer, director*

Mckinleyville
†Byrd, Joseph *composer*

Menlo Park
Baez, Joan Chandos *folk singer*

Mill Valley
Padula, Fred David *filmmaker*

Mission Viejo
†Burke, Kathleen J. *music director, writer*

Montecito
Schwartz, Norman Benjamin *theatre director*

Moorpark
†Kessner, Dolly Eugenio *music educator, musician*

Moraga
Gordon, David Jamieson *tenor*

Mountain View
†Sultanov, Namig, 2d Baronet, *musician, music educator*

Murrieta
†Cloud, Mark F. *video producer, director, writer, musician*

Nipomo
Stock, Kim H. *dance studio owner, choreographer*

North Hollywood
Balmuth, Bernard Allen *retired film editor*
Downey, Roma *actress*
Gallardo, Sandra Silvana *producer*
Grasso, Mary Ann *theater association executive*
Kantor, Igo *film and television producer*
†Milliken, Susan *film director, human services administrator*
Reynolds, Debbie (Mary Frances Reynolds) *actress*
†Stone, Sharon *actress*
Toplitt, Gloria H. *voice educator, singer, actress*

Northridge
Loudon, Craig Michael *video specialist*

Norwalk
†Kiss, Boglarka *music educator*
†Schreiner, Gregory Lee *music educator*

Oakland
Crocker, Joy Laksmi *concert pianist and organist, composer*
DeFazio, Lynette Stevens *dancer, choreographer, educator, chiropractor, author, actress, musician*
†Elliott, Jack *folk musician*
Jackson, Marjorie *musician*
Lake, Suzanne *singer, teacher*
Perlmutter, Martin Lee *interactive media producer, consultant, writer, educator*
Randle, Ellen Eugenia Foster *opera and classical singer, educator*
†Richmond, William O'Neal *retired music educator*

Oceanside
Swoger, James Wesley *magician*

Ojai
Cusumano, James Anthony *filmmaker, retired pharmaceutical company executive, former recording artist*
Paxton, Glenn Gilbert *composer*

Orange
†Matthews, Joseph Virgil *pianist, music educator*

Orinda
†Anderson, Barbara Jeanne *music educator*

Pacific Palisades
Kirkgaard, Valerie Anne *retired media group executive, syndicated talk radio host, writer, producer, consultant*

Palm Springs
Gordon, Stewart Lynell *musician, educator*
†Ingelson, Brian Charles *music educator, director*

Palmdale
Luther, Amanda Lisa *producer*

Palo Alto
†Ta, Christopher Nguyen *performing arts educator*
Tirschwell-Newby, Kathy Ann *events production company executive*

Palos Verdes Estates
Chary, Erika M. *music educator*

Pasadena
Hicklin, Ronald Lee *music production company executive*
Horak, Jan-Christopher *film studies educator, curator*
Marien, Robert *producer, director, naturalist, photographer, designer*
Ubovich, Ben A. *music educator*
Wilcox, Roberta Moat *music educator*
Worby, Rachael Beth *conductor*

Pine Mountain
Edwards, Sarah Anne *radio, cable TV personality, clinical social worker*

Pleasanton
†Goddard, John Wesley *cable television company executive*

Pomona
†Kopplin, David F. *music educator, composer*

Port Hueneme
Schneider, Arthur Paul *retired videotape and film editor, author*

Redlands
†Auerbacher, Mary Jane *church organist*
Niks, Inessa *piano teacher*

Redondo Beach
Reed, John E. *producer, consultant*

Reedley
Walter Jr., Burl Leroy *retired music educator*

Reseda
Turner, Lloyd Daniel *musician*

Richmond
Lasseter, John P. *film director, computer animator*

Sacramento
Mazzaferro, James Joseph *music educator*
Nice, Carter *conductor, music director*
†Piper, Jami Kathleen *music educator, composer*
†Tarrant, Kevin Theodore *music educator*

San Diego
Bales, Dorothy Johnson *violinist, educator*
Bonn, Ronald Sheldon *TV news producer, journalism educator*
Burge, David Russell *concert pianist, composer, piano educator*
Campbell, Ian David *opera company director*
Engle, Robert Irwin *music educator, musician, composer, writer, translator*
†Eulert, Corneaux H *drama therapist, educator*
Flettner, Marianne *opera administrator*
Langer, Eva Marie *video specialist*
Overton, Marcus Lee *performing arts administrator, actor, writer*
Pagan, Keith Areatus *music educator, academic administrator*
†Pfiffner, Patrick Meehan *musician, educator*
†Ransom, Bryan Kenneth *music educator*
†Soria, Merja T. *music educator*
Ward-Steinman, David *composer, music educator, pianist*
†Wyatt, Roland Gratts *music educator, voice educator, consultant*

San Dimas
Peters, Joseph Donald *filmmaker*

San Francisco
Caniparoli, Val William *choreographer, dancer*
Dupont, Colyer Lee *television and film producer, video and film distributing company executive*
Festinger, Richard *music educator, composer*
Frey, Adam Lewis *performing company executive*
Gondek, Juliana *soprano soloist, music educator*
†Gregory, Sara Susan *musician, lyricist, poet*
†Gropman, Saul I. *music educator*
Hastings, Edward Walton *theater director*
Kennedy, Matthew Lawry *film historian, anthropologist*
King, Alonzo *artistic director, choreographer*
LeBlanc, Tina *dancer*
Magie, Gregory Alden *music educator*
†Neve, Victoria J *music educator*
Nichols, William J. *film studies educator*
†Peterson, Wayne Turner *composer, pianist*
†Rosenberg, Pamela *conductor*
†Runnicles, Donald *conductor*
Schechter, Joel *magazine editor, writer, educator*
Smuin, Michael *choreographer, director, dancer*
Stowell, Christopher R. *choreographer, retired dancer*
Talbot, Stephen Henderson *television producer, documentary filmmaker, writer*
Tiano, Anthony Steven *television producer, book publishing executive*
†Tomasson, Helgi *dancer, choreographer, dance company executive*

San Gabriel
Keeling, Geraldine Ann *musicologist, educator*

San Jose
Archibeque, Charlene Paullin *music educator*
Dalis, Irene *mezzo-soprano, opera company administrator, music educator*
Slater, Stewart Eugene *theatre producer*
Weiner, Claire Zundell *theatrical director*

San Juan Capistrano
Pece, Robert Frank *filmmaker, artist*
Sibbio, Michael Gregory *promoter, concept developer, inventor technical consultant*

San Luis Obispo
†Snell, Keith Oren *musician, educator*
†Swanson, Clifton Eric *music educator, orchestra conductor*

San Marcos
†Glasson, Frank Michael *musician (classical and jazz), music educator*
Houk, Benjamin Noah *artistic director, choreographer*

San Rafael
†Brubeck, David Warren *musician*
Lucas, George W., Jr., *film director, producer, screenwriter*

†Santana, Carlos *guitarist*

Santa Ana
Freeman, James Michael *musician, vocalist*
Sudbeck, Robert Francis *music educator, philosophy educator*

Santa Barbara
†Brant, Henry *composer*
Brodhead, James E(aston) *actor, writer*
Howorth, David *producer, director*
Roads, Curtis *music educator, composer*
Sebastian, Suzie *producer*

Santa Clarita
†Mumford, Lawrence R. *composer, educator*

Santa Cruz
Martinez, Alma R. *actor, director, educator*
Winston, George *solo pianist, guitarist, harmonica player*

Santa Monica
Angel, Steven *musician*
Angier, Joseph *television producer, writer*
Bruckheimer, Jerry *producer*
†Burrell, Orville Richard (Shaggy) *popular musician*
†Cameron, James *film director, screenwriter, producer*
Chartoff, Robert Irwin *film producer*
Fisher, Frances *actress*
†Kaminski, Janusz *cinematographer*
†LaBelle, Patti (Patricia Louise Holt) *singer*
Leaf, Paul *producer, director, writer*
Lohner, Henning *composer, filmmaker*
†Marin, Mindy *casting agent, entrepreneur, film producer, writer*
Redford, Robert (Charles Robert Redford) *actor, director*
Roberts, Tony (David Anthony Roberts) *actor*
Rose, Michael Leonard *film, television and video producer*
Suschitzky, Peter *cinematographer*
Sussman, Peter Alan *entertainment company executive*
†Tinturin, Peter *composer*
Toussaint, Christopher Andre *video producer, director, editor, writer*
†Watson, Doc (Arthel Lane Watson) *vocalist, guitarist, banjoist, recording artist*
Wexler, Haskell *film producer, cameraman*
York, Michael (Michael York-Johnson) *actor*

Santa Rosa
Conway, Lois Lorraine *piano teacher*
Daniel, Gary Wayne *motivation and behavior consultant*

Seal Beach
Harkey, Verna Rae *piano, educator*

Sebastopol
†Boatright, Ann Long *dancer, pianist, music educator, choreographer*

Sherman Oaks
†Bergman, Alan *lyricist, writer*
Clark, Susan (Nora Goulding) *actress*
Foldes, Lawrence David *film producer, director, writer*
Gibbs, Antony (Tony Gibbs) *film editor*
†Goldenthal, Elliot *composer*
Heffner, Daniel Jason *film producer*
†Horner, James *composer*
Karras, Alex *actor, former professional football player*
†Norwood, Brandy *singer, actress*
†Serova, Nina *music educator, accompanist*
Sertner, Robert Mark *producer*
†Tesoro, Robert Aaron White *vocalist, actor, photographer*

Sonoma
Clynes, Manfred *musician, neuroscientist, inventor*

Sonora
†Carter, John Robert *music educator*

Soquel
Bidelman, Mark *music educator*

South Lake Tahoe
†Williams, Mark Didrik *music educator, composer*

Stanford
Cohen, Albert *musician, educator*

Stockton
†Haffner, James W., Jr., *opera educator, director*
†Hung, Li-shan *music educator*

Studio City
Boyle, Peter *actor*
†Carsey, Marcia Lee Peterson *television producer*
Gautier, Dick *actor, writer*
Kenney, H(arry) Wesley, Jr., *producer, director*
Lamothe, Irene Elise *television producer, distributor*
Rubin, Saul *producer, writer, labor and civil rights organizer*
Steinberg, Roy Bennett *television producer, director, educator*
von Dassanowsky, Elfi (Elfriede Maria von Dassanowsky) *film producer, educator, vocalist*
†Werner, Tom *television producer, professional baseball team executive*

Sun Valley
Taesch, Richard Edmond *music educator*

Sylmar
Foster, Dudley Edwards, Jr., *musician, educator*

Tarzana
Richman, Peter Mark *actor, painter, writer, producer*

Temple City
Robbins, William Curtis, Jr., *television and motion picture producer, director, writer, news reporter, cameraman*
Weidaw, Kenneth Roe *musician, educator, consultant*

Thousand Oaks
Donenfeld, Alice R. Greenbaum *producer, broadcast executive*
Loren, Sophia *actress*
†Rooney, Mickey (Joe Yule Jr.) *actor*
Sloane, J.P. *television producer, writer, entertainer, theologian*

Toluca Lake
Morton, Hugh Wesley *producer, director*

Tulare
†Speckman, Virginia Wilson *music educator*

Turlock
Klein, James Mikel *music educator, associate dean*

Tustin
Kollias, Jim Harry *music educator*

Universal City
Crow, Sheryl *singer/songwriter, musician*
Kingi, Henry Masao *actor, stuntman*
Meyer, Ron *agent*
†Rapke, Jack *agent*
†Reitman, Ivan *film director, producer*
†Wolf, Dick (Richard A. Wolf) *television producer, film company executive*

Upland
Robertson, Carey Jane *musician, educator*

Vacaville
Luther, Richard S. *music educator*

Valencia
LeBaron, Alice Anne *musician*
Windsor, William Earl *consulting engineer, sales representative*

Valley Center
Fry, Eva Margaret *entertainer, writer*

Venice
Bill, Tony *producer, director*

Ventura
Gay, Marilyn Fanelli Martin *television producer, writer, talk show hostess, journalist*

Villa Park
†Murphy, Patrick Christopher *music educator*

West Hollywood
Annakin, Kenneth Cooper *film director, writer*
Bloom, Claire *actress*
†Cage, Nicolas (Nicolas Coppola) *actor*
†De Palma, Brian Russell *film director, writer*
Harper, Robert *actor*
Innes, Laura *actress*
Jaglom, Henry David *actor, director, writer*
Madonna, (Madonna Louise Veronica Ciccone) *singer, actress, producer*
Shaye, Robert Kenneth *cinema company executive*
Sherman, Robert B(ernard) *composer, lyricist, screenwriter*
Stein, Benjamin J. *television personality, writer, lawyer, economist*

Whittier
Korf, Jean Prinz *retired theater educator*
Korf, Leonard Lee *theater arts educator*

Woodland Hills
†Berger, Phil *musician*
Homer, Raymond Rodney *film producer, director*
Levy, Norman *motion picture company executive*
†O'Connor, Brian D.A. *music educator, musician*

Yucca Valley
Styles, Beverly (Juanita Robins Carpenter) *entertainer, composer, musician*

COLORADO

Aspen
Ewing, Wayne Hilley *film producer, director, writer*
Roth, Don *music executive*

Aurora
Hughes, Christopher Adam *conductor, educator*

Avon
Laub, David L. *music educator*

Boulder
Boydston, James Christopher *composer*
Burge, Catherine Alice *musician, educator*
Duckworth, Guy *musician, pianist, educator*
†Ellsworth, Oliver Bryant *music educator, writer*
Fink, Robert Russell *music theorist, former university dean*
†Goldstein, Tamara Beth *musician*
†Korevaar, David *musician, educator*
Mooney, William Piatt *actor*
†Reinhold, Karen *music educator*
†Riis, Thomas Laurence *music educator*
Sable, Barbara Kinsey *former music educator*
Sarson, John Christopher *television producer, director, writer*
†Wallace, Brett *music educator, musician*

Colorado Springs
†Borgen, Irma R. *music educator*
†Massey, Russell Alvia *music educator*

Peckham, Jeffrey William *music educator*

Denver
†Albig, Irina S. *music educator*
†Alsop, Marin *conductor*
Bearden, Thomas Howard *news program producer, correspondent*
Burshtan, John Willis *television producer*
Ceci, Jesse Arthur *violinist*
Coe, Judith Anne *music educator, composer, performer*
†Davenport, Mark *music educator, musician*
Fredmann, Martin *ballet artistic director, educator, choreographer*
†Lee, Joo-Mee *musician, music educator*
Robinson, Cleo Parker *artistic director*
Schwartz, Cherie Anne Karo *storyteller, writer*
Van Arsdale, Kathy *music educator*

Englewood
Davis, Mary Georgia *music educator*

Estes Park
Bridges, Douglas M. *musician, small business owner*

Evergreen
White, John David *composer, theorist, cellist*

Fort Collins
Johnson, Neil Arthur *composer, educator*
†Kraus, David (Dirk) Bruce *musician, educator*
Wilber, Clare Marie *musician, educator*

Grand Junction
†Elias, Carlos Enoc *music educator, conductor*

Highlands Ranch
Fiess, Stephen Charles Edward *musician, music educator*
†Mezey, Richard R. *music educator, organist*

Lakewood
Berg Oram, Stephanie *music educator*

Littleton
†Alykova, Valentina *musician, music educator*
†Johansson, Alicia Barbara *musician*
Keats, Donald Howard *composer, educator*
Zwilling, Mark C. *music director*

Loveland
Balsiger, David Wayne *television-video director, researcher, producer, writer*

Monte Vista
Guadagnoli, Michael John *music educator*

Morrison
†Dorn, Mark S. *music educator, musician*

Niwot
†Buss, Kathleen E. *music educator*

Pritchett
†Hall, Carol Ann *music educator*

Pueblo
†Chi, Jacob *music educator*

Telluride
Tatum, Thomas Deskins *film and television producer, director*

Walsenburg
†Mellott, George Kenneth *retired music educator*

Westminster
Callier, Maria Cecile *writer, actress*

Windsor
†Landon, Jack Leonard *music educator*

CONNECTICUT

Avon
De Moura Castro, Luiz C. *musician, educator*
†Fantozzi, Donald Robert *music educator*

Berlin
†Kelly, Robert A. *music educator*

Branford
Smith, Richard Emerson (Dick Smith) *make-up artist*

Bridgeport
†Salyer, Douglas W *music educator*

Chaplin
Wood, Wendy Deborah *filmmaker*

Colchester
Winter, John Dawson, III, *blues guitarist, singer*

Cos Cob
Beliveau Muchnicki, Margaret Anne *television producer*

Danbury
Humphreville, James Edwin *conductor*
Jennings, Alfred Higson, Jr., *music educator, actor, singer*

Durham
Holahan, John Michael *music educator, researcher*

East Haddam
Borton, John Carter, Jr., (Terry Borton) *theatrical producer*

East Hartford
†Giardina, David Vincent *music educator*
Rivers, Loretta J. *film producer, film director, consultant*

Hartford
Lyman, Peggy *artistic director, dancer, choreographer, educator*
Mc Lean, Jackie *jazz saxophonist, educator, composer, community activist*
Stewart, James George *producer, director, video executive*
†Wood, Margaret *performing company executive*

Lakeville
Restout, Denise *musician*

Ledyard
Hammond, Russell Paul *music educator*

Madison
Lucas, Shari *musician, educator*

Mystic
Bobruff, Carole Marks *radio producer, radio personality*

New Canaan
Richardson, Dana Roland *technology consultant*

New Haven
Garvey, Sheila Hickey *theater educator*
Jordan, Paul *music director*
†Morgan, Robert P. *music theorist, educator*
Nolan, Victoria *theater director*
Piehler, Wendell Howard *organist, choir director, fund raiser*
Schlusberg, Julian Simon *theater educator, theater director, writer*
Tirro, Frank Pascale *music educator, author, composer*
†Warshaw, Marvin D. *conductor, educator, musician*

New London
Dygert, James Lloyd, Jr., *music educator, musician*
Vinson, Danny Steve *musician, music educator*

New Preston Marble Dale
Grizzard, George *actor*

Newtown
Carroll, Thomas Lawrence, Jr., *film and video producer*

Ridgefield
Kantor, James Graham *music educator, composer*

Southport
Walker, Charles Dodsley *conductor, organist*

Stamford
Karp, Steve *producing director*
†Novikova, Tatyana *music educator*
Preiss-Harris, Patricia *music educator, composer, pianist*
Schnitzer, Robert C. *theater administrator*

Storrs
Crow, Laura Jean *design educator, costume designer*

Storrs Mansfield
†MacDonald, Earl Murray *musician, educator*

Stratford
Rock, William Booth *producer, announcer*

Vernon Rockville
Susi, Anthony J *music educator, composer*

Washington
†Shay, Christopher King *music educator*

Washington Depot
Tracy, Michael Cameron *choreographer, performer, educator*
Wolken, Jonathan *performing company executive*

Waterford
White, George Cooke *theater director, foundation executive*

Watertown
†Thompson, Thomas James *music educator*

West Hartford
Gryc, Stephen Michael *composer, music educator*
Yueh, Chai-Lun *voice educator, opera singer*

Weston
Fredrik, Burry *theatrical producer, director*

Westport
Solum, John Henry *flutist, educator, author*

Wilton
Eriksen, Dan Oluf *film director*
Horgan, Susan Bedsow (Susan Merril Taylor) *producer, writer*

Woodbridge
Just, Jennifer Ramsay *television and video producer, writer*

DELAWARE

Dover
†Dean, Thomas Eugene *music educator, consultant*

Hockessin
†Faulcon, Clarence Augustus *musician*

Lewes
†Buchert, Stephanie Nicole *music educator*

Wilmington
Bettinger, Judith Pedersen *soprano, voice educator*
Brown Leatherberry, Thomas Henry *gospel music company executive, clergy member*
†Butterfield, Margaret Anne Davis *music educator, vocalist*
Cason, June Macnabb *musician, educator, arts administrator, fundraiser*
Gunzenhauser, Stephen Charles *conductor*
Lassman, Martin R. *musician, educator*
Wesler, Ken *performing arts company executive*

DISTRICT OF COLUMBIA

Washington
Barr, Cyrilla Patricia *music educator*
Battis, Emery John *actor*
†Baumgarten, Jonathan *flutist*
†Bowen, Jose Antonio *music educator*
Bradley, Barbra Bailey *musician, educator, accompanist*
Byers, Paul Heed *television news producer, consultant*
Crawford-Mason, Clare Wootten *television producer, journalist*
Crosby, Thomas Anthony *radio producer, broadcaster*
Crowther, G. Rodney, III, *television production company executive, writer, photographer*
Day, Mary *artistic director, ballet company executive*
Dodge, Judith C. *musician*
†Domingo, Placido *tenor*
Findley, Mary Baker *violinist*
†Fischer, Elizabeth (Betsy) *television producer*
Forrest, Sidney *clarinetist, music educator*
†Gersh, Darren *television correspondent*
Giusto, Thomas Michael *broadcast journalist*
†Hamlisch, Marvin *composer, conductor, pianist, entertainer*
Harpham, Virginia Ruth *violinist*
Kahn, Michael *stage director*
Kaiser, Michael M. *performing company executive*
Kaltchev, Ivo *musician, educator*
†Keyes, Alan L. *radio and talk show host, former federal government official*
Konstantinov, Tzvetan Krumov *musician, concert pianist, educator*
Makris, Andreas *composer*
Massey, Jeanne Kelly *music festival producer*
Mosettig, Michael David *television producer, writer*
Raphael, Nan Helene *musician*
Royle, David Brian Layton *television producer, journalist*
Russell, Mark *comedian*
†Sankaran, Shubha Silver *musician, music educator, consultant*
Smith, Stephanie Zaharoudis *producer*
Sonneborn, Daniel Atesh *composer, ethnomusicologist, producer, author*
Staton, Candi Maria *singer*
Taft, John Thomas *television producer, writer*
†Webre, Septime *ballet company artistic director, choreographer*
Weidenfeld, Sheila Rabb *television producer, author*
†Yurko, Michiko Kathleen *music educator, writer*

FLORIDA

Anna Maria
Moerk, Alice Anne *music educator, composer*

Apopka
Reinecke, William T. *conductor, educator*

Bayonet Point
Errington, Norman *television producer, photographer*

Boca Raton
Dower Gold, Catherine Anne *music history educator*
Fengler, John Peter *television producer, director, advertising executive*
St. Clair, James Earl *music educator*
Yelin, Robert Bruce *musician, recording artist, composer, lyricist*

Boynton Beach
†Corbière, Paul *music educator*
†Horowitz, Fedora Cohen *music educator, pianist*

Bradenton
Lister, Thomas Mosie *composer, lyricist, publishing company executive, minister*
Lorentzen, Robert Roy, Jr., *producer*
†Sarakatsannis, Leonidas Nicholas *musician, music educator, composer, conductor*

Cape Coral
Wendel, Joan Audrey *music educator*

Clermont
Levy, David Walton *music educator*

Coconut Grove
†Dominguez, Ramon Emilio *composer, visual artist*

Coral Gables
†Pilar, Nobleza G. *vocalist*

Dade City
†Wickersheim, Michael Edward *music educator*

Davie
†Marino, Dan, Jr., *sports broadcaster, retired professional football player*
O'Farrill, Alan John *music educator*

Daytona Beach
Picott, Jr., Jerry Lee *music educator*

Deland
†Musco, Lynn Ann *music educator*
†Robinson, Stephen A. *music educator*
Sorensen, Jacki Faye *choreographer, aerobic dance company executive*

Delray Beach
Fedder, Norman J. *retired theater educator, playwright*
Spyker, Harry A., III, *music educator*

Dunedin
Flemm, Eugene William *concert pianist, educator, conductor, chamber musician*

Englewood
Brainard, Paul Henry *musicologist, retired music educator*
Dickson, Katharine Hayland *dance educator*

Eustis
Alfrey, Lydia Jean *musician educator*

Fort Lauderdale
Holland, Beth *actress*
LeRoy, Miss Joy *model, apparel designer*
Randi, James (Randall James Hamilton Zwinge) *magician, writer, educator*
†Rieder, Christopher Anton *music educator*

Fort Myers
Diers, Hank H. *drama educator, playwright, director*
†Eccles, David Fitzgerald *conductor, educator*
†Renfroe, W. Douglas *musician, conductor, music educator*

Fort Pierce
Norton, Robert Howard *entertainer, musical arranger, author*

Fort Walton Beach
†Lindegren, Cecile Keyser *music educator*

Gainesville
Paul, Ouida Fay *music educator*
Poe, Gerald Dean *music educator, consultant*

Graceville
Cox, Buford E. *music educator*

Green Cove Springs
Davidson, Joy Elaine *mezzo-soprano*

Hallandale
†Vaserstein, Ludmila *music educator*

Highland Beach
Settler, Eugene Brian *record company executive*

Hobe Sound
†Pierpoint, Paula Jean *music educator*

Hollywood
Border, Gladys Louise *piano educator*

Jacksonville
Clifton, Rachel Letter *music educator, performing arts educator*
†Greene, Barry *music educator, writer*
†Huber, Mary Susan *music educator*
Stanley, Helen Camille *composer, musician*
Stewart, Sandra Kay *music educator*
†Taylor, Gavin Hall *music educator*

Key West
Mitchell, John Dietrich *theatre arts institute executive*

Lake Buena Vista
†Sereno, Keala *musician*

Lake City
Freeby, Stephen John, Jr., *music educator*
†Montgomery, June C. *musician, composer*
†Poplin, William L., Jr., *retired music educator*

Lake Helen
Finn, Stephen Martin *producer*

Lake Worth
†Volkman, Barry M. *conductor, music educator*

Lakeland
†Pranno, Arthur James *music educator*

Largo
Meredith, Bradford L. *musician, educator*

Lecanto
Max, Buddy (Boris Max Pastuch) *musician*

Longwood
Chernak, Jerald Lee *television executive*

Madison
Shaw, Kathleen Bentley *violist*

Melbourne
Kreines, Joseph Melvin *conductor*

Miami
Allen, Charles Norman *television, film and video producer*
†Batson, Dawn Kirsten *music educator, cultural consultant*
Berman, Mona S. *actress, playwright, theatrical director and producer*
†Betancourt, Conchita *music educator*
†Coro, Edys *music educator*
Hardy, Michael C. *performing arts administrator*
Heuer, Robert Maynard, II, *opera company executive*
Jacobson, Claire E. *music therapist*
Kwiat, David Mark *educator, actor*
†Letona-Holloway, Maria E. *music educator*
Madurga, Gonzalo F. *artistic director, actor, singer*
Reed, Alfred *composer, conductor*
†Secada, Jon *musician*
Stephan, Egon, Sr., *cinematographer, film equipment company executive*
†Thomas, Lowell Richard *music educator*
Yaklich, Richard E. *music educator*

Miami Beach
Gardiner, Pamela Nan *performing arts company executive*
Gibb, Robin *vocalist, songwriter*

Miami Shores
†Mowad, Louis Francis *musician, educator*

Milton
†Arnold, Margaret Morelock *music specialist, educator, performer*
Losee, Michael Patrick *music director*

Miramar
Besteni, Barbara Amnerys *video producer, editor, director*
Walsh, Thomas Francis, Jr., *producer, writer, director*

Naples
Kirby, Charles William, Jr., *dancer, choreographer*
White, Roy Bernard *theater executive*

North Palm Beach
†Hayman, Richard Warren Joseph *conductor*

Ocala
†Satterfield, Sarah Watkins *music educator*

Odessa
Cobb, Terri Reamer (Ceci Cobb) *film and video producer*

Okeechobee
Tolbert, Danny Lee *music producer, songwriter*

Orange Park
Walsh, James Anthony (Tony Walsh) *theater and film educator*

Orlando
Arman Gelenbe, Deniz *concert pianist*
†Boyd, Kenneth Andrew *music educator*
Feliciano, José *entertainer*
Schultz, Victoria L. *entertainer, music teacher*
†Smisek, James J. *music educator*
†Warfield, Scott *music educator, writer*
†Yonetani, Ayako *music educator, entertainer*

Ormond Beach
Hodkinson, Sydney Phillip *composer, educator*

Palm Harbor
Katzen-Guthrie, Joy *performance artist, engineering services executive*
Kessler-Hodgson, Lee Gwendolyn *actress, corporate executive*
†Krawczynski, Tony Edward *music educator*

Panama City Beach
Fejer, T. William *pianist, composer, architect, furniture designer*

Pensacola
†Gonçalves, Pitagoras L. *music educator*
Rubardt, Peter Craig *conductor, educator*
†Stecchi, Nathan John *music educator*

Pinellas Park
†Benedict, Gail Cleveland *music educator*

Pompano Beach
Eger, Joseph *conductor, music director*

Port Richey
†Fry, Ronald Sylvan *music educator, director*

Riviera Beach
†Feller, Thomas Richard, Jr., *music educator*

Ruskin
Smith, Calvin Douglas *music educator, musician*

Saint Petersburg
Blankstein, Mary Freeman *violinist*
Carroll, Charles Michael *music educator*

Sarasota
†Carstens, Charlene B. *composer, music educator*
McCollum, John Morris *tenor*
†Mizer, Joyce Taylor *music educator*
Ramsier, Paul *composer, psychotherapist*
†Schwartz, Francis *music educator, composer*
Serrie, Gretchen Ihde *retired symphony executive director*

Shalimar
Sublette, Julia Wright *music educator, performer, adjudicator*

Silver Springs
Parks, Sherri Lou *ballet dancer, thoroughbred handler*

Spring Hill
Burnim, Kalman Aaron *theatre educator emeritus*

Stuart
†Ballinger, Richard L. *orchestra director*

Summerland Key
†Dallas, Joseph Anthony, Jr., *music educator*

Tallahassee
Bridger, Carolyn Ann *pianist, music educator*
Elder, Joan Elizabeth *music educator, consultant*
Harsanyi, Janice *soprano, educator*
†Nalley, James H., II, *music educator, musician*
Perry-Camp, Jane *music educator, pianist*
†Stebleton, Michelle Marie *music educator, musician*
Streem, James Kenneth *musician, educator*
†Wright, Thomas G. *music educator, musician*

Tampa
†Dickson, Tim F. *music educator*
Edberg, Judith Florence *music educator*
Hankenson, E(dward) Craig, Jr., *performing arts executive*
Hankins, Phillip R. *music educator*
Khokhlov, Vladimir Abramovich *pianist, educator*
Manieri, Michele Dawn *musician, educator*
Norton, Kenneth Frederick *band director*
†Scialdo, Mary Ann *music educator, musician*

Tarpon Springs
†Barfield, Robert Elliott *music educator*

Titusville
Davis, Thomas Paul *music educator, choral director*

Treasure Island
Dunn, Craig Andrew *entertainer, conductor, composer, writer, educator*

Venice
Gabriele, Charles *composer, educator*

Wellington
†Gonzalez, Juan Carlos *music educator, musician*

West Palm Beach
†Bezerra, Márcio *musician, educator*
Escalante, Juan *performing company executive*
Hale, Marie Stoner *artistic director*
†Lappin, Bob *music director, conductor*
†Phillips, Kenneth Wayne *music educator*
†Rander, JoAnn Corpaci *musician, music educator*
Robinson, Raymond Edwin *musician, music educator, writer*
Rosenberg, Leslie Karen *media buyer*
Snyder, Gary Michael *music educator*
†Uzan, Bernard *artistic director*

Winter Springs
†McKinney, Frank *music educator*

GEORGIA

Alpharetta
Baugh, Charles H. *music educator, actor*

Athens
†Crowell, Allen *music educator*
Lee, Margaret Kendig *music educator*
Staub, August William *drama educator, theatrical producer, director*
†Stipe, Michael *musician*

Atlanta
†Crist, Stephen Alan *music educator*
Domingo, Esther *music educator*
†Everett, G. Steven *music educator*
†Flannery, James William *performing arts educator*
Kingsbury, Michael Bryant *organist, retired elementary and secondary education educator*
McFall, John *artistic director*
†McKnight, Terrance Thales *music educator*
†McRaney, James Thomas *choral music educator*
Patterson, James Hardy *entertainer, conductor, musician, educator, arranger, composer*
Rouse, Terrie Suzitte *performing arts association administrator, museum director, consultant*
Spano, Robert *conductor*
Tullis, Bill *sound recording engineer, music producer*

Augusta
Bradberry, Edward *opera company executive*
Floyd, Rosalyn Wright *pianist, accompanist, educator*

Bainbridge
†Lucas, Tammi Michelle *music educator*

Buchanan
Rainey, Terry Lee *music educator, director*

Canton
Forsh, Frederick Douglas *music educator*
Lokey, Linda H. *music educator*

Carrollton
Bakos, Daniel Frank *music educator, organist, composer*

Cave Spring
Boehm, John Charles *music educator*

Columbus
Campbell, Edward Wilson (Ned Campbell) *theater director, actor*
†Cobos, Patricio *music educator*

Conyers
Waters, Roger Allen *music educator*

Cordele
Helms, Bobby Gillespie *music educator, consultant*

Dahlonega
Broman, John Michael *music educator*

Decatur
Cartman, Shirley Eleise *retired music educator*
Downs, Jon Franklin *drama educator, director, writer*
Hamilton, Frank Strawn *jazz musician, folksinger, composer and arranger, educator*

Duluth
†Brasher, Earlene D. *music educator, church organist*
†McClung, Samuel Brenton *music educator, consultant*

Dunwoody
Clark, Faye Louise *drama and speech educator*

East Point
Bridgewater, Herbert Jeremiah, Jr., *radio host*
†Fields, Warren C. *music educator, minister*

Fayetteville
†Hood, Barbara W. *musician, educator*

Flowery Branch
Congdon, Jon Harvey *music educator*

Fort Valley
†Stripling, Allen James *music educator*

Gainesville
McCord, Gloria Dawn Harmon *music educator, choral director, organist*
†Santander, Andrew Michael *music educator, researcher*

Hampton
Williams, Owen Brian *music educator*

Kennesaw
Adams, Dean (Lewis Adams) *theater director*
†Doke, David Reed *musician, musician*
Kruger, Harry *retired conductor, retired music educator*
Tuttle, Marshall *musician, educator*
Vandewalker, David W. *music educator*

Lagrange
†Anderson, Toni P. *music educator, vocalist*

Loganville
Spurgeon, Barbara *music educator*

Macon
†Bell, Andrew C. *music educator*

Marietta
†Howell, Roger Eugene *music educator, musician*
Leonard, Steven K. *orchestra director, educator*
†Morisco, Jerid Simon *music educator, conductor*
Poor, Andrew Ford *music educator*
Wells, Palmer Donald *performing arts executive*
†Willoughby, Eric Alan *music educator*
†Wimberly, Linda Roberts *music educator, artist*

Moultrie
McLendon, Richard Charles *music educator*

Mount Berry
†Davis, John Edward *music educator, musician*

Mount Vernon
†Eernisse, Glenn P. *music educator*

Peachtree City
†Green, Franklin Pasco *music educator*

Rome
†Jeffrey, Therber Kent *music educator*
Potts, Glenda Rue *music educator*

Roswell
Lawler-Johnson, Dian L. *singer, instructor of voice, vocal technician*
Siepi, Cesare *opera singer*

Saint Simons
Cedel, Melinda Irene *music educator, violinist*

Savannah
Cooper, Lynda Shepard *music educator*
Greenberg, Philip B. *symphony orchestra conductor and music director*
Simmonds, Jimmie Neil *theatre educator*

Smyrna
Rife, Elizabeth *musician, music educator*

Statesboro
Bryan, Carolyn J. *music educator, saxophonist*
†Harbour, James William *theater educator*
Whitaker, Mical Rozier *theater director, educator*

Stone Mountain
†Render, Nelson Leon *music educator, musician*

Suwanee
†Frey, Glenn *songwriter, vocalist, guitarist*

Swainsboro
Hundley, Frederick Eugene, Jr., *music educator, consultant*

Sylvester
Bean, Craig Baylor *music educator*

Tallapoosa
Ramsey, Paul Randall *band director*

Thomaston
Pitts, Charles Carey *music educator*

Toccoa Falls
Stufft, William David *music educator*

Valdosta
†Farwell, Doug George *music educator*

Moss, Kirk D. *music educator*

Waleska
Naylor, Susan Embry *music educator*

Woodstock
†Soh-Harbin, Julie *music educator*

HAWAII

Ewa Beach
Kea, Jonathan Guy *instrumental music educator*
Lewis, Mary Jane *film producer, director, scriptwriter*

Honolulu
Abe, Gregg Koyei *music educator*
Langhans, Edward Allen *drama and theater educator*
Moulin, Jane Ann Freeman *ethnomusicology educator, researcher*
Nakamura, Ross Hideo *educator, band director, musician*
Smith, Barbara Barnard *music educator*

Kapolei
†Dudley, Doris S. *music educator, small business owner*

IDAHO

Boise
Holt, Isabel Rae *radio program producer*
†Mathie, David Gordon *music educator*
†Parkinson, Del R. *music educator, pianist*
†Schiller, Paul Omar *pianist, technical consultant*
†Totorica, Ted Francisco *music educator*

Caldwell
†Houle, Arthur Joseph *music educator*

Coeur D Alene
Phillips, James W. *music educator*

Idaho Falls
Dresen, Steven Paul *music educator*

Moscow
†Miralis, Yiannis Christos *music educator*

Nampa
Waller, Deloris Amy *musician, educator*

Pocatello
Keezer, James Robert *music educator*

Rexburg
†Wayne, Barbara Ann *music educator, classical guitar performer*

Twin Falls
Halsell, George Kay *music educator*
Yost, Kelly Lou *pianist*

ILLINOIS

Aledo
Ruggles, Rusty L *music educator*

Arlington Heights
†Lim, Cheryl Cheon-Ae *music educator*

Aurora
Halfvarson, Lucille Robertson *music educator*
†McCarthy, Mary Elizabeth (Beth) Constance *conductor, educator, music educator*

Berwyn
Levin, Michael David *musician, educator*

Bloomington
Brown, Jared *theater director, educator, writer*
Casey-Beich, Micheal Louanna *theater director, artist*
†Hining, Michael Lynn *music educator, conductor*
†Setchell, Charles Marshall *music educator, consultant*
Vayo, David Joseph *composer, music educator*

Bourbonnais
†Ball, Karen Michele *music educator, musician, composer*

Braidwood
Steinacher, Ronald *music educator*

Burlington
Nesseth, Jeffrey David *music educator*

Carbondale
†Townsend, Gregory Williams *music educator*

Carterville
†Bryant-Sala, Karen *music educator*

Carthage
†Ward, Roger Allen *music educator, musician*

Champaign
†Allen, David Joseph *music educator*
Fredrickson, L(awrence) Thomas *composer*

Charleston
Ignazito, Madeline Dorothy *music educator, composer*
Rossi, Richard Robert *music educator, conductor, performer, composer*

Chicago
Akos, Francis *violinist, conductor*
Arpino, Gerald Peter *performing company executive*

†Berkhout, Bjorn Haldane *composer, music educator*
†Brauer, Sasha Gerritson *church musician, music educator*
†Conte, Lou *artistic director, choreographer*
Davis, Katherine Helene *vocalist, educator*
DeMiles, Edward *agent*
Duell, Daniel Paul *artistic director, choreographer, lecturer*
Eaton, John C. *composer, educator*
†Emmons Jr., Charles N. *music educator*
†Falls, Robert Arthur *artistic director*
Florine, Albert Allen *musicology educator*
Fogel, Henry *orchestra administrator*
†Glaser, Katherine *pianist*
Hansen, Jack Winsor *musician, educator*
†Heider, Anne Harrington *music educator*
Kalver, Gail Ellen *dance company executive, musician*
†Katsman, Zinaida *musician, music educator*
Kenas-Heller, Jane Hamilton *musician*
†Lazar, Ludmila *concert pianist, music educator, pedagogue*
†Mason, William *general director of opera company*
Matesky, Elisabeth Anne *international solo violinist, educator, composer, arranger*
May, Aviva Rabinowitz *music educator, linguist, musician*
Moffatt, Joyce Anne *performing arts executive*
†Myers-Rami, Masequa *theatrical company executive, theater producer*
Naegele, Elizabeth Marie *musician, educator*
Naudzius, Aldona Kanauka *pianist, music educator*
Padberg, Helen Swan *violinist*
Palermo, James W. *artistic director*
Pokorni, Orysia *musician, educator*
†Rami, Pemon *theatrical company executive, theater producer*
Ran, Shulamit *composer*
Ratner, Carl Joseph *theater director*
Renard, Paul Steven *music educator*
†Sato, Junichi Steven *musician, music educator*
Schmitt, Natalie Crohn *theatre educator*
Schwan, David Paul *radio personality, radio producer, writer*
Scott, Stephen Brinsley *theater producer*
Sedelmaier, John Josef *filmmaker*
†Silverstein, Harry *theater director, music educator*
†Stonehouse, Kimber J. *music educator, artist*
†Tallchief, Maria *ballerina*
Tyson, Terri Lynn *television programming producer, consultant*
†Vincent, Jim *performing company executive*
Wang, Albert James *violinist, educator*
Winfrey, Oprah *television talk show host, actress, producer*
Wyszynski, Richard Chester *musician, writer, conductor, educator*
Yost, Emery Joseph *music industry producer, educator*
Zajicek, Jeronym *music educator*

Chicago Heights
†Reed, Scott C. *music educator, writer*

Coal City
Major, Mary Jo *dance school artistic director*

Country Club Hills
McClelland, Helen *music educator*

Crystal Lake
Christensen, Kenneth Ashley *composer, tenor, music educator*

DeKalb
†Goldenberg, William Bruce *music educator, musician*

Deerfield
†Gillette, Deborah Jean *music educator*

Dixon
Hertel, William John *music educator*

East Peoria
Curtright, Toby Arthur *music educator*

East Saint Louis
†Dunham, Katherine *choreographer, dancer, anthropologist*

Edwardsville
†Schultz, Norbert J. *retired music educator*

Elgin
Dodohara, Jean Noton *music educator*
Jakle, Kenneth Richard *broadcasting executive*

Elk Grove Village
Roberts, Verna Dean *music educator*

Evanston
Eberly, Helen-Kay *opera singer, classical record company executive, poet*
Fitzgerald, Mary Joan *music educator*
Hemke, Frederick L. *music educator, university administrator*
Karlins, M(artin) William *composer, educator*
Kujala, Walfrid Eugene *musician, educator*
McDonough, Bridget Ann *music theatre company director*
Peters, Gordon Benes *retired musician*
Yoder, John Clifford *producer, consultant*
Zimmerman, Mary *performing arts educator*

Flossmoor
Day, Gregory Lynn *music educator*

Galesburg
†Polay, Bruce *music director, music educator*

Geneva
Gallagher, Kent Grey *theater arts educator*

Klenke, Deborah Ann *band director, choral director, department chairman*

Glen Ellyn
Dewald, Brian L *music educator*

Glencoe
†Boyell, Gloria *musician, music educator*

Grayslake
†Carter, Jeanie *performing company executive*

Greenville
Weiss, Louise Annette *music educator*

Gurnee
†Myren, Allen W(illiam) *music educator*

Hazel Crest
Thies, Julie Ann *music educator*

Hickory Hills
†Haustein, Janis M. *musician, music educator*

Hillsboro
Dal Pozzo, Mark Brian *music educator, director*

Homewood
Villari, Jack C. *performing arts executive, arts entrepreneur*

Jacksonville
†Hayter, John Eldon *music educator*

Joliet
†Chalupnik, Steven Andrew *music educator*
†Liley, Thomas *music educator*

Lake Forest
Wasson, Jeffrey *music educator*

Lake Zurich
†Holdhusen, J. David *music educator*

Lisle
Vitson, Robyn Stanko *piano teacher, singer, pianist*

Lombard
†Devany, Donald Joseph, II, *music educator*

Macomb
Julstrom, Rosa Drake *music educator*
†Romig, James *composer, educator*

Manteno
†Conrad, David L *music educator*

Melrose Park
Hillert, Richard Walter *composer, educator, author*

Metamora
†Degenhart, Anne Elizabeth *music educator*

Monmouth
White, Perry D. *music educator*

New Baden
Blue, Myrna Kay *retired music educator*

New Lenox
†Carlson, Tammi Clair *music educator, musician*

Niles
Kessell, Charles Arthur *music educator, musician*

Normal
Luginbuhl, Benjamin Ryan *music educator*
†Morenus, Carlyn G. *music educator*
†Steele, Stephen K. *music educator*

North Aurora
Kuhl, Christopher Fanelli *music educator*

Northbrook
Kaiserman, David Norman *music educator*
Meyer, Carl James *music educator*
Slattery, James Joseph (Joe Slattery) *actor*

Oak Park
†Leitch, Stuart *music educator, musician*

Palos Hills
Porter, Joyce Klowden *theatre educator and director*

Pana
Waddington, Irma Joann *music teacher*

Paris
†Gill, Joseph F. *music educator*

Park Forest
Billig, Etel Jewel *theater director, actress*

Park Ridge
Barnett, Patrick Shawn *music educator*
†Eubank, Edward J. *music educator*

Paxton
Kirk, Colleen Jean *retired conductor, educator*

Peoria
Price Boday, Mary Kathryn *choreographer, small business owner, educator*
†Twitty, Susan Kay *music educator*
Wessler, Peter *music educator*

Plano
Krieghbaum, Douglas Matthew *music educator*

Port Byron
†Reece, Matthew Lynn *music educator*

Quincy
†Bohn, Donna May *music educator*

Rantoul

Holmes, Lois Rehder *composer, piano and voice educator*
Wolters, Paul Henry *music educator, musician*

River Forest

Prendergast, Carole Lisak *musician, educator*

Rockford

Hendershott Love, Arles June *television community relations director*
†Heuer, Beth Lee *music educator, composer*
Larsen, Steven *orchestra conductor*
Masters, Arlene Elizabeth *singer*
†Olson, Lynne Diane *music educator*
Pape, Sheri *music director, educator, artist*
Robinson, Donald Peter *musician, retired electrical engineer*
Steurer, Jeffrey M *music educator*

Rockton

Gregoire, Eugene Harold *music educator*

Round Lake Beach

Brown, Jeffrey Don *musician*

Saint Charles

Kull, James Arthur *music educator*
†Stovall, April Leanne *music educator*

Saint Jacob

Carter, Dennis R. *music educator, band director, musician*

Schaumburg

Tipps, Gregory Paul *music educator*

Shorewood

Lombardo, David Albert *actor, writer, speaker, aviation educator*

Smithton

Hostetler, Elsie J. *musician, music educator*

South Holland

Bourgeois, Marilyn Ann *piano educator, pianist*

Springfield

Ellis, Michael Eugene *documentary film producer, writer, director, marketing executive*
Rogers, James Allan *music director, hymnologist, author, editor*
Schrader, Andrew Robert *music educator*

Urbana

†Davis, Ollie Watts *musician, educator*
Di Virgilio, Nicholas *voice music educator*
Ehlen, Timothy John *music educator, musician*
Hedlund, Barbara Smith *musician, educator, music publisher*
Hedlund, Ronald *baritone*
†Oehlers, Paul A. *composer, music educator*
†Schleis, Thomas Henry *music educator, organist*
†Tsitsaros, Christos *composer, musician*
†Von Gunden, Heidi *music educator*
Weidner, Robert Wright *musician, music educator, musicologist*

Vernon Hills

†Lee, Jungok Paik *music educator*

Villa Park

Antonelli, Joseph K. *musician, educator*

Washington

Miller, Jennifer Renee *music educator, composer, writer*

Westmont

†Nyien, Patricia *music educator*

Wheaton

Horn, Daniel Paul *music educator, concert pianist*

Wilmette

Butz, Bradley Mitchell *music educator*
Delaplane, Sister Marjorie Marie *music educator*
†Jampole, Michael *music educator, composer*
Merrier, Helen *actress, writer*
Miller, Frederick Staten *retired music educator, academic administrator*
†Montgomery Tobias, Karen Twerdahl *music educator*

Winnetka

Hausfeld, James Frank *executive director*

INDIANA

Bloomington

†Biss, Paul Martin *music educator*
†Brown, A. Peter *music educator, researcher*
Brown, Keith *musician, educator*
Klotman, Robert Howard *music educator*
Phillips, Harvey *musician, soloist, music educator, arts consultant*
Pratt, Stephen W. *music educator, conductor*
†Schwartzkopf, Michael L. *music educator, conductor*
†Spera, Dominic Gregorio *music educator, writer*
Strickholm, Peter William *composer, environmentalist*
Svetlova, Marina *ballerina, choreographer, educator*
Wittlich, Gary Eugene *music theory educator, college administrator*
†Zeani-Rossilemeni, Virginia *music educator, soprano*

Carmel

Thomas, John David *musician, composer, arranger, graphic designer, recording engineer, producer*

Columbus

†Groves, Richard Thomas, III, *conductor, minister*

Crawfordsville

Everett, Cheryl Ann *music educator, pianist*
Fisher, A. James *theater educator, director, actor*

Elkhart

Niederer, William Glenn *music educator*

Evansville

Savia, Alfred *conductor*

Fort Wayne

Sack, James McDonald, Jr., *radio and television producer, marketing executive*

Frankfort

†Burrows, John (Jack) Newton *music educator*

Goshen

†Hovan, Rebecca S. *music educator*
†Roberts, Mary Lois *music educator*

Greencastle

Irwin, Stanley Roy *music educator, singer, conductor*

Hagerstown

Sherry, Priscilla Mae *retired music educator*

Hanover

†Batchvarova, Madlen Todorova *music educator, conductor*

Highland

†Loos, Phillip Adam *music educator, musician*

Indianapolis

Aliev, Eldar *artistic director, choreographer, educator*
Bolin, Daniel Paul *music educator*
Coomer, Steven Robert *music educator*
†Everly, Jack *conductor*
†Grubb, William *musician, music educator*
Hanford, Pat *performing company executive*
Johnson, David Allen *singer, songwriter, investment advisor, minister*
Pugh, Daniel Wilbert *theatre educator, costume designer*
†Sowers, Jodi Louise *music educator*
Suzuki, Hidetaro *violinist*
Turner, Barbara A. *former dance company executive*
Venzago, Mario *conductor*
Zurick, John *consultant, former dance company director*

Kingsport

Herron, Charles Kyle *music educator*

Knox

Weiss, Randall A. *television and radio producer, supermarket executive*

Lafayette

Dure, Robert Samuel *music educator*

Martinsville

James, Timothy Dale *music educator*

Middlebury

Bowen, Derek Tyrone *music educator*

Muncie

†Atherton, Leonard James Archibald *musician, conductor*
Grill, Richard Louis *music educator*
Larson Mattern, Julia A. *music educator, musician*
McColley, Ruth Ann *music teacher, band director*
Palmer, Robert Christopher *music educator, musician*
†Scheib, John W. *music educator, conductor*
Seidel, Lizbeth J. *pianist, educator*
Whitaker, Sandra Sue *soprano, educator*
Zhong, Mei *music educator*

Munster

†Woods, William George *music educator*

Richmond

Bordo, Guy Victor *conductor*

Royal Center

†Blume, Craig Lee *music educator*

South Bend

Lampkin, Ralph, Jr., *vocalist, nightclub consultant, producer, writer, coach*

Tell City

†Rutherford, Michael Francis *retired music educator*

Terre Haute

Damer, Linda K. *music educator*
Feinsod, Arthur Bennett *theatre arts educator*

Upland

†Parker, Richard Allan *music educator*

Valparaiso

†Bognar, Joseph Andrew *music educator, musician*

Vincennes

†Jackson, Sharon Sue *music educator*
Spurrier, James Joseph *theater educator*

West Lafayette

Lefever, Maxine Lane *music educator*

IOWA

Ames

†Bovinette, James Thomas *musician, educator*
†Forrest, Paula Sue *musician, music educator*
Work, George Paul *cellist*

Anita

Everhart, Robert Phillip (Bobby Williams) *entertainer, songwriter, recording artist*

Bettendorf

Hamburg, David D. *music educator*

Cedar Falls

Fanelli, Michael Paul *music educator*
Floyd, Angeleita Stevens *flutist*
Hedden, Debra Gordon *music educator*

Cedar Rapids

†Foust, LeAnne *voice educator, vocalist*
Hall, Kathy L. *orchestra executive*
†Nassif, Gary Tannus *singer and entertainer, art and special education educator, sculptor*
Tiemeyer, Christian *conductor*

Council Bluffs

†Kurt, Johnny Thomas *music educator*

Davenport

Dcamp, Charles Barton *educator, musician*
Schleicher, Donald *music director*
Willett, Lance *orchestra executive*

Des Moines

Blank, Myron Nathan *theater executive*
Erickson, Elaine Mae *composer, poet*
Giunta, Joseph *conductor, music director*
Mill, Jeth *performing company executive*

Dubuque

Hemmer, Paul Edward *musician, composer, broadcasting executive*
†Hughes, Brian Lee *music educator*

Fort Dodge

Cassady, Daniel Bennet *music educator*

Fort Madison

†Chapman, Allen D. *music educator*

Indianola

Larsen, Robert LeRoy *artistic director*
Mace, Jerilee Marie *opera company executive*
Songayllo, Raymond Thaddeus *music educator*

Iowa City

Kottick, Edward Leon *music educator, harpsichord maker*
Mather, Roger Frederick *music educator, writer*
†Paredes, Robert Wesley *music educator*
Thompson, Basil F. *ballet master*

Iowa Falls

Sherve-Ose, Anne *music educator*

Le Mars

Cottrell, David Milton *sound recording engineer*

Mount Pleasant

†Johnson, David Allen *music educator*

Sioux Center

Ringerwole, Joan Mae *musician, recitalist*

Sioux City

Huldeen, Gerald Alvin *retired music educator*
†Storm, Christopher *music educator*

Solon

de Salme, John W. *retired music educator, music association administrator*

Sumner

†Wright, James Timothy *music educator, composer*

Tipton

Farwell, Walter Maurice *vocalist, educator*

Van Horne

Arndt, James Edward *music educator, musician*

Washington

Hazell, Patrick James *musician, producer*

West Liberty

Woodley, Jason Lynn *music educator*

Wheatland

Knoll, August E. *retired music educator*

KANSAS

Caldwell

Robinson, Alice Jean McDonnell *retired drama and speech educator*

El Dorado

†Mack, Valerie Lippoldt *music educator, performing arts educator, freelance/self-employed choreographer*

Hays

Conger, Robert B. *music educator*

Highland

Casey, Brian Lee *music educator*

Hutchinson

Wendelburg, Norma Ruth *composer, pianist, educator*

Kansas City

Horseman, Barbara Ann *church musician, voice educator*

Lawrence

†Castle, Joyce M *mezzo soprano*
†Daugherty, James Franklin *music educator*
Duerksen, George Louis *music educator, music therapist*
Hilding, Jerel Lee *music and dance educator, former dancer*
Pozdro, John Walter *music educator, composer*
Tsubaki, Andrew Takahisa *theater director, educator*

Manhattan

Littrell, David A. *music educator, conductor*
Mortenson, Kristin Oppenheim *violinist*

Mcpherson

†Selack, Laurene E. *music educator*

Offerle

Herrmann, Lorena Joyce *retired music educator*

Olathe

†Dunn, Dwayne Earle *music educator*
Epp, Garrett Wayne *music educator*
Smith, Katheryn Jeanette *music educator*

Osage City

Wooge, Daniel Lee *music educator*

Ottawa

Hoge, Medora Davidson *dance educator*

Overland Park

Asner, Marie A. *classical musician*
†Lamb, Gordon Howard *music educator*
Ofverstedt, Margaret Elise *music educator, library and information scientist*
†Pretzel, Mark William *musician*
Ruperd, Theresa *music educator*

Pittsburg

†Berger, Reena *musician, music educator*

Rossville

†Budden, Frederick Richard *music educator*

Salina

Allen, Milton D. *music educator*

Shawnee

Beck, Jeff L. *music educator*

Shawnee Mission

†Talley, Douglas Eric *music educator*

Topeka

Rivers, Julie Elaine *concert pianist, composer, recording industry executive*
†Schultz, LeAnne *violinist, performer, music educator*

Wichita

Berman, Mitchell A. *orchestra executive*
†Fear, Judith A. *music educator, director*
Johnson, C. Nicholas *dance company executive*
Johnson, Guy Charles *music educator, musician*
Sewell, Andrew *music director*

KENTUCKY

Berea

Turner, Charles Robert, Jr., *music educator*

Campbellsville

†Gaddis, John Robert *music educator*
†Imes, Daniel Alan *music educator*
†McArthur, Lisa R. *music educator*
†Roberts, M. Wesley *musician, educator*

Elizabethtown

†Hill, Camille Crunelle *music educator*

Frankfort

Fletcher, Winona Lee *theater educator emeritus*
†Griffith, Patricia Barnes *music educator, pianist*

Grayson

†Golightly, John Wesley *music educator*

Hickory

†Murphy, George Ray *music educator*

Highland Heights

†Forman, Sandra H. *theater educator*

Hopkinsville

Estes, Scott Elliott *music educator*
Knob, Steven Edward *band director, composer*

Lexington

Stone, Martha Jane *musician*
Zack, George J. *conductor, music director*

Louisville

†Atz, Sarah J. *music educator*
Doane, Christopher Philip *music educator*
Dugger, Richard Charles *music educator*
Foster, Teresa E. *choral director, piano teacher*
Ganoe, Bob (robot) *model, actor*
†Hernandez, John E. *musician, music educator*
Hinson, Grady Maurice *music educator*
†Kee, Brenda Eltrine *music educator, concert pianist*
King, Tim *orchestra executive*
†Littleway, Lorna *theater producer, theater educator, theater director*
Mitchell, Charlie Henry *music educator, performer, church musician*
Mowery, Ward Franklin *retired music educator*
Oliphant, Naomi Joyce *music educator, performer*

†Robinson, Dennis Shea *music educator*
Segal, Uriel *music director*
Shaver, Karen *performing company executive, educator, design educator*
Sherman, Mildred Mozelle *music educator, singer, actress, opera director*
Tofteland, Curt L. *producer, director*
Whittington, Denise Lynn *music educator*

Morehead
†Detweiler, Greg Jeffrey *music educator*

Murray
Dycus, Mark *music educator*
Johnson, Dennis L. *conductor, music educator*
†Leslie, Tracy Fortson *music educator*
Steffa, John Amon *music educator, composer*
Wilkins, Margaret Nell Stamper *music educator, musician*

Richmond
†Crosby, Richard Allen *music educator*

Williamsburg
†Smoak, Jeff C., Jr., *music educator*

Wilmore
†Bell, Vicki P. *music educator, organist*

LOUISIANA

Alexandria
†Burns, Ronald C. *music educator*
Thomason, Teresa *musician, educator*

Baton Rouge
†King, Roy Michael *music educator*
Lusted, Dona Sanders *music educator, consultant, organist*
Mathews, Sharon Walker *artistic director, secondary school educator*
McCoy, Wesley Lawrence *musician, conductor, educator*
Norem, Richard Frederick, Sr., *musician, music educator*
†Pitombeira, Liduino *composer, educator*
†Smith, Richard James *retired music educator*
Willett, Anna Hart *composer, painter*
†Zibilich, Louise Anna *television news producer*

Destrehan
†Toups, Byron Joseph *musician, educator*

Grambling
†Simpson, Arthur Earl *music educator, assistant principal*

Hammond
Couret, Keiron Leigh *performing arts presenter*
Hemberger, Glen James *university band director, music educator*
†Johansen, David Alan *musician, educator*

Iowa
Kuykendall, Richard G. *music educator*

Jennings
Golden, Willie Malcome, Jr., *band director, music educator*

Lafayette
Ducrest, Willis Francis *retired music educator*
Springer, Leonard *musician, educator*

Lake Charles
†Gates, Keith R. *music educator*

Leesville
†Davis, Gene H. *music educator*

Metairie
Horton, Shearon Smith *piano educator*
†Shikhris, Alexandra K. *music educator*

Natchitoches
†Thompson, J. Mark *music educator*

New Orleans
Angeles, Louis Dean *conductor*
†Erb, Helen K. *musician, educator*
Guma, Michael Joseph *music educator, band director, musician*
Litwin, Sharon *orchestra executive*
†St. Julien, Thais Mary *soprano*
Seibel, Klauspeter *conductor*

Saint Amant
Millet, Craig Steven *music educator*

Scott
Richard, Zachary *singer, songwriter, poet*

Shreveport
†Andress, Will K. *music educator, conductor*
†Conley, Dayspring Linder *retired music educator*
James, Newell E. *music educator, musician*
Simons, Dennis *performing company executive*

Slidell
Cotton, Joseph L *music educator*

Thibodaux
Basham, Kay *music teacher*

West Monroe
White, Coralie Heard *music educator*

Westlake
†Yarbrough, Frances Carole *music educator*

MAINE

Augusta
†Jenkins, Pamela Lynn *music educator*

Bangor
Moreau, James William *stuntman*

Belfast
Coller, Robert Burton *music educator, musician*

Bethel
Farrar, Susan Clement *choreographer, performing company executive, writer*

Blue Hill Falls
Stookey, Noel Paul *folksinger, composer*

Brunswick
†Antolini, Anthony Frederick *music educator, editor*
Schwartz, Elliott Shelling *composer, author, music educator*

Camden
Jenks, Glenn Arnold *musician, educator*

Castine
Davis, Peter Frank *filmmaker, author*
Hall, David *sound archivist, writer*

Dover Foxcroft
†Poland, Arnold Livermore *music educator*

East Blue Hill
†Weinberg, Holly Bartlett *music educator*

Monmouth
Greenham, David *theater administrator*

Newcastle
Waterman, Charles Albert *actor, director, retired sales executive*

Oakland
Rhein, Kevin Douglas *music educator*

Orono
MacDonald, Elizabeth Helen *bassoonist, educator*

Portland
Bucci, Thomas Vincent *music educator, pianist, composer*
Miller, Buffy *dancer*
†Russell, Robert Jackson *music educator, conductor*

Scarborough
†Shulman, Richard *musician, composer, recording industry executive*

Surry
Sopkin, George *cellist, music educator*

Vassalboro
Schad, Vicki Jean Reynolds *piano teacher*

Waterville
†Desrosiers, Muriel C. *music educator, retired nursing consultant*

West Baldwin
Simmonds, Rae Nichols *musician, composer, educator*

MARYLAND

Baltimore
†Carver, Kathryn Louise *music educator*
Drucker, Arno P. *music educator*
†Gubernatis, Mary Loretto *filmmaker, agent, writer*
†Hall, Marian M. *retired music educator*
†Harrison, Michael *opera company executive*
Huggins, Amy Branum *music educator*
†Huntoon, Ann Kristen *performing arts association administrator, music educator*
†Jeffcoat, Cathleen Merle *musician, educator*
†Moran, John Gregory *musician*
Rauschenberg, Dale Eugene *music educator*
†Temirkanov, Yuri *music director*

Bel Air
Kramer, Keith Allan *music educator, composer*

Bethesda
Burkhalter, Susan Shively *music educator, organist*
Hallsted, Nancy Ruth Everett *pianist, music educator*
Hartman, Matthew G. *music educator*
Robinson, Peter Bullene *musician, composer, songwriter*

Bowie
†Gottlieb, Sylma R. *music educator, performing arts educator*
†Parr-Corretjer, Polly *singer, music educator*

Chestertown
Clarke, Garry Evans *composer, educator, musician, administrator*
†Wharton, Keith Alan *music educator, musician*

Columbia
†Brown, Ronald *music educator*
Spicknall, Joan *music educator*
Weems, Helen Rachel *piano teacher, accompanist*

Elkridge
†Matthews, Lois Marr *musician, music educator*

Ellicott City
Benjamin, Thomas Edward *music educator, composer, conductor*
Melaro, Constance Loraine *pianist, organist, instructor*
†Wann, Michael Stephen *music educator*

White, Robert, Jr *McKay musician, consultant, musician, educator*

Frederick
Lester, Noel K. *music educator, concert pianist*
†McKewen Amato, Mary Patricia *musician*

Gambrills
†White, Elizabeth G. *music educator*

Germantown
Harris, William Norman *music educator*
Hartley, James R. *musician, writer*

Hagerstown
†Domenico, Anthony Wayne *music educator*
Perry, Cinda *music educator*
†Sanders, Korby Moss *music educator*

Highland
Varga, Deborah Trigg *music educator, entertainment company owner*

Hyattsville
Dukes, Rebecca Weathers (Becky Dukes) *musician, singer, songwriter*

Jefferson
Ward, Susan Annette *music teacher*

Lanham Seabrook
†Moore, Erica *band director*

Largo
Mahaffey, Redge Allan *movie producer, director, writer, actor, scientist*

Potomac
Dyer, Rosemary *musician*
Murow, Christine *music educator*
Wang, An-Ming *composer*

Reisterstown
†Goethe, Elizabeth Hogue *music educator*

Rockville
Cain, Karen Mirinda *musician, educator*
†Chang, Ya-Ting *pianist, music educator, educator*
Kurkul, Wenyi Wang *musician, educator, administrator*
Middleton, Wanda Karen Lee *songwriter, poet, minister*
O'Donnell, Duck Hee *cellist, music teacher*

Saint Marys City
†Hooper, Michael Wayne *music educator, director*

Silver Spring
†Boeringer, James Leslie *music educator*
†Conger, Virginia Day *music educator, educator*
†Gordon, Joy *music educator*
Korth, Thomas A. *musician, educator*
Mallory, Joan Matey *music educator, composer*
Markey, Paul Victor *videographer, videotape editor, production manager*
Neumann, Alfred John *music director*
Secular, Sidney *writer, weather forecaster, actor, model, voiceover specialist, fundraiser, small business and mailorder marketing consultant*
Smith, A(rletta) Renee *agent*
†Stanic, Inja *music educator*

Sykesville
†Smith, George Allen, III, *music educator*

Woodstock
Wells, Christine Valerie *music educator*

MASSACHUSETTS

Allston
†Burton, Gary *musician*

Amherst
Brandon, Liane *filmmaker, educator*
May, Ernest Dewey *university administrator, musician, executive*
Plaček, Roman *cellist, music educator*

Belmont
†Gabrieli, Anna *voice educator*

Billerica
Snowden, B(ertha) J(eanne) *composer*

Boston
†Amlin, Martin Dolph *music educator*
Anderson, Jewelle Lucille *musician, educator*
Bacon, A. Smoki *television host*
†Beatty, Carl *music educator*
Charnas, Fran Elka *theatre director, educator, author*
Del Sesto, Janice Mancini *opera company executive*
Hagan, David *musician, educator*
†Harvey, Mark Sumner *composer, minister, educator, musician*
Jochum, Veronica *pianist*
Lesser, Laurence *musician, educator*
Lockhart, Keith Alan *conductor, musician, teacher*
†Lowell, Richard Lee *music educator, musician*
†McPhee, Jonathan *music director, conductor, composer, interim artistic coordinator*
Mitchell, Jon Ceander *music educator, conductor*
Moriarty, John *opera administrator, artistic director*
Nissinen, Mikko Pekka *dancer*
Rotenberg, Sheldon *violinist*
Simpson, George Eugene *music educator, director*
†Sonnenschein, David *music educator, composer*
†Takenaka, Makoto *music educator*
†Tronzo, David R. *music educator, entertainer*

Vila, Robert Joseph *television host, designer, real estate developer*
†Wahlberg, Mark *actor*
Weeks, Clifford Myers *musician, educational administrator*
Wheeler, W(illiam) Scott *composer, conductor, music educator*
Woodard, Jr., Fredrick James *music educator, musician*
Young, Laura *dance educator, choreographer*
Zander, Benjamin *conductor, educator*

Bridgewater
Nicholeris, Carol Angela *music educator, composer, conductor*

Brimfield
Curtis, William Edgar *conductor, composer*

Brookline
Epstein, Alvin *actor, director, singer, mime*
Kliman, Sylvia May Stern *film executive, editor, realtor*
†Kroll, Mark *music educator*
†Rizzi, Marguerite Claire *music educator*

Burlington
Reagan, Stevan Ray *cable company executive*

Cambridge
Beers, Deborah Yardley *musician*
†Chin, Wayman *musician, educator*
Cleary, David Michael *composer, critic, library assistant*
†Clement McKinley, Sandi *performing arts association administrator, not-for-profit fundraiser*
†Connick, Harry, Jr., *jazz musician, actor, singer*
de Varon, Lorna Cooke *choral conductor*
Erdely, Stephen Lajos *music educator*
†Fitch, Frances Conover *music educator*
Glaser, Victoria Merrylees *music educator, retired*
Hoyt, Herbert Austin Aikin *television producer*
Leach, Brenda Lynne *conductor, music educator, organist*
†Lifson, Ludmilla V. *music educator, musician*
Martino, Donald James *composer, clarinetist, educator*
Orchard, Robert John *theater producer, educator*
Pinkham, Daniel *composer*
Russell, George Allen *composer, theoritician, author, conductor*
Sims, Ezra *composer*

Concord
Gomberg, Sydelle *dancer educator*

Dedham
Firth, Everett Joseph *timpanist*

Fairhaven
Young, Bryan Alan *musician, educator*

Fall River
Lynds, Lucinda *music educator*

Fitchburg
†Caniato, Michele *music educator, composer, conductor*

Framingham
Bogard, Carole Christine *lyric soprano*

Franklin
Ferguson, Dennis Edward *music educator, musician*

Great Barrington
Curtin, Phyllis *music educator, former dean, operatic singer*

Greenfield
Damon, Steven William *music educator*
†Nix, Michael Charles *musician, educator*

Groton
Clark, Susan Frances *theater educator*

Lexington
†O'Connell, Brian Morgan *music educator*

Lincoln
Giles, Allen *pianist, composer, music educator*

Littleton
Crandall Hollick, Julian Bernard Hugh *radio producer*

Lowell
†Lloyd, Gerald Joseph *music educator*

Lynnfield
†Hodgkins, Douglas Wendell *music educator*

Marblehead
Kennedy, Elizabeth Mae *musician*

Medford
Anderson, Thomas Jefferson, Jr., *composer, educator*

Nantucket
Rorem, Ned *composer, author*

Needham
Di Domenica, Robert Anthony *musician, composer*
Donahue, Arthur Thomas *television producer*

New Bedford
†Harrison, John, III, *music educator*

New Town
Capestro, Susan *musician, educator, composer*

Newburyport
†Lazarus, Penny Cyd *music educator*

Newton
Bavicchi, John Alexander *music educator*
Brilliant, Barbara *television host, producer, columnist, consultant, journalist, communications and media consultant, musician*
Chan, Jennie M. *retired music educator*
†Li, Fan *pianist, music educator*

Newton Center
Schuller, Gunther Alexander *composer*

Newtonville
Zimmardi, James Anthony *musician, music educator, record producer*

North Attleboro
Russo, Steven P. *television producer, actor*

North Dartmouth
†Lamoureux, Ann Margaret *music educator*
†Noel, Barbara Hughes McMurtry *retired music educator*

North Easton
†Keogh, Martin Jay *dancer, educator*

Northampton
Levy, Ralph Jacob, Jr., *retired theater educator*
Naegele, Philipp Otto *violinist, violist, music educator*
†Snedeker, James Peter *music educator*
Wheelock, Donald F. *music educator, composer*

Peabody
Simmons, Jon L. *music educator*

Plymouth
Gregory, Dick *comedian, civil rights activist*

Prides Crossing
†Fish, Richard VanCortlandt, Jr., *music educator*

Salem
Melby, John B. *composer, educator*

Shrewsbury
†McCluskey, James Francis *music educator*

Somerset
†Girard, Jonathan Richard *conductor*
Schaefer, Ira Marc *music educator, musician*

South Weymouth
Edwards, Eleanor Mattiasich *singer, voice educator*

Southbridge
Rutanen, Roy Stewart *producer, television personality*

Stockbridge
MacDonald, Sharon Ethel *dancer, choreographer, administrator*
Silverstein, Joseph Harry *conductor, musician*

Tyngsboro
Dascomb, Audrey Lynn *dance educator*

Waltham
Boykan, Martin *composer, music educator*
†Chasalow, Eric David *composer, educator*
Wyner, Yehudi *composer, pianist, conductor, educator*

Watertown
Langstaff, John Meredith *musician*

Wellesley
†Yun, Elise Hae-Ryung *music educator*

Weston
Tenney, Sarah G. *music educator*

Williamstown
Shainman, Irwin *music educator, musician*

Winchester
Kleinschmidt, Carol C. (Carol C. Fieleke) *pianist, educator*

Woburn
†Freeman, Jeanne Marie *music educator, writer*

Worcester
†Hagar, Richard Joseph *music educator, musician*
Lamothe, Donat Romeo *music educator*
†McGinn, John Richard *composer, educator*
†Rifkah, Eve *performing company executive*

Worthington
Schrade, Rolande Maxwell Young *composer, pianist, educator*

MICHIGAN

Allendale
Chen, Chin-Chin *music educator*
†Reichert, Aviram *concert pianist, educator*

Ann Arbor
Aikman, James Whitton *composer, music educator*
†Benamou, Catherine Laure *filmmaker, educator*
†Bengtsson, Erling Blöndal *classical cellist, educator*
Bolcom, William Elden *musician, composer, educator, pianist*
Borders, James Matthew *music educator, dean*
†Jeffrey, Timothy Michael *film director*
†Matjias, Christian *music educator, musician*
†Meier, Gustav *conductor*

Scavarda, Donald Robert *composer, artist*

Battle Creek
Matthews, Wyhomme S. *retired music educator, college administrator*

Beverly Hills
Tolias, Linda Puroff *music educator*

Bloomfield Hills
Haidostian, Alice Berberian *concert pianist, civic volunteer and fundraiser*
Swift, Jonathan *educator, television host, tenor*

Cadillac
Whitmer, Walter Glenn *band director*

Canton
†Caraballo, Dimas J. *music educator*

Cedar
Kunkel, Dorothy Ann *music educator*

Clarkston
†Chapman, Clifford Kenneth *music educator*

Dearborn
†D'Alessio, Gina Maria *music educator*
Dzuiblinski, Gerard Arthur *theatre educator, artistic director*

Detroit
Calarco, N. Joseph *theater educator*
†Di Chiera, David *general director of opera company*
†Duensing, Dorothy Jean *music educator, vocalist*
Gulley, James Clarence, Jr., *television producer, marketing specialist, internet consultant*
Kang, Emil J. *orchestra executive*

East Lansing
Draper, Penny Kaye Pekrul *music educator, piano technician*
Kirk, Edgar Lee *musician, educator*
Whiting-Dobson, Lisa Lorraine *video production educator, producer, director*

Farmington Hills
Goslin, Gerald Hugh *concert pianist, educator*

Fremont
Johnson, Bernadine *piano educator, composer*

Gladwin
†Budai, William H. *music educator*

Grand Blanc
†Byerly, Carl Wesley *music educator, academic administrator*

Grand Rapids
†Horn, Joyce Elaine *music educator*
Lockington, David *conductor*
Ryberg, William A. *orchestra executive*
Schmidt, Gordon Peirce *artistic director*
†Taylor, Mark Lyman *music educator*

Hillsdale
†Flaskerud-Rathmell, Susan Marie *musician, music educator*
†Knecht, Melissa *music educator, musician*

Interlochen
Masterson, Wendy Lynn *choreographer, dance educator, arts administrator*

Kalamazoo
†Spradling, Robert Ledford *music educator, conductor*

Lake Ann
Kumjian, John Charles *musician, educator*

Lansing
Kluge, Len H. *director, actor, theater educator*

Lapeer
Parrish, Patrick Michael *music educator*

Livonia
†Custer, Gerald Stockton *conductor*

Mason
†Yoakam, Lynn Kelly *harpist, educator*

Monroe
Brodie, Catherine Anne *music educator*
Nuechterlain, James Howard *music educator*

Mount Pleasant
Orlik, Christina Bear *music educator*

Muskegon
Swartz, Wilma Jeanne *music educator*

Nashville
Pash, Teresa A. *piano teacher, performer*

Northport
Scripps, Douglas Jerry *music educator, conductor, director*

Olivet
†Humphrey, Roger Gavin *music educator*

Rochester Hills
†Thoma, August John *music educator*

Roscommon
†Carton, Gary L. *performing arts association administrator*

Saginaw
†Leppert-Largent, Anna M. *church musician*

South Branch
Savard, Christine Elizabeth *music educator*

Sterling Heights
Bajor, James Henry *musician, jazz pianist*

Swartz Creek
Russell, Charles Harry *music educator, restaurant manager*

Traverse City
†Faulmann, Roger R. *music educator*

Troy
Okun, Maury *dance company executive*

MINNESOTA

Apple Valley
Becker, Bruce Warren *music educator*

Bagley
Ragan, Stephen T. *music educator*

Bemidji
Bradley, Terrance Lee *retired music educator*
Logan, P. Bradley *music educator, church musician*
†Wettstein, Shannon Leigh *music educator*

Bloomington
Smith, Henry Charles, III, *symphony orchestra conductor*

Blue Earth
Ellingsen, Michael O. *music educator, theater educator*

Brainerd
Wannamaker, Mary Ruth *music educator*

Champlin
†Lyons, Steven Gerard *music educator*

Chanhassen
Prince, (Prince Rogers Nelson) *musician, actor*

Crookston
Houske, Sister Virginia *music educator, organist*

Duluth
Fields, Allen *artistic director*
Hanson, Curtis James *music educator, composer*
†Osborn, Vincent Owen *music educator, musician*
†Vasquez, Ramon Francisco *music educator*

Eden Prairie
De Bono, Luella Elizabeth *music educator*

Frazee
Haugen, Troy Marlin *music educator*

Inver Grove Heights
†Vogel, Steven Norman *music educator*
Wetli, Peggy Marie *performing company executive*

Jackson
McConnell, Timothy Irvin *voice educator, gymnastics coach*

Mahtomedi
†Pontious, Robert Wayne *music educator*

Maple Grove
Shmidov, Anna *music educator, piano teacher*

Mapleton
†Ek, Jon Merrill *music educator*

Milaca
Wig, Robert Curtis *retired music educator, conductor*

Minneapolis
Doepke, Katherine Louise Guldberg *retired music educator*
Felker, William H. (B. C. Stuvinski) *filmmaker, videomaker*
Fetler, Paul *retired composer*
Fleezanis, Jorja Kay *violinist, educator*
†Jackson, Donna Cardamone *music educator*
†Kaess, John Philip *music educator, choir director*
Lamb, Deborah Kathleen *music educator, vocal, choral consultant, fiber artist*
Nash, Elizabeth Hamilton *music and theater educator, vocalist, writer*
Nortwen, Patricia Harman *music educator*
Porter, Jennifer Madeleine *producer, director*
Rousseau, Eugene Ellsworth *musician, music educator, consultant*
†Severinsen, Doc (Carl H. Severinsen) *conductor, musician*
Skrowaczewski, Stanislaw *conductor, composer*
Thurman, Virgil Leon *voice educator*
†Vanska, Osmo *theater director*
†Williams, Yolanda Yvette *music educator*
Wollan, Curtis Noel *theater producer, theater director*

Minnetonka
†Brunk, Sara J. *music educator*
Fisk, Gail Marie *music educator*
Jarvis, Linda Marie *music director, music educator*

Moorhead
†Eyler, David Paul *music educator*
†Houglum, Bruce Monroe *music educator*
Rothlisberger, Rodney John *music educator*
Ruzicka, Charles Edward *music educator, director*

Plymouth
Werden, David Ray *music educator*

Rochester
Lofgren, Anne Elizabeth *musician, educator*

Rosemount
Dick, Herbert James *music educator*

Saint Paul
†Calkins, Mark R. *tenor, educator*
Coppock, Bruce *orchestra executive*
†Costanzi, Marianne *retired music teacher*
†Dahlberg, Eric Ross *music executive*
Hanley, Mary Ann *music educator, pianist, writer*
†Kolarov, Nickolai Atanassov *musician, educator*
Lange, Richard Alan *music educator*
Nice, Pamela Michele *theater director, educator, film director, educator*
†Orzolek, Douglas C *music educator*
†Sawyer, Timothy Kenneth *music educator*
†You, Yali *music educator*

Saint Peter
McKay, John Robert *concert painist*

Staples
†Iverson, Jeffrey G. *music educator, director*

Stillwater
†Huelsmann, Thomas J. *retired music educator*

Vadnais Heights
†Martinez, Kathryn Marie *music educator*

Wheaton
†Lanter, Martin Luther *music educator*

Windom
†Blackstad, Mildred Mae *retired music educator*

Winona
†Draayer, Suzanne Rhodes *music educator, writer*
O'Shea, Patrick Michael *conductor, music educator*
†Ramsdell, Bruced D *music educator*

Woodbury
Fraher, Elaine Adel *retired music educator*

MISSISSIPPI

Cleveland
†Pettway, Keith *music educator*

Clinton
Durham, Carol Elise *musician, educator*
Sclater, James Stanley *music educator, composer, musician*
†Young, Craig S. *music educator, conductor*

Corinth
Gray, Janet D. *piano teacher, organist*

Fulton
Myers, Jeffery Mark *music educator, musician*

Grenada
Dugan, Cindy *music educator, organist*
Thomas, Ouida Power *music educator*

Hattiesburg
De Chiaro, John Paul *music educator*
Treybig, Joel Andrew *musician, educator*
†Vail, Kathryn G *music educator*
†Wooton, John Andrew *music educator*

Itta Bena
Goldman, Lawrence *music educator*

Jackson
Beck, Crafton *music director*
Bobo, Len Davis *musician, educator*
Keary, David *artistic director*
Moak, Elizabeth *performing pianist*
Somekawa, Mina C. *pianist, educator*

Laurel
Giles, Mamye Ruth *genealogy consultant, music voice educator*
Stringer, Lorrie Steen *pianist, educator*

Moss Point
†Barnes, Anthony Clarke *music educator*

Raymond
†Bee, Anna Cowden *dance educator*
†Ingwerson, John C. *music educator*

Senatobia
†Ungurait, John Bentley *music educator, consultant*

University
†Steel, David Warren *music history educator*

MISSOURI

Arrow Rock
Bollinger, Michael *artistic director*

Ballwin
†Rothermich, Gayla *music educator, director*

Bolivar
†Harrison, Carol L. *music educator*
Hooper, William Loyd *music educator, university administrator*
†Thaller, Gregg P. *music educator*

Bowling Green
Bruce, Judith Esther *retired music educator, elementary education educator*

Branson
Bradley, Leon Charles *musician, educator, consultant*
Vinton, Bobby (Stanley Robert Vinton) *entertainer*

Chesterfield
Logue, Jean Evelyn *music educator, educator*

Columbia
Hook, Martin Lawrence *music educator, director*
Middleton, James Allen *music educator*
Sevier, Jacob Thomas *music educator*

Dixon
†Jackson, David Williams *music educator*

Doniphan
McCann, Lawrence Alton *music educator*

Herculaneum
Jackson, Kirk Allan *music educator, director*

Jefferson City
Greene, Thomasina Talley *concert pianist, educator*

Joplin
†Mahn, Timothy W. *music educator*

Kansas City
Andersen, Jerry Rae *music educator*
Bentley, Jeffrey *performing company executive*
Bolender, Todd *choreographer*
Buford, Ronetta Marie *music educator*
Colaianni, Louis Edward *voice educator*
Davis, Mary Bronaugh *music educator*
Dibble, Cameron Shawn *music educator, concert pianist*
Londré, Felicia Mae Hardison *theater educator*
Louis, William Joseph (Jonn Garvie Monks) *theater educator, actor, director, artist, poet*
Manson, Anne *music director*
Parcell, John Cleo *music educator*
†Reinschmidt, Laura Pilioglos *choreographer, educator*
Rich, Ruthanne *musician, educator*
Robertson, Kenneth Carl *music educator*
†Schaeffer, Ronald Lee *theatre production manager*
Valliere, Roland Edward *performing company executive*
Weirich, Robert Wayne *musician, educator*
Werner, Betty Jean *music educator*
Whitener, William Garnett *dancer, choreographer*

Lees Summit
†Hardy-Parcell, Cathy Kay *music educator, department chairman*

Liberty
Harriman, Richard Lee *performing arts administrator, educator*
Warnex, Paul David *music educator*

Marshall
†Lines, Kevin Lee *music educator*
Sayer, Ronald J. *composer, educator*

Maryville
Kramer, Ernest Joachim *music educator, composer*
Schultz, Patricia Bowers *vocal music educator, performer*

Mound City
Reiter, David G. *music educator, musician*

Peculiar
†Turley, William Homer *music educator*

Point Lookout
†Hardin, Garry Joe, II, *music educator*

Richmond
Seward, Nancy H. *retired band director, composer*

Saint Charles
Burns, Betty X. *music educator*

Saint James
Stevens, Helen Jean *retired music educator*

Saint Joseph
Glise, Anthony LeRoy *musician, composer, writer*

Saint Louis
Boddie, Don O'Mar *recording company executive, producer, recording artist*
†Carlin, Seth A. *music educator, musician*
†Colson, Kirby Lewis *music educator*
Di Bisceglie, Laureen Gail *pianist, educator*
Eichhorn, Arthur David *music director*
Haley, Johnetta Randolph *musician, educator, university official*
Hirsch, Arthur (Buzz Hirsch) *film producer, educator*
Hylton, John Baker *music educator, university administrator*
Macdonald, Hugh John *music educator, writer*
†Montgomery, Alice Elizabeth *vocalist, speech pathologist*
Radentz, Michael Grey *recording engineer, producer, composer, musician*
Schindler, Laura Ann *piano teacher, accompanist*
Stewart, John Harger *music educator*
Stumpf, Earlwayne Schwarze *actor, advertising executive*
Wolf, Jonathon Edward *music educator*

Salem
Jessen, Chris Michael *music educator*

Springfield
Boland, Beverly Joyce *music educator*
Echols, Carol Avery *music educator*
Hawkins, Kevin Andrew *music educator*
†Henry, Jack Allen, Jr., *music educator*
†McClellan, Norma D. *music educator*
Morris, Gregory W *music educator*

Moulder, T. Earline *musician*
†Parsons, James *music educator*
Quebbeman, Robert C. *conductor, educator*
†Shirley, George William *retired music educator, farmer*
Spicer, Holt Vandercook *retired speech and theater educator*
†Thomassen, Roger Clifford *music educator*

Wentzville
†Mason, Bryan *music educator*

MONTANA

Billings
Barnea, Uri N. *music director, conductor, composer, violinist*

Bozeman
Vick, Jeffrey Harrison *music educator, musician*

Glendive
†Shields, Lisa A. *music educator*

Great Falls
Johnson, Gordon James *artistic director, conductor*

Malta
†Engebretson, Erik John *music educator, director*

Missoula
Gillett, Gary Lee *music educator*
Knowles, William Leroy (Bill Knowles) *television news producer, journalism educator*

Whitefish
DeFranco, Boniface Ferdinand Leonard (Buddy DeFranco) *clarinetist, bandleader*

NEBRASKA

Columbus
Micek, Isabelle *music educator*

Crete
†Monson, Larry Lee *music educator*

Grand Island
Hesterman, Phillip Karl *music educator*

Hastings
Freed, Donald Callen *vocal and choral musician, educator*

Kearney
Buckner, Nathan Andrew *music educator, musician*
†Schnoor, Neal Henry *music educator*
†Svoboda, Aaron Michael *music educator*

Lincoln
†Barnes, Paul Edwin *concert pianist, music educator*
Collier, Nathan Morris *musician, music educator*
Dixon, Wheeler Winston *film and video studies educator, writer*

Lyons
Rose, Dwight Dean *music educator*

North Platte
Mueller, Wayne Dennis *music educator*

Omaha
Barker, Rex J. *music educator*
Cleary, Pamela Ann *symphony executive*
Johnson, James David *concert pianist, organist, educator*
Saker, James Robert *music educator*
Soh, Lip-Khoon (Kenneth Soh) *music educator, musician*
†Tyrance, Geraldine Vaughan *music educator*
Yampolsky, Victor *conductor*
Yontz, Timothy Gene *music educator*

Seward
†Blersch, Jeffrey Neal *music educator, composer*
†Kuhn, William Frank *music educator*

South Sioux City
Dailey, Michael Patrick *music educator*
†Wagner, R. Eugene *music educator*

York
Roush, Clark Alan *music educator, conductor*
Wilson, Gary Paul *music educator*

NEVADA

Boulder City
†Schultheis, Adam John *music educator, consultant*

Carson City
†Bugli, David *conductor, arranger, composer*

Henderson
Devin, Richard *casino gaming host*
DeVol, Luana *dramatic soprano, consultant, arts administrator*
Riske, William Kenneth *producer, cultural services consultant*

Las Vegas
Borovicka, Marsha Lorraine *music educator*
Castro, Joseph Armand *music director, pianist, composer, orchestrator*
Davies, Alma (Alma Rosita) *producer, playwright, lyricist, composer, designer, sculptor*
†Gjurich, Michael John *music educator*
Gold, Hyman *cellist*

†Gordon, Lonny Joseph *choreographer, dance and fine arts educator*
Goulet, Robert Gerard *singer, actor*
Healy, Mary (Mrs. Peter Lind Hayes) *singer, actress*
Kalb, Benjamin Stuart *television producer, director*
Knight, Gladys (Gladys Maria Knight) *singer*
†Letourneau, De Ann Marie *musician*
Lewis, Jerry (Joseph Levitch) *comedian*
Lovern, Terrance Lee *production manager*
Wiemer, Robert Ernest *film and television producer, writer, director*

North Las Vegas
†Kennedy, Brenda S. *performing arts center executive, theatrical light designer*

Reno
†Ake, David Andrew *music educator*
†Hudson, Karen Ann Sampson *music educator*
†Lee, H. Helen *music educator*
†Munc, Joel Xander *orchestra director, musician*

Sparks
†McKenzie, Jr., Wesley Melvin *music educator, composer*

NEW HAMPSHIRE

Alstead
Holloway, Robert Charles *orchestrator, arranger, composer*

Bath
†Page, Patti (Clara Ann Fowler) *vocalist*

Bradford
Lettvin, Theodore *concert pianist*

Colebrook
Killam, David E. *retired music educator*

Concord
Church, Gail Graham *television producer, consultant*

Durham
†Kempster, William Geoffrey *conductor, music educator*

Hanover
†Dong, Kui *music educator, composer*
Ehrlich, David Gordon *film director, educator*

Keene
Martin, Thomas Russell *music educator, musician*

Manchester
Carkin, Gary Bryden *performing arts educator*

New London
Twombly, Jean Sawyer *musician, educator*

Northwood
Lynne-O'Brien, Vincent *stage manager, director, actor*

Orford
Karol, John J., Jr., *producer, filmmaker*

Plymouth
†Bourgelais, Paul *music educator*
†Dionne, Aubrie Anne *music educator*
†Graff, Carleen *music educator*

Somersworth
Tully, Hugh Michael *music educator*

Walpole
Burns, Kenneth Lauren *filmmaker, historian*

NEW JERSEY

Allendale
Ruth, Rodney *musician, music consultant, contractor, educator*

Allenhurst
†Tognoli, Era M. *performing company executive, artistic director*

Atco
Blackford, Alan Ralph *music educator*

Atlantic City
Marks, Robert Bosler *television producer, consultant*

Bayonne
McMahon, Eileen Marie *artist agent*

Bergenfield
Kupp, John C. *music educator*

Brick
Grotto, Douglas Thomas Matthew *music educator*

Brookside
†Schaberg, Eric L. *music educator*

Caldwell
†Childress Orchard, Nan L. *music educator*

Cherry Hill
Clauser, Donald Roberdeau *musician*

Clayton
Bertenshaw, William Howard, III, *radio and television producer*

Cliffside Park
Perhacs, Marylouise Helen *musician, educator*

Closter
Stein, Ellen F. *music therapist, songwriter*

Colts Neck
Borisov, George P. *music educator*

Denville
Fisher, Sharon Mary *musician*
†Veech, Lynda Anne *musician, educator*

Dumont
Chiandusse, Richard Stephen *music educator*

East Brunswick
Hurst, Gregory Squire *director, producer, investment executive*
†Savio, Frances Margaret Cammarotta *music educator*
Yttrehus, Rolv Berger *composer, educator*

East Hanover
†Iovel, Alla *music educator, writer, pianist*

East Orange
Oderman, Stuart Douglas *pianist, composer, playwright*

Englewood
†Svezia, Vera Tisheff *concert pianist*
Zwilich, Ellen Taaffe *composer*

Florham Park
Atkins, Richard Bart *film, television producer*

Fort Lee
Amara, Lucine *opera and concert singer*
Houston, Whitney *vocalist, recording artist*
†Thomopoulos, Michael *music educator*

Freehold
†Cheng, Grace Zheng-Ying *music educator*

Glassboro
Robinette, Joseph Allen *theater educator, playwright*

Hackettstown
†Bratten, William P. *music educator*

Hamilton
Pucciatti, Sandra Milstein *opera company director*

Jackson
†McCormick, Harold J. *music educator*

Jersey City
Stinchcomb, Albert Monroe *producer, designer/realtor*

Lawrenceville
†Frantz, Charles Frederick *music educator*
†Vaccaro, Kimberly Ann Chandler *performing arts educator, consultant, writer*

Leonia
Deutsch, Nina *musician, vocalist*
†Dondysh, Victoria *pianist*
Silverman, Lawrence Ira *music educator, musician*
†Victoria, Dondysh L. *piano educator*

Lincroft
Benham, Helen *music educator*

Lodi
†Arella, Ann Marietta *music educator, vocalist*

Long Valley
†Landis, Daniel Scott *music educator*

Madison
Monte, Bonnie J. *performing company executive, director, educator*
†Silvestri, Michael Anthony *music educator*

Margate City
Rose, Jodi *opera company founder and artistic director*

Marlton
Shapiro, Ellen Goldberg *music educator*

Mays Landing
Seigel, Andrew Mark *music educator, consultant*

Medford
†Saltus, Phyllis Borzelliere *music educator*

Monmouth Junction
†Lien, Ting-Ting *music educator*

Montclair
Walker, George Theophilus, Jr., *composer, pianist, music educator*
†Wasko, James W *music educator*

Mount Holly
†Basmajian, Thomas Stephen *actor, performing arts association administrator*

Mount Laurel
Torres, Robert Alvin *dancer, singer, actor, sign language interpreter*

New Brunswick
Ledgin, Stephanie P. *music journalist, educator*

New Milford
Filardi, Eldonna Marie *music educator, accompanist*

Newark
†Macal, Zdenek *conductor*

†Martin, Henry John *music educator, composer*
Monty, Gloria *former television producer, film executive*
Silipigni, Alfredo *opera conductor*
Storrer, William Allin *consultant*

North Bergen
†Schumacher, Barret *motion picture propman, writer*

Old Tappan
†Ebersole, Curt *music educator*

Paramus
Gordon, Scott (Harry Scott Buehlmeier) *entertainer, actor*

Perth Amboy
Richardson-Melech, Joyce Suzanne *music educator, singer*

Pitman
Carpenter, Hoyle Dameron *music educator emeritus*

Pompton Lakes
McHugh, Robert Ernest (Bob McHugh) *pianist, composer*

Princeton
Artzt, Alice Josephine *classical guitarist, writer*
Cheadle, Louise *concert pianist, educator*
†Kawarsky, Jay A. *music educator, conductor, composer*
Levy, Kenneth *music educator*
Lustig, Graham *artistic director*
Orphanides, Nora Charlotte *ballet educator*
Vizzini, Carol Redfield *symphony musician, music educator*

Raritan
Bower, David Norman *music educator, researcher*

Red Bank
Hughes, Barnard *actor*

Rivervale
Moderacki, Edmund Anthony *music educator, conductor*

Rockaway
Laine, Cleo (Clementina Dinah Dankworth) *singer*

Rumson
Topham, Sally Jane *ballet educator*

Runnemede
Adams, Robert *music educator*

Secaucus
Pinsker, Penny Collias (Pangeota Pinsker) *television producer*

Shamong
Knight, Margaret Elizabeth *music educator*

Skillman
†Hackel, Adam William *music educator*

Somers Point
†Hagerthey, Gwendolyn Irene *retired music educator*

South Hackensack
Belinfante, Geoffrey Warren *television producer*

Stanhope
Ferrara, Dominick John, IV, *music educator*

Stratford
†Giacabetti, Thomas *musician, educator*

Teaneck
Bullough, John Frank *organist, music educator*

Totowa
Wesp, Wendy Louise *vocalist, songwriter*

Trenton
Iszard, Calvin Oscar, Jr., *television production executive, public relations manager, former county freeholder*

Upper Montclair
Bergen, Christopher Brooke *opera company administrator, translator, editor*

Warren
Maull, George Marriner *music director, conductor*

Wayne
†Kresky, Jeffrey *music educator, writer, composer*

West Long Branch
Tripold, David Michael *music educator*

West Milford
Both, Robert Allen *recording engineer, record producer*

West New York
Abbadessa, Constance Immaculata *music educator, vocal artist*

Westfield
Gajewski, Ferdinand John *music educator, musician, musicologist*
Schlosberg, Theodore K. *music educator*

Woodbridge
†Qiu, Li-Hui *music educator, actress*

NEW MEXICO

Albuquerque
†Block, Steven D. *music educator, composer*
Cook, Marcella Kay *retired theater educator*
Ellen, Jane *composer, music educator, researcher*
Evans, Bill (James William Evans) *dancer, choreographer, educator, arts administrator*
Guerrant, Mary Thorington *music educator*
Jordan, Keith M *band director, musician*
Rice, Linda Angel *music educator*
Schacht, Catherine Ann *classical violinist, pianist, mezzo-soprano*
Smyer, Myrna Ruth *drama educator*
†Steinbach, Falko *musician, music educator*
†Weagel, Deborah Fillerup *composer*

Edgewood
Hamilton, Jerald *musician*

Farmington
Smith, Mark Edward *music educator*

Portales
Dal Porto, Mark Daniel *music educator*
†Wozencraft-Ornellas, (Betty) Jean *singer, music educator*

Rio Rancho
†Huff, Jay *music educator*
†Schulz, Robert *music educator, musician*

Roswell
Hedin, Edna Jenks *musician, educator*
Lee, Mike *music educator*

Santa Fe
Ballard, Louis Wayne *composer*
†Gaddes, Richard *performing arts administrator*
†McIntosh, Kathleen Ann *music educator*
Rubenstein, Bernard *orchestra conductor*
Zlatoff-Mirsky, Everett Igor *violinist*

NEW YORK

Akron
Allen, Sue Fay *music educator, conductor*

Albany
†Burian, Jarka Marsano *performing arts educator*

Amherst
Braun, Kazimierz Pawel *theatrical director, writer, educator*

Annandale On Hudson
Gibbs, Christopher Howard *musicologist, educator*

Armonk
Scotto, Renata *soprano*

Astonia
Carroll, David Joseph *stage manager*

Auburn
†Correll, Janet Moore *music educator*

Averill Park
†Blostein, Michael David *music educator*

Babylon
Kroll, Brian Walter Thomas *music educator*

Baldwin
Abram, Blanche Schwartz *music educator, pianist*

Bayport
†Hurst, Matthew Thomas *music educator*

Bayside
Zinn, William *violinist, composer, business executive*

Bedford
Chase, Chevy (Cornelius Crane Chase) *comedian, actor, author*

Binghamton
†Biggers, Jonathan Edward *music educator, consultant*
†Reitz, Margaret Anne *musician, educator*

Bohemia
Leddy, John Joseph, Jr., *music educator*

Briarcliff Manor
Kennell, Richard Wayne *recording artist, business manager*

Brockport
Halquist, Shawn A. *music educator*

Bronx
†Murillo, Emilio *filmmaker, writer, poet*
Sherman, Judith Dorothy *producer, recording company owner, recording engineer*
Somary, Johannes Felix *conductor*
Verrett, Shirley *soprano*

Bronxville
Biscardi, Chester *composer, educator*

Brooklyn
Babcock, Jonathan Paul *music educator, conductor*
Contino, Rosalie Helene *historian, playwright*
Ham, Karen *musician, music educator*
†Hausman, Jill Susan *cantor, vocalist, lyricist, poet, composer*
Hopkins, Karen Brooks *performing arts executive*
Moorman, Joyce Solomon *music educator*
Morris, Mark William *choreographer*

Niesen, James Louis *theater director*
†Prescod, Roy A. *musician, educator*
Richmond, Eero *composer, music librarian*
Salzman, Eric *composer, writer*
Schlemowitz, Joel *film studies educator, film director*
Skrobela, Katherine Creelman *music producer*
†Smith, Bernadine M. *television producer, director, writer*
Thomson, David *dancer, vocalist*
Vidal, Maureen Eris *theater educator, actress*
Zabriskie, Sherry LaFollette *filmmaker, author, actress*

Buffalo
Boyar, Benjamin *music educator*
Cantrick, Robert Birdsall *music educator, academic administrator*
Flood, James Duncan *music educator*
Kordinak, Irma L. *piano teacher, musician*

Camillus
†Alvaro, Anthony Joseph *music educator*

Carmel
Calegari, Maria *ballerina*

Churchville
†Ciarvella, David R. *music educator, plastics company executive*

Clifton Park
Orsini, Paul Vincent *music educator*

Commack
Ohman, Franklin Eric *ballet educator, choreographer, choreographer*

Coram
Celella, Karen Ann *music teacher, author*
†Gale, Diane *music educator*

Deer Park
D'Amore, Victor *director, choreographer, dance educator*

Dexter
DeVito, Shawn Joseph *music educator*

Dix Hills
Mymit, Chuck W. *music educator, musician*

Dobbs Ferry
Briskin, Efrem *music educator*

Dover Plains
Rand, Christopher Edward *music educator*

East Hampton
Dello Joio, Norman *composer*

East Islip
†Levy, Joel Michael *music educator*

East Syracuse
Besten, Jr., John Joseph *music educator*

Elma
†Gastle, Timothy Anthony *music educator*

Elmsford
Mulrain, Andrea E. *talent scout*

Fairport
Rowe, Howard, Jr., *composer, arranger*
Stewart, Barbara Dean *writer, musician, educational consultant*

Flushing
Smaldone, Edward Michael *composer*

Forest Hills
Ashvil-Bibi, Sigalit *musician, artist*
Polakoff, Abe *baritone*
†Rosenhaus, Steven L. *composer, conductor, music educator*

Fredonia
Piorkowski, James Paul *music educator, composer, guitarist*
†Rudge, David Thomas *music educator, conductor*

Geneva
†Oberbrunner, John W. *music educator, musician*

Germantown
Farberman, Harold *conductor, composer*
Rollins, Sonny (Theodore Rollins) *composer, musician*

Gilbertsville
Roos, Casper *actor*

Glen Cove
†Carbuto, Nicholas *music educator*

Greenfield Center
Conant, Robert Scott *harpsichordist, music educator*

Greenlawn
†Starost, Diane Joan *music educator*

Greenvale
Senft, Mason George *musician*

Hamburg
†Voto, James Anthony *music educator*

Hamilton
†Cheng, Marietta N. *conductor, educator*

Hartsdale
McMann, Edith Brozak *performance artist, visual artist*

Hastings On Hudson
D'Antoni, Philip *producer*
Del Colle, Paul Lawrence *communications administrator, educator*
Happel, Dorothy *violinist, concertmaster*
Sharpe, Robert Kent *writer, director, producer, photographer*
Wolfe, Stanley *composer, educator*

Hempstead
Chapman, Ronald Thomas *musician, educator*
Graffeo, Mary Thérèse *music educator, performer*
Hettrick, William Eugene *music educator*

Hewlett
Wolff, Eleanor Blunk *actress*

Homer
Bull, Beverly Jane *piano and voice educator*

Hopewell Junction
†Mione, Anna J. *music educator, writer*

Horseheads
†Peters, Linda S. *musician, music educator*

Hunter
Khanzadian, Vahan *tenor*

Hurley
LaRusso, Joseph *retired musician*

Islip
†Romeo, Anthony M., III, *music educator*

Ithaca
†Aiosa, Vincent Nestor *music educator*
Arquit, Nora Harris *retired music educator, writer*
†Borden, David *composer, educator*
Husa, Karel *composer, conductor, educator*

Jackson Heights
Morrow, Nana Kwasi Scott Douglas *choreographer, writer, filmmaker, educator*
Stevenson, Amanda (Sandy Stevens) *librettist, composer, document examiner*

Jamaica
Lee, Joseph *musician, educator*
Moser, Martin *retired music educator*
†Retzel, Frank *music educator, composer*
Tedesco, Anne Cavolo *music educator, concert pianist*

Katonah
Brownlee, Delphine *actress, musician*

Kingston
†Abrams, Bruce D *music educator*

Lake Katrine
Shaut, Robert William *music educator, composer*

Larchmont
Swire, Edith Wypler *music educator, musician, violist, violinist*

Latham
LeRoy, Beth Seperack *jazz musician, piano teacher*

Levittown
†Romano, Joseph Scott *music educator*

Lindenhurst
Farrell Logan, Vivian *actress*
Lazarek, John Willliam *music educator, musician*

Little Neck
Hettrick, Jane Schatkin *music educator, classical musician*

Liverpool
Coggiola, Jill Angela *musician, educator*

Lockport
Pregmon, Stephen Kenneth *music educator, musician*

Locust Valley
†Peek, William DeWitt, Jr., *music educator*

Long Eddy
Hoiby, Lee *composer, concert pianist*

Long Island City
Rosenstein, Ira H. *radio producer, poet, writer*

Manhasset
Brand, Oscar *folksinger, writer, educator*

Manlius
†Koch, Catherine Ann *music educator, musician*

Massapequa
†Turk, Elizabeth Ann *music educator*

Massena
Scholl, Edwin John *retired secondary educator, stage director*

Mastic Beach
Merolla, Michael B. *secondary school music educator*

Melville
Sobol, Elise Schwarcz *music educator*

Merrick
Sardo, Sanford *music educator*

Millbrook
Flexner, Josephine Moncure *musician, educator*

Millerton
Hastings, Donald Francis *actor, writer*

Mineola
Lelyveld, Gail Annick *actress*

Mount Vernon
†Lemos, Arthur *retired music educator*

Narrowsburg
†Krause, Gloria Rose *music educator*

New
†Goines, Victor Louis *music educator*

New Paltz
†Schempf, Ruthanne *music educator, musician*

New Rochelle
Cleary, James C. *audio-visual producer*

New York
†Adams, John Coolidge *composer, conductor*
Adler, Richard *composer, lyricist*
Affleck, Ben *actor*
Aguilera, Christina *vocalist*
†Ahrens, Lynn *lyricist*
†Ailes, Roger Eugene *television producer, consultant*
Alenikoff, Frances *choreographer, performer, writer, dancer, artist*
Alexander, Jane *actress, former federal agency administrator, producer, author, theater educator*
Allen, Betty (Mrs. Ritten Edward Lee III) *mezzo-soprano*
Alpert, Mark Zachary *performing arts executive*
†Alt, Carol A. *actress, model, entrepreneur*
Altman, Robert B. *film director, writer, producer*
Amelan, Bjorn G. *choreographer*
Anagnost, Dino *artistic director*
†Ananiashvili, Nina *ballerina*
†Andrade, Andres *vocalist, educator*
†Arnon, Baruch *pianist, educator*
Asakawa, Takako *dancer, dance teacher, director, choreographer*
Avgerakis, George Harris *film director*
Avins, Styra *musician, writer*
Ax, Emanuel *pianist*
†Bacall, Lauren *actress*
Banks, Helen Augusta *singer, actress*
Barber, Russell Brooks Butler *television producer*
Barbour, Catherine Jean *actress, director, mime, set designer*
Barker, Edwin Bogue *musician*
Barrios, Soledad *dancer*
Barsalona, Frank Samuel *theatrical agent*
Bart, Roger *actor*
Barth, Diana *actress, playwright, journalist, editor*
Bashkow, Jack Simon *musician*
Bednar, Rudy *television producer, director*
Beeson, Jack Hamilton *composer, educator, writer*
Belotserkovsky, Maxim *dancer*
Bennett, Tony (Anthony Dominick Benedetto) *entertainer*
Benton, Nicholas *theater producer*
†Bergen, Polly *actress*
Bergstein, Eleanor *filmmaker, writer*
Bernardi, Mario *conductor*
†Besterman, Douglas *composer, orchestrator*
Bikel, Theodore *actor, singer*
Birkenhead, Thomas Bruce *theatrical producer and manager, educator*
†Blakemore, Michael Howell *theatre and film director*
Bolotowsky, Andrew Ilyitch *flutist, composer*
Bonazzi, Elaine Claire *mezzo-soprano*
Borree, Yvonne *dancer*
†Boston, Gretha *vocalist, actress*
Bowden, Sally Ann *choreographer, teacher, dancer*
†Bowman, Carl Byron *music educator, composer*
Boxill, Edith Hillman *music therapist, educator, writer*
Braden, Martha Brooke *concert pianist, educator*
Bradford, Robert Ernest *motion picture producer, financier*
†Brady, Mark A. *cinematographer, photographer*
Braxton, Toni *popular musician*
Brecker, Michael *saxophonist*
Brendel, Alfred *concert pianist*
Brewster, Robert Gene *concert singer, educator*
†Brohn, William David *conductor, orchestrator*
Brothers, Joyce Diane *television personality, psychologist*
Brown, David *motion picture producer, writer*
Brown, Trisha *dancer*
†Brunkhurst, William Lee, Jr., *music educator*
†Butt, Sameer *filmmaker, writer*
Button, Richard Totten *television and stage producer, former figure skating champion*
Byer, Diana *performing arts company executive*
Calabrese, Rosalie Sue *arts management consultant, writer*
Caldwell, Zoe *actress, director*
†Cammisa, Rebecca *filmmaker, photographer*
Cantrell, Lana *actress, singer, lawyer*
Capalbo, Carmen *theater director and producer*
Caples, Richard James *dance company executive, lawyer*
†Carlisle, Kitty *actress*
Carlson, Marvin Albert *theater educator*
Carney, Michael *orchestra leader*
†Carpenter, Mary Chapin *singer, songwriter*
Carter, Elliott Cook, Jr., *composer*
Carthay, R. Jon *hand model, actor*
Castel, Nico *tenor, educator*
Cazeaux, Isabelle Anne Marie *retired musicology educator*
†Cesar, Kamala *dancer, educator*
Chang, Marian S. *filmmaker, composer*
Chappell, Wallace *performing company executive*
Charnin, Martin *theatrical director, lyricist, producer*

Chenoweth, Kristin *actress*
Chesler, Gail *arts organization development executive*
Christensen, Dieter *ethnomusicologist*
†Ciarrocchi, Maya *dancer*
Colbath, Brian (Brian Colbath Watson) *actor, script and live performance writer*
Coleman, Cy *pianist, composer, producer*
Coleman, George Edward *tenor, alto and soprano saxophonist*
Collins, Phil (Philip David Charles Collins) *singer, songwriter, drummer, record producer*
Comissiona, Sergiu *conductor*
Conway, Kevin *actor, director*
†Cooper, Kenneth *harpsicordist, pianist, music educator, conductor, musicologist*
Cooperman, Alvin *television and theatrical producer*
Corbin, Patrick *dancer*
Corsaro, Frank Andrew *theater, musical and opera director*
Cory, Jeffrey *television, film, stage, event and creative director*
†Costello, Elvis (Declan Patrick McManus) *musician, songwriter*
†Craven, Frank John *actor, writer*
Creshevsky, Noah Ephraim *composer, music educator*
†Cruz, Celia *vocalist*
†Cullman, Joan *theatrical producer*
Cunningham, Merce *dancer*
Curtis, Paul James *mime director*
D'Addario, Edith *performing company executive*
d'Amboise, Jacques Joseph *former dancer, choreographer, educator, director*
Danitz, Marilynn Patricia *choreographer, videographer*
Daraio, Robert Reid *technical director*
David, Hal *lyricist*
Davidovsky, Mario *composer*
Davis, Leonard *violist*
†DeFord, Ruth I. *music educator*
de Kenessey, Stefania Maria *composer*
De Luca, Eva *vocalist, writer, composer, entrepreneur, designer, inventor*
†Dendy, Mark *choreographer*
†Dickson, James Edward *actor*
Diggins, Peter Sheehan *arts administrator*
†Dion, Celine *musician*
Dissette, Alyce Marie *television multimedia and theatrical producer, non-profit foundation executive*
†Di Vittorio, Salvatore *music educator, composer, conductor*
Dlugoszewski, Lucia *artistic director*
Dodson, Daryl Theodore *ballet administrator, arts consultant*
Dodson, Helen Zrake *television news producer*
†Domino, Fats (Antoine Domino) *pianist, singer, songwriter*
Donelian, Armen *pianist, composer, author*
Doty, Shayne Taylor *organist*
Dowd, Irene *dance educator, choreographer*
†Downs, Hugh Malcolm *radio and television broadcaster*
Drake, Laura *theater director, performer*
Duchin, Peter Oelrichs *musician*
†Dutoit, Charles *conductor*
†Dylan, Bob (Robert Allen Zimmerman) *singer, composer*
†Edmunds, Kenny (Babyface) *popular musician*
†Ellis, Scott *theatrical director*
Entremont, Philippe *conductor, pianist*
Erdman, Jean *dancer, choreographer*
†Eschenbach, Christoph *conductor, pianist*
†Espina-Ruiz, Oskar *clarinet, educator*
†Eterovich Maguire, Karen Ann *actress, writer*
Evans, Albert *dancer*
Falletta, Jo Ann *musician*
Farley, Carole *soprano*
Feit, Barberi Paull *composer, lyricist, psychotherapist, author*
Feld, Eliot *dancer, choreographer*
†Feldman, Marion *musician, music educator*
Feuer, Cy *motion picture and theatrical producer, director*
Fichandler, Zelda *director*
†Flaherty, Stephen *composer, orchestrator*
Fleming, Renée L. *opera singer*
Fontana, Thomas Michael *producer, scriptwriter*
Foreman, Richard *theater director, playwright*
Formento, Daniel *radio company executive, writer*
Foster, Sutton *actress*
Frankel, Gene *theater director, writer, producer, educator*
†Franklin, Aretha *singer*
†Freeman, Morgan *actor*
Freizer, Louis A. *radio news producer*
Frisell-Schröder, Sonja Bettie *opera producer, stage director*
Frith, Michael Kingsbury *artistic director, illustrator, writer, production company executive, actor*
†Gaines, Boyd *actor*
Garcia, Andy *actor*
Garniez, Nancy Caballero *pianist, educator*
Gillies, Trent Donald *television producer*
Giraldi, Robert Nicholas *film director*
Glass, Philip *composer, musician*
Goines, Leonard *music educator, consultant*
Goldsmith, Merwin *actor, theater director*
Goodman, Roger Mark *television director*
Gordon, Mark *actor, theater director, theater educator*
†Graziano, John Michael *music educator*
†Griffel, L. Michael *music educator, researcher*
Guettel, Henry Arthur *retired arts executive*
Hagen, Uta Thyra *actress*
†Haimes, Todd *artistic director*
†Halmi, Robert *film producer, television producer*
†Hample, Henry *music educator, musician*
Hancock, Gerre Edward *musician, educator*
Hardee, Lewis Jefferson, Jr., *theater educator*
Harmon, Jane *producer*
Harris, Julie (Julie Ann Harris) *actress*

Harrow, Nancy (Mrs. Jan Krukowski) *jazz singer, songwriter, editor*
Harth, Robert James *performing arts executive*
Hartley, Hal *film director*
†Hartley, Sean Joseph *composer, lyricist, music educator*
Hayes, Isaac *rhythm and blues singer, composer*
Hebert, Bliss Edmund *opera director*
Herrera, Paloma *dancer*
Hewitt, Don S. *television news producer*
Heyward, Andrew John *television producer*
Hill, Lauryn *vocalist, actress*
Holmes, Anna-Marie *ballerina, ballet mistress*
†Horn, Shirley *vocalist, pianist*
†Horne, Marilyn *mezzo-soprano*
Hurlin, Dan *actor, theater director*
†Hutchinson, Lynda Ronette (Billie Holiday Jr., Princess of Jazz, Munchie) *vocalist, musician, comedian*
†Imus, Don *radio host*
Intilli, Sharon Marie *television director, small business owner*
†Isaacs, Robert *conductor, director*
Ivory, James Francis *film director*
Jablonsky, Stephen *music educator, composer, artist, writer*
Jackson, Anne (Anne Jackson Wallach) *actress*
Jacobs, Jim *actor, playwright, composer, lyricist*
Jacobson, Lawrence Seymour *television executive producer*
Jamison, Judith *dancer*
Jasperse, John *performing company executive*
†Jewel, (Jewel Kilcher) *folk singer, songwriter*
Jung, Doris *dramatic soprano*
Kahane, Jeffrey *conductor, pianist*
Kamlot, Robert *performing arts executive*
Karchin, Louis Samuel *composer, educator*
Kassel, Virginia Weltmer *television producer, writer*
†Kellogg, Paul *general & artistic director opera company*
Kent, Julie *ballet dancer, actress, model*
Kent, Linda Gail *dancer*
Kern, Heath Thayer *producer*
Khasday, Alyce Field *literary and film agent, psychic consultant, business owner, investment coach*
Kinberg, Judy *television producer, director*
†King, B. B. (Riley B. King) *singer, guitarist*
†Kiser, Molly *musician*
Kitt, Eartha Mae *actress, singer*
Kline, Kevin Delaney *actor*
Kono, Toshihiko *cellist*
Kowroski, Maria *dancer*
Kraut, Harry John *music producer, consultant*
Kulin, Keith David *cinematographer*
Lane, Kenneth Robert *producer, distributor*
Lansbury, Edgar George *theatrical producer*
Last, Ruth Edith *actress*
†Lawergren, Bo *music educator*
Leach, Robin *producer, writer, television host*
†LeCompte, Elizabeth *theater director*
Lee, Dai-Keong *composer*
†Lee, Iara *filmmaker*
Legrand, Michel Jean *composer*
†LePage, William *composer*
Leppard, Raymond John *conductor, harpsichordist*
Leritz, Lawrence R. *choreographer, singer, actor, dancer, producer*
†Leslee, Ray *composer*
†Letterman, David *television personality, producer, comedian, writer*
Levine, James *conductor, pianist, artistic director*
Li, Qin *television anchor, reporter, director, producer*
Libin, Paul *theatre executive, producer*
LiBretto, John Charles *television director*
Liebermann, Lowell *composer, pianist, conductor*
†Limbaugh, Rush Hudson *radio and talk show host*
Loney, Glenn Meredith *drama educator*
Lopez-Cobos, Jesus *conductor*
Loudon, Dorothy *actress*
Lubovitch, Lar *dancer, choreographer*
Lucas, James E(vans) *operatic director*
Lucci, Susan *actress*
Lynn, Judith *opera singer, artist, voice teacher*
Ma, Yo-Yo *cellist*
†Maazel, Lorin *conductor, composer, violinist*
Macurdy, John Edward *basso*
Malkin, Barry *film editor, consultant*
Mamlok, Ursula *composer, educator*
†Manahan, Anna *actress*
†Mandabach, Caryn *television producer*
Mansouri, Lotfollah (Lotfi Mansouri) *retired general director of opera company*
Maraynes, Allan Lawrence *filmmaker, television producer*
Margolis, Mark Neal *actor*
Marks, Robert *music director, composer, educator*
Marshall, John Richard *opera director*
†Marshall, Robert *film director, television director, theater director, choreographer*
Martin, Elliot Edwards *theatrical producer*
Martini, Richard K. *theatrical producer*
†Martins, Peter *ballet master, choreographer, dancer*
Massey, Andrew John *conductor, composer*
Maysles, Albert H. *filmmaker*
Mazzola, John William *former performing arts center executive, consultant*
†McDonald, Audra Ann *actress*
McKenzie, Kevin Patrick *artistic director*
McLachlan, Sarah *composer, musician*
Meadow, Lynne (Carolyn Meadow) *theatrical producer and director*
†Meltzer, Harold *performing company executive, composer*
Merchant, Ismail Noormohamed *film producer, film director*
Meunier, Monique *dancer*
†Meyer, Edgar *musician, composer*
Michaels, Lorne *television writer, producer*

Miller, Bebe *choreographer*
†Miller, Erika *on-air business news reporter*
Mintz, Shlomo *conductor, violist, violinist*
Mitchell, Arthur *dancer, choreographer, educator*
†Mold, David F. *performing arts educator, director*
Monk, Meredith Jane *artistic director, composer, choreographer, filmmaker, director*
Moore, Michael Watson *musician, educator*
Morath, Max Edward *entertainer, composer, writer*
Morris, John *composer, conductor, arranger*
†Morton, Joëlle *musician, editor*
Moyers, Judith Davidson *television producer*
Muller, Jennifer *choreographer, dancer*
Muradian, Vazgen *musician, composer*
†Murphy, Donna *actress*
Murphy, Rosemary *actress*
Nederlander, James Morton *theater executive*
Nelson, Edwin Stafford *actor, educator*
†Nelson, Stanley *film director, writer, film producer*
Nugent, Nelle *theater, film and television producer*
Nussbaum, Jeffrey Joseph *musician*
O'Brien, Conan *writer, performer, talk show host*
Ohira, Kazuto *theatre company executive, writer*
O'Neal, Hank *entertainment producer, business owner*
†Osbourne, Ozzy (John Osbourne) *vocalist*
Palackal, Joseph Joseph *researcher, musician*
Palmer, Wayne Lewis *television director and producer*
†Paranosic, Milica *composer, educator*
Parker, Alice *composer, conductor*
†Parks, Gordon Roger Alexander *film director, author, photographer, composer*
Parsons, Estelle *actress*
†Paul, Les *entertainer, inventor*
Pavarotti, Luciano *lyric tenor*
Payton-Wright, Pamela *actress*
Perahia, Murray *pianist*
Peress, Maurice *symphony conductor, musicologist*
†Perlman, Itzhak *violinist*
Perlmutter, Alvin Howard *television and film producer*
Perry, Douglas *opera singer*
Peters, Bernadette (Bernadette Lazzara) *actress*
†Peters, Roberta *soprano*
†Philbin, Regis *television personality*
†Pier, Stephen McKay *dancer, educator, choreographer*
†Plant, Robert Anthony *singer, composer*
Poor, Peter Varnum *producer, director*
Porter, Karl Hampton *orchestra musical director, conductor*
Porter, Stephen Winthrop *stage director*
Posin, Kathryn Olive *choreographer*
Powers, Scott *producer, actor*
†Price, Leontyne *concert and opera singer, soprano*
Prince, Harold *theatrical producer*
Queler, Eve *conductor*
†Ramirez, Tina *artistic director*
Ramsay, Gustavus Remak *actor*
Randolph, David *conductor*
Raphael, Sally Jessy *talk-show host*
Raps, Gena *pianist*
Rauch, Paul David *television producer*
Reich, Steve *composer*
Reinking, Ann H. *actress, dancer*
Renick, Kyle *artistic director*
Rennie, Milbrey Tower *television news producer*
Reuben, Gloria *actress*
Rhodes, Samuel *violist, educator*
Rice, Barbara Lynn *stage manager*
†Richard, Ellen *theater executive*
†Richards, Keith *musician*
Richards, Lloyd George *theatrical director, university administrator*
†Richards, Martin *theatrical producer*
Rigg, Dame Diana *actress*
Ringer, Jennifer *dancer*
Rivera, Chita (Conchita del Rivero) *actress, singer, dancer*
Rivera, Geraldo *television personality, journalist*
Robertson, Andrew *dancer*
Rosen, Nathaniel Kent *cellist*
Rostropovich, Mstislav Leopoldovich *conductor, music director, musician*
Rothschild, Amalie Randolph *filmmaker, producer, director, digital artist, photographer*
Rouse, Christopher Chapman, III, *composer, educator*
Rudel, Julius *conductor*
†Rudin, Scott *film and theatre producer*
Rupcich, Matthew William *music educator*
†Saddler, Donald Edward *choreographer, dancer*
Salerno-Sonnenberg, Nadja *violinist*
Salomon, Frank Ernest *classical music administrator*
†Salonen, Esa-Pekka *conductor*
†Sanders, B. Lamar *film educator, scriptwriter*
Sarandon, Susan Abigail *actress*
†Schachter, Sandra R. *actress, film producer, poet*
Schafer, Milton *composer, pianist, educator*
Schechner, Richard *theater director, author, educator*
Scheeder, Louis *theater producer, director, educator*
Schifrin, Lalo *composer*
Schoonmaker Powell, Thelma *film editor*
Schorer, Suki *ballet teacher*
Schrade, Robert Warren *classical pianist, educator*
Schuhart, Anne Dashley (Susan Schuhart Zito) *actress*
Scorsese, Martin *film director, writer*
†Seal, *popular musician*
Seary, Lawrence Anthony *cinematographer, news assignment editor, field operations administrator*
†Seeger, Pete *folk singer, songwriter*
Seldes, Marian *actress*
Seligson, Gary Marc *musician*

PROFESSIONAL INDEX 6199 ARTS: PERFORMING

Seltzer, Leo *documentary filmmaker, educator, lecturer*
Serebrier, José *musician, conductor, composer*
†Sergel, Ruth *filmmaker*
Severs, William Floyd *actor*
Shane, Rita *opera singer, educator*
Sheik, Duncan *musician, writer*
Shelley, Carole *actress*
Sherman, Arthur *theater educator, writer, actor, composer, sculptor*
Shuman, Earl Stanley *songwriter, music publisher*
Siegel, Marc Monroe *television and film producer, writer, director*
Silver, Joan Micklin *film director, screenwriter*
Silvers, Sally *choreographer, performing company executive*
†Simon, Abbey *pianist*
Sitomer, Sheila Marie *television producer, director*
Smith, Malcolm Sommerville *bass*
Snyder, Arlen Dean *actor*
†Soley, David Benjamin *composer*
Solomon, Maynard Elliott *music historian, former recording company executive*
Solomons, Gus, Jr., (Gustave Martinez) *choreographer, dancer, writer*
Solov, Zachary *choreographer, ballet artist*
Somogyi, Jennie *dancer*
†Soto, Jock *dancer*
Soyer, David *cellist, music educator*
Spacey, Kevin *actor*
Speller, Robert Ernest Blakefield, Jr., *choreographer*
Stang, Arnold *actor, director, writer*
Stang, Rolf Kristian *vocalist, actor, educator, writer, advertising executive*
†Stern, Howard Allan *radio personality, television show host*
Stern, Isaac *violinist, performing arts executive*
Stevens, Risë *performing arts company administrator*
Stiefel, Ethan *dancer*
Sting, (Gordon Matthew Sumner) *musician, songwriter, actor*
Stocker, Jeffrey David *film acting coach*
Stoltzman, Richard Leslie *clarinetist*
†Stoney, George Cashel *film educator*
Storch, Arthur *theater director*
Strasfogel, Ian *stage director,playwright*
Stratechuk, Michael *musician, educator*
†Stroman, Susan *choreographer*
Sult, Jeffery Scot *performing company executive, playwright, director, actor*
Sutherland, Dame Joan *retired soprano*
Swan, William *actor*
Talmi, Yoav *conductor, composer*
†Taylor, Paul B. *choreographer*
†Taylor, Timothy Dean *music educator*
Taymor, Julie *theater, film and opera director and designer*
Thomas, Richard *actor*
Thorne, Francis *composer*
†Tilson Thomas, Michael *symphony conductor*
Tischler, Judith Blanche *retired music publishing executive, educator*
†Torres, Dalys E. *music educator, consultant*
Tree, Michael *violinist, violist, educator*
Tucker, Allan Marc *mastering engineer*
Turturro, John *actor*
Tuttle, Ashley *dancer*
Uggams, Leslie *entertainer*
†Ulrich, Lars *drummer*
Uppman, Theodor *concert and opera singer, voice educator*
†Van Halen, Eddie *guitarist, rock musician*
†Vedder, Eddie *singer*
†Volpe, Joseph *opera company general manager*
Vonk, Hans *retired conductor*
†Wadsworth, Oliver *actor, playwright*
Wagner, Alan Cyril *television and film producer, consultant, performing arts educator*
Wagner, Susan Jill *producer*
Wallach, Eli *actor*
Warrick, Ruth *actress*
†Waxman, Anita *producer*
†Weaver, John Borland *organist, composer*
Weaver, Marianne Gruhn *flutist*
Wedgeworth, Ann *actress*
Weese, Miranda *dancer*
†Wilcox, T.J. *filmmaker*
Wile, Joan *composer, lyricist, singer*
Wilhjelm, Christian *conductor, artist*
†Williams, Arthur Joseph *film editor*
Williams, Lucinda *country musician*
Williams, Montel *television talk show host*
Wilson, Morrow *actor, theater producer, writer, television producer, radio producer*
Wisnosky, Thomas R. *television director*
Wittstein, Edwin Frank *stage and film production designer*
†Wolfe, George C. *theater director, producer, playwright*
Wood, Frank *actor*
Wuorinen, Charles Peter *composer*
†Yamaguchi, Masaya *musician, educator*
Yellin, Victor Fell *composer, music educator*
Zane, Arnie *performing company executive, choreographer*
Zhu, Ai-Lan *opera singer*
Zipay, Joanne Margaret *theatre educator, director, dramaturge*
Zosike, Joanie Fritz *theater director, actor*
Zucker, Stefan *tenor, writer, editor, radio broadcaster*
Zukerman, Pinchas *concert violinist, violist, conductor*

Newcomb
Chatzky, Herbert *music educator*

Niskayuna
†Hughes, Eric Scott *music educator*

North Bangor
†Hastings, Ralph B. *music educator*

North Massapequa
Felker, Gerald Lee *music educator, musician*

Nyack
†Kenote, Marie Herseth *music educator*
†Lum, Tammy Kar-Hee *concert pianist, education educator*

Oakfield
Mikulski, John Michael *music educator*

Oceanside
Glass, Noah F. *music educator, web site designer*

Orangeburg
†Wagoner, Russell A. *music educator*

Orchard Park
Geiger, Loren Dennis *classical musician*
†Staebell, William A. *music educator*

Oswego
Lisk, Edward Stanley *musician, educator, conductor*

Palisades
Krainin, Julian Arthur *film director, producer, writer, cinematographer*

Patterson
Jaffee, Kay *musician, musicologist*

Pawling
Jones, James Earl *actor*
Utter, Donald L. *music educator*

Pelham
†Borzova, Alla Aleksandra *composer, conductor*
Weiss, Stuart Lloyd *television and radio producer, tax attorney*

Penfield
†Bagale, John R. *music educator*

Pine City
†Stepulis, Vincent G. *retired music educator*

Pittsford
Benson, Warren Frank *composer, educator*

Pleasant Valley
Avakian, Helen Ross *musician, educator*
Becofsky, Arthur Luke *arts administrator, writer*

Pleasantville
†Maceli, Anthony G *music educator*

Poughkeepsie
†Osborne, Robert Michael *music educator, vocalist*
Wilson, Richard Edward *composer, pianist, music educator*

Purchase
Bannon, Nancy *performing arts educator*
Magaziner, Elliot Albert *musician, conductor, educator*
†Mizelle, Dary John *composer, educator*

Putnam Valley
Amram, David Werner *composer, conductor, musician*

Ravena
†Andrews, Scott Michael *music educator*

Rochester
†Antonova, Natalya *music educator, musician*
†Atkins, Carl J. *conductor, educator*
†Blades-Zeller, Elizabeth L. *music educator, vocologist*
Diamond, David Leo *composer*
Grunow, Richard F. *music educator*
Kowalke, Kim H. *music educator, musicologist, conductor, foundation executive*
Marcellus, John Robert, III, *trombonist, educator*
Reynolds, Verne *musician, retired music educator*
†Scatterday, Mark Davis *conductor, educator*
†Sholl, Martha *music educator*
Toribara, Masako Ono *voice educator*
†Webber, Carol S. *music educator, soprano*
Weiss, Howard A. *violinist, concertmaster, conductor, music educator*

Roslyn
Rosegarten, Rory *talent manager, television and theater producer*

Rye
Fumasoli, John *music educator*

Rye Brook
†Levy, Howard Alan *music educator*

Saratoga Springs
Porter, David Hugh *pianist, classicist, academic administrator, liberal arts educator*
†Rosengarten, Lewis Bart *composer, educator*
†Van Wye, Benjamin David *conductor*

Sayville
Bernstein, Neil Howard *music educator*

Scarsdale
Machover, Wilma Simon *musician*

Schenectady
Hermance, Jr., Myron E. *conductor, educator*
†McCafferty, Dennis A. *composer, musician*
†Szokody, Aniko *pianist, educator*
†Wery, Brett Lars *music educator, conductor*

Schroon Lake
†Williams, Wayne M. *music educator*

Sea Cliff
Mourashkin, Boris V. *composer, sound therapist, poet, performer, producer*
Popova, Nina *dancer, choreographer, director*

Sherburne
Dodd, Mary Ann *organist, educator*

Smithtown
Ayrovainen, Robert Michael *music educator*

South Salem
†Knijff, Jan-Piet *musician, educator*
Rosenbaum, Harold L. *conductor, music educator*

Sparkill
Dahl, Arlene *actress, writer, designer, cosmetic executive*

Sparrow Bush
Murray, William Bruce *opera singer*

Spencer
Grunberg, Slawomir *film and television producer and director, director of photography*

Spencerport
Jones, Alan D. *music educator*

Staten Island
Cross, Ronald *musicologist, educator*
Miller, Wayne *actor, designer, producer, impresario*
Robison, Paula Judith *flutist*
†Schulenberg, David Louis *musician, educator*
Thomas, Charles Columbus *educator, artist*

Syracuse
Elms, Ben *actor, director*
Wolff, Catherine Elizabeth *opera company executive*

Tarrytown
Frisch, Celia *violinist, chamber music coach, educator*

Troy
Isaacs, Andrea *editor, publisher, dancer, choreographer, former educator*

Verona
Smith, Kathy Ann *music educator*

Wallkill
†Strauser, Susan Parkyn (Susan Parkyn Strauser) *performing arts educator*

Warwick
†Emery, James Patrick *composer, musician*

Weedsport
†English, Richard Paul *music educator*

West Hempstead
†Petorak, Bryan Thomas *music educator, musician*

West Hurley
Martucci, Vincent James *composer, pianist*

West Islip
Keller, Joyce *television and radio host, counselor, writer*

White Plains
Eckfeld, William Grover *music educator, composer, musician*
Sedelmaier, J. J. *filmmaker*
Teck, Katherine *musician, writer*
Wedge, Chris *animation director, studio executive*

Williamstown
Mixon, Kevin Anthony *music educator, composer*

Willow
Bley, Carla Borg *jazz composer*

Woodmere
†Ronis, Gwendlyn *music educator, musician*

Woodside
Beeks, Delisco James (Delisco) *vocalist, actor, poet*

Yonkers
Baumel, Herbert *violinist, conductor*
Brickman, Miriam *concert pianist*
Stattel, Robert John *music educator, musician*

NORTH CAROLINA

Asheville
Weed, Maurice James *composer, retired music educator*

Banner Elk
Tilden, Ralph Fulton *retired music educator, organist*

Bladenboro
Cameron, Fred E. *band director, composer*

Boiling Springs
Vaughan, Ted Wayne *music and communications educator, musician*

Boone
Cole, Susan Stockbridge *theatre educator*

Bostic
Prince, Anna Lou *composer, music publisher, construction company executive*

Brevard
Effron, David Louis *conductor, music director*

Buxton
Froeber, Sarah Marjorie *actor, playwright, educator*

Cary
Bruce, Brenda *pianist*

Chapel Hill
Adamson, Judy *theater educator*
Hammond, David Alan *stage director, educator*
Lytle, Stephen Charles *music educator*
Parker, Scott Jackson *theatre manager*
Powell, Carolyn Wilkerson *music educator*

Charlotte
Bonnefoux, Jean-Pierre *artistic director, choreographer, dancer*
†Bulow, Harry Timothy *music educator*
†Iley, Martha Strawn *music educator*
Reese, Annette Evelyn *music educator*
†Thompson, Gregory Thomas *music educator, musician*

Cherokee
†Hotelling, Kurt Paul *music educator, writer*

Cherryville
Barger, Linda Kale *choral director*

Concord
†Price, Randy S. *music educator*

Creedmoor
Cross, June Crews *retired music educator*

Durham
Nakarai, Charles Frederick Toyozo *music educator, adjudicator*
Ward, Robert *composer, conductor, educator*
†Williams, Frank Earl *music educator*

Elizabeth City
†Harrison, Thomas R. *music educator*

Fayetteville
†Cook, James Wesley *music educator*
Curtis, Marvin Vernell *music educator*
†Hall, Phoebe Jean *theater educator*
†Skorich, John Jovan *music educator*
†Warner, James Alex *music educator*

Franklinton
†Elmore, Cenieth Catherine *music educator*

Greensboro
†Brotherton, Jonathan Paul *music educator*
Middleton, Herman David, Sr., *theater educator*
Styles, Teresa Jo *producer, educator*

Greenville
†Kramar, John Shaw *voice educator, vocalist*

Hickory
†Kiser, Daniel *music educator, musician*

High Point
Burnette, Marie (Helen Marie Burnette) *music educator*
†Huss, Donald Edwin, Jr., *musician*

Lexington
†Carter, Jason Wayne *music educator*
†Harris, Ricky E. *music educator*

Mars Hill
†Corley, Alton L. *music educator*
†Lamberson, Carolyn H. *music educator*
†Newton, Paul George *musician, retired librarian*

Mount Holly
Price, Jr., Dwight Richard *musician, educator*

Murfreesboro
†McIntire, Dennis Kean *music educator*

Newport
Mundine, Rachel Quinn *music educator*

Raleigh
†Albert, David Saleeba *music educator*
†Brown, Marilyn Shull *music educator*
†Entzi, John A. *music educator*
Greene, David Beckwith *music educator*

Rougemont
Nilsson, Mary Ann *music educator*

Salisbury
†Falocco, Joe *theater educator, actor*
†Higbee, Dale (Strohe) *musician, retired psychologist*
†Julian, Rose Rich *music educator, director*

Statesville
Wright, David Alan *music educator*

Swannanoa
Whittington, Lorin Dale *music educator*

Tuckasegee
Lominac, Harry Gene *retired theater educator, designer*

Wake Forest
†Markoch, Andrew Richard *music educator*

Warrenton
Weddington, Elizabeth Gardner (Liz Gardner) *actress, editor*

Wilmington
Adams, Veronica Wadewitz *musician*
Cameron, Kay *conductor, music director, arranger*

Kelley, Virginia Wiard (Judy Kelley) *dance educator*

Wingate
†Bostic, Ronald David *music educator*

Winston Salem
†Capitano, Nicholas *television producer*
Chumbley, Robert Edward *performing arts association administrator*
†Mchugh, David Joseph *music educator, composer*
Mitchener, John Edward *music educator, musician*
Mueller, Margaret S. *musician, educator*
Trautwein, George William *conductor, educator*

Youngsville
†Riggs, Susan Dunnagan *music educator, musician*

NORTH DAKOTA

Bismarck
†Baumann, Jon Paul *music educator, director*
Lundberg, Susan Ona *musical organization administrator*
Tornow, L. William *musician*
Wellin, Thomas *music director*

Edmore
Sampson, Valerie K. Morman *music educator*

Fargo
†Sondrall, Pat *music educator*

Grand Forks
Gallo, Sergio Roberto *music educator, researcher*
Werpy, Steve *music educator, conductor*

Lakota
†Hoerth, Kenneth D. *music educator*

Zeeland
Wolf, Trudy J. Fraase *music educator, librarian*

OHIO

Akron
†Barlowe Bodman, Amy *violinist, composer*
Flick, Lynette Lowry *piano teacher*
Kazle, Elynmarie *producer, performing arts executive*
†Wilding, James *music educator, composer*

Alliance
DeStefano, L. Timothy *music educator, conductor*

Antwerp
†Schmidt, John R. *music educator*

Ashland
†Goodwin, Richard Charles *performing arts association administrator, actor*

Athens
Condee, William Faricy *theater educator, writer*
†Stomberg, Eric W *musician*

Bluffton
Schattschneider, Adam James *music educator*
Sycks, David Brent *band director, musician*

Bowling Green
Fung, Chi-Keung Victor *music educator, researcher*
Skoog, William Melvin *music/voice educator*
†Trantham, Gene Starr *music educator*
Wolcott, Nancy Bookout *music director*

Bratenahl
DesRosiers, Anne Booke *performing arts administrator, consultant*

Burton
†Fuller, David William *music educator*

Canfield
Volenik, James Edward *music educator*

Canton
†Klotz, Leora Nylee *retired music educator, vocalist*

Cedarville
Anderson, Connie *music educator*
Hoffmann, Kenneth Michael *music educator*

Chillicothe
Donahue, Jeffrey David *music educator*

Cincinnati
†Adams, David Hardy *voice educator, concert singer*
†Bell, David Maxwell *music educator, consultant*
†Brown, Lillie Harrison *music educator*
†Costigan-Kerns, Louise E. *musician*
†de Mallet Burgess, Thomas *opera director, music educator*
Galloway, Lillian Carroll *modeling agency executive, consultant*
Hills, Alan *performing company executive*
Hoffman, Joel Harvey *composer, educator*
Huber, Henry B. *retired music educator*
†Jarvi, Paavo *conductor*
Kunzel, Erich, Jr., *conductor, arranger, educator*
Monder, Steven I. *orchestra executive*
Morgan, Victoria *performing company executive, choreographer*
Paavo, Jarvi *conductor*
Smith, Timothy W. *musician*
Tocco, James *pianist*

Cinncinati
†Leavitt, Tod John *music educator, musician*

Cleveland
Adams, H. Leslie *composer*
Ciarlillo, Marjorie Ann *musician, educator*
Erb, Donald *composer*
†Field, Jonathon Hugh *theater director, theater educator*
Giannetti, Louis Daniel *film educator, film critic*
Janson, Patrick *singer, actor, conductor, educator*
Krausz, Susan *musician, pianist, composer*
Lawrence, Estelene Yvonne *musician, transportation executive*
Morris, Thomas William *symphony orchestra administrator*
†Nahat, Dennis F. *artistic director, choreographer*
Teissonniere, Gerardo *musician, educator*
†Vieaux, Jason Brian *musician, music educator*
Weir, Dame Gillian Constance *concert organist, harpsichordist*
Welser-Möst, Franz *conductor*

Columbus
Allen, Lois Arlene Height (Mrs. James Pierpont Allen) *musician*
Charles, Gerard *performing company executive, choreographer*
Drvota, Mojmir *cinema educator, author*
†Grega, Andrew Michael *music educator*
Harris, Donald *composer*
Hart, Daniel *orchestra executive*
Johnson, Rebecca Grooms *music educator*
†Mollenhauer, Jude *music educator, musician*
Rosenstock, Susan Lynn *orchestra administrator*
†Satoh, Yuko *music educator*
Siciliani, Alessandro Domenico *conductor*
Wagner, Robert Walter *photography, cinema and communications educator, media producer, consultant*
†Wang, Tianshu *music educator*

Dayton
†Atkins, Laura Jane *music educator*
Leung, Jackson Yi-Shun *music educator*
†Mullinix, Susan Carlock *musician, educator*
Walters, Jefferson Brooks *musician, retired real estate broker*
†Wasson, Steven *music educator, piano technician*

Delaware
Jamison, Roger W. *pianist, piano educator*
†Remlinger, Rolf *music educator, cartoonist*

Delphos
†Stearns, David Allen *music educator*

Dublin
†Gray, James H., Jr., *music educator*
Laurence, Amy Rebecca *music educator, composer*
†Ma, Hengwei *music educator*

East Cleveland
Soule, Lucile Snyder *pianist, music educator*

Findlay
†Benedict, A. Joan *music educator*
†Hanson, David Alan *music educator*

Geneva
†Carrel, Marianne Eileen *music educator*

Grove City
†Traini, Thomas Albert *music educator*

Hamilton
Glass, Robert Edward *retired music educator*

Hiram
Bane, James Wallace *music educator*

Holland
Conlin, Thomas *conductor*

Kent
Prioleau, Darwin E. *dance educator, choreographer*

Kirtland
†Brown, Robert Loran *music educator*
†Petrone, John R. *music educator, composer*

Lafayette
Dellifield, Dennis L. *conductor*

Lexington
†Maxwell, Mark *music educator*

Lima
Casey, Rebecca Lynn *music educator*
†Grim, Brian Keith *music educator*

London
Lloyd, John *composer, educator*

Lorain
Tucker, Thomas Edward *music educator*

Malvern
†Crum, Clarence F. *music educator, school system administrator*

Mansfield
Bernhardt, Carol Ann *musician, educator*
†Ellis, Mark Carlton *music educator*
†Mitchell, Sheron Lynn *music educator*

Medina
Liauba, Danute *music educator*

Middlefield
†Jaite, Gail Ann *music educator*

Mineral Ridge
Czifra, Lisa Takacs *piano educator*
Yaksich, John Joseph *music educator*

Mount Vernon
†Tocheff, Robert Dale *music educator*

Newark
Sanders, Paul David *music educator*

Norton
Becker, Janet Sue *musician*

Oberlin
†Lee, Kyung Sun *music educator*
†Rejto, Peter Alan *music educator*
Rutstein, Sedmara Zakarian *piano educator, concert pianist*

Ottoville
Bowery, Warren E. *music educator*

Oxford
†Papanikolaou, Eftychia *music educator*

Parma
†Laycock, Randolph Philip *music educator, conductor*

Peninsula
Shaw, Doris Beaumar *film and video producer, executive recruiter, management consultant*

Pickerington
†Parulekar, Marc Samir *music educator*

Port Clinton
Bixler, Thomas L. *music educator*

Roseville
Carney, Karen Rose *music educator, pianist*

Sandusky
†Kowalski, Anthony Albert *music educator*

Sidney
Fahrer, Franklin James *music educator*

Springfield
†Chen, Peng-Hsin *composer, music educator*
†Faber, Trudy *music educator*
†Winteregg, Steven Lee *composer, musician, educator*

Stoutsville
Wernick, Edith Elaine *pianist, educator*

Tipp City
†Ahmed, Gail R. *music educator*

Toledo
Bell, Robert *orchestra executive*
Duling, Edward Burger *music education educator*
†Girgis-Hanna, Mary Fahim *music educator*
Knorr, John Christian *entertainment executive, bandleader, producer*

Vandalia
†Korte, Genevieve L *music educator*

Wadsworth
Mayes, Samuel William *music educator*
†Ross, Jane Arlene *music educator*

Wapakoneta
Lusk, Mary Margaret *music educator*

Warren
Seachrist, Denise *music educator*

Warrensville Heights
Stephenson, Samuel Floyd, Jr., *music educator*

Waverly
†McNelly, Charles Wesley *music educator*

Waynesville
†Lenney, Shawn Edward *music educator*

West Chester
†Pease, Stacey Lyn *music educator*

Westerville
Clamme, Marvin Leslie *recording engineer, electronic engineer*
†Swinehart, Timothy E. *music educator*

Whitehouse
Boyle, Daniel Robert *musician, delivery service executive*

Willoughby
Baker, Charles Stephen *music educator*
†Primavera, Fred Joseph *music educator*

Wooster
†Gallagher, Jack B(urt) *composer, music educator*
Ling, Stuart James *music educator, composer*

Youngstown
Schwers, Dorothy Jean *retired music educator*

Zanesville
Brown, Karen Rima *orchestra manager, Spanish language educator*

OKLAHOMA

Ada
Mornhinweg, Claudia Beth Jones *music educator*

Bethany
†Ballweg, David Brent *music educator, conductor*
†Halpain, Sue R. *music educator, musician*

Choctaw
Howard, David L. *music educator, conductor*

Claremore
†Smith, David M. *music educator*

Corn
Regier, Charles E. *music educator*

Durant
Christy, David Hardacker *music educator, consultant*

Edmond
Charoenwongse, Chindarat *pianist, educator, school administrator*

Enid
†Record, Donald D. *music educator, literature educator*
Russell, Rhonda Cheryl *piano educator, recording artist*
Seem, Evelyn Ashcraft *music educator*

Frederick
Clayton, Ann Allman *music educator, minister*

Grove
†Illgen, Joel R. *music educator*

Guthrie
†Tickle, Jona *music educator*

Lawton
Klein, Scott Richard *acting and directing educator*

Mcalester
†Smith, Jason Richard *music educator*

Miami
†Lawson, Wayne A. *voice educator, minister*

Mounds
Fellows, Esther Elizabeth *musician, music educator*
Halsey, James Albert *international entertainment impresario, theatrical producer, talent manager*

Norman
†Daniel, Sean *voice educator, baritone, artist*
†Enrico, Eugene Joseph *music educator*
†Griffith-Barbara, Martha Jayne *music educator*
Herstand, Theodore *theatre artist, educator*
Magrath, Jane *music educator*
Malick, Eldon Roy *music educator, musician*
†Matlick, Eldon R. *music educator*
†Meiller, James R. *music educator*
Ross, Allan Anderson *music educator, university official*

Oklahoma City
Adams, Mary Lou *piano teacher*
Boyles, S. Kay *pianist, music educator*
†Holeman, Lora White *music educator*
Levine, Joel *music director, conductor*
†Mailman, Matthew *conductor*
Moore, Billy Don *video scriptwriter, producer*
Payne, Gareld Gene *vocal music educator, medical transcriptionist*
Pitts, Bryan *performing company executive*
Thomas, Gary Wayne *actor*
Twyman, Nita (Venita Twyman) *music educator*

Sapulpa
†Weinstock Rad, Katheryn Louise *music educator*

Shawnee
Clark, Don Eugene *music educator*
†Tyler, Jeannie E. *music educator*

Stillwater
Foster, Gayla Catherine *musician*
King, Marilyn Sodowsky *music educator*
Lanners, Thomas Martin *music educator*
Smeyak, Gerald Paul *telecommunication educator*
†te Velde, Rebecca Groom *organist, music educator, composer*

Tonkawa
†Fiscus, Linda Kay *music educator*

Tulsa
Angelini, Marcello *artistic director*
†Cottingham, Barbara J. *music educator*
Geary, Barbara Ann *recital and concert pianist, music educator*
Huff, Rosemary Bowers *music and voice educator*
Moore, David Arthur *composer, music educator*
Owens, Jana Jae *entertainer*
Reed, Robert A. *performing arts executive*
Saied, James Guy *conductor, consultant*
Slaucitajs, Andrew Paul *videographer, video producer*
Sowell, Laven *retired music educator*

Vinita
Lollman, Matthew Tobias *music educator*

Weatherford
†Widen, Dennis Charles *music educator*

OREGON

Aloha
†Sheykman, Bella *music educator*

Bend
Gillem, Elise (Marie) (Elise Michaels) *radio and television personality*
Seed, Brian Bruce *music educator*

Burns
Peckham, Kendall I. *music educator*

Pawtucket
Orson, Barbara Tuschner *actress*

Providence
Barnhill, James Orris *theater educator*
Dempsey, Raymond Leo, Jr., *radio and television producer, moderator, writer*
Hutchinson, Park William, Jr., *theatre educator*

SOUTH CAROLINA

Andrews
Pittman, Joey Jay *music educator*

Beaufort
Horn, Lois Burley *pianist, educator*

Chapin
†Mills, James H. *music educator*

Charleston
†Bonds, John Bledsoe *musician, educator*
Cantwell, Don *artistic director*
Edwards, Darrell *orchestra executive*

Cleveland
†Balent, Andrew *composer, musician*

Clinton
†Stokes, James Porter, II, *music educator*

Columbia
†Bell, Isaac, Jr., *music educator*
Cleveland, Elbin L. *theatre design and technology educator*
†Douglas, Samuel Osler *musician, educator*
†Headrick, John David *music educator*
†Ingram, Jonathan Hall *music educator*
†Jesselson, Robert *musician, educator*
†Leaman, Clifford Lynn *saxophone educator*
†Olenchak, Frank Richard *music educator, musician*
†Shearer, Ellen Marie *music educator*
Starrett, William *dancer, artistic director*
†Summer, Munson *music educator*

Cowpens
†Bishop, Alan Douglas *music educator*

Due West
Warren, John Floyd *music educator*

Edisto Island
Van Metre, Margaret Cheryl *artistic director, dance educator*

Florence
Jones, Michael Stuart *music educator*

Gaffney
Sweeney, Christopher Robert *music educator, researcher*

Greenville
†Cochran, Kathy Holcombe *music educator, conductor*
Purtle, Jeffery Allan *music educator*
Tchivzhel, Edvard *music director*

Hilton Head Island
†Kimbell, David Lawrence *music educator*

Isle Of Palms
Lorince, L(ois) Margaret *music educator*

Johnston
†McKinney, Steven Dallas *music educator*

Lexington
†Gatch, Jerald V. *music educator*

Meggett
†Stoots, Leigh Henderson *music educator*

Murrells Inlet
Washburn, John Lee *music educator*

North Charleston
†Spitler, John Robert *music educator, musician*

Pickens
†White, Leeanne J. *music educator*

Rock Hill
†Dickert, Lewis, Jr. H. *music educator, musician*
Wishert, Jo Ann Chappell *music educator, elementary and secondary education educator*

Spartanburg
Bolton, Calvin *music educator*
Lucktenberg, Jerrie Cadek *music educator*
†Robbins, Malcolm Scott *composer, education educator*
Smithey, Pamela *consultant, organist, freelance accompanist*

Summerville
†Capps, Phillip Lewis *music educator*
Shakibanasab, Lauren Vorwerk *music director, educator*

Taylors
†Riddle, Thad (Tad) W., III, *music educator, webmaster*

Walterboro
Meshach, Joseph Robert *music educator*

SOUTH DAKOTA

Aberdeen
†Manhart, Grant Lee *music educator*
†Wieland, William John *music educator, composer*

Brookings
†Crowe, Don Raymond *music educator, consultant*

Canton
Kaufman, Angela J. *music educator*

Herreid
†Schumacher, Michelle Kelly *music educator*

Marion
†Nielson, Helen M. *music educator*

Mitchell
Almjeld, Paul F. *conductor, music educator*

Sioux Falls
Bennett, Thomas *orchestra executive*
†McDowell, Robert James *music educator, composer*

Volin
Aiello, Frank John *music educator*

TENNESSEE

Antioch
Ely, Joe *singer, songwriter*

Athens
†Dannel, James Micheal *voice educator*

Bristol
†Flannagan, William Patrick *music educator*

Chattanooga
Bernhardt, Robert *music director, conductor*
Butler, David Alfred *music educator*
Fouquet, Anne (Judy Fuqua) *musician, music educator*
†Tsai, Sin-Hsing *musician, music educator*
†Wilkes, Gary S. *music educator*
†Winham, Richard Paul *radio director, English and communications educator*

Columbia
†Scheusner, Ronald L. *music educator*

Cordova
Griffin, Walton W. *performing company executive*
Pugh, Dorothy Gunther *artistic director*

Covington
Key, Thomas Marshall *music educator*
Kinningham, Alan Goodrum *music educator, composer/arranger*

Dandridge
Martin, Earl Richard *theology educator*

Dayton
†Luther, Sigrid *music educator*

Fairview
†Hutchison, Barbara Bailey *singer, songwriter*

Fayetteville
Bone, Lawson Mitchell *songwriter, poet*

Franklin
Bull, Sandy (Alexander Benjamin Bull) *musician, composer*
†Smith, Michael W. *popular musician*

Henderson
†Hay, Thomas Franklin *music educator*

Hendersonville
Clark, Alan Martin *band director*
Miller, Creighton Herbert *music educator*
†Skaggs, Ricky *country musician*

Jackson
Gatwood, Dianne N. *music educator*
†McRoberts, Terry Allan *music educator*
†Weimer, Lee J. *music educator*

Jefferson City
Dunn, Lynda M. *music educator*

Johnson City
Champouillon, David Charles *music educator, musician*
Jenrette, Thomas Shepard, Jr., *music educator, choral director*
†Rice-See, Lynn *music educator*
†Self, Jimmie Everette *music educator, musician*

Knoxville
†Baldwin, Wesley Hale Barrick *music educator*
Jacobs, Kenneth A. *composer, educator*
†Milligan, Robert Spencer *music educator*
Powell, Edwin Charles *music educator, conductor, musician*
†Sousa, Gary D. *music educator*
†Speas, Bruce Orburn *theater educator*
Trevor, Kirk David Niell *orchestra conductor, cellist*
†Wentzel, Andrew Neal *vocalist, voice educator*

Lawrenceburg
†Hayes, Sylvia Richmond *music educator*

Lebanon
Daniels, Charlie *musician, songwriter*

Martin
†Bowman, Joseph Leonard *music educator*
Wade, Reba *music teacher, pianist*

Memphis
†Chester, James A. *music educator*
Ching, James Michael *artistic director opera company, composer, conductor*

†Dixon, Samuel B *retired comedian, film director, film producer*
Head, Willis Stanford *music educator, performer*
Holland, Nicholas V., III, *music educator*
Huddleston, Jeffrey Lawrence *music educator*
Lane, Sheryl Leanne *music educator, organist, violinist, pianist*
Piazza, Marguerite *opera singer, actress, entertainer*
†Simpson, Timothy Young *music educator*
Williams, David Russell *retired music educator*

Morristown
†Rowland, Kyla Faye *gospel songwriter*

Mount Juliet
†Dent, Cedric Carl *musician, educator*
Garvey, Pat *vocalist, composer, actor, novelist*

Murfreesboro
†Dougan, John *music educator*

Nashville
Autry, Philip Earl *music educator, musician*
†Cleveland, Ashley *musician*
Estrin, Kari (Karen Ruth Estrin) *artist and tour manager, agent, consultant*
Fabian, Jane *former ballet company executive*
†Fleck, Bela *country musician*
James, H. Neal *video, record, movie producer, director*
Kahan, Sheldon Jeremiah (Christopher Reed) *musician, singer*
Kaine, Paul *performing company executive*
†Krauss, Alison *country musician*
Lee, Douglas A. *music educator*
McDonald, Reginald Adrian *musician, educator*
Schermerhorn, Kenneth *music director*
Twain, Shania *country musician*
Valentine, Alan Darrell *symphony orchestra executive*
Vasterling, Paul *artistic director*

Pigeon Forge
Parton, Dolly Rebecca *singer, composer, actress*

TEXAS

Abilene
†Eaves, Stephen R. *music educator*
Ellis, Laura Renee *music educator*
†Puckett, Lauren Joy *music educator*
†Scarbrough, Michael *music educator*
Springer, Lorene Hargrove *music educator*
†Tolosa, Gustavo Alberto *music educator*
†Westman, Lanie Jo *music educator, performing company executive, performing arts educator*

Amarillo
†Busch, Mildred Moorman *music educator*
†Laur, Noel Paul Douglas *music educator*

Arlington
Bruton, Carole Diane *music educator*
Carey, Milburn Ernest *musician, educator*
†Lau, Irene B. *music educator*
Sky-Eagle, Melissa Jean *musician, pianist*
†Thomas, Lois C. *organist, music educator*
†Turcotte, Karen M. *music educator*

Aubrey
†Pizzamiglio, Albert Theodore (Al Pierson) *conductor*
Pizzamiglio, Nancy Alice *performing company executive*

Austin
Adair, Dwight Rial *film director, educator*
Antokoletz, Elliott Maxim *music educator*
Aubery, Stephen Royston Edmund *film producer*
Bradford, Mary Pinkney *music educator*
Brockett, Oscar Gross *theatre educator*
Burnaman, Stephen Paul *music educator*
†Gilmson, Sophia *music educator*
†Gimble, Johnny *country musician*
†Henley, Paul Thomas *music educator, researcher*
Holtzman, Joan King *musician, composer*
†Hopkins, Mitchell Shade *music educator*
Kennan, Kent Wheeler *composer, educator*
Lary, Banning Kent *video producer, publisher*
MacDonald, Martha Frances *clarinetist, music educator*
Marse, Linda Moody *music educator*
Mills, Stephen *artistic director*
Mueller, Peggy Jean *dance educator, choreographer, rancher*
Murphy, Michele Sandra *musician, educator*
†Neubert, Bernard David *music educator*
Robbins, Mary *concert pianist*
Ruiz, Cookie *performing company executive*
†Scott, Laurie P. *music educator*

Beaumont
Brailsford, June Evelyn *musician, educator*

Beeville
†Switzer, Linda Thrall *music educator*

Belton
†Wood, Connie Garrison *music educator*

Borger
Allen, Bessie Malvina *music educator, church organist*

Brenham
†Plaag, Joel Fredrick *music educator, director*

Brownsville
†Stone, Michael John *music educator, conductor*

Brownwood
†Banks, Patricia Anne *music educator, minister*

Canyon
†Sheffield, Jovonna Michele *music educator*

Carthage
†Brumley, Larry Gene *music educator*

Commerce
†Chang, Fenia I-fen *music educator, pianist*

Conroe
†Harrison, Paula Jean *music educator*
Taylor, Mary Curtis Smith *musician*

Corpus Christi
Allison, Joan Kelly *music educator, pianist*
†Ellison, Bobbie Dilworth *retired music educator, composer*
†Wojcik, John Casimir *music educator, director*

Dallas
†Atkinson, Bill *artistic director*
Bronstein, Fred *orchestra executive*
Croskell, Madelon Byrd *music educator, classical vocalist*
†Etgen, Ann *ballet educator, artistic director, choreographer*
Foutch, Michael James *actor, dancer, lighting designer, producer*
†Freiberger, Katherine Guion *composer, retired piano educator*
Johnson, Mary Elizabeth *music educator, pianist*
†Karayanis, Plato Steven *opera company executive*
Litton, Andrew *musical director*
†Palmer, Christine (Clelia Rose Venditti) *operatic singer, performer, pianist, vocal instructor, lecturer, entertainer*
Pell, Jonathan Laurence *artistic administrator*
†Stone, Karen *theater director*
Thomas, Paul Lindsley *composer, organist, music director*
Turocy, Catherine *performing company executive*

Deer Park
†Wester, R. Glen *music educator, director*

Denison
O'Toole, Dennis P. *music educator, musician*

Denton
Bonduris, Thad Santikos *music educator*
Cohen, Nicki Sandra *music educator, music therapist*
†Couturiaux, Clay James *musician*
†Eustis, Lynn Eleanor *music educator, vocalist*
Latham, William Peters *composer, former educator*
McTee, Cindy *classical musician, educator*
†Nestler, Eric M. *music educator*
Paul, Pamela Mia *concert pianist*
†Phipps, Graham H. *music educator*
†Reikofski, Helen Dewey *musician, educator*

Desoto
Tyrer-Ferraro, Polly Ann *music instructor, software developer*

Edinburg
†Grossman, Morley Keith *music educator*
†Mizener, Charlotte Lynn Pearson *music educator, musician*

Farmers Branch
Walsh, Elizabeth Jameson *musician*

Flower Mound
Wells, Margaret Ann *piano educator*

Fort Worth
Cliburn, Van (Harvey Lavan Cliburn Jr.) *concert pianist*
Danilow, Deborah Marie *singer, songwriter, musician, rancher, realtor*
†Dressler, Oscar H. *music educator*
Faherty, David Miles *musical instrument repairman*
Fritz, Mary Ann *music educator*
†Harth-Bedoya, Miguel *conductor*
Lipkin, Seymour *pianist, conductor, educator*
Mallette, David *performing company executive*
Patteson, Charles Lynn *musician, retired music educator*
Raessler, Kenneth Ray *music educator*
Tarpenning, Emily *music educator*
Whillock, David Everett *communication educator, dean, consultant*
†Wilson, Echo Maurer *music educator*
†Yacante, Maria Lucy *music educator, researcher*

Fredericksburg
Gibson, Frances Ernst *music educator*

Fulshear
†Grantham, Nan L. *music educator, writer*

Galena Park
†Sonnier, Erich Joseph *music educator*

Georgetown
Teat, Herbert Leroy *retired music educator*

Gonzales
†Ince, Laurel T. *music educator*

Houston
Adams, Daniel Clifford *music educator*
Baranovich, Diana Lea *music educator*
Brown, Glenda Ann Walters *ballet director*
Buyse, Leone Karena *orchestral musician, educator*
Clark, Ron D(ean) *cosmetologist*
Conner, Cecil C., Jr., *performing company executive*
Douglas, P C *producer, director, reporter, editor*
Englesmith, Tejas *actor, producer, curator*
†Fischer, Norman Charles *music educator*
Gearhart, John Wesley, III, *musician, educator*
Girouard, Peggy Jo Fulcher *ballet educator*
†Gockley, David (Richard David Gockley) *opera director*

Graf, Hans *conductor*
Guilliouma, Larry Jay, Jr., *performing arts administrator, music educator*
†Gutierrez, Edith G. *freelance/self-employed music educator, composer, lyricist*
Halen, Walter John *music educator, composer*
Herring, Linda *pianist, music educator*
Jackson, Donna Ann *musician, piano instructor*
Jenkins, Jerry Wayne *musician*
Jones, Florence M. *music educator*
†Krajewski, Michael *conductor*
Ledford, Tanner O'Brain *music educator*
Lindemulder, Laurie *piano educator, concert pianist*
Ostrow, Stuart *theatrical producer, educator, writer*
†Perkyns, Jane Elizabeth *music educator, composer, actress*
†Pollack, Howard J. *music educator, writer*
Sing, Doris Anne *music educator*
Stevenson, Ben *artistic director*
†Talbert, Arthur Thomas *music educator*
†Welch, Stanton *performing company executive*

Huntsville
Cesario, Robert James *music educator, performer*
†McInturf, William Matthew *music educator*
†Plugge, Scott Douglas *music educator, saxophonist*
Russell, George Haw *video production company executive*

Irving
Allen, Barbara Ann *musician, educator, personnel contractor*
Milgrim, Samuel G. *television producer*
†Tonelli, Mark Louis *performer, composer, music educator*

Katy
†Golka, Anna Maria *musician, educator*

Keene
Beary, Shirley Lorraine *retired music educator*

Kilgore
†Neal, Paul *music educator*

Killeen
†Bryan, Arthur Lee *music educator*

Kingsville
Hessong, Cindy Hoch *music educator*

Kingwood
†Hagen, Barbara C. *music educator*

Lewisville
Mebane, Barbara Margot *artistic director, choreographer*

Livingston
Gordon, Pamela Ann Wence *pianist*

Longview
Haymes, Jerry Lynn *entertainment industry executive*

Lorena
Maricle, Robyn LuAnn (Ford) *band director, choir director*

Lubbock
Aker, Suzanne Deverse *physical movement educator*
†Chung, Ya-Li *music educator*
†Dolter, Gerald Thomas *voice educator*
Killian, Janice Kay Nelson *music educator, researcher*
Lucas, Don John *music educator*
†Ode, Arthur Henry, III, *music educator*
van Appledorn, Mary Jeanne *composer, music educator, pianist*

Marshall
†Snowden, James W. *music educator, musician*

Meadowlakes
†Wilcox, Mary Reba *music educator*

Midland
Celia, George *composer, writer*
Powers, Patricia Kennett *piano and organ educator*

Mineral Wells
Warfield, Gerald Alexander *composer, writer*

Nacogdoches
†Jacobsen, Jeffrey Richard *music educator*

Pampa
Cooley, Loralee Coleman *professional storyteller*

Pasadena
Gilley, Mickey Leroy *musician*

Plano
Frock, Scott Joseph *music educator*
Sexton, Karen Kay *piano teacher, singer, actress*
Thompson, Joshua A. *music educator*

Prairie View
†Wyatt, Lucius Reynolds, Sr., *music educator*

Richardson
Anderson, John Kerby *talk show host*
†Murphy, Priscilla Parrish *music educator*
†Riccio, Thomas Patrick *theater director*

Rockwall
Wallace, Mary Elaine *opera director, author*

San Angelo
†Curtin, David *music educator*

San Antonio
†Carroll, John Arthur *musician, educator*
Dowdy, Eugene Brown *music educator*
†Hornsby, David McMillan *musician, music educator*
†Jiménez, Leonardo *popular accordionist*
Masinter, Thomas Alan *composer*
†Noble, Ron Raymond *musician, educator*
Oppenheim, Martha Kunkel *pianist, educator*
Peters, Richard Spencer *musician*
Robertson, Sterling Clifton *music educator, pianist*
Wilkins, Christopher Putnam *conductor*
Worman, James Vincent *music educator*

San Marcos
†Laumer, Jack C *music educator, trumpet player*
†Nelms, Morris Howard *musician, educator*
†Schmidt, John Charles *music educator*

Sherman
Duhaime, Ricky Edward *music educator, woodwind specialist*

Snyder
†Tune, Barbara Ann *music educator*

Spring
Howard, Gerry Rea *music educator, singer, classical musician*

Stephenville
†Legan, Pamela June *music educator, elementary school educator*

Sugar Land
Milner, Matthew A. *music educator*

The Woodlands
Blume, Shane L. *music educator*
Crain, Richard Charles *school district music director, retired*

Tyler
†Cooper, Kelli D. *music educator*
Hatfield, James Allen *theater arts educator, administrator*
Rogers, Cheryl Lynn *music and dance educator*
†Rumbley, Philip Lee *music educator, musician, photographer*

Waco
Colvin, Herbert, Jr., (Otis Herbert Colvin) *musician, educator*
†Ullman, Beth Robin *vocalist, voice educator*

Waxahachie
†Fulmer, Daniel A. *music educator, composer*
†Gallo, Tony Giovanni *musician, educator*

Webster
Dickard-Green, Roxanne Lynn *choreographer, dance educator*

Wharton
†George, Lila Gene Plowe Kennedy *music educator*
†Giovanoni, Stephen Francis *music educator*

Whitehouse
Baker, Rebecca Louise *musician, music educator, consultant*

UTAH

Bountiful
†King, Chad Lavere *music educator*

Cedar City
Leibovit, Arnold L. *film producer, director*

Kaysville
Hendricks, Steven Ron *music educator*

Ogden
†Yang, Yu-Jane *music educator*

Orem
Hatch, David Glen *musician, educator*
Soelberg, Diane *music educator*

Park City
†Huhnke, Jr., Billy Gene *music educator*

Provo
†Brown, Shauna Kirsti *music educator, researcher, composer*
†Clayton, April Diane *music educator, flutist*
†Durham, Thomas L. *music educator, director*
Jaccard, Jerry-Louis *music educator, translator*

Salt Lake City
†Conner, Heather J. *music educator*
†Goodro, Julie Nichols *music educator*
†Graham, Patricia Kelsey *music educator, writer, composer*
Morey, Charles Leonard, III, *theatrical director*
Osborne, Christine Megan *musician, educator*
†Roens, Steven Thomas *music educator, dean*
†Romney-Manookin, Elaine Clive *music educator, composer*

Sandy
George, Mary Gae *music educator*

Springdale
Bimstein, Phillip Kent *composer*

Sundance
Grant, Raymond Thomas *arts administrator*

Woods Cross
†Blackley, Cheryl Ann *freelance/self-employed music educator, musician*
†Hendriksen, Neil Evan *music educator*

VERMONT

Brattleboro
Brofsky, Howard *musician, music educator*

Burlington
†Schneider, Wayne J. *music history educator, organist*
†Toner, Donald Thomas *music educator*

Johnson
Whitehill, Angela Elizabeth *artistic director*

Marlboro
†Brelsford, Edmund Munger, III, *musician, educator*

Middlebury
†Clemmons, Francois Scarborough *vocalist*
Varricchio, Louis *radio and television producer, science writer, personality, journalist, journalist*

North Bennington
Neuman, Maxine Darcy *cellist, educator*

Norwich
Stetson, Eugene William, III, *film producer*

Shelburne
†Chukhman, Nella *music educator*

Tunbridge
Stewart, Donald George *musician, music industry executive, composer*

Weston
Stettler, Stephen F. *performing company executive*

VIRGINIA

Afton
Edwards, Virginia Davis *music educator, concert pianist*

Alexandria
†Meserole, Lisa Christine *music educator*

Annandale
Hudson, William L. *conductor*

Arlington
Mc Donald, Gail Faber *musician, educator*
†Orkis, Lambert *musician, music educator*
Southern, Hugh *retired performing arts manager*

Burke
Ward, Barry Lee *music educator, musician*

Charlottesville
Bishop, Ruth Ann *coloratura soprano, voice educator*
Chapel, Robert Clyde *stage director, theater educator*
†Ross, Walter Beghtol *music educator, composer*

Chesapeake
†Grifa, Robert James *music educator*
Hoster-Burandt, Norma J. *musician, fundraiser*

Chester
Gray, Frederick Thomas, Jr., ('Rick Gray) *actor, educator, playwright*

Fairfax
Hilbrink, William John *violinist*
†Kim-Yi, Sungsook *music educator, pianist*
†Mann, Laura A. *soprano*
†Miller, Patricia A. *music educator, opera and concert artist*
Negron, Jaime *performing arts center administrator, real estate agent*

Falls Church
Butler, Quincy Gasque *musician*
Inzana, Barbara Ann *professional musician, educator*

Farmville
†Kinzer, Charles Edward *music educator*

Hampton
Edmonds, Michael Darnell *music educator, educator*
†Harris, Carl G. *music educator*

Harrisonburg
Arthur, Thomas Hahn *theater educator, director*
Hedrick, Eric Todd *musician, educator*
†Reid, Susan L. *conductor*

Herndon
†Walker, Lawrence Howard, Jr., *music educator, department chairman*

Lancaster
Spiers, Robert Franklin *music educator*

Leesburg
†Mahood, Ken *music educator*

Lexington
†Brodie, John *music educator*
Young, Bruce Kenneth *film director*

Lynchburg
†Kerr, Stephen Paul *music educator*
Quakenbush, Brian Clay *music educator*

Manassas
†Cznadel, John Paul *music educator*

Martinsville
Kidd Hill, Leonice Thompson *musician, writer*

Mc Lean
Skantze, Pat *model, consultant*
Youngs, William Ellis *motion picture engineer, projectionist*

Mechanicsville
McEntire, Jean Reynolds *music educator*

Midlothian
McCarney, William Christopher *music educator*
†Yohe, David Edward *music educator*

Moneta
Pfeuffer, Robert John *musician*

Newport News
†Crane, Martha Beavers *music educator*
†Trachuk, Lillian Elizabeth *music educator*

Norfolk
Braswell, Ronald Lee *music educator, tenor*
†Broadbent, Arthur, III, *music educator*
†Kasparov, Andrey R. *composer, pianist, conductor, educator*
Mark, Peter *director, conductor*
Musgrave, Thea *composer, conductor*
†Myers, Ronald J. *music educator*
†Nixon, Patricia Saunders *music educator, performer*

Oak Hill
†Ritter, Elza K. *music educator*

Oakton
Drummond, Carol Cramer *voice educator, singer, artist, writer*

Radford
Camphouse, Mark David *music educator, composer, conductor*
James, Clarity (Carolyne Faye James) *mezzo-soprano*
†Phillips, David B. *music educator, composer*

Reston
Hepworth-Woolston, Connie Jo *choreographer*
Thayer, Edwin Cabot *musician*

Richmond
†Bray, Patricia Shannon *music educator, musician, small business owner*
Campbell, Neal Franklin *music educator*
Carlton, Buzz (Clyde Gordon Carlton Jr.) *singer, songwriter, entertainer, recording artist*
Hammel, Alice Maxine *music educator*
Lohuis, Ardyth June *musician, educator*
†Riehl, Jeffrey S. *music educator*
Winslett, Stoner *artistic director*

Roanoke
Hartless, Keith D. *music educator*
Milam, Michael Ray *music educator*
Sitton, Michael *musician, educator*

Salem
†Crowder, Rebecca Byrum *music educator, elementary school educator*

Springfield
Eastman, Donna Kelly *composer, music educator*

Staunton
Balsley, Philip Elwood *entertainer*

Stephens City
†Amos, George *music educator, coach*

Sterling
Jefferson, Sandra Traylor *choreographer, ballet coach*

Stuart
Coleman, Lawrence Gerald, II, *music educator*

Sweet Briar
Green, Jonathan David *music educator, composer, conductor*

Vienna
Kinsolving, Sylvia Crockett *musician, educator*

Virginia Beach
†Hardy, Romayne Adams *music educator*
Krudop, Donald W. *music educator, choral director*
Panoff, Stephen Edward *music educator*
†Prescott, David L. C., Jr., *music educator*
Rigg, Richard Lee *church musician, composer, music educator*

Williamsburg
Williamson, Michael Allen *music educator*

Winchester
Dumm, Robert Wayne *musician, educator, writer*
†Ruiz-Bernal, Gabriel *concert pianist, music educator*
Russell Jr., John Wallace *composer, educator*
†Suverkrop, Bard *vocalist, voice educator*

WASHINGTON

Auburn
†Thornton, Laird Michael *music educator, baritone*

Bellingham
Larner, Daniel M. *theater educator, playwright, author*
Whyte, Nancy Marie *performing arts educator*

Blaine
Cox, Gregory Allen *musician*

Bothell
McConnell, Sarah Stacey *film producer, French language educator*

Bremerton
Welle, Talman Jamison *music educator*

Centralia
†Fast, Linda Lee *music educator*
†Hansen, Bruce Lynn *retired music educator*

Clarkston
Torgerson, Linda Belle *music educator*

Cle Elum
Wampler, Stephen George *music educator*

East Wenatchee
†Marion, Sarah Kathleen *music educator*

Ellensburg
†Snedeker, Jeffrey Leighton *music educator*

Endicott
Ray, Billy John, Jr., *music educator*

Everett
Rimbach, Evangeline Lois *retired music educator*

Freeland
Berg, Doris Veron (Doris Veron McKinstry) *musician, educator*

Issaquah
Hunt, Robert William *theatrical producer, arts management consultant*

Kirkland
Toy, Mary L. *music educator*

Lacey
Louis, Glenn *music educator*

Mercer Island
Barlin, L. Paul *dance director*
†Huling, Timothy Oliver *composer, educator*

Port Angeles
†Gailey, Douglas Mitchell *music educator*
†Grier, George Edward *music educator, musician*

Pullman
Kelley, Margaret Mary *music educator, musician*
†Tseng, Chi-Ting *music educator*
†Yasinitsky, Gregory Walter *music educator*

Quincy
†Silk, Michael Loren *music educator*

Seattle
Beale, Jane Guthrie *music publisher, music educator, pianist*
Chilgren, D. Dianne *concert pianist, piano teacher*
Chung, Sung-Sook (Yoojin) *music educator*
†Demorest, Steven McGregor *music educator*
†Denke, Conrad William *motion picture producer*
Elyn, Mark *retired opera singer, educator*
Forbes, David Craig *musician*
Humphries, Edna Bevan *music educator, choir director*
Jenkins, Speight *opera company executive, writer*
Jones, Samuel Leander *conductor*
Loso, Christi Ball *television producer*
†Matesky, Nancy Lee *music educator*
Moore, Benjamin *theatrical producer*
†Mull, Robert W. *filmmaker, curator*
Ozaki, Nancy Junko *performance artist, performing arts educator*
Russell, Francia *ballet director, educator*
Ryder, Hal *theater educator, director*
Staryk, Steven Sam *violinist, concertmaster, educator*
†Stowell, Kent *ballet director*
Talachian, Reza *filmmaker*
Van Lierop, John Henry, Jr., *music educator*

Shoreline
†Kim, Steve *music educator, musician*
†Reid, Doug B. *music educator*

Silverdale
†Raum, Mary Beth *ballet educator*

Snohomish
Philpott, Larry La Fayette *horn player*

South Hill
†Minkler, Douglas Glen *music educator*

Spokane
†Baker, Sylvia Halldorson *music educator*
Coffee, Gale Furman *musician, educator*
Fowler, Betty Janmae *dance company director, editor*
†Halvorson, Marjory *opera director*
Phillips, John Grant (Jack Phillips) *theatre director*
Pugh, Kyle Mitchell, Jr., *musician, retired music educator*
Strauch, Richard C. *music educator*

Tacoma
Reid, Clement Michael *composer, educator, musician*

Vancouver
†Hobbs, Gary G *music educator*

Washougal
Harness, William Edward *tenor*

Wenatchee
Rappé, Teri Wahl *piano educator*

Woodinville
Sanders, Richard Kinard *actor*

WEST VIRGINIA

Athens
Westbrook, Gary Wayne *music educator, consultant*

Bethany
†Collaros, Pandel Lee *music educator*

Charleston
†Brightbill, Janet M. *music educator*
Cooper, Grant *composer, conductor, music educator*
Helfrich, Paul A. *orchestra executive*

Fairmont
O'Connor, John Edward *theater educator, director*

Inwood
Rizzetta, Carolyn Teresa *musical instrument, sound recording entrepreneur*

Mannington
Schumacher, Theresa Rose (Terry Schumacher) *singer, musician, legal assistant*

Morgantown
Kinsey, Donna Lee *music educator*
Wilson, Mary Alice *violinist, music teacher*

Parkersburg
Gunter, Norma *artistic director*

Salem
Raad, Virginia *pianist, lecturer*

Shenandoah Junction
Showen Jr., Donald Eugene *music educator*

Spanishburg
Jenks, William Robert *music educator*

WISCONSIN

Antigo
Dewey, Jeff D. *music educator*

Appleton
†Boncher, Austin J. *music educator, director*

Aurora
†Thurlow, Stephen *music educator, department chairman*

Cadott
Blair, David Chalmers Leslie *composer, writer*

Cameron
†Joosten, Michael John *music educator*

Cashton
†Johnson, David Paul *music educator*

De Pere
Tepe, Judith Mildred *vocal music teacher, choral director*

Delavan
Lepke, Charma Davies *musician, educator*

Dodgeville
Dentinger, Ronald Lee *comedian, speaker, freelance writer*

Dunbar
†Gerdt, Barry Lee *music educator*
†Habing, Brett William *music educator*

Eau Claire
Cecchini, Penelope Crawford *piano educator*
Heidel, Richard Mark *music educator*
Patterson, Donald Lee *music educator*
†Yasuda, Nobuyoshi *music educator*
†Young, Jerry Allen *music educator*

Fall River
†Barker, David Matthew *music educator*

Fond du Lac
†Demerath, Julie Ellen *music educator*

Green Bay
Welhouse, Lucille Marie *musician, educator*

Greenfield
McKillip, Patricia Claire *operatic soloist*

Horicon
Gasner, Donn Allan *music educator*

Kenosha
Crowley, James Francis *composer, educator*
†Saucedo, Matthew Dan *college band director, counselor*

La Crosse
Schorr, Timothy Brian *music educator, concert pianist*

Madison
De Main, John *orchestra musical director*
Faulkner, Julia Ellen *opera singer*
Mackie, Richard H. *orchestra executive*
†Manoogian, Vartan *musician, educator*
Rosser, Annetta Hamilton *composer*
†Wengler, Michael J. *music educator*

Menasha
Anderson, Kenneth Fritz *dramatic arts educator*

Menomonee Falls
Chicorel, Ralph *composer, lyricist, playwright*

Middleton
Erichsen-Hubbard, Isabel Janice *music educator*
Semmes, Sally Peterson *choreographer, educator*
†Taylor, Christopher Philip *pianist*

Milwaukee
Beliavsky, Yuri *violinist, educator*
Blau, Richard Miles (Dick Blau) *performing arts educator, photographer, film director*
†Cheatham, Wallace McClain *music educator*
Cook, Wayne Evans *music educator*
Crocker, Ray Dean *musician, musical director*
Delfs, Andreas *conductor, musical director*
Downey, John Wilham *composer, pianist, conductor, educator*
Harris, Christine *dance company executive*
Jirovec, Mary Ann *music educator*
Mannisto, Richard Todd *music educator*
†Pink, Michael *performing company executive*
Rosenblatt, Suzanne Maris *performance artist, poet, visual artist*
Samson, Richard Max *theatre director, investment/real estate executive*
Uecker, Bob *actor, radio announcer, former baseball player, TV personality*
Verhaalen, Marion *music educator*

Neenah
†Orm, Sally S. *music educator, consultant*

New Berlin
Duszynski-Waldbillig, Cynthia *piano teacher, performer, adjudicator*

Oregon
Latimer, James Harold *percussionist, conductor, composer, consultant, educator*

Oshkosh
McWilliams, Robert Lindsay *music educator, musician, conductor*

Platteville
Dennis, Gregory James *music educator, secondary school educator*

Racine
Schoening, Ruth Irene *retired music educator, musician*

Reedsburg
Miotke, David Roy *music educator*

Rice Lake
Strong, Linda Louise *music educator*

River Falls
Hedahl, Gorden Orlin *theatre educator, university dean*

Stevens Point
†Holland, Patricia Christine *music educator, musician*
†Teeple, Scott D. *conductor, music educator, director*

Superior
McKnight, Patricia Gayle *musician, artist, writer, educator*

Sussex
†Ryan, Sandra C. *music educator, musician*

Washington Island
Schweikert, Norman Carl *retired musician*

Watertown
†Townsend, Rick David *music educator, writer*

Whitewater
†Ellenwood, Christian Kent *music educator*

WYOMING

Casper
†Cowell, Jennifer M. *music educator*
Unruh, Eric W. *music educator, academic administrator*

Cheyenne
†Hoffman, Steven Arlie *musician*
Woodman, Lucy Rhodes *music educator*

Dubois
Glasser, Pamela Jean *musician, music educator*

Lander
†Bakke, Luanne Kaye *music educator*

Torrington
Hamer, Jeanne Marie Huntington *soprano, retired voice educator*
†Bly, Carl Anthony *retired music educator*

TERRITORIES OF THE UNITED STATES

PUERTO RICO

Bayamon
Ortiz, William *composer, music educator*

San Juan
Guilermo, Figueroa *conductor*
San Miguel, Lolita *artistic director*

CANADA

ALBERTA

Calgary
Monk, Allan James *baritone*
Raeburn, Andrew Harvey *performing arts association executive, record producer*

BRITISH COLUMBIA

Vancouver
Murray, Anne *singer*

Victoria
Turner, Robert Comrie *composer*

MANITOBA

Winnipeg
Birtwhistle, Tara *dancer*
Chang, Johnny W. *dancer*
Corrales, Jesús *dancer*
Lewis, André Leon *artistic director*
Reyes, Reyneris *dancer*
Vargas, Arionel P. *dancer*

ONTARIO

Kitchener
Coles, Graham *conductor, composer*
Eldred, Gerald Marcus *retired performing arts association executive*

London
†Brian, Jackson *artistic director*
William, David *director, actor*

Ottawa
Gillingham, Bryan Reginald *music educator*

Saint Catharines
Oliphant, Betty *retired ballet school director*

Toronto
Antonijevic, Aleksandar *dancer*
Beckwith, John *musician, composer, educator*
Bertram, Victoria Elaine *dancer*
Boorne, Ryan *ballet dancer*
†Bradshaw, Richard James *general director of opera company*
Colgrass, Michael Charles *composer*
Egoyan, Atom *film director*
Eklof, Svea Christine *ballet dancer*
Freedman, Harry *composer*
Goh, Chan Hon *ballerina*
Hodgkinson, Greta *dancer*
Hon Goh, Chan *dancer*
Israelievitch, Jacques H. *violinist, conductor*
Kudelka, James *choreographer, artistic director*
Marrié, William *dancer*
Nan Yu, Xiao *dancer*
†Oundjian, Peter *conductor*
Rasky, Harry *producer, director, writer*
Rodriguez, Sonia *dancer*
Schramek, Tomas *ballet dancer, educator*
Shaw, Andrew R. *performing arts association administrator*
†Shearing, George Albert *pianist, composer*
Sirman, Robert *performing company executive*
Staines, Mavis Avril *artistic director, ballet principal*
Stefanschi, Sergiu *dancer*
Van Der Wyst, Geon *dancer*
Yu, Xiao Nan *dancer*

QUEBEC

Montreal
Bissonnette, Anik *dancer*
Girard, Francois *film director*
Guérard, Geneviève *dancer*
Gulkin, Harry *arts administrator, film producer*
†Lacombe, Jacques *conductor, music director*
Lagacé, Bernard *performing company executive*
†Pankov, Gradimir Krunislav *ballet artistic director*
Radacovský, Mário *dancer*
Von Gencsy, Eva *dancer, choreographer, educator*

Calgary
†Grand-Maitre, Jean *performing company executive*

Montreal
†Labadie, Bernard *performing company executive*
†Lock, Edouard *performing company executive*
†Moss, David *conductor*

MEXICO

Mexico City
Soberon Kuri, Alejandro *performing company executive*

AUSTRALIA

Clayton
De Wilde, Craig James *music educator, researcher*

Darlinghurst
Davis, Judy *actress*

Collins, Joan Henrietta *actress*
Collins, Kathleen Anne *artistic director*
Collins, Sandra Kay *pianist, composer, music educator*
†Compton, Michael *music educator*
Cone, Dennis Allen *music educator*
Cone, Edward Toner *composer, emeritus music educator*
†Connors, Loren M. *composer, guitarist*
Consoli, Marc-Antonio *composer*
Constantine, Michael *actor*
Coogan, Mary Ellen *musician, educator*
Cooper, Hal *television director*
†Coppola, Francis Ford *film director, producer, writer*
†Cordell, Bobbie B. *music educator*
†Cordell, Philip Granvile *music educator, musician*
Corto, Diana Maria *lyric-coloratura, producer, educator*
Corvino, Ernesta *ballet dancer*
Cosby, Bill *actor, entertainer*
Cosenza, Arthur George *opera director*
Cossa, Dominic Frank *baritone*
Costa-Gavras, (Constantin Gavras) *director, writer*
Cotrubas, Ileana *opera singer, retired lyric soprano*
Coukis, Peter George *musician, composer*
Cox, Richard Garner *music educator*
†Cromwell, James *actor*
Crosby, Julie Lynne *theater industry executive, educator*
Crosby, Norman Lawrence *comedian*
†Cross, Richard B. *bass, educator*
†Crotty Guile, Julianne Marie *musician, educator, composer, writer*
Crouse, Lindsay *actress*
†Crow, Todd William *pianist*
Cruise, Tom (Tom Cruise Mapother IV) *actor*
Cruz-Romo, Gilda *soprano*
†Cuaron, Alfonso *film director*
Cummins, Wilma Jeanne *actress*
Cunningham, Michael Gerald *composer, music educator*
Currier, Ruth *dancer, choreographer and educator*
†Curry, Daniel Francis Myles *filmmaker*
Curson, Theodore *musician*
†Curtis, Linda S *vocal instructor*
†Curtis, Peter Andrew *music educator, musician*
Dabbs, Henry Erven *television and film producer, educator*
Dafoe, Willem *actor*
Dailey, Irene *actress, educator*
Dalberg, Anabelle Hanson *church organist, piano and organ teacher*
Danaher, Mallory Millett (Mallory Jones) *actress, photographer, film producer, theater producer*
†Danes, Claire *actress*
Daniels, Ronald George *theater director*
Daniels, Sydney Robert *theater director, educator*
D'Arcangelo, Marcia Diane *educational media producer*
Darling, Robert Edward *designer, stage director*
†Davis, Carla Mia *music educator*
†Deal, Gordon Richard *music educator, musician, real estate agent*
De Angelis, Rosemary Eleanor *actress*
de Blasis, James Michael *artistic director, producer, stage director*
Debus, Eleanor Viola *retired business management company executive*
De Felitta, Frank Paul *producer, writer, director*
de Lattre, Candace Lorraine *singer, voice teacher*
†Demissie, Yemane I. *filmmaker*
Dench, Judith Olivia *actress*
†Denny, Jera Cecilia Jane Elizabeth *musician, graphics designer*
De Rossi, Julie Anne *music promoter, entrepreneur, freelance editor, retail consultant*
Deutsch, Didier (Delaunoy Deutsch) *music producer, writer*
Deutsch, Herbert Arnold *music educator*
Deutz, Natalie Rubinstein *actress, consultant*
Devlin, Michael Coles *bass-baritone*
†DeVries, Linda Jane *music educator*
Diaz, Oscar, Jr., *voice educator, music company executive*
†DiCaprio, Leonardo *actor*
Dick, James Cordell *concert pianist*
Diemer, Emma Lou *composer, music educator*
DiGirolamo, Glen Francis *actor*
†Ding, Ai-Yue *conductor, music educator*
Dishy, Bob *actor*
Dixon, William Robert *musician, composer, educator*
†Dobrzanski, Slawomir *music educator*
Donaldson, Myrtle Norma *music educator, musician*
Dornin, Catharine Quillen *music educator, concert pianist*
†Dorsky, Nathaniel *filmmaker*
†Downs, Leslie G *music educator, musician*
†Dowty, Marcus Duaine *music educator*
Doyle, Gillian *actress*
Drake, Ervin Maurice *composer, author*
Drozd, Leszek Stanislaw *composer, performer*
Duigan, John *film director*
Dunkerley, Erna Lee *musician*
Dunlap, Richard Donovan *artistic director*
Dyal, Edith Colvin *retired music educator*
Dysart, Richard A. *actor*
Eagle, Jack *commercial actor, comedian*
Easterly, Susan *music and humanities educator*
Ebb, Fred *lyricist, librettist*
†Edwards, Anthony *actor*
Edwards, Ryan Hayes *baritone*
Ehrling, Sixten *orchestra conductor*
†Eisenberg, Daniel *filmmaker*
†Elfman, Jenna *actress*
Elgart, Larry Joseph *orchestra leader*
Elikann, Lawrence S. (Larry Elikann) *television and film director*
Elizondo, Hector *actor*
Ellsworth, Frederick Lee *music educator*
Epcar, Richard Michael *actor, writer, director*
Erbe, Yvonne Mary *music educator, marketing specialist, guidance counselor*
†Escobar, Elaine Ofelia *television producer, writer*
†Evans, Teresa Rinaldi *music educator, vocalist*
Evdokimova, Eva *prima ballerina assoluta, choreographer, director, producer, actress*
†Everett, Aubrey Leigh *musician*
Everett, Tom *actor*
†Fabian, D'Arline D. *music educator*
Fairleigh, James Parkinson *music educator*
†Fan, Cong *music educator*
†Fare, Elizabeth Carol *music educator*
Feinstein, Martin *performing arts consultant, art director*
Fennell, Tracy Lee *music educator, composer*
†Field, Sally *actress*
Fields, Freddie *producer, agent*
†Fiennes, Ralph Nathaniel *actor*
Filerman, Michael Herman *television producer*
First, Craig Patrick *composer, educator*
Fischer, Clare *composer*
Fischer, William Samuel *composer, lecturer*
Fish, Brian R *music educator*
†Fleming, Brian Anthony *musician, educator*
Fleming, Rhonda *actress, singer, humanitarian*
†Floyd-Hooper, Carol Ann *musician, educator*
Foglia, Stephen Phillip *musician, recording industry executive*
Foldi, Andrew Harry *retired singer, educator*
Folsom, Virginia Jean *music educator*
†Fonda, Peter *actor, director, producer*
†Ford, Harrison *actor*
Ford, Nancy Louise *composer, scriptwriter*
Forest, Eva Brown *songwriter, producer, performer, publisher*
Forsythe, Henderson *actor*
Foss, Lukas *composer, conductor, pianist*
†Foster, Sonja Marguerite *musician, educator*
Franciosa, Anthony (Anthony Papaleo) *actor*
Frankish, Brian Edward *film producer, director*
†Freston, Thomas E. *cable television programming executive*
Fried, Emanuel Joseph *actor, writer*
†Friedrich, Su G. *filmmaker, educator*
Friendly, Ed *television producer*
†Fucuals, Ronald H. *conductor, director*
Fuerstner, Fiona Margaret Anne *ballet company executive, ballet educator*
†Fukasawa, Natsuki *music educator*
Fullenwider, Nancy Vrana *music composer, dance educator, pianist*
Galante, Jane Hohfeld *pianist, music historian*
Galt, John William *actor, writer*
Garber, Victor *stage and film actor*
Gardner, Wanda Joyce *harpist, business owner, home educator*
Garniss, Joan Brewster *musician, educator*
†Gascoine-Molina, Jill Viola *actress, writer*
†Gazaway, Barbara Ann *music educator, art educator*
Gegelmann, Sharon Fay *piano teacher*
Gehm, Denise Charlene *ballerina, arts administrator*
Geller, Norman Harvey *music arranger, conductor*
Gelman, Larry *actor, film director*
†Gere, Richard *actor*
†Giannascoli, B. Greg *musician, entrepreneur*
Gilbert, Melissa *actress*
†Glover, Eryn M. *music educator*
Glynn, Carlin (Carlin Masterson) *actress*
Godsey, Jeffrey Lynn *actor, educator*
†Goen, Bob *television show host*
†Goetzinger, Laurel Eldredge *music educator*
Goldberg, Alan Michael *music educator*
†Goldberg, Whoopi (Caryn Johnson) *actress*
Goldin, Marion Freedman *television news producer, reporter*
Goldman, Mia *film editor*
†Gonzales, Gregory *music educator*
Goodman, Erika *dancer, actress*
Gordon, Marjorie *lyric coloratura soprano, opera producer, teacher*
Grant, Alexander Marshall *ballet director*
Grant, Merrill Theodore *producer*
Graves, Lorraine Elizabeth *dancer, educator, coach*
Great, Don Charles *composer, music company executive*
†Greco, Christopher Jon *musician, composer, educator*
Greenberg, Marvin *retired music educator*
†Greer, Suzanne Michelle *music educator*
Gregory, Claire Distelhorst *television producer*
†Grimes, Gary A. *music educator*
Grody, Donald *actor, judge, lawyer, arbitrator*
Grosbard, Ulu *director*
Groskopf, Aubrey Bud *motion picture television executive, lawyer*
Gruen, Margaret *actress*
†Gulledge, Irene O. *retired music educator*
Gustafson, Craig Thomas *theatrical director, playwright, graphic artist*
Guter, James L. *music educator*
Gutierrez, Gerald Andrew *theatrical director*
†Gyuras, Brian Joseph *music educator*
†Haar, Franklin Duane *musician, writer*
†Hain, Patricia A. *music educator*
Hajost, James E. *music educator, conductor, composer*
Hall, James Stanley *jazz guitarist, composer*
Hall, Monty *television producer, actor*
†Haney, Marlene Carol *music educator*
Hankin, Lawrence Alan *actor*
†Harding, Laura J. *music educator*
Harlow, Elizabeth Mary *retired music educator*
Harper, Richard Henry *film producer, director*
Harris, Robert A. *retired music educator*
Harris, Theodore Clifford *songwriter, music publisher*
Hathcock, John Edward *vocalist*
Hathorne, Gayle Gene *musician, family historian*
Hay, George Austin *actor, artist, musician, director*
†Hayek, Salma *actress*
†Heche, Anne *actress*
Helgenberger, Marg *actress*
Heller, George Norman *music educator*
Hendl, Walter *conductor, pianist, composer*
Henes, Donna *celebration artist, ritualist, writer*
Herbig, Günther *conductor*
Hergo, Jane Antoinette *piano educator, composer*
Herson, Arlene Rita *producer, journalist, television program host, radio commentator and panelist*
Hicks, Ronald Alvin *music educator*
Hicks, William Hampton *pianist, conductor, voice coach*
Hill, Stan Wayne *video producer*
Hingle, Pat *actor*
Hodges, Ann *actress, singer, dancer*
Hoggard, Lara Guldmar *conductor, educator*
Holland, Samuel Stinson *music educator, writer, musician*
Holliday, Polly Dean *actress*
Holm, Celeste *actress*
Holm, Sir Ian *actor*
Holman, Bill *composer*
Holsinger, Adena Seguine *music educator, community volunteer*
Hooper, Josh *screen actor, director, media producer, writer*
Hooper, Robert Alexander *television producer, international educator*
Hopkins, Cynthia *composer*
Hopkins, Robert Elliott *music educator*
Horisberger, Don Hans *conductor, musician*
†Hornyak, Roy Robert *music educator, minister*
Horsman, Lenore Lynde (Eleanora Lynde) *soprano, educator, actress*
Horton, Patricia Mathews *artist, violist and violinist*
Horvath, Imre Gabor *television producer and director*
Hosman, Sharon Lee *music educator*
†Hostetter, Elizabeth A. *music educator*
†Houghton, Diane Murley *actor, vocalist*
Houghton, Katharine *actress*
Howard, David *ballet school administrator*
†Howell, Neil *music educator*
†Howell, Thomas Lee *composer, writer*
Hubbard, Elizabeth *actress*
Hudson, Alan C.H. *music educator, tropical fruit farmer*
†Hudson, Kate *actress*
Hughes, Michaela Kelly *actress, dancer*
Hundley, Carol Marie Beckquist *music educator*
Huning, Devon Gray *actress, dancer, audiologist, veterinary technician, photographer, video producer and editor*
†Hymer, Tabitha Kim *music educator, writer, photographer*
†Ibergs, Harry *musician, educator, music company executive*
Ichino, Yoko *ballet dancer*
Indenbaum, Dorothy *musician, researcher*
Inglesi, Noreen Mary *music educator, poet, composer*
Intravaia, Toni *dance educator, journal editor*
Irey, Charlotte York *dance educator*
Irving, George Steven *actor*
Issari, M(ohammad) Ali *film producer, writer, consultant*
Jackson, Michael Joseph *singer*
Jackson, Nagle *stage director, playwright*
†Jackson, Samuel L. *actor*
Janis, Conrad *actor, jazz musician, art dealer, film producer, director*
Jansen, John Carl *recording producer and engineer*
Jarmusch, Jim *director, actor*
Jarrett, Keith *pianist, composer*
Jarvi, Neeme *conductor*
Jeffreys, Rebecca Elizabeth *professional flutist*
†Jelsma, Elizabeth Barbara *music educator*
Jenkin, James Thomas *videotape editor*
Jensen, Nancy Daggett *music educator*
†Johns, Leslie A. *music educator*
Johnson, John Henry *film director, producer, photographer, educator*
†Johnson, Shaun Darrin *music educator*
Jones, Shirley *actress, singer*
†Jones, Tommy Lee *actor*
†Jordan, Bruce Leslie *music educator, musician*
Jordania, Vakhtang *conductor, educator*
†Kåge, Jonas *ballet company artistic director*
Kaiser, Keith Allen *music educator, researcher, conductor*
Kamm, Laurence Richard *television producer, director*
Kane, Michael Joseph *director*
†Kantor, Mary Louise *music educator*
Kaplan, Richard James *producer, director, writer, educator, consultant*
Kasdan, Lawrence Edward *film director, screenwriter*
†Kaspar, Frances Wolf *music educator*
Kavanaugh, Frank James *film producer, educator*
Kaylan, Howard Lawrence *musical entertainer, screenwriter, composer*
Keim, Betty Lou *actress, literary consultant*
Kellaigh, Kathleen *conservatory artistic director*
†Kempskie, Jeffrey T. *music educator*
†Kennedy, Kathleen *film producer*
†Kennedy, Linda Dale *music educator, pianist, organist*
†Kenny, H. Sharie *music educator*
Kent, Gary Warner *film director, writer*
†Kernochan, Sarah M. *film director, scriptwriter, composer*
Kernodle, Robert Gary *dance and exercise ecucator*
Kerr, Forrest David *actor, writer, producer*
†Keysar, Krista Lynn *music educator*
†Kiefer, Anna Jacquelynn *music educator*
†Kietzman, Kris *music educator*
†Kim, Hwa-Jin *music educator*
†Kim, Nicole Y. *music educator, pianist*
Kimball, Spencer D. *music educator, small business owner*
King, Deborah Simpkin *music, choral, vocal educator*
Kirby, Frank Eugene *musicology educator, author, editor*
Kirchner, Lisa Beth *vocalist, actress*
Kirkland, Geoffrey Alan *motion picture production designer*
†Klampe, Craig Allen *music educator*
Klein, Stephen Thomas *performing arts executive*
Kline, James Edgar *actor*
†Knieser, Catherine *music educator*
†Koch, Michael Arthur *music educator*
Koerber, Dolores Jean *music educator, musician*
Komlos, Peter *violinist*
Kopelson, Arnold *film producer*
Koszarski, Richard *film historian, writer*
Kriegsman, Sali Ann *arts executive, artistic director, writer, consultant*
Kroll, David Lee *music educator*
†Krueger, Karli Ann *music educator*
Kudrow, Lisa *actress*
†Kuo, Michelle Chen (Chou-hsia Chen) *musician, educator*
Kupferman, Meyer *composer*
†Kurahashi, Yuko *theater educator*
†Kurdi, Ramsey *music educator*
Kutrzeba, Joseph S. *theatrical and film producer, director*
Lacey, Aaron Michael *actor, director, screenwriter, executive producer*
Ladd, Diane Rose *actress*
†Lane, Diane *actress*
Langley, Joellen S. *music educator*
Leatto, Renne *director, writer*
†LeBlanc, Matt *actor*
†Lee, Anne *music educator*
Lee, Christopher Frank Carandini *actor, author, singer*
Lee, Cynthia *television producer, playwright, filmmaker*
Lee, Gwendolin Kuei *retired ballet educator*
Leeves, Jane *actress*
Lefferts, George *producer, writer, director*
†Leiber, Jerry *songwriter*
Leoni, Tea (Elizabeth Tea Pantaleoni) *actress*
Lepage, Robert *actor, director, playwright*
Lesser, Felice A. *choreographer, dancer, playwright, screenwriter, filmmaker*
Leventhal, Nathan *performing company executive, lawyer, municipal official*
†Levine, Alan J. *entertainment company executive*
Levitas, Miriam C. Strickman *documentary filmmaker, designer, consultant intergenerational relationships*
Lewis-Griffith, Dorothy Ellen *music educator, pianist*
Lewitzky, Bella *choreographer*
Leybourn, Carol *musician, educator*
Lichtenstein, Harvey *performing arts executive*
†Light, April Gene *music educator*
†Lim, Jerry Teik-Chuan *composer, music educator*
Lind, Lanette Mina *piano teacher*
†Linden, Gordon L. *music educator*
Lindorff, Joyce Zankel *harpsichordist*
†Lipke, William Alan *music educator, musician*
Lister, Linda Joanne *music educator, composer, vocalist*
Little, Loren Everton *musician, ophthalmologist*
Little, Mildred Miller *music educator, soloist*
†Liu, Kexi *music educator*
Liu, Margaret C. *music educator*
†Livengood, Stanley *music educator, conductor*
Livingstone, Trudy Dorothy Zweig *dancer, educator*
Lockhart, Aileene Simpson *retired dance, kinesiology, physical education educator and editor*
Loffredi, Deborah Lynn *music educator, actress*
†Lomax, Elisabeth Louise *music educator*
Longstreet, Renee Schonfeld *television writer, producer*
Loring, Gloria Jean *singer, actress*
Lovecchio, Joseph A. *music educator, conductor*
LoVetri, Jeannette Louise *voice educator*
†Lovett, David M. *musician, acoustical engineer*
Lubin, Steven *concert pianist, musicologist*
†Lubman, Brad *conductor, composer, music educator*
†Lucas, Joan Dawson *music educator*
Lucas, Nancy Broome *music educator*
Ludwig, Christa *mezzo-soprano*
†Lukasiewicz, Paul Manus *music educator*
Lupu, Radu *pianist*
Lynn, Bonnie Jane *music educator*
†Lynn, Enid *retired artistic director*
Mabee, Sandra Ivonne *timpanist, percussionist, educator, clergyman*
†Macan, Edward L. *music educator*
Madeira, Francis King Carey *conductor, educator*
Magno, Gil D. *music educator*
Magor, Louis Roland *conductor*
Maher, Robert Raymond, Jr., *music educator*
†Mahoney, John *actor*
†Malloy, Michael Dennis *radio personality*
Malouf-Cundy, Pamela Bonnie *film editor, video editor*
†Mancell, Donald Wayne *music educator*
†Mancusi, Roberto Francesco Costantino *vocalist, educator*
Mannes, Elena Sabin *film and television producer, director*
Manson, David Joseph *producer, director*
†Marderosian, Armena Pearl *music educator*
Mardis, Richard Lyle *television producer and director, production manager*
†Mariska, Bradley Clayton *composer, musicologist*
Mark, Michael Laurence *retired music educator*
Marks, Bruce *artistic director, choreographer*
†Marsalis, Wynton *musician*
Marsee, Susanne Irene *mezzo-soprano*
Marsh, Joan Knight *educational film, video and computer software company executive, publisher children's books*
Marshall, Peter *actor, singer, game show host*
Martin, James Richard *music educator*
Martin, Leonard Austin, II, *music educator*

Ziegler, Evan Frank *music educator*
†Ziemba, Karen *actress*
†Zohn, Andrew Eliot *musician, music educator*

ARTS: VISUAL

UNITED STATES

ALABAMA

Birmingham
Carmichael, Mary Alice *artist, genealogist*
Keller, Armor *artist, arts advocate*
Price, Rosalie Pettus *artist*

Hayden
Berry, Chris David *artist, writer*

Huntsville
†Simpson, Debra Brashear *artist*

Madison
†Johnson, Kathy Virginia Lockhart *art educator*

Marion
Street, Deborra Lynn *director of fine arts*

Mobile
Clausell, Deborah Deloris *artist, songwriter*

Normal
Dawkins, Jimmie Angela *art educator*

Trussville
Best, Frederick Napier *artist, designer, educator*

ALASKA

Anchorage
Shadrach, Jean Hawkins (Martha Shadrach) *artist*
Smith, Isaac Danial *artist*

Fairbanks
Murakami, Gael Baxley *artist*
Nakoneczny, Michael Martin *artist*

Juneau
DeRoux, Daniel Grady *artist*

ARIZONA

Carefree
Chase, James Keller *retired artist, museum director, educator*

Chino Valley
†Casey, Bonnie Mae *artist, educator*

Clarkdale
Eide, Joel Sylvester *art consultant, appraiser*

Flagstaff
Edgerton, Debra *artist, educator*

Green Valley
de Soto, Ernest Frank *artist, publisher*
Page, John Henry, Jr., *artist, educator*

Lake Montezuma
Burkee, Irvin *artist*

Oracle
Rush, Andrew Wilson *artist*

Paradise Valley
Maxey, Diane Meadows *artist*
McCall, Louise Harrup *artist*

Patagonia
La Noue, Terence David *artist, educator*

Payson
Salomon, Marilyn *artist*

Peoria
Willard, Garcia Lou *artist*

Phoenix
deMatties, Nicholas Frank *artist, art educator*
Dignac, Geny (Eugenia M. Bermudez) *sculptor*
Lewis, Carl Edwin *artist, photographer, designer*
Schaumburg, Donald Roland *art educator, ceramic artist*
Stone, Hazel Anne Decker *artist*

Prescott
Stasack, Edward Armen *artist*

Prescott Valley
Decil, Stella Walters (Del Decil) *artist*

Scottsdale
Fratt, Dorothy *artist*
Gray, Don *artist*
Kleppe, Shirley R. Klein *artist*
Lang, Margo Terzian *artist*
Lloyd, Sally-Heath Fahnestock *artist*
Scholder, Fritz *artist*
Vanier, Jerre Lynn *art director*

Sedona
Darrow, Jane *artist*
Garrison, Gene Kirby *artist, writer, photographer*
Vayanian, Solara Zakeli *artist, educator*

Sun City
Blanchet, Jeanne Ellene Maxant *artist, educator, performer*

Sunsites
Datcu, Ioana *visual artist*

Tempe
Meissinger, Ellen Murray *artist, educator*

Tucson
Conant, Howard Somers *artist, educator*
Constantino, Valerie *artist, writer, art educator*
Flint, Willis Wolfschmidt (Willi Wolfschmidt) *artist, sculptor*
Fountain, Ellen Allgaier *artist, educator*
Hamilton, Ruth Hellmann *design company owner*
Lascelles, Susan *artist*
Matthew, Neil Edward *artist, educator*
Root, Nile *photographer, educator*
Schaffer, Richard E(nos) *artist, registrar*

ARKANSAS

Ashdown
Edmonson, Phyllis Denty *artist*

Berryville
Brown, Frances Louise (Grandma Fran) *artist, art gallery owner*

El Dorado
Cameron-Godsey, Melinda A. Brantley *artist*

Fayetteville
Cockrill, Sherna *artist*
Wilson, Charles Banks *artist*

Garfield
Campbell, Patricia Ann *artist*

Jonesboro
†Allen, William Julius *art history educator*

North Little Rock
Paulsen, Darlyne Evelyn *artist, residential and commercial architectural designer, interior decorator*

State University
Lindquist, Evan *artist, educator*

CALIFORNIA

Acampo
Eger, Marilyn Rae *artist*

Altadena
Bockus, Herman William, Jr., *artist, educator, writer*

Anaheim
†Barkemeijer de Wit, Jeanne Sandra *graphic artist, illustrator, writer, multimedia consultant*
Bennett, Genevieve *artist*
Nelipovich, Sandra Grassi *artist*

Arcadia
Danziger, Louis *graphic designer, educator*

Atascadero
Meyer, Lois Kathryn *graphic artist*

Auburn
Rothwell, Elaine B. *artist*

Bakersfield
Reep, Edward Arnold *artist*

Belmont
Pava, Esther Shub *artist, educator*

Ben Lomond
Johnson-Grauer, Lois Eileen *artist*

Berkeley
Bendix, Jane *artist, author, anthropological illustrator*
Cantor, Rusty Sumner *artist*
Casida, Kati *artist*
Genn, Nancy *artist*
Hack, Elizabeth *artist*
Hartman, Robert Leroy *artist, educator*
Jones, Patricia Bengtson *sculptor*
Kasten, Karl Albert *painter, printmaker, educator*
McNamara, John Stephen *artist, educator*
Miyasaki, George Joji *artist*
Moore, Frank James *artist, educator*
†Polos, Iris Stephanie *artist, art educator*
Rapoport, Sonya *artist*
Simpson, David William *artist, educator*
Sussman, Wendy Rodriguez *artist, educator*
Tanahashi, Kazuaki *artist, writer*
Washburn, Stan *artist*
Webster, Mary Hull *artist, writer*

Beverly Hills
Lewis, Helen Natalie *visual arts advisor*

Bodega
Hedrick, Wally Bill *artist*

Bodega Bay
†Fruiht, Dolores Giustina *artist, educator, poet*

Bolinas
Harris, Paul *sculptor*
Okamura, Arthur Shinji *artist, educator, writer*

Boonville
Hanes, John Ward *sculptor, civil engineer consultant*

Brentwood
Peters, William Frank *art educator*

Cambria
Harden, Marvin *artist, educator*
†Price, Stephen Earl *artist*

Canoga Park
Rosenfeld, Sarena Margaret *artist*

Carmel
Adams, Tracey Linden *artist, educator*
Hobbs, C. Fredric *artist, filmmaker, author*
†Jacobs, Ralph, Jr., *artist*

Carmel Valley
Sands, Sharon Louise *graphic design executive, art publisher, artist*

Carpinteria
Hansen, Robert William *artist, educator*

Carson
Hirsch, Gilah Yelin *artist, writer*

Castro Valley
Erwin, Frances Suzanne *artist*
Knight, Andrew Kong *visual artist, educator*
McLean, Richard Thorpe *artist*

Chico
Hornaday, Richard H. *artist, retired art educator*
Patton, Thomas Edward *artist, educator*

Claremont
Benjamin, Karl Stanley *artist, art educator*
Blizzard, Alan *artist*
Casanova, Aldo John *sculptor*
†Dunye, Cheryl *artist, film maker*
Zornes, Milford *artist*

Corona Del Mar
Delap, Tony *artist*

Coronado
Hubbard, Donald *marine artist, writer*

Costa Mesa
†Bartletti, Don *photographer, editor*
Muller, Jerome Kenneth *photographer, art director, editor*

Crescent City
Swart, Bonnie Blount *artist*

Crestline
Noble, Lawrence Alan *artist*

Culver City
†Gordon, Florence Irene *graphic artist, illustrator*
Grant, Joan Julien *artist, poet*
Wilson, David *artist*

Cupertino
Carnie, Kay C. *artist, educator*

Cypress
Bloom, Julian *artist, editor*

Daggett
Bailey, Katherine Christine *artist, writer*

Daly City
Kennedy, Gwendolyn Debra *artist, scriptwriter, playwright*

Davis
DePaoli, Geri M. (Joan DePaoli) *artist, art historian*
†Powers, Gay Havens-Monteagle *artist*

Del Mar
†Mullen, George D. *artist*

Desert Hot Springs
†Laws, Maurice Wesley *set decorator, museum exhibit designer*

El Cajon
†Jordan, Jack D. *art educator*

El Cerrito
Hargis, Barbara Louise *artist*

Emeryville
Fineman, Jeanette Krulevitz *retired artist*

Encinitas
Breslaw, Cathy Lee *artist, educator*

Escondido
†Carey, Catherine Anita *artist, art educator*

Eureka
Marak, Louis Bernard, Jr., *artist, educator*

Fair Oaks
Dorf, Eve Buckle *artist*

Fallbrook
Ragland, Jack Whitney *artist*

Flintridge
Johnston, Oliver Martin, Jr., *animator*

Folsom
Campbell, Ann Marie *artist*

Fremont
Ko, Hyunok *artist, sculptor*

Fresno
Shmavonian, Gerald S. *philanthropist, art collector*
Stuart, Dorothy Mae *artist*

Fullerton
Bell, Melodie Elizabeth *artist, massage therapist*
†Coronel, Raul Angulo *sculptor*

Galt
Nunes, Judy Omai *artist*

Glendale
Ferren, Bran *graphics designer*

Half Moon Bay
Harris, David Jack *artist, painter, educator*

Hayward
Perrizo, James David *art and sculpture educator, forestry pilot*

Hollister
†Miller, Alisa Dorothy Norton *artist*

Hollywood
†Bird, Topanga *artist, writer*

Huntington Beach
Berry, Kim Lauren *artist*
†Isabelle, Beatrice Margaret *artist*
Neal, Anita *artist*

Indio
Zorick, Nancy Lee *artist, actress*

Inverness
Welpott, Jack Warren *photographer, educator*

Irvine
Belić Weiss, Zoran *artist, designer, educator*

Kelseyville
Fletcher, Leland Vernon *artist*

La Jolla
Imana, Jorge Garron *artist*
Low, Mary Louise (Molly Low) *documentary photographer*
Merrim, Louise Meyerowitz *artist, actress*
Whitaker, Eileen Monaghan (Eileen Monaghan) *artist*

Lafayette
Monheit, Molly Jane *artist, writer*

Laguna Beach
Powers, Runa Skötte *artist*

Laguna Hills
Block, Amanda Roth *artist*

Laguna Niguel
Zagon, Laurie *artist, writer*

Lagunitas
Holman, Arthur Stearns *artist*

Loleta
Schoenfeld, Diana Lindsay *photographer, educator*

Loma Linda
Worley, Margaret Ann *apparel designer, writer*

Long Beach
Nielsen, Pamela Jeanne *artist, writer*
Vernon, Alejandra *artist*
Viola, Bill *artist, writer*

Los Alamitos
Rippo, Olga Alicia *art director*

Los Altos
Sharpe, Kathryn Peck *artist*
Sherwood, Patricia Waring *artist, educator*
Spangler, Dorothy Benita *artist*

Los Angeles
Apple, Jacki (Jacqueline B. Apple) *artist, writer, educator*
Apt, Charles *artist*
Caroompas, Carole Jean *artist, educator*
Caryl, Naomi *artist*
Curran, Darryl Joseph *photographer, educator*
†De Larios, Dora *artist*
Dismukes, Valena Grace Broussard *photographer, former physical education educator*
Di XX Miglia, Gabriella *artist, conservationist*
Galanos, James *retired fashion designer*
Hamilton, Patricia Rose *art dealer*
Hess, Frederick Scott *artist*
Hockney, David *artist*
Janowski, Karyn Ann *artist*
Johnston, Ynez *artist, educator*
Krupp, Robin Rector *illustrator, author*
Kupper, Ketti *artist*
Lark, Raymond *artist, art scholar*
Layton, Harry Christopher *artist, lecturer, consultant*
Lee, Cecilia Hae-Jin *artist, writer*
Lem, Richard Douglas *painter*
Mears, Linda Shaw *artist*
Park, Lee (Lee Parklee) *artist*
†Pastor, Jennifer *sculptor*
Porter, Bonnie *artist, photographer*
Rankaitis, Susan *artist*
Serafin, Thomas Joseph *photographer, writer*
†Siguenza, Herbert Orlando *artist*
†Smith, Vernon *artist, educator*
Stone, George *artist, art educator*
Swildens, Karin Johanna *sculptor*
†Wells, Annie *photographer*
†Williams, Clarence J, III, *photographer*

Los Banos
Peterson, Stanley Lee *artist*

Los Gatos
†Carson, Sol Kent *artist, educator*

Ricklin, Elaine Paula *artist, educator*
†Shwayder, Elizabeth Yanish *sculptor*

Dolores
Winterer, Barbara Jean *designer, author*

Durango
Vogl, Laurel Covington *artist, educator*

Englewood
Kristin, Karen *artist*
Lamb, Darlis Carol *sculptor*

Grand Junction
†Erickson, Mary Evelyn *artist, writer*

Greeley
Jenkins, Virginia *visual arts educator, artist*
Ursyn, Anna *computer graphics artist, educator*

Greenwood Village
Cocklin, Ruth Ellen *artist*

Hotchkiss
Blackstock, Virginia Harriett *artist*

Jamestown
Craigo, Christina Ila *artist, educator*

Lake George
Norman, John Barstow, Jr., *designer, educator*

Littleton
Nesheim, Dennis Warren *art educator, artist, writer, instructional materials producer, special education educator*

Loma
Young, David Bennion *artist*

Longmont
King, Jane Louise *artist*

Loveland
Weimer, Dawn *sculptor*
Weresh, Thelma Faye *sculptor, artist*

Montrose
Pitcher, Helen Ione *advertising director*

Snowmass Village
Casebeer, Douglas Kelley *artist, ceramist, consultant*

Steamboat Springs
Zabel, Curtis Lee *artist, rancher*

Westcliffe
Merfeld, Gerald Lydon *artist*

Westminster
†Carol Ann, *artist, educator*

Woodland Park
Cockrille, Stephen *art director, business owner*

CONNECTICUT

Avon
Drapeau, Suzanne Eva *art educator, artist*

Berlin
Pulito, Francis N. *artist*

Branford
LeVasseur, Lee Allan *fine artist*
Milgram, Judith Lee *art educator, administrator, artist*

Bridgeport
Hofbauer, Michele Pace *illustrator, writer*

Bristol
†Raymond, Kathy Ann *graphics designer, poet*

Brookfield
Rowe, Edward Lawrence, Jr., *graphic designer*

Colebrook
Ash, Hiram Newton *graphic designer*

Cos Cob
Kane, Margaret Brassler *sculptor*
Neal, Irene Collins *artist, educator*

Danbury
Saghir, Adel Jamil *artist, painter, sculptor*

Darien
Black, Lisa *artist*
Ossi, James Matthew *artist*

East Haddam
Conant, Jan Royce *artist*

East Hartford
Soppelsa, George *artist*

Fairfield
Bullard, Roger Perrin *artist*
Everett, Wendy Ann *toy designer*
Khachian, Elisa Arpenia *artist, educator*

Falls Village
Cronin, Robert Lawrence *sculptor, painter*

Georgetown
Roberts, Priscilla Warren *artist*

Greenwich
DeNigris, Carole Dell Cato *artist*
Perless, Robert L. *sculptor*
Pope, Ingrid Bloomquist *sculptor, poet*
Sandbank, Henry *photographer, film director*

Guilford
Pease, David Gordon *artist, educator*

Hartford
Carey, Ellen *artist*
Del Giudice, Leon Louis *auctioneer*
Hammer, Alfred Emil *artist, educator*
Martin, Ionis B *artist, educator*
Shuler, Scott Corbin *art education administrator*

Ivoryton
Jensen, Leo *artist*
Osborne, Judith Barbour *artist, art educator*

Madison
Nebel, Sara Drought *artist, poet*

Meriden
Bertolli, Eugene Emil *sculptor, goldsmith, designer, consultant*

Milford
Curt, Denise Morris *artist, limner, photographer*

Monroe
Cote-Beaupre, Camille Yvette *artist, educator*

Mystic
Rooney, Maria Dewing *photographer*

Naugatuck
†Chrzanowski, Rose-Ann Cannizzo *art educator*
Mannweiler, Mary-Elizabeth *painter*

New Canaan
Christensen, Donna Radovich *needlecraft designer, consultant, educator*
Kovatch, Jak Gene *artist*
Rendl-Marcus, Mildred *artist, economist*
Richards, Walter DuBois *artist, illustrator*
Sweeny, Kenneth S. *graphic design consultant*

New Fairfield
Mann, Jean Adah *artist*

New Haven
Bailey, William Harrison *artist, educator*
Cooke, Edward Strong, Jr., *art educator*
†Feinstein, Rochelle *artist, educator*
Grausman, Philip *sculptor*
Johnson, Lester Fredrick *artist*
Lindroth, Linda (Linda Hammer) *artist, curator, writer*
Papageorge, Tod *photographer, educator*

New Milford
Page, Alice Cecilia *artist, educator*

North Grosvenordale
Kornbluth, Frances Helen Schachter *artist*

Norwalk
Babcock, Catherine Evans *artist, educator*

Old Lyme
Chandler, Elisabeth Gordon (Mrs. Laci De Gerenday) *sculptor, harpist*

Redding
Isley, Alexander Max *graphic designer, lecturer*

Ridgefield
Kromer, Ann Marie *artist*

Riverside
Dunn, Virginia *artist, community volunteer*

Roxbury
†Kelsey, Sterett-Gittings *sculptor*

Sherman
Goodspeed, Barbara *artist*

Stamford
Roberts, Victoria Lynn P. *antique expert*
Rudman, Joan Eleanor *artist, educator*

Stonington
Elliott, Inger McCabe *designer, textile company executive, design consultant*

Torrington
McKenzie, Kathleen Julianna *artist*

Voluntown
Caddell, Foster *artist*

Wallingford
Lauttenbach, Carol *artist*

Washington
Grimes, Margaret Whitehurst *artist, educator*
Renouf, Edda *artist*

Waterford
Patnode, Mark W. *artist, graphic designer*

West Cornwall
Prentice, Tim *sculptor, architect*

West Hartford
Uccello, Vincenza Agatha *artist, director, educator emerita*

Weston
Bleifeld, Stanley *sculptor*
Reinker, Nancy Cooke *artist*
Williams, Paul Alan *artist*
Wilson, Melissa Anne *sculptor*

Westport
Chernow, Ann Levy *artist, art educator*
Fisher, Leonard Everett *artist, writer, educator*
†Malloy, Susan Rabinowitz *artist*
†McTague-Stock, Nancy A. *painter, printmaker*
Reilly, Nancy (Anne Caulfield Reilly) *painter*
Siff, Marlene Ida *artist, designer*

Wilk, Barbara *artist, educator*

Woodbury
Martin, M. Gertrude *artist*

DELAWARE

Greenville
†Cooch, Nancy duPont (Mrs. Edward W. Cooch Jr.) *sculptor*

Lewes
Costigan, Constance Frances *artist, educator*
Laub-Novak, Karen *artist, writer, sculptor*
Visbal, Kristen Elizabeth *sculptor*

New Castle
Almquist, Don *illustrator, artist*

Newark
Brown, Hilton *visual arts educator, artist, writer*
Holmes, Larry Wayne *artist, educator*
Rowe, Charles Alfred *artist, designer, educator*

Rockland
Harvey, Andre *sculptor*

Wilmington
Bounds-Seemans, Pamella J. *artist*
Lewis, Mary Therese *artist*

DISTRICT OF COLUMBIA

Washington
†Allard, William Albert *photographer*
Basch, Richard Vennard *photographer, producer, writer, director*
Baughman, J. Ross *photographer, writer, educator*
†Benoh, Ibrahim *artist, art educator*
Biddle, Catharina Baart *artist*
Blair, James Pease *retired freelance photographer*
Boucher, Jack Edward *architectural photographer, writer*
Bowman, Dorothy Louise *artist*
Brown, Pamela Wedd *artist*
Colton Skolnick, Judith A. *artist*
Coppola, John Francis *exhibits director*
DiPerna, Frank Paul *photographer, educator*
†Elson, Beverly Lynn *art educator*
†Ferrell, James T. *sculptor*
Forrester, Patricia Tobacco *artist*
Giles, Patricia Cecelia Parker *retired art educator, graphic designer*
†Gordon, Dorothy K. *silversmith, goldsmith*
Gumpert, Gunther *artist*
†Kapikian, Catherine Andrews *artist*
Kelso, Gwendolyn Lee *silver appraiser, consultant*
†Kobersteen, Kent *photographer, director, editor-in-chief*
Koller, Shirley Leavitt *sculptor*
†Maletsky, Alfred F. *sculptor, engraver*
†Mercanti, John M. *sculptor, engraver*
Millon, Henry Armand *fine arts educator, architectural historian*
†Nemeth, Norman E. *sculptor, engraver*
†Olson, Randy *photographer*
Oxman, Mark *sculptor, educator*
Polan, Annette Lewis *artist, educator*
†Ravenal, Carol Bird Myers *artist, art historian*
Shinolt, Eileen Thelma *artist*
Steadham, Richard Lynn *magazine art director*
Summerford, Ben Long *retired artist, educator*
Tacha, Athena *sculptor, educator*
Truitt, Anne Dean *artist*
†Weaver, Donna L. *engraver*

FLORIDA

Alachua
Tilton, John Ellsworth *ceramic artist*

Atlantic Beach
Gartland, Alice Johnson *artist*

Bal Harbour
Bernay, Betti *artist*

Boca Raton
Ortlip, Paul Daniel *artist*
Wertheimer, Esther *sculptor*

Bonita Springs
McNamara-Ringewald, Mary Ann Thérèse *artist, educator*

Bradenton
Boudreau, Alice Benjamin *artist, educator*
McClish, Jerry Franklin *artist*
McMullan, Kathryn Oatman *watercolor painter, promotion specialist*
Voorhees, Stephanie Robin Faught *retired art educator*

Citra
Parisi, Marita *artist, art gallery director*

Clearwater
Slade, Roy *artist, college president, museum director*

Clermont
Morris, Helen Julia *artist*

Cocoa
Ollie, Pearl Lynn *artist, singer, songwriter*

Cocoa Beach
Blum, June *artist, curator*
Herbstman, Loretta *sculptor, painter*

Coconut Creek
†Marshak, Arthur *artist, sculptor*

Dania
Satin, Claire Jeanine *sculptor, book artist*

Davie
†Pittle, Jeffrey Robert *artist*

Daytona Beach
Frank, Robert Edwin *artist*

Daytona Beach Shores
Dalia, Vesta Mayo *artist*

Debary
†Pelosi, Haydee *sculptor*

Delray Beach
Mills, Agnes Eunice Karlin *artist, printmaker, sculptor*
Ross, Beatrice Brook *artist*

Dunedin
Allison, Brooke Hastings *artist, educator*

Fernandina Beach
DelPesco Thornton, Nancy Rose *artist, educator*

Flagler Beach
Cornelius, Aleta *artist, designer, restorer, educator, judge*

Fort Lauderdale
Ambrose, Judith Ann *designer*
Duke, James T *art educator, consumer products company executive*

Fort Myers
Dean, Jean Beverly *artist*
Frank, Elizabeth Ahls (Betsy Frank) *art educator, artist*
Schwartz, Carl Edward *artist, printmaker*
Weiss, Susette Maré *technical and photographic consultant, mass communications and media relations specialist, investor*

Fort Pierce
Cassens, Susan Forget *artist*
Peterson, Barbara Owecke *artist, nurse, realtor*

Gainesville
Collins, Harvey Arnold *art educator, retired*
Kerslake, Kenneth Alvin *artist, printmaker, art educator*
Morgan, Anne Margaret Barclay *artist, author, psychologist*
Murray, Kate Shakeshaft *artist*

Hialeah
Gil de Gibaja, Susana *artist, small business owner*

Hobe Sound
Houser, Jim (James Cowing Houser Jr., Jim Houser) *painter, art educator*

Holly Hill
Perman, Carrie Lee *artist, educator*

Hollywood
Sadowski, Carol Johnson *artist*

Indian Harbor Beach
Traylor, Angelika *stained glass artist*

Indian Harbour Beach
†Rains, Baxter Smith *sculptor, consultant*

Jacksonville
Eden, F. Brown *artist*
Schultz, Nancy Reilly *artist*

Jensen Beach
Gruppe, Charles Camille *artist*

Key Largo
Fundora, Thomas *artist, journalist, composer*
Kennedy, Mary Sussock *artist*

Key West
McIntosh, Jon Charles *illustrator, graphic designer*
†Taylor, Victoria *sculptor*

Lake Mary
Bachmann, Bill *photographer*
†Reagan, Bettye Jean *artist*

Lake Worth
Melvin, Pamela Lee *artist*

Lakeland
†Rogers, James Gordon, Jr., *art educator*
Stark, Bruce Gunsten *artist*

Longboat Key
Molles, Emily DeMartino *artist, real estate broker*

Marathon
Giffen, Lois Key *artist, psychosynthesis counselor*

Melbourne
Conneen, Mari M. *artist*

Melrose
Harley, Ruth *artist, educator*

Miami
Balás, Irene Barbara *artist*
Bannard, Walter Darby *artist, art critic*
Chambers, Elenora Strasel *artist*
Dorn, Gordon Joseph *artist, art educator*
Fleisher, Betty *artist, educator*
Kislak, Jean Hart *art educator*

Kitner, Jon David *art educator*
Mendieta, Raquelín Maria de la Concepción *artist*
†Moran, Kate *sculptor, photographer*
†Pietrocarlo, Nick *artist, consultant*
Salinas, Baruj *artist, architect*

Micco
Christoph, Frances *painter*

Mount Dora
Kirton, Jennifer Myers *artist*

Naples
†Demko, Cathy *artist, art educator*
Eldridge, David Carlton *art appraiser*
†Gifford, Nancy (Mumtaz) *artist, poet*
York, Tina *painter*

New Port Richey
Bell, Sandra Cheever *artist*

Nokomis
Robinson, Mary Catherine *artist*

Okeechobee
Mercer, Frances deCourcy *artist, educator*

Orange Park
Hunt, J(ulian) Courtenay *artist*

Orlando
Haxton, David *filmmaker, photographer*
Warren, Dean Stuart *artist*

Osprey
Gross, Marilyn Agnes *artist, business owner, speech audiologist*

Palm Beach
Gilbertson, Bernice Charlotte *artist*
Krois, Audrey *artist*
†Ness, Evaline (Mrs. Arnold A. Bayard) *illustrator, writer*

Palm Beach Gardens
Samuels, Fern Jacqueline *artist, educator*

Palm City
Sloan, Richard *artist*

Palm Harbor
Giavis, Theodore Demetrios *commercial illustrator, artist*

Pensacola
Burke-Fanning, Madeleine *artist*
Desposito, Martha Sheats *artist, educator*
Maki, Hope Marie *artist, sculptor, illustrator, poet, educator*

Plantation
Ballantyne, Maree Anne Canine *artist*

Port Charlotte
Leslie, John *artist, designer, fine art photographer, sculptor*

Safety Harbor
Banks, Allan Richard *artist, art historian, researcher*
Banks, Holly Hope *artist*

Saint Augustine
Connaway, Robert Wallace *artist, computer programmer*
Quirke, Lillian Mary *retired art educator*

Saint Petersburg
Christiano, Melissa *artist, educator*
Grastorf, Jean Elizabeth Hancock *artist, educator*
†Mancuso, Vincent *artist, art educator*
†Reilly, Thomas *museum exhibit designer, artist, writer*
Stedman, R VanGorden *artist, art historian radio and television personality*

Sanibel
Keogh, Mary Cudahy *artist*

Sarasota
Altabe, Joan Augusta Berg *artist, writer, art and architecture critic*
Krate, Nat *artist*
Melançon, Joseph Herman *artist, educator*
Plunket, Dolores *art and archaeology educator*
Winterhalter, Dolores August (Dee Winterhalter) *art educator*

Satellite Beach
Osmundsen, Barbara Ann *sculptor*

Sebastian
Pieper, Patricia Rita *artist, photographer*

Sunrise
Mason, Sherilyn Sue *artist*

Tallahassee
Hicken, Russell Bradford *art dealer, appraiser*

Tampa
Cardoso, Anthony Antonio *artist, educator*

Temple Terrace
Kashdin, Gladys Shafran *painter, educator*

Venice
Callari, Emily Dolores *artist*
†Girman, Dee-Marie *iconographer, artist*

Vero Beach
Billeci, Andre George *art educator, sculptor*
Krupp, Barbara D. *artist*
Sautner, Barry Robert *artist*

West Palm Beach
†Baker, Dina Gustin *artist*
Brody, Carol Z. *artist, educator*
Gronlund, Robert B. *art collector, fund raising consultant*
Longhofer, Gordan Allen *art educator, performance artist*
Lozito, Gilda Lelia *artist, painter*

Weston
Deleuze, Margarita *artist*
Napp, Gudrun F. *artist*

Winter Springs
San Miguel, Manuel *painter, historian, composer, poet, art collector*

GEORGIA

Alpharetta
Bolton, Robin Jean *artist, painter*

Athens
Clements, Robert Donald *sculptor*
DeZurko, Edward Robert *retired art educator*
Herbert, James Arthur *artist, filmmaker*
Kaufman, Glen Frank *art educator, artist*
Mullins, W. Stan *artist, cultural ambassador*
Olsen, Richard James *artist, educator*
Paul, William Dewitt, Jr., *artist, educator, photographer, videographer, museum director*

Atlanta
Alexander, Constance Joy (Connie Alexander) *stone sculptor*
Brown, Sarah M. *artist, gallery owner, educator, publisher*
†Dongoski, Craig R. *art educator*
Farmer, Mary Bauder *artist*
Fouché, Helen Strother *editorial design executive*
†Gibson, Michael *artist*
Guberman, Sidney *painter, writer*
Longobardi, Pamela Scott Dodgen *artist, educator*
Malone, James Hiram *graphic artist, painter, writer*
McLean, James Albert *artist, educator*
Nesin, Barbara *artist, art educator*
†Parrish, Carl E. *artist, educator*
Richards, Jacqueline *artist, curator*
†Rodríguez, Rocío *artist*
Schreiber, Barbara *artist*
Wilmer, Mary Charles *artist*

Augusta
†Hand, Maryanne Kelly *artist, educator*
Rosen, James Mahlon *artist, art historian, educator*

Columbus
†Nix, Jeffrey Alan *photographer*

Dalton
Pritchett, Deborah Kaye *artist*

Darien
Davis, Ann Richardson *artist, sculptor, book dealer, writer*

Decatur
Bleser, Katherine Alice *artist*
Morrison, Margaret L. *artist, educator, consultant*

Franklin Springs
†Pettyjohn, Emma Kennedy *fine arts educator*

Jasper
Sutter, Jean *sculptor*

Lagrange
†Greene, Annie Lucille *artist, retired art educator*

Lawrenceville
Hobbs, Robert Ellice, Jr., *artist*

Macon
Weaver, Jacquelyn Kunkel Ivey *artist, educator*

Marietta
Lahtinen, Silja Liisa *artist*

Meansville
Hankins, Patricia L. *ceramic artist, educator*

Mount Berry
Mew, Thomas Joseph, III, (Tommy Mew) *artist, educator*

Rockmart
Hardin, Sherrie Ann Asfoury *commercial photographer*

Rome
†Bell, Allen D. *art director, writer*

Roswell
Christopher, Lin *artist*

Savannah
Aja-Herrera, Marie *fashion designer, educator*
Aquadro, Jeana Lauren *graphic designer, educator*
Boylston, Scott Thomas *graphic design educator*
Fell, Cheryl Cookmeyer *artist, art educator*
Foley, Marilyn Lorna *artist*

Scottdale
Borochoff, Ida Sloan *artist*

Stone Mountain
Bundy, Jane Bowden *artist, educator*
Lori-Gene, *artist, educator*

Tybee Island
Pearce, Mallory *artist, educator, ecologist*

HAWAII

Honolulu
†Belknap, Jodi Parry *graphic designer, writer, business owner*
Betts, Barbara Stoke *artist, educator*
Chang, Rodney Eiu Joon *artist, dentist*
Guthrie, Edgar King *artist*
Pickens, Frances Jenkins *jewelry/metal artist, art educator*
Uhl, Philip Edward *artist, photographer, cinematographer*
Wolfe, Suzanne L. *artist, art educator*

Kapaa
duPont, Nicole *artist*

Kapaau
Jankowski, Theodore Andrew *artist*

Kihei
Galesi, Deborah Lee *fine artist*

Kurtistown
Charon, Kenneth Arnold, Jr., *artist*

Waikoloa
Lyon, Henry Clarence *artist*

IDAHO

Boise
Williams, DeWayne Arthur, Jr., *artist*

Harrison
Carlson, George Arthur *artist*

Lewiston
Scott, Linda Byrne *artist*

Meridian
Shaffer, Mary Louise *art educator*

Osburn
Bardelli, Frederick Ketchell *artist, art educator*

ILLINOIS

Aurora
Hegarty, Carol Irene *painter, writer*

Bourbonnais
Wilkey, Elmira Smith *illustrator, artist, publisher, author, educator*

Champaign
Jackson, Billy Morrow *artist, retired art educator*
Kotoske, Roger Allen *artist, educator*

Chicago
Aiello, Susan *artist, illustrator, educator*
Altman, Edith G. *sculptor*
Aubin, Barbara Jean *artist*
Buxbaum, Alexandra *photographer*
†Campos-Pons, Maria Magdalena *artist*
Castillo, Mario Enrique *artist, educator*
†Coffey, Susanna Jean *artist, educator*
Crane, Barbara Bachmann *photographer, educator*
Gallagher, Blanche Marie *art and spirituality educator, nun*
Gray, Richard *art dealer, consultant, holding company executive*
†Gunning, Tom *art educator*
Hards, Richard Charles *artist*
Himmelfarb, John David *artist*
Kearney, John Walter *sculptor, painter*
Kearney, Lynn Marilyn Haigh *arts administrator, curator*
†Kenney, Estelle Koval *artist, educator*
King, Andre Richardson *architectural graphic designer*
Klopack, Kenneth Barthon *art educator, artist*
Kolkey, Gilda *artist*
McGrail, Jeane Kathryn *artist, educator, poet, curator*
Nixon, Emily *art advisor, curator*
Phelan, Mary Helen *artist, educator*
Sigler, Hollis *artist, educator, author*
Smith, Harry Buchanan, Jr., *graphic designer, painter, photographer, writer*
Tessing, Louise Scire *graphic designer*
Thall, Robert *photographer, educator*
Workman, Robert Peter *artist, cartoonist*
Zgoda, Lawrence *artist*

Crystal Lake
Salvesen, B. Forbes *artist*

Dekalb
Byrum, Linda Kluber *artist*
Merritt, Helen Henry *retired art educator, ceramic sculptor, art historian*
Tió, Adrian Ricardo *artist, art educator*

Des Plaines
Banach, Art John *graphic artist*
Henrikson, Arthur Allen *political cartoonist, educator*

Dixon
Huber, Marianne Jeanne *art dealer, appraiser*

East Dundee
Simons, Gail S. *artist, educator, librarian*

Edwardsville
Hampton, Phillip Jewel *artist, educator*
Malone, Robert Roy *artist, art educator*

Elmhurst
Schultz, Evelyn Ecale *artist*
Weber, John Pitman *artist, educator*

Evanston
Conger, William Frame *artist, educator*
Hirshfield, Pearl *artist*
Rasco, Kay Frances *antique dealer*

Galena
Jackman, Levon Merchant O'Day *artist*

Geneva
Mishina, Mizuho *artist*

Glenview
Reuter, Linda N. *corporate design executive*

Gurnee
Wulfers, Monika *artist*

Hawthorn Woods
Brooks, Susan Louise *artist*

Highland Park
Slavick, Ann Lillian *retired art educator*

Hudson
Mills, Frederick VanFleet *art educator, educator, watercolorist*

Lake Forest
†Van Ella, Kathleen E. *fine art consultant*
Weston, Dawn Thompson *artist, researcher*

Lawrenceville
Dooley, David Inskeep *artist, educator*

Lombard
Ahlstrom, Ronald Gustin *artist*
Hudson, Samuel Campbell, Jr., *art educator, artist, sculptor, portraitist*

McHenry
Chisu, Ioan *artist*

Naperville
Finzer, Carolyn Lauing *artist, speaker*

Normal
Mau, Benjamin *artist*

Oak Lawn
Jachna, Joseph David *photographer, educator*

Olympia Fields
Sandlin, Dorothy *artist*

Palatine
Fortunato, Nancy *artist*
Miletto, David Gregory *artist*

Park Forest
Cribbs, Maureen Ann *artist, educator*

Park Ridge
Charewicz, David Michael *photographer*
Orlow, Daniel John *photographer*

Peoria
Nelson, Lisa Louise *artist*

River Forest
Sloan, Jeanette Pasin *artist*

Rockford
Apgar, Jean E. *artist, consultant*
Argraves, Hugh Oliver *poet, artist, playwright*
Baxter, Jeffrey Q. *graphic artist, sculptor*
Tregay, Susan Webb *artist, educator*

Scales Mound
Lieberman, Archie *photographer, writer*

South Holland
Fota, Frank George *artist*

Table Grove
Thomson, Helen Louise *artist*

Techny
Vanderstappen, Harrie Albert *Far Eastern art educator*

Warrenville
†Benson, Valerie A. *artist, writer*

Wheaton
Lowrie, Pamela Burt *educator, artist*

Willowbrook
Burrows, Donald Albert *artist, painter, photographer, dean*

Winnetka
Plowden, David *photographer*

INDIANA

Albany
Patrick, Alan K. *artist*

Anderson
Day, Sandy J. *painter, writer*

Beverly Shores
Collins, Moira Ann *graphics and communications company executive, calligrapher*

Bloomington
Baldner, Karen A. *artist, art educator*
Connally, Sandra Jane Oppy *retired art educator, artist*
Markman, Ronald *artist, educator*

O'Hearn, Robert Raymond *stage designer*
†Stines, Betty Irene *artist*

Burlington
†Roussakis, Dorothy Ferguson *artist*

Crown Point
Scheub, Richard Herman *photographer*

Evansville
†Brown, William Fredrick *art educator*
Roth, Carolyn Louise *art educator*
Worman, Sylvia Easler *artist*

Indianapolis
†Davis, Mary Ann *graphic artist*
Hayes, Brenda Sue Nelson *artist*
Jacobson, Marc Peter *art educator, educator*
Rutledge, Joanne *artist, consultant*

Kokomo
Ranney, Sandra Kay *artist, humanities educator*

Marion
Shepler, Debra Lynn *artist, secondary education educator*

Martinsville
Cupka, Nancy Irvine *artist, educator*

Merrillville
Hoffman, Robert Joseph *artist, art educator*

Milltown
Chapman, Sue Turner *artist*

Morgantown
Siddiq, Patricia Kay *artist*

Munster
Dompke, Norbert Frank *retired photography studio executive*

Nashville
Brown, Peggy Ann *artist*
Kriner, Sally Gladys Pearl *artist*
Tracy, James Leon *artist*

Richmond
Kennedy, Barbara Ellen Perry *art therapist*

Terre Haute
Lamis, Leroy *artist, retired educator*

Unionville
†Lyle, Melanie S. *web developer*

Valparaiso
Olson, Lynn *sculptor, painter, writer*

West Lafayette
Bannatyne, Mark William McKenzie *technical graphics educator*
Ichiyama, Dennis Yoshihide *design educator, consultant, administrator*

Winamac
Ligocki, Gordon Michael *artist, educator*

IOWA

Ames
Paschke, Teresa Ann *artist, educator*

Britt
Castillo, Leanne Marlow *artist, nurse*

Coralville
Allen, (Edwin) Lee *artist*

Davenport
Jecklin, Lois Underwood *art corporation executive, consultant*

Des Moines
Reece, Maynard Fred *artist, author*
Truck, Frederick John *artist*

Fort Dodge
Hanson, Richard James *art educator, artist*

Iowa City
†Green, Carin Margreta *art educator*
Hettmansperger, Sue *artist, art educator*
Merkel-Hess, Mary Lynne *artist*
Myers, Virginia Anne *art educator*
Schmidt, Julius *sculptor*

Le Grand
Hildebrandt, Willis Harvey *artist, educator*

Marion
Prall, Barbara Jones *artist*

Mount Pleasant
Scarff, Hope Dyall *photographer*

Waverly
Frick, Arthur Charles *art educator*

KANSAS

Chase
Stull, Evalyn Marie *artist*

Dodge City
Rosel, Carol Ann *artist*

Emporia
Henry, Elaine Olafson *artist, educator*

Kansas City
†Amundson, Beverly Carden *artist*

Lawrence
Dooley, Patrick John *graphic designer, design educator*
Hermes, Marjory Ruth *machine embroidery and arts educator*
†Nam, Yoonmi *artist, art educator*
Shimomura, Roger Y. *artist, educator*

Leawood
Kordash, Dorothy Mae *artist*

Ottawa
Howe, William Hugh *artist*

Overland Park
†Benjamin, Peggy-Ann Biel *artist*

Shawnee
Smokorowski, Peter *retired artist*

Topeka
Navone, Edward William *artist, educator*
Peters, Barb Waterman *artist, educator*

Wichita
Riegle, Robert M. *art dealer, retired architect*

KENTUCKY

Corinth
Wilson, Genevieve Adkins *artist*

Fort Wright
Sullivan, Connie Castleberry *artist, photographer*

Lexington
Boyer, Lillian Buckley *artist, educator*
Sandoval, Arturo Alonzo *art educator, artist*
Snowden, Ruth O'Dell Gillespie *artist*

Louisville
Brugioni, David Michael *graphic designer, illustrator, artist*
†Chan, Ying Kit *artist, educator*

Richmond
Springate, Karen Spears *artist*

LOUISIANA

Alexandria
Jeffress, Charles H. *retired art educator*

Cecilia
†Girouard, Tina *artist, curator*

Choudrant
Ford, John Charles *artist*

Covington
Rohrbough, Elsa Claire Hartman *artist*

Franklin
Trosclair, Kattina T. *graphics designer*

Gonzales
Noonan, Robert Harry *art and music educator*

Houma
Babin, Regina-Champagne *artist, educator, consultant*

Lafayette
Barry, Mildred Castille *artist*

Lake Charles
Dentler, Anne Lillian *artist*
Roy, Donald *artist, poet*

Metairie
Ales, Beverly Gloria Rushing *artist*
Crosby, Deborah Berry *artist*
Killeen, Edward Joseph *actor, designer*

New Orleans
Bailey, Barry Stone *sculptor, educator*
Best, Susan Marie *artist, educator*
†Emery, Lin *sculptor*
†Gertjejansen, Doyle *artist, educator*
Simons, Dona *artist*
Thornell, Jack Randolph *photographer*
Wegmann, Mary Katherine *art director*

Shreveport
Hughes, Mary Sorrows *artist*
Wray, Geraldine Smitherman (Jerry Wray) *artist*

Slidell
†Neale, Zahidi Sahaj *artist, educator*

Thibodaux
Robichaux, John Wayne *art educator, writer*

MAINE

Bar Mills
Buchanan, Bruce *functional metal artist, photographer*

Biddeford
†Riley, Pamela Janerico *artist*

Boothbay Harbor
Cavanaugh, Tom Richard *artist, antiques dealer, retired art educator*

Camden
Daly, Daniel Ánthony *artist, illustrator*

Castine
Mancuso, Leni *artist, poet, educator*

Cushing
Magee, A. Alan *artist*

East Boothbay
Peters, Andrea Jean *artist*

Gorham
Bearce, Jeana Dale *artist, educator*

Lincolnville
Swanson, Harry Frederick *artist*

New Harbor
Lyford, Cabot *sculptor*

Ogunquit
Carpenter, George Robert *artist*
West, Norman Ellsworth *artist*

Scarborough
Warg, Pauline *artist, educator*

Stratton
Gray, R(obert) J(ames), Jr., *printmaker, editor*

Tenants Harbor
Quint-Rose, Marylin Iris *artist*

Trevett
Bettinson, Brenda *artist, educator*
Mathias, Cordula *art dealer*

Wells
Hero, Barbara Ferrell *visual and sound artist, writer*

West Southport
Barker, Walter William, Jr., *artist, waiter*

York
Hallam, Beverly (Beverly Linney) *artist*

MARYLAND

Annapolis
Alderdice, Cynthia Lou *artist*
Fry, Virginia Milne *artist, poet*
Thoms, Josephine Bowers *artist, illustrator*

Arnold
Kellogg-Smith, Peter *sculptor, educator*
Kolb, Joyce Diana *artist, educator*

Baltimore
Carper, Gertrude Esther *artist, marina owner*
Duncan, Lionel Sebastian *artist, educator*
Massey, Allyn Frances *artist, educator*
Parsons, Ivy *artist, sculptor, educator*
†Tapper, Leona (Leela) Siff *artist*
Zaruba, Allen Scott Harmon *sculptor, educator*

Barnesville
Pearcy, Susan Beth Due *artist, printmaker*

Bethesda
Dox, Ida *author, medical illustrator*
Elliott, George Armstrong, III, *artist, journalist*
Fleming, Patricia Stubbs *artist*
Koenig, Elizabeth Barbara *sculptor*
Larson, Jane Warren *ceramist*
Lee, Dora Fugh *artist*
Prevots, Naima *art educator, writer*
Sarnoff, Lili-Charlotte (Lolo Sarnoff) *artist, executive*
Tanenbaum, Jill Nancy *graphic designer*

Boonsboro
Zeleny, Ann Douglas *sculptor*

Cabin John
†Bergfors, Constance Marie *artist, educator*

Centreville
Amos, James Lysle *photographer*

Chestertown
†Scott, Joanne *artist, painter*

Chevy Chase
Duvall, Bernice Bettum *artist, exhibit coordinator, jewelry designer*
Wright, Frank *artist, educator*

Columbia
Kurlander, Honey Wachtel *artist, educator*

Crisfield
Ryan, Jerome Francis *artist*

Crofton
Andrysiak, Frank Louis *videographer*

Denton
Doster, Rose Eleanor Wilhelm *artist*

Ellicott City
†Kushnir, Andrei *artist, consultant*

Gaithersburg
Jevtic, Milomir *artist, sculptor*

Galena
†Hunsperger, Elizabeth Jane *art and design consultant, educator*

Germantown
Bu, Rulei *artist, educator*

Glen Echo
Stevenson, A. Brockie *retired artist*

Hyattsville
Raines, Charlotte Austine Butler *artist, poet*

Kensington
Frederikse, Yolanda Rossi *painter, printmaker, art educator*

Laurel
Logsdon, Roslyn *artist, educator*

Lutherville
Kissel, William Thorn, Jr., *sculptor*

Owings
Oring, Stuart August *visual information specialist, publisher, writer, photographer, researcher*

Oxford
Zachai, Dohrn Dorian *artist*

Port Deposit
Burch, G. David *sculptor*

Potomac
Keil, Marilyn Martin *artist*

Quantico
Scott, David Winfield *artist, museum consultant*

Severna Park
Hopkins, Edith Rose *artist*

Shady Side
Nadolski, Stephanie Lucille *artist, designer*

Silver Spring
Barkin, Robert Allan *graphic designer, newspaper executive, consultant*
Neuhäuser, Mary Helen *artist, writer, playwright*
Peiperl, Adam *kinetic sculptor, photographer*
Woolard, Connie Ward *artist, retired art gallery manager*

Woodbine
Nuss, Barbara Gough *artist*

MASSACHUSETTS

Amherst
Anderson, Ronald Trent *artist, educator*
Dabrowski, Thaddeus E. *art educator, art consultant, painter*
Feshbach, Oriole Farb *artist*
Hendricks, James Powell *artist*
†Kimball, Justin *photographer, educator*
Liebling, Jerome *photographer, educator*
Yarde, Richard Foster *art educator*

Auburn
Berg, G. Vivian *artist*

Belmont
Hilt, Mary Louise *artist*

Beverly
Manheim, Michael Philip *photographer*
Roy, Robert William *artist, educator*

Boston
Ablow, Joseph *artist, educator*
Ablow, Roz Karol (Roz Ablow) *painter, curator*
Avison, David *photographer*
Filer, Crist N. *artist, chemist*
Fink, Aaron *artist*
†Gallagher, Ellen *artist*
Gibran, Kahlil *sculptor*
†MacLean, Alex Stokes *aerial photographer*
Manning, William Frederick *wire service photographer*
McDaniel, Joyce L. *artist, educator*
Parker, Olivia *photographer*
†Purvis, Philip Alston Willcox *art educator*
Sichel, Kim Deborah *art history educator*
†Wiesner, David *illustrator, children's writer*
Yang, Sue *artist*

Brookfield
Couture, Ronald David *art administrator, design consultant*

Brookline
Barron, Ros *artist*
Kawada, Janet Hansen *artist, educator*
Kay, Reed *artist, educator*
Schiller, Sophie *artist, graphic designer*
†Swirnoff, Lois *artist, color theorist*

Burlington
DeCrosta, Susan Elyse *graphic designer*

Cambridge
Ackerman, James Sloss *fine arts educator*
Alcalay, Albert S. *artist, design educator*
Bakanowsky, Louis Joseph *visual arts educator, architect, artist*
Chandler, Fay Martin *artist*
Feininger, Theodore Lux *artist*
Handford, Martin John *illustrator, author*
Jones, Timothy Mark *graphic designer, painter*
Mazur, Michael *artist*
Mc Kie, Todd Stoddard *artist*
Slosburg-Ackerman, Jill Rose *artist, educator*
†Thompson, Samuel G. *artist*
†Wodiczko, Krzysztof *artist, architect, educator*

Chatham
Patten, Nicholas Frederick *artist*

Chicopee
Costanzo, Nanci Joy *art educator*

Chilmark
Geyer, Harold Carl *artist, writer*
Low, Joseph *artist*

Concord
Ihara, Michio *sculptor*

Gowen, Leo Francis *artist*
Hansman, Robert G. *art educator, artist*
Sago, Janis Lynn *photography educator*
Stanton, Frank Lawrence, Jr., *graphic designer, illustrator, educator*
†Ward-Brown, Denise *sculptor, educator*

Saint Peters
Gilman, Patricia Ann *artist, educator*

Sedalia
Berry, Jean Stanfield *artist, retired art educator*

Sibley
Morrow, Elizabeth Hostetter *sculptress, museum administrator, farmer, educator*

Sikeston
Tesseneer-Street, Susan *photographer, artist, writer*

Springfield
Thompson, Wade S. *artist, art and design educator, administrator*

Stover
Reynolds, Sallie Blackburn *artist, civic volunteer*

Vandalia
Berry, Rebecca Diane *artist, art educator*

Webster Groves
Gergeceff-Cooper, Lorraine *artist, consultant*
Osver, Arthur *artist*

MONTANA

Billings
Deschner, Jane Waggoner *photo artist, public relations consultant*
Snell, Alma Hogan *artist*

Bozeman
Selyem, Bruce Jade *freelance/self-employed photographer*
†Wiltsie, Gordon H. *photographer*

Great Falls
Becker, Julia Margaret *artist, educator*
Gallagher, Sherry E. *artist*

Helena
Clarkson, Robert Noel *commercial photographer, magician*
Cleary, Shirley Jean *artist, illustrator*
†Kilgore, Tulasi *artist, art educator*

Hot Springs
Erickson, James Gardner *retired artist, cartoonist*

Kalispell
von Krenner, Walther G. *artist, writer, art consultant and appraiser*

Missoula
Scamman, Frederick L. *retired tool and die maker*

NEBRASKA

Amelia
Jellico, Nancy Rose *painter, sculptor*

Lincoln
†Ayoub, Roula G. *artist*
Eckersley, Richard Hilton *graphics designer, educator*
Rogge, Kathleen Ruth *domestic engineer, art educator, nurse*

Omaha
Burkholder, Roger Glenn *artist, author*
Seng, Jeffrey Frazier *artist, poet*

NEVADA

Carson City
†Sins, Denise M. *art educator*

Fallon
†Venturacci, Toni Marie *artist, substitute educator*

Henderson
Hara-Isa, Nancy Jeanne *graphic designer, county official*

Incline Village
Ealy, Cynthia Pike *artist, realtor*

Las Vegas
Badik, Eleanore *artist*
Gideon-Hawke, Pamela Lawrence *fine arts small business owner*
Goldblatt, Hal Michael *photographer, accountant*

Mesquite
Alcorn, Karen Zefting Hogan *artist, art educator, journalist*

Reno
Goin, Peter Jackson *art educator*
Harder, Kelsie T. *artist, educator*
Hilts, Ruth *artist*
Newberg, Dorothy Beck (Mrs. William C. Newberg) *portrait artist*

NEW HAMPSHIRE

Bennington
Willis, Barbara Florence *artist*

Canaan
†Taussig, Margaret C. *artist*

Concord
Winterling, Ann *artist*

Dover
Mitchell, William Clark *printmaker, graphic artist*

Etna
Judson, J. Richard *retired art educator, historian*

Freedom
Lummus, Carol Travers *artist, printmaker*

Hancock
Pollaro, Paul Philip *artist*

Hanover
Boghosian, Varujan Yegan *sculptor, educator*
Moss, Ben Frank, III, *art educator, painter*

Jaffrey
Press, Fred *artist*

Lyme
†Wise, Joanne Herbert *artist representative*

Manchester
Groulx, Aimé René *artist, photographer*
Ronalter, Chelsea Maria *artist, graphic designer*

Nashua
Marie, Linda *artist, photographer*

New Ipswich
Stirnweis, Shannon *illustrator, painter*

Newport
Gayvoronsky, Ludmila *artist, educator*

North Hampton
August, June *artist, educator*

Plaistow
Collins, James Francis *wildlife artist*

Stoddard
Whitney, Richard Wheeler *artist, educator*

Stratham
Green, Catherine Cooper *artist*
Terry, Elizabeth Hays *calligrapher, needlepoint designer*

Winchester
Tandy, Jean Conkey *art educator*

Wolfeboro
Bonin, Suzanne Jean *artist*
Croteau, Jan Helling *artist*

NEW JERSEY

Annandale
Konrad, Adolf Ferdinand *artist*

Asbury Park
Myers, Dorothy Roatz *artist*

Atlantic Highlands
Tice, George A(ndrew) *photographer*

Basking Ridge
Frediani, Diane Marie *graphic designer, interior designer*

Bayonne
Gorman, William David *artist, graphic artist*

Beach Haven
Schreiber, Eileen Sher *artist*

Belmar
Swett, Stephen Frederick, Jr., *artist, educator*

Bernardsville
Spofford, Sally (Sally Hyslop) *artist*

Blairstown
Bean, Bennett *artist*

Bridgeton
Williams, Jennifer Margaret *freelance artist, substitute teacher*

Bridgewater
Glesmann, Sylvia-Maria *artist*

Browns Mills
DeWitt, Edward Francis *artist*

Caldwell
Palombo, Lisa *artist*

Califon
†Clipsham, Jacqueline Ann *artist*
Rosen, Carol Mendes *artist*

Cedar Grove
Anderson, Robert Raymond *artist, consultant*

Chatham
Glover, Janet Briggs *artist*

Cliffside Park
De Pol, John *artist*

Collingswood
Poacelli, Dolores *fine artist, graphic designer*

Cresskill
Smyth, Craig Hugh *fine arts educator*

Edison
Arakawa, Peter Stanhope *artist, educator*

Englewood
Anuszkiewicz, Richard Joseph *artist*
Valenti, Paula Anne (Pelak) *art educator, assistant principal*

Essex Fells
Thummel, Rosa *artist*

Ewing
Sanders, Philip F., Jr., *artist, computer art educator*

Fairfield
de Smet, Lorraine May *artist*

Fairview
Park, Chung *painter, educator, computer software developer*

Fort Lee
Nemser, Robert Solomon *visual communications consultant, art director, creative director, designer, writer, educator*

Franklin Lakes
Baker, Cornelia Draves *artist*

Harmony
Van Rensselaer, Miles *artist, sculptor*

Hasbrouck Heights
Walsh, Virginia *artist, educator*

Hazlet
Wunsch, Anna Catherine Mary O'Brien Horton *artist, consultant*

Highland Park
Chamberlin-Davis, Ann Elizabeth *artist, writer*

Hightstown
Howard, Barbara Sue Mesner *artist*

Hoboken
Frankenthal, Danielle *painter, sculptor*
Rose, Roslyn *artist*

Holmdel
Slovik, Sandra Lee *retired art educator*

Jersey City
Barney, Christine J. *artist*
†Bruso, Arthur *artist*
Gurevich, Grigory *visual artist, educator, mime*

Keasbey
Hari, Kenneth Stephen *painter, sculptor, writer*

Lambertville
Goodyear, John L. *artist, educator*

Laurel Springs
Roma, Aida Clara *artist*

Lawrenceville
Naar, Harry I. *fine arts educator, artist*

Lebanon
DeBevoise, Francine (Franke DeBevoise) *artist*

Leonia
Wilson, Marcia Sandmeyer *artist*

Long Branch
Stamaty, Clara Gee Kastner *artist*

Marlton
Cullen, Mary Lynne *artist*

Medford
Mayer, Joyce Harris *artist*

Metuchen
Adlerman, Kimberly Marie *illustrator, writer, graphics designer*
†Arbeiter, Joan *artist, educator*

Monroe Township
Liebson, Milt *sculptor, educator, author*

Montclair
Beerman, Miriam *artist, educator*
Phillips, Ann Y. *art advisor*

Morristown
Prince, Leah Fanchon *art educator and research institute administrator*

Neptune
Ventura, Anthony Paul *artist, fine art educator*

New Brunswick
Goffen, Rona *art educator, educator*
Ortiz, Raphael Montañez *performance artist, educator*

New Providence
†Rivo, Shirley Winthrope *artist*

Newark
D'Astolfo, Frank Joseph *graphic designer, educator*
†Rainey, Matt *photographer*

North Plainfield
Stroppel, Betty MacNair *artist, educator*

Northvale
Heslin, Cathleen Jane *artist, designer, entrepreneur*

Oakland
Dressel, Margaret Jane *artist, art educator*

Oldwick
Svoboda, Joanne Dzitko *artist, educator*

Oradell
†Bassis, Aileen *artist*
Struck, Norma Johansen *artist*

Phillipsburg
Richards, Jay Claude *commercial photographer, news service executive, historian*

Picataway
†Pardo, Janette M. *multimedia editor, archivist, librarian*

Piscataway
Kivetz, Michael Adam *artist, sculptor*
Rosalsky, Barbara Ellen *artist, home health aide*
Scher, Karen Maria *illustrator, multimedia specialist, systems engineer*

Princeton
Benarde, Anita Estelle *artist*
Boretz, Naomi Messinger *artist, educator*
Bunnell, Peter Curtis *photography and art educator, museum curator*
†Diller, Elizabeth E. *artist, educator*
George, Thomas *artist*
Grabar, Oleg *retired art educator*
Seawright, James L., Jr., *sculptor, educator*
Wilmerding, John *art history educator, museum curator*

Princeton Junction
Smith, Peter Edward (Pietro del Fabro) *sculptor, artist*

Rahway
Appezzato, Marc Robert *graphic artist*

Ringwood
Day, Ann Elizabeth *artist, educator*

Rutherford
Petrie, Ferdinand Ralph *illustrator, artist*

Salem
Carpenter, Margaret S. (Molly Carpenter) *artist, sculptor*

Somerset
Young, James Earl *ceramics educator, educational administrator*

South Bound Brook
Weir, Sonja Ann *artist*

Sparta
Rosser, Alvin Raymon *artist*

Springfield
Baker, Alden *artist*
DeVone, Denise *artist, educator*
Marino, Natalie Marie *artist*

Stockton
Mahon, Robert *photographer*
†Schoenherr, John (Carl) *artist, illustrator*
Taylor, Rosemary *artist*

Summit
Rousseau, Irene Victoria *artist, sculptor*

Teaneck
Indick, Janet *sculptor, educational administrator*

Tenafly
Koons, Irvin Louis *design and marketing executive, graphic artist, consultant*
Schoenberg, Coco *sculptor*

Toms River
Unger, Howard Albert *artist, photographer, educator*

Trenton
Brearley, Candice *fashion designer*
Chavooshian, Marge *artist, educator*
†Leipzig, Melvin *art educator*

Union
David, Ivo *artist, poet, real estate broker*
Korn, Neal Mark *painter, art educator*
Samer, Bill Fred Carl *illustrator, writer, cartoonist*

Union City
Erbe, Gary Thomas *artist*

Ventnor City
Robbins, Hulda Dornblatt *artist, printmaker*

Verona
Ayaso, Manuel *artist*

Waldwick
Samuelson, Billie Margaret *artist*

Wayne
Cetrulo, Jerry *artist, sculptor*
Katz, Leandro *artist, filmmaker*

West End
Tesser, Dorothy *artist*

West Paterson
Seiffer, Neil Mark *photographer*

Westwood
Vandeburgt, Hendrik Jozef *designer*

Whippany
Petitto, Barbara Buschell *artist*

Woodbridge
Scolamiero, Peter *retired artist*

NEW MEXICO

Albuquerque
Antreasian, Garo Zareh *artist, lithographer, art educator*
Barry, Steve *sculptor, educator*
Coleman, Barbara McReynolds *artist*
Culpepper, Mabel Claire *artist*
De Jong, Constance A. *artist*
Dunn, Dennis Steven *artist, illustrator*
Feinberg, Elen Amy *artist, educator*
Green, Mae Maera *artist*
Haight, Cathy *artist*
Hovel, Esther Harrison *art educator*
Keating, David *photographer*
†Loss, Lynne Franklin *artist, volunteer*
Miera, Lucille Catherine Miera *artist, retired educator*
Multhaup, Merrel Keyes *artist*
Nelson, Mary Carroll *artist, writer*
Nevin, Jean Shaw *artist*
Peterson, Gwen Entz *artist*
†Steider, Doris *artist*
Witkin, Joel-Peter *photographer, poet*

Alto
Zeitelhack, Gloria Jeanne *artist*

Belen
Chicago, Judy *artist*

Bernalillo
Pritchard, Betty Jean *retired art educator*

Carrizozo
Mack, James Willard *artist, educator*

Cerrillos
Harnack, Barbara Wood *artist, sculptor*

Corrales
Eaton, Pauline *artist, educator*

Deming
De Mott, Marianne *educator, artist, craftsperson, space designer*

Farmington
Peters, Evelyn Joan *artist*

Gallup
Cattaneo, Jacquelyn Annette Kammerer *artist, educator*

Hobbs
Ebler, Marilyn Ann *graphic designer, educator*
Garey, Patricia Martin *artist*

Pinos Altos
Rogers, Linda Lee *artist*

Ranchos De Taos
Marx, Nicki Diane *sculptor, painter*

Rio Rancho
†Qualley, Charles Albert *art educator*

Roswell
Avery, Keith Willette *artist, educator*
Wiggins, Kim Douglas *artist, art dealer*

Ruidoso Downs
Templeton, Ann *artist, educator*

Sandia Park
Weitz, Jeanne Stewart *artist, educator*

Santa Fe
Bauer, Betsy (Elizabeth Bauer) *artist*
†Harroun, Dorothy Summer *painter, educator*
Herdman, Susan *art educator, artist*
Hudson, Noel *artist*
Kingsley, Judith *artist*
†Lippincott, Janet *artist, art educator*
Malone, Roxanne Enyeart *artist, educator*
Orduno, Robert Daniel *artist, painter, sculptor*
Perroni, Carol *artist, painter*
Racuya-Robbins, Ann Elizabeth *artist*
Randolph, Somers *sculptor*
†Salas Stone, Susan *artist, poet, web site designer*
Shubart, Dorothy Louise Tepfer *artist, educator*
Silverman, Sherri Lynn *artist, educator*
†Villela, Khristaan David *art educator*

Silver City
McCray, Dorothy Westaby *artist, printmaker, educator*

Taos
Bell, Larry Stuart *artist*
Berkeley, Seamus Osborne *artist*
†Harmon, Barbara Sayre *artist*
Martin, Agnes *artist*
Price, Brenda Chloè *artist, entrepreneur*

Tesuque
Novak, Joe *artist*

Truchas
Breuer, Mala Klee *artist*

Vadito
Patten, Christine Taylor *artist, writer*

NEW YORK

Afton
Schwartz, Aubrey Earl *artist, educator*

Albany
Herrick, Kristine Ford *graphic design educator*
Lawton, Nancy *artist*
Shankman, Gary Charles *art educator*

Alfred
Higby, Wayne (Donald Higby) *artist, educator*

Amenia
Hale, Nathan Cabot *sculptor, artist, poet*

Ancramdale
Weinstein, Joyce *artist*

Ardsley
Sokolow, Isobel Folb *sculptor*

Armonk
†Tantillo Elton, Nina *artist, graphics designer, educator*

Babylon
Haley, Priscilla Jane *artist, printmaker*

Batavia
Grieger, Donald L. *artist*

Bearsville
Ruellan, Andree *artist*
Whitman, Karen *artist*

Bedford Hills
Jensen-Carter, Philip Scott *photographer, photographer*

Berne
†Skiff, Colleen Fraser *art educator, art gallery director, recreational therapist*

Binghamton
Rosko, Keith Allan *art educator, illustrator*
†Weissman, Ann Paley *art educator, artist, consultant*

Brainard
†Johnsen, May Ann *artist, sculptor, graver*

Brentwood
Oshypko, John *artist, set designer*

Briarcliff Manor
Lew, Leslie *artist*

Bridgehampton
Goff, Kimberly (Kimberly Knollenberg) *art dealer, painter, writer*
Smith, Christine Chew *artist, educator*

Brockport
Hickerson, Dianne *artist, former educator*

Bronx
Adams, Alice *sculptor*
Behnken, William Joseph *art educator, artist*
Brickner, Alice *painter, illustrator*
Gonzalez, Rose A-Navarro *artist*
Greenberg, Arline Francine *artist, photographer*
Juszczyk, James Joseph *artist*
Kassoy, Hortense (Honey Kassoy) *artist, sculptor, painter, printmaker*
Kitt, Olga *artist*
Schwam, Marvin Albert *graphic design company executive*
Terner, Ron M. *artist, photographer*

Brooklyn
Allman, Avis Asiye *artist, poet, Turkish and Islamic culture educator, human rights activist*
Amendola, Sal John *artist, teacher, writer*
Biondi, Florence *artist, cantor*
Brody-Lederman, Stephanie *artist*
Burns, Josephine Dora *artist*
Carlile, Janet Louise *artist, educator*
Colette, Lois Marie *artist*
Dantzic, Cynthia Maris *artist, educator*
Davidek, Annette Marie *artist*
Del Rosario, Mariano Boras, Jr., *artist*
Del Valle, Cezar Jose *artist, writer, theatre historian*
Diamond, Jessica *artist*
Dinnerstein, Harvey *artist*
Dinnerstein, Simon Abraham *artist, educator*
Fischer, R. M. *sculptor*
Gabris, George Steven *sculptor, welder*
Gianlorenzi, Nona Elena *painter, art dealer, educator*
†Giusti, Karin F. *artist, educator*
Grado, Angelo John *artist*
Haber, Ira Joel *artist, art educator*
Hauft, Amy Gilbert *artist*
†Henning, Roni Anita *printmaker, artist*
Hoepfner, Karla Jean *designer, artist*
Jemisin, Noah *artist, educator*
Jones, Susan Emily *fashion educator, administrator, educator emeritus*
Kemp, James William *graphic artist*
Kessler, Linda Joan *artist, educator*
Kjok, Sol *artist, art historian, linguist, government authorized translator*
†Lanzillotto, Ann Rachele *performance artist, writer*
Machell, Iain Hugh *artist educator*
Marcano, Soraya *visual artist*
McClintock, Jane *sculptor, painter*
Moore, Anne Frances *arts administrator, consultant, educator, art appraiser*
†Moylan, Donna Jean *artist*
Neaderland, Louise Odes *artist, educator, professional society executive*
Otterness, Tom *artist*
Pearlstein, Seymour *artist*
Peker, Elya Abel *artist*
Pitynski, Andrzej Piotr *sculptor*
†Rauschenbusch, Stephanie *artist, educator, poet*
Schaefer, Marilyn Louise *artist, writer, designer*
Shaw, Kendall (George Shaw) *artist, educator*
Shechter, Laura Judith *artist*
Silverstein, Louis *art director, designer, editor*
Swirsky, Judith Perlman *arts administrator, consultant, educator*
von Rydingsvard, Ursula Karoliszyn *sculptor*
Walker, Joy *visual artist*

Alfred
†Woodham, Joseph Ed *artist, art educator*
Yamada, Takeshi *artist, language and cultural consultant, educator, writer*
Zakanitch, Robert Rahway *artist*
Zhang, Robert *painter*
Zinnes, Alice Fich *artist, educator*
†Zweig, Janet *artist, sculptor*

Buffalo
†Houseknecht, Stephen *artist, educator*
Kazmierczak, Elzbieta Teresa *graphic designer, illustrator, educator, semiotician*
†McKibbin, William Alex *artist*
Naylon, Betsy Zimmermann *artist*
†Parker, Catherine B. *artist, art educator*
Paterson, Tony Ralph *sculptor, educator*
Rogovin, Milton *documentary photographer, retired optometrist*
St. Pierre, Cheryl Ann *retired art educator*

Buskirk
Johanson, Patricia Maureen *artist, architect, park designer*

Campbell Hall
Greenly, Colin *artist*

Canaan
Knebel, Constance *potter, ceramist*
Walker, William Bond *painter, retired librarian*

Catskill
†Green, Barbara R. *artist*
Green, Francis Eugene *artist, educator*

Central Square
BuMann, Sharon Ann *sculptor*

Chatham
Squier, Rita Ann Holmberg *graphic designer*

Clarence
Hubler, Julius *artist*

Climax
Adler, Lee *artist, educator, marketing executive*

Copake
Wahlers, Linda Ann Ford *writer*

Corning
Buechner, Thomas Scharman *artist, retired glass manufacturing company executive, museum director*

Cortlandt Manor
Croft, Michele Izzo *graphic designer, artist*
Rosenberg, Marilyn Rosenthal *artist, visual poet*

Croton On Hudson
Johann, Anne Dorothy *visual artist, painter, printmaker, graphic artist*
Rubinfien, Leo H. *photographer, filmmaker*

Cutchogue
Dank, Leonard Dewey *medical illustrator, audio-visual consultant*
†Pugliese, Ralph James, Jr., *freelance/self-employed photographer*
Strimban, Robert *graphic designer*

Deer Park
Martone, Jeanette Rachele *artist*

Denver
Koutroulis, Aris George *artist, educator*

Dix Hills
Fouladvand, Hengameh *artist*

East Hampton
Banks, Monica *sculptor*
Delson, Elizabeth *artist*
Jaudon, Valerie *artist*
Petersen, Ellen Anne *artist*

East Setauket
Badalamenti, Fred Leopoldo *artist, educator*

Eastchester
Gottschall, Edward Maurice *graphic arts company executive*

Elmhurst
Matos Morales, Germán Joseph *art and antiques dealer, advocate, fundraiser*

Fayetteville
Hadyk-Wepf, Sonia Margaret *artist, real estate manager*

Flushing
Belden, Ursula *set designer*
Bertoni, Mae *artist*
Bezrod, Norma R. *artist*
Carlson, Cynthia Joanne *artist, educator*
Flechner, Roberta Fay *graphic designer*
Goldstein, Milton *art educator, printmaker, painter*
Hammerman, Pat Jo *artist, educator*
Yeo, Kim Eng *artist*

Fly Creek
Dusenbery, Walter Condit *sculptor*

Forest Hills
†Tsay, Chwen Wen *artist*
Wolpert Richard, Chava *artist*

Franklin Square
Indiviglia, Salvatore Joseph *artist, retired naval officer*

Fredonia
Booth, Robert Alan *artist, educator*
†Conradi, Janet K. *art educator*

Freehold
Maltzman, Stanley *artist*

Freeport
Terris, Albert *metal sculptor*

Gilbertsville
†Greefkes, Roland Cornelis *artist*

Glen Oaks
†Luger, Louise *photographer*

Great Neck
Blanda, Sandi *artist*
Dennett, Lissy *sculptor*
Eckstein, Ruth *artist*
Lande, Ruth Harriet *photographer, language educator*
Seidler, Doris *artist*

Greenwich
Fung, Paul, Jr., *cartoonist, illustrator*

Hamburg
Dor, Caplyn *artist*

Hastings On Hudson
Goldstein, Eleanor *artist, social worker*

Hempstead
Nelson, Vivienne E. *artist, office manager*

Hillsdale
Richards, Joseph Edward *artist*

Hudson
Artschwager, Richard Ernst *artist*

Hudson Falls
Leary, Daniel *artist*

Huntington
Maglione, Lili *fine artist, art consultant*
Tar, Laszlo *artist*
Twardowicz, Stanley Jan *artist, photographer*

Irvington
Rainer, Renata Urbach *artist, photographer, lecturer, educator*

Ithaca
Garrison, Elizabeth Jane *artist*
Grippi, Salvatore William *artist*
McCue, Arthur Harry *artist, educator*
Mikus, Eleanore Ann *artist*
Poleskie, Stephen Francis *artist, retired educator, writer*
Resnick, Minna *artist, educator*
Squier, Jack Leslie *sculptor, educator*

Jackson Heights
†Dacey, Paul *artist*

Jamaica
Cade, Walter, III, *artist, musician, singer, actor*
Cocchiarelli, Maria *artist, educator*
Jones, Cynthia Teresa Clarke *artist*

Jeffersonville
Craft, Douglas Durwood *artist*
Harms, Elizabeth Louise *artist*

Jordanville
Durham, Jeanette Randall *artist, educator*

Kiamesha Lake
†Cash, Jeffrey Marc *commercial artist, photographer*

Lagrangeville
Liccione, Alexander Anthony *artist*

Locust Valley
DeRegibus, William *artist*

Long Island City
Donneson, Seena Sand *artist*
Munro, Roxie Jean *artist, educator, illustrator, writer*
†Popian, Lucia *artist*

Mahopac
Gonzalez-Tornero, Sergio *artist*

Malverne
Gavalás, Alexander Beary *artist*

Mamaroneck
Pugh, Grace Huntley *artist*

Manhasset
Catchi, (Catherine Oeland Childs) *artist*

Marcellus
Baker, Bruce Roy *retired art educator, artist*

Medford
Tafuri, William *sculptor*

Merrick
Cariola, Robert Joseph *artist*

Miller Place
Sanger, Eileen *artist*

Monroe
†Centeno-Dainty, Sonia Margarita *artist*

Mount Kisco
Michael, Creighton *artist, educator*

Napanoch
†Kooistra, Andrew J. *painter, sculptor*

Naples
Gelder, Donald Clifford Barnard *artist*

New Hampton
†Sinnard, Elaine Janice *painter, sculptor*

New Paltz
Azank, Roberto *artist*
†Goodell, Kathy Susan *artist, educator*

New Rochelle
†Schwartz, Peri *artist*
Slotnick, Mortimer H. *artist*

New York
Abish, Cecile *artist*
Adams, Dennis Paul *artist*
Adams, Edward Thomas (Eddie Adams) *photographer*
Adri, (Adri Steckling Coen) *fashion designer*
†Aitken, Doug *artist*
Allner, Walter Heinz *designer, painter, art director*
Alpert, William Harold (Bill Alpert) *artist, painter*
†Alvarado-Juárez, Francisco *visual artist*
Anastasi, William Joseph *artist*
Andre, Carl *sculptor*
Anthony, William Graham *artist*
Antonakos, Stephen *sculptor*
Aptekar, Ken *painter*
Arrons-Lane, Marion Jean *artist, educator*
†Ashkin, Michael *artist*
Avedon, Richard *photographer*
Bachner, Barbara LaVerdiere *artist*
Backstedt, Roseanne Joan *artist*
Banerjee, (Bimal Banerjee) *artist, educator*
Barnes, Jhane Elizabeth *fashion design company executive, designer*
Barnet, Will *artist, educator*
Bastidas, Hugo Xavier *painter*
Baumgardner, Matthew Clay *artist*
Beck, Rosemarie *artist, educator*
Bee, Susan *artist, editor, designer*
Belag, Andrea Susan *artist*
Ben-Haim, Zigi *artist*
Berlind, Robert Elliot *artist, educator*
Berman, Ariane R. *artist*
Berthot, Jake *artist*
Beveridge, Stephen D *freelance/self-employed artist*
Bhavsar, Natvar Prahladji *artist*
Blechman, R. O. *artist, filmmaker*
Bloodworth, Sandra Gail *artist, arts administrator*
Boardman, Seymour *artist*
Bordiga, Lord Benno *art dealer*
Borgatta, Isabel Case *sculptor*
†Bourgeois, Louise *sculptor*
Boutis, Tom *artist, painter, print maker*
Bradley, Lisa M. *artist*
Bradshaw, Dove *artist*
Brett, Nancy Heléne *artist*
Brodsky, Beverly *artist*
Brown, Alice Dalton *artist*
Brown, Charlotte *artist*
Bruder, Harold Jacob *artist, educator*
Brumer, Miriam *artist, educator*
Bull, Helen May *artist, writer*
Bunts, Frank Emory *artist*
Byron, Eric Howard *sculptor, museum researcher and administrator*
Cajori, Charles Florian *artist, educator*
Campbell, Ronald Neil *retired magazine designer*
Cardile, Paul Julius *fine arts dealer*
Carmi, Giora *illustrator*
Casella, Margaret Mary *artist, photographer*
Castoro, Rosemarie *sculptor*
†Celmins, Vija *artist, photographer*
Cesarani, Sal *fashion designer*
Chermayeff, Ivan *graphic designer*
Cherry, Vivian *photographer*
Chodes, John Jay *photographer, writer*
Chwast, Seymour *graphic artist*
Chwatsky, Ann *photographer, educator*
Clutz, William (Hartman Clutz) *artist, educator*
Cohen, Cora *artist*
Cole, Sylvan, Jr., *art dealer*
†Cole, Willie *artist*
Colp, Norman Barry *photographic artist, curator*
Colquhoun, Peter Lloyd *artist, educator*
†Conelli, Maria Ann *art educator, dean, architectural historian*
Cooper, Mark Frederick *artist, sculptor, art educator*
Cooper, Paula *art dealer*
Cortor, Eldzier *artist, printmaker*
Cowles, Charles *art dealer*
Coyle, Terence *artist*
†Crean, Hugh *art educator*
Dana, F(rank) Mitchell *theatrical lighting designer*
Daphnis, Nassos *artist*
Davidson, Marilyn *artist*
Davidson, Nancy Brachman *artist, educator*
Davis, Doris Rosenbaum (Dee Davis) *artist, writer*
Davis, Lisa Corinne *artist*
de Champlain, Vera Chopak *artist, painter*
Deem, George *artist*
deGroat, Diane *illustrator, author children's books*
de la Renta, Oscar *fashion designer*
DeMonte, Claudia Ann *artist, educator*
Denes, Agnes C. *environmental artist*
Dennis, Donna Frances *sculptor, art educator*
des Rioux, Deena Victoria Coty *computer artist, digital graphics artist*
†Di Corcia, Philip-Lorca *artist, photographer*
Di Meo, Dominick *artist, sculptor, painter*
Dobbs, John Barnes *artist, educator*
Dodd, Lois *artist, art educator*
Dombrowski, Bob *artist, publisher*
†Donegan, Cheryl *artist*
Drexler, Joanne Lee *art appraiser*
†Drum, Sydney Maria *artist*
Duff, John Ewing *sculptor*
Dunkelman, Loretta *artist*
Dyyon, Mario (LeRoy Frazier) *artist*
†Egielski, Richard *illustrator*
Eins, Stefan *painter, conceptual artist, sculptor, arts curator*
Eisenberg, Sonja Miriam *artist*
Eisner, Carole Swid *artist*
Ellis, Richard *artist, writer*
Elman, Naomi Geist *artist, producer*
Enders, Elizabeth McGuire *artist*
Estes, Richard *artist*
†Fazal, Sheikh *photographer*
Feigen, Richard L. *art dealer, collector, writer*
Feinman, Stephen Erwin *art dealer, consultant, appraiser*
Feltus, Alan Evan *artist*
Ferri, David *lighting designer*
Feuerman, Carole A. *sculptor, artist*
Findlay, Michael Alistair *art dealer, poet*
Fiore, Joseph Albert *artist*
Fischer, Carl *graphic designer, photographer, actor*
†Foley, Maura *picture editor*
Foster, Kim *art dealer, gallery owner*
Fraser, Pamela *artist*
Fredericks, Wendy Ann *graphic designer*
Fugate-Wilcox, Tery *artist*
Gage, Beau *artist*
Geismar, Thomas H. *graphic designer*
Geissbuhler, Stephan *graphic designer*
Georges, Paul Gordon *artist, educator*
Gibson, Ralph H(olmes) *photographer*
Giffuni, Flora B. *artist, educator*
Ginzel, Andrew H. *artist*
Gittler, Wendy *artist, art historian, writer*
Goell, Abby Jane *painter, collage artist, artist*
Goertz, Augustus Frederick, III, *artist*
Goings, Ralph *artist*
Gold, Albert *artist*
Gold, Lois Meyer *artist*
Gold, Sharon Cecile *artist, educator*
Goldin, Leon *artist, educator*
Goldsmith, Caroline L. *arts executive*
†Gordon, Douglas *artist*
Gourevitch, Jacqueline *artist*
Graves, Thomas Vincent *sculptor*
Gray, George *mural painter*
Griefen, John Adams *artist, educator*
†Gursky, Andreas *artist*
Gutman, Robert William *retired educator*
Haacke, Hans Christoph Carl *artist, educator*
Haessle, Jean-Marie Georges *artist*
Halaby, Samia Asaad *artist, educator, computer artist*
Hamoy, Carol *artist*
†Harbutt, Sarah *photographer, director*
†Hauser, Sarah B. *artist*
Henselmann, Caspar Gustav Fidelis *sculptor*
Henson Scales, Jeffrey C. *photographer, photo editor*
†Herrera, Arturo *artist*
Herrera, Carmen *painter*
†Herring, Oliver *artist*
Highstein, Jene Abel *sculptor*
Hill, Clinton *artist*
†Holder, Donald *lighting designer*
Holtz, Itshak *artist*
Houghtelling, Ayres *artist, architect, engineer*
Hull, Cathy *artist, illustrator*
Hultberg, John *artist*
†Ichikawa, Akiko *artist, editor*
Incandela, Gerald Jean-Marie *artist*
Ireland, Patrick *artist*
Iwamoto, Ralph Shigeto *artist*
Jacquette, Yvonne Helene *artist*
Jenkins, Paul *artist*
Jerins, Edgar *artist, painter*
†Jetter, Frances S. *illustrator, educator, artist*
Johnson, Harmer Frederik *art appraiser*
Jones, Kristin Andrea *artist*
†Joo, Michael *artist, educator*
Kahn, Wolf *artist*
Kaish, Luise Clayborn *sculptor, former educator*
Kaish, Morton *artist, educator*
Kamali, Norma *fashion designer*
Kan, Diana Artemis Mann Shu *painter, art educator, writer*
Karan, Donna (Donna Faske) *fashion designer*
†Kardon, Dennis *artist,, educator*
Katz, Alex *artist*
Keech, Pamela *artist, curator*
†Kersels, Martin *artist*
†Khedoori, Toba *artist*
†King, Marcia Gygli *artist*
Kinstler, Everett Raymond *artist*
Kirsch, Marilyn *artist*
Klein, Calvin Richard *fashion designer*
Klein, Gloria *artist, retired educator*
Koppelman, Chaim *artist, educator*
Koppelman, Dorothy Myers *artist, consultant*
Korot, Beryl *artist*
Krementz, Jill *photographer, author*
Kuehn, Frances *painter*
Kushner, Robert Ellis *artist*
Kusmierski, Janet Louise *painter, illustrator, graphic designer*
Kutosh, Sue *artist*
†LaChapelle, David *photographer*
Lang, Daniel S. *artist*
Lash, Stephen Sycle *auction company executive*
Lasker, Jonathan Lewis *artist*
Lauren, Ralph *fashion designer*
Lavedan, Christiane *artist, researcher*
Lee, Catherine *sculptor, painter*
Lee, Leslie Enders *artist*
†LeGrady, George *photographer, educator*
Leinwand, Freda *photographer*
†Leonard, Zoe *artist*
Levine, David *artist*
LeWitt, Sol *artist*
Lighter, Jeremiah B. *book designer, artist, illustrator, educator*
Lipsky, Pat *artist*
Loengard, John Borg *photographer, editor*
Lord, Richard Dennis *photographer*
Loring, John Robbins *artist, writer*
†Lou, Liza *artist*
Lovell, Whitfield *artist*
†Lytle, Ellen Wendy *artist*
†Mackie, Robert Gordon *costume and fashion designer*
Mackler, Tina *artist*
Madsen, Loren Wakefield *sculptor*
†Manglano-Ovalle, Inigo *artist, sculptor*
Mann, Frank Bert *visual artist, painter*
Marcus, Gwen Ellen *sculptor*
Marden, Brice *artist*
†Marello, Matthew *artist*
Margolin, Jean Spielberg *artist*
Marinoff, Elaine *artist*
Maryschuk, Olga Yaroslava *artist, executive assistant*
†Mathias, Thelma *sculptor, video artist, curator*
Mayer, Rosemary *artist*
McCormick, Pamela Ann *artist, sculptor*
McCredie, James Robert *fine arts educator*
McDarrah, Fred William *photographer, editor, writer, photography reviewer*
Mc Gowin, William Edward *artist*
McHugh, Caril Eisenstein Dreyfuss *art dealer, gallery director, consultant*
McKenzie, Mary Beth *artist*
McKinley-Haas, Mary *artist*
Meiselas, Susan Clay *photographer*
Mendelson, Haim *artist, educator, art gallery director*
Miller, Harry Brill *scenic designer, actor, director, acting instructor, lyricist, interior designer*
Miller, Joan Leff *artist*
Miller, Richard Kidwell *artist, actor, educator*
Miller, Richard McDermott *sculptor*
Milonas, Minos *artist, designer, poet*
Minotti, Diana Lynn *art appraiser, consultant*
Morgan, Jacqui *illustrator, painter, educator, writer*
Mori, Mariko *artist*
†Mullarkey, Maureen *artist, critic*
Neiman, LeRoy *artist*
Nemec, Vernita Ellen (Vernita N'cognita) *artist, curator*
Newman, Arnold *photographer*
Niccolini, Dianora *photographer*
Noda, Takayo *artist*
Notarbartolo, Albert *artist*
O'Beil, Hedy *artist*
Obuck, John Francis *artist*
Ohlson, Douglas Dean *artist, educator*
Okuhara, Tetsu *artist, photographer*
Okumura, Lydia S. *painter, sculptor*
Ono, Yoko *conceptual artist, singer, recording artist*
†Opie, Catherine *photographer*
†Orozco, Gabriel *artist*
Ortman, George Earl *artist*
†Osorio, Pepon *artist*
Pace, Stephen Shell *artist, educator*
Parker, Nancy Winslow *artist, writer*
Pascual, Carlota *painter*
Pask, Scott *display designer*
Pavone, Joseph Anthony *display designer, artist*
Pearson, Henry Charles *artist*
Peckolick, Alan *painter, graphic designer*
Pepi, Vincent *artist*
Pionk, Richard Cletus *artist, educator*
†Piper, J.E. *artist, photographer, historian*
Plavinskaya, Anna Dmitrievna *artist*
†Polsky, Cynthia Hazen *artist, collector, philanthropist*
Poons, Larry *artist*
Porter, Liliana Alicia *artist, photographer, painter, print and filmaker*
†Prager-Kamel, Nancy Ann *artist, investment banker, business development firm executive*
†Prieto, Monique N. *artist*
†Pujol, Ernesto *artist*
Quackenbush, Robert Mead *artist, author, psychoanalyst*
Rabinowitch, David George *sculptor*
Rachko, Barbara Gail *artist*
Radunsky, Alexander *lighting designer*
Rankin-Smith, Pamela *photographer*
†Rauschenberg, Robert *artist*
Reddy, Krishna Narayana *artist, educator*
Redmond, Catherine *artist, educator*
Reiback, Earl Martin *artist*
Reininghaus, Ruth *retired artist*
Remington, Deborah Williams *artist*
Resika, Paul *artist*
Ringgold, Faith *artist*
Rivelli, William Raymond Allan *photographer*
Robb, Carole *artist*
Robbins, Carrie F(ishbein) *costume designer, educator*
Rodriguez, Geno (Eugene Rodriguez) *artist, arts administrator*
Roosevelt, Ruth Barrons *international trading consultant, artist*
†Rose, Aaron *artist*
Rose, Leatrice *artist, educator*
Rosenberg, Alex Jacob *art dealer, curator, fine arts appraiser, educator*
Ross, Charles *artist*
Ross, John T. *artist, educator*
†Ruscha, Edward *artist*
Russotto, Paul *artist, educator*
Ryman, Robert Tracy *artist*
Saez Guillermo, Francisco Eduardo *photographer*
St. Lifer, Jane M. *art appraiser*
Sand Lee, Inger *artist*
Saru, George *artist*
†Schimmel, Avigail *freelance/self-employed photographer*
Schneider, JoAnne *artist*
Schneider, Martin Aaron *photojournalist, ecologist, engineer, writer, artist, TV director, filmmaker, public advocate, educator, university instructor, lecturer, inventor*
Schwartz, Daniel Bennett *artist*
Seborovski, Carole *artist*
†Shambroom, Paul *artist, photographer*
Shapiro, Joel Elias *artist*
Sharp, Anne Catherine *artist, educator*
Sherin, Robin *artist*
†Shurdut, Jeffrey Hayden *artist*
†Sikander, Shahzia *artist*
Silverman, Burton Philip *artist*
Simonds, Charles Frederick *artist*
Simonelli, Maggie *artist*
Singer, Barbara Helen *photographer*
Size, Dennis Michael *lighting and scenery designer*
Skupinski, Bogdan Kazimierz *artist*
Slavin, Arlene *artist*
Sleigh, Sylvia *artist, educator*
Slone, Sandi *artist*
Slonem, Hunt *artist*
†Smith, Kiki *artist*
†Smith, Mimi *artist*
Smith, Shirley *artist*
Smith, Vincent DaCosta *artist*
Sobell, Nina R. *artist*
Solman, Joseph *artist*
Sonneman, Eve *artist*
Sopanen, Jeri Rainer *photography director*
Southworth, Linda Jean *artist, critic, educator, poet*
†Souto, Gustavo *painter*
Sperakis, Nicholas George *artist*
Starr, Steven Dawson *photographer*
Sterling, David Mark *graphic designer*
Stewart, Jack *artist, educator, writer*
Stine, Catherine Morris *artist*
Stone, Caroline Fleming *artist*
Storrs, Immi Casagrande *sculptor*
†Sullivan, Graeme Leslie *art educator*
Sullivan, Jim *artist*
Surrey, Milt *artist*
Swain, Robert *artist*
Swartz, Burton Eugene *artist, actor, theater director, writer, educator*
†Tagliarino, Salvatore *set designer, educator*
†Thomasos, Denyse *artist*
Throckmorton, Spencer S., III, *art dealer*
†Tiravanija, Rirkrit *sculptor*
Tooker, George *artist*
Tscherny, George *graphic designer*
Unruh, Richard Greenwood, III, *artist*
Upright, Diane Warner *art dealer*
Vass, Joan *fashion designer*
†Von Betzen, Valerie *artist*
Wald, Sylvia *artist*
†Walker, Kara *artist*
Wall, Susan Lee *artist*
Walton, Anthony John (Tony Walton) *theater and film designer, book illustrator*
†Wang, Vera *fashion designer*
Ward, Elaine *artist*
Wechsler, Gil *lighting designer*
†Weeeng, Joy *artist*
Weems, Carrie Mae *photographer*
Weiner, Lawrence Charles *artist*
Weitz, John *designer, writer*
†Welish, Hester *artist*
Wenegrat, Saul S. *arts administrator, art educator, consultant*
Wesley, John Mercer *artist*
Wesser, Yvonne *artist*
White, Roger L., Jr., *graphic designer, art director*
†Williams, Sue *artist*
†Williamson, Philemona *artist*
Willis, Thornton Wilson *painter*
†Wilson, Robert Frank *graphics designer, property manager*
Winer, Jessica Daryl *artist*
Winter, Roger *artist*
†Winters, Terry *artist*
†Wixom, Max Valentine *artist*
†Wright, Faith-dorian *artist*
Wunderman, Jan Darcourt *artist*
Wurmfeld, Sanford *artist, educator*
†Wyeth, James Browning *artist*
Zann, Nicholas T. *artist*
Zimmerman, Kathleen Marie *artist*
Zlowe, Florence Markowitz *artist*

Newark
Hughes, Owen Willard *artist*
Williams, Wayne Francis *art educator, sculptor*

Newburgh
Ochs, Richard Wayne *artist, gallery owner*

Northport
Wingerter, John Parker *artist, photographer*

Oakdale
†Iberti, Elissa Tatigikis *painter, costume designer, educator, independent curator*

Odessa
Stillman-Myers, Joyce L. *artist, educator, writer, illustrator, consultant*

Old Westbury
†Tiscornia, Ana Maria *artist, educator, writer*

Oneonta
Michaelsen, Niels Henrik *painter, illustrator*
Wentworth, Murray Jackson *artist, educator*

Orchard Park
Mariani, David Frank *artist*

Ossining
†Hill, Nils Arvid *artist, educator*

Oswego
Baitsell, Wilma Williamson *artist, educator, lecturer*
Fox, Michael David *retired art educator*

Owego
McCann, Jean Friedrichs *artist, educator*

Oyster Bay
Mooney, James David, Jr., *aerial photographer*
Prey, Barbara Ernst *artist*

Palisades
Knowlton, Grace Farrar *sculptor, photographer, painter*

Koshkin-Youritzin, Victor *art educator*

Okemah
DeShields, Elizabeth Peggy Bowen *artist, educator, poet*

Oklahoma City
Alaupovic, Alexandra Vrbanic *artist, educator*
Boston, Billie *costume designer, costume history educator*
Jordan, Beth McAninch *artist, educator*
Sorrin, Mary Louise *artist, nurse*
Whitener, Carolyn Raye *artist*
Zanoni de los Santos, Jacqueline M. *artist, curator*

Shawnee
Hicks, Steve L. *artist, art educator*

Tulsa
Frazier, Mary Ann *artist*
†Hess, Stanley O. *retired art educator*
Neal, E(verett) G(ilbert) *small business owner*

Vinita
Castor, Carol Jean *artist, teacher*

OREGON

Ashland
†Kostka, Robert Anton *artist, educator*

Bandon
Lindquist, Louis William *artist, writer*

Bend
Acosta, Cristina Pilar *artist*

Cannon Beach
Greaver, Harry *artist*

Cheshire
Antikajian, Sarkis Serop *artist, retired pharmacist*

Coos Bay
Van Allen, Katrina Frances (Katrina Frances) *painter*

Dillard
Gugel, M. Sue *artist*

Grants Pass
Remington, Mary *artist, author*
Roberts, Susan Sturgeon *art educator, writer*

Hillsboro
Hurley, Bruce Palmer *artist*

Jacksonville
Johnson, Morgan Burton *artist, writer*

Medford
Morris, Judy *artist*

Newberg
Keith, Pauline Mary *artist, illustrator, writer*

Newport
Gilhooly, David James, III, *artist*

Portland
Burritt, Barbara *artist*
Cwik, Lawrence John *artist, lawyer*
†Finch, Rob *photographer*
Hall, Mike Burt (Marshall B. Hall) *artist, educator*
Hinckley, Gregory Keith *software industry executive*
†Lilly, Susan Martin *costume designer, educator*
Lorenz, Nancy *artist*
Mazzola, Michael *lighting designer*
Montone, Kenneth Alan *art director, creative director, consultant*
Parsons, Lisa Kay *artist, writer*
Ramsby, Mark Delivan *lighting designer and consultant*
Thompson, Terrie Lee *graphic designer*

Roseburg
Comerford, Susan Marie *artist*

Salem
Pierre, Joseph Horace, Jr., *commercial artist*

Silverton
†Stone, Jane Buffington *artist, writer*

Sisters
Givot, Winnie *artist, educator*

PENNSYLVANIA

Allentown
Battle, Turner Charles, III, *art educator, educational association administrator*

Ardmore
Rodriguez, Kathleen Moore *art educator*

Audubon
Trone, Jacquelyn Lee *artist*

Bala Cynwyd
Blumberg, June Beth *artist*

Bally
Bertoia, Val *artist*

Bellefonte
Stevens-Sollman, Jeanne Lee *artist*

Berwyn
Dobie, Jeanne H. *artist*

Bethlehem
Ackerman, Rudy Schlegel *artist, educator*
Grainger, Nessa *artist*
Sossiadis, Katina *artist, filmmaker*

Boyertown
Stires, Midge *artist, painter*
Woods Coggins, Alma *artist*

Butler
Patterson, Patricia Lynne *artist, educator*

Camp Hill
Rowe, Michael Duane *artist*

Canadensis
Lima, Jacqueline Dutton *artist, educator*

Chadds Ford
Gaadt, Suzanne DeMott *graphic designer*

Cochranville
Sazegar, Morteza *artist*

Devon
Santoleri, Nicholas Peter *artist, art publishing company executive*

East Stroudsburg
Lane, Miharu Qualkinbush *artist, educator*

Easton
Delong, Ronald *artist, educator*

Elkins Park
Erlebacher, Martha Mayer *artist, educator*
†Romberg, Osvaldo *artist*
Schatz, Charlotte Asness *artist, educator*

Erdenheim
Murphy, Mary Marguerite *artist*

Exton
Webber, Helen *artist, designer*

Fairless Hills
Marable, Simeon-David *artist*

Glen Mills
Turner, Janet Sullivan *painter, sculptor*

Glenshaw
Guentner, James Francis, Jr., *art educator, artist*

Glenside
Frudakis, Zenos Antonios *sculptor, artist*
Medel, Rebecca Rosalie *artist*

Glenwillard
Milne, Christopher McQuiston Wilmoth *photographer, journalist*

Hawley
Persche, Henry-Peter *art consultant, artist*

Huntingdon Valley
Edelman, Janice *artist, educator*

Indiana
†LaRoche, Lynda *artist, educator*

Jessup
Karluk, Lori Jean *craft designer, copy editor*

Kimberton
Williams, Lawrence Soper *photographer*

Kinzer
Blake, Richard E. *sculptor, art educator*

Lancaster
Galligan, Carolyn M.B. *artist, educator*
Kent, Charles Imbrie, III, *artist, former university official*
Kermes, Constantine John *artist, industrial designer*
Stewart, Arlene Jean Golden *designer, stylist*

Lederach
Hallman, H(enry) Theodore, Jr., (Ted Hallman) *artist, textile designer*

Ligonier
†Lear, M. Kathleen *artist, music educator, small business owner*

Lumberville
Katsiff, Bruce *artist*

Mechanicsville
Bye, Ranulph DeBayeux *artist, author*

Media
†Steinhardt Gutman, Bertha *artist, educator*
Turner, Letitia Rhodes *artist*

Millersville
†Bensur, Barbara Jean *art educator, researcher*
Giblin, Claire L. *artist*

Moon Township
Bacher, Lutz *film, video and photography educator*

Narberth
†Pollack, Sonya A. *artist*

New Hope
Brandes, Doris *artist, art administrator, journalist*

Newtown Square
Vela, Laurie Story *illustrator, writer, publisher, producer*

Norristown
Gerdes, Michelle Ann *designer*

Philadelphia
Camp, Donald Eugene *experimental photographer, educator*
†Di Falco, Gerard A. *visual artist*
Druckrey, Inge Heide *graphic designer, educator*
Faraghan, George Telford *photographer*
Fine, Miriam Brown *artist, educator, poet, writer*
Le Clair, Charles George *artist, retired university dean*
Levy, Rochelle Feldman *artist*
McCormick, Rod *sculptor, art educator*
Paone, Peter *artist*
†Saul, April *photographer*
Schaff, Barbara Walley *artist*
Spandorfer, Merle Sue *artist, educator, author*
Willet, E(verett) Crosby *artist*
Williams, James Boughton *artist, art educator*
Yaros, Constance Greenberg *painter, sculptor*

Pittsburgh
Bickel, Minnette Duffy *artist*
Burgess, David Lowry *artist*
Foucart Vincenti, Valerie *retired art educator*
Kamienska-Carter, Eva Hanna *designer, artist*
Schwalb, Harry *artist*
Spalding, Rita Lee *artist*
Wilkins, David George *fine arts educator*

Pottstown
Mitchell, Eric Ehrman *photographer, stock broker*

Reading
†Bush, George Arthur *illustrator*

Scranton
Alexander, Steven *artist, educator*

Selinsgrove
Connolly, Elma Troutman *artist, contractor, designer*

Shickshinny
Luksha, Rosemary Dorothy *art educator*

Shippensburg
Sturtz-Davis, Shirley Zampelli *artist, retired arts administrator/educator, fashion archivist*

Slippery Rock
Bruya, John Robert *art educator*

Solebury
Anthonisen, George Rioch *sculptor, artist*

Spring Grove
Helberg, Shirley Adelaide Holden *artist, educator*

Villanova
Beck, Christine Safford *photographer, publisher, volunteer*

Washington
Maloney, Patricia Diana *artist, educator*

Wellsboro
Driskell, Lucile G. *artist*

West Grove
Allman, Margo Hutz *sculptor, painter*

Wynnewood
Buffum, Kathleen D. *artist*

Yardley
Ahrens, Henry William *art educator, consultant, puppeteer*
Finn, Marie Frances *artist*
Harris, Charney Anita *painter, sculptor*

York
Laucks, Therese Elaine *commercial art instructor*

RHODE ISLAND

Carolina
O'Neill, Lawrence T. *artist, poet*

Chepachet
Pentleton, Carol June *visual communications designer*

Hope Valley
Devin, Carl Eric *artist*

Jamestown
Worden, Katharine Cole *sculptor*

Lincoln
Volmer, Suzanne *artist*

Narragansett
Bentley-Scheck, Grace Mary *artist*

Newport
Liotus, Sandra Mary *lighting designer, business owner, consultant*
Nash, Karen Marsteller Myers *sculptor, designer, systems analyst*
†Newman, Howard H. *painter, sculptor, artist*
Rogers, Rita *artist, conservator*

North Kingstown
Kilguss, Elsie Schaich *artist, gallery owner*

Pawtucket
Boghossian, Joan Thompson *artist*

Providence
Grimaldi, Vince *artist*
Harman, Carole Moses *retired art educator, artist*
Heyman, Lawrence Murray *printmaker, painter*

Howes, Lorraine de Wet *fashion designer, educator*
Immonen, Gerald Matthew *artist*
Spalter, Anne Morgan *artist*
Wunderlich, Alfred Leon *artist, art educator*

Smithfield
Kosowski, Mary *artist, educator*

Wakefield
Leete, William White *artist*

SOUTH CAROLINA

Camden
Buckley, Claude Langford *artist*

Central
Smith-Cox, Elizabeth Shelton *art educator*

Chapin
McNinch, Michel Cottingham *artist, educator*

Charleston
Kitner, Harold *artist, educator*

Clover
Easter, Jr., Willie *artist, writer*

Columbia
Elkins, Toni Marcus *artist, art association administrator*
Hansen, Harold John (Harry Hansen) *artist, educator*
Thompson, Charles Otis *lighting designer*

Georgetown
Robinson, Betty Hefner *artist*

Gray Court
†West, Jack *art dealer*

Greenville
McCune, Linda Williams *artist, educator*

Hilton Head Island
Shepard, Steven Louis *graphic artist, painter*

Lexington
Holland, Gene Grigsby (Scottie Holland) *artist*

Mc Cormick
Hofer, Ingrid *artist, educator*

Mount Pleasant
Ayres, Paul Erdman *artist*

Murrells Inlet
Howard, Joan Alice *artist*

Seneca
Oppenheimer, Nancy Bea *artist*

SOUTH DAKOTA

Huron
Clatworthy, Catherine Lynn *educational trainer, graphics designer*

Rosebud
†MacKichan, Margaret Anna *artist, art educator*

Sioux Falls
Aldern, Robert Judson *architectural, liturgical and landscape artist*
DeGeus, Wendell Ray *photographer*
Peters, John Henry *artist*

Spearfish
Termes, A. Dick *artist*

TENNESSEE

Chattanooga
Martin, Chester Y. *sculptor, painter*
Mills, Olan, II, *photography company executive*
Swanger, Daniel Anthony-Ignatius *artist*

Kingston
Worden, Marny *artist, musician*

Knoxville
Drinnon, Janis Bolton *artist, poet, volunteer*
Sublett, Carl Cecil *artist, educator*

La Follette
Stormer, Barbara Jean *artist*

Lookout Mountain
†Wyeth, Andrew *artist*

Memphis
Burton, Fred Clifford *visual artist, educator*
Carroll, Billy Price *artist*
Crawford, Sheila Jane *elementary education librarian, reading consultant*
De Mere-Dwyer, Leona *medical illustrator*
McPherson, Larry E(ugene) *photographer, educator*
Riss, Murray *photographer, educator*

Nashville
†Albright, Julia Szur *artist*
Chandler, Nettie Johnson *artist*
Chenicek, Laura *artist, educator*
Oates, Sherry Charlene *portraitist, artist, photographer*
Porter, Ronald *artist, educator*
Sharp, Katherine Street *artist, business owner*

Oak Ridge
†Regan-Stanton, Christa Maria *artist*

Rockvale
†Ritter, Sparkle Whitaker *lighting designer, educator*

Sewanee
Ende, Arlyn Ruth *textile artist, arts administrator*
Warburton, Minnie *writer, artist*

TEXAS

Austin
Fearing, William Kelly *art educator, artist*
Goldstein, Peggy R. *sculptor*
Guerin, John William *artist*
Hatgil, Paul Peter *artist, sculptor, educator*
High, Timothy Griffin *artist, educator, curator, writer*
Long, Bert Louis, Jr., *artist*
Mayer, Susan Martin *art educator*
†Moreno, David *artist*
Reese, Claudia *artist*
Robinson, Priscilla Jane *artist*
Sawyer, Margo Lucy *artist, educator*
Smith, Jeffrey Chipps *art educator*
Weismann, Donald Leroy *art educator, artist, filmmaker, writer*

Bellaire
Lundy, Anstis Burwell *artist*

Brownsville
Gómez, Carlos Guillermo *artist, educator, curator*

Cedar Hill
Moore, Jacquelyn *art educator, artist*

Cleburne
†Arnold, Sandra Ruth Kouns *photographer*

College Station
Stone, Mary Elizabeth *artist*

Commerce
Seawell, Thomas Robert *artist, retired educator*

Conroe
Ballard, Carrie *artist*

Corpus Christi
Goode, Jane Kinney *artist*
Ullberg, Kent Jean *sculptor*

Corrigan
†Jeffrey, J. Jann *artist, educator*

Corsicana
Senkarik, Mikki *oil painter*

Dallas
Blessen, Karen Alyce *artist, writer*
†Dealey, Lynn Townsend *artist*
Gantz, Ann Cushing *artist, educator*
Kochan, Patricia Ann *artist*
†Lawrence, Annette *artist*
Norman, Bobby Don *artist, writer, theologian*

Denton
Cox, Barbara Claire *costume designer, educator*

Duncanville
Terry, Martin Michael *visual artist, art therapist*

El Paso
Cox, Helen Adelaide (Holly Cox) *artist, writer*

Elgin
Hallenbeck, Pomona Juanita *artist*

Euless
Leding, Anne Dixon *artist, educator*

Fort Worth
Allen, William Marion, III, *retired graphic designer, artist*
Durham, Jo Ann Fanning *artist*
Kellerman, Shirley Rose *artist*
Phillips, Mary Ann *artist, writer, retired legal secretary*
Procknow, Margot *artist*
Rickett, Carolyn Kaye Master *artist, criminologist*

Houston
Camfield, William Arnett *art educator, educator*
†Davenport, Bill *sculptor*
Hamilton, Jacqueline *art consultant*
Honeycutt, George Leonard *photographer, retired*
Jackson, Susanne Leora *retired creative placement firm executive*
Matalon, Marlene *artist*
O'Neil, John *artist*
Orr, Carole *artist*
Parkerson, John E. (Sandy) *art dealer*
Reid, Katherine Louise *artist, educator, author*
Saks, Judith-Ann *artist*
Shelley, Clyde Burton *artist*

Huntsville
Lea, Stanley E. *artist, educator*

Katy
Huffaker, E. Wayne *artist*

Kerrville
Chance, F. Earlayne *artist*
Frudakis, Evangelos William *sculptor*

Lakehills
Spears, Diane Shields *artist, retired art academy administrator*

Laredo
Watson, Helen Richter *educator, ceramic artist*

Lometa
Thompson, Mary Koleta *sculptor, non-profit organization management consultant*

Lufkin
Mott, Earl *artist, poet, writer*

Mabank
Smith, Thelma Tina Harriette *gallery owner, artist*

Marfa
Meyer, Ellen Adams *arts and small business development specialist*

Midland
King, Mary Lou *artist, medical technologist*

Mission
McClendon, Maxine Nichols *artist*

New Braunfels
Alexander, Anna Margaret *artist, writer, educator*

Odessa
Phillips, Barry *artist, educator*

Plano
Cotter-Smith, Cathleen Marie *art educator, artist*
†Kuddes, Kathryn M. *fine arts director*

Port Aransas
Van Baalen, Donna Gale *artist, retired pharmacist*

Post
Killian, Lawrence Harding, II, (Larry H. Killian) *sculptor*

San Angelo
Mobley, Nancy Elizabeth *artist, art educator*

San Antonio
Elder, Gene Wesley *artist*
Garza, Xavier *artist, writer*
Hammond, Linda *artist*

Spring
Wilbanks, Mary *artist*

Waco
Kagle, Joseph Louis, Jr., *artist, arts administrator, art educator*

Wimberley
Troester, Waltraud *artist, graphic designer, consultant*

UTAH

American Fork
Reinhold, Allen Kurt *graphic design educator*

Bountiful
†Peterson, Rose Ann *artist*

Castle Valley
Zavada, Barbara Johanna *artist*

Logan
Rasmuson, Brent J. *photographer, graphic artist, lithographer*

Monroe
Kirby, Orville Edward *potter, painter, sculptor*

Salt Lake City
Dibaiyan, Fatemeh Mariam *artist*
Hougaard, Todd Lamont *photographer*
Maxwell, George Russell *scenic designer*

Springville
Francis, Rell Gardner *artist, photographer, writer*

Stansbury Park
Moyer, Linda Lee *artist, educator, author*

West Jordan
Wyness, Steven Charles *illustrator*

VERMONT

Belvidere Center
Lipke, Kathryn *artist, educator*

Bristol
Dendler, Royce *painter, sculptor, writer*

Cavendish
Shapiro, David *artist, art historian*

Charlotte
Robinson, Sally Winston *artist*

Danby
Peel, Harris *art gallery owner, retired diplomat*

East Calais
de Gogorza, Patricia *sculptor, educator*

Enosburg Falls
Svendsen, Alf *artist, art educator*

Essex Junction
Tedd, Monique Micheline *artist*

Hardwick
Holtz, Laurence *artisan, photographer*

Manchester Center
Armstrong, Jane Botsford *sculptor*

Milton
Vreman, Anna Aurora *artist, technical writer*

Newark
Van Vliet, Claire *artist*

Newbury
McGarrell, James *artist, educator*

North Pomfret
Shepherd, Gaal *artist*

Pownal
Leavey, John Christopher *artist*

Randolph
Zimet, Matthew *graphic arts and science educator*

Springfield
Thayer, Rosealyce Cullen *painter*

Weston
Kasnowski, Chester Nelson *artist, educator*

Winooski
Essman, Robert Norvel *artist, graphic designer*

VIRGINIA

Alexandria
Flood, Sandra Wasko *artist, educator*
Huddy, Margaret *artist, writer, educator*
Kim, Sook Cha *artist*
Tesler, Diane Elaine *artist*
Wasko-Flood, Sandra Jean *artist, educator*
†Whitson, Elizabeth Temple *graphics designer*

Annandale
Smith, Ralph *artist*

Arlington
†Lurry, Michael Christopher *graphics designer, writer*
†McCoart, Janice Greenberg *art educator*
Reed, Paul Allen *artist*

Blacksburg
Davis, Carole Carrera *watercolor artist*
Gablik, Suzi *art educator, writer*

Burgess
Krebs, Rockne *artist*

Charlottesville
Gladstone, Arthur M. *artist, author*
†Norment, Rachel Gobbel *artist, educator, writer*
Priest, Hartwell Wyse *artist*
Weinberger, Adrienne *artist, appraiser*

Chesapeake
Katz, MaryAnne *artist, educator*

Chincoteague
Payne, Nancy Sloan *retired visual arts educator*

Clifton
Hennesy, Gerald Craft *artist*

Colonial Heights
Grizzard-Barham, Barbara Lee *artist*

Draper
Whitehurst, Mary Tarr *artist, poet, writer*

Fairfax
Krupinski, Christine Margaret *artist*

Falls Church
Harshfield, Neil Alan *sculptor, educator*

Flint Hill
Forbush, Sandra M. *artist, educator*

Fredericksburg
Herndon, Cathy Campbell *artist, educator*
Nikolic, Jean *artist*
Schmutzhart, Berthold Josef *sculptor, educator, art and education consultant*

Front Royal
†Armstrong, Hamilton Reed *sculptor, educator*

Harrisonburg
Theodore, Crystal *artist, retired educator*

Independence
Craig, James Hicklin *fine arts consultant*

Leesburg
†Robertson, Ruth *artist, art gallery owner*

Leon
Han, Nong *artist, sculptor, painter*

Lynchburg
Hudson, Walter Tiree *artist*
Massie, Anne Adams Robertson *artist*

Mc Lean
Freyer, Victoria C. *fashion and interior design executive*
Kipniss MacDonald, Betty Ann *artist, educator*
Rugala, Karen Francis (Karen Francis) *painter, television producer*
Safer, John *artist, lecturer, banker, real estate developer*
Scott, Concetta Ciotti *artist, art educator*

Middleburg
Robinson, Michael Francis *private art dealer and appraiser*

Midlothian
Kellum, Betsy M. *artist, educator*

New Hope
Hough, Michael James *sculptor, educator*

Newport News
Abbott, Beverly Stubblefield *artist*
Camp, Hazel Lee Burt *artist*
Hoffman, Nannette Hertz Schweig *artist, poet, educator*
†Kyte, Shannan Dyan *multimedia designer*

Norfolk
Frieden, Jane Heller *art educator*

Oak Hill
Adler, Dale Atkins *artist*

Petersburg
†Abbott-Ryan, Pat *painter, writer*

Radford
Kessler, Kendall Seay Feriozi *artist*

Reston
Deremer, Susan René *artist*

Richmond
Bohannan, Jay Kirby *artist*
Freed, David Clark *artist*
Kevorkian, Richard *artist*
Savedge, Anne Creery *artist, photographer*
Vaughn, Ann Marie *art educator, artist*

Roanoke
Osterhaus, Greg S. *artist, graphic designer*

Swoope
Avery, Robert Newell *sculptor*

Vienna
Milton, Carol Lynne *artist*
Yamaguchi, Yuriko Fujita *artist*

Virginia Beach
Drozda, Donna Jean *artist, educator, inventor*
Ruben, Leonard *retired art educator*
Schroff, Lois Grunwell *artist, color researcher*

Wachapreague
Wilkins, Guy (Ira Wilkins) *painter, art teacher*

Williamsburg
Coleman, Henry Edwin *art educator, artist*
Lorenz, Hans Ernest *photographer*
Robinson, Jay (Jay Thurston Robinson) *artist*

WASHINGTON

Anacortes
Mc Cracken, Philip Trafton *sculptor*

Bainbridge Island
Burns, Shirley M. *artist, educator*
Carlson, Robert Michael *artist*
Grisham, Jeannie *artist*

Battle Ground
Hansen, James Lee *sculptor*

Belfair
Cooper, Shirley Ruth *artist, illustrator*

Camano Island
Thayer, Thomas Manor, Jr., *artist*

Cheney
Feeney, Kendall Greer *art director, music educator*

Edmonds
Deering, Anne-Lise *artist, retired real estate salesperson*
Johnson, d'Elaine Ann Herard *artist, consultant*

Ellensburg
†Loper, Patte *art educator, artist*

Everett
Krahn, Thomas Frank *photographer*

Goldendale
Musgrave, Lee *artist, museum administrator*

Issaquah
Parker-Fairbanks, Dixie *artist*

Kent
Pierce, Danny Parcel *artist, educator*

Kirkland
Bibaud, Rene *artist, performer, consultant*

Leavenworth
†Caemmerer, Richard Rudolph *art educator*

Lilliwaup
McGrady, Corinne Young *design company executive*

Mercer Island
Langhout-Nix, Nelleke *artist*

Ocean Park
Lee, Martha *artist, writer*

Olympia
Fitzgerald, Betty Jo *artist, educator, curator*
Haseltine, James Lewis *artist, consultant*
John, Yvonne Maree *artist, designer*
Randlett, Mary Willis *photographer*
Thomas-John, Yvonne Maree *artist, interior designer*

Palouse
Russman, Irene Karen *artist*

Richland
Ristow, Gail Ross *art educator, paralegal, children's rights advocate*
Sinerius-Rupp-Bloor, Sharon Kay *sculptor*

Seattle
†Berger, Paul Eric *artist, photographer*
Brody, David *artist, educator*
Bruch, Barbara Rae *artist, educator*
Calderon, Mark A. *artist, sculptor*
Dailey, Michael Dennis *painter, educator*
De Alessi, Ross Alan *lighting designer*
†Farbanish, Thomas *sculptor*
Feldman, Roger Lawrence *artist, educator*
Gardiner, T(homas) Michael *artist*
Gault, Rosette Ford *artist, writer, composer, inventor*
Kangas, Matthew Arvid *art critic, curator*
Safonov, Alexandre Anatolevich *artist*
Scott, Samuel Joseph *art educator, artist*
Tift, Mary Louise *artist*
Washington, James Winston, Jr., *artist, sculptor*

Sequim
Belson, Patricia A. *artist*
Guilmet, Glenda Jean *artist*

Snohomish
Guzak, Karen Jean Wahlstrom *artist*

Tacoma
Harris, Robert Gaylen *art director, graphic designer, illustrator*

Vancouver
Hulburt, Lucille Hall *artist, educator*
Tower, Sue Warncke *artist*

Vashon
Ingalls, Pamela Lynn *artist, educator*

WEST VIRGINIA

Bluefield
Brown, Sheri Lynn *artist, poet, educator*

Buckhannon
Oiler, Dorilou Wemlinger *artist*

Charleston
Moore, Jeanne *retired arts educator and administrator*

Institute
Moore, Mark Tobin *art educator, artist, retired museum curator*

Parkersburg
Gilbert, Kenneth G. *art educator*

Wheeling
Phillis, Marilyn Hughey *artist*

WISCONSIN

Appleton
Amm, Sophia Jadwiga *artist, educator*

Elkhorn
Herr, Richard Joseph *sculptor, educator*

Germantown
Hargan, Charles James *retired lithographer, village official*

Gordon
La Liberte, Ann Gillis *graphic artist, consultant, designer, educator*

Grafton
Duback, Sally Wood *artist, educator*

Hartland
Stamsta, Jean F. *artist*

Hollandale
Colescott, Warrington Wickham *artist, printmaker, educator*

Iola
Rosenberger, Carolyn Ann *art educator*

Janesville
Detert-Moriarty, Judith Anne *graphic artist, educator, civic activist*

Madison
Becker, David *artist, educator*
Cooper, Peggy (Mary Margaret) *artist, educator, poet, composer, choreographer*

Marshfield
Gardner, Ella Haines *artist*

Mc Farland
Deniston-Trochta, Grace Marie *educator, artist*

Milwaukee
Biller, Geraldine Pollack *art consultant, curator*
Michaels-Paque, Joan Marie *artist, educator*
Paque, Joan Michaels *multimedia artist, author, educator*
†Spransy, Celeste Bower *artist*
Thrall, Arthur Alvin *artist, educator*
Weisner, David *illustrator*

New Richmond
†Schwan, LeRoy Bernard *artist, retired educator*

Oconomowoc
Conrader, Constance Ruth *artist, writer, librarian*
†Driscoll, Virgilyn Mae (Schaetzel) *retired art educator, artist, consultant*
Vespa, Ned Angelo *photographer*

Oshkosh
Hu, Li *art educator*
Smith, Merilyn Roberta *art educator*

Redgranite
Borchardt, Betsy Olk *artist*

South Milwaukee
Knoll, Gregg A. *artist, printmaker, educator*

Superior
Grittner, James Russell *artist, educator, department chair*

Whitewater
Arntson, Amy Ellen *artist, art educator*
Gauger, Michele Roberta *photographer, studio administrator, corporate executive*

WYOMING

Casper
†Navarro, Christopher J. *artist*
Ryan, Linda Lee *sculptor, art educator*

Centennial
Russin, Robert Isaiah *sculptor, educator*

Cheyenne
Moore, Mary French (Muffy Moore) *potter, community activist*

Cody
Jackson, Harry Andrew *artist*

Jackson
Roll-Preissler, Audrey *artist*

Laramie
Griffin, Leah G. *art specialist*
Reif, David (Frank David Reif) *artist, educator*

TERRITORIES OF THE UNITED STATES

PUERTO RICO

San Juan
Luna Padilla, Nitza Enid *photography educator*

CANADA

ALBERTA

Calgary
Besant, Derek Michael *artist, educator*

BRITISH COLUMBIA

Duncan
Hughes, Edward John *artist*

Salt Spring Island
Raginsky, Nina *artist*

Vancouver
†Bonifacho, Bratsa *artist*
Grauer, Gay Meredith (Sherrard Grauer) *artist*

Victoria
Harvey, Donald *artist, educator*

MANITOBA

Winnipeg
Eyre, Ivan *artist, educator*

NEWFOUNDLAND

Corner Brook
Coyne, John Michael *artist, educator*

Portugal Cove
Creates, Marlene Ruth *artist*

Torbay
Dabinett, Diana Frances *visual artist*

NOVA SCOTIA

Halifax
Kulyk, Karen Gay *visual artist*

Wolfville
Bartkiw, Roman *artist*
Colville, David Alexander *artist*

ONTARIO

Etobicoke
Aska, Warabé (Takeshi Masuda) *artist, writer*

Kincardine
Braswell, Paula Ann *artist*

London
Livick, Stephen *fine art photographer*

Mississauga
Sabelis, Huibert *artist*

Peterborough
Dumas, Michael Godfrey Joseph *artist*

Red Lake
Zaikow, Larry J. James *painter*

Scarborough
Cetín, Anton *artist*

Toronto
Astman, Barbara Ann *artist, educator*
Bolley, Andrea *artist*
Downing, Robert James *artist*
Elder, Richard Bruce *artist, writer*
Jaworska, Tamara *painter, tapestry maker*
Kooluris Dobbs, Linda Kia *artist*
Kramer, Burton *graphic designer, educator*
Semak, Michael William *photographer, educator*
Tolmie, Kenneth Donald *artist, author*
Winter, Frederick Elliot *fine arts educator*

Waterloo
Urquhart, Tony *artist, educator*

QUEBEC

Beaconsfield
Harder, Rolf Peter *graphic designer, painter*

Longueil
Archambault, Louis *sculptor*

Montreal
Charney, Melvin *artist, architect, educator*
Hopkins, Tom *artist*
Krausz, Peter Thomas *artist, gallery director, educator*

Saint-Adele
†Rousseau-Vermette, Mariette *artist*

SASKATCHEWAN

Saskatoon
Bornstein, Eli *artist, sculptor*

MEXICO

Mexico City
†De La Riva, Myriam Ann *artist*
Friedeberg, Pedro *painter, sculptor, designer*

Mich
di Cori, Pat Miller *painter, sculptor*

AUSTRALIA

Hawthorn
Base, Graeme Rowland *illustrator, author*

Malanda
Cooper, William Thomas *natural history artist*

AUSTRIA

Vienna
Higgins, William Woods *painter, art educator*
Mag Walz, Günther *artist*

BELGIUM

Brussels
Nelson, Marcella Simonetta *artist*

EGYPT

Cairo
Basilious, Nagi Moussa *artist, painter*
Morsi, Abd el Wahab *artist*

ENGLAND

Chiswick
Adams, Norman *artist, educator*

London
†Brotherston, Lez *set designer, costumer*
Edwards, Sylvia Ann *artist*
Hiller, Susan *artist*
Mendoza, Ryan *artist*
Ramos, Theodore Sanchez de Piña *artist, educator*
Vicari, Andrew *artist*

Oaker
Pickering, Pollyanna *artist*

Richmond Surrey
Armfield, Diana Maxwell *artist, educator*

FRANCE

Arles
Clergue, Lucien Georges *photographer*

Maine et Loire
Wilkinson, Una McCann *artist*

Paris
Lacroix, Christian Marie Marc *fashion designer*
Langley, Joseph Jeremiah *artist, poet*
Levee, John Harrison *artist, designer*
Ungaro, Emanuel Matteotti *fashion designer*

Saint Ceols
Saisselin, Remy Gilbert *fine arts educator*

GERMANY

Berlin
Iannone, Dorothy *visual artist, writer*
Meckseper, Friedrich *painter, printermaker*

Frankfurt
Ammann, Jean-Christophe *art director*

ISRAEL

Ariel
Alexenberg, Mel (Mel Alexenberg Menahem) *artist, art educator*

Jerusalem
Menses, Jan *artist, draftsman, etcher, lithographer, muralist*

ITALY

Camaiore
Lavatelli, Carla *sculptor, weaver*

Florence
Cecil, Charles Harkless *artist, educator*

Milan
Honegger, Federico *artist*

Pietrasanta
Marinsky, Harry *artist*
Swarz, Sahl *sculptor*

JAPAN

Kanagawa
Kato, Tomiko *artist*

NEW ZEALAND

Auckland
Cuba, Ivan *artist*

PAKISTAN

Lahore
Geoffrey, Iqbal (Mohammed Jawaid Iqbal Jafree) *artist, educator, lawyer*

POLAND

Warsaw
Abakanowicz, Magdalena *artist, sculptor*

SAINT LUCIA

Gablewoods Mall
Branch, Winston Patrick *artist*

SPAIN

Macharaviaya
Harvey, Robert Martin *artist*

Seville
Sanchez, Leonedes Monarrize Worthington (His Royal Highness Duke de Leonedes of Spain Sicily Greece) *fashion designer*

SWEDEN

Bralanda
Emilson, Henry Bertil *artist*

SWITZERLAND

Geneva
Fetherston, Marianne Renee *artist, painter*

TUNISIA

Carthage
Sehili, Mahmoud *artist*

TURKEY

Atakoy
Donma, Hatice *artist*

WEST INDIES

Grand Cayman Island

Ronald, Pauline Carol *retired art educator*

ADDRESS UNPUBLISHED

Abbe, Elfriede Martha *sculptor, graphic artist*
Abbott, Linda Joy *stained glass artisan, educator, photographer*
Abeles, Kim Victoria *artist*
Abeles, Sigmund M. *painter, printmaker, sculptor*
Aber, Ita *multimedia designer, conservator, historian*
Absher, Donna Atkins *textile designer*
†Adler, Posy (Roslyn) *artist, educator*
Albano, Maureen Teresa *artist*
Aldredge, Theoni Vachliotis *costume designer*
Alexander, Marjorie Anne *artist, hand papermaker, art consultant*
Anasazi, Maria *artist, educator*
Ancona, George Efrain *photographer, author*
Andrade, Edna *artist, art educator*
Andrews, Jean *artist, writer*
Archer, Dave *artist*
Arnold, Gloria Malcolm *artist, educator*
Aronson, Jan *artist, educator*
Aronson, Marc *artist*
†Arrigo, Jan Elizabeth *photographer, writer*
Arrott, Patricia Graham *artist, art instructor*
Aschheim, Eve Michele *artist, educator*
Ascone, Teresa Palmer *artist, educator*
Assael, Alyce *artist*
Astaire, Carol Anne Taylor *artist, educator*
Atkin, Edith *artist, poet*
August, Robert William *designer, educator*
Auwarter, Brian William *sculptor*
†Babailov, Igor V. *artist, educator*
Bader, Lorraine Greenberg *textile stylist, designer, consultant*
Baker, Suzanne Martin *artist, rancher*
Baldassano, Vincent J. *artist*
Ballaine, Jerrold Curtis *artist*
Barlow, Jean *art educator, painter*
†Barolini, Nicoletta E. *artist*
†Barreto, Bernardo *artist*
Barrow, Thomas Francis *artist, educator*
†Barsky, Irene J. *graphics designer*
Barth, Frances *artist*
Bartholomew, Dennis *sculptor, fine arts company executive*
Bateman, Robert McLellan *artist*
Bauman, Marilyn Adrienne *artist, educator*
Beard, Audrey Lucille *artist, art educator*
Becker, Jon Andrew *arts and education consultant*
Behr, Marion Ray *artist, writer, business executive*
Bellamy, Jennifer Wiggins *artist*
†Beloff, Zoe *artist, educator*
Benzle, Curtis Munhall *artist, art educator*
Berman, Eleanore *artist*
Bermann, Nancy Stewart *artist*
†Berridge, Mary Lloyd *photographer*
Berryhill, Georgia Gene *web designer, photographer, educator*
Bierman, Sandra *artist*
Birchard, Catherine Suzanne Sieh *artist*
†Bishop, Delores Ann *artist, educator*
Blair, Warren *artist, educator*
Blinder, Janet *art dealer*
Blitt, Rita Lea *artist*
†Block, Thomas Alan *artist, educator*
†Bloodgood-Abrams, Jane Marie *artist*
Blue, China *artist*
Blumenfeld, Rochelle S. Reznik *artist*
Bockus, Kimmerle *photographer, consultant*
Bogdanowicz, Loretta Mae *artist, educator*
Bonassi, Jodi *artist, marketing consultant*
Boni, Miki *artist*
Bowen-Forbes, Jorge Courtney *artist, author, poet*
Bowman, Fay Louise *artist*
Brach, Paul Henry *artist*
Bradford, Peter Corey *design consultant*
Braudy, Dorothy McGahee *artist, educator*
Brearey, Susan Winfield *artist, art educator*
†Brennan, Sara Jean *retired artist*
Brenton, Hatice *painter, graphics designer*
Brigeois, Evelyne Brigitte *artist, publisher*
Bronkar, Eunice Dunalee *artist, art educator*
Brown, Alice Elste *artist*
Brown, Carol *artist*
†Brown, James Justin *artist*
Browne, Diana Gayle *artist, social services*
Buck, John E. *sculptor, print maker, educator*
†Buell, Dexter *artist, sculptor*
Bundi, Renee *art director, graphic designer*
Burkett, Rosemary L. *artist*
Burns, Leslie Kaye *artist*
Burton, Sigrid *artist*
Busch, Nancy Elizabeth *artist, educator*
Butterfield, Deborah Kay *sculptor*
Byrd, Marc Robert *designer, florist*
Cabot, Hugh, III, *painter, sculptor*
Calabrese, Karen Ann *artist, educator*
Calamar, Gloria *artist*
Campbell, Demarest Lindsay *artist, interior designer, writer*
Campbell, Patton *stage designer, educator*
Campello, Florencio Lennox *artist*
†Cape, Francis *artist*
Caplan, Susan Robin *artist, writer, educator*
†Carl, Susan Marie *photographer, photojournalist*
Carroll, Marie-Jean Greve *retired educator, artist*
Carter, Nanette Carolyn *artist*
Caseiras, Jo Ann Striga *artist, educator*
Casey, Thomas Warren *graphic design company executive, architect*
Cassara, Frank *artist, printmaker*
Chapin, Deborah *artist*
Charney, Sharon Renee *artist*
Chase, Doris Totten *sculptor, video artist, filmmaker*
Child, Judith *artist*
Chinni, Peter Anthony *artist, poet*
Clague, John Rogers *sculptor*
†Claiborne, Liz (Elisabeth Claiborne Ortenberg) *fashion designer*
Clark, Sara M. *artist, art educator*
Cobb, Ruth *artist*
Cofer, Deborah End *artist*
Cogan, John Dennis *artist*
Colbert, Margaret Matthew *artist*
Colker, Edward *artist, educator*
Conklin, Eric Linwood *artist*
Conroy, Tamara Boks *artist, special education educator, former nurse*
Cooper, Elva June *artist, writer*
Cooper, Rebecca *art dealer*
Coover, Doris Dimock *artist*
Corcoran, David *designer, artist*
†Corey, Claire *artist*
Coughlin, Jack *printmaker, sculptor, art educator*
Cox, Pat *artist*
Cramer, Richard Charles *artist, educator*
Craw, Freeman (Jerry) *graphic artist*
Cummings, David William *artist, educator*
†Curington, Thomas Franklin, III, *photographer, writer*
Curnutte, Mary E. *artist, restorer of painting, educator*
Currie, Steven Ray *artist*
Dailey, Daniel Owen *artist, educator, designer*
D'Alessio, Valaida Corrine *artist, consultant*
Daley, Sandra *retired artist, filmmaker, photographer*
Dangremond, David W. *fine arts educator*
Davidson, Jeannie *costume designer*
†Davis, Courtney A. *artist, educator*
Debevoise, A. Clay *artist*
De Blasi, Tony (Anthony Armando De Blasi) *artist*
Dechar, Peter Henry *artist*
DeGraff, Helen Marie *artist*
DeHority, Miriam A. (Miriam Newman) *artist*
DeJack, Jacqueline Elvadeana *artist, educator*
DeLoyht-Arendt, Mary Isobel *artist*
Dennick, Lori Ann (Loranden) *artist, model, actress*
Despres, Patrick John *artist, art educator*
Dickau, Keith Michael (Mike Dickau) *artist, secondary school educator*
DiEdwardo, Mary Ann Pasda *artist, writer*
Di Giacomo, Fran *artist*
Dill, Laddie John *artist*
Di Suvero, Mark *sculptor*
Dixon, Michael Wayne *designer, writer, researcher*
Dogançay, Burhan C. *artist, photographer, sculptor*
Dominguez, Eddie *artist*
Donath, Therese *artist, author*
Downes, Rackstraw *artist*
Doyle, Tom *sculptor, retired educator*
Drasler, Gregory John *artist*
Du Boise, Kim Rees *artist, photographer, art educator*
Dunbar, Bruce Stephen *photographer, gallery administrator*
Duval-Carrié, Edouard *artist*
Easterson, Sam *artist*
Ebata, Masako *artist*
Eddy, Don *artist*
Edmo, Jean Umiokalani *artist, poet*
Elcik, Elizabeth Mabie *fashion illustrator*
Engle, Steve Eugene *artist*
†Erden, Sybil Isolde *artist*
Evans, Judith Ann Futral *artist*
Ewing, Edgar Louis *artist, educator*
Fahey-Cameron, Robin *artist, photographer, writer*
Falconer, Marguerite Elizabeth *artist*
Farrar, Elaine Willardson *artist*
Favorite, Malaika *artist*
Faxon, Alicia Craig *art educator, department chairman*
Feiler, Jo Alison *artist*
Ferreira, Armando Thomas *sculptor, educator*
Ferri, Ronald Domenico *artist, painter*
Fetherston, Brian Lloyd *artist, painter, sculptor*
Field, Charles Twist *artist, retired art educator*
†Fields, Tina Rae *artist, ecopsychologist*
Fiks, Yevgeniy *artist, critic*
Fillmore, John Dillon *artist*
Finn, Mary Ralphe *artist*
Firestein, Cecily Barth *artist*
Fish, Janet Isobel *artist*
†Fisher, Margaret *artist, researcher*
Fitzgerald, Daniel R. *artist, consultant*
Fleming, Susan F. *artist*
Foster, Fredericka *artist*
Foti, Joanne Erminia *painter, textile designer, educator*
Fox, Jennifer Joy *artist, educator*
†Frank, JoAnn *photographer*
Frank, Leona *artist*
Fraser, Frederick Ewart *art educator*
Frauenhoffer, Rose Marie *visual artist, cosmetologist*
Frederick, Elizabeth Eleanor Tatum *watercolor artist, retired educator*
Freeland, Aaron Leonard *painter, printmaker*
Freilicher, Jane *artist*
Friday, Katherine Orwoll *artist*
Friedman, Betsy Sue *artist*
Friedman, Marcia L *photographer, writer*
†Fruisen, Catherine Myler (Violet LeMay) *illustrator*
Fumagalli, Barbara Merrill *artist, printmaker*
†Furth, Karen J. *artist, art educator*
Gallagher, Cynthia *artist, educator*
Galvis y Assmus, Patricia *computer animator, educator, filmmaker*
Gamble, Desirata *artist, poet*
Gard, Judy Richardson *artist, educator*
Gardner, Elizabeth Ann Hunt *artist, poet, genealogist*
Gedroc, Maria *artist*
George, Cecelia G. *photographer, writer, artist, musician*
†Gerhardt, Carol Ashby *visual artist*
Gillespie, Adrienne Amalia *artist, editor, researcher*
Glasson, Lloyd *sculptor, educator*
Glen, Niki *artist*
†Gloman, David J. *artist*
Godbee, Gary Russell *artist*
Gold, Betty Virginia *artist*
Goldberger, Blanche Rubin *sculptor, jeweler*
Goldblatt, Eileen Witzman *art director, director, management consultant*
Golden, Judith Greene *artist, educator*
Goldsmith, Elsa M. *painter, graphic artist*
Goolsby, Charles William *artist, educator*
Graham, K(athleen) M. (K. M. Graham) *artist*
Grames-Lyra, Judith Ellen *retired artist, building plans examiner*
†Grams, Diane M. *artist, educator*
Gray, Barbara May *artist*
Greenberg, Albert *art director*
Greene, Lynne Jeannette *fashion designer*
Gregson, Merry Chris (Merry Smith) *artist*
Griffin, Linda French *artist, activist, consultant*
Grim, Ellen Townsend *artist, retired art educator*
Guevarra, Manuel Robinson *artist, retired military officer*
Gurwitz-Hall, Barbara Ann *artist*
Gutiérrez, Mary Carmen *artist*
Hajikano, Maki *artist*
Haley, Sally Fulton *artist*
†Hall, Douglas Erskine *artist, educator*
Hall, Susan Laurel *artist, educator, writer*
Hamel, Louise *artist, writer, muralist*
†Hamilton, Ann Katherine *artist*
Hammond, Mary Sayer *art educator*
Hanan, Laura Molen *artist*
†Hannaman, Alberta Anna *artist*
Hanson, Janice Crawford *artist, financial analyst*
Hanson, Jo *artist, lecturer, writer*
Harper, James Robert *graphic designer, sculptor*
Hartley, Corinne *painter, sculptor, educator*
Hasen, Burton Stanley *artist*
Hasson, Raymond Edward, III, *artist, writer*
Havens, Keith Cornell *artist*
Hawkins, Cynthia *artist, educator*
Hayes, David Vincent *sculptor*
Hecht, Irene *artist, educator*
Heginbotham, Jan Sturza *sculptor*
Helander, Bruce Paul *artist*
Heller, Dorothy *artist*
Heller, Jules *artist, writer, educator*
†Hemmila, Linda-Kay *graphics designer*
Henson Scales, Meg D(iane) *artist, writer, publisher*
Herman, David Henry *artist, violin restorer and dealer*
†Hermann, Mildred L. *artist*
Herranen, Kathy *artist, graphic designer*
Herzberg, Thomas *artist, illustrator*
†Hickman, Patricia *artist, craftswoman*
Higgins, Margaret Christie *photographer*
Hill, Catherine Stanton *freelance artist*
†Hofmann, George W. *artist, educator*
Holden, Rebecca Lynn *artist*
Holt, Rochelle Lynn *writer, lecturer*
Holter, Patra Jo *artist, art education consultant*
†Holton, William *artist*
Holzer, Jenny *artist*
Hornick, Katherine Joyce Kay *artist, small business owner*
Huber, Colleen Adlene *artist*
Huffington, Anita *sculptor*
Hughes, Michael Patrick *artist*
Hull, Margaret Ruth *artist, educator, consultant*
†Humann, Richard *artist*
Hummel, Marian *retired art teacher, photographer*
Hunt, Charlotte Dumaresq (Demi) *artist, writer*
Hunt, Mary Melinda *artist*
Huo, Bonnie Kwan *artist*
Hurcomb, Laura Grace *visual artist*
Iannaccone, Cynthia Jean *painter, illustrator*
Jackson, Lola Hirdler *art educator*
Janko, May *graphic artist*
Jansen, Angela Bing *artist, educator*
Jarcho, Judith Lynn *artist, art educator*
Jay, Norma Joyce *artist*
†Johnson, Elaine Lucille *artist, director*
Jones, Jane *artist*
Jones, John Harding *photographer*
Josephson, Kenneth Bradley *artist, retired educator*
Kahn, Susan *artist*
Kannenstine, Margaret Lampe *artist*
Kaplan, Phyllis *artist, composer*
Karnofsky, Mollyne *artist, poet*
Katchor, Ben *cartoonist, artist, writer*
Kauffman, Kaethe Coventon *art educator, artist, author*
†Kazan, Alexandra Khan *photographer, web site designer*
Kearney, Nancy Jean *artist*
Kearns, Ellen Veronica *artist*
Kearns, James Joseph *artist*
Kehew, George Mansir *artist*
Kehlmann, Robert *artist, critic*
Kemp, Flo *artist*
Kidder, Craig Stephen *artist, digital photographer*
Kipniss, Robert *artist*
Kiritani, Saeri *artist*
Kirsch, Roslyn Ruth *art educator, painter, printmaker*
Kiskadden, Robert Morgan *artist, educator*
Kleiman, Alan Boyd *artist*
Klein, Lynn Ellen *artist*
Klement, Vera *artist*
Knapp, Candace Louise *sculptor*
†Knapp, Lucretia A *artist, educator*
Kolbe, Stephanie Jill *artist*
Komar, Vitaly *artist*
Korn-Davis, Dottie *artist, educator, consultant*
Kreiter-Foronda, Carolyn *poet, artist*
Krienke, Kendra Cliver (Kendra Daniel) *art dealer, artist*
Krulik, Barbara S. *director, writer, curator*
Kumao, Heidi Elizabeth *artist, educator*
†LaCroix, Sophia Marie *artist*
Lafleur, Laurette Carignan *artist*
Lahmann, Robert Oscar *retired artist*
Laisure, Thomas James *artist, sculptor*
LaMantia, Paul Christopher (W. Zombek) *artist*
La Moy, June Inez *graphic designer*
Lancaster, Michael Dean *artist, marketing executive*
Landi, Diane Marie *graphics designer, consultant*
Lanzl, Christina Anna *visual artist, arts coordinator*
La Rocca, Isabella *artist, educator*
Larson, Ada Copp *artist*
Lassiter, Kenneth T. *photography educator, consultant*
Laufer, William Hervey *artist, printmaker*
Lawrence, Mary Josephine (Josie Lawrence) *artist, retired library official*
Leak, Nancy Marie *artist*
Lebensohn, Jeremy *sculptor*
Leeds, Nancy Brecker *sculptor, lyricist*
LeFevre, Edmund Arthur, Jr., *scenic designer*
Lefranc, Margaret (Margaret Schoonover) *artist, illustrator, editor, writer*
Legere, Kathy Ann *artist, poet*
Lehman, Todd Wilson *artist*
Lehrer, Leonard *artist, educator*
Leiber, Judith Maria *designer, manufacturer*
Leikhim, Nance *artist*
Leipzig, Arthur *photographer, educator emeritus*
†Leiva, Nicolas *artist*
Lerner, Ilya *artist*
LeRoy, G. Palmer *art dealer*
Levi, Josef Alan *artist*
Levin, Morton D(avid) *artist, printmaker, educator*
Levin, Steven James *artist*
Levine, Jack *artist*
Lieberman, Louis (Karl Lieberman) *artist*
Liljegren, Frank Sigfrid *artist, art association official*
Liman, Ellen *painter, writer, arts advocate*
†Lindley, Cheryl A. *artist, writer*
Linhares, Judith Yvonne *artist, educator*
Lionetti, Frank Carmine *graphic design executive*
Littleton, Harvey Kline *artist*
Liu, Katherine Chang *artist, art educator*
†Liu, Yaozen *artist*
Lockart, Barbetta *fabric designer, textile and fine artist, jeweler, art educator*
Logan, Earl Steven *artist*
Loomis, Janice Kaszczuk *artist*
Lopez, Luz-Maria *visual artist*
†Lopez Heredia, Hubert *artist*
Lowenthal, Susan *artist, designer, retired finance executive*
Ludwig, Allan Ira *photographer, artist, author*
Lund, David Nathan *artist*
Lundgren, Cissi *painter, poet*
†Lundine, Lucinda R. *artist, horse rancher, interior designer*
Lurye, Helen *artist*
†Lutzen, Sherry Lynn Blanco *art educator*
†Lynd, Phyllis *artist, educator*
Lynn, Genevieve *artist*
Lyshak-Stelzer, Frances *artist*
Mady, Beatrice M. *artist*
Magoni, Despo *artist*
Mallet, Marlys Kaye *artist*
Malloy, John Edward *media artist, writer*
Mangold, Sylvia Plimack *artist*
Marci-Mariani, Anita *designer, illustrator, fine artist, educator*
†Marks, Terry *artist*
Marlowe, Willie *artist, fine arts educator*
Marsh, Merrilyn Delano *sculptor, painter*
†Marti, Virgil *artist*
Martin, Noel *graphic design consultant, educator*
Martinez, Rey Antonio *artist, writer*
Martyl, (Mrs. Alexander Langsdorf Jr.) *artist*
Mason, Lois E. (J. Day Mason) *painter, poet, actress, educator*
Massey, Stephen Charles *rare books and manuscripts appraiser, auctioneer*
Mathieu, Georges Victor Adolphe *artist*
Matlow, Linda M. *photographic agency executive, publishing executive*
Mauney, Thomas Lee *theater designer*
McBride, Sharon Sue *artist*
McCargar, Eleanor Barker *portrait painter*
McCully, Emily Arnold *illustrator, writer*
McCurdy, Michael Charles *illustrator, author*
McFarlane, James L. *artist, educator*
†McGee, Carrie L. *artist*
†McHugh, Sean Paul *artist, writer*
McKay, Renee *artist*
McKnight, Thomas Frederick *artist*
McMillen, Elizabeth Cashin *artist*
McPeters, Sharon Jenise *artist, writer*
McVicker, Jesse Jay *artist, educator*
†Mead, Elizabeth *artist*
Meneeley, Edward Sterling *artist*
Menefee, Linnea-Norma *antique dealer*
Merritt, Eleanor Lynette *artist, educator*
Middaugh, Robert Burton *artist*
Minami, Robert Yoshio *artist, graphic designer*
Misrach, Richard Laurence *photographer*
Monczewski, Maureen R. *secondary art educator, visual artist*
†Moore, Mary Carroll *artist*
Morning, John *graphic designer*
Mowry, Elizabeth *artist*
Murdock, Chloe Conger *artist*
Murray, Ernest Don *artist, educator*
Murray, Robert Gray *sculptor*
Muslin, Lee *artist*
Nash, Mary Harriet *artist, educator*
Natkin, Robert *painter*
†Neff, Jennifer Ellen *painter, computer graphics designer*
Nemec-Kessel, Charlene *artist, educator*
Nemiroff, Maxine Celia *art educator, gallery owner, consultant*

Neuwirth, Allan Charles *designer, director, screenwriter*
Newman, Bruce Murray *antiques dealer*
Newman, Muriel Kallis Steinberg *art collector*
Ng, Woon Lam *artist, educator*
Nichols, Iris Jean *illustrator*
†Nix, Patricia *artist*
Noffke, Jane Bunge *sculptor, writer*
Noland, Kenneth Clifton *artist*
Nuss, Joanne Ruth *sculptor, artist*
Obrant, Susan Elizabeth *artist, illustrator*
†O'Donnell, Kathleen C. *artist*
Okoshi-Mukai, Sumiye *artist*
Oldenburg, Claes Thure *artist*
Olitski, Jules *artist*
Olkinetzky, Sam *artist, retired museum director and educator*
Ord, Linda Banks *artist*
Oritsky, Mimi *artist, educator*
Owen, Carol Thompson *artist, educator, writer*
Owen, June Lois *artist*
Oxell, Loie Gwendolyn *fashion and beauty educator, consultant, columnist*
Pack, Susan Joan *art consultant*
Palmer, George Thomas *artist*
Passlof, Pat *artist, educator*
Pate, Virginia Frances *artist, educator*
Paul, Arthur *artist, graphic designer, illustrator, art and design consultant*
Pazlamatchev, Ivan Gueorguiev *artist, art restorer*
Pearlstein, Philip *artist*
Peckham, Ellen *artist, poet*
Péladeau, Marius Beaudoin *art consultant, retired museum director*
Pellman, James Carl *artist*
Pepin, Yvonne Mary *artist, writer*
Perrin, Lisa C. *fiber artist*
Peterson, Martha *artist*
Petterson, Margo *artist*
Philipp, Jeanne *artist*
Phillips, Ronald Edward *artist, sales executive*
Pidgeon, Leslea Sharon *artist, writer*
Pierce, Hilda (Hilda Herta Harmel) *painter*
Piniat, Shirley Zina *artist, educator*
Porter, Charles Henry *photographer*
Porter, Nora Roxanne *freelance graphic designer*
†Potter, Scott Michael *artist, writer*
Pozzatti, Rudy Otto *artist*
Provensen, Alice Rose Twitchell *artist, author*
Puckett, Terry Gay *art educator, artist*
Purcell, George Richard *artist, postal employee*
Puryear, Rachelle Marie *artist, educator*
Putnam, Marlene Evans *artist*
Putterman, Florence Grace *artist, printmaker*
Qian, Zifen *artist, researcher*
†Quayle, Jackie M. *artist*
Raash, Kathleen Forecki *artist*
Rankin, Scott David *artist, educator*
Rath, Ed *artist, educator*
Raymond, Susan Grant *sculptor*
†Reding, Barbara Grace *artist*
Reed, Angelica Denise *sculptor, writer, illustrator*
†Rees, Michael S. *sculptor, educator*
Reid, Geraldine Wold (Geraldine Reid Skjervold) *artist*
Rendal, Camille Lynn *artist*
†Reynolds, Robert (Gary) *artist, educator*
Reynolds, Wade *artist*
Richards, Patricia Jones *artist, poet*
Richardson, Robert John *producer, director animation*
Richenburg, Robert Bartlett *artist, retired art educator*
Rinaldi, Robert R., Jr., *artist, photographer, publisher*
Rizk, Mysoon *art historian, artist, educator*
Robbins, Jack *artist*
†Roberts, Russell L. *artist*
Roberts, Suzanne Catherine *artist*
Robinson, Lynda Hickox *artist*
Robinson, Maura *artist*
Rock, Mary Ann *fine artist, educator, consultant*
Rockall, Arthur Allison *automotive designer*
Rockburne, Dorothea Grace *artist*
Roe, Wanda Jeraldean *artist, retired educator, lecturer*
Rohm, Robert Hermann *sculptor, educator*
†Rose, Mildred Virginia *artist, writer, adult nurse practitioner*
Rose, Patricia *artist, educator*
Rosen, Diane *artist*
Rosenbaum, Belle Sara *appraiser, interior designer, museum director, educator*
Rosenberg, Carole *art dealer, real estate broker, foundation executive*
Rosenberg, Herb *sculptor, educator*
Ross, Molly Owings *gold and silversmith, jewelry designer/sculptor, small business owner*
Rossman, Ruth Scharff *artist, educator*
Rowe, Bobby Louise *art educator*
Rowlett, Kimberly Jayne *artist, photographer*
Rubello, David Jerome *artist*
Rubin, Sandra Mendelsohn *artist*
Rubinstein, Eva (Anna Rubinstein) *photographer*
Ruffo, Michael *painter*
Rush, Julia Ann Halloran (Mrs. Richard Henry Rush) *artist, writer*
Rutherford, Doreen *artist, excavating company executive*
†Sabraw, John Collier *artist, educator*
†Sacks, Glen *artist, web site designer*
St. Pierre, Joyce Bourré *art educator*
Sakai, Kiyoko *artist*
Sakaoka, Yasue *artist, educator*
Sakson, Robert George *artist*
Salerno, Cherie Ann (C. S. Mau) *artist*
Sanabria, Sherry Zvares *artist*
†Santini, Debrah Ann *artist, educator*
Santoso, Irene *art director, graphics designer*
Saseen, Sharon Louise *artist, painter, educator*
Schabner, Dawn Freeble *artist, educator*
Scharf, William *artist*
Schefman, Robert Bankle *artist, educator*
Schmalz, Carl Nelson, Jr., *artist, educator, printmaker*
Schmitz, Barbara *art preservationist*
Schulte, Gregory Alan *art educator*
Schultz, Eileen Hedy *graphic designer*
Schwartz, Lillian Feldman *artist, filmmaker, art analyst, writer, nurse*
Schwegman, Monica Joan *artist*
†Scofidio, Ricardo *artist*
†Scott, Rosa Mae *artist, educator*
Searles, Edna Lowe *artist, illustrator, composer*
Seliger, Mark Alan *photographer*
Seligson, Judith *artist*
Sfirri, Mark Stephen *artist, educator*
Shaughnessy, Marie Kaneko *artist, business executive*
Shaw, Gloria Doris *art educator*
Sheets, Nelda *artist*
Sheridan, Sonia Landy *artist, retired art educator*
Sherman, Ruth Tenzer *artist, fixtures company executive*
Sherr, Sylvia *artist, educator*
Sherrie, Laurel Elizabeth *artist*
†Sherwood, Gloria N. *graphic and literary artist, genealogy researcher*
Shom, Jean *artist*
Shore, Stephen *photographer*
Shulman, Mildred *artist, inventor*
†Siegel, Fran *artist*
Siejka, George John *artist*
Simmons, Karen Elaine *artist*
†Sims, Pauline Andrée Villarico *artist*
Smith, Karen Ann *visual artist*
Smith, Leila Hentzen *artist*
†Smith, Leonard Glenn *artist, educator*
Smith, Leonore Rae *artist*
Smith, Mary Elizabeth *retired art historian*
†Smith, Serafina Gangemi *artist, drug counselor*
Smith, Susan Porter *artist, environmentalist*
Smits, Kathleen Curran *artist, educator*
Snelson, Kenneth Duane *sculptor*
†Sniffen, Frances P. *artist*
†Snowden, Ruth *artist, educator, legal secretary*
†Softic, Tanja *artist*
Sorel, Edward *artist*
Souders, Jean Swedell *artist, educator*
Spence, Andrew *artist, painter*
†Spicer, Kathleen *artist*
Stanley, Robert Anthony
Steckel, Anita *artist*
Stern, Marilyn *photographer, writer, picture editor*
Stevens, May *artist*
Stewart, Heather Meri *painter, sculptor*
†Stinnett, William Leeon *artist, writer*
Stinsmuehlen-Amend, Susan *artist*
Stockar, Helena Marie Magdalena *artist*
Stover, Laura Elkins *artist*
Strider, Marjorie Virginia *artist, educator*
Stripling, Betty Keith *artist, medical/surgical nurse*
Stroud, Betsy Dillard *artist*
Struble, Susan C. *artist, volunteer art therapist*
Stuart, Signe Margaret *artist*
Studer, Carol A. *creative director, graphic designer, consultant*
Styler, Anda Jasamine *artist, educator*
Sukopp, Karl Martin *sculptor, painter, graphic artist*
Sullivan, Barbara Jean *artist*
Sunward, Justin Hugo *artist, writer*
Swanner, Barbara Melson *artist*
Swensen, Mary Jean Hamilton *graphic artist*
Switzer, Toccoa *artist*
Taddei, Lois Annette Magowan *artist, decorator*
Taft, Nellie Leaman *artist*
Tagliente, Josephine Marlene *artist*
Tardos, Anne *artist, writer, composer*
Taylor, Margaret Turner *clothing designer, architectural designer, economist, writer, planner*
Taylor-Brown, Cameron Ann *artist, educator, consultant*
Teal, Monika Josepha *artist*
Tejada, Audrey Dolar *artist, writer*
Thielen, Jean Rose *artist*
†Tirello, Maria Eugenia Duke *artist*
Tomash, Diane *painter, educator*
Tomkow, Gwen Adelle *artist*
Torak, Elizabeth Lichtenstein *artist*
Tougias, Mark A. *artist*
Toussaint, Mauricio *painter*
Townsend, Alvin Neal *artist*
Tresslar, Nola V. *artist, retired foundation administrator, marketing professional*
Tsai, Wen-Ying *sculptor, painter, engineer*
Tuchscherer, Marsha Smith *visual artist, university official*
Turner, Bonese Collins *artist, educator*
Turner, Bracha *Naive Landscape painter*
Turner, Florence Frances *ceramist*
Turner, Peggy Ann *graphics designer, artist, educator*
†Tyrrell, Lilian *craftsperson, artist*
Tytla, Peter T. *artist*
Unithan, Dolly *visual artist*
Vahradian, Melinda *fine artist*
Van Bruggen, Coosje *artist, writer*
†Vanderbilt, Gloria Morgan *artist, actress, fashion designer*
†Van Hooser, Patricia Lou Scott *art educator*
Van Lone Trieschman, Janet Anne *graphic arts educator*
Vergano, Lynn (Marilynn Bette Vergano) *artist*
†Vergara, Camilo José *photographer*
Vero, Radu *freelance medical and scientific illustrator, educator, writer, consultant*
Versch, Esther Marie *artist*
Vollmer, Howard Robert *artist, photographer*
VonSchulze-Delitzsch, Marilyn Wandling (Lady VonSchulze-Delitzsch) *artist, writer*
Walker, Debra *artist*
Walker, John Seibels *artist*
WalkingStick, Kay *artist, art educator*
Wallach-Levy, Wendee Esther *astrophotographer*
Walsh, Nan *fine artist, painter, sculptor, consultant*
†Waltner, Beverly Ruland *artist*
Warach, Marie *artist*
†Ward, Nari *sculptor*
Wasserman, Helene Waltman *art dealer, artist*
†Watkins, Wendy R. *artist*
Watts, Ginny (Virginia C. Watts) *artist*
Weld, Alison Gordon *artist*
Wendel, Christopher Mark *environmental experience designer*
Westbie, Barbara Jane *retired graphics designer*
Westfall, Carol Ann *artist, educator*
Wexler, George *retired art educator, artist*
†Whitehill, Mary Evelyn *artist, retired librarian*
Whitson, Angie *artist*
Wilde, John *artist, educator*
Willenbecher, John *artist*
Williams, Eleanor Claflin (Claffy Williams) *artist*
Wilson, Jane *artist*
Wilson, Melissa Elizabeth *artist, educator*
Winokur, Neil *photographer*
Wiseman, Jay Donald Donald *photographer, inventor, mechanical designer and contractor, land developer, writer*
Witt, Nancy Camden *artist*
Wofford, Terry *artist*
Wood, Kate *artist*
Woodard, Deana Safford *artist, travel consultant*
Woskow, Catherine Rose *artist*
Wylan, Barbara *artist*
Wynn, Karla Wray *artist, agricultural products company executive*
†Yates, Steven A. *artist, curator*
Ynda, Mary Lou *artist, educator*
Zaleski, Jean *artist*
Zapf, Hermann *book and type designer*
Zeir, Nell *artist*
Zekman, Terri Margaret *graphic designer*
Zelinsky, Paul O. *illustrator, painter, author*
Zentz, Patrick James *artist, rancher*
Zercher, D. Lowell *artist*
Zex, Damon *artist*
Zheutlin, Dale *sculptor, educator*
Zorn, Elizabeth C. *artist*
†Zwerling, Lisa *painter, educator*

ASSOCIATIONS AND ORGANIZATIONS *See also* specific fields

UNITED STATES

ALABAMA

Birmingham
Bonfield, Barbara Goldstein *non-profit organization administrator*
Carter, Frances Tunnell (Fran Carter) *fraternal organization administrator*
Connors, Marty *political party administrator, small business owner*
Diasio, Ilse Wolfartsberger *volunteer*
Kirkley, D. Christine *non-profit organization administrator*
Masters, Jeffrey D. *association executive*
Newton, Don Allen *real estate broker, economic development consultant*
†Rynearson, W. John *foundation administrator*

Huntsville
Motz, Kenneth Lee *former farm organization official*

Mobile
Livers, Thomas Henry *fundraiser for nonprofit organizations*
McCann, Clarence David, Jr., *special events coordinator, museum curator and director, artist*

Montgomery
Pitt, Redding *political organization administrator*

Mooresville
Reeder, Edward Cameron *association executive, clergyman*

ALASKA

Anchorage
Jones, Jewel *social services administrator*
Jones, Mark Logan *educational association executive, educator*
Ruedrich, Randy *political party official*
Sterling, Scott *political party official*
Thorsness, Julia Marie *hospice administrator*
Thrasher-Livingston, Kara Scott *program director*
Wilkniss, Peter E. *foundation administrator, researcher*
†Williams, Deborah Lee *foundation administrator*

ARIZONA

Chandler
†Rossi, Mark Antony *political consultant, writer*

Parker
Carnicom, Gene E. *health services administrator*

Phoenix
Dorland, Byrl Brown *retired civic worker*
Fannin, Paul Robert *political party official*
Genrich, Mark L. *foundation administrator*
Hays, E. Earl *youth organization administrator*
Karnas, Fred G., Jr., *non-profit organization executive*
Pederson, Jim *political party official*
Rodriguez, Leonard *foundation and nonprofit administrator*
Swartz, Jack *chamber of commerce executive*
Waas, Andrea Sue *nonprofit foundation administrator*

Prescott
Garvey, Daniel Edward *foundation administrator, educator, academic administrator*

Scottsdale
Ferree, John Newton, Jr., *fundraising specialist, consultant*
Jacobson, Frank Joel *cultural organization administrator*
Lorrance, Arleen *foundation administrator*
Marshall, Jonathan *charitable foundation administrator, journalist*
Milanovich, Norma JoAnne *training and development company executive*
Mohraz, Judy Jolley *foundation administrator*
Morrison, James William, Jr., *lobbyist, government relations consultant*
Nelson, Florence Ely *civic leader*
O'Meara, Sara *nonprofit organization executive*

Sedona
Sasmor, Jeannette Louise *educational consulting company executive*

Sierra Vista
Hessler, Thomas John *community activist*

Tucson
†Alley, Steven E. *foundation administrator*
Grand, Marcia *civic worker*
Hechler, Pauline Urbano King *fundraiser*
†Johnson, Robert Bruce *company director*
Lauver, Edith Barbour *nonprofit organization administrator*
Lovejoy, Jean Hastings *social services counselor*
Marr, Steve *foundation executive*
Riggs, Lew *foundation executive*
Schevill, Edward *social services agency director*
Sickel, Joan Sottilare *foundation administrator*
Tirrell, John Albert *organization executive, consultant*

ARKANSAS

Fort Smith
Howard, Jeff David *volunteer, retired military officer*

Heber Springs
Niehaus, Sherry M. *social welfare administrator*

Little Rock
Adams, Rose Ann *nonprofit administrator*
Malone, David Roy *educational association administrator, director*
Moore, W. David *charitable foundation executive, minister*
Oliver, Ron *political party official*
Ryall, Marty *political organization administrator*
Walden, Catherine Jane *not-for profit director, social worker, consultant*

CALIFORNIA

Alameda
†Kohgadai, Shukrullah *foundation administrator, editor*

Albany
Thomsen, Peggy Jean *educator, mayor, council member*

Anderson
†Wittmann, Jane Gordon *volunteer*

Avila Beach
Dvora, Susan (Susan Bernstein) *non-profit organization professional*

Belvedere Tiburon
Collins, Dennis Arthur *foundation executive*

Berkeley
Chew, Linda Lee *fundraising management executive*
Felix, Susan Duhan *consultant, community development specialist, artist*
McLaughlin, Sylvia Cranmer *community volunteer, environmentalist*
Myers, Miles Alvin *educator, educational association administrator*
Odermatt, Diana B. *development consultant*
Pope, Alexander H. *former lawyer, county assessor and non-profit administrator*

Beverly Hills
†Khaladjan, Mikhail Nikolaevich *educator, song writer*
Pavlik, John Michael *performing arts association executive*
†Schaff, Manya *foundation administrator*
Siciliano, Rocco Carmine *institute executive*

Brea
Tamura, Cary Kaoru *consultant*

Burbank
Rawlinson, Joseph Eli *foundation executive, lawyer*
Steel, Shawn *political party official*

Canoga Park
Lederer, Marion Irvine *cultural administrator*

Capistrano Beach
Sheedy, Evelyn Mardelle *nonprofit corporation executive*

Carlsbad
†Muth, Dorothy Dudley *volunteer*

Caspar
Schooley, Caroline Naus *retired laboratory supervisor*

Chico
Burks, Rocky Alan *independent living center executive, consultant*

Chula Vista
Reinhart, Roderick Lester *non-profit organization consultant*

Citrus Heights
Leisey, Donald Eugene *educational materials company executive, educator*

Claremont
Pendleton, Othniel Alsop *fundraiser, clergyman*

Concord
Misner, Charlotte Blanche Ruckman *retired community organization administrator*

Coronado
Hinsvark, Don George *social services agency professional*

Covina
White, Rebecca E. *advocate*

Culver City
Netzel, Paul Arthur *fund raising management executive, consultant*

Cypress
Friess, Donna Lewis *children's rights advocate*

Daly City
†Malifrando, Frank *foundation executive director, theater producer, consultant*

Davis
Wydick, Judith Brandli James *volunteer*

Downey
†del Calvo, Alberto C. *educational association administrator, lawyer*

El Monte
Last, Marian Helen *social services administrator*

Elk Grove
McIntyre, Mary Maureen *social services consultant*

Encino
Baker, William Morris *cultural organization administrator*

Fairfax
Urquhart, Karin May *foundation administrator, environmentalist*

Fairfield
Phelps, Joseph Alfred *social services administrator, small business owner*

Folsom
Peck, Raymond Charles, Sr., *driver behavior research specialist and research consultant*

Fremont
Maloney, Cheryl Ann *foundation, consultant, business executive*

Fullerton
Sadrudin, Moe *humanitarian organization executive*

Granite Bay
Cornwell, Jimmy Lee *fundraising executive, retired air force officer*

Irvine
†Goldman, Doris Toran *not-for-profit developer*

Keene
†Rodriguez, Arturo Salvador *labor union official*

Kentfield
Blum, Joan Kurley *fundraising executive*

La Jolla
Knox, Elizabeth Louise *community volunteer, travel consultant*
Schimmel, Cleo Ritz *civic worker*

Laguna Hills
Wheatley, Lucile Maris *civic worker*

Lancaster
†Groom, Diane V. *not-for-profit developer*

Lodi
Nusz, Phyllis Jane *not-for-profit fundraiser, consultant, educational consultant*

Loma Linda
Pendergraft, Janice Gayle *volunteer*

Long Beach
†Heggeness, Julie Fay *foundation administrator, lawyer*
Herman, Elaine *non-profit theatre artistic director*
Warder, Michael Young *non-profit executive*

Los Altos
Wilbur, Colburn Sloan *foundation consultant and trustee, former executive*

Los Angeles
Baker, Carolyn *non-profit executive, fundraiser*
Christopher, James Roy *executive director*
†Cislowski, Joseph A. *association executive*
Erichsen, Peter Christian *foundation administrator*
Harris, Barbara Hull (Mrs. F. Chandler Harris) *social agency administrator*
†Hirsch, Daniel Oren *nonprofit nuclear policy organization executive*
Hubbs, Donald Harvey *foundation executive*
Khalsa, Shakti Parwha Kaur *not for profit foundation executive*
Lindley, F(rancis) Haynes, Jr., *foundation executive, lawyer*
†Lumaroa, Joseph Matthew *foundation administrator*
Mack, J. Curtis, II, *civic organization administrator*
Marshall, Mary Jones *civic worker*
Meier, Stephen Charles *foundation executive*
Munitz, Barry *arts and foundation administrator*
Orsatti, Alfred Kendall *organization executive*
Poole, Robert William, Jr., *foundation executive*
Shakely, John Bower (Jack Shakely) *foundation executive*
Smith, Jean Webb (Mrs. William French Smith) *civic worker*
†Smith, LaShawn Renee *not-for-profit fundraiser, consultant*
Wachtell, Wendy *foundation administrator*
†Williams, Harold Marvin *foundation official, former government official, former university dean, former corporate executive*
Wlaschin, Ken *cultural organization administrator, writer*

Malibu
Walla-Murphy, Meghan Anne *foundation administrator*

Manhattan Beach
Devitt-Grasso, Pauline Virginia *civic volunteer, nurse*

Menlo Park
†Collins, Nancy Whisnant *foundation administrator*
Goerz, Mary Elizabeth Larsen *civic worker*
Nichols, William Ford, Jr., *foundation executive, business executive*
Smith, Marshall Savidge *foundation executive*

Mill Valley
Burke, Kathleen J. *foundation administrator*

Modesto
Barnes, William David *non-profit charities consultant, publisher*
Mattos, William Harold *trade association executive, newspaper publisher*
Whiteside, Carol Gordon *foundation executive*

Monterey Park
Besen, Jane Phyllis Triptow *retired civic worker*

Morongo Valley
Lindley, Judith Morland *cat registry administrator*

Mount Shasta
Mann, Karen *consultant, educator*

Mountain View
Bills, Robert Howard *political party executive*
Serra, Patricia Janet *social services administrator*

Napa
Loar, Peggy Ann *foundation administrator, museum administrator*

Oakland
†Hawkins, Robert B. *think tank executive*
Lazar, John Edward *administrator non-profit organization*
Macmeeken, John Peebles *foundation executive, educator*

Oceanside
Roberts, James McGregor *retired professional association executive*

Orinda
Fisher, Robert Morton *foundation administrator, university administrator*

Oxnard
Tolmach, Jane Louise *community activist, municipal official*

Pacific Grove
†Adamson, Kathleen Frances *not-for-profit developer, educator*

Pacific Palisades
Holberg, Eva Maria *volunteer*

Palo Alto
†Brown, Charles Dickson *not-for-profit fundraiser, consultant*
Lee, Virginia Fern *community volunteer*
Robinson, Agnes Claflin *educational administrator*

Palos Verdes Peninsula
†Vanderlip, Elin Brekke *philanthropic executive*

Pasadena
Salandra, Helen E. *volunteer, retired nurse*
Staehle, Robert L. *foundation executive*

Pleasanton
Whisnand, Rex James *association housing executive*

Porterville
Mullen, Rod *nonprofit organization executive*

Rancho Mirage
Wyatt, Lenore *civic worker*

Redding
Potter, James Vincent *association executive*

Redwood City
McFarland, Kevin John *foundation administrator*
Spangler, Nita Reifschneider *volunteer*

Riverside
Smith, Richard Charles *not-for-profit administrator, educator*

Sacramento
Alberson, Barbara *health services professional*
Hayward, Fredric Mark *social reformer*
Meyer, Rachel Abijah *foundation director, artist, theorist, poet*
Patino, Douglas Xavier *foundation, government agency, and university administrator*

Salinas
Chester, Lynne *foundation executive, artist*

San Andreas
Breed, Allen Forbes *correctional administrator*

San Bernardino
Traynor, Gary Edward *association administrator*

San Diego
Beattie, Geraldine Alice (Geri Beattie) *advocate*
Boersma, Lawrence Allan (Larry Allan) *animal welfare administrator, photographer*
Gallison, H(arold) Bailey, Sr., *youth agency administrator, public relations and marketing consultant*
Grosser, T.J. *administrator, developer, fundraiser*
Krejci, Robert Harry *non-profit organizations development consultant*
Lane, Gloria Julian *foundation administrator*
Repetti, Anamaria *healthcare foundation executive*
Rossi, Norma J. *not-for-profit executive, advocate*
Sheldon, Lois Elizabeth *social services administrator*
Spira, Patricia Goodsitt *association executive*
Swanson, Mary Catherine *educational reform program founder*
Wojcik, Martin Henry *foundation development official*

San Francisco
†Barzelatto, Jose S. *social welfare organization executive*
Bitterman, Mary Gayle Foley *foundation executive*
Brown, Bernice Leona Baynes *foundation consultant, educator, consultant*
Canales, James Earl, Jr., *foundation administrator*
†Catalano, Richard *retired educational association administrator*
Chen, Kevin B. *arts organization executive, artist*
Eastham, Thomas *foundation administrator*
Egan, Patricia Jane *foundation executive, former university development director, writer*
†Fields, Jerri Lynn *foundation administrator*
Giovinco, Joseph *nonprofit administrator, writer*
Grose, Andrew Peter *foundation executive*
Hoganson, Susan Cook *non-profit organization executive*
Kong, Gail Mildred *foundation executive*
Lord, Mia W. *world peace and disarmament activist*
Madson, David John *fundraising executive*
†Maracek, Leigh *association administrator*
Mattern, Douglas James *foundation administrator*
Metz, Mary Seawell *foundation administrator, retired academic administrator*
Nee, D. Y. Bob *think tank executive, engineering consultant*
Newirth, Richard Scott *cultural organization administrator*
†Pipes, Sally C. *think-tank executive*
†Pope, Carl *professional society administrator*
†Soler, Esta *foundation administrator*
Tobin, Gary Allan *cultural and community organization educator*
Wolfe, Burton H. *non-profit organization executive*

San Jose
Sidener, Margaret Weil Leathers *foundation administrator*

San Luis Obispo
Jamieson, James Bradshaw *foundation administrator*

San Pedro
Daniels, Kathleen Angela *educational administrator*

Santa Ana
Zepeda, Susan Ghozeil *foundation executive*

Santa Barbara
†Altschuler, Allan Bruce *society administrator*
McCoy, Lois Clark *emergency services professional, retired county official, magazine editor*
Shreeve, Susanna Seelye *educational planning facilitator*
Walker, Sally C. *fundraising consultant*

Santa Clarita
†Boyer, Carl, III, *non-profit organization executive, former mayor, city official, secondary education educator*

Santa Cruz
†Lenox, Catherine Corneau *volunteer*
McLean, Hulda Hoover *volunteer, conservationist, naturalist, artist*
Wasson, Eleanor Walsh *volunteer*

Santa Monica
Abarbanel, Gail *social service administrator, educator*
Cretin, Shan *activist*
Foley, Jane Deborah *foundation administrator*
†Greene, C. Michael *art association administrator*
Hosie, Stanley William *foundation executive*
Klowden, Michael Louis *think-tank executive*
Rich, Michael David *research corporation executive, lawyer*
Thirtle, Michael Robert *community activist, consultant*
Thomson, James Alan *research company executive*

Santa Rosa
Feissel, Gustave *former international organization official*

Sonora
Coffill, Marjorie Louise *civic leader*

Standish
Klaseen-Eagle, Virginia *retired volunteer*

Stanford
Lyman, Richard Wall *foundation and university executive, historian*

Stockton
Blodgett, Elsie Grace *retired association executive*

Studio City
Frumkin, Simon *political activist and columnist*

Sun City
Peterson, Arthur Laverne *foundation administrator*

Susanville
McCoy, Douglas Michael *social services administrator, clergyman*

Sylmar
Froelich, Beverly Lorraine *foundation director*

Temecula
Angel, Michael Gonzalez *cultural organization administrator*

Torrance
Blumenfeld, Anita *community relations director*
Carey, Kathryn Ann *foundation administrator, editor, consultant*
Kallman, Burton Jay *foods association director*

Trinidad
Marshall, William Edward *historical association executive*

Valencia
Anguiano, Lupe *business executive*
Harvey, Rufus William *nonprofit organization administrator*

Ventura
Downs, Floella McIntyre *civic worker, ferry pilot, instructor and flight examiner*

Visalia
Keenan, Robert Joseph *trade association executive*
Taylor, Helen Shields *civic worker*

Watsonville
Cane, William Earl *nonprofit organization executive*

West Hollywood
Hoffenblum, Allan Ernest *political consultant*

Whittier
Harvey, Patricia Jean *special education administrator, retired*
Meardy, William Herman *retired educational association administrator*

Woodside
Patterson, Francine G. P. *foundation administrator*

Yorba Linda
Stavropoulos, Rose Mary Grant *community activist, volunteer*

COLORADO

Arvada
Leafgreen, Lisa Diane *education coordinator*
Meiklejohn, Mindy June (Lorraine Meiklejohn) *political organizer, realtor*

Boulder
†Forstrom, June Rochelle *professional society administrator*
Heath, Josephine Ward *foundation administrator*
Hess, John Warren *professional society administrator*
Johnston, Laurance Scott *foundation director*

Centennial
Bryan, A(lonzo) J(ay) *retired service club official*

Colorado Springs
Deiotte, Margaret Williams Tukey *nonprofit consultant, grants writer*
†Farr, David C.M. *non-profit organizational business development, consultant*
Hawley, Nanci Elizabeth *association administrator*

Killian, George Ernest *educational association administrator*
Miller, Zoya Dickins (Mrs. Hilliard Eve Miller Jr.) *civic worker*
Rochette, Edward Charles *association executive*
†Slason, Judith A. *not-for-profit developer*

Denver
Anders, Tisa Maree *social justice minister*
†Covey, Herbert Cecil *social services administrator, sociologist*
†DeGroot, Mary A. *social welfare administrator*
Fevurly, Keith Robert *educational administrator*
Gloss, Lawrence Robert *fundraising executive*
†Groff, JoAnn *organization administrator*
Hirschfeld, Arlene F. *civic worker, homemaker*
Hogan, Curtis Jule *union executive, industrial relations consultant*
Jones, Jean Correy *organization administrator*
Knaus, Tim *political organization administrator*
Low, Merry Cook *civic worker*
†Nelson, Bernard William *foundation executive, educator, physician*
Raughton, Jimmie Leonard *education consultant, public administrator, urban planner*
Simpson, Diane Jeannette *school social worker, counselor, adoption home study worker*
Ward, Lester Lowe, Jr., *arts executive, lawyer*

Englewood
Jessee, William Floyd *executive*
†Keesling, Ruth Morris *foundation administrator*
Lessey, Samuel Kenric, Jr., *foundation administrator*

Estes Park
Cope, James Dudley *retired trade association executive*

Fort Collins
Cummings, Sharon Sue *state extension service youth specialist*

Greeley
Schrenk, Gary Dale *foundation executive*

Greenwood Village
Chesser, Al H. *union official*

Guffey
Ward, Larry Thomas *social program administrator*

Littleton
Doty, Della Corrine *organization administrator*
Keogh, Heidi Helen Dake *advocate*

Longmont
Flanders, Eleanor Carlson *community volunteer*

Louisville
Jonsen, Richard Wiliam *retired educational administrator*

Louviers
Murdock, John T., II, *academic organization administrator, publishing company executive*

Loveland
†Rosa, Linda *advocate*

Mancos
Brown, Joy Alice *social services administrator*

Snowmass
Lovins, L. Hunter *public policy institute executive*

Westminster
Campagna, Timothy Nicholas *institute executive*

CONNECTICUT

Avon
Schatz, Norma H. *volunteer*

Bridgeport
Pagano, Celeste Ann *social services coordinator*

Burlington
Nelson, Linda Beatrice D'Andrea *volunteer worker*

Canaan
Kettenhofen, Gretchen Maria *development executive*

Chester
Spencer, William Courtney *foundation executive, international business executive*

Danbury
Meyers, Abbey S. *foundation administrator*

Fairfield
Evans, Margaret A. *volunteer*
Ford, Maureen Morrissey *civic worker*

Falls Village
Toomey, Jeanne Elizabeth *animal activist*

Greenwich
Bjornson, Edith Cameron *foundation executive, communications consultant*
Kovner, Kathleen Jane *civic worker, portrait artist*
Stauffer, Valerie Vilas *civic volunteer*
Tomikawa, Soji *educational institute administrator*

Groton
Kennedy, Evelyn Siefert *foundation executive, textile specialist*

Guilford
Macy, Terrence William *social services administrator*

Hartford
†Decko, Kenneth Owen *trade association administrator*
Huie, Georgette Lynn *social services administrator*

Lakeville
Nickerson, Bee Davis *social services executive, volunteer*

Madison
Houghton, Alan Nourse *association executive, educator, consultant*

Manchester
McHaelen, Robin Passariello *executive*

Milford
Myers, David Richard *youth organization financial executive*

New Canaan
Lindstrom, Janet Elena *non-profit executive*
McNamara, Francis Joseph, Jr., *retired foundation executive, lawyer*

New Haven
Anderson, Carl Albert *association executive, lawyer*
†Regan, Frederick E. *foundation administrator*

North Branford
Logan, John Arthur, Jr., *retired foundation executive*

Old Lyme
Bond, Niles Woodbridge *cultural institute executive, former foreign service officer*

Riverside
Coulson, Robert *retired association executive, arbitrator, author*

Rocky Hill
Olsen, John William *political organization administrator*

Simsbury
Calvert, Lois Wilson *civic worker*

South Windsor
Carman, Gary Olen *child welfare company executive*

Stamford
Brakeley, George Archibald, Jr., *fundraising consultant*
†Chisholm, Andrea Lynne *business association administrator, foundation administrator*
Hathaway, Lynn McDonald *education advocate, administrator*
Sharp, Daniel Asher *foundation executive*
Stillings, Irene Ella Grace Cordiner *foundation executive*

Vernon Rockville
Roden, Jon-Paul *retired educator and labor union organizer, educational consultant*

Waterbury
Harper, Barbara Clara *counselor, educational program administrator, counselor*
McIntyre, Kaye *non-profit organization executive, consultant*

Wilton
Forger, Robert Durkin *retired professional association administrator*

DELAWARE

Bethany Beach
Gale, Robert L. *educational association administrator, consultant*

Dover
Friedland, Billie Louise *former human services administrator*
Ornauer, Richard Lewis *retired educational association administrator*

Lewes
Spence, Sandra *retired professional administrator*
Warden, Richard Dana *government labor union official*

Montchanin
Hall, Robert Paul *social services administrator*

New Castle
Bayard, Richard H. *political party official*

Newark
†Roller, Cathy M. *educational association administrator*

Wilmington
Battaglia, Basil Richard *company executive, former political party official*
Emmert, Richard Eugene *retired industrial and professional association executive*
Milbury-Steen, Sally Louise (Sarah Milbury-Steen) *not-for-profit association administrator, advocate*
Peterson, Russell Wilbur *former association executive, former state governor*
Spence, Janet Blake Conley (Mrs. Alexander Pyott Spence) *civic worker*

DISTRICT OF COLUMBIA

Washington
Able, Edward H. *association executive*
Alberts, Bruce Michael *research organization executive*
Alexander, Richard C. *association administrator*
Arlook, Ira Arthur *non-profit association executive*
†Armacost, Michael Hayden *research institution executive, ambassador*
Arnold, William Edwin *health advocate, consultant*
Auerbach, Stuart Charles *development loan fund administrator, journalist*
Babby, Ellen Reisman *education administrator*
Backas, James Jacob *foundation administrator*
†Bahr, Morton *trade union executive*
†Barry, John J. *labor union leader*
Bartlett, Charles Leffingwell *foundation executive, former newspaperman*
Bednash, Geraldine Polly *association executive*
†Bell, Jerry Alan *science education association administrator*
Bender, David Ray *library association executive*
†Berry, Morrell John *cultural organization administrator*
Binkley, Marilyn Rothman *educational research administrator*
Blair, Louis Helion *foundation executive*
Boaz, David Douglas *foundation executive*
Bode, Barbara *Internet entrepreneur, foundation executive, freelance/self-employed writer*
Bonosaro, Carol Alessandra *professional association executive, former government official*
Bookbinder, Hyman H(arry) *public affairs counselor*
Brady, Patricia G. *volunteer*
Bray, Sarah Hardesty *newspaper editor, writer*
Brightup, Craig Steven *lobbyist*
Brintnall, Michael Arthur *association executive, political scientist*
Brobeck, Stephen James *consumer advocate*
Brown, Ann W. *not-for-profit developer*
Calhoun, John Alfred *social services administrator*
Calingaert, Michael *nonprofit organization executive*
Callahan, Debra Jean *professional society administrator*
Case, David Randall *trade association executive*
Chase, Robert F. *educational association executive*
Chavez-Thompson, Linda *labor union administrator*
Clymer, John Marion *think-tank executive*
Colbert, Robert Ivan *education association administrator*
Crane, Edward Harrison, III, *institute executive*
Damgard, John Michael *trade association executive*
Daroff, William Clayton *political organization executive, lawyer*
Deal, Timothy *association executive, former diplomat*
DeKuyper, Mary Hundley *non-profit consultant*
Dennis, Kimberly Ohnemus *philanthropy consultant*
Dettke, Dieter M. *foundation executive*
DiConti, Michael Andrew *trade organization executive*
Dolibois, Robert Joseph *trade association administrator*
Donahue, Thomas Reilly *trade union official*
Dooley, Betty Parsons *educational association administrator*
Dorsey, David Byard *non-profit executive*
DuBois, Paul Martin Joseph *non-profit organization executive*
Edwards, Steve *attorney, former political organization executive*
Eisenberg, Pablo Samuel *non-profit organization executive*
Ekman, Richard *association executive, educator*
Elliott, Thomas Michael *retired association executive, educator, consultant*
Elsey, George McKee *retired foundation administrator*
Emely, Mary Ann *association executive*
Evans, Joy *foundation administrator*
Evans, Marsha Johnson *non-profit association administrator, former career officer*
Fai, Ghulam Nabi *cultural organization administrator*
Feldman, Sandra *labor union executive*
Fineberg, Harvey Vernon *professional society administrator*
Fink, Matthew Pollack *trade association executive, lawyer*
Finkle, Jeffrey Alan *professional association executive*
†Fisher, William Pierre *association executive*
Flippo, Karen Francine *social welfare administrator*
Floyd, Jeanne *professional society administrator*
Foard, Douglas W. *educational association administrator*
Forkan, Patricia Ann *foundation executive*
Foster, Serrin Marie *non-profit organization executive*
†Fried, Bruce Merlin *health services director*
Fries, Helen Sergeant Haynes *civic leader*
Fuller, Kathryn Scott *environmental association executive, lawyer*
Futrell, John William *environmental agency executive, lawyer*
†Gallant, Carol Daniels *not-for-profit fundraiser, consultant*
†Garner, Mary Cox *not-for-profit developer*
Goldman, Neil *association administrator*
Golodner, Jack *labor association official*
Gorham, William *organization executive*
Gough, Samuel Nathanael, Jr., *fund-raising executive*
Grant, Donald Marcus *alcohol policy specialist*
Griffenhagen, George Bernard *trade association executive*
Grimm, Mary M. *development professional*
Hamilton, Lee Herbert *educational organization administrator, former congressman*
†Handman, Bobbie (Barbara Handman) *foundation executive*
Hanley, Frank *labor union official*
Harrison, Monika Edwards *business development executive*
Harrison, Ronald O. *association administrator*
Hartman, Chester Warren *public interest organization executive*
Hawkinson, Brian Patrick *professional association executive*
Heinz, Teresa F. *foundation administrator*
Hense, Donald Langford *educational association administrator*
Herbert, James Charles *educational association administrator*
Higgins, Kathryn O'Leary *non-profit organization executive*
†Hill, Edwin D. *trade association administrator*
Hills, John Merrill *educational administrator, consultant, former public policy research center executive*
Hoehn, Richard Albert *association executive, clergyman*
Hoffa, James P. *labor union administrator*
Hollis, Nicholas Everett *trade association executive*
Holmer, Alan Freeman *trade association executive, lawyer*
Hoppe, John David *political organization worker*
Howard, Glen Scott *foundation executive, lawyer*
Hoyt, John Arthur *humane society executive*
Huband, Frank Louis *educational association executive*
Hudnut, William Herbert, III, *senior resident fellow, political scientist*
Hughes, Sharon Mary *trade association executive*
Hughes, Thomas Lowe *foundation executive*
Ingram, Richard Thomas *educational association executive*
Ireland, Patricia *not-for-profit developer*
Jacobson, Michael Faraday *consumer advocate, writer*
†Jarboe, Kenan Patrick *think-tank executive, researcher*
†Jensen, James E. *director congressional and government affairs*
Johnson, Victor Charles *association executive*
Kamber, Victor Samuel *political consultant*
Kane, Cheryl Marie *education program developer*
Karpinski, Gene Brien *non-profit group administrator, think tank executive*
Kauffman, Amy *political organization worker*
Kavanaugh, Everett Edward, Jr., *trade association executive*
Kearns, Kevin Lawrence *political association executive, lawyer*
Keeny, Spurgeon Milton, Jr., *association executive*
†Kelly, John A. (Jack Kelly) *lobbyist*
Kerr, Sterling, III, *social and advocacy administrator*
Kim, Charles Changyoung *trade association executive, lawyer*
†King, Jacqueline Elizabeth *policy analyst, researcher*
Knapp, Richard Maitland *association executive*
Knippers, Diane LeMasters *association executive*
Kolb, Charles Chester *humanities administrator*
Kovach, Bill *educational foundation administrator*
Kreig, Andrew Thomas *trade association executive*
Lampl, Peggy Ann *public policy administrator*
Langfeld, Patricia Ann *trade association executive, marketing and event planner*
La Sala, James *labor union administrator*
Lasher, Craig Richard *policy analyst*
Leibold, Peter McCloskey *professional association executive*
Lenn, Marjorie Peace *education association administrator, consultant*
Leshner, Alan Irvin *science administrator*
Leskes, Andrea *academic administrator, educator*
Levin, George Martin *association and organization administrator, aeronautical engineer*
Lewis, Henry Donald *fundraising consultant*
Liroff, Richard Alan *environmental association executive*
Loge, Peter Martin *organization administrator*
Low, Stephen *foundation executive, educator, former diplomat*
Lucas, C. Payne *development organization executive*
Lynch, Robert L. *art association administrator*
Magrath, C. Peter *educational association executive*
†Majors, Melynda Elizabeth *not-for-profit organization administrator*
Makins, Christopher James *foreign policy institute administrator*
Mariotte, Michael Lee *environmental activist, environmental publication director*
Marshall, Brian Laurence *trade association executive*
Martin, Jerry Lee *organization executive, educator*
Masters, Edward E. *association executive, former foreign service officer*
Maynes, Charles William *foundation executive*
McCarron, Douglas J. *labor union administrator*
McClintic, Howard Gresson *foundation executive*
McEntee, Gerald W. *labor union official*
Mc Kay, Emily Gantz *civil rights professional*
†McLaughlin, David *foundation administrator*
McNulty, Robert Holmes *non-profit executive*
†Meyerson, Adam *foundation administrator*
Michael, Terry P. *foundation executive, educator*

PROFESSIONAL INDEX 6225 ASSOCIATIONS AND ORGANIZATIONS

Moore, Jacquelyn Cornelia *labor union official, editor*
Mueller, Sharon Lee (Sherry Mueller) *educational organization executive*
Muir, Patricia Allen *professional association administrator*
Murphy, Gerard Norris *trade association executive*
Murray, James Joseph, III, *association executive*
Musil, Robert Kirkland *professional society administrator*
†Nader, Ralph *consumer advocate, lawyer, author*
Neverson, Norman Carl *political organization administrator*
†Nicholson, Jim *political organization administrator*
Nicholson, Richard Selindh *educational association administrator*
O'Flaherty, James Daniel *council executive*
†Ohlke, Amanda Anne *museum association administrator, museum educator*
O'Kane, Margaret E. *non-profit organization executive*
Ottley, William Henry *professional association director, consultant*
Parkel, James G. *health association administrator*
Pearson, Roger *organization executive*
Pelavin, Sol Herbert *research company executive*
Petito, Margaret L. *foundation administrator*
Pierce, David R. *educational administrator*
Platts, Howard Gregory *scientific, educational organization executive*
Puryear, Jeffrey Merrill *cultural association administrator*
Radin, Alex *former association executive, consultant*
Rasmus, John Charles *trade association executive, lawyer*
†Ray, J. Ram *foundation administrator*
Reger, Lawrence Lee *trade association administrator*
Reich, Alan Anderson *executive*
Reinsch, William Alan *association executive, educator*
Repa, Edward William *waste management association executive, hydrologist*
Rice, Edmund Burke *trade association executive*
Rich, Dorothy Kovitz *writer, educational administrator*
Richardson, Ann Bishop *foundation executive, lawyer*
Ridings, Dorothy Sattes *association executive*
Riehle, B. Hudson *trade association executive*
Rodgers, Clifton Eugene, Jr., *trade association administrator, lobbyist*
Rodman, Peter Warren *government official*
†Roessel, Faith *Indian arts and crafts administrator*
†Romero, Jesse Charles *political organization worker*
Roos, Barbara Diane *association administrator*
Rosenstein, Peter D. *educational association administrator*
Ruskin, Robert Sterling *association executive*
Russell, William Joseph *educational association administrator*
Salisbury, Dallas L. *research institute executive*
†Satloff, Robert B. *think-tank executive*
Saunders, Harold Henry *foundation administrator*
Scanlon, Terrence Maurice *public policy foundation administrator*
Schlicht, James P. *pharmaceutical executive, lobbyist*
Schroeder, Patricia Scott *trade association administrator, retired congresswoman*
Scruggs-Leftwich, Yvonne *association executive*
Sewell, John Williamson *research association executive*
Shelby, Richard David *trade association executive*
Sieverts, Frank Arne *association executive*
Simmons, Caroline Thompson *civic worker*
Slade, John Danton *lobbyist*
Small, Sarah Mae *volunteer*
Smerling, Thomas Robert *think-tank executive, consultant*
Smith, Elise Fiber *international non-profit development agency administrator*
†Smith, Jessie P. Dowling *retired social services administrator*
Smith, Lloyd David *community activist*
†Smith, William S., Jr., *education association administrator*
Snyder, John Michael *lobbyist, public relations director*
Sombrotto, Vincent R. *postal union executive*
Sparks, Kenneth R. *association executive*
Splete, Allen Peterjohn *association executive, educator*
†Staats, Elmer Boyd *foundation executive, former government official*
Stebbins, Leroy Joseph (Lee Stebbins) *not-for-profit organization executive*
Stephens, John Frank *association executive, researcher*
Stern, Andrew L. *labor union administrator*
†Stern, Paula *international trade advisor*
Stone, Alec J. *healthcare lobbyist*
Strong, Henry *foundation executive*
Stump, E. Gordon *association administrator*
Sweeney, John Joseph *labor union administrator*
Swenson, Sue *foundation administrator, former health and education administrator*
†Teare, Richard Wallace *educational administrator*
Teich, Albert Harris *professional society administrator*
Theodore, Eustace D. *educational advancement consultant, management consultant*
Tipton, E. Linwood *trade association executive*
Tobias, Robert Max *labor leader, lawyer*
Tolu, Tolu *foundation administrator*
Tong, Chiling *trade and commerce administrator*
Tonkin, Leo Sampson *educational foundation administrator*
Townsend, Ann Van Devanter *foundation administrator, art historian*
Tracy, Alan Thomas *trade association administrator*
†Trumka, Richard Louis *labor leader, lawyer*
Tse, Man-Chun Marina *educational association administrator*
Unsell, Lloyd Neal *energy organization executive, former journalist*
Vanderryn, Jack *philanthropic foundation administrator*
Van Lare, Barry Lee *social welfare executive*
Veatch, Elizabeth Wilson *educational administrator*
von Kann, Clifton Ferdinand *aviation and space executive, software executive*
Votaw, Carmen Delgado *civic association executive*
†Walker, Barbara Dodson *cultural organization administrator, consultant, lecturer, researcher*
Warren, David Liles *educational association executive*
Weinstein, Kenneth R. *think-tank executive*
Werronen, Betsy Warren *political organization administrator*
Wertheimer, Fredric Michael *public policy advocate*
Wesley, LaTonya Rashawn *legislative assistant*
Weyrich, Paul Michael *political organizations executive*
Wilhelm, John W. *labor union administrator*
Williams, Eddie Nathan *research institution executive*
Williams, Jody *political organization administrator*
Williams, Lawrence Floyd *conservation organization official*
Wise, William Harvey, IV, *human service executive*
Wiseman, Laurence Donald *foundation executive*
Yost, Paul Alexander, Jr., *foundation executive, retired coast guard officer*
Zielinski, Paul Bernard *grant program administrator, civil engineer*

FLORIDA

Altamonte Springs
Pesut, Timothy Scott *wealth advisor, professional speaker, lifestyle coach*

Atlantis
Chittick, Elizabeth Lancaster *women's rights activist*

Bal Harbour
Ash, Dorothy Matthews *civic worker*

Boca Raton
Dembowski, Frederick Lester *educational administrator, educator, consultant*
Jessup, Jan Amis *arts volunteer, writer*

Bonita Springs
Feldblum, Sandra Faye Neuman *communal worker, nurse*

Boynton Beach
Rogers, John S. *retired union official*

Bradenton
Eppinger, James Edward *educational administrator*

Cantonment
†Hoskins, John Royce, Jr., *organization program specialist*

Coconut Grove
Martinez-Carbonell, Karelia *not-for-profit fundraiser*

Coral Gables
Landon, Robert Kirkwood *philanthropist, retired insurance company executive*
Lynch, Catherine Gores *social work administrator*

Coral Springs
Burg, Ralph *art association executive*

Debary
Pajama, Helen *advocate*

Delray Beach
Stewart, Patricia Carry *foundation administrator*

Destin
De Revere, David Wilsen *retired professional society administrator*

Englewood
Schultz, Arthur Joseph, Jr., *retired trade association executive*

Estero
Brown, William Robert *association executive, consultant*

Fort Lauderdale
Bowen, Judith Reina *fundraising executive*
Calhoun, Peggy Joan *fundraising executive*

Fort Pierce
Stock, Grace Emma *civic volunteer*

Gulf Breeze
Rainwater, Freddie Barrett *volunteer worker*
Walker, Peggy Jean *retired social work agency administrator*

Hialeah
Phelps, Dorothy Frink *civic worker*

Hillsboro Beach
Donoho, Tim Mark *charity founder and executive, entrepreneur*

Holmes Beach
Dunne, Nancy Anne *retired social services administrator*

Indialantic
Krasny, Charlotte Althea *volunteer*

Jacksonville Beach
Morris, Max King *foundation executive, former naval officer*

Key West
Haskell, Monica M. *art association administrator*

Lady Lake
Akins, Zane Vernon *association executive*

Lake Mary
Southward, Patricia C. *volunteer*

Lake Worth
Goldstein, Jerome Charles *professional association executive, surgeon, otolaryngologist*

Lakeland
Spencer, Mary Miller *civic worker*

Lauderdale By The Sea
Wynne, Brian James *former association executive, consultant*

Longboat Key
Dorsey, Eugene Carroll *former foundation and communications executive*

Maitland
Lovelace, Dorothy Louise *volunteer*

Marathon
†Vail, Elizabeth Forbus *volunteer*

Marco Island
Hollenbeck, Karen Fern *foundation consultant*

Melbourne
†Dean, Michael J. *lobbyist, consultant*
Thursfield, Fred Falconer, II, *foundation administrator*

Merritt Island
Anderson, Mary Helen Steed *volunteer*

Miami
Angones, Georgina Alfonsin *educational association administrator*
Bennett, Olga Salowich *civic worker, graphic arts researcher, consultant*
Blanco, Josefa Joan-Juana (Jossie Blanco) *social services administrator*
Cullom, William Otis *trade association executive*
†Culmer, Leome Frances *volunteer*
Dickason, John Hamilton *retired foundation executive*
Todd, Betty Clare *organization executive*
VanBrode, Derrick Brent, IV, *trade association administrator*

Miami Beach
Hair, Gilbert Martin *foundation administrator*

Naples
Rowe, Herbert Joseph *retired trade association executive*

New Port Richey
Wolf, Marilyn *volunteer*

Nocatee
Turnbull, David John (Chief Piercing Eyes-Penn) *cultural association executive*

North Miami
Gordon, Jack David *foundation administrator, real estate company officer*

North Palm Beach
Crawford, Roberta *association administrator*
Woodard, Wallace William, III, *quality advocate*

Okeechobee
Bishop, Sid Glenwood *union official*

Orlando
†Murrah, Ann Ralls Freeman *historical association executive*

Osprey
Harrington, Nancy O'Connor *volunteer*
Holec, Anita Kathryn Van Tassel *civic worker*

Palm Beach
†Elson, Suzanne Goodman *community activist*
Hope, Margaret Lauten *civic worker*
†Levine, Audrey Pearlstein *foundation administrator*
Mandel, Carola Panerai (Mrs. Leon Mandel) *foundation trustee*
Rinker, Ruby Stewart *foundation administrator*

Palm Beach Gardens
Falk, Bernard Henry *trade association executive*

Palm Coast
Cook, Gloria Houston *civic leader*

Palm Harbor
Angier, Carol C. *volunteer*

Pembroke Pines
Vayda, Rose K. *community volunteer*

Pensacola
Furlong, George Morgan, Jr., *museum foundation consultant, retired naval officer*

Pinellas Park
West, Wallace Marion *cultural organization administrator*

Ponte Vedra Beach
Slayton, Gus *foundation administrator*
Watson, John Lawrence, III, *former trade association executive*

Port Saint Lucie
†Weber, Alban *association executive, lawyer*

Punta Gorda
Clinton, Mariann Hancock *educational association administrator*

Saint Petersburg
Allshouse, Merle Frederick *educational organization administrator*
Beaman, Ann Thomson *volunteer*
Leach, Jane Riley *fundraiser*

Sanibel
Ball, Armand Baer *former association executive, consultant*

Sarasota
Bausch, James John *foundation executive*
Dobosz, Mark Joseph *fundraiser*
Gustafson, Karin Elisabeth *foundation executive*
Johnson, Leland "Lee" Harry *social services administrator*
Paru, Marden David *fundraising executive*
Rilla, Donald Robert *retired social services administrator*
Spencer, Lonabelle (Kappie Spencer) *political agency administrator, lobbyist*

Sebring
Maire, Barbara Jean *volunteer*

Stuart
Hutchinson, Janet Lois *historical society administrator*

Sunrise
Kolker, Sondra G. *fund raising, special events executive*

Tallahassee
Bishop, Barney Tipton, III, *political commentator, analyst, lobbyist, consultant*
†Campbell, Frances Harvell *foundation administrator*
Hammer, Marion Price *association executive*
Humphrey, Louise Ireland *civic worker, equestrienne*
Turnbull, Marjorie Reitz *foundation executive, former state legislator*

Tallevast
Celorie, Dennis Jay *not-for-profit executive*

Temple Terrace
Callan, Joseph Patrick *social service administrator*

West Palm Beach
†Coppock, Mark Stephen *not-for-profit fundraiser*
†Solomon, Louis B. *planned giving professional, professional association executive*

Windermere
Russell, Robert Leonard *professional association executive*

Winter Park
Olsson, Nils William *former association executive*

GEORGIA

Americus
Fuller, Millard Dean *charitable organization executive, lawyer*

Atlanta
Birdsong, Alta Marie *volunteer*
Drake, Stanley Joseph *association executive*
Gray, Phenessa Antoinette *not-for-profit developer*
Kelly, William Watkins *educational association executive*
†King, Coretta Scott (Mrs. Martin Luther King Jr.) *educational association administrator, lecturer, writer, concert singer*
†King, Dexter Scott *foundation administrator*
Lehfeldt, Martin Christopher *nonprofit association executive*
Mays, Jill Duncan *social services administrator, counselor*
†McCallum, John Arthur *foundation executive*
McTier, Charles Harvey *foundation administrator*
Smyre, Calvin *political organization executive, state legislator*
Spillett, Roxanne *social services administrator*
Weatherly, Alvis Morrison, Jr., *retired association developer*
Williams, Loraine Plant *civic worker*

Augusta
Grier, Leamon Forest *social services administrator*

Bonaire
Rustin, Varie Beatrice *community volunteer*

Clayton
Martinez, Susan Barbara *human rights advocate, journalist*

Conyers
Houchard, Michael Harlow *retired organization executive*

Decatur
Davis, Laura Ann *executive coach, trainer, facilitator*

Duluth
Reed, Ralph Eugene, Jr., *political party official*

Evans
Large, Mary Mitchell Westall *volunteer*

Gainesville
†Rivera, Cindy L. *social services administrator, medical/surgical nurse*

Lagrange
Gresham, James Thomas *foundation executive*

Peachtree City
Pulin, Carol *fine arts organization administrator*

Roswell
Hill, I. Kathryn *medical certification, licensing and education consultant*

Saint Simons
Bell, Ronald Mack *university foundation administrator, consultant*

Sautee Nacoochee
Hill, Ronald Guy, Sr., *non-profit organization consultant*

Savannah
Beals, L(oren) Alan *association executive*
†Flynn, Laura D *foundation administrator, consultant, educator*
†Thomson, Audrey Shire *volunteer*

Summerville
Spivey, Suzan Brooks Nisbet *association administrator, medical technologist*

Tucker
McNair, Nimrod, Jr., *foundation executive, consultant*

West Point
Barnwell, Madge Owen *volunteer*

HAWAII

Honolulu
Furuyama, Renee Harue *association executive*
Hack, Randolph C. *advocate, educator, counselor*
†Kahikina, Michael Puamamo *social services administrator, state legislator*
Kane, Micah *political party official*
†Mindo, Romeo *labor union administrator*
Morrison, Charles E. *think-tank executive*
†Noji, Deborah Teruko *not-for-profit fundraiser*
Ogburn, Nancy Wrenn *civic volunteer*
Robinson, Robert Blacque *foundation administrator*
White, Emmet, Jr., *retirement community administrator*
Witeck, John Joseph *labor union representative, educator*

Kihei
Corell, Marcella Anne *community worker, retired educator*

IDAHO

Boise
Blackwell, David C. *foundation administrator*
Boyce, Carolyn *political organization administrator*
Craig, Kara Lynn *children's home administrator*
Olson, A. Craig *foundation administrator, former retail executive, retail executive*
Sandy, John A. *political organization administrator, state legislator*

Hailey
Liebich, Marcia Trathen *community volunteer*

Saint Anthony
Williams, Joanne Merle *volunteer hospice coordinator*

Sandpoint
Nelson, Marcella May *volunteer*

ILLINOIS

Arlington Heights
Nerlinger, John William *retired trade association administrator*

Barrington
Dykla, K.H.S. Edward George *retired social services administrator*

Belvidere
Luhman, William Simon *community development administrator*

Carbondale
Trescott, Kathleen Marie *cultural association administrator*

Carlinville
Bellm, Joan *civic worker*

Chicago
Benedict, Kennette Mari *foundation executive, researcher*

Bindenagel, James Dale *foundation executive*
Bourdon, Cathleen Jane *professional society administrator*
Brandt, Gene Stuart *fundraising consultant*
Brown, Joan Phillips (Abena Joan Brown) *foundation administrator*
Cameron, Catherine Isabella *community volunteer*
Chacko, Samuel *association official*
Chappell, Kathleen Diane *fundraising executive*
Clevenger, Penelope *international business consultant*
†Colker, David *trade association administrator*
†Dan, Bernard W. *trade association administrator*
Dolan, Thomas Christopher *professional society administrator*
Donnell, Harold Eugene, Jr., *professional society administrator*
†Donohue, Craig S. *trade association administrator*
English, Henry L. *not-for-profit association executive*
†Franke, Richard James *arts advocate, former investment banker*
Frazin, Rhona Sondra *non-profit executive*
†Hanson, Monique Shiraz *not-for-profit fundraiser*
†Hart, Reginald *advocate, writer, adult education educator*
†Harvey, Katherine Abler *civic worker*
Helpingstine, Daniel Wallace *organization official, freelance writer*
Huff, John Gardner *child welfare specialist, state official*
†Hunter, Mattie *human services executive*
Klimley, Nancy Lee *volunteer*
Lerner, Alexander Robert *association executive*
MacDougal, Gary Edward *corporate director, foundation trustee*
†Mayer, Beatrice Cummings *civic worker*
McDonald, William Brice *educational association administrator*
Minow, Josephine Baskin *civic volunteer*
Munger, Benson Scott *former professional society administrator*
Murphy, Ellis *association management executive*
Nebenzahl, Paul *fundraising executive, museum executive*
Olsen, Rex Norman *trade association executive*
†Page, Mary Robertson *foundation administrator*
Perry, James E. *not-for-profit development executive*
Ree, Donna *social services administrator, educator*
Richman, Harold Alan *social welfare policy educator*
Rielly, John Edward *educational association administrator*
Rodgers, James Foster *association executive, economist*
Scherer, Karla *foundation executive, venture capitalist*
Schimberg, Barbara Hodes *organizational development consultant*
Sigmon, Joyce Elizabeth *professional society administrator*
Skolnick, Sherman Herbert *media host/producer, researcher, court reformer*
Smith, Kent Ernest *non-profit organization executive*
†Termondt, M. James *foundation administrator*
Valentine, Valerie *volunteer*
Vogelzang, Jeanne Marie *professional association executive, lawyer*
†Wilson, Cleo Francine *entertainment company executive*
Wright, Helen Kennedy *retired professional association administrator, publisher, editor, librarian*
Wyant, Carol Shumaker *not for profit management consultant*

Crystal Lake
Chamberlain, Charles James *railroad labor union executive*

Dekalb
Folgate, Cynthia A. *social services administrator*

Des Plaines
Quellmalz, Frederick *foundation executive, editor*
Womack, Doug C. *labor union representative*

East Saint Louis
†Harrison, Patricia Ann *educational association administrator*

Elgin
Kelly, Matthew Edward *association executive, retired*
Mason, Stephen Olin *nonprofit association administrator*

Evanston
Abnee, A. Victor *trade association executive*
Arrington, Michael Browne *foundation administrator*
Gordon, Julie Peyton *foundation administrator*
Thrash, Patricia Ann *educational association administrator*
Wener, Maureen G. *association executive*

Galena
Hermann, Paul David *retired association executive*

Glen Carbon
Martinez, Steven Frank *organization executive*

Jacksonville
†Mathews, Jack Sherman *foundation administrator, retired insurance company executive*
Randall, Catherine Horn *advocate*

Joliet
†Farmer, Marilyn *volunteer*

La Grange Park
Brown, Helen Sauer *fund raising executive*

Lake Bluff
Schreiber, George Richard *association executive, writer*

Lake Forest
Fetridge, Bonnie-Jean Clark (Mrs. William Harrison Fetridge) *civic volunteer*
Morell, William Nelson, Jr., *foreign trade association executive, government agency administrator*

Lansing
McKeown, Mary Elizabeth *educational administrator*

Macomb
North, Teresa Lynn *student services administrator*

Marion
†Aikman, Elflora Anna *senior citizens center administrator*

Mooseheart
†Ross, Donald Hugh *fraternal organization executive*

Mount Prospect
Mirsky, Howard *social services administrator, pharmacist*

Naperville
†Hilt, Meredith Dykstra *foundation administrator*
L'Allier, James Joseph *educational multimedia company executive, instructional designer*

Northbrook
†Siegal, Judy A. *social services administrator*

Oak Brook
John, Richard C. *enterprise development organization executive*

Orion
Magee, Elizabeth Sherrard *civic organization volunteer*

Orland Park
Herbert, Victor James *foundation administrator*

Ottawa
Thornton, Edmund B. *philanthropist*

Palatine
Walker, Sally Y. *educational association administrator*

Palos Park
Maxwell, Dorothea Bost Andrews *civic worker*

Park Ridge
Ewald, Robert Frederick *insurance association executive*

Peoria
Kroehler, Ralph S. *association executive*
Laible-White, Sherry Lynne *welfare reform administrator*
Quanstrom, Roy Fred *non-profit organization executive*

Percy
Rice, Charles Dale *labor relations specialist, writer*

Riverside
Dengler, Robert Anthony *professional association executive, educator*

Rock Falls
Julifs, Sandra Jean *community action agency executive*

Rockford
Heinke, Warren E. *social services administrator*

Rolling Meadows
†Bassi, Suzanne Howard *volunteer*

Rosemont
Good, William Allen *professional society executive*
Rosenthal, Lawrence Edward *association executive*

Schaumburg
Little, Bruce Washington *professional society administrator*
Tompson, Marian Leonard *professional society administrator*

Skokie
Gleason, John Patrick, Jr., *trade association executive*
Weidmann, K. Timothy *not-for-profit fundraiser, writer*

Springfield
Blackman, Jeanne A. *community program manager*
†Ramirez-Campbell, Christine M. *art council administrator*

Sycamore
Stone, Van Courtright *professional society administrator*

Urbana
†Bodmer, Paul Herbert *professional society administrator*
Ikenberry, Judith Life *social and charitable organization volunteer, writer*
Lazarus, Betty Ross *retired civic activist*
Roley, Jeff W. *foundation representative*

Sturtevant, William T. *fundraising executive, consultant*

Vernon Hills
Michalik, John James *legal educational association executive*

Waukegan
Drapalik, Betty R. *volunteer, artist, educator*

Wheaton
Votaw, John Frederick *educational foundation executive, educator*

Wilmette
Brink, Marion Francis *trade association administrator*
Hansen, Andrew Marius *retired library association executive*

Winnetka
Schechter, Gail Helene *social services administrator, educator*

INDIANA

Bloomington
Brinkman, Paul Del(bert) *foundation executive, university administrator*
†Ikranagara, Kay *educational association administrator, educator*
†Wells, Kimberly K. *not-for-profit organization executive*

Columbus
†Brunner, Ellen Margaret *not-for-profit fundraiser*

Elkhart
Harrington, Lori Lynn *social services administrator*

Evansville
Early, Judith K. *social services director*

Fishers
Gatto, Louis Constantine *educational association administrator*

Fort Wayne
Neuman, Paula Anne Young *cultural organization administrator*

Francesville
†Wilson, Kathy Kay *foundation executive*

Hagerstown
Bex, Brian William Louis *educational administrator*

Hanna
Stephenson, Dorothy Maxine *volunteer*

Indianapolis
Alvarez, Thomas *foundation administrator, writer, consultant*
Barcus, Robert Gene *retired educational association administrator*
Blaydes, June Louise *volunteer*
Braun, Robert Clare *retired association and advertising executive*
Chamness, Charles Morris *professional society administrator*
Finley, Katherine Mandusic *professional society administrator*
Maxwell, Florence Hinshaw *civic worker*
McLaughlin, Sherry *association administrator*
Palmer, Robert P. *professional association executive*
Santos, Richard J. *association administrator*
Shaffer, Alfred Garfield (Terry Shaffer) *service organization executive*
†Sparks, Donald Eugene *interscholastic activities association executive*
Stein, Carole Ruth *social services administrator, researcher*
Sweezy, John William *political party official*
Vereen, Robert Charles *retired trade association executive*

Lafayette
†Scaletta, Helen Marguerite *volunteer*

Lawrenceburg
Edwards, Marie D. *social services administrator*

Martinsville
†Smith, Peg L. *foundation administrator*

Muncie
†Bakken, Douglas Adair *foundation executive*
Shoemaker, Helen E. Martin Achor *civic worker*

Noblesville
†Emswiller, Julie L. *not-for-profit developer*

Terre Haute
Aldridge, Sandra *civic volunteer*

West Lafayette
Baumgardt, Billy Ray *professional society administrator, agriculturist*
Watlington, Sarah Jane *community volunteer, retired military officer*

IOWA

Ames
Swanson, Florine Mary *foundation administrator*

Cedar Rapids
Arnold-Olson, Helen B. *nonprofit consultant*
Huber, Rita Norma *civic worker*
Whipple, William Perry *foundation administrator*

Decorah
Gray, Phyllis *educational administrator*

Des Moines
Blake, Darlene Evelyn *political worker, consultant, educator, author*
Hutchison, Charlotte Pancoast (Sherry Hutchison) *civic worker*
McGuire-Riggs, Sheila *chairman Democratic party*
Nelson, Charlotte Bowers *public administrator*

Iowa City
Rockel, Viana Eileen *university fundraiser, consultant*

Sioux City
Waller, Ephraim Everett *retired association executive*

KANSAS

Atwood
Okeson, Dorothy Jeanne *educational association administrator*

Kansas City
Benjamin, Janice Yukon *development executive*
Campbell, Joseph Leonard *trade association executive*
Steineger, Margaret Leisy *non-profit organization officer*

Lawrence
Bowman, Laird Price *retired foundation administrator*

Leawood
Puppe, Gerald Clarence *trade association executive*

Shawnee
†Wilson, Eugene Rolland *foundation executive*

Shawnee Mission
Green, John Lafayette, Jr., *education executive*

South Hutchinson
Armstrong, Larry Don *activist, association administrator*

Topeka
Frahm, Sheila *association executive, former government official, academic administrator*

Wichita
Lowrey, Annie Tsunee *retired cultural organization administrator*
Myers, John Moore *fraternal organization administrator*
Rueb, Sheree A. *social services administrator*
Timmerman, Dora Mae *community volunteer, art advocate*

Winfield
Gray, Ina Turner *fraternal organization administrator*

KENTUCKY

Frankfort
Patton, Nicki *former political organization executive*
Underwood, John Thomas, IV, *trade association executive, lobbyist*
Williams, Ellen C. *political party official*
Williamson, Deborah McKibben *social services administrator, educator*

Hardin
Morrow, Bruce William *educational administrator, business executive, consultant, author*

Lexington
Ehmann, Nancy Gallagher *civic worker*
†Hamilton, C. Todd *lobbyist*
Lewis, Robert Kay, Jr., *fundraising executive*
Sexton, Robert Fenimore *educational organization executive*

Louisville
Appleberry, James Bruce *higher education consultant*
Early, Jack Jones *foundation executive*
Hoffer, Debra Humes *educational association administrator*

LOUISIANA

Alexandria
Bradford, Louise Mathilde *social services administrator*

Baton Rouge
Brister, Pat *political party executive*
Jeffers, Ben *political organization executive*
McDaniel, Barry Lynn *educational association administrator*

Franklin
Domingue, Michael W. *community developer*

Lafayette
Ceballos, Jacqui Michot *feminist activist, organizer, administrator*
Dickie, Shirley Dalme *vocational rehabilitation counselor and consultant*

Mandeville
Landry, Joseph L., Jr., *retired affirmative action specialist*

New Orleans
Benjamin, Adelaide Wisdom *community volunteer and activist, retired lawyer*
Cody, Wilmer St. Clair *retired educational administrator, educational policy consultant*
†Cramer, Cheryl Quave Wilson *not-for-profit developer, consultant*
Rathke, Dale Lawrence *community organizer and financial analyst*
Sullivan, Daniel Edmond *fundraising executive*

Shreveport
Goodman, Sylvia Klumok *volunteer*
Magness, Nan Jean *social services professional*

MAINE

Augusta
Gervais, Paul Nelson *foundation administrator, psychotherapist, public relations executive, author*
Phillips, Gwethalyn *political organization administrator*
†Raths, Barbara *political organization worker*

Bangor
†Coffman, Michael S. *international organization official*

Brunswick
Rosser, Richard Franklin *higher education consultant*

Caribou
Bosse, Denise Frances *educational administrator, education educator*

Georgetown
Chapin, Maryan Fox *civic worker*

Pemaquid
Howell, Jeanette Helen *retired cultural organization administrator*

Portland
†Boyle, John Edward Whiteford *cultural organization administrator*
Konkel, Harry Wagner *civic volunteer, retired career officer*

Rockport
Merrill, Mary Lee *professional society administrator*

South Portland
Harris, Penny Smith *fundraising consultant*

Spruce Head
Bird, Mary Alice *fund raising consultant*

Waterford
Stockwell, William F. *fundraiser, management consultant*

Windham
Mulvey, Mary Crowley *retired adult education director, gerontologist, senior citizen association administrator*

York
Smart, Mary-Leigh Call (Mrs. J. Scott Smart) *civic worker*

York Harbor
Rust, Libby Karen *fundraising and public relations counsel*

MARYLAND

Aberdeen Proving Ground
Tobin, Aileen Webb *educational administrator*

Annapolis
†Kane, John *political organization administrator*
Rogers, Wayne L. *political organization administrator*
Stahl, David Edward *trade association administrator, retired*

Arnold
Yarrow, C. W. *fund raiser*

Baltimore
Deffenbaugh, Ralston H., Jr., *immigration agency executive, lawyer*
Dickinson, Jane W. *social services administrator*
Ephross, Paul Hullman *social work educator*
Fuentealba, Victor William *professional society administrator*
Manno, Bruno Victor *foundation administrator*
†Mfume, Kweisi *civil rights advocate, former congressman*
Pinkard, Anne Merrick *foundation administrator*
Ridgeway, Dominic Charles *advocate*
Rosen, Wendy Workman *arts management and publishing executive*
Safran, Linda Jacqueline *fundraiser*
Silberg, Carol Ann Schwartz *cultural organization administrator, educator*
Weber, Nancy Walker *charitable trust administrator*

Bethesda
Augustine, Norman Ralph *organization executive, educator*
Cleary, Timothy Finbar *professional society administrator*
Dangremond, Dale Joan *executive director, chief operating officer, consultant*
Day, Mary Louise *volunteer*
Day, Robert Dwain, Jr., *foundation executive, lawyer*
Dulin, Maurine Stuart *volunteer*
Grady, Patricia A. *health institute director, researcher*
Grau, John Michael *trade association executive*
Guenther, Kenneth Allen *business association executive, economist*
Hershaft, Alex *organization executive*
Jonas, Gary Fred *philanthropy executive*
Kochanski, Lois Whidden *foundation administrator*
Oddis, Joseph Anthony *associations executive*
Salisbury, Tamara Paula *foundation executive*
Saunders, Charles Baskerville, Jr., *retired association executive*
Sprott, Richard Lawrence *foundation administrator, researcher*
Stearman, William Lloyd *military association executive, author*
Stone, Jeremy Judah *public interest activist*
Tape, Gerald Frederick *former association executive*
Weinstein, Allen *educator, historian, non-profit administrator*
Young, Ina Weinstein *association administrator*

Bowie
Francois, Francis Bernard *retired association executive, lawyer, transportation consultant*

Chevy Chase
Hunt, Frederick Talley Drum, Jr., *association executive*
Pogue, Mary Ellen E. (Mrs. L(loyd) Welch Pogue) *youth and community worker*
Wright, Helen Patton *professional society administrator*

College Park
Stover, Carl Frederick *foundation executive*
Unsell, Lloyd Neal, Jr., *association executive*

Columbia
Bailey, John Martin *retired transportation planner, educator*
†Purcell, James Nelson, Jr., *international organization administrator*
Rogers, Thomas Francis *foundation administrator*

Crofton
Ross, E(dwin) Clarke *association executive, educator*

Damascus
Nelligan, William David *professional association executive*

Edgewater
Hammer, Jane Amelia Ross *advocate*

Elkton
Scherf, Christopher N. *trade association administrator*

Ellicott City
Woodcock, Cynthia Hardin *program development strategic planning*

Fort Washington
Coffey, Matthew B. *trade association executive*

Frederick
Keefe, Arthur Thomas, III, *non-profit fund raising executive*

Gambrills
Messner, Howard Myron *professional association executive*

Germantown
Searles, Thomas Daniel *society administrator*

Greenbelt
Miller, Alwin Vermar *educational advisor, consultant*

Lanham Seabrook
Littlefield, Roy Everett, III, *association executive, legal educator*

Lexington Park
Sprague, Edward Auchincloss *retired association executive, economist*

Mitchellville
Ball, Robert M(yers) *social security, welfare and health policy specialist, writer, lecturer*

Montgomery Village
Avedisian, Archie Harry *community organization executive*

Mount Airy
Wagner, Doris Walkling *volunteer, director*

North Bethesda
Chilcote, Samuel Day, Jr., *trade association administrator*
Rogul, June Audrey *fundraising executive, government relations specialist*
Sherman, Deane Murray *culture organization administrator*

Owings Mills
Tapp, Mamie Pearl *educational association administration*

Port Republic
Sugarman, Jule Meyer *children's services consultant, former public administrator*

Potomac
Gelatt, James Prentice *nonprofit management consultant*
Johnson, Anne Hale *educational association administrator, director*
Marincola, Elizabeth Mark *scientific society executive*
Rosenberg, Sarah Zacher *institute arts administration executive, humanities administration consultant*

Randallstown
Hatch, Sally Ruth *foundation administrator, writer, consultant*

Rockville
†Futrovsky, Cheryl Jean *foundation administrator, performing company executive*
Kline, Raymond Adam *professional organization executive*
Marcuccio, Phyllis Rose *retired association executive, editor*
Spahr, Frederick Thomas *association executive*
Standing, Kimberly Anna *educational researcher*
Sumberg, Alfred Donald *professional association executive*

Severna Park
Hall, Marcia Joy *non-profit organization administrator*

Silver Spring
†Camphor, James Winky, Jr., *educational administrator*
Fanelli, Joseph James *retired public affairs executive, consultant*
Fockler, Herbert Hill *foundation executive*
†Grosso, Stacia Strouss *foundation administrator*
Hayman, Harry *association executive, electrical engineer*
Hermanson Ogilvie, Judith *foundation executive*
Roth, Harriet Steinhorn *educator, public speaker*
Smedley, Lawrence Thomas *retired organization executive*
Winston, Michael Russell *foundation executive, historian*
Zakheim, Barbara Jane *development professional*

Sykesville
Crist, Gertrude H. *civic worker*

Takoma Park
Lancaster, Alden *educational and management consultant*
Richie, Robert Douglas *not-for-profit executive*

Upper Marlboro
Buffenbarger, R. Thomas *labor union administrator*
†Salter, Carol A. *not-for-profit executive*

MASSACHUSETTS

Acton
Hamel, Elizabeth Cecil *volunteer, educator*

Amesbury
Bartnicki, Karen Jo *social services administrator*

Attleboro
Tuniewicz, Mark Anthony *political activist, corporate credit executive*

Ayer
Anthony, Sylvia *social welfare organization executive*

Bedford
Kampits, Eva *accrediting association administrator, educator*

Boston
†Brennan, Timothy William *not-for-profit fundraiser*
Cabot, Louis Wellington *foundation trustee*
Franks, Peter John *educational administrator*
Glass, Renée *educational health foundation executive*
Jackson, Patience Kenney *grants adminstrator, library consultant*
Jennings, Jon Paul *nonprofit foundation executive*
Knight, Norman *philanthropist, former broadcast executive*
Leff, Deborah *government executive*
McClung, William Alexander *foundation administrator, educator*
Shea, Dermot P. *consumer advocate, lawyer*
Sullivan, James Leo *organization executive*
†Tate, Randall J. (Randy Tate) *former congressman*
Trumbull, David Lewis Kitchen *trade association executive*
Walsh, Peter L. *arts administrator, writer, consultant, researcher, art critic*

Brookline
†Neumann, Deborah Brochi *not-for-profit fundraiser*

Cambridge
†Bloomfield, Steven B. *think-tank executive*
Brown, Lloyd David *association executive, management educator*
†DiGiustini, Antonetta Anna *educational association administrator, educator*
Forbes, John Malcolm *non-profit administrator*
Glazier, Raymond Earl, Jr., *social research executive, disability policy analyst*
†Harris, William Wolpert
Hyman, Steven Edward *federal agency administrator, psychiatrist, educator*
Tucker, Louis Leonard *retired historical society administrator*

Chelmsford
Elwell, Barbara Lois Dow *community organizer*

Dorchester
Smith, Survilla Marie *social services administrator, artist, poet*

Fitchburg
Niemi, Beatrice Neal *social services professional*

Framingham
Harrington, Joseph Francis *educational company executive, history educator*

Great Barrington
Witt, Susan Carreer *environmental educator, society administrator*

Greenfield
Hutcheson, Thomas Worthington *trade association official*

Groton
Searle, Andrew Barton *fund raising consultant*

Hull
Anderson, Timothy Christopher *educational association administrator*

Ipswich
Bryant, Edward Curtis *college admissions consultant*
Munro, Donald William, Jr., *non-profit organization executive*
Wilson, Doris H. *volunteer*

Lexington
Garing, Ione Davis *civic worker, club woman*

Lincoln
Kane, Melissa L. *fundraiser*

Malden
Guild, Richard Samuel *trade association management company executive*

Medford
O'Connell, Brian *community organizer, public administrator, writer, educator*

Middleboro
Cacciatore, Sharen Wendy *educational administrator*

Milton
Corcoran, Robert Joseph *fund raising executive*

Nantucket
Pollard, Margaret Louise *association administrator*

New Bedford
Bullard, John Kilburn *educational association administrator*

Newton
Chalfen, Judith Resnick *community activist*

Northampton
Diehl, Timothy Jerel *social services administrator*

Orleans
Bast, James Louis *retired trade association executive*
Marquand, Jean MacMurtry *educational administrator*
Putnam, Allan Ray *association executive*

Peabody
Marshall, Laurence Paul *social services administrator*

Quincy
†Holway, David *association administrator*
Wilson, Blenda Jacqueline *foundation administrator*

Salem
Haskell, James Thompson *cultural organization administrator*

Sharon
Reilley, Dennen *research agency administrator, educator*

South Boston
Adams, Rita Fuerst *management and fundraising consultant*

Springfield
Faerber, Kent William *foundation administrator, consultant*

Wakefield
†Crate, Darrell *political organization administrator*
Inman, Jean A. *political party official*

Watertown
†Boland, Elizabeth *social services company financial executive*

Wayland
Humphrey, Diana Young *fund raiser*

Wellesley
Henderson, Mary Louise *civic worker*
Tagge, Anne *writer, not-for-profit organization administrator*

West Barnstable
†Tollefsen, Astrid *not-for-profit fundraiser*

West Yarmouth
Crist, Bainbridge *volunteer*

Westford
†Geary, Marie Josephine *art association administrator*

Weston
Daly, Charles Ulick *foundation executive*

Westwood
Provost, Lura Swift *civic volunteer*

Winchester
Reno, John F. *foundation administrator*

MICHIGAN

Ann Arbor
Diana, Joseph A. *retired foundation executive*
Kennedy, David Boyd *foundation executive, lawyer*
Porter, John Wilson *education executive*
Radock, Michael *foundation executive*
†Ramírez-Betances, Beatriz Eugenia *student activist*
Ware, Richard Anderson *foundation executive*

Battle Creek
Baldwin, Susan Olin *community service administrator*
Davis, Laura Arlene *retired foundation administrator*
Wendt, Linda M. *educational association administrator*

Beaver Island
Thompson, Sarah Ellen *grants consultant*

Bloomfield Hills
Kyes, Helen G. (Mrs. Rogers M. Kyes) *volunteer*
†Levin, Carolyn Bible *volunteer*

Dearborn Heights
Donoian, George *education executive*

Detroit
Neithercut, Mark Edward *foundation executive*
Noland, Mariam Charl *foundation executive*
†Palmer, Keturah *association administrator*
Ryder, James Lee *missionary, community-based agency official*

Dowagiac
Ott, C(larence) H(enry) *citizen ambassador, accounting educator*

Flint
Belcher, Max *social services administrator, college dean*
†Munerlyn, Lorraine *administrative secretary, writer*
White, William Samuel *foundation executive*

Grand Rapids
†Sieger, Diana R. *foundation administrator*

Grosse Ile
Meyer, Rosalind Mae *community volunteer*

Holt
Wiltse, Richard Allan *association executive*

Howell
Heinel, Robert Steven *social services administrator*

Kalamazoo
Petersen, Anne C.(Cheryl) *foundation administrator, educator*

Lansing
Lobenherz, William Ernest *container company/association executive, lawyer*
McKeague, Nancy Palmer *trade association executive*
Porter, Karen Collins *non-profit administrator*
Tucker, John Andrews *association executive*

Manistee
Behring, Daniel William *educational and business professional, consultant*

Oak Park
Piper, Annette Cleone *social services administrator, researcher*

Okemos
Belyea, Karlene Boyes *professional association executive*
Luecke, Eleanor Virginia Rohrbacher *civic volunteer*

Saint Clair Shores
Smith, Frank Earl *retired association executive*

Traverse City
Keilitz, Gene Martin *retired association administrator*

Troy
Marshall, John Elbert, III, *foundation executive*

Waterford
Laing, James Thomas *retired not-for-profit developer*

MINNESOTA

Chaska
†Burke, Steven Francis *organization executive*
Casselman, Barry *political correspondent, nonprofit administrator, author*

Glencoe
Beneke, Millie Stong *civic worker, author*

Minneapolis
Fawcett, Marie Ann Formanek (Mrs. Roscoe Kent Fawcett) *civic leader*
Herbison, Priscilla Joan *public policy and law educator, consultant*

Johnson, John Warren *retired association executive*

Rochester
†Riggs, Jeanette Templeton *civic worker*

Roseville
Hughes, Jerome Michael *education foundation executive*

Saint Paul
Anderson, Gordon Louis *foundation administrator*
Archer, Joan M. *trade association administrator*
†Bila, Thomas A. *not-for-profit fundraiser*
Bruener, James William *fundraiser*
Eibensteiner, Ron *political organization administrator, venture capitalist*
†Franey, Billie Nolan *political activist*
Kurtz, Harold Paul *foundation executive*
Pampusch, Anita Marie *foundation administrator*
Skillingstad, Constance Yvonne *social services administrator, educator*
Smith, Mary Hill *volunteer*

Saint Peter
Nelsen, William Cameron *educational association administrator, retired academic administrator*

St Paul
†Ta, Minh Tuan *lobbyist, consultant*

MISSISSIPPI

Bay Saint Louis
†Latham, Terry L. *social services administrator*

Crystal Springs
†Bates, Lura Wheeler *retired trade association executive*

Fayette
La Salle, Arthur Edward *historic foundation executive*

Jackson
†Cole, Ricky *political organization worker*
Hegwood, Barbara H.
Herring, James H. *political organization administrator, lawyer*
†Marks, Michael *association administrator*
Risley, Rod Alan *education association executive*
†Sullivan, Bettye Yarborough *foundation administrator*

Long Beach
Kanagy, Steven Albert *foundation administrator*

Madison
Hiatt, Jane Crater *arts agency administrator*

Meridian
†Rosenbaum, Ike Alfred *foundation administrator*

Tougaloo
†Whittington, Felicia Trenise *social services administrator, educator*

MISSOURI

Blue Springs
Sauer, Richard John *retired non-profit executive*

Bolivar
Rice, Cindy G. *estate planning associate*

Bridgeton
Kenison, Raymond Robert *fraternal organization administrator, director*

Chesterfield
†Henderson, William J. *association executive*

Columbia
McDermott, Dennis Michael *trade association executive*

Defiance
LeMaster, Sherry Renee *fundraising administrator, foundation administrator, consultant*

Earth City
Anderhalter, Oliver Frank *educational organization executive*

Florissant
Schutzius, Mary Jane *volunteer activist*

Independence
Mallinson, Sarah Jane *volunteer civic activities*
Potts, Barbara Joyce *retired historical society executive*

Jefferson City
†Ridenhour, Cory Todd *association executive, consultant, accountant*
Wagner, Ann *political organization executive*

Kansas City
Benner, Richard Edward, Jr., *community service volunteer, investor*
Bugher, Robert Dean *professional society administrator*
Paden, John Bruce *community resource executive*
Switzer, Samuel Thomas *non-profit administrator*

Kirksville
French, Michael Francis *non-profit education agency administrator*

Lees Summit
Carter, William Gerald *non-profit corporation executive*

Richmond Heights
Chandler, James Barton *international education consultant*

Saint Louis
Bascom, C. Perry *retired foundation administrator*
Blood, Milton Ray *association executive*
Brauer, Camilla Thompson (Kimmy Thompson Brauer) *civic leader*
Duhme, Carol McCarthy *civic worker*
Hall, Mary Taussig *professional volunteer*
Hunter, Earle Leslie, III, *retired professional association executive*
Kimmey, James Richard, Jr., *foundation administrator*
Melman, Joy *civic volunteer*
†Nelson, Ronald Erwin *not-for-profit fundraiser*
Pope, Robert E(ugene) *fraternal organization administrator*
†Porter, Paul Robert *foundation administrator*
Reck, Carleen Joan *social welfare administrator*
Robins, Marjorie McCarthy (Mrs. George Kenneth Robins) *civic worker*
Silverman, Victoria Lillian *not-for-profit fundraiser*
Wright, Gary Kennedy *educational administrator*

Salem
Sheriff, Kenneth Wayne *social services administrator*

Springfield
Morris, Ann Haseltine Jones *social welfare administrator*

MONTANA

Billings
†Gilluly, Mary Seana *not-for-profit executive*
Sample, Joseph Scanlon *foundation executive*

Bozeman
Gibson, David Frederic *foundation executive, engineering educator*

Helena
Porter, Jeanne Smith *civic worker*
Ream, Bob *political organization administrator*

Missoula
Amundson, Eva Donalda *civic worker*
Earls, Joy R. Shulman *professional society administrator*
Kemmis, Daniel Orra *cultural organization administrator, author*

NEBRASKA

Bellevue
Hoell, Kathy *disability rights advocate*

Eagle
Krutz, Jonathan Lawrence *non-profit association administrator*

Grand Island
Abernethy, Irene Margaret *civic worker, retired county official*

Harrison
Coffee, Virginia Claire *civic worker, former mayor*

Lincoln
†Nelson, Sara June *victim advocate*
Rosenow, John Edward *foundation executive*

Ogallala
Bourque, Richard Michael *foundation administrator*

Omaha
Burris, Janice Elaine *educational administrator*
Cheloha, John Anthony *city lobbyist, lawyer*
Humlicek, Evelyn Clarice *volunteer, retired nursing educator*
Strawhecker, Paul Joseph *fundraising consultant*

Seward
Vrana, Verlon Kenneth *retired professional society administrator, conservationist*

NEVADA

Carson City
Ayres, Janice Ruth *social services administrator*

Henderson
Freyd, William Pattinson *fund raising executive, consultant*

Incline Village
Johnston, Bernard Fox *foundation executive, writer*

Las Vegas
†bolognini, Dorothy Barber *not-for-profit developer*
Martin, Myron Gregory *foundation administrator*
Nicholson, R. Stephen *organization administrator*
Reid, Rory *former political organization administrator*
Wunstell, Erik James *non-profit organization administrator, communications consultant*
Zucker, Blanche Myra *civic worker*

Pahrump
†Hersman, Marion Frank *professional administrator, lawyer*
Nowell, Linda Gail *organization executive*

NEW HAMPSHIRE

Hollis
Merritt, Mary Jane *community volunteer*

Manchester
Sullivan, Kathleen N. *political organization administrator, lawyer*

North Sandwich
Penrose, Charles, Jr., *professional society administrator*

Peterborough
Eppes, William David *arts/humanities supporter*

Pike
Teschner, Douglass Paul *project administrator*

Randolph
Bradley, William Lee *retired foundation executive, educator*

Somersworth
Furbush, Mary Chapman *clubwoman*

NEW JERSEY

Atlantic City
Jamieson, John Edward, Jr., *social services administrator, minister, bioethicist*

Basking Ridge
Probert, Edward Whitford *foundation executive, volunteer*

Bloomfield
McCulloch, George McQuillan *retired foundation executive, fundraiser*

Bound Brook
†Blumberg, Adele Rosenberg *volunteer*

Cherry Hill
Moyer, Cheryl Lynn *non-profit administrator*

Cliffside Park
Pushkarev, Boris S. *research foundation director, writer*

East Brunswick
Goldberg, Bertram J. *social agency administrator*

East Orange
Caldwell, Toni Lucille

Englewood
Hantgan, George *social services administrator*

Glen Ridge
Pendley, Donald Lee *association executive*

Glen Rock
†D'Angelo, Thomas J. *not-for-profit developer, financial consultant*
Sirower, Bonnie Fox *fundraising executive*

Haddonfield
Podgorski, Miriam Coder *volunteer*

Highland Park
Kolodzei, Natalia A. *art foundation administrator, art historian, curator*

Hightstown
Bramwell, Katharine Hone Emmet *civic worker*

Jersey City
Conner, Ruth (Edone) *not-for-profit developer*

Keyport
Gilmartin, Clara T. *volunteer*

Lambertville
Mackey, Philip English *non-profit organization consultant*

Lebanon
O'Neill, Elizabeth Sterling *trade association administrator*

Linwood
Moss, Andrea *fundraiser, community service volunteer*

Locust
Freeman, David Forgan *retired foundation executive*

Mercerville
Wentz, Debra Linowitz *professional association executive*

Metuchen
Madden, John Francis *fundraising executive*

Montclair
Campbell, Stewart Fred *foundation executive*
Mason, Lucile Gertrude *fundraiser, consultant*

New Providence
Wilderotter, Peter Thomas *non-profit executive*

New Vernon
Dugan, John Leslie, Jr., *foundation executive*

Newark
Morris-Yamba, Trish *educational and social service association director*

Pennington
Calvo, Roque John *professional society administrator*
Mitchell, Janet Aldrich *fund raising executive, reference materials publisher*

Plainsboro
McGeady, Kathleen Birmingham *grant administrator*

Princeton
De Lung, Jane Solberger *independent sector executive*
Freeman, Bruce George *fundraising consultant*
Kassof, Allen H. *foundation administrator*
Kenyon, Regan Clair *educational research executive*
Orrill, Robert Thomas *foundation executive, former history educator*
Plaks, Livia Basch *foundation executive*
†Silverman, Jane Aresty *not-for-profit organizational consultant*
Some, Steven Edward *lobbyist, public affairs consultant*
Stern, Gail Frieda *historical association director*

Ridgefield
†Halvorson, Milton Hunter *association administrator, retired*

Ridgewood
Kahlenberg, Jeannette Dawson *retired civic organization executive*

Rumson
Brenner, Theodore Engelbert *retired trade association executive*

Scotch Plains
McCleary, Paul Frederick *voluntary agency executive*
Ungar, Manya Shayon *volunteer, education consultant*

Shiloh
Garrison, John Raymond *organization executive*

Short Hills
Friedman, Frances Wolf *political fund raiser*

Somerset
Lawrence, Barbara *not-for-profit development consultant*

South Orange
†Friedman, Susan R. *foundation administrator, consultant*
Stringile, Marie Elizabeth *educational administrator*
Terry, Myra *administration administrator*

Upper Montclair
Blooston, Roselee *cultural organization administrator, writer*

West Caldwell
Giblin, Thomas Patrick *labor union administrator, political organization administrator*

West Orange
Rinsky, Judith Sue Lynn *foundation administrator, educator consultant*

Whippany
†Price, Deborah Kantor *educational association administrator*

NEW MEXICO

Albuquerque
Dendahl, John *political organization administrator*
Foster, Margaret Anne *volunteer worker*
Koch, Jamie *political party official*
Roberts, Dennis William *association executive*

Nogal
Hume, Patsy Diseker *politician*

Roswell
Anderson, Sally Midgette *social services administrator, linguist*

Santa Fe
Charles, Cheryl *non-profit and business executive*
Lukac, George Joseph *not-for-profit fundraiser*

NEW YORK

Albany
Bellizzi, John J. *law enforcement association administrator, educator, pharmacist*
Hobart, Thomas Yale, Jr., *union president*
Rogers, James Thomas *trade association executive*

Amagansett
Frankl, Jeanne Silver *association executive, lawyer*

Amherst
Clark, Donald Malin *professional association executive*

Arkville
Downing, Darlene L. *non-for-profit organization executive*

Bayside
Madden, Joseph Daniel *trade association executive*

Bedford Hills
Waller, Wilhelmine Kirby (Mrs. Thomas Mercer Waller) *civic worker, organization official*

Bellport
Straus, Oscar S., II, *foundation executive*

Breesport
Peckham, Joyce Weitz *foundation administrator, former secondary education educator*

Bronx
Kheel, Ann Sunstein *civic worker*
Stevenson, Gelvin Lee *not-for-profit developer*
†Vassel, Lee Hylton *urbanist, social services administrator, writer*

Brooklyn
Crawford, Patricia Alexis Ann *social justice advocate, writer*
Frank, Marjorie Slavick *educational curriculum specialist, composer*
Herman, Allen Ian *foundation administrator*
†Lovett, Edward Richardson *not-for-profit developer, writer*
†Maslow, Jeffrey R. *not-for-profit fundraiser*
Morgan, Mary Louise Fitzsimmons *fund raising executive, lobbyist*

Buffalo
Clarkson, Elisabeth Ann Hudnut *volunteer*
Spengler, Paul Albert *grants and foundation administrator*

Centereach
Chassman, Karen Moss *educational administrator*

Central Islip
Wiggins, Gloria *nonprofit organization administrator, television producer*

Chappaqua
de Janosi, Peter Engel *research manager*

Clinton
Couper, Richard Watrous *foundation executive, educator*

Commack
†Price, Amelia Ruth *not-for-profit foundation president, artist, small business owner*

Congers
Commanday, Peter Martin *educator*

Corning
Cicerchi, Eleanor Ann Tomb *fundraising executive*

Cross River
†Lang, Robert Mays, Jr., *foundation administrator, controller*

Croton On Hudson
Katzowitz Shenfield, Lauren *philanthropic consultant, foundation executive*

Dobbs Ferry
Miss, Robert Edward *fundraiser*

East Hampton
Hope, Judith H. *former political organization administrator*

East Quogue
Weiss, Elaine Landsberg *community development management official*

Elmhurst
Matsa, Loula Zacharoula *social services administrator, educator*

Endicott
Englehart, Joan Anne *consultant*

Flushing
Fichtel, Rudolph Robert *retired association executive*

Germantown
Callanan, Laura Patrice *foundation executive*

Great Neck
†Sterling, Lorraine *volunteer*

Hampton Bays
†Komoski, Paul Kenneth *community activist, educational research executive*

Harrison
Wadsworth, Frank Whittemore *foundation executive, literature educator*

Hauppauge
†Tublisky, Marcy *association administrator*

Hawthorne
†Cantor, Arnold *labor relations official*

Hudson
Hanvik, Jan Michael *arts promoter, writer*
Miner, Jacqueline *political consultant*

Ithaca
Grainger, Mary Maxon *civic volunteer*
Pinstrup-Andersen, Per *educational administrator*

Jamaica
Keys, Martha McDougle *educational administrator*

Jamestown
Thompson, Birgit Dolores *civic worker, writer*

Larchmont
Hinerfeld, Ruth G. *civic organization executive*

Locust Valley
Chapman, Judith Coste *charitable institution volunteer administrator*

Manhasset
Foerst, John George, Jr., *retired fundraising executive*

Montauk
Butler, Thomas William *retired health and social services administrator*

Mount Kisco
Keesee, Patricia Hartford *volunteer*

Mount Marion
Berg, Miriam Rosemary *association executive*

New Rochelle
Black, Page Morton *civic worker*
Sarro, Michael Thomas *not-for-profit fundraiser*

New York
Aborn, Richard Mark *organization executive, lawyer*
Allmendinger, Paul Florin *retired engineering association executive*
Amitin, Mark Hall *cultural organization administrator, educator, writer, actor, director*
Anderson, Richard Theodore *association executive, urban planner*
Annan, Kofi A. *international organization official*
Appel, Marsha Ceil *association executive*
Aronson, Esther Leah *retired foundation administrator, psychotherapist*
Baird, Zoë *foundation president, lawyer*
Baker, William W. *nonprofit company executive*
Beardsley, Theodore S(terling), Jr., *professional society administrator*
Belden, David Leigh *professional association executive, engineering educator*
Bellamy, Carol *international organization executive*
Bergman, Charles Cabe *foundation executive*
Bertini, Catherine Ann *international organization official*
Bird, Mary Lynne Miller *professional society administrator*
Bishop, Frances Blackburn *civic worker*
Booth, Barbara Ribman *civic worker*
Braverman, Robert Jay *international consultant, public policy educator*
Brindle, Lewis Carver *administrator, fundraiser, consultant*
Bristol, Barbara Kammer *foundation administrator*
Brown, Mark Malloch *international organization official*
Brown, Terrence Charles *art association executive, researcher, lecturer*
Buckman, Thomas Richard *foundation executive, educator*
Calhoun, Craig Jackson *social scientist, educator*
†Carlson, Donna *art association administrator, director*
Carroll, David Paul *social welfare administrator*
Cassella, William Nathan, Jr., *retired organization executive*
Catley-Carlson, Margaret *not-for-profit developer*
Cavanagh, Carroll John *business advisor, lawyer, art services consultant*
Chapin, Schuyler Garrison *cultural affairs executive, university dean*
Chatfield-Taylor, Adele *historic preservationist*
Christensen, Kathleen Elizabeth *foundation administrator*
†Coffin, Anne Gagnebin *educational association editor, consultant*
†Collins, J. Robert *trade association administrator*
Coly, Lisette *foundation executive*
Conarroe, Joel Osborne *foundation administrator, educator, editor*
Cook, John Wesley *foundation administrator*
Cornell, Thomas Charles *peace activist, writer*
Dajani, Virginia *arts association administrator*
Dauer, Sheila A. *human rights program director*
Davis, Karen *fund executive*
Davis, Kathryn Wasserman *foundation executive, writer, lecturer*
Delaney, Pamela DeLeo *foundation administrator*
Dennis, Everette Eugene, Jr., *foundation executive, educator, writer*
†Desai, Nitin Dayalji *international organization official*
Dewhurst, David Litchfield *university administrator*
Drake, Owen Burtch Winters *association administrator*
†Easum, Donald Boyd *consultant, educator, former institute executive, diplomat*
Eisenberg, Alan *professional society administrator*
Elliott, Eleanor Thomas *foundation executive, civic leader*
Engelhardt, Sara Lawrence *organization executive*
Erdman, Sol *non-profit organization administrator*
Fay, Joseph Bartlett *not-for-profit marketing executive*
Ferry, Martha Morton *nonprofit executive*
Feuerstein, Paul Bruck *social services agency executive*
Finberg, Barbara Denning *not-for-profit developer*
†Flicker, John *foundation executive*
†Fowler, Dona Sylvia B. *trade union executive*

Fox, Daniel Michael *foundation executive, author*
Foxman, Abraham Henry *advocacy organization administrator*
Franklin, Phyllis *professional association administrator*
Goldberg, Beverly *foundation administrator, consultant*
†Goldman, Fatima *social services administrator*
Grabois, Neil Robert *foundation administrator, former college president*
Greene, Frank Edward Wade *writer, philanthropy adviser*
Greenwood, Ted Ronald Ivan *foundation administrator*
Gregorian, Vartan *foundation administrator*
Grimaldi, Nicholas Lawrence *fundraising executive*
Guenther, Paul Bernard *volunteer*
Hanley, William Herbert *association executive*
Harris, David Alan *not-for-profit organization executive*
Hart, Kitty Carlisle *arts administrator*
Hatter, Richard Wayne *foundation administrator, artist*
Helton, Arthur Cleveland *advocate, lawyer, scholar, writer*
Henderson, Maxine Olive Book (Mrs. William Henderson III) *foundation executive*
Hesselbein, Frances Richards *foundation executive, consultant, editor*
Hester, James McNaughton *foundation administrator, artist*
†Heyzer, Noeleen *international organization official*
Hochbaum, Martin *trade association administrator*
Hoffman, Linda R. *social services administrator*
Holman, Margaret Mezoff *fundraising consultant*
Horowitz, Sara *labor organizer*
Ilchman, Alice Stone *foundation administrator, former college president, former government official*
Innis, Roy Emile Alfredo *organization executive*
Iselin, John Jay *foundation president*
Jacobsen, Theodore H. (Ted H. Jacobsen) *labor union administrator, secondary school educator*
Josephson, Diana Hayward *not-for-profit company executive*
Kaggen, Lois Sheila *non-profit organization executive*
Kahan, Marlene *professional association executive*
Kahn, Alfred Joseph *social worker and policy scholar, educator*
Kaskell, Peter Howard *association executive, lawyer*
Kramberg, Ross *arts administrator*
Kuyper, Joan Carolyn *foundation administrator*
Labunski, Stephen Bronislaw *professional society administrator*
†Lamberg, Carol *housing fund executive*
Landy, Joanne Veit *foreign policy and health policy reform analyst*
Lawson-Johnston, Peter Orman *foundation executive*
Lee, Clement William Khan *trade association administrator*
†Lee, David Hee-Don *trade association administrator, educator*
Levy, Gerald Dun *nonprofit organization administrator*
Lewis, Richard A. *educational association administrator, writer*
Linder, Bertram Norman *foundation administrator, horse-breeder, actor*
Long, Donna Elaine *fundraising executive*
Luce, Henry, III, *foundation administrator*
Luckman, Sharon Gersten *arts administrator*
Luers, Wendy Wilson Woods *non-profit foundation executive*
Luers, William Henry *foundation administrator, former art museum administrator*
Luks, Allan Barry *executive director*
Mahoney, Margaret Ellerbe *foundation executive*
Mangan, Mona *association executive, lawyer*
Manuell, Lynn Marie *booking agent, singer, actress*
Marchi, Lorraine June *social services administrator*
†Matsui, Connie L. *youth organization executive*
Maynard, Virginia Madden *charitable organization executive*
McCrary, Eugenia Lester (Mrs. Dennis Daughtry McCrary) *civic worker, writer*
McNamara, Mary E. *nonprofit executive, asset manager, minister*
†McPherson, Mary Patterson *charitable foundation executive*
Milbank, Jeremiah *foundation executive*
Miller, Harvey S. Shipley *foundation trustee, private investor*
Millett, Kate (Katherine Murray Millett) *political activist, sculptor, artist, writer*
Moran, Martin Joseph *fundraising company executive*
Morehouse, Ward *human rights organization executive, publisher*
†Obaid, Thoraya Ahmed *international organization official*
Odenweller, Robert Paul *philatelist, association executive, retired airline pilot*
O'Neil Bidwell, Katharine Thomas *fine arts association executive, performing arts executive*
Osborn, Frederick Henry, III, *foundation executive*
Ovadiah, Janice *cultural institute executive*
Park, Leslie Desmond *health organization executive*
†Parrott, James Alfred *city economist*
Paul, James Albert *public policy organization executive, author*
Phillips, Russell Alexander, Jr., *retired foundation executive*
Polin, Jane L. *foundation official*
Qiang, Xiao *advocate*
†Rabin, Elliott Ira *educational administrator*
Redd, J. Diane *professional fundraiser and grants management executive*
Rich, Donna Bonem *fundraising consultant*
Robertson, William, IV, *foundation administrator*
Robinson, Nan Senior *not-for-profit organization consultant*
Rockefeller, Laurance S. *philanthropist*
Rose, Joanna Semel *cultural activist*
†Rosenthal, Jacob (Jack Rosenthal) *foundation executive*
†Rosenthal, Joel Howard *think-tank executive*
Roth, Kenneth *human rights advocate*
Rowe, Elizabeth Webb *community volunteer*
Sard, Susannah Ellen *non-profit executive*
Sasman, Irene Deak Handberg *educational publishing executive*
Shelp, Ronald Kent *non-profit, business and trade association executive, author, lecturer, consultant*
†Short, Thomas C. *theatre union executive*
Sidamon-Eristoff, Anne Phipps *community trust executive*
Sitruk-Ware, Régine *research organization executive, educator*
Slutsky, Lorie A.(Ann) *foundation executive*
Smith, Barry Hamilton *foundation administrator, physician*
Snyder, Jack L. *international relations educator*
Solomon, Deborah Antoinnette *volunteer*
Spero, Joan Edelman *foundation president*
Spindler, James Andrew *not-for-profit executive*
Steedman, Doria Lynne Silberberg *organization executive*
†Stein, Marcia *not-for-profit executive*
Steuer, Gary Paul *art association administrator*
Strang, John *association executive*
Strauss, Carol Kahn *institute executive director, editor, consultant*
Sussman, Leonard Richard *foundation executive*
Sweeley, Michael Marlin *foundation executive, public relations executive*
†Symonette, Lys *foundation executive, musician, writer*
Szymkowiak, Mary L. *non-profit organization administrator*
Tapia, Mario Eduardo *cultural organization administrator*
†Tobin, Eugene Marc *foundation administrator, retired academic administrator*
Tudryn, Joyce Marie *professional society administrator*
Turnbaugh, Douglas Blair *arts administration executive, author*
†Van de Bovenkamp, Sue Erpf *charitable organization executive*
†Wade, Shawan Monique *cultural organization administrator*
Wadsworth, Deborah *foundation administrator*
†Wang, John *not-for-profit company executive*
Wanner, Eric *foundation executive*
Wattleton, Faye (Alyce Faye Wattleton) *educational association administrator*
Weisl, Edwin Louis, Jr., *foundation executive, lawyer*
Weissman, Susan *social services professional*
†Wheatley, Steven Charles *educational association administrator*
Whiteside, Duncan *disability and child welfare foundation executive*
Wiener, Malcolm Hewitt *foundation executive*
†Wilson, Marie C. *foundation administrator*
†Zelin, Madeleine *think-tank executive*

Oakland Gardens
†Freeley, James *labor union administrator*

Oyster Bay
Russell, Mary Wendell Vander Poel *non-profit organization executive*

Potsdam
Stevens, Sheila Maureen *teachers union administrator*

Poughkeepsie
Wygan, Dorothy Camilla *foundation administrator*

Red Hook
†Cranna, Christina M. *social services specialist*

Rochester
Fleischmann, Ruth H. *foundation executive*
Lebman, Robert Richard *social services administrator*
Pacala, Leon *retired association executive*
Robbins, Nancy Slinker *volunteer*

Roslyn Hts.
†Malekoff, Andrew *social services administrator, writer*

Saranac
Smith, J. Kellum, Jr., *foundation executive, lawyer*

Saratoga Springs
Carey, Margot Beckmann *fundraiser*

Scarborough
Taylor, Nell Cochrane *non-profit association executive*

Scarsdale
Bruck Lieb Port, Lilly *retired consumer advisor, broadcaster, columnist*
Johnson, Katharyn Price (Mrs. Edward F. Johnson) *civic worker*
Stamas, Stephen *not-for-profit administrator*

Spring Valley
†Cacciola, Patrick Barry *art association administrator*

Staten Island
Behnke, Henryk Jorg *marketing and fundraising executive*
Lutkenhouse, Anne *non-profit executive*
Vinet, George Ellsworth, Jr., *foundation administrator*

Stony Brook
Brandwein, Ruth Ann *social welfare educator, administrator, author*

Syracuse
Furze, Edward William *fundraising consultant*

Tarrytown
Bergson, Henry Paul *professional association administrator*

Tonawanda
Glickman, Marlene *non-profit organization administrator*

Troy
Carovano, John Martin *not-for-profit administrator, conservationist*

Upton
Melucci, Richard Charles *research institute administrator*

Valley Stream
Haies, Evelyn S(olomon) *fundraiser, educator, writer*

White Plains
Altman, S. Morton *community center executive*
David, Miles *association and marketing executive*
Heimerdinger, John Frederick *association executive*
†Howse, Jennifer Louise *foundation administrator*
Stalerman, Ruth *civic volunteer, poet*

Yonkers
†Karpatkin, Rhoda Hendrick *consumer information organization executive, lawyer*
Neal, Leora Louise Haskett *social services administrator*

NORTH CAROLINA

Asheville
Brooker, Lena Epps *human relations diversity management consultant*
Fobes, John Edwin *international organization official*
Jones-Rafferty, Brenda Anne *personal growth and development company executive*

Bethel
Speir, Betty Smith *consultant, retired foundation administrator*

Black Mountain
Hibbard, Carl Roger *social services administrator*

Butner
†Crowell, Rosemary Elaine *criminal justice professional*

Cary
Martin, William Royall, Jr., *retired association executive*

Chapel Hill
Ferris, William Reynolds *humanities organization administrator, folklore educator*
Grayson, Mark *organization executive*
Krasno, Richard Michael *foundation executive, educator*
Wicker, Marie Peachee *civic worker*

Charlotte
Locke, Elizabeth Hughes *foundation executive*
McClure, Howard Jean, Jr., *advocate*
McIntyre, Jane London *association administrator*
Pyle, Gerald Fredric *medical geographer, educator*

Clinton
Griffin, Betty Lou *not-for-profit developer, educator*

Durham
Bevan, William *retired foundation executive*

Greensboro
Kornegay, Horace Robinson *trade association executive, former congressman, lawyer*

Hendersonville
Mankoff, Albert William *cultural organization administrator, consultant, writer*

Raleigh
Allen, Barbara Kirkman *politcal organization administrator*
Cobey, William Wilfred, Jr., *political organization administrator*
Daubert, Erik Joseph *organization administrator*
Graham, Kent Hill *philanthropist, museum guide*

Research Triangle Park
Miller, Robert Reese *trade association executive*

Waynesville
†Cole, James Yeager *foundation administrator*

Wilmington
Dickman, Catherine Crowe *retired human services administrator*
Nubel, Marianne Kunz *cultural administrator, writer, composer*

Seapker, Janet Kay *museum and architectural history consultant*

Wingate
Dodd, John Robert *non-profit organization administrator*

Winston Salem
Carter, Henry Moore, Jr., *retired foundation executive*

Woodland
Wilson, Lloyd Lee *organization administrator*

NORTH DAKOTA

Bismarck
Thompson, Vern *political organization executive*

OHIO

Akron
Collier, Alice Elizabeth *retired community organization executive*
Donehey, Marilyn Moss *social services executive*
Frank, John V. *foundation executive*
Juriga, Rosemarie *social services administrator*

Athens
Rudy, Joel S. *retired fraternal organization administrator*

Canton
Lyon, James Hugh *education specialist, legislative consultant*

Chagrin Falls
Vail, Iris Jennings *civic worker*

Chardon
Reinhard, Sister Mary Marthe *educational organization administrator*

Cincinnati
Adlard, Carole Rechtsteiner *health education agency executive*
Aft, Richard Nathaniel *professional society admnistrator, consultant*
Church, Jane Evelyn *executive director, counselor*
Hoyt, Lupé Ann González *social services administrator*
Johnson, Ronda Janice *professional not-for-profit fundraiser*
Marx, Marjorie McCullough *service organization executive*
McAusland, Randolph M. N. *arts consultant*
†Parker, Linda Bates *professional development organization administrator*
Ruehlmann, Virginia Juergens *foundation creativity director, writer*
Sowder, Fred Allen *foundation administrator, alphabet specialist*
Tenbosch, Gerald John *fundraising executive*
†Wilson, Arthur Henry *charitable institution executive*

Cleveland
Begala, John Adelbert *human service administrator*
Bender, Peggy Wallace *charitable gift planning consultant*
Buescher, Thomas Paul *labor market analyst*
Calabrese, Leonard M. *social services administrator, director*
Calkins, Hugh *foundation executive*
Carter, John Dale *organizational development coordinator*
Distelhorst, Garis Fred *trade association executive*
Faller, Dorothy Anderson *international agency administrator*
Garrison, William Lloyd *cemetery executive*
Hartley, Duncan *fundraising executive*
Jenson, Jon Eberdt *association executive*
Lord, James Gregory *organizational and philanthropic counsel to consultants*
Pike, Kermit Jerome *cultural organization administrator*
Smythe Zajc, M. Catherine *not-for-profit developer, consultant*

Columbus
Akers, Saundra Ruth *disability rights advocate*
Arnold, Dale Robert *farm bureau association executive*
Brandes, Marciana Watson *civic worker*
Newman, Diana S. *development consultant*
Patrick, Jane Austin *association executive*
Selby, Diane Ray Miller *fraternal organization administrator*
Sharp, Paul David *institute administrator*
Staten, Beverly Janet *political action administrator*
†Thompson, Linda Lezius *foundation administrator, consultant*
†White, Dennis L. *political organization administrator*

Cuyahoga Falls
Smith, Margaret A. (Maggie Carroll Smith) *community volunteer*

Dayton
Daley, Robert Emmett *retired foundation executive*
Mathews, David *foundation executive*
McDonald, Bronce William *community activist, advocate*
Ponitz, Doris Humes *volunteer*
Thomas, Marianna *volunteer community activist, writer, speaker*
Williams, Walker Richard, Jr., *social services administrator*

Dublin
Needham, George Michael *association executive*

Fairfield
Gruenwald, James Howard *association executive, consultant*

Hillsboro
Carson, Jean Hopkins Kessel *civic worker*

Lakewood
†Olson, Carol Joan *foundation administrator, consultant*

Marietta
†Bicoy, Bret Nalani *think-tank executive*

Oberlin
Cartier, Brian Evans *association executive*
Shaeffer, Ruth Gilbert *retired nonprofit corporation executive*

Oxford
Becker, Stephen Bradbury *fraternal organization administrator*
Miller, Robert James *educational association administrator*

Richfield
Lewis, Sylvia Davidson *foundation executive*

Shaker Heights
Brucken, Lois Gilbert *volunteer*

Westerville
Newkirk, Peggy Rose Wills *civic volunteer*

Westfield Center
Edington, Patricia Ann *social services administrator*

Yellow Springs
Graham, Jewel Freeman *social worker, lawyer, educator*

Zoar
Fernandez, Kathleen M. *cultural organization administrator*

OKLAHOMA

Enid
McCobb, Allan Paul *not-for-profit organization executive*

Oklahoma City
†Blochowiak, Mary Ann *cultural organization administrator, writer*
Brooks, Gene (Leslie Gene Brooks) *cultural association administrator*
Coates, Eleanor Smith *civic worker*
Dutcher, Brandon Tyler *think tank research director, columnist*
Kerr, Lou C. *foundation administrator*
McLaughlin, Lisa Marie *educational administrator*
Parmley, Jay *political organization administrator*

Sallisaw
Crowson, Watie Dee *foundation administrator*

Tulsa
Wagner, Clarence H., Jr., *charitable organization administrator*

OREGON

Bandon
Millard, Esther Lound *foundation administrator, educator*

Bend
Evers-Williams, Myrlie *cultural organization administrator*

Corvallis
Wilkins, Caroline Hanke *consumer agency administrator, political worker*

Eugene
Cone, June Elizabeth *civic worker*
Hale, Dean Edward *social services administrator*

Grants Pass
Boling, Judy Atwood *civic worker*

Junction City
Humphry, Derek *association executive, writer, speaker*

Lake Oswego
Miller, Barbara Stallcup *development consultant*

Lincoln City
Decker, Mary Duryea *retired educator, community volunteer*

Medford
†Boldt, Susan Luques *not-for-profit developer*
Sours, James Kingsley *association executive, former college president*

Portland
Collins, Maribeth Wilson *foundation president*
Edmunson, James L. *political organization administrator*
Henderson, George Miller *foundation executive, former banker*
Holt, Mavis Murial *parents group executive*
Krenk, Christopher Joseph *human services professional*
Milton, Catherine Higgs *social service entrepreneur*

Patterson, Beverly Ann Gross *fund raising consultant, grant writer, federal grants administrator, social services administrator, poet*
Pine, William Charles *foundation executive*
Rooks, Charles S. *foundation administrator*

Salem
Atkinson, Perry *political organization administrator*
Frank, Gerald Wendel *civic leader, journalist*

Summerville
Hopkins, Gerald Frank *trade association administrator*

Tualatin
Bruce, John Allen *foundation executive, educator*

PENNSYLVANIA

Allison Park
Wood, Edward Manning *fund raising counsel*

Ambler
Curry, Susan Margaret *not-for-profit administrator, writer*

Ardmore
Ginsburgh, Brook *association executive*

Ben Avon
Gibson, Samuel Norris *educational organization executive, retired clergy*

Berwyn
Reed, Clarence Raymond *retired association executive*

Bethlehem
Orr, Sandra Jane *civic worker, pharmacist*

Blue Bell
Root, Joan Schimpf *civic worker, museum trustee*

Bryn Mawr
Carroll, Mary Colvert *corporate executive*
Cooney, Patricia Ruth *civic worker*

Carlisle
Anderson, Howard Wayne, Jr., *training company executive*
Renaud, Robert (Edwin Renaud) *college administrator*

Chadds Ford
King, M. Jean *association executive*

Chambersburg
†Lesher, Richard Lee *association executive, retired*

Chester
Ciociola, Cecilia Mary *development specialist*

Darby
Wardell, Lindy Constance *nonprofit organization administrator*

Dillsburg
Bowers, Glenn Lee *retired professional society administrator*

Drexel Hill
Schiazza, Guido Domenic (Guy Schiazza) *educational association administrator*

Easton
Danjczek, Michael Harvey *social service administrator*

Elizabethtown
Madeira, Robert Lehman *professional society administrator*

Elkins Park
Pak, Hyung Woong *community advocate*

Erie
Hauck, Barbara Jean *fund raising executive, writer, artist*

Gettysburg
Nelson-Small, Kathy Ann *foundation administrator*

Gibsonia
Haas, Eileen Marie *homecare advocate*

Glenside
Block, Isaac Edward *professional society administrator*

Greensburg
Hager, Edward Paul *development executive*

Harleysville
Bell, Michael G. *trade association administrator*

Harrisburg
Breslin, Michael Joseph, III, *social services administrator, educator*
Novak, Alan P. *political organization administrator*
†Rooney, Terence Joseph (T.J.) *political organization worker, state legislator*
Ross, Sheila Moore *philanthropic executive*
Staub, Shalom David *cultural organization administrator*
Wissler-Thomas, Carrie *professional society administrator, artist*

Hershey
Pincock, Garry LaMar *association administrator*

Hollidaysburg
Savage, Patricia Werner *nonprofit health and human service agency executive*

Huntingdon
†Tuten, James H. *educational association administrator, educator*

Indiana
Steelman, Sara Gerling *art association administrator*

Kingston
Benovitz, Madge Klein *civic volunteer*
Friedman, Pauline Poplin *civic worker, consultant*
Van Scoy, Gary *social services administrator*

Lancaster
Jordan, Lois Wenger *foundation official*

Lewisburg
Neuman, Nancy Adams Mosshammer *civic leader*
†Schlegel, Richard LaMar *advocate, writer*

Macungie
Farr, Lona Mae *non-profit executive, business owner*

Mechanicsburg
Gibbons, Miles Joseph, Jr., *foundation administrator*
McBeth, David Paul *fundraising consultant*

Media
†Derby, Steven R. *foundation administrator*

Merion Station
Freeze, James Donald *administrator, clergyman*

Monroeville
Skolnick, Marilyn *civic worker*

New Cumberland
†Wilson, Wanda Mae French *animal association administrator*

New Oxford
Arnold, Ellen Holt *continuing care retirement community administrator*

Newtown
Keenan, Terrance *foundation executive*

Penn Valley
Newhall, John Harrison *retired non profit company executive*

Philadelphia
Bodine, James Forney *retired civic leader*
†Chung, Jennifer M. *not-for-profit executive*
Connor, Nancy L. *foundation executive*
Foti, Margaret *association executive, publisher, editor, lecturer*
Friedman, Murray *civil rights official, historian*
Gambescia, Stephen Francis *higher education administrator*
Hamilton, Antonia Wallace *foundation administrator*
†Henderson, L(eona) Harriette *retired social work administrator, consultant*
Hochberg, Mark Stefan *professional society administrator, cardiac surgeon*
Holst, Arthur Matthew *government affairs executive*
Horwitz, Joy A. *foundation administrator*
Klein, Arthur *foundation executive*
Makous, Bruce B. *fundraiser*
Mallery, David *education association executive, consultant*
Meyerson, Margy Ellin *urbanist, civic volunteer*
Ray, Evelyn Lucille *arts facilitator, small meetings planner*
Reed, Sally Gardner *cultural organization administrator*
Stevenson, Josiah, IV, *cultural arts administrator*
Tucker, Cynthia Delores Nottage (Mrs. William M. Tucker) *political party official, former state official*
†Vredenburgh, Judy *youth organization executive*
Watson, Bernard Charles *educator, foundation administrator*
Wing, Kennard Thompson *educational organization official*

Pittsburgh
Aronson, Mark Berne *retired attorney, consumer advocate*
Becker, George *labor union administrator*
Cheever, Meg *non-profit organization administrator*
Dybeck, Alfred Charles *labor arbitrator*
†Gerard, Leo W. *trade association administrator*
Ketchum, David Storey *retired fundraising executive*
Lloyd, Robert Albert *retired foundation administrator*
Petersen, Jean Snyder *association executive*
Ziegler, Arthur P., Jr., *foundation executive*

Reading
Bennett, Richard Clark *fundraising consultant*
Dietrich, Renée Long *fund raising executive*
Mattern, Donald Eugene *retired association executive*
Murphy, Kevin Keith *foundation executive*

Red Lion
Hartman, Charles Henry *not-for-profit developer, education educator, consultant*

Saint Marys
Quirk, Gail Elizabeth Manz *community services administrator*

Spring Grove
†Sterner, Deborah Kay *volunteer*

State College
Book, Edward R. *consultant, retired association executive*
Phillips, Janet Colleen *retired educational association executive, editor*

Uniontown
†Eberly, Robert Edward *foundation administrator*

Upper Saint Clair
Van Dusen, Margaret Davis *community volunteer, consultant*

Villanova
Friend, Theodore Wood, III, *foundation executive, historian, writer*
Smith, Standish Harshaw *non-profit company executive*

Warren
†Johnson, Newkirk Lynn *not-for-profit developer*

Warrendale
Rumbaugh, Max Elden, Jr., *professional society administrator*
Scott, Alexander Robinson *engineering association executive*

Wayne
Etris, Samuel Franklin *trade association research consultant*

West Grove
†Cornell, Suzanne *youth services executive*

Williamsport
Schultz, Carole Lamb *community volunteer*

York
Binder, Mildred Katherine *retired public welfare agency executive*
Russell, Stephen Speh *lawyer*

RHODE ISLAND

Kingston
Taylor, Suzanne S. *educational association administrator, educator*

North Providence
Maciel, Patricia Ann *development professional*

Providence
Klyberg, Albert Thomas *historical society administrator*

Warwick
Jennings, Julianne *cultural organization administrator*
Worthington, Samuel Andrew *social welfare administrator*

West Warwick
Lancellotta, John Jerry-Louis *foundation administrator*

SOUTH CAROLINA

Aiken
Ely, Duncan Cairnes *non profit/human services executive, civic leader*

Anderson
Bailey, Jake Schultz *volunteer, retired electrical engineer*

Charleston
Bailey, Dawn Marie *fund raising systems consultant*
Crossley, Gary Exley *organization executive*
Ferguson, Esther B. *philanthropist*
Hughes, Blake *retired architectural institute administrator, publisher*

Columbia
†Dawson, Katon *political organization administrator*
†McGill, Jennifer Houser *non-profit association administrator*

Green Pond
Ittleson, H(enry) Anthony *foundation executive*

Greenville
Algary, Ruth Wilkins *community volunteer*
Hendrix, Susan Clelia Derrick *civic worker*

Lancaster
Bundy, Charles Alan *foundation executive*

Spartanburg
Glassick, Charles Etzweiler *academic foundation administrator*
Richards, Marty Grover *university foundation director*

Surfside Beach
Turner, Gloria Townsend Burke *social services association executive*

Taylors
†Erwin, Joseph Arnold *political organization worker, advertising executive, creative director*

West Columbia
Moxon, Barbara Wischan *volunteer*

Winnsboro
McMaster, Mary Rice *civic worker*

Woodruff
Childers, Bob Eugene *educational association executive*

SOUTH DAKOTA

Aberdeen
Eldredge, Robert John *social services administrator, psychologist*

Crazy Horse
Ziolkowski, Ruth *foundation administrator, postmistress*

Pierre
Collins-Adler, Catherine Kay *social services professional*
†Frederick, Randall Davis *political organization administrator, state legislator*

Sioux Falls
Wegner, Mary Josephine *civic volunteer, farmer*

TENNESSEE

Athens
Brown, Sandra Lee *art association administrator, watercolorist*

Brentwood
Lodowski, Charles Alan *business association executive*

Chattanooga
McNeill-Murray, Joan Reagin *volunteer consultant*
Piatt, Albert Earl *educator, researcher, consultant*
Tracy, Carol Cousins *association executive, former educator*

Cleveland
Lockhart, Madge Clements *educational organization executive*

Columbia
Tamberrino, Frank Michael *professional association executive*

Franklin
Jowdy, Jeffrey William *development executive*

Jackson
Tolley, Jim *not-for-profit administrator*

Knoxville
†Adaku, Chioma *non-profit organization administrator*
Barger, Don P. *conservation association administrator*
Froula, James DeWayne *national honor society executive, engineer*

Lafayette
Carter, Anna Dean *volunteer*

Lebanon
Howard, Lounita Cook *nonprofit executive director*

Memphis
†Jalenak, Peggy Eichenbaum *volunteer*
McConnico, Nancy Mann *civic worker*
Sanford, Susan Haspel *not-for-profit executive*
Whitesell, Dale Edward *retired association executive, natural resources consultant*

Nashville
Beaty, Sandy *lobbyist, lawyer*
Farmer, William H. *political organization worker, lawyer*
Harwell, Beth H. *political organization worker*
Henderson, Milton Arnold *professional society administrator*
†Hoffman, Cheri *social services administrator*
Johnson, Hollis Eugene, III, *foundation executive*
Saltsman, John B. *former political party executive, commissioner*
Siegfried, John *association officer*
Turk, Thomas Liebig *arts consultant*

Sparta
Mitchell, Annie-Martin *volunteer civic worker*

TEXAS

Amarillo
Berry, Jacob Obadiah *not-for-profit developer, rancher*
Crain, Mary Tom *volunteer*
Utterback, Will Hay, Jr., *retired labor union administrator, genealogist*

Austin
Banks, Virginia Anne (Ginger Banks) *association administrator*
Bonjean, Charles Michael *foundation executive, sociologist, educator*
Bright, Garry Michael *executive*
Cleaves, Peter Shurtleff *foundation official*
Dougherty, Molly Ireland *organization executive*
Fisk, Doris Rosalie Scanlan *volunteer*
Green, Shirley Moore *retired public affairs and communications executive*
Malcolm, Molly Beth *political party official, counselor*
Mathias, Reuben Victor (Vic Mathias) *chamber of commerce executive, real estate investor*
Mc Kinney, Michael Whitney *trade association executive*
Middleton, Harry Joseph *foundation administrator*
Weddington, Susan *political party official*

White, Alice Virginia *college campaign program administrator*

Breckenridge
Jones, Karen Annette *civic volunteer*

Carrollton
Hart, Elizabeth Ann *foundation administrator*

Colleyville
Love, Ben Howard *retired organization executive*
Tigue, Virginia Beth (Ginny Tigue) *volunteer*

Corpus Christi
French, Dorris Towers Bryan *volunteer*

Dallas
†Braun, Susan *foundation administrator*
†Clary, Rebecca Kristen *social services administrator*
Cockerham, Sidney Joe *professional society administrator*
Evans, Dvorah A. *organization executive, professional organizer*
†Falk, James Nathan *not-for-profit organization administrator, consultant*
†Hamilton, Wendy *foundation administrator*
Hay, Betty Jo *civic worker*
Juergens, Bonnie Kay *not-for-profit company executive*
Wassenich, Linda Pilcher *retired health policy analyst, fund raiser*
Wilson, Jean Marie Haley *civic worker*

El Paso
Fox, Ronnie Ilaine *volunteer educator, densitometry technician*
Goodman, Gertrude Amelia *civic worker*

Fort Worth
Davis, Alan Tucker *foundation administrator, philanthropist, minister*
†Dilley, Carol *association administrator*
Prather, Robert Franklin *fund administrator*
†Saenz, Nancy Elizabeth King (Mrs. Michael Saenz) *civic worker*
Strasser, Jack C. *association professional*

Galveston
Baker, Robert Ernest, Jr., *retired foundation executive*

Georgetown
Busfield, Roger Melvil, Jr., *retired trade association executive, educator*

Houston
Anderson, Helen Sharp *civic worker*
Black, Marilyn Hammer *non-profit organization executive*
Grayson, Charles Jackson, Jr., *research association executive*
Heckler, Walter Tim *association executive*
†Henry, Louise L. *educational association administrator*
McCleary, Beryl Nowlin *civic worker, travel agency executive*
Meredith, John *non-profit executive*
Nelson, David Leon *foundation administrator, lawyer, accountant*
Tarlov, Alvin Richard *former philanthropic foundation administrator, physician, educator, researcher*
Wuenschel, Peter Cyril *educational association administrator, social worker*

Irving
Olson, Herbert Theodore *trade association executive*
Steele, C. William *scouting organization administrator*

Lubbock
Baiza, Mary Pesina *development management consultant*

Odessa
Boyd, Claude Collins *educational specialist, consultant*

Plano
Carver, Rita *fundraising consultant*

San Antonio
†Atherton, Flora Cameron *volunteer*
Jacobson, Helen Gugenheim (Mrs. David Jacobson) *civic worker*
†Krier, Joseph Roland *chamber of commerce executive, lawyer*
Moder, John Joseph *non-profit administrator*

Shallowater
Thompson, Carol Joyce Hinkley *philanthropy consultant, motivational speaker, writer*

Sugar Land
Hosley, Marguerite Cyril *civic worker*

Weatherford
Bergman, Anne Newberry *civic leader*

UTAH

Brigham City
Bishop, Robert *former political organization administrator, secondary school educator*

Ogden
Pappas, Leah Aglaia *civic worker, political consultant*

Orem
Hatch, Steven Graham *foundation administrator*

Provo
Jensen, Elouise Henrie *volunteer*

Salt Lake City
Clark, Deanna Dee *civic leader and volunteer*
Holbrook, Meghan Zanolli *fundraiser, public relations specialist, political organization chairman*
Landa, Esther Rosenblatt *retired volunteer*
Lee, Blaine Nelson *executive consultant, educator, author*

Woods Cross
Ingles, Joseph Legrand *social services administrator, political science educator*

VERMONT

Bennington
Perin, Donald Wise, Jr., *former association executive*

Bondville
Ambach, Gordon Mac Kay *educational association executive*

Brattleboro
Beal, Donna Lee *association executive*

Montpelier
Barbieri, Christopher George *professional society administrator*
Metcalf, Cindy W. *political organization administrator*

Peacham
Barnes, Harry G., Jr., *human rights activist, conflict resolution specialist, retired ambassador*

Shelburne
Ryerson, William Newton *non profit organization executive*

VIRGINIA

Abingdon
Jones, Mary Trent *endowment fund trustee*

Alexandria
Bachus, Walter Otis *retired army general, former association executive*
Baroody, Michael Elias *trade association executive*
Belmont, Barbara S. *association executive*
Bezold, Clement *think tank executive*
Bolger, Robert Joseph *retired trade association executive*
Carter, Gene Raymond *professional association executive*
Cline, Michael Patrick *association executive*
Cooper, David Earl Kaleoikaika *foundation executive*
Crane, Stephen Charles *professional society administrator*
Culkin, Charles Walker, Jr., *retired trade association administrator*
De Barbieri, Mary Ann *nonprofit management consultant*
Engler, Brian David *association executive*
Farrell, William Christopher *lobbyist*
Greenstein, Ruth Louise *research institute executive, lawyer*
Henton, Melissa Kaye *analyst*
†Jordan, Carole Jean *political organization administrator*
Kolar, Mary Jane *trade and professional association executive*
LeBlanc, James Leo *business executive, consultant*
†Lendsey, Jacquelyn L. *foundation administrator*
Lenz, Edward Arnold *trade association executive, lawyer*
Magazine, Alan Harrison *association executive, consultant*
McCulloch, William Leonard *trade association administrator*
†Murray, Robert John *think-tank executive*
Murtagh, William John *preservationist, educator*
Noland, Royce Paul *association executive, physical therapist*
Rabun, John Brewton, Jr., *criminal justice agency administrator*
Rector, John Michael *association executive, lawyer*
Reed, Leon Samuel *policy analyst, writer, photographer*
Richman, Arleen *professional society administrator*
Schubert, Richard Francis *consultant*
Turner, Mary Jane *educational administrator*

Annandale
Herbst, Robert LeRoy *organization executive*

Arlington
Anderson, Dean William *educational administrator*
Asbell, Fred Thomas *health industry association executive*
Becker, Fred Reinhardt, Jr., *association executive, lawyer, retired military officer*
Ericsson, Sally Claire *not-for-profit organization administrator*
Frame, Kathleen S. *non-profit education association administrator*
Fujito, Wayne Takeshi *international business company executive*
Gilmore, Marjorie Havens *civic worker, lawyer*
Goetze, Richard B., Jr., *association administrator*
Hendrickson, Daniel C. *association administrator*
Hickman, Elizabeth Podesta *retired counselor, educator*
Hunter, Jody Jean *association executive, naturalist*

Hunter, J(ohn) Robert *insurance consumer advocate*
Isaacson, Jeffrey Alan *think-tank executive, physicist*
Lampe, Margaret Sanger *community activist*
Langworthy, Everett Walter *association executive, natural gas exploration company executive*
McKee, Thomas J. *association administrator*
McKinnon, Russel Francis Daniel *professional society administrator*
O'Day, Paul Thomas *trade association executive*
Paynter, Harry Alvin *retired trade association executive*
Politi, John J. *association administrator*
Price, Jack C. *association administrator*
†Rubottom, George Milton *foundation administrator, chemist*
Shannon, Thomas Alfred *retired educational association administrator emeritus*
Stolgitis, William Charles *professional society executive*
Taylor, Robert William *professional society administrator*
†Tugwell, Franklin *think-tank executive*
Uncapher, Mark Elson *lawyer, trade association administrator*
Watson, Alexander Fletcher *organization executive, former ambassador*
Wilson, Minter Lowther, Jr., *retired officers association executive*

Basye
†Stanley, Robert Warren *association executive*

Boston
Fisher, John Morris *association official, business executive, educator*

Burke
Wood, C(harles) Norman *former association executive, military officer*
Woodruff, C(harles) Roy *consultant, retired professional association executive*

Chantilly
Sroka, John Walter *trade association executive*
Zirkle, William Vernon *philanthropist*

Charlottesville
Friedman, Susan Lynn Bell *economic development professional*
Hendrickson, Jerome Orland *trade association executive, lawyer*
Jordan, Daniel Porter, Jr., *foundation administrator, history educator*
Wilson, Mitchell B. *fraternal organization administrator*

Colonial Heights
Thomson, Gary R. *political organization administrator, accountant*

Fairfax
Cullison, Alexander C. (Doc Cullison) *mediator, arbitrator*
†Gray, William H., III, *association executive, former congressman*
Hollans, Irby Noah, Jr., *retired association executive*
Jones, George Fleming *international consultant*
Matthews, Stephen Philip *trade association administrator*
Roberts, Cecil Edward, Jr., *labor union administrator*
Robinson, Kayne B. *lobbyist, former political organization officer*

Fairfax Station
Graul, Faye Anne *lobbyist*

Falls Church
Jones, Linda R. Wolf *company executive*
Reilly, Patrick John *nonprofit executive*
Thomsen, Samuel Borron *non-profit executive, consultant*
Wali, Sima *foundation administrator*
Work, Jane Magruder *retired professional society administrator*

Flint Hill
Dietel, William Moore *former foundation executive*
Williamson, Richard Hall *association executive*

Franktown
Holcomb, Caramine Kellam *volunteer worker*

Garrisonville
Emely, Charles Harry *trade association executive, consultant*

Glen Allen
Spitzer, William John *healthcare social work administrator, educator*

Great Falls
DiBona, Charles Joseph *retired trade association executive*
Klimczuk, Stephen John *business executive, foundation director*

Harrisonburg
Helmuth, Les N. *fund raising executive, non-profit consultant*

Keswick
Nosanow, Barbara Shissler *art association administrator*

Lexington
Adams, James Lamont *educational foundation executive*

Louisa
Small, William Edwin, Jr., *association and recreation executive*

Lynchburg
Johnson, Robert Bruce *historic preservationist*

Manassas
Cypess, Raymond Harold *bioscience organization executive*

Mc Lean
Canes, Michael Edwin *research economist*
†Kargbo, Ranya *educational association administrator*
Lovaas, John L. *foreign aid executive, community activist*
McInerney, James Eugene, Jr., *trade association executive*
Stackpole, Kerry Clifford *association executive*
Trout, Margie Marie Mueller *civic worker*

Merrifield
Earley, Mark Lawrence *not-for-profit administrator, former state attorney general*

Middleburg
Sodolski, John *retired association administrator*

Newport News
Mazur, Rhoda Himmel *community volunteer*

Norfolk
Meslang, Susan Walker *educational administrator*

Oakton
Rees, Clifford Harcourt, Jr., (Ted Rees) *retired association executive, retired air force officer*

Reston
Brennan, Norma Jean *professional society publications director*
†Carroll, Terence Evan *professional society administrator*
Chattman, Raymond Christopher *foundation executive*
Gates, James David *retired association executive, consultant*
Hope, Samuel Howard *accreditation organization executive*
†Mahlmann, John James *music education association administrator*
Minton, Joseph Paul *retired safety organization executive*

Richmond
Brackenridge, N. Lynn *not-for-profit developer*
Bryan, Lisa Margaret Stevenson *volunteer*
DeWitt, Brydon Merrill *development consultant*
†Framme, Lawrence Henry, III, *political organization administrator, lawyer*
Rada, Heath Kenneth *social service organization executive*
Wood, Jeanne Clarke *charitable organization executive*

Roanoke
Schlegel, Beverly Faye *private club administrator*

Spotsylvania
Clower, William Dewey *retired trade association executive*
Hardy, Dorcas Ruth *business and government relations executive*

Springfield
Bartlow, Gene Steven *association executive, retired air force officer*
Kratovil, Jane Lindley *think tank associate, developer/fundraiser*
Larson, Reed Eugene *foundation administrator*
Nelson, Kimberly Susan *not-for-profit fundraiser*

Stafford
Sedlak, James William *organization administrator*

Sterling
Munger, Paul David *company executive, educational administrator*

Upperville
Smart, Edith Merrill *civic worker*

Vienna
Gerson, Elliot Francis *foundation administrator*
Marx, Gary Dean *international education consultant, association executive*
†Quarles, Orage, III, *professional society administrator*
Spiro, Robert Harry, Jr., *foundation and business executive, educator*
†Sturm, John F. *trade association administrator*
Thompson, Louis Milton, Jr., *association executive, horse breeder*

Virginia Beach
Reece-Porter, Sharon Ann *international human rights educator*

Warrenton
Fox, Raymond Graham *educational technologist*

Weems
Merrick, Roswell Davenport *educational association administrator*

Williamsburg
Campbell, Colin Goetze *foundation president*
Haufe, Bonnie Campbell *foundation affiliate*
Sass, Arthur Harold *educational executive*

Woodbridge
Garon, Richard Joseph, Jr., *political organization worker*

WASHINGTON

Bainbridge Island
Oechsli, Christopher George *foundation executive, business executive*
Rosner, Robert Allan *advocate*

Battle Ground
Fineran, Diana Lou *association administrator*

Bellevue
Arnold, Ronald Henri *nonprofit organization executive, consultant*
Kiest, Alan Scott *social services administrator*

Des Moines
Ray, Marianne Yurasko *social services administrator*

Edmonds
Monroe, James Walter *retired organization executive*

Everett
Sherwood, Sharon Dee *association executive*

Kenmore
Patten, Richard E. *not-for-profit developer, director*

Olympia
Olson, Steven Stanley *social service executive*
Stohl, Esther A. *senior citizen advocate*

Port Townsend
Woolf, William Blauvelt *retired association executive*

Puyallup
Muchmore, Don Moncrief *retired museum, foundation, educational, financial fund raising and public opinion consulting firm administrator, banker*

Redmond
De Blasi, Camille E. *advocate, counselor*

Seattle
Arthur, William Lynn *environmental/political program director*
Berendt, Paul *political organization worker*
Davidson, Robert William *not-for-profit executive*
Farrell, Anne Van Ness *foundation executive*
†Foster, Barry Alan *cultural organization researcher, educator*
Friedman-Barone, Ronnie Eva
Martínez, Yolanda R. *social services administrator*
†Vance, Christopher *political organization worker*

Spokane
Coker, Charlotte Noel *political activist*
Falkner, James George, Sr., *foundation executive*
†Herzer, Marian Day *not-for-profit developer, educator*

Tacoma
Graybill, David Wesley *chamber of commerce executive*
†Hinkley, Nancy Emily Engstrom *foundation administrator, educator*

Vancouver
†Erickson, Sally Alice *social welfare administrator*
Smith, Sam Corry *retired foundation executive, consultant*

WEST VIRGINIA

Bethany
†Dunbar, Jeffrey Bartlett *social services administrator*

Charleston
Chapman, John Andrew *retired chamber of commerce executive*
Maroney, Thomas P. *lawyer, political party executive*

Fairmont
Ford, Alma Regina *union official, educator*

Oak Hill
Janney, Sally Baggs *civic worker*

South Charleston
Warner, Kris *political organization administrator*

Webster Springs
†Moore, Alma Merle *association executive*

Wheeling
Hogan, Susan Cox *association executive*

WISCONSIN

Altoona
James, Henry Thomas *former foundation executive, educator*

Balsam Lake
Mattson, Carol Linnette *social services administrator*

Hales Corners
Wesener, Barbara A. *association executive*

Kenosha
Adler, Seymour Jack *social services administrator*

La Crosse
Schumacher, Philip Gerard *fundraising executive*

Madison
Heim, Marcy Lynn Schultz *foundation executive*
Higby, Gregory James *historical association administrator, historian*
Honold, Linda Kaye *political organization executive, human resources development executive*
Schmidt, Martha Bubeck *educator, counselor*

Manitowoc
Behnke, Elizabeth Doelker *community volunteer, retired nurse*

Milwaukee
Brever, Michael Stephen *non-profit executive director, alderman*
Frey, James Severin *educational association executive*
Ritz, Esther Leah *civic worker, volunteer, investor*
Schneider, Thomas Paul *non-profit agency administrator*
Zeidler, Frank P. *former association administrator, mayor, arbitrator, mediator, fact-finder*

Onalaska
Pertzsch, Evelyn Maria *civic worker*

Oshkosh
Khan, Zillur Rahman *foundation executive*

Pewaukee
†Carlson, Kathleen *not-for-profit fundraiser, writer, journalist*

Shawano
Lyon, Thomas L. *agricultural organization administrator*

Stevens Point
†Piotrowski, Cynthia Louise *not-for-profit developer*

Whitewater
Connor, James Richard *retired foundation administrator*
Kolda, Thomas Joseph *non-profit organization executive*

WYOMING

Casper
Constantino, Becky *political organization administrator*
Stoval, Linda *political party official*

Cheyenne
Noe, Guy *retired social services administrator*

Gillette
Jennings, Linda Sturgill *volunteer*

Laramie
Darnall, Roberta Morrow *association executive*
Hanson, Mary Louise *retired social services administrator*

Yellowstone National Park
Cole, Patricia Eisenbise *educational organzation executive*

TERRITORIES OF THE UNITED STATES

GUAM

Agana
†San Agustin, Joe Taitano *political organization worker*

PUERTO RICO

Hato Rey
†Ferre, Luis A. *political organization administrator*

CANADA

ALBERTA

Calgary
Roberts, John Peter Lee *cultural advisor, administrator, educator, writer*

NEW BRUNSWICK

Fredericton
Lewell, Peter A. *international technology executive, researcher*

Saint John
Mowatt, E. Ann *women's voluntary leader, lawyer*

NOVA SCOTIA

Wolfville
Elliott, Robbins Leonard *consultant*

ONTARIO

Ottawa
Ecroyd, Lawrence Gerald *trade association administrator*
†Rodger, Ginette *professional association executive, nurse*
Wilson, Ian Edwin *cultural organization administrator, archivist*

Toronto
†Goodenow, Robert W. *labor union administrator*
†Stymiest, Barbara *trade association administrator*

QUEBEC

Outremont
Letourneau, Jean-Paul *business association executive and consultant*

Rosemere
Hopper, Carol *meeting and incentive trip administrator*

MEXICO

Mexico City
Bruton, John Macaulay *trade association executive, consultant*

ARGENTINA

Buenos Aires
Levy, Joseph Bruno *foundation administrator, educator*

AUSTRALIA

Altona
Daniel-Dreyfus, Susan B. Russe *civic worker*

AUSTRIA

Salzburg
Angermüller, Rudolph *music foundation executive*

Vienna
al-Omair, Saleh *trade association administrator*

BELGIUM

Brussels
Berna, Marie-Rose *international organization executive*
Maroy, Michel *European affairs consultant*

BERMUDA

Saint George
Saadian, Javid *cultural organization administrator, consultant*

CZECH REPUBLIC

Prague
†Gubta, Indrajit *trade association administrator*
†Tu, Nguyen Van *former trade association administrator*
Zharikov, Alexander Nikolaevich *trade union federation executive*

DENMARK

Copenhagen
Holm, Erik *foundation director, political scientist, economist*

ENGLAND

Henley-on-Thames
Ashbrook, Kate Jessie *charitable organization director*

London
Brierley, Peter William *charitable foundation administrator*
Chadwick, Derek James *foundation administrator*
Funnell, Christina Mary *non-profit consultant*
Hazell, Robert John Davidge *policy institute director, government educator*
Nelson, Elizabeth Hawkins *public association administrator*
Sharif, Khalid *educational association administrator*

Petts Wood
Bompas, Donald George *charitable organization executive, consultant*

FRANCE

Paris
Janicot, Daniel Claude Emmanuel *foundation administrator*

Mestrallet, Gérard *professional society administrator*

GERMANY

Hamburg
Lüst, Reimar *foundation president*

Mayen
Gartz, Rolf Fritz *foundation administrator*

Munich
Magill, Samuel Wallace *international relations specialist*

HUNGARY

Budapest
Rózsa, György *academy library foundation president*

ISRAEL

Herzlia
Gruder, Yaron E. *foundation administrator*

ITALY

Rome
Wilson, George Peter *international organization executive*

JAMAICA

Nassau
†Denison, Barry Reed *human rights association executive*

JAPAN

Minato-ku Tokyo
Scullion, Tsugiko Yamagami *non-profit organization executive*

NORTHERN IRELAND

Belfast
†Corrigan-Maguire, Mairead *peace worker*

NORWAY

Trondheim
Lunde, Øivind *cultural organization administrator, archaeologist*

PHILIPPINES

Paranaque
Mabasa, Teresa Albar *social welfare association administrator*

POLAND

Warsaw
Rotfeld, Adam Daniel *research institute administrator, government official*

REPUBLIC OF KOREA

Seoul
Park, Won Kuk *foundation administrator*

SCOTLAND

Turnberry
Kerr, William Revill *housing association executive*

SWEDEN

Stockholm
Altéus, Åke *foundation administrator*
Sohlman, Michael *foundation administrator*

SWITZERLAND

Bern
Leavey, Thomas Edward *international organization administrator*

Brig
Guntern, Gottlieb *foundation executive, physician*

Geneva
†Rossier, William *world trade organization*
Schweitzer, Theodore Gottlieb, III, *United Nations administrator*
Sommaruga, Cornelio *humanitarian services organization administrator, diplomat*

ADDRESS UNPUBLISHED

Aitchison, Anne Catherine *environmental activist, retired*
Allerton, John Stephen *association executive*
Almond, Lincoln *lobbyist, former governor*
Anderson, Ned, Sr., *Apache tribal chairman*
Andrassy, Timothy Francis *trade association executive*
Andringa, Patricia Perkins *fundraiser, consultant*
Anson, Wayne Melvin *social welfare administrator*
†Apfel, Meri F *not-for-profit developer*
Aron, Peter Arthur *charitable foundation executive, private investor*
Ashman, Alicia Koninska *civic activist*
Atchison, Richard Calvin *trade association director*
Babb, Roberta Joan *educational administrator*
Bales, Susan Ford *social service spokesperson*
Balter, Frances Sunstein *civic worker*
Bard, Marjorie *social welfare administrator*
Barr, Marlene Joy *volunteer*
Barrow, Robert Earl *retired agricultural organization administrator*
Bashore, Irene Saras *art association administrator*
Beatty, Frances *civic worker*
Beck, Irene Clare *educational consultant, writer*
†Beggan, Robert M. *non-profit executive*
†Berenbeim, Jane Rosen *not-for-profit developer*
Berger, Arthur Seymour *organization executive, city official*
Berger, Joyce Muriel *foundation executive, author, editor*
Berley, Marc S. *foundation administrator, English educator*
Berresford, Susan Vail *philanthropic foundation executive*
Blair, Fred Edward *social services administrator*
Blair, Kathie Lynn *social services worker*
Bland, Marybeth *volunteer, artist*
Blum, Barbara Meddock *retired association executive*
Blumstein, Susan Bender *fundraiser*
Boal, Dean *retired arts center administrator, educator*
Bond, Julian *civil rights leader*
Bordner, Marjorie Rich *educator, civic worker*
†Boysen, Thomas Cyril *educational association administrator*
Brawer, Catherine Coleman *foundation executive, curator*
Brent, Rebecca Kemp *volunteer, calligrapher and textile artist*
Brim, Orville Gilbert, Jr., *former foundation administrator, author*
Briscoe, Marianne Grier *development professional, educator*
Brooke, Francis John, III, *foundation administrator*
†Brooks, Gilbert Gil *association development director*
Brown, Anne Rhoda Wiesen *civic worker*
Brown, Bruce Maitland *philanthropy consultant*
Brownsberger, Mary Grace *social services administrator, consultant*
Brundtland, Gro Harlem *international organization executive*
Brune, Eva *fundraiser*
†Buhl, Cynthia Maureen *foreign policy educator and advocate*
Bundy, Cheryl LaSota *non-profit executive, consultant*
Burki, Fred Albert *labor union official*
Bush, Barbara Pierce *former First Lady of the United States, volunteer*
Bush, Richard Clarence, III, *think-tank associate*
Butcher, Harry William *educational administrator, educator, historian*
Campbell, Edwin Denton *consultant*
†Carey, Ronald *former labor union leader*
Carley, Michael John *organization official, playwright, actor*
Carr, Larry Dean *not-for-profit company executive*
Carroll, Brenda Sandidge *volunteer civic worker*
Carter, Hodding, III, (William Hodding Carter) *foundation executive, former journalist, public official and educator*
Cesnik, James Michael *union official, newspaperman, printer, consultant*
†Chapman, Dennis Earl *social services administrator*
†Charles-Kay, Joy *not-for-profit fundraiser*
Chassman, Leonard Fredric *labor union administrator, retired*
Chernish, Lelia Margaret *fundraiser*
Childers, Andrew Aisle *educational association administrator*
†Chowdhury, Anwarul Karim *international organization official*
Clark, Alicia Garcia *political party official*
Clark, Stan *association executive*
Cohn, Marianne Winter Miller *civic activist*
Collyer, Robert B. *trade association administrator*
Connell, Hugh P. *foundation executive*
Connor, Joseph E. *former international organization official*
Cooper, Charles Donald *association executive, editor, retired career officer*
Cooper, Josephine Smith *trade association and public relations executive*
Corder, Steven Lee *non-profit organization executive*
Cordwell, Arthur George *not-for-profit fundraiser*
Covell, Christopher Greene *management executive*
Curry, John Joseph *professional organization executive*
Dechant, Virgil C. *retired fraternal organization administrator*
Dees, Bowen Causey *institute executive, retired*
DeVries, Robert Allen *foundation administrator*
Dickey, Sally Ann *retired cultural organization administrator*
Dickinson, Carol Rittgers *arts administrator, writer, executive director*
Diehr, David Bruce *retired social service administrator*
Dorman, Richard Frederick, Jr., *association executive, consultant*
Dowling, Michael Paul *foundation administrator*
Drennen, William Miller, Jr., *cultural administrator, film executive, producer, director, mineral resource executive*
†Dunn, Peter Colt *not-for-profit developer*
Easton, Michelle *foundation executive*
Eberhard, Franz Valentin *association executive*
Egerer, Karen Ann *association executive*
†Eliot, Theodore Lyman, Jr., *international consultant*
Ellis, Anne Elizabeth *fundraiser*
†Elliston, Kristine *not-for-profit fundraiser*
Engstrom, Marlene M. *volunteer*
Epperson, Margaret Farrar *civic worker*
Erlichson, Miriam *fundraiser*
Evans, Rosemary Hall *civic worker*
Fahlbeck, Douglas Alan *corporate development executive*
Farinella, Paul James *retired arts institution executive*
Filer, Emily Symington Harkins *retired foundation administrator, writer*
Finner, Stephen Lawrence *labor union administrator*
Fluth, John Adam *educational administrator*
Flynn, Paul Bartholomew *foundation executive*
Forbes, Marjorie Webster *volunteer counselor*
Forry, Steven *not-for-profit fundraiser*
Foshay, Maxine Valentine Shottland *civic worker, public relations executive*
Foster, Charles Henry Wheelwright *former foundation officer, consultant, author*
Frederick, Robert Melvin *retired farm organization executive*
Freeman, Glenn *political organization worker, retired non-commissioned military officer*
Fuchs, Betty Corcoran *retired fundraising consultant*
Fulbright, Harriet Mayor *educational association administrator*
Gabria, Joanne Bakaitis *health and education volunteer, former information processing systems equipment company executive*
Gallagher, John Paul *association administrator*
Gammon, Samuel Rhea, III, *association executive, former ambassador*
Garner, Carlene Ann *fundraising consultant*
Gasper, Jo Ann *consulting firm executive*
Gereau, Mary Condon *political corporate executive*
Gertenbach, Robert Frederick *medical research organization executive, accountant, lawyer*
Gilchrest, Thornton Charles *retired association executive*
Glasgow, Agnes Jackie *social welfare administrator, therapist*
Goldberg, Norma Lorraine *retired public welfare administrator*
Goldman, Rachel Bok *civic volunteer*
Goldstein, Laurence Alan *trade association executive*
Green, Laura Lorraine *foundation administrator*
Greenfield, James M. *retired fund raiser*
Grell, Lewis Adam *retired association executive*
Gunderson, Judith Keefer *golf association executive*
Guzik, Estelle Marion *professional society administrator*
Hadas, Julia Ann *social services administrator*
Hamilton, Shirley Siekmann *arts administrator*
Hammett, Louise Barfield *community service volunteer, artist, historian, playwright*
Hanford, George Hyde *retired educational administrator*
Hardin, Martha Love Wood *civic leader*
Hardy, Clarence Earl, Jr., *government, nonprofit and corporate sector executive*
Harrison, John Raymond *foundation executive, retired newspaper executive*
Harvey, Glenn Francis *association manager*
Heinz, Susan Goldin *educational association administrator*
Helm, DeWitt Frederick, Jr., *consultant, professional association administrator*
Hendrickson, Louise *retired association executive, retired social worker*
Henricks, Roger Lee *retired social services administrator*
Hicks, Dolores Kathleen (De De Hicks) *foundation director*
Hill, Dale Stewart *volunteer*
Himes, Diane Adele *buyer, fundraiser, actress, lobbyist*
Hoffheimer, Minette Goldsmith *community service volunteer*
†Hogsett, Joseph H. *political organization worker, former state official*
Holloway, James Lemuel, III, *foundation executive, retired naval officer*
†Horn, Howard M. *labor union administrator, consultant*
Howitt, Pamela Tesler *development and philanthropy association administrator*
†Huber, Mark *foundation administrator*
Huggins, Robert Brian *nonprofit organization official*
Hyatt-Smith, Ann Rose *non-profit organization executive, consultant*
Isaacson, Edith L. *civic leader*
†Jacobowitz, Chana M. *cultural organization administrator*
Jacoby, Thomas S. *cultural organization administrator*
Jaffeson, Richard Charles *association executive administrator*
Jeansonne, Mary Scanlan *not for profit developer*
Johnson, Marlene M. *nonprofit executive*
Jones, Dorothy Joanne *social services professional*
†Julander, Paula Foil *health care and political consultant, state senator*
†Jump, Sharyl A. *special events coordinator*
Kabat, Linda Georgette *civic leader*
Kahmann, Sarah Stuber *retired foundation administrator*
Kahrmann, Robert George *educational administrator*
Kaskowitz, Edwin *social services executive*
Keil, M. David *retired international association executive*
Kelly, Cheryl Ann *healthcare administrator*
Kelly, Nancy Folden *arts administrator*
King, Jane Cudlip Coblentz *volunteer educator*
King, Rosalyn Mercita *social science researcher*
Klarich, David John *political organization executive, lawyer*
Klopfleisch, Stephanie Squance *social services agency administrator*
Knauer, Virginia Harrington (Mrs. Wilhelm F. Knauer) *consumer consultant, former government official*
†Koerner, Joshua David *foundation administrator*
Korologos, Ann McLaughlin *public policy, communications executive*
Kristensen, Hans M. *think-tank executive, researcher*
Kuczynski, Les Stanislaus *non-profit organization administrator*
Kunstadter, Geraldine Sapolsky *foundation executive*
Kurtz, Dolores May *civic worker*
Kussrow, Nancy Esther *educational association administrator*
Labbe-Webb, Elizabeth Geralyn *arts administrator, theatre artist*
Lancaster, Sally Rhodus *retired non-profit executive and consultant*
Langer, Edward L. *trade association administrator*
LaPidus, Jules Benjamin *educational association administrator*
Lawton, Jean Margaret *volunteer*
Ledwig, Donald Eugene *association executive, former broadcasting executive, former naval officer*
Leggett, Roberta Jean (Bobbi Leggett) *retired social services administrator*
Leimas, Carol Ann *women's association consultant*
LePome, Penelope Marie *rehabilitation counselor, educator*
Lester, Virginia Laudano *education administrator*
Liddell, Jane Hawley Hawkes *civic worker*
Livingston, Margaret Gresham *civic leader*
Lord, Kathleen Virginia Anderson *fundraising executive, educator*
†Losey, Michael Robert *retired professional society administrator*
Low, Louise O. *civic volunteer*
Luckey, Doris Waring *civic volunteer*
MacCarthy, Talbot Leland *civic volunteer*
MacCarthy, Timothy Charles *association executive*
MacCullagh, Bruce Scott *fund raiser, software designer*
Mack, Charles Daniel, III, *labor union executive*
Mahoney, Ann Dickinson *fundraiser*
Marler, Larry John *nonprofit organization administrator*
Marquardt, Sandra Mary *activist, lobbyist, researcher*
†Marshall, William Ross *professional society administrator*
Maxwell, Patricia Joy *fund raising executive*
Mazur, Jay J. *trade union official*
Mazza, Terilyn McGovern *finance executive*
McCloskey, J(ohn) Michael *retired association administrator*
McDaniel, Mike *former political association executive*
McDaniel, Sue Powell *cultural organization administrator*
McDonald, Douglas Robert *non profit agency executive*
McFate, Kenneth Leverne *trade association administrator*
McFate, Patricia Ann *foundation executive, scientist, educator*
McIntyre, Carol Chrisman *social services administrator*
McLauchlan, Sylvia June *charity organization executive*
†McMahon, John E. *not-for-profit fundraiser*
McMullen, Ralph Edgar *convention center administrator*
McWethy, Patricia Joan *educational association administrator*
†Medina, Janie *not-for-profit fundraiser*
Mende, Robert Graham *retired engineering association executive*
Metcalf, Karen *retired foundation executive*
Miller, Jay Alan *retired civil rights association executive*
Minges, John Franklin, III, *non-profit management consultant*
Miracle, Nancy *foundation administrator*
Mitchell, Carolyn Cochran *foundation administrator's executive assistant*
Moore, Robert William *professional organization executive*
†Morckel, Sandy *not-for-profit fundraiser, consultant*
Morgali, Diane *retired non-profit corporation administrator*
Morrison, Barbara Haney *educational administrator*
Morse, Jean Avnet *higher education administrator, lawyer*
Muller, H(enry) Nicholas, III, *retired foundation administrator*
†Murphy-Pilon, Monica *cultural organization administrator*
Neel, Judy Murphy *association executive*
Neely, Marion Victoria *community volunteer*
Nell, James Leo *association administrator*
Niemiec, Edward Walter *professional association executive*

ATHLETICS

---

†Quann, Megan *Olympic athlete*
Rouse, Jeff *Olympic athlete, swimmer*
†Shealy, Courtney *Olympic athlete*
†Torres, Dara *Olympic athlete*
†Woolridge, Orlando *former professional basketball coach, Olympic coach*

Denver
Alomar, Sandy, Jr., (Santos Velazquez Alomar) *professional baseball player*
†Balboa, Marcelo *professional soccer player*
†Bell, David Gus (Buddy Bell) *professional baseball manager*
Beuerlein, Steve Taylor *professional football player*
Evans, Mike *professional basketball coach*
Forsberg, Peter *professional hockey player*
†Hardaway, Timothy Duane *basketball player*
Helton, Todd *professional baseball player*
Hurdle, Clint *professional athletics manager*
†McDyess, Antonio *professional basketball player*
†Myernick, Glenn *professional soccer coach*
Sakic, Joseph Steve *professional hockey player*
Walker, Larry Kenneth Robert *professional baseball player*

Englewood
Bowlen, Pat(rick)(Dennis) *professional sports team executive, holding company executive, lawyer*
Davis, Terrell *former professional football player*
Griese, Brian *football player*
McGlockton, Chester *professional football player*
Plummer, Jason Steven (Jake Plummer) *professional football player*
Shanahan, Mike *professional football coach*
†Smith, Neil *professional football player*
Smith, Rod *football player*

Greeley
Hilgenkamp, Kathryn Darline *exercise and sport psychologist, health educator*

U S A F Academy
†DeBerry, Fisher *college football coach*

CONNECTICUT

Cos Cob
†Leamy, Nancy M. *professional athletics coach*

Hamden
Barberi, Matthew *physical education and health educator*

New London
Pinhey, Frances Louise *retired physical education educator*

Stamford
Johnson, Dwayne Douglas (The Rock) *professional wrestler, actor*
Valentine, Robert John (Bobby Valentine) *former professional baseball manager*

West Hartford
Spencer, Priscilla James *physical education educator*

Wethersfield
†DiCicco, Tony *soccer coach*

Willimantic
Williams, Neil Franklin *physical education educator*

DELAWARE

Newark
Cairns, Sara Albertson *physical education educator*

DISTRICT OF COLUMBIA

Washington
†Bullett, Vicky *basketball player*
Chin, Allen E., Sr., *athletic administrator, educator*
Ewing, Patrick Aloysius *professional basketball coach*
Hamilton, Richard Clay *basketball player*
Holdsclaw, Chamique Shaunta *professional basketball player*
†Jagr, Jaromir *professional hockey player*
†McCray, Nikki Kesangame *basketball player*
†McEnroe, John Patrick, Jr., *former professional tennis player, commentator*
†Oakley, Charles *professional basketball player*
Pollin, Abe *professional basketball team executive, builder*
Shriver, Sargent *sports association executive*
Shriver, Timothy P. *sports association executive*
†Upshaw, Gene *sports association executive*

FLORIDA

Clearwater
McGann, Michael Geyer *martial arts instructor, protection expert*

Coral Springs
†Singh, Vijay *professional golfer*

Davie
†Gailey, Thomas Chandler *professional football coach*
Madison, Sam A., Jr., *football player*
Mare, Olindo Franco *football player*
Martin, Tony Derrick *professional football player*

†McDuffie, Otis James (O.J. McDuffie) *professional football player*
Seau, Junior (Tiana Seau Jr.) *professional football player*
†Thomas, Thurman Lee *football player*
Thomas, Zach Michael *football player*
Williams, Ricky *professional football player*

Daytona Beach
Andrews Reeves, Donna *professional golfer*
Barrett, Tina *professional golfer*
†Bodine, Brett *race car driver*
†Bodine, Geoff *race car driver*
France, William Clifton, Jr., *professional sports team executive*
†Gordon, Jeff *race car driver*
Helton, Mike *professional sports team executive*
†King, Betsy *professional golfer*
†Pak, Se Ri *professional golfer*
†Rudd, Ricky *race car driver*
†Schrader, Ken *race car driver*
Steinhauer, Sherri *professional golfer*
†Votaw, Ty M. *golf association commissioner*
†Wallace, Rusty *race car driver*
Whitworth, Kathrynne Ann *professional golfer*
†Yarborough, William Caleb *retired race car driver*

Deerfield Beach
†King, Don *boxing promoter*

Fort Lauderdale
†Lassiter, Roy *soccer player*
†Melo, Welton *professional soccer player*
Searcy, Leon, Jr., *football player*

Gainesville
†Donovan, Billy *university basketball coach*
Varnes, Jill Tutton *university official, health educator*

Hollywood
King, Alma Jean *former health and physical education educator*

Indialantic
Rose, Peter Edward *former professional baseball player and manager*

Jacksonville
Brady, Kyle James *football player*
Brunell, Mark Allen *professional football player*
†Del Rio, Jack *professional football coach, former professional football player*
Smith, Jimmy, Jr., *football player*
Taylor, Fred *professional football player*

Lady Lake
Hartzler, Genevieve Lucille *physical education educator*

Miami
†Brondello, Sandy *professional basketball player*
Fiedler, Jay *football player*
McKeon, John Aloysius (Jack McKeon) *professional baseball manager*
†Meadors, Marynell *former professional basketball coach, sports team executive*
†Mourning, Alonzo *professional basketball player*
Riley, Patrick James *professional basketball coach*
†Rothstein, Ronald *professional basketball coach*
†Strickland, Rodney *professional basketball player*

Miami Beach
Shula, Don Francis *former professional football coach, team executive*

Naples
Frazer, John Howard *tennis association executive*

Opa Locka
Beckett, Joshua Patrick *baseball player*
Castillo, Luis Antonio Donato *professional baseball player*
†Kotsay, Mark Steven *baseball player*
Lee, Derrek Leon *baseball player*
†Perez, Tony *former baseball player*

Orlando
Hill, Grant *professional basketball player*
†Janzen, Lee *professional golfer*
Johnson, Shannon *professional basketball player*
Rivers, Glenn Anton (Doc Rivers) *professional basketball coach, former basketball player*

Ormond Beach
Wendelstedt, Harry Hunter, Jr., *umpire*

Palm Beach
Floyd, Raymond Loran *professional golfer*

Palm Beach Gardens
†Awtrey, Jim L. *sports association executive*
†Couples, Frederick Steven *professional golfer*
†Duval, David Robert *professional golfer*
†Henninger, Brian Hatfield *professional golfer*
†Leonard, Justin (Justin Charles Garret Leonard) *professional golfer*
†Love, Davis Milton, III, *professional golfer*
†Maggert, Jeffrey Allan *professional golfer*
†Mickelson, Phil(ip Alfred) *professional golfer*
†Miller, John Laurence *professional golfer*
†O'Meara, Mark *professional golfer*
†Stankowski, Paul Francis *professional golfer*
†Strange, Curtis Northrop *professional golfer*
†Verplank, Scott Rachal *professional golfer*
†Watson, Thomas Sturges *professional golfer*
†Westwood, Lee *professional golfer*
†Woods, Tiger (Eldrick Woods) *professional golfer*

Palm City
Mc Hale, John Joseph *baseball club executive*

Ponte Vedra Beach
Agassi, Andre Kirk *professional tennis player*
†Faxon, Brad *professional golfer*
Finchem, Tim *sports association executive*
Pavin, Corey Allen *professional golfer*
†Sluman, Jeff (Jeffrey George Sluman) *professional golfer*
Stricker, Steve *golfer*
Triplett, Kirk Allen *golfer*
†Wadkins, Lanny *professional golfer*
†Washington, MaliVai *professional tennis player*

Saint Petersburg
Alvarez, Wilson Eduardo *baseball player*
†Gooden, Dwight Eugene *professional baseball player*
†McGriff, Fred (Frederick Stanley McGriff) *baseball player*
Vaughn, Gregory Lamont *professional baseball player*
Wilson, Paul *baseball player*

Sunrise
Keenan, Mike *professional hockey team coach*
†Larionov, Igor *hockey player*
Ozolinsh, Sandis *hockey player*
Torrey, William Arthur *professional hockey team executive*
Worrell, Peter *professional hockey player*

Tallahassee
Bowden, Bobby *university athletic coach*
Hamilton, J. Leonard *collegiate basketball coach, former professional basketball coach*

Tampa
Alstott, Michael Joseph (Mike Alstott) *professional football player*
Brooks, Derrick Dewan *football player*
Christy, Jeff *football player*
†Dudley, Rick *professional hockey coach*
†Gruden, Jon *professional football coach*
†Hankinson, Tim *soccer coach*
Johnson, Brad *football player*
Johnson, Keyshawn *professional football player*
Khabibulin, Nikolai *professional hockey player*
Kubina, Pavel *professional hockey player*
Lecavalier, Vincent *professional hockey player*
Lynch, John Terrence *football player*
McCardell, Keenan *football player*
McDaniel, Randall Cornell *retired professional football player*
Modin, Fredrik *professional hockey player*
Sapp, Warren Carlos *football player*

GEORGIA

Athens
Dishman, Rodney King *physical education educator*

Atlanta
†Aaron, Hank (Henry L. Aaron) *professional baseball team executive*
Arani, Ardy A. *professional sports marketing executive, lawyer*
Babcock, Peter Heartz *professional sports executive*
Bellamy, Walter *retired basketball player*
Cox, Bobby (Robert Joe Cox) *professional baseball manager*
Hartley, Bob *professional hockey coach*
Heatley, Dany *hockey player*
Jones, Andruw Rudolf *professional baseball player*
Jones, Larry Wayne "Chipper", Jr., *baseball player*
Kovalchuk, Ilya *hockey player*
Kozlov, Vyacheslav *hockey player*
Kruger, Lon *coach*
Maddux, Gregory (Gregory Alan Maddux) *professional baseball player*
Rhodes, Damian *hockey player*
†Schuerholz, John Boland, Jr., *professional baseball executive*
†Smoltz, John Andrew *professional baseball player*
Thompson, Wallace Reeves, III, *physical education educator*

Flowery Branch
Blank, Arthur M. *professional sports team executive, retired home and lumber retail chain executive*
Dunn, Warrick *football player*
†Reeves, Daniel Edward *professional football coach*
Vick, Michael *football player*

Marietta
Devigne, Karen Cooke *retired amateur athletics executive*

Suwanee
Anderson, Jamal Sharif *professional football player*

Waverly Hall
Merritt, Martin David *counselor, tennis professional, educator, musician*

IDAHO

Twin Falls
Studebaker, William Vern *sports and literature educator, writer*

ILLINOIS

Belleville
†Connors, Jimmy (James Scott Connors) *former professional tennis player*

Chicago
†Agoos, Jeff *professional soccer player*
†Akers, Michelle Anne *soccer player*
Alou, Moises *professional baseball player*
†Arena, Bruce *professional soccer coach*
Artest, Ron *professional basketball player*
†Baker, Dusty (Johnnie B. Baker Jr.) *professional baseball team manager*
Baylor, Don Edward *former professional baseball manager*
†Bradley, Bob *professional soccer coach*
Buehrle, Mark *baseball player*
Cartwright, Bill *professional basketball coach*
Daze, Eric *professional hockey player*
†Fawcett, Joy Lynn *soccer player*
Fleury, Theoren *hockey player*
†Foudy, Julia Maurine *soccer player*
†Gabarra, Carin Leslie *professional soccer player, professional soccer coach*
Girardi, Joseph Elliott *baseball player*
†Hamm, Mariel Margaret *soccer player*
Housley, Phil F. *professional hockey player*
†Jones, Cobi *professional soccer player*
Konerko, Paul *baseball player*
†Lilly, Kristine Marie *soccer player*
†MacMillan, Shannon Ann *soccer player*
Mercer, Ron *professional basketball player*
†Milbrett, Tiffeny Carleen *professional soccer player*
Ordonez, Magglio *professional baseball player*
†Overbeck, Carla Werden *soccer player, coach*
†Parlow, Cynthia Maria *soccer player*
Pizer, Howard Charles *sports and entertainment executive*
Reinsdorf, Jerry Michael *professional sports teams executive, real estate executive, lawyer, accountant*
†Reyna, Claudio *soccer player*
Rose, Jalen *professional basketball player*
Schwartz, Alan Gifford *sport company executive*
†Schwoy, Laurie Annette *soccer player*
†Scurry, Briana Collette *soccer player*
†Sobrero, Kathryn Michele *soccer player*
Sosa, Samuel (Sammy Sosa) *professional baseball player*
Thomas, Frank Edward *professional baseball player*
†Venturini, Tisha Lea *professional soccer player*
†Whalen, Sarah Eve *soccer player*
Zelepukin, Valeri *hockey player*

Elk Grove Village
Meyer, Raymond Joseph *former college basketball coach*

Glendale Heights
Spearing, Karen Marie *physical education educator, coach*

Glenview
King, Billie Jean Moffitt *former professional tennis player*

Lake Forest
Chandler, Christopher Mark (Chris Chandler) *professional football player*
Hampton, Daniel Oliver *professional football player*
Jauron, Dick *professional football coach*
McCaskey, Michael B. *professional football team executive*
Stewart, Kordell *professional football player*

Libertyville
Trzyna, Chris *physical education educator*

Lincolnshire
Schauble, John Eugene *physical education educator*

Mahomet
Thompson, Margaret M. *physical education educator*

Mundelein
Carr, Bonnie Jean *professional ice skater*

Naperville
†Gems, Gerald Robert *physical education educator*

Sterling
Moran, Joan Jensen *physical education and health educator*

Urbana
†Sydnor, Synthia *kinesiology educator*

Wheaton
Miller, Lynn Breckenfelder *health and physical education educator*

INDIANA

Evansville
Wilson, Gregory Scott *kinesiology educator, coach*

Granger
Thomas, Debi (Debra J. Thomas) *ice skater*

Indianapolis
Abdul-Jabbar, Karim *retired professional football player*
†Bird, Larry Joe *professional athletics manager, former professional basketball coach*
†Buford-Bailey, Tonja Yevette *Olympic athlete*
Carlisle, Rick *professional basketball coach*
Catchings, Tamika *professional basketball player*
†Colander-Richardson, LaTasha *Olympic athlete*
†Dawes, Dominique *Olympic athlete*
Dimas, Trent *Olympic athlete, gymnast*
†Drummond, Jon *Olympic athlete*
Dungy, Tony *professional football coach*

Cooperstown
†Yount, Robin *retired professional baseball player*

Flushing
†Alomar, Roberto Velazquez *professional baseball player*
Bell, Derek *professional baseball player*
Glavine, Tom (Thomas Michael Glavine) *professional baseball player*
†Leiter, Alois Terry (Al) *professional baseball player*
†Piazza, Michael Joseph *professional baseball player*
†Vaughn, Mo (Maurice Samuel Vaughn) *professional baseball player*
Zeile, Todd Edward *professional baseball player*

Garden City
Berka, Marianne Guthrie *health and physical education educator*

Hempstead
Beasley, Aaron Bruce *football player*
Chrebet, Wayne *professional football player*
Edwards, Herman *professional football coach*
Johnson, Robert Wood, IV, *sports team executive*
Martin, Curtis *professional football player*
Testaverde, Vincent Frank (Vinny Testaverde) *professional football player*
Yashin, Alexei *hockey player*

Lake Placid
†Bakken, Jill *Olympic athlete*
†Gale, Tristan *Olympic athlete*
†Grimmette, Mark *Olympic athlete*
†Martin, Brian *Olympic athlete*
Rossi, Ronald Aldo *sports association administrator, Olympic athlete*

Mohegan Lake
Ettinger, Jayne Gold *physical education educator*

New York
Ackerman, Valerie B. *sports association executive*
†Adubato, Richard Adam (Richie Adubato) *professional basketball coach*
Bettman, Gary Bruce *sports league official, lawyer*
Blazejowski, Carol *sports team executive, retired basketball player*
Bure, Pavel *hockey player*
Capriati, Jennifer Maria *professional tennis player*
Chaney, Don *professional basketball coach*
†Granik, Russell T. *sports association executive*
†Gulati, Sunil *sports administrator*
†Hampton, Kym *basketball player*
Holik, Bobby *hockey player*
†Houston, Allan Wade *professional basketball player*
Jackson, Reggie (Reginald Martinez Jackson) *former professional baseball player*
†Johnson, Larry Demetric *professional basketball player*
Katz, Jane *swimming educator*
Kovalev, Alexei *professional hockey player*
†Lalas, Alexi *retired professional soccer player*
Layden, Scott *professional sports team executive*
Leetch, Brian Joseph *hockey player*
Lindros, Eric Bryan *hockey player*
†Logan, Douglas George *sports commissioner*
†Louganis, Greg E. *Olympic athlete, researcher, actor*
Martin, Michael Townsend *racing horse stable executive, sports marketing executive*
Messier, Mark Douglas *hockey player*
Ruta, Thomas V. *professional sports team executive, accounting executive*
Sampras, Pete *retired professional tennis player*
Scott, Dale Allan *major league umpire*
†Selig, Allan H. (Bud Selig) *professional sports league executive*
†Sprewell, Latrell Fontaine *professional basketball player*
†Steinfeld, Allan *sports association administrator*
†Stern, David Joel *basketball association executive*
†Tagliabue, Paul John *national football league commissioner*
Weatherspoon, Teresa Gaye *professional basketball player*
Zahnd, Richard H. *professional sports executive, lawyer*

Orchard Park
Bledsoe, Drew *professional football player*
Moulds, Eric Shannon *professional football player*
Williams, Gregg *professional football coach*

South Setauket
Berger, H. Jean *retired physical education educator*

Syracuse
Christian, David Michael *athletic director, parochial school educator*
Duerr, Dianne Marie *educator, sports medicine consultant*

Uniondale
†Arbour, Alger *professional hockey coach*
Hamrlik, Roman *professional hockey player*
†Osgood, Chris *hockey player*
Peca, Michael *hockey player*
Wang, Charles B. *professional sports team executive*

White Plains
Davenport, Lindsay *professional tennis player*
Frazier, Amy *professional tennis player*
†Gambill, Jan-Michael *professional tennis player*
†Garrison-Jackson, Zina *retired tennis player*
†Gilbert, Bradley *professional tennis coach, former professional tennis player, former Olympic athlete*
†Gimelstob, Justin *professional tennis player*
†Grossman, Ann *professional tennis player*
†McEnroe, Patrick *former professional tennis player, sports commentator*
†McNeil, Lori Michelle *professional tennis player*
Raymond, Lisa *tennis player*
†Reneberg, Richard (Richey Reneberg) *professional tennis player*
Rubin, Chanda *professional tennis player*
†Schnyder, Patty *professional tennis player*
†Wheaton, David *professional tennis player*
Williams, Serena *professional tennis player*
Williams, Ted Vaughnell *physical education educator*
Williams, Venus *professional tennis player*

NORTH CAROLINA

Chapel Hill
†Guthridge, Bill *university basketball coach*
Smith, Dean Edwards *university basketball coach*

Charlotte
Bates, Michael *professional football player, former Olympic athlete, track and field*
Fox, John *professional football coach*
Johnson, Jimmie *race car driver*
Long, Jim *racing team crew chief*
Means, Natrone Jermaine *professional football player*
†Metcalf, Eric Quinn *professional football player*
Muhammad, Muhsin, II, *football player*
Nadeau, Jerry *race car driver*
Robinson, Shawna *race car driver*
Staley, Dawn *basketball player*
Stinson, Andrea Maria *professional basketball player*
Walls, Wesley (Charles Wesley Walls) *football player*
Weinke, Chris *football player*

Concord
Biffle, Greg *race car driver*
Busch, Kurt *race car driver*
Elder, Christian *race car driver*

Conover
†Jarrett, Dale *race car driver*

Durham
†Goestenkors, Gail *head basketball coach*
†Krzyzewski, Mike *university athletic coach*

Fairview
Bradley, Edward William *sports foundation executive*

Harrisburg
Hendrick, Ricky *race car driver*
†Labonte, Terry *race car driver*
Sprague, Jack *race car driver*

High Point
†Burton, Ward *professional race car driver*
Stricklin, Hut *race car driver*
Wimmer, Scott *race car driver*

Huntersville
McLaughlin, Mike *race car driver*
†Stewart, Tony *professional race car driver*

Mooresville
Atwood, Casey *race car driver*
Blaney, Dave *race car driver*
Compton, Stacy *race car driver*
†Cope, Derrike *race car driver*
†Earnhardt, Dale, Jr., *race car driver*
Earnhardt, Kerry *race car driver*
Foyt, Larry *race car driver*
Keller, Jason *race car driver*
LaJoie, Randy *race car driver*
†Little, Charles Glen, Jr., *professional race car driver*
†Marlin, Sterling *race car driver*
†Martin, Mark *race car driver*
†Mayfield, Jeremy *race car driver*
Nemechek, Joe *race car driver*
Newman, Ryan *race car driver*
Park, Steve *race car driver*
Riggs, Scott *race car driver*
Wallace, Mike *race car driver*
†Waltrip, Michael *professional race car driver*

Morrisville
Francis, Ron *professional hockey player*
Maurice, Paul *professional hockey coach*

Raleigh
Brind'Amour, Rod Jean *hockey player*
Irbe, Arturs *professional hockey player*
O'Neill, Jeff *professional hockey player*
†Rutherford, Jim *professional sports team executive*

Randleman
Andretti, John *professional race car driver*

Statesville
Evernham, Ray *race team owner*

Summerfield
Brueckmann, Robin M. *riding instructor, horse show judge*

Trinity
†Labonte, Bobby *race car driver*

Welcome
Gordon, Robby *race car driver*
Green, Jeff *race car driver*
Harvick, Kevin *race car driver*
Purvis, Jeff *race car driver*
Sauter, Johnny *race car driver*
†Skinner, Mike *professional race car driver*

OHIO

Berea
Campo, Dave *professional football coach*
†Clark, Dwight Edward *sports team executive, former professional football player*
Davis, Butch *professional football coach*
Policy, Carmen A. *professional sports team executive*

Cadiz
Hoffman, Barbara Jo *health and physical education educator, athletic director*

Canton
Elliott, Peter R. *retired athletic organization executive*
†Long, Howie *former pro football player*
†Mack, Tom *retired professional football player*
†Shaw, Billy *retired professional football player*

Cincinnati
Brown, Mike *professional sports team executive*
Dillon, Corey *professional football player*
Griffey, Ken, Jr., (George Kenneth Griffey Jr.) *professional baseball player*
Huggins, Bob *college basketball coach*
Kitna, Jon *football player*
Larkin, Barry Louis *professional baseball player*
Smith, Akili *professional football player*
Warrick, Peter *football player*

Cleveland
†Baranova, Elena *basketball player*
†Faldo, Nick (Nicholas Alexander Faldo) *professional golfer*
Fryman, David Travis *professional baseball player*
Gardocki, Christopher *professional football player*
†Hart, John *professional sports team executive*
Hill, Tyrone *professional basketball player*
†Johnston, Alastair J. *sports association executive*
Lopez, Nancy *professional golfer*
Manuel, Charlie Fuqua, Jr., *professional baseball manager*
Moceanu, Dominique *retired Olympic athlete*
†Nemcova, Eva *professional basketball player*
Pierce, Mary *professional tennis player*
Seles, Monica *professional tennis player*
Silas, Paul *professional basketball coach*
Thome, Jim *professional baseball player*
Vizquel, Omar Enrique *professional baseball player*

Columbus
†Cooper, John *university football coach*
†McBride, Brian *soccer player*
†O'Brien, Jim *university basketball coach*
Sanderson, Geoff *hockey player*

Gahanna
†Douglas, James (Buster) *boxer*

Hilliard
†Herta, Bryan *race car driver*

Oxford
Pont, John *football coach, educator*

Shaker Heights
Eakin, Thomas Capper *sports promotion executive*

Tiffin
Spellerberg, Elinor M. *riding instructor*

Westlake
†FitzRandolph, Casey *Olympic athlete*
†Ohno, Apolo Anton *Olympic athlete*
†Parra, Derek *Olympic athlete*

Worthington
Whitney, Ray *hockey player*

Youngstown
†DeBartolo, Edward John, Jr., *professional football team owner, real estate developer*

OKLAHOMA

Enid
Abdul-Jabbar, Kareem (Lewis Ferdinand Alcindor) *professional basketball coach*

OREGON

Portland
Daniels, Antonio *professional basketball player*
†Dunleavy, Michael Joseph *professional basketball coach*
†Hargrove, Linda *professional basketball coach*
†Kemp, Shawn T. *professional basketball player*
Patterson, Steve *professional basketball team executive*
Pippen, Scottie *professional basketball player*

PENNSYLVANIA

Clifton Heights
Pagano, Richard Donald *physical education educator, researcher*

Delmont
Mock, Robert Allen *professional figure skating coach, editor*

Easton
†Holmes, Larry, Jr., *retired professional boxer*

Millersville
Kabacinski, Stanley Joseph *health and physical education educator, consultant, speaker*

Philadelphia
Abreu, Bobby *professional baseball player*
Bowa, Lawrence Robert (Larry Bowa) *professional baseball manager*
†Branche, Anna Louise *physical education educator, performing arts educator, religious studies educator*
†Clarke, Robert Earle (Bobby Clarke) *hockey executive*
Croce, Pat *author, fitness trainer, former sports team executive*
Fish, Elizabeth Ann *physical education educator*
Francona, Terry Jon *professional baseball manager*
Iverson, Allen *basketball player*
†Kukoc, Toni *professional basketball player*
LeClair, John Clark *hockey player*
Levens, Dorsey (Herbert Levens) *professional football player*
Lurie, Jeffrey *professional sports team executive*
McNabb, Donovan *football player*
†Mutombo, DiKembe (Dikembe Mutombo Mpolondo Mukamba Jean Jacque Wamutombo) *professional basketball player*
Primeau, Keith *hockey player*
Reid, Andy *professional football coach*
Roenick, Jeremy *hockey player*
Rollins, James Calvin *baseball player*
Snider, Edward Malcolm *professional hockey club executive*
†Vanbiesbrouck, John *hockey player*
Van Horn, Keith *professional basketball player*
Wallace, Rasheed *professional basketball player, marketing professional*

Pittsburgh
Berenato, Agnus McGlade *women's basketball coach*
Bettis, Jerome Abram *professional football player*
†Constantine, Kevin *professional hockey coach*
Cowher, Bill *professional football coach*
Giles, Brian Stephen *baseball player*
Lemieux, Mario *professional sports team executive, professional hockey player*
Mathis, Terance *professional football player*
McClatchy, Kevin S. *professional sports team executive*
†Perkins, Kenneth Alan *physical education educator*
Rooney, Daniel M. *professional football team executive*
Straka, Martin *hockey player*

Reading
†Unser, Alfred, Jr., *race car driver*

Rydal
Fernberger, Marilyn Friedman *events organizer, consultant, civic leader*

Youngstown
Palmer, Arnold Daniel *professional golfer*

SOUTH CAROLINA

Mount Pleasant
Mixon, Janet Sandhoff *physical education educator*

TENNESSEE

Greeneville
Ford, Sally J. *physical education educator*

Memphis
†Williams, Jason *professional basketball player*

Nashville
Cunningham, Gunther *professional football coach*
Fisher, Jeff *professional football coach*
George, Eddie *professional football player*
Johnson, Greg *professional hockey player*
Kearse, Jevon *football player*
Legwand, David *hockey player*
Mason, Derrick *football player*
McNair, Steve LaTreal *professional football player*
Trotz, Barry *professional hockey coach*
†Voight, Michael Lee *physical education educator*
Wycheck, Frank *football player*

TEXAS

Arlington
Alvarez, Juan M. *baseball player*
Guerin, Bill *professional hockey player*
Palmeiro, Rafael Corrales *professional baseball player*
†Ryan, Nolan *former professional baseball player*
Showalter, Buck (William Nathaniel Showalter III) *major league baseball team manager*

Austin
†Armstrong, Lance *professional cyclist*
†Barnes, Richard Dale *college basketball coach*
†Crenshaw, Ben *professional golfer*

Clutch City
†Rice, Glen Anthony *professional basketball player*

College Station
Slocum, Richard Copeland (R.C. Slocum) *university athletic coach*

Dallas
†Dir, Dave *professional soccer coach*
Hamilton, David Lee *sports association administrator, conservationist*
Hudel, Chestella Alvis *athletics educator*
Modano, Michael *hockey player*

Wagner, Richard *athletics consultant, former baseball team executive*
†Waltrip, Darrell Lee *race car driver*
†West, Jerry Alan *professional basketball team executive*
Williams, Erik George *professional football player*
Williams, Matt (Matthew Derrick Williams) *former professional baseball player*
Wilpon, Fred *professional baseball team executive, real estate developer*
Wilson, Ralph Cookerly, Jr., *professional football team executive*
Wooden, John Robert *former basketball coach*
Woosnam, Ian Harold *professional golfer*
Yamaguchi, Kristi Tsuya *ice skater*

BUSINESS *See* FINANCE: INDUSTRY

COMMUNICATIONS *See* COMMUNICATIONS MEDIA; INDUSTRY: SERVICE

COMMUNICATIONS MEDIA *See also* ARTS: LITERARY

UNITED STATES

ALABAMA

Anniston
Ayers, Harry Brandt *editor, publisher, columnist*

Birmingham
Crichton, Douglas Bentley *editor, writer*
Francavilla, Donna T. *journalist*
Galloway, Catherine Black *publishing executive*
†Griffin, Eleanor *magazine editor*
Hanson, Victor Henry, II, *newspaper publisher*
Hickson, Marcus Lafayette, III, *communication educator, consultant*
Kennedy, Joe David, Jr., (Joey Kennedy) *editor*
†Powell, Larry *communications educator*
Seitz, Karl Raymond *editor*
†Sheppard, Scott *magazine publisher*
†Stephens, James T. *publishing executive*

Cullman
†Brunck, Terri Lee *journalist*

Gadsden
Coakley, Deirdre *writer*
Smothers, Jimmy *editor, sportswriter*

Jacksonville
Merrill, Martha *library media educator*

Madison
Cazavan, Larry O. *television executive*

Mobile
Clark, Veronica Ann Wilds (Ronni Patriquin Clark) *journalist*

Montgomery
Hertenstein, Myrna Lynn *publishing executive*

Pelham
Harvey, James Mathews, Jr., *communications specialist*

Tuscaloosa
Reinhart, Kellee Connely *journalist*
Ross, Daniel J.J. *publishing executive*
Thomson, H. Bailey *editor, educator*

Vina
†Cayson, Joyce Scallorn *editor, small business owner*

ALASKA

Anchorage
Cohn, Gary Dennis *journalist*
Hill, Erik Bryan *newspaper photographer*
Pearson, Larry Lester *journalism educator, internet presence provider*

Fairbanks
Berry Bertram, Kathryn *editor in chief science publication*
Crawford, Sarah Carter (Sally Carter Crawford) *broadcast executive*

Homer
Beach, Geo *journalist, poet*

ARIZONA

Bisbee
Arrowsmith, Nancy *journalist*
Eppele, David Louis *columnist, author*

Gilbert
Kenney, Thomas Frederick *broadcasting executive*

Glendale
Joseph, Gregory Nelson *media critic, writer, actor*

Green Valley
Macafee, Susan Diane *reporter*

Paradise Valley
Harnett, Lila *retired publisher*

Phoenix
†Bushee, Ward *newspaper editor*
Clark-Johnson, Susan *publishing executive*
Edens, Gary Denton *broadcasting executive*
Grafe, Warren Blair *broadcast executive*
Gunty, Christopher James *newspaper editor*
Leach, John F. *editor, journalism educator*
Moyer, Alan Dean *retired newspaper editor*
Pyle, Thomas Alton *instructional television and motion picture executive*
Schatt, Paul *newspaper editor*
Steckler, Phyllis Betty *publishing company executive*
Turi, Louis *publishing executive*
Weil, Louis Arthur, III, *retired newspaper publishing executive*

Prescott
Anderson, Parker Lynn *editorial columnist, playwright*

Scottsdale
Faer, A.M. *magazine publishing consultant, poet*
Murian, Richard Miller *book company executive*
Reidy, Richard Robert *publishing company executive*

Sedona
Chicorel, Marietta Eva *publishing company executive, consultant*
Sasmor, James Cecil *publishing representative, educator*

Tempe
Peterson, Michael R. *music company executive*
Rankin, William Parkman *educator, former publishing company executive*
Richards, Gale Lee *communication educator*
Sabine, Gordon Arthur *educator, writer*

Tucson
Grimes, James Cahill *retired publishing executive, advertising executive*
Hale, William Bryan, Jr., *newspaper editor*
Hutchinson, Charles Smith, Jr., *book publisher*
Martin, June Johnson Caldwell *journalist*
Roos, Nestor Robert *consultant*
†White, Jane See *journalist*

ARKANSAS

Arkadelphia
†Addington, Ronald Paul *mass media educator*

Cedarville
Whitaker, Ruth Reed *state legislator, retired newspaper editor*

Fayetteville
Smith, Stephen Austin *communications educator*

Harrison
Mathis, Kevan Eugene *journalist*

Hot Springs Village
Smith, W. Preston *publishing executive, educator, real estate broker*

Little Rock
Bell, James Winfred *retired publishing executive*
Greenberg, Paul *editor*
Hussman, Walter E., Jr., *publishing executive*
Portis, Charles McColl *reporter, writer*
Smith, Griffin *editor*

Magnolia
Reppert, James Eugene *mass communications educator*

Rogers
Angleman, Sharon Ann *journalist*

CALIFORNIA

Agoura Hills
Chagall, David *journalist, writer*
Teresi, Joseph *publishing executive*

Alhambra
Duke, Donald Norman *publishing executive*

Alpine
Greenberg, Byron Stanley *newspaper and business executive, consultant*

American Canyon
†Downer, Eugene Debs, Jr., *editor, publisher*

Anaheim
†Laderman, Kathleen Ann *magazine publisher*

Arcadia
Belnap, David F. *journalist*

Arcata
Swanson, Carolyn Rae *news reporter, counselor*

Atascadero
Rios, Evelyn Deerwester *columnist, musician, artist, writer*

Belvedere
Benet, Carol Ann Levin *journalist, teacher*

Berkeley
Bagdikian, Ben Haig *journalist, emeritus university educator*
Browne, G.M. Walter Shawn *journalist, publisher, organizer*
Cook, Geoffrey Arthur *editor, writer*
Helson, Henry Berge *publisher, retired mathematics educator*
Hertelendy, Paul *critic, writer, poet*
Lesser, Wendy *editor, writer, consultant*
Matthews, Mildred Shapley *scientific editor, freelance writer*
Selvin, David F. *retired editor, journalist*
Witt, Melvin Sylvan *periodical editor, publisher*

Beverly Hills
Blackwell, Michelle S. *media company executive*
Bland, Janeese Myra *editor*
Boyle, Barbara Dorman *motion picture company executive*
Bradshaw, Terry *sports announcer, former professional football player*
Corwin, Stanley Joel *book publisher*
Farhat, Carol Sue *motion picture company executive*
Friedman, Robert Lee *film company executive*
†Gerber, William Norman *motion picture executive*
†Grazer, Brian *film company executive*
†Grushow, Sandy *broadcast executive*
Hefner, Hugh Marston *editor-in-chief*
Heller, Paul Michael *film company executive, producer*
†Hill, David *broadcast executive*
Immerman, William Joseph *film company executive*
Lond, Harley Weldon *editor, publisher*
Paul, Gregory Marshall *motion picture and television executive*
Rosenzweig, Richard Stuart *publishing company executive*
†Rothman, Thomas Edgar *production executive*
Schneider, Charles Ivan *newspaper executive*
Stambler, Irwin *publishing executive*
Wolper, David Lloyd *motion picture and television executive*
†Zanuck, Richard Darryl *motion picture company executive*

Brisbane
Daniels, Caroline *publishing company executive*

Burbank
Ancier, Garth Richard Richard *television broadcast executive*
†Bishop, Debbie *publishing executive, book designer, writer*
Brogliatti, Barbara Spencer *television and motion picture executive*
†Daniels, Susanne *broadcast executive*
†DiBonaventure, Lorenzo *film company executive*
Eisner, Michael Dammann *entertainment company executive*
Iger, Robert A. *broadcast executive*
†Jonas, Tony *television executive*
†Kellner, Jamie *broadcasting executive*
Michel, Donald Charles *editor*
†Robertson, Richard Trafton *entertainment company executive*
†Roth, Joe *motion picture company executive*
Roth, Peter *broadcast executive*
†Sassa, Scott M. *broadcast executive*
†Schneider, Peter *film company executive*
†Schumacher, Thomas *film company executive*
Shriver, Maria Owings *news correspondent*
†Thyret, Russ *recording industry executive*
†Zucker, Jeffrey *broadcast executive*

Burlingame
Mendelson, Lee M. *film company executive, writer, producer, director*

Carlsbad
Allison, Stephen Galender *broadcast executive*
Howard, Robert Staples *newspaper publisher*

Carmel
Bohannon-Kaplan, Margaret Anne *publisher, lawyer*
Koeppel, Gary Merle *publisher, art gallery owner, writer*
Mollman, John Peter *book publisher, consultant electronic publishing*

Carson
†Rashkin, Elissa Joy *editor, writer*

Century City
†Braun, Lloyd *broadcast executive*

Chico
Stout, Robert Joe *freelance journalist*

Chino Hills
Hemenway, Stephen James *record producer, author*

Chula Vista
Blankfort, Lowell Arnold *newspaper publisher*

Coronado
Carrier, Lynne Thomson *journalist*

Cottonwood
†Fernandez, Joseph Jacob *sportscaster, basketball announcer*

Culver City
†Calley, John *motion picture company executive, film producer*
†Feltheimer, Jon *entertainment company executive*
Fisher, Lucy *motion picture company executive*
†Harris, Mel *broadcast executive*
Jarmon, Lawrence *developmental communications educator*
†Michaels, Helene *broadcast executive*
Pascal, Amy *film company executive*

†Wigan, Gareth *film company executive*

Daly City
Batlin, Robert Alfred *retired newspaper editor*

Davis
Motley, Michael Tilden *communication educator*

Downey
Wayman, Joseph McKelden *editor, researcher*

El Cerrito
Doyle, William Thomas *retired newspaper editor*

El Dorado Hills
Schlachter, Gail Ann *publishing company executive*

El Segundo
†Carey, Chase *broadcast executive*
Conrad, Paul Francis *editorial cartoonist*

Encino
Holman, Harland Eugene *retired motion picture company executive*
Rawitch, Robert Joe *journalist, educator*
Weitzman, Bernard *film company executive, consultant*

Fair Oaks
Stewart, William Thomas *communications educator*

Fall River Mills
Caldwell, Walter Edward *editor, small business owner*

Fallbrook
†Seelye, Gloria Walls *retired newswriter, public relations executive*

Fresno
Wilson, James Ross *communications educator, broadcasting executive*

Glendale
Benedict, Chuck (Charles J. Benedict Jr.) *writer, broadcaster, editor, producer*
†Katzenberg, Jeffrey *motion picture studio executive*
Kaye, Jhani *radio station manager, owner production company*
†O'Connor, (Robert) Patrick *editor*

Hanford
Harris, Mildred Staeger *retired broadcast executive*

Hollywood
†Perth, Rod *network entertainment executive*

Huntington Beach
De Massa, Jessie G. *media specialist*

Imperial
Lokey, Frank Marion, Jr., *broadcast executive, consultant*

Inglewood
Sludikoff, Stanley Robert *publisher, writer*

Irvine
Bartkus, Richard Anthony *magazine publisher*
Kaplan, Arline Ray *editor, writer*
Lesonsky, Rieva *editor*
Power, Francis William *newspaper publisher*
Stein, M(eyer) L(ewis) *journalist, magazine editor, writer*

La Jolla
Copley, David C. *newspaper publishing company executive*
Freedman, Jonathan Borwick *journalist, writer, lecturer, educator*
Hall, TennieBee M. *editor*
†Hallin, Daniel Clark *communications educator*
Harris, T. George *editor*
Hornaday, Aline Grandier *publisher, independent scholar*
Jones, Charlie *television sports announcer*

Lafayette
Alexander, Kenneth Lewis *editorial cartoonist*

Linden
Smith, Donald Richard *editor, publisher*

Loma Linda
Bell, Denise Louise *newspaper reporter, photographer, paralegal, librarian, life agent*

Long Beach
Adler, Jeffrey D. *political consultant, public affairs consultant, crisis management expert*
Bond, Frances Curtis *retired editor*
Ellis, Harriette Rothstein *editor, writer*

Los Angeles
Amos, Brice Allen *film company executive, writer*
Askin, Richard Henry, Jr., *entertainment company executive*
Bernstein, William *film company executive*
†Berry, Stephen Joseph *reporter*
†Bloomberg, Stu *broadcast executive*
†Bouju, Jean-Marc *photojournalist*
Carroll, John Sawyer *newspaper editor*
†Chernin, Peter *motion picture company executive*
†Churgin, Amy *publishing executive*
Clarke, Peter *communications and health educator*
Del Olmo, Frank *newspaper editor*
†DeLuca, Michael *film company executive*
Delugach, Albert Lawrence *journalist*
DeMartini, Frank Thomas *film company executive, lawyer*

PROFESSIONAL INDEX 6241 COMMUNICATIONS MEDIA

Dwyre, William Patrick *journalist, public speaker*
Fein, Irving Ashley *television and motion picture executive*
Field, Ted (Frederick Field) *film and record industry executive*
Findley, John Allen, Jr., *publishing executive*
Flanigan, James J(oseph) *journalist*
Gross, Larry Paul *communications educator*
Harnisch, Lawrence M. *editor*
Hart, John Lewis (Johnny Hart) *cartoonist*
†Herzog, Doug *broadcast executive*
Horowitz, David Charles *consumer commentator, newspaper columnist*
†Iovine, Jimmy *recording industry executive*
Jacobson, Sidney *editor*
Jones, Quincy *producer, composer, arranger, conductor, trumpeter*
Knittle, William Joseph, Jr., *media executive, psychologist, religious leader, management and marketing consultant, educator*
Kranwinkle, Conrad Douglas *broadcast executive*
Kristof, Kathy M. *journalist*
Langguth, Arthur John *writer, journalism educator*
Larson, Gary *cartoonist*
Lazarus, Mell *cartoonist*
†Levine, Jesse E. *publishing executive*
Maltin, Leonard *television commentator, writer*
Mann, Wesley F. *editor, writer, reporter*
†McCluggage, Kerry *television executive*
Mestres, Ricardo A., III, *motion picture company executive*
Miles, Jack (John Russiano) *journalist, educator*
†Nazario, Sonia *reporter*
Nelson, Bryce Eames *journalist, educator*
O'Reilly, Richard Brooks *journalist*
Parks, Michael Christopher *journalist*
Perlmutter, Donna *music and dance critic*
Philips, Chuck *journalist*
Phillips, Geneva Ficker *academic editor*
Plate, Thomas Gordon *newspaper columnist, educator*
Puerner, John P. *newspaper publishing executive*
Raksin, Alex *reporter*
Reich, Kenneth Irvin *journalist*
†Rense, Paige *editor, publishing company executive*
Rich, Alan *music critic, editor, author*
Rust, Patricia Joan *television/film production company executive, writer, producer*
Saltzman, Joseph *journalist, producer, educator*
Sarnoff, Thomas Warren *television executive*
†Selvin, Molly *journalist, historian*
Shaw, David Lyle *journalist, columnist*
†Shea, Fran *broadcast executive*
Shuster, Alvin *journalist, newspaper editor*
Siegel, Barry *reporter*
Sigband, Norman Bruce *management communication educator*
Sinay, Hershel David *publishing executive*
Sipchen, Bob *reporter*
Somerson, Paul *editor-in-chief*
Stern, Leonard Bernard *television and motion picture production company executive*
†Ut, Huynh Cong *photojournalist*
†Valentine, Dean *broadcast executive*
Zwick, Barry Stanley *newspaper editor, speechwriter*

Marina Del Rey
Lindheim, Richard David *television company executive, university official*

Menlo Park
Lynch, Kevin J. *publishing executive, media planner*

Mill Valley
Cohn, Bruce *film and television company executive*
Leslie, Jacques Robert, Jr., *journalist*
McNamara, Stephen *newspaper executive*

Modesto
Smith, Chester *broadcasting executive*

Monterey
Gotshall, Cordia Ann *publishing company executive, distributing executive*
†Miller, Richard Connelly *publishing executive, writer*

Monterey Park
Stapleton, Jean *journalism educator*

Mount Shasta
Stienstra, Stephani Ann *editor, writer*

National City
Beauchamp, Miles Philip *newspaper editor, columnist, education consultant*

Newport Beach
Bryant, Thomas Lee *magazine editor*
Dean, Paul John *magazine editor*
Weber, Mark Edward *editor, historian*

Northridge
Dart, John Seward *journalist, author*

Oakland
Brevetti, Francine Clelia *journalist*
Buzaljko, Grace Wilson *retired editor*
Dailey, Garrett Clark *publisher, lawyer*
George, Donald Warner *online columnist and editor, freelance writer*
Haiman, Franklyn Saul *author, communications educator*
Kelso, David William *artist, fine arts publishing executive*
McKinney, Judson Thad *broadcast executive*
Sample, Herbert Allan *reporter*
Schrag, Peter *editor, writer*
Stewart, Leslie Mueller *editor, writer*

Wood, Larry (Mary Laird) *journalist, author, university educator, public relations executive, environmental consultant*

Oceanside
Beck, Marilyn Mohr *columnist*
Villasenor, Barbara *book publisher*

Ontario
Rappaport, Michael Paul *columnist*

Pacific Grove
Davis, Robert Edward *retired communication educator*

Pacific Palisades
Hadges, Thomas Richard *media consultant, consultant*
Price, Frank *motion picture and television company executive*

Pacifica
Kelly, Kevin *editor*

Palm Desert
Ayling, Henry Faithful *writer, editor, consultant*
Godfrey, Alden Newell *communications educator*

Palm Springs
Gerard, James Wilson *publishing consultant*
Mann, Zane Boyd *editor, publisher*

Palo Alto
†Diamond, Diana Louise *editor, graphic artist*
Hamilton, David Mike *publishing company executive*
†Moran, Amanda Marie *acquisitons editor*

Pasadena
Carey, Keith Grant *editor, publishing executive*

Paso Robles
Brown, Benjamin Andrew *journalist*

Placentia
Zweifel, Donald Edwin *newspaper editor, lobbyist, consultant*

Pomona
Wirsig, Woodrow *magazine editor, trade organization executive, business executive*

Rancho Mirage
Sheldon, Deena Lynn *television camera operator*

Rancho Palos Verdes
Hillinger, Charles *journalist, writer*

Rancho Santa Fe
McNally, Connie Benson *magazine editor, publisher, antiques dealer*

Redlands
Heiss, David James *editor*

Redwood City
†Hearst, William Randolph, III, *newspaper publisher*
Martone, Massimiliano Max *telecommunications consultant*

Riverside
McLaughlin, Leighton Bates, II, *journalism educator, former newspaperman*
McQuern, Marcia Alice *newspaper publishing executive*
Robbins, Karen Diane *editor*
Sokolsky, Robert Lawrence *journalist, entertainment writer*

Sacramento
Baltake, Joe *film critic*
Belyn, David Neves *journalist, editor*
Block, Alvin Gilbert *publishing executive*
Glackin, William Charles *arts critic, editor*
Heaphy, Janis Besler *newspaper executive*
Jones, Mark Alan *broadcast technician*
†Knudson, Thomas Jeffery *journalist*
LaVally, Rebecca Jean *research editor, journalist*
†Locker, Raymond Duncan *editor*
Lundstrom, Marjie *newspaper editor and columnist*
Proud, Robert Donald (Robert Payton) *broadcast executive*
Rodriguez, Rick *newspaper executive editor*
Shaw, Eleanor Jane *newspaper editor*
Walsh, Denny Jay *reporter*

San Diego
†Bell, Gene *newspaper publishing executive*
†Benedyk, Mika Ono *editor, writer*
Borden, Diane Lynn *communications educator*
Fike, Edward Lake *newspaper editor*
Kaufman, Julian Mortimer *broadcasting company executive, consultant*
Klein, Herbert George *newspaper editor*
Krulak, Victor Harold *newspaper executive*
Kyle, Robert Campbell, II, *publishing executive*
Manifold, Gregory Lee *sportswriter*
Morgan, Neil *writer, newspaper editor, lecturer, columnist*
Owen, Charles Theodore *journalist, publisher*
Pincus, Robert Lawrence *art critic, cultural historian*
Rowe, Peter A. *newspaper columnist*
Steen, Paul Joseph *retired broadcasting executive*
Willis, Norman Hunt *author, writer, director, producer*
Winner, Karin E. *editor*

San Francisco
Bentley, Lisa *publisher*
Berlandt, Herman Joseph *editor, publisher*
Blakey, Scott Chaloner *journalist, writer*
Bronstein, Phil *executive editor*
Cameron, Heather Anne *publishing executive*
Chapin, Dwight Allan *columnist, writer*
Chase, Marilyn *journalist*
Dickey, Glenn Ernest, Jr., *sports columnist*
Duscha, Julius Carl *journalist*
Eastwood, Susan *medical scientific editor*
Elmore, Matthew Bret *radio, television announcer*
Falk, Steven B. *newspaper publishing executive*
Garchik, Leah Lieberman *journalist*
German, William *newspaper editor*
Graysmith, Robert *political cartoonist, author*
Hale, Cecil *communications educator, finance educator*
Hochschild, Adam *writer, commentator, journalist*
Johns, Roy (Bud Johns) *publisher, writer*
Mason, Greg *publishing executive*
McKean, Kevin S. *editor-in-chief, editor, writer*
†Pazour, Don *publishing executive*
Perlman, David *science editor, journalist*
†Riggenbach, Jeff *journalist*
Risser, James Vaulx, Jr., *journalist, educator*
Rogoff, Alice Elizabeth *writer, editor*
†Rosen, Evan Mark *executive communication advisor, journalist*
Rubenstein, Steven Paul *newspaper columnist*
Rusher, William Allen *writer, commentator*
Schwarz, Glenn Vernon *newspaper editor*
Sias, John B. *former multi-media company executive, newspaper publisher, publishing executive*
Susskind, Teresa Gabriel *publishing executive*
†White, Timothy *newspaper publisher*
Winn, Steven Jay *critic*

San Gabriel
Fry, Donald Owen *broadcasting company executive*

San Jose
Carey, Peter Kevin *reporter*
†Ceppos, Jerome Merle *newspaper editor*
Doctor, Kenneth Jay *publishing executive*
†Harris, Jay Terrence *communications educator*
†Ingle, Robert D. *newspaper editor, newspaper executive*
Natoli, Joe *newspaper publishing executive*
Rockstroh, Dennis John *journalist*
†Schneider, Hilary A. *publishing executive*
Woldt, Harold Frederick, Jr., *newspaper publishing executive*

San Mateo
†Nizard, Michael *editor-in-chief*

San Pedro
Bowling, Lance Christopher *record producer, publishing executive*

San Rafael
Sansweet, Stephen Jay *journalist, author, marketing executive*

Santa Ana
Anderson, N. Christian, III, *newspaper publisher*
†Balzer, Robert Lawrence *journalist*
†Gudea, Darlene *publishing company executive*
Katz, Tonnie *newspaper editor*
Kinosian, Janet Marie *journalist*
†Lehrer, John *editor*

Santa Barbara
Ackerman, Marshall *publishing company executive*
Brantingham, Barney *journalist, writer*
Brilliant, Ashleigh Ellwood *writer, cartoonist, publisher, educator*
Brown, J'Amy Maroney *journalist, media relations consultant, investor*
Campbell, William Steen *publishing executive, writer, speaker*
Dubroff, Henry Allen *newspaper editor, publisher*
Gibney, Frank Bray *publisher, editor, writer, foundation executive*
Roberts, Jerry *newspaper editor*

Santa Cruz
Young, Gary Eugene *editor, poet*

Santa Monica
Baer, Walter S. *research executive*
†Block, Bill *film company executive*
Halperin, Stuart *entertainment company executive*
Israel, David *journalist, screenwriter, producer*
†Lewis, Leslie Joy *music company executive, artist*
†Littlefield, Warren *television executive*
†Malin, Amir *film company executive*
†Mancuso, Frank G. *entertainment and communications company executive*
†McGurk, Christopher *film company executive*
Palmatier, Malcolm Arthur *editor, consultant*
†Rifkin, Arnold *film company executive*
Rush, Herman E. *television executive*
†Whalley, Tom *recording industry executive*
†Yemenidjian, Alex *film company executive*

Santa Rosa
Callum, Myles *magazine editor, writer*
Person, Evert Bertil *newspaper and radio executive*
Swofford, Robert Lee *newspaper editor, journalist*

Sausalito
Hansen, Charles Morton *editor, retired military officer*

Seal Beach
Caesar, Vance Roy *newspaper executive*

Seaside
†May, James Harvey *communications educator*

Sherman Oaks
Yasnyi, Allan David *communications company executive*

Sierra Madre
Dewey, Donald William *magazine publisher, editor, writer*

Sonoma
Beckmann, Jon Michael *publishing company executive*

South Pasadena
Mantell, Suzanne Ruth *editor*

Stanford
Andreopoulos, Spyros George *writer*
Baker, Patricia Ann *publishing executive*
Breitrose, Henry S. *communications educator*
Kennedy, Donald *editor, environmental scientist, educator*
Roberts, Donald Frank, Jr., *communications educator*

Stockton
Lovell, Emily Kalled *retired journalist*

Summerland
Cannon, Louis Simeon *journalist, author*
Hall, Lee Boaz *publishing company consultant, author*

Sunnyvale
†Coleman, Gregory G. *former magazine publisher*

Tehachapi
Mitchell, Betty Jo *writer, publisher*

Thousand Oaks
Ames, Steven Edmund *journalist, educator*
Ferber, Samuel *publishing executive*

Toluca Lake
Ragan, Ann Talmadge *media and production consultant, actor*

Torrance
Sperling, Irene R. *publishing executive*

Tujunga
Loehwing, Rudi Charles, Jr., *publicist, radio broadcasting executive, journalist*

Ukiah
Martin-Gall, Jennie Marie *editor*

Universal City
†Fleishman, Susan Nahley *media consultant*
Geffen, David *recording company executive, producer*
†Mulligan, Brian *film company executive*
Snider, Stacey *film company executive*

Valley Springs
Anema-Garten, Durlynn C. *communications educator, counselor, writer*

Van Nuys
†Becker, Frawley *film company executive*

Ventura
Greig, William Taber, II, *publishing company executive*
Kirman, Charles Gary *photojournalist*

Vista
Linhart, Letty Lemon *editor*

Walnut Creek
Anderberg, Roy A. *journalist*
Borenstein, Daniel Asa *newspaper political editor*
Pfeiffer, Phyllis Kramer *publishing executive*
Satz, Louis K. *publishing executive*
Trousdale, Stephen Richard *newspaper editor*

Watsonville
Condon, Thomas Joseph *editor, writer*

West Hollywood
†Kaplan, Andy *broadcast executive*

Whittier
Loughrin, Jay Richardson *mass communications educator, consultant*

Wilton
Harrison, George Harry, III, (Hank Harrison) *publishing executive, author*

Woodland Hills
Anastasi, Michael Anton *journalist*
Deters, Thomas C. *editor-in-chief, educator*
DeWitt, Barbara Jane *journalist*
†Harris, Barbara S. *publishing executive*
Schueler, John R. *newspaper executive*
Shuster, Fred Todd *journalist, commentator*

Yreka
Smith, Vin *sports editor, business owner, novelist*

COLORADO

Aspen
Hayes, Mary Eshbaugh *editor, writer*

Berthoud
Davis, Donald Alan *news correspondent, writer, lecturer*

Boulder
Birosik, PJ *music company executive*
Clos, Lynne Mobley *magazine publisher, paleontologist*
Horii, Naomi *editor*
†Kellogg, Dale M *editor*
Rienner, Lynne Carol *publishing executive*

Centennial
Ulevich, Neal Hirsh *photojournalist*

Cherry Hills Village
Stapleton, Katharine Hall (Katie Stapleton) *food broadcaster, writer*

Colorado Springs
†Brander, Bruce George *international journalist, author*
Mansfield, Roger Leo *astronomy and space publisher*
Mehlis, David Lee *publishing executive*
Zapel, Arthur Lewis *book publishing executive*

Denver
Barbour, Alton Bradford *human communication studies educator*
Brom, Libor *journalist, educator*
†Clarkson, Richard Clair *publisher, editor, photographer*
Dance, Francis Esburn Xavier *communication educator*
Drake, Sylvie (Jurras Drake) *theater critic*
†Elliman, Donald M., Jr., *magazine publisher and executive*
Engdahl, Todd Philip *editor*
Grilly, Gerald E. *publishing executive*
Milstead, John David *reporter*
Moore, Gregory L. *editor*
Mowry, Frank Henry *journalist, photojournalist*
Price, Kathleen McCormick *book editor, writer*
Rothman, Paul Alan *publishing executive*
Saltz, Howard Joel *newspaper editor*
Singleton, Dean *publishing executive*
Temple, John R. *publishing executive*
Weinberg, Hedy Leah *journalist*
Willbanks, Roger Paul *publishing and book distributing company executive*
Zimmer, Larry William, Jr., *sports announcer*

Durango
Ballantine, Morley Cowles (Mrs. Arthur Atwood Ballantine) *newspaper editor*
Van Mols, Brian *publishing executive*

Evergreen
Dobbs, Gregory Allan *journalist*

Fort Collins
†Buddenbaum, Judith M. *communications educator, writer*
Christiansen, Norman Juhl *retired newspaper publisher*
Hallahan, Kirk Edward *journalism educator*
MacLauchlin, Robert Kerwin *communications artist, educator*
May, Stephen James *communications educator, writer*
Sons, Raymond William *journalist*

Georgetown
Stern, Mort(imer) P(hillip) *journalism and communications educator, academic administrator, consultant*

Golden
Baron, Robert Charles *publishing executive*
Henderson, Sabrina Nicole *journalist*

Granby
Johnson, William Potter *newspaper publisher*

Gunnison
Venturo, Frank Angelo *communications educator, college offical*

Littleton
Bennett, Janice Lynn *publisher, educator*
†Ergen, Charles *communications professional*
†Ingui, Nicolle Eileen *journalist*
Udevitz, Norman *publishing executive*

Longmont
Pattyn, Sue *publishing executive*

Morrison
Myers, Harry J., Jr., *retired publisher*

Pueblo
Rawlings, Robert Hoag *newspaper publisher*

Westminster
Wirkkala, John Lester *cable company executive*

CONNECTICUT

Bethel
Shepard, Jean Heck *publishing company consultant, author, agent*

Bridgeport
Henderson, Albert Kossack *publishing company executive, dairy executive, consultant*
Simoneau, Cynthia Lambert *newspaper editor, journalism educator*

Bridgewater
Crooke, Robert Andrew *media consultant, writer, educator*

Bristol
†Bodenheimer, George *broadcast executive*
Eisen, Rich *reporter*

Brookfield
Reynolds, Jean Edwards *publishing executive*

Chester
Frost-Knappman, Elizabeth (Linda Elizabeth Frost-Knappman) *editor, author, executive*

Cos Cob
Barnard, Charles Nelson *editorial consultant, author*
Hauptman, Michael *broadcasting company executive*

Danbury
Bascom, Lionel Cyril *writer, educator*

Darien
Bigelow, Jonathan Lehr *editor, publishing executive*
Brooke, Avery Rogers *publisher, writer*

Deep River
Cobb, Hubbard Hanford *magazine editor, writer*

Easton
Enos, Randall *cartoonist, illustrator*
Lorenz, Lee Sharp *cartoonist*

Fairfield
Eigel, Marcia Duffy *editor*
Hodgkinson, William James *publishing executive*
Kaff, Albert Ernest *journalist, author*
Spence, Barbara E. *publishing company executive*
Wright, Robert *broadcasting executive*

Greens Farms
Deford, Frank *sportswriter, television and radio commentator, author*

Greenwich
Angel, Jack Easton *publishing executive*
Collins, Richard Lawrence *magazine editor, publisher, author*
Engstrom, Erik *private equity investor*
Keogh, James *journalist*
Moffly, John Wesley, IV, *magazine publishing executive*
Rukeyser, Louis Richard *economic commentator*
Sweeney, Michael Andrew *newspaper editor*
van Rosendaal, John *journalist*

Hartford
Davis, Jack Wayne, Jr., *publishing executive*
Englehart, Robert Wayne, Jr., *cartoonist*
Harden, Jon Bixby *publishing executive*
Keating, Christopher Patrick *reporter*
Noel, Don Obert, Jr., *retired newspaper columnist*
Pach, Peter Barnard *newspaper columnist and editor*
Toolan, Brian Paul *newspaper editor*

Ivoryton
Bendig, William Charles *editor, artist, publisher*

Lakeville
Estabrook, Robert Harley *journalist*

Madison
Egbert, Emerson Charles *retired publisher*
Falk, Peter Hastings *publishing company executive, author, art dealer*
Purcell, Bradford Moore *publishing company executive*

Mansfield Center
Petrus, Robert Thomas *internet business owner, real estate investor*

Middletown
Balay, Robert Elmore *editor, reference librarian*

Moodus
Cumming, Robert Emil *editor, writer*

New Britain
†Martin, Vivian Bonita *journalist, educator*

New Haven
Caplan, Lincoln *journalist*
†Donatich, John E *publishing executive, writer*
McClatchy, J. D. *editor, writer, educator*
Ryden, John Graham *publishing executive*

New Milford
†Nadeau, Coni (Concetta) *editor, writer*

Newington
Zeldes, Edith R. *freelance journalist*

Newtown
Cayne, Bernard Stanley *editor*

Norfolk
†Smith, Patrick Lawrence *journalist*

Norwalk
DeCesare, Donald E. *broadcasting executive*
†White, Rick *publishing executive*

Old Greenwich
Dixon, John Morris *magazine editor*

Ridgefield
Richard, David Dean *publishing executive*

Sharon
Gordon, Nicholas *broadcasting executive*

Sherman
Valeriani, Richard Gerard *news broadcaster*

Southbury
Barry, Edward William *retired publisher*
Vega, Marylois Purdy *journalist*
†Wolsch, Robert Allen *communication educator*

Stamford
Beck, Angel C. *columnist, screenwriter, educator, film director*
Britt, Glenn Alan *media company executive*
Chisholm, Colin Alexander Joseph, III, *media professional*
Fein, Ronnie *writer, journalist*
Harrington, Richard J. *information business executive*
Kisseberth, Paul Barto *retired publishing executive*
Wilensky, Julius M. *publishing company executive*

Stonington
Elliott, Osborn *journalist, educator, urban activist, former dean*

Storrs Mansfield
Maier, Romulus *journalist*

Stratford
Cox, Richard Joseph *former broadcasting executive*

Torrington
Di Russo, Terry *communications educator, writer*

Trumbull
†Binder, Steven F. *publishing executive*
†Fox, Mitchell B. *magazine publisher*
Harty, Thomas H. *publishing executive*
Seitz, Nicholas Joseph *magazine editor, journalist*

Vernon Rockville
Orr, Jim (James D. Orr) *editor, writer*

Waterbury
Pape, William James, II, *newspaper publisher*

Waterford
Walsh, Peter Joseph *multimedia marketing professional*

West Haven
Ellis, Lynn Webster *management educator, telecommunications consultant*

Weston
Wiseman, Carter Sterling *editor, writer, educator*

Westport
Abel, Alan Irwin *film company executive*
Kramer, Sidney B. *publisher, lawyer, literary agent*
McCormack, Donald Paul *newspaper consultant*
Murphy, Thomas John *publishing executive*
Ross, John Michael *editor, magazine publisher*
Stern, Robert D. *publishing executive*
Woog, Dan *journalist*

Wethersfield
†Jenks, Dennis *publishing executive*
†Osborne, Louise *publishing executive*

Wilton
†Tarde, Gerard (Jerry) *magazine executive*

DELAWARE

Dover
†Lewis, Larry *communications educator, video producer*
Smyth, Joel Douglas *newspaper executive*

Millsboro
Kettinger, David John *broadcast executive*

New Castle
Cansler, Leslie Ervin *retired newspaper editor*
Henley, Deborah *newspaper editor*

Newark
†Jackson, M.(arvin) Dennis *journalism educator, writer*

DISTRICT OF COLUMBIA

Washington
Adams, Robert Edward *journalist*
Aguirre-Baca, Francisco *publisher, consultant*
Allen, William Kent *journalist*
†Allen, William L. *editor*
Amolsch, Arthur Lewis *publishing executive*
Andrews, John Frank *editor, author, educator*
Apple, Raymond Walter, Jr., *journalist*
Arana, Marie *editor, writer*
†Archibald, George *reporter*
Arena, Kelli *news correspondent*
Arnold, Gary Howard *film critic*
Arnovitz, Benton Mayer *editor*
Asker, James Robert *magazine editor*
†Atcheson, Richard *editor*
†Atkinson, Lawrence Rush, IV, (Rick Atkinson) *journalist*
Atlas, Terry *journalist*
Bailey, Charles Waldo, II, *journalist, author*
Bandow, Douglas Leighton *editor, columnist, policy consultant*
Barber, Ben Bernard Andrew *journalist*
Beach, Walter Eggert *retired publishing organization executive*
Beale, Betty (Mrs. George K. Graeber) *columnist, writer*
Bern, Paula Ruth *columnist*
Bird, Kai *journalist, historian*
Bohannon, Camille *news anchor*
†Boo, Katherine *newswriter*
Boyce, Clayton Winfred *magazine publisher, editor*
Boyle, Patrick Kevin *journalist*
Bradlee, Benjamin Crowninshield *executive editor*
Branegan, James Augustus, III, *journalist*
Brant, Donna Marie *journalist*
Braverman, Jordan *columnist*
Brazaitis, Thomas Joseph *journalist*
Broder, David Salzer *reporter, writer*
Brown, John Patrick *newspaper executive, financial consultant*
Bruzelius, Nils Johan Axel *journalist*
Butterworth, Ritajean Hartung *broadcast executive*
Canning, Michael Paul *movie reviewer, film essayist*
Clift, Eleanor *magazine correspondent*
Clurman, Michael *newspaper publishing executive*
Clymer, Adam *newspaper correspondent*
Cocco, Marie Elizabeth *journalist*
†Cohen, Richard Edward *journalist*
Cohen, Sarah *reporter*
Coll, Stephen Wilson *editor*
Conroy, Sarah Booth *columnist, novelist, speaker*
Cook, Charles Edward, Jr., *editor, political analyst*
Cook, David *editor*
Cosby, Rita Karen *newscaster*
Cosgrove, John Patrick *editor*
Cowan, Edward *journalist, editor*
Cowen, Eugene Sherman *broadcasting executive*
Crenshaw, Albert Burford *journalist*
Crewdson, John Mark *journalist, author*
Crock, Stanley Miles *journalist*
Curtiss, Richard Holden *magazine editor, writer*
Cutler, Bernard Joseph *editor-in-chief, writer*
Cutler, Carol Ann *food writer, consultant*
Dalglish, Arthur Ray *journalist*
Davidson, Lee Howard *reporter*
Davidson, Susan Bettina *editor, writer*
Davis, Evelyn Y. *editor, writer, publisher, investor*
Davis, Garry (S. Gareth Davis)
de Borchgrave, Arnaud *editor, writer, lecturer*
Deeb, Mary-Jane *editor, educator*
Denlinger, John Kenneth *journalist*
Devens, Richard Mather *publishing executive, economist*
Dillin, John Woodward, Jr., *retired newspaper editor, correspondent*
Doan, Michael Frederick *editor*
Donaldson, Samuel Andrew *journalist*
Donlan, Thomas Garrett *journalist*
Donohoe, Cathryn Murray *journalist*
Dorn, James Andrew *editor*
Dowd, Maureen *columnist*
Downie, Leonard, Jr., *editor, writer*
Drew, Elizabeth *television commentator, journalist, author*
†Duffy, Brian *editor*
Dujack, Stephen Raymond *editor*
Eaton, Sabrina Catherine Elizabeth *journalist*
Eby, Lloyd Martin *editor, writer, educator, filmmaker*
Edsall, Thomas Byrne *reporter*
Edwards, Bob (Robert Alan Edwards) *radio news anchor*
Elfin, Mel *magazine editor*
Elsasser, Glen Robert *journalist*
Elsberg, John William *editor-in-chief*
Epstein, Sidney *retired editor*
Faherty, Robert Louis *publishing executive*
†Fahey, John M., Jr., *book publishing executive*
Feld, Karen Irma *columnist, journalist, broadcaster, public speaker*
Fhanks, Hershel *editor, writer*
Fields, Suzanne Bregman *syndicated columnist*
Flattau, Edward *columnist*
Flintoff, Corey Alan *radio newscaster, writer*
Franzen, Byron T. (John Franzen) *media specialist*
†Friedman, Thomas Loren *foreign correspondent*
†Fritts, Edward O. *broadcast executive*
Galloway, Joseph Lee, Jr., *writer, journalist*
Garrish, Theodore John *publishing executive*
Gart, Murray Joseph *journalist, consultant*
Geyer, Georgie Anne *syndicated columnist, educator, author, biographer, TV commentator*
Gibson, Florence Anderson *talking book company executive, narrator*
Gillis, Justin Howard *journalist*
Glaser, Vera Romans *journalist*
Glass, Andrew James *newspaper editor*
Glassman, James Kenneth *editor, writer, publishing executive*
Graham, Donald Edward *publishing company executive*
Greenhouse, Linda Joyce *journalist*
Greenwood, William Warren *journalist*
Gregory, Bettina Louise *journalist*
Groner, Jonathan Jacob *periodical editor, freelance writer, lawyer*
†Grosvenor, Gilbert Melville *journalist, educator, business executive*
Gutman, Roy William *reporter*
Guzy, Carol *photojournalist*
Gwaltney, Corbin *editor, publishing executive*
†Hailu, Brook *media analyst, analyst*
Halsey, Ashley, III, *newspaper editor*
Halton, David Campbell *journalist*
Harper, Jennifer *journalist, entertainer*
Hartman, Carl (Howard Carl Hartman) *reporter*
Hecht, Marjorie Mazel *editor*
Hennig, Bertrand Randy *journalist, commentator*
Henry, John Cooper *journalist*
Herman, Andrea Maxine *newspaper editor*
Herman, George Edward *radio and television correspondent*
†Hiatt, Fred *editorial editor*
Hiebert, Ray Eldon *educator, author, consultant*
Higham, Scott *reporter*
Hinden, Stanley Jay *newspaper editor*
Hoagland, Jimmie Lee *newspaper editor*
Horwitz, Sari *reporter*
Hoyt, Clark Freeland *journalist, newspaper editor*
Hume, Brit (Alexander Britton Hume) *journalist*
†Hunt, Albert R. *newspaper executive*
†Hunter, Stephen *film critic, writer*
Irvine, Reed John *media critic, corporation executive*
James, Bruce Richard *information specialist*
Jaschik, Scott P. *editor*
Jepsen, Peter Lee *court reporter*
Johnson, Richard Kent *publishing executive*
†Johnson, Robert Louis *cable television company executive*
Jones, Boisfeuillet, Jr., *publishing executive*

Joo, Douglas D.M. *newspaper and video production executive*
Jordan, Anne E. Dollerschell *journalist*
†Jordan, Mary *editor-in-chief, reporter*
Joyce, Anne Raine *editor, director of publications*
Kaiser, Robert Greeley *newspaper editor*
Kempley, Rita A. *film critic, editor*
Kilborn, Peter Thurston *journalist*
Kilian, Michael David *journalist, columnist, writer*
†King, Colbert Isaiah *editor*
King, Larry (Larry Zeiger) *broadcaster, radio personality*
King, Llewellyn Willings *publisher, lecturer, journalist, commentator*
Kiplinger, Knight A. *journalist, publisher*
Kirk, Donald *journalist*
Klass, Philip Julian *technical journalist, electrical engineer*
Klose, Kevin *broadcast executive*
Knight, Athelia Wilhelmenia *journalist*
Koppel, Ted *broadcast journalist*
Kristol, William *editor, political analyst*
Laessig, Walter Bruce *publishing executive*
†Lamb, Brian P. *broadcast executive*
Lambro, Donald Joseph *columnist*
Lardner, George, Jr., *journalist, author*
Larson, George Charles *magazine editor, writer*
Lawson, Jennifer *broadcast executive*
†Lazado, Carlos Edvardo *journalist*
LeBrecht, Thelma Jane Mossman *reporter*
†Lee, Debra L. *broadcast executive*
Leeds, Charles Alan *publishing executive*
Leubsdorf, Carl Philipp *publishing executive*
Levey, Robert Frank *newspaper columnist*
Lewis, Charles Joseph *journalist*
Lewis, Robert David Gilmore *retired editor*
Lindberg, Tod Marshall *editor, writer*
Lorsung, Thomas Nicholas *news service editor*
Lubar, Jeffrey Stuart *journalist, trade association executive*
Luxenberg, Steven Marc *newspaper editor*
†Lyden, Jacki Lyn *journalist, writer*
†Mankiewicz, Frank F. *journalist, writer*
Margolis, Doris May Rosenberg *editor, writer*
McBee, Susanna Barnes *retired journalist*
McCaslin, John Larson *political columnist*
McFeatters, Ann Carey *journalist*
†Means, Marianne *political columnist*
Melendy, David Russell *broadcast journalist*
Melton, Carol A(nne) *corporate executive*
Merry, Robert William *publishing executive*
†Miller, Alan *newswriter*
Mitchell, Andrea *journalist*
Moore, Miles David *journalist*
†Moser, Donald Bruce *magazine editor*
Moss, Madison Scott *editor*
Mowlana, Hamid *international relations and communication educator*
†Nesmith, Jeff *journalist*
Novak, Robert David Sanders *newspaper columnist, television commentator*
O'Brien, Soledad *newscaster, news anchor*
O'Brien, Timothy Andrew *writer, journalist, lawyer, educator*
Oka, Takashi *journalist, consultant, educator*
Ottaway, David Blackburne *journalist*
†Page, Clarence E. *newspaper columnist*
Page, Tim *music critic, writer, producer*
Peck, Louis Moses *editor*
Peirce, Neal R. *journalist*
Perkins, Lucian *photographer*
Peters, Charles Given, Jr., *editor*
Pincus, Walter Haskell *editor*
Putzel, Michael *journalist, entrepreneur*
Randell, Cortes W. *news service executive*
Rankin, Robert Arthur *journalist*
Ridgeway, James Fowler *journalist*
Rogers, Warren Joseph, Jr., *journalist*
Rosen, Gerald Robert *editor*
Russert, Timothy John *broadcast journalist, executive*
Safire, William *journalist, author*
Salant, Jonathan D. *reporter*
Samsot, Robert Louis *newspaper editor, consultant*
Satin, Mark *editor, lawyer*
Scheibel, Kenneth Maynard *journalist*
Schieffer, Bob *broadcast journalist*
Schram, Martin Jay *journalist*
Scoblic, J. Peter *journalist*
Seidman, L(ewis) William *television commentator, publisher*
Shanks, Judith Weil *editor*
Shannon, Donald Hawkins *retired editor*
Shapiro, Walter Elliot *political columnist*
Sheehan, Neil *reporter, scholarly writer*
Shenon, Philip *journalist*
Shosky, John Edwin *communications consultant, speechwriter*
Sidey, Hugh Swanson *correspondent*
Siegel, Robert Charles *broadcast journalist*
Silver, Brian Quayle *broadcast journalist, musician, educator*
Simons, Carol Lenore *magazine editor*
†Slafka, Kristi Lynne *journalist*
Smith, Dean *communications advisor, arbitrator*
Smith, Stephen Grant *communications executive*
Snow, Robert Anthony *journalist*
Sperling, Godfrey, Jr., *journalist*
Stern, Carl Leonard *former news correspondent, federal official*
†Sullivan, Kevin *editor-in-chief, reporter*
Tabor, Mary Leeba
Terzian, Philip Henry *journalist*
Theis, Paul Anthony *publishing executive*
Thomas, Helen A. (Mrs. Douglas B. Cornell) *newspaper bureau executive*
Tiede, Tom Robert *journalist*
Tolchin, Martin *retired newspaper reporter, author*
Toledano, Ralph De *columnist, author, poet*
Toles, Thomas Gregory *editorial cartoonist*
Tolson, John J. *writer, editor*
Totenberg, Nina *journalist*
Trafford, Abigail *columnist, editor, writer*
Turner, Douglas Laird *writer, editor, columnist*
Turner, Ted (Robert Edward Turner) *former television executive, philanthropist*
Utley, Jon Basil *think tank director, journalist*
†Valenti, Jack Joseph *motion picture executive*
Warren, Albert *publishing executive*
Warren, Clay *communication educator*
Watson, William Hughes *news service publisher, network executive*
Weinberger, Caspar Willard *publishing executive, former secretary of defense*
†Weymouth, Elizabeth Morris Graham (Lally Weymouth) *editor, columnist*
†White, Keith Andrew *publishing executive, writer*
White, Robert M., II, *newspaper executive, editor, publisher*
Whitelaw, Kevin John *journalist*
Wiener, Leonard *journalist*
Williams, Earl Patrick, Jr., *editor, freelance writer*
†Williams, James R., III, *broadcast executive*
Winfrey, Carey Wells *journalist, magazine editor*
Winter, Thomas Swanson *editor, newspaper executive*
Witcover, Jules Joseph *newspaper columnist, author*
Woodruff, Judy Carline *broadcast journalist*
Woodward, Robert Upshur *newspaper reporter, writer*
Yardley, Jonathan *journalist*
Young, Thomas Wade *journalist, pilot*
Zwadiuk, Oleh *radio executive*

FLORIDA

Amelia Island
Britt, David Van Buren *retired educational communications executive*

Aventura
Babson, Irving K. *publishing company executive*
Perkel, Robert Simon *photojournalist, educator*

Big Pine Key
Harris, Douglas Clay *retired newspaper executive*

Boca Grande
Heffernan, John William *retired journalist*

Boca Raton
Coz, Steve *editorial director*
Levine, Irving Raskin *news commentator, university dean, author, lecturer*
McQueen, Scott Robert *broadcasting company executive*

Boynton Beach
Kempner, Marvin A. *broadcasting corporation executive*
Klein, Bernard *publishing company executive*
Oppler, Ralph Leo *retired publishing executive, advertising executive*

Bradenton
Crouthamel, Thomas Grover, Sr., *editor, consultant*
McFarland, Richard Macklin *retired journalist*
White, Dale Andrew *journalist*

Clearwater
VanMeer, Mary Ann *publisher, writer, researcher, webmaster*
†Warden, Jo Ann Griffith *retired journalist*

Coral Gables
Roberts, Samuel Smith *television news executive*

Coral Springs
†Medina-Salinas, Elizabeth *publishing executive, writer*

Daytona Beach
Davidson, Herbert M., Jr., (Tippen Davidson) *newspaper owner*

Deerfield Beach
†Drucker, Lisa K. *editor*

Delray Beach
Robinson, Brenda Kay *editor, public relations professional*
Salsberg, Arthur Philip *publishing company executive*
Siegel, Ira T. *publishing executive*

Dover
Pearson, Walter Donald *editor, columnist*

Fort Lauderdale
Bolanos, Michael Templeton *new media executive*
Eisner, Will *publishing company executive*
Gremillion, Robert *publishing executive*
Markus, Robert Michael *journalist, retired*
Maucker, Earl Robert *newspaper editor, newspaper executive*
Skellings, Edmund *communications educator, poet*
Williamson, William Paul, Jr., *journalist*

Fort Myers
Barbour, William Rinehart, Jr., *retired book publisher*

Gainesville
Barber, Charles Edward *newspaper executive, journalist*
Bedell, George Chester *retired publisher, educator, priest*
Hollien, Harry Francis *speech and communications scientist, educator*
Kaid, Lynda Lee *communications educator*
Kaplan, John *photojournalist, educator, consultant*
Kelly, Kathleen S(ue) *communications educator*
Maple, Marilyn Jean *educational media coordinator*
†Ross, Melanie Fridl *journalist, writer*

Hallandale
Schatken, Nancy Leah *medical editor*
Yigit, Nuyan *journalist*

Hialeah
†Hernandez, Roland *broadcast executive*

Highland Beach
Zagoria, Sam D(avid) *reporter, government official, educator*

Hillsboro Beach
Gibbons, Celia Victoria Townsend (Mrs. John Sheldon) *editor, publisher*

Hollywood
†Alfano, Jorge *music company executive, counselor*
Blakley, John Clyde *telecommunications consultant*

Holmes Beach
McCartney, James Harold *newspaper columnist, educator, journalist*

Jacksonville
Barrow, Sally Settle *media specialist, librarian*
Brown, Lloyd Harcourt, Jr., *newspaper editor*
Davis, Fred *journalist, educator*
Hartmann, Frederick William *newspaper editor*
Koeppel, Mary Sue *communications educator*
Vincent, Norman Fuller *broadcasting executive*
Walters, John Sherwood *retired newspaperman*

Key Biscayne
Smith, Harrison Harvey *journalism consultant*

Lake Worth
Asher, Kathleen May *communications educator*

Lakeland
Perez, Louis Michael *newspaper editor*

Largo
Szep, Paul Michael *editorial cartoonist*

Longboat Key
Gilbert, Hamlin Miller, Jr., *publishing executive*

Longwood
O'Keefe, Maurice Timothy *editor, author, photographer, educator*

Lutz
Kolb, Richard Maurice *sports writer, sportscaster*

Marco Island
†Sinoradzki, Felicia Teresa *journalist*
Wheeler, Warren G(age), Jr., *retired publishing executive*

Melbourne
Eberle, Terry R. *editor, newspaper executive*

Miami
Barry, Dave *columnist, author*
Birsh, Arthur Thomas *publishing executive*
Black, Creed Carter *newspaper executive*
Chapman, Alvah Herman, Jr., *newspaper executive*
Dahlburg, John-Thor Theodore *newspaper correspondent*
de Leon, Lidia Maria *magazine editor*
†Diaz, Alan *photojournalist*
Fichtner, Margaria *journalist*
†Fiedler, Tom *editor-in-chief*
Foster, Kathryn Warner *newspaper editor*
†Garvin, Glenn *journalist, writer*
Hampton, John Lewis *retired newspaper editor*
Ibarguen, Alberto *newspaper executive*
Lawrence, David, Jr., *journalist, early childhood development advocate*
Lew, Salvador *radio station executive*
Lewis, John Milton *cable television company executive*
Miller, Gene Edward *newspaper reporter and editor*
Muir, Helen *journalist, author*
Pope, John Edwin, III, *newspaper sports editor, columnist*
Russell, James Webster, Jr., *newspaper editor, columnist*
Savage, James Francis *editor*
Wax, William Edward *photojournalist*

Middleburg
King, Leo *journalist*

Naples
Blevins, Charles Russell *publishing executive*
Breitenstein, David E. *newswriter*
Burdick, Robert W. *newspaper editor*
Clapp, Roger Howland *retired publishing executive*
Cobb, Brian Eric *broadcasting executive*
Dill, John Francis *retired publishing company executive*
†Miller, Donald *art critic, writer*
Penniman, Nicholas Griffith, IV, *retired newspaper publisher*
Taishoff, Lawrence Bruce *publishing company executive*

North Miami
Kopenhaver, Lillian Lodge *journalism educator*

North Palm Beach
Edwards, William James *broadcasting executive*
Lavine, Alan *columnist, writer*

North Port
Coe, Laurie Lynne Barker *photojournalist, artist*
Hill, Wallace Harry *sports television consultant*

Ocala
Stock, Stephen Michael *broadcast journalist*

Orlando
†Bredin, Brenda Ann *communications educator*
Dunn, William Bruna, III, *journalist*
†Franklin, Timothy A. *editor-in-chief, editor*
Healy, Jane Elizabeth *newspaper editor*
Waltz, Kathleen M. *publishing executive*

Ormond Beach
Phillips, Marti *editor*

Palm Beach
Monath, Norman *publishing company executive*
Pryor, Hubert *editor, writer*
Rukeyser, M.S., Jr., *television consultant, writer*

Palm Beach Gardens
†Kline, Adrienne Marie *news producer*
Rigby, Paul Crispin *artist, cartoonist*

Palm Coast
Franco, Annemarie Woletz *editor*

Palm Harbor
Barker, Larry Lee *communications educator, educator*

Parrish
Wood, Rev. Dr. Benton *retired editor, priest*

Pensacola
Bowden, Jesse Earle *newspaper editor, author, cartoonist, journalism educator*

Pompano Beach
Roen, Sheldon R. *publisher, psychologist*

Port Saint Lucie
Sommers, Robert Thomas *editor, publisher, author*

Punta Gorda
Miles, Frank Charles *retired newspaper executive*

Saint Augustine
Nolan, Joseph Thomas *journalism educator, communications consultant*

Saint Petersburg
Barnes, Andrew Earl *newspaper executive*
Belich, John Patrick, Sr., *journalist*
Benbow, Charles Clarence *retired writer, critic*
†Buchan, Russell Paul *publisher, gas company executive, entrepreneur*
Corty, Andrew P. *publishing executive*
Favre, Gregory *publishing executive*
Haiman, Robert James *newspaper editor, journalism educator, media consultant*
Hooker, Robert Wright *journalist*
Jenkins, Robert Norman *reporter, editor*
Johnson, Pam *former newspaper editor, communications educator*
Leavell, William A. *publisher, editor*
Naughton, James Martin *journalist*
Patterson, Eugene Corbett *retired editor, publisher*
Petty, Marty *publishing executive*
Pittman, Robert Turner *retired newspaper editor*
Stark, Brandy B. *news correspondent, educator, artist*
Tash, Paul Clifford *editor, publishing executive*

Sanibel
Ray, Charles Albert *photojournalist*

Sarasota
Allen, George Howard *publishing management consultant*
Hughes, Allen *music critic*
Jackel, Lawrence *publishing company executive*
Marino, Eugene Louis *publishing company executive*
North, Marjorie Mary *columnist*
Proffitt, Waldo, Jr., *newspaper editor*
Stevens, Elisabeth Goss (Mrs. Robert Schleussner Jr.) *writer, journalist, graphic artist*
Wetstone, Janet Meyerson *designer, journalist*

Satellite Beach
†Covault, Craig *editor*

Sebring
DeWitt, Carol A. *publishing executive, writer*

Steinhatchee
Grubbs, Elven Judson *retired newspaper publisher*

Tallahassee
Dadisman, Joseph Carrol *newspaper executive*
Morgan, Lucy Ware *journalist*
Pettijohn, Fred Phillips *retired newspaper executive, consultant*
Sanchez, Robert Francis *journalist*

Tampa
†Culpepper, Mary Kay *publishing executive*
Friedlander, Edward Jay *journalist, educator*
Roberts, Edwin Albert, Jr., *newspaper editor, journalist*
Thelen, Gil *newspaper publisher*
Tully, Darrow *newspaper publisher*
Weaver, Steven M. *publishing executive*

Tarpon Springs
Leisner, Anthony Baker *publishing company executive*

Venice
Corrigan, William Thomas *retired broadcast news executive*

Vero Beach
Parkyn, John William *editor, writer*

West Palm Beach
Bergmann, Arthur M. *writer, former county official, former newspaperman*
Flaxman, Fred *broadcast executive*
Howard, Jean Catherine Hart *photojournalist, educator*
Passy, Charles *arts critic*
Sears, Edward Milner, Jr., *newspaper editor*

GEORGIA

Athens
Agee, Warren Kendall *journalism educator*
Corey, Stephen Dale *magazine editor, poet, educator*
Feldman, Edmund Burke *art critic*
Fink, Conrad Charles *journalism educator, communications consultant*
Holder, Howard Randolph, Sr., *broadcasting company executive*

Atlanta
†Anstrom, Decker *broadcast executive*
Behrens, William Blade *television program syndication executive*
Bernhardt, Jay Michael *health communications researcher, educator*
Bisher, James Furman *journalist, author*
†Bruner, Michael Lane *communications educator*
Campbell, Colin McLeod *journalist*
Chambers, Anne Cox *newspaper executive, former diplomat*
Charles, Cory Anne *television guest booking director*
Collier, Diana Gordon *publishing executive*
Connelly, Terrence John, Sr., *television and cable station executive*
Davis, Sterling Evan *television executive*
Dobson, Bridget McColl Hursley *television executive and writer*
Ellis, Elmo Israel *broadcast executive, consultant, columnist*
†Furnad, V. Robert (Bob Furnad) *television news executive*
†Johnson, W. Thomas, Jr., *media executive*
Jones, J. Kenley *journalist*
Kaplan, Richard N. *broadcast executive, cable*
†Kennedy, James C. *publishing and media executive*
†Kintzel, Roger *publishing executive*
Kloer, Philip Baldwin *popular culture critic*
Merdek, Andrew Austin *publishing/media executive, lawyer*
Neil, Robert F. *broadcast executive*
Polk, James Ray *journalist*
Robelot, Jane *anchor*
Rosenfeld, Arnold Solomon *retired newspaper editor*
Roth, Teresa Ann *broadcast executive*
†Sack, Kevin *news correspondent*
†Sansone, Victor *broadcast executive*
Schwartz, Sandy *publishing executive*
Sloan, Mary Jean *retired media specialist*
Stewart, Michael McFadden *professional speaker*
Subramanian, Mani *communications educator, consultant*
Teepen, Thomas Henry *newspaper editor, journalist*
Toner, Michael F. *journalist*
Walden, Philip Michael *recording company executive, publishing company executive*
Wallace, Julia Diane *newspaper editor*
†Waters, Lou *anchorman, correspondent*
Whitt, Richard Ernest *reporter*
Wussler, Robert Joseph *broadcasting executive, media consultant*

Decatur
Knight, Walker Leigh *editor, publisher, clergyman*
Shaw, Jeanne Osborne *editor, poet*
Veach, Daniel Lee *editor*

Fayetteville
Turnipseed, Barnwell Rhett, III, *journalist, public relations consultant*

Fort Valley
Archer, Lloyd Daniel *communications educator*

Jekyll Island
Bentley, James Luther *former journalist*
McKinley, Douglas Webster (Webb McKinley) *consultant*

Mableton
Rowe, Bonnie Gordon *music company executive*

Macon
Savage, Randall Ernest *journalist*

Marietta
Dunwoody, Kenneth Reed *magazine and book editor*
Hays, Robert William *communications consultant, educator, writer*
Opre, Thomas Edward *magazine editor, film company executive, corporate travel company executive*

Oxford
Sitton, Claude Fox *newspaper editor*

Roswell
Eckert, Michael Joseph *television executive, media specialist*
Peterson, Donald Robert *magazine editor, vintage automobile consultant*

Savannah
Edeawo, Gale Sky *publishing company executive, writer*
Jackel, Stephanie Deck *publisher, editor, publishing executive*

HAWAII

Honolulu
Black, Cobey *journalist, corporate executive*
Jellinek, Roger *editor*
Parma, Florence Virginia *magazine editor*
Rexner, Romulus *publishing executive*
Simonds, John Edward *retired newspaper editor*
Sparks, Robert William *retired publishing executive*
Tehranian, Majid *political economy and communications educator*
Wageman, Virginia Farley *editor, writer*
Willes, Mark Hinckley *media industry executive*

Kahului
Yamamoto, Irwin Toraki *editor, publisher investment newsletter*

Kailua
Bone, Robert William *writer*

Kaneohe
McGlaughlin, Thomas Howard *publisher, retired naval officer, marine surveyor*

Pahoa
Lewis, Jack (Cecil Paul Lewis) *publishing executive, editor*

IDAHO

Boise
Boren, Robert Reed *communication educator*

Hailey
Bailey, Susan Mary *editor, writer*

Idaho Falls
Harris, Darryl Wayne *publishing executive*

Moscow
Anderson, Clifton Einar *writer, communications consultant*

Twin Falls
Tario, Terry C(harles) *broadcasting executive*

ILLINOIS

Addison
Klemens, Thomas Lloyd *editor*
McFadden, Fred Lee *publishing executive*

Arlington Heights
Baumann, Daniel E. *retired newspaper executive*
Frisbie, Richard Patrick *communications consultant, author*
Lampinen, John A. *newspaper editor*
Ray, Douglas Kent *newspaper executive*

Barrington
Bash, Philip Edwin *publishing executive*

Belleville
Richmond, Richard Thomas *journalist*

Berwyn
Forst, Edmund Charles, Jr., *communications educator, administrator, consultant*

Bloomington
Merwin, Davis Underwood *newspaper executive*

Carol Stream
Franzen, Janice Marguerite Gosnell *magazine editor*
Taylor, Kenneth Nathaniel *publishing executive, writer*

Champaign
Hays, Robert Glenn *journalism educator*
Kroner, Fred L. *journalist*
McCulloh, Judith Marie *editor*
Meyer, August Christopher, Jr., *broadcasting company executive, lawyer*
Thomas, Jo *journalist*
Turquette, Frances Bond *editor*
Watts, Robert Allan *publisher, lawyer*
Yates, Ronald Eugene *newspaper editor, journalist, educator, author*

Chicago
†Adams, Rosemary Kathleen *publishing executive*
Agema, Gerald Walton *publishing executive*
Allen, Richard Blose *legal editor, lawyer*
Anderson, Jon Stephen *newswriter*
Anderson, Karl Stephen *editor*
Borysewicz, Mary Louise *editor*
Bratcher, Juanita *journalist*
Breen, Neil Thomas *publishing executive*
Brumback, Charles Tiedtke *retired newspaper executive*
Brummel, Mark Joseph *magazine editor*
Callaway, Karen A(lice) *journalist*
Camper, John Jacob *speech writer*
Cappo, Joseph C. *journalist, writer*
Carvajal, Arthur Gonzalez *editor, lawyer*
Claiborne, William *journalist*
Connors, Dorsey *television and radio commentator, newspaper columnist*
Cooke, Michael *editor-in-chief*
Cross, Robert Clark *journalist*
Curwen, Randall William *journalist, editor*
Darby, Edwin Wheeler *retired newspaper financial columnist*
Dee, Ivan Richard *book publisher*
Dold, Robert Bruce *journalist*
Epstein, David M. *publishing executive*
Fair, Hudson Randolph *recording company executive*
Feder, Robert *television and radio columnist*
Fetridge, Clark Worthington *business executive*
Field, Marshall *business executive*
Flock, Jeffrey Charles *news bureau chief*
Francuch, Paul Charles *broadcast journalist*
Fuller, Jack William *writer, publishing executive*
Goldsborough, Robert Gerald *publishing executive, author*
†Grant, Dennis *newspaper publishing executive*
Greising, David Walter *columnist*
Grossman, Kate Nadia *journalist*
†Grumman, Cornelia *newswriter*
Hallinan, Joseph Thomas *journalist, author*
Harvey, Paul *news commentator, author, columnist*
Hast, Adele *editor, historian*
Hefner, Christie Ann *multi-media entertainment executive*
Hlavacek, Roy George *publishing executive, magazine editor*
Huntley, Robert Stephen *newspaper editor*
†Jones, Linda *communications educator*
†Jones, Wayne Allen *publisher*
Judge, Bernard Martin *editor, publisher*
Kelly, Curtis Hartt *retired publishing executive*
Kelly, Maura Anne *reporter*
Kisor, Henry Du Bois *newspaper editor, critic, columnist, writer*
†Klatt, Wayne Roy *editor, writer*
Klaviter, Helen Lothrop *magazine editor*
Kleiman, Kelly (Ruth B. Kleiman) *journalist, lawyer*
Koppes, Steven Nelson *science writer, editor*
†Kotulak, Ronald *newspaper science writer*
Krueger, Bonnie Lee *editor, writer*
Kupcinet, Irv *columnist*
†Leckey, Andrew A. *financial columnist*
Lenehan, Michael Daniel *editor, writer*
Lewis, Michael Ray *encyclopedia editor*
Lindberg, Richard Carl *editor, author, historian*
Lipinski, Ann Marie *newspaper editor*
Loesch, Katharine Taylor (Mrs. John George Loesch) *communication and theatre educator*
Longworth, Richard Cole *journalist*
Madigan, John William *publishing executive*
McDaniel, Charles-Gene *journalism educator, writer*
McNally, Andrew, IV, *publishing executive, director*
Migala, Lucyna J. *journalist, arts administrator, radio station executive*
Nault, William Henry *publishing executive*
Neubauer, Charles Frederick *investigative reporter*
Parisi, Joseph (Joseph Anthony Parisi) *magazine editor, writer-consultant, educator*
Peerman, Dean Gordon *magazine editor*
Peres, Judith May *journalist*
Pitt, Judson Hamilton *publisher, author*
Plotnick, Harvey Barry *publishing executive*
Plotnik, Arthur *author, columnist*
Pope, Kerig Rodgers *magazine executive*
Price, Henry Escoe *broadcast executive*
Primm, Earl Russell, III, *publishing executive*
Radler, Franklin David *publishing holding company executive*
Ream, Davidson *law publications administrator, writer*
Reardon, Patrick Thomas *newspaper reporter*
Reich, Howard Leonard *journalist*
†Rice, Linda Johnson *publishing executive*
Rice, William Edward *newspaper columnist*
Roeser, Thomas Francis *columnist, commentator*
Ross, Michael Neil *publishing executive*
Roth, Robert A. *newspaper executive*
Rynkiewicz, Stephen Michael *journalist*
Scanlan, Thomas Cleary *publishing executive, editor*
Schultz, Paul Neal *electronic publishing executive*
Smith, Sam *columnist, author*
Towers, Kenneth Dale *journalism educator*
Tyner, Howard A. *publishing executive, newspaper editor, journalist*
Venson, Lily Pagratis *journalist, lecturer*
von Rhein, John Richard *music critic, editor*
Wade, Nigel *former editor in chief*
Wasiolek, Edward *literary critic, language and literature educator*
Weinberg, Lila Shaffer *writer, editor*
Weintraub, Joseph Barton *publishing executive*
Wier, Patricia Ann *publishing executive, consultant*
Wille, Lois Jean *retired newspaper editor*
Wilson, Gahan *cartoonist, author*
Wolfe, Sheila A. *journalist*
Youngman, Owen Ralph *newspaper executive*

Crystal Lake
Keller, William Francis *publishing consultant*

Des Plaines
Clapper, Marie Anne *magazine publisher*
Decker, William Alexander *editor*
Henrikson, Lois Elizabeth *photojournalist*

Evanston
†Abrahamson, David Stephen Rodler *journalism educator, writer, management consultant*
Borcover, Alfred Seymour *journalist*
Buck, Tom *journalist*
Deming, Thomas Edward *publishing company executive*
Downing, Joan Forman *editor, writer*
Dreier, David Louis *editor, writer*
Felknor, Bruce Lester *editorial consultant, writer*
Galvin, Kathleen Malone *communication educator*
Hannan, Bradley *educational publishing consultant and executive*
Jacobs, Norman Joseph *publishing company executive*
Jones, Robert Russell *magazine editor*
Kuenster, John Joseph *editor*
Larson, Roy *journalist, publisher*
McCarron, John Francis *editor*
McCleary, Elliott Harold *magazine editor*
Otwell, Ralph Maurice *retired newspaper editor*
Peck, Abraham *editor, writer, educator, magazine consultant*
Wefler, Wilson Daniel *publisher, management consultant*
Wilhelm, Frank Leo *publisher, writer*
Wills, Garry *journalist, educator*
Ziomek, Jonathan S. *journalist, educator*

Franklin Park
Duncanson, Donald George *retired encyclopedia editor*

Glen Ellyn
Beers, V(ictor) Gilbert *publishing executive*
Murphy, Jerome Eugene *retired communications consultant*

Glenview
Mabley, Jack *newspaper columnist, communications consultant*
Martin, James Frederick *media consultant*

Highland Park
Johnson, Curtis Lee *publisher, editor, writer*
Pattis, S. William *publishing executive*
Rutenberg-Rosenberg, Sharon Leslie *retired journalist*

Huntley
Balk, Alfred William *journalist*

Kenilworth
Cook, Stanton R. *media company executive*
Ewing, Raymond Peyton *educator, author, management consultant*
Hayes, M. M.M. *publishing executive*

La Salle
Vickrey, Robert Fischer *publishing executive, broadcast executive*

Lake Forest
Schulze, Franz, Jr., *critic, educator*

Lake In The Hills
Kay, Dennis Matthew *retired publishing company official*

Libertyville
True, Raymond Stephen *writer, editor, analyst, consultant*

Litchfield
Jackson, David Alonzo *retired newspaper editor*

Morris
†Fabian, Karen *publishing executive, small business owner*

Mount Vernon
Withers, W. Russell, Jr., *broadcast executive*

Mount Zion
Burns, B. Thomas *broadcasting executive*

Naperville
Spiotta, Raymond Herman *editor*

Northbrook
Pesmen, Sandra (Mrs. Harold William Pesmen) *editor*
Snader, Jack Ross *publishing company executive*

Northfield
Hotze, Charles Wayne *publisher, printer*
Quaal, Ward Louis *broadcast executive*

Oak Brook
Biedron, Theodore John *newspaper advertising executive*

Oregon
Haynes, Gary Allen *photographer, journalist, newspaper editor*

Paw Paw
Heim, Alberta Jane *publishing executive, writer*

Pekin
Dancey, Charles Lohman *newspaper executive*

Peoria
Harkrader, Alan Dale, Jr., *photojournalist*
McConnell, John Thomas *newspaper executive, publisher*
Murphy, Sharon Margaret *educator*

Peru
Carus, Milton Blouke *publisher children's periodicals*

Plainfield
Diercks, Eileen Kay *educational media coordinator, elementary school educator*

Prospect Heights
Robinson, Martin (Marty Robinson) *television and radio broadcaster, media consultant*

Quincy
Moritz, Betty Ann *retired editor*

Rockford
†Fleming, Thomas J. *editor, publishing executive*
Jacobi, Fredrick Thomas *newspaper publisher*

Tinley Park
German, Frank William *broadcaster*

University Park
McMaster, Michele *communications educator*

PROFESSIONAL INDEX 6245 COMMUNICATIONS MEDIA

Urbana
Christians, Clifford Glenn *communications educator*
Dash, Leon DeCosta, Jr., *journalist*
Hansen, Kathryn Gertrude *editor, former state official*

Westmont
Hansen, Donald Marty *journalist, retired accountant*

Wheaton
Taylor, Mark Douglas *publishing executive*

Wheeling
Kuennen, Thomas Gerard *journalist*

Winnetka
†Burke, John Edward *communications editor*

INDIANA

Angola
†Jones, Donald Paul *communications educator, consultant*

Atlanta
Poindexter, Beverly Kay *media and communications professional*

Bloomington
†Cookman, Claude *journalist, educator*
Hogan, Jeremy Robert *photojournalist*
Jacobi, Peter Paul *journalism educator, author*
Lee, Don Yoon *publisher, academic researcher and writer*
Schurz, Scott Clark *journalist, publisher*
Walling, Donovan Robert *educational book editor*
Weaver, David Hugh *journalism educator, communications researcher*

East Chicago
Platis, Mary Lou *media specialist*

Fort Wayne
Green, Lisa R. *journalist*
Klugman, Stephan Craig *newspaper editor*
Oxley, Ann *television executive*
Pellegrene, Thomas James, Jr., *editor, researcher*
Sandeson, William Seymour *cartoonist*
Skufca, Sherry Lee *newspaper editor*

Franklin
Nuwer, Henry Joseph (Hank Nuwer) *journalist, educator*

Harlan
Jackson, Dean Michael *broadcaster, writer*

Huntington
Lindsey, Jacquelyn Maria *editor*

Indianapolis
Caperton, Albert Franklin *retired newspaper editor*
Clanin, Douglas Edward *editor, researcher*
Coffey, Charles Moore *communication research professional, writer*
Fleming, Marcella *journalist*
Garmel, Marion Bess Simon *retired journalist*
Henry, Barbara A. *publishing executive*
Lyst, John Henry *former newspaper editor*
McKeand, Patrick Joseph *newspaper publisher, educator*
Nancrede, Sarah Elizabeth (Sally Nancrede) *reporter*
Robertson, Jean Ellis *art critic, art history educator*
Russell, Frank Eli *retired newspaper publishing executive*
†Ryerson, Dennis *editor*
Schilling, Emily Born *editor, association executive*
SerVaas, Beurt Richard *corporate executive*
Smiley, Wynn Ray *nonprofit corporation executive*
†Wheeler, Daniel Scott *management executive, editor*
Wright, David Burton *retired newspaper publishing company executive*

Lafayette
Finch, Robert Jonathan *communications engineering consultant*
Renzetti, Phyllis Jean *retired technical editor*

Muncie
Bell, Stephen Scott (Steve Bell) *journalist, educator*
Ingelhart, Louis Edward *journalism educator, retired*
Massé, Mark Henry *journalism educator*

Munster
Neff, Bonita Dostal *communication development facilitator*
Potempa, Philip Matthew *entertainment journalist, columnist, communications educator*

Poseyville
Joos, Steven Lee *sports editor*

Rushville
Moore, Helen Elizabeth *reporter*

South Bend
JOnes, E. Michael *editor, writer*
Schurz, Franklin Dunn, Jr., *media executive*
Smith, E. Berry *television and radio consultant*
Wensits, James Emrich *newspaper editor*

Terre Haute
Chesebro, James William *communication educator*

Tipton
Lewis, Richart Drake *columnist*

IOWA

Cedar Rapids
Keller, Eliot Aaron *broadcasting executive*
Quarton, William Barlow *broadcasting company executive*

Davenport
Phelps, Michael Edward *publishing executive*
Preston, Ann Elizabeth *media and communication educator*

Des Moines
Gartner, Michael Gay *editor, television executive, baseball executive*
†Graham, Diane E. *newspaper editor*
Kerr, William T. *publishing and broadcasting executive*
Kruidenier, David *newspaper executive*
Leach, Dave Francis *editor, musician*
Myers, Mary Kathleen *publishing executive*
Stier, Mary *publishing executive*
Van Zante, Shirley M(ae) *magazine editor*
Witke, David Rodney *retired newspaper editor, consultant*

Dubuque
Kolz, Beverly Anne *publishing executive*

Iowa City
Campion, Daniel Ray *editor*
Peters, John Durham *communications educator, writer*

Mason City
Collison, Jim *business executive*

Moville
Baker, Kent Alfred *broadcasting, publishing company executive*

Sioux City
Olson, Cal Wallace *editor*

Spirit Lake
Hedberg, Paul Clifford *broadcast executive*
van der Linden, John Edward *newspaper broker, consultant*

Urbandale
Alumbaugh, JoAnn McCalla *magazine editor*

West Des Moines
Dooley, Donald John *retired publishing executive*

KANSAS

Abilene
†Sadowski, Vivien Lavonne *editor, publishing executive, consultant*

Fort Scott
Emery, Frank Eugene *publishing executive*

Hutchinson
Baumer, Beverly Belle *journalist*
Buzbee, Richard Edgar *retired newspaper editor*

Iola
Lynn, Emerson Elwood, Jr., *retired newspaper editor/publisher*

Lawrence
Dickinson, William Boyd, Jr., *editorial consultant*
Hale, Richard Lee *magazine editor*
Pickett, Calder Marcus *retired journalism educator*
Simons, Dolph Collins, Jr., *newspaper publisher*

Manhattan
Seaton, Edward Lee *editor, publishing executive*

Marion
Meyer, Bill *newspaper publisher, editor*

North Newton
Snider, Marie Anna *syndicated columnist*

Overland Park
†Dodd, James B. *internet executive*

Salina
Hansen, Donna Lauren *court reporting educator*

Shawnee Mission
Martin, Donna Lee *publishing company executive, retired*
Meiners, Phyllis Bloom *publishing executive, writer, not-for-profit developer*

Topeka
Sipes, Karen Kay *newspaper editor*
†Zaharopoulos, Thimios *media specialist, educator*

Wichita
Hatteberg, Larry Merle *photojournalist*
Zimmerman, Melva Jean *writer, retired media specialist, educator*

KENTUCKY

Carlisle
Wolf, John Howell *retired publisher*

Frankfort
Cross, Alvin Miller (Al Cross) *political columnist, writer*
Taylor, Livingston Vernon *retired newspaper reporter*

Georgetown
Allison, James Claybrooke, II, *broadcasting executive*
†Chi, Keon Soo *editor, educator, researcher*

Goshen
Strode, William Hall, III, *photojournalist, publisher*

Lexington
Donohew, Robert Lewis, Sr., *communications educator*
Keeling, Larry Dale *journalist*
Kelly, Timothy Michael *newspaper publisher*
Kissling, Fred Ralph, Jr., *publishing executive, insurance agency executive*
†Noar, Seth Michael *communications researcher*

London
Giles, William Elmer *retired newspaper editor*

Louisville
Ferré, John Patrick *communications educator*
Hall, Jill Watkins *communications educator*
Ivory, Bennie *editor*
Landau, Herman *newspaperman retired*
Manassah, Edward E. *publishing executive*
Naslund, Alan Joseph *communications educator*
Scheu, Lynn McLaughlin *scientific publication editor*
Towles, Donald Blackburn *retired publishing executive*
†Walker, Kandi *communications educator*

Paducah
Stice, Dwayne Lee *broadcasting company executive*

Pewee Valley
Gill, George Norman *newspaper publishing company executive*

LOUISIANA

Alexandria
Smith, Joe Dorsey, Jr., *retired newspaper executive*

Baker
Roberson, Patt Foster *mass communications educator*

Baton Rouge
Gilmore, Clarence Percy *writer, magazine editor*
Jenkins, Louis (Woody) *television executive, state legislator*
Lee, Jean Clarisse *editor, writer*

Gonzales
Young, David Nelson *media and communications consultant*

Jonesboro
Arrington, James Henry *journalist*

La Place
Fiffie Proctor, JoAnn *media and technology specialist*

Lake Charles
Beam, James Carroll (Jim Beam) *retired newspaper editor*
Stacey, Truman *journalist, consultant*

New Orleans
Amoss, Walter James (Jim), III, *editor*
Corey, Orlin Russell *publisher, editor*
Crumley, David Oliver *publisher, author, foundation executive*
Curry, Dale Blair *journalist*
Ferguson, Charles Austin *retired newspaper editor*
Gebauer, August William *editor, writer*
Jacobs, Wendy *editor, writer, translator*
Kemp, John Randolph *journalist, author*
†Manalla, Christine Labourdette *editor*
Phelps, Ashton, Jr., *newspaper publisher*
Pope, John M. *journalist*
†Roberts, Shauna S. *editor, writer*
Roesler, Robert Harry *media consultant*

Shreveport
Beaird, Charles T. *former publishing executive*
Lazarus, Allan Matthew *retired newspaper editor*
Robinson, Garry Lewin *television news executive*

Thibodaux
Delahaye, Alfred Newton *retired journalism educator*

MAINE

Bangor
†Warren, Richard Jordan *newspaper publisher*

Belfast
Griffith, Patricia King *journalist*

Camden
Fisher, Craig Becker *film and television executive*

Damariscotta
Blake, Bud (Julian Watson) *cartoonist*

Georgetown
Ludgin, Donald Hugh *editor*

Kennebunkport
Ray, Virginia H. S. *columnist, writer*

Lincoln
Kneeland, Douglas Eugene *retired newspaper editor*

Portland
Firestone, Deborah Ilene *publishing executive*

Presque Isle
†Cunningham, Shawn Petrice *TV anchor*

Sebago Lake
Murray, Wallace Shordon *publisher, educator*

Sedgwick
Schroth, Thomas Nolan *editor*

Sunset
Knowlton, Leslie Brooks *journalist*

York Beach
Foerster, Richard Alfons *editor, poet*

MARYLAND

Annapolis
Casey, Edward Dennis *newspaper editor*
Chambers, Ronald D. *book publishing executive*
Holston, A. Frank *retired broadcaster, communications educator*
Nelson, Charles Arthur *publisher, author*

Baltimore
Berger, Daniel *retired newswriter*
Broening, Walter Stephens, Jr., *journalist, history educator*
Dorsey, John Russell *journalist*
Giuliano, Michael Philip *arts journalist, educator*
Glasgow, Jesse Edward *newspaper editor*
Hirsh, Allan Thurman, Jr., *publishing executive*
†Kesselring, Linda J. *medical editor, writer*
Marimow, William Kalmon *journalist*
†Murphy, Frances Louise, II, *retired newspaper publisher*
Nichols, Edith Rothman *publications director, editor*
Palmer, Denise *publishing executive*
†Pollak, Lisa *columnist*
†Price, Larry C. *photojournalist*
Rousuck, J. Wynn *theater critic*
Scott, Frederick Isadore, Jr., *editor, business executive*
Sterne, Joseph Robert Livingston *newspaper editor, educator*
†Sugg, Diana K. *reporter*
Sullam, Brian Eliot *journalist*
Waller, Michael E. *publishing executive*

Bethesda
Chronister, Gregory Michael *newspaper editor*
Cornish, Edward Seymour *magazine editor*
Frank, Richard Sanford *retired magazine editor*
Hartmann, Robert Trowbridge *newspaperman, presidential counselor*
†Hendricks, John S. *broadcast executive*
Herman, Edith Carol *journalist*
Hoover, Roland Armitage *publisher, printer*
†Kesaris, Paul *publishing executive*
Larrabee, Donald Richard *publishing company executive*
Nelson, John Howard (Jack Howard Nelson) *journalist*
Orthmann, Rosemary Ann *editor*
Pickerell, James Howard *photojournalist*
Pratt, Dana Joseph *publishing consultant*
Prendergast, Curtis Walker *journalist*
†Rodgers, Johnathan *broadcast executive*
Rooney, William Richard *magazine editor*
Schaeffer, Charles Perry *newswriter, editor*
Wagner, Cynthia Gail *editor, writer*
Walsh, Trudy Catherine *journalist*

Bowie
Nwokeafor, Cosmas Uchenna *communications educator*
Towle, Laird Charles *book publisher*

Butler
Hardie, Thomas Gary *journalist, editor, business executive*

Cheverly
Miller, Mark Karl *journalist*

Chevy Chase
Adler, James Barron *publishing executive*
Armbrister, Trevor *journalist, author*
Bruno, Harold Robinson, Jr., *retired journalist, writer*
Jones, Philip Howard *broadcast journalist*
Kingsley, Nathan *journalist, consultant, educator*
Kriegsman, Alan M. *retired critic*
Shipler, David Karr *journalist, correspondent, author*
Shogan, Robert *news correspondent*
Toth, Robert Charles *retired polling consultant, journalist, writer*

College Park
Beasley, Maurine Hoffman *journalism educator, historian*
Gomery, Douglas *communications educator, writer*
Grunig, James Elmer *communications educator, researcher, public relations consultant*
Johnson, Haynes Bonner *author, journalist, television commentator*
Martin, L(eslie) John *retired journalism educator and dean*
Winik, Jay B. *writer, political scientist, consultant*

Columbia
Beckenstein, Myron *journalist*

Easton
Potter, Blair Burns *editor*

Frederick
Delaplaine, George Birely, Jr., *newspaper editor, cable television executive*

Gaithersburg
Wicklein, John Frederick *journalist, educator*

Garrett Park
Franklin, Benjamin A. *editor, reporter*

Hollywood
Powledge, Fred Arlius *freelance writer*

Kensington
Dugua, Pierre-Yves *journalist*

Landover
†Maduka, Chikezie *journalist*

Lanham
Godwin, Mary Jo *editor, librarian consultant*
Lyons, James Edward *publishing executive*

Lanham Seabrook
†Hill, Ben *broadcast executive*

Lutherville Timonium
Cedrone, Louis Robert, Jr., *critic*

North Potomac
Lide, David Reynolds *handbook and database editor*

Odenton
†Aho, Brien *photojournalist*

Owings Mills
Holdridge, Barbara *book publisher*

Potomac
Christian, John Kenton *organization executive, publisher, writer, marketing consultant*
Fox, Arthur Joseph, Jr., *editor*
Karnow, Stanley *journalist, writer*
Rehns, Marsha Lee *magazine editor, writer*

Rockville
Hoar, William Patrick *editor, author*
Kohlmeier, Louis Martin, Jr., *newspaper reporter*
Langley, Roger Richard *editor*
Miller, Claire Ellen *children's writer, editor, educator*

Salisbury
†Kleiman, Gary Howard *broadcast, advertising and cellular communications consultant*

Severna Park
Moore, John Leo, Jr., *journalist, writer, editor*

Silver Spring
Bennett, Carol(ine) Elise *retired reporter, retired actress*
Carson, Steven Lee *newspaper publisher*
†Eiserer, Leonard Albert Carl *publishing executive*
†Kurata, Phillip Cedomir *journalist*
Mooney, James Hugh *newspaper editor*
Speights, Michael David *newsletter editor*
Vernon, Weston, III, (Wes Vernon) *broadcaster, writer, actor*
Wooster, Martin Morse *author, editor*

Street
Spangler, Ronald Leroy *retired television executive, aircraft executive, automobile collector*

Sykesville
Born, Roscoe Conklin *writer*

Towson
†Roome, Dorothy Maud *media specialist, educator*

MASSACHUSETTS

Acton
Kittross, John Michael *retired communications educator*

Allston
Becton, Henry Prentiss, Jr., *broadcasting company executive*

Arlington
Thomas, Patricia Joanne *journalist, writer*

Bedford
Goodman, William Beehler *editor, literary agent*

Beverly
†Daya, Jackie *publishing company executive*

Boston
Baughman, James Carroll *information and communication educator*
Bennett, Clay *cartoonist*
Bourne, Katherine Day *journalist, educator*
Buckingham, Virginia *editor*
Caldwell, Gail *book critic*
Cohen, Rachelle Sharon *journalist*
Collins, Monica Ann *journalist*
Costello, Andrew F. *newspaper editor*
Daly, Christopher Burke *journalist, educator*
Davison, Peter Hubert *editor, poet*
DeFleur, Margaret H. *communications educator*
Donovan, Helen W. *newspaper editor*
Eder, Richard Gray *newspaper critic*
Feder, Donald Albert *syndicated columnist*
Flaherty, Lois Talbot *editor, psychiatrist, educator*
Gibson, Barry Joseph *magazine editor*

Gilman, Richard H. *newspaper publishing executive*
Godine, David Richard *publishing company executive*
Grimes, Heilan Yvette *publishing executive*
Harris, Roy Jay, Jr., *editor, business journalist*
Hillery, Thomas Hungiville *journalist, financial consultant*
Hoffman, Stanley Marc *editor, composer*
Hostetter, Amos Barr, Jr., *cable television executive*
Kikel, Rudy John *editor, writer*
Kimball, George Edward, III, *sports columnist*
Klarfeld, Jonathan Michael *journalism educator*
Krakoff, Robert Leonard *publishing executive*
Kuttner, Robert Louis *editor, columnist*
Larkin, Michael John *newspaper editor, journalist*
Lawrence, Merloyd Ludington *editor*
Lee, Donald Young (Don Lee) *publishing executive, editor, writer*
Leland, Timothy *retired newspaper executive*
Lyman, Henry *retired publisher, marine fisheries consultant*
Manning, Robert Joseph *editor*
Mason, Charles Ellis, III, *magazine editor*
McNamee, Linda Rose *broadcast executive*
Menzies, Ian Stuart *newspaper editor*
Morris, Gerald Douglas *newspaper editor*
Norment, Eric Stuart *newspaper editor*
Purcell, Patrick Joseph *newspaper publisher*
Raeder, William Munro *publishing executive*
Rhoads, Linda Smith *editor*
Schulz, John Joseph *communications educator*
Schwartz, Lloyd *music critic, poet*
Sigman, Stuart J. *communications educator*
Stevens, Marilyn Ruth *editor*
Taylor, William Osgood *newspaper executive*
Whitworth, William A. *magazine editor*
Williams, James Francis *professional baseball manager*

Brookline
†McCracken, Natalie Jacobson *editor, writer*
Storin, Matthew Victor *retired newspaper editor*

Cambridge
Aronson, Michael Andrew *editor*
Bane, Bernard Maurice *publishing company executive*
Bove, Victor Michael, Jr., *media arts and sciences educator, researcher*
Durham, Bradley Paul *financial publisher*
Effron, Seth Alan *editor, journalist*
Giles, Robert Hartmann *journalist, educator*
†Greenberg, David *columnist, historian, educator*
Jones, Alex S. *journalist, writer, broadcaster*
Lenger, John Richard *journalism educator*
Nordell, Hans Roderick *journalist, retired editor*
Urbanowski, Frank *publishing company executive*
Wilcox, Maud *editor*

Chestnut Hill
†Casey, Amy L. *communications educator, film producer*

Cohasset
Replogle, David Robert *publishing company executive*

Dorchester
†Baron, Martin *editor*
Brelis, Matthew Dean Burns *journalist*
Goodman, Ellen Holtz *journalist*

Easton
Chichetto, James William *editor, educator*

Fall River
Dion, Marc Munroe *newspaper columnist*

Forestdale
Bissell, Phil (Charles P. Bissell) *cartoonist*

Framingham
†Kenealy, Patrick *publishing company executive*
Ostrow, Robert *publishing executive*
Sleeper, Thomas F. *journalist, consultant, insurance investigator*

Franklin
Maril, David C. *editor*

Gardner
Koller, John Dryden *media educator, scriptwriter*

Hudson
†Osoff, Jeffrey Arlin *media executive*

Hyannis
Makkay, Albert *broadcast executive*
Makkay, Maureen Ann *broadcast executive*

Ipswich
†Brooks, Sam *publishing executive*

Jamaica Plain
†Howland, Llewellyn, III, *publishing executive, writer*

Leeds
Deane, James Garner *magazine editor, conservationist*

Lincoln
Nenneman, Richard Arthur *retired publishing executive*

Marblehead
Quigley, Stephen Howard *executive editor*

Medford
†Lundquist, Eric *editor-in-chief*
†Seymour, Sloan *publishing executive*

Needham
Davis, Sidney L. *journalist*
Greenway, Hugh Davids Scott *journalist*
†Kardon, Brian *music company executive*

Newton
Hume, Ellen Hunsberger *media analyst, journalist*

Newton Highlands
Swain, Roger Bartlett *editor, writer, television host*

Newton Upper Falls
Kaufmann, Andrew Stone *music journalist*

North Adams
Thurston, Donald Allen *broadcasting executive*

Northampton
Garvey, Richard Conrad *journalist*

Norwell
Rolnik, Zachary Jacob *publishing company executive*

Oxford
Holbrook, Jay Mack *publishing company executive*

Pittsfield
Bahlman, Dudley Rhodes *journalist*
Rich, Philip Dewey *publishing executive*

Quincy
Chung, Cynthia Norton *communications specialist*
Lippincott, Joseph P. *photojournalist, educator*

Roslindale
Driscoll, Kathleen J. *writer*

Salisbury
Berggren, Dick *editor*

Sandwich
Porter, John Stephen *retired television executive*

Springfield
Mish, Frederick Crittenden *editor*
Starr, David *newspaper editor, publisher*

Sudbury
Hillery, Mary Jane Larato *columnist, producer, television host, reserve army officer*

Waltham
†Davis, Robert J. *internet company executive*

Wayland
Huff, William Braid *retired publishing company executive*

Wellesley
Caso, Adolph *publishing company executive*
Myers, Arthur B. *journalist, author*

Wellfleet
Limpitlaw, John Donald *retired publishing executive, clergyman*

West Falmouth
King, Richard Hood *newspaper executive*

Westfield
Gardner, Thomas Neville *communications educator*

Weston
Sanzone, Donna S. *publishing executive*

Westport
Gormley, Robert John *publishing executive*

Westwood
Borgman, George Allan *journalist*

Williamstown
Bleezarde, Thomas Warren *retired magazine editor*

Winchester
Ockerbloom, Richard C. *newspaper executive*
Totosy de Zepetnek, Steven *editor, educator*

Winthrop
Lutze, Ruth Louise *retired textbook editor, public relations executive*
Vettel, Niki Marcia (Monica Marcia Scher) *broadcasting executive*

MICHIGAN

Ann Arbor
Beaver, Frank Eugene *communication educator, film critic and historian*
Bedard, Patrick Joseph *editor, writer, consultant*
Csere, Csaba *magazine editor*
Eisendrath, Charles Rice *journalism educator, manufacturer, farmer, consultant*
Fitzsimmons, Joseph John *publishing executive*
Hessler, David William *information and multimedia systems educator*
Kennedy, George Francis *publishing executive*
Lewis, Robert Enzer *lexicographer, educator*
Mangouni, Norman *publishing executive*

Bear Lake
Richard, Timothy C. *journalist, editor*

Birmingham
Berman, Laura *journalist, writer*

Bloomfield Hills
James, William Ramsay *cable television executive*

Bloomfield Township
Brown, Lynette Ralya *journalist, publicist*

Clinton
Anderson, Denice Anna *editor*

Dearborn
Hogan, Brian Joseph *editor*

Detroit
Alpert, Daniel *television executive*
Ashenfelter, David Louis *reporter*
Blomquist, David Wels *journalist*
Colby, Joy Hakanson *critic*
Dickerson, Brian *columnist*
Hutton, Carole Leigh *newspaper editor*
Kelleher, Timothy John *publishing company executive*
Meriwether, Heath J. *newspaper publisher*
Smyntek, John Eugene, Jr., *editor*
Teagan, John Gerard *newspaper executive*
Waldmeir, Peter Nielsen *journalist*
†White, Joseph B. *reporter*

Durand
Cook, Bernadine Fern *book publisher, writer*

East Lansing
Freedman, Eric *journalist, educator, writer*
Greenberg, Bradley Sander *communications educator*
Maran, Michael Joseph *publisher, writer, lawyer*
Morton, Jerry Lee *journalist*
Ralph, David Clinton *communications educator*

Farmington Hills
Harwell, William Earnest (Ernie Harwell) *broadcaster*
Olendorf, Donna *editor*

Flint
†Samuel, Roger D. *newspaper publishing executive*

Grand Rapids
Fortner, Robert Steven *media educator, researcher*
Kaczmarczyk, Jeffrey Allen *journalist, classical music critic*
Mayo, David Wayne *sportswriter*
Scott, Barbara June *editor, writer*
Wheeler, Kathryn S. *editor*

Grosse Pointe
Hill, Draper *editorial cartoonist*
Ruffner, Frederick G., Jr., *book publisher*
Whittaker, Jeanne Evans *former newspaper columnist*

Grosse Pointe Farms
Christian, Edward Kieren *broadcasting station executive*

Grosse Pointe Park
Elsila, David August *editor*

Grosse Pointe Woods
McWhirter, Glenna Suzanne (Nickie McWhirter) *retired newspaper columnist*

Kalamazoo
Carver, Joan Willson *publishing executive, artist*
Jamison, Frank Raymond *independent video producer, retired communications educator*

Lansing
Brown, Nancy Field *editor*
Graham, Lester Lynn *radio journalist*

Manistee
Trussell, Charles Tait *columnist*

Marion
†Jager, Mark Alan *publishing executive, writer*

Marquette
Manning, Robert Hendrick *media consultant*

Mears
Binder, L. James *magazine editor, retired, journalist*

Midland
Messing, Carol Sue *communications educator*

Mount Pleasant
Petrick, Michael Joseph *journalism educator*

Petoskey
Vernon, Doris Schaller *retired writer*
Winter, Kenneth Michael *newspaper editor, publisher*

Royal Oak
Bohy, Ric *magazine editor, consultant, broadcast commentator*
†Maurus, Marc Allen *writer, publisher*

Saginaw
Chaffee, Paul Charles *newspaper editor*
Killingbeck, Janice Lynelle (Mrs. Victor Lee Killingbeck) *journalist*

Saint Clair Shores
Shine, Neal James *journalism educator, former newspaper editor, publisher*

Southfield
Thomas, Judy Janet *reporter, health services professional*

Sturgis
Hair, Robert Eugene *editor, writer, historian*

Troy
†Lorencz, Mary *media relations administrator*
Moore, Oliver Semon, III, *publishing executive, consultant*

Ypsilanti
Evans, Gary Lee *communications educator and consultant*

MINNESOTA

Bloomington
Johnson, Leslie Carole *editor, publisher*

Chanhassen
†Martin, Brett Stephan *editor, writer*

Circle Pines
†Barott, Pat Robert *broadcast technician*

Dayton
†Ostroot, Kathleen Ann *editor, writer, adult nurse practitioner*

Duluth
Latto, Lewis M. *broadcasting company executive*

Eagan
Miller, Alan M. *editor, educator, writer*

Edina
Bisping, Bruce Henry *photojournalist*
Steinberg, Michael *music critic, educator*

Melrose
Larson, Michael Len *newspaper editor, hospital administrator*

Minneapolis
Bednar, R. Craig *magazine and book publisher*
Cope, Lewis *journalist*
Cowles, John, Jr., *publisher, women's sports promoter*
Crosby, Jacqueline Garton *newspaper editor, journalist*
†Fine, Pam *newspaper editor*
Flanagan, Barbara *journalist*
Hill, Gary D. *journalist*
Johnson, Gary L. *publishing executive*
Jones, Will(iam) (William Arnold Jones) *writer, former newspaper columnist*
Kalman, Marc *radio station executive*
†Kramer, Joel Roy *journalist, newspaper executive*
Laing, Karel Ann *magazine publishing executive*
Lerner, Harry Jonas *publishing company executive*
†Martin-Estudillo, Luis *editor, researcher*
McGuire, Tim *editor*
Meador, Ron *newspaper editor, writer*
†Moyer, Keith J. *publishing executive*
Murphy, Joseph Edward, Jr., *broadcast executive*
Rajkumar, Roshini Anne *reporter*
Randall, Roger David *publishing executive*
Roloff, Marvin L. *publishing executive*
Salyer, Stephen Lee *media executive*
Scallen, Thomas Kaine *broadcasting executive*
†Werner, Lawrence H. *editor*
White, Robert James *newspaper columnist*
†Whittemore, Brian *broadcast executive*
Wright, Frank Gardner *retired newspaper editor*

Minnetonka
Swartz, Donald Everett *television executive*
Thompson, Sally Ann *newspaper editor*

Moorhead
Holtan, Merrie Sue *communications educator*

Rochester
†Shampo, Marc Anthony *medical editor, writer, retired*

Rushford
Schober, Myron Jerome *newspaper editor and publisher*

Saint Cloud
Porter, Laurinda Wright *communications educator, consultant*

Saint Joseph
Rowland, Howard Ray *mass communications educator*

Saint Paul
Aggergaard, Steven Paul *journalist, educator, musician*
Amidon, Paul Charles *publishing executive*
Bree, Marlin Duane *publisher, author*
Burkart, Jeffrey Edward *communications educator*
Clark, Ronald Dean *retired newspaper editor*
†Griffin, Michael Scott *communications educator, writer*
Hubbard, Stanley Stub *broadcast executive*
Kling, William Hugh *broadcasting executive*
Oliver, Marlys Mae *retired editor, writer*
Sadowski, Richard J. *former publishing executive*
Wehrwein, Austin Carl *newspaper reporter, editor, writer*

Sartell
Dominik, John Julius *retired advertising company executive*

Two Harbors
McMillion, John Macon *retired newspaper publisher*

West Saint Paul
Cento, William Francis *retired newspaper editor*

Winona
Bures, Frank Adolph *journalist, writer*

MISSISSIPPI

Greenwood
Jones, Carolyn Ellis *publisher, retired employment agency and business service company owner*

Hattiesburg
Hickman, Ronald Lee *media broker, broadcast executive*

Jackson
McWilliams Morse, Anne Washburn *retired journalist, writer*

Kosciusko
Shoemaker, William C. *journalist*

Leland
Ayres, Mary Jo *professional speaker, writer, composer*

Liberty
†Stratton, Richard Howard *publishing executive*

Ocean Springs
Baughn, Mary Alice Jackson *journalist*

Oxford
Hoar, Jere Richmond *journalism educator, writer*

Yazoo City
Brown, Marion Lipscomb, Jr., *publisher, photographer, writer, retired chemical company executive*

MISSOURI

Aurora
Jay, Jerry Leon, Sr., *retired publishing executive, industrial engineer*

Chesterfield
Gill, Suzanne *software book publisher*
Higgins, Edward Aloysius *retired newspaper editor*

Clinton
Wentz, Wendell Franklin *columnist, writer*

Columbia
Helvey, William Charles, Jr., *communications specialist*
Loory, Stuart Hugh *journalist*
Sanders, Keith Page *journalism educator*
Winfield, Betty Houchin *communications educator*

Cuba
Pascoe, Percy Willard *newspaper publisher*

Harrisonville
James, Mary Lee *human resources specialist, retired*

Hartsburg
Flink, Jane Duncan *columnist*

Higginsville
Rhodes, Robert Charles *cable company executive, consultant*

Hunt Valley
Guthrie, Phillip Patrick *division production manager*

Jefferson City
†Benson, Joseph Fred *journalist, legal historian*

Joplin
Massa, Richard Wayne *retired communications educator*

Kansas City
Anderson, James Keith *retired magazine editor*
Batiuk, Thomas Martin *cartoonist*
Brisbane, Arthur Seward *newspaper publisher*
Busby, Marjean (Marjean Busby) *retired journalist*
Davis, James Robert *cartoonist*
Diguid, Lewis Walter *newspaper executive, columnist*
Gusewelle, Charles Wesley *journalist, writer, documentary maker*
Mc Meel, John Paul *newspaper syndicate and publishing executive*
McSweeney, William Lincoln, Jr., *retired publishing executive*
Oliphant, Patrick *cartoonist*
Palmer, Cruise *newspaper editor*
Stein, Allison *media specialist*
Tammeus, William David *journalist, columnist*
Thornton, Thomas Noel *publishing executive*
Van Buren, Abigail (Jeanne Phillips) *columnist, lecturer*
Williams, Randy G. *community relations executive, communication professional*
Zieman, Mark *newspaper editor*

Kirksville
Presley, Paula Lumpkin *editor*

Marshall
Roberts, David Lowell *journalist, educator*

Saint Louis
Barnes, Harper Henderson *movie critic, editor, writer*
Cuoco, Lorin (Jean) *editor, writer*
Domjan, Laszlo Karoly *newspaper editor*
Egger, Terrance C.Z. *publishing executive*

Ehrlich, Ava *television executive*
Elkins, Ken Joe *retired broadcasting executive*
Engelhardt, Thomas Alexander *editorial cartoonist*
Ferguson, Gary Warren *retired public relations executive*
Gauen, Patrick Emil *newspaper correspondent*
Goldberg, Norman Albert *music publisher, writer*
Green, Joyce *book publishing company executive*
Hays, Howard H. (Tim Hays) *editor, publisher*
Killenberg, George Andrew *newspaper consultant, former newspaper editor*
Martínez-Solís, Luis Fernando *journalist, writer, historian*
Masinelli, Anthony Dean *journalist, writer*
Perkins, Norris Lynwood, III, (Terry Perkins) *columnist and writer*
Pollack, Joe *retired newspaper critic and columnist, writer*
Randolph, Jennings, Jr., (Jay Randolph) *sportscaster*
Regnell, Barbara Caramella *retired media educator*
Rice, Patricia Jane *journalist*
Soeteber, Ellen *journalist, newspaper editor*
Waters, Richard *retired publishing company executive*

Springfield
Boardman-Fite, Linda Irene *speaker, management consultant*
Champion, Norma Jean *communications educator, state legislator*
Glazier, Robert Carl *publishing executive*
Harris, Ralph William *religious journalist*

Warrensburg
†Jones, Robert Claude *editor*

Wentzville
†Duncan, Aaron W. *media specialist, minister*

MONTANA

Havre
Gallus, Charles Joseph *retired journalist*

Whitefish
James, Marion Ray *magazine founder, editor*

NEBRASKA

Friend
De Bevoise, Lee Raymond *editor, writer*

Hastings
Bush, Marjorie Evelynn Tower-Tooker *educator, media specialist, librarian*

Lincoln
Botts, Jack Chester *journalist*
Dyer, William Earl, Jr., *retired newspaper editor*

Norfolk
Huse, Eugene Franklin *newspaper publisher*

Omaha
Batchelder, Anne Stuart *retired publisher, political party official*
†Gottschalk, John E. *newspaper publishing executive*
King, Larry *editor*
Lipschultz, Jeremy Harris *communication educator*

York
Baker, John I., III, *communications educator*
Givens, Randal Jack *communications educator*

NEVADA

Fernley
Weniger-Phelps, Nancy Ann *media specialist, photographer*

Henderson
Kelley, Michael John *newspaper editor*
Wills, Robert Hamilton *retired newspaper executive*

Incline Village
Diederich, J(ohn) William *internet publisher*

Las Vegas
Frederick, Sherman *publishing executive*
Jaffe, Herb *retired newspaper editor, columnist*
Magliocco, Peter Anthony *editor, writer*
Miller, Valerie Carol *journalist*
Mitchell, Thomas *editor*
Scherf, Dietmar *publishing executive, artist, minister*
Steckler, Larry *publisher, editor, writer*
Tash, Martin Elias *publishing company executive*
†Wooten, Glen Donovan *media consultant*

Reno
Hengstler, Gary Ardell *publisher, editor, lawyer*
Miller, Newton Edd, Jr., *communications educator*

NEW HAMPSHIRE

Concord
Brown, Tom Christian *newspaper publisher*
Fahey, Patricia Anne *editor*

Deering
Hunter, Beatrice Trum *editor*

Dover
Wentworth, William Edgar *retired journalist*

Dublin
†Carlton, Michael *magazine editor*
Hale, Judson Drake, Sr., *editor, writer*

Hooksett
Di Stefano, Julia Mary *communications educator*

Lebanon
Linnell, Robert Hartley *editor-in-chief*

Lyme
Dwight, Donald Rathbun *newspaper publisher, corporate communications executive*

Manchester
Perkins, Charles, III, *newspaper editor*

Merrimack
Kotelly, George Vincent *editor, writer, electrical engineer*

Newport
Hill, Evan *retired journalism educator, writer*

Peterborough
Twombly, Stephen Doane *magazine publisher*

Portsmouth
Hopkins, Jeannette Ethel *book publisher, editor*
Thornhill, Arthur H., Jr., *retired book publisher*

Salem
Smith, Laurence Roger *journal editor*

NEW JERSEY

Allendale
DiBlasi, Dianne Clark *editor*
†Long, Jo-Nelle Desmond *editor, consultant, historian*

Blackwood
Cloyd, Thomas Earl *broadcast designer, consultant*

Caldwell
Mann, Robert Christopher *communications educator, television host, producer*

Cape May
Fox, Matthew Ignatius *publishing company executive*

Chatham
Meagher, James Proctor *editor*

Cherry Hill
Gutin, Myra Gail *communications educator*
Rudman, Solomon Kal *magazine publisher*
†Sullivan, Eileen Alison *reporter*

Cranbury
Yoseloff, Julien David *publishing company executive*

Deal
Becker, Richard Stanley *music publisher*

Delran
Parker, Michael J. *editor, writer, researcher*

Dover
Kassell, Paula Sally *editor, publisher*

Dumont
Sadock, Karen *editor, writer*

East Brunswick
Ollwerther, William Raymond *newspaper editor*

East Windsor
†Adams, Stephen M. *publishing company executive*

Edison
Hunter, Michael *publishing executive*

Englewood
Hoexter, Corinne Rosenfelder Katz *author, editor*

Englewood Cliffs
Haltiwanger, Robert Sidney, Jr., *book publishing executive*
Lipsitz, Lawrence Irwin *publishing executive*
†Saible, Stephanie Irene *magazine editor*
†Vane, Dena *magazine editor-in-chief*

Fair Haven
Wyndrum, Ralph William, Jr., *communications executive consultant*

Fair Lawn
Mazel, Joseph Lucas *publishing executive, consultant*

Fanwood
Berger, Ivan Bennett *magazine editor, writer*
Whitaker, Joel *publisher, editor, elected public official*

Flemington
Thomas, Anne Moreau *former newspaper owner*

Florham Park
Marshall, William Jeffrey *journalist, author*

Fords
Blond, Stuart Richard *newsletter editor*

Fort Lee
Bolster, William Lawrence *broadcast executive*
Cohn, Scott *television news correspondent*
Dobrzynski, Judith Helen *journalist, commentator*
Fischel, Daniel Norman *publishing consultant*

Fisher, Andrew, IV, *newswriter, television producer*
Stuart, Carole *publishing executive*
Stuart, Lyle *publishing company executive*

Gillette
Nathanson, Linda Sue *publisher, author, technical writer*

Hackensack
Ahearn, James *newspaper columnist*
Borg, Malcolm Austin *publishing executive*
Margulies, James Howard *editorial cartoonist*

Haworth
Biesel, David Barrie *publishing executive*
Biesel, Diane Jane *editor, publishing executive*

Highland Lakes
Ludwig, Gregory Brian *editor, writer*

Hightstown
Wham, George Sims *retired publishing executive*

Hillsborough
Yuster-Freeman, Leigh Carol *broadcasting executive*

Hoboken
Berzinski, Patrick Anthony *media consultant*
Ubell, Robert Neil *editor, publisher, educator, consultant*

Jackson
Wagner, Edward Kurt *publishing company executive*

Jersey City
Brandes, Joel R. *consultant, publisher, writer*
Levine, Richard James *publishing executive*
Solomon, Mack Busch *retired newspaper editor*

Lakewood
Forbes, Gordon Maxwell *sports journalist, commentator*

Leonia
Greenwald, Martin *publishing company executive*

Linden
Ball, William Lee (Atley Fall) *sportswriter*

Little Falls
Glasser, Stephen Andrew *publishing executive, lawyer*

Long Branch
Lagowski, Barbara Jean *writer, book editor*

Lumberton
Brown, Hershel M. *retired newspaper publisher*

Madison
Goodman, Michael B(arry) *communications educator*

Mantua
†Holt, Robert Donald *columnist, auditor*

Maplewood
Laramee, Elaine R. *magazine editor*

Marlton
Cheney, Daniel Lavern *retired magazine publisher*

Martinsville
Squire, Laurie Rubin *media consultant*

Middletown
Bishop, Gordon Bruce *journalist*

Monmouth Junction
Prestbo, John Andrew *newspaper editor, journalist, author*

Monroe Township
Miller, Isadore *television executive, consultant*
Reichek, Morton Arthur *retired magazine editor, writer*

Montclair
Gollob, Herman Cohen *retired publishing company, editor*
Jacoby, Tamar *journalist, author*

Montvale
Dowden, Mark Vincent *editor, publishing company executive*
Politi, Beth Kukkonen *publishing services company executive*

Montville
Coleman, Earl Maxwell *publishing company executive*
Teubner, Ferdinand Cary, Jr., *retired publishing company executive*

Morris Plains
O'Neill, Robert Edward *business journal editor*

Mountainside
Horner, Shirley Jaye *columnist, writing and publishing consultant*

Neptune
†Breen, Stephen P. *editorial cartoonist*

Neptune City
Axelrod, Glen Scott *publishing company executive, pet product company executive*

New Brunswick
Horowitz, Irving Louis *publisher, educator*
Katz, James E. *communications educator*

Kubey, Robert William *media educator, developmental psychologist, television analyst and researcher*
Taliaferro, James Hubert, Jr., *communications educator*
Wilson, Donald Malcolm *publishing executive*

New Providence
Barnes, Sandra Henley *publishing company executive*
†Cooper, Carol Diane *publishing company executive*
Esser, Joseph Allen *editor*
†Hollister, Dean *publishing company executive*

Newark
Aregood, Richard Lloyd *editor*
Dennery, Linda *newspaper publishing executive*
Everett, Richard G. *newspaper editor*
Newhouse, Mark William *publishing executive*
Willse, James Patrick *newspaper editor*

North Bergen
Mongelli, Thomas Guy *broadcast executive, radio personality*

Oldwick
Snyder, Arthur *publishing executive*

Oradell
Nesoff, Robert (Bob) *newspaper publisher*

Paterson
Deffaa, Chip *jazz critic*

Piscataway
Fogiel, Max *publishing executive*

Plainfield
Allen, Stuart (Stuart Allen Sup) *film and television company executive*
Johnson, Lonnie L., Jr., *information specialist*

Pleasantville
Applewhite, Kim *music company executive, educator*

Princeton
Buttenheim, Edgar Marion *publishing executive*
Crawford, Franklin David *publishing company executive*
Lippincott, Walter Heulings, Jr., *publishing executive*
Nied, Thomas H. *media company executive*
O'Donnell, Laurence Gerard *editorial consultant, former managing editor The Wall Street Journal*
Sandman, Peter M. *risk communication consultant, speaker*
Weiss, Renée Karol *editor, writer, musician*

Ramsey
Underwood, Steven Clark *publishing executive*

Ridgefield Park
D'Avella, Bernard Johnson, Jr., *publishing company executive, lawyer*

Ridgewood
Mitgang, Lee David *journalist, author, lecturer, foundation manager*

Rockaway
†Kurtz, Ellen R. *journalist*

Saddle River
Noyes, Robert Edwin *publisher, writer*

Secaucus
Pedersen, Darlene Delcourt *publishing executive, psychotherapist*
Williams, Brian *news anchor, correspondent*

Short Hills
Soderlind, Sterling Eugene *newspaper industry consultant*
Winter, Ruth Grosman (Mrs. Arthur Winter) *journalist*

Skillman
Eiger, Richard William *retired publisher*

Somerville
Dunbar, Holly Jean *communications and public relations executive*

South Amboy
†Burkard, Thomas Robert *publishing executive, writer*

Southampton
Callaway, Ben Anderson *journalist*

Sparta
Scianna, Irene F. *film company executive, photography executive*
Spence, Robert Leroy *publishing executive*

Spring Lake
McGreal, Joseph A., Jr., *publishing company executive*

Stockholm
dePaolo, Ronald Francis *editor, writer*

Summit
Buchanan, Andrew Simpson *writer*

Teaneck
Ehrenfeld, Phyllis Rhoda *editor, playwright, book reviewer*
Goldman, Eric A. *film company executive*

Tenafly
Vaughan, Samuel Snell *editor, author, publisher*

Titusville
†Klim, Christopher *editor, publishing executive, writer*

Toms River
Leone, Judith Gibson *educational media specialist, video production company executive*

Trenton
Christopherson, Elizabeth Good *broadcast executive*
Joseph, Edith Hoffman *retired editor*

Weehawken
Hobson, Burton Harold *publishing executive*

West Caldwell
Reboli, John Anthony *publishing executive*

Westfield
Jannotti, Gene Patrick *business consultant, telecommunications professional*

Woodcliff Lake
Jacobs, Charles Nathan *editor, writer*

NEW MEXICO

Albuquerque
†Allen, Hubert A., Jr., *publishing executive, writer, statistician, consultant*
Brooks, Alan *publications editor, writer*
Danziger, Jerry *broadcasting executive*
Hadas, Elizabeth Chamberlayne *editor*
Lang, Thompson Hughes *publishing company executive*
Moskos, Harry *writer, former newspaper editor*
Rhetts, Paul Fisher *publishing executive*
Walz, Kent *publishing executive*

Belen
Perry, Charles *photo-illustrator, writer, researcher*

Las Cruces
Merrick, Beverly Georgianne *journalism, communications educator*

Los Alamos
Mendius, Patricia Dodd Winter *editor, educator, writer*

Raton
Carroll, William *publishing company executive*

Santa Fe
Burke, Lawrence J. *editor-in-chief*
Dirks, Lee Edward *newspaper executive*
Groseclose, Everett Harrison *retired editor*
Lichtenberg, Margaret Klee *publishing company executive*
Stieber, Tamar *journalist*

Silver City
Fryxell, David Allen *publishing executive*

NEW YORK

Albany
Cornell, Ralph Lawrence, Jr., *publishing executive*
†Morga Bellizzi, Celeste *editor*
Mueller, I. Lynn *strategic planning and communications consultant*
Ortloff, George Christian, Sr., (Chris Ortloff) *journalist, state legislator*
Poe, Suzy Crowbar *publisher, author*
Rosenfeld, Harry Morris *editor*

Amherst
Paul, Laurence Johnson *retired journalist*

Bainbridge
Goerlich, Shirley Alice Boyce *publishing executive, educator, media consultant*

Ballston Lake
Silverman, Gerald Bernard *journalist*

Beacon
Mc Keown, William Taylor *magazine editor, author*

Bedford
Bowman, James Kinsey *publishing company executive, rare book specialist*

Bellport
Sutton-Straus, Joan M. *journalist*
Townsend, Terry *publishing executive*

Bethpage
Dolan, Charles Francis *media, entertainment company executive*
Mahony, Sheila Anne *cable television executive*
†McEnroe, Kate *broadcast executive*

Binghamton
Marella, Philip Daniel *broadcasting company executive*

Bohemia
Maccarone, Frances Mary *publishing executive*

Brewster
Simon, Andrew L. *educational publishing executive*

Bridgehampton
Phillips, Warren Henry *publishing executive*

Bronx
Ahmose, Nefertari A. *journalism educator*

Lomke, Evander *publishing executive*
Stein, Bernard L. *journalist*
Strate, Lance Adam *communications educator*
Zalaznick, Sheldon *editor, journalist*

Bronxville
Lombardo, Philip Joseph *broadcasting company executive*
Rosenthal, Lucy Gabrielle *writer, educator, editor*

Brooklyn
Bianco, Anthony Joseph, III, *newswriter*
†Chambers, William Edmond *telephone techician, writer*
Daly, Joe Ann Godown *publishing company executive*
Davis, Lawrence James *editor, writer*
De Lisi, Joanne *media consultant, educator*
†Donnelly, Timothy B. *editor, writer*
Downes, Nicholas Street *cartoonist*
†Ensminger, John J. *publishing executive, lawyer*
†Fink, Jennifer Natalya *publishing executive, educator*
Michaud, Christopher *journalist*
Newbauer, John Arthur *editor*
Ortner, Everett Howard *magazine editor, writer*
Quick, Walter Curtis *music company executive*
Reynolds, Nancy Remick *editor, writer*
Sanford, David Boyer *writer, editor*
Walsh, George William *publishing company executive, editor, author*
Wiener, Hesh (Harold Frederic Wiener) *publisher, editor, consultant*

Buffalo
Goldhaber, Gerald Martin *communication educator, author, consultant*
Halpert, Leonard Walter *retired editor*
Lee, Genevieve Bruggeman *publishing company executive*
Robinson, David Clinton *reporter*
†Sullivan, Margaret M. *editor*
Trotter, Herman Eager, Jr., (Herman Trotter) *retired music critic*
Urban, Henry Zeller *newspaperman*
Vogel, Michael N. *journalist, writer, historian*

Campbell Hall
Austin, Danforth Whitley *newspaper executive*
Ottaway, James Haller, Jr., *newspaper publisher*

Chappaqua
Ujifusa, Grant Masashi *editor*

Cherry Valley
Sapinsky, Joseph Charles *magazine executive, photographer*

Clinton
Behrens, John (Jack) *editor, writer, columnist, educator*

Cortland
Hartsock, John C. *communications educator and scholar*

Croton On Hudson
Plummer, Samuel Craig *editor*
Straka, Laszlo Richard *publishing consultant*
Turner, David Reuben *publisher, author*

Dobbs Ferry
Anbinder, Paul *publishing company executive*
Simon, Lothar *publishing company executive*
Smith, Charles Carter, Jr., *publishing executive*

East Rochester
Lilly, Eugene Francis *retired publishing company executive*

Elba
Kauffman, William Joseph *writer, editor*

Elmira
Horton, Martha Heim *retired newspaper editor, writer*

Elmsford
Miranda, Robert Nicholas *publishing company executive*

Flushing
Cathcart, Robert Stephen *mass media consultant*
Chook, Paul Howard *publishing executive*

Forest Hills
†Acain, Angeline Ramos *publishing executive*
Prager, Alice Heinecke *music company executive*
Reis, Don *publishing executive*

Fresh Meadows
†Cohen, Robert L. *editor*

Garden City
Egan, Frank T. *writer, editor*
Rhein, John Hancock Willing, III, *publishing executive*

Glen Head
Fairman, Joel Martin *broadcasting executive*

Great Neck
Fiel, Maxine Lucille *journalist, behavioral analyst, lecturer*
Kahn, David *editor, author*
Panes, Jack Samuel *publishing company executive*
Roth, Harvey Paul *publishing executive*
Rubin, Karen Beth *publishing, marketing executive*

Hamilton
Edmonston, William Edward, Jr., *publisher, educator*

†Klein, Laura *publishing executive*
Klepper, Anne *journalist, speechwriter*
†Klingensmith, Michael *publishing executive*
Knopf, Alfred, Jr., *retired publisher*
Kolatch, Myron *magazine editor*
Korman, Lewis J. *entertainment/media company executive, entrepreneur*
†Korvin, Catherine Madeleine *editor*
†Koslow, Sally *editor-in-chief*
Kosner, Edward A(lan) *editor and publisher*
Koster, Elaine Landis *publishing executive*
Koteff, Ellen *periodical editor*
Krajick, Kevin Rudolph *freelance/self-employed journalist*
†Kravitz, Lee *editor*
Kristof, Nicholas Donabet *journalist*
Kroft, Steve *news correspondent, editor*
†Kunes, Ellen *editor-in-chief*
†Kupper, William P., Jr., *publishing executive*
†LaBarge, Joan Sheridan *publishing executive*
†Lack, Andrew *broadcast executive*
†Lafavore, Michael J. *magazine editor*
Lamm, Donald Stephen *publishing company executive*
Lamont, Lansing *journalist, public affairs executive, author*
Landau, Sidney Ivan *lexicographer*
Lane, Nancy *editor, human rights activist*
Lapham, Lewis Henry *editor, author, television host*
Larsen, Jonathan Zerbe *journalist*
Lauer, Matt *broadcast journalist*
Laventhol, David Abram *newspaper editor*
†Lawhon, Charla *editor*
†Laybourne, Geraldine *broadcasting executive*
†Leahey, Lynn *editor-in-chief*
Leahy, Michael Joseph *newspaper editor*
LeDoux, Harold Anthony *cartoonist, painter*
Lee, Bruce *editor, writer*
Lee, Frances Helen *editor*
Lee, Sally A. *editor-in-chief*
Lees, Alfred William *writer, former magazine editor*
Lehmann-Haupt, Christopher Charles Herbert *book reviewer*
†Lehmkuhl, Lynn *publishing executive*
†Leive, Cindi *editor-in-chief*
Lelyveld, Joseph Salem *writer, retired newspaper editor, correspondent*
†Lemann, Nicholas B. *journalist, writer*
Levin, Alan M. *television journalist*
Levin, Martin P. *publishing executive, lawyer*
†Levine, Ellen R. *magazine editor*
Levinson, Warren Mitchell *broadcast journalist*
Levitz, Paul Elliot *publishing executive*
Levy, Alan Joseph *editor, journalist, writer*
†Levy, Clifford J. *reporter*
†Lewis, Russell T. *publishing executive*
Lingeman, Richard Roberts *editor, writer*
Linz, Werner Mark *international publishing executive*
Lipscomb, Thomas Heber, III, *media executive*
Loeb, Marshall Robert *journalist*
Logan, Don *publishing executive*
†Long, David L. *former magazine publisher*
Loomis, Robert Duane *publishing company executive, author*
Lopez, Kathryn Jean *editor, reporter*
Lord, Robert Wilder *retired editor and writer*
†Love, Robert *editor*
Low, Richard H. *broadcasting executive, producer*
Lublin, Joann Sandra *journalist*
Lundberg, George David, II, *medical editor in chief, pathologist*
Lurie, Ranan Raymond *political cartoonist, political analyst, artist, lecturer*
†Lynne, Michael *film company executive*
Lyons, Nick *publishing executive*
Mabrey, Vicki *news correspondent, anchor*
MacGowan, Sandra Firelli *publishing executive, publishing educator*
Macri, Theodore William *book publisher*
Malamed, Seymour H. *motion picture company executive*
†Mann, Maria *photojournalist, director*
Mapes, Glynn Dempsey *newspaper editor*
†Mardin, Arif *music industry executive, musician*
Martin, Judith Sylvia *journalist, author*
Martin, Paul Ross *editor*
†Marzorati, Gerald *editor*
Mathews, Jack Wayne *journalist, film critic*
Mazzola, Anthony Thomas *editor, art consultant, designer, writer*
†McCarrick, Edward R. *magazine publisher*
McCarthy, Patrick *magazine publishing executive*
McCarty, V.K. *publisher, chaplain, librarian*
†McConnico, John *photojournalist*
McCormack, Thomas Joseph *playwright, retired publishing company executive*
McCrie, Robert Delbert *editor, publisher, educator*
McDonell, Robert Terry *magazine editor, novelist*
†McDonell, Terry *editor*
McFadden, Robert Dennis *reporter*
McFeely, William Drake *publishing company executive*
†McGill, Jay *magazine publisher*
McGrath, Judith *broadcast executive*
McGraw, Harold Whittlesey, Jr., *publishing executive*
†McPherson, David *music company executive*
†Mehta, A. Sonny *publishing company executive*
Melloan, George Richard *editor, columnist, writer*
Melvin, Russell Johnston *magazine publishing consultant*
Mencher, Melvin *journalist, retired educator*
†Mercado-Valdes, Frank *broadcast executive*
Metz, Robert Roy *publisher, editor*
Meyer, Karl Ernest *journalist*
Meyer, Pucci *newspaper editor*
Meyers, John Allen *magazine publisher*
†Michaels, Alan Richard *sports commentator*
Mikita, Joseph Karl *broadcasting executive*
Miller, Caroline *editor-in-chief*
Miller, Darcy M. *publishing executive*
Miller, Michael Jeffrey *editor, columnist*
Minick, Michael *publishing executive*
†Moldow, Susan *publishing executive*
†Moonves, Leslie *television company executive*
Moore, Ann S. *magazine executive*
†Morehouse, Ward, III, *theater critic, playwright*
†Morgan, Mary E. *publishing executive*
Morgenson, Gretchen C. *reporter*
†Morris, David *publishing executive*
†Morris, Douglas Peter *recording company executive*
Moskin, John Robert *editor, writer*
†Moss, Adam Wender *editor*
Mottola, Thomas *entertainment company executive*
†Moyers, Bill D. *journalist*
Moylan, Steve *publishing executive*
†Murdoch, Lachlan Keith *publishing executive*
†Murphy, Ann Pleshette *magazine editor-in-chief*
Murphy, Helen *recording industry executive*
Nagourney, Herbert *publishing company executive*
Nathan, Paul S. *editor, writer*
Navasky, Victor Saul *magazine editor, publisher*
†Newcomb, Jonathan *publishing executive*
Newhouse, Nancy Riley *newspaper editor*
Norris, Floyd Hamilton *financial journalist*
Novitz, Charles Richard *television executive*
Novogrod, Nancy Gerstein *editor*
Nyren, Neil Sebastian *publisher, editor*
O'Brien, Geoffrey Paul *editor, writer*
†Oldham, Joe *editor*
†Olson, Peter *publishing executive*
Orwell, Mark Peter *magazine editor*
†Osgood, Charles *news broadcaster, journalist*
Osnos, Peter Lionel Winston *publishing executive*
Ostling, Richard Neil *journalist, author*
Pace, Eric Dwight *journalist, writer*
†Packard, George Randolph *journalist, educator*
†Palsho, Dorothea Coccoli *information services executive*
Paneth, Donald Joseph *editor, writer*
Parisotto, Gloria *publishing executive, poet*
Paul, Kenneth *newspaper editor*
Pearlstine, Norman *editor*
Peck, Thomas *newspaper publishing executive*
Penn, Stanley William *journalist*
†Pennington, William Mark *sportswriter*
Pesin, Ella Michele *journalist, public relations professional*
Petersen, Barry Rex *news correspondent*
Petzal, David Elias *editor, writer*
Pfeiffer, Jane Cahill *former broadcasting company executive, consultant*
Phillips, Reneé *editor-in-chief, author, public speaker*
Phillips, Stone *television journalist*
Piel, Gerard *science editor, publisher*
Pines, Burton Yale *media executive*
†Plagemann, Susan *publishing executive*
Podd, Ann *newspaper editor*
Pope, Liston, Jr., *writer, journalist*
Porterfield, Christopher *magazine editor, writer*
Post, David Alan *media and internet technology executive*
Potter, Ned *science journalist, writer*
Pressman, Gabe Stanley *television reporter*
Prozes, Andrew *publishing executive*
Quinn, Jane Bryant *journalist, writer*
Quinson, Bruno Andre *publishing executive*
Ragan, David *publishing company executive*
Rather, Dan *broadcast journalist*
Rauch, Rudolph Stewart, III, *periodical editor, arts education executive*
Rawson, Eleanor S. *publishing company executive*
Ray, C. Claiborne *editor, columnist*
Raymond, Jack *journalist, public relations executive, foundation executive*
†Regan, Judith Terrance *publishing executive*
†Regazzi, John James, III, *publishing executive*
Reice, Sylvie *columnist, editor, author*
Reichl, Ruth Molly *editor*
Reilly, William Francis *media company executive*
Remnick, David J. *journalist, editor*
Rescigno, Richard Joseph *editor*
Reuther, David Louis *children's book publisher, writer*
Reynolds, Warren Jay *retired publisher*
Rhoads, Geraldine Emeline *editor, consultant*
Rhone, Sylvia *recording industry executive*
Rich, Frank Hart *journalist, author*
†Riggio, Leonard *book publishing executive*
Rigney, Jane *copy editor, writer*
†Roach, Margaret *editor-in-chief*
Roberts, John *news anchor*
†Roberts, Madelyn Alpert *publishing executive*
†Robinson, Janet *publishing executive*
†Robinson, Janet L. *publishing executive*
Rogin, Gilbert Leslie *editor, author*
Roland, John *newscaster*
Ronson, Raoul R. *publishing executive*
†Rosado, Rossana *publishing executive, editor-in-chief*
Rose, Charles *television journalist*
†Rosengarten, Frank *retired communications educator, writer*
Rosset, Barnet Lee, Jr., *publishing executive*
Rothberg, Gerald *editor, publisher, editor-in-chief*
†Rubenstein, Atoosa Behnegar *editor-in-chief*
Rubin, Harry Meyer *entertainment and software industry executive*
Rudin, Max Allen *publishing executive*
Ruhlmann, William James *music critic*
†Rusell, Anne M *publishing executive*
Sabat, Robert Hartman *magazine editor*
Sabino, Catherine Ann *magazine editor*
Safer, Morley *journalist*
†Safian, Robert *managing editor*
Salembier, Valerie Birnbaum *publishing executive*
Sanders, Richard Louis *executive editor*
Sandler, Irving Harry *art critic, art historian*
Sawyer, Diane (L. Diane Sawyer) *television journalist*
Saxon, Wolfgang Erik Georg *journalist*
†Scannell, Herb *broadcast executive*
Scarborough, Charles Bishop, III, *broadcast journalist, writer*
Schlosser, Herbert S. *broadcasting company executive*
Schmemann, Serge *journalist*
Schmertz, Mildred Floyd *editor, writer*
Schoell, William Robert *editor, author*
Schrader, Michael Eugene *columnist, editor*
Schuman, Patricia Glass *publishing company executive, educator*
Schwartz, Gail Garfield *media consultant*
Scribner, Charles, III, *publisher, art historian, lecturer*
†Seelig, Jill *publishing executive*
Segal, Jonathan Bruce *editor*
Seligman, Daniel *editor*
†Seligman, Nicole K. *broadcast executive, lawyer*
Semple, Robert Baylor, Jr., *newspaper editor, journalist*
Servodidio, Pat Anthony *broadcast executive*
Seymour, Lesley Jane *magazine editor-in-chief*
Shaine, Frederick Mordecai *newspaper executive, consultant*
Shanbacker, Frank Morse, III, *television news producer*
†Shanks, David *publishing executive*
Shapiro, Gary Evan *newspaper journalist*
†Shapiro, Neal *broadcast executive, television producer*
Sheinman, Mort *editor, consultant, writer, photographer*
Shepard, Stephen Benjamin *journalist, magazine editor*
†Shepard, Thomas Rockwell, III, *advertising sales executive*
Sheward, David John *newspaper editor and critic*
Shewchuk, Robert John *television executive*
Shier, Shelley M. *production company executive*
Shnayerson, Robert Beahan *editor, consultant*
Shortz, Will *puzzle editor*
Shull, Mikki *media consultant*
Siegal, Allan Marshall *newspaper editor*
Siegel, Joel Steven *television news correspondent*
Siegel, Marvin *newspaper editor*
Sifton, Elisabeth *book publisher*
†Sigmund, Stephen Hale *broadcast executive*
Sikorsky, Robert Bellarmine *syndicated columnist*
Silverman, Al *editor*
Silvers, Robert B. *editor*
†Simmons, Russell *recording industry executive*
Simon, Bob *news correspondent, anchor*
†Simon, Peter J. *editor*
Singer, Niki *media consultant*
Singleton, Donald Edward *journalist*
Sivy, Michael *journalist*
†Skinner, Peter Graeme *publishing executive, lawyer*
Sleed, Joel *columnist*
Sloan, Allan Herbert *journalist*
Smith, Corlies Morgan *publishing executive*
Smith, Dennis (Edward Smith) *author, publisher*
†Smith, Harry *newscaster*
Smith, Joseph Phelan *film company executive*
Smith, Liz (Mary Elizabeth Smith) *newspaper columnist, broadcast journalist*
Smith, Patrick John *editor, writer*
†Smith, Richard Mills *editor-in-chief*
Soriano, Nancy Mernit *editor-in-chief*
Soto, Roberto Fernando Eduardo *journalist*
Speller, Robert Ernest Blakefield *publishing executive*
Spence, James Robert, Jr., *television sports executive, educator*
Spring, Michael *editor, writer*
Stahl, Lesley R. *news correspondent*
Stanger, Ila *writer, editor*
†Steck, Jodi *photojournalist*
Steiger, Paul Ernest *newspaper editor, journalist*
†Stephanopoulos, George Robert *reporter*
†Stern, Mitchell *broadcast executive*
Stern, Roslyne Paige *magazine publisher*
Steves, Gale C. *marketing professional, writer, retired editor-in-chief, publishing executive*
†Storm, Hannah *newscaster*
Stringer, Howard *media executive*
†Studin, Jan *publishing executive*
Sturtevant, Peter Mann, Jr., *television news editor*
Sugihara, Kenzi *publishing executive*
Sugiyama, Kazunori *music producer*
Sulzberger, Arthur Ochs, Jr., *newspaper publisher*
†Susskind, Emily H. *broadcast executive*
Sussman, Gerald *publishing company executive*
Sweed, Phyllis *publishing executive*
Sweeting, Charles Harvard *columnist, film director*
†Syler, Rene *newscaster*
Tarr, Robert Joseph, Jr., *publishing executive, retail executive*
Taylor, Chris *journalist, writer*
Taylor, Sherril Wightman *broadcasting company executive*
Taylor, Terry R. *editor, educator*
†Teren, Marc *publishing executive*
†Tetlezi, Rick *editor*
Thomas, Brooks *publishing company executive*
Thompson, Martin Christian *news service executive*
Thorn, Rod *professional basketball executive*
Tober, Barbara D. (Mrs. Donald Gibbs Tober) *editor*
Toff, Nancy Ellen *book editor*
Tomlinson, James Francis *retired news agency executive*
†Toussaint, Allen Richard *recording studio executive, composer, pianist*
Townsend, Alair Ane *publisher, municipal official*
†Townsend, Charles H. *publishing executive*
†Trauthwein, Christina *editor-in-chief*
Tuchman, Phyllis *critic*
†Turnley, David Carl *photojournalist*
Uchitelle, Louis *journalist*
†Umansky, Diane *publishing executive*
†Ungaro, Susan Kelliher *magazine editor*
Valand, Theodore Lloyd *media company executive*
†Velez, Phillip Luis *communications specialist, researcher*
Vick, James Albert *publishing executive, consultant*
†Vitale, Alberto Aldo *retired publishing company executive*
†Vlamis, Susan (Suzanne) Anne *editor, photographer*
Voorhees, David William *editor, historian*
Wald, Richard Charles *broadcasting executive*
Walker, Christopher T. *newswriter, commentator*
Walker, Mort *cartoonist*
†Wallace, Carol *editor at large*
Wallace, Mike *television interviewer and reporter*
Wallace, Thomas C(hristopher) *editor, literary agent*
Walters, Barbara *television journalist*
Wang, Arthur Woods *retired publisher*
Warner, Peter David *publishing executive*
Washburn, Deborah Field *publishing executive*
Weber, Robert Maxwell *cartoonist*
Weber, Samuel *editor, retired*
†Weinstein, Harvey *film company executive*
†Weinstein, Robert *film company executive*
†Weiss, Barry *recording industry executive*
Wells, Linda Ann *editor-in-chief*
†Wenner, Jann Simon *editor, publisher*
Wetschler, Ed *editor*
Whitaker, Mark Theis *magazine editor*
†White, Kate *editor-in-chief*
Whitney, Craig Richard *journalist*
Wilford, John Noble, Jr., *science news correspondent*
†Wilkins, Amy P. *publishing executive*
Williams, Ian George *writer*
Willis, Ellen *journalist, educator*
Willis, John Alvin *editor*
Wilson, James Reid, Jr., *publishing executive*
Windsor, Laurence Charles, Jr., *publishing executive, writer*
Winship, Frederick Moery *journalist*
Wogan, Robert *broadcasting company executive*
Wolper, Allan *journalist, educator*
Woodcock, Les *editorial director*
Woodruff, Mark Reed *magazine editor*
†WuDunn, Sheryl *journalist, correspondent*
Yablon, Leonard Harold *publishing company executive*
Young, Genevieve Leman *publishing executive, editor*
Zackheim, Adrian Walter *editor*
†Zagat, Nina *publishing executive*
†Zagat, Tim *publishing executive*
Zerman, Melvyn Bernard *publishing company executive, author*
Zimmerman, William Edwin *newspaper editor, publisher, writer*
†Zinczenko, David *publishing executive*
†Zuckerman, Mortimer Benjamin *publisher, editor, real estate developer*

North Salem
Burlingame, Edward Livermore *book publisher*

Nyack
Flood, H(ulda) Gay *editor, consultant*
Oursler, Fulton, Jr., *editor, writer*

Old Westbury
O'Brien, Adrienne Gratia *communications educator*

Oswego
Loveridge-Sanbonmatsu, Joan Meredith *communication studies and women's studies educator, poet*
Messere, Frank *communications educator*

Palisades
Polk, Milbry Catherine *media specialist*

Pine Plains
Janitschek, Hans *journalist*

Pleasantville
Leo, Jacqueline M. *editor-in-chief, Internet company executive*
†McEwen, Laura *publishing executive*
†Reddicliffe, Steven *periodical editor-in-chief*
†Schrier, Eric *publishing executive*
†Willcox, Christopher Patrick *magazine editor*

Port Washington
Candido, Arthur Aldo *publishing and distribution company executive*
Jay, Frank Peter *writer, lexicographer, educator*

Poughkeepsie
Kim, David Sang Chul *publisher, evangelist, retired seminary president*

Remsenburg
Billman, Irwin Edward *publishing company executive*

Rhinebeck
Swift, Paul *editor*

Richmondville
†Bartholomew, Debra Lee *publishing executive*

Riverdale
Chimsky, Mark Evan *publishing consultant*

Riverhead
Roland, David Leonard *retired broadcast production educator*

Rochester
†Kaidy, Mitchell *journalist, writer, legislative staff member*

PROFESSIONAL INDEX 6251 COMMUNICATIONS MEDIA

Lank, Edith Handleman *columnist, educator*
Pitoniak, Scott Michael *sportswriter*
Prosser, Michael Hubert *communications educator*

Rome
Waters, George Bausch *newspaper publisher*

Rye
Iarocci, Kent Alexander *newswriter, home improvement contractor*
Nelson, Vita Joy *editor, publisher*
Pearson, Nathan Williams *communications and investment executive*
Schmitz, Robert Allen *publishing executive, investor*

Sag Harbor
Clemente, Vince *journalist, retired English educator, historian*
Epstein, Jason *publishing company executive*

Scarborough
Byrne, Robert Eugene *chess columnist*

Scarsdale
Goodman, Jordan Elliot *journalist*
Heese, William John *music publishing company executive*
O'Neill, Michael James *editor, author*
Pope, Leavitt Joseph *broadcast company executive*
Shaw, Grace Goodfriend (Mrs. Herbert Franklin Shaw) *publisher, editor*
Toff, Ruth Bluthenthal *editor*
Topping, Audrey Ronning *photojournalist, author*
Topping, Seymour *author, educator*

Schenectady
Pearson, Timothy Alfred *newspaper circulation executive*

Selkirk
†Christoph, Peter Richard *historical editor, archivist*

Setauket
Dunaief, Leah S. *newspaper editor, publisher, writer*
Robinson, Richard M. *technical communication specialist*

Sleepy Hollow
Flynn-Connors, Elizabeth Kathryn *editor*

Somers
Cohn, Howard *retired magazine editor*

South Ozone Park
Banks, Robert Lee *publisher, author, jazz guitarist, composer, arranger*

South Setauket
Poli, Kenneth Joseph *editor, writer, photographer*

Southampton
Graham, Howard Barrett *publishing company executive*

Staten Island
†Choo, Kristin E. *journalist*
†Kahn, Jim *former magazine publisher*
†Newhouse, Donald E. *newspaper publishing executive*
†Newhouse, Samuel I., Jr., *publishing executive*

Stony Brook
Booth, George *cartoonist*
Harvey, Christine Lynn *publishing executive*

Stony Point
Carter, Richard *publisher, writer*

Syracuse
Bunn, Timothy David *newspaper editor*
†Fischler, Alan Bernard *communications educator*
LaRue, William David *television critic*
†Thompson, Robert James *media specialist, educator*

Tarrytown
Ashburn, Anderson *magazine editor*
†Bunton, Phil *editor-in-chief*
†LeGrice, Stephen *magazine editor*
Neill, Richard Robert *retired publishing company executive*
Stein, Sol *publisher, writer, editor in chief*

Troy
Friedman, Sue Tyler *technical publications executive*

Utica
Donovan, Donna Mae *newspaper publisher*

Valhalla
Lombardi, Don Dominick *art critic, artist*

Valley Cottage
Lazecko, David John *broadcast executive*

Waccabuc
Krefting, Robert J(ohn) *publishing company executive*

Wading River
Budd, Bernadette Smith *lawyer, newspaper executive, public relations consultant*

Wainscott
Henderson, William Charles *editor*

Warwick
Simon, Dolores Daly *copy editor*

Watertown
Brett, James Clarence *retired journalism educator*
Johnson, John Brayton *editor, publisher*

Yonkers
Denver, Eileen Ann *magazine editor*
Dudley, Don *broadcast journalist, communications consultant*
Kagan, Julia Lee *magazine editor*

Yorktown Heights
Wade, James O'Shea *editor and writer*

NORTH CAROLINA

Asheboro
†Cunningham, Laine *editor, educator, writer, consultant*

Asheville
Damtoft, Walter Atkinson *editor, publishing executive, consultant*
De Bruhl, A. Marshall *writer, editor, publishing consultant*

Battleboro
Hardy, Linda Lea Sterlock *media specialist*

Boone
Aluri, Rao *book publisher*

Brevard
Phillips, Euan Hywel *publishing executive*

Burlington
Buckley, J. Stephen *newspaper publisher*

Chapel Hill
Bailey, Herbert Smith, Jr., *retired publisher*
Edwards, Dale Leon *communications educator*
Gaither, Thomas K. *communications consultant*
Guillory, John Ferrel *journalism educator*
Lauder, Valarie Anne *editor, educator*
Ravenel, Shannon *book publishing professional*

Charlotte
Barrows, Frank Clemence *editor*
Buckner, Jennie *newspaper editor*
Curtis, Mary Cecelia *journalist*
Ethridge, Mark Foster, III, *writer, publisher, media consultant*
Haines, Kenneth H. *sports television broadcasting and marketing executive*
†Horner, Bob *broadcast executive*
†Jones, Amos Nathanael *journalist, violist*
Powell, Dannye Romine *news columnist*
†Ridder, Peter B. *publishing executive*
†Turner, Kathleen J. *communications educator, consultant*

Durham
Cooper, Charles Howard *photojournalist, newspaper publishing company executive*
Fiske, Edward B. *editor, journalist, educational consultant*
Harrell, Carlton (Benjamin Carlton Harrell) *writer, retired editor*
Hawkins, William E. N. *newspaper editor*
Mallette, Malcolm Francis *newspaper editor, educator*
Rollins, Edward Tyler, Jr., *newspaper executive*
Rossiter, Alexander, Jr., *news service executive, editor*

Greensboro
Blackwell, William Ernest
Gill, Evalyn Pierpoint *editor, writer, publisher*
Herman, Roger Eliot *professional speaker, consultant, futurist, writer*
Jellicorse, John Lee *communications and theatre educator*
McKissick-Melton, S. Charmaine *mass communications educator*

Greenville
Eribo, Festus *mass communication educator, journalist*

Hampstead
Unger, Stephen Allan *publishing executive, editor*

Harrisburg
Economaki, Chris Constantine (Christopher Economaki) *publisher, editor*

Hillsborough
Bolduc, Jean Plumley *journalist, education activist*

Jefferson
Franklin, Robert McFarland *book publisher*

Laurel Springs
Gilbert-Strawbridge, Anne Wieland *journalist*

Lawndale
†Williams, Robert Leonard *publishing executive, photographer*

Lincolnton
Kempster, Norman Roy *journalist*

Newton
Harris, Gerald Wayne *retired radio advertising sales executive*

Pembroke
Jordan, Chester I. *communication educator, theater educator*

Pisgah Forest
Rierson, Robert Leak *retired broadcasting executive, television writer*

Pittsboro
Hauser, Charles Newland McCorkle *newspaper consultant*

Raleigh
Crisp, Fred *retired publishing executive*
†Daniels, Frank Arthur, Jr., *newspaper publisher*
Entman, Robert Mathew *communications educator, consultant*
Kauffman, Terry *broadcast and creative arts communication educator, artist*
McKinney, Donald Lee *magazine editor*
Parker, Joseph Mayon *printing and publishing executive*
Paschal, Beth Cummings *journalist, editor*
Reeves, Ralph Bernard, III, *publisher, editor*
Sill, Melanie *editor*

Research Triangle Park
Greenwell, Arnold *associate editor, photographer*

Saluda
McCutcheon, John Tinney, Jr., *retired journalist*

Sanford
Harrington, Anthony Ross *radio announcer, educator*

Spindale
Trautmann, Patricia Ann *communications educator, storyteller*

Vaughan
†Jordan, Paul Richard *journalist, writer*

Waxhaw
Lamparter, William C. *printing and publishing consultant, digital printing and information systems specialist*

Wilmington
Swain, Mary Margaret *editor, marketing consultant*

Winston Salem
Graybeal, Barbara *editor, writer*
King, Wayne Edgar *journalist, educator*
Somerville, Atwell Wilson, Jr., *medical editor*

Wrightsville Beach
Mc Ilwain, William Franklin *newspaper editor, writer*

NORTH DAKOTA

Finley
Devlin, William Russell *newspaper owner*

Grand Forks
Glassheim, Eliot Alan *editor, state legislator*

OHIO

Akron
Tyrity, Kathy Milica *reporter, editor*

Ashland
Reidenbach, Faith E. *medical editor, writer*

Athens
Metters, Thomas Waddell *sports writer*
Sanders, David *university press administrator*
Scott, Charles Lewis *photojournalist*
Stempel, Guido Hermann, III, *journalism educator*

Beachwood
†Cozzarin, James Robert *editor, writer*
Mendel, Roberta *editor, publisher, writer*
Wells Bradley, Charlena Renee *editor, writer*

Bowling Green
Clark, Robert King *communications educator emeritus, lecturer, consultant, actor, model*

Canton
Maxwell, John Alexander, Jr., *retired newspaper editor, consultant*

Chagrin Falls
Lange, David Charles *journalist*

Cincinnati
Beckwith, Barbara Jean *journalist*
Burleigh, William Robert *newspaper executive*
Callinan, Tom *editor*
Gelfand, Janelle Ann *music critic*
Irwin, Miriam Dianne Owen *book publisher, writer*
King, Margaret Ann *communications educator*
McMullin, Ruth Roney *publishing executive, trustee, management fellow*
Mechem, Charles Stanley, Jr., *former broadcasting executive, former golf association executive*
Petty, Priscilla Hayes *writer, columnist, producer*
Silvers, Gerald Thomas *retired publishing executive*
Steinberg, Janet Eckstein *journalist*
Wasnak, Lynn *publishing executive, writer*
Whipple, Harry M. *newspaper publishing executive*

Cleveland
†Appling, Christopher Michael *columnist, writer*
Bingham, Richard Donnelly *journal editor, director, educator*
Brandt, John Reynold *editor, journalist*
†Clark, Gary R. *newspaper editor*
Clifton, Douglas C. *newspaper editor*
Conrad, Robert David *broadcast executive, educator*
Dolgan, Robert Joseph *journalist*
Fabris, James A. *journalist*
†Hanson, Karen Lynn *editor*
Jindra, Christine *editor*
Kanzeg, David George *radio station executive*
Lebovitz, Harold Paul (Hal Lebovitz) *journalist*
Lee, Jae-won *journalism educator, political campaign consultant*
Lowry, Joan Marie Dondrea *broadcaster*
Machaskee, Alex *newspaper publishing company executive*
Miller, Arnold *retired newspaper editor*
Molyneaux, David Glenn *newspaper travel editor*
O'Hara, Thomas Patrick *managing editor*
Pascarella, Perry James *author, editor, speaker*
†Raven, Hyacinthe L. *publishing executive, editor*

Columbus
Barry, James P(otvin) *writer, editor*
Charles, Bertram *radio broadcasting executive*
Cox, Mitchel Neal *editor*
Dervin, Brenda Louise *communications educator*
Gribble, Charles Edward *editor, Slavic languages educator*
Grossberg, Michael Lee *theater critic, writer*
Kefauver, Weldon Addison *publishing executive*
†Krumm, Tahlman, Jr., *communications educator*
Langholz, Armin Paul *communications educator*
Lowe, Clayton Kent *radio film critic, educator*
Massie, Robert Joseph *publishing company executive*
Sherrill, Thomas Boykin, III, *retired newspaper publishing executive*

Columbus Grove
Thiede, Richard Wesley *retired communications educator*

Cuyahoga Falls
Hamilton, Donald Dow Webb *publisher, freelance writer*

Dayton
Duncan, Richard Leo *communications educator*
Elliott, Scott Emory *reporter*
†Gaines, Elliot *communications educator*
Hamlin, Tom *sportscaster*
Matheny, Ruth Ann *editor*
†Rucker, Mary L *communications educator*
Tillson, John Bradford (Brad), Jr., *newspaper publisher*

Dublin
Wang, Andrew Hsing-Jen *information marketing executive, journalist, librarian*

Elyria
Coleman, D. Christian *journalist*

Kent
†Springer, Barbara Hipsman *journalism educator*
†Tiene, Drew *communications educator, consultant*

Kirtland
Ryan, William Joseph *multimedia and distance education designer, information technology executive*

Lakewood
Condon, George Edward *journalist*

Lancaster
†Crandall, Margaret Elizabeth *editor*

Mason
Smith, C. LeMoyne *publishing company executive*

Newcomerstown
Komorowski, Anne Marie *freelance journalist, paralegal*

Orville
†Long, Elizabeth Valk *former magazine publisher*

Oxford
Sanders, Gerald Hollie *communications educator, educator*

Pataskala
Caw, Thomas William *retired publisher and editor*

Pepper Pike
O'Neill, Katherine Templeton *journalist, museum administrator, former nursing educator*
†Vail, Thomas Van Husen *retired newspaper publisher and editor*

Reynoldsburg
Powell, Edward Lee *broadcasting company executive*

Seaman
Cartaino, Carol Ann *editor*

Sidney
Laurence, Michael Marshall *magazine publisher, writer*
†Marlow, Meme Elizabeth *journalist*
Mintchell, Gary Alan *editor*
Stevens, Robert Jay *magazine editor*

Toledo
Block, John Robinson *newspaper publisher*
Block, William K., Jr., *newspaper executive*
Brickey, Suzanne M. *editor*
Royhab, Ronald *journalist, newspaper editor*
Willey, John Douglas *retired newspaper executive*

Westerville
DeVassie, Terry Lee *publishing executive*

Wilberforce
Oluyitan, Emmanuel Funso *communications educator*

Willoughby
Corrigan, Faith *journalist, educator, historian*

Wooster
August, Robert Olin *journalist*

Yellow Springs
Cawood, Albert McLaurin (Hap Cawood) *retired newspaper editor*

OKLAHOMA

Ada
Reese, Patricia Ann *retired editor, columnist*

Bethany
Engle, Richard Victor *publishing executive*
Murrow, Wayne Lee *retired communications educator, dean*

Chouteau
Sasser, Charles Wayne *journalist, educator, writer*

Edmond
McCoy, William Ulysses *journalist*
Pydynkowsky, Joan Anne *journalist*

Midwest City
Lesko-Bishop, Julia *editor*

Norman
Dary, David Archie *journalism educator, author*
Drayton, John N. *publishing executive*
Kennedy, Gregory Dustin *journalist*
Morton, Linda P. *journalism educator*

Oklahoma City
Gourley, James Leland *editor, publishing executive*
Gourley, Vicki Clark *publishing executive*
McGuigan, Patrick Bruce *editor, educator*
Mitrovgenis, James William, Jr., *journalist*
†Thompson, David *publishing executive*
Triplett, E. Eugene *editor*

Ponca City
Collins, Walter Lloyd George *editor*

Sallisaw
Mayo, James Watie (Jim Mayo) *publishing executive*

Tulsa
Beck, Robert James *editor, energy economist, author, consultant*
Bender, John Henry, Jr., (Jack Bender) *editor, cartoonist*
Fleming, Ken *publishing executive*
Haring, Robert Westing *newspaper editor*
Jones, Jenk, Jr., *editor, educator*
Jones, Jenkin Lloyd *retired newspaper publisher*
Lorton, Robert E., Jr., *publishing executive*
Major, John Keene *radio broadcasting executive*
†Scott, John Prosser *television program producer, management consultant*
Upton, Howard B., Jr., *management writer, lawyer*

Wewoka
Trimble, Vance Henry *retired newspaper editor*

OREGON

Albany
Wood, Kenneth Arthur *retired newspaper editor, writer*

Corvallis
Hall, Don Alan *editor, writer*
Zwahlen, Fred Casper, Jr., *journalism educator*

Eugene
Baker, Alton Fletcher, III, *newspaper editor, publishing executive*
Baker, Bridget Downey *newspaper executive*
Baker, Edwin Moody *retired newspaper publisher*
Bassett, Carol Ann *journalism educator, writer*
Glaspey, Terry W. *publishing executive, writer*
Green, Paul John *independent critic*
Tykeson, Donald Erwin *broadcast executive*

Medford
Ryder, Stephen Willis *retired newspaper publisher*

Portland
Bhatia, Peter K. *newspaper editor, journalist*
Bunza, Linda Hathaway *editor, writer, composer, institution director*
Crabbs, Roger Alan *publisher, consultant, small business owner, educator*
Dolan, William J. *media executive*
Hart, Jack Robert *newspaper editor*
Johnston, Virginia Evelyn *retired editor*
Mapes, Jeffrey Robert *journalist*
Nokes, John Richard *retired newspaper editor, writer*
Pippi, Mikel Eugene *media specialist, director, academic administrator*
Rowe, Sandra Mims *editor*
Stickel, Frederick A. *publishing executive*
Stickel, Patrick Francis *publishing executive, newspaper*
Walth, Brent David *journalist, writer*

Salem
Hall, Mark Everett *editor, writer*

Wallowa
Wizard, Brian *publisher, author*

PENNSYLVANIA

Ardmore
Gerbner, George *communications educator, university dean emeritus*

Bala Cynwyd
Perkins, Russell Alexander *publisher, consultant*

Bensalem
Kang, Benjamin Toyeong *writer, clergyman*

Berwyn
Baxter, John Michael *editor*

Bloomsburg
Bertelsen, Dale Alan *communications educator*
Brasch, Walter Milton *journalist, educator*
Schwartz, Susan R. *reporter*
Strine, Harry Cornelius, III, *communications educator*

Butler
Hawk, Kathleen Patricia *broadcast consultant*

Carlisle
Fish, Chester Boardman, Jr., *retired editor*
Talley, Carol Lee *newspaper editor*

Clarion
Siddiqui, Dilnawaz Ahmed *communications educator, consultant*

Clearfield
Krebs, Margaret Eloise *publishing executive*

Du Bois
Bonavita, Dennis Joseph *newspaper publisher*

East Stroudsburg
Rosenblum, Stewart Irwin *recording industry executive*

Easton
Bader, Cal Joseph, Jr., *broadcast executive*
Stitt, Dorothy Jewett *journalist*

Emmaus
†Bricklin, Mark Harris *magazine editor, publisher*
†Favorule, Denise *publishing executive*
†Rodale, Ardath Harter *publishing executive*

Felton
Shoemaker, Eleanor Boggs *television production company executive*

Flourtown
Lee, Adrian Iselin, Jr., *journalist*

Forest City
Kameen, John Paul *newspaper publisher*

Gettysburg
Gritsch, Ruth Christine Lisa *editor*

Gwynedd Valley
Strasburg, William Edward *retired newspaper publisher*

Harrisburg
Antoun, Annette Agnes *newspaper editor, publisher*
DeKok, David *writer, reporter*
Gover, Raymond Lewis *retired newspaper executive*

Hellertown
McCullagh, James Charles *publishing executive*

Henryville
†Dittmer, Luther Albert *publisher, educator*

Holland
Hosey, Sheryl Lynn Miller *educator, editor, theater director*

Honesdale
Clark, Christine May *editor, author*

Horsham
†Dariano, Joseph *publishing company executive*
†Fisher, Darryl *information services company executive*

Kennett Square
Landstrom, Elsie Hayes *retired editor*

King Of Prussia
Broido, Arnold Peace *music publishing company executive*

Lancaster
Shaw, Charles Raymond *journalist*
Shenk, Willis Weidman *newspaper executive*

Leola
Gehman, Terry Lee *music industry professional*

Levittown
Halberstein, Joseph Leonard *retired associate editor*

Marshalls Creek
†Johnson, Loren Charisse *publishing executive, writer*

Mechanicsburg
Davis, Frank Daniel *retired journalist*
Stouffer, Nancy Kathleen *publishing company executive*

Montoursville
Woolever, Naomi Louise *retired editor*

New Kensington
Demmler, Albert William, Jr., *retired editor, metallurgical engineer*

Philadelphia
Bennett, Amanda *editor*
Biddle, Daniel R. *editor, reporter*
Binzen, Peter Husted *columnist*
Carey, Arthur Bernard, Jr., *editor, writer, columnist*
Cohen, David Michael *newspaper editor, journalist*
Cooper, Richard Lee *newspaper editor, journalist*
Gordon, Anne Kathleen *editor*
Gruliow, Rebecca Agnes Lindsay *editor, translator, artist*
Hall, Robert J. *newspaper executive*
Halpern, Eric Franklin *university publishing director*
Hillgren, Sonja Dorothy *journalist*
Hochman, Stanley Richard *journalist*
Jackson, Harold *journalist*
Klein, Julia Meredith *freelance/self-employed journalist*
Leiter, Robert Allen *journalist, magazine editor*
Lent, John Anthony *journalist, educator*
Libkind, Jean Sue Johnson (Jean Sue Johnson-Libkind) *publishing executive*
Lundy, Walker *newspaper editor*
Lyon, William Carl *sports columnist*
†Nalle, Peter Devereux *publishing company executive*
Othmer, David Artman *television and radio consultant*
Parry, Lance Aaron *newspaper executive*
Rorer, John Whiteley *publisher, consultant*
Saline, Carol Sue *journalist*
Stalberg, Zachary *newspaper editor*
†Vitez, Michael *reporter*
Wilkinson, Signe *cartoonist*
Winfrey, Marion Lee *retired television critic*

Pittsburgh
Apone, Carl Anthony *journalist*
†Claussen, Dane Sherman *newspaper consultant, journalism educator*
†Froehlich, Fritz Edgar *communications educator, telecommunications scientist*
Graham, Laurie *editor, writer*
Harrell, Edward Harding *newspaper executive*
Heindl, Mary Lynn *magazine editor*
Leo, Peter Andrew *newspaper columnist, writing educator*
†Lopes, Jerry *broadcast executive*
†Rial, Martha *photographer*
Ross, Madelyn Ann *newspaper editor*
†Shribman, David Marks *editor*
Webb, Geneá Lynetta *journalist*

Reading
†Creasy, Dana Eugene *communications educator*

Saint Davids
Denenberg, Herbert Sidney *journalist, lawyer, former state official*

Scottdale
†Brittain, Paul S. *editor*

Scranton
Lynett, William Ruddy *publishing, broadcasting company executive*

Shippenville
†Fortis, Marie-Jose *editor*

South Sterling
Bancroft, Peggy *editor*

Spring House
†Hurley, Kevin *publishing executive*

State College
Kowalczyk, Kim Jan *editor, writer*

University Park
Jackson, Ronald L., II, *communications educator*

Warrendale
Snyder, Linda Ann *editor*

Warrington
Ward, Hiley Henry *journalist, educator*

Wayne
Fabbri, Anne R. *art critic, curator*
Youman, Roger Jacob *editor, writer*

West Chester
Gallagher, Terrence Vincent *editor*
Lenfest, Harold Fitz Gerald *former cable television executive, lawyer*
Mahoney, William Francis *editor/author*

Williamsport
Rosebrough, Carol Belville *cable television company executive*

Wynnewood
Bernfeld, Gerald E. *editor, writer, retired nursing educator*
Brown, Michael John *publishing executive*
Harrison, Donald *newspaper editor*

Yardley
Zulker, Charles Bates *broadcasting company executive*

York
Kodadek, William F(rancis) *communication educator*

RHODE ISLAND

Charlestown
Ungaro, Joseph Michael *newspaper publishing executive, consultant*

Cranston
Parravano, Amelia Elizabeth (Amy Beth Parravano) *recording industry executive*

Middletown
Cooper, Michele F. *writer, editor, analyst*

Newport
Uhlig, Frank, Jr., *editor, writer*

Portsmouth
Needham, Richard Lee *magazine editor*
Parker, Nancy Knowles (Mrs. Cortlandt Parker) *retired publishing executive*

Providence
Dujardin, Richard Charles *journalist*
Farmer, Susan Lawson *broadcasting executive, former secretary of state*
Forliti, Amy Marie *reporter*
Israel, Kay Frank *communications educator*
Levin, Leonard Irving *newspaper editor*
Rosenberg, Alan Gene *newspaper editor*
Sutton, Howard G. *publishing executive*

Wakefield
Wyman, James Vernon *newspaper executive*

Warwick
Halperson, Michael Allen *publishing executive*
Hamilton, Andrew David *publishing company executive, writer*

West Kingston
Haring, Howard Jack *newsletter editor*

Woonsocket
Eno, Paul Frederick *editor, writer*

SOUTH CAROLINA

Barnwell
Nichols, M(arian) Theresa *radio station executive*

Bennettsville
Kinney, William Light, Jr., *newspaper editor, publisher*

Blackstock
King, Robert Thomas *editor, freelance writer*

Cayce
McElveen, William Lindsay *broadcasting executive, lecturer*

Charleston
Langley, Lynne Spencer *newspaper editor, columnist*
Reed, Stanley Foster *editor, author, publisher, lecturer*
Schreadley, Richard Lee *writer, retired newspaper editor*
Tarleton, Larry Wilson *editor*
Williams, Barbara Stambaugh *editor*

Clemson
Denham, Bryan Errol *communications educator*

Columbia
Breedin, Berryman Brent *journalist, public relations, historian, consultant*
Lett, Mark *editor*
Mott, Frederick B., Jr., *publishing executive*
Smith, W. Thomas, Jr., *author, journalist*

Conway
Shaw, M. Beatryce *retired publishing executive, writer*

Easley
Failing, George Edgar *editor, clergyman, educator*

Greenville
Eskew, Rhea Taliaferro *newspaper publisher*
Hipp, William Hayne *broadcast executive*

Hilton Head Island
†Shaheen, Jack George *communications educator*

Mount Pleasant
Abbott-Lyon, Frances Dowdle *journalist, civic worker*

Orangeburg
Creekmore, Verity Veirs *media specialist*
Sims, Edward Howell *editor, publisher*

Piedmont
Davis, Robert Barry *technician, religious studies educator*

Simpsonville
Gilstrap, Leah Ann *media specialist*
Hamilton, Martha Jean Anderson *media specialist*
Kanzler, George *journalist, critic*

SOUTH DAKOTA

Martin
Kampfe, Nancy Lee *communications educator*

Mobridge
Hall, Jo(sephine) Marian *newspaper editor, photographer*

PROFESSIONAL INDEX 6253 COMMUNICATIONS MEDIA

Sioux Falls
Garson, Arnold Hugh *publishing executive*
†Masters, Lee *broadcast executive*

Spearfish
Wishard, Della Mae *former newspaper editor*

TENNESSEE

Brentwood
Flanagan, Van Kent *journalist*

Chattanooga
Holmberg, Albert William, Jr., *retired publishing company executive*
Lutgen, Robert Raymond *newspaper editor*
Sachsman, David Bernard *communications educator*

College Grove
Battle, William Robert (Bob Battle) *retired newspaper executive*

Franklin
Duduit, Michael *editor, university administrator*

Jonesborough
Rose, Anita *journalist, minister*

Kenton
†Jenkins-Brady, Terri Lynn *publishing executive, journalist*

Knoxville
Hartmann, Bruce *publishing executive*
Hooper, William Edward *broadcast journalist*
Howard, Herbert Hoover *broadcasting and communications educator*
McElroy, Jack *editor*
Rukeyser, William Simon *journalist*
Siler, Susan Reeder *communications educator*
Teeter, Dwight Leland, Jr., *journalism educator*

Lewisburg
Poole, Rhonda Ann *editor, reporter*

Maryville
Bradford, Tutt Sloan *retired publisher*

Mc Minnville
Martin, Ron *editor, superintendent of schools, consultant, minister*

Memphis
Brooks, Kathleen *journalist*
Kushma, David William *journalist*
Stokes, Henry Arthur *journalist*
Vetscher, Timothy John *reporter, anchor on TV news show*

Murfreesboro
Roose-Church, Lisa Ann *reporter, secondary school educator*

Nashville
Bart, Teddy *journalist*
Boyd, Theophilus Bartholomew, III, *publishing company executive*
†Du Bois, Tim *recording industry executive*
Giallombardo, Leslie *publishing executive*
Green, Lisa Cannon *online editor*
Hargrave, James Lee *editor, consultant*
Mayhew, Aubrey *music industry executive*
Policinski, Eugene Francis *newspaper editor, foundation executive, radio producer, television producer*
Rayburn, Ted Rye *newspaper editor*
Rogers, Barbara Jean (B.J. Rogers) *writer, editor*
Shaw, Carole *editor, publisher*
Sherborne, Robert *editor*
Stone, Lawrence Mynatt *publishing executive*
Sutherland, Frank *publishing executive, editor*

TEXAS

Abilene
Boyll, David Lloyd *broadcasting company executive*
Marler, Charles Herbert *journalism educator, historian, consultant*

Arlington
Otto, Ludwig *publisher, educator, consultant, evangelist*
†White, Alisa *communications educator, consultant*

Austin
†Carmical, Phil *editor*
Conine, Ernest *newspaper commentator, writer*
Danielson, Wayne Allen *journalism and computer science educator*
Dorsch, Jeffrey Peter *journalist*
Klym, Kendall *journalist, dancer, educator, choreographer*
†Laosa, Mike *publishing executive*
Mark, Marion Thorpe *writing educator*
†Matthews, Jay Arlon, Jr., *publisher, editor*
Mayes, Wendell Wise, Jr., *broadcasting company executive*
Oppel, Richard Alfred *newspaper executive*
Rodden, John Gallagher *communications educator, writer*
Spielman, Barbara Helen New *editor, consultant*
Williamson, Thomas Arnold *publishing company executive*

Beaumont
Baker, Mary Alice *communication educator, consultant*
†Roth, Lane *communications educator*

Brownfield
Denison, James Dickey *broadcasting executive*

Burleson
Lisi, Lori A. (Lori Fredeking) *freelance/self-employed editor, writer*

Canyon
Williams, Donald Mace *newswriter, writer*

Carrollton
Daily, Ellen Wilmoth Matthews *technical publications specialist*

College Station
†Priddy, Sharon *television producer*
Wegener, Robert Paul *communications educator*

Crockett
Gibbs, James Howard *broadcast executive*

Dallas
Bailon, Gilbert *newspaper editor*
Bleiberg, Lawrence Russell *journalist*
Burns, Scott *columnist*
Cantrell, Scott *newspaper music critic*
Cummins, James Duane *correspondent, media executive*
Decherd, Robert William *newspaper and broadcasting executive*
Dillon, David Anthony *journalist, lecturer*
Dufner, Edward Joseph *editor*
Fields-Hill, Valerie *journalist*
Glines, Carroll Vane, Jr., *magazine editor*
Holmes, Bert Otis E., Jr., *retired editor*
Johnson, Kevin Orlin *publishing executive, writer*
Kutner, Janet *art critic, book reviewer*
†Maddoux, Marlin *broadcast executive, journalist, author*
†Malone, Dan F. *journalist*
Maza, Michael William *newspaper editor, columnist*
Moroney, James M., III, *publishing executive, broadcast executive*
Osborne, Burl *newspaper publisher, editor*
Patterson, Ronald Paul *publishing company executive, clergyman*
Pederson, Rena *newspaper editor*
Siegfried, Tom *newspaper editor*
Smith, David Lee *newspaper editor*
Smith, Sue Frances *newspaper editor*
Weinkauf, William Carl *instructional media company executive*

Denton
Millay, Kathleen Kriner *communication disorders educator*
Shelton, James Keith *journalism educator*
Staples, Donald Edward *radio, film and television educator*

El Paso
Treadwell, Hugh Wilson *publishing executive*

Fort Worth
Peipert, James Raymond *journalist*
Price, Michael Howard *journalist, critic, composer, cartoonist, theatrical operator*
Record, Phillip Julius *journalist*
Tinsley, Jackson Bennett *newspaper editor*
Turner, Wesley R. *publishing executive*
Witt, Jim *editor*

Galveston
Bremer, Joanna Charles *journalist*

Garland
†Driver, Jennifer *communications educator*

Houston
Barlow, Jim B. *retired columnist*
Bischoff, Susan Ann *newspaper editor*
Cohen, Jeff *editor*
Downing, Margaret Mary *newspaper editor*
George, Deveral D. *editor, journalist, advertising consultant*
Hammond, Ken *newspaper magazine editor*
Hawes, William Kenneth *communication educator, author*
Hobby, William Pettus *broadcast executive, retired*
Holmes, Ann Hitchcock *journalist*
Johnson, Richard James Vaughan *newspaper executive, retired*
Johnston, Marguerite *journalist, author*
†Loftis, Jack D. *newspaper editor, newspaper executive*
McDavid, George Eugene (Gene Mc David) *retired newspaper executive*
Oren, Bruce Clifford *newspaper editor, artist*
Osgood, Christopher Mykel *radio sales executive*
Osterberg, Susan Snider *communications educator, farmer*
Powers, Hugh William *newspaper executive*
Read, Michael Oscar *editor, consultant*
Sweeney, Jack *publishing executive*
Taylor, James Sheppard *communications educator*
Thomas, Katherine Jane *magazine and newspaper columnist*
Tice, Pamela Paradis *scientific editor, writer*
Walbridge, Willard Eugene *broadcasting executive*
Walls, Martha Ann Williams (Mrs. B. Carmage Walls) *newspaper executive*
Ward, David Henry (Dave Ward) *television news reporter, anchorman*

Irving
Halter, Jon Charles *magazine editor, writer*
Young, J. Warren *magazine publisher*

Jacksonville
Thrall, Gordon Fish *publishing executive*

Kerrville
Dozier, William Everett, Jr., *newspaper editor and publisher*

Kyle
Saunders, Patricia Gene *freelance writer, editor*

Lewisville
Vacca, John Joseph, Jr., *television executive*

Liberty Hill
West, Felton *retired journalist, councilman*

Magnolia
Gray, Robert Steele *publishing executive, editor, writer*

New Braunfels
Bryant, Dennis Michael *publisher, educator*

Palestine
Sellers, Wayne Chadick *newspaper publisher, editor, retired*

Richardson
Patrick, James Nicholas, Sr., *radio, television, newspaper commentator, consultant*
Senderling, Jon Townsend *journalist, public affairs specialist*

San Angelo
Garza, Adolph Aranda *broadcast engineer, consultant*

San Antonio
Clark, Robert Phillips *newspaper editor, consultant*
Gwathmey, Joe Neil, Jr., *broadcasting executive*
Heloise, *columnist, lecturer, broadcaster, author*
Lenke, Joanne Marie *publishing executive*
Marbut, Robert Gordon *communications, electronic security and broadcast executive, investor*
†Mays, L(ester) Lowry *broadcast executive*
Michaels, Willard A. (Bill Michaels) *retired broadcasting executive*
Walker, W. Lawrence, Jr., *newspaper publishing executive*
Wilkinson, Kenton Todd *communications educator*
Yerkes, Susan Gamble *newspaper columnist*

Spring
Jackson, Guida Myrl *writer, magazine editor, book editor, publisher*
Mohalley, Patricia JoAnn *library media specialist*

Sugar Land
Smithers, Donald Lee *telecommunication consultant*

Sweetwater
Adams, Brenda Kay *publishing executive*

The Woodlands
Logan, Mathew Kuykendall *journalist*
Pistorius, Alvin William, Jr., (Bill Miller) *communications educator*

Tomball
Ham, Sommy L. *publisher, writer*

Tulia
†Irlbeck, Amber Rose *journalist, scriptwriter*

Tyler
Brock, Dee Sala *television executive, educator, writer, consultant*

Waco
Kramer, Denny B. *professional communication educator*

Wharton
Jackson, Larry C. *publishing executive*

Woodway
†McCorkle, William Littleton *journalism educator, writer*

UTAH

Midway
Zenger, John Hancock *training company executive*

Morgan
†Chaston, Deanne Winterton *editor*

Murray
Carter, Paul Edward *publishing company executive*

North Salt Lake
Meitzler, Leland Keith *publishing executive*

Ogden
†Trundle, W(infield) Scott *publishing executive newspaper*

Park City
Gallivan, John William *publishing executive*

Provo
Szucs, Loretto Dennis *internet publishing executive, editor*
Tata, Giovanni *publishing executive*

Salt Lake City
Brown, Carolyn Smith *communications educator, consultant*
Conway, Nancy Ann *newspaper editor*
Fehr, J. Will *newspaper editor*
Gregersen, R(oald) George *newspaper publishing executive*
Hatch, George Clinton *television executive*
Hatch, Wilda Gene *broadcast company executive*
Newell, Clayton Coke *media professional, writer*
Shelledy, James Edwin, III, *newspaper editor*
Smith, Donald E. *broadcast engineer, manager*
Welch, Dominic *publishing consultant*

VERMONT

Bennington
Burkhardt, Frederick Henry *editor*

Brookfield
†Newton, Earle Williams *editor, museum director, library and museum consultant*

Burlington
Liley, Elizabeth Ellen *journalist, educator*

Charlotte
Monsarrat, Nicholas *newspaper editor, writer, educator*

Hartland Four Corners
Brady, Upton Birnie *editor, literary agent*

Lincoln
Kompass, Edward John *consulting editor*

North Pomfret
Crowl, John Allen *retired publishing company executive*

Norwich
†Paine, Walter Cabot *journalist, consultant*

Perkinsville
Harris, Christopher *publisher, designer, editor*

Randolph
Ryerson, Marjorie Gilmour *journalist, educator, poet, photographer*

Sheffield
Holladay, Martin John *editor*

South Burlington
Stoddert, Sandra Smith *media director*

Woodstock
Goulazian, Peter Robert *retired broadcasting executive*

VIRGINIA

Alexandria
Barbato, Joseph Allen *writer*
Brownfeld, Allan Charles *columnist*
Cromley, Raymond Avolon *syndicated columnist*
Fichenberg, Robert Gordon *newspaper editor, consultant*
Fleming, Douglas Riley *journalist, publisher, public affairs consultant*
Foxwell, Elizabeth Marie *editor, writer*
Francis, Samuel Todd *columnist*
Hobbs, Michael Edwin *broadcasting company executive*
Jolly, Bruce Overstreet *retired newspaper executive*
Mathews, Thomas Jay *reporter, columnist, writer*
Morse, Burnham Spottswood *broadcast executive*
Radewagen, Fred *publisher, organization executive*
Rosenfeld, Stephen Samuel *newspaper editor*
Snyder, James P. *audio and digital television engineer, videographer, editor*
Tarpley, James Douglas *journalism educator, magazine editor*
Yoder, Edwin Milton, Jr., *columnist, educator, editor, writer*

Annandale
Blodgett, Todd Alan *publisher, marketing executive*

Arlington
Bowers, Ray Landis *editor*
Clayton, James Edwin *journalist*
Fleischman, Phil *radio news executive*
Goodman, Mark *journalist, educator*
†Goodpasture, Bruce *retired editor, publisher, social sciences educator*
Holt, Pat Mayo *journalist*
Lehrer, James Charles *television journalist*
Lester, Barnett Benjamin *editor, retired foreign affairs officer*
MacDougall, William Lowell *magazine editor*
MacNeil, Robert Breckenridge Ware *retired broadcast journalist, writer*
†Mazzarella, David *newspaper editor*
McWethy, John Fleetwood *journalist*
Mears, Walter Robert *journalist*
Mirrielees, James Fay, III, *publishing executive*
Myers, Elissa Matulis *publisher, association executive*
Neikirk, William Robert *journalist*
Obermayer, Herman Joseph *newspaper publisher*
Quinn, John Collins *publishing executive, newspaper editor*
Reiss, Susan Marie *editor, writer*
†Rockefeller, Sharon Percy *broadcast executive*
Seamans, Andrew Charles *editorial and public relations consultant, columnist, author*
Simonson, David C. *retired newspaper association executive*
Stelter, Paul James *editor, freelance writer*
Tyrrell, Robert Emmett, Jr., *periodical editor, writer*

Bridgewater
Bittel, Muriel Albers *managing editor*

Charlottesville
Daniel, Leon *journalist, newspaper columnist, editor*
Foard, Susan Lee *editor*

Kaiserlian, Penelope Jane *publishing company executive*
†**Koester**, Robert James *publishing executive, educational consultant*
Loo, Beverly Jane *publishing company executive*
Parrish, David Walker, Jr., *legal publishing company executive*
Worrell, Anne Everette Rowell *newspaper publisher*

Chesapeake
Collins, Carolyn Herman *school media specialist, legislative aide*
Green, Barbara Marie *publisher, journalist, poet*

Clifton
Gibbs, Hope Katz *journalist*

Covington
Rohr, Dwight Mason *news director, radio marketing consultant*

Dulles
Desmond, Ned *editor, writer*

Fairfax
McAllister, William Howard, III, *newspaper reporter, columnist, public relations executive*

Fairfax Station
Abuzaakouk, Aly Ramadan *publishing executive*

Falls Church
Aukofer, Frank Alexander *journalist*
Cromley, Allan Wray *journalist*
Kaplow, Herbert Elias *journalist*

Great Falls
Garrett, Wilbur (Bill Garrett) *magazine editor*

Hampton
Barnes, Myrtle Sue Snyder *editor*
Brauer, Harrol Andrew, Jr., *broadcasting executive*

Harrisonburg
Rollman, Steven Allan *communication educator*

Herndon
Berry, Fred Clifton, Jr., *author, magazine editor, book packager*
Miller, Donald Lane *publishing executive*
Shevis, James Murdoch *journalist*

Keswick
Halfen, David *retired publishing executive*

Lexington
†**Cumming**, Douglas O. *journalist, educator*
Luecke, Pamela *professor, former editor*
Paxton, Matthew White, IV, *newspaper publisher*

Luray
Burzynski, Norman Stephen *editor*

Lynchburg
†**Simmons**, Tracy Lee *editor, writer*
Vaughn, Susan Marie *journalist, educator*

Manassas
Wilson, Robert Spencer *magazine editor*

Marion
Elledge, Glenna Ellen Tuell *journalist*

Mason Neck
Mc Curdy, Patrick Pierre *editor, consultant*

Mc Lean
Bullard, Marcia *publishing executive*
Carlson, Richard Warner *journalist, diplomat, federal agency administrator, broadcast executive*
Feller, Mimi *newspaper publishing executive*
Gniewek, Raymond Louis *newspaper editor*
Hope, Melissa B. *radio and television correspondent*
Jurgensen, Karen *newspaper editor*
Mathews, Linda McVeigh *newspaper editor*
†**Moon**, Craig *publishing executive*
Parshall, Gerald *journalist*
Taylor, Priscilla Sheppard *editor*
Ullmann, Owen *journalist*

McLean
†**Gallagher**, Brian *editor-in-chief*

Midlothian
Chapman, Gilbert Whipple, Jr., *publishing company executive*
Crutchfield, George Thomas *journalism educator*
Pearson, Gregory David *publisher, media specialist*

Mount Vernon
Brownson, Anna Louise Harshman *publishing executive, editor*

Norfolk
Addis, Kay Tucker *newspaper editor*
Barry, Richard Francis, III, *publishing executive*
Carpenter, Dee *publishing executive*
Griffin, O. Daniel, Jr., *reporter, writer, photographer, audio engineer, videographer*
Ruehlmann, William John *communications educator*
Sizemore, William Howard, Jr., *journalist*

Orange
Burke, Robert Lawrence *consultant*

Paeonian Springs
Sloyan, Patrick Joseph *journalist*

Reston
Clapp, Stephen Caswell *journalist*
Powell, Anne Elizabeth *editor*

Richmond
Ashe, Reid *publishing executive*
Bryan, John Stewart, III, *newspaper publisher*
†**Curley**, John J. *diversified media company executive*
Fletcher, Paul Edwin, III, *publishing executive, editor-in-chief*
Goodykoontz, Charles Alfred *newspaper editor, retired*
Seals, Margaret Louise *newspaper editor*
Smith, Ted Jay, III, *mass communications educator*

Roanoke
Beagle, Benjamin Stuart, Jr., *columnist*
Garrett, Lee (Homer Simmons Holcomb) *retired broadcaster*
Warren, William Kermit *retired media company executive*
Zomparelli, Wendy *newspaper publisher*

Saint Paul
Gregory, Ann Young *editor, publisher*

Sedley
Briggs, Martha Wren *publishing executive, writer*

Springfield
Green, Gerald *editor, consultant*
Hillis, John David *television news executive, producer, writer*
Rankin, Jacqueline Annette *communications expert, educator*

Sterling
Sanfelici, Arthur H(ugo) *editor, writer*

Tazewell
Garner, June Brown *journalist*

Vienna
Mc Arthur, George *journalist*
McElveen, Joseph James, Jr., *journalist, author, educator, mass media executive*
Ogrean, David William *sports executive*
Roellig, Paul David *publishing executive*

Virginia Beach
†**Benson**, Robert A. *photojournalist*
Wicker, Richard Fenton, Jr., *editor*

Warrenton
Brimelow, Peter *journalist*

Waynesboro
Kerby, Robert Browning *media consultant*

Winchester
Byrd, Harry Flood, Jr., *newspaper executive, former senator*

WASHINGTON

Bellevue
Wilson, Johnny Lee *publishing executive*

Bellingham
Hansen, Leonard Joseph *writer, journalist, editor, communications executive*

Blaine
Miller, Ronald *writer, critic*

Edmonds
Owen, John *retired newspaper editor*

Kirkland
Welke, Elton Grinnell, Jr., *publisher, writer*

Lynnwood
Araki, Takaharu *editor, mineralogist, crystallographer, consultant*
Krause, Thomas Evans *record promotion and radio consultant*

Olympia
McClelland, Kamilla Kuroda *news reporter, proofreader, book agent*

Port Angeles
Brewer, John Charles *journalist*

Port Ludlow
†**Trzaska**, Joyce Anne *publishing executive*

Port Orchard
Bonsell, Thomas Allen *journalist, publisher*
Huber, Virginia Rollo *photojournalist, educator, artist*

Port Townsend
Buhler, Jill Lorie *editor, writer*
MacLean, Barbara Hutmacher *author, retired journalist*

Redmond
Kinsley, Michael E. *magazine editor*

Seattle
Blethen, Frank A. *newspaper publisher*
Boardman, David *newspaper editor*
Buckner, Philip Franklin *newspaper publisher*
Duncan, Dale A. *publishing executive*
Ellegood, Donald Russell *publishing executive*
Fancher, Michael Reilly *newspaper editor, newspaper publishing executive*
Godden, Jean W. *columnist*
Gouldthorpe, Kenneth Alfred Percival *publisher, state official*
Gwinn, Mary Ann *newspaper reporter*
Hills, Regina J. *journalist*
†**Horsey**, David *editorial cartoonist*
Johnson, Wayne Eaton *writer, editor, former drama critic*

Medved, Michael *film critic, author, talk show host*
†**Nalder**, Eric Christopher *investigative reporter*
Oglesby, Roger *publishing executive*
Pascal, Naomi Brenner *editor-at-large, publishing executive*
Payne, Ancil Horace *retired broadcasting executive*
†**Sharify**, Shahab John *journalist*
†**Sizemore**, Herman Mason, Jr., *newspaper executive*
Strahilevitz, Meir *inventor, researcher, psychiatry educator*
Turner, Wallace L. *reporter*

Spokane
Cowles, William Stacey *newspaper publisher*
Gray, Alfred Orren *retired journalism educator*
Kafentzis, John Charles *journalist, educator*
Kunkel, Richard Lester *public radio executive*
Steele, Karen Dorn *journalist*

Tacoma
Brenner, Elizabeth (Betsy Brenner) *publishing executive*
Gilbert, Ben William *retired newspaper editor*
Mowery, Gerald Eugene *publisher, writer*
Zeeck, David *newspaper editor*

Tukwila
Lamb, Ronald Alfred *editor*

Vancouver
Oppegaard, Brett *journalist*

Vashon
Mann, Claud Prentiss, Jr., *retired television journalist*

Woodinville
Alvarez, Bryan *newsletter editor, writer*

Yakima
Ramsey, Douglas Arthur *journalist, writer, critic, foundation executive*

WEST VIRGINIA

Buckhannon
Johnson, Danette Ifert *communication educator*

Bunker Hill
Marple, Thomas Franklin *columnist, reporter*

Charleston
Chilton, Elizabeth Easley Early *newspaper executive*
Grimes, Richard Stuart *editor, writer*
Haught, James Albert, Jr., *journalist, newspaper editor, author*

Greenville
Warner, Kenneth Wilson, Jr., *editor, association and publications executive*

Huntington
Ritchie, Garry Harlan *television broadcast executive*

Shepherdstown
Hresan, Sally L. *journalism educator*
Snyder, Joseph John *editor, historian, author, lecturer, consultant*

Weston
Billeter, Robert James *newspaper publisher*

WISCONSIN

Appleton
Oppmann, Andrew James *newspaper editor*

Berlin
†**Schwersenska**, Sarah Elizabeth *broadcast executive*

Black River Falls
Michaels, Marion Cecelia *writer, editor, news syndicate executive*

Brookfield
Fibich, Howard Raymond *retired newspaper editor*

Cedar Grove
Feider, Gary Joseph *newspaper editor*

Fort Atkinson
Knox, Brian Victor *newspaper publisher and editor*
Knox, William David *publishing company executive*
Meyer, Eugene Carlton *retired editor*

Green Bay
Daley, Arthur James *retired magazine publisher*

Greendale
Kaiser, Ann Christine *magazine editor*

Iola
Krause, Chester Lee *publishing company founder*
Van Ryzin, Robert Richard *magazine editor*

Janesville
Fitzgerald, James Francis *cable television executive*

Kenosha
Brown, Howard Jordan *media executive*

La Crosse
Thomas-Williams, Pamela Rae *publishing executive, writer*

Madison
Denton, Frank M. *newspaper editor*
Drechsel, Robert Edward *journalism educator*
Dunwoody, Sharon Lee *journalism and communications educator*
Gruber, John Edward *editor, railroad historian, photographer*
Hachten, William Andrews *journalism educator, author*
Haslanger, Philip Charles *journalist*
Hopson, James Warren *publishing executive*
Hoyt, James Lawrence *journalism educator, athletic administrator*
McNelly, John Taylor *journalist, educator*
†**Miller**, Frederick William *publisher, lawyer*
Wolman, J. Martin *retired newspaper publisher*
Zweifel, David Alan *newspaper editor*

Menomonie
Cutnaw, Mary-Frances *emeritus communications educator, writer, editor, publisher*

Milwaukee
Armstrong, Douglas Dean *journalist*
Auer, James Matthew *art critic, journalist*
Behrendt, David Frogner *retired journalist*
†**Enk**, Scott *editor, researcher, activist*
Farris, Trueman Earl, Jr., *retired newspaper editor*
Foster, Richard *journalist*
Garbaciak-Bobber, Joyce Katherine *news anchor*
Hoffmann, Gregg J. *journalist, author, publisher*
Kaiser, Martin *newspaper editor*
Kritzer, Paul Eric *media executive, communications lawyer*
Leonard, Richard Hart *journalist, educator*
Spore, Keith Kent *newspaper executive*

Monroe
Wilcox, Winton Wilfred, Jr., *communications specialist, consultant*

Pewaukee
Lee, Jack (Jim Sanders Beasley) *broadcast executive*

Racine
†**Miller**, Yolanda *publisher, writer*

Superior
Billig, Thomas Clifford *publishing executive, marketing professional*

Waukesha
Dreyfus, Lee Sherman *international speaker*
Larson, Russell George *magazine publisher*

West Bend
Fraedrich, Royal Louis *magazine editor, publisher*

WYOMING

Cheyenne
Schliske, Rosalind Routt *journalism educator, journalist*

Kelly
Harrice, Cy (Nicholas Psiharis) *commercial radio and television announcer*

Riverton
Peck, Robert A. *newspaper publisher, state legislator*

TERRITORIES OF THE UNITED STATES

GUAM

Agana
George, Duane M. *editor*

PUERTO RICO

San Juan
†**Sepúlveda**, Sandra *communications educator*

VIRGIN ISLANDS

Saint John
Walker, Ronald R. *writer, editor, educator*

CANADA

ALBERTA

Calgary
†**Shaw**, Jim, Jr., *broadcast executive*

Edmonton
Hughes, Linda J. *newspaper publisher*

BRITISH COLUMBIA

Vancouver
Yaffe, Barbara Marlene *journalist*

MANITOBA

Winnipeg
Wreford, David Mathews *magazine editor*

†Heins, John *publishing executive*
Heller, Richard H. *writer, editor, book critic, publisher*
Hemperly, Rebecca Sue *publishing manager*
Henig, Robin Marantz *journalist*
Henry, Frances Ann *journalist, educator*
Herguth, Robert John *columnist*
Hering, Doris Minnie *dance critic*
Hey, Robert Pierpont *retired editor*
Hieb, Mario Kirk *broadcast engineer, inventor, writer, consultant*
Himmelfarb, Milton *editor, educator*
Hinshaw, Edward Banks *retired broadcasting company executive*
Hodges, Sharon Green *editor, consultant, writer*
Holaday, Susan G. *editor*
Holland, David Thurston *former editor*
Hollis, Janice Denise *publishing executive, minister*
Hopkins, Philip Joseph *journalist, information technology executive*
Horn, Lee Shawn *sports analyst*
Horne, Alexander Douglas *journalist*
†Hottenstein, Erin *journalist*
Hubley, Reginald Allen *publishing executive*
Huey, Ward L(igon), Jr., *retired media executive*
†Hunn, Max W. *freelance/self-employed photojournalist*
Hurd, Byron Thomas *retired publishing executive*
Huston, Margo *journalist*
Idaszak, Jerome Joseph *economic journalist*
†Ireland, Timothy *media consultant*
Ismach, Arnold Harvey *retired journalism educator*
Jacobson, Kenneth Mark *journalist, writer, editor*
Jenkins, Billie Beasley *film company executive*
Jenkins, Jeffrey Eric *theater critic, educator*
Jensen, Michael Charles *journalist, lecturer, author*
Jinks, Robert Larry *retired newspaper publisher*
John, Mertis, Jr., *record company executive*
Johnson, John *broadcast journalist*
Johnson, Micah William *television newscaster, director*
Jones, David Rhodes *consulting editor*
Jones, Leonade Diane *media publishing company executive*
Jones, Stephanie J. *photojournalist, artist*
Jordan, Marvin Evans, Jr., *record company executive*
Joseph, Michael Thomas *broadcast consultant*
Kamin, Blair Douglass *newspaper critic*
Karol, Michael Alan *editor*
Karr, Norman *communications consultant, public relations executive*
Kaye, Daniel Theodore *editor*
Kayfetz, Victor Joel *writer, editor, translator*
†Kelly, Michael Joesph, II, *publishing executive*
Key, Ted *cartoonist*
†Khawaja, Irfan Ahmad *columnist, philosopher, educator*
Killgore, Le *journalist, political columnist*
Kilpatrick, James Jackson, Jr., *columnist, writer*
Kimes, Beverly Rae *editor, writer*
King, Glen (Lenard Glen King) *broadcasting educator, composer*
King, John Charles Peter *newspaper editor*
Kiser, Jo Ann *editor*
Klein, Edward Joel *editor, author, lecturer*
Klein, William Francis *social ecologist, multimedia publisher, producer, musician, writer*
Klinghoffer, David *journalist*
Koehler, George Applegate *broadcasting company executive*
†Kontos, Gregory Edward *film company executive, sculptor*
Koplovitz, Kay *television network executive*
Koren, Edward Benjamin *cartoonist, educator*
Kramer, Donovan Mershon, Sr., *newspaper publisher*
Kraslow, David *retired newspaper publishing executive, reporter, author, consultant*
Kuehn, James Marshall *newspaper editor*
Kyles-Omari, Cynthia Lee *editor, career consultant*
Laidlaw, Robert Richard *publishing company executive*
LaMotta, Connie Frances *communications consultant, executive coach*
Landes, William Alan *publishing executive*
Langer, Ralph Ernest *journalist, newspaper executive and editor*
†Lang-Piaseki, Vera Jean *former publishing company executive*
Lape, Robert Cable *broadcast journalist*
Lashner, Marilyn Auerbach *communication content analyst, forensic expert*
Leach, Janet C. *publishing executive*
Leason, Jody Jacobs *newspaper columnist*
Lee, Robert W(illiam) *journalist, researcher*
Lehrman, Nat *magazine editor*
Leonard, Carolyn Branch *publisher, editor, writer*
Lepkowski, Wil (Wilbert Charles Lepkowski) *journalist*
Lesly Stevens, Elizabeth *journalist*
Levine, David M. *newspaper editor*
Lewin, Rhoda Greene *editor, historian, columnist*
Lewis, Anthony *newspaper columnist*
Liberman, Gail Jeanne *editor*
Lipman, David *retired journalist, multimedia consultant*
Littleford, William Donaldson *retired publishing executive*
Littlewood, Thomas Benjamin *retired journalism educator*
Lively, John Pound *magazine editor, publisher*
Lloyd, Michael Jeffrey *recording producer*
Logan, Douglas Orr *magazine editor*
Love, Nancy Lorene *communication and political strategist, educator*
Lucier, P. Jeffrey *publishing consultant*
Lumpkin, Anne Craig *retired television and radio company executive*
†Lynch, Patricia Gates *broadcasting organization executive consultant, former ambassador*
Maharidge, Dale Dimitro *journalist, educator, writer*
Maher, Lisa Krug *editor*
Main, Robert Gail *communications educator, training consultant, television and film producer, former army officer*
Mallo-Garrido, Josephine Ann *advertising agency owner*
Malloy, Michael Terrence *journalist, newspaper editor*
Malott, Adele Renee *editor*
Mandell, Arlene Linda *communications educator*
Manley, Joan A(dele) Daniels *retired publisher*
Marcus, Greil Gerstley *critic*
†Marino, Richard J. *publishing executive*
Marken, William Riley *magazine editor*
Marmer, Nancy *editor*
Martarella, Franc David *television executive, not-for-profit fundraiser*
Martin, John Joseph *journalist*
Martin, Marilyn Mann *retired library media specialist*
Martz, Lawrence Stannard *retired periodical editor*
Masih, Tara Lynn *book editor, writer*
Masket, Edward Seymour *television executive*
Mason, John Oliver *freelance journalist, poet, community activist*
Mayer, Allan *crisis communications consultant, writer*
McCarty, Thomas Joseph *publishing company executive*
McCauley, Jane Reynolds *journalist*
McDarrah, Gloria Schoffel *editor, author*
McEachran, Angus *retired editor*
†McEwen, James Wallace, Jr., *former publishing executive*
McGuirk, Terrence *former broadcasting company executive*
McIntosh, Amy Bennett *publishing/internet company executive*
McIntyre, Bruce Herbert *media and marketing consultant*
McKenna, John Francis *media executive*
McKinney, Jerry Wayne *retired journalist*
McManus, Jason Donald *editor, retired*
†Mechanic, William M. *former television and motion picture industry executive*
Medavoy, Mike *motion picture company executive*
Medina, Kathryn Bach *book editor*
Mellema, Donald Eugene *retired radio news reporter and anchor*
Melody, Michael Edward *publishing company executive*
†Mermelstein, Paula *broadcasting executive*
Mesrobian, Arpena Sachaklian *publisher, editor, consultant*
Mettee, Stephen Blake *publishing executive*
†Meyer, Andrew W. *retired publishing executive*
Michel, Daniel John *broadcast educator, writer, photographer, artist*
Michels, Dia Loren *publishing executive, writer*
Miller, Carole Ann Lyons *editor, publisher, video and marketing specialist, writer, producer*
†Miller, Deanna *editor, writer*
Miller, Donald LeSessne *publishing executive*
Miller, Norman Charles, Jr., *editor, reporter*
Miller, Robert Branson, Jr., *retired newspaper publisher*
†Milliron, Tim *film company executive*
Mills, Dale Douglas *journalist*
†Mitchell, Patricia Edenfield *television executive*
†Mkrtschjan, Simona A. *editor*
Moen, Margaret *print company editor*
Monacelli, Gianfranco *publishing executive*
†Montgomery, Cliff Wilson *journalist, writer, researcher*
Moore, Thomas Paul *retired broadcast executive*
Morgan, Anne Marie G. *broadcast journalist, educator*
Morgan, Clara McMahon *publishing consultant*
Morgans, Susan Fleming *editor*
Morton, George Thomas *reporter*
Mossman, Thomas Mellish, Jr., *broadcasting consultant*
Mudd, Roger Harrison *news broadcaster, educator*
†Mullenneaux, Lisa *journalist, publishing executive*
Myers, Shirley Diana *art book editor*
Nachman, Gerald Weil *columnist, critic, author*
Neff, Donald Lloyd *news correspondent, writer*
Neitzel, Lisa Ann *newscaster, reporter*
Nelson, Martha Jane *magazine editor*
Nelson, Robert Charles *retired publishing executive*
Newman, Rachel *magazine editor*
Nibley, Andrew Mathews *editorial executive*
Nichols, Cherie L. *songwriter, art publishing executive, artist representative*
†Nichols, Wendalyn R. *publishing executive*
†Niedermeier, Donna M. *newswriter, lyricist*
Noeth, Louise Ann *journalist*
Norton, Wayne Anderson *public information officer, retired journalism educator, public relations specialist*
Novick, Julius Lerner *theater critic, educator*
Oakley, Andrew Arthur *journalist, educator*
Ochs, Michael *editor, librarian, music educator*
†O'Donnell, Maureen Stacey *editor*
Olive, David Michael *magazine writer, magazine editor*
Oppedahl, John Frederick *newspaper publisher, publishing executive*
†Opperman, Dwight Darwin *publishing company executive*
Orr, Carol Wallace *book publishing executive*
†Osberg, Gregory John *publishing company executive*
Osborn, Susan Titus *editor*
Osterhaus, William Eric *television executive*
Otis, Denise Marie *editor, writer*
Otto, Jean Hammond *journalist*
Pakenham, Rosalie Muller Wright *magazine and newspaper editor*
Palmer, Bradley Beran *sportscaster*
Palvino, Jack Anthony *broadcasting executive*
Papirno, Elissa *journalist, newspaper editor*
Parker, Mel *editor*
Parkhurst, William Michael *media consultant*
Pasher, Victoria Sonshine *journalist*
Pauley, Jane *television journalist*
Paulson, Kenneth Alan *journalist, lawyer, foundation executive*
Peacock, Mary Willa *magazine editor*
Peeples, Rufus Roderick, Jr., (Roddy Peeples) *farm and ranch news radio broadcaster*
Pendleton, Gail Ruth *newspaper editor, writer, educator*
Perkins, Anthony B. *editor-in-chief, writer, educator*
Perreca, Michael Andrew *artistic director, freelance editor, theater director*
Peters, Mary Catherine *journalist, researcher, announcer*
Peterson, Kevin Bruce *newspaper editor, publishing executive*
Philipson, Morris *university press director*
Phillips, Glynda Ann *editor*
Picower, Warren Michael *editor*
Pi-González, Amaury Francisco *announcer, journalist*
Plangere, Jules Leon, Jr., *retired media company executive*
Pletcher, Eldon *editorial cartoonist*
Podhoretz, Norman *magazine editor, writer*
Poling, Jerome Paul *journalist*
†Portale, Carl *retired publishing executive*
Povich, Lynn *journalist, magazine editor, internet executive*
†Prady, Norman *journalist, writer, advertising executive, marketing consultant*
Preddy, Raymond Randall *retired newspaper publisher, educator*
Press, Aida Kabatznick *former editor, writer, poet*
†Presto, Catherine Ann (Kay Presto) *media specialist, consultant*
Price, Nelson (John Nelson Price) *author, journalist*
Price, Tom *journalist*
Quade, Vicki *editor, writer, playwright, producer*
Quinn, Charles Nicholas *journalist*
Quint, Bert *journalist*
Radcliffe, Redonia (Donnie Radcliffe) *journalist, author*
Radlauer, Steve *freelance writer, journalist, producer*
Ramsay, Karin Kinsey *publisher, educator*
Ramsey, Jerry Virgil *educator, financial planner, radio broadcaster*
Randinelli, Tracey Anne *magazine editor*
Rapoport, Ronald Jon *journalist*
Rash, Wayne, Jr., *journalist*
Rawlins, Christopher John *publishing executive, director*
Ray, William Melvin *newsletter publishing consultant*
Raymond, Catherine M. *editor*
Rayner, William Alexander *retired newspaper editor, author*
Read, Richard Eaton *newspaper reporter*
Reed, James Donald *journalist, author*
†Reed, JoyLynn Hailey *communications educator, consultant*
Reidenbaugh, Lowell Henry *retired sports editor*
Reidenberg, June Wilson *editor, writer*
Remelius, Roger Martin *broadcasting and licensing executive*
Richards, Wesley Jon *newscaster, writer, producer*
Richman, Alan *magazine editor*
Ricklefs, Roger Ulrich *retired newspaper editor*
Ridder, Paul Anthony *newspaper executive*
Rieselman, Deborah Sue *editor*
Riggs, Michael David *writer, editor*
Roberts, Corinne Boggs (Cokie Roberts) *correspondent, news analyst*
Roberts, Delmar Lee *editor*
Roberts, Margaret Harold *editor, publisher*
Rohn, David Riis *reporter, columnist, educator*
Rohse, Elaine Dahl *newswriter*
Rojany, Lisa Adrienne *publishing company executive, writer*
Rollins, Lisa L. *journalist*
Rosen, Yereth Josette *journalist*
Rosenberg, Shirley Sirota *publications executive*
Rosenkrantz, Linda *writer*
Rosenthal, Arthur Jesse *publishing executive*
Rosenthal, Robert Jon *newspaper editor, journalist*
Rubin, William *editor*
†Ruff, Kerry *communications educator, consultant*
Rugaber, Walter Feucht, Jr., *interim university president, newspaper executive*
Runck, Robert Ridgway *publishing executive*
Rushnell, Squire Derrick *author, speaker, television executive*
Russell, Dick *journalist*
Rust, Robert Francis *retired publishing executive*
Ryan, Allan James *publishing executive, editor*
Salinger, Pierre Emil George *journalist*
†Salvatore, Diane J. *editor*
Sandberg-Morgan, Barbara *retired communication and women's studies educator*
Sanders, Marlene *anchor, journalism educator*
Sanford, Geraldine Agnes *retired editor, retired English language educator*
Sapsowitz, Sidney H. *entertainment and media company executive*
Sarris, Andrew George *film critic*
Schleuning, Jay James *reporter*
Schmidt, Diane Joy *photographer, author, educator*
Schorr, Daniel Louis *broadcast journalist, author, lecturer*
Schrand, Richard Henry *broadcaster, writer*
Schulz, Ralph Richard *publishing consultant*
†Schwartz, Debra Ann *journalist, educator*
Schwartz, Sharon Linda *publisher, writer, educator*
Scogin, Troy Pope *publishing company executive, accounts executive*
Seigenthaler, John Lawrence *retired newspaper executive*
Serwatka, Walter Dennis *publishing executive*
†Seymore, James W., Jr., *magazine editor*
Shacter, James Detmers *editor, writer*
Shao Collins, Jeannine *magazine publisher*
Shapiro, Richard Charles *publishing sales and marketing executive*
Shelton, Stephani *broadcast journalist, consultant*
Shere, Dennis *retired publishing executive*
†Shome, Raka *communications educator*
Shreiner, Curt *educational technologist, consultant*
Shugrue, James Leonard *bookseller, writer, educator*
Shuler, Sally Ann Smith *retired media consultant*
Shulgasser-Parker, Barbara *writer*
Sifton, David Whittier *retired magazine editor*
Silvey, Anita Lynne *editor*
Simms, Maria Kay *writer, non-profit organization executive*
Simon, Peter E. *publishing executive*
Simons, Lewis Martin *journalist*
Simonson, Lee Stuart *broadcast company executive*
†Simpson, Hugh L *news correspondent, newswriter*
Sinclair, Carole *publisher, editor, author*
Singer, Kurt Deutsch *news commentator, writer, publisher*
Singer, Renata *publisher, writer, editor*
Skinner, Thomas *broadcasting and film executive*
†Smardz, Zofia Jadwiga *editor, writer*
Smith, A. Robert *editor, author*
†Smith, Angela Elsie *media relations executive, interior designer*
Smith, George Drury *publisher, editor, collagist, writer*
Smith, Hedrick Laurence *journalist, television producer, correspondent, author, lecturer*
Smith, Martin Bernhard *journalist*
Solomon, Goody Love *journalist, editor*
Spitaleri, Vernon Rosario *newspaper publisher, manufacturing company executive*
Stamaty, Mark Alan *cartoonist, writer, artist*
Stamper, Malcolm Theodore *publishing company executive*
Stanley, Scott, Jr., *editor*
Stanton, John Jeffrey *editor, writer, print and broadcast journalist, government programs director, analyst, professional society administrator*
Stauderman, Albert Philip, Jr., *media consultant*
Stauffer, Stanley Howard *retired newspaper and broadcasting executive*
Steiner, Shari Yvonne *publisher, editor, journalist*
Stennett, William Clinton (Clint Stennett) *television station executive, state legislator*
Stephens, Edward Carl *communications educator, writer*
Stiff, Robert Martin *newspaper editor*
Stolley, Richard Brockway *journalist*
Stotsenberg, Dorothy Danskin *free-lance journalist*
Strothman, James Edward *editor*
Strutton, Larry D. *former newspaper executive*
Stuart, Nancy Rubin (Nancy Zimman Stetson) *journalist, author, writer, producer*
Stutz, Pearl Hewlett *retired photojournalist*
Sullivan, Daniel Joseph *theater critic*
Sustendal, Diane *media executive*
Swanson, David Elmer *editor*
Switzer, Maurice Harold *journalist*
†Talent, Ronnie *publishing executive, writer*
†Tarses, Jamie *television network executive*
Taylor, George Frederick *newspaper publisher, editor*
Teison, Herbert J. *editor, publisher*
Terry, Clifford Lewis *journalist*
Tharpe, Frazier Eugene *journalist*
Thomas, Patricia Goodnow *journalist*
†Thomopoulos, Anthony D. *retired motion picture company executive*
Thompson, Michael Alan *political cartoonist*
Threlkeld, Richard Davis *broadcast journalist*
Tiedge-Lafranier, Jeanne Marie *editor*
Toay, Thelma M. *columnist, poet*
Todd, Jay Marlyn *retired editor*
†Tomassetti, Carmen Richard *entertainment company executive, composer*
Triece, Anne Gallagher *magazine publisher*
Trueman, William Peter Main *broadcaster, newspaper columnist*
Twigg-Smith, Thurston *newspaper publisher*
Ucciardo, Frank Joseph *television journalist, reporter*
Uman, Sarah Dungey *editor*
Urdang, Laurence *lexicographer, publisher*
Vandenberg, Peter Ray *magazine publisher*
†Van Susteren, Greta Conway *news anchor, lawyer*
Varro, Barbara Joan *retired editor*
Verdery, David Norwood *broadcast programming executive*
Vincent, Charles Eagar, Jr., *sports columnist*
Wagman, Robert John *journalist, author*
Wagner, Durrett *former publisher, picture service executive*
Wagner, Julia A(nne) *retired editor*
†Waitz, Michael Louis *editorial trainer*
Wakefield, Dawn Lee *communications and fundraising consultant*
Walker, Fred Elmer *broadcasting executive*
†Walker, Ronald C. *retired magazine publisher*
Walls, Carmage Lee, Jr., *newspaper publisher/executive, consultant*
Waters, Betty Lou *newspaper reporter, writer*
Watkins, William David *editor, writer, consultant, mentor*
Watson, George Henry, Jr., *journalist, broadcaster*
Wearn, Wilson Cannon *retired media executive*
†Weaver, Franklin Thomas *retired newspaper executive*
Weaver, Howard C. *newspaper executive*
Weaver, Leah Ann *journalist, speech writer*

Weckesser, Ernest Prosper, Jr., *publisher, educator*
Weissman, Jack (George Anderson) *retired editor*
Welsome, Eileen *journalist*
Werman, Thomas Ehrlich *record producer*
Westphal, Ruth Lilly *educational media company*
Whipple, Judith Roy *book editor*
Whitesell, John Edwin *retired motion picture company executive*
Whittell, Polly (Mary Kaye Whittell) *editor, journalist*
Wicker, Thomas Grey *retired journalist*
Wies, Barbara *editor, publisher*
Wiessler, David Albert *news correspondent*
Wilcox, Robert Kalleen *journalist*
Wilhoit, G. Cleveland *journalism educator*
Wille, Wayne Martin *retired editor*
Wilson, Matthew Frederick *former newspaper editor*
Wilson, Richard George *journalism educator*
†Winterbottom, Goddard Williams *retired editor*
†Wittebols, James Henry *communications educator*
Wittman, Allan Henry *publishing executive*
Woestendiek, John, Jr., (William John Woestendiek) *newspaper reporter*
Wolaner, Robin Peggy *internet and magazine publisher*
Wolfman, Ira Joel *editor, writer*
Wollman Rusoff, Jane Susan *journalist, writer*
Wood, Marian Starr *publishing company executive*
Woodruff, Virginia *broadcast journalist, writer*
†Woods, Alison *publisher*
Woods, David Lyndon *publishing and broadcast executive, former federal agency executive*
Woodward, John Russell *motion picture production executive*
Wright, Donald Franklin *retired newspaper executive*
Wyche, Samuel D(avid) *sportscaster*
Yack, Patrick Ashley *editor*
Young, Jennifer Law *photojournalist, documentary producer*
Young, Patrick *writer, editor*
Young, Richard Alan *association executive*
Zappe, John Paul *city editor, educator, newspaper executive*
†Zeilig, Nancy Meeks *magazine editor*
Ziegler, Jack (Jack Denmore) *cartoonist*
Zucker, Herbert *retired publishing executive*

EDUCATION *See also* specific fields for postsecondary education

UNITED STATES

ALABAMA

Alpine
Hartman, Donald Dewayne *retired secondary education educator, writer*

Arab
Black, Daniel Hugh *retired secondary school educator*

Auburn
†Brewer, Jesse Wayne *education educator, entomologist*
†Eaves, Ronald Clark *special education educator*
Galbraith, Ruth Legg *retired university dean, home economist*
Gropper, Daniel Michael *college assistant dean, business educator*
Miller, Wilbur Randolph *university educator and administrator*
†Osei, Joseph *education educator, minister*
Philpott, Harry Melvin *former university president*
Vazsonyi, Alexander Thomas *education educator*
Voitle, Robert Allen *college dean, physiologist*

Auburn University
†Boosinger, Timothy R. *dean*
†Dodge, Timothy de K. *college librarian*
†Winn, John Emmett *education educator*

Bessemer
Stephens, Betsy Bain *retired elementary school educator*

Birmingham
Berte, Neal Richard *academic administrator*
Branham, Grady Eugene *principal*
Carter, John Thomas *retired educational administrator, writer*
Corts, Thomas Edward *university president*
Coyne, Edward James, Sr., *international business educator*
Deal, William Brown *physician, educator, author, medical school dean*
†Drentea, Patricia *educator, researcher*
Goldman, Renitta Librach *special education educator, consultant*
†Mayne, Richard *educator*
Mc Callum, Charles Alexander *university official*
†Reynolds, W. Ann *academic administrator*
Reynolds, W(ynetka) Ann *academic administrator, educator*
Sloan, Albert *college president*
Wheeler, Ruric E. *educator*
Wood, Clinton Wayne *middle school educator*

Daphne
Henson, Pamela Taylor *secondary education educator*

Decatur
†Smith, Trina *academic administrator*

Dothan
†Fell, Elizabeth P. *education educator*
Fletcher, Sarah Lee *retired elementary school educator*
Flowers, V. Anne *academic administrator emerita*

Enterprise
Holdman, Bettie *retired elementary school educator*

Eufaula
Vandenberg, Donald *retired education educator, philosopher*

Florence
Barfield, Kenny Dale *religious school administrator*
Potts, Robert Leslie *academic administrator*

Gadsden
Massaro, Traci Lynn *special education educator*

Guntersville
Patterson, Harold Dean *retired superintendent of schools*
Sparkman, Brandon Buster *educator, writer, consultant*

Hanceville
Galin, Jerry Dean *college dean*

Hartselle
Smith, Pamela Rodgers *elementary education educator*

Houston
Lafontaine, Diane Elaine *retired elementary education educator, computer specialist*

Huntsville
Dimmock, John Oliver *university research center director*
Evans, Darrell J. *higher education educator*
Franz, Frank Andrew *university president, physics educator*
Hawley, Harold Patrick *educational consultant*
Hoppe, Lea Ann *elementary education educator*
Lundquist, Charles Arthur *university official*
Morgan, Beverly Hammersley *middle school educator, artist*
Quick, Jerry Ray *academic administrator, retired*

Jacksonville
Boswell, Rupert Dean, Jr., *retired academic administrator, math educator*
Dunaway, William Preston *retired educator*
McCrary, Judy Hale *education educator*

Jasper
†Rowland, David Jack *academic administrator*

Livingston
Green, Asa Norman *university president*

Mobile
Byrd, Mary Jane *education educator*
Kreisberg, Robert A. *dean, medical educator*
†Phan, Anh-Vu *adult education educator, researcher*
Rewak, William John *former academic administrator, clergyman*

Montgomery
Bigham, Wanda Durrett *college president*
Brannan, Eulie Ross *educational consultant*
†Dybczak, Zbigniew Wladyslaw *dean, educator, mechanical engineer*
Kline, John Alvin *academic administrator*
May, Cecil Richard, Jr., *academic administrator*
†Reilly, Erin Rene *education educator*
Ritvo, Roger Alan *vice chancellor, health management-policy educator*
Walker, Annette *retired counseling administrator*

Normal
†Hall, Doris Spooner *educator*
†Lane, Rosalie Middleton *extension specialist*

Odenville
Whitten, Joseph Lee *retired school librarian, elementary educator*

Phenix City
Jinright, Noah Franklin *vocational school educator, security executive*

Prattville
Burrows, Henry Peter, III, *secondary education educator*

Scottsboro
McGill, Judy Annell McGee *early childhood and elementary educator*

Seale
Lishak, Lisa Anne *secondary education educator*

Troy
Davidson, Barry Sheldon *academic administrator, education educator*

Tuscaloosa
Bills, Robert E(dgar) *emeritus psychology educator*
†Chalmers, Jon D. *director*
†Pittman, Kathleen M. *education educator, consultant*
Searcy, Jane Berry *retired educational administrator, counselor*
Southern, James Terry *secondary education educator*
†Temimi, Akram *education educator*
Thomas, Joab Langston *retired university president, biology educator*

Tuscumbia
Hutchens, Eugene Garlington *college administrator*

Tuskegee
Green, Elbert P. *retired university official*
Payton, Benjamin Franklin *college president*

ALASKA

Anchorage
†Alsua, Carlos J. *educator*
Byrd, Milton Bruce *college president, former business executive*
Collins, Michael Paul *secondary school educator, earth science educator, consultant*
†Comeau, Carol Smith *educator*
†DeTerra, Sandra Lee Shivers *secondary school educator*
Gorsuch, Edward Lee *chancellor*
Matsui, Dorothy Nobuko *elementary education educator*
Mitchell, Michael Kiehl *elementary and secondary education educator, minister*
†Narang, Deborah Lynn *education educator*
North, Douglas McKay *academic administrator*
Skladal, Elizabeth Lee *retired elementary school educator*
Wedel-Cowgill, Millie Redmond *secondary school educator, performing arts educator*
Widdicombe, Richard Toby *educator*

Fairbanks
Alexander, Vera *dean, marine science educator*
Doran, Timothy Patrick *educational administrator*
Hamilton, Mark R. *academic administrator*
Johnson, Diane *educator*
Lewis, Carol E. *academic administrator, management consultant*
Lind, Marshall L. *academic administrator*
Reichardt, Paul Bernard *provost, chemistry educator*

Juneau
Pugh, John Robert *chancellor, former state health administrator*

Kotzebue
O'Brien, Annmarie *education educator, educator*

Palmer
†Holbert, Carolyn D. *education educator, writer*

Sitka
Ross, Dona Ruth *education program director, retired*

Tuntutuliak
Daniel, Barbara Ann *retired elementary school educator*

ARIZONA

Arizona City
Donovan, Willard Patrick *retired elementary education educator*

Camp Verde
†Wagner, Gary Wayne *educational administrator*

Casa Grande
Landers, Patricia Glover *reading specialist*

Chandler
Barnard, Annette Williamson *elementary school principal*
Rowe, Ernest Ras *education educator, academic administrator*
Stewart, Nancy Sue Spurlock *educator*
VanderVeen, Joseph Richard *special education administrator*

Chinle
†Quell, Margaret Anne *special education educator*
Reed, Leonard Newton *secondary school educator*

Douglas
†Britton, Ruth Ann Wright *elementary educator*

Flagstaff
†Baron, Patricia Burrell *university director*
Haeger, John Denis *academic administrator*
Lovely, Cynthia Jane *reading educator*
Reyhner, Jon Allan *education educator*

Florence
Puglia, Frank Alan *academic administrator*

Fort Huachuca
Adams, Frank *education specialist*

Fountain Hills
Humes, Charles Warren *counselor, educator*
Wright, C. T. Enus *former academic administrator*

Gilbert
Peoples, Esther Lorraine *elementary education educator, writer, publisher*

Glendale
†Avila, Lidia D. *principal*
Cole, James W. *academic administrator*
Edwards, Vicki Ann *elementary school principal*
†Staczek, John Joseph *academic administrator, consultant*
Stauffer, Thomas Michael *former university president*
†Sweat, Lynda Sue *cooking instructor, catering company owner, deaconess*
Woods, Cyndy Jones *secondary educator, researcher*

Green Valley
Shafer, Susan Wright *retired elementary school educator*
Smith, Raymond Lloyd *former university president, consultant*
Turner, Harold Edward *education educator*

Holbrook
Passer, Gary Louis *college president*

Kingman
McAfee, Susan Jacqueline *educator*

Mesa
Carter, Sally Packlett *elementary education educator*
†Christiansen, Larry K. *college president*
Garwood, John Delvert *former college administrator*
Lingle, Muriel Ellen *retired elementary education educator*
Mead, Linda McCullough *secondary education educator, adult education specialist*
†Yates, Cheryl Ann *home economist, educator*

Oro Valley
Scoville, Lynda Sue *special education educator, writer*

Paradise Valley
Moya, Sara Dreier *educator*

Phoenix
Bickford, David Lawrence *librarian, educator*
Coor, Lattie Finch *university president*
Culnon, Sharon Darlene *reading specialist, special education educator*
Fleenor, Geneva Lucille *retired elementary school educator*
Karabatsos, Elizabeth Ann *career counseling services executive*
†Klor de Alva, Jorge *education company executive*
McConnell, Albert Lynn *dean*
McGrath, Jane Lee *education educator, writer*
Minor, Willie *college department chair*
Noone, Palmer *academic administrator*
Rajyaguru, Mahesh Shantilal *education educator*
†Roselle, Ann *school librarian*
Thompson, Bonnie Ransa *education consultant*
†Thorne, Ann LaRayne *secondary school educator*
†Udall, Vesta Hammond *special education educator*
†Yamamoto, Alice M. *educator*

Picacho
Cortright, Lewis Stephen *elementary educator*

Prescott
Clancy, Lynn Roger, Jr., *retired educational administrator, educator*
Forbes, Judie *university official*
Halvorson, Mary Ellen *education educator, writer*
Rheinish, Robert Kent *university administrator*
Waterer, Bonnie Clausing *retired high school educator*

Rio Verde
Vanselow, Neal Arthur *university administrator, physician*

San Manuel
Hawk, Dawn Davah *secondary education educator*
Hawk, Floyd Russell *secondary school educator*

Scottsdale
Churchill, William DeLee *retired education educator, psychologist*
Esquer, Deborah Anne *elementary school educator*
Hill, Louis Allen, Jr., *former university dean, consultant*
Linderman, William Earl *elementary school educator, writer*
Mayer, Robert Anthony *retired college president*
Stone, Alan Jay *retired college administrator*

Sedona
†Mastor, Helen *career planning administrator, educator*

Sierra Vista
†Childers, John R. *education educator*
†Plummer, Val J. *education educator, chaplain*

Sun City West
Cohen, Abraham J. (Al Cohen) *educational administrator*

Sun Lakes
Johnson, Marian Ilene *education educator*
Smith, Eleanor Jane *university chancellor, retired, consultant*
Thompson, Loring Moore *retired college administrator, writer*

Sun Valley
Hamilton, Jimmy Ray *secondary education educator*

Tempe
†Askland, Andrew *academic administrator, educator*
Codell, Julie Francia *academic administrator, educator*
Crow, Michael *academic administrator*
Haggerson, Nelson Lionel, Jr., *education educator*
Krahenbuhl, Gary Stuart *university administrator*
Rivers, Patrick A. *education educator, researcher*
Wills, J. Robert *academic administrator, drama educator, writer*

Tucson

Arzoumanian, Linda Lee *early childhood educator*
Chandola, Anoop C. *educator, writer*
Dyer-Raffler, Joy Ann *special education diagnostician, educator*
Evans, Arthur Haines, Jr., *educational consultant, researcher*
Heins, Marilyn *college dean, pediatrics educator, writer*
Humphrey, John Julius *university program director, historian, writer*
Johnson, John Gray *retired university chancellor*
Kaltenbach, C(arl) Colin *dean, educator*
Larson, L. Jean *educational administrator*
†Leafgren, John Robert *education educator*
Leavitt, Jerome Edward *childhood educator*
Lemley, Diane Claire Beers *principal*
Likins, Peter William *university administrator*
†Peirce, Karen Patricia *education educator*
Stoffle, Carla Joy *university library dean*
†Studer, Jeannette R. *dean*
Thomson, Donald Arthur *education educator*
Tombaugh, Dorothy Elve *retired secondary school educator, author, lecturer*
Vincent, Thomas Lange *educator*
Wood, Christopher Todd *educator*

Window Rock

†Deschinny, Isabel *elementary school educator*

ARKANSAS

Arkadelphia

†Dunn, Charles DeWitt *academic administrator*
Elrod, Ben Moody *academic administrator*
Grant, Daniel Ross *retired academic administrator*

Barton

Murphree, Kenneth Dewey *elementary school educator*

Booneville

Dyer, V. Jeffrey *educational administrator*

Camden

Bradshaw, Otabel *retired primary school educator*
Greene, Darlene *elementary education educator*

Dardanelle

Wilkins, Melinda Ann *director university program, educator*

De Valls Bluff

Arnold, Elliott O. (Bill Arnold) *secondary school educator*

El Dorado

†Daymon, Joy Jones *school psychology specialist*

Fayetteville

†Ferritor, Daniel E. *chancellor*
†Hanlin, Todd Campbell *education educator*
†Jones, Louis, Jr., (Bucky Jones) *academic administrator*
Schoppmeyer, Martin William *education educator*
Smith, Robert Victor *university administrator*
Van Patten, James Jeffers *education educator*
Williams, Doyle Z. *university dean, educator*

Fort Smith

†Buchanan, L A *band director, music educator*
Gooden, Benny L. *school system administrator*

Harrison

Street, Susan Lee *elementary school educator*

Hartford

Roller Hall, Gayle Aline *gifted and talented education educator*

Hot Springs National Park

Farris, Jefferson Davis *university administrator*
Stein, Karen Louise *elementary music education educator, composer*

Jonesboro

Smith, Eugene Wilson *retired university president and educator*

Little Rock

†Anderson, Joel E., Jr., *university administrator*
Bass, Evelyn Elizabeth *educator*
Branon, M. Susan *school system administrator*
Caldwell, Bettye McDonald *education educator, director*
Chesser, Thelma Jo Sykes *early childhood educator, administrator*
Fribourgh, James Henry *university administrator*
Hathaway, Charles E. *academic administrator*
†Holzer, Linda Ruth *education educator*
O'Neal, Nell Self *retired principal*
†Robison, Judy A. *grants officer, research administrator*
†Smith, Mary Scott *elementary school educator, education educator*
Truex, Dorothy Adine *retired university administrator*
†Wilson, I. Dodd *dean*

Rogers

Spainhower, James Ivan *retired college president*

Russellville

Morris, Lois Lawson *education educator*

Springdale

Cordell, Beulah Faye *special education educator*
Hill, Peggy Sue *principal*

State University

†Wyatt, Leslie *academic administrator*

White Hall

Scott, Vicki Sue *school system administrator*

CALIFORNIA

Alameda

Acker, Cindy Sherlinda Bernice *preschool administrator*
Carter, Roberta Eccleston *therapist, counselor*

Alhambra

†Schuster, Darleen Victoria *director*

Aliso Viejo

†Carroll, Adeline F. *special education educator*
Jeung, Albert *secondary school educator*

Alta Loma

Haskvitz, Alan Paul *elementary education educator, consultant*

Anaheim

Guajardo, Elisa *counselor, educator*

Antioch

†Thomson, Sondra K. *secondary school educator*

Aptos

Bohn, Ralph Carl *educational consultant, retired educator*
Hirsch, Bette G(ross) *college administrator, foreign language educator*

Arcadia

Baltz, Patricia Ann (Pann Baltz) *elementary education educator*
†Endrusick, Rose Marie *secondary school educator*
Meysenburg, Mary Ann *principal*

Arcata

McCrone, Alistair William *retired academic administrator*

Atherton

Lane, Joan Fletcher *educational administrator*

Azusa

Gray, Paul Wesley *university dean*

Bakersfield

Arciniega, Tomas Abel *university president*
Hancock, Tapp *elementary school educator*
Thornton, Pauline Cecilia Eve Marie Suzanne *special education educator*

Banning

Finley, Margaret Mavis *retired elementary school educator*
Gladden, Garnett Lee *educator, health consultant, psychologist*

Beaumont

Mayer, Harvey Ethan *educator*

Belmont

†Sansing, Lucille H. *academic administrator*

Belmont Shore

Fleming, Jane Williams *retired educator, writer*

Ben Lomond

Sikora, James Robert *educational business consultant, financial analyst*

Berkeley

Bastrenta, Brigitte Elisabeth *school administrator*
Berdahl, Robert Max *academic administrator, historian, educator*
Bowker, Albert Hosmer *retired university chancellor*
†Buchanan, Bob Branch *education educator*
Cieslak, William *academic administrator*
†Davis, Maggie L. *elementary teacher*
†De Jonghe, Lutgard C. *educator*
†Fletcher, Daniel A. *adult education educator*
†Hinshaw, Stephen P. *education educator*
Johnson, Mary Katherine (Katie Johnson) *elementary education educator*
Kay, Herma Hill *education educator*
Kerr, Clark *academic administrator emeritus*
LaBelle, Thomas Jeffrey *academic administrator*
Leonard, Thomas *dean, educator, librarian*
†Liu, Xin *education educator*
Maslach, George James *former university official*
McCoy, Charles Sherwood *university president, former theology educator*
McPhail-Geist, Karin Ruth *secondary education educator, realtor, musician*
Merrill, Richard James *educational director*
Miles, Raymond Edward *former university dean, organizational behavior and industrial relations educator*
Ralston, Lenore Dale *academic policy and program analyst*
Rice, Robert Arnot *school administrator*
Shortell, Stephen Michael *dean, health services researcher*
†Ullman, Dana Gregory *educational administrator, publisher, author*
†Wetzel, David *education educator*

Beverly Hills

Grant, Michael Ernest *educational administrator, institutional management educator*

Big Bear City

Pipes, Doris Perry *secondary school educator, consultant*

Boulevard

Charles, Blanche *retired elementary education educator*

Brea

Hall, Linda Sue Bohannon *special education educator*

Brentwood

Groseclose, Wanda Westman *retired elementary school educator*

Buena Park

Turkus-Workman, Carol Ann *educator*

Burbank

Nielsen, Kenneth Ray *academic administrator*
Walters, Kenneth C. *retired educator*

Camarillo

Rush, Richard R. *academic administrator*

Campbell

Kaipa, Prasad Lakshmi Narasimha *educational researcher and consultant*

Campo

Jermini, Ellen *educational administrator, philosopher*

Carmel

Faul, June Patricia *education specialist*

Carson

Garcia, Angélica María *elementary education educator*
Mori, Allen Anthony *academic administrator, consultant*

Castaic

Ashton, Tamarah M. *special education educator, consultant*

Castro Valley

Lee, Joyce Y. *educational administrator*

Cathedral City

Satcher, Clement Michael *elementary school educator*

Chico

Esteban, Manuel Antonio *academic administrator, language educator*
Houpis, James Louis Joseph *dean, biologist*
Robinson, Beulah Lobdell *retired educator*

Chino

Forsyth, Barbara Jean *elementary reading specialist, writer, poet*

Claremont

Alexander, John David, Jr., *college administrator*
Bekavac, Nancy Yavor *academic administrator, lawyer*
†Cumberbatch, Ellis *education educator, researcher*
†Dewey, Thomas Gregory *dean, physical chemist, educator*
Douglass, Enid Hart *educational program director*
Gann, Pamela Brooks *academic administrator*
†Kurita, Kyoko *education educator*
Liggett, Thomas Jackson *retired seminary president*
Maguire, John David *academic administrator, educator, writer*
Platt, Joseph Beaven *former college president*
Riggs, Henry Earle *academic administrator, engineering educator*
Stanley, Peter William *former academic administrator*
Strauss, Jon Calvert *academic administrator*
†Wettack, F. Sheldon *academic administrator*

Cool

Sheridan, George Groh *elementary education educator, teacher educator, English educator*

Corcoran

Martines, Eugenia Belle *elementary school educator*

Corona

Clark, Nanci *elementary education educator*

Corte Madera

Dalpino, Ida Jane *retired secondary education educator*

Costa Mesa

Dempster, Murray Wayne *academic administrator, religion educator, minister*
Tillman, Barbara Ann *education educator, consultant*

Covina

Aguilar, Gladys Maria *counselor, educator*

Culver City

Maxwell-Brogdon, Florence Morency *school administrator, educational adviser*

Cupertino

†Lyon, Mary Lou *educator*

Cypress

†Henrickson, Leslie Ann *educational consultant, educator*

Danville

Cross, Christopher T. *education consultant*

Davis

Carey, James Robert *educator*
Carter, Colin Andre *education educator*
†Hall, John Ross *educator*
†Kraft, Rosemarie *dean, educator*
Norton, Donald Alan *retired adult education educator*
†Osburn, Bennie I. *dean*

Pritchard, William Roy *former university system administrator*
†Sandoval, Jonathan Hough *education educator*
Springer, Sally Pearl *university administrator*
Vanderhoef, Larry Neil *academic administrator*

Downey

Brooks, Lillian Drilling Ashton (Lillian Hazel Church) *adult education educator*
Ruecker, Martha Engels *retired special education educator*

Earlimart

†White, Kathleen *director*

El Cajon

Ostermeyer, Maryann *secondary school educator, writer*
Thomas, Esther Merlene *elementary education educator*

El Centro

Kussman, Eleanor (Ellie Kussman) *retired educational superintendent*

El Cerrito

Herzberg, Dorothy Crews *secondary education educator*

Elk Grove

Landon, JoJene Babbitt *special education educator*
†Moe, Janet Anne *elementary school educator, musician*
Sparks, Jack Norman *college dean*

Encino

Bach, Cynthia *educational program director, writer*
†O'Riley, Karen E. *principal*

Escondido

†Duguid, Iain Moir *education educator*
Friedman, Alan Howard *writer, educator*
†Hannam-Oosterbaan, Maria Gertrude *educator*
Moore, Marc Anthony *university administrator, writer, retired military officer*
Sanders, Adrian Lionel *educational consultant*

Fair Oaks

Lemke, Herman Ernest Frederick, Jr., *retired elementary education educator, consultant*

Fairfield

Kirkorian, Donald George *retired college official, management consultant*

Folsom

Jantzen, J(ohn) Marc *retired education educator*
†Sample, Winona Elliott *educational consultant*
†Sarraf, Shirley A. *secondary school educator*

Fontana

Donica, Cheryl Marie *elementary education educator*

Forestville

Kielsmeier, Catherine Jane *school system administrator*

Foster City

Berman, Daniel K(atzel) *educational consultant, university official*

Fountain Valley

†Olivadoti, Victoria Ruth *educational consultant*
Otto, Marie (Bertha Otto) *educational administrator, educational consulting company executive*
Purdy, Leslie *community college president*

Fremont

Le, Thuy Trong *educator, researcher*

Fresno

Coleman, Donald Gene *education educator*
Dandoy, Maxima Antonio *education educator emeritus*
†Fields, Jill S. *education educator*
Girvin, Shirley Eppinette *retired elementary education educator, journalist*
Klassen, Peter James *academic administrator, history educator*
Welty, John Donald *academic administrator*

Fullerton

Donoghue, Mildred Ransdorf *education educator*
Fischer, Robert Blanchard *university administrator, researcher*
O'Donnell, Edith J. *educational and information technology consultant, writer, musician*
Smith, Ephraim Philip *academic administrator, former university dean, educator*
Snider, Jane Ann *elementary school educator*

Gardena

†Harvey, Cyril Leslie *education educator*

Glendale

Edwards, Kathryn Inez *educational technology consultant*
Whalen, Lucille *retired academic administrator*

Glendora

Schiele, Paul Ellsworth, Jr., *education business owner, writer*
†Solheim, Bruce Olav *education educator*

Grass Valley

McDaniel, Carolyn Marie (Lynn) *secondary education educator*

Hanford

†Hazen, William A. *secondary school educator*
Park, Penny Sheran *elementary school educator, writer*

Hawthorne
Brann, Donald Lewis, Jr., *school superintendent*
†Perry, Lucinda B. *retired elementary school educator, writer*

Hayward
Getz, Melissa B. *secondary education educator*
Laycock, Mary Chappell *gifted and talented education educator, consultant*
McCune, Ellis E. *retired university system chief administrator, higher education consultant*
Rees, Norma S. *academic administrator*

Hemet
Knapp, Lonnie Troy *elementary education educator*

Hollister
Turpin, Calvin Coolidge *retired university administrator, educator*
†Zuniga, James R. *director, music educator, conductor, composer*

Huntington Beach
†Agadjanyan, Michael Grant *education educator*
Davidson-Shepard, Gay *secondary education educator*

Idyllwild
Smith, Robert Bruce *college administrator*

Indian Wells
†Trotter, F(rederick) Thomas *retired academic administrator*

Inglewood
†Cato, Gloria Maxine *retired secondary education educator, school program administrator*
Logan, Lynda Dianne *elementary education educator*

Inyokern
Norris, Lois Ann *elementary school educator*

Irvine
Cesario, Thomas Charles *dean*
Chen, Chuansheng *education educator*
Cicerone, Ralph John *academic administrator, geophysicist*
Fleischer, Everly Borah *academic administrator*
†Grandone-LLorente, Maria Elisa *dean, consultant*
McCubbin, Sharon Anglin *elementary school educator*
Peltason, Jack Walter *foundation executive, educator*
Tengs, Tammy Ora *educator*

Kelsey
Rankin, Graham M. *educator, consultant*

La Canada Flintridge
Lamson, Robert Woodrow *retired school system administrator*

La Crescenta
Klint, Ronald Vernon *secondary school educator, financial consultant*

La Jolla
Carty, Heidi Marlene *educator, researcher*
Cavenee, Webster K. *director*
†Chandler, Marsha *academic administrator, professor*
Henig, Suzanne *retired educator, writer, editor*
Holmes, Edward W. *dean, physician, medical educator*
Masys, Daniel Richard *medical school director*
North, Kathryn E. Keesey (Mrs. Eugene C. North) *retired educator*
Stefan, Vladislav Alexander *academic administrator, educator, research scientist, writer*

La Mesa
Black, Eileen Mary *retired elementary school educator*
Charleton, Margaret Ann *child care administrator, consultant*
†Espinosa, Ruben *education educator, consultant*

La Quinta
Farber, Patricia Ann *secondary education educator*
†Tebbs, Carol Ann *secondary education educator, academic administrator*

La Verne
†Ebersole, Helen Brownsberger *elementary school educator*
Fleck, Raymond Anthony, Jr., *retired university administrator*
Morgan, Stephen Charles *academic administrator*

Laguna Beach
Fry, Edward Bernard *education educator, retired*

Laguna Hills
Powers, Janet F. *special education educator*

Laguna Niguel
Teitelbaum, Marilyn Leah *special education educator*

Laguna Woods
Strong, Winifred Hekker *educational counselor, consultant*

Lakeside
†Walker, Wanda Medora *retired elementary school educator, consultant*

Lakewood
Bogdan, James Thomas *secondary education educator, electronics researcher and developer*

De Lorca, Luis E. *public school administrator, educator, speaker*

Lancaster
Walsh, Patricia Maack *special education educator*

Lemon Grove
Mott, June Marjorie *school system administrator*

Lincoln
Oscarson, Kathleen Dale *retired writing assessment coordinator, educator*

Livermore
Roshong, Dee Ann Daniels *dean, educator*

Lodi
Bishop-Graham, Barbara *secondary school educator, journalist*

Loma Linda
Goodacre, Charles J. *academic administrator*
Klooster, Judson *academic administrator, dentistry educator*

Long Beach
Blazey, Michael Alan *educator*
†Collins, Jr., Aristide J. *academic administrator*
Cook, Karla Joan *elementary education educator*
Cotner, Douglas Monroe *provost, mathematics and environmental science educator*
Culton, Paul Melvin *retired counselor, educator, interpreter*
Dublin, Stephen Louis *secondary school educator, singer, musician*
Duran, Matias Martin *adult education educator*
Hellmer, Lynne Beberman *education educator*
Knudson, Ruth Esther *education educator*
Lathrop, Irvin Tunis *retired academic dean, educator*
Lauda, Donald Paul *university dean*
†Lofland, Patricia Lois *educator*
†Mandarino, Candida Ann *education educator, consultant*
†Maxson, Robert C. *university president*
Oviatt, Larry Andrew *retired secondary school educator*
†Reed, Charles Bass *chief academic administrator*
†Reichard, Gary Warren *university administrator, history educator*
†Singhal, Meena *education educator*

Los Altos
Keller, James Warren *college administrator*
Welsh, Doris McNeil *early childhood education specialist*

Los Angeles
Agnew, John A. *education educator*
†Anastos, Rosemary Park *retired higher education educator*
Armstrong, Lloyd, Jr., *university official, physics educator*
†Banner, Lois Wendland *education educator, writer*
†Baum, Geoffrey Leo *director*
Bice, Scott Haas *dean, lawyer, educator*
Carnesale, Albert *academic administrator*
†Coker, Sybil Jane Thomas *counseling administrator*
Darmstaetter, Jay Eugene *secondary education educator*
Dewey, Donald Odell *dean, academic administrator*
Erickson, Frederick David *education and anthropology educator*
Fitz-Carter, Aleane *elementary education educator, composer*
Gilbert, Richard Keith *education educator, researcher*
Gothold, Stuart Eugene *school system administrator, educator*
†Greenland, Sander *education educator*
†Gurval, Robert Alan *education educator*
Hagedorn, Linda Serra *education educator, researcher*
Haley, Roslyn Trezevant *educational program director*
Harris, F. Chandler *retired university administrator*
Harvey, James Gerald *educational counselor, consultant, researcher*
Hayes, Robert Mayo *university dean, library and information science educator*
Heath, Berthann Jones *education administrator*
Hubbard, John Randolph *retired academic administrator*
†Idini, Antonio Gionvanni *education educator*
Kaback, Elaine *career counselor, family therapist, consultant*
Keddie, Nikki R. *education educator*
Kleingartner, Archie *founding dean, educator*
†Koo, Eun-Hee *education educator*
†LeBeau, Mary Delle *education educator, writer, dancer*
Lee, William Bradley *education educator*
Lieber, David Leo *university president*
Lim, Larry Kay *university official*
Lucente, Rosemary Dolores *retired educational administrator, consultant*
Lynch, Beverly Pfeifer *education and information studies educator*
Mandel, Joseph David *academic administrator, lawyer*
Martin, Shane Patrick *education educator, consultant*
McCabe, Edward R. B. *academic administrator, educator, physician*
McCloskey, Mark *educator*
McGee, Lynda Plant *guidance counselor*
McLinn, Anna Ruth *educator*
†Mitchell, Theodore Reed *academic administrator*
Money, Ruth Rowntree *infant development and care specialist, consultant*
Moore, Donald Walter *academic administrator, school librarian*

†Morisky, Donald E. *director, medical educator*
Park, No-Hee *academic administrator*
Parks, Debora Ann *private school director*
Pierskalla, William Peter *university dean, management-engineering educator*
†Rider, Elizabeth Ann Cottrell *elementary school educator*
Rosser, James Milton *academic administrator*
Ryan, Stephen Joseph, Jr., *ophthalmology educator, university dean*
Sample, Steven Browning *university executive*
Shearer, Derek Norcross *international studies educator, diplomat, administrator*
Simun, Patricia Bates *education educator, consultant*
Small, Gary W. *academic administrator, psychiatrist, educator*
Sohaili, Monira *special education educator, writer*
Steinberg, Warren Linnington *school principal*
Strippoli, William Peter *academic administrator*
Taylor, Leigh Herbert *college dean*
Tsebelis, George *educator*
Wagner, William Gerard *university dean, physicist, consultant, information scientist, investment manager*
Wang, Jia *educator*
Wazzan, A(hmed) R(assem) Frank *engineering educator, dean*
†Yip, Andy Ming-Ham *education educator, researcher*
†Yu, Pauline Ruth *dean, East Asian languages educator*
Zexter, Eleanor M. *secondary education educator*

Los Banos
†Ellington, Karen Renae *secondary education resource specialist*

Los Gatos
†Ferrari, L. Katherine *speaker, consultant, entrepreneur*

Malibu
†Benton, Andrew Keith *university administrator, lawyer*
†Cardoso, Dinora Caridad *education educator*
Phillips, Ronald Frank *university administrator*
Raine, Melinda L. *library manager*

Marina
Hill, Karen Caecilia *education educator*

Menifee
Balow, Irving Henry *retired education educator*

Menlo Park
Chapin, June Roediger *education educator*
Raffo, Susan Henney *elementary education educator*
Studley, Jamienne Shayne *former academic administrator, lawyer*
†Walker, George Edward *academic administrator, physicist*
†Zercher, Craig Allen *special education educator, researcher*

Mill Valley
Maubert, Jacques Claude *retired school superintendent*

Mission Viejo
Hodge, Kathleen O'Connell *academic administrator*

Modesto
Harrison-Scott, Sharlene Marie *elementary school educator*
Tidball, Lee Falk *elementary school educator, writer*

Mojave
Shelby, Tim Otto *secondary education educator*

Montebello
†Bucey, Constance Virginia Russell *retired elementary school educator, education educator*
Dible, Rose Harpe McFee *special education educator*

Monterey
†Boger, Gail Lorraine Zivna *reading specialist*
Di Girolamo, Rosina Elizabeth *education educator*
Oder, Broeck Newton *school emergency management consultant*

Moreno Valley
†Wittwer, Marc Wayne *secondary school educator, football coach*

Newport Beach
Dean, John F. *retired school system administrator*

North Hills
†Deets, Richard M. *secondary school educator, consultant*

North Hollywood
Burman, Sheila Flexer Zola *special education educator*

Northridge
Brotman, Carol Eileen *adult education educator, advocate*
Curzon, Susan Carol *university administrator*
Falk, Heinrich Richard *theater and humanities educator*
†Kranz, Jack *university librarian, educator*
†McHenry, Leemon Benton *education educator, writer*
Mitchell, James Andrew *education educator*
Syms, Helen Maksym *educational administrator*

Norwalk
Matsuura, Kenneth Ray *counselor, articulation officer*

Novato
Jaeger, Patsy Elaine *retired secondary education educator, artist*
Patterson, W. Morgan *college president*

Oakland
Anderson, Brother Timothy Mel *academic administrator*
Atkinson, Richard Chatham *university president*
Diaz, Sharon *education administrator*
Dibble, David Van Vlack *visually impaired educator, lawyer*
Dynes, Robert C. *academic administrator*
Eykamp, Paul W. *academic administrator*
Gomes, Wayne Reginald *academic administrator*
Griffin, Betty Jo *elementary school educator*
Heydman, Abby Maria *academic executive*
†Holmgren, Janet L *college president*
Howatt, Sister Helen Clare *former human services director, former college library director*
Hwang, Michael Tian-Chung *university president*
Isaac Nash, Eva Mae *educator*
†King, C. Judson *academic administrator*
Stewart, John Lincoln *university administrator*

Oceanside
†LaRosa, John Paul *education educator*
Pena, Maria Geges *academic services administrator*

Ojai
Shagam, Marvin Hückel-Berri *private school educator*

Ontario
Kennedy, Mark Alan *secondary school educator*

Orange
†Cooper, Steven Harold *education educator*
Hamilton, Harry Lemuel, Jr., *educator*
Tuggle, Francis Douglas *dean, consultant*

Orinda
Glasser, Charles Edward *university president*

Oxnard
Auston, David Henry *former academic administrator, electrical engineer, educator*
Rosales, Sandra Johnson *school system administrator*

Pacific Grove
Longman, Anne Strickland *special education educator, consultant*

Pacific Palisades
Georges, Robert Augustus *emeritus educator, researcher, writer*

Palm Desert
Baxter, Betty Carpenter *educational administrator*
Hoffmann, Joan Carol *retired academic dean*
Porter, Priscilla *elementary education educator*
Sexson, Stephen Bruce *education writer, educator*

Palm Springs
†Fitzgerald, Jack Lyon *education educator, writer*
Gill, Jo Anne Martha *middle school educator*
Hartman, Rosemary Jane *retired special education educator*

Palo Alto
†Bohrnstedt, George William *educational researcher*
Gong, Mamie Poggio *elementary education educator*
Loveless, Edward Eugene *education educator, musician*

Palos Verdes Estates
Lazzaro, Anthony Derek *university administrator*

Paramount
Williams, Vivian Lewie *retired counseling administrator*

Pasadena
Almore-Randle, Allie Louise *special education educator*
Baltimore, David *academic administrator, microbiologist, educator*
Brooks, Edward Howard *college administrator*
Everhart, Thomas Eugene *retired university president, engineering educator*
Gilman, Richard Carleton *retired college president*
Hoffman, Philip Thomas *university educator*
Kimbrough, Lorelei *elementary education educator*
Lingenfelter, Sherwood Galen *university provost, anthropology educator*
Meye, Robert Paul *retired seminary educator, administrator, writer*
Pings, Cornelius John *educational consultant, director*
†Scoonover, Frank Miller, Jr., *retired secondary school educator*
Siemon-Burgeson, Marilyn M. (Marilyn Burgeson) *education administrator*
Stolper, Edward Manin *secondary education educator*

Paso Robles
Gruner, George Richard *retired secondary education educator*

Penn Valley
†Longan, Suzanne M. *retired elementary school educator*

Nehls, Robert Louis, Jr., *school system financial consultant*

Pinole
Grogan, Stanley Joseph *educational and security consultant*

Placerville
†Miller, Edna Rae Atkins *educator*

Pleasanton
Lucas, Linda Lucille *dean*

Pomona
Ambrose, William Wright, Jr., *dean, academic administrator*
†Callaway, Linda Marie *special education educator*
Demery, Dorothy Jean *secondary school educator*
†Fremont, Ronald H., II, *academic administrator, consultant*
†Kinsey, Gary W. *education educator*
Lenz, Craig *academic administrator*
Rhodes, Rhonda Lynn *business educator*
Tunison, Elizabeth Lamb *education educator*

Porterville
Hayes, Shirley Ann *special education educator*

Quartz Hill
Nettelhorst, Robin Paul *academic administrator, writer*

Rancho Cordova
Hendrickson, Elizabeth Ann *retired secondary education educator*

Red Bluff
Hoofard, Jane Mahan Decker *retired elementary school educator*
Kennedy, James William, Jr., (Sarge Kennedy) *special education administrator, consultant*

Redlands
Burgess, Charlotte Gaylord *academic administrator*
Gogolin, Marilyn Tompkins *language pathologist, retired educational administrator*
Healy, Daniel Thomas *secondary education educator*
Huntley, William Barney *educator*

Redwood City
Jones, Brenda Gail *school district administrator*

Reedley
†Heise, Clarence Buddy *secondary school educator, real estate developer*

Rialto
Bauza, Christine Diane *special education educator*
Jackson, Betty Eileen *music and elementary school educator*

Riverside
Bulloch, Kathleen Louise *educational professional*
†Deese, E(thel) Helen *English educator*
†d'Encarnacao-Bradley, Aja A. *supervisor*
Finan, Ellen Cranston *secondary education educator, consultant*
†Fischer, John Martin *education educator, researcher*
†Fontana, Sandra Ellen Frankel *special education educator*
Hendrick, Irving Guilford *education educator*
Lacy, Carolyn Jean *elementary education educator, secondary education educator*
Prosser, Michael Joseph *college librarian*
Yacoub, Ignatius I. *university dean*

Rocklin
Hyde, Geraldine Veola *retired secondary school educator*

Rohnert Park
Arminana, Ruben *academic administrator, educator*
Babula, William *university dean*

Rolling Hills Estates
Ingerson, Nancy Nina Moore *special education educator*

Roseville
French, Leura Parker *secondary educator*

Ross
Matan, Lillian Kathleen *educator, designer*

Sacramento
Gerth, Donald Rogers *university president*
Grimes, Pamela Rae *retired elementary school educator*
†Lam, Siuwa Monica *education educator, consultant*
Menebroker, Ann *special education educator, writer*
Mogull, Robert G. *educator, researcher*
O'Leary, Marion Hugh *university dean, chemist*
Ramey, Felicenne Houston *dean*
Reed-Graham, Lois L. *eeducation consultant, author, management organizer*
Sanborn, Kathy *career planning administrator, consultant*
Shoemaker, Cameron David James *dean, educator*
Silva, Joseph, Jr., *dean, medical educator*
Zaidi, Emily Louise *retired elementary school educator*

San Anselmo
†Harpham, Heather Elise *educator*

San Bernardino
Caballero, Sharon *academic administrator*
Crowell, Samuel Marvin, Jr., *education educator*
Norton, Ruth Ann *education educator*

San Bruno
†White, Frances LaVonne *academic administrator*

San Carlos
Patnode, Darwin Nicholas *retired academic administrator, professional parliamentarian*

San Diego
Donley, Dennis Lee *school librarian*
Early, Teri Wilson (Denise Wilson) *elementary education educator*
Feinberg, Lawrence Bernard *university dean, psychologist*
Golding, Brage *university president*
†Gundersen, Larry Edward *academic administrator*
†Idos, Rosalina Vejerano *secondary school educator*
James, Helen Foster *education director*
†Kahan, David Michael *education educator*
†Lyons, Mary E. *academic administrator*
Mayer, George Roy *educator*
Moss, Barbara Gae *education educator*
Perrault, Jacques *educator*
Schade, Charlene Joanne *adult and early childhood education educator*
Schwartz, Alfred *university dean*
Travaglini, Joseph *educational consultant*
†Uribe, Jennie Ann *elementary school educator*
†Vartanian, Pershing *education educator*
Walker, Donald Ezzell *retired academic administrator*
Weber, Stephen Lewis *university president*

San Dimas
†Cameron, Judith Lynne *secondary education educator, hypnotherapist*
Lindly, Douglas Dean *elementary/middle school educator, administrator*

San Francisco
Albino, Judith Elaine Newsom *university president*
Baxter-Lowe, Lee Ann *educator*
Corrigan, Robert Anthony *academic administrator*
Davis, James Wesley *university program administrator, artist, writer, composer*
Finocchiaro, Penny Morris *secondary school educator*
Fleishhacker, David *school administrator*
Goldstine, Stephen Joseph *college administrator*
Hudson, Suncerray Ann *analyst, research grants manager*
Kane, Mary Kay *dean, law educator*
Kikukawa, Randall Hiroyuki *university administrator*
Kleinberg, David Lewis *education administrator*
Kopel, Stephen *educator*
Kozloff, Lloyd M. *university dean, educator, scientist*
Kuriloff, Effie Hannah *education educator*
†Lane, Mary B. *education educator, writer*
Laret, Mark R. *school system administrator*
Naegele, Carl Joseph *university academic administrator, educator*
†Newacheck, Paul W. *education educator, researcher*
Rowe, Mary Ann Gunder *education educator*
†Rumjahn, Diana *academic administrator*
Stephens, Elisa *college president*
Tantum, James Kent *educational facilitator, publisher*
Ury, Claude Max *educational consultant, book reviewer*
Zhu, Bo-qing *cardiovascular research specialist*
†Zingale, Donald Paul *academic administrator, educator*

San Gabriel
Tomich-Bolognesi, Vera *educator*

San Jose
†Abbott, Rexford J. *secondary school educator, mechanical engineer*
Cryer, Rodger Earl *educational administrator*
Elsorady, Alexa Marie *secondary education educator*
Holyer, Erna Maria *adult education educator, writer, artist*
Jordan, Bernice Bell *retired elementary school educator*
Lobig, Janie Howell *special education educator*
Martin, Bernard Lee *former college dean*
Merriam, Janet Pamela *special education educator*
Okerlund, Arlene Naylor *university official*
Pflughaupt, Jane Ramsey *secondary school educator*
†Struckman, Christina Kennedy *education educator, consultant*
Whitney, Natalie White *primary school educator*
Wiens, Beverly Jo *educator*

San Juan Capistrano
†Larwood, Susan Elizabeth *elementary school educator*

San Leandro
Chohlis, Dana Marie *educator, theatre director*

San Luis Obispo
Bailey, Philip Sigmon, Jr., *university official and dean, chemistry educator*
Baker, Warren J(oseph) *university president*
Ericson, Jon Meyer *academic administrator, rhetoric theory educator*
Haile, Allen Cleveland *educator and administrator*
Kennedy, Robert Edwin *university administrator*

San Marcos
Lilly, Martin Stephen *university dean*

San Marino
Footman, Gordon Elliott *educational administrator*

San Pablo
Collier, Judith Brandes *elementary education educator*

San Pedro
Gaines, Jerry Lee *retired secondary education educator*

San Rafael
Adcock, Muriel W. *special education educator*
Fink, Joseph Richard *academic administrator*
Henry, Joseph Louis *university dean*

Santa Ana
†Austin, Marie A. *academic administrator*
†Beal, Dennis *academic administrator*
Kato, Terri Emi *elementary school and gifted and talented educator*
Watts, Judith-Ann White *secondary school educator*

Santa Barbara
Allaway, William Harris *retired university official*
†Barry, Robert Michael *education educator*
Boyan, Norman J. *retired education educator*
Cirone, William Joseph *educational administrator*
†Cortijo, Antonio *education educator*
Hong, Sehee *education and psychology educator*
†Lewandowski, Leon Scott *elementary school educator*
O'Dowd, Donald Davy *retired university president*
Sinsheimer, Robert Louis *retired university chancellor and educator*
Yang, Henry T. *academic administrator, educator*

Santa Clara
Ling, Nam *educator*
Locatelli, Paul Leo *academic administrator*

Santa Clarita
Grishman, Lee Howard *college program administrator*
Lavine, Steven David *academic administrator*
Ungar, Roselva May *primary and elementary educator*

Santa Cruz
Jackson, Kingsbury Temple *educational contract consultant*
Mirk, Judy Ann *retired elementary educator*

Santa Paula
Leeds-Horwitz, Susan Beth *director*

Santa Rosa
Cheung, Judy Hardin *retired special education educator*
Foster, Lucille Caster *school system administrator, retired*
†Mann, Jennifer E. *education development coordinator*
Webb, Charles Richard *retired university president*

Santee
Morris, Henry Madison, Jr., *education educator*

Saratoga
Houston, Elizabeth Reece Manasco *correctional education consultant*

Seaside
†Paget, Ruth Lois *academic administrator, educator, writer*

Selma
Rezac, Debra Dowell *bilingual educator*

Shasta Lake
Parsons, Debra Lea *elementary school educator*

Sherman Oaks
O'Neill, Sallie Boyd *educational consultant, business owner, sculptor*

Signal Hill
Vandament, William Eugene *retired academic administrator*

Silverado
Mamer, James Michael *secondary education educator*

Simi Valley
Robison, Marsha Gail *career planning administration*

Solana Beach
†Beck-von-Peccoz, Michele *retired secondary school educator, writer*

Sonoma
Hobart, Billie *education educator, consultant*

South Pasadena
†Fuller, Kathy J. *special education educator, consultant, researcher*
Yett, Sally Pugh *elementary school educator, art educator*

Stanford
†Evers, Williamson Moore *education policy analyst, political scientist*
Gross, Richard Edmund *education educator*
Grossman, Pamela Lynn *education educator*
†Hausman, Warren Howard *educator*
Hennessy, John L. *academic administrator*
Henriksen, Thomas Hollinger *university official*
Kays, William Morrow *university administrator, mechanical engineer*
Kirst, Michael Weile *education educator, researcher*
†Levy, Doron *educator*
Palm, Charles Gilman *university official*
Perry, William James *educator, former federal official*
†Raisian, John *academic administrator, economist*
Spence, A(ndrew) Michael *dean, finance educator*
Stone, William Edward *academic administrator, consultant*
Strober, Myra Hoffenberg *education educator, consultant*

Stockton
†Cooper, Iva Jean *special education educator*
DeRicco, Lawrence Albert *college president emeritus*
Fung, Rosaline Lee *educator*
Haines, Joybelle *retired elementary school educator*
Kareem, A'isha *educational consultant, counselor*
Sorby, Donald Lloyd *university dean*

Sun Valley
Mayhue, Richard Lee *provost, dean, pastor, writer*

Thousand Oaks
Gillette, Dennis C. *academic administrator, mayor*
†Kuzmanovic, Jane Violet *director*
Powe, Larry Kenneth *clinical researcher*

Torrance
†Carlini, Piero Eliso *secondary school educator*
Kuc, Joseph A. *education educator, consultant*
Lewis, Eric Stephen *elementary school educator*
McNamara, Brenda Norma *secondary school educator*
Roney, Raymond G. *educator, publisher*
†Ulrich, Vera Elizabeth *educator*

Trinidad
Conant, Ralph Wendell *educator, consultant, author*

Tustin
Greene, Wendy Segal *special education educator*

Upland
Doyle, Michael James *educator, organist*

Vallejo
Murillo, Carol Ann *secondary school educator*
Purificacion, Dennis Torres *secondary school educator, lecturer, theologian*
Zeliger, Bernard *dean*

Van Nuys
Altshiller, Arthur Leonard *secondary education educator*

Ventura
Moffatt, Mindy Ann *educator, educational training specialist*
Zuber, Norma Keen *career counselor, educator*

Visalia
†Daniels, Joan Frances *private school educator*
Goulart, Janell Ann *elementary education educator*
Singh, Daljit *dean, business and public administration educator*

Walnut
Spencer, Constance Marilyn *secondary education educator*

Walnut Creek
Carver, Dorothy Lee Eskew (Mrs. John James Carver) *retired secondary education educator*
Fielding, Elizabeth Brown *education educator*
†Lilly, Luella Jean *academic administrator*
Wolf, Harry *retired dean and educator*

Waterford
Reed, Thomas W. *secondary education educator*

Weimar
Kerschner, Lee R(onald) *academic administrator, political science educator*

Westlake Village
Doerr, Patricia Marian *elementary and special education educator*
Steadman, Lydia Duff *symphony violinist, retired elementary school educator*

Whittier
Drake, E. Maylon *academic administrator*

Woodland Hills
Zeitlin, Herbert Zakary *retired academic administrator, real estate consultant*

Yorba Linda
Lunde, Dolores Benitez *retired secondary education educator*
Sternitzke-Holub, Ann *elementary school educator*

Yountville
Bedell, Jay Dee *educator, writer*

Yucaipa
Gomez, Louis Salazar *college president*
Marks, Sharon Lea *primary school educator, nurse*
Matsuda, Stanley Kazuhiro *secondary education educator*

COLORADO

Arvada
Bert, Carol Lois *retired educational assistant*
Reed, Joan-Marie *special education educator*

Aurora
Beckman, L. David *university chancellor*
Halford, Sharon Lee *college administrator, advocate, educator*
†Jarvis, Mary Grace *principal*
Kellogg Fain, Karen *retired history and geography educator*
Lassen, Betty Jane *educator*
Newman, John Henry *educational researcher*
Sorenson, Katherine Ann *elementary school educator*
Walker, Joyce Marie *secondary school educator*

Bailey
Wright, Dixie Lee *special needs persons consultant*

Boulder
Anderson, Ronald Delaine *education educator*
†Buchanan, Mary Estill *education trustee*
†Buechner, John C. *academic administrator*
†Burke, Thomas Sebastian, Jr., *educator, writer*
†Byyny, Richard Lee *academic administrator, physician*
Dawson, Roy Edward *academic advisor*
Enarson, Harold L. *retired academic administrator*
†Mahajan, Roop L. *dean, engineering educator*
McGuinness, Aims Chamberlain, Jr., *higher education policy analyst*
†Park, Wounjhang *adult education educator*
Sirotkin, Phillip Leonard *education administrator*
Swenson, Ann-Marie *education educator*
Vigil, Daniel Agustin *academic administrator*
Williams, James Franklin, II, *university dean, librarian*

Broomfield
Burns, James Scotte, II, *secondary school educator*

Calhan
Henderson, Freda LaVerne *elementary education educator*

Cheyenne Wells
Palmer, Rayetta J. *technology coordinator, educator*

Colorado Springs
Adams, Bernard Schroder *retired college president*
†Cascaval, Radu Cristian *education educator*
†Celeste, Richard F. *academic administrator, former ambassador, former governor*
Guy, Mildred Dorothy *retired secondary school educator*
Hinkle, Betty Ruth *educational administrator*
Kettner-Polley, Richard Brian *director*
†Klingner, Donald E. *educator, consultant*
Ruch, Marcella Joyce *retired educator, biographer*

Commerce City
Baker, Maria Luise *retired secondary school educator*

Denver
Augustine, Rosemary *vocational counselor, writer*
Bautista, Michael Phillip *school system administrator*
Bosworth, Bruce Leighton *school administrator, educator, consultant*
Brown, Hank *foundation administrator, former university administrator, former senator*
†Burrows, Bertha Jean *retired academic administrator*
†Clark, Thomas Arthur *education educator, consultant*
Driggs, Margaret *educator*
†Du, Yiping P. *education educator*
Ellis, Sylvia D. Hall *development and library education consultant*
Fielden, C. Franklin, III, *early childhood education consultant*
Gibson, Elisabeth Jane *retired principal*
Halgren, Lee A. *academic administrator*
†Horton, Frank Elba *university official, geography educator*
†Jarles, Ruth Sewell *education educator*
Kaplan, Sheila *academic administrator*
Landesman, Howard M. *academic administrator*
Lane, Peggy Lee *educator*
Leitinger, Christiane *educator*
Messer, Donald Edward *theological school president, theology educator*
Parsell, Roger Edmund *retired educator, civic worker*
†Pointer, Marsha G. *principal*
Ritchie, Daniel Lee *academic administrator*
Shaeffer, Thelma Jean *primary school educator*
Vogel, Robert Lee *college administrator, clergyman*

Durango
†Mann, Rochelle Gayl *education educator, writer*

Englewood
Nelson, Barbara Louise *secondary education educator*
Shields, Marlene Sue *elementary school educator*
Whiteaker, Ruth Catherine *retired secondary education educator, counselor*

Estes Park
†Easton, Lois Brown *educational consultant*
Guest, Linda Sand *education educator*

Fort Collins
†Baldwin, Lionel Vernon *retired university president*
Fotsch, Dan Robert *elementary education educator*
Harper, Judson Morse *university administrator, consultant, educator*
Linden, James Carl *educator, consultant*
Maher, Thomas George *academic administrator, producer, media educator*
†Perryman, Lance *dean*
Yates, Albert Carl *academic administrator, chemistry educator*

Fort Morgan
Raines, Louis Edward *school administrator*

Golden
Bickart, Theodore Albert *university president emeritus*
Klug, John Joseph *secondary education educator, director of dramatics*
Shea, Dion Warren Joseph *university official, fund raiser*
†Truly, Richard H. *academic administrator, former federal agency administrator, former astronaut*

Grand Junction
Moberly, Linden Emery *educational administrator*
†Woodworth, Sandra Sue *communications educator*

Greeley
Duff, William Leroy, Jr., *university dean emeritus, business educator*

Greenwood Village
Lynn, Patricia Anne *student services representative*

Highlands Ranch
Erickson, Linda Rae *educator*

Lakewood
Binns, Cathleen Isabel *retired secondary school educator*
McBride, Guy Thornton, Jr., *college president emeritus*

Littleton
Bush, Stanley Giltner *secondary school educator*
Greenberg, Elinor Miller *university official, consultant*
Kennedy, Jack *secondary education journalism educator*
Lesh-Laurie, Georgia Elizabeth *university administrator, biology educator, researcher*
Marion, John Martin *academic administrator*
†Panetta, Sandra Jean *education coordinator*
Pardue, Karen Reiko *elementary education educator*
Rockwell, Kay Anne *elementary education educator*
Rothenberg, Harvey David *educational administrator*
Shelton, Olga-Jean *school counselor*

Longmont
Blackwood, Lois Anne *elementary education educator*
†Venrick, Kristie Lund *educator*

Loveland
Lee, Evelyn Marie *elementary and secondary education educator*

Nederland
Lutz, Frank Wenzel *education administration educator*
†Morrison, K. Jaydene *education counseling firm executive*

Parker
Fedak, Barbara Kingry *retired technical center administrator*

Pueblo
Sisson, Ray L. *retired dean, author*

Steamboat Springs
†Farmer, Debra *academic administrator, educator*

Trinidad
†Veltri, Sandra Kay *education educator*

U S A F Academy
†Casebeer, William D. *adult education educator*

United States Air Force Academy
†Heidler, Jeanne Twiggs *adult education educator*

Westminster
Eaves, Stephen Douglas *educator, vocational administrator*

Wiggins
†Kammerzell, Susan Jane *elementary school educator, music educator*

Yuma
Pfalmer, Charles Elden *secondary school educator*

CONNECTICUT

Bloomfield
D'Annolfo, Suzanne Cordier *educational administrator, educator*
Foster, Benjamin, Jr., *educational administrator*

Bolton
Marshall, James Hilton *retired secondary education educator*

Branford
Milgram, Richard Myron *music school administrator*
Thomas, Lisa Francine *secondary school educator, assistant principal*

Bridgeport
Hendricks, Edward David *education director, consultant, speaker, trainer*
†Lanci, Janet Mead *academic administrator, educator*

Bristol
Copeland, Karin A. *training director*
Roberts, Alida Jayne *elementary school educator*

Columbia
Vance, Carmen Lee *retired university official*

Cos Cob
McElwaine, Theresa Weedy *academic administrator, artist*
Sorese, Denise Powers *reading and language arts consultant, educator*

Coventry
Halvorson, Judith Anne (Judith Anne Devaud) *elementary education educator*

Danbury
Arbitelle, Ronald Alan *elementary school educator*
Bernasconi, Stacey Christine *project data manager*
Hawkes, Carol Ann *academic administrator*
Jensen-Ruopp, Helga Spitko *school program administrator, consultant*
†Nair, Vijay *school librarian*
†Roach, James Richard *university president*
Weiner, Patricia Hermann *performing arts administrator, concert manager, artist manager*

Fairfield
Hauck, Madeline (Agnes Hauck) *special and adult basic education educator*
†Howell, Karen Jane *private school educator*
Kalapos, Felicia Zera *elementary school educator, writer*
Kelley, Aloysius Paul *university administrator, priest*
Miles, Leland Weber *university president*
Paolini, Claire Jacqueline *dean, educator*

Falls Village
Purcell, Mary Louise Gerlinger *retired adult education educator*

Farmington
Cutler, Leslie Stuart *academic administrator and medical educator*
Deckers, Peter John *dean*
Jestin, Heimwarth B. *retired university administrator*
Paplauskas, Leonard Paul *academic administrator, health science educator*

Gales Ferry
Wilson, Margaret Elizabeth *educator*

Groton
English, James Fairfield, Jr., *former college president*

Guilford
Speth, James Gustave *dean, environmental studies educator, lawyer*

Hamden
Brown, Jay Marshall *retired secondary school educator*
Sola, Janet Elaine *secondary school educator*

Hartford
†Borus, David Murray *college dean*
Cibes, William Joseph, Jr., *chancellor, educator*
Frost, James Arthur *former university president*
†Painter, Borden W. *academic administrator*
Reynolds, Scott Walton *academic administrator*
Rosa, Peter Manuel *university administrator, researcher, education educator*

Meriden
Brandt, Irene Hildegard *retired secondary education educator*

Middletown
Bennet, Douglas Joseph, Jr., *university president*

Milford
†Palm, April H. *special education educator*
†Sullivan, Christine Anne *secondary school educator*

Monroe
Gleason, Mary Rena *secondary education educator*

Naugatuck
Stauffer, Elizabeth Clare *elementary education educator, music choral director, consultant*

New Branford
Peterkin, Albert Gordon *retired education educator*

New Britain
Higgins, Jane Margaret *university official*
Judd, Richard Louis *academic administrator*
†Lunn, Charles Paul *elementary school educator*

New Fairfield
Lambrech, Régine M. *college program administrator, language educator*

New Haven
†Diaz, Sebastian R. *education educator*
†Dimitrov, Ivan Kolev *education educator, researcher*
†Gaudiani, Claire Lynn *retired academic administrator*
Green, Donald Philip *education educator*
†Hennah, Vivian Lisa *school system administrator*
Kessler, David A. *dean, medical educator*
†Krasner, David *education educator*
Kronman, Anthony Townsend *law educator, dean*
Lamar, Howard Roberts *educational administrator, historian*
Levin, Richard Charles *academic administrator, economist*
Neisler, Otherine Johnson *education educator, consultant*
†Pierson, W. Lee *retired headmaster, foundation administrator*
†Podnar, Hrvoje *education educator*
†Soderstrom, Edward Jonathan *academic administrator, consultant*
Waxman, Merle *dean*
Yandle, Stephen Thomas *dean*

New London
†Fainstein, Norman *college president*
Olsen, Robert C., Jr., *academic administrator, military officer*

Newington
Vassar, Barbara Ellen *educational consultant*

Norfolk
Potter, Elizabeth Stone *academic administrator*

North Branford
Ward, Frederick Champion *retired educator*

North Haven
Fuggi, Gretchen Miller *education educator*

North Stonington
Keane, John Patrick *retired secondary education educator*

Norwalk
Ratchford, Roger Lionel *retired secondary education educator*

Old Greenwich
Hayden, Anthony *secondary and elementary educator*
Pursley, Carol Roberts *admissions director*

Old Lyme
Osborne, Frederick Spring, Jr., *academic administrator, artist*
Peagler, Owen Fair *retired college dean*

Orange
Gyorgyey, Clara M. *educator, writer*

Prospect
Thornley, Wendy Ann *retired educator, sculptor*

Ridgefield
Brewster, Carroll Worcester *former academic administrator*
Leonard, Sister Anne C. *superintendent, education director*
Lindsay, Dianna Marie *educational administrator*

Rowayton
Nelson, Paula Morrison Bronson *educator*

Shelton
Bonina, Sally Anne *secondary school educator*
Fedornak, Mary *school counselor, educator*

Simsbury
Barnicle, Stephan Patrick *secondary school educator*
DiCosimo, Patricia Shields *secondary school educator*

Stonington
Friedman, Malcolm *consultant*

Storrs
†Higonnet, Margaret Randolph *education educator*
†Liu, Lanbo *adult education educator*
†Siegle, Del *education educator*

Storrs Mansfield
Austin, Philip Edward *university president*
Gilbert, Margaret P. *university educator, researcher*
Kerr, Kirklyn M. *university administrator, veterinary pathologist, researcher*
Lee, Tsoung-Chao *education educator*
MacDonald, John Thomas *educational administrator*
Nieforth, Karl Allen *university dean, educator, retired*

Stratford
†Schimpf, William Paul *university administrator*

Trumbull
†Lang, James Richard *education consultant*
Nevins, Lyn (Carolyn A. Nevins) *educational supervisor, trainer, consultant*
Norcel, Jacqueline Joyce Casale *educational administrator*

Waterbury
Aucella, Laurence Frank *counseling administrator, educator*

West Hartford
Coleman, Winifred Ellen *academic administrator*
Dunn, Robert Elbert *education consultant, principal*
Harrison, Walter Lee *university president*
Malone, Thomas Francis *academic administrator, meteorologist*

†Schindelman, Sylvia *education educator*
Tonkin, Humphrey Richard *academic administrator, educator*

West Haven
DeNardis, Lawrence J. *academic administrator*
Farquharson, Patrice Ellen *primary school educator*
†Singh, Parbudyal *dean, educator*

Wethersfield
Gallicchio, David Michael
Gaudreau, Gayle Glanert *computer resource educator*

Willimantic
Carter, David George, Sr., *university administrator*
Eshoo, Barbara Anne Rudolph *academic official*
Stoloff, David L. *education educator, academic administrator, web site designer*
Wilson, Margaret Sullivan *retired executive dean, consultant*

Windsor Locks
Coelho, Sandra Signorelli *secondary school educator, consultant*

DELAWARE

Bear
McLain, William Tome *principal, educator*
Stewart, Shirley Anne *educational administrator*

Dover
Braverman, Ray Howard *secondary school educator*
Delauder, William B. *academic administrator*
Gorum, Jacquelyne W. *dean, social work educator*
Sessoms, Allen Lee *academic administrator, former diplomat, physicist*
Wagner, Nancy Hughes *secondary school educator, state legislator*

Ellendale
Davis, Mark Lofland, II, *retired educator, farmer, photographer, financial consultant*

Georgetown
†Tuman, Rhonda Helene *director, advocate*

Hockessin
Hounsell, Jillann Cusick *secondary education educator*

Millsboro
Derrickson, Shirley Jean Baldwin *elementary school educator*

New Castle
Brownson, Kenneth C. *university dean*
Martin, Jean Ann *educator*

Newark
Carter, Mae Riedy *retired academic official, consultant*
Clayton, John Middleton, Jr., *development officer*
Gehrlein, William Vincent *business education educator*
Hockersmith, Charles Edwin *information technology educator*
Lemay, J(oseph) A(lberic) Leo *American literature educator*
Nelson, Marilyn (Marilyn Nelson Waniek) *education educator, poet*
Prodan, James Christian *university administrator*
Roselle, David Paul *university president, mathematics educator*

Wilmington
Chagnon, Lucille Tessier *workforce development and literacy specialist*
†Evans, Margaret Utz *secondary school educator*
Fletcher, Lawrence Francis *guidance counselor*
Higgins, Roxanne Snelling *educational consultant*
Olson, Leroy Calvin *retired educational administration educator*
Renshaw, John Hubert *retired secondary education educator*

DISTRICT OF COLUMBIA

Washington
Alatis, James Efstathios *university dean emeritus*
Allan, Ronald Gage *university research coordinator*
Alpert, Eugene J. *academic administrator*
Anderson, Beverly Jacques *academic administrator*
Arnez, Nancy Levi *educational leadership educator*
Baldi, Stéphane *education researcher, sociologist*
†Baldwin, Elizabeth Ann *academic administrator*
Barrett, Richard David *university director, consultant, bank executive*
Battle, Lucius Durham *retired educational institution administrator, former diplomat*
Beckham, Edgar Frederick *educational consultant*
Biggs, Jeffrey Robert *educator*
Boggs, George Robert *academic administrator*
†Brown, Dorothy M. *academic administrator*
Bulger, Roger James *academic health center executive*
Burgin, Walter Hotchkiss, Jr., *educational administrator*
Burris, James Frederick *federal research administrator, educator*
†Chamberlain, Mary *retired academic administrator, translator*
Christian, Mary Jo Dinan *educator*
Churchill, John Hugh *college academic administrator*
†Cleland, Joseph Maxwell (Max Cleland) *education educator, retired state official*
Collins, Herbert, Jr., *retired elementary education educator*
Collins, Michael John *dean*
DeGioia, John J. *university president*
Detweiler, Richard Allen *college president*
Dixon, Michel L. *educational administrator*
Duffey, Joseph Daniel *academic administrator*
†Elliott, Emerson John *education consultant, policy analyst*
Felbinger, Claire Louise *research administrator*
†Fernandes, Jane *academic administrator, educational consultant, sign language professional*
Fisher, Miles Mark, IV, *education and religion educator, minister*
French, Roderick Stuart *university chancellor*
Halperin, Samuel *education and training policy analyst*
Happel, Stephen P. *university dean*
Hayes, Kevin Gregory *university administrator*
Ingold, Catherine White *academic administrator*
Jordan, Irving King *university president*
Kang, Young Woo *special education educator, dean*
†Katsapis, Christine C. A. *university research administrator*
Keeley, Robert Vossler *retired academic administrator, retired ambassador*
Klaits, Joseph Aaron *education program director, historian*
†Kochhar-Bryant, Carol Anne *education educator*
Ladner, Benjamin *university president*
Lebel, Gregory Galen *educator, consultant*
Lovett, Clara Maria *university administrator, historian*
Luttwak, Edward Nicolae *academic administrator, educator, policy and business consultant*
†Mallon, William T. *education educator, researcher*
Malveaux, Floyd Joseph *dean*
Manley, Audrey Forbes *retired academic administrator, pediatrician, military officer*
Mantyla, Karen *distance learning consultant*
Martas, Julia Ann *special education administrator*
†Miller, Mary Rita *former college educator*
†Mohrman, Kathryn J *academic administrator*
Nwagbaraocha, Joel Onukwugha *academic administrator, educator*
O'Donovan, Leo Jeremiah *former academic administrator, priest, theologian*
Peck, Malcolm Cameron *educational exchange specialist*
Porter, John Weston *counselor, consultant, administrator*
†Ramos, Flavia Sales *education educator, consultant*
Ranck, Edna Runnels *academic administrator, researcher*
Reddel, Carl Walter *educational administrator*
†Reese, La Tanya Lynn *academic administrator*
†Riccards, Michael Patrick *academic administrator*
Ryan, Sheila A. *nursing educator, former dean*
Sanders, Charles F. *dean*
†Santoro, Miléna *education educator*
Savukinas, Robert Steven *educator*
Smith, Abbie Oliver *college administrator, educator*
Smuckler, Ralph Herbert *dean, political scientist, educator*
Solomon, Henry *university dean*
†Statom, Laurena Edith *retired special education educator*
Steigman, Andrew L. *academic dean*
†Stewart, Debra Wehrle *academic administrator*
Swygert, Haywood Patrick *university president, law educator*
Thompson, Bernida Lamerle *principal, consultant, educator*
Timpane, Philip Michael *education educator, policy analyst*
Trachtenberg, Stephen Joel *university president*
†Trenkle, Amy Barba *secondary school educator*
Tucker, Marc Stephen *education policy analyst, author*
Van Ummersen, Claire A(nn) *academic administrator, biologist, educator*
Ward, David *academic administrator, educator*
Weiss, Charles, Jr., *educator*
†Weitzel, Ronald L. *secondary school educator*
Wiesel, Sam W. *dean, educator, department chairman*
Williams, Katherine *educational consultant, artist, poet*
Zhao, Quansheng *university administrator, educator*

FLORIDA

Altamonte Springs
Huyett, Debra Kathleen *elementary education educator*

Bartow
Mercadante, Anthony Joseph *special education educator*

Belle Glade
Clay, Irene Gibson *community activist, retired educational administrator, educator*

Boca Raton
Arden, Eugene *retired university provost*
Connor, Frances Partridge *retired education educator*
Connor, Leo Edward *special education administrator*
†Decker, Larry E *education educator*
Leary, William James *educational administrator*
†Levy, Ralph *elementary school educator*
Miller, Eugene *university official, business executive*
†Rosen, Harriet R. *elementary school educator*
Tennies, Robert Hunter *headmaster*
†Warshaw, Carole Klein *education educator, consultant*

Bokeelia
Adams, Alfred Hugh *retired college president*
Vilardi, Charles Ronald *principal*

Bonita Springs
Becker, Richard Charles *retired college president*
Johnson, Franklyn Arthur *academic administrator*

Boynton Beach
Costa, Terry Ann *principal*
Kobliner, Richard *secondary school educator*

Bradenton
Driscoll, Constance Fitzgerald *educator, writer*
Pedersen, Norman Arno, Jr., *retired headmaster, literary club director*

Cocoa
Gamble, Thomas Ellsworth *academic administrator*

Cocoa Beach
Coppola, Phyllis Gloria Cecire *retired special education educator*

Coconut Creek
Brenner, Egon *university official, education consultant*
Rogge, James Alan *education educator*

Cooper City
Stabile, Christopher Michael *secondary school educator*

Coral Gables
Schmitt, Peter Harlan *educator*
Shalala, Donna E. *university administrator, former federal official, political scientist, educator*
Yarger, Sam Jacob *dean, educator*

Crawfordville
Black, B. R. *retired educational administrator, consultant*

Dania
Fernander, Karen Geneine *secondary school educator*

Davie
Childrey, John A., Jr., *literacy educator*

Daytona Beach
Cool, Mary L. *education specialist*
Ebbs, George Heberling, Jr., *university executive*
Green, Betty Nielsen *education educator, consultant*
Hartsell, Horace Ed *college president*
Libbey, James K. *education educator*
Sharples, D. Kent *college administrator*

De Leon Springs
Price, Artis J. *retired secondary education educator*

DeLand
†ElAarag, Hala *adult education educator*

Deland
Bear, Frederick Thomas *educator*
Brakeman, Louis Freeman *retired university official*
Dascher, Paul Edward *university dean, accounting educator*
Gill, Donald George *education educator*
†Juusela, Kari Henrik *dean*
Langston, Paul T. *music educator, university dean, composer*
Lee, Howard Douglas *academic administrator*
Morland, Richard Boyd *retired educator*

Deltona
Neal, Dennis Melton *middle school administrator*

Destin
Asher, Betty Turner *academic administrator*

Dunedin
†Banome, Lydia M. *elementary school educator*
†Gamblin, Cynthia MacDonald *mathematics educator, loybbist*

Estero
Brush, George W. *college president*

Fort Lauderdale
Edmund, Norman Wilson *educational researcher*
Fischler, Abraham Saul *educator, retired university president*
Ginn, Vera Walker *director*
†Guest, Suzanne Mary *adult education educator, artist*
Hanbury, George Lafayette, II, *academic administrator*
McCan, James Lawton *education educator*
Spungin, Charlotte Isabelle *retired secondary education educator, writer*
Sydnor, William Andrew *special education educator, writer*
†Tolchin, Karen Rebecca *adult education educator*
†Trubey, Lillian Priscilla *secondary education educator, retired*

Fort Myers
Canham, Pruella Cromartie Niver *retired educator*
†Elliott, Elizabeth Marie *education educator*
Frank, Mary Lou *retired elementary education educator*
Gauvey, Ralph Edward *educational consultant*
Pouliot, Assunta Gallucci *retired business school owner and director, consultant*

Fort Pierce
Arnold, Donna F. *business educator*

Fort Walton Beach
†Register, Annette Rowan *reading educator*
Sanders, Jimmy Devon *public administration and health services educator*

Gainesville
†Aydede, Murat *education educator*
Brodeur, Michael Stephen *dean*
Bryan, Robert Armistead *university administrator, educator*
Challoner, David Reynolds *university official, physician*
Chambers, Robert Hunter, III, *college president, American studies educator, consultant*
Cheek, Jimmy Geary *university administrator, agricultural education and communications educator*
†DiPietro, Joseph A. *dean, educator*
Dolan, Teresa A. *dean, educator, researcher*
Gets, Lispbeth Ella *educational administrator*
†Li, Yue Irene *education educator*
Lowenstein, Ralph Lynn *university dean emeritus*
Neims, Allen Howard *university dean, medical scientist*
Phillips, Winfred Marshall *dean, biomedical research executive, mechanical engineer, educator*
Price, Donald Ray *university official, agricultural engineer*
Renner, Richard Roy *education educator, educator*
Rosenberger, Margaret Adaline *retired elementary school educator, writer*
Steele, Jere Randall *elementary school educator*
Viessman, Warren, Jr., *civil engineering educator emeritus, researcher*
York, E. Travis *academic administrator, former university chancellor, consultant*
Young, Charles Edward *academic administrator*
†Zlotecki, Robert Alan *education educator*

Goulds
Cooper, Kenneth Stanley *principal, educator, finance company executive*

Graceville
Kinchen, Thomas Alexander *college president*

Hernando
Saxe, Thelma Richards *secondary school educator, consultant*

Hialeah
Agrawal, Piyush C. *school system administrator*
†Palacios, Olga *director*

Hollywood
Budnik, Patricia McNulty *retired elementary education educator*

Holmes Beach
Dunne, James Robert *academic administrator, management consultant, business educator*

Homestead
Davis, Scott Michael *director, music educator*
Horton, Thelma White *educational administrator, author*

Inverness
†Hawk, Pauletta Browning *student elementary school educator*

Jacksonville
Alexander, Edna M. DeVeaux *elementary education educator*
Carver, Joan Sacknitz *academic administrator*
†Cornelius, Jacquelyn H. *high school principal, educator*
Corse, John Doggett *university official, lawyer*
†Dumbleton, Duane Dean *college president, educator*
†Fine, Cory R. *education educator, consultant*
†Grundig, John Patrick *director*
Jamrich, John Xavier *retired university administrator*
Kinne, Frances Bartlett *chancellor emeritus*
Leonard, Thomas Michael *university program director, educator*
Main, Edna Dewey (June Main) *education educator*
Osborn, Marvin Griffing, Jr., *educational consultant*
Sandercox, Robert Allen *college official, clergyman*
†Simms, Jacqueline Kamp *secondary education educator*
†Smith, Stephen Mark *special education educator, music educator*
†Vadnal, John Louis *dean, mathematician, educator*
Wiles, Jon W(hitney) *education educator, consultant*

Jupiter
McGee, Lynne Kalavsky *principal*
Moseley, Karen Frances Flanigan *educational consultant, retired school system administrator, educator*
Sproull, Robert Lamb *retired university president, physicist*

Kennedy Space Center
Feldman, Stephen *academic administrator*

Key Largo
Stern, Joanne Thrasher *elementary school educator*

Kissimmee

Evans-O'Connor, Norma Lee *secondary education educator, consultant*
Haynes, Ulric St. Clair, Jr., *dean*
Jablon, Elaine *education consultant*
Rattie, Margaret Elizabeth (Beth Rattie) *educator*
†Severance, Jeri-Lynne White *elementary school educator*
Toothe, Karen Lee *elementary and secondary school educator*

Lake Park

Portera, Alan A. *parochial school educator*

Lake Worth

Taylor, Clifford Otis *retired principal*

Lakeland

†Herron, Robert Wilburn, Jr., *academic administrator, educator*
Mooney, Burton Lee *secondary school educator, editor*
Tate, Robert Hale *academic administrator*
Wade, Ben Frank *college administrator*

Lecanto

Mathia, Mary Loyola *parochial school educator, nun*

Leesburg

†Whalen, Norma Jean *special education educator*

Longwood

Brown, Barbara Jean *special and secondary education educator*
†Johnson, Nancy Plattner *secondary education educator*

Lutz

Pfeuffer, Dale Robert *secondary school social studies educator*

Manalapan

Phipard, Nancy Midwood *retired special education educator, poet*

Marco Island

Lovely, Erna Susan *retired primary school educator*

Marianna

Ledbetter, Eugene Floyd, Jr., *vocational education coordinator*

Melbourne

Cahill, Gerard Albin *university educator*
Catanese, Anthony James *academic administrator*
Hollingsworth, Abner Thomas *university dean*
McCay, Thurman Dwayne *university official*
†Scheuerer, Diane Thomspon *home economics educator*
Stark, Norman *secondary school educator*
Weaver, Lynn Edward *academic administrator, consultant, editor*

Merritt Island

†Galeano, Sharon J. *institutional advancement director*
McClanahan, Leland *university director*
Thompson, Hugh Lee *academic administrator*
Walter, George Anthony *elementary education educator*

Miami

Bachmeyer, Steven Allan *secondary education educator*
†Beers, Mayra E. *academic administrator*
Brenner, Esther Hannah *elementary school educator*
Brooten, Dorothy *nursing educator, former dean*
Brotherson, Mary Lou Nelson *education educator*
Butterworth, Robert A. *dean, former state attorney general*
Castro, Feinberg Rosa *education educator*
Clarkson, John G. *academic administrator, ophthalmologist*
†Cortes, Carol Solis *school system administrator*
†Engen, John Scott *academic administrator, consultant*
†Fischl, Margaret A. *education educator, researcher*
Foote, Edward Thaddeus, II, *university president, lawyer*
Geis, Tarja Pelto *educational coordinator, consultant, counselor, teacher, professor*
Halberg, F. David *principal*
†Johnson, Channey *elementary school educator*
†Jones, Janice Cox *elementary education educator, writer*
†Jones-Koch, Francena *school counselor, educator*
Kaplan, Betsy Hess *school board member*
Lee, J. Patrick *academic administrator*
†Maidique, Modesto Alex *academic administrator*
McCabe, Robert Howard *college president*
†Miyazaki, Anthony D. *adult education educator, consultant*
Nelson, Florence G. *retired secondary school educator*
†Patrouch, Joseph Francis *education educator*
†Scarborough, Jack William *business education administrator*
Stiehm, Judith Hicks *university official, political science educator*
Stolzenberg, Lisa Ann *education educator*
†Vielot, Alain J. *elementary school educator*
Warren, Emily P. *retired secondary and adult school educator*
†Williams, Patrick Anthony *elementary school educator, consultant*
Wright, Pamela Jean *administrator*

Miami Beach

Gitlow, Abraham Leo *retired university dean*

Miramar

†Stephens, Sallie L. *retired assistant principal, commissioner*

Mount Dora

Pahman, David A. *principal*
Scharfenberg, Margaret Ellan *retired elementary educator*

Naples

Finger, Iris Dale Abrams *elementary school educator*
Nelson, John Charles *retired educator*
Post, Barbara Joan *elementary school educator*

New Port Richey

Dormeyer, LaVon *school counselor*

Newberry

Thornton, J. Ronald *technology consultant*

Nokomis

Lockledge, Jack E. *retired principal*

North Miami

Pierre-louis, Rosaire *elementary school educator, educator*

Oakland Park

Krauser, Janice *special education educator*

Ocala

Gatison, Karen Ann *private school educator*
Kinney, Thomas J. *adult education educator*
Ovrebo, Judith *retired physical education educator*
Renda, Rosa A. *special education educator*
Simon, Margaret B(allif) *elementary school educator, writer*
†Westbrook, Rebecca Vollmer *secondary school educator*

Opa Locka

Harley, Rafael Emanuel *secondary school educator*
†Wilson, Isabel Gomez *elementary school educator, consultant*

Orange Park

Miller, Martin Eugene *school system consultant, negotiator, lobbyist*
Tracanna, Kim *elementary and secondary physical education educator*

Orlando

Ady, Laurence Irvin *academic administrator*
Baggott, Brenda Jane Lamb *elementary educator*
Clinton, Stephen Michael *academic administrator*
Colbourn, Trevor *retired university president, historian*
Crawford, Patricia Ann *education educator*
Guzman, Marie Elvira *school guidance counselor*
†Hitt, John Charles *academic administrator*
Johns, Elizabeth Jane Hobbs *educational administrator*

Ormond Beach

†Hodges, Elizabeth Swanson *educational consultant, tutor*

Osprey

Weathermon, Sidney Earl *elementary school educator*

Oviedo

MacKenzie, Charles Sherrard *academic administrator*

Palatka

†Embree, Mary Evelyn *retired secondary school educator*

Palm Bay

Boley, Andrea Gail *secondary school educator*
Colman, Charles Kingsbury *academic administrator, criminologist*

Palm Beach

†Robb, Babette *retired elementary school educator*

Palm Beach Gardens

Orr, Joseph Alexander *educational administrator*

Palm Coast

Dickson, David Watson Daly *retired college president*

Pembroke Pines

†Blanco, Jana M. *assistant principal*
DeBiagi, Anna Lillian *retired educator*
Embergher, Mary Louise *elementary educator*

Pensacola

†Broxton, Randall *education educator, researcher*
Leach, Luann Marie *elementary school educator*
Sisk, Rebecca Benefield *retired secondary school educator, small business owner*

Plantation

Young, William Benjamin *retired special education educator*

Pompano Beach

Adams, Nancy Ann *retired school system administrator*
Bookbinder, Robert Max *superintendent of schools*
†Gill, Robert Jerome *education educator*
Johnson, Dorothy Curfman *elementary education educator*

Ponte Vedra Beach

Hartzell, Karl Drew *retired university dean, historian*

Patterson, Oscar, III, *university program administrator*
- †Tyler, Diane Lazzelle *elementary school educator*

Port Charlotte

Hill, Richard Earl *academic administrator*
Peterson, Elaine Grace *retired technology director*
Whittaker, Douglas Kirkland *school system administrator*

Port Saint Lucie

Guglielmino, Lucy Margaret Madsen *education educator, researcher, consultant*
†Guglielmino, Paul Joseph *educator*
Keeley, Ethel S. *workforce development trainer*

Punta Gorda

Goodman, Donald C. *university administrator*
Klarik, Bela William James Clark *retired school system administrator*
Spaulding, Mar *retired special education educator, therapist*

Rockledge

Sutton, Betty Sheriff *elementary education educator*

Safety Harbor

†Patterson, Sylvia K. *elementary school educator, writer*

Saint Augustine

†Lando, Joseph P., Jr., (Louis Lento) *at-risk educator, writer, retired executive*
Proctor, William Lee *college chancellor*
Sullivan, Mary Jean *elementary school educator*

Saint Petersburg

Armacost, Peter Hayden *academic administrator*
†Dunlap, Karen F. Brown *academic administrator*
†Gregg, Kathy Kay *school system administrator*
Kuttler, Carl Martin, Jr., *academic administrator*
†McArdle, Barbara Virginia *elementary school educator*
Meyer, Robert Allen *human resource management educator*
Runde, Craig Eric *academic director*
†Sebastien, Anya Celita *academic administrator, consultant*
Southworth, William Dixon *retired education educator*
†Williams, Minnie Caldwell *retired educator*

Sanford

Scott, Mellouise Jacqueline *educational media specialist*

Sarasota

Atwell, Robert Herron *higher education executive*
Brassard, Virginia *educator*
Christ-Janer, Arland Frederick *college president*
Cleland, Sherrill *college president*
Feldhusen, Hazel Jeanette *elementary education educator*
Lee, Ann McKeighan *curriculum specialist*
Pillot, Gene Merrill *retired school system administrator*
Reagan, Larry Gay *college vice president*
Stevens, Leonard Berry *educational consultant*
Thompson, Annie Figueroa *academic director, educator*
Williams, Julia Rebecca Keys *secondary school educator*

Sebastian

Mauke, Otto Russell *retired college president*

Seminole

Riedling, Ann Marlow *education educator*

Spring Hill

Hopkins, Thomas Charles *behavior specialist*
Mericle, Suzanne Eleanor *retired secondary school educator*
Rojas, Victor Hugo Macedo *retired vocational education educator*
Wood, Shelton Eugene *college educator, consultant, minister*

Sun City Center

Gummere, Walter Cooper *educator, consultant*
Stanton, Vivian Brennan (Mrs. Ernest Stanton) *retired educator*

Tallahassee

†Bailey, Theresa L. *director, consultant*
Burkman, Ernest, Jr., *education educator*
Burnette, Ada M. Puryear *educational administrator*
Crew, Andrew Jackson *retired secondary school educator, band director*
D'Alemberte, Talbot (Sandy D'Alemberte) *academic administrator, lawyer*
†Fiorito, Jack Thomas *education educator*
†Friedman, Max Paul *education educator*
Gomory, Tomi *educator*
Grant, Sydney R. *education educator, consultant*
Lick, Dale Wesley *educational leadership educator*
Losh, Susan Carol *education educator, researcher*
Mills, Belen Collantes *early childhood education educator*
Morgan, Robert Marion *educational research educator*
†Oseroff, Andrew Bell *assistant dean*
†Pierce, Michael Jack *education specialist*
Riley, Kenneth Jerome *athletic director*
†Sliger, Bernard Francis *academic administrator, economist, educator*

Tampa

†Adams, Lowell P. *assistant principal, music educator*

†Barrow, Frederica Harrison *education educator, social worker*
Bondi, Joseph Charles, Jr., *education educator, consultant*
Brookes, Carolyn *early childhood education educator*
Daugherty, Robert Melvin, Jr., *dean, medical educator*
Givens, Paul Ronald *former university chancellor*
Harlow, Carol Jean *prospect researcher*
Hegarty, Thomas Joseph *academic administrator, history educator*
Kaywell, Joan *education educator*
Luddington, Betty Walles *library media specialist*
McCook, Kathleen de la Peña *university educator*
McIntosh, Martha Ann *retired educator, religious education director*
Meisels, Gerhard George *academic administrator, chemist, educator*
Olson, Candy *school system administrator*
Sanchez, Mary Anne *retired secondary school educator*

Tarpon Springs

Byrne, Richard Hill *counselor, educator*

Tierra Verde

Schmitz, Dolores Jean *primary education educator*

Titusville

Barnes, Jacqueline C. Linscott *education consultant, retired educator*

Venice

†Finlay, Susan Sparling *education educator*
Thomas, David Ansell *retired university dean*

West Palm Beach

Corts, Paul Richard *college president*
Jividen, James Carl *educational administrator*
†Mims, Lloyd Lee *dean, conductor, vocalist*

Wewahitchka

Stryker, Terence Wayne *secondary school educator*

Winter Garden

Gillet, Pamela Kipping *special education educator*

Winter Haven

Peck, Maryly VanLeer *retired academic administrator, chemical engineer*

Winter Park

Bornstein, Rita *academic administrator*
†Sinclair, Gail D. *education educator*

Zephyrhills

†Barron, Ilona Eleanor *reading educator, consultant*

GEORGIA

Adel

Darby, Marianne Talley *elementary school educator*

Albany

Carter-Wommack, Barbara *retired educator*
†Ellis, Mark E. *school librarian*
Forsyth, Rosalyn Moye *middle school educator*
†Hill, Kenderson *career systems development executive, city councilman*
†Shields, Portia Holmes *academic administrator*
Stanley-Chavis, Sandra Ornecia *special education educator, consultant*

Americus

Capitan, William Harry *university president emeritus*
Stanford, Henry King *college president*

Athens

Adams, Michael Fred *university president, political communications specialist*
Algeo, John Thomas *retired educator, association executive*
Amstutz, Margaret *academic administrator*
Andrews, Grover Jene *adult education educator, administrator*
†Baggett, Rebecca Gaye *academic advisor, poet*
†Boehmer, Robert G. *academic administrator, educator*
Cole, David Akinola *educational administrator, educator*
Coley, Linda Marie *retired secondary school educator*
Crowley, John Francis, III, *university dean*
David, Martha Lena Huffaker *educator*
Golembiewski, Robert Thomas *educator, management consultant*
Henderson, Alma *educator*
Herrman, Margaret Susan *university official, sociologist*
Mixon, Deborah Lynn Burton *elementary school educator*
†Prasse, Keith W. *dean*
Smagorinsky, Peter *education educator*
West, Marsha *elementary school educator*
Wraga, William Gerard *educator*

Atlanta

Aaberg, Thomas Marshall, Sr.,
Alexander, Cecil Abraham *college official, architect, consultant*
†Ayhan, Hayriye *educator*
†Beik, William H. *education educator, writer*
Bright, David Forbes *academic administrator, classics and comparative literature educator*
†Clough, Gerald Wayne *academic administrator*

Cole, Thomas Winston, Jr., *chancellor, college president, chemist*
D'Andrea, Frances Mary *special education educator*
†Denmark, Darron B. *compliance specialist*
Ferris, James Leonard *academic administrator*
Flanigan, Robert Daniel, Jr., *academic administrator*
†Galloway, Thomas D. *dean*
†Geil, Mark D. *education educator*
Harris, Sidney Eugene *dean, management educator*
Henry, Ronald James Whyte *university official*
Hogan, John Donald *retired college dean, finance educator*
†Hunter, Howard Owen *academic administrator, law educator*
Ignatonis, Sandra Carole Autry *special education educator*
†Jackson, Lawrence P. *education educator*
Jones, Sherman J. *academic administrator, management educator, investment executive*
Keiller, James Bruce *college dean, clergyman*
Lawley, Thomas J. *dean, medical educator*
Lee, Hamilton H. *education educator*
Lovewell, Marjorie Klingensmith *secondary school educator*
McQueen, Sandra Marilyn *educator, consultant*
Meredith, Thomas C. *academic administrator*
Meyer, Ellen L. *academic administrator*
†Meyer, Richard W. *school librarian*
†Myrick, Cecilia Jane *education educator, consultant*
Nentwich, Michael Andreas Erhart *educator, consultant*
Patton, Carl Vernon *academic administrator, educator*
Richey, Russell E. *university dean*
Rogers, Brenda Gayle *educational administrator, educator, consultant*
Sacks, Michael Alan *educational consultant, educator*
Wagner, James Warren *academic administrator, engineering educator*
Walker, Carolyn Smith *college services administrator, counselor*
Yancey, Carolyn Dunbar *educational policy maker*
†Zhao, Yichuan *education educator*

Augusta
Bloodworth, William Andrew, Jr., *academic administrator*
†Jackson, Rosa M. *educator*
Lewis, Shirley Ann Redd *college president*
Potter, Brad J. *dean, researcher, educator*
Puryear, Joan Copeland *academic administrator*
Stern, David M. *dean, educator*
Tedesco, Francis Joseph *university administrator*

Austell
Vance, Sandra Johnson *secondary school educator*

Barnesville
Barnard, John Phillip *technology educator*

Bishop
Bower, Douglas William *pastoral counselor, psychotherapist, clergyman*

Brunswick
†Spencer, Shirley Ann *secondary school educator, speech educator, literature educator*

Carrollton
Brewer, A. Bruce *university administrator*
Butler, Jody Talley *gifted education educator*
Ferling, John E. *history educator*
Morgan, Harry New *education educator*
Sethna, Beheruz Nariman *university president, marketing, management educator*

Chatsworth
Witherow, Jimmie David *secondary school educator*

Cleveland
Raznoff, Beverly Shultz *education educator*

Cochran
Halaska, Thomas Edward *academic administrator, director, engineer*

College Park
Ferguson, Wendell *private school educator*

Columbus
Abrahamson, William Gene *retired school counselor*
Averill, Ellen Corbett *secondary education science educator, administrator*
†Conklin, Jeffrey T. *director*
Edmondson, Michael Herman *secondary school educator*
Montgomery, Anna Frances *elementary school educator*
Newton, Gwendolyn Stewart *elementary school educator*
Riggsby, Dutchie Sellers *education educator*
Ripple, Rochelle Poyourow *educational administrator, educator*
†Tidd, Joyce Carter *etiquette educator*

Conyers
Bouchillon, John Ray *education coordinator*
Griffey, Karen Rose *special education educator*

Cumming
Benson, Betty Jones *retired school system administrator*
†Muirhead, Brent *secondary school educator*

Dahlonega
Boggan, Jeffrey Scott *college administrator*
Hansford, Nathaniel *academic administrator, lawyer*

Dalton
Frerichs, Joy Roberta *elementary education educator*

Danielsville
Bond, Joan *retired elementary school educator*

Decatur
Baker, Stephen Monroe *school system administrator*
†Wilbur, Roger *education educator, poet*

Douglas
Pugh, Joye Jeffries *educational administrator*

Douglasville
Eddy, Julia Veronica *educator*
†Hall, Mary Hugh *retired secondary school educator*
Jackson, Cynthia Williford *special education educator*

Dublin
Fatum, Delores Ruth *school counselor*

Duluth
Pickett, Christa Langford *elementary school counselor*

East Point
Harris, Carlos Ortez *elementary school educator*
Johnson, Hardwick Smith, Jr., *school psychologist*
†Warren, Barbara Denise *special education educator*

Folkston
Knowles, Julie Nall *secondary school educator*

Franklin
Lipham, William Patrick *principal, educator*

Gainesville
Burd, John Stephen *academic administrator, music educator*
Fish-Lacey, Helen Therese *educator, author*

Homer
Rylee, Gloria Genelle *educator*

Jonesboro
Ziegler, Robert Oliver *retired music and special education educator*

Kennesaw
†Graham, Dorothy H. *education educator*
†Siegel, Betty Lentz *university president*

La Fayette
Hendrix, Bonnie Elizabeth Luellen *retired elementary school educator*

Lagrange
Ault, Ethyl Lorita *special education educator, consultant*

Lawrenceville
†Crain, Mary Ann *elementary school educator*

Lilburn
Cline, Sandra Williamson *retired elementary school educator*
Wagner, Douglas Alan *secondary school educator*

Locust Grove
Bomar, Robert Linton *assistant principal*

Lookout Mountain
Dreger, D. C. *academic administrator*

Macon
†Godsey, R(aleigh) Kirby *university president*
†Hester, D. Micah *education educator*
Hunnicutt, Victoria Anne Wilson *educator*
Jobe, Ann Connor *dean, educator*
Parrish, Carmelita B. *retired secondary school educator*
Steeples, Douglas Wayne *retired university dean, consultant, researcher*
†Williams, Carol Kennedy *college administrator*

Madison
Short, Betsy Ann *elementary education educator*

Manchester
Ellison, Betty D. *retired elementary educator*

Marietta
Houston, Dorothy Middleton *elementary education educator*
Laframboise, Joan Carol *middle school educator*
Rivers, Alma Faye *secondary education educator*
Rossbacher, Lisa Ann *university president, geology educator, writer*
Segerhammar, Sharon K. *special education administrator*
†Spain, Sheryl Scarbrough *school counselor, educator*

Metter
Farmer, DeWayne Mark *director, photographer*

Mount Berry
†Bissonnette, Victor L. *education educator*

Mount Vernon
†Smith, David Robert *higher education administrator, minister, writer*
Williamson, C. Dean *university official*

Patterson
Cunningham, Raymond Carol, Jr., *elementary school educator*

Peachtree City
Barnes, Marylou Riddleberger *retired academic administrator, educator*

Riverdale
Lambert, Ethel Gibson Clark *secondary school educator*

Rome
†Sheeley, Steven M. *academic administrator, minister, education educator*
†Wingo, Willie Bruce *secondary school educator*

Roopville
†Huckeba, Emily Causey *retired elementary school educator*

Roswell
Hoskinson, Carol Rowe *middle school educator*

Saint Marys
Hall, Lois Bremer *retired educator, volunteer*

Saint Simons Island
Mathis, Luster Doyle *college administrator, political scientist*

Savannah
Brown, Carlton E. *college president*
Leighton, Richard Frederick *retired dean*
†Polite, Evelyn C. *retired middle school educator, counselor, evangelist*
†Presley, Susan Franklin *secondary school educator, department chairman*
†Rowan, Paula S. *academic administrator*
Taggart, Helen M. *adult education educator, nurse*
†Zhang, Weihua *education educator*

Smyrna
Bean, Susan Montgomery *secondary education educator*

Statesboro
†Glover, Sheena *academic administrator*
Pearsall, Thomas Armstrong *educator*

Stockbridge
Sprayberry, Roslyn Raye *retired secondary school educator*

Stone Mountain
Dees, Julian Worth *retired academic/research administrator*

Suwanee
Gerson, Martin Lyons *secondary school educator*
Trice, Mary Sue Williams *guidance counselor*

Swainsboro
†Edenfield, Cynthia Smith *education educator*

Thomaston
†Brown, June Dyson *elementary education educator, administrator*

Toccoa Falls
Alford, Paul Legare *college and religious foundation administrator*
Gardner, Donna Rae (Diehl) *education educator*

Tucker
Stewart, Connie Ward *academic administrator*

Valdosta
†Aronson-Friedman, Amy Ilene *education educator*
Bailey, Hugh Coleman *university president*
Krotseng, Marsha Van Dyke *higher education administrator*

Waleska
†Robertson, Eddie B. *education educator*

Warner Robins
Owens, Helen Dawn *elementary school educator, reading consultant*

Washington
†Dukes, Patrick Ryan *secondary school educator*

West Point
†Hart, Brenda Rebecca *retired gifted and talented educator*

Winterville
Anderson, David Prewitt *retired university dean*

Woodstock
Baumann, Sara Margaret Culbreth *retired elementary school educator*

Zebulon
Bizzell Yarbrough, Cindy Lee *school counselor*

HAWAII

Hilo
Larson, Mary Bea *elementary education educator*
O'Brien, Sally K. *secondary school educator, consultant*
Tseng, Rose *academic administrator*

Honolulu
Bogart, Louise Berry *education educator*
Cadman, Edwin Clarence *dean, health facility administrator, medical educator*
Dobelle, Evan Samuel *academic administrator*
Doi, Dorothy Mitsue Yano *educator, consultant*
Gee, Chuck Yim *dean*
†Gonsalves, Margaret Leboy *elementary school educator*
Kaiser-Botsai, Sharon Kay *early childhood educator*
Keith, Kent Marsteller *YMCA leader, academic administrator, corporate executive, government official, lawyer, author*
King, Arthur R., Jr., *education educator, researcher*
Masters, Elaine *educator, writer*
†Migimoto, Fumiyo Kodani *retired secondary education educator*
Mortimer, Kenneth P. *retired academic administrator*
Neubauer, Deane *academic administrator*
†Ng, Blythe Yuri Monzen *elementary school counselor*
Pacific, Joseph Nicholas, Jr., *educator*
Perkins, Frank Overton *university official, marine scientist*
Pickens, Alexander Legrand *retired education educator*
Schimmelfennig, Ladona Beth *special education educator, management analysis and compliance specialist*
Walsh, Janice Maureen *counselor, educator*
Wesselkamper, Sue *academic administrator*
Wright, Chatt Grandison *academic administrator*

Kailua Kona
Clewett, Kenneth Vaughn *college official*
Diama, Benjamin *retired educator, artist, composer, writer*
Spitze, Glenys Smith *retired educator*

Kaneohe
†Ko, Seung Kyun *educator, consultant*

Kaneoke
Tokuno, Kenneth Alan *college administrator, poet*

Kapaa
Outcalt, David Lewis *academic administrator, mathematician, educator, consultant, musician*

Keaau
Repp, Andrew Scott *secondary school educator*

Laie
James, Mark Olov *education educator*
Shumway, Eric *academic administrator*

IDAHO

Boise
Andrus, Cecil Dale *academic administrator*
Ellis-Vant, Karen McGee *elementary and special education educator, consultant*
Griffin, Sylvia Gail *reading specialist*
Kaupins, Gundars Egons *education educator*
Maloof, Giles Wilson *academic administrator, educator, author*
Ruch, Charles P. *academic administrator*
Wentz, Catherine Jane *elementary education educator*

Caldwell
Hendren, Robert Lee, Jr., *academic administrator*
Hoover, Robert Allan *university president*

Coeur D Alene
Dunnigan, Mary Ann *former educational administrator*

Kimberly
Coonts, Janet Rodman *education educator*
†McGregor, Wendolyn Suzanne *elementary school educator, mathematician*

Lewiston
Duley, Charlotte Dudley *vocational counselor*
Thomas, Dene *academic administrator, educator*

Menan
Webb, Marilyn McCoy *middle school educator*

Middleton
Brown, Ilene De Lois *special education educator*

Moscow
Jankowska, Maria Anna *librarian, educator*
†Sebald, Jama Lynn *academic administrator*

Mountain Home
Graves, Karen Lee *counselor*

Nampa
Hagood, Richard A. *academic administrator, educator*

Ola
Farr, Reeta Rae *special education administrator*

Pocatello
Bowen, Richard Lee *academic administrator, political science educator*
Eichman, Charles Melvin *school counselor, career assessment educator*
Lawson, Jonathan Nevin *university official*
Pemberton, Cynthia Lee A. *educational leadership educator*

Saint Anthony
Blower, John Gregory *special education educator*

Sandpoint
Rigas, Anthony Leon *university department director*

Sun Valley
Cassell, William Comyn *retired college president*

Twin Falls
†Gentry, James Robert *education educator*

PROFESSIONAL INDEX 6265 EDUCATION

Wayan
Carney Nelson, Ellen B. *elementary school educator*

Wendell
†Anderson, Marilyn Nelle *elementary education educator, librarian, counselor*

ILLINOIS

Addison
†Jares, Daniel John *secondary school educator*

Andalusia
Gilliland, Rick E. *elementary education educator*

Argonne
†Vivio, Frank Michael *education educator, researcher*

Arlington Heights
Placek-Zimmerman, Ellyn Clare *school system administrator, educator, consultant*

Aurora
Holinger, Richard *secondary school educator, writer*
Settles, William Frederick *secondary and university educator, administrator*

Barrington
Roland, Regina E. *elementary school educator*

Belleville
Tinoco, Patricia Ann *elementary education educator*

Bethalto
†Sabaj, Nancy J. *secondary school educator*

Bloomington
Gregor, Marlene Pierce *primary education educator, elementary science consultant*
Kistner, Richard Warren *university administrator*

Cambridge
Nicholson, Tom Cotton *school district administrator*

Carbondale
Covington, Patricia Ann *university administrator*
Dixon, Billy Gene *academic administrator, educator*
†Eaton, William Edward *education educator*
†Hammond, Charles E *education educator*
Humphreys, Kendra Sue *adult education educator*
Mead, John Stanley *university administrator*
Snyder, Carolyn Ann *education educator, librarian*

Carlinville
Pride, Miriam R. *college president*

Carterville
†Payne, Deborah Hindman *dean*

Caseyville
Dayton, Jean *elementary school principal*

Catlin
Asaad, Kolleen Joyce *special education educator*

Champaign
Cammack, Trank Emerson *retired university dean*
†Cantor, Nancy *academic administrator*
Creamer, Bruce Cunningham *retired safety educator, property manager*
Dulany, Elizabeth Gjelsness *university press administrator*
Espeseth, Robert D. *park and recreation planning educator*
Farmer, James Alexander, Jr., *retired education educator*
Ikenberry, Stanley Oliver *education educator, former university president*
†Loeb, Jane Rupley *university administrator, educator*
Osborne, Margery Diane *education educator*
Schowalter, William Raymond *college dean, educator*
Spodek, Bernard *early childhood educator*
Ward, James Gordon *education administration educator*
Wicks, Eugene Claude *college president, art educator*

Charleston
Johnson, Sarah Lynn (Lewis) *librarian, editor*
Moler, Donald Lewis *educational psychology educator*
†NeSmith, Richard A. *education educator, consultant*
Rives, Stanley Gene *university president emeritus*
Surles, Carol D. *academic administrator*
Thornburgh, Daniel Eston *retired university administrator, journalism educator*

Chicago
Adelman, Pamela Bernice Kozoll *education educator*
Allen, Julie Michelle *secondary education educator*
†Amarasekare, Priyanga *education educator*
Andreoli, Kathleen Gainor *dean, nurse*
Ayman, Iraj *educational consultant*
†Bartel, Barbara M. *educator*
†Bell, Dean Phillip *dean*
†Blecic, Deborah Diana *school librarian, educator*
Blumenthal, Carlene Margaret *vocational-technical school and language arts educator*
Bordage, Georges *physician, medical education educator*
Bouton, Marshall Melvin *academic administrator*
Bowman, Barbara Taylor *early childhood educator*
†Cafferty, Pastora San Juan *public policy educator*
Casazza, Martha Ellen *developmental education educator*
Coleman, Roy Everett *secondary education educator, computer programmer*
Collens, Lewis Morton *university president, legal educator*
Cooper, Wylola *retired special education educator*
Coy, Patricia Ann *special education director, consultant*
Craine, Thomas Knowlton *non-profit administrator*
Crockett, George Ephriam *secondary education educator*
Culverwell, Rosemary Jean *principal, elementary education educator*
†Desombre, Nancy Cox *academic administrator, consultant*
Di Prima, Stephanie Marie *educational administrator*
Drechney, Michaelene *secondary education educator*
Driskell, Claude Evans *college director, educator, dentist*
Dunlap, Patricia Pearl *elementary school educator*
Einoder, Camille Elizabeth *retired secondary education educator*
Ellison, Jeffrey Alan *educator*
Fish, Stanley Eugene *university dean, English educator*
Gajic, Ranka Pejovic *educator*
Gantz, Suzi Grahn *special education educator*
Graham, Bruce S. *dean, educator*
†Graner, Evan *academic administrator*
†Green, Richard M. *academic administrator, internist*
Gross, Theodore Lawrence *university administrator, author*
Hamada, Robert S(eiji) *educator, economist, entrepreneur*
Hawkins, Loretta Ann *retired secondary school educator, playwright*
Hayes, Alice Bourke *academic administrator, biologist, educator*
Helms, Byron Eldon *academic administrator*
Johnson, Barbara Elaine Spears *retired education educator*
Johnson, Mary Ann *vocational school owner*
Jones, Trina Wood *special education educator*
Kim, Mi Ja *dean, academic administrator*
†Kubistal, Patricia Bernice *educational consultant*
Madara, James Lee *dean, epitheliologist, pathologist, educator*
Mason, Gregory Wesley, Jr., *secondary education educator*
Matasar, Ann B. *former dean, business and political science educator*
McDowell, Orlando *secondary education educator*
McPherson, Michael Steven *former academic administrator, economist*
Merwin, Peter Matthew *secondary school educator, writer*
†Miceli, William Cyril, Sr., *director*
Mindes, Gayle Dean *education educator*
†Minogue, John P. *academic administrator, priest, educator*
Mirza, Leona Lousin *educator*
Monaghan, M. Patricia *educator, writer, poet*
Morris-Rogers, Cheryl-Ann *daycare provider, director, educator*
Moss, Gerald S. *dean, medical educator*
†Nucci, Larry P. *education educator, psychologist, educator*
Orden, Alex *management science educator emeritus*
O'Reilly, Charles Terrance *university dean*
†Ornstein, Allan Charles *education educator*
Pappas, David Wayne *guidance counselor, consultant*
Petitan, Debra Ann Burke *educator, education counselor, design engineer, writer, author*
Petrak, Cliff Matthew *secondary school educator*
Piderit, John J. *university educator*
†Powers, William Bryan *academic administrator*
Randel, Don Michael *academic administrator, musicologist*
†Rawal, Viresh *education educator*
Roberts, Jo Ann Wooden *school system administrator*
Robillard, James L. *educator*
Rosenbluth, Marion *educator, consultant, psychotherapist*
Schieser, Hans Alois *education educator*
Schubert, William Henry *curriculum studies educator*
Schwarzkopf, Gloria A. *education educator, psychotherapist*
Scribner, Margaret Ellen *educational consultant, consultant*
†Scrimshaw, Susan Crosby *dean*
Sebring, Penny Bender *education educator, researcher*
Shahidehpour, Mohammad *dean, academic administrator, engineering educator*
Shaver, Joan Louise Fowler *adult education educator*
Sinha, Raj P. *education educator, researcher*
Skiba, Aurelia Ellen *private school educator*
Snodgrass, Klyne Ryland *seminary educator*
Snyder, Edward Adams *dean, economics educator*
Spearman, David Leroy *elementary education educator, administrator*
Standberry, Herman Lee *school system administrator, educational consultant*
†Stovall, Patricia *elementary school educator, writer*
Strong, Dorothy Swearengen *educational administrator*
†Sulkin, Howard Allen *college president*
Swanson, Don Richard *university dean*
†Tukes, Jamu Wayne *educator*
†Vaughn, Michael *education educator*
Wasan, Darsh Tilakchand *university official, chemical engineer educator*
Wham, David Buffington *secondary school educator*
Yamakawa, Allan Hitoshi *academic administrator*
†Youm, Yoosik *education educator*
Young, Lauren Sue Jones *education educator*

Country Club Hills
Scherer, George Robert *secondary education educator*

Crystal Lake
Davidson, Shirley Jean *elementary and secondary educator*

DeKalb
†Rode, Denise Lynn *education educator, director*
Stahl, Norman A. *educator*

Decatur
†Munoz, Joseph Mark *education educator, consultant*
†Rinchiuso, Diana Lynn *academic administrator*

Deerfield
Meyer, Mara Ellice *special education consultant, principal*

Dekalb
Healey, Robert William *school system administrator*
James, Marilyn Shaw *secondary education educator, social service worker*
Monat, William Robert *university official*
†Plue, Cynthia *education educator*

Des Plaines
Coburn, James LeRoy *educational administrator*

Dixon
†Behrendt, Richard Louis *academic administrator*

Downers Grove
LaRocca, Patricia Darlene McAleer *middle school mathematics educator*
Nichols, Karen *academic administrator*
Punt, Leonard Cornelis *educational services company executive*
†Purcell, Joann *secondary school educator*
Soder-Alderfer, Kay Christie *counseling administrator*

Dundee
Ghrist, John Russell *audio/visual technician*

East Moline
Polios, Nancy Louise *secondary school educator*

East Saint Louis
Wright, Katie Harper *educational administrator, journalist*

Edwardsville
May, Mary Louise *elementary education educator*
†Sachtleben, Holly Rae *director*

Effingham
Kessler, Lynne Marie *secondary education educator*
Pickett, Steven Harold

Elgin
†Roberts, Elaine J. *academic administrator*
Turnquist, Jerry L. *teacher, journalist*

Elk Grove Village
Edmiston, Cheryl Lee *educator, clergywoman*
†Yeates, Donovan B. *education educator, researcher*

Elmhurst
Begando, Joseph Sheridan *retired university chancellor, educator*
Hillman, Carole Dorothy *education educator, educator*

Eureka
Hearne, George Archer *academic administrator*

Evanston
Birge, John Roberts *university administrator*
Boye, Roger Carl *academic administrator, journalism educator, writer*
Christian, Richard Carlton *university dean, former advertising agency executive*
Jacobs, Donald P. *dean emeritus, banking and finance educator*
Lafont, Cristina *educator*
Lewis, Dan Albert *education educator*
McCoy, Marilyn *university official*
Musa, Samuel Albert *university executive*
Nicholson, Eleanor Ann *education educator*
†Rubin, Jill M. *director*
Weber, Arnold Robert *academic administrator*

Fox Lake
Vida, Diane *high school administrator*

Freeport
Baumgartner, Reuben Albert *retired school administrator*

Galesburg
Haywood, Bruce *retired academic administrator*
Sunderland, Jacklyn Giles *former alumni affairs director*

Geneva
Weigand, Jan Christine *elementary education educator, computer specialist*

Glen Carbon
Lazerson, Earl Edwin *academic administrator emeritus*

Glen Ellyn
Gage, Nancy Elizabeth *college administrator, accountant, educator*
Patten, Ronald James *university dean*

Glenview
Corley, Jenny Lynd Wertheim *elementary education educator*
Livingston, Richard Alan *retired secondary education educator*

Godfrey
†Zilm, Karl Miller *education educator*

Granite City
Eftimoff, Anita Kendall *educational consultant*
Humphrey, Owen Everett *retired education administrator*

Grayslake
Choice, Priscilla Kathryn Means (Penny Choice) *educational director, international consultant*
Taylor, Sharen Rae (Sharen McCall) *special education educator*

Greenfield
Weller, Robin Lea *elementary school educator, secondary school educator*

Gurnee
Belluomini, Ronald Joseph *secondary education educator, poet*
Hutten, Angela Clare *special education educator*

Hartford
†Shelton, Michael Patrick *principal*

Harvey
Jackson, Richard Perry *secondary school educator*

Hazel Crest
Freed, Melvyn Norris *retired higher education administrator and educator, writer*

Highland Park
Hoffman, Sharon Lynn *adult education educator*

Hinsdale
Taylor, Ronald Lee *academic administrator*
Taylor, T(homas) Roger *educational consultant, educator*

Homewood
Schillings, Denny Lynn *retired history educator, educational and grants consultant*

Ingleside
Currie, Leah Rae *special education educator, retired*
Krentz, Eugene Leo *university president, educator, minister*

Jacksonville
Anderson, Michael R. *elementary school educator, writer*
Johns, Beverley Anne Holden *special education administrator*
Moe-Fishback, Barbara Ann *counseling administrator*

Joliet
Caamano, Kathleen Ann Folz *gifted and talented educator*
Hodgman, Vicki Jean *retired school system administrator*

Kankakee
Peters-Lambert, Betty A. *assistant principal*

Kewanee
Golby, James L. *school system administrator*
Lotspeich, Ellin Sue *elementary education educator*

Kildeer
Muffoletto, Mary Lu *retired school program director, consultant, editor*

Kirkland
†Olson-McGee, Pat M. *guidance counselor*

La Grange
Jaffe-Notier, Peter Andrew *secondary education educator*

Lake Forest
Feinberg, Jeffrey Enoch *educator, author*
Ferrari, Michael Richard, Jr., *university administrator*
Herron, Orley R. *college president*
Hotchkiss, Eugene, III, *retired academic administrator*

Lemont
Urban, Patricia A. *former elementary school educator*

Lincoln
†Schilling, Anthony Ronald *academic administrator*

Lincolnshire
Nehring, Lisa Marie *secondary school educator*

Lincolnwood
Greenblatt, Deana Charlene *elementary education educator*

Lisle
Huffman, Louise Tolle *middle school educator*

Macomb
Kyllonen Rose, Julie Frances *college program administrator*
Witthuhn, Burton Orrin *retired university official*

Madison
Purdes, Alice Marie *retired adult education educator*

Maple Park
†Callaghan, Barney *secondary school educator*

Marengo
Van Horn, John Henry *secondary school educator*

Marion
Coil, Carolyn Chandler *educational consultant*
Glasco, Sue Alice *retired educator*

Markham
Peacock, Marilyn Claire *primary education educator*

Maywood
Libka, Robert John *educational director, consultant*

Moline
Mitchell, Lucille Anne *retired elementary school educator*

Momence
†Holland, Leslie Ann *special education educator*

Morton
Corey, Judith Ann *retired educator*

Murphysboro
Barrette, Linda Jones *dean*
Hall, James Robert *secondary education educator*

Naperville
†Briseno, Kathleen *education educator*
Heuer, Michael Alexander *dean, endodontist educator*
Martin, Joan Ellen *secondary education educator*
Rosenthal, Edward Leonard *secondary school educator*
†Staley, Charles Walter, Jr., *secondary school educator*
Wilde, Harold Richard *college president*

Normal
†Alstrum, James Joseph *education educator*
†De Santis, Christopher Charles *education educator, writer*
†Hickrod, George Alan Karnes Wallis *educational administration educator*
Matsler, Franklin Giles *retired education educator*
Miller, Wilma Hildruth *education educator*
Parette, Howard P. *school system administrator, special education educator*
Parry, Sally Ellen *academic administrator, English educator*
Presley, John Woodrow *academic administrator*
†Temple, Mark Allen *adult education educator, consultant*
†Wortham, Anne Estelle *education educator*

North Aurora
Butcher, Ann Patrice *elementary school educator*

North Chicago
Kovacek, Duane Michael *secondary school educator*

Northbrook
Beljan, John Richard *university administrator, medical educator*

O Fallon
Herrington, James Patrick *secondary education educator*

Oak Brook
Baar, John Greenfield, II, *school educator*

Oak Lawn
Jandes, Kenneth Michael *superintendent of schools*

Oak Park
Adelman, William John *university labor and industrial relations educator*
Venerable, Shirley Marie *gifted education educator*

Oakbrook Terrace
Cason, Marilynn Jean *technological institute official, lawyer*
Levine, Norman M. *academic administrator*

Olney
Boyer, A(deline) Nadine *guidance counselor*

Ottawa
Benning, Joseph Raymond *principal*

Palatine
Ross, Mary Ann *principal*

Pekin
Schurter, Richard Allen *secondary school history educator*

Peoria
†Diaz, Maria E. *director*
Kelly, Grace Dentino *secondary education educator*
McMullen, David Wayne *education educator*
Nielsen, Eloise Wilma Soule *elementary education educator*

Peoria Heights
Bergia, Roger Merle *school system administrator*

Richton Park
†Pierce, Mary E. *retired educator, public relations consultant*

River Forest
Bush, Gail *library educator, school librarian*
Coe, Donald Kirk *retired university official*
McDonald, Glena June *school counselor*

River Grove
Stein, Thomas Henry *social science educator*

Rock Island
Adams, Stewart Lee *special education educator*
Horstmann, James Douglas *college official*
Tredway, Thomas *college president*

Rockford
Hart-Nolan, Elsie Faye *elementary education educator*
Howard, John Addison *former college president, institute executive*
Johnson, Elizabeth Ericson *retired educator*
Pribbenow, Paul C. *higher education administrator, consultant*
Steele, Carl Lavern *academic administrator*

Schaumburg
Hlousek, Joyce B(ernadette) *school system administrator*
Westlund, Maribeth *secondary school educator*

South Holland
Larsen, Mary Ann Indovina *counselor, educator*

Springfield
Bretz, William Franklin *retired elementary and secondary education educator*
†Daugherty, Phyllis Lyn *secondary school educator*
Dorsey, J. Kevin *dean*
Poorman, Robert Lewis *education consultant, former college president*

Sterling
Donahue, Shirley Ohnstad *elementary education educator*

Sugar Grove
Burch, Susan Ann *human resource developer, educator*

Swansea
Chambers, Jerry Ray *school system administrator*

Sycamore
†Goodman, Kenneth Alan *secondary school educator*
Johnson, Yvonne Amalia *elementary education educator, science consultant*

Table Grove
†Reller, Kristi Jo *secondary school educator*

Tinley Park
Baker, Betty Louise *retired secondary education educator*

University Park
Keys, Paul Ross *university provost/academic affairs official*

Urbana
†Carter, Nicholas Carter *education educator*
Glick, Karen Lynne *college administrator*
†Goldman, Dara Ellen *education educator*
Goodman, David G. *Japanese, comparative literature educator, writer*
Haziyu, Wallace Muleya *secondary school educator*
†Leggett, Anthony J. *education educator*
Livingstone, Carol *academic administrator*
McConkie, George Wilson *educational psychology educator*
†Stukel, James Joseph *academic administrator, mechanical engineering educator*
†Whiteley, H. E. *dean*

Vernon Hills
Cho, Yong Hyo *public administrator, educator*

Villa Park
Smith, Barbara Ann *gifted education coordinator*

Washington Park
Krause, Richard John (RJ) *elementary school educator, coach*

Waverly
Stahr, Ellen Marie *secondary school educator*

Wayne City
†Blank, Stanley Bruce *secondary school educator*

Wheaton
†Buswell, James Oliver, III, *retired education educator, retired academic administrator*
Potter, Janice Baber *retired school superintendent, educator*

Wilmette
†Mantrala, Murali K. *education educator, researcher, marketing professional*
Rhoad, Richard Arthur *secondary school educator, writer*

Winnetka
Bundy, Blakely Fetridge *early childhood educator, advocate*
Fink, Eloise Bradley *educator, writer, editor*
Huggins, Charlotte Susan Harrison *secondary school educator, author, travel specialist*
†Kucharski, Thomas Edward *secondary school educator*
Schwartz, Daniel Joel *education administrator*

Woodstock
Levandowski, Barbara Sue *educational administrator*

Zion
Baule, Steven Michael *principal*

INDIANA

Anderson
Neidert, David Lynn *administrator*
Nicholson, Robert Arthur *college president*

Bloomington
Arnove, Robert Frederick *education educator*
Barnes, A. James *academic dean*
Bornholdt, Laura Anna *university administrator*
†Chafel, Judith Ann *educator*
†Fernhaber, Stephanie Ann *grant administrator*
Herbert, Adam William, Jr., *academic administrator, educator*
†Hinds, Leonard Dale *education educator, research scientist*
†Johnson, Kevin LaMont *educator*
Mehlinger, Howard Dean *education educator*
Mobley, Tony Allen *foundation executive, former university dean, recreation educator*
Ryan, John William *academic administrator*
Smith, Carl Bernard *education educator*
†Sprouse, Rex A. *education educator*
Webb, Charles Haizlip, Jr., *retired university dean*

Carmel
Brooks, Patricia Scott *principal*
†Pescovitz, Ora H. *education educator*
†Rand, Leon *academic administrator*

Cicero
Lay, Andrew Sean *secondary school educator, elementary school educator*

Columbus
Robbins, Mary Ann *secondary school educator*

Crawfordsville
Ford, Andrew Thomas *academic administrator*
Servies, Richard L. *retired secondary education educator, mathematician*
Spurgeon, Nannette SuAnn (Susie Spurgeon) *special education educator*

Crown Point
Harder, Heather Anne *education educator*

East Chicago
Fortenberry, Delores B. *dean*

Elberfeld
Bernhardt, Richard C. *secondary school educator, band director*

Evansville
Dean, K. Matthew *elementary school educator*
Huff, Sheila Lindsey *secondary education educator, coach*
Jennings, Stephen Grant *academic administrator*
†Lasser, Bradley D. *academic administrator*

Fort Wayne
Andorfer, Donald Joseph *university president*
Barksdale, Jacqueline Yvonne *elementary school educator*
Carter, George Edward *education educator*
†Cummins, Kathleen K. *retired elementary school educator*
Hamrick, Linda L. *educator*
†Hickey, M. Gail *education educator*
Stebbins, Vrina Grimes *retired elementary school educator, counselor*

Franklin
Bender, Larry Wayne *vocational educator*

Gary
Hall, James Rayford, III, *adult educator*
Smith, Vernon G. *education educator, state representative*
Walker, Juanita Moffett *retired middle school educator*
†Woodson, Rudolph *secondary school educator*

Georgetown
Dailey, Donald Harry *adult education educator, volunteer*

Goshen
Meyer, Albert James *educational researcher*
†Stoltzfus, Victor Ezra *retired university president*
Weaver, Henry David *retired educational administrator, consultant*

Granger
Morgan, Ardys Nord *school improvement consultant*

Greencastle
Bottoms, Robert Garvin *academic administrator*

Greenfield
†Bollinger, Mark W. *school system administrator*

Hammond
Delph, Donna Jean (Donna Maroc) *education educator, consultant, university administrator*
†Fehring, Mary Ann *secondary education educator*
Kadow, Cathi *academic counselor*
†Weber, Elsa Koenig *pre-school educator*
Woodson, Adrianne Marie *secondary school educator and coordinator*

Huntington
†Urschel, Linda Kathleen *English educator*

Indianapolis
Bepko, Gerald Lewis *university administrator, law educator, lecturer, consultant, lawyer*
Brand, Myles *academic administrator*
Brater, D. Craig *dean, educator*
†Broman, Per Fredrik *education educator*
Cilella, Mary Winifred *director*
Clark, Charles M., Jr., *medical school administrator*
†Donle, Harold P. *director, advocate*
Dykstra, Clifford Elliot *chemistry educator, researcher*
Evenbeck, Scott Edward *university official, psychologist*
Fletcher, Brady Jones *vocational education career specialist*
Fox, Patricia Sain *academic administrator*
Goldblatt, Lawrence *dean, educator, researcher*
Gooldy, Patricia Alice *retired elementary education educator*
Huffman-Hine, Ruth Carson *adult education administrator, educator*
†Kennedy, Russell Edward *academic administrator*
Kovacik, Karen Marie *university educator*
Metzner, Barbara Stone *university counselor*
Ney, Michael Vincent *university administrator*
†Osgood, Robert Lincoln *education educator*
Solomon, Marilyn Kay *educator, consultant*
Speth, Gerald Lennus *education and business consultant*
Stookey, George Kenneth *retired director, retired dental educator*
Watkins, Sherry Lynne *elementary school educator*
Wolfe, Elaine Claire Daughetee *junior high school educator*
Woody, John Frederick *retired secondary education educator*

Kokomo
Person, Ruth Janssen *academic administrator*

Kouts
Miller, Sarabeth *secondary education educator*

LaPorte
Johnson, Bruce Ross *elementary education educator*

Lafayette
†Lusk, Jayson L. *education educator, researcher*
Troutner, Joanne Johnson *school technology administrator, educator, administrator, consultant*

Lincoln City
Blessinger, Timothy Louis *secondary school educator*

Logansport
Thacker, Jerry Lynn *school administrator*

Madison
Stoner, David A. *elementary school educator, consultant*

Merrillville
†Protho, Jessie *educator*

Monroeville
Sorgen, Elizabeth Ann *retired educator*

Muncie
Brownell, Blaine Allison *university administrator, history educator*
Felsenstein, Frank Arjeh *educator*
Holt, Gerald Wayne *retired counseling administrator*
†Kitchens, Frederick Lynton, III, *education educator, researcher*
Linson, Robert Edward *university administrator emeritus*
Stewart, Rita Joan *academic administrator*
Swetnam, Ruth E. Danglade *curriculum director*
Wiedmer, Terry Lynn *educational administration educator, consultant*

Munster
Fies, James David *elementary education educator*
Platis, Chris Steven *educator*

New Albany
Riehl, Jane Ellen *education educator*

New Harmony
†Rice, David Lee *university president emeritus*

North Manchester
†McFadden, Renée Fancher *education educator*
Switzer, Jo Young *academic administrator, dean*

Notre Dame
†Bederman, Gail *education educator, historian*
Crosson, Frederick James *former university dean, humanities educator*
Francis, Michael Jackson *educational administrator*
Hyder, Anthony K. *academic administrator, science educator*
Malloy, Edward Aloysius *academic administrator*
O'Meara, Onorato Timothy *academic administrator, mathematician*
†Shin, Hojung *education educator*

Plainfield
Lucas, Georgetta Marie Snell *retired educator, artist*

Plymouth
Jurkiewicz, Margaret Joy Gommel *secondary education educator*

Portland
Downing, Barbara Kay *school system administrator*

Purdue University
†Vitter, Jeffrey Scott *academic administrator, computer science educator, researcher*

Richmond
Robinson, Dixie Faye *educator*

Shelbyville
†Clark, Rose Sharon *elementary school educator*

South Bend
†Cerny, William *retired education educator, musician*
Charles, Isabel *university administrator*
†Colborn, Nancy Wootton *school librarian*
Knight, Ida Brown *retired elementary educator*
†McGuire, Gail Marie *education educator*
†Redmond, Mark Leroy *secondary school educator*

Spencer
†Coley, Brenda Ann *elementary education educator*

Terre Haute
Hulbert, Samuel Foster *college president*
Hunt, Effie Neva *former college dean, former English language educator*
Landini, Richard George *university president emeritus, English educator*
Leach, Ronald George *educational administration educator*
†Miller, Maurice Dean *special education educator*
†Olsen, Christopher John *education educator*
Van Til, William *education educator, writer*

Upland
Harbin, Michael Allen *religion educator, writer*
Jessup, Dwight Wiley *academic administrator, educator*
Kesler, Jay Lewis *academic administrator*
Kitterman, Joan Frances *education educator, educator*

Valparaiso
Harre, Alan Frederick *academic administrator*
Mundinger, Donald Charles *retired college president*
Schnabel, Robert Victor *retired academic administrator*

Vincennes
Holcomb, Michelle K. *elementary education educator*

Walkerton
Snakenberg, Sharon Ann *special education educator*

Warren
Pattison, Deloris Jean *retired counselor, university official*

West Lafayette
Asher, J. William *education and psychology educator*
Beering, Steven Claus *academic administrator, medical educator*
Cosier, Richard A. *dean, business educator, consultant*
Frick, Gene Armin *university administrator*
Gennett, Timothy *academic administrator*
Jischke, Martin C. *academic administrator*
†Mejias, ROBERT, Dr. J. *education educator, consultant, researcher*
†Mocioalca, Oana *educator*
Moskowitz, Herbert *management educator*
†Rebar, Alan H. *dean*
Ringel, Robert Lewis *university administrator*
Shertzer, Bruce Eldon *education educator*
Tilton, Mark Campbell *educator*

Winona Lake
†Henry, Ronald O. *academic administrator*
Plaster, David Roy *college executive*

Winslow
McKinney, Shannon J. *retired secondary school educator*

IOWA

Ames
Crabtree, Beverly June *retired college dean*
Ebbers, Larry Harold *education educator*
Geoffroy, Gregory L. *academic administrator, educator*
Green, Detroy Edward *retired dean*
Herwig, Joan Emily *developmental education educator, researcher*
Manatt, Richard *retired education educator*
Mattila, Mary Jo Kalsem *elementary and art educator*
Meeks, Carol Jean *educator*
†Premkumar, Prem *educator*
Schuh, John Howard *higher education educator, academic administrator*

Bettendorf
Hanzelka, Richard Louis *education educator*

Burlington
Lundy, Sherman Perry *secondary school educator*

Cascade
Peryon, Charleen D. *education educator, consultant*

Cedar Falls
†Lettow, Lucille Jane *school librarian, education educator*

Cedar Rapids
Haines, Cathy Jean *middle school education educator*
Hutton, Mary J. *guidance counselor*
Rosberg, Merilee Ann *education educator*
Smith, Cindy Thompson *special education educator*
Stirler, Karen Sue *special education educator, adult education educator*

Davenport
Hudson, Celeste Nutting *education educator, reading clinic administrator, consultant*
†McAulay, Brian J. *director*
McGuire, John Francis *retired English educator, consultant*
Sanborne, Lewis W. *director, English educator*

Des Moines
Davilla, Donna Elaine *school system administrator*
Gaines, Ruth Ann *educator*
†Maxwell, David E. *academic executive, educator*
†Rieck, Michael Quentin *educator*
Teitelbaum, Howard S. *academic administrator*
Webb, Mary Christine *reading recovery educator, in-class reading specialist*

Dubuque
†Keller, Robert Scott *education educator*
Peterson, Walter Fritiof *academic administrator*
Toale, Thomas Edward *school system administrator, priest*

Early
Myers, Kenneth L(eRoy) *secondary education educator*

Emmetsburg
Wells, Martha Johanna *elementary education educator*

Epworth
†Wozniak, John S. *dean*

Fairfield
Joshi, Prabhakar G. *educator*

Fort Dodge
Pratt, Diane Adele *talented and gifted education educator*

Grinnell
Osgood, Russell King *academic administrator*

Harlan
†Wilson, Annette Sigrid *educator*

Hopkinton
Pounds, Buzz R. *educator*

Indianola
Pearson, Walter Stephen *adult learning educator*

Iowa City
Boyd, Willard Lee *academic administrator, educator, museum administrator, lawyer*
Brennan, Robert Lawrence *educational director, psychometrician*
Buckwalter, Kathleen C. *academic administrator, educator*
Davis, Julia McBroom *college dean, speech pathology and audiology educator*
Dreher, Melanie Creagan *dean, nursing educator*
Duffy, William Edward, Jr., *retired education educator*
Feldt, Leonard Samuel *university educator and administrator*
†Gray, George Trumon *test development professional*
Hines, N. William *dean, law educator, administrator*
†McGovern, Jennifer Anne *education educator*
†Porter, Nancy Lefgren *reading recovery educator*
Roe, Gerald Bruce *director, writer*
Saterfiel, Thomas Horne *education researcher, administrator*
Skorton, David Jan *academic administrator*
Spriestersbach, Duane Caryl *academic administrator, speech pathology/audiology services professional, educator*
Venzke, Kristina Lea *academic administrator*
Walker, Joye A. *secondary school educator*

Janesville
Jarosh, Colleen Marie *educator, mediator, consultant*

Jefferson
Said, Clifford Everett *seminar company executive, speaker, author*

Keokuk
Hardy, Julia Irene *elementary school educator*

Morning Sun
†Byers, Elizabeth *education educator*

New Sharon
Sullivan, Mary Jane *elementary school educator*

Newton
Jamison, Elywn Paul *secondary education educator*
Ponder, Marian Ruth *retired mathematics educator*

Oelwein
†Flaucher-Falck, Velma Ruth *retired special education educator*

Oskaloosa
Burrow, Paul Irving *secondary education educator*
Clovis, Samuel Harvey *academic administrator*

Pacific Junction
†Krogstad, Jack Lynn *associate dean, accounting educator*

Pella
Iverson, Thomas Edwin *retired academic administrator, mathematician, educator*

Sheldon
†Gifford, Carla J. *education educator*

Sioux Center
†Kornelis, Benjamin Douglas *education educator*

Sioux City
Deeds, William Charles *university dean, executive*
Dillman, Kristin Wicker *elementary and middle school educator, musician*
Hamilton, Ruth Milton Green *retired college administrator, consultant*
†Rants, Carolyn Jean *college official*

Sloan
Ullrich, Roxie Ann *special education educator*

Spirit Lake
Wilson, Wendy Melgard *kindergarten and special education educator*

Storm Lake
†Klavano, Ann Marie *school librarian*

Waterloo
Hasek, Jane Ellen *academic administrator*
Kober, Arletta Refshauge (Mrs. Kay L. Kober) *supervisor*

Waverly
Fredrick, David Walter *academic administrator*
†Langan, Patrick William *education educator, consultant*

Woodward
†Jenkins, Alice Marie *secondary school educator*

KANSAS

Americus
Grimsley, Bessie Belle Gates *retired special education educator*

Anthony
Carr, Cynda Annette *elementary education educator*

Baxter Springs
O'Neal, Vicki Lynn *elementary education educator*

Bushton
Cooper, Sharon Kay *school media specialist*

Clearwater
†Taverner, Pamela Johnson *educator*

Dodge City
Sapp, Nancy L. *educational administrator*

El Dorado
Fangmann, Heather Ann *secondary educator, English*

Emporia
Mallein, Darla J. *educator*
Mehring, Teresa Ann *dean, education educator*

Frontenac
†Wilson, Donald Wallin *academic administrator, communications educator*

Garden City
†Thomas, Gregory Hall *educator*

Hays
Harbin, Calvin Edward *retired educator*

Hutchinson
Green, Thereasa Ellen *elementary education educator*
Stevens, Leota mae *retired elementary education educator*

Kansas City
Atkinson, Barbara F. *dean, medical educator, academic administrator*
Hagen, Donald Floyd *university administrator, former military officer*
†Warne, Alan M. *adult education educator, consultant*
Williams, Shirley J. *daycare provider, educator, writer*

Lawrence
Berry, James Lee *retired educator*
†Capps, Jason Scott *education educator, researcher*
Frederickson, Horace George *former college president, public administration educator*
Greenberg, Marc Leland *education educator*
†Hemenway, Robert E. *academic administrator, language educator*
Locke, Carl Edwin, Jr., *academic administrator, engineering educator*
Rury, John Leslie *education educator*
Turnbull, Ann Patterson *special educator, consultant, research director*
Wiechert, Allen LeRoy *educational planning consultant, architect*

Liberal
Wilkerson, Rita Lynn *special education educator, consultant*

Manhattan
†Amtoft, Torben *adult education educator, researcher*
Coffman, James Richard *academic administrator, veterinarian*
†Lei, Shuting *adult education educator*
Muir, William Lloyd, III, *academic administrator*
†Richardson, Ralph C. *dean*
†Schumm, Walter Richard *family researcher, educator*
†Shanklin, Carol Williams *academic administrator, researcher*
†Stoney, BeEtta Lorranine *education educator*

Mankato
Wiest, Donald Edwin *secondary education educator*

Marysville
Herman, J. Clayton *retired adult education educator*

Meade
Brannan, Cleo Estella *retired elementary education educator*

Mulvane
George, Donald Richard *retired principal*

Nickerson
Kirschner, Rod *secondary education educator*

North Newton
Ediger, Marlow *education educator*

Olathe
Dennis, Patricia Lyon *adult education educator*
†Hackler, Ruth Ann *retired educator*
Stevens, Diana Lynn *elementary education educator*

Overland Park
Whelan, Richard J. *retired academic administrator*

Pittsburg
†Runyan, Charles Kent *education educator*

Pomona
Gentry, Alberta Elizabeth *elementary education educator*

Prairie Village
Breidenbach, Monica Eileen *educator, career counselor*

Saint John
Wibright, Eddy Ann *secondary education educator*

Salina
Dubuc-Schindler, Deborah Jo *special education educator*

Sublette
Swinney, Carol Joyce *secondary education educator*

Topeka
Greene, Jane *health educator*
Jennings, Nancy Ann *retired elementary education educator*
Smith, Loran Bradford *educator*
Varner, Robert Bernard *counselor, educator*

Wichita
Huber, Tonya *teacher educator, writer*
Kindrick, Robert LeRoy *academic administrator, dean, English educator*
†Mau, Wei-Cheng Joseph *education educator*
Mitchell, Linda Marlene *education educator*
Platt, George Milo *university administrator*
Sherwood, Joan Karolyn Sargent *retired career counselor*
Van Arendonk, Susan Carole *elementary school educator*

KENTUCKY

Berea
Krug, John Carleton (Tony Krug) *college administrator, library consultant*

Bowling Green
†Atwell, Nedra Wheeler *education educator, consultant*
Blair, John Paul *academic administrator*

Campbellsville
Conner, Jeanette Jones *elementary school educator*
Skaggs, Karen Gayle *elementary school educator*

Clinton
Clark, Linda Wilson *educational administrator*

Columbia
Brown, Billy Charlie *secondary school educator*

Covington
Berg, Lorine McComis *retired guidance counselor*

Danville
Breeze, William Hancock *college administrator*
Kennan, Elizabeth Topham *former university president and history educator*
†Roush, John A *academic administrator*

Ekron
†Hamilton, Amelia Wentz (Amy Wentz) *elementary school educator*

Frankfort
†Shabazz, David Lorenzo *vocational school educator*

Harlan
Greene, James S., III, *school administrator*

Henderson
Wayne, Bill Tom *secondary school educator, coach*

Highland Heights
†Kurk, Katherine Chenault *education educator*

Lexington
Assael, Leon A. *dean, educator*
Cole, Henry Philip *educational psychology educator*
Crouch, Dianne Kay *secondary school guidance counselor*
Hurley, Janet Lee *university health service administrator*
Lindle, Jane Clark *educator*
Logan, Joyce Polley *education educator*
†Robinson, Thomas Christopher *academic administrator, educator*
Taylor, Paul Franklin *college dean*
Thelin, John Robert *academic administrator, education educator, historian*
Wethington, Charles T., Jr., *academic administrator*
Wilson, Emery Allen *university dean, obstetrician-gynecologist, educator*
Wolff, L. Thomas *medical director*

Louisville
Bratton, Ida Frank *retired secondary school educator*
†DeVitis, Joseph L. *education educator*
Kaplan, Joel A. *dean*
†Kmetz, Donald R. *retired academic administrator*
†Knox, Michael John *academic administrator*
Martin, Janice Lynn *special education educator*
Mohler, Richard Albert, Jr., *academic administrator, theologian*
Newby, Elizabeth Ann *elementary education educator*
†Ryan-Kessler, Michael Lewis *secondary school educator*
Schneider, Jayne Bangs *school librarian*
Swain, Donald Christie *retired university president, history educator*
Taylor, Robert Lewis *management educator*
†Wagoner, Ruth R *education coach*
Watts-Wilson, Denise *secondary school educator*
Williams, John N. *dean*

Masonic Home
Schweichler, Mary Ellen *childhood education educator, consultant*

Murray
†Russell, Mary Ann *secondary school educator*

Newport
Clinkenbeard, James Howard *principal*

Nicholasville
†Burton, Malinda Daugherty *school librarian*

Owensboro
Roberts, Brian Wayne *middle school educator, minister*

Richmond
†Blanchard, Paul *academic administrator, educator*
Newby, Earl Fernando *educator*

Russell Springs
Ackerman, Anthony Wayne *secondary school educator, band director*

Shelbyville
†Hedrick, William David *secondary school educator, musician, educator*

Vanceburg
Phillips, Susan Diane *secondary school educator*

Whitley City
Stephens, Robert Ernest *retired educator*

Williamsburg
†Trickett, Paula J. *assistant principal*

LOUISIANA

Alexandria
†Marivani, Syrous *education educator*
Vandersypen, Rita DeBona *guidance counselor, academic administrator*
Wesse, David Joseph *higher education administrator, consultant*

Baton Rouge
Bensman, Stephen J. *school librarian, researcher*
Caffey, H(orace) Rouse *university official, agricultural consultant*
Conerly, Evelyn Nettles *educational consultant*
†Freedman, Carl Howard *education educator*
†Garretson, Judith Anne *education educator*
†Giger, Andreas *education educator*
†Groves, Michael G. *dean*
†Guy, Matthew Wayne *education educator, writer*
Hamilton, John Maxwell *university dean, writer*
Harrelson, Clyde Lee *retired secondary school educator*
Jones, Mary Elizabeth *school counselor*
†Litton, Nancy Joan *education educator*
†Marchand, Suzanne Lynn *education educator*
Maxcy, Spencer John *education educator*
Mc Cameron, Fritz Allen *retired university administrator*
Perkins, Huel Davis *academic administrator*
Prestage, James Jordan *university chancellor*
†Smith, Michael *college president*

Benton
Hudson, Marguerite W. *secondary school educator*

Chalmette
Williamson, Ramona Diane *special education educator*

Franklin
Fairchild, Phyllis Elaine *school counselor*

Grambling
Favors, Steve Alexander *academic administrator*
Porter, Wilma Jean *educational consultant*
†Stentiford, Barry Maxfield *education educator, military officer*
Warner, Neari Francois *university president*

Gramercy
Deroche, Kathleen Samrow *elementary educator, mathematics consultant*

Gretna
†Weekley, Judy Liddington *special education educator*

Hammond
†Kulkin, Heidi Sharon *education educator*
Nauman, Ann Keith *education educator, department chairman*
Parker, Clea Edward *retired university president*
†van der Jagt, Johan *special education educator*

Iowa
Leonard, Linda Faye *secondary education educator*

Kenner
Regan, Siri Lisa Lambourne *gifted education educator*

Lafayette
Authement, Ray P. *college president*
†Clark, Bradd Evans *dean, mathematician, educator*
Petry, Ruth Vidrine *principal*
Rieck, William Albert *secondary school educator and administrator, professor*

Lake Charles
Fields-Gold, Anita *retired dean*
†Hebert, Robert D. *academic administrator*
Leder, Sandra Juanita *retired elementary school educator*

Mandeville
†Huie, Roland Eugene, Jr., *director, music educator*

Marrero
Blanchard, Bruce Roy *principal, minister*

Merryville
†Joslin, Joe Edward, Jr., *secondary school educator*

Metairie
†Andersson, Billie Venturatos *school learning specialist*
Chambers, Thomas Edward *college president, psychologist*
†St. John, Bridgette Alayne *secondary school educator*

Monroe
†Long, Derle Ray *education educator*

Natchitoches
Wolfe, George Cropper *retired private school educator, artist, writer*

New Orleans
†Autin, Nancy Pellerin *secondary school educator*
Baudoin, Larry Anthony *academic administrator*
†Bayer, Thora Ilin *professor*
Carter, James Clarence *university administrator*
Cowen, Scott S. *academic administrator*
†DeLarge, Marie P. *director*
†Dinsmore, Jennifer J. *student affairs professional*
Gery, John Roy Octavius *secondary school educator, poet*
Gordon, Joseph Elwell *university official, educator*
Grubb, Wendy Standley *school counselor*
Hamlin, James Turner, III, *university dean, physician*
Hebert, Thomas Joseph *university educator*
Lomax, Michael Lucius *college president*
Longstreet, Wilma S. *curriculum and instruction educator*
McCall, John Patrick *college president, educator*
†McFarland, James W. *academic administrator*
†Mosier, John *education educator, writer*
Novakov, George John, Jr., *gifted and talented educator, consultant, administrative assistant*
†Puri, Pratap *educator, researcher*
Ross, Brenda Marie *elementary school educator*
Taylor, Ian Logan *dean*
Washington, Brian Keith *secondary school educator, music educator*

Newllano
Boren, Lynda Sue *gifted education educator*

Port Allen
†Goins, Sheila Lewis *elementary school educator, researcher*

Quitman
Davis, Ella Delores *special education educator, elementary school educator*

Ruston
Freasier, Aileen W. *special education educator*
†Gooch, John Casey *education educator, consultant*
Maxfield, John Edward *retired university dean*
Taylor, Foster Jay *retired university president*

Shreveport
†Bogue, Ernest Grady *academic administrator, educator*
Driscoll, Barbara Hampton *special education educator*
Joshua, Percy *English educator*
Knight, Diane *special education educator*
Morehead, Deborah Elizabeth Betts *gifted and talented educator, music educator*
Smith, Harriet Gwendolyn Gurley *secondary school educator, writer*
Thomas, Bessie *primary education educator*
†Watts, Jessica Milan *director*
†Wood, Julienne Louise *school librarian, historian*

Slidell
Hendricks, Donald Duane *retired school librarian*
Sanders, Georgia Elizabeth *secondary school educator*

Thibodaux
Hulbert, Stephen Thompson *academic administrator*

Westwego
Brehm, Loretta Persohn *secondary art educator, librarian, consultant*

MAINE

Auburn
Umpierre, Luz María *women studies educator, foreign language educator*

Augusta
Huffman, Durward Roy *college system official, electrical engineer*
Lyons, Charles M. *academic administrator*

Bangor
MacTaggart, Terrence Joseph *professor, former university chancellor*
McKinnon, Carolyn Ann *child care center director*
Westphal, Joseph W. *academic administrator*

Bar Harbor
Krevans, Julius Richard *university administrator, physician*
Swazey, Judith Pound *academic administrator, sociomedical science educator*

Biddeford
Featherman, Sandra *university president, political science educator*
Shannon, Stephen Curtis *dean, occupational health physician*

Bremen
Wilson, Linda Smith *academic administrator*

Brownfield
Kloskowski, Vincent John, Jr., *educational consultant, writer, educator*

Brunswick
Greason, Arthur LeRoy, Jr., *retired university administrator*

Bucksport
Williams, Christine Hewes *elementary education educator*

Camden
Smith, J(ames) Brian *education specialist and researcher, writer*

Cumberland Foreside
Dill, William Rankin *college president*

Ellsworth
Eaton, Candace Johnson *program director*

Farmington
Kalikow, Theodora June *university president*

Hartland
†Gard, Trudy May *pre-school educator, writer*

Islesboro
Rogers, William Raymond *college president emeritus, psychology educator*

Lewiston
Hansen, Elaine T. *academic administrator*
†Harward, Donald West *retired academic administrator*

Lubec
Hudson, Miles *retired special education educator*

Mount Desert
Singleton, Francis Seth *international educator*

New Harbor
†Woolf-Wade, Sarah Jane *retired elementary school educator, writer*

North Haven
White, Jerry T. *academic administrator*

North Yarmouth
Fecteau, Rosemary Louise *educational administrator, educator, consultant*

Oakland
Asmussen, J. Donna *retired educational administrator, researcher, artist*

Old Town
Alex, Joanne DeFilipp *educator Montesorri school*

Orono
†Estler, Suzanne E. *education educator*
†Hess, Charles T. *education educator*
Hoff, Peter Sloat *academic administrator*
†MacDougall, Pauleena Mary *education educator, researcher*
Rauch, Charles Frederick, Jr., *retired university official and business educator*
†Rice, Edward Perry *secondary school educator*
Wiersma, G. Bruce *dean, forest resources educator*

Palermo
Robbins, Marjorie Jean Gilmartin *elementary education educator*

Portland
Braithwaite, Karl Royden *dean*
Gilmore, Roger *college consultant*
Pattenaude, Richard Louis *university administrator*

Rockport
†Hinrichs, Stephen Ernest *education educator, consultant*

Scarborough
†Durham, Dona Anita *special education educator*

Skowhegan
†Ross, James Owen *education educator, researcher*

South Paris
Martin, Charles Seymour *middle school educator*

Veazie
Kennedy, Robert Alan *educational administrator*

Waterville
Adams, WilliaM D. *academic administrator*
Cook, Susan Farwell *associate director planned giving*

Wells
Hanrahan, Joyce Yancey *educational consultant, antiquarian bookseller*

Yarmouth
Bischoff, David Canby *retired university dean*
Hart, Loring Edward *academic administrator*

MARYLAND

Adamstown
Church, Martha Eleanor *retired academic administrator, scholar*

Adelphi
Heeger, Gerald Arthur *university president*

Annapolis
†Brann, Eva Toni Helene *educator*
†Jacobs, Linda Joan *educator*
Stern, Margaret Bassett *retired special education educator, author*

Arnold
†Irwin, Jennifer Vogel *education educator*

Baltimore
Allan, Janet D. *dean*
Behm, Mark Edward *university administrator, consultant*
Bradshaw, Cynthia Helene *educational administrator*
Breazeale, Helene *arts administrator, educator*
Brewer, Nevada Nancy *elementary education educator*
Brewster, Gerry Leiper *educator, lawyer*
Brody, William Ralph *academic administrator, radiologist, educator*
†Browne, Lovetie W. *special education educator, small business owner*
Buser, Carolyn Elizabeth *correctional education administrator*
Donovan, Sharon Ann *educator*
Ellis, Brother Patrick (H. J. Ellis) *academic administrator*
Follet, Robert Edward *music librarian*
†Freedman, Janet Whittle *retired academic administrator, writer*
Gifford, Donald George *legal educator*
Gleichmann, Frances Evangeline *retired elementary educator*
†Goldenberg, Mikhail *mathematics*
Haine, Thomas William Nicholas *educator*
Heller, Barbara R. *former dean, nursing educator*
Howland, Kristine Nelson *college administrator*
Hrabowski, Freeman Alphonsa, III, *university president*
†Hsu, Cornelia Wang Mei-Chih *education educator*
†Isable, Alisha *elementary school educator*
Jackson, Stanley Edward *retired special education educator*
Jones, Dan L. *academic administrator*
Keller, George Charles *higher education consultant, writer*
Kemp, Suzanne Leppart *elementary education educator, clubwoman*

Kessler, Wallace Frank *school director, tour developer*
Klitzke, Theodore Elmer *former college dean, arts consultant*
Lazarus, Fred, IV, *college president*
†Margolis, Frank L. *education educator, research scientist*
Maun, Caroline Cherie *writing educator*
McPartland, James Michael *university official*
†Norris, Karen W. *grants specialist*
Ranney, Richard Raymond *dental educator, researcher*
Reinhart, Walter Josef *educator*
†Richardson, Earl Stanford *university president*
†Roby, Mary Lorraine *special education educator*
Ross, Richard Starr *medical school dean emeritus, cardiologist*
Sawyer, David Jonathan *educator*
Simmons, Howard L. *education educator*
Sugiyama, Toku Mary *retired school administrator*
†Takacs, Laszlo *adult education educator, physicist*
Wilson, Donald Edward *dean, medical educator, physician*

Bel Air
†Larsen, Kevin Wayne *education educator*
Nye, Daniel William *retired elementary school educator*
Phillips, Bernice Cecile Golden *retired vocational education educator*

Berlin
†Auxer, Cathy Joan *elementary school educator*

Bethesda
Bradley, Damon Frederic *headmaster*
Buccino, Alphonse *university dean emeritus, consultant*
Corn, Milton *academic dean, physician*
Gleazer, Edmund John, Jr., *retired education educator*
Hemming, Val G. *university dean*
Jameson, Sanford Chandler *education educator*
Laughlin, Larry W. *academic administrator, military officer*
Sanoff, Alvin Paul *education consultant, writer*

Brookeville
Rowe, Joseph Charles *elementary school educator, principal*

Brooklandville
Brandt, Gregory Alan *secondary school educator*

Catonsville
†Smith, F. Louise *elementary school educator*

Cheverly
LaRoche, Gérard Laurent *adult education educator, writer*

Chevy Chase
Mathis, Laurelle Sheedy *academic administrator, volunteer*
Ostar, Allan William *academic administrator, higher education consultant*
Towsner, Cynthia Merle *educator, administrator*

Clarksville
Peirce, James Walter *secondary school educator, historian, educator*

College Park
Amershek, Kathleen *education educator*
†Destler, William W. *academic administrator*
Dieter, George Elwood, Jr., *university official*
Hey, Nancy Henson *educational administrator*
Langenberg, Donald Newton *retired academic administrator, physicist*
Modarres, Mohammad *education educator*
Mote, Clayton Daniel, Jr., *university president, mechanical engineer, educator*
†Ramsey, S. Robert *education educator*
Schwab, Susan Carroll *dean*
Souza, Gilvan Castro *operations and management educator*
Stewart, Teresa Elizabeth *elementary school educator*
Stumpff, Robert Thomas *academic administrator*
Szymanski, Edna Mora *dean*
Toll, John Sampson *university president, physics educator*

Columbia
Bruley, Duane Frederick *academic administrator, consultant, engineer*
Davis, Janet Marie Gorden *secondary education educator*
Hartman, Lee Ann Walraff *educator*
Jones-Wilson, Faustine Clarisse *education educator emeritus*
Strain, Lucille Bewton *education educator, researcher*
Whiting, Albert Nathaniel *former university chancellor*

Edgewater
†Masson Brinsley, Margaret W. *university official, historian*

Elkton
Howe, Patricia Moore *adult education educator*

Fort Washington
Diercks, Elizabeth Gorman *elementary education educator*

Frostburg
†Childs, William Parker *education educator*
Root, Edward Lakin *education educator, university administrator*

Garrett Park
†Stites, M(ary) Elizabeth *educator*

Germantown
†McDougle, Loella *educational consultant*
Smith, Ann Hess *guidance counselor*

Hagerstown
Spruill, Howard Vernon *former academic administrator, minister*
Warner, Charles David, III, *academic administrator*

Hanover
Schmidt, Sandra Jean *secondary school educator*

Hunt Valley
†Collier, Stephen N *educational consultant*

Indian Head
†Price, Teresa Annette *elementary school educator*

Joppa
Bates, Charles Benjamin *elementary school administrator*

Kennedyville
Schiff, Gary Stuart *academic administrator, educator, consultant*

Kensington
Holloway, William Jimmerson *retired educator*
†Palacios, Gonzalo T. *education educator*

Largo
Wootten, Patricia Eileen *adult education educator*

Laurel
Cornett, Richard Orin *research educator, consultant*
Coursey, Sharon Martin *adult education educator, consultant*
Dorsey, John Wesley, Jr., *university administrator, economist*

Lusby
Ladd, Culver Sprogle *secondary education educator*

Lutherville Timonium
Booth, Penelope Partridge *educator, school principal, author*

Marion Station
†Handy, Mary Thomas *retired elementary school educator*

Ocean Pines
Crawford, Norman Crane, Jr., *academic administrator, consultant*

Owings Mills
Barton, Dawn Kanani *elementary school educator*
Berg, Barbara Kirsner *health education specialist*
†Reihl, Donna L. *director*

Oxon Hill
†Scott, Frances Fisher Markoe *retired secondary school educator*

Port Republic
Karol, Eugene Michael *school system administrator*

Potomac
Au, Mary Lee *school system administrator*
Bremenstuhl, David P. *elementary school educator*
Kuykendall, Crystal Arlene *educational consultant, lawyer*

Prince Frederick
Karol, Victoria Diane *educational administrator*

Princess Anne
McKinney, Frances Hathaway *university program administrator*

Rockville
Cooperman, Susan *educator*
Rankin, Rachel Ann *retired media specialist*
Sparks, David Stanley *university administrator*
Stansfield, Charles W. *educational administrator*
Wall, Janet E. *assessment, testing, evaluation, and career development professional*
Woodhouse, Kathryn Andersen *counselor, educator*

Saint Marys City
Stover, Lois T. *education educator, department chairman*

Saint Michaels
Feisel, Lyle Dean *retired dean, electrical engineer, educator*

Salisbury
†Barzilai, Harel *education educator*
Woolford, Dornell Larmont *academic administrator*

Severna Park
†Chatelaine, Kenneth Leo *education educator, psychoanalyst*

Silver Spring
Bonner, Bester Davis *school system administrator*
Boykin, Nancy Merritt *academic administrator*
Coles, Anna Louise Bailey *retired university official, nurse*
Fromberg, Jean Stern *school system administrator*
Jackson, Mary Jane McHale Flickinger *principal*
Latson, Richard Charles *retired audio-visual specialist*

McGinn, Cherie M. *secondary education educator*
Roshwald, Mordecai Marceli *educator, writer*
Schick, Irvin Henry *academic administrator, educator*
Whalen, John Philip *retired educational administrator, clergyman, lawyer*

Stevenson
Hyman, Mary Bloom *science education programs coordinator*
Manning, Kevin James *academic administrator*

Suitland
Speier, Peter Michael *mathematics educator*

Swanton
Cummins, Delmer Duane *academic administrator, historian*

Towson
†Baltzley, Patricia Creel *secondary mathematics educator*
Boucher, Laurence James *educator, chemist*
Caret, Robert Laurent *academic administrator*
Hoch, David Allen *athletic director*
†Lund, Mark Fifield *secondary school educator*
Silverman, Linda L. *elementary educator*

Union Bridge
Hannah, Judy Challenger *private education tutor*

Westminster
Coley, Joan Develin *education educator*
†Dundes, Lauren *education educator*
Rosenthal, Michael Ross *academic administrator, consultant*

Wye Mills
†Schisler, Amy MacWilliams *school librarian, graphics designer*
Woods, Willie G. *dean, English language and education educator*

MASSACHUSETTS

Agawam
Schilling-Nordal, Geraldine Ann *retired secondary school educator*

Amherst
†Immerman, Neil *academic administrator, computer scientist*
Lombardi, John V. *university administrator, historian*
MacKnight, Carol Bernier *educational administrator*
†Marx, Anthony W. *academic administrator*
Prince, Gregory Smith, Jr., *academic administrator*

Andover
Wise, Kelly *private school educator, photographer, critic*

Arlington
Fulmer, Vincent Anthony *retired college president*
Winfield, Cynthia Lees *middle school educator*

Ashburnham
†Von Deck, Joseph Francis *secondary school educator, researcher*

Ashfield
Gabriel, Peter Paul *educator*

Attleboro
Rounds, Hollis A. *secondary school educator*

Auburndale
†Doran, Kathleen Brewer *dean, consultant*

Bedford
Wasson, Lila Elizabeth *educational consultant*

Belmont
Dober, Richard Patrick *campus and facility planner, writer*

Beverly
Eastman, W. Dean *secondary school educator*
Hart, Claire-Marie *educator*
Lennox, Jo Stewart *college relations and external affairs director*
Murray, Mary *educational consultant*
Smith, Merelyn Elizabeth *elementary and middle school educator*

Billerica
Furlong, Patrick David *educator, researcher*

Boston
†Athanassiou, Nicholas *education educator*
Banks, Henry H. *academic dean, physician*
†Boodram, Mohan David *academic administrator*
Caldwell, Ann Wickins *academic administrator*
Cass, Ronald Andrew *dean*
Chobanian, Aram *medical school dean, cardiologist*
†Chou, Laisheng *education educator*
Coleman, K(atherine) Ann *behavioral psychology educator*
Cotter, William Reckling *foundation president*
Daukantas, George Vytautas *counseling practitioner, educator*
Davies, Don *education educator*
DePaola, Dominick Philip *academic administrator*
Dluhy, Deborah Haigh *college dean*
Doyle, Mathias Francis *university president, political scientist, educator*
†Fitzmaurice, Garrett Martin *education educator, researcher*
Freeland, Richard Middleton *academic affairs administrator, historian*

Gora, JoAnn M. *university chancellor*
†Grant, Barbara Hurwitz *educator*
Greene, Robert Allan *former university administrator*
Harden, Patricia Keegan *financial aid officer*
†Harris, Andrew Michael *director*
Hedlund, Ronald David *academic administrator, researcher, educator*
†Henderson, Jeffrey J. *dean, educator*
Kaplan, Robert Samuel *educator*
Kirkpatrick, Edward Thomson *college administrator, mechanical engineer*
Klafter, Craig Evan *university administrator, legal historian*
†Matarazzo, James M. *dean, educator*
Morris, Robert *educator*
Norris, Lonnie Harold *dean*
Novotny, Vladimir *educator, consultant*
†Pei, Lowry Cheng-Wu *education educator, writer*
Penney, Sherry Hood *university president, educator*
Ronayne, Michael Richard, Jr., *academic dean*
Silber, John Robert *university chancellor, philosophy and law educator*
Silverman, Robert Alan *college official, historian*
†Steketee, Gail *education educator, researcher*
Thacker, Strom Cronan *educator*
Tilchin, William Neal *educator*
Tornow, Barbara *academic administrator*
Tyler, John W. *private secondary school educator, editor*
†Upton, Nancy Marie *education educator, researcher*
Van Domelen, John Francis *academic administrator*
Vernon, Heidi *international business educator*
Westling, Jon *university administrator*
Wilson, Elaine Louise *academic administrator*
†Xu, Xiping *adult education educator, director*
†Yarborough, Nellie Constance *principal, minister*
Yoffie, David B. *educator*

Brewster
†Kanis, Mersh Lubel *special education educator, writer*

Bridgewater
Nelson, Marian Emma *education educator*
Thompson, Andrew Ernest *secondary school educator*
Tinsley, Adrian *college president*
Witherell, Nancy Louise *education educator*

Brookline
Ruthchild, Rochelle Goldberg *education educator*

Cambridge
Avakian, Laura Ann *academic administrator*
Baumgartner, Mary Anne Sgarlat *academic administrator, entrepreneur*
Bruce, James Donald *academic administrator*
Cazden, Courtney B(orden) *education educator*
Clay, Phillip L. *academic administrator*
†Erlick, June Carolyn *director*
Eurich, Nell P. *educator, author*
Fischer, Kurt Walter *education educator*
Fox, John Bayley, Jr., *university dean*
Graham, Patricia Albjerg *education educator*
Gray, Paul Edward *academic official*
Greyser, Linda Lorraine *education educator*
Harris, Joseph C. *education educator*
Howitt, Arnold Martin *university administrator, educator*
Johnson, Howard Wesley *former university president, business executive*
Khoury, Philip S. *academic administrator*
Lagace, Paul Alfred *college educator*
Lagemann, Ellen Condliffe *history and education educator*
Litant, William T. G. *director*
McKenna, Margaret Anne *university president*
†Mitchell, Robert Cameron *education educator, consultant*
†Mitchell, William J. *dean, architecture educator*
†Mullainathan, Sendhil *education educator, researcher*
†Power, Samantha *academic administrator, writer*
Ray, Stephen Alan *academic administrator, lawyer*
Reimers, Fernando Miguel *education educator*
Rowe, Mary P. *organizational ombudsman, management educator*
Schmalensee, Richard Lee *dean, economist, former government official, educator*
Thiemann, Ronald Frank *dean, religion educator*
Thompson, William Irwin *educational consultant, writer*
†Vest, Charles Marstiller *academic administrator*
White, Alan Frederick *academic administrator*
Whitlock, Charles Preston *former university dean*

Centerville
Kiernan, Owen Burns *educational consultant*

Chesterfield
†Schiffman, Lawrence H. *adult education educator*

Chestnut Hill
Altbach, Philip *director, educator*
Bando, Patricia Alice *director*
†Gaiser, Ted Joseph *academic administrator, minister*
Leahy, William P. *academic administrator, historian, educator*
Monan, James Donald *university chancellor*

Chicopee
Chelte, Judith Segzdowicz *secondary education educator*
Czerwiec, Irene Theresa *gifted education educator*

Concord
Lilien, Elliot Stephen *secondary education educator*

Danvers
Clark, Sharon Jackson *private school administrator*

Dighton
Buote, Rosemarie Boschen *retired special education educator*

East Sandwich
Clarendon, John Marsden *counselor, youth program director*

Fairhaven
Goes, Kathleen Ann *secondary education educator, choral director*
Rose, Anita Carroll *retired educator*

Fitchburg
†Kemp, Deborah K. *secondary school educator*
Mara, Vincent Joseph *college president*

Framingham
LeDuc, Karen Lorain Leacu *elementary and middle school education educator*

Gardner
Marceau, Judith Marie *retired elementary school educator*

Great Barrington
†Thalheimer, Anne N. *residence director*

Greenfield
Davis, Allen Jeffrey *academic administrator*

Haverhill
Kelley, David Brian *community college dean, educator, consultant*

Holland
†McGrory, Mary Kathleen *retired college president*

Housatonic
Charpentier, Gail Wigutow *private school executive director*

Hyde Park
Harris, Emily Louise *special education educator*

Lakeville
Barry, Marilyn White *retired special education educator, dean*

Leominster
Cucchiara, Sandra Chiavaras *special education educator*

Lexington
France-Litchfield, Ruth A. *reading and early literacy specialist*
Kilson, Marion *college dean*
McFarland, Philip James *educator, writer*
†Roos, Albert Q. *secondary school educator*

Longmeadow
Katz, Barbara S. *special education educator*
Leary, Carol Ann *academic administrator*

Lowell
Goodwin, Susan Ann *academic administrator*
Hayes, Donald Paul, Jr., *elementary and secondary education educator*
†Kuhn, Sarah *educator, consultant*
LeBaron, John Francis *education educator*
†McAfee, Noelle Claire *education educator*

Lunenburg
Schnakenberg, Lori Ann *secondary school educator*

Lynn
Astuccio, Sheila Margaret *educational administrator*
Ryder, Edward Francis *secondary education educator*

Malden
Marques, Paul Joseph *secondary school educator, consultant*
Murphy, Mary Agnes (Meg Murphy) *adult education coordinator, artist*

Marblehead
Tamaren, Michele Carol *special education educator*

Marion
†Latham, Christopher Robert *alumni and development director*

Marstons Mills
Martin, David Standish *education educator*

Mashpee
Searle, William Ross *academic administrator, artist, educator*

Mattapoisett
Andersen, Laird Bryce *retired university administrator*

Maynard
Holway, Ellen Twombly Hay *primary education educator*

Medfield
Herbeck, Dale Alan *educator*

Medford
Bacow, Lawrence Seldon *academic administrator, environmental educator*

Gittleman, Sol *university official, humanities educator*

Methuen
Stanley, Malchan Craig *school system administrator, psychologist*

Milton
Warren, John Coolidge *private school administrator, history educator*
Wengler, Marguerite Marie *educational therapist*

Needham
Zambone, Alana Maria *special education educator, consultant*

Newbury
Hamond, Karen Marie Koch *secondary education educator*

North Waltham
†Liu-Constant, Brian *educational consultant, educator*

Northampton
†Christ, Carol Tecla *academic administrator*
Gounaridou, Kiki *higher education educator*

Norton
Marshall, Dale Rogers *college president, political scientist, educator*

Norwood
†Reilley, Margaret Randall *secondary school educator*

Oakham
Poirier, Helen Virginia Leonard *elementary education educator*

Plymouth
Paul, Carol Ann *retired academic administrator, biology educator*

Plympton
Smith, Robert Rutherford *university dean, communication educator*

Provincetown
Wolfman, Brunetta Reid *education educator*

Quincy
Adams, Ronald G. *middle school educator*
Short, Janet Marie *principal*

Reading
Terilli, Joseph Anthony *secondary education educator*

Revere
Ferrante, Olivia Ann *retired educator, consultant*

Rockport
Bakrow, William John *college president emeritus*

Salem
†Carroll, Gregory Joseph *education educator*

Saugus
Austill, Allen *dean emeritus*

Scituate
Spangler, Stanley Eugene *international relations educator*

Sheffield
Russell, Hilary Francis *secondary education educator*

Shrewsbury
Onorato, Nicholas Louis *retired program director, economist*

South Dartmouth
Ward, Richard Joseph *university dean, educator, author*

South Hadley
Creighton, Joanne Vanish *academic administrator*

Springfield
Caprio, Anthony S. *academic administrator*
Cleland, Thomas Edward, Jr., *secondary school educator*
†Cook, Kathryn Anne *secondary school educator*
Courniotes, Harry James *academic administrator*
†Mariani, Marita C. *secondary school educator*
Miller, Leroy Paul, Jr., *secondary English educator*
†Schmutte, Gregory Thomas *dean, consultant*

Sudbury
†Thompson, Mary Lou *elementary school educator*

Tewksbury
DeAngelis, Michele F. *school system administrator*

Turners Falls
†Finley-Morin, Kimberley K. *educator*

Tyngsboro
Lee, Joan Roberta *elementary education educator*

Waltham
Adamian, Gregory Harry *academic administrator*
†Bernstein, Melvin *provost*
Mc Menimen, Kathleen Brennan *secondary education educator*
Reinharz, Jehuda *academic administrator, history educator*
Reis, Arthur Henry, Jr., *university administrator*
†Schwarz, Gerald Walter *adult education educator*

Shonkoff, Jack P. *dean, educator*

Wareham
Gustafson, Deborah Lee *educational administrator, educator*

Watertown
Mason, Linda Anne *daycare administrator*

Wayland
†Anderson, Monica Luffman *school librarian, educator, real estate broker*

Wellesley
Auerbach, Jerold S. *university educator*
Baum, Laura *educator*
†Heartt, Charlotte Beebe *university official*
Ragone, David Vincent *former university president*
Tucker, John Avery *retired academic administrator, electrical engineer*
Walsh, Diana Chapman *academic administrator, sociologist, educator*

Wenham
†Beauregard, John *school librarian, consultant*

West Boylston
†Benestad, Kelly Ann *secondary school educator*

Westborough
Antalek, Eileen Elizabeth *educational consultant*

Westfield
Dunphy, Maureen Milbier *educator*

Whitman
Anderson, Beth Ellen *English literature and composition educator*

Wilbraham
Woloshchuk, Candace Dixon *secondary school educator, artist, consultant*

Williamstown
Chandler, John Wesley *educational consultant*
†Schapiro, Morton Owen *university administrator*

Winchester
Irving, Gitte Nielsen *secondary education educator*

Woburn
Tramonte, Michael Robert *education educator*

Woods Hole
Farrington, John William *academic administrator, dean, research scientist*

Worcester
Bassett, John E. *academic administrator, English educator*
Bowen, Alice Frances *school system administrator*
Brooks, John Edward *college president emeritus*
†Brunell-Joiner, Karlea *academic administrator, educator*
Bunuan, Josefina Santiago *early childhood education educator, graduate program coordinator*
Johnson, Nancy Ann *education educator, educator*
Lazare, Aaron *dean, psychiatrist*
Loew, Franklin Martin *college president, biologist, consultant*
†Mardilovich, Ivan P *education educator*
McFarland, Michael C. *academic administrator*
Palmer, John Anthony, III, *secondary education educator*
†Toomey, Sister Cathleen *academic administrator*

Yarmouth Port
Hall, James Frederick *retired college president*

MICHIGAN

Adrian
Caine, Stanley Paul *college administrator*
†Lamprecht, Elizabeth Ann *educator*

Algonac
Paquet, Gary Lee *elementary school educator*

Alma
Swanson, Robert Draper *college president*

Alpena
Lancour, Karen Louise *secondary education educator*

Ann Arbor
Alfred, Richard Lincoln *education educator, educational association administrator, consultant, researcher*
†Beutler, Suzanne A. *retired middle school educator, artist*
†Chin, Chen Ooi *dean*
Cole, David Edward *university administrator*
Copeland, Carolyn Abigail *retired university dean*
Duderstadt, James Johnson *academic administrator, engineering educator*
Dumas, Rhetaugh Etheldra Graves *university official*
Ellis, Charles Norman *professor, researcher*
†Fabian, Hans J. *education educator*
Fishback, Robert Lawrence *retired secondary education educator*
Fleming, Robben Wright *retired educator*
Fleming, Suzanne Marie *university official, chemistry educator*
Hinshaw, Ada Sue *dean, nursing educator*
Kelch, Robert Paul *former dean, pediatric endocrinologist*
†La Fountain-Stokes, Lawrence M *education educator*

†Moje, Elizabeth Birr *education educator*
Omenn, Gilbert Stanley *academic administrator, physician*
Paul, Ara Garo *university dean*
Perkins, George *educator, writer*
Porretta, Louis Paul *education educator*
Rounds, William C. *educator*
Sears, JoAnn Marie *academic librarian*
Sullivan, Thomas Patrick *academic administrator*
Warner, Robert Mark *university dean, archivist, historian*
White, B. Joseph *dean, business educator*

Armada
Kummerow, Arnold A. *superintendent of schools*

Auburn Hills
De Martin, Colleen Dianne *college official, interior designer, consultant*

Bay City
Zuraw, Kathleen Ann *special education and physical education educator*

Belmont
Delnick, Martha Joyce *retired elementary education educator*

Benzonia
Acker, Nathaniel Hull *retired educational administrator*

Berrien Springs
Lesher, William Richard *retired academic administrator*
†Lundgren, Dennis D. *intermediate school educator*

Bloomfield Hills
Hitchcock, Lillian Dorothy Staw *educator, actress, artist*
Thompson, Richard Thomas *academic administrator*
Wermuth, Mary Louella *secondary school educator*

Buchanan
Falkenstein, Karin Edith *elementary school principal*
Stromswold, Dorothy *retired secondary educator, book reviewer*

Cadillac
Whitmer, Gretchen Sue *secondary school educator*

Clarkston
Mousseau, Doris Naomi Barton *retired elementary school principal*

Clinton Township
Fontanive, Lynn Marie *special education administrator*
Stone, Beverly Ann *retired counselor*
Syropoulos, Mike *retired school system director*

Clio
McCabe, Donald James *educational research director*

Commerce Township
Boynton, Irvin Parker *retired educational administrator*

Dearborn
Dziuba, Henry Frank *retired university official*
Fair, Jean Everhard *retired education educator*

Detroit
Abel, Ernest Lawrence *education educator*
Barrett, Nancy Smith *university administrator*
†Booth, Betty Jean *daycare administrator, poet*
†Braunschweig, Karl David *education educator, performing arts educator, humanities educator*
Connellan, William Wesley *higher education educator*
Corbitt, Eumiller Mattie *education educator, special education educator*
†Ebenezer, Jazlin V. *adult education educator*
Edelstein, Tilden Gerald *university official, history educator*
†Edison, Jonathan E. *assistant principal, motivational speaker*
†Green, Charles Adam *retired education educator, psychologist*
†Johnson, Steven Carl *educational consultant*
Jones, James Allen *secondary education educator*
Jordan, Napoleon Bonaparte *educational consultant*
Mika, Joseph John *library school director, educator, consultant*
Penn, Maggie Scott *school counselor, mental health therapist, small business owner*
Pettapiece, Bob (Mervyn Arthur Pettapiece) *education educator*
Pietrofesa, John Joseph *education educator*
Rogers, Richard Lee *educator*
Semanik, Anthony James *instructional technology supervisor*
†Spiller, Alan Clark *director, consultant*
Steinman, H. Robert *dean*
†Wadlington, Lorna Jackie Jones *school system administrator*

Dowagiac
Gourley, Everett Haynie *educator*
Mulder, Patricia Marie *education educator*

East Lansing
Brophy, Jere Edward *education educator, researcher*
Byerrum, Richard Uglow *college dean*
Fernandez, Ramona Esther *adult education educator*
†Gift, David Ayres *academic administrator*

Harrison, Jeremy Thomas *dean, law educator*
Honhart, Frederick Lewis, III, *academic director*
†Jackson-Elmoore, Cynthia *dean, educator*
†King, Lonnie J. *dean*
McPherson, Melville Peter *academic administrator, former government official*
†Noverr, Douglas Arthur *academic administrator, educator*
†Petropoulos, Evangelos *former health institute director, educator*
†Schwille, John Robert *education educator, researcher*
Snoddy, James Ernest *education educator*
Strampel, William *dean, medical educator*
Velicer, Janet Schafbuch *retired elementary school educator*

Escanaba
†Bennett, Kathleen Marourneen *elementary school educator*

Farmington
Rowen, Samuel Frederick *education educator*

Farmington Hills
Sparrow, Laura *secondary educator*

Flint
Duckett, Bernadine Johnal *retired elementary principal*
Lorenz, John Douglas *college official*

Franklin
Reinhart, Anne Christine *special education educator, consultant*

Gaylord
Magsig, Judith Anne *retired early childhood education educator*

Grand Rapids
Diekema, Anthony J. *college president emeritus, educational consultant*
Kunze, Linda Joye *educator*
Lubbers, Arend Donselaar *retired academic administrator*
†Pauley, Garth Ernest *education educator*
†Riekse, Robert James *education educator, researcher, writer*
†VanHarn, Gordon Lee *college administrator and provost*
Yarington, David Jon *retired educator*

Gwinn
Lasich, Vivian Esther Layne *secondary education educator*

Hancock
Puotinen, Arthur Edwin *college president, clergyman*
†Smith, Stephen Alan *secondary school educator*

Harbor Springs
Cappel, Constance *educational consultant, writer*

Haslett
Hotaling, Robert Bachman *community planner, educator*
Warrington, Willard Glade *former university official*

Hillsdale
†Grassl, Wolfgang *adult education educator*
Kline, Faith Elizabeth *college official*

Holland
Nyenhuis, Jacob Eugene *college official*
Schieringa, Paul Kenneth *special education educator, entertainer*
Van Wylen, Gordon John *former college president*

Houghton
Tompkins, Curtis Johnston *academic administrator*

Jackson
Straayer, Carole Kathleen *retired elementary education educator*
Trap, Jennifer Josephine *special education administrator*

Kalamazoo
Bailey, Judith Irene *university official, consultant*
Burns, James W. *education educator*
Cody, Frank Joseph *secondary school educator*
Gordon, Alice Jeannette Irwin *secondary and elementary education educator*
Haenicke, Diether Hans *academic administrator emeritus, educator*
Jones, James Fleming, Jr., *academic administrator, Roman language and literature educator*
†Lewis, James Eldon, Jr., *education educator*
Mingus, Matthew Scott *public administration educator*
†Ott, Jennifer Hubbell *education educator*
Ransford, Sherry *secondary education educator*
Stufflebeam, Daniel LeRoy *education educator*

Kentwood
Yovich, Daniel John *educator*

Lake Orion
Brewer, Judith Anne *special education educator, consultant*
†Leonard, Jacquelyn Ann *retired elementary school educator*

Lansing
Butcher, Amanda Kay *retired university administrator*
†Kissling, Paul Joseph *academic administrator, religious studies educator, minister*
Marazita, Eleanor Marie Harmon *retired secondary education educator*
Piveronus, Peter John, Jr., *education educator*

†Straus, Kathleen Nagler *education administrator, consultant*

Lapeer
Spray, Pauline Etha Mellish *retired elementary educator, writer*

Lawrence
Fudge, Mary Ann *vocational school educator*

Ludington
Puffer, Richard Judson *retired college chancellor*

Macomb
Farmakis, George Leonard *education educator*

Maple City
Morris, Donald Arthur Adams *college president*

Marquette
Saville, Kathleen Jo *instructional technologist*

Midland
Barker, Nancy Lepard *university official*

Mount Pleasant
Carlson, Charles Evans *university official*

Pentwater
†Noffke, Frank Edward *educational planner, writer, educator*

Pinckney
Duquet, Suzanne Frances *special education educator*

Pleasant Ridge
Sneed, Marie Eleanor Wilkey *retired secondary education educator*

Pontiac
Decker, Peter William *academic administrator*
Love, Sharon Irene *elementary education educator*

Portland
Rainey, Derek Rexton *educator, sculptor*

Presque Isle
Kinney, Mark Baldwin *educator*

Richmond
Wood, Virginia Ann *educator*

Riverview
Thompson, LaVerne Elizabeth Thomas *college official*

Rochester
†Gallagher, Edward Arthur *retired academic administrator, real estate developer*
Packard, Sandra Podolin *education educator, consultant*
†Russi, Gary D. *academic administrator*

Rochester Hills
Mills, Helene Audrey *education educator*

Rockford
Pappas, William John *principal, educator*
Teliczan, Casimir Joseph *secondary school educator*

Royal Oak
Pricer, Wayne Francis *counseling consultant*

Saginaw
Sudhoff, Virginia Rae *retired elementary education educator*

Saint Clair
Kocan, Ronald Robert *secondary school educator*

Saint Clair Shores
Kavadas-Pappas, Iphigenia Katherine *preschool administrator, educator, consultant*

Saugatuck
Blair, John Raymond *educational psychology educator*

Sault Sainte Marie
†Fields, Polly Stevens *educator, writer, researcher*

Sidney
Rice, Sharon Jean *secondary school educator*

South Bend
†Demmon, Terri Lynn *educational consultant, educator*

Southfield
Chambers, Charles MacKay *university president*
Hartman-Abramson, Ilene *adult education educator*
Lee, James Edward, Jr., *educational consultant*
Ragan, Stephen C. *academic administrator*

Spring Lake
†Bussard, Janice Wingeier *retired educator, inventor*

Stanton
Winchell, George William *curriculum and technology educator*

Traverse City
Zimmerman, Paul Albert *retired college president, minister*

Trenton
Beebe, Grace Ann *retired special education educator*
Wukovits, John Francis *secondary school educator, writer*

Troy
Maierle, Bette Jean *director nursery school*

University Center
Gilbertson, Eric Raymond *academic administrator, lawyer*

Walled Lake
Peal, Christopher John *educational administrator*

Warren
Cutter, Jeffrey S. *secondary education educator, music educator*
Quay, Gregory Harrison *retired secondary school educator*

Waterford
Anderson, Francile Mary *secondary education educator*

Wayne
Carpenter, Arthur Lloyd *education educator*

Wellston
Spain, Frederick William *secondary school educator, writer*

West Bloomfield
Simpson, Robert Lee *university official, biology educator*

Westland
Mullinix, Barbara Jean *special services director*

Williamston
Johnson, Tom Milroy *academic dean, medical educator, physician*

Ypsilanti
Boone, Morell Douglas *information and communications technology educator*
Griffin, Carolyn Leigh *English educator, genealogist*
Gwaltney, Thomas Marion *education educator, writer*
Hafter, Daryl M. *educator*
Robbins, Jerry Hal *educational administration educator*
†Stevens, Lizbeth Jane *special education educator, researcher*

MINNESOTA

Ada
Sillerud, Arlen Roger *retired educator*

Albert Lea
Rechtzigel, Sue Marie (Suzanne Rechtzigel) *child care center executive*

Bemidji
Forseth, William J. *retired education educator*
†Rogers, Patricia Louise *education educator, consultant*

Bloomington
Allen, Mary Louise Hook *secondary education educator*

Cloquet
Ellison, David Charles *special education educator*

Cushing
Perfetti, Robert Nickolas *educational consultant*

Duluth
Stevenson, Jean Myers *education educator*
Ziegler, Rick *dean, science educator*

Edina
Meyer, Warren George *vocational educator*

Fridley
Larson, Marilyn J. *retired elementary music educator*

Grand Marais
Kreitlow, Burton William *retired adult education educator*

Hopkins
Zins, Martha Lee *elementary education educator, media specialist*

Hutchinson
†Pasche, Steven Frederick *secondary school educator, football coach*

Lakeland
Helstedt, Gladys Mardell *vocational education educator*

Litchfield
†Huselid, Boyd Lynn *secondary school educator*

Long Lake
Lowthian, Petrena *academic administrator*

Mankato
Hustoles, Mary Jo *elementary education educator*
Nickerson, James Findley *retired educator*

Maple Lake
Haack, John Scott *special education educator, historian*

Marine On Saint Croix
Gavin, Robert Michael, Jr., *education consultant*

Marshall
Danahar, David C. *academic administrator, historian, educator*

Minneapolis
Atwood, John Brian *dean*
Avella, Joseph Ralph *university executive*
Bowie, Norman Ernest *university official, educator*
Buggey, Lesley JoAnne *education educator, consultant*
†Cerra, Frank Bernard *dean*
†Cline, Richard Ryan *education educator*
Coskran, Kathleen Anne *principal*
DiGangi, Frank Edward *academic administrator*
Eckberg, E. Daniel *secondary education educator*
†Gardebring, Sandra S. *academic administrator*
†Houe, Poul *education educator*
†Johnson, David Chester *university chancellor, sociology educator*
Jorgensen, Daniel Fred *academic executive*
Lindell, Edward Albert *former college president, religious organization administrator*
Matson, Wesley Jennings *educational administrator*
O'Keefe, Thomas Michael *academic administrator*
Osander, John *secondary school educator*
Polverini, Peter *dean*
Porter, Jeannette Upton *elementary education educator*
†Ransom, Lakeesha Krotonya *academic administrator*
Rogers, Karen Beckstead *gifted studies educator, researcher, consultant*
Schuh, G(eorge) Edward *university dean, agricultural economist*
Southall, Francis Geneva *retired education educator music*
†Sullivan, Alfred Dewitt *academic administrator*
Svendsbye, Lloyd August *college president, clergyman, educator*
Veldey, Bonnie *special education educator*
Wehrwein-Hunt, Jeri Lynn *elementary education educator*
†Wilhelm, Gretchen *retired secondary school educator, volunteer*

Minnetonka
Vanstrom, Marilyn June Christensen *retired elementary education educator*

Moorhead
Benson, John Steven *education educator*
Dille, Roland Paul *college president*
Emmel, Bruce Henry *retired secondary education mathematics educator*
O'Hara, Sabine U. *academic administrator, dean, economist, educator*
Treumann, William Borgen *university dean*
†Zhang, Haimeng *education educator*

Morris
†Ng, Peh H. *education educator*

Mounds View
Calvin, Stafford Richard *academic administrator*

Northfield
†Oden, Robert A., Jr., *academic administrator*
Rand, Sidney Anders *retired college administrator*

Ortonville
Schrom, Elizabeth Ann *educator*

Owatonna
Larson, Diane LaVerne Kusler *principal*

Preston
Hokenson, David Leonard *secondary school educator*

Proctor
Scheibe, Margaret Helen *elementary school educator, librarian*

Remer
McNulty-Majors, Susan Rose *special education administrator*

Richfield
Reilly, Jill Marlene *school system administrator*

Rochester
Sherman, Thomas Francis *education educator*
Windebank, Anthony J. *dean*

Rosemount
Trygestad, JoAnn Carol *secondary education educator*

Rushford
Stras, Penny Lynn *director*

Saginaw
Stauber, Marilyn Jean *retired secondary and elementary school*

Saint Cloud
Reha, Rose Krivisky *retired business educator*
Saigo, Roy Hirofumi *academic administrator*
Wertz, John Alan *retired secondary school educator*

Saint James
Jones, Patricia Louise *elementary counselor*

Saint Paul
Brushaber, George Karl *college-theological seminary president, minister*
Dickel, Michael Huf *higher education administrator, writer*
Dykstra, Robert *retired education educator*
Gabrick, Robert William *secondary education educator*
Graham, Charles John *university educator, former university president*
Huber, Sister Alberta *college president*
†Klausner, Jeffrey *dean*

Magnuson, Roy William *secondary school educator*
Pinn, Anthony Bernard *educator*
†Rosenberg, Brian C *academic administrator*
Stroud, Rhoda M. *elementary education educator*

Saint Peter
Mosbo, John Alvin *dean*

Savage
Loutzenhiser, Carolyn Ann *retired elementary education educator*

Shoreview
Nolting, Earl *retired academic administrator*

Ulen
Harmon, Kay Yvonne *elementary education educator*

Waseca
Frederick, Edward Charles *university official*

West Saint Paul
†Kassulke, Paul Robert *secondary school educator*

Winona
Boseker, Barbara Jean *education educator*
Krueger, Darrell William *academic administrator*
Nasstrom, Roy Richard *retired education educator, consultant*

MISSISSIPPI

Ackerman
Coleman, Frances McLean *secondary school educator*

Alcorn State
Bristow, Clinton, Jr., *academic administrator*
†Conner, Deondra *education educator*
†Felder-Wright, Pamela Theresa Evans *education educator*
†Iheanacho, Vitalis A *education educator, researcher*

Batesville
Neal, Joseph Lee *vocational school educator*

Belden
Whitehead, Zelma Kay *special education educator*

Biloxi
Brown, Sheba Ann *elementary education educator*
Manners, Pamela Jeanne *middle school educator*

Brandon
Okojie, Felix A. *research administrator*

Braxton
†Skiffer-Robinson, Danielle K. *guidance counselor*

Clinton
Whitlock, Betty *secondary education educator*

Columbus
†Limbert, Claudia A. *academic administrator, writer*

Courtland
Lindgren, Carl Edwin *educational consultant, antiquarian, historian*

Drew
†Morris, DeVoyce Campbell *school system administrator*

Gautier
Baggett, James Lamar *anatomy, physiology and microbiology educator*

Glen
†Wigginton, Lisa Benderman *elementary school educator*

Hattiesburg
Gunther, William David *university administrator, economics educator*
Lucas, Aubrey Keith *retired university president*
Noonkester, James Ralph *retired college president*
†Slade, Barbie Evette Delk *special education educator*

Hazlehurst
Blakeney, Margaret Elizabeth Fleming *counselor, educator*

Holly Springs
Beckley, David Lenard *academic administrator*

Holly Springs,
†Frederick, Richard John *education educator*

Itta Bena
†Ahanonu, Chukwuma Smart *education educator*

Iuka
†Barnes, Betty Jean *educational administrator*

Jackson
Anglin, Linda McCluney *retired elementary school educator*
Collins, Deloris Williams *secondary school educator*
Harmon, George Marion *academic administrator*
Hupp, James R. *academic administrator*
†Iraki, Waithaka Njuguna *educator, journalist*
McLeod, Stephen Glenn *education educator, language educator*
Rogers, Oscar Allan, Jr., *college president*

Long Beach
White, Edith Roberta Shoemake *elementary school educator*
Williams, James Orrin *university administrator, educator*

Meridian
Phillips, Patricia Jeanne *retired school system administrator*

Mississippi State
Hughes, Patricia Newman *academic administrator*
Mabry, Donald Joseph *university administrator, history educator*
Rabideau, Peter Wayne *university dean, chemistry educator*
Rent, Clyda Stokes *academic administrator*

Natchez
Marion, Ann *school psychologist, educator*
Profice, Rosena Mayberry *elementary school educator*

Noxapater
Sumner, Margaret Elizabeth *elementary school educator*

Oxford
Moorhead, Sylvester Andrew *education educator retired*
Walton, Gerald Wayne *retired university official*

Pascagoula
McKee, Ronald Gene *vocational education educator*

Perkinston
Mellinger, Barry Lee *community college president, vocational educator*

Starkville
Dampier, Caryn *self-defense instructor*
Martin, Theodore Krinn *former university administrator (deceased)*

University
†Khayat, Robert Conrad *academic administrator*
Martin, Jeanette St. Clair *adult education educator*

Vicksburg
Keulegan, Emma Pauline *special education educator*

Yazoo City
Hawthorne, Minnie *elementary school educator*

MISSOURI

Blue Eye
Anderson, Ruth G. *retired education educator, educational consultant*

Blue Springs
Shover, Joan *retired secondary school educator*

Camdenton
Hosman, Sharon *elementary education educator*

Cape Girardeau
†Eom, Sean Bock *education educator, researcher*
McMahan, Gale Ann Scivally *education educator*

Cassville
Sheats, Rachel Gay *computer and reading educator, videographer*

Chesterfield
Cox, Glenda Jewell *retired elementary school educator*
Finley, Marlynn Holt *elementary educator consultant*
Jordan, Thomas E. *retired academic researcher*
McLain, Donald J. *educational consultant*
Shepperd, Susan Abbott *special education educator*

Columbia
†Ballard, Bruce W. *philosophy educator, religious studies educator*
†Duan, Dongsheng *education educator, researcher*
George, Melvin Douglas *retired university president*
Gysbers, Norman Charles *education educator*
Kierscht, Marcia Selland *academic administrator, psychologist*
†Klein, Cerry Martin *operations research and industrial engineering educator, consultant*
Miller, Paul Ausborn *adult education educator*
Pacheco, Manuel Trinidad *academic administrator*
Payne, Thomas L. *university official*
†Wallace, Richard Lee *chancellor*

Farmington
Massie, Maureen Teresa *elementary school educator*

Fayette
Inman, Marianne Elizabeth *college administrator*

Florissant
Carman, Robert Eugene *secondary school educator*

Fulton
Lamkin, Fletcher M., Jr., *academic administrator*

Gallatin
Wilsted, Joy *elementary education educator, reading specialist, parenting consultant*

Grandview
Daugherty, Tonda Lou *special education educator*

Hannibal
Carty, Raymond Wesley *academic administrator*
Dugger, Tommy Ray *academic administrator*

Hillsboro
Adkins, Gregory D. *higher education administrator*

Imperial
Usher, Mary Margaret *special education educator*

Independence
†Henley, Patricia Joan *principal*
Marlow, Lydia Lou *elementary education educator*

Jefferson City
Gonder, Sharon *special education educator*
Henson, David B. *university administrator*
Novotney, Donald Francis *superintendent of schools*

Jennings
Robards, Bourne Rogers *elementary education educator*

Joplin
Allman, Margaret Ann Lowrance *counseling administrator*

Kansas City
Bové-DeWald, Marylou Goodman *university director, educator*
Caulfield, Joan *director, educator*
†Churchman, Michael Steele Bright *educational consultant, educator*
Doyle, Wendell E. *retired band director, educator*
Drees, Betty *dean, educator*
Eubanks, Eugene Emerson *education educator, consultant*
Hamilton, Richard Alfred *university administrator, marketing educator*
McCollum, Clifford Glenn *college dean emeritus*
†Schuchman, Philip Melchor *education educator*
†Shaw, Willie G. *adult education educator*
Sizemore, William Christian *retired academic administrator, county official*
Slaughter, Rochelle Denise *elementary school educator*
Wilkins, Arthur Norman *retired college administrator*
Willsie, Sandra K. *dean, physician, medical educator*

Kirksville
†Dixon, Barbara Bruinekool *provost*
†Grow-Maienza, Janice *education educator*
Koutstaal, Cornelis W. *university administrator*

Kirkwood
†Hoglen, Jewel Pamela *retired secondary school educator*
Pittman, Shepard Clifton *secondary principal*

Lees Summit
†Linder, Beverly L. *educator*
Smith, Dwyane *university administrator*

Liberty
Armstrong, Susan J. *academic administrator*
Tanner, Jimmie Eugene *retired dean*

Marshall
Huff, Jane Van Dyke *secondary education educator*

Maryville
†Hubbard, Dean Leon *university president*
Primm, David John *middle school educator*

O Fallon
Brungard, Daniel V. *small business owner, city official*

Plato
Wood, Joetta Kay *special education educator*

Raytown
†Coppenbarger, Cecelia Marie *special education educator*

Rolla
Thomas, Gary L. *academic administrator*
Wan, Kai-tak *education educator*
Warner, Don Lee *dean emeritus*

Saint Charles
Newcomb, Carolyn Jeanne *special education educator*
†Segelhorst, Cindy Marie *early childhood educator*

Saint Joseph
Comerford, John Leo *college official*

Saint Louis
†Bassoppo-Moyo, Sheila *elementary school educator*
†Biondi, Lawrence *university administrator, priest*
†Boyer, Patricia Grace *education educator*
Briggs, Cynthia Anne *educational administrator, clinical psychologist*
Bubash, Patricia Jane *special education educator*
Byrnes, Christopher Ian *academic dean, researcher*
Cain, James Nelson *arts school and concert administrator*
†Careklas, John Orestes *secondary school educator*
Danforth, William Henry *retired academic administrator, physician*
†Evans, Johnnie P. *retired elementary school educator*
†Foy, Betsy D. *counseling administrator, educator*
George, Thomas Frederick *academic administrator*
†Gilligan, Sandra Kaye *private school director*
†Grant, Michele Byrd *secondary school educator*
Jacobi, Jan de Greeff *school administrator*
†Kalyanaraman, Ramki *education educator, researcher*
†Keeling, Robert E. *secondary school educator*
Kennelly, Sister Karen Margaret *retired academic administrator, church administrator, nun*
Koff, Robert Hess *academic administrator*
Lackey, Kayle Diann *elementary education educator*
Leonard, Judith Price *educational advisor*
Lovin, Keith Harold *academic administrator, philosophy educator*
Luebbert, Karen Merritt *academic administrator*
Mahan, David James *retired university official*
Martens Balke, Patricia Frances *adult education educator*
Maupin, Stephanie Zeller *educator, consultant*
†McGlothlin, Erin Heather *education educator*
†Mitchell, Louise Tyndall *special education educator*
Monteleone, Patricia *dean*
†Nickolai, Beatrice Rose *education educator*
O'Neill, Sheila *principal*
Payuk, Edward William *elementary education educator*
Ramming, Michael Alexander *retired school system administrator*
Reid, Lorene Frances *middle school educator*
Sableman, Lynn *educator*
†Scheffing, Dianne Elizabeth *special education educator*
Seligman, Joel *dean*
Thomas, Pamela Adrienne *special education educator*
Watkins, Hortense Catherine *middle school educator*
Weiss, Robert Francis *former academic administrator, religious organization administrator, consultant*
†Williams, Nellie James Batt *secondary education educator*
†Williamson, Marilyn *retired secondary school educator*
Wiltenburg, Robert Edward *university dean*

Saint Peters
Huckshold, Wayne William *elementary education educator*

Sedalia
Hazen, Elizabeth Frances *retired special education educator*

Springfield
Allcorn, Terry Alan *principal, educator*
†Fritts, Josephine Ann *education educator*
Good, Stephen Hanscom *academic administrator*
†Hess, John *education educator, counselor*
Keiser, John Howard *academic administrator*

Theodosia
Johnson, Larry Robert *education educator*

Unity Village
Boehm, Toni Georgene *seminary dean, nurse*

Verona
Youngberg, Charlotte Anne *education specialist, clergywoman*

Warrensburg
Limback, E(dna) Rebecca *vocational education educator*
†Myers, Michelle E. *education educator, consultant*

Waynesville
Learmann, Judith Marilyn *secondary school educator*

Webb City
James, Kathryn A. *secondary education educator*

Webster Groves
Carr, Margaret *educator*

Windyville
Clark, Laurel Jan *adult education educator, author, editor, minister, counselor*
Condron, Daniel Ralph *academic administrator, metaphysics educator*

MONTANA

Billings
Gardiner, Steve E. *secondary school educator, writer*
†Guha, Sujata *education educator*

Bozeman
†Creel, Scott *adult education educator, researcher*
Gamble, Geoffrey *academic administrator*
†Large, David Clay *education educator, writer*

Butte
Sherrill, Barbara Ann Buker *elementary school educator*

Crow Agency
Pease-Pretty On Top, Janine B. *community college administrator*

Darby
†Haugen, Margaret Ellen *daycare administrator*

Dayton
Catalfomo, Philip *retired university dean*

Havre
Lanier, William Joseph *college program director*

Helena
Crofts, Richard A. *academic administrator*

Kalispell
Klang, Mary Margaret *secondary school educator*

Livingston
Beland, Charlet Sue *secondary school educator*

Missoula
Brown, Perry Joe *university dean*
Dennison, George Marshel *academic administrator*
†Kuhn, Thomas B *education educator*
Rowland, Paul McDonald *education educator*
†Vogelsberg, Ross Timm *education educator, researcher*

Victor
Stewart, JoAnne *director*

NEBRASKA

Auburn
Winegardner, Rose Mary *special education educator*

Barneston
March, Darlene J. *secondary school educator, news correspondent*

Bellevue
Kayne, Jon Barry *industrial psychologist*
Muller, John Bartlett *university president*
Wydeven, Joseph Jude *university dean, educator*

Blair
Christopherson, Myrvin Frederick *college president*

Doniphan
Alcorn, Donald J. *secondary school educator, band and choral director*

Grand Island
Howard, John Kenneth *secondary school educator*
†Weseman, Vicki Lynne *elementary school educator*
Zichek, Shannon Elaine *retired secondary school educator*

Gretna
Druliner, Marcia Marie *education educator*

Hayes Center
Fornoff, Ann Lynette *secondary school educator*

Kearney
†Johnston, Gladys Styles *university official*

Lincoln
Bradley, Richard Edwin *retired college president*
†Epp, Dianne Naomi *secondary educator*
Grew, Priscilla Croswell *university official, geology educator*
Hendrickson, Kent Herman *university administrator*
Hermance, Lyle Herbert *retired college official*
Janzow, Walter Theophilus *retired college administrator*
Milligan, Cynthia Hardin *university dean, lawyer*
Nelson, Darrell Wayne *university administrator, scientist*
†Owens, John C. *academic administrator*
Reinhardt, John W. *dean, educator, researcher, consultant*
Smith, Lewis *academic administrator, educator*
†Stensaas, Starla A. *education educator, artist*
†Trainin, Guy *education educator*

Norfolk
Mortensen-Say, Marlys *school system administrator*
Timmer, Margaret Louise (Peg Timmer) *educator*

North Platte
Boerner, Sheila Gertrude *secondary education educator*
†Wohler, Ruth *education educator*

Omaha
Barkmeier, Wayne W. *academic administrator*
†Destache, Christopher J. *education educator, researcher*
†Fyfe, Doris Mae *elementary school educator*
Haselwood, Eldon LaVerne *retired education educator*
Hill, John Wallace *special education educator*
Ho, David Kim Hong *educator*
Juel, Twila Eileen *elementary education educator*
Krecklow, Douglas Earl *secondary education educator, coach*
Newton, John Milton *academic administrator, psychology educator*
O'Brien, Richard L(ee) *medical educator, academic administrator, physician, cell biologist*
†Ross, Larry *education educator, researcher*
Schlegel, John P. *academic administrator*
Schlessinger, Bernard S. *retired university dean*
†Schulz, Merryellen Towey *education educator*
†Temple, Eloise *school system administrator*

Papillion
James, Geneva Behrens *secondary school educator*
Mueller, Suzanne *secondary school educator*

Scottsbluff
Baltensperger, David Dwight *education educator, researcher*

Stuart
Larabee, Brenda J. *secondary education educator*

NEVADA

Carson City
Wadman, William Wood, III, *educational director, technical research executive, consulting company executive*

Elko
Lovell, Walter Benjamin *secondary education educator, radio broadcaster*

Fallon
Dwyer, Doris Dawn *adult education educator*

Gardnerville
†Smith, Roderick Joel *behavioral consultant, researcher, educator*

Henderson
Chairsell, Christine *academic administrator*
Moore, Richard *former academic administrator, educator*
†Sigman, Kevin Andrew *director*
Thomas, James Patrick *special education educator*

Incline Village
Timinsky, Dale *academic administrator*

Las Vegas
Ananias, José *retired school system administrator*
Carroll, Rossye O'Neal *college administrator*
Ferrillo, Patrick J., Jr., *academic dean, endodontist*
Gaspar, Anna Louise *retired elementary school educator, consultant*
Hair, Kittie Ellen *secondary educator*
Harter, Carol Clancey *university president, English language educator*
Holmes, BarbaraAnn Krajkoski *secondary education educator*
Horner, Sandra Marie Groce (Sandy Heart) *educator, poet, songwriter, lyricist*
†Lieberman, Joel David *education educator*
Miller, Susan Peterson *special education educator*
Patricks, Edward John *elementary education educator*
Phillips, Karen *secondary education educator*
Pierce, Thresia Korte (Tish Pierce) *primary school educator*
Shuman, R. Baird *academic program director, writer, English language educator, educational consultant*
Singer, Kathryn J. *assistant principal*
Skoll, Pearl A. *retired mathematics and special education educator*
Williams, Jane Marie *special education educator*

North Las Vegas
†Kelly, Christopher Pat *dean, educator*
†Redd, Virginia Lee *elementary school educator*
†Taylor, William L., Jr., *academic administrator, educator*

Reno
Cathey-Gibson, Sharon Sue Rinn *school principal, college administrator*
Crowley, Joseph Neil *university president, political science educator*
Humphrey, Neil Darwin *retired university president*
Lilley, John Mark *academic administrator, dean*
McFarlane, Stephen C. *dean, researcher*
Walen, Joanne Michele *secondary education educator, consultant*

Sparks
Salls, Jennifer Jo *secondary school educator, consultant*
†Tran, Can Ngoc *educator, researcher*

NEW HAMPSHIRE

Alton Bay
Scott, Susan Shattuck *secondary education educator*

Bedford
Seidman, Alan *educational administrator*

Claremont
Evensen, Edward Arthur *elementary school educator*

Concord
Colby, Virginia Little *retired elementary school educator*

Dover
Pelletier, Marsha Lynn *secondary school educator, poet*

Durham
†Berona, David A. *computer systems librarian, educator*
DeMitchell, Todd Allan *education educator, educator*
Greenberg, Arthur *dean, chemist*
Hart, Ann Weaver *educational administration educator*
†Sugerman, Deborah Ann *education educator, consultant*

Exeter
†Cole, Donald Barnard *education educator*
Ganley, Albert C. *retired private school educator, writer*

Hanover
Danos, Paul *dean, finance educator*
Dmitrovsky, Ethan *dean, cancer physician, medical educator, researcher, oncologist*
†Dycus, Elizabeth Rasmussen *academic administrator*
Freedman, James Oliver *former university president, lawyer*
Hennessey, John William, Jr., *academic administrator, educator*
Wright, James Edward *academic administrator, historian, educator*

Hollis
†Castner Jr., Theodore G. *education educator*

Keene
Hickey, Delina Rose *retired education educator*

Lebanon
Tinker, Averill Faith *special education educator*

Lempster
Jillette, Arthur George, Jr., *school system administrator, educator*

Manchester
Desrosiers, Aprylle Lynn *director, consultant*

Nashua
Auclair, Louise A. *education educator*
†Connell, Diane Jacobs *education educator*
†La Salle, Cathy *education educator*
Mitsakos, Charles Leonidas *education educator, consultant*
†Sabin, Mihaela *education educator*

New Durham
†Wellman, Helen M. *administrative secretary*

New London
Mc Laughlin, David Thomas *academic administrator, business executive*
†Muyskens, Judith A. *academic administrator, dean, language educator*
Vulgamore, Melvin L. *retired college president*

Newmarket
Forcier-Delgadillo, Jennifer Libby *Spanish language educator*

North Haverhill
Brown, Susan Elizabeth S. *secondary school educator*
Charpentier, Keith Lionel *school system administrator*

Plaistow
Wilder, Dwight Safford *academic administrator*

Plymouth
Brook, Carol Ann *retired guidance director, school counselor*
†DeCotis, Ruth Janice *career planning administrator, educator*
†McCormack, Louise Samaha *education educator*

Rindge
Dangelantonio, Sarah Teresa *academic administrator, educator*

Rochester
Albert, Carole Annette *elementary school educator*

West Lebanon
Halperin, George Bennett *education educator, retired naval officer*
†Malik, Shazia Mumtaz *education educator, researcher*

Wilton
Potter, Robert Wallace, Jr., *educator*

NEW JERSEY

Allenhurst
Teicher, Henry Earl *retired education educator*

Asbury Park
Avella, John Thomas *educational administrator*

Atlantic City
Logan-Sutton, Floretta R. *educator*

Basking Ridge
Giglio, William Vito *secondary education educator*
Lachenauer, Robert Alvin *retired school superintendent*

Bayonne
Wanko, Michael Andrew *school system administrator*
Zuckerman, Nancy Carol *learning disabilities specialist, consultant*

Bayville
Kropinack, John Frank *secondary education educator*

Berkeley Heights
Older, Richard Samuel *elementary school music educator*

Bernardsville
Cooperman, Saul *educational administrator*
Robinson, Maureen Loretta *retired secondary school educator*

Salinger, Anthony Wilshire *educator, organization consultant*

Beverly
Taylor, Lyn Ann *principal*

Bloomfield
Rivera, Ruth Ellen *special services director*

Bogota
Oldenhage, Irene Dorothy *retired elementary school educator*

Bridgewater
Baldwin, Dorothy Leila *secondary school educator*
Ford, Frederic Hugh *secondary school educator*

Brigantine
Kickish, Margaret Elizabeth *elementary school educator*

Browns Mills
Di Nunzio, Dominick *educational administrator*

Caldwell
Ott, Walter Richard *academic administrator*
Werner, Patrice (Patricia Ann Werner) *college president*

Camden
†Beck, Susan J. *school librarian*
Gordon, Walter Kelly *retired provost, English language educator*
Lawrence, Francis Leo *university president, language educator*

Cherry Hill
Brenner, Lynnette Mary *reading specialist, educator*
Bryan, Henry Collier *clergyman, retired secondary school educator*
Rovner, Leonard Irving *education educator*

Chester
†Di Battista, Anthony Paul *secondary school educator*
Fluker, Jay Edward *middle school visual arts educator*

Clifton
Charsky, Thomas Robert *elementary education educator*
Giordano, Sandra L. *elementary school educator*

Cranford
†Vazquez, Felipe Miguel *educator*

Dover
Byrnes, Robert William *secondary school educator*

East Brunswick
Meningall, Evelyn L. *educational media specialist*

East Hanover
Tamburro, Peter James, Jr., *secondary school educator*

East Orange
Jones-Gregory, Patricia *secondary art educator*

East Windsor
†Orenstein, Fran M. *director, writer*

Edison
†Kushinsky, Jeanne Alice *SAT tutor*
Maeroff, Gene I. *academic administrator, journalist*
Robinson, Donald Warren *educator, artist*
Wolfthal, Michael Edward *director*

Egg Harbor Township
Sykes, Paula Marie *school counselor*

Elmwood Park
DeCondo, Anthony Paul, Sr., *elementary school educator*

Englewood
Glass, Janet Levine *primary and secondary education educator*

Ewing
Hamm, Claire Rose *development information services administrator*
†Meola, Marc *school librarian*

Fair Lawn
Aitchison, Suann *elementary school educator*
Wallace, Mary Monahan *elementary and secondary schools educator*

Fort Lee
Sugarman, Alan William *educational consultant, national speaker*

Frenchtown
Fogelson, Brian David *educational administrator*

Garfield
Kobylarz, Joseph Douglas *secondary education educator*

Glassboro
D'Augustine, Robert *university administrator, lawyer*
Davis, Ronald P. *secondary school administrator*
Gephardt, Donald Louis *university official*
Holdcraft, Janet Rulon *academic administrator*
James, Herman Delano *college administrator*
Margolis, Jeffrey Allen *program specialist*
†Walpole, MaryBeth *education educator*

Green Brook
Balsamello, Melissa (Marley) *educator*

Hackensack
Cicchelli, Joseph Vincent *principal*
Parisi, Cheryl Lynn *elementary school educator*

Hackettstown
†Grigsby, Byron Lee *dean*

Haddon Heights
Gwiazda, Stanley John *retired university dean*
†Weinberg, Ruthmarie Louise *special education educator, researcher*

Haledon
†Finkelstein, Ronald *assistant principal, director*

Hamburg
Kane, James Patrick *superintendent of schools*

Highland Park
†Feuerwerker, Elie *secondary school educator*

Highlands
†Lofstrom, Arlene Katherine *primary school educator*

Hoboken
†Hultin, Jerry MacArthur *dean, lawyer*
Moeller, Joseph John, Jr., *university official*
Raveché, Harold Joseph *university administrator, physical chemist*
Woodward, Holly Lowell *educator, writer*

Irvington
Alston, Goldie Venessa *early childhood educator*

Jackson
Carney, Rita J. *educational administrator*
Wedderman, Wayne Allan *elementary school educator*

Jersey City
Farrior, Evan Bell *special education educator, writer*
Miller, Adele Engelbrecht *educational administrator*
Shaik, Fatima *college official, writer*

Kenilworth
Fargey, Michael Andrew *special education educator*

Lakewood
Williams, Barbara Anne *college president emerita*

Lawrenceville
Leonard, Patricia Louise *education educator, consultant*
†Rozanski, Mordechai *academic administrator*
Stehle, Edward Raymond *secondary education educator, school system administrator*
Tharney, Leonard John *education educator, consultant*

Linden
Bedrick, Bernice *retired science educator, consultant*

Lindenwold
Kish, Elissa Anne *educational administrator, consultant*

Linwood
Sutman, Francis Xavier *university dean*

Little Falls
Blanton, Lawton Walter *retired dean*

Long Branch
Hecht, Patricia Layton *elementary school educator, writer, consultant*
Rassas, Beverly *educator, consultant*

Madison
Mertz, Francis James *university president*

Mahwah
Geiling, Louise Elizabeth *elementary school educator, secondary school educator*

Manalapan
Barratt, Donna Lee *elementary school educator*

Maple Shade
Bryant, Walter *secondary school educator*

Marlboro
†Francisco, Deborah Antosh *educational administrative professional*
Kayafas, Stephanie Ann *special education educator, consultant, supervisor, actress*

Marlton
Benjamin, Leni Bernice *elementary education educator*
Cheney, Eleanora Louise *retired secondary education educator*

Martinsville
†Raby, John Cornelius *secondary school educator*

Matawan
Liggett, Twila Marie Christensen *academic administrator, public television executive*

Medford
Kapfer, Miriam Bierbaum *technical documentation and training specialist*
Murphy, David Thomas *secondary school educator*

Mendham
Posunko, Barbara *retired elementary education educator*
Posunko, Linda Mary *retired elementary education educator*

Middletown
Shields, Patricia Lynn *educational broker, consultant*

Midland Park
Varallo, D. Vincent *educator*

Millville
†Bunting, John L. *counseling administrator, insurance agent*

Montclair
Cole, Susan A. *university president, English language educator*
Gregory, Maughn Rollins *education educator*
†Ju, Semmy *educational administrator*
Weischadle, David Emmanuel *education educator*

Mount Holly
†Mancini, Lois Jean *elementary education educator*

New Brunswick
Durnin, Richard Gerry *education educator*
Garner, Charles William *educational administration educator, consultant*
Henry, Paula Louise (Paula Louise Henry Coover) *academic administrator*
†Idler, Ellen Louise *education educator*
Jenkins, Alyce Mitchem *secondary school educator, writer*
Kansfield, Norman J. *seminary president*
Kantor, Paul *information scientist, educator*
McCormick, Richard Levis *academic administrator*
†Mears, David R. *education educator, consultant*
Miskiewicz, Susanne Piatek *educational administrator*
Nelson, Jack Lee *education educator*
†Nixon, Kenneth Elmer *academic administrator*
Paz, Harold Louis *dean, medical educator, internist*
Strickland, Dorothy *education educator*
Tanner, Daniel *curriculum theory educator*

New Milford
†Rosato, Melissa Anne *educator*

New Monmouth
Santos, Sharon Lee *parochial school educator*

Newark
Bergen, Stanley Silvers, Jr., *retired university president, physician*
Docarmo, Jerry Soares *academic administrator*
†Eljabiri, Osama M. *education educator, director*
Fenster, Saul K. *university president emeritus*
Flagg, E(loise) Alma Williams *educational administrator*
Givens, Theartis Tina Mansfield *primary school educator*
Hollander, Toby Edward *education educator*
Jackson, Nancy Lee *geography educator*
Joffe, Russell T. *dean*
Pfeffer, Edward Israel *educational administrator*
†Ryan, Lisa Kathleen *education educator, consultant*
Schachter, Hindy Lauer *public management educator*
Valyo, Judy Ann *dean*

Newton
Clymer, Jerry Alan *educational administrator*
Koerber, Joan C. *retired educator*
MacMurren, Margaret Patricia *secondary education educator, consultant*

North Arlington
Batshaw, Marilyn Seidner *education administrator*

North Brunswick
Kahrmann, Linda Irene *child care supervisor*

North Haledon
Onove, Daniel James *elementary educator*

Nutley
Bukovec, Joseph Aloysius *special education educator*

Oakland
Butterfield, Charles Edward, Jr., *educational consultant*

Oceanport
Meibauer, Amery Filippone *special education educator*

Old Tappan
Gaffin, Joan Valerie *secondary school educator*

Paramus
†Agresta, Anthony John *academic administrator, educational consultant, language educator*
†Hendel, Elisa Beth *special education educator, writer*
Younie, William John *special education educator, researcher*

Penns Grove
Graham, Albert Darlington, Jr., *educational administrator*

Pennsauken
Curry, Emma Beatrice *secondary education and college educator*

Piscataway
Cargill, Ursula Bardot *university official*
Colaizzi, John Louis *college dean*
Coppola, Sarah Jane *special education educator*
Dill, Ellis Harold *university dean*
†Epstein, Yakov M *education educator, psychologist*
Klein, Michael Tully *university dean, chemical engineer, consultant*
†Pae, Kook Dong *education educator*

Pitman
Lamey, Mary Cocove *elementary guidance counselor*
Lloyd, David Dilsworth Talbott *emeritus educator*

Plainfield
Montford, Claudian Hammond *retired gifted and talented education educator*
†Reeder, Hubert *elementary school educator*
Thomas, William Joseph *secondary school educator, administrator*

Pleasantville
London, Charlotte Isabella *secondary education educator, reading specialist*

Pomona
Colijn, Geert Jan *academic administrator, political scientist*
Comfort, Priscilla Maria *retired college official, human resources professional*
†Dagavarian-Bonar, Debra Aghavni *college administrator, consultant*

Princeton
Cooper, Michael R. *dean*
Gillespie, Thomas William *theological seminary administrator, religion educator*
Howarth, William (Louis Howarth) *education educator, writer*
Krulewicz, Rita Gloria *special education educator*
Lavizzo-Mourey, Risa Juanita *academic administrator, medical association administrator*
Malkiel, Nancy Weiss *dean, historian, educator*
Sandoval, Amada *education program director*
Shapiro, Harold Tafler *former academic administrator, economist*
Tilghman, Shirley Marie *academic administrator, biology educator*
Trussell, James *dean*

Randolph
Zulauf, Sander William *educator, poet*

Ridgefield Park
Finch, Carol Anne *former secondary education educator*

Rockaway
Allen, Dorothea *secondary education educator*

Roseland
Bolger, Mary Phyllis Judge *special education educator*

Roselle
Bizub, Barbara L. *elementary school educator*
Di Marco, Barbaranne Yanus *special education educator*

Roselle Park
Scarpelli, Vito *adult education educator, administrator*

Saddle River
Lehmann, Doris Elizabeth *elementary education educator*

Short Hills
Robbins-Wilf, Marcia *educational consultant*

Sicklerville
Miller, Audrey Thornton *retired educational administrator*

Skillman
Rhett, Haskell Emery Smith *educator*

Somerville
†Fesq, Jacqueline *education educator*

South Amboy
Moskal, Anthony John *former dean, professor, management and education consultant*

South Bound Brook
Simpson-Steeber, Marybeth *educator*

South Orange
†Deyrup, Marta Mestrovic *school librarian, writer*
Gokcekus, Omer *education educator*
Gruenwald, Renee *special education educator*
Hanbury, Kevin M. *dean, priest*
†Hu, Shouping *education educator*
Sheeran, Robert *academic administrator*

Stratford
Gallagher, R. Michael *academic administrator*

Summit
McGuire, Catherine Frances *elementary education educator*
Rossey, Paul William *school superintendent, university president*
Starks, Florence Elizabeth *retired special education educator*

Teaneck
Dewey, Ralph Jay *school system administrator*
Graham, Aaron Richard *school superintendent*
†Lewis, Karen Ann *director*
Mahoney, Maureen E. *retired secondary education educator*
Pischl, Adolph John *school administrator*
Smith, Susan Elizabeth *guidance director*
Walker, Lucy Doris *secondary school educator, writer*

Toms River
Moffet, Jane Humes *retired school principal*

Trenton
Mintz, Herman *adult education educator*
Pruitt, George Albert *college president*
Smallwood, Robert Albian, Jr., *secondary education educator*
Thurber, John Peter *academic administrator, lawyer*
Troyanovich, Stephen John *educational program director, poet*

Union
Lederman, Susan Sturc *public administration educator*
Lersch, Arthur David *director, educator*

Union City
Bull, Inez Stewart *special education, gifted music educator, coloratura soprano, pianist, editor, author, curator*
Makar, Nadia Eissa *secondary education educator, educational administrator*
Sheehy, Janice Ann *education technology coordinator*

Upper Montclair
Narrett, Carla Marie *university administrator*
Ververs, Beverly Joan *career development administrator*

Vernon
Megna, Steve Allan *secondary school educator*

Verona
Monacelli, Jeffrey Paul *elementary education educator*

Vineland
Vivarelli, Daniel George, Sr., *special education and learning disabilities educator, consultant*

Voorhees
Carter, Catherine Louise *retired elementary and middle school educator*

Waldwick
Greenberg, Rita Moffett *special education educator, consultant*
Lynch, Carol *director special services, psychologist*

Warren
Hennings, Dorothy Grant (Mrs. George Hennings) *education educator*

Washington
De Sanctis, Vincent *college president*

Wayne
Garcia, Ofelia *dean*
Lelyveld, David Simon *university administrator, historian*

West Long Branch
Bass, Mary Lee *education educator, administrator*
Gaffney, Paul Golden, II, *academic administrator, military officer*
Lutz, Francis Charles *university dean, civil engineering educator*
†Sarsar, Saliba *academic administrator*

West New York
Rosenberg, Raymond David *special education educator, consultant*

West Orange
Pollara, Joanne *learning disabilities educator consultant*

Westwood
Wright, Norman Albert, Jr., *middle school educator*

Willingboro
Denslow, Deborah Pierson *primary education educator*

Woodbridge
Paugh, Nancy Adele *elementary and secondary education educator*

Woodbury
Banks, Theresa Ann *retired elementary education educator*

Woodstown
†Rader, Jeanann Rose *secondary school educator*
Tatnall, Ann Weslager *reading educator*

NEW MEXICO

Alamogordo
Lee, Joli Fay Eaton *elementary education educator*
McFadin, Helen Lozetta *retired elementary education educator*

Albuquerque
Abraham, Karen A. *university administrator*
Anaya, Rudolfo *educator, writer*
†Betts, Dorothy Anne *elementary school educator*
†Brodeur, Helen Antionette *elementary school educator*
†Caldera, Louis Edward *academic administrator, former federal official*
Caplan, Edwin Harvey *university dean, accounting educator*
Edwards, Louise Wiseman *career counselor, educator*
Garcia, F. Chris *academic administrator, political science educator, public opinion researcher*

Floral Park
Ford, Donald Herbert *retired educator, consultant*

Flushing
Erickson, Raymond *music historian, musician*
Roberts, Kathleen Joy Doty *secondary education educator*
Swell, Lila *education educator*
†Totakura, Satyanarayana Raju *secondary school educator*

Frankfort
Conigilaro, Phyllis Ann *retired elementary education educator*

Franklinville
Kurzdorfer, Peter John *chess educator, writer, editor*

Fredonia
Collingwood, Tracy Lynn *career counselor*

Freeport
Burkett, Lloyd A. *secondary education educator and administrator, automotive engineer*
Martorana, Barbara Joan *secondary education educator*
†Walker, Lula Noriega *secondary administrator*

Fresh Meadows
†Castellano, Joseph P. *assistant principal*

Garden City
Gorin, Robert Murray, Jr., *history educator*
Scott, Robert Allyn *academic administrator*
Shuart, James Martin *retired academic administrator*
†Siegfried, Robert Michael *education educator*
†Snauwaert, Dale T. *education educator*
Webb, Igor Michael *academic administrator*

Geneva
Best, Sharon Louise Peckham *college administrator*
†Stranahan, Patricia *dean*

Grand Island
Kutlina, Mary Louise *elementary education educator*
Schultz, Susan Marie *special education administrator*

Great Neck
Fried, Belle Warshavsky *education educator*
Gross, Beatrice Schaap *education educator, consultant, writer*
Hecht, Marie Bergenfeld *retired educator, author*

Greenport
†Monsell, Thomas Oliver *secondary English educator, writer*

Greenvale
†Maillet, Lucienne *educator*
Megay-Nespoli, Karen Patricia *elementary school educator*
Shenker, Joseph *academic administrator*
Steinberg, David Joel *academic administrator, historian, educator*
Westermann-Cicio, Mary Louise *academic administrator, library studies educator*

Greenwood
Rollins, June Elizabeth *elementary education educator*

Hamburg
Witt, Dennis Ruppert *secondary school mathematics educator*

Hamilton
Chopp, Rebecca S. *university president*
Jones, Howard Langworthy *retired educational administrator, consultant*
Karelis, Charles Howard *former academic administrator*

Harrison
Northcutt, Marie Rose *educator*

Hartsdale
Aker, Susan K. *elementary education educator*

Hempstead
Berliner, Herman Albert *university provost and officer, economics educator*
Gold, Ruth Forman *education educator*

Hicksville
Moshoyannis, Phillip Demetri Alexander *educator*

Highland Mills
Gazzaniga, Antonette J. *secondary school educator*

Himrod
Preska, Margaret Louise Robinson *education historian, administrator*

Holbrook
Watkins, Linda Theresa *educational researcher*

Holland
Loockerman, William Delmer *educational administrator, retired*

Honeoye
Blackmer, Sally *secondary education educator*

Houghton
Chamberlain, Daniel Robert *college president*
Luckey, Robert Reuel Raphael *retired academic administrator*

Howard Beach
Iorio, John Emil *retired education educator*
Watnick, Rochelle *principal*

Hudson
Vile, Sandra Jane *leadership training educator*

Huntington
D'Addario, Alice Marie *school administrator*

Huntington Station
Boxwill, Helen Ann *primary and secondary education educator*
Devlin, Jean Theresa *educator, storyteller*

Hurley
Opdahl, Viola Elizabeth *secondary education educator*

Inwood
Soffer, Grace Florey *retired elementary school educator, artist*

Ithaca
Ben Daniel, David Jacob *entrepreneurship educator, consultant*
Firebaugh, Francille Maloch *university official*
†Gockley, Daniel L. *academic administrator*
Green, Edward Thomas, Jr., *education educator*
Halpern, Bruce Peter *academic administrator, researcher, educator*
Lehman, Jeffrey Sean *college president, educator*
†Lovelace, Richard Van Evera *education educator, research scientist*
McCarroll, Earl *educator, director*
Michael, M. Todd *university educator*
Nesheim, Malden C. *academic administrator, nutrition educator*
Rawlings, Hunter Ripley, III, *academic administrator, classicist*
Rhodes, Frank Harold Trevor *university president emeritus, geologist*
Sass, Stephen Louis *education educator*
Scott, Norman Roy *academic administrator, agricultural engineering educator*
Seibert, Mary Lee *college official*
†Smith, Donald F. *dean*
Streett, William Bernard *retired university dean, engineering educator*
Swieringa, Robert Jay *dean, accountant, educator*
Wavle, Elizabeth Margaret *college official*
Weinstein, Leonard Harlan *institute program director, educator*

Jackson Heights
†Gall, Lenore Rosalie *educational administrator*

Jamaica
Cline, Janice Claire *education educator*
Davis-Jerome, Eileen George *principal, educational consultant*
Delener, Nejdet *college dean, marketing and international business educator*
Faust, Naomi Flowe *education educator, poet*
Harrington, Donald James *university president*
Mangru, Basdeo *secondary education educator*
†Nedwek, Brian *director, consultant*
Sciame, Joseph *university administrator*
†Skirde, Edward George *academic administrator, consultant*

Jeffersonville
†Hoering, Helen G. *elementary educator*

Johnson City
Kopuz, Kasim *educator, consultant*

Kendall
Rak, Linda Marie *elementary education educator, consultant*

Kings Point
†Mazek, Warren F(elix) *academic administrator, economics educator*

Krumville
Nagi, Catherine Raseh *retired educational administrator, financial planner*
†Schuckman, Nancy Lee *retired principal*

Lake Placid
Reiss, Paul Jacob *college president*

Lake Ronkonkoma
Spahr, Clinton S., Jr., *retired elementary education educator*

Lancaster
Kappan, Sandra Jean *elementary education educator*

Latham
McGoldrick, William Patrick *educational consultant*

Lawrence
†Press, Marlyn Rothman *special education educator*

Levittown
Schettino, Maria Carmen *preschool educator*

Lewiston
Presutti, Robert Michael *secondary education educator*
Shimer, Alice Marie *retired educator*

Lido Beach
†Shear, Richard Gary *education administrator*

Lindenhurst
Sanna, Catherine Lee *special education educator*

Liverpool
Williams, John Alan *secondary education educator, coach*

Lockport
March, Cathleen Case *education educator*

Locust Valley
Mathews, Walter Michael *educational consultant*

Long Beach
Thompson, Dorothy Barnard *elementary school educator*

Loudonville
Toal, James Francis *academic administrator*

Malverne
†Alesse, Judith *special education educator*

Mamaroneck
†Feigin, Nancy J. *guidance counselor*

Manhasset
†Lankevich, George J. *history, writer*

Marcy
Rishel, Kenn Charles *school superintendent*

Massapequa
Kurtz, Judith Marsha *elementary education educator*
McCann, Susan Lynn *elementary education educator*

Mastic Beach
Pagano, Alicia I. *education educator*

Medford
Haig, Monica Elaine Nachajski *special education educator*

Melville
Atkins, William Allen *academic administrator*

Merrick
Auteri, Rose Mary Patti *school system administrator*
Garfinkel, Lawrence Saul *academic administrator, educator, television producer*

Middle Island
Sanfilippo, Stephen Nicholas *educator*

Middletown
McCord, Jean Ellen *secondary art educator, coach*
Moore, Virginia Lee Smith *elementary education educator*

Millwood
Durst, Carol Goldsmith *educator*

Monsey
Schaefer, Rhoda Pesner *elementary school educator*

Montrose
Matthias, George Frank *retired educator*

Nanuet
Miney, Maureen Elizabeth *middle school educator*

New Kingston
St. George, Joyce *conflict and crisis management educator, writer*

New Paltz
Edwards, Peter *educator, writer*
Emanuel-Smith, Robin Lesley *special education educator*
Flanagan Kelly, Anne Marie *academic administrator*

New Rochelle
Cohen, Saul Bernard *former college president, geographer*
Conte, Susan *secondary school counselor*
Donahue, Richard James *secondary school educator*
Gallagher, John Francis *education educator*
†Reddington, Mary Jane *retired secondary school educator*
Sweeny, Stephen Jude *academic administrator*

New York
Alfano, Michael Charles *dental school dean*
Arndt, Cynthia *educational administrator*
Barber, Benjamin R. *director, educator*
Barron, Marlene *education educator*
†Benhabib, Jess *adult education educator*
Bloomgarden, Karenne Jo *elementary special education educator, company president*
Bollinger, Lee Carroll *academic administrator, law educator*
†Brown, Joyce F. *academic administrator*
Buckley, Robert John *academic research administrator*
Budig, Gene Arthur *former chancellor, professional sports executive*
†Burns, Red *academic administrator*
Burton, John Campbell *university dean, educator, consultant*
Caputo, David Armand *university president, political scientist educator*
Charendoff, Mark Stuart *educator*
Claster, Jill Nadell *university administrator, history educator*
Cochran, Raymond Martin *university auditor*
Cohen, Steven Alan *program director*
Consagra, Sophie Chandler *academy administrator*
Daly, George Garman *college dean, educator*
†Damianakos, Phaedra Vasiliki *secondary school educator*
†Davidson, Anthony R. *education educator, consultant*
Denes, Ronni Carol *academic administrator*
Dimino, Sylvia Theresa *elementary and secondary educator*
Dobrinsky, Herbert Colman *university administrator*
Durkin, Dorothy Angela *university official*
Elster, Samuel Kase *college dean, medical educator, physician*
Essandoh, Hilda Brathwaite *kindergarten educator*
Etzkowitz, Henry *educator, consultant*
Fabian, Larry Louis *university administrator*
Feldberg, Meyer *university dean*
Finegold, Amy Beth *elementary school educator, consultant*
†Fraiman, Nelson *educator*
Gatto, John Taylor *educational consultant, writer, speaker*
Gerety, Tom *academic administrator, lawyer, educator, philosopher*
Giblin, Jean-Ellen Dorsey *university administrator, economics educator*
Gillespie, John Thomas *university administrator*
Goldstein, Matthew *academic administrator*
†Gorelick, Steven Michael *academic administrator, writer*
Gottschalk, Alfred *retired college chancellor, museum executive*
Grant, Sonia Vivienne *secondary school educator*
†Guttmacher, Sally Jeanne *education educator*
Haffner, Alden Norman *university official*
Hayes, Joyce Merriweather *secondary education educator*
Herter, Frederic Pratt *university administrator*
Hoffner, Marilyn *university administrator*
†Hood, Donald Charles *university administrator, psychology educator*
Horowitz, Frances Degen *academic administrator, psychology educator*
Howard, David *educational administrator*
Huppauf, Bernd Rudiger *educator*
Ilchman, Warren Frederick *university administrator, foundation director, educator*
Jelinek, Vera *university director*
Jeynes, Mary Kay *college dean*
†Joel, Richard Marc *academic administrator, law educator, dean*
Kampel, Donne *academic administrator, educator*
Kastan, David Scott *university educator, writer*
†Kelley, Robin D. G. *education educator, writer*
Kerrey, Bob (J. Robert Kerrey) *academic administrator, former senator*
King, Kathleen Palombo *adult education educator, consultant*
Konner, Joan Weiner *university administrator, educator, publisher, broadcasting executive, television producer*
Koshi, Annie K. *education educator, researcher*
Kozlowski, Cheryl M. *principal*
†Kurman, Juta *educator*
Lamm, Norman *academic administrator, rabbi*
Lange, Phil C. *retired education educator*
†Lao, Joseph R. *education educator, researcher*
Laruccia, Stephen Dominic *university official*
†Leebron, David Wayne *dean, law educator*
Levine, Naomi Bronheim *academic administrator*
Little, Nancy Jane *art school director*
Lloyd, Jean *early childhood educator*
Lynch, Gerald Weldon *academic administrator, psychologist*
Macchiarola, Frank Joseph *academic administrator, educator*
Marcuse, Adrian Gregory *academic administrator*
Marks, Lillian Shapiro *secretarial studies educator, author*
†Maurrasse, David J. *educator, consultant*
Melnick, Ralph *library director, secondary school educator,*
†Mills, Barry *academic administrator, lawyer*
Mitterand, Henri C. *education educator, writer*
†Mora, Raimundo *academic administrator, educator*
Morgan, Arlene Notoro *university administrator*
Morreale, Joseph Constantino *higher education administrator, public administration educator, economic and financial consultant*
Nelson, Iris Dorothy *retired guidance and rehabilitation counselor*
Nurse, Sir Paul M. *academic administrator*
Oliva, Lawrence Jay *former academic administrator, history educator*
Oreskes, Susan *private school educator*
Palmeri, Marlaina *school executive*
Pawliczko, George Ihor *academic administrator*
†Perelman, Michael A *education educator, psychologist*
Polisi, Joseph W(illiam) *academic administrator*
Prager, Leslie Beth *career counselor*
†Prutzman, Penelope Elizabeth *educator*
Pulanco, Tonya Beth *special education educator*
Reutter, Eberhard Edmund, Jr., *education and law educator*
Robinson, Joyce McPeake *administrator*
Rosensaft, Jean Bloch *university administrator*
Rowland, Esther E(delman) *retired college dean*
Rubino, Victor Joseph *academic administrator, lawyer*
Rudenstine, Neil Leon *former academic administrator, educator*
Rupp, George Erik *not-for-profit administrator*
Scaffidi, Judith Ann *academic administrator*
Seidenberg, Rita Nagler *education educator*
Seitz, Frederick *former university administrator*
Selby, Cecily Cannan *dean, educator, scientist*
Sexton, John Edward *academic administrator, law educator*
Shapiro, Judith R. *academic administrator, anthropology educator*
Shaver, Judson Rayford *academic administrator*
Shields, James Joseph *education administrator, educator, author*
Silverman, Martin Morris Bernard *secondary education educator*
Socol, Sheldon Eleazer *university official*
Takamura, Jeanette Chiyoko *dean*
†Tschumi, Bernard *dean*

Magill, Samuel Hays *academic administrator, higher education consultant*
†McCoy, William O. *former academic administrator, retired telecommunications executive*
Mc Kean, John Rosseel Overton *university dean*
Moeser, James Charles *university chancellor, musician*
Nord, Warren Allen *university official*
†Pardun, Carol J *education educator*
Roper, William Lee *dean, physician*
Satterfield, John Roberts, Jr., *retired college president and music educator*

Charlotte
†Bobbitt, Warren Leslie, Sr., *director*
†Bradley, Dana Burr *education educator, consultant*
Colvard, Dean Wallace *emeritus university chancellor*
Eppley, Frances Fielden *retired secondary education educator, author*
Fretwell, Elbert K., Jr., *retired university chancellor, consultant*
†Mercer, Evelyn Lois *retired guidance counselor*
Payne, Ronald Dean *secondary school educator, music educator* *
Phillips, Sandra Allen *retired primary school educator*
Stephens, Kitty Frances *academic administrator*
Tyson, Cynthia Haldenby *academic administrator*
Woodward, James Hoyt *academic administrator, engineer*
†Yancy, Dorothy Cowser *academic administrator*

Clayton
Jenkins, Elaine Parker *secondary school educator*

Clyde
Rogers, Frances Nichols *assistant principal*

Conover
Sims, Janette Elizabeth Lowman *educational director*

Cramerton
†Kim, Paul DongUk *academic administrator, religious organization administrator, minister*

Cullowhee
†Bardo, John William *university administrator*
Coulter, Myron Lee *retired academic administrator*
Reed, Alfred Douglas *retired academic administrator*

Davidson
Spencer, Samuel Reid, Jr., *education consultant, former university president*
†Vagt, Robert F. *academic administrator*

Dobson
Smith, Richard Jackson *elementary education educator*

Dunn
Overton, Elizabeth Nicole *elementary school educator, aerobics instructor*

Durham
Dowell, Earl Hugh *university dean, aerospace and mechanical engineering educator*
Feaver, Peter Douglas *political science educator, consultant, defense analyst*
†Gaines, Roland H. *academic administrator*
†Grocott, Hilary Peter *adult education educator*
Huestis, Charles Benjamin *former academic administrator*
†Jeffreys, Arcelia Taylor *education educator*
Keller, Thomas Franklin *business administration educator*
Keohane, Nannerl Overholser *university president, political scientist*
Kuniholm, Bruce Robellet *university administrator*
O'Briant, Margaret Denny *retired elementary school educator*
Schmalbeck, Richard Louis *university dean, lawyer*
†Takahashi, Toku *education educator, researcher*
†Wescott, Joseph Warren, II, *academic administrator, education educator*
Williams, R. Sanders *dean, academic administrator, educator, researcher*

Elizabeth City
White, Leon Samuel *college administrator*

Elon College
Tolley, Jerry Russell *university administrator*

Fayetteville
Friedman, Deborah Leslie White *educational administrator*
Jordan, Karla Salge *early childhood education educator*
Watt, Willis Martin *academic administrator, communications, adult education, leadership educator*

Gibsonville
Crawford, Kathrine Nelson *special education educator*

Greensboro
Baldwin, Jason Holt *secondary school educator*
†Bynum, Magnolia Virginia Wright *retired secondary school educator*
Cole, Johnnetta Betsch *university president, educator*
Felts, John Winfred, Jr., *school librarian, educator*
Godard, Jerry Holton Caris *psychology educator, college dean*
†Hayes, Robert Banks, II, *assistant principal*

Miller, Robert Louis *university dean, chemistry educator*
Moran, William Edward *academic administrator*
Sullivan, Patricia A. *academic administrator*

Greenville
Bearden, James Hudson *university official*
Eakin, Richard Ronald *academic educator, mathematics educator*
Howell, John McDade *retired university chancellor, political science educator*
Kragel, Peter J. *academic administrator*
Leggett, Donald Yates *academic administrator*
Leggett, Nancy Porter *university administrator*
†Lewis, Nell J. *director, consultant*
Muse, William Van *academic administrator*
Stuart, Andrew Michael *educator*
Thompson, Robert Joseph *university administrator, educator*

Hendersonville
Payne, Gerald Oliver *retired elementary education educator*

High Point
Howard, Lou Dean Graham *elementary education educator*
Martinson, Jacob Christian, Jr., *academic administrator*

Kannapolis
Whitley, Walter Ralph *educator*

Kernersville
Litton, Daphne Napier Rudhman *special education educator*

Kinston
Petteway, Samuel Bruce *college president*
Scott, Stephen Carlos *academic administrator*

Lake Junaluska
Stanton, Donald Sheldon *academic administrator*

Laurinburg
Deegan, John, Jr., *academic administrator, researcher*

Monroe
Rorie, Nancy Catherine *retired elementary and secondary school educator*

Mount Airy
Short, Linda Matthews *retired elementary education educator*

Mount Olive
Raper, William Burkette *retired college president*

Murfreesboro
Whitaker, Bruce Ezell *college president*

Pembroke
Meadors, Allen Coats *health administrator, educator*

Raleigh
Baker, Stanley Beckwith *education educator*
†Bruck, Robert Ian *education educator*
Burris, Craven Allen *retired college administrator, educator*
Dolce, Carl John *education administration educator*
Dornan, John Neill *public policy center professional*
Fletcher, Oscar Jasper, Jr., *college dean*
Howell, Bruce Inman *academic administrator*
Jarrett, Polly Hawkins *secondary education educator, retired*
Mac Cormac, Earl Ronald *retired education educator*
Maidon, Carolyn Howser *teacher education director*
Page, Anne Ruth *gifted education educator, education specialist*
Parramore, Barbara Mitchell *education educator*
Penick, John E. *education educator*
Robinson, Prezell Russell *academic administrator*
Sardi, Elaine Marie *special education educator*
Shaw, Talbert O. *university president*
Steed, Michelle Elnora *special education educator, counselor*
Winstead, Nash Nicks *university administrator, phytopathologist*

Salisbury
†Freeman, Algeania Warren *academic administrator*
Hall, Telka Mowery Elium *retired educational administrator*

Sanford
York, Carolyn Pleasants Stearns *English educator*

Shelby
Edgar, Ruth R. *retired educator*

Smithfield
Wiggs, Shirley JoAnn *retired secondary school educator*

Southern Pines
Kaufmann, Rachel Norsworthy *educator*

Spruce Pine
Rensink, Jacqueline Biddix *secondary school educator*

Taylorsville
Leonhardt, Debbie Ann *counselor, writer, minister*

Wake Forest
Buchanan, Edward A. *education educator*

Washington
Alligood, Lola Jane Lurvey *retired educator*

Waynesville
Carpenter, Margaret Mary *state legislator, information technology manager*

Whiteville
Godwin, Kipling Eliga *academic administrator*

Williamston
†Mobley, Jackie *elementary school educator*

Wilmington
†DePaolo, Rosemary *dean, academic administrator*
Rorison, Margaret Lippitt *reading consultant*
†Wiseman, Cindy R. *education educator*

Winston Salem
Brown, David G. *academic administrator*
Crowder, Lena Belle *retired special education educator*
Gordon, William Charles *college administrator*
Harris, Frederick Holladay deBrosche *business educator*
Hearn, Thomas K., Jr., *university president*
Hobgood, E(arl) Wade *college chancellor*
†Horne, Aaron *academic administrator*
Jarrell, Iris Bonds *elementary school educator, business executive*
†Linster, Michelle Lynn *education educator, consultant*
Roth, Marjory Joan Jarboe *special education educator*
Schexnider, Alvin J. *academic administrator*
Suttles, Donald Roland *retired academic administrator, business educator*
Thrift, Julianne Still *academic administrator*
Volz, Annabelle Wekar *learning disabilities educator, consultant*
Williams, Frances Elizabeth *retired secondary education educator*
Zubov, Lynn *special education educator, researcher*

NORTH DAKOTA

Beulah
Maize, Linda Lou *elementary education educator*

Bismarck
Barrett, Carole A. *American Indian studies educator*
Evanson, Barbara Jean *middle school education educator*
†Joersz, Fran Woodmansee *secondary education educator*
Sanstead, Wayne Godfrey *school system administrator*

Devils Lake
Tande, Teresa Lyn *secondary educator*

Dickinson
†Medlar, Deborah Starkey *secondary school educator*

Ellendale
Schlieve, Hy C. J. *school administrator*

Fargo
Sanford, Glenda Levonne *educational administrator*

Glenfield
Spickler, JoAnn Dorothy *secondary education educator*

Grand Forks
†Alfonso, Peter J. *educator*
Ashe, Kathy Rae *special education educator*
†Aune, Adonica Schultz *education educator, consultant*
†Kupchella, Charles Edward *academic administrator, author, educator*
Wilson, H. David *dean*

Mandan
Novak, Laura J. *secondary school educator*

Minot
Jermiason, John Lynn *elementary school educator, farmer, rancher*
Shaar, H. Erik *academic administrator*

West Fargo
Boutiette, Vickie Lynn *educator, reading specialist*

OHIO

Ada
Baker, Kendall L. *academic administrator*
Freed, DeBow *college president*

Akron
†Akhigbe, Aigbe *education educator, researcher*
Auburn, Norman Paul *university president*
Barker, Harold Kenneth *former university dean*
Buzzelli, Charlotte Grace *educator*
†Davis, Theresa Mary *education educator, artist*
Dietz, Margaret Jane *retired public information director*
†Duan, Zhong-Hui *education educator, researcher*
†Jana, Sadhan C *education educator, researcher*
Ruebel, Marion A. *university president*

Amherst
†Gerstenberger, Valerie *media coordinator*

Andover
Mathay, John Preston *elementary education educator*

Ashland
†Baker, David Weston *education educator*
Kerr, Margaret Ann *elementary education educator*
Shelly, Ann Converse *education educator, administrator*
†Suggs, Robert Chinello *academic administrator, educator*

Athens
Bruning, James Leon *academic administrator, educator*
Bugeja, Michael Joseph *educator, writer*
Glidden, Robert Burr *academic administrator, musician, educator*
†Mantione, Meryl E. *director, education educator*
Neiman, Gary S. *university administrator*
†Tymas-Jones, Raymond *dean*
†Van Hook, Cheryl W. *education educator*

Austintown
Kope, Joseph B. *retired humanities educator, consultant*

Avon
Smolen, Cheryl Hosaka *special education educator*

Avon Lake
Mick, Deborah West Fairchild *elementary education educator*

Batavia
Muskopf, Beth A. *curriculum consultant*
Nichols, Marci Lynne *gifted education coordinator, educator, consultant*

Bath
Bowman-Dalton, Burdene Kathryn *education testing coordinator, computer consultant*

Bay Village
Woods, Dennis Craig *school superintendent*

Bedford
Hodakievic, James Joseph *retired secondary education educator*

Bergholz
Goddard, Sandra Kay *elementary education educator*
McElwain, Edwina Jay *retired elementary school educator*

Bexley
Beller, Stephen Mark *university administrator*

Bowling Green
Dobb, Linda Sue *university official, librarian*
Zwierlein, Ronald Edward *athletics director*

Broadview Heights
Jergens, Maribeth Joie *school counselor*

Brunswick
Zahs, David Karl *secondary school educator, educational administrator*

Bryan
Stevens, Muriel Kay *elementary educator*

Cedarville
†Dugle, Vivian Rachelle *education educator*

Centerville
Geier, Sharon Lee *special education educator*

Chagrin Falls
Brown, Jeanette Grasselli *retired university official*

Chillicothe
Atwood, Joyce Charlene *curriculum and instruction administrator, consultant*
Leedy, Emily L. Foster (Mrs. William N. Leedy) *retired education educator, consultant*

Cincinnati
Ashley, Lynn *educator, consultant, administrator*
Backherms, Kathryn Anne *parochial school educator*
Barton, Keith Casey *college educator*
Boothe, Leon Estel *academic administrator emeritus, consultant*
Briggs, Henry Payson, Jr., *headmaster*
†Dionysiou, Dionysios Demetriou *adult education educator, researcher*
Fischer, Patricia Ann *middle school educator*
Greengus, Samuel *academic administrator, religion educator*
Harrison, Donald Carey *university official, cardiology educator*
Hess, Marcia Wanda *retired educator*
†Jin, Li *education educator*
†Johnson, Betty Lou *secondary education educator*
Kamp, Cynthia Lea *elementary education educator*
Kelz, Rochelle Shelle K. *academic administrator*
Kohl, David *dean,emeritus librarian*
Martin, William J., II, *academic administrator*
†McFarlan, Rebecca Collins *secondary school educator, consultant*
Morrow, Ardythe Luxion *adult education educator, researcher*
Nester, William Raymond, Jr., *retired academic administrator and educator*
Smith, Gregory Allgire *college administrator*
Steger, Joseph A. *university president*
Sturwold, Sister Rita Mary *educational administrator*
Tomain, Joseph Patrick *dean, law educator*

Winkler, Henry Ralph *retired academic administrator, historian*
Zimpher, Nancy Lusk *academic administrator*

Circleville
†McGuire, James Kavanaugh *education and history educator*

Cleveland
Ainsworth, Joan Horsburgh *university development director*
Berger, Nathan Allen *academic administrator*
†Cavanagh, Peter Robert *academic administrator, department chairman, science educator, researcher*
Goldberg, Jerold S. *dean*
†Grabowski, John Joseph *education educator, researcher*
†Hansman, Catherine Ann *adult education educator, researcher*
†Hundert, Edward M. *academic administrator*
†Jaffe, Marcia Weissman *elementary education educator*
Johnson, Victoria Houston *elementary school educator, poet*
Kay, Irene Pramisloff *school system administrator*
Kennedy, Frederick Morgan *retired secondary school educator*
McArdle, Richard Joseph *academic administrator, retired*
McCullough, Joseph *college president emeritus*
Neal, Bennie F. *secondary school administrator*
Nickerson, Gary Lee *secondary education educator*
Parker, Robert Frederic *university dean emeritus*
Queen, Joyce Ellen *elementary school educator*
Quigney, Theresa Ann *special education educator*
Sabik, Joseph Andrew *psychometrist, counselor*
Schmidt, Patricia Jean *special education educator*
†Smith, Beverly Harriett *elementary school educator*
Smith, Mieko Kotake *education educator*
Spicer, Michael William *university educator*
Thomas, Faye Evelyn J. *elementary and secondary school educator*
Weidenthal, Maurice David (Bud Weidenthal) *educational administrator, journalist*
Wykle, May L. *dean, educator, researcher*

Columbia Station
Goll, Paulette Susan *education educator*

Columbus
†Alexander, Rudolph *education educator*
†Antony, Louise Marie *education educator*
Armes, Walter Scott *vocational school administrator*
†Barsky, Constance Kay *education educator*
Blankenship, Dolores Moorefield *principal, music educator, retired*
Cole, Clarence Russell *college dean*
Culbertson, Jack Arthur *education educator*
Evans, David Charles *retired elementary school educator*
Hart, Mildred *retired counselor*
Heinlen, Daniel Lee *alumni organization administrator*
Heron, Timothy Edward *special education educator, consultant*
†Hoffsis, Glen F. *dean*
Jackson, John Charles *retired secondary education educator, writer*
†Kerns, Allen Franklin *education educator*
Koenigsknecht, Roy A. *education administrator*
†Kozobarich, Jeri L. *director*
Kronmiller, Jan E. *academic administrator*
†Lee, Robert J. *education educator, consultant*
Leitzel, Joan Ruth *university president emerita*
Magliocca, Larry Anthony *education educator*
Mathis, Lois Reno *retired elementary education educator*
McCracken, John David *education educator*
Meuser, Fredrick William *retired seminary president, church historian*
Miller, Wayne Clayton *student services administrator, notary public*
†O'Hanlon, Nancyanne *school librarian, educator*
Otte, Paul John *academic administrator, consultant, trainer*
Oxley, Margaret Carolyn Stewart *elementary education educator*
Rezin, Andrew Anthony *academic administrator, educator*
Riedinger, Edward Anthony (Ted Riedinger) *international educator, Brazilianist*
Ritchey, Kenneth William *administrator*
Stephens, Thomas M(aron) *education educator*
Stewart, Mac A. *educator*
†Stull, Gary Evan *secondary school educator, writer*
Warmbrod, Catharine Phelps *educational researcher, consultant*
Willke, Thomas Aloys *university official, statistics educator*

Copley
Cox, Hillery Lee *retired primary school educator*

Cuyahoga Falls
Harr, Jeffrey Alan *secondary school educator*

Dayton
Allen, Rose Letitia *special education educator*
Calico, Robert A. *dean*
Carter, Harold Lloyd *secondary education educator*
Crowe, Shelby *educational specialist, consultant*
Goldenberg, Kim *academic administrator, internist*
Lasley, Thomas J., II, *education educator*
Part, Howard M. *dean*
Ponitz, David H. *former academic administrator*
Taylor, Elisabeth Coler *retired secondary school educator*

Uphoff, James Kent *education educator*
Wagner, Samuel, V, *secondary school English language educator, college counselor*
Welly, Michael Anthony *elementary school educator*
Williams, Charles Vernon, III, *education administrator*
†Zhan, Qiwen *education educator, consultant*

Delaware
Courtice, Thomas Barr *academic administrator*
Pettigrew, Carolyn Landers *theological school official, minister*

Delta
Miller, Beverly White *past college president, education consultation*

Dublin
Bordelon, Carolyn Thew *elementary school educator*
Conrad, Marian Sue (Susan Conrad) *special education educator*

East Palestine
Patterson, Paula Jeanne *secondary education educator*

Euclid
Keay, Charles Lloyd *elementary school educator*
†Powaski, Ronald E. *education educator, writer*

Fairborn
Russell-Rader, Kathleen *secondary school educator*

Fairview Park
†Flynn, Patricia M. *director, special education educator, gifted and talented educator*

Findlay
Norris, Neal Albert *academic administrator*

Franklin
Foley, Harriet Elizabeth *retired school librarian*

Gambier
†Nugent, S. Georgia *academic administrator*

Garfield Heights
Chamberlin, Joan Mary *school system administrator*

Gates Mills
Altman, Leslie Joan *secondary school educator*
O'Malley, Mary Kay *elementary education educator*

Hamilton
Royer, Diana Amelia *educator*

Highland Hills
†Sender, Maryann *director*

Hiram
Oliver, G(eorge) Benjamin *educational administrator, philosophy educator*

Hudson
Goheen, Janet Moore *counselor, sales professional*

Ironton
†Crawford, James G. *director*
†Curry, Estella Roberta *education educator, consultant*

Kent
Buttlar, Rudolph Otto *retired college dean*
Gaston, Paul Lee *academic administrator, language educator*
†Lilly, Erica Barditch *academic librarian*
†McCormick, Edgar Lindsley *education educator, writer*
†Odell-Scott, David Winfield *education educator*

Kettering
Collins, Jo Anne Dilworth *secondary school educator*
Denlinger, Vicki Lee *secondary school physical education educator*
Hoffman, Sue Ellen *elementary education educator*
Martin, Margaret Gately *elementary school educator*

Lakewood
†Pecot, Mark Andre *education educator*

Lancaster
†Young, Paul Garlin *principal*

Lewis Center
Strip, Carol Ann *gifted education specialist, educator*

Lorain
Brownson, Roger James *university official, photographer*
†Comer, Brenda Warmee *educator, real estate company executive*
Trelka, Janice Margaret Nace *retired secondary school educator*

Maineville
Cook, Janice Eleanor Nolan *retired elementary school educator*

Mansfield
Ash, Thomas Phillip *superintendent of schools*
Gregory, Deirdre Dianne *secondary educator*
Riedl, John Orth *university dean*

Marietta
Montgomery, Jerry Lynn *retired education educator*

Marion
Badertscher, Doris Rae *elementary education educator*

Mechanicsburg
Maynard, Joan *education educator*

Medina
†DeMars, Judith M. *elementary educator*
Feola, David Craig *secondary school administrator*
Graham, Stanley Belding *retired secondary school educator, writer*
Hunter, Brinca Jo *education specialist*
†Ilg, Christopher Paul *secondary school educator, music educator*
†Neiman, Marcus Lawrence *educational consultant*

Middleburg Heights
Molnar, Bela *school administrator*

Middletown
Ewers, James Benjamin, Jr., *director*

Millersburg
Yoder, Anna A. *elementary school educator*

Mogadore
Kelly, Janice Helen *elementary school educator*

Moreland Hills
Hardie, James Carl *college administrator, consultant*

Mount Vernon
Bennett, Marguerite Hildreth *college administrator, mathematics educator*
Shriver, William Russell *secondary education educator*

Munroe Falls
†Clawson, Judith Louise *middle school educator*

New Bremen
Wierwille, Marsha Louise *elementary education educator*

New Matamoras
Brown, Blanche Y. *secondary education educator, genealogy researcher*

New Philadelphia
Doughten, Mary Katherine (Molly Doughten) *retired secondary education educator*
Goforth, Mary Elaine Davey *secondary education educator*

New Washington
†Blum, Joseph R. *secondary school educator, emergency nurse practitioner*

Newark
Paul, Rochelle Carole *special education educator*
†Simpson, Linda Sue *elementary educator*
Van Dervort, Sharyn L. *secondary education educator*

North Olmsted
†Schuttenberg, Ernest M. *education educator*

Norton
Kun, Joyce Anne *secondary education educator, small business owner*

Norwood
Tubbs, Robin Lee *secondary education educator*

Oberlin
Brown, John Lott *educator*
Dye, Nancy Schrom *academic administrator, historian, educator*
MacKay, Alfred F. *dean, philosophy educator*
MacKay, Gladys Godfrey *adult education educator*

Oregon
Crain, John Kip *school system administrator*

Orrville
†Hennell, Robert William, III, *secondary school educator*
Warner, Patricia Ann *secondary school educator*

Orwell
†Strong, Marcella Lee *music specialist, educator*

Oxford
Shriver, Phillip Raymond *academic administrator*
Thompson, Bertha Boya *retired education educator, antique dealer and appraiser*

Painesville
Blyth, Ann Marie *secondary education educator*
Davis, Barbara Snell *college educator*
†Sachwartz, David Allen *secondary school educator*

Parma
Hall, Clara Jean *special education educator*
†Scheffel, Donna Jean *elementary school educator*
Shirey, Connie Mae *secondary school educator*
Tener, Carol Joan *retired secondary education educator*

Patriot
Riggle, Patricia Carol *special education educator*

Pickerington
Collins, Arlene *secondary education educator*
Young, Glenna Asche *elementary education educator*

Plymouth
†Hartman, Ruth Campbell *educator*

Port Clinton
Randels, David George *secondary school educator*

Portsmouth
†Johnson, Janice E *education educator, writer*
Turner, Elvin L. *retired educational administrator*

Proctorville
†Barnett, Steven R. *director, music educator*

Ravenna
Drugan, Cornelius Bernard *retired school administrator, retired psychologist, musician*
Felton, Robert O'Neil, II, *secondary education educator*

Richmond
Martin, Clara Rita *elementary school educator*

Rio Grande
Shibley, Ralph Edwin, Jr., *special education and career-technical education*

Rootstown
Nora, Lois Margaret *medical college administrator, dean*

Sagamore Hills
Harvuot, Cathleen Mary *elementary school educator, consultant*

Sardinia
Evans, C(aroline) Sue *educator*
Stratton, Sondra Kay *primary school educator*

Shaker Heights
Brachna, Gabor (Samuel) *elementary school educator*
Trefts, Joan Landenberger *retired educator, administrator*

Shelby
Gilbert, Michelle Dawn *middle and secondary school educator*

Sidney
Seitz, James Eugene *retired college president, freelance writer*

Springfield
Dominick, Charles Alva *college official*
Kinnison, William Andrew *retired university president*
Stelzer, Patricia Jacobs *retired secondary school educator*

Strongsville
†Berkey, Donald Frederick *counseling administrator*
Chidsey, Ronald Grant *counseling*
Shambaugh, Catherine Anne *elementary education educator*

Sylvania
Sampson, Earldine Robison *education educator*

Toledo
Billups, Norman Fredrick *college dean, pharmacist, educator*
Braithwaite, Margaret Christine *retired elementary education educator*
†Condon, Elizabeth M. *education educator*
†Cuckovic, Zeljko *education educator*
†Escobar, Isabel Cristina *education educator*
Flaskamp, Ruth Ehmen Staack *retired elementary education educator*
†Goldstein, Margaret Franks *special education educator*
Gutteridge, Thomas G. *academic administrator, consultant and labor arbitrator*
†Knuth, Marya Danielle *special education educator*
†Martin, Geoffrey Kimball *academic administrator, mathematician*
Pham, David Lan *secondary school educator, writer*
Rabideau, Margaret Catherine *retired media center director*
Romanoff, Marjorie Reinwald *retired education educator*
†Salyers, Kathleen Marie *education educator*
Weinblatt, Charles Samuel *university administrator, employment consultant*

University Heights
Glynn, Edward *college administrator*
Seaton, Shirley Smith *academic administrator, consultant*
Starcher-Dell'Aquila, Judy Lynn *special education educator*

Valley View
Miller, Susan Ann *school system administrator*

Vermilion
†Baughman, Walter David *parochial school educator*

Vincent
Meek, Barbara Susan *elementary education educator*

Washington Court House
Fichthorn, Fonda Gay *gifted and talented educator, retired principal*

Waverly
Lovett, Francis William, Jr., *adult education educator*

Westerville
Diersing, Carolyn Virginia *educational administrator*
Husarik, Ernest Alfred *educational administrator*
Kerr, Thomas Jefferson, IV, *academic official*

Van Sant, Joanne Frances *academic administrator*

Westfield Center
Spinelli, Anne Catherine *elementary education educator*

Wilberforce
George, Larry Darnell *dean, educator*
Williamson, Vikki Lyn *university official, financial executive*

Willoughby
Grossman, Mary Margaret *elementary education educator*

Wooster
Shepherd, Mary Anne *elementary education educator*
†Woods, Susanne *educator, academic administrator*

Worthington
Vankeerbergen, Bernadette Chantal *educator*

Wright Patterson Afb
Kankey, Roland Doyle *educator*

Youngstown
Atwater, Tony *provost,dean, educator*
Loch, John Robert *university administrator*
Zorn, Robert Lynn *education educator*

OKLAHOMA

Ada
Dennison, Ramona Pollan *special education educator*
†Frye, Linda Beth (Linda Beth Hisle) *elementary, secondary education educator*

Bartlesville
Chambers, Imogene Klutts *school system administrator, financial consultant*

Bethany
†Berryman, Warren *dean*
Crabtree, John Michael *college administrator, consultant*

Billings
†Matthiesen, Robert L. *education educator, farmer, rancher*

Broken Arrow
†Huckeby, Ed D. *academic administrator, composer, conductor*

Choctaw
Uselton, Bill W. *secondary education educator*

Dale
Capps, Larry Lynn *school librarian*

Disney
Hamilton, Carl Hulet *retired academic administrator*

Durant
†Spencer, Mark Benner *education educator*

Edmond
Graves, Paul Matthew *secondary school educator, choir director*
Powers, G. Kay *lawyer, mathematics educator*
†Spigner, Terry E. *special education educator*
Zabel, Vivian Ellouise *secondary education educator*

Enid
Hamilton, Lisa Dawn *secondary education educator*

Healdton
Lewis, Reba Jolene *secondary school educator, consultant*

Kansas
Pemberton, Merri Beth Morris *educator*

Langston
Holloway, Ernest Leon *university president*

Lawton
Cates, Dennis Lynn *education educator*
Gardner, Carol Elaine *elementary school educator*
Smiley, Frederick Melvin *education educator, consultant*

Maramec
Blair, Marie Lenore *retired elementary school educator*

Midwest City
Saulmon, Sharon Ann *college librarian*

Mooreland
†Eilers (Bowers), Betty Sue *elementary school educator, writer*

Muskogee
†Edwards, Terri Lyn Wilmoth *education educator*
†Ehlers, Deborah Layne *educator, dramaturg, director*

Norman
Croft, Janet Brennan *academic librarian*
Havlicek, Joseph Paul *educator*
Jones, Charlotte *principal*
†Kidwell, Clara Sue *education educator*
†Martin, Leisa Ann *educational consultant*
Pappas, James Pete *university administrator*
†Ragep, F. Jamil *academic administrator, educator*

Sharp, Paul Frederick *former university president, education consultant*
Zapffe, Nina Byrom *retired elementary education educator*

Nowata
Moore, Jeannie Marie *education educator, writer*

Oklahoma City
Alexander, Patrick Byron *university administrator*
Boomer, Dennis Keith *college official, clergyman*
Brown-Kuykendall, Donita *early childhood educator*
Forni, Patricia Rose *dean, nursing educator*
†McCook, Matt *education educator*
Noakes, Betty LaVonne *retired elementary school educator*
†Sibley, William Arthur *academic administrator, physics educator, consultant*
†Voth, Douglas W. *dean*
Woods, Pendleton *college director, author*
Young, Stephen K. *academic administrator*

Pawhuska
Holloway, Sharon Kay Sossamon *vocational/secondary school educator*

Ponca City
Gallagher, Gary W(ayne) *educational services executive*
Rice, Sue Ann *dean, industrial and organizational psychologist*
Surber, Joe Robert *assistant superintendent of schools*
Tatum, Betty Joyce *secondary school educator*

Prague
Stefansen, Peggy Ann *special education educator*

Pryor
Burdick, Larry G. *school system administrator*

Sallisaw
Buckner, JoAnn *special education educator, consultant*

Shawnee
†Hackett, Patricia Jo *academic administrator, dean*
Hill, Bryce Dale *school administrator*
Wilks, Jacquelin Holsomback *campus ministries director*
Zuhdi, Omar *secondary education educator*

Stillwater
†Chung, Jong-Moon *education educator*
Curl, Samuel Everett *university dean, agricultural scientist*
Evans, Cheryl Lynn *elementary school principal*
Halligan, James Edmund *university administrator, chemical engineer*
†Vestal, Theodore Merrill *education educator*

Tahlequah
†Grant, Kay Lallier *early childhood education educator*
†Howard, James Kenton *academic administrator, journalist*
Sumner, Delores Titchywy *school librarian, educator*

Tulsa
Cardwell, Sandra Gayle Bavido *university admissions professional*
†Donaldson, Robert Herschel *university administrator, educator*
Knaust, Clara Doss *retired elementary school educator*
Kukura, Rita Anne *pre-school educator*
Lawless, Robert William *academic administrator*
Roger, Jerry Lee *academic administrator*
Trennepohl, Gary Lee *university administrator, finance educator*
Undernehr, Laura Lee *elementary education educator*
Wood, Emily Churchill *educator, educational consultant*

Weatherford
†Aspedon, Mary D. *education educator*
Vanderslice, Ronna Jean *education educator*

OREGON

Ashland
Kreisman, Arthur *higher education consultant, humanities educator emeritus*

Beaverton
†Nikolich-Zugich, Janko *biomedical scientist, educator*

Bend
Nelson, Douglas Michael *school system administrator, educator*

Cannon Beach
Wismer, Patricia Ann *retired secondary education educator*

Clackamas
Woods, Dennis Oliver *headmaster, market and political research analyst*

Corvallis
Arnold, Roy Gary *academic administrator*
Byrne, John Vincent *higher education consultant*
Davis, John Rowland *university administrator*
Healey, Deborah Lynn *education administrator*
†McKee-Ryan, Frances M *education educator*
Parker, Donald Fred *college dean, human resources management educator*
Risser, Paul Gillan *academic administrator, botanist*

Verts, Lita Jeanne *university administrator*
Young, Roy Alton *university administrator, educator*

Eagle Point
†Blanchard, Shirley Lynn *primary school educator, consultant*

Eugene
Christian, Sonya *college dean*
†Foley, Charles Bradford *university dean, music educator*
Frank, David Anthony *educator*
Frohnmayer, David Braden *academic administrator*
Gall, Meredith Damien (Meredith Mark Damien Gall) *education educator, writer*
Matthews, Esther Elizabeth *education educator, consultant*
McMillan, Adell *retired educational administrator*
†Moseley, John Travis *university administrator, research physicist*
Pickett, Stephen Wesley *university official, lecturer and consultant*
Piele, Philip Kern *education infosystems educator*
Tobin, Tary Jeanne *educational consultant, researcher*
Warpinski, Terri L. *academic administrator, artist*
Womack, James Errol *college president*
Wood, Daniel Brian *educational consultant*

Florence
de Sá e Silva, Elizabeth Anne *secondary school educator*

Gold Beach
Shockley, James Jay *elementary school administrator, choir director, technology specialist*

Gresham
Light, Betty Jensen Pritchett *former college dean*
Light, Kenneth Freeman *college administrator*
Webb, Donna Louise *academic director, educator*

Hillsboro
Curry, Everett William, Jr., *college official, minister*

Jacksonville
Langworthy, William Clayton *college official*

Joseph
Gilbert, David Erwin *retired academic administrator, physicist*

La Grande
†Woodward, Ralph Frederick, Jr., *elementary school educator, consultant*

Lake Oswego
Lenderman, Joanie *elementary school educator*
Meltebeke, Renette *career counselor*

Madras
Hillis, Stephen Kendall *secondary education educator*

Mcminnville
Bull, Vivian Ann *college president*
McGillivray, Karen *retired elementary school educator*
Walker, Charles Urmston *retired university president*

Medford
Dixon, Andrew Derart *retired academic administrator*
Tracy, Harold Dewayne *secondary education educator, retired*

Merrill
Porter, Roberta Ann *counselor, educator, school system administrator*

Monmouth
†Dunn, Doris Marjory *retired educator, volunteer*

Newberg
Johnson, Thomas Floyd *former academic administrator, educator*

Oceanside
Wadlow, Joan Krueger *academic administrator*

Portland
†Bartlett, Thomas Alva *educational administrator*
Bennett, Charles Leon *vocational and graphic arts educator*
Blumel, Joseph Carlton *university president*
Braun, Stephen Baker *academic administrator*
Cantelon, John Edward *retired university chancellor*
Cox, Joseph William *former academic administrator , education educator*
†Deming, Willoughby Howard *education educator*
Diver, Colin S. *academic administrator, educator*
Fawcett, Lee C. *retired dean*
Frolick, Patricia Mary *retired elementary school educator*
Hartman, Cherry *clinical social worker*
Jarvis, Richard S. *academic administrator*
†Kinsella, David *education educator*
†Kohn, Art *education educator*
†Lanker, Stefan *education educator*
Leupp, Edythe Peterson *retired education educator*
McClave, Donald Silsbee *academic administrator*
Mooney, Michael Joseph *college president*
Potempa, Kathleen *dean, nursing educator*
Shaff, Beverly Gerard *education administrator*
†Tabor, Joshua Hamilton *academic administrator*

†Thao, Yer *education educator*
Tufts, Robert B. *academic administrator*
Tyson, David T. *academic administrator*
†Unger, Karen Virginia *director*
†Weiss, Tiffany L. *director*
†Whitlow, Lillian *retired elementary school educator, poet*
†Wiest, William Marvin *education educator, psychologist*
†Wilson, Thomas Dale *philanthropic fundraising consultant*
Yatvin, Joanne Ina *education educator*

Roseburg
Johnson, Doris Ann *educational administrator*

Salem
†Bauer, James Richard *academic administrator*
Hoff, Reno R. *academic administrator*
†Pelton, M Lee *academic administrator*

The Dalles
†Crawley, Cheryl K. *school system administrator*

Yachats
Robeck, Mildred Coen *educator, writer*

PENNSYLVANIA

Abington
†Montemurro, Elizabeth A *education educator*
Scheuer, Donald William, Jr., *educational administrator*

Aliquippa
Drobac, Nikola (Nick Drobac) *educator*

Allentown
Hausman, Keith Wayne *secondary school educator*
†McGuire, Linda E. *education educator*

Allison Park
Guffey, Barbara Braden *elementary education educator*

Altoona
Larsen, Carlton Keith *academic administrator*
†Love, Sharon RedHawk *education educator*
Vreeland-Flynn, Tracy Lynn *elementary education educator*

Annville
McGill, William James, Jr., *university official, writer*

Aspers
Saltzman. Charles McKinley *educational consultant*

Athens
Luther-Lemmon, Carol Len *elementary school educator*

Bala Cynwyd
Oswald, James Marlin *education educator*
Sutnick, Alton Ivan *dean, educator, researcher, physician*

Bally
Kelsch, Joan Mary *elementary education educator*

Bangor
Pensack, Susan *elementary education educator*

Beaver
Sefton, Mildred McDonald *retired educator*
†Strock, Robert S. *retired education educator*

Beaver Falls
†Siple, Samuel D. *academic administrator*

Bellefonte
Dupuis, Victor Lionel *retired curriculum and instruction educator*

Bensalem
Klingerman, Karen Nina *elementary school educator, teacher consultant, course coordinator*

Bethel Park
Douds, Virginia Lee *elementary education educator*

Bethlehem
Bergethon, Kaare Roald *retired college president*
Farrington, Gregory C. *university administrator*
Grenestedt, Joachim Lennart *educator*
†Tannenbaum, Nicola B. *education educator*
Weisman, Melody *special education guidance counselor*

Biglerville
†Marks, Nora Maralea *retired secondary school educator*

Bloomsburg
†Kozloff, Jessica S. *university president*
Liu, Hsien-Tung *dean*
†Perner, Darlene E. *special education educator, consultant, editor*
Traugh, Donald George, III, *secondary education educator*

Blue Bell
Brendlinger, LeRoy R. *academic administrator*
Rizzo, Gary Edward *academic administrator*

Brownsville
Martin, Richard H. *principal*

Bryn Mawr
†Opendak, Irene *academic administrator*
Salisbury, Helen Holland *education educator*

Smith, Nona Coates *academic administrator*
Vickers, Nancy J. *academic administrator*

Butler
†Ameduri, Michael A *education educator, consultant*
Rettig, Carolyn Faith *educator*

Cambridge Springs
Learn, Richard Leland *corrections classification program manager*

Canonsburg
Mascetta, Joseph Anthony *principal*

Carbondale
†Morcom, Gregory Lee *elementary school educator*

Carlisle
†Durden, William G. *academic administrator*
†Tuttle, James Brooks, II, *education educator, researcher*

Carnegie
†Ferro, Vincent Anthony *elementary school educator, music educator*

Center Valley
Bartolacci, Paulette Marie *middle school educator, aerobics instructor*
†Turner, Brian Allen *sport management director, educator*

Chalfont
†Detwiler, Christine Wendler *special education educator*

Chester
Bruce, Robert James *retired academic administrator*
Buck, Lawrence Paul *academic administrator, educator*
†Carnwath, Thomas Howlan *academic administrator*
Harris, James Thomas, III, *college administrator, educator*
McFarland, Ella Mae Gaines *secondary school educator, elementary school educator*
Rozycki, Edward George *education educator*
Wepner, Shelley Beth *education educator, software developer*

Christiana
Fitzgerald, Susan Helena *elementary educator*

Clarion
Dingle, Patricia A. *education educator, artist*

Clarks Summit
King, Carol Brennan *dean*
Sylvester, Robert J. *academic administrator*

Coatesville
Smith, Patricia Anne *special education educator*

Cochranton
Miller, Carl F. *secondary school educator*

Collegeville
Richter, Richard Paul *academic administrator*

Columbia
McTaggart, Timothy Thomas *secondary education educator*

Cooperstown
Hogg, James Henry, Jr., *retired education educator*

Cranberry Township
Moyer, Christina Beth *retired elementary education educator, reading specialist*

Dallas
Hunter, Todd Lee *secondary school music educator*
†Madras, Diane Elizabeth *education educator, physical therapist*

Dayton
Patterson, Madge Lenore *elementary education educator*

Devon
Garbarino, Robert Paul *retired administrative dean, lawyer*

Dillsburg
Holmes, David James *elementary school educator*

Downingtown
Hemingway, David C. *elementary school principal*

Doylestown
Rodenbaugh, Marcia Louise *retired elementary school educator*
Somers, Sarah Pruyn *retired elementary school educator*

Drexel Hill
Student, John Michael *secondary school educator*

Drums
Frask, Robin Ann Kostanesky *secondary school educator*

Dunmore
Krogh-Jespersen, Mary-Beth *academic administrator*
†McDonald, Nancy E. *retired secondary school educator*

Eagles Mere
Sample, Frederick Palmer *former college president*

East Stroudsburg
Dillman, Robert John *academic administrator*

Easton
Rothkopf, Arthur J. *college president*
†Sanborn, Joshua A. *education educator*

Edinboro
Cox, Clifford Laird *retired academic administrator*

Elkins Park
Burnley, June Williams *secondary school educator*

Enola
Myers, Alfred Frantz *retired state education official, educator*

Erie
†Belfiore, Phillip Joseph *education educator, researcher*
Drexler, Nora Lee *retired educator, writer, illustrator*
Eberlin, Richard D. *education educator*
Ferretti, Silvia *dean*
†Henry, Martin Daniel *university president*

Exton
Shollenberger, Sharon Ann *secondary school educator*

Fayetteville
Taylor, Margaret Uhrich *educational administrator*

Flourtown
Lambert, Joan Dorety *elementary education educator*

Fort Washington
Elliott, Bruce Roger *secondary education educator, artist*

Franklin
Moore, Mary Julia *educator*

Gettysburg
†Haaland, Gordon Arthur *psychologist, university president*
Kile, Marcia Ann *education consultant*
†Schneider, Katherine P. *retired elementary school educator*

Gibsonia
Korchnak, Lawrence C. *educational administrator, consultant, writer*

Glenside
Sacks, Robert D. *educational administrator, fund raiser*

Greensburg
Neff, Mary Ellen Andre *retired elementary school educator*

Greenville
†Parmiter, Karen Lynn *education educator*

Hanover
Clark, Sandra Marie *school administrator*

Harleysville
Hauber, Patricia Anne *educator*

Harrisburg
Brown, John Walter *vocational education supervisor*
Burns, Rebecca Ann *educator, librarian*
Partin, Daniel Ray *secondary school educator*
Popnik, Marlene Alita *school librarian, retired*

Harrison City
McWilliams, Samuel Robert *secondary education educator*

Hatfield
Jesberg, Robert Ottis, Jr., *educational consultant, science educator*
Madden, Theresa Marie *elementary education educator*

Haverford
†Brownlow, Donald Grey *private school educator*
Gruen, Jane Swan *retired educator, lecturer*
†Stuard, Susan Mosher *education educator*
Tritton, Thomas Richard *academic administrator, biologist, educator*

Havertown
Beck, Elaine Kushner *elementary and secondary school educator*
†Wright, Cecilia Powers *gifted and talented educator*

Hellertown
Claps, Judith Barnes *educational consultant*

Hermitage
Garay, Stephen R. *secondary school educator*

Hershey
†Jones, Marshall Bush *education educator, researcher*
Kirch, Darrell Gene *academic administrator, dean*
Ruth, Edward B. *supervisor*
†Sumera, Sherry A. *secondary school educator*

Honesdale
Barbe, Walter Burke *education educator*

Houston
†Briggs, Rich *secondary school educator*

Hummelstown
Moffett, Dawn Schulten *retired elementary education educator*

Huntingdon
Kepple, Thomas Ray, Jr., *college administrator*
†Wang, Xinli *education educator*

Indiana
Bowers, Fredalene Barletta *education educator, consultant*
Kulis, Ellen Mae *elementary education educator*
Pettit, Lawrence Kay *university president*
Rife, John Merle, Jr., *retired educator, pilot*
Thibadeau, Eugene Francis *education educator, consultant*

Jermyn
Crotti, Rose Marie *special education educator*

Jewkintown
†Jih, Chang-Shin *education educator*

Johnstown
Alcamo, Frank Paul *retired educational administrator*
Grove, Nancy Carol *academic administrator*
Lovingood, Rebecca Britten *elementary school educator*
†Puto, Anne-Marie *reading specialist*
Van Blerkom, Dianna L. *education educator*

King Of Prussia
Gallis, Carole Campbell *secondary education educator*
Hawes, Nancy Elizabeth *mathematics educator*

Kingston
Marko, Andrew Paul *school system administrator*

Knox
Rupert, Elizabeth Anastasia *retired university dean*

Kutztown
Watrous, Robert Thomas *academic director*

La Plume
Boehm, Edward Gordon, Jr., *college administrator, educator*

Lafayette Hill
Delacato, Janice Elaine *learning consultant, educator*
King, Diane Averbach *teacher educator*

Lake Ariel
Casper, Marie Lenore *middle school educator*

Lancaster
Baylor, Scott Allen *chemistry educator*
Drum, Alice *academic administrator, educator*
Ebersole, Mark Chester *emeritus college president*
Kane, Edward Joseph *educator*
†Kneedler, Richard (Alvin Kneedler) *former academic administrator*
Linton, Joy Smith *primary school educator*
Teague, Peter Wesley *college president*
Young, Mary Frances Braccio *educational consultant*

Langhorne
Babb, Wylie Sherrill *college president*

Lebanon
Synodinos, John Anthony *academic administrator*

Lehman
†Ivanov, Anatoli F. *education educator*
Williams, Thomas Alan *elementary education educator, coach*

Lewisburg
Hetherington, Bonita Elizabeth *elementary education educator*
†Roberts, Ruth W. *retired elementary school educator*
†Rogers, Steffen H. *academic administrator*

Lincoln University
†Babatunde, Emmanuel Debo *education educator*
†Chapp, Jeffrey A *education educator, artist*
Nelson, Ivory Vance *academic administrator*

Lock Haven
Almes, June *retired education educator, librarian*
†Moyer, Anna Blackburn *retired secondary and elementary school educator*
Willis, Craig Dean *academic administrator*

Macungie
Rubin, Arthur Herman *retired university official, consultant*

Manheim
Frederick, Susan Louise *preschool educator*

Maple Glen
Weaver-Stroh, Joanne Mateer *education educator, consultant*

Marietta
Jones, Shannon Shawna Marie *elementary guidance counselor*

Martinsburg
Neff, Robert Wilbur *academic administrator, educator, minister*

Mc Murray
Cmar, Janice Butko *home economics educator*

Meadville
Dixon, Armendia Pierce *school program administrator*

Media
Coyle, Edward J. *physical education coordinator*
DiRosa, Steven Joseph *primary and secondary school educator*
Strunk, Betsy Ann Whitenight *education educator*

Mercersburg
Tompkins, Christopher Robin *director, educator*

Merion Station
Pearcy, Lee Theron *secondary education educator, writer*

Mertztown
Allison, Robert Harry *school counselor*

Milford
Reynolds, Edwin Wilfred, Jr., *retired secondary education educator*

Monroeville
Baker, Faith Mero *retired elementary education educator*
†Sehring, Hope Hutchison *library science educator*

Moon Township
Tannehill, Darcy Anita Bartins *academic administrator*

Nanticoke
Dalmas-Brown, Carmella Jean *special education educator*
Donohue, Patricia Carol *academic administrator*

New Castle
Denniston, Marjorie McGeorge *retired elementary school educator*
Roux, Mildred Anna *retired secondary school educator*

New Galilee
†McKim, James O., Jr., *secondary school educator*

New Hope
Knight, Douglas Maitland *educational administrator, optical executive, writer*

New Kensington
†Kalavar, Jyotsna Mirle *education educator*

New Wilmington
†Magyary, Cynthia Marie *elementary school educator, music educator*

Newtown
†Conrad, Stephen Edward *secondary school educator*

Northumberland
Wert, Barbara J. Yingling *special education consultant*

Oakdale
Gilden, Robin Elissa *elementary education educator*

Oil City
†Sabousky, Richard Anthony *adult education educator*

Patton
†Pompa, Louise Elaine *secondary school educator*

Perkasie
Ferry, Joan Evans *school counselor*

Philadelphia
Aversa, Dolores Sejda *educational administrator*
Bass, Aaron *school system administrator*
Bates, James Earl *academic administrator*
Blumberg, Baruch Samuel *academic research scientist*
†Brucker, Paul C. *academic administrator, physician*
†Capers, Gregg *secondary school educator, musician*
Cohen, David Walter *academic administrator, periodontist, educator*
Cooperman, Barry S. *educational administrator, educator, scientist*
†Cromarty, G. Geoffrey *academic administrator*
Davidson, Rhonda Elizabeth *preschool educator*
†Doherty, Roger Davidge *adult education educator, consultant*
Drake, Jayne Kribbs *university administrator, English educator*
Fernandez, Happy Craven (Gladys Fernandez) *academic administrator*
Goldman, Richard Paul *educational administrator*
Gusoff, Patricia Kearney *retired elementary education educator*
Hack, Gary Arthur *dean*
†Kelly, Alan M. *dean*
†Korsh, James F. *educator*
Liacouras, Peter James *academic administrator, educator, lawyer, arbitrator*
Ludwig, Kurt James *residence director*
Lynch, William Francis, Jr., *secondary mathematics educator*
McNamara, Kevin John *academic administrator*
Meyerson, Martin *university educator, urban and regional planner*
Padulo, Louis *university administrator*
Papadakis, Constantine N. *university executive*
Powers, Michael Roland *educator, insurance consultant*

Presseisen, Barbara Zemboch *retired educational director, researcher*
Reid, Mary Wallace *retired secondary education educator*
Rodin, Judith Seitz *academic administrator, psychology educator*
Romer, Daniel *university official, psychologist, educator*
†Rost, Gregory Stuart *academic administrator*
Rubenstein, Arthur Harold *medical school official, physician*
Rudczynski, Andrew B. *academic administrator, medical researcher*
Samway, Patrick H. *secondary education educator*
Savoie, James Anthony *university official*
†Schaubroeck, John Michael *education educator, academic administrator*
†Scheele, Dorothy R. *secondary school educator*
Shakespeare, Edward Oram, III, *retired secondary school educator*
Sibolski, Elizabeth Hawley *higher education administrator*
Slaughter-Defoe, Diana Tresa *education educator*
Solmssen, Peter *academic administrator*
Swan, Ralph Edward *education educator*
Toto, Mary *elementary and secondary education educator*
Veit, Kenneth *dean, educator*
Wachman, Marvin *former university president and chancellor*
Zheng, Robert Zhiwei *educational technology educator*
Zimmer, Janie Louise *mathematics educator, administrator*

Philipsburg
Genesi, Susan Petrovich *educator, consultant*

Phoenixville
†Harkin, Ann Winifred *elementary school educator, psychotherapist*

Pittsburgh
†Balach, Claudia Ann *director*
†Bandix, George C. *dean, chemist, educator*
Barazzone, Esther Lynn *academic administrator, educator*
Bouldin, Chapman Whitfield, Jr., *educator, consultant*
Boyce, Doreen Elizabeth *lecturer, civic development foundation executive*
Braun, Thomas W. *academic administrator*
†Brockmann, Stephen Matthew *education educator*
Carney, Ann Vincent *retired secondary education educator*
Cohon, Jared L. *academic administrator*
Curry, Nancy Ellen *educator, psychoanalyst, psychologist*
†Davis, Diane J. *director, educator*
Dempsey, Jacqueline Lee *special education director*
Dougherty, Charles John *university administrator, philosophy and medical ethics educator*
Eckert, Jean Patricia *elementary education educator*
†Faigen, Anne Gussin *secondary school educator, writer*
†Ford, Amanda Melody *director*
Gal-Or, Esther *educator*
†Giannoukakis, Nick *educator*
†Kamlet, Mark *provost*
Kimm, Sue Young Sook *academic medical researcher*
Laughlin, Patricia *university dean*
†Linke, Erika C. *school librarian*
†Livi, Ivan David *retired educational administrator*
Logsdon, Marge A. *education educator*
Lorensen, Frederick Hamilton *educational administrator, consultant*
McHoes, Ann McIver *academic administrator, computer systems consultant*
†Michalopoulos, George Konstantine *academic administrator*
Packard, Rochelle Sybil *elementary school educator*
†Praytor, Kent Dwayne *career planning administrator*
Rago, Ann D'Amico *university official, public relations professional*
†Richard, Jean-Francois *education educator, consultant*
Smartschan, Glenn Fred *school system administrator*
†Sobehart, Helen C *academic administrator, educator*
Spohn, Janice *elementary education educator, consultant*
Sullivan, Loretta Roseann *elementary education educator*
Van Dusen, Albert Clarence *university official*
Weidman, John Carl, II, *education educator, consultant*
Wilson, George David *school administrator*

Pottstown
Nash, William Lewis, III, *retired music education educator*

Punxsutawney
Graffius, Richard Stewart, II, *middle school educator*

Quarryville
Armerding, Hudson Taylor *retired college president, consultant*
Schreiner, Helen Ann *special education educator*

Reading
Bowles, Patricia Mary *secondary education educator*
White, Thomas David, II, *academic administrator*
†Yoder, James Dale *adult education educator*

Red Lion
Van Kouwenberg, Martha Nester *secondary education educator*

Robesonia
Fuhrman, Gwendolyn Sue *secondary school educator*

Russellton
Curtis, Paula Annette *elementary and secondary education educator*

Saint Davids
Baird, John Absalom, Jr., *retired college official*
Chang, Heewon *education educator, Electronic Journal Editor*

Saltsburg
Pidgeon, John Anderson *headmaster*

Schnecksville
Kiechel, Barbara Bernadette *vocational school educator*

Scranton
Nee, Sister Mary Coleman *college president emeritus*
Passon, Richard Henry *English language educator, former administrator*

Shickshinny
Geffken, Meg Comstock *secondary education educator*

Shippensburg
Miller, Linda Lou *education administrator, communications specialist*

Shohola
Williams, Carolyn Woodworth *retired elementary education educator, consultant*

Slippery Rock
Smith, Grant Warren, II, *university administrator, physical sciences educator*
Smith, Robert Mason *academic administrator*

Spring City
Middleton, Dawn E. *education educator*

Springboro
Lillie, Marshall Sherwood *college safety and security director, educator*

Springfield
Carter, Frances Moore *educator, writer, foundation executive*

State College
Aitken, Ruth Elaine Willson *educational and career/job search consultant*
Hoffa, Harlan Edward *retired university dean, art educator*
Max, Elizabeth *educator*
McKeel, Lillian Phillips *retired education educator*
Remick, Forrest Jerome, Jr., *former university official*
Tehie, Janice Beveridge *education educator*
Toombs, William Edgar *professor*

Stroudsburg
Kratz, Charles E., Jr., *dean*
Macmillan, Robert Francis *director university service*
Weitzmann, William Henry *education educator, photographer*

Summerdale
†Zeiders, Jeffrey Alan *secondary school educator, historian, educator*

Sunbury
Maue, Leta Jo *special education administrator*

Swarthmore
†Bloom, Alfred Howard *academic administrator, educator*

Swiftwater
†Braithwaite, Barbara J. *secondary school educator*

Swissvale
Skrbin, Aaron T. *assistant principal*

Titusville
Campasino, Ellen Marie *elementary school educator*

Tyrone
Spewock, Theodosia George *principal, elementary school educator*

Unionville
Martin, Helen Elizabeth *educational consultant*

University Park
Askov, Eunice May *adult education educator*
Bazirjian, Rosann V. *dean, librarian*
Chander, Subhash *educator*
†De Jong, Gordon Frederick *education educator, consultant*
†Edmondson, Jacqueline *education educator*
†Erickson, Rodney Allen *university executive, provost*
Felson, Richard Barnet *educator*
†Goulias, Konstadinos G. *director*
†Herr, Edwin Leon *educator, academic administrator*
†Ibrahim, Ibrahim Awad *adult education educator*
Ivanov, Kostadin Nikolov *educator*
Larson, Russell Edward *university provost emeritus, consultant agriculture research and development*
†McNeese, Michael D. *educator*

Nicely, Robert Francis, Jr., *education educator, administrator*
Spanier, Graham Basil *university president*
Yoder, Edgar Paul *education educator*

Upper Darby
Hudiak, David Michael *academic administrator, lawyer*
Leiby, Bruce Richard *secondary education educator, writer*

Verona
Bruno, Louis Vincent *special education educator*

Villanova
†Caverly, Robert *adult education educator*
Clement, Barbara Koltes Sadtler *academic administrator*
Dobbin, Edmund J. *university administrator*
Fitzpatrick, M. Louise *dean, nursing educator*
Savitz, Fred *education educator*

Warminster
Ciao, Frederick J. *school system administrator, educator*

Wayne
Howard, Harold Charles *provost, strategic planner, consultant*

Wernersville
Panuska, Joseph Allan *academic administrator*

West Aliquippa
Peya, Prudence Malava *retired elementary education educator*

West Chester
Bove, Patrice Magee *elementary education educator*
Hammonds, Jay A. *retired secondary education educator, administrator*
†Heston, Thomas J. *education educator*
Hickman, Janet Susan *college administrator, educator*
Morgan, John David *middle school educator*

West Mifflin
†Archey, Mary Frances Elaine (Onofaro) *academic administrator, educator*

Westtown
Jackson, Katherine Church *former elementary school educator, reading educator*

Wexford
Hutchinson, Barbara Winter *elementary school educator*

Wilkes-Barre
†Reboli, Denise M. *education educator*

Williamsport
Williams, Robert L. *principal*

Yardley
Breitenfeld, Frederick, Jr., *retired educational consultant, former public broadcasting executive*
Elliott, Frank Nelson *retired college president*
Watson, Joyce Leslie *elementary educator*

York
Aarestad, James Harrison *retired educational administrator, army officer*
†Gill, Sukhdeep *education educator, researcher*
Owens, Marilyn Mae *elementary school educator, secondary school educator*

RHODE ISLAND

Barrington
Graser, Bernice Erckert *elementary school principal, educational consultant, psychologist*

Bristol
†Berman, Garrett L *education educator*
†Camara, Joan Ellen *dean*

Central Falls
Leclerc, Leo George *guidance counselor*

Kingston
Carothers, Robert Lee *academic administrator*
†Klein, Maurice (Maury) Nickell *education educator, writer*
†Park, Eugene *education educator, consultant*
Stark, Dennis Edwin *university official*

Middletown
Jackson, John Edward *educator, logistician, retired naval officer*

Narragansett
Pierson, Douglas H. *special education educator*

Newport
Flowers, Sandra Joan *elementary education educator*
†Maurer, John Henry *education educator*
Wood, Berenice Howland *educator*

North Kingstown
Resch, Cynthia Fortes *secondary education educator*

Providence
†Blume, Jeffrey David *adult education educator, researcher*
†Blumstein, Sheila Ellen *former academic administrator, linguistics educator*
†Cervone, Laureen Avery *educational consultant, researcher*
Deal, Joseph Maurice *academic administrator, art educator, photographer*

Duncan, David Frank *community health specialist, educator*
Gaebe, Morris J. *academic administrator*
Greer, David S. *university dean, physician, educator*
†Mandle, Earl Roger *design school president, former museum executive*
Marsh, Donald Jay *medical school dean, medical educator*
Nazarian, John *academic administrator, mathematics educator*
O'del, John Nicholas *educator*
Shapiro, Raquel *school psychologist, educator, counselor*
Simmons, Ruth J. *academic administrator*
Smith, Philip A. *academic administrator*
Waite-Franzen, Ellen Jane *academic administrator*
†Yena, John A. *academic administrator*

Saunderstown
Donovan, Gerald Alton *retired academic administrator, former university dean*

Warwick
Izzi, John *educator, author*

Wood River Junction
Carlson-Pickering, Jane *gifted education educator*

Woonsocket
Stubbs, Donald Clark *secondary education educator*

SOUTH CAROLINA

Aiken
Salter, David Wyatt *secondary school educator*

Anderson
Martin, Terrell Owen *retired university administrator*
Whitaker, Evans Parker *academic administrator*

Barnwell
Miller, Elizabeth Jane *secondary education educator*

Beaufort
Raines, Karen Cornell *secondary education educator*
Shaw, Danny Wayne *educational consultant, musician*

Blythewood
Daniels, James Douglas *retired academic administrator*

Central
†Holcombe, Joseph Steven *academic administrator, educator*

Charleston
Appleget, Terri Lynn *elementary education educator*
Coleman, Dorothy Zipper *retired educational administrator*
Gay, Frances Marion Welborn *private school educator*
Greenberg, Raymond Seth *academic administrator, educator*
Gunn, Morey Walker, Jr., *secondary education educator, choir director, organist*
Henson, Kenneth Tyrone *education educator*
Morris, Valerie Bonita *performing arts administrator*
O'Bryant-Seabrook, Marlene Loretta Linton *retired educator*
†Quinn, E. Moore *adult education educator, researcher, consultant*
Sanders, Tence Lee Walker *elementary education educator*
Suggars, Candice Louise *special education educator*
Sutusky, John Charles *higher education educator*
Worthington, Ward Curtis, Jr., *university dean, anatomy educator*

Chesterfield
Shields-Cassidy, Gloria Ann *adult education educator, poet*

Clemson
Bailey, Beatrice Naff *researcher and educator in English*
†Felder, Frankie Ottowiess *academic administrator*
†Juang, Charng Hsein *adult education educator*
Kelly, John William, Jr., *university administrator*
†Kimmel, Robert Michael *education educator, consultant*
Nilson, Linda Burzotta *academic administrator*
†Sluss, Dorothy Louise *education educator, researcher*
Vogel, Henry Elliott *retired university dean and physics educator*

Clinton
Griffith, John Vincent *academic official*

Columbia
Aelion, C. Marjorie *adult education educator*
Akhavi, Shahrough *educator*
†Bellon, Michael Kenneth *director, music educator*
Faulkner, Larry R. *dean, educator, researcher, writer*
Feldman, Daniel Charles *adult education educator*
†Fields, Harriet Gardin *counselor, educator, consultant*
Friedman, Myles Ivan *education educator*
†Lowery, John Wesley *education educator*
Luna, Gene Irving *academic administrator, education educator*

Murray, George William *university president*
Palms, John Michael *academic administrator, physicist*
Petty, Donna Matthews *middle school educator*
Sorensen, Andrew Aaron *university president*
†Swinton, David Holmes *academic administrator*
Tetreault, Donald Richard *education educator*
Tunstall, Dorothy Fiebrich *early childhood educator*

Conway
†Dozier, Etrulid Pressley *school librarian*
Johnson-Leeson, Charleen Ann *former elementary school educator, insurance agent, insurance consultant, regional executive assistant*
Squatriglia, Robert William *university dean, educator*
Wiseman, Dennis Gene *academic administrator*

Due West
Koonts, Jones Calvin *retired education educator*

Easley
Cole, Lois Lorraine *retired elementary school educator*

Elgin
Peake, Frank *middle school educator*

Florence
Carter, Luther Fredrick *university president*
†Fitzkee, Thomas L. *education educator*
Rutherford, Vicky Lynn *special education educator*

Gaffney
Suttle, Helen Jayson *retired education educator*

Gilbert
McGill, Cathy Broome *gifted and talented education educator*

Greenville
Alford, Robert Wilfrid, Jr., *elementary school educator*
Hill, Grace Lucile Garrison *education educator, consultant*
†Jones, Bob, III, *academic administrator*
†Myers, Daniel Thomas *educational consultant, consultant, writer*
†Shi, David E. *academic administrator, historian*
Smith, Philip Daniel *academic administrator, education educator*

Greenwood
Jackson, Larry Artope *retired college president*
Williams, Sylvester Emanual, III, *educator, consultant*

Hilton Head Island
Fleischman, Kathryn Agnes *secondary education educator*
Wallace, Arthur, Jr., *retired college dean*

Iva
Gentry, Margaret Burton *retired elementary school teacher*

Kiawah Island
Warren, Russell Glen *academic administrator*

Ladson
Cannon, Major Tom *special education educator*

Laurens
Sheppard, Anne Thomson *retired secondary school educator*

Leesville
Covington, Tammie Warren *elementary education educator*

Little River
Sarvis, Elaine Magann *retired assistant principal*

Marion
Kirkpatrick, Donald Robert *secondary school educator*

Moore
Parris, Michael Lynn *academic administrator*

Mount Pleasant
Gilbert, James Eastham *academic administrator*

North Charleston
Reilly, David Henry *university dean*

Orangeburg
Hill, Howard Darnell *educator, university administrator*
Robinson, Ruth Hubbard *retired elementary school educator*
†Vincent, Elaine Sistare *academic administrator, psychologist, educator*

Pawleys Island
Proefrock, Carl Kenneth *academic medical administrator*

Piedmont
Winter-Neighbors, Gwen Carole *art and special education educator, consultant*

Prosperity
Hause, Edith Collins *college administrator*

Richburg
Cox, Kevin Monterey *school administrator*

Rock Hill
†Abdel-Aal, Hisham A *adult education educator*

Simpsonville
Furrow, John Mayo *secondary school educator*

Spartanburg
Doyle, Sharon Thomas *school system administrator*
Gray, Nancy Ann Oliver *college administrator*
McDaniel, Thomas Robb *academic administrator, educator*
McGehee, Larry Thomas *university administrator*
Stephens, Bobby Gene *college administrator, consultant*

Sumter
Blair, Charlie Lewis *elementary school educator*

Timmonsville
McDonald, Robert Irving *secondary education mathematics educator*

Westminster
Duncan, Gwendolyn McCurry *elementary education educator*

York
Clinch, Nicholas *assistant principal*

SOUTH DAKOTA

Aberdeen
Geier, Constance B. *education educator*
†Houge, Timothy Todd *education educator*
Omland, Jacqueline Leigh-Knute *secondary school educator, small business owner*
Ruud, Jay Wesley *dean*
Tebben, Sharon Lee *education educator*

Brookings
Iverson, John Wilfred *educator*
Miller, Peggy Gordon Elliott *university president*

Kadoka
Stout, Maye Alma *educator*

Madison
Tunheim, Jerald Arden *academic administrator, physics educator*

Pierre
Perry, Robert Tad *educational official*

Rapid City
Hughes, William Lewis *former university official, electrical engineer*
Schleusener, Richard August *college president*

Selby
Akre, Donald J. *school system administrator*

Sioux Falls
Balcer, Charles Louis *college president emeritus, educator*
Talley, Robert Cochran *medical school dean and administrator, cardiologist*

Spearfish
Thie, Genevieve Ann Robinson *retired secondary school educator*

Vermillion
Dahlin, Donald C(lifford) *academic administrator*

Yankton
Crandall, Terrence Lee *counseling administrator*
Foster, James Caldwell *academic dean, historian*

TENNESSEE

Big Sandy
Hancock, Sandra Olivia *secondary school educator, elementary school educator*

Bristol
Anderson, Jack Oland *retired college official*
Gaines, John Strother *retired educator, writer, municipal official*

Chapel Hill
Christman, Luther Parmalee *retired dean, dean, consultant*

Chattanooga
Bartoo, Eugene Chester *academic administrator, educator*
Foster, Edwin Powell, Jr., *educator, structural engineer*
Obear, Frederick Woods *academic administrator*
†Willimon, William Parker *academic administrator*

Clarksville
†Schutz, Gregory John *academic administrator*
†Stoddard, Peter Hawkins *education educator, consultant*

Cleveland
†Garren, Sanford M. *secondary school educator*
Suttles, David Clyde *educator*

Columbia
Cantrell, Sharron Caulk *principal*

Cookeville
Alfred, Suellen *English education educator*
Elkins, Donald Marcum *dean, agronomy educator*
Peters, Ralph Martin *academic administrator*
Volpe, Angelo Anthony *former university president, chemistry educator*

Eads
Dwyer, John Thomas, Jr., *educator, researcher*

Elkton
Newman, Sharon Lynn *elementary education educator*

Franklin
†Bouldin-Payor, Elizabeth Gai *educator (K-12)*
Daniel, Cathy Brooks *tutor, educational consultant*
Garey, Mark Edward *secondary school educator, band director*
Guthrie, Glenda Evans *academic counselor, development specialist*

Germantown
Wiatr, Jeanne Malecki *education educator, educator*

Goodlettsville
Vatandoost, Nossi Malek *art school administrator*

Greeneville
Casteel, DiAnn Brown *principal*

Hermitage
Quaintance, Alice Lynn *elementary school media specialist*

Houston
†Reynolds, Jeffrey Wayne *secondary school educator*

Jackson
Agee, Bob R. *academic administrator, educator, minister*
†Freeman, Sherry *education educator*
†Hearn, Beverly Jean *secondary education educator, librarian*
†Myatt, Dottie Woodard *education educator*

Johnson City
Alfonso, Robert John *university administrator*
Bishop, Wilsie Sue *dean, nursing educator*
Franks, Ronald Dwyer *university dean, psychiatrist, educator*

Kingsport
Davis, Tammie Lynette *assistant principal*

Kingston
Alexander, Deborah Radford *elementary education administrator*

Knoxville
Armistead, Willis William *university administrator, veterinarian*
Boling, Edward Joseph *university president emeritus, educator*
†Brockett, Ralph Grover *adult education educator*
Crabtree, Loren William *chancellor, academic administrator, history educator*
Galligan, Thomas C., Jr., *dean, law educator*
†Gilley, James Wade *university president*
Harris, Roland Arsville, Jr., *director program or activities, sociologist*
†Hatton, Barbara R. *academic administrator*
†Joshi, Hem Raj *educator*
Kelley, Paul Lewis *retired educator*
†Kim, Hyunjoong *education educator*
Mankel, Francis Xavier *former principal, priest*
Moran, James D., III, *university administrator*
Ratliff, Eva Rachel *elementary education educator*
Royse, Sue Marion *special education educator*
†Snyder, William T. *university chancellor*
†South, Stephen A. *academic administrator*
Srinivasan, Mandyam Mudumbai *management educator, researcher*
Walsh, Joanne Elizabeth *retired educator, librarian*
Yeomans, Gordon Allan *retired educator*

Martin
McCracken, Kenneth Donald *retired education educator*

Mc Minnville
Henry, Mary Lou Smelser *elementary education educator*

Memphis
†Bond, Beverly Greene *education educator, writer*
Booth, Linda Leigh *vocational educator, homemaker*
Champion, Herman Daniel, Jr., *college dean*
Crist, William Miles *dean, physician*
Daughdrill, James Harold, Jr., *academic administrator*
†Diener, Andrew M. *educator*
Dunathan, Harmon Craig *college dean*
Faudree, Ralph J. *academic administrator, mathematician, educator*
Gourley, Dick R. *college dean*
Herrod, Henry Grady, III, *dean, allergist, immunologist*
Hord, Pauline Jones *primary school educator, educator*
Hunt, James Calvin *academic administrator, physician*
Moffitt, Carolyn Mullins *university official*
Pezeshki, S. Reza *educator*
Ranta, Richard Robert *university dean*
Sigler, Lois Oliver *retired educator*
†Stegall, Susan Elizabeth *elementary school educator*
†Troutt, William Earl *academic administrator*
Werle, Robert Geary *academic administrator*

Mount Juliet
Bauernfeind, James Charles *secondary education educator*

Murfreesboro
†Diaz-Ortiz, Oscar A. *education educator, researcher*
Doyle, Delores Marie *retired principal*

Nashville
†Bader, David Mansfield *education educator*
Beasley, John Snodgrass, II, *university administrator*
Chambers, Carol Tobey *elementary school educator*
Chaney, Sharon Henderson *secondary education educator, consultant*
Collins, Joe Lena *retired educator*
Coney, PonJola *dean, researcher, educator*
Conway-Welch, Colleen *dean, nurse midwife*
Gee, Elwood Gordon *academic administrator*
†Hazelip, Herbert Harold *academic administrator*
Heard, Alexander *retired educator and chancellor*
Longhurst, Robert Russell *retired secondary school educator*
Loper, Linda Sue *special collections librarian*
†Manning, Charles W. *university chancellor*
McMurry, Idanelle Sam *educational consultant*
Porter, Andrew Calvin *academic administrator, psychologist, educator*
Ramer, Hal Reed *academic administrator*
†Rivera, Maximiano Marquez *academic administrator, writer*
†Schoenfeld, Michael *academic administrator, education educator*
†Singh, Surendra P. *educator*
Swan, Patricia Brintnall *research administrator*
Treible, Kirk *retired academic administrator, foundation administrator*
Wyatt, Joe Billy *academic administrator*

Newport
Ball, Travis, Jr., *educational consultant, editor*
Runnion, Cindie J. *elementary school educator*

Oliver Springs
Heacker, Thelma Weaks *retired elementary school educator*

Pinson
Bailey, James Andrew *principal*

Pleasant Hill
Hull, Charles William *retired special education educator*

Rogersville
Fairchild, Dorcas Sexton *English educator*

Sewanee
Croom, Frederick Hailey *academic administrator, mathematician, educator*
Cunningham, Joel Luther *university president, vice-chancellor*
Patterson, William Brown *university dean, history educator*

Signal Mountain
Swasey, Martha Gracy *school administrator*

Smyrna
Faules, Barbara Ruth *retired elementary education educator*

Sneedville
Dodson, Danita Joan *secondary school educator, consultant*

Sparta
Langford, Jack Daniel *elementary school educator*

Strawberry Plains
†Blanchard, Pamela Snyder *special education educator*

Telford
Mashburn, Donald Eugene *educator*

TEXAS

Abilene
†Christopher, Mary M. *education educator, consultant*
Crymes, Mary Cooper *secondary school educator*
McCaleb, Gary Day *university official*
†Roy, Wayne Morris *academic administrator*
†Turner, Stafford *education educator, baritone*

Alice
†Thomas, Katherine Carol *educator*

Allen
Anderson, Robin Marie *secondary education educator*
Williams, Bryan *university dean, medical educator*

Alpine
Morgan, Raymond Victor, Jr., *university administrator, mathematics educator*
†Snyder, John Edward, Jr., *education educator*

Alvin
Roberson, Deborah Kay *secondary school educator*

Amarillo
†Stapleton, Claudia Ann *dean*

Arlington
†Ausbrooks, Carrie Y. Barron *education educator, researcher*
Sobol, Harold *retired dean, manufacturing executive, consultant*
Sorber, Charles Arthur *academic administrator*

Austin
Auvenshine, Anna Lee Banks *school system administrator*
Ayres, Robert Moss, Jr., *retired university president*

Brewer, Thomas Bowman *retired university president*
Cannon, William Bernard *retired university educator*
Cardozier, Virgus Ray *higher education educator*
Cunningham, William Hughes *former academic administrator, marketing educator*
†DuBose, Gaylan Ray *elementary school educator, musician, writer*
Ehrlich, Stacy Wheeler *school fundraiser, administrator*
Faulkner, Larry Ray *university official, chemistry educator*
Franklin, G(eorge) Charles *retired academic administrator*
Harris, Ben M. *education educator*
†Herrin, David Leslie *educator*
Hetzler, Susan Elizabeth Savage *educational administrator*
Hunter, Brother Eagan (Donald J. Hunter) *retired education educator*
Johnson, Sandra Lynn Terry *education consultant*
Jordan, Bryce *retired university president*
Lafferty, Joyce G. Zvonar *retired middle school educator*
Lehmann-Carssow, Nancy Beth *secondary school educator, coach*
Lewis, Nancy Louine Lambert *school counselor*
Livingston, William Samuel *university administrator, political scientist*
Rogers, Lorene Lane *university president emeritus*
Roueche, John Edward, II, *education educator, leadership program director*
Roueche, Suanne Davis *university administrator*
Royal, Darrell K. *university official, former football coach*
†Shiff, Richard Allen *director, art historian*
Shilling, Roy Bryant, Jr., *academic administrator*
Warner, David Cook *public affairs educator*
Wurzbach, Linda *educational consultant*

Bastrop
Carpenter, Delbert Stanley *educational administration educator*

Baytown
Black, Sarah Joanna Bryan *secondary school educator*

Beaumont
Brentlinger, William Brock *college dean*
Gagne, Mary *academic administrator*

Bedias
Williamson, Norma Beth *adult education educator*

Belton
Andreason, George Edward *university administrator*
†Gary, Jonathan Mark *academic administrator*
†Guess, David Lynn *education educator*

Blanco
Dudley, Brooke Fitzhugh *educational consultant*

Boerne
Daugherty, Linda Hagaman *private school executive*
Goode, Bobby Claude *retired secondary education educator, writer*

Brownfield
†McNamara, Derek Michael *education educator, minister*

Brownsville
†Boze, Betsy Vogel *university dean, marketing educator*
†Garcia, Juliet Villarreal *university administrator*
Santa-Coloma, Bernardo *secondary school educator, counselor*

Bryan
Hubert, Frank William Rene *retired university system chancellor*

Bryan
Hanks, Clay David *academic administrator*

Buchanan Dam
Miloy, Leatha Faye *university program director*

Buffalo Gap
Simpson, Patricia Elaine *education educator, dean*

Canyon
Long, Russell Charles *academic administrator*
†Nix, Susan Jenkins *principal, education educator*

Carrollton
Fricke, Raymond W. *religious school administrator*

Channelview
Wallace, Betty Jean *elementary school educator, lay minister*

College Station
†Adams, H. Richard *dean*
Adkisson, Perry Lee *university system chancellor*
†Bowen, Ray Morris *academic administrator, engineering educator*
Byrne, C. William, Jr., *athletics program director*
Calhoun, John C., Jr., *academic administrator*
Erlandson, David Alan *education administration educator*
Lynn, Laurence Edwin, Jr., *university administrator, educator*
Monroe, Haskell Moorman, Jr., *retired university educator*
†Paprock, Kenneth Edward *education educator, consultant*
Reinarz, Alice G. *academic administrator*
Sadoski, Mark Christian *education educator*
Vandiver, Frank Everson *institute administrator, former university president, author, educator*
Zhao, Wei *academic administrator*

Colleyville
Hodgell, Murlin Ray *university dean*

Comanche
Droke, Edna Faye *elementary school educator, retired*

Commerce
McLemore, Matthew Hunter *education educator*
Scott, Joyce Alaine *university official*

Coppell
†Griffin, Jim *secondary school educator*
Smothermon, Peggi Sterling *middle school educator*

Corpus Christi
Cassidy, Jack *academic administrator, educator*
Chodosh, Robert Ivan *retired middle school educator, coach*
Furgason, Robert Roy *university president, engineering educator*
Harper, Sandra Stecher *university administrator*
†McEndree, Phillip *education educator*

Corsicana
Orsak, Charles George *college district official*

Crockett
LaClair, Patricia Marie *physical education director, paramedic*

Dallas
Alpern, Robert J. *dean, medical educator*
†Blankenbaker, Zarina *adult education educator, consultant*
Campaigne, Linda Mary *special education educator*
Cirilo, Amelia Medina *educational consultant, supervisor*
Cole, James S. *academic administrator*
Cook, Gary Raymond *university president, clergyman*
†Cooper, Lamar Eugene, Sr., *academic administrator, minister*
Davis, Patricia M. *educator*
Dumerer, Lorraine JoAnne Lori *social studies educator, clinician, consultant*
†Early, James *education educator*
†Flowers, Terry James *headmaster*
Friedheim, Jan V. *education administrator*
Friedheim, Stephen Bailey *educational consultant*
Gajewski, Ronald S. *consulting and training company executive*
†Giggleman, Gene Felton *academic administrator, veterinarian*
Haayen, Richard Jan *university official, insurance company executive*
Harrison, Frank *former university president*
Hester, Linda Hunt *retired dean, counseling administrator*
Hill-Foster, Ialine *retired secondary school educator*
Kesterson, Ray Brent *college dean, retired air force officer*
McCartor, Sheila Smith *secondary school educator*
†Mittelstet, Stephen *academic administrator*
Savannah, Mildred Thornhill *public school educator*
Schulz, Sandra E. *secondary art educator*
Scott, John Roland *business law educator*
Shambaugh, Irvin Calvin, Jr., *aptitude test firm executive*
Spooner, Bernard Myrick *dean*
Turner, Robert Gerald *university president*
Wenrich, John William *college president*
†Wilkerson, Patricia Helen *director child development center*
Wrucke-Nelson, Ann C. *elementary education educator*

Denton
†Abunasser, Rima Jamil *education educator*
†Bean, Judith Mattson *academic administrator, educator*
†Boukerchi, Azzedine *adult education educator, computer scientist, researcher*
Carlson, William Dwight *college president emeritus*
Cobb, Jeanne Beck *education educator, researcher, consultant*
Hurley, Alfred Francis *historian, academic administrator emeritus, retired air force officer*
McDonald-West, Sandi MacLean *headmaster, consultant*
Smith, Howard Wellington *education educator, dean emeritus*
Swigger, Keith *dean*

Edgewood
Cates, Sue Sadler *educational diagnostician*

Edinburg
Nevarez, Miguel A. *academic administrator*
†Zeng, Liang *education educator*

Edna
Schrimsher, Joanne Johnson *professional counselor*

Egypt
Wynn, John Thomas *retired college president, farming executive, economic consultant, oil and gas producer*

El Paso
Erskine, William Crawford *academic administrator, accountant, health facility administrator*
†Gijon, José Enrique *special education educator*
Gordon, Erline Schecter *educational administrator*
Hernandez, Roberto Reyes *secondary school educator, educator*
†Martinez, Luis E. *education educator, consultant*
Natalicio, Diana Siedhoff *academic administrator*
Patty, William Robert *educator, administrator*
†Riter, Stephen *university administrator, electrical engineer*
Small, Ray *university administrator*
Tess, Alice Charlene *writer, retired secondary school educator*
von Tungeln, George Robert *retired university administrator, economics consultant*

Elgin
Shelby, Nina Claire *special education educator*

Floresville
Vontur, Ruth Poth *retired elementary school educator*

Fort Sam Houston
Robinson, Naomi Jean *educational training systems educator*

Fort Worth
†Alexander, Elizabeth Urban *education educator*
Bickerstaff, Mina March Clark *university administrator*
Collins Block, Cathy *education educator, writer, educational consultant*
Helton, Lucille Henry Hanrattie *academic administrator*
Kitchens, Larry Edwin *university administrator*
Saenz, Michael *college president*
†Slater, Carmen Rochelle *elementary school educator*
Tucker, William Edward *academic administrator, minister*
Wilson-Webb, Nancy Lou *education administration consultant, rancher*
Zaslavsky, Robert *secondary school educator*

Fredericksburg
Chase, John David *university dean, physician*

Freeport
Baskin, William Gresham *counselor, music educator, vocalist*

Fresno
Shaw, Teshetesa S. *pre-school educator*

Frisco
Reedy, Nancy Sue *elementary school educator*

Galveston
Banet, Charles Henry *academic administrator, clergyman*
Carrier, Warren Pendleton *retired university chancellor, writer*
Clayton, William Howard *retired university president*
Goodwin, Sharon Ann *academic administrator*
Hawkins, Ida Faye *elementary school educator*
Heins, Sister Mary Frances *educator, nun*
†Rajarathnam, Krishna *education educator, researcher*
†Stobo, John David *dean, physician, educator*

Garland
Michaels, Cindy Whitfill (Cynthia G. Michaels) *educational consultant*

Georgetown
Abegg, Martin Gerald *retired academic administrator*

Grand Prairie
†Puckett, Mary Alice *primary school educator, consultant*

Grapevine
Hirsh, Cristy J. *principal*

Hale Center
Courtney, Carolyn Ann *school librarian*

Hartley
Cooley, Regina Kae *educational administrator*

Henderson
†Rhoades, Eva Yvonne *retired elementary school educator*

Houston
†Arowosafe, Muyi *education educator*
Brinkley, William R. *dean*
Bui, Khoi Tien *college counselor*
Burgos-Sasscer, Ruth *chancellor emeritus*
Butler, William Thomas *college chancellor, physician, educator*
Caram, Dorothy Farrington *educational consultant*
Carroll, Michael M. *academic dean, mechanical engineering educator*
Darst, Mary Lou *secondary school educator*
Davis, Bruce Gordon *retired principal*
Djerejian, Edward Peter *institute administrator, former diplomat*
Douglas, James M. *university president*
Feigin, Ralph David *medical school administrator, pediatrician, educator*
Fisher, Janet Warner *secondary school educator*
Geisinger, Kurt Francis *university administrator, psychometrician*
Gillette, Lynn G. *dean*
†Gillis, Malcolm (Stephen Gillis) *academic administrator, economics educator*
Hammond, DeAnna *educator*
Ho, Yhi-Min *university dean, economics educator*
Hoffman, Philip Guthrie *former university president*
†Issa, Jean-Pierre J *education educator, medical educator*
Jackson, Wanda Britton *educator*
Jimmar, D'Ann *elementary education educator, fashion merchandiser*
Johnson, Sandra Ann *educator, counselor*
†Kapadia, Asha Seth *education educator, consultant*
Kinnaird, Susan Marie *special education educator*
†Kono, Junichiro *adult education educator*
Ligon-Borden, Betty Lee *academic director*
Mansell, Joyce Marilyn *special education educator*
McIntire, Mary *university administrator*
Miller, Harry Freeman *university administrator*
†Moran, Maria D. *elementary school educator*
Paul, Alida Ruth *arts and crafts educator*
Pickering, James Henry, III, *academic administrator, educator*
Pinson, Artie Frances *retired elementary school educator*
Poats, Lillian Brown *education educator*
Rice, Emily Joy *retired secondary school and adult educator*
Roos, Sybil Friedenthal *retired elementary school educator*
Sayer, Coletta Keenan *gifted education educator*
Shaffer, Anita Mohrland *counselor, educator*
Sharp, Douglas Andrew *secondary school educator, educator*
Smith, Arthur Kittredge, Jr., *academic administrator, political science educator*
Smythe, Cheves McCord *dean, medical educator*
Stryker, Daniel Ray *adult education educator*
Timpani, Nancy Evelyn *elementary school educator*
Trichel, Mary Lydia *middle school educator*
†Tyson, Carla Lea *director*
Untermeyer, Charles Graves (Chase Untermeyer) *academic administrator*
Urbina, Febe Gloria *elementary school principal*
van Cleave, Kirstin Dean (Kit van Cleave) *martial arts educator, writer, educator, publishing executive*
Wagner, Paul Anthony, Jr., *education educator*
†Ward, Stephanie G. *education educator*
Webb, Marty Fox *principal*
Whitaker, Gilbert Riley, Jr., *academic administrator, business economist*
Whiting, Martha Countee *retired secondary education educator*
†Wiley, Shirley Winona Walters *adult education educator, artist*
Williames, Lee John *university official, history educator*

Huntsville
Hopper, Margaret Sue *academic administrator, educational diagnostician, consultant*
Payne, David Emer *university administrator*
Ward, Richard Hurley *university dean, writer*
Warner, Laverne *education educator*

Hurst
Dodd, Sylvia Bliss *special education educator*

Iowa Park
Harvill, Melba Sherwood *retired university librarian*

Irving
Bielss, Otto William, Jr., *secondary school educator*
Chase, Pearline *adult education educator*
Clark, Priscilla Alden *retired elementary education educator*
Martin, Thomas Lyle, Jr., *academic administrator*
McVay, Barbara Chaves *secondary education mathematics educator*
†Rutledge, Deborah Jean *secondary school educator, music educator*

Johnson City
†Pollock, Margaret Landau Peggy *elementary school educator*

Katy
Gibert, Charlene West *gifted education educator*

Kingsville
Wiley, Millicent Yoder *realtor, pianist, accompanist, retired secondary school educator*

La Porte
†Svambera, Beatrice Alice *secondary school educator*

Lake Creek
Smith, Shirley Ann Nabors *retired secondary school educator*

Lake Jackson
Tasa, Ken *college dean*

Laredo
Black, Clifford Merwyn *academic administrator, sociologist, educator*
Fierros, Ruth Victoria *retired secondary school educator*
†Keck, Ray Marvin, III, *academic administrator*

Lewisville
Myers, Madeleine Becan *secondary school educator*

Livingston
Horner, Jennie Linn *retired educational administrator, nurse*

Longview
Fouse, Anna Beth *education educator*
Gentry, Vernessa Diana *principal, consultant*
LeTourneau, Richard Howard *retired college president*

†Roller, Robert H. *dean, finance educator*

Los Fresnos
Martin, José Ginoris *education administrator*

Lubbock
Askins, Billy Earl *education educator, consultant*
Burns, John Mitchell *academic administrator*
†Gelca, Razvan *education educator*
Haragan, Donald Robert *university administrator, geosciences educator*
Hisey, Lydia Vee *educational administrator*
Nelson, Toza *retired elementary school educator, church administrator*
Nugent, Connie *elementary education educator*
†Porrua, Enrique J. *adult education educator*
Schmidly, David J. *university president, biology educator*
†Schneider, Andreas *education educator, researcher*
Yoder-Wise, Patricia Snyder *educator*

Luling
†Collie, Paula Renea *secondary school educator*

Magnolia
Esmond, Cheri Sue *secondary school educator*

Marfa
Chambers, Johnnie Lois (Tucker Chambers) *elementary school educator, rancher*
†Edge, Daniel *education educator, artist, consultant*

Marshall
Shaw, Dianne Elizabeth *school administrator*

Maxwell
Peters, Carol Ann *secondary school educator*

Mcallen
Gonzalez, Rolando Noel *secondary school educator, religion educator, photographer*
Sands, Norman Earl *elementary school educator, composer*

Mesquite
†Gant, Linda Gayle *elementary school educator*
†Holt, Mildred Frances *educator*
Kessner, Micheal J. *elementary school educator*
Patrick, Pamela Ann *research consultant*
Pratt, Sharon L. *retired secondary and elementary education educator*
Vaughan, Joseph Lee, Jr., *education educator, consultant*

Mineola
Tabor, Beverly Ann *retired elementary school educator*

Moody
Judah, Frank Marvin *retired school system administrator*

Nacogdoches
Wagner, William Michael *academic administrator*

New Braunfels
Oestreich, Charles Henry *retired university president*

Odessa
Grubbs, Donald Ray *educational director, educator, welder*
Rasor, Doris Lee *retired secondary education educator*

Orange
Odom, Sarah Bernice *elementary school educator*

Pasadena
Blue, Monte Lynn *college president*
Fogo, Peter C. *educator, novelist, poet*
Hall, Georganna Mae *elementary school educator*

Perryton
Doerrie, Bobette *secondary education educator*

Plano
Fleming, Christina Samusson *special education educator*
Haggard, Geraldine Langford *primary school educator, adult education educator, consultant*
McWilliams, Chris Pater Elissa *elementary school educator*
†Philips, Coby Nelson *education educator, special education educator*
Reisner, Elena Mackay *retired educational administrator*
Rhodes, Doris Chaney *freelance/self-employed secondary school educator*

Prairie View
Gonzalez, Antonio *academic administrator, mortgage company executive*
Hines, Charles A. *academic administrator*

Rancho Viejo
Garza, Roberto Jesus *retired education educator*

Richardson
Bray, Carolyn Scott *education educator*
†Downey, Margie Lee Cooper *educator, writer*
Dunn, David E. *university dean*
Kelly, Rita Mae *academic administrator, researcher*

Rockdale
Estell, Dora Lucile *retired educational administrator*

Roscoe
†Beeks, Cheryl Elaine *elementary school educator*

Round Rock
Ledbetter, Sharon Faye Welch *retired educational consultant*

Rusk
†Hendrick, Zelwanda *drama and psychology educator*

San Angelo
Davison, Elizabeth Jane Linton *education educator*
Mowrer, Robert Ranck *educator*
Smith, Karen B. *educational consultant*

San Antonio
Barrera, Elvira Puig *counselor, therapist, educator*
Bennett, Sister Elsa Mary *retired secondary education educator*
Brazil, John Russell *academic administrator*
Chance, Truett Lamar *retired secondary school educator*
Garner, Jo Ann Starkey *retired elementary and special education educator*
Goelz, Paul Cornelius *university dean*
Hall, Denise *special education educator*
Henderson, Dwight Franklin *dean, educator*
†Hogan, Donna Helen *school librarian, educator*
Horowitz, Rosalind *education educator, researcher*
†King, Kandi J. *secondary school educator, consultant*
Ledvorowski, Thomas Edmund *secondary education educator*
Madrid, Olga Hilda Gonzalez *retired elementary education educator, association executive*
Massey, Patti Chryl *elementary school educator*
Maxwell, Diana Kathleen *early childhood education educator*
McBee, Lucy Armijo *retired elementary education educator, administrator, singer, actress, writer*
Orange, Carolyn *education educator*
Persellin, Diane Y. Cummings *music education educator*
Robertson, Samuel Luther, Jr., *special education educator, therapist, researcher*
†Sobre, Judith Berg *education educator*
Tomkewitz, Marie Adele *elementary school educator*
Wartman, Steven *dean, educator*
White, Charles B. *academic administrator*
Young, James Julius *university administrator, retired army officer*

San Diego
Pena, Modesta Celedonia *retired principal*

San Juan
†Guzmán, Belinda F. *elementary school educator*

San Marcos
Barragán, Celia Silguero *junior high school educator*
Clayton, Katy *elementary education educator*
Fite, Kathleen Elizabeth *education educator*
Fox, Frank G. *school librarian, writer*
†McCall, Carolyn Murphy *education educator*
Moore, Betty Jean *retired education educator*

Sherman
Carnes, La Zetta *educator*
Jarma, Donna Marie *secondary education educator*
Page, Oscar C. *academic administrator*

Southlake
Somerstein-Campbell, Jasmine Aurora Abrera *preschool administrator, educator*

Spade
Davis, Thomas Pinkney *secondary school educator*

Sugar Land
Ramos, Rose Mary *elementary school educator*

Sulphur Springs
†Clayton, Pamela Sanders *special education educator*
Gibson, Jannette Poe *educator, consultant*

Temple
Kreitz, Helen Marie *retired elementary education educator*
Staten, Donna Kay *elementary school educator*

Texarkana
†Austin, Sandra Jenelle *school librarian, language educator*
†Davis-Sutton, Rosiland *secondary school educator*

The Woodlands
Sharman, Diane Lee *secondary school educator*

Trophy Club
Hardy, Vicki *elementary school principal*

Tyler
Davidson, Jack Leroy *academic administrator*
†Dunlap, Martha McKinzie *elementary school educator*
Waller, Wilma Ruth *retired secondary school educator and librarian*

Victoria
Haynes, Karen Sue *academic administrator, educator*

Waco
Belew, John Seymour *academic administrator, chemist*
Brooks, Roger Leon *university president*
†Girouard, Tandy Denise *special education educator, psychology educator*

Hollingsworth, Martha Lynette *secondary school educator*
Lindsey, Jonathan Asmel *university official, librarian, educator*
Reynolds, Herbert Hal *academic administrator*

Weatherford
Colton, James Patrick *community college administrator*
Estes, Carolyn Ann Hull *retired elementary school educator*
†Miller, Dixie Davis *elementary school educator*

West Columbia
†Walker, Phyllis LeVonne *elementary school educator*

Wichita Falls
Haff, Guy Gregory *exercise science educator, researcher*
†Leavell, Landrum Pinson, II, *seminary administrator, clergyman, educator*
Rodriguez, Louis Joseph *academic administrator, economist, educator*
Stange, Terrence V. *education educator*

UTAH

Bountiful
Rawlins, Jan *principal*

Cedar City
Templin, Carl Ross *college dean, educator*

Logan
Ahlstrom, Callis Blythe *university official*
Emert, George Henry *former academic administrator, biochemist*
Gay, Charles W., Jr., *academic administrator*
†Hall, Kermit Lance *academic administrator, historian, educator*
Hunsaker, Scott Leslie *gifted and talented education educator*
McKell, Cyrus M. *retired college dean, plant physiologist*
Merrill, M. David *education educator*
Shaver, James Porter *education educator, university dean*

Ogden
Thompson, Paul Harold *university president*

Orem
Cook, Bradley James *academic administrator*
Romesburg, Kerry D. *university president, former state education administrator*

Provo
†Bergeson, Scott D. *education educator*
Boyter, Scott M. *academic administrator*
Bullough, Robert Vernon, Jr., *educator*
Densley, Colleen T. *principal*
Dyches, Tina Taylor *special education educator, consultant*
Hansen, H. Reese *dean, educator*
†Samuelson, Cecil O. *academic administrator*
Shirts, Randall Brent *chemistry educator, researcher*
Stahmann, Robert F. *education educator*
Whatcott, Marsha Rasmussen *elementary education educator*

Saint George
†Cahoon, Beth Ann *special education educator*

Salem
Hahn, Joan Christensen *retired secondary education educator, travel agent*

Salt Lake City
Bassis, Michael Steven *academic administrator*
†Bennion, John Warren *urban education educator*
Betz, A. Lorris *dean, pediatrician, educator, consultant*
†Brown, Hugh Auchincloss, III, *education educator*
Christensen, Bruce LeRoy *former academic administrator, commercial broadcasting executive*
Donaldson, Rebecca S. *elementary education educator, reading specialist*
Drew, Clifford James *university administrator, special education and educational psychology educator*
Gough, Eugene V. *vocational education educator*
†Huefner, Dixie Snow *special education educator*
Kim, Sung Wan *educator*
Machen, J. Bernard *academic administrator*
Markham, Reed B. *education educator, consultant*
McCleary, Lloyd E(verald) *education educator*
Pickering, AvaJane *specialized education facility executive*
Stock, Peggy A(nn) *college president, educator*

Sandy
Pierce, Ilona Lambson *educational administrator*
Sabey, J(ohn) Wayne *academic administrator, consultant*

West Jordan
Shepherd, Paul H. *elementary school educator*

VERMONT

Bennington
Rector, Liam *university program director*

Brattleboro
Stewart-Smith, David *adult education educator, historian, researcher*

Burlington
Allard, Judith Louise *secondary education educator*

†Helzer, John Earl *academic administrator, educator, psychiatrist*
†Murakami, Kentaro *education educator, neuroscientist*
Warshaw, Joseph Bennett *dean, pediatrician*
Willis, Russell Edward *academic administrator*

Colchester
†Ashline, George Lawrence *education educator*
Kenney, John Peter *dean, educator*
vanderHeyden, Marc A. *academic administrator*

East Corinth
Freeman, Carole Cook *education educator*

Lower Waterford
Burnham, Robert Alan *academic administrator, educator*

Ludlow
Davis, Vera *elementary school educator*

Manchester Center
Sossi, Marie Frances *elementary education educator*

Middlebury
McCardell, John Malcolm, Jr., *academic administrator*
O'Brien, George Dennis *retired academic administrator*

Northfield
Schneider, Richard William *academic administrator*

Poultney
Benson, Thomas Luther *academic administrator*
Cooper, Charleen Frances *special and elementary education educator*
Pentkowski, Raymond J. *principal*

Rutland
Lucci, William Ralph, Jr., *school system administrator*

South Hero
Bisson, Roger *middle school educator*

South Royalton
Doria, Anthony Notarnicola *college dean, educator*

Strafford
Williams, William Magavern *headmaster*

Swanton
Chaim, Linda Susan *special education adminsistrator*

Williston
†Foss, Jean Mitchell *school system administrator*

VIRGINIA

Alexandria
Bartlett, Elizabeth Susan *audio-visual specialist*
Dubin, Martin Steven *principal*
Edgell, Karin Jane *reading specialist, special education educator*
Jenkins, John Smith *retired academic dean, lawyer*
†Johnson, Marlys Marlene *elementary school educator*
Pastin, Mark Joseph *association executive*
Smith, Harold Allen *education administrator, researcher, educator*
Stevens, Alice Marie *educational consultant*

Amherst
Campbell, Catherine Lynn *elementary school educator*
†Copp, Cindy Pierce *education educator*
Herbert, Amanda Kathryn *special education educator*

Annandale
Bohen, Dolores Boylston *retired school administrator*
Veney, M. Beatrice *professional counselor*
Wilhelmi, Mary Charlotte *education educator, college official*

Arlington
†Bawa, Raj *education educator, educator, biodefense specialist, biotechnology company executive, patent agent*
Berg, Sister Marie Majella *president emerita*
Davis-Imhof, Nancy Louise *retired elementary school educator*
†Finta, Frances Mickna *secondary school educator*
Hill, Donald Wain *education accreditation commission executive*
†McTique, Maurice P. *director*
Ramaley, Judith Aitken *former university president, endocrinologist*
Rogers, Sharon J. *education consultant*
Rosenblatt, Louise Michel *emerita educator*
Simms, Frances Bell *retired elementary education educator*
Stout, Mary Webb *education program specialist*
Trombley, Edward Francis, III, *educational administrator*

Ashland
Martin, Roger Harry *college president*
†Rice, Adrian Clifford *education educator*

Blacksburg
Barksdale, Mary Alice *education educator*
Brown, Gregory Neil *university administrator, forest physiology educator*
†Eyre, Peter *dean*
Hirt, Joan B. *education educator*
King, Stephen Emmett *educational administrator*

Pearson, Ronald Earl *educator, researcher*
Porter, Duncan MacNair *editor, educator*
Smoot, Raymond D., Jr., *academic administrator*
Steger, Charles William *university administrator*
Tillar, Thomas Cato, Jr., *university alumni relations administrator, consultant*
Torgersen, Paul Ernest *academic administrator, educator*
Wall, Robert Thompson *secondary school educator*

Boyd Tavern
Darden, Donna Bernice *special education educator*

Bridgewater
†Barkley, Terrell Wayne *school librarian, museum curator*
†Geisert, Wayne Frederick *educational consultant, retired administrator*

Burke
Emery, Vicki Morris *school library media administrator*

Charlottesville
Casteen, John Thomas, III, *university president*
†Frey, Jr., Sherwood Charles *education educator, consultant*
Garson, Arthur, Jr., *dean, medical educator*
†Greville, Florence Nusim *secondary school educator, mathematician*
Hine, Jonathan Trumbull, Jr., *educator, translator*
†Keith, Delorese Parker *elementary school educator*
Matson, Robert Edward *public management educator, leadership consultant*
Miller, Margaret Alison *education educator*
†O'Neil, Robert Marchant *university administrator, law educator*
†Patashnik, Eric Mark *education educator*
Reynolds, Robert Edgar *academic administrator, physician*
Roots, Keith Dyland *academic administrator*
Smith, Clyde Ray *dean*
Thompson, Kenneth W(inifred) *educational director, writer, editor, administrator, social science educator*

Chesapeake
Carson, Michael *secondary school educator, music educator*
Clarkson, Phyllis Owens *early childhood educator*
Lewter, Helen Clark *elementary education educator, retired*
†Potter, Cynthia M. *art educator, artist*

Chester
Law, Thomas Melvin *college president*
Spindler, Judith Tarleton *elementary school educator*

Christiansburg
Patty, Anna Christine *tax specialist*

Danville
Aaron, Larry Gene *secondary education educator, writer, minister*
†Habich Wolf, Lynn Charlotte *education educator, department chairman, educational consultant*
Pfau, Richard Anthony *university president*

Dulles
Hegarty, George John *university rector, English educator*

Fairfax
Crouch, Toni L. *principal*
Dykstra, Vergil Homer *retired academic administrator*
Kettlewell, Gail Biery *academic administrator*
Longin, Thomas Charles *retired academic administrator*
Reeves, Tracey Elizabeth *director*
†Silcox, Gordon Bruce *career management consultant*
†Tichy, Susan *education educator, writer*

Falls Church
Copes, Marvin Lee *college president*
Johnson, William David *retired university administrator*
†Parson, Stephen Richard *education educator, consultant*
†Teodorovic, Dusan *educator*
Todd, Shirley Ann *school system administrator*

Fort Belvoir
Ainsley, James Robert *academic administrator*

Fort Lee
Simmonds, Robert Maurer *education educator*

Fredericksburg
Emory, Samuel Thomas *retired educator*
Hedke, Richard Alvin *retired gifted education educator*
Jenks-Davies, Kathryn Ryburn *retired daycare provider and owner, civic worker*

Gainesville
Burke, Marjorie Tisdale *retired special education educator*
Tuck, Russell R., Jr., *former college president*

Great Falls
Andrews, Betty Bauserman *retired secondary school educator, property manager*

Grundy
Davis, W. Jeremy *dean, law educator, lawyer*

Hampton
Harvey, William Robert *university president*
†Makagon, Andrzej Leszek *education educator*
†Moser, Eugene Paul, Jr., *retired secondary school educator*
†Satterthwaite, Janice Ursula *academic administrator*

Harrisonburg
Carrier, Ronald Edwin *academic administrator, director*
†Wang, Greg G. *education educator, consultant*

Heathsville
Sisson, Jean Cralle *retired middle school educator*

Herndon
†Jones, Reba (Becki) Pestun *elementary school educator, music educator*

Hillsville
Becker, Elizabeth Anne *secondary education educator*

Keswick
Fletcher, John Caldwell *bioethicist, educator*

Lansdowne
Green, May Clayman *early childhood educator and administrator*

Leesburg
†Alwani, Ahmed J. *dean, consultant*

Lexington
†Ball, Gordon Victor *adult education educator, writer, editor, photographer*
Burish, Thomas Gerard *academic administrator*
Partlett, David F. *dean, law educator*
†Squire, James C *adult education educator, engineer, consultant*
Thelin, John Robert *academic administrator, writer*
Young, Kenneth Evans *educational consultant*

Lynchburg
Husted, Stewart Winthrop *dean, marketing educator, consultant*
†Schewel, Rosel Hoffberger *education educator*

Manassas
Archer, Chalmers, Jr., *retired education educator*

Marion
Greer, Carole Kilby *reading specialist*

Mc Dowell
Harkleroad, Jo-Ann Decker *special education educator*

Mc Lean
Michalowicz, Karen Dee *secondary education educator*
Scribner, Sherlie Ann *educator*

Mechanicsville
†Gorman, Joseph Batterton *elementary school educator*
Henshaw, William Raleigh *retired middle school educator*
†Watkins, Carol A. *special education educator*

Middleburg
Coven, Robert Michael *secondary school educator, researcher, writer*
Kaplan, Jean Gaither (Norma Kaplan) *reading specialist, retired educator*

Midlothian
Smith, Alma Davis *elementary education educator*

Moneta
Wiatt, Carol Stultz *elementary education educator*

Monterey
†Blanchard, Julia Smith *secondary school educator*

Newport News
Eastman, John Robert *educator*
Hightower, John Brantley *arts administrator*
Powell, Jouett Lynn *college dean, philosophy and religious studies educator*

Norfolk
Bucher, Katherine Toth *education educator, librarian*
Combs, Charles Donald *academic administrator*
DiCroce, Deborah Marie *college president*
†Epplein, Lawrence Elliott *hospitality management educator*
Farmer, Evan R. *academic administrator, dermatologist, researcher*
Jones, Franklin Ross *education educator*
Koch, James Verch *academic administrator, economist*
Notti, Donna Betts *special education educator*
†Opfer, Steven Earl *education educator, researcher*
Ritz, John Michael *education educator*
Runte, Roseann *academic administrator*
Sebren, Lucille Griggs *retired educator*
Steele, James Eugene *retired school system administrator*
Stepanovich, Paul *management educator*
Strait, Patricia Bellin *organizational management educator*
†Taylor Claud, Andrea *educational consultant*

Orange
Daniel, Daniele Mallison *elementary school educator*

Petersburg
Miles, Ruby Williams *secondary education educator*

Poquoson
Parry, Thomas Herbert, Jr., *school system administrator, educational consultant*

Portsmouth
Williams, Lena Harding *educational administrator*

Quantico
Cann, John Pearce, III, *educator*

Radford
Templeton, Dennie, III, *educational administrator, consultant*

Rapidan
Powers, Evelyn Mae *education educator*

Reston
Keefe, James Washburn *educational writer, researcher, consultant*

Richlands
†Claytor, Katherine W. Moss *secondary education educator*

Richmond
†Archer, Kellie Jo *education educator*
Blank, Florence Weiss *literacy educator, editor*
Boudinot, Frank Douglas *dean*
Budd, Richard Wade *university official, communications scientist, priest*
Christenbury, Leila *education educator*
Cooper, William Edwin *university president, educator*
Drain, Cecil B. *university dean, nurse anesthetist educator, retired army officer*
Ellis, Anthony John *education educator*
Hamel, Dana Bertrand *academic administrator*
†Heilman, E. Bruce *academic administrator*
Hunt, Ronald J. *academic administrator*
James, Allix Bledsoe *retired university president*
Jones, Jeanne Pitts *pre-school administrator*
McGhee, Annette Booker *educator*
†Miles, Donna Jones *education educator*
Miles, Donna Regina *educator, researcher*
Minor, Marian Thomas *elementary and secondary school educational consultant*
Newsome, Heber H. *academic administrator*
Trani, Eugene Paul *university president, educator*

Roanoke
Cole, Evelyn Marie *day care administrator*

Springfield
Insalaco-De Nigris, Anna Maria Theresa *middle school educator*
†Kropp, Edward H. *education educator, consultant*
†Leavitt, Mary Janice Deimel *special education educator, civic worker*

Stafford
Lambert, Linda Margaret *reading specialist*

Staunton
Hagen, Agnes Mary *adult education educator, writer*

Sterling
†Bridwell, Carolyn Elizabeth *elementary school educator*

Surry
Sprouse, Earlene Pentecost *special education educator*

Urbanna
Salley, John Jones *university administrator, oral pathologist*

Vienna
Colosi, Thomas R. *educator, mediator*

Virginia Beach
Jones, Robert Clair *middle school educator*
Kawczynski, Diane Marie *elementary and middle school educator, composer*
Morgan, Raymond Franklin *education educator*
Selig, William George *university official*

Waynesboro
Dillon, William Henry *retired secondary school educator*

West Springfield
Sproul, Joan Heeney *elementary school educator*

Williamsburg
Aldrow-Liput, Priscilla Reese *retired elementary education educator*
†Bell, Christine Marie *secondary educator*
Birney, Robert Charles *retired academic administrator, psychologist*
Calver, Richard Allen *retired college dean*
Chandler, Kimberley Lynn *educational administrator*
Cross, Dennis Wayne *academic administrator*
†Palmer, Jonathan Wold *education educator, academic administrator*
Reveley, Walter Taylor, III, *dean*
Smith, James Brown, Jr., *secondary school educator*
†Tschannen-Moran, Megan *education educator*

Winchester
Pleacher, David Henry *secondary school educator*

Wise
Smiddy, Joseph Charles *retired academic administrator*

Woodbridge
Packard, Mildred Ruth *middle school educator*

Yorktown
Rogers, Sheila Wood *elementary and secondary school educator*

WASHINGTON

Anacortes
Felger, Ralph William *educator, retired military officer*

Bellevue
Clark, Richard Walter *education consultant*
Westergaard, George Henry *secondary education educator*

Benton City
†Kromminga, An-Marie *special education educator*

Bothell
Banks, Cherry Ann McGee *education educator*

Bremerton
Fischer, Mary E. *special education educator*
Milander, Henry Martin *educational consultant*

Centralia
Kirk, Henry Port *academic administrator*

Cheney
Jordan, Stephen M. *university president*
†Stearns, Susan A *education educator*

Chimacum
Hollenbeck, Dorothy Rose *principal*

College Place
†Anderson, Clarence Glen *dean*

Davenport
Harper, Rob *secondary school educator*

Ellensburg
McIntyre, Jerilyn Sue *academic administrator*
†Nethery, Vincent Michael *adult education educator*

Everett
Callaghan, Mary Anne *secondary school educator*
Hundley, Ronnie *academic administrator*

Federal Way
Duggan, Edward Martin *secondary science education educator*

Gig Harbor
Minnerly, Robert Ward *retired headmaster*

Goldendale
Nygaard, Mary Payne *primary school education*

Greenacres
†Peterson, Carol L. *school system administrator, education educator*

Issaquah
Newbill, Karen Margaret *elementary school educator, education educator*

Kelso
Janke, John Eric *secondary educator*

Kenmore
Jennerich, Edward John *university official and dean*

Kennewick
Merkel, Patricia Mae *retired school system administrator*

Kirkland
Argue, Don Harvey *college president, minister*
Ballinger, Sandra Lynn *secondary education educator*
Rich, Clayton *retired university official and educator*
Tyllia, Frank Michael *university official, educator*

Lacey
Chen, Huabin *education educator*
Kuniyasu, Keith Kazumi *secondary education educator*

Lakewood
Oakes, DuWayne Earl *retired principal*
Walker, Doris Ann *education educator*

Leavenworth
Smith, G(odfrey) T(aylor) *retired academic administrator*

Mill Creek
Corbally, John Edward *adult education educator*

Nine Mile Falls
Payne, Arlie Jean *parent education administrator*

Olympia
†Vavrus, Michael J. *education educator, researcher*

Otis Orchards
Coffin, Mary Ann *elementary school educator*

Port Angeles
Kane, Patrick J. *high school principal*

Pullman
†Lewis, Norman G. *academic administrator, researcher, consultant*
Rawlins, V. Lane *university president*
Shrope, Nancy Ruth *research administrator*

Richland
†Baker, Timothy Kevin *education educator*
Miller, James Vince *university president*

Seattle
Abbott, Robert Dean *education scientist*
Baker, Roland Jerald *educator*
Banks, James Albert *educational research director, educator*
Carlson, Dale Arvid *university dean*
Coulter, John Arthur *academic administrator*
Cox, Frederick Moreland *retired university dean, social worker*
Denny, Brewster Castberg *retired university dean*
†Fetterly, Mary E. *counseling administrator*
Gardiner, John Jacob *leadership educator, writer, philosopher, speaker*
Gerberding, William Passavant *retired university president*
Goodlad, John Inkster *education educator, writer*
Grembowski, David Emil *educator, researcher*
Halferty, Frank Joseph *middle school music educator*
Hampton, Shelley Lynn *hearing impaired educator*
Hegyvary, Sue Thomas *nursing school dean, editor, nursing educator*
†Huntsman, Lee *university provost, academic administrator*
†Katsov, Kirill *education educator, researcher*
Ostrom, Katherine Elma *retired educator*
Plotnick, Robert David *educator, economic consultant*
Proctor, Richard Macfarlane *art educator, artist, writer, gallery owner*
Ralston, Charles Philip *elementary school educator*
Ramsey, Paul Glenn *dean, internist*
Ray, Charles Kendall *retired university dean*
Silver, Michael *school superintendent*
Somerman, Martha J. *academic administrator*
Stringer, William Jeremy *university official*
Sundborg, Stephen V. *academic administrator*
Terrell, W(illiam) Glenn *university president emeritus*
†Voegtlin-Anderson, Mary Margaret *secondary school educator, music educator*
Warlum, Michael Frank *training, consulting and writing company executive*
†Wasley, Patricia A. *dean*
Woods, Nancy Fugate *dean, women's health nurse*

Sequim
McGee, Jane Marie *retired educator*

Spanaway
†Parker, Lynda Christine Rylander *secondary education educator*

Spokane
Baker, Danial Edwin *director, consultant, pharmacy educator*
†Danke, Virginia *educator, travel consultant*
†Helgeson, James G. *education educator*
Hosking, Neville John *educational administrator*
Matters, Clyde Burns *former college president*
McManus, Patrick Francis *educator, writer*
Nyman, Carl John, Jr., *university dean and official*
Robinson, William P. *academic administrator, consultant, speaker*
Spitzer, Robert J. *academic administrator*
†Watson, William M *director*

Sumner
Wickizer, Cindy Louise *retired elementary school educator*

Tacoma
Baldassin, Michael Robert *secondary school educator*
Davis, Albert Raymond *secondary education educator*
King, Gundar Julian *retired university dean*
Lewis, Jan Patricia *education educator*
†Wu, Dane Wenzhen *educator*

Toppenish
Ross, Kathleen Anne *college president*

Vancouver
†Tuttle, Marcia *retired elementary school educator, music educator*

Walla Walla
Cronin, Thomas Edward *academic administrator*

WEST VIRGINIA

Athens
Marsh, Joseph Franklin, Jr., *emeritus college president, educational consultant*

Beckley
Brownlee, Sarah Hale *elementary special education educator*
†Carpenter, J.D. *academic administrator*

Belmont
†Drane, A. D. *adult education educator*

Bluefield
Blevins, Thomas E. *college administrator, educator*
Loundmon-Clay, Juanita L. *educator, academic administrator*
Patsel, E. Ralph, Jr., *retired registrar, research director*

Charleston
Arrington, Carolyn Ruth *education consultant*
Davis, Billie Johnston *school counselor*
Manning, Sherry Fischer *college president emeritus, business executive*

Welch, Edwin Hugh *academic administrator*

Clarksburg
†Leuliette, Connie Jane *secondary educator*

Dunbar
†Given, Melissa Ann *elementary school educator, educational consultant*
Russell, James Alvin, Jr., *college administrator*

Fairmont
Hardway, Wendell Gary *retired academic administrator*

Glen Jean
Beverly, Laura Elizabeth *special education educator*

Glenville
†Schmetzer, Frances Myers *secondary school educator*

Harpers Ferry
Bailey, Nancy Joyce *educator*

Huntington
†Anderson, Lorraine Pearson *dean*
Gould, Alan Brant *academic administrator*
Hayes, Robert Bruce *former college president, educator*
Hooper, James William *educator*
Kent, Calvin Albert *university administrator*
McKown, Charles Henry *dean*
Shondel, William J. *academic administrator*

Lewisburg
Adelman, Michael *dean*

Martinsburg
Wendel, Joseph Arthur *retired secondary education educator*

Morgantown
Allamong, Betty D. *academic administrator*
†Bajura, Richard Albert *university administrator, engineering educator*
Biddington, William Robert *university administrator, dental educator*
Bucklew, Neil S. *educator, past university president*
D'Alessandri, Robert M. *dean*
Douglas, Stephen Lane *academic administrator*
Drvar, Margaret Adams *vocational education educator*
Haggett, Rosemary Romanowski *academic administrator*
Hardesty, David Carter, Jr., *university president*
Levine, Ann Mebane *university administrator*
†Mei, Betty Muichi *director*
Nellis, M. Duane *dean, geography educator*
Stewart, Guy Harry *university dean emeritus, journalism educator*

Mt. Gay
†Pierce, Calisa A. *director*

New Martinsville
†Francis, Elizabeth Romine *secondary school educator, theater director*

Nitro
Lucas, Panola *elementary education educator*

Parkersburg
Meadows, Lois Annette *elementary education educator*

Saint Albans
Smith, Robert Carlisle *department administrator, welding educator*

Shepherdstown
†Wilson, Rebecca Ann *English and special education educator, retired*

Vienna
†Terry, Ralph Bruce *education educator*

Walton
Parker, Theresa Ann Boggs *special education educator, music educator*

West Liberty
Forrester, James Ronald *educator*

Wheeling
Campbell, Clyde Del *academic administrator*
Welker, William Andrew *reading specialist*

WISCONSIN

Appleton
Meidl, Kevin *secondary education educator*
Warch, Richard *academic administrator*

Barron
Johnson, Eleanor Mae *education educator*

Beloit
†Blake, Kenneth Wayne, III, *principal, music educator*
Burris, John Edward *academic administrator, biologist, educator*
Melvin, Charles Alfred, III, *superintendent of schools*
†Wheeler, Karla *education educator*

Burlington
†Roeschen, Marlene Y. *retired elementary school educator*

Cedarburg
Tamsen, Christi Marie Wagner *secondary school educator, coach*

De Forest
O'Neil, J(ames) Peter *computer software designer, educator*

Delafield
Kurth, Ronald James *university president, retired naval officer*

Eau Claire
Brill, Donald Maxim *educator, writer, researcher*
†Brummer, James J. *adult education educator, writer*
Clark, Mark William *dean, educator*
Joos, Winnie J. *home and community educator*
Kozbial, Richard James *retired elementary education educator*
Mash, Donald J. *college president*
†Richards, Jerry Lee *academic administrator, religious educator*

Elkhorn
Reinke, Doris Marie *retired elementary education educator*

Fort Atkinson
†Schumacher, Mabel G. *director, consultant*

Fox Point
Stahl, Mary Gail *elementary educator*

Freedom
†Moscinski, David Joseph *educational administrator, school psychologist*

Glendale
Schenker, Eric *university dean, economist*

Green Bay
†Perkins, Mark L. *university chancellor*
†Shepard, W. Bruce *academic administrator*
Weidner, Edward William *university chancellor, political scientist*

Hales Corners
Michalski, Wacław (Żur-Żurowski Wacł Michalski) *adult education educator*

Holmen
Meyer, Karl William *retired university president*

Hudson
Dahle, Johannes Upton *retired academic administrator*

Janesville
Thomas, Margaret Ann *educational administrator, art educator*

Kenosha
†Arif, Mohammed *education educator*
Armstrong, Leona May Bottrell *retired counselor, educator*
Campbell, F(enton) Gregory *college administrator, historian*
†Eigenberger, Martin E *education educator*
Levis, Richard George *secondary school educator*

La Crosse
†Harwood, Larry D. *education educator*
†Lentz, Kirby Warren *academic administrator*
Medland, William James *university president*
Wallin, Susan Marie *secondary school counselor*

Madison
Aberle, Elton David *dean*
Arenas, Andrea Teresa *academic administrator*
Bell-Jackson, Marianne Jeanne *elementary and secondary education educator*
Berggren-Moilanen, Bonnie Lee *education educator*
Busby, Edward Oliver *retired dean*
Fermanich, Mark Leon *education researcher, consultant*
†Jackson, Jerlando F.L. *education educator*
Kreuter, Gretchen V. *academic administrator*
Lyall, Katharine C(ulbert) *academic administrator, economics educator*
Mertens, Diane K. *secondary education educator*
Odden, Allan Robert *education educator*
†Reilly, Kevin P. *academic administrator*
†Suri, Jeremi A. *education educator*
†Wiley, John D. *academic administrator*
Yuill, Thomas MacKay *academic administrator, microbiology educator*

Malone
Tyunaitis, Patricia Ann *elementary school educator*

Manitowoc
Schuh, Martha Schuhmann *mathematics educator*

Mayville
†Schabel, Lorie Ann *pre-school educator*

Menomonee Falls
Hinnrichs-Dahms, Holly Beth *middle school educator*
Schlagel, David Mark *academic administrator*

Mequon
Bell, Scott William *private school educator, principal*
Dohmen, Mary Holgate *retired primary school educator*
Ellis, William Grenville *academic administrator, management consultant*

Middleton
Conaway, Jane Ellen *elementary education educator*

Milwaukee
Aman, Mohammed Mohammed *dean, library and information science educator*

Barth, Karl Luther *retired seminary president*
†Benesh, Sara C. *adult education educator*
Conner, David Lee *secondary educator*
Dunn, Michael J. *dean*
Fonner, Kelly S. *educational technologist, consultant*
†Gagliani, William Dennis *school librarian*
†Gonzalez, Jorge Antonio *education educator*
Hansen, John Herbert *university administrator, accountant*
Iaquinta, Leonard Phillip *university official*
Jenkins, Clarence William, Jr., *academic administrator*
Read, Sister Joel *academic administrator*
Reed, John Kennedy Emanuel *elementary school teacher*
Rheams, Annie Elizabeth *education educator*
Rhoten, Juliana Theresa *retired school principal*
Roberson, Reniti Renea *elementary school educator*
Sankovitz, James Leo *retired development director, lobbyist*
Schroeder, John H. *university chancellor*
Setright, Mildred Alberta *educator*
Viets, Hermann *college president, consultant*
Wake, Madeline Musante *academic administrator, nursing educator*
Wild, Robert Anthony *university president*
†Yakovlev, Vladislav *education educator, researcher*

Nekoosa
†Ramirez, Mary Catherine *retired secondary school educator*

New Glarus
Etter, Peter Erich *retired school district administrator*

New London
Fitzgerald, Laurine Elisabeth *university dean, educator*

Oak Creek
Thomae, Mary Joan Pangborn *special education educator*

Oconomowoc
Reich, Rose Marie *retired art educator*

Oconto
Watson-Boone, Rebecca A. *library and information studies researcher, educator*

Osceola
Finster, James Robert *library media specialist*

Oshkosh
†Earns, Lane Robert *academic administrator, historian, educator*
Herzog, Barbara Jean *secondary school educator, administrator*
Kerrigan, John E. *academic administrator*
Olejniczak, Bernard Charles *education educator*
†Ristow, Thelma Frances *elementary educator*

Palmyra
Hammiller, Ruth Ellen *school official and psychologist*

Platteville
Lindahl, Thomas Jefferson *retired university dean*
†Markee, David James *university official, education educator*

Racine
†Baldukas, Ann-Mari Peirce *dean*
†Bradley, Paul N. *special education educator*

Rhinelander
Mussehl, Allan Arthur *program director*

River Falls
†Lydecker, Ann Marie *college administrator*
Thibodeau, Gary A. *academic administrator*

Salem
Hayes, Doris Ann *elementary education educator, consultant*

Sheboygan
†Abbay, Alemseged *education educator*

Shorewood
Lietz, Jeremy Jon *educational administrator, writer*

Spencer
†Herder, Paul O. *secondary school educator*

Sun Prairie
Schmidt, Glenn Norbert *special education educator*
Sveum, Steven John *secondary school educator*

Superior
Peterson, Charlene Marie *educational administrator*

Thiensville
Hobbs, Walter Clarence *retired educator*

Valders
Lindholm, William Robert *elementary school educator*

Watertown
Henry, Helga Irmgard *liberal arts educator*

Waukesha
†Gustafson, Mardel Emma *secondary school educator, writer*
†Ringhand, Ryan Randall *career planning administrator, educator*
†Satterlee, William Thomas *career planning administrator, consultant*

Trebon, Thomas *academic administrator*

Wausau
Switalski, Michael Mathew *secondary educator, lawyer*

Wauwatosa
Dupuis, Kateri Theresa *retired elementary education educator*

West Bend
Christianson, Marcia LaRaye *middle school educator*

Whitefish Bay
†Pustejovsky, Susan F. *education educator*

Whitewater
Busse, Eileen Elaine *special education educator*
Greenhill, H. Gaylon *retired academic administrator*
†Gwalla-Ogisi, Nomsa *education educator, consultant*
†Kolb, Sharon Marie *educator, cognitive disabilities specialist*
Zbikowski, John Michael *education educator*

Wisconsin Rapids
Kronholm, Martha Mary *elementary education educator*
Olson-Hellerud, Linda Kathryn *elementary school educator*
Pahl, Randall *principal, parochial school educator*

WYOMING

Buffalo
Urruty, Katherine Jean *secondary school educator*

Casper
†Moler, Mary *secondary school educator*
†Richardson, Bruce Alan *academic administrator*
Wilkes, Shar (Joan Charlene Wilkes) *elementary education educator*

Cheyenne
Hart, Kerry *college administrator, music educator*
Rice, Wallace William *secondary education educator*
Richardson, Earl Wilson *elementary education educator, retired*
Weigner, Brent James *secondary education educator*

Ethete
†Tepper, Marcy Elizabeth *drug education director*

Green River
†Albers, Dolores M. *secondary education educator*

Jackson
Massy, William Francis *education educator, consultant*
Ninnemann, Thomas George *secondary education educator*

Laramie
Chatton, Barbara Ann *education educator*
Dubois, Philip Leon *university administrator, political science educator*
†Landis, Bruce Chapman *academic administrator*
McBride, Judith *elementary education educator*
Schmitt, Diana Mae *elementary education educator*

Riverton
Pickinpaugh, Richard Neal *assistant principal, educator*

Rock Springs
Arambel, Phyllis Ann *elementary education educator*

TERRITORIES OF THE UNITED STATES

GUAM

Talofofo
Taylor, James John *academic administrator*

NORTHERN MARIANA ISLANDS

Saipan
†Kaufer, Connie Tenorio *retired reading specialist*

PUERTO RICO

Bayamon
Rosa, Helen *dean*

Cayey
†Acevedo-Loubriel, Suzette *adult education educator*

Ramey
†Aponte, Abraham *secondary school educator*

San German
Mojica, Agnes *academic administrator*

San Juan
Carreras, Francisco José *retired university president, foundation executive*
Joglar, Francisco *academic administrator*

Lopez, Angel R. Pagan *dean, dentist*
Matheu, Federico Manuel *university chancellor*
†Pedreira, Mark Alan *education educator*

VIRGIN ISLANDS

Frederiksted
Petrait, Brother James Anthony *secondary education educator, clergy member*

St Thomas
†Kean, Orville *academic administrator*
†Morse, Theodore Freeman *dean, writer*

CANADA

ALBERTA

Athabasca
McGreal, Rory Patrick *university official*

Calgary
Neale, E(rnest) R(ichard) Ward *retired university official, consultant*
Watanabe, Mamoru *former university dean, physician, researcher*
White, Terrence Harold *academic administrator, sociologist*

Edmonton
Adams, Peter Frederick *university president, civil engineer*
†Tyrrell, D. Lorne J. *university dean*

BRITISH COLUMBIA

Cobble Hill
Cox, Albert Reginald *academic administrator, physician, retired*

Kelowna
Muggeridge, Derek Brian *dean, engineering consultant*

Langley
Van Brummelen, Harro Walter *education educator*

Vancouver
Finnegan, Cyril Vincent *retired university dean, zoology educator*
Haycock, Kenneth Roy *educator, consultant, administrator*
McNeill, John Hugh *pharmaceutical sciences educator*
Webber, William Alexander *university administrator, physician*

Victoria
Welch, S(tephen) Anthony *university administrator, Islamic studies and arts educator*

MANITOBA

Winnipeg
Poettcker, Henry *retired academic administrator*
Stalker, Jacqueline D'Aoust *academic administrator, educator*

NEWFOUNDLAND

Saint John's
May, Arthur W. *retired academic administrator, educator*

NOVA SCOTIA

Halifax
†Jaeger, Leslie Gordon *university administrator*
Murray, Thomas John (Jock Murray) *medical humanities educator, medical researcher, neurologist*
Ozmon, Kenneth Lawrence *retired university president, educator*

Nova Scotia
Sweet, William *educator, author, administrator*

Timberlea
Verma, Surjit Kumar *retired school system administrator*

Wolfville
Ogilvie, Kelvin Kenneth *university president, chemistry educator*

ONTARIO

Arnprior
†Shideler, Janet L. *adult education educator*

Belleville
Buckley, Edward Joseph *retired academic dean*

Gloucester
Malouin, Jean-Louis *university educator*

Hamilton
Shaw, Denis Martin *university dean, former geology educator*

London
Davenport, Paul *academic administrator, economics educator*

Ottawa
Brombal, Douglas Nereo *retired university official, consultant*
Jordan, Joseph Louis *education educator, government official*
Kroeger, Arthur *former university chancellor, former government official*
Labarge, Margaret Wade *medieval history educator*
Philogene, Bernard J. R. *academic administrator, science educator*
†Prevost, Roxane Lise *music theory educator*

Peterborough
Theall, Donald Francis *retired university president*

Thunder Bay
Locker, J. Gary *university official, civil engineering educator*

Toronto
Evans, John Robert *former university president, physician*
Hayhurst, James Frederick Palmer *career and business consultant, inspirational speaker, author*
Knowlton, Thomas A. *university dean, retired food products executive*
Kushner, Eva *academic administrator, educator, author*
Macdonald, Hugh Ian *university president emeritus, economist, educator*
†Marks, Ray *education educator, researcher*
Ostry, Sylvia *academic administrator, economist*
†Sessle, Barry John *adult education educator, researcher*

Waterloo
Berczi, Andrew Stephen *academic administrator, educator*
Smith, Rowland James *educational administrator*
Wright, Douglas Tyndall *business executive, university executive emeritus*

Willowdale
†Wolfe, Rose *former academic administrator*

QUEBEC

Brossard
Allen, Harold Don *mathematics educator, science writer, monetary historian*

Montreal
Freedman, Samuel Orkin *university official*
French, Stanley George *university dean, philosophy educator*
Granger, Luc Andre *university dean, psychologist*
Lowy, Frederick Hans *academic administrator, psychiatrist*

Saint-Laurent
†Jundi, Bilal *principal*

SASKATCHEWAN

Regina
Barber, Lloyd Ingram *retired university president*

Saskatoon
Knott, Douglas Ronald *college dean, agricultural sciences educator, researcher*

MEXICO

Oaxaca de Juárez
Hallberg, Thomas Boone *education educator*

San Pedro Garza García
†Defiore, Perry Dennis *academic administrator, business owner*

AUSTRALIA

Armadale
Searby, Richard Henry *academic administrator, lawyer*

Canberra
Harris, Stuart Francis *educator, researcher*
Thayer, Carlyle Alan *educator*

Karrinyup
Young, Deidra Jane *educational researcher*

Sydney
Encel, Solomon *education educator, consultant*

BELGIUM

Shape
Gates, Sheree Hunt *counseling administrator, educator, writer*

CHINA

Jinan Shandong
Fan, Xijun *education educator*

DENMARK

Copenhagen
Koktvedgaard, Mogens *education educator*

EGYPT

Cairo
Miller, Harry George *education educator*

Damietta
†Mansour, Ahmed Hamed *educational technology educator, academic administ*

ENGLAND

Brighton
Hirst, Paul Heywood *retired education educator*

Durham
Galloway, David Malcolm *retired education educator*

London
Tizard, Barbara *education and child development researcher*

Richmond-upon-Thames
Smith, Norman Raymond *academic administrator*

Saint Albans Herts
Thomas, Norman *education educator*

FINLAND

Jyväskylä
Kari, Jouko *education educator*

FRANCE

Lyon
Brown, James Chandler *college administrator*

Paris
†Edwards, John David *university educator*

GERMANY

Bielefeld
Dehmlow, Eckehard Volker *education educator, educator*

Bochum
Meyers, Albert Thomas Marie *academic counsellor*

Braunschweig
Fricke, Reiner *education educator*
Rass, Hans Heinrich *politics educator*

Dortmund
Vogt, Hartmut *education educator*

Koblenz
†Harbusch, Karin Maria *education educator, researcher*

Tübingen
Flitner, Andreas Hermann *education educator*

GREECE

Athens
†Hoesly, Eileen M. *academic administrator, educator*
Panayiotis, Chinas *school psychologist, consultant*

GUATEMALA

Guatemala City
Harris, Randy Jay *university official, finance executive*

HONG KONG

Shatin
Wong, Ngai Ying *educator*

IRELAND

Limerick
Flood, Patrick Christopher *business educator, researcher, corporate speaker*

ITALY

Rome
Chang, Hiang-Chu Ausilia *education educator, researcher*

JAPAN

Sayama-shi Saitama-Ken
Hazelrigg, Meredith Kent *education consultant*

Tokyo
Nakajima, Hiroshi *education educator*

Tsukuba-shi
Shimizu, Kazuhiko *education educator*

NETHERLANDS

Nymegen
Braaksma, Johanna *educational consultant, researcher*

NORWAY

Trondheim
Søvik, Nils *education educator*

POLAND

Gdańsk
Mokrzecki, Lech Marian *history of education educator*

Poznan
Skrzypczak, Jozef Aleksander *education educator*

REPUBLIC OF KOREA

Sodaemoon-ku Seoul
Lee, Sungho H. *education educator, consultant, dean*

RUSSIA

Moscow
Khaladjan, Nikolai Nikolaevich *academic administrator*

SCOTLAND

Nottingham
Newman, Judith Alice *education educator, educator*

SENEGAL

VA

Dulles
†Tall, Aliou *secondary school educator, researcher*

SINGAPORE

Bopry, Jeanette *education educator*

SOUTH AFRICA

Parklands
Koekemoer, Carl Lodewicus *college official, business consultant*

Port Elizabeth
Botha, Maria Magdalena *education educator, researcher*

SWEDEN

Karlstad
Lindqvist, Gunilla *education educator*

Stockholm
Lindström, Lars Ernst Simon *education educator*

THAILAND

Bangkok
Kruck, Donna Jean *special education educator, consultant*

VIETNAM

Da Lat
†Ha, Quan Manh *adult education educator*

ADDRESS UNPUBLISHED

Aaslestad, Halvor Gunerius *college dean, retired*
Aczel, Mollie Goodman *educational consultant*
Adams, Renee Bledsoe *retired elementary school educator*
Adamson, Jane Nan *retired elementary school educator*
†Adams-Passey, Suellen S. *elementary education educator*
Agar, John Russell, Jr., *school district administrator*
Aiken, Michael Thomas *former academic administrator*
Albers, Edward James, Sr., *retired secondary school educator*
Alexander, Doris Muriel *humanities educator, writer*
Alfano, Edward Charles, Jr., *elementary education educator*
Allen, Charles Eugene *university administrator, agriculturist, educator*
Allgrim, Caroline Denham *retired college official*
Alligood, Elizabeth Ann Hiers *retired special education educator*
Alves, Kyrin Jean *association executive, educator*
†Amaya, Carlos C. *education educator, researcher*
Ammeraal, Brenda Ferne *secondary school educator*
†Amos, Linda K. *academic administrator*
Anderson, Donna Elaine *elementary and secondary school educator*
†Anderson, Gregory Thomas *secondary school educator, researcher, historian*
Anderson, Iris Anita *retired secondary education educator*
†Anderson, Jock Robert *adult education educator, consultant*
†Andretti, Daniel *secondary school educator*
Andrews, Carol *primary education educator*
†Applegate, Edward C. *education educator, researcher, writer*
†Apps, Jerold Willard *adult education educator, writer*
Archer-Sorg, Karen S. *secondary school educator*
Armacost, Mary-Linda Sorber Merriam *former academic administrator, consultant*
Armstrong, Karen Lee *special education educator*
Armstrong-Law, Margaret *school administrator*
Arnold, Leslie Ann *special education educator*
Arnold, P. A. *special education educator*
Arnold, Ruth Ann *elementary education educator*
Attig, John Clare *secondary education educator, consultant*
†Austin, Robyn Michelle *development administrator, speech professional*
†Avant, Gayle *political science educator*
Babbitt, Samuel Fisher *retired university official*
Bachtel, Ann Elizabeth *educational consultant, researcher, educator*
Bade, Carl August *retired secondary education educator*
Baird, Donald Robert *retired secondary school educator*
Baker, C. B. *retired day care director, organizer, communicator*
Baker, Carol Ann *elementary school educator*
Baker, Eva Lee *education educator, researcher*
Baker, Katherine June *elementary school educator, minister, artist*
†Baldwin, Marie Hunsucker *retired educator*
Balis, Jennifer Lynn *academic administrator, computer technology educator*
Ball, Howard Guy *education specialist educator*
Ball, Margie Barber *elementary school educator*
Bannister, Geoffrey *university president, geographer*
Barnes, Robert Vincent *retired elementary and secondary school art educator*
Barone, John Anthony *academic administrator emeritus*
Barrett, Evelyn Carol *retired secondary education educator*
Barrett, Janet Tidd *academic administrator*
Bavington, Bette Anne *special needs educator*
Baxter, Cecil William, Jr., *retired college president*
†Baxter, Judith Lee *academic administrator, mathematician*
Bayard, Susan Shapiro *adult education educator, small business owner*
†Beach, Nancy Ann Helen *special education educator, educator*
Bearg, Esther Marilyn *retired school counselor, educational consultant*
Beck, Barbara Nell *elementary school educator*
Becker, Elizabeth Wallace *elementary school guidance counselor*
Becker, Walter Heinrich *vocational educator, planner*
Beckwith, Sidney Johnson *director special programs, curriculum administrator*
†Beery, Barbara Faye *secondary school educator*
Belanger, Cherry Churchill *elementary school educator*
†Belcher, Charles William *education educator*
†Bell, Elva Glenn *retired secondary school educator, retired counseling administrator, interpreter*
†Benson, Ellen Marie *elementary school educator*
Berger, Deborah Kornbluth *educator, educational consultant*
†Berger-Knorr, Lawrence *education educator, information technology manager*
Bergman, Hermas John (Jack Bergman) *retired college administrator*
Bernstein, I. Melvin *university official and dean, materials scientist*
Bert, Clara Virginia *retired home economics educator, administrator*
Beston, Rose Marie *retired college president*
†Beyer, La Vonne Ann *special education educator*
Beyersdorf, Marguerite Mulloy *educator*
†Bhanot, Karan *education educator*
†Bianconi, Marcelo *education educator*
Birkmayer, Donald Tefft *retired college official*
Birman, Linda Lee *retired elementary school educator*
Bishop, Charles Edwin *university president emeritus, economist*
Bishop, Sue Marquis (Ina Sue Marquis Bishop) *dean, psychiatric and mental health nurse educator, researcher*
Bivens, Lynette Kupka *director*
†Black, Rebecca Leree *special education educator*
†Black, Recca Marcele *educator*
Blackledge, David William *retired academic administrator*
Blazey, Judith Leiston *school district administrator*
Blecke, Arthur Edward *retired principal*
Bloch, Julia Chang *educator, former ambassador, former bank executive*
Blood, Peggy A. *college administrator*
Bloodworth, Gladys Leon *educator*
Boesch, Diane Harriet *retired elementary education educator*
Boise, Audrey Lorraine *retired special education educator*
Bolek, Catherine *university research director*
†Bolton, Marie *elementary school educator, minister*
†Bonura, Jacqueline *special education educator*
†Borchert, Carol Ann *school librarian*
Borntrager, John Sherwood *principal*
Borst, Philip West *academic administrator*
Bosse, Margaret Fisher Ishler *education educator*
Bost, Raymond Morris *retired college president*
Boswell, Tommie C. *retired middle school educator*
†Bower, Laurel Lee *education educator, researcher*
Boyenga, Cindy A. *secondary education educator*
Bragdon, Paul Errol *educator*
Brain, George Bernard *university dean*
Brandt, Mitzi Marianne *retired educational specialist*
†Brannman, Ward Scott *elementary school educator*
Brawner, Sharon Lee *bilingual education educator, researcher*
Brennan, Elizabeth Lane *educator, program director*
†Brester, Gary W. *educator*
Brewer, Carey *retired academic administrator*
Brown, Beulah Louise *retired elementary educator*
Brown, David Richard *school system administrator, minister*
†Brown, Diana L. *elementary education educator*
Brown, Lillie McFall *elementary school principal*
Brown, Ronald Miles *retired academic administrator*
Brownlee, Paula Pimlott *higher education consultant, former academic administrator*
†Brown-Zekeri, Lolita Molanda *elementary school educator*
Bryan, Lawrence Dow *college president*
Bryant, Janice Ann *special education department administrator*
Buckler, Marilyn Lebow *school psychologist, educational consultant*
Bullock, Molly *retired elementary school educator*
Burbridge, Ann Arnold *music educator, choir director*
†Burchett, Michael Henry *education educator*
Burch-Martinez, Berkeley Alison *primary education educator*
Burke, Joseph C. *former university official*
Burnett, Howard Jerome *academic administrator emeritus*
Burnley, Kenneth Stephen *school system administrator*
Burns, Brenda Carolyn *retired special education administrator, chemical dependence counselor*
Burns, James Milton *retired educator*
Burns, Marie T. *retired secondary education educator*
†Bursley-Hamilton, Susan *secondary school educator*
Burton, Lavon D. *education educator*
Busch, Kyle *counseling administrator*
†Bush, Janice *principal*
Bush, Sandi Tokoa *elementary school educator*
Butler, Orton Carmichael *earth science educator, climatologist*
Cahill, Charles L. *retired university administrator, chemistry educator*
Caldwell, William Edward *educational administration educator, arbitrator*
Callan, Richard John *elementary school educator*
†Calvert, Laura Cristina *private school educator*
Cameron, J. Elliot *retired parochial educational system administrator*
Cameron, Lucille Wilson *retired dean of libraries*
Campbell, Sarah *elementary education educator, special education specialist*
†Campbell, Stanley Clinton *retired school system administrator, retired military officer*
Canelli, Jeanne *early childhood educator*
†Caputo, Joseph Anthony *retired university president*
Carey, John Jesse *academic administrator, religion educator*
Carlin, Betty *educator*
†Carlin, Phyllis Eva Scott *education educator*
†Carpenter, Rosalie T. *education educator, consultant*
Carr, Bessie *retired middle school educator*
Carrell, Heather Demaris *school system administrator*
Carter, Herbert Edmund *former university official*
Carter, Julia Marie *secondary education educator*
Casler, Frederick Clair, Sr., *academic administrator, law enforcement educator*
Casper, Gerhard *former academic administrator, law educator*
Castellanos-Brandon, Alba G. *secondary school educator*
Cepielik, Elizabeth Lindberg *educator*
Chace, William Murdough *former university administrator*
Chandler, Alice *higher education consultant, university president*
†Chapman, David Arthur *education educator*
Chappell, Annette M. *higher education consultant, minister*
Chase, James Richard *retired college president*
Chatelain, Dalia de la Paz *elementary education educator, counselor*
Chatman, Eleanor Louise *secondary school educator*
Chaudoir, Jean Hamilton (Jean Hamilton) *educator*
Cheek, Barbara Lee *college reading program director, educator*
Childers, Lawrence Jeffrey *superintendent of schools, personnel director*
Childers, Susan Lynn Bohn *special education educator, administrator, human resources and transition specialist, consultant*
Christensen, Caroline "Connie" *vocational educator*
Church, Jo Hall *retired adult education educator*
Cioffi, Eugene Edward, III, *retired educational administrator*
Clark, James Milford *college president, retired*
Clarke, Lambuth McGeehee *retired academic administrator*
Clawson, Roxann Eloise *college administrator, computer company executive*
†Clements, Cathy J. *education educator*
†Clements, Michael Taylor *academic administrator, educator*
Cline, Pauline M. *educational administrator*
†Close, Thomas James *school administrator*
Clough, Lauren C. *retired special education educator*
Cochrane, Walter E. *academic administrator, music educator, conductor*
Coffee, Joseph Denis, Jr., *retired college chancellor*
†Colage, Beatrice Elvira *education educator*
Cole, Nancy Stooksberry *educational research executive*
Coleman, Gary William *retired elementary school educator*
Coleman, Mary Sue *academic administrator*
Colgate-Lindberg, Catharine Pamella *educator*
Collier, Herman Edward, Jr., *retired college president*
Collinson, Vivienne Ruth *education educator, researcher, consultant*
Coluccio, Josephine Catherine *primary and elementary school educator*
Compton, Norma Haynes *retired university dean, artist*
†Compton, Robert *private school educator*
Connell, George Edward *former university president, scientist*
Conover, Nancy Anderson *retired secondary school counselor*
Conway, Edward Gerald, Jr., *university educational technology administrator*
Cook, Edward Joseph *college president*
Cook, Iva Dean *education educator*
Cook, Sister M(ary) Mercedes *educator, educational administrator*
Cook, Michelle Westerman *special education educator*
Cooke, Thomas Paul *education educator*
Cooper, James Michael *education educator*
Cooper, Kathy Stegall *school counselor*
Copeland, Henry Jefferson, Jr., *former college president*
†Copeland, Phillips Jerome *former academic administrator, former air force officer*
Craig, Bradford *retired secondary school educator*
Cramer, Robert Vern *retired college administrator, consultant*
Crawford, Kenneth Charles *educational institute executive, retired government official*
Crissman, John D. *dean, physician*
Crook, Alison Laura *academic administrator*
Crosby, Janet Halley *retired secondary school educator*
Crosby, Marena Lienhard *retired college administrator*
Cross, Kathryn Patricia *education educator*
Crotty, Jerome T. *educator*
Crouse, Carol K. Mavromatis *elementary education educator*
†Crozier, Jane E. *educational consultant, researcher*
Cummings, Carole Edwards *retired special education educator*
Cusimano, Adeline Miletti *educational administrator*
Cutler, Sarah Taylor *educator, enamelist*
Cyphers, Christopher John *academic administrator*
Darke, Charles Bruce *academic administrator, dentist*
Daus, Jonathan Michael *secondary education educator*
Davenport, Lawrence Franklin *school system administrator*
Davey, Mark Ellis *secondary school educator, band director*
Davies-McNair, Jane *retired educational consultant*
Dávila, Rafael Angel, III, *college counselor, educator*
Dávila, Susan *guidance counselor*
Davion, Ethel Johnson *school system administrator, curriculum specialist*
Davis, Anna Jane Ripley *elementary education educator*
†Davis, Deborah *education educator, actor*
†Davis, Diann Holmes *educator*
Davis, Hiram Joe *public school administrator*
Davis, Jonni K. *secondary school educator, writer*
Davis, Joseph Lloyd *educational administrator, consultant*
Davis, Nathan Joseph *academic administrator, music educator*
†Davis, Sue Ellen H. *elementary and secondary music educator*
†Davison, Helen Irene *secondary education educator, counselor*
de Abreu, Sue *elementary educator*
Debs, Barbara Knowles *former college president, consultant*
†DeCourcey, Catherine Maureen *special education educator*
†de Fee, Nicole Reneé *education educator*
Delahanty, Rebecca Ann *school system administrator*
DeLong, Janice Ayers *education educator*
†del Rosario, Anna Antonio *director*

†Denham, Carolyn Hunter *academic administrator, statistics educator*
Denton, Joan Cameron *reading consultant, former educator*
Derrickson, Denise Ann *secondary school educator, educator*
Detwiler, Christina LeFevre *elementary school educator*
DeVera, Gertrude Quenano *education educator*
Dey, Carol Ruth *secondary education educator*
Diamond, Richard *retired secondary education educator*
Diamond, Robert Mach *higher education administrator*
Diamond, Stuart *business executive, educator, lawyer, consultant*
DiBiaggio, John A. *university president*
Dickeson, Robert Celmer *retired university president, foundation executive, political science educator*
Dickinson, Gail Krepps *educator*
Dike, Margaret Hopcraft *retired education administrator*
DiSalle, Michael Danny *secondary education educator*
Dittman, Duane Scott *registrar*
Dobler, Donald William *retired college dean, consultant, corporate executive*
Dockery, J. Lee *retired medical school administrator*
Dodds, Linda Carol *special education educator*
Donaldson, Wilma Crankshaw *elementary education educator*
†Doren, Bonnie E. *special education educator, researcher*
†Douglas, Mary Younge Riley *secondary education educator*
†Douglas, Maurice LaJohn *private school educator, music educator*
Douglas, Roxanne Grace *secondary school educator*
†Doviak, Ingrid Ellinger *elementary school educator*
Dowling, Paul Dennis *bilingual special education educator*
Drake, George Albert *college president, historian*
Dresbach, Mary Louise *state educational administrator*
Dritschilo, William *educator*
Dubé, Ronald Norman *elementary school educator*
Dubois, Nancy Q. *elementary school educator*
Duckworth, Paula Oliver *secondary school educator, freelance artist, writer, photographer*
Dudycha, Anne Elizabeth *retired special education educator*
Duff, John Bernard *college president, former city official*
Duffy, John Joseph *retired academic administrator, history educator*
Duncan, Pope Alexander *college administrator*
Dunham, Rebecca Betty Beres *school administrator*
†Dunlap, Paul Edward *secondary school educator, writer*
†Dunn, Helen Elizabeth *retired secondary school educator*
Dunworth, John *retired college president*
Duplessis, Audrey Joseph *school system administrator*
Dutson, Thayne R. *university dean*
DuVall, Patricia Arlene *secondary education educator*
Dwinell, Ann Jones *retired special education educator*
†Dye, Linda Kaye *elementary school educator*
†Dzwik, Leigh Settlemair *director*
Eaton, Dorel *elementary school educator*
†Eaton, Emma Parker *special education educator*
Ecklund, Judith Louise *academic administrator*
Edelman, Norman Herman *medical educator, university dean and official*
Edens, Betty Joyce *reading recovery educator*
Edwards, Ardis Lavonne Quam *retired elementary education educator*
Edwards, June Caroline *retired education educator*
†Edwards, Robert Hazard *retired college president*
†Edwards-Mitchum, Lillian (Red the Poet) *secondary school educator, writer*
Ekey, Carrie Rae *elementary education educator*
†Elfers-Mabli, Linda M. *educational consultant, educator*
Eliot, Charles William John *former university president*
Elliott, Tommy *secondary school educator*
Endicott, Jennifer Jane Reynolds *education educator*
Enfield, Susan Ann *secondary school educator*
Erfani, Shervin *academic administrator, engineering educator*
Ertl, Rita Mae *elementary education educator*
†Espiricueta, Sylvia *counseling administrator*
Essa, Lisa Beth *elementary school educator*
†Essegaier, Skander *education educator, researcher*
Essig, Kathleen Susan *university official, management consultant*
Evans, Bonita Dianne *adult education educator*
Evans, Geraldine Ann *academic administrator*
Evans, James Handel *university administrator, architect, educator*
†Ewald, Laura Anne *school librarian*
†Ewanchuk, Michael *retired school system administrator*
Fair, Marcia Jeanne Hixson *retired educational administrator*
Falk, Marshall Allen *retired university dean, physician*
Farquhar, Robin Hugh *former university president*
Farrar, Richard Bartlett, Jr., *school system administrator*
†Faucette, Merilon Cooper *retired elementary educator*
Feldman, Lillian Maltz *early childhood education consultant*
Feldstein, Joshua *educational administrator*
Felicetti, Daniel A. *academic administrator, educator*
Fernández-Velazquez, Juan Ramon *university chancellor*
Field, Michael Jay *education educator*
Fife, Jonathan Donald *higher education educator*
Filchock, Ethel *education educator, poet*
†Fink, Alma *retired elementary education educator*
†Fischer, Harald Maximilian *education educator, researcher*
†Fishwick, Marshall W. *education educator*
†Fitzpatrick, Kathleen G. *education educator, accountant*
Fitzpatrick, Ruth Ann *education educator*
†Flanagan, Kathleen Theresa *education educator*
Fleetwood, Mary Annis *education association executive*
†Fleming, Horace Weldon, Jr., *educator, former university president*
Fodrea, Carolyn Wrobel *educational researcher, publisher, consultant*
Foltiny, Stephen Vincent *special education educator*
Folz, Kathleen Louise *elementary education educator*
Forister, Jean Whitby *retired guidance counselor, consultant*
Forney, Ronald Dean *elementary school educator, consultant, educational therapist*
†Forster, Donald R. *vocational school educator*
Forsyth, Ben Ralph *academic administrator, medical educator*
Fountain, Andre Ferchaud *academic program director*
Fowler, Hugh Charles *charter school consultant & developer*
†Frankel, Albert J. *registrar*
Franklin, Billy Joe *international higher education specialist*
Franklin, Mary Ann Wheeler *educator, higher education and management consultant*
Freeman, Meredith Norwin *former college president, education educator*
Frey, Katie Manciet *education educator*
Frey, Margo Walther *career counselor, columnist*
Frick, Ivan Eugene *college president emeritus, education consultant*
Fricklas, Richard Leon *roofing educator, educational institute administrator*
†Frieden, Brenda Joyce *secondary school educator*
Frost, Everett Lloyd *anthropologist, academic administrator*
Fuller, Maxine Compton *retired secondary school educator*
Fullerton, Gail Jackson *university president emeritus*
Gabel, Katherine *retired academic administrator*
Galdi-Weissman, Natalie Ann *secondary education educator*
Galliher, Clarice A. Andrews *secondary education educator*
Gamsky, Neal Richard *academic administrator, psychology educator*
†Garcia, Julia Theresa *secondary school educator*
Garcia, Marietta Kaye *elementary school educator, writer*
Garcia-Mely, Rafael *retired education educator*
Gardner, David Chambers *adult education educator, psychologist, business executive, author*
Garner, Doris Traganza *educator*
†Gass, Saul Irving *educator*
Gavin, Joan Elaine *special education educator*
Gehring, Donald D. *education educator*
Gemming, Mary Frances *college educator, writer, astrologer*
Gentilcore, Eileen Marie Belsito *elementary school principal*
Giblett, Phylis Lee Walz *middle school educator*
Gibson, Orpha Ray *educator*
Gibson, Patricia *family educator*
Gillin, Carol Ann *middle school educator*
†Gilmore, Connie Sue *educator*
Gitner, Deanne *retired school system administrator*
Gittman, Elizabeth *retired educator*
Giusti, Joseph Paul *retired academic administrator, consultant*
Gladstone, Carol Lynn *education educator*
†Glasgow, Karen *principal*
Glaze, Lynn Ferguson *development consultant*
Glennen, Robert Eugene, Jr., *retired university president*
Gleue, Lorine Anna *elementary education educator*
Glismann, Clementine *elementary school educator, researcher*
Goerke, Glenn Allen *university administrator*
Goertz, Roger Lamar *retired education counselor*
Goetz, Jack Ralph *dean*
Goff, Jane E. *secondary school educator*
Goldfarb, Helene Diane *school counselor, retired*
†Golemon, Patricia Lynn *education educator, writer*
Gonzalez, John M. *educator*
Good, Linda Lou *elementary education educator*
Goode, Janet Weiss *elementary school educator*
†Goodman, Rebecca Gruver *education educator, writer*
Goodrich, Kenneth Paul *retired college dean*
Goodsell, Charles True *retired educator*
†Gorder, Jennifer LeAnn *special education educator*
Gordis, David Moses *academic administrator, rabbi*
Goron, Mara J. *social studies educator, assistant principal*
Graham, Sylvia Swords *secondary school educator, retired*
Graves, Ruth Parker *educational executive, educator*
Graves, Wallace Billingsley *retired university executive*
†Gray, Hazel Irene *retired special education educator, counselor, consultant*
Gray, Richard Moss *retired college president*
Grebstein, Sheldon Norman *university administrator*
Green, Nancy Loughridge *newspaper executive*
Green, Patricia Pataky *school system administrator, consultant*
Greenway, Joan M. *dean*
Gregory, Mary Sharon *educator*
Grey, Robert Dean *academic administrator, biology educator*
Grier, Dorothy Ann Pridgen *secondary education specialist*
Griffie, Gayle G. *retired principal*
Griffin, Gloria Jean *retired elementary school educator*
Griffin, Laura Mae *retired educator*
Grine, Florence May *secondary education educator*
Grove, Myrna Jean *elementary education educator*
Gruberg, Cy *educational administrator*
†Gruchot, Linda *secondary school educator*
Gurspan, Susan Judith *English as Second Language educator, consultant*
Guskin, Alan E. *university president*
Gustafson, Richard Alrick *university president*
Gustafson, Sandra Lynne *retired secondary school educator*
Haak, Harold Howard *university president*
Haas, Carolyn Buhai *elementary education educator, publisher, writer, consultant*
Habkirk, Sue Ann *education educator, consultant*
Haden, Clovis Roland *university administrator, engineering educator*
Hadley, William Melvin *retired dean*
Haeberle, Rosamond Pauline *retired educator*
Hagan, Joseph Henry *higher education consultant*
Hageman, Katherine Elizabeth *secondary school educator*
Hageman, Richard Philip, Jr., *educational administrator*
Hall, Zach Winter *academic administrator*
†Hamm, Aurolyn Melba *elementary school educator, writer*
†Hammond, John Baptiste, III, *academic administrator*
†Hampton, Nanette Davina *private school educator, writer*
Hamrock, Margaret Mary *retired educator, writer*
†Han, Xianlin *education educator, consultant*
Haneke, Dianne Myers *retired education educator*
Hansen, Sally Jo *educational consultant*
Hanshaw, Leann Viala *counseling administrator*
Hardage, Page Taylor *elementary education educator*
Hardin, Clifford Morris *retired university chancellor, cabinet member*
Harding, Robert William *academic administrator*
Harding, Susan Kathleen *early childhood and elementary school educator, writer, poet*
Hare, Norma Q. *retired school administrator*
Harper, Janet Sutherlin Lane *retired educational administrator, writer*
Harrington, Jean Patrice *college president*
Harris, Ann *elementary school teacher*
Harris, Delmarie Jones *elementary education educator*
Harris, Dolores M. *academic administrator*
Harris, Merle Wiener *college administrator, educator*
Harrison, Earl Grant, Jr., *educational administrator*
Harrod, Lois Marie *secondary school educator, poet*
Hart, James Warren *retired academic administrator, retired football player*
Hartley, Philip. L. *academic administrator, psychology educator*
Harvey, Judith Gootkin *elementary school educator, real estate agent*
Harville, Martha Louise *special education educator*
Haskin, Larry Allen *academic administrator, geochemist, educator*
Hasselmo, Nils *academic administrator, linguistics educator*
Haugland, Susan Warrell *education educator, consultant*
†Hawkins, Brian L. *academic administrator, educator*
Hawkins, Jacquelyn *elementary and secondary education educator*
†Hawks, Shelley Drake *educator*
†Haynes, Cheryl Lynn *secondary school educator*
Hazard, John W., Jr., *secondary school educator*
†Hazel, Mary Belle *university administrator*
Heaggans, Raphael Chesare *education educator*
Heap, Sylvia Stuber *educator*
Heath, Jerome Bruce *information systems educator*
Hebert, Christine Anne *elementary education educator*
Heebner, Amy L. *educator, writer, artist*
Heestand, Diane Elissa *education educator, medical educator*
Helman, Alfred Blair *retired college president, education consultant*
Henderson, Catherine Lynn *retired secondary education educator, writer*
Henderson, William Eugene *education educator*
Henley, Robert Lee *school system administrator*
Henry, Donna Edwards *educator*
†Henry, Robert E. *dean, educator*
†Henry, Stephen Ray *director*
†Henry-Beauchamp, Leah Alexandra *special education educator*
†Herge, Donna Carol *secondary school educator*
Herge, Henry Curtis, Sr., *education educator, dean emeritus*
Herold, Rochelle Snyder *early childhood educator*
†Hersh, Richard H. *academic administrator*
Hertel, Suzanne Marie *training and development specialist*
Hestad, Marsha Anne *educational administrator*
Hibbs, Dawn Wilcox *elementary school educator*
Hickey, Sharon Marie *middle school educator*
Higgins, Dorothy Marie *academic dean*
Hill, Emita Brady *academic administrator, consultant*
†Hill, Jerry Dean *secondary school educator*
Hill, Virgil Lusk, Jr., *academic administrator, naval officer*
†Hillery, Susie Moore *retired elementary school educator*
Hilsabeck, Larry L. *education educator*
Hines, Voncile *special education educator*
Hing, Barbara Lim *elementary school educator, assistant principal*
Hinman, Eve Caison *retired academic administrator*
Hinton, Karolyn Kay *retired elementary school educator*
Hitchcock, Walter Anson *educational consultant, retired educational administrator*
Hoffman, Judy Greenblatt *preschool director*
Hoffman, Neil James *academic administrator*
†Hogan, Martha A. *academic administrator, educator*
Hogue, James Larry *retired academic administrator, business executive*
†Holcomb, Mildred Geneva Comrie *elementary education educator*
Holmes, Susan G. *educator*
Holtkamp, Susan Charlotte *elementary education educator*
Hood, Luann Sandra *special education educator*
Hooper, Henry Olcott *retired academic administrator, physicist*
†Hopkins, Kevin W *education educator*
†Hopping, Richard Lee *college president emeritus*
Horner, Matina Souretis *retired college president, corporate executive*
†Horton-Wright, Alma Irene *educator*
†House, Ernest Robert *education educator, educational evaluator*
Houseman, Ann Elizabeth Lord *educational administrator, state official*
Hoy, Harold Joseph *marketing educator, retail executive, writer, military officer, editor, management consultant*
Huff, Janet House *special education educator*
Huffman, Carol Koster *retired elementary school educator*
Huie, Carol P. *information systems educator*
Hull, Louise Knox *retired elementary educator, administrator*
Hull, McAllister Hobart, Jr., *retired university administrator*
Hulsey, Rachel Martinez *secondary school educator, columnist*
Hummel, Marilyn Mae *elementary education educator*
Hunt-Clerici, Carol Elizabeth *retired academic administrator, counselor*
Hutchinson, Elaine Frances *secondary education educator*
†Huth, Brian Justin *ESL educator, poet*
Huttenback, Robert Arthur *academic administrator, educator*
Jack, Patricia Ann *assistant principal*
†Jackson, Grace Louise *education educator, writer*
Jackson, Heather *secondary school educator*
Jackson, Miles Merrill *retired university dean*
Jacobs, Linda Rotroff *elementary school educator*
Jacobson, Eugene Donald *educator, administrator, researcher*
Jakubauskas, Edward Benedict *college president*
Janeway, Richard *university official*
†Jefferson, Kathleen Henderson *retired secondary education educator*
Jenkins, Brenda Gwenetta *early childhood and special education specialist*
Jennings, Charles Robert *educator*
†Jensen, N. Jean *special education educator, secondary school educator*
Jervis, Jane Lise *college official, science historian*
Jimmink, Glenda Lee *retired elementary school educator*
Johnson, Alice Elaine *retired academic administrator*
†Johnson, Bryn K. *academic administrator, consultant*
Johnson, Duane P. *retired academic administrator, consultant*
Johnson, Julie Ann *career planning administrator*
†Johnson, Julie Elizabeth Sillin *educator*
Johnson, Kirsten Denise *elementary education educator*
Johnson, LaVerne St. Clair *retired elementary school educator*
Johnson, Olin Chester *education educator*
Johnson, Sylvia Sue *university administrator, educator*
†Johnson-MIller, Charleen V. *teacher coordinator*
Jones, Lawrence Neale *university dean, minister*
Jordan, James Lowell *educator, writer*
Jurasek, Randall John *educational consultant*
Kachur, Betty Rae *elementary education educator*
Kaltvedt, Larry Dean *elementary school educator*
†Kalu, Kalu Ndukwe *public administration educator, researcher, consultant*
†Kanada, Gary N. Kahaho'omalu *adult education educator*
Kane, Sydell *elementary school principal*
†Kappner, Augusta Souza *academic administrator*
Kasper, Victor, Jr., *economics educator*
Kaspin, Susan Jane *child care specialist*
Kazmarek, Linda Adams *secondary education educator*
Keebler, Lois Marie *elementary school educator*
Keiper, Marilyn Morrison *elementary education educator*

Rinehart, Alice Day Duffy *retired education educator*
Rinsland, Roland DeLano *retired university official*
Rittel, Kathleen Ann Maurer *educator*
Rivero, Andria *education educator*
Roaden, Arliss Lloyd *retired higher education executive director, former university president*
Roberts, Maura M. *retired secondary school educator*
Roberts, Patricia Lee *education educator*
Robertson, Wyndham Gay *university official, journalist*
Robinson, Nancy Nowakowski *academic administrator*
†Robles-Cereceres, Oscar F. *adult education educator, writer*
Rochelle, Lugenia *academic administrator*
Rodgers, Geraldine Ellen *retired elementary school educator*
†Rogers, Olivia Johnson *elementary school counselor*
Rohan, Virginia Bartholome *college development director*
Rohrer, Jane Carolyn *retired gifted education specialist, academic administrator, poet, consultant*
Ronco, Wilma Lilley *chief operating officer*
Root, Janet Greenberg *private school educator*
Rosenblum, Estelle H. *retired dean, nursing educator*
†Rossen-Knill, Deborah F. *academic administrator, English educator*
†Rossi, Michelle Renee *elementary school educator*
†Rossman, G. Parker *education educator*
Roth, Loretta Elizabeth *retired educator*
Rowell, Barbara Caballero *junior college official*
†Rozell, Todd B. *education educator*
Rudden, Jane Frances *education educator*
Rusie, Ruth Louise *literacy educator*
†Russell, Attie Yvonne *academic administrator, dean, pediatrics educator*
Ryan, Daniel John *university administrator*
Ryan, Ione Jean Alohilani Rathburn *retired educator, counselor*
Ryan, Kenneth J. *academic administrator, educator*
Sacchetti, Karen *creative arts educator*
Sachitano, Sheila Marie *secondary school educator, small business owner*
Salgado, Lynn Enza Grant *educator*
†Salisbury, Fayann Annie *elementary school educator*
†Santangelo, Gaspare Charles *education educator, retired principal*
†Savercool, Susan Elisabeth *elementary school educator*
Scaffidi-Wilhelm, Gloria Angelamarie *elementary education educator*
Scala, Marilyn Campbell *literacy and inclusion consultant, writer*
Scandary, E. Jane *special education educator, consultant*
†Scarborough, Ann Barlow *secondary school educator*
Schmidt, B. June *education educator*
Schmidt, Ruth Ann *academic administrator emerita*
Schmidt, Sara Marie *English educator*
Schneider, Mary Louise *retired elementary education educator*
†Schofield, Barbara Curtright *retired school administrator*
Schrage, Rose *educational administrator*
†Schuckman, Gregory A. *academic administrator*
Schumacher, Cynthia Jo *retired elementary and secondary education educator*
Schure, Alexander *university chancellor*
†Schwartz, Eleanor Brantley *academic administrator*
†Scott, Steven Lee *education educator*
†Sealey-Ruiz, Yolanda *education educator, marketing professional, consultant, writer*
Seeligson, Molly Fulton *professional life coach, education consultant, academic administrator*
Seigler, Elizabeth Middleton *retired counselor*
Sestini, Virgil Andrew *retired biology educator*
†Shaffer, Lisa Marie *academic administrator*
Shanahan, Eileen Frances *secondary education educator*
Shannon-Hallam, Isabelle Louise *education director*
†Shavender, Marilyn Faye *elementary school educator*
†Shaw, Fran *education educator, writer*
†Shearer, Charles Livingston *academic administrator*
Shen, Jianping *education educator*
†Sherman, Dana M. *educator, consultant*
Sherratt, Gerald Robert *retired academic administrator*
Sherrer, Charles David *college dean, clergyman*
Shields, Rana Colleen *special education educator*
Shoun, Ellen Llewellyn *retired secondary school educator*
Shutler, Mary Elizabeth *academic administrator*
†Siddeeq, Baiyinah Nawal Rubye *secondary school educator*
Singleton, Robert Culton *graduate school administrator, Bible educator*
Siper, Cynthia Dawn *special education educator*
Sizemore, Barbara Ann *Black studies educator*
Skaggs, Bebe Rebecca Patten *college dean, clergywoman*
Slaydon-Wolbert, Jeanne Miller *secondary school educator*
†Sliwa, Krzysztof *education educator, researcher*
†Smith, Clodus Ray *retired academic administrator*
†Smith, Debbie Ilee Randall *elementary school educator*
Smith, Dwight L., III, *academic administrator*
Smith, Hoke LaFollette *university president*
Smith, Joyce Ann *secondary school educator*
Smith, Martha Virginia Barnes *retired elementary school educator*
†Smith, Samuel Howard *academic administrator, plant pathologist*
Snortland, Howard Jerome *education financial consultant*
Sonnenschein, Hugo Freund *academic administrator, economics educator*
Sosnick, Fay Maxine *retired educator, volunteer*
Soto-Fernandez, Liliana *education educator*
Southworth, Jamie MacIntyre *retired education educator*
Spadafora, David Charles *adult education educator*
†Spencer, Rex LeRoy *retired secondary school educator*
Spiesicke, Margrit Herma *retired counselor*
†Spires, Michael *academic administrator, writer*
Squires, Connie Jo *special education educator*
Stafford, Rebecca *academic administrator, sociologist*
Staresnick, Julie Chih *school psychologist*
Stark, Joan Scism *education educator*
Starnes, Susan Smith *elementary education educator*
Starr, Ila Mae *educator*
Starr, Joyce Ives *special education educator*
Stecich, Rita Louise *secondary education educator*
†Stegall, Joel Ringold *university administrator*
Steigmeier, Roger James *adult educator, poet*
Stellar, Arthur Wayne *educational administrator*
Stewart, Dorothy K. *educator, librarian*
†Stewart, Joan Hinde *academic administrator*
Stewart, John Wray Black *college dean*
Stewart, Lucille Marie *retired special education coordinator*
Stomfay-Stitz, Aline Maria *education educator*
Stopp, Donald L. *retired educator, retired business owner*
Stuckey, Helenjean Lauterbach *counselor educator*
Stuckwisch, Clarence George *retired university administrator*
Sugnet, Linda A'Brunzo *elementary education educator*
Sullivan, Charles *dean, educator, author*
†Sutton, Julia Zeigler *retired special education educator*
†Suzuki, Bob H. *retired academic administrator*
Swecker, John H. *secondary school educator*
Tanner, Laurel Nan *education educator*
Tarbi, William Rheinlander *secondary education educator, curriculum consultant, educational technology researcher*
Taylor, Mary Lee *retired college administrator*
†Teng, Xiaolin *education educator, researcher*
TenHoeve, Thomas *academic administrator*
Tepper, Howard *partner*
Therrien, Anita Aurore *elementary school educator*
Thomas, Beverly Irene *special education educator, educational diagnostician, substance abuse counselor*
†Thomas, Meltonia Antionette *secondary school educator, music educator*
Thompson, Ana Calzada *secondary education educator, mathematician*
Thueme, William Harold *educator*
Tiedeman, David Valentine *education educator*
†Tiemann, Barbara Jean *special education educator*
Timmons, Sharon L. *retired elementary education educator*
Toledo, Victor *educational consultant*
†Tolson, David Edward *education consultant, education educator*
Tonjes, Marian Jeannette Benton *education educator*
†Tooms, Autumn Kennedy *education educator*
†Touhill, Blanche Marie *university chancellor, history-education educator*
Traicoff, George *retired academic administrator*
Trammell, John Kent *educator*
Troupe, Marilyn Kay *educational administrator*
†Trusdell, Mary Louise Cantrell *retired state educational administrator*
†Tuckson, Reed V. *academic administrator*
Tudor, Mary Louise Drummond *retired elementary school educator*
Turnbull, Vernona Harmsen *retired residence counselor, education educator*
Turoczy, D. Ann *counseling administrator, educator*
Tzimopoulos, Nicholas D. *educational administrator*
Uehling, Barbara Staner *educational administrator*
Underwood, Evelyn B. *elementary and secondary educator, consultant, counselor*
Usher, Nancy Spear *retired language arts educator*
†Uttech, Melanie Renée *qualitative research methodology educator*
†Valentine, Phyllis Louise *counseling administrator*
Van der Tuin, Mary Bramson *headmistress*
Van Ness, John Ralph *university official, educator*
Van Scotter, Richard Dale *education policy executive, writer*
Van Tassel, Daniel Ellsworth *academic administrator, consultant, educator*
Vaughan, Gary David *history and government educator*
†Velkley, Richard Lee *educator, journal editor*
†Veverka, Ruth Tonry *retired educator*
Vichiola, Christopher Michael *educator, writer*
Vickers, Mark Stephen *business educator, travel industry executive, sculptor, painter*
Vinson, James Spangler *academic administrator*
Volkering, Mary Joe *special education educator*
Volpe, Edmond L(oris) *college president*
Volpe, Eileen Rae *retired special education educator*
Von Burg, Frederick E., Sr., *secondary school educator, writer*
Vonderbrink, Gerald William *retired academic administrator, property manager*
Von Herrmann, Denise Keefer *educator*
Wagner, Marilyn Faith *retired elementary school educator*
Walker-Williams, Hope Denise *administrator, business consultant*
Walsh, Dolores Ann Gonczo (Lorry Walsh) *special education educator*
Walters, Donald Lee *education educator*
Walters-Lucy, Jean Marie *personal growth educator, consultant*
Warder, Richard Currey, Jr., *dean, mechanical aerospace engineering educator*
Waskow, Joyce Ann *school administrator*
Waters, Donald Eugene *academic administrator*
Watson, Marilyn Kaye *elementary education educator*
Watts, John Ransford *university administrator*
Watts, Mary Ann *retired elementary education educator*
Weaver, Charles Horace *educator*
Weintraub, Sam *reading educator*
Weir, Morton Webster *retired academic administrator, educator*
Weitzman, Stephen Michael *educator*
Welch, Michael Francis *educator, author*
†Weliver, Phyllis Rebecca *education educator*
Weller, Debra Anne *elementary educator*
Wendt, Marilynn Suzann *elementary school educator, principal*
†Werner, J., II, *secondary school educator*
Werner, Robert Joseph *college dean, music educator*
Westbrook, Michael George *secondary school educator*
†Westerberg, Mary L. *retired secondary school educator*
†Westfall, Jeffrey N. *education educator*
†Westfall, Ralph *educator*
Wheeler, David Laurie *university dean*
White, Florence May *learning disabilities specialist*
White, John Wesley, Jr., *retired academic administrator*
Wilhoit, Carol Diane *retired special education educator*
Wilkening, Laurel Lynn *academic administrator, planetary scientist*
Wille, Rosanne Louise *higher education administrator*
†Williams, Bobbretta M. *educational company executive*
Williams, Cheryl A. *secondary education educator*
†Williams, Deberrah Deithrisha *elementary school educator, researcher*
Williams, Harriette Flowers *retired school system administrator, educational consultant*
Williams, Lewis T. (Rusty Williams) *education educator*
Williams-Monegain, Louise Joel *retired science educator, ethnographer*
Wilson, Doris Fanuzzi *learning disabilities consultant, educator*
Wilson, Robin Scott *retired academic administrator, writer*
†Wimmer, Kathryn *retired elementary school educator*
Wingham, Erma Doris *secondary education educator*
Winterstein, James Fredrick *academic administrator*
Wiseman, Douglas Carl *education educator, department chairman, dean*
Wittich, John Jacob *retired academic administrator, business executive*
Wolf, Edith Maletz *retired educator*
†Wolfe, James Michael *education educator, researcher*
Woltering, Margaret Mae *retired secondary school educational consultant*
†Wolverton, Susan E. Quinn *secondary school educator*
Wong, David Yue *academic administrator, physics educator*
†Wood, Margo *academic administrator*
Woodsworth, Anne *university administrator, librarian*
Woolworth, Susan Valk *primary school educator*
Workman, Kayleen Marie *special education and adult education educator*
Worthen, John Edward *retired academic administrator*
Wulf, Janie Scott McIlwaine *gifted and talented education educator*
Wyatt, Susan Melinda Clough *career counselor, writer*
Wynne, Terry Lynne *career counselor, trainer, writer*
Yannella, Donald *educator*
Yannuzzi, Giuseppe Alberto *elementary education educator, writer*
Yates, William Tennyson, II, *educational consultant, management consultant*
Yitts, Rose Marie *nursery school executive*
Yoder, Anna Mary *reading educator*
Yoder, Myron Eugene *secondary school educator*
Yool, George Richard *dean*
†Yost, Randy *secondary school educator*
Young, George R. *educator*
Young, Margaret Chong *elementary education educator*
Young, Michael Kent *dean, lawyer, educator*
Young, Ruth Brooks *retired elementary education educator*
Young, Teresa Gail Hilger *adult education educator*
Young, Virgil Monroe *education educator*
Youngs, Diane Campfield *learning disabilities specialist, educator*
Zacharias, Donald Wayne *academic administrator*
Zahner, Dorothy Simkin *elementary education educator*
†Zampara, Angela Spentzakis *secondary school educator*
Zarzour, Robin Ann *special education educator*
Zauner, Christian Walter *university dean, exercise physiologist, consultant*
Zdanis, Richard Albert *academic administrator*
Zeilinger, Elna Rae *elementary educator, gifted-talented education educator*
Zilbert, Allen Bruce *education educator, computer consultant*
†Zufryden, Fred S. *academic administrator, marketing educator, researcher*
Zuiches, James Joseph *academic administrator*

ENGINEERING

UNITED STATES

ALABAMA

Athens
Gatlin, Tony Franklin *electrical engineer*

Auburn
†Baskiyar, Sanjeev *engineering educator*
Cicci, David Allen *aerospace engineer, educator*
Cochran, John Euell, Jr., *aerospace engineer, educator, lawyer*
Haneman, Vincent Siering, Jr., *consulting engineer, educator, university dean*
Irwin, John David *electrical engineering educator*
Jaeger, Richard Charles *electrical engineer, educator, science center director*
Kandhal, Prithvi Singh *civil engineer, manager*
Niu, Guofu *electrical engineer, educator*
Rainer, Rex Kelly *civil engineer, educator*
†Sforzini, Richard Henry *aerospace engineer, educator*
Turnquist, Paul Kenneth *agricultural engineer, educator*
Yoo, Chai Hong *civil engineering educator*

Birmingham
Bunt, Randolph Cedric *mechanical engineer*
†Crump, Michael David *electrical engineer*
Edmonds, William Fleming *retired engineering and construction company executive*
Flakes, Larry Joseph *civil engineer*
Goldman, Jay *industrial engineer, educator, former dean*
Goodrich, Thomas Michael *engineering and construction executive, lawyer*
Grantham, Charles Edward *broadcast engineer*
Jones, Albert Cecil *consulting engineer*
†Parma, Edward Scott *engineer, surgeon*
Potter, John Leith *mechanical and aerospace engineer, educator, consultant*
Sain, Charles (Hack Sain) *civil engineer, surveyor*
Scott, Owen Myers, Jr., *nuclear engineer*
Segner, Edmund Peter, Jr., *civil engineer, educator*
Uddin, Nasim *civil engineer, educator*

Daphne
†Jeffreys, Elystan Geoffrey *geological engineer, petroleum consultant and appraiser, gemologist*

Decatur
Smith, Troy Alvin *aerospace research engineer*

Florence
Badger, Phillip Charles *agricultural engineer*
Barrier, John Wayne *engineer, management consultant*

Hoover
Schaffhausen, Robert Joseph *retired structural engineer*

Huntsville
Balint, David Lee *engineering company executive*
Buckelew, Robin Browne *aerospace engineer*
Chassay, Roger Paul, Jr., *engineering executive*
Componation, Paul Joseph *industrial and systems engineer, educator*
Daussman, Grover Frederick *electrical engineer, consultant*
Hammond, Walter Edward *aerospace engineer*
†Hartline, Thomas William *aerospace engineer*
Hunter, Herbert Erwin *aerospace engineer*
Kim, Young Kil *aerospace engineer*
†Madewell, Charles David *aerospace engineer*
Mazumder, Sandip *engineer, researcher*
Mc Donough, George Francis, Jr., *retired aerospace engineer, consultant*
Moore, Fletcher Brooks *retired engineering company executive*
Morgan, John Derald *electrical engineer*
†Muth, William Donald *aeronautical engineer*
Pastrick, Harold Lee *aeronautical engineer*
Pittman, William Claude *electrical engineer*
†Reddy, Chintareddy Vidya Sagar *electrical engineer*
Schroer, Bernard Jon *industrial engineering educator*
†Stephenson, Arthur G. *aerospace engineer*
Stevens, Dale Marlin *civil engineer*
Theisen, Russell Eugene *electrical engineer*
Vaughan, Otha H., Jr., *retired aerospace engineer*
Vinz, Frank Louis *electrical engineer*
Watson, Raymond Coke, Jr., *engineering executive, academic administrator*
Wieland, Paul Otto *environmental control systems engineer*

Wu, Susan Ying Chu Lin (Ying-chu Lin) *engineering company executive, engineer*

Loachapoka
Schafer, Robert Louis *agricultural engineer, researcher*

Madison
Adams, Gary Lee *systems engineering supervisor*
†Brown, Daniel Morris *lens designer, consultant*
Dannenberg, Konrad K. *aeronautical engineer*
Emerson, William Kary *engineering company executive*
Lilly, Julius Quentin *engineering researcher*

Mobile
Hamid, Michael *electrical engineering educator, consultant*
†Hsiao, Kuang-Ting *mechanical engineer educator, researcher*
Perry, Nelson Allen *retired radiation safety engineer, radiological consultant*

Montgomery
Pan, Chai-Fu *engineering educator*

Pike Road
Schuetzenduebel, Wolfram Gerhard *retired engineering executive*

Spanish Fort
van Aken, John Henry *retired marine surveyor, engineer, consultant*

Thomasville
Davis, Gene *retired civil engineer*

Tuscaloosa
Barfield, Robert F. *retired mechanical engineer, educator, dean*
Bryan, Colgan Hobson *aerospace engineering educator*
†Chou, Kevin *mechanical engineer, educator*
Fonseca, Daniel J. *engineering educator*
†Greene, Timothy James *industrial engineering educator*
†Griffin, Marvin Anthony *industrial engineer, educator*
Morley, Lloyd Albert *electrical engineering educator*
Moynihan, Gary Peter *industrial engineering educator*
Polites, Michael Edward *aerospace engineer, educator*
Turner, Daniel Shelton *civil engineering educator*
Warren, Garry Wilbur *engineering educator*

ALASKA

Anchorage
Baker, Grant Cody *civil engineering educator*
†Coran, Joshua D. *mechanical engineer*
Mandell, Gordon Keith *aerospace engineer*
Pressley, James Ray *electrical engineer*
Thomas, Howard Paul *civil engineer, consultant*

Fairbanks
Ma, Zhongguo (John Ma) *engineering educator, researcher*
Milne, Clark Roger *civil engineer*
Tilsworth, Timothy *retired environmental/civil engineering educator*

ARIZONA

Apache Junction
†Campbell, John Carl *retired engineering educator*

Chandler
Fordemwalt, James Newton *microelectronics engineering educator, consultant*
Myers, Gregory Edwin *aerospace engineer*

Flagstaff
Collins, Galen Robert *technology educator*

Gilbert
Pendleton, Winston Kent, III, *aerospace engineer, physics educator*

Golden Valley
Davis, Richard Ernest *engineer*

Goodyear
Bailey, Thomas Everett *engineering company executive*

Hereford
Hirth, John Price *metallurgical engineering educator*

Mesa
Baxter, Gene Kenneth *mechanical engineer, company executive*
†Burgess, Robert Kingsley *aeronautical engineer*
†Raymond, Robert Joseph *mechanical engineer*
Rummel, Robert Wiland *aeronautical engineer, writer*

Paradise Valley
Ratkowski, Donald J. *mechanical engineer, consultant*
Russell, Paul Edgar *electrical engineering educator*

Phoenix
Bachus, Benson Floyd *mechanical engineer, consultant*
Banerjee, Ajoy Kumar *engineer, constructor, executive*
Blevins, Willard Ahart *electrical engineer*

Cai, Weizhong (Will Cai) *electronics engineer, researcher, physicist*
†Crawford, Neil Robert *mechanical engineer, researcher*
Freyermuth, Clifford L. *structural engineering consultant*
Fullmer, Steven Mark *engineering executive*
†Graham, LeRoy Cullen *retired electrical engineer*
†Kramer, Kevin William *aerospace engineer*
Liaw, Hang Ming *engineer*
Miller, Michael Jon *survey engineer, local government manager*
Morrison, John Haddow, Jr., *engineering company executive*
Quddus, Mohammed Tanvir *electrical engineer, researcher*
Sochacki, Andrzej *mechanical engineer, researcher, tourism educator*
Wiley, William David *engineer, hydrologist*

Prescott
Bieniawski, Zdzislaw Tadeusz Richard *engineering educator emeritus, writer, consultant*
Chesson, Eugene *civil engineering educator, consultant*
Kahne, Stephen James *systems engineer, educator, academic administrator, engineering executive*

Scottsdale
†Berry, Kenneth Jay, Jr., *aerospace engineer, consultant*
Cazier, Barry James *electrical engineer, software developer*
Fisher, John Richard *engineering consultant, former naval officer*
Gilson, Arnold Leslie *retired engineering executive, consultant*
Gookin, Thomas Allen Jaudon *civil engineer*
Jeffe, Sidney David *automotive engineer*
Kiehn, Mogens Hans *aviation engineer, consultant*
Lee, Dennis Turner *civil engineer, construction executive*
Miller, Harry *mechanical engineer*
Newman, Marc Alan *electrical engineer*

Sun City
Davies, Percy (Pete) Charles *mechanical engineer*
Lackey, James Franklin, Jr., *retired civil engineer*

Sun City West
Brown, Ruth Geisler *engineering supervisor*
Coté, Ralph Warren, Jr., *mining engineer, nuclear engineer*
Schlabach, Leland A. *electrical engineer*
Woodruff, Neil Parker *agricultural engineer*

Surprise
Ybarra, Kathryn Watrous *systems engineer*

Tempe
Balanis, Constantine Apostle *electrical engineering educator*
Berman, Neil Sheldon *chemical engineering educator*
Chawla, Nikhilesh *engineering educator*
Chiriac, Victor Adrian *aerospace engineer, researcher*
Collins, Richard Augustine *mechanical engineer*
Duhnke, Robert Emmet, Jr., *retired aerospace engineer*
Ferry, David Keane *electrical engineering educator*
†Freeman, Gary Eugene *civil engineer, researcher*
Harris, Warren Lynn *computer engineer*
Karady, George Gyorgy *electrical engineering educator, consultant*
Laananen, David Horton *mechanical engineer, educator*
Matthias, Judson Stillman *civil engineering educator, consultant*
Mays, Larry W. *civil engineering educator, hydrologist*
Robertson, Samuel Harry, III, *transportation safety research engineer, educator*
Schroder, Dieter Karl *electrical engineering educator*
Shah, Jami J. *mechanical engineering educator, researcher*
Shaw, Milton Clayton *mechanical engineering educator*
Stephenson, Frank Alex *engineer, consultant*
Tseng, Ampere An-Pei *mechanical engineer, educator, administrator*

Tonopah
Brittingham, James Calvin *nuclear engineer*

Tucson
Arnell, Walter James William *engineering educator, consultant*
Bjorhovde, Reidar *civil engineer, educator, researcher, consultant*
Brunton, Daniel William *mechanical engineer*
Buras, Nathan *hydrology and water resources educator*
Chapman, Richard Grady *engineer*
Coates, Wayne Evan *agricultural engineer*
Contractor, Dinshaw N. *civil engineer, educator*
Cook, Paul Christopher *engineering psychologist*
Cuello, Joel L. *biosystems engineer, educator*
Davis, Roswita Beate *architectural engineer*
Denney, Dwight Lee *engineer*
Edwards, John Womer *aerospace systems engineer*
Eigel, James Anthony *environmental engineer*
Gaither, William Samuel *civil engineering executive, consultant*
†Ganapol, Barry Douglas *nuclear engineering educator, consultant, aerospace engineer, mechanical engineer*
Gill, Rebecca LaLosh *aerospace engineer*

Harrington, Roger Fuller *electrical engineering educator, consultant*
Kececioglu, Dimitri Basil *reliability engineering educator, consultant*
Kerwin, William James *electrical engineering educator, consultant*
Lavu, Rana Pratap *engineer*
Mense, Allan Tate *research and development engineering executive*
Ogilvie, T(homas) Francis *engineer, educator*
Prince, John Luther, III, *engineering educator*
Rubendall, Richard Arthur *civil engineer*
Slack, Donald Carl *agricultural engineer, educator*
Smerdon, Ernest Thomas *engineering educator*
Szilagyi, Miklos Nicholas *electrical and computer engineering educator*
Wyant, James Clair *engineering company executive, educator*

ARKANSAS

Black Rock
Plunkett, Joseph Charles *electrical engineer, consultant*

Fayetteville
Andrews, John Frank *civil and environmental engineering educator*
Gaddy, James Leoma *chemical engineer, educator*
LeFevre, Elbert Walter, Jr., *civil engineering educator*
†Rossetti, Manuel David *engineering educator, consultant*

Hot Springs National Park
Brown, Dennis James *industrial engineer, consultant*
Ray, Arliss Dean *retired environmental consultant*

CALIFORNIA

Aliso Viejo
Boeckmann, Alan L. *engineering company executive*

Alpine
Doliber, Darrel Lee *retired engineering consultant, hotel executive*

Alta Loma
Bordner, Gregory Wilson *chemical engineer*

Altadena
Coles, Donald Earl *retired aeronautics educator*
Stewart, Homer Joseph *engineering educator*
Webster, Jeffery Norman *engineer*

Anaheim
†Elchert, Kenneth Clarence *aerospace engineer*
Phelan, Patrick John *engineer*
Uyehara, Otto Arthur *mechanical engineering educator emeritus, consultant*
Watson, Oliver Lee, III, *aerospace engineering manager*

Antioch
Granik, Vladimir *mechanics researcher, educator*

Arroyo Grande
Hoffmann, Jon Arnold *retired aeronautical engineer, educator*

Atherton
Morel-Seytoux, Hubert Jean *civil engineer, educator*

Auburn
Aro, Glenn Scott *environmental and safety executive*

Azusa
Lau, Henry *mechanical engineer, consultant*

Bakersfield
Gilmore, Gordon Ray *engineering executive*

Belmont
Hollis, Mary Frances *aerospace educator*

Benicia
Farnham, Timothy *training and education administrator*

Berkeley
Berger, Stanley Allan *mechanical and biomechanical engineering educator*
Birdsall, Charles Kennedy *electrical engineer*
Bogy, David B(eauregard) *mechanical engineering educator*
Cairns, Elton James *chemical engineering educator*
Chopra, Anil Kumar *civil engineering educator*
Dornfeld, David Alan *engineering educator*
Finnie, Iain *mechanical engineer, educator*
Frisch, Joseph *mechanical engineer, educator, consultant*
Fuerstenau, Douglas Winston *mineral engineering educator*
Garrison, William Louis *civil engineering educator*
Greif, Ralph *mechanical engineer, educator*
Grossman, Lawrence Morton *nuclear engineering educator*
Hodges, David Albert *electrical engineering educator*
Horvath, Arpad *engineering educator*
Kastenberg, William Edward *engineering educator, science educator*
Kuh, Ernest Shiu-Jen *electrical engineering educator*
Leitmann, George *mechanical engineer, educator*

Lewis, Edwin Reynolds *biomedical engineering educator*
May, Adolf Darlington *civil engineering educator*
†McMains, Sara A. *engineering educator*
Monismith, Carl Leroy *civil engineering educator*
Muller, Richard Stephen *electrical engineer, educator*
Nazaroff, William W. *engineering educator*
Newman, John Scott *chemical engineer, educator*
Ott, David Michael *engineering company executive*
Pagni, Patrick John *mechanical and fire safety engineering science educator*
Pawsey, Stuart Frederick *structural engineer, retired*
Penzien, Joseph *structural engineering educator*
Pigford, Thomas Harrington *nuclear engineering educator*
Pister, Karl Stark *engineering educator*
Polak, Elijah *engineering educator, computer scientist*
Prausnitz, John Michael *chemical engineer, educator*
Radke, Clayton J. *chemical engineer, educator*
†Rakas, Jasenka Milan *aerospace engineer, researcher, aerospace engineer, educator*
Susskind, Charles *engineering educator, writer, publishing executive*
†Szeri, Andrew John *mechanical engineer, educator*
†Tien, Chang-Lin
Tomizuka, Masayoshi *mechanical engineering educator, researcher*
Whinnery, John Roy *electrical engineer, educator*
White, Richard Manning *electrical engineering educator*
Wiegel, Robert Louis *consulting engineering executive*
†Yeung, Ronald Wai-Chun *engineering educator*

Berry Creek
Miller, Joseph Arthur *retired manufacturing engineer, educator, consultant*

Beverly Hills
†Dragan, Alexandra *mechanical engineer, consultant, environmental engineer, researcher, engineering educator*

Bonsall
Jeffredo, John Victor *aerospace engineer, manufacturing company executive, inventor*

Brea
Brown, Ronald Malcolm *engineering corporation executive*

Brentwood
Rawson, Eric Gordon *optical engineer*

Buellton
Porter, Bruce Jackman *military engineer, computer software engineer, application developer, investment broker, civil engineer*

Buena Park
Wiersema, Harold LeRoy *aerospace engineer*

Calabasas
Moule, William Nelson *electrical engineer, consultant*

Camarillo
MacAlister, Robert Stuart *petroleum engineer, consultant*
MacDonald, Norval (Norval Woodrow MacDonald) *safety engineer*

Camino
Van Klaveren, Nico *engineer, consultant*

Campbell
Levy, Salomon *mechanical engineer*
Ross, Hugh Courtney *electrical engineer*

Canoga Park
†Egermeier, Robert Paul *retired engineer, retired lawyer*

Canyon Country
Hawkins, Dale Cicero *aviator, educator, engineer*

Carlsbad
Nahavandi, Amir Nezameddin *retired engineering firm executive*
Plachno, Ronald John *electrical engineer*

Carmel
Alsberg, Dietrich Anselm *electrical engineer, consultant*

Castaic
†Rouzbehani, Anousheh *engineering executive, consultant*

Cayucos
Theurer, Byron W. *aerospace engineer, business owner*

Cerritos
El-Sayed, Khalil Mohamad *aerospace engineer*
Subramanya, Shiva *aerospace systems engineer*

Chatsworth
†Wimberly, Doug J. *design engineer, consultant*

Chico
Allen, Charles William *mechanical engineering educator*
Learned, Vincent Roy *electrical engineer, educator*

Chula Vista
Rusconi, Louis Joseph *marine engineer*

Claremont
Acosta, Nelson John *civil engineer*
Dym, Clive Lionel *engineering educator*
Molinder, John Irving *engineering educator, consultant*
Monson, James Edward *electrical engineer, educator*
Presecan, Nicholas Lee *environmental and civil engineer, consultant*
Tanenbaum, Basil Samuel *engineering educator*

Clovis
†Brahma, Chandra Sekhar *civil engineering educator*

Compton
Wang, Charles Ping *engineering executive*

Concord
Crandall, Ira Carlton *consulting electrical engineer*
Lee, Low Kee *electronics engineer, consultant*
Middleton, Michael John *civil engineer*

Cool
Trybul, Theodore Nicholas *engineering educator*

Corona
Tillman, Joseph Nathaniel *engineering executive*

Corona Del Mar
Richmond, Ronald LeRoy *aerospace engineer*

Coronado
Crilly, Eugene Richard *engineering consultant*

Corralitos
Short, Harold Ashby *imaging engineer*

Costa Mesa
Buchtel, Michael Eugene *optical mechanical engineer*
Carpenter, Frank Charles, Jr., *retired electronics engineer*

Coto De Caza
Sheehy, Jerome Joseph *electrical engineer*

Crockett
Leporiere, Ralph Dennis *retired quality engineer*

Cupertino
Chung, Jin Soo *ocean mining and ocean engineer*
Edson, William Alden *electrical engineer, researcher*
Fan, Chien *aerospace engineer, researcher*
Fenn, Raymond Wolcott, Jr., *retired metallurgical engineer*
Finnemore, (Erhardt) John *civil engineer, educator*
Lam, Cheung-Wei *electrical engineer*
Szczerba, Victor Bogdan *electrical engineer, sales engineer*
†Zhang, Ming *engineering researcher*

Daly City
Mobley, Clarence Fowler *retired civil engineer*

Dana Point
Easton, Richard Allen *electrical engineer*
Olvera, Carlos Nelson *mechanical engineer, executive*

Davis
Akesson, Norman Berndt *agricultural engineer, emeritus educator*
Brandt, Harry *mechanical engineering educator*
Chancellor, William Joseph *agricultural engineering educator*
Chang, Daniel Pan Yih *environmental engineering educator*
Cheney, James Addison *civil engineering educator*
Dorf, Richard Carl *electrical engineering and management educator*
Gates, Bruce Clark *chemical engineer, educator*
Ghausi, Mohammed Shuaib *electrical engineering educator, university dean*
†Hess, Ronald Andrew *aerospace engineer, educator*
Kavvas, M. Levent *civil engineering educator*
Larock, Bruce Edward *civil engineering educator*
Marino, Miguel Angel *engineering educator*
†Pan, Ning *engineering educator*
†Sperling, Daniel *engineering educator, transportation studies director*
Tchobanoglous, George *civil engineering educator*
Wang, Shih-Ho *electrical engineer, educator*

Del Mar
Wilkinson, Eugene Parks *nuclear engineer, director*

Desert Hot Springs
Halasz, Stephen Joseph *retired electro-optical systems engineer*

Diamond Bar
Mirisola, Lisa Heinemann *air quality engineer*

Dinuba
Leps, Thomas MacMaster *civil engineer, consultant*

Downey
Baumann, Theodore Robert *aerospace engineer, consultant, army officer*

El Segundo
†Abbassian-Kashi, Mandana *industrial engineer, systems engineer*

†Agrawal, Suphal P. *engineering company executive*
Bauer, Jerome Leo, Jr., *chemical engineer*
Chang, I-Shih *aerospace engineer*
Daughaday, Douglas Robert *computer engineer*
Hollander, Sidney *computer systems engineer*
Jacobs, Michael Moises *aerospace engineer, consultant*
Lantz, Norman Foster *electrical engineer*
McDonald, Rosa Nell *engineering executive*
†Puckett, Allen Emerson *aeronautical engineer*
†Rosen, Harold A. *retired aeronautical engineer*

Emeryville
†Deeb, Rula Anselmo *environmental engineer*
Zwoyer, Eugene Milton *retired consulting engineering executive*

Encinitas
Frank, Michael Victor *risk assessment engineer*

Encino
Friedman, George Jerry *aerospace engineer, executive*
Knuth, Eldon Luverne *engineering educator*

Escondido
Ellenberger, William Joseph *retired engineering consultant*
Ghandhi, Sorab Khushro *electrical engineering educator*
Grew, Raymond Edward *mechanical engineer*
†Kennedy, Robert Philip *civil engineer*
Pantos, William Pantazes *mechanical engineer, consultant*

Fair Oaks
Agerbek, Sven *mechanical engineer*
Jackson, Fred Lester *retired civil engineer*

Folsom
Ettlich, William F. *electrical engineer*
†Ryu, Woong Hwan *electrical engineer*

Fountain Valley
†Tu, John *engineering executive*

Fremont
Mian, Guo *electrical engineer*
Ramirez-Mireles, Fernando *electrical engineer*
Unsal, Cem *electrical engineer, educator*
Wang, Huai-Liang William *mechanical engineer*
Wu, James Chen-Yuan *aerospace engineering educator*

Fresno
Huffman, David George *electrical engineer*

Fullerton
Bradburn, David Denison *engineer, retired air force officer*
Gunness, Robert Charles *retired chemical engineer*
†Rao, Prasada *engineering educator*
Tehrani, Fleur Taher *electrical engineer, educator, researcher*

Gardena
†Stuart, Jay William *retired engineer*

Gilroy
Hart, William Carl *retired civil engineer*

Glendale
Cutts, Stephen Paul *civil engineer, linguistics researcher*
Knoop, Vern Thomas *civil engineer, consultant*

Glendora
Haile, Benjamin Carroll, Jr., *retired chemical engineer, retired mechanical engineer*

Goleta
Cork, Donald Burl *electrical engineer*
†Lea, Wayne Adair *electrical engineer, linguist*
†Sullivan, Kevin Joseph *mechanical engineer*

Granite Bay
Hunnicutt, Richard Pearce *metallurgical engineer*

Hacienda Heights
Love, Daniel Joseph *consulting engineer*

Hawthorne
†McRuer, Duane Torrance *aerospace engineering executive*

Hayward
Kimbell, Marion Joel *retired engineer*

Hollywood
Mkhitarian, Marine *chemical engineer*

Huntington Beach
De Veirman, Geert Adolf *engineer*
†Duong, Cong Nghiep *aeronautical engineer*
Grooms, Henry Randall *civil engineer*
Harsha, Philip Thomas *aerospace engineer*
Nash, Richard Eugene *aerospace engineer*
Nguyen, Han Van *mechanical engineer*
Nowlan, Daniel Ralph *engineering executive*
Stillman, Alfred William, Jr., *electrical engineer*

Indian Wells
Jorgensen, Gordon David *retired engineering company executive*

Irvine
Back, Lloyd H. *mechanical engineer, researcher*
Chelapati, Chunduri Venkata *civil engineering educator*
Chen, Chungte William *optical engineer*
Khalessi, Mohammad R. *structural engineer, researcher*
Kumar, Anil *nuclear engineer*

Orme, Melissa Emily *mechanical engineering educator*
Rangel, Roger Henrique *mechanical and aerospace engineering educator*
Samueli, Henry *electrical engineering educator, entrepreneur*
Sandu, Constantine *process development engineer*
Sharbaugh, W(illiam) James *plastics engineer, consultant*
Sirignano, William Alfonso *aerospace and mechanical engineer, educator*
Smedley, Keyue Ma *engineering educator, researcher*
Ting, Albert Chia *bioengineering researcher*
Villaverde, Roberto *civil engineer*
Zabsky, John Mitchell *engineering executive*

Irwindale
Lu, Guiyang *electrical engineer*
Miao, Rongsheng *mechanical and thermal engineer*

Kensington
Oppenheim, Antoni Kazimierz *mechanical engineer*

La Canada
Ruskin, Arnold Milton *engineer, educator*

La Canada Flintridge
Price, Humphrey Wallace *aerospace engineer*

La Jolla
Chang, William Shen Chie *electrical engineering educator*
Coler, Myron A(braham) *chemical engineer, educator*
Counts, Stanley Thomas *aerospace consultant, retired naval officer, retired electronics company executive*
†Elgamal, Ahmed *geotechnical and structural engineering educator*
Fung, Yuan-Cheng Bertram *bioengineering educator, writer*
Hall, Harold Robert *retired computer engineer*
Karin, Sidney *computer science and engineering educator*
†Lanza Di Scalea, Francesco *engineering educator*
Levy, Ralph *engineering executive, consultant*
Milstein, Laurence Bennett *electrical engineering educator, researcher*
†Morrow, Esther M. *aerospace engineer, researcher*
Nemat-Nasser, Sia *engineering educator, researcher*
Penner, Stanford Solomon *engineering educator*
Rudee, Mervyn Lea *engineering educator, researcher*
Rudolph, Walter Paul *engineering research company executive*
†Saldivar, Enrique *bioengineer, researcher*
Schmid-Schoenbein, Geert Wilfried Wilfried *biomedical engineer, educator*
Williams, Forman Arthur *engineering science educator, combustion theorist*

La Mesa
Threlkeld, Steven Wayne *civil/environmental engineer*

La Mirada
Kong, Xiangli (Charlie Kong) *mechanical and control engineer, educator*

Lafayette
Krueger, Robert Edward *manufacturing executive, mechanical engineer*
Peirano, Lawrence Edward *civil engineer*

Laguna Hills
Hammond, R. Philip *chemical engineer*

Laguna Niguel
Chen, Shoei-Sheng *retired mechanical engineer*

Laguna Woods
Green, Leon, Jr., *mechanical engineer*

Lancaster
Hodges, Vernon Wray *mechanical engineer*

Lincoln
Chiang, George Djia-Chee *retired engineer, educator*

Livermore
Ambrose, William Patrick *engineer*
Brereton, Sandra Joy *engineer*
Chen, Er-Ping *engineering executive*
Johnson, Roy Ragnar *electrical engineer, researcher*
Judge, James Carl *quality assurance officer, information systems specialist*
King, Ray John *electrical engineer, educator, business executive*
Martovetsky, Nicolai N. *mechanical engineer, researcher*

Lomita
Balcom, Orville *engineer*

Lompoc
Means, James Andrew *engineer*

Long Beach
Button, Glenn Marshall *aeronautical engineer*
Cummings, Darold Bernard *aircraft engineer*
Davis, Mark Hezekiah, Jr., *electrical engineer*
†de Soto, Simon *mechanical engineer*
Dillon, Michael Earl *engineering executive, mechanical engineer, educator*
Elliott, John Gregory *aerospace design engineer*
Jager, Merle LeRoy *aerospace engineer*
Kumar, Rajendra *electrical engineering educator*
†Madan, Ram Chand *aeronautical engineer*

Moroso, Michael Joseph *aerospace engineer*
Yang, Xinjian (Sam Yang) *environmental engineer*

Los Alamitos
Eckelman, Richard Joel *engineering specialist*

Los Altos
Carlson, Warren Ore *civil engineer*
Gough, William Cabot *engineer*
Moll, John Lewis *electronics engineer, retired*
Peterson, Victor Lowell *aerospace engineer, management consultant*
Sharpe, Roland Leonard *structural engineer, consultant*
Zebroski, Edwin Leopold *risk management consultant*

Los Altos Hills
Fondahl, John Walker *civil engineering educator*

Los Angeles
†Ballhaus, William Francis, Jr., *aerospace industry executive, research scientist*
Buffington, Gary Lee Roy *safety engineer, construction executive*
Carman, Greg *mechanical engineer, educator*
Cheng, Tsen-Chung *electrical engineering educator*
Chobotov, Vladimir Alexander *aerospace engineer, educator*
Cosner, Christopher Mark *engineer*
Crombie, Douglass Darnill *aerospace communications system engineer*
Dorman, Albert A. *consulting engineer executive, architect*
Erman, Andrew David *civil engineer*
Friedlander, Sheldon Kay *chemical engineering educator*
Gildersleeve, Thomas Henry *retired civil engineer, consultant, photographer*
Hovanessian, Shahen Alexander *electrical engineer, educator, consultant*
Huang, Sung-cheng *electrical engineering educator*
Incaudo, Joseph August *engineering company executive*
Itoh, Tatsuo *engineering educator*
†Jacobson, Marcus J. *retired mechanical engineer*
Jacoby, Neil Herman, Jr., *astronautic engineer, consultant*
Johnston, Roy G. *consulting structural engineer*
Kelly, Robert Edward *engineer, educator*
Kim, Jeongbin John *mechanical engineering educator*
Klinger, Allen *engineering and applied science educator*
Kuehl, Hans Henry *electrical engineering educator*
Lin, Tung Hua *civil engineering educator*
MacKenzie, John Douglas *engineering educator*
Marmarelis, Vasilis Zissis *engineering educator, writer, consultant*
Martin, J(ohn) Edward *architectural engineer*
Masri, Sami F(aiz) *civil and mechanical engineering educator, consultant*
Meecham, William Coryell *engineering educator*
Mendel, Jerry Marc *electrical engineering educator*
Mirza, Zakir Hussain *aerospace company consultant*
Mortazavian, Harold *electrical engineer, researcher, mathematician*
Muntz, Eric Phillip *aerospace and mechanical engineering and radiology educator, consultant*
Nathanson, Theodore Herzl *aeronautical engineer, architect*
†Newman, Richard G. *engineering company executive*
Nobe, Ken *chemical engineering educator*
Okrent, David *engineering educator*
O'Neill, Russell Richard *engineering educator*
Orchard, Henry John *electrical engineer*
Parker, Alice Cline *computer engineering educator, consultant*
Perrine, Richard Leroy *environmental engineering educator*
Ramo, Simon *retired engineering executive*
Rauch, Lawrence Lee *aerospace and electrical engineer, educator*
Roden, Martin S. *engineering educator, writer*
Rubinstein, Moshe Fajwel *engineering educator*
Russell, Joseph Allen *instrumentation and controls engineer, consultant*
†Safadi, M. Oussama *engineering educator*
Safonov, Michael George *electrical engineering educator, consultant*
Scholtz, Robert Arno *electrical engineering educator*
Settles, F. Stan, Jr., *engineering educator, manufacturing executive*
Shung, Koping Kirk *engineering educator*
Sklansky, Jack *electrical and computer engineering educator, researcher*
Stenstrom, Michael Knudson *civil engineering educator*
Udwadia, Firdaus Erach *engineering educator, consultant*
Urena-Alexiades, Jose Luis *electrical engineer*
Wagner, Christian Nikolaus Johann *materials engineering educator*
Welch, Lloyd Richard *electrical engineering educator, communications consultant*
Willner, Alan Eli *electrical engineer, educator*
†Wilson, Karen *engineer*
Yang, Fan *electrical engineering research scientist*
Yen, Teh Fu *civil and environmental engineering educator*

Los Banos
York, Courtney Carter *retired engineering executive, genealogist*

Los Gatos
Kazan, Benjamin *research engineer*

PROFESSIONAL INDEX 6295 ENGINEERING

Naymark, Sherman *consulting nuclear engineer*
Rosenheim, Donald Edwin *electrical engineer*

Malibu
Ancker, Clinton James, Jr., *emeritus systems and industrial engineering educator*
Bedrosian, Edward *electrical engineer*

Marina Del Rey
Philpott, Lindsey *civil engineer, researcher, educator*

Menlo Park
Abdou, Ikram Escandar *engineering consultant*
Honey, Richard Churchill *retired electrical engineer*
Jeffries, Robin *computer engineer*
McCarthy, Roger Lee *mechanical engineer*
Ross, Bernard *engineering consultant, educator*
Shah, Haresh Chandulal *civil engineering educator*

Milpitas
†Wang, Shao *tribologist, senior hard disk drive engineer*

Mission Hills
Cramer, Frank Brown *engineering executive, combustion engineer, systems consultant*

Mission Viejo
Drozdowski, Miladin Peter Ljubicic *consulting engineer*

Moffett Field
†Bilimoria, Karl D. *aerospace engineer*
†Denery, Dallas G. *aeronautical engineer, researcher*
Eodice, Michael Thomas *aerospace engineer, biomedical engineer*
†Park, Chul *aerospace engineer*
Statler, Irving Carl *aerospace engineer*

Monarch Beach
Dougherty, Elmer Lloyd, Jr., *retired chemical engineering educator, consultant*

Monrovia
Edwards, Kenneth Neil *chemical engineering executive*
†Liu, Wenhai *optical engineer*
Mac Cready, Paul *aeronautical engineer*
Pray, Ralph Emerson *metallurgical engineer*

Monterey
Butler, Jon Terry *computer engineering educator, researcher*
Dutta, Indranath *metallurgical engineer, educator*
Marto, Paul James *retired mechanical engineering educator, consultant, researcher*
Newberry, Conrad Floyde *aerospace engineering educator*

Monterey Park
Zheng, Dawei *process integration engineer, materials scientist*

Moorpark
Bahn, Gilbert Schuyler *retired mechanical engineer, researcher, novelist*

Morro Bay
Wagner, Peter Ewing *physics and electrical engineering educator*

Mountain View
Aron, Mohit *software engineer*
Chandramouli, Ramamurti *electrical engineer*
Johnson, Conor Deane *mechanical engineer*
Perrella, Anthony Joseph *electronics engineer*
Savage, Thomas Warren *engineering director*
Unangst, Gregory John *aerospace engineer*

Murrieta
Geffe, Philip Reinhold *electrical engineer, consultant*

Napa
Grambow, Richard F. *construction engineer, consultant*

Nevada City
Symes, Peter David *engineer*

Newport Beach
Kraus, John Walter *former aerospace engineering company executive*
Lorti, Daniel Caesar *engineer*

North Hollywood
de la Houssaye, Brette Angelo-Pepe *electronics engineer, researcher*

Northridge
Bekir, Nagwa Esmat *electrical engineer, educator, consultant*
Bradshaw, Richard Rotherwood *engineering executive*
Kiddoo, Robert James *engineering service company executive*
Stout, Thomas Melville *control systems engineer*
Torgow, Eugene N. *electrical engineer*

Oakland
King, Cary Judson, III, *chemical engineer, educator, university official*
Musihin, Konstantin K. *electrical engineer*
Tsztoo, David Fong *civil engineer*
Youngs, Robert Riggs *engineer*

Occidental
Rumsey, Victor Henry *electrical engineering educator emeritus*

Oceanside
McLean, Arthur Frederick *mechanical engineer*
Yurist, Svetlan Joseph *mechanical engineer*

Orange
Demarchi, Ernest Nicholas *retired aerospace executive*
Fisk, Edward Ray *retired civil engineer, author, educator*
Jones, Cleon Boyd *research engineer*
Toeppe, William Joseph, Jr., *retired aerospace engineer*
Vice, Charles Loren *electromechanical engineer, consultant*

Oxnard
Zhou, Sophia Huai *biomedical engineering scientist*

Pacific Palisades
Herman, Elvin E. *retired consulting electronic engineer*

Palm Desert
Copperman, William H. *value engineer, consultant*
Morrison, Robert Thomas *aerospace engineering and marketing consultant*
Osborne, Bartley Porter, Jr., *aeronautical engineer*

Palo Alto
Bright, Peter Bowman *scientist, engineer, researcher*
Brown, David Randolph *electrical engineer*
†Casati, Fabio *engineer*
Hodge, Philip Gibson, Jr., *mechanical and aerospace engineering educator*
Jung, Henry Hung *mechanical engineer*
†Kapoor, Ashok Kumar *engineer*
Kim, Wan Hee *electrical engineering educator, business executive*
Luh, Howard H. *aerospace engineer*
McHugh, Stuart Lawrence *materials engineer*
Taylor, John Joseph *nuclear engineer, researcher*
†Vassar, Richard Holt *aerospace engineer*
Watson, David Colquitt *electrical engineer, educator*
Youngdahl, Paul Frederick *mechanical engineer*

Palos Verdes Estates
Abbott, A. Dwight *retired astronautical engineer*
Perry, Robert Michael *engineering company executive*
Raue, Jorg Emil *electrical engineer*
Yarbrough, Allyson Debra *electrical engineer*

Palos Verdes Peninsula
Denke, Paul Herman *retired aircraft engineer*
Mirels, Harold *aerospace engineer*
Seide, Paul *civil engineering educator*

Pasadena
Arik, Baha Engin *engineering executive*
†Bobba, Kumar Manoj *engineer, researcher*
Bridges, William Bruce *electrical engineer, researcher, engineering educator*
Chiang, Wen-Li *hydrodynamicist*
Dallas, Saterios (Sam Dallas) *aerospace engineer, researcher, consultant*
†Elachi, Charles *aerospace engineer*
Farr, Donald Eugene *engineering scientist*
Hatheway, Alson Earle *mechanical engineer*
Hilbert, Robert S(aul) *optical engineer*
Hornung, Hans Georg *aeronautical engineering educator, science facility administrator*
†Housner, George William *retired civil engineering educator, consultant*
Jacobs, Joseph John *engineering company executive*
Jennings, Paul Christian *civil engineering educator, academic administrator*
Knowles, James Kenyon *applied mechanics educator*
†Lamassoure, Elisabeth Sylvie *aerospace engineer*
†Liebe, Carl Christian *aerospace engineer, researcher*
List, Ericson John *environmental engineering science educator, engineering consultant*
Losh, Samuel Johnston *engineering administrator*
Newell, Michael Alfred *electrical engineer*
Otoshi, Tom Yasuo *electrical engineer, consultant*
Perez, Reinaldo Joseph *electrical engineer*
Poon, Peter Tin-Yau *engineer, physicist*
Roshko, Anatol *aeronautic engineer*
Sabersky, Rolf Heinrich *mechanical engineer*
Schlinger, Warren Gleason *retired chemical engineer*
†Scott, Ronald Fraser *civil engineering educator, engineering consultant*
Seinfeld, John Hersh *chemical engineering educator*
Shimada, Katsunori *retired electrical engineer*
Smith, Michael Robert *electro-optical engineer, physicist*
Stelzried, Charles Thomas *engineer*
Tekippe, Rudy Joseph *civil engineer*
Weisbin, Charles Richard *nuclear engineer*
Wood, Lincoln Jackson *aerospace engineer*
Yariv, Amnon *electrical engineering educator, scientist*
Yeh, Paul Pao *electrical and electronics engineer, educator*

Penn Valley
Morgenthaler, John Herbert *chemical engineer*
Throner, Guy Charles, Jr., *engineering executive, scientist, engineer, inventor, consultant*

Penryn
Bryson, Vern Elrick *nuclear engineer*

Piedmont
Schell, Farrel Loy *transportation engineer*

Pleasant Hill
Hopkins, Robert Arthur *retired industrial engineer*

Pleasanton
†Cheng, Shide *engineer, researcher*
Jarnagan, Harry William, Jr., *project manager*
Novak, Randi Ruth *engineer, computer scientist*
Van Dreser, Merton Lawrence *ceramic engineer*

Pomona
Teague, Lavette Cox, Jr., *systems educator, consultant*

Poway
Pugay, Jeffrey Ibanez *mechanical engineer*

Rancho Cordova
Carleone, Joseph *business executive*

Rancho Cucamonga
Alvarez, Tirso Reyes, Jr., *engineer*

Rancho Mirage
Kramer, Gordon *mechanical engineer*

Rancho Palos Verdes
Frassinelli, Guido Joseph *retired aerospace engineer*

Redlands
Chandler, David Leslie *engineer*

Redondo Beach
Brodsky, Robert Fox *aerospace engineer, educator, author*
†Grzesik, Jan Alexander *electronics engineer, mathematician*
†Johnson, Dan R. *engineering executive*
†Kich, Rolf *communications scientist, consultant*

Riverside
Balandin, Alexander A. *electrical engineer, educator*
Beni, Gerardo *electrical and computer engineering educator, robotics scientist*
Hackwood, Susan *electrical and computer engineering educator*
Mulchandani, Ashok Kimatrai *chemical engineer, educator*
†Ozkan, Mihri *engineering educator*

Rodeo
Emmanuel, Jorge Agustin *chemical engineer, environmental consultant*

Rohnert Park
Lord, Harold Wilbur *electrical engineer, electronics consultant*

Rolling Hills Estates
Diaz-Zubieta, Agustin *nuclear engineer, engineering executive*
Wong, Sun Yet *engineering consultant*

Roseville
Jacks, Bruce William *civil engineer*

Running Springs
Liddle, Sidney George *retired mechanical engineer, researcher*

Sacramento
Cavigli, Henry James *petroleum engineer*
Crimmins, Philip Patrick *metallurgical engineer, lawyer*
Forsyth, Raymond Arthur *civil engineer, consultant*
Kerri, Kenneth Donald *civil engineering educator*
Kumar, B. Preetham *engineering educator, researcher*
†Roberts, James E. *civil engineer*
Simeroth, Dean Conrad *chemical engineer*
Yousif, Salah M. *electrical engineer, educator, electrical engineer, consultant*

Salinas
†Michener, John Russell *electrical engineer*

San Bernardino
Bauer, Steven Michael *cost containment engineer*
Golondzinier, Theodore Matthew *civil engineer*
Kirkland, Bertha Theresa *project engineer*

San Bruno
Amick, Collin Hal *civil engineer, consultant*

San Carlos
Symons, Robert Spencer *electronic engineer*

San Clemente
Nguyen, Ky Duc *electrical engineer*
White, Stanley Archibald *research electrical engineer*

San Diego
†Anderson, Karl Richard *aerospace engineer, consultant*
Anderson, Paul Maurice *electrical engineering educator, researcher, consultant*
Auld, Robert Henry, Jr., *biomedical engineer, educator, consultant, author*
Beyster, John Robert *engineering company executive*
Chen, Carlson S. *mechanical engineer*
Conly, John Franklin *engineering educator, researcher*
Crocker, Valerie Marian *mechanical engineer*
Crook, Sean Paul *aerospace systems division director*
†Dai, Liang *electrical engineer*
Davenport, Roger Lee *research engineer*
Day, Robert William *geotechnical engineer*
Dean, Richard Anthony *mechanical engineer, engineering executive*
Evans, Ersel Arthur *consulting engineer executive*
Foreman, John Patrick *electrical engineer*
Fraitag, Leonard Alan *product development engineer*
Frederick, Norman L., Jr., *electrical engineer*
Friedman, Arthur Daniel *electrical engineering and computer science educator, investment management company executive*
Gilleland, John Rogers *technology company executive*
Gross, Jeffrey *software engineer*
Gupta, Madhu Sudan *electrical engineering educator*
Ito, Carl Susumu *computer engineer*
Larson, Arvid Gunnar *electrical engineer*
Levi, Victor H. *retired electrical engineer*
McLeod, John Hugh, Jr., *mechanical and electrical engineer*
Paget, John Arthur *mechanical engineer*
Poppendiek, Heinz Frank *engineering executive*
Robbins, Arthur M. *retired aerospace engineer*
St. Clair, Hal Kay *electrical engineer*
†Schmidt, Thomas Charles *biomedical engineer, researcher*
Schryver, Bruce John *safety engineer*
†Schultz, Kenneth Robert *nuclear engineer, researcher*
Sell, Robert Emerson *electrical engineer*
Slate, John Butler *biomedical engineer*
Suycott, Mark Leland *systems engineer, retired naval flight officer*
Tartz, Robert Scott *engineering executive*
Thomas, Kevin Anthony *biomedical engineer*
Tricoles, Gus Peter *electromagnetic engineer, physicist, consultant*
Ward, Charles Raymond *systems engineer*
Youngs, Jack Marvin *cost engineer*

San Francisco
Bechtel, Riley Peart *engineering company executive*
Bechtel, Stephen Davison, Jr., *engineering company executive*
Bell, Chester Gordon *computer engineering company executive*
Cheng, Wan-Lee *mechanical engineer, industrial technology educator*
Dolby, Ray Milton *engineering company executive, electrical engineer*
†Eliaz, Rom Ezer *chemical engineer, educator*
Gerwick, Ben Clifford, Jr., *construction engineer, educator*
†Hillier, Wynship West *systems engineer*
Holtz, Klaus Erich *computer engineer*
Kammerer, Ann Marie *geotechnical engineer*
Keller, Edward Lowell *electrical engineer, educator*
Koffel, Martin M. *engineering company executive*
Lin, Tung Yen *civil engineer, educator*
Luft, Rene Wilfred *civil engineer*
Tang, Man-Chung *engineer, administrator*
Vreeland, Robert Wilder *retired electronics engineer*
Wong, Stephen T.C. *radiology, neurology, computer scientist, and bioengineer educator*
Yuan, Shao Wen *aerospace engineer, educator*

San Jose
Antweiler, Dennis Francis *mechanical engineer*
Chamberlin, Donald Dean *computer engineer*
Contos, Paul Anthony *engineer, investment consultant*
Dennison, Ronald Walton *engineer*
Eastburn, Martin Howard *engineer*
Gill, Hardayal Singh *electrical engineer*
Hoang, Loc Bao *electrical engineer*
Israel, Paul Neal *computer design engineer, writer*
Jacobson, Albert Herman, Jr., *industrial and systems engineer, educator*
Jain, Raj *engineering educator*
Jonaris, George G. *electrical engineer, computer engineer*
Kirk, Donald Evan *electrical engineering educator, dean*
Kring, Charles Udell *retired civil engineer*
†Luo, Yuhao *electrical engineer*
Morimoto, Carl Noboru *computer system engineer, crystallographer*
Sankar, Subramanian Vaidya *aerospace engineer*
Shaw, Charles Alden *engineering executive*
Tran, Jack Nhuan Ngoc *gas and oil reservoir engineer*
Tretz, Christophe Robert *electrical engineer*
Watson, Guy Edwards *mechanical engineer, consultant*
Wu, Dongping (Don Wu) *optical laser and electrical engineer*
Yuan, Xiao Jie *high technology professional*
Zhang, G. Z. (Guangzhi Zhang) *electro-optics engineer*
Zobel, Jon D., Jr., *electrical engineer*

San Lorenzo
Thompson, Lyle Eugene *electrical engineer*

San Luis Obispo
Anderson, Warren Ronald *electrical engineering educator*
Cummings, Russell Mark *aerospace engineer, educator*
Goel, Rakesh K. *engineering educator*

San Luis Rey
Melbourne, Robert Ernest *civil engineer*

San Marcos
Purdy, Alan Harris *biomedical engineer*

San Mateo
Hur, Stephen Ponyi *civil engineer, management consultant, educator*

San Pedro
Chamberlain, Thomas Eugene *mechanical engineer*
Ellis, George Edwin, Jr., *chemical engineer*

McCarty, Frederick Briggs *electrical engineer, consultant*

San Rafael
Douglas, James *construction engineering educator*
Wright, Frederick Herman Greene, II, *computer systems engineer*

San Ramon
Morrison, Cheryl Lynn *petroleum engineer, project manager*
Schlitt, William Joseph, III, *metallurgical engineer*

Sand City
†Coile, Russell Cleven *electrical engineer, consultant*

Santa Ana
Amoroso, Frank *retired communication system engineer, consultant*
Bauer, Bruce F. *former aerospace engineer*
Kelly, James Patrick, Jr., *retired engineering and construction executive*
Sethi, Sandeep *environmental engineer*
Waaland, Irving Theodore *retired aerospace design executive*

Santa Barbara
Bruch, John Clarence, Jr., *engineer, educator*
Coldren, Larry Allen *engineering educator, consultant*
†Culler, Glen *retired electrical engineer, electrical engineer, educator*
Edebo, Ralph Bertil *engineer, economist*
Gilbert, Paul Thomas *chemical development engineer*
Iselin, Donald Grote *civil engineering and management consultant*
Kokotovic, Petar V. *electrical and computer engineer, educator*
Kramer, Edward John *materials science and engineering educator*
Kroemer, Herbert *electrical engineering educator*
Lawrance, Charles Holway *retired civil and sanitary engineer*
†Leedham, Clive Douglas *retired electrical engineer*
Mitra, Sanjit Kumar *electrical and computer engineering educator*
Parhami, Behrooz *engineering educator, consultant*
Russell, Charles Roberts *chemical engineer*
Sensiper, Samuel *electrical engineer*
Swalley, Robert Farrell *retired structural engineer, consultant*
Theofanous, Theo G. *engineering educator, consultant*
Thomas, Bertram David *retired chemical engineer*
Wade, Glen *electrical engineer, educator*

Santa Clara
Aitken, Robert Campbell *engineer*
Chakravarty, Sreejit *computer engineer, researcher*
Chan, Shu-Park *electrical engineering educator*
Chen, Wai-Kai *electrical engineering and computer science educator, consultant*
Hoagland, Albert Smiley *electrical engineer, researcher*
†Kamal, Abu Hena M. *electrical engineer, researcher*
Kaneda, David Ken *electrical engineering company executive*
Kelley, Robert Suma *network engineer*
†Liu, Kevin *structural engineer*
Nevins, Bryan Dexter *integrated circuit design engineer*
Nguyen, Luu Thanh *engineering executive*
Parden, Robert James *engineering educator, management consultant*
†Pease, Robert Allen *electrical engineer*
†Vakanas, George P. *process engineer, research scientist, consultant, entrepreneur*
Vu, Quat Thuong *electrical engineer*
Weinberg, William Henry *chemical engineer, chemical physicist, educator*
Yan, Pei-Yang *electrical engineer*
Zecevic, Aleksandar I. *engineering educator*

Santa Clarita
Garcia, Andrew B. *chemical engineer*

Santa Cruz
Kang, Sung-Mo (Steve Kang) *electrical engineering educator*
†Mantey, Patrick Edward *engineering educator, consultant*
Wiberg, Donald Martin *electrical engineering educator, consultant*

Santa Monica
Gritton, Eugene Charles *nuclear engineer, director*
Kayton, Myron *engineering company executive*
McGuire, Michael John *environmental engineer*
Rhodes, Carl Anthony *engineer*
Roney, Robert Kenneth *retired aerospace company executive*
Sherman, Zachary *civil and aerospace engineer, consultant*

Santa Rosa
Grundy, Richard David *engineer*

Santee
Kropotoff, George Alex *civil engineer*

Saratoga
Brown, Paul Fremont *aerospace engineer, educator*
Johnson, Noel Lars *biomedical engineer*
Syvertson, Clarence Alfred *engineering and research management consultant*

Seal Beach
†Robinson, Michael R. *aeronautical engineer*

Sebastopol
Norman, Arnold McCallum, Jr., *engineer*

Sonoma
Muchmore, Robert Boyer *engineering consultant executive*
Sasaki, Y(asunaga) Tito *engineering executive*
Scott, John Walter *chemical engineer, research management executive*

South Pasadena
Glad, Dain Sturgis *aerospace engineer, consultant*
Kopp, Eugene Howard *electrical engineer*

South San Francisco
Lipsky, Ian David *business executive*

Stanford
Aziz, Khalid *petroleum engineering educator*
Boudart, Michel *chemical engineer, chemist, educator, consultant*
Bracewell, Ronald Newbold *engineering educator*
Bryson, Arthur Earl, Jr., *retired aerospace engineering educator*
Cannon, Robert Hamilton, Jr., *aerospace engineering educator*
†Cornell, Carl Allin *civil engineering educator*
Cox, Donald Clyde *electrical engineering educator*
Eshleman, Von Russel *electrical engineering educator*
Eustis, Robert Henry *mechanical engineer*
Goodman, Joseph Wilfred *electrical engineering educator*
Gray, Robert M(olten) *electrical engineering educator*
Harris, Stephen Ernest *electrical engineering and applied physics educator*
Herrmann, George *mechanical engineering educator*
Hesselink, Lambertus *electrical engineering and physics educator*
†Hillier, Frederick Stanton *industrial engineer, educator*
†Iglehart, Donald Lee *engineering educator*
Jin, Xuecheng *engineering researcher*
Kailath, Thomas *electrical engineer, educator*
Kane, Thomas Reif *engineering educator*
Kino, Gordon Stanley *electrical engineering educator*
Kruger, Paul *nuclear civil engineering educator*
†Landau, Ralph *chemical engineer*
Levitt, Raymond Elliot *civil engineering educator*
Linvill, John Grimes *engineering educator*
Macovski, Albert
McCarty, Perry Lee *civil and environmental engineering educator*
Nelson, Drew Vernon *mechanical engineering educator*
Ortolano, Leonard *civil engineering educator, water resources planner*
Ott, Wayne Robert *environmental engineer*
Parkinson, Bradford Wells *astronautical engineer, educator*
Paulson, Boyd Colton, Jr., *civil engineering educator*
Springer, George Stephen *mechanical engineering educator*
Steele, Charles Richard *biomedical and mechanical engineering educator*
Street, Robert Lynnwood *civil, mechanical and environmental engineer*
Van Dyke, Milton Denman *aeronautical engineering educator*
Vincenti, Walter Guido *aeronautical engineer, emeritus educator*
White, Robert Lee *electrical engineer, educator*
†Zahedi, Sina *electrical engineer, researcher*
Zhou, Ping *physical engineer*

Stockton
Cassens, Nicholas, Jr., *ceramics engineer*
Fletcher, David Quentin *civil engineering educator*

Sunnyvale
Blish, Richard Clark, II, *reliability engineering manager*
Mittal, Manmohan *design and technology engineer*
†Petersen, Kurt Edward *electrical engineer, researcher, entrepreneur*
Puckett, W. Greer *engineer*
Robbins, James Edward *electrical engineer*
†Roy, Abhra *process engineer, researcher*
Siddiqee, Muhammad Waheeduddin *electrical engineer*
†Tabatabaei, Ali *analog designing engineer*
†Xu, Songlin *engineering executive*

Sylmar
Bridges, Robert McSteen *mechanical engineer*
Kroll, Mark William *electrical engineer*
Madni, Asad Mohamed *engineering executive*

Tarzana
Hansen, Robert Clinton *electrical engineering consultant*
Larson, Edward William *civil engineering educator, aerospace engineer*
Macmillan, Robert Smith *electronics engineer*
Portney, Joseph Nathaniel *retired aerospace executive, navigation consultant*

Temecula
†Bathaee, Soussan *engineering technician*
Minogue, Robert Brophy *retired nuclear engineer*
Petersen, Vernon Leroy *communications and engineering corporations executive*

Thousand Oaks
Chang, Jie (Jay Chang) *power electronics and control specialist*

Torrance
David, Guy Albert *electrical engineer*
Hicks, Jerry *retired systems engineer*
Kucij, Timothy Michael *engineer, minister, musician*
Lee, Francis Cho-Kuen *aerospace engineering analyst*
Mende, Howard Shigeharu *mechanical engineer*
Sorstokke, Susan Eileen *systems engineer*
Wylie, Richard Thornton *aerospace engineer*

Tustin
Prasad, Birendra (Brian) *mechanical engineer*

Ventura
Gaynor, Joseph *chemical engineer, technical-management consultant*

Victorville
Sedeño, Eugene Raymond *electronics engineer, consultant*
†Szasz, Lorant (ZAS) *industrial engineer, poet*

Walnut Creek
Cassidy, John Joseph *hydraulic and hydrologic engineer*
Hanson, Robert Duane *civil engineering educator*
Van Maerssen, Otto L. *aerospace engineer, consulting firm executive*

Watsonville
Brown, Alan Charlton *retired aeronautical engineer*

Westlake Village
†Baumheinrich, Thorsten Frank *electrical engineer*
Caligiuri, Joseph Frank *retired engineering executive*

Westminster
Armstrong, Gene Lee *systems engineering consultant, retired aerospace company executive*

Whittier
Hartling, Earle Charles *environmental engineer*

Wilmington
Hatch, Ronald Ray *engineer*

Wilton
Felts, Margaret "George" Clemen *environmental engineer, consultant*

Woodland Hills
Hokana, Gregory Howard *engineering executive*
Piersol, Allan Gerald *mechanical engineer*

Wrightwood
Caudron, John Armand *accident reconstructionist, forensic examiner*

Yorba Linda
Lynch, Frank Thomas *aeronautical engineer, consultant*
Porcello, Leonard Joseph *engineering research and development executive*

COLORADO

Arvada
Ferguson, Lloyd Elbert *retired manufacturing engineer*

Aurora
Fisk, Charles Carroll *retired civil engineer, consultant*
Osterberg, Jorj O. *retired civil engineer*
Robertson, James Mueller *civil engineer, educator*
Schwartz, Lawrence *aeronautical engineer*
Vallado, David Anthony *aerospace engineer*

Bayfield
Haug, Edward Joseph, Jr., *retired mechanical engineering educator, simulation research engineer*

Boulder
Barnes, Frank Stephenson *electrical engineer, educator*
Breddan, Joe *systems engineering consultant*
Cathey, Wade Thomas *retired electrical engineering educator*
Corotis, Ross Barry *civil engineering educator, academic administrator*
Hanna, William Johnson *electrical engineering educator*
Hauser, Ray Louis *research engineer, entrepreneur*
Hill, David Allan *electrical engineer*
Joy, Edward Bennett *electrical engineer, educator*
Kompala, Dhinakar Sathyanathan *chemical engineering educator, biochemical engineering researcher*
Lemp, John, Jr., *telecommunications engineer*
Mulhern, Martin Robert *engineer*
Peters, Max Stone *chemical engineer, educator*
Ramirez, W. Fred *chemical engineering educator*
Reitsema, Harold James *aerospace engineer*
Rodriguez, Juan Alfonso *technology corporation executive*
Sani, Robert LeRoy *chemical engineering educator*
Smith, Ernest Ketcham *electrical engineer*
Sodal, Ingvar Edmund *electrical engineer, scientist*
Sture, Stein *civil engineering educator*
Timmerhaus, Klaus Dieter *chemical engineering educator*
Uberoi, Mahinder Singh *aerospace engineer, educator*
†Zable, Jack Louis *mechanical engineer, educator*

Broomfield
Andreiev, Yura (George Andreiev) *electronics engineer*
Arnesen, Tore Olav *structural engineer, inventor*
Crawford, Caren Lee *computer engineer*

Centennial
Ballard, Jack Stokes *engineering educator*
Brown, Steven Harry *engineering executive*
Goughnour, Roy Robert *civil engineer, consultant*

Colorado Springs
Adnet, Jacques Jim Pierre *astronautical and electrical engineer, consultant*
Heilman, John Edward *engineering consultant*
James, Wayne Edward *electronic engineer*
McMillan, Larry Donald *engineering executive*
Morris, Steven Lynn *engineering consultant, retired career officer*
Prochaska, Frank Joseph *industrial engineer, educator*
Sidman, Michael David *control systems engineer, consultant*
Watts, Oliver Edward *engineering consultancy company executive*
White, Gayle Clay *aerospace company executive*
Ziemer, Rodger Edmund *electrical engineering educator, consultant*

Craig
Violette, Glenn Phillip *transportation engineer*

Denver
†Abu-Hejleh, Naser M. *civil engineer, researcher*
Bialasiewicz, Jan Tadeusz *electrical engineering educator*
Chamberlain, Adrian Ramond *transportation engineer*
Chugh, Ashok Kumar *civil engineer*
Colvis, John Paris *aerospace engineer, mathematician, scientist*
Devitt, John Lawrence *consulting engineer*
Emery, Henry Alfred *petroleum engineer*
Fay, Richard James *mechanical engineer, executive, educator*
†Guo, James Chwen-Yuan *civil engineer, educator*
†Haliw, Jerome Michael *civil engineer*
Holmquist, Darrel Vernon *geotechnical engineer*
Kelly, William States *data network engineer*
Long, Francis Mark *retired electrical engineer*
McCandless, Bruce, II, *aerospace engineer, former astronaut*
Poirot, James Wesley *engineering company executive*
Smith, William French, II, *safety engineer, special projects administrator*
Stephens, Larry Dean *engineer, consultant*
Walker, Radford *computer system architect*
Yuan, Shen-Chuan *civil and structural engineer, consultant*

Durango
Langoni, Richard Allen *civil engineer*

Englewood
Barbezat, Eugene LaVar *computer systems engineer, retired air force officer*
Ervin, Patrick Franklin *nuclear engineer*
†Oberhelman, Todd W. *aerospace engineer, consultant*
†Peterson, Ralph Randall *engineering executive*

Estes Park
Ojalvo, Morris *civil engineer, educator*
Webb, Richard C. *engineering company executive*

Evergreen
Frobel, Ronald Kenneth *geosynthetic engineer, consultant*
Rodolff, Dale Ward *engineer, sales executive, consultant*

Fort Collins
Abt, Steven R. *civil engineering educator, dean*
Cermak, Jack Edward *engineer, educator*
Charlie, Wayne Alexander *civil engineering educator*
Emslie, William Arthur *electrical engineer*
Evans, Norman Allen *retired civil engineering educator*
Johnson, Bruce Allan *engineering executive*
Kaufman, Harold Richard *mechanical engineer and physics educator*
Matthies, Frederick John *civil and environmental engineer*
Mesloh, Warren Henry *civil and environmental engineer*
Moore, Charles E. *engineer*
Morgan, David Allen *electronic engineer*
Nassar, Carl Rudolph *engineering executive, psychotherapist*
Richardson, Everett Vern *hydraulic engineer, educator, administrator, consultant*
Roesner, Larry August *civil engineer*
Sandborn, Virgil Alvin *civil engineer, educator*

Golden
Fanchi, John Richard *physicist, educator, industrial technologist*
Illangasekare, Tissa Harischandra *engineering educator, researcher*
Lane, William Lewis *civil engineer*
Loomis, Christopher Knapp *metallurgical engineer*
Myers, Daryl Ronald *engineer*
Sloan, Earle Dendy, Jr., *chemical engineering educator*
Yarar, Baki *mining and metallurgical engineering educator*

Delray Beach
Smith, Charles Oliver *engineer*
Zepnick, Seymour *civil engineer, consultant*

Destin
†Harmuth, Henning F. *electrical engineer, educator*

Dunedin
Goodale, Arthur Worthington *civil engineer, researcher*

Dunnellon
Miller, Kenneth Edward *mechanical engineer, consultant*

Fernandina Beach
Lilly, Wesley Cooper *marine engineer, surveyor*

Fort Lauderdale
Cassidy, Terrence Patrick, Jr., *engineering consultant*
King, Jenn L. *civil engineer*
Schear, Betty Z. *engineering executive, consultant*

Fort Myers
Mergler, Harry Winston *engineering educator*
Moeschl, Stanley Francis *electrical engineer, management consultant*
Scott, Kenneth Elsner *mechanical engineering educator*
Sechrist, Chalmers Franklin, Jr., *electrical engineering educator*

Gainesville
Abbaschian, Reza *materials science and engineering educator*
Anderson, Timothy J. *chemical engineering educator*
Balabanian, Norman *electrical engineering educator*
Bilgili, Ecevit Atalay *chemical engineer, researcher*
Capehart, Barney Lee *industrial and systems engineer*
†Cristescu, Nicolaie Dan *engineering educator*
Delfino, Joseph John *environmental engineering sciences educator*
Fossum, Jerry George *electrical engineering educator*
Isaacs, Gerald William *retired agricultural engineering educator, consultant*
Kurzweg, Ulrich Hermann *engineering science educator*
Law, Mark Edward *electrical engineer, educator*
Lee, Kyu-pil *electrical engineer, researcher*
†Li, Sheng-San *engineering educator*
McDougal, William George *civil engineering educator*
Papila, Melih *aeronautical engineer, researcher, aerospace engineer*
Peebles, Peyton Zimmermann, Jr., *electrical engineer, educator*
Polasek, Edward John *retired electrical engineer, consultant*
Rakov, Vladimir A. *electrical and computer engineering educator*
Ruth, Byron Edward *civil engineering educator*
Schmertmann, John Henry *civil engineer, educator, consultant*
Sheng, Yea-Yi Peter *oceanographic engineer, educator, researcher*
Sherif, S. A. *mechanical engineering educator*
Shyy, Wei *aerospace and mechanical engineering researcher, educator*
Taylor, James Daniel *consulting engineer*
Tia, Mang *civil engineering educator*
Tulenko, James Stanley *nuclear engineer, educator*
Verink, Ellis Daniel, Jr., *metallurgical engineering educator, consultant*
Westphal, Roger Allen *electrical engineer*
Wise, William R. *engineering educator*

Indialantic
MacNeill, John Harmon *mechanical engineer*

Jacksonville
Arbogast, Gordon Wade *systems engineer, educator, consultant , retired military officer*
Costin, Rea-Silvia *civil engineer*
Enns, John Benjamin *polymer scientist*
Joyce, Edward Rowen *retired chemical engineer, educator*
Mueller, Edward Albert *retired transportation engineer executive*
Reagan, James Raymond *safety and ergonomics consultant*
Russell, David Emerson *mechanical engineer, consultant*

Jacksonville Beach
Mahorner, James M. *engineer*

Jensen Beach
Blettner, James Donald *engineering company executive*

Juno Beach
Mathavan, Sudershan Kumar *nuclear power engineer*
McCloud, Paul Duane *chemical engineer*
Migliaro, Marco William *electrical engineer*

Jupiter
Callahan, Edward William *chemical engineer, retired manufacturing executive*
Elwell, Howard Andrew *safety engineer*
Wolff, Edward Alvin *electronics engineer*
Yinh, Victor Marius *electrical engineer*

Keystone Heights
Ohanian, Mihran Jacob *nuclear engineering educator, research dean*

Lady Lake
Dore, Stephen Edward, Jr., *retired civil engineer*
Granger, Robert Alan *mechanical and aerospace engineering educator*

Lake Placid
Rew, William Edmund *civil engineer*

Lake Worth
Cohen, Edward *civil engineer*

Largo
Nixon, Wayne Robert *engineering manager*

Lauderhill
†Swisher, Charles Francis *electrical engineer, consultant*

Lighthouse Point
Farho, James Henry, Jr., *mechanical engineer, consultant*

Longboat Key
Workman, George Henry *structural engineering consultant*

Longwood
McIntosh, John Osborn *engineering consultant*

Margate
†Valdes, Ramon F. *electrical engineer, consultant, math educator*

Melbourne
Baylis, William Thomas *systems engineering specialist, writer*
Ciubotaru, Alexandru Aurelian *electronics engineer*
Cosentino, Paul John *civil engineering educator*
†Maloratsky, Leo G. *electrical engineer*
†Russell, John Masters *aerospace engineer, educator*

Melbourne Beach
Belefant, Arthur *engineer*

Merritt Island
Dean, Dorsey Edward *retired engineer*

Miami
Barthel, William Frederick, Jr., *engineer, electronics company executive*
Chang-Mota, Roberto *electrical engineer*
Daub, S. Spencer
de la Guardia, Mario Francisco *electrical engineer*
Fry, David Donald *civil engineer, consultant*
Gomez, Nancy *engineer, architect*
Jones, William Kinzy *materials engineering educator*
†Linn, Richard John Kuei-hsiung *engineering educator, researcher, engineering educator, consultant*
Sanchez, Javier Alberto *industrial engineer*
Torres, Milton John *industrial engineering educator*
Ural, Oktay *civil engineering educator*
Wolfenson, Azi U. *electrical, mechanical and industrial engineer, consultant*
Worth, James Gallagher *engineer, chemist*

Miami Beach
Milne, Edward Lawrence *biomedical engineer*

Naples
Johnson, James Robert *ceramic engineer, educator*
Leverenz, Humboldt Walter *retired chemical research engineer*
Lynn, Larry (Verne Lauriston Lynn) *engineering executive*
Sowman, Harold Gene *ceramic engineer, researcher*
Suziedelis, Vytautas A. *engineering corporation executive*
Tanner, Robert Hugh *engineer, consultant*
Thampi, Mohan Varghese *environmental health and civil engineer*
Williams, George Earnest *engineer, retired business executive*

New Smyrna Beach
Claridge, Richard *structural engineer*

Nokomis
Beck, George William *retired industrial engineer*
Brisbin, Sterling G. *engineering executive, consultant*
Novak, Robert Louis *civil engineer, pavement management consultant*

North Miami Beach
Roif, Henry Irving *aeronautical engineer, electronic engineer*

North Palm Beach
Sooy, William Ray *electrical engineer, systems analyst*

Orlando
Abdel-Aty, Mohamed A. *engineering educator*
Bauer, Maria Casanova *computer engineer*
Bevc, Frank Peter *electrical engineer*
Dovel-Cash, Michelle *engineer*
†Figner, William James *instructional systems designer, consultant*
Fournier, Donald Joseph, Jr., *mechanical engineer, consultant, educator*
†Ha, Yonggang *optical engineer*
†Landaeta, Rafael Ernesto *industrial engineer, researcher*
Marsh, Malcolm Roy, Jr., *electronics engineer*
†Pet-Armacost, Julia Johanna Agricola *engineering educator, academic administrator*
Rattman, William John *electronics and electro-optic engineer*
Whitehouse, Gary *industrial engineer, educator*

Wu, Thomas Xinzhang *engineering educator, researcher*

Osprey
Boldt, Heinz *aerospace engineer*

Oviedo
Reynolds, Samuel D., Jr., *metallurgical engineer, consultant*

Palm City
Taylor Dye, Judy Angie *engineer, consultant*

Palm Harbor
Warfield, John Nelson *retired engineering educator, consultant*

Panama City
D'Arcy, Gerald Paul *engineering executive, consultant*
Gould, Gerald G. *electrical engineer*
†Priest, Adam Taft *civil engineer*

Patrick AFB
†Beauregard, Adam *aerospace engineer*

Pensacola
Mazzeo, Daniel Patrick *aerospace engineer, aviation consultant*
Olsen, Richard Galen *biomedical engineer, consultant*

Plantation
Chou, Chung-Kwang *bio-engineer*

Port Charlotte
Kok, Hans Gebhard *consulting engineer*

Port Orange
Millar, Gordon Halstead *mechanical engineer, agricultural machinery manufacturing executive*

Riverview
Morshed, Md Moqbul *civil and environmental engineer*

Saint Augustine
Hibbard, Walter Rollo, Jr., *retired engineering educator*
Lund, Frederick Henry *aerospace and electrical engineer*

Saint Cloud
Everett, Woodrow Wilson *electrical engineer, educator*

Saint Petersburg
Collins, Carl Russell, Jr., *industrial engineer*
Gross, Geoffrey Fries *systems engineer*
Huang, Ben (Haibin Huang) *chemical engineer, researcher*
Hussain, Basit *computer engineer, writer*
Styve, Orloff Wendall, Jr., *electrical engineer*
†Tabakovic, Dragan *electrical engineer, researcher*

Sarasota
Deutsch, Sid *bioengineer, educator*
†Jones, George Steven *civil engineer*
Long, Robert Radcliffe *fluid mechanics educator*
Metzger, Sidney *retired communications engineer*
†Michejda, Oskar *civil engineer, structural engineer, consultant*
Mitchell, John Noyes, Jr., *retired electrical engineer*
Pender, Michael Roger *engineering consultant*
Rosenkoetter, Gerald Edwin *engineering and construction company executive*
Ross, Gerald Fred *engineering executive, researcher*
Stumm, Brian J. *mechanical engineer, researcher*

Satellite Beach
Clark, John F. *aerospace research and engineering educator*
Nunnally, Stephens Watson *civil engineer*
Van Arsdall, Robert Armes *engineer, retired air force officer*

Seminole
Wilson, Marc Burt *engineer*

Sun City Center
Edwards, Paul Beverly *retired science and engineering educator*
Jeffries, Robert Joseph *retired engineer, educator, business executive*

Sunny Isles Beach
Brunetto, Frank *electrical engineer*

Tallahassee
†AbdelRazig, Yassir A. *engineering educator*
Anderson, John Roy *grouting engineer*
Coloney, Wayne Herndon *civil engineer*
De Forest, Sherwood Searle *agricultural engineer, agribusiness services executive*
Eggebraaten, Gary Bruce *software engineer, consultant*
Hall, Houghton Alexander *electrical engineer, city official*
Harrison, Thomas James *electrical engineer, educator*
Huang, Dongzhou *civil engineer, researcher, engineering educator*
†Islam, A.K.M. Anwarul *civil engineer, consultant*
Prusty, Rabin *environmental engineer*
Roberts, Rodney Glen *electrical engineering educator*
Wekezer, Jerzy Wladyslaw *civil engineering educator*

Tampa
Aguinaldo, Jorge Tansingco *chemical engineer, water treatment specialist*

†Ayoub, Ashraf S. *engineering educator*
Carnahan, Robert Paul *civil engineer, educator, researcher, consultant*
†Centeno, Grisselle *industrial engineer*
Furland, Loren P. *civil and environmental engineer*
Henning, Rudolf Ernst *electrical engineer, educator, consultant*
Hunter, Larry Lee *retired electrical engineer*
†Jain, Vijay K. *electrical engineer, educator*
Kaw, Autar Krishen *mechanical engineer, educator*
Safavi, Hadi Akbar *tranportation planner*
Sen, Rajan *civil engineer, educator*
Stephens, Robert David *environmental engineering executive*

Tavares
Kaiser, Robert Lee *engineering executive, retired*

Temple Terrace
Schmaltz, Lawrence Gerard *engineer, consultant*

Titusville
Stewart, David Witherington *aerospace engineer*

Venice
Concordia, Charles *consulting engineer*
Miller, Richard Walter *consulting engineer*

Vero Beach
Torres, Terry Terol *mechanical engineer, general contractor*

West Palm Beach
Aaron, M. Robert *electrical engineer*
D'Angelo, Andrew William *retired civil engineer*
Davis, Paul B. *mechanical engineer, civil engineer, retired*
De Mastry, John A. *engineer*

Winter Haven
Johnson, Gordon Selby *consulting electrical engineer*

Winter Park
Granberry, Edwin Phillips, Jr., *safety engineer, consultant*
Kerr, James Wilson *engineer*

GEORGIA

Albany
Marbury, Ritchey McGuire, III, *engineering executive, surveyor*

Alpharetta
Miller, Robert Allen *software engineer, consultant*

Athens
Marlar, John Thomas *environmental engineer*
Nelson, Stuart Owen *agricultural engineer, researcher, educator*
Tollner, Ernest William *agricultural engineering educator, agricultural radiology consultant*

Atlanta
Abdel-Khalik, Said Ibrahim *nuclear and mechanical engineering educator*
Agrawal, Pradeep Kumar *chemical engineer, educator*
Aral, Mustafa Mehmet *civil engineer educator*
Armanios, Erian Abdelmessih *aerospace engineer, educator*
Bacon, Louis Albert *retired consulting civil engineer*
Baldwin, Daniel Flanagan *mechanical engineer, researcher, educator*
Barksdale, Richard Dillon *civil engineer, educator*
Bellanca, Joseph Paul *engineering construction executive*
†Bendelius, Arthur George *engineering firm executive*
Bevins, Karl Alten *retired engineer, musician, educator*
Caseman, Austin Bert *civil engineering educator*
Coble, William Carroll *computer engineer*
Damken, John August *computer systems engineer*
Eckert, Charles Alan *chemical engineering educator*
Ellingwood, Bruce Russell *structural engineering researcher, educator*
Fitzgerald, John Edmund *civil engineering educator*
Gentry, David Raymond *textile engineer*
Giddens, Don Peyton *engineering educator, researcher*
Hess, Dennis William *chemical engineering educator*
Hodges, Dewey Harper *aerospace engineer, educator*
Johnson, Roger Warren *chemical engineer*
Koros, William John *chemical engineering educator*
Lehrer, Robert Nathaniel *retired educator, executive, consultant*
†Loewy, Robert Gustav *aeronautical engineering executive, engineering educator*
Loven, Andrew Witherspoon *environmental engineering company executive*
McDowell, David Lynn *mechanical engineering educator*
Meindl, James Donald *electrical engineering educator, administrator*
Neitzel, George Paul *engineer, educator*
Nemhauser, George L. *industrial, systems engineer, operations research educator*
Nerem, Robert Michael *engineering educator, consultant*
O'Kon, James Alexander *engineering company executive*
Pence, Ira Wilson, Jr., *material handling research executive, engineer*

Piper, Samuel O'Dell *engineer*
Porter, Alan Leslie *industrial and systems engineering educator*
Price, Edward Warren *aerospace engineer, educator*
Rincón-Mora, Gabriel Alfonso *electrical engineer, educator*
Rodenbeck, Sven Erich *environmental engineer*
Rouhani, Shahrokh *civil engineering/environmental consultant, educator*
Rouse, William Bradford *systems engineering executive, researcher, educator*
†Ryan, Charles E., Jr., *electrical engineer, researcher*
Salant, Richard Frank *mechanical engineer, educator*
Schafer, Ronald William *electrical engineering educator*
Scovil, Roger Morris *international business consultant*
Simitses, George John *retired engineering educator, consultant*
Sommerfeld, Jude Thomas *chemical engineer, educator*
Stacey, Weston Monroe, Jr., *nuclear engineer, educator, physicist*
Stancell, Arnold Francis *chemical engineering educator, retired oil executive*
Su, Kendall Ling-Chiao *engineering educator*
Teja, Amyn Sadrudin *chemical engineering educator, consultant*
Tentzeris, Emmanouil Manos *engineering educator, researcher*
Thuesen, Gerald Jorgen *industrial engineer, educator*
Ueng, Charles En-Shiuh *engineering educator, consultant*
Vachon, Reginald Irenee *mechanical engineer*
Winer, Ward Otis *mechanical engineer, educator*
†Yu, Jianjun *electrical engineer, researcher*
Zhang, Zhuomin *mechanical engineering educator*

Buford
†Garwood, Robert Ashley, Jr., *systems engineer*
†Napolitano, Mary Elizabeth *nuclear engineer*

Clayton
Ritter, Guy Franklin *structural engineer*

Columbus
†Cummins, James Donald *retired electrical engineer*
†Gibbons, Dona Alden Coe *electrical engineer*
Sweeney, Robert David *communications engineer*

Decatur
Gueller, Samuel *civil and environmental engineer*
Holtzman, Mary *engineering company executive*
Tan, Li-Zhe *engineering educator, researcher*

Doraville
Wempner, Gerald Arthur *engineering educator*

Duluth
Colwell, Gene Thomas *engineering educator*
Luger, Donald R. *engineering company executive*

Gainesville
Jones, William Benjamin, Jr., *electrical engineering educator*

Jesup
Li, Jian *chemical engineer, educator*

Lawrenceville
Allen, Julian Myrick, Jr., *industrial engineer*

Locust Grove
Smith, Al Jackson, Jr., *environmental engineer, lawyer*

Macon
Aldridge, Melvin Dayne *engineering educator*
Mines, Richard Oliver, Jr., *civil and environmental engineer*

Marietta
Garrett, Joseph Edward *aerospace engineer*
Miles, Thomas Caswell *aerospace engineer*
Ranu, Harcharan Singh *biomedical scientist, administrator, orthopaedic biomechanics educator*
Sanner, George Elwood *electrical engineer*
Tatnall, Peter Coolidge *civil engineer*
Wassel, Thomas Shelly *engineering executive*

Murrayville
Morris, Donald G. *engineering company executive*

Norcross
Feeney, Michael Thomas *civil engineer*
Harrison, Gordon Ray *engineering executive, consultant, research scientist*
Moore, Christopher Barry *industrial engineer*
Storey, Bobby Eugene, Jr., *electrical engineer, engineering consultant*

Peachtree City
Liang, Yue *engineer*
Snyder, Franklin Farison *hydrologic engineering consultant*

Robins AFB
Hedden, Kenneth Forsythe *chemical engineer*
Manley, Nancy Jane *environmental engineer*

Rome
Lewis, Wayne Walton *industrial engineer*

Savannah
Belles, Martin Russel *manufacturing engineer*
Billet, Donald Franklin *civil engineer, consultant*
De Agostino, Sergio *engineering educator*
Hsu, Ming-Yu *engineering educator*
Nawrocki, H(enry) Franz *propulsion technology scientist*
†Salamone, Joseph Anthony *mechanical engineer*

Smyrna
†Michelson, Robert C. *engineering educator, researcher*

Statesboro
†Wu, Yan *engineering educator*

Suwanee
Stevenson, Michael E. *metallurgical engineer*

Thomaston
Beohm, Richard Thomas *safety engineering consultant*

Townsend
Hicks, Harold Eugene *chemical engineer*

Warner Robins
DePriest, C(harles) David *engineering executive, retired military officer*

HAWAII

Honolulu
Chen, Wai-Fah *civil engineering educator*
†Coimbra, Carlos F.M. *mechanical engineering educator, fluid dynamicist*
Cox, Richard Horton *civil engineering executive*
Graf, Edward Dutton *grouting consultant*
Hamada, Harold Seichi *civil engineer, educator*
Kohloss, Frederick Henry *retired consulting engineer*
Koide, Frank Takayuki *electrical engineering educator*
Saxena, Narendra K. *marine research educator*
Wang, Jaw-Kai *bioengineering educator*
White, Gary Richard *electrical engineer, plant operator*

Kahului
Adachi, Athan Ken *civil engineer*

Kaneohe
Hanson, Richard Edwin *civil engineer*

Kapaau
McFee, Richard *electrical engineer, physicist*

Kilauea
McDowell, Edward R. H. *chemical engineer*

Puunene
Tocho, Lee Frank *mechanical engineer*

Wahiawa
Camery, John William *computer engineer*

IDAHO

Boise
Cory, Wallace Newell *retired civil engineer*
True, Leland Beyer *civil engineer, consultant*

Idaho Falls
Epstein, Jonathan Stone *mechanical engineer, lawyer*
Jacobsen, Richard T. *mechanical engineering educator*
Miller, Gregory Kent *structural engineer*
†Pillay, Gautam *chemical engineer, electrochemist*
Riemke, Richard Allan *mechanical engineer*

Inkom
Ambrose, Tommy W. *chemical engineer, executive*

Moscow
DeShazer, James Arthur *biological engineer, educator, administrator*
Jackson, Melbourne Leslie *chemical engineering educator and administrator, consultant*
Johnson, Brian Keith *electrical engineering educator*

Pocatello
Ross, Keith A. *electrical engineer*
Valentine, Ralph Schuyler *chemical engineer, research director*

ILLINOIS

Argonne
†Chang, Yoon Il *nuclear engineer*
Choi, Stephen U.S. *mechanical engineer*
Kumar, Romesh *chemical engineer*
Miller, Shelby Alexander *chemical engineer, educator*
Myles, Kevin Michael *metallurgical engineer*
Yoo, Bong *mechanical engineer, researcher, structural engineer, researcher*

Aurora
Hoefle, Ronald Anthony *civil engineer*
Koopman, Richard Nelson *engineer, consultant*

Belleville
Thien-Stasko, Vicki Lynn *civil engineer technician*

Bolingbrook
Relwani, Nirmal Murlidhar (Nick Relwani) *mechanical engineer*

Carbondale
Mohanty, Manoj K. *mineral engineer, educator*
Nicklow, John William *civil engineer, educator*
†Paul, Souren *engineer, researcher*

Carthage
Erbes, John Robert *engineering executive*

Champaign
Davisson, Melvin Thomas *consulting engineer*
Korst, Helmut Hans *mechanical engineer, educator*
Sohn, Chang Wook *energy systems researcher, educator*

Chicago
Babcock, Lyndon Ross, Jr., *environmental engineer, educator*
Banerjee, Prashant *industrial engineering educator*
†Ben-Arie, Jezekiel *electrical engineer, computer scientist, educator*
Breyer, Norman Nathan *metallurgical engineering educator, consultant*
Brown, Teion O'Dell *engineering executive*
Cheng, Paul Hung-Chiao *civil engineer*
Chung, Paul Myungha *mechanical engineer, educator*
Darvodelsky, Alexander *structural engineer*
Dix, Rollin C(umming) *mechanical engineering educator, consultant*
Epstein, Raymond *engineering and architectural executive*
Fahnestock, Jean Howe *retired civil engineer*
Fortuna, William Frank *architectural engineer, architect*
Garg, Vijay Kumar *telecommunications engineer*
Gerstner, Robert William *structural engineering educator, consultant*
Gupta, Krishna Chandra *mechanical engineering educator*
Guralnick, Sidney Aaron *civil engineering educator*
Hartnett, James Patrick *engineering educator*
He, Bin *biomedical engineer, educator*
Herckis, Charles Y. *civil engineer*
Hoffman, Albert Adam, Jr., *retired structural engineer, educator*
Jaramillo, Carlos Alberto *civil engineer*
Jones, R(oger) Kent *civil engineer, educator*
Kennedy, Lawrence Allan *mechanical engineering educator*
Kiefer, John Harold *chemical engineering educator*
Lin, James Chih-I *biomedical and electrical engineer, educator*
Linden, Henry Robert *chemical engineer, researcher*
†Liu, Derong *engineering educator, electrical/computer engineer*
Miller, Irving Franklin *chemical engineering educator, biomedical engineering educator, academic administrator*
Minkowycz, W. J. *mechanical engineering educator*
Minneste, Viktor, Jr., *retired electrical company executive*
†Mohammadian, Abolfazl *civil engineer, educator*
Munoz, Mario Alejandro *civil engineer, retired consultant*
Murata, Tadao *engineering and computer science educator*
†Nassos, George P. *chemical engineer, educator*
Nehorai, Arye *electrical engineering educator, researcher*
Nickel, Melvin Edwin *metallurgical engineer*
Omosheyin, Rotimi *electronics specialist, real estate company executive*
Oskouie, Ali Kiani *chemical and environmental engineer*
Rikoski, Richard Anthony *engineering executive, electrical engineer*
Russo, Gilberto *engineering educator*
†Schieber, Jay Donald *chemical engineer, educator*
Stoller, Patricia Sypher *structural engineer, engineering executive*
Wang, Yaoyu *electrical engineer*
Wong, Thomas Tang Yum *engineering educator*
†Wyslotsky, Ihor *engineering company executive*
Yeldandi, Veeraînder Antiah *engineer, consultant*

Chicago Heights
†Kavis, George *engineer, photographer*

Clarendon Hills
Moritz, Donald Brooks *mechanical engineer, consultant*

Crete
†Cosme, Luke George *retired structural engineer*

Crystal Lake
Dabkowski, John *electrical engineering executive*

Darien
Hanson, Martin Philip *mechanical engineer, farmer*

Decatur
Graf, Karl Rockwell *nuclear engineer*
Koucky, John Richard *metallurgical engineer, manufacturing executive*

Deerfield
Saida, Toyoyasu *chemical and biochemical engineer*

Dekalb
Azad, Abul Kashem Mohammod *engineer*
Wolfgram, Kenneth Charles *agricultural engineer*

Des Plaines
†Gahan, Brian C *petroleum engineer, researcher*
†Galperin, Leonid Boris *petroleum engineer, chemical engineer, researcher*
Lyu, Seung Won *metallurgical engineer, environmental scientist*

Dunlap
Reinsma, Harold Lawrence *design consultant, engineer*

Edwardsville
†Gu, Keqin *mechanical engineering educator*

Elmhurst
Burton, Darrell Irvin *engineering executive*
Eck, Bernard John *engineer*
Parker, James John *engineering and marketing manager*

Evanston
Achenbach, Jan Drewes *engineering educator, scientist*
Bazant, Zdenek Pavel *structural and materials engineering educator, scientist, consultant*
Belytschko, Ted *civil and mechanical engineering educator*
Bobco, William David, Jr., *consulting engineering company executive*
Brazelton, William Thomas *chemical engineering educator*
Carr, Stephen Howard *materials engineer, educator*
Cheng, Herbert Su-Yuen *mechanical engineering educator*
Daskin, Mark Stephen *civil engineering educator*
Fessler, Raymond R. *metallurgical engineering consultant*
Fine, Morris Eugene *materials engineer, educator*
Fourer, Robert Harold *industrial engineering educator, consultant*
Frey, Donald Nelson *industrial engineer, educator, retired manufacturing executive*
Goldstick, Thomas Karl *biomedical engineering educator*
Haddad, Abraham Herzl *electrical engineering educator, researcher*
Keer, Leon Morris *engineering educator*
Kliphardt, Raymond A. *engineering educator*
Krizek, Raymond John *civil engineering educator, consultant*
†Li, Zhifeng *industrial engineer, researcher*
Liu, Wing Kam *mechanical engineering educator*
Murphy, Gordon John *electrical engineer, educator*
Ottino, Julio Mario *chemical engineering educator, scientist*
Patankar, Neelesh Ashok *mechanical engineer, educator*
Rubenstein, Albert Harold *industrial engineering and management sciences educator*
Sahakian, Alan Varteres *electrical engineer, educator*
Shah, Surendra Poonamchand *engineering educator, researcher*
Smith, Spencer Bailey *engineering and business educator*
Sobel, Alan *electrical engineer, physicist*
Taflove, Allen *electrical engineer, educator, researcher, consultant*
Van Ness, James Edward *electrical engineering educator*
†Wachs, Alan L *quality assurance engineer*

Fairview Heights
Wu, Yunying *engineer, researcher*

Gilman
Ireland, Herbert Orin *retired engineering educator*

Glencoe
Dean, H. Clark *retired civil engineer, professional genealogist*

Glendale Heights
Rawal, Darshan Lal *civil, structural engineer, consultant*

Glenview
Logani, Kulbhushan Lal *civil and structural engineer*
Panarese, William C. *civil engineer*
Sowa, Paul Edward *research engineer*
Van Zelst, Theodore William *civil engineer, natural resource exploration company executive*

Gurnee
Sommerlad, Robert Edward *environmental research engineer*

Highland
Orthwein, William Coe *mechanical engineer*

Hillside
†Hayes Jr., Richard J. *engineering company executive*

Hoffman Estates
Compton, David Bruce *software engineer*

Joliet
Vandevender, Robert Lee, II, *nuclear engineering consultant*

Kankakee
Dodson, Carl Edward *nuclear engineer, real estate agent, executive, minister, assistant superintendent*

La Grange
Mehlenbacher, Dohn Harlow *civil engineer, consultant*

Lake Forest
Lambert, John Boyd *chemical engineer, consultant*

Lemont
†Deen, James Robert *nuclear engineer*

Libertyville
Gallopoulos, Nicholas Efstratios *chemical engineer*

Lincolnwood
Rokach, Abraham Jacob *structural engineering and computer software consultant*

Lisle
†Joung, John J. *chemical engineer, researcher*

Mahomet
Sundy, George Joseph, Jr., *retired engineering executive*

Manhattan
Cramer, Brian Starkweather *electrical engineer*

Moline
Harrington, Roy Edwards *agricultural engineer, author*

Morton Grove
Blanchard, James Arthur *engineer, computer systems specialist, marketing professional*

Mount Prospect
Scott, Norman Laurence *engineering consultant*

Naperville
Chengalvarayan, Rathinavelu *engineering researcher*
†Curry, David Gordon *engineer, consultant*
Koeppe, Eugene Charles, Jr., *electrical engineer*
Kotynek, George Roy *mechanical engineer, educator, marketing executive*
McCaul, Joseph Patrick *chemical engineer*
Vora, Manu Kishandas *chemical engineer, quality consultant*

Normal
†Devinatz, Victor Gary *industrial relations educator*

Northbrook
Adler, Robert *electronics engineer*
Boettcher, Robert Walter *civil engineer*
Ghosh, Satyendra Kumar *structural engineer, educator*

O Fallon
†Gilroy, Joseph M. *civil engineer*

Oak Brook
Degerstrom, James Marvin *retired engineering executive*

Oak Forest
Kogut, Kenneth Joseph *consulting engineer*

Oak Park
Clark, John Peter, III, *engineering consultant*

Oakbrook Terrace
Samet, Dean Henry *safety engineer*

Olympia Fields
Menees, John Robert *mechanical engineer*

Orland Park
Mockus, Joseph Frank *electrical engineer*

Palatine
Kieft, Gerald Nelson *mechanical engineer*

Paris
Anders, Larry Ermel Fagg *mechanical engineer*

Park Forest
Williams, Jack Raymond *civil engineer*

Peoria
Kroll, Dennis Edwards *industrial engineering educator*

Plainfield
Chakrabarti, Subrata Kumar *marine research engineer*

Rock Island
Kowalczyk, Paul Alan *civil engineer*

Rockford
Casagranda, Robert Charles *industrial engineer*
Eliason, Jon Tate *electrical engineer*
Hornby, Robert Ray *mechanical engineer*
Shepler, John Edward *engineering executive*

Rolling Meadows
Eckel, James J. *flight test engineer*

Roscoe
Jacobs, Richard Dearborn *consulting engineering company executive*

Roselle
Marshall, James Andrew *civil engineer, real estate developer*

Sauget
Baltz, Richard Arthur *chemical engineer*

Schaumburg
De Lerno, Manuel Joseph *electrical engineer*
Gyorfi, Julius Steven *electrical engineer, researcher*
Hambley, Douglas Frederick *geological and environmental engineer*

Sherman
Boyd, Marvin G. *electrical engineer*

Skokie
Corley, William Gene *engineering research executive*
Siegal, Rita Goran *engineering company executive*

Springfield
†Chen, Eden Hsien-chang *engineering consultant*
Hahin, Christopher *metallurgical engineer, corrosion engineer*
Porter, William L. *retired electrical engineer*

Sullivan
Holder, Lonnie Edward *engineering administrator, design engineer*

Tinley Park
†West, David Wayne *mechanical engineer*

Urbana
Addy, Alva Leroy *mechanical engineer*
Axford, Roy Arthur *nuclear engineering educator*
Basar, Tamer *electrical engineering educator*
Benekohal, Rahim Farahnak *civil engineering educator, researcher, consultant*
Bergeron, Clifton George *ceramic engineer, educator*
Blahut, Richard Edward *electrical and computer engineering educator*
†Bombardelli, Fabián Alejandro *hydraulic engineer, researcher*
Chao, Bei Tse *mechanical engineering educator*
Chato, John Clark *mechanical and bioengineering educator*
Coleman, James J. *electrical engineer, educator*
Coleman, Paul Dare *electrical engineering educator*
Conry, Thomas Francis *mechanical engineering educator, consultant*
Cusano, Cristino *mechanical engineer, educator*
Daniel, David Edwin *civil engineer, educator*
Dick, William Allen *engineering educator*
Eden, James Gary *electrical engineer, educator, physicist, researcher*
Gaddy, Oscar Lee *electrical engineering educator*
†Georgiadis, John G. *mechanical engineer, educator*
Hall, William Joel *civil engineer, educator*
Hannon, Bruce Michael *engineer, educator*
Hanratty, Thomas Joseph *chemical engineer, educator*
Hess, Karl *electrical and computer engineering educator*
Holonyak, Nick, Jr., *electrical engineering educator*
Huang, Thomas Shi-Tao *electrical engineering educator, researcher*
Jones, Benjamin Angus, Jr., *retired agricultural engineering educator, administrator*
Kumar, Panganamala Ramana *electrical and computer engineering educator*
Larson, Carl Shipley *engineering educator, consultant*
May, Walter Grant *chemical engineer, educator*
Mayes, Paul Eugene *engineering educator, technical consultant*
Miley, George Hunter *nuclear and electrical engineering educator*
Miller, Robert Earl *engineer, educator*
Pearlstein, Arne Jacob *engineer, educator*
Phinney, Leslie Mary *mechanical engineering educator*
Rao, Nannapaneni Narayana *electrical engineer*
Robinson, Arthur Richard *civil engineer, educator*
Sauer, Peter William *electrical engineering educator*
†Snoeyink, Vernon L. *civil engineer, educator*
Stallmeyer, James Edward *engineer, educator*
Swenson, George Warner, Jr., *electronics engineer, radio astronomer, educator*
Walker, William Hamilton *civil engineering educator*
Wert, Charles Allen *metallurgical and mining engineering educator*
Yoerger, Roger Raymond *agricultural engineer, educator*

Washington
Hallinan, John Cornelius *mechanical engineering consultant*

Waukegan
Srinivasa, Venkataramaniah *engineer*

Wheaton
Astrup, Jens Leo *retired civil engineer*

Wheeling
Ebeling, Arthur William *mechanical engineer*

Wilmette
Muhlenbruch, Carl W. *civil engineer*
Wadden, Richard Albert *environmental engineer, educator, science administrator, consultant*

INDIANA

Albany
†White, William Richard *manufacturing engineer, consultant*

Angola
†Meeks, Kenneth W. *civil engineer, educator*

Avon
Shartle, Stanley Musgrave *consulting engineer, land surveyor*

Carmel
Ashcraft, Nancy Olson *mining engineer*
Kalwara, Joseph John *engineer*

Chesterfield
Fry, Meredith Warren *civil engineer, consultant*

Columbus
†Duan, Xin-Ran *mechanical engineer, educator*
Hercamp, Richard Dean *chemical engineer*

Matthews, Drexel Gene *quality control executive*
†Richardson, Dan Earl *power cylinder engineer*

Corydon
Speth, Camille *engineer*

Crane
Waggoner, Susan Marie *electronics engineer*

Crown Point
Ceroke, Clarence John *engineer, consultant*

East Chicago
Bhattacharya, Debanshu *metallurgical engineer*

Evansville
†Heathcotte, Barry W. *mechanical engineer, consultant*
†Stamps, Douglas *mechanical engineer, educator*

Fort Wayne
Hannigan, John Dennis *logistics engineer*
Lyons, Jerry Lee *mechanical engineer*
†Sharp, William Edward *engineering executive, researcher*
Streeter, Robert Davenport *electrical engineer, consultant*
Weatherford, George Edward *civil engineer*

Goshen
Heap, James Clarence *retired mechanical engineer*

Hammond
Neff, Gregory Pall *mechanical engineering educator, consultant*
Pierson, Edward Samuel *engineering educator, consultant*

Indianapolis
Battle, Joe David *engineer*
Collins, James Duffield *marine engineer, editor*
Evans, Richard James *mechanical engineer*
†James, Sunil *aerospace engineer*
†Ramos, Jose A. *engineering educator*
Selby, Ronald Jay *electrical engineer*
Vlach, Jeffrey Allen *environmental specialist*

Kokomo
Bukowski, Eugene Raymond *electrical engineer*
Miller, Robert Frank *retired electronics engineer, educator*
Nierste, Joseph Paul *software engineer*
Ray, Tuhin *computer engineer*

Lafayette
†Caldwell, Barrett Scott *industrial engineering educator*
Carneiro, Mervyn Joseph *mechanical engineer*
Etzel, James Edward *environmental engineering educator*
Fox, Robert William *mechanical engineering educator*
Geddes, Leslie Alexander *bioengineer, physiologist, educator*
Gustafson, Winthrop Adolph *aeronautical and astronautical engineering educator*
Liley, Peter Edward *retired mechanical engineering educator*
Lindenlaub, John Charles *electrical engineer, educator*
Ott, Karl Otto *nuclear engineer, consultant*
Ransom, Victor Harvey *engineering educator*
Revankar, Shripad T. *nuclear engineering educator*

Leavenworth
Kreisle, William Eckman *civil engineer, surveyor, research cartographer, writer*

Mount Vernon
Moll, Joseph Eugene *chemical engineer, chemical company executive*

Muncie
Jarvis, David Alan *engineer*
Seymour, Richard Deming *technology educator*

Noblesville
Monical, Robert Duane *consulting structural engineer*

Notre Dame
Incropera, Frank Paul *mechanical engineering educator*
Jerger, Edward William *mechanical engineer, university dean*
Michel, Anthony Nikolaus *electrical engineering educator, researcher*
Mueller, Thomas James *engineering educator, researcher*
†Renaud, John E. *engineering educator, aerospace engineer, mechanical engineer*
Schmitz, Roger Anthony *chemical engineer, educator, academic administrator*
Varma, Arvind *chemical engineering educator, researcher*

Peru
Einselen, Kenneth Lee *civil engineer*
McMinn, William Lowell, Jr., *engineer*

Syracuse
Blakesley, Wayne Lavere, Jr., *retired production engineer*

Terre Haute
Malooley, David Joseph *electronics and computer technology educator*
Wheelock, Larry Arthur *retired engineer, consultant*

West Lafayette
†Abraham, John *mechanical engineer, engineering educator*
Albright, Lyle Frederick *chemical engineering educator*

Altschaeffl, Adolph George *civil engineering educator, retired*
Andres, Ronald Paul *chemical engineer, educator*
Barany, James Walter *industrial engineering educator*
Cohen, Raymond *mechanical engineer, educator*
Delleur, Jacques William *civil engineering educator*
Drnevich, Vincent Paul *civil engineering educator*
Eckert, Roger E(arl) *chemical engineering educator*
Frankenberger, Jane Rossing *agricultural engineer*
Friedlaender, Fritz Josef *electrical engineering educator*
†Frosch, Robert J. *civil engineer, educator*
Greenkorn, Robert Albert *chemical engineering educator*
Harding, Bruce Alan *engineering technology educator*
Landgrebe, David Allen *electrical engineer*
†Li, Zongzhi *engineer, researcher*
Lin, Pen-Min *electrical engineer, educator*
Marshall, Francis Joseph *aerospace engineer*
Mc Laughlin, John Francis *civil engineer, educator*
Miyamoto, Jun *nuclear engineer*
Ong, Chee-Mun *engineering educator*
Rao, Ramachandra Adiseshappa *civil engineering educator*
Salvendy, Gavriel *industrial engineer, educator*
Schneider, Steven Philip *aerodynamics educator*
Schwartz, Richard John *electrical engineering educator, researcher*
Taber, Margaret Ruth *electrical engineering technology educator, electrical engineer*
†Tawarmalani, Mohit *engineering educator*
†Thomas, Marlin Uluess *industrial engineering educator, academic administrator*
Tomovic, Mileta Milos *mechanical engineer, educator*
Viskanta, Raymond *mechanical engineering educator*
Wankat, Phillip Charles *chemical engineering educator*
Williams, Theodore Joseph *engineering educator*
Yao, Bin *mechanical engineering educator*
Yih, Yuehwern *engineering educator*

IOWA

Ames
Anderson, Robert Morris, Jr., *electrical engineer*
Basart, John Philip *electrical engineering and remote sensing researcher*
Baumann, Edward Robert *environmental engineering educator*
Black, James Robert *industrial engineer*
Brown, Robert Grover *engineering educator*
Buchele, Wesley Fisher *retired agricultural engineering educator*
Bullen, Daniel Bernard *mechanical engineering educator*
Cleasby, John LeRoy *civil engineer, educator*
Colvin, Thomas Stuart *agricultural engineer, farmer*
Johnson, Howard Paul *agricultural engineering educator*
Jones, Edwin Channing, Jr., *electrical and computer engineering educator*
Lane, Orris John, Jr., *retired engineer*
Larsen, William Lawrence *materials science and engineering educator*
Mischke, Charles Russell *mechanical engineering educator*
Okiishi, Theodore Hisao *mechanical engineering educator*
Sanders, Wallace Wolfred, Jr., *civil engineer*
Sheble, Gerald B. *engineering educator, consultant*
Somani, Arun Kumar *electrical engineer, educator*
†Sung, Shihwu *environmental engineer, educator*
Vaughn, Richard Clements *engineering educator*
Venkata, Subrahmanyam Saraswati *electrical engineering educator, electric energy and power researcher*
Wheelock, Thomas David *professor chemical engineering*
Wilder, David Randolph *materials engineer, consultant*

Belmond
Johnson, Roger Christie *environmental engineer*

Bettendorf
Heyderman, Arthur Jerome *engineer, civilian military employee*

Cedar Falls
†Rao, Posinasetti Nageswara *manufacturing engineering educator*

Cherokee
Clark, Larry Dalton *civil engineer*

Davenport
Chowdhury, Ali Asraf *electrical engineer, researcher*
Pedersen, Karen Sue *electrical engineer*
Tsau, William Wen-Shiung *civil engineer, consultant, structural engineer*

Des Moines
Riekenberg, Warren Glenn *civil engineer*

Iowa City
†Andersland, Mark Steven *electrical and computer engineering educator*
Lonngren, Karl Erik *electrical and computer engineering educator*
Marshall, Jeffrey Scott *mechanical engineer, educator*

Odgaard, Anders Jacob civil and environmental engineer, educator
Park, Joon Bu biomedical engineer, researcher, educator
Patel, Virendra Chaturbhai mechanical engineer, educator

Madrid
Handy, Richard Lincoln civil engineer, educator

Monona
Johnson, Milton Lee civil engineer

Muscatine
Stanley, Richard Holt consulting engineer
Thomopulos, Gregs G. consulting engineering company executive

Orange City
Hancock, Albert Sidney, Jr., engineering executive

Storm Lake
Bergendoff, Robert Perry retired civil engineer

KANSAS

Andover
Whiteside, Glenn G. manufacturing engineer

Burlington
Dingler, Maurice Eugene civil engineer

Colby
Lamm, Freddie Ray research agricultural engineer

Fort Leavenworth
Brown, Richard Francis command and control systems engineer, military officer

Independence
Osborn, Ralph J. retired electrical engineer

Lawrence
Benjamin, Bezaleel Solomon architecture and architectural engineering educator
Darwin, David civil engineering educator, researcher, consultant
Green, Don Wesley chemical and petroleum engineering educator
Grzymala-Busse, Jerzy Witold engineering educator
Haugh, Dan Anthony mechanical engineer
†Luchies, Carl W engineering educator, researcher
McCabe, Steven Lee structural engineer
Moore, Richard Kerr electrical engineering educator
Muirhead, Vincent Uriel retired aerospace engineer
Roskam, Jan aerospace engineer
Rowland, James Richard electrical engineering educator
Vossoughi, Shapour chemical and petroleum engineering educator

Leawood
Karmeier, Delbert Fred consulting engineer, realtor

Manhattan
Johnson, William Howard agricultural engineer, educator
Lee, E(ugene) Stanley engineer, mathematician, educator
†Pei, Zj engineer, educator, researcher
Russell, Eugene Robert, Sr., engineering educator, administrator
Simons, Gale Gene nuclear and electrical engineer, educator

Mcpherson
Grauer, Douglas Dale civil engineer

Overland Park
Cassidy, John Lemont retired engineering executive
†Kuppuswamy, Carthy network engineer
Tubbs, David Eugene mechanical engineer, marketing professional
Voeller, John George engineer

Paola
†Norland, Richard Strand mechanical engineer

Salina
†Sigai, A. Gary engineer

Shawnee Mission
Bartlett, Roger Danforth engineering executive

Topeka
Berry, Michael Wayne civil engineer
†Nason, Barry Mark systems engineer, mathematician, educator
Sutherland, John Bennett chemical engineer

Wellington
Montgomery, Robert Louis retired chemical engineer

Wichita
Dietz, David William structural engineer
Kice, John Edward engineer, consultant, engineer, educator
McKee, George Moffitt, Jr., civil engineer, consultant
Shue, Shyh-Pyng Jack aerospace engineer, electrical engineer, researcher, consultant
Siginer, Dennis A. mechanical engineering educator, university dean
Wilhelm, William Jean civil engineering educator

KENTUCKY

Baughman
†Jackson, Donnie Ray electrical engineer, researcher

Bellevue
Lemlich, Robert chemical engineer, educator

Lexington
Baker, Merl engineering educator
Brock, Louis Milton, Jr., engineering educator, researcher
Caroland, William Bourne structural engineer
Chen, Zhi electrical engineering educator
Drake, Vaughn Paris, Jr., electrical engineer, retired telephone company executive
Male, Alan Thomas engineering educator, association executive
McDonough, James Michael engineer, educator
Poh, Churn K. chemical engineer, researcher
Steele, Earl Larsen electrical engineering educator

Louisville
Clark, John Hallett, III, consulting engineering executive
Cornelius, Wayne Anderson electrical and computer engineering consultant
Edward, David Andrew environmental engineer
Garcia, Rafael Jorge retired chemical engineer
Hanley, Thomas Richard engineering educator
Longuet, Gregory Arthur automation engineer, consultant
Siewert, Robin Noelle planning engineer
Smith, Robert F., Jr., civil engineer
Taylor, G. Don industrial engineering educator
Tran, Long Trieu industrial engineer
†Wang, Chung-Hsiao industrial engineer

Murray
Bernard, Tracey Marie ergonomics educator, industrial engineer

Prospect
Donahoo, Leonard E. retired engineer
Kehlbeck, Joseph H. software developer and consultant

Union
Hochstrasser, John Michael environmental engineer, industrial hygienist

West Paducah
†Dowell, Jennifer Ann mechanical engineer

Wickliffe
Gray, Carol Hickson chemical engineer

Winchester
Studebaker, John Milton utilities engineer, consultant, educator

LOUISIANA

Baker
†Cross, James Edward electrical engineering educator

Baton Rouge
Arman, Ara civil engineering educator
Avent, Raymond Richard, Jr., civil engineering educator
Bengtson, Richard Lee agricultural engineer, educator
†Bernhard, James M., Jr., engineering executive
Chen, Peter Pin-Shan electrical engineering, computer science and internet/web educator, data processing executive
Constant, William David chemical engineer, educator
†de Queiroz, Marcio S. engineering educator
Gammon, Malcolm Ernest, Sr., surveying and engineering executive
†Helms, Jack Elwin, Jr., mechanical engineer, educator
Khonsari, Michael M. mechanical engineering educator
Moody, Gene Byron engineering executive, small business owner, minister
Pike, Ralph Webster chemical engineer, educator, university administrator
†Podlaha-Murphy, Elizabeth Josephine chemical engineer, educator
Reible, Danny David environmental chemical engineer, educator
Schroeder, Rolf Robert retired chemical engineer
Scronce, Gary Wayne engineer
Sinclair, Glenn Bruce mechanical engineering educator, researcher
Tipton, Kenneth Warren agricultural administrator, researcher
Tumay, Mehmet Taner geotechnical consultant, educator, research administrator
Valsaraj, Kalliat Thazhathuveetil chemical engineering educator
Voyiadjis, George Zino civil engineer, educator

Destrehan
Bishop, David Nolan electrical engineer

Dubach
Straughan, William Thomas engineering educator

Elm Grove
Livingston, John H. retired engineer, retired military officer

Geismar
†Comeaux, Erick J. chemical engineer

Hammond
Parish, Richard Lee engineer, consultant

Homer
Guenther, Gordon P. mechanical engineer

Kenner
Hallila, Bruce Allan welding engineer
Siebel, Mathias Paul mechanical engineer, consultant

Kinder
Arnold, Rinee' Stephen petroleum engineer

Lacombe
Mangus, Carl William technical safety and standards consultant, engineer

Lafayette
Domingue, Emery consulting engineering company executive, retired
Fang, Cheng-Shen chemical engineering educator
Marshak, Alan Howard electrical engineer, educator
Misra, Devesh K. engineering educator
Rickey, Horace B., Jr., retired engineer
Salters, Richard Stewart engineering company executive
†Sibille, Mark Stephen mechanical design engineer

Lake Charles
Levingston, Ernest Lee engineering company executive

Mandeville
Lanclos, Ritchie Paul petroleum engineer

Metairie
Nicoladis, Michael F. engineering company executive

New Orleans
Boh, Robert Henry civil engineer, construction company executive
Lannes, William Joseph, III, electrical engineer
Li, Xiao-Rong electrical engineer, educator
Lintinger, Gregory John electrical engineer, educator
McCorquodale, J. Alexander civil and environmental engineer, educator
Michaelides, Efstathios Emmanuel mechanical engineer
Nelson, Waldemar Stanley civil engineer, consultant
O'Connor, Kim Claire chemical engineering and biotechnology educator, researcher, inventor
Solomonow, Moshe biomedical engineer, scientist, educator

Pearl River
Gernon, Clarke Joseph, Sr., mechanical and forensic engineering consultant

Ruston
Sterling, Raymond Leslie civil engineering educator, researcher, consultant
†Thompson, Ronald H. chemical engineer, educator

Slidell
Tewell, Joseph Robert, Jr., electrical engineer

Vivian
Collier, Samuel Melvin aerospace engineer

MAINE

Auburn
Bastow, Richard Frederick civil engineer, educator, surveyor

Bangor
Hsu, Yu Kao aerospace scientist, mathematician, educator

Eastport
Kennedy, Robert Spayde electrical engineering educator

Falmouth
Rohsenow, Warren Max retired mechanical engineer, educator

Greenville
Pepin, John Nelson materials research and design engineer

Portland
Watts, Helen Caswell civil engineer

Scarborough
Raisbeck, Gordon systems engineer, consultant

Waterville
Laurence, Robert Lionel chemical engineering educator

Westbrook
†Hammond, Jeremy Marshall engineer, educator

Wiscasset
Plante, Paul Joseph metallurgical engineer

MARYLAND

Aberdeen Proving Ground
†Berry, Patrick Lowell chemical engineer
Cozby, Richard Scott electronics engineer, military officer
Gupta, Aaron Das mechanical engineer
†Howard, Stephen L. chemical engineer

Adelphi
†Mait, Joseph N. electrical engineer, educator
Torrieri, Don Joseph electronics engineer, mathematician, researcher

Annapolis
DiAiso, Robert Joseph civil engineer
Johnson, Bruce engineering educator
Mumford, Willard Royal engineering educator, educational consultant
Rogers, David Freeman aerospace engineering educator
Trescott, Sara Lou water resources engineer
Tuttle, Kenneth Lewis engineering educator, consultant
Zhu, Jian Zhong computational engineer

Ashton
Lundsager, Christian Bent retired mechanical engineer, consultant

Baltimore
Bero, Joseph Martin manufacturing engineer
Braddy, Vanessa F. civil engineer
Busch-Vishniac, Ilene Joy mechanical engineering educator, researcher
Emerick, Norman Cooper consulting engineer
Grayson, Richard Andrew aerospace engineer
Haynes, Gregory Kent engineer
Heselton, Kenneth Emery energy engineer
Hirsch, Richard Arthur retired mechanical engineer
Jelinek, Frederick electrical engineer, educator
Katz, Joseph Louis chemical engineer, educator
†Kavdia, Mahendra chemical engineer, researcher
Kelman, Gary F. environmental engineer
Knoedler, Elmer L. retired chemical engineer
Lemer, Andrew Charles engineer, economist
Nathanson, Harvey Charles electrical engineer
†O'Melia, Charles Richard
Thakor, Nitish Vyomesh biomedical engineering educator
†Tsoukias, Nikolaos chemical engineer, biomedical engineer, researcher
Wang, Hong engineer, researcher
†Washington, Strother Lee, Jr., mechanical engineer, design engineer

Bel Air
Powers, Doris Hurt retired engineering company executive

Bethesda
Burdeshaw, William Brooksbank engineering executive
Di Marzo, Marino engineering researcher, educator
Freedman, Joseph sanitary and public health engineering consultant
Fuller, Joseph, Jr., aeronautical engineer
Koltnow, Peter Gregory engineering consultant
Kutemeyer, Peter Martin industrial engineering executive
Meyerson, Martin aerospace engineer
Saville, Thorndike, Jr., coastal engineer

Burtonsville
Mitchell, Keith Christopher software engineer

California
Jessup, Edwin Harley, III, aerospace engineering executive

Chevy Chase
Cheng, David Keun engineering educator
Cooley, William Crockett mechanical engineer, retired educator
Hirschhorn, Joel Stephen engineer
Lebow, Irwin Leon communications engineering consultant
Rockwell, Theodore nuclear engineer
Short, Steve Eugene engineer

Claiborne
Guinness, Kenelm L. civil engineer

Cockeysville Hunt Valley
Barr, Irwin Robert retired aeronautical engineer

College Park
Aggour, Mohamed Sherif civil engineer, educator
Anderson, John David, Jr., aerospace engineer
Ayyub, Bilal M. civil engineering educator, researcher, executive
Barbe, David Franklin electrical engineer, educator
Granatstein, Victor Lawrence electrical engineer, educator
Gupta, Ashwani Kumar mechanical engineering educator
Levine, William Silver electrical engineering educator
†Lin, Hung C. electrical engineer educator
Marcus, Steven Irl electrical engineering educator
Newcomb, Robert Wayne electrical engineer educator
Qi, Jianwei mechanical engineer, researcher
Raghavan, Srinivasa Ramamurthy chemical engineer, educator
Rao, Jaganmohan Boppana Lakshimi electrical engineer
Taylor, Leonard Stuart engineering educator, consultant
Tseng, Chung-Li engineering educator

Columbia
Doi, Yutaka electrical engineer
Du Toit, Cornelis Frederik electronic engineer
Moulton, Paul Douglas (Pete Moulton) information technology consultant
Straja, Sorin Radu chemical engineer, mathematician, computer programmer
†Van Buiten, Robert D. aerospace engineer

Crofton
Laurenson, Robert Mark mechanical engineer
†Tyler, Craig Alan weather satellites engineer

Cumberland
Bernstein, Louis *civil engineer*

Easton
Brodt, Burton Pardee *retired chemical engineer, writer, researcher*

Elkton
Chen, Oliver Tsung-Yu *chemical engineer, researcher*

Ellicott City
Bers, Eric Lawrence *civil engineer*

Finksburg
Konigsberg, Robert Lee *electrical engineer*

Fort Washington
Caveny, Leonard Hugh *mechanical engineer, aerospace scientist, consultant*

Frederick
Bryan, John Leland *retired engineering educator*
Narula, Ram Gopal *engineer*
Nayyar, Mohinder Lal *mechanical engineer*
Vincoli, Jeffrey Wayne *safety and environmental engineering executive*

Gaithersburg
Bement, Arden Lee, Jr., *engineering educator*
Cookson, Alan Howard *electrical engineer, researcher*
Ferrell, Charles Madison *retired nuclear engineer, health physicist*
Gorin, Barney Franklin *spacecraft systems, propulsion and robotics engineer*
†Grotenhuis, Marshall *retired nuclear engineer*
†Hesterberg, Larry Allen *aerospace engineer*
Jahanmir, Said *materials scientist, mechanical engineer*
Levine, Robert Sidney *chemical engineer, consultant*
Marin, Cynthia Myers (Cheryl Marin) *systems engineer*
Presser, Cary *research engineer*
Shyam-Sunder, Sivaraj *structural engineer, researcher*
Stever, Horton Guyford *aerospace scientist and engineer, educator, consultant*
Ulbrecht, Jaromir Josef *chemical engineer*
Wang, Francis Wei-Yu *biomedical materials scientist, researcher*
Wiederhorn, Sheldon Martin *materials scientist engineer*
Wright, Richard Newport, III, *retired civil engineer*

Glen Arm
Harris, Benjamin Louis *chemical engineer, consultant*

Greenbelt
Bryant, Paul T. *electronics engineering manager*
Cooper, Robert Shanklin *engineering executive, former government official*
Ferrara, Jeffrey Francis *electronics engineer*
†Healey, John Joseph *engineering executive, civil engineer*
Kolasinski, John Richard *electrical engineer*
Ku, Jentung *mechanical and aerospace engineer*
Levitt, Gerald Steven *engineering services executive*
Steiner, Mark David *systems engineer*
Tilton, James Charles *computer engineer*
Vranish, John Michael *electrical engineer, researcher*

Havre De Grace
Huang, Yung-Hui *chemical engineer*

Hunt Valley
Kinstlinger, Jack *engineering executive, consultant*
Plaks, Albert I. *electrical engineer, educator*

Hyattsville
Kirk, James Allen *mechanical engineering educator*
Pierce, Melvin Andrew *engineer*

Indian Head
Latimer, Paul Jerry *non-destructive testing engineer*

Joppa
Morgenstern, Hans George *consulting engineer*

Lanham
Criscimagna, Ned Henry *reliability engineer*
Pendley, Rex Dale *systems engineer*

Lanham Seabrook
Reupke, William Albert *engineer*

Laurel
Bowman, Bruce Alan *civil engineer*
Dallman, Paul Jerald *engineer, writer*
†Darrell, Charles G. *engineer*
Eaton, Alvin Ralph *aeronautical and systems engineer, research and development administrator*
Lombardo, Joseph Samuel *acoustical engineer*
†Mulich, Terrence Joseph, Jr., *aerospace engineer*
Westhaver, Lawrence Albert *electronics engineer, consultant*

Linthicum
Banuk, Ron Edward (Ron Banuk) *mechanical engineer*

Linthicum Heights
Skillman, William Alfred *consulting engineering executive*

Owings Mills
Whittle, Joseph F., Jr., *engineering executive, consultant*

Patuxent River
Adams, Richard Eugene *aerospace engineer, project manager*
Frazier, William Edward *materials engineer*
Tipton, Thomas Wesley *retired aerospace engineer*

Phoenix
Harclerode, Howard Charles, II, (Skip Harclerode) *chemical engineer*

Potomac
Cutler, Robert Sumner *engineering educator*
Kirkendall, Thomas D. *aerospace engineer, materials scientist*
Lawrence, Robert Edward *electrical engineer*
Peters, Frank Albert *retired chemical engineer*
Schleckser, James Henry *engineering executive, sales executive*
Williams, Peter MacLellan *nuclear engineer*

Queenstown
Corn, Morton *environmental engineer, educator*

Rockville
Burdick, William MacDonald *biomedical engineer*
Davies-Venn, Christian *environmental engineer*
McDonald, Capers Walter *biomedical engineer, corporate executive*
Menendez, Adolfo *engineering company executive*
Reddy, Thikkavarapu Ramachandra *electrical engineer*
Seagle, Edgar Franklin *environmental engineer, consultant*
Sorensen, John Noble *mechanical and nuclear engineer*
Souto, Carlos Dias *engineer*

Saint Inigoes
Dorsey, William Walter *aerospace engineer, engineering executive*
Masters, George Windsor, Jr., *electrical engineer, educator*

Severna Park
Davis, John Adams, Jr., *electrical engineer, roboticist, corporate research executive*

Silver Spring
Gabi, Mark *engineering and management educator, consultant, researcher*
†Halvorsen, Harald Wayne *electronics engineer*
Hermach, Francis Lewis *consulting engineer*
Mok, Carson Kwok-Chi *structural engineer*
†Okigbo, Franklin C. *engineering company executive*
Scipio, L(ouis) Albert, II, *former aerospace science engineering educator, architect, military historian*
Shalowitz, Erwin Emmanuel *civil engineer*
White, Edmund William *chemical engineer*
†Yang, Jing-Shyang *structural engineer*
†Yanushevsky, Rafael Tovie *electromechanical engineer, scientist, consultant, educator*

Suitland
†Brooks, Richard C. *electrical engineer, federal government executive*
Cheng, Jian-Yu *mechanical engineer, researcher, application developer*

Towson
Huang, Joseph Chen-Huan *civil engineer*

Upper Marlboro
Freeman, Ernest Robert *engineering executive*

West Bethesda
Sevik, Maurice *acoustical engineer, researcher*
Su, Jen-Houne Hannsen *mechanical engineer*

MASSACHUSETTS

Acton
Hicks, Walter Joseph *electrical engineer*
Tuttle, David Bauman *electrical engineer*

Amherst
Abbott, Douglas Eugene *engineering educator*
Franks, Lewis E. *electrical and computer engineering educator, researcher*
Koren, Israel *electrical and computer engineering educator*
Krishnamurty, Sundar *mechanical engineer*
Nash, William Arthur *civil engineer, educator*
Schaubert, Daniel Harold *electrical engineering educator*
Swift, Calvin Thomas *electrical and computer engineering educator*
†Terpenny, Janis P. *engineering educator, researcher*
Vogl, Otto *polymer science and engineering educator*

Andover
Jakes, William Chester *electrical engineer*

Arlington
†Lala, Jaynarayan Hotchand *computer engineer*

Attleboro
†Sogge, Dale R. *automotive sensor engineer*

Attleboro Falls
†Kulwicki, Bernard Michael *ceramics engineer, researcher*

Ayer
†Palis, Michael Richard *mechanical engineer, systems engineer*

Bedford
†An, Hong *engineer*
Fante, Ronald Louis *engineering scientist*
Jelalian, Albert V. *electrical engineer*
Labudovic, Marko *research scientist, consultant*
Lackoff, Martin Robert *engineer, physical scientist, researcher*
Winter, David Louis *systems engineer, human factors scientist, retired*
Zhang, Yanwu *electrical engineer*

Belmont
Durgin, Frank Herman, II, *aeronautical engineer*
Haralampu, George Stelios *electric power engineer, former engineering executive electric utility company*
Merrill, Edward Wilson *chemical engineering educator*

Billerica
Kinsman, Robert Preston *biomedical plastics engineer*

Boston
Agnello, David John *civil engineer*
Baillieul, John Brouard *aerospace engineering and applied mathematics educator*
Buchanan, Walter Woolwine *electrical engineer, educator, academic administrator*
Chen, Chih-Fan *electrical engineer*
De Luca, Carlo John *biomedical engineer, educator*
Frank-Kamenetskii, Maxim D. *biomedical engineer*
Gilbert, Arthur Charles *aerospace engineer, consulting engineer*
Hoffman, Andrew John *environmental management educator*
Langer, Robert Martin *retired chemical engineering company executive, consultant*
Miaoulis, Ioannis Nikolaos *mechanical engineer, educator*
Moore, Richard Lawrence *structural engineer, consultant*
Mulukutla, Sarma S. *engineering educator, consultant*
Paschalidis, Ioannis *engineering educator*
Pierce, Allan Dale *engineering educator, researcher, editor*
Rappaport, Carey Milford *electrical engineering educator*
Teich, Malvin Carl *electrical engineering educator*
Wiegner, Allen Walter *biomedical engineering educator, researcher*
†Willey, Ronald J. *chemical engineer, educator*

Boxford
Yates, John Robert, Jr., *engineer, educator*

Boylston
Healy, Patrick James *civil engineer*

Brockton
Park, Byiung Jun *textile engineer*

Brookline
Eden, Murray *electrical engineer, emeritus educator*
Jacobson, Murray M. *chemical engineer*
Perkins, James R. *manufacturing engineering educator, researcher*

Burlington
Kim, Nam-Deuk *electrical engineer, researcher*
Wilson, Daniel Donald *engineering executive*

Cambridge
Abernathy, Frederick Henry *mechanical engineering educator*
Baron, Judson Richard *aerospace educator*
Battin, Richard Horace *astronautical engineer*
Beér, János Miklós *engineering educator*
Ben-Akiva, Moshe Emanuel *civil engineering educator*
†Benedict, Manson *chemical engineer, educator*
Beranek, Leo Leroy *acoustical consultant*
Bras, Rafael Luis *engineering educator*
Brenner, Howard *chemical engineering educator*
Brown, Robert Arthur *chemical engineering educator*
Carmichael, Alexander Douglas *engineering educator*
Chen, Sow-Hsin *nuclear engineering educator, researcher*
Cohen, Morris *engineering educator*
Cohen, Robert Edward *chemical engineering educator, consultant*
Colton, Clark Kenneth *chemical engineering educator*
†Costantino, Henry Raymond *chemical engineer, researcher*
Covert, Eugene Edzards *aerospace engineer, physics educator*
Crandall, Stephen Harry *engineering educator*
de Neufville, Richard Lawrence *engineering educator*
Dewey, Clarence Forbes, Jr., *engineering educator*
DiBerardinis, Louis Joseph *health and safety professional, industrial hygiene engineer, consultant, educator*
Drake, Elisabeth Mertz *chemical engineer, consultant*
Duffy, Robert Aloysius *aeronautical engineer*
Dugundji, John *aeronautical engineer*
Eagleson, Peter Sturges *civil engineer, environmental engineer, educator*
Fay, James Alan *mechanical engineering educator*
Flemings, Merton Corson *engineering educator, materials scientist*
Gallager, Robert Gray *electrical engineering educator*
Gatos, Harry Constantine *engineering educator*
†Green, William H., Jr., *chemical engineer, educator*
Greitzer, Edward Marc *aeronautical engineering educator, consultant*
†Griffith, Peter *mechanical engineering educator, researcher*
Hansen, Kent Forrest *nuclear engineering educator*
†Hansman, Robert John, Jr., *aeronautics and astronautics educator*
Harleman, Donald Robert Fergusson *environmental engineering educator*
Harris, Wesley L. *aeronautical engineer, educator*
Heywood, John Benjamin *mechanical engineering educator*
†How, Hoton *electrical engineer*
Ippen, Erich Peter *electrical engineer, educator, physicist*
Kamm, Roger Dale *biomedical engineer, educator*
Kazimi, Mujid Suliman *nuclear engineer, educator*
Ladd, Charles Cushing, III, *civil engineer, educator*
Latanision, Ronald Michael *materials science and engineering educator, consultant*
†Magee, Christopher L. *systems engineer*
Mann, Robert Wellesley *biomedical engineer, educator*
Marini, Robert Charles *environmental engineering executive*
Markey, Winston Roscoe *aeronautical engineering educator*
Marks, David Hunter *civil engineering educator*
McGarry, Frederick Jerome *civil engineering educator*
Mei, Chiang Chung *civil engineer, educator*
Milgram, Jerome H. *marine and ocean engineer, educator*
Mitter, Sanjoy K. *electrical engineering educator*
Nightingale, Deborah Seifert *systems engineer, consultant*
Penfield, Paul Livingstone, Jr., *electrical engineering educator*
Peraire, Jaume *aeronautical engineering educator*
Pian, Theodore Hsueh-Huang *engineering educator, consultant*
Powers, Michael Kevin *architectural and engineering executive*
Probstein, Ronald Filmore *mechanical engineering educator*
Reid, Robert Clark *chemical engineering educator*
Remington, Paul James *mechanical engineer, educator*
Rogers, Peter Phillips *environmental engineering educator, city planner*
Roos, Daniel *engineering educator*
Ruina, Jack Philip *electrical engineer, educator*
Russell, Kenneth Calvin *metallurgical engineer, educator*
Satterfield, Charles Nelson *chemical engineer, educator*
Smith, Henry Ignatius *engineering educator*
Smith, Kenneth Alan *chemical engineer, educator*
Staelin, David Hudson *electrical engineering educator, consultant*
Stevens, Kenneth Noble *electrical engineer, educator*
Suh, Nam Pyo *mechanical engineering educator*
Todreas, Neil Emmanuel *nuclear engineering educator*
Triantafyllou, Michael Stefanos *ocean engineering educator*
Trilling, Leon *aeronautical engineering educator*
Troxel, Donald Eugene *electrical engineering educator*
Ungar, Eric Edward *mechanical engineer*
Vander Velde, Wallace Earl *aeronautical and astronautical educator*
Vicens, Guillermo Juan *engineering executive*
White, David Calvin *electrical engineer, energy educator, consultant*
Whitman, Robert Van Duyne *civil engineer, educator*
Williams, James Henry, Jr., *mechanical engineer, educator, consultant*
Wuensch, Bernhardt John *ceramic engineering educator*
Yannas, Ioannis Vassilios *polymer scientist, educator*

Carlisle
Drew, Philip Garfield *consultant engineering company executive*

Centerville
Boulay, Marc Norman *civil engineer, engineering executive*

Concord
Davidson, Frank Paul *macroengineer, lawyer*
Villers, Philippe *mechanical engineer*
Woll, Harry J. *electrical engineer*

Danvers
†Shenai, Deodatta Vinayak *chemical engineer*

Dartmouth
†Notaros, Branislav M *electrical engineer, educator*

Dedham
Ghosh, Asish *control engineer*

Dover
Kovaly, John Joseph *consulting engineering executive, educator*

Foxboro
Devenis, Keistutis Peter *civil engineer, consultant*
Ryskamp, Carroll Joseph *retired chemical engineer*

Framingham
Crossley, Frank Alphonso *former metallurgical engineer*

PROFESSIONAL INDEX 6303 ENGINEERING

Lindsay, Leslie *packaging engineer*
Wulf, Stanley Arthur *engineering executive*

Franklin
Tsivinsky, Vladimir George *systems engineer*

Gloucester
†Baxter, Larry K. *electrical engineer, consultant*

Groveland
Sims, Andrew Harley, Jr., *engineering executive, public administrator*

Hanscom AFB
Lemieux, Jerome Anthony, Jr., *electrical engineer, computer engineer*
Schmitt, Stephen Richard *electronics engineer*

Holbrook
Crandlemere, Robert Wayne *engineering executive*

Holyoke
Gan, Deqiang *engineer*

Hopkinton
Berthiaume, Wayne Henry *electrical engineer*

Jamaica Plain
Shapiro, Ascher Herman *mechanical engineer, educator, consultant*

Lancaster
Richter, Henry Andrew *electrical engineer*

Leicester
Rogers, Randall Lloyd *mechanical engineer*

Lenox
Coffin, Louis Fussell, Jr., *mechanical engineer*
Gela, George *electrical engineering researcher*

Lexington
Aldrich, Nancy Cook *engineer, administrator*
Aronin, Lewis Richard *metallurgical engineer*
Bailey, Fred Coolidge *retired engineering consulting company executive*
†Beusch, John Ulrich *engineer, researcher*
Brookner, Eli *electrical engineer*
Bussgang, Julian Jakub *electronics engineer*
Colby, George Vincent, Jr., *electrical engineer, consultant*
†Elanayar, Sunil K. *research and development engineer*
Freed, Charles *engineering consultant, researcher*
Glaser, Peter Edward *mechanical engineer, consultant*
Haldeman, Charles Waldo, III, *aeronautical engineer*
Keicher, William Eugene *electrical engineer*
Kerr, Thomas Henderson, III, *electrical engineer, researcher*
†Lafrey, Raymond Richard *electrical engineer*
†Lyons, W. Gregory *electrical engineer, researcher*
Martinez, David R. *electrical engineer, science educator*
Morrow, Walter Edwin, Jr., *electrical engineer, university laboratory administrator*
Smith, Steven Thomas *signal processing engineer*
Sussman, Martin Victor *chemical engineering educator, inventor, consultant*
von Braun, Curt *aerospace engineer*

Lincoln
†Kerrebrock, Jack Leo *aeronautics and astronautics engineering educator*
Kusik, Charles Lembit *chemical engineer*

Longmeadow
Lemnios, Andrew Zachery *aerospace engineer, educator, researcher*

Lowell
†Kazmer, David Owen *engineering educator*
Liu, Fenghai *engineer*

Lynn
Chow, Humphrey Wai *mechanical engineer*
D'Entremont, Edward Joseph *infosystems engineer, educator*
Kiley, Thomas Francis *civil engineer, lawyer*

Manchester
Arntsen, Arnt Peter *engineer, consultant*

Mansfield
Jellows, Tracy Patrick *software engineer*

Marlborough
Bennett, C. Leonard *consulting engineer*
Hunt, Philip Charles *engineer, consultant*

Medford
Astill, Kenneth Norman *mechanical engineering educator*
Greif, Robert *mechanical engineering educator*
Howell, Alvin Harold *engineer, company executive, educator*
Kreifeldt, John Gene *mechanical engineering educator*
Nelson, Frederick Carl *mechanical engineering educator*
Uhlir, Arthur, Jr., *electrical engineer, university administrator*

Medway
Hoag, David Garratt *aerospace engineer*

Milford
Carson, Charles Henry *microwave engineer*

Nantucket
Kales, Paul Albert *engineering educator, cartoonist*

New Bedford
Soares, Carl Lionel *quality control engineer, metrologist*

Newton
Waggener, Thomas Barrow *research bioengineer*
Ward, William Weaver *retired electrical engineer*

Newton Center
Mark, Melvin *consulting mechanical engineer, educator*

North Andover
Spring, Gary Stephen *civil engineer, educator, consultant*
Walters, Donald Benjamin, Jr., *civil engineer*

North Attleboro
†Shareef, Nazeer Hussain *mechanical engineer*

North Dartmouth
Law, Frederick Masom *engineering educator, structural engineering firm executive*

Northborough
Jeas, William C. *aerospace engineering executive, consultant*

Norwood
De Noto, Thomas J. *chemical engineer*
Sheingold, Daniel H. *electrical engineer*

Oxford
Moshegov, Nikolay *engineer*

Peabody
Goldberg, Harold Seymour *electrical engineer, educator*
Peters, Leo Francis *environmental engineer*

Pittsfield
Feigenbaum, Armand Vallin *systems engineer, systems equipment executive*
Shammas, Nazih Kheirallah *environmental engineering educator, consultant*

Plymouth
Wiederhold, Pieter Rijk *instrument company executive*

Quincy
Colgan, Sumner *manufacturing engineer, chemical engineer*
Kelley, James Francis *civil engineer*
Roma, John Richard *civil engineer, executive*

Reading
Melconian, Jerry Ohanes *engineering executive*

Silver Spring
†Kaplan, Arkady *optical engineer, researcher*

Somerset
†Bower, John *retired fluid mechanics engineer, commissioner*

South Deerfield
Waluk, Stanley Peter *corporate engineering official*

South Wellfleet
Bargellini, Pier Luigi *electrical engineer*

South Yarmouth
Towns, Donald Lionel *engineering executive*

Springfield
Parthasarathy, Gautham *chemical engineer, researcher*

Stow
Clayton, John *retired engineering executive and consultant*

Sudbury
Fowler, Charles Albert *electronics engineer*

Swampscott
Kaufman, William Morris *engineer consultant*

Waban
Christian, John Thomas *civil engineer*

Walpole
Allman, Mark C. *engineer, physicist*

Waltham
Gumpertz, Werner Herbert *structural engineering company executive*
†Liu, Huamin Patrick *communications engineer, researcher*

Watertown
Linden, Lynette Lois *bioelectrical engineer*
True, Edward Keene *architectural engineer*

Wellesley
Weil, Thomas Alexander *electronics engineer, retired*

Westborough
Gionfriddo, Maurice Paul *aeronautical engineer, research and development manager*
Mehta, Jatin Vinodrai *biomedical engineer*

Weston
Katz, William Emanuel *chemical engineer*
Kendall, Julius *consulting engineer*

Westport Point
Bennett, Bruce Anthony *civil engineer*

Westwood
Foster, Arthur Rowe *mechanical engineering educator*
Old, Bruce Scott *chemical and metallurgical engineer*

Wilmington
Akhavan, Farhad *electrical engineer*
Eldada, Louay A. *fiber optic engineer*

Winchester
Hansen, Robert Joseph *civil engineer*
Koppel, Lowell B. *chemical engineer*

Woburn
Gelb, Arthur *electrical and systems engineering executive*
Tijmann, Willem Bert *civil engineer, consultant*

Worcester
Clarke, Edward Nielsen *engineering science educator*
Fragala, Guy Andrew *safety engineer, educator*
Katz, Robert Nathan *ceramic engineer, educator*
Parrish, Edward Alton, Jr., *electrical and computer engineering educator, academic administrator*
Rencis, Joseph John *engineering educator, mechanical and civil engineer*
Rong, Yiming *manufacturing engineering educator*
Wilbur, Leslie Clifford *mechanical engineering educator*
Zwiep, Donald Nelson *mechanical engineering educator, administrator*

Wrentham
Bittenbender, Brad James *safety and health engineer*

Yarmouth Port
Stott, Thomas Edward, Jr., *retired engineering executive*

MICHIGAN

Adrian
Coleman, John Wesley *fluid mechanics engineer, heat transfer engineer*

Ann Arbor
Adamson, Thomas Charles, Jr., *aerospace engineering educator, consultant*
Becher, William Don *electrical engineer, engineering educator, writer*
Bej, Shyamal K *chemical engineer, researcher*
Bilello, John Charles *materials science and engineering educator*
Bitondo, Domenic *engineering executive*
Director, Stephen William *electrical and computer engineering educator, academic administrator*
England, Anthony Wayne *electrical engineering and computer science educator, astronaut, geophysicist*
Faeth, Gerard Michael *aerospace and mechanical engineering educator, researcher*
Friedmann, Peretz Peter *aerospace engineer, educator*
Gerlitz, Frank Edward *engineer*
Gibala, Ronald *metallurgical engineering educator*
Gilbert, Elmer Grant *aerospace engineering educator, control theorist*
Goovaerts, Pierre Etienne *agriculture engineering educator*
Green, Paul Allan *scientist, engineer, educator*
†Harris, Robert Blynn *civil engineer, educator*
Hayes, John Patrick *electrical engineering and computer science educator, consultant*
Johnson, Neil Monroe *test engineer*
Kauffman, Charles William *aerospace engineer*
Kozma, Adam *electrical engineer*
Leith, Emmett Norman
Lyons, Harvey Isaac *mechanical engineering educator*
Martin, William Russell *nuclear engineering educator*
Mazumder, Jyotirmoy *mechanical and materials engineering educator*
†McClamroch, N. Harris *aerospace engineering educator, consultant, researcher*
Meitzler, Allen Henry *electrical engineering educator, automotive scientist*
Meyer, John Frederick *engineering and computer science educator, researcher, consultant*
Michalowski, Radoslaw Lucas *civil engineer, educator*
Pan, Jwo *engineering educator*
Pehlke, Robert Donald *materials and metallurgical engineering educator*
†Perlin, Marc *engineering educator*
Petrick, Ernest Nicholas *mechanical engineer, researcher*
Pollock, Stephen Michael *operations research engineer, educator, consultant*
Root, William Lucas *electrical engineering educator*
Rumman, Wadi (Saliba Rumman) *civil engineer, consultant*
Saitou, Kazuhiro *engineering educator*
Schwank, Johannes Walter *chemical engineering educator*
Scott, Norman Ross *electrical engineering educator*
Senior, Thomas Bryan A. *electrical engineering educator, researcher, consultant*
Solomon, David Eugene *engineering company executive*
Sovani, Sandeep Dinkar *mechanical engineer, educator, researcher*
Tai, Chen-To *electrical engineering educator*
Willmarth, William Walter *aerospace engineering educator*
Wilson, Richard Christian *engineering firm executive*
Yagle, Andrew Emil *engineering educator*
Ye, Cang *electrical engineer*
Young, Edwin Harold *chemical and metallurgical engineering educator*

Auburn Hills
Bahman, Mujibur *engineer*
Nusholtz, Guy Samuel *executive consultant*

Augusta
Barr, William Robert *industrial engineer, consultant*

Bingham Farms
Gratch, Serge *mechanical engineering educator*

Bloomfield Hills
Cuffe, Stafford Sigesmund *engineering company executive, consultant*
Gabriel, Martin George *engineering consultant*
†Kollins, Michael Jerome *automotive engineer, historian, writer*
Putchakayala, Hari Babu *engineering company executive*
Roy, Ranjit Kumar *mechanical engineer*
Stivender, Donald Lewis *mechanical engineering consultant*

Buchanan
Riches, Kenneth William *nuclear regulatory engineering manager*

Canton
Cattani, Luis Carlos *manufacturing engineer*

Dearborn
Atkin, Rupert Lloyd *retired engineer*
Bautz, Jeffrey Emerson *mechanical engineer, educator, researcher*
Bugli, Neville Jimmy *mechanical engineer*
Cairns, James Robert *mechanical engineering educator*
Chen, Weigang *applied mechanics scientist, research engineer*
Gu, Jianmin *mechanical engineer, researcher*
†Irick, Brett D *manufacturing engineer*
Jie, Min *mechanical engineering educator, researcher*
Kendall, Laurel Ann *geotechnical engineer*
Li, Guosong *mechanical engineering educator*
Libertiny, Susan Fryc *mechanical engineer*
Linnansalo, Vera *engineer*
Little, Robert Eugene *mechanical engineering educator, materials behavior researcher, consultant*
Olson, Richard Gottlieb *nuclear engineer*
†Raghava, Ram Singh *polymer scientist*
Tallio, Kevin Verne *engineering supervisor*
Wagner, Harvey Arthur *nuclear engineer, consultant*
Wang, Dexin *research engineer*
Yang, Guangbin *engineer*

Detroit
Babar, Raza Ali *industrial engineer, utility consultant, futurist, management educator, marketing strategist, author, publisher*
Batcha, George *retired mechanical and nuclear engineer*
Berri, Mohamad Hussein *electrical and computer engineer, educator, researcher*
Dong, Zhong *biomedical scientist*
Fu, Gongkang *civil engineering educator*
Harden, Daniel Alexander, Jr., *chemical engineer*
Holness, Gordon Victor Rix *engineering executive, mechanical engineer*
Kline, Kenneth Alan *mechanical engineering educator*
Kummler, Ralph H. *chemical engineer, educator, dean*
Putatunda, Susil Kumar *metallurgy educator*
Trim, Donald Roy *consulting engineer*

East Lansing
Andersland, Orlando Baldwin *civil engineering educator*
Chen, Kun-Mu *electrical engineering educator*
Cutts, Charles Eugene *civil engineering educator*
Foss, John Frank *mechanical engineering educator*
Goodman, Erik David *engineering educator*
Lloyd, John Raymond *mechanical engineering educator*
Matuana, Laurent Malanda *engineering educator, researcher*
Pierre, Percy Anthony *engineering educator*
†Salem, Fathi M. *electrical engineer, educator*
Saul, William Edward *civil engineering educator*
†Udpa, Satish S. *electrical engineering educator, researcher*
von Bernuth, Robert Dean *agricultural engineering educator, consultant*
Von Tersch, Lawrence Wayne *electrical engineering educator, university dean*
Xi, Ning *engineering educator, researcher*

Eastport
Tomlinson, James Lawrence *mechanical engineer*

Farmington
Chou, Clifford Chi Fong *research engineering executive*
Neyer, Jerome Charles *consulting civil engineer*

Farmington Hills
Hurd, Mary K. *civil engineer, writer*

Flint
Echempati, Raghu *mechanical engineering educator, consultant*

Galesburg
Russell, Josette Renee *industrial engineer*

Grand Blanc
Riley, Ronald Jim *industrial engineer, consultant*

Grand Rapids
Garver, Frederick Merrill *industrial engineering executive*

Sandmore, Donald Robert *research and development engineer*

Greenbush
Paulson, James Marvin *engineering educator*

Grosse Pointe
Beltz, Charles Robert *retired engineering executive*

Hartland
Ellis, Robert William *materials engineer, consultant*

Holland
Mills, Charles Anthony *engineering company executive*
Stynes, Stanley Kenneth *retired chemical engineer, educator*

Houghton
Crittenden, John Charles *civil and environmental engineering educator*
Heckel, Richard Wayne *metallurgical engineering educator*
Huang, Eugene Yuching *civil engineer, educator*
Pelc, Karol Ignacy *engineering and technology management educator, researcher*
White, Calvin Lamont *engineer*

Kalamazoo
Ahmad, Shah Mahmood *chemical engineer, consultant*
Dinculescu, Antonie *chemical engineer, scientist*
Engelmann, Paul Victor *plastics engineering educator*
†Litynski, Daniel Mitchell *engineering educator, retired military officer*
Mangalaramanan, Sathya Prasad *mechanical engineer, researcher*
†Sampath, Arun *chemical engineer, consultant*

Lansing
Shirtum, Earl Edward *retired civil engineer*

Laurium
Pippenger, John Junior *fluid power engineer*

Leland
Soutas-Little, Robert William *mechanical engineer, educator*

Livonia
†Hinsch, James Erwin *retired chemical engineer*
Uicker, Joseph Bernard *retired engineering company executive*

Madison Heights
Xia, Jiding *chemical engineering educator*

Marquette
Curtis, Mark Allen *engineering educator, author, consultant*

Mason
Midgley, John W. *civil engineer, consultant*
Toekes, Barna *chemical engineer, polymer consultant*

Midland
Carson, Gordon Bloom *retired engineering executive*
Leng, Douglas Ellis *chemical engineer, scientist*
Meister, Bernard John *chemical engineer*
Robbins, Lanny Arnold *chemical engineer*

North Branch
Stevenson, James Laraway *communications engineer, consulting*

Okemos
Giacoletto, Lawrence Joseph *electronics engineering educator, researcher, consultant*

Petersburg
Hicks, George William *mechanical engineer, automotive engineer*

Plymouth
Champa, John Joseph *telecommunications engineer, consultant*

Pontiac
Hampton, Philip Michael *consulting engineering company executive*

Portage
†Dasgupta, Rathindra *metallurgical engineer*

Rochester
†Yang, Lianxiang *optical engineer, educator*

Rochester Hills
Meldrum, Richard James *electrical engineer*
Shah, Jayprakash Balvantrai *civil engineer*
Szetela, Rebecca E. Coombe *engineer*

Royal Oak
Smith, John William Hugh *civil engineer*

Saint Joseph
Maley, Wayne Allen *engineering consultant*

Shelby Township
Jacovides, Linos Jacovou *electrical engineer, researcher*
Nagy, Louis Leonard *engineering executive, researcher*

Southfield
Hanisko, John-Cyril Patrick *electronics engineer, physicist*
McKeen, Alexander C. *retired engineering executive, foundation administrator*

Sterling Heights
Burke, Thomas Joseph *civil engineer*

Troy
Haryadi, Satish Govindaram *structural engineer, researcher*
Pulkkinen, Jyrki Tuomo Juhani *structural engineer*

Walled Lake
Kaldobsky, Phoebus Reeveman *retired transportation engineer, retired management consultant*
†Williams, Sam B. *engineering executive*

Warren
Lett, Philip W. *defense consultant*
†Li, Jingshan *electrical engineer, researcher*
Nefske, Donald Joseph *engineer*
†Papasavva, Stella *research engineer*

Washington
Chatterley, James Philip *retired automotive development engineer*

MINNESOTA

Aitkin
Prickett, Gordon Odin *mining, mineral and energy engineer*

Burnsville
Lai, Juey Hong *chemical engineer*

Chanhassen
Thorson, John Martin, Jr., *electrical engineer, consultant*

Coleraine
Iwasaki, Iwao *engineering educator*

Eden Prairie
Higgins, Robert Arthur *electrical engineer, educator, consultant*

Grand Marais
Napadensky, Hyla Sarane *engineering consultant*

Lakeville
Setterholm, Jeffrey Miles *systems engineer*

Le Sueur
†Yang, Mengyan *research scientist*

Madison
Husby, Donald Evans *engineering company executive*

Minneapolis
Abi-Ghanem, Georges Victor *engineer, scientist*
Anderson, John Edward *mechanical engineering educator*
Bae, Seongtae *electrical engineer*
Bakken, Earl Elmer *electrical engineer, bioengineering company executive*
Cussler, Edward Lansing, Jr., *chemical engineer, educator*
Davis, Howard Ted *engineering educator*
Fletcher, Edward Abraham *engineering educator*
Galambos, Theodore Victor *civil engineer, educator*
Goldstein, Richard Jay *mechanical engineer, educator*
Gulliver, John Stephen *civil engineering educator, consultant*
†Guo, Meiwen *structural engineer*
Hillstrom, Thomas Peter *engineering executive*
Johnson, Walter Kline *civil engineer*
Joseph, Daniel Donald *aeronautical engineer, educator*
Keller, Kenneth Harrison *engineering educator, science policy analyst*
Kulacki, Francis Alfred *engineer, educator*
Kvalseth, Tarald Oddvar *mechanical engineer, educator*
Lambert, Robert Frank *electrical engineer, consultant*
Luzhansky, Dmitry M. *chemical engineer, researcher*
Ogata, Katsuhiko *engineering educator*
Oriani, Richard Anthony *metallurgical engineer, educator*
Persson, Erland Karl *electrical engineer, engineering executive*
Pfender, Emil *mechanical engineering educator*
Rauenhorst, Gerald *architectural engineer, construction and development executive*
Sapiro, Guillermo *engineering educator, consultant*
Schlentz, Robert Joseph *biomedical, electromagnetic compatibility, regulatory, reliability and safety engineer*
Sheikh, Suneel Ismail *aerospace engineer, researcher*
Shulman, Yechiel *engineering educator*
Sparrow, Ephraim Maurice *mechanical engineering scientist, educator*
Stelson, Kim Adair *mechanical engineering educator*
Svärd, N. Trygve *electrical engineer*
Tennyson, Joseph Alan *engineering executive*
†Viegas, Herman Hermogio *mechanical engineer*
Wilkinson, Jeffrey David *engineer*

Minnetonka
Johnson, Lennart Ingemar *materials engineering consultant*

Mounds View
†Brandt, Dean Myron *design engineer*

New Brighton
Karls, Nicholas James *engineering executive*

Oakdale
Tran, Nang Tri *electrical engineer, physicist*

Plymouth
Park, Gyoungwon *electrical engineer, research scientist*
Peterson, Donn Neal *forensic engineer*

Rochester
Huffine, Coy Lee *retired chemical engineer, consultant*
O'Hare, Daniel John *electrical engineer*

Saint Cloud
Korde, Umesh Arvind *ocean engineer, researcher, educator*

Saint Paul
†Baker, Lawrence Alan *environmental engineer, researcher*
Boyle, Bradley Charles *civil engineer*
†Hennessey, Michael Peter *mechanical engineer, educator*
Lampert, Leonard Franklin *mechanical engineer*
Myren, David James *aeronautical engineer*
Nam, Sehyun *polymer engineer*
†Webster, Steven Craig *engineer*
Yin, Kewen Karen *chemical engineer, educator*

Shoreview
Liu, Benjamin Young-hwai *engineering educator*

South Saint Paul
Fairhurst, Charles *civil and mining engineering educator*

Welch
Solymossy, Joseph Martin *nuclear engineer*

Woodbury
Benforado, David M. *environmental engineer*
Exe, David Allen *electrical engineer*

MISSISSIPPI

Bay Saint Louis
†Rahman, Shamim A. *engineering executive*

Brandon
Guthrie, Michael Steele *magnetic circuit design engineer*

Diamondhead
Brinsmade, Akbar Fairchild *chemical engineering consultant*

Lorman
Hylander, Walter Raymond, Jr., *retired civil engineer*

Meridian
Miller, Cliff *engineer*

Mississippi State
Bumgardner, Joel David *biomedical engineer, educator*
Cliett, Charles Buren *aeronautical engineer, educator, academic administrator*
†Taylor, Clayborne Dudley *engineering educator*
Truax, Dennis Dale *civil engineer, educator, consultant*

Ocean Springs
Ales, Michael Raymond *engineering educator*

Oxford
Costner, Charles Lynn *retired civil engineer*
Horton, Thomas Edward, Jr., *mechanical engineering educator*

Starkville
Carley, Charles Team, Jr., *mechanical engineer*
Jacob, Paul Bernard, Jr., *electrical engineering educator*

University
Chen, Wei-Yin *chemical engineering educator, researcher*
†Cheng, Alexander Hung-Darh *engineering educator, consultant*
Smith, Allie Maitland *engineering educator*
Wang, Sam Shu-Yi *hydraulic and mechanical engineer, educator*

Vaiden
Murphy, Ben Carroll *engineering company executive*

Vicksburg
McRae, John Leonidas *civil engineer, consultant*

Waveland
Briggs, Leslie Ray *retired mechanical engineer*

MISSOURI

Ava
Murray, Delbert Milton *manufacturing engineer*

Ballwin
Arantes, José Carlos *industrial engineer, educator*
Cornell, William Daniel *mechanical engineer*

Chesterfield
Mak, Sioe Tho *retired engineer*
Metzler, Paul Raymond *electrical engineer, consultant*
Rathore, Anurag Singh *chemical engineer*
†Wohl, Martin H. *retired chemical engineer, business executive*

Columbia
Frisby, James Curtis *agricultural engineering educator*
Ho, Dominic KC *electrical engineering educator*
†Keyvan, Shahla *nuclear engineer, educator*
O'Connor, John Thomas *civil engineering educator*
Pringle, Oran Allan *mechanical and aerospace engineering educator*
Schuder, John Claude *biomedical engineer*
†Shende, Rajesh V. *chemical engineer, materials scientist, researcher*
Tzou, Robert Da *engineering educator*
Waidelich, Donald Long *electrical engineer, consultant*
Welshons, Wade Vincent *biomedical sciences educator*
†Wu, Bin *industrial engineering, professor*
Yasuda, Hirotsugu Koge *chemical engineering professor*

Ferguson
Bruns, Billy Lee *electrical engineer, consultant*
Fieldhammer, Eugene Louis *civil engineer*

Florissant
Stevens, Robert Edward *engineering company executive*
Tomazi, George Donald *retired electrical engineer*
Ziemer, John Robert *software engineer*

Fortuna
Ramer, James LeRoy *civil engineer*

Four Seasons
Bivins, Susan Steinbach *systems engineer*

Innsbrook
Ruwwe, William Otto *retired automotive engineer*

Kansas City
Acheson, Allen Morrow *retired engineering executive*
Das, Dilip Kumar *chemical engineer*
Davis, F(rancis) Keith *civil engineer*
Green, Frank Earl *civil engineer*
Heisey, Raymond K. *civil engineer*
†Jennings, Michael C. *engineer, designer, psychologist, consultant*
O'Bannon, Deborah Jean *civil engineering educator*
†Rodman, Leonard C. *civil and communication engineering executive*
Wade, Robert Glenn *engineering executive*

Kirkwood
Holsen, James Noble, Jr., *retired chemical engineer*

Lake Lotawana
†Heineman, Paul Lowe *consulting civil engineer*

Maryland Heights
Goldfarb, Marvin Al *retired civil engineer*
Ramanuja, Teralandur Krishnaswamy *retired structural engineer*

Rocheport
Basye, Charles Benjamin *engineering educator*

Rolla
†Barr, David John *civil, geological engineering educator*
Belarbi, Abdeldjelil *civil engineering educator, researcher*
Chen, Genda *engineering educator*
Crosbie, Alfred Linden *mechanical engineering educator*
Dagli, Cihan Hayreddin *engineering educator*
DuBroff, Richard Edward *electrical engineer, educator*
Finaish, Fathi Ali *aeronautical engineering educator*
Grayson, Robert Larry *mining engineering educator, mining executive*
Lehnhoff, Terry Franklin *mechanical engineering*
Leighly, Hollis Philip, Jr., *metallurgical engineering educator, researcher*
†Mendoza, Cesar *civil engineer, educator, civil engineer, researcher*
Mishra, Rajiv Sharan *metallurgical engineer, educator*
†Padhi, Radhakant *engineer*
Prakash, Shamsher *retired civil engineering educator, consultant*
Saperstein, Lee Waldo *mining engineering educator*
Sarangapani, Jagannathan *embedded systems and networking engineer, educator*
Sauer, Harry John, Jr., *mechanical engineering educator, university administrator*
†Wagner, Harold Willis, Jr., *civil engineer, educator*
Yu, Wei-Wen *retired engineering educator*

Saint Charles
Martin, Edward Brian *electrical engineer*

Saint Joseph
Laderoute, Charles David *engineer, economist, consultant*

Saint Louis
Amini, Amir Arsham *biomedical engineering researcher, educator*
Antonacci, Anthony Eugene *engineer*
Birman, Victor Mark *mechanical and aerospace engineering educator, academic administrator*
Brasunas, Anton de Sales *retired metallurgical engineering educator*
Briggs, William Benajah *aeronautical engineer*
Cairns, Donald Fredrick *engineering educator, management consultant*
Cox, Jerome Rockhold, Jr., *electrical engineer*
Dreifke, Gerald Edmond *electrical engineering educator*
†Duchek, Michael Gerard *mechanical engineer*
Dudukovic, Milorad P. *chemical engineering educator, consultant*
Foley, Deborah Ann *civil engineer*

PROFESSIONAL INDEX 6305 ENGINEERING

Goldstein, Julius Lester *biomedical engineer, consultant*
Gould, Phillip Louis *civil engineering educator, consultant*
Izuchukwu, John Ifeanyichukwu *industrial engineer, mechanical engineer*
Jacks, Sidney *engineer*
Luecke, Kenn Robert *software engineer*
McKelvey, James Morgan *chemical engineering educator*
Olsen, Tava Maryanne Lennon *industrial and operations engineering educator*
Orton, George Frederick *aerospace engineer*
Peters, David Allen *mechanical engineering educator, consultant*
Richardson, Thomas Hampton *design consulting engineer*
Rogers, John Russell *manufacturing company executive, engineer*
Ross, Monte *electrical engineer, researcher*
Shrauner, Barbara Wayne Abraham *electrical engineer, educator*
Spielman, Barry E *electrical engineer, educator, department chairman*
Sullentrup, Michael Gerard *fracture mechanics engineer, consultant*
Sutera, Salvatore Philip *mechanical engineering educator*
Szabo, Barna Aladar *mechanical engineering educator, mining engineer*
Thompson, William Charles *civil engineer*
Trout, Keith William *electrical engineer*
Winter, David Ferdinand *electrical engineering educator, consultant*
Zaidi, Riaz Haider *aircraft engineer, consultant*
Zurheide, Charles Henry *consulting electrical engineer*

Springfield
Brady, Steven L. *civil engineer, consultant*
Hansen, John Paul *retired metallurgical engineer*
Maples, Jimmie Kay *mechanical engineer*

University City
McVey, Francis Daniel *mechanical engineer, software developer, educator*

Webb City
Nichols, Robert Leighton *civil engineer*

West Plains
Fugate, Charles Royce, Sr., *civil engineer*

MONTANA

Billings
Gerlach, Thurlo Thompson *electrical engineer*

Bozeman
Billau, Robin Louise *engineering and consulting executive*
Cokelet, Giles Roy *biomedical engineering educator*
Nehrir, M. Hashem *electrical engineer, educator*
Sanks, Robert Leland *environmental engineer, emeritus educator*
†Sobek, Durward Kenneth, II, *engineering educator*
Stanislao, Joseph *consulting engineer, educator*

Butte
Jensen, Roger Christian *industrial engineer*
†Nikoli-Tirkas, Bojana *aerospace engineer, researcher*

Great Falls
Walker, Leland Jasper *civil engineer*

Harlem
Brekke, Alan Lee *industrial engineer*

Helena
Johnson, David Sellie *civil engineer*

Missoula
Rice, Steven Dale *electronics educator*
Robertson, Gregory Howard *civil engineer*

NEBRASKA

Alliance
Riemenschneider, Albert Louis *retired engineering educator*

Clay Center
Hahn, George LeRoy *agricultural engineer, biometeorologist*

Crete
Hoback, Ronald Dean *retired engineer*

Lincoln
Bahar, Ezekiel *electrical engineering educator*
Burnham, Stephen John *civil engineer*
Edison, Allen Ray *electrical engineer, educator*
Edwards, Donald Mervin *biological systems engineering educator, university dean, emeritus*
Gitelson, Anatoly Avraam *engineering educator*
Hoffman, Glenn Jerrald *retired agricultural and biological engineering educator, consultant*
Lagerstrom, Thomas Jay *engineering executive*
†Mohebbi, Esmail *industrial engineer*
Ramamurthy, Byravamurthy *computer engineer, educator*
Splinter, William Eldon *agricultural engineering educator*
Woollam, John Arthur *electrical engineering educator*

Omaha
†Durham, Charles William *civil engineer, director*
Howard, Walter Burke *chemical engineer*
Kostecki, Martin Paul *industrial engineer*
Kotan, Richard Marvin *engineer*
Rossbach, Philip Edward *civil engineer*
Sokolof, Phil *industrialist, consumer advocate*
Tunnicliff, David George *civil engineer*

Scottsbluff
Jensen, Christopher Douglas *civil engineer*

NEVADA

Boulder City
Wyman, Richard Vaughn *engineering educator, exploration company executive*

Carson City
Hughes, Robert Merrill *control system engineer*
Klippert, Richard Hobdell, Jr., *engineering executive*

Dayton
Clements, Linda L. *materials engineer, educator, journalist*

Henderson
†Wennerstrom, Arthur John *aeronautical engineer*

Incline Village
Merdinger, Charles John *civil engineer, naval officer, academic administrator*
Thompson, David Alfred *industrial engineer*

Las Vegas
Culp, Gordon Louis *consulting engineer*
Dastin, Samuel J. *aerospace engineer, consultant*
Fraser, Gale William, II, *civil engineer*
Haas, Robert John *aerospace engineer*
Herzlich, Harold J. *chemical engineer*
Massier, Paul Ferdinand *mechanical engineer*
Messenger, George Clement *engineering executive, consultant*
Mulvihill, Peter James *fire protection engineer*
Ramos, Albert A. *electrical engineer*
Snaper, Alvin Allyn *engineer*
Swallow, Kristina Louise *civil engineer*

Minden
Bently, Donald Emery *electrical engineer*

Reno
Byrd, Ronald Dallas *civil engineer*
Danko, George *engineering educator*
Haupt, Randy Larry *electrical engineering educator*
Kleppe, John Arthur *electrical engineering educator, business executive*
Krenkel, Peter Ashton *engineer, educator*
Saiidi, Mehdi *engineering educator*
Sanders, David H. *civil engineering educator*
Trzynadlowski, Andrzej Maria *electrical engineering educator*
Whiting, Wallace Burton, II, *chemical engineer, educator*

Silver City
Bloyd, Stephen Roy *environmental manager, educator, consultant*

Sparks
Lagasse, Bruce Kenneth *retired structural engineer*

Zephyr Cove
Barnett, Arthur Lyn *land use and environmental planner*

NEW HAMPSHIRE

Atkinson
Hess, David Graham *engineering administrator*

Concord
Caswell, William Stephen, Jr., *civil engineer*

Durham
Sivaprasad, Kondagunta N. *electrical engineering educator*

Farmington
†Panek, William Dominick *systems engineer executive*

Grantham
Crane, Robert Kendall *engineering educator, researcher, consultant*

Hanover
Graves, Robert John *industrial engineering educator*
Hutchinson, Charles Edgar *engineering educator*
Long, Carl Ferdinand *engineering educator*
Queneau, Paul Etienne *metallurgical engineer, educator*

Hillsboro
Pearson, William Rowland *retired nuclear engineer*

Lebanon
†Hartov, Alexander *engineering educator*
Thaker, Amish A. *engineer*

Manchester
Dorwart, Brian Curtis *geotechnical engineer, consultant*
Hower, Philip Leland *semiconductor device engineer*
†Kamen, Dean *biomedical engineer*

Marlow
Lindholm, Ulric Svante *engineering research institute executive, retired*

Merrimack
Drobny, Jiri George *chemical engineer*
Malley, James Henry Michael *industrial engineer*

Nashua
Fallet, George *civil engineer*
Seifer, Arnold David *systems engineer*
Woodruff, Thomas Ellis *electronics consulting executive*

New Castle
Klotz, Louis Herman *structural engineer, educator, consultant*

Peterborough
Farnham, Sherman Brett *retired electrical engineer*

Portsmouth
Lambert, Eugene Louis *engineer, manufacturing executive*

Salem
Bonacorsi, Gregory James *mechanical engineer*

West Lebanon
Sullivan, Charles R. *engineering educator*

Wolfeboro
Hutchins, Carleen Maley *acoustical engineer, consultant*

NEW JERSEY

Aberdeen
Smith, Marvin Frederick, Jr., *chemical engineer, consultant*

Annandale
Bhagat, Phiroz Maneck *mechanical engineer*
Matsen, John Morris *retired engineer*

Atco
Beard, Richard Burnham *engineering educator emeritus, researcher*
Conrad, George John *retired design engineer, planner*

Audubon
Sconyo, Philip *engineering consultant*

Basking Ridge
Drewry, Don Neal *fire protection engineer*

Bedminster
David, Edward Emil, Jr., *electrical engineer, business executive*

Berkeley Heights
Rabiner, Lawrence Richard *electrical engineer, educator*

Bloomingdale
Janow, Chris *mechanical engineer*

Bloomsbury
Williams, James Richard *human factors engineering psychologist*

Burlington
Kennedy, Christopher Robin *ceramic engineer, director*

Caldwell
Stanton, George Basil, Jr., *engineering executive, chemical engineer*

Camden
Madan, Deepak Sheelmohan *engineer*

Cherry Hill
Batterman, Steven Charles *engineering mechanics and bioengineering educator, forensic engineering and biomechanics consultant*
Deppa, Timothy Wayne *electrical engineer*
Fuentevilla, Manuel Edward *chemical engineer*
Melick, George Fleury *mechanical engineer, educator*

Cliffside Park
Bedian, Maral Papazian *civil and geotechnical engineer*

Clinton
†Swift, Richard J. *engineering company executive*

Columbus
Litman, Bernard *electrical engineer, consultant*

Cranbury
Palócz, István *electrical engineer, educator*

Cranford
Schink, Frank Edward *electrical engineer*

Denville
Tilak, Avinash G. *industrial engineer, management consultant*

Dumont
†Raffa, Stanley William *engineer*

Dunellen
Richmond, Ernest Leon *research engineer, consultant*

East Brunswick
Liebowitz, Larry Arnold *chemical engineer*

East Orange
Masucci, Nicholas J. *engineering company executive*

Eatontown
Rapka, James Richard *electronics engineer*

Elmwood Park
Semeraro, Michael Archangel, Jr., *civil engineer*

Englewood
Deresiewicz, Herbert *mechanical engineering educator*

Essex Fells
Yu, Yi-Yuan *mechanical engineering educator*

Ewing
Brunda, Daniel Donald *retired aerospace engineer, consultant, inventor*

Fairfield
Govic, Rudolf *structural engineer*
Purcell, Fenton Peter *engineering consultant*

Farmingdale
Kalnins, Andis Imants *civil engineer*

Florham Park
†Kim, Hong Kook *electrical engineer, researcher*

Fort Lee
Cheng, David Hong *mechanical engineering educator*
Screpetis, Dennis *retired nuclear engineer, consultant*

Fort Monmouth
Kosinski, John August *electrical engineer, civilian military employee*
Mandelbaum, David Michael *electrical engineer*
Perlman, Barry Stuart *electrical engineering executive, researcher*
†Su, Wei *electrical engineer*
Tobias, John Michael *electronics engineer*

Freehold
†Christ, Duane Marland *computer systems engineer*
Schwartz, Perry Lester *information systems engineer, consultant*
Stirrat, William Albert *electronics engineer*

Frenchtown
†Heck, Ronald Marshall *chemical engineer*

Glassboro
Dusseau, Ralph Alan *civil and environmental engineering educator*
†Kadlowec, Jennifer *engineering educator*

Green Village
Castenschiold, René *engineering company executive, author, consultant*

Hackensack
Zimmerman, Marlin U., Jr., *chemical engineer*

Haddonfield
Eklund, Thor Ignatius *aeronautical engineer, consultant*
Siskin, Edward Joseph *engineering and construction company executive*

Hamilton Square
Bloor, W(illiam) Spencer *electrical engineer, consultant*

Helmetta
†Gabay, Eleonora V. *mechanical engineer, educator*

Hewitt
Selwyn, Donald *engineering administrator, researcher, inventor, educator*

Hightstown
Johnson, Ernest Frederick *chemical engineer, educator*
Johnson, Walter Curtis *electrical engineering educator*

Hoboken
Babko-Malyi, Sergei Vladimirovitch *process engineer, researcher*
Boesch, Francis Theodore *electrical engineer, educator*
Bruno, Michael Stephen *ocean engineering educator, researcher*
Fernandez, Fernando Lawrence *aeronautical engineer, research company executive*
Griskey, Richard George *chemical engineering educator*
Kalyon, Dilhan M(ehmet) *chemical engineering educator*
†Li, Hongbin *electrical engineer*
Savitsky, Daniel *engineer, educator*
Sisto, Fernando *mechanical engineering educator*
Tang, Hansong *computational fluid dynamics researcher*

Holmdel
Boyd, Gary Delane *electro-optical engineer, researcher*
Lang, Howard Lawrence *electrical engineer*
Mondal, Kalyan *engineering executive*
Papadias, Constantinos Basil *electrical engineer*
Ross, Ian Munro *electrical engineer*
†Valenzuela, Reinaldo A. *communications engineer, researcher*
Yu, Charles X. *optical engineer, researcher*

Hopewell
VanMarcke, Erik Hector *civil engineer, educator*

Jersey City
Adlershteyn, Leon *naval architect, engineer, educator, researcher*
Klyatis, Lev Matusovich *test engineer*

Kearny
Shin, John Joongsung *mechanical nuclear engineer, consultant*

Kinnelon
Haller, Charles Edward *engineering consultant*

Lawrenceville
Enegess, David Norman *chemical engineer*

Lincroft
Heirman, Donald Nestor *training engineering company executive, consultant*

Little Falls
Viil, Heino *retired engineer*

Livingston
Daman, Ernest Ludwig *mechanical engineer*
DeGhetto, Kenneth Anselm *engineering executive, construction executive*

Madison
Chang, Darwin Ray *civil engineer*

Mahwah
Grgin, Joseph Michael *environmental engineer*
†Rakotobe-Joel, Thierry *engineering educator, researcher*

Manasquan
Abate, John E. *electrical and electronic engineer, communications consultant*

Matawan
Swett-Brasefield, Susan *chemical engineer*

Middletown
Cooley, Sidney Elizabeth Ann *engineer*
Granstrom, Marvin Leroy *civil and sanitary engineering educator*
Hernon, Richard Francis *civil engineer*
Luo, Wei *electronics engineer*
†Noel, Eric *electrical engineer*
O'Neill, Eugene Francis *retired communications engineer*

Millburn
Wilkinson, Clifford Steven *civil engineer*

Monroe Township
Rosenthal, Louis Aaron *electrical engineer*

Montclair
Clech, Jean Paul Marie *mechanical engineer*
Eager, George Sidney, Jr., *electrical engineer, business executive*

Montvale
Mantell, Keith C. *chemical engineer*

Moorestown
Atilgan, Timur Faik *structural engineer*
Lipscomb, Thomas Heber, Jr., *retired civil engineer*

Morris Plains
Slaby, Louis Richard *civil and mechanical engineer*

Morristown
Kagan, Val Alexander *engineer, researcher, educator*
Lieberman, Lester Zane *engineering company executive*
†Pavlovich, John Stephen *civil engineer*
Rainal, Attilio Joseph *retired electronics engineer, researcher*
Raziq, Yaqub *telecommunications engineer*
Sincoskie, W. David *computer engineer*

Murray Hill
†Divakaran, Ajay *electrical engineer, research and development company executive*
Garfias, Luis Francisco *chemical engineering researcher*
Morgan, Dennis Raymond *electrical engineer*

Neptune
Zurick, Jack *electrical engineer, consultant*

New Brunswick
Awan, Ahmad Noor *civil engineer*
Jaluria, Yogesh *mechanical engineering educator*
Smith, Fredric Charles *electrical engineer, consultant*
Weng, George Jueng-Cious *engineering educator*

New Providence
Bair, Harvey Edward *polymer scientist*
Chen, Yudong *engineer, researcher*
Cho, Alfred Yi *electrical engineer*
Savari, Serap Ayse *electrical engineer, researcher*
Smith, George Artell *chemical engineer*
†Yaghubian, Arman Rugo *industrial engineer*

Newark
Armenante, Piero M. *chemical engineering educator*
Bar-Ness, Yeheskel *electrical engineer, educator*
Carpinelli, John Dominick *computer engineering educator*
Dhawan, Atam Prakash *engineering educator, dean*
Friedland, Bernard *engineer, educator*
Hanesian, Deran *chemical engineer, chemistry and environmental science educator, consultant*
Hrycak, Peter *mechanical engineer, educator*
Khera, Raj Pal *civil and environmental engineering educator*
Pignataro, Louis James *engineering educator*
Rosato, Anthony Dominick *mechanical engineer, educator*
†Shi, Yun Qing *electrical engineer*
†Shishkin, Dimitri Victor *mechanical engineer, consultant*
Spillers, William Russell *civil engineering educator*
Ziavras, Sotirios George *computer and electrical engineer, educator*

Newfoundland
Van Winkle, Edgar Walling *retired electrical engineer, computer consultant*

North Caldwell
Stevens, William Dollard *consulting mechanical engineer*

Norwood
Barbini, Richard John *chemical engineer, marketing manager*

Nutley
Gudema, Norman H. *civil engineer*

Ocean
Reich, Bernard *retired telecommunications engineer*

Ocean City
†Weir, William Thomas *retired engineering educator*

Ocean Grove
Gabriel, Edwin Zenith *consulting engineer*

Oradell
Roe, W. Barton *engineering executive*

Parsippany
Marscher, William Donnelly *engineering company executive*

Passaic
Lindholm, Clifford Falstrom, II, *engineering executive, mayor*

Pennington
Kelly, Quentin Thorn *water company executive, inventor, writer*

Pennsauken
Alday, Paul Stackhouse, Jr., *retired mechanical engineer*

Pine Brook
Schwiederek, William Neil *engineering executive*

Piscataway
†Balaguru, Perumalsamy *civil engineering educator*
Benaroya, Haym *aerospace engineer, educator, researcher*
Boucher, Thomas Owen *engineering educator, researcher*
†Chen, Jian *engineer*
Elsayed, Elsayed Abdelrazik *industrial engineer, educator*
Flanagan, James Loton *electrical engineer, researcher, engineering educator*
Freeman, Herbert *computer engineering educator*
Frenkiel, Richard Henry *retired systems engineer, consultant*
Guo, Qizhong *engineering educator, researcher, consultant*
Hsiao, Michael S. *electrical engineer, educator*
†Langrana, Noshir A. *mechanical engineer, educator, research scientist*
Mammone, Richard James *engineering educator*
Poses, Frederic M. *engineering company executive*
Welkowitz, Walter *biomedical engineer, educator*
Zhang, Li *engineer, researcher*
Zhao, Jian Hui *electrical and computer engineering educator*

Plainsboro
Sorensen, Henrik Vittrup *electrical engineering educator*

Princeton
Bartolini, Robert Alfred *electrical engineer, researcher*
Billington, David Perkins *civil engineering educator*
Blair, David William *mechanical engineer*
Curtiss, Howard Crosby, Jr., *mechanical engineer, educator*
Debenedetti, Pablo Gaston *chemical engineering educator*
File, Joseph *research physics engineer*
Fusillo, Thomas Victor *environmental engineer*
Galloway, Patricia Denese *civil engineer*
Gillham, John Kinsey *chemical engineering educator*
Glassman, Irvin *mechanical and aeronautical engineering educator, consultant*
Hough, Robert Alan *civil engineer*
Jackson, Roy *chemical engineering educator*
†Ju, Yiguang *engineering educator*
Kalafut, Michael Francis *civil engineer*
Lechner, Bernard Joseph *consulting electrical engineer*
Liu, Bede *electrical engineering educator*
Lo, Arthur Wu-nien *electrical engineering educator*
Miles, Richard Bryant *mechanical and aerospace engineering educator*
Poor, Harold Vincent *electrical engineering educator*
†Rowley, Clarence W. *engineering educator*
Russel, William Bailey *engineering educator*
Stengel, Robert Frank *engineering and applied science educator*
Stevens, Allan Woodard *electrical engineer*
Sundaresan, Sankaran *engineering educator, consultant*
Tsui, Daniel C. *electrical engineer, physicist*
Vahaviolos, Sotirios John *electrical engineer, researcher, engineering executive*
Verdu, Sergio *engineering educator*
Wei, James *chemical engineering educator, academic dean*
Whipple, William, Jr., *government policy consultant, writer*
Wolf, Wayne Hendrix *electrical engineering educator*
Zatz, Irving J. *structural engineer*
Zubry, Boris *mechanical engineer, writer*

Princeton Junction
Bair, William Alois *engineer*
Denlinger, Edgar Jacob *electronics engineering research executive*
Haddad, James Henry *chemical engineering consultant*
Lull, William Paul *engineering consultant*
Snedeker, Richard Stockton *research engineer*

Ramsey
Young, C(ornelius) B(ryant), Jr., *electronics engineer*

Red Bank
Lucky, Robert Wendell *electrical engineer*
Schneider, Sol *electronic engineer, consultant, researcher*

Rumson
Rowe, Harrison Edward *electrical engineer*

Scotch Plains
Domeshek, Sol *aeronautical engineer*
Marlowe, Chris Sean *safety engineer*

Sea Bright
Plummer, Dirk Arnold *chemical, electrical, and electronics engineer*

Short Hills
Wharton, Lennard *engineering company executive*

Skillman
Brill, Yvonne Claeys *engineer, consultant*
Shah, Hash N. *plastics technologist, researcher*

Somerset
Chaudhary, Bharat Indu *chemical engineer*
Peng, Xiaoyuan *optical engineer*

Somerville
†Andjelic, Sasa *engineer, polymer scientist*

South Plainfield
†Gopalakrishnan, Suresh *computer engineer*
Kennedy, John William *engineering company executive*

Sparta
Truran, William Richard *electrical engineer*

Springfield
Perilstein, Fred Michael *electrical engineer, consultant*

Summit
Auerbach, Andrew B *polymer engineer, chemist*
Fukui, Hatsuaki *electrical engineer, art historian*

Swedesboro
Lovell, Theodore *electrical engineer, consultant*

Teaneck
Ehrlich, Ira Robert *mechanical engineering consultant*
Mirza, Muhammad Zubair *product development company executive, researcher, engineering consultant, inventor*
Pfeffer, Robert *chemical engineer, academic administrator, educator*

Tinton Falls
†Robinson, Bruce Thomas *systems engineer, mathematics educator*
Tague, Charles Francis *retired engineering, construction and real estate development company executive*

Titusville
Cooper, Paul *retired mechanical engineer, research director*

Toms River
Fanuele, Michael Anthony *retired electronics engineer, research engineer*

Trenton
Anderson, Bruce James *electrical engineer, consultant*

Union
Manz, August Frederick *welding technology and safety consultant*
Newman, Stephen Alexander *chemical engineer, thermodynamicist*

Upper Saddle River
Wallace, William, III, *engineering executive*

Ventnor
†Larky, Arthur Irving *electrical engineer, educator, computer engineer, consultant*

Wallington
Kisciras, Ross Peter *chemical engineer, plant manager*

Warren
Ellerbusch, Fred *environmental engineer*

Watchung
Michaelis, Paul Charles *engineering physicist executive*
Tornqvist, Erik Gustav Markus *chemical engineer, research scientist*

Wayne
Meeldijk, Victor Anthony *engineering professional*
Schmidt, Barnet Michael *communications and electronic engineer*

Whippany
Xu, Hao *electrical engineer*

Woodbridge
Morris, David *retired electrical engineer*

NEW MEXICO

Albuquerque
Anderson, Lawrence Keith *electrical engineer, consultant*
Byrne, Raymond Harry *electrical engineer*
Chen, Jinn-Kuen *mechanical engineer*
Davis, Jon L. *logistics consultant*
†de Ríos, María Estela *engineering company executive*
Dorato, Peter *electrical and computer engineering educator*
Eichel, Paul Herman *electrical engineer*
Gross, William Allen *mechanical engineer*
Haddad, Edward Raouf *civil engineer, consultant*
Hall, Jerome William *research engineering educator*
†Herrera, Gilbert Victor *engineering executive*
Hulsbos, Cornie Leonard *civil engineering educator*
Lee, David Oi *engineer*
†Milloy, John Arthur *structural engineer*
Moulds, William J. *retired aeronautical engineer*
Peck, Ralph Brazelton *civil engineering educator, consultant*
Plough, Charles Tobias, Jr., *retired electronics engineering executive*
Rand, Ruth A. *science and computer educator*
Reuter, Robert Carl, Jr., *retired engineering scientist*
†Rush, Eric Palmer *civil engineer*
Santhanam, Balu *engineering educator*
Warren, Thomas Lynn *mechanical engineer*

Belen
Toliver, Lee *mechanical engineer*

Carlsbad
Hayes, Robert Bruce *radiological engineer*

Cerrillos
Lutz, Raymond Price *retired industrial engineer, educator*

Cloudcroft
Hadfield, Michael James *electrical engineer*

Embudo
Rogers, Benjamin Talbot *former consulting engineer, solar energy consultant*

Farmington
Caldwell, John Winston, III, *petroleum engineer*
Lewis, Homer Dick *retired nuclear engineer*

Holloman AFB
†Minto, David W. *aeronautical engineer*

Kirtland Afb
Baum, Carl Edward *electromagnetic theorist*

Las Cruces
Ford, Clarence Quentin *mechanical engineer, educator*

Los Alamos
Baskes, Michael I. *materials engineer*
Dudziak, Donald John *nuclear engineer, educator*
Durkee, Joe W(orthington), Jr., *nuclear engineer*
Edeskuty, Frederick James *engineer, consultant*
Jackson, James F. *nuclear engineer, educator*
McDonald, Thomas Edwin, Jr., *electrical engineer*
Morel, Jim E. *nuclear engineer, researcher*
Nunz, Gregory Joseph *aerospace engineer, program manager, educator, entrepreneur*
Peratt, Anthony Lee *electrical engineer, physicist*
†Popa-Simil, Liviu I. *nuclear engineer, researcher*
Sicilian, James Michael *research engineer*
Stoddard, Stephen Davidson *ceramic engineer, former state senator*
Van Tuyle, Gregory Jay *nuclear engineer*
†Wilson, William Bradley *nuclear engineer*

Placitas
Hidy, George Martel *chemical engineer, executive*

Rio Rancho
Delahanty, Carlos Anthony *industrial engineer*
Ives, John Milton *retired engineer*
Sei, Ibrahim *process engineer*

Roswell
Kelly, J. Michael *petroleum consultant*

Sandia Park
Pinkus, Oscar *mechanical engineer, writer*

Santa Fe
Amtmann, Hans Henry *aeronautical engineer, naval architect*
Davidson, James Madison, III, *retired engineer, technical manager*
†Goorley, John Timothy *nuclear engineer*
Miller, Edmund Kenneth *retired electrical engineer, educator*

Santa Teresa
Pinzon, Brian William *inventor, consultant*

Socorro
Bond, Robert Harold *electrical engineering educator*

White Sands Missile Range
Arthur, Paul Keith *electronic engineer*

NEW YORK

Albany
Duncan, Jeffrey Burt *computer systems engineer*
Fanuele, Frank John *engineering executive*
Happ, Harvey Heinz *electrical engineer, educator*
Roy, Rob J. *biomedical engineer, anesthesiologist*
Saridis, Panayota Dimarogona *civil engineer*

Alfred
Pian, Carlson Chao-Ping *mechanical engineering educator, researcher*
Spriggs, Richard Moore *ceramic engineer, research center administrator*

Amherst
†Hu, Yun Hang *chemical engineer*
†Kutsin, Leonid *engineering educator, researcher*

Ballston Lake
Fiedler, Harold Joseph *electrical engineer, consultant*

Ballston Spa
†Cameron Jr, Edward John *engineer*

Bethpage
Conti, James Joseph *chemical engineer, educator*
†Whiteside, James Brooks *mechanics engineer, researcher*

Big Flats
Orsillo, James Edward *computer systems engineer, company executive*

Binghamton
Cornacchio, Joseph Vincent *engineering educator, computer researcher, consultant*

Bohemia
Baglio, Vincent Paul *engineering executive*

Brewster
Nadel, Norman Allen *civil engineer*

Bronx
Reynolds, Joseph Patrick *chemical engineering educator, consultant*

Bronxville
Brunale, Vito John *aerospace engineer*

Brooklyn
Beaufait, Frederick W(illiam) *civil engineering educator*
Bertoni, Henry L. *electrical engineering educator*
Birenbaum, Leo *retired engineering educator*
Cambel, Joseph Andrew *design engineer*
†Crânganu, Constantin *engineer*
†Czarkowski, Dariusz *electrical engineer*
Das, Nirod K. *engineering educator*
Goodman, Alvin S. *engineering educator, consultant*
Helly, Walter Sigmund *engineering educator*
Kempner, Joseph *aerospace engineering educator*
†McLean, William Ronald *retired electrical engineer, consultant*
Mijovic, Jovan *chemical engineering educator*
Nakanishi, Yuko Julie *engineering educator, consultant*
Ortiz, Mary Theresa *biomedical engineer, educator*
Parlamis, Michael Frank *civil engineer, construction company executive*
Shaw, Leonard Glazer *electrical engineering educator, consultant*

Buffalo
Anderson, Wayne Arthur *electrical engineering educator*
Deppe, Paul Richard *electrical engineer, engineering test pilot*
Frandina, Philip Frank *civil engineer, consultant*
†Hughes, Timothy F. *mechanical engineer, consultant*
Karwan, Mark Henry *engineering educator, dean*
Landi, Dale Michael *industrial engineer, academic administrator*
Meredith, Dale Dean *civil engineering educator*
Metzger, Ernest Hugh *aerospace engineer, scientist*
†Nichita, Constantin Camil *industrial engineer, researcher*
Reinhorn, Andrei M. *civil structural engineering educator, consultant*
Reismann, Herbert *engineer, educator*
Ruckenstein, Eli *chemical engineering educator*
Shaw, David Tai-Ko *electrical and computer engineering educator, university administrator*
Shelton, Peter Arthur *retired civil engineer*
Weber, Thomas William *chemical engineering educator*
Weller, Sol William *chemical engineering educator*
Wozniak, Richard Anthony *computer engineer*

Cambridge
Eissenberg, David Martin *retired engineering executive*

Canandaigua
Hansen, Widmer Case *retired weapons systems engineer, analyst*

Cato
†Sheckler, Ross David *engineering executive*

Chappaqua
Deutsch, Alina *electrical engineer, researcher*
O'Neill, Robert Charles *inventor, consultant*
Pomerene, James Herbert *retired computer engineer*

Clarence
Greatbatch, Wilson *biomedical engineer*

Clifton Park
Mathur, Devesh *chemical engineer, researcher*

Clinton
Pagani, Albert Louis *aerospace system engineer*

Cold Spring
Pugh, Emerson William *electrical engineer*

Coram
Uh, David Keun *civil engineer*

Corning
†Ahuja, Sanjay *engineer, project manager, educator*

Delmar
Campas, Anna Penelope *civil engineer, architect*
Shen, Thomas To *environmental engineer*

East Amherst
Soong, Tsu-Teh *engineering science educator*

East Norwich
Rosen, Meyer Robert *chemical engineer*

East Syracuse
Wiley, Richard Gordon *electrical engineer*

Endicott
Powers, Steven Eugene *procurement engineer*
Schwartz, Richard Frederick *electrical engineering educator*

Farmingdale
†Bandyopadhyay, Amitabha *engineering educator*

Fayetteville
Dosanjh, Darshan S(ingh) *aeronautical engineer, educator*

Flushing
Kopp, Ilya Zinovij *energy and environmental researcher*
Salgo, Michael Nicholas *civil engineer, consultant*
Stahl, Frank Ludwig *civil engineer*
Unsal-Tunay, Nuran *geological engineer, researcher*

Franklin Square
Cantilli, Edmund Joseph *safety engineering educator, translator, writer, consultant*

Garden City
†Wang, Ping-chan *engineering educator*

Glen Cove
Makris, Constantine John *infosystems engineer*

Glenham
Douglas, Fred Robert *cost engineering consultant*

Glenville
Anderson, Roy Everett *retired electrical engineer*

Goshen
Lanc, John Jan *civil and geodetic engineer, land surveyor*

Greenlawn
Bachman, Henry Lee *electrical engineer, engineering executive*

Harrison
Schulz, Helmut Wilhelm *chemical engineer, environmental executive*

Hauppauge
Buckley, Robert Matthew *electrical engineer*

Hempstead
Goldstein, Stanley Philip *engineering educator*

Hewlett
Haralick, Robert Martin *electrical engineering educator*

Hicksville
Notaro, Anthony *software engineer*

Holtsville
Katz, Joseph *research and development executive*

Homer
MacNeill, John Sears, Jr., *civil engineer*

Hopewell Junction
Gluschenkov, Oleg *electrical engineer*
Kirihata, Toshiaki *VLSI design engineer, researcher*
†Park, Byeongju *engineer*
†Sikka, Kamal K. *engineering executive*

Horseheads
Shabanowitz, Harry *electronics engineer, educator*

Huntington
Chmelev, Vsevolod *engineer, consultant*
Christiansen, Donald David *electrical engineer, editor, publishing consultant*
LaTourrette, James Thomas *retired electrophysics, electrical engineering and computer science educator*

Huntington Station
Agosta, Vito *mechanical and aerospace engineering educator*

Ithaca
Berger, Toby *electrical engineer, educator*
Carlin, Herbert J. *electrical engineering educator, researcher*
De Boer, Pieter Cornelis Tobias *mechanical and aerospace engineering educator*
Dick, Richard Irwin *environmental engineer, educator*
Eastman, Lester Fuess *electrical engineer, educator*
†Finn, Robert Kaul *retired biochemical engineering educator*
Gouldin, Frederick Caskey *mechanical and aerospace engineering professor*
Harriott, Peter *chemical engineering educator*
Leibovich, Sidney *engineering educator*
Linke, Simpson *electrical engineering educator*
Loucks, Daniel Peter *environmental systems engineer*
Maxwell, William Laughlin *retired industrial engineering educator*
McCartney, Elaina *space mission planner*
McGuire, William *civil engineer, educator*
Meyburg, Arnim Hans *transportation engineer, educator, consultant*
O'Rourke, Thomas Denis *civil engineer, educator*
Phelan, Richard Magruder *mechanical engineer*
Rodríguez, Ferdinand *chemical engineer, educator*
Shuler, Michael Louis *biochemical engineering educator, consultant*
Stedinger, Jery Russell *civil and environmental engineer, researcher*
Wang, Kuo-King *manufacturing engineer, educator*

Jackson Heights
Olmsted, Robert Amson *civil engineer*
Parascos, Edward Themistocles *engineering consultant*

Jamaica
Goldenshteyn, Vladimir Lev *civil engineer*

Jamestown
Leising, David Michael *industrial engineer*

Jericho
Shinners, Stanley Marvin *electrical engineer*
†Tafaghodi, Hamid *civil engineer*

Katonah
Bashkow, Theodore Robert *electrical engineering consultant, former educator*

Kew Gardens
†Chipkin, Frederick *textile designer, consultant*

Kings Point
Maclean, Walter Marcus *engineering educator, retired*

Kingston
Dennison, Robert Abel, III, *civil engineer*

Lakewood
Brown, Melvin Henry *retired chemical engineer*

Lansing
Dalman, Gisli Conrad *electrical engineering educator*

Liverpool
Shubsda, Stanley Richard *retired computer engineer*

Long Island City
Barbanel, Sidney William *engineering consulting firm executive*
Theodoru, Stefan Gheorghe *civil engineer, writer*

Manlius
Jefferies, Michael John *retired electrical engineer*

Maspeth
Merjan, Stanley *civil engineer, inventor*

Melville
Bongiorno, Joseph John, Jr., *electrical engineering educator*
Bultan, Aykut *communications systems engineer*
Scire, Frank Jackson *retired radar scientist*
Sullivan, Kenneth W. *engineer*
Taub, Jesse J. *electrical engineering researcher*

Mineola
Lizardos, Evans John *mechanical engineer*
Newman, Malcolm *mechanical and civil engineering consultant*

Mohegan Lake
Paik, John Kee *structural engineer*

Montrose
Reber, Raymond Andrew *retired chemical engineer*

Mount Kisco
Green, Paul Eliot, Jr., *optical communications consultant*

New Hartford
Shieh, Wei T. *senior hardware design engineer*

New Hyde Park
†Huebscher, Herbert *electrical engineer, educator*
Hyman, Abraham *electrical engineer*

New Paltz
†Chikwendu, Sunday C. *engineering educator, mathematician, educator*
González, Julio Jorge *electrical engineering educator*
Izadi, Baback A. *engineering educator*

New Rochelle
Schwarz, Ralph Jacques *retired engineering educator*

New York
Acrivos, Andreas *chemical engineering educator*
Aghassi, William J. *mechanical engineer, consultant*
Ahmad, Jameel *civil engineer, researcher, educator*
Baum, Richard Theodore *engineering executive*
Boley, Bruno Adrian *engineering educator*
Bove, John Louis *chemistry and environmental engineering educator, researcher*
Brazinsky, Irv(ing) *chemical engineering educator*
Briskman, Robert David *engineering executive*
Chang, Jenghwa *biomedical and electrical engineer, medical physicist*
Chen, Tak-Ming *civil engineer, consultant*
Christie, Richard Wallace *retired structural engineer*
Cowin, Stephen Corteen *biomedical engineering educator, consultant*
Daniel, Charles Timothy *transportation engineer, consultant*
Denn, Morton Mace *chemical engineering educator*
DiMaggio, Frank Louis *civil engineering educator*
Fawcett, Christopher Babcock *civil engineer, construction and water resources company executive*
†Fennell, Thomas Edward, Jr., *engineering educator*
Fogel, Irving Martin *consulting engineer*
Friedman, Y. Zak *process control consultant*
Gambs, Gerard Charles *consulting engineer*
†Goldfarb, Donald *industrial engineering educator*
†Gong, Su *computer engineer*
Greenfield, Seymour Stephen *mechanical engineer*
Haratunian, Michael *engineering company executive*
Hasan, Nausherwan *civil engineer, consultant*
Hennessy, John Francis, III, *engineering executive, mechanical engineer*
Herrmann, Andrew William *consulting engineer*
Jarvik, Robert K. *biomedical research scientist*
†Kaufman, Lawrence Jesse *computer engineer*
Kitsopoulos, Sotirios C. *electrical engineer, management consultant*
Knobler, Alfred Everett *ceramic engineer, manufacturing company executive, publisher*
Koshar, Louis David *civil engineer*
Lai, W(ei) Michael *mechanical engineer, educator*
Lammie, James Louis *engineering executive, retired military officer*
†Levy, Matthys Paul *structural engineer*
†Londorenko, Oksana G. *computer engineer*
Manassah, Jamal Tewfek *electrical engineer, educator, management consultant*
Morfopoulos, V. *metallurgical engineer, materials engineer*
Mow, Van C. *engineering educator, researcher*
†Nasr, George Elias *electrical engineer, consultant, computer engineer, educator*
†O'Neill, Thomas J. *engineering company executive*
Paaswell, Robert Emil *civil engineer, educator*
†Patel, Jyotindra H. *civil engineer*
Perez, Julie Anna *audio engineer*
Riazi, Kambiz *civil engineer*
Rubenstein, Leonard *engineering company executive*
Rumschitzki, David Sheldon *chemical engineering educator*
Sadegh, Ali M. *mechanical engineering educator, researcher, consultant*
Schoenfeld, Robert Louis *biomedical engineer*
Schwartz, Mischa *electrical engineering educator*
See, Saw-Teen *structural engineer*
†Shinnar, Reuel *chemical engineering educator, industrial consultant*
Sivakumaran, Kumaraswamy *civil engineer, consultant, lawyer*
Smith, Gordon H. *civil engineer, consultant, forensic engineer consultant*
Soejima, Daisuke *international trade engineer, economist*
Stypulkowski, Jacek Bogdan *geotechnical engineer*
Subak-Sharpe, Gerald Emil *electrical engineer, educator*
Tamaro, George John *consulting engineer*
Tsividis, Yannis P. *electrical engineering educator*
†Villela, Daniel Antunes Maciel *electrical engineer, researcher*
Vogelman, Joseph Herbert *scientific engineering company executive*
Weinbaum, Sheldon *biomedical engineer*
Weinstein, Herbert *chemical engineer, educator*
Yao, David Da-Wei *engineering educator*
Yao, Y. Lawrence *engineering educator*
Yapijakis, Constantine *environmental engineering educator, consultant*
Yegulalp, Tuncel M. *mining engineer, educator*
Zuck, Alfred Christian *consulting mechanical engineer*

Niskayuna
†Chupp, Raymond Edward *mechanical engineer, researcher*
Fitzroy, Nancy deLoye *engineering executive, mechanical engineer*
Huening, Walter Carl, Jr., *retired consulting application engineer*
†Kapur, Ajay *systems engineer*

North Babylon
Tipirneni, Tirumala Rao *metallurgical engineer*

North Syracuse
Roberts, Robert *engineering organization executive, think-tank executive*

Northport
Weber, Ray Everett *engineering executive, consultant*

Norwich
Palahnuk, Donald Walter, Jr., *chemical engineer*

Norwood
Church, Richard Dwight *electrical engineer, scientist*

Oakdale
Carnevale, Louis *civil engineer, inventor*

Old Bethpage
Buzzelli, Dennis Kevin *mechanical engineer*

Orangeburg
Ye, Biqing *biomedical engineer, researcher*

Ossining
Sri-Jayantha, Sri Muthuthamby *mechanical engineer*

Owego
Feavearyear, John Edgar *aerospace systems engineer*

Phoenix
Ackerman, Roger G. *ceramic engineer*

Plainview
Snyder, Joel Bennett *engineering executive, educator*

Plattsburgh
Treacy, William Joseph *electrical and environmental engineer*

Pleasantville
Pike, John Nazarian *optical engineering consultant*
Urban, Joseph Jaroslav *engineer, consultant*

Port Jefferson
Gilmore, Arthur Warham *retired aeronautical engineer*

Port Washington
Gaddis, M. Francis *mechanical and marine engineer, environmental scientist*

Potsdam
Campbell, Gregory August *engineering educator, consultant*
Chin, Der-Tau *chemical engineer, educator*
Mochel, Myron George *mechanical engineer, educator*
†Rengaswamy, Raghunathan *chemical engineering researcher, educator*
Shen, Hung Tao *hydraulic engineering educator*

Poughkeepsie
Chen, Zhaoqing *electronics engineer*
Katopis, George A. *electrical engineer*
Logue, Joseph Carl *electronics engineer, consultant*
†Simons, Robert Edward *mechanical engineer, consultant*
Turgeon, Paul R. *computer program manager*

Riverhead
Thompson, Marie Angela *computer engineer, consultant*

Rochester
Carstensen, Edwin Lorenz *biomedical engineer, biophysicist*
Drummond, Malcolm McAllister *electronics engineer*
Freckleton, Jon Edward *engineering educator, consultant, retired military officer*
Hetnarski, Richard Bozyslaw *mechanical engineering educator*
Joos, Felipe Miguel *mechanical engineer, researcher*
Loewen, Erwin G. *precision engineer, educator, consultant*
Loui, Alexander C.P. *electrical engineer, researcher*
Oldshue, James Y. *chemical engineering consultant*
Parker, Kevin James *electrical engineer, educator*
Ressel, Howard Robert *civil engineer*
Sackett, David Harrison *electrical engineer*
Schmidhammer, Robert Howard *environmental executive, engineering consultant*
Setchell, John Stanford, Jr., *color systems engineer*
Shah, Ramesh Keshavlal *researcher, engineering educator*
Stratton, John Alfred *electrical engineer, educator*
†Wright, David Allen *mechanical engineer, councilman*

Rye
Lehman, Lawrence Herbert *consulting engineering executive*

Rye Brook
†Landegger, George F. *engineering executive*

Scarsdale
Borg, Robert Frederic *civil engineer*
†Florman, Samuel Charles *civil engineer*

Schenectady
Baskous, Athan A. *retired civil engineer*

Fischer, Michael David *civil engineer*
Jones, Edward Allen *engineer*
Mikata, Yozo *mechanical engineer, application developer*
Ringlee, Robert James *consulting engineering executive*
Solomon, Harvey Donald *engineer, educator*

Scotia
Mosteller, Henry W. *retired electrical engineer*

Setauket
Irving, A. Marshall *retired marine engineer*
Levine, Sumner Norton *industrial engineer, educator, editor, author, financial consultant*

Smithtown
Austerlitz, Howard *electronics engineer, writer*
Rockensies, John William *mechanical engineer*

Somers
Anderson, John Erling *chemical engineer*
Terman, Lewis Madison *electrical engineer, researcher*

South Setauket
Richardson, Charles Marsh *electrical engineer, educator*

Staten Island
Garzi, John Joseph *maintenance engineer*
Johansen, Robert John *electrical engineer*
Simkhovich, Semen Lasarevich *engineering educator, researcher*

Stony Brook
Gambino, Richard Joseph *materials science engineering*
Zemanian, Armen Humpartsoum *electrical engineer, mathematician*

Syracuse
Drucker, Alan Steven *mechanical engineer*
Hamlett, James Gordon *electronics engineer, management consultant, educator*
Levy, Alan Joseph *mechanical engineer, educator*
Mandel, James A. *civil engineer, educator*
Sargent, Robert George *engineering educator*

Tarrytown
Bacaloglu, Radu *chemical engineer*
Farrell, Gregory Alan *biomedical engineer*

Tonawanda
Drozdziel, Marion John *aeronautical engineer*
Rovison, John Michael, Jr., *chemical engineer*

Troy
†Arcak, Murat *engineering educator, consultant*
Belfort, Georges *chemical engineering educator, consultant*
Bergles, Arthur Edward *mechanical engineering educator*
Block, Robert Charles *nuclear engineering and engineering physics educator*
Boyina, Ramana Prasad Venkata *civil engineering educator, researcher*
Desrochers, Alan Alfred *electrical engineer*
Duquette, David Joseph *materials science and engineering educator*
Feeser, Larry James *civil engineering educator, researcher*
Gerhardt, Lester A. *engineering educator, dean*
Gill, William Nelson *chemical engineering educator*
Glicksman, Martin Eden *materials engineering educator*
Hsu, Cheng *decision sciences and engineering systems educator*
Jordan, Mark Henry *retired consulting civil engineer*
Kliman, Gerald Burt *electrical engineer*
Lahey, Richard Thomas, Jr., *nuclear engineer, fluid mechanics engineer*
†Linton, Jonathan D *management researcher, educator*
Littman, Howard *chemical engineer, educator*
McDonald, John Francis Patrick *electrical engineering educator*
Messac, Achille *mechanical engineer, aerospace engineer*
Nelson, John Keith *electrical engineer, educator*
Sanderson, Arthur Clark *engineering educator*
Saridis, George Nicholas *electrical, computers and system engineering educator, robotics and automation researcher*
†Shephard, Mark Scott *civil and mechanical engineering educator*
Shuey, Richard Lyman *engineering educator, consultant*
Stoloff, Norman Stanley *materials engineering educator, researcher*
Tien, James M. *engineering educator, consultant*
Woods, John William *electrical, computer and systems engineering educator, consultant*
Zimmie, Thomas Frank *civil engineer, educator*

Uniondale
Gillin, John F. *quality engineer*

Upton
Foerster, Conrad Louis *project engineer*
Fthenakis, Vasilis *chemical engineer, consultant, educator*
Steinberg, Meyer *chemical engineer*

Verona
Smith, Michael Allen *mechanical engineer*

Wanakena
Hunter, William Schmidt *engineering executive, environmental engineer*

Wantagh
Young, Morris *electrical engineering consultant*

Watertown
Dimmick, Kris Douglas *civil engineer*

Watervliet
Underwood, John H. *research engineer*

Webster
McWilliams, C. Paul, Jr., *engineering executive*
Scherer, John V. *computing and instrumentation laboratory manager*

Wellsville
†Fuller, Bruce E. *mechanical engineer*
Tezak, Edward George *mechanics educator*

West Hurley
Krembs, George Michael *computer and electrical engineer*

West Kill
Dwon, Larry *retired electrical engineer, educator, consultant*

West Point
†Burk, Roger Chapman *engineering educator*
†Leamy, Michael Joseph *mechanical engineer, educator*

Westbury
Fleisig, Ross *aeronautical engineer, engineering manager*

Westhampton Beach
Ozero, Brian John *chemical engineer*

White Plains
Foster, John Horace *consulting environmental engineer*
Freed, Arthur *civil engineer*
Haines, Daniel Webster *engineering consultant, educator*
Mitchell, Robert Dale *consulting engineer*
Westerhoff, Garret Peter *environmental engineer, executive*

Woodstock
Smith, Albert Aloysius, Jr., *electrical engineer, consultant*

Yorktown Heights
Dennard, Robert Heath *engineering executive, scientist*
Hong, Se June *computer engineer*
Zwick, Thomas *electrical engineer*

NORTH CAROLINA

Asheville
Born, Robert Heywood *consulting civil engineer*
Jaslow, Howard *engineer*
Lowery, Douglas Lane *retired environmental engineer*
Moubray, John Mitchell *engineering company executive*
Mustin, Bob *retired civil engineer, writer*

Boonville
Crump, Gwyn Norman *engineer*

Bunn
Boblett, Mark Anthony *civil engineering technician*

Cary
Conrad, Hans *materials engineering educator*
Khan, Masrur Ali *nuclear and chemical engineer, physicist*
Miranda, Constancio Fernandes *civil engineering educator*
Odum, Jeffery Neal *mechanical engineer*
Vick, Columbus Edwin, Jr., *retired civil engineering design firm executive*

Chapel Hill
Kuhn, Matthew *retired engineering company executive*
†Kusy, Robert Peter *biomedical engineering and orthodontics educator*
†Leith, David *engineering educator*
Lucas, Carol Lee *biomedical engineer*
McKinney, Ross Erwin *civil engineering educator*
Okun, Daniel Alexander *environmental engineering educator*
Singer, Philip Charles *environmental engineer, educator*
Stidham, Shaler, Jr., *operations research educator*

Charlotte
Driscoll, John Paul *civil engineer*
Fitzpatrick, James Ward, Jr., *engineering technology educator*
Foss, Ralph Scot *mechanical engineer*
Griffith, Dewey Maurice *mechanical engineer, investor*
Jones, James Richard *mechanical engineer*
Keanini, Russell Guy *mechanical engineering educator, researcher*
King, L. Ellis *civil engineer, educator, consultant*
Rodite, Robert R.R. *engineering scientist*
Valasquez, Joseph Louis *industrial engineer*

Columbus
Brooks, Jerry Claude *safety engineer, educator*

Cullowhee
†Lusky, Jason Francis *electronics engineer*

Durham
†Brady, David Jones *engineering educator, entrepreneur*
Casey, H(orace) Craig, Jr., *electrical engineering educator*

†Gavin, Henri Philippe *engineering educator, researcher*
Guilak, Farshid *biomedical engineering researcher, educator*
Hamaker, Richard Franklin *engineer*
Harman, Charles Morgan *mechanical engineer*
Islam, Farhad Fuad *electronics and computer research engineer*
†Pamula, Vamsee K. *electrical engineer, researcher*
Petroski, Henry *engineer educator, writer*
Plonsey, Robert *electrical and biomedical engineer*
Utku, Senol *civil engineer, computer science educator*
Vatavuk, William Michael *chemical engineer, author*
Wilson, Blake Shaw *electrical engineer, researcher*

Fayetteville
Carwile, Billy Price *computer engineer, civilian military employee*

Flat Rock
Davidson, Clayton Leslie *chemical engineer*

Granite Falls
Humphreys, Kenneth King *engineer, educator, association executive*

Greensboro
Adewuyi, Yusuf Gbadebo *chemical engineering educator, researcher, consultant*
Cazel, Hugh Allen *industrial engineer, educator*
Meyers, Carolyn Winstead *mechanical engineer, educator*
Pai, Devdas Mizar *engineering educator*
Shivakumar, Kunigal Nanjundaiah *aerospace engineer, educator*

Hendersonville
†Thomas, Stephen *retired industrial engineer*

Hickory
Auten, George Robert, Jr., *civil engineer*

Mocksville
Smith, Mark Eugene *architectural engineering service company executive*

Morrisville
†Briggs, Joseph Jay *communications engineer*

Mount Airy
Ratliff, Robert Barns, Jr., *mechanical engineer*

Murphy
Kerr, Walter Belnap *retired missile instrumentation engineer, English language researcher, consultant*

New Bern
Addabbo, Nunzio Philip *civil engineer*
Baughman, Fred Hubbard *aeronautical engineer, former naval officer*
Love, Darryl Lewis *quality engineer*
Moeller, Dade William *environmental engineer, educator*
Painter, Jack Timberlake *civil engineer*
Whitehurst, Brooks Morris *chemical engineer*

Raleigh
†Barrett, Rolin Farrar, Jr., *mechanical engineer, consultant*
Beatty, Kenneth Orion, Jr., *chemical engineer, educator*
Bitzer, Donald Lester *electrical engineering educator, retired research laboratory administrator*
Bourham, Mohamed Abdelhay *nuclear and electrical engineering educator*
Cooper, Stuart Leonard *chemical engineering educator, researcher, consultant*
Dzieduszko, Janusz Wladyslaw *electrical engineer*
Gardner, Robin Pierce *engineering educator*
Hale, Francis Joseph *engineering educator, consultant, retired military officer*
Hauser, John Reid *electrical engineering educator*
Havner, Kerry Shuford *civil engineering and solid mechanics educator*
Hendricks, Leonard Loyed *industrial engineer, public hearing officer*
Hinton, David Owen *retired electrical engineer*
Holton, William Coffeen *electrical engineering executive*
Kolbas, Robert Michael *electrical engineering educator*
Larsen, Ralph Irving *environmental research engineer*
†Lorenc, Steven J. *mechanical engineer*
†Ma, Nancy *mechanical engineer, educator*
Meier, Wilbur Leroy, Jr., *industrial engineer, educator, former university chancellor*
Nelson, Cynthia Kaye *infrastructure security engineer*
Noori, Mohammad Noori *mechanical engineering educator*
Poole, Marion Ronald *civil engineering executive*
Pourbeik, Pouyan *power engineering consultant*
Skaggs, Richard Wayne *agricultural engineering educator*
Sneed, Ronald Ernest *engineering educator emeritus*
Turinsky, Paul Josef *nuclear engineer, educator*
†Velev, Orlin D. *chemical engineer, educator*
Wahls, Harvey Edward *civil engineer, educator*
Wehring, Bernard William *nuclear engineering educator*
Williams, Hugh Alexander, Jr., *retired mechanical engineer, consultant*

Research Triangle Park
Johnson-Payton, Lori Renee *systems engineer*

PROFESSIONAL INDEX 6309 ENGINEERING

Sunset Beach
Mattson, Clarence Russell *safety engineer*

Swannanoa
Stuck, Roger Dean *electrical engineering educator*

Washington
Hackney, James Acra, III, *industrial engineer, consultant, retired manufacturing company executive*

Willow Spring
Grantham, Donald James *chemical engineer, educator, author*

Winston Salem
†Bayram, Ersin *electrical engineer, researcher*
Bourne, Henry Clark, Jr., *electrical engineering educator, former academic official*
Henderson, Richard Martin *retired chemical engineer*

NORTH DAKOTA

Fargo
†Danescu, Radu Ioan *engineering educator*
Helweg, Otto Jennings *civil engineer, educator*
Li, Kam Wu *mechanical engineer, educator*
†Lin, Wei *civil engineer, educator*
Rogers, David Anthony *electrical engineer, educator, researcher*
Varma, Amiy *civil engineer, educator*

OHIO

Akron
Brown, David Rupert *engineering executive*
Fatemi, Ray S. *mechanical engineer, consultant*
Fertis, Demeter George *civil engineering educator*
Haritos, George Konstantinos *engineer, educator, military officer*
Isayev, Avraam Isayevich *polymer engineer, educator*
Pipes, Robert Byron *mechanical engineer, educator*
Sancaktar, Erol *engineering educator*
Symens, Ronald Edwin *electrical engineer, consultant*

Athens
†Bayless, David J. *engineer*
Dinos, Nicholas *engineering educator, administrator*
Irwin, Richard Dennis *electrical engineering educator*
McFarland, Richard H. *engineering educator, pilot*
Robe, Thurlow Richard *engineering educator, university dean*

Aurora
Kirchner, James William *retired electrical engineer*

Barberton
Kitto, John Buck, Jr., *mechanical engineer*
Wietzke, Donald *industrial engineer*

Batavia
Bower, Kenneth Francis *electrical engineer*

Brecksville
†Forsyth, T. Henry *plastic researcher*

Canton
Pedoto, Gerald Joseph *supplier quality analyst*

Chandlersville
Herron, Janet Irene *industrial manufacturing engineer*

Cincinnati
Agrawal, Dharma Prakash *engineering educator*
Bahr, Donald Walter *retired chemical engineer*
†Barrett, William Martin *environmental engineer, chemical engineer, researcher*
Bluestein, Paul Harold *management engineer*
†Bruno, David Joseph, Jr., *chemical engineer, researcher*
Greenberg, David Bernard *chemical engineering educator*
Hantush, Mohamed M. *hydrologist, researcher*
Hersman, Fernando William (Ferd Hersman) *retired engineering executive*
Hodge, Bobby Lynn *mechanical engineer, manufacturing executive*
Isaacs, S. Ted *engineering executive*
Kowel, Stephen Thomas *electrical engineer, educator*
Lim, Teik C. *engineering educator, consultant*
Liu, Yijun *engineering educator, researcher*
†Madson, Philip Ward *engineering executive, consultant*
Martin, John Bruce *chemical engineer*
Morgan, William Richard *mechanical engineer*
Pan, Zigang *engineering educator*
Pancheri, Eugene Joseph *chemical engineer*
Ratliff, Thomas Asbury, Jr., *retired engineer*
Rubin, Stanley Gerald *aerospace engineering educator*
Toftner, Richard Orville *engineering executive*
Vinciguerra, Thomas Michael *chemical engineer*
Weisman, Joel *nuclear engineering educator, engineering consultant*
†Wisler, David Charles *aerospace engineer, educator*

Cleveland
Angus, John Cotton *chemical engineering educator*
Anthony, Donald Barrett *engineering executive*
Bahniuk, Eugene *mechanical engineering educator*
Burghart, James Henry *electrical engineer, educator*
†Choi, Sung Rak *mechanical engineer, researcher*
†DellaCorte, Christopher *engineer, tribologist*
†Del Rosario, Ruben *mechanical engineer, researcher*
Fernandez, René *aerospace engineer*
Gyekenyesi, John Paul *mechanical engineer*
Harkins, Richard Wesley *marine engineer, naval architect*
Heuer, Arthur Harold *ceramics engineer, educator*
†Hottel, Jerry W. *engineering executive, consultant*
Jaczkowski, Frank Stanislaus *retired civil engineer*
Ko, Wen-Hsiung *electrical engineering educator*
Madden, James D. *forensic engineer*
Merat, Francis Lawrence *engineering educator*
†Olson, Sandra *aerospace engineer*
Olson, Sandra Lee *aerospace engineer, research scientist*
†Oyama, Akira *aerospace engineer, researcher*
Papachristou, Christos A. *engineering educator*
†Povinelli, Louis A. *aeronautical engineer*
Reshotko, Eli *aerospace engineer, educator*
Rudy, Yoram *biomedical engineer, biophysicist, educator*
Saada, Adel Selim *civil engineer, educator*
Savinell, Robert Francis *engineering educator*
Seikel, George R. *research engineer*
Tavakoli, Amir *civil engineer, educator*
Wilson, Jack *aeronautical engineer*
Xiong, Fuqin *electrical engineering educator*

Cleveland Heights
Mofflin, Lionel Hugh (Harry Mofflin) *biomedical engineer, physician*

Columbus
†Adeli, Hojjat *engineer, educator, computer scientist*
Alexander, Carl Albert *ceramic engineer, educator*
Altan, Taylan *engineering educator, mechanical engineer, consultant*
Arps, David Foster *electronics engineer*
Bailey, Cecil Dewitt *aerospace engineer, educator*
Bechtel, Stephen E. *mechanical engineer, educator*
Bhushan, Bharat *mechanical engineer*
Brodkey, Robert Stanley *chemical engineering educator*
Catalyurek, Umit Veysel *computer engineer, researcher*
Cruz, Jose Bejar, Jr., *engineering educator, educator*
Duckworth, Winston Howard *retired ceramic engineer*
Ensminger, Dale *mechanical engineer, electrical engineer*
Farson, Dave Forest *engineering educator*
Fenton, Robert Earl *electrical engineering educator*
Gozon, Jozsef Stephan *engineering educator*
Grant, Michael Peter *electrical engineer*
Gutman, Richard *electrical engineer*
Hadipriono, Fabian Christy *engineering educator, researcher*
Harris, Ronald David *chemical engineer*
Houser, Donald Russell *mechanical engineering educator, consultant*
Jacox, John William *retired mechanical engineer and consulting company executive*
Keaney, William Regis *engineering and construction services executive, consultant*
Ksienski, Aharon Arthur *electrical engineer*
Malguarnera, Salvatore Chris *mechanical engineer*
Miller, Don Wilson *nuclear engineering educator*
Moulton, Edward Quentin *civil engineer, educator*
†Ogras, Umit Yusuf *electrical engineer*
Ozkan, Umit Sivrioglu *chemical engineering educator*
Peters, Leon, Jr., *electrical engineering educator, research administrator*
Rapp, Robert Anthony *metallurgical engineering educator, consultant*
Rich, Joseph William *engineering educator, consultant*
Rubin, Alan J. *environmental engineer, chemist, photgrapher*
St. Pierre, George Roland, Jr., *materials science and engineering administrator, educator*
Singh, Rajendra *mechanical engineering educator*
Smith, Philip John *industrial and systems engineering educator*
Taiganides, E. Paul *agricultural and environmental engineer, consultant*
Uotila, Urho Antti Kalevi *geodesist, educator*
Volakis, John Leonidas *engineering educator*
Ware, Brendan John *retired electrical engineer and utility executive*
Whitlatch, Elbert Earl, Jr., *engineering educator, consultant*
†Xie, Chunlei *applied mechanics researcher*
Zakin, Jacques Louis *chemical engineering educator*
Zhu, Xiankui *mechanical engineer, researcher*

Concord
†Kushalkumar, M. Baid *chemical engineer*

Continental
Dranchak, Lawrence John *retired mechanical engineer*

Dayton
Bogner, Fred Karl *civil engineering educator*
Carson, Richard McKee *chemical engineer*
Cowden, Roger Hugh, II, *systems engineer*
Houpis, Constantine Harry *electrical engineering educator*
Kazimierczuk, Marian Kazimierczuk *electrical engineer, educator*
Kumar, Binod *materials engineer, educator*
†Mukhopadhyay, Sharmila Mitra *materials engineer, educator*
Phillips, Chandler Allen *biomedical/human factors engineer*
Repperger, Daniel William *electrical engineer*
Schmitt, George Frederick, Jr., *materials engineer*
Soon, Boon Yi *engineer*

Delaware
Arnold, Jay *retired engineering executive, educator*

Dublin
Major, Coleman Joseph *chemical engineer*

Eastlake
Spohn, Wayne Robert *mechanical engineer*

Elyria
Dunaevsky, Valery *mechanical engineer, researcher*

Fairborn
Conklin, Robert Eugene *electronics engineer*

Fairfield
†Walsh, Thomas James *environmental engineer, consultant*

Gates Mills
Enyedy, Gustav, Jr., *chemical engineer*
Pace, Stanley Carter *retired aeronautical engineer*

Lakeside Marblehead
Haering, Edwin Raymond *chemical engineering educator, consultant*

Logan
Carmean, Jerry Richard *broadcast engineer*

Mansfield
Burnell, Elvin Wallace *industrial engineer, security specialist*
Miller, Kenneth William, II, *research and development engineering executive*
Sheridan, Mark William *mechanical engineer, strategic planner*
Stander, Richard Ramsay, Sr., *retired civil engineer and construction engineer*

Marysville
Baik-Kromalic, Sue S. *metallurgical engineer*

Mayfield Heights
Grants, Valdis *engineering manager*

Medina
Kenat, Thomas Arthur *chemical engineer, consultant*

Mentor
†Benjamin, Michael Anthony *engineer*

Miamisburg
Haigh, Peter Leslie *software company executive, consultant*

Middletown
Newby, John Robert *metallurgical engineer*

North Olmsted
Bluford, Guion Stewart, Jr., *engineering company executive*
Lundin, Bruce Theodore *engineering and management consultant*

Ostrander
Smith, Rick A. *mechanical engineer, consultant*

Oxford
Ward, Roscoe Fredrick *engineering educator*

Perrysburg
Khan, Amir U. *agricultural engineering consultant*

Poland
Murphy, Thomas Michael *civil engineer*

Rocky River
Masters, Albert Townsend *mechanical engineer*

Shauck
Garvick, Kenneth Ryan *broadcast engineer, announcer, educator*

Springboro
Saxer, Richard Karl *metallurgical engineer, retired air force officer*

Springfield
Moore, Florian Howard *retired electronics engineer*

Strongsville
Mills, S. Loren *product safety manager, engineer*

Tallmadge
Turner, Richard L. *retired computer software engineer*

Toledo
Benham, Linda Sue *civil engineer*
Diehl, Dean R. *engineering company executive*
†Fetzer, Derek *industrial engineer, consultant*
Randolph, Brian Walter *civil engineer, educator*
Wolfe, Robert Kenneth *engineering educator*
Wolff, Edwin Ray *retired construction engineer, consultant*

Wadsworth
Atwood, Glenn Arthur *engineer, educator*
Brumbaugh, John A., Jr., *electrical engineer*

West Chester
Mital, Anil *engineering educator*

Westerville
Bigg, Donald Michael *chemical engineer*
Giannamore, David Michael *electronics engineer*

Westlake
Huff, Ronald Garland *mechanical engineer*

Wickliffe
Scott, Christopher G. *metallurgical engineer, researcher*

Wilberforce
†Elali, Taan *engineering and computer science educator*

Wooster
Marathe, Bhaskar *development engineer*

Worthington
Compton, Ralph Theodore, Jr., *electrical engineering educator*
Wu, Tien Hsing *civil engineering educator, consulting engineer*

Wright Patterson Afb
†Babish, Charles A., IV, *aerospace engineer*
Blasch, Erik Philip *research engineer, Air Force officer*
Goltz, Mark Neil *environmental engineer*
†Mall, Shankar *engineering mechanics educator, researcher*
Wallace, Robert Luther, II, *engineer*

Yellow Springs
Trolander, Hardy Wilcox *engineering executive, consultant*

Youngstown
†Cernica, John N. *engineering educator, civil engineer, consultant*
Fok, Thomas Dso Yun *civil engineer*
Kenner, Marilyn Sferra *civil engineer*
Lacivita, Michael John *safety engineer*

OKLAHOMA

Bartlesville
Gao, Hong Wen *retired chemical engineer*
Johnson, Marvin Merrill *chemical engineer, chemist*
Lai, Young-Jou *industrial engineer*
Mihm, John Clifford *chemical engineer*
Olsen, David K. *engineer, chemist*

Bethany
Arnold, Donald Smith *chemical engineer, consultant*

Buffalo
Anthony, Jack Ramon *mechanical engineer, retired*

Collinsville
Councilman, Richard Robert *product development engineer*

Jenks
Leming, W(illiam) Vaughn *electronics engineer*

Midwest City
Smith, Wayne Calvin *chemical engineer, consultant*

Muskogee
Tobin, Thomas Edward, Jr., *civil engineer*

Norman
Aligizaki, Kalliopi K. *civil engineer, educator*
Altan, M(ustafa) Cengiz *mechanical engineering educator*
Atiquzzaman, Mohammed *engineering educator*
Bagajewicz, Miguel *engineering educator*
Bert, Charles Wesley *mechanical and aerospace engineer, educator*
Campbell, John Morgan *retired chemical engineer*
Hughes, Richard Gary *engineering educator*
Mallinson, Richard Gregory *chemical engineering educator*
O'Rear, Edgar Allen, III, *chemical engineering educator*
†Striz, Alfred Gerhard *aerospace engineer, educator*
Zelby, Leon Wolf *electrical engineering educator, consulting engineer*

Oklahoma City
Kindschuh, Jeffery Alan *civil engineer*
Lovelace, George David, Jr., *quality engineer*
Mikkelson, Dean Harold *geological engineer, writer*
Miller, Herbert Dell *petroleum engineer*

Park Hill
Lindsey, James Kendall *civil engineer*

Perry
Gard, Michael Floyd *research engineer*

Ponca City
Gong, Xiaoyi *engineer*

Stillwater
Brusewitz, Gerald Henry *agricultural engineering educator, researcher*
Hoberock, Lawrence Linden *mechanical engineer, educator*
Komanduri, Ranga *engineering educator*

†Lu, Hongbing *aerospace engineer, consultant*
Mize, Joe Henry *industrial engineer, educator*
Ndegwa, Pius Mwangi *agricultural engineer, researcher*
Thompson, David Russell *engineering educator, academic dean*

Tulsa
Allwein, Robert William *mechanical engineer*
Baukal, Charles Edward, Jr., *mechanical engineer*
Blenkarn, Kenneth Ardley *mechanical engineer, consultant*
Cobbs, James Harold *engineer, consultant*
Earlougher, Robert Charles, Sr., *petroleum engineer*
Ferrell, Howard Hulen *retired petroleum engineer*
Fleifil, Mahmoud Mohamed *acoustics engineer, researcher*
McAdams, Jason David *mechanical engineer*
Parker, Robert Lee, Sr., *petroleum engineer, drilling company executive*
Prayson, Alex Stephen *design engineering educator*
Williams, John Horter *civil engineer, oil, gas, telecommunications and allied products distribution company executive*

OREGON

Beaverton
Cassidy, Richard Arthur *environmental engineer, governmental water resources specialist*
Chartier, Vernon Lee *electrical engineer*
Edlich, Richard French *biomedical engineering educator*

Bend
Amber, Rich *manufacturing engineer*
†Löffler, Daniel G. *chemical engineer, researcher*

Brookings
Nolan, Benjamin Burke *retired civil engineer*

Corvallis
Engelbrecht, Rudolf *electrical engineering educator*
Forbes, Leonard *engineering educator*
Howland, James Chase *retired engineer, consultant*
Miner, John Ronald *bioengineer*
Rapier, Pascal Moran *chemical engineer, physicist*
Temes, Gabor Charles *electrical engineering educator*

Eugene
Richards, James William *electromechanical engineer*

Florence
Ericksen, Jerald Laverne *retired engineering scientist, educator*

Hillsboro
†Jones, Robert Brent *electrical engineer*
†Moon, In-Ho *electrical engineer, researcher*

Hood River
†Hederstrom, Matt *engineer*

Klamath Falls
Lomas, Charles Gardner *engineering educator, retired, psychotherapist*
Woodall, David Monroe *research engineer, dean*

Lake Oswego
Gehrig, Edward Harry *electrical engineer, consultant*
Kovtynovich, Dan *civil engineer*

Medford
Horton, Lawrence Stanley *electrical engineer, apartment developer*

Myrtle Point
Walsh, Don *marine consultant, executive*

Portland
Chrzanowska-Jeske, Malgorzata Ewa *electrical engineering educator, consultant*
Kennedy, R(obert) Evan *engineering executive, consultant, retired structural engineer*
Khalil, Mohammad Aslam Khan *environmental science and engineering educator, physics educator*
Kocaoglu, Dundar F. *engineering management educator, industrial and civil engineer*
Lall, B. Kent *civil engineer, educator*
McCoy, Eugene Lynn *civil engineer*
Perkowski, Marek Andrzej *electrical engineering educator*
Pham, Kinh Dinh *electrical engineer, educator, administrator*
Yamaguchi, Tadanori *electrical engineer*
Yamayee, Zia Ahmad *engineering educator, dean*

Salem
Butts, Edward Perry *civil engineer, environmental consultant*
Dixon, Robert Gene *retired manufacturing engineering educator, retired mechanical engineering company executive*

Springfield
Pearson, John Mark *civil and structural engineer*

Sunriver
Clough, Ray William, Jr., *civil engineering educator*

Tualatin
Webster, Merlyn Hugh, Jr., *manufacturing engineer, information systems consultant*

Wilsonville
Isberg, Reuben Albert *radio communications engineer*

Woodburn
Oliver, Madison E. *retired engineering executive, mechanical engineer*

PENNSYLVANIA

Acme
Randza, Jason Michael *engineer*

Alcoa Center
Yeh, Jieh Ren *engineer*

Allentown
Agrawal, Rakesh *industrial researcher*
Buck, Daniel Michael *engineering executive*
Foster, Edward Paul (Ted Foster) *process industries executive*
†Gaensler, Tomas Fritz *engineering executive*
Gewartowski, James Walter *retired electrical engineer*
Hansel, James Gordon *engineer, educator*
Lesak, David Michael *safety engineer, educator, consultant*
Linden, David Hugh *engineering executive*
†Moore, Robert Byron *chemical engineer, consultant*

Allison Park
†Lagnese, Joseph F. *environmental engineer*
Preik, Michelle Letitia Petruna *engineer*

Annville
Carlson, Scott Henery *electrical engineer*

Apollo
Musselman, Larry L. *chemical engineer*

Bala Cynwyd
Staley, Kenneth Bernard *civil engineer*

Beaver
Vogeley, Clyde Eicher, Jr., *engineering educator, artist, consultant*

Beaver Falls
Shaw, David William *engineering educator*

Berwyn
Lund, George Edward *retired electrical engineer*

Bethel Park
Korchynsky, Michael *metallurgical engineer*
O'Donnell, Thomas P. *mechanical engineer*

Bethlehem
Anderson, David Martin *environmental health scientist, environmental engineer*
Beedle, Lynn Simpson *civil engineering educator*
Chen, John C. *chemical engineering educator*
Durkee, Jackson Leland *civil engineer*
Fisher, John William *civil engineering educator*
Frey, Doug R. *electrical engineering educator, consultant*
Jain, Himanshu *materials science engineering educator*
Karakash, John J. *engineering educator*
McGeady, Leon Joseph *engineer, educator*
Mirro, John *engineering company executive*
Neti, Sudhakar *mechanical engineering educator*
Ostapenko, Alexis *civil engineer, educator*
Pense, Alan Wiggins *metallurgical engineer, academic administrator*
Roberts, Richard *mechanical engineering educator*
Tuzla, Kemal *mechanical engineer, scientist*
Wachs, Israel Ephraim *chemical engineering educator*

Birdsboro
Mengle, Tobi Dara *mechanical engineer, consultant*

Blue Bell
Staplin, David Earl *civil engineer*

Boalsburg
Gettig, Martin Winthrop *retired mechanical engineer*

Bridgeville
Andersen, Theodore Selmer *engineering manager*

Carnegie
Moretti, Edward Charles *environmental engineer, consultant*

Chadds Ford
Isakoff, Sheldon Erwin *chemical engineer*

Chalfont
†Brown, Richard Eric *electrical engineer, consultant*

Cheltenham
Weinstock, Walter Wolfe *systems engineer*

Cheswick
Nair, Bala Radhakrishnan *engineer*

Clearfield
Singh, Shiwendra Prasad *civil engineer*

Cooksburg
Meley, Robert Wayne *structural and storage tank engineer*

Coopersburg
Bolle, Donald Martin *retired engineering educator*

Matulevicius, Edward *engineering company executive, consultant*
Peserik, James E. *electrical, controls and computer engineer, consultant, forensics and safety engineer, fire cause and origin investigator*
Siess, Alfred Albert, Jr., *engineering executive, management consultant*

Coraopolis
Aichbhaumik, Dibyajyoti *metallurgical engineer*
Kay, George Paul *environmental engineer*

Cuddy
Pearlman, Seth Leonard *civil engineer*

Danville
†Cheung, Joseph Yat-Sing *biomedical scientist, nephrologist*

Easton
Viscomi, B. Vincent *civil engineer*

Ebensburg
Ramsdell, Richard Adoniram *marine engineer*

Edinboro
Patterson, John Keith *civil engineer, consultant*

Erie
Crankshaw, John Hamilton *mechanical engineer*
Dockstader, Emmett Stanley *engineer, construction executive*
Gruenwald, Geza *plastics consultant*

Fort Washington
Visek, Albert James *semi-retired computer engineer*

Glen Mills
Churchill, Stuart Winston *chemical engineering educator*

Glenside
Hargens, Charles William, III, *electrical engineer, consultant*

Harrisburg
Dietz, John Raphael *consulting engineer executive*

Hershey
†Collins, Christopher Michael *engineering educator*

Huntingdon Valley
†Abend, Kenneth *electrical engineer*
Goff, Kenneth Wade *electrical engineer*
West, A(rnold) Sumner *chemical engineer*

Indiana
Soule, Robert D. *safety and health educator, administrator*

Irwin
Kuhn, Howard Arthur *engineering executive, educator*

Jamison
Touhill, C. Joseph *environmental engineer*

Jeannette
LaFave, Richard *engineer, consultant*

Johnstown
†Depra, Alan Jay *mechanical engineer*

King Of Prussia
Abbott, Henry James *electro-mechanical engineer*
Hegedus, L. Louis *chemical engineer, research and development executive*
†Lee, Robert *engineer*
Spielvogel, Lawrence George *engineer*

Kulpsville
DiDomizio, Robert Anthony, Jr., *mechanical engineer*

Kutztown
Messics, Mark Craig *civil engineer*

Lancaster
Ebersole, J. Glenn, Jr., *engineering, marketing, management and public relations executive*
Hoffer, Roy *forensic electrical engineer, fire and explosion analyst*

Lewisburg
Aldrich, Robert Adams *agricultural engineer, consultant*
Kim, Jai Bin *civil engineering educator*
Knisely, Charles William, Jr., *engineering educator, researcher, consultant*
Lowe, John Raymond, Jr., *mechanical engineer*
Orbison, James Graham *civil engineer, educator*

Ligonier
Mattern, Gerry A. *engineering consultant*

Lower Burrell
Nordmark, Glenn Everett *civil engineer*

Macungie
Dwyer, John James *mechanical engineer*

Meadville
Gilles, Bruce Carlson *civil engineer*

Mechanicsburg
Murphy, Stephan David *electrical engineer*

Media
McDonnell, Leo Francis *engineer, consultant*

Mercer
Zellers, Robert Charles *materials engineer, consultant, speaker*

Merion Station
Coppa, Anthony Patrick *engineer, consultant*

Monroeville
Di Gioia, Anthony Michael, Jr., *civil engineer, business executive*
Hribar, John Anthony *civil engineer, consultant*
Jacobi, William Mallett *nuclear engineer, consultant*
Mandel, Herbert Maurice *civil engineer*
Schlesser, Thomas Piper *civil engineer*

Montgomeryville
Potsko, Maureen Kathryn *chemical engineer*

Moon Township
Rabosky, Joseph George *engineering consulting company executive*

Morrisville
Stabenau, Walter Frank *systems engineer*

Murrysville
McWhirter, James Herman *consulting engineering business executive, financial planner*

Nazareth
Bader, William Alan *computer engineer*

New Alexandria
Ackerman, Robert Lloyd *chemical engineer, environmental tree farmer*

New Kensington
Jarrett, Noel *chemical engineer, researcher*

Newtown
Schroeder, Alfred Christian *electronics research engineer*
Woods, Howard James, Jr., *civil engineer*

Newtown Square
Lang, Lothar A. *engineer*
Perrone, Nicholas *mechanical engineer, business executive*

Norristown
†Dat, Manabendra Nath *civil engineer, consultant*

North Wales
Napier, Thomas M. *electrical engineer*

Petersburg
White, Elizabeth Loczi *academic researcher, civil engineer*

Philadelphia
Bajscy, Ruzena *computer engineer*
Barsoum, Michel W. *materials engineer, educator*
Brooks, Robert Mark *civil engineer, educator*
Byer, Harold George *civil/environmental engineer*
Cohen, Ira Myron *aeronautical and mechanical engineering educator*
El-Sherif, Mahmoud A. *electrical engineering educator*
Engheta, Nader *electrical engineering educator, researcher*
Falkie, Thomas Victor *mining engineer, mining executive*
Flicker, Eric Lee *civil engineer, consultant*
Hahn, Peter Mathias *electrical engineer, consultant*
Jaron, Dov *biomedical engineer, educator*
Koch, Carl Mark *environmental engineering executive*
Kritikos, Haralambos Nicholas *electrical engineering educator*
Kunkel, George A., Jr., *civil engineer*
Kuruvilla, Kollanparampil *electrical engineer*
Lawley, Alan *materials engineering educator*
†Lepore, John Anthony *engineering educator*
Lewin, Peter Andrew *electrical engineer, educator*
Litt, Mitchell *chemical engineer, educator, bioengineer*
Morlok, Edward Karl *engineering educator, consultant*
Mulford, Richard Albert *mechanical engineer, professional society administrator*
Ponte-Castañeda, Pedro *mechanical engineering educator*
Popovics, Sandor *civil engineer, educator, researcher*
Quinn, John Albert *chemical engineering educator*
Rumpf, John Louis *civil engineer, consultant*
Schwan, Herman Paul *electrical engineering and physical science educator, research scientist*
†Seider, Warren D. *engineering educator*
Siderer, Jack Philip *engineering executive*
Sun, Hun H. *electrical engineering and biomedical engineering educator*
Terzian, Karnig Yervant *civil engineer*
Tomiyasu, Kiyo *consulting engineer*
Van der Spiegel, Jan *engineering educator*
Winey, Karen I. *engineering educator, researcher*

Phoenixville
Rippel, Harry Conrad *mechanical engineer, consultant*

Pittsburgh
Bergmann, Carl Adolf *chemical engineer, researcher*
Bloom, William Millard *furnace design engineer*
†Borovetz, Harvey Selwyn *biomedical engineer, educator*
Casasent, David Paul *electrical engineering educator, data processing executive*

†Cendes, Zoltan Joseph *electrical engineer, educator*
Charap, Stanley Harvey *electrical engineering educator*
Chelemer, Harold *engineering educator, consultant*
Chiu, Chao-Lin *civil engineer*
Conti, Ronald Samuel *electronics engineer, fire prevention engineer*
†Desai, Niranjan A. *chemical engineer*
Dubaniewicz, Thomas H., Jr., *electrical engineer, bioengineer*
Griffin, Donald Spray *mechanical engineer, consultant*
Grossmann, Ignacio Emilio *chemical engineering educator*
Hendrickson, Chris Thompson *civil and environmental engineering educator, researcher*
Hoburg, James Frederick *electrical engineering educator*
Humphrey, Watts Sherman *technical executive, author*
Jordan, Angel Goni *electrical and computer engineering educator*
†Kadow, Clemens Martin Joachim *engineer, researcher*
Kitzes, Arnold S. *retired chemical engineer, retired nuclear engineer*
Kryder, Mark Howard *computer and electrical engineering executive, educator, consultant*
Kumar, Vijaya Bhagavatula *electrical engineering educator, consultant*
Li, Ching-Chung *electrical engineering and computer science educator*
Mann, Alfred N. *chemical engineer*
McAvoy, Bruce Ronald *engineer, consultant*
Meiksin, Zvi H. *electrical engineering educator*
Mickle, Marlin Homer *electrical engineer, educator*
Milnes, Arthur George *electrical engineer, educator*
Morrison, L. Warren *computer engineer*
Moura, José Manuel Fonseca *electrical engineer, educator*
Nastac, Laurentiu *materials and metallurgy engineer*
Neuman, Charles P. *electrical and computer engineering educator*
O'Donnell, William James *engineering executive*
Pease, Robert Barnard *civil engineer*
Peterson, Robert Scott *electrical engineer*
Pettit, Frederick Sidney *metallurgical engineering educator, researcher*
Pohland, Frederick George *environmental engineering educator, researcher*
Quimpo, Rafael Gonzales *civil engineering educator*
†Rabin, Yoed *biomedical engineer, consultant*
Reznik, Alan A. *petroleum engineering educator*
Russell, Alan James *chemical engineering and biotechnology educator*
Schultz, Jerome Samson *biochemical engineer, educator*
Simaan, Marwan *electrical engineering educator*
Stahl, Laddie L. *electrical engineer, manufacturing company executive*
Tierney, John William *chemical engineering educator*
†Trumble, Dennis Robert *biomedical engineer*
Wesner, John William *engineering educator*
Westerberg, Arthur William *chemical engineering educator*
Williams, Lisle Edward *civil, planning and structural engineer*
†Woo, Savio Lau-Yuen *bioengineering educator*
Yang, Wen-Ching *chemical engineer*

Radnor
McCluskey, Gayla Jacque *health, safety and environmental executive*

Reading
Hollander, Herbert I. *consulting engineer*
Lacki, Allan Vincent *industrial engineer*
Moriarty, John Klinge *electronics engineer, consultant*

Ridgway
Redmount, Melvin Berr *chemical engineer, consultant*

Shady Grove
†Schoonmaker, Stephen J. *mechanical engineer*

Shillington
†Lidman, William G. *mechanical engineer, consultant*

Shippensburg
White, David Lawrence *marketing professional*

Spring Grove
Todorovic, John *chemical engineer*

State College
Barnoff, Robert Mark *civil engineering educator*
Cannon, Frederick Scott *water engineer, educator, consultant*
Foderaro, Anthony Harolde *nuclear engineering educator*
Grimes, Dale Mills *physics and electrical engineering educator*
Maneval, David Richard *mineral engineering consultant*
†Mutmansky, Jan M. *retired engineering educator, consultant*
Olson, Donald Richard *mechanical engineering educator*
Petrie, Howard Lane *engineer, researcher*
Shaikh, Nazrul Islam *industrial engineer, researcher*
Sibul, Leon Henry *electrical engineer*
†Sinha, Sunil K. *engineer, educator*

Swarthmore
Krendel, Ezra Simon *systems and human factors engineering consultant*

Tionesta
Martincic, John Edward *engineering executive*

Trout Run
Nelson, Richard Lloyd *systems engineer, consultant*

University Park
Aplan, Frank Fulton *metallurgical engineering educator*
Austin, Leonard George *mineral engineer*
Bose, Nirmal Kumar *electrical engineering, mathematics educator*
Brown, John Lawrence, Jr., *electrical engineering educator*
†Danner, Ronald Paul *chemical engineering educator*
Davids, Norman *engineering science and mechanics educator, researcher*
Duda, John Larry *chemical engineering educator*
†Ertekin, Turgay *petroleum engineer educator, researcher, consultant*
Feng, Tse-yun *computer engineer, educator*
Grimes, Craig Alan *electrical engineering educator*
†Guo, Ruyan *engineering educator, researcher*
Holl, John William *engineering educator*
Kabel, Robert Lynn *chemical engineering educator*
Knott, Kenneth *engineering educator, consultant, expert witness*
Lauchle, Gerald Clyde *acoustics educator*
McCormick, Barnes Warnock *aerospace engineering educator*
McDonnell, Archie Joseph *environmental engineer*
Mentzer, John Raymond *electrical engineer, educator*
†Modest, Michael Fritz *mechanical engineering educator*
Nisbet, John Stirling *electrical engineering educator*
Ramani, Raja Venkat *mining engineering educator*
Rotz, C. Alan *agricultural engineer, educator*
Ruud, Clayton Olaf *engineering educator*
Scanlon, Andrew *structural engineering educator*
Thompson, William, Jr., *engineering educator*
†Tikalsky, Paul J. *civil engineering educator, structural engineer*
Tittmann, Bernhard Rainer *engineering science and mechanics educator*
Vannice, M. Albert *chemical engineering educator, researcher*
†Vennam, Venkata Surya Prakash *engineering educator, researcher*
Ventura, Jose Antonio *industrial engineer, educator, researcher*
Webb, Ralph Lee *mechanical engineering educator*
Witzig, Warren Frank *nuclear engineer, educator*
Wysk, Richard A. *engineering educator, researcher*

Verona
Koch, Robert Wotring *chemical engineer*

Villanova
McLaughlin, Philip VanDoren, Jr., *mechanical engineering educator, researcher, consultant*
Ray, Eva Konig *biomedical consultant*
Tomlinson, J. Richard *engineering services company executive*

Wallingford
Parker, Jennifer Ware *chemical engineer, researcher*

Warminster
Sibley, Lewis Branch *engineering executive*
Tatnall, George Jacob *aeronautical engineer*

Waynesboro
Martin, Harold G. *engineering consultant*

West Conshohocken
Hochreiter, Joseph Christian, Jr., *engineering company executive*

West Grove
Fuller, Jack Glendon, Jr., *retired plastics engineer*

West Mifflin
Ardash, Garin *mechanical engineer*
Aumiller, David *nuclear engineer*

West Point
Buckland, Barry Christopher *chemical engineer*
†Lee, Jonghwi *chemical engineer, researcher*

Wexford
Hartwig, Thomas Leo *civil engineer, environmental engineer, sports association administrator*
Reid, Robert H. *engineering consultant*

White Haven
Velzy, Charles O. *mechanical engineer*

Willow Grove
Chatterjee, Hem Chandra *electrical engineer*

York
Clautice, Edward Wellmore *retired industrial engineer*
Horn, Russell Eugene *engineering executive, consultant*
Miller, Donald Kenneth *engineering consultant*

RHODE ISLAND

Bristol
Danzberger, Alexander Harris *chemical engineer, consultant*

Fiskeville
Mc Feeley, John Jay *chemical engineer*

Kingston
Lee, Kang-Won Wayne *engineer, educator*

Newport
Ehrlich, Stanley Leonard *acoustical engineer, consultant*
†Korolenko, Kyrill V. *electrical engineer*
Lynch, Robert Stephen, Jr., *electrical engineer, researcher and developer*

North Kingstown
Andraka, Raymond Joseph *digital electronics design engineer, consultant*

Pawtucket
Bose, Kingshuk *research engineer*

Portsmouth
Becken, Bradford Albert *engineering executive*

Providence
Dobbins, Richard Andrew *engineering educator, researcher*
Freund, Lambert Ben *engineering educator, researcher, consultant*
Furland, Joseph *engineering educator*
Glicksman, Maurice *engineering educator, former dean and provost*
Hazeltine, Barrett *electrical engineer, educator*
Khrushchev, Sergei Nikitich *engineering educator, educator*
Needleman, Alan *mechanical engineering educator*
Richman, Marc Herbert *forensic engineer, educator*
Suuberg, Eric Michael *chemical engineering educator*
Symonds, Paul Southworth *mechanical engineering educator, researcher*
Weiner, Jerome Harris *mechanical engineering educator*

Wakefield
†Boothroyd, Geoffrey *industrial and manufacturing engineering educator*

Warwick
Baffoni, Frank Anthony *biomedical engineer, consultant, internist*
Berube, Richard Henry *electrical engineering educator, consultant*

SOUTH CAROLINA

Aiken
Hootman, Harry Edward *retired nuclear engineer, consultant*
Murphy, Edward Thomas *engineering executive*
Silton, Ronald Helmut *electrical engineer*
Zirps, George Thomas *marine engineer, consultant*

Anderson
Rich, Linvil Gene *civil engineering educator*

Beaufort
†Fielder, William James, III, *electrical engineer, consultant*
Pinkerton, Robert Bruce *mechanical engineer*

Blythewood
Falcone, Anthony *mechanical engineer*

Camden
†Sindler, Allan Jay *chemical engineer, sculptor, educator*

Central
Jalili, Nader *mechanical engineer, educator*

Charleston
Bolin, Edmund Mike *electrical engineer, franchise engineering consultant*
Chapman, Howard Reed *city and county transportation engineer, consultant*

Clemson
Amirkhanian, Serji N. *civil engineering educator*
Golan, Lawrence Peter *mechanical engineering educator, energy researcher*
Goodwin, James Gordon, Jr., *engineering educator, consultant, researcher*
Grady, C.P. Leslie, Jr., *engineering educator*
†Harrell, William Rodney *electronics engineer*
Leonard, Michael Steven *industrial engineering educator*
Mino, Michael George *engineering executive*
Paul, Frank Waters *mechanical engineer, educator, consultant*
Pursley, Michael Bader *electrical engineering educator, communications systems research and consulting*
Williamson, Robert Elmore *engineering educator*
Xu, Xiao-Bang *engineering educator*
Zumbrunnen, David Arnold *mechanical engineering and materials science educator, consultant*

Columbia
Baskin, C. R. *retired civil engineer, physical scientist*
Gadala-Maria, Francis Arturo *chemical engineering educator*
Gibbons, Joseph Harrison *engineering educator, farmer*
†Graulty, Robert Thomas *engineer, consultant*
Linyard, Samuel Edward Goldsmith *retired civil engineer*
Reid, Claude G. *engineer, consultant*
Shatalov, Maxim S. *electrical engineer, researcher*
†Weidner, John Walter *chemical engineer, educator*
White, Ralph Edward *chemical engineer, educator*

Edisto Island
Cannon, David C. *mechanical engineer, consultant*

Elgin
Ladmer, William Edward *food product engineering executive*

Goose Creek
Floss, Mark Thaddeus *civil engineer, computer scientist*

Greenville
Omidvar, Bijan *structural engineer, researcher*
Plumstead, William Charles *quality engineer, consultant*
Wang, Ming De *engineer*

Hartsville
Menius, Espie Flynn, Jr., *electrical engineer*

Hilton Head Island
†Bruun, Per Moller *civil engineer, consultant*
Huckins, Harold Aaron *chemical engineer*
Shea, Gerald Patrick *engineering executive*
Smith, Paul David *electrical engineer, administrator*
Windman, Arnold Lewis *retired mechanical engineer*

Jenkinsville
Loignon, Gerald Arthur, Jr., *nuclear engineer*

North Charleston
Fei, James Robert *engineering executive, consultant*

Orangeburg
Graule, Raymond (Siegfried) *metallurgical engineer*
Hong, Jae-Dong *industrial engineering educator*

Pawleys Island
Alexander, William D., III, *civil engineer, consultant, former army air force officer*

Salem
†Darnell, William Headen *chemical engineer, medical/surgical nurse, nursing educator*

Simpsonville
Seaman, Duncan Campbell *civil engineer*

Surfside Beach
Edwards, George Henry *retired aeronautical engineer*

West Union
Klutz, Anthony Aloysius, Jr., *health, safety and environmental manager*

SOUTH DAKOTA

Brookings
Melby, Paul Elliott *electrical engineer*

Rapid City
Ramakrishnan, Venkataswamy *civil engineer, educator*
Scofield, Gordon Lloyd *mechanical engineer, educator*

Watertown
Hanson, Dorene Kay *engineering draftsman*

Yankton
†Ostergaard, David Arne *mechanical engineer*

TENNESSEE

Arnold AFB
Davis, John William *government science and engineering executive*

Chattanooga
Campbell, William Buford, Jr., *materials engineer, chemist, forensic consultant*
Duckworth, Jerrell James *electrical engineer*
Hensley, Marble John, Sr., *civil engineer, consultant*
†Sacks, Richard *electrical engineer*

Cleveland
Knight, Sandra Norton *civil engineer*
Lewis, Charlton Scott *civil engineer*

Cookeville
Black, Gary William *industrial engineer*
Chowdhuri, Pritindra *electrical engineer, educator*
†Jackson, Mark James *engineering educator*
Sissom, Leighton Esten *engineering educator, dean, consultant*

Crossville
Bell, Charles Eugene, Jr., *industrial engineer*

Fairfield Glade
Pitt, Woodrow Wilson, Jr., *engineering educator, educator*

Greenbrier
Newell, Paul Haynes, Jr., *engineering educator, former college president*

Kingsport
Siirola, Jeffrey John *chemical engineer*

Knoxville

Badiru, Adedeji Bodunde *industrial engineer*
Bose, Bimal Kumar *electrical engineering educator*
Bressler, Marcus Nathan *consulting engineer*
Brown, Donald Vaughn *technical educator, engineering consultant*
Cliff, Steven Burris *engineering executive*
El-Ghazaly, Samir *electrical engineering educator*
Garrison, Arlene Allen *engineering executive, engineering educator*
Greene, David Lloyd *transportation researcher*
Howlader, M. Mostofa Kamal *engineering educator*
Hull, Dwight Sigworth, II, *engineer*
Hung, James Chen *engineer, educator, consultant*
LeVert, Francis Edward *nuclear engineer, researcher*
Mc Dow, John Jett *agricultural engineering educator*
Mise, Jesse Sherden *structural engineer, consultant*
Oakes, Thomas Wyatt *environmental engineer, computer engineer*
†Prados, John William *engineering educator*
Roth, J(ohn) Reece *electrical engineer, educator, researcher, inventor*
Schuler, Theodore Anthony *retired civil engineer, retired city official*
Uhrig, Robert Eugene *nuclear engineer, educator*

Loudon

Lownsdale, Gary Richard *mechanical engineer*

Maryville

Oakes, Lester Cornelius *retired electrical engineer, consultant*

Memphis

Bhattacharya, Syamal Kanti *biomedical scientist, educator*
Forster, Hamish *engineer*
Fountain, Robert Allen *organizational management executive*
Grace, Wesley Gee, Jr., *engineer*
Iftekharuddin, Khan M. *engineering educator, researcher*
†Widjanarko, Taufiq *engineering educator*
Williams, Edward F(oster), III, *environmental engineer*

Morristown

Marz, Loren Carl *environmental engineer, chemist, meteorologist*

Mountain Home

Lucas, R. Robert *finance engineer, corporate tax planner*

Nashville

Auld, Bernie Dyson *civil engineer, consultant*
Basu, Prodyot Kumar *civil engineer, educator*
Cadzow, James Archie *engineering educator, researcher*
Collett, Walter Lee *electrical engineer*
Galloway, Kenneth Franklin *engineering educator*
Hahn, George Thomas *materials engineering educator, researcher*
Harris, Thomas Raymond *biomedical engineer, educator*
†LeVan, Martin Douglas *chemical engineering educator*
Schnelle, Karl Benjamin, Jr., *chemical engineering educator, consultant, researcher*
Speece, Richard Eugene *civil engineer, educator*
Tanner, Robert Dennis *chemical engineering educator*

Oak Ridge

Dixon, Warren Everett *robotics engineer*
†Fox, Janie *environmental engineer*
Hu, Michael Z. *chemical engineer, educator*
†Kress, Thomas Sylvester *engineer, consultant*
Lee, Donald William *mechanical engineer, researcher*
Mosko, Sigmund Weiner *electrical engineer, researcher*
Rivera, Angel Luis *chemical engineer*
Rosenthal, Murray Wilford *chemical engineer, science administrator*
Zinkle, Steven John *engineer, researcher*

Ooltewah

Culpepper, Richard Groom *engineer*

Signal Mountain

†Makansi, Munzer *chemical engineer, researcher*

South Pittsburg

Cordell, Francis Merritt *instrument engineer, consultant*

Tullahoma

Hill, Susan Sloan *safety engineer*
Smith, L. Montgomery *electrical engineering educator*

TEXAS

Allen

†Desthieux, Bertrand M. *optical engineer, editor-in-chief*
Lim, Jae Doeg *systems engineer, researcher*

Alpine

Kittlitz, Rudolf Gottlieb, Jr., *chemical engineer, researcher*

Amarillo

Elkins, Lloyd Edwin, Sr., *petroleum engineer, energy consultant*
Keaton, Lawrence Cluer *safety engineer, consultant*

Von Eschen, Robert Leroy *electrical engineer, consultant*

Argyle

Stallings, Frank, Jr., *industrial engineer, realtor*

Arlington

Anderson, Dale Arden *aerospace engineer, educator*
Clark, Dayle Meritt *civil engineer*
†Everard, Noel J. *structural engineer, educator*
Imrhan, Sheik Nazir *industrial engineer, educator*
Lewis, Frank Leroy *electrical engineer, educator, researcher*
Liu, Hanli *biomedical engineer, educator*
†Rollins, Albert Williamson *civil engineer, consultant*
†Shiakolas, Panayiotis Stavros *mechanical engineering educator, researcher*
Stevens, Gladstone Taylor, Jr., *industrial engineer*

Austin

Abraham, Jacob A. *computer engineering educator, consultant*
Akins, Vaughn Edward *retired engineering company executive*
Al-Omari, Ra'ed M. *computer engineer, consultant, computer scientist, researcher*
Armstrong, Neal Earl *civil engineering educator*
Baker, Lee Edward *biomedical engineering educator*
Banerjee, Sanjay Kumar *electrical engineer, director*
Bhat, Chandra R. *engineering educator, consultant*
Brannon-Peppas, Lisa *chemical engineer, researcher*
Breen, John Edward *civil engineer, educator*
Brock, James Rush *chemical engineering educator*
Bronaugh, Edwin Lee *electromagnetic compatibility engineer, consultant*
Burns, Ned Hamilton *civil engineering educator*
Carlton, Donald Morrill *research, development and engineering executive*
Castaldi, Frank James *environmental engineer, consultant*
Cywar, Adam Walter *management engineer*
Dougal, Arwin Adelbert *electrical engineer, educator*
Ell, Travis Eugene *electronics engineer*
Epright, Charles John *retired aerospace engineer*
†Erengil, Mehmet Erdal *aeronautical engineer, researcher*
Evans, Walter Reed *retired engineering executive, consultant*
Fair, James Rutherford, Jr., *chemical engineering educator, consultant*
Fowler, David Wayne *architectural engineering educator*
†Furlong, Richard W. *structural engineer, educator*
Gavande, Sampat Anand *agricultural engineer, soil scientist*
Gibson, George Edward, Jr., *civil engineering educator, consultant, researcher*
Gloyna, Earnest Frederick *environmental engineer, educator*
Gomes, Norman Vincent *retired industrial engineer*
Goodenough, John Bannister *engineering educator, research physicist*
Grimm, Clayford Thomas *architectural engineer, consultant*
Harris, Richard Lee *engineering executive, retired army officer*
Himmelblau, David Mautner *chemical engineer*
Hixson, Elmer L. *retired engineering educator*
Howell, John Reid *mechanical engineering educator*
Hull, David George *aerospace engineering educator, researcher*
Kockelman, Kara Maria *engineering educator*
Koen, Billy Vaughn *mechanical engineering educator*
Koepsel, Wellington Wesley *electrical engineering educator*
Krishna, Hari J. *engineer*
Lamb, Jamie Parker, Jr., *retired mechanical engineer, educator*
Landsberger, Sheldon *nuclear engineer, educator, radiation engineer, educator*
Luedecke, William Henry *mechanical engineer*
†Manthiram, Arumugam *materials science and engineering educator*
Mc Ketta, John J., Jr., *chemical engineering educator*
Murthy, Vanukuri Radha Krishna *civil engineer*
Nicastro, David Harlan *forensic engineer, consultant, author*
Nichols, Steven Parks *mechanical engineer, lawyer, educator*
O'Connor, James T. *civil engineering educator*
Oden, John Tinsley *engineering educator, mathematician, consultant*
O'Geary, Dennis Traylor *retired contracting/engineering company executive*
Paul, Donald Ross *chemical engineer, educator*
Peppas, Nikolaos Athanassiou *chemical and biomedical engineering educator, consultant*
Reese, Lymon Clifton *civil engineering educator*
Rossen, William R. *engineering educator*
Rylander, Henry Grady, Jr., *mechanical engineering educator*
Sanchez, Isaac Cornelius *chemical engineer, educator*
Sandberg, Irwin Walter *electrical and computer engineering educator*
Saunders, Jimmy Dale *aerospace engineer, physicist, naval officer*
Sciance, Carroll Thomas *chemical engineer*
Smith, Daniel Montague *engineer*
Steinfink, Hugo *chemical engineering educator*
Streetman, Ben Garland *electrical engineering educator*

Swartzlander, Earl Eugene, Jr., *engineering educator, former electronics company executive*
†Tesar, Delbert *machine systems and robotics educator, researcher, manufacturing consultant*
Thurston, George Butte *mechanical and biomedical engineering educator*
Touba, Nur Ali *electrical engineering educator*
Walton, Charles Michael *civil engineering educator*
Welch, Ashley James *engineering educator*
Wittliff, Danny Joe *environmental engineer*
Woodson, Herbert Horace *retired electrical engineering educator*
†Yoon, SungPil *aerospace engineer, researcher*

Baird

Rodenberger, Charles Alvard *aerospace engineer, consultant*

Bangs

Whiteley, James Morris *retired aerospace engineer*

Baytown

†Loyka, Jeffrey J. *environmental engineer*

Beaumont

Hopper, Jack Rudd *chemical engineering educator*
Jao, Mien *civil engineer educator*
Koehn, Enno *engineering educator, researcher*
Morales, Emmitt *mechanical consultant*
Myler, Harley Ross *electrical engineer, educator*

Bellaire

Wisch, David John *structural engineer*

Big Spring

Fryrear, Donald William *agricultural engineer, researcher*

Boerne

Mitchelhill, James Moffat *retired civil engineer*

Brooks AFB

Polhamus, Garrett Douglas *biomedical engineer*

Brownsville

†Gilbert, Marilyn del Bosque *architectural engineer*

Bryan

Samson, Charles Harold, Jr., (Car Samson) *retired engineering educator, consultant*

Carrollton

Ades, Bruce Allan *engineering executive, researcher*
Councill, William Thomas, III, *computer engineer, consultant*
Henderson, William David *mechanical engineer*
Laurent, Duane Giles *memory design engineer*

College Station

Adams, Marvin Lee *nuclear engineer, researcher*
Button, Joe Wade *civil engineer, researcher, consultant*
Cochran, Robert Glenn *nuclear engineering educator*
†Cohen, Aaron *aerospace engineer*
Ehsani, Mehrdad (Mark Ehsani) *electrical engineering educator, consultant*
†Entchev, Pavlin Borissov *aerospace and mechanical engineer*
Fletcher, Leroy Stevenson *mechanical engineer, educator*
Godbey, Luther David *architectural and engineering executive*
Hall, Kenneth Richard *chemical engineering educator, consultant*
Hann, Roy William, Jr., *civil engineer, educator*
Holste, James Clifton *chemical engineering educator*
Isdale, Charles Edwin *chemical engineer*
†Kirk, Ivan Wayne *agricultural engineer*
Kunze, Otto Robert *retired agricultural engineering educator*
Kuo, Way *industrial engineer, researcher*
Lee, William John *petroleum engineering educator, consultant*
Lowery, Lee Leon, Jr., *civil engineer*
Lu, Mi *computer engineer, educator*
Lytton, Robert Leonard *civil engineer, educator*
Mannan, M. Sam *chemical engineer, educator, consultant*
Mathewson, Christopher Colville *engineering geologist, educator*
Mercer, Melvin Ray *electrical engineer, educator*
Page, Robert Henry *engineer, educator, researcher*
Painter, John Hoyt *electrical engineer*
Parlos, Alexander George *systems and control engineering educator*
Patton, Alton DeWitt *electrical engineering consultant*
Reddy, J. N. *mechanical engineering educator*
Reinschmidt, Kenneth Frank *engineering and construction executive, educator*
Richardson, Herbert Heath *mechanical engineer, educator, institute director*
Riskowski, Gerald Lee *engineering educator*
Serpedin, Erchin *electrical engineering educator, researcher*
Wurbs, Ralph Allen *civil engineering educator, consultant*

Coppell

Robinson, Charles Emanuel *systems engineer, consultant*

Corpus Christi

Bockhop, Clarence William *retired agricultural engineer*
Brennecke, Henry Martin *chemical engineer, researcher*

Elarba, Nagib A. *mechanical engineer, consultant*
Nadkarni, Ashok B. *electrical engineer*

Dallas

Bailey, Calvin Dean *audio engineer*
Bruene, Warren Benz *electronic engineer*
Chadbourne, John Frederick, Jr., *engineering executive*
Cruikshank, Thomas Henry *energy services and engineering executive*
Dasgupta, Udayan *electrical engineer, researcher*
Eberhart, Robert Clyde *biomedical engineering educator, researcher*
Fix, Douglas Martin *electrical engineer*
Fontana, Robert Edward *electrical engineering educator, retired air force officer*
†Gray, Peter Frederick *software engineer, educator*
Hammerlindl, Donald James *petroleum consultant*
Kilby, Jack St. Clair *electrical engineer*
Lersch, DeLynden Rife *computer engineering executive*
McLane, William Delano *mechanical engineer*
Ramsey, Jennifer Christa *civil engineer, consultant*
Schulze, Richard Hans *engineering executive, environmental engineer*
Szygenda, Stephen A. *electrical and computer engineering educator, researcher*
†Talla, Deependra *systems engineer*
†Taylor, Richard L., Jr., *engineer, consultant*
Williams, Charles Edward *engineer*
Zimmerman, S(amuel) Morton (Mort Zimmerman) *engineering executive*

Deer Park

Sandstrum, Steve D. *engineering executive*

Denton

†Golding, Terry David *engineering educator, researcher*

El Paso

Diong, Billy Ming *energy control engineering researcher*
Fahy, Michael P. *civil and environmental engineer*
Grieves, Robert Belanger *engineering educator*
Heide, John Wesley *engineering executive*
Nava, Patricia Ann *electrical engineering educator, researcher*
Peterscheck, Walter Hermann *chemical engineer*

Fair Oaks Ranch

Dixon, Robert James *aerospace consultant, former air force officer, former aerospace company executive*

Fort Worth

Billingsley, David Stuart *chemical engineer, researcher, software developer*
Buckner, John Kendrick *aerospace engineer*
Cunningham, Atlee Marion, Jr., *aeronautical engineer*
Nichols, James Richard *civil engineer, consultant*
Palmer, Jeffery Dean *systems engineering executive, consultant*
†Poth, Aimee Nicolle *systems engineer*
Pray, Donald George *retired aerospace engineer*
†Roberson, Janet L. *aircraft manufacturing company official*
Thornton, Anthony L *aerospace engineer*

Galveston

Brown, Karl Beck *civil engineer*
Otis, John James *civil engineer*
†Schein, Catherine H. *biomedical engineer, researcher*
†Wang, Zhishun *biomedical engineer, consultant*

Garland

Christensen, Allan Robert *electrical engineer, enrolled agent*

Georgetown

Moore, Pat Howard *engineering and construction company executive*

Grapevine

†Blair, Sylvia H. *computer engineer, small business owner*
Killebrew, James Robert *architectural engineering firm executive*

Hollywood Park

Smith, Richard Thomas *retired electrical engineer*

Houston

Allen, John Timothy *mechanical engineer*
Bai, Yong *engineering executive, educator*
Bovay, Harry Elmo, Jr., *retired engineering company executive*
Bozeman, Ross Elliot *engineering executive*
Cheatham, John Bane, Jr., *retired mechanical engineering educator*
Chiquelin, David Bryan *mechanical engineer*
†Colborn, Jack P. *engineering company executive*
Devoy, Stephen Douglas *marine engineer*
Duerr, David *civil engineer*
Dutta, Nripendu *stress analyst, consultant*
Eichberger, LeRoy Carl *mechanical engineer, consultant, stress analyst*
†Fassihi, Mohammad Reza *engineering executive*
Focht, John Arnold, Jr., *geotechnical engineer*
Fossati, Humberto Mario *electrical engineer, researcher*
Frankhouser, Homer Sheldon, Jr., *engineering and construction company executive*
Geer, Ronald Lamar *mechanical engineering consultant, retired oil company executive*
†Ghayour, Kaveh *aeronautical engineer*
Gilbert, David Wallace *retired aerospace engineer*
Gunsel, Selda *chemical engineer, researcher*

PROFESSIONAL INDEX 6313 ENGINEERING

Halyard, Raymond James *aerospace engineer, mathematics educator*
Hellums, Jesse David *chemical engineering educator and researcher*
Henley, Ernest Justus *chemical engineering educator, consultant*
Hsu, Thomas Tseng-Chuang *civil engineer, educator*
Huang, Hsien-Lu *electrical engineer*
Huang, Shawn Shaoping *engineer*
Itaketo, Umana Thompson *systems and control engineer*
Karger, Walter *mechanical engineer*
†Lammers, Michael Lee *aerospace engineer*
Lienhard, John Henry, IV, *mechanical engineer, educator*
Litvinov, Dmitri *advisory development engineer*
Luss, Dan *chemical engineering educator*
Maligas, Manuel Nick *metallurgical engineer*
Matthews, Charles Sedwick *petroleum engineering consultant, research advisor*
McIntire, Larry Vern *biomedical engineering educator*
McLeod, Harry O'Neal, Jr., *petroleum engineer, consultant*
Miele, Angelo *engineering educator, researcher, consultant, author*
Mo, Yi-Lung *structural engineering educator*
Morris, Owen Glenn *engineering corporation executive*
†Nachlinger, R. Ray *marine engineer, consultant, mechanical engineer, educator*
Nance, Weldon Bailey *petroleum engineer*
Nelson-Thorpe, Carlon Justine *engineering and operations executive*
Nichols, Mark Edward *aerospace engineer*
Nordgren, Ronald Paul *engineering educator, researcher*
Ouyang, Liangbiao *petroleum engineer, researcher, petroleum engineer, educator*
Peng, Liang-Chuan *mechanical engineer*
Powell, Alan *scientist-engineer*
Prats, Michael *petroleum engineer, educator*
Rhodes, Allen Franklin *engineering executive*
†Samman, Mahmod *engineering educator, consultant*
Spanos, Pol Dimitrios *engineering educator*
Talapatra, Dipak Chandra *aerospace engineer*
Tezduyar, Tayfun Ersin *engineering educator*
Tiras, Herbert Gerald *engineering executive*
Tsai, Tom Chunghu *chemical engineer*
†Vipulanandan, Cumaraswamy *civil engineer, educator*
Wang, Xiaozhi *structural engineer*
†Wiesner, Mark Robert *environmental engineer, educator*
Williams, Curtis Chandler, III, *retired chemical engineer, consultant*
†Wilton, Donald Robert *engineering educator*
Wren, Robert James *aerospace engineering manager*
Yiu, Fang *structural engineer, researcher*
Yu, Aiting Tobey *engineering executive*
†Zhao, Zhongshan *structural engineer, researcher*

Humble
†Brown, Samuel Joseph, Jr., *engineer, scientist*

Ingleside
Naismith, James Pomeroy *civil engineer*

Irving
Adams, Charles Paul *communications engineer, consultant*
Lee, Michael Wayne *structural engineer, consultant*
McCormack, Grace Lynette *civil engineering technician*
Papakostas, Achilleas *telecommunications engineer, researcher*
Potter, Robert Joseph *technical and business executive*
Walley, James Marvin, Jr., *engineering and real estate executive, management consultant*

Kerrville
Matlock, Hudson *civil engineer, educator*

Kingsville
†Li, Shuhui *engineer, educator*

Kingwood
Bowman, Stephen Wayne *quality assurance engineer, consultant*

League City
Kanuth, James Gordan *chemical engineer*

Livingston
Hayes, Gordon Glenn *civil engineer*

Longview
Winn, Walter Terris, Jr., *civil and environmental engineer*

Lubbock
Archer, James Elson *engineering educator*
Dudek, Richard Albert *engineering educator*
Giesselmann, Michael *engineering educator*
Kiesling, Ernst Willie *civil engineering educator*
Kristiansen, Magne *electrical engineer, educator*
Levitas, Valery *mechanics and materials educator, researcher*
McMillen, Robert Paul *agricultural engineer*
†Nikishin, Sergey A. *electrical engineering educator, researcher*
Roberts, Evan Elijah, Jr., *structural engineer, architect*
Zhang, Hong-Chao *manufacturing engineer, educator*

Mc Kinney
Gill, David Brian *electrical engineer, educator*

Mesquite
†Ellison, John Vogelsanger *retired engineer*

Midland
Maha, Callen Dale *project manager engineer*

New Braunfels
Belzung, Paul Edward *engineering executive*

Pampa
Alexander, Steven Ray *chemical engineer*

Pasadena
Martinez, Fernando V. *civil engineer*

Pearland
Claridge, Elmond Lowell *retired engineering educator, consultant*

Pflugerville
Carlsen, John Richard *engineer*

Plano
Davani, Bahman Faghaie *telecommunications engineer*
†Hiegel, James Edward *mechanical engineer*
†Naimi-Tajdar, Reza *petroleum engineer*
Seals, Ryan Brown *electronics engineer*

Port Aransas
Lehmann, William Leonardo *electrical engineer, educator*

Richardson
Duan, Xiaodong *engineer*
Nosratinia, Aria *engineering educator, researcher*
†Paranchych, David Walter *electrical engineer*
Rogers, Mal David, Jr., *chemical engineer*

Richmond
Johanson, Knut Arvid, Jr., *retired engineering executive*

Rockport
Minor, Joseph Edward *civil engineer, educator*
†Stachiw, Jaroslaw (Jerry) Drahomyr *mechanical engineer, consultant*

Rockwall
Griffith, James William *systems engineer, consultant*

Rosenberg
Tourtellotte, Mills Charlton *mechanical and electrical engineer*

San Antonio
Abramson, Hyman Norman *engineering and science research executive*
Atchley, Curtis Leon *mechanical engineer*
Fischer, Marsha Leigh *civil engineer*
†Painter, Scott L. *engineer, researcher*
Qian, Chunjiang *engineering educator, researcher*
Quiroga, Cesar Augusto *transportation engineer*
Shadaram, Mehdi *electrical engineering educator*
Singh, Yesh Pal *mechanical engineering educator, consultant*
Wang, Xiaodu *engineering educator*
Weinbrenner, George Ryan *aeronautical engineer*

Sour Lake
Presley, Dale Mark *electrical engineer*

Spring
Ho, Hwa-Shan *engineering executive, civil engineer, consultant, drilling engineer*
Szymczak, Edward Joseph *mechanical engineer*

Stafford
Cizek, John Gary *safety and fire engineer*

Sugar Land
Westphal, Douglas Herbert *retired engineering company executive*

Temple
Carroll, Irwin Dixon *engineer*
Dowdy, William Louis *consulting and engineering company executive*
Patureau, Arthur Mitchell *chemical engineer, consultant*

The Woodlands
Saikowski, Ronald Alexander *consulting engineer*

Tyler
Morgan, Freeman Louis, Jr., *engineer, consultant*
Trent, Warren C. *mechanical engineer*

Waco
Farison, James Blair *electrical biomedical engineer, educator*
Skains, Timothy Karl *electrical engineer*
Solomon, Charles Francis *electronics educator*

Webster
Kobayashi, Herbert Shin *electrical engineer*

Wharton
Schulze, Arthur Edward *biomedical engineer, researcher*

UTAH

Bluffdale
†Bliss, Rick Wayne *engineer*

Brigham City
Krejci, Robert Henry *aerospace engineer*
Tolle, Melinda Edith *engineer, scientist*

Dugway
†Benson, Morgan *energy engineer, military officer*

Fort Duchesne
Cameron, Charles Henry *supervisory petroleum engineer*

Logan
Bowles, David Stanley *engineering educator, engineering consultant*
Clyde, Calvin Geary *civil engineer, educator*
Hargreaves, George Henry *civil and agricultural engineer, researcher*
Keller, Jack *agricultural engineering educator, consultant*
†Subprasom, Kitti *civil engineer*

Murray
Volberg, Herman William *electronics engineer, consultant*

Ogden
Davidson, Thomas Ferguson *chemical engineer*
Haygarth, John Charles *industrial scientist*

Orem
Harris, Michael James *software engineer*

Provo
Losee, Ferril Andrew *retired electrical engineer*
Merritt, LaVere Barrus *engineering educator, civil engineer*
Youd, T. Leslie *civil engineer*

Salt Lake City
Anderson, Charles Ross *civil engineer*
Barney, Kline Porter, Jr., *engineering company executive, consultant*
Bousfield, Kenneth Harold *civil engineer*
De Vries, Kenneth Lawrence *mechanical engineer, educator*
Gandhi, Om Parkash *electrical engineer*
Ghosh, Sambhunath (Sam Ghosh) *civil engineering educator, environmental engineer*
Hereth, Lyle George *electrical engineering technologist*
Judd, Thomas Eli *electrical engineer*
Kopecek, Jindrich *biomedical scientist, biomaterials and pharmaceutics educator*
Pershing, David Walter *chemical engineering educator, researcher*
Sandquist, Gary Marlin *engineering educator, researcher, consultant, writer*
Seader, Junior DeVere (Bob Seader) *chemical engineering educator*
Silver, Barnard Joseph Stewart *mechanical and chemical engineer, consultant, inventor*
Sohn, Hong Yong *chemical engineer, educator, metallurgical engineer, educator*
Stringfellow, Gerald B. *engineering educator*

Sandy
Jorgensen, Leland Howard *aerospace research engineer*

VERMONT

Burlington
Dorwart, Roger Wilson *retired civil engineer*
Outwater, John Ogden *mechanical engineering educator*
Pinder, George Francis *engineering educator, scientist*

Charlotte
Pricer, Wilbur David *electrical engineer, educator*

Essex Junction
Aitken, John Malcolm *engineer, educator*
Ishaq, Mousa Hanna *materials engineer*
Lee, Mankoo *device engineer, scientist*

Jericho
Bolin, Henry Robert *retired engineer*

Shelburne
Anderson, Richard Louis *electrical engineer*

Underhill
Panner, Jeannie Harrigan *retired electrical engineer*

VIRGINIA

Abingdon
Pratt, Mark Ernest *retired mechanical engineer*

Afton
Anderson, Donald Norton, Jr., *retired electrical engineer*

Alexandria
Brandell, Sol Richard *electrical power and control system engineer, research mathematician*
Cook, Charles William *aerospace engineer, consultant, educator*
Cooper, Henry Franklyn *engineering, technology and national security affairs consultant*
Eckhart, Myron, Jr., (Max Eckhart) *retired marine engineer*
Glynn, Ernest B. *civil engineer, environmental engineer*
Gould, Phillip *engineer*
Jokl, Alois Louis *electrical engineer*
Kemble, James Richard *retired engineering services executive*
Lasser, Howard Gilbert *chemical engineer, consultant*
Mandil, I. Harry *nuclear engineer*
Murray, Russell, II, *aeronautical engineer, defense analyst, consultant*
Poehlein, Gary Wayne *retired chemical engineering educator*
†Rebman, Jack Arthur *communications engineer*

Taylor, William Brockenbrough Newton *engineer, consultant, management consultant*
Thomas, Carlton Eugene (Sandy Thomas) *electrical engineer, researcher*
Weisberg, Leonard R. *engineering executive, researcher, retired*
Wilcox, David Eric *electrical engineer, educational consultant*

Annandale
Geiger, Richard Bernard *engineer, retired federal agency administrator*
Hagn, George Hubert *electrical engineer, researcher*
Ochs, Walter J. *civil engineer, drainage adviser*

Arlington
Allen, David *systems engineer*
Atkins, Walter J. *electrical engineer*
Beck, Buddy *systems engineer*
Bordogna, Joseph *engineer, educator*
Breckinridge, James Bernard *optical engineer*
Brown, Gardner Russell *engineering executive*
Facklam, Roger Lee *engineer, physicist*
Hall, Carl William *agricultural and mechanical engineer*
†Hazelrigg, George Arthur, Jr., *systems engineer, educator*
Heineken, Frederick George *biochemical engineer*
Henderson, Robert Earl *mechanical engineer, educator, consultant*
†Hidalgo, Henry *aerospace engineer, consultant*
Kappaz, Michael H. *engineering and energy executive*
Katona, Peter Geza *biomedical engineer, educator*
Kim, John Chan Kyu *electrical engineer*
†Kinsey, John Allen *systems engineer, director*
†Kumar, Srikanta Ponnathpur *electrical engineer, researcher*
MacDonald, Paul Edward *electrical engineer*
Rahman, Muhammad Abdur *mechanical engineer*
Reagan, Lawrence Paul, Jr., *systems engineer*
Salmon, William Cooper *mechanical engineer, engineering academy executive*
Seedlock, Robert Francis *engineering and construction company executive*
Sewell, William George, III, *electronics engineer*
Shortal, Terence Michael *systems company executive*
Stevens, Donald King *retired aeronautical engineer, consultant*
Stuart, Charles Edward *electrical engineer, oceanographer*

Ashburn
†Torrico, Saúl A. *electrical engineer, engineering educator*

Bedford
Ramsey, Forrest Gladstone, Jr., *retired engineering company executive*
Turpin, Richard Ben *civil engineer*

Blacksburg
Batra, Romesh Chander *engineering mechanics educator, researcher*
Boardman, Gregory Dale *environmental engineer, educator*
Brown, Gary Sandy *electrical engineering educator*
de Wolf, David Alter *electrical engineer, educator*
Disney, Ralph L(ynde) *retired industrial engineering educator*
Easterling, William Samuel *structural engineering educator*
Fabrycky, Wolter Joseph *engineering educator, author, industrial and systems engineer*
Glasser, Wolfgang Gerhard *chemical engineering wood science researcher, educator*
Gray, Festus Gail *electrical engineer, educator, researcher*
Grisso, Robert Dwight, Jr., *engineering educator*
Haugh, Clarence Gene *agricultural engineering educator*
Inman, Daniel John *mechanical engineer, educator*
Lee, Fred C. *electrical engineering educator*
Mitchell, James Kenneth *civil engineer, educator*
Nayfeh, Ali Hasan *mechanical engineering educator*
Pearce, David Harry *biomedical engineer, consultant*
Perumpral, John Verghese *agricultural engineer, administrator, educator*
Phadke, Arun G. *electrical engineering educator*
Randall, Clifford Wendell *civil engineer, educator*
†Schetz, Joseph Alfred *aerospace engineer, educator*
Squires, Arthur Morton *chemical engineer, educator*
Stutzman, Warren Lee *electrical engineer, educator*
†Vikesland, Peter John *environmental engineering educator, researcher*
Walker, Richard David *civil engineer, educator*

Blue Ridge
Elmore, Walter A. *electrical engineer, consultant*

Boyce
Murray, Arthur Joseph *engineering executive, speaker*

Burke
Lynch, Charles Theodore, Sr., *materials science engineering researcher, consultant, educator*

Chantilly
Evans, Richard Taylor *aerospace engineer, consultant*

Charlottesville
Bly, Charles Albert *nuclear engineer, research scientist*
†Brewer, Philip Warren *retired civil engineer*
Gaden, Elmer Lewis, Jr., *chemical engineering educator, retired*
Haimes, Yacov Yosseph *systems and civil engineering educator, consultant*
Hoel, Lester A. *civil engineering educator*
Hudson, John Lester *chemical engineering educator*
Inigo, Rafael Madrigal *retired electrical engineering educator*
Iwasaki, Tetsuya *engineering educator*
Krzysztofowicz, Roman *systems engineering and statistical science educator, consultant*
Lin, Zongli *electrical engineering educator*
McGinnis, Charles Irving *civil engineer*
Morton, Jeffrey Bruce *aerospace engineering educator*
Reynolds, Albert Barnett *nuclear engineer, educator*
Theodoridis, George Constantin *biomedical engineering educator, researcher*
Thompson, Anthony Richard *electrical engineer, astronomer*
Townsend, Miles Averill *aerospace and mechanical engineering educator*
White, K(ing) Preston, Jr., *systems engineering educator, researcher, consultant*

Chesapeake
Hampton, John Philip *systems engineer, retired naval officer*

Dulles
†Lovell, Robert R(oland) *engineering executive*

Fairfax
Bornmann, John Albert, Jr., *electrical engineer*
Chen, Chun-Hung *engineering educator*
Cook, Gerald *electrical engineering educator*
Gertler, Janos John *electrical engineer, educator*
Gollobin, Leonard Paul *chemical engineer*
Hatch, Ross Riepert *weapon system engineering executive*
Larsen, Phillip Nelson *electrical engineer*
Levis, Alexander Henry *systems engineer, educator, consultant*
Lott, Wayne Thomas *systems engineer*
Roser, Robert Hutchins, Jr., *systems engineer*

Fairfax Station
Coaker, James Whitfield *mechanical engineer*
Duff, William Grierson *electrical engineer, educator*

Fairfield
Harrawood, Paul *civil engineering educator*

Falls Church
Jones, Russel Cameron *civil engineer, educator*
Lorenzo, Michael *engineer, government official, real estate broker*
May, Carol Lee *mechanical engineer*
†Poza, Hugo Bernardo *aerospace company executive*
Villarreal, Carlos Castañeda *engineering executive*
Woo, Dah-Cheng *hydraulic engineer*

Fort Belvoir
Barnholdt, Terry Joseph *chemical, industrial, and general engineer*

Fredericksburg
Anderson, Roberta June *computer engineer*
†Hasenfus, Harold Joseph *retired mechanical engineer, naval technical director*
Medding, Walter Sherman *retired environmental engineer*

Front Royal
†Cosby, Lynwood A. *electrical engineer*

Great Falls
Hesse, Richard Joseph *construction engineer*
Skeen, David Ray *systems engineer, consultant, engineering executive, educator*

Hampton
Bartels, Robert Edwin *aerospace engineer*
Joshi, Suresh Meghashyam *research engineer*
Krueger, Ronald *aerospace engineer*
Meyers, James Frank *electronics engineer*
Singleterry, Robert Clay, Jr., *aerospace technologist, physicist, NASA administrator*
Sobieski, Jaroslaw *aerospace engineer*
†Spearman, Morris Leroy *aeronautics and aerospace researcher*
Tessler, Alexander *aerospace engineer*
Weiser, Erik Saul *materials research engineer, project manager*

Huddleston
Kopp, Richard Edgar *electrical engineer*

Leesburg
Kelsey, Ronald Grant *environmental engineer*

Lynchburg
Barkley, Henry Brock, Jr., *research and development engineering executive*
Groshner, Maria Star *nuclear engineer*

Mc Lean
Carnicero, Jorge Emilio *aeronautical engineer, business executive*
Chase, Emery John, Jr., *nuclear engineer, researcher*
Dobson, Donald Alfred *retired electrical engineer*
Halik, Eugene Egon *engineering consultant*
Klopfenstein, Rex Carter *electrical engineer*
McCambridge, John James *civil engineer*
Metters, Samuel *engineering executive*
Mohleji, Satish Chandra *electrical engineer*

Reichenbach, Roy Earl *engineering executive*
Rosenbaum, David Mark *engineering executive, consultant, educator*
Schauer, Franz Peter *civil and nuclear engineer, educator*
Schmeidler, Neal Francis *engineering executive*
Sonnemann, Harry *electrical engineer, consultant*
Walsh, John Breffni *aerospace consultant*

McLean
†Park, Sunwoo *engineer*
†Staats, Richard Charles *computer engineer*

Mechanicsville
Galloway, Joseph Edward, Jr., *retired highway engineer*

Middleburg
Langley, Rolland Ament, Jr., *retired engineering technology company executive*

Newport News
Donaldson, Coleman duPont *aeronautical engineer, consultant, aerospace engineer, consultant*
Hubbard, Harvey Hart *aeroacoustician, noise control engineer, consultant*
Laroussi, Mounir *electrical engineer*
Noblitt, Nancy Anne *aerospace engineer*

Norfolk
Donohue, David Patrick *engineering executive, retired navy rear admiral*
Estes, Edward Richard, Jr., *engineering consultant, engineer, retired educator*
Leavitt, Sheldon Joseph *civil engineer, architect, consultant*
†Samuels, John M., Jr., *industrial engineer*
Wei, Benjamin Min *engineering educator*
Wiltse, James Clark *civil engineer*

Oakton
Curry, Thomas Fortson *electronics engineer, defense industry executive*
Divone, Louis Vincent *aerospace engineer, educator, federal official, author*

Palmyra
Avers, Carl Dennison *computer engineer*

Penhook
Coar, Richard John *mechanical engineer, aerospace consultant*

Reston
Choi, Michael Kamwah *aerospace engineer, mechanical engineer, researcher*
Cramond, Richard, Jr., *structural and systems engineer, diversified aerospace company executive*
Harvey, Aubrey Eaton, III, *industrial engineer*
†Kahn, Robert E. *electrical engineer*
Lanfear, Kenneth Joseph *engineering administrator, hydrologist*

Richmond
Aiken, Peter Haynes *systems engineer, educator*
Compton, Olin Randall *consulting electrical engineer, researcher*
Gad-el-Hak, Mohamed *aerospace and mechanical engineering educator, scientist*
Hamlett, Robert Barksdale *systems engineer*
Lingerfelt, Alan Thomas *civil engineer, real estate executive*
Ludden, George Clemens *engineer*
Mattauch, Robert Joseph *electrical engineering educator*
Reed, Christopher Robert *civil engineer*
Rowe, James William, Sr., *engineer*
Sprinkle, William Melvin *audio-acoustical engineer, engineering administrator*

Roanoke
Goad, Danny Harlan *mechanical engineer*
Landis, John William *engineering and construction executive, government advisor*
McKenna, John Dennis *environmental testing engineer*
†Stadler, Donald Arthur *management engineer*

Salem
Shaffner, Patrick Noel *retired architectural engineering executive*

Spotsylvania
Kozloski, Lillian Terese D. *history of aerospace technology educator*

Springfield
Casazza, John Andrew *electrical engineer, business executive, educator*
Galvin, Cyril Jerome, Jr., *coastal engineer*
Meikle, Philip G. *engineer, retired government agency executive*
Schlegelmilch, Reuben Orville *electrical engineer, consultant*
Thompson, Morris Mordecai *civil engineer, researcher, consultant*

Stafford
Tallent, Robert Glenn *chemical and environmental engineer, entrepreneur*

Staunton
Dixon, Corbin *retired electrical engineer, conservationist*
Smith, Rodney Wike *engineering executive*

Sterling
Coulter, David Creswell *research engineer*

Vienna
Benton, Stephen Richard *civil and mechanical engineer*
Keiser, Bernhard Edward *engineering company executive, consulting telecommunications engineer*

Mott, Charles Davis *civil engineer*
Mujumdar, Vilas Sitaram *structural engineer, trade association administrator*
Salah, Sagid *retired nuclear engineer*
Tennyson, Edson Leigh *transportation engineer*
Woodward, Kenneth Emerson *retired mechanical engineer*

Virginia Beach
Denyes, James Richard *industrial engineer*
Spivak, Maurice Sidney *chief project management, consultant*

Williamsburg
Aaron, Bertram Donald *engineering executive, management consultant*
Dunn, Ronald Holland *civil engineer, management executive, consultant*
Shoosmith, John Norman *retired aerospace engineer*

Woodbridge
Kreipke, Merrill Vincent *civil engineer, consultant*

Zacata
Gardiner, William Ralph *electrical engineer, consultant*

WASHINGTON

Anacortes
†Bacani, Nicanor-Guglielmo Vila *civil and structural engineer, consultant*

Auburn
Whitmore, Donald Clark *retired engineer*

Bainbridge Island
Eber, Lorenz *aeronautical engineer, civil engineer, inventor*

Bellevue
Faris, Charles Oren *civil engineer*
Hibbard, Richard Paul *industrial ventilation consultant, educator*
Killgore, Mark William *civil engineer*
†Neuzil, Dennis R. *civil engineer*
Shushkewich, Kenneth Wayne *structural engineer*
Wang, Xing *power systems engineer*
Zhu, Jizhong *engineering educator*

Bellingham
Albrecht, Albert Pearson *electronics/systems engineer, consultant*
Jansen, Robert Bruce *consulting civil engineer*

Black Diamond
Morris, David John *mining engineer, consultant, mining executive*

Chehalis
Nichols, James Raymond, Jr., *civil engineer*

Clinton
Jacobs, Harold Robert *mechanical engineering educator, practitioner*

Dupont
Pettit, Ghery St. John *electronics engineer*

Edmonds
Peckol, James Kenneth *consulting engineer*
Schmit, Lucien André, Jr., *structural engineer*
Terrel, Ronald Lee *civil engineer, business executive, educator*

Ellensburg
Bates, Dwight Lee *retired mechanical engineer*

Everson
Schmitz, Eugene Gerard *engineer*

Federal Way
Gates, Thomas Edward *civil engineer, waste management administrator*
Holman, Kermit Layton *chemical engineer*
Mast, Robert Frederick *structural engineer*
Studebaker, Irving Glen *mining engineering consultant*

Greenbank
Prochaska, Charles Roland *aerospace engineer*

Issaquah
Reid, John Mitchell (Jack Reid) *biomedical engineer, researcher, consultant*
Wright, Theodore Otis *forensic engineer*

Kenmore
Guy, Arthur William *electrical engineering educator, researcher*

Kennewick
Henager, Charles Henry *civil engineer*

Kingston
Longwell, John Ploeger *chemical engineering educator*

Kirkland
Forsen, Harold Kay *retired engineering executive*
Malcolm, David John *structural engineer, researcher*
Szablya, John Francis *electrical engineer, consultant*

Lummi Island
Ewing, Benjamin Baugh *environmental engineering educator, consultant*

Lynnwood
Schneider, Robert Kerry *electric utility engineer*
†Wicks, Patrick Heath *chemical engineering consultant*

Marysville
McClure, Allan Howard *materials engineer, space contamination specialist, space materials consultant*

Mercer Island
Bridgforth, Robert Moore, Jr., *aerospace engineer*

Mill Creek
Sengupta, Mritunjoy *mining engineer, educator*

Mukilteo
Bohn, Dennis Allen *electrical engineer, executive*

Nine Mile Falls
Maus, John Andrew *computer systems engineer, consultant*

Olympia
Das, Tapas Kumar *chemical and environmental engineer*
Sesonske, Alexander *nuclear and chemical engineer*

Port Ludlow
Pihl, James Melvin *electronic engineer*

Port Townsend
Wald, Quentin Roosevelt *research aerodynamics and hydrodynamics engineer*

Preston
Fadden, Delmar McLean *retired electrical engineer*

Pullman
Funk, William Henry *retired environmental engineering educator*
Katona, Michael George *civil engineer, educator*
Scheer, Gary Werner *electrical engineer*
Stock, David Earl *mechanical engineering educator*

Redmond
Egner, John David *electrical engineer*
Gorin, Ralph Edgar *software engineer, consultant*
Willard, H(arrison) Robert *electrical engineer*

Renton
†Majors, James Edward *electrical engineer*

Richland
Madni, Imtiaz K. *mechanical engineer*
Piper, Lloyd Llewellyn, II, *engineer, government and service industry executive*
Stenner, Robert David *environmental and health research engineer, toxicologist*

Seattle
Babb, Albert Leslie *biomedical engineer, educator*
Bowen, Jewell Ray *chemical engineering educator*
Burges, Stephen John *civil engineer, hydrologist*
Christiansen, Walter Henry *aeronautics educator*
Clark, Robert Newhall *electrical and aeronautical engineering educator*
Coleman, Debra Lynn *electrical engineer*
Davis, Earl James *chemical engineering educator*
Dreisbach, Rodney Lewis *structures engineer, researcher*
Drumheller, Kirk *retired engineering company executive*
Erickson, Virginia Bemmels *chemical engineer*
Finlayson, Bruce Alan *chemical engineering educator*
Gilbert, Paul H. *engineering executive, consultant*
Grisham, Andrew Fletcher *aerospace engineer, consultant*
Hands, Eric William *civil engineer, general engineer, researcher*
Hertzberg, Abraham *aeronautical engineering educator, university research scientist*
Hoffman, Allan Sachs *chemical engineer, educator*
Ishimaru, Akira *electrical engineering educator*
Kaplan, Laurence Scott *computer engineer*
Kapur, Kailash Chander *industrial engineering educator*
Kippenhan, Charles Jacob *mechanical engineer, retired educator*
Kobayashi, Albert Satoshi *mechanical engineering educator*
Mc Feron, Dean Earl *mechanical engineer, educator*
Montgomery, David Randolph *aeronautical engineer*
Murphy-Daniels, Karen Ilene *environmental, safety and health professional*
Oman, Henry *retired electrical engineer, engineering executive*
Parker, Donald Edward *aeronautics and aerospace educator*
Ratner, Buddy Dennis *bioengineer, educator*
†Roeder, Charles William *structural engineering educator*
Rojas, Eddy M. *engineering educator*
Sleicher, Charles Albert *chemical engineer*
Spindel, Robert Charles *electrical engineering educator*
Stephenson, Gary Van *electro-optics systems engineer*
Sutter, Joseph F. *aeronautical engineer, consultant, retired aircraft company executive*
Wenk, Edward, Jr., *civil engineer, policy analyst, educator, writer*
Wood, Stuart Kee *retired engineering manager*
Yeh, Ying Chin *electrical engineer*

Snohomish
Meister, John Edward, Jr., *technical educator, systems administrator*

South Bend
Heinz, Roney Allen *civil engineering consultant*

Spokane
Nandagopal, Mallur R. *engineer*

Sumner
Olson, Ronald Charles *aerospace executive*

Tacoma
Sloan, Daniel Kay *electrical engineer*

Vancouver
Taylor, Carson William *electrical engineer*

Woodland
Mairose, Paul Timothy *mechanical engineer, consultant*

Yelm
Kelley, Richard Allen, Jr., *software engineer*

WEST VIRGINIA

Charleston
Koleske, Joseph Victor *chemical engineer, consultant*
Lewis, Charles Raymond, II, *traffic engineer, consultant*
Sterling, Donald Eugene *civil engineer*

Fairmont
Richardson, Tia Maria *civil engineer, educator*

Huntington
Fischer, Robert Lee *engineering executive, educator*

Montgomery
Gourley, Frank Arnett, Jr., *engineering educator*
Sathyamoorthy, Muthukrishnan *engineering researcher, educator*

Morgantown
Eck, Ronald Warren *civil engineer, educator*
Gray, Donald Dwight *civil engineering educator*
Guthrie, Hugh Delmar *chemical engineer*
Kemp, Emory Leland *civil engineering educator*

Parkersburg
†Sperati, Carleton Angelo *retired industrial scientist*

South Charleston
Nielsen, Kenneth Andrew *chemical engineer*

Washington
Pace, John Edward, III, *chemical engineer*

Weirton
Adamczyk, Edmond David *metallurgical engineer*

WISCONSIN

Brookfield
Curfman, Floyd Edwin *engineering educator, retired*
Thomas, John *mechanical engineer, research and development*

Edgerton
Peck, David Blackman *electrical engineer*

Genoa
†Parkyn, John Duwane *nuclear engineer*

Green Bay
Panchalavarapu, Poornachandra Rao *industrial engineer, consultant*

Kenosha
Turner, Michael D. *chemical engineer*

La Crosse
Davy, Michael Francis *civil engineer, consultant*

Madison
Beachley, Norman Henry *mechanical engineer, educator*
Berthouex, Paul Mac *civil and environmental engineer, educator*
Bird, Robert Byron *chemical engineering educator, author*
Boyle, William Charles *civil engineering educator*
Carbon, Max William *nuclear engineering educator*
Converse, James Clarence *agricultural engineering educator*
Dietmeyer, Donald Leo *retired electrical engineer, educator*
Duffie, John Atwater *chemical engineer, educator*
Edil, Tuncer Berat *civil and environmental engineering educator*
†El-Guebaly, Laila Ahmed *nuclear engineer*
Emmert, Gilbert Arthur *engineer, educator*
Grogan, Paul J. *retired engineering educator*
Hill, Charles Graham, Jr., *chemical engineering educator*
Kulcinski, Gerald LaVerne *dean*
†Langer, Stanley Harold *chemical engineer, educator*
Lasseter, Robert Haygood *electrical engineering educator, consultant*
†Lee, Mark Charles *engineer*
Lightfoot, Edwin Niblock, Jr., *retired chemical engineering educator*
Long, Willis Franklin *electrical engineering educator, researcher*
Loper, Carl Richard, Jr., *metallurgical engineer, educator*

Lovell, Edward George *mechanical engineering educator*
Malkus, David Starr *retired mechanics educator, applied mathematician*
Nembhard, David A. *engineering educator, researcher*
Novotny, Donald Wayne *electrical engineering educator*
Skiles, James Jean *electrical and computer engineering educator*
†Smith, Michael James *industrial engineering educator*
Stewart, Warren Earl *chemical engineer, educator*
†Sun, Hongyu *electrical engineer, researcher*
†Vanderheiden, Gregg C. *engineering educator, research scientist*
Webster, John Goodwin *biomedical engineering educator, researcher*

Milwaukee
Chandler, Edward William *communication systems engineer, electrical engineer, electrical engineering educator*
Christensen, Erik Regnar *engineering educator, researcher*
Cutler, Verne Clifton *engineering educator, consultant*
Demerdash, Nabeel Aly Omar *electrical engineer*
Fournelle, Raymond Albert *engineering educator*
Gaggioli, Richard Arnold *mechanical engineering educator*
Graef, Luther William *civil engineer*
Heinen, James Albin *electrical engineering educator*
Horowitz, Alan Joel *civil engineer, educator*
†Kadel, Lee A. *computer engineer*
Landis, Fred *mechanical engineering educator*
Laubenheimer, Jeffrey John *civil engineer*
Li, Jin *environmental engineer, educator*
Vairavan, Kasivisvanathan *electrical engineering and computer science educator*
†Wen, Haifang *transportation engineer*
Widera, Georg Ernst Otto *mechanical engineering educator, consultant*
Wilsdon, Thomas Arthur *product development engineer, administrator*
Zuperku, Edward John *biomedical engineering educator*

Oconomowoc
Dupies, Donald Albert *retired civil engineer*

Racine
Stephens, James Linton *mechanical engineer*

Richland Center
Heinen, John Timothy *environmental engineer*

Waukesha
Mielke, William John *civil engineer*

Wauwatosa
Bub, Alexander David *acoustical engineer*

Wisconsin Rapids
Drew, Richard Allen *retired electrical and instrument engineer*

WYOMING

Casper
Hinchey, Bruce Alan *environmental engineering company executive, state legislator*

Cheyenne
Stoughton, Herbert Warren *geodetic engineer*

Laramie
Bellamy, John Cary *civil engineer, meteorologist*
Rechard, Paul Albert *retired civil engineering company executive, consultant*
Wright, Cameron Harrold Greene *electrical engineer*

Wilson
Lawroski, Harry *nuclear engineer*

TERRITORIES OF THE UNITED STATES

PUERTO RICO

Bayamon
†Ocasio, Luis Alberto *mechanical engineer, consultant*

MILITARY ADDRESSES OF THE UNITED STATES

PACIFIC

Apo
Turner, David Lowery *system safety engineer*

CANADA

ALBERTA

Calgary
†Dumbrava, Adrian *chemical engineer, process engineer*
Glockner, Peter G. *civil and mechanical engineering educator*

Heidemann, Robert Albert *chemical engineering educator, researcher*
Hovdestad, Wayne Roy *petroleum engineer*
Lam, Galen Ka-Ron *electrical engineer*
Malik, Om Parkash *electrical engineering educator, researcher*
McDaniel, Roderick Rogers *petroleum engineer, researcher*
†Skulmoski, Gregory James *project management engineer*
Telitchev, Igor Yevgenievich *aerospace engineering educator, researcher*

Edmonton
Lock, Gerald Seymour Hunter *retired mechanical engineering educator*
McDougall, John Roland *civil engineer*
Morgenstern, Norbert Rubin *civil engineering educator*
Offenberger, Allan Anthony *electrical engineering educator*
Otto, Fred Douglas *chemical engineering educator*
Zuo, Ming Jian *industrial engineering educator*

BRITISH COLUMBIA

Vancouver
Crawford, Carl Benson *retired civil engineer, government research administrator*
Grace, John Ross *chemical engineering educator*
Salcudean, Martha Eva *mechanical engineer, educator*
Young, Lawrence *electrical engineering educator*

Victoria
Antoniou, Andreas *electrical engineering educator*
Lind, Niels Christian *civil engineering educator*

Westbank
Wedepohl, Leonhard Martin *electrical engineering educator*

MANITOBA

Winnipeg
†Cohen, Harley *civil engineer, science educator*
Morrish, Allan Henry *electrical engineering educator*
Mufti, Aftab A. *civil engineering educator*

NEW BRUNSWICK

Fredericton
Bray, Dale Irving *civil engineering educator*

NEWFOUNDLAND

Saint John's
†Clark, Jack Ivor *civil engineer, researcher*
Meisen, Axel *chemical engineering educator, university dean*

NOVA SCOTIA

Kentville
Baker, George Chisholm *engineering executive, consultant*

ONTARIO

Burks Falls
Cameron, Gordon Murray *chemical engineer*

Burlington
Harris, Philip John *engineering educator*

Hamilton
Bandler, John William *electrical engineering educator, consultant*
Campbell, Colin Kydd *electrical and computer engineering educator, researcher*
Crowe, Cameron Macmillan *chemical engineering educator*
Gershman, Alexei *electrical engineer, researcher*
†Ghosh, Raja *engineering educator*
Wong, Kon Max *electrical engineering educator*

Kingston
Batchelor, Barrington de Vere *civil engineer, educator*
†Fam, Amir Z. *engineering educator, researcher*
Lewis, William John *aerospace engineer*

London
Davenport, Alan Garnett *civil engineer, educator*
Inculet, Ion I. *electrical engineering educator, research director, consultant*

Mississauga
Foda, Rabiz Nasir *industrial engineer, electrical engineer*
†Gupta, Rajesh *engineer, consultant*
John, Leonard Keith *aerospace and mechanical engineer*
Rygiel, Edward K. *chemical engineer*

North York
Buzacott, John Alan *engineering educator*
Tse, Philip Kui *airport engineering maintenance consultant*

Oakville
Yeom, Choong Kyun *chemical engineer, researcher*

Oshawa
Esmailzadeh, Ebrahim *mechanical engineering educator, consultant*

Ottawa
†Bozozuk, Michael *civil engineer*
Georganas, Nicolas D. *electrical engineering educator*
Moore, William John Myles *electrical engineer, researcher*
Seydnejad, Saeid Reza *engineering educator, consultant*

Saint Catharines
Picken, Harry Belfrage *aerospace engineer*

Toronto
Davison, Edward Joseph *electrical engineering educator*
Endrenyi, Janos *research engineer, educator*
Ganczarczyk, Jerzy Jozef *civil engineering educator, wastewater treatment consultant*
Goring, David Arthur Ingham *chemical engineering educator, scientist*
Janischewskyj, Wasyl *electrical engineering educator*
Kunov, Hans *biomedical and electrical engineering educator*
Meagher, George Vincent *mechanical engineer*
Rimrott, Friedrich Paul Johannes *engineering educator*
Runnalls, Oliver John Clyve (John Runnalls) *nuclear engineering educator*
Salama, C. Andre Tewfik *electrical engineering educator*
Sedra, Adel Shafeek *electrical engineering educator, academic administrator*
Semlyen, Adam *electrical engineering educator*
†Sennah, Khaled M. *structural engineering educator, consultant*
Slemon, Gordon Richard *electrical engineering educator*
Smith, Peter William Ebblewhite *electrical engineering educator, scientist, physicist*
Venetsanopoulos, Anastasios Nicolaos *electrical engineer, educator*
Wonham, Walter Murray *electrical engineer, educator*
Zeng, Hong *audio system architect, researcher*

Waterloo
Penlidis, Alexander *chemical engineering educator*
Vlach, Jiri *electrical engineering educator, researcher*

Windsor
Hackam, Reuben *electrical engineering educator*
†Kennedy, John Baptist *civil engineer*

QUEBEC

Montreal
Couture, Armand *civil engineer*
Dealy, John Michael *chemical engineer, educator*
Haccoun, David *electrical engineering educator*
Ladanyi, Branko *civil engineer, educator*
Lamarre, Bernard *engineering, contracting and manufacturing advisor*
Paidoussis, Michael Pandeli *mechanical engineering educator*
Ramachandran, Venkatanarayana Deekshit *electrical engineering educator*
Saint-Pierre, Guy *engineering executive*
Selvadurai, Antony Patrick Sinnappa *civil engineering educator, applied mathematician, consultant*

Quebec
Tavenas, François *civil engineer, educator*

Saint-Lambert
Terreault, Charles *engineer, management educator, researcher*

Sainte-Anne-de-Bellevue
Broughton, Robert Stephen *irrigation and drainage engineering educator, consultant*

Sainte-Foy
LeDuy, Anh *engineering educator*

Sillery
La Rochelle, Pierre-Louis *civil engineering educator*

Varennes
Bartnikas, Raymond *electrical engineer, educator*

Westmount
Kalaycioglu, Serdar *space robotics engineer, manager*

SASKATCHEWAN

Regina
Mollard, John Douglas *engineering and geology executive*

Saskatoon
Billinton, Roy *engineering educator*
†Smith, C. D. *civil engineering educator*

MEXICO

Mexico City
Olechnowicz Fridman, Elias *civil engineer*
Porraz, Mauricio Jimenez Labora *civil engineer, researcher*
Thomas, Zdeněk *retired civil engineer, researcher*

AUSTRALIA

Bankstown
Kruckenberg, Teresa May *research engineer, consultant*

Cammeray
Besley, Morrish Alexander (Tim Besley) *civil engineer*

BELGIUM

Ghent
Vandepitte, Daniël Camille Cornelis *civil engineering educator*

Roeselare
Libbrecht, Gaspar Joseph *civil engineer, educator*

CHINA

Beijing
Shu, Wenlong *environmental engineer, educator*

Shanghai
Yun, Liang *marine engineer, educator*

DENMARK

Copenhagen
Nielsen, Jens Evald *retired engineer*

Lyngby
Sumer, B. Mutlu *civil engineer, educator, researcher, consultant*

Vedbaek
Svensson, Sven Eilif *civil engineer, consultant*

ENGLAND

Ascot
Monk, Anthony John *engineer*

Coulsdon
Vijayaratnam, Kanapathipillai *civil and environmental engineer, consultant, director, educator*

Godalming
Port, Stanley Robert *civil engineer, data management engineer*

Grimsby
Burgess, John Richard *engineer*

Liverpool
Sawko, Felicjan *civil engineering educator*

London
Wolf, Peter Otto *civil engineer, consultant*

Southampton
Brebbia, Carlos Alberto *educator, engineering consultant*

Warwick
Cowlishaw, Michael Frederic *electronic engineer*

Westminster
Broers, Sir Alec Nigel *engineering educator*

FRANCE

Carriéres s/Seine
Saunier, Bernard-Marie *civil engineer*

Pantin
Limantour, Philippe *computer science research executive, educator*

Paris
Robillard, Alain Richard *civil engineer*

GERMANY

Aachen
Pischinger, Franz Felix *engineer, researcher*

Braunschweig
Duddeck, Heinz Werner *civil engineering educator*

Ilmenau
Schuller, Gerald Diedrich Thomas *electrical engineer*

Spraitbach
Kaffenberger, Ernst Wilhelm *engineer*

HONG KONG

Hong Kong
Kao, Charles Kuen *electrical engineer, educator*

Tai Po NT
Pien, Shyh-Jye John *mechanical engineer*

HUNGARY

Budapest
Nagy, Imre V. *civil engineer, educator*

Starosolszky, Ödön *civil engineer*
Tóth-Orowan, Lóránt Miklós *civil engineer*

INDIA

Calcutta
Garai, Gautam *engineer, researcher*

IRELAND

Dublin
Dooge, James Clement Ignatius *civil engineer, hydrologist, former senator*

Limerick
Parnas, David Lorge *engineering educator, computer scientist*

ISRAEL

Beer Sheva
Brosilow, Coleman Bernard *chemical engineering educator*

Tel Aviv
Eliaz, Noam *materials engineer, researcher*

ITALY

Milan
De Miranda, Fabrizio

Padua
Schrefler, Bernhard Aribo *civil engineering educator*

JAPAN

Nagoya
Sendo, Takeshi *mechanical engineering educator, researcher, author*

Shizuoka
Anma, So *engineer consultant*

Tokyo
Hori, Yukio *engineering educator, scientific association administrator*
Kato, Shuichi *information engineering educator*
Nishiwaki, Takeo *structural engineering educator*
Saito, Shuzo *electrical engineering educator*
Sakuta, Masaaki *engineering educator, consultant*

PAKISTAN

Lahore
Rai, Maqbool Ahmad *civil engineer, consultant*

PERU

Lima
Suazo, Miguel *civil engineer, consultant*

PORTUGAL

Algés
Horta, José Carlos de Oliveira Sousa *civil engineering consultant*

Lisbon
Serôdio, Ilídio de Ayala *civil engineer*

QATAR

Doha
†Zednik, Jay Juraj *marine engineer*

REPUBLIC OF KOREA

Pusan
Ha, Chang Sik *polymer science educator*

Taejon
Kang, Kyungin *electronics engineer, researcher*
Park, Seok-Kyun *civil engineer, educator*

SAUDI ARABIA

Riyadh
Alsubaie, Abdulaziz Mohamed *civil engineer*

SCOTLAND

Edinburgh
Sinha, Brajraman Prasad *civil engineer, educator*

SINGAPORE

Singapore
†Zhou, Wei *engineer, educator*

SLOVAKIA

Bratislava
Fristacky, Norbert *computer engineering educator, researcher*

SPAIN

Alcobendas
†Pumares, Luis Jose *industrial engineer*

SWEDEN

Askim
Bakhuizen, Willem Anthonie Hendrik Johannes *civil engineer*

Bromma
Orrje, Olle *civil engineer, jazz musician, poet*

Gothenburg
Wallmark, John Torkel *scientist, educator*

Göteborg
Bornstein, Jan Martin *computer engineer*

Uppsala
Wörman, Anders Lars Edvard *civil engineering educator*

SWITZERLAND

Zurich
Gazzetta, Moreno Augusto *engineer*
Morari, Manfred *chemical engineer, educator*

TAIWAN

Tainan
Huang, Ting-Chia *chemical engineering educator, researcher*
Lin, Jiin-Huey Chern *engineering educator*

TURKEY

Bilkent Ankara
Akman, Varol *computer engineer, educator*

UNITED ARAB EMIRATES

Abu Dhabi
Dajani, Jarir Subhi *civil engineer, consultant*

WALES

Gwynedd
Kuncheva, Ludmila Ilieva *engineering educator*

Porthmadog
Owen, Walter Shepherd *materials science and engineering educator*

ZIMBABWE

Harare
Salahuddin, Ahmad *civil engineer, educator*

ADDRESS UNPUBLISHED

Aasen, Arne *civil engineer, researcher, artist*
Abetti, Pier Antonio *consulting electrical engineer, technology management and entrepreneurship educator*
†Adam, Paul James *mechanical engineer*
†Agins, Barnett Robert *electrical engineer, educator*
Aguinsky, Richard Daniel *electrical engineer, administrator*
Ahmer, Inam
†Albin, Woodrow Ross *civil engineer*
Allen, Alfred William *chemical engineer, consultant*
Allison, John McComb *retired aeronautical engineer*
†Alvarez-Gomariz, Husayn *simulation engineer, physicist*
Amancio, Ruth Carson *safety engineer*
Amann, Charles Albert *mechanical engineer, researcher*
Anderson, John Gaston *electrical engineer, consultant*
Anderson, Thomas Patrick *mechanical engineer, educator*
Andersson, Per Lennart *computer engineer, consultant*
Andrea, Mario Iacobucci *engineer, scientist, gemologist, appraiser*
Archer, Hugh Morris *consulting engineer, retired manufacturing executive*
Arcot, Prakash Kumar B *engineer, consultant*
Arenberg, Jonathan William *engineer*
Armaingaud, Franck *engineer*
†Azad, Gm Salam *engineer, researcher*
Azadeh, Mohammad *electrical engineer, researcher*
†Azar, Fred S. *biomedical engineer, researcher*
†Babcock, James William *geotechnical engineer*
Baddour, Raymond Frederick *chemical engineer, educator, entrepreneur*
Bailey, Michael Wallace *aerospace engineer*

†Baker, Jack Thomas *design engineer, environmental scientist, consultant*
Bakht, Baidar *civil engineer, researcher, educator*
†Ballhaus, William Louis *engineering executive*
Baltazzi, Evan Serge *engineering research consulting company executive*
Bamberger, Joseph Alexander *mechanical engineer, educator*
Banerjee, Kaustav *electrical and computer engineering educator*
Barbee, Steven George *engineer*
Bar-Cohen, Avram *mechanical engineering educator*
Baron, Barton Leonard *engineer*
Bartlett, Desmond William *engineering company executive*
Battaglia, Francine *mechanical engineering educator, researcher*
Batzer, John L. *systems engineer*
Bauer, Richard Carlton *nuclear engineer*
Beard, Leo Roy *retired civil engineer*
Beckjord, Eric Stephen *nuclear engineer, energy researcher*
Beckwith, Larry Edward *mechanical engineer*
Bellow, Donald Grant *mechanical engineering educator*
Berger, Frederick Jerome *electrical engineer, educator*
Bergeron, Elmo P. *chemical engineer, consultant*
Bergfield, Gene Raymond *engineering educator*
Bers, Abraham *electrical engineering and physics educator*
Bershad, Neil Jeremy *electrical engineering educator*
†Bescher, Eric Pascal *engineering educator, researcher*
Beumer, Richard Eugene *engineer, architect, construction firm executive*
†Bhatia, Rajan *engineer, physicist, researcher*
Bierley, Paul Edmund *aeronautical engineer, musician, author, publisher*
Bigham, James George *structural engineer*
Bishop, Paul Leslie *civil and environmental engineering educator, environmental engineering consultant*
Bjorndahl, David Lee *electrical engineer*
Bloch, Erich *retired electrical engineer, former science foundation administrator*
Bodensieck, Ernest Justus *mechanical engineer*
Boedo, Stephen *mechanical engineer, consultant*
†Bonato, Paolo *electrical engineer, educator*
Boppe, Charles William *aeronautical engineering educator*
Bornhorst, Kenneth Frank *electromagnetics and systems engineer*
Bose, Anjan *electrical engineering educator, academic administrator*
Boundy, David Eric *patent lawyer, computer engineer*
Bowman, Charles Hay *retired engineering educator, petroleum company executive*
Boyle, Bryan Douglas *computer and network systems architect*
Bradshaw, Peter *engineering educator*
Brar, Berinder Pal Singh *engineer*
Brennan, Lawrence Edward *electronics engineer*
Brickell, Charles Hennessey, Jr., *marine engineer, retired military officer*
Bridger, Baldwin, Jr., *electrical engineer*
Briggs, James Henry, II, *engineering administrator*
†Bronson, Robert Lee *engineering company inventor, retired*
Brown, Donald Richard *capacitor engineer*
Brozowski, Laura Adrienne *mechanical engineer*
Brubaker, James Edward *mechanical engineer*
Brungraber, Robert J. *civil engineer, educator*
†Brustman, Richard D. *civil engineer, consultant*
†Bueno, Pablo Cesar *aeronautical engineer, educator*
Bugno, Walter Thomas *civil engineer*
Bunch, Jennings Bryan, Jr., *electrical engineer*
Burchard, John Kenneth *retired chemical engineer*
Burhans, Frank Malcolm *mechanical engineer*
Burns, Richard Francis *mechanical engineer*
Bush, Marilyn Wolin *management consultant, software engineer*
†Butler, Sheryl L. *systems engineer, consultant*
Buttz, Gabriela I *chemical engineer, artist*
Byrd, Lloyd Garland *civil engineer*
Caffey, James Enoch *civil engineer*
Calder, Robert Mac *aerospace engineer*
Callanan, Kathleen Joan *retired electrical engineer*
Cao, L. Charlie *structural engineer, consultant*
Carlson, Robert Codner *industrial engineering educator*
Carlton, Doug A. *standards engineer*
†Carreau, Pierre *chemical engineering educator*
Carreker, John Russell *retired agricultural engineer*
†Carroll, Philip Joseph, Jr., *engineering company executive*
Cassidy, Kevin Andrew *retired engineering company executive*
Cech, Joseph Harold *retired chemical engineer*
Cerny, Louis Thomas *civil engineer, railway engineering consultant*
Cha, Soyoung Stephen *mechanical engineer, educator*
Chance, Kenneth Donald *engineer*
Chandra, Abhijit *engineering educator*
†Chang, Nelson Liang An *electrical engineer, researcher*
Charwat, Andrew Franciszek *engineering educator*
†Chen, Chin-Jung *mechanical engineer*
Cheng, Liang *electrical engineer, researcher*
Cheng, Liangsheng *engineer, researcher, educator*
Cheston, Theodore C. *electrical engineer*
Childress, Dudley Stephen *biomedical engineer, educator*

Raven, Francis Harvey *mechanical engineering educator*
Rea, James Jason *engineer*
Reaves, Ray Donald *civil engineer*
Rector, William David *civil engineer*
Rehm, Leo Frank *civil engineer*
Reid, Robert Lelon *retired mechanical engineering educator, dean*
Reinfelds, Juris *computer engineer, educator*
Reitan, Daniel Kinseth *electrical and computer engineering educator*
Remer, Donald Sherwood *engineering educator, engineering economist, cost estimator, management consultant*
Ren, Chung-Li *engineer*
†Ren, Ying *engineer*
†Reynerson, Charles *aerospace engineer, educator*
Reynik, Robert John *materials scientist, research and education administrator*
Richards, Earl Frederick *electrical engineer, educator*
Richards-Barnard, Sandra L. *control systems engineer, computer graphics consultant*
Riden, Michael David *nuclear engineer*
Riffe, Delmar Ray *engineer*
Rinder, Herbert Roy *retired electrical engineer*
†Roberts, George Edward *retired systems engineer*
Rockefeller, Harry Andrew *software engineer*
Rodgers, Billy Russell *chemical engineer, research scientist*
Rogo, Kathleen *safety engineer, researcher*
Rohr, Davis Charles *aerospace consultant, business executive, retired air force officer*
Rolewicz, Robert John *estimating engineer*
†Rollins, Andrew Martin *biomedical engineer, educator*
Rooke, Allen Driscoll, Jr., *civil engineer, consultant*
Rosen, Bernard *engineer, engineering company executive*
Rosenburgh, Dwayne Maurice *electronics engineer*
Ross, Donald Edward *engineering company executive*
Rudd, D(ale) F(rederick) *chemical engineering educator*
Rusen, Theodore, Jr., *civil engineer*
Russo, Roy Lawrence *retired electronic design automation engineer*
Saeks, Richard Ephraim *engineering executive*
Saha, Arun Kumar *engineering educator, researcher*
Saiff, Joshua M. *mechanical engineer*
Sainani, Ram Hariram *civil engineer*
†Sajda, Paul *biomedical engineer, educator*
Salamon, Miklos Dezso Gyorgy *mining engineer, educator*
Salkind, Michael Jay *technology administrator*
Salvatorelli, Joseph J. *engineer, consultant*
Satterlee, George Leonard, Jr., *retired civil engineer, consultant*
Savage, Richard Mark *retired systems engineer*
Savrun, Ender *engineering executive, researcher, engineer*
†Saxena, Vishal *mechanical engineer*
Sazawal, Vijay Kumar *engineering executive*
Schaefer, Robert Paul *software engineer*
Schell, Allan Carter *retired electrical engineer*
Scherrer, George M. *electrical engineer*
Schloesslin, Mark Edward *software quality engineer*
Schmidt, Robert *retired mechanics and civil engineering educator*
Schnelle, Phillip David *electrical engineer, consultant*
Schoen, Allen Harry *retired aerospace engineering executive*
Schrader, Henry Carl *retired civil engineer, consultant*
Schultz, Albert Barry *engineering educator*
Schurmeier, Harris McIntosh *aeronautical engineer*
Schuster, Robert Conrad *consulting engineer*
Scott, Charles David *chemical engineer, consultant*
Scott, Ralph Gordon *retired engineer, association editor*
Seaden, George *civil engineer*
Seamans, Robert Channing, Jr., *astronautical engineering educator*
Seldner, Betty Jane *environmental engineer, consultant, aerospace company executive*
Sells, Kevin Dwayne *marine engineer*
Senyard, Corley Price, Jr., *engineering executive, consultant*
†Sepanloo, Al *electrical engineer*
Seymour, Frederick Prescott, Jr., *industrial engineer, consultant*
Shaffer, Bernard William *mechanical and aerospace engineering educator*
Shangguan, Dongkai *mechanical engineer*
Shank, Maurice Edwin *aerospace engineering executive, consultant*
Sharp, Pamela Ann *quality assurance engineer*
Sheaffer, Richard Allen *electrical engineer*
Sheem, Sang Keun *fiber optics engineering professional*
Sheridan, Thomas Brown *mechanical engineering and applied psychology educator, researcher, consultant*
Sherman, Frank William *engineer*
Shur, Michael *electrical engineer, educator, consultant*
Shuster, John A. *civil engineer*
Siljak, Dragoslav D. *engineering educator, researcher*
†Silsby, Graham Forbes *mechanical engineer, consultant*
Simon, Marvin Kenneth *electrical engineer, consultant*
Simpson, Murray *engineer, consultant*
†Singhal, Rajan *engineering executive, consultant*
Sitnyakovsky, Roman Emmanuil *scientist, writer, inventor, translator*
Skeels, Stephen Glenn *civil engineer*

Skelland, Anthony Harold Peter *chemical engineering educator*
Skov, Arlie Mason *petroleum engineer, consultant*
Skromme, Lawrence H. *consulting agricultural engineer*
Sloan, Jason Gerard *aerospace engineer*
Smally, Donald Jay *consulting engineering executive*
Smith, Frank Neale *materials and corrosion engineer*
Smith, Kevin S. *civil engineer*
Smith, Virgil Baker *retired electrical engineer*
Somasundaran, Ponisseril *surface and colloid engineer, applied science educator*
Sormaz, Dusan Nedeljko *industrial engineer, educator, researcher*
Sorrells, Frank Douglas *retired mechanical engineer*
Sowers, William Armand *civil engineer*
Spanovich, Milan *retired civil engineer*
Speciner, Michael *computer engineer*
Spelson, Nicholas James *engineering executive, retired*
Spoeri, Laura Lenhardt *industrial engineer, consultant*
†Sponable, Jess M. *astronautical engineer, physicist*
Stafford, James Polk, Jr., *civil engineer*
Stallings, Viola Patricia Elizabeth *systems engineer, educational systems specialist, retired information technology manager*
†Stanboulian, Hovig Jean *electrical engineer, director*
Stephens, John Joseph, Jr., *materials engineer*
Stevenson, Warren Howard *mechanical engineering educator*
Stewart, Albert Elisha *safety engineer, industrial hygienist*
Stiffler, Jack Justin *electrical engineer*
Stoica, Susana *computer/electrical engineer, scientist, author, healer*
†Strange, Nathan John *aerospace engineer*
Stratton, Roy Franklin *retired electronics engineer*
Stumpe, Warren Robert *county official, retired scientific, engineering and technical services company executive*
Suarez, Michael Anthony *civil engineer, consultant*
†Subbarao, Kamesh *aeronautical engineer*
Subramanian, R. Shankar *chemical engineer, educator*
Subramanian, Ravi *electrical engineer*
Sullivan, Gregory Patrick, Sr., *research engineer*
Sullivan, Paul Andrew *retired research electrical engineer*
†Sun, Yi *optical engineer, researcher*
Sundaram, Ramakrishnan *engineering educator*
Sutton, Nigel James *aeronautical engineer, test flight officer*
†Svatek, Patrick Lawrence *aerospace engineer*
Swalm, Thomas Sterling *aerospace executive, retired military officer*
Swift, Jill Anne *industrial engineer, educator*
Swisher Harnetty, Stacey Elaine *mechanical engineer*
Tachau, Herman *structural engineer*
†Tate, Raymond Grant *research and consulting executive*
Taylor, David Spencer *engineer*
†Teshirogi, Jerry Takahide *aerospace engineer*
Tetelbaum, Solomon David *research engineer*
Thackston, Edward Lee *engineer, educator*
†Thomas, Matthew Shawn *civil engineer*
Thomason, Harry Jack Lee, Jr., *mechanical engineer*
Todd Copley, Judith A. *materials and metallurgical engineering educator*
Tokerud, Robert Eugene *retired electrical engineer*
Tontiruttananon, Channarong *electrical engineer, researcher*
Trauger, Donald Byron *nuclear engineering laboratory administrator*
Treinavicz, Kathryn Mary *software engineer*
Trujillo-Cuthrell, Loretta Marie *chemical engineer*
†Tsygan, Leonid Iosifovich *civil engineer, writer*
Tumbleson, Arthur Louis *civil engineer, contractor*
Turchi, Peter John *aerospace and electrical engineer, physicist, educator*
Turner, Leland S., Jr., (Lee Turner) *civil engineer, consultant, former utilities executive*
Uht, Augustus Kinzel *computer engineering researcher*
Underwood, Ralph Edward *computer engineer*
Upatnieks, Juris *retired optical engineer*
Urbanik, Thomas, II, *civil engineering educator, researcher*
Vega, J. William *aerospace engineering executive, consultant*
†Velev, Miroslav N. *electrical engineer, educator*
Vér, István László *acoustical engineer, consultant*
Verbov, Lev Falkovich *metallurgical engineer, writer, translator*
Viest, Ivan M(iroslav) *consulting structural engineer*
Voldman, Steven Howard *electrical engineer*
Wagner, John Philip *safety engineering educator, science researcher*
Wakeman, Thomas Herbert, III, *civil engineer, regional administrator*
Walasek, Otto Frank *chemical engineer, biochemist, photographer*
Walker, Loren Haines *electrical engineer*
Walton, Harold Vincent *former agricultural engineering educator, academic administrator*
Wang, Leon Ru-Liang *civil engineer, educator*
Wang, Qigui *materials engineer, researcher*
Wang, Qin *computer engineer, researcher*
Wang, Wanlong *engineer, researcher*
†Wang, Xi Cheng (David Wang) *mechanical engineer*
†Washington, Donna Janel *engineer*

Waxman, Ronald *computer engineer*
Weinberger, Arnold *retired electrical engineer*
Weingarten, Joseph Leonard *aerospace engineer*
Weiss, Alvin Harvey *chemical engineering educator, catalysis researcher and consultant*
Weldon, William Forrest *electrical and mechanical engineer, educator*
Wentz, William Henry, Jr., *aerospace engineer, educator*
Wheeler, George Charles *materials and processes engineer*
Whitcomb, Richard Travis *aeronautical consultant*
Whitehead, Nelson Peter *engineering company executive, consultant*
Wicke, Dallas Clyde *retired aerospace engineer*
Wilde, Daniel Underwood *computer engineering educator*
Wilhoit, Darrel Loel *chemical engineer*
†Willard, John Charles, Sr., *computer engineer, educator*
Williams, Charles Wesley *technical executive, researcher*
Williams, Howard Walter *aerospace engineer, executive*
Williams, Ronald Oscar *defense systems engineer*
Wilson, Melvin Edmond *civil engineer*
Winston, Thomas George *engineering educator, consultant*
Wintle, Rosemarie *biomedical electronics engineer*
†Witkowski, Allen *aeronautical engineer*
Wong, Kainam Thomas *electrical engineer*
Wood, Allen John *electrical engineer, consultant*
†Woodland, N. Joseph *retired optical engineer, retired mechanical engineer*
Woodward, Clinton Benjamin, Jr., *civil engineering educator*
†Wright, Brian Theodore *retired engineering executive*
†Xiao, Jizhong *engineering educator, researcher*
Yadav, Sunil *mechanical engineer*
Yang, Xiaoping *engineering researcher*
Yao, James Tsu-Ping *retired civil engineer*
Ye, Nan *engineer*
Yeager, Kurt Eric *research institute official*
Yeh, Jung-Hua *senior mechanical engineer*
†Yen, Bing Cheng *retired civil engineer, retired engineering educator*
Yen, Wen Liang *retired aerospace engineer*
Yerion, Michael Ross *civil engineer*
†Yin, Zhiping *engineer*
Ying, Jackie *chemical engineer, educator*
†Yocam, Eric Wayne *engineer*
Yong, Raymond Nen-Yiu *civil engineering educator*
†Yoon, Sei Seung *engineer*
Young, Leo *electrical engineer*
Yue, Alfred Shui-choh *metallurgical engineer, educator*
Yun, James Kyoon *electrical engineer*
Zajta, Aurel Joseph *software engineer, mathematician*
Zanjacomo, Paulo Regis *engineering executive*
Zeitlin, Gerald Mark *electrical engineer*
†Zeleke, Assefa *electrical engineer*
Zelinski, Joseph John *engineering educator, consultant*
†Zhang, Huanlin *electrical engineer*
†Zhou, Yuanxin *mechanical engineer, educator*
Zimmerman, Roger Max *civil engineer*

FINANCE: BANKING SERVICES
See also **FINANCE:
INVESTMENT SERVICES**

UNITED STATES

ALABAMA

Atmore
Garrard, John, Jr., *bank executive, city councilman*

Birmingham
†Horsley, Richard David *banker*
†Jones, Carl E., Jr., *bank executive*
Jones, D. Paul, Jr., *banker, lawyer*
Morgan, Hugh Jackson, Jr., *bank executive*
†Northen, Charles Swift, III, *retired banker*
Powell, William Arnold, Jr., *retired bank executive*
Stone, Edmund Crispen, III, *banker*
Weatherly, Robert Stone, Jr., *banker*

Daphne
†Spybey, Amanda N. *mortgage company executive*

Dothan
Peterson, M. Roger *community bank executive, retired international investment banker, retired manufacturing executive, retired Air Force officer*

Locust Fork
Edwards, Sheila M. *banker, educator*

Mobile
Coker, Donald William *economic, management, banking, evaluation, healthcare, international business and real estate consultant, stock trader*

Montgomery
Hoffman, Richard William *banker*
Taylor, Watson Robbins, Jr., *investment banker*

ALASKA

Anchorage
Cuddy, Daniel Hon *bank executive*
Rasmuson, Edward Bernard *banker*
†Reed, Frank Metcalf *bank executive, director*

ARIZONA

Fort Smith
†Detary, Timothy James *banking and health care executive*

Gilbert
Duran, Michael Carl *bank executive*

Paradise Valley
Unruh, James Arlen *banking executive*

Phoenix
Holman, John Foster *investment banker*

Scottsdale
Carpenter, Peter Rockefeller *retired bank executive*
Garfield, Ernest *bank consultant*

Surprise
Koessel, Donald Ray *retired banker*

Tubac
Miller, Frederick Robeson *banker*

Tucson
Bradley, Gilbert Francis *retired banker*
Markman, Sherman *investment banker, venture capitalist*

ARKANSAS

Bentonville
Walton, Alice L. *bank executive*

Forrest City
Stipe, John Ryburn *bank executive*

Little Rock
Bowen, William Harvey *banker, lawyer*
Franks, Candace Ann *bank executive*
Gulley, Wilbur Paul, Jr., *retired savings and loan association executive*

CALIFORNIA

Arcadia
Kalm, Arne *investment banker*
Ulrich, Peter Henry *banker*

Bakersfield
Sawyer, Nelson Baldwin, Jr., *credit union executive*

Beverly Hills
†Conner, Lindsay Andrew *investment banker*
Goldsmith, Bram *banker*
Matzdorff, James Arthur *investment banker, internet marketing professional*
Spivak, Jacque R. *bank executive*
Walker, William Tidd, Jr., *investment banker*

Burbank
Miller, Clifford Albert *merchant banker, business consultant*

Carmel
Barton, Hugh Perry *bank executive*
Dobey, James Kenneth *banker*

Concord
Miller, John Nelson *banker*

Davis
Kaplan, Douglas Allen *financial care company executive*

Escondido
Newman, Barry Ingalls *retired banker, lawyer*

Fallbrook
David, Ward S. *bank officer, retired federal agency executive*

Folsom
Hennessey, David Patrick *banker*

Fresno
Smith, Richard Howard *banker*

Glendale
Cross, Richard John *banker*

Huntington Beach
MacCauley, Hugh Bournonville *banker*

Irvine
Giannini, Valerio Louis *investment banker*
Jamshidipour, Yousef *bank executive, economist, financial advisor*

La Mesa
Schmidt, James Craig *retired bank executive*

La Palma
†Sinard, Gary *mortgage company executive*

Lafayette
Dethero, J. Hambright *banker*

Laguna Hills
Pelton, Harold Marcel *mortgage broker*

Lake Arrowhead
Fitzgerald, John Charles, Jr., *investment banker*

†Kincaid, Richard D. *bank executive*
Logan, David Samuel *investment banker*
Lorenz, Katherine Mary *banker*
McKay, Neil *banker*
Pollock, Alexander John *banker*
Roberts, Theodore Harris *banker*
Schulte, David Michael *investment banker*
Scully, John Edward, Jr., *banker*
Seaman, Irving, Jr., *banker*
Stepke, Russ *investment banker, lawyer*
Stirling, James Paulman *investment banker*
Swift, Edward Foster, III, *investment banker*
Theobald, Thomas Charles *banker*
Thomas, Richard Lee *banker*
Vander Wilt, Carl Eugene *banker*
Varwig, David Lee *merchant banker*
Williams, Edward Joseph *banker*

Dundee
Weck, Kristin Willa *bank executive*

Evanston
Scholten, Menno Nico *mortgage banker*

Fox River Grove
Abboud, Alfred Robert *banker, consultant, investor*

Glenview
Jacobson, Earl James *lawyer, investment banker*

Golf
Fellingham, Warren Luther, Jr., *retired banker*

Highwood
Brown, Lawrence Haas *banker*

Hinsdale
Kinney, Kenneth Parrish *retired banker*

Hoffman Estates
Weston, Roger Lance *banker*

Hopedale
Birky, John Edward *banker, consultant, financial advisor*

Kenilworth
Corrigan, John Edward, Jr., *banker, lawyer*

Lake Forest
McCormack, Robert Cornelius *investment banker*
Rahe, Maribeth Sembach *bank executive*
Ross, Robert Evan *bank executive*

Moline
Parise, Marc Robert *banker*

Northbrook
Gratalo, John, Jr., *mortgage banker, business owner*
Keehn, Silas *retired bank executive*

Oak Brook
Iles, Eileen Marie *bank executive*

Oak Park
Kinzie, Raymond Wyant *banker, lawyer*

Palatine
Hershenhorn, Robert Gene *bank executive*

Peoria
Bussone, Frank Joseph *bank executive, television broadcaster*

Tinley Park
Keenan, Robert Arthur *bank executive, consultant*

Washington
Blumenshine, Mahlon *banker*

Wilmette
†Griffiths, Robert Pennell *banker*

Winnetka
Fenton, Clifton Lucien *investment banker*
Klapperich, Frank Lawrence, Jr., *investment banker*

INDIANA

Columbus
Abts, Henry William *banker*
Nash, John Arthur *bank executive*

Fort Wayne
Shaffer, Paul E. *retired banker*

Greenwood
†Broscoe, Peter A. *mortgage banker, consultant*

Indianapolis
Meyer, William Michael *mortgage banking executive*

Muncie
Anderson, Stefan Stolen *banker*
†Sursa, Charles David *banker*

Ogden Dunes
Gasser, Wilbert, Jr., (Wilbert Warner Gasser Jr.) *retired banker*

South Bend
†Jones, Wellington Downing, III, *banker*

Terre Haute
Smith, Donald E. *banker*

IOWA

Cedar Rapids
Nebergall, Donald Charles *rural consultant*

Wax, Nadine Virginia *retired banker*

Des Moines
Edwards, Richard Alan *banker*

Missouri Valley
Johnson, Michael Randy *bank executive*

KANSAS

Coldwater
Adams, Elizabeth Herrington *banker*

Leawood
Gregory, Lewis Dean *trust company executive*

Manhattan
Stolzer, Leo William *bank executive*

Overland Park
De Vries, Robert John *investment banker*

Pratt
Loomis, Howard Krey *banker*

Shawnee Mission
McEachen, Richard Edward *banker, lawyer*

Tonganoxie
Torneden, Connie Jean *bank officer*

Topeka
Bunten, William Daniel *retired banker*

KENTUCKY

Georgetown
White, Mary Ann *bank executive*

Inez
Duncan, Robert Michael *banker, lawyer, Republican national committeeman*

Lexington
Savage, William Earl *savings and loan executive, religious educator*

Louisville
Guillaume, Raymond Kendrick *banker*

Owensboro
Johnston, Barry Algene *housing loan administrator*

Shepherdsville
Pike, Burlyn *retired bank director, lawyer*

LOUISIANA

Alexandria
Bolton, Robert Harvey *banker*

Covington
Blossman, Alfred Rhody, Jr., *banker*

Lafayette
Stuart, Walter Bynum, III, *banker*

New Orleans
†Milling, R(oswell) King *bank executive, lawyer*

MAINE

Andover
Ellis, George Hathaway *retired banker and utility company executive*

Bangor
Bullock, William Clapp, Jr., *banker*

Cape Elizabeth
Cotter, Joseph Francis *retired hotel and bank executive*

MARYLAND

Annapolis
Gavian, Peter Wood *investment banker*
McGuirk, Ronald Charles *retired banker, economic advisor*
Schleicher, Nora Elizabeth *banker, treasurer, accountant*

Baltimore
Baldwin, Henry Furlong *banker*
Barnhill, Gregory Hurd *investment banker*
Dunn, Edward K., Jr., *banker*
Kent, Edgar Robert, Jr., *investment banker*
Liberto, Joseph Salvatore *retired banker*
Morrel, William Griffin, Jr., *banker*
Murphy, Shaun Edward *bank executive*
Schaefer, Robert Wayne *banker*
Wieler, Scott Alan *investment banker*

Bethesda
Rosenbaum, Greg Alan *merchant banker, consultant*
Saul, B. Francis, II, *bank executive, director*

Darnestown
†Lightner, Gene Cleek *investment banker*

Frederick
Hoff, Charles Worthington, III, *banker*

Owings Mills
Sanner, George Bradley *bank executive*

Potomac
Martinez, Miguel Eduardo *development bank executive*
Schonholtz, Joan Sondra Hirsch *banker, civic worker*

Rockville
Meyer, F. Weller *bank executive*

Sparks Glencoe
†Swackhamer, Gene L. *bank executive*

MASSACHUSETTS

Boston
Alden, Vernon Roger *corporate director, trustee*
Aquilino, Daniel *banker*
Brown, William L. *banker*
†Comeau, Susan *bank executive*
Finnegan, Neal Francis *banker*
Gifford, Charles Kilvert *banker*
Hoffer, David Paul *investment banker, lawyer*
Mullin, Patricia Jones *banker*
Phillips, Daniel Anthony *trust company executive*
†Szostak, M. Anne *bank executive*

Cambridge
Edgerly, William Skelton *banker*

Dover
Aldrich, Frank Nathan *banker*

Duxbury
Safe, Kenneth Shaw, Jr., *fiduciary firm executive*

Gloucester
Fioravanti, Nancy Eleanor *retired banker*

Lenox
Newton, Frank George *bank executive*

Longmeadow
Lo Bello, Joseph David *bank executive*

Methuen
Simoes, Ronald Alan *mortgage company executive*

Natick
Weisberg, Bruce Steven *bank executive*

Newburyport
MacWilliams, Kenneth Edward *investment banker*

Newton
Teig, Marlowe Gilman *investment banker*

Norwood
Carpenter, Pamela Prisco *bank officer, foreign language educator*

Reading
Burbank, Nelson Stone *investment banker*

Salem
McLaughlin, Michael Angelo *mortgage consultant, author*

Wellesley
Mailer-Howat, Patrick Lindsay Macalpine *investment banker*
Small, Parker Adams, III, *investment banker*

Westport
Nichols, C. Walter, III, *retired trust company executive*

Westwood
Riley, Henry Charles *banker*

Winchester
Brennan, Francis Patrick *banker*

Worcester
Hunt, John David *retired banker*
Spencer, Harry Irving, Jr., *retired banker*

MICHIGAN

Ann Arbor
†Nelson, Jason Craig *company executive*

Bay City
Van Dyke, Clifford Craig *retired banker*

Bloomfield Hills
Colladay, Robert S. *trust company executive, consultant*
†McQueen, Patrick M. *bank executive*
†Miller, Eugene Albert *retired bank executive*

Clarkston
†Snow, Sandra Inez *mortgage company executive*

Detroit
Babb, Ralph W., Jr., *banker*
†Buttigieg, Joseph J. *banking executive*
Greenwood, Harriet Lois *environmental banker, researcher*

Farmington Hills
Heiss, Richard Walter *former bank executive, consultant, lawyer*

Frankfort
Foster, Robert Carmichael *banker*

Grand Rapids
Canepa, John Charles *banking consultant*

Grosse Pointe Farms
Surdam, Robert McClellan *retired banker*

Grosse Pointe Park
Harmon, Phyllis Darnell *mortgage banker*

Saginaw
Evans, Harold Edward *banker*

Saint Joseph
Wallace, Jon Robert *mortgage company executive, marketing professional*

Southfield
Shields, Robert Emmet *merchant banker, lawyer*

Suttons Bay
Whitney, William Chowning *retired banker, financial consultant*

Waterford
Houston, E. James, Jr., *bank officer, consultant*

MINNESOTA

Chanhassen
Severson, Roger Allan *bank executive*

Duluth
Madich, Bernadine Marie Hoff *savings and loan executive*

Minneapolis
Campbell, James Robert *retired bank executive*
†Cooper, William Allen *banking executive*
†Griffith, Sima Lynn *investment banker, consultant*
Grundhofer, Jerry A. *bank executive*
Grundhofer, John F. *banking executive*
Morrison, Clinton *banker*
Rahn, Alvin Albert *former banker*
Walters, Glen Robert *banker*
†Zona, Richard A. *bank executive*

Saint Paul
Rothmeier, Steven George *merchant banker, investment manager*

Wayzata
Rich, Willis Frank, Jr., *banker*

MISSISSIPPI

Gulfport
Thatcher, George Robert *banker, columnist, author*

Tupelo
Patterson, Aubrey Burns, Jr., *banker*
Ramage, Martis Donald, Jr., *banker*

MISSOURI

Clayton
Kemper, David Woods, II, *banker*

Kansas City
Green, Jerry Howard *investment banker*
†Kemper, Jonathan McBride *banker*

Saint Louis
Barksdale, Clarence Caulfield *banker*
Bryant, Ruth Alyne *banker*
Costigan, Edward John *investment banker*
David, Lynn Allen *banking executive*
Dohr, John Michael, Jr., *banker*
Joyner, Dee Ann *bank official*
†Leonard, Eugene Albert *banker*
Maurer, Frederic George, III, *banker*
Poole, William *bank executive*
Rasche, Robert Harold *banker, retired economics educator*
Stoecker, David Thomas *banker*

Springfield
Budzinsky, Armin Alexander *investment banker*
Imhoff, Richard James *trust company executive, financial planner*
McCartney, N. L. *investment banker*

Villa Ridge
Kling, S(tephen) Lee *banker*

Walker
Martin, Phillip Dwight *bank consulting company executive, mayor*

NEBRASKA

Lincoln
Lundstrom, Gilbert Gene *banker, lawyer*
Stuart, James *banker, broadcaster*
Young, Dale Lee *banker*

Omaha
†Jacobsen, Jon Anthony *bank officer, lawyer*

NEVADA

Las Vegas
Hansen, Janet M. *bank executive*
Latusky, William John *investment banker*
Thomas, Keith Vern *bank executive*

Logandale
Smiley, Robert William, Jr., *investment banker*

Reno
Binns, James Edward *retired banker*
Day, Kevin Thomas *banker, community services director*

PROFESSIONAL INDEX 6321 FINANCE: BANKING SERVICES

NEW HAMPSHIRE

Sanbornville
Berg, Warren Stanley *retired banker*

Silver Lake
Tregenza, Norman Hughson *investment banker*

NEW JERSEY

Bay Head
O'Brien, Robert Brownell, Jr., *investment banker, consultant, yacht broker, opera company executive*

Burlington
Denbo, Alexander *retired bank executive*

Chatham
Leonett, Anthony Arthur *banker*

Cherry Hill
Agasar, Ronald Joseph *mortgage banker*

Cinnaminson
Johnson, Victor Lawrence *banker*

Cliffside Park
Goldstein, Howard Bernard *investment banker, advertising and marketing executive*

Fair Lawn
Wall, Mark Emanuel *banker, engineer, consultant*

Florham Park
O'Keefe, Robert James *retired banker*

Jackson
Gasparro, Madeline *banker*

Jersey City
Goldberg, Arthur Abba *merchant banker, financial advisor*

Madison
Armstrong, Richard William *bank executive, management consultant*

Manasquan
Sbarbaro, Robert Arthur *banker*

Marmora
Graves, Thomas Browning *investment banker*

Morristown
Kearns, William Michael, Jr., *investment banker*
Moore, Milo Anderson *banker*
Morrissey, Michael Joseph *investment banker*

Princeton
Ganoe, Charles Stratford *banker, consultant*
Mills, Bradford *merchant banker*
Semrod, T. Joseph *banker*

Red Bank
Dale, Madeline Houston McWhinney *banker*

Short Hills
Good, Allen Hovey *investment banker, real estate broker, business consultant*
Klemme, Carl William *banker*
Lohse, Austin Webb *banker*

Shrewsbury
Jones, Charles Hill, Jr., *banker*

Spring Lake
D'Luhy, John James *investment banker*

Summit
Lewis, Donald Emerson *banker*
Mueller, Paul Henry *retired banker*

Tenafly
Levy, Norman Jay *investment banker, financial consultant*

Vineland
†Bracken, Thomas *bank executive*

NEW MEXICO

Albuquerque
Constantineau, Constance Juliette *retired banker*
†Gunn, Gordon McKay, III, *retired investment banker, retired entrepreneur*

Deming
Rogers, Alice Louise *retired bank executive, writer, researcher*

Santa Fe
Clyde, Larry Forbes *banker*
Dreisbach, John Gustave *investment banker*

NEW YORK

Albany
Robinson, John Bowers, Jr., *bank holding company executive*

Bedford
Chia, Pei-Yuan *banking executive*
Philip, Peter Van Ness *former trust company executive*

Bolton Landing
Crosby, John Griffith *investment banker*

Brooklyn
Bottiglia, Frank Robert *bank executive*
†Cohen, Alan *investment banker*
Hamm, Charles John *banker*

Buffalo
Wilmers, Robert George *banker*

Cherry Valley
Humes, Graham *investment banker*

Elmira
Henbest, Robert LeRoy *retired bank and insurance company executive*

Elmont
Cusack, Thomas Joseph *retired banker*

Farmingville
Olson, Gary Robert *banker*

Garden City
Lovely, Thomas Dixon *banker*

Great Neck
Katz, Edward Morris *banker*

Hartsdale
Katz, John *investment banker*

Ithaca
Smith, Robert Samuel *banker, former agricultural finance educator*

Katonah
Grunebaum, Ernest Michael *investment banker*

Lake Success
Gould, Arthur Paul *investment banker*

Larchmont
Kaufmann, Henry Mark *mortgage banker*

Melville
Newman, Samuel *retired trust company executive*

Miller Place
Leedom, E. Paul *banker*

New Paltz
Smith, Kathleen Tener *bank executive*

New York
Abdelnour, Ziad Khalil *international investment banker, financier, venture capitalist, lobbyist*
Adams, John Brett *investment banker, company executive*
Aigrain, Jacques A. *banker*
Allen, Claxton Edmonds, III, *investment banker*
Arens, Nicholas Herman *bank executive*
Baird, Douglas James *investment banker*
Ballard, Charles Alan *investment banker*
Barbeosch, William Peter *bank executive, lawyer*
Barrett, William Joel *investment banker*
Barry, Nancy Marie *bank executive*
Beale, Christopher William *banker*
Beim, David Odell *investment banker, educator*
Bellanger, Serge René *bank executive*
†Biglari, Hamid *investment banker*
Blitzer, Judi Rappoport *retired bank executive, consultant*
Boothby, Willard Sands, III, *bank executive*
Brown, G(lenn) William, Jr., *bank executive*
Burke, James Joseph, Jr., *investment banker*
Carey, Francis James *investment banker*
Carey, William Polk *investment banker*
Casey, Karen Anne *banker*
Casey, Thomas Jefferson *business executive, investment banker, venture capitalist, environmental entrepreneur*
Castellanos, Julio J. *banker*
Castle, John Krob *merchant banker*
Cayne, James E. *investment banker*
Chester, Norman Charles *bank executive*
Childs, John Farnsworth *consultant, retired investment banker*
Clayton, Jonathan Alan *banker*
Clifford, Stewart Burnett *banker*
Cohen, Jonathan Little *investment banker*
†Cohn, Bertram Josiah *investment banker*
Collins, Adriana Delia *banker*
Comfort, William Twyman, Jr., *banker*
Corrigan, E(dward) Gerald *investment banker*
Cromwell, Oliver Dean *investment banker*
Curtis, John Walter *investment banker*
David-Weill, Michel Alexandre *investment banker*
Davin, James Manson *investment banker*
Davis, George Linn *banker*
Davis, Thomas W. *investment bank executive*
Davison, Daniel P. *retired banking executive*
Debs, Richard A. *investment banker*
DeGroff, Ralph Lynn, Jr., *investment banker*
DeNunzio, Ralph Dwight *investment banker*
Djeddah, Richard Nissim *investment banker*
Douglass, Robert Royal *banker, lawyer*
†Dublon, Dina *bank executive*
†DuGan, Gordon F. *investment banker*
Dwek, Cyril S. *bank executive*
Ehrlich, Susan Patricia *banking executive*
Farley, Terrence Michael *banker*
Feder, Harry Simon *bank executive*
†Feldberg, Chester Ben *banker, lawyer*
Fischer, Stanley *bank executive, economist, educator*
Fisher, Richard B. *investment banker*
Flinn, Michael de Vlaming *investment banker, former state legislator*
†Flynn, Elizabeth E. *bank executive*
Frank, Frederick *investment banker*
†Frankel, Judith Leibholz *bank executive*
Fredericks, David Michael *merchant banker, venture capitalist*
†Friedberg, Barry Sewell *investment banker*
Friedman, W. Robert, Jr., *investment banker*
Fruitman, Frederick Howard *investment banker*
Furman, Roy Lance *investment banker*
Gambee, Robert Rankin *investment banker*
Gamble, Theodore Robert, Jr., *investment banker*
Gant, Donald Ross *investment banker*
Garner, Albert Headden *investment banker*
Gatto, Joseph Daniel *investment banker*
Gellert, Michael Erwin *investment banker*
†Golden, Marc Alan *investment banker*
Goldmark, Peter Francis *banker*
Gonzalez, Eugene Robert *investment banker*
Goodwin, Todd *banker*
Gossett, Robert Francis, Jr., *merchant banker*
†Greenhill, Robert Foster *investment banker*
Greenstein, Abraham Jacob *mortgage company executive, accountant*
Griffith, Alan Richard *banker*
Halpern, Merril Mark *investment banker*
Harlan, Leonard Morton *merchant banker*
Harrison, Gilbert Warner *investment banker*
Hedstrom, Mitchell Warren *banker*
Heimann, John Gaines *investment banker*
Herregat, Guy-Georges Jacques *banker*
Hill, J(ames) Tomilson *investment banker*
†Hilliard, Landon *banker*
Horowitz, Gedale Bob *investment banker*
†Hricik, Lorraine E. *bank executive*
Hurley, Dean C. *bank executive, lawyer*
Janiak, Anthony Richard, Jr., *investment banker*
Jeffries, David Hamilton *investment banker*
Johnson, Thomas Stephen *banker*
Jones, Thomas E. *bank executive*
†Kahn, Jason S. *investment banker, consultant*
Kaiser, Suzanne Billo *investment banker*
Kardon, Robert *mortgage company executive*
Kaufmann, Mark Steiner *banker*
Kennedy, John Joseph *bank financial officer*
Kirdar, Nemir Amin *banker*
Krimendahl, Herbert Frederick, II, *investment banker*
Lattin, Albert Floyd *banker*
Lavine, Lawrence Neal *investment banker*
Layton, Donald Harvey *banker*
LeBlond, Richard Knight, II, *banker*
Leighton, Lawrence Ward *investment banker*
Levinson, Harlan Shaw *investment banker*
Lewis, Donna Cunningham *banker, communications consultant*
Lewis, Sherman Richard, Jr., *investment banker*
Lucander, Henry *investment banker*
Manges, James Horace *investment banker*
Mathews, Michael Stone *investment banker*
Maughan, Sir Deryck *bank executive*
Maxwell, Anders John *investment banker*
McCleary, Benjamin Ward *investment banker*
†McDonald, Stephen Douglas *banker*
Mc Gillicuddy, John Francis *retired banker*
McMullan, William Patrick, III, *investment banker*
Meachin, David James Percy *investment banker*
Mendell, Oliver M. *banking executive*
Menschel, Robert Benjamin *investment banker*
Merriss, Philip Ramsay, Jr., *banker*
Miller, Edward Daniel *financial services executive*
Mintz, Norman Nelson *investment banker, educator*
Myerberg, Marcia *investment banker*
Necarsulmer, Henry *investment banker*
Needham, George Austin *investment banker*
Newbold, John Lowe *banker, financial consultant*
†Newman, Frank Neil *retired bank executive*
Nolan, William Joseph, III, *banker*
Nuzum, John M., Jr., *banker*
Ostrander, Thomas William *investment banker*
Patterson, Edward *investment banker*
Patterson, Ellmore Clark *banker*
Petrie, Donald Joseph *banker*
Pincus, Lionel I. *private equity investor*
Poll, Robert Eugene, Jr., *bank executive*
Potter, William James *investment banker*
†Prince, Charles O., III, *bank executive*
Prizzi, Jack Anthony *investment banking executive*
Prountzos, Tina *investment banker*
Purse, Charles Roe *real estate investment banker*
Rainis, Eugene Charles *banking executive*
Ramsey, Peter Christie *bank executive*
Reckford, Samuel Philip *investment banker*
Rhodes, William Reginald *banker*
Rines, John Randolph *investment banker*
Rizzi, Joseph Vito *banker*
Roberts, Donald Munier *retired banker, trust company executive*
†Roby, Joe Lindell *investment banker*
Rockefeller, David *banker*
Roosevelt, Theodore, IV, *investment banker*
Rubin, Robert Samuel *investment banker*
Sacerdote, Peter M. *investment banker*
Scaturro, Philip David *investment banker, university chancellor*
Schiff, David Tevele *investment banker*
Schless, Phyllis Ross *investment banker*
Schumacher, Robert Denison *banker*
Schupak, Donald *merchant banker, strategic planner, lawyer*
Scott, Margaret Simon *retired mortgage broker*
Selby, Frederick Peter *investment banker*
Shipley, Walter Vincent *retired bank executive*
Shore, Jennifer Ann *bank officer*
Singer, Eric T. *investment banker*
Slusser, William Peter *investment banker*
Smith, Hilary Cranwell Bowen *investment banker*
Spangler, Arnold Eugene *investment banker*
Spielvogel, Sidney Meyer *investment banker*
Stainrook, Harry Richard *retired banker*
Stakias, G. Michael *merchant banker*
Stein, Howard S. *banker*
Stern, James Andrew *investment banker*
Stewart, James Montgomery *banker*
Straton, John Charles, Jr., *investment banker*
Stupin, Susan Lee *investment banker*
Svenson, Charles Oscar *investment banker*
Tagliaferri, Lee Gene *investment banker*
Tanner, Harold *investment banker*
Tarnopol, Michael Lazar *bank executive*
†Thornburgh, Richard E. *bank executive*
Tovey, Joseph *investment banker*
Towbin, A(braham) Robert *investment banker*
Trachtenberg, Matthew J. *bank executive*
Urkowitz, Michael *banker*
Van Dine, Vance *investment banker*
van Hengel, Maarten *banker*
†Van Saun, Bruce *banking executive*
von Fraunhofer-Kosinski, Katherina *bank executive*
Walters, Milton James *investment banker*
Warner, Miner Hill *investment banker*
†Webster, Lesley Daniels *bank executive*
Weil, Frank A. *investment banker, lawyer*
Weill, Sanford I. *bank executive*
Weinberg, John Livingston *investment banker*
Wellin, Keith Sears *investment banker*
West, Blair *investment banker, consultant*
Whitcomb, James Howard, Jr., *investment banker*
White, Keith Gordon *bank executive, artist*
Whitehead, John Cunningham *bank executive, diplomat, philanthropist*
Whiting, Gordon James *investment banker*
Whittemore, Laurence Frederick *private banker*
Wigmore, Barrie Atherton *investment banker*
Wolff, William F., III, *investment banker*
Wolitzer, Steven Barry *investment banker*
Wriston, Walter Bigelow *retired banker*
Yancey, Richard Charles *investment banker*
Young, George Haywood, III, *investment banker*
†Zheng, Changguang K. *investment banker*

Oyster Bay
Schwab, Hermann Caspar *banker*
Walsh, Charles Richard *retired banker*

Plandome
Williams, Morgan Lloyd *retired investment banker*

Queensbury
Mead, John Milton *banker*

Quogue
Hines, William Eugene *banker*

Ridgewood
Jones, Harold Antony *banker*
Meehan, Richard Andrew *investment banker*

Rochester
Wayland-Smith, Robert Dean *retired banker*

Saratoga Springs
Wait, Charles Valentine *banker*

Scarsdale
Abbe, Colman *investment banker*

Shelter Island
Dowd, David Joseph *banker, builder*

Southampton
†Atkins, Victor Kennicott, Jr., *investment banker*
Brokaw, Clifford Vail, III, *investment banker, business executive*

Stamford
Bergleitner, George Charles, Jr., *investment banker*

Syracuse
Gray, Charles Augustus *banker*

Tonawanda
Haller, Calvin John *banker*

West Harrison
Verano, Anthony Frank *retired banker*

Westbury
Tulchin, Stanley *banker, lecturer, author, business reorganization consultant*

White Plains
Bober, Lawrence Harold *retired banker*
Bushkin, Merle Jerome *investment banker*
†Cohn, John L. *merchant banker*

Yonkers
Philipps, Edward William *banker, real estate appraiser*
Singer, Cecile Doris *bank executive, state legislator*

NORTH CAROLINA

Charlotte
†Erwin, Betty *bank executive*
Hance, James Henry, Jr., *bank executive*
†Lehman, Alice *bank executive*
Lewis, Kenneth D. *bank executive*
McColl, Hugh Leon, Jr., *bank executive*
Thompson, G. Kennedy *bank executive*

Cornelius
Giblin, Patrick David *retired banker*

Fairmont
Byrne, James Frederick *banker*

Gastonia
Teem, Paul Lloyd, Jr., *bank executive*

Greenville
Wilkerson, William Holton *banker*

Highlands
Sheehan, Charles Vincent *investment banker*

Raleigh
Hardin, Eugene Brooks, Jr., *retired banker*
†Holding, Lewis R. *banker*

Wilson
Stewart, Burton Gloyden, Jr., *retired banker*

Winston Salem
Allison, John Andrew, IV, *bank executive*
Cramer, John Scott *retired banker*

†Kelly, Robert P. *banking executive*
McNair, John Franklin, III, *banker*
Medlin, John Grimes, Jr., *banker*
Runnion, Howard J., Jr., *banker*
Wanders, Hans Walter *banker*

NORTH DAKOTA

Fargo
Mengedoth, Donald Roy *commercial banker*

OHIO

Canton
Carpenter, Noble Olds *retired bank executive*

Chagrin Falls
Obert, Charles Frank *retired banker*

Cincinnati
Kramer, Randolph John *bank executive*
Schaefer, George A., Jr., *bank executive*

Cleveland
Daberko, David A. *banker*
Glickman, Carl David *banker*
Lenn, Stephen Andrew *investment banker*
Rupert, John Edward *retired savings and loan executive, business and civic affairs consultant*
Sparber, Dale Paul *banker*
Warren, Russell James *investment banker, consultant*

Columbus
†Glaser, Gary A. *bank executive*
†Johnson, Julia F. *bank executive*
Manning, Ronald Lee *banker*
McCoy, John Bonnet *retired banker*
Page, Linda Kay *banking executive*

Newark
McConnell, William Thompson *commercial banker*

Pepper Pike
Mc Call, Julien Lachicotte *banker*

Rocky River
O'Brien, John Feighan *investment banker*

Solon
Macko, David *retired bank adjustor*

Sylvania
Bergsmark, Edwin Martin *mortgage bank executive*

Toledo
Carson, Samuel Goodman *retired banker, company director*
Koppus, Betty Jane *retired savings and loan association executive*
Kunze, Ralph Carl *retired savings and loan executive*

Willoughby
Abelt, Ralph William *bank executive*

OKLAHOMA

Bartlesville
Doty, Donald D. *retired banker*

Oklahoma City
Brown, Kenneth Ray *banker*
Browne, John Robinson *banker*
†Rainbolt, H. E. *bank executive*
Trost, Louis Frederick, Jr., *banker, financial planner*

Tulsa
Hawkins, Francis Glenn *banker, lawyer*

OREGON

Eugene
Drennan, Michael Eldon *banker*

Lincoln City
Morrow, James Thomas *investment banker, financial executive*

Wilsonville
McKay, Laura L. *banker, consultant*

PENNSYLVANIA

Bala Cynwyd
Bausher, Verne C(harles) *banker*

Buckingham
Hover, John Calvin, II, *banker*

Canonsburg
Prado, Gerald M. *investment banker*

Devon
Boehne, Edward George *banker*

Eagles Mere
Gruver, William Rolfe *investment banker*

Erie
Bracken, Charles Herbert *banker*

Harleysville
Daller, Walter E., Jr., *banking executive*

Harrisburg
Campbell, Carl Lester *banker*

---

†Zuern, David Ernest *bank executive*

Lancaster
Ashby, Richard James, Jr., *bank executive, lawyer*

Lansdale
Fawley, John Jones *retired banker*

Malvern
Bedrosian, Gregory Ronald *investment banker*

Mendenhall
Frangopoulos, Zissimos A. *banker*

Philadelphia
Foulke, William Green *retired banker*
Murdoch, Lawrence Corliss, Jr., *retired banker, economist*
Reintzel, Warren Andrew *trust company executive*
Santomero, Anthony M. *bank executive, public policymaker*

Pittsburgh
Alexander, Andrew James *investment banker*
Fisher, Henry *investment banker*
†Gulley, Joan Long *banker*
Hansen, Stephen Christian *banker*
†Haunschild, Robert L. *bank executive*
Jefferson, Joseph Murray *banker*
Lahey, Regis Henry *bank executive*
McGrath, Edward Leo *banker*
Milsom, Robert Cortlandt *banker*
Rohr, James Edward *banker*

Radnor
Eagleson, William Boal, Jr., *banker*

Reading
Roesch, Clarence Henry *banker*
†Snyder, Clair Allison *banker*

Saint Davids
Pollard, Edward Ellsberg *banker*
Sheftel, Roger Terry *merchant banker*

Scranton
Janoski, Henry Valentine *investment advisor, former banker*

Sewickley
Ostern, Wilhelm Curt *retired holding company executive*

Souderton
Hoeflich, Charles Hitschler *banker*

West Chester
Swope, Charles Evans *bank president, lawyer*
Taylor, Bernard J., II, *banker*

West Conshohocken
Boenning, Henry Dorr, Jr., *investment banker*

Wyomissing
Moll, Lloyd Henry *banker*

RHODE ISLAND

East Greenwich
Hunter, Garrett Bell *investment banker*

Little Compton
Middendorf, J. William, II, *investment banker*

Newport
Sands, Harold Winthrop *banker, financial adviser*

Providence
Burns, Robert E. *bank executive*
†Lohrum, Frederick *bank executive*

SOUTH CAROLINA

Columbia
Boggs, Jack Aaron *banker, publisher, municipal government official*
Hollis, Charles Eugene, Jr., *savings and loan association executive*

Greenville
Whittle, Mack Ira, Jr., *banking executive*

Greenwood
Boxx, Rita McCord *banker*

SOUTH DAKOTA

Sioux Falls
Engen, Lee Emerson *retired savings and loan executive*

TENNESSEE

Cleveland
Miles, Doris Cooper *bank executive*

Clinton
Birdwell, James Edwin, Jr., *retired banker*

Knoxville
Barker, Keith Rene *investment banker*
†Blake, Gerald Rutherford *banker*

Maryville
Lawson, Fred Raulston *banker*

Memphis
Horn, Ralph *bank executive*

Murfreesboro
Ford, William F. *banker*

Nashville
Andrews, Holdt *investment banker*
Burch, John Christopher, Jr., *investment banker*
Daane, James Dewey *banker*
Harrison, Clifford Joy, Jr., *banker*
Shell, Owen G., Jr., *retired banker*

TEXAS

Abilene
Bentley, Clarence Edward *savings and loan executive*

Alamo
Fellenstein, Cora Ellen Mullikin *retired credit union executive*

Austin
Carner, William John *banker*
Deal, Ernest Linwood, Jr., *banker*
Howard, John Loring *retired trust banker*
Lemens, William Vernon, Jr., *banker, finance company executive, lawyer*
West, Glenn Edward *investment banking executive*

Corpus Christi
Bexley, James Byron *banker*

Dallas
†Bishop, Gene Herbert *financial corporate executive*
Brown, Gloria Vasquez *central banker*
Cameron, Glenn Nilsson *mortgage company executive*
Cochran, George Calloway, III, *retired bank executive, lawyer*
Fritz, Terrence Lee *investment banker, strategic consultant*
Gumbiner, Anthony Joseph *investment banker, lawyer*
†Jacobs, Andrew F. *mortgage company executive*
Mason, Barry Jean *retired banker*
McTeer, Robert D., Jr., *banker*
Philipson, Herman Louis, Jr., *investment banker*
Reid, Langhorne, III, *merchant banker*

Houston
Anderson, William, Jr., (William Albion Anderson Jr.) *investment banker*
Elkins, James Anderson, Jr., *banker*
Elkins, James Anderson, III, *investment professional*
Friedman, Janet Teri *mortgage company executive*
†Knapp, David Hebard *banker*
Neuhaus, Philip Ross *investment banker*
Tilghman, Richard Granville *bank executive*

Kingwood
†Ribeiro, Frank Henry *banker, energy consultant*

Pasadena
Moon, John Henry, Sr., *banker*

San Antonio
†Condos, J. Alexander *mortgage company executive*
Crichton, John Hayes *investment banker*
Duncan, A. Baker *investment banker*
Keyser-Fanick, Christine Lynn *banking executive, marketing, strategic planning, investments and insurance professional*
Post, Gerald Joseph *retired banker, retired air force officer*

Tyler
Blasingame, Donald Ray (Don Blasingame) *banker*

Victoria
Stubblefield, Page Kindred *banker*

UTAH

Saint George
Beesley, H(orace) Brent *bank executive*

VERMONT

Lyndon Center
Dame, William Page, III, *bank executive, educational administrator*

Manchester
Carey, James Henry *banker*

VIRGINIA

Alexandria
Birely, William Cramer *investment banker*
Furash, Edward Elliott *banker, investment company executive, writer, lecturer, theater producer*

Arlington
Leland, Marc Ernest *trust advisor, lawyer*
Rogers, James Frederick *banker, management consultant*
Watkins, Birge Swift *investment banker*

Ashburn
Pavsek, Daniel Allan *banker, educator*

Charlottesville
Bull, George Albert *retired banker*

Falls Church
Bowman, Richard Frederick *banker*
Geithner, Paul Herman, Jr., *retired banker*

Lynchburg
Quillian, William Fletcher, Jr., *retired banker, former college president*

Mc Lean
†Baumann, Martin F. *savings and loan association executive*
†Parseghian, Gregory J. *savings and loan association executive*
†Paul, Peterson T. *savings and loan association executive*

Norfolk
Cutchins, Clifford Armstrong, III, *banker*

Richmond
Black, Robert Perry *retired banker, executive*
Broaddus, John Alfred, Jr., *bank executive, economist*
Epperson, Wallace W., Jr., *investment banker*
Jones, Catesby Brooke *retired banker*
†Miller, Lewis Nelson, Jr., *banker*
Moore, Andrew Taylor, Jr., *banker*
Powell, Kenneth Edward *investment banker*
Talley, Charles Richmond *commercial banking executive*

Salem
Ramsey, Lloyd Brinkley *retired savings and loan executive, retired army officer*

Urbanna
†Garey, Francis Benjamin *retired merchant banker*

Virginia Beach
Harrison, William Wright

WASHINGTON

Kirkland
Melby, Orville Erling *retired banker*

Lakewood
Owen, Thomas Walker *banker, broker*

Mercer Island
Spitzer, Jack J. *banker*

Oak Harbor
Piercy, Gordon Clayton *bank executive*

Olympia
Alfers, Gerald Junior *retired banker*

Seattle
Andrew, Lucius Archibald David, III, *bank executive*
Arnold, Robert Morris *banker*
Campbell, Robert Hedgcock *investment banker, lawyer*
Cockburn, John F. *retired bank executive*
Cullen, James Douglas *banker, finance company executive*
Fetters, Norman Craig, II, *banker*
†Green, Joshua, III, *retired banker*
Killinger, Kerry Kent *bank executive*

Sequim
Laube, Roger Gustav *retired trust officer, financial consultant*

Spokane
McWilliams, Edwin Joseph *banker*

Tacoma
Anderson, Lynn L. *trust company executive*

Walla Walla
Oliver, Dan David *banker*

WISCONSIN

Delafield
Walters, Ronald Ogden *mortgage banker*

Pewaukee
Long, Robert Eugene *banker*

Zenda
Sills, William Henry, III, *investment banker*

WYOMING

Cheyenne
Knight, Robert Edward *banker*

CANADA

BRITISH COLUMBIA

Vancouver
Gardiner, William Douglas Haig *bank executive, director*
Lyons, Terrence Allan *merchant banking, investment company executive*

ONTARIO

Hamilton
Robinson, Daniel Baruch *retired banker*

Mississauga
Palmer, Patrick Asa *former banker, lecturer*

Peoria
Molinsky, Bert *tax consultant*

Phoenix
†Castleberry, W. Thomas *financial company executive*
Daniel, James Richard *accountant, computer company financial executive*
Jungbluth, Connie Carlson *wealth strategist*
Khan, Ahmed Mohiuddin *finance, insurance executive*
Linxwiler, Louis Major, Jr., *retired finance company executive*
Mullen, Daniel Robert *finance executive*
Scozzari, Albert *portfolio manager, inventor*
Smith, James Parker *accountant*
Upson, Donald V. *financial executive, retired*
Van Fleet, David Dominic *finance educator*
†Yu, Angie *auditor, music educator*

Scottsdale
Hansen, Donald W. *insurance and financial services executive*
Jensen, Dale Finnlay *accountant*
Washburn, Jerry Martin *accountant, corporate executive*
Weil, John David *financial executive*

Sun City
Larkin, Mary Sue *financial planner*

Sun City West
Person, Robert John *financial management consultant*
Schrag, Adele Frisbie *business education educator*

Tempe
Kaufman, Herbert Mark *finance educator*
†Makri, Marianna *finance educator, researcher*
Pany, Kurt Joseph *accounting educator, consultant*
Poe, Jerry B. *financial educator*
†Reckers, Philip Merle *accounting and business educator*
Roy, Asim *business educator*

Tucson
Cain, Vernon *retired information services executive*
Carleton, Willard Tracy *retired finance educator*
Crawford, Richard Eben, Jr., *former investment advisor*
†Fajardo, Sarah Elizabeth Johnson *financial consultant*
†Hellon, Michael Thomas *tax consultant, political party official*
Nixon, Robert Obey, Sr., *business educator*
†Ruscher, Charles B. *finance educator, consultant*
Seay, Suzanne *financial planner, educator*
Taveggia, Thomas Charles *business educator*

ARKANSAS

Arkadelphia
Webster, Robert Lee *accounting educator, researcher*

Conway
Horton, Finis Gene *management services company executive*
Horton, Joseph Julian, Jr., *economics and finance educator*
McNew, Bennie Banks *retired finance educator*
Moore, Herff Leo, Jr., *management educator*

Fayetteville
Cook, Doris Marie *accountant, educator*
†Fuentes-Henriquez, Fernando Neftali *finance educator, researcher*
Hay, Robert Dean *retired management educator*
Rosenberg, Leon Joseph *marketing educator*

Fort Smith
Craig, David Clarke *financial advisor*
Hembree, Hugh Lawson, III, *diversified holding company executive*

Little Rock
Flournoy, Jacob Wesley *internal audit director*
Goodner, Norman Wesley *governmental relations specialist*
Hanson, Jeanne Sutley *accountant*
Scivally, Bart Murnane *accountant, auditor*

Mena
Wiles, Betty Jane *accountant*

North Little Rock
George, James Edward *accountant*

Paragould
Humway, Ronald Jimmie *accountant, former state agency administrator*

Siloam Springs
Hill, James Robert *accountant*

CALIFORNIA

Alameda
Hudkins, James Allen *accountant*

Anaheim
Lano, Charles Jack *retired financial executive*

Aptos
Garcia, Louis Lawrence *financial executive*

Atherton
Barker, Robert Jeffery *financial executive*

Bakersfield
Bacon, Leonard Anthony *accounting educator*

Bell Canyon
Labbett, John Edgar *senior financial executive*

Berkeley
Blume, James Beryl *financial advisor*
Bucklin, Louis Pierre *business educator, consultant*
Staubus, George Joseph *accounting educator*

Beverly Hills
McGagh, William Gilbert *financial consultant*
Widaman, Gregory Alan *financial executive, accountant*

Brea
Oh, Tai Keun *business educator*

Brentwood
Defield, Charleen K. *accountant*
Fridley, Saundra Lynn *private investigator*

Buena Park
Kristy, James E. *financial management consultant*

Burbank
Gold, Stanley Phillip *diversified investments executive*
Marinace, Kenneth Anthony *financial advisor*
Murphy, Peter E. *corporate financial officer*
Thornton, Cameron Mitchell *financial planner*

Burlingame
Doyle, William B. *investment executive*

Calabasas
Goldfield, Emily Dawson *finance company executive, artist*
Mozilo, Angelo R. *diversified financial services company executive*

Canoga Park
Brandenburg, Stanley C. *financial company executive*

Carmichael
Areen, Gordon E. *finance company executive*

Cathedral City
Konwin, Thor Warner *financial executive*

Claremont
Christian, Suzanne Hall *financial planner*
Lipman-Blumen, Jean *public policy and organizational behavior educator*

Clovis
Kellam, Becky *business educator, consultant*

Corona Del Mar
Helphand, Ben J. *actuary, consultant*

Coronado
†Edison, Thomas Robert *management educator, retired military officer*

Costa Mesa
Kolanoski, Thomas Edwin *financial company executive*
Metzger, Vernon Arthur *management educator, consultant*
Rayner, Linda Calix *financial analyst*

Covina
Cottrell, Janet Ann *controller*

Culver City
Abarbanell, Gayola Havens *financial planner*
Eckel, James Robert, Jr., *financial planner*
Marcus, Richard Andrew *accountant, mayor*
Richardson, John Edmon *marketing educator*

Davis
Naik, Prasad Anand *marketing educator*
Tsai, Chih-Ling *management educator*

Encino
†Dor, Yoram *accountant*
Luna, Barbara Carole *financial analyst, accountant, appraiser*
Ribac, Catalino Tagatac *retired accountant*

Fallbrook
Freeman, Harry Lynwood *retired accountant*

Fountain Valley
Penderghast, Thomas Frederick *business educator*

Fremont
Jensen, Paul Edward Tyson *business educator, consultant*

Fresno
Tellier, Richard Davis *management educator*

Granada Hills
Lehtihalme, Larry K. (Lauri Lehtihalme) *financial planner*

Grass Valley
†Connell, Will *financial consultant*

Hayward
†Staudohar, Paul David *economics educator, labor arbitrator*

Hemet
Rowe, Mary Sue *accounting executive*

Huntington Beach
Canyon, Steven *financial officer*
Hamilton, Allen Philip *financial advisor*
Strutzel, J(od) C(hristopher) *escrow company executive*

Indian Wells
Harding, James Warren *retired finance company executive*

Irvine
Craig, Karen Lynn *accountant, controller*
Farrar, Donald Keith *retired financial executive*
Feldstein, Paul Joseph *management educator*
Tripoli, Masumi Hiroyasu *financial consultant*
Vines, Henry Ellsworth, III, *accountant, lawyer, financial planner*

La Canada
Tookey, Robert Clarence *consulting actuary*

La Crescenta
Fisk, Irwin Wesley *financial investigator*

La Habra
Schoppa, Elroy *accountant, financial planner*

La Jolla
Brimble, Alan *business executive*
Bruggeman, Terrance John *financial corporate executive*
Dorsey, Dolores Florence *retired corporate treasurer, business executive*
Jeub, Michael Leonard *financial consultant*
Purdy, Kevin Moore *estate planner*
Simon, Ronald I. *financial executive*

La Verne
†Driebe, Michael D. *corporate financial executive*

Laguna Beach
Pories, Muriel H. *business executive, loan consultant*

Laguna Niguel
†Bauer, Barbara A. *financial consultant*

Lakewood
Bogdan, Carolyn Louetta *financial specialist*

Larkspur
Ramos, Charles Joseph (Joe Ramos) *wealth management consultant*

Lincoln
Dorn, Mary Ann *retired auditor*

Long Beach
Hunt, Herbert Gage, III, *accounting and tax educator*
Nwokogba, Isaac *financial analyst*
Walker, Linda Ann *financial planner*

Los Altos
†Yu, Oliver Shukiang *corporate executive, educator, technology strategist*

Los Angeles
Allen, Suzanne *financial planning executive, insurance agent, writer*
Allison, Laird Burl *business educator*
Anderson, John Edward *diversified holding company executive, lawyer*
Anderson, Kenneth Jeffery *financial planner, accountant, lawyer*
Becraft, Stephen Jay *accountant*
Bennis, Warren Gameliel *business administration educator, writer, consultant*
Borsting, Jack Raymond *business administration educator*
Broad, Eli *financial services executive*
Caskie, William Wirt *accountant, securities broker*
Chan, David Ronald *tax specialist, lawyer*
Crowell, Donald W. *diversified financial services company executive, financial consultant*
Diamond, Lindy S. *financial executive*
Drummond, Marshall Edward *business educator, university administrator*
Ellsworth, Frank L. *business executive*
Goedde, Alan George *financial company executive*
†Karmarkar, Uday Sadashiv *management educator*
Lin, Thomas Wen-shyoung *accounting educator, researcher, consultant*
More, Philip Harvey Birnbaum *business administration educator*
Morrison, Donald Graham *business educator, consultant*
Morrow, Winston Vaughan *financial executive*
Mosich, Anelis Nick *accountant, writer, educator, consultant*
†O'Brien, Rosanne P. *corporate financial executive*
†Ogden, Devika *accounting executive*
†Ownbey, Vance Scott *corporate financial executive*
Roth, Gary Neal *accountant*
Roussey, Robert Stanley *accountant, educator*
Stancill, James McNeill *finance educator, consultant*
Stewart, David Wayne *marketing educator, psychologist, consultant*
Tellis, Gerard J. *business educator*
Walendowski, George Jerry *accounting and business educator*
Weston, John Frederick *business educator, consultant*
Williams, Julie Ford *mutual fund officer*

Malibu
Baskin, Otis Wayne *business educator*
Hill, Lawrence Sidney *finance educator*

Manhattan Beach
Pettersen, Thomas Morgan *accountant, finance executive*

Marina Del Rey
Allmon, Michael Bryan *financial consultant*

Marysville
†Larson, Billy Dell *finance company executive*

Menlo Park
McDonald, Warren George *accountant, former savings and loan executive*
†Messmer, Harold Maximilian, Jr., *financial services executive*

Midway City
McCawley, William Dale, II, *accountant, writer, ethnohistorian*

Mill Valley
Mumford, Christopher Greene *corporate financial executive*
Ware, David Joseph *financial consultant*

Montebello
Orr, Stanley Chi-Hung *financial executive*

Napa
Gillespie, Marcia Lou *accountant, tax preparer, musician*
Hennings, Dorothy Ann *financial advisor*

New Orleans
Ford, Gerald J. *finance company executive*

Newbury Park
†Keller, James Robert *business development director*

Newport Beach
Gross, William H. *financial analyst, investment company executive*
Hoffman, George Bernard *estate planner*
Randolph, Steven *financial advisor*
Tracy, James Jared, Jr., *accountant, financial executive, law firm administrator*

North Hollywood
†Boulanger, Donald Richard *financial services executive*
Chang, Wung *business advisor, researcher, lecturer*

Northridge
Roberts, Teri Alane *accountant, educator, civic activist*
Ruley, Stanley Eugene *cost analyst*

Oakland
Lee, Jong Hyuk *accountant*
McKeever, Michael Pierce, Sr., *economics and business educator*
Randisi, Elaine Marie *accountant, educator, writer*
Tyndall, David Gordon *business educator*

Oceanside
Garfin, Louis *retired actuary*
Taverna, Rodney Elward *financial services company executive*

Ontario
Coney, Carole Anne *accountant*

Palo Alto
†Druyan, Lara Catherine *financial consultant*
Herrick, Tracy Grant *fiduciary*
Ivy, Benjamin Franklin, III, *financial and real estate investment advisor*
Rehman, Saifur *business executive*
Wong, Michael Anthony *financial analyst*

Palos Verdes Peninsula
Barab, Marvin *financial consultant*
Manning, Christopher Ashley *finance educator, consultant*

Pasadena
Axelson, Charles Frederic *retired accounting educator*
†Azinfar, Fatemeh *financial analyst, writer, finance educator*
Gillis, Christine Diest-Lorgion *financial planner, stockbroker*
†Jalbert, Janelle Jennifer *financial consultant, educator*

Pittsburg
Williams, Elizabeth A. *financial planner, business consultant*

Pollock Pines
Johnson, Stanford Leland *marketing, international business educator*

Pomona
Cosgrove, William James *business educator, researcher*
Lin, Lianlian *management educator, researcher*
Patten, Thomas Henry, Jr., *management, human resources educator*

Poway
Mueller, Gerhard G(ottlob) *retired financial accounting standard setter, retired educator*
Uke, Alan Kurt *company executive*

Rancho Mirage
Steele, Charles Glen *retired accountant*

Rancho Palos Verdes
Hughs, Mary Geraldine *accountant, social service specialist*

Rancho Santa Margarita
Parth, Frank R. *consulting company executive, educator*

Redlands
Pick, James Block *finance educator*

Redwood City
†Moore, Nicholas G. *finance company executive*

Wilton
Hersh, Ira Paul *tax and financial planning consultant*
McNear, Barbara Baxter *retired financial communications executive, consultant*

DELAWARE

Dover
Beugre, Constant D. *management educator, researcher*
Kim, Dae Ryong *management information systems educator*
Masland, Charles Henry, IV, (Chad Masland) *financial services executive*

Greenville
Daney, Bernard Joseph *accountant, consultant*

Newark
†Davis, Darwin Jacob *finance educator*
Sawyer, John Edward *management educator*
Solano, Paul (Paul Leonard Solano) *finance educator*

Wilmington
Copeland, Tatiana Brandt *accountant*
†Griffin, Jo Ann Thomas *retired financial planner, tax specialist*
Mand, Martin G. *financial executive*
Moore, Brian Clive *actuary*
Porter, Kenneth Wayne *actuary*
Rogoski, Patricia Diana *financial executive*

DISTRICT OF COLUMBIA

Washington
Aguirre-Sacasa, Rafael Eugenio *international consultant*
†Anjaria, Shailendra J. *international finance official*
Armstrong, Alexandra *financial advisor*
Arnold, G. Dewey, Jr., *accountant*
Arundel, John Howard *financial consultant*
Campbell, Ruth Ann *budget analyst*
Czinkota, Michael Rudolf *business educator*
Donaldson, William Henry *financial executive, insurance company executive*
Droms, William George *finance educator, investment advisor*
DuCran, Claudette Deloris *retired financial analyst*
Ellison, Michael Scott *former financial executive, sailing coach*
Emmons, William Monroe, III, *business educator, consultant*
Fischetti, Michael Joseph *accounting educator*
†Howard, J. Timothy *finance company executive*
Hubbard, Helen Mitchell *accountant, lawyer*
Johnson, James A. *financial organization executive*
†Knight, Linda K. *financial company executive*
Larsen, Richard Gary *accounting firm executive*
Le Goc, Michel Jean-Louis *business educator*
Levy, Michael B. *business educator*
Lister, Harry Joseph *finance company executive*
†Logan, Ann D. *financial company executive*
Logue-Kinder, Joan *consultant*
Malek, Frederic Vincent *finance company executive*
Maul, Kevin Jay *financial consultant*
†McGuire, Stephen J.J. *business educator*
Merrifield, Dudley Bruce *business educator, former government official*
Mosso, Lyle David *financial executive*
Myers, Donald Lee *university chief financial officer*
Parde, Duane Arthur *association executive*
Parrish, Edgar Lee *financial services executive*
Schaal, Pamela Marguerite *program evaluation analyst*
†Springer, Linda *portfolio manager, controller*
Stekler, Herman O. *finance educator*
Stowe, Alexis Mariani *accountant, consultant*
Taylor, David Kerr *international business educator, consultant*
Walker, David A(lan) *finance educator, educator*
Wolfensohn, James David *finance company executive*
†Zeidman, Fred S. *corporate financial executive*

FLORIDA

Apopka
Rufenacht, Roger Allen *accounting educator*

Aventura
Fishel, Peter Livingston *accounting business executive*
Kliger, Milton Richard *financial services executive*

Avon Park
Dutton, Carol Tyminski *accounting and business educator*

Belleview
Bellis, Arthur Albert *financial executive, government official*

Boca Grande
de Saint Phalle, Thibaut *investment banker, educator, lawyer, financial consultant*

Boca Raton
Jessup, Joe Lee *business educator, management consultant*
Karmelin, Michael Allen *financial executive*
Litvak, Isaiah A. *business educator, consultant*
Miles, Jesse Mc Lane *retired accounting company executive*
Ortiz, Jaime *business educator*
Peterson, Mark F. *business educator*

Pradere, Sonia *accounting administrator*
Rosenberg, Lee Evan *financial planner*
Sigel, Marshall Elliot *financial consultant*

Boynton Beach
Bartholomew, Arthur Peck, Jr., *accountant*
Van Den Brande, Rene Albert *retired accountant*

Clearwater
Campolettano, Thomas Alfred *international contract manager*
Conwell, Theresa Gallo *financial services representative*
Crites, Richard Ray *financial planner, investment advisor, financial services company executive*
Loos, Randolph Meade *financial planner*

Cocoa Beach
Kennedy, Thomas Patrick *financial executive*
Wirtschafter, Irene Nerove *tax specialist, consultant*

Coral Springs
Becker, Edward A. *accounting educator, consultant*
†MacDonald, Laurianne *accountant, poet*

Crestview
Scott, George Gallmann *accountant*

Crystal River
Schlumberger, Robert Ernest *accountant*

Deerfield Beach
Moran, Patricia Genevieve *corporate executive*
Siegel, Steven L. *finance company executive, consultant*

Deland
Horton, Thomas Roscoe *business advisor*

Delray Beach
Bryan, Robert Fessler *former investment analyst*

Fort Lauderdale
†Abraham, Rebecca Jacob *finance educator*
Bamberg, Louis Mark *wealth management specialist*
Castro, Stephanie L. *business management educator*
Cobb, David Keith *business executive*
Feldman, Les J. *finance educator*
Lampert, Wayne Morris *corporate financier*
Shoemaker, William Edward *financial executive*
Tobias, Benjamin Alan *portfolio manager, financial planner*
Vasquez, William Leroy *business educator, consultant*

Fort Myers
Adams, Todd Porter *financial and investment advisor*
†Kleman, Charles J. *finance company executive*
Oligario, Max *retired accountant*

Green Cove Springs
Dasher, Bonita Ann *accountant*

Hialeah
Shaw, Steven John *retired marketing educator, academic administrator*

Hollywood
†Harkin, Daniel John *controller*
Mendelson, Laurans Adam *accountant*
Sim, Robert Wilson *accountant*

Jacksonville
Adams, Scott Leslie *accountant*
Allen, Ronald Wesley *financial executive*
Edwards, Marvin Raymond *investment counselor, economic consultant*
Swartz, Stephen Arthur *corporate financial executive*
Talbot, Peter Jennings *financial services executive*
Tomlinson, William Holmes *management educator, retired army officer*
Vane, Terence G., Jr., *finance company executive, lawyer*

Lake City
Moore, Emma Sims *finance educator*

Lake Wales
Luing, Gary Alan *financial management educator*

Largo
Shillinglaw, Gordon *accounting educator, consultant*

Lauderdale By The Sea
†Kennedy, Beverly (Kleban) Burris *financial advisor, tv and radio talk show host*

Lighthouse Point
Shein, Jay Lesing *financial planner*

Longboat Key
Van Dyke-Cooper, Anny Marion *retired financial company executive*

Maitland
Plane, Donald Ray *management science educator*

Manalapan
†Gatewood, Robert Payne *financial planning executive, retired*

Melbourne
Roub, Bryan R(oger) *financial executive*

Miami
Boccagna, David Louis *finance company executive*

Capraro, Franz *accountant*
Coton, Carlos David *finance manager*
Day, Kathleen Patricia *financial planner*
Ehrlich, Morton *international finance executive*
Forgione, Dana Anthony *healthcare accounting educator*
†Ibler, Gerold *finance company executive, consultant*
†Javier-Dejneka, Amelia Luisa *accountant*
†King, Joseph *finance educator, consultant*
Lavin, David *accountant, educator*
Nunez-Lawton, Miguel G. *international finance specialist*
Pomeranz, Felix *accounting educator*
†Samlut, Carlos *accountant*
†Scully, Robert Edmund *management educator, consultant*

Miami Shores
Diener, Betty Jane *finance educator*

Naples
Berry, Donald Lee *accountant*
Handy, Charles Brooks *accountant, educator*
Madigan, Joseph Edward *financial executive, consultant, director*
Ordway, John Danton *retired pension administrator, lawyer, accountant*
Thomas, Gary Lynn *financial executive*

Neptune Beach
Forrest, Allen Wright *tax and financial services firm executive, accountant, financial planner*

New Port Richey
Assini, Vincent Paul *financial executive*

Nokomis
Meyerhoff, Jack Fulton *financial executive*

North Miami
Tate, Stanley G. *diversified business executive, expert witness*

North Miami Beach
†Katzman, Chaim *finance company executive*

North Palm Beach
Frevert, James Wilmot *financial planner, investment advisor*

Ocklawaha
Silagi, Barbara Weibler *corporate administrator*

Ocoee
Davis, Elena Denise *accountant*

Orlando
Armacost, Robert Leo *management educator, former coast guard officer*
Deli, Steven Frank *business investment and development executive*
Gray, Anthony Rollin *retired finance company executive*
†Whyte, Ann Marie *finance educator*

Oviedo
Drummer, Donald Raymond *financial services executive*

Palm Beach
Fitilis, Theodore Nicholas *portfolio manager, financial analyst, retired*

Palm Beach Gardens
Howard, Melvin *financial executive*

Palm Coast
Owens, Garland Chester *accounting educator*

Palmetto
Patton, Ray Baker *financial consultant, real estate broker*

Pensacola
Carper, William Barclay *management educator*
Sjolander, Richard James *marketing and economics educator*

Ponte Vedra Beach
Roland, Melissa Montgomery *accountant*

Punta Gorda
Hughes, Spencer Edward, Jr., *retired financial executive, consultant*

Saint Augustine
†DeLaughter, Thomas Glenn *finance educator, consultant, academic administrator*

Saint Petersburg
Bryant, Timothy Clark *investment brokerage executive*
Freeburg, Richard Gorman *financial derivatives company executive*
Putnam, J. Stephen *financial executive*
Wasserman, Susan Valesky *accountant, artist, yoga instructor*

Sarasota
Arreola, John Bradley
Bailey, Robert Elliott *financial executive*
Berman, Lewis Paul *financial executive*
Drake, Diana Ashley *financial planner*
Dryce, H. David *accountant, consultant*
Kendig, Calvin Fridy, Jr., *financial consultant, electrical engineer, consultant*
Miles, Arthur J. *financial planner, consultant*
Morris, Gordon James *financial company executive, consultant*
Roberts, Don E. *accountant*

Tallahassee
Keister, Beverly Jane *accountant*
†Teague, James Calvin, Jr., *finance educator*

Tampa
Aldrich, David Alan *accountant, consultant*
Alexander, William Olin *finance company executive*
Bear, Marca Marie *business educator, management consultant*
Becatti, Lance Norman *financial consultant*
Bradish, Warren Allen *internal auditor, operations analyst, management consultant*
DeVane, Mindy Klein *financial planner*
Henard, Elizabeth Ann *controller*
Hernandez, Gilberto Juan *accountant, auditor, management consultant*
Lebouitz, Martin Frederick *financial services industry executive, consultant*
Nord, Walter Robert *business administration educator, researcher, consultant*
Schine, Jerome Adrian *retired accountant*
Sendrow, Jerrold B. *financial services executive*
Shah, Sameer Naren *financial advisor, management consultant*
†Taylor, Thomas S. *diversified financial services company executive*

Vero Beach
Conway, Earl Cranston *business educator, retired manufacturing company executive*
Danforth, Arthur Edwards *finance executive*
Fetter, Robert Barclay *retired administrative sciences educator*
Koontz, Alfred Joseph, Jr., *financial and operating management executive, consultant*
Riefler, Donald Brown *financial consultant*
Satuloff, Barth *accounting executive, dispute resolution professional, investment strategist, publisher*
Simon, Donald John *employee benefits administrator, insurance and investment broker*

Wesley Chapel
Mendelsohn, Louis Benjamin *financial analyst*

West Palm Beach
Capasso, Robert *financial executive*
Eppley, Roland Raymond, Jr., *retired financial services executive*
†Fowler, Steven Lane *compliance officer*
Herrick, John Dennis *financial consultant, former law firm executive, retired food products executive*
Livingstone, John Leslie *accountant, management consultant, business economist, educator*

Weston
Holtzman, Gary Yale *retired administrative and financial executive*

Winter Haven
Goodman, Karen Lacerte *financial services executive*

Winter Park
†Alon, Ilan *international business educator*
Matulich, Serge *accounting educator, author*
Mishra, Chandra S. *finance educator, consultant*
Pearson, R. Scott *investment advisor, editor*

Winter Springs
Bevc, Carol-Lynn Anne *accountant*

GEORGIA

Alpharetta
Kurtz, Robert Arthur *finance company executive*

Athens
†Ayers, Benjamin C. *finance educator*
Miller, Herbert Elmer *accountant*

Atlanta
Ackerman, Arlene Alice *accountant, business consultant, artist, writer*
†Appeadu, Charles Edward *finance educator, researcher*
Bowman, Douglas *business educator*
Chambers, Robert William *financial company executive*
Cook, Don Lloyd *marketing educator, lawyer, consultant*
Craig, Anna Maynard *financial educator, consultant*
Dial, Carmen Miranda *financial counselor, evangelist*
Gross, Stephen Randolph *accountant*
Grove, Denise Whitlock *accounting and financial professional*
Gundersen, Mary Lisa Kranitzky *finance company executive*
Hanna, Frank Joseph, Jr., *credit company executive*
Hays, William Grady, Jr., *corporate financial and bank consultant*
Hogan, William Jephtha, Jr., *financial consultant*
Kimball, Curtis Rollin *financial analyst*
Kringelis, Kurt *portfolio manager*
Lobb, William Atkinson *financial services executive*
Norwood, Samuel Wilkins, III, *financial consultant*
O'Haren, Thomas Joseph *financial services executive*
Parsons, Leonard Jon *marketing educator, consultant*
Roberts, Bradley Edward *finance company executive*
Robertson, Sandra Dee (Graen) *tax director*
Seto, William Roderick *public accounting company executive*
Sheth, Jagdish Nanchand *business administration educator*
Taylor, Richard Bertrom *accountant*
Villwock, Kenneth James *procurement executive*
Whitmer, William Eward *retired accountant*

Whittington, Frederick Brown, Jr., *business administration educator*

Buford
Stubbs, Thomas Hubert *company executive*

Columbus
Bowman, Donald Campbell *accountant*

Conyers
Spearman, Maxie Ann *financial analyst, administrator*

Cuthbert
Hinds, Glester Samuel *financial consultant*

Dalton
Winter, Larry Eugene *accountant*

Decatur
Anderson, Jonpatrick Schuyler *financial consultant, therapist, archivist*
Myers, Clark Everett *retired business administration educator*

Duluth
Bell, Tonya Lynn *auditor*

Fayetteville
†Brown, L(arry) Eddie *tax practitioner, business accountant, real estate broker, financial planner*

Hinesville
Wise, Carl Stamps *accounting educator*

Kennesaw
Robinson, Kenneth Charles *management educator*

Lagrange
†Hawkins, Frances Pam *finance educator*
Turner, Fred Lamar *accountant, lawyer*

Marietta
Bruce, Thomas Allen *financial consultant*
Edwards, Charles Mundy, III, *financial consultant*
Kiger, Ronald Lee *contract negotiator*
Simmons, Stephen Gregory *accountant*

Milledgeville
†Campbell, Scott Kenneth *management educator*
Engerrand, Doris Dieskow *business educator*

Norcross
†Massey, Lewis *finance company executive*

Oakwood
Martin, Johnny Benjamin *accountant*

Peachtree City
Moulder, Wilton Arlyn *financial management consultant*

Riverdale
Minter, Jimmie Ruth *accountant*

Roswell
Teets, Charles Edward *international business consultant, lawyer*

Statesboro
Murkison, Eugene Cox *business educator*

Thomasville
Stepanek, David Leslie *financial services company executive*

Tybee Island
Smith, Elizabeth Mackey *financial consultant*

Valdosta
Campbell, J(ohn) Jette *corporate finance executive*

Washington
Mansfield, Norman Connie *bookkeeper*

Woodstock
Austin, John David *retired financial executive*

HAWAII

Honolulu
Fukushima, Barbara Naomi *financial advisor*
Haig, David M. *property and investment manager*
Hook, Ralph Clifford, Jr., *business educator*
Kam, Thomas Kwock Yung *accountant educator*
Liu, Roger Kim Sing *accountant*
Ng, Wing Chiu *accountant, educator, application developer, lawyer, educator, advocate*
Palia, Aspy Phiroze *marketing educator, researcher, consultant*
Solidum, James *finance and insurance executive*
Sterrett, James Melville *accountant, business consultant*

Laie
†Bradshaw, James R. *business educator*

Wailuku
Yoshida, Lisa M.T. *accountant*

IDAHO

Boise
Ingram, Cecil D. *accountant, state legislator*
Mock, Stanley Clyde *certified financial planner, investment advisor*

Hayden
Morris, Mary Ann *bookkeeper*

Idaho Falls
Riddoch, Hilda Johnson *accountant*

ILLINOIS

Abbott Park
Silva, Cheryl Lynn *financial economist*

Aurora
Halloran, Kathleen L. *financial executive, accountant*

Bartlett
Lawrence, Madalena Joan Vignocchi *accountant*

Bellwood
Miller, Denyce Karlina *tax specialist*

Bloomington
Friedman, Joan M. *accounting educator*

Buffalo Grove
Johnson, Craig Theodore *portfolio manager*
Leonetti, Michael Edward *financial planner*
Yacktman, Donald Arthur *financial executive, investment counselor*

Cahokia
Healy, Steven Michael *accountant, city official*

Carbondale
Mathur, Ike *finance educator*
Mihalopulos, Gus, Jr., *accountant*

Carterville
Lake, Tracy Marie Grace *accountant*

Champaign
Brighton, Gerald David *accounting educator*
Michael, Steven Craig *business educator*
Perry, Kenneth Wilbur *accounting educator*
†Schmidt, Jeffrey Brian *finance educator*
Schoenfeld, Hanns-Martin Walter *accounting educator*

Charleston
Bagwell, Kim Diane *accountant*
Cooper, George Kile *business educator*

Chicago
Almeida, Richard Joseph *finance company administrator*
Baniak, Sheila Mary *accountant, educator*
Berardino, Joseph Francis *accounting company executive*
Carlson, Richard Gregory *accountant*
Chromizky, William Rudolph *accountant*
Dobrev, Stanislav James *educator, researcher*
Fitzgerald, Robert Maurice *financial executive*
†Fleming, Richard H. *finance executive*
Forbes, John Edward *financial consultant*
†Forehand, Joseph W. *finance company executive*
Garrigan, Richard Thomas *finance educator, consultant, editor*
†Gluth, Robert C. *management company executive*
†Goodman, Robert Stanley *management educator*
Hansen, Claire V. *financial executive*
Haydock, Walter James *banker*
Herting, Claireen LaVern *financial planner*
Hicks, Cadmus Metcalf, Jr., *financial analyst*
†Hooton, James G. *finance company executive*
†Ibbotson, Roger G. *financial educator*
†Kackley, James R. *former financial services executive*
Kamerick, Eileen Ann *corporate financial executive, lawyer*
Kamin, Kay Hodes *financial planner, journalist, lawyer, entrepreneur, educator, financial columnist*
Knowles, Thomas William *business educator, consultant*
Kullberg, Duane Reuben *accounting firm executive*
Lorie, James Hirsch *business administration educator*
Mallory, Robert Mark *controller, finance executive*
Mayer, Raymond Richard *business administration educator*
†McDonnell, David Croft *diversified financial services company executive*
†Medvin, Harvey Norman *diversified financial services company executive, treasurer*
Miller, Heidi G. *diversified financial company executive*
Morisato, Susan Cay *actuary*
Nelson, Thomas George *consulting actuary*
Novak, Harry R. *financial consultant*
†Perlmutter, Norman *finance company executive*
Prosnitz, David J. *cost control company executive*
Pump, Bernard John *finance company executive, consultant*
Rappaport, Anna M *actuary*
Ryan, Patrick G. *diversified financial services company executive, director*
Saltiel, Natalie *accountant*
Schornack, John James *accountant*
†Sjogren, Bengt B *corporate financial executive*
Smith, Marcia Jean *accountant, tax specialist, financial consultant*
Sorgel, Sylvia *financial services executive*
†Stirling, D. Leslie *corporate financial executive*
Sullivan, Bernard James *accountant*
Velisaris, Chris Nicholas *corporate financial executive*
Verschoor, Curtis Carl *business educator, consultant*
Vitale, Gerald Lee *financial services executive*
Weil, Roman Lee *accounting educator*
†Wittenberg, Jon Albert *accountant*
Young, Scott Thomas *business management educator*
Zimmerman, Martin E. *financial executive*

Zorko, Mark A. *financial executive*

Crestwood
Cowie, Norman Edwin *credit manager*

Decatur
Decker, Charles Richard *investment executive*

Deerfield
Boyd, Joseph Don *financial services executive*
Heiman, Marvin Stewart *finance company executive*
Lifschultz, Phillip *financial and tax consultant, accountant, lawyer*
Serwy, Robert Anthony *accountant*

Dekalb
Hanna, Nessim *marketing educator*

Des Plaines
Koller, Marita Ann *accountant*

Elgin
Freeman, Corwin Stuart, Jr., *financial planner, investment advisor, consultant*

Elk Grove Village
Bandel, David Brian *accountant*

Evanston
†Chernev, Alexander *marketing educator, researcher*
Dranove, David *business educator, consultant, economist*
†Gulati, Ranjay *finance educator*
Prince, Thomas Richard *accountant, educator*
Scott, Walter Dill *management educator*
Seaman, Jerome Francis *actuary*
†Skoulakis, Georgios *finance educator*
Stern, Louis William *marketing educator, consultant*

Geneva
Young, Jack Allison *financial executive*

Glen Ellyn
Garrett, Paul James *financial planner*

Glencoe
Silver, Ralph David *financial consultant and arbitrator*

Glenview
Faig, Kenneth Walter *actuary, publisher*
Levin, Donald Robert *business and finance executive, motion picture producer, professional sports team owner*
Mack, Stephen W. *financial planner*

Hickory Hills
Schultz, Barbara Marie *investment advisor representative*

Hinsdale
Ciccarone, Richard Anthony *financial executive*
Self, Madison Allen *finance company executive*
Urbik, Jerome Anthony *financial consultant*

Jacksonville
Kirchhoff, Michael Kent *economic development executive*

Joliet
Colonna, William Mark *accountant*

Kenilworth
Bott, Harold Sheldon *accountant, management consultant*

Lincolnshire
Hays, Thomas Chandler *holding company executive*

Lisle
†Tenkasi, Ramkrishnan V. *finance educator, researcher*

Macomb
Bauerly, Ronald John *marketing educator*

Mattoon
Finley, Gary Roger *financial company executive*

Mchenry
Koehl, Camille Joan *accountant*

Moline
Meredith, Lynnette Ann Logan *accountant*

Mount Prospect
Epstein, Stephen Roger *financial executive*

Naperville
Tan, Li-Su Lin *accountant, insurance executive, investment consultant*

North Riverside
Perkins, William H., Jr., *finance company executive*

Northbrook
Afterman, Allan B. *accountant, educator, researcher, consultant*
Feibel, Frederick Arthur *financial consultant*
†Hale, Danny Lyman *financial executive*
Mandel, Karyl Lynn *accountant*
Newman, Lawrence William *financial executive*

Northfield
Mathieson, Michael Raymond *controller*
Shillestad, John Gardner *financial services company executive*

Oak Brook
Baillie-David, Sonja Kirsteen *controller*
Koufis, John Theodore *accountant*

Oakbrook Terrace
Catalano, Gerald *accountant*
Keller, Dennis James *management educator*

Palatine
Butler, John Musgrave *financial consultant, consultant*
Spinner, Lee Louis *accountant*

Park Ridge
Russell, William Steven *finance executive*

Peoria
Goitein, Bernard Joel *management educator, researcher*
Vaughan, David John *corporate financial executive*

Prospect Heights
Aldinger, William F., III, *diversified financial services company executive*

Quincy
Mallory, Troy L. *accountant*

Riverdale
Hoekwater, James Warren *treasurer*

Rockford
Albert, Janyce Louise *human resources specialist, retired business educator, banker, consultant, human resources specialist*
Petru, Suzanne Mitton *health care finance executive*
Wallem, Paul Sigurd *financial planner*

Roselle
†Waite, Darvin Danny *accountant*

Schaumburg
Aitken, Rosemary Theresa *financial planner, consultant*
†Devonshire, David W. *financial executive*

Skokie
†Lang, Louis I. *state legislator, lawyer*

Spring Grove
York, Karen Kay *accountant, farmer*

Springfield
Kuhn, Kathleen Jo *accountant*
†Reents, Ray Edward *banking and stock consultant*
Travis, Lawrence Allan *accountant*

Westchester
Morefield, Michael Thomas *financial executive*

Westmont
Moor, Roy Edward *finance educator*

Wheaton
Diersen, David John *financial consultant*
Holman, James Lewis *financial and management consultant*

Wilmette
†Beck, Ralph *financial consultant*
Wishner, Maynard Ira *retired finance company executive, lawyer*

Winnetka
Mathers, Thomas Nesbit *financial consultant*

INDIANA

Beech Grove
Clapper, George Raymond *retired accountant, computer consultant*

Bloomington
Belth, Joseph Morton *retired business educator*
DeHayes, Daniel Wesley *management executive, educator*
Gordon, Paul John *management educator*
Hustad, Thomas Pegg *marketing educator*
MacKay, David B.
Wentworth, Jack Roberts *business educator, consultant*

Carmel
Kellison, Donna Louise George *accountant, educator*
Wendt, Gary Carl *finance company executive*

Columbus
†Binkley, John Frey, Jr., *financial consultant, writer*
Miller, William Irwin *finance company executive*

Evansville
Gaither, John Francis *accountant, consultant*
McGuire, Brian Lyle *educator, consultant*
Moers, Joyce Ann *bookkeeper, day camp administrator*

Fort Wayne
†Gutreuter, Jill Stallings *financial consultant, financial planner*
†Owen, Dave A. *finance executive*

Franklin
Link, E. G. (Jay Link) *corporate executive, family wealth counselor*

Goshen
Whitcraft, James Richard, Jr., *accountant*

Indianapolis
Berkey, Jeffrey Alan *project manager*
Braham, Delphine Doris *accountant, government official*
†Brewer, Ryan Matthew *financial analyst*

Carey, Edward Marshel, Jr., *accounting company executive*
Carlock, Mahlon Waldo *financial consultant, former high school administrator*
Davit, Frank Torino *accountant*
Day, M. Joanna *accountant, foundation administrator*
Fisher, Gene Lawrence *financial executive*
Furlow, Mack Vernon, Jr., *retired financial executive, treasurer*
Goodwin, William Maxwell *financial executive*
Gutermuth, Scott Alan *accountant, pharmaceutical company executive*
Israelov, Rhoda *financial planner, writer, entrepreneur*
Kaufman, Barton Lowell *financial services company executive*
Larsen, Glen Albert, Jr., *finance educator*
Long, Clarence William *accountant*
†Planeaux, Christopher Sean *financial analyst, educator*
Strycker, Steve Lynn *accountant*
Williams, Gregory Keith *accountant*
Winemiller, James D. *accountant*

Kokomo
†Pati, Niranjan *finance educator*

Lafayette
Helmuth, Ned D. *certified financial planner*
McCormick, Teresa D. *accountant*

Madison
†Helms, Rebecca J. *finance educator*

Merrillville
†Reitmeister, Noel William *certified financial planner, investment and insurance professional, author, columnist, television host and producer, educator*

Notre Dame
Huang, Roger Dominic *finance educator*
Reilly, Frank Kelly *business educator*
Shannon, William Norman, III, *marketing and international business educator, food service executive*
Vecchio, Robert Peter *business management educator*

Pendleton
Corby, Francis Michael, Jr., *financial executive*

Rensselaer
†Slaby, Frank *financial executive*

Sellersburg
†MacEva, Carol Ann *accountant*

South Bend
Agbetsiafa, Douglas Kofi *financial and management consultant*
Cohen, Ronald S. *accountant*
Harriman, Gerald Eugene *retired business administrator, economics educator*
†McDonnell, G. Darlene *retired business educator*

West Lafayette
Cooper, Arnold Cook *management educator, researcher*
Lewellen, Wilbur Garrett *management educator, consultant*
Plante, Robert Donald *management educator, university dean*

IOWA

Adel
Hougham, Norman Russell *financial services company executive*

Ames
Hunger, J(ohn) David *business educator*

Bettendorf
Nolte, Jacqueline *accountant*

Davenport
Asadi, Anita Murlene *business educator*

Des Moines
Smith, Diana Marie *business educator*

Dubuque
Lisk, Alan Robert *finance educator, consultant*

Fonda
Tamm, Eleanor Ruth *retired accountant*

Iowa City
Collins, Daniel W. *accountant, educator*
Riesz, Peter Charles *marketing educator, consultant*

Ottumwa
Lang, Janelle J. *accountant*

West Des Moines
McNamara, David Joseph *financial and tax planning executive*
Sather, Everett Norman *accountant*

KANSAS

Atchison
DeMeritt, Kelly Anne *accountant*

Emporia
Hashmi, Sajjad Ahmad *business educator, university dean*
†Hindi, Nitham M. *finance educator, department chairman*

Kansas City
Globoke, Joseph Raymond *accountant*

Lawrence
Beedles, William LeRoy *finance educator, financial consultant*
Conard, John Joseph *financial official*

Leawood
Byrum-Sutton, Judith Miriam *accountant*
White, Shanon Kathleen *accountant, consultant*

Manhattan
Sheu, Chwen *finance educator*
Swanson, Diane L. *finance educator, researcher*

Mcpherson
Hull, Robert Glenn *retired financial administrator*

Olathe
Tast, Marci *business analyst*

Overland Park
Guckenheimer, Daniel Paul *financial advisor*
Lucas, James Raymond *business executive, leadership consultant, author, speaker*
Surbaugh, Dolores Sayas *accounting and professional development educator*
Zinke, Michael Duane *finance and accountancy manager*

Pittsburg
Darling, John Rothburn, Jr., *business educator*

Shawnee Mission
Hoffman, Alfred John *retired mutual fund executive*
Robinson, Mary Lu *retired accountant, artist*

Topeka
Reser, Elizabeth May (Betty Reser) *bookkeeper*

Wichita
Sullivan, Mitzi *accountant*
Wolff, James August August *finance educator, researcher*

KENTUCKY

Bowling Green
Rahim, M. Afzalur *management educator, editor*

Fort Thomas
Hill, Esther Dianne *business education educator*

Frankfort
Hatchett, Edward Bryan, Jr., *state auditor, lawyer*

Lexington
Stone, Dan N. *accounting educator*

Louisville
Dalton, Jennifer Faye *accountant*
†Johnson, Adria Elaine *financial analyst, accountant*
†McKim, Ruth Ann *financial planner*
Min, Hokey *business educator*

Madisonville
Kington, Barry Clark *investor, consultant*

Prospect
Katsianis, John Nick *financial executive*

LOUISIANA

Alexandria
Morris, Rebecca Ann Brittain *accountant*

Baton Rouge
Bedeian, Arthur George *business educator*
Carlson, Orville James (Skip Carlson) *accountant, financial planner*
Crumbley, Donald Larry *accounting educator, writer, consultant*
DeVille, Donald Charles *accountant*
Thomas, Jeffrey Cone *financial executive, consultant*
Wild, Dirk Jonathan *accountant*

Bogalusa
†Wood, Helen Chamblee *accountant*

Gonzales
McGarr, Charles Taylor *accountant*

Hammond
LaFargue, Melba Faye Fulmer *financial manager, real estate consultant*

Keithville
Duraczynski, Donna Moore *retired accountant*

Kenner
McShan, Clyde Griffin, II, *financial executive*
Scherich, Edward Baptiste *retired diversified company executive*

Leesville
Wimberly, Beadie Reneau (Leigh Wimberly) *financial services executive*

Metairie
Doody, Louis Clarence, Jr., *accountant*
†Evans, Pat Terrell *financial consultant*

New Orleans
†Fisk, Raymond Paul *marketing educator*
Ledbetter, Linda Carol *pension fund executive, professional organization executive*

Pearl River
Haas, Edward Norbert *financial consultant, writer*

Pineville
†Conway, Evelyn Atkinson *accountant, financial analyst*

Ruston
Posey, Clyde Lee *business administration and accounting educator*
Pullis, Joe Milton *business administration educator, writer*

Saint Rose
Lennox, Edward Newman *holding company executive*

Shreveport
Lenard, Lloyd Edgar *financial consultant*
†Lin, Binshan *management educator*

Thibodaux
Fairchild, Joseph Virgil, Jr., *accounting educator*

MAINE

Bangor
Albrecht, Ronald Lewis *financial services executive*
Bennett, Rondi Kim Albrecht *financial services executive*

Camden
Dyer, Barbara F. *retired accountant, writer*

Orono
Mahon, John Francis *management policy educator*

South Portland
Martin, Joseph Robert *corporate financial executive*

MARYLAND

Adelphi
Sutherland, Alan Roy *business educator*

Annapolis
Ames, Steven Reede *financial planner*

Baltimore
Beasley, Robert Scott *financial executive*
Duke, George Wesley *financial executive*
Fontanazza, Franklin Joseph *accountant, business executive*
Hilgenberg, John Christian *corporate financial executive, consultant*
Jacobs, Richard James *banker, educator*
Kues, Irvin William *health care financial executive*
Langmead, Joseph Michael *accountant, consultant, educator*
†Lucas, Leyland Mervyn *finance educator, consultant*
Quinn, Michael Desmond *diversified financial services executive*
Roupe, James Paul *accountant*
Tringali, Joseph *financial planner, accountant*
†Vemuganti, Ramakrishan R. *business educator*

Bethesda
Castelli, Alexander Gerard *accountant*
Klote, James Denver *financial consultant*
Nason, Charles Tuckey *diversified financial services company executive*
Petty, John Robert *financier*
Schwarz, Louis Jay *financial advisor*
Soffer, Lowell Charles *financial executive*
†Wardinski, Bruce David *hotel chain executive*

Chestertown
Scout, Terrence Houser *business educator*

Chevy Chase
Smith, Peter Leonard *diversified financial services company executive*

College Park
Fu, Michael C. *management science educator*
†Gannon, Martin John *finance educator*
Gordon, Lawrence Allan *accounting educator*
†Maksimovic, Vojislav *finance educator*
Sims, Henry P., Jr., *management educator*

Columbia
†Hyde, Rebecca Medwin *financial consultant*
Kurlander, Neale *accounting and law educator, lawyer*
Walrath, Michelle Taylor *accountant*

Easton
Fredrick, Susan Walker *tax company manager*
Higgins, Michael Edward *finance executive*

Ellicott City
Clive, Craig N. *compensation executive*
†Tinsley, Perin Delano *tax specialist, real estate agent*

Frederick
Orzechowski, Alice Louise *accountant*

Gaithersburg
Johnson, George H. *financial services company executive*
Ruth, James Perry *financial planning executive*

Glenn Dale
Helfers, Eric C. *financial analyst*

Greenbelt
Stehman, Betty Kohls *financial and management consultant*

Joppa
Kott, Beverly Parat *financial counselor, community activist*

Kensington
Murray, Thomas James *financial planner, publisher*

Lusby
Hutchins, Edith Elizabeth *accountant*

Lutherville Timonium
Gray, Dahli *accounting educator and administrator*
Klasons, Ilona *accountant, consultant*

Pasadena
Dubke, Marie E. *business educator*

Potomac
Patel, Vinod Motibhai *accountant*

Rock Hall
Lang, Lillian Owen *retired accountant*

Rockville
Burt, Marvin Roger *financial advisor, investment manager*
Edwards, Bert Tvedt *accountant*
Kamerow, Martin Laurence *accountant*

Salisbury
†Adams, Stephen Bernard *finance educator, consultant*
†Parente, Ronaldo *business educator, consultant*

Silver Spring
Grubbs, Donald Shaw, Jr., *retired actuary*
Yasher, Michael *retired accountant*

Sykesville
Vreeland, Russell Glenn *accountant, consultant*

Trappe
Blades, G(ene) Granville *accountant*

Waldorf
Gregan, John Patrick *finance executive, small business owner*

Woodstock
Price, John Roy, Jr., *financial executive*

Wye Mills
Schnaitman, William Kenneth *finance company executive*

MASSACHUSETTS

Acton
†Coughlin, Cornelius Edward *accounting company executive*

Allston
Mills, Daniel Quinn *business educator, consultant, author*

Amherst
Manz, Charles C. *management educator*
Roberts, Chris *strategy and finance educator, researcher*

Ashland
Pettinella, Nicholas Anthony *financial executive*

Auburndale
Vaccaro, Joseph Pascal *retired marketing educator, marketing consultant*

Babson Park
Goldstein, Michael Aaron *finance educator*

Belmont
Fuller, Stephen Herbert *business administration educator*
Rich, Sharon Lee *financial planner*

Boston
Aber, John William *finance educator*
Baker, Charles Duane *business administration educator, former management executive*
Bower, Joseph Lyon *business administration educator*
Boyd, David Preston *business educator*
Bruns, William John, Jr., *business administration educator*
Cardinal, Roger Joseph *tax specialist*
Christenson, Charles John *retired business educator*
Cody, Alan Morrow *financial consultant*
Colburn, Kenneth Hersey *financial executive*
Elfner, Albert Henry, III, *retired mutual fund management company executive*
Farb, Thomas Forest *financial executive*
Gifford, Nelson Sage *financial company executive*
†Hansen, Morten T. *management educator*
Hayes, Robert Herrick *technology management educator*
Hayes, Samuel Linton, III, *business educator*
Hudson, Bradford Taylor *management educator*
Ives, J. Atwood *financial executive*
Johnson, Edward Crosby, III, *financial company executive*
Lawrence, Paul Roger *retired organizational behavior educator*
Lodge, George C(abot) *business administration educator*
Marshall, James Peter *accountant, educator*
Marshall, Martin Vivan *business administration educator, business consultant*

McArthur, John Hector *business educator*

†McCraw, Thomas Kincaid *business history educator, editor, author*

McFarlan, Franklin Warren *business administration educator*

Park, William H(erron) *financial executive*

Pitts, James Atwater *financial executive*

Reiling, Henry Bernard *business educator*

†Robertson, Christopher John *management educator*

Schnitzer, Iris Taymore *finance company executive, lawyer, arbitrator, mediator*

Sloane, Carl Stuart *educator and management consultant*

†Spooner, John D. *financial planner, writer*

Stevenson, Howard Higginbotham *business educator*

Stobaugh, Robert Blair *business educator, business executive*

Tucker, Richard Lee *financial executive*

Vatter, Paul August *business administration educator, dean*

Widmann, John Andrew *account administrator, musician*

†Winn, Joseph Lampher *financial officer*

Young, David William *management educator*

Brockton
Clark, Carleton Earl *tax consultant*

Brookline
Reedy, Harry Lee *financial services executive*

Buzzards Bay
Daley, Michael Edward *financial consultant*

Cambridge
Deshpandé, Rohit *business educator*
†French, Kenneth Ronald *finance educator*
Hauser, John Richard *marketing and management science educator*
Hax, Arnoldo Cubillos *management educator, industrial engineer*
Kochan, Thomas A. *business educator*
Kothari, Sriprakash *business educator*
Leonard, Herman Beukema (Dutch Leonard) *public finance and management educator*
Little, John Dutton Conant *management scientist, educator*
†Mohamed, Mustafa A. *management educator*
†Norrman, Lena Elisabeth *accountant*
Pounds, William Frank *management educator*
†Rosenbloom, Richard Selig *business administration educator*
von Hippel, Eric Arthur *innovation educator*

Canton
Kurzman, Stephen Alan *accountant, educator*
Rankin, James *financial services company executive*

Chelsea
Jenkins, Alexander, III, *business executive*

Chestnut Hill
†Torbert, William Rockwell *finance educator, researcher*
Woodside, Arch G. *marketing educator, researcher*

Concord
Collis, David John *management educator*
Smith, Peter Walker *finance executive*
Weiss, James Michael *financial analyst, portfolio manager*

Dartmouth
Wang, Shouhong *business educator*

Eastham
Souther, Jean Lorraine *accounting and management educator, accountant*

Fitchburg
†Kim, Kwahng Soo *finance educator*

Foxboro
Bush, Raymond T. *accountant, corporate professional*
Karelitz, Richard Alan *financial executive, lawyer*

Gloucester
Means, Elizabeth Rose Thayer *financial consultant, writer, lawyer*

Leominster
Ford, John Stephen *treasurer*

Lexington
†Goglia, Richard A. *corporate financial executive*
Klein, Lawrence Allen *accounting educator*
†Pliner, Edward S. *corporate financial executive*

Lowell
Teague, Bernice Rita *accountant*

Marblehead
Snow, George Bartlett *city official, accountant*

Medford
Goldberg, Pamela Winer *finance educator, director*

Monson
Krach, Mitchell Peter *retired financial services executive*

Nantucket
Louderback, Peter Darragh *accountant, consultant*

Needham
Safran, Edward Myron *financial consultant, banking executive*

Newton
Buff, Gayle Helene *financial advisor*
Julian, Raymond Charles *financial planner, investment company executive*
Lueders, Carl L. *finance executive*
Temkin, Robert Harvey *accountant*

North Chatham
Wilson, E. B. *business executive, consultant, writer*

North Easton
Bestgen, William Henry, Jr., *financial planner*

Osterville
Silk, Alvin John *business educator, management consultant*

Pittsfield
Keator, David P. G. *stockbroker, financial consultant*

Quincy
Britt, Margaret Mary *finance educator*
Somers, Susan Eileen *business educator*

Randolph
Cammarata, Richard John *financial advisor*

Salisbury
Camacho, Henry Francis *accountant*

Spencer
Goldman, Ethan Harris *finance executive*

Springfield
O'Connell, Robert John *diversified financial services company executive*

Sudbury
Buono, Anthony Francis *business educator*
Meltzer, Donald Richard *treasurer*

Swansea
Hjerpe, Edward Alfred, III, *finance and banking executive*

Tewksbury
Black, Richard Bruce *business executive, consultant*

Waban
Tofias, Allan *accountant*

Wakefield
†Coffman, Dallas Whitney *financial consultant*

Waltham
Jones, Clark Powell, Jr., *financial services executive*
McClary, Loretta Mary *accountant*
O'Connell, Jeanne *financial planner, insurance broker*
Syron, Richard Francis *financial executive, economist*

Wellesloy
Maxwell, J. B. *financial consultant, marketing professional, consultant*

Weston
Valente, Louis Patrick (Dan Valente) *business and financial executive*

Woburn
†Offermann, Peter *financial executive*

Worcester
Chaison, Gary N. *labor relations educator, researcher*
Greenberg, Nathan *accountant*
Marconi, Peter Paul, Jr., *financial analyst*
†Zeng, Amy Z. *finance educator, engineering educator*

MICHIGAN

Ada
Mathews, George Meprathu *accounting executive*

Ann Arbor
Elger, William Robert, Jr., *accountant*
Foster, Alan Herbert *financial consultant, educator*
Kim, E. Han *finance and business administration educator*

Auburn Hills
Drexler, Mary Sanford *financial executive*

Big Rapids
Slaymaker, Adrianne Lee E. *accountant, educator*

Birmingham
Helppie, Charles Everett, III, *financial consultant*
McCuen, John Joachim *business executive, columnist and lecturer*

Bloomfield Hills
†Ebert, Douglas Edmund *corporate financial executive*
Poth, Stefan Michael *retired sales financing company executive*

Canton
Lee, Kamee Angela *financial analyst*

Dearborn
Lee, Hei Wai *finance educator, researcher*

Detroit
Anderson, Thomas Caryl *financial and administrative systems professional*
Cavanagh, Gerald Francis *business educator*

Kahalas, Harvey *business educator*

East Lansing
Krishnan, Ranjani *finance educator*

Farmington Hills
Holforty, Pearl Martha *accountant*
Smith, Isabel Francis *financial planner*

Grand Rapids
Hermann, William M. *finance company executive*
†Mavima, Paul *finance educator*
Parrish, Kenneth Dale *treasurer, accountant*
Thauer, Edwin William, Jr., *financial services executive*

Grosse Pointe Farms
Weingart, Robert Paul *financial consultant*

Lansing
Feight, Theodore J. *financial planner*
Prout, Carolyn Ann *controller, personnel administrator*

Livonia
Valerio, Michael Anthony *financial executive*

Maple City
Duff, James George *retired financial services executive*

Marquette
Camerius, James Walter *marketing educator, corporate researcher*
Carnahan, George Richard *business educator, consultant*

Muskegon
DeLong, Donald R. *accountant*

Orchard Lake
Rauwerdink, William Jay *accountant*

Plymouth
Zilincik, Jerome Matthew *financial analyst*

Portage
Zhang, Charles C. *financial planner*

Portland
Rich, Joseph John *accountant*

Rochester
Giordano, Joseph, Jr., *financial planner, investment consulting firm executive*

Southfield
Boyce, Daniel Hobbs *financial planning company executive*
Selis, Stuart L. *financial consultant, underwriter*

Traverse City
Taylor, Donald Arthur *marketing educator*

Troy
Rappleye, Richard Kent *financial executive, consultant, educator*

University Center
Hall, David McKenzie *business and management educator*

West Bloomfield
Meyers, Gerald Carl *educator, author, expert witness, consultant*

MINNESOTA

Crookston
Shol, Kim Durand *accountant, computer programmer*

Duluth
Feroz, Ehsan Habib *accounting educator, researcher, writer*
Nelson, Dennis Lee *finance educator*

Elk River
Goss, Cynthia Lee *tax specialist*

Mankato
Janavaras, Basil John *business educator, consultant*
†Schreier, Bradley *finance company executive*

Minneapolis
Benson, Donald Erick *holding company executive*
Berryman, Robert Glen *accounting educator, consultant*
Bromelkamp, David John *investment officer*
Chandy, Rajesh K. *business educator*
Elm, Dawn Rae *business educator*
Goldberg, Luella Gross *corporation executive*
Hoffmann, Thomas Russell *business management educator*
Kinney, Earl Robert *mutual funds company executive*
Martin, Frederick Kane *portfolio manager, investor*
†Mohanty, Sunil K. *finance educator, researcher*
†Moller, Andrew K. *finance company executive*
Montgomery, Henry Irving *financial planner*
Petersen, Douglas Arndt *financial development consultant*
Picconatto, Evelyn Clara *accountant*
Pillsbury, George Sturgis *investment adviser*
†Prange, Michael J. *finance company executive*
†Schroeder, Roger Glenn *management educator*
Schwartz, Howard Wyn *business/marketing educator, consultant*
Stenberg, Adam W. *financial advisor, investment company executive*
†Zellmer-Bruhn, Mary Elizabeth *management educator*

Minnetonka
Wesselink, David Duwayne *finance company executive*
†Woo, Benson *financial executive*

Moorhead
†Keup, Linda C. *management educator*

Nevis
Stibbe, Austin Jule *accountant*

Nisswa
Marmas, James Gust *retired business educator, retired college dean*

Plymouth
Chadwick, John Edwin *financial consultant*
†Hauser, Elloyd *finance company executive*

Saint Paul
Dresbach, David Philip *financial consultant, educator*
†Henning, Angela E. *controller*
Rudelius, William *marketing educator*

Sleepy Eye
Ruddy, James Vincent, Jr., *tax advocate*

Winona
Haas, James Wayne *accountant*

Worthington
Meyer, Helen Bernadine *financial services company executive*

MISSISSIPPI

Clarksdale
Walters, William Lee *accountant*

Hattiesburg
Duhon, David Lester *business educator, management consultant*

Jackson
†Fuller, Phillip Roland *finance educator*

Meadville
Ikerd, Shirley Temple *financial planner*

Meridian
Thomas, Kenneth Eugene *auditor*

Mississippi State
Chrisman, James Joseph *management educator*
Vance, David A. *information systems educator*

Starkville
George, Ernest Thornton, III, *financial consultant*
Thomas, Garnett Jett *accountant*

Tupelo
Nash, Henry Warren *marketing educator*

University
†Bougnol, Marie-Laure *finance educator*
Flesher, Dale Lee *accounting educator, dean*
Gardner, William Lansing, III, *business educator*
†Guidice, Rebecca Monette *strategic management educator*

MISSOURI

Ballwin
Bond, Dennis Earl *auditor*

Canton
Janney, DellAnn *accountant, educator*

Cape Girardeau
Haugland, Jerry Lee *accounting educator*

Chesterfield
Armstrong, Theodore Morelock *financial executive*
Driscoll, Charles Francis *financial services company executive, investment adviser*
Hunter, Buddy D. *holding company executive*

Columbia
Geiger, Mark Watson *management educator*
†Gopalakrishna, Srinath *finance educator*
†Horner, Stephen VanDyke *finance educator*
Nikolai, Loren Alfred *accounting educator, writer*
Stockglausner, William George *accountant*
Wagner, William Burdette *business educator*

Farmington
Lees, William Glenwood *finance executive, retail executive*

Grain Valley
†Love, Gary Duane *financial consultant*

Kansas City
Bloch, Henry Wollman *tax preparation company executive*
Boysen, Melicent Pearl *finance company executive*
De Lurgio, Stephen Anthony *management educator*
†Ernst, Mark A. *diversified financial services company executive*
Johnson, Sondra Lea *accountant*
Jones, Charles Calhoun *estate and business planning consultant*
Latza, Beverly Ann *accountant*
Lock, Robert Joseph *accountant*
Mustard, Mary Carolyn *financial executive*
Pruitt, Stephen Wallace *finance educator*
Rowland, Landon Hill *diversified holding company executive*

Rozell, Joseph Gerard *accountant*
Shaw, Richard David *marketing and management educator*
Stevens, James Hervey, Jr., *retired financial advisor*

Kearney
Shrimpton, James Robert *controller*

Lees Summit
Foudree, Charles M. *retired financial executive*

Neosho
Weber, Margaret Laura Jane *retired accountant*

Poplar Bluff
Henson, Elizabeth K. *accountant*

Saint Charles
Pring, Robert Bradford *financial consultant*

Saint Louis
Arthur, Charles Gemmell, IV, *accountant*
Badalamenti, Anthony *financial planner*
Benson, Jim *finance company executive*
Brockhaus, Robert Herold, Sr., *business educator, consultant*
Burch, Stephen Kenneth *financial services company executive, real estate investor*
Carlson, Arthur Eugene *accounting educator*
Crider, Robert Agustine *international financier, law enforcement official*
Folz, Carol Ann *financial analyst*
Horwitz, William J. *treasurer*
James, William W. *financial consultant*
Koehler, Colleen M. *accountant*
Liggett, Hiram Shaw, Jr., *retired diversified industry financial executive*
Lock, Albert Larry, Jr., *financial services company executive*
†Novik, Steve *finance company executive*
O'Donnell, Mark Joseph *accountant*
Osborn, John David *credit union executive*
Ricks, David Artel *business educator, editor*
†Ronen, David *logistics and operations management educator, consultant*
Ruth, David Allen *accountant*
Sandbach, Charlie Bernard *accountant*
Schmidt, Charles, Jr., *finance executive*
Seibert, Earl Henry, Jr., (Si Seibert) *diversified financial services company executive*
Shepperd, Thomas Eugene *accountant*
†Supanvanij, Janikan *finance educator*
Tyree, Donald Andrew *financial educator*
Wiggins, Dewayne Lee *financial executive*
Wildhaber, Michael Rene *accountant*
Winter, Richard Lawrence *financial and health care company executive*

Springfield
†Knotts, Tami Leigh *finance educator*
†Scroggins, Wesley Allen *finance educator, researcher*

MONTANA

Billings
Stanfill, Patricia Mae *accountant*

Bozeman
Davis, Nicholas Homans Clark *finance company executive*

Dillon
Sethi, A. S. (Jim Sethi) *business educator*

Great Falls
Christiaens, Chris (Bernard Francis Christiaens) *financial analyst, state legislator*
Knowles, Randall Gene *financial planner*

Helena
Craig, Mary Lauri *accountant*

Troy
Sherman, Signe Lidfeldt *portfolio manager, former research chemist*

NEBRASKA

Beaver City
†Hall, Jay De *finance educator, consultant*

Fremont
Dunklau, Rupert Louis *personal investments consultant*

Hastings
†Nelson, Ricky Eugene *financial executive*

Lincoln
Digman, Lester Aloysius *management educator*
Lee, Sang M. *management educator*
Lienemann, Delmar Arthur, Sr., *accountant, real estate developer*

Norfolk
Wehrer, Charles Siecke *business and education educator*

Ogallala
Rausch, Paul Matthew *financial executive*

Omaha
Erickson, James Paul *retired financial service company executive*
Miller, Larry Thomas *accountant*

Papillion
Miller, Drew *financial management company executive*

Pierce
Thieben, Barbara Esther *accountant, tax professional*

Scottsbluff
DiBacco, T(had) Jay *financial services planner, career reserve officer*

Wayne
Nelson, Jeryl L. *financial consultant, educator, portfolio manager*

NEVADA

Boulder City
Omelianowich, Janet Anne *accountant*

Elko
†Ballew, Kathy I. *controller*

Las Vegas
†Assane, Djeto *finance educator*
Bovee, Courtland Lowell *business educator*
Duva-Mikhail, Donna Marie *financial executive*
Goldin, Martin Bruce *financial executive, consultant*
Hobbs, Guy Stephen *financial executive*
Nold, Aurora Ramirez *business and economics educator*
Rogers, David Hughes *finance executive*
Sand, Stephanie Jo *accountant, consultant*

Reno
Garcia, Katherine Lee *controller, accountant*
Neidert, Kalo Edward *accountant, educator*

NEW HAMPSHIRE

Amherst
Atwater, Verne Stafford *finance educator*

Center Harbor
Smith, Paul Thomas *financial services company executive*

Gilmanton
Osler, Howard Lloyd *retired controller*

Goffstown
Martel, Eva Leona *accountant*

Hanover
Anthony, Robert Newton *management educator emeritus*
†Pauwels, Koen Hendrik *finance educator*

Manchester
†Maloney, Simone *accountant*

Meredith
Lovett, Miller Currier *management educator, clergyman*

Nashua
Hemming, Walter William *business financial consultant*

New Castle
Levin, Harvey Jay *financial institution design and construction specialist, developer, auctioneer*

Peterborough
McCarthy, John Robert *tax consultant, hospital consultant*

NEW JERSEY

Avon By The Sea
Bruno, Grace Angelia *accountant, retired educator*

Bloomfield
Conta, Richard Vincent *actuary*

Bridgewater
Accardi, Joseph Ronald *accountant*

Budd Lake
Bauer, Jean Marie *accountant*

Camden
Foley, Eugene Arthur *accountant, consultant*
Homan, Kenneth Lewis *auditor*
Jones, Larry Darnell *tax specialist*

Chatham
Bugen, David Henry *financial advisor*
Earle, Jean Buist *finance executve*

Cherry Hill
Newell, Eric James *financial planner, tax consultant, former insurance executive*

Clifton
Klein, Hubert *accountant*

Cranbury
Campbell, Joseph John *financial services executive*
Kemmerer, Peter Ream *financial executive*

East Brunswick
Yahya, Muhammad Javaid *financial consultant, economist*

Edison
Barcun, Gail E. *forensic economics executive*
Cangemi, Michael Paul *accountant, financial executive, writer*
Hecht, William David *accountant*

Elizabeth
Lisa, Janis P. *finance manager, auditor*

Fair Lawn
Kourkoumelis, Nick *financial analyst, consultant, finance educator*

Fairfield
Byer, Theodore Scott *accountant*

Florham Park
Bossen, Wendell John *retired financial consultant*
Sinnett, William McNair *finance researcher*

Gladstone
Caspersen, Finn Michael Westby *diversified financial services company executive*

Hackensack
Donahoe, Maureen Alice *accounting consultant*

Haddonfield
Newell, Russell Anderson *financial planner*

Haworth
Posner, Roy Edward *retired finance executive*

Ho Ho Kus
Deupree, Marvin Mattox *accountant, business consultant*

Hoboken
†Mankin, Robert Stephen *financial executive*

Jersey City
Ezrati, Milton Joseph *investment manager, economist, writer*
Raffelson, Michael *financial executive*
Vogel, Nadine Orsoff *finacial services marketing executive*

Lawrenceville
†Lorenzet, Steven Joseph *management educator, consultant*

Little Falls
Armellino, Michael Ralph *retired asset management executive*
Birnberg, Jack *financial executive*

Lyndhurst
Brzezanski, Jay Marian *financial executive*

Manasquan
Branco, James Joseph *estate planner*

Marlton
Brown-Buchanan, Deborah Ann *financial consultant*
Gorenberg, Charles Lloyd *financial services executive*

Mendham
Hesselink, Ann Patrice *financial executive, lawyer*

Middletown
Meyler, William Anthony *financial executive*

Monmouth Beach
Herbert, LeRoy James *retired accounting firm executive*

Montclair
George, Nashwa E. *accountant, educator*
Luftglass, Murray Arnold *corporate financial executive*

Montvale
Fontana, John Arthur *employee benefits specialist*
Showalter, David Scott *accounting executive*

Montville
Klapper, Byron D. *financial company executive*

Morganville
Sternfeld, Marc Howard *finance educator*

Morristown
Cregan. Frank Robert *financial executive, consultant*
Flynn, Marie Cosgrove *portfolio manager, corporate financial executive*

Mount Laurel
Laubach, Roger Alvin *accountant*
Mann, Louis Eugene *financial planner*

New Brunswick
†Onwuchekova, Michael O. *accountant, educator*

Newark
Arabie, Phipps *marketing educator, researcher*
Clymer, Brian William *diversified financial services company executive, former state official*
Contractor, Farok *business and management educator*
Darr, Walter Robert *financial analyst*
McElwee, Bernard *management educator*
Seiglie, Carlos *finance educator*

Nutley
Henning, Neil Scott *financial consultant*

Oakhurst
Fasthuber-Grande, Traudy *financial services company executive*

Oldwick
Kellogg, C. Burton, II, *financial analyst*

Paramus
Balter, Leslie Marvin *business communications educator*

Parsippany
Pedescleaux-Muckle, Gail *business analyst, writer*
Wechter, Ira Martin *tax specialist, financial planner*

Pennington
Kaschak, David James *accountant*

Point Pleasant
†Albano, Pasquale Charles *management educator, management and organization development consultant*

Princeton
Cleary, Lynda Woods *financial advisor, consultant*
Goldfarb, Irene Dale *retired financial planner*
Hamburger, Jeffrey Allen *financial planner*
Harvey, Norman Ronald *retired finance company executive*
King, Alfred Meehan *financial executive*

Princeton Junction
Cohen, Florence Emery *retired financial services executive*

Red Bank
Oberst, Robert John *financial analyst*
Rose, Arthur Royal *financial planner, tax consultant*

River Edge
Gass, Manus M. *accountant, business executive*

Rivervale
Becker, Murray Leonard *corporate financial consultant, consulting actuary*

Short Hills
Gibson, William Lee *financial consultant*
Mebane, William Black *controller, financial consultant*
Sangiuliano, Barbara Ann *tax consultant*

Skillman
Wheelock, Keith Ward *retired consulting company executive, educator*

Somers Point
Berenato, Anthony Francis *financial executive*

Somerset
Gruchacz, Craig M. *financial executive*

Somerville
Cohen, Walter Stanley *accountant, financial consultant*

South Orange
Amar, A. D. *finance educator, management consultant*

South Plainfield
Pappas, Michael *financial services company executive*

Southampton
Knortz, Walter Robert *accountant, former insurance company executive*

Spring Lake
O'Connor, Francis X. *financial executive*
Wrege, Charles Deck *management educator*

Summit
Hickman, J. Kenneth *accounting company executive*

Toms River
Boisseau, Jerry Philip *financial services company executive*

Warren
Hartman, David G. *actuary*

Wayne
Boronico, Jess Stephen *management science educator, academic dean*
Li, Fuan *marketing educator, researcher*

West Orange
Weiner, Mervyn *retired mergers and acquisitions executive*
Zimmerman, David Carl *controller, corporate financial executive*

Woodbridge
Ayub, Yacub *financial consultant*
DeMatteo, Gloria Jean *financial counselor*

NEW MEXICO

Albuquerque
Capaldi, Larry Sylvestro *business educator*
†Gallegos, Aileen Arroyo *financial consultant*
Kaehele, Bettie Louise *accountant*

Las Cruces
Bell, M. Joy Miller *financial planner, real estate broker*
Cochrun, John Wesley *financial consultant*
Constantini, Louis O. *financial consultant, stockbroker*
Peterson, Robin Tucker *marketing educator*
Rosile, GraceAnn *business management educator*
Snare, Carl Lawrence, Jr., *retired accountant, financial planner*

Mesilla Park
Gibson, Dianna R. *financial consultant*

Niagara Falls
Askins, Arthur James *accountant, finance management and auditing executive*

Niagara University
†Kidwell Jr., Roland E. *finance educator, writer, researcher*

Nyack
Brecht, Warren Frederick *retired business executive*
†Laski, John N. *finance educator*

Oakdale
†Fayez, Mehanni Samuel *finance educator*

Old Westbury
Barbera, Anthony Thomas *accountant, educator*

Orchard Park
Keenan, John Paul *management educator, consultant, psychologist*
Oliver, Dominick Michael *business educator*

Patchogue
Barna, Douglas Peter *collection agency executive*

Pearl River
Bryant, Karen Worstell *financial advisor, investment company executive*

Pittsford
Green, Martin Lincoln *financial analyst, consultant*
Herge, Henry Curtis, Jr., *consulting firm executive*

Plainview
Feller, Benjamin E. *actuary*

Plattsburgh
Dossin, Ernest Joseph, III, *credit consulting company executive*

Pleasant Valley
Odescalchi, Edmond Péry *international financial consultant, author*

Pleasantville
Reps, David Nathan *finance educator*

Pomona
Landau, Lauri Beth *accountant, tax consultant*

Port Washington
Phelan, Arthur Joseph *financial executive*

Poughkeepsie
Handel, Bernard *accountant, actuarial and insurance consultant, lawyer*
Hansen, Karen Thornley *accountant*

Pound Ridge
Darcy, Keith Thomas *finance company executive, educator*

Purchase
Papaleo, Louis Anthony *accountant*
Sacco, John Michael *accountant*

Queensbury
Bitner, William Lawrence, III, *retired banker, educator*

Rego Park
Thomas, James Edward *accountant*

Riverdale
Lee, Dong Hwan *business administration educator*

Rochester
Garg, Devendra *financial executive*
Goyer, Virginia L. *accountant*
Schwert, G(eorge) William, III, *finance educator, educator*
Watts, Ross Leslie *accounting educator, consultant*

Rye
Finnerty, John Dudley *financial consultant*

Saratoga Springs
Dickinson, Richard Henry *accountant*

Scarsdale
Fenichel, Alvin Henry *financial executive*
Gollin, Stuart Allen *accountant*

Schenectady
Barber, Nicholas Carl *tax specialist, consultant, real estate executive*

Sleepy Hollow
Ferguson, Douglas Edward *financial executive*

Somers
Gulick, Donna Marie *accountant*

Southampton
Needham, James Joseph *retired financial services executive*

Spencertown
Hawkins, Robert Garvin *management educator*

Staten Island
Clark, Sylvia Dolores *business educator*
Fung, Amy Shu-Fong *accountant*
Gelbein, Jay Joel *accountant*
†Matveev, Alexei V. *business educator*
Storberg, Eric Philip *financial planner*

Syracuse
Doty, Duane Harold *business educator*
Marcoccia, Louis Gary *accountant, university administrator*

Tarrytown
Ferrari, Robert Joseph *business educator, former banker*
Hyman, Leonard Stephen *financial consultant, economist, writer*

Troy
Phan, Phillip Hin Choi *business educator, consultant*
St. John, William Charles, Jr., *business educator, administrator*

Valley Stream
Ellis, Bernice *financial planning company executive, investment advisor*

Vestal
Horwitz, Bertrand Nathan *accounting and finance educator*
Piaker, Philip Martin *accountant, educator*

Wappingers Falls
Hogan, Edward Robert *financial services executive*
Kells, Albert John *financial consultant*

Water Mill
Kreimer, Michael Walter *financial planner, investment company official*

Waterloo
†Schreck, Richard Thomas *accountant*

Webster
Laschenski, John Patrick *accountant*
McCormack, Stanley Eugene *financial consultant*
Nicholson, Douglas Robert *accountant*
Southard, Paul Raymond *financial executive*

Westbury
Goldstein, Fred *accountant*
Mondello, John Paul *financial consultant*

White Plains
Beldock, Donald Travis *corporate financial executive*
Gillingham, Stephen Thomas *financial planner*
†Isaak, Robert Allen *international management and political economy educator, writer*
Keegan, Warren Joseph *business educator, consultant*
Zuckerman, Marc Abraham *accountant, educator*

Whitestone
Brill, Steven Charles *financial advisor, lawyer*

Windsor
Warner, Roberta Arlene *accountant, financial services executive*

Yonkers
Alessi, George Anthony *financial advisor, consultant*
Johansen, Robert Joseph *consulting actuary*

York
Coleman, David Cecil *financial executive*

Yorktown Heights
Donovan, Andrew Joseph *financial consultant*

NORTH CAROLINA

Advance
Herpel, George Lloyd *marketing educator*

Asheville
†Mack, Carole *financial consultant*
Scully, Bonnie Diane *financial planner*

Beaufort
Pagano, Filippo Frank *financial broker, commercial loan consultant*

Bolivia
Brooks, Lithia Esther *finance executive*

Boone
Bowden, Elbert Victor *banking, finance and economics educator, author*
Krug, Jeffrey Alan

Cary
Bowen, Chester Edward *financial consultant, financial planner*
Bradley, Elizabeth Clay *financial planner, educator*
Coderre, Nancy Adele *financial analyst*
Hagan, John Aubrey *financial executive, retired*

Chapel Hill
Chapman, Robert Lee, III, *fund administrator, real estate developer*
Perreault, William Daniel, Jr., *business administration educator*
Rondinelli, Dennis A(ugust) *business administration educator, researcher*
Rosen, Benson *business administration educator*
Roth, Aleda Vender *business educator*
Whybark, David Clay *business educator, researcher*
†York, Anne Stewart *finance educator*

Charlotte
Anderson, Gerald Leslie *financial executive*
Burke, Peggy Hudgins (Margaret Hudgins Burke) *auditor*
Halas, Paul Anthony, Jr., *business appraisal and valuation specialist, consultant*
Labardi, Jillian Gay *financial planner, insurance agent*
†Larsen, Marshall O. *corporate financial executive*
Schulz, Walter Kurt *accountant, information technology consultant*

Clemmons
Taquey, Antony *accountant*

Dunn
Robison, Frederick Mason *financial executive*

Durham
Bettman, James Ross *management educator*
Staelin, Richard *business administration educator*

Fayetteville
Trull, Timothy Lane *financial services executive*

Greensboro
Black, Sylvia Sloan *business educator*
Compton, John Carroll *accountant*
Jones, Thomas Owen, Jr., *business educator, military officer*
†Lloyd, Lila G. *finance educator*
†Nemati, Hamid R. *management educator*
Starling, Larry Eugene *auditor*

Greenville
Krpata, Steven Allen *accountant, real estate company executive*

Havelock
Lindelof, William Christian, Jr., *financial company executive*

Hendersonville
Daubert, Madeline J. *accountant, educator*

High Point
Min, Sung Sik *accountant*

Pittsboro
Smith, Edith L'Engle Graham *accountant*

Raleigh
Aldridge, Adrienne Yingling *accountant, financial analyst*
Gower, Dana W. *financial consultant*
Hill, Hulene Dian *accountant*
Jessen, David Wayne *accountant*
McLawhorn, William Benjamin *audit administrator*
Mowrey, Timothy James *investment manager, financial planner*

Rock Hill
Cornick, Michael F(rederick) *accounting educator*

Rockingham
Spencer, Walter Jesse *accountant, consultant*

Southern Pines
Matney, Edward Eli *fretired securities company executive*

Tryon
Flynn, Kirtland, Jr., *accountant*

Wake Forest
Arnold, Eric Daniell *budget analyst, security supervisor*

Wilkesboro
Thomas, David Lloyd *accountant, consultant*

Wingate
Pitts, E. Hampton *business educator, dean*

Winston Salem
Gallo, Vincent John *financial planner*
Mecimore, Charles Douglas *retired accounting educator*
Middaugh, Jack Kendall, II, *management educator*
Moyer, R. Charles *finance educator, consultant*

NORTH DAKOTA

Fargo
Ness, Gary Gene *accountant*
†Shi, Zhengzhong *finance educator*

Grand Forks
†Tangsrud, Robert Raymond, Jr., *finance educator*

OHIO

Ada
Cooper, Ken Errol *retired management educator*

Akron
†Brouthers, Lance Eliot *finance educator*
Burg, H. Peter *financial executive*

Amelia
Hayden, Joseph Page, Jr., *company executive*

Ashland
Heimann, Beverly Ann *business educator, consultant*

Athens
†Senteney, David L. *accountant, educator*

Avon
Grmek, Dorothy Antonia *accountant*

Beachwood
Youdelman, Robert Arthur *financial executive, lawyer*

Berea
Keller, Tiffany Lee *business educator*

Bowling Green
Lunde, Harold Irving *management educator*

Brooklyn
Spahnie, Michelle Marie *accountant*

Brunswick
Reed, Jane Garson *eldercare/disability consultant*

Cincinnati
Allen, Anna Marie *financial executive*
Conaton, Michael Joseph *financial service executive*
Di Benedetto, Ann Louise *accounting administrator*
Dougherty, Charlotte Anne *financial planner, insurance and securities representative*
Gyuro, Paula Candice *financial planner*
Huenefeld, Thomas Ernst *financial consultant, retired banker*
Johnson, Norma Louise *accountant*
Krishnan, Hema A. *finance educator*
Lawson, Randall Clayton, II, *financial executive*
Linder, Carl H., III, *diversified financial services company executive*
Lintz, Robert Carroll *retired financial holding company executive*
Mantel, Samuel Joseph, Jr., *management educator, consultant*
Miles, John Bill *accountant, tax advisor*
Rand, Carolyn *financial executive*
Rebel, Jerome Ivo *financial planner*
Scruggs, Catherine Lynn *financial manager*
Wulker, Laurence Joseph *portfolio manager, educator, financial planner*

Cleveland
Chester, Russell Gilbert, Jr., *accountant, auditor*
†Holland, Brian Joseph *corporate financial executive*
Johnson, Michael Lee *accountant, controller*
Key, Helen Elaine *accountant, consulting company executive, educator*
Krulitz, Leo Morrion *financial executive*
Lemmo, Roberta June *financial advisor*
Lynn, Leonard Harvey *business educator*
Manley, David Thomas *employee benefits plan administration executive*
Mayne, Lucille Stringer *finance educator*
†Morgenthaler, David Turner *venture capitalist*
Noetzel, Arthur Jerome *business administration educator, management consultant*
Petina, David Anthony *industry analyst*
Pierson, Marilyn Ehle *financial planner*
Poza, Ernesto *business consultant, educator*
Roberts, James Owen *financial planning executive, consultant*
Seaton, Robert Finlayson *retired finance company executive*
Skolnik, David Erwin *financial analyst*
Stratton-Crooke, Thomas Edward *financial consultant*
Thomas, Richard Stephen *financial executive*
Vickers, Mary Louise *financial analyst*
Webb, James R. *finance educator, consultant*
Yetmar, Scott Andrew *accountant, educator*

Columbus
Berry, William Lee *business administration educator*
Eaton, Michael Christopher *accounting technician*
Ellis, Greg Evan *investment sales executive, consultant*
Fidler, Carol Ann *accountant*
Kasper, Larry John *accountant, litigation support consultant*
Kreager, Eileen Davis *administrative consultant*
LaLonde, Bernard Joseph *educator*
Levin, Richard Allen *auditor, consultant*
Milligan, Glenn Wesley *business educator*
Raabe, William Alan *tax writer, business educator*
Rennix, Paul Donley *accountant*
†Rosholt, Robert A. *financial executive*
Ruhlin, Peggy Miller *investment adviser, financial planner*
Schneider, Cindy E. Gower (Lones) *financial advisor*
Sestina, John E. *financial planner*

Cuyahoga Falls
Moses, Abe Joseph *international financial consultant*

Dayton
Hoge, Franz Joseph *accounting firm executive*
†Kanet, John Joseph *management educator*
Singhvi, Surendra Singh *finance and strategy consultant*

East Liverpool
Feldman, Marvin Herschel *financial consultant*
Gailey, Joan Dale *retired finance educator*

Geneva
Clement, Daniel Roy, IV, *accountant, assistant nurse, small business owner, tax preparation consultant*

Greenville
Franz, Daniel Thomas *financial planner*

Harrison
Kocher, Juanita Fay *retired auditor*

Hudson
†Szefcyk, Renee Marie *financial services executive*

Independence
Boyle, Kammer *estate planner, financial analyst*

Jackson
Moore, Jimmie Lee *accountant*

Lake Milton
Healy, Joanne P. *accounting educator*

PROFESSIONAL INDEX 6333 FINANCE: FINANCIAL SERVICES

Lancaster
Voss, Jack Donald *international business consultant, lawyer*

Mansfield
Shah, James M. *actuary*

Mason
Roemer, John Alan *financial executive*

Middletown
Wainscott, James Lawrence *accountant*

North Canton
Lynham, C(harles) Richard *company executive*

North Olmsted
Cotman, John Martin *accountant*
McCafferty, Owen Edward *accountant, dental-veterinary practice consultant*

Oxford
Snavely, William Brant *management educator and consultant*

Poland
†Horton, Barbara Louise *business educator*

Reynoldsburg
Gunnels, Lee O. *retired finance and management educator, manufacturing/research company director, inventor*

Shaker Heights
Donnem, Sarah Lund *financial analyst, non-profit and political organization consultant*

Springboro
Walden, James William *accountant, educator*

Stow
Hessler, William Gerhard *tax consultant*

Strongsville
Pinkerton, Richard LaDoyt *retired management educator*

Sylvania
†Sampson, Wesley Claude *auditor, software inventor*

Tiffin
Debbink, Thomas Mason *management educator*

Toledo
Chang, Kathryn Jinmei *accountant*
Eberly, William Somers *financial consultant*
Geisler, Nathan David *financial consultant*
Hartmann, Ann W. *financial planner*
†Pullins, Ellen Bolman *finance educator*

Warren
Robbins, Robert Marvin *accountant*

West Chester
Ulrich, Jody L. *accountant*

Wilberforce
†Omolewu, Gabriel Adebayo *business educator, researcher*

Willoughby
Trennel, Lawrence William *accountant, educator*

Worthington
Barbe, Betty Catherine *retired financial analyst*

OKLAHOMA

Ada
Parham, Betty Ely *credit bureau executive*

Durant
England, Dan Benjamin *accountant*

Enid
Curtis, Albert Bradley, II, *financial planner, tax specialist*
Rider, John Allen, II, *business educator, paralegal*

Moore
Lee, Myung Woo *financial secretary, accountant*

Muskogee
Slattery, Jeffrey *management educator, consultant*

Norman
Tihanyi, Laszlo *management educator, researcher*

Oklahoma City
Cassel, John Elden *accountant*
†Crites, Carl D. *auditor*
Harrington, Gary Burnes *retired controller*

Stillwater
†DeGroot, Timothy *finance educator*
†Dooley, Robert S. *finance educator*

Tulsa
Candreia, Peggy Jo *financial analyst*
Duncan, Maurice Greer *accountant, consultant*
Gaddis, Richard William *management educator*
Hoe, Richard March *insurance and securities consultant, writer*
Jones, Michael Lynn *financial consultant, branch operations manager*
Kaiser, George B. *corporate financial executive*
†Wolfe, Joseph Allen *finance educator, consultant*

OREGON

Ashland
Chatfield, Michael *accounting educator*

Beaverton
Kaplan, Bradley S. *corporate financial executive*

Clackamas
Love, Susan Denise *accountant, consultant, small business owner*

Eugene
†Bergquist, Timothy M. *business educator, researcher*
Hamren, Nancy Van Brasch *bookkeeper*
Lindholm, Richard Theodore *economics and finance educator*
Smith, Vangy Edith *accountant, consultant, writer, artist*

Grants Pass
Smith, Barnard Elliot *management educator*

Lake Oswego
McPeak, Merrill Anthony *business executive, consultant, retired officer*
Mylnechuk, Larry Herbert *financial executive*

Marylhurst
Applegate, Charles G. *financial professional*

Newberg
McMahon, Paul Francis *finance company executive*

Portland
Arnold, Ralph Leo, III, *valuation analyst, consultant*
Epperson, Eric Robert *company executive, film producer*
Finley, Lewis Merren *financial consultant*
Johnson, H. Thomas *business educator*
Petersen, Devi Lynne *accountant*
Stewart, Marlene Metzger *financial planning practitioner, insurance agent*
Watne, Donald Arthur *accountant, educator, retired*
Weber, George Richard *financial and internet marketing executive, writer*
White, Roberta Lee *financial analyst*
Workman, Norman Allan *accountant, graphic arts consultant*

West Linn
Luchterhand, Ralph Edward *financial advisor*

PENNSYLVANIA

Allentown
Balog, Ibolya *accountant*
Coyle, Charles A. *marketing educator*
Fortune, Robert Russell *financial consultant*
Heitmann, George Joseph *business educator, consultant*

Allison Park
LaDow, C. Stuart *retired consultant financial services*

Bala Cynwyd
Bronson, Christopher Herbert *financial service company executive, planner*
Cohen, Rachel Rutstein *financial planner*
Isdaner, Lawrence Arthur *accountant*
McGill, Dan Mays *insurance business educator*
Miller, L. Martin *accountant, financial planning specialist*

Beaver Falls
Fox, Michael F. *controller*

Bethlehem
Barsness, Richard Webster *management educator, administrator*
Hobbs, James Beverly *business administration educator, writer*
†Sivakumar, K. *marketing educator*

Blue Bell
Zucchi, Donna Marie *financial services executive*

Boyertown
Stephen, Dennis John *financial planner*

Braddock
Slack, Edward Dorsey, III, *financial systems professional, consultant*

Bryn Mawr
Daly, Donald Francis *consultant, retired investment counsel*
Duska, Brenda Shay *accountant, academic financial administrator*
Giese, William Herbert *tax accountant*
Moyer, F. Stanton *financial executive, advisor*

Butler
Coleman, Arthur Robert *retired accountant*

Carlisle
Robinson, Ronald Michael *financial executive, financial consultant*

Center Valley
†McGorry, Susan Yacapsin *finance educator*

Chester
DiAngelo, Joseph Anthony, Jr., *finance educator, dean*
McCloskey, Donna Weaver *business educator*
Saad, Germaine H. *finance educator, researcher*

Chester Springs
Dallas, Noelle Marie *financial analyst*

Collegeville
Maco, Teri Regan *accountant, engineer*

Doylestown
†Gauer, Linette-Jean Crete *accountant*
Kohlhepp, Edward John *financial planner*

Drexel Hill
†Bay, Joann Reeder *financial planner*

Du Bois
Forsythe-Adamson, Velma Brown *accountant, consultant, English language educator*

Dunmore
Pencek, Carolyn Carlson *treasurer, educator*

Erie
†Janikowski, Stanley M. *retired tax specialist, advocate*
Monahan, Thomas Andrew, Jr., *accountant*

Flourtown
Christy, John Gilray *financial company executive*

Glen Riddle Lima
Newett, Edward J., Jr., *accountant*

Glenside
Ralston, Steven Philip *portfolio manager, financial analyst*

Greencastle
†Horst, Carolyn Diane *accountant*

Harrisburg
Ellenbogen, Elisabeth Alice *retired accountant*
Reigel, Timothy John *accountant*
Willow, Judith Ann Loye *tax preparer*

Haverford
Merrill, Arthur Alexander *financial analyst*

Havertown
Brinker, Thomas Michael *finance executive*

Horsham
Johnson, G. Carol *financial services executive*

Hughesville
Bellmore, Lawrence Robert, Jr., *financial planner*

Kennett Square
Bell, Philip Wilkes *accounting and economics educator*

King Of Prussia
Anderson, Jerry Allen *financial analyst*
de La Morandiere, Brice *finance executive*

Kutztown
Ogden, James Russell *marketing educator, consultant, lecturer, writer*

Lafayette Hill
King, Leon *financial services executive*

Lancaster
Fisher, Sarah Young *money manager, financial adviser*
Freeman, Clarence Calvin *financial executive*
Showers, Krista Ann *accountant*

Latrobe
Fazzi, Charles *accounting educator*

Macungie
Moore, Joyce Kristina *financial planner, director*

Malvern
Hendrix, Stephen C. *financial executive*

Meadowbrook
Baeckstrom, Marianne *actuary*

Media
Hemphill, James S. *investment management executive, financial advisor*

Middletown
Culpan, Refik *finance educator*

Mohnton
Hart, LeRoy Banks *financial software executive*
Konnick, Dianne Cheryl *financial executive*

Monaca
Nutter, James Randall *management educator*

Narberth
Estefan, Nabil *finance and business executive*

Newry
LaBorde, Terrence Lee *audit consultant, negotiator*

Newtown
Fiore, James Louis, Jr., *public accountant, educator, professional speaker, trainer consultant*

Newtown Square
Graf, Arnold Harold *employee benefits executive, financial planner*

North Huntingdon
Brazer, Barbara Roback *accountant*

Paoli
Gotshall, Jan Doyle *financial planner*

Parkesburg
Zevtchin, J. Mark *financial executive, consultant*

Philadelphia
Alexander, Elmore Rosebur, III, *business educator, dean*
Alexander, William Herbert *business educator, former construction executive*
Anderson, Rolph Ely *finance educator*
Andrisani, Paul J. *business educator, management consultant*
Babbel, David Frederick *finance and insurance educator*
Blume, Marshall Edward *finance educator*
Booth, Anna Belle *accountant*
Brittain, Willard Woodson, Jr., (Woody Brittain) *diversified financial services company executive*
Friedman, Sidney A. *financial services executive*
Goldsmith, Nancy Carrol *business and health services management educator*
Joglekar, Prafulla Narayan *information systems management educator, consultant*
Keim, Donald Bruce *finance educator*
†Kim, Seung-Lae *accounting educator, researcher*
Kimberly, John Robert *management educator, consultant*
Kozlowski, Bette Marie *accountant*
Ksansnak, James Edward *service management company executive*
Kurokawa, Susumu *management educator, researcher*
Leimkuhler, Gerard Joseph *financial holding company executive*
Lodish, Leonard Melvin *marketing educator, entrepreneur*
Mazzarella, James Kevin *business administration educator*
Micko, Alexander S. *financial executive*
Moore, Faye L. Mitchell *financial executive*
Rosenbloom, Bert *marketing educator, consultant, writer*
†Rosenthal, Edward Charles *management science educator*
Rowan, Richard Lamar *business management educator*
Sanyour, Michael Louis, Jr., *diversified financial services company executive*
Saul, Ralph Southey *financial service executive*
Scogno, Stacie Joy *financial services company executive*
Selles, Robert Hendrikus *actuary, consultant*
Shils, Edward B. *management educator, lawyer, arbitrator and mediator*
Staloff, Arnold Fred *financial executive*
Stambaugh, Robert F. *finance educator*
Webber, Ross Arkell *management educator*
Weidner, C. Ken, II, *management and business ethics educator, consultant*
Ziegler, Donald Robert *accountant*
Zucker, William *retired business educator*

Pittsburgh
Bernt, Benno Anthony *business executive, entrepreneur and investor*
Bly, James Charles, Jr., *financial services executive*
Cornuejols, Gerard Pierre *operations research educator*
Costel, Daniel Eugene *financial analyst*
Franklin, Kenneth Ronald *franchise company executive, consultant*
†Galletta, Dennis F. *business administration educator, consultant*
Giliberti, Michael Richard *financial planner*
†Haley, Roy W. *finance company executive*
Heitzenroder, David August *financial services professional, investment advisor, investment banker*
Ijiri, Yuji *accounting and economics educator*
†Inman, John Jeffrey *finance educator*
†King, William Richard *business educator, consultant*
Kriebel, Charles Hosey *management sciences educator*
Lewis, Richard Allan *financial planner, business consultant*
Means, Dwight Bardeen, Jr., *financial consultant, educator*
†Reed, William Ferguson *corporate financial executive*
Saykiewicz-Sajkiewicz, Jan Napoleon *marketing educator*
Smrekar, Karl George, Jr., *financial planner*
Stevens, William Talbert *financial services executive*
Thorne, John Reinecke *business educator, venture capitalist*

Radnor
Stearns, Milton Sprague, Jr., *financial executive*

Reading
McVey, Diane Elaine *accountant*

Richboro
Higginbotham, Kenneth James *financial services executive*

Saint Davids
Bertsch, Frederick Charles, III, *business executive*
Rogers, James Gardiner *accountant, educator*

Sayre
Brittain, Nancy Hammond *accountant*

Scranton
Eckersley, Richard Laurence *accountant*

Sewickley
Jehle, Michael Edward *financial executive*

Slippery Rock
†Mukherjee, Pracheta *management educator, researcher, consultant*

University Park
Kelley, Eugene John *retired business educator*

McKeown, James Charles *accounting educator, consultant*
Muscarella, Christopher James *finance educator*
†Rangaswamy, Arvind *marketing educator, consultant*

Valley Forge
Phelizon, Jean Francois *business executive*

Villanova
Cox-Klaczak, Karen Michelle *marketing educator, computer company official*

Volant
Moore, Janet Marie *accountant, state official*

Wayne
Mestre, Oscar Luis *financial consultant*

West Chester
Blasiotti, Robert Vincent *accountant, consultant*
Handzel, Steven Jeffrey *accountant*

Wilkes Barre
McHale, Maureen Bernadette Kenny *controller*

Wynnewood
Frankl, Razelle *management educator*
Robinson, Robert L. *former financial service company executive, lawyer*

Wyomissing
Gebbia, Robert James *tax executive*
Spatcher, Dianne Marie *finance executive*

Yardley
Gilmour, D(avid) James *financial analyst, systems analyst*

York
Day, Ronald Richard *retired financial executive*

RHODE ISLAND

Cranston
Ahlgren, Charles Stephen *educator, business and public policy consultant*
Langlois, Michael A. *financial adviser, consultant*

East Providence
Tripp, Michael Windsor *accountant*

Kingston
Mazze, Edward Mark *marketing educator, consultant*

Lincoln
Carter, Wilfred Wilson *financial executive, controller*

Providence
McNeil, Paul Joseph, Jr., *employment security interviewer*
Satterthwaite, Franklin Bache, Jr., *management educator, executive coach, author*

Warwick
Ribezzo, John Steven *business administration educator, accountant*

SOUTH CAROLINA

Charleston
Adelson, Gloria Ann *financial executive*
Franklin, Paul Deane *financial services executive, investor*
Prewitt, William Chandler *finance company executive*
Rhea, Marcia Chandler *accountant*

Columbia
Edwards, James Benjamin *accountant, educator*
Luoma, Gary A. *accounting educator*
Monahan, Thomas Paul *accountant*
Outin, Mary Louise *business, multi-cultural history and geneology educator*
Powell, J(ohn) Key *estate planner, consultant*
Pritchett, Samuel Travis *finance and insurance educator, researcher, consultant*

Conway
†Nale, Robert D. *finance educator*

Darlington
Bischoff, Frederick Christopher, III, *retired accountant*

Georgetown
Bowen, William Augustus *financial consultant*
McGrath, James Charles, III, *financial services company executive, lawyer, consultant*

Graniteville
Learnard, James Michael *middle school educator, former finance company executive, special education educator*

Greenville
Rogers, Jon Martin *financial consultant, financial company executive*
Smythe, Thomas Ira, Jr., *finance educator, researcher*

Lancaster
Carnes, Laura *financial analyst*

Seneca
Fairleigh, Marlane Paxson *retired management educator*

Spartanburg
†Pate, John Gillis, Jr., *financial consultant, accounting educator*

Summerville
Sexton, Donald Lee *retired business administration educator*

Sumter
Van Bulck, Hendrikus Eugenius *accountant*
van Bulck, Margaret West *accountant, financial planner, educator*

West Columbia
Byars, Merlene Hutto *accountant, visual artist, writer, publisher*

Williamston
Alewine, James William *financial executive*

SOUTH DAKOTA

Aberdeen
Hollingsworth, John Arthur *business educator*

Platte
Pennington, Beverly Melcher *financial services company executive*

Rapid City
†Collins, Rey *financial analyst*

TENNESSEE

Alamo
Finch, Evelyn Vorise *financial planner*

Brentwood
Jordan, Robert Andrew *accountant*
McClary, Jim Marston *accounting executive, consultant*

Brighton
Iles, Roger Dean *business educator*

Chattanooga
†Dawson, Gail Alesia *management educator*
Matherley, Steve Allen *cost accountant*
†Russell, Lynn Mawk *actuary*

Cookeville
Swanson, Gale Alden *accountant, educator*

Crossville
Lansford, Edwin Gaines *accountant*

Elizabethton
Taylor, Wesley Alan *accountant, consultant*

Franklin
Sloan, W(ilson) Keith *actuary*

Goodlettsville
Tongate, Darrel Edwin *accountant*

Jackson
Holt, Michael Kenneth *management and finance educator, consultant, city councilman*

Jefferson City
Driver, Phyllis Nelke *accountant, educator*

Johnson City
†Driver, Michaela Claudia *organizational behavior and development educator*
†Morgan, Robert George *accounting educator, researcher*

Knoxville
†Naoumova, Irina Yevgenievna *finance educator, consultant*

Martin
†Lemons, Mary A. *finance educator*

Mc Kenzie
†Blasick, James David *finance educator*

Memphis
Brandon, Elvis Denby, Jr., *financial planner*
Brandon, Elvis Denby, III, *financial planner*
Brandon, Raymond Wilson *financial planner, securities principal*
Umholtz, Clyde Allan *financial analyst*

Munford
Harrington, Herbert H. *accountant*

Nashville
Brophy, Jeremiah Joseph *former financial company official, former army officer*
†Christie, William Gary *finance educator, dean*
Dykes, Archie Reece *financial services executive*
Freudenthal, Ernest Guenter *technology and business educator*
Gore, Steven Lowell *financial consultant*
Manning, David Lee *financial executive*
Richmond, Samuel Bernard *management educator*
Saunders, Ted Elliott *accountant*
Sircy, Bob C., Jr., *accountant, financial executive*
Ullestad, Merwin Allan *tax services executive*
Weingartner, H(ans) Martin *finance educator, educator*

Soddy Daisy
Swafford, Douglas Richard *corporate credit executive*

TEXAS

Allen
Plum, Charles Walden *retired business executive and educator*

Amarillo
Ingraham, Joseph Edwin *financial officer*

Martin, Luan *accountant, payroll and timekeeping supervisor*

Argyle
Pettit, John Douglas, Jr., *management educator*

Arlington
Dickinson, Roger Allyn *business administration educator*
Reilly, Michael Atlee *financial company executive, venture capital investor*
Swanson, Peggy Eubanks *finance educator*

Austin
Alpert, Mark Ira *marketing educator*
Anderson, Urton Liggett *accounting educator*
Crum, Lawrence Lee *banking educator*
†Cundiff, Edward William *marketing educator*
Doenges, Rudolph Conrad *finance educator*
Granof, Michael H. *accounting educator*
Graydon, Frank Drake *retired accounting educator, university administrator*
Hagerty, Polly Martiel *financial analyst, construction executive*
Kane, James Robert *financial executive*
Kimberlin, Sam Owen, Jr., *financial institutions consultant*
Larson, Kermit Dean *accounting educator*
Leeds, Sanford J., III, *financial executive, educator*
Parrino, Robert *finance educator*
Peterson, Robert Allen *marketing educator*
Rasbury, Julian George *financial services company executive*
Wolf, Harold Arthur *finance educator*

Beaumont
Ellsworth, Myrna Ruth *accountant*

Brenham
Rothermel, James Douglas *retired finance educator*

Brownwood
Bell, Mary E. Beniteau *accountant*

Burleson
Just, Philip Ray *auditor*

Cedar Hill
Ebozue, Benson Obian *financial analyst*
Shower, Robert Wesley *financial executive*

College Station
Bierman, Leonard *management educator*
Cocanougher, Arthur Benton *business administration educator*
Wichern, Dean William *business educator*

Commerce
Avard, Stephen Lewis *finance educator*

Corpus Christi
Vaughan, Alice Felicie *accountant, real estate executive, tax consultant*
†Vokurka, Robert John *finance educator, researcher, finance educator, consultant*

Cypress
Hlozek, Carole Diane Quast *business executive*

Dallas
Bayne, James Elwood *investor and financial consultant*
Caldwell, Thomas Howell, Jr., *accountant, financial management consultant*
Coldwell, Philip Edward *financial consultant*
Eads, John A. *accountant*
Garner, Paul Trantham *auditor*
Grant, Joseph Moorman *finance executive*
Guthrie, M. Philip *corporate financial executive*
Gyemant, Robert Ernest *diversified financial services company executive, merchant*
Harris, Lucy Brown *accountant, consultant*
Hay, Jess Thomas *retired finance company executive*
†Hoyt, Rosemary Ellen *trust advisor*
Jobe, Larry Alton *financial company executive*
Lam, Chun Hung *finance educator, consultant*
McElvain, David Plowman *retired manufacturing company financial executive*
McElyea, Jacquelyn Suzanne *accountant, real estate consultant*
Moore, Thomas Joseph *financial company executive*
Peiser, John George *accountant, consultant*
Shimer, Daniel Lewis *corporate executive*
†Sobol, Marion Gross *business educator*
Solender, Robert Lawrence *real estate executive, retired newspaper executive*
Tannebaum, Samuel Hugo *accountant*
Walker, Gordon Beverley Moore, Jr., *business educator*
Wilbur, Janis A. *financial consultant, sales professional*
†Zimmermann, Walter Halen *finance company executive*

Denton
Prybutok, Victor Ronald *business educator*
Wallace, William Hall *economic and financial consultant*

Dripping Springs
†Guess, Aundrea Kay *accounting educator*

Duncanville
Trotter, Ide Peebles *financial planner, investment manager*

El Paso
Beard, Jane Alida *retired accountant*
Kelley, Sylvia Johnson *financial services firm executive*
†Showery, Charles George, Jr., *financial services company executive, consultant*

Flower Mound
Zoellner, Sandra Ann *accountant*

Fort Worth
Clark, Emory Eugene *financial planning executive*
Clifton, Gregory Todd *financial services company executive*
Dominiak, Geraldine Florence *accounting educator, retired*
†Hendricks, Scott *corporate budget specialist*
Karnes, Keith Dale *portfolio manager*
Low, George Solon *business educator, consultant*
Pappas-Speairs, Nina *financial planner, educator*

Friendswood
Thomas, James Raymond *accountant*

Frisco
Bloskas, John D. *financial executive*

Galveston
Selig, Oury Levy *port financial consultant*
Welch, Ronald J. *actuary*

Garland
Lord, Jacqueline Ward *accountant, photographer, artist*
McGill, Maurice Leon *financial executive*

Georgetown
Sellers, Fred Evans *accounting educator*

Hondo
†Bryant, Jannie *accountant*

Houston
Ayadi, Olusegun Felix *finance educator*
Barnett, Donald Blake *corporate financial executive*
Bartunek, Kenneth Steven *financial consultant*
Braden, John Alan *accountant*
†Chatterjee, Amitava *finance educator, consultant*
Clark, Geoffrey *accountant*
D'Agostino, James Samuel, Jr., *financial executive*
Getz, Lowell Vernon *financial advisor*
Goldberg, William Jeffrey *accountant, financial planner*
Griffith, Martha *controller*
Hargrove, James Ward *financial consultant*
Harris, Venita Van Caspel *retired financial planner*
Horvitz, Paul Michael *finance educator, educator*
Janssens, Joe Lee *controller, consultant*
Jones, Eli, III, *marketing/sales educator*
Knauss, Robert Lynn *international business educator, corporate executive*
Mahadeva, Manoranjan *financial executive, accountant*
Malone Watkins, Lisa R. *accountant, scheduler*
Rawson, Jim Charles *accountant, executive*
†Salam, Debera Jean *accounting company executive*
Starkey, Elizabeth LaRuffa *accountant*
Van Dusen, Glenn T. *business executive*
Wang, Fu-kuo Albert *finance educator*
Weisgarber, Robert Lee *corporate financial executive*
†Windsor, Oliver Duane *business and public administration educator*
Zeff, Stephen Addam *accounting educator*

Irving
Forson, Norman Ray *controller*
Martin, Stacey *accountant*
Sambaluk, Nicholas Wayne *auditor, educator*
Whitaker, Heidi Sue *accountant, auditor, information systems specialist*
Whittington, James Leland *management educator*

Keene
†Stembridge, Allen Frederick *management educator*

Keller
†Flournoy, Edward Brian *financial consultant, consultant*

Laredo
Mayfield, Jacqueline Rowley *business educator, department chairman*

Lubbock
Sears, Robert Stephen *finance educator, university dean*
Stem, Carl Herbert *business educator*
Wolfe, Verda Nell *pension consultant, financial planner*

Mc Kinney
Goldstein, Lionel Alvin *personal financial and investment advisor*
Kessler, John Paul, Jr., *financial planner*
Williams, James Lee *financial industries executive*

Midland
Groce, James Freelan *financial planning specialist*
Tom, James Robert *accountant*

New Braunfels
Griffin-Thompson, Melanie *accounting firm executive*

Plano
Bode, Richard Albert *retired financial executive*

Port Aransas
Beimers, George Jacob *financial executive*

Richardson
Burke, Thomas William *executive benefits consulting company official*

PROFESSIONAL INDEX 6335 FINANCE: FINANCIAL SERVICES

Neely, Vicki Adele *accountant, legal assistant, poet*

Rosharon
Jenkins, Judith Alexander *bank consultant*

Round Rock
Puri, Rajendra Kumar *business and tax specialist, consultant*

San Antonio
Carroll, William Marion *financial services executive*
Fonseca, Joseph Mojica, Jr., *financial analyst, educator*
Fuhrmann, Charles John, II, *strategic and finance consultant*
Hannah, John Robert, Sr., *accountant*
†Herres, Robert Tralles *financial services executive*
Jones, James Richard *business administration educator*
†Lomeli, Ruth M. *accountant*
Marvin, Catherine A. *financial consultant*
Stevens, Dennis Max *audit director*
Sun, Minghe *business educator*
†Turner, Whick Darrin *controller*
Volk, Thomas *accountant*
Weber, William Wesley *accountant*
Wilson, Bennie James, III, *business educator*

San Marcos
Palmer, Roger Raymond *accounting educator*
Taylor, Ruth Arleen Lesher *marketing educator*

Spring
†Kehoe, John Kimball *management educator, management consultant*

Stephenville
Collier, Boyd Dean *finance educator, management consultant*

Sugar Land
Keefe, Carolyn Joan *tax accountant*

Sweetwater
†Woodrow, Natile Latreece *accountant, educator*

Victoria
†Lee, Yong-Gyo *accountant, educator*

Waco
Davis, Charles Elliot *accounting educator*
Rose, John Thomas *finance educator, department chairman*
Teal, Elisabeth Jane *business educator, researcher*

Waring
†Leslie, Wendyl Keith *financial consultant*

Wichita Falls
Silverman, Gary William *financial planner*

Wimberley
Skaggs, Wayne Gerard *financial services company executive, retired*

UTAH

Bountiful
Brooke, Edna Mae *retired business educator*

Provo
Hunt, H(arold) Keith *business management educator, marketing consultant*

Salt Lake City
Leibsla, Melvin Donald *audit executive*
Nelson, Roger Hugh *management educator, corporate consultant, business executive*
†Nicolatus, Stephen Jon *financial consultant*

VERMONT

Burlington
Harrison, David Michael *finance educator, consultant*

Rutland
Haley, John Charles *financial executive*
Norris, Richard Anthony *accountant, waste systems company executive*

Shelburne
Giles, Scott Andrew *finance company executive*

Woodstock
Churchill, James Garton *retired international finance consultant*

VIRGINIA

Abingdon
Graham, Howard Lee, Sr., *financial services company executive*

Alexandria
Brickhill, William Lee *international finance consultant*
Coryell, Glynn Heath *financial services executive*
Henderson, Paul Bargas, Jr., *economic development consultant*
Inman, Stephen Eugene *finance officer*
†Smith, Robert Luther *management educator*
Wesberry, James Pickett, Jr., *financial management consultant, auditor, international organization executive*

Annandale
Connair, Stephen Michael *financial analyst*

Arlington
Bianchi, Charles Paul *technical and business executive, money manager, financial consultant*
Lewis, Hunter *financial advisor, publisher*
McClure, William Earl *financial advisor*
Page, Harry Robert *business administration educator*

Blacksburg
Brozovsky, John A. *accounting educator*
Moore, Laurence John *business educator*
Patterson, Douglas MacLennan *finance educator*

Broad Run
Kube, Harold Deming *retired financial executive*

Chantilly
Carlson, Robert Charles *financial advisor, writer*

Charlottesville
Davis, Edward Wilson *business administration educator*
Ellett, John Spears, II, *retired taxation educator, accountant, lawyer*
Kehoe, William Joseph *educator, researcher, writer, consultant*
†Laseter, Timothy Marks *finance educator*
Minehart, Jean Besse *tax accountant*
Scott, Charlotte H. *business educator*
Shenkir, William Gary *business educator*
Sihler, William Wooding *finance educator, educator*
Thompson, David William *business educator*
Verstegen, Deborah A. *policy and finance educator*
Wheeler, David Wayne *freelance/self-employed accountant*

Chesapeake
Shirley, Charles William *insurance and investment advisor, farm owner*

Chester
Roane, David James, Jr., *information technology auditor*

Crozet
Rosenblum, John William *finance educator*

Fairfax
Bowden, Howard Kent *accountant*
Cramer, H. R. *financial officer*
Kalas, Frank Joseph, Jr., *financial, information systems consultant*
Kautt, Glenn Gregory *financial planner, consultant*
†Meamber, Laurie Ann *finance educator*
Van Eeckhoudt, Marc Victor Celestin *purchasing manager*

Falls Church
Bruck, William *business executive*
Hahn, Thomas Joonghi *accountant*
Purvis, Ronald Scott *financial counselor, real estate professional*
Rosenberg, Theodore Roy *financial executive*
Vodra, Richard Earle *financial planner*

Hampton
Douglass, James Frederick *business administration educator*
Wiedman, Timothy Gerard *management educator*

Haymarket
Phillips, Robert Benbow *financial planner*

Keswick
Pochick, Francis Edward *financial consultant*

Keysville
Nipper, Patricia Diane *accounting and economics educator*

Lexington
DeVogt, John Frederick *management science and business ethics educator, consultant*

Lynchburg
Kulp, James *finance company executive*

Mc Lean
Drew, K. *financial advisor, management consultant*
Edgar, Janelle Diane Ward *financial services executive*
Fairbank, Richard D. *diversified financial services company executive*
Pho, Long Ambrose Ba *business educator, consultant*
Young, Loretta Ann *auditor*

Newport News
Le Mons, Kathleen Ann *securities company executive, investment officer, portfolio manager*

Norfolk
McKee, Timothy Carlton *taxation educator*
Shumadine, Anne Ballard *financial advisor, lawyer*

Palmyra
Sahr, Morris Gallup *financial planner*

Reston
Fox, Edward A. *business executive*
Palumbo, James Fredrick *financial services company executive*
Polemitou, Olga Andrea *accountant*

Richmond
Dye, David Ray *tax accountant, financial advisor*
Harris, Ruth Hortense Coles *retired accounting educator*
Hull, Rita Prizler *retired accounting educator*
King, Robert Leroy *business administration educator*
Mann, Stephen Ashby *financial counselor*
Narula, Subhash Chander *management science and statistics educator*
Scott, Sidney Buford *financial services company executive*
Thompson, Francis Neal *financial services consultant*

Roanoke
Hudick, Andrew Michael, II, *finance executive*

Staunton
Huffer, Melissa Wynne Clem *accountant*

Upperville
Smart, Stephen Bruce, Jr., *business and government executive*

Vienna
Kumar, Verinder *accountant, financial executive*
Townsend, Irene Fogleman *accountant, tax specialist*
Urbanas, Alban William *estate planner*
Zoeller, Jack Carl *financial executive*

Virginia Beach
†Crawford-Harris, Patrice Ann *accountant, financial consultant*
DiCarlo, Susanne Helen *financial analyst*
Lawson, Beth Ann Reid *strategic planner*
Martin, William Raymond *retired financial manager*
O'Brien, Robert James *financial consultant, business owner*
Price, Alan Thomas *business and estate planner*

Waterford
Harper, James Weldon, III, *finance consultant*

Williamsburg
Holstein, William Kurt *business administration educator*
Kottas, John Frederick *business administration educator*
McLennan, Barbara Nancy *international tax specialist*
Messmer, Donald Joseph *business management educator, marketing consultant*
O'Connell, William Edward, Jr., *finance educator*

Woodbridge
†Denison, Cynthia Lee *accountant, tax specialist*
Dillaber, Philip Arthur *budget and resource analyst, economist, consultant*

WASHINGTON

Bellevue
Graham, John Robert, Jr., *financial executive*

Bellingham
Ross, Steven Charles *business administration educator, consultant*

Bremerton
Holk, George Bertwell *accountant*

Edmonds
Kasama, Hideto Peter *international business and investment advisor*

Kirkland
†Etcheson, Warren Wade *business administration educator*

Medical Lake
Grub, Phillip Donald *business educator*

Mount Vernon
Gaston, Margaret Anne *retired business educator*

Mukilteo
Brown, Bruce Baden *accountant*

Olympia
Myers, Sharon Diane *auditor*

Pullman
Nofsinger, John *finance educator, consultant*

Seattle
Awasthi, Vidya Nidhi *accounting educator*
Collett, Robert Lee *financial company executive*
Evans, Richard Lloyd *financial services company executive*
Feiss, George James, III, *financial services company executive*
Fry, John Craig, Jr., *portfolio manager*
Gaskill, Herbert Leo *accountant, engineer*
Harder, Virgil Eugene *business administration educator*
Judie, Joyce Fox *tax specialist, educator*
Klein, Jonathan D. *finance company executive*
MacLachlan, Douglas Lee *marketing educator*
Patterson, Beverley Pamela Grace *accountant*
Pitts, Barbara Towle *accountant, painter*
Sandstrom, Alice Wilhelmina *accountant*
Saxberg, Borje Osvald *management educator*
Sundem, Gary Lewis *accounting educator*

Sequim
Walker, Raymond Francis *business and financial consulting company executive*

Shoreline
Hanson, Kermit Osmond *business administration educator, university dean emeritus*

Spokane
Cameron, Alex Brian *accounting educator*
Teets, Walter Ralph *accounting educator*

Vancouver
†Rama, Shelby R. *accountant, finance educator, researcher*

WEST VIRGINIA

Charleston
Lamb, Patrick John *financial consultant, state official*
McKee, William Herman, Jr., *accountant*

Huntington
Wenzel, Loren Alvin *accounting educator*

Lewisburg
Kennedy, Leila *accounting educator*

WISCONSIN

Appleton
Fisher, Robert Warren *accountant*

Beloit
Kaplan, Kenneth Franklin *manufacturing company financial executive*
Rodeman, Frederick Ernest *accountant*

Brookfield
Breu, George *accountant*
Hundt, Paul Anthony *financial planner*

De Pere
Rueden, Henry Anthony *accountant*

Eau Claire
Weil, D(onald) Wallace *business administration educator*

Franklin
Akhter, Syed H. *business educator*
Schutte, Richard David *diversified financial services company executive*

Germantown
Boegel, Nick Norbert *accountant, lawyer*

Kenosha
Infusino, Achille Francis *financial and administrative support executive*
†Manion, Michael T. *finance educator*
Wright, David Jonathan *finance educator*

Madison
Aldag, Ramon John *management and organization educator*
†Durcan, Deborah Ann *finance company executive*
Eisler, Millard Marcus *financial executive*
Hickman, James Charles *finance educator, dean*
Nevin, John Robert *business educator, consultant*
Reuschlein, Robert William *accountant, researcher*

Mequon
Berry, William Martin *financial consultant*

Middleton
Baron, Alma Fay S. *management educator*

Milwaukee
Ertel, Gary Arthur *accountant*
Franklin, Scott Bradley *accountant, lawyer*
Grabowski, Michael Joseph *financial executive*
†Kendall, Leon Thomas *finance and real estate educator, retired insurance company executive*
Nystrom, Paul Clifdon *business educator*
Redlin, Bruce Michael *financial consultant*
Schnoll, Howard Manuel *financial consultant, investment company executive*
Simoneau, Daniel Robert *accountant, watercolorist, educator, application developer*
Stefaniak, Norbert John *business administration educator*
†Zore, Edward John *financial services executive*

Oconomowoc
Kneiser, Richard John *accountant*

Superior
Robek, Mary Frances *business education educator*

Verona
Brachman, Richard John, II, *financial services consultant, banking educator*

Waupun
Wendt, Thomas Gene *finance executive*

Wausau
†Hering, Helen Dora *controller*

West Bend
†Rodee-Schneider, Robin *marketing educator*
VanBrunt-Kramer, Karen *business administration educator*

WYOMING

Cody
†Riley, Victor J., Jr., *financial services company executive*

Laramie
Konstantinov, Vassil Alexandrov *finance educator*
Spiegelberg, Emma Jo *business education educator, academic administrator*

Riverton
Clark, Stanford E. *accountant*

Sheridan
†Pilch, Margaret L. *grant consultant*

Ryan, Michael Louis *controller*

Wheatland
Whitney, Ralph Royal, Jr., *financial executive*

TERRITORIES OF THE UNITED STATES

PUERTO RICO

Hato Rey
Vilches-O'Bourke, Octavio Augusto *accounting company executive*

MILITARY ADDRESSES OF THE UNITED STATES

PACIFIC

Fpo
Tarpeh-Doe, Linda Diane *controller*

CANADA

ALBERTA

Calgary
Cruess, Leigh Saunders *financial executive*

BRITISH COLUMBIA

Salt Spring Island
Kandler, Joseph Rudolph *financial executive*

Vancouver
Mattessich, Richard Victor (Alvarus) *business administration researcher*

MANITOBA

Winnipeg
†McCallum, John Stuart *finance educator, columnist*

NEW BRUNSWICK

Saint Andrews
Anderson, John Murray *operations executive, former university president*

ONTARIO

Ancaster
Smith, Newman Donald *retired financial executive*

Arva
Weldon, David Black *company director*

London
Osbaldeston, Gordon Francis *business educator, former government official*

Mississauga
Turnbull, Adam Michael Gordon *financial executive, consultant*

Oakville
Patterson, David Hibbert *corporate financial executive*

Toronto
Butt, William *corporate financial executive*
Cockwell, Jack Lynn *business executive*
Cook-Bennett, Gail *pension fund administrator*
Cunningham, Gordon Ross *financial executive*
Evans, Martin G. *management educator*
Hirst, Peter Christopher *consulting actuary*
Lowe, Robert Edward
Mann, George Stanley *real estate and financial services corporation executive*
Martin, Roger Lloyd *educator, management consultant*
Mercier, Eileen Ann *corporate financial executive*
Morneau, Bill *financial consultant*
Oliphant, Randall *financial executive*
Pollock, Samuel *diversified financial services company executive*
Poprawa, Andrew *financial services executive, accountant*
†Price, Timothy R. *accountant*
Schwartz, Gerald Wilfred *financial executive*
Silk, Frederick C.Z. *financial consultant*
Sloan, David Edward *retired corporate executive*
†Weston, W. Galen, Sr., *diversified holdings executive*

Willowdale
Sze, Michael Ming-Chih *actuary, consultant*

QUEBEC

Montreal
Crowston, Wallace Bruce Stewart *management educator*
Daly, Gerald *accountant*
Desmarais, Paul *holding company executive*
Gratton, Robert *diversified financial services company executive*

Laurin, Pierre *finance company executive*
†Picard, Laurent A(ugustin) *retired management educator, administrator, consultant*
Saumier, Andre *finance executive*
Speirs, Derek James *diversified corporation financial executive*
Thompson, John Douglas *financier*
Weir, Stephen James *financial executive*

Verdun
Lessard, Michel M. *finance company executive*

SASKATCHEWAN

Saskatoon
Irvine, Vernon Bruce *accounting educator, administrator*

MEXICO

Puebla
Powell, Benjamin Loomis *government management analyst*

AUSTRALIA

Melbourne
Batrouney, Clive M. *corporate financial executive*

Sydney
Guthrie, James Ernest *accounting educator*

THE BAHAMAS

Nassau
Crone, John Thomas, IV, *portfolio manager, financial analyst*

CAYMAN ISLANDS

Chehalis
Hughey, David Vaughn *business administration educator, educational consultant*

CYPRUS

Nicosia
Aloneftis, Andreas *financial and investment executive*

ENGLAND

Coventry
Thomas, Howard *business educator*

Doncaster
Warde-Norbury, William George Antony *financial executive*

London
Akin, Steven Paul *financial company executive*
Ellis, Claud M. Buddy *diversified financial services company executive*
Ettinghausen, Thomas Andrew David *investment banker, writer*
†Eustace, Dudley Graham *diversified financial services company executive*
Lamaze, Jean-Hugues de *equity analyst executive*
Melling, John Kennedy *accountant*
Mitchell, Geoffrey Bentley *accountant*
Sarkis, Ziad Joseph *private equity executive*
Shmueli, Alfred *accountant, educator*
Sinclair, David Grant *accountant*
Waldegrave, Lord (Lord Waldegrave of North Hill) *financial services company executive*

Stokenchurch
Barratt, Eric George *accountant*

FRANCE

Paris
†Messier, Jean-Marie *corporate financial executive*

GREECE

Athens
Baltas, George *finance educator*

HONG KONG

Hong Kong
Pacter, Paul Allan *accounting standards researcher*

Shatin
†Luo, Jessica Chaoying *actuary*

Wanchai
Iwasawa, Isoo (Francis Iwasawa) *accountant, management consultant*

INDIA

Calcutta
Kothari, Amitav *accountant*

ISRAEL

Jerusalem
Shrensky, Don Steven *accountant, consultant*

JAPAN

Kumatori
Ohashi, Shoichi *business administration educator*

Tokyo
Makihara, Minoru *diversified corporation executive*
†Nishimura, Masao *diversified financial services company executive*
Yamamoto, Yoshiro *former diversified financial services company executive*

Yokohama
Tokutani, Masao *risk management educator*

NIGERIA

Umuahia Abia State
Ukaegbu, David Okwukanmanihu *accountant, management consultant*

SCOTLAND

Dundee
Lee, Thomas Alexander *accountant, educator*

SINGAPORE

Singapore
Frank, Ronald Edward *marketing educator*

SOUTH AFRICA

Rivonia
Machuca, Carlos R. *financial, management consultant*

SWEDEN

Bjuv
Persson, Ronny Anders *accountant, historian*

TAIWAN

Taipei
Tsung, Christine Chai-yi *financial executive*

ADDRESS UNPUBLISHED

Abbott, Edward Leroy *finance executive*
Abdelaal, Ahmed Tharwat *marketing educator, marketing professional, consultant*
Adler, Ruth Gratt *financial planner, securities arbitrator*
Alberternst, Judith Ann *pension administrator*
Allbritton, Joe Lewis *diversified holding company executive*
Alper, Merlin Lionel *finance company executive*
Anderson, Christopher Ralston *financial consultant*
Arenberg, Julius Theodore, Jr., *retired accounting company executive*
†Ashby, Franklin Charles, Jr., *business executive, author*
Ashcraft, Charles Olin *business educator*
Astill, Robert Michael *credit manager*
Atcheson, Sue Hart *business educator*
Austin, Robert Daniel
†Balakrishnan, P.V. (Sundar) *finance educator*
Barbee, George E.L. *financial services and business executive*
Bare, Steven Wayne *consulting services company executive*
Barney, Austin Dunham, II, *estate planner*
Barr, Michael Charles *financial journalist*
Barton, Ann Elizabeth *retired financial executive*
Bauman, Winfield Scott *finance educator*
Beller, Luanne Evelyn *accountant*
Belluomini, Frank Stephen *accountant*
Benenson, Claire Berger *investment and financial planning educator, finance educator*
Bennett, Peter Dunne *retired marketing educator*
†Benussi, Elena *financial consultant*
Berran, Lawrence Charles *finance company executive*
Bertucelli, Robert Edward *accountant, educator*
Betts, James William, Jr., *financial analyst, consultant*
Black, David deLaine *retired investment consultant*
Block, Lynne Wood *accountant*
Bobbitt, Juanita Crawford *international organization executive*
Bolt, Dawn Maria *financial coach*
Borum, Rodney Lee *financial business executive*
†Boswell, Wendy R. *finance educator, researcher*
Bowne, Shirlee Pearson *finance and housing consultant*
Boxer, Alan Lee *accountant*
Boyd, Danny Douglass *financial counselor*
Brainard, Melissa *accountant*
Branson, Harley Kenneth *finance executive*
Brdlik, Carola Emilie *retired accountant*
Breitling, Julius *financial executive*

Brennan, Ciaran Brendan *accountant, oil industry executive*
Bridges, Eileen *marketing educator*
Broome, Oscar Whitfield, Jr., *accounting educator, administrator*
Brown, Henry Bedinger Rust *financial management company executive*
Brown, James Nelson, Jr., *retired accountant*
Brown, Michael Robert *finance specialist*
Burdett, James Richard *treasurer*
Butrimovitz, Gerald Paul *financial planner, securities analyst, investment advisor*
†Callaway, Julienne Morriss *financial consultant*
Campagna, Richard Samuel *investment management executive*
Canfield, Constance Dale *retired accountant, retired medical/surgical nurse*
Carter, Richard Duane *business educator*
Casey, Micheal William *portfolio manager*
Cavill, Ronald William *financial planner*
Charlton, Jesse Melvin, Jr., *management educator, lawyer*
Chattin, Gilbert Marshall *financial analyst*
Chen, Eric Yen-Po *accountant, consultant*
†Chow, I-Shang Jackson *mutual fund company executive*
Clapp, Beverly Booker *accountant*
Clayton, Richard Reese *retired holding company executive*
Coates, Shirley Jean *finance educator, secondary school educator*
†Cohen, William Alan *marketing educator, author, consultant*
Coleman, Henry James, Jr., *management educator, consultant*
Collette, Frances Madelyn *retired tax consultant, lawyer*
†Conner, William J. *diversified financial services company executive*
Conti, Indalicio Palomar *accountancy educator*
Contillo, Lawrence Joseph *financial and computer company executive*
Cook, Christopher L. *accountant*
Cooper, John Arnold *financial analyst*
Coulter, Jack Benson, Jr., *financial planner*
Cramp, Lori Angell *finance executive*
Crook, Robert Wayne *retired mutual funds executive*
Cullen, Robert John *financial planner, investment advisor*
Cummings, Erika Helga *business consultant*
Danner, Paul Kruger, III, *financial services executive*
Davis, Charles William *certified public accountant*
Denn, Cyril Joseph *financial advisor*
†Denning, Karen Craft *finance educator*
Derchin, Michael Wayne *portfolio manager and financial analyst*
DeRosa, David Francis *finance educator, trading company executive*
Dickman, James Earl *financial services executive*
Dickson, Eva Mae *credit manager*
Doherty, Thomas Joseph *financial services industry consultant*
Dolan, Peter J. *corporate financial consultant*
Doty, Philip Edward *accountant*
Downing, M. Scott *budget systems analyst*
Dozier, Glenn Joseph *diversified financial services company executive*
Duncan, Robert Bannerman *strategy and organizations educator*
Eggan, Hugh Melford *retired accountant*
English, Christine A. *accountant, business development manager*
Estrin, Herbert Alvin *financial consultant, entertainment company executive*
Farrall, Harold John *retired accountant*
Faucette, Gloria Marie *accountant, educator*
Fitzpatrick, Lorraine *accountant*
Folker, Cathleen Ann *business educator*
†Forbush, Robert Raymond, Sr., *financial consultant, small business owner, educator*
†Fortune, Annetta *management educator, accountant*
Fox, Kelly Diane *financial adviser*
Frago-Zito, Ivy Marie *accountant*
Frank, Charles Raphael, Jr., *financial advisor*
Frank, Edgar Gerald *retired financial executive*
Frank, Edmund Paul, Jr., *accountant*
Fredrickson, Sharon Wong *accountant, controller*
Freeman, Kevin David *portfolio management executive, entrepreneur*
†Freimark, Jeffrey Philip *corporate financial executive*
Frimerman, Leslie *retired financial services company executive*
Furst, E. Kenneth *accountant*
Gabriel, Rennie *financial counselor, author, publisher*
Gaiber, Lawrence Jay *financial company executive*
Gallagher, Lindy Allyn *banker, financial consultant*
Garpow, James Edward *retired financial executive*
Gehrke, Karen Marie *retired accountant*
Geissinger, Frederick Wallace *finance company executive*
Genét, Barbara Ann *accountant, travel counselor*
†Giaquinto, Jane Schneider *finance executive*
Giles, James Francis *financial executive*
Goehring, Maude Cope *retired business educator*
Goldberger, George Stefan *finance company executive*
Goodson, Raymond Eugene *business educator, former automotive executive*
Graf, Robert Arlan *retired financial services executive*
Graham, Claxton A. *business systems analyst*
†Green, Tracy V. *financial consultant, management consultant*
Grey, Francis Joseph *accountant, accounting company executive, educator*
Griffin, Carleton Hadlock *accountant, educator*
†Griffith, David A *marketing educator, consultant*
Griffith, Madlynne Veil *college administrator*

Griggs, John Robert financial and consumer credit services executive
Gruber, Fredric Francis financial planning and investment research executive
†Hacker, Michelle Wendy auditor, researcher, finance educator
Haddock, Harold, Jr., retired accounting firm executive
Hand, Herbert Hensley finance educator, writer, entrepreneur
Handy, Edward Otis, Jr., retired financial services executive
Hanford, Agnes Rutledge retired financial adviser
Hanson, Carl Malmrose financial company executive
†Hanson, J. Donald retired diversified financial services company executive
Harper, W(alter) Joseph financial consultant
Harrison, John Alexander financial executive
Heller, H(einz) Robert financial executive
Henry, William Ray business administration educator
†Hepburn, Laird financial consultant
Hickson, Ernest Charles financial executive
Hild, Matthias finance educator
†Holloran, Thomas Edward business educator
Holtmeier, Robert J. accountant
Holton, Grace Holland accountant
Horwitz, Ronald M. business administration educator
Howard, John Kenneth accountant, consultant
Hubbe, Henry Ernest financial forecaster, funds manager
Hudak, Thomas F(rancis) finance company executive
Ivezaj, Viktor N. auditor, consultant
Jabs, Jennifer financial planner
Jamison, John Callison business educator, investment banker
Johnson, Freda S. public finance consultant
Johnson, Margaret Kathleen business educator
Jones, Kacy Douglas accountant
†Jong, Nancy financial consultant
Kaplan, Leonard Eugene accountant
†Karabell, Zachary economic analyst
Kass, David Norman accountant, lawyer
Kessler, Roslyn Marie financial analyst
†Khuong, Loc Huu corporate financial executive
Kidd, Robert Hugh financial executive, accountant
Kilmann, Ralph Herman business educator
King, Algin Braddy retired marketing educator
King, Ronald Lee accountant, government agency official
Kingsbery, Walton Waits, Jr., retired accounting firm executive
Kirk, Donald James accountant, consultant
Kreitzer, Lois Helen personal investor
Kroeger, Susan Jean accountant
Kruse, Rosalee Evelyn accountant, auditor, executive
Kulak, Daryl Wayne holistic health business educator
Kushmar, Neal accountant
Kuska, John Joseph, Jr., accountant, management consultant
La Blanc, Robert Edmund consulting company executive
Lamont, Alice accountant, consultant
Latta, Jean Carolyn financial analyst
Lavengood, Lawrence Gene management educator, historian
†Leaptrott, John accountant
†Leibler, Kenneth Robert financial service executive
Lerner, Herbert J. tax consultant
Lester, Alicia L. financial analyst
Leventhal, Ellen Iris portfolio manager, financial services executive
Levy, Louis Edward retired accounting firm executive
Lewis, James Lee, Jr., actuary
†Li, Bingguang business educator
Lieberman, Anne Marie retired financial executive
Loken, Barbara marketing educator, social psychologist
Longden, Claire Suzanne retired financial planner, investment advisor
Long-Ignaszewski, Joan accountant
Louderback, Tom auditor
Macdonald, Sheila de Marillac company executive
Magnano, Salvatore Paul retired financial executive, treasurer
Magoon, Donald W. retired business educator
†Marker, David Carl finance educator
Marks, Leonard, Jr., retired corporate financial executive
Marot, Lola retired accountant
†Martin, Preston financial services writer
Mason, George Henry business educator
Massura, Edward Anthony accountant
Mauser, Kevin Edward finance executive
Maxwell, Raymond Roger retired accountant
May, Phyllis Jean financial executive
Mayoras, Donald Eugene corporate executive, writer, consultant, educator
McBride, Jack J. financial services executive
McClinton, Donald George retired diversified holding company executive
†McGovern, John Francis former financial executive
McLennan, Robert Gordon asset management company executive
†Measelle, Richard Leland accountant
Mednick, Robert accountant
Mero, Marjorie Anne retired compensation specialist
Meyer, Sandra Palmer financial executive
Miller, Donald Muxlow accountant
Miller, Jane Andrews accountant
Miselson, Alex J. (Jacob Miselson) portfolio manager, securities analyst, investment theorist
Mitchem, Cheryl E. accounting educator
Mobley, William Hodges management educator, researcher, author, executive
Moore, Robert Henry financial services executive
Morgan, Robert Arthur accountant
Morse, Richard Alan accountant
Mosler, John retired financial planner
Moyer, Jerry Mills financial services company executive
Mudry, Michael pension and benefit consultant
Mull, Dawn Kathleen accountant, auditor
Munhall, Ruth Beatrice business and financial consultant
Munlu, Kamil Cemal finance educator
Myers, Miller Franklin finance company executive, retail executive
Naito, Michiro financial analyst
Needles, Belverd Earl, Jr., accountant, educator
Nelson, Mary Ellen Dickson retired actuary
†Neureuther, Brian business educator, researcher
Newill, James Wagner accounting executive
Newman, Jay Hartley financial company executive
North, John Adna, Jr., accountant, real estate appraiser
Norton, Karen Ann accountant
Norwood, B.J. Scott business and management educator, Russian studies, pro bono public service
Oldman, Alfred Maurice accountant, management consultant
†Ortiz-Walters, Rowena management educator
Osborn, Kenneth Louis financial executive
Paleveda, Carl August accountant
Palmer, Gary Andrew portfolio manager
Paonessa, M. Suzanne budget analyst
Park, Patricia Weill controller
Parker, Susan Joellyn controller
Paulose, Anil Chiramel financial market data/trading systems software infrastructure consultant
Payton, Thomas William corporate finance consultant executive
Pefley, Norman Gordon consultant
Peruzzo, Albert Louis actuary, accountant
Pfeister, Raymond Lynn diversified financial services company executive
Phillips, Charles Alan accounting firm executive
Pierre, Natasha Unada accountant
Plimpton, Peggy Lucas trustee
Powers, Michael J. retired financial company executive
Powless, David Griffin accountant
Pratt, Michael Gerard management educator
Puryear, Alvin Nelson management educator
†Putnam, Kristen Margaret consulting company executive
Pyle, Robert Milner, Jr., financial consultant
Quant, Harold Edward retired financial services company executive, rancher
Quirk, Kenneth Paul accountant
Rachlin, Ellen Joan financial and risk analyst
†Ragland, William C. accountant
Rail, Kathy Lynn Parish accountant
Raines, Franklin Delano finance company executive
Ramchander, Sanjay finance educator
Ray, Richard Stanley accountant
Reeves, Peggy Lois Zeigler accountant
Reynolds, Billie Iles financial representative and counselor, former national association executive director
Rhea, Jerry Dwaine director consumer lending
Rich, David Barry financial executive, accountant, entertainer
Richardson, Margaret Milner former accounting firm executive, lawyer
Rickard, David Lawrence fundraising consultant
†Riles, Jesse tax examiner, writer
Ritchey, Paul Andrew accountant
Robertson, A. Haeworth actuary, benefit consultant, foundation executive
Robertson, Jack Clark accounting educator
Robison, William Christopher management accountant
Rodriguez, Elena Garcia retired pension fund administrator
Rogan, Robert William management educator, consultant, osteopath, psychiatrist
Rogers, Kathie Anne accountant
Roller, David Isaac financial services company executive
Roth, Marilyn Green retired accountant
Rowe, William Davis financial services company executive
Rowland, Kathleen O'Shea accountant
Rush, Richard Henry financial executive, writer, lecturer
Rutherford, Reid finance company executive
Ryan, Leo Vincent business educator
Sagafi-Nejad, Tagi business educator
Sales, Angel Rodolfo financial executive
Saniga, Erwin Martin educator, painter
Saunders, Donna M. accountant
Saunders, James Harwood accountant
Sayles, Leonard Robert management educator, consultant
Scanlon, Peter Redmond accountant
Scheel, Nels Earl financial executive, accountant
Schellenberger, Robert Earl retired management educator and department chairman
Schoen, William Jack financier
Schulte Shields, Mary Ann finance executive
Schulz, Marianne accountant
Schwyn, Charles Edward retired accountant
†Sexton, Carol Burke consultant
Shankar, Gautham associate, financial services & sales trader
Shannon, Jimmie L. retired accountant
Sheridan, Patrick Michael finance company executive, retired
Sherman, Barnet financial services executive
Sherman, Howard D. financial consultant
Shon, John J. accounting executive, researcher
Shore, Harvey Harris business educator
Short, George Oscar, III, accountant
Shultis, Robert Lynn finance educator, cost systems consultant, retired professional association executive
Skinner, Alastair retired accountant
Smith, Harold Charles private pension fund executive
Smith, John Joseph, Jr., financial management executive
Smith, Linda Ann Glidewell accountant
Smith, Ronald Emory financial executive
Snelling, Robert Orren, Sr., franchising and employment executive
†Sonnier, Patricia Bennett business management educator
Spritzer, Samuel Lewis financial executive, computer consultant
Srinivasan, Venkataraman marketing and management educator
Stanfill, Dennis Carothers business executive
Stawnychy, Zoriana Maria financial executive
Stevens, Jesse financial executive
Stiles, Donald Alan retired financial company executive
Stofferson, Terry Lee financial officer
Strong, John Scott finance educator
†Stucky, Katherine Ann finance educator, small business owner
Talarico, Maria Theresa tax accountant
Taliaferro-Regonini, Yvon Rochelle accountant, consultant
Taylor, Linda Rathbun investment manager
Taylor, Wilson H. retired diversified financial company executive
Thimm, Alfred Louis management educator
Thomson, Alexander Bennett, Jr., financial planner, tax and management consultant
Tilford, Tricia J. accountant
Tongue, Paul Graham financial executive
Trail, Margaret Ann retired employee benefits company executive, beef cattle producer, sterling silver merchant
Trent, Robert Harold retired business educator
Treynor, Jack Lawrence financial advisor, educator
Turner, Henry Brown finance executive
Tyler, Richard James personal and professional development educator
Tyler, W(illiam) Ed finance company executive
†Vadaparty, Kumar Venkata finance company executive, director
Vago, Anthony Scott investment representative
van Hengel, Maarten R. financial executive
Vega, Alberto Leon financial executive
Vitale, Paul accountant
Vogel, Julius retired consulting actuary
von Ber, Ina management educator, clinical psychologist
Vronskiy, Vadim Viktorovich financial company executive
Vu, Joseph Duong financial educator
Wachbrit, Jill Barrett accountant, tax specialist
Wain, Christopher Henry Fairfax Moresby actuary, insurance and investment consultant
Wald, Mary S. retired risk management and personal finance educator
Wall, M. Danny financial services company executive
Wells, Pauline M. accountant
Wilhelmsen, Harold John accountant, operations controller
Wilkinson, Harry Edward management educator and consultant
Williams, Helen Margaret retired accountant
Wilson, Robert M. business executive
Wolf, Frank business educator, consulting executive
†Woods, Cheryl financial analyst
Wright, Judith Rae retired accountant
Yingling, Robert Granville, Jr., accountant
Yost, Paula Lynn accountant
†Zalon, Rick financial consultant, educator, writer
†Zenios, Stefanos management educator, consultant
Zick, John Walter retired accounting company executive
†Zimmerman, Helene Loretta retired business educator

FINANCE: INSURANCE

UNITED STATES

ALABAMA

Anniston
Currie, Larry Lamar insurance agent

Foley
Russell, Ralph Timothy insurance company executive, mayor

Mobile
Robinson, Kenneth Larry insurance company executive

Tuscaloosa
Bickley, John S. insurance association executive, educator, writer
Edgeworth, Emily retired insurance agency executive-antique dealer

ALASKA

Anchorage
Trevithick, Ronald James underwriter

ARIZONA

Bullhead City
Shervheim, Lloyd Oliver insurance company executive, lawyer

Green Valley
Brissman, Bernard Gustave retired insurance company executive

Phoenix
†Foley, William Patrick, II, title insurance company executive
Fugiel, Frank Paul insurance company executive

Prescott
Osborn, DeVerle Ross insurance company executive

Scottsdale
Burr, Edward Benjamin life insurance company executive, financial executive
Prisbrey, Rex Prince retired insurance agent, underwriter, consultant
Tyner, Neal Edward retired insurance company executive
Vairo, Robert John insurance company executive
Wise, Paul Schuyler insurance company executive

Sedona
†French, Richard Edmund insurance company executive

Tempe
Asadi, Robert Samir insurance company executive

Tubac
Fey, John Theodore retired insurance company executive

Tucson
Haney, Robert Locke retired insurance company executive
Martin, Paul Edward retired insurance company executive
Ziehler, Tony Joseph insurance agent

ARKANSAS

Cherokee Village
Payne, Howard James retired insurance company executive

El Dorado
Hardy, Charlotte B. insurance agent

Jonesboro
Calaway, Dennis Louis insurance company executive, real estate broker, financial executive

Sherwood
Keaton, Frances Marlene insurance sales representative

CALIFORNIA

Auburn
Jeske, Howard Leigh retired life insurance company executive, lawyer

Calabasas
Christensen, Donn Wayne insurance executive

Camarillo
Halperin, Kristine Briggs insurance sales and marketing professional

Cupertino
Knapp, George Griff Prather retired insurance executive

Dana Point
Lang, George Frank insurance executive, consultant, lawyer

Danville
Grager, Steven P. investment consultant

Encino
Parrott, Dennis Beecher retired insurance executive
Seiden, Paul insurance agent, consultant

Garden Grove
Williams, J(ohn) Tilman insurance executive, real estate broker, city official

Glendale
Dudash, Linda Christine insurance executive

Gold River
Gray, Myles McClure retired insurance company executive

Hermosa Beach
Winthrop, Kenneth Ray insurance executive

La Mesa
Schlador, Paul Raymond, Jr., insurance agent

La Quinta
Adolph, Diane Joyce retired underwriter

Los Angeles
Bernstein, Samuel insurance company executive
Gurash, John Thomas insurance company executive
Houston, Ivan James insurance company executive
Inman, James Russell claims consultant
Johnson, E. Eric insurance executive

McNamara, Aida Shahid *insurance executive*

Monrovia
Lim, SallyJane *insurance company executive, financial consultant, diversified financial services company executive*

Mountain View
Harrison, Wendy Jane Merrill *insurance company executive*

Newark
†Gupta, Anju *risk management consultant*

Newman
Carlsen, Janet Haws *retired insurance company owner, mayor*

Newport Beach
Cosgrove, Cameron *insurance company executive*
Fries, Arthur Lawrence *life health insurance broker, disability claim consultant*
Gerken, Walter Bland *insurance company executive*
Marcoux, Carl Henry *former insurance executive, writer, historian*
†Schafer, Glenns *insurance company executive*
Sutton, Thomas C. *insurance company executive*

Oakland
Ching, Eric San Hing *health care and insurance administrator*

Orange
Godeke, Raymond Dwight Cook *insurance company executive, accountant*

Paso Robles
Webster, David Arthur *retired life insurance company executive*

Pismo Beach
Brisbin, Robert Edward *insurance agency executive*

Rancho Cordova
Alenius, John Todd *retired insurance executive*

Rancho Mirage
Fromm, Erwin Frederick *retired insurance company executive*

San Diego
Baxter, Robert Hampton *insurance executive*
Hayes, Robert Emmet *retired insurance company executive*
Jeffers, Donald E. *retired insurance executive, consultant*
Purcifull, Robert Otis *insurance company executive*
Rotter, Paul Talbott *retired insurance executive*

San Francisco
Drexler, Fred *insurance executive*
Enfield, D(onald) Michael *insurance company executive*
Lamberson, John Roger *insurance company executive*

San Rafael
Keegan, Jane Ann *insurance executive, consultant*

Santa Barbara
Evans, Thomas Edgar, Jr., *title insurance agency executive*

Sherman Oaks
Holden, William Willard *insurance executive*
Milgrim, Darrow A. *insurance broker, recreation consultant*

Thousand Oaks
Gregory, Calvin *insurance service executive*

Vista
Fuhlrodt, Norman Theodore *retired insurance executive*

Woodside
Freitas, Antoinette Juni *insurance company executive*

COLORADO

Aurora
Nelson, Marvin Ray *retired life insurance company executive*

Denver
O'Connell, Richard J. *insurance adviser*
Volpe, Richard Gerard *insurance accounts executive, consultant*

Englewood
Conroy, Thomas Francis *insurance company consultant*
Hardy, Wayne Russell *insurance and investment broker*
Manley, Richard Walter *insurance executive*

Fort Collins
Schendel, Winfried George *insurance company executive*

Littleton
Moore, Dan Sterling *insurance executive, sales trainer*
Rotherham, Larry Charles *insurance executive*

Superior
Forshee, Gladys Marie *writer, insurance agent*

CONNECTICUT

Danbury
Gogliettino, John Carmine *insurance broker*

Essex
Miller, Walter Neal *insurance company consultant*

Greenwich
Berkley, William Robert *insurance holding company executive*
Clements, Robert *insurance executive*
Fuller, Theodore *retired insurance executive*

Hartford
Ayer, Ramani *insurance company executive*
†Fiondella, Robert William *insurance company executive*
Mullane, Denis Francis *insurance executive*
Reynolds, Stephen H. *insurance safety and loss prevention consultant*
Rowe, John Wallis *health insurance executive, medical executive*
Sargent, Joseph Denny *insurance executive*
Scully, John Carroll *life insurance marketing research company executive*
Wilde, Wilson *insurance company executive*

Marlborough
White, Harold R. *insurance and health care information company executive*

Mystic
Spakoski, Marcia *insurance agent*

New Canaan
Cohen, Richard Norman *insurance executive*
Ylvisaker, James William *insurance executive*

Norwalk
Hickey, Kevin Francis *healthcare executive*

Southington
Rudolph, Kathleen Ann *insurance company executive*

Stamford
Block, Ruth *retired insurance company executive*
Chickering, Howard Allen *insurance company executive, lawyer*
Ferguson, Ronald Eugene *reinsurance company executive*
Hudson, Harold Jordon, Jr., *retired insurance executive*
Schiff, Jayne Nemerow *underwriter*

Tolland
Simons, Sir Barry *underwriter, insurance consultant*

Trumbull
†Berg, Charles G. *insurance company executive*

Vernon Rockville
Wolff, Gregory Steven *insurance company executive*

Weatogue
Wise, Richard Evans *corporate executive*

Weston
Thompson, N(orman) David *insurance company executive*

DELAWARE

Hockessin
Dombeck, Harold Arthur *insurance company executive*

DISTRICT OF COLUMBIA

Washington
Canapary, Herbert Carton *insurance company executive*
Howes, Theodore Clark *claims examiner*
†Nicely, Olza M. (Tony) *insurance company executive*
Oakley, Diane *insurance executive, benefit consultant*
Simpson, Louis A. *insurance company executive*
Snider, Virginia L. *antitrust consultant*

FLORIDA

Boca Raton
Deppe, Henry A. *insurance company executive*
Kaye, Barry *insurance company executive*
Knudsen, Rudolph Edgar, Jr., *insurance company executive*
Richardson, R(oss) Fred(erick) *insurance executive*

Boynton Beach
Bryant, Donald Loyd *insurance company executive*
Caras, Joseph Sheldon *life insurance company executive*

Bradenton
Phelan, John Densmore *insurance executive, consultant*

Coral Springs
Miller, Karl Frederick *insurance professional*

Daytona Beach
Adams, John Carter, Jr., *insurance executive*

Destin
Linn, James Eldon, II, *insurance company executive*

Fort Lauderdale
Hull, Richard Franklin *insurance brokerage executive*
Lilley, Mili Della *insurance company executive, entertainment management consultant*
Rough, Herbert Louis *insurance company executive*

Fort Myers
†Blomquist, Robert Oscar *retired insurance company executive*
Dockins, George Joel *retired insurance and securities company executive*
Mc Queen, Robert Charles *retired insurance executive*
Pearson, Paul Holding *insurance company executive*

Gainesville
Boothroyd, Herbert J. *insurance company executive*
Niblack, Nancy Lee Parham *insurance agent, financial consultant, social worker*
Robertson, James Cole *consultant*

Gulf Breeze
DeBardeleben, John Thomas, Jr., *retired insurance company executive*

Hollywood
†Martinez, Carlos *insurance adjuster, company manager*

Jacksonville
†Glover, Gene Alan *banking risk analyst*
Lyon, Wilford Charles, Jr., *insurance executive*
Rader, David *insurance company executive*

Juno Beach
Holmes, Melvin Almont *insurance company executive*

Key Largo
Daenzer, Bernard John *insurance company executive, legal consultant*

Lady Lake
Rossbacher, John Robert *retired insurance broker, musician, writer*

Longwood
Brown, Donald James, Jr., *insurance company executive*

Miami
Gabor, Frank *insurance company executive*
George, Stephen Carl *reinsurance executive, educator, medical and life consultant, expert witness, expert witness*
Gindy, Benjamin Lee *insurance company executive*
Heggen, Arthur William *insurance company executive*
Shusterman, Nathan *underwriter, financial consultant*
Van Wyck, George Richard *insurance company executive*

Naples
Clark, William James *retired insurance company executive*

New Port Richey
Hanahan, James Lake *retired insurance executive*

Ocean Ridge
Bates, Edward Brill *retired insurance company executive*

Oldsmar
Caronis, George John *insurance executive*

Orlando
Kellison, Stephen George *actuarial consultant*

Ormond Beach
Burt, Wallace Joseph, Jr., *insurance company executive*

Oviedo
Brethauer, William Russell, Jr., *claim investigator*

Palatka
Ginn, John Arthur, Jr., *insurance agent*

Plant City
Feola, Ralph Leonard *insurance agent*

Ponte Vedra Beach
MacKowski, John Joseph *retired insurance company executive*

Punta Gorda
McDaniel, Norwood Allan *insurance broker*

Redington Beach
Alpert, Barry Mark *insurance company and banking executive*

Saint Augustine
Witty, Robert Wilkes *insurance services company executive*

Saint Petersburg
Fraser, John Wayne *insurance executive, consultant, underwriter*

Sarasota
Best, Jerry Lavon *insurance consultant*
Bushey, Alan Scott *retired insurance holding company executive*
Eller, Warren Bernson *retired insurance company executive*

Spring Hill
Vanderburg, Paul Stacey *insurance executive, consultant*

Tallahassee
Gabor, Jeffrey Alan *insurance and financial services executive*
Gunter, William Dawson, Jr., (Bill Gunter) *insurance company executive, consultant*
Hunt, John Edwin *insurance company executive, consultant*

Tamarac
Gould, Bernard Howard *insurance agent*

Tampa
Sullivan, Joseph Peter *risk and insurance management consultant*

Vero Beach
Burton, Arthur Henry, Jr., *insurance company executive*
Feagles, Robert West *retired insurance company executive*

Winter Park
Kraft, Kenneth Houston, Jr., *insurance agency executive*

GEORGIA

Alpharetta
Fowler, Vivian Delores *insurance company executive*
Horton, Rosalyn *underwriter*

Atlanta
†Atkinson, A. Kelley *insurance company executive*
Black, Kenneth, Jr., *retired insurance executive and educator, author*
Gregory, Mel Hyatt, Jr., *retired insurance company executive*
Peacock, George Rowatt *retired life insurance company executive*

Columbus
Amos, Daniel Paul *insurance company executive*
Cloninger, Kriss, III, *insurance company executive*

Duluth
Burns, Carroll Dean *insurance company executive*
Denney, Laura Falin *insurance company executive*

Gainesville
Clary, Ronald Gordon *insurance agency executive*

Lagrange
Hudson, Charles Daugherty *insurance executive*

Savannah
Dodge, William Douglas *insurance company consultant*
Standbridge, Peter Thomas *retired insurance company executive*

Smyrna
Buck, Lee Albert *retired insurance company executive, evangelist*

HAWAII

Honolulu
Kanehiro, Kenneth Kenji *insurance educator, risk analyst, consultant*

ILLINOIS

Algonquin
Barilich, Thomas Anthony *loss control specialist*

Bloomington
Curry, Alan Chester *insurance company executive*
Johnson, Earle Bertrand *insurance executive*
Joslin, Roger Scott *insurance company executive*
Rust, Edward Barry, Jr., *insurance company executive, lawyer*
Ward, Jon David *insurance company executive*

Champaign
Wills, Bart Francis *insurance company executive*

Chicago
Bartholomay, William C. *insurance brokerage company executive, professional baseball team executive*
Beemster, Joseph Robert *risk management consultant*
†Bolger, David P. *insurance company executive*
DeMoss, Jon W. *insurance company executive, lawyer*
Hinkelman, Ruth Amidon *insurance company executive*
Janecek, Lenore Elaine *insurance specialist, consultant*
Lorenz, Hugo Albert *retired insurance executive, consultant*
Mc Caskey, Raymond F. *insurance company executive*
O'Halleran, Michael D. *insurance company executive*
Parcells, Frederick R. *underwriter*
Preble, Robert Curtis, Jr., *insurance executive*
†Tyree, James C. *insurance company executive*
Zucaro, Aldo Charles *insurance company executive*

Kansas City
Mc Gee, Joseph John, Jr., *former insurance company executive*

Saint Louis
Cramer, Michael William *insurance executive*
Haberstroh, Richard David *insurance agent*
Mullens, William Reese *retired insurance company executive*
Werner, Burton Kready *insurance company executive*

MONTANA

Whitefish
Hemp, Ralph Clyde *retired reinsurance company executive, consultant, arbitrator, umpire*

NEBRASKA

Holdrege
Hendrickson, Bruce Carl *life insurance company executive*

Lincoln
Angle, John Charles *retired life insurance company executive*

Omaha
Jetter, Arthur Carl, Jr., *insurance company executive*
Lechowicz, Lisa Marie *insurance executive*
Sigerson, Charles Willard, Jr., *insurance agency executive*
Strevey, Guy Donald *insurance company executive*
Sturgeon, John Ashley *insurance company executive*
Weekly, John William *insurance company executive*

NEVADA

Carson City
Marangi, Vito Anthony, Sr., *claim administrator*

Las Vegas
Zervoudakes, Annette Dian *reinsurance specialist*

NEW HAMPSHIRE

Dover
Bergerson, Nancy Dahl *life and health underwriter, paralegal*

Grantham
Smith, Dudley Renwick *retired insurance company executive*

Kingston
Saunders, Janet McGee *small business owner, healthcare administrator*

Portsmouth
Ward, Bonnie J. *insurance company executive*

Rochester
Dworkin, Gary Steven *insurance company executive*

NEW JERSEY

Augusta
Martin, Richard L. *retired insurance executive*

Berkeley Heights
Gottheimer, George Malcolm, Jr., *insurance executive, educator*

Bloomfield
Feldman, Max *insurance executive*

Bridgewater
Klinck, James William *insurance company executive*

Cranford
Crow, Lynne Campbell Smith *insurance company representative*

East Brunswick
Todd, Edward Francis, Jr., *risk management consultant, insurance broker*

Englewood
†Volk, Austin N. *insurance company executive*

Fort Lee
Adler, Earl *insurance executive*

Glen Rock
Mc Elrath, Richard Elsworth *retired insurance company executive*

Little Silver
Redden, Harral Arthur, Jr., *broker*

Lumberton
Friedberg, Thomas Harold *insurance company executive*

Madison
Calligan, William Dennis *retired life insurance company executive*
Parker, Henry Griffith, III, *insurance executive*

Morristown
Munson, William Leslie *insurance company executive*

Mountain Lakes
Cook, Charles Francis *insurance executive*

New Brunswick
Mills, George Marshall *insurance consultant*

New Vernon
McCormack, John Joseph, Jr., *insurance executive*

Newark
Marino, William J. *insurance executive*
Ryan, Arthur Frederick *insurance company executive*

Princeton
Fleetwood, Rex Allen *insurance company executive*

Rumson
Creamer, William Henry, III, *retired insurance company executive*

Short Hills
MacKinnon, Malcolm D(avid) *retired insurance company executive*

Somerset
Brophy, Joseph Thomas *information company executive*

Spring Lake
Bonhag, Thomas Edward *insurance company executive, financial consultant, financial planner*

Summit
Gerathy, E. Carroll *former insurance executive, real estate developer*

Warren
Chubb, Percy, III, *insurance company executive*
†Finnegan, John D. *insurance company executive*
O'Hare, Dean Raymond *insurance company executive, director*

Whitehouse Station
Fiscus, Philip Wayne *underwriter*

NEW MEXICO

Albuquerque
Liss, Norman Richard *insurance executive*
Wainio, Mark Ernest *insurance company consultant*

Santa Fe
Glotzbach, George Linus *retired insurance executive*

NEW YORK

Albany
Cole, John Adam *insurance executive*

Amityville
Imbert, Richard Conrad *insurance company executive, real estate developer*

Armonk
†Dunton, Gary C. *insurance company executive*

Binghamton
Best, Robert Mulvane *insurance company executive*

Bronx
Elkins, Alfred David *insurance company administrator*

Brooklyn
Faison, Seth Shepard *retired insurance broker*

Cobleskill
Wilson, Lewis Lansing *insurance executive*

Cohocton
Sarfaty, Wayne Allen *insurance agent, financial planner*

Dryden
Baxter, Robert Banning *insurance company executive*

Elmira
Henbest, William Harrison *insurance agent*

Lindenhurst
Hungerford, Gary A. *insurance executive, columnist, author, editor*

Lockport
Salen, Wayne Louis *risk management consultant*

Long Island City
Corry, James Michael *insurance executive, educator*

Malverne
Knight, John Francis *retired insurance company executive*

Merrick
Cherry, Harold *insurance company executive*

Mineola
Gibson, William Shepard *insurance company executive*
Miller, Loring Erik *insurance agent, broker*

New York
†Baker, George R. *insurance industry executive*
Benmosche, Robert H. *insurance company executive*
Berdick, Leonard Stanley *insurance broker*
Biggs, John Herron *retired insurance company executive*
Borelli, Francis J(oseph) (Frank Borelli) *insurance brokerage and consulting firm financial executive*
Burns, John Joseph, Jr., *financial and insurance holding company executive*
Crystal, James William *insurance company executive*
Devlin, Robert Manning *insurance company executive*
Dolan, Raymond Bernard *insurance executive*
Earls, Kevin Gerard *insurance company executive*
Gammill, Lee Morgan, Jr., *retired insurance company executive*
†Gamper, Albert R., Jr., *insurance executive*
Greenberg, Maurice Raymond *insurance company executive*
Harris, David Henry *retired life insurance company executive*
Hohn, Harry George *retired insurance company executive, lawyer*
Hutchings, Peter Lounsbery *retird insurance company executive, director*
Kaplan, Theodore Norman *insurance company executive*
Leaf, Robert Jay *dental insurance consultant*
MacDonald, Ronald Francis *financial services company executive*
†Manning, Dennis J. *insurance company executive*
Manton, Edwin Alfred Grenville *insurance company executive*
Martino, Cheryl Derby *insurance company secretary*
Melone, Joseph James *retired insurance company executive*
Murray, Richard Maximilian *insurance executive*
Nagler, Stewart Gordon *insurance company executive*
Olsen, David Alexander *insurance executive*
Piccione, Tal P. *insurance company executive*
Rein, Catherine Amelia *insurance executive, lawyer*
Sandler, Robert Michael *insurance company executive, actuary*
Sargent, Joseph Dudley *insurance executive*
Schwartz, Robert George *retired insurance company executive*
Slavutin, Lee Jacob *life insurance executive*
Smith, Howard I. *insurance company executive*
Somers, John Arthur *insurance company executive*
Sternberg, Seymour *insurance company executive*
Stocker, Michael A. *health insurance company executive*
Toppeta, William John *insurance company executive, lawyer*
Underhill, Jacob Berry, III, *retired insurance company executive*
Vidal, David Jonathan *insurance company executive, journalist*
Wisner, Frank George *insurance company executive, former ambassador*
Wolf, James Anthony *insurance company executive*
Yalen, Gary N. *retired insurance company executive*

Northport
†Miller, Philip John *insurance consultant*

Oceanside
Rubin, Hanan *retired insurance company executive*

Point Lookout
Stack, Maurice Daniel *retired insurance company executive*

Saratoga Springs
Ford, Dexter *retired insurance company executive*

Scarsdale
Decaminada, Joseph Pio *retired insurance company executive*

Schenectady
Murray, Edward Rock *insurance broker*

Staten Island
Gavrity, John Decker *insurance company executive*

Syosset
Barry, Richard Francis *retired life insurance company executive*
Kniffin, Paula Sichel *insurance sales executive*

Utica
Austin, Michael Charles *insurance company executive*

Valley Stream
Brunell, Jerry Albert *insurance executive*

White Plains
Greer, Robert E. *insurance executive, retired*

Yonkers
Wolfson, Irwin M. *insurance company executive*

Youngstown
Wolfang, Joan Winter *insurance company executive*

NORTH CAROLINA

Burlington
Blevins, James Ray *lawyer, insurance company claims executive*

Camden
Hammond, Roy Joseph *reinsurance company executive*

Chapel Hill
Fine, J(ames) Allen *insurance company executive*
Stewart, Richard Edwin *insurance consulting company executive*
Webb, James Okrum, Jr., *insurance company executive*

Charlotte
Maday, Clifford Ronald *insurance professional*
Mendelsohn, Robert Victor *insurance company executive*

Durham
Bachini, Peter P. *insurance company executive*
Clark, Arthur Watts *insurance company executive*

Greensboro
Hall, William Edward, Jr., *insurance agency executive*
Soles, William Roger *insurance company executive, director*

Pfafftown
Walker, Wendy K. *healthcare risk consultant*

Pinehurst
O'Loughlin, John Kirby *retired insurance executive*

Pineville
Dunn, Kenneth Ralph *insurance company executive*

Winston Salem
Beardsley, Charles Mitchell *retired insurance company executive*
Jesseph, Steven Austin *risk management consultant*

NORTH DAKOTA

Grand Forks
Wogaman, George Elsworth *insurance executive, financial consultant*

OHIO

Canton
Caswell, Linda Kay *insurance agency executive*
Repp, Ronald Stewart *insurance company executive*
Schauer, Thomas Alfred *insurance company executive*

Cincinnati
Klein, Jerry Emanuel *insurance and financial planning executive*
Krohn, Claus Dankertsen *insurance company executive*
Scheineson, Irwin Bruce *insurance and investment company executive*

Cleveland
†Lewis, Peter Benjamin *insurance company executive*
†Renwick, Glenn M. *insurance company executive*

Columbus
Barnes, Galen R. *insurance company executive*
Cook, John Roscoe, Jr., *insurance executive*
Duryee, Harold Taylor *insurance consultant*
Fullerton, Charles William *retired insurance company executive*
†Jurgensen, W.G. *insurance company executive*
†McFerson, Dimon Richard *insurance company executive*
Wilhelmy, Odin, Jr., *insurance agent*

Grove City
Purdy, Dennis Gene *insurance company executive, education consultant*

Highland Heights
Shumate, Minerva *risk management analyst*

North Canton
Jackson, David Lee *insurance company executive*

Powell
Emanuelson, James Robert *retired insurance company executive*

Rocky River
Riedthaler, William Allen *risk management professional*

Shreve
Denman, Nicholas Werner *insurance executive*

Upper Sandusky
Waggy, Corrina Jeanne *insurance agent*

Westfield Center
†Blair, Robert Cary *insurance company executive*

OKLAHOMA

Bartlesville
†White, Joy Kathryn *claims consultant, artist*

Oklahoma City
Hamilton, Thomas Allen *independent insurance agent, securities representative*
Ille, Bernard Glenn *insurance company executive, director*
Lee, Ellen Faith *insurance company associate*

Perry
Doughty, Michael Dean *insurance agent*

Tulsa
Watson, Eric N. *corporate executive*

OREGON

Portland
Blachly, Beverly Jean *vocational and insurance consultant*
Clemens, Charles Joseph *insurance agent*
Hill, James Edward *insurance company executive*
Lang, Philip David *former state legislator, insurance company executive*
Timpe, Ronald Ernest *insurance company executive*

Tigard
Yates, Keith Lamar *retired insurance company executive*

Tualatin
Chambers, Lois Irene *insurance automation consultant*

Waldport
Ginter, Carolyn Augusta Romtvedt (Carol Augusta Romtvedt Ginter) *retired bond underwriter*

West Linn
Dunstan, Larry Kenneth *insurance company executive*

PENNSYLVANIA

Bala Cynwyd
Shepard, Geoffrey Carroll *insurance executive*

Berwyn
McIntyre, James Owen *insurance executive*

Bethlehem
Schumacher, Susan Louise *underwriter*

Bushkill
Garretto, Leonard Anthony, Jr., *insurance company executive*

Camp Hill
Mead, James Matthew *insurance company executive*

Hatboro
Quigley, Robert Charles *insurance industry consultant*

Jenkintown
†O'Neill, Judith Jones *insurance agent*

King Of Prussia
Katz, Arnold Martin *insurance brokerage firm executive*
Volpe, Ralph Pasquale *insurance company executive*

New Cumberland
Gorman, Ida Niebauer *HMO outsourcing company executive*

Newtown Square
Staats, Dean Roy *retired reinsurance executive*

Philadelphia
Boscia, Jon Andrew *insurance company executive*
Hanway, H. Edward *insurance company executive*
Hart, William C. *underwriter, educator, writer*
Hochberg, Edward S. *insurance executive*
Phillips, Fred Ronald *insurance company executive*
Welch, Patrick *health insurance company executive*
Wolf, Gregory H. *insurance company executive*

Ridgway
Aiello, Gennaro C. *insurance company executive*

Spring House
van Steenwyk, John Joseph *health care plan consultant, educator*

Wayne
Yoskin, Jon William, II, *insurance company executive*

Wynnewood
Waber, Harry Edward *insurance agency executive*

SOUTH CAROLINA

Columbia
Averyt, Gayle Owen *retired insurance executive*

Johns Island
Schenck, Benjamin Robinson *insurance consultant*

Murrells Inlet
Schumaker, William Thomas *retired insurance company executive*

Spartanburg
Stewart, James Charles, II, *insurance agent*

SOUTH DAKOTA

Aberdeen
Stoia, Viorel G. *life underwriter*

Mitchell
Widman, Paul Joseph *insurance agent*

TENNESSEE

Nashville
Carson, Paul Eugene *insurance examiner*
Dedman, Bertram Cottingham *retired insurance company executive*
Gaultney, John Orton *life insurance agent, consultant*
Howell, John Floyd *insurance company executive*

Seymour
Steele, Ernest Clyde *retired insurance company executive*

TEXAS

Austin
Ellis, Glen Edward, Jr., *insurance agent, financial planner*
Golden, Edwin Harold *insurance company executive*
Mullen, Ron *insurance company executive*
Payne, Tyson Elliott, Jr., *retired insurance executive*
Spielman, David Vernon *retired insurance, finance and publications consultant*
Watson, Brenda Bennett *insurance company executive*

Bryan
†Valdez-Flores, Ciriaco *risk management consultant*

Corpus Christi
Vargas, Joe Flores *insurance claims executive*

Dallas
Caperton, Bob W. *risk manager*
Cline, Bobby James *insurance company executive*
Hogan, Thomas Victor *insurance company executive*
Madden, Teresa Darleen *insurance agency owner*
Rinne, Austin Dean *retired insurance company executive*
Weakley, Clare George, Jr., *insurance executive, theologian, entrepreneur*

Fort Worth
Blackburn, Wyatt Douglas *insurance executive*
Cooper, Alcie Lee, Jr., *entrepreneur, former insurance executive*
Faherty, John Kevin *insurance broker, consultant*
Kern, Edna Ruth *insurance executive*
Mitchell, Robert Joseph *insurance executive*
St. John, Evert Eugene *insurance company executive*

Houston
Alexander, Harold Campbell *insurance consultant*
Couch, Jesse Wadsworth *retired insurance company executive*
Davis, Rex Lloyd *insurance company executive*
Dean, Robert Franklin *insurance company executive*
Harris, Richard Foster, Jr., *insurance company executive*
Hook, Harold Swanson *former management consulting executive*
Lindsey, John Horace *insurance agency executive*
Lyons, Phillip Michael, Sr., *insurance accounting and real estate executive*
Martin, Kenneth Frank *insurance company executive*
Poulos, Michael James *insurance company executive*

Irving
Eudaly, Nathan H. *insurance company executive*

Lake Jackson
Elbert, James Peak *independent insurance agent, minister*

Mcallen
Whisenant, B(ert) R(oy), Jr., *insurance company executive*

North Richland Hills
Mutz, Gregory Thomas *insurance company executive*

Richardson
White, Irene *insurance professional*

San Antonio
Colyer, Kirk Klein *insurance executive, real estate investment executive*
Davis, Robert G. *insurance executive*
†Reid, Demetra Adams *insurance company executive*
Wellberg, Edward Louis, Jr., *insurance company executive*

Temple
Gillett, Victor William, Jr., *title insurance company executive*

Tyler
Guin, Don Lester *insurance company executive*

Waco
Rapoport, Bernard *life insurance company executive*

UTAH

Ogden
Buckner, Elmer La Mar *insurance executive*

Salt Lake City
Allen, Roy Verl *retired life insurance company executive*

Sandy
Macumber, John Paul *insurance company executive*

VERMONT

East Calais
Harding, John Hibbard *retired insurance company executive*

Moscow
Kende, Stephen James *insurance sales executive*

White River Junction
Kemp, Karl Thomas *insurance company executive*

VIRGINIA

Charlottesville
Long, Charles Farrell *insurance company executive*

Fairfax
Tringale, Anthony Rosario *insurance executive*

Lynchburg
McRorie, William Edward *lawyer, retired life insurance company executive*

Norfolk
Dungan, William Joseph, Jr., *insurance broker, economics educator*

Penhook
Hahn, John William *retired insurance company executive*

Richmond
Payne, William Sanford *insurance company executive*

Williamsburg
Herrmann, Benjamin Edward *former insurance executive*
†Sisk, Albert Fletcher, Jr., *retired insurance agent*

Woodstock
Walker, Charles Norman *retired insurance company executive*

WASHINGTON

Auburn
Colburn, Gene Lewis *insurance and industrial consultant*

Bellevue
Clay, Orson C. *insurance company executive, director*

Kennewick
Stevens, Henry August *insurance agent, educator*

Kirkland
McDonald, Joseph Lee *insurance broker*

Redmond
English, Donald Marvin *loss control representative*

Seattle
Duckworth, Tara Ann *insurance company executive*
†Eigsti, Roger Harry *retired insurance company executive*
LaPoe, Wayne Gilpin *retired business executive*
McGavick, Michael S. *insurance and financial services company executive*
Robb, Bruce *former insurance company executive*

Walla Walla
Perry, Louis Barnes *retired insurance company executive*

Woodland
Hansen, Walter Eugene *insurance executive*

WISCONSIN

Eau Claire
Rusch, Gerald Allen *financial representative*

Green Bay
Fischer, Robert Leo *insurance agent, financial consultant*

Madison
DuRose, Stanley Charles, Jr., *insurance executive*
Larson, John David *insurance company executive, lawyer*
Pierce, Harvey R. *insurance company executive*
Sims, Terre Lynn *insurance company executive*
Waldo, Robert Leland *retired insurance company executive*

Merrill
Gebhardt, Suzanne Marie *insurance company executive*

Whitburn, Gerald *insurance company executive*

Milwaukee
Johannes, Kay L. *insurance company executive*
Trytek, David Douglas *insurance company executive*

Nashotah
Vincent, Norman L. *retired insurance company executive*

Sun Prairie
Rollette, Harold Henry *insurance company executive*

WYOMING

Glenrock
Bennington, Leslie Orville, Jr., *insurance agent*

CANADA

ALBERTA

Calgary
Libin, Alvin G. *business executive*

ONTARIO

Etobicoke
Howe, James Tarsicius *retired insurance company executive*

Toronto
D'Alessandro, Dominic *financial executive*

BERMUDA

Hamilton
Kramer, Donald *insurance executive*

CHILE

La Reina Santiago
Beshears, Charles Daniel *insurance executive*

FRANCE

Paris
Peugeot, Patrick *insurance executive*

HONG KONG

Hong Kong
Mak, Wing Kwong Tony *life insurance executive, training consultant*
Tse, Edmund Sze-Wing *insurance company executive*

ADDRESS UNPUBLISHED

Adam, John, Jr., *insurance company executive emeritus*
Allison, Dianne J. Hall *retired insurance company official*
†Alpert, Ann Sharon *retired insurance claims examiner*
Armstrong, F(redric) Michael *retired insurance company executive, consultant*
Balkcom, Carol Ann *insurance agent*
Bare, Bruce *retired life insurance company executive*
Bellamy, James Carl *retired insurance company executive*
Bertrand, Frederic Howard *retired insurance company executive*
Borda, Richard Joseph *retired insurance company executive*
Bovey, Terry Robinson *insurance executive*
Briggs, Philip *insurance company executive*
Broome, Burton Edward *former insurance company executive*
†Brown, Joseph W., Jr., (Jay Brown) *insurance company executive*
Buck, Earl Wayne *insurance investigator, motel owner*
Carey, Edward John *insurance company executive*
Carver, Kendall Lynn *insurance company executive*
Chandler, J. Harold *insurance company executive*
Clark, Edgar Sanderford *insurance broker, consultant*
Coleman, Ronald Lee *insurance claims executive*
Conrad, Donald Glover *insurance executive*
Cooper, Charles Gordon *insurance consultant, former executive*
Deering, Fred Arthur *retired insurance company executive*
DiPiazza, Michael Charles *insurance company executive*
Doyle, Patrick Lee *retired insurance company executive*
Emek, Sharon Helene *risk management consultant*
Fibiger, John Andrew *life insurance company executive*
Fox, Lloyd Allan *insurance company executive*
Goodstone, Edward Harold *retired insurance company executive*
Goulet, Charles Ryan *retired insurance company executive*

Green, Robert Bailey *insurance executive, retired*
Gulko, Paul Michael *insurance executive*
Gummere, John *insurance company executive, director*
Hardy, Thomas Cresson *insurance company executive*
Hartsell, Samuel David *insurance agent*
Hawk, Carole Lynn *retired insurance company executive, research analyst*
Haynes, Marcia Margaret *insurance agent*
Hensley, Stephen Allan *insurance executive*
Hibner, Rae A. *risk management consultant, director, nursing*
Hinds, Edward Dee *insurance and investment professional, financial planner*
Hirst, Heston Stillings *former insurance company executive*
Hudson, William Mark *insurance company executive, owner*
Impellizzeri, Anne Elmendorf *insurance company executive, non-profit executive*
Jacobs, James Paul *retired insurance executive*
Jacobson, James Bassett *insurance executive*
Johnson, Glendon E. *retired insurance company executive*
Johnson, William Ray *insurance company executive*
†Jones, Lupe Sirena *insurance agent*
Kamen, Harry Paul *retired life insurance company executive, lawyer*
Karlin, Gary Lee *insurance executive*
Klingensmith, James M. *health insurance executive*
Knizeski, Justine Estelle *insurance company executive*
Knotts, Robert Lee *retired insurance company executive*
Kolde, Richard Arthur *insurance company executive, consultant*
Lacey, Cloyd Eugene *retired insurance company executive*
Ladd, Joseph Carroll *retired insurance company executive*
Lamel, Linda Helen *professional society executive, former insurance company executive, former college president, lawyer*
†Leatherdale, Douglas West *insurance company executive*
Long, John D. *retired insurance educator*
Maatman, Gerald Leonard *insurance company executive*
Maloney, Therese Adele *insurance company executive*
Mathieson, Garrett Alfred *insurance brokerage executive*
McKenna, Terence Patrick *retired insurance company executive*
McLaughlin, Michael John *retired insurance company executive*
Mehdizadeh, Parviz *insurance company executive*
Milam, June Matthews *life insurance agent*
Morrill, Thomas Clyde *insurance company executive*
Moses, Michael James *insurance company executive*
Moynahan, John Daniel, Jr., *retired insurance executive*
Nelson, Walter Gerald *retired insurance company executive*
Newman, Steven Harvey *insurance company executive, director*
Nichols, John David *insurance agent*
Norris, Darell Forest *retired insurance company executive*
Papa, Vincent T. *insurance company executive*
Pool, John Thomas *risk management consultant*
Porter, Dixie Lee *insurance company executive, consultant*
Resnick, Myron J. *retired insurance company executive, lawyer*
Reynolds, John Francis *insurance company executive*
Roark, Robert Cameron *insurance broker*
Rodino, Vincent Louis *insurance company executive*
Rondepierre, Edmond Francois *insurance executive*
Rowell, Lester John, Jr., *retired insurance company executive*
Ryan, James *insurance company executive*
Sanders, Franklin D. *retired insurance company executive*
Schwartz, Marina Malia *insurance company official, dancer*
Sharick, Merle Dayton, Jr., *retired insurance executive, auctioneer, broker*
†Smith, Debra A. *insurance company medical director*
Smith, Floyd Leslie *insurance company executive*
Smith, Michael Alan *retired insurance industry analyst*
Snyder, William Burton *insurance company executive*
Stewart, Gordon Curran *association executive*
Strong, John David *insurance company executive*
†Turner, John Gosney *insurance company executive, director*
Van Houten, James Forester *educator, consultant, retired insurance company executive*
Vasholz, Lothar Alfred *retired insurance company executive*
Viscardi, Peter G. *risk management and environmental affairs executive*
Weber, John Walter *insurance company executive*
Wentz, Sidney Frederick *insurance company executive, foundation executive*
Westervelt, James Joseph *retired insurance company executive*
Whiteley, Benjamin Robert *retired insurance company executive*
Wills, William Ridley, II, *former insurance company executive, historian*

†Zupsic, Matthew Michael *insurance company executive*

FINANCE: INVESTMENT SERVICES

UNITED STATES

ALABAMA

Birmingham
Comer, Donald, III, *investment company executive*
Marks, Charles Caldwell *retired investment banker, retired industrial distribution company executive*
Massey, Richard Walter, Jr., *retired investment counselor*
Tucker, Thomas James *retired investment manager*

Montgomery
Blount, Winton Malcolm, III, *investment executive*

Thomasville
†Corzealious, Forrest Lee *entrepreneur*

ALASKA

Anchorage
Hickel, Walter Joseph *investment firm executive, forum administrator*
Rose, David Allan *investment manager*

Homer
Oberstein, Sally *entrepreneur, not-for-profit fundraiser*

ARIZONA

Paradise Valley
Doede, John Henry *investment company executive*

Payson
Crom, Thomas LeRoy, III, *venture capitalist, accountant*

Phoenix
Hedberg, John Charles *investor*
Salmonson, Marty Lee *stockbroker, consulting engineer*
Scarbrough, Ernest Earl *stockbroker, financial planner*
Stern, Richard David *investment company executive*
Taylor, Elizabeth Jane *investment consultant, real estate and international marketing executive*
Tribble, Richard Walter *brokerage executive*

Scottsdale
Getz, Bert Atwater *investment company executive*
Luke, David Kevin *investment company executive*

Sierra Vista
Hasney, Christopher William *retired investment company executive, educator*

Tucson
Lomicka, William Henry *investor*
Schannep, John Dwight *brokerage firm executive*

Tumacacori
Myers, Clay *retired investment management company executive*

ARKANSAS

Little Rock
Good, Mary Lowe (Mrs. Billy Jewel Good) *investment company executive, educator*
Heath, Richard Raymond *investment company executive, retired*
Light, Jo Knight *stockbroker*
Reeves, Rosser Scott, III, *retired investment company executive*
Whiteside, Charles B., III, *investment company executive*

CALIFORNIA

Alamo
Bouret, Pierre George *brokerage house executive*

Antioch
Archuleta, Keith Anthony *entrepreneur, business and management consultant*

Arcadia
Berkus, David William *venture capitalist*

Atherton
Sollman, George Henry *venture capitalist*

Belvedere Tiburon
Rayner, Arno Alfred *investment company executive, consultant*

Benicia
Szabo, Peter John *investment company executive, financial planner, mining engineer, lawyer*

Beverly Hills
Evans, Louise *investor*
Gambrell, Thomas Ross *investor, retired physician, surgeon*
King, Lori Suzanne *entrepreneur*
Seidel, Joan Broude *stockbroker, investment advisor*

Burlingame
Most, Nathan *mutual fund executive*

Camarillo
Sullivan, Michael Evan *investment and management company executive*

Carlsbad
†Smith, Benjamin Eric *venture capitalist*

Chico
Houx, Mary Anne *investments executive*

Chino Hills
Ofner, William Bernard *investor*

Coronado
Smith, Albert Cromwell, Jr., *investments consultant*

Costa Mesa
Kiang, Assumpta (Amy Kiang) *brokerage house executive*

Fresno
Armey, Douglas Richard *investment consultant*
Dauer, Donald Dean *investment executive*

Glendale
Kinney, Paul William *investment company executive*

Hollywood
Marshall, Conrad Joseph *entrepreneur*

Irvine
†Boris, James R. *investment company executive*
Jones, Joie Pierce *entrepreneur, acoustician, educator, writer, scientist*

La Jolla
Grave de Peralta, Armando Rene *venture capitalist*
Stone, Donald Diamond *investment and sales executive*

Lake Elsinore
Shears, Roger Hammond *investment company executive*

Lancaster
Houck, John Dudley *investment adviser, educator*

Livermore
Grant, Alan J. *business executive, educator*

Los Altos
Carsten, Jack Craig *venture capitalist*
Ilstad, Geir Are *venture capitalist*

Los Angeles
Angeloff, Dann Valentino *investment banking executive*
Baxter, Frank Edward *brokerage executive*
Bernstein, Arthur Harold *venture capital executive*
Binder, Gordon M. *venture capitalist*
Dennison, Terry Alan *investment consultant*
Gordy, Berry *entrepreneur, record company executive, motion picture executive*
†Gores, Tom T. *investment company executive*
Hemingway, George Francis *investment company executive, lawyer*
Hsi, Denise Chur-Yee Tso *investment consultant*
Hurt, William Holman *investment management company executive*
Larkin, Thomas Ernest, Jr., *investment management company executive*
Lewis, Basil *investment company executive*
Maher, William James *investment executive*
Mann, Nancy Louise (Nancy Louise Robbins) *entrepreneur*
Ratliff, James Conway *investor, consultant*
Schmitz, Clarence T. *investment company executive*
Tennenbaum, Michael Ernest *investor*
†Trumbull, Stephen Michael *entrepreneur*

Menlo Park
Davies, Paul Lewis, III, *venture capitalist*
Fenton, Noel John *venture capitalist*
Lucas, Donald Leo *investor*
Lynch, Charles Allen *investment executive, corporate director*
†McCown, George E. *venture banking company executive*
†Raab, Michael George *venture capital investor*
Santry, Barbara Lea *venture capitalist*
Walsh, William Desmond *investor*
Wolfson, Mark Alan *investor, business educator*

Moraga
Ittner, Helen Louise *entrepreneur*

Napa
Strock, David Randolph *brokerage house executive*

Newport Beach
Hinshaw, Ernest Theodore, Jr., *private investor, former Olympics executive, former finance company executive*
Thorp, Edward Oakley *investment management company executive*

Novato
Bibeault, Donald Bertrand *business executive, investor*

Oakland
Alford, Joan Franz *entrepreneur*
Al Malek, Amir Isa *entrepreneur, business consultant, musician*
Dunn, David Cameron *entrepreneur, business executive*

Orinda
Danvers, David Bell *equity broker*

Palm Desert
Krallinger, Joseph Charles *entrepreneur, business advisor, author*

Palo Alto
Renda, Patrick Blake *investment company executive*

Palos Verdes Estates
Mennis, Edmund Addi *investment management consultant*

Pasadena
Arnott, Robert Douglas *investment company executive*
Corby, John Meade *investment company executive*
Fredericks, Ward Arthur *venture capitalist, food industry consultant*
Liebau, Frederic Jack, Jr., *investment manager*

Pinedale
Falcone, Patricia Jeanne Lalim *investor, foundation administrator*

Rancho Santa Fe
Kessler, A. D. *business, financial, investment and real estate advisor, consultant, lecturer, author, broadcaster, producer*
Polster, Leonard H. *investment company executive*
Robinson, Lawrence Brandon *investment company executive*

Ross
Rosenbaum, Michael Francis *securities dealer*

San Diego
Dunn, David Joseph *financial executive*
Ellsworth, Robert Fred *investment executive, former government official*
Huberman, Jonathan Serge *venture capitalist*

San Francisco
Brown, Cabot *investment company executive*
Buckner, John Knowles *investor*
Dachs, Alan Mark *investment company executive*
Da Silva, Delio P. *investment advisor*
†DeFeo, Phillip D. *brokerage house executive*
Dunn, Richard Joseph *retired investment counselor*
Hagenbuch, John Jacob *investor, real estate company executive*
Halliday, John Meech *investment company executive*
Hellman, F(rederick) Warren *investment advisor*
Kahn, Ronald N. *investment researcher*
Mahoney, Michael James *investment and software executive*
Mc Kee, Allen Page *investment company executive*
Pfau, George Harold, Jr., *investment advisor*
Pottruck, David Steven *brokerage house executive*
Redo, David Lucien *investment company executive*
Rock, Arthur *venture capitalist*
Rosenberg, Claude Newman, Jr., *investment adviser*
Schwab, Charles R. *brokerage house executive*
†Steinberg, David M. *securities analyst*
Turner, Ross James *investment corporation executive*
Wolf, Christopher Robin *investment executive*

Santa Barbara
Bartlett, James Lowell, III, *investment company executive*
Emmeluth, Bruce Palmer *investment company executive, venture capitalist*
Sipprelle, Dudley Gene *investor*

Santa Monica
Unterman, Thomas *venture capitalist, lawyer*

Sausalito
Apatoff, Michael John

Sherman Oaks
Koonce, John Peter *investment company executive, educator*

Signal Hill
Schinnerer, Alan John *entrepreneur*

South Pasadena
Zimmerman, William Robert *entrepreneur, engineering based manufacturing company executive*

Tarzana
Lauter, James Donald *retired stockbroker*
Neece, Olivia Helene Ernst *investment company executive, consultant*

Torrance
Enright, Stephanie Veselich *investment company executive, financial consultant*

Truckee
Turner, George Pearce *consulting company executive*

West Covina
Tuck, Edward Fenton *venture capitalist*

Westlake Village
Valentine, Gene C. *securities dealer*

Wildomar
Wells, James T. *development and brokerage executive, consultant*

Woodland Hills
Feiman, Thomas E. *investment manager*

Woodside
Markkula, A.C., Jr., *entrepreneur, computer company executive*

COLORADO

Arvada
Simon, Marvin B. *investment company executive, real estate broker*

Aurora
†Ton, Paul *investor, educator*

Boulder
Mehalchin, John Joseph *entrepreneur, finance executive*

Canon City
Alexander, Arline *entrepreneur, writer, real estate consultant*

Cherry Hills Village
Sutton, Robert Edward *investment company executive*

Denver
Gampel, Elaine Susan *investment company executive, consultant*
Stephenson, Arthur Emmet, Jr., *corporate and investment company executive*
Wagner, Judith Buck *investment firm executive*
Welch, J(oan) Kathleen *entrepreneur*

Englewood
Keegan, James Joseph *financial executive*
Van Loucks, Mark Louis *venture capitalist, business advisor*

Estes Park
Marr, J(ames) Joseph *venture capitalist*

Evergreen
Jackson, William Richard *entrepreneur*

Grand Junction
Skogen, Haven Sherman *investment company executive*

Kersey
Guttersen, Michael *ranching and investments professional*

Lakewood
Finnie, Doris Gould *investment company executive*

Littleton
Burgess, Larry Lee *commercial investment executive*

Placerville
Kickert, Juliana Arlene *investor*
Monferrato, Angela Maria *investor, writer, designer*
Treat, John Elting *entrepreneur*

CONNECTICUT

Collinsville
Whitney, Carol Marie *securities sales professional*

Darien
†Koontz, Carl Lennis, II, *investment counselor*
Moltz, James Edward *investment brokerage company executive*
Morse, Edmond Northrop *investment management executive*

Farmington
Halligan, Howard Ansel *investment management company executive*
Jones, Mary Jeanne A. *investment adviser*

Glastonbury
Orr, Richard Clayton *financial modeler, futures trader*

Greenwich
Dickerson, Thomas Pasquali *investment banker, lawyer*
Erlanger, Richard Alan *investment executive*
Miller, Donald Keith *venture capitalist, asset management executive*
Schneider, John Arnold *investor*
Swarz, Jeffrey Robert *securities analyst, neuroscientist*
Winkler, Charles Howard *investment company executive*

Litchfield
Sherva, Dennis G. *retired investment company executive*

New Canaan
Bisbee, Gerald Elftman, Jr., *investment company executive*
Gilbert, Steven Jeffrey *venture capitalist, screenwriter*
Grace, Julianne Alice *investor relations firm executive*
Lione, Susan Garrett *consultant*
Mountcastle, Kenneth Franklin, Jr., *retired stockbroker*

Penny, Susan Caroline Voelker *investment manager*
Pike, William Edward *business executive*

Norwalk
Alderman, Rhenus Hoffard, III, *investment company executive*
Hathaway, Carl Emil *investment management company executive*
Maisano, Phillip Nicholas *investment company executive*

Riverside
Crawford, R. George *investment manager, educator*

Southport
Wilbur, E. Packer *investment company executive*

Stamford
Hawley, Frank Jordan, Jr., *venture capital executive*

West Hartford
Bigler, Harold Edwin, Jr., *retired investment company executive*

Weston
Miller, Christopher Edward *investment advisor*
Wayne, Neil Russell *investment management company executive*

Westport
Frey, Dale Franklin *financial investment company executive, manufacturing company executive*
O'Keefe, John David *investment specialist*
Rudd, Nicholas *investor, consultant*
Walton, Alan George *venture capitalist*

DELAWARE

Greenville
DeWees, Donald Charles *securities company executive*

Millsboro
Lasher, Hiram Nelson *international biological consultant, entrepreneur*

Wilmington
Kalil, James, Sr., *investment executive*

DISTRICT OF COLUMBIA

Washington
†Akerson, Daniel F. *investment company executive*
Ansary, Cyrus A. *investment company executive, lawyer*
Bonde, Count Peder Carlsson *investment company executive*
Caldwell, John L. *international company executive*
Coreth, Joseph Herman *investment advisor*
Darman, Richard *investor, educator*
Farr, Michael Keogh *investment company executive*
Fisher, Robert Dale *stockbroker, retired naval officer*
Flügelman, Máximo Enrique *financier, composer*
Gibson, Paul Raymond *international trade and investment development executive*
Hartwell, Stephen *investment company executive*
Kelly, Charles J., Jr., *investment company executive*
Kent, Jill Elspeth *entrepreneur, art dealer, lawyer*
Lurton, Horace VanDeventer *brokerage house executive*
Macomber, John D. *investment company executive*
McIlwain, John Knox *housing policy fellow*
Morrissey, Elizabeth R. *investment company executive*
Nordlinger, Gerson *investor*
Rahming, John Christopher *investment company executive, consultant*
Selin, Ivan *entrepreneur*
Shrier, Adam Louis *investment firm executive, consultant*
Szymanski, Christopher John *consulting company executive*
Tomlinson, Alexander Cooper *investment banker, consultant*
Wortley, George Cornelius *government affairs consultant, investor*

FLORIDA

Alva
Darlow, George Anthony Gratton *investor*

Boca Raton
Barbarosh, Milton Harvey *merchant banking executive*
Batmasian, Marta Tersakian *investment company owner*
Bloomberg, Judith *stockbroker*
Land, Judith Broten *stockbroker*

Boynton Beach
Allison, Dwight Leonard, Jr., *investor*

Bradenton
Nelson, Ralph Erwin *investment company executive, coin dealer*

Clearwater
Grala, Jane M. *securities firm executive*
Sassouni, Chris Garo *investment advisor*

Coral Gables
Nunez-Portuondo, Ricardo *investment company executive*
Steinberg, Alan Wolfe *investment company executive*

Coral Springs
Brown, Ted Leon, Jr., *investment company executive*

Delray Beach
†Schaffer, Marvin W. *investor*

Englewood
Simis, Theodore Luckey *investment banker, information technology executive*

Fort Lauderdale
Huizenga, H. Wayne *entrepreneur, professional sports team executive*
Landry, Michael Gerard *investment company executive*
Sands, Roberta Alyse *real estate investor*
Vladem, Paul Jay *investment advisor, broker*

Highland Beach
Lane, James McConkey *retired investment executive*

Hobe Sound
Parker, H. Lawrence *investor, rancher, retired investment banker*

Jacksonville
Monsky, John Bertrand *investment banking executive*
Schultz, Frederick Henry *investor, former government official*

Jupiter
Kulok, William Allan *entrepreneur, venture capitalist*
Malm, Rita H. *securities executive*

Longboat Key
Levitt, Irving Francis *investment company executive*

Longwood
Goddard, Edward Dean *stockbroker, accountant*

Marco Island
Blackwell, John Wesley *securities industry executive, consultant*
Pettersen, Kjell Will *stockbroker, consultant*

Merritt Island
Thomas, Albert W *investment company executive, financial analyst*

Miami
Batcheller, Joe Ann *entrepreneur*
Bishopric, Karl *investment banker, real estate executive, advertising executive*
Dorion, Robert Charles *entrepreneur, investor*
†Ferré, Maurice A. *entrepreneur*
Kuczynski, Pedro-Pablo *investor*
†Mitchell, Virginia Ann *investment company executive*

Miami Lakes
Zwigard, Bruce Albert *brokerage house executive*

Miramar
Bruckenstein, Joel P. *investment company executive, financial planner*

Naples
Elliott, Edward *investment executive, financial planner*
Frantzen, Henry Arthur *retired investment company executive*
Gulda, Edward James *business acquisitions executive*
Oliver, Robert Bruce *retired investment company executive*
Presley, Brian *investment company executive*
Taillon, James Howard *investment advisor*

North Palm Beach
Jaffe, Melvin *securities company executive*
Xanthopoulos, Philip, Sr., *brokerage house executive*

Palm Beach
Bagby, Joseph Rigsby *financial investor*
Gundlach, Heinz Ludwig *investment banker, lawyer*
Johnson, Theodore Mebane *investment executive*
McCarter, Thomas Nesbitt, III, *investment counseling company executive*

Palm Beach Gardens
Kleinberg, Lawrence H. *investor, consultant*
Mergler, H. Kent *investment counselor*

Pompano Beach
Rifenburgh, Richard Philip *investment company executive*

Ponte Vedra Beach
Keeler, Ross Vincent *securities company executive*

Saint Petersburg
Emerson, William Allen *retired investment company executive*
Godbold, Francis Stanley *investment banker, securities firm executive*
Scott, Lee Hansen *retired holding company executive*

Sarasota
Balliett, John William *entrepreneur, real estate executive*

Tampa
Harriman, Malcolm Bruce *investment advisor, financial consultant*
Meek, Mark Alan *investment executive*
Michaels, John Patrick, Jr., *investment banker, media broker*
Sigety, Charles Birge *investment company executive*

Tavernier
Hawkins, Frank Nelson, Jr., *investor relations consultant, writer*

Tierra Verde
Gaffney, Thomas Francis *private investor*

Vero Beach
Clawson, John Addison *financier, investor*
Thompson, William David *investment banking executive*
Wilson, Robert James Montgomery *investment company executive*

West Palm Beach
Robertson, Sara Stewart *private investor, entrepreneur*

Winter Park
Holland, Robert Debnam, Sr., *investment company executive*

GEORGIA

Alpharetta
Christy, Robert Allen *investment advisor*

Atlanta
†Chandra, Vinay *entrepreneur*
Dees, Lafon Carabo *brokerage house executive*
Dietz, Arthur Townsend *investment counseling company executive*
Green, Holcombe Tucker, Jr., *investment executive*
Jackson, Geraldine *entrepreneur*
Keough, Donald Raymond *investment company executive, director*
McMahon, Donald Aylward *investor, corporate director*
Moss, Dan, Jr., *stockbroker*
Ottley, John K., Jr., *entrepreneur*
Prater, Robert Stanley, Jr., *broker*
Roberts, Thomasene Blount *entrepreneur*
Whitman, Homer William, Jr., *retired investment counseling company executive*
Willett, Chris Godwin *securities company executive, consultant*
Williams, Ralph Watson, Jr., *retired securities company executive*

Austell
†Orr, Zellie *entrepreneur, educator, writer, researcher*

Cleveland
Lewis, Richard, Sr., *securities broker, consultant*

Columbus
Diaz-Verson, Salvador, Jr., *investment advisor*

Cumming
Drew, Paul S. *entrepreneur*

Duluth
Street, David Hargett *investment company executive*

Marietta
Lee, Raymond William, III, *institutional stockbroker*

Roswell
Huntley, William Thomas, III, *investor, consultant*

HAWAII

Hilo
Merk, Elizabeth Thole *investment company executive*

Honolulu
Haight, Warren Gazzam *investor*
Kubo, Kimberly Annette *entrepreneur*

Kailua
†Amos, Wally *entrepreneur*

IDAHO

Boise
Hendren, Merlyn Churchill *investment company executive*

ILLINOIS

Alton
Greenwood, John E. *stock brokerage executive*

Barrington
Leon, Edward *investor*
Porter, Stuart Williams *investment company executive*

Burr Ridge
Clarke, Philip Ream, Jr., *retired investment banker*

Champaign
†Spice, Dennis Dean *venture capitalist, consultant*

Chicago
Beitler, Stephen *private equity and venture capital executive*
Bergonia, Raymond David *venture capitalist*
Block, Philip Dee, III, *investment counselor*
Brodsky, William J. *options exchange executive*
Chaleff, Carl Thomas *brokerage house executive*
Cloonan, James Brian *investment executive*
Crown, James Schine *investment executive*
†Duffy, Terrence A. *brokerage house executive*
Gilbert, Debbie Rose *entrepreneur*
Goldstein, William A. *investment counsel*
Gorchow, Bruce D. *investment company executive*
Harris, Irving Brooks *investor, director*
†Herron, David K. *brokerage house executive*
Hickey, Jerome Edward *investment company executive*
Hinrichs, Todd Aaron *securities executive*
Kelly, Arthur Lloyd *management and investment company executive*
Kirsch, Jeffrey Scott *securities executive*
Kneen, John W. *venture capitalist*
Kuhn, Ryan Anthony *information industry investment banker*
Lenhardt, Benjamin F., Jr., *investment management executive*
Lewis, Charles A. *investment company executive*
†McCausland, Thomas James, Jr., *brokerage house executive*
Miner, Thomas Hawley *international entrepreneur*
Nash, Donald Gene *commodity investigator*
†Neubauer, Nickolas J. *brokerage house executive*
Oliver, Harry Maynard, Jr., *retired brokerage house executive*
Pero, Perry R. *investment company executive*
Rasin, Rudolph Stephen *corporate executive*
Reece, Beth Pauley *commodities broker*
Renslow, Charles George *entrepreneur*
Rosenberg, Sheli Z. *investment company executive*
Slansky, Jerry William *investment company executive*
Stead, James Joseph, Jr., *securities company executive*
Stearns, Neele Edward, Jr., *investment executive*
†Towson, Thomas D. *securities trader*
Underwood, Robert Leigh *venture capitalist*
†Walsh, Matthew M. *investment company executive*
Weinberg, David B. *investor*
Weiner, Gerald Arne *stockbroker*
Weitzman, Robert Harold *investment company executive*
Whitesides, Lawson Ewing, Jr., *investment management executive*
Wilmouth, Robert K. *commodities executive*
Woods, Robert Archer *investment counsel*
Zeid, Paula Klein *metals broker*

Deerfield
Bagley, Thomas Steven *private equity investor*
Howell, George Bedell *equity investing and managing executive*
†Jordan, John W., II, *holding company executive*

Downers Grove
Smith, James C. *entrepreneur*

Highland Park
Uhlmann, Frederick Godfrey *commodity and securities broker*

Hinsdale
Peckenpaugh, Robert Earl *investment advisor*

Lake Forest
Young, Ronald Faris *commodity trader*

Lincolnshire
Aldrich, Susan Miller *entrepreneur*

Long Grove
Othman, Talat Mohamad *financial consultant, investment banker*

Naperville
Burchfield, Bruce Allen *entrepreneur*
Penisten, Gary Dean *entrepreneur*
Vanagas, Rimantas Andrius (Ray Vanagas) *entrepreneur*

Northbrook
Colburn, David Dunton *investment manager*
Edelson, Ira J. *venture banker, trade finance executive*

Oak Forest
Jashel, Larry Steven (L. Steven Rose) *entrepreneur, media consultant*

Park Ridge
†Albert, Elizabeth Franz (Mrs. Henry B. Albert) *investor, artist, conservationist*

Quincy
Taylor, Judith Caroline *entrepreneur*

River Forest
Wirsching, Charles Philipp, Jr., *retired brokerage house executive, private investor*

Rock Island
†Griffin-Brown, Dianna Lynn *entrepreneur, educator*

Schaumburg
Balasa, Mark Edward *investment consultant*

Villa Park
Tang, George Chickchee *investment company executive*

Wheaton
Back, Robert Wyatt *investment executive, pharmaceutical company executive consultant*

Wilmette
Albright, Townsend Shaul *investment banker, government benefits consultant*
Ryan, Mike *investment advisor, consultant*

Winnetka
Sick, William Norman, Jr., *venture capital company executive*

INDIANA

Bloomington
Mann, David O'Brien *venture capitalist, military officer*

Evansville
Brill, Alan Richard *entrepreneur*
Frary, Charles O., III, (Chuck Frary) *venture capitalist*

Greenwood
Grube, Elizabeth *investment company executive*

Indianapolis
Cox, Archibald, Jr., *investment company executive*
King, Kay Sue *investment company executive*

Munster
Shields, Robert Francis *stockbroker*

West Lafayette
Phillips, Terry LeMoine *investment advisor*

IOWA

Bettendorf
Rathje, James Lee *broker*

Johnston
Shoafstall, Earl Fred *entrepreneur, consultant*

Storm Lake
Franker, Stephen Grant *investment executive*

KANSAS

Overland Park
Miller, Mark William *investment advisor, writer*

Shawnee Mission
Braude, Michael *retired commodity exchange executive*

Topeka
Hedrick, Lois Jean *retired investment company executive, state official*

KENTUCKY

Louisville
Porter, Henry Homes, Jr., *investor*
Saunders, Robert Samuel *venture capital executive*

Murray
Boston, Betty Lee *investment company executive, financial consultant, financial planner*

Pikevill
Smith, Roger Keith *investment executive*

LOUISIANA

Mandeville
†Colomb, Marjorie Monroe *investor, volunteer*

New Orleans
Dahlberg, Carl Fredrick, Jr., *entrepreneur*
Flower, Walter Chew, III, *investment counselor*
Gensler, Philip, Jr., *investment counselor*

MAINE

Cumberland Center
Thomas, Charles Carroll *retired investment management executive*

Manchester
Moody, Stanley Alton *entrepreneur, financial consultant*

Portland
Anderson, Stephen Mills *investment broker*
Boyson, Michael Andrew *investment consultant*
†Harte, Christopher McCutcheon *investment manager*
Henshaw, Nathaniel Venable *venture capitalist*

MARYLAND

Annapolis
Smith, Robert Myron *investment company executive*

Arbutus
Maloney, Charles Wayne *gunsmith*

Baltimore
Bowman, Donald Eugene *investment counselor*
Curley, John Francis, Jr., *mutual fund executive*
Hardiman, Joseph Raymond *securities industry executive*
Himelfarb, Richard Jay *investment firm executive*
Hopkins, Samuel *retired investment banker*

Riepe, James Sellers *investment company executive*
Shaeffer, Charles Wayne *investment counselor*

Bethesda
Biddle, Albert George Wilkinson, III, (Jack Biddle) *venture capitalist*
Drazin, Lisa *real estate and corporate investment banker, financial consultant*
Koonce, Calvin Scott *brokerage firm executive, physicist*

Chevy Chase
Freeman, Harry Louis *investment executive*

Hagerstown
Baer, John Metz *entrepreneur*

Riverdale
Guetzkow, Daniel *technology company entrepreneur*

Rockville
Frazier, Walter Ronald *real estate investment company executive*
Freedman, Marc Allan *investment advisory executive*
Jacques, Joseph William *investment advisor*
Proffitt, John Richard *business executive, educator*
Tripp, Frederick Gerald *investment advisor*

Towson
McManus, Walter Leonard *investment executive*
Young, William Sherban *investment broker*

Westminster
Yingling, Jacob Matthias *independent investor*

MASSACHUSETTS

Bedford
Boghani, Ashok Balvantrai *entrepreneur*

Boston
Aikman, William Francis *venture capitalist*
Bailey, Richard Briggs *investment company executive*
Beck, Robert Randall *investment management executive*
Bennett, George Frederick *investment manager*
Beyerl, Scott Alan *investment company executive*
Cantella, Vincent Michele *stockbroker*
Carey, John Andrew *investment company executive*
de Burlo, Comegys Russell, Jr., *investment advisor, educator*
Estin, Hans Howard *investment executive*
Gozonsky, Edwin O. O. *investment broker*
Hale, Martin de Mora *investor*
†Higgins, Harriet Pratt *investment advisor*
†Johnson, Abigail *investment company executive*
Johnstone, C. Bruce *investment company executive*
Jonas, Stephen P. *investment company executive*
Lee, David Stoddart *retired investment counselor*
Lovell, Francis Joseph *investment company executive*
Markoff, Gary David *investment executive*
McCullen, Joseph T., Jr., *venture capitalist*
Metcalfe, Murray Robert *venture capitalist*
Morrison, Gordon Mackay, Jr., *investment company executive*
Morton, William Gilbert, Jr., *stock exchange executive*
Oates, William Armstrong, Jr., *investment company executive*
Philbin, Ann Margaret *brokerage house executive*
Rice, William Phipps *investment counselor*
Tempel, Jean Curtin *venture capitalist*
Towles, Stokley Porter *commercial and investment banking executive*
†Waite, Charles Prescott *entrepreneur*

Burlington
†Foxlin, Eric Michael *entrepreneur, researcher*

Cambridge
Davis, Paul Robert *investment manager, portfolio manager*
Lloyd, Boardman *investment executive*

Carlisle
Fohl, Timothy *consulting and investment company executive*

Concord
Schiller, Pieter Jon *venture capital executive*
Wickfield, Eric Nelson *investment company executive*

Falmouth
Preston, Mark I. *retired investment company executive*

Groveland
deNapoli, Paul Frederick *investment manager*

Lincoln
Holberton, Philip Vaughan *entrepreneur, educator, professional speaker*

Middleborough
†Maddigan, Bill *entrepreneur*

Newton
Saffran, Kalman *entrepreneur, venture capitalist*
Svrluga, Richard Charles *entrepreneur*

Norwell
Markham, Charles Rinklin *financial executive, tax accountant*

Quincy
Moran, James Joseph, Jr., *insurance executive*

Scituate
Keating, Margaret Mary *entrepreneur, business consultant*

Siasconset
†Albani, Thomas J. *investor*

South Dartmouth
Greene, William Caswell *investment company executive*

Stockbridge
Fitzpatrick, Jane *entrepreneur*

Stoneham
Mc Donald, Andrew Jewett *securities firm executive*

Taunton
Ricciardi, Louis Michael *brokerage house executive*

Waltham
Cox, Howard Ellis, Jr., *venture capitalist*
Ederle, Douglas Richard *investment adviser*
Elfers, William *retired investment company director*
Spoon, Alan Gary *venture capital company executive*

Westborough
Burdick, George Harold *investment company executive*

Weston
Alcock, George Lewis, Jr., (Peter Alcock) *investor, business strategist*

Westwood
Gillette, Hyde *retired investment banker*

MICHIGAN

Beulah
Auch, Walter Edward *securities company executive*

Bloomfield Hills
Rom, Martin (Melvyn Rom) *investor*

Farmington Hills
Ellmann, Sheila Frenkel *investment company executive*

Grand Rapids
Vandercook, Keith D. *investment company executive*

Grosse Pointe
Mengden, Joseph Michael *retired investment banker*

Grosse Pointe Park
Pankin, Jayson Darryl *entrepreneur, biotechnologist, venture capitalist, e-mail system developer*

Madison Heights
Janke, Kenneth *investment consultant*

Monroe
Nowitzke, Gary Earl *investment company executive*

Muskegon
Cirona, Jane Callahan *investment company executive*

Oak Park
Novick, Marvin *investment company executive, former automotive supplier executive, accountant*

Trenton
†Tang, Cyrus *investment company executive*

West Bloomfield
Mamut, Mary Catherine *retired entrepreneur*

MINNESOTA

Anoka
Ward, Bart James *investment executive*

Minneapolis
Dale, John Sorensen *investment company executive, portfolio manager*
†Fauth, John J. *venture capitalist*
Gallagher, Gerald Raphael *venture capitalist*
†Horsager, Kent *brokerage house executive*
†Lindau, Philip *commodities trader*
†Piper, Addison Lewis *securities executive*
Sit, Eugene C. *investment executive*

Saint Paul
Heyman, William Herbert *financial services executive*

Savage
Bean, Glen Atherton *entrepreneur*

Stillwater
Horsch, Lawrence Leonard *venture capitalist, corporate revitalization executive*

Waubun
Christensen, Marvin Nelson *venture capitalist*

Wayzata
Wyard, Vicki Shaw *investment and insurance company executive*

MISSOURI

Jefferson City
Beatty, Grover Douglas *stockbroker*

Joplin
Huffman, Patricia Nell *entrepreneur*
McReynolds, Allen, Jr., *retired investment company executive*

Kansas City
Latshaw, John *entrepreneur, director*
Morgison, F. Edward *investment broker*
†Petersen, Robert R. *brokerage house executive*
†Spady, Michael Benjamin *entrepreneur*

Lees Summit
Korschot, Benjamin Calvin *investment executive*

Saint Louis
Bachmann, John William *securities firm executive*
Bernstein, Donald Chester *brokerage company executive, lawyer*
Bickel, Floyd Gilbert, III, *investment counselor*
Critchfield, Scott A. *investment broker*
Keffler, Karl Joseph *investment company executive, lawyer*
†Losos, Joseph *investment advisor*
†Mendel, Mark J. *venture capitalist*
Moore, Patricia Kay *investor, public relations director*
O'Neill, Eugene Milton *mergers and acquisitions consultant*
†Walker, George Herbert, III, *investment banking company executive, lawyer*

Springfield
O'Block, Robert *entrepreneur, publishing executive*

MONTANA

Missoula
Liston, Albert Morris *investor, administrator, educator*

Polson
Marchi, Jon *former investment brokerage executive, cattle rancher, exporter, venture capitalist*

NEBRASKA

Lincoln
Knox, Arthur Lloyd *investor*

Omaha
Buffett, Susan Thompson *investment company executive*
Buffett, Warren Edward *entrepreneur*
Cross, W. Thomas *investment company executive*

NEVADA

Carson City
Reid, Belmont Mervyn *brokerage house executive*

Henderson
Stanton, Benjamin R. *investment company executive*

Las Vegas
Di Palma, Joseph Alphonse *investment company executive, lawyer*
Jabara, Michael Dean *technology and business development entrepreneur*

Reno
Newberg, William Charles *stock broker, real estate broker, automotive engineer*

Sparks
Holder, Harold Douglas, Sr., *investor, brokerage house executive, hotel executive*

NEW HAMPSHIRE

Derry
†Sapareto, Frank Vincent, II, *investment advisor, state legislator*

Dover
Parks, Joe Benjamin *entrepreneur, former state legislator*

Manchester
Levins, John Raymond *investment advisor, management consultant, educator*

NEW JERSEY

Avenel
Berg, Louis Leslie *investment executive*

Bridgewater
†Lowman, Tyrone David *entrepreneur*

Cranford
Bardwil, Joseph Anthony *investments consultant*

Cresskill
Uehling, Gordon Alexander, Jr., *investment company executive*

Fort Lee
Lippman, William Jennings *investment company executive*

Franklin Lakes
Baker, Philip Douglas *consultant, retired investment banker*

Hackensack
Heilborn, George Heinz *investor*

Hoboken
Breuer, Ronald Karl, Sr., *investment banking executive*

Jersey City
Alliton, Vaughn *brokerage executive*
Mak, Ken Ping *brokerage executive*
Tang, C. Mark *investment advisor, investment banker, venture capitalist, writer*

Lawrenceville
Galloway, Bonnie J. *investor, sociologist*

Lincoln Park
Sichuk, George *entrepreneur, theoretical biologist*

Little Egg Harbor Township
Dinges, Richard Allen *entrepreneur*

Little Silver
Turbidy, John Berry *investor, management consultant*

Livingston
Levine, Harry Bruce *stockbroker*

Madison
Johnson, William Joseph *investment manager*

Mendham
Kirby, Allan Price, Jr., *investment company executive*
Pierson, Robert David *investor*

New Brunswick
Mills, Dorothy Allen *investor*

North Brunswick
Mahajan, Sanjiv Rai *entrepreneur*

Parsippany
Ferris-Waks, Arlene Susan *compliance officer*

Plainsboro
Schreyer, William Allen *retired investment firm executive*

Princeton
Chamberlin, John Stephen *investor, former cosmetics company executive*
Fernholz, Erhard Robert *investment executive*
Gund, Gordon *venture capitalist, professional sports team executive*
Johnston, Robert Fowler *venture capitalist*
Schafer, Carl Walter *investment executive*
Treu, Jesse Isaiah *venture capitalist*

Ramsey
†Moch, Kenneth Ian *entrepreneur*

Red Bank
Hertz, Daniel Leroy, Jr., *entrepreneur*

Ridgewood
O'Leary, Paul Gerard *investment executive*
Tuthill, Jay Dean, II, *investment executive*

Roseland
Golden, Robert Charles *financial services executive*

Rumson
Strong, George Hotham *private investor, consultant*

Scotch Plains
Bishop, Robert Milton *former stock exchange official*
Plumeri, Joseph James, II, *financial executive*

Short Hills
Howe, James Everett *investment company executive*

Skillman
Tenenbaum, Bernard Hirsh *entrepreneur, educator*

Summit
Keith, Garnett Lee, Jr., *investment executive*
Malin, Robert Abernethy *investment management executive*

Teaneck
Lehmann, Esther Strauss *investment company executive*

Toms River
Boyd, Roger Allen *investment consultant*

Upper Saddle River
Oolie, Sam *manufacturing and investment company executive*

Westfield
Simon, Martin Stanley *commodity marketing company executive, economist*

NEW MEXICO

Alamogordo
Green, Francis William *investment consultant, former missile scientist*

Corrales
Eisenstadt, Pauline Doreen Bauman *investment company executive, state legislator*

Santa Fe
Colvin, Greta Wilmoth *entrepreneur*
Davis, Shelby Moore Cullom *investment executive, consultant*
†Schuyler, Robert Len *investment company executive*

Taos
Lipscomb, Anna Rose Feeny *entrepreneur, arts organizer, fundraiser*

NEW YORK

Albany
Leichman, Kenneth William *investment executive*

Ardsley
Jacobs, Sheldon *investment advisor*

Babylon
Brackett, Ronald E. *investment company executive, lawyer*

Bay Shore
Williams, Tonda *entrepreneur, consultant*

Bedford Corners
Singer, Craig *entrepreneur, investor, consultant*

Brooklyn
Wilson, Robert Warne *philanthropist, investor*

Buffalo
Irwin, Robert James Armstrong *investment company executive*
Littlewood, Douglas Burden *business brokerage executive*

Cooperstown
Gavey, James Edward *investment company executive*

Forest Hills
Flowers, Cynthia *investment company executive*

Glen Cove
Pettersen, Kevin Will *investment company executive*

Glens Falls
Pearsall, Glenn Lincoln *brokerage house executive*

Great Neck
Appel, Gerald *investment advisor*
Hampton, Benjamin Bertram *brokerage house executive*

Greenwich
Smethurst, E(dward) William, Jr., *brokerage house executive*

Holtsville
Braff, Howard *brokerage house executive, financial analyst, solar energy consultant*

Ithaca
Cornish, Elizabeth Turverey *stockbroker*
†Hojnowski, Jules Austin *entrepreneur*

Long Island City
†Falk, Charles H. (Harry Falk) *brokerage house executive*

Mamaroneck
Topol, Robert Martin *retired financial services executive*

Manhasset
Calvin, Donald Lee *business executive, stock exchange consultant*
Gardner, Robert *financial services executive*

Melville
Clinard, Joseph Hiram, Jr., *securities company executive*

Merrick
Poppel, Seth Raphael *entrepreneur*

New Hyde Park
Richards, Bernard *investment company executive*

New York
Acampora, Ralph Joseph *brokerage firm executive*
†Allison, Herbert Monroe, Jr., *investment firm executive*
Andersen, K(ent) Tucker *investment executive*
Araiz, Joseph Michael *securities company executive*
Aronson, Edgar David *venture capitalist*
Asch, Arthur Louis *investment company executive*
Barry, Thomas Corcoran *investment counselor*
Beinecke, Frederick William *investment company executive*
Bell, Martin Allen *investment company executive*
Bellas, Albert Constantine *investment banker, advisor*
Bendelac, Roger E. *investment executive, financial consultant*
†Bennett, Paul B. *brokerage house executive, economist*
Berg, Jonathan Albert *investment company executive*
Berkowitz, Brad Alan *stock analyst*
Bewkes, Eugene Garrett, Jr., *investment company executive, consultant*
Birkelund, John Peter *investment banking executive*
Blalock, Sherrill *investment advisor*
Boyd, Michael Alan *investment company executive, lawyer*
Bradsher, Neal Clifton *investment company executive*
Brittenham, Raymond Lee *investment company executive*
†Britz, Robert G. *stock exchange executive*
Britz Lotti, Diane Edward *investment company executive*
Brody, Alan Jeffrey *investment company executive*
Brody, Eugene David *investment company executive*
Brown, Ronald *retired stockbroker*
Brown, Valerie Sharice *venture capitalist*
Bruce, Duncan Archibald *investor, writer*
Brunie, Charles Henry *investment manager*
Buckles, Robert Howard *retired investment company executive*
Bulow, George Mitchell *entrepreneur*
Carpenter, Michael *financial services executive*
Cecil, Donald *retired investment company executive*
Chapman, Peter Herbert *investment company executive*
Cohen, Claire Gorham *investors service company executive*
Cole, Carolyn Jo *brokerage company executive*
Collins, Timothy Clark *holding company executive*
Condron, Christopher (Kip Condron) *investment company executive*
Conway, Richard Francis *investment company executive*
Cortez, Ricardo Lee *investment management executive*
Dallen, Russell Morris, Jr., *investment company executive, lawyer, publishing company executive*
Daly, John Neal *investment company executive*
D'Angelo, Ernest Eustachio *brokerage house executive*
Dantzker, David Roy *venture capitalist*
Darlington, Henry, Jr., *investment broker*
Darst, David Martin *investment company executive, educator, writer*
Dhore, Prasanna G. *mutual fund executive*
Dimond, Thomas *investment advisory company executive*
Dorsett, Burt *investment company executive*
Edlow, Kenneth Lewis *securities brokerage official*
Ehinger, Albert Louis, Jr., *securities trader*
Eig, Norman *investment company executive*
Ercklentz, Alexander Tonio *investment executive*
Evnin, Anthony Basil *venture capital investor*
Fahey, James Edward *brokerage house executive*
Feeley, Michael John *investment counselor*
Filimonov, Mikhail Anatolyevitch *investment company executive*
Fort, Randall Martin *investment banking executive*
France, Joseph David *securities analyst*
Franklin, Edward Ward *international investment consultant, lawyer, actor*
Freidheim, Stephen C. *investment company executive*
Friedenberg, Daniel Meyer *financial investor, writer*
Friedman, Alvin Edward *investment executive*
Friedman, Robert Laurence *investment professional*
Gero, Anthony George *securities and commodities trader*
Goelet, Robert G. *investment executive*
Gold, Jeffrey Mark *investment banker, financial adviser*
Goldfarb, David *investment banking executive*
Goldstein, Michael Lewis *investment strategist*
Gottesman, David Sanford *investment executive*
Gray, James L. *investment company executive*
Grusky, Robert R. *investor*
Haas, Eleanor A. (Mrs. Peter Ralph Haas) *business advisor*
Haggerty, Rosanne *entrepreneur*
Hansmann, Ralph Emil *investment executive*
Hart, Gurnee Fellows *investment counselor*
Haskell, John Henry Farrell, Jr., *investment banking company executive*
Healey, Thomas J. *former government official, brokerage house executive*
†Helsby, Keith R. *brokerage house executive*
Herbst, Edward Ian *brokerage firm executive*
Herrmann, Lacy Bunnell *investment company executive, financial entrepreneur, venture capitalist*
Hilton, Andrew Carson *investor, management consultant, former manufacturing company executive*
Holland, Michael Francis *investment company executive*
House, Karen Elliott *company executive, former editor, reporter*
Howard, Nathan Southard *investment banker, lawyer*
†Hurst, Robert Jay *securities company executive*
Hyman, Seymour *capital and product development company executive*
Ilacqua, Rosario Salvatore *securities analyst*
Jacobs, Harry Allan, Jr., *investment firm executive*
James, Robert Gregory *investment company executive*
Janney, Stuart Symington, III, *investment company executive*
Jepson, Hans Godfrey *investment company executive, director*
Johnson, Johnnie Dean *investor relations consultant*
Jones, Abbott C. *investment banking executive*
Kehoe, John P. *investor relations and corporate development consultant*
Kelly, William Michael *investment executive*
†Kinney, Catherine R. *stock exchange executive*
Klein, Jeffrey Peter *investor*
†Kolm, Petter N. *investment advisor, mathematician*
Krekorian, James Edmund *stock options trader*
Kressel, Henry *venture capitalist*

Lakatos, Susan Carol *investment banker, artist*
Lamle, Hugh Roy *investment advisor, consultant*
Lamport, Anthony Matthew *investments and venture capitalist*
Lang, Everett Francis, Jr., *brokerage house executive*
Langone, Kenneth *investment company executive*
Lasser, Joseph Robert *investment company executive*
Lau, Joseph James *investment analyst*
Lawrence, Bryan Hunt *investment banking executive*
Levy, Matthew Degen *investment banking technology and operations company executive, consumer products business development and planning executive, management consultant*
Linburn, Michael Richard *investment company executive*
Lipper, Kenneth *investment banker, author, producer*
Loeb, John Langeloth, Jr., *investment counselor*
Logan, J. Murray *investment manager*
Luke, Douglas Sigler *business executive*
Mager, Ezra Pascal *investment management company executive*
Main, Patricia Englander *investor*
Mariotti, Steve J. *entrepreneur, financial educator, president and founder NFTE*
Mayer, William Emilio *investor*
McGlynn, William Charles *brokerage house executive*
†McKay, Geoff *private equity investor*
Metz, Emmanuel Michael *investment company executive, lawyer*
Miller, Corbin Russell *investment company executive*
Mintz, Walter *investment company executive*
Morris, William Charles *investor*
Morrissey, Dolores Josephine *investment executive*
Morse, Robert Parker *investment company executive*
†Murphy, Donald B. *investment company executive*
Murphy, John B. *investment advisor*
Murphy, John Joseph, Jr., *investment company executive*
Nabi, Stanley Andrew *investment executive*
Nadelberg, Eric Paul *brokerage house executive*
Nazem, Fereydoun F. *venture capitalist*
Nichols, Carol D. *real estate professional*
Niemiec, David Wallace *investment management executive*
Obernauer, Marne, Jr., *business executive*
Obolensky, Ivan *investment banker, foundation consultant, writer, publisher*
Offit, Morris Wolf *investment advisory executive*
O'Grady, Beverly Troxler *investment executive, counselor*
Okun, Melanie Anne *venture capitalist*
Olinger, Chauncey Greene, Jr., *investment executive, editorial consultant*
†O'Neal, Stanley *investment company executive*
O'Neill, George Dorr *investment company executive*
Orben, Jack Richard *investment company executive, director*
Owen, Thomas Llewellyn *investment executive*
Pados, Frank John, Jr., *investment company executive*
Pappas, Milton J. *venture capitalist*
Paulson, Henry Merritt, Jr., *venture capitalist, investment company executive*
Perlmutter, Louis *investment banker, lawyer*
Peterson, Peter G. *investment company executive*
Pettit, William Dutton, Sr., *investment executive, consultant*
Pittman, Robert Warren *investor*
Pollack, Stephen J. *stockbroker*
Pouschine, John Laurence *private equity investment executive*
Quick, Peter *former brokerage firm executive*
Quick, Thomas Clarkson *brokerage house executive*
Quirk, John James *investment company executive*
Rand, Lawrence Anthony *investor, financial relations executive*
†Reed, John Shepard *investment company executive*
†Robinson, Jeffrey Arnold *entrepreneur*
Rogers, James Beeland, Jr., *investment company executive*
Rogers, Theodore Courtney *investment company executive*
Rose, Robert Neal *brokerage house executive*
Rosenbloom, Daniel *investment banker, lawyer*
Rothfeld, Michael B. *theatrical productions executive, investor*
Rothstein, Gerald Alan *investment company executive*
Schaeffer, Peter Neal *investment banking executive*
Schick, Harry Leon *investment company executive*
Schoen, Rem *investment executive*
Shalom, Liliane Winn *investment company executive, consultant*
Shapiro, Robert Frank *investment banking company executive*
†Shern, Stephanie Marie *investment company executive, accountant*
Siebert, Muriel *brokerage house executive, former state banking official*
Smith, Malcolm Bernard *investment company executive*
†Sodano, Salvatore F. *stock exchange executive*
Sorte, John Follett *investment firm executive*
Spira, Robert Alan *securities company executive*
†Stead, Jerre L. *investment company executive*
Stein, Bernard *stockbroker*
Stein, David Fred *investment executive*
Steinberg, Saul Phillip *holding company executive*
Sterling, Robert Lee, Jr., *investment company executive*
Stern, Walter Phillips *investment executive*
Stevens, Jerome Hebert *entrepreneur*

Stewart, E(dward) Nicholson *investment management executive*
Stoddard, George Earl *investment company financial executive*
†Taylor, Richard William *investment banker, securities broker*
Tizzio, Thomas Ralph *brokerage executive*
Tozer, W. James, Jr., *investment company executive*
Train, John *investment counselor, writer, government official*
Trapp, Peter Jarl Rudolf *investment manager, farmer*
Turner, Patrick Noel Waddington *fund manager*
Ule, Guy Maxwell, Jr., *stockbroker*
Updike, Helen Hill *investment manager, financial advisor*
Viniar, David *investment company executive*
Volk, Stephen Richard *company executive, lawyer*
Wages, Robert Coleman *equity investor*
Wareham, Raymond Noble *investment professional*
Williams, Dave Harrell *investment executive*
Wit, Harold Maurice *investment banker, lawyer, investor*
Wolff, Alexander Nikolaus *writer*
Xia, Lulin *private equity investor*
Yeager, George Michael *investment counsel executive*
Zeuschner, Erwin Arnold *investment advisory company executive*
Zirkle, William Denman *investment company executive*
Zoullas, Deborah Decotis *private investor, entrepreneur*
Zwickler, Allen *investment advisor, educator*

Oceanside
Rosenbaum, Frances (Phran Ginsberg) *entrepreneur*

Plainview
McCaffrey, John Anthony *brokerage house executive*

Rochester
Rulison, Joseph Richard *investment advisor*

Rockville Centre
Rogers, Eugene Charles *retired investment firm executive*

Rye Brook
†Schorer, Marianne T. *entrepreneur, consultant*

Southampton
Culp, Michael Bronston *investor, writer, publisher*

Syosset
Schiff, Peter Grenville *venture capitalist*

Uniondale
Brustein, Martin *financial adviser*

Wantagh
Zinder, Newton Donald *stock market analyst, consultant*

Westbury
Fogg, Joseph Graham, III, *investment banking executive*

White Plains
†Eisner, Alan Bradley *entrepreneur*

Woodstock
Ober, Stuart Alan *investment consultant, book publisher*

Yonkers
Smith, Aldo Ralston, Jr., *brokerage house executive*

NORTH CAROLINA

Charlotte
Grimaldi, James Thomas *investment fund executive*
May, Benjamin Tallman *securities specialist, administrator*
Ragan, Robert Allison *private investment executive, financial consultant*

Denton
Tuttle, Bynum R., Jr., *brokerage house executive*

Flat Rock
Childress, Richard Thomas *investment company executive*

Greensboro
Johnson, Marshall Hardy *investment company executive*

High Point
Phillips, Earl Norfleet, Jr., *diplomat, financial services executive*

North Wilkesboro
Pardue, Dwight Edward *venture capitalist*

Raleigh
McKinney, Charles Cecil *investment company executive*
Sandlin, James Delacy, III, *investment broker*

Wilmington
Toth, Susan Smith *investment executive*

Winston Salem
Strickland, Robert Louis *former retail company executive*

NORTH DAKOTA

Fargo
Tallman, Robert Hall *investment company executive*

Grand Forks
†Bateman, Connie Rae (Hanson) *entrepreneur, finance educator*
Gjovig, Bruce Quentin *entrepreneur coach, consultant, entrepreneur*

OHIO

Alpha
James, Francis Edward, Jr., *investment counselor*

Bay Village
Hook, John Burney *investment company executive*

Cincinnati
Anning, Robert Doan Hopkins *brokerage company executive*
James, George Barker, II, *investment executive*
Lucke, Robert Vito *merger and acquisition executive*
†Sanford, Jimmie *securities trader, investor*

Cleveland
Brentlinger, Paul Smith *venture capital executive*
Charnas, Michael (Mannie Charnas) *investment company executive*
Gelfand, Ivan *investment advisor*
†O'Donnell, Thomas Michael *former brokerage firm executive*
Shepard, Ivan Albert *securities and insurance broker*

Columbus
Barthelmas, Ned Kelton *investment and commercial real estate developer*
Pointer, Peter Leon *investment executive*

Dayton
Klein, Sophia H. *entrepreneur*

Delaware
Hamre, Gary Leslie William *entrepreneur*

Franklin
Wilkey, Mary Huff *investor, writer, publisher*

Galion
Cobey, Ralph *industrialist*

Hudson
Ashcroft, Richard Carter *investment company executive*
Kempe, Robert Aron *venture management executive*

Kent
Juvan, Dennis Paul *securities trader*

Pomeroy
Edwards, John David *investment executive*

Westerville
Barr, John Michael *investor, management consultant*

OKLAHOMA

Edmond
Munhollon, Samuel Clifford *investment brokerage house executive*

Tulsa
Healey, David Lee *investment company executive*
Neas, John Theodore *investment company executive*
Sanditen, Edgar Richard *investment company executive*

OREGON

Depoe Bay
Fish, Barbara Joan *investor, small business owner*

Lebanon
Stewart, Thomas Clifford *trading and investment company executive*

Medford
Hennion, Carolyn Laird (Lyn Hennion) *investment executive*

Portland
Rutherford, William Drake *investment executive*

PENNSYLVANIA

Alburtis
†Sullivan, Edward W. *entrepreneur*

Ambler
Cannon, John *investment consultant*

Bensalem
Graf, William J. *entrepreneur*

Bethlehem
Stella, John Anthony *investment company executive*

Blue Bell
Giordano, Nicholas Anthony *stock exchange executive*

Camp Hill
Custer, John Charles *investment broker*

Collegeville
Barnes, Jo Anne *investment advisor*

Ephrata
Sager, Gilbert Landis *investment company executive*

Gladwyne
Geisel, Cameron Meade, Jr., *investment professional*

King Of Prussia
Cannon, Lynne Marple *investment management company executive*

Lancaster
Carlisle, James Patton *entrepreneur*

Ligonier
Mellon, Seward Prosser *investment executive*

Moscow
Shotko, Kurt Joseph *entrepreneur, music entertainer*

Murrysville
Maurer, Richard Michael *investment company executive*

New Hope
Sergey, John Michael, Jr., *investment company executive*

Newtown Square
Lewis, James Earl *financier*

Paoli
Denny, William Murdoch, Jr., *investment management executive*

Philadelphia
†Cunningham, Jessie Jerome *entrepreneur*
†Frucher, Meyer S. (Sandy Frucher) *brokerage house executive*
Greenwald, Burton Jay *investment company executive, financial consultant*
Neff, P. Sherrill *venture capitalist*
Nobel, Glenn Lloyd *investment group director, arbitrator, mediator*
Palmer, Russell Eugene *investment executive*
Savitz, Samuel J. *actuarial consulting firm executive*
Simpson, Carol Louise *investment company executive*
Wilde, Norman Taylor, Jr., *investment banking company executive*
Wolitarsky, James William *securities industry executive*
Woosnam, Richard Edward *venture capitalist, lawyer*

Pittsburgh
Casturo, Don James *venture capitalist*
Donahue, John Francis *investment company executive*
Hillman, Henry L. *investment company executive*
Hyman, Lewis Neil *investment company executive, investment advisor*
Walton, James Mellon *investment company executive*

Quarryville
Bird, L. Raymond *investor*

Radnor
Buck, James Mahlon, Jr., *venture capital executive*

Valley Forge
Bogle, John Clifton *investment company executive*

West Chester
Branman, M. Jeffrey *investment fund company executive*

West Conshohocken
Taylor, Martha Elizabeth (Betsy Taylor) *investment company executive*

West Grove
Seder, Jeffrey A. *entrepreneur*

Williamsport
McDonald, Peyton Dean *brokerage house executive*

York
Thornton, George Whiteley *investment company executive*
White, Timothy Paul *brokerage house executive*

RHODE ISLAND

East Greenwich
†Raykhman, Alexander M. *entrepreneur, consultant*

Newport
Stone, Edward Luke *private equity investor, realtor*

Providence
Joukowsky, Artemis A. W. *private investor*

Wakefield
Mason, Scott MacGregor *entrepreneur, inventor, consultant*

Brussels
Buysse, Paul Henri Maria *trading company executive*

CHANNEL ISLANDS

Guernsey
Hunter, John Graham *investment management company executive*

CHINA

Beijing
Melville, Richard Allen *investment company executive*

Hong Kong
Li, Ka-Shing *international entrepreneur*

ENGLAND

Keynsham
Obolensky, Nicholas *entrepreneur*

London
Fleming, Robert *investment company executive*
Flint, Douglas J. *business executive*
†Furse, Clara *stock exchange executive*
Moon, Peter Geoffrey *investment executive*
Parry, Roger George *entrepreneur, writer*
Scheinman, Stanley Bruce *international financial executive, lawyer*
†Seardino, Marjorie *investment company executive*
†Willett, Joseph T. *investment company executive*

Slough
Mobbs, Sir Gerald Nigel *property investment executive*

FRANCE

Nedules
Masurel, Jean-Louis Antoine Nicolas *investment company executive*

GERMANY

Frankfurt am Main
von Rosen, Rüdiger *stock exchange executive*

Heidelberg
Swanson, Barry Ernest *securities company executive*

ITALY

Milan
DeBenedetti, Carlo *entrepreneur*

JAPAN

Tokyo
†Fukuma, Toshikatsu *investment banking executive*
†Kondo, Masanobu *investment company executive*
†Kusamichi, Masatake *investment company executive*
†Ohmura, Nobuaki *investment company executive*
†Ueshima, Shigeji *investment company executive*
†Yasutake, Shiro *investment/commodities company executive*
Yonezu, Takehiko *retired investment company executive*

MONGOLIA

Ulaanbaatar
Mandel, Leslie Ann *investment advisor, business owner, author*

NEW ZEALAND

Wellington
von Kohorn, Baron Ralph Steven *retired investment banker, author*

REPUBLIC OF KOREA

Seoul
†Hyun, Myung-Kwan *investment company executive*

SAUDI ARABIA

Riyadh
†Al-Saud, Alwaleed Bin Talal Bin Abdulaziz *investment company executive*

SINGAPORE

Singapore
Bay, Yew Chuan *conglomerate company executive*

SLOVENIA

Ljubljana
†Rotar, Tomaz *stock exchange executive*
Veselinovič, Draško *stock exchange executive*

SRI LANKA

Colombo
Kannangara, Vijith Julian *entrepreneur*

SWITZERLAND

Geneva
Farman-Farmaian, Ghaffar *investment company executive*

Zurich
Leite de Faria, Hernani J. *investment analyst*

TURKEY

Istanbul
Tugcu, Nejat *investment consultant, information systems expert*

ADDRESS UNPUBLISHED

†Ackerman, Don Eugene *venture capital executive*
Ackerman, Melvin *investment company executive*
Albers, Charles Edgar *investment manager*
Aljian, James Donovan *investment company executive*
Allen, Donald Vail *investment executive, writer, concert pianist*
Apel-Brueggeman, Myrna L. *entrepreneur*
Arp Lotter, Donna *venture capitalist, investor*
Aurin, Robert James *entrepreneur*
Bacharach, Melvin Lewis *retired venture capitalist*
Bacon, Caroline Sharfman *investor relations consultant*
Bagwill, John Williams *retired pension fund company executive*
Bailey, Rita Maria *investment advisor*
Bantry, Bryan *entrepreneur, producer, director*
Becker, Paul Albert *investment executive*
Berkley, Stephen Mark *computer industry entrepreneur and investor*
Berlin, Howard Richard *investment advisory company executive*
Beyman, Jonathan Eric *information officer*
Blum, Barbara Davis *investor*
Bowles, Barbara Landers *investment company executive*
Bratt, Nicholas *investment management and research company executive*
Brown, Samuel *retired corporate executive*
†Buck, James E. *financial exchange executive*
Burns, Barbara Belton *investment company executive*
Burns, Donald Snow *registered investment advisor, financial and business consultant*
Callard, David Jacobus *investment company executive*
Carr, Harold Noflet *investment corporation executive*
Casey, Gavin *former stock exchange executive*
Cassidy, Donald L. *investment analyst*
Chen, Philip Minkang *investment banker, corporate executive, lawyer, engineer*
Chryssis, George Christopher *entrepreneur*
Comegys, Ethel Blanche *brokerage house administrator*
Conrad, David Paul *business broker, retired restaurant chain executive*
Cox, Marvin Melvin, Jr., *finance executive, corporate officer*
Crutchfield, Alexander *investor, investment banker, venture capitalist*
Czarnecki, Gerald Milton *investment banker, venture capitalist*
Daie, Jaleh *investment company executive*
†D'Arcy, John P. *investment company executive*
Dean, Edwin Becton *entrepreneur*
De Lutis, Donald Conse *investment adviser, consultant*
de Neufville, Pierre *retired brokerage house executive*
Doherty, Charles Vincent *investment counsel executive*
Drake, Rodman Leland *investment company executive, consultant*
Dunn, John Raymond, Jr., *stockbroker*
Edgreen, Robert J. *equity company executive*
Fehribach, Ronald Steven *investment executive*
Fitts, Catherine Austin *investment advisor*
Fiumefreddo, Charles A. *investment management company executive*
Frankenberger, Bertram, Jr., *investor, consultant*
Freeman, Ralph Carter *investment banker, management consultant*
Froehlke, Robert Frederick *financial services executive*
Fuld, Richard Severin, Jr., *investment banking executive*
Glasberg, Laurence Brian *private investor, business executive*
Godwin, Pamela June *financial services executive*
†Goldberg, Arthur H. *brokerage services company executive*
Goldberg, David Alan *investment banker, lawyer*
Goldman, Alan Ira *investment banking executive*
Good, Walter Raymond *investment executive*
Gouletas, Evangeline *investment executive*
Grasso, Richard A. *stock exchange executive*
Greene, Frank Sullivan, Jr., *investment management executive*
Grijns, Laine *investment company executive*
†Hansen, Hal T. *retired investment company executive*
Hanson, John C. *investment company executive*
Hapner, Mary Lou *securities trader and dealer*
Hartness, Sandra Jean *venture capitalist*
†Heaton, Larry Cadwalder *securities company executive*
Heine, Leonard M., Jr., *investment executive*
Hentic, Yves Frank Mao *investment banker, industrial engineer*
Herzog, John E. *securities dealer*
Hitz, Duane Everett *brokerage executive*
Hochheimer, Frank Leo *brokerage executive*
Holte, Debra Leah *investment executive, financial analyst*
Hom, Doris Soo *consultant, investment manager*
Howard, James Webb *investment banker, lawyer, engineer*
Hudson, Donald J. *retired stock exchange executive*
Ihlanfeldt, William *investment company executive, consultant*
Jerrytone, Samuel Joseph *financial broker*
Johnson, Michael Warren *international relations specialist*
Kahn, Herta Hess (Mrs. Howard Kahn) *retired securities trader*
†Kaveripatnam, Sandesh *venture capitalist*
Kawano, James Conrad *investment analyst*
Keithler, John William *investment executive*
Kimmel, Mark *author, venture capital company executive*
Kisak, Paul Francis *venture capitalist, consultant*
†Korins, Leopold *stock exchange executive*
Krefetz, Gerald Saul *investment counselor, writer*
Kuhens, Brian Scott *investment company executive, publishing company executive*
†Lafair, Theodore *investment company executive, financial consultant*
Lambert, Rebecca Fotouhi *investment company executive*
Landis, Robert Kumler, III, *investment banker, lawyer*
Landsman, Richard *investment company executive, finance educator*
Lavington, Michael Richard *venture capital company executive*
†Lee, Courtney *investment company executive, educator*
Levens, Joseph David *investment company executive*
†Levitt, Arthur, Jr., *investment company executive*
Lewis, Brock *investment company executive*
Lieberman, Gail Forman *investment company executive*
Liu, Ralph Yieh-Min *investment management and banking executive*
Logan, Dan *investor, writer*
Lohrer, Richard Baker *investment consultant*
Luk, Tei Lewis *financial company executive*
Lynch, Thomas Peter *securities executive*
Mace, Stephen Alan *investment advisor*
Madison, T. Jerome *business executive*
Marshall, Julie W. Gregovich *investor relations executive*
Martin, George J. *investment banker, financial consultant*
Mathias, Julian Robert *investment manager*
Mayer, Anthony John *investment company executive*
Mc Lendon, Heath Brian *securities investment company executive*
†McNeill, Robert Patrick *investment counselor*
Messens, Mark Richard *entrepreneur*
Mikitka, Gerald Peter *investment banker, financial consultant*
Millsaps, Fred Ray *investor*
Moran, Charles A. *securities executive*
Mordecai, David K. A. *brokerage house executive, editor*
Morgenroth, Earl Eugene *entrepreneur*
Myers, John Herman *investment company executive*
Nadel, Elliott *investment firm executive*
Niehoff, Karl Richard Besuden *financial executive*
†O'Sullivan, Lawrence Joseph *retired investment counselor*
Page, Jonathan Roy *investment analyst*
Paladino, Albert Edward *venture capitalist*
Patrick, Thomas H. *investment company executive*
Pauken, Thomas Weir *venture capital executive, mediator*
Paup, Martin Arnold *real estate and securities investor*
Petrillo, Leonard Philip *retired corporate securities executive, lawyer*
Pinkney, D. Timothy *investment company executive*
†Polimeno, Mark Anthony *entrepreneur, music educator*
Pope, Dale Allen *investment company executive*
Pulling, Thomas Leffingwell *investment advisor*
Rathnam, Lincoln Yesu *investment company executive*
Renouf, Anne *technology commercialization financier*
Rider, Gregory Ashford *investment company executive*
Robertson, Mark Wayne *investment specialist*
Robinson, Annettmarie *entrepreneur*
Rondeau, Doris Jean *entrepreneur, consultant*
Ross, Darius Alexander *arbitrager and commodities trader, philanthropist, investment banker*
†Ross, Joe *commodities trader, educator*
Rydén, Bengt Gunnar *retired stock exchange executive*
Sallen, Marvin Seymour *investment company executive*
Scharff, Monroe Bernard *investor relations consultant*
Schloss, Claudia Z. *investment executive*
Sells, Boake Anthony *private investor*
Sener, Joseph Ward, Jr., *securities company executive*
Shinn, George Latimer *investment banker, consultant, educator*
†Shivers, Mitchell Everett *investment advisor*
Shuler, Jon Emmett *securities industry professional*
Snyder, Nathan *entrepreneur*
Sojka, Sandra Kay *investor, livestock conservator*
†Solberg, Ronald Louis *investment adviser*
Steen, Carlton Duane *private investor, retired food products executive*
Stephens, Donald R(ichards) *investor*
Stiles, Thomas Beveridge, II, *retired investment banking executive*
Stuart, Gerard William, Jr., *investment company executive, city official*
Tansor, Robert Henry *investor*
Thomas, James Edward, Jr., *brokerage house executive*
Tull, C. Thomas *investment advisor*
Turnbull, E.R. (Ned Turnbull) *venture capitalist*
Uchida, Prentiss Susumu *entrepreneur, management executive*
Urato, Barbra Casale *entrepreneur*
Urciuoli, J. Arthur *investment executive*
Uys, Jurgen Peter Brinker *securities analyst*
Wadsworth, Jacqueline Dorèt *private investor*
Ward, Anthony G. *stock, options and futures exchange consultant*
Washburn, Dorothy A. *entrepreneur*
Wruble, Brian Frederick *private investor*
†Zarb, Frank Gustave *investment executive*
Zeviar-Geese, Gabriole *stock market investor, lawyer*

GOVERNMENT: AGENCY ADMINISTRATION

UNITED STATES

ALABAMA

Birmingham
Bailey, Jeffrey Wayne *law enforcement educator, consultant*

Cullman
Munger, James Guy *protective services executive*

Huntsville
Schumann, J. Paul *federal agency administrator*

Mobile
Cunningham, Julian Antonia *retired protective services official*

Montgomery
Mandry, Christine M. *public adminstator*

ALASKA

Anchorage
Burke, Marianne King *state agency administrator, financial executive, consultant*
Lacy, Gregory Lawrence *protective services official*

ARIZONA

Glendale
Goforth, Nathan Dan *protective services official*

Goodyear
Carlson, Norman A. *government official*

Mesa
†Nielson, Theo Gilbert *protective services official, university official*

Phoenix
†Brunacini, Alan Vincent *protective services official*
Houseworth, Richard Court *state agency administrator*
Moriarty, Karen *state agency administrator*

Tucson
Smith, David Mitchell *fire and explosion consultant*

ARKANSAS

Jonesboro
Fair, Everett Neil *public administrator*

Little Rock
†Green, Johnnie D. *government agency administrator, finance educator*
Greene, Tristan Dorian *state agency administrator*

CALIFORNIA

Castaic
†Burkhart, Stephanie Gloria *protective services official, writer*

Castro Valley
Palmer, James Daniel *protective services official*

Corona
Hall, Harlan *federal agency administrator*

Holmstead, Jeffrey Ralph *federal agency administrator*
Horinko, Marianne Lamant *federal agency administrator*
Horn, Wade Frederick *federal agency administrator*
Horner, Constance Joan *federal agency administrator*
Howard, John *federal agency administrator*
Hunt, Earl Stephen *federal agency administrator*
Huntsman, Jon Meade, Jr., *federal agency administrator*
Hutchinson, Asa *federal agency administrator*
Hutchison, Claude B., Jr., *federal agency administrator*
Iklé, Fred Charles *former federal agency administrator, policy advisor, defense expert*
Iverson, Kristine Ann *federal agency administrator*
Jackson, Alphonso *federal agency administrator*
Jackson, Beverly Roberson *state agency administrator, consultant*
Jackson, Michael P. *federal agency administrator*
Jacobs, David Ernest *federal agency administrator*
James, Kay Coles *federal agency administrator*
Jarrett, Jeffrey D. *federal agency administrator*
Jen, Joseph Jwu-Shan *federal agency administrator*
Jennings, Jerry D. *federal agency administrator*
Jenson, William G. *federal agency administrator*
Jochum, James J. *federal agency administrator*
Johnson, Allen Frederick *federal agency administrator*
Johnson, Arlene Lytle *government agency official*
Johnson, Stephen L. *federal agency administrator*
Jones, A. Elizabeth *federal agency administrator*
†Jones, Kelley Raylin *labor relations specialist*
Juarbe, Frederico, Jr., *federal agency administrator*
Juster, Kenneth Ian *federal agency administrator*
Kansteimer, Walter H., II, *federal agency administrator*
Kassinger, Theodore William *federal agency administrator*
Keane, Kevin *federal agency administrator*
Keegan, Richard *federal agency administrator*
†Keisler, Peter Douglas *federal agency administrator, lawyer*
Kelly, Paul V. *federal agency administrator*
Keys, John W., III, *federal agency administrator*
Kicklighter, Claude Milton *federal agency administrator, retired army officer*
Kicza, Mary E. *federal agency administrator*
Kilgore, Edwin Carroll *retired government official, consultant*
Kincannon, Louis *federal agency administrator*
Kinney, Anne *federal agency administrator*
Klein, Dale Edward *federal agency administrator*
Korsmo, John Thomas *federal agency administrator*
Kroszner, Randall Scott *federal agency administrator, economist*
Langfeld, Stanley Chaitt *government executive*
Lash, William Henry, III, *federal agency administrator, law educator, lawyer*
Laurie, Rich M. *federal agency administrator*
Lawson, Kenneth *federal agency administrator*
Leahy, Daniel F. *federal agency administrator*
Leary, Thomas Barrett *federal agency administrator*
Ledbetter, Kenneth W. *federal agency administrator*
Legg, Hilda Gay *federal agency administrator*
Lengyel, David *federal agency administrator*
Lenkowsky, Leslie *federal agency administrator*
Lentini, Joseph Charles *government agency management analyst*
Levinson, Daniel Ronald *federal agency administrator, lawyer*
Libutti, Frank *federal agency administrator*
Lipnic, Victoria A. *federal agency administrator*
Liu, Michael Minoru Fawn *federal agency administrator*
Lloyd, James D. *federal agency administrator*
Locke, Thomas Bernard *retired federal agency administrator, security firm executive*
Lockhart, James Bicknell, III, *federal agency administrator*
Lozada, Jacob *federal agency administrator*
Luck, Andrew Peter *federal agency administrator*
Luther, Michael R. *federal agency administrator*
Mackay, Leo Sidney, Jr., *federal agency administrator*
Maco, Paul Stephen *securities and exchange administrator*
Magaw, John W. *former federal agency administrator*
Magnee, Tom *federal agency administrator*
Mahone, Glenn *federal agency administrator*
Mainella, Frances P. *federal agency administrator*
Maizel, Roy *federal agency administrator*
Mansfield, Gordon H. *federal agency administrator*
Manson, Harold Craig *federal agency administrator*
Marburger, John Harmen, III, *federal agency administrator*
Marin, Rosario *federal agency administrator*
Marshall, John *federal agency administrator*
Martin, Jack *federal agency administrator*
Martin, Kevin J. *federal agency administrator*
Martin, Robert Sidney *federal agency administrator*
Mason, Eileen B. *federal administrator*
Maxwell, David Ogden *former government official and financial executive*
†Mayeaux, Maxwell Hayden Edward *government agency administrator*
Mc Afee, William *government official*
McCaleb, Neal *federal agency administrator*
McCallum, Robert D., Jr., *federal agency administrator*
McClain, Tim S. *federal agency administrator*
McCutchen, Tommy Dee *federal agency administrator*
McFarland, Patrick E. *federal agency administrator*
McLaughlin, John E. *federal agency administrator*
McLean, Donna *federal agency administrator*
McNamara, Robert M., Jr., *federal agency administrator, lawyer*
McPherson, Edward Russell *federal agency administrator*
McSlarrow, Kyle E. *federal agency administrator*
McTaggart, Timothy Robert *state agency administrator, lawyer*
Mead, Kenneth Minor *federal agency administrator*
Meadows, Vickers B. *federal agency administrator*
Mehan, George Tracey, III, *federal agency administrator*
Mehlman, Bruce P. *federal agency administrator*
Mendelowitz, Allan Irwin *federal agency administrator*
Mlay, Marian *retired government official*
Mok, Samuel T. *federal agency administrator*
Montelongo, Michael *federal agency administrator, career officer*
Moore, Powell Allen *federal government official*
Mora, Alberto *federal agency administrator, councilman*
Morales, Diane K. *federal agency administrator*
Morello, Steven J. *federal agency administrator, lawyer*
Morse, Jerome Samuel *government administrator, trade specialist*
Moseley, James R. *federal agency administrator, farmer*
Mosley, Everett L. *federal agency administrator*
Mosley, Raymond A. *federal agency administrator*
Mosley, William Harry, Jr., *public affairs specialist*
Mueller, Robert Swan, III, *federal agency administrator, lawyer*
Mulville, Daniel R. *federal agency administrator*
Murano, Elsa A. *federal agency administrator*
Muris, Timothy Joseph *federal agency administrator*
Myers, William Gerry, III, *federal agency administrator*
Natsios, Andrew *federal agency administrator*
Navas, William Antonio, Jr., *federal agency administrator, retired military officer*
Neal, Darwina Lee *government official*
Nedelkoff, Richard R. *federal agency administrator*
†Nelligan, Jeffrey Parnell *public information officer*
Nelson, Kimberly Terese *federal agency administrator*
†Nesmith, Steven B. *congressional and intergovernment relations secretary*
Nethery, John Jay *government official*
Neuman, Susan B. *federal agency administrator*
Newman, Constance Berry *federal agency administrator*
Newsome, James E. *federal agency administrator*
†Nicholson, John W. *federal agency administrator*
†Noriega, Roger Francisco *federal agency administrator*
Novak, Michael John *government analyst*
O'Connor, Eileen J. *federal agency administrator*
Ohl, Joan E. *federal agency administrator*
O'Hollaren, Sean B. *federal agency administrator*
O'Keefe, Sean Charles *federal agency administrator*
Oliver, LeAnn Michelle *government official*
Olsen, Josephine *federal agency administrator*
Olsen, Kathie Lynn *federal agency administrator*
Olson, Theodore Bevry *federal agency administrator, lawyer*
Parker, Michael (Mike Parker) *federal agency administrator*
Pastorek, Paul G. *federal agency administrator*
Patron, June Eileen *former government official*
Patterson, Sally Jane *government affairs consultant*
Perper, Michael Joseph *federal agency administrator*
Peters, Mary E. *federal agency administrator*
Peterson, E. Anne *federal agency administrator*
Pizzella, Patrick *federal agency administrator*
†Pope, Anne B. *government agency administrator, department chairman*
Posner, Paul Leonard *government official*
Potok, Nancy Ann Fagenson *federal agency administrator*
Powell, Donald E. *federal agency administrator*
†Powell, Michael K. *federal agency administrator*
Prosper, Pierre-Richard *federal agency administrator*
Quello, James Henry *government official*
Railton, William Scott *federal agency administrator*
Raley, Bennett W. *federal agency administrator*
Ramsey, Charles H. *protective services official*
Recchia, Christopher *state agency administrator*
Reese, George W. *federal agency administrator*
Rey, Mark E. *federal agency administrator*
Reynolds, Gerald *federal agency administrator*
Richlen, Scott Lane *federal government program administrator*
Riegler, Guenter *federal agency administrator*
†Rivlin, Alice Mitchell *federal agency administrator, economist*
Roberson, Jessie Hill *federal agency administrator*
Rocca, Christina B. *federal agency administrator*
Rogan, James E. *federal agency administrator, former congressman*
Roseboro, Brian Carlton *federal agency administrator*
Rosendhal, Jeffrey David *federal science agency administrator, astronomer*
Rosenfeld, Arthur F. *federal agency administrator*
Rosenfeld, Ronald A. *federal agency administrator*
Rosenker, Mark Victor *federal agency administrator*
Roswell, Robert H. *federal agency administrator*
Roth, Stanley Owen *federal agency administrator*
Rottman, Ellis *public information officer*
Runge, Jeffrey William *federal agency administrator*
Rush, Jeffrey, Jr., *federal agency administrator*
Russell, Richard M. *federal agency administrator*
Rutledge, Peter J. *federal agency administrator*
Rutter, Alan *federal agency administrator*
Saleeba, David A. *federal agency administrator*
Sambur, Marvin *federal agency administrator*
Sampson, David Allan *federal agency administrator*
Sansonetti, Thomas L. *federal agency administrator*
Scarlett, Patricia Lynn *federal agency administrator*
†Schapiro, Mary *federal agency administrator, lawyer*
†Schaumber, Peter C. *government agency administrator*
Schieck, Frederick W. *federal agency administrator*
Schneider, Mark Lewis *government official*
Schubert, William G. *federal agency administrator*
Scolese, Christopher *federal agency administrator*
Scully, Thomas A. *federal agency administrator*
Sebejais, Melanie *federal agency administrator*
Sessions, William Steele *former government official, lawyer*
Shane, Jeffrey Neil *state agency administrator, lawyer*
Shapiro, Michael Henry *government executive*
Shearer, Paul Scott *government relations professional*
Sibolski, John Alfred, Jr., *educational association executive*
Silverman, Leslie E. *federal agency administrator*
Simmons, Emmy B *federal agency administrator*
Simon, James M. *federal agency administrator*
Slater, Eve *federal agency administrator*
Smith, Carl Michael *federal agency administrator, lawyer*
Sontag, Ed *federal agency administrator*
Sorrels, Carrie L. *federal agency administrator*
Spear, Chris *federal agency administrator*
Springer, Michael Louis *federal agency administrator*
Stadd, Courtney *federal agency administrator*
Steele, Ana Mercedes *former government official*
Stenbit, John Paul *federal agency administrator*
Stevenson, Katherine Holler *federal agency administrator*
Stillman, Robert Donald *government official*
Stoner, John Richard *federal government executive*
Stroup, Sally *federal agency administrator*
†Sturgell, Robert A. *government agency administrator*
Styles, Angela B. *federal agency administrator*
Sullivan, Thomas M. *federal agency administrator*
†Swimmer, Ross Owen *federal agency administrator*
Swinton, Sonya DeVonne *government agency administrator*
Taft, William Howard, IV, *federal agency administrator*
Tamargo, Mauricio J. *federal agency administrator*
Tarplin, Richard J. *federal agency administrator*
Tarrants, William Eugene *government official*
Taylor, John Brian *federal agency administrator, economist, educator*
Teets, Peter B. *federal agency administrator*
Tenet, George John *government agency official*
Tether, Anthony J. *government agency administrator*
Thompson, Larry Dean *federal agency administrator, lawyer*
Thompson, Lawrence Hyde *federal agency official*
Thompson-Curry, Dorothy *federal agency administrator*
Tinsley, Nikki Lee *federal agency administrator*
Tomb, Diane Lenegan *federal agency administrator*
†Townsend, Frances Fragos *federal agency administrator*
Tuck, John Chatfield *former federal agency administrator, public policy advisor*
Turner, John Freeland *federal agency administrator*
Van de Water, Read *federal agency administrator*
Van Tine, Kirk Kelso K. *federal agency administrator*
Vasquez, Gaddi *federal agency administrator*
Venneri, Samuel L. *federal agency administrator*
Victory, Nancy *federal agency administrator*
Walker, Mary L. *federal agency administrator, lawyer*
†Walsh, Dennis P. *government agency administrator*
†Walsh, John F. *government agency administrator*
Washburn, Abbott McConnell *government official*
Washburn, Kathryn Hazel *government agency executive*
Waters, Mary Brice Kirtley *federal agency administrator*
Watson, Harlan L(eroy) *federal official, physicist, economist*
Watson, Peter S. *federal agency administrator*
Watson, Rebecca Wunder *Federal Agency Administrator, Lawyer*
Wayne, Earl Anthony *federal agency administrator*
Weicher, John Charles *federal agency administrator*
Weiler, Edward J. *federal agency administrator*
Weinberger, Mark *federal agency administrator*
Weiner, Robert Stephen *federal agency administrator*
Wenzel, Bob *federal agency administrator*
Whitaker, Scott *federal agency administrator*
Williams, B. John, Jr., *federal agency administrator, lawyer*
Williams, David C. *federal agency administrator*
Williams, Steven A., Jr., *federal agency administrator*
Wilson, Joanne *federal agency administrator*
Winkenwerder, William, Jr., *federal agency administrator*
Winn, Morris X. *federal agency administrator*
Winter, Michael Alex *federal agency administrator*
Winter, Roger Paul *federal agency administrator*
Wolanin, Thomas Richard *educator, researcher*
Wolff, Otto *federal agency administrator*
Wood, Patrick Henry, III, *federal agency administrator*
Worden, Robert L. *government agency administrator, researcher*
†Yeager, Brooks Birdwell *policy and international affairs administrator*
Young, Frank Edward *former federal agency administrator, religious organization administrator*
Zaffos, Gerald *federal agency executive*
Zaragoza, Lawrence Jay *government manager*
Ziglar, James W. *investment banker, lawyer, educator*

FLORIDA

Cocoa
Baker, David Allen *protective services official*

Delray Beach
Schenkel, Suzanne Chance *retired natural resource specialist*

Fort Lauderdale
Etling, Terry Douglas *state agency administrator*

Fort Pierce
Belcher, Dorothy S. *state correctional department administrator*

Gulf Stream
Nalen, Craig Anthony *government official*

Indian Rocks Beach
DeLucia, Gene Anthony *government administrator, computer company executive*

Jacksonville
†Glover, Nathaniel, Jr., *sheriff*

Lake Worth
Heessel, Eleanor Lucille Lea *retired state agency administrator*

Niceville
Culver, Dan Louis *federal agency administrator*

Pensacola
Larson, Kurt Paul *fire chief*

Pinellas Park
Cramer, Kenneth Lee *protective services official, consultant*

Plantation
Gay, John Marion *federal agency administrator, organization-personnel analyst*

Saint Petersburg
Burnette, Charles Galyon *protective services official*
Simpson, Lisa Ann *government agency administrator, physician*

Stuart
Laska, Paul Robert *protective services official, writer, educator*

Tallahassee
Ashler, Philip Frederic *international trade and development advisor*
Buford, Barbara Fest *retired state agency employee*
Drayton, Carey M. *police administrator*
†Hood, Glenda E. *state agency administrator*
Milligan, Robert Frank *state agency administrator*
†Struhs, David B. *state agency administrator*
Thomas, James Bert, Jr., *government official*

GEORGIA

Atlanta
Binder, Sue *federal agency administrator*
†Finley, Michael Valton *foundation executive*
Gerberding, Julie Louise *federal agency administrator*
Hakes, Jay Edward *federal agency administrator*
Jaffe, Harold W. *federal agency administrator*
†Palmer, James I. *government agency administrator*
Rucker, Kenneth Lamar *law enforcement officer, educator, military officer*
Walker, Thomas H. *federal agency administrator*

Augusta
Cheng, Wu C. *retired patent examiner*

MINNESOTA

Minneapolis
Aanerud, Melvin Bernard *state agency administrator*

Saint Paul
Hall, Beverly Joy *police officer*

MISSISSIPPI

Clarksdale
Johnson, P. H. *federal agency administrator*
†Schmidt, John Frederick, III, *government agency administrator, consultant*

MISSOURI

Blue Springs
Snyder, James Robert *protective services official, educator*

Clayton
Davenport, Dennis Lynn *protective services official*

Creve Coeur
Luzio, Timothy Joseph *protective services official*

Jefferson City
Forbis, Bryan Lester *state agency administrator*
Mahfood, Stephen Michael *governmental agency executive*

Kansas City
†English, R(obert) Bradford *marshal*
Parker, Dennis Gene *former sheriff, martial arts instructor*

Saint Louis
Berkel, Edwin Martin *fire marshal*
Domahidy, Mary Rodgers *public policy educator*
Scheffrug, Donald George *county government administrator*
Warner, Susan *federal agency administrator*

Springfield
Gruhn, Robert Stephen *retired parole officer*

Wheeling
Roe, Mary Ann *postmaster*

MONTANA

Great Falls
Hodge, Glenn Roy *retired postmaster*

NEBRASKA

Lincoln
Texel, Timothy J. *state agency director*

Omaha
Patrick, Erline M. *federal agency administrator*

Oneill
Hedren, Paul Leslie *national park administrator, historian*

NEVADA

Henderson
†Perkins, Richard D(ale) *police official, state legislator*
Wood, Benjamin Carroll, Jr., *senior loss prevention consultant*

Las Vegas
†Anthony, Stavros *protective services official*
Chevers, Wilda Anita Yarde *former state official and educator*
Lally, Norma Ross *retired federal agency administrator*
Wieting, Gary Lee *federal agency executive*

Reno
Griffin, Jeff *federal agency administrator, mayor*
Svahn, John Alfred *government official*

NEW HAMPSHIRE

Brentwood
Micklos, Janet M. *state agency administrator, human services director*

Concord
Brunelle, Robert L. *retired state education director*
Day, Russell Clover *state agency administrator*
Lohmann, Keith Henry *police department official, consultant*
Mevers, Frank Clement *state archivist, historian*

NEW JERSEY

Absecon
Byrne, Shaun Patrick *law enforcement mediator*

Adelphia
Carter, Harry Robert *fire protection consultant*

Bordentown
Lowery, William Odell *personnel services executive*

Cape May Court House
Pierson, Jeffrey Lynn *protective services officer*

East Orange
†Ilogienboh, Caroline O. *protective services official, publishing executive*

Hawthorne
Schlachman, Edwin *retired state agency administrator*

Lawrenceville
Hunt, Wayne Robert, Sr., *state government official*

Maplewood
Rabadeau, Mary Frances *protective services official*

Mays Landing
Connor, Wilda *government health agency administrator*

Monroe Township
Wolfe, Deborah Cannon Partridge *government education consultant, educator, clergy*

Mountainside
Weigele, Richard Sayre *police officer*

Pompton Lakes
Kubas, Christine *retired law enforcement officer*

Toms River
Luzky, Leonard *law enforcement official, national guard officer, educator*
Rupert, Wayne Richard *protective services official*

Trenton
Tucci, Mark A. *state agency administrator*

Willingboro
Greene, Natalie Constance *protective services official*

NEW MEXICO

Albuquerque
†Eichenberg, Peter Thompson *state agency administrator*
Gutierrez, Sidney M. *federal agency administrator*
Jaramillo, Mari-Luci *retired federal agency administrator*
Montoya, Patricia T. *federal agency administrator*
†Varma, Roli *public administration educator*
Williams, Marion Lester *government official*

Santa Fe
†Kelly, Ruth *state agency administrator*
Knapp, Edward Alan *retired government agency administrator, scientist*
Saurman, Andrew (Skip Saurman) *state agency executive*

NEW YORK

Albany
Borys, Theodor James *state agency data center administrator*
Bradley, Edward James *state official, computer programmer and analyst*
Cross, Robert Francis *commissioner*
†Gilliam, Marsha Sampson *state agency administrator*
Hilton, Joseph D. *state agency administrator*
Novello, Antonia Coello *state health commissioner, former surgeon general*
Shields, Robert Michael *state agency administrator*

Baldwin
†Zeitlin, Joan *federal agency administrator*

Bronx
Sedacca, Angelo Anthony *protective services official, educator*

Brooklyn
Von Essen, Thomas *protective services official*

Flushing
Ghazarbekian, Sahak *retired civil servant, consultant*

Great Neck
Blumberg, Barbara Salmanson (Mrs. Arnold G. Blumberg) *retired state housing official, housing consultant*

Jamaica
Reid, Michelle Marie Brady *government official*

Liverpool
Naum, Christopher John *fire protection management and industrial safety specialist, training consultant, educator*

New York
Beausoleil, Doris Mae *federal agency housing specialist*
Cremer, Leon Earl *federal agent, lawyer*
Drake, Paul *detective agency owner*
Fisher, David Robert *forensic scientist*
†FitzGerald, Gerald P. *state agency executive*
Holzer, Harold *public affairs officer, historian, writer*
†Kenny, Jane Marie *government agency administrator*
Leichter, Franz S. *federal agency administrator*
Rosa, Margarita *agency chief executive, lawyer*

Russell, Andrew James *government agency official, diplomat*
Sorensen, Gillian Martin *United Nations official*
Talbot, Phillips *Asian affairs specialist*
Turso, Vito Anthony *government and public affairs executive*
Varmus, Harold Eliot *health science administrator, educator, science researcher*

Oneida
†Walsh, Gregory E. *protective services official*

Schenevus
Fielder, Dorothy Scott *retired postmaster*

Scotia
Graper, William Earl *state agency administrator*

Stony Point
Ricci, Daniel Michael *protective services official*

Valhalla
Czarnecki, Anthony J. *correction administrator, educator*

Woodside
Johnson, Davy L. *protective services official, minister, writer*

NORTH CAROLINA

Burlington
Kee, Walter Andrew *former government official*

Canton
Roberts, Bill Glen *retired fire chief, investor, consultant*

Charlotte
Wright, Wayne Kenneth *federal agency statistician*

Corolla
Schrote, John Ellis *retired government executive*

Durham
Peele, Anne Marie *government relations administrator*

Franklinton
Moran, John Bernard *government official, retired*

Greensboro
Nunn, Robert William *sentencing services official*
Reed, William Edward *government official, educator*

Raleigh
Maness, Edwin Clinton, III, *highway patrol officer, video coordinator*
Neenan, Peter Anthony *state agency administrator*

Waynesville
†Ingle, Marti Annette *protective services official, educator*

Wilmington
†Clinton, Lottie Dry Edwards *retired state agency administrator*

OHIO

Centerville
Baver, Roy Lane *retired protection services official, consultant*

Cincinnati
†Finney, Michael Douglas *public safety consultant*
Hardwick, Kevin Dale *retired protective services official*

Cleveland
Grabow, Raymond John *mayor, lawyer*
Jettke, Harry Jerome *retired government official*

Columbus
Gillmor, Karen Lako *state agency administrator*
McInturff, Floyd M. *retired state agency administrator*
Metzler, Eric Harold *retired state agency administrator, researcher*

Cuyahoga Falls
Shane, Sandra Kuli *postal service administrator*

Dayton
Cannon, Cris A. *protective services official*

Galloway
Barner, Bruce Monroe *former state agency administrator, not-for-profit company chairman*

Montpelier
Deckrosh, Hazen Douglas *retired state agency educator and administrator*

Newark
Billy, Gerry Dee *protective services official*

Reynoldsburg
Dailey, Fred L. *state agency administrator*
D'Onofrio, Peter Joseph *protective services official, educator*

Springfield
†Woodhouse, Elizabeth C. *retired government agency administrator*

Toledo
Smith, Robert Nelson *former government official, anesthesiologist*

Zanesville
O'Sullivan, Christine *retired executive director social service agency, consultant*

OKLAHOMA

Oklahoma City
Bush, William Arden *federal agency administrator*
Clark, Gary Ray *licensing board executive*
Collins, William Edward *aeromedical administrator, researcher*
Harbour, Robert Randall *state agency administrator*
Jenkins, LeAnn *government executive*
Pratt, Billy Kenton *police officer*

Tulsa
Deihl, Michael Allen *federal agency administrator*

PENNSYLVANIA

Butler
Rickard, Dennis Clark *sheriff, educator*

Camp Hill
Nowak, Jacquelyn Louise *state agency administrator, artist, realtor, consultant*

Carlisle Barracks
Metz, Steven Kent *federal agency administrator, writer*

Gettysburg
Roach, James Clark *government official*

Harrisburg
†Margolis, David Leslie *government agency administrator*

Lancaster
Hudak, Joseph David *forensic engineer, educator, police investigator*

Philadelphia
Brown, Betty Marie *government agency administrator*
†Hackney, Sheldon *former federal agency administrator, history educator*
Hairston, Harold B. *protective services official*
†Moreno, Michele R. *court reporter*
†Welsh, Donald S. *government agency administrator*

Pittsburgh
Marshall, Meriam Doris *federal agency administrator*

University Park
Lee, Robert Dorwin *public affairs educator, administrator*

Wallingford
Cook, Harvey Carlisle *law enforcement official*

York
Jacobs, Laura *probation/parole officer*

RHODE ISLAND

Saunderstown
Knauss, John Atkinson *former federal agency administrator, oceanographer, educator, former university dean*

SOUTH CAROLINA

Chapin
Freitag, Carol Wilma *state official, political scientist*

Charleston
Gaillard, John Palmer, Jr., *former government official, former mayor*

Columbia
Duffie, Virgil Whatley, Jr., *retired state agency administrator*
Inkley, Scott Russell, Jr., *state agency administrator*
Ringer, Keith William *state education professional, consultant*

Hopkins
Garrett, Robin Scott *public information officer*

Lexington
Resch, Mary Louise *town agency administrator*

Swansea
Inabinet, George Walker, Jr., *retired state agency administrator*

SOUTH DAKOTA

Pierre
Olson, Judith Mary Reedy *retired public information officer, former state senator*

TENNESSEE

Knoxville
Baxter, William *federal agency administrator*

Memphis
Knight, H. Stuart *law enforcement official, consultant*

Goldoff, Anna Carlson *public administration educator*
Gordon, Peter Lowell *federal agency administrator*
†Green, Richard James *federal agency administrator, aerospace engineer*
Grossman, Marc *federal agency administrator*
Guay, Gordon Hay *federal agency administrator, marketing educator, consultant*
Guild, Nelson Prescott *retired state education official*
†Hall, James Evan *lawyer*
Helms, J. Lynn *former government agency administrator*
Hervey, Homer Vaughan *retired federal agency administrator*
Heyman, Ira Michael *federal agency administrator, museum executive, law educator*
Hubbard, Robert Glenn *former federal agency administrator*
†Hundt, Reed Eric *information industry advisor, lawyer*
Jameson, Patricia Marian *government agency administrator*
Jiler, Linda Cerise *retired fire and aviation program support specialist, fire emergency dispatcher, consultant, researcher, writer*
Keene, Mary Ellen *federal agency executive*
Keilty, Bryan T. *government agency administrator*
Kelley, Edward Watson, Jr., *former federal agency administrator*
Kelso, John Hodgson *former government official*
†Kemble, Penn *government official*
Kezer, Pauline Ryder *state government executive, management consultant*
†King, Rosemary M. *protective services official, poet*
Knox, Deborah Carolyn *state information systems administrator*
Kott, Alan *state agency administrator*
Kutscher, Ronald Earl *retired federal government executive*
LaBarre, Carl Anthony *retired government official*
†Lau, Fred H. *protective services official*
Lawler, Thomas Comerford *intelligency agency official, government agency administrator*
LeDoux, John Clarence *retired law enforcement official*
Lewis, Samuel Winfield *retired government official, former ambassador*
Lines, Sandra Ramsey *forensic document examiner*
†Lissakers, Karin Margareta *former federal agency administrator*
Livingstone, Susan Morrisey *consultant, former federal agency administrator*
Lovelace, Rose Marie Sniegon *federal space agency administrator*
†Low, Paul Charles *protective services specialist*
Loy, Frank Ernest *retired government official*
Lyding, John Frederick *retired government administrator, editor*
McClain, Lena Alexandria *protective services official*
Mc Coy, Tidal Windham *former government official*
McDowell, Elaine *retired federal government executive, educator*
Mc Fee, Thomas Stuart *retired government agency administrator*
McGarry, Marcia *retired community service coordinator*
†Metzenbaum, Shelley H. *public information officer*
Moody, Nelson Leon *protective services official, writer*
Morgan, Linda Joan *former federal agency administrator*
Murr, James Coleman *retired federal government official*
Nyquist, Maurice Otto *federal agency administrator, scientist*
Palmieri, Rodney August *retired state agency administrator, pharmacist*
Panetta, Michael Jon *retired state agency administrator, educator, writer, researcher*
†Philippus, Al A. *protective services official*
Pitt, Harvey Lloyd *former federal agency administrator*
Polisar, Joseph Michael *protective services official*
Rehnquist, Janet *federal agency administrator*
Reilly, Edward Francis, Jr., *federal agency administrator, former state senator*
Rhodes, Karren *public information officer*
†Rockett, John Alexander *fire safety consultant*
Rossotti, Charles Ossola *former federal agency administrator*
Saddler, George Floyd *government economic adviser*
Schoenberger, James Edwin *retired federal agency administrator*
Schrenko, Linda C. *state agency administrator*
Scott, Jeffrey Lyle *protective services official*
Shasteen, Donald Eugene *government official*
Shelton, Henry H. *former chairman of joint chiefs*
Shirzad, Faryar *federal agency administrator*
Shuman, Thomas Alan *protective services official, consultant*
Shute, Richard Emil *government official, engineer*
Skaff, Joseph John *retired state agency administrator, army officer*
Sloat, Jane Roberts DeGraff *government official, civic worker, consultant*
†Smith, Marcia K. *government agency administrator*
Smith, Nancy Angelynn *federal agency administrator*
Smith, Wendy Haimes *federal agency administrator*
Sorter, Bruce Wilbur *federal program administrator, educator, consultant*
Stagliano, Vito Alexander *federal agency administrator, utilities executive*
Sweedler, Barry Martin *transportation safety consultant*
Thomas, Cherryl T. *former federal agency administrator*
Thomas, Larry Dee *retired corrections administrator, poet*
Truesdale, John Cushman *government executive*
van Schilfgaarde, Jan *retired agricultural engineer, government agricultural research service administrator*
Walker, Gordon Davies *former government official, writer, lecturer, consultant*
White, Thomas E. *former federal agency administrator*
Williamson, Rushton Marot, Jr., *information technology project manager*
†Young, Edwin S. W. *federal agency official*
Zaltman, Mark Allen *federal agency administrator*
Ziese, Dennis Russell *protective services official, retired military officer*

GOVERNMENT: EXECUTIVE ADMINISTRATION

UNITED STATES

ALABAMA

Birmingham
Boomershine, Donald Eugene *bureau executive, development official*
Wheeler, Cathy Jo *government official*

Dothan
†Turkoski, William Steve *workforce development consultant*

Mobile
Bostwick, Robert Otis *municipal staff member*
Higginbotham, Prieur Jay *city official*

Montgomery
†Baxley, Lucy *lieutenant governor*
Bennett, James Ronald *state official*
†Bright, Bobby *mayor*
Campbell, Maria Bouchelle *state official*
Harris, Joseph Lamar *state official*
Pryor, William Holcombe, Jr., *state attorney general*
Riley, Robert *governor*
Williamson, Donald Ellis *state official*
†Worley, Nancy L. *secretary of state*
†Young, Caron L *county official*

Semmes
Phelps, James Franklin *retired county official*

ALASKA

Anchorage
Brown, Dean Naomi *state official, geologist*
Knowles, Tony *former governor*
†Leman, Loren Dwight *lieutenant governor, civil engineer*

Juneau
Meacham, Charles P. *president, capital consulting*
Murkowski, Frank Hughes *governor*
†Renkes, Gregg *state attorney general*
Ulmer, Frances Ann *former lieutenant governor*
Whistler, Bradley James *state government official*

Kodiak
Selby, Jerome M. *mayor*

ARIZONA

Chandler
Dunn, Boyd *mayor, lawyer*

Glendale
Brewer, William E. *city materials manager*
Scruggs, Elaine M. *mayor*

Mesa
Brown, Wayne J. *former mayor*
Hawker, Keno *mayor, trucking company executive*
†Wong, Willie *former mayor, automotive executive*

Phoenix
Bentheim, Wendy J. *municipal official*
†Brewer, Janice Kay *state official*
Curcio, Christopher Frank *city official*
†Fernandez, Helen Agnes *municipal official*
†Goddard, Terry *state attorney general*
McClennen, Miriam J. *former state official*
Miel, Vicky Ann *city official*
Napolitano, Janet Ann *governor*
†Quayle, Dan (James Danforth Quayle) *former vice president United States, entrepreneur*
Rimsza, Skip *mayor*

Scottsdale
Manross, Mary *mayor*

Sun Lakes
Sharpless, Joseph Benjamin *retired county official*

Tempe
Giuliano, Neil Gerard *mayor, academic administrator*

Tucson
Updike, John R. *municipal administrator*
Walkup, Robert E. *mayor*

ARKANSAS

Alexander
Hunter, Carl Glenn *retired commissioner*

Bella Vista
Medin, Myron James, Jr., *city manager*

Conway
Polk, William Allen *city planner, architect*

Heber Springs
Rawlings, Paul C. *retired government official*

Little Rock
Beebe, Mike *state attorney general*
Cheek, James Richard *ambassador*
Huckabee, Michael Dale *governor*
Priest, Sharon Devlin *secretary of state*

Magnolia
Barnard, Anna Marion *county official*

CALIFORNIA

Anaheim
Hill, Harry David *city official, human resources professional*
†Pringle, Curt *mayor*

Aptos
Trounstine, Philip John *communications consultant, institute administrator*

Bakersfield
Hall, Harvey L. *mayor, medical transportation company executive*
†Mc Quiston, Jonathan Alan *county official*
Mosby, Dorothea Susan *retired municipal official*

Bellflower
†Bermudez, Rudy *state official*

Belvedere Tiburon
Rice, Edward Earl *former government official, author*

Benicia
von Studnitz, Gilbert Alfred *state official*

Berkeley
Hamilton, Randy Haskell *city manager*
Taylor, John Lockhart *former city official*
†Yellen, Janet Louise *government official, economics educator*

Beverly Hills
Covitz, Carl D. *state official, real estate and investment executive*

Brea
†Daucher, Lynn M. *state official*

Carson
†Oropeza, Jenny *state official*

Cathedral City
†Garcia, Bonnie *state official*

Chino Hills
†Lascurain, Randolph *county official*

City Of Industry
†Pacheco, Robert *state official*

Claremont
Pedersen, Richard Foote *diplomat and academic administrator*

Coronado
Hostler, Charles Warren *former ambassador, international affairs consultant*

Costa Mesa
†Maddox, Ken *state official*

El Cajon
Pollock, Richard Edwin *former county official*
Thigpen, Mary Cecelia *city official, consultant*

Encinitas
Miller, Kerry Lee *city manager*

Fall River Mills
Reed, Eva Silver Star *chieftain*

Felicity
Istel, Jacques Andre *mayor*

Folsom
Peck, Ellie Enriquez *retired state administrator*

Fremont
Morrison, Gus (Angus Hugh Morrison) *mayor, engineer*

Fresno
Autry, Alan *mayor, actor, former professional football player, film company executive*

Fullerton
†Sa, Julie *councilwoman*

Garden Grove
Broadwater, Bruce A. *mayor*

Gardena
Hardison, Dee *former mayor*

Grass Valley
Cassella, Dennis Gene *retired county official*

Hayward
Cooper, Roberta *mayor*

Huntington Beach
†Harman, Thomas *state official*

Inglewood
†Horton, Jerome E. *state official*

Irvine
Agran, Larry *mayor, lawyer*
†Campbell, John B. T., III, *state official*
Shea, Christina *former mayor*

La Jolla
Shakespeare, Frank *ambassador*

La Mesa
†La Suer, Jay *state official*

Laguna Niguel
†Bates, Patricia C. *state official*

Laguna Woods
Hussey, William Bertrand *retired foreign service officer*

Long Beach
†Lowenthal, Alan *state official*
O'Neill, Beverly Lewis *mayor, former college president*
Sato, Eunice Noda *former mayor, consultant*

Los Angeles
Antonovich, Michael Dennis *county official*
†Davis, Michael Rico *county official*
Griffiths, John Liebig *retired foreign service officer, marketing consultant*
Hahn, James Kenneth *mayor, lawyer*
Reagan, Nancy Davis (Anne Francis Robbins) *wife of former President of United States, volunteer*
Reagan, Ronald Wilson *40th President of the United States*
Riordan, Richard J. *former mayor, lawyer*
Toman, Mary Ann *federal official*
Torres-Gil, Fernando M. *federal official, academic administrator*

Marina
Mettee-McCutchon, Ila *municipal official, retired career officer*

Mckinleyville
Schoettger, Theodore Leo *city official*

Menlo Park
Lane, Laurence William, Jr., *retired ambassador, publisher*

Mission Viejo
Wilson, Eleanor McElroy *county official*

Modesto
Sabatino, Carmen *mayor*

Monrovia
†Mountjoy, Dennis Lee *state official*

Montclair
†Negrete McLeod, Gloria *state official*

Montebello
†Calderon, Ronald *state official*

Monterey Park
Smith, Betty Denny *county official, administrator, fashion executive*

Moreno Valley
White, Charles R. *former mayor*

Murrieta
McClellan, Barry Dean *city manager*

Napa
Battisti, Paul Oreste *retired county supervisor*

Oakland
Brown, Jerry (Edmund Gerald Brown Jr.) *mayor, former governor*

Oceanside
Lyon, Richard *mayor emeritus, retired naval officer*

Ontario
Ovitt, Gary C. *mayor*

Orange
†Spitzer, Todd *state official*

Oroville
Curry, William Sims *county official*
Davis, Frederick Charles *county official*

Oxnard
Lopez, Manuel M. *mayor*
Takasugi, Nao *state official, business developer*

Pasadena
Bean, Maurice Darrow *retired diplomat*
Bogaard, William Joseph *mayor, lawyer, educator*

Pearblossom
Benedict, Lawrence Neal *foreign service officer*

Penn Valley
†Holmes, Genta Hawkins *diplomat*

Pomona
Cortez, Edward S. *mayor*

Rancho Cucamonga
†Dutton, Robert D. *state official*

Rancho Mirage
Ford, Betty Bloomer (Elizabeth Ford) *former First Lady of United States, health facility executive*
†Ford, Gerald Rudolph, Jr., *38th President of the United States*

Redlands
Hanson, Gerald Warner *retired county official*

Riverside
†Benoit, John *state official*
Stewart, Richard A. *former mayor*

Sacramento
Betts, Bert A. *former state treasurer, accountant*
Burns, John Francis *state official, educator*
†Burton, John *state official*
Bustamante, Cruz M. *lieutenant governor*
Cahill, Virginia Arnoldy *lawyer*
DeYoung, David Jeffrey *state official*
Dunnett, Dennis George *retired state official*
Fargo, Heather *mayor*
Garth-Lewis, Kimberley *state official, political scientist*
Hodgkins, Francis Irving (Butch Hodgkins) *county official*
Hunter, Patricia Rae (Tricia Hunter) *state official*
Lockyer, Bill *state attorney general*
Olson, Timothy Allan *state official*
Pettite, William Clinton *public affairs consultant*
†Schwarzenegger, Arnold Alois *governor*
Shirey, John Frederick *local government administrator, lecturer, consultant*
Tubbs, William Reid, Jr., *public service administrator*

Salinas
Solis, Gilberto, Jr., *county official*
Wong, Walter Foo *county official*

San Bernardino
Valles, Judith *mayor, former academic administrator*

San Diego
Bliesner, James Douglas *municipal/county official, consultant*
Freeman, Myrna Faye *county schools official*
Golding, Susan *former mayor*
†Kehoe, Christine T. *state official*
Murphy, Dick *mayor, former superior court judge*
†Plescia, George A. *state official*
Robinson, David Howard *lawyer*

San Francisco
Achtenberg, Roberta *former federal official*
Brown, Willie Lewis, Jr., *mayor, former state legislator, lawyer*
Frank, Anthony Melchior *federal official, former financial executive*
Low, Donald *diplomat, financial investor*

San Jose
Edwards, Frances Lavinia *city official*
Gonzales, Ron *mayor, former county supervisor*

San Luis Obispo
Shlaudeman, Harry Walter *retired diplomat*

Santa Ana
†Correa, Lou *state official*
Daly, Tom *county official, mayor*
Pulido, Miguel Angel *mayor*

Santa Monica
Aaron, David L. *diplomat, author*
Rice, Donald Blessing R. *business executive, former secretary of air force*

Santa Paula
Kay, Hazel T. *local commissioner*

Seaside
Panetta, Leon Edward *federal official, former congressman*

Solana Beach
Beard, Ann Southard *diplomat, government official, travel company executive, oil company executive, consultant, event planner, writer, educator*
Gildred, Theodore E. *former diplomat, real estate developer*

South Gate
†Firebaugh, Marco Antonio *state official*

Stanford
Shultz, George Pratt *former government executive, economics educator*

Stockton
Lewis, Mark Earldon *city manager*
Podesto, Gary A. *mayor*

Torrance
Walker, Dan *mayor, business consultant*

Ventura
Smith, Bill *city manager*

Vista
†Wyland, Mark *state official*

West Covina
Manners, Nancy *retired mayor*

West Hollywood
Prang, Jeffrey *mayor*

Yuba City
Kemmerly, Jack Dale *retired state official, aviation consultant*

Yucaipa
†Bogh, Russell *state official*

COLORADO

Aurora
Sheffield, Nancy *city agency administrator*
Tauer, Paul E. *mayor, educator*

Colorado Springs
†Chestnutt, Ellen Joanne *state official*
Makepeace, Mary Lou *former mayor*
Milton, Richard Henry *retired diplomat, children's advocate*
†Rivera, Lionel *mayor*

Denver
Brown, Keith Lapham *retired ambassador*
Cohen-Vader, Cheryl Denise *municipal official*
Cuba, Stanley L. *government official*
Davidson, Donetta *state official*
Gallagher, Dennis Joseph *municipal official, state senator, educator*
Galloway, Judy A. *deputy commissioner*
†Hickenlooper, John W. *mayor*
Himmelmann, William Charles *municipal official*
†Norton, Jane E. *lieutenant governor*
Owens, Bill *governor*
Rogers, Joe *former lieutenant governor*
†Romer, Roy R. *former governor*
Salazar, Kenneth L. *state attorney general*
†Walcher, Jennifer Lynne *city official*
Webb, Wellington E. *former mayor*

Golden
Fahey, Barbara Stewart Doe *public agency administrator*

Grand Junction
Achen, Mark Kennedy *city administrator, management consultant*

Lakewood
Burkholder, Steve *mayor*

Littleton
Geringer, James E. *former governor*

Pueblo
Occhiato, Michael Anthony *city official*

CONNECTICUT

Bantam
Privitera, Joseph F. *retired foreign service officer, writer-researcher*

Canton Center
Humphrey, Samuel Stockwell *town official, physicist*

Darien
McIntire, William Tredick, II, *municipal official, investment banker*

East Hartford
Dubin, Joseph William *federal mediator*

Easton
Meyer, Alice Virginia *state official*

Hamden
Westerfield, Carolyn Elizabeth Hess *city planner*

Hartford
Blumenthal, Richard *state attorney general*
Bysiewicz, Susan *secretary of state*
Killian, Robert Kenneth *former lieutenant governor*
Perez, Eddie A. *mayor*
Rell, M. Jodi *lieutenant governor*
Rowland, John G. *governor, former congressman*

Meriden
Kemp, Roger Lark *city manager, writer*

New Canaan
Lucas, Norman Arthur *retired town manager*

Norwalk
Brown, Otha Nathaniel, Jr., *political official, retired educator*
†Willcox, Roger *city planner, consultant*

Southington
Weichsel, John *town manager*

Stamford
Dennies, Sandra Lee *city official*
Malloy, Dannel Patrick *mayor*

DELAWARE

Dover
Carney, John C., Jr., *lieutenant governor*
Minner, Ruth Ann *governor*
†Windsor, Harriet Smith *state official*

Lewes
Bookhammer, Eugene Donald *state government official*

Newark
Freel, Edward J. *former state official*
Woo, S. B. (Shien-Biau Woo) *former lieutenant governor, physics educator*

Wilmington
Brady, M. Jane *state attorney general*
Ianni, Francis Alphonse *state official, former army officer*
Morris, Ronald Anthony *county official*
Sholl, Howard George, Jr., *state official*

DISTRICT OF COLUMBIA

Washington
Abraham, Spencer *secretary of energy*
Abrams, Elliott *governmental official*
Abshire, David Manker *diplomat, research executive*
Andersen, Robert Allen *retired government official*
Anthony, Sheila Foster *government official*
Armitage, Richard Lee *federal government official*
Ashcroft, John David *attorney general*
Atherton, Charles Henry *federal commission administrator*
†Atkins, Paul S. *commissioner*
†Austin, Roy L. *ambassador*
Ayres, Mary Ellen *government official*
†Baasan, Ragchaa *diplomat*
Babbitt, Bruce Edward *former federal official, lawyer*
Baldyga, Leonard J. *retired diplomat, international consultant*
†Bandar, Prince bin Sultan bin Abd al-Aziz Al Saud *Saudi Arabian ambassador to United States*
Bandler, Donald K. *diplomat*
Barbosa, Rubens Antonio *Brazilian ambassador*
Barnes, Shirley Elizabeth *foreign service officer*
Baroody, Judith Raine *federal official, educator*
Barringer, Philip E. *retired government official*
Bassin, Jules *foreign service officer*
†Battle, Vincent M. *ambassador*
Bellows, Michael Donald *foreign service officer*
Berg, Stephen Warren *government official*
†Bernstein, Stuart A. *ambassador*
†Blackwill, Robert D. *ambassador*
†Blankenship, J. Richard *ambassador*
Block, John Rusling *former secretary of agriculture*
†Blust, Steven R. *commissioner*
Boehm, Peter Michael *ambassador, diplomat*
†Bolten, Joshua Brewster *federal official*
†Braceras, Jennifer C. *commissioner*
Bragg, Lynn Munroe *federal commissioner*
Brazeal, Aurelia Erskine *former ambassador*
†Bremer Martino, Juan Jose *ambassador*
Brewster, Robert Charles *diplomat, consultant*
†Bridgewater, Pamela E. *ambassador*
Brown, Elizabeth Ann *foreign service officer*
Brown, Gordon Stewart *diplomat, business association administrator, writer*
†Brownfield, William R. *ambassador*
Buck, Carolyn J. *federal official*
†Bujon de L'Estang, Francois *diplomat*
Burns III, Matthew J. *diplomat*
†Burson, Charles W. *federal official, former state attorney general*
Bush, George Herbert Walker *41st President of the United States*
†Campos, Roel C. *commissioner*
†Card, Andrew H., Jr., *federal official*
Chao, Elaine L. *secretary of labor*
Cheney, Richard B. (Dick Cheney) *Vice President of the United States*
Chesser, Judy Lee *municipal official*
Chrétien, Raymond A.J. *ambassador*
Chrobog, Juergen *ambassador*
Chuang, Yii-Der *diplomat*
Churchill, Malcolm Hughes *retired diplomat, financial analyst*
Cohen, William Sebastian *consultant, former federal official, former senator*
Collins, James Franklin *retired ambassador*
Collins, Keith *federal executive*
Cook, Michael Blanchard *government executive*
Coy, Curtis L. *federal official*
Craner, Lorne Whitney *federal official*
Crock, Jonathan Mark *diplomat*
Crocker, Chester Arthur *diplomat, scholar, federal agency administrator*
Cropp, Linda W. *city official*
Cutler, Walter Leon *diplomat, foundation executive*
†Damelin, Harold *federal official*
†Danzig, Richard Jeffrey *former government official, lawyer*
Dawson, Horace Greeley, Jr., *former diplomat, government official*
†Dell, Christopher William *ambassador*
†Deming, Rust M. *ambassador*
†DeThomas, Joseph Michael *ambassador*
Duelfer, Charles A. *diplomat*
Duemling, Robert Werner *diplomat, museum director*
†Duffy, Michael F. *commissioner*
Eastham, Alan Walter, Jr., *foreign service officer, lawyer*
Eddy, John Joseph *diplomat*
Einaudi, Luigi Roberto *diplomat, educator*
Eizenstat, Stuart Elliot *ambassador, lawyer*
Eliasson, Jan K. *Swedish ambassador*
†Elnakib, Hesham Moussa *diplomat*
Ely-Raphel, Nancy *diplomat*
Ensenat, Donald Burnham *ambassador, lawyer*
Evans, Donald L. *secretary of commerce*
Federspiel, Ulrik *diplomat*
Feierstein, Mark Barry *pollster*
Fishel, Andrew S. *director, federal*
†Fishman, Len *state commissioner*
FitzGerald, William Henry G. *diplomat, corporation executive*
Fleisher, Eric Wilfrid *retired foreign service officer*
Franco, Omar *governmental relations administrator*
†Frankel, Emil H. *transporation policy secretary*
Frawley Bagley, Elizabeth *government advisor, ambassador*
†Freeman, Russell Fuller *ambassador*
†Fried, Daniel *ambassador*
Fritsche, Claudia *diplomat, ambassador*
†Gadsden, James Irvin *ambassador*
†Gallis, Paul Eugene *government executive*
†Gantt, Harvey B. *former mayor*
Garthoff, Raymond Leonard *diplomat, diplomatic historian*
Gatons, Anna-Marie Kilmade *government official*
Gaull, Erik Samuel *municipal official*
Gaviria Trujillo, Cesar *international organization administrator, former president of Colombia, economist*
Gelbard, Robert Sidney *ambassador*
Gerry, Dale Francis *defense adviser, legislative administrator*
Gessaman, Donald Eugene *government executive, federal official, consultant*
Giffin, Gordon D. *former ambassador, lawyer*
Gilliom, Judith Carr *government official*
†Ginsberg, Marc C. *former diplomat, investment company executive*
†Glassman, Cynthia A. *commissioner*
Gregorian, Raffi *diplomat*
Grove, Brandon Hambright, Jr., *diplomat*
†Hall, Kathryn Walt *ambassador*
†Hammond, Anthony *commissioner*
Harrop, William Caldwell *retired ambassador, foreign service officer*
Hawke, John Daniel, Jr., *United States Comptroller of the Currency*
Hayes, Allene Valerie Farmer *government executive*
†Hecklinger, Richard E. *ambassador*
Heivilin, Donna Mae *government executive*
†Herbst, John Edward *diplomat*
Herman, Alexis M. *former labor secretary*
†Hernreich, Nancy *federal official*
Horowitz, Herbert Eugene *retired diplomat*
†Hull, Edmund J. *ambassador*
Hunter, Michael James *state government official, lawyer, educator*
†Ilkin, Baki *diplomat*
Indyk, Martin S. *diplomat*
†Ivry, David *diplomat*
†Jacobs, Susan S. *ambassador*
†Jarque Uribe, Carlos *former federal official*
Jee, Justin Soonho *government official*
Jensen, Donald Norman *diplomat, writer*
†Jeter, Howard F. *diplomat*
Jones, Brian W. *federal official*
Jones, James Robert *ambassador, former congressman, lawyer*
Joseph, James Alfred *ambassador*
Kaiser, Philip Mayer *retired diplomat*
†Kampelman, Max M. *former ambassador, lawyer*
Kattouf, Theodore E. *ambassador*
Kauzlarich, Richard Dale *retired ambassador, political scientist, consultant*
Keating, Francis Anthony, II, *former governor, lawyer*
Keating, Robert B. *ambassador*
†Killgore, Andrew Ivy *former ambassador*
Koempel, Michael L. *government official, researcher*
Koskinen, John Andrew *government executive*
†La Rocque, Gene Robert *retired naval officer, government official, author*
Larson, Alan Philip *federal official*
Lastowka, James Anthony *former federal agency executive, lawyer*
†Lee, Hongkoo *diplomat*
Lilly, William Eldridge *government official*
Livingood, Wilson S. *law enforcement official*
†Loftis, Robert G. *ambassador*
Lovell, Malcolm Read, Jr., *public policy institute executive, educator, former government official, former trade association executive*
Lowe, Mary Frances *federal government official*
Lowenstein, James Gordon *former diplomat, international consultant*
Lucas, James Walter *federal government official*
†Lukken, Walt *commissioner*
†MacKay, Kenneth Hood, Jr., (Buddy MacKay) *federal official*
Magee, Charles Thomas *international consultant, retired diplomat*
Maisto, John F. *ambassador*
†Malinowski, Michael E. *ambassador*
†Malott, Frank Stephen *foreign service officer*
Marcotte, Michael Steven *municipal administrator*
†Martinez, Carmen M. *ambassador*
Martinez, Melquiades R. (Mel Martinez) *secretary of housing and urban development*
Mathews, Jessica Tuchman *executive, foreign policy expert*
McCamman, John William *federal official*
McCargar, James Goodrich *diplomat, writer*
†McDonald, Jackson *ambassador*
†McElveen-Hunter, Bonnie *ambassador*
†McHale, Paul F., Jr., *federal official, former congressman*
McMichael, Guy H., III, *federal official*
†McQueary, Charles E. *federal official*
†Meece, Roger A. *ambassador*
Meyer, Armin Henry *retired diplomat, author, educator*
Meyer, Laurence Harvey *former federal official*
†Michaud, Michael Alan George *diplomat, writer*
Milam, William Bryant *former ambassador, economist*
Miller, Candice S. *former state official*
†Miller, Marcia E. *federal government official*
Miller, William Green *ambassador*
Mineta, Norman Yoshio *secretary of transportation*
†Moorefield, Kenneth P. *ambassador*
Morrissey, Patricia A. *commissioner*
†Moschella, William Emil *state attorney general*
†Myers, Richard B. *chairman Joint Chiefs of Staff*
Myrick, Bismarck *diplomat*
†Nesbitt, Wanda L. *ambassador*
Newhouse, Alan Russell *federal government executive*
Nitze, William Albert *government official, lawyer, not-for-profit developer*
Norland, Donald Richard *retired foreign service officer*

Norton, Gale Ann *secretary of interior*
Nurnberger, Ralph D. *public affairs executive*
†Olson, Lyndon Lowell, Jr., *ambassador*
†Ordway, John *ambassador*
Orr, Bobette Kay *diplomat*
Owen, Henry *former ambassador, consultant*
†Oyarzabal, Antonio *diplomat*
Paige, Roderick R. *secretary of education*
†Parris, Mark Robert *ambassador*
Passage, David *diplomat*
Pendleton, Miles Stevens, Jr., *diplomat*
Perle, Richard Norman *former government official*
†Peters, F. Whitten *lawyer, former federal official*
Phillips, James D. *retired diplomat*
Phillips, Jeanne L. *ambassador*
†Pibulsonggram, Nitya *diplomat*
†Piccininno, Anthony Ray *government administrative executive*
Pierce, Margaret Hunter *government official*
Placke, James A(nthony) *foreign service officer, international affairs consultant*
Plaisted, Joan M. *diplomat*
Powell, Colin Luther *secretary of state, retired military officer, author, public speaker*
Principi, Anthony Joseph *secretary of veterans affairs*
Quainton, Anthony Cecil Eden *diplomat*
†Quinn, Maureen E. *ambassador*
Ransom, David Michael *retired ambassador*
Reed, John Hathaway *former ambassador*
Reef, Grace *government official*
†Reyes Heroles, Jesus *former Mexican government official*
Rice, Condoleezza *national security advisor*
Ridge, Thomas Joseph *secretary of homeland security*
†Rivers, Beverly D. *secretary of the district*
Rogers, Thomasina *federal commissioner*
Rogowsky, Robert Arthur *trade commission operations director, professor*
Romani, Paul Nicholas *government official*
†Rossin, Lawrence G. *ambassador*
†Rostker, Bernard *federal official*
†Rove, Karl Christian
Rumsfeld, Donald Henry *secretary of defense*
Ryan, Mary A. *diplomat*
Sacksteder, Frederick Henry *former foreign service officer*
Sakoda, Robin (Sak Sakoda) *government administrator*
Saleh, Ali-Abdullah *state official*
Saliba, George *Maltese government official*
†Salleo, Ferdinando *Italian diplomat*
†Sanderson, Janet A. *ambassador*
Sarros, P. Peter *diplomat, consultant*
Sayre, Robert Marion *ambassador*
Scarbrough, Frank Edward *government official*
Scott-Finan, Nancy Isabella *government administrator*
Seck, Mamadou Mansour *ambassador, career officer*
Sellin, Theodore *foreign service officer, consultant*
†Sharpless, Mattie R. *ambassador*
†Shiner, Josette Sheeran *ambassador*
Shinn, David Hamilton *educator, former diplomat*
Shumate, John Page *diplomat*
†Silverstein, Martin J. *ambassador*
Simmons, Anne L. *federal official*
Slater, Rodney E. *former federal official, lawyer*
Smith, Elaine Diana *foreign service officer*
†Smith, Pamela Hyde *ambassador*
Snow, John William *secretary of treasury*
Somerville, Walter Raleigh, Jr., *government official*
Sommerfelt, Soren Christian *foreign affairs, international trade consultant, former Norwegian diplomat, lawyer*
Sonnenfeldt, Helmut *former government official, educator, consultant, author*
Spiegelman, James Michael *international affairs expert*
†Stadtler, Walter Edward *diplomat*
†Stapleton, Craig Roberts *ambassador*
Steinberg, Donald Kenneth *diplomat*
Sutter, Eleanor Bly *retired diplomat*
†Teal, Arabella W. *state attorney general*
†Tefft, John *ambassador*
†Terpeluk, Peter, Jr., *ambassador*
Thawley, Michael *diplomat*
†Thomas, Gerald E. *ambassador*
Thomas, Ralph Charles, III, *federal official*
Thomas, Scott E. *federal government executive, lawyer*
Thompson, Tommy George *secretary of health and human services, former governor*
†Toner, Michael E. *commissioner*
Truman, Edwin Malcolm *federal official*
†Unlu, Tuba *diplomat, researcher*
Ushakov, Yuri Viktorovich *diplomat*
Veneman, Ann M. *secretary of agriculture*
Verville, Elizabeth Giavani *federal official*
†Vos, Joris Michael *diplomat*
†Wahba, Marcelle M. *ambassador*
Walker, David Michael *federal official*
†Walker, Edward S., Jr., *diplomat*
Walston, Roderick Eugene *federal official*
Walters, John P. *federal official*
Watson, Arthur Dennis *federal official*
Wayne, Stephen J. *government educator, writer*
†Weintraub, Ellen L. *commissioner*
West, Togo Dennis, Jr., *lawyer, former cabinet member, former aerospace executive*
Wheat, J. Marc *federal official*
Whiting, Meredith Armstrong *public affairs executive*
Williams, Anthony A. *mayor*
†Wills, E. Ashley *ambassador*
Wilson, Joseph Charles, IV, *ambassador*
Witajewski, Robert M. *diplomat*
Wolf, John S. *ambassador, federal agency administrator*
Wolfowitz, Paul Dundes *federal official, former ambassador to Indonesia*
Won, Delmond Jack Hing *commissioner*

Wulf, Norman *federal official*
Yanai, Shunji *former diplomat*
†Yates, Mary Carlin *ambassador*

FLORIDA

Bal Harbour
Horton, Jeanette *municipal government official*

Boca Raton
Brogan, Frank T. *former lieutenant governor*

Bonita Springs
Mehuron, William Otto *government official*

Boynton Beach
Polinsky, Janet Naboicheck *retired state official, former state legislator*

Brooksville
Anderson, Richard Edmund *city manager, management consultant*

Clearwater
Henderson, Janet Lynn *city commissioner, real estate broker*

Daytona Beach
Betancourt, Ralph Ernest *mayor*

Fort Lauderdale
Burleigh, A. Peter *ambassador*
†King, Donald Charles *fire rescue battalion chief*

Gainesville
Heflin, Martin Ganier *foreign service officer, international political economist*
Jones, Elizabeth Nordwall *county government official*

Hollywood
Giulianti, Mara Selena *mayor, civic worker*

Jacksonville
Delaney, John Adrian *mayor*

Jensen Beach
Peterson, David Frederick *government agency executive*

Kennedy Space Center
Banks, Lisa Jean *government official*

Merritt Island
Thomas, James Arthur *retired government official, electrical engineer*

Miami
Bouri, Michael *civil servant*
Diaz, Manuel A. *mayor*
Grist, John *retired government official, engineering consultant*
†Penelas, Alex *mayor*
Pinder, Renee Monique *diplomat*

Naples
†Edwards, Jennifer J. *county official*

Orlando
Mausser, Albert *municipal official*

Ormond Beach
Burton, Alan Harvey *city official*

Palm City
Henry, David Howe, II, *retired diplomat*

Palmetto
Angulo, Charles Bonin *foreign service officer, lawyer*

Punta Gorda
Smith-Mooney, Marilyn Patricia *city government official, management consultant and facilitator*

Saint Augustine
Borchardt, Duke *federal labor relations professional*
Bourne, John David *retired city finance executive*

Saint Petersburg
Mussett, Richard Earl *city official*

Sarasota
Hennemeyer, Robert Thomas *diplomat*
Morrow, William Earl *retired government official*

Sebastian
Eddy, Elsbeth Marie *retired government official, statistician*

Tallahassee
Bush, John Ellis (Jeb Bush) *governor*
†Crist, Charles (Charlie Crist) *state attorney general*
Hetrick, Charles Brady *county official*
Jennings, Toni *lieutenant governor*
Mortham, Sandra Barringer *former state official*
Smith, James Cloudis *secretary of state, former state attorney general*

Tampa
Freedman, Sandra Warshaw *former mayor*
Studer, William Allen *county official*

Vero Beach
Cochrane, William Henry *former city official*

GEORGIA

Atlanta
Baker, Thurbert E. *state attorney general*
Bell, Griffin B. *lawyer, former attorney general*

†Bowers, Michael Joseph *former state attorney general*
Broadnax, Walter D. *public policy educator*
Carter, Jimmy (James Earl Carter Jr.) *39th President of the United States*
Cox, Cathy *state official*
Franklin, Shirley Clarke *mayor*
†Howard, Pierre *former state official*
Laney, James Thomas *former ambassador, educator*
†Perdue, George (Sonny Perdue) *governor, state legislator*
Streeb, Gordon Lee *diplomat, economist*
Taylor, Mark *lieutenant governor*

Cartersville
Harris, Joe Frank *former governor*

Conyers
Kelly, John Hubert *diplomat, business executive*

Decatur
Gay, Robert Derril *public agency director*

Saint Simons
Douglas, William Ernest *retired government official*

Statesboro
Wood, George Ambos *city manager*

Woodland
Carter, James *mayor, educator, tax consultant, real estate agent*

HAWAII

Honolulu
†Aiona, James R., Jr., *lieutenant governor*
†Bennett, Mark J. *state attorney general*
†Bronster, Margery S *state attorney general*
Harris, Jeremy *mayor*
Hirono, Mazie Keiko *lieutenant governor*
Lingle, Linda *governor*
†Shaw, Abelina Madrid *state official*

Kailua
Sullivan, Karen Lau *real estate company executive, campaign consultant, federal commissioner*

IDAHO

Boise
Hawkins, James Victor *former state official*
Kempthorne, Dirk Arthur *governor*
Risch, James E. *lieutenant governor, former state legislator, lawyer*
†Wasden, Lawrence *state attorney general*
Wilson, Jack Fredrick *retired federal government official*

Idaho Falls
King, Ronald Amos *federal official, communications professional, retired*

Post Falls
Riggs, Jack Timothy *emergency physician, former state lieutenant governor*

ILLINOIS

AMF Ohare
Walker, Thomas Ray *city aviation commissioner*

Bloomington
Dick, Philip Wiens *county official*

Carbondale
Cole, Brad *mayor*

Chicago
Bey, Lee *municipal official*
Cherry, Robert Steven, III, *municipal administrator*
†Cullerton, John James *state senator, lawyer*
Daley, Richard Michael *mayor*
†Emmanuel, Rahm *former federal official, investment banker*
Enenbach, Mark Henry *community action agency executive, educator*
Harris, Gregory Scott *municipal official*
Johnson, Donald Harry, Jr., *government official, educator*
Keryczynskyj, Leo Ihor *county official, educator, lawyer*
†Madigan, Lisa *state attorney general*
Natarus, Burton F. *lawyer, municipal legislator*
Olk, Frederick James *county official, paralegal*
Olson, Roy Arthur *government official*
†Quinn, Patrick *lieutenant governor*
Robbins, Audrey *county official*

Decatur
Garman, Stephen Louis *city manager*

Downers Grove
Jacklin, William Thomas *retired county official, educator*

Glencoe
Morris, Robert Barrett *city manager*

Lake Zurich
Dixon, John Fulton *village manager*

Quincy
Points, Roy Wilson *municipal official*

Springfield
Blagojevich, Rod R. *governor, former congressman*
Gamble, Douglas Irvin *state official, educator*

Schmidt, Mark James *state public health official*
White, Jesse *state official*

Urbana
†Edgar, Jim *former governor*

Vernon Hills
†Ryg, Kathleen Schultz *municipal government official*

Westchester
Crois, John Henry *local government official*

INDIANA

Columbus
Carter, Pamela Lynn *former state attorney general*

Fort Wayne
Helmke, Paul (Walter Paul Helmke Jr.) *mayor, lawyer*
Lee, Timothy Earl *international agency executive, paralegal*

Huntington
Brown, Robert Clark, Jr., *county official*

Indianapolis
Carter, Steve *state attorney general*
Nass, Connie Kay *state auditor*
Peterson, Bart *mayor*
Usher, Phyllis Land *state official*

IOWA

Cedar Rapids
Novetzke, Sally Johnson *former ambassador*
Wright, Walter Edward *county official, retired army officer*

Des Moines
Anderson, Eric Anthony *city manager*
Bergman, Bruce E. *municipal official*
Corning, Joy Cole *former state official*
Culver, Chester J. *state official, educator*
Miller, Thomas J. *state attorney general*
Odell, Mary Jane *former state official*
Pederson, Sally *lieutenant governor*
Vaughan, Therese Michele *insurance commissioner*
Vilsack, Thomas *governor*

Hiawatha
Pate, Paul Danny *mayor*

Nevada
Bilyeu, Gary Edward *government official*

Oelwein
McFarlane, Beth Lucetta Troester *former mayor*

Waterloo
Johannsen, Sonia Alicia *retired county official*

West Des Moines
†Branstad, Terry Edward *former governor, lawyer*

KANSAS

Arkansas City
†Bruton, Rebecca Ann *mayor, commissioner*

Coffeyville
Garner, Jim D. *state official*

El Dorado
Adkins, William Lloyd *state official*

Hays
Gustafson, Randall Lee *city manager*

Hutchinson
†Kerr, Dave *state official, marketing professional*

Shawnee
Chaffee, Paul David *city official*

Topeka
Glasscock, Joyce H. *state official*
†Kline, Phillip D. *state attorney general*
†Moore, John Eddy *lieutenant governor*
†Sebelius, Kathleen Gilligan *governor*
†Thornburgh, Ron E. *secretary of state*

Wichita
†Knight, Robert G. *mayor, investment banker*

KENTUCKY

Bowling Green
Cooper, Davis A. *city official*

Frankfort
Brown, John Y., III, *state official*
Chandler, Albert Benjamin, III, *state attorney general*
Henry, Stephen Lewis *lieutenant governor, orthopedic surgeon, educator*
Palmore, Carol M. *state official*
Patton, Paul E. *governor*
Sonego, Ian G. *assistant attorney general*

Lexington
Miller, Pamela Gundersen *mayor*
Whitmer, Leslie Gay *federal official*

Richmond
Schwendeman, Kenneth David *government official, consultant*

LOUISIANA

Alexandria
Richmond, Angie Anna Alice Murray *government official*

Baton Rouge
Blanco, Kathleen Babineaux *lieutenant governor*
Bohlinger, Lewis Hall *state government official*
Foster, M. J., Jr., (Mike Foster) *governor*
Ieyoub, Richard Phillip *state attorney general*
McKeithen, Walter Fox *secretary of state*

New Orleans
Gates, Audrey Castine *city government administrator*
Hunter, Sue Persons *former state official*
Nagin, C. Ray *mayor*
Ortique, Revius Oliver, Jr., *city official, retired state supreme court justice*
Stansbury, Harry Case *state commissioner*

Slidell
Dearing, Reinhard Josef *city official*

MAINE

Augusta
Baldacci, John Elias *governor, former congressman*
Gwadosky, Dan A. *secretary of state*
Ketterer, Andrew *state commissioner, former state attorney general*
Rowe, G. Steven *state attorney general*

Brunswick
King, Angus S., Jr., *former governor*

Portland
†O'Leary, John *ambassador*

MARYLAND

Annapolis
†Aumann, R. Karl *state official, lawyer*
Coulter, James Bennett *state official*
Ehrlich, Robert L., Jr., *governor, former congressman*
Meima, Ralph Chester, Jr., *retired diplomat, corporate executive*
†Steele, Michael *lieutenant governor*

Baltimore
Curran, J. Joseph, Jr., *state attorney general*
Jones, Raymond Moylan *strategy and public policy educator*
Mazur, John *city administrator*
O'Malley, Martin Joseph *mayor, former councilman, lawyer*
Willis, John T. *former secretary of state*

Bel Air
O'Bryon, James Fredrick *defense executive*

Bethesda
Ackerman, Michael J. *government executive*
Bowsher, Charles Arthur *retired government official, business executive*
Gallagher, Hubert Randall *government consultant*
Green, Jerome George *federal government official*
Hempstone, Smith, Jr., *diplomat, journalist*
Ingraham, Edward Clarke, Jr., *retired foreign service officer*
Kirby, Harmon E. *retired ambassador*
Laingen, Lowell Bruce *diplomat*
Morgan, John Davis *consultant*
Neill, Denis Michael *international consultant*
North, William Haven *foreign service officer*
Peck, Edward Lionel *retired foreign service officer, corporate executive*
Rowell, Edward Morgan *retired foreign service officer, lecturer*
†Schiff, Stanley D. *diplomat, consultant*
Sober, Sidney *retired diplomat, educator*
Spector, Melbourne Louis *retired foreign service officer*
Stoddard, Philip Hendrick *foreign affairs analyst, writer*
Vest, George Southall *retired diplomat*

Burkittsville
Aughenbaugh, Deborah Ann *mayor, retired educator*

Chevy Chase
Albright, Raymond Jacob *government official*
Bush, Frederick Morris *federal official*
Lewis, Jon Roderick *political advisor*
Lukens, Alan Wood *retired ambassador and foreign service officer*
Sampas, Dorothy Myers *retired government official*

College Park
Benedick, Richard Elliot *diplomat*

Columbia
Cargo, William Ira *retired ambassador*
Scates, Alice Yeomans *former government official, consultant*

Crownsville
Hanna, James Curtis *state official*

Ellicott City
Stough, Liza Boyle *government official*

Fort Washington
Smoot, Burgess Howard *federal official*

Frederick
†Baker, Joanne Evelyn *retired government official*

Gaithersburg
French, Judson Cull *government official*
Watson, Royce Andrew *retired federal official*

Grasonville
Andrews, Archie Moulton *government official*

Kensington
Rosenthal, Alan Sayre *government official*

La Plata
Fisher, Gail Feimster *government official*

Leonardtown
Smalley, Robert Manning *government official*

Lexington Park
Morgan, Dennis Alan *retired federal official*

North Bethesda
Szabo, Daniel *government official*

Owings Mills
Nes, David Gulick *retired diplomat*

Oxford
Shepard, William Seth *government official, diplomat, writer*

Potomac
Kernan, Barbara Desind *senior government executive*
Roesser, Jean Wolberg *state official*

Rockville
Chiogioji, Melvin Hiroaki *former government official, entrepreneur*
Corley, Rose Ann McAfee *government official*
Epps, Leon Anthony *government official*
Ewing, Blair Gordon *federal official*
Sacchet, Edward Michael *foreign service officer*
Woodcock, Janet *federal official*

Silver Spring
Goott, Daniel *government official, consultant*
Kelly, John Joseph, Jr., *government executive*
Ware, Thaddeus Van *government official*

Takoma Park
Lott, Alfred Davis *assistant city manager*

Towson
McGrain, John William, Jr., *county government official*

MASSACHUSETTS

Amesbury
Parker, William H., III, *federal official*

Boston
Galvin, William Francis *state official*
†Healey, Kerry Murphy *lieutenant governor*
Menino, Thomas M. *mayor*
Reilly, Thomas F. *state attorney general*
†Romney, W. Mitt *governor*
Shattuck, John *diplomat, civil rights lawyer, educator*

Bridgewater
Heffernan, Peter John *state official*

Cambridge
Herold, Jill Mehlhop *public administrator*
†Hunt, Swanee G. *public policy educator, former ambassador*
Kelman, Steven Jay *management educator*
Porter, Roger Blaine *government official, educator*
Seidel, Samuel Learned Richard Cartun *governmental researcher*

Canton
Fuchs, Lawrence Howard *government official, educator*

Concord
Rathore, Naeem Gul *retired United Nations official*

Dartmouth
Connors, Robert Leo *city official*

Fitchburg
Railsback, David Phillips *former state official, lawyer*

Ipswich
Phillips, Christopher Hallowell *retired diplomat*

Littleton
Crory, Mary *town official*

Lowell
Donoghue, Eileen M. *former mayor*
Natsios, Nicholas Andrew *retired foreign service officer*

Lynn
McManus, Patrick J. *mayor, lawyer, accountant*

Medford
Bosworth, Stephen Warren *ambassador*

Salem
Prokopy, John Alfred *government consultant*

Sherborn
Kennedy, Chester Ralph, Jr., *former state official, art director*

Springfield
Albano, Michael J. *mayor*

Taunton
Lopes, Maria Fernandina *commissioner*

West Hyannisport
Devine, Nancy *postmaster*

Worcester
Murray, Timothy P. *mayor*

Yarmouth Port
Nichols, Robert Lyman *retired foreign service officer, lecturer*

MICHIGAN

Ann Arbor
Sheldon, Ingrid Kristina *former mayor of Ann Arbor, bookkeeper*

Bloomfield Hills
Fauver, John William *mayor, retired business executive*

Cadillac
Walker, Dale Maxwell *city official*

Dearborn
†Lin, Paul kuang-Hsien *assemblyman, educator*

Detroit
Bell Wilson, Carlotta A. *state official, consultant*
†Kilpatrick, Kwame *mayor*

Fennville
Kamman, Curtis Warren *retired ambassador*

Grand Rapids
Logie, John Hoult *mayor, lawyer*

Howell
Wagoner, William Douglas *public administrator, urban/regional planner*

Lansing
†Cannon, Patrick D. *federal offical, broadcaster*
†Cherry, John D., Jr., *lieutenant governor*
Christian, Sandra Svec *retired state official*
†Cox, Mike *state attorney general*
Granholm, Jennifer Mulhern *governor*
Hills, Rusty *state official*
Johnson, Rick *state official*
Posthumus, Richard Earl *former lieutenant governor, farmer*

Mount Clemens
Kolakowski, Diana Jean *county commissioner*

Muskegon
Roy, Paul Emile, Jr., *county official*

Negaunee
Friggens, Thomas George *state official, historian*

Pinckney
Davis, Robert Leach *retired government official, consultant*

MINNESOTA

Chisholm
Peterson, Marjorie *former mayor*

Crosslake
Beaupre, Elaine Marcia Kenow *retired chamber of commerce executive*
†Larson, Paul Michael *city planner*

Golden Valley
Leppik, Margaret White *municipal official*

Minneapolis
Carlson, Arne Helge *former governor*
Mondale, Joan Adams *wife of former Vice President of United States*
Quinlan, C. Patrick *retired diplomat, educator*
Rybak, R.T. *mayor*
Swan, Wallace Kent *county official*

Northfield
Flaten, Robert Arnold *former ambassador*
Levin, Burton *diplomat*

Saint Paul
Hatch, Mike *state attorney general*
Kiffmeyer, Mary *state official*
†Molnau, Carol *lieutenant governor*
†Pawlenty, Tim *governor*

MISSISSIPPI

Gulfport
Dickerson, Monar Steve *city official*
Mc Call, Jerry Chalmers *retired government official*

Jackson
Clark, Eric C. *state official*
Moore, Mike *state attorney general*
Musgrove, David Ronald *governor*
Tuck, Amy *lieutenant governor*
Winter, William Forrest *former governor, lawyer*

Long Beach
Easton, Jill Johanna *state official*

Wesson
Pickering, Garry Marlon *state official*

MISSOURI

Bridgeton
Brauer, Stephen Franklin *diplomat, manufacturing company executive*

Columbia
Lubensky, Earl Henry *diplomat, anthropologist*

Jefferson City
Blunt, Matt *secretary of state*
Holden, Bob *governor*
Maxwell, Joe Edwin *lieutenant governor*
Nixon, Jeremiah W. (Jay Nixon) *state attorney general*

Kansas City
Barnes, Kay *mayor*
Davis, Richard Francis *city government official*
Price, Charles H., II, *former ambassador*
Stroup, Kala Mays *educational alliance administrator, former state higher education commissioner*

Queen City
Wilson, Roger Byron *former governor, school administrator*

Saint Louis
Geary, Daniel Patrick *postal service worker*
Harmon, Clarence *former mayor, law educator*
Slay, Francis G. *mayor*

Springfield
Montgomery, Linda Stroupe *county official*

MONTANA

Billings
Larsen, Richard Lee *former mayor and city manager, business, municipal and labor relations consultant, arbitrator*

Clancy
Ekanger, Laurie *retired state official, contractor*

Fairfield
Graf, Ervin Donald *municipal official*

Helena
Brown, Robert J. (Bob Brown) *state official*
Cooney, Mike *former secretary of state*
Mazurek, Joseph P. *lawyer, former state legislator*
McGrath, Mike *attorney general, lawyer*
Ohs, Karl *lieutenant governor*

NEBRASKA

Lincoln
Beermann, Allen J. *former state official*
Boyle, Anne C. *state commissioner*
†Bruning, Jon Cumberland *state attorney general*
Gale, John A. *secretary of state*
Hasselbalch, Marilyn Jean *state official*
Heineman, David *lieutenant governor*
Johanns, Michael O. *governor*
Novoa, Yanira *diplomat*

North Platte
Hawks, James Wade *county highway superintendent, county surveyor*

Omaha
Daub, Hal *former mayor, former congressman*
Fahey, Mike *mayor*
Moore, Scott *former state official*
Pirsch, Carol McBride *county official, former state senator, community relations manager*

NEVADA

Carson City
Guinn, Kenny C. *governor*
Heller, Dean *state official*
Hunt, Lorraine T. *lieutenant governor*
†Sandoval, Brian *state attorney general*

Henderson
Gibson, James B. *mayor*
McKinney, Sally Vitkus *state official*

Las Vegas
Goodman, Oscar Baylin *mayor, lawyer*
†Hammargren, Lonnie L. *former lieutenant governor*
Vandever, Judith Ann *county official*

Reno
Fregulia, Jeanette Marie *county official*

NEW HAMPSHIRE

Concord
Benson, Craig Robert *governor*
Gardner, William Michael *state official*
Taylor, Stephen H. *state commissioner*

Durham
Selig, Todd Irving *municipal official*

Grantham
Feldman, Roger Bruce *government official*

Hanover
Haselton, Mary Michelson *retired foreign service officer, artist*

Hooksett
Denaco, Parker Alden *state official, lawyer, arbitrator*

Keene
†Heed, Peter W. *state attorney general*

Munsonville
Kirk, Jane Seaver *municipal government administrator*

New Durham
Herman, William George *municipal government executive*

NEW JERSEY

Camden
Uhler, Walter Charles *government official, writer, reviewer*

Cape May Point
Fraser, Malcolm Cavanagh *mayor*

Clifton
Anzaldi, James Anthony *mayor*

East Orange
Corbitt, Ann Marie *municipal official*

Elizabeth
Bollwage, J. Christian *mayor*

Freehold
Vernick, Jeffrey Francis *county official*

Irvington
Paden, Harry *municipal official*

Jackson
Washington, William Nicolai *government official*

Jersey City
Schundler, Bret Davis *former mayor*

Kearny
John, Ricky *state official*

Little Ferry
†Navarro-Steinel, Catherine A. *municipal official*

Morristown
MacKinnis, Ann Phelps *municipal government and land use management executive*

Newark
Davis, Yvonne D. *county official*
Martin, James Hanley *deputy state attorney general*

Princeton
†Doyle, Michael W. *federal official*
Matlock, Jack Foust, Jr., *diplomat*

Rockaway
Catlin, Robert Thomas *city planning consultant*

Sea Isle City
Tull, Theresa Anne *retired ambassador*

Somerset
Soaries, DeForest B., Jr., *former state official*

Trenton
Castro, Ida L. *state official, former federal official*
Farmer, John J. *state commissioner, former state attorney general*
†Harvey, Peter C. *state attorney general*
McGreevey, James E. *governor*
†Thomas, Regena L. *secretary of state*

Vincentown
Trainor, Lillian (Midge Trainor) *elections official, campaign consultant*

NEW MEXICO

Albuquerque
Giller, Edward Bonfoy *retired government official, retired air force officer*

Los Alamos
†Gonzales, Stephanie *state official*

Mesilla
Lewis, Delano Eugene *ambassador, former broadcast executive*

Santa Fe
Bradley, Walter D. *lieutenant governor, real estate broker*
Denish, Diane D. *lieutenant governor*
Madrid, Patricia A. *state attorney general*
†Richardson, William Blaine *governor*
Vigil-Giron, Rebecca *state official*

NEW YORK

Albany
Berman, Carol *commissioner*
†Chretien, Margaret Cecilia *public administrator*
Clarey, Donald Alexander *government affairs consultant*
Croce, Alan J. *government agency executive*
Daniels, Randy A. *secretary of state*
Donohue, Mary *lieutenant governor*
Herman, Robert S. *former state official, economist, educator*
Pataki, George E. *governor*
Spitzer, Eliot *state attorney general*
Toren, Mark *state official, econometrician*
Treadwell, Alexander F. *former state official, political party chairman & leader*

Ballston Lake
Cotter, William Donald *former state commissioner, former newspaper editor*

Brewster
Bates, Barbara J. Neuner *retired municipal official*

Buffalo
Giambra, Joel Anthony *county executive*
†Masiello, Anthony M. (Tony Masiello) *mayor*
Nowak, Carol Ann *city official*

Canandaigua
Barden, George V. *county official, watershed specialist*

Chappaqua
Laun, Louis Frederick *government official*

Elmira
Olthof, Randy James *commissioner*

Floral Park
Corbett, William John *government and public relations consultant, lawyer*

Flushing
Rusu, Sir Andrew Peter (Sir Andrew Rusu Baron Rochefort) *ambassador, lawyer*

Hempstead
Parola, Frederick Edson, Jr., *state official*

Laurelton
Goodman, Robert Merrill *United Nations executive, artist*

Middle Village
Rowan, John Patrick *city official*

Monticello
Sorensen, Alan John *county official*

New York
Abulhasan, Mohammad Abdulla *ambassador*
†Aguilar Zinser, Adolfo Miguel *diplomat*
†Alzamora, Carlos *ambassador*
Anderegg, Julius Fidelis *diplomat, consul general*
†Arias, Inocencío F. *diplomat*
Arystanbekova, Akmaral Khaidarovna *diplomat*
†Atsada, Chaiyanam *diplomat*
Blinken, Donald *ambassador, investment banker*
Bloomberg, Michael Rubens *mayor*
Boisson, Jacques Louis *diplomat, ambassador*
Bowles, Erskine *White House staff member*
Bowles, Newton Rowell *United Nations executive*
Carlson, Mitchell Lans *international technical advisor*
Chaves, Jose Maria *diplomat, foundation administrator, lawyer, educator*
Clinton, William Jefferson (Bill Clinton) *42d President of the United States*
Cohn, David Herc *retired foreign service officer*
Corwin, Jules Arthur *civil servant*
Cunningham, James Blair *ambassador*
Curley, Walter Joseph Patrick *diplomat, investment banker*
†Dangue Rewaka, Denis *diplomat*
Dayson, Diane Harris *superintendent, park ranger*
†Dejammet, Alain *diplomat*
Doherty, Patrick William *municipal official*
Dos Santos, Carlos *ambassador*
Eisenstadt, G. Michael *diplomat, writer, educator, researcher*
Enkhsaikhan, Jargalsaikhan *ambassador*
Finauri, Graciela Maria *foreign service professional*
†Fowler, Robert Ramsay *former Canadian government official*
Gambari, Ibrahim Agboola *diplomat*
Gardner, Richard Newton *diplomat, lawyer, educator*
Gartner, Alan P. *municipal official*
Gelb, Bruce Stuart *city commissioner, consultant*
Giuliani, Rudolph W. *former mayor, consultant, lawyer*
Grunwald, Henry Anatole *ambassador, editor, writer*
Guillot, Cyril Etienne *international organization administrator*
Heimbold, Charles Andreas, Jr., *ambassador*
Holbrooke, Richard Charles Albert *ambassador, government official, investment banker, author*
Ingolfsson, Thorsteinn *diplomat*
Katz, Abraham *retired foreign service officer*
†Kavan, Jan *UN General Assembly official, former Czech Republic government official*
Kennedy, Patrick F. *federal official*
Koch, Edward I. *former mayor, lawyer*
Lavrov, Sergei Viktorovich *ambassador*
Lehman, Orin *retired state official*
Mabilangan, Felipe Hugo, Jr., *Philippine diplomat*
McKenna, George Norton *government educator*
†Morial, Marc Haydel *former mayor, association executive*
Murphy, Richard William *retired foreign service officer, Middle East specialist, consultant*
Neewoor, Anund Priyay *ambassador*
Negroponte, John Dimitri *ambassador*
Okun, Herbert Stuart *diplomat, educator*
Platt, Nicholas *Asia specialist, retired ambassador*
Rabiu, Badru I.O. *federal official*
Ranald, Ralph Arthur *former government official, educator*
†Rapoport, Miles S. *state official*
Rohatyn, Felix George *ambassador*
Saleh, Mohammed *diplomat*
Schlesinger, Stephen Cannon *educator*
Segesváry, Victor Györö *retired diplomat*
Shearer, Walter Christians *diplomat*
Sheehan, Michael Andrew *diplomat*

Shelley, Sally Swing *United Nations official, broadcaster*
Siv, Sichan Aun *ambassador*
Swing, William Lacy *ambassador*
†Tello Macias, Manuel *diplomat*
Townsend, Kathleen Kennedy *former lieutenant governor*
Urroz-Rapold, Patricia Julia S. *retired diplomat, writer*
†Vural, Volkan *Turkish representative to UN*
Wastberg, Olle M. *diplomat*
†Wibisono, Makarim *diplomat*
Williamson, Richard Salisbury *ambassador*
Wyzner, Eugeniusz *diplomat*

Newburgh
Zarutskie, Andrew John *town official*

Newtonville
Conroy-LaCivita, Diane Catherine *city administrator*

Ogdensburg
Krol, John Casimir *city manager, municipal planner*

Plainview
Bell, James Thomas *housing authority official*

Port Jefferson
Strong, Robert Thomas *former mayor, middle school educator*

Riverdale
Mendez, Ruben Policarpio *diplomat, educator, economist*

Romulus
Ostrander, Robert Edwin *retired United Nations interregional advisor, petroleum company executive*

Syracuse
Driscoll, Matthew J. *mayor, restaurant manager, real estate developer*
Ortiz, Fernando, Jr., *commissioner*
Sullivan, Michael Joachim *financial executive*

Troy
St. Hilaire, David William *county official, financial manager*

Watertown
Coe, Benjamin Plaisted *retired state official*

Williamsville
Danni, F. Robert *town official*

Yonkers
Dinanzio, Philip Joseph *city official*

NORTH CAROLINA

Charlotte
Brynn, Edward Paul *former ambassador*
McCrory, Patrick *mayor*

Clinton
Hobbs, Jerry Dean *county manager*

Conover
Carmichael, Richard E. *government official, financial manager, educator*

Durham
Kerckhoff, Sylvia Stansbury *mayor*

High Point
Moore, Jeffrey A. *municipal official*
Pate, William Patrick *city manager*

Merritt
de Vos, Peter Jon *ambassador*

Mill Spring
Saunders, Barry Wayne *state official*

New Bern
Perdue, Beverly E. *lieutenant governor, geriatric consultant*

Pittsboro
Cotter, Michael William *retired ambassador, business consultant*

Raleigh
Boyles, Harlan Edward *former state official*
Cooper, Roy Asberry, III, *state attorney general, lawyer*
Easley, Michael F. *governor*
Johnston, Linda Tidwell *municipal official*
Marshall, Elaine Folk *state official*

Southern Pines
Toon, Malcolm *former ambassador*

Wilson
Wyatt, Edward Avery, V, *city manager*

NORTH DAKOTA

Bismarck
Clark, Tony *state commissioner*
Dalrymple, Jack *lieutenant governor*
Gilmore, Kathi *state treasurer*
Hoeven, John *governor*
Jaeger, Alvin A. (Al Jaeger) *secretary of state*
Stenehjem, Wayne Kevin *state attorney general, lawyer*

Edinburg
Myrdal, Rosemarie Caryle *state official, former state legislator*

Mandan
Heitkamp, Heidi *former state attorney general*
Paul, Jack Davis *retired state official, addictions consultant*

OHIO

Akron
Plusquellic, Donald L. *mayor*

Cedarville
Wiggins, Robert Ray *criminal justice educator*

Cincinnati
Kelley, Cleophus O. *city official*
†Reis, Peggy D. *township official*

Cleveland
Campbell, Jane Louise *mayor*
Chema, Thomas V. *consultant, government official, lawyer*
Robiner, Donald Maxwell *lawyer, former federal official*
†White, Michael Reed *former mayor*

Columbus
Blackwell, J(ohn) Kenneth *state official*
†Bradley, Jennette *lieutenant governor*
Coleman, Michael B. *mayor*
Draghi, Raymond Amadea *retired postal worker*
Householder, Larry *state official, small business owner*
Lashutka, Gregory S. *mayor, lawyer*
Montgomery, Betty Dee *state auditor, former state attorney general, former state legislator*
Petro, James Michael *state attorney general*
Speck, Samuel Wallace, Jr., *state official*
Taft, Bob *governor*

Dayton
Lashley, William Bartholomew *county official*

Gahanna
†Sherman, Ruth Todd *government advisor, counselor, consultant*

Mentor
Traub, Ronald Matthew *municipal administrator*

Toledo
†Finkbeiner, Carlton S. (Carty Finkbeiner) *mayor*

Walton Hills
†Thellmann, Edward L. *mayor*

Wright Patterson Afb
Caudill, Tom Holden *governmental policy and analysis executive*

OKLAHOMA

Ada
Anoatubby, Bill *governor of Chickawaw Nation*

Bethany
Hendrick, Howard H. *state government administrator*

Lawton
Ellenbrook, Edward Charles *county official, small business owner*

Norman
Corr, Edwin Gharst *ambassador*
Perkins, Edward J. *diplomat*
Price, Linda Rice *community development administrator*

Oklahoma City
Edmondson, William Andrew *state attorney general*
Fallin, Mary Copeland *lieutenant governor*
†Henry, C. Brad *governor*
Humphreys, Kirk *mayor*
†Jenkins, Sherry L. *state accounting manager*
McKenzie, Clif Allen *Indian tribe official, accountant*
Savage, Susan M. *state official, former mayor*

Tulsa
LaFortune, Bill *mayor*

OREGON

Eugene
Bascom, Ruth F. *retired mayor*
Torrey, James D. *mayor, communications executive, consultant*

Lake Oswego
Campbell, Colin Herald *former mayor*

Monmouth
Khe, Sriram *planning educator*

Portland
Church-Gaultier, Lorene Kemmerer *retired government official*
Katz, Vera *mayor, former college administrator, state legislator*
Kitzhaber, John Albert *former governor, physician, former state senator*
Kleim, E. Denise *city official*

Salem
Bradbury, William Chapman, III, *state official*
Kulongoski, Theodore Ralph *governor, former judge*
Myers, Hardy *state attorney general, lawyer*

PROFESSIONAL INDEX 6359 GOVERNMENT: EXECUTIVE ADMINISTRATION

PENNSYLVANIA

Allentown
Glaessmann, Doris Ann *former county official, consultant*

Camp Hill
Besch, Nancy Adams *county official*

Chambersburg
Ross, Larry Michael *county economic development official*

Donora
Todd, Norma Ross *retired government official*

Fort Washington
Saurman, George Edwin *legislator, retired*

Girardville
Dempsey, Thomas Joseph *retired postmaster*

Glen Mills
Dunion, Celeste Mogab *consultant, township official*

Harrisburg
†Baker Knoll, Catherine *lieutenant governor*
Fisher, D. Michael *state attorney general*
Hafer, Barbara *state official*
Jubelirer, Robert C. *lieutenant governor*
O'Connor, Charles Edward, Jr., *state government official, lawyer*
Pizzingrilli, Kim *state official*
Reed, Stephen Russell *mayor*
Rendell, Edward Gene *governor, former mayor, lawyer*
Wolfe, Gary Donald *library commissioner, retired state education official*

Lititz
Koch, Bruce R. *diplomat*

Newtown
Brennan, Thomas John *city and state official, consultant, educator*

Norristown
Biondi, Anthony *municipal official*

Philadelphia
Goldenberg, Nancy Ann *city planner*
Harris, Raymond Jesse *retired government official*
Latsios, Barbara Lynn *government official*
Schweiker, Mark S. *former governor*
Wolfe, J. Matthew *lawyer*

Pittsburgh
Crawford, Robin Yvette *county caseworker*
Donahoe, David Lawrence *state and city official*
Mitchell, George Charles *diplomat, international consultant, mediator, educator, writer*
Murphy, Thomas J., Jr., *mayor*
O'Neill, Paul Henry *former government official*
Simpson, Daniel H. *ambassador*

Sayre
†Smith, Robin L. *municipal official*

State College
Lamb, Robert Edward *retired diplomat, professional society administrator*

West Chester
Dinniman, Andrew Eric *county commissioner, history educator, academic program director, international studies educator*

York
Wiles, William Wharton *retired federal government official*

RHODE ISLAND

Kingston
Sundlun, Bruce *former governor*

Narragansett
O'Keefe, Beverly Disbrow *state official, federal official*

Pawtucket
†McGill, Kenneth R. *mayoral aide*
Metivier, Robert Emmett *retired mayor*

Providence
†Carcieri, Donald L. *governor*
Fogarty, Charles Joseph *lieutenant governor*
†Lynch, Patrick C. *state attorney general*
†Pine, Jeffrey Barry *lawyer, former state attorney general*
Younkin, Richard Ambrose *state official, air quality specialist*

Warwick
Darlington, David Alan *government relations professional*

SOUTH CAROLINA

Charleston
Lader, Philip *lawyer, government official, diplomat, business executive, university president*

Columbia
†Bauer, R. Andre *lieutenant governor*
McMaster, Henry Dargan *state attorney general*
Morris, John Allen, Jr., *state government administrator, educator*
Sanford, Marshall (Mark Sanford) *governor, former congressman*
Waites, Candy Yaghjian *former state official*

Edgefield
Gambrell, Olin Eric, III, *municipal official*

Lexington
Morris, Earle Elias, Jr., *retired state official, business executive*

Sumter
Moore, Verna *county official*

SOUTH DAKOTA

Brookings
Burge, Steven Donald *city administrator*

Pierre
†Daugaard, Dennis M. *lieutenant governor*
†Long, Larry *state attorney general*

Rapid City
Eccarius, Scott *state official, eye surgeon*
Hillard, Carole *former lieutenant governor*

Sioux Falls
Justman, Dick Joseph *public works administrator*

TENNESSEE

Alcoa
Dunlap, Bill *municipal administrator*

Memphis
Herenton, Willie W. *mayor*

Nashville
Bredesen, Philip Norman *governor*
Darnell, Riley Carlisle *state government official, lawyer*
Gore, Tipper (Mary Elizabeth Gore) *wife of the former vice president of the United States*
Summers, Paul *state attorney general*
Thomas, Hazel Beatrice *state official*
†Wadley, Fredia Stovall *state commissioner*
Wilder, John Shelton *lieutenant governor*

Oak Ridge
†Holloway, Jacqueline *county commissioner*

Springfield
Nutting, Paul John *city manager*

Tazewell
Herrell, Virgil Lee *county official*

Townsend
Sundquist, Don *former governor, former congressman, sales corporation executive*

TEXAS

Arlington
Hall, Anna Christene *retired government official*

Austin
Abbott, Greg Wayne *state attorney general, former state supreme court justice*
Cooke, Carlton Lee, Jr., *mayor*
†Dewhurst, David *lieutenant governor*
Gates, Charles Woodley, Sr., *city official*
Johnson, Lady Bird (Mrs. Claudia Alta Taylor) *wife of former President of United States*
Perry, Rick *governor*
Ratliff, William *former stae senator; lieutenant governor, civil engineer*
Richards, Ann Willis *former governor*
†Todd, Bruce M. *public affairs executive, former mayor*
Townsend, Richard Marvin *government insurance executive, city manager, consultant*
†Wynn, Will *mayor*

Beaumont
Lord, Evelyn Marlin *mayor*

Brenham
Pipes, Paul Ray *county commissioner*

Buffalo
Standley, John Robert *city official*

Dallas
Baker, James Edward *city planner*
Campos, Nora *government official*
Jackson, Jimmy Lee *commissioner*
Lake, Joseph Edward *ambassador*
Miller, Laura *mayor, journalist*
Rubottom, Roy Richard, Jr., *retired diplomat and educator, consultant*

El Paso
Caballero, Raymond Cesar *former mayor*
†Wardy, Joe *mayor*

Gainesville
Broyles, Stephen Douglas *public administrator*

Harlingen
Matz, James Richard *municipal official*

Houston
Brown, Lee P. *mayor*
Brown, Lee Patrick *mayor, city official, law enforcement educator*
Kendrick, Robert Warren *county official*
Sipahioglu, Hatice Elcin *diplomat, interpreter/translator*

La Feria
Philip, Sunny Koipurathu *municipal official*

Lago Vista
Barrett, Archie Don *retired federal official, educator*

Laredo
†Gonzalez, Rene *government executive*

Lubbock
Stuart, Frank Adell *county official*

New Braunfels
Krueger, Robert Charles *former ambassador, former senator, congressman*

Plano
Daley, William M. *former federal government official*

Port Isabel
Pon-Salazar, Francisco Demetrio *diplomat, educator, deacon, counselor*

Richardson
Lee, Jimmy Che-Yung *city planner*

San Antonio
Catto, Henry Edward *former government official, former ambassador*
Garza, Ed *mayor*
Henderson, Connie Chorlton *city planner, artist and writer*

UTAH

North Salt Lake
Johnson, Frank *educator, retired state official*

Salt Lake City
Alter, Edward T. *state treasurer*
Anderson, Ross Carl *mayor, lawyer*
Corradini, Deedee *mayor*
Deamer, Michael Lynn *mayor, lawyer, accountant*
Leavitt, Michael Okerlund *governor*
Quinn, Eugene Frederick *foreign service officer, clergyman*
Schow, Terry D. *state official*
Shurtleff, Mark L. *state attorney general*
Sorenson, Roger A. *international relations consultant*
Stephens, Martin R. *state official*
Walker, Olene S. *lieutenant governor*

VERMONT

Burlington
Clavelle, Peter *mayor*
Dean, Howard *former governor*
Glitman, Maynard Wayne *foreign service officer*

Calais
Levin, Herbert *retired diplomat, retired foundation executive*

Middlebury
Kunin, Madeleine May *former ambassador to Switzerland, former governor*

Montpelier
†Douglas, James Holley *governor*
†Dubie, Brian E. *lieutenant governor*
Markowitz, Deborah Lynn *state government official*
Racine, Douglas A *former lieutenant governor*
Sorrell, William H. *state attorney general*

Peacham
Engle, James Bruce *ambassador*

South Londonderry
Spiers, Ronald Ian *diplomat*

Waterbury
Morse, James L. *commissioner, former state supreme court justice*

VIRGINIA

Alexandria
Brotzman, Donald Glenn *government official, lawyer*
Costagliola, Francesco *retired government official*
Ensslin, Robert Frank, Jr., *retired association executive and military officer*
Fitton, Harvey Nelson, Jr., *former government official, publishing consultant*
Freeman-Wilson, Karen *former attorney general, prosecutor, educational association administrator*
Havens, Harry Stewart *former federal assistant comptroller general, government consultant*
Helman, Gerald Bernard *government official*
Hurley, John Arthur *national security advisor*
McCaffrey, Barry Richard *federal official, retired army officer*
McGuire, Roger Alan *retired foreign service officer*
McNicol, David Leon *federal official, consultant*
†Morris, Warren Frederick *retired government agency executive*
Pringle, Robert Maxwell *diplomat*
Saloom, Joseph A., III, *diplomat*
Skoug, Kenneth Nordly, Jr., *diplomat*
Tucker, Alvin Leroy *retired government official*

Annandale
Christianson, Geryld B. *government relations consultant*
Rogers, Stephen Hitchcock *former ambassador*

Arlington
Aggrey, Orison Rudolph *former ambassador, university administrator*
Allison, Graham Tillett, Jr., *federal government official*
Bolster, Archie Milburn *retired foreign service officer*
Boster, Davis Eugene *retired ambassador*
Bune, Karen Louise *criminal justice official*
Douglass, John W. *commissioner*
Edmondson, William Brockway *retired foreign service officer*
Galloway, William Jefferson *former foreign service officer*
†Itoh, William H. *former ambassador*
†Katzen, Jay Kenneth *foundation administrator, consultant, former foreign service officer*
Krys, Sheldon Jack *retired foreign service officer, career minister*
Mc Donald, John Warlick *diplomat, global strategist*
Ochmanek, David Alan *defense analyst*
Pickering, Thomas Reeve *diplomat*
Schneider, William, Jr., *commissioner*
Smith, Myron George *former government official, consultant*
Taggart, G. Bruce *government program executive*
Umminger, Bruce Lynn *government official, scientist, educator*
Winter, Harvey John *retired government official*
Wood, Heidi *commissioner*

Burke
Pfister, Cloyd Harry *consultant, former career officer*

Chantilly
Pajak, Roger F. *federal official, policy adviser, lecturer, writer*

Charlottesville
Newsom, David Dunlop *foreign service officer, educator*

Chesapeake
Ward, William E. *mayor*

Dublin
Lineberry, Rebecca J. *municipal official, treasurer*

Dulles
Huddle, Franklin Pierce, Jr., *diplomat*
†Minikes, Stephan Michael *ambassador, lawyer, banker*
Montgomery, William D. *ambassador*
Yates, John Melvin *retired ambassador*

Dumfries
Wolle, William Down *foreign service officer*

Fairfax
Beckler, David Zander *government official, science administrator*
Haskett, Dianne Louise *former mayor, lawyer, consultant*
Pyatt, Everett Arno *government official*
†Ruedy, Ralph H. *diplomat, consultant*

Falls Church
Beeman, Josiah Horton *diplomat*
†Beyer, Donald Sternoff, II, *state official*
Ward, George Frank, Jr., *ambassador*

Franklin
Fleming, June Helena *retired city manager*

Front Royal
Stanley, Douglas Parnell *county planner, administrator*

Haymarket
Doolittle, Warren T. *retired federal official*

King George
Newhall, David, III, *former government official*

Lynchburg
Davenport, James Robert *retired city official, retired utility executive*
Stephens, Bart Nelson *former foreign service officer*

Manassas
Nemfakos, Charles Panagiotis *defense industry executive*
Storing, Paul Edward *retired foreign service officer*

Mathews
Busby, Morris D. *former ambassador*

Mc Lean
Cahill, Harry Amory *diplomat, educator*
Cannon, Mark Wilcox *government official, business executive*
Chaplin, Stephen Michael *retired diplomat*
Gregus, Linda Anna *government official*
Healy, Theresa Ann *former ambassador*
Keevey, Richard Francis *government official, educator*
Malley, Raymond Charles *retired foreign service officer, industrial executive*
Newman, William Bernard, Jr., *government consultant*
Russell, Theodore Emery *diplomat*
Smith, Russell Jack *former intelligence official*
Trout, Maurice Elmore *diplomat*

Midlothian
Perkins, Raymond Lamont *retired government official*

Norfolk
Andrews, Mason Cooke *mayor, obstetrician, gynecologist, educator*

Oakton
Farwell, Albert Edmond *retired government official, consultant*
Pratsch, Lloyd Wilmer *government official*

Richmond
Adiele, Moses Nkwachukwu *state official*
Hager, John Henry *state official, former lieutenant governor*
Jones-Atkins, DeBorah Kaye *state official*
Kaine, Timothy M. *lieutenant governor*
Kilgore, Jerry *state attorney general*
Linkonis, Suzanne Newbold *probation officer, counselor*
†McCollum, Rudolph C., Jr., *mayor*
Petera, Anne Pappas *state official*
†Warner, Mark R. *governor*
Wilder, L(awrence) Douglas *former governor*

Springfield
Hunt, Robert Gayle *former government official*
Stottlemyer, David Lee *government official*

Stafford
Williams, Carlisle M., Jr., *municipal official*

Stanardsville
Keel, Alton Gold, Jr., *ambassador*

Suffolk
Hope, James Franklin *mayor, civil engineer, consultant*

Susan
Ambach, Dwight Russell *retired foreign service officer*

The Plains
Gibbons, John Howard Howard (Jack Gibbons) *government official, physicist*

Vienna
Almaguer, Frank *ambassador*
DeWitt, Charles Barbour *federal government official*

Virginia Beach
Davies, George Patrick *city official*
Friedman, Andrew Mitchell *director housing and neighborhood preservation*
Oberndorf, Meyera E. *mayor*
Smith, Ruth Hodges *city clerk*

Washington
Skowronski, Frank Stanley *foreign service officer, consulting executive*

WASHINGTON

Bellevue
Mosher, Charles D. *mayor, real estate manager*

Chattaroy
Ezelle, Robert Eugene *diplomat*

Edmonds
Thyden, James Eskel *diplomat, educator, lecturer*

Olympia
Chopp, Frank *state official*
Gregoire, Christine O. *state attorney general*
Hagens, William Joseph *state official, public health educator*
Locke, Gary *governor*
Markham, J. David *educator, writer, historical consultant*
O'Brien, Robert S. *state official*
Owen, Bradley Scott *lieutenant governor*
Reed, Sam *secretary of state*

Seattle
Carlsen, Russell Arthur *county official*
Covington, Germaine Ward *municipal agency administrator*
Kennedy, Mary Virginia *diplomat*
Krochalis, Richard F. *municipal government official*
Nickels, Greg *mayor*
Schell, Paul E.S. *former mayor*
†Zumeta, William Mark *public policy educator*

Sequim
Huntley, James Robert *government official, international affairs scholar and consultant*
Huston, Harriette Irene Otwell (Ree Huston) *retired county official*
McMahon, Terrence John *retired foreign service officer*

Spokane
Powers, John T., Jr., *mayor*

Sumas
Hemry, Larry Harold *former federal agency official, writer, inventor*

Tacoma
Ebersole, Brian *former mayor*
Vlasak, Walter Raymond *state official, human resource manager*

Vancouver
†McDonnell, Patrick John *city manager*
Ogden, Daniel Miller, Jr., *government official, educator*

WEST VIRGINIA

Charleston
Hechler, Ken *former state official, former congressman, political science educator, writer*
†Manchin, Joe, III, *secretary of state*
Mc Graw, Darrell Vivian, Jr., *state attorney general*
†Melton, G. Kemp *former mayor*
Wise, Robert Ellsworth, Jr., (Bob Ellsworth) *governor, former congressman*

Harpers Ferry
Cooley, Hilary Elizabeth *county official*

WISCONSIN

Appleton
Lillge, Eugene Francis *state official*

Ashland
Smith, Jane Schneberger *retired city administrator*

Eau Claire
Juett, Samuel Joseph *administrative officer, consultant*

Elm Grove
Steen Crawford, Andrea *village manager*

Janesville
Blazkowski, Phillip *community development and planning official*

Juneau
Carpenter, David Erwin *county planner*

Madison
Bauman, Susan Joan Mayer *mayor, lawyer*
Doyle, James E(dward) *governor*
Earl, Anthony Scully *former governor of Wisconsin, lawyer*
La Follette, Douglas J. *secretary of state*
†Lautenschlager, Peggy A. *state attorney general*
†Lawton, Barbara *lieutenant governor*
Malinowski, Dennis Edmund *government consultant*
Narveson, Joyce Ann *public services administrator*
Saunders, Charles David *state official*
Thompson, Barbara Storck *state official*
†Voight, Jack C. *state official*

Milwaukee
Norquist, John Olaf *mayor*
Schmitz, Francis David *lawyer*

Pewaukee
Farrow, Margaret Ann *former state official*

Pleasant Prairie
Pollocoff, Michael R. *village administrator*

River Hills
Tollaksen, Thomas William *village manager*

WYOMING

Casper
Sullivan, Michael John *ambassador, former governor*

Cheyenne
†Crank, Pat *state attorney general*
†Freudenthal, David D. *governor*
Meyer, Joseph B. *state official, former academic administrator*
Thomson, Thyra Godfrey *former state official*
Woodhouse, Gay Vanderpoel *former state attorney general, lawyer*

Laramie
Dickman, Francois Moussiegt *former foreign service officer, educator*
Brown, Carroll *diplomat, association executive, consultant*

TERRITORIES OF THE UNITED STATES

AMERICAN SAMOA

Pago Pago
†Faalevao, Aviata Fano *attorney general, political organization worker*
†Mailo, Toetagata Albert *territory attorney general*
†Sunia, Aitofele Toese F. *lieutenant governor*
†Sunia, Muagututia Fiti *American Samoa attorney general*
Tulafono, Togiola T.A. *governor*

GUAM

Anigua
†Moylan, Kaleo *lieutenant governor*

Hagatna
†Camacho, Felix Perez *governor*
Gutierrez, Carl T. C. *former governor*
†Moylan, Douglas *state attorney general*

NORTHERN MARIANA ISLANDS

Saipan
†Benavente, Diego T. *lieutenant governor*
†Manglona, Ramona V. *state attorney general*
†Tenorio, Pedro Pangelinan *former governor*

PUERTO RICO

San Juan
Calderón, Sila M. *governor*
†Garcia, Marc Anthony *diplomat*
Mercado-Ramos, Ferdinand *secretary of state*
Rodriguez, Annabelle *state attorney general*
†Santini, Jorge *mayor*

VIRGIN ISLANDS

Charlotte Amalie
Stridiron, Iver Allison *attorney general*

Christiansted
James, Gerard Luz Amwur, II, *former lieutenant governor*
†Richards, Vargrave A. *lieutenant governor*

Saint Thomas
Turnbull, Charles W. *governor*

MILITARY ADDRESSES OF THE UNITED STATES

ATLANTIC

Apo
Bond, Clayton Alan *foreign affairs fellow*
†Danilovich, John J. *ambassador*
†Jett, Dennis Coleman *foreign service officer*

EUROPE

APO
Webster, Christopher White *foreign service officer*

Apo
Carson, Johnnie *ambassador*
Cejas, Paul L. *diplomat, executive*
†Fowler, Wyche, Jr., *ambassador*
Gnehm, Edward W., Jr., *ambassador*
†Kurtzer, Daniel *ambassador*
McGowan, Gerald S. *diplomat*
†Romero, Edward L. *diplomat, environmental engineering executive*
Schoonover, Brenda B. *ambassador*

Fpo
Klosson, Michael *foreign service officer*
Neumann, Ronald Eldredge *diplomat*

PACIFIC

Apo
Ray, Charles Aaron *foreign service officer*

Fpo
Bishop, Donald Michael *foreign service officer*

CANADA

BRITISH COLUMBIA

Vancouver
Chan, Raymond *Canadian government minister*
Harcourt, Michael Franklin *retired premier of Province of British Columbia, lawyer, educator*
†Owen, Stephen *member of parliament, secretary of state*

Victoria
Gardom, Garde Basil *lieutenant governor of British Columbia*
†Halsey-Brandt, Greg *mayor*

MANITOBA

Winnipeg
Curtis, Charles Edward *Canadian government official*
Filmon, Gary Albert *Canadian provincial premier, civil engineer*
Liba, Peter Michael *Canadian provincial government official*

NOVA SCOTIA

Waverley
Grady, Wayne J. *government official*

ONTARIO

Downsview
Eggleton, Arthur C. *former Canadian government official, member of Parliament*

Nobleton
Embleton, Tony Frederick Wallace *retired Canadian government official*

Ottawa
Anderson, David Leslie *member of parliament*
Angus, W. David *Queen's Counsel*
Armstrong, Henry Conner *former Canadian government official, consultant*
Augustine, Jean *member of parliament*
Austin, Jacob (Jack Austin) *Canadian government official*
†Axworthy, Lloyd *Canadian government official*
Bailey, Roy H. *member of parliament*
†Baker, George S. *federal official*
Bélisle, Paul C. *Canadian government official*
Blaikie, William *government official*
Buchanan, John MacLennan *Canadian provincial official*
Caplan, Elinor *Canadian provincial legislator, former cabinet minister*
Cauchon, Martin *Canadian government official*

Cellucci, Argeo Paul *ambassador, former governor*
Chrétien, Jean (Joseph Jacques Jean Chrétien) *prime minister of Canada, lawyer*
Clarkson, Adrienne *Governor General of Canada*
Collenette, David Michael *Canadian government official*
Dawson, Mary E.
Day, Stockwell Burt *government official*
†Dhaliwal, Herb *Canadian government official*
Dion, Stéphane *federal official*
Fairbairn, Joyce *Canadian government official*
Giroux, Robert-Jean-Yvon *retired Canadian government official*
Gold, Lorne W. *Canadian government official*
Goodale, Ralph E. *Canadian government minister*
Graham, B. Alasdair *government official*
Gray, Herbert Eser (The Right Honourable Herbert Gray) *former federal official*
Grey, Deborah Cleland *Canadian government official*
Harb, Mac *Canadian government official*
Kingsley, Jean-Pierre *government official*
Kirkwood, David Herbert Waddington *Canadian government official*
Laliberte, Rick *member of parliament*
Lalonde, Francine *member of parliament*
MacAulay, Lawrence A. *Canadian government official, legislator*
MacDonald, Flora Isabel *Canadian government official*
Manley, John *Canadian government official*
Marleau, Diane *Canadian government official*
Martin, Paul *Canadian government official*
McLellan, A. Anne *Canadian government official*
McLure, John Douglas *government relations*
Mifflin, Fred John *Canadian government official*
Mills, Bob *member of parliament*
Minna, Maria *member of parliament*
Mitchell, Andy *Canadian federal official*
Nystrom, Lorne *member of parliament*
†Pagtakhan, Rey *member of parliament*
Pankiw, Jim *member of parliament*
†Peterson, Jim *member of parliament*
Poulin, Marie *Canadian government official*
Proctor, Dick *member of parliament*
Robillard, Lucienne *Canadian government official*
Rock, Allan Michael *Canadian government official*
Roland, Anne *registrar Supreme Court of Canada*
†Scott, Andy *government official*
Silverman, Ozzie *consulting strategist*
†Southam, G(ordon) Hamilton *former Canadian government official*
Stanford, Joseph Stephen *diplomat, lawyer, educator*
†Stewart, Christine Susan *Canadian government official*
Vanclief, Lyle *federal official, legislator*
Yalden, Maxwell Freeman *Canadian diplomat*
Yeomans, Donald Ralph *Canadian government official, consultant*

Toronto
†Bartleman, James K. *lieutenant governor*
Gotlieb, Allan E. *former ambassador*
Holyday, Douglas Charles *city councillor*
Lastman, Melvin D. *mayor*
MacLaren, Roy *retired federal official*
Turner, John Napier *former prime minister of Canada, legislator*

QUEBEC

Chelsea
Warren, Jack Hamilton *former diplomat and trade policy adviser*

Hull
Blondin-Andrew, Ethel *Canadian government official*
Bradshaw, Claudette *federal government official, parliamentarian*
Copps, Sheila *Canadian government official*
Gagliano, Alfonso *Canadian government official*
Stewart, Jane *Canadian government minister*

Montreal
Mulroney, Brian (Martin Brian Mulroney) *former prime minister of Canada*

Pointe-Claire
Lapointe, Lucie *Canadian government official*

SASKATCHEWAN

Regina
Clayton, Raymond Edward *government official*
Haverstock, Lynda M. *lieutenant governor*

Saskatoon
Blakeney, Allan Emrys *Canadian government official, lawyer*

MEXICO

Col Centro
Gil Diaz, Francisco *minister of finance for Mexico*

Col Cordesa
†Blanco Mendoza, Herminio *Mexican government official*

Col Jardines Montana
†Carabias Lillo, Julia *government official*

Colonia Cuauhtemoc
†Garza, Antonio O. *ambassador*

Distrito Federal
de la Fuente Ramirez, Juan Ramon *Mexican government official, academic administrator*

Mexico City
†Abascal Carranza, Carlos Maria *secretary of labor and social planning for Mexico*
†Barrio Terrazas, Francisco *government official of Mexico*
†Cerisola y Weber, Pedro *secretary of communications and transportation for Mexico*
†Creel Miranda, Santiago *secretary of the interior for Mexico*
†Derbez Bautista, Luis Ernesto *secretary of foreign affairs of Mexico*
†Fox, Vicente (Vicente Fox Quesada) *President of Mexico*
†Gurria Trevino, José Angel *former Mexican government official*
†Herrera Tello, Maria Teresa *secretary of agrarian reform for Mexico*
†Lichtinger, Victor *secretary of environment, natural resources and fisheries for Mexico*
†Macedo de la Concha, Rafael *attorney general of Mexico*
†Navarro, Leticia *Mexican government official*
Ortiz, Guillermo *banker*
†Peyrot Gonzalez, Marco A. *secretary of the navy of Mexico*
†Tamez Guerra, Reyes S. *secretary of public education for Mexico*
†Usabiaga Arroyo, Javier *secretary of agriculture, livestock and rural development for Mexico*
†Vazquez Mota, Josefina *secretary of social development for Mexico*
†Vega Garcia, Gerardo Clemente R. *secretary of defense for Mexico*
†Zedillo Ponce de León, Ernesto *former president of Mexico*

Piso
†Tellez Kuenzler, Luis *government official*
†Arroyo Marroquin, Romárico *former federal official*
†Carrasco Altamirano, Diódoro *former federal official*
†Farell Cubillas, Arsenio *former Mexican government official*
†Limón Rojas, Miguel *former Mexican government official*
†Lorenzo Franco, José Ramón *former Mexican government official*
†Martens Rebolledo, Ernesto *secretary of energy for Mexico, glass products company executive*
†Robledo Rincón, Eduardo *former federal official*

ARGENTINA

Buenos Aires
†Green Macias, Rosario *ambassador*
Gutierrez, Lino *diplomat*
†Rocha, Manuel *diplomat*

AUSTRALIA

Camberwell
Peterson, Douglas Pete (Pete Peterson) *ambassador, former congressman*

Double Bay
Peacock, Penne Korth *ambassador*

BANGLADESH

Dhaka
†Thomas, Harry K., Jr., *ambassador*

BELARUS

Minsk
Sychov, Alyaksandr *diplomat*

BELGIUM

Brussels
Kerber, Frank John *diplomat*

BRAZIL

70403-900
†Hrinak, Donna Jean *ambassador*

Brasília
Amorim, Celso Luiz Nunes *government official*

CHAD

N'Djamena
Goldthwait, Christopher E. *ambassador*

CHILE

Santiago
Wilkey, Malcolm Richard *retired ambassador, former federal judge*

CHINA

Bangkok
†Johnson, Darryl Norman *ambassador*

COSTA RICA

San José
Arias Sanchez, Oscar *former president of Costa Rica*

DEMOCRATIC REPUBLIC OF CONGO

Kinshasa
†Hooks, Aubrey *ambassador*

DENMARK

Copenhagen
Lage, Cristina *secretary general*

EGYPT

Cairo
Elaraby, Nabil A. *Egyptian diplomat*
Pendleton, Mary Catherine *foreign service officer*
†Welch, David C. *ambassador*

ENGLAND

London
Elizabeth, Her Majesty , II, (Elizabeth Alexandra Mary) *Queen of United Kingdom of Great Britain and Northern Ireland, and her other Realms and Territories, head of the Commonwealth, Defender of the Faith*
†Farish, William S. *U.S. ambassador to United Kingdom*
Meyer, Sir Christopher J.R. *former diplomat*
†Navarrete, Jorge Eduardo *ambassador*
Paulus, Michael John *government official, bank executive, economist*

Oxford
Robinson, Mary *former U.N. high commissioner for human rights*

FRANCE

Paris
Dean, John Gunther *diplomat*
Myerson, Jacob Myer *retired diplomat*

GREECE

Athens
Burns, R. Nicholas *federal official*

HONG KONG

Hong Kong
†Randt, Clark Thorp, Jr., *ambassador, lawyer*

INDIA

New Delhi
Anderson, Michael Hugh *diplomat*

INDONESIA

Jakarta Pusat
†Boyce, Ralph L. *ambassador*

ITALY

Rome
†Bartholomew, Reginald *diplomat*
Creagan, James Francis *diplomat, academic administrator*
†Fulci, Francesco Paolo *diplomat*
Sisulu, Sheila Violet Makate *diplomat*
Skodon, Emil Mark *diplomat*

JAPAN

Tokyo
†Baker, Howard Henry, Jr., *ambassador, former senator, lawyer*
†Foley, Thomas Stephen *diplomat, former speaker House of Representatives*
Manz, Johannes Jakob *Swiss diplomat*

NETHERLANDS

The Hague
Schneider, Cynthia Perrin *ambassador, art historian, educator*
Tomka, Peter *Slovakian diplomat, lawyer, judge*

NORWAY

Oslo
Ong, John Doyle *ambassador, retired manufacturing executive*

OMAN

Medinat Qaboos
Craig, John Bruce *ambassador*

PAKISTAN

Islamabad
†Powell, Nancy J. *ambassador*

PHILIPPINES

Manila
†Ricciardone, Francis *diplomat*

REPUBLIC OF KOREA

Seoul
†Hubbard, Thomas C. *ambassador*

RUSSIA

Moscow
Vershbow, Alexander R. *diplomat*

SLOVENIA

Ljubljana
Rupel, Dimitrij *diplomat*

SOUTH AFRICA

Johannesburg
Dunn, David B. *ambassador*

Pretoria
†Hume, Cameron R. *ambassador*

SPAIN

Canary Islands
Wells, Melissa Foelsch *foreign service officer*

Palafrugell, Girona
Carner, George *foreign service executive, economic strategist*

SWEDEN

Stockholm
Wachtmeister, Count Wilhelm H. F. *diplomat*

SWITZERLAND

Bern
Gonzalez, Guillermo Enrique *diplomat*

Geneva
Brown, Kent Newville *ambassador*
Marchi, Sergio Sisto *Canadian government official*
†Ogata, Sadako *United Nations official*

Versoix
†Frenk, Julio Jose *secretary of health for Mexico, health systems researcher, consultant*
Boutros-Ghali, Boutros *former U.N. secretary general*

TAIWAN

Taipei
Chang, Parris Hsu-cheng *law-maker, political science educator, writer*

TURKEY

Ankara
†Edelman, Eric Steven *ambassador*
†Pearson, W. Robert *ambassador*

UKRAINE

Kiev
†Pascual, Carlos *ambassador*

VIETNAM

Hanoi
†Burghardt, Raymond Francis, Jr., *ambassador*

ADDRESS UNPUBLISHED

Abramowitz, Morton I. *former ambassador*
Adams, Edwin Melville *former foreign service officer, actor, author, lecturer*
Adams, James Blackburn *former state government official, former federal government official, lawyer*
Addo, Charles Kwame *municipal official*
Albertson, Susan L. *retired federal government official*
Albright, Madeleine Korbel *former secretary of state*
Allen, Edgar Burns *records management professional*
Allukian, Myron, Jr., *government administrator, public health educator, dental educator*
†Amato Chiaramonte Bordonaro, Baron Carlo Camillo *ambassador, consultant*
†Anderson, David *Canadian government official*
Anzai, Earl I. *former state attorney general*
Arcos, Cresencio S. *ambassador*
Armstrong, Anne Legendre (Mrs. Tobin Armstrong) *former ambassador, corporate director*
†Arrington, Richard, Jr., *former mayor*
Atwater, Phyllis T. *municipal administrator*
Baca, Jim *former mayor*
Barkley, Richard Clark *ambassador*
Barnes, Roy Eugene *former governor, lawyer*
Barnett, Mark William *former state attorney general*
Barr, Kenneth L. *former mayor*
Bayless, Betsey *state official*
†Beasley, David Muldrow *former governor, consultant*
†Bentsen, Lloyd *former government official, former senator*
Berlincourt, Marjorie Alkins *government official, retired*
Betti, John Anso *federal official, former automobile manufacturing company executive*
†Binsfeld, Connie Berube *former state official*
Bishop, Oliver Richard *retired state official*
Blood, Archer Kent *retired foreign service officer*
Bolen, David Benjamin *ambassador, former corporation executive*
Bomer, Elton *former state official*
Botelho, Bruce Manuel *former state attorney general, mayor*
Boyatt, Thomas David *former ambassador*
Breed, Henry Eltinge, III, *diplomat, educator*
Broadrick-Allen, Sandra Carol *retired city manager, consultant, civic worker*
Brown, June Gibbs *retired government official*
†Bryant, Winston *former state attorney general*
Burchman, Leonard *government official*
Bush, George Walker *43d President of the United States*
Bushnell, Prudence *diplomat, management consultant*
Carr, Elizabeth Davis-Jackson *municipal manager*
Carter, Rosalynn Smith *wife of former President of United States*
Castaneda, Jorge G. *former government official, political scientist*
Cayetano, Benjamin Jerome *former governor, former state senator and representative*
Cenarrusa, Pete T. *retired state official*
Chen, Stephen S. F. *retired diplomat*
Christie, Walter Scott *retired state official*
Chung, Caroline *foreign service officer*
Clark, William, Jr., *political advisor*
Clarke, Henry Lee *foreign service officer, former ambassador*
Cohen, Roberta Jane *government executive*
Coles, H. Brent *former mayor*
Condayan, John *foreign service officer, diplomat, consultant*
Condon, Charles Molony *former state attorney general*
Connell, Marion Fitch *retired government official, management consultant*
Cook, Rebecca McDowell *former state official*
Coop, Frederick Robert *retired city manager*
Coppie, Comer Swift *retired state official*
Corkery, James Caldwell *retired Canadian government executive, mechanical engineer*
Cornell, Robert Arthur *retired international government official, consultant*
Cornish, Richard Joseph *international affairs consultant, retired diplomat*
Cosman, Francene Jen *former government official*
Cougill, Roscoe McDaniel *mayor, retired air force officer*
Dalsimer, Anthony Stearns *retired foreign service officer, educator*
†Dalton, John Howard *former secretary of the navy, financial consultant*
Daly, Paul Sylvester *mayor, retired academic administrator, management consultant*
David, Ronald Bryan *county official*
Davis, Gray (Joseph Graham Davis) *former governor*
Del Papa, Frankie Sue *former state attorney general*
Dillon, Robert Sherwood *retired government official*
Dyrstad, Joanell M. *former lieutenant governor, consultant*
Ebert, Dorothy Elizabeth *retired county clerk*
Egan, Wesley William *former ambassador*
Eisenhower, John Sheldon Doud *former ambassador, author*
Elson, Edward Elliott *diplomat*
Emmons, Robert Duncan *diplomat*
Engler, John *governor*
Eu, March Fong *ambassador, former state official*
Evatt, Parker *former state commissioner, former state legislator*
Ewing, Raymond Charles *retired ambassador*
Fiddick, Paul William *government official, broadcasting executive*

Fisher, Allan Michael *government official, educator*
†Foglietta, Thomas Michael *former diplomat, former congressman*
Ford, Ford Barney *retired government official*
†Fordice, Kirk (Daniel Kirkwood Fordice Jr.) *former governor, construction company executive, engineer*
Fowler, Robert Asa *diplomat, consultant, business director*
Franke, Wayne Thomas *retired government affairs director, consultant*
Fraser, Donald MacKay *former mayor, former congressman, educator*
Fréchette, Louise *international organization official*
Garcia, Gus *former mayor*
Gawf, John Lee *foreign service officer*
Geisel, Harold Walter *diplomat*
Gilroy, Sue Anne *state official*
Glendening, Parris Nelson *former governor, political science educator*
Goldsmith, Aaron Clair *retired federal government executive, dean*
†Gore, Albert, Jr., *former Vice President of the United States*
Graham, Jan *former state attorney general*
Graves, William Preston *governor*
Haley, George W. *ambassador*
Hall, Keith R. *retired federal official*
Hanmer, Stephen Read, Jr., *retired government executive*
Harder, Robert Clarence *state official*
Havel, Vaclav *former president of Czech Republic, playwright*
Hazeltine, Joyce *former state official*
†Henry, Sherrye P. *former political advisor*
Hester, Nancy Elizabeth *county government official*
Hett, Joan Margaret *ecological consultant*
Heydt, William *former mayor*
Hilsman, Roger *government educator*
Hodges, Jim *former governor*
Holiday, Edith Elizabeth *former presidential adviser, cabinet secretary*
Holmes, Henry Allen *government official*
Howard, Robert Elliott *former federal official, consultant, educator*
Huenemann, Rodney Karl *state administrator, executive*
Hull, Jane Dee *former governor, former state legislator*
Inman, Edward Salisbury, III, *former secretary of state, secondary school educator*
†James, Fob, Jr., (Forrest Hood James) *former governor*
Johnson, Gary Earl *former governor*
Johnson, Karla Ann *county official*
Jones, Bill *former state official, rancher*
Joseph, Geri Mack (Geraldine Joseph) *former ambassador, educator, journalist*
†Kastrup, Dieter *diplomat*
Kelley, Wayne Plumbley, Jr., *retired federal official*
Kendig, William Lamar *retired government official, accountant*
Kernan, Joseph E. *governor*
Kissinger, Henry Alfred *former secretary of state, international consulting company executive*
Kniesler, Frederick Cornelius *retired municipal official*
Kulstad, Guy Charles *public works official*
Lance, Alan George *former state attorney general*
Leader, Joyce E. *ambassador*
Ledogar, Stephen J. *retired diplomat*
Lee, James Matthew *Canadian politician*
Levy, Leah Garrigan *federal official*
Loiello, John Peter *diplomat*
†Lungren, Daniel Edward *former state attorney general*
MacIsaac, John Anthony *retired municipal official*
MacMillan, Hoke *former state attorney general*
Maestrone, Frank Eusebio *diplomat*
Maguire-Zinni, Deirdre *federal community development management analyst*
Mariano, Raymond V. *former mayor*
Martin, James Kay *government official*
Martz, Judy Helen *governor*
Marvin, William Glenn, Jr., *former foreign service officer*
Masa, George John *retired regional director*
Mattingly, Mack Francis *former ambassador, former senator, entrepreneur*
Mazankowski, Donald Frank *Canadian government official*
McCallum, Scott *former governor*
McClinton, James Leroy *city administrator*
McCoy, Mary Ann *state official*
McLean, Hon. Walter Franklin *consultant, pastor, legislator*
Miles, Jim *state official*
Miller, Susan Smith *state official*
†Milne, James F. *former secretary of state*
Modisett, Jeffrey A. *lawyer, state attorney general, business executive*
Mohler, Brian Jeffery *diplomat*
Mondale, Walter Frederick *former Vice President of United States, diplomat, lawyer*
Morris, Robert G(emmill) *retired foreign service officer*
Motyl, Alexander John *political science educator*
Munro, Ralph Davies *state official*
Murphy, Gerald *retired government official, consultant*
Neal, Robert Lee, Jr., *government official*
Nelson, Norman Daniel *government official*
†Normand, Gilbert *government official*
Obermann, Richard Michael *governmental technology and policy analyst*
Ortiz, Francis Vincent, Jr., *retired ambassador*
Owada, Hisashi *government official*
Paliwal, Dinesh Kumar *diplomat, educational administrator*
Palmerlee, April Wahlestedt *diplomat*
Partridge, William Russell *retired federal executive*
Patterson, James *former mayor*
†Peak, Howard W. *former mayor*
Pearl, Laurence Dickson *retired federal government executive*
Peeler, Bob *lieutenant governor*
†Peña, Federico Fabian *retired federal official*
Peters, Michael P. *former mayor*
Petrequin, Harry Joseph, Jr., *foreign service officer*
†Peyton, John *mayor*
Pies, Ronald E. *retired city official*
Price, Robert Otis *former mayor*
Pridmore, Roy Davis *government official*
Propp, Steven H. *analyst*
Purcell, Bill *mayor*
†Qualls, Roxanne *mayor*
†Ramirez, Carlos Moises *former mayor*
Raynolds, Harold, Jr., *retired state education commissioner*
Reinhardt, John Edward *former international affairs specialist*
Reno, Janet *former attorney general*
Rice, Richard Campbell *retired state official, retired army officer*
Rickert, Jonathan Bradley *retired foreign service officer*
Ridgway, James Mastin *retired government official*
Ridgway, Rozanne LeJeanne *retired diplomat, executive*
Robinson, Laurie Overby *former assistant attorney general*
Rockefeller, Winthrop P. *lieutenant governor*
Rosenthal, James D. *retired federal official, former ambassador, government and foundation executive*
†Rossello, Pedro *former governor*
Rubin, Robert E. *former secretary of treasury*
Rudin, Anne *former mayor, nurse*
Ruggiero, Renato *former Italian government official*
Rundio, Joan Peters (Jo Rundio) *public administrator*
Ryan, George H. *former governor, pharmacist*
Ryan, James E. *former state attorney general*
Salmaggi, Guido Godfrey *former diplomat, opera agent*
Savocchio, Joyce A. *former mayor*
Scanlan, John Douglas *foreign service officer, former ambassador*
Schafer, Edward T. *former governor, real estate company executive*
†Schmoke, Kurt L. *mayor*
Schoettler, Gail Sinton *former ambassador*
Schunk, Mae *former state official*
Seale, Robert L. *former state treasurer*
Shaheen, C. Jeanne *former governor*
Sherrer, Gary *former state lieutenant governor, bank executive*
Siegelman, Don Eugene *former governor*
Simms, John William *retired foreign service officer, consultant*
†Smith, Jean Kennedy *former ambassador*
Smith, Robert Powell *former ambassador, former foundation executive*
Smith, Robert William *state official, educator*
Smith, Stanford Sidney *former state treasurer*
Snider, L. Britt *government executive*
†Solomon, Connie Scott *chief of staff*
Sotirhos, Michael *ambassador*
Stevens, Kenneth Allen *retired defense department worker*
Stovall, Carla Jo *former state attorney general*
Street, John F. *mayor*
Sudanowicz, Elaine Marie *government executive*
Swett, Richard Nelson (Dick Swett) *diplomat, former congressman*
Swift, Jane Maria *former governor*
Swoap, David Bruce *government affairs consultant*
Talbott, John *mayor*
Tambs, Lewis Arthur *diplomat, historian, educator*
Tarkowski, Larry Michael *town official*
Teater, Dorothy Seath *retired county official*
Tibshraeny, Jay *former mayor*
Tienken, Arthur T. *retired foreign service officer*
Tomlinson, Keith *state claims examiner*
Tooley, Lowell James *city manager*
Turner, Lisa Hill *county official*
Underwood, Cecil H. *former governor, company executive*
Ventura, Jesse (James Janos) *former governor*
Warner, Shauna Ruth *city official*
Watkins, James David *federal official, military officer*
Wendt, E. Allan *international affairs consultant*
Whitman, Christine Todd *former governor*
Whitney, Jane *foreign service officer*
†Wilson, Pete *former governor*
Windom, Stephen Ralph *former leutenant governor, lawyer*
†Witt, James Lee *business executive*
Wolf, Dale Edward *state official*
Wood, Corinne *former state official*
Zischke, Douglas Arthur *foreign service officer*
Zoellick, Robert Bruce *federal official*

GOVERNMENT: LEGISLATIVE ADMINISTRATION

UNITED STATES

ALABAMA

Birmingham
Allen, Maryon Pittman *former senator, journalist, lecturer, interior and clothing designer*
Hilliard, Earl Frederick *congressman, lawyer*

Jasper
†Bevill, Tom *retired congressman, lawyer*

Mobile
Edwards, Jack *former congressman, lawyer*

Montgomery
†Barron, Lowell Ray *state legislator*
Dixon, Larry Dean *state legislator*
Hammett, Seth *state legislator*

Tuscumbia
Heflin, Howell Thomas *former senator, lawyer, former state supreme court chief justice*

ALASKA

Eagle River
Cotten, Samuel Richard *fisheries consultant, former state legislator*

Juneau
Kohring, Victor H. *state legislator*
†Kott, Pete *state representative*
†Therriault, Gene *state senator*

North Pole
James, Jeannette Adeline *state legislator, accountant*

ARIZONA

Phoenix
Burns, Brenda *state senator*
Weiers, Jim *state representative*

Scottsdale
Salmon, Matt *former congressman, communications company executive*

Tempe
Smith, Carol Estes *retired city councilman*

Tucson
Bartlett, David Carson *state legislator*

Waddell
Turner, Warren Austin *state legislator*

ARKANSAS

Dumas
Schexnayder, Charlotte Tillar *state legislator*

Greenwood
Walters, Bill *former state senator, lawyer*

Little Rock
†Hill, Jim B. *state legislator*

Morrilton
Johnson, Bob W. *state senator*

Paris
†Cleveland, Herschel *state representative*

CALIFORNIA

Alamo
†Baker, William P. (Bill Baker) *former congressman*

Arcadia
†Margett, Bob G. *state legislator*

Bakersfield
†Ashburn, Roy *state senator*
†Florez, Dean R. *state senator*

Brentwood
†Houston, Guy Spencer *state legislator*

Chico
†Keene, Rick *state legislator*

Chula Vista
†Moreno-Ducheny, Denise *state senator*

Compton
Dymally, Mervyn Malcolm *retired congressman, international business executive*

El Cajon
†Hollingsworth, Dennis *state senator*

Eureka
†Berg, Patty *state legislator*

Fremont
†Dutra, John A. *state legislator*

Garden Grove
†Dornan, Robert Kenneth *former congressman*

Glendale
†Moorhead, Carlos J. *former congressman*

Glendora
Harmsen, Mark Spaulding *legislative aide*

Inglewood
†Vincent, Edward *state legislator*

Long Beach
†Karnette, Betty *state senator*

Los Altos
Thurber, Emily Forrest *political consultant*

Los Angeles
†Cedillo, Gilbert A. *state senator*

Martinez
†Canciamilla, Joseph *state legislator*
†Torlakson, Tom A. *state senator*

Merced
†Denham, Jeffrey *state senator*

Monterey
†Browder, John Glen *former congressman, educator*

Nevada City
†Aanestad, Samuel Mark *state legislator*

Ontario
†Soto, Nell *state senator*

Palm Desert
†Battin, James F., Jr., *state legislator, sales executive*

Pasadena
†Scott, Jack Alan *state senator*

Redding
†La Malfa, Doug *state representative*

Redondo Beach
Harman, Jane *congresswoman*

Roseville
†Oller, Thomas R. *state senator*

Sacramento
†Aghazarian, Greg G. *state representative*
Alpert, Deirdre Whittleton (Dede Alpert) *state legislator*
†Brulte, James L. *state legislator*
†Cogdill, David *state representative*
†Cohn, Rebecca *state representative*
†Cox, Dave *state legislator*
Detwiler, Peter Murray *legislative staff member, educator*
†Diaz, Manny *state representative*
†Dunn, Joseph *state legislator*
†Escutia, Martha *state senator*
†Figueroa, Liz *state senator*
†Frommer, Dario F. *state representative*
Holmes, Robert Eugene *legislative staff member, journalist*
Horton, Shirley A. *state legislator, former mayor*
†Johnson, Ross *state legislator*
Knight, William J. (Pete Knight) *state legislator, retired air force officer*
†Koretz, Paul *state representative*
†Kuehl, Sheila James *state legislator*
†Levine, Lloyd E. *state representative*
†Lieber, Sally J. *state representative*
†Liu, Carol *state representative*
†Machado, Michael J(ohn) *state legislator, farmer*
†Maze, Bill *state representative*
†McCarthy, Kevin *state representative*
†McPherson, Bruce *state legislator*
†Montanez, Cindy *state representative*
†Morrow, Bill *state legislator*
†Murray, Kevin *state legislator*
†Nunez, Fabian *state representative*
†Ortiz, Deborah V. *state legislator*
†Parra, Nicole M. *state representative*
†Pavley, Fran J. *state representative*
†Perata, Don *state legislator*
†Poochigian, Charles *state legislator*
†Reyes, Sarah *state representative*
†Richman, Keith Stuart *state representative*
†Romero, Gloria *state senator*
†Runner, Sharon *state representative*
†Simitian, Joe *state representative*
†Speier, Jackie *state senator*
†Steinberg, Darrell S. *state legislator*
†Strickland, Anthony *state representative*
Torres, Art *former state legislator*
Wesson, Herb J. *state representative*
Wilson, E. Dotson *legislative staff member*

San Francisco
†Leno, Mark *state legislator*

San Jose
†Sher, Byron D. *state legislator, law educator*
†Vasconcellos, John *state legislator*

San Mateo
†Mullin, Gene *state legislator*

Santa Rosa
†Chesbro, Wesley *state senator*
King, Gwendolyn Bair *former government staff member, public speaker*

Stockton
†Matthews, Barbara *state legislator*

Thousand Oaks
†McClintock, Tom *state senator*

Torrance
†Kuykendall, Steven Thomas *former congressman*

Vacaville
†Wolk, Lois *state legislator*

Van Nuys
†Alarcon, Richard *state legislator, former councilman*
Hertzberg, Robert M. *former state legislator*
Westall, Andrew Jon *legislative staff member, urban planner*

West Covina
Torres, Esteban Edward *former congressman, business executive*

†Miller, Ralph Bradley *congressman*
Miller, Zell Bryan *senator, former governor*
Mitchell, George John *former senator, lawyer*
Mollohan, Alan B. *congressman*
Monagan, John Stephen *retired congressman and lawyer, writer, lecturer*
Moore, Dennis *congressman*
Moran, James Patrick, Jr., *congressman, stockbroker*
Moran, Jerry *congressman*
†Murkowski, Lisa *senator*
†Murphy, Timothy F. *congressman*
Murray, Patty *senator*
Murtha, John Patrick *congressman*
†Musgrave, Marilyn N. *congresswoman*
Nadler, Jerrold Lewis *congressman, lawyer*
Napolitano, Grace F. *congresswoman*
Nardi Riddle, Clarine *legislative staff member*
Neal, Richard Edmund *congressman, former mayor*
Nelson, Benjamin *senator, former governor, lawyer*
Nelson, Bill *senator, former state treasurer*
Nelson, Gaylord Anton *former senator, association executive*
Nethercutt, George Rector, Jr., *congressman, lawyer*
†Neugebauer, Randy *congressman*
Ney, Robert W. *congressman*
Nickles, Don (Donald Nickles) *senator*
Northup, Anne Meagher *congresswoman*
Norton, Eleanor Holmes *congresswoman, lawyer, educator*
Norwood, Charles W., Jr., *congressman*
†Nunes, Devin *congressman*
Nussle, James Allen *congressman*
Oberstar, James L. *congressman*
Obey, David Ross *congressman*
Olver, John Walter *congressman*
Ortiz, Solomon P. *congressman*
Osborne, Tom *congressman, former college football coach*
Ose, Douglas *congressman*
Otter, Clement Leroy (Butch Otter) *congressman*
Owens, Major Robert Odell *congressman*
Oxley, Michael Garver *congressman*
Pallone, Frank, Jr., *congressman*
Pascrell, William J., Jr., *congressman*
Pastor, Edward *congressman*
†Paxon, L. William *former congressman*
Payne, Donald M. *congressman*
†Pearce, Steve *congressman*
†Pease, Edward *former congressman*
Pelosi, Nancy *congresswoman*
Pence, Michael Richard *congressman*
Peterson, Collin C. *congressman*
Peterson, John E. *congressman*
Petri, Thomas Evert *congressman*
Phelps, David D. *former congressman, government agency administrator*
Pickering, Charles W., Jr., *congressman*
Pitts, Joseph R. *congressman*
Platts, Todd Russell *congressman, state legislator*
Pombo, Richard *congressman, rancher, farmer*
Pomeroy, Earl R. *congressman, former state insurance commissioner*
Poppleton, Janet Waters *legislative staff member*
Porter, John Edward *former congressman*
†Porter, Jon Christopher *congressman*
Portman, Rob *congressman*
†Pressler, Larry *former senator*
Price, David Eugene *congressman, educator*
Pryce, Deborah D. *congresswoman*
Pryor, Mark Lunsford *senator*
Putnam, Adam Hughes *congressman, farmer, rancher*
Quinn, Jack *congressman, English language educator, sports coach*
Radanovich, George P. *congressman*
Rahall, Nick Joe, II, (Nick Rahall) *congressman*
Ramstad, James *congressman, lawyer*
Rangel, Charles Bernard *congressman*
Reed, John Francis (Jack Reed) *senator*
Regula, Ralph *congressman, lawyer*
Rehberg, Dennis R. *congressman*
†Renzi, Rick *congressman*
Reynolds, Thomas M. *congressman*
Roberts, Charles Patrick (Pat Roberts) *senator*
Rockefeller, John Davison, IV, (Jay Rockefeller) *senator, former governor*
†Rodriguez, Ciro Davis *congressman*
Roemer, Timothy J. *former congressman, lawyer*
Rogers, Harold Dallas (Hal Rogers) *congressman*
†Rogers, Mike *congressman*
Rohrabacher, Dana *congressman*
Ros-Lehtinen, Ileana *congresswoman*
Ross, Mike *congressman*
Rothman, Steven R. *congressman*
Roybal-Allard, Lucille *congresswoman*
Royce, Edward R. (Ed Royce) *congressman*
†Rudman, Warren Bruce *former senator, lawyer, think tank executive*
†Ruppersberger, Charles Albert, III, *congressman*
Rush, Bobby L. *congressman*
Ryan, Paul *congressman*
†Ryan, Timothy *congressman*
Ryun, James Ronald *congressman*
Sabo, Martin Olav *congressman*
†Sanchez, Linda T. *congresswoman*
Sanchez, Loretta *congresswoman*
Sanders, Bernard (Bernie Sanders) *congressman*
Sandlin, Max Allen, Jr., *congressman*
Santorum, Rick *senator*
Sarbanes, Paul Spyros *senator*
Saxton, H. James *congressman*
Schaffer, Robert (Bob Schaffer) *former congressman*
Schakowsky, Janice *congresswoman*
Schiff, Adam Bennett *congressman, lawyer*
Schrock, Edward L. (Ed Schrock) *congressman, former state senator*
Schumer, Charles Ellis *senator*
†Scott, David Albert *congressman*
Scott, Robert Cortez *congressman, lawyer*
Sensenbrenner, F(rank) James, Jr., *congressman*
Serrano, Jose E. *congressman*
Sessions, Jefferson Beauregard, III, *senator*
Shadegg, John B. *congressman*
Shaw, E. Clay, Jr., (Clay Shaw) *congressman*
Shays, Christopher *congressman*
Shelby, Richard Craig *senator, former congressman*
Sherman, Bradley James *congressman*
Sherwood, Donald Lewis *congressman*
Shimkus, John Mondy *congressman*
Shuster, William (Bill Shuster) *congressman*
Simmons, Robert Ruhl *congressman*
Simpson, Michael K. *congressman*
Skeen, Joseph Richard *congressman*
Skelton, Isaac Newton, IV, (Ike Skelton) *congressman*
†Slaughter, Louise McIntosh *congresswoman*
Smith, Christopher Henry *congressman*
Smith, D. Adam *congressman*
Smith, Gordon Harold *senator*
Smith, Lamar Seeligson *congressman*
Smith, Nick *congressman, farmer*
Snowbarger, Vince *former congressman*
Snowe, Olympia J. *senator*
Snyder, Vic *congressman, physician*
Solis, Hilda Lucia *congresswoman, educational administrator*
Souder, Mark Edward *congressman*
Specter, Arlen *senator*
Spratt, John McKee, Jr., *congressman, lawyer*
Stabenow, Deborah Ann *senator, former congresswoman*
Stark, Fortney Hillman (Pete Stark) *congressman*
Stearns, Clifford Bundy *congressman, business executive*
Stenholm, Charles W. *congressman*
Stevens, Theodore Fulton *senator*
Stokes, Louis *former congressman, lawyer*
Strickland, Ted *congressman, clergyman, psychology educator, psychologist*
Stupak, Bart T. *congressman, lawyer*
Sullivan, John A. *congressman*
Sununu, John E. *senator*
Sweeney, John E. *congressman*
Tancredo, Thomas G. *congressman*
Tanner, John S. *congressman, lawyer*
Tauzin, W. J. Billy, II, (Wilbert J. Tauzin) *congressman*
Taylor, Charles H. *congressman*
Taylor, Gene *congressman*
†Tenorio, Pedro A. *resident representative*
Terry, Lee R. *congressman, lawyer*
Thomas, Craig *senator*
Thomas, William Marshall *congressman*
Thompson, Bennie G. *congressman*
Thompson, C. Michael *congressman*
Thornberry, Mac *congressman*
Thurman, Karen L. *congresswoman*
Tiahrt, W. Todd *congressman, former state senator*
Tiberi, Patrick J. *congressman, former state legislator*
Tierney, John F. *congressman, lawyer*
Toomey, Patrick J. *congressman*
Towns, Edolphus *congressman*
Turner, James *congressman*
†Turner, Michael *congressman*
Udall, Mark *congressman*
Udall, Thomas (Tom Udall) *congressman*
†Underwood, Robert Anacletus *former congressman, university official*
Upton, Frederick Stephen *congressman*
†Van Hollen, Christopher, Jr., *congressman*
Vazirani-Fales, Heea *legislative staff member, lawyer*
Velazquez, Nydia M. *congresswoman*
Visclosky, Peter John *congressman, lawyer*
Vitter, David *congressman*
Voinovich, George V. *senator, former mayor and governor*
Walden, Greg *congressman*
Walker, Robert Smith *former congressman*
Walsh, James Thomas *congressman*
Wamp, Zach *congressman*
Warner, John William *senator*
Waters, Maxine *congresswoman*
Watson, Diane Edith *congresswoman*
Watt, Melvin L. *congressman, lawyer*
Waxman, Henry Arnold *congressman*
Weldon, David Joseph, Jr., *congressman, physician*
Weldon, W(ayne) Curtis (Curt Weldon) *congressman*
Weller, Gerald C. *congressman*
Wexler, Robert *congressman*
Whitfield, Edward (Wayne Whitfield) *congressman*
Wicker, Roger F. *congressman, lawyer*
Wilson, Addison Graves (Joe Wilson) *congressman, former senator, lawyer*
†Wilson, Charles *former congressman*
Wilson, Heather Ann *congresswoman*
Wolf, Frank R. *congressman, lawyer*
Woolsey, Lynn *congresswoman*
Wu, David *congressman*
Wyden, Ron *senator*
Wynn, Albert Russell *congressman*
Young, C. W. (Bill Young) *congressman*
Young, Donald E. *congressman*

FLORIDA

Fernandina Beach
Smeeton, Thomas Rooney *governmental affairs consultant*

Miami
Cosgrove, John Francis *lawyer, state legislator*

Pensacola
Hutto, Earl *retired congressman*

Tallahassee
†Byrd, Johnnie, Jr., *state legislator*
†King, James E. "Jim", Jr., *state legislator, personnel executive, consultant*

Tampa
Davis, Helen Gordon *former state senator*

GEORGIA

Atlanta
†Coleman, Terry Lewis *state legislator*
Holmes, Robert Alexander *state legislator*
†Nunn, Samuel (Sam Nunn) *former senator, lawyer*
Purcell, Ann Rushing *state legislator, office manager medical business*
Starr, Terrell *state senator*

Lawrenceville
Wall, Clarence Vinson *state legislator*

Savannah
†Johnson, Eric B. *state legislator*

Smyrna
Atkins, William Austin, Sr., (Bill Atkins) *former state legislator*

Snellville
Cleland, Max *former senator*

HAWAII

Hilo
Ushijima, John Takeji *state legislator, lawyer*

Honolulu
†Aduja, Melodie Williams *state senator*
†Arakaki, Dennis A. *state representative*
†Bukoski, Kika G. *state representative*
Bunda, Robert *state legislator*
†Caldwell, Kirk *state representative*
†Chun Oakland, Suzanne Nyuk Jun *state legislator*
†English, J. Kalani *state senator*
†Espero, William (Willie C.) *state senator*
Fasi, Frank Francis *state legislator*
Fong, Hiram Leong *former senator*
†Fox, Galen W. *state representative*
†Fukunaga, Carol A. *state legislator, lawyer*
†Hale, Helene H. *state representative*
†Hanabusa, Colleen *state legislator, lawyer*
†Hemmings, Fred *state senator*
†Hogue, Bob *state senator*
†Ige, David Y. *state legislator*
†Ihara, Les, Jr., *state legislator*
†Inouye, Lorraine R. *state legislator*
†Ito, Ken *state representative*
†Kanno, Brian M. *state legislator, volunteer worker*
†Kawakami, Bertha C. *state representative*
†Kawamoto, Calvin Kazuo *state legislator*
†Kim, Donna Mercado *state senator*
†Kokubun, Russell S. *state senator*
†Lee, Marilyn B. *state representative*
†Leong, Bertha F.K. *state representative*
†Magaoay, Michael Y. *state representative*
†Menor, Ron *state legislator*
†Moses, Mark S. *state representative*
†Ontai, Guy Po'olanui *state representative*
Say, Calvin *state legislator*
†Slom, Samuel M. *state legislator*
Takumi, Roy Mitsuo *state legislator*
†Taniguchi, Brian T. *state senator*

Kailua
Young, Jacqueline Eurn Hai *former state legislator, consultant*

Kapolei
†Sakamoto, Norman Lloyd *state legislator, civil engineer*

Wailuku
Baker, Rosalyn Hester *state senator*

IDAHO

Boise
Black, Pete *retired state legislator, educator*
†Geddes, Robert L. *state legislator*
Newcomb, Bruce *state legislator, farmer, rancher*

ILLINOIS

Aurora
Etheredge, Forest DeRoyce *former state senator, former university administrator*

Belleville
†Holbrook, Thomas Aldredge *state legislator*

Bloomington
†Brady, William E. *state legislator*

Carbondale
†Bost, Mike *state legislator*
†Poshard, Glenn W. *former congressman*
Simon, Paul *former senator, educator, writer*

Champaign
†Winkel, Richard J., Jr., *state legislator*

Chicago
Berman, Arthur Leonard *retired state senator*
Bugielski, Robert Joseph *state legislator*
†Burke, Daniel J. *state legislator*
†Capparelli, Ralph C. *state legislator*
Cohen, Ira *legislative staff member*
Davis, Danny K. *congressman*
†DeLeo, James A. *state legislator*
†Dillard, Kirk Whitfield *state legislator, lawyer*
Doherty, Brian Gerard *alderman*
†Feigenholtz, Sara *state legislator*
†Giles, Calvin Lamont *state legislator*
†Hendon, Ricky *state legislator*
†Jones, Emil, Jr., *state legislator*
†Molaro, Robert S *state legislator, lawyer*
Moore, Joseph Arthur *alderman, lawyer*

Coal City
†O'Brien, Mary Kathleen *state representative, lawyer*

Collinsville
†Hoffman, Jay C. *state legislator*

Crestwood
†Rita, Robert *state representative*

East Alton
†Davis, Steve *state legislator*

East Moline
†Jacobs, Denny *state legislator*

East Saint Louis
†Clayborne, James F., Jr., *state legislator*
†Younge, Wyvetter Hoover *state legislator*

Effingham
†Hartke, Charles A. *state legislator*

Elmhurst
†Biggins, Robert A. *state legislator*
†Cronin, Dan *state legislator*

Gilson
†Moffitt, Donald L. *state legislator*

Greenville
†Watson, Frank Charles *state legislator*

Jacksonville
Findley, Paul *former congressman, author, educator*

Joliet
†Cross, Thomas H. *former state legislator*
†McGuire, John C. *state legislator*

La Grange
†Lyons, Eileen *state legislator*

Lincolnwood
Carroll, Howard William *lawyer, retired state senator*

Macomb
†Myers, Richard P. *state legislator*

Mount Vernon
†Jones, John O. *state legislator*

Peoria
†Leitch, David R. *state legislator*

Quincy
†Tenhouse, Art *state representative, farmer*

Romeoville
†Hassert, Brent *state legislator*

Schaumburg
†Wojcik, Kathleen Louise *state representative*

Springfield
†Beaubien, Mark H., Jr., *state representative*
†Black, William B. *state legislator*
†Boland, Michael Joseph *state legislator*
†Bomke, Larry K. *state legislator*
†Bradley, Richard T. *state representative*
†Brady, Daniel P. *state representative*
†Collins, Annazette R. *state representative*
†Collins, Jacqueline Y *state senator*
†Crotty, M. Maggie *state senator*
†Cultra, Shane *state representative*
Currie, Barbara Flynn *state legislator*
Daniels, Lee Albert *state legislator*
†Davis, Monique D. (Deon Davis) *state legislator*
†Del Valle, Miguel *state legislator*
†Demuzio, Vince Thomas *state legislator*
†Dunn, Joe *state representative*
†Eddy, Roger L. *state representative*
†Flowers, Mary E. *state legislator*
†Forby, Gary F. *state representative*
†Fritchey, John A. *state representative*
†Garrett, Susan *state senator*
†Geo-Karis, Adeline Jay *state legislator*
†Granberg, Kurt *state legislator, lawyer*
†Haine, William R. *state senator*
†Halvorson, Debbie DeFrancesco *state legislator*
†Hamos, Julie E. *state representative*
†Hannig, Gary L. *state representative*
†Howard, Constance A. *state representative*
†Jakobsson, Naomi D. *state representative*
†Jefferson, Charles E. *state representative*
†Jones, Lovana S. *state legislator*
†Jones, Wendell E. *state legislator*
†Kelly, Robin L. *state representative*
†Kosel, Renée *state representative*
†Krause, Carolyn H. *state legislator, lawyer*
†Kurtz, Rosemary *state representative*
†Lauzen, Christopher J. *state legislator*
†Lightford, Kimberly A. *state legislator*
†Link, Terry *state legislator*
†Luechtefeld, David *state legislator*
†Lyons, Joseph M. *state representative*
Madigan, Michael Joseph *state legislator*
†Martinez, Iris *state senator*
†Mathias, Sidney H. *state representative*
†McCarthy, Kevin A. *state representative*
†McKeon, Larry J. *state representative*
†Meeks, James T. *state senator*
†Miller, David E. *state representative*
†Mitchell, Gerald Lee *state legislator*
†Mulligan, Rosemary Elizabeth *legislator*
†Munoz, Antonio *state legislator*
†Nekritz, Elaine *state representative*
†Obama, Barack A. *state legislator*
†Pankau, Carole *state legislator*

†Erdman, Philip *state legislator, farmer*
†Exon, J(ohn) James *former senator*
†Foley, Mike *state legislator*
Kramer, David J. *state representative, lawyer*
Kristensen, Douglas Allan *former state legislator*
Landis, David Morrison *state legislator*
†Maxwell, Chip *state legislator*
†Robak, Jennie *state legislator*
Schimek, DiAnna Ruth Rebman *state legislator*
Stuhr, Elaine Ruth *state legislator*

NEVADA

Carson City
†Amodei, Mark E. *state legislator, lawyer*
O'Connell, Mary Ann *state legislator, business owner*

Las Vegas
Care, Terry *state legislator, lawyer*
Ensign, John E. *senator, former congressman*
Wiener, Valerie *state senator, writer, positioning strategist, communications executive*

Reno
Raggio, William John *state legislator*

Yerington
Dini, Joseph Edward, Jr. *state legislator*

NEW HAMPSHIRE

Bartlett
Chandler, Gene G. *state legislator*

Bow
Sytek, Donna P. *former state legislator*

Concord
Arnold, Thomas Ivan, Jr., *state legislator*
Cote, David Edward *state legislator*
Dunlap, Patricia C. *state legislator*
†Eaton, Thomas *state legislator*
Eaton, Thomas R. *state legislator, retired funeral director*
Hager, Elizabeth Sears *state legislator, social services organization administrator*
Hollingworth, Beverly A. *state legislator*
Pignatelli, Debora Becker *state legislator*
Richardson, Barbara Hull *state legislator, social worker*

Derry
Katsakiores, George Nicholas *state legislator, retired restauranteur*

Dover
Pelletier, Arthur Joseph *state legislator, educator*

Durham
Wheeler, Katherine Wells *retired state legislator*

Etna
Copenhaver, Marion Lamson *former state legislator*

Hanover
Crory, Elizabeth L. *former state legislator*
Guest, Robert Henry *state legislator, management educator*

Lancaster
Pratt, Leighton Calvin *state legislator*

Manchester
Arnold, Barbara Eileen *state legislator*

Plaistow
Senter, Merilyn P(atricia) *former state legislator and freelance reporter*

Randolph
Bradley, Paula E. *former state legislator*

Windham
Arndt, Janet S. *state legislator*
†Delahunty, Joseph Lawrence *state senator, business investor*

NEW JERSEY

Atlantic Highlands
†Corodemus, Steven James *state legislator, lawyer*

Bayonne
Doria, Joseph V., Jr., *state legislator*

Bordentown
†Malone, Joseph R. *state legislator*

Brick
†Ciesla, Andrew R. *state legislator*
†Wolfe, David W. *state legislator*

Camden
†Bryant, Wayne Richard *state legislator*

Cresskill
†Cardinale, Gerald *state legislator*

Deal
†Palaia, Joseph A. *state legislator*

Delran
†Conaway, Herb(ert) C., Jr., *assemblyman*

Denville
†Bucco, Anthony R. *state legislator*

Edison
†Barnes, Peter J., Jr., *assemblyman*
†Buono, Barbara *state legislator*

Egg Harbor Township
†Blee, Francis J. *state legislator, chiropractor*

Elizabeth
†Cohen, Neil M. *state legislator*
†Lesniak, Raymond J. *state legislator*
†Suliga, Joseph *state legislator*

Emerson
†Rooney, John Edward *state legislator, electrical company executive*

Ewing
†Turner, Shirley Kersey *state legislator*

Flemington
Lance, Leonard *state legislator*

Forked River
†Connors, Christopher J. *state legislator*
†Moran, Jeffrey W., Jr., *state legislator*

Franklin
†Littell, Robert E. *state legislator*

Freehold
Bennett, John O. *state legislator*
†Farragher, Clare M. *state legislator*

Gloucester City
†Roberts, Joseph J. *former state legislator*

Hackensack
†Baer, Byron M. *state legislator*

Hackettstown
†Gregg, Guy R. *state legislator*

Hamilton
†Inverso, Peter A. *state legislator*

Hawthorne
†Girgenti, John Alexander *state legislator*

Hoboken
†Kenny, Bernard F. *state legislator, lawyer*

Irvington
†Stanley, Craig A. *state legislator*

Jackson
†Dancer, Ronald S. *assemblyman*

Jersey City
†Quigley, Joan Marie *state legislator*

Lodi
†Heck, Rose *state legislator*

Matawan
†Thompson, Samuel Donald *assemblyman*

Mays Landing
†Gormley, William L. *state legislator*

Middletown
†Azzolina, Joseph *state legislator, grocery executive*

Midland Park
†Russo, David C. *state legislator*

Monroe
†Greenstein, Linda R. *assemblywoman*

Montclair
Gill, Nia H. *state legislator*

Morris Plains
†DeCroce, Alex *state legislator*
†Martin, Robert J. *state legislator*

Morristown
†Carroll, Michael Patrick *assemblyman*

Mount Laurel
†Bark, Martha W. *state legislator*
†Bodine, Francis L. *state legislator*
†Chatzidakis, Larry *assemblyman*

New Brunswick
Franks, Robert D. (Bob Franks) *former congressman*

Newark
†Caraballo, Wilfredo *assemblyman*
James, Sharpe *mayor, state legislator*
Martini, William J. *former congressman, state commissioner, judge*
†Payne, William D. *assemblyman*
†Rice, Ronald L. *state legislator*
†Tucker, Donald *assemblyman*

Newton
†McHose, Alison Littell *assemblywoman*

Ocean City
Hughes, William John *former congressman, diplomat*

Paramus
†Ahearn, Matthew J. *assemblyman*

Paterson
†Pou, Nellie *assemblywoman*
†Steele, Alfred E. *assemblyman*

Plainfield
Green, Gerald B. *state legislator*

Red Bank
†Arnone, Michael John *state legislator, dentist*

Rutherford
†DiGaetano, Paul *state legislator*

Secaucus
†Impreveduto, Anthony Neil *state legislator*

Short Hills
Ogden, Maureen Black *retired state legislator*

Somerset
†Chivukula, Upendra J. *assemblyman, electrical engineer*

Somerville
†Bateman, Christopher (Kip Bateman) *state legislator*
†Biondi, Peter J. *assemblyman*
†Kavanaugh, Walter J. *state legislator*

South Orange
†Hackett, Mims, Jr., *state legislator*

Teaneck
Weinberg, Loretta *state legislator*

Trenton
†Allen, Diane Betzendahl *state legislator*
Ben-Asher, Daniel Lawrence *legislative researcher, writer*
†Charles, Joseph, Jr., *state legislator*
†Codey, Richard J. *state legislator*
†Coleman, Bonnie Watson *assemblywoman*
Collins, Jack *retired state legislator*
†Connors, Leonard T. *state legislator*
†Geist, George F. *state legislator*
†Gusciora, Reed *assemblyman*
Kyrillos, Joseph M. *state legislator, political organization worker*
†Sacco, Nicholas J. *state legislator*
†Singer, Robert W. *state legislator*
†Vandervalk, Charlotte *state legislator*
†Watson-Coleman, Bonnie *state legislator*

Turnersville
Matheussen, John J. *state legislator*

Union
†Cryan, Joseph P. *assemblyman*

Union City
†Fraguela, Rafael J. *assemblyman*

Vineland
†Asselta, Nicholas *state legislator*

Washington
†Myers, Connie *assemblywoman*

West New York
Sires, Albio *legislative staff member, business owner*

Wildwood
†Cafiero, James S. *state legislator, lawyer*

Woodbridge
†Friscia, Arline M. *assemblywoman*
†Vitale, Joseph F. *state legislator*

Wyckoff
†McNamara, Henry P. *state legislator*

NEW MEXICO

Albuquerque
†Gorham, Ramsay L. *state legislator, political organization administrator*
†Romero, Richard M. *state legislator, educator*
Rutherford, Thomas Truxtun, II, *county commissioner, former state senator*
Sanchez, Raymond G. *former state legislator*

Hobbs
Reagan, Gary Don *state legislator, lawyer*

Los Alamos
†Redmond, Bill *former congressman, minister*
Wallace, Jeannette Owens *state legislator*

Santa Fe
Lujan, Ben *state representative*

NEW YORK

Albany
†Bruno, Joseph L. *state legislator, senate majority leader*
Canestrari, Ronald *state legislator*
Ferrara, Donna *state legislator*
†Treadwell, Sandy *legislative staff member, political organization administrator*
Volker, Dale Martin *state legislator, lawyer*

Bayside
Goldes, Jordan *legislative staff member, press secretary*

Brooklyn
Weiner, Anthony David *congressman*

Clifton Park
DeLong, Lawrence Albert *former legislative official*

Glendale
Maltese, Serphin Ralph *state legislator, lawyer*

Huntington
Israel, Steve *congressman*

Jamaica
†Flake, Floyd Harold *former congressman*

Mount Kisco
Matusow, Naomi C. *state legislator*

New Windsor
Gilman, Benjamin Arthur *former congressman, lawyer*

New York
†Farrell, Herman Denny, Jr., *state legislator, political organization worker*
†Fazio, Vic *former congressman*
Gramm, William Philip (Phil Gramm) *former senator, economist*
†Silver, Sheldon *state legislator, lawyer*

Pearl River
Karben, Ryan Scott *state legislator*

Port Chester
Oppenheimer, Suzi *state legislator*

Rego Park
†Manton, Thomas Joseph *former congressman*

Rochester
John, Susan V. *state representative*

NORTH CAROLINA

Advance
Cochrane, Betsy Lane *state senator*

Burlington
Holt, Bertha Merrill *state legislator*

Charlotte
Myrick, Sue *congresswoman, former mayor*

Clinton
†Faircloth, Duncan McLauchlin (Lauch Faircloth) *former senator, businessman, farmer*

Pinehurst
Funderburk, David Britton *former congressman and ambassador, consultant*

Raleigh
Basnight, Marc *state senator, small business owner, construction executive*
Black, James M. *state representative, optometrist*
Lancaster, H(arold) Martin *former congressman, former presidential advisor, academic administrator*
Shaw, Robert Gilbert *state senator, restaurant executive*
Stevens, Richard Yates *state senator*
Tally, Lura Self *state legislator*

Winston Salem
Ward, Marvin Martin *retired state senator*

NORTH DAKOTA

Ashley
Kretschmar, William Edward *state legislator, lawyer*

Bismarck
†Dever, Dick *state legislator*
Heigaard, William Steven *state senator*
Traynor, Daniel M. *state representative*
†Urlacher, Herbert *state legislator*

Cavalier
Trenbeath, Thomas L. *state legislator, lawyer*

Dickinson
Wald, Francis John *state legislator*

Edgeley
Schimke, Dennis J. *former state legislator*

Fargo
Bernstein, LeRoy G. *state legislator*
Mathern, Tim *state legislator*

Fessenden
Streibel, Bryce *state senator*

Grand Forks
DeMers, Judy Lee *former state legislator, university dean*
†Espegard, Duaine C. *state legislator*
†Polovitz, Michael *state legislator*

Lehr
†Erbele, Robert S. *state legislator*

Minnewaukan
†Every, Michael A. *state legislator*

Williston
Rennerfeldt, Earl Ronald *state legislator, farmer, rancher*
Yockim, James Craig *former state senator, foundation administrator*

OHIO

Akron
Seiberling, John Frederick *former congressman, law educator, lawyer*

Aurora
Herington, Leigh Ellsworth *state legislator, lawyer*

Columbus
†Austria, Steve *state legislator*
Davidson, Jo Ann *former state legislator*
†Glenn, John Herschel, Jr., *former senator, astronaut*
†Hollister, Nancy *state legislator*
Kearns, Merle Grace *state representative*
Wachtmann, Lynn R. *state legislator*
†White, Doug *state legislator*

Dayton
Reid, Marilyn Joanne *state legislator, lawyer*

OKLAHOMA

Muskogee
Coburn, Tom A. *former congressman*

Oklahoma City
†Adair, Larry E. *state representative*
Ford, Charles Reed *state legislator*
Garrett, Kathryn Ann Byers (Kitty Garrett) *legislative clerk*
†Hobson, Calvin J., III, *state legislator, real estate firm executive*
Mass, Michael D. *state legislator*
Taylor, Stratton *state legislator, lawyer*

Tulsa
Wiland, George William, Jr., *legislative staff member, consultant*

OREGON

Grants Pass
Adams, Brady *bank executive, former state legislator*

Hillsboro
†Furse, Elizabeth *former congresswoman, small business owner*

Portland
†Hatfield, Mark Odom *former senator*
Hunt, David G. *state representative, coalition executive*

Salem
Brown, Kate *state legislator*
†Courtney, Peter C. *state legislator*
†Minnis, Karen *state representative*
Simmons, Mark *state representative*

PENNSYLVANIA

Abington
Poth, Jodie Megan *legislative staff member*

Erie
Boyes, Karl W. *state legislator*

Harrisburg
Czikowsky, Leon Lawton *legislative aide*
†Gerlach, James William *congressman*
†Greenleaf, Stewart John *state legislator*
Herman, Lynn Briggs *state legislator*
†Kukovich, Allen Gale *state legislator, lawyer*
Miller, Sheila *state legislator*
†Perzel, John Michael *state legislator*
Tartaglione, Christine M. *state legislator*
†Wenger, Noah W. *state legislator*

Lewisberry
Smith, Bruce I. *state legislator*

Monroeville
Klink, Ron *former congressman, reporter, newscaster*

Philadelphia
†Josephs, Babette *legislator*
Muntean, Andrei Mihai *legislative staff member, educator*
Roebuck, James Randolph, Jr., *state legislator*

Reading
Kiehne, Frank Charles, Jr., *foreign affairs adviser*

Wayne
Rubley, Carole A. *state legislator*

Wellsboro
Baker, Matthew Edward *state legislator*

RHODE ISLAND

Providence
Ajello, Edith H. *state legislator*
Algiere, Dennis Lee *state legislator*
Gibbs, June Nesbitt *state legislator*
Graziano, Catherine Elizabeth *state legislator, retired nursing educator*
†Murphy, William J. *state legislator*

Rumford
†Irons, William V. *state legislator*

Warwick
Revens, John Cosgrove, Jr., *state legislator, lawyer*

SOUTH CAROLINA

Clover
Kirsh, Herb *state legislator*

Columbia
Courson, John Edward *state legislator, insurance company executive*
Harvin, Charles Alexander, III, *state legislator, lawyer*
Leatherman, Hugh Kenneth, Sr., *state legislator, business executive*
†McConnell, Glenn F. *state legislator, lawyer, art gallery executive*
Wilkins, David Horton *state legislator*

Greenville
†Inglis, Robert D. (Bob Inglis) *former congressman, lawyer*
Manly, Sarah Letitia *retired state legislator, ophthalmic photographer, angiographer*
Mann, James Robert *former congressman*

Mc Cormick
Clayton, Verna Lewis *retired state legislator*

SOUTH DAKOTA

Black Hawk
Maicki, G. Carol *former state senator, consultant*

Brandon
Hunt, Roger *former state legislator*

Brookings
†Brown, Arnold M. *state legislator*
McClure-Bibby, Mary Anne *former state legislator*

Miller
Morford, JoAnn (JoAnn Morford-Burg) *state senator, investment company executive*

Mud Butte
Ingalls, Marie Cecelie *former state legislator, retail executive*

Pierre
†Diedtrich, Elmer *state legislator*
Pederson, Gordon Roy *state legislator, retired military officer*

Sioux Falls
Paisley, Keith Watkins *former state senator, retired small business owner*

TENNESSEE

Kingsport
†Quillen, James Henry (Jimmy Quillen) *former congressman*

Memphis
Ford, Harold Eugene *consultant, former congressman*

Nashville
†Graves, Jo Ann *state legislator*
Naifeh, James O. (Jimmy Naifeh) *state legislator, speaker of the house*
Person, Curtis S., Jr., *state legislator, lawyer*

TEXAS

Austin
Denny, Mary Craver *state legislator, rancher*
†Lucio, Eduardo Andres, Jr., *state legislator*
Shea, Gwyn *secretary of state*

Beaumont
Brooks, Jack Bascom *former congressman*

Dallas
Bryant, John Wiley *former congressman*

Fort Worth
†Geren, Pete (Preston Geren) *former congressman*
Harris, Christopher J. *state legislator, lawyer*
Willis, Doyle Henry *state legislator, lawyer*

Garland
Driver, Joe L. *state legislator, insurance agent*

Hale Center
Laney, James Earl (Pete Laney) *state representative, speaker of the house, farmer*

Laredo
Zaffirini, Judith *state legislator, small business owner*

Lubbock
Montford, John Thomas *state legislator, academic administrator, lawyer*

Midland
Craddick, Thomas Russell *speaker of state house of representatives*

Temple
Jones, Grant *retired state legislator, lawyer, insurance agent*

UTAH

Bountiful
Burningham, Kim Richard *former state legislator*

Corinne
Ferry, Miles Yeoman *former state legislator*

Logan
Hillyard, Lyle William *state legislator, lawyer*

Midvale
Mansell, L. Alma *state legislator*

Provo
Cannon, Christopher Black *congressman*
Valentine, John Lester *state legislator, lawyer*

Salt Lake City
Black, Wilford Rex, Jr., *former state senator*
Carnahan, Orville Darrell *retired state legislator, retired college president*
Shepherd, Karen *former congresswoman*

Tremonton
Kerr, Kleon Harding *former state senator, educator*

VERMONT

Bellows Falls
Obuchowski, Michael J. *state legislator*

Brattleboro
Milkey, Virginia A. *state legislator*

Montpelier
Paquin, Edward H., Jr., *former state legislator, non-profit organization executive*

Putney
†Darrow, Steve *state legislator*

Rutland
Ferraro, Betty Ann *state senator, corporate administrator*

Waterbury
Steele, Karen Kiarsis *retired state legislator*

White River Junction
Bohi, Lynn *state legislator*
†Welch, Peter F. *state legislator*

VIRGINIA

Alexandria
Collins, Cardiss *former congresswoman*
Goodling, William F. *former congressman*
Montgomery, Gillespie V. (Sonny Montgomery) *former congressman*
Ticer, Patricia *state senator*
Wofford, Harris *former senator, national service executive*

Arlington
Davis, Sharon Eileen *congressional staff member*
Robb, Charles Spittal *former senator, former governor, lawyer, educator*
Zanfagna, Philip Edward *government executive, urban planner*

Fairfax
Miller, Emilie F. *former state senator, consultant*

Fredericksburg
Goolrick, John Cole *congressional staff member, writer, consultant*

Leesburg
Mims, William Cleveland *state legislator, lawyer*

Mc Lean
Burke, Sheila P. *federal administrator*
Callahan, Vincent Francis, Jr., *state legislator, publisher*
Kim, Jay *former congressman*
Paul, Andrew Robert *defense and legislative consultant*

Newport News
Keator, Margaret Whitley *legislative aide*
Trible, Paul Seward, Jr., *former United States senator*

Norfolk
Miller, Yvonne Bond *state legislator, educator*

Reston
Plum, Kenneth Ray *state legislator*

Richmond
Chichester, John H. *state legislator*
†Howell, William James *state legislator*
Putney, Lacey Edward *state legislator*
Rimler, Anita A. *secretary of state*
Schaar, Susan Clarke *state legislative staff member*

Roanoke
†Larkin, Peter S. *legislative aid*

Vienna
Higginbotham, Wendy Jacobson *political adviser, writer*

WASHINGTON

Langley
Metcalf, Jack *former congressman, retired state senator*

Olympia
Ballard, Clyde *state legislator*
Cook, Tony Michael *legislative staff member*
Kessler, Lynn Elizabeth *state legislator*
Long, Jeanine Hundley *retired state legislator*
†Winsley, Shirley J. *state legislator, insurance agent*

Tumwater
†Satran, Jill Marie *policy analyst, lawyer*

Vancouver
Benton, Donald Mark *state legislator, political organization chairman*
†Smith, Linda A. *former congresswoman*

WEST VIRGINIA

Charleston
Helmick, Walt *state legislator*
†Kiss, Robert *state legislator*
Tomblin, Earl Ray *state legislator*

Shinnston
Spears, Jae *state legislator*

WISCONSIN

Black Earth
†Klug, Scott Leo *former congressman*

De Pere
†Lasee, Alan J. *state legislator*

Madison
Barish, Lawrence Stephen *nonpartisan legislative staff administrator*
Gunderson, Scott Lee *state legislator*
Risser, Fred A. *state legislator*
Roessler, Carol Ann *state legislator*
Turner, Robert Lloyd *state legislator*
Whitney, Lori Ann *legislative staff member*
Young, Rebecca Mary Conrad *state legislator*

Peshtigo
†Gard, John *state legislator*

WYOMING

Casper
Donley, Russell Lee, III, *former state legislator*
Tempest, Rick *state representative*

Cheyenne
†Kunz, April Brimmer *state legislator, lawyer*
†Parady, Fred *state representative*

Cody
Coe, Henry H. R. *state legislator*
Shreve, Peg *retired state legislator, retired elementary school educator*
Simpson, Alan Kooi *former senator, lawyer*

Douglas
Twiford, Jim *former state legislator*

Jackson
LaLonde, Robert Frederick *state senator, retired*

Lander
Tipton, Harry Basil, Jr., *state legislator, physician*

Laramie
Hansen, Matilda *former state legislator*
Maxfield, Peter C. *state legislator, law educator, lawyer*

TERRITORIES OF THE UNITED STATES

GUAM

Agana
Bordallo, Madeleine Mary (Mrs. Ricardo Jerome Bordallo) *congresswoman*

NORTHERN MARIANA ISLANDS

Saipan
Babauta, Juan Nekai *governor*

PUERTO RICO

San Juan
Romero-Barceló, Carlos Antonio *former congressman, former governor of Puerto Rico, former mayor of San Juan*

CANADA

BRITISH COLUMBIA

Vancouver
McWhinney, Edward Watson *Canadian government legislator*

ONTARIO

Brampton
Malhi, Gurbax Singh *legislator*

Ottawa
Bevilacqua, Maurizio *member of Canadian parliament*
Boudria, Don *Canadian government official*
Catterall, Marlene *Canadian legislator*
Coderre, Denis *legislator*
Kilgour, David *Canadian member of parliament*
Maheu, Shirley *Canadian legislator*
Mills, Dennis Joseph *member of parliament*
Murray, Lowell *Canadian senator*
Nault, Robert D. *legislator*
Penson, Charlie Frederick *member of parliament*
Pettigrew, Pierre S. *politician, member of parliament*
Ritz, Gerry *member of parliament*
St. Hilaire, Caroline *member of parliament*
Skelton, Carol *member of parliament*
Telegdi, Andrew *member of parliament*
Vellacott, Maurice *member of parliament*
Whelan, Susan *member of parliament*
Yelich, Lynne *member of parliament*

Toronto
Eyton, John Trevor *senator, business executive*

SASKATCHEWAN

Regina
Spencer, Larry *member of parliament*

GERMANY

Bonn
†Coats, Daniel Ray *former senator*

ITALY

Rome
Hall, Tony P. *ambassador, former congressman*

ADDRESS UNPUBLISHED

Armey, Richard Keith (Dick Armey) *former congressman*
Barrett, Thomas M. *congressman*
Barrett, William E. *former congressman*
Barton, Joe Linus *congressman*
Beals, Nancy Farwell *former state legislator*
Benson, Loyd *retired state legislator*
Bilbray, Brian P. *former congressman*
Bilbray, James Hubert *former congressman, lawyer, consultant*
Binienda, John J. *state legislator*
†Bradley, Bill *former senator*
Brightbill, David John *state legislator, lawyer*
†Brown-Waite, Virginia (Ginny Brown-Waite) *congresswoman*
Bryant, Edward *former congressman, lawyer*
Callahan, Sonny (H.L. Callahan) *former congressman*
Campbell, Tom *former congressman, dean*
Carnahan, Jean *former senator*
Carstairs, Sharon *state legislator*
Charlton, Betty Jo *retired state legislator*
Chenoweth-Hage, Helen P. *former congresswoman*
†Chrysler, Richard R. *former congressman*
Churchill, Robert Wilson *state legislator, lawyer*
Clay, William Lacy *former congressman*
Clement, Bob *former congressman*
Clinger, William Floyd, Jr., *retired congressman*
Coble, Howard *congressman, lawyer*
Cochran, Thad *senator*
Combest, Larry Ed *retired congressman*
Condit, Gary Adrian *former congressman*
Connelly, Elizabeth Ann *retired state legislator*
Cook, Merrill A. *former congressman, explosives industry executive*
†Coyne, William Joseph *former congressman*
Crippen, Bruce D. *former state legislator, real estate manager*
Danner, Patsy Ann (Mrs. C. M. Meyer) *former congresswoman*
De Gette, Diana Louise *congresswoman, lawyer*
DeMint, James Warren *congressman, marketing professional*
Dickey, Jay W., Jr., *former congressman, lawyer*
Doderer, Minnette Frerichs *retired state legislator*
Eisenberg, Albert Charles *senior government official*
Ewing, Thomas William *former congressman, lawyer*
Federing, Eric K. *congressional communications director, motion picture preservationist, educator, public policy advisor*
†Fields, Cleo *state legislator*
Finestone, Sheila *legislator, state official*
Forbes, Michael Patrick *former congressman*
†Fox, Jon D. *former congressman*
Ganske, J. Greg *former congressman, plastic surgeon*
Gekas, George William *former congressman*
Gordly, Avel Louise *state legislator, community activist*
†Grams, Rodney D. *former senator, former congressman*
Granger, Kay *congresswoman*
Groscost, Jeff *former state legislator, small business owner*
Hammerschmidt, John Paul *retired congressman, lumber company executive*
Hatch, Orrin Grant *senator*
Haytaian, Garabed (Chuck Haytaian) *state legislator*
Hearn, Joyce Camp *retired state legislator, educator, consultant*
Heath, Roger Charles *state senator, writer*
Helms, Jesse *retired senator*
Henry, Margaret Rose *state legislator*
Hickey, Winifred E(spy) *former state legislator, social worker*
Hill, Anita Carraway *retired state legislator*
Hill, Rick Allan *former congressman*
Hilleary, Van *former congressman, lawyer*
Holliday, Robert Kelvin *corrections officer, retired state senator, former newspaper executive, educator*
Horn, Stephen *congressman, political science educator*
Hunter, Duncan Lee *congressman*
Hutchison, Kay Bailey *senator*
†Johnson, Jay Withington *former congressman*
†Kasich, John R. *former congressman*
Kerns, Brian D. *former congressman*
Konnyu, Ernest Leslie *former congressman*
La Falce, John Joseph *former congressman, lawyer*
Largent, Steve *former congressman, former professional football player*
Lazio, Rick A. *former congressman, lawyer, association administrator*
Maloney, James Henry *former congressman*
Maroney, Jane P. *former state legislator, consultant*
Martinez, Matthew Gilbert *former congressman*
Mascara, Frank R. *former congressman*
Matsunaka, Stanley T. *former state legislator*
†Mautino, Frank J. *state legislator*
May, Edgar *former state legislator, nonprofit administrator*
Mc Collum, Ira William, Jr., (Bill Mc Collum) *former congressman*
†McDade, Joseph Michael *former congressman*
McKay, John M. *former state senator*
Meek, Carrie P. *former congresswoman*
Meshel, Harry *state senator, political party official*
Mikulski, Barbara Ann *senator*
Mizuguchi, Norman *former state senator*
†Moseley-Braun, Carol *former senator, former ambassador*
Murphy, Thomas Bailey *retired state legislator*
Myers, John Thomas *retired congressman*
Nielsen, Linda Miller *city councilwoman*
†Novak, John Philip *state legislator*
Packard, Ronald C. *former congressman*
†Pappas, Michael *former congressman*
Pascoe, Patricia Hill *former state legislator*
Patrick, Michele Mary *government official*
Patterson, Elizabeth Johnston *former congresswoman*
Paul, Ron *congressman*
Pell, Claiborne *former senator*
Pettis-Roberson, Shirley McCumber *former congresswoman*
Pevear, Roberta Charlotte *retired state legislator*
Philip, James (Pate Philip) *retired state legislator*
†Poe, Donald Raymond *state legislator*
Pond, Phyllis Joan Ruble *state legislator, educator*
Powers, Ray Lloyd *former state senator, dairy farmer, rancher*
Quinby, Harold Eugene *retired councilman*
Redwine, John Newland *state legislator, physician*
Reid, Harry *senator*
Reyes, Silvestre *congressman*
Rivers, Lynn N. *former congresswoman*
Roukema, Margaret Scafati *former congressman*
Rudy, Ruth Corman *former state legislator*
St. Germain, Fernand Joseph *retired congressman*
Satterthwaite, Helen Foster *retired state legislator*
Saucier, Gene Duane *retired state legislator*
Sawyer, Thomas C. *former congressman*
Scarborough, Joe *former congressman*
†Schaefer, Dan L. *former congressman*
Searle, Rodney Newell *state legislator, farmer, insurance agent*
Sessions, Pete *congressman*
Shows, Ronnie *former congressman*
†Shuster, Bud *former congressman, lobbyist*
Skinner, Patricia Morag *state legislator*
Smith, Robert Clinton *former senator*
Snelling, Barbara W. *retired state legislator*
Soles, Ada Leigh *former state legislator, government advisor*
Sorensen, Sheila *state legislator*
Stickney, Jessica *former state legislator*
Sykora, Barbara Zwach *state legislator*
Tauscher, Ellen O. *congresswoman*
Taylor, Casper R., Jr., *lobbyist, former state legislator*
Thompson, Fred Dalton *former senator*
Thune, John *former congressman*
Torricelli, Robert G. *former senator*
Treppler, Irene Esther *retired state senator*
Van Engen, Thomas Lee *state legislator*
Vellenga, Kathleen Osborne *retired state legislator*
†Viverito, Louis Samuel *state legislator*
†Vucanovich, Barbara Farrell *retired congressman*
†Wait, Ronald A. *state legislator*
Warnstadt, Steven H. *state legislator*
Watkins, Wesley Wade *retired congressman*
Watts, J. C., Jr., *former congressman, retired football player*
White, Douglas Allan *legislative aide, data archivist*
†Winters, David Forrest *state legislator*
Zimmerman, Harold Samuel *retired state legislator, newspaper editor and publisher, state administrator*

HEALTHCARE: DENTISTRY

UNITED STATES

ALABAMA

Birmingham
Fullmer, Harold Milton *dentist, educator*
King, Charles Mark *dentist, educator*

Huntsville
Yarbrough, Isabel Miles *dentist, educator*

Mobile
Langley, Barry Lynn *dentist*

ARIZONA

Glendale
Hanhila, Matt Oscar, Jr., *orthodontist*

Tucson
Davis, Richard Calhoun *dentist*
Hawke, Robert Francis *dentist*
Kassman, Andrew Lance *orthodontist*
†Mondragon, Marc *dentist, pharmacist, consultant*
Pearson, Gary Dean *dentist*

CALIFORNIA

Arcadia
Gamboa, George Charles *retired oral surgeon, educator*

Bellflower
Davis, W. Howard *retired oral and maxillofacial surgeon*

Costa Mesa
Okamoto, Vicki E. *orthodontist*

Irvine
Kim, Han Pyong *dentist, researcher*

Loma Linda
†Rungcharassaeng, Kitichai *dentist*

Los Angeles
Drury, Gerald Irwin *periodontist, educator*
Dummett, Clifton Orrin *dentist, educator*
Friedlander, Arthur Henry *oral and maxillofacial surgeon, researcher*
†Ting, Kang *orthodontist, education educator*
†Younai, Fariba Simhai *dental educator, researcher*

Manteca
Tonn, Elverne Meryl *pediatric dentist, dental benefits consultant, forensic odontologist*

Merced
†Dylina, Timothy Joseph *dentist, educator*

Northridge
Logan, Lee Robert *orthodontist*

Pasadena
Mc Carthy, Frank Martin *oral surgeon, surgical sciences educator*

Richmond
Anderson, Vera Strong *retired dentist*

San Diego
Milder, David Geoffrey *oral and maxillofacial surgeon*

San Francisco
Bensinger, David August *dentist, university dean*
†Bertolami, Charles *oral surgeon*
Dugoni, Arthur A. *orthodontics educator, university dean*
†Gekelman, Diana *dentist, dental educator, researcher*
Greenspan, Deborah *dental educator*
Khosla, Ved Mitter *oral and maxillofacial surgeon, educator*
Olsen, Steven Kent *dentist*

San Jose
†Lee, Stanley Tak *dentist*
Yoshizumi, Donald Tetsuro *dentist*

San Rafael
Greene, John Clifford *dentist, former university dean*
Gryson, Joseph Anthony *orthodontist*

Santa Barbara
Lee, Glen K. *dentist*

Scotia
Hise, Mark Allen *dentist*

Toluca Lake
Bitting, Kevin Noel *pediatric craniofacial orthotist, researcher*

Vacaville
Dedeaux, Paul J. *orthodontist*
Welton, Michael Peter *dentist*

Whittier
Lowe, Oariona *dentist*

COLORADO

Denver
Patterson, Daniel William *dentist*

Golden
Christensen, Robert Wayne *oral maxillofacial surgeon, minister*

CONNECTICUT

Avon
†Boucher, Louis Jack *retired dentist, educator*
Weiss, Robert Michael *dentist*

Brookfield
Cohen, Mark Steven *dentist*

Middletown
Valentine, George Edward *dentist*

Orange
Dileone, Carmel Montano *dental hygienist*

Sharon
Nweeia, Martin Thomas *dentist, musician, composer, anthropologist*

Southbury
Hopf, Frank Rudolph *retired dentist*

Vernon Rockville
†Putnam, Richard *dentist, educator*

West Hartford
Liftig, S. Rick *dentist, author*

DELAWARE

Wilmington
Wachstein, Joan Martha *dental hygienist*

DISTRICT OF COLUMBIA

Washington
Calhoun, Noah Robert *oral maxillofacial surgeon, educator*
†Richeson, James G., Jr., *dentist*
Sinkford, Jeanne Craig *dental association administrator, dentist, retired dean, educator*

FLORIDA

Bay Harbor Islands
Rosenbluth, Morton *periodontist, educator*

Boca Raton
Eckelson, Robert Alan *orthodontist*
Lerner, Theodore Raphael *dentist*

Boynton Beach
Kronman, Joseph Henry *orthodontist, educator*

Bradenton
Engelman, Melvin Alkon *retired dentist, business executive, scientist*

Clearwater
Stewart, Michael Ian *orthodontist*

De Leon Springs
Price, Harry Mackey *dentist*

Fort Lauderdale
Dorn, Samuel O. *endodontist*
†Garcia-Godoy, Franklin *dental educator*
Oliet, Seymour *endodontics educator, dean, dentist*
†Siegel, Michael Alan *dental educator*

Fort Myers
Laboda, Gerald *oral and maxillofacial surgeon*

Gainesville
Tomar, Scott Lance *dentist*
Widmer, Charles Glenn *dentist, researcher*

Jupiter
Nessmith, H(erbert) Alva *dentist*

Madison
†Shaw, Roderick Kirkpatrick, III, *dentist*

Melbourne
†Elder, Stewart Taylor *dentist, retired naval officer*

Miami
Higley, Bruce Wadsworth *orthodontist*
Parnes, Edmund Ira *oral and maxillofacial surgeon, educator*

Naples
Rehak, James Richard *orthodontist*

Pembroke Pines
†Eisenstein, Sam *pediatric dentist*

Pinellas Park
Frantzis, Theodosios George *periodontist*

Tampa
Pasetti, Louis Oscar *retired dentist*
Perret, Gerard Anthony, Jr., *orthodontist*

Vero Beach
Glenn, Frances Bonde *retired dentist*

Winter Park
Bush, Christine Gay *dental hygienist*
McKean, Thomas Wayne *dentist, retired naval officer*

GEORGIA

Atlanta
Freedman, Louis Martin *dentist*

Augusta
Rippert, Eric Theodore *oral and maxillofacial surgeon*
Rogers, Michael Bruce *orthodontist*
Shrout, Michael Kirby *dental educator, researcher*

Calhoun
Edgmon, Gary Martin *orthodontist*

Macon
Holliday, Peter Osborne, Jr., *dentist*
Walton, DeWitt Talmage, Jr., *dentist*

Tucker
Osborne, Thomas Eugene *oral and maxillofacial surgeon*

HAWAII

Honolulu
George, Peter T. *orthodontist, consultant*
Nishimura, Pete Hideo *oral surgeon*
Scheerer, Ernest William *dentist*

Pearl City
Sue, Alan Kwai Keong *dentist*

IDAHO

Boise
Houston, William Orris, Jr., *oral and maxillofacial surgeon*

ILLINOIS

Bloomington
Milligan, Michael Lee *dentist*

Chicago
Barr, Sanford Lee *dentist*
†Barrows, Michael John *endodontist, educator*
Diefenbach, Viron Leroy *dental, public health educator, university dean*
Glenner, Richard Allen *dentist, dental historian*
Graber, Thomas M. *orthodontist, researcher*
Hardaway, Ernest, II, *oral and maxillofacial surgeon, public health official*
Hirsch, Martin *dentist*
Jackson, Gregory Wayne *orthodontist*
Litch, C(hristopher) Scott *dental association executive, lawyer*
†Reisberg, David J. *prosthodontist, director*
Santangelo, Mario Vincent *dentist*
Yale, Seymour Hershel *dental radiologist, educator, university dean, gerontologist*

Elburn
Willey, James Lee *dentist*

Geneva
Kallstrom, Charles Clark *dentist*
Lazzara, Dennis Joseph *orthodontist*

Godfrey
King, Ordie Herbert, Jr., *oral pathologist*

Hinsdale
Szeremeta-Browar, Taisa Lydia *endodontist*

Jacksonville
Loughary, Thomas Michael *dentist*

Kenilworth
Edson, Wayne E. *retired dentist, consultant*

Lake Forest
Jones, Gordon Kempton *dentist*

Naperville
Grimley, Jeffrey Michael *dentist*

Northbrook
Williams, David Allan *dentist, educator*

Park Ridge
Kenney, John Patrick *dentist*

INDIANA

Columbus
Arthur, Jewell Kathleen *dental hygienist*

Elkhart
Bryan, Norman E. *dentist*

Evansville
Fritz, Edward Lane *dentist*

Fishers
Behner, Elton Dale *dentist*

Gary
Stephens, Paul Alfred *dentist*

Indianapolis
Christen, Arden Gale *dental educator, researcher, consultant*
Roberts, Wilbur Eugene *dental educator, research scientist, wine importer*
Standish, Samuel Miles *oral pathologist, college dean*

Lafayette
Buckles, Judith Ann *dental educator, program administrator*

Peru
Davidson, John Robert *dentist*

Terre Haute
Roshel, John Albert, Jr., *orthodontist*

IOWA

Ankeny
†Weigel, Ollie J. *dentist, former mayor*

Iowa City
Bishara, Samir Edward *orthodontist*
Bjorndal, Arne Magne *endodontist*
Olin, William Harold *orthodontist, educator*
†Vargas, Kaaren Giselle *pediatric dentistry, molecular biologist*

KANSAS

Hays
Wagner, Paul Dean *oral and maxillofacial surgeon*

Topeka
Fyler, Carl John *dentist*
Stroud, Herschel Leon *retired dentist*

Wellington
Willis, Robert Addison *dentist*

Wichita
Huntley, Diane E. *dental hygiene educator*

KENTUCKY

Danville
†Morris, Alvin Leonard *retired dentist, educational administrator*

Lexington
Chance, Kenneth Bernard *endodontist, educator, university official*

Louisville
Gist, William Claude, Jr., *retired dentist*
Jacobs, Amelia Carol *orthodontist*
Parkins, Frederick Milton *dental educator, university dean*

LOUISIANA

Shreveport
Lloyd, Cecil Rhodes *pediatric dentist*

MAINE

Kennebunkport
Mulvihill, James Edward *periodontist, educator*

MARYLAND

Baltimore
McCauley, H(enry) Berton *retired public health dentist*

Bethesda
Kruger, Gustav Otto, Jr., *oral surgeon, educator*
Ogbureke, Kalu Ugwa Emmanuel *oral surgeon, oral and maxillofacial pathologist, molecular biologist*
Sazima, Henry John *retired oral and maxillofacial surgery educator*

Columbia
Lorton, Lewis *researcher, computer executive, dentist*
Rovelstad, Gordon H. *dentist, researcher*

Gaithersburg
Frome, David Herman *dentist*

Potomac
Cotton, William Robert *retired dentist*
Rosenberg, Jacob Joseph *orthodontist*

Rockville
†Chohayeb, Aida A. *dentist, educator*

Simpsonville
Altschuler, Bruce Robert *research dentist*

MASSACHUSETTS

Bedford
Eagles, Eugene, III, *orthodontist*

Boston
Frankl, Spencer Nelson *dentist, university dean*
Goldhaber, Paul *dental educator*
Johansen, Erling *retired dental educator and dean*
Shklar, Gerald *oral pathologist, periodontist, educator*
†White, George Edward *pedodontist, educator*

Chestnut Hill
Segelman, Allyn Evan *dentist, researcher, insurance executive*

Dorchester
Lee, June Warren *dentist*

Rockport
Gavelis, Jonas Rimvydas *dentist, educator*

Watertown
Berk, Harold *dentist, consultant, educator*

Wellesley
Birnbaum, Nathan Simcha *dentist*

Weston
Kim, Young Ho *orthodontist*

MICHIGAN

Ann Arbor
Ash, Major McKinley, Jr., *dentist, educator*
Brown, William Ernest *dentist*
Christiansen, Richard Louis *orthodontics educator, research director, former dean*
Craig, Robert George *dental science educator*
Giannobile, William Victor *periodontist, educator*
Millard, Herbert Dean *dentist*

Dearborn
Sarkisian, Edward Gregory *dentist*

Grand Rapids
†Yamusah, Aretha *dentist, writer*

Warren
Woehrlen, Arthur Edward, Jr., *dentist*

MINNESOTA

Kenyon
Jacobson, Lloyd Eldred *retired dentist*

Mankato
Dumke, Melvin Philip *dentist*

Minneapolis
†Brosky, Mary Elizabeth *dental educator, dentist*
†Doroschak, John Z. *dentist, consultant*
Martens, Leslie Vernon *dentistry educator, consultant*
Shapiro, Burton Leonard *oral pathologist, geneticist, educator*

Saint Paul
Jensen, James Robert *dentist, educator*

MISSOURI

Chesterfield
Biebel, Curt Fred, Jr., *dentist*
Selfridge, George Dever *retired dentist, retired naval officer*

Kansas City
Blanchaert, Remy Henry, Jr., *oral and maxillofacial surgeon*
Burk, Norman *retired oral surgeon*
Moore, Dorsey Jerome *dentistry educator, maxillofacial prosthetist*

Mexico
Rice, Marvin Elwood *dentist*

Saint Louis
Isselhard, Donald Edward *dentist*
Osborn, Mark Eliot *dentist*

MONTANA

Hardin
MacClean, Walter Lee *dentist*

NEBRASKA

Fremont
Roesch, Robert Eugene *dentist*

Lincoln
Johnson, William W. *dental educator*

Omaha
Lynch, Benjamin Leo *oral surgeon educator*
Zaiman, K(oichi) Robert *dentist*

NEVADA

Las Vegas
†Rawson, Raymond D. *dentist, state legislator*

Reno
Waltz, Marcus Ernest *retired prosthodontist*

NEW HAMPSHIRE

Bedford
Twarjan, Colleen Ann *dental hygienist*

Portsmouth
McArdle, Barry Francis *dentist*

NEW JERSEY

Chatham
Hurley, Allyson Kingsley *dentist*

Cherry Hill
Jacobson, Gerald *orthodontist*

Englewood
Schwartz, Howard Alan *periodontist*

Fair Haven
Di Turi, Christopher *dentist, maxillofacial prosthodontist, educator, researcher*

Fort Lee
Kiriakopoulos, George Constantine *dentist*

Freehold
†Greenstein, Gary *periodontist, dental educator*

Hackensack
Rosenbloom, Donald Theodore *orthodontist, sleep disorders specialist*

Hackettstown
Wiedemann, Charles Louis *dentist*

Ho Ho Kus
Van Slooten, Ronald Henry Joseph *dentist*

Kearny
Perricci, Jeffrey Michael *dentist*

Lakewood
Brod, Morton Shelvin *oral surgeon*

Maple Shade
Gordon, Paul *retired dentist, artist*

Marmora
Ingaglio, Diego Augustus *dentist*

Montclair
†Bolden, Theodore Edward *dentist, consultant, dental educator*

Newark
Feldman, Cecile Arlene *dentist*
Kantor, Mel Lewis *dental educator, researcher*

Oakland
Maccario, Maurice Malcolm *oral and maxillofacial surgeon, consultant*

Princeton
McClelland, Richard Lee *dentist*

Ridgewood
Lucca, John James *retired dental educator*

Sparta
Alberto, Pamela Louise *oral and maxillofacial surgeon, educator*

Voorhees
†Piermatti, Jack *dentist*

West New York
Steinberg, Louis Marshall *dentist, researcher*

Westfield
Feret, Adam Edward, Jr., *dentist*

Woodbridge
Galkin, Samuel Bernard *orthodontist*

NEW MEXICO

Farmington
Graham, Warren Kirkland *dentist*

NEW YORK

Albany
Sbuttoni, Michael James *orthodontist, building contractor*

Bay Shore
Goldstein, Leonard Barry *dentist, educator*

Bellport
Graskemper, Joseph Peter *dentist*

Bronx
†Ferraro, Marie *dental hygienist*

Brooklyn
†Bedrick, Anthony Edward *oral surgeon, educator*
Meyler, Mark Zinovyevich *dentist*
Schweikert, Edgar Oskar *dentist*
†Segelnick, Stuart Lawrence *periodontist*

Buffalo
†Drinnan, Alan John *oral pathologist*
Ortman, Harold Rodebaugh *retired prosthodontist*

Elmira
Bellohusen, Ronald Michael *orthodontist, educator*

Grand Island
Hennigar, William Grant, Jr., *dentist*

Great Neck
Elkowitz, Lloyd Kent *dental anesthesiologist, dentist, pharmacist*

Hempstead
Ancrum, Cheryl Denise *dentist*

Huntington
†Sforza, Alfred Vincent *dentist, educator, writer*

New York
Arvystas, Michael Geciauskas *orthodontist, educator*
Ashkinazy, Larry Robert *dentist*
Brzustowicz, Stanislaw Henry *clinical dentistry educator*
Di Salvo, Nicholas Armand *dental educator, orthodontist*
Kaslick, Ralph Sidney *dentist, educator*
Klatell, Jack *dentist, department chairman*
La Bruna, Vincent Vito *orthodontist*
Mandel, Irwin Daniel *dentist*
Marder, Michael Zachary *dentist, researcher, educator*
Scarola, John Michael *dentist, educator*
Wank, Gerald Sidney *periodontist, educator*
†Weinberg, Mea Arlene *dental educator, researcher, consultant*

Ossining
Maloney, William James *dentist, educator*

Rochester
Bowen, William Henry *dental researcher, dental educator*

Schenectady
DeLuke, Dean M. *oral surgeon*

Shelter Island
Moran, Daniel Thomas *dentist, poet*

Stony Brook
Sreebny, Leo M. *oral biology and pathology educator*

Tarrytown
Andreen, Aviva Louise *dentist, researcher, academic administrator, educator*

West Hempstead
Tartell, Robert Morris *retired dentist*

Yonkers
Torrese, Dante Michael *prosthodontist, educator*

NORTH CAROLINA

Boone
†Warren, Robert Lee *dentist, educator*

Chapel Hill
Proffit, William Robert *orthodontics educator*
White, Raymond Petrie, Jr., *dentist, educator*

Charlotte
Freedland, Jacob Berke *dentist, endodontist*
Misiek, Dale Joseph *oral and maxillofacial surgeon*
Owen, Kenneth Dale *orthodontist, real estate broker*
Twisdale, Harold Winfred *dentist*

Durham
†Mofidi, Mahyar *dental educator*

NORTH DAKOTA

Williston
Bekkedahl, Brad Douglas *dentist*

OHIO

Beachwood
Robertson, Edward Neil *dentist*

Canton
Osborne, Harry Alan *orthodontist*

Cincinnati
Gehlert, Sally Oyler *dental hygienist, consultant*

Cleveland
De Marco, Thomas Joseph *periodontist, educator*

Columbus
Austin, David George *dentist*
Buchsieb, Walter Charles *orthodontist, director*
†Carr, Michele Paige *dental hygienist, educator*
†Goorey, Nancy Jane *dentist*
Jolly, Daniel Ehs *dental educator*
Stevenson, Robert Benjamin, III, *prosthodontist, writer*
Vermilyea, Stanley George *prosthodontist, educator*
†Wee, Alvin Gerard *dental educator*

Cuyahoga Falls
†Barsan, Robert Blake *dentist*

Fairfield
Cutter, John Michael *dentist*

Hilliard
Relle, Attila Tibor *dentist*

Marion
Beals, Clem Kip, III, *dentist*

Milford
Creath, Curtis Janssen *pediatric dentist*

Pepper Pike
Goodman, Donald Joseph *dentist*

Powell
†Chen, Chia-En John *dentist*

Toledo
Kastner, Michael James *dentist*
Krakoff, Kenneth B. *dentist, consultant*

Uniontown
Naugle, Robert Paul *dentist*

Youngstown
Rose, Ernst *dentist*

OKLAHOMA

Calera
Young, James Oliver *dentist, communication company executive*

Mcalester
Bartheld, Robert Lyle *dentist*

Oklahoma City
Shillingburg, Herbert Thompson, Jr., *dental educator*

OREGON

Portland
Bartley, Murray Hill *retired dental educator*

PENNSYLVANIA

Allison Park
Conway, James Claude *periodontist*

Bryn Mawr
Sylvis, Robin *dental hygiene educator*

Chambersburg
Scarlata, Paul Anthony *oral surgeon*

Clarion
Foreman, Thomas Alexander *dentist*

Danville
Lessin, Michael Edward *oral-maxillofacial surgeon*

Doylestown
Slade, Edwin Walter, Jr., *oral surgeon, lawyer*

Harrisburg
Prioleau, Sara Nelliene *dentist*

Lancaster
Bentman, Julius *periodontist*

Lansdale
Strohecker, Leon Harry, Jr., *orthodontist*

Lebanon
Gallaher, William Marshall *dental laboratory technician*

Mc Kees Rocks
Barczynski, John Leslie *periodontist*

Mount Pleasant
Juriga, Raymond Michael *dentist*

Norristown
Steinberg, Arthur Irwin *periodontist, educator*

Philadelphia
†Appleby, David Curtis *dentist, educator*
Breitman, Joseph B. *prosthodontist, dental educator*
Fielding, Allen Fred *oral and maxillofacial surgeon, educator*
Fonseca, Raymond J. *dental medicine educator*
†Pappas, Charles Nicholas, III, *dentist, educator*
Winkler, Sheldon *dentist, educator*

Pittsburgh
†Galey, R. Kent *oral surgeon*
Ismail, Yahia Hassan *dentist, educator*
†Melnick, Michael S. *dentist, educator*
Miller, Charles Jay *dentist*
Schleyer, Titus Karl Ludwig *dental educator*

Washington
Balta, Andrew Stephen *oral and maxillofacial surgeon*

Wayne
Guernsey, Louis Harold *retired oral and maxillofacial surgeon, educator*

Whitehall
Tufton, Janie Lee (Jane Tufton) *dental hygienist, animal rights lobbyist, activist*

RHODE ISLAND

Providence
Mehlman, Edwin Stephen *endodontist*

SOUTH CAROLINA

Charleston
Johnson, Dewey E(dward), Jr., *dentist*

Columbia
Witherspoon, Walter Pennington, Jr., *orthodontist, philanthropist*

SOUTH DAKOTA

Howard
Hattervig, Robin Lynn *dentist*

TENNESSEE

Chattanooga
Carden, Zachary Frank, Jr., *dentist*

Memphis
Butts, Herbert Clell *retired dentist, educator*
Cannon, Joe Louis *retired orthodontist*
Fields, W(ade) Thomas *dental educator*
Harris, Edward Frederick *orthodontics educator*
Jurand, Jerry George *periodontology educator, researcher*
Lynch, Denis Patrick *dentist, educator*
McCullar, Bruce Hayden *oral and maxillofacial surgeon*

Nashville
Martin, James Larence *dentist, educator*
Medwedeff, Fred Marshall *dentist*

TEXAS

Cypress
Heath, Frank Bradford *retired dentist*

Dallas
Alexander, Roger Eugene *oral and maxillofacial surgeon, educator*
Buschang, Peter Heinz *dental educator*
McWhorter, Kathleen *orthodontist*

Flower Mound
Kolodny, Stanley Charles *oral surgeon, air force officer*

Houston
†Hobdell, Martin Howard *dental educator, researcher*
Sweet, James Brooks *oral and maxillofacial surgeon*

Lackland A F B
†Dunn, William Jackson *dental educator, researcher*
†Mealey, Brian L *periodontist, military officer*

Missouri City
Chang, Jeffrey Chai *dentist, educator, researcher*

Mount Pleasant
McCauley, Dan Paul *dentist*

Plainview
Crawford, Felix Conkling *dentist*

Plano
Findley, John Sidney *dentist*
Taylor, Paul Peak *pediatric dentist, educator*

Salado
Willingham, Douglas Barton *dentist*

San Antonio
†Bauerle, James Ernest *oral surgeon*
†Bsoul, Samer A. *dentist, educator*
Palmer, Hubert Bernard *dentist, retired military officer*
†Schmitz, John Phillip *maxillofacial surgeon, researcher*

VERMONT

Essex Junction
Lampert, S. Henry *retired dentist*

Shelburne
Sawabini, Wadi Issa *retired dentist*

VIRGINIA

Clifton
Bowes, Arlene Dannenberg *dentist*

Pearisburg
Morse, F. D., Jr., *dentist*

Petersburg
Boyd, Herbert Reed, Jr., *dentist*

Richmond
Laskin, Daniel M. *oral and maxillofacial surgeon, educator*

Sterling
Block, Robert Michael *endodontist, educator, researcher*

Virginia Beach
Lowe, Cameron Anderson *dentist, endodontist, educator*

WASHINGTON

Bellevue
Carlson, Curtis Eugene *orthodontist, periodontist*
Page, Roy Christopher *periodontist, scientist, educator*

Everett
Oliver, William Donald *orthodontist*

Seattle
Dworkin, Samuel Franklin *dentist, psychologist*
Herring, Susan Weller *dental educator, oral anatomist*
Hollender, Lars Gösta *dental educator*
†Johnson, Marcia J. *dental hygienist*

Spokane
Kolsrud, Henry Gerald *dentist*
Steadman, Robert Kempton *oral and maxillofacial surgeon*

WISCONSIN

Beloit
Green, Harold Daniel *dentist*

Madison
Wanek, Ronald Melvin *orthodontist*

Milwaukee
Scrabeck, Jon Gilmen *dental educator*

New Glarus
Sippy, David Dean *dentist*

Racine
Sikora, Suzanne Marie *dentist*

Shawano
Swetlik, William Philip *orthodontist*

Wisconsin Rapids
Sheker, William Clyde *dentist*

WYOMING

Casper
Keim, Michael Ray *dentist*

CANADA

QUEBEC

Fossambault Sur Le Lac
Maranda, Guy *retired oral maxillofacial surgeon, Canadian health facility executive, educator*

Montreal
Bentley, Kenneth Chessar *oral and maxillofacial surgeon, educator*

MEXICO

Toluca
†Tapia Reyes, Gustavo *prosthodontist*

GERMANY

Witten
Gaengler, Peter Wolfgang *dentist, researcher*

ADDRESS UNPUBLISHED

†Ambard, Alberto J *prosthodontist*
Armstrong, Edward Bradford, Jr., *oral and maxillofacial surgeon, educator*
Beagrie, George Simpson *dentist, educator, dean emeritus*
Bogdan, Glendon Joseph *retired orthodontist*
Brooke, Ralph Ian *dental educator*
†Bulan, Liana *dentist*
†Collins, Frank, Jr., *dentist, educator*
†Elzay, Richard Paul *retired dental school administrator*
†Farrell, Edward Wagner *retired dentist, educator*
†Fehrenbach, Margaret Jean *dental hygienist, educator*
Garnick, Jerry Jack *periodontist, educator*
Geistfeld, Ronald Elwood *retired dental educator*
Goepp, Robert August *dental educator, oral pathologist*
Grewe, John Mitchell *orthodontist, educator*
Gugino, Carl Frank *orthodontist, educator*
Hammer, Wade Burke *retired oral and maxillofacial surgeon, educator*
Herman, David Jay *orthodontist*
Hoffman, Jerry Irwin *retired dental educator*
Johnson, John Edwin *orthodontist*
Kula, Katherine Sue *dentist*
Lambert, Joseph Parker *retired dentist*
Ligotti, Eugene Ferdinand *retired dentist*
Lippert, Christopher Nelson *dentist, consultant*
Listgarten, Max Albert *periodontics educator*
Löe, Harald *retired dentist, educator, researcher*
Martens, Donald Mathias *orthodontist*
Meffert, Roland Matthew *periodontist, educator*
†Molinaro, Joseph Daniel *dentist*
Mundorff Shrestha, Sheila Ann *cariologist*
Nabers, Claude Lowrey *retired periodontist, writer*
Okada, Geoffrey Toshio *endodontist*
†Paris, David Andrew *dentist*
Park, Jon Keith *dentist, educator*
Rodin, Howard Alan *periodontist*
Simaie, Joseph R. *dentist*
Slaughter, Freeman Cluff *retired dentist*

HEALTHCARE: HEALTH SERVICES

UNITED STATES

ALABAMA

Andalusia
Cross, Charlotte Lord *retired social worker, artist*

Birmingham
Booth, Rachel Zonelle *nursing educator*
Brannan, Stephen E. *health services administrator*
Crawford, Edwin Mac *health facilities executive*
Crittenden, Martha A. *disability specialist*
Devane, Denis James *health care company executive*
Gibbs, Sydney Royston *health facility administrator*
Holmes, Suzanne McRae *nursing supervisor*
Jones, Moniaree Parker *legal nurse consultant*
O'Connor, Stephen James *healthcare educator*
Perry, Helen *medical/surgical nurse, secondary school educator*
Quintana, Jose Booth *health care executive*
Roth, William Stanley *hospital foundation executive*
†Sathiakumar, Nalini *public health educator, researcher, epidemiologist, pediatrician*
Stephens, Deborah Lynn *health company executive*
Tieszen, Ralph Leland, Sr., *hospital administrator*

Chelsea
Culpepper, Michael Irving *researcher, educator*

Cullman
†Thornton, Nancy Freebairn *psychotherapist, consultant, military officer*

Daphne
Curreri, Peter William *health policy consultant*

Dauphin Island
Levenson, Maria Nijole *retired medical technologist*

Decatur
Mardis, Elizabeth Williams *occupational health nurse*

Fairhope
Radtke, Dawn Eleanor *clinical social worker*

Emeryville
Finney, Lee *social worker, negotiator*
Goldstein, Jack *health science executive, microbiologist*

Encino
House-Hendrick, Karen Sue *nursing consultant*
Vogel, Susan Carol *nursing administrator*

Escondido
†Garcia, Luis F. *social worker, photographer*
Gentile, Robert Dale *optometrist, consultant*
Kelley, George Lorenze *psychologist, consultant*
Rich, Elizabeth Marie *nursing educator*

Fort Irwin
Shuler, George Nixon, Jr., *social worker, writer*

Foster City
†Denny, James M. *health care services company executive*
Nugent, Denise *holistic nurse consultant and educator*

Fountain Valley
Curl, Wade, Jr., (Mack Curl Jr.) *health facility administrator, consultant*

Fremont
Sahatjian, Manik *nurse, psychologist*
Squiers, Elizabeth C. *healthcare administrator*

Fresno
†Cole, Jessie Mae *nursing assistant, writer*
Ezaki-Yamaguchi, Joyce Yayoi *dietitian*
Schroeder, Rita Molthen *retired chiropractor*
†Scott, David Allen *mental health services professional, writer*

Glendale
Ebert, Gerard (Gerry Ebert) *hypnotherapist, freelance/self-employed writer*

Glendora
Lasko, Allen Howard *pharmacist*

Greenbrae
Neuharth, Daniel J., II, *psychotherapist*

Hawthorne
Fila, John Charles *psychoanalyst*

Hemet
Lawrence, Paula Denise *physical therapist*

Hermosa Beach
Barr, Warren Paul *optometrist*

Highland
Tacal, Jose Vega, Jr., *retired public health official, veterinarian*

Huntington Beach
Carey, Shirley Anne *nursing consultant*
Solomon, Susan Carol *hospital administrator, marketing specialist*

Inglewood
Epstein, Marsha Ann *public health administrator, physician*

Irvine
Ruttenberg, Susann I. *health sciences administrator*

Kingsburg
Quaday-Gray, Ailene Diann *retired speech pathologist*

La Crescenta
†Gray, Velma LeVan *medical surgical nurse*

La Jolla
Covington, Stephanie Stewart *psychotherapist, writer, educator*
Hazzard, Mary Elizabeth *nurse, educator*
Richard, Rae Linda *nurse practitioner, vascular access specialist*
Rosenblatt, Adylin Isabelle *social worker*

La Mirada
Graybill, Ruth Ann *social worker*

Laguna Beach
Frenzel, Frances Johnson *registered nurse, educator, lecturer, poet, real estate broker*
†Jensen, Gloria Veronica *adult nurse practitioner*

Laguna Hills
Banuelos, Betty Lou *rehabilitation nurse*

Laguna Niguel
Carr, Bernard Francis *hospital administrator*
Smith, Leslie Roper *hospital and healthcare administrator*

Laguna Woods
Leonard, Elizabeth Adney *social worker*

Lake Elsinore
Young, Patricia Janean *speech pathologist*

Lake View Terrace
McCraven, Eva Stewart Mapes *health service administrator*

Lakewood
Woodson-Glenn, Yolanda *social worker*

Lincoln
Helzer, James Dennis *retired hospital executive*

Lodi
Bernhoft, Franklin Otto *psychotherapist, psychologist*

Loma Linda
Bleidt, Barry Anthony *pharmacy educator*
Bullock, Weldon Kimball *health facility administrator, pathologist, pathology educator*
Snyder, John Joseph *retired optometrist*

Lompoc
Boone, Donna Clausen *physical therapist, biostatistician, researcher*
Wagner, Geraldine Marie *nursing educator, consultant*

Long Beach
Brown, Lester B. *social worker, educator*
Kingore, Edith Louise *retired geriatrics and rehabilitation nurse*
Mullins, Ruth Gladys *nurse*
†Welch, Ronnie Scott *health facility administrator*

Los Altos
McCreary, Deborah Dennis *oncology nurse*
Spiller, Gene Alan *nutritionist, health facility administrator*

Los Angeles
Andersen, Ronald Max *health services educator, researcher*
Ash, Lawrence Robert *public health educator, administrator*
Baron, Melvin Farrell *pharmacy educator*
†Barsugli, Jesse Benjamin *lab administrator*
Blakeney, Karen Elizabeth *social service and community health program executive, consultant*
†Brodwin, Martin George *counselor, educator*
Chen, Peter Wei-Teh *mental health services administrator*
Dyoniziak, Adama *health agency administrator*
Goodlaw, Edward *retired optometrist*
Greene, Albert Lawrence *healthcare executive*
Horowitz, Ben *health facility administrator*
Jin, Yan *university educator, researcher, consultant*
Johns, Karen Louise *nurse, psychotherapist*
Karpf, Michael *health facility administrator, director*
Katchur, Marlene Martha *nursing administrator*
Katzin, Carolyn Fernanda *nutritionist, consultant*
Kwon, Oh Chae *researcher*
Lewis, Mary Ann *nursing educator*
Lloyd-Jones, Dadiva Bocobo *nursing assistant, writer*
Looney, Claudia Arlene *healthcare administrator*
†Manalo, Victor A. *social work educator*
Mass-Achs, Sharon *social worker, educator*
Nichols, Gerald *counselor, hypnotist*
Parham, Linda Diane *occupational therapist, researcher, educator*
Priselac, Thomas M. *health facility administrator*
Que Hee, Shane Stephen *environmental health educator*
Roberts, Robert Winston *social work educator, dean*
†Soo Hoo, Guy W. *health facility administrator*
Swartz, Allan Joel *hospital administrator*
Taylor, Darla Jean *nurse*
Territo, Mary C. *health facility administrator, oncologist*
Thompson, Judith Kastrup *nursing researcher*
Tulloch-Reid, Elma Deen *nurse, consultant*
†Valente, Sharon McBride *mental health nurse*
van Dam, Heiman *psychoanalyst*
Ver Steeg, Donna Lorraine Frank *nurse, sociologist, educator*
White-Whitfield, Lisa Denise *social worker, grant writer*
Williams, Bradley Robert *pharmacy and gerontology educator, consultant*

Los Gatos
Westendorf, Elaine Susan *social worker*

Malibu
Palacio, June Rose Payne *nutritional science educator*

Marina Del Rey
Nizze, Judith Anne *retired physician assistant*

Martinez
†Baird, Laurel Cohen *clinical nurse*
†St. James, Holly (Saundra Manning) *social worker*

Marysville
Gray, Katherine *marriage, family and child therapist, writer, educator*
Myers, Elmer *psychiatric social worker*

Menlo Park
Reamy, Michaelin *marriage and family therapist, educator, consultant*

Middletown
Selandia, Elizabeth *acupuncturist, Oriental medicine physician*

Mill Valley
Taylor, Rose Perrin *social worker*

Mission Viejo
Shah, Shirish Anantlal *pharmacist*

Modesto
Lipomi, Michael Joseph *health facility executive*
Smith, Heather Lynn *psychotherapist, recreational therapist*

Monrovia
†Salaman, Maureen Kennedy *nutritionist*

Monterey Park
†Ly, Allan Q. *medical technician*

Moorpark
Young, Victoria E. *occupational health and pediatrics nurse practitioner, lawyer*

Moraga
Allen, Richard Garrett *healthcare and education consultant*

Moreno Valley
Gull, Paula Mae *adult nurse practitioner*

Mount Shasta
Mariner, William Martin *chiropractor*

Napa
Lee, Margaret Anne *psychotherapist, social worker*
Wilhelm-Hass, Elaine *operating room nurse*

Newhall
†Stone, Susan Foster *mental health services professional, psychologist*

North Highlands
Emburg, Kathryn Maria *social worker, writer*

North Hollywood
Charis, Barbara *nutritionist, consultant, health researcher*

Northridge
†Hedge, Thomas Lyle, Jr., *rehabilitation services professional*

Novato
Kratka-Schneider, Dorothy Maryjohanna *psychotherapist*

Oakland
Cole, Joan Hays *social worker, clinical psychologist*
Gaál, Violetta *retired social worker, massage therapist*
King, Janet Carlson *nutrition educator, researcher*
Miller, Barry *research administrator, psychologist*
†Miller, Steven Lamont *neuroscience company executive, researcher*
O'Hara, Delia Iglauer *family nurse practitioner*
Okazawa-Rey, Margo *social worker, educator*

Oceanside
Downer, William John, Jr., *retired hospital administrator*

Ontario
Hull, Jane Laurel Leek *retired nurse, administrator*

Orange
Todsen, Dana Rognar *health care executive*

Pacific Palisades
Bilson, Wesley *healthcare company executive*

Palm Springs
Alameda, Russell Raymond, Jr., *radiologic technologist*
Boyajian, Timothy Edward *public health officer, educator, consultant*

Palmdale
Kinzell, La Moyne B. *school health services administrator, educator*

Palo Alto
Mutch, James Donald *health therapist*

Pasadena
Brotman, Richard Dennis *counselor*

Pebble Beach
Ference, Helen Marie *nursing consultant, consultant*

Perris
Zimmer, Paul Gerald, II, *retired community care licensing professional*

Petaluma
Angress, Dina Dasberg *retired social worker*

Placerville
Wall, Sonja Eloise *nurse administrator*

Pleasanton
Shen, Mason Ming-Sun *medical center administrator*

Portola Valley
Harper, Elizabeth A. *retired occupational therapist*

Ramona
Cooper, James Melvin *healthcare executive, consultant*

Rancho Mirage
Kiser, Roberta Katherine *medical records administrator, education educator*

Red Bluff
Purdy, Carol Ann *psychotherapist*

Redlands
Coleman, Arlene Florence *retired nurse practitioner*

Redondo Beach
Cardin, Suzette *nursing educator*
Dennis, Helen Marion *gerontologist, educator*

Reseda
†Hoover, Pearl Rollings *nurse*

Richmond
Terrill, Karen Stapleton *retired medical planning consultant*

Riverside
Chang, Sylvia Tan *health facility administrator, educator*
†Leifer, Gloria *pediatrics nurse, writer, educator*

Rohnert Park
Johnson, Herman Leonall *research nutritionist, retired*

Roseville
Wright, Carole Yvonne *chiropractor*

Running Springs
Fangerow, Kay Elizabeth *nurse*

Sacramento
Childress, Dori Elizabeth *nursing consultant*
†Dager, William Erling *pharmacist specialist, educator*
Drachnik, Catherine Meldyn *recreational therapist, artist, counselor*
Farrell, Francine Annette *psychotherapist, educator, author*
†Jasperson, John Arthur *public health service educator, consultant*
Johnson, Van R. *health facility administrator*
Merwin, Edwin Preston *healthcare educator, consultant*
†Rowland, Shirley K. *alcohol/drug abuse services professional, educator, mental health services professional, consultant*
Ryan, Patricia Ellen *healthcare executive*
Sato-Viacrucis, Kiyo *nurse, inventor, entrepreneur, consultant*

San Andreas
†Cretan, Donna *neonatal nurse, lactation consultant*

San Anselmo
Ellenberger, Diane Marie *nurse, consultant*
Motz, Julie Ann *energy healer, author*

San Bernardino
Neighbors, Ira Arthell *social work educator*

San Diego
Bakko, Orville Edwin *retired health care executive, consultant*
Batey, Sharyn Rebecca *clinical research scientist*
Covert, Michael Henri *healthcare facility administrator*
†Doan, Tai Danh *social worker, director*
Eastham, John Howard *pharmacist, educator*
Edwards-Tate, Laurie Ellen *human services administrator, educator*
Johnson, Kenneth Owen *retired audiologist*
Klamerus, Karen Jean *pharmacist, researcher*
†Larson, Vernon Dale *audiologist, researcher*
McDonough, Mark *neuropsychologist, forensic consultant*
Nenner, Victoria Corich *nurse, educator*
Norling, Richard Arthur *health care executive*
Roberts-DeGennaro, Maria *social work educator*
Rodgers, Janet Ahalt *nursing educator, dean*
Rymer, Thérèse Elizabeth *family practice nurse practitioner*
Schmidt, Terry L. *health care executive*
Smith, Raymond Edward *retired health care administrator*
Stein, Franklin Joseph *youth counselor*
Stewart, Jean Catherine *critical care and neuroscience emergency trauma nurse, educator*
Whittington, Anne Elizabeth *diabetes educator*

San Francisco
Auerback, Sandra Jean *social worker*
Boone, Anthony Gerard *healthcare educator*
Dibble, Suzanne Louise *nurse, researcher*
Dunlap, Margi *social worker, non-profit executive*
Eng, Catherine *health care facility administrator, physician, medical educator*
Formichi, Virginia Jeanne *retired social welfare administrator*
†Foster, Stephen William *mental health nurse*
Harrington, Charlene Ann *sociology and health policy educator*
†Robinson, Effie *social worker, educator*
Rosales, Suzanne Marie *hospital coordinator*
Roth, Charles Philip *psychotherapist*
Solday, Alidra (Linda Brown) *psychotherapist, psychoanalyst, filmmaker*
Ventura, Jacqueline N. *retired nurse, researcher*
Wu-Chu, Stella Chwenyea *nutritionist, consultant*

San Jose
Luna, Michael Donovan *speech language pathologist*
Morales, Steven Roque *social worker*
†Yi, Jeonghee *researcher*

San Leandro
Becker, Anne Margaret *neonatal nurse, clinical nurse specialist*

San Luis Obispo
Smith, Joey Spauls *mental health nurse, home health nurse, biofeedback therapist, consultant, educator*

San Marcos
Ball, Betty Jewel *retired social worker, consultant*
Knight, Edward Howden *retired hospital administrator*
†Whitney, Stan *marriage and family therapist*

San Mateo
Richens, Muriel Whittaker *marriage and family therapist, educator*

San Pedro
McMullen, Sharon Joy Abel *marriage and family therapist*

PROFESSIONAL INDEX 6373 HEALTHCARE: HEALTH SERVICES

†Montgomery, Thom Mathew *health program administrator, counselor*

San Rafael
Amada, Gerald *psychotherapist*
Friesecke, Raymond Francis *health company executive*

Santa Ana
Chenhalls, Anne Marie *nurse, educator*
Oberstein, Marydale *geriatric specialist*
†Schmitz, Stephen E. *mental health specialist, writer*

Santa Barbara
†Fetter, Trevor *healthcare industry executive*
Focht, Michael Harrison *health care industry executive*

Santa Cruz
†Smith, Darin Scott *marriage and family therapist*

Santa Fe Springs
Hanzel, Mimi S. *psychotherapist*

Santa Maria
Phillips, Dorothy Lowe *nursing educator*
†Walton, Maurine Isabel *social worker*

Santa Monica
Brook, Robert Henry *health services researcher, physician, educator*
†Deffry, Frank M. *retired marriage and family therapist*
Magnabosco-Bower, Jennifer Lynn *mental health professional*
Reichmann, Susan Helene *psychotherapist*
Silbergeld, Carol A. *clinical social worker, psychotherapist*

Santa Rosa
Bruner-Welch, Ann S. *physician assistant*
Cornett, Donna J. *counselor, alcohol moderation administrator*
Nickens, Catherine Arlene *retired nurse, freelance writer*
Provost, Rhonda Marie *nurse anesthetist*

Santa Ynez
†Jensen, Regina Brunhild *psychotherapist*
O'Grady, Barbara Vinson *community health nurse, administrator, retired*
Walker, Burton Leith *psychotherapist, engineering writer*

Sausalito
Groah, Linda Kay *nursing administrator, educator*
Seymour, Richard Burt *health educator*

Sepulveda
Burton, Paul Floyd *social worker*

Simi Valley
Slonaker, Dena Meckler *occupational therapist, rehabilitation consultant*
Trager, D. David *retired pharmacist, general consultant*

Sonoma
Markey, William Alan *health care administrator*

Stanford
Marks, Michael Paul *medical administrator*
Marsh, Martha *hospital administrator*
Mc Namara, Joseph Donald *researcher, retired police chief, novelist*

Stockton
†Gregory, Philip J. *pharmacist, editor*
Norton, Linda Lee *pharmacist, educator*
†Ravnan, Susan LaShelle *pharmacist, educator*
†Shek, Allen *pharmacist, educator*

Studio City
Stoughton, W. Vickery *healthcare executive*

Sun City
†Olim, August Souza *counselor*

Sunnyvale
Gordon, Marc Stewart *pharmacist, scientist*

Sunol
Rebello, Marlene Munson *speech pathologist*

Tarzana
Rinsch, Maryann Elizabeth *occupational therapist*

Temecula
Keenan, Retha Ellen Vornholt *retired nursing educator*

Thousand Oaks
Emerson, Alton Calvin *retired physical therapist*
†Gaus, Clifton R. *healthcare executive*
Herman, Joan Elizabeth *healthcare company executive*
Mulkey, Sharon Renee *gerontology nurse*
Schaeffer, Leonard David *healthcare executive*

Torrance
Ebeling, Vicki *marriage and family therapist, psychotherapist, educational therapist*
Medley, Nancy May *nurse*
Moy, Gwendolyn C.I. *nursing administrator, nursing educator*

Trabuco Canyon
Jessup, R. Judd *health care executive*

Truckee
Todd, Linda Marie *circulation manager, nutrition researcher, financial consultant, pilot, newspaper professional, pilot*

Union City
Glueck, Mary Audrey *retired psychiatric and mental health nurse*

Upland
Boswell, Dan Alan *health maintenance organization executive, health care consultant*
†Likens, John David *rehabilitation services professional*

Vandenberg AFB
Huggins, Elaine Jacqueline *nurse, retired army officer*

Ventura
Bircher, Andrea Ursula *psychiatric nurse practitioner*

Victorville
McGulpin, Elizabeth Jane *nurse*

Visalia
Phillipe, Chester Tolleson *alcohol/drug abuse services professional, educator, substance abuse facility administrator*
Ryan-Halley, Charlotte Muriel *oncology clinical specialist, family nurse practitioner*

Walnut Creek
Burns, Francis Raymond *medical facility administrator, researcher*
Nolan, Janiece Simmons *health care company executive*

West Covina
Adams, Sarah Virginia *psychotherapist, family counselor*

West Hills
Cheney, Anna Marie Jangula *retired medical-surgical nurse*

Westminster
Hannah, JaNellyn Bender *public health nurse*

Whittier
Renteria, Juana *community health educator*

Woodland
Clement, Katherine Robinson *retired social worker*
Ramirez, Graciela *women's health nurse*

Woodland Hills
Funari, Robert Glenn *health care services executive*
Goldberg, Bruce Edward *hypnotherapist*
Pettit, John W. *administrator*
Yates, Gary L. *marriage and family therapist*

Yountville
Jones, Thomas Robert *social worker*
Sedlock, Joy *social worker*

COLORADO

Aurora
Brown, Anne Sherwin *speech pathologist, educator*
Gardner, Sandra Lee *nurse, outreach consultant*
King Calkins, Carol Coleman *health sciences administrator*
Starr, Nancy Barber *pediatric nurse practitioner*

Boulder
Arnold, Janet Nina *health care consultant*
Braddock, David Lawrence *health science educator*
Holdsworth, Janet Nott *women's health nurse*
Kelley, Bruce Dutton *pharmacist*
Middleton-Downing, Laura *psychiatric social worker, artist, small business owner*

Broomfield
Lybarger, Marjorie Kathryn *nurse*

Buena Vista
Herb, Edmund Michael *optometrist, educator*

Canon City
Honaker, Charles Ray *health facility administrator*

Colorado Springs
Birkhead, John Andrew *health services professional, mental health counselor*
DiPadova, Regina Maria *counselor*
Driscoll, David Lee *chiropractor*
Haas, Julian L. *researcher, educator*
Lokken, Steven Lee *chiropractor, nutritionist, internist*
Moorhouse, Mary Frances *rehabilitation nurse*
Olson, Kenneth Paul *vocational consultant*
Strickland, Sylvia Raye *social worker*
Williams, Ruth Lee *clinical social worker*

Commerce City
Hollomon, Carol Howell *social worker*

Denver
Backus, Susan *clinical social worker, educator*
Edelman, Joel *medical center executive*
†Hotchkiss, Heather A. *social worker, consultant*
Hunsaker, Jill Ann *public health administrator*
Jennett, Shirley Shimmick *home care management executive, nurse*
Joyce, Mary Holt *retired social worker*
Judson, Franklyn Nevin *physician, educator*
Kirkpatrick, Charles Harvey *physician, immunology researcher*
Kraizer, Sherryll A. *child safety and interpersonal violence prevention educator*
Levine, Joel Seth *medical school administrator, educator*
Lofton, Kevin Eugene *medical facility administrator*
Lyons, Cherie Ann *researcher, writer*
Miller, Jill Marie *psychoanalyst*
Parker, Catherine Susanne *psychotherapist*
Plummer, Ora Beatrice *nursing educator, trainer*
Rael, Henry Sylvester, Sr., *retired health administrator, financial and management consultant*
†Robinson, Charles Andrew *audiology services professional*
Schoeneberger, Marlies Luise *alcohol/drug abuse services professional, gerontologist, sociologist*
Solano, Janine T. *physician assistant*
Spilka, Bernard *psychology educator*
†Švec, Jan G. *voice scientist, researcher*
†Thomas, Enolia *nutritionist, educator*
†Thompson, Cathy Joanne *nursing educator, consultant, acute care nurse practitioner*
Wilkinson, Joan Kristine *nurse, pediatric clinical specialist*
Witt, Catherine Lewis *neonatal nurse practitioner, writer*

Englewood
Bradshaw, Beverly Jean *psychotherapist, consultant, educator*
Carroll, Kim Marie *nurse*

Fort Collins
Gubler, Duane J. *research scientist, administrator*
Hultgren, Glenn M. *chiropractor*
Sedei Rodden, Pamela Jean *therapist*
Smith, Nina Maria *mental health nurse, administrator, consultant*
Tyler, Gail Madeleine *nurse*

Grand Junction
Pantenburg, Michel *hospital administrator, health educator, holistic health coordinator*
Van Horn, O. Frank *retired counselor, consultant*

Greeley
Gritts, Gerald Lee *home health nurse, AIDS care nurse, AIDS educator*
Linde, Lucille Mae (Lucille Jacobson) *motor-perceptual specialist*
Ross, Rosann Mary *psychotherapist, educator*

Guffey
McCaslin, Kathleen Denise *child abuse educator*

Highlands Ranch
Allen, Roberta Jane *social worker*
Sandoval, Lisa Ann *occupational therapist*

Idledale
Brown, Gerri Ann *physical therapist*

Johnstown
Williams, Matt Eugene *chiropractor, educator*

Lakewood
Brinkmeyer, Dotty Stewart *maternal/child nurse*
Burnett, Elizabeth (Betsy Burnett) *counselor*

Las Animas
DeKrey, Ramona *medical/surgical nurse, educator*

Littleton
Benkert, Mary Russell *pediatrics nurse, researcher*
Goebel, Kathryn Mary *nurse*
Hagman, Sally Wingchong *physical therapist*
Miller, Betty Sue *counselor*

Longmont
Jones, Beverly Ann Miller *nursing administrator, retired patient services administrator*
Melendez, Joaquin *retired orthopedic assistant*
Ralston Thompson, Paula Jane *nurse*

Loveland
Hartsock, Jane Marie *nurse, educator*
Jones, Janis Sue *women's health nurse*

Parker
Haas, Bradley Dean *pharmacy director, clinical pharmacist, consultant*

Peyton
†Dunn, Doris *retired critical care nurse, artist, rancher*

Yuma
Hertneky, Randy Lee *optometrist*

CONNECTICUT

Beacon Falls
Holub, Barbara Ann *rehabilitation nurse*

Bloomfield
Hamilton, Thomas Stewart *physician, hospital administrator*

Bridgeport
†McAuliffe, Catherine A. *counselor, psychology educator, psychotherapist*
Payson, Norman C. *healthcare services company executive*
Trefry, Robert J. *healthcare administrator*

Canterbury
Brown, Philip Henry *psychiatric social worker*

Chaplin
Gunn, Bert Dennis *social worker*

Cheshire
Pettine, Linda Faye *physical therapist*
Sherman, Barbara Jane *social worker*

Clinton
Douglas, Hope M. *psychotherapist, forensic hypnotist*
Harris, Doris Ann *medical/surgical nurse*
Kingsbury, Katherine Duffield *social worker*

Cromwell
†Stiber, Julie Anne *social worker*

Derby
Jekel, James Franklin *physician, public health educator*

Durham
Russell, Thomas James *critical care supervisor*

East Hartford
†Young, Albert Frederick Antonio *grants coordinator*

Fairfield
Mead, Philomena *mental health nurse*

Farmington
Dellaripa, Christine M. *nursing care administrator*
Houchin, John Frederick, Sr., *human services administrator*

Glastonbury
Pudlo, Virginia Mary *medical surgical nurse*

Greenwich
Hirschberg, Ruth *retired social worker*
Kleinman, Noela MacGinn *family nurse practitioner*
Krauser, Robert Stanley *health care executive*
Langley, Patricia Coffroth *retired psychiatric social worker*

Guilford
Pãquin, Trudy *gerontological nurse*

Hamden
Cofrancesco, Donald George *health facility administrator*
Cole-Schiraldi, Marilyn Bush *occupational therapy educator*

Hartford
Inniss-Brewer, Yvonne *nurse, insurance company administrator*
McCormack, Katherine McGrath *nursing administrator*
Smith, Francis Xavier *nurse*
Young, Sara Ann *women's health nurse*

Higganum
Gillmor, Rogene Godding *retired medical technologist*

Meriden
Molder, Sybil Ailene *retired occupational health nurse*

Middlefield
Rammler, Linda Hope *human services consultant*

Middletown
Brogan, Mary Rose *public mental health facility administrator, psychologist*
Sage, Elderia Franckling *social worker*

Milford
Muth, Eric Peter *ophthalmic optician*

New Canaan
Johansen, Barbara B. *social worker, consultant*

New Haven
Ahern, Jo Ann *diabetes clinical nurse specialist*
Armbruster, Paula *child mental health educator, university director*
Benfer, David William *hospital administrator*
†Breny Bontempi, Jean M. *health educator*
†Carroll, Deirdre Holden *psychiatric nurse practitioner, clinical researcher, educator*
Clark, Susan Atkinson *clinical social worker, educator*
De Rose, Sandra Michele *psychotherapist, educator, supervisor, administrator*
Gaynor, Mark Leslie *clinical social worker*
†Gilliss, Catherine Lynch *nursing educator*
†Irwin, Melinda Liggett *healthcare educator, researcher*
Krauss, Judith Belliveau *nursing educator*
Reyes, Marcia Stygles *medical technologist*
Ritvo, Samuel *psychoanalyst, researcher, educator*

New London
†Allen, Carol Marie *radiologic technologist*
Larson, Richard Everett *lab technician*

Newington
Zeldes, Benjamin *optometrist*

North Branford
Womer, Charles Berry *retired hospital executive, management consultant*

North Haven
Hogan, James Carroll, Jr., *public health administrator, research biologist*

Norwalk
Boles, Lenore Utal *nurse psychotherapist, educator*
Macdonald, Karen Crane *occupational therapist, geriatric counselor*

Old Lyme
†Algiere, Scott G. *health facility administrator*
Kraus, Janice *social worker, educator*

Orange
Douskey, Theresa Kathryn *health facility administrator*

Putnam
Desaulniers, Rene Gerard Lesieur *retired optometrist*

Redding
Benyei, Candace Reed *psychotherapist*

Simsbury
Dumais, Arlene *psychiatric mental health and critical care nurse*
Long, Ann Marie *health facility administrator*

Stamford
Bostin, Marvin Jay *hospital and health services consultant*
†Moore, Sharon Helen Scott *gerontological nurse*
Scott, Gregory Alan *pharmacist, writer*
Smith-Young, Anne Victoria *health services coordinator*

Storrs Mansfield
Jensen, Helene Wickstrom *retired nutritionist, educator*
Jensen, Robert Gordon *nutritionist, consultant*
Suits, Alice-Mae *retired school social worker*

Stratford
Probert, Dorothy Wittman *retired social worker*

Suffield
Bianchi, Maria *critical care specialist, adult and acute care nurse practitioner, nursing administration*

Vernon Rockville
Gallien, Sandra Jean *social worker*

Wallingford
Spero, Barry Melvin *medical center executive*

Waterbury
Semple, Donita C. *nurse*

West Hartford
Gebo, Susan Claire *consulting nutritionist*
Gitterman, Alex *social work educator*
Gobes, Landy *psychotherapist*
Hugg, Geraldine Bertha Novotny *retired gerontology specialist, journalist*
Leshem, Osnat Alice *healthcare administrator*

West Haven
Levinson Miller, Carolyn *mental health services professional, researcher*

DELAWARE

Claymont
Johnson, Lois Ann *patient educator*

Dover
Gambardella, Robert Edward *retired medical social services consultant*
Millon-Wisneski, Sharon Marie *critical care nurse, educator*

Hockessin
Croyle, Barbara Ann *health care management executive*

Lewes
Fried, Jeffrey Michael *health care administrator*

Newark
Doberenz, Alexander R. *nutrition educator, chemist*
Protokowicz, Nora Jane *nursing administrator*
Talbert, Dorothy Georgie Burkett *social worker*

Wilmington
†Creekmore, Joseph R. *pharmacist, researcher*
Gleeson, Roslyn M. *pediatric clinical nurse specialist/practitioner*
Jones, Priscilla Lee *community health nurse, counselor*
McDonough, Kenneth Lee *pharmaceutical company medical administrator*
Schmerling, Erwin Robert *counselor, retired physicist*
Souney, Paul Frederick *pharmacist*
Thureau, Lani Carole *speech and language pathologist*

DISTRICT OF COLUMBIA

Washington
†Acord, Bobby *health science association administrator*
Altman, Beth Lee *social worker*
Alward, Ruth Rosendall *nursing consultant*
Angotti, Catherine Marie *occupational health director*
Arling, Donna Dickson *social worker*
Bailar, John Christian, III, *retired public health educator, physician, statistician*
Bale, Judith R. *health science association administrator*
Beale, Susan Yates *social worker*
Blocker-Burnette, Maxine Peterson *social worker*
Burger, Edward James, Jr., *health care policy executive*
Corless, Dorothy Alice *nurse educator*
Curtis, Carolyn Anne Bernardette *nurse midwife*
Cushman, Margaret Jane *home care executive, nurse*
Delgado, Jane *health executive, writer*
Eckenhoff, Edward Alvin *health care administrator*
Engle, Jane *research nurse, artist*
Fitzgerald, Helen Teresa *grief therapist, writer*
Flax, Jane *psychotherapist, educator*
Foley, Virginia Sue Lashley *counselor, international training consultant*
Francke, Gloria Niemeyer *pharmacist, editor, publisher*
Frederickson, Jon Julius *social worker*
Gaston, Marilyn Hughes *health facility administrator*
Golden, Olivia A. *human service agency administrator*
Goldstein, Murray *health organization official*
Gray, Bradford Hitch *health policy researcher*
Green, Edward Crocker *research scientist*
Grob, George Frederick *health, social services association administrator*
Gutierrez, Guillermo *human services administrator, medical educator*
Hannett, Frederick James *healthcare consulting company executive*
Hartmann, Robert Sankey *hospital administrator, communications and fundraising executive*
Heller, (Douglas) Brian *human services administrator*
Hendrickson, Constance C. *social worker*
Henney, Jane Ellen *health administrator, oncologist*
Hudson, Timothy Leon *nursing educator*
Jones, Stanley Boyd *health policy analyst, priest*
†Kenner, Bridget Agatha *mental health services professional*
Lee, Shew Kuhn *retired optometrist*
Leidinger, William John *clinic administrator*
Lombardo, Fredric Alan *pharmacist, educator*
Mahaffey, Kathryn Rose *risk assessor*
Martinez, Rose Marie *health facility administrator*
Masi, Dale A. *research company executive, social work educator*
McCarter, Katherine Sauter *association executive*
Mewani, Rajshree Ramchand *researcher*
Michnich, Marie E. *health facility administrator, consultant, educator*
†Mickalide, Angela Denise *public health educator*
Muth, William Henry Harrison, Jr., *medical/surgical nurse, nurse practitioner*
Nightingale, Stuart Lester *physician, public health officer*
Njie, Veronica P.S. *nurse educator, clinical nurse*
Obrams, Gunta Iris *medical officer*
O'Neill, Joseph F. *health science association administrator*
Orlans, F(lora) Barbara *bioethics researcher*
Peart, Laverne T. *retired nursing assistant, poet*
†Pestell, Richard G. *health facility administrator, medical educator*
Pope, Andrew *medical organization administrator*
Rheintgen, Laura Dale *research center official*
Richman, Joseph Herbert *retired public health services official*
Satcher, David *public health service officer, federal official*
Schorr, Lisbeth Bamberger *child and family policy analyst, author, educator*
Sheavly, Robert Bruce *social worker*
†Spencer, Harrison Clark, Jr., *public health administrator, educator*
Stark, Nathan J. *medical administrator, health policy consultant, lawyer*
Stoiber, Susanne A. *health science organization administrator*
Theiss, Patricia Kelley *public health researcher, educator*
Walder, Debby Jean *program director, quality manager, nursing service administrator, nurse, educator*
Wells, Samuel Fogle, Jr., *research center administrator*
Wiener, Joshua Mark *public health service officer, researcher*
Yoder, Mary Jane Warwick *psychotherapist*

FLORIDA

Altamonte Springs
LeBlanc, Janet M. *addictions and relationship counselor*
†Melvin, Margaret *nurse, consultant*

Archer
Lockwood, Rhonda J. *mental health services professional*

Bay Pines
†Nolan, Marilyn Ann *health facility administrator*
Weaver, Thomas Harold *health facility administrator*

Boca Raton
Barnett, Judy Jannette *healthcare technology company executive, consultant*
Fels, Robert Alan *psychotherapist*
Jacobson, Susan Bogen *psychotherapist*
Rothberg-Blackman, June Simmonds *retired nursing educator, psychotherapist, psychoanalyst*

Bokeelia
Grottanelli, Pamala N. *nursing administrator, educator*

Bonita Springs
Megee, Geraldine Hess *social worker*

Boynton Beach
Machtiger, Harriet Gordon *retired psychoanalyst*

Bradenton
Aerts, Cindy Sue *nurse*
Taylor, Carol *rehabilitation nurse*

Brandenton
†Miles, Elizabeth Jane *social worker*

Brandon
Thompson, Venita Brant *nutritionist, diet technician*

Cape Coral
Buthman, Nancy Smith *nurse practitioner, critical care nurse*

Clearwater
Barry, Joyce Alice *dietitian*
Fenderson, Caroline Houston *psychotherapist*
Whedon, George Donald *medical administrator, researcher*

Cocoa
Malvey, Donna M. *health sciences educator*

Coral Gables
Weiner, Ruth Eileen Blower Kassewitz *retired public relations executive*

Crystal River
Stone, Fred Lyndon *retired human resources administrator*

Dade City
Smith, Howell Jackson, III, *physician assistant*

Daytona Beach
Cardwell, Harold Douglas, Sr., *retired rehabilitation specialist*
Martin, Kimberly Sue *critical care nurse, educator*
Rogers, Patricia June *clinical social worker*

Deerfield Beach
Areskog, Donald Clinton *retired chiropractor*
Schaefer, Robert Joseph *counselor*
Solomon, Barry Jason *healthcare administrator*

Delray Beach
Erenstein, Alan *emergency room nurse, medical education consultant*
Weiner, Anne Lee *social worker*

Deltona
Bondinell, Stephanie *counselor, academic administrator*

Dunedin
McIntosh, Roberta Eads *retired social worker*

Edgewater
Henderson, Janice Elizabeth Wilson *respiratory therapist*
†Lawson, Bonnie Hulsey *psychotherapist, consultant*

Ellenton
Edson, Herbert Robbins *retired foundation and hospital executive*

Englewood
Curtis, Caroline A. S. *community health and oncology nurse*

Fernandina Beach
Kurtz, Myers Richard *hospital administrator*

Fort Lauderdale
Alpert, Martin Jeffrey *chiropractor*
Blumenfeld, Harry *retired social worker*
Dickens, Joyce Rebecca *addictions therapist, educator*
Easton, Robert Morrell, Jr., *optometric physician*
Geronemus, Diann Fox *social work consultant*
Leasher, Janet Louise *optometric physician*
Lister, Mark Wayne *clinical laboratory scientist*
Marine, Michael R. *healthcare company executive*
†McCarthy, James Peter *marine safety officer, management consultant*
Miller, Barry M. *child care administrator*
Phillips, Linda Darnell Elaine Fredricks *retired psychiatric and geriatrics nurse*
Rentoumis, Ann Mastroianni *psychotherapist*
Silva, Joanne Rizzo *family nurse practitioner*
Sundel, Sandra Stone *social worker*
Sutton, Douglas Hoyt *nurse*
Zikakis, John P. *life scientist, biochemist, nutritionist, educator*

Fort Myers
Elliott, Luella Lee *retired women's health nurse, educator*
Giebels, Sharon J. *human services manager*
Housel, Natalie Rae Norman *physical therapist*
Johnson, Sally A. *nurse, educator*
Newland, Jane Lou *nursing educator*
†Nolan, Anne Maria *nursing educator, director*
†Nugent, Timothy Scott *alcohol/drug abuse services professional*
Williams, Suzanne *pediatric nurse practitioner*
Woodbridge, Norma Jean *registered nurse, writer*

Fort Pierce
Eastmond-Robinson, June Patricia *public health nurse*

Fort Walton Beach
Villecco, Judy Diana *substance abuse, mental health counselor, director*

Gainesville
Brushwood, David Benson *pharmacy educator, lawyer*
†Chmielewski, Terese Lynn *physical therapist, educator*
Detweiler, Nancy Logan *social worker*
†Doering, Paul Louis *pharmacist, educator*
Gamble, Kathryn *nurse*
Kersey, Talana S. *mental health counselor*
Malasanos, Lois Julanne Fosse *nursing educator*
Marohn, Ann Elizabeth *health information management professional*
Puckett, Ruby Parker *nutritionist, hospital administrator, consultant, author*
Randall, Malcom *health care administrator*
Ray, Timothy Britt *social worker, lawyer, administrator*
Schwartz, Michael Averill *pharmacy educator, consultant*
†Sheu, Jiunn-Jye *healthcare educator, researcher*
Small, Natalie Settimelli *pediatric mental health counselor*
Sugarman, Bahira *clinical social worker*
Thompson, Neal Philip *food science and nutrition educator*
Watson, Robert Joe *hospital administrator, retired career officer*

Graceville
Tilbe, Linda MacLauchlan *nursing administrator*

Hialeah
Perez, Leyanee C. *nutritionist, consultant*

Hillsboro Beach
Marshall, Jo Taylor *social worker*

Hollywood
Shane, Doris Jean *respiratory therapist, administrator*

Hypoluxo
Ferguson, Paula Irene *nursing administrator*

Inverness
Dowdell, Michael Francis *critical care nurse, forensic and anesthesia nurse practitioner*
Mavros, George S. *clinical laboratory director*
Robinson, Charlene G. *mental health nurse, educator*

Jacksonville
Akers, James Eric *health facility administrator*
Cherry, Barbara Waterman *speech and language pathologist, physical therapist*
Copley, William McKinley, III, *counselor, counseling administrator, consultant*
Fulton-Quindoza, Debra Ann *nurse practitioner*
†Haley, Donald Robert *health facility administrator*
Langford, Cecilia Motes *nurse educator*
Longino, Theresa Childers *nurse*
Pavlick, Pamela Kay *nurse, consultant*
Rubens, Linda Marcia *home health services administrator*
Sanders, Marion Yvonne *retired geriatrics nurse*
Scarborough, Marion Nichols *nutritionist, recreational facility executive*
Yamane, Stanley Joel *optometrist, consultant*

Jensen Beach
Gamble, Raymond Wesley *marriage and family therapist, clergyman*

Key West
Burns, William Joseph *audiologist, speech-language pathologist*

Lakeland
Balish, Ruth Reitz *retired community health nurse*
Barber, Gerard Reno *pharmacist, writer*
Hixon, Andrea Kaye *healthcare quality specialist*
Moffitt, Tony Lee *family practice nurse practitioner*

Largo
Hamlin, Robert Henry *public health educator, management consultant*
Haumschild, Mark James *pharmacist*
Simmons, Deborah Jo *pharmacy executive*

Longwood
Andrews, Diane Randall *nursing administrator, critical care nurse*
Laven, David Lawrence *nuclear and radiologic pharmacist, consultant*

Melbourne
Hughes, Ann Nolen *psychotherapist*
MacDonald, Michael Joseph *physician, administrator*
Miner, Lynne Shirley *nurse midwife, educator*

Merritt Island
Babcock, Hope Smith *counselor, educator, program designer*

Miami
Cekauskas, Cynthia Danute *social worker*
Cherry, Andrew Lawrence, Jr., *social work educator, researcher*
Chisholm, Martha Maria *dietitian*
Clark, Ira C. *hospital association administrator, educator*
Dann, Oliver Townsend *psychoanalyst, psychiatrist, educator*
Durkin, Diane L. *nurse*
Getz, Morton Ernest *medical facility director, gastroenterologist*
Jones-Wills, Eunice Stephanie *mental health nurse, researcher*
Kooima, Linda Kay *neonatal and pediatrics nurse*
Lee, Nellie Greenberg *social worker, educator, counselor*
Nadeau, Joseph Eugene *health care management consultant, information systems consultant*
†Newton, Terry Fernando *health information specialist, writer*
Osinski, Martin Henry *healthcare consultant*
Potocky-Tripodi, Miriam *social worker, educator*
†Sari, Nazmi *economist, healthcare educator*
Strinko, Thomas Edward *medical services administrator*
†Teicher, Morton Irving *social worker, anthropologist, educator*

Miami Beach
Blassingame, Ronald Jay *social worker*

Milton
Mack, Susan Prescott *practical nursing educator*

PROFESSIONAL INDEX 6375 HEALTHCARE: HEALTH SERVICES

Mount Dora
†Crone, Eugene N. *addictions counselor, retired educator*
Moretto, Jane Ann *nurse, public health officer, consultant*
Shyers, Larry Edward *mental health counselor, educator*

Naples
Barkley, Marlene A. Nyhuis *nursing educator*
Brown, Cindy Lynn *family nurse practitioner, critical care nurse*
Seavey, Christopher Gordon *psychotherapist, addiction counselor*
Sekowski, Cynthia Jean *corporate executive, contact lens specialist*

New Port Richey
Charters, Karen Ann Elliott *critical care nurse, health facility administrator*
Hlad, Gregory Michael *psychometrist, institutional test administrator, career assessment and testing manager*

North Palm Beach
Ackerman, Paul Adam *pharmacist*

North Port
Galterio, Louis *healthcare information executive*

Oakland
Purrone, Scott *physician assistant*

Oakland Park
Gannon, Marc Jay *optometrist*

Ocala
Blakeman, Carol Ann *medical/surgical nursing educator*
Fontaine, Laura Ann *social worker*
Kelly, Edward John, V, *counselor*
Michelson, Edward Harlan *retired medical educator*
Roberts, Mary Belle *clinical social worker*

Oldsmar
†Smith, Nicole A. *development coordinator, not-for-profit fundraiser, realtor*

Orange Park
Rice, Ronald James *hospital administrator*

Orlando
Brock, Barry James *health services administrator, educator, consultant*
Fottler, Myron David *health services educator*
Jacinto, George Anthony *social worker, counselor, educator, consultant*
Morgan, Robert Miles *paramedic, educator*
Scott, Kathy Lynn *peri-operative nurse*
†Sharp, Christina Krieger *nursing educator, researcher*
†Vanryckeghem, Martine *speech pathology/audiology services professional, educator*
Walker, Deborah Lynne *nurse practitioner*
Witty, John Barber *health care executive*

Palm Bay
Jones, Mary Ann *geriatrics nurse*

Palm Beach Gardens
Holloway, Edward Olin *human services manager*
†Marciano, Rico *health and fitness professional*

Palm Harbor
†Rivelli, Susan Veronica *nurse*

Palmetto
Carter, Elizabeth Wackerman *retired mental health nurse*

Panama City
Griffin, Donald Scott *physician assistant*
Nelson, Edith Ellen *dietitian*
Reedy-Dewey, Madeline Anne *retired occupational therapist*

Parkland
Brancaleone, Salvatore Joseph *nutritionist, consultant*

Pembroke Pines
Ferris, Rita Bernadette *social worker*
Sobong, Loreto Calibo *nursing researcher*

Pensacola
Loesch, Mabel Lorraine *social worker*
Maygarden, Jerry Louis *health care foundation executive*
Raisler, Mary E. *nurse*
Shimmin, Margaret Ann *women's health nurse*
Taggart, Linda Diane *women's health nurse*
Van Atta, Cheri Marie *massage therapist*

Pineland
Donlon, Josephine A. *diagnostic and evaluation counseling therapist, educator*

Pinellas Park
Tower, Alton G., Jr., *pharmacist*

Placida
Wood, Yvonne McMurray *retired nursing educator*

Plant City
Henry, J. Myrle *pharmacist*

Plantation
Burnett, Barbara Diane *social worker*
Carmichael, Robert William *medical group administrator*
Gonshak, Isabelle Lee *nurse, civic worker*
Patterson, Janice Pauline *community and geriatrics health nurse*

Pompano Beach
Goldberg, Lois D. *health facility administrator, disability analyst*

Port Charlotte
Gendzwill, Joyce Annette *retired health officer*
†Holt, Barbara Lynn *school nurse practitioner*

Port Saint Lucie
Beatrice, Ruth Hadfield *hypnotherapist, retired educator, financial administrator*
Hogan, Roxanne Arnold *nursing consultant, risk management consultant, educator*
Holloman, Marilyn Leona Davis *nurse non profit administrator, health products executive*
Verfaillie, Roland Bruce *mental health professional*

Punta Gorda
Beasom, Nancy Ann *occupational therapist, consultant*
O'Donnell, Mary Murphy *retired medical/surgical nurse*

Ruskin
LaComb-Williams, Linda Lou *community health nurse*

Saint Cloud
Potts, Carol Jean Fox *geriatrics nurse, quality assurance coordinator*

Saint Petersburg
Conover, Dorothy Nancy Lever *medical practice administrator, nurse*
Freeman, Corinne *financial services, former mayor*
Jarrard, Marilyn Mae *nursing consultant, nursing researcher*
Jaworski, Dolores Daley *advanced nurse practitioner*
Keller, Natasha Matrina Leonidow *nursing administrator*
McCluskey, Charles James, Jr., *physician assistant*
Piscani, Kathleen Folkerts *clinical psychiatric nurse*
Ratzlaff, Donna Cheryl *social worker*
Siska, Mary Noreen *nursing administrator*
Walker, Francis Roach *rehabilitation consultant*

Sanibel
†LaCombe, David M. *emergency medical services educator, consultant*
Simontacchi, Carol Nadine *nutritionist, writer*

Sarasota
Benedick, James Michael *psychotherapist*
Carr, Patricia Ann *community health nurse*
Ceo, Barbara Ann *speech-language pathologist, educator*
Dearden, Robert James *pharmacist*
Harris, Judith Ann White *health occupations vocational educator, nurse*
Middleton, Norman Graham *social worker, psychotherapist*
Tucci, Steven Michael *health facility administrator, physician, recording industry executive*

Sebastian
Mauke, Leah Rachel *retired counselor*

South Miami
Bauman, Sandra Spiegel *nurse practitioner, mental health counselor*

Spring Hill
†Thompson, Connie Ann *nurse*

Stuart
Cocoves, Anita Petzold *psychotherapist*

Sun City Center
Ward, Jacqueline Ann Beas *nurse, healthcare administrator*

Tallahassee
Molinari, Joseph Francis *oculist*
Rice, Nancy Marie *nursing consultant*
Soliman, Karam Farah Attia *pharmacy educator*

Tamarac
Krause, John L. *optometrist*

Tampa
†Berarducci, Adrienne *nursing educator, researcher*
Boutros, Linda Nelene Wiley *medical/surgical nurse*
Clendinen, Cynthia A.A. *healthcare professional, compliance specialist*
Collins, Gwendolyn Beth *health administrator*
Liller, Karen DeSafey *public health educator*
Mahan, Charles Samuel *public health educator*
Russell, Diane Elizabeth Henrikson *career counselor*
Shern, David Len *educator, dean*
†Wolfson, Jay *public health and medical educator, researcher, consultant, lecturer, lawyer*

Tarpon Springs
Georgiou, Ruth Schwab *retired social worker*

Tavares
Osborne, Glenna Jean *social and health services administrator*

Trenton
Ivey, James Frederick, Jr., *physician, health facility administrator*

Valrico
Carlucci, Marie Ann *nursing administrator, nurse*

Venice
Barritt, Evelyn Ruth Berryman *nurse, educator, university dean*

Vero Beach
Bonny, Helen Lindquist *music therapist*
Cobb, Ronald David *pharmacist, educator*
Fielding, Inez Victoria Brown *community health nurse*
Kepley, Stephen Richard *optometrist*
McCrystal, Ann Marie *community health nurse, administrator*

West Palm Beach
Bernhardt, Marcia Brenda *mental health counselor*
Bohn, Barbara Ann *retired laboratory director*
Davis, Shirley Harriet *social worker, editor*
Glinski, Helen Elizabeth *operating room nurse*
Rafaidus, David Martin *health and human services planner*

Winter Haven
Porter, Howard Leonard, III, *health and education policy consultant*

Winter Park
Douglas, Kathleen Mary Harrigan *retired psychotherapist, educator*
Jernigan, Donald *hospital administrator*
Werner, Thomas Lee *hospital administrator*
Wisler, Willard Eugene *retired health care management executive*

Zephyrhills
Ayres, Jayne Lynn Ankrum *community health nurse*

GEORGIA

Albany
†Gates, Roberta Pecoraro *nursing educator*

Alpharetta
McBride, Vickie Darlene *geriatrics nurse*
Mock, Melinda Smith *orthopedic nurse specialist, consultant*
White, Carl Edward, Jr., *pharmaceutical administrator*

Athens
Posey, Loran Michael *pharmacist, editor*

Atlanta
†Anderson, Barbara Allen
Baird, Mariann Saunorus *critical care clinical nurse specialist, administrator*
†Bales, Virginia Shankle *health administrator*
Barker, William Daniel *hospital administrator*
Beaton, Rebecca Andrea *psychotherapist*
Blasini-Alcivar, Lydia M. *health education specialist, consultant*
Chandler, Robert Charles *healthcare consultant*
Cox, Lynetta Frances *neonatal nurse practitioner*
†Datz, Kimberly Malaika *health facility administrator, consultant*
Ganzarain, Ramon Cajiao *psychoanalyst*
†Grummer-Strawn, Laurence M. *public health service officer, researcher*
Hardegree, Gloria Jean Fore *health services administrator*
Honaman, J. Craig *health facility administrator*
Huff, Sara Davis *nursing manager*
†Isaac, Yvonne Renee *construction company executive*
Johnson, Carl Frederick *marriage and family therapist*
Jowers, Ronnie Lee *university health sciences center executive*
†Kolbe, Lloyd Joseph *health facility administrator*
Marks, James S. *public health service administrator*
Martin, David Edward *health sciences educator*
Orenstein, Walter Albert *health facility administrator*
Press, Christopher E. *health facility administrator*
Salmon, Marla E. *nursing educator, dean*
Seffrin, John Reese *health science association administrator, educator*
†Shafey, Omar *health facility administrator*
Shaunnessy, George Daniel *medical company executive*
Tkaczuk, Nancy Anne *cardiovascular services administrator*
Walton, Carole Lorraine *clinical social worker*
Weed, Roger Oren *rehabilitation services professional, educator*
†Whitley, Deborah Marie *social worker, educator*

Augusta
Feldman, Elaine Bossak *medical nutritionist, educator*
Gillespie, Edward Malcolm *hospital administrator*
Kuhn, Walter F. *emergency medicine physician*
Sansbury, Barbara Ann Pettigrew *nursing administrator*
Stark, Nancy Lynn *critical care nurse*
Tucker, Jessie L., III, *health facility administrator, educator*
Whittemore, Ronald Paul *hospital administrator, retired army officer, nursing educator*

Brunswick
Herndon, Alice Patterson Latham *public health nurse*
Hopwood, Vicki Jeane *medical center official*
Mitchell, Dorothy Harvey *healthcare administrator*

Calhoun
Parman, Debra Lanette *physical therapist*

Canton
Sperin, Amelia Harrison *medical/surgical nurse, obstetrics/gynecological nurse*

Carrollton
Alexander, Mary Gerette Blaydes *child therapist*

Columbus
†Boothby, Lisa Anne *pharmacist, drug information specialist*

Cordele
Jordan, Randall Warren *optometrist*

Dahlonega
Edmondson, Joanne Holt *counselor, educator*
†Miller, Carol Ann *physical therapist, educator*

Dallas
Schafer, Sandra Lee *geriatric nurse practitioner, educator*

Decatur
Dade, Joann *critical care nurse, small business owner*
Hagood, Susan Stewart Hahn *clinical dietitian*
Hawkins, Janice Edith *medical/surgical clinical nurse specialist*
Hinman, Alan Richard *public health administrator, epidemiologist*
Rosenberg, Mark L. *health agency administrator*
Ross, Valdor Wendell *operating room nurse*

Douglasville
Wilson, Keith Mark *health services administrator*

Dublin
Doster, Daniel Harris *retired counselor, minister*
Folsom, Roger Lee *healthcare administrator*

Duluth
Weldon, Thomas David *medical products manufacturer*

Evans
Fournier, Joseph Andre Alphonse *nurse, social worker, psychotherapist*
Perry, Sarah Teresa Anderson (Teri Perry) *nursing administrator*

Fayetteville
Cokuslu, Lynda Elizabeth McCord *medical assistant*
Harris, Glenda Stange *medical language specialist, proofreader, writer*

Grayson
Mitchell, Laura Anne Gilbert *family nurse practitioner*
Nease, Judith Allgood *marriage and family therapist*

Hiawassee
Bayless, Carolyn Cotton *nurse*

Jonesboro
Dame, Laureen Eva *nursing administrator, educator*
Finley, Sarah Maude Merritt *social worker*

Kennesaw
Hetrick, Joan Willette *critical care nurse, administrator*
Munoz, Steven Michael *physician associate*

La Fayette
Lim, Esteban, Jr., *medical facility administrator, physician*
Muerth, Cherie Anne *social worker*

Lagrange
Davidson, Joeline Dillard *laboratory services administrator*
Rhodes, Eddie, Jr., *medical technologist, phlebotomy technician, educator*

Lithonia
Wilson, Veta Emily *community health nurse*

Lyons
Frey, Bob Henry *psychotherapist, sociologist, educator, poet, canon lawyer*

Macon
Drysdale, Joyce A *substance abuse counselor*
Keating, Thomas Patrick *health care administrator, educator*

Marietta
Biehle, Karen Jean *pharmacist*
Billingsley, Judith Ann Seavey *oncology nurse*
Dobrzyn, Janet Elaine *quality management professional*
†Kearney, Colleen Ann *occupational therapist*
Petit, Parker Holmes *health care corporation executive*

Norcross
Irons, Isie Iona *retired nursing administrator*
Wolkow, Alan Edward *chiropractic physician*

Peachtree City
Crutchfield, Carolyn Ann *physical therapy educator*

Quitman
McElroy, Annie Laurie *nursing educator, administrator*

Rockmart
Holley, Tammy Dannette Fennell *critical care nurse*

Rome
Kines, Joan Elaine *human services administrator, consultant*

Massing, Virginia Reeves *surgical nurse and administrator*

Savannah
Baker, Brinda Elizabeth Garrison *infectious disease nurse*
DiClaudio, Janet Alberta *health information administrator*

Senoia
Bradley, Sally Sue *registered nurse*

Statesboro
Beasley, John Julius *child and family development educator*

Stockbridge
Curtis, Joycelyn *social worker*

Union Point
Miller, Bryant Davis *healthcare administrator*

Warner Robins
Beck, Rhonda Joann *paramedic, educator, writer*

Woodstock
Smith, Jeanne Hawkins *critical care nurse*

HAWAII

Hilo
Lu, Christopher Dah-Cheng *nutritionist, educator, university dean*
Skorikov, Vladimir B *researcher, educator*

Honolulu
Adams, Nancy R. *nurse, military officer*
Chung, Richard S. *health facility administrator*
Dockham-Leong, Sondra Marguerite *social worker*
Fischer, Joel *social work educator*
Flannelly, Laura T. *mental health nurse, nursing educator, researcher*
Ho, Stuart Tse Kong *health facility administrator*
Kadohiro, Jane K. *educator, nurse, diabetes consultant*
Katz, Alan Roy *public health educator*
Kennedy, Faye *retired social worker, author*
Lacey, Roberta Balaam *emergency room nurse, pediatrics nurse*
Lum, Jean Loui Jin *nursing educator*
†Miyawaki, Edison Hiroyuki *health care executive, physician*
Roberson, Kelley Cleve *health care administrator*
Schneider, Thomas Richard *hospital administrator*
Simon, Gary B. *health care manager, investor*
Wilson, William James *healthcare executive*

Kailua
Lundquist, Dana Richard *healthcare executive*
Saavedra Garcia, Katherine Andrews *health group executive director*
Westerdahl, John Brian *nutritionist, health educator*

Kaneohe
Lange-Otsuka, Patricia Ann *nursing educator*

Kihei
Chin, Barbara *massage therapist*

Laupahoehoe
Kroll, Sandra L. *retired healthcare facility administrator*

Makawao
Tanner, Barbara Ann *pediatrics nurse*

IDAHO

Boise
Blonshine, Sheena Kay *medical, surgical nurse*
Townsend, Sandra Lynnette *nurse*

Burley
King, Janet Felland *family nurse practitioner*

Eagle
†Wickman, Patricia Ann *retired social worker*

Hope
Meyers, Marlene O. *retired health facility administrator*

Idaho Falls
Lee, Glenn Richard *medical administrator, educator*
Leverett, Margaret Ann *women's health nurse practitioner*

Naples
Soss, Daniel Lee *social work educator*

Payette
Bragg, Darrell Brent *nutritionist, consultant*

Pocatello
†Heberlein, Alice LaTourrette *healthcare educator, physical education educator, coach*

Post Falls
Hamman, Steven Roger *vocational rehabilitation specialist*

Twin Falls
Becker, Tamara Sue *nursing administrator*

ILLINOIS

Alton
Kessler, William Eugene *health care executive*

Antioch
Dahl, Laurel Jean *human services administrator*

Arlington Heights
Baptist, Allwyn J. *healthcare consultant*
Telleen, Judy *counselor*

Aurora
Buffum, William Erwin *social worker, educator*

Barrington
Schaefer, Mary Ann *health facility administrator, consultant*

Bartonville
Lewis, Georgia Eileen *counselor, school counselor*

Berwyn
Gordon, Dolores Joan *retired emergency medical technician*
Hudik, Martin Francis *hospital administrator, educator, consultant, writer*

Bloomington
Hunt, Roger Schermerhorn *healthcare administrator*
Passetti, Lora Linda *alcohol/drug abuse services professional, researcher*
White, Marilea *school social worker*

Bolingbrook
Price, Theodora Hadzisteliou *individual, child and family therapist*

Carbondale
Dick, Steven Joseph *researcher, educator*
Kawewe, Saliwe Moyo *social work educator, researcher*

Cary
Blevins, Steven W. *chiropractor*

Champaign
Schiro-Geist, Chrisann *rehabilitation counselor*

Charleston
Drake, Anne Kelly *social worker, educator*
Hedges, Edith Rittenhouse *nutrition and family and consumer sciences educator*

Chatham
Chew, Keith Elvin *healthcare services administrator*
Powell, Carol Sue *pediatric special education educator, nursing consultant*

Chicago
Abrohams, Janice Elaine *social work supervisor*
Baron, Richard L. *health services administrator*
†Bauman, Jerry L. *pharmacy researcher, educator*
Benson, Irene M. *nurse*
Bracken, Kathleen Ann *nurse*
Bristo, Marca *human services administrator*
Brown, Charles Eric *health facility administrator, biochemist*
†Chong, Pang Hyon *pharmacist, consultant*
Conlon, Patrick C. *family nurse practitioner, pediatric nurse practitioner*
Crawford, Jean Andre *clinical therapist*
D'Andrea, Deborah Dawn *nursing consultant, critical care nurse*
Davis, Concelor Dominguez *marriage and family therapist*
Dickerson, Martha Ann *health facility administrator*
Elson, Miriam *social work educator*
†Gaynes, Bruce Ira *optometrist, pharmacist, educator*
Goldsmith, Ethel Frank *medical social worker*
Kaleba, Richard Joseph *healthcare consultant*
Kleinpell-Nowell, Ruth *nursing educator and researcher, medical writer*
Kopytko, Edwin Edward *nursing administrator*
Levin, Arnold Murray *social worker, psychotherapist*
Ling, Kathryn Wrolstad *health association administrator*
Magoon, Patrick M. *healthcare executive*
Massura, Eileen Kathleen *family therapist*
McDermott, Mary Ann *nursing educator*
Mecklenburg, Gary Alan *hospital executive*
Peters, Elizabeth Anne *nutrition educator*
Popowski, Karen Joyce *social worker*
Reed, Vastina Kathryn (Tina Reed) *child and adolescent psychotherapy, family development specialist*
Reilly, Joan Rita *nurse practitioner, educator, school nurse*
Riordan, Michael C. *hospital administrator*
Rosenheim, Margaret Keeney *social welfare policy educator*
Rudnick, Ellen Ava *health care executive*
Sauer, Kathy R. *health information administrator*
Schwartz, John Norman *human services administrator*
†Scott, Nancy L. *health facility administrator, consultant*
Simon, Bernece Kern *social work educator*
Smalley, Penny Judith *healthcare technology consultant*
Spergel, Irving Abraham *social worker, researcher*
Telser, Sylvia Ruth *retired family life educator, social worker*
Trierweiler, Robert Louis *rehabilitation counselor*
Turner, Bernice Cooper *social worker*
Vigen, Kathryn L. Voss *nursing administrator, educator*
Walton, Carmelita Noreen *retired nurse*
Witrod, Sister Mary Rosalita *nursing home administrator*
Zander Schrage, Maryanne Elizabeth *physician assistant*
Zimmermann, Polly Gerber *emergency nurse*

Collinsville
†Sabbert, Anne Ward *vision therapist, consultant*

Decatur
Litchfield, Jean Anne *nurse*

Deerfield
Sanner, John Harper *retired pharmacologist*

Dekalb
Banovetz, James M. *public administration educator, consultant*
Bukonda, Ngoyi K. Zacharie *health care management educator*

Des Plaines
Miraglio, Angela Maria *dietitian*

Downers Grove
Thomas, Daniel J. *health services executive*

Dupo
Gallamore, Betty Lou *nurse*

East Moline
Burns, John Richard *chiropractor, educator*

Edwardsville
Adkerson, Donya Lynn *clinical counselor*
Svoboda, Donna Lee *neonatal nurse*

Effingham
Heth, Diana Sue *therapist*

Elgin
Beyer, Karen Haynes *social worker*

Elmhurst
Fry, Evelyn Leona *clinical social worker*

Evanston
Aronson, Judith *clinical social worker*
Prasad, Pottumarthi Vara *health facility administrator*
Summers, Renee Ann *clinical social worker*
Tarnoff, Eileen Feldman *social worker*

Fairfield
Thomason, Nola Faye *critical care-emergency supervisor*

Flossmoor
Herring, Marsha Kathline *health services marketing administrator*

Forest Park
Mack, William Joseph *psychotherapist, rehabilitation specialist*

Freeport
Weaver, Michael Glenn *pharmacist*
Wise, Sarajane Goers *community education nurse*

Galena
Alexander, Barbara Leah Shapiro *clinical social worker*

Galesburg
Kowalski, Richard Sheldon *hospital administrator*
Taylor Swisher, Debora Dianne *home health nurse*

Glenview
Coulson, Elizabeth Anne *physical therapy educator, state representative*
Garber, Betty Kahn *social worker*

Grand Ridge
Goodchild, Rosina Ann *community health nurse*

Grayslake
Patterson, D(ouglas) Reid *pharmaceutical scientist*

Harrisburg
Rushing, Philip Dale *retired social worker*

Herrin
Buckley, John Joseph, Jr., *health care executive*

Highland Park
Boutet, Jane Gilmour *retired social worker*
Eldridge, Amy Helene *clinical social worker, academic dean*
Mervis, Bonnie Aaron *social worker*
Zywicki, Cindy Mary *nurse*

Hines
Hagarty, Eileen Mary *pulmonary clinical nurse specialist*
Weaver, Frances M. *research career scientist, health services researcher*

Homewood
Ramirez, Ralph Henry *nurse, corporate executive*

Irvington
Van Cleve, Sandra Rose *retired nursing educator*

Joliet
Lynch, Priscilla A. *nursing educator, therapist*

Kampsville
Schumann, Alice Melcher *medical technologist, educator, sheep farmer*

Kankakee
Ross, Julie Anne *social worker*

La Grange
Mahoney, Donna Marie *psychotherapist*

Lake Forest
Damico, Joseph F. *medical company executive*

Lewistown
Shank, Glenna Kaye *medical and surgical nurse, nursing educator*

Lincolnwood
Lewitz, Amy Mae *clinical nurse specialist, geriatrics psychiatry nurse*

Litchfield
Deaton, Beverly Jean *nursing administrator, educator*

Lombard
Holgers-Awana, Rita Marie *electrodiagnosis specialist*

Macomb
Hopper, Stephen Rodger *hospital administrator*

Manteno
Balgeman, Richard Vernon *radiology administrator, alcoholism counselor*

Mapleton
Hayes, Debra Troxell *family nurse practitioner*

Markham
Burkes-Rawlins, Sarah *nutritional elementary school educator, counselor*

Matteson
van der Hoek, Sherry A. *counselor*

Maywood
Hindle, Paula Alice *nursing administrator*

Mchenry
Duel, Ward Calvin *retired health care consultant*

Moline
Williamsen, Dannye Sue *personal development educator, health facility administrator*

Monmouth
Moore, Richard Alan *optometrist*

Morrison
Galbreath, Joseph C. *pharmacist*

Morton Grove
†Labunski, Alma Joel *nursing educator*

Mount Prospect
O'Connor, Nan G. *social worker*
†Rueggeberg, Erna M. *nursing consultant, nursing administrator, researcher*

Mundelein
Strauss, Jeffrey Lewis *healthcare executive*

Murphysboro
Young, Linda Diane *speech pathology/audiology services professional*

Naperville
Dhar, Promila *researcher*

Neoga
Davis, Sharon Gail *nursing assistant*

Normal
Liechty, Daniel *social worker, educator*
Parton, Thomas Albert *speech-language pathologist*

Northbrook
Betz, Ronald Philip *pharmacist*
Brandeisky, Kathleen Sexton *social worker, consultant*
Hicks, Judith Eileen *nursing administrator*
Kahn, Sandra S. *psychotherapist*
Lever, Alvin *health science association administrator*
Morris, Marilyn Ann *social worker*
†Noeth, Carolyn Frances *speech and language pathologist*

Northfield
Lubawski, James Lawrence *health care consultant*

Oak Brook
Baker, Robert J(ohn) *hospital administrator*
Bower, Barbara Jean *nurse*
Schultz, Karen Rose *clinical social worker, author, publisher, speaker*

Oak Park
Jones, Rebecca Alvina Patronis *nurse*
Varchmin, Thomas Edward *environmental health administrator*

Oakbrook Terrace
Berry, Lynn Marina *healthcare researcher*

Onarga
Wilken, Caroline Doane *critical care, emergency, recovery room, and medical/surgical nurse*

Oregon
Hayes, Randy Alan *family therapist*

Palatine
Sharpee, Rhoda Anderson *social worker*

Palos Heights
Lysen, Lucinda Katherine *nutrition support nurse, dietitian*

Palos Hills
Healy, Judith Ann *school social worker*

Pana
Evans, Marsha Jo Anne *nursing administrator*

PROFESSIONAL INDEX 6377 HEALTHCARE: HEALTH SERVICES

Park Ridge
†Boe, Gerard Patrick *health science association administrator, educator*
Campbell, Bruce Crichton *hospital administrator*

Peoria
Hellhake-Hall, Gerri Ann *critical care nurse, cardiology nurse*
McCollum, Jean Hubble *medical assistant*
Tietjen, Suzanne Davenport *critical care nurse*
Walker, Philip Chamberlain, II, *health care executive*

Plainfield
Cook, Bruce Lawrence *research analyst*
Schinderle, Robert Frank *retired hospital administrator*
Vandevender, Deborah Ann *critical care nurse*

Quincy
Fecht, Lorene *surgical nurse*
Franklin, Diana Jeanne *chiropractor*

Rockford
Cadigan, Elise *social worker*
Mahlburg, Norine Elizabeth *retired nurse*
Maysent, Harold Wayne *hospital administrator*

Rockton
Pennell, Danny Joe *social worker*

Rolling Meadows
Theis, Steven Thomas *public health service officer*

Round Lake
†Abdullah, Bashar Y. *pharmacist, researcher*
†Dalzell, Kimberly Kay *nutritionist*

Saint Anne
Holtzman, Michael *alcohol abuse professional*

Saint Charles
†Abts, Gwyneth Hartmann *dietitian*

Saint Francisville
Harezi, Ilonka Jo *medical technology research executive*

Shorewood
Petrella, Mary Therese *community health and women's health nurse*

Silvis
Bobb, Harold Daniel *chiropractor, consultant*

Skokie
Fan, Tai-Shen Liu *dietitian*
Langguth, Margaret Witty *health facility administrator*
McCarthy, Michael Shawn *health care company executive, lawyer*

Smithfield
Corsaw, Ardith *geriatrics nurse, administrator*

Springfield
Bartolo, Donna Marie *health association executive, retired nurse*
Campbell, Kathleen Charlotte Murphey *audiology educator, administrator, researcher*

Tinley Park
Daniels, Kurt R. *speech and language pathologist*
Haley, David Alan *healthcare executive*
Mulquin, Kimberly Ann *nurse*
Taylor, Marva Jean Shipman Foulks *social worker*

University Park
Leftwich, Robert Eugene *oncological and adult nursing educator*

Urbana
Baker, David Hiram *nutritionist, nutrition educator*
Clark, Jimmy Howard *nutrition educator*
Siedler, Arthur James *nutrition and food science educator*

Vernon Hills
Curns, Eileen Bohan *counselor, author, speaker*

Waterloo
Poschel, James Edward *mental health services administrator, psychotherapist*

Waukegan
Martis, Leo *healthcare researcher*

Westchester
Shaffer, Susan E. *nutrition specialist*

Western Springs
Walsh, Robert Joseph *psychotherapist*

Westville
Hammer, John Henry, II, *hospital administrator*

Wheaton
Blair, Rosemary Kasul *social work educator*
Boudreau, Beverly Ann *health care professional*
Harper, Joannalee O. *dietician*
Pape, Patricia Ann *social worker, consultant*

Wheeling
Sheeley, Harriet Spiegel *social worker*

Wilmette
Ellis, Helene Rita *social worker*

Winfield
Young, Quentin Hayse *family counselor*

Winnetka
Peck, Annette Biemond *retired social worker, writer*
Day, Mary Ann *medical/surgical nurse*

INDIANA

Anderson
Pleninger, Susan Elaine *women's health and pediatrics nurse*
Whitaker, Audie Dale *hospital laboratory medical technologist*

Beech Grove
Byrkett, Gary Lee *hospital engineer*

Berne
Habegger, Cynthia A. *medical/surgical nurse*

Bloomington
Austin, Joan Kessner *mental health nurse*
Bartleson, Amy Aileen *psychotherapist*
Torabi, Mohammad R. *healthcare educator*

Carmel
Haddad, Freddie Duke, Jr., *hospital development administrator*

Depauw
Baggett, Alice Diane *critical care nurse*

East Chicago
Psaltis, Helen *medical and surgical nurse*

Elkhart
Williams, Pauline M. *psychiatric-mental and community health nurse*

Evansville
Elpers, Kathleen Margaret *social work educator*

Fishers
Chojnacki, Paul Ervin *pharmacist, pharmaceutical company official*

Fort Wayne
Harwood, Virginia Ann *retired nursing educator*
Kennedy, Elizabeth *health facility administrator*
Lewton, Diane Kay *nurse practitioner*
†Mueller, Carla Lynn *nursing educator*
†Rhoad, Richard E. *healthcare executive*
Ridderheim, Mary Margaret *psychotherapist*

Gary
Bennett, Richard Carl *social worker*
†Hardin, Gregory *rehabilitation services professional*
†Woodson, Porsha Marie *speech pathology/audiology services professional*

Goshen
Loomis, Norma Irene *marriage and family therapist*

Hammond
Chandler, Melanie Lynn *surgical technologist, paralegal*
Randazzo, Rebecca Ann *nursing administrator*

Hobart
Wilson, Donna Marie *health information services executive*

Hope
Golden, Eloise Elizabeth *community health nurse*

Huntingburg
Heim, Tonya Sue *nurse, small business owner*

Indianapolis
Archer, Sarah Ellen *public health and humanitarian assistance consultant*
Barker, Orel O'Brien *retired activity and social service director*
Buhner, Byron Bevis *health science facility administrator*
Cowles, Lois Anne Fort *social worker, educator*
Davis, Edgar Glenn *science and health policy executive*
Fox, Donald Lee *mental health counselor, consultant*
Gantz, Nancy Rollins *hospital administrator, nursing administrator, consultant*
Handel, David Jonathan *health care administrator*
Harden, Anita Joyce *nurse*
Hitchens, William Randolph (Randy Hitchens) *health care executive*
†Loveday, William John *hospital administrator*
Moelhman, Amy Jo *social worker*
Murray, Michael Dennis *pharmacist*
Peebles, Julian T. *health education administrator*
Pesut, Daniel J. *nursing educator*
Riegsecker, Marvin Dean *pharmacist, state senator*
†SerVaas, Cory *health sciences association administrator*
†Shi, Lizheng *health economist*
Smith, Donald Eugene *healthcare facility management administrator owner*
Stern, Phyllis Noerager *nursing educator*
Stone, Cynthia Lawson *nursing educator*
Storm, Janet S. *psychiatric social worker*
Tisdale, James Edward *pharmacy educator, pharmacotherapy researcher*
Torres, Judith *lab administrator*
Walther, Joseph Edward *health facility administrator, retired physician*
Waymire, Bonnie Gladine *nursing administrator*
†Yip-Schneider, Michele Terrell *researcher*

Jasper
Aronoff, Donald Matthew *mental health facility administrator*

Jeffersonville
Walburn, John Clifford *mental health services professional*

Kokomo
Coppock, Janet Elaine *mental health nurse*

La Porte
Morris, Leigh Edward *retired hospital executive officer*

Lafayette
Geddes, LaNelle Evelyn *nurse, physiologist*
Hall, Dorothy Susan *nurse, educator*
McBride, Angela Barron *nursing educator*
Miller, Jolene K. *healthcare educator*

Michigan City
Brown, Arnold *physical therapy consultant*

Mishawaka
Bays, June Marie *counselor, social worker*
Erdel, Sally Elizabeth *nurse*

Muncie
Hoffman, Mary Catherine *retired nurse, anesthetist*
Terrell, Pamela Sue *pharmacist*

New Albany
Rhodes, Betty Fleming *rehabilitation services professional, nurse*

New Haven
Frantz, Dean Leslie *psychotherapist*

Noblesville
Tank, Rod Gaillard *orthopaedic physical therapist*

Plymouth
Stiver, James Frederick *pharmacist, health physicist, administrator, scientist*

Portage
Michael, John William *prosthetist orthotist*

Rockport
Davis, Karen Sue *hospital nursing supervisor*

Schererville
Castor, Christina Pelayo *critical care nurse*

Seymour
Benter Brock, Teresa Ann *health facility administrator*
Lake, Nancy Jean *nursing educator, operating room nurse*
Norrell, Mary Patricia *nursing educator*

South Bend
Bella, Dantina Carmen Quartaroli *human services consultant*
Szigeti, Michelle Marie *critical care nurse*

Terre Haute
†Cockrell, Jan Meyer *recreation therapist*
Hightower, Jeanne Jackson *nursing administrator*
Tomey, Ann Louise Marriner *nursing educator*
Williams, Joseph Claude *physician assistant*

Valparaiso
White, Linda Sue *cardiology technician*

West Lafayette
Belcastro, Patrick Frank *pharmaceutical scientist*
Christian, John Edward *health science educator*
Clifton, Christopher W. *researcher, educator*
Evanson, Robert Verne *pharmacy educator*
Kirksey, Avanelle *nutrition educator*
Means, Catherine Elizabeth *nurse*
Peck, Garnet Edward *pharmacist, educator*

IOWA

Ainsworth
Sellars, Arlene Judy *gerontology nurse*

Altoona
Berkenes, Joyce Marie Poore *social worker*

Ames
Kaplan, Murray Lee *nutritionist, educator*

Ankeny
Kapler, Jeanne Marie *occupational therapist*

Bettendorf
Mosby, John Singleton, Jr., *chiropractor, educator, consultant*

Cedar Rapids
Brandt, John Edward *human services administrator*
Brooks, Debra L. *healthcare executive, neuromuscular therapist*
Stephens, Ralph Renne *massage therapy educator*
Ziese, Nancylee Hanson *social worker*

Des Moines
Abbott, Aloris Jean *operating room nurse, administrator*
Bell, Edward Allen *pharmacy educator*
Dukes, Vanessa Johnson *dietitian*
Eichner, Kay Marie *mental health nurse*
Hall, Donald Vincent *social worker*
Lund, Doris Hibbs *retired dietitian*
Ramsden, Mary Catherine *substance abuse specialist*
Tormey, Jerome Marshall *human services administrator*

Glenwood
Campbell, William Edward *mental hospital administrator*

Hudson
Mettlin, Connie Ann *social worker, educator*

Iowa City
Banker, Gilbert Stephen *industrial and physical pharmacy educator, administrator*
Berg, Mary Jaylene *pharmacy educator, researcher*
Colloton, John William *university health care executive*
Cyphert, Stacey Todd *health facilities administrator*
Guillory, J. Keith *pharmacist, educator*
Kelley, Patricia Lou *social work educator*
Kelsay, Danielle Marie Rubino *audiologist*
†Landsman, Miriam Joy *social worker, educator, social worker, researcher*
†Muir, Ruth Brooks *counselor, substance abuse service coordinator*
Nesbitt, John Arthur *recreation service educator, recreation therapy educator*
Wurster, Dale Eric *pharmacy educator*
Wurster, Dale Erwin *pharmacy educator, university dean emeritus*

Johnston
Schumacher, Larry P. *health facility administrator*

Keokuk
Lowenberg, Lorraine Lynette *psychiatric and mental health nurse*

Knoxville
Taylor, Mary Kay *medical, surgical nurse*

Oskaloosa
Gleason, Carol Ann *mental health nurse, educator*

Shenandoah
Hanna, Suzanne Louise *nurse*

Waterloo
Haskell, Brenton Ernest *health facility administrator*
†Moore, Marilyn Ulfers *social worker*

West Des Moines
Goldsmith, Janet Jane *retired pediatric nurse practitioner*
Zimmerman, Jo Ann *health services and educational consultant, former lieutenant governor*

KANSAS

Courtland
Johnson, Dorothy Phyllis *retired counselor, art therapist*

Emporia
Frogge, Beverly Ann *nurse, consultant*
Madore, Joyce Louise *gerontology nurse*

Fort Leavenworth
Oliver, Thornal Goodloe *health care executive*

Goddard
Picotte, Susan Gaynel *geriatrics nurse, nursing educator, rehabilitation nurse*

Hays
†Bustos, Rudolph R. *health facility administrator*

Humboldt
Finney, Paul David *acupuncturist, Chinese herbologist, entrepreneur*

Kansas City
Boal, Marcia Anne Riley *clinical social worker, administrator*
Eldredge, Peggy *oncological nurse*
Godwin, Harold Norman *pharmacist, educator*
Jerome, Norge Winifred *nutritionist, anthropologist*
†Sanders-Hall, Patricia E. *health facility administrator*
†Starling, Carol King *nursing educator*
Taunton, Roma Lee *nurse educator and researcher*
Ternus, Jean Ann *nursing educator*

Larned
Davis, Mary Elizabeth *speech pathologist, educator, counselor*
Zook, Martha Frances Harris *retired nursing administrator*

Lawrence
Canda, Edward R. *social work educator*
Mc Coin, John Mack *social worker*
Searles, Lynn Marie *nurse*
Siemsen, Susan Anne *physician assistant*

Leavenworth
Heim, Dixie Sharp *family practice nurse practitioner*

Leawood
Tonkens, Rebecca Annette *maternal/women's health nurse*

Manhattan
†Crowe, Linda K. *speech pathology/audiology services professional, educator*
Morrison, Lisa Ann *psychiatric nurse practitioner*
Moss, Larry W. *nursing administrator, quality management consultant*

Mission
Bonci, Andrew S. *chiropractor*

Olathe
Jones, Robert Lyle *emergency medical services leader, financial planner, educator*

Overland Park
Bronaugh, Deanne Rae *home health care administrator, consultant*

Pratt
Westerhaus, Catherine K. *social worker*

Shawnee
Hudson, Tajquah Jaye *managed health care executive*
Lehmkuhl, Margie Mae *occupational health nurse*

Shawnee Mission
Breen, Katherine Anne *speech and language pathologist*
Jones, George Humphrey *retired healthcare executive, hospital facilities and communications consultant*
Picciano, R.J. *renal technician*
Shalinsky, Joseph George *pharmacist, pharmaceutical executive*

Topeka
Reymond, Patricia Ann *social worker*
Sheffel, Irving Eugene *psychiatric institution executive*
Varner, Charleen LaVerne McClanahan (Mrs. Robert B. Varner) *nutritionist, educator, administrator, dietitian*

Valley Center
Bryan, Paul Edward *pharmacist*

Wheaton
Willis, Joan Ellen *nurse*

Wichita
Dorr, Stephanie Tilden *psychotherapist*
Guthrie, Diana Fern *nursing educator*
Hicks, M. Elizabeth (Liz Hicks) *pharmacist*
Korf, Clifford Dean *physician assistant*
Park, Chan Hyung *cell biologist, physician*
Rogers, Rita Doris Luck *family nurse practitioner*

Winfield
Laws, Carolyn Marie Roderick *medical/surgical nurse, pediatrics nurse*

KENTUCKY

Albany
†Tallent, Brenda Colene *social worker, psychotherapist*

Bowling Green
Pierce, Verlon Lane *pharmacist, small business owner*

Calvert City
Butler, Sheila Morris *occupational health nurse*

Corbin
Mahan, Shirley Jean *nursing educator*

Covington
Bush, Sister Mary Kathleen *social worker*

Edgewood
Rue, Nelson B. *hospital administrator*

Frankfort
Dringenburg, Duane Clinton *health services executive*
Fleming, Juanita Wilson *nursing education, university official*

Glasgow
†Mortimer, Beverly Jo *medical/surgical nurse, director*

Goshen
Dahl, Marilyn Gail *psychotherapist, nurse*

Hartford
Brown, Russell Jay *nurse*

Henderson
Logan, John A., III, *hospital administrator*

Kings Mountain
Gill, Allen (Dale Gill) *environmental management service*

Lexington
Braun, Janet Larson *nurse*
DeLuca, Patrick Phillip *pharmaceutical scientist, educator, administrator*
Farrar, Donna Beatrice *hospital official*
Hasan, Saiyid Zafar *social work educator*
Kelso, Lynn A. *acute care nurse practitioner*
Leukefeld, Carl George *researcher, educator*
Walize, Reuben Thompson, III, *health research administrator*

Louisville
Anderson, Linda Jean *critical care and psychiatric nurse practitioner*
Berger, Barbara Paull *social worker, marriage and family therapist*
†Bloem, James H. *managed health care executive*
Holmes, Gary Lee *medical/surgical nurse*
†Jones, David Allen *health facility executive*
Kuntz, Edward Lawrence *health care executive*
Lunsford, W. Bruce *health facility administrator, health and medical products executive*
Mather, Elizabeth Vivian *healthcare executive*
†Matuschka, Paul R. *pharmacist*
McCallister, Michael B. *managed health care executive*
Rose, Judy Hardin *nursing administrator*
Tully, Carol Thorpe *social work educator, administrator*
Zechman, David Mark *health system executive, educator*

Middlesboro
Money, Max Lee *family nurse practitioner*

Mount Olivet
Dorton, Truda Lou *medical, surgical and geriatrics nurse*

Mount Sterling
Kukulinsky, Nancy Elaine *health care consultant*

Owensboro
Oberst, Charlotte L. *physical therapist, nurse*

Paducah
Wurth, Susan Winsett *clinical nurse specialist*

Rousseau
Bach, Betty Jean *health services educator*

Russellville
Harper, Shirley Fay *nutritionist, educator, consultant, lecturer*

LOUISIANA

Abbeville
Hebert, Margaret Burns *social worker*

Alexandria
Jones, Syble Thornhill *dietitian*
Slipman, Ronald (Samuel Slipman) *hospital administrator*
Sneed, Ellouise Bruce *nursing educator emeritus*

Baton Rouge
Finan, John Joseph *hospital administrator*
Slaybaugh, Janet Louise *social worker*
Vaeth, Agatha Min-Chun Fang *clinical nurse, nursing administrator, consultant*

Bossier City
Fry, Randy Dale *emergency medical technician, paramedic*
Wheelahan, Timothy Michael *physical therapist*
Winham, George Keeth *retired mental health nurse*

Carencro
Ford, Deborah Hardy *nursing administrator*

Chalmette
Brown, Courtney Allison *social worker*

Covington
Burton, Barbara Able *psychotherapist*

Cut Off
Adams, Laura Ann *critical care nurse*

Houma
Bridges, Gerald Jackson *social worker*

Jackson
Payne, Mary Alice McGill *behavior management healthcare quality consultant*

Lake Charles
Campbell, Carol Sue *sociology, social work, psychology, and criminal justice educator*

Leesville
Gutman, Lucy Toni *school social worker, educator, counselor*

Mandeville
Franke, Kathleen Eleanor *medical social worker*
Pittman, Jacquelyn *retired mental health nurse, nursing educator*
Treuting, Edna Gannon *retired nursing administrator*

Metairie
Evans, Carol Rockwell *nursing administrator*
Friedman, Lynn Joseph *counselor*

Monroe
McClanahan, Patsy Hitt *women's health nurse practitioner*

Natchitoches
Egan, Shirley Anne *retired nursing educator*

New Orleans
Belsom, John Anton (Jack Belsom) *writer, researcher*
†Culbertson, Richard Allen *healthcare educator, health system director*
Ducote, Charlotte Anne *allied health services administrator*
Edmonds, Velma McInnis *nursing educator*
Grace, Marcellus *pharmacy educator, university dean*
Hackman, Gwendolyn Ann *private duty nurse*
Ibanez, Jane Bourquard *management training consultant, lecturer*
Isaacson, Julanne R. *social worker, retired*
Layman, Kim Florinda Marie *pharmacist, writer*
†LeBan, Levon Aldon *counselor, secondary school educator*
Le Blanc, Alice Isabelle *public health program, academic program administrator*
Marier, Robert L. *dean, hospital administrator*
Oliver, Ronald *retired medical technologist*
Rigby, Perry Gardner *medical center administrator, educator, former university dean, physician*
Rogers, Joan Lisso *social worker, psychotherapist*
†Sterling, Yvonne Marie *nursing educator, consultant*
Weiner, Roy Samuel *medical educator, health facility administrator*
White, Dana Eileen *public health prevention specialist*

Pineville
McAllister, Ann Marie *social worker, educator*
Williams, Karen Olivia *nurse manager, maternal/child health nurse*

Shreveport
†Bellew, James William, Jr., *physical therapist, educator*
Heacock, Donald Dee *social worker*
Hummel, Kay Jean *physical therapist*
St. Aubyn, Ronald Anthony *pediatrics nurse*

Slidell
†Jacob, Susan Marie *nurse*
†Laurent, Lynn Margaret *nurse*

Winnfield
Jones, Susie Mathis *social worker*

MAINE

Augusta
Crate, Stephen Church *vocational rehabilitation specialist, consultant, author, politician*

Bangor
Ballesteros, Paula Mitchell *nurse*
Beaupain, Elaine Shapiro *psychiatric social worker*

Belgrade Lakes
Kany, Judy C(asperson) *health policy analyst, former state senator*

Biddeford
Crockett, Ann Hemenway *psychotherapist*
Kimball, Judith Giencke *occupational therapist, educator*

Blue Hill
Evans, Howard Morgan *acupuncturist, zero balancer*

Brooklin
Schmidt, Lynda Wheelwright *psychotherapist*

Brunswick
Fiori, Michael J. *pharmacist*

Canton
Parsons, Lorraine Leighton *nurse, child care professional*

Caribou
Swanson, Shirley June *emergency room nurse, travel nurse, adult education educator*

Cumberland Center
Brewster, Linda Jean *family nurse practitioner*

Damariscotta
Swanson, Karin *hospital administrator, consultant*

East Boothbay
Eldred, Kenneth McKechnie *acoustical consultant*

Fort Fairfield
Shapiro, Joan Isabelle *laboratory administrator, nurse*

Gorham
Fall, Marijane Eaton *counselor educator*

Gray
Nickerson, Bruce Donald *medical services administrator*

Hampden
Karlson, Donna Mae *clinical social worker*

Kittery
Clark, Sandra Ann *clinical social worker*

Lewiston
Le, Phuoc Hong *internist, consultant*

Limerick
Stewart, Harold T. *social worker, consultant*

Medway
Klein, Kathryn Ann *social worker*

Newburgh
Berardelli, Catherine Marie *women's health nurse, nurse educator*

North Yarmouth
Kuhrt, Sharon Lee *nursing administrator*

Perry
Breckinridge, Michael Frederick *pharmacist*

Pittsfield
†Eliopoulos, Barbara J. *health facility administrator, medical/surgical nurse*

Portland
Fenton, Clarence Asa *healthcare facility administrator*

Presque Isle
Barrett, Paul J. *pharmacist*

Scarborough
Connolly, Elaine Alexander Paterson *nurse*

South Portland
Cotton, Joyce E. Doherty *mental health nurse*

Starks
Medeiros, M. Joyce *community health educator*

Waterville
Tormollan, Gary Gordon *health facility administrator, physical therapist*

MARYLAND

Aberdeen Proving Ground
Sommer, Valerie Kulis *occupational health nurse*

Adamstown
Munson, John Christian *acoustician*

Annapolis
Castleyoung, Brenda *social worker, mental health nurse*
Core, Mary Carolyn W. Parsons *health facility administrator*
Kushner, Jack *retired physician executive*
Otte, Lynda Ellen *neonatal nurse*
Palmer, Timothy Trow *safety and health consultant*
Swan, William Irving *nutritionist*

Arnold
Brandimore, Wadie Miller *retired pediatrics nurse*
France, Mary Pearre *rehabilitation nurse, consultant*

Baltimore
Beilenson, Peter Lowell *public health official*
†Biser-Rohrbaugh, Ann K. *physician assistant*
†Block, James A. *hospital administrator, pediatrician*
Brieger, Gert Henry *medical historian, educator*
Buccino, Daniel L. *psychotherapist, consultant*
Campbell, Jacquelyn C. *community health nurse*
†Chin, Katherine Moy *nutritionist, consultant*
Cohen, Eric *optometrist*
Dickler, Howard Byron *biomedical administrator, research physician*
Donaldson, Sue Karen *nursing educator, researcher*
†Dowling, Thomas C. *pharmacist, educator, pharmacist, researcher*
Flanigan, Lynn Flournoy *nurse, social worker and administrator*
Greif, Geoffrey Leonard *social work educator*
Gross, Kathleen Albright *interventional radiology nurse, educator, writer*
Haines, Stuart Tilman *pharmacist. educator*
Howard, Bettie Jean *surgical nurse*
†Hwang, Wenke *health services researcher*
Jenkins, Louise Sherman *nursing researcher, educator*
Kaplan, Abner J. *social worker, public relations executive*
Kelleher, Catherine Patricia *nursing educator*
†Keyser, Randall E. *exercise physiologist*
Korniewicz, Denise M. *nursing educator*
Lashley, Mark Alan *physician assistant*
Merrill, Earlene Brown *nurse educator*
Moses, Gloria *nurse*
Palley, Howard A. *social worker, educator*
Palumbo, Francis Xavier Bernard *pharmacy educator*
Peterson, Ronald R. *health service administrator*
†Pointer, Michelle Phillips *counselor, educator, consultant*
Pruce, Rhoda Posner *social worker*
†Sachs, Murray B. *audiologist, educator*
Sallese, Paula Marie *critical care, resuscitation nurse*
Santamaria, Barbara Matheny *retired nurse practitioner*
Schneewind, Elizabeth Hughes *social worker*
Schreter, Carol Ann *social worker, gerontologist, writer*
†Steinwachs, Donald Michael *public health educator*

Bel Air
Haupt, Sheri Lynn *pharmacist*
Osborne, Lisette Kirstie *neonatal nurse practitioner, nursing administrator*

Beltsville
Bloch, Bobbie Ann *nurse, educator*
Levin, Gilbert Victor *health information, services and products*

Berwyn Heights
Kirchknopf, Matthew Bela *research laboratory manager*

Bethesda
Atwell, Constance Woodruff *health services executive, researcher*
Dyer, Doris Anne *nursing consultant*
Ehrenfeld, Ellie (Elvera Ehrenfeld) *health science association administrator*
Fauci, Anthony Stephen *health facility administrator, physician*
Gabelnick, Henry Lewis *medical research director*
†Govern, Frank Stanley *health facility administrator, consultant, healthcare educator, writer*
Graeff, Alan S. *health association executive*
Greenwood, Naomi *social worker*
†Hood, Maureen N *medical/surgical nurse, researcher*
Hoyer, Mary Louise *social worker, educator*
Keusch, Gerald T. *health services administrator*
†Kinsel, Jane F. *health science association administrator*
Koslow, Stephen Hugh *science administrator, pharmacologist*

PROFESSIONAL INDEX 6379 HEALTHCARE: HEALTH SERVICES

Marino, Pamela Anne *health sciences administrator*
Mattson, Margaret Ellen *health research administrator*
†McCray, Alexa T. *health science association administrator, director*
Metzger, Henry *federal research institution administrator*
Mulhauser, Lynda Cahan *clinical social worker, educator, administrator*
Nakamura, Richard *mental health services professional*
Nee, Linda Elizabeth *social science analyst*
Onufrock, Richard Shade *pharmacist, researcher*
Polsby, Gail K. *psychotherapist*
Robinson, Sharon Beth *health science association administrator*
Rodríguez-Franson, Julie Isabel *counselor*
Sevin-Rodgers, Imogene *occupational and environmental health sciences consultant*
Taylor, Lindsay David, Jr., *health care executive*
Tracy, Thomas Miles *international health organization official*
Wang, Chin-Hua *rehabilitation service professional*
Wheeler, Beverly B. *cardiology and cardiothoracic nurse specialist*
Willoughby, Anne *health facility administrator, researcher, educator*
†Wolman, Sandra R. *health science association administrator, pathologist, geneticist*

Bowie
Rupp, Monica Cecilia *nursing administrator*
Speller-Brown, Barbara Jean *pediatric nurse practitioner*

California
Barnes, Stuart Robert *physician assistant*

Catonsville
Woolley, Alma Schelle *nursing educator*

Cheverly
Wilkes, Deborah Ann *neonatal intensive care nurse*

Chevy Chase
Meltzer, Rae *social worker*

Chillum
Malbon, Louise *registered, nurse, hypnotherapist writer, publisher*

Clarksville
Hung, Mei-Jong Chow *social worker*

Clinton
Dandy, Roscoe Greer *clinical psychotherapist, educator, public health analyst*

College Park
Anderson, Randi Laine *occupational therapist*
†MacDonald-Wilson, Kim Lorraine *psychiatric rehabilitation counselor*
Morris, Joseph Anthony *health science association administrator*
Younger, Deirdre Ann *pharmacist*

Colora
Borland, Raymond M. *researcher*

Columbia
Abel, Florence Catherine Harris *social worker*
Chaiklin, Harris *retired social work educator*
Crivelli, Kenneth John *physical therapist, athletic trainer*
Gull, Hazel Joy (Connie Gull) *retired nursing administrator*
Lenz, Lois Martin Elser *psychiatric and mental health nurse*
Margolis, Vivienne O. *psychotherapist, educator*

Crofton
Boland, Gerald Lee *health facility financial executive*

Cumberland
Wolford, Nancy Lou *medical and surgical nurse*

Easton
Whitten, Nancy Bimmerman *clinical social worker, marriage therapist*

Elk Mills
Dorsman, Jerry *addictions therapist, writer*

Elkridge
Szilagyi, Sherry Ann *psychotherapist, lawyer*

Fallston
Lewis, Howard Franklin *chiropractor*

Fort Washington
Isom, Virginia Annette Veazey *retired nursing educator*

Frederick
†Devineni, Mohan *pharmacist*
Wickizer, Stephen Wesley *pharmacist*

Gaithersburg
Dowd, Carolyn Lay *social worker*
Johnson, Betty Marie *retired nursing educator*
Peele, Roger *hospital administrator*
Quraishi, Mohammed Sayeed *retired health scientist, administrator*
Reynolds, Frank Miller *retired government administrator*
Tenney, Lisa Christine Gray *healthcare administrator*

Glen Burnie
†Hepburn, Jeanette C. *home health nurse*

Hagerstown
Harrison, Lois Smith *hospital executive, educator*

Hanover
Rochdi, Myriam *pharmacist, researcher*

Hyattsville
Sondik, Edward J. *health science administrator*

Kensington
Hayunga, Mary Ann *women's health nurse*

La Plata
Bivens, Kenneth Edward *physician assistant*

Lanham Seabrook
Cook, Linda Kay *critical care nurse*
Pleasant-Jackson, Tonya *therapist, consultant*

Laurel
Landis, Donna Marie *nursing administrator, women's health nurse*

Leominster
†Markham, John Thomas *social worker, educator*

Marriottsville
Strange, Donald Ernest *health care company executive*

Mitchellville
Chilman, Catherine Earles Street *social welfare educator, author*

Montgomery Village
Bingham, Raymond Joseph *neonatal/perinatal nurse practitioner*

Oakland
McClintock Fost, Donna *social worker*

Ocean City
O'Hanlon, Richard Thomas *counseling educator*

Olney
Michael, Jerrold Mark *public health specialist, former university dean, educator*
Weller, Jane Kathleen *emergency nurse*
Westerman, Rosemary Matzzie *nurse, administrator*

Owings Mills
Ryan, Judith W. *geriatrics consultant, adult nurse practitioner, educator, researcher*

Patuxent River
Kennedy, David L. *social worker, military officer*

Perry Point
Yackley, Luke Eugene *nursing educator*

Port Tobacco
†Smith, Sheila Robertson *laboratory technician*

Potomac
Anfinsen, Libby Esther Shulman *social worker, clinical administrator*
Heller, Peggy Osna *psychotherapist, poetry therapist*
Leva, Neil Irwin *psychotherapist, hypnotherapist*
Leva, Susan Mary *social worker*
Wolman, Eric *health care consultant*

Rockville
†Baine, William Brennan *public health service officer, internist*
Chiacchierini, Richard Philip *healthcare consultant*
Clark, H. Westley *health facility administrator*
Covington, Sharon Nickel *social worker, psychotherapist*
Duke, Elizabeth M. *health facility administrator*
Feigal, David W., Jr., *health science association administrator*
Greenberg, Jerrold Selig *health education educator*
Howard, Lee Milton *international health consultant*
Hsia, David *health services researcher, administrator*
Kacuba, Alice Marie *nurse*
Leach, Lynnetta Jane *social worker, consultant*
Lewis, Benjamin Pershing, Jr., *pharmacist, public health service officer*
Long, Cedric William *health research executive*
†McCormick, Kathleen Ann Krym *geriatrics nurse, information scientist, federal agency administrator*
O'Donnell, James Francis *retired health science administrator*
Parham, Deborah *health facility administrator*
Peyser, Hedy Jeanette *social worker*
Rasmussen, Caren Nancy *hospital executive*
Rimer, Barbara K. *health facility administrator, educator*
Scully, Martha Seebach *speech and language pathologist*
Shekar, Sam *health facility administrator*
Smith, Shelagh Alison *public health educator*
Trujillo, Michael H. *administrator*
Uppoor, Rajendra *pharmaceutical scientist, pharmacist, educator, researcher, private pilot*
Wallach, Harold Charles *health policy and health services research administrator, educator*
Weinel, Pamela Jean *nurse administrator*

Sabillasville
McCulloch, Anna Mary Knott *pharmacy technician*

Saint Michaels
Young, Donald Roy *pharmacist*

Salisbury
Cugler, Carol Marie Miller *retired mental health services professional*

Severna Park
Daly, Charles Arthur *health services administrator*
Simonds, Valerie Deverse *prehospital educator*

Silver Spring
Aukamp, Ann Walkley North *social worker, consultant, small business owner*
Ledley, Christian Salvesen *retired social worker*
Lizanich-Aro, Suzanne *health care consultant*
Mashin, Jacqueline Ann Cook *medical sciences administrator, nursing administrator*
Nevans, Laurel S. *rehabilitation counselor*
O'Connell, Mary Ita *psychotherapist*
Waldmann, Katharine Spreng *public health physician*

Takoma Park
Stephenson, Patricia Ann *public health researcher, educator*

Towson
Serpick, Arthur Allen *health facility administrator, physician*
Sheredos, Carol Ann *rehabilitation clinical specialist*

Towson,
†Evangeliou, Christos C. *researcher, educator*

Westminster
Lippy, Karen Dorothy Fethe *nurse psychotherapist*

Westover
Carter, Carolyn Marie *social work executive*

MASSACHUSETTS

Acton
Brody, Leslie Gary *social worker, sociologist*

Andover
Feinberg, Linda Sones *social worker, artist, writer*
Whidden, Robert Lee, Jr., *healthcare consultant*

Arlington
†Carvotta, Crystal Champaigne *nursing administrator, consultant*
Casey, Ellen Patricia *obstetric and gynecological nurse*

Attleboro
Bischoff, Marilyn Brett *clinical social worker, personal life coach*

Auburndale
Kibrick, Anne *retired nursing educator and university dean*

Bedford
Taylor, Cora Hodge *social worker*

Belmont
Hanfling, Sue Carol (Suki Hanfling) *social worker*
Junger, Miguel Chapero *acoustics researcher*

Berkley
Mills, Carol Andrews *mental health administrator*

Beverly
DeVore, Dale Paul *scientific research organization executive*

Boston
Bacigalupe, Gonzalo Manuel *family therapist, educator*
†Bebo, Joseph Anthony *counselor, educator*
Blendon, Robert Jay *health policy educator*
†Board, Rhonda M. *pediatrics nurse, researcher*
Cohen, Alan Barry *researcher, educator*
DeJong, H. William *health educator*
Delahanty, Linda Michele *dietitian*
Drought, James Henry *healthcare business owner, exercise physiologist*
Fava, Maurizio *hospital administrator, researcher*
Fein, Rashi *health sciences educator*
†Fowler, Floyd Jackson, Jr., *researcher*
Frank, Richard G. *health educator*
Glod, Carol Ann *nursing educator*
Hemenway, David *public health educator*
Kasper, Dennis Lee *health facility administrator, educator*
Millar, Sally Gray *nurse*
Milton, Donald Kirby *occupational and environmental health researcher*
Portney, Leslie Gross *physical therapist*
Reinherz, Helen Zarsky *researcher, social services educator*
Restuccia, Joseph D. *healthcare educator*
Slavin, Peter L. *hospital administrator, medical association administrator*
†Stevens, Joyce West *social worker, educator, social worker, researcher*
Weinstein, Milton Charles *health policy educator*
Williams, Mary Margaret *nurse administrator*
Winkelman, James Warren *hospital administrator, pathology educator*
Woods, Cathi L. *human services administrator*

Boxboro
Evdokimoff, Merrily Weber *nursing administrator, community health nurse*

Boxford
Siegert, Barbara (Barbara Marie Siegert) *health care administrator*

Boylston
Larson, Roland Elmer *health care executive*

Brockton
Anderson, Ernest Robert, Jr., *pharmacist*
Moore, Mary Johnson *nurse*
Sherman, Beverly Robin *medical, surgical, pediatric, and maternity nurse*

Brookline
Erick, Miriam Anna *dietitian, medical writer*
Gewirtz, Mindy L. *organizational and human relations consultant*

Cambridge
Botkin, James W. *leadership and life coach*
Burns, Virginia *social worker*
Clifton, Anne Rutenber *psychotherapist, educator*
Lima, Kristine Roop *clinical social worker*
Russell, Mason Webster *healthcare economist, educator*
†Young, Vernon Robert *nutrition, biochemistry educator*

Canton
Bihldorff, John Pearson *hospital director*
Sawtelle, Carl S. *psychiatric social worker*

Centerville
Rieber, Jesse Alvin *psychotherapist*

Chestnut Hill
Barry, Joan *clinical researcher*
Boskin, Claire *psychotherapist*
†Burgess, Ann Wolbert *nursing educator*
Hawkins, Joellen Margaret Beck *nursing educator*
Newman, Morton B. *psychoanalyst, psychiatrist*
†Vessey, Judith Ann *nursing educator*

Chicopee
Dame, Catherine Elaine *acupuncturist*

Concord
Brentani, Patricia Brodie *social worker*
Domar, Carola Rosenthal *social worker*

Dedham
Winder, Alvin Eliot *public health educator, clinical psychologist*

Dorchester
†Weaver, Mark Franklin *social worker, pastor*
Worgaftik, Susan Carol *social worker*

Dracut
Brousseau, Catherine Dalton *retired school health services director*

Fairhaven
Merolla, Michele Edward *chiropractor, broadcaster*

Fall River
†Bessette, Heidi Dee *adult nurse practitioner*
Frost, Carol A. *clinical social worker, consultant*

Foxboro
Kaul, Alan Franklin *healthcare consultant, pharmacist*

Framingham
Austin, Sandra Ikenberry *nurse educator, consultant*
Vermette, Raymond Edward *clinical laboratories administrator*
Willinger, Rhonda Zwern *optometrist*

Gloucester
Scanlan, Esther Meader *psychiatric social worker*

Great Barrington
Berryhill, Mary Finley *emergency nurse*
Drohan, Margo Angela *pediatric nurse practitioner*

Green Harbor
Gaffey, Virginia Anne *retired nurse anesthetist*

Greenfield
Curtiss, Carol Perry *health care consultant*
Sternberg, Harriet Elaine *psychiatric social worker*

Haverhill
Rubinstein, Nancy G. *social worker, consultant*
Walker, Robert Ross *social worker*

Holden
Ciance, Karin Lori (Ohs) *medical/surgical nurse*

Holyoke
Dearborn, Maureen Markt *speech and language clinician*

Hyannis
Nicholson, Ellen Ellis *clinical social worker*

Lawrence
Walker, Gail Flanagan *pediatrics nurse, women's health nurse, nursing administrator*

Lenox
Lewis, Marianne H. *psychiatric nurse practitioner*

Lexington
Densmore, Ann *speech pathology/audiology services professional, audiologist, writer*
Otten, Jeffrey *former hospital administrator*
Perez, Carol Anne *rehabilitation services professional, consultant*

Lowell
Baskin, Frank Ellis *social worker, educator*

Lynn
Donovan, Elaine F. *social worker*

Malden
†Kemp, Loretta Christine *human services administrator*

Marion
McPartland, Patricia Ann *health educator and administrator*

Medford
Roth, Sallyann *social worker*

Medway
Civitella, Corine Antoinette *retired health facility administrator*

Methuen
Jean, Patricia Anne *medical center administrator*

Milton
Desmond, Patricia Lorraine *psychotherapist, writer, publisher*

Monterey
Frye-Moquin, Marsha Marie *social worker*

Nantucket
Giddings, Lucille Cassell *nurse*

Natick
Bower, Kathleen Anne *nurse consultant*
Lebowitz, Charlotte Meyersohn *social worker*
O'Bannon, Jacqueline Michele *geriatrics and mental health nurse*

Needham
Ryan, Una Scully *health sciences professional, medical educator*

Newton
Adler, Jill S. *psychiatric social worker, psychotherapist*
Benedict, Mary-Anne *nursing educator, consultant*
Micklitsch, Christine Nocchi *health care administrator*

Newton Center
Pill, Cynthia Joan *social worker*

Newton Centre
Kaneko, Sylvia Yelton *clinical social worker, educator*

North Dartmouth
†Xing, Liudong *researcher, educator*

Northampton
Payne, Marilyn Ann *physical therapist*

Oak Bluffs
Rose, Kathleen Nolan *health facility administrator*

Osterville
Weber, Adelheid Lisa *former nurse, chemist*
Williams, Ann Meagher *retired hospital administrator*

Peabody
Baures, Mary Margaret *clinical psychotherapist, author*

Pembroke
Egan, Denise *home health nurse*

Quincy
Wise, Carol Lewis *occupational therapist*

Rockland
†LaFerney, Michael C. *mental health nurse, counselor*

Rockport
Reardon, Bea *social worker*

Salem
Hudson, Christopher Giles *social worker, educator*

Shrewsbury
Falter, Robert Gary *nursing home administrator, educator*

Somerset
Fletcher, Dorothy *community health and primary home care nurse*

South Boston
Nalbandian, E. Carolyn *social worker*

South Dartmouth
LaPorte, Adrienne Aroxie *nursing administrator*

South Dennis
Stiefvater, Pamela Jean *chiropractor*

South Harwich
Finn, Nita Ann *social worker*

Southbridge
Anderson, Ross Barrett *healthcare environmental services manager*
Mangion, Richard Michael *health care executive*

Springfield
†Evans, Elizabeth E. *physical therapist, educator*
Gross, Donalyn Ann *counselor*
Saia, Diane Plevock DiPiero *nutritionist, educator, legal association administrator*

Sterling
Garafalo, Lynne Mary *audiologist, speech and language pathologist*

Swampscott
Smith, Carl Dean, Jr., *marriage and family therapist*

Taunton
Anderson, Peter D. *pharmacist, forensic scientist*

Tewksbury
Herlihy-Chevalier, Barbara Doyle *mental health nurse*

Tiverton
†Brock, Dawn Marie *counselor*

Vineyard Haven
Knowles, Christopher Allan *healthcare executive*

Walpole
Cotter, Douglas Adrian *healthcare executive*

Waltham
†Bleicher, Paul Alan *health facility administrator*
Fleming, Samuel Crozier, Jr., *healthcare executive*
Gray-Nix, Elizabeth Whitwell *occupational therapist*
Liljestrand, James Stratton *physician administrator, internist*

Ware
Zwemke, Katharine Priscilla *dietitian, diabetes educator*

Watertown
Amsler, Karen Marie *medical technologist, scientist*

Wayland
Budner, Ruth Stern *social worker*

Wellesley
Montague, Joel Gedney *public health officer*

West Newton
†Logan, Georgiana Marie *psychotherapist*

West Roxbury
Rogers, Brenda Ann *community health clinical specialist*

West Springfield
Ballard, Mildred Louise *retired adult nurse practitioner*

Westborough
Gordon, Betty L. *health services administrator*

Westwood
Donahue, Charles Lee, Jr., *health network executive*

Williamstown
Conklin, Susan Joan *psychotherapist, educator, corporate staff developer, TV talk show host*

Woburn
†Conway, James Bernard *hospital administrator, consultant*
Crowley, Dean Timothy *occupational therapist*
Goela, Jitendra Singh *researcher, consultant*

Worcester
Capriole, Sister Carmen Maria *geriatric nurse*
Cashman, Suzanne Boyer *health services administrator, educator*
Hand, Paul Desautels, Sr., *social work educator*
Joshi, Harihar S. *medical laboratory executive*
Snyder, L. Michael *hospital administrator*
Stempsey, William Edward *medical philosopher*

Yarmouth Port
Ierardi, Anne Marie *pastoral counselor, artist*
McGill, Grace Anita *retired occupational health nurse, case manager*
†Phelps, Judson Hewett *health facility administrator*
Terrill, Robert Carl *hospital administrator*

MICHIGAN

Ada
Bandemer, Norman John *healthcare consulting executive*

Allen Park
Kirby, Dorothy Manville *social worker*

Ann Arbor
Allen-Meares, Paula G. *social work educator, dean*
†Bashshur, Rashid L. *health facility administrator, educator*
Clark, Noreen Morrison *behavioral science educator, researcher*
Gordinier, Terri Klein *speech-language pathologist*
Griffith, John Randall *health services administrator, educator*
Henrickson, Christine Guldager *social worker*
†Huston, Sally Ann *pharmacist*
Kalisch, Beatrice Jean *nursing educator, consultant*
Leong, Sue *retired community health and pediatrics nurse*
Lucy, Dlorah Rae *medical/surgical nurse*
Meezan, William Alan *social work educator, consultant*
Mowbray, Carol Beatrice (Thiessen) *social worker, educator, mental health services professional, researcher*
Romani, John Henry *health administration educator*
Rupp, Ralph Russell *audiologist, educator, author*
†Samons, Sandra Lea *psychotherapist*

Sasaki, Joseph Donald *optometrist*
Schweitzer, Pamela Bifano *psychiatric and mental health nurse practitioner*
Zarley, Karlta Rae *Healing Touch practitioner, nurse consultant*

Bay City
Bosco, Jay William *optometrist*
†Deskin, William C. *healthcare educator*

Benton Harbor
Alsbro, Donald Edgar *health educator*

Central Lake
Hocking, Marian Ruth *women's health nurse*

Charlotte
Herrick, Kathleen Magara *social worker*

Chesterfield
Burnett, Gary Main *social work administrator, crisis counselor*

Dearborn
†Barnhart, Mary C. *health facility administrator*
†Beauford, Sandra *registered nurse, data processing executive*
Ibbotson, Patricia Ann *nurse, author*

Detroit
Abramson, Hanley Norman *pharmacy educator*
†Bell, Sue Ellen *research analyst, administrator, nursing educator*
Berke, Amy Turner *health science association administrator*
Garriott, Lois Jean *clinical social worker, educator*
Heppner, Gloria Hill *medical science administrator, educator*
†Jacox, Ada Kathryn *nurse, educator*
Klurfeld, David Michael *nutritionist, pathologist*
Krouse, Helene June *nursing educator*
†McGinnity, John G. *physician assistant, medical educator*
Redman, Barbara Klug *nursing educator*
Sims-McCallum, Rosalyn Patrice *pharmacist*
†Tran, Alison Ha *pharmacist, educator*

Dexter
†Hanamey, Rosemary T. *nursing educator*

East Lansing
Schemmel, Rachel Anne *food science and human nutrition educator, researcher*

Farmington
Burns, Sister Elizabeth Mary *hospital administrator*

Farmington Hills
Cooper, Elaine Janice *physical therapist*

Flint
Alarie-Anderson, Peggy Sue *physician assistant*
Williams, Veronica Myres *psychotherapist, social worker*

Franklin
Sax, Mary Randolph *speech and language pathologist*

Fruitport
Anderson, Frances Swem *nuclear medical technologist*

Gaylord
Hoshield, Susan Lynn *pediatric nurse practitioner*
Schafer, Philip Nicholas *physician assistant*

Grand Blanc
Shaw, Randy Lee *human services administrator*

Grand Haven
†Disbrow, Sidney Arden, Jr., *chiropractor*

Grand Ledge
Evert, Sandra Florence (Sandra Wheeler) *medical/surgical nurse*

Grand Rapids
Chase, Sandra Lee *clinical pharmacist, consultant*
Gemmell-Akalis, Bonni Jean *psychotherapist*
Jackson, Wendy S. Lewis *social worker*
Kramer, Carol Gertrude *marriage and family counselor*
McFadden, Emily Jean *social work educator, consultant*

Grosse Pointe
Marshall, Douglas William *medical administrator, educator*

Grosse Pointe Farms
Couzens, Linda Lee Anderson *oncology nurse*

Grosse Pointe Park
Knapp, Mildred Florence *retired social worker*

Hastings
Adrounie, V. Harry *public health administrator, scientist, educator, environmentalist*

Holland
Franken, Darrell *counselor, writer, publisher*

Holt
Henning, Sandra Jean *social worker*

Houghton Lake
Marra, Samuel Patrick *retired pharmacist, small business owner*

Howell
Metz, Patricia Anne *school social worker*

Huntington Woods
Kirschner, Esther Green *social worker*

Jackson
Klingel, Patti Jean *health facility administrator*
Silva Potts, Margarita *counseling administrator*

Kalamazoo
†Aduroja, Amos Oladipo *healthcare educator, consultant*
Bennett, Arlie Joyce *clinical social worker emeritus*
†Dirette, Diane Kay *occupational therapist, educator*
Fredericks, Sharon Kay *nurse's aide*
Hamilton, Diane Bronkema *nursing educator*
Hoffman, Penelope Joan (Penny Hoffman) *adult nurse practitioner, administrator*
Lander, Joyce Ann *nursing educator, medical/surgical nurse*
Lawson, Gary D. *audiology educator*
Maurer, Edward Lance *chiropractor, radiologist*
Ortiz-Button, Olga *social worker*
†Price, Kim Denise *counselor*
Scholfield, Arlene R. *social worker*
†VandenBussche, Heather Lynne *pharmacist*
Voshel, Elizabeth Harbeck *social worker, educator*
Walker, Kay S. *geropsychiatric nurse*
Wijnberg, Marion Holley *social work educator*

Lansing
Barnes, Carla Leddy *social worker, developmental psychologist*
Frisosky, Rosarita Marie *volunteer nurse*
Loftus, Kay Douglas Colgan *social worker*

Leland
Hamelin, Paul Robert *pharmacist, pharmaceutical executive, consultant*

Lincoln Park
Russell, Harriet Shaw *social worker*

Linden
Tomaszewski, Kathleen Bernadette *social worker, educator*

Livonia
Gepford, Barbara Beebe *retired nutrition educator*

Midland
Black, Jacinth Baublitz *clinical social worker*
†Lile, James Michael *pharmacist, educator*

Muskegon
Sciba, JoAnn *social worker*

North Muskegon
Heyen, Beatrice J. *psychotherapist*

Novi
Abramowitz, Harriet C. *social worker*
Ragatzki, Paul A. *internist, administrator, educator*

Okemos
Tuttle, Mary Celia Putnam *social worker, retired*

Pinckney
McNamara, Ann Dowd *medical technologist*

Plymouth
Stewart, Katherine Hewitt *advanced practice nurse*

Redford
Aubertin, Madeline Katherine *retired nursing educator, medical/surgical nurse, mental health services professional*

Rochester Hills
Romero, Josefino Tabernilla *nurse anesthetist*

Royal Oak
Franklin, Barry Allan *health facility administrator, physiologist*

Saginaw
Gaffney, Karen Elizabeth *clinical social worker*
Mielke, Susan Kay *mental health nurse*
Shackelford, Martin Robert *social worker*

Southfield
Bennett, Helen *social worker*
Denes, Michel Janet *physical therapist, rehabilitation consultant*
Fennell, Christine Elizabeth *healthcare system executive*
Martin, Marcella Edric *retired community health nurse*
Sedler, Rozanne Friedlander *social worker, educator*
Wagner, Muriel Ginsberg *nutrition therapist*

Sparta
†Miller, Barbara Jean *health facility administrator*

Standish
Lamson, Evonne Viola *therapist, health care administrator, consultant, pastor, Christian educator*

Sterling Heights
Hammond-Kominsky, Cynthia Cecelia *optometrist*
Rosenfeld, Martin Jerome *healthcare executive, educator*

Traverse City
VanderKolk, Mary DeDecker *nursing educator*

Troy
Arking, Lucille Musser *nurse, epidemiologist, nursing administrator*
Hunter, Lorie Ann *women's health nurse*

Taber, Frances Kathryn *geriatrics nurse, administrator*

West Bloomfield
Barr, Martin *health care and higher education administrator*
Myers, Kenneth Ellis *hospital administrator*

Westland
Coates, Dianne Kay *social worker*

Ypsilanti
Brown-Chappell, Betty L. *social worker, educator*
Rainville, Alice Johannah *dietitian*

Zeeland
Mast, Mae Jerene *nurse*

MINNESOTA

Bemidji
Martinson, Ida Marie *nursing educator, nurse, physiologist*

Bloomington
Nichols, Donna Mardell *nurse anesthetist*

Brainerd
McTernan, Ann Cibuzar *adult nurse practitioner*

Cambridge
Lahr, John William *optometrist*

Circle Pines
Davis, Richard Carlton *rehabilitation services administrator*

Cottage Grove
Glazebrook, Rita Susan *nursing educator*

Crookston
Ring, K(arin) Elisabeth *physician assistant, registered nurse*

Duluth
Dillon, Herb Lester *critical care and emergency room nurse*
Gallinger, Lois Mae *medical technologist*

Edina
Jones-Gromacki, Lisa Dawn *health facility administrator*

Elysian
Thayer, Edna Louise *medical facility administrator, nurse*

Golden Valley
Nager, Elizabeth Eileen *clinical social worker*

Hastings
Blackie, Spencer David *physical therapist, administrator*

Mankato
†Shellum, Renee Elise *audiologist, education educator*

Maple Grove
Manthei, Robin Dickey *project coordinator*

Minneapolis
Ackerman, F. Kenneth, Jr., *health facility administrator*
Budd, Elaine *social worker*
Dahl, Gerald LuVern *psychotherapist, educator*
Dillon, Helen Kaye *obstetrics staff nurse*
Durdahl, Carol Lavaun *psychiatric nurse*
†Feldman, Nancy Jane *health organization executive*
†Franz, Marion J. *dietician, consultant*
Freese, Richard Bradley *health care executive*
Gerdner, Linda Ann *nursing researcher, educator*
Goldner, John Darrol *retired pharmacist*
Grant, David James William *pharmacy educator*
Idiyatullin, Djaudat Shavkatovich *research associate*
†Kralewski, John Edward *health service research educator*
LaValleur, June *obstetrician/gynecologist*
†Mathews, Kathleen Ann *social worker, psychotherapist*
Morrison, John M. *hospital administrator, bank executive*
Murphy, Edrie Lee *laboratory administrator*
†Stang, Jamie Sue *dietician, consultant*
Steen-Hinderlie, Diane Evelyn *social worker, musician*
Suryanarayanan, Raj Gopalan *researcher, consultant, educator*
Toscano, James Vincent *medical institute administration*
Woldt, Gerald D. (Jay Woldt) *nurse anesthetist*

Minnetonka
Joseph-Kordell, Shelley M. *geriatric care administrator*

Monticello
Wollan, Christine R. *clinical social worker*

New Brighton
Appel, William Frank *pharmacist*

Palisade
Kilde, Sandra Jean *nurse anesthetist, educator, consultant*

Pipestone
Appeldorn, Claudia J. *nursing administrator, editor*

Robbinsdale
Anderson, Scott Robbins *hospital administrator*

Rochester
Canan, Elizabeth Levy *health facility administrator*
Flaaten, Ruby Cheryl *nurse manager*
Gervais, Sister Generose *hospital consultant*
†Kummeth, Patricia Joan *nursing educator*
†Stelck, Mickie Joann *technologist*
Stewart, Karen Meyer *pediatrics nurse, nursing manager*
Verbout, James Paul *recreational therapist*
Williams, Arthur Ross *health service and public administrator*

Saint Louis Park
†Croll, Jillian Kathleen *dietician, researcher*

Saint Paul
Gilgun, Jane Frances *social work educator*
Hollister, Clifton David *social work educator*
Indritz, Mary Eloise Stoikes *pharmacy researcher*
Joyce, Michael Daniel *personal resource management therapist and consultant, neurolearning therapist*
Kilbourne, Barbara Jean *health and housing executive*
McChesney, Margaret Lee *clinical social worker*
Victor, Lorraine Carol *critical care nurse*
†Wendler, M. Cecilia *nursing educator*

Stillwater
Rescigno, Aldo *pharmacokinetics educator*

Thief River Falls
Reeves, Bruce *social worker*

White Bear Lake
Rogers, Megan Elizabeth *mental health therapist*

MISSISSIPPI

Biloxi
Erickson, Georganne Morris *nursing administrator, nursing educator, psychiatric-mental health consultant*
Gentry, Nancy O'Pry *medical/surgical nurse*

Brandon
Baltz, Richard Jay *health care company executive*
Jones, Helene Rasberry *nursing educator*
Parker, Rhonda Walker *nurse, administrator*

Byhalia
†Tackett, Maresa D. *medical technician*

Centreville
Nelson, Janie Rish *hospital executive*

Cleveland
Taylor, Donna Buescher *marriage and family therapist*

Gulfport
†Bosarge, Rick Anthony *health facility administrator*

Hattiesburg
Saucier Lundy, Karen *nursing educator*

Itta Bena
Newsome, Moses *social work educator*

Jackson
Brooks, Jean Evelyn *social work educator*
Buckner-Brown, Joyce *allied health instructor*
Deschamp, Clyde *emergency medical technician*
Dickson, Betsy G. *social worker*
Malloy, James Matthew *health management executive, healthcare consultant*
Roberts, Kristie *researcher*
Tchounwou, Paul Bernard *environmental health specialist, toxicologist, educator*
Thornton, Larry Lee *psychotherapist, author, educator, minister*
†Zisman, Stuart *healthcare educator, social worker, counselor*

Lauderdale
Van Doren, Henrietta Lambert *nurse, anesthetist*

Meridian
†Rackley, Emmerll *psychiatric nurse practitioner*

Mississippi State
Crudden, Adele Louise *social work research educator*

Ocean Springs
Lee, Kathleen Mary *administration and nursing executive*

Olive Branch
Harmon Brown, Valarie Jean *hospital laboratory director, information systems executive*

Pass Christian
Henrion, Rosemary P. *mental health professional*

Raleigh
Price, Tommye Jo Ensminger *community health nurse*

Tupelo
Zurawski, Jeanette *rehabilitation services professional*

MISSOURI

Arcadia
†Davis, Jo *nurse, aromatherapist, writer, professional speaker, small business owner*

Arnold
Freukes, Patricia E. *pediatrics nurse, nursing supervisor*

Belton
Brown, Doris Jane *nursing aide*

Boonville
Omer, Robert Wendell *hospital administrator*

Branson West
Peterson, Sharon Lynn Craig *medical care manager, cost containment specialist*

Brookfield
Sutton, Joyce Elaine *medical records director*

Cape Girardeau
Mohd Zain, A(hmad) Zaidy *counselor, educator*

Chesterfield
Baumann, Carol Kay *clinical nurse specialist*

Clinton
Boarman, Marjorie Ruth *prevention specialist, manufacturing company executive*

Columbia
†Beaujean, A. Alexander *researcher*
Brinegar, Elizabeth Anne *critical care nurse, educator*
Hensley, Elizabeth Catherine *nutritionist, educator*
Parmeley, Jerry Paul *software support analyst*
Stewart, Bobby Gene *laboratory director*

Crystal City
Sita, Michael John *pharmacist, educator*

Dexter
Owens, Debra Ann *chiropractor*

Fayette
Burres, Carla Anne *medical technologist*

Grandin
Wallace, Louise Margaret *nurse*

Greenwood
Dickinson, Lois Jean Berwanger *adult nurse practitioner, nurse staff officer*

Holts Summit
Melton, June Marie *nursing educator*

Hurley
Feazell, Johnny Ray *physicians assistant*

Independence
Sturges, Sidney James *pharmacist, educator, investment and development company executive*

Jefferson City
Chang, Yi-Shih Joshua *health researcher*
Dey, Charlotte Jane *retired community health nurse*
Winegar, Anthony C. *health care worker*

Kansas City
†Begleiter, Michael L. *genetic counselor*
Butler, Alice Claire *rehabilitation nurse*
DeParle, Nancy-Ann Min *former federal agency administrator, lawyer*
Eddy, Charles Alan *chiropractor*
Galloway, Margaret Elinor *social worker*
Harris, Roxanna Marie *emergency room nurse*
Piepho, Robert Walter *pharmacy educator, researcher*
Steffens, John Howard *cytotechnologist*
Thompson, Catherine Rush *physical therapist, educator*
Tunley, Naomi Louise *retired nurse administrator*
Worrall, Judith Rae *health and welfare plan consultant*

Kirbyville
†McPhillen, Beverly Louise *registered nurse*

Lake Ozark
DeShazo, Marjorie White *occupational therapist*

Lebanon
Caplinger, Patricia Ellen *family nurse practitioner*

Liberty
Samuel, Robert Thompson *optometrist*

Linn Creek
Waldon, Marja Parker *mental health nurse*

Marshfield
Gloe, Donna *systems change manager*

Maryville
Gorman, Karen Machmer *optometric physician*

Neosho
Gartner, Jessie Lee *family nurse practitioner*

Nevada
Wassenberg, Evelyn M. *medical and surgical nurse, nursing educator*

Osborn
Findley, Delpha Yoder *retired public health nurse*

Saint Ann
Gardner, Carla Deneen *social worker*
†Jamison, Darlene *geriatrics nurse*

Saint Charles
Drucker, Barry Jules *environmental health specialist*

Saint Joseph
Brown, Jean Gayle *social worker*

Saint Louis
Alessi, Mary Jean *family life educator*
Ashworth, Ronald Broughton *health facility executive, accountant*
Baum, M(ary) Carolyn *occupational therapist*
Bell, Laura Jeane *retired nurse*
Borders, John Gillespie *psychotherapist, former corporate executive*
Bryan, Jean Marie Wehmueller *nurse*
Campbell, Cheryl Ann *social worker*
Chignoli, C(elso) William *health care center administrator*
Cima, Cheryl Ann *medical/surgical nurse*
Cook, Cynthia Ann Loveland *health and mental health educator*
Ezenwa, Josephine Nwabuoku *social worker*
Fitch, Rachel Farr *health policy analyst*
French, Douglas Dewitt *medical facility administrator*
Friedberg, Michael A. *healthcare executive*
Gacem, Debra Ann *critical care nurse*
Herzfeld-Kimbrough, Ciby *mental health educator*
†Karoll, Brad R. *psychotherapist, researcher*
Manne, Deborah Sue *oncology nurse, consultant, dental hygienist*
Meyersick, Sharon Kay *nurse, insurance administrator*
Molloff, Florence Jeanine *speech and language therapist*
Munkel, Wayne Irvin *social worker*
Ozawa, Martha Naoko *social work educator*
†Schmitt, David E. *health facility administrator, music therapist*
Schoenhard, William Charles, Jr., *health care executive*
Smith, Gladys Ann *counselor, military medic*
Stencer, Mark Joseph *healthcare administrator, consultant*
Stratton, Sharon Elizabeth Spahn *mental and women's health nurse, nurse supervisor*
Stretch, John Joseph *social work educator, management and evaluation consultant*
Virgo, Katherine Sue *health services researcher*
Zucchero, Frederic Joseph *medical director*

Sedalia
Miller, Toni M. Andrews *critical care nurse, educator*

Springfield
†Gardner, Steven *health insurance specialist*

St Louis
Betsinger, Peggy Ann *retired oncological nurse*

Warrensburg
Collins, John W. *nurse practitioner, lecturer*

Webb City
Rose, Terri Kaye *obstetrical gynecological nurse practitioner, forensic exam nurse*

Whitewater
Sahlfeld Bunger, Kimberly Katherine *speech language pathologist*

MONTANA

Billings
Glenn, Lucia Howarth *retired mental health services professional*
Letz, Eileen Korber *retired community health nurse*
Martinez, Bonnie Yvonne *retired social services worker*

Great Falls
Ledesma-Nicholson, Charmaine *psychotherapist*

Hamilton
Soden, Ruth M. *geriatrics nurse, educator*

Poplar
Gabrielson, Shirley Gail *nurse*

NEBRASKA

Crofton
Bogner, Darlene Ruth *retired social worker*

Fremont
Winans, Anna Jane *dietitian*

Fulerton
†Brugman, Jacquelyn Joy *physician assistant*

Gering
Zach, Debra Jean *social worker*

Grand Island
Etheridge, Margaret Dwyer *medical center director*

Kearney
Wittman, Connie Susan *oncology clinical nurse specialist*

Lincoln
Donovan, Gregory Stearn *human services administrator*
†Steffan, Judy Mae *medical/surgical nurse*

Newman Grove
†Anderson, Joyce Lorraine *nurse aid*

Norfolk
Hibl, Veronica Katherine *physician assistant*

Offutt A F B
Johnson, Daniel E. *university educator, dean*

Omaha
†Ansingkar, Kamlesh G. *health facility administrator, otolaryngologist*
Baldwin, Jeffrey Nathan *pharmacy educator*
Brick, Shirley Jean *rehabilitation nurse*
†Brown, Sandra Dean *counselor*
Graves, Maureen Ann *self esteem and spirituality consultant*
Johnson, Christine Ann *nurse*
†Koperski, Nanci Carol *health care administrator, women's health nurse*
Leininger, Madeleine Monica *nursing educator, anthropologist, therorist, editor, writer*
Malone, Patrick Michael *pharmacist, educator*
†Mu, Keli *occupational therapist, researcher, educator*
Penke, Cynthia Marie *critical care nurse*
Thies, Margaret Diane *nurse*

Papillion
Rees, Patricia Glines *occupational health nurse, consultant, educator*

Scottsbluff
Hippe, Anne Elaine *nursing educator*
Olson, Ernestine Lee *nurse*
Shoemaker, Troy *hazardous materials response team coordinator, firefighter*

Wilcox
Ziebarth, Lisa Marie *medical/surgical nurse*

NEVADA

Carson City
†Ayers, Janice R. *social service administrator*
Hull, Dennis Jacques *counselor*

Elko
Alleman, Kurt G. *optometrist*

Henderson
†Henkelman, Wallace James *critical care nurse, educator*
Van Noy, Terry Willard *health care executive*

Las Vegas
Francis, Timothy Duane *chiropractor*
Gage, Miriam Betts *retired nutritionist*
Gilchrist, Ann Roundey *hospice nurse*
Israel, Joan *social worker*
Ivy, Berrynell Baker *critical care nurse*
Jagodzinski, Ruth Clark *retired nursing administrator*
Kowalski, Susan Dolores *critical care nurse, educator*
Leake, Brenda Gail *enterostomal therapist nurse practitioner*
Mastrini, Jane Reed *social worker, consultant*
Michel, Mary Ann Kedzuf *nursing educator*
Pelton, Leroy Howard *social work educator*
Ramsey, Nancy Lockwood *nursing educator*
Sweeten, Edward Drew *administrator*

Reno
Bramwell, Marvel Lynnette *mental health nurse, social worker*
Burkholder, Joyce Lynn *clinical social worker*
Graham, Denis David *marriage and family therapist, educational consultant*
McGary, Rita Rose *social worker*
Middlebrooks, Deloris Jeanette *nurse, educator*
Pinson, Larry Lee *pharmacist*

NEW HAMPSHIRE

Amherst
Buff, Margaret Anne *psychiatric nurse practitioner*

Bedford
Demers, Nancy Kae *nursing educator*
†Werner, R. Robert, Jr., *healthcare policy analyst, political organization manager*

Campton
Scrimshaw, Nevin Stewart *physician, nutrition and health educator*

Concord
Arnstein, Paul Michael *nurse practitioner, pain specialist, educator*
Freeman, Rose Brodeur *retired nursing educator*
MacKay, James Robert *psychiatric social worker, mayor, educator*
White, Jeffrey George *healthcare consultant*

Danville
Girotti, Robert Bernard *medical and surgical nurse*

Enfield
Gamache, Kathleen Smith *retired psychotherapist*

Hanover
Burgess, Robert Sargent *retired human services consultant*

Intervale
Baker, Mary Jane *social worker*

Lebanon
Boardman, Maureen Bell *community health nurse, educator*
Fishman, Joan Roslyn *clinical information analyst*
Moore, Frederick Appel *administrator*
†Stephenson, Jane Finkeldey *social worker*
Varnum, James William *hospital administrator*

Londonderry
Parten, Priscilla M. *medical and psychiatric social worker, educator*

Manchester
†Bolduc, Diane Eileen Mary Buchholz *psychotherapist*
Ellerin, Thelma Ruth *psychiatric social worker*
Telles, Marelyn V. Taylor *psychiatric clinical nurse specialist*

Nashua
Descoteaux, Carol J. *health facility administrator*
Gale, Sylvia Elizabeth *child protection professional*

Newbury
Koehler, Paul Burrell *retired medical administrator*

North Hampton
†Jones, Leroy Welwood (Wry Welwood) *mental health services professional*

Ossipee
Bartlett, Diane Sue *clinical mental health counselor, family therapist*

Sandown
Densen, Paul Maximillian *former health administrator, educator*

Tilton
Wolf, Sharon Ann *psychotherapist*

NEW JERSEY

Asbury
Gardner, Janette Lynn *critical care nurse, educator*
Oostdyk, Arlene Rosa *natural health educator, nurse*

Atlantic Highlands
Royce, Paul Chadwick *medical administrator*

Basking Ridge
Smith, Irmhild Wrede *public health nurse coordinator*

Belle Mead
Sarle, Charles Richard *health facility executive*

Belvidere
Walsh, John Alfred *retired social worker*

Berlin
Lewis, Michael Seth *health care executive*

Blackwood
Breve, Franklin Stephen *pharmacist*

Bradley Beach
†Parry, Ronald *massage therapist*

Brick
Sanseigne, Mary Josephine *nurse anesthetist*

Bridgewater
Weingast, Marvin *laboratory executive*

Budd Lake
Davis-Kalugin, Dorinne Sue *audiologist*

Burlington
Rowlette, Henry Allen, Jr., *social worker*

Carneys Point
Baker, Natalie Michele *child therapist*

Chatham
Murphy, Joseph James *chiropractic physician*

Cherry Hill
†Berman, Steven Eric *audiologist*
Betchen, Stephen Jay *marital, family and sex therapist*
Israelsky, Roberta Schwartz *speech pathologist, audiologist*
McCormick, Donna Lynn *social worker*

Cinnaminson
†Lafragola, Margherita Raffaelina *pharmacist*

Clark
Kinley, David *physical therapist, acupuncturist*

Columbus
Lasorda-Sivieri, Helen Marie *school social worker*

Dayton
Bassett, Alton Herman *health care company executive*

East Orange
Vasey, James Anthony *psychotherapist, consultant*

Eatontown
†Manzo-Goral, Carmen M. *critical care nurse*
O'Hare-VanMeerbeke, Anne Marie *dietitian*

Edison
†Islam, Naushad S. *pharmacist, government agency administrator*

Elizabeth
Lunt, Alan Nicholas *psychiatric rehabilitation counselor*

Emerson
†Gariolo, Richard *psychotherapist*

Englewood
Koch, Randall Glory *hospital administrator*
Salzer, Linda Parsons *clinical social worker*

Ewing
Steen, John *health policy company executive, consultant*

Fair Lawn
Shain-Alvaro, Judith Carol *physician assistant*

Fort Lee
†Schirmer, Helga *retired chiropractor*

Franklin Lakes
Ludwig, Edward J. *medical technology company executive*
†Mohtashemi, Paymon *physician assistant*

Freehold
Wilson, Nancy Jeanne *laboratory consultant, medical technologist*

Green Brook
Spoeri, Randall Keith *healthcare company executive*

Hackensack
Ferguson, John Patrick *medical center executive*
Shapiro, Sylvia *psychotherapist*

Hamilton
Nashif, Taysir N. *researcher*
Reid-Merritt, Patricia Ann *social worker, educator, author, performing artist*

Hamilton Square
†Ridolfi, Dorothy Porter Boulden *nurse*

Harrington Park
Salmon, Margaret Belais *nutritionist, dietitian*

Haworth
Mango, Christina Rose *psychiatric art therapist*

Highland Park
Grady, Joyce (Marian Joyce Grady) *psychotherapist, consultant*
Marin-Garcia, Jose *researcher, cardiologist*

Hillsborough
Gulko, Edward *health care executive, consultant*
Weinman, Steven Alan *emergency nurse, researcher, writer, educator, consultant*

Hillsdale
Kohan, Lois Rae *community health nurse*

Jersey City
Catalano, James Anthony *social worker, consultant*
†Milton, Barbara Ella, II, *psychotherapist*

Kenilworth
†Yang, Tsong-Toh (T.T.) *pharmacist, researcher*

Kinnelon
Preston, Andrew Joseph *pharmacist, drug company executive*

Lakewood
Biasini, Virginia *social worker*

Landing
Wolahan, Caryle Goldsack *nursing educator*

Lincoln Park
Byrnes, Jo Ann *professional relations administrator*

Linwood
Cohen, Diana Louise *psychology, educator, psychotherapist, consultant*

Livingston
Adelsberg, Harvey *hospital administrator*

Lumberton
Losse, Catherine Ann *pediatric nurse, critical care nurse, educator, clinical nurse specialist, family nurse practitioner*

Madison
Ellenbogen, Leon *nutritionist, pharmaceutical company executive*
Foy, Martin Thomas, Jr., *pharmacist*

Marlton
Letizia, Dorothy *nursing educator*

Millville
Caldwell, Linda E. *critical care nurse*

Montclair
O'Malley, Eileen (Eileen Ann O'Malley) *medical/surgical nurse*

Montville
Leeson, Lewis Joseph *research pharmacist, scientist*

Morganville
Kellner, Millicent H. *social worker, researcher*
Lechtanski, Cheryl Lee *chiropractor*

Morris Plains
Inez, Donna Lee *hospital administrator*

Mount Freedom
Allen, B. Marc *managed care executive*

Mount Laurel
Panichi-Egberts, Michele A. *healthcare facility manager*

New Brunswick
Brilliant, Eleanor Luria *social work educator*
Greenberg, Michael Richard *urban studies and community health educator*
Momah, Ethel Chukwuekwe *women's health nurse*

New Providence
Kelleher, James Raymond *health care corporation executive*

Newark
†Boyd, Kanisha *nurse manager*
Cunningham-Stevens, Vandetta Antoinette *practical nurse, poet*
Hudson-Zonn, Eliza *nurse, psychologist*
Nehring, Wendy Marie *pediatrics nurse*
Stevenson, Joanne Sabol *older adults care provider, educator, researcher*

Newfield
Dreher, Jr., Frank H. *retired optician*

Newton
Worman, Linda Kay *nursing administrator*

North Brunswick
Shapiro, Marsha N. *social worker*
Spears, Marcia Hopp *nursing educator, health facility administrator*

North Haledon
McGill, Kenneth, Jr., *mental health services professional*

Nutley
Andreula-Ortiz, Jo-Ellen *pharmaceutical company administrator, cosmetologist*
Romanoski, Barbara Ann *neonatology nurse*

Oakland
Weiner, Marc V. *health services facility executive*

Oaklyn
Johnson, Mark Kevin *operating room nurse*

Ocean City
Szczepaniak, Jane Camille *childbirth educator*

Paramus
De La Cruz, Carolina *pharmacist*

Parsippany
†Gannon, Peter M. *healthcare executive*

Paterson
Daniels, Cheryl Lynn *pediatrics nurse, case manager*

Pennington
DeMontigney, James Morgan *health services administrator*

Phillipsburg
Borah, Kripanath *pharmacist*
Souders, Nicole Elizabeth *oncological nurse, researcher*

Plainfield
Holdorf, Harry Hulbert *health services administrator*

Plainsboro
†Dezii, Christopher Michael *medical researcher, organ transplant nurse*
Gould, Susan Eileen *social worker, elementary school educator*

Pleasantville
†Etim, Terris *geriatrics nurse*

Pomona
Bukowski, Elaine Louise *physical therapist, educator*

Princeton
Bergman, Richard Isaac *health information company executive*
†Durdanovic, Igor *researcher*
Franze, Anthony James *pharmacist, lawyer*
†Gu, Henry Hongsheng *pharmacist, researcher*
†Khanna, Ashish *pharmacist*
Logue, Judith Felton *psychoanalyst, educator, professional coach*
Lucas, Lorraine J. *regulatory affairs professional, clinical research scientist, epidemiologist consultant*
Woodfield, Denis Buchanan *retired healthcare company executive*

Rahway
Tice, Kirk Clifford *health facility administrator*

Red Bank
Alburtus, Mary Jo *social worker, consultant*
Brown, Valerie Anne *psychiatric social worker, educator*
Gutentag, Patricia Richmand *social worker, family counselor, occupational therapist*
Howson, Agnes Wagner *health educator*

Ridgewood
Arnt, Georgia Lee *psychiatric social worker*
Clements, Lynne Fleming *family therapist, programmer*

Roseland
Malafronte, Donald *health executive*

Saddle Brook
Clifton, Nelida *social worker*

Scotch Plains
Palmer, Teresa Anne *nurse practitioner*
Touretzky, Muriel Walter *nursing educator*

Sewell
Aldover-Ayon, Marta *critical care nurse*

Skillman
Prestbo, Darlene (Martha Darlene Prestbo) *licensed clinical social worker*
Schirber, Annamarie Riddering *speech and language pathologist, educator*

Somers Point
Miller, W. Denise Saunders *community health nurse*

Somerset
†James, Anthony F. *social worker*
Patel, Tarun R. *pharmaceutical scientist*

South Orange
Hansell, Phyllis Shanley *nursing educator, administrator, researcher, consultant*
Hecht, Marion B. *mental health counselor, mental health therapist*

Springfield
Gottlieb, Helen *social worker, legal immigration consultant*

Summit
Mitchell, Peter William *addictions counselor*

Teaneck
Alperin, Richard Martin *clinical social worker, psychoanalyst*
Erlich Penchuk, Sara *social worker, psychotherapist*
Hollman, Barbara Carol *psychoanalyst, psychotherapist, consultant*

Tenafly
Brown, Shirley Ann *speech-language pathologist*

Teterboro
Freeman, Kenneth W. *laboratory executive*

Toms River
Hines, Patricia *social worker, educator*

Trenton
Cruz, Nelson Xavier *healthcare executive*
Fordyce, Theresa Rose *mental health nurse*
Kelman, Marybeth *health care consultant, health policy analyst*
Kulkosky, Chris James *social worker*
Lerner, Carol Menzel *social worker*
Martin, Linda Ann *geriatrics nurse, educator*
Miller, Velvet G. *healthcare administrator*

Union
Kaplan, Doris Weiler *social worker*
Nesoff, Irwin *social work educator, management consultant*
†Valentine, John Vartan *physical education and health educator*
Williams, Carol Jorgensen *social work educator*

Vineland
Popp, Charlotte Louise *health development center administrator, nurse*

Warren
Kozberg, Donna Walters *rehabilitation administration executive*

Washington Township
Bilz, Laurie S. *nursing educator*

West Caldwell
Schiff, Robert *healthcare consulting company executive*

West Long Branch
†McCaffrey, Jane Carol *addiction recovery counselor, medical/surgical nurse, consultant*
Ward, Kelly *social worker, educator*

West Milford
Colflesh, Gertrude Patterson (Trudy P. Colflesh) *counselor*

West New York
Kelly, Lucie Stirm Young *nursing educator*

West Orange
Bornstein, Lester Milton *retired medical center executive*
Chiaravalloti, Nancy Donofrio *neuropsychologist*
De Lisa, Joel Alan *rehabilitation physician, rehabilitation research executive*
Katz, Alix Martha *respiratory care practitioner*

Westfield
Roll, Marilyn Rita Brownlie *social worker*

Westmont
†Stiefel, Bernard M. *psychotherapist*

Willingboro
Green, Riva Lee *social worker, minister*

Woodbury
O'Bryant, Cathy *retired social worker, evangelist*
Szgalsky, Helen A. *pediatric nurse practitioner, school nurse*

NEW MEXICO

Albuquerque
†Belinsky, Steven Alan *health science association administrator*
Boshier, Maureen Louise *health facilities administrator*
†Burrows, Kathy S. *health facility administrator*
Clark, Teresa Watkins *psychotherapist, clinical counselor*
Feldman, Miriam Bernice *social worker*
†Gupchup, Gireesh Vijay *pharmacist, educator*
Hancock, Don Ray *researcher*
Harbert, Kenneth Ray *health care educator , physician*
†Jones, Rondall Eugene *lab administrator*
Lowrance, Muriel Edwards *program specialist*
Manzitto, Arthur Sebastian *nursing and hospital administrator*
Mateju, Joseph Frank *hospital administrator*

Moody, Patricia Ann *psychiatric nurse, artist, small business owner*
†Pasternacki, Linda Lea *critical care nurse*
Solomon, Arthur Charles *pharmacist*
Stambaugh, Harriett McCardell (Harriett Wynn McCardell) *social worker*

Carlsbad
Speed, Lynn Elizabeth *nurse practitioner*

Edgewood
†Villagomez, Deborah Lynn *medical/surgical nurse, horse breeder*

Farmington
†Thompson, Joseph T., Jr., *health facility administrator*

Gallup
Fuhs, Terry Lynn *emergency room nurse, educator*

Hobbs
†Landers, Billy N., Jr., *medical and surgical nurse, administrator*

Las Cruces
Adaime, Hamed Nazin *counselor*
Mata, Josefina *health education coordinator, educator*
Welsh, Mary McAnaw *family mediator, educator*

Milan
Kanesta, Nellie Rose *chemical dependency counselor*

Mountainair
†Woodruff, Joan Leslie *occupational therapist, counselor*

Raton
Charriez, Blanca Noelia *social worker*

Roswell
Johnston, Mary Ellen *retired nursing educator*

Santa Fe
Feist-Fite, Bernadette *international health education consultant*
Melnick, Alice Jean (AJ Melnick) *counselor*
Pulitzer, Roslyn Kitty *social worker, psychotherapist*
Sakara, Marilyn Judith *social worker*

Truth Or Consequences
Rush, Domenica Marie *health facilities administrator*

Tyrone
Wilson, Johnnie Lou *social work educator, retired*

NEW YORK

Albany
†Curry, Robert Richard *health facility administrator*
DeNuzzo, Rinaldo Vincent *pharmacy educator*
Lane, Nancy Lucille *mental health and critical care nurse*
Loneck, Barry Martin *social work researcher, educator*
Miesing, Paul *university educator, consultant, researcher*
Pasquariello, Julius Anthony *pharmacist*
Reaulo, Arthur Robert *mental health specialist, advocate*
Reid, William James *social work educator*
Travers, W. Lawrence *healthcare executive*

Ardsley
Mohl, Allan S. *social worker*

Astoria
Matheson, Linda *retired clinical social worker*

Auburn
Trapani, Janet Leigh *physical therapist*

Ava
Hicks, Phyllis Ann *retired medical, surgical nurse*

Baldwin
Zuckerman, Jackie Lynn *social worker*

Ballston Spa
Knight, Jane Miller *nurse midwife, retired air force officer*

Batavia
Small, Bruce Michael *health facility administrator*

Bay Shore
Sampino, Michele *physician assistant*

Bayside
†Du Mont, Allen André *pyschotherapist, educator*

Bedford
D'Angelo, Gonda *retired social worker*
Margolin, Carl M. *psychotherapist*

Binghamton
†Gilroy, Eileen M. *speech pathology/audiology services professional, educator*
†Rowe, Steven L. *mental health nurse*
Terriquez-Kasey, Laura Marie *emergency nurse*

Bohemia
†Talbot, Sandra Ann *medical-surgical nurse*

Boston
Connors, Linda Marie *community health nurse*

Bronx
Alfrey, Larry Robert *physician assistant*
Clary, Roy *hospital administration executive*
Cubeñas, José Antonio *social worker, consultant*
Gang, Vanessa Noble *health facility administrator, researcher, nursing consultant*
†Heath, Cedric Alexander *nurse, health services administrator, real estate agent, insurance agent, financial analyst*
Iezza, Anita Kay *physician assistant*
Pompa Pillai, Donna Ann *social worker, educator, psychotherapist*
Smith-Alnimer, Marie Margaret Cella *mental health nurse*
Weiner, Richard Lenard *hospital administrator, educator, pediatrician*
Yadeka, Theophilus Adeniyi *hospital administrator*

Brooklyn
†Abraham, Teena *pharmacist, educator*
Astwood, William Peter *psychotherapist*
†Baker, Kristina Marie *family practice nurse practitioner*
Bizzoco, Drew Frank *chiropractor*
†Brenner, Beryl H. *arts therapist*
Capaccio, Matteo *social worker, health facility administrator*
Donovan, Rita R. *nurse anesthetist, trauma and critical care nurse, educator*
†Eliasi, Jennifer Rebecca *dietician, consultant*
Giordano, Catherine Kowkabany *nurse*
†Gonsalves, Patricia E. *surgical nurse*
Graham, RosaLind Carlies *nursing educator*
Gross, Stephen Mark *pharmacist, academic dean*
Gustin, Mark Douglas *hospital executive*
Harris, Fred *prosthetist*
†Harris-Olayinka, Verda (Lorraine Harris-Olayinka) *health agency administrator, cultural consultant*
Heisler, Norma Boodman *psychotherapist*
Kamen, Cheryl L. Heiberg *social worker*
Marsala-Cervasio, Kathleen Ann *medical/surgical nurse, administrator*
McDuffie, Minnie *nursing administrator, community health nurse*
Morales, Jose *psychotherapist, writer*
Murillo-Rohde, Ildaura Maria *marriage and family therapist, consultant, educator, dean*
†Nadler, Nona Jean *social worker*
Peters, Mercedes *psychoanalyst*
Phillips, Gretchen *social worker*
Pine, Bessie Miriam *social worker, editor, columnist*
Radice, Beatrice Rosemarie *family nurse practitioner*
Safian, Harriet Sara *social worker*
†Samuel, Carren C. *hospital administrator*
Stellman, Jeanne Mager *public health educator*
Stepherson, Brian Edward *psychological social worker, artist, writer*
Strauss, Dorothy Brandfon *marital, family, and sex therapist*
Tronolone, Tracey Ann *social worker*
Wachewski, Robert Thomas *health facility administrator*
Wilkes, David Ross *therapist*
Zukowski, Barbara Wanda *clinical social work psychotherapist*

Buffalo
Blane, Howard Thomas *research institute administrator*
Deck, Judith Z. *adult nurse practitioner*
†Dickson, Stanley *speech pathology/audiology services professional, educator*
Hoffman, Faith Louise *social worker*
†Jusko, William Joseph *pharmaceutical scientist, educator*
McGuire, William Dennis *health facility administrator*
Perry, J. Warren *health sciences educator, administrator*
Schentag, Jerome John *pharmacy educator*
Seller, Steven Mark *pharmacist*
Silver, Kathleen Frances *rehabilitation counselor*
Simonson, Patricia Lou Hoffman *director health, fitness and recreation programs, grants writer*

Cedarhurst
Lipsky, Linda Ethel *business executive*

Center Moriches
Miller-Roseman, Linda Sarah *critical care, emergency room nurse*

Chappaqua
Boal, Lyndall Elizabeth *social worker*

Chatham
Fiorillo, John A(nthony) *health care executive*

Cheektowaga
Richmond, Allen Martin *speech pathologist, educator*

Clinton Corners
McDermott, Patricia Ann *nursing administrator*
Sylvester, John Edward *social worker*

Colonie
Mallory, Doris Ann Bourgeois *social worker, counselor*

Commack
Jaiswal, Dinesh Kumar *pharmaceutical scientist, educator*

Cooperstown
Fullington, Cynthia Janette *pediatric nurse*

Cornwall
Smerek, Gay *pharmacist*

Craryville
Kaufman, Michele Beth *clinical pharmacist, educator*

Delmar
Pember, John Bartlett *social worker, educator*

Dix Hills
Katzberg, Jane Michaels *health care administrator, consultant, educator*
†Ruhl, Vincent *psychotherapist, writer*

East Meadow
Hinson, Gale Mitchell *social worker*

Eastchester
Giuliano, Robert Paul *pharmacist*

Elmira
Cerio, Milissa Bausch *social worker*
Gulati, Teresa Antoinette *nursing educator*
Wright, Linda Ellen *nursing educator*

Far Rockaway
Shonek, Arlene *dietitian*

Floral Park
Brancaleone Kenna, Laurie Ann *social worker*
Calodny, Alan Lee *retired pharmacist*

Flushing
†Kovalyov, Mikhail *researcher, educator*
Tarasko, Alexandra *nursing educator*

Forest Hills
Alsapiedi, Consuelo Veronica *psychoanalytic psychotherapist, consultant*
Glassmann, Marvin Jean *marriage and family therapist*
Gold, Roslyn *social worker, educator*

Garden City
Klainberg, Marilyn Blau *community health educator*
†Nicklin, George Leslie, Jr., *psychoanalyst, educator, physician, author*
Scollard, Patrick John *hospital executive*

Glens Falls
†Tucker, Bernadine *patient registrar*
Vitvitsky, Jack *physician assistant*

Grand Central
†Freedman, Mollie Cecille *researcher*

Great Neck
Feldman, Gary Marc *nutritionist, consultant*
Haber, Diane Lois *psychotherapist, clinical specialist*
Mayer, Susan Lee *nurse, educator*

Greenfield Center
Dittner, Deborah Marie *nurse practitioner in family health*

Hamburg
Iafallo, Deborah Lynn *geriatrics nurse*
Kuhn, Merrily A. *nursing educator*

Hastings On Hudson
Stillman, Jeanne Betsock *public health administrator, consultant*

Hemlock
Doty, Dale Vance *educator, psychotherapist, hypnotherapist*

Hempstead
Ades, Janet *social worker*

Howard Beach
Miller, Theresa Valentini *social worker, psychotherapist*

Huntington Station
Williams, Una Joyce *psychiatric social worker*

Hurley
Petruski, Jennifer Andrea *speech and language pathologist*

Hyde Park
Rider, Kathleen Mary *dietitian*

Ionia
Paddock, Paula J. *geriatrics nurse*

Islandia
†Gorman, Marcy *health care administrator*

Ithaca
Feinstein, Rosalind Deborah *social worker*
Haas, Jere Douglas *nutritional sciences educator, researcher*
Habicht, Jean Pierre *healthcare educator, nutritionist*
Leicht, Susan Dale *occupational therapist*
Mueller, Betty Jeanne *social work educator*
Pagliarulo, Michael Anthony *physical therapy educator*
Rasmussen, Kathleen Maher *nutritional sciences educator*
Strassberg, Marilyn *social worker*
Zall, Robert Rouben *food scientist, educator*

Jackson Heights
Chang, Lydia Liang-Hwa *social worker, educator*

Jamaica
Ahmed, Jimmie *health facility administrator*
De La Paz, Lucia *social worker, consultant*
Morrill, Joyce Marie *social worker, educator*
Waisman, Warner *retired pharmacist*

Kew Gardens
Klein-Scheer, Cathy Ann *social worker*

Kingston
Dalbo, Joanne *social worker, writing teacher, secondary educator, poet*

Matturro, Peter John *social worker*

Latham
Caruso, Aileen Smith *managed care consultant*

Little Falls
Feeney, Mary Katherine O'Shea *retired public health nurse*

Long Island City
Henick, Nita Halpern *retired social worker*

Lynbrook
Kassimatis, Loretta Eileen *clinical social worker*

Manhasset
Cavaliere, Terri Angela *neonatal nurse practitioner*

Manlius
Gibson, Judith W. *clinical therapist*
Vasile, Gennaro James *health care executive*

Massapequa
Margulies, Andrew Michael *chiropractor*

Massapequa Park
Blair, Carol *social worker, therapist*

Medford
Brower, Robert Charles *rehabilitation counselor, small business owner*

Melville
Johns, Michael Douglas *health care corporate executive, former federal official, writer, former federal government offical*

Middletown
Radeboldt-Daly, Karen Elaine *medical nurse*

Millbrook
Turndorf, Jamie *psychotherapist*

Monsey
Schore, Robert *social worker, educator, consultant*

Monticello
Vamvaketis, Carole *health services administrator*

Mount Vernon
Coombes, David Harrison *health facility administrator*
Giammartino, Frank Arnold *chiropractor*

New Baltimore
Buono, Kathleen Ann Cleary *nursing specialist*

New Hartford
Benzo-Bonacci, Rosemary Anne *health facility administrator*

New Hyde Park
Francischine, Janice Marie *pediatrics nurse*

New Paltz
Pine, Patricia Palmer *aging services administrator*

New Rochelle
Rothstein, Ann Laurel *clinical social worker, consultant*
Wolf, Robert Irwin *psychoanalyst, art therapist, art therapy educator, sculptor, photographer*

New Windsor
Hammond, Judith Anne *family nurse practitioner*

New York
Agard, Emma Estornel *psychotherapist*
Alderson, Marjorie Jean *healthcare administrator, nurse*
Barker, Sylvia Margaret *nurse*
Barnum, Barbara Stevens *writer, retired nursing educator*
Barrett, Elizabeth Ann Manhart *nursing educator, psychotherapist, consultant*
†Batavia, Mitchell *physical therapist, educator*
†Bendor, Susan Julia *social worker, educator*
Billig, Robert Emmanuel *psychiatric social worker*
Blau, John *retired social worker*
†Boufford, Jo Ivey *health and human services administrator*
Bradley, Courtney Jene *researcher*
Brownell, Patricia Jane *social worker, educator*
Buehler, Thomas *psychotherapist, expressive therapist, artist*
Campbell, David James *hospital administrator*
Caroff, Phyllis M. *social work educator*
Carroll, Linda Marie *vocologist*
Caruana, Joan *educator, psychotherapist, nurse*
Carver, John H. *medical science organization administrator*
Cavanagh-McKee, Kathryn *nurse*
Chu, Benjamin K. *hospital administrator*
Chu-Zhu, Janice Gail *social worker*
Connolly, John Joseph *health care company executive*
Constable, Simon James *hospital administrator*
Corwin, Steven *hospital administrator*
†Cox, Carole Beth *social worker, educator*
Daines, Richard *health services executive*
†Daniel, Samuel J. *hospital administrator, medical educator*
Daniel, Samuel Michael *social worker, psychotherapist*
Dinerman, Miriam *social work educator*
Dorn, Sue Bricker *consultant, retired hospital administrator*
Eagan, Marie T. (Ria Eagan) *chiropractor*
Edelstein, Joan Erback *physical therapy educator*
Ethan, Carol Baehr *psychotherapist*
Farrell, Eileen Marie *nurse, administrator*
Feldman, Ronald Arthur *social work educator, researcher*

Fenchel, Gerd H(erman) *psychoanalyst*
Fewell, Christine Huff *psychoanalyst, alcohol counselor*
Fink, Matthew E. *health facility executive, educator*
Francoeur, Richard Benoit *social worker, educator*
†Gaynor, Suzanne Marie *health care executive, researcher*
Giordano, Bill A. *psychotherapist*
Giorlando, Jeanne A. *labor and delivery nurse*
Goerdt, Ann Renee *physical therapist, consultant*
Goff, Robert Edward *health care executive*
Gold, William Elliott *health care management consultant, educator*
Goldberg, Franklin H. *psychotherapist*
Goldrich, Stanley Gilbert *optometrist*
Grandizio, Lenore *social worker*
Green, Barbara Strawn *psychotherapist*
†Haseley, Dennis *psychoanalyst, writer*
†Hoffman, Jennifer Anne *vascular technician, director*
Hoffman, Madelyn Kay *psychoanalyst, social worker*
†Horvath, Annette *home care health administrator*
†Hoskins, Carol Noll *nursing educator, researcher*
Isaacs, Richard B. *investigative and protective services professional*
Johnson, Evan Kenneth *physical therapist, educator*
Jorjani, Maryam *psychotherapist*
Kalayjian, Anie *psychotherapist, nurse, educator, consultant*
Kamerman, Sheila Brody *educator, social worker*
†Kapoor, Neera *optometrist*
Kassel, Catherine M. *community, maternal, and women's health nurse, consultant*
Katz, Cheryl Ann *human services manager, social worker*
Kent, Deborah Warren *hypnotherapist, consultant, lecturer*
Kove, Miriam *psychotherapist*
Krasilovsky, Gary Wayne *physical therapist, educator*
Lawrence, Lauren *writer, dreams expert, psychoanalytical theorist, psychoanalyst*
Laznick, Hope *physical therapist*
Lederman, Sally Ann *nutrition researcher*
Lehrer, Ruth Jeannette *social work supervisor*
Levitt, Harry *speech and hearing scientist*
Lopez, Pedro Felipe *social worker, educator, playwright, writer*
Mandracchia, Violet Ann Palermo *psychotherapist, educator*
Marrone, Stephen Richard *critical care nurse, educator*
Marshak, Hilary Wallach *psychotherapist, owner, small business owner*
Matseoane, Carol *social worker*
Mattson, Marlin Roy Albin *health facility administrator, psychiatry educator*
McGonagle, Duncan Francis *mental health nurse, substance abuse counselor*
Miller, Joseph Anthony *healthcare executive, psychotherapist*
Mishne, Judith Marks *social work educator, psychotherapist*
†Moskowitz, Harry *pediatrics educator*
Mulvihill, William J. *former health science association administrator*
Naegle, Madeline Anne *mental health nurse, educator*
Neubauer, Peter Bela *psychoanalyst*
Niles, Barbara Elliott *psychoanalyst*
O'Brien, Patricia Grace *psychiatric nurse, clinician and administrator*
Pakter, Jean *maternal and child health consultant*
Pandolfi, Frances *health facility administrator*
Patterson Dehn, Cathleen *pediatrics administrator*
Paulson, Loretta Nancy *psychoanalyst*
Pennisi, Liz *women's health nurse*
Perez, Carlos F. *health facility administrator*
Pfaffle, Antony *healthcare analyst*
Pilcz, Maleta *psychotherapist*
Piombino, Nicholas *psychotherapist*
Rabinowitz, Joan Karen *social worker*
Rehr, Helen *social worker*
Resnick, Rhoda Brodowsky *psychotherapist*
Richard, Elaine *educational therapist*
†Roccosalvo, Joseph C. *psychotherapist*
Roglieri, John Louis *health facility administrator*
Rosenthal, Donna Myra *social worker*
†Saffar, Jean-Marc *healthcare consultant*
Salwen, Marie (Manya Salwen) *social worker, psychotherapist*
†Sandler, Susan Silverstein *dietician, nutritionist*
Scherman, Susan Louise *nurse*
Schiffmann, Robert Frank *research and development executive*
Scott, Adrienne *social worker, psychotherapist*
Scott, Mimi Koblenz *psychotherapist, actress, publicist, journalist, playwright*
Shohen, Saundra Anne *health care communications and public relations executive*
Sigety, Cornelius Edward *family office manager*
†Solomon, Libertina *pharmacist, educator*
Spriggs, David Randall *healthcare administrator, educator*
Stark, Robin Caryl *psychotherapist, consultant*
†Steichen, Joanna T(aub) *psychotherapist, writer*
Stich, June Jeacoma *psychotherapist*
Storm, Jackie *nutritionist, health education specialist*
Teich, Stephen S. *forensic psychiatrist*
†Trachtman, Richard *psychotherapist, mediator*
Turner, Sandra Goodspeed *social worker, psychotherapist, educator*
Turo, Joann K. *psychoanalyst, psychotherapist, consultant*
Urman, Rhoda M. *social worker, psychotherapist*
Van Etten, Peter Walbridge *foundation executive*
†Victor, Jack *former health association executive, consultant*

Vladeck, Bruce Charney *health services administrator, policy educator*
Williams, Alexander Hazard, III, *health care executive, consultant*
Wolin, James Michael *health services executive*
Yoshiuchi, Ellen Haven *health educator, clinical counselor*
Yousef, Mona Lee *psychotherapist*
Zagoren, Joy Carroll *health facility director, researcher*

Newburgh
Schwake, Torsten *chiropractor*
Weintraub, Arthur E. *health service association executive*

North Tonawanda
Coleman, Kimberlee Michele *critical care nurse*

Norwich
Garzione, John Edward *physical therapist*

Nyack
Carey, Lois J. *psychotherapist*

Olean
Horn, Daniel Joseph *pharmacist*

Oneonta
Lapidus, Patricia Jean *social worker*

Ontario
Nevil, Linda *nursing administrator*

Orangeburg
Harvey, Virginia Marie *nurse, administrator*

Ossining
Robinson, Karen Vajda *clinical dietitian*

Ozone Park
Catalfo, Betty Marie *health service executive, nutritionist*

Painted Post
Ogden, Anita Bushey *nursing educator*

Palmyra
Hartman, Susan Margaret *community mental health nurse*

Patchogue
†Fawcett, Bernadine L. *marriage and family counselor*

Peekskill
Jackson, Linda B. *social worker*

Pittsford
Mooney, Lillian Harnett *social worker, consultant*
Taub, Aaron Myron *healthcare administrator, consultant*

Pomona
DeMaio, Barbara Patricia *social worker*

Port Chester
Harris, Elisabeth Tamlyn *psychiatric social worker*

Port Washington
Levy, Marlene Lois *clinical social worker*

Potsdam
Gruda, Benjamin Joseph *pharmacist*

Poughkeepsie
Heller, Mary Bernita *psychotherapist*
Henley, Richard James *health facility administrator*

Purchase
Fink, Judy Smolka *social worker*

Rexford
Kresge, Jennifer Alison *physician assistant*

Rochester
Agrawal, Govind Prasad *optics educator*
Aydelotte, Myrtle Kitchell *retired nursing administrator*
†Braley, Oleta Pearl *home health care provider*
Coon, Penny K. *human services administrator*
Hoffman, Nancy Yanes *medical author, patient educator, writer, editor, health care consultant, lecturer*
†Horowitz, Bruce *social worker, photographer, musician*
Hurlbut, Robert Harold *health care services executive*
Huston, Samuel Richard *health facility executive*
†Kates, Cheryl L. *legal nursing consultant*
King, Kathleen Bernadette *nursing educator*
LaSpagnoletta, Susan Ann *nurse*
Marriott, Marcia Ann *health facility administrator, finance educator*
Moellering, Helen S. *retired social worker*
Moore, Duncan Thomas *optics educator*
Ryan, Diane Phyllis *nurse*

Rockville Centre
Erland, Shirley May *nurse*

Romulus
†Treahy, John P *human services administrator*

Roslyn
Epstein, Arthur Barry *optometrist*

Rye
Davis, Samuel *hospital administrator, educator, consultant*
Newburger, Howard Martin *psychoanalyst*

Sabael
Morrill-Cummins, Carolyn *social worker, consultant*

Saint James
†Richards, Fran W. *social worker*

Salt Point
Lackey, Mary Michele *physician assistant*

Saranac Lake
Brown, Jonathon Andrew *healthcare executive*
Caguiat, Carlos Jose *health care administrator, Episcopal priest*

Scarsdale
Lieberman, Florence *clinical social worker, educator*
Rogalski, Lois Ann *speech and language pathologist*
Young, Pamela Ruth *social worker, consultant, therapist*

Schenectady
O'Baire, Marika *community health nurse, writer*
Sager, Robert Wendell *retired social work administrator*
Weiner, Clare Frances *social worker, psychotherapist*

Scottsville
Reitz, JoAnne Bellam *health information executive*

Seaford
†Kulpa, Aldona *pharmacist*
Tuzil, Teresa Jordan *clinical social worker, psychotherapist*

Seneca Falls
Norman, Mary Marshall *educator, counselor, therapist*

Shortsville
Rosati, Sharon Wetmore *social worker*

Slingerlands
Jacobs, Karen Louise *medical technologist*

Spencerport
Cassin, Sandra Jane *social worker*

Staten Island
De Luca, Anthony James *psychoanalyst, theologian*
Kennedy, Colleen Geralyn *nurse, social worker*
†Norberg, Tilda Ann *psychotherapist*
Parente, Louise *social worker*
Spada, Dominick *pharmacist*

Stony Brook
Greene, William Harris *hospital administrator*
Lurie, Abraham *social worker, educator*
Mundie, Gene E. *nursing educator*

Suffern
Raven, Luisa Antonia *nurse, psychotherapist*

Syosset
Doerfler, Leo G. *audiology educator*

Syracuse
Carlton, Carole Gassett *medical/surgical nurse*
Fitzgerald, Harold Kenneth *social work educator, consultant*
†Fluck, Robert R., Jr., *respiratory therapy technician, educator*
Guharoy, Roy *pharmacy director, medical educator*
Mulcahy, Kathleen Lynn *neonatal and pediatric nurse practitioner*
Rabuzzi, Daniel D. *medical administrator*

Tarrytown
Gutheil, Irene A. *social work educator, researcher*
Safian, Keith Franklin *hospital administrator*
Singh, Brahma Nand *pharmaceutical scientist*

Tillson
Giordano, Sondra Britchky *nursing educator, medical and surgical nurse*

Troy
†Clause, Steven Lee *pharmacist, researcher*

Tuckahoe
Offner, Roxane *retired social worker*

Utica
De Iorio, Lucille Theresa *social worker*
†Noviasky, John A *pharmacist*
Plumley, Danielle L. *social worker*

Vestal
Zinner, Faith Orloff *social worker, consultant, psychotherapist*

Wantagh
Engros, Elaine *nurse, case manager*
Kushner, Aileen *medical/surgical nurse*

Watertown
Fredriksen, Maryellen *physician assistant*

West Bloomfield
Charron, Helene Kay Shetler *retired nursing educator*

Westbury
Lelonek, David *optometrist*

White Plains
Dvorak, Roger Gran *health facility executive*
†Fowlkes, Nancy Lanetta Pinkard *social worker*
Leung, Betty Brigid *nursing administrator*

PROFESSIONAL INDEX 6385 HEALTHCARE: HEALTH SERVICES

Newman, Barney David *medical administrator, internist*
Russo, Donna Lee *social worker*

Whitesboro
Campbell, Joann Cavo *social worker*

Whitestone
Fischer, Eugene *medical administrator, educator*

Williamsville
Altman, David J *pharmacist, consultant*

Woodside
VanArsdale, Diana Cort *social worker*

Wyandanch
Hodges-Robinson, Chettina M. *nursing administrator*

Yaphank
Digilio, Jr., John Thomas *health care executive, consultant*

Yonkers
Lawson, Beverly Elaine *nursing administrator*
Roberson, Doris Jean Herold *retired social worker*

NORTH CAROLINA

Aberdeen
Marcham, Timothy Victor *pharmacist*

Advance
Walser, Sandra Teresa Johnson *rehabilitation nurse, preceptor*

Ahoskie
Weiss, Stephen Max *healthcare administrator, surgeon, educator*

Apex
Olson, Jean Lounsbury *social worker*

Asheville
McKeown, Peter Philip *medical center administrator, medical educator, cardiothoracic surgeon*
Teutsch, Monica *health services administrator*

Boone
†Clark, Heather *speech pathology/audiology services professional, educator*

Buies Creek
Blalock, Mary Wright *counselor*

Burlington
Kernodle, Lucy Hendrick *school system nurse*
Knesel, Ernest Arthur, Jr., *diagnostic company executive*
Powell, James Bobbitt *biomedical laboratories executive, pathologist*

Chapel Hill
Bowen, Gary Lee *social work educator, researcher*
Kahn, Annette Lee *clinical social worker, psychotherapist*
Mann, Billie Arnell *neuroscience nurse, radiologic technologist*
Martikainen, A(une) Helen *retired health education specialist*
Palmer, Gary Stephen *health services administrator*
†Soltys, Florence Gray *social worker*
†Turner, John B. *social worker, educator, retired dean*
Usher, Charles Lindsey *social work educator, public policy analyst*
Willingham, Emagene Emanuel *social worker*

Charlotte
Lowrance, Pamela Kay *medical/surgical nurse*
Mallinson, James A., Jr., *student health services administrator*
Martin, James Grubbs *medical executive, former governor*
McNeal, Jeannette Johnson *social worker*
†Sharts, Thomas *human services administrator, social sciences educator, consultant*

Cullowhee
Drew, Ruby Louise *speech-language pathologist, consultant*

Davidson
Plyler, John Laney, Jr., *retired healthcare management professional*

Durham
Brantley, Jeffrey Garland *health science facility administrator*
Burgess, Paula Lashenske *health facility administrator*
Colvin, O. Michael *medical director, medical educator*
†Demark-Wahnefried, Wendy *nutritionist, researcher*
Gosselin, Tracy Karen *nursing administrator*
Harrison, Dean Thomas *physician assistant*
†Richardson, Lily Pendarvis *retired occupational health nurse*
†Smith, Effie Barnette *caregiver*
†Ware, Ruth Winchester *social worker*
Wilson, Ruby Leila *nurse, educator*

Elizabeth City
Deaton, Fae Adams *clinical social worker, counselor*

Fayetteville
†Berryhill, Maurice Judd *human services administrator*
Jansen, Michael John *healthcare executive*

Greensboro
Brown, Hazel Fay Nixon *women's health nurse, educator, administrator*
Carlyon, Diane Claire *nurse*
†Penley, Virginia Long *social worker*
Schwenn, Lee William *retired medical center executive*
Shotwell, Sheila Murray *medical/surgical nurse*
Tredinnick, Laurel Christine *social worker*

Hendersonville
Cochran, Linda Thornthwaite *psychotherapist, social worker, consultant*
Heil, Mary Ruth *former counselor*

Hickory
†Leger-Scott, Debbie *critical care nurse*

High Point
Bailey, William Nathan *nutritionist, consultant*

Hillsborough
Richmond, Donna *speech-language pathologist*

Kinston
Welch, Alexis B. *nursing administrator*

La Grange
†Cannon, Alice Grace *counselor*

Lenoir
Moore, Mary Ellen *community health, hospice nurse*

Marshall
Jatinen, Jane Ellen *social worker, educator*

Monroe
Kwetkauskie, John A. *medical technologist*

Morganton
Singleton, Stella Wood *nurse*

Murphy
Dickey, Jeannetta Burkett *social worker*

New Bern
†Pierce, Judy Capel *nursing educator*
Smith, Larry Wayne *medical/surgical nurse*

Newland
Lustig, Susan Gardner *occupational therapist*

Oxford
Harvey, Gloria-Stroud *physician assistant*

Pinehurst
Fleming, Doris Aven *mental health nurse*

Raleigh
Bailey, Mary Beatrice *retired nursing information systems director*
Berry, Joni Ingram *hospice pharmacist, educator*
Ciraulo, Stephen Joseph *nurse, anesthetist*
†Cromwell, William C. *health facility administrator, researcher*
Ferrell, Dorothy Dobransky *social worker*
Geller, Janice Grace *nurse*
Johnson, Janet Gray Andrews *clinical social worker*
Malling, Martha Hale Shackford *social worker, educator*
Stewart, D. Jane *nursing educator, researcher*
Webster, Debbie Ann *social worker*

Research Triangle Park
†Kunka, Robert L. *pharmacist, researcher*
Olden, Kenneth *science administrator, researcher*

Rockingham
Evans, Patricia McCormick *clinical therapist*

Rocky Mount
Davis, Barbara Judy *counselor, mental health educator*
Stokes, Angela Cohoon *pharmacist*

Rougemont
Cooney, M(uriel) Sharon Taylor *medical and surgical nurse*

Roxboro
Broyles, Bonita Eileen *nursing educator*

Southport
Richmond, Jonathan Y. *public health administration officer*

Spindale
Blanton, Madge Brantley *family practice nurse practitioner*

Stokes
Reynolds, Betty Jane *retired nursing administrator and educator*

Sylva
Babel, Deborah Jean *social worker, paralegal*

Tarboro
Andrews, Claude Leonard *psychotherapist*

Weaverville
Hauschild, Douglas Carey *optometrist*

Whiteville
Gilmore, Robin Harris *nursing administrator*

Wilkesboro
Boyd, Robert Giddings, Jr., *health facility administrator*

Wilmington
Israel, Margie Olanoff *psychotherapist*

Wilson
Batchelor, Ruby Stephens *retired nurse*

Morris, Sharon Louise Stewart *emergency medical technician, paramedic*
Setliffe, Charles David *hospital administrator*

Winston Salem
Dawson, Paula Dayl *oncological nurse*
Gibson, Christina Renee *radiation therapist*
Walters, Doris Lavonne *pastoral counselor, counseling services facility administrator*
Yeatts, Dorothy Elizabeth Freeman *nurse, retired county official, educator*

Wrightsville Beach
McDonald, Wylene Booth *former nurse, pharmaceutical sales professional*

NORTH DAKOTA

Bismarck
Oldenburger, Norma Jane *medical/surgical nurse*

Dickinson
Kessel, Lloyd R. *nursing administrator, educator*

Fargo
Miller, Donald R. *pharmacist, educator*
Nickel, Janet Marlene Milton *geriatrics nurse*
Rice, Jon Richard *managed care administrator, physician*

Grand Forks
Nielsen, Forrest Harold *research nutritionist*
†Ransom, Michael T. *counselor*

Hazen
Lorenz, Denise Eileen *physician assistant*

Maddock
Aadland, Kathleen A. *counselor, army intelligence officer*

Pettibone
Flanders, Paula L. *director public health*

Williston
†Benson, Robert John *physical therapist, department chairman, massage therapist*

OHIO

Akron
Lesner, Sharon A. *audiologist, educator*
O'Brien, Gayle Ann *nurse*
Webb, Adele Ann *nursing administrator*
West, Michael Alan *retired hospital administrator*

Amelia
Hensley, Kimberly Sue *counselor*
Ullman, Susan Joyce Feldman *social worker*

Ashtabula
Hornbeck, Harold Douglas *psychotherapist*

Avon Lake
Stives, William Robert *retired pharmacist*

Bath
Hoffer, Alma Jeanne *nursing educator*

Beachwood
Wilkes, Angela Biggs *mental health consultant*

Beavercreek
Rinta, Christine Evelyn *nurse, air force officer*

Bowling Green
†Scherer, Ronald Callaway *voice scientist, educator*

Bratenahl
Jones, Trevor Owen *biomedical industry executive, management consultant*

Brecksville
Meyer, Karin Zumwalt *pharmacist, consultant*

Bucyrus
Cooper, April Helen *family nurse practitioner*

Canfield
†Weiss, Susan Ellen *adult nurse practitioner, educator*

Canton
Bartlette, Donald Lloyd *social worker, counselor, educator*
Lindesmith, Dixie Lou *retired geriatrics nurse*

Cedarville
Firmin, Michael Wayne *psychology educator*

Cincinnati
Angeline, Michael E. *social worker, bereavement facilitator*
Derstadt, Ronald Theodore *health care administrator*
Goldstein, Sidney *pharmaceutical scientist*
Hensgen, Herbert Thomas *medical technologist*
Knapp, Judy Ann *pharmacist*
Lang, Jackie Ann *nursing consultant*
Lichtin, Leon (Judah Leon Lichtin) *pharmacist*
Lippincott, Jonathan Ramsay *healthcare executive*
Matulewicz, Patricia Ann *social worker*
Miller, Catherine Ann *nursing administrator*
Monroe, Erin *psychiatric nurse practitioner*
Powley, Elizabeth Ann *health facility administrator*
Rudney, Bernice Snider *social worker, psychotherapist*
Shapiro, Judith *social worker*
Shertzer, Howard Grant *health educator*
Stinson, Mary Florence *retired nursing educator*
†Trofe, Jennifer *pharmacist, educator*

Cleveland
Anders, Claudia Dee *occupational therapist*
Baker, Melvin *hospital pharmacy administrator*
Bersin, Susan Joyce-Heather (Reignbeaux Joyce-Heather Bersin) *critical care nurse, police officer*
Blum, Arthur *social work educator*
†Bridges, John Francis Patrick *healthcare educator, researcher*
Cotleur, Mark A. *hospital administrator*
Crispin, Patricia Lynnette *social worker*
†Curran, Phyllis Marie *counselor*
Curtis, Susan Virginia *social worker*
Dadley, Arlene Jeanne *sleep techologist*
Dylag, Helen Marie *healthcare administrator*
Freire, Gloria Medonis *social worker*
†Gallagher, Lisa Marie *music therapist*
Goodman, Glenn David *occupational therapist, educator*
Hokenstad, Merl Clifford, Jr., *social work educator*
Hudak, Christine Angela *nursing informatics educator, specialist nursing informatics*
Hulme, Mary Ann Prim Kumm *women's health nurse, administrator*
Johnson, Mattiedna *nurse, retired diaconal minister*
Joseph, Eleanor Ann *health science association administrator, consultant*
Kohn, Mary Louise Beatrice *nurse*
Mantzell, Betty Lou *school health administrator*
Mazgalev, Todor Nikolov *health science association administrator, research scientist*
O'Brien, Margaret Ann *obstetrics nurse, community health nurse*
†Romaniuk, Jaroslaw Richard *social worker, neuroscientist*
Schlotfeldt, Rozella May *nursing educator, educator*
Schorr, Alvin Louis *social worker, educator*
Schrott, Norman *retired clinical social worker*
Schultz, Jeffrey Eric *optometrist*
Shakno, Robert Julian *hospital and social services administrator*
†Simmons, Clinton Craig *human resources executive*
Stark, George Robert *health science association administrator*
Taylor, Harris C. *consultant endocrinologist, diabetologist*
Walcott, Robert *healthcare executive, priest*
†Womack, John W. *pharmacist*

Columbus
Anderson, Carole Ann *nursing educator, academic administrator*
Bachman, Sister Janice *healthcare executive*
Banasik, Robert Casmer *nursing home administrator, educator*
†Bauldoff, Gerene S. *nursing researcher, educator*
Beckholt, Alice *clinical nurse specialist*
Bilderback, George Garrison, III, *alcohol/drug abuse services professional*
Blom, Dave *healthcare industry executive*
Carter, Cheryl A. *endoscopy nurse*
Lewis, Nina *social worker*
†Lindsay, Ronald Lee *health facility administrator, pediatrician*
Murden, Robert A. *medical administrator, physician*
Pitzer, Martha Seares *nursing educator*
Schuller, David Edward *cancer center administrator, otolaryngologist*
Shipley, Martha Theresa *social worker, educational and program consultant*
Sims, Richard Lee *hospital administrator*
Smith, Ann Marie *rehabilitation nurse*
†Tripodi, Tony *social work educator, author, editor*

Copley
Smith, Joan H. *retired women's health nurse, educator*

Dayton
Ctvrtnicek, Scarlett Jane *physician assistant*
Gillen, Patrick Bernard *nurse*
Kiser, Sharon Ann *health facility professional*
Nixon, Charles William *acoustician*
O'Malley, Patricia *critical care nurse*
Stefanics, Charlotte Louise *retired mental health nurse*
Versic, Linda Joan *nurse educator, research company executive*

Elyria
Manner, Jennifer Fouse *social worker*

Fairfield
Goodman, Myrna Marcia *school nurse*

Fairlawn
Kurzweil, Alan Dennis *social worker, marriage and family therapist, consultant*

Findlay
Reamsnyder, Margaret Elizabeth *nurse*
Stephani, Nancy Jean *social worker, journalist*

Gahanna
Kaye, Gail Leslie *healthcare consultant, educator*

Gallipolis
Niehm, Bernard Frank *mental health center administrator, retired*
Wilcox, Victoria Lynn *nurse*

Hamilton
Fein, Linda Ann *nurse anesthetist, consultant*
Johnson, Pauline Benge *nurse, anesthetist*

Hudson
†Pollino, Sandra Michelle *psychotherapist, educator*

Wooldredge, William Dunbar *health facility administrator*

Independence
Meredith, Thomas Brian *healthcare consultant*
Van Kirk, Robert John *nursing case manager, educator*

Kent
†Biordi, Diana L. *healthcare educator, dean*

Lakewood
Burton, Kathleen T. *mental health services professional*

Lancaster
Varney, Richard Alan *medical center administrator*

Lebanon
Osborne, Quinton Albert *psychiatric social worker, inspector of institutional services*

Lewis Center
Ball, Kay Atkinson *health services consultant*

Lima
Miller, Roy Raymond *optician, oculist*
Palmer, Arthur Eugene *retired nursing home administrator*

Little Hocking
Corbin, David P. *counselor*

Logan
Yeagley, Kathleen Lux *community health nurse, educator*

Malta
Peyton, Sharon Anne Reed *geriatrics nurse*

Marietta
Scanlan, Carla R. *researcher, educator*

Mason
Clements, Michael Craig *health services consulting executive, retired renal dialysis technician*
Erbe, Janet Sue *medical surgical, orthopedics and pediatrics nurse*
Jackobs, Miriam Ann *dietitian*
†Wekselman, Kathryn *pharmaceutical researcher*

Massillon
Kidder, J. Penelope *consultant, mental health services administrator*

Mc Comb
Ewing, Mary Eileen *radiologic technologist*

Medina
Calhoun, Lyla Lea *clinical social worker, consultant*
Miller, Randal Howard *health science association administrator*

Mentor
Core, Harry Michael *psychiatric social worker, mental health therapist and administrator*
Russell, Brenda Sue *critical care nurse*

Middleburg Heights
Hartman, Lenore Anne *physical therapist*

Middletown
Gordon, Sandy Gale Combs *medical/surgical nurse, community health nurse*
Redding, Barbara J. *nursing administrator, occupational health nurse*

New Albany
Rusk, Karla Marie *nurse practitioner*

New Carlisle
Leffler, Carole Elizabeth *mental health nurse, women's health nurse*
Peters, Elizabeth Ann Hampton *retired nursing educator*

New Philadelphia
Zinkon, Lana Sue *occupational health nurse*

North Royalton
Shimandle, Sharon Anne *nurse anesthetist*

Northfield
Cartier, Charles Ernest *alcohol and drug abuse services professional*

Oberlin
†Pagliai, Valentina *researcher, educator*

Olmsted Falls
†Semple, Jane Frances *health facility administrator*

Oxford
†Weinrich, Barbara Diane *speech pathology/audiology services professional, educator*

Perrysburg
Billnitzer, Bonnie Jeanne *nurse, gerontology specialist*
Murdock, Nanci C. *women's health nurse*

Poland
Donatelli, Daniel Dominic, Jr., *medical/surgical and oncological nurse*
Mike-Nard, Beverly Jean *nurse*

Portsmouth
Murphy, Pearl Marie *medical and surgical nurse*

Ravenna
Turcotte, Margaret Jane *retired nurse*

Reynoldsburg
Odor, Richard Lane *mental health administrator, psychologist*

Rootstown
Gibson, Denise Dawn *social worker, educator*

Saint Clairsville
Hahn, David Bennett *hospital administrator, marketing professional*
Zavacky-DeBertrand, Lynette Michele *women's health nurse*

Sandusky
Freehling, Harold George, Jr., *respiratory therapist, consultant*
Sokol, Dennis Allen *hospital administrator*

Sebring
Kelley-Hall, Maryon Hoyle *retired social worker*

Shaker Heights
Salomon, Elizabeth Lowenstein *social worker*

Spencer
Snyder, Teresa Ann *medical/surgical nurse*

Stow
Kase-Janowski, Kristen Marian *healthcare educator*

Strongsville
†Lamberton, Jacquelyn E. *psychotherapist*
†Taghizadeh, Georgeanne Marie *medical/surgical nurse, diagnostic cardiac sonographer*

Sylvania
Verhesen, Anna Maria Hubertina *social worker*

Tallmadge
Kaul, Mohan Lal *social worker, educator*

Toledo
Hyman, Melvin *speech-language pathologist, consultant*
Lessick, Mira Lee *nursing educator*
Luckner, Kleia Raubitschek *nursing administrator, lawyer, nurse midwife*
†Marco, Alan Paul *hospital administrator, anesthesiologist*
Ormond, Paul A. *health facility executive*
†Overmyer, Janet Elaine *counselor*
Talmage, Lance Allen *obstetrician/gynecologist, career military officer*
Toczynski, Janet Marie *oncological nurse*
†Weikel, Malcolm Keith *healthcare company executive*

Troy
Enright, Georgann McGee *healthcare educator*

Upper Arlington
Williams, Cathy Lynn *nurse*

Urbana
Meyers, Marsha Lynn *retired social worker*

Warren
VanAuker, Lana *recreational therapist, educator*

Westerville
Strapp, Naomi Ann *women's health nurse*
Williams, John Michael *physical therapist, sports medicine educator*

Westlake
Coeling, Harriet Van Ess *nursing educator, editor*
Lahiff, Marilyn J. *nursing administrator*
†Schroth, Joyce Able *social worker*

Worthington
Bernhagen, Lillian Flickinger *retired school health consultant*
Lentz, Edward Allen *consultant, retired health administrator*

Youngstown
Hassell, Jean Treverton *dietetics educator*
Lambert, Jean Marjorie *health care executive*
McClelland, Marleen Iannucci *physical therapist, educator*
Valenta, Janet Anne *substance abuse professional*

Zanesville
Ray, Susanne Gettings *counselor*

OKLAHOMA

Ada
Davenport, Ann Adele Mayfield *retired home care agency administrator*

Bartlesville
Byfield, Rita Rae *nursing educator, family nurse practitioner*

Broken Arrow
Cruzan, Clarah Catherine *dietitian*

Claremore
McCall, Charles Barnard *health facility administrator, educator*
McClain, Marilyn Russell *counselor*

Edmond
Lewis, Gladys Sherman *nurse, educator*

El Reno
Buendia, Imelda Bernardo *clinical director, physician*

Lawton
†Dishman, Bob N. *pharmacist*

†Jurgensen, Monserrate *clinical nurse, consultant*
Mayes, Glenn *social worker*
†Reece, Juliette M. Stolper *community health and mental health nurse*

Mangum
Bronson, William Cavolt, Jr., *counselor*

Muskogee
Diede, Nancy *nursing educator*

Newkirk
Newport, L. Joan *clinical social worker, retired psychotherapist*

Norman
Gaskins-Clark, Patricia Renae *dietitian*
Javellas, Ina June *social worker*
Tackwell, Elizabeth Miller *social worker*
Weber, Jerome Charles *education and human relations educator, former academic dean and vice-provost*

Oklahoma City
Adams, Warren Lynn *alcohol/drug abuse services professional, consultant*
Arbuckle, Averil Dorothy (Cookie Arbuckle) *healthcare facility administrator*
Bishop, Wanda Caroline *geriatrics nurse, medical/surgical nurse*
Dean, Chrystell Fetty *women's health nurse, educator*
Greiner, Kenneth Donald, Jr., *nursing home company executive*
Harper, Robbie Jane *critical care nurse, administrator*
Holder, Lee *human services administrator*
Jones, Renee Kauerauf *health care administrator*
McClellan, Mary Ann *pediatrics nurse, educator*
McEwen, Irene Ruble *physical therapy educator*
Mustion, Alan Lee *pharmacist*
†Nakagawara, Van B. *optometrist, researcher*
O'Steen, Randy A. *nursing administrator*
Paris, Wayne *social worker, researcher*
†Rathbun, Robert Christopher *pharmacy educator*
Schroyer, Michael Kevin *critical care nurse and hospital administrator*
Sookne, Herman Solomon (Hank Sookne) *retirement services executive*
Spencer, Melvin Joe *hospital administrator, lawyer*
Tillinghast, Jon Dalton *public health physician*
Williamson, Marvel *dean, sexologist, nursing administrator, author, speaker*

Sand Springs
†Biggoose, Charles *counselor*

Stillwater
Bahr, Beverly Katherine *critical care nurse*
†Hendrix, Charles C. *marriage and family therapist, educator*

Tahlequah
Edmondson, Linda Louise *optometrist*

Tulsa
Arrington, Rebecca Carol *occupational health nurse*
Davis, Annalee Ruth Conyers *clinical social worker*
Gray, Karen Kay *counselor*
Joice, Nora Lee *clinical dietitian*
Lewis, Corinne Hemeter *psychotherapist, educator*
†Redfearn, Charlotte Marie *nursing administrator*

OREGON

Albany
Chowning, Orr-Lyda Brown *dietitian*

Ashland
Masters, Robert Edward Lee *psychotherapist, neural researcher, human potential educator, philosopher*

Bend
†Irwin, Kerri Lynne *pharmacist, writer, small business owner*
Sabatella, Elizabeth Maria *clinical therapist, educator, mental health facility administrator*
Thompson, Mari Hildenbrand *medico-legal and administrative consultant*

Central Point
Brown, Christopher Patrick *health care administrator, educator*

Eugene
Acker, Martin Herbert *psychotherapist, educator*
Camp, Delpha Jeanne *counselor*
Hibbard, Judith Hoffman *health services researcher*

Forest Grove
Randolph, Harry Franklin, III, (Randy Randolph) *health facility administrator, educator, physician assistant*

Klamath Falls
Klepper, Carol Herdman *mental health therapist*

Lake Oswego
Tyler, Darlene Jasmer *retired dietitian*

Medford
Linn, Carole Anne *dietitian*

Milwaukie
†Orloff, Barbara-Lee Marguerite Hewitt *social worker*

Newberg
Jordan, Karin Balten-Babkowski *health facility administrator*

Purcell, Kevin Brown *special education services professional*

Pendleton
Smiley, Richard Wayne *researcher*

Phoenix
Dodd, Darlene Mae *nurse, retired air force officer*

Portland
Busch, Ann Marie Herbage *medical/surgical nurse*
Cereghino, James Joseph *health facility administrator, neurologist*
Fritz, Barbara Jean *occupational health nurse*
Giffin, Sandra Lee *nursing administrator*
Greenlick, Merwyn Ronald *health services researcher*
†Korb, Christine Ann *music therapist, researcher, educator*
McDonald, Robert Wayne *cardiac sonographer*
Olson, Roger Norman *retired health service administrator*
Pfeifer, Larry Alan *public health service coordinator*
Pladel, John Gerald *psychiatric nurse practitioner, psychologist, psychotherapist*
Plonski, Halina Maria *pharmacist*
Powell, Roberta A. *medical social worker*
Rooks, Judith Pence *midwifery, public health consultant*
Rummell, Helen Mary *critical care and pediatrics nurse*
Shireman, Joan Foster *social work educator*
†Sims, Kathleen Marie Eichner *nursing educator*
Uliano, Anthony, Jr., *industrial hygienist, educator*

Rhododendron
Williamson, Diana Jean *nurse*

Salem
Callahan, Marilyn Joy *social worker*
Casey, Patricia Carolyn *retired social worker*
Edge, James Edward *health care administrator*
Fore, Ann *counselor, educator, country dance instructor*
Zumwalt, Roger Carl *hospital administrator*

The Dalles
Cooper, Rickey Eugene *medical transcriptionist, educator*

Tillamook
Rand, Merthel Luretta *family nurse practitioner*

White City
Williams, Kevin Leonard *clinical social worker, marriage and family therapist*

PENNSYLVANIA

Abington
Mabry, Sondra B. *nurse educator and practitioner*
Roediger, Paul Margerum *hospital administrator*

Acme
Babcock, Marguerite Lockwood *addictions treatment therapist, educator, writer*

Allentown
Berman, Muriel Mallin *optometrist, humanities lecturer*
Brownback, Linda Mason *health company executive*
Flores, Robin Ann *social worker, social services administrator*
Saylor, Kathleen Marie *pediatric nurse practitioner*
†Zocco, Patricia Elizabeth *human services manager, cardiac ultrasound technologist*

Auburn
Johnson, Barbara Jean *rehabilitation nurse, gerontology nurse*

Bala Cynwyd
Peret, Karen Krzyminski *health service administrator*

Bensalem
Quinn, Holli Jo Bardo *social worker, educator*

Berwick
Smith, Clara Jean *retired nursing home administrator*

Bethel Park
Buyny, Marianne Jo *eating disorders therapist, addictions counselor*

Bethlehem
Herrenkohl, Roy Cecil *psychology educator*
Watsula, Linda Marie *social worker*

Blue Bell
Harmon-Weiss, Sandra Rhoads *physician administrator*

Brodbecks
McMenamin, Helen Marie Foran *home health care, pediatric, and maternal nurse*

Bryn Mawr
Maehl, Jane Cecilia *social worker, administrator*

Butler
Klemens, Jonathan Mark *pharmacy educator, writer*

California
Syphers, James Edgar *retired social worker*

Camp Hill
Crider, Rudyard Lee *psychotherapist*

Carbondale
Niles, John Southworth, III, *counselor, farmer*

Chambersburg
Mehrmann, CraigAnn *nurse practitioner*

Cheltenham
Kuziemski, Naomi Elizabeth *counselor, education consultant*

Clarks Summit
†Bass, Suzanne *social worker*

Cogan Station
Sander, Theresa Marie *nurse practitioner*

Collegeville
†Dragalin, Vladimir *research statistics director*
Witman, Philip Alan *pharmaceutical researcher, epidemiologist*

Columbia
Gillmore, Vicki Longenecker *health care administrator*

Conneaut Lake
Starn, Barbarajean *healthcare administrator*

Cresson
Clark, Threese Anne *occupational therapist, disability analyst*
Grady, Janet Laura *nurse, educator*

Dallas
Baltimore, Ruth Betty *social worker*
Moran, Michael Lee *physical therapist, gerontologist*

Danville
Savitsky, Maureen Elizabeth *pharmacist*

Downingtown
Skrajewski, Dennis John *health care executive*

Doylestown
King, Robert Edward *retired pharmacy educator*
†Meyer, Diane Christine *social worker*

Dresher
Michael, Dorothy Ann *nursing administrator, naval officer*

Dushore
Getz, Mary E. *medical/surgical nurse*

East Stroudsburg
Boyd, Katherine Ann *clinical therapist*

Easton
Pysher, Zane Kermit *counselor*

Edinboro
Paul, Charlotte Patricia Peggram *nursing educator*
Thompson, Richard W. *retired health facility administrator*

Elizabethville
Rippon-Lovett, Dodie *social worker*

Elkins Park
Verma, Satya Bhushan *optometrist, educator*

Erie
Gagliano, Christine Louise *social worker*
Nihill, Karen Bailey *nursing home executive, nurse clinician*
Sensor, Mary Delores *hospital official, consultant*
Steckler, Jessica Ann *continuing nursing education educator*

Export
Carter, Linda Whitehead *oncology nurse, educator, consultant, researcher*

Fairview Village
†Filippini, Christine Marie *counselor*

Forty Fort
Olerta, Leslie Anne *nuclear medicine technologist*

Gladwyne
Cathcart, Harold Robert *hospital administrator*

Glenside
Crivelli-Kovach, Andrea *public health and nutrition consultant, educator*

Grantham
†Kreamer, Carolyn Lee *nursing educator, community health nurse*

Greensburg
Sumner, Christine Marie *counselor*

Grove City
Sellers, Patricia Ann *home health nurse*

Hamburg
Schappell, Abigail Susan *speech, language, hearing and massage therapist*

Hanover
Conway, Samuel Anthony *retired chiropractor*
Davis, Ruth Carol *pharmacy educator*

Harleysville
Kwortnick, Linda Marie *emergency nurse*

Harrisburg
O'Donnell, John Joseph, Jr., *optometrist*
Patrick, David Bruce *chiropractor*
Plawsky, Bernard Morris *retired social work administrator*
Stwalley, Brian David *pharmacist*
Tyson, Gail L. *health federation administrator*
†West, Eileen M. *caseworker*

Harveys Lake
Wolensky, Joan *occupational therapist, interfaith minister*

Hawley
Vierra, Deborah *critical care, community health nurse*

Herman
Dittmer, Sylvester Stephen Wess *retired nursing administrator*

Hermitage
Mayne, Ruth E. *medical nurse*

Hershey
Anderson, Allan Crosby *hospital executive*
†Christensen, Dawn Michelle *family practice nurse practitioner, consultant*
Lindenberg, Steven Phillip *counselor, consultant*
Michel, Nancy Claire *physician assistant*
Moskowitz, Jay *health sciences educator*
†Nickolaus, Michelle J *family practice nurse practitioner*
Ozereko-deCoen, Mary T. *therapeutic recreation specialist and therapist*

Hidden Valley
Betta, Pamela Albers *community health nurse, administrator, educator*

Hulmeville
Jackson, Mary L. *health services executive*

Hunker
Bromke, Cindy Rose *geriatrics, rehabilitation and home health nurse*

Huntingdon Valley
Isard, Phillip Isaac *medical nutritionist, consultant*

Jenkintown
Lowry, Karen M. *biomedical research scientist, pharmacist*

Johnstown
Babik, Dennis Allen *social worker, consultant*
Hull, Patricia Ann *nursing administrator*
Keiper, Jeffrey Lynn *counselor, therapist, lawyer*

King Of Prussia
Miller, Alan B. *hospital management executive*

Lafayette Hill
Hess, Wanda Jean *health facility administrator*

Lancaster
Brunner, Lillian Sholtis *nurse, writer*
Groff, Tracey Anne *social worker*
Saganich, Bonnie Sue *medical/surgical nurse*

Langhorne
Bishop, Ann Shorey *oncological nurse*
Boyce, Andrea Zygmunt *nurse*

Lansdale
Habecker, Sandra K. *retired nurse*

Leola
Wedel, Paul George *retired hospital administrator*

Levittown
Ferraro, Ronald Louis *health facility administrator*

Lincoln University
Racine, Linda Jean *college health nurse*

Lititz
Hartz, Brian David *physical therapist, educator, small business owner*

Lock Haven
Hartline, Darrell G. *retired healthcare executive*
Ivory, Patrick J. *physician assistant*

Loretto
Sackin, Claire *retired social work educator*

Malvern
Stuckey, Susan Jane *perioperative nurse, consultant*

Martinsburg
Keith, Tammy Leah *geriatrics nurse*

Meadville
McGuigan, Charles James *rehabilitation therapist*

Mechanicsburg
Wagner, Tanya Suzanne Lineberry *health facility administrator*

Media
Allen, Anne Norgaard *social worker*

Midland
Vosler Petrella, Brenda Gayle *family nurse practitioner, educator, researcher*

Millersville
Heintzelman, Carol Ann *social work educator*

Monaca
Jaskiewicz, David Walter *optometrist*

Moon Township
Hagar, Joanne Marie *physician assistant*

Mount Pleasant
Morgan, Joyce Kaye *social worker*

Nazareth
Halberstadt, Robert Bilheimer *optometrist*

Newtown
Derivan, Mary Collins *nursing consultant, oncological nurse*

Newtown Square
Sacks, Susan Bendersky *mental health clinical specialist, educator*

Norristown
Hunter, Patricia Phelps *physician assistant*

Oakmont
Bryce, Marguerite Maher *social worker, educator*

Paoli
†Rosenblatt, Barbara S. *educator, writer*

Parkesburg
Procyson, Mary G. Walton *critical care nurse*

Patton
Reed-Gates, Mary Louise *natural health professional*

Perkasie
Laincz, Betsy Ann *nurse*

Philadelphia
Aiken, Linda Harman *nurse, sociologist, educator*
Anyanwu, Chukwukre *alcohol and drug abuse facility administrator*
†Austan, Frank Acosta *clinician, educator*
Bamberger-Herrmann, Julia Kathryn *social worker*
Blissitt, Patricia Ann *nurse*
Borislow, Alan Jerome *hospital dental department chairman*
Brewer-Smyth, Kathleen *nursing researcher, nursing educator*
†Broytman, Vladislav I. *hygenist*
Carpenter, Nathaniel Dennard *resident health services director*
Casey, Rita Jo Ann *nursing administrator*
†Charney, Natalie J. *behavioral health services administrator, researcher*
Clarke, Sean Patrick *nursing researcher, educator*
Clarkin, John Francis *health care management executive*
†Corprew, Helen Barbara *mental health services professional*
†Donaher, Joseph G *speech pathology/audiology services professional, director*
Drozdis, Marie Trese *crisis intervention nurse*
Fagin, Claire Mintzer *nursing educator, administrator*
Fernandez, Mike *healthcare company executive*
†Freeman, Sharon Elizabeth *psychiatric nurse practitioner*
Hand, Virginia Saxton *home health nurse*
Holman, Larry Dean *health care administrator*
Jemmott, Loretta Sweet *nursing educator*
Lane, Vivian Pryce *educational counselor*
Lang, Norma M. *nursing educator*
Lauck, Donna L. *mental health nurse*
Lichtman, Joan *healthcare researcher, author, accountant, consultant*
Maplesden, Carol Harper *marital and family therapist, music educator*
Meleis, Afaf Ibrahim *nurse sociologist, educator, clinician, researcher*
Micozzi, Marc Stephen *health executive, physician, educator*
Miller Calandra, Linda Marguerita *pediatric nurse practitioner*
Paulus, Ronald Alan *health executive, physician*
Payne, Deborah Anne *medical company officer*
Peck, Susan Nell *pediatric nurse*
Piccolo, Joseph Anthony *hospital administrator*
Potter, Alice Catherine *clinical laboratory scientist*
Rothrock, Robert William *physician assistant*
Sands, Roberta G. *social work educator*
Sayed, M. Gary *healthcare administrator, educator, scientist*
Scheib, Garry L. *hospital administrator*
Schultz, Jane Schwartz *health research administrator*
Schwartz, Arthur *social worker*
Shapiro, Paula *retired maternal/women's health nurse*
Solomon, Phyllis Linda *social work educator, researcher*
Souders, Beryl V. *medical/surgical and rehabilitation-detox nurse*
Sovie, Margaret Doe *nursing administrator, educator, clinician, researcher*
†Steinberg, Janet DeBerry *optometrist, educator, researcher*
Tate, Loretta Clara *health educator*
Tegenu, Mesfin *health services administrator, consultant*
Warnick, Patricia Ann *healthcare consultant, nurse ethicist*
Williams, Sankey Vaughan *health services researcher, internist*

Pittsburgh
Bauccio, Lisa Valentine *obstetric nurse, high-risk perinatal nurse*
Bell, Lori Jo *crisis counselor, psychiatric nurse*
Benson, Jeryl Disanti *occupational therapist*
Brennen, Carole J. *researcher in human services*
Constantino-Bana, Rose Eva *nursing educator, researcher, lawyer*
†Fink, Bruce *psychoanalyst, educator*
Friede, Samuel A(rnold) *health care executive*
George, John Anthony *health corporation executive*
Germanowski, Janet *women's health and medical surgical nurse, educator, researcher*
Goertzen, Irma *hospital executive*
Goldstein, Bernard David *physician, educator*
Grubbs, Arlene Busse *social worker, consultant*
Heinecke, Deborah Ann *pediatrics nurse*
Herleman, Laura Ann *nursing administrator*
Hudachek, Susan Marie *contracts specialist; consultant*
Jakub, Kathleen Ann *medical/surgical nurse*
Maguire, Lambert *social worker, educator*
†Maiolini, Gloria J. *nurse case manager, poet, writer*
Martich, Dawna *nurse*
Matzke, Gary Roger *pharmacist, educator*
Missiriotis, Irene *geriatric services professional, artist*
Mitchell, Ann Margaret *nursing educator, psychiatric nurse practitioner*
Mokotoff, Michael *pharmaceutical sciences educator*
Moore, Pearl B. *nursing educator*
Omiros, George James *medical foundation executive*
†Pennell, Daniel Mark *researcher*
Romoff, Jeffrey Alan *health care executive*
Rubin, Deborah Jean *social worker*
Sessoms, Sandra Lea *hospital administrator*
Steele, Cheryl A. *oncology nurse*
Trapani-Hanasewych, Marybeth Ann *speech language pathologist*
Young, Eveline *social worker*
Zanardelli, John Joseph *healthcare services executive*
Zdilla, Robyn Lynn *occupational therapist*

Quakertown
Ambrus, Lorna *medical/surgical nurse, geriatrics nurse*

Reading
Bell, Frances Louise *medical technologist*
Shultz, Lois Frances Casho *nursing supervisor*
Weiland, Jonathon A. *nursing and rehabilitation facility administrator*

Scranton
Borja, Marianne E. *healthcare educator*
†Farrell, Marian Louise *nursing educator*
Lemoncelli, Lorine Barbara *counselor, elementary school educator*
Maislin, Isidore *hospital administrator*
Shovlin, Joseph Patrick *optometrist*
Turock, Jane Parsick *nutritionist*

Shohola
Harding, Linda Otto *gerontological nurse, diabetes educator*

Slippery Rock
Fulton, Jane *health science institution administrator*

Souderton
Moyer, June Faye *retired critical care nurse*

South Park
Kokowski, Palma Anna *nurse consultant*

Spring Grove
Alcon, Sonja L. *retired medical social worker*

State College
Henshaw, Beverly Ann Harsh *women's health nurse, consultant*
Moon, Marla Lynn *optometrist*

Stroudsburg
Miller, Nancy A. *nursing administrator*

Taylor
Champagne, Cecile Belisle *nursing educator, maternal/child health nurse*

Temple
VonNieda, Jean Lorayne *infection control practitioner*

Transfer
Larson, Sharon Lynn *oncological nurse*

Tunkhannock
McNabb, Leonard Matthew *clinical social worker, administrator*

Uniontown
Prescott, Janelle *medical and surgical nurse, emergency room nurse, psychiatric nurse*

University Park
Mayers, Stanley Penrose, Jr., *public health educator*
†Murray-Kolb, Laura Elaine *nutritionist, researcher*
Rolls, Barbara Jean *nutritionist, educator, director*
†Rosen, Scott Lowell *researcher*

Valencia
Hill, Ellen Brockett Brown *emergency medicine nurse, geriatrics services professional*

Villanova
Beletz, Elaine Ethel *nurse, educator*
Cordes, Eugene Harold *pharmacy and chemistry educator*
Zhang, Yimin *researcher*

Wallingford
McCarthy, Carol A. *pediatric nurse practitioner*

Warren
Crone, John Rossman *pharmacist*

Warrington
Miller, Lynne Marie *critical care nurse, administrator*

Washington
Robinson, Jennifer Lynn *nursing educator*

Washington Bord
†Snyder, John Jacob *researcher*

Wayne
Grace, Thomas Lee *health facility administrator, emergency nurse practitioner*

West Chester
Abbott, Ann Augustine *social worker, educator*
Patin Falini, Nancy Marie *dietitian*

Whitehall
Budd, Patricia Jean *counselor*

Wilkes Barre
Brady, Patricia Marie *nurse*
Campbell, Sophie Ann Oriszko *manager and senior health care consultant*
†Legg, Timothy James *nursing educator*
†Stokes, Kimberly Ann *counselor*

Willow Grove
Yuan, Joan Reynolds *community health nurse*

Windber
Ott, Clarice Jean *social worker*

Wyncote
Schaffner, Roberta Irene *retired medical, surgical nurse*

Wynnewood
†Khurana, Poonam *neonatologist*

York
Bartels, Bruce Michael *health care executive*
Chronister, Virginia Ann *school nurse, educator*
Keiser, Paul Harold *retired hospital administrator*
Rosen, Raymond *health facility executive*

RHODE ISLAND

East Greenwich
Jordan, Ronald P. *pharmacist, pharmaceutical executive, consultant*
Schibler, John J. *health facility administrator, consultant, educator*

Kingston
Katzanek, Robin Jean *physical therapy educator*

Narragansett
Menihan, Cydney Afriat *nurse midwife, medical sonographer*

Newport
Mullaney, Joann Barnes *nursing educator*

North Providence
†Bain, Marissa *social worker*

Pawtucket
Tarpy, Eleanor Kathleen *social worker*

Providence
Kane, Steven Michael *psychotherapist, educator*
Lamond, Sharon Ann *health administrator*
Marek, Kiersten L. *social worker*
Metrey, George David *social work educator, academic administrator*
Monteiro, Lois Ann *medical science educator*
Murphy, Christine *medical facility administrator*
Pivin, Jeanette Eva *psychotherapist*

Warwick
Galamaga, Donald Peter *health and mental health systems consultant*

SOUTH CAROLINA

Aiken
Felkel, Charlene Campbell *family nurse practitioner, nursing educator*
Madory, James Richard *hospital administrator, former air force officer*
Voss, Terence J. *human factors scientist, educator*

Anderson
George-Lepkowski, Sue Ann *retired echocardiographic technologist*
Meador, Valerie Lane *clinical dietitian*
Pruitt, Rosanne Harkey *nursing educator, human services researcher*

Cayce
Paynter, Vesta Lucas *pharmacist*

Charleston
Cheng, Kenneth Tat-Chiu *pharmacy educator*
†Fricano, Scott D. *counselor*
Garro, Susan Ann *adult nurse practitioner*
Hines, Judith Albergotti *social worker, management consultant*
Hollis, Bruce Warren *experimental nutritionist, industrial consultant*
Infinger, Gloria Altman *retired nursing administrator*
Killeen, Therese *therapist*
Lavelle, Mary Lee Demetre *psychiatric nursing educator*
Leonard, Mary Eileen *retired medical technologist, educator*

Columbia
Amidon, Roger Lyman *retired health administration educator*
†Bowman, Ned David *medical administrator*
Bristow, Thomas Cole, Jr., *social work educator*
†Bryant, Douglas E. *public health service official*
Ettel, Zita Moak *nursing administrator, food services executive*
Fowler, Linda McKeever *hospital administrator, management educator*
Ginsberg, Leon Herman *social work educator*
Heiney, Sue Porter *psychosocial oncology nurse*
Leaphart, Ashley Regan *pharmacist*
Pickens, Randi Ellen *social worker*
Rabb, Gael Caution *mental health consultant*
Ramsey, Bonnie Jeanne *mental health facility administrator, psychiatrist*
†Voris, John Charles *pharmacy educator*

Conway
Nale, Julia Ann *nursing educator*

Gaffney
†Howie, Henry S., III, *social worker, educator*

Gaston
†Taylor-Mcbride, Briggette *surgical technologist, writer*

Greenville
Boone, William Rogers *health facility administrator, educator, researcher*
Cargill, Paula Marie *social worker, gerontologist*

Hilton Head Island
Hardin, Bryan David *occupational safety and health specialist*
Kearney-Nunnery, Rose *nursing administrator, educator, consultant*
Scovel, Mary Alice *retired music therapy educator*
Wesselmann, Glenn Allen *retired hospital executive*

Lexington
†Blind, Joy Bailey *women's health nurse*

Little River
Green, Beverly Jean *nurse*

Marion
Inabinet, Lawrence Elliott *retired pharmacist*

Myrtle Beach
Fowler, Marilyn S. Atlas *social worker*

Pendleton
Fehler, Polly Diane *neonatal nurse, educator*

Rock Hill
†Bessinger, Raymond Carlton *dietician, educator*

Seneca
Grant, Martha F. *social worker*

Spartanburg
Browning, Kathryn Whelchel *psychiatic nurse, corporate compliance officer*
Fields, Ricky Edward *counselor*
Jones, William Osborne, II, *physician assistant*

Summerville
Bukala, Phyllis *social worker*

Tamassee
Martof, Mary Taylor *retired nursing educator*

SOUTH DAKOTA

Aberdeen
Pesicka, Harlene Neave *mental health services professional*

Brookings
Brandt, Linda Ann *social worker*

Pierre
†Weyer, Dianne Sue *health facility administrator*

Rapid City
Corwin, Bert Clark *optometrist*

Sioux Falls
Koepsell, Pamela Ann *nursing educator*
McMillin, Joan Austin *social worker*
Nygaard, Lance Corey *nurse, data processing consultant*
Richards, LaClaire Lissetta Jones (Mrs. George A. Richards) *social worker*
Rossing, William Osmund *healthcare administrator*
VanDemark, Michelle Volin *critical care, neuroscience nurse*

Watertown
Niemann, Jody Marie *occupational therapist*

TENNESSEE

Bluff City
Vaughn, JoAnn Wolfe *family nurse practitioner*

Brentwood
White, Michael James *healthcare facilities administrator*

Broomfield
†Scott, John Atwood, Jr., *hypnoanalyst, psychologist, marriage and family therapist*

Camden
Burchum, Jacqueline Rosenjack *family nurse practitioner*
Carter, Tamera Lynnette *clinical nurse specialist*
†Jasper, Doris J. Berry *nurse*

Chattanooga
†Holmes, Everlena McDonald *health science administrator, consultant, retired dean*
Parker, Christine Wright *medical director*
Scott, Mark Alden *hospital network executive*
Weinmann, Judy Munger *nurse*

Cleveland
†Preston, Forrest L. *health care executive*
Watson, S. Michele *school nurse*

Clinton
Seib, Billie McGhee Rushing *nursing administrator, consultant*

Cookeville
Musacchio, Marilyn Jean *nurse midwife, educator, administrator*

Franklin
Eddy, Mark James *healthcare industry executive*
Miller, Dennis Edward *health medical executive*

Germantown
Nolly, Robert J. *hospital administrator, pharmaceutical science educator*

Goodlettsville
Harper, Jewel Benton *pharmacist*

Greeneville
Bowman, Betsey Jean *social worker*

Hendersonville
Davis, Robert Norman *hospital administrator*
Linville, Mary Todd *family nurse practitioner*

Hixson
Twitty, H. R. *hospital official*

Jackson
Stutts, Gary Thomas *clinical analyst*

Jellico
Hausman, Keith Lynn *hospital administrator, physical therapist*

Johnson City
Becker, Teresa Ann *neonatal nurse practitioner*
Dabbs, John Morris, II, *health facility administrator, director*
Olsen, Martin E. *obstetrician, medical educator*

Kingsport
Coffman, Wilma Martin *women's health nurse, educator*

Knoxville
Brown, Janet Witucki *nursing educator, geriatric researcher*
†Erickson, Mary (Molly) Louise *speech pathology/audiology services professional, educator*
Harlan, Mary Jane *nursing administrator*
†Mackey, Debbie L. *researcher, educator*
McGuire, Sandra Lynn *nursing educator*
Menefee-Greene, Laura S. *psychiatric nurse*
Parker-Conrad, Jane E. *nursing consultant*
Reynolds, Marjorie Lavers *nutrition educator*
†Skinner, Amy Liddell *rehabilitation services professional, educator*
Taylor, Lee *organization development practitioner*
Trout, Monroe Eugene *hospital systems executive*

Kodak
Walker, Patricia D. *critical care nurse*

Lewisburg
Gonzalez, Raquel Maria *pharmacist*

Lexington
Swatzell, Marilyn Louise *nurse*

Linden
Mitchell, Elizabeth Marelle *family nurse practitioner, nursing educator, medical, surgical nurse*

Louisville
McReynolds, David Hobert *hospital administrator*

Memphis
Allen, Laurie Louise *retired medical social worker*
†Boucher, Bradley Albert *pharmacist, educator*
Carter, Michael Allen *nursing educator*
Crain, Frances Utterback *retired dietitian*
Diggs, Walter Whitley *health science facility administrator*
Foster, Stephan Lyle *pharmacist, educator*
Getske, Kathrine *psychiatric social worker*
Gourley, Greta Ann Kimbrough *pharmaceutical sciences educator*
Jarvis, Daphne Eloise *laboratory administrator*
Mendel, Maurice *audiologist, educator*
†Mirvis, David Marc *health administrator, cardiologist, educator*
Reynolds, Stephen Curtis *hospital administrator*
Shorb, Gary Seymour *hospital administrator*
Strauser, David Ross *healthcare educator*
Van Arsdale, Stephanie Kay Lorenz *cardiovascular clinical specialist, nursing educator, researcher*
Wicks, Mona Newsome *medical/surgical nurse, educator*
Winters, Darcy LaFountain *medical management company executive*

Nashville
Carlson, Robert Marshall *hospital professional services official*
Dalton, James Edgar, Jr., *health facility administrator*
Dauser, Kimberly Ann *physician assistant*
Doyal, Linda E. *clinical pharmacist*
Frist, Thomas Fearn, Jr., *hospital management company executive*
†Johnson, Anita Rochelle *mental health specialist*
Johnson, David *medical administrator*
Jones, Evelyn Gloria *medical technologist, educator*
Land, Rebekah Ruth *marriage and family therapist*
McKeel, Sheryl Wilson *pharmacist*
McPhee, Scott Douglas *occupational therapist, educator*
O'Reilly, Susan Whitee *health facility administrator*
†Ricketts, Todd *researcher, educator*
Sergent, John S. *hospital administrator, medical educator*
†Silver, Heidi Jaye *nutritionist, educator, researcher*
Sloan, Reba Faye *dietitian, consultant*
Urmy, Norman B. *hospital administrator*
†Warner, Tokesha L *health facility administrator*

Oak Ridge
Jones, Virginia McClurkin *retired social worker*
Slusher, Kimberly Goode *researcher*

Oliver Springs
Davis, Sara Lea *pharmacist*

Ooltewah
Mixon, Valorie Johnson *physician assistant*

Paris
Wiedemann, Ramona Diane *occupational therapist*

Pulaski
Calvert, Lois Prince *health facility administrator, geriatrics nurse*

Rockwood
Raymond, Betty Jean *critical care nurse*

Signal Mountain
Wakim, Judith *nursing educator*

Soddy-Daisy
†Payne, Deborah Sue *radiation technologist*

Trenton
McCullough, Kathryn T. Baker *social worker*

Tullahoma
Keele, Jean A. *medical, surgical, geriatrics and home health nurse*

TEXAS

Abilene
Baughn, Cynthia J. *human services administrator*
Campbell, Lillie Spurgin *social worker*
Cawood, Jenny Lind *social worker, poet*
Godsey, Martha Sue *speech-language pathologist*
Morrison, Shirley Marie *nursing educator*

Allen
Garner, Julie Lowrey *occupational therapist*
Gilliland, Mary Margarett *healthcare consultant*

Amarillo
Arnold, Winnie Jo *retired mental health nurse, nursing administrator*
Simpson, Chad W. *pharmacist, educator*

Arlington
Adams, Phyllis Curl *nursing educator*
Jordan, Catheleen *social worker, educator*
†McIntyre, Corwin L. *pharmacist*

Austin
Abel, Robert L. *healthcare quality improvement professional*
Attal, Gene (Fred Eugene Attal) *hospital executive*
Austin, David Mayo *social work educator*
Davis, Donald Robert *nutritionist, researcher, consultant*
Dennis, Elizabeth P. *social worker, therapist, consultant*
Dirienzo, Margaret Helen *nursing administrator*
Doluisio, James Thomas *pharmacy educator*
Durbin, Richard Louis, Sr., *healthcare administration consultant*
Easley, Christa Birgit *nurse, researcher*
Fletcher, Robin Mary *health care administrator*
Gardner, Joan *medical, surgical nurse*
Gionfriddo, Paul *healthcare executive*
Golden, Kimberly Kay *critical care, flight nurse*
Hall, Beverly Adele *nursing educator*
Hayes, Patricia Ann *health facility administrator*
Herrington-Borre, Frances June *sign language school director*
Hutchins, Karen Leslie *psychotherapist*
Kirk, Lynda Pounds *biofeedback therapist, neurotherapist, counselor*
Larkam, Beverley McCosham *clinical social worker, family therapist*
Lauchner, Kathryn Ann *nursing educator*
Martin, Frederick Noel *audiology educator*
Rider, Katherine Loveta Thompson *clinical social worker*
Smith, Bert Kruger *retired mental health services professional*

Beaumont
Tucker, Gary Wilson *nursing educator*

Bedford
Hamstra, Christine Josephine *social worker*

Benbrook
Margolis, Susan Ellen *psychiatric clinical nurse specialist, artist*

Big Spring
Wylie, Mary Ann *critical care nurse*

Brenham
Dalrymple, Christopher Guy *chiropractor*

Bryan
†Guitry, Loraine Dunn *community health nurse*
Helpert-Nunez, Ruth Anne *clinical social worker, psychotherapist*
Parrott, Thena Elizabeth *nurse educator*

Bulverde
†Donbavand, James Joseph, Jr., *medical facility administrator*

Carrollton
Withrow, Lucille Monnot *nursing home administrator*

Chillicothe
Brock, Helen Rachel McCoy *retired mental health and community health nurse*

College Station
†Logan, Erin Nicole *researcher*

Colleyville
Collins, Stephen Barksdale *retired health care executive*
Donnelly, Barbara Schettler *retired medical technologist*

Conroe
Bruce, Rachel Mary Condon *retired nurse practitioner*
Sowers, Amelia Barnet *speech and language pathologist*

Converse
Droneburg, Nancy Marie *geriatrics nurse*

Copperas Cove
Haas, Lu Ann *counselor*

Corpus Christi
Clark, Joyce Naomi Johnson *retired nurse, counselor*
Jones, Audrey Beyer *dietitian*
Stetina, Pamela Eleanor *nursing educator*

Dallas
†Bair, Donna Marlene *medical laboratory administrator*
†Baker, James Guy *health facility administrator*
Blome, Dorothy Carter *pediatrics nurse*
Bradley, John Andrew *hospital management company executive*
†Brucker, Mary C. *nurse midwife*
Byrd, Ellen Stoesser *school nurse administrator*
Collins, Lynn M. *oncology clinical nurse specialist*
Dykes, Virginia Chandler *occupational therapist, educator*
France, Newell Edwin *former hospital administrator, consultant*
Goldmann, James Allen *healthcare consultant*
Grange-Maasoumi, Lynette Danielle *community health nurse, educator*
†Harris, Hazel Lynn *medical/surgical nurse*
†Hastings, Beverly Ann *alcohol/drug abuse services professional*
Hitt, David Hamilton, Sr., *retired hospital executive*
Holl-Matthews, Dee Lynn *career counselor, psychotherapist, nutrition coach*
Johnson, Murray H. *optometrist, researcher, consultant, lecturer*
Key, Tara Ann *clinical social worker*
Mancini, Mary Elizabeth *nursing executive*
McLean, Lynne Marie *social worker*
Miller, Jo Carolyn Dendy *family and marriage counselor, educator*
O'Bannion, Mindy Martha Martin *nurse*
Shelton, James D. *hospital administrator*
Smith, William Randolph (Randy Smith) *health care management executive*
Staber, Dorothee Beatrice *lab administrator*
Taulbee, Thomas Lester *psychotherapist, educator*
Wheeler, M. Cass *health science association administrator*

Deer Park
Fotsch, George Bernard, III, *chemical addiction counselor*

Denton
Cissell, William Bernard *health studies educator*
Mathes, Dorothy Jean Holden *occupational therapist*
Ryan, Melbagene T. *retired food and nutrition service director*
†Wilhite, Barbara C. *recreational therapist, educator*

Deport
Sawyer, Mary Catherine *retired hospital administrator*

Dublin
Johnson, Nancy Ruth *nurse*

Edinburg
Wilson, Bruce Keith *men's health nurse*

El Paso
Allen, Anna J. *chiropractor*
Bartlett, Janet Sanford (Janet Walz) *school nurse*
DiNardo-Ekery, Dorothy Maria *retired internist, cardiologist, educator*
Dombrowski, Frank Paul, Jr., *pharmacist*
Hedrick, Wyatt Smith *pharmacist*
†Ituah, Martins O. *pharmacist*
Juarez, Antonio *psychotherapist, consultant, counselor, educator*
Mitchell, Paula Rae *nursing educator, college dean*
Olvera, Joe Enrique *alcohol/drug abuse services professional*
Salewski, Ruby Marie Graf *nursing educator*

Fairview
Chapdelaine, Perry Anthony, Jr., *public health and preventive medicine physician, educator*

Fort Sam Houston
Nelson, James Harold *health sciences administrator*

Fort Worth
Beveridge, Jo-Anne Fay *laboratory director*
Brockman, Leslie Richard *social worker*
Brown, Janet McNalley *social worker*
Caddy, Deborah Carol Runyan *social worker*
Ford, Kathleen Marie *home health nurse, nursing administrator*
†Goates, Pat LaNetta *social worker, consultant*
Isik, Tela Mae *obstetrical/gynecological nurse practitioner*
Lemke, Henry Robert *physician assistant*
McNairn, Peggi Jean *speech pathologist, educator*
Rockemann, David Douglas *health services administrator*
Smaistrla, Jean Ann *family therapist*

Frisco
Bomberger, Audrey Shelley *health facility administrator*

Galveston
Glaister, Judy Alane *nursing educator*
Lemon, Stanley M. *hospital administrator*
Watkins, Joanne Patricia *clinical social worker*

Granbury
McCuistion, Robert Wiley *hospital administrator, management consultant, lawyer*

Grand Prairie
Amil-Barker, Jana Kay *social worker*
Loo, Maritta Louise *nurse, national guard officer*

Hermleigh
Barnes, Maggie Lue Shifflett (Mrs. Lawrence Barnes) *nurse*

Hockley
†Patterson, Maria Riland *medical technician, writer*

Houston
Altman, William Carl *health facility administrator, merger and acquisitions specialist, investment manager, consultant*
†Arcilla, Demetrio Ballares, Jr., *health facility administrator, rehabilitation services professional, writer, genealogist*
Armentrout, Debra Catherine *neonatal nurse practitioner*
Bahl, Saroj Mehta *nutritionist, educator*
Battin, R. Ray (Rosabell Harriet Ray) *audiologist, neuropsychologist*
Blasingim, Charlotte Oren DeShazor *counselor, consultant*
Bowers, Paula Jean *medical/surgical nurse*
Callender, Norma Anne *psychology educator, counselor*
Cheung, Kam-Fong Monit *social worker, educator*
Chima, Felix O. *social work educator*
Cunningham, Terence Thomas, III, *hospital administrator*
Dimachkie, Mazen Mohammad *health care educator*
Duncan, Cheryl L. *critical care and cardiac catherization nurse*
Ferguson, J. Scott *quality management coordinator*
Florian-Lacy, Dorothy *therapist, educator*
Gerhart, Glenna Lee *pharmacist*
Golinkin, Webster Fowler *healthcare executive, media consultant*
†Grimes, Richard Michael *public health educator*
Gunn, Joan Marie *health care administrator*
Hanrahan, Lawrence Martin *healthcare consultant*
†Hempfling, Linda Lee *nurse*
Hilkemeyer, Renilda Estella *nurse*
Holmes, Harry Dadisman *health facility administrator*
Ingersoll, Maryann E. Patterson *health educator, holistic nurse*
Jhin, Michael Kontien *health care executive*
Koerner, Jo Ellen *health facility administrator*
Latting, Jean Kantambu *social worker, educator*
Lenox, Angela Cousineau *healthcare consultant*
Lewis, Nelda Conner *social worker, therapist*
†Mallia, Marianne Hagar *medical writer*
Minton, Melanie Sue *neuroscience nurse*
Moore, Lois Jean *health science facility administrator*
Munsell, Debra S. *physician assistant, educator*
Nora, Hope *healthcare consultant*
Park, Cheryl Antoinette *women's health nurse, educator*
Pate, Patricia Ann *women's health nurse*
Peabody, Arlene L. Howland Bayar *retired, nurse*
†Piech, Ruth Diane *nursing administrator*
Potluri, Venkateswara Rao *medical facility administrator*
Reed, Kathlyn Louise *occupational therapist, educator*
†Rives, Terry Edward *public health service officer, researcher, epidemiologist*
Robbins, Susan Paula *social work educator*
Ruppert, Susan Donna *acute/critical care nursing educator, family and adult nurse practitioner*
Schiflett, Mary Fletcher Cavender *retired health facility executive, researcher, educator*
Smith, J. Thomas *mental health consultant*
Turner, Kelley Bailey *non-profit consultant, volunteer program administrator*
Wagner, Donald Bert *health care consultant*
Windle, Pamela Evelyn *surgical nurse*
Wisecup, Barbara Jean *retired medical and surgical nurse*

Huntsville
Vick, Marie *retired health science educator*

Irving
Hicks, Allen Morley *hospital administrator*

Karnes City
Davis, Troy Arnol *reflexologist, hypnotherapist*

Keller
Patterson, Ronald R(oy) *health care systems executive*

Kerrville
Rhodes, James Devers *psychotherapist*

Killeen
Rappaport, Claudia Diane *social worker, educator*

Kingsville
Robins, James Dow *counselor*

La Porte
Levi, Janice Lawan *counselor*

Lago Vista
Garcia y Carrillo, Martha Xochitl *pharmacist*

Lake Dallas
Richardson, Wanda Louise Gibson *nurse*

Leander
Johnson, Vicki Valeen *paramedic, technical advisor movie studios*

Lubbock
Allison, Jane Shawver *medical school administrator, management consultant*
Broselow, Linda Latt *medical office technician, aviculturist*
McBeath, Don B. *health administrator*
Shaw, Gwen Ellen Grose *social worker*
Young, Teri Ann Butler *pharmacist*

Lufkin
Williams, Mary Hickman *social worker*

Mc Kinney
Thompson, Jeannine Lucille *community health nurse*

Mcallen
Tupper, Ron *public health, policy, and management educator*

Memphis
†Mahato, Ram Ishwar *pharmacist, educator*

Mesquite
Williamson, Barbara Jo *retired community health nurse, educator*

Mexia
Chambers, Linda Dianne Thompson *social worker*

Midland
Bradshaw, Troy Wayne *nurse educator*
Sullivan, Patricia G. *maternal, child and women's health nursing educator*
Syed, Elizabeth Chance *health facility administrator, critical care nurse*

Midlothian
Esberger, Karen Ann *school nurse*

Montgomery
Gooch, Carol Ann *psychotherapist consultant*

Nacogdoches
Brennan, Thomas George, Jr., *audiologist, speech-language pathologist*
Migl, Donald Raymond *therapeutic optometrist, pharmacist*

Normangee
Rector, M. Eugene *community pharmacist*

Odessa
Knox, Glenda Jane *retired health and safety specialist, educator*
Pokky, Eric Jon *clinical pharmacist*

Panhandle
Sherrod, Lloyd Bruce *nutritionist*

Pasadena
Kenagy, Cheri Lynn *nurse*
Smith, Oscar William *nursing home administrator*

Pflugerville
Schroer, Jane Hastings *nurse practitioner*

Port Arthur
Vinecour, Oneida Agnes *nurse*

Post
Warren, Jennifer Elizabeth *family nurse practitioner*

Red Oak
Jones, Genia Kay *emergency supervising nurse, consultant*

Richardson
Avadhut, HitendranandaAcarya *spiritual counselor, yoga teacher*
†Huesca Dorantes, Patricia *researcher*
†Krauss, Henry Frederick, Jr., *optometrist*
†Wylie, Mary Lucinda *healthcare administrator*

Richmond
Eversole, Sandra Joy *operating room nurse*

Roanoke
Kleinkort, Joseph Alexius *physical therapist, consultant*

Rockwall
Crooks, Patricia Kay *counselor*

Rosebud
Mey, Rindy *physician assistant*

Rusk
Cart-Rogers, Katherine Cooper *emergency nurse, nurse consultant*

San Angelo
Rivero, Magda *counselor*

San Antonio
Adcox, Mary Sandra *dietitian, consultant*
Beverly, Zylphia Marie *mental health services professional*
Bunten, Brenda Arlene *geriatrics nurse*
Champion, Michael Edward *physician assistant, clinical perfusionist*
Crabtree, Ben C. *neuromuscular therapy clinic director*
†Dacbert-Friese, Sharyn Varhely *social worker, evangelist*
†Davis, Sarah Jane *health care professional*
Fisher, Dierdre Denise *mental health nurse, administrator, educator*
Gilliland, Irene Lydia *nursing educator*
Gonzalez, Hector Hugo *nurse, educator, consultant*
Jackson, Earl, Jr., *medical technologist, retired*
†Junek, Heather Diane *medical/surgical nurse*
McCuistion, Peg Orem *hospice administrator*
Pysher, Alan Guy *nurse anesthetist*
Rojo, Ruth M. *nutritionist, alternative medicine consultant*
Schwab, Therese Mathes *nursing educator*
Skelley, Dean Sutherland *clinical laboratory administrator*
Swansburg, Russell Chester *medical administrator educator*
Walker, Mary Erline *critical care nurse*
Wood, Thomas Willard *health care industry executive*

San Marcos
Mooney, Robert Thurston *health care educator*
Watkins, Ted Ross *social work educator*

Scurry
Newkirk, Trixie Darnell *family nurse practitioner*

Southlake
Gelinas, Marc Adrien *healthcare administrator*

Sulphur Springs
Morris, Diane Baker *nurse*

Temple
Frost, Juanita Corbitt *retired hospital foundation coordinator*
Tobin, Margaret Ann *cardiac medical critical care nurse*

The Woodlands
Martineau, Julie Peperone *social worker*

Tyler
Gonzalez-Byrd, M. Teresa *physician assistant*
†Mastern, Dean Scott *personal growth and development consultant*
West, Syntha Jane Traughber *mental health services professional*

Universal City
Lamoureux, Gloria Kathleen *nurse, retired air force officer, consultant*

Victoria
†Nguyen, PeterMinh V. *pharmacist*

Waco
Corley, Carol Lee *retired school nurse*
Scott, Richard Elton *health facility administrator*

Wharton
†Medina, Debra Parker *medical/surgical nurse, consultant*

Whitney
Williams, Margaret Lu Wertha Hiett *nurse*

Willow Park
Bynumn, Jeanette Lynn *holistic health nurse*

Wortham
Lee, Gordon Kenneth *physician assistant*

Yoakum
Leahy, Lawrence Marshall *health care administrator, marketing consultant*

UTAH

Kaysville
Ashmead, Allez Morrill *speech, hearing, and language pathologist, orofacial myologist, consultant*

Layton
Hendren, Debra Mae *critical care nurse*

Logan
Wade, Kenneth Alan *physician assistant*

Ogden
Jones, Galen Ray *physician assistant*

Phelps, Robin McCann *clinical social worker*
Seager, Dauna Gayle Olson-Stokes *speech therapist*

Orem
Sauter, Gail Louise *speech pathologist*

Park City
Hallowell Schemmer, Shannon *nurse anesthetist*

Provo
Nance, Richard J. *health facility administrator, social worker*

Saint George
Chilow, Barbara Gail *social worker*

Salt Lake City
Barusch, Amanda Smith *social welfare educator, researcher*
Hull, Grafton Hazard, Jr., *social work educator*
Jorgensen, Lou Ann Birkbeck *social worker*
Kelen, Joyce Arlene *social worker*
Loewy, Kathy *social worker, therapist*
†Morris, Elizabeth Treat *physical therapist*
Schutz, Roberta Maria (Bobbi Schutz) *social worker*
Wolf, Harold Herbert *pharmacy educator*

Taylor
Atwater, Julie Demers *critical care nurse*

VERMONT

Brattleboro
Bussino, Melinda Holden *human services administrator*
Cramer, Janet French *social worker, marriage and family therapist*
Smiley, Carol Anne *home health administrator, sculptor*

Burlington
†Erno, Margaret Jean *social worker, consultant*
Mead, Philip Bartlett *healthcare administrator, obstetrician, educator*
Milliard, Aline *retired social worker*

East Thetford
Cummings Rockwell, Patricia Guilbault *psychiatric nurse*

Guilford
Gregg, Michael B. *health science association administrator, epidemiologist*

Montpelier
Erskine, Kali (Wendy Colman) *psychoanalyst*

North Ferrisburg
Tulin, Marna *psychotherapist*

Saint Johnsbury
Moore, Lisa Lynn (Lisa Lynn Marceau) *geriatrics nurse*

Shaftsbury
Dalton, Steven Paul *physician assistant*

Winooski
†Higgins, Margaret Ann *home health nurse, operating room nurse*

Woodstock
Hallock-Bannigan, Suzy *counselor, consultant, counselor educator*

VIRGINIA

Alexandria
Fisher, Donald Wayne *medical association executive*
Gormley, Dennis Michael *research scholar*
Graham, John H., IV, *health science association administrator*
Hutchison, Elizabeth Doran *social worker, educator*
†Mathias, Melvin Merle *nutrition scientist*
Penrose, Cynthia C. *retired health care consultant*

Annandale
Abdellah, Faye Glenn *retired public health service executive*

Appomattox
Morris, Dorothea Louise *nurse midwife*

Arlington
Adreon, Beatrice Marie Rice *pharmacist*
Behney, Clyde Joseph *health policy researcher*
Downing, Diane Virginia *community health nurse*
Lurie, Nicole *former health science association administrator*
May, Sterling Randolph *health association executive*
†McKeown, Marilyn Godlewski *coronary care nurse, public health researcher, consultant*
†Pfister, Karstin Ann *human services administrator*
Schneider, Clara Garbus *dietitian, nursing consultant*
Tabibi, S. Esmail *pharmaceutical researcher, educator*

Aroda
Nisly, Loretta Lynn *medical and surgical nurse, geriatrics nurse*

Ashburn
Walsh, Geraldine Frances *nursing administrator*

Big Island
Durham, Betty Bethea *therapist*

Blacksburg
Redican, Kerry John *health education educator*

Burke
Werfel, Sandra Diane *clinical social worker*

Charlottesville
Cook, Lynn J. *nursing educator*
Durr, Leslie Martina *nurse, psychotherapist*
Hanft, Ruth S. Samuels (Mrs. Herbert Hanft) *health care consultant, economist*
Hawkins, Deborah Craun *community health nurse, family practice nurse practitioner*
Hinnant, Clarence Henry, III, *health care executive*
Lyder, Courtney Harvey *nursing educator, consultant*
Pate, Robert Hewitt, Jr., *counselor educator*
†Wiggins, Barbara Sue *pharmacy clinical specialist, educator*

Chesapeake
Martin, Angela Carter *nursing educator*
Ternus, Mona Pearl *critical care nurse, flight nurse, educator*

Chester
Sadler, Charles Benjamin, Jr., *pharmacist, real estate associate, marketing professional*

Chesterfield
†Morrow, Kenneth Albert *substance abuse counselor, self-employed*

Cross Junction
Dettloff, Donna Jean *psychiatric social worker*

Culpeper
Goddard, Frances Byrd *clinical social worker*

Danville
Johnson, Gerald Lee *health facility administrator*

Duffield
Orr, Emma Jane *pharmacist, educator*

Fairfax
Knee, Ruth Irelan (Mrs. Junior K. Knee) *social worker, health care consultant*
Monahan, Danielle Joan *renal nutritionist*
Nelson, Joan Marie *social worker*
Robertson, Patricia Aileen *adult and geriatric nurse practitioner*

Fairfax Station
†Barringer, Joan Marie *counselor, educator, artist, writer*
Cary, Ann Hagan *nurse, educator, health facility administrator*

Falls Church
†Chester, Linnes Lee, Jr., *healthcare association administrator*
Fink, Charles Augustin *behavioral systems scientist*
French, John Lawrence *university educator, researcher*
Grabenstein, John Douglas *pharmacist, army officer*
Halpern, Judith *social worker*
Nulty, Mary Anne *clinical social worker*
Seifert, Patricia Clark *cardiac surgery nurse, educator, consultant*

Farmville
Terry, Wayne Gilbert *healthcare executive, hospital administrator*

Fredericksburg
Adams, Cynthia Ann *nursing administrator*
Speirs, Carol Lucille *nurse, naval officer*

Hampton
Kostel, Laura Everitt *social worker*
Kulp, Eileen Bodnar *social worker*
Reid, Anna Louise *nurse anesthetist*

Harrisonburg
Larson, Kenneth Oscar *occupational therapist*

Hopewell
Vartanian, Isabel Sylvia *retired dietitian*

Keswick
Johansen, Eivind Herbert *special education services executive, former army officer*

Lynchburg
Weimar, Robert Henry *clinical hypnotherapist*

Manassas
Lytton, Linda Rountree *marriage and family therapist, test consultant*

Mc Lean
Cuffe, Robin Jean *nursing educator*
Filerman, Gary Lewis *health educator*
Gladeck, Susan Odell *retired social worker*
Martin, Raymond S. *international health consultant*
Smith, Carey Daniel *acoustician, undersea warfare technologist*
Walsh, Marie Leclerc *nurse*

Newport News
Moore, Mildred Thorpe *dietician*
Warren, Daniel Churchman *health facility administrator*

Norfolk
Davis, Russell Haden *consultant*
Martin, Wayne A. *clinical social worker*
Rogers, Candace Marie *nursing educator*

Petersburg
Watkins, Sherry Ligon *medical facility data executive, nurse*

Radford
Carter, Kimberly Ferren *nursing educator*
Scartelli, Joseph Paul *music therapy educator, dean*

Reston
Harmon, Robert Gerald *health company executive, educator*
Kader, Nancy Stowe *nurse, consultant, bioethicist*
Norris, Susan Elizabeth *social worker*

Richmond
Barker, Thomas Carl *retired health care administration educator, executive*
Beaman, Mary Anina *psychiatric nurse, educator*
Becker, Herman Eli *retired pharmacist*
Beckett, Joyce *educator, social worker*
Bentley, Kia Jean *social worker, educator*
Cafaro, Patricia L. *nurse practitioner, nurse, clinical administrator*
†Dennis, Shay *social worker*
Fischer, Carl Robert *retired health care facility administrator*
Freund, Emma Frances *medical technologist*
†Galbis-Reig, David *health facility administrator, physician, consultant, researcher*
Gandy, Gerald Larmon *rehabilitation counseling educator, psychologist, writer*
Hardy, Richard Earl *rehabilitation counseling educator*
Johnson, Katherine Anne *health research administrator, lawyer*
McCarthy, Charles R. *bioethicist, consultant*
Neal, Gail Fallon *physical therapist, educator*
Riddick, Joseph Robert *health analyst, columnist*
Sheehan, Kathy Renee *quality improvement administrator*
White, Kenneth Ray *health administration educator, consultant*

Roanoke
Dagenhart, Betty Jane Mahaffey *nursing educator, administrator*
Duff, Doris Eileen (Doris Shull) *critical care nurse*
Kinzie, Brenda Asburry *counselor*

South Hill
Clay, Carol Ann *family nurse practitioner*

Springfield
Dake, Marcia Allene *retired nursing educator, university dean*
Williams, Cecilia Lee Pursel *optometrist*

Suffolk
†Glasson, Linda *hospital security and safety official, healthcare*

Vienna
Welters, Anthony *health services executive*

Virginia Beach
Denzler, James Wyatt *pharmacist*
Eleuterius, Nancy Lea *health administrator*
Guckert, Nora Jane Gaskill *medical and surgical nurse, hospice nurse, holistic consultant*
Wilson, Angela Saburn *nursing educator*

Wallops Island
†Myatt, Sue Henshaw *nursing home administrator*

Warrenton
Rodgers, Lynne Saunders *women's health nurse*

Williamsburg
Cappetta, Pamela Guyler *counselor*
Farrar, John Thruston *health facility administrator*
Wilson, Catherine Ann *critical care nurse, educator, health policy analyst*
Yocum, Tonia Sheets *physician assistant*

Woodbridge
Flori, Anna Marie DiBlasi *nurse anesthetist, educational administrator*
†Phillips-LeSane, Fay M. *mental health professional*

Woodstock
Kabriel, Marcia Gail *psychotherapist*

WASHINGTON

Anacortes
Kuure, Bojan Marlena *operating room nurse*

Auburn
Blum, Sarah Leah *nurse psychotherapist*
Ketchersid, Wayne Lester, Jr., *medical technologist*

Bellevue
Edwards, Kirk Lewis *medical services company executive*

Bothell
McDonald, Michael Lee *clinic administrator, retired naval officer*

Camano Island
Hartley, Celia Love *nursing consultant, writer, retired nursing educator, nursing administrator*

Centralia
Gimbel, Hervey Willis *public health physician, medical administrator*

Chehalis
Burrows, Robert Paul *optometrist*

Federal Way
Mail, Patricia Davison *public health specialist*

Gig Harbor
Larson, Maureen Inez *rehabilitation consultant*

Issaquah
Duncan, Elizabeth Charlotte *retired marriage and family therapist, educational therapist, educator*

Kennewick
†Fann, Margaret Ann *counselor*

Kirkland
Gerstman, Hubert Louis *healthcare risk manager, speech and language pathologist, audiologist, otolaryngology educator*

Lacey
Shkurkin, Ekaterina Vladimirovna (Katia Shkurkin) *social worker, educator*

Langley
Cammermeyer, Margarethe *retired medical/surgical nurse*

Long Beach
McClintock, William Thomas *long term health care administrator*

Mill Creek
O'Connell, Michael Alexander *social worker*

Oak Harbor
Miller, Robert Scott *mental health administrator, social worker*

Olympia
Boruchowitz, Stephen Alan *health policy analyst*
Coolen, Phyllis Rose *community health nurse*
Inverso, Marlene Joy *optometrist*

Port Angeles
†Barker, Barbara *registered nurse, medical researcher*
Muller, Carolyn Bue *physical therapist, volunteer*
Richmond, Mardell C. *family nurse practitioner*

Port Townsend
†Jamison, Margaret Ruth *psychotherapist, freelance/self-employed writer*

Poulsbo
Carle, Harry Lloyd *social worker*

Pullman
Baugh, Bradford Hamilton *occupational and environmental health advisor*
†Chermak, Gail D. *audiologist, educator*
†Hu, Ming *pharmaceutical scientist*

Redmond
Oaks, Lucy Moberley *retired social worker*
Sasenick, Joseph Anthony *animal health and food safety company executive*

Renton
†Darrin, Karen Irene *medical/surgical nurse, nursing administrator*
St. Hilaire, Cherie Ann *pharmacist*

Sammamish
†Marsh, B. Duane *researcher*

Seattle
†Aspinall, Cassandra Louise *social worker, researcher*
Berni, Rosemarian Rauch *rehabilitation and oncology nurse*
†Blomstrand, Doreen Kathryn *retired physician assistant*
Carter, Becky Sue *neonatal/perinatal nurse practitioner, consultant*
Czarny, Ph.D., Frank Silvey *social problems specialist, human and organizational systems consultant*
Dear, Ronald Bruce *social work educator*
de Tornyay, Rheba *nurse, former university dean, educator*
Dorpat, Theodore Lorenz *psychoanalyst*
Johnston, William Frederick *emergency services administrator*
Kolbeson, Marilyn Hopf *holistic practitioner, educator, artist, advertising executive*
Larson, Eric B. *hospital administrator*
Law, Marcia Elizabeth *counselor aide*
Monsen, Elaine Ranker *nutritionist, educator, editor*
Northen, Helen E(sther) *retired social work educator, consultant*
Perkin, Gordon Wesley *international health executive*
Perrin, Edward Burton *health services researcher, biostatistician, public health educator*
Sandahl, Bonnie Beardsley *health services executive and provider, educator*
Sellick, Kathleen A. *hospital administrator*
Thompson, Arlene Rita *nursing educator*
Wilmering, Katharine Jean *social worker, clinical nurse specialist*
Wylie, Laurie Jean *health care executive, nurse practitioner*

Seaview
McNeil, Helen Jo Connolly *nursing educator, public health administrator*

Spanaway
Campbell, Thomas J. *chiropractor, legislator*

Spokane
Cope, Kathleen Adelaide *critical care and parish nurse, educator*
Hendershot, Carol Miller *physical therapist*
Johnson, Alan M. *optometric physician*
Robinson, Herbert Henry, III, *educator, psychotherapist*

Tacoma
†Hawk, Marsha K. *health facility administrator*
Maloney, Patsy Loretta *nursing educator*
Neff Balch, Betty Marie *retired nursing educator*
Powell, Laurel Ann *social worker*

University Place
Reim, Ruthann *career and personal counselor, corporate trainer*

Vancouver
Hanbey, Teresa *healthcare executive, consultant*
Simpson, Carolyn Marie *critical care nurse*
Woodward, Jonathan Morgan *mental health specialist*

Yakima
Simonson, Susan Kay *hospital clinical care coordinator*

WEST VIRGINIA

Beckley
†Finch, Melody Renee *nurse*

Bethany
Shelek-Furbee, Katherine *social worker educator*

Bluefield
Jessee, Deborah Williams *nursing administrator*

Bridgeport
Gainer, Earl Mark *pharmacist*

Fort Gay
Napier, Michelle H. *nursing educator*

Huntington
Engle, Jeannette Cranfill *medical technologist*
Henderson, Dan W. *psychiatric therapist, educator*

Institute
†Richards, John Dale *social worker, educator, counselor*

Kearneysville
Lotze, Evie Daniel *psychodramatist*

Morgantown
Barba, Roberta Ashburn *retired social worker, writer*
Beresford, Annette Diana *researcher*
Rock, Gail Ann *obstetrical and gynecological nurse*
Smart, Suzanne D. *social worker*

Parkersburg
†Bush, Roberta B. *psychotherapist, accountant*

Princeton
Barker, Donald Dewayn *psychotherapist*

Ranson
Rudacille, Sharon Victoria *medical technologist*

Vienna
Arthur, Margaret Ferne *nurse, insurance paramedic*

Weirton
Wojnakowski, Mary Melissa *nurse anesthetist, researcher*

West Liberty
Young, Patricia Jean Hedrick *mental health nurse, educator*

Wheeling
Fox, Thomas George *health science educator*
Tucker, Gina Louise *women's health nurse*
Urval, Krishna Raj *health facility administrator, educator*

Williamsburg
Scott, Pamela Moyers *physician assistant*

WISCONSIN

Berlin
McShane, Franklin John, III, *nurse anesthetist*

Burlington
†Oestmann, Mary Jane *retired senior radiation specialist*

Chippewa Falls
Copeland, Christine Susan *therapist*

Columbus
Brinkman, Michael Owen *health care consultant, educator*

De Pere
Dykes, Kathryn A. *community health nurse, educator, administrator, gerontological nurse practitioner*

Eau Claire
Biegel, Eileen Mae *retired hospital executive*
Lippold, Judith Rosenthal *retired occupational therapist*

Franklin
†Rauschenberger, Margaret Ann *nursing educator*

Germantown
Reichert, Julie Anne *registered nurse, medical transcriptionist*

Green Bay
Manske, Lynn Darlene *surgical nurse*
Mervilde, Michael John *clinical social worker*

Greendale
Bull, Margaret Jane *nurse educator*

Greenfield
Nelson, Kay Ellen *speech and language pathologist*

Highland
Kreul, Carol Ann *nurse*

Madison
Berven, Norman Lee *counselor, psychologist, educator*
Brennan, Patricia Flatley *nursing educator, systems engineering educator*
Derzon, Gordon M. *hospital administrator*
Faith, Tristan *counselor*
Gavin, Mary Jane *medical and surgical nurse*
†Gurney, Mary Kathleen *pharmacist*
Johnson, Jean Elaine *nursing educator*
Maersch, Nancy Kay *health facility administrator*
Migas, Rosalie Ann *social worker*
Schmidt, Cheryl A. Zeise *family practice nurse practitioner*
Wertsch, Paul Anthony *family physician, medical administrator*

Manawa
Koehler, Carol Jean *nurse*

Manitowoc
Shimek, Rosemary Geralyn *medical/surgical nurse*

Marshfield
McCarty, John Edward *medical clinic administrator*
Wesbrook, Frederic P. *health facility administrator, physician*

Menasha
Mahnke, Kurt Luther *psychotherapist, clergyman*

Menomonee Falls
DeBoer, Bernice Mary *nurse*
Janzen, Norine Madelyn Quinlan *medical technologist*

Mequon
Beaudry, Diane Fay Puta *medical quality management executive*

Milwaukee
Brideau, Leo Paul *healthcare executive*
Cohn, Lucile *psychotherapist, nurse*
Coogan, Frank Neil *health and social services administrator*
Dye, Sharon Elizabeth Herndon *speech pathologist*
Ferguson, Nancy L. *social worker, psychotherapist*
†Fluharty, George Mark *speech pathology/audiology services professional*
Frank, Dennis *psychotherapist, educator*
Frittitta, Peter Anthony *health maintenance organization executive*
Harvieux, Anne Marie *psychotherapist*
Heim, Kathryn Marie *psychiatric nurse, author*
Herr, Sister Annette Ellen *pharmacist*
Murphy, Josephine Mancuso *critical care nurse, adult nurse practitioner*
†Platt, Jeb Buchanan *health facility administrator*
Silverman, Franklin Harold *speech pathologist, educator*
†Tillett, Jacquelynn *nurse midwife*
Waller, Mary Bellis *psychotherapist, education educator, consultant*

Minocqua
Jaye, David Robert, Jr., *retired hospital administrator*

New Berlin
Winkler, Dolores Eugenia *retired health facility administrator*

Oconomowoc
Schacht, Ruth Elaine *nursing educator*

Port Washington
Kettling, Virginia *health facility administrator*

Racine
Singh, Susan Marie *medical/surgical nurse*

Rhinelander
Van Brunt-Bartholomew, Marcia Adele *social worker*

River Falls
Hayden, Paul Allan *speech pathology educator, consultant, researcher*

Superior
Rodne, Kjell John *healthcare administrator*

Tomah
Hillman, Lin (Linda Lou Hillman) *nursing administrator*

Verona
Moynihan, Carolyn Jean *clinical social worker*

Watertown
Degnitz, Dorothy Elsie *retired nurse*

Waukesha
Wallskog, Joyce Marie *nursing educator, psychologist*

Wausau
Gau-Krueger, Susan Marie *social worker*

West Allis
Fiorelli, Karen Lynn *registered nurse*

West Bend
Dries, Kathleen Marie *social worker*

Whitefish Bay
Nortman, M. Judith Haworth *geriatrics nurse*

Whitehall
Nordhagen, Hallie Huerth *nursing home administrator*

Whitewater
Kirst-Ashman, Karen Kay *social work educator*

WYOMING

Aladdin
Brunson, Mabel (Mabel Dipper) *researcher*

Bondurant
Ellwood, Paul Murdock, Jr., *health policy analyst, consultant*

Hanna
Turner, Lillian Erna *retired nurse*

Jackson Hole
Farkas, Carol Garner *nurse, administrator*

Laramie
Renaud, Paula Marie *researcher*

Rock Springs
Garrison, Kathleen Marie *social worker*

TERRITORIES OF THE UNITED STATES

GUAM

Yigo
Duenas, Laurent Flores *health and nursing consultant*

PUERTO RICO

Bayamon
†Quinones, Areliz *counselor*

Fajardo
Millan, Alvin *speech pathology/audiology services professional, educator*

Luquillo
Pinney, Frances Bailey *art therapist, artist, consultant*

San Juan
Gonzalez, Michael John *nutrition scientist, nutriologist*

VIRGIN ISLANDS

Saint Thomas
Clark, Jessie Dona *social worker*

CANADA

ALBERTA

Calmar
Tomaszeski, Josephine Gallas *retired nursing educator*

Edmonton
Fields, Anthony Lindsay Austin *health facility administrator, oncologist, educator*

BRITISH COLUMBIA

Burnaby
Yip, Chi Yan Toby *social worker, journalist, researcher*

Vancouver
Gilbert, John Humphrey Victor *speech scientist, educator*
Riedel, Bernard Edward *retired pharmaceutical sciences educator*

NEW BRUNSWICK

Sussex
Secord, Lloyd Douglas *healthcare administrator*

ONTARIO

Brantford
Inns, Harry Douglas Ellis *retired optometrist*

Etobicoke
Scholefield, Peter Gordon *health agency executive*

Owen Sound
Jones, Phyllis Edith *nursing educator*

Red Lake
McGeorge, Ronald Kenneth *hospital executive*

Toronto
McRae, Marion Eleanor *critical care nurse*
Phillips, Robert Allan *scientist, administrator*

QUEBEC

Montreal
Messing, Karen *occupational health researcher*
Scriver, Charles Robert *medical scientist, human geneticist*

MEXICO

Reynosa
†Asomoza, Miguel A. *researcher, educator*

AUSTRALIA

Perth
Riley, Richard Haydn *anaesthetist, researcher*

CHANNEL ISLANDS

Guernsey
Schere, Jean *researcher*

COLOMBIA

Cali
Rao, Idupulapati Madhusudana *plant nutritionist, plant physiologist*

DENMARK

Vejle
Vagn-Hansen, Carsten Peter Mathias *health consultant, physician*

ENGLAND

Bournemouth
Pritchard, Colin *social work educator*

Greenwich London
de Savorgnani, Adriane Aldrich *health care administrator, nurse*

Liverpool
Barr, Wally *social worker, researcher*

Oxford
†Da'Luz Vieira, Lorraine Christine C. *acupuncturist, researcher*

Tunbridge Wells
Singer, Norbert *health services professional, education consultant*
Kingsley, James Gordon *college administrator*

ISRAEL

Jerusalem
Macarov, David *former social work educator*
Pantel-Bakst, Sharon S. *social worker*

JAPAN

Abiko Chiba
Sakaguchi, Takehiro *health educator, researcher*

Chofu Tokyo
Sayama, Hiroki *researcher*

Nagoya
Kojima, Akinori *public health counselor, pathologist*

Tokyo
†Murray, Julia Kaoru (Mrs. Joseph E. Murray) *occupational therapist*

REPUBLIC OF KOREA

Taegu
Kim, Doohie *retired public health educator*

SWITZERLAND

Geneva
Maglacas, A. Mangay *nursing researcher, educator*

Versoix
Mahler, Halfdan Theodor *physician, health organization executive*

TAIWAN

Kaohsiung
Chien, Yie W. *pharmaceutical science educator, university dean*

Taipei
†Huang, Hertz *market researcher, statistician*

ZAMBIA

Nangoma
Hansen, Florence Marie Congiolosi (Mrs. James S. Hansen) *social worker*

ADDRESS UNPUBLISHED

†Aalberts, Nola Jean *social worker, administrator*
Abbott, Regina A. *neurodiagnostic technologist, consultant, business owner*
Abernathy, Ronald Fittz *pharmacist*
Abernathy, Vicki Marie *retired nurse*
Ackerson, Barry James *social worker*
Adams, Corlyn Holbrook *nursing facility administrator*
†Adams, Jocelia *oncological nurse, educator*
Adducci, Regina Marie *medical/surgical nurse*
Adekson, Mary Olufunmilayo *therapist, counselor educator*
Alberico, Salvatore J. *psychiatric social worker, educator, researcher*
†Alberts, Renée Miller *substance abuse and mental health professional*
Alcantara, Felicisima Garcia *dietitian, nutrition consultant*
Alfonso, Roberta Jean *emergency room nurse*
Allen, Bonnie Lynn *optometrist*
Allen, Jocleta Dalton *retired social worker, writer*
Allen, Joyce Doyle *social worker, preschool and elementary educator*
Allison, Donna M. (Donna Maughan) *critical care nurse*
Alvarez-Galloso, Roberto C. *mental health professional*
Ambrosi, Sandra Elizabeth *retired nurse, educator*
Ambrosio, Deborah Ann *critical care nurse*
Amspacher, John Clair Elder *retired human services manager*
Anderson, Dorothy Fisher *social worker, psychotherapist*
Anderson, Laurie Ann *critical care nurse*
Anderson, Lois D. *nursing administrator, mental health nurse*
Andes, Phoebe Cabotaje *retired women's health nurse, educator*
Andrau, Maya Hedda *physical therapist*
†Angermeier, Patricia *occupational therapist*
Angst, Karen K. *mental health nurse, hospice nurse*
Angus, Robert Carlyle, Jr., *naturopathic physician, health administrator*
Antoun, Mikhail *medicinal chemistry and pharmacognosy educator*
Appelbaum, Michelle Gellman *family nurse practitioner*
Arnold, Deborrah Ann *human services director*
Arnold, Jean Ann *health science facility administrator*
Atal, Bishnu Saroop *retired speech research executive*
Atamian, Susan *nurse*
Autrey, Kathy W. *social worker*
Babitzke, Theresa Angeline *health facility administrator*
Backer, Joanne Arlene *case manager*
Baeza, Cheryl Anne *psychiatric social worker*
Bagstad, Kristin Kim *pediatric nurse practitioner*
Baier, Edward John *former public health official, industrial hygiene engineer, consultant*
Bailey, Carla Lynn *nursing administrator*
Bailey-Stein, Deena Tamara *health care administrator*
Bain, Diane Martha D'Andrea *clinical nurse specialist in critical care*
Baldwin, Deanna Louise *dietitian*
Baldwin, William Russell *optometrist, foundation executive*
Ball, John Robert *healthcare executive*
Banks, David Russell *former health care executive*
Barbakow, Jeffrey C. *former healthcare industry executive*
Barfield, Stewart Bayne *counseling therapist*
Barker, Virginia Lee *nursing educator*
Barrett, Jessica (Donna Ann Nipert) *psychotherapist*
Barrett, Lisa Marie *acupuncture physician, herbologist, hypnotherapist*
Barshis, Victoria R. Garnier *social worker*
Bartels, Betty Jane *nurse*
Bartlett-Powers, John David *social worker, elementary education educator*
Basinger, Karen Lynn *renal dietitian*
Bass, Lynda D. *retired medical/surgical nurse, retired nursing educator*
Batalden, Paul Bennett *pediatrician, health care educator*
Baumann-Sinacore, Patricia Lynn *nursing administrator*
†Baxter, Decima Christine *hospital administrator, military officer*
†Bear, Geraldine M. *nursing assistant, poet*
Beaton, Meredith *enterostomal therapy clinical nurse specialist*
Becich, Raymond Brice *healthcare consultant, mediator, trainer, educator*
Belco, Karen Marie *cardiology nurse*
Bell, Dorothy Frances *nurse, educator*
Bell, Karen June *critical care nurse*
Bell, Rebecca *psychotherapist, journalist*
Bell, Susan Jane *nurse*
Belles, Donald Arnold *pastoral therapist, mental health counselor*
Belmont, Larry Miller *retired public health executive*
Belonick, Cynthia Ann *psychiatric-mental health nurse*
Benford, Anne Michele (Anne Sass) *pediatric nurse practitioner, clinical nurse specialist*
Bennett, Geraldine Eudora (Jerrie Bennett) *mental health services professional, nursing educator*
Bennett, Harriet Cook *social worker, educator*
Bennett, R. Dawn *social worker*
Berger, Anita Hazel *psychotherapist, adult educator, organizational consultant*
Berger, Miriam Roskin *creative arts therapy director, educator, therapist*
Berger-Kraemer, Nancy *speech and language pathologist, artist*
Berkley, Gail Winnick *psychotherapist*
Berman, Richard Angel *health and educational administrator*
Bern, Lynda Kaplan *women's health and pediatric nurse*
Berner, Judith *mental health nurse*
Berry, Leora Mary *school nurse*
Berry, Omega Makeece *nursing assistant*
†Berry, Winifred L. *medical technologist*
Bertram, Susan *rehabilitation counselor*
Biegel, David Eli *social worker, educator*
Bieron, Louise T. *physician placement executive*
†Bizzell, Mary Ann *counselor*
Blacher, Joan Helen *psychotherapist, educator*
Blackson, Benjamin F(ranklin) *clinical social worker*
Blauvelt, Barbara Louise *nutritionist*
Bloom, Jill Elizabeth *physician assistant*
Blumberg, Mark Stuart *health services researcher*
Blume, Arthur Walter, IV, *addictive behaviors researcher, therapist*
Blummer, Kathleen Ann *counselor*
Blunck, Klaire Darlene *nurse*
Bockius, Ruth Bear *nursing educator*
Boggs, Robert Wayne *human services administrator, consultant*
Boldt, Patricia C. *social worker*
Bolton, Julia Gooden *human services administrator*
Borg, Ruth I. *home nursing care provider*
Borgstahl, Kaylene Denise *health facility administrator*
†Borish, Irvin Max
Boyd, Robert Carr, Jr., *fire fighter, paramedic, graduate student*
Boyle, Marylou Olsen *nursing administrator*
Bradford, David Paul *psychotherapist*
Bragiel, Sue A. *social work educator, clinical practitioner*
Brame, Marillyn A. *hypnotherapist*
†Brauer, Donna Jeanne *nursing educator, researcher*
Brault, G. Lorain *healthcare executive*
Braun, Mary Lucile Dekle (Lucy Braun) *therapist, consultant, counselor, educator*
Brawner, Nancy Jayne *social worker, psychotherapist*
Breen, Janice DeYoung *health services executive, community health nurse*
Breslin, Evalynne Louise Wood-Robertson *retired psychiatric nurse*
Breza, Kevin S. *wellness consultant, writer*
Briggs, Janet Marie Louise *nurse practitioner*
Bristol, Louise Fitzgerald *educator, retired nurse*
Brodie, Alice Velma *health and ethics advocate*
†Bronson, Carol E. *administrative health facility coordinator*
†Bronzi, Philip A. *social worker, educator*
Brosz, Margaret Headley *pediatrics nurse*
†Broten, Robert Gary *optician, writer*
Brouse, Virginia May (Ginny Brouse) *retired rehabilitation nurse*
†Brown, April Schlea *pharmacist*
Brown, Barbara June *hospital and nursing administrator*
Brown, Billye Jean *retired nursing educator*
Brown, Deborah A. *social worker, therapist*
Brown, Geraldine *nurse, freelance writer*
Brown, Lynda Nell *nursing educator*
Brown, Stephen Hayze, Jr., *human services caseworker*
Brown, Steven Bernard *counselor*
†Brownlee, June McGaugh *health facility administrator*
Bruno, Barbara Altman *social worker*
Bryant, Bertha Estelle *retired nurse*
†Bryant, Veronica Maria *hospital administrator, writer*
Buchbinder, Sharon Bell *health care management educator*
Bullough, Vern LeRoy *sexologist, historian, nursing educator, researcher*
Bundy, Mary Lothrop *retired clinical social worker*
Burke, Grace Dora Reynolds *medical/surgical nurse*
Buzard, James Albert *healthcare management consultant*
Byers, Steven John *health facility administrator*
Byington, Diane B. *social work educator*
†Byrd, Lorenda Sue *nursing administrator*
Byrne, Carol Cunkle *medical/surgical nurse*
Cabanas, Elizabeth Ann *nutritionist, educator*
Calsbeek, Franklin *health promotion educator*
Cameron, Mary Emily *pediatrics nurse, nursing researcher*
Campbell, Claire Patricia *nurse practitioner, educator*
Campbell, Edward Wallace *nutritionist*
Canarina, Opal Jean *nurse, administrator, educator, consultant, lecturer*
†Capozziello, Martha M. *medical/surgical nurse*
Carlson, Deanna Lynn *social worker*
Carman, Susan Hufert *nurse coordinator*
†Carrington, Arese U. *medical doctor, public health consultant*
Carruthers, Claudelle Ann *occupational and physical therapist*
†Carson, Mary Silvano *career counselor, educator*
Carson, Regina E. *healthcare administrator, geriatric specialist, pharmacist, educator*
Cash, Deanna Gail *retired nursing educator*
Cason, Nica Virginia *nursing educator*
Caspy, Barbara Jane *social worker*
Castleman, Breaux Ballard *health management company executive*
Cates, Coral J. Hansen *nurse practitioner, respiratory therapist*
Cauthorne-Burnette, Tamera Dianne *family nurse practitioner, healthcare consultant*
Ceasor, Augusta Casey *medical technologist, microbiologist, research scientist*
Cecil, Maxine *critical care nurse*
Centafont, Lucy Ann Alexander *occupational therapy consultant*
Cesario, Sandra Kay *women's health nurse, educator, researcher*
Chait, Fay Klein *health administrator*
Chambers, Judith Tarnpoll *speech pathologist, audiologist*
†Chambers-Steinberg, Wanda *researcher*
Chamings, Patricia Ann *nurse, educator*
†Chazhur, Bess John *health facility administrator*
Child, Carroll Cadell *research nursing administrator*
Chin, Jennifer Young *public health educator*
Chirikos, Thomas N. *healthcare economics educator*
Chodorow, Nancy Julia *psychotherapist*
Chojnowski, Donna Applegate *cardiac nursing administrator*
Cholewka, Patricia Anne *health services administrator*
Chow, Rita Kathleen *nursing consultant*
Christiansen, David K. *healthcare administrator*
Christman, Virginia Reece *physician assistant*
Clark, Patricia Maye *oncology nurse*
Clauser, Angela Frances *medical surgical, pediatrics and geriatrics nurse*
Clayton, Paul Douglas *health care administrator*
Clecak, Dvera Vivian Bozman *psychotherapist*
Coate, David Edward *acoustician, consultant*
†Coffey, Mary Margaret *pharmacist*
Cohen, Norman Girard *retired social worker*
Colangelo, James Joseph *psychotherapist*
Colburn, Nancy Douglas *social worker, educator*
Coleman, Jean Black *nurse, physician assistant*
Colline, Marguerite Richnavsky *maternal, women's health and pediatrics nurse*
Collins, E. Dorlee (E. Dorlee Woodyard) *business counselor*
Collins, Melissa Ann *oncological nurse*
Condry, Robert Stewart *retired hospital administrator*
Conley, Sarah Ann *health facility administrator*
Conley Riedy, Mary Therese *peri-operative nurse*
Conner, Natalie Ann *community health nurse specialist*
Consiglio, Helen *nursing educator and consultant*
Cook, Chequetta Lynn Favors *nurse*
Cooper, Erlyne S. *social worker*
Cooper, Eugene Bruce *speech, language pathologist, educator*
Cooper, Signe Skott *retired nurse educator*
Cortright, Louise Vera *retired medical technologist, small business owner*
†Cosby, Stephanie Bennett *health services professional*
Coté, Kathryn Marie *psychotherapist, stress management educator*
Cotruvo, Joseph Alfred *environmental and public health consultant*
Couch, Daniel Michael *healthcare executive*
Couchman, Robert George James *human services consultant*
Courtney, Sheryl *rehabilitation nurse, consultant*
Cox, John Curtis *healthcare and educational administrator*
Cox, William Frederick *hospital executive*
Craig, Carol Mills *marriage, family and child counselor*
†Crimlisk, Janet Therese *pulmonary clinical nurse specialist, educator*
Crocker, Barbara Jean *clinical nurse specialist*
Cromwell, Florence Stevens *occupational therapist*
†Cushman, Oris Mildred *retired nurse, hospital education director*
da Fonseca, Augusto J. *social worker*
†Dahl, Corey Shane *physical therapist*
Daly-Gawenda, Debra *health facility administrator, nursing educator*
Danto, Elizabeth Ann *social worker, educator*
Darkovich, Sharon Marie *nurse administrator*
Daus, Victoria Lynn *nurse midwife*
Davidow, Jenny Jean *counselor, writer*
Davidson, Ardeth Anderson *nurse, poet, writer*
†Davis, Ada Romaine *nursing educator*
Davis, Carolyne Kahle *health care consultant*
†Davis, Elba Lucila *veterans affairs nurse*
Davis, Margaret Thacker *retired critical care, medical and surgical nurse*
Davis, Teresann Weller *social worker*
Dawson, Karen Oltmanns *nursing educator*
Day, Angela Riddle *occupational health nurse, educator*
Day, Anne White *retired nurse*
De Antoni, Edward Paul *lab administrator*
DeBello, Marguerite Catherine *oncological nurse*
DeBrincat, Susan Jeanne *nutritionist*
Decker, Cynthia J. Schafer *community and occupational health nurse*
Deely, Maureen Cecelia *community health nurse*
Deemer, Albert Earl *social worker, director*
Dejewski, Deborah Elizabeth *pharmacist*
Dell, Thomas Charles *nurse anesthetist*
†DeMille, Dale Esther *medical/surgical nurse, educator*
De Roest, Jan Marie *mental health counselor*
DeShazer, Ruth Shomler *health facility administrator, consultant*
Desselle, Debra Duke *social worker*
Dianto, Linda Christine *therapeutic activities coordinator, administrator*
†Diaz-Zubieta, Ana Maria *social worker*
DiCarlo, Laurette Mary *nurse*
Dickens, Alycia Thompson *nurse practitioner*
Diedrick, Geraldine Rose *retired nurse*
DiMatteo, Rhonda Lynn *speech-language pathologist, audiologist*
†Dimengo, Josephine *medical/surgical nurse*
Dincecco, Jennie Elizabeth Williams *healthcare administrator, mentor, volunteer*
Dodds, Brenda Kay *nurse*
Dogoloff, Lee Israel *clinical social worker, psychotherapist, consultant*
Donahue, Patricia Toothaker *retired social worker, administrator*
Doniger, Jay *health information executive*
†Donnelly, Paja Lee *nursing educator and nurse practitioner*
Donnelly-Kempf, Moira Ann *nursing administrator*
Donovan, Dorothy Diane *adult nurse practitioner*
Donovan, Marion Conran *school social worker*
Doorenbos, Judy Tucker *cardiology critical care nurse*
Doucette, Betty *public and community health and geriatrics nurse*
Dove, Lorraine Faye *gerontology nurse*
Downs, Kathleen Anne *health facility administrator*
Dozier, Nancy Kerns *retired geriatrics nurse*
Dressel, Irene Emma Ringwald *alcoholism and family therapist*
Drews, Jürgen *pharmaceutical researcher*
Dreyfuss, John Alan *retired health facility administrator*
Dudash, Karen Shreffler *community health nurse*
Duffy, Mary Kathleen *neonatal nurse*
Dukes, Deborah Feagans *counselor, administrator*
Dumas, Sandra Lee *medical technologist, microbiologist*
Duncombe, Patricia Warburton *retired social worker*
Dungan, Gloria Kronbeck *critical care nurse*
Dunmeyer, Sarah Louise Fisher *retired health care consultant*
Dunn, Patricia C. *retired social work educator*
Dyer, Wayne Walter *psychologist, writer, radio and television personality*
†Eason, Karen E. *public health service officer, researcher*
†Eaton, Shirley M. *medical/surgical nurse*
Eaves, Sandra Austra *social worker*
Edelsberg, Sally Comins *physical therapy educator and administrator*
Edelstein, Rosemarie (Rosemarie Hublou) *medical/surgical nurse, educator, medical and legal consultant*
Edrington, Sue Ellen *critical care nurse*
Edwards, Sharon Jane *nurse*
Eichel, Edward William *psychotherapist, painter*
Eimers, Jeri Anne *retired therapist*
Eisner, Eleanor *social worker*
Elliott-Zahorik, Bonnie *nurse, administrator*
Ellstrom-Calder, Annette *research consultant*
Emerson, Ann Parker *dietitian*
Emma, Lynne Anne *healthcare administrator*
†Empey, Kerry McGarr *pharmacist*
Ernzen, Mary Anne *women's health nurse, clinical nurse specialist*
†Esparza, Monica *nursing administrator*
Farrington, Bertha Louise *retired nursing administrator*
Feathers, Gail M. Wratny *social worker*
†Fecht-Gramley, Mary E. *trauma specialist, health facility educator*
Fehr, Lola Mae *health organization administrator*
Felhofer, Marylouise Katherine *nursing administrator*
Ferreira, Linda Doreen *long term, acute care and rehabilitation nurse*
Fields, Velma Archie *medical/surgical nurse*
Finder-Stone, Patricia Ann *nurse, health educator, volunteer*
†Findling, Rhonda Barbara *psychotherapist*
Fischer, Linda Marie *nursing educator*
Fittro, Ronald G., Jr., *healthcare executive, consultant*
Fitts, Janet Sue *emergency nurse practitioner, educator, homeschool educator, cosmetics executive, consultant*
Fitzgerald-Verbonitz, Dianne Elizabeth *healthcare executive*
Fiume, Barbara Parenty *social worker*
†Fogelman, Ann Florence *nutritionist, consultant*
Fountain, Linda Kathleen *health science association executive*
Franciosa, Joseph Anthony *health care consultant*
Fredericks, Joan DeLanoy *retired health science administrator*
Fredrichs, Anne Marie Johnson *pediatric nurse practitioner*
Freese, Barbara Tapp *nursing educator*
Frohlichstein, Alan *retinal angiographer*
†Froiland, Kathryn Grace *nursing educator*
Fuller, Margaret Jane *medical technologist*
Fuller, Richard Kenneth *retired alcohol/drug abuse services professional*
Gabriel, Judith A. *bodywork therapist, educator, writer*
Gallaher, Frederick Blake *public health specialist*
Gandy, Bonnie Sergiacomi *oncological and intravenous therapy nurse*
Garbacz, Patricia Frances *school social worker, therapist*
Gardner, Clyde Edward *healthcare executive, consultant, educator*
Gardner, Nancy Augustine *researcher*
Garrett, Roberta Kampschulte *nurse*
Garrett, Shirley Gene *nuclear medicine technologist*

†Ongkingco, Florence Kagahastian *health facility educator*
O'Quinn, Nancy Diane *nurse, educator, consultant*
†Osborn, Alison *nurse midwife*
Otis, Jack *social work educator*
Owens, John Franklin *health care administrator, consultant, nurse*
Oxyer, Mina Jane Stevens *nurse*
Ozbolt, Judy G. *nursing educator*
Paine, Susan Mary *pharmacist*
Palombo, Joseph *clinical social worker*
Papadopoulos, Patricia Marie *healthcare professional*
Pargament, Frances P. *social worker, psychotherapist*
†Parker, Christopher Shannon *public health service officer, writer*
Parker, Joyce Steinfeld *social worker*
Parker, Susan Brooks *healthcare executive*
Parkman, Cynthia Ann *medical and surgical nurse, nursing educator*
Paskawicz, Jeanne Frances *pain specialist*
Pastizzo, Gary F. *physician assistant*
Patton, Susan Oertel *clinical social worker, educator*
Paul, Evelyn Rose *critical care nurse*
Peabody, Sylvia Rockwood *retired community health nurse, agency administrator*
Pegues, June Allen *social work educator*
Pelletier, Nancy Anne *obstetrical and gynecological nurse, educator*
Penachio, Anthony Joseph, Jr., *psychotherapist, hypnotherapist, behavioral therapist*
Pepelea, Kimberli Rae *case manager*
Pepper, Dorothy Mae *nurse*
Perinelli, Marguerite Rose *women's health nurse, educator*
Peters, Carol Ann Dudycha *counselor*
Peters, Douglas Alan *medical-legal consultant, appeals analyst*
Peterson, Sharon L. *community health nurse*
Petow, Joan Claudia *orthopedic nurse*
Phillips, Juanita M. *maternal/women's health and neonatal nurse*
Phillips, Marrise Mason *clinical research coordinator*
Pierce, Benedict Enol *social worker*
†Pierce, John Thomas *industrial hygienist, clinical toxicologist*
Pierce, Shaheeda Laura *midwife, consultant*
†Pike, Mary L. *school nurse practitioner*
Pipchick, Margaret Hopkins *advance practice nurse, marriage and family therapist*
Pippin, Linda Sue *pediatrics nurse, educator*
Pisciotta, Vivian Virginia *psychotherapist*
Pitasi, Judy *nurse*
Pitts, Deborah Krueger *healthcare consultant*
Plummer, Carol Ann *social worker*
†Poleshuk, Alicia L. *alcohol/drug abuse services professional*
Poulton, Roberta Doris *nurse, consultant*
Pozek, Kathleen Dianne *nurse*
Pratt, Barbara Dahl *nurse*
Preszler, Sharon Marie *psychiatric home health nurse*
Prettyman-Baker, Sheila *pediatrics, neonatal nurse*
†Price, Donna B. *special education services professional*
Price, J(ohn) Douglas *human services administrator*
†Prince, Jonathan *medical technician*
Prisco, Frank J. *psychotherapist*
Prominski, Eileen Alice *school nurse, educator*
Przybylski, Sandra Marie *speech pathologist*
Ptasinski, Carol Mary *nurse, educator*
Pucek, Anthony J. *psychiatric nurse practitioner*
Puderbaugh, Kathleen Annette *maternal/women's health nurse practitioner*
Pursley-Crotteau, M. Suzanne *psychiatric nurse, substance abuse professional*
Quaife, Marjorie Clift *retired nursing educator*
Quattrone-Carroll, Diane Rose *clinical social worker*
†Quilala, Joanna Caneda *physician assistant, researcher*
Quiroz, Carole Elizabeth *nurse anesthetist*
Ragsdale, Richard Elliot *healthcare management executive*
Rainey, Claude Gladwin *retired health care executive*
Rand, Joella Mae *retired nursing educator, counselor*
†Randolph, Donald Phillip *nurse anesthetist*
Rawls, Nancy Lee Stirk *nursing educator*
Reber, Cheryl Ann *consultant, social worker, trainer*
Recine, Judy Ann *medical/surgical nurse*
Redburn, Amber Lynne *nurse*
Reed, Scott Warren *respiratory therapist, consultant*
Reeves, Nancy Alice *critical care nurse*
†Reichert, Marc G. *pharmacist*
Reilly, Robert Joseph *counselor*
Reisch, Michael Stewart *social work educator, political organization worker*
Repko, Lisa *medical/surgical nurse*
Requénez, Eunice Loida *medical, surgical, and community nurse*
Reynolds, Elizabeth Burson *social worker*
Reynolds, Ellen Aaker *pediatric nurse practitioner*
Reynolds, Louise Maxine Kruse *retired school nurse*
Ricci, Mary Jean *community health nurse, educator*
Richburg, Billy Keith *healthcare manager, consultant, entrepreneur*
Riddle, Marnita Marie *medical nurse*
Ries, Barbara Ellen *alcohol and drug abuse services professional*
Riikonen, Charlene Boothe *international health administrator*
Rindone, Joseph Patrick *clinical pharmacist, educator*
Ringo, Betty Penfold *hypnotherapist*
Rinker, Marianne Marie *rehabilitation nurse*
Ritter, Elise Dawn *therapist, clinical social worker, writer*
Ritter, Madeliene *practical nurse, surgical technologist*
Rizzi, Teresa Marie *speech and language pathologist*
Robbins, Dennis Alan *health services executive, educator*
Robinette, Betty Lou *retired occupational health and infection control nurse*
Robinson, Angela Tomei *clinical laboratory technologist, laboratory manager*
Robinson, Gail Patricia *retired mental health counselor*
Robinson, Glenda Carole *pharmacist*
Robinson, William Andrew *health service executive, physician*
Rochette, Ann Robinson *clinical manager*
Rock, Barry David *social work educator*
Rodriguez, Donna Jeanne Anglin *dietitian, writer*
Roesler, Rose Pieper *retired geriatrics nurse*
Rohde, Tamera Annette *oncological nurse*
Roper, Sally Ann *health facility administrator*
Rose, Joan Marie *medical/surgical nurse*
Rosenblum, Elizabeth Parker *retired statistical consultant, nurse*
Rosenstein, Mary Elisabeth Mallory *retired clinical social worker*
Rosenthal, Carla *medical/surgical nurse*
†Ross, Wendi N. *women's health nurse*
Rothman, Juliet Cassuto *social work educator, writer*
Rothstein, Gloria *social worker*
Rountree, Ruthann Louise *social worker, lecturer*
Rowles, Arlene Beverly *geriatric social program administrator*
Ruskaup, Calvin *therapist, history professor*
Saad, Barbara T. *occupational health nurse, administrator*
Saari, Joy Ann *family nurse practitioner, geriatrics medical and surgical nurse*
Sabatini, Nelson John *health care executive*
Sacaccio, Margaret Mary *critical care, geriatrics nurse*
Sadler, Sallie Inglis *psychotherapist*
Sailer, Ruth Luckenbill *retired women's health nurse*
Salatino, David *critical care nurse*
Salerno, Sister Maria *nursing educator, adult and gerontological nurse*
Salts, Nancy Lee *critical care, emergency nurse*
Samuels, Marc *health care consultant*
Sanders, Judith Brown *clinical nurse specialist*
†Sandorsen, Cassiopeia *public health service officer*
Santina, Dalia *nutritionist, writer*
Santos, Lisa Wells *critical care nurse*
Sardeson, Lynda Schultz *nurse, parish nurse, diabetes educator*
Sastrowardoyo, Teresita Manejar *nurse*
Savoy, Suzanne Marie *advanced practice nurse*
Sawyer-Morse, Mary Kaye *nutritionist, educator*
Scala, James *health care industry consultant, writer*
†Scarlett, Novlin Rose *public health nurse, educator*
Schlachter, Kathleen *community health administrator, director*
Schoenberg, April Mindy *nursing administrator*
Schuch, Cynthia Silleck *nurse*
Schulte, Timothy J. *psychologist, counselor, educator, consultant*
Schwartz, Ilene *psychotherapist*
Schwartz, Michael Robinson *health facility administrator*
Schwartz, Stephen Wayne *critical care, emergency and recovery room nurse*
Scott, Justine Ford *counselor, educator*
Seeman, Isadore *human services administrator, consultant*
Shanks, Kathryn Mary *health care administrator*
Shannon, Mary Lou *adult health nursing educator*
Shapiro, David Benjamin *researcher*
Shapiro, Marcia Haskel *speech and language pathologist*
Shaw, Ann *social worker, educator*
Sheaffer, Suzanne Frances *geriatrics nurse*
Shedlock, Kathleen Joan Petrouskie *community health and research nurse*
Shippy, Cynthia Leslie *mental health nurse*
Shrembek, Carol Rose *critical care nurse, writer*
Siebenaler, Rita Reilly *clinical social worker, consultant*
Siegel, Mary-Ellen *social worker, psychotherapist, author*
Sievers, Ann Elisabeth Furiel *clinical nurse specialist in otolaryngology*
Silverman, Ellen-Marie *speech and language pathologist*
Silvers, Ann *peri-operative nurse, educator*
†Silvio, Heather *social worker*
Simms, Maria Ester *health services administrator*
Simonson, Steven Neil *psychotherapist*
Simpson, Jack Benjamin *medical technologist, business executive*
Simpson, John Noel *healthcare administrator*
Sinclair, Sara Voris *health facility administrator, nurse*
Skarda, Richard Joseph *clinical social worker*
Skoglund, Elizabeth Ruth *marriage and family therapist*
Skrocki, Edmund Stanley, II, *health fair promoter, executive*
Slaughter, Djuanique Naté *healthcare analyst, consultant*
Smith, Barbara Anne *healthcare management company consultant*
Smith, Barbara Dail *school nurse*
Smith, Ethel Farrington *retired social worker, genealogist, writer*
Smith, Helen Marie *social worker, hospital administrator*
Smith, Melissa Christine-Mary *flight nurse*
Smith, Paula Marion *urology and medical/surgical nurse*
Sneider, Joyce Pappachristou *dietitian, educator*
Snyder, Dorothy Z. *social worker*
Sollars, Candis Kay *social worker, therapist*
Solomon, Risa Greenberg *clinical social worker, child and family therapist, former entertainment industry executive*
Somes, Joan Marie *emergency nurse*
Sommerfeld, Marianna *retired social worker, writer*
Sovde-Pennell, Barbara Ann *sonographer*
Spagnuolo, Pasqualina Marie *rehabilitation nurse*
Speer, Nancy Girouard *health care administrator*
Spelios, Lisa Garone *nurse, educator*
Spence, Marjorie A. *medical/surgical nurse*
Spencer, Heidi Honnold *psychotherapist, writer, educator*
Spero, Maddalena Ann *nurse*
Spiegel-Hopkins, Phyllis *psychotherapist*
Splane, Richard Beverley *social work educator*
Stadler, Selise M. *laboratory and x-ray technician*
Stancil, Irene Mack *family counselor*
Stanley-Hermanns, Melinda Louise *mental health nurse*
Stansil, Sheryl *medical/surgical nurse*
Starnes, Jane Smith *women's health nurse*
Stash, Susan Michele *critical care nurse*
Statz, Shelly Rose *social worker*
Stauber, Cynthia B. *medical/surgical nurse*
†Steinbock, Dan *researcher, consultant*
Stevens, Elizabeth *psychotherapist, consultant*
Stillings, Dennis Otto *research association administrator, consultant*
Stocks, Mary Lee *social worker, social services administrator*
Stoddard, M. Anita *psychiatric nurse*
Stohlman, Connie Suzanne *obstetrical gynecological nurse*
Stratton, Mariann *retired naval nursing administrator*
†Strother - Stewart, Georgia Rae *emergency medical technician*
Stumpf, Mary Rita *administrator, executive director*
Stutzman, Sandra Louise *advanced nurse practitioner*
Suber, Robin Hall *former medical and surgical nurse*
Suhr, Geraldine M. *medical/surgical nurse*
Suter, Susan Virginia *retired social worker*
Svikla, Alius Julius *pharmacist*
Svoboda, Janice June *nurse*
†Swan, Beth Ann *nursing administrator*
Swaters, Cherie Lynn Butler *nurse*
Swist, Marian Irene *emergency nurse*
Szantai, Linda Marie *speech and language therapist*
Tack, Theresa Rose *women's health nurse*
Talavera, Francisco *pharmacist, writer*
Tanner, Peggy *retired nurse*
Tarnow, Malva May Wescoe *post-anesthesia care nurse*
Tarzian, Anita Jeanne *nurse, researcher, ethicist*
Tauber, Sonya Lynn *nurse*
Taylor, Edna Jane *retired employment program counselor*
Taylor, Karen Annette *mental health nurse*
Taylor, Nathalee Britton *nutritionist*
Taylor, Pamela Ann *social worker*
†Terry, Barbara L. *human services administrator*
†Tewfik, Diane Burak *occupational therapist, educator*
Thiel, David Brian *physician assistant*
†Thios Jr., John Thomas *marriage and family therapist, information technology manager*
Thomas, Adrian Wesley *laboratory director*
Thomas, Robert Rene *physician assistant, athletic trainer*
†Thomas, Stephen Crawford *social worker*
Thomas, Vickie Mueller *medical laboratory director*
Thompson, Theodis *retired healthcare executive, health management consultant*
Thrasher, Rose Marie *critical care and community health nurse*
Timm, Deborah A. *critical care nurse*
Timmons, Barbara Alice *retired geriatrics nurse*
Tinner, Franziska Paula *social worker, artist, designer, educator, entrepreneur*
Tolliver, Glenda Reeder *social worker*
Toter, Kimberly Mrowiec *nurse*
Trachtenberg, Howard Alan *retired medical center administrator, educator*
Tracy, Susanne Mary *nurse educator*
Trautman, Alta Louise *nurse, funeral director, author*
Travis, Marlene O. *healthcare management executive*
Tucceri, Ellen Lee *medical/surgical nurse*
Tucci, Janis A(nn) *health unit administrator*
Tucker, Constance A. *critical care nurse*
Uemura, Teruki *child brain developmentalist*
Ullmann, Barbara *maternal/child health and community health nurse*
Ullrich, Linda J. *medical technologist*
Unison-Pace, Wendy Jane *hospital administrator*
†Urpina-Arca, Raquel *pharmacist, education educator*
Valentine, Constance *health service program analyst, researcher*
Van Alstine, Ruth Louise *medical language specialist, writer*
†VanderLee, Louise Dianne *cardiopulmonary rehabilitation critical care nurse*
Varney, Suzanne Glaab *health facility administrator*
Voelker, Margaret Irene (Meg Voelker) *gerontology, medical, surgical nurse*
Vogel, H. Victoria *psychotherapist, trauma, post-traumatic stress disorder and addiction recovery counselor and educator, author*
Vohs, James Arthur *health care program executive*
Wallschlaeger, Josephine Ingeborg *mental health nurse*
Walston, Lola Inge *dietitian*
Ward, Vicki Dawne *family nurse practitioner, rural health specialist*
Wargowsky, Robin Kay *nurse*
Waring, Mary Louise *retired social worker*
Warner, Heidi Celeste *clinical trials consultant*
Warres, Margie Black *social work administrator emerita*
†Warwick, Margaret Ann *health science facility administrator, consultant*
Washburn, Caryl Anne *occupational therapist*
†Weaver, Agnes Jin Ai *medical/surgical nurse*
Weber, Ellen Schmoyer *pediatric speech pathologist*
Webster, John Kingsley Ohl, II, *health administrator, rehabilitation manager*
Weightman, Esther Lynn *emergency trauma nurse*
Weil, Thomas P. *health services consultant*
Weimer, Gary W. *academic medical center development executive*
Weiss, Joan Oppenheimer *social worker, educator*
†Welch, Janet L. *nursing educator*
Wendland, Claire *nursing administrator, geriatrics nurse*
Westphal, William Henry *staff nurse*
Westrick, Heidi Lynn *medical/surgical nurse*
Whalen, Alberta Dean *retired community health nurse*
Wheatley, George Milholland *medical administrator*
Whildin, Donna *retired medical/surgical nurse*
White, Eugene Vaden *retired pharmacist*
White, Sarah Jowilliard *counselor*
Wiebe, Leonard Irving *radiopharmacist, educator*
Wieland, William Dean *healthcare consulting executive*
Wiese, Neva *critical care nurse*
Wilke Montemayor, Joanne Marie *nursing administrator*
Williams, Athanasia Maria *perinatal nurse specialist*
†Williams, Mosi Omari *counselor, educator*
Williams-Barnard, Carol Lou *mental health nurse*
Williams Maddox-Brown, Janice Helen *nurse*
Wills, Ritchie Jean *hospital administrator*
Wilson, Linda Ann *renal dialysis nurse*
Wilson, Mary Elizabeth *geriatrics nurse*
†Wilson, Zara D *speaker, consultant*
Winters, Sheila *family nurse practitioner*
Winton, Howard Phillip *retired optometrist*
†Wise, Allen F. *health care administrator*
Wolfberg, Melvin Donald *optometrist, educational administrator, consultant*
Wood, John Arthur *nurse*
Wood, Norma J. *nurse practitioner*
Worrell, Cynthia Celeste *school nurse*
†Wright, Dell *residential care and treatment facility executive,*
Wykoff, Beverly Young *social worker*
Yarbrough, Kathryn Davis *public health nurse*
†Yielding, (Mildred) Louise *maternal/infant nurse*
†York, Robert Lee, Jr., *health facility administrator*
Young, Deborah (Deborah Ayling Yanowitz) *social worker, librarian*
Young, Kim Ann *health facility administrator*
Younger, Betty Nichols *social worker*
Zevola, Donna Ruth *critical care nurse, educator*
Zimmerman, Lydia *retired community health nurse, consultant*

HEALTHCARE: MEDICINE

UNITED STATES

ALABAMA

Alexander City
Tyler, Eric Owen *pediatrician*

Auburn
Kam, Frederick Anthony *internist, physician*
Parsons, Daniel Lankester *pharmaceutics educator*

Birmingham
Allman, Richard Mark *physician, gerontologist*
Avent, Charles Kirk *medical educator*
Bashir, Khurram *neurologist*
Bell, David Samuel Henry *medical educator*
Bridgers, William Frank *retired physician*
Bueschen, Anton Joslyn *physician, educator*
†Bunchman, Timothy Edward *nephrologist, educator*
Callahan, Alston *physician, author*
Carlo, Waldemar A. *neonataologist*
Clayton, Orville Woolford *surgeon*
Cooper, Max Dale *pediatrician, researcher*
Davis, Richard Oliver *obstetrician-gynecologist, educator*
de la Torre, Jorge Ignacio *plastic surgeon, educator*
Diethelm, Arnold Gillespie *surgeon*
Elewski, Boni Elizabeth *dermatologist, educator*
†El-Galley, Rizk *urologist, educator*
†Eloubeidi, Mohamad Ali *gastroenterologist, internist*
Falkson, Carla Isadora *medical oncologist*
Finney, James Owen, Jr., *cardiologist*
Fix, R. Jobe *plastic surgeon, reconstructive hand surgeon*
Geer, Jack Charles *retired pathology educator*
Greene, Ernest Rinaldo, Jr., *anesthesiologist, chemical engineer*

Hirschowitz, Basil Isaac *physician*
Honan, Michael Benjamin *cardiologist*
†Kiefe, Catarina Isabel *medical educator*
Kirby, Russell Stephen *epidemiologist, statistician, geographer*
†Kirklin, John Webster *surgeon*
Koopman, William James *medical educator, internist, immunologist*
Lochridge, Stanley Keith *cardiovascular and thoracic surgeon*
Meezan, Elias *pharmacologist, educator*
Meredith, Ruby Frances *radiation oncologist, researcher, educator*
Mowry, Robert Wilbur *pathologist, educator*
Nepomuceno, Cecil Santos *physician*
Nettelbeck, Dirk Manfred *biomedical researcher*
Oakes, Walter Jerry *pediatric neurosurgeon*
Omura, Emily Fowler *dermatologist, educator*
Omura, George Adolf *medical oncologist*
Oparil, Suzanne *cardiologist, educator, cardiologist, researcher*
Pacifico, Albert Dominick *cardiovascular surgeon*
Pittman, James Allen, Jr., *physician, educator*
†Read, Russell W. *ophthalmology educator*
Rousso, Daniel Elliott *facial plastic surgeon, educator*
Russell, Richard Olney, Jr., *cardiologist, educator*
Schroeder, Harry William, Jr., *physician, scientist*
†Schwacha, Martin G. *biomedical researcher*
†Shaneyfelt, Terrence M *physician, researcher*
Siegal, Gene Philip *pathology educator*
Skalka, Harold Walter *ophthalmologist, educator*
Stevenson, Edward Ward *retired physician, surgeon, otolaryngologist*
Strickler, Howard Martin *physician*
Vargas, Pilar *physician, consultant*
†Wells, Alan Hilary *biomedical researcher*
Wright, Amos Jasper, III, *medical librarian*

Decatur
Sims, William Arthur *orthopedist*

Fairhope
McBrearty, Michael Leigh *family physician*
Mozley, Paul David *retired obstetrics and gynecology educator*
Ottensmeyer, David Joseph *retired neurosurgeon, retired healthcare executive*

Gadsden
Brown, Andrew M. *otolaryngologist, allergist*

Gulf Shores
Appelt, Glenn David *pharmacologist, consultant, medical educator*

Guntersville
Zahn, Allan Lee *emergency physician*

Hoover
Sobhan, Tanveer *physician*

Huntsville
Burg, Fredric David *physician, university dean*
Corman, Lourdes C. *physician, educator*
Huber, Donald Simon *physician*
Nuessle, William Raymond *surgeon*
Robinson, Helen Margaret *emergency physician, internist*
Tietke, Wilhelm *gastroenterologist, educator*

Madison
Maladkar, Madan Ananda Rao *internist*

Mobile
Atkinson, William James, Jr., *retired cardiologist*
Brandon, Jeffrey Campbell *physician, interventional radiologist, educator*
Brogdon, Byron Gilliam *physician, radiology educator*
Cohen, Michael Victor *cardiologist*
DeBakey, Ernest George *physician, surgeon*
Eichold, Samuel *medical educator, medical museum curator*
†Gremse, David Albert *pediatrician, educator*
Guarino, Anthony Michael *pharmacologist, educator, consultant, counselor*
Horenstein, Marcelo Gabriel *pathologist, educator*
†Hutchens, Dennis Wade *anesthesiologist*
†Lee, Ron Rafael, Jr., *physician, medical educator, researcher*
Littleton, Jesse Talbot, III, *radiology educator*
†LoCicero, Joseph *thoracic surgeon, researcher*
Outlaw, Kitti Kiattikunvivat *plastic surgeon*
Rodning, Charles Bernard *surgeon*
Smith, Jesse Graham, Jr., *dermatologist, educator*

Montgomery
Adams, Robert Barry *pathologist*
Barnes, Harrey McGwinn, III, *internist, oncologist*
Frazer, David Hugh, Jr., *allergist*
†Givhan, Edgar Gilmore *physician, writer*
Hunker, Fred Dominic *internist, medical educator*
Kirschenfeld, J. J. *retired physician, educator*
Lee, Harry Antonius *allergist, immunologist*
Maya, Ivan Dario *internist*
Myers, Ira Lee *physician*
Shashy, Paul Moses *urologist*

Orange Beach
Conrad, Marcel Edward *hematologist, educator*

Pelham
Nuckols, Frank Joseph *psychiatrist*

Tuscaloosa
Aldridge, Kenneth William *physician*
Keeton, J. E. *retired psychiatrist*
Koger, Michael Pigott *physician, writer*
Lumpkin, Thomas Riley *physician, educator*

Moody, Maxwell, Jr., *retired physician*
Newsom, Barry Douglas *cardiovascular and thoracic surgeon*
Pieroni, Robert Edward *internist, educator, military officer*

ALASKA

Anchorage
†Ballew, Carol *epidemiologist, researcher*
Finley, John Clifford *cardiologist*
Park, Gloria *family physician, consultant*
Rogers, Donald Robert *retired pathologist*

Fairbanks
Bergeson, Marvin Ernest *pediatrician*
Gianni, Keith Brian Michael *internist*
Hess, Richard Christian, Jr., *obstetrician/gynecologist, educator*

ARIZONA

Avondale
Manning-Weber, Claudia Joy *medical education consultant, author*

Carefree
Hook, William Franklin *locum tenens radiologist*

Casa Grande
Kapsos, Philip John *anesthesiologist*
Khan, Habib Urrehman *neurologist*

Chandler
Devi, Talluri S. *retired obstetrician/gynecologist*
Mönkemüller, Klaus Erik *physician, researcher, clinician*

Flagstaff
Braunstein, Ethan Malcolm *skeletal radiologist, paleopathologist, educator*
Lewicky, Roman Taras *orthopedic surgeon*

Fountain Hills
Gifford, Ray Wallace, Jr., *retired physician, educator*

Gilbert
Eitner, James William *physician, medical consultant, administrator*

Glendale
†Lysik, Melanie Alison *pharmacologist, educator*
Michael, Cecil Francis, Jr., *pediatrician*

Green Valley
Moser, Robert Harlan *physician, educator, writer*

Mesa
Boren, Kenneth Ray *endocrinologist, nephrologist*
Bunchman, Herbert Harry, II, *plastic surgeon*
Fiorino, John Wayne *podiatrist*
Hagen, Nicholas Steward *medical educator, consultant*
McGill, John J. *radiologist*
Thompson, Ronald MacKinnon *former family physician, artist, writer*

Paradise Valley
Burkholder, Peter Miller *physician, educator*
Calkins, Jerry Milan *anesthesiologist, educator, administrator, biomedical engineer*
Lorenzen, Robert Frederick *ophthalmologist*
Targovnik, Selma E. Kaplan *physician*

Phoenix
†Allison, Rebecca Anne *cardiologist, writer*
†Ammon, John Richard *anesthesiologist*
Bodensteiner, John Burton *neurologist*
Borel, James David *anesthesiologist*
Buffmire, Donald K. *internist*
Charlton, John Kipp *pediatrician*
Cole, Daniel John *anesthesiologist, educator*
†Dib, Nabil *cardiologist, researcher*
Felicetta, James Vincent *endocrinologist, educator*
Fishburne, John Ingram, Jr., *obstetrician/gynecologist, educator*
Goldberg, Morris *internist*
Hamilton, Gillian *geriatrician*
Holman, Paul David *plastic surgeon*
Hotz, Jeffrey Alan *anesthesiologist, educator*
Koppenbrink, Walter Edwin, III, *internist*
Laufer, Nathan *cardiologist*
Lawrence, William Henry, Jr., *neurologist*
McLoone, James Brian *psychiatrist, educator*
Merlin Kearfott, DuVal *health consultant*
Nilsen, Laurance Beckwith *retired endocrinologist*
Pittman, Hal Watson *neurosurgeon*
Reed, Wallace Allison *anesthesiologist*
Rodriguez-Lopez, Julio Arnaldo *surgeon, researcher*
Roth, Sanford Harold *rheumatologist, health care administrator, educator*
Rudd, Gerald Patrick *ophthalmologist*
Sage, Webster LeGene, Jr., *ophthalmologist*
Singer, Jeffrey Alan *surgeon*
Stern, Stanley *psychiatrist*
Swafford, Leslie Eugene *physician assistant, consultant*
†Underwood, Paul Lester *cardiologist*
Vu, Eric Tin *neurobiologist, researcher*
Walters, Carrie Lou *neurosurgeon*
Wright, Richard Oscar, III, *pathologist, educator, clinical ethicist*
Zerella, Joseph T. *retired pediatric surgeon*

Scottsdale
†Cawley, Leo Patrick *pathologist, immunologist*
Chaurasia, Vishal *physician, writer, computer programmer*
†Dahl, Mark Victor *dermatologist, educator*

Dlugie, Paul David *physician*
Donnelly, Richard E. *physician assistant, educator*
Ellis, Frank Russell *retired pathologist*
Evans, Tommy Nicholas *obstetrician/gynecologist, educator*
French, Lyle Albert *surgeon*
Friedman, Shelly Arnold *cosmetic surgeon*
Garcia-Buñuel, Luis *neurologist*
George, Frank Richard *science and technoloty officer*
Heigh, Russell Irwin *gastroenterologist*
Huston, Christopher Worth *rehabilitation medicine physician*
Kandell, Howard Noel *pediatrician*
Kübler-Ross, Elisabeth *physician*
Leighton, William D. *plastic and reconstructive surgeon*
†Lillo, Joseph Leonard *osteopath, family practice physician*
Nadler, Henry Louis *pediatrician, geneticist, medical educator*
Novicki, Donald Edward *urologic surgeon*
Orford, Robert Raymond *consulting physician*
Reznick, Richard Howard *pediatrician*
Sanderson, David R. *physician*
Starr, Phillip Henry *psychiatrist, educator*
Watkins, Eugene Leonard *surgeon, educator*
Weisman, Avery *psychiatrist*
†Whitaker, Michael D. *endocrinologist, consultant*
White, Alexander B. *retired internist*

Sedona
Briney, Allan King *retired radiologist*
Hawkins, David Ramon *psychiatrist, writer, researcher, religious studies educator*
Metzner, Richard Joel *psychiatrist, psychopharmacologist, educator*
Mikles, Devin Alaric *physician, educator*
Reno, Joseph Harry *retired orthopedic surgeon*
Shors, Clayton Marion *cardiologist*

Sun City
Buchman, Elwood *internist, pharmaceutical company medical director*
Filek, Allan August *physician*

Sun City West
†Wasmuth, Carl Erwin *physician, lawyer*

Tempe
Anand, Suresh Chandra *physician*
Rowley, Beverley Davies *medical sociologist*

Tubac
Brandon, Gary Kent *physician, health facility administrator*

Tucson
Abrams, Herbert Kerman *physician, educator*
Acosta, Ruben *surgeon*
Ahern, Geoffrey Lawrence *behavioral neurologist*
Alberts, David Samuel *physician, pharmacologist, educator*
Alpert, Joseph Stephen *physician, educator*
Ben-Asher, M. David *physician*
Brown, Howard Mark *physician*
Capp, Michael Paul *physician, educator*
Carter, L. Philip *neurosurgeon, consultant*
†Cherrick, Ruth E. *medical researcher, researcher*
Cisler, Theresa Ann *osteopath, former nurse*
†Comiter, Craig Vance *urologist*
Copeland, Jack G. *cardiac surgeon, researcher*
Dalen, James Eugene *cardiologist, educator*
DeLuca, Dominick *medical educator, researcher*
†Elliott, Sean P. *pediatrician, infectious disease specialist*
Ewy, Gordon Allen *cardiologist, clinician, researcher, educator*
†Fass, Ronnie *gastroenterologist, director*
Galloway, James Malcolm *cardiologist*
Goldfarb, Robert Paul *neurological surgeon*
Graham, Anna Regina *pathologist, educator*
Hamilton, Allan J. *neurosurgeon*
Harris, David Thomas *immunology educator*
Hatch, Kenneth Deroy *gynecologist, oncologist*
Hattery, Robert Ralph *radiologist, educator*
Houser, Harold Byron *epidemiologist*
†Huestis, Douglas William *physician, pathologist*
Hunter, Tim Bradshaw *radiologist, educator*
Katakkar, Suresh Balaji *hematologist, oncologist*
†Kershner, Robert M. *ophthalmologist, educator, research scientist*
†Khouzam, Rami Nadim *physician*
King, Joseph Willet *child psychiatrist*
Kischer, Clayton Ward *human embryologist, educator*
Kittredge, John Russell *physician*
Koshkarian, Gregory Merrill *physician*
Levenson, Alan Ira *psychiatrist, physician, educator*
Levine, Norman *physician*
†Lien, Yeong-Hau Howard *nephrologist, researcher*
Marcus, Frank Isadore *cardiologist, educator*
Nugent, Charles Arter *internist, educator*
Patton, Dennis David *radiologist, educator*
Pollack, Irwin William *psychiatrist, educator*
Sampliner, Richard Evan *physician*
Sanan, Abhay *physician*
Schumacher, Michael John *allergist*
†Slepian, Marvin J. *cardiologist, consultant*
Smith, Josef Riley *internist*
Stearns, Elliott Edmund, Jr., *retired surgeon*
Wahl, Richard Alan *pediatrician, educator*
Weil, Andrew Thomas *physician, educator*
Westerband, Alex *surgeon, educator*
Whaley, Joseph S. *physician*
Witte, Marlys Hearst *internist, educator*
Woolfenden, James Manning *nuclear medicine physician, educator*
Woosley, Raymond *pharmacology and medical educator*

Vail
Reichlin, Seymour *physician, educator*

Yuma
Martin, James Franklin *physician, lawyer*
Meyer, Andrew Hoyt *physician*

ARKANSAS

Arkadelphia
Fullerton, John C., III, *surgeon*

Batesville
Bess, Lloyd George *radiologist*

Bella Vista
Rose, Donald L. *physician, educator*

Conway
Fleisher, Homer Luther, III, *surgeon*
McCarron, Robert Frederick, II, *orthopedist, surgeon*

El Dorado
Tommey, Charles Eldon *retired surgeon*

Fayetteville
Fink, William James *retired surgeon*

Fort Smith
†Coleman, Michael Dortch *nephrologist*
Drolshagen, Leo Francis, III, *radiologist, physician*
Hinkle, Richard Allen, Jr., *internist*
Snider, James Rhodes *radiologist*

Hot Springs National Park
Brunner, John Harry *surgeon*

Jonesboro
Jones, Kenneth Bruce *surgeon*

Little Rock
†Anand, Kanwaljeet Singh *pediatrician, researcher*
Bates, Joseph Henry *physician, educator*
Bissada, Nabil Kaddis *urologist, educator, researcher, author*
†Brodsky, Michael Carroll *ophthalmologist, educator*
Bruce, Thomas Allen *physician, educator*
Campbell, Gilbert Sadler *surgery educator, surgeon*
Cone, John Baxter *trauma surgeon, medical researcher*
Culp, William Combs *radiologist*
Ferrer, Thomas John *surgeon*
Hart, Ronald Wilson *radiobiologist, educator, toxicologist, researcher, government research executive*
Henderson, Victor Warren *behavioral and geriatric neurologist, researcher, educator*
Jansen, G. Thomas *dermatologist*
Kemp, Stephen Frank *pediatric endocrinologist, educator, composer*
†Kumar, Udaya *urologist*
Lang, Nicholas Paul *surgeon*
Logan, Charles Wilbur *urologist*
Lucy, Dennis Durwood, Jr., *neurologist, educator*
Mehta, Jawahar Lal *cardiologist*
Mrak, Robert Emil *neuropathologist, educator, electron microscopist*
Nagarajan, Radhakrishnan *medical researcher*
Peters, Phillip Joseph *endocrinologist, educator*
Reece, E. Albert *dean, obstetrician, gynecologist, perinatologist*
Sherman, Jerome Kalman *retired anatomy educator*
Simmons, Caroline Jennermann *biomedical researcher, writer*
Simmons, Debra Lynn *physician, educator*
†Stowe, Cindy D. *pharmacologist, educator*
Strode, Steven Wayne *physician*
Suen, James Yee *otolaryngologist, educator*
Ward, Harry Pfeffer *physician, retired university chancellor*
†Wenger, Galen Rosenberger *pharmacology educator*
Westbrook, Kent Coleman *surgeon, educator*

North Little Rock
Biondo, Raymond Vitus *retired dermatologist*
†Clothier, Jeffrey Lane *neuropsychiatrist, educator*
†Pyne, Jeffrey Mark *psychiatrist, researcher*

Pine Bluff
Jacks, David Clinton *urologist*

Rogers
Wood, Charles Earl *obstetrician, gynecologist*

Scranton
Uzman, Betty Ben Geren *pathologist, retired educator*

Searcy
Simpson, James Albert *surgeon*

CALIFORNIA

Agoura Hills
deCiutiis, Alfred Charles Maria *oncologist, television producer*
Havlicek, Michael *medical association administrator*

Alameda
Whorton, M. Donald *occupational and environmental health physician, epidemiologist*

Alhambra
Kilburn, Kaye Hatch *medical educator*
Mabee, John Richard *physician assistant, educator*

Anaheim
Carvajal, Jorge Armando *endocrinologist, internist*

Arcadia
Fisher, Alan J. *otolaryngologist, plastic surgeon*

Artesia
Dhamija, Kailash Raj *physician, consultant*

Atherton
Oakes, David Duane *medical educator*

Auburn
Henrikson, Donald Merle *forensic pathologist*
†Werner, Terry Scott *otorhinolaryngologist*

Bakersfield
Abdou, Wafik Andrew *anesthesiologist*
†Prunes, Fernando *plastic surgeon, educator*
†Senining, Randolph Del Castillo *internist, infectious diseases consultant*
†Sio, Jimmy Ong *embryologist*

Bellflower
Kivuls, Juris *plastic surgeon*
Lee, Paul Yue-Yan *surgeon*

Belvedere
Wallerstein, Robert Solomon *psychiatrist*

Belvedere Tiburon
Behrman, Richard Elliot *pediatrician, neonatologist, university dean*
Kilgore, Eugene Sterling, Jr., *former surgeon*

Berkeley
†Abbott, Myles Bruce *pediatrician*
Abel, Carlos Alberto *immunologist*
†Budinger, Thomas Francis *radiologist, educator*
Buffler, Patricia Ann *epidemiologist, educator, retired dean*
Diamond, Marian Cleeves *anatomy educator*
Duhl, Leonard *psychiatrist, educator*
Falkner, Frank Tardrew *physician, educator*
Grossman, Elmer Roy *pediatrician*
Josephian, Jenny Adele *acupuncturist, artist*
Mohle-Boetani, Janet Carol *epidemiologist*
Policoff, Leonard David *physician, educator*
Seitz, Walter Stanley *cardiovascular research consultant*
†Syme, Sherman Leonard *epidemiologist, educator*
Tempelis, Constantine Harry *immunologist, educator*
Winkelstein, Warren, Jr., *physician, educator*

Beverly Hills
Allen, Howard Norman *cardiologist, educator*
Arieff, Allen Ives *physician*
Bao, Katherine Sung *pediatric cardiologist*
Caster, Andrew Ian *ophthalmologist*
Catz, Boris *endocrinologist, educator*
Crandall, Earle Ellsworth *neurosurgeon, educator*
Fein, William *ophthalmologist*
Fox, Joyce Naness *dermatologist*
Goodman, Mark Paul *physician*
†Haworth, Randal Digby *plastic surgeon*
Karpman, Harold Lew *cardiologist, educator, writer*
Klein, Arnold William *dermatologist*
Kure, Katsuhiro *plastic surgeon*
†Marshak, Harry *plastic surgeon*
Menkes, John Hans *pediatric neurologist*
Rabens, Steven Fisher *dermatologist, educator*
Rodman, Francis Robert *psychoanalyst, writer*
Saperstein, Harry W. *physician, dermatologist*
Seiff, Stephen S. *ophthalmologist*
Stolinsky, David C. *physician*
Weinstein, Irwin Marshall *internist, hematologist*
Yuan, Robin Tsu-Wang *plastic surgeon*

Bishop
Clark, D. Scott *surgeon*

Bolinas
Remen, Rachel Naomi *pediatrician, integrative medicine physician*

Bonita
Covarrubias-Lugo, Irma *physician*

Borrego Springs
†Scallen, Terence Joseph *retired medical educator*
†Strong, John Oliver *plastic surgeon, educator*

Brawley
Jaquith, George Oakes *ophthalmologist*

Burbank
Renner, Andrew Ihor *surgeon*
Tran, Lawrence Delano *family physician, educator*

Calabasas
Bursten, Stuart Lowell *physician, biochemist*

Campbell
Tran, Nam Van *health education specialist*

Carlsbad
Chopra, Deepak *preventive medicine physician, writer*
Crooke, Rosanne M. *pharmacologist*

Carmel
Felch, William Campbell *internist, editor*
Flanagan, Michael Brendan *obstetrician/gynecologist*
Janko, Albert Bela *physician*

Carmel Valley
Chapman, Robert Galbraith *retired hematologist, administrator*

Carmichael
Marino, Joseph Thomas *physician*
Wagner, Carruth John *physician*

Chico
Lobosky, Jeffrey *physician, neurosurgeon*
Ritter, Dale William *obstetrician, gynecologist*
Ward, Chester Lawrence *physician, consultant*

Chula Vista
Allen, Henry Wesley *biomedical researcher, consultant*
Cohen, Elaine Helena *pediatrician, pediatric cardiologist, educator*
Gongora, Eduardo *plastic surgeon*
Otten, Richard Heuse *physician*

Claremont
Johnson, Jerome Linné *cardiologist, educator*

Clovis
Chang, Stanley F. *gastroenterologist*

Colton
Greene, Gerald R. *pediatrician*
†Seifert, Mark R. *pathologist*

Concord
Jothi, Rishyur K. *surgeon*
Latner, Barry P. *pathologist*
Paterson, Bruce Foote *internist, allergist*
†Rohra, Srikrishin Assardas *cardiologist*

Corona
Shaffer, Audrey Jeanne *health information administrator, educator*

Corona Del Mar
†Dougherty, Jocelyn *retired neurologist*
Tobis, Jerome Sanford *physician*

Coronado
Mock, David Clinton, Jr., *internist*

Corte Madera
Epstein, William Louis *dermatologist, educator*
Serber, William *radiation oncologist, educator*

Costa Mesa
Steinberg, Russell Max *behavioral pediatrician, educator*

Cypress
Waite, Verner Stuart *surgeon, retired*

Davis
†Bloom, Heather Lynn *physician*
Cardiff, Robert Darrell *pathology educator*
Enders, Allen Coffin *anatomy educator*
Gardner, Murray Briggs *pathologist, educator*
Hance, Anthony James *retired pharmacologist, educator*
Jensen, Hanne Margrete *pathology educator*
Palmer, Philip Edward Stephen *radiologist*
Richman, David Paul *neurologist, educator, researcher*
Schenker, Marc Benet *preventive medicine educator*
Williams, Hibbard Earl *medical educator, physician*

Deer Park
Hodgkin, John E. *pulmonologist*

Del Mar
†Engler, Robert L. *retired cardiologist*
Lesko, Ronald Michael *osteopathic physician*

Delano
Salmassi, Sadegh *family practice physician*

Downey
†Chui, Helena Chang *physician*
Gong, Henry, Jr., *physician, researcher*
Hackney, Jack Dean *physician*
Mishal, Devadatt M. *obstetrician/gynecologist*
Swyden, Robert Gene *family practice physician*

Duarte
Comings, David Edward *physician, medical genetics scientist*
Fung, Henry Chi-hang *physician, medical researcher*
†Li, Jian Jian *medical educator*

El Cajon
Turk, Robert Louis *radiologist*

El Dorado Hills
Sparks, Robert Dean *medical administrator, physician*

El Macero
Andrews, Neil Corbly *surgeon*
Stowell, Robert Eugene *pathologist, retired educator*

Eldridge
†Mason, William H. *podiatrist*

Emeryville
†Bonci, Antonello *neurologist*
Donnelly, John James, III, *immunologist*
Hurst, Deborah *pediatric hematologist*
Penhoet, Edward *medical association administrator, biochemicals company executive, former dean*

Encinitas
Chavez, Cesar T. *ophthalmologist, cosmetic surgeon*

Encino
Dosik, Gary M. *internist, oncologist, hematologist, educator*

Escondido
Everton, Marta Ve *retired ophthalmologist*
Steele, John Thomas *surgeon, military officer*

Fairfield
Martin, Clyde Verne *psychiatrist*
Munn, William Charles, II, *psychiatrist*

Folsom
Anderson, Jeffrey Lee *physician, anesthesiologist, consultant*
Ewing, Russell Charles, II, *physician*

Fontana
†Johna, Samir *surgeon*

Fremont
Steinmetz, Seymour *pediatrician*

Fresno
Chandler, Bruce Frederick *internist*
Garza, Alvaro *physician*
Holmes, Albert William, Jr., *physician*
Khouzam, Hani Raoul *psychiatrist, physician, educator*
Leigh, Hoyle *psychiatrist, educator, writer*
Patton, Jack Thomas *family practice physician*
Salzman, Barnett Seymour *psychiatrist*
Shigyo, Tetsuo Ted *emergency physician*
Smith, V. Roy *neurosurgeon*
Thompson, Leonard Russell *pediatrician*
Welch, Jack Hamill *retired internist*
†Zweifler, John Andrew *physician, educator*

Fullerton
†Aston, Edward Ernest, IV, *dermatologist*
Nitta, Douglas *family practice physician*
Sugarman, Michael *physician, rheumatologist*

Glendale
Spring, Carl Chaffee, Jr., *medical writer*
Wang, James K. *internist, medical administrator*

Grass Valley
†Ely, Parry Haines *dermatologist, educator*

Greenbrae
Levy, S. William *dermatologist, educator*
Parnell, Francis William, Jr., *otolaryngologist*
Ramirez, Archimedes *neurosurgeon, educator*

Gualala
Ring, Alice Ruth Bishop *retired physician*

Half Moon Bay
Robertson, Abel L., Jr., *pathologist*

Hanford
Gamboa, Lucito G. *physician, pathologist*

Harbor City
Ackerson, Bradley Kent *physician*
Kwan, Benjamin Ching Kee *ophthalmologist*

Hayward
Bachicha, Joseph Alfred *physician, educator*
Waller, Marilyn Jean *podiatric surgeon, educator*

Hemet
Galletta, Joseph Leo *physician*
Mata, David Joseph *physician*

Hillsborough
Kraft, Robert Arnold *retired medical educator, physician*
Packard, Peter *medical educator, retired internist*

Huntington Beach
Appelbaum, Bruce David *physician*
Nichter, Larry Steven *medical educator, plastic surgeon*
†Pacino, Frank George *physician, educator*
†Sebag, Jerry *ophthalmologist, surgeon*
Welsh, William Daniel *geriatric medicine family practice physician*

Inglewood
Sukov, Richard Joel *radiologist*

Irvine
de la Maza, Luis M. *pathology educator*
Friedenberg, Richard Myron *radiology educator, physician*
Gupta, Sudhir *immunologist, educator*
Hubbell, Floyd Allan *physician, educator*
Miledi, Ricardo *neurobiologist*
Olek, Michael Joseph *medical educator*
Pirkle, Hubert Chaillé *pathologist, educator*
Quilligan, Edward James *obstetrician, gynecologist, educator*
Ribak, Charles Eric *anatomy educator*
Smith, Harold Raymond *neurologist, sleep medicine specialist, educator*
Stone, David Mark *plastic surgeon*
Tetef, Merry Lynn *internist, oncologist*
Weinstein, Gerald D. *dermatology educator*
Werlin, Lawrence B. *obstetrician, gynecologist, reproductive endocrinologist*

Kentfield
Bruyn, Henry Bicker *physician*
Freed, Thomas Alexander *retired radiologist*

La Canada Flintridge
Byrne, George Melvin *physician*

La Jolla
Bailey, David Nelson *pathology educator, university official*
†Ball, Edward David *hematologist, oncologist*
Barlow, Carrolee *physician, scientist, educator*
Barrett-Connor, Elizabeth Louise *epidemiologist, educator*
Beutler, Ernest *physician, research scientist*
†Blanchard, Daniel G. *cardiologist*
Block, Melvin August *surgeon, educator*
Brown, Stuart I. *ophthalmologist, educator*
Carmichael, David Burton *physician*
Dalessio, Donald John *internist, neurologist, educator*
Diamant, Joel Charles *internist*
Dixon, Frank James *medical scientist, educator*
†Edgington, Thomas S. *pathologist, educator, molecular biologist, vascular biologist*
Edwards, Charles Cornell *surgeon, research administrator*
Friedmann, Theodore *physician*
Garland, Cedric Frank *epidemiologist, educator*
Gascoigne, Nicholas Robert John *immunologist, researcher*
Gerber, Michael Lewis *cardiac surgeon*
Gill, Gordon N. *medical educator*
Gittes, Ruben Foster *urological surgeon*
†Glass, Christopher Kevin *physician*
Golomb, Beatrice Alexandra *physician, medical researcher*
†Grise, Mark Andrew *cardiologist*
†Han, Jiahuai *medical researcher*
Hench, Philip Kahler *physician*
Hendler, Sheldon Saul *internist, educator, biochemist, writer*
Hofmann, Alan Frederick *biomedical researcher, educator*
Hostetler, Karl Yoder *internist, endocrinologist, educator*
Joris-Quinton, Liesbet *internal medicine physician*
Katzman, Robert *medical educator, neurologist*
†Kripke, Daniel Frederick *psychiatrist, educator*
Masouredis, Serafeim Panagiotis *pathologist, educator*
†Mayer, John M *medical researcher, educator*
Mendoza, Stanley Atran *pediatric nephrologist, educator*
Nakamura, Robert Motoharu *pathologist*
Nyhan, William Leo *pediatrician, educator*
Rapaport, Samuel I. *educator, physician*
Rearden, Carole Ann *clinical pathologist, educator*
Resnik, Robert *medical educator*
Rosenfeld, Michael G. *medical educator*
†Rubin, Lewis J *physician, researcher*
†Schneider, Gerald L. *plastic surgeon*
Shapiro, William Maurice *emergency medicine physician, administrator, researcher*
†Singer, Robert *plastic surgeon*
†Stein, Murray Brent *psychiatrist, researcher*
Steinberg, Daniel *preventive medicine physician, educator*
Takabe, Kazuaki *gastroenterology surgeon, research scientist*
Tan, Eng Meng *immunologist, biomedical scientist*
Teirstein, Paul Shepherd *physician, health facility administrator*
Terry, Robert Davis *neuropathologist, educator*
Walker, Richard Hugh *orthopaedic surgeon*
Yen, Samuel S(how)-C(hih) *obstetrics and gynecology educator, reproductive endocrinologist*

La Mesa
Behrend, Albert James *surgeon*
†Boghairi, Anoushiravan *cardiologist*
Kafka, John Abraham *pediatrician*

La Quinta
Calvin, James Willard *thoracic and vascular surgeon*
Pitkin, Roy Macbeth *retired obstetrician, educator*

Lafayette
Cobb, George Edward *surgeon*

Laguna Beach
Foltz, Eldon Leory *neurosurgeon, educator*
Richard, Robert Max *cardiologist*

Laguna Hills
†Alva, Alejandro *psychiatrist*
Widyolar, Sheila Gayle *dermatologist*
Wrobel, Lance J. *orthopedic surgeon*

Laguna Woods
Berk, Jack Edward *gastroenterologist, educator*
Ross, Mathew *medical educator*

Lake Forest
Larsen, Robert Ray *healthcare executive, surgeon*

Lincoln
McKay, Thomas Frederick *retired radiologist*

Livermore
Seward, James Pickett *internist, educator*

Loma Linda
Armon, Carmel *neurologist*
†Ballard, Jeffrey Lawrence *surgeon, educator*
Behrens, Berel Lyn *physician, academic and healthcare administrator*
Bull, Brian Stanley *pathology educator, medical consultant, business executive*
Bunnell, William Paul *orthopaedic surgery educator*
Coggin, Charlotte Joan *cardiologist, educator*
Condon, Stanley Charles *gastroenterologist*
†Dayes, Lloyd Albert *neurosurgeon, minister*
†Edwards, Lincoln Paul *pharmacologist, educator*
Herrmann, Paul C. *physician, chemist*
Krick, Edwin Harry, Sr., *medical educator, internal medicine physician*
Llaurado, Josep G. *nuclear medicine physician, scientist*
Mace, John Weldon *pediatrician*
†Razzouk, Anees Jacob *surgeon*
Reeve, Ivan Leon *physician*
Roberts, Walter Herbert Beatty *anatomist, educator*
Slater, James Munro *radiation oncologist*
†Smith, Aida Marissa *medical reference librarian*

PROFESSIONAL INDEX 6397 HEALTHCARE: MEDICINE

Strother, Allen *biochemical pharmacologist, researcher*
†Wareham, Ellsworth Edwin *cardiothoracic surgeon, educator*
Wong, Raymond Y. *physician, educator*

Long Beach
†Aguilar, Félix *public health physician, educator*
Berke, Irving *obstetrician-gynecologist, military officer*
Fagan, Frederic *neurosurgeon*
Friis, Robert Harold *epidemiologist, health science educator*
Kwaan, Jack Hau Ming *retired physician*
Macer, George Armen, Jr., *orthopedic hand surgeon*
Marks, Melvin I. *physician, educator, health services consultant*
Mills, Don Harper *pathology and psychiatry educator, lawyer*
†Nageotte, Michael Patrick *obstetrician*
Stemmer, Edward Alan *surgeon, educator*
White, Katherine Elizabeth *retired pediatrician*
Worcester, Howard Lester *internist*

Los Altos
Abrams, Arthur Jay *physician*
Martin, Leonardo S.J. *urologist, surgeon*

Los Angeles
†Agarwal, Sanjay Kumar *physician*
Aguas, Ruben Tech *otolaryngologist*
Agus, David Bernard *physician*
†Alkalay, Arie L. *pediatrician, neonatologist*
Alkon, Ellen Skillen *physician*
Anderson, Kathryn D. *surgeon*
Apt, Leonard *physician*
Archie, Carol Louise *obstetrician and gynecologist, educator*
Ardehali, Abbas *physician, surgeon*
Ashley, Sharon Anita *pediatric anesthesiologist*
Askanas-Engel, Valerie *neurologist, educator, researcher*
Barker, Wiley Franklin *surgeon, educator*
Beart, Robert W., Jr., *surgeon, educator*
Beckson, Mace *psychiatrist*
Bernstein, Sol *cardiologist, educator*
Bessman, Samuel Paul *pediatrician, biochemist*
Beydoun, Said R. *physician, neurology educator*
†Bhidayasiri, Roongroj *neurologist, researcher*
Biles, John Alexander *pharmacology educator, chemistry educator*
Blahd, William Henry *physician, nuclear medicine physician*
Bloch, Saul K. *obstetrician-gynecologist*
Bodey, Bela *immunologist, pathologist, oncologist*
Bondareff, William *psychiatry educator*
Borenstein, Daniel Bernard *psychiatrist, educator*
Boyarsky, Igor *emergency physician*
†Brackmann, Derald E. *otolaryngologist*
Braunstein, Glenn David *physician, educator*
Breslow, Lester *physician, educator*
Brooks, Philip G. *obstetrician-gynecologist*
Brynes, Russell Kermit *pathologist, educator*
Burgess, J. Wesley *neuropsychiatrist*
Chandor, Stebbins Bryant *pathologist*
Cherry, James Donale *pediatrician*
Chopra, Inder Jit *physician, endocrinologist*
Cicciarelli, James Carl *immunology educator*
Clemente, Carmine Domenic *anatomist, educator*
Cochran, Sachiko Tomie *radiologist, educator*
Cook, Ian Ainsworth *psychiatrist, researcher, educator*
Cooper, Edwin Lowell *anatomy educator*
Cote, Richard James *pathologist, researcher*
Danoff, Dudley Seth *surgeon, urologist*
†Datar, Ram Hemant *pathologist, educator*
Davidson, Ezra C., Jr., *physician, educator*
De Cherney, Alan Hersh *obstetrics and gynecology educator*
†Derebery, Mary Jennifer *otolaryngologist*
Detels, Roger *epidemiologist, physician, former university dean*
Dignam, William Joseph *obstetrician, gynecologist, educator*
Dixit, Vivek *biomedical scientist, medical educator*
†Duckwiler, Gary Ross *physician*
Durfee, Michael John *child psychiatrist*
Edgerton, Bradford Wheatly *plastic surgeon*
Enstrom, James Eugene *epidemiologist*
†Eshagian, Joseph *ophthalmologist*
Ettenger, Robert Bruce *physician, nephrologist*
Feig, Stephen Arthur *pediatrics educator, hematologist, oncologist*
Ferrante, F. Michael *anesthesiologist, internist*
Figlin, Robert Alan *hematologist, oncologist*
†Fishbein, Michael Claude *physician, pathologist*
Fonkalsrud, Eric Walter *pediatric surgeon, educator*
†Francis, Charles K. *medical educator*
Fukushima, Teiichiro *obstetrician, educator, gynecologist*
Gabriel, Ronald Samuel *child neurologist*
Geller, Kenneth Allen *otolaryngologist*
Geller, Stephen Arthur *pathologist, educator*
Giannotta, Steven Louis *neurosurgery educator*
Giesser, Barbara Susan *neurologist, educator*
Gonick, Harvey Craig *nephrologist, educator*
Goodwin, Scott Craig *interventional radiologist*
Gordon, Kenneth Lee *ophthalmologist*
Gorney, Roderic *psychiatry educator*
Grody, Wayne William *physician*
Haas, Neil B. *psychiatrist*
†Hahn, Bevra Hannahs *medical educator*
†Hallegua, David Samuel *internist, rheumatologist, educator*
Hance, Darwood B. *radiologist*
Hartman, Rita Maria *psychiatrist*
Haywood, L. Julian *physician, educator*
Helsper, James Thomas *surgical oncologist, researcher, educator*
Henriksen, Eva H. *former anesthesiology educator*
†Herbst, Karen Louise *endocrinologist, researcher*
Hirai, Denitsu *surgeon*
Hoang, Duc Van *theoretical pathologist, educator*
†Hofmann, Wolf K *internist, researcher*
Holland, Gary Norman *ophthalmologist, educator*
Holland, Harold Mervin *urologist*
Hollander, Daniel *gastroenterologist, medical educator*
Horwitz, David A. *physician, scientist, educator*
House, John William *otologist*
Huang, Sheng He *medical educator*
†Hubbell, Wayne Lester *ophthalmologist, educator, chemist, educator*
†Huerta, Sergio *physician, researcher*
Ignarro, Louis J. *pharmacology educator*
Itabashi, Hideo Henry *neuropathologist*
Jadvar, Hossein *nuclear medicine physician, biomedical engineer*
Jalali, Behnaz *psychiatrist, educator*
Jarvik, Lissy F. *psychiatrist*
Jelliffe, Roger Woodham *cardiologist, clinical pharmacologist*
Johnson, Arthur Ingram *obstetrician and gynecologist*
Johnson, Cage Saul *hematologist, educator*
Jones, Neil Ford *surgeon, educator*
Jones, Peter Anthony *medical research administrator*
Kagan, Bruce Laurence *psychiatrist, scientist*
Kahn, Fredrick Henry *internist*
Kamil, Elaine Scheiner *pediatric nephrologist, educator*
Kaplan, Samuel *pediatric cardiologist*
Kattlove, Herman Ely *oncologist*
Katz, Ronald Lewis *physician, educator*
Kaunitz, Jonathan Davidson *physician*
Kelly, Arthur Paul *physician*
Kleeman, Charles Richard *medical educator, nephrologist, researcher*
Kloner, Robert A. *cardiologist, researcher, educator*
Koch, Richard *retired pediatrician, educator*
Korsch, Barbara M. *pediatrician*
Kramer, Barry Alan *psychiatrist, educator*
Kraus, Robert *physician*
Lamb, H. Richard *psychiatry educator*
Lawrence, Sanford Hull *physician, immunochemist, author*
Lazareff, Jorge Antonio *neurosurgeon, researcher*
†Le, Bach Trong *maxillofacial surgeon*
Lechago, Juan *pathologist, educator*
Levey, Gerald Saul *dean, internist, educator*
Lewin, Klaus Jonathan *pathologist, educator*
Lewis, Charles Edwin *epidemiologist, educator*
Liberman, Robert Paul *psychiatry educator, researcher, writer*
Lubman, Richard Levi *physician, educator, research scientist*
†Macavinta-Tenazas, Gemorsita *family physician*
Maloney, Robert Keller *ophthalmologist, medical educator*
Mandal, Ashis K. *cardiothoracic surgeon*
Marder, Stephen R. *psychiatrist, educator*
Markham, Charles Henry *neurologist*
Marmor, Judd *psychiatrist, educator*
Maronde, Robert Francis *internist, clinical pharmacologist, educator*
Martinez, Miguel Acevedo *urologist, consultant, lecturer*
Mellinkoff, Sherman Mussoff *medical educator*
Mihan, Richard *retired dermatologist*
Miles, Samuel I(srael) *psychiatrist, educator*
†Miller, Timothy Alden *plastic and reconstructive surgeon*
†Mintz, Jim *psychiatrist, educator*
Mishell, Daniel R., Jr., *obstetrician, gynecologist, educator*
Monforte-Muñoz, Hector L. *pathologist*
Moshfegh, Moussa *surgeon*
Moxley, John Howard, III, *internist*
Moy, Ronald Leonard *dermatologist, surgeon*
Naqvi, Tasneem Zehra *cardiologist, researcher, consultant*
Nathwani, Bharat N. *pathologist, consultant*
Nelson, Marvin Dale, Jr., *radiologist, educator*
Newman, Anita Nadine *surgeon*
Nissenson, Allen Richard *physician, educator*
Noble, Ernest Pascal *pharmacologist, biochemist, educator*
Parmelee, Arthur Hawley, Jr., *pediatric medical educator*
Patzakis, Michael J. *orthopaedic surgeon, educator*
Pisegna, Joseph Rocco *gastroenterologist*
†Preston-Martin, Susan *epidemiologist, educator*
Rachelefsky, Gary Stuart *medical educator*
Raghavan, Derek *oncologist, medical researcher and educator*
Rao, Jian Yu *physician, cancer biologist, educator*
Reynolds, Charles Patrick *pediatric oncologist, researcher*
Richters, Arnis *medical educator, researcher*
Rimoin, David Lawrence *physician, geneticist*
Rivin, Arthur Udell *medical educator*
†Rosenbaum, Arthur L. *ophthalmologist*
Roy-Burman, Pradip *molecular biology and virology educator*
Salamon, Georges M. *radiologist*
Salem, Hadi *thoracic surgeon*
†Sarma, Radha J. *cardiologist, educator*
Sarnat, Bernard George *plastic surgeon, educator, researcher*
Sattin, Albert *psychiatry and neuropharmacology educator*
Sawyer, Charles Henry *anatomist, educator*
Scheibel, Arnold Bernard *psychiatrist, educator, research director*
Schelbert, Heinrich Ruediger *nuclear medicine physician*
Schiff, Martin *physician, surgeon*
Schneider, Edward Lewis *medicine educator, research administrator*
Seri, Istvan *physician, researcher*
Shapiro, Martin Frederick *internist, educator*
Shapiro, Nina Lisbeth *pediatric otolaryngologist*
†Sherman, Randolph *plastic and reconstructive surgeon, educator*
Shtengold, Yefim Shelichovich *medical educator, researcher*
Siegel, Michael Elliot *nuclear medicine physician, educator*
Siegel, Sheldon C. *pediatrician, allergist, immunologist*
Siegel, Stuart Elliott *physician, pediatrics educator, cancer researcher*
†Small, Kent Wilson *ophthalmologist, educator*
Solomon, David Harris *geriatrician, educator*
Stein, Tomiko *infectious disease specialist*
Stern, Walter Eugene *neurosurgeon, educator*
Stiehm, E. Richard *pediatrician, educator*
Straatsma, Bradley Ralph *ophthalmologist, educator*
Sullivan, Stuart Francis *anesthesiologist, educator*
Sutterby, Larry Quentin *internist*
Tabachnick, Norman Donald *psychiatrist, educator*
Tache, Yvette France *neurogastroenterologist*
Tasini, Miriam Finder *medical educator, psychiatrist, psychoanalyst*
Taylor, Andrew T. *medical association administrator*
Titus, Edward Depue *psychiatrist, administrator*
Tompkins, Ronald K. *surgeon*
Van Der Meulen, Joseph Pierre *neurologist*
†Vierling, John Moore *physician*
Vredevoe, Donna Lou *research immunologist, microbiologist, educator*
Wallach, Howard Frederic *psychiatrist*
†Walts, Ann E. *pathologist*
Wasterlain, Claude Guy *neurologist*
Weiner, Leslie Philip *neurology educator, researcher*
Weiss, Martin Harvey *neurosurgeon, educator*
Wilkinson, Alan Herbert *nephrologist, medical educator*
Williams, Roberta Gay *pediatric cardiologist, educator*
Wincor, Michael Z. *psychopharmacology educator, clinician, researcher*
Winet, Howard *medical educator*
Withers, Hubert Rodney *radiotherapist, radiobiologist, educator*
Woodley, David Timothy *dermatology educator*
Wu, Shi-Qi (Samuel Wu) *medical geneticist*
Yaffe, Sumner Jason *pediatrician, educator*

Los Gatos
Cohen, James Robert *oncologist, hematologist*
Naughten, Robert Norman *pediatrician*

Malibu
Jenden, Donald James *pharmacologist, educator*
Moore, John George, Jr., *medical educator*
Morgenstern, Leon *surgeon*

Manteca
Miller, Max William *emergency physician*

Martinez
Barnard, William Marion *psychiatrist*
McKnight, Lenore Ravin *child psychiatrist, educator*

Mcclellan AFB
Chong, Vernon *surgeon, physician, air force officer*

Mendocino
Felton, Jean Spencer *physician*

Menlo Park
Hoffman, Thomas Edward *dermatologist*
Holmquest, Donald Lee *physician, astronaut, lawyer*
Kovachy, Edward Miklos, Jr., *psychiatrist, consultant*
Marton, Laurence Jay *researcher, educator, clinical pathologist*
Wachtel, John Steven *obstetrician, gynecologist*
Woodrow, Kenneth M. *psychiatrist*

Mill Valley
Harris, Jeffrey Saul *physician, executive, consultant*
Kolb, Felix Oscar *physician*
†Newman, Nancy Marilyn *ophthalmologist, educator*

Millbrae
Ferrer, Adelardo Manuel *physician*

Milpitas
Chiu, Peter Yee-Chew *physician*

Mission Viejo
Mruthyunjaya, G.T. *pediatrician*

Modesto
Boyce, Dennis Wayne *radiologist*
Cimino, Lewis R., Jr., *surgeon*
Khanna, Kanwal *rheumatologist*
Lewis, Marshall Edward *psychiatrist, administrator, educator*
†Suntra, Charles Ratapol *surgeon, educator*

Moffett Field
Dismukes, Robert Key *medical scientist*

Monrovia
Deliman, Robert Michael *surgeon*

Monterey
Bhaskar, Surindar Nath *pathologist, periodontist*
Black, Robert Lincoln *pediatrician, educator*
Sunde, Douglas *plastic surgeon*

Monterey Park
Chang, Jonathan Lee *orthopedist, educator*

Moreno Valley
Garcia, Ariel H. *plastic surgeon*

Morgan Hill
Tan, Lucas G. *anesthesiologist*

Mountain View
†Abel, Elizabeth A. *dermatologist*
Fischman, Stanley Edwin *psychiatrist*
Ivy, Edward Joseph *plastic surgeon*
†Lowen, Robert Marshall *plastic surgeon*
Piazza, Duane Eugene *biomedical researcher*
Urman, Jeffrey David *physician, educator*
Warren, Richard Wayne *obstetrician, gynecologist*

Napa
Anderson, Richard Elliott *internist, educator*
†Morgese, Vincent John *neurosurgeon*

National City
Morgan, Jacob Richard *cardiologist*

Nevada City
André Kildare, Michel Walter *neurosurgeon*

Newbury Park
Bleiberg, Leon William *surgical podiatrist*

Newhall
†Stein, Karl N. *plastic and reconstructive surgeon*

Newport Beach
Amyes, Edwin Westby *neurosurgeon*
Blinder, Barton Jerome *physician, psychiatrist, psychoanalyst, educator*
Connolly, John Earle *surgeon, educator*
Robinson, Hurley *surgeon*
Shohet, Jack A. *otolaryngologist*
Williams, Donald Edward *endocrinologist*
Zubrin, Jay Ross *surgeon*

Norwalk
Armstrong, David Ligon *psychiatrist*
Bao, Joseph Yue-Se *orthopedist, microsurgeon, educator*
Khajawall, Ali Mohamad *psychiatrist*

Oak Park
Caldwell, Stratton Franklin *kinesiology educator*

Oakland
Collen, Morris Frank *medical association administrator, physician, medical researcher*
Dell, Stephen Owen *neurosurgeon*
Hilsinger, Raymond L., Jr., *otolaryngologist*
†Hsu, John *physician scientist*
Killebrew, Ellen Jane (Mrs. Edward S. Graves) *cardiologist, educator*
Ng, Lawrence Ming-Loy *pediatrician*
†Osmond, Dennis Hubert *epidemiologist*
Rice, Frances Mae *physician*
Sharpton, Thomas *physician*
Sun, Peter P. *neurosurgeon*
Teufel, William Lockwood *emergency physician*
†Victorino, Gregory Peter *trauma surgeon*
†Weinmann, Robert Lewis *neurologist*
Wiesenthal, Andrew Michael *physician*

Oceanside
Curtin, Thomas Lee *ophthalmologist*
Haley, Thomas John *retired pharmacologist*

Orange
Barr, Ronald Jeffrey *dermatologist, pathologist*
Berman, Michael Leonard *gynecologic oncologist*
Calvert, Jay Wynn *plastic surgeon*
Chang, Jae Chan *hematologist, oncologist, educator*
†Cinat, Marianne Eva *surgeon*
Crumley, Roger Lee *surgeon, educator*
Evans, Gregory Randolph Dean *plastic surgeon, educator*
Fischel, Richard Jeffrey *thoracic surgeon*
Fisher, Mark Jay *neurologist, neuroscientist, educator*
Kim, Moon Hyun *endocrinologist, educator*
†Klassen, Henry John *ophthalmologist*
Lippa, Linda Susan Mottow *ophthalmologist*
Lott, Ira Totz *pediatric neurologist*
Meshkinpour, Hooshang *gastroenterologist, educator*
Milliken, Jeffrey *cardiothoracic surgeon*
Monk, Bradley James *gynecologic oncologist, researcher, educator*
Morgan, Beverly Carver *pediatrician, educator*
Mosier, Harry David, Jr., *physician, educator*
Rowen, Marshall *radiologist*
Schneider, Max Alexander *physician, educator*
Schoon, Doris Vivien *ophthalmologist*
Simjee, Aisha *ophthalmologist, educator*
Stamos, Michael Jerry *surgeon, educator*
†Stratton, Samuel Joe *emergency physician, researcher*
Sundine, Michael James *plastic surgeon*
Vatcher, James Gordon *retired physician*
Vaziri, Nosratola Dabir *internist, nephrologist, educator*
Wilson, Archie Fredric *medical educator*
Wilson, Samuel Eric *vascular and general surgeon*
Yu, Jen *medical educator*

Oroville
Chandy, Mammen G. *surgeon*

Oxnard
Young, Ronald Frederick *neurosurgeon*

Pacific Palisades
Beck, John Christian
Claes, Daniel John *physician*
Newmark, Harris, III, *diagnostic radiologist*
Tourtellotte, Wallace William *neurologist, educator*

Palm Desert
Warren, Joan Leigh *pediatrician*

Palm Springs
Gaede, James Ernest *physician, medical educator*
Kern, Donald Michael *internist*
Wilson, Myron Robert, Jr., *retired psychiatrist*

Palo Alto
Adamson, Geoffrey David *reproductive endocrinologist, surgeon*
Alexander, Steven Roy *pediatric nephrology educator*
Bagshaw, Malcolm A. *radiation oncologist, educator*
Bensch, Klaus George *pathology educator*
Britton, M(elvin) C(reed), Jr., *physician, rheumatologist*
Byrd, Thomas Russell *medical educator*
Chen, Stephen Shi-hua *pathologist, biochemist*
†Dement, William Charles *medical researcher, medical educator*
Farquhar, John William *physician, educator*
†Forno, Lysia S. *neuropathologist*
Fortmann, Stephen Paul *medical educator, researcher, epidemiologist*
Fries, James Franklin *internal medicine educator*
Goldstein, Mary Kane *physician*
Halamek, Louis Patrick *neonatologist*
Harris, Edward Day, Jr., *physician*
Hays, Marguerite Thompson *nuclear medicine physician, educator*
Holman, Halsted Reid *medical educator, physician*
Hubert, Helen Betty *epidemiologist*
†Illes, Judy *medical researcher, radiologist*
Lane, Alfred Thomas *medical educator*
Linna, Timo Juhani *immunologist, researcher, educator*
Maffly, Roy Herrick *medical educator, retired*
Murovic, Judith Ann *neurosurgeon*
Pizzo, Philip A. *pediatrics educator, university administrator*
Salvatierra, Oscar, Jr., *transplant surgeon, urologist, educator*
Schrier, Stanley Leonard *hematologist, educator*
Shuer, Lawrence Mendel *neurosurgery educator*
Silverman, Norman Henry *cardiologist, educator*
Strober, Samuel *immunologist, educator*
†Tune, Bruce Malcolm *pediatrics educator, renal toxicologist*
Urquhart, John *medical researcher, educator*
Weng, Wen-Kai *physician, medical researcher*
Wong, Nancy L. *dermatologist*
†Wren, Sherry M. *surgeon*
Zarins, Christopher Kristaps *surgery educator, vascular surgeon*

Palos Verdes Peninsula
Haynes, Moses Alfred *physician*
Thomas, Claudewell Sidney *psychiatry educator*

Panorama City
Jacob, Peter James *obstetrician-gynecologist*

Paradise
Haws, Hale Louis *medical consultant*

Paramount
Cohn, Lawrence Steven *physician, educator*

Pasadena
Buck, Francis Scott *pathologist, educator*
Carregal, Enrique J. *anesthesiologist, educator*
Girod, Erwin Ernest *internist*
Harvey, Joseph Paul, Jr., *orthopedist, educator*
Holmes, Louis Ira *physician assistant, educator, photojournalist*
†Judd, Stephen Alan *biomedical researcher, educator, marketing professional*
Lake, Kevin Bruce *medical association administrator*
Lee, Fred Arthur *radiologist, educator*
Magnes, Harry Alan *physician*
Miklusak, Thomas Alan *psychiatrist, psychoanalyst*
†Newman, Marjorie Yospin *psychiatrist*
Rosenfeld, Harold Lee *plastic surgeon*
Shaw, Anthony *physician, pediatric surgeon*
Short, Elizabeth M. *physician, educator, federal agency administrator*
Soleimani, Massoud *internist, rheumatologist*
Wang, Jin-Chen Camilla *physician, geneticist*
Wong, Raymond Shiu-Loong *radiologist*

Paso Robles
Allison, Ralph Brewster *psychiatrist*

Piedmont
Hughes, James Paul *physician*
Reich, Stanley Benjamin *radiologist, medical educator*

Pinole
Naughton, James Lee *internist*

Placerville
Bonser, Quentin *retired surgeon*
Vandenberg, Byron F. *cardiologist*

Pleasant Hill
Hollister, Arthur Clair, Jr., *epidemiologist, public health officer*

Pleasanton
†Auker, Todd Alan *ophthalmologist, surgeon*

Poway
Conrad, Alan John *internist*

Rancho Mirage
†Ausman, James I. *neurosurgeon, educator*
Shaeffer, Charlie Willard, Jr., *cardiologist*

Rancho Santa Fe
Affeldt, John Ellsworth *retired physician*
Carr, David Turner *physician*
Rockoff, S. David *radiologist, physician, educator*

Redding
Shadish, William Raymond *retired plastic surgeon*
Stone, William Kenneth *surgeon*

Redlands
Adey, William Ross *physician*
Bangasser, Ronald Paul *physician*
Skoog, William Arthur *former oncologist, educator*

Redwood City
Ellis, Eldon Eugene *surgeon*
Shmagranoff, George L. *physician*

Richmond
†Arnon, Stephen Soulé *epidemiologist, research scientist*
†Shenoy, Surendra *internist*

Riverside
Bricker, Neal S. *physician, educator*
Chang, Janice May *lawyer, naturopathic doctor, psychologist*
Chen, Adam I. *physician*
Froehly, Bertram Martin, Jr., *neurologist*
Jung, Timothy Tae Kun *otolaryngologist*
Linaweaver, Walter Ellsworth, Jr., *physician*
Shoji, Hiromu *orthopedic surgeon, educator*
Stone, Herman Hull *internist*

Rolling Hills Estates
Bellis, Carroll Joseph *surgeon, educator*
Page, Phyllis Eleanor *physician*

Roseville
Haugen, David Lee *surgeon*
Jammal, Joseph Jamil *cardiologist*

Rowland Heights
Hsu, John *anesthesiologist*

Sacramento
†Battistella, Felix D. *physician, educator*
Bogren, Hugo Gunnar *radiology educator*
Chapman, Michael William *orthopedist, educator*
Cunningham, Mary Elizabeth (Mary Cunningham-Lusby) *physician*
Davis, Brian Adam *physician*
Dobie, Robert Alan *otologist*
†Ellis, William Gene *neuropathologist*
Evans, David Alun *otolaryngologist*
Evrigenis, John Basil *obstetrician/gynecologist*
†Hilty, Donald M *psychiatrist, educator*
†Lilla, James A. *plastic surgeon*
†Lim, Alan Young *plastic surgeon*
Lippold, Roland Will *surgeon*
Lynch, Peter John *former dermatologist*
Malkin, Harold Marshall *medical researcher*
†Parsons, Gibbe Hull *medical educator*
Richards, John Ray *emergency physician, educator*
†Sciammarella, Maria Graciela *internist, cardiologist*
Shapero, Harris Joel *pediatrician*
Sharma, Arjun Dutta *cardiologist*
Spann, Lawrence Henry (Chip Spann) *physician associate*
Stevenson, Thomas Ray *plastic surgeon*
Styne, Dennis Michael *physician, educator*
†Tung, Prabhas *plastic surgeon*
Watson, Robert D. *allergist, immunologist, pediatric rheumatologist*
West, Irma Marie *retired occupational health physician*
†Wisner, David Hamilton *surgeon, educator*
Wolfe, Bruce McLaren *surgery educator*
Wolfman, Earl Frank, Jr., *surgeon, educator*
Wolkov, Harvey Brian *oncologist, researcher*
Woo, Karen *physician*
Zil, J. S. *psychiatrist, physiologist*

Salinas
†Phillips, John P(aul) *retired neurosurgeon*

San Bernardino
De Haas, David Dana *emergency physician*

San Bruno
Bradley, Charles William *podiatrist, educator*

San Clemente
Gialamas, Gus G. *orthopedic surgeon*
Kim, Edward William *ophthalmic surgeon*

San Diego
†Alksne, John F. *medical educator, former dean*
Backer, Matthias, Jr., *obstetrician, gynecologist*
†Bookstein, Joseph J. *radiologist, educator*
Bot, Adrian Ion *immunologist*
Chambers, Henry George *orthopedic surgeon*
Cosman, Bard Clifford *surgeon, educator*
DeMaria, Anthony Nicholas *cardiologist, educator*
Demeter, Steven *neurologist, medical publishing company executive*
Drummond, John C. *anesthesiologist, educator*
Friedman, Lawrence Stuart *internist, pediatrician, educator*
Friedman, Paul Jay *radiologist, educator*
Garfin, Steven R. *orthopedic surgeon*
Goltz, Robert William *physician, educator*
Grant, Igor *psychiatrist*
Hoffer, Michael E. *otolaryngologist, naval officer*
Hunt, Robert Gary *medical consultant, oral and maxillofacial surgeon*
Intriere, Anthony Donald *retired internist, gastroenterologist*
Jacoby, Irving *physician*
Jamieson, Stuart William *surgeon, educator*
Jones, Clyde William *anesthesiologist*
Kaback, Michael *medical educator*
Kaplan, George Willard *urologist*
†Keramati, Shahin *cardiologist*
Levy, Jerome *dermatologist, retired naval officer*
Levy, Michael Lee *neurosurgeon*
Lynch, Frank P. *pediatric surgeon*
McCarberg, Bill Harold *physician*
Meerson, Felix Zalmanovich *cardiologist*
Mercola, Daniel A. *medical researcher*
Merrill-Nach, Suzanne Marie *obstetrician, gynecologist*
Mills, Paul J. *psychiatry educator*
Moossa, A. R. *surgery educator*
Moss, Gene Richard *psychiatrist*
†Naviaux, Robert *pediatrician, educator*
Neuman, Tom S. *emergency medical physician, educator*
O'Malley, Edward *psychiatrist, consultant*
Peebles, Carol Lynn *immunology researcher*
Perlman, Richard Donald *orthopedic surgeon*
Pitt, William Alexander *cardiologist*
Ray, Albert *family physician*
†Reid, Robert Tilden *medical association administrator, internist*
†Ross, John, Jr., *cardiologist, educator*
†Sakamoto, Kyoko *surgeon, educator*
Schmidt, Joseph David *urologist*
Schuckit, Marc Alan *psychiatry educator, researcher*
Seagren, Stephen Linner *oncologist*
Silverstone, Leon Martin *neuroscientist, cardiologist, educator, researcher*
Van Gorder, Chris *medical executive*
Wallace, Helen Margaret *physician, educator*
Wasserman, Stephen Ira *physician, educator*
Yuan, Jason Xiao-Jian *medical researcher, educator*

San Francisco
Amend, William John Conrad, Jr., *physician, educator*
Ascher, Nancy Louise *surgeon*
Bachman, David Christian *orthopedic surgeon*
Bainton, Dorothy Ford *pathology educator, researcher*
Barkovich, Anthony James *pediatric neuroradiologist, educator, researcher*
Baron, Barry Camp *otolaryngologist*
Barondes, Samuel Herbert *psychiatrist, educator*
Benet, Leslie Zachary *pharmacokineticist, educator*
Berg, Bruce O. *child neurologist, educator*
Bishop, John Michael *biomedical research scientist, educator*
Boles, Roger *otolaryngologist*
†Brown, Donald Malcolm *plastic surgeon*
Brown, Eric Joel *biomedical researcher, researcher*
Busch, David Frederick *internist*
Campbell, André Renay *surgical educator, internist*
Clever, Linda Hawes *physician*
†Crawford, Michael Howard *cardiologist, educator, researcher*
David, George *psychiatrist, economic theory lecturer*
Deicken, Raymond Friedrich *neuropsychiatrist, clinical neuroscientist*
†Deng, Donna Y. *urologist, surgeon*
Denys, Eric Heli *neurologist*
†Dillon, William Patrick *neuroradiologist, radiologist*
Engleman, Ephraim Philip *rheumatologist*
Epstein, Charles Joseph *physician, medical geneticist, pediatrics and biochemistry educator*
Epstein, Ervin Harold, Jr., *dermatologist, educator, researcher*
Epstein, John Howard *dermatologist*
Erskine, John Morse *surgeon*
†Fessel, Walford Jeffrey *rheumatologist*
Feuerstein, Burt Gary *medical educator, geneticist*
Fields, Kathy Ann *dermatologist*
Finberg, Laurence *pediatrician, educator, dean*
Fletcher, John C. *physician*
Foye, Laurance Vincent *physician, hospital administrator*
Frick, Oscar Lionel *physician, educator*
Fu, Karen King-Wah *radiation oncologist*
Gellin, Gerald Alan *dermatologist*
Gibbs, Patricia Hellman *physician*
Goode, Erica Tucker *internist*
Gooding, Charles Arthur *radiologist, physician, educator*
†Gotway, Michael B. *radiologist, health facility administrator*
Gradinger, Gilbert Paul *plastic surgeon*
Greenspan, Francis S. *physician*
Grossman, William *medical researcher, educator*
Hauser, Stephen L. *medical educator*
Havel, Richard Joseph *physician, educator*
Henderson, Isaac Craig *oncologist, researcher*
Herbert, Chesley C. *psychiatrist, educator*
Hering, William Marshall *medical organization executive*
Heyman, Melvin Bernard *pediatric gastroenterologist*
Higashida, Randall Takeo *radiologist, neurosurgeon, medical educator*
Hinman, Frank, Jr., *urologist, educator*
Hoffman, Julien Ivor Ellis *pediatric cardiologist, educator*
Hsu, John Chao-Chun *retired pediatrician*
†Ikeda, Clyde Junichi *plastic and reconstructive surgeon*
Jacobson, Lester Barry *cardiologist*
†Jacobson, Mark Andrew *epidemiologist, educator, physician*
Jaffe, Robert Benton *obstetrician, gynecologist, reproductive endocrinologist*
Jonsen, Albert R(upert) *retired medical ethics educator*
†Kakar, Sanjay *gastrointestinal and liver pathologist*
Kallet, Richard Hubbard *medical researcher*
Kan, Yuet Wai *hematologist, educator*
†Kashani-Sabet, Mohammed *physician*
Katz, Hilliard Joel *physician*
Katzung, Bertram George *pharmacologist*
†Kenyon, Cynthia *medical researcher*
Kerman, Barry Martin *ophthalmologist, educator*
King, Talmadge E. *physician*
Kline, Howard Jay *cardiologist, educator*
†Koo, John Ying Ming *dermatologist*
†Lawton, Michael Thomas *neurosurgeon*
Lee, Philip Randolph Randolph *medical educator*
Liu, Xiao *ophthalmologist, neurobiologist*
Low, Randall *internist, cardiologist*
Lu, Francis Gordon *psychiatrist, educator*
Lucia, Marilyn Reed *physician*
Lull, Robert John *nuclear medicine physician, educator*
Maibach, Howard I. *dermatologist*
†Margolin, Frederick Ronald *radiologist, educator*
Mason, Dean Towle *cardiologist*
Massie, Barry Michael *cardiologist*
McAninch, Jack Weldon *urological surgeon, educator*
McClure, Thomas Allan *physician*
McGrath, Mary Helena *plastic surgeon, educator*
†Messina, Louis Michael *vascular surgeon, educator*
Miller, Walter Luther *pediatrician, educator*
Mustacchi, Piero *preventive medicine physician, educator*
Navarro, J. Renee *anesthesiologist*
Owsley, John Quincy, III, *plastic surgeon, educator*
Palmer, Bonita Ann *physician, healing minister, marriage and family therapist*
†Pan, Edward *neuro-oncologist*
†Parer, Julian Thomas *obstetrics and gynecology educator*
†Peterlin, Boris Matija *physician*
Petrakis, Nicholas Louis *epidemiologist, medical researcher, educator*
Phillips, Theodore Locke *radiation oncologist, educator*
Raskin, Neil Hugh *neurology educator*
Reilly, Linda M. *surgeon*
Ristow, Brunno *plastic surgeon*
Roe, Benson Bertheau *surgeon, educator*
Rosenbaum, Ernest Harold *internist, oncologist, educator*
†Rosenthal, Philip *gastroenterologist*
Rosinski, Edwin Francis *medical educator*
Rudolph, Abraham Morris *pediatrician, educator*
Schiller, Francis *neurologist, medical historian*
Schmid, Rudi (Rudolf Schmid) *internist, educator, academic administrator*
Schmidt, Robert Milton *physician, scientist, educator, administrator*
Schrock, Theodore R. *surgeon*
Schroeder, Steven Alfred *medical educator*
Seebach, Lydia Marie *physician*
Shaw, Richard Eugene *cardiovascular researcher*
Shinefield, Henry Robert *pediatrician*
Smith, David Elvin *physician*
Smith, Lloyd Hollingsworth *physician*
Speidel, John Joseph *obstetrician, educator*
Spivey, Bruce E. *ophthalmologist, integrated healthcare delivery systems management executive*
Stamper, Robert Lewis *ophthalmologist, educator*
Straube, Barry Maynard *physician executive*
†Suba, Eric John *physician*
Terr, Abba Israel *allergist, immunologist*
Terr, Lenore Cagen *psychiatrist, writer*
Thompson, Charlotte Ellis *pediatrician, educator, author*
Tseng, Elaine Evelina *cardiothoracic surgeon*
Turek, Paul Jacob *urological surgeon*
†Verghese, Vino John *gastroenterologist*
Volberding, Paul Arthur *academic physician*
Volpe, Peter Anthony *surgeon*
Wallerstein, Ralph Oliver *physician*
Watts, Malcolm S(tuart) M(cNeal) *physician, medical educator*
Way, E(dward) Leong *pharmacologist, toxicologist, educator*
Wescott, William Burnham *oral maxillofacial pathologist, educator*
Wilson, Charles B. *neurosurgeon, educator*
Woeber, Kenneth Alois *physician*
Wolff, Sheldon *radiobiologist, educator*
Wolkowitz, Owen Mark *physician, psychiatrist, researcher*
Zippin, Calvin *epidemiologist, educator*

San Gabriel
Chen, John Calvin *child and adolescent psychiatrist*
Ko, Cheng Chia Charles *obstetrician-gynecologist*

San Jose
Avakoff, Joseph Carnegie *medical consultant, law consultant*
Boldrey, Edwin Eastland *retinal surgeon, educator*
Doty, Jeffrey Edward *surgeon*
Gale, Arnold David *pediatric neurologist, consultant*
Joshi, Janardan Shantilal *surgeon*
Kagawa, Frank Takeshi *critical care physician*
Kramer, Richard Jay *gastroenterologist, educator*
Nguyen, Thinh Van *internist*
Pulley, Douglas Boyd *ophthalmologist*
Shatney, Clayton Henry *surgeon*
Stein, Arthur Oscar *pediatrician, small business owner, retired pediatrician*
†Stevens, David Alec *medical educator*

San Juan Capistrano
Braunstein, Herbert *pathologist, educator*
Fisher, Delbert Arthur *physician, educator*
Zalta, Edward *otorhinolaryngologist, physician*

San Luis Obispo
Pinkel, Donald Paul *pediatrician*
Weaver, Karl E. *psychiatrist*

Greeley
Cook, Donald E. *pediatrician, educator*
Ebomoyi, William Ehigie *epidemiologist*

Greenwood Village
†Klasco, Richard *emergency physician, information technology executive*

Highlands Ranch
Bublitz, Deborah Keirstead *pediatrician*

La Junta
Williams, Ronald Lee *retired pharmacologist*

Littleton
Brega, Kerry Elizabeth *physician, researcher*
Forstot, Stephan Lance *ophthalmologist*

Lonetree
Washington, Reginald Louis *pediatric cardiologist*

Montrose
Boice, Judith Lynette *physician, writer, educator*

Morrison
Pettee, Daniel Starr *retired neurologist*

Pueblo
Lewallen, William Marvin, Jr., *ophthalmologist*

Snowmass Village
Neumann, Bruce Russell *emergency physician*

Vail
Bevan, William Arnold, Jr., *emergency physician*
Chow, Franklin Szu-Chien *obstetrician, gynecologist*
McFadden, Joseph Tedford *retired neurosurgeon, writer*

Wheat Ridge
Brown, Steven Brien *radiologist*

CONNECTICUT

Ansonia
Dvoretzky, Israel *dermatologist*

Avon
Hinz, Carl Frederick, Jr., *physician, educator*

Bloomfield
Goldenberg, Philip Theodore *physician*

Branford
Cronin, Michael Thomas Ignatius *pathologist, educator*
†Tchernev, Velizar Tzvetanov *biomedical scientist*
Vietzke, Wesley Maunder *internist, educator*

Bridgeport
Bernstein, Larry Howard *clinical pathologist*
Hanley, Hilda Christina *endocrinologist*
Lobdell, David Hill *pathologist*
Nijensohn, Daniel Edgardo *neurosurgeon*
Rosenman, Stephen David *obstetrician and gynecologist*
†Salam, Adil *pulmonary critical care physician*
Skowron, Tadeusz Adam *physician*
Slepian, Jacob Zeiger *otolaryngologist*

Cos Cob
Duncalf, Deryck *retired anesthesiologist*

Danbury
Bristol, Josephine Hart *psychiatrist*
Falkenstein, Ralph Jay *ophthalmologist*
Hulnick, Donald H. *radiologist*
Keller, Barry R. *physician*
Kurien, Santha T. *psychiatrist*
Mashman, Jan Howard *neurologist, educator, rehabilitation administrator*
Miller, Jeffrey David *allergist*
Taweh, Ziad Michael *internist*
Walker, Michael James *surgeon*

Darien
Newman, Fredric Alan *plastic surgeon, educator*

East Haven
Conn, Harold O. *physician, educator*

East Lyme
Levin, Robert Earl *clinical rheumatologist*

Essex
Burris, Harriet Louise *emergency physician*
Goff, Christopher Wallick *pediatrician*

Fairfield
Burd, Robert Meyer *hematologist, oncologist, educator*
Clements, Hana Joan *physician*
Levinson, Stephen Ronald *retired otolaryngologist*
Mauer, Kenneth Ray *gastroenterologist, educator*
Pinto, Edward Ralph *internist, cardiologist*

Farmington
†Arnold, Andrew *medical researcher, physician*
Cone, Robert Edward *immunologist, educator*
Cooperstein, Sherwin Jerome *medical educator*
Donaldson, James Oswell, III, *neurology educator*
Grunnet, Margaret Louise *pathology educator*
Liebowitz, Neil Robert *psychiatrist*
McCawley, Austin *psychiatrist, educator*
†Metersky, Mark L. *physician*
Moskowitz, Harold *radiologist*
Rothfield, Naomi Fox *physician*
Schenkman, John Boris *pharmacologist, educator*
Walker, James Elliot Cabot *physician*

Georgetown
Einstein, Eric Brandt *internal medicine physician*

Glastonbury
Juda, Richard John *anesthesiologist, critical care specialist*
Singer, Paul Richard *ophthalmologist*

Greenwich
Blumberg, Joel Myron *cardiologist*
Camel, Mark Howard *neurological surgeon*
Kalan, Gary Edward *anesthesiologist*
Kopenhaver, Patricia Ellsworth *podiatrist*
Rosenberg, Arthur Henry *internist*
Wolfson, Ellen N. *physician*

Groton
†Fossa, Anthony Andrea *pharmacologist*
Harrigan, Edmund Patrick *physician, researcher*

Guilford
Langdon, Robert Colin *dermatologist, educator*
Springgate, Clark Franklin *physician, researcher*

Hamden
Nuland, Sherwin *surgeon, author*

Hartford
Banever, Thomas Clark *surgeon, educator*
Blair, Charles Lee *physician, educator*
Brauer, Rima Lois *psychiatrist*
Brennan, Tracy Elizabeth *physician*
Cole, Solon Robert *pathologist, educator*
Dobkin, Eric David *critical care surgeon, educator*
Dworkin, Paul Howard *pediatrician*
Gibbons, John Martin, Jr., *physician, educator*
Gillam, Linda Dawn *cardiologist, researcher*
Herzog, Alfred *psychiatrist, health facility executive*
Humphrey, Chester Bowden *cardio-thoracic surgeon*
Jahiel, Rene Ino *physician*
Jeresaty, Robert Michel *cardiologist, educator*
Joshi, Vijay V. *pathologist, educator*
Jung, Betty Chin *epidemiologist, research analyst, educator, medical/surgical nurse*
†Kirton, Orlando Cecilio *surgeon, educator*
Klimek, Joseph John *physician, educator*
Krause, Peter James *pediatrician, researcher, educator*
Lyons, Robert William *medical educator, infectious disease consultant*
Pachter, Lee M. *pediatrician*
Pastuszak, William Theodore *hematopathologist*
Powers, Robert David *physician*
Rosenberg, Eric Lee *internal medicine physician, educator*

Lyme
Bloom, Barry Malcolm *pharmaceutical consultant*

Madison
Snell, Richard Saxon *anatomist*

Manchester
Jacobson, Charles Edward, Jr., *urologist*
Klipstein, Arnold Lloyd *gastroenterologist*
Schwartz, Robert G. *physician*

Meriden
Combs, Jerome Thomas *pediatrician, consultant*
Horton, Paul Chester *psychiatrist*
†Perricone, Nicholas V. *dermatologist*

Middlebury
Arnold, William Parsons, Jr., *retired internist*

Middletown
Miller, Donald Edwin *physician*
Narad, Joan Stern *psychiatrist*
Rabuffo, Jeffrey Vincent *urologist*
Torop, Paul *psychiatrist*

Mystic
Burrow, Gerard Noel *physician, educator*

New Britain
Bernene, James Louis *physician*
Owens, Guy *neurosurgeon*

New Canaan
Ackerman, Sigurd Howard *psychiatrist*
Coughlin, Francis Raymond, Jr., *surgeon, educator, lawyer*

New Haven
Aghajanian, George Kevork *medical educator*
†Andriole, Vincent Thomas *medical educator, researcher*
Arons, Marvin Shield *plastic and hand surgeon*
Askenase, Philip William *medicine and pathology educator*
Barash, Paul George *anesthesiologist, educator*
†Bartoshuk, Linda J. *otolaryngologist, educator*
†Bazzy-Asaad, Alia *pediatrician, pulmonologist, academic administrator*
Behrman, Harold Richard *endocrinologist, physiologist, educator*
Boyer, James Lorenzen *physician, educator*
Braverman, Irwin Merton *dermatologist, educator*
Cohen, Donald Jay *pediatrics, psychiatry and psychology educator, administrator*
Cohen, Lawrence Sorel *physician, educator*
Collins, William F., Jr., *neurosurgery educator*
Comer, James Pierpont *psychiatrist, educator*
Cooper, Dennis Lawrence *oncologist, educator*
Cooper, Jack Ross *pharmacology educator, researcher*
Davey, Lycurgus Michael *neurosurgeon*
Dunkle, Lisa Marie *pharmaceutical research executive*
Fei, Yijian *ophthalmologist, biomedical researcher*
†Fikrig, Erol *rheumatologist, medical educator*

†Forster, Susan H. *ophthalmologist, educator*
Freedman, Gerald Stanley *radiologist, healthcare administrator, educator*
Friedlaender, Gary Elliott *orthopedist, educator*
Genel, Myron *pediatrician, educator*
Glaser, Gilbert Herbert *neuroscientist, physician, educator*
Goodrich, Isaac *neurosurgeon, educator*
†Haddad, Gabriel G. *pediatrician, educator*
Heninger, George Robert *psychiatry educator, researcher*
†Hockfield, Susan *medical educator*
†Horwich, Arthur L. *medical educator*
Inouye, Sharon K. *physician, educator*
Jatlow, Peter I. *pathologist, medical educator, researcher*
Kashgarian, Michael *pathologist, physician*
Kernan, Walter Newberry *physician*
Kirchner, John Albert *retired otolaryngology educator*
†Kosten, Thomas R. *psychiatrist, educator*
Kushlan, Samuel Daniel *physician, educator, hospital administrator*
Lannin, Donald Rowe *oncologist, surgeon*
Laub, Dori *psychiatrist*
Lee, Sin Hang *pathologist, educator*
Leffell, David Joel *dermatologist, surgeon, health facility administrator, educator, writer*
Lentz, Thomas Lawrence *biomedical educator, dean, researcher*
Levine, Robert John *physician, educator*
Lewis, Melvin *psychiatrist, pediatrician, psychoanalyst*
Lytton, Bernard *urology educator*
Madigan, Janet A. *psychiatrist, child psychiatrist, educator*
Mark, Harry Horst *ophthalmologist, researcher*
†Mason, Graeme Finlay *biophysicist, researcher, educator*
†Matthay, Richard A. *pulmonary and critical care physician, educator*
McCarthy, Paul Louis *pediatrics educator*
Mukherjee, Sandip Kumar *cardiologist*
Musto, David Franklin *physician, educator, historian, consultant*
Naftolin, Frederick *physician, reproductive biologist educator*
Niederman, James Corson *physician, educator*
Nwangwu, John Tochukwu *epidemiologist, public health educator*
Persing, John Arthur *surgeon*
†Porter, George Arthur, Jr., *pediatric cardiologist, researcher*
†Powsner, Seth *psychiatry educator, medical computing researcher*
Prusoff, William Herman *biochemical pharmacologist, educator*
†Richerson, George Bradley *neurologist, educator*
Ritchie, J. Murdoch *pharmacologist, educator*
Romero-González, Guido Mauricio *psychiatrist, educator, consultant*
†Safriel, Yair *neuroradiologist*
Sartorelli, Alan Clayton *pharmacologist, educator*
Sasaki, Clarence Takashi *surgeon, medical educator*
Schowalter, John Erwin *child and adolescent psychiatry educator*
Schwartz, Peter Edward *physician, gynecologic oncology educator*
Seashore, Margretta Reed *physician*
Shaywitz, Bennett Arthur *medical educator*
†Shulman, Gerald I. *physician, scientist, educator*
Siegel, Norman Joseph *pediatrician, educator*
Silverstone, David Edward *ophthalmologist*
†Smith, Brian Richard *hematologist, oncologist, pathologist*
Spinner, Gary Frederick *physician assistant, healthcare administrator*
Spiro, Howard Marget *physician, educator*
Stern, Robert *psychiatrist*
Sze, Gordon *neuroradiologist*
Tamborlane, William V., Jr., *physician, biomedical researcher, pediatrics educator*
†Volkmar, Fred Robert *psychiatrist, educator*
†Waxman, Stephen George *neurologist, neuroscientist*
Weiss, Robert M. *urologist, educator*
†Werdiger, Norman *neurologist*
Wessel, Morris Arthur *retired pediatrics educator*
Wright, Hastings Kemper *surgeon, educator*
Yanagisawa, Eiji *otolaryngologist, educator*
Zaret, Barry Lewis *cardiologist, medical educator*

New London
Bobruff, Jerome *physician*
Schoenberger, Steven Harris *physician, research consultant*
Urbanetti, John Sutherland *internist, consultant*

New Milford
Battista, John Robert *psychiatrist*

Niantic
Douglas, Robert Gordon, Jr., *physician*

Norwalk
Atlas, Ernest *physician*
Conoscenti, Craig Stephen *physician*
Floch, Martin Herbert *physician*
Greenberg, Sheldon Burt *plastic and reconstructive surgeon*
Rose, Gilbert Jacob *psychiatrist, writer, psychoanalyst*
Tracey, Edward John *physician, surgeon*

Norwich
Chakrabarti, Jai *internist, cardiologist*

Old Lyme
Cook, Charles Davenport *pediatrician, educator*

Orange
Granata, Attilio Vincent *medical educator, physician executive*

Plainville
Petit, William Arthur, Jr., *endocrinologist*

Putnam
Day, John Anthony, Jr., *pulmonologist*

Ridgefield
†Egan, Kenneth J. *dermatologist*

Sharon
Gottlieb, Richard Matthew *psychiatrist, consultant*
Jensen, Philip Bailey *urologist*

Southington
Byeff, Peter David *hematologist, oncologist*

Stamford
†Besser, Gary Steven *obstetrician, gynecologist, surgeon*
Cook, Colin Burford *psychiatrist*
Goodhue, Peter Ames *obstetrician and gynecologist, educator*
Klein, Neil Charles *physician*
Walsh, Thomas Joseph *neuro-ophthalmologist*
Waxberg, Jonathan Abel *urologic surgeon, oncologist*
†Yap, Jesus F., Jr., *cardiologist*

Storrs Mansfield
Skauen, Donald Matthew *retired pharmaceutical educator*

Stratford
Feinberg, Dennis Lowell *dermatologist*
Trapasso, Robert Louis *surgical pathologist*

Trumbull
Beres, Milan *surgeon*

Wallingford
Kailasam, Mala Trichur *physician*
†Sanchez, Ramiro, Jr., *pharmaceutical physician*

Waterbury
Bobowick, A. Roger *neurologist*
DeFrancesco, Mark Stephen *physician*
deLuise, Vincent Paul *ophthalmologist*
Dudrick, Stanley John *surgeon, scientist, educator*
Fischbein, Charles Alan *pediatrician*
Garsten, Joel Jay *gastroenterologist*
Getnick, Richard Alan *ophthalmologist*
Knight, David Clough *physician*
Peterson, W(alter) Scott *ophthalmic surgeon*
Shetty, Jayakara *surgeon*

Waterford
Pierson, Anne Bingham *physician*

Watertown
Sherwood, James Alan *physician, scientist, educator*

West Hartford
Silver, Herbert *physician*
Stavola, John Joseph *retired obstetrician-gynecologist*
Thompson, Howard King, Jr., *retired physician, educator*

Westport
Burns, John Joseph *pharmacology educator*
Clausman, Gilbert Joseph *retired medical librarian*
Dakofsky, LaDonna Jung *radiation oncologist, educator*
Lacouture, Peter George *medical researcher*
Lopker, Anita Mae *psychiatrist, researcher*
Meinke, Alan Kurt *surgeon*
Sacks, Herbert Simeon *psychiatrist, educator, consultant*

Woodbridge
Arnold, Philip Bruno *physician*
Bondy, Philip Kramer *physician, educator*
Yesner, Raymond *pathologist, consultant*

Woodbury
Dressler, David Michael *psychiatrist*

DELAWARE

Dover
Wilson, Samuel Mayhew *surgeon*

Hockessin
Kramer, Janet Phillips *physician*

Lewes
Adams, John Pletch *orthopaedic surgeon*

Milford
Quinn, Edward Francis, III, *orthopedic surgeon*

Newark
Breslin, Nancy Ann *psychiatrist, photographer, educator*
†Collier, Virginia Upchurch *internist*
Dadmarz, Kewmars Ebrahim *physician, educator*
Esterly, Katherine Louise *pediatrician*
Lemole, Gerald Michael *surgeon*
Lieberman, Joseph Aloysius, III, *physician, educator*
Phoon, Wai Wor *physician*
Reider, Martha Crawford *industrial immunologist*

Rockland
Levinson, John Milton *obstetrician, gynecologist*

Seaford
Campbell, Eugene Paul *retired public health administrator*

Wilmington
Benes, Solomon *biomedical scientist, physician*
Cornelison, Floyd Shovington, Jr., *retired psychiatrist, former educator*
†Dalziel, Sean Mark *pharmaceuticals researcher*
Frelick, Robert Westcott *physician, consultant*
Goldberg, Morton Edward *pharmacologist*
Gonzalez, Ricardo *surgeon, educator*
Greenblatt, Hellen Chaya *immunologist, microbiologist*
Gupta, Rakesh Kumar *internist*
Hammond, Isaac William *physician, epidemiologist*
Harley, Robison Dooling *physician, educator*
Inselman, Laura Sue *pediatrician, educator*
†Mandell, Gerald A. *nuclear medicine physician*
Morgan, Craig Douglas *orthopaedic surgeon*
Pahnke, Greg Randolph *surgeon*
Pell, Sidney *epidemiologist*
Schwartz, Marshall Zane *pediatric surgeon*
Wallace, Jesse Wyatt *pharmaceutical scientist*

DISTRICT OF COLUMBIA

Washington
†Aaron, Henry J. *medical association administrator*
Abel, Anne Elizabeth Sutherland *pediatrician*
Ahlgren, James David *oncologist*
Al-Kawas, Firas H. *physician*
Anthony, Virginia Quinn Bausch *medical association executive*
Arling, Bryan Jeremy *internist*
Armaly, Mansour F(arid) *ophthalmologist, educator*
Ascensão, João Luis Afonso *physician, researcher*
Atkinson, Richard Lee, Jr., *internal medicine educator*
August, Gilbert Paul *physician*
Bachman, David M. *ophthalmologist*
Benjamin, Georges Curtis *emergency physician, consultant*
Bernstein, Lionel M. *gastroenterologist, educator*
Biebuyck, Julien Francois *medical educator, administrator*
Blumenthal, Susan J. *physician*
†Blumenthal, Susan Jane *psychiatrist, educator, public health agent*
Boisvert, Marc Edward *surgeon, researcher*
Borenstein, David Gilbert *physician, author*
Bourne, Peter Geoffrey *physician, educator, author*
Bryant, Thomas Edward *physician, lawyer*
Burklow, Thomas Ray *pediatric cardiologist*
Burris, Boyd Lee *psychiatrist, psychoanalyst, physician, educator*
Callaway, Clifford Wayne *physician*
Callender, Clive Orville *surgeon*
Catoe, Bette Lorrina *physician, health educator*
Chamberlain, John Loomis, III, *retired pediatrician, educator*
Cheng, Tsung O *cardiologist, educator*
Chester, Alexander Campbell, III, *physician*
Chiapella, Anne Page *epidemiologist*
†Chiappinelli, Vincent Alexander *pharmacology educator*
Cohen, Jordan Jay *medical association executive*
Collea, Joseph Vincent *perinatologist, educator*
Collins, Robert Ellwood *surgeon*
Cooper, Byron Stanley *physician, educator*
Curfman, David Ralph *neurological surgeon, civic leader, musician*
†Cytowic, Richard Edmund *neurologist*
Dave, Harish Pranlal *hematologist*
Davidson, Richard J. *medical association administrator*
Davis, David Oliver *radiologist, educator*
Delaney, Morgan D. *physician, educator*
Dennis, Gary C. *neurosurgeon, educator*
Deutsch, Stanley *anesthesiologist, educator*
Dey, Radheshyam Chandra *cytologist*
Dritschilo, Anatoly *radiologist, educator*
Dublin, Thomas David *retired physician*
†Durakovic, Asaf *nuclear medicine physician, consultant*
Earll, Jerry Miller *internist, educator*
Ein, Daniel *allergist*
Epps, Roselyn Elizabeth Payne *pediatrician, educator*
Evans, Charles Hawes, Jr., *immunologist, health science educator*
Fairbanks, David Nathaniel Fox *physician, surgeon, educator*
Fallon, Harold Joseph *physician, pharmacology and biochemistry educator*
Fenton, Wayne S. *psychiatrist*
Ficarra, Bernard Joseph *former surgeon, legal medicine and bioethics consultant*
Finkelstein, James David *physician, educator*
Fowler, Paul Raymond *physician, lawyer*
Freis, Edward David *physician, medical researcher*
†Freishtat, Robert J. *pediatrician, researcher*
Galbis, Ricardo *psychiatrist*
Gelmann, Edward Paul *oncologist, educator*
Gobern, Camita Antoinette *internist*
Goldson, Alfred Lloyd *oncologist, educator*
Goodwin, Frederick King *psychiatrist*
Gordon, James Samuel *psychiatrist*
†Granados, Francisco D. *physician*
Gray, Sheila Hafter *psychiatrist, psychoanalyst*
†Gupta, Ashmit *otolaryngologist, researcher*
Hamburg, Margaret Ann (Peggy Hamburg) *public health administrator*
†Harris, Patricia Flora *epidemiologist*
Harvey, John Collins *physician, educator*
Hauser, Gabriel Jacob *pediatrician*
†Helman, Donald Lee *physician, military officer*
Herdman, Roger C. *physician, policy analyst*
Holden, Raymond Thomas *physician, educator*
Hollinshead, Ariel Cahill *research oncologist, educator*
Hussain, Syed Taseer *biomedical educator, researcher*
†Ishak, Kamal George *pathologist, consultant, pathologist, researcher, pathologist, educator*
Jani, Sushma Niranjan *pediatric psychiatrist*
Johnston, Gerald Samuel *physician, educator*
Kallakury, Bhaskar Venkata Satya *pathologist, educator*
Kamerow, Douglas Biron *epidemiologist, physician*
Kaplan, Keith Jacob *physician*
†Khachemoune, Amor *physician*
Kizer, Kenneth Wayne *physician, educator, researcher, consultant, administrator*
†Korn, David *educator, pathologist*
†Kuehl, Karen Simpson *cardiologist, researcher*
Kung, David *plastic surgeon*
Kupersmith, Joel *physician, medical school dean*
Kwart, Arnold Martin *urologic surgeon*
Kwik-Kostek, Christine Irene *physician, retired air force officer*
Landau, Emanuel *epidemiologist*
Leach, Berton Joe *medical educator*
Leffall, LaSalle D(oheny), Jr., *surgeon*
Lessin, Lawrence Stephen *hematologist, oncologist, educator*
Luessenhop, Alfred John *neurosurgeon, educator*
Lundergan, Conor Francis *cardiologist*
Majd, Massoud *radiology and nuclear medicine educator*
Mandel, H(arold) George *pharmacologist, educator*
Mann, Marion *physician, educator*
Mann, Oscar *retired physician, internist, educator*
Marcus, Devra Joy Cohen *internist*
Massaro, Donald John *medical educator, medical researcher*
Mattsson, Ake *psychiatrist, physician*
McGill, Willis Alexander *anesthesiologist*
McLean, Ian William *ophthalmic pathologist, researcher*
Miller, Richard N. *medical association administrator*
Murray, Robert Fulton, Jr., *physician*
†Musgrave, Franklyn Garfield *obstetrician, gynecologist*
Natarajan, Aruna *physician, educator, researcher*
Nelson, Alan Ray *internist, medical association administrator*
Novitch, Mark *physician, retired pharmaceutical executive*
Nowak, Judith Ann *psychiatrist*
†Nsouli, Talal Mounir *physician, allergist, immunologist*
Pahira, John Joseph *urology educator*
Pasternack, Stefan Alan *psychiatrist, psychoanalyst*
Paulson, Jerome Avrom *pediatrician*
Payne, Fred J. *physician, educator*
Pellegrino, Edmund Daniel *physician, educator, academic administrator*
†Peña, Maria Teresa *surgeon, educator, otolaryngologist*
Perkins, Joseph S. *medical association administrator*
Phillips, Michael M. *gastroenterologist*
Pichard, Augusto D. *medical educator*
Pincus, Jonathan Henry *neurologist, educator*
Pincus, Stephanie Hoyer *dermatologist, educator*
†Pinkerson, Alan Lee *physician*
Pollack, Murray Michael *physician, medical services administrator*
Potter, Barry M. *radiologist, medical educator*
†Puchalski, Christina M. *physician, medical educator*
Quivers, Eric Stanley *physician*
†Rabin, David L. *medical educator*
†Ramphele, Mamphela A. *medical educator*
Ramsey, Robert Leslie *oncologist*
Rapp, Michael Thomas *emergency physician*
Reaman, Gregory Harold *pediatric hematologist, oncologist*
Redman, Robert Shelton *pathologist, dentist*
†Rennert, Wolfgang Peter *pediatrician, educator*
Rhodes, Lee Ann *anesthesiologist*
Richert, John Rolin *neuroimmunologist, educator*
Robinowitz, Carolyn Bauer *psychiatrist, educator*
Ruckman, Roger Norris *pediatric cardiologist*
Ruehle, Charles Joseph *pathologist, military officer*
Rushton, Harry Gil *pediatric urologist, educator*
†Sable, Craig *physician, cardiologist*
†Sabshin, Melvin *psychiatrist, educator, medical association administrator*
Sandler, Sumner Gerald *medical educator*
Sawin, Clark Timothy *endocrinologist*
†Schubert, Richard D. *medical educator, physician*
Shanahan, Sheila Ann *pediatrician, educator*
Shepherd, Mary Elizabeth *dermatologist*
Shrier, Diane Kesler *psychiatrist, educator*
Simon, Gary Leonard *internist, educator*
†Slonim, Anthony Daniel *pediatrician, internist*
Sly, Ridge Michael *physician, educator*
Smith, Lee Elton *surgery educator, retired military officer*
Spagnolo, Samuel Vincent *internist, pulmonary specialist, educator*
Spear, Scott Lawrence *plastic surgeon*
Steinberg, Paul Jay *psychiatrist*
†Stephan, Dietrich A. *pediatrician, educator, geneticist*
Stolley, Paul David *medical educator, researcher*
Stratton, Kathleen R. *medical association administrator*
Taler, George Abraham *medical educator*
Tavassoli, Fattaneh Abbas-zadeh *pathologist, consultant*
Thura, Peter *emergency physician*
Tosi, Laura Lowe *orthopaedic surgeon*
†Valachovic, Richard W. *medical association administrator*
Valadez, Joseph James *epidemiologist, researcher*
Vane, John Robert *pharmacologist*
†Vernalis, Marina *osteopath*
Vittone, Bernard John *psychiatrist, researcher*
Walton, Tracy Matthew, Jr., *radiologist*
Wartofsky, Leonard *medical educator*
Webster, Thomas Glenn *psychiatrist, educator*
Werkman, Sidney Lee *psychiatry educator*
Wilensky, Robert J. *plastic surgeon, historian*
Williams, John Franklin *anesthesiologist educator and administrator*
Willis, Arnold Jay *urologic surgeon, educator*
Wyngaarden, James Barnes *physician*
Yates, Allison A. *scientific organization administrator*
Young, Donald Alan *physician*
Zaleske, David Joseph *surgeon, scientist, health administrator*
Zinberg, Stanley *physician, educator*
Zook, Bernard Charles *pathology educator, administrator, researcher*

FLORIDA

Amelia Island
Schiebler, Gerold Ludwig *pediatrician, educator*

Atlantic Beach
Walker, Richard Harold *pathologist, educator*

Atlantis
†Borzak, Steven *cardiologist*
Louie, Steven J. *allergist, immunologist*
Lysaker, Earl C., Jr., *internist*

Aventura
Kovanic, Peter H. *pathologist, educator*

Bal Harbour
Katz, Shmuel *surgeon*

Bay Pines
Law, David Hillis *physician*
†Shettigar, Udipi R. *cardiologist, researcher*
Stewart, Jonathan Taylor *psychiatrist, educator*

Belleair
Lasley, Charles Haden *cardiovascular surgeon, health and fitness consultant*

Boca Raton
Friend, Harold Charles *neurologist*
Kramer, Cecile E. *retired medical librarian*
Levenson, David Irwin *endocrinologist*
Levine, Richard A. *physician*
Marcus, Harold *retired physician, health facility administrator*
Michel, Stephen Lewis *physician*
Plosker, Harvey *anesthesiologist*
Weiner, Howard Marc *physician*
Zaleznak, Bernard D. *physician*
Zuckerman, Sidney *retired allergist, immunologist*

Bonita Springs
Dougherty, James *orthopedic surgeon, educator, author*

Boynton Beach
Glickman, Franklin Sheldon *dermatologist, educator*
Lemanski, Larry Fredrick *medical educator, university administrator*
Pataky, Paul Eric *ophthalmologist*
Srinath, Latha *physician*

Brandon
Mack, Arthur Neal *emergency medicine and family practice physician*

Cape Coral
Martin, Benjamin Gaufman *ophthalmologist*

Celebration
Pollack, Robert William *psychiatrist*

Clearwater
Blumencranz, Peter William *surgeon*
Brown, Richard Christopher *retired epidemiologist*
Goldenfarb, Paul Bennett *internist, oncologist*
Heid, Michael Patrick *surgeon*
Horowitz, Harry I. *podiatrist*
Thomas, Patrick Robert Maxwell *oncology educator, academic administrator*
†Zbella, Edward Andrew *obstetrician, educator*

Coral Gables
Perez, Josephine *psychiatrist, physician, educator*
Quillian, Warren Wilson, II, *pediatrician, educator*

Coral Springs
Swiller, Randolph Jacob *internist*

Dade City
†Feld, Harvey Joel *pathologist*

Daytona Beach
Brown, Benjamin Thomas *urologist, educator*
Di Nicolo, Roberto *allergist*
Erickson, Larry Ray *dermatologist*

Debary
Barry, Wayne Stephen *physician, educator*

Deerfield Beach
†Bader, Robert S. *dermatologist*
Bruno, Andrew Felix *ophthalmologist*

Deland
Goldberg, Paul Bernard *gastroenterologist, clinical researcher*

Delray Beach
Baine, Stuart Allan *cardiologist*
Ehrlich, S(aul) Paul, Jr., *physician, consultant, former government official*
†Ellsweig, Phyllis Leah *retired psychotherapist*
Kronish, Jan Warren *ophthalmologist*
Rosenfeld, Steven Ira *ophthalmologist*
Sherwood, Louis Maier *physician, scientist, pharmaceutical company executive*
Sonnenblick, Bernard *obstetrician-gynecologist*

Englewood
Sanders, W(illiam) Eugene, Jr., *physician, educator*

Fernandina Beach
Barlow, Anne Louise *pediatrician, medical research administrator*

Fort Lauderdale
Chernow, Bart *critical care physician*
Crikelair, George Francis *retired plastic surgeon, educator, researcher*
Fernandez, Bernardo B., Jr., *physician*
Lerner, Lauren Lipshutz *physician*
Lodwick, Gwilym Savage *radiologist, educator*
Robb, James Arthur *pathologist*
Rubinson, Howard Alan *physician*
Silvagni, Anthony Joseph *dean, osteopath*
Singer, Caren Bebchuck *physician*
Thomas, John Melvin *retired surgeon*
†Wand, Paul Henry *neurologist, researcher*

Fort Myers
Arnall, Robert Esric *physician, medical administrator*
Pascotto, Robert Daniel *cardiovascular/thoracic surgeon*
Simmons, Vaughan Pippen *medical consultant*
Vera, Enrique *psychiatrist*
Zeldes, Ilya M. *forensic scientist, lawyer*

Fort Pierce
Partenheimer, Robert Chapin *emergency physician*
Starner, Don Edward *radiologist, educator*

Fort Walton Beach
Fleischer, Leslie Raymond *cardiologist*

Gainesville
Antonelli, Patrick Joseph *otolaryngologist, educator*
†Aranda, Juan M., Jr., *cardiologist, medical educator*
Bandarchi-Chamkhaleh, Bizhan *pathologist*
Berns, Kenneth Ira *physician*
Black, David Joseph *physician*
Caffee, H. Hollis *plastic surgery educator*
Cance, William George *surgery educator*
Cassisi, Nicholas John *otolaryngologist, dean*
Cluff, Leighton Eggertsen *physician*
Copeland, Edward Meadors, III, *surgery educator*
Donnelly, William Henry *pathology educator*
Freund, Gerhard *medical educator*
Gold, Mark Stephen *psychopharmacologist, physician*
Gossinger, Gary Thomas *physician, psychiatrist, educator*
Greenberg, Samuel I. *psychiatrist, psychoanalyst*
Greer, Melvin *medical educator*
Heuer, Marvin Arthur *physician, research and industry consultant*
Idris, Ahamed H. *emergency medicine physician*
LeVeen, Robert Frederick *radiologist*
Limacher, Marian Cecile *cardiologist*
Mazzaferri, Ernest Louis *physician, educator*
†Meakin, Faith Anne *medical library diector*
Modell, Jerome Herbert *anesthesiologist, educator*
†Morey, Timothy E. *anesthesiologist, medical researcher*
Newman, Robert C. *urologist, educator*
Palovcik, Reinhard Anton *research neurophysiologist*
Pfaff, William Wallace *medical educator*
Reynolds, Richard Clyde *physician, educator*
Rhoton, Albert Loren, Jr., *neurological surgery educator*
Rosenbloom, Arlan Lee *physician, educator*
Rubin, Melvin Lynne *ophthalmologist, educator*
Ryerson, Gene Grove *internist*
†Saxonhouse, Matthew Adam *pediatrician, researcher*
†Seaberg, David Charles *emergency physician, educator*
Seeger, James M. *vascular surgeon*
Small, Parker Adams, Jr., *pediatrician, educator*
Suzuki, Howard Kazuro *retired anatomist, educator*
Uthman, Basim Mohammad *neurologist, epileptologist, consultant*
Victorica, Benjamin Eduardo *pediatrician, educator*

Grassy Key
Mankowitz, Barry Joel *surgeon*

Greenacres
Goldfarb, Arthur A. *allergist and immunologist, educator*

Gulf Breeze
Couch, John Alexander, Sr., *biomedical researcher*
Pettyjohn, Frank Schmermund *cardiology and emergency medicine educator*

Hallandale
Sielczak, Marek Wlodzimierz *pathologist, researcher*

Hialeah
Economides, Christopher George *pathologist*
Koreman, Dorothy Goldstein *physician, dermatologist*

Hollywood
Duffner, Lee R. *ophthalmologist*
Hochberg, Victor I. *retired neurologist*
Novak, Stephen Bruce *endocrinologist*

Schonfeld, Wayne Brent *gastroenterologist*
Vaicys, Ceslovas *neurosurgeon*

Hudson
Hirschauer, David R. *physician*

Indialantic
MacDonald, Stephen Hugh *physician, reserve naval officer*

Inverness
Esquibel, Edward V. *psychiatrist, clinical medical program developer*

Jacksonville
†Achem, Sami Rene *internist, medical educator*
†Bosworth, William Posey *physician, physical education educator*
Camacho, George *internist*
Cangemi, John Richard *physician*
Chalam, Kakarla Venkata *physician, educator*
†Deen, Hugh Gordon *physician, neurological surgeon*
†DeOrio, James Keith *orthopedic surgeon*
Earle, J.D. *physician*
Feinglass, Neil Gordon *anesthesiologist*
Gonwa, Thomas Arthur *nephrologist, transplant physician, educator*
Hecht, Frederick *physician, researcher, writer, educator, consultant*
Johnson, Douglas William *physician, radiation oncologist*
Kelalis, Panayotis *pediatric urologist*
Kimmich, Haydee Javier *orthopedist, consultant*
Krueger, Ross T. *gastroenterologist*
Lewis, Richard Harlow *urologist*
Margileth, Andrew Menges *physician, former naval officer*
Mizrahi, Edward Alan *allergist*
Narayan, Vaduvur Srinivasan *preventive medicine physician*
Nuss, Robert Conrad *oncologist*
Oldenburg, Warner Andrew *vascular surgeon*
Owusu, Akua *psychiatrist*
Paryani, Shyam Bhojraj *radiologist*
†Raynor, Eileen Margolies *otolaryngologist, educator*
Rhatigan, Ronald Merlin *pathologist*
†Safford, Robert Eugene *cardiologist, health facility administrator, educator*
Smallridge, Robert Christian *endocrinologist*
Stephenson, Samuel Edward, Jr., *retired physician*
Thorsteinsson, Gudni *physiatrist*
Threlkel, Robert Hays *pediatrician*
Tucker, N(imrod) H(olt), III, *physician*
Van Cleve, Robert Baldwin *cardiologist*
Wharen, Robert Ellsworth, Jr., *neurosurgeon, educator*

Jensen Beach
†Zuber, Shantung E., III, *physician, pastor*

Jupiter
Small, Melvin D. *physician, educator*

Kennedy Space Center
Darwood, John Joseph *physician*
Myers, Kenneth Jeffrey *physician*

Key Biscayne
Aleniewski, Monica Irene *retired anesthesiologist*
Palmer, Roger Farley *pharmacology educator*

Key West
Elwood, William Norelli *medical educator*

Kissimmee
Rajyaguru, Vrajlal Laljibhai *anesthesiologist*

Lake Worth
Kieval, Joshua *cardiologist, educator*
Stone, Ross Gluck *orthopedic surgeon*
†Zeltzer, Jack *vascular surgeon*

Lakeland
Glotfelty, John William *ophthalmologist*
Jennings, Ralph Henry, Jr., *physician*
Sklenicka, Russell Charles *orthopaedic surgeon*
Spoto, Angelo Peter, Jr., *internist, allergist*
Tripi, Vincent James *physician*

Largo
Grove, Jeffrey Scott *family practice physician*
Wheat, Myron William, Jr., *cardiothoracic surgeon*

Lecanto
Mchedlishvili, Gela *physician*

Loxahatchee
Foucauld, Jean *cardiologist*

Lutz
†Cualing, Hernani Del Mundo *physician, researcher*

Madeira Beach
Medins, Gunars *surgeon*

Marco Island
Krause, Charles Joseph *otolaryngologist*
†Sundberg, Ruth Dorothy *physician, educator*

Margate
Ory, Steven Jay *physician, educator*

Melbourne
Pocoski, David John *cardiologist*

Miami
Abraira, Carlos *endocrinologst, physician*
Allington, Gloria Jean Ham *medical education administrator*
Alvarez, Raul Alberto *internist*
†Anderson, Douglas Richard *ophthalmologist, educator, scientist, researcher*
Beck, Morris *allergist*
†Bejarano, Pablo A. *physician, consultant, medical educator*
Block, Norman Louis *physician, medical educator*
Bolooki, Hooshang *cardiac surgeon*
†Burke, George William, III, *surgery educator*
†Burrows, Suzetta Cecile *medical librarian*
Cassel, John Michael *plastic surgeon*
Chakko, Simon C. *cardiologist, educator*
†Ciancio, Gaetano *transplant surgeon, urologist*
Civantos, Francisco *pathologist, educator*
Cutler, Robert Brian *medical educator, researcher*
†Davis, Richard Edmund *facial plastic surgeon*
†Duchowny, Michael S. *physician, educator*
Eftekhari, Nasser *physiatrist*
Eisdorfer, Carl *psychiatrist, health care executive*
Engle, Mary Allen English *physician*
Freshwater, Michael Felix *plastic surgeon, educator*
Furst, Alex Julian *thoracic and cardiovascular surgeon*
Ganz, William Israel *radiology educator, medical director, researcher*
Gelman, Barry *pediatrician, educator*
Ginsberg, Myron David *neurologist*
Goldberg, Lee Dresden *endocrinologist, medical educator*
†Goldstein, Burton Jack *psychiatrist*
Goodwin, W. Jarrard *otolaryngologist, educator*
Heros, Roberto Cosme *neurosurgeon*
Howell, Ralph Rodney *pediatrician, educator, geneticist*
†Irvin, George Lee, III, *surgeon*
†Johnson, Thomas Edward *plastic and reconstructive surgeon*
Kaiser, Gerard A. *senior vice president*
Karl, Robert Harry *cardiologist*
†Khan, Danyal Mushtaq *pediatric cardiologist*
Lasseter, Kenneth Carlyle *pharmacologist*
†Lebwohl, Nathan Howard *orthopedist, surgeon*
Lemberg, Louis *cardiologist, educator*
Leyva, Luis Pablo, Jr., *obstetrician/gynecologist*
Malinin, Theodore *medical educator, researcher*
Martínez, Luís Osvaldo *radiologist, educator*
Maulion, Richard Peter *psychiatrist, physician, neurolinguist*
Mc Kenzie, John Maxwell *physician*
McLaughlin, Gwenn Elizabeth *pediatrician, educator*
†Medina, Luis Santiago *radiologist, researcher*
†Mendez, Luis Eduardo *medical educator, researcher*
Miguez-Burbano, Maria-Jose *medical immunologist*
Millard, Max *pathologist*
Mintz, Daniel Harvey *endocrinologist, educator, academic administrator*
Mizel, Mark Stuart *orthopedic surgeon*
Morrison, Glenn *neurosurgeon*
†Munoz, Oscar *cardiologist*
†Nadji, Mehrdad *pathologist, educator*
†Nishida, Seigo *surgeon, educator*
Nouri, Keyvan *dermatologic surgeon*
Pacin, Michael P. *internist, allergist*
Page, Larry Keith *neurosurgeon, educator*
†Palmberg, Paul Frederic *ophthalmologist, educator*
Parrish, Richard Kenneth, II, *medical educator*
Pefkaros, Kyriacos C. *internist, cardiologist*
Pham, Si Mai *cardiothoracic surgeon, medical educator*
Porter, Wayne Randolph *dermatologist*
Potter, James Douglas *pharmacology educator*
Puliafito, Carmen Anthony *ophthalmologist, healthcare executive*
Quencer, Robert Moore *neuroradiologist, researcher*
Raez, Luis Estuardo *physician*
Raines, Jeff *biomedical scientist, medical research director*
†Razdan, Sanjay *urologist*
†Regev, Arie *gastroenterologist, researcher, hepatologist*
Reisman, Terry Milton *gynecologist*
Roberts, Jonathan S. *interventional cardiologist*
Roth, Michael Stewart *obstetrician-gynecologist*
Sanchez de Leon, Roberto J. *physician, educator, writer*
Schachner, Lawrence Alan *pediatric dermatologist*
Scheinberg, Peritz *neurologist*
Schiff, Eugene Roger *medical educator, hepatologist*
Schwade, James Gary *radiation oncologist*
Sequeira, Rafael Francis *cardiologist, medical educator*
Smith, Stanley Bertram *clinical pathologist, allergist, immunologist, anatomic pathologist*
Struhl, Theodore Roosevelt *surgeon*
Sugarbaker, Everett Van Dyke *surgical oncologist*
†Sussmane, Jeffrey Brett *pediatrician*
Tejada, Francisco *physician, educator*
†Telischi, Fred *otolaryngologist, researcher*
Temple, Jack Donald, Jr., *physician, medical educator*
Tzakis, Andreas Gerasimos *surgeon, educator*
†Vilasuso, Francisco X. *anesthesiologist*
Wheeler, Steve Dereal *neurologist*
Wolff, Grace Susan *pediatrician*
Wolfson, Aaron Howard *radiation oncologist, educator*

Miami Beach
Lamas, Gervasio Antonio *cardiologist, educator*
Lazović, Gavrilo *internist*
Mandri, Daniel Francisco *psychiatrist*
Nash, Seymour Cy *surgeon, urologist*

Naples
Brooks, Joae Graham *psychiatrist*
Carneiro, Ronaldo Dos Santos *surgeon*
Cohen, Mark George *retired cardiologist*
Doyle, Joseph Thomas *preventive health physician*
Gehring, David Austin *physician, cardiologist, administrator*
Grove, William Johnson *physician, surgery educator*
Muir, John Douglass *physician*
Randall, Neil Warren *gastroenterologist*
Temple, Donald *retired allergist and dermatologist*
†Wallace, Edward L. *biomedical researcher, consultant*
Wiegenstein, John Gerald *physician*

New Port Richey
Hauber, Frederick August *ophthalmologist*

North Miami Beach
†Benjamin, Yukhanan *physician*

North Palm Beach
Fierer, Joshua Allan *pathology educator*
Stein, Mark Rodger *allergist*

Ocala
Altenburger, Karl Marion *allergist, immunologist*
Stone, Ira Michael *internist, cardiologist*

Oldsmar
Rogers, James Virgil, Jr., *retired radiologist and educator*

Orange Park
Fetchero, John Anthony, Jr., *otorhinolaryngologist*

Orlando
Carson, Thomas P. *pediatric cardiologist*
Guerriero, David John *physician*
Hoff, Theodore Francis *neurological surgeon*
†Magsino, Marissa Estiva *internist, pediatrician*
Marsh, Ella Jean *pediatrician*
Moore, Wistar *cardiovascular surgeon*
Norris, Franklin Gray *thoracic and cardiovascular surgeon*
Okun, Neil Jeffrey *vitreoretinal surgeon*
Taitt, Earl Paul *psychiatrist, army officer*
Wells, Natalie Clarke *anesthesiologist*

Ormond Beach
Cromartie, Robert Samuel, III, *thoracic surgeon*
Rubin, Mark Stephen *ophthalmic surgeon*

Osprey
Gross, James Dehnert *pathologist*

Palm Beach
Fredericks, Lillian Elizabeth *anesthesiologist*
Lee, Robert Earl *retired physician*
Seggev, Meir *radiologist, educator*
Simon, Harold *radiologist*

Palm Beach Gardens
Dedo, Douglas Donald *physician*
Ginsberg, Stanley Arthur *retired urologist, consultant*
Seaman, William Bernard *physician, radiology educator*
Skinner, Margaret Sheppard *pathologist*

Palmetto
Dielman, Ray Walter *radiologic scientist, natural hygienist, medical herbalist*

Pembroke Pines
Patel, Manish M. *physiatrist*
Robinson, Howard Neil *plastic surgeon*

Pensacola
Canady, Alexa Irene *pediatric neurosurgeon*
†Chhoeu, Austin H. *surgeon*
Dillard, Robert Perkins *pediatrician, educator*
Gill, Becky Lorette *retired psychiatrist*
Porter, Henry Olin *neurologist*
Ricketson, George Manning, III, *retired surgeon*
Telle, Lewis Donald *surgeon*
†Valdez, Michael R. *physician*
Vuksta, Michael Joseph *surgeon*

Plantation
†Levine, Tara Elise *physician*
Morris, James Bruce *internist*
Nickelson, Kim René *internist*
Patterson, Michael Milton *neuropsychologist, educator*
†Wick, Mitchell A. *physician*

Pompano Beach
Bliznakov, Emile George *biomedical research scientist*
Bowsher, Dennis James *internist, cardiologist, pharmacologist*
†Searle, Bernard G. *pharmacologist, dental educator*
Sichewski, Vernon Roger *physician*

Ponte Vedra Beach
Nadler, Sigmond Harold *physician, surgeon*
ReMine, William Hervey, Jr., *surgeon*

Port Charlotte
Al-Khatib, Tareq *surgeon*
McMullen, G. Arthur *physician, cardiologist*

Safety Harbor
†Kaplan, Kerry Joseph *internist, cardiologist*

Saint Petersburg
Bercu, Barry Bernard *pediatric endocrinologist*
Betzer, Susan Elizabeth Beers *family physician, geriatrician*
Collins, Paul Steven *vascular surgeon*
Kaiser, Greg Christopher *pediatric gastroenterologist*
†Lacson, Atilano G. *pathologist*
Linhart, Joseph Wayland *retired cardiologist, educational administrator*
Root, Allen William *pediatrician, educator*
Rosenblum, Martin Jerome *ophthalmologist*
Schmidt, Paul Joseph *physician, educator*
Williams, Larry Ross *surgeon*
Witt, Jeffrey R. *cardiologist*

Sanford
Octaviani, Hector *pediatrician*
Oostwouder, Peter Henry *family physician*

Sanibel
Davie, Joseph Myrten *physician, pathology and immunology educator, science administrator*

Sarasota
Bowers, Charles Richard *surgeon*
Cavanagh, Denis *physician, educator*
Colina, Ramon Enrique *gastroenterologist*
Cummings, Martin Marc *medical educator, physician, scientific administrator*
El Shahawy, Mahfouz *internist, cardiologist, educator*
Giordano, David Alfred *retired internist, gastroenterologist*
Iverson, Robert Louis, Jr., *internist, physician*
Jelks, Mary Larson *retired pediatrician*
Krumholz, Richard A. *physician*
Magenheim, Mark Joseph *physician, epidemiologist, educator*
Marks, Charles *surgeon, educator*
O'Malley, Thomas Anthony *gastroenterologist, internist*
Robinson, Bruce Eugene *physician, educator, researcher*
Sturtevant, Ruthann Patterson *anatomy educator*
Yonker, Richard Aaron *rheumatologist*
Zavon, Mitchell Ralph *occupational medicine physician*
Zentner, Arnold Stuart *psychiatrist*

Sebring
Ibrahim, George W. *physician, health facility administrator*

South Miami
Skolnik, Phyllis *dermatologist*

Spring Hill
Finney, Roy Pelham, Jr., *urologist, surgeon, inventor*

Stuart
Maldonado, Carlos Manuel *surgeon*

Summerfield
Shahmiri, Anis Ahmad *internist*

Sun City Center
Crow, Harold Eugene *physician, family medicine educator*

Tallahassee
Conti, Lisa Ann *epidemiologist, veterinarian*
Deal, Charles Raymond *anesthesiologist*
Deeb, Larry Charles *pediatric endocrinologist, epidemiologist*
†Hernandez, Jose Yolando Balagtas *physician, surgeon*
Maguire, Charlotte Edwards *retired physician*
†Shamsham, Fadi Michel *cardiologist*

Tampa
Afield, Walter Edward *psychiatrist, service executive*
Barness, Lewis Abraham *physician*
Bedford, Robert Forrest *anesthesiologist*
Belsole, Robert John *surgeon*
Bowen, Thomas Edwin *cardiothoracic surgeon, retired army officer*
Branch, William Terrell *urologist, educator*
Brantley, Stephen Grant *pathologist*
Bukantz, Samuel Charles *physician, educator*
Donelan, Peter Andrew *dermatologist*
†Dwornik, Julian Jonathan *anatomist, researcher*
Ebel, Theron Arthur *physician*
Eichberg, Rodolfo David *physician, educator*
Evangelista, Allan *podiatrist, medical researcher*
Fabri, Peter J. *surgeon, educator*
Figueroa, Tomas *internist*
Freeman, Thomas Benedict *neurosurgery educator*
Frias, Jaime Luis *pediatrician, educator*
Gambone, Victor, Jr., *internist, geriatrician*
Gilbert Barness, Enid *medical educator*
Gilbert-Barness, Enid F. *pathologist, pathology and pediatrics educator*
Greenfield, George B. *radiologist*
Haas, Robert Lance *surgeon, consultant*
Habal, Mutaz Billah *plastic surgeon*
Hartmann, William Herman *pathologist, educator*
Hoffman, Mitchel Scott *gynecologic oncologist, educator*
Holfelder, Lawrence Andrew *pediatrician, allergist*
Jacobs, Timothy Andrew *epidemiologist, international health consultant, medical missionary*
Jacobson, Howard Newman *obstetrics and gynecology educator, researcher*
Julien, Terrence Darryl *neurosurgeon, researcher*
Kohler, William Curtis *sleep specialist, neurologist*
Lakdawala, Sharad R. *psychiatrist*
Ledford, Dennis Keith *physician*
Lockey, Richard Funk *allergist/immunologist, educator*
Louis, Kenneth Maliq *neurosurgeon, educator*
Malafa, Mokenge Peter *surgeon*
Malone, John I. *pediatrics educator, biomedical researcher*
Martin, Robert Leslie *physician*
Muroff, Lawrence Ross *nuclear medicine physician, educator*
Murtagh, Frederick Reed *neuroradiologist, educator*

Nagera, Humberto *psychiatrist, psychoanalyst, educator, author*
Nord, H. Juergen *gastroenterologist*
Norman, T. Gail *family practice physician*
Older, Jay Justin *ophthalmic plastic surgeon*
Olson, Robert Eugene *physician, biochemist, educator*
†Orlowski, James Phillip *pediatrician*
Pfeiffer, Eric Armin *psychiatrist, gerontologist, writer*
Pollara, Bernard *immunologist, educator, pediatrician*
†Pomerance, Herbert Hart *pediatrician*
Powers, Pauline Smith *psychiatrist, educator, researcher*
Reading, Anthony John *physician, department chairman*
†Rifkin, Stephen *nephrologist*
Rowlands, David Thomas *pathology educator*
Shenefelt, Philip David *dermatologist*
Shephard, Bruce Dennis *obstetrician, educator, medical writer*
Siegel, Richard Lawrence *allergist, immunologist*
Silbiger, Martin L. *radiologist, medical educator, college dean*
Spellacy, William Nelson *obstetrician, educator, gynecologist, educator*
Sullebarger, John Thompson *internist, cardiologist, educator*
Troxel, David B. *president*
Trunnell, Thomas Newton *dermatologist*
Watkins, Joan Marie *osteopath, occupational medicine physician*
Weathers, Laura Sue *pediatrician*

Tarpon Springs
Mueller, Willys Francis, Jr., *retired pathologist*

Treasure Island
Hemadeh, Ossama Sharif *surgeon*

University Park
Wurlitzer, Fred Pabst *surgeon*

Venice
Hrachovina, Frederick Vincent *osteopathic physician and surgeon*
Ross, Robert Roy, Jr., *urologic surgeon*

Vero Beach
Christopher, Robert Paul *retired physician*
Schwarz, Berthold Eric *psychiatrist*

Viera
Duffy, John Charles *psychiatric consultant*

Wellington
Elmquist, John Gunnar *plastic surgeon, general surgeon*

West Melbourne
Grenevicki, Lance Francis *surgeon*

West Palm Beach
Brumback, Clarence Landen *physician*
Kapnick, S. Jason *oncologist*
Khouri, George George *ophthalmologist*
Lichtstein, Daniel M. *medical educator*
Mendelow, Gary N. *physician, emergency consultant*
Newmark, Emanuel *ophthalmologist*
Pottash, A. Carter *psychiatrist, hospital executive*
†Stambaugh, Reginald Jack *ophthalmologist*
Turner, Robert Alexander, Jr., *rheumatologist, consultant*
Whitfield, Graham Frank *orthopedic surgeon*
Wisnicki, Jeffrey Leonard *plastic surgeon*

Weston
Malave, Andres *pharmacologist, educator*
McAuliffe, John Anthony *hand surgeon*
†Tuchman, Roberto Fabian *neurologist*
Weiss, Eric Glenn *physician*

Wimauma
Palmer, Louis Thomas *pathologist*

Winter Haven
Cassell, Robert Holland *internist, oncologist*
Honer, Richard Joseph *surgeon*
Radocha, Richard Francis *plastic surgeon*
Warner, Nelson Alfred *dermatologist*

Winter Park
Acierno, Louis Joseph *medical educator, researcher*
Pineless, Hal Steven *neurologist*

Zephyrhills
Finnerty, Nancy Wells *family physician*

GEORGIA

Albany
Mayher, William Edgar, III, *neurosurgeon*

Alpharetta
Bridgers, John David *retired pediatrician*
Harris, James Herman *pathologist, neuropathologist, consultant, educator*

Ashburn
†Swygert, Leslie Ann *epidemiologist, consultant*

Athens
Erwin, Goodloe Y. *physician, land company executive*
Masters, Orlan Vincent Wade *gynecologist*

Atlanta
Affronti, John Paul *medical educator*
Alexander, Robert Wayne *medical educator*
Allen, Robert Charles *pathologist*
Ambrose, Samuel Sheridan, Jr., *urologist, educator*
Amin, Mahul B. *physician, researcher, educator, consultant*
†Anderson, Lynda A *geriatrician, behavioral scientist*
Baker, Edward L., Jr., *physician, science facility executive*
Barnett, Crawford Fannin, Jr., *internist, educator, cardiologist, travel medicine specialist*
Beasley, Ernest William , Jr., *endocrinologist*
Berga, Sarah Lee *women's health physician, educator*
Berkelhamer, Jay Ellis *pediatrician*
Block, Peter Carl *internist, cardiologist*
Branch, William Thomas, Jr., *medical educator*
Brandenburg, David Saul *gastroenterologist, educator*
†Bremner, James Douglas *psychiatrist, researcher, education educator*
†Brody, Harold Joseph *dermatologist*
Casarella, William Joseph *physician*
Cohen, Stanley Allen *pediatric gastroenterologist*
Cooper, Gerald Rice *clinical pathologist*
Cordero, Jose Fernando *pediatrician, federal agency administrator*
Correa-Villaseñor, Adolfo *epidemiologist, physician*
†Curran, James W. *epidemiologist, educator, academic administrator*
Davis, Lawrence William *radiation oncologist*
Davis, Michael *medical educator*
Dawood, Mohamed Yusoff *obstetrician, gynecologist*
Dion, Jacques Edgar *physician, neuroradiologist*
Dobes, William Lamar, Jr., *dermatologist, educator*
†Dowda, William F. *internist*
Dutt, Kamla *medical educator*
†Earles, Kathi Amille *pediatrician*
Farhi, Diane C. *pathologist and researcher*
Fermanis, Ernest George *urologic surgeon*
Fleming, Sidney Howell *psychiatrist, educator*
†Franch, Harold August *nephrologist, researcher*
Ganaway, George Kenneth *psychiatrist, psychoanalyst*
Gayles, Joseph Nathan, Jr., *administrator, fund raising consultant*
Godwin, John Thomas *pathologist, nuclear medicine specialist*
Gonzalez, Emilio Bustamante *rheumatologist, educator*
Gordon, Frank Jeffrey *medical educator*
Gude, Albert Valdemar *retired anesthesiologist*
Hanson, Victor Arthur *surgeon*
Harris, Eon Nigel *dean, rheumatologist, internist*
Hatcher, Charles Ross, Jr., *surgeon, health facility administrator*
Haynes, Ralph Lewis *internist, pulmonary diseases, consultant*
†Houry, Debra *emergency physician, educator*
†Hsu, Vincent P *epidemiologist*
Hug, Carl Casimir, Jr., *anesthesiology and pharmacology, educator*
Hughes, James Mitchell *epidemiologist*
†Hutchens, Wayne Goode *anesthesiologist*
Israili, Zafar Hasan *scientist, clinical pharmacologist, educator*
Jackson, Richard Joseph *epidemiologist, public health physician, educator*
†Jarvis, William Robert *epidemiologist, educator*
Jurkiewicz, Maurice John *surgeon, educator*
Karp, Herbert Rubin *neurologist, educator*
Kaul, Pushkar Nath
Kell, Michael Jon *physician, researcher*
Kellermann, Arthur L. *medical educator*
†Khuri, Fadlo Raja *oncologist, educator*
Kimani, Grace Alexandra *internist*
†Klein, Luella Voogd *obstetrics-gynecology educator*
Kokko, Juha Pekka *physician, educator*
†Kopelman, Harry Arvin *physician*
Koplan, Jeffrey Powell *physician*
†Ku, David Nelson *medical educator*
Letton, Alva Hamblin *surgeon, educator*
Lipman, John Crawford *endovascular surgeon*
Louard, Rita Jean *endocrinologist, educator*
Lubin, Michael Frederick *physician, educator*
Lui, Victor King Shing *pediatrician*
Lybarger, Jeffrey Allen *epidemiology research administrator*
Majesté, Richard Michael *pathologist*
Majmudar, Bhagirath *medical educator*
Mandel, Jack Sheldon *epidemiologist, educator*
Mantella, Tino J. *medical association administrator*
Matsuura, John Henry *surgeon*
†Mattox, Douglas E. *otolaryngologist*
Miller, Daniel Lee *surgeon*
Minneman, Kenneth Paul *pharmacology educator*
Monitz, Theodore Allan *cardiologist*
Morgan, Anne Hutchinson *medical association administrator, consultant*
†Murphy, Ana Alvarez *obstetrician, gynecologist*
Nemeroff, Charles Barnet *neurobiology and psychiatry educator*
O'Brien, Mark Stephen *pediatric neurosurgeon*
†Olansky, Sidney *retired dermatologist*
Oyesiku, Nelson Mobolanle *neurosurgeon, neuroscientist*
Peacock, Lamar Batts *retired physician*
Pederson, Linda Lue *epidemiologist, researcher*
Pickering, Larry Kenneth *pediatrician, researcher*
†Pollard, Zane F. *ophthalmologist*
Reed, James Whitfield *physician, educator*
Rich, Robert Regier *immunology educator, physician*
Salomone, Jeffrey Paul *surgeon, educator*
Semaan, Salaam J. *healthcare researcher*
Sessions, George Purd *physician*
Sherman, Roger Talbot *surgeon, educator*
Shore, Steven L. *pediatrician*
Sills, Eric Scott *infertility surgeon, reproductive endocrinologist*
Smith, Robert Boulware, III, *vascular surgeon, educator*
†Sola, Augusto *pediatrician, educator*
†Spangler, Dennis Lee *physician*
Steinhaus, John Edward *physician, medical educator*
Stillwagon, Gary Bouldin *radiation oncologist*
†Strikas, Raymond Algimantas *medical epidemiologist*
Tait, C(olumbus) Downing, Jr., *physician, medical educator*
Thacker, Stephen Brady *medical association administrator, epidemiologist*
Tissue, Mike *medical educator, respiratory therapist*
Toledo, Andrew Anthony *obstetrician, gynecologist*
Van Assendelft, Onno Willem *hematologist*
Wang, Richard Y. *emergency physician, osteopath*
Weintraub, William Seth *epidemiologist*
Wenger, Nanette Kass *cardiology educator, cardiologist, researcher*
Willis, Isaac *dermatologist, educator*
Woodruff, Bradley Allen *epidemiologist*
†Wulkan, Mark Lewis *pediatrician, surgeon*
Xi, Hongkang *medical sciences researcher*
Yancey, Asa Greenwood, Sr., *physician*
†Zhong, Hua *medical educator, researcher*
Zumpe, Doris *ethologist, researcher, educator*

Auburn
Hutchinson, Leslie Julian *preventive medicine physician*

Augusta
Chandler, Arthur Bleakley *pathologist, educator*
Cundey, Paul Edward, Jr., *cardiologist*
Dolen, William Kennedy *allergist, immunologist, pediatrician, educator*
Gambrell, Richard Donald, Jr., *endocrinologist, educator*
Given, Kenna Sidney *surgeon, educator*
Guill, Margaret Frank *pediatrics educator, medical researcher*
Gujral, Jaspal Singh *physician, internist*
†Hess, David Charles *neurologist, educator*
†Horuzsko, Anatolij *medical research scientist*
Imig, John David *medical educator*
Krauss, Jonathan Seth *pathologist*
Luxenberg, Malcolm Neuwahl *ophthalmologist, educator, retired*
Manganiello, Louis Otto Joseph *retired neurosurgeon*
Mansberger, Arlie Roland, Jr., *surgeon*
†McDaniel, George M. *pediatrician*
Mode, Donald G. *urologist, medical director*
Nesbit, Robert Raymond, Jr., *surgeon*
Ottinger, Mary Louise *podiatrist*
Ownby, Dennis Randall *pediatrician, educator, allergist, researcher*
†Pallas, Christopher William *cardiologist*
Parrish, Robert Alton *retired pediatric surgeon, educator*
Prisant, L(ouis) Michael *cardiologist*
Pryor, Carol Graham *obstetrician, gynecologist*
Rivner, Michael Harvey *neurologist*
Ryan, James Walter *physician, medical researcher*
Smith, Randolph Relihan *plastic surgeon*
Talledo, Oscar Eduardo *medical educator*
Tikare, Satyanarayana K. *retired internist*
Wilde, James Alfred *pediatrician, educator*
Wray, Betty Beasley *allergist, immunologist, pediatrician*

Austell
Halwig, J. Michael *allergist*

Brunswick
Perniciaro, Charles Vincent *dermatologist, educator, entrepreneur*

Buford
Byrd, Larry Donald *behavioral pharmacologist*

Colquitt
San Jose, Angel Molina *surgeon*

Columbus
Chan, Philip *dermatologist, retired army officer*

Dalton
†McKay, William Paul *oncologist, health facility administrator*

Decatur
Bain, James Arthur *pharmacologist, educator*
Brown, William Virgil *internal medicine educator*
Gann, Joyce Ann *obstetrician-gynecologist*
Heller, John Gaylord *orthopaedic surgery educator*
Henderson, Ralph Hale *physician*
Matthews, Frank *retired pathologist*
Rausher, David Benjamin *internist, gastroenterologist*
†Rimland, David *epidemiologist, researcher*
Udoff, Eric Joel *diagnostic radiologist*

Douglas
Newland, Hillary Reid *pathologist*

Dublin
†Nellis, Noel *thoracic surgeon, educator*

Fort Benning
Glushko, Gail Marie *physician, military officer*

Fort Valley
Swartwout, Joseph Rodolph *obstetrics and gynecology educator, administrator*

Gainesville
Givogre, John Lee *pain medicine specialist, anesthesiologist*
Turner, John Sidney, Jr., *retired otolaryngologist, educator*
Vaughn, Betty Jean *obstetrician/gynecologist*

Jasper
Webster, Robert McNaught *physician, researcher*

Kennesaw
Barnett, Benjamin Lewis, Jr., *retired physician, educator*

Lagrange
Copeland, Robert Bodine *internist, cardiologist*
West, John Thomas *retired surgeon*

Lawrenceville
Elsey, James Kevin *vascular surgeon, educator*
Fetner, Robert Henry *radiation biologist*

Mableton
Armour, Christopher E. *physician*

Macon
Bagley, Cathy Lorraine *obstetrician, gynecologist*
Etheridge, John Green *retired pathologist*
†Hash, Robert Bruce *medical educator*
Robinson, Joe Sam *neurosurgeon, educator*
Scheetz, Allison Paige *medical educator*
Skelton, William Douglas *physician*
Young, Henry E. *tissue engineering medical educator*

Marietta
†Chastain, Mark Alan *dermatologist, otolaryngologist, educator*
Drake, Alison Brooks *physiatrist*
Hagood, Murl Felton *surgeon*
Meyer, Roger Albert *surgeon*
Wheatley, Joseph Kevin *physician, urologist*
†Wheelock, Argil J. *urologist, medical company executive*
Yonkosky, Reena Ann *emergency physician*

Martinez
Colborn, Gene Louis *anatomy educator, researcher*
Nesbitt, Robert Edward Lee, Jr., *physician, educator, scientific researcher, writer, poet*

Mcdonough
Amarasinghe, Amarasinghe A.W. *psychiatrist, consultant*

Milledgeville
Velimirovich, Boris *urologist*

Newnan
Burns, Matthew Lynwood *surgeon*

Norcross
Nardelli-Olkowska, Krystyna Maria *ophthalmologist, educator*
†Yeboah, George Kwame *medical researcher, public health service officer*

Quitman
Baum, Joseph Herman *retired biomedical educator*

Reidsville
†Saad, Fathy Zaki *medical association administrator, physician*

Richmond Hill
Byrnes, Thomas Raymond, Jr., *osteopath*

Roswell
McCloud, Melody Theresa *obstetrician-gynecologist, surgeon*

Savannah
Ham, O(scar) Emerson, Jr., *neurologist*
Hoskins, William John *obstetrician, gynecologist, educator*
Krahl, Enzo *retired surgeon*
†Spitalnick, Benjamin David *pediatrician*
Taylor, Roslyn Donny *family physician*
Wirth, Fremont Philip, Jr., *neurosurgeon, educator*
Zoller, Michael *otolaryngologist, head and neck surgeon, educator*

Smyrna
Huttenbach, Dirk Erik *psychiatrist*

Snellville
Dhara, Venkata Ramana *physician, educator*

Statesboro
†Williamson, Matthew Allen *anatomist, educator, physiologist, anthropologist*

Stockbridge
Friedman, Robert Barry *physician*
Sharpe, Terry Lynn *dermatologist*

Stone Mountain
Gotlieb, Edward Marvin *pediatrician*

Suwanee
Shih, John Yozen *osteopathic physician*

Thomaston
Brewton, Samuel Alton, Jr., *urologist*
Harris, David Frederick *pathologist*

Tifton
Dorminey, Henry Clayton, Jr., *allergist*

Tucker
Brown, William Michael *scientist, consultant, writer, editor, lawyer*

Valdosta
Greer, Mack Varnedoe *retired physician*
Von Taaffe-Rossmann, Cosima T. *physician, writer, inventor*

Warm Springs
Stefenelli, George Edward *physician*

Warner Robins
Cleary, Cathleen Ann *psychiatrist*
†Klein, William Brent *surgeon*

Watkinsville
Johnson, Norman James *physician, lawyer, medicological consultant*

Winder
Souther, Joseph Carroll *family practice physician*

HAWAII

Aiea
†Kokame, Gregg Takashi *medical educator, researcher*

Honaunau
Schultz-Ross, Roy Andrew *forensic psychiatrist, educator, writer*

Honolulu
Ahmed, Iqbal *psychiatrist, consultant*
Bauman, Kay A. *physician*
Brady, Stephen R.P.K. *physician*
Chee, Percival Hon Yin *ophthalmologist*
Ching, Baron Kwai Fong *internist*
Chock, Clifford Yet-Chong *family practice physician*
Crowell, David Harrison *retired biomedical researcher, consultant*
Edwards, John Wesley, Jr., *urologist*
Fitz-Patrick, David *endocrinologist, educator*
Fong, Bernard W.D. *physician, educator*
Gandy, Hortense M. *retired endocrinologist*
Goldstein, Sir Norman *dermatologist*
Goodhue, William Walter, Jr., *forensic pathologist, military officer, educator*
†Hay-Roe, Victor *plastic surgeon*
Ho, Reginald Chi Shing *medical educator*
†Ishii, Clyde Hideo *plastic surgeon*
Kane, Thomas Jay, III, *orthopaedic surgeon, educator*
Lau, H. Lorrin *obstetrician/gynecologist, inventor*
Lee, Yeu-Tsu Margaret *surgeon, educator*
Lindes, Dorothyann Marlene *physician*
Linman, James William *retired physician, educator*
Liu, Alfred Jitfu *otolaryngologist*
McCarthy, Laurence James *physician, pathologist*
Moreno-Cabral, Carlos Eduardo *cardiac surgeon*
Murray, Kevin Dennis *surgeon*
Nelson, Marita Lee *anatomist, educator*
Oishi, Stephen Masato *physician*
†Parsa, Fereydoun Don *plastic surgeon*
Schatz, Irwin Jacob *cardiologist, educator*
Sharma, Santosh Devraj *obstetrician/gynecologist, educator*
†Sia, Calvin Chia Jung *pediatrician*
Stevens, Stephen Edward *psychiatrist*
Sugiki, Shigemi *ophthalmologist, educator*
†Takanishi, Jr., Danny M. *medical educator, department chairman*
Tseng, George Shihchi *anesthesiologist*
Vogel, Carl-Wilhelm Ernst *biomedical scientist, clinical pathologist*
†Wallach, Stephen Joseph *cardiologist*

Kailua Kona
Wohl, Armand Jeffrey *cardiologist*

Kamuela
Mc Dermott, John Francis, Jr., *psychiatrist, physician*
Morgan, Andrew Lane *urologist, educator*

Kawaihae
Place, Virgil Alan *physician, pharmaceutical researcher*

Koloa
Donohugh, Donald Lee *physician*

Lihue
Culliney, John James *radiologist, educator*

Mililani
Gardner, Sheryl Paige *gynecologist*
Okita, George Torao *pharmacologist educator*

Tripler Army Medical Center
Cordts, Paul Roger *surgeon*

Wahiawa
Hazenfield, Hugh Norman *surgeon*

Waikoloa
Copman, Louis *radiologist*

IDAHO

Blackfoot
Peterson, Grant Mark *obstetrician, gynecologist*

Boise
†Charan, Nirmal B. *pulmonologist, educator*
Hoffman, William Kenneth *retired obstetrician, gynecologist*
Huntington, Thomas Robert *surgeon*
Redshaw, James Douglas *neurologist*
Stevens, Dennis Leroy *physician, researcher*

Coeur D Alene
Gumprecht, Jane Caroline Doering *retired physician*

Pocatello
Risinger, Fred Owen *pharmacologist*

Rupert
Ditmore, Harry B. *surgeon*

Twin Falls
Shuss, John Logan *surgeon*

ILLINOIS

Alton
Kisabeth, Tim Charles *obstetrician, gynecologist*

Anna
Berube, Paul E. *obstetrician-gynecologist*

Arcola
Arrol, Robert N. *family physician*

Arlington Heights
DeDonato, Donald Michael *obstetrician, gynecologist*
Herskovic, Arnold Manfred *physician, oncologist*

Aurora
Witanowski, Michael Frank *surgeon*

Bannockburn
Cohn, Arnold Keith *orthopedic surgeon*

Belleville
Megahy, Diane Alaire *physician*
Ulven, Matthew Eric *family practice physician, educator*

Benton
Khan, Saeed Ahmad *internist, cardiologist*

Berwyn
†Galinsky, Dennis Lee *radiation oncologist, educator*

Bloomington
Efaw, David Scott *surgeon*
Skillrud, David Mark *pulmonologist, sleep specialist*
Trefzger, Richard Charles *surgeon*

Bolingbrook
Malicay, Manuel Alaban *physician*

Carol Stream
Schmerold, Wilfried Lothar *dermatologist*

Champaign
Freedman, Philip *physician, educator*
Risken, Jared Cleveland *physician*

Chester
Felthous, Alan Robert *psychiatrist*

Chicago
Abcarian, Herand *surgeon, educator*
Abelson, Herbert Traub *pediatrician, educator*
Abramowicz, Jacques Sylvain *obstetrician, perinatologist, educator*
Adler, Solomon Stanley *internist, oncologist, hematologist*
†Adomavicius, Jonas *gastroenterologist, writer*
Andersen, Burton Robert *physician, educator*
Backer, Carl Lewis *pediatric cardiac surgeon, educator*
Baldwin, DeWitt Clair, Jr., *physician, educator*
Balk, Robert A. *medical educator*
Barker, Walter Lee *thoracic surgeon*
Barkin, Robert Lyn *pharmacologist, pharmacist*
Barton, John Joseph *obstetrician, gynecologist, educator, researcher*
Baumann, Gerhard Paul *endocrinologist, educator*
Beck, Robert N. *nuclear medicine educator*
Becker, Michael Allen *physician, educator*
Beedle, Dennis Dean *psychiatrist, educator*
Beigl, William *physician, hypnotist, acupuncturist, consultant*
Bell, Carl Compton *psychiatrist, researcher*
Benditzson, David Jerome *physician, educator*
Benzon, Honorio Tabal *anesthesiologist*
Berendi, Erlinda Bayaua *physician surgeon*
Betts, Henry Brognard *physician, health facility administrator, educator*
Beutel, Ernest William *thoracic surgeon*
Bienias, Julia Louise *medical researcher, statistician*
†Black, Henry Richard *internist*
Boddie, Arthur Walker, Jr., *surgeon, cancer researcher*
Boggs, Joseph Dodridge *pediatric pathologist, educator*
Bonow, Robert Ogden *medical educator*
Boshes, Louis D. *physician, scientist, educator, historian, author*
Bowman, James Edward *physician, educator*
Brandman, James Franklin *internist, oncologist*
Bransfield, James Joseph *surgeon*
Brendler, Charles Burgess *urologist, educator*
Bryant, James *pathologist*
Bunn, William Bernice, III, *physician, lawyer, epidemiologist*
†Burck, Joseph Russell *medical educator, consultant, minister*
Burd, Laurence I. *obstetrician-gynecologist*
†Byun, Michael *plastic surgeon*
Calenoff, Leonid *radiologist*
Calvin, James Eldon, Jr., *cardiologist, educator, researcher*
Caro, William Allan *physician, educator*
Catalona, William *surgeon, urologist, educator, researcher*
Chan, Lawrence Siu-Yung *dermatologist, educator*
Chappidi, Prasad V. *neurologist*
Charles, Allan G. *physician, educator*
Chatterton, Robert Treat, Jr., *reproductive endocrinology educator*
†Chaudhary, Kamran *internist*
Coe, Fredric L. *physician, educator, researcher*
Cohen, Melvin R. *physician, educator*
†Colley, Karen J. *medical educator, medical researcher*
Conway, James Joseph *radiologist, educator*
†Costa, Erminio *pharmacologist, cell biology educator*
Cugell, David Wolf *medical educator*
†Curry, Raymond Howard *physician*
Curtis, Arthur William *otolaryngologist*
Davison, Richard *physician, educator*
Degroot, Leslie Jacob *medical educator*
Deorio, Anthony Joseph *surgeon*
†deRegnier, Raye-Ann Odegaard *physician, researcher*
Derlacki, Eugene L(ubin) *otolaryngologist, physician*
Deutsch, Thomas Alan *ophthalmologist, educator*
Diamond, Seymour *physician*
Diamond, Shari Seidman *law and psychology educator, researcher*
Dobyns, William B. *human geneticist, pediatrician, neurologist*
Dunaif, Andrea Elizabeth *endocrinologist*
Dunea, George *nephrologist, educator*
†Eiser, Arnold Robert *internist, bioethicist, nephrologist*
Erdös, Ervin George *pharmacology and biochemistry educator*
Espat, N. Joseph *surgeon*
Evans, Thelma Jean Mathis *internist*
†Farhadi, Ashkan *physician, researcher*
Fennessy, John James *radiologist, educator*
†Fintel, Dan James *cardiologist*
Fitch, Frank Wesley *pathologist educator, immunologist, educator, administrator*
Fragen, Robert Joseph *physician, anesthesiologist*
Frederiksen, Marilynn C. *physician*
Frohman, Lawrence Asher *endocrinology educator, scientist*
Funk, Phillip E. *immunologist, biology educator*
Galante, Jorge Osvaldo *orthopedic surgeon, educator*
Garden, Jerome M. *physician*
†Gecht, Martin Louis *physician, bank executive*
Geha, Alexander Salim *cardiothoracic surgeon, educator*
Gerbie, Albert Bernard *obstetrician, gynecologist, educator*
Gewertz, Bruce Labe *surgeon, educator*
Giovacchini, Peter Louis *psychoanalyst*
Glagov, Seymour *physician, educator, research scientist*
Glass, Richard McLean *psychiatry educator, medical editor*
†Glassenberg, Myron *neurologist*
Goldberg, Arnold Irving *psychoanalyst, educator*
Golomb, Harvey Morris *oncologist, educator*
Gonzalez-Crussi, Frank *pathologist, author, essayist*
Grayhack, John Thomas *urologist, educator*
Hahn, Yoon Sun *pediatric neurosurgeon, educator*
Hambrick, Ernestine *retired colon and rectal surgeon*
Hanauer, Stephen Brett *medical educator*
†Hasnain, Memoona *medical educator, medical researcher*
Hast, Malcolm Howard *medical educator, biomedical scientist*
Head, Louis Rollin *surgeon*
Hekmatpanah, Javad *neurosurgery educator*
Hellman, Samuel *radiologist, physician, educator*
Hendel, Robert Charles *medical educator*
Hendrix, Ronald Wayne *physician, radiologist*
Herbst, Arthur Lee *obstetrician, gynecologist*
†Hersch, Bryan L. *surgeon*
Holst, Ruth Mary *medical librarian*
Honig, George Raymond *pediatrician*
†Horgan, Santiago *surgeon*
Houston, Thomas Price *family physician, medical association official*
Hrycelak, George J. *surgeon*
Hsueh, Wei *pathologist, educator*
Huckman, Michael Saul *neuroradiologist, educator*
Hughes, John Russell *physician, educator*
Husain, Aliya Noor *pathologist*
†Hutchinson, Mark Robert *orthopaedic surgeon*
Ivankovich, Anthony D. *anesthesiologist, educator*
†Jeevanandam, Valluvan *surgeon, educator*
Jensen, Harold Leroy *medical liability insurance administrator, physician*
Jilhewar, Ashok *gastroenterologist*
Jones, Richard Jeffery *internist, educator*
Katz, Adrian Izhack *physician, educator*
†Katz, Ben Z. *pediatrician, educator*
Kavey, Rae-Ellen Webb *pediatric cardiologist*
†Kelly, James Paul *neurologist*
†Keshavarzian, Ali *gastroenterologist, educator*
†Kessler, John Allen *physician, biomedical researcher*
Kinslow, Monica M. *forensic scientist*
Kirschner, Barbara Starrels *pediatric gastroenterologist*
Kirsner, Joseph Barnett *physician, educator*
Kittle, Charles Frederick *surgeon*
Kowal-Vern, Areta *pathology and pediatrics educator*
†Kushner, Robert F *physician*
†Kuzel, Timothy Michael *hematologist, oncologist, consultant*
†Lamont, Elizabeth Bernier *physician, educator*
Landsberg, Lewis *dean, endocrinologist, medical researcher*
Langman, Craig Bradford *nephrologist*
Lara-Valle, Julio *medical educator, physician*
Lauth, William Brian *emergency physician, internist, educator*
Lee, Raphael Carl *plastic surgeon, biomedical engineer*
Leff, Alan Richard *medical educator, researcher*
Lelyveld, Steven *pediatric emergency physician*
Leventhal, Bennett Lee *psychiatry and pediatrics educator, administrator*
Levinson, Dennis Joel *internist, rheumatologist, educator*
Lichtor, Terry *neurosurgeon, neuro-oncologist*
Lipman, Laurie S. *psychiatrist*
Macdonald, Robert Loughlin *neurosurgeon, educator*
Malkinson, Frederick David *dermatologist, educator*
Marciniak, Christina Maria *physician*
Marcus, Joseph *child psychiatrist*
Martin, Gary Joseph *medical educator*
Massad, Malek George *surgeon, researcher*
Maves, Michael Donald *medical association executive*
McDermott, Raymond, Jr., *physician*
McDonald, Larry William *neuropathologist educator*
McLawhon, Ronald William *pathology educator, biochemist*
Mehlman, David Joel *physician, cardiologist, medical educator*
Meltzer, David Owen *internist, educator, economist*
†Merk, Bradley Robert *orthopedic surgeon*
Metz, Charles Edgar *radiology educator*
Metzger, Boyd Ernest *endocrinologist, educator*
Meyer, Paul Reims, Jr., *orthopedic surgeon*
†Milad, Magdy Peter *physician*
Miller, Albert J. *cardiologist, internist*
Millichap, Joseph Gordon *neurologist, educator*
Mirkin, Bernard Leo *clinical pharmacologist, pediatrician*
†Moen, Ronald S. *medical association administrator*
†Mokhlesi, Babak *critical care physician*
Moore, Vernon John, Jr., *pediatrician, lawyer, medical consultant*
Morris, Naomi Carolyn Minner *medical educator, administrator, researcher, consultant*
†Morrow, Monica *medical educator*
Mullan, John Francis (Sean Mullan) *neurosurgeon, educator*
Naclerio, Robert Michael *otolaryngologist, educator*
†Nadler, Robert B. *medical educator*
Nahrwold, David Lange *surgeon, educator*
Narahashi, Toshio *pharmacology educator*
†Naryzhny, Elena V. *physician*
Noskin, Gary Alan *physician*
Nyhus, Lloyd Milton *surgeon, educator*
Onsager, David Ralph *cardiothoracic surgeon, educator*
Page, Ernest *medical educator*
Pappas, George Demetrios *anatomy and cell biology educator, scientist*
†Pasche, Boris Claude Roger *physician*
Penn, Richard Deren *neurosurgeon, researcher, educator*
Pensler, Jay Michael *plastic surgeon, educator*
Polatnick, Lois Ann *neuro-ophthalmologist*
Pollock, George Howard *psychiatrist, psychoanalyst*
Poma, Pedro Alfonso *obstetrician, gynecologist*
Porter, Kimberly René *epidemiologist*
Poznanski, Andrew Karol *pediatric radiologist*
Prinz, Richard Allen *surgeon*
Rafeyan, Roueen *psychiatrist, educator*
Reid, Orien *medical association administrator*
Replogle, Robert Lee *cardiovascular and thoracic surgeon*
Rhone, Douglas Pierce *pathologist, educator*
Rice, Charles Lane *surgical educator*
Robinson, June Kerswell *dermatologist, educator*
Romeo, Anthony Albert *orthopedic surgeon*
Rosen, Steven Terry *oncologist, hematologist*
Rosenbush, Stuart William *cardiologist*
Rosenfield, Robert Lee *pediatric endocrinologist, educator*
Rotman, Carlotta H. *physician*
Rotmensch, Jacob *gynecologic oncology*
Rowley, Janet Davison *physician*
Rudnicki, Marek *surgeon*
Rudy, Lester Howard *psychiatrist, educator*
†Russell, Thomas R. *medical association administrator*
Sabbagha, Rudy E. *obstetrician, gynecologist, educator*
Sandlow, Leslie Jordan *physician, educator*
Savage, Edward Bruce *surgeon*
Schafer, Michael Frederick *orthopedic surgeon*
Schilsky, Richard Lewis *oncologist, researcher*
†Schnaper, H. William *pediatrician, educator*
Schneidman, Barbara Sue *psychiatrist*
Schulman, Sidney *neurologist, educator*
Sciarra, John J. *physician, educator*
Scommegna, Antonio *physician, educator*
Seeler, Ruth Andrea *pediatrician, educator*
†Sequeira, Winston *medical educator, researcher*
Shannon, Iris Reed *health consultant*
†Shapiro, Charles Michael *physician, consultant*
Shapiro, Richard Alan *surgeon*
†Sheagren, John Newcomb *physician, educator*
Shields, Thomas William *surgeon, educator*
Siegler, Mark *internist, educator*
Silverman, Morton Mayer *psychiatrist, educator*
†Silverstein, Jonathan Charles *surgeon, researcher*
Slavin, Konstantin Vladimirovich *neurosurgeon*
Smith, Earl Charles *nephrologist, educator*
Socol, Michael Lee *obstetrician, gynecologist, educator*
Sorensen, Leif Boge *physician, retired educator*
Sparberg, Marshall Stuart *gastroenterologist, educator*
Spargo, Benjamin H. *educator, renal pathologist*
Straus, Francis Howe *pathologist, educator*
Swerdlow, Martin Abraham *physician, pathologist, educator*
†Szerlag, Chester Theodore *oncologist, consultant, academic administrator*
Tachauer, Allan Dinu *internist*
Taraszkiewicz, Waldemar *physician*
Tatar, Arnold Marshall *internal medicine physician, educator*
Telfer, Margaret Clare *internist, hematologist, oncologist*
Thomas, Leona Marlene *health information educator*
Tomar, Russell Herman *pathologist, educator, researcher*

Anderson
King, Charles Ross *physician*
†Williams, Paul Allan, Jr., *psychiatric social worker, educator*

Bedford
Hunter, Harlen Charles *orthopedic surgeon*

Bloomington
Matthews, Leland Ray *obstetrician-gynecologist*
Moore, Ward Wilfred *medical educator*
Rink, Lawrence Donald *cardiologist*

Bluffton
Pitts, Neal Chase *rheumatologist*

Carmel
Van Tassel, Charles Jackson *physician, urologist*

Chesterton
Martino, Robert Salvatore *orthopedic surgeon*

Columbus
Kinsey, Helen Joan *physician*

Corydon
Kelty, Paul David *physician, educator*

Elkhart
Lankford, Neill Stacy *urologist*

Evansville
Faw, Melvin Lee *retired physician*
Green, Robert Frederick *physician, photographer*
Heimburger, Irvin LeRoy *retired surgeon*
Matheson, Gordon Keith *neuroanatomist, educator, neuroendocrinologist*
Penkava, Robert Ray *radiologist, educator*
Sartore, J. Christopher *family practice physician*

Fishers
Baach, Michael L. *internist*

Fort Wayne
Eastlund, Marvin Eugene *physician*
Heger, James Joseph *internist, cardiologist*
Lee, Shuishih Sage *pathologist*
McMurray, Stephen D. *nephrologist*
Richardson, Joseph Hill *physician, medical educator*

Gary
Zunich, Janice *pediatrician, geneticist, educator, administrator*

Hammond
Ashbach, David Laurence *internist, nephrologist*

Highland
Steen, Lowell Harrison *retired physician*

Indianapolis
Agarwal, Rajiv *physician*
Allen, Stephen D(ean) *pathologist, microbiologist*
Atkins, Clayton H. *family physician, epidemiologist, educator*
Beltz, Homer Ferguson *radiologist, healthcare executive*
Bergstein, Jerry Michael *pediatric nephrologist*
Besch, Henry Roland, Jr., *pharmacologist, educator*
Biller, Jose *neurologist*
Bjerke, H. Scott *surgeon*
Bloch, Richard *physician*
Bonaventura, Leo Mark *gynecologist, educator*
Brandt, Ira Kive *pediatrician, medical geneticist*
Brickley, Richard Agar *retired surgeon*
Brown, Edwin Wilson, Jr., *physician, educator*
†Brown, John W. *pediatric cardiothoracic surgeon*
Broxmeyer, Hal Edward *medical educator*
Burr, David Bentley *anatomy educator*
Cheng, Liang *pathologist*
†Choplin, Robert Hanley *physician, radiologist*
Chuang, Tsu-Yi *dermatologist, epidemiologist, educator*
Coleman, John Joseph, III, *surgery educator*
†Corkins, Mark R. *physician, pediatric gastroenterologist*
Cramer, Harvey M. *cytopathologist*
Croop, James Merrill *pediatrician, educator*
Daly, Walter Joseph *physician, educator*
Dere, Willard Honglen *internist, educator*
Eble, John Nelson *pathologist, oncology researcher*
Eigen, Howard *pediatrician, educator*
Eisenberg, Paul Richard *cardiologist, consultant, educator*
Eriksen, Erik Fink *endocrinologist, osteoporosis researcher*
†Feng, Gen-sheng *medical educator, researcher*
Geisler, Hans Emanuel *gynecologic oncologist*
Ghetti, Bernardino Francesco *neuropathologist, neurobiology researcher*
Green, Morris *physician, educator*
Greist, Mary Coffey *dermatologist*
Grosfeld, Jay Lazar *surgeon, educator*
Hansell, Richard Stanley *obstetrician, gynecologist, educator*
Heath, Hunter, III, *endocrinologist, researcher*
Helveston, Eugene McGillis *pediatric ophthalmologist, educator*
Holden, Robert Watson *radiologist, educator, university dean*
Inui, Thomas Spencer *physician, educator*
Irwin, Glenn Ward, Jr., *medical educator, physician, university official*
Jackson, Valerie Pascuzzi *radiologist, educator*
Johnston, Cyrus Conrad, Jr., *medical educator*
Kaye, Gordon Israel *pathologist, anatomist, educator*
Knoebel, Suzanne Buckner *cardiologist, medical educator*
Lemberger, Louis *pharmacologist, physician*
Luerssen, Thomas George *pediatric neurosurgeon, educator*

Lumeng, Lawrence *physician, educator*
MacDougall, John Duncan *surgeon*
Madura, James Anthony *surgical educator*
Mahomed, Yousuf *physician, cardiothoracic surgeon*
Manders, Karl Lee *neurosurgeon*
†McCarthy, Leo Joseph *pathologist*
Miyamoto, Richard Takashi *otolaryngologist*
Molitoris, Bruce Albert *nephrologist, educator*
†Moore, Gregory Powell *emergency physician, consultant*
Mouser, Robert Winston *physician*
Namyslowski, Jan *physician, interventional radiologist*
Norins, Arthur Leonard *physician, educator*
Pande, Prakash Narain *cardiologist, educator, consultant*
Pratt, George Byington, III, *pediatric radiologist*
Rescorla, Frederick John *pediatric surgeon, educator*
Rogers, Robert Ernest *medical educator*
Ryder, Kenneth William *pathologist, educator*
Schadow, Gunther *medical information scientist*
†Schamberger, Marcus S. *pediatric cardiologist*
Schlegel, Donald Max *retired surgeon*
Schmetzer, Alan David *psychiatrist*
†Small, Joyce Graham *psychiatrist, educator*
Smith, James Warren *pathologist, microbiologist, parasitologist*
†Subramanian, Usha *medical researcher, educator, clinician*
Surawicz, Borys *physician, educator*
Sutton, Gregory Paul *obstetrician, gynecologist*
Ware, J(oe) Anthony *cardiologist*
Weber, George *oncology and pharmacology researcher, educator*
Weinberger, Myron Hilmar *medical educator*
Wilson, Fred M., II, *ophthalmologist, educator*
Winters, Peter Lee *dermatologist*
Woolling, Kenneth Rau *vascular internist*
Yee, Robert Donald *ophthalmologist*
Yune, Heun Yung *radiologist, educator*
Zipes, Douglas Peter *cardiologist, researcher*

Kokomo
†Charlot Jr, Joseph Leonce *preventive medicine physician*

La Porte
Thordarson, Smari *diagnostic radiologist*

Lafayette
†Ash, Stephen R. *nephrologist*
Frey, Harley Harrison, Jr., *anesthesiologist*
Maickel, Roger Philip *pharmacologist, educator*
McPherson, Richard Clark *surgeon*
Poulos, James Thomas *endocrinologist, educator*
Rosen, Arthur David *neurobiology educator*
Wagner, Lindley Heath *physician, medical educator*

Logansport
Brewer, Robert Allen *physician*
Hall, James Alan *obstetrician-gynecologist*

Madison
Snodgrass, Robert Eugene *psychiatrist*

Marion
Fisher, Pierre James, Jr., *physician*
Lau, Patrick Hing-Leung *radiologist, educator*

Merrillville
Cristea Salberg, Richard Litz *neurologist, health facility administrator*
Doumanian, Heratch Ohannes *radiology*
Nguyen, Thach Ngoc *cardiologist*
Yu, Peter Legaspi *rehabilitation physician*

Michigan City
Mothkur, Sridhar Rao *radiologist*

Monrovia
Bennett, James Edward *retired plastic surgeon, educator*

Muncie
McDowell, Lucy Jane *allergist, immunologist, pediatrician*
Roch, Lewis Marshall, II, *ophthalmic surgeon, medical entrepreneur*
Zemtsov, Alexander *dermatology and biochemistry educator, inventor*

Munster
Jano, Ghassan *oncologist, hematologist*
Singh, Manmohan *orthopedic surgeon, educator*

Nappanee
Borger, Michael Hinton Ivers *osteopathic physician, educator*

New Albany
Chowhan, Naveed Mahfooz *oncologist*

New Castle
†Stone, Joy Lynne *internist*

Newburgh
Byrne, Jeffrey Edward *pharmacology researcher, educator, consultant*

Purdue University
Rutledge, Charles Ozwin *pharmacologist, educator*

Rockville
Swaim, John Franklin *physician, health care executive*

Scottsburg
Kho, Eusebio *surgeon*

South Bend
Agostino, Michael Anthony *otolaryngologist*
Anderson, Kenneth Paul *nephrologist, administrator*

Beker, Bernardo Enrique *anesthesiologist*
Creps, Philp Lloyd *child psychiatrist*
White, Robert Dennis *pediatrician, director*

Sullivan
Chavez, Mary Ann *osteopathic family physician*

Terre Haute
Kunkler, Arnold William *retired surgeon, educator*
Sawyer, Thomas Harrison *health, physical education and recreation director*
Siebenmorgen, Paul *retired family physician, lay church worker*

Valparaiso
Kobak, Alfred Julian, Jr., *obstetrician, gynecologist*
Poracky, Bernard Francis *radiologist*

Walton
Chu, Johnson Chin Sheng *retired physician*

West Lafayette
†Bergstrom, Donald E. *medical educator*
Borowitz, Joseph Leo *pharmacologist, educator*
Johns, Janet Susan *physician*
†Robinson, Farrel Richard *pathologist, toxicologist*
Shaw, Stanley Miner *nuclear pharmacy scientist*
Tacker, Willis Arnold, Jr., *medical educator, researcher*

IOWA

Ames
Fleming, Jon Lee *gastroenterologist*

Cedar Rapids
Houmes, Blaine V. *emergency physician, county medical examiner*
Norris, Albert Stanley *psychiatrist, educator*
Toluie, Kamran *cardiologist, electrophysiologist*

Clinton
Vidal, Ronald Anthony *otolaryngology*
Woodman, Grey Musgrave *psychiatrist*

Clive
Neis, Arthur Veral *healthcare and development company executive*

Davenport
Arnold, David Alan *surgeon*
Edgerton, Winfield Dow *retired gynecologist*
Shammas, Nicolas Wahib *internist, cardiologist*

Des Moines
Brown, Loren Dennis *internist, educator*
†Clark, Craig Boyd *cardiologist*
Elmets, Harry Barnard *retired osteopath, dermatologist*
Ely, Lawrence Orlo *retired surgeon*
†Freeman, Denise *podiatrist, educator*
Goodin, Julia C. *forensic pathologist, state official, educator*
Pray, Ralph Rustin *internist*
Rodgers, Louis Dean *retired surgeon*
Song, Joseph *pathologist, educator*
Wattleworth, Roberta Ann *physician, medical educator*
Zagoren, Allen Jeffrey *surgeon*

Dubuque
Chapman, John Stephen *retired internist, medical administrator*

Fort Dodge
Delucca, Leopoldo Eloy *otolaryngologist, head and neck surgeon*

Iowa City
Afifi, Adel Kassim *physician*
Anderson, Barrie *gynecologic oncologist*
Andreasen, Nancy Coover *psychiatrist, educator, neuroscientist*
Apicella, Michael Allen *physician, educator*
Bedell, George Noble *physician, educator*
Buckwalter, Joseph Addison *orthopedic surgeon, educator*
Burns, C(harles) Patrick *hematologist-oncologist*
Butler, John Edward *biomedical sciences educator, consultant*
†Choi, Kent Choung *surgeon, researcher*
Clifton, James Albert *physician, educator*
Cooper, Reginald Rudyard *orthopedic surgeon, educator*
Dyken, Mark Eric *physician*
Eckstein, John William *physician, educator*
Erkonen, William E. *radiologist, medical educator*
Fellows, Robert Ellis *medical educator, medical scientist*
Folk, James Calvin *ophthalmologist, researcher*
Galask, Rudolph Peter *obstetrician and gynecologist*
Gantz, Bruce Jay *otolaryngologist, educator*
Grose, Charles Frederick *pediatrician, infectious disease specialist*
Hammond, Harold Logan *oral and maxillofacial pathologist, educator*
Hein, Herman August *physician*
Heistad, Donald Dean *cardiologist*
Helms, Charles Milton *medical educator, consultant*
†Johlin, Frederick Carl, Jr., *medical educator*
Johnson, Cynda Ann *physician, educator*
Kardon, Randy H. *ophthalmologist, researcher*
Kerber, Richard E. *cardiologist*
Kisker, Carl Thomas *physician, medical educator*
Lakshman, Venkatesh *gastroenterologist, researcher, educator*
Lariviere, Gene Robert *surgeon*
LeBlond, Richard Foard *internist, educator*
†Mahoney, Larry T. *pediatrician, cardiologist*

Markham, Sanford Max *obstetrician-gynecologist, educator*
Mason, Edward Eaton *surgeon*
Morriss, Frank Howard, Jr., *pediatrics educator*
Morriss, Mary Jeannette Hagan *pediatric cardiologist, educator*
Muller, Barbara Ann *allergist*
Nelson, Herbert Leroy *psychiatrist*
†Noyes, Russell, Jr., *psychiatrist*
†Oetting, Thomas Andrew *medical association administrator, medical educator, educator*
†Peloso, Paul Michael *medical educator*
Ponseti, Ignacio Vives *orthopaedic surgery educator*
Rao, Satish *medical educator, physician scientist*
Richerson, Hal Bates *physician, internist, allergist, immunologist, educator*
†Schulz-Stübner, Sebastian Hans Wolfgang *anesthesiologist, critical care specialist, pain specialist, psychotherapist, medical quality manager*
Sivitz, William Irving *endocrinologist*
Smoker, Wendy Rue Kartinos *neuroradiologist, consultant, educator*
†Snyder, Peter M. *medical educator, medical researcher*
†Sontheimer, Richard D. *dermatology educator, researcher*
Spector, Arthur Abraham *physician, educator*
Strauss, John Steinert *dermatologist, educator*
Sutphin, John E. *ophthalmologist, educator*
Tephly, Thomas Robert *pharmacologist, toxicologist, educator*
Thompson, Herbert Stanley *neuro-ophthalmologist*
Van Gilder, John Corley *neurosurgeon, educator*
Wallace, Robert B. *medical educator*
Weinberger, Miles M. *physician, pediatric educator*
Weiner, George Jay *internist*
Weingeist, Thomas Alan *ophthalmology educator*
Weinstein, Stuart Leslie *orthopaedic surgeon*
Ziegler, Ekhard Erich *pediatrics educator*

Johnston
Thoman, Mark Edward *pediatrician*

Marshalltown
Cassidy, Eugene Patrick *pathologist*
Thomas, David Llewellyn *family practice physician*

Mason City
†Tatkon-Coker, James Edward *cardiologist*

West Des Moines
Alberts, Marion Edward *physician*

KANSAS

Augusta
Baker, Tracy McKenzie *family practice physician*

Coffeyville
Hawley, Raymond Glen *pathologist*

Concordia
Fowler, Wayne Lewis, Sr., *internist*

Fort Scott
Weddle, Douglas Paul *family practice physician*

Great Bend
Jones, Edward *pathologist*

Hutchinson
Crater, Timothy Andrews *internist*
Graves, Kathryn Louise *dermatologist*

Kanas City
Pehlivanov, Nonko Dimitrov *gastroenterologist, researcher*

Kansas City
Anderson, Harrison Clarke *pathologist, educator, biomedical researcher*
Arakawa, Kasumi *physician, educator*
Damjanov, Ivan *pathologist, educator*
Dunn, Marvin Irvin *physician*
†Fiskin, Arthur Max, Jr., *medical educator*
Godfrey, Robert Gordon *physician*
Hite, Pamela Rene *emergency medicine physician*
Hudson, Robert Paul *medical educator*
Johnson, Joy Ann *diagnostic radiologist*
Krantz, Kermit Edward *physician, educator*
Lawrence, Walter Thomas *plastic surgeon*
Lee, Kyo Rak *radiology educator*
Mathews, Paul Joseph *health educator*
Mathewson, Hugh Spalding *anesthesiologist, educator*
McCallum, Richard Warwick *medical researcher, clinician, educator*
Meyers, David George *internist, cardiologist, educator*
Milligan, Donald Bruce *physician, educator*
Mohn, Melvin Paul *anatomist, educator*
†Neuberger, John Stephen *preventive medicine and epidemiology educator*
Pahwa, Rajesh *physician*
Rawitch, Allen Barry *medical educator, academic administrator*
Schloerb, Paul Richard *surgeon, educator*
Sciolaro, Charles Michael *cardiac surgeon*
Skikne, Barry S. *hematologist, educator*
Varghese, George *physician, educator*
Voogt, James Leonard *medical educator*
Waxman, David *physician, university consultant*
Ziegler, Dewey Kiper *neurologist, educator*

Lawrence
†Buck, Henry William, Jr., *obstetrician-gynecologist*
Miller, Don Robert *surgeon, educator*

Leavenworth
Poulose, Kuttikatt Paul neurologist

Manhattan
Durkee, William Robert retired physician
Oehme, Frederick Wolfgang medical researcher and educator

Newton
Dyck, George psychiatry educator

Olathe
Sternberg, David Edward psychiatrist

Overland Park
Dockhorn, Robert John physician, educator
Finley, Jennifer Ellen physical medicine and rehabilitation physician
Goodale, Sean Douglas healthcare administrator, consultant
Landry, Mark Edward podiatrist, researcher
Sawkar, Laxmidas Anant retired internist, oncologist

Pittsburg
Sullivan, William John osteopath

Shawnee Mission
Bell, Deloris Wiley physician
Fairchild, Robert Charles pediatrician
Hartzler, Geoffrey Oliver retired cardiologist
Henley, Douglas E. medical association administrator
Price, James Gordon physician, educator
Thomas, Christopher Yancey, III, surgeon, educator

Topeka
Huaman-Mejia, Antonio pathologist
Lacoursiere, Roy Barnaby psychiatrist
Menninger, William Walter psychiatrist
Roy, William Robert physician, lawyer, former congressman

Westwood
Hart, Paul Vincent, Jr., emergency and family medicine physician, inventor

Wichita
Baumann, Paul Arthur radiation oncologist
Burket, George Edward, Jr., retired family physician
Cummings, Richard J. retired otologist
French, James Edward surgeon
Gorecki, John Paul neurosurgeon, educator
Guthrie, Richard Alan physician
Kellerman, Rick Dean physician, academic administrator
McKenzie, Harry James cardiothoracic surgeon, surgical researcher
†Oxley, Dwight K(ahala) pathologist

KENTUCKY

Ashland
Roth, Oliver Ralph radiologist

Berea
Lamb, Irene Hendricks medical researcher

Bowling Green
Buono, Frank Louis orthopedic surgeon

Cynthiana
Harpel, Gerald Robert obstetrician and gynecologist

Edgewood
Martin, Kevin Douglas surgeon

Elizabethtown
Rahman, Rafiq Ur oncologist, educator

Elkton
Manthey, Frank Anthony physician, director

Fort Knox
Nagorski, Leonard Edward radiologist

Fort Thomas
Gultekin, Ebru Kadriye pediatrician

Henderson
Esser, James Mark cardiovascular and interventional radiologist

Lancaster
Vandiviere, H. Mac medical educator

Lexington
Anderson, James Wingo physician
Avant, Robert Frank physician, educator
Baumann, Robert Jay child neurology educator
Burki, Nausherwan pulmonologist
Clawson, David Kay orthopedic surgeon
Davey, Diane Davis pathologist, educator
Ferguson, James Edward, II, obstetrician, gynecologist, maternal-fetal medicine specialist
Fried, Andrew Michael radiologist, educator
Friedell, Gilbert Hugo pathologist, hospital administrator, educator, cancer center director
Gilliam, M(elvin) Randolph retired urologist, educator
Glenn, James Francis urologist, educator
Hagen, Michael Dale family physician educator
Holsinger, James Wilson, Jr., physician
Kang, Bann C. immunologist
Kaplan, Martin P. allergist, immunologist, pediatrician
Mayer, Lloyd Dewald allergist, immunologist, physician, medical educator
Mentzer, Robert Melvin, Jr., surgeon
Poundstone, John Walker preventive medicine physician
Rowland, Randall G. urologist
†Van Meter, Woodford Spears ophthalmologist, surgeon
Villaran, Yuri physician, medical educator
Von Unrug, Thomas Paul physician, lab administrator
†Weitzel, William David psychiatrist
†Whayne, Thomas French, Jr., cardiologist, educator
†Woodring, John Howell radiologist
Young, Paul Ray medical board executive, physician

Louisa
Cataldi, Patricia Lee surgeon

Louisville
Amin, Mohammad urology educator
Andrews, Billy Franklin pediatrician, educator
Austin, Erle Harris pediatric cardiac surgeon
Bloemer, Gary Fred orthopedic surgeon, educator
Cai, Lu biomedical scientist
Callen, Jeffrey Phillip dermatologist, educator
Chien, Sufan surgeon, educator
Cook, Christine L. endocrinologist, gynecologist, educator
Cook, Larry Norman pediatrician, neonatologist, educator
Corwin, Hal Michael neurologist
Danzl, Daniel Frank emergency physician
DeMunbrun-Harmon, Donne O'Donnell retired family physician
Elin, Ronald John pathologist, educator
Fallat, Mary Elizabeth pediatric surgeon
Farman, Allan George radiologist, oral pathologist, educator
Galandiuk, Susan colon and rectal surgeon, educator
Gall, Stanley Adolph physician, immunology researcher
Garver, David L. psychiatrist
Griffin, Larry Paul obstetrician-gynecologist, educator
Haddy, Richard Ian family physician, educator
Harrell, Frank William family physician
Haynes, Douglas Martin physician, educator
Holt, Homer Anthony, Jr., urologist, educator
Kaplan, Henry Jerrold ophthalmologist, educator
Kutz, Joseph Edward hand surgeon, educator
La Rocca, Renato Vincenzo medical oncologist, clinical researcher
Lei, Zhenmin endocrinologist, reproductive biologist, researcher
Parker, Joseph Corbin, Jr., pathologist, educator
Pereira, Edgard Luiz physician
Polk, Hiram Carey, Jr., surgeon, educator
Raff, Martin Jay internist, infectious diseases educator, lawyer
Rao, Ch. V. endocrinologist, educator
Richardson, James David surgeon
Schwab, John Joseph psychiatrist, educator
Scott, Ralph Mason physician, radiation oncology educator
Spratt, John Stricklin surgeon, educator, researcher
Syed, Ibrahim Bijli medical educator and physicist, author, philosopher, theologist, public speaker, writer
†Tanguay, Peter Eugene child and adolescent psychiatry educator
Tasman, Allan psychiatry educator
†Thongboonkerd, Visith nephrologist, researcher
Waddell, William Joseph pharmacologist, toxicologist
Weakley-Jones, Barbara Ann forensic pathologist, educator
Whitelaw, Christine Cappelle pediatrician, educator
Wright, Jesse Hartzell psychiatrist, educator
Zimmerman, Thom Jay ophthalmologist, educator

Madisonville
Stulc, Jaroslav Peter surgeon, educator

Mayfield
Viles, Henry pathologist

Radcliff
Flores, George H. obstetrician and gynecologist

Russellville
Arshad, Abrar Mehmood physician
†Desai, Maulik Bharat emergency physician

Whitesburg
†Garimella, Satya V. cardiologist

LOUISIANA

Alexandria
Butler, Robert Moore, Jr., podiatrist
†Hanley, Henry Gorman cardiologist
Myers, Charles Lawrence anesthesiologist

Arcadia
Cummings, Kenneth Ila coroner, medical examiner

Baton Rouge
Bray, George August physician, scientist, educator
Cherry, William Ashley surgeon, state health officer
DiBenedetto, Robert Lawrence retired obstetrician, gynecologist, insurance company executive
Dunlap, Wallace Hart pediatrician
Gettys, Thomas Wigington medical researcher
Kidd, James Marion, III, allergist, immunologist, naturalist, educator
Kisner, Wendell Howard, Jr., plastic surgeon
Le Vine, Jerome Edward retired ophthalmologist
Puyau, Francis Albert retired physician, radiology educator
Scollard, David Michael research pathologist

Bogalusa
Hussain, Hamid physician

Bossier City
Lim, Diana Magpayo internist

Gretna
Long, Daniel A. ophthalmologist

Houma
Eschete, Mary Louise internist
Ferguson, Thomas Glen internist

Kenner
Fouchi, Dana Ray physician

Lafayette
Jolissaint, Stephen Lacy pathologist
Rolfes, Leonard Joseph pediatrician
Stephan, Mark Tyler radiologist
Wyatt, Charles H. cardiovascular surgeon

Lake Charles
Clement, Richard Joseph obstetrician-gynecologist
Drez, David Jacob, Jr., orthopedic surgeon, educator
Gunderson, Clark Alan orthopedic surgeon
Mocklin, Kevin Etienne physician, medical educator

Longville
Royer, Linda Bates medical case manager

Marrero
†Kushner, Frederick Gary cardiologist, medical educator
†Leftwich, Owen B. ophthalmologist

Metairie
Dugan, Fortune Anthony cardiologist, consultant
Edisen, Clayton Byron physician
Lake, Wesley Wayne, Jr., internist, allergist, educator
Ochsner, Seymour Fiske radiologist, editor
Rietschel, Robert Louis dermatologist

New Orleans
Agrawal, Krishna Chandra pharmacology educator
Arshad, M. Kaleem psychiatrist
Beck, David Edward surgeon
Berenson, Gerald Sanders physician
Bhattacharyya, Ashim Kumar pathology and physiology educator, researcher
Brazda, Frederick Wicks pathologist, educator
Campeau, Richard John, Jr., internal medicine and radiology educator
Carey, Michael Emmett neurosurgeon, educator
Cefalu, Charles A. medical educator
†Chan, Albert W. cardiologist
Cohn, Isidore, Jr., surgeon, educator
Connolly, Edward S. neurological surgeon
Corrigan, James John, Jr., pediatrician, dean
Daniels, Robert Sanford psychiatrist, administrator
Dildy, Gary Andrew, III, maternal fetal medicine physician, educator
Domingue, Gerald James medical scientist, microbiology, immunology and urology educator, researcher, clinical bacteriologist
Doucet, Hosea Joseph, III, pediatrician
Duncan, Margaret Caroline physician
Easson, William McAlpine psychiatrist, educator
Ensenat, Louis Albert surgeon
Epstein, Arthur William physician, educator
Ewin, Dabney Minor surgeon
Farris, Charles, Jr., obstetrician, gynecologist
Fisher, James William medical educator, pharmacologist
Fonseca, Vivian Andrew physician
Frohlich, Edward David medical educator
Fuselier, Harold Anthony, Jr., physician, urologist
Garcia, Carlos Arturo medical educator
Gatipon, Betty Becker medical educator, consultant
†Gitlin, Melvin Charles anesthesiologist, educator
Graham, H. Devon, III, otolaryngologist, plastic surgeon
Howard, Richard Ralston, II, medical health advisor, researcher, financier
Hyman, Albert Lewis cardiologist, educator
Incaprera, Frank Philip internist
Jaffe, Bernard Michael surgeon, department chairman
Kewalramani, Laxman Sunderdas surgeon, consultant
Kline, David Gellinger neurosurgery educator
Kolinsky, Michael Allen emergency physician
Lewy, John Edwin pediatric nephrologist
Locke, William retired endocrinologist
Mancuso, Donna Mariene psychiatrist
Martin, David Hubert physician, educator
McKinnon, William Mitchell Patrick surgeon
Meekers, Dominique Armand health and demographics researcher
Miller, Robert Harold otolaryngologist, educator
Millikan, Larry Edward dermatologist
Mushatt, David Michael medical educator
†Nelson, Steve pulmonologist, researcher
Nichols, Ronald Lee surgeon, educator
Ochsner, John Lockwood thoracic-cardiovascular surgeon
Olubadewo, Joseph Olanrewaju pharmacologist, educator
Pankey, George Atkinson internist, educator, researcher
Pfister, Richard Charles physician, radiology educator
Plavsic, Branko Milenko radiology educator
Puschett, Jules B. medical educator, nephrologist, researcher
†Rayford, Walter urology educator
Reisin, Efrain nephrologist, researcher, educator
Reyes, Raul Gregorio surgeon
Reza, Ali Hajmohammad cardiologist
Richardson, Donald Edward neurosurgery educator
Riddick, Frank Adams, Jr., physician, medical association administrator
Rock, John Aubrey gynecologist and obstetrician, educator
Rodriguez, Fred Henry, Jr., pathologist, educator
Salatich, John Smyth retired cardiologist, internist
Schabelman, Sergio Eduardo cardiologist, educator
Schally, Andrew Victor endocrine oncologist, researcher
Schneider, George T. obstetrician-gynecologist
†Simakajornboon, Narong physician
Stewart, Gregory Wallace physician
Straumanis, John Janis, Jr., psychiatry educator
†Strong, Jack Perry pathologist, educator
Sullivan, Jerry Warner educator, physician
Szepeshazi, Karoly Istvan pathologist
†Tiel, Robert Lyons neurosurgeon
Timmcke, Alan Edward physician and surgeon
Tracy, Richard E. medical educator
Udall, John Nicholas, Jr., pediatric gastroenterologist
Usdin, Gene Leonard physician, psychiatrist
Ventura, Hector Osvaldo cardiologist
Waring, William Winburn pediatric pulmonologist, educator
†Warrier, Raj P. pediatrician, educator
Webb, Watts Rankin surgeon
Welsh, Ronald Arthur physician, educator
Willis, Gladden Williams pathologist, scientific photographer, tree farmer
Winstead, Daniel Keith psychiatrist
Wong, Joaquin pediatric neurologist

Opelousas
Lafleur, Kenneth Charles ophthalmologist
Pinac, André Louis, III, obstetrician, gynecologist

Raceland
Conrad, Harold Theodore psychiatrist

Scott
Bergeron, Wilton Lee physician

Shreveport
Albores-Saavedra, Jorge pathologist, educator
†Brannon, Guy Emilio physician
Conrad, Steven Allen critical care and emergency physician, biomedical engineer, educator
Dhanireddy, Ramasubbareddy neonatologist, researcher
Fort, Arthur Tomlinson, III, physician, educator
Fort, Juliana Melody psychiatrist
†Fowler, Marjorie Ellen Rees pathologist
Freeman, Arthur Merrimon, III, psychiatry educator, dean
Gallagher, Patrick Timothy emergency physician
Ganley, James Powell ophthalmologist, educator
†German, Jeffrey Allen physician
Ghafourifar, Pedram pharmacologist
Griffith, Robert Charles allergist, educator, planter
Jones, Kenneth B., Jr., surgeon
Levine, Steven Neil endocrinologist
Li, Benjamin Dunlop surgeon, researcher
London, Steve Norman obstetrician-gynecologist, educator
Mancini, Mary Catherine cardiothoracic surgeon, researcher
McDonald, John Clifton surgeon
Misra, Raghunath Prasad physician, educator
O'Neal, Barron Johns surgeon
Shelby, James Stanford cardiovascular surgeon
Van Savage, John G. pediatric urologic and reconstructive surgeon
Wolf, Robert Edward physician, educator

Slidell
McBurney, Elizabeth Innes physician, educator
Muller, Robert Joseph gynecologist

Springfield
Annable, Charles Roy pathologist

MAINE

Auburn
McCann, Dervilla Mairin physician, consultant

Augusta
Cheng, Hsueh Ching physician
Ehrenkrantz, David medical researcher, researcher

Bangor
Bostwick, George Wallace family practice physician, geriatrician
Long, John Michael neuroradiologist
Moulton, Paul Rush ophthalmologist
Rosen, Clifford James internist
Segal, Harvey Mordecai physician
Shubert, Dennis L. neurosurgeon, medical administrator

Belfast
Kennedy, Ronald Craig anesthesiologist

Biddeford
Ford, Charles Willard health science educator

Deer Isle
Smith, Gardner Watkins physician

Falmouth
Singer, Richard Bunker physician, medical risk consultant
Sommer, Robert Georg dermatologist

Freeport
†Nass, Meryl J. physician, writer, research scientist

Kennebunk
Sholl, John Gurney, III, physician

Kingfield
†Collins, H(erschel) Douglas retired physician

Lubec
Hayes, Ernest M. podiatrist

Orono
Weiss, Robert Jerome psychiatrist, educator

Portland
Clark, David Eugene surgeon
Clark, Gordon Hostetter, Jr., physician
†Groom, Robert Craig perfusionist
Hotelling, David Rawson endocrinologist, educator
Kaplan, David K. emergency physician, educator
Smith, Robert Pease, Jr., physician

Sanford
Collins, Thomas Michael surgeon

Scarborough
Devlin, John Tobey physician, educator

South Portland
Wheeler, Hewitt Brownell surgeon, educator

Topsham
Arnold, Charles Burle, Jr., psychiatrist, writer

Waterville
Bhatnagar, Hemendra Narain otolaryngologist

Yarmouth
Mansmann, Paris Taylor medical educator

York
Lauter, M. David family physician

MARYLAND

Annapolis
Essandoh, Louis Kofi cardiologist
Halpern, Joseph Alan physician
Hoyer, Leon William physician, educator
Libber, Samuel Mogul pediatrician
Prout, George Russell, Jr., medical educator, urologist
Walman, A. Terry physician, lawyer
Welch, Robert Bond ophthalmologist, educator

Arnold
Harris, Roger Clark psychiatrist, consultant

Baltimore
Adkinson, N. Franklin, Jr., clinical immunologist
†Alberg, Anthony J. epidemiologist
Albuquerque, Edson Xavier pharmacology educator
Alpern, Linda Lee Wevodau health agency administrator
Baker, R. Robinson surgeon
Baker, Susan P. public health educator
Baker, Timothy Danforth physician, educator
Baramki, Theodore Atallah gynecologist, reproductive endocrinologist
†Barnes, Kathleen Carole medical educator
Bartlett, John Gill infectious disease physician
Baumgartner, William Anthony cardiac surgeon
Bayless, Theodore M(orris) gastroenterologist, educator, researcher
†Benitez, Robert Michael medical educator, cardiologist
Berger, Bruce Warren physician, urologist
Bergey, Gregory Kent neurology educator, neuroscientist
Bever, Christopher Theodore, Jr., neurologist
Bigelow, George E. psychology and pharmacology scientist
Brem, Henry neurosurgeon, educator, researcher
†Brodie, Angela M. biomedical researcher, educator
Brody, Eugene Bloor psychiatrist, educator
†Brushart, Thomas Marshall hand surgeon, neuroscience researcher
Brusilow, Saul pediatrics researcher
†Califano, III, Joseph physician
Carducci, Michael Anthony oncologist, educator
†Carrier, France medical educator
Carson, Benjamin Solomon neurosurgeon
†Chai, Toby C. urologic surgeon, research scientist
Chen, Yu acupuncturist, Chinese herbologist
†Childs, Barton retired physician, educator
Chiu, William Chien-Chen surgeon
†Civelek, A. Cahid nuclear medicine physician, medical researcher
Connaughton, James Patrick psychiatrist
Crain, Barbara Jean pathologist, educator
Cundiff, Geoffrey William physician
Dang, Chi Van hematology and oncology educator
Dannenberg, Arthur Milton, Jr., experimental pathologist, immunologist, educator
Davidson, Nancy Ellen oncologist
†Dawson, Ted Murray neurologist, educator
†DeAngelis, Catherine D. pediatrics educator
DeLateur, Barbara Jane medical educator
Dellon, A. Lee plastic surgeon
Dilsizian, Vasken cardiologist, nuclear medicine physician
Drachman, Daniel Bruce neurologist, educator
Dubin, Norman Harold endocrinologist
Dubowitz, Howard pediatrician
Durso, Samuel Christopher physician, educator, academic administrator
Eagan, James William, Jr., pathologist, educator
Edelman, Martin Joseph medical educator, oncologist, researcher
Eisenberg, Howard Michael neurosurgeon
Eldefrawi, Amira Toppozada medical educator, toxicologist, pharmacologist, neuroscientist
†Ellerkmann, Richard Marcus gynecologist, educator, surgeon, educator
†Ettinger, David Seymour medical oncologist
Faden, Ruth R. medical educator, ethicist, researcher
Felsenthal, Gerald physiatrist, educator
Ferencz, Charlotte pediatrician, epidemiology and preventive medicine educator
†Ferentz, Kevin Scott physician
Fishbein, Ronald Harrison surgeon
Fishman, Elliot Keith medical educator, medical consultant, diagnostic radiologist
†Fleg, Jerome Louis physician, research cardiologist
Foldberg, Morton Falk ophthalmologist, educator
Fox, Harold Edward obstetrician, gynecologist, educator, researcher
Freeman, John Mark pediatric neurologist
Gallant, Joel Emanuel physician
Gambert, Steven Ross geriatrician, internist
Gimenez, Luis Fernando physician, educator
Godenne, Ghislaine Dudley physician, psychoanalyst, educator
Golden, Archie Sidney pediatrician
Goldman, Lynn Rose medical educator
Gordis, Leon physician
Greenough, William Bates, III, medical educator
Griffith, Lawrence Stacey Cameron cardiologist, educator
Grossman, Stuart Alan oncologist, medical educator
†Gustafson, Thomas administrator
Hamilton, Bruce Peter Milburn endocrinologist, educator
Hanley, Daniel F., Jr., neurologist, educator
Harmon, John Watson surgeon, educator
Harris, James Carol Overton, Jr., psychiatrist, pediatrician
Hecker, Erwin retired obstetrician/gynecologist
Hellmann, David Bruce medical educator
Henderson, Donald Ainslie public health educator
Hoffman, Elmer surgeon
Hofkin, Gerald Alan gastroenterologist
Horn, Janet physician
Hruban, Ralph Harvey pathologist, educator
Hungerford, David Samuel orthopedic surgeon, educator
Hutchins, Grover MacGregor pathologist, educator, consultant
Jabs, Douglas Alan ophthalmology educator, researcher
Johns, Richard James physician, educator
Johnson, Richard Tidball neurology, microbiology and neuroscience educator, research virologist
Kaczka, David Walter physician, biomedical engineer
Karp, Judith Esther oncologist, science administrator
Kastor, John Alfred cardiologist, educator
Kessler, Irving Isar epidemiologist, consultant
Korzick, Karen Anne pulmonary, critical care physician
Kowarski, Allen Avinoam endocrinologist, educator
†Krasna, Mark Jonathan thoracic surgeon, researcher
†Krugman, Scott Daniel pediatrician, educator
Krumholz, Allan medical educator
†Kuppusamy, Periannan medical educator, medical researcher
Kwon, Chul Soo psychiatrist
Lawrence, Robert Swan physician, educator
Lawson, Edward Earle neonatologist
Lazarus, Gerald Sylvan physician, dean
Lehmann, Christoph Ulrich pediatrician, neonatologist, medical informatician
Lewison, Edward Frederick surgeon
Lichtenstein, Lawrence Mark allergy, immunology educator, physician
Lion, John René psychiatrist, educator
†Litrenta, Frances Marie psychiatrist
Long, Donlin Martin surgeon, educator
†Matheson, Nina W. medical researcher
Matjasko, M. Jane anesthesiologist, educator
Maumenee, Irene H. ophthalmology educator
McHugh, Paul R. psychiatrist, neurologist, educator
McKhann, Guy Mead physician, educator
McMillan, Julia A. pediatrician
Migeon, Barbara Ruben pediatrician, geneticist
Migeon, Claude Jean pediatrics educator
Miller, Michael physician, educator
†Mirvis, Stuart E. radiologist, educator
Molmenti, Ernesto P. surgeon
†Morford, Thomas administrator
Moser, Hugo Wolfgang physician
Mower, Morton Maimon cardiologist
Mulligan, Michael Eugene physician, radiologist
Myslinski, Norbert Raymond medical educator
†Nahabedian, Maurice Y. plastic surgeon
Napolitano, Lena Marie surgeon, educator
Noar, Mark David internist, gastroenterologist, therapeutic endoscopist, consultant, inventor
†Noga, Stephen Joseph oncologist, researcher
Norman, Philip Sidney physician
†Oldach, David epidemiologist, researcher
†Park, Adrian E. surgeon
Pass, Carolyn Joan dermatologist
Patz, Arnall ophthalmologist
†Peralta, Ligia pediatrician
Perman, Jay Allan pediatrician, educator
Pierce, Nathaniel Field medical researcher, educator
Proctor, Donald Frederick otolaryngology educator, physician
†Pronovost, Peter J. anesthesiology educator, health facility administrator
Rayson, Glendon Ennes internist, preventive medicine specialist, writer
Rennels, Marshall Leigh neuroanatomist, biomedical scientist, educator
Rose, Noel Richard immunologist, microbiologist, educator
†Rosenstein, Beryl Joel physician
Rubin, Haya Rahel physician, researcher
Safer, Daniel J. psychiatrist
Samet, Jonathan Michael epidemiologist, educator
Sarles, Richard M. medical educator
Saudek, Christopher D. medical association administrator, medical educator
Schoenrich, Edyth Hull internal and preventive medicine physician
Schuster, Marvin Meier retired physician, educator
Shi, Leiyu educator, researcher
Shuldiner, Alan Rodney physician, endocrinologist, educator
Silbergeld, Ellen Kovner environmental epidemiologist, researcher, toxicologist
Silverberg, Steven George pathologist, educator
Silverstein, Arthur Matthew ophthalmic immunologist, educator, historian
Sirithara, Ramanather cardiologist
Slavney, Phillip Richard psychiatrist
Smith, Stephen Ross endocrinologist
†Snitker, Soren biomedical researcher, educator, physician
Snyder, Solomon Halbert psychiatrist, pharmacologist
Sommer, Alfred medical educator, scientist, ophthalmologist
Staats, Peter S. pain medicine physician, surgeon
Starfield, Barbara Helen pediatrician, educator
†Sun, Chen-Chih J. pathologist, educator
Talalay, Paul pharmacologist, physician
Tamargo, Rafael J. neurological surgeon, educator
Taylor, Carl Ernest physician, educator
Tso, Mark On-man ophthalmologist
Udebiuwa, Oparaugo Ihentuge psychiatrist
Udvarhelyi, George Bela neurosurgery educator emeritus, cultural affairs administrator
Vinores, Stanley Anthony ophthalmology educator
Vogelstein, Bert oncology educator
†Wagner, Henry Nicholas, Jr., physician
Wahl, Richard Leo radiologist, educator, nuclear medicine researcher
Walker, Wilbur Gordon physician, educator
Wallach, Edward Eliot physician, educator
Walser, Mackenzie physician, educator
Waterbury, Larry physician, educator
Weisfeldt, Myron Lee physician, educator
Weiss, James Lloyd cardiology educator
Welker, James Anthony physician
Wharam, Moody DeWitt, Jr., physician, medical educator
Woodward, Theodore Englar medical educator, internist
Wu, Albert W. medical educator
Yen, Michael C. physician
Yossif, George psychiatrist
Young, Barbara psychiatrist, psychoanalyst, psychiatry educator, photographer
Zacur, Howard Ardlen reproductive endocrinologist
Zenilman, Jonathan Mark medical educator
Zizic, Thomas Michael physician, educator

Bel Air
Thompson, Sandra Fay psychiatrist

Bethesda
Alexander, Duane Frederick pediatrician, research administrator
Apud, Jose Antonio psychiatrist, psychopharmacologist, educator
Arons, Bernard S. psychiatrist, educator, health services director
Atkinson, Arthur John, Jr., pharmacologist, educator
Axelrod, Julius pharmacologist, researcher
Barrett, J. Carl cancer researcher, molecular biologist
†Belyakov, Igor M. immunologist, researcher
†Berrigan, David epidemiologist
Billingsley, Frank S. gynecologist, obstetrician, educator
Brodine, Charles Edward physician
Brown, Dudley Earl, Jr., psychiatrist, educator, health executive, former federal agency administrator, former naval officer
Brunell, Philip Alfred physician, educator
Carney, William Patrick medical educator
†Chanock, Robert Merritt pediatrician
Charney, Dennis S. psychiatrist
Chase, Thomas Newell neurologist, researcher, educator
Cohen, Robert Abraham retired physician
Cohen, Sheldon Gilbert physician, historian, immunologist
Coleman, C. Norman radiation and medical oncologist, researcher, educator
Crout, J(ohn) Richard physician, pharmaceutical researcher
†D'Agnillo, Felice biomedical researcher, physiologist
Danforth, David Newton, Jr., physician, scientist
Datiles, Manuel Bernaldes, III, ophthalmologist, researcher
Dietrich, Robert Anthony pathologist, medical administrator, consultant
†Farci, Patrizia medical educator, researcher
Farmer, Richard Gilbert physician, foundation administrator, medical advisor, healthcare consultant
Fleisher, Thomas Arthur physician
Friedman, Robert Morris pathologist, molecular biologist
Gastwirth, Glenn Barry medical association administrator
Gershengorn, Marvin Carl physician, scientist, educator
Gottesman, Michael Marc biomedical researcher, researcher
Greenwald, Peter physician, government medical research director
Haffner, William H.J. obstetrician, gynecologist
Hallett, Mark physician, neurologist, health researcher
†Harlan, Linda Carol epidemiologist
†Harris, Curtis C. physician
Hasan, Ahmed Abul Kashem biomedical researcher, research scientist
Haseltine, Florence Pat obstetrician, gynecologist, research administrator
Herman, Mary Margaret neuropathologist
Hodes, Richard J. immunologist, researcher
Hutton, John Evans, Jr., surgery educator, retired military officer
Hwang, Paul Mingyou cardiologist
Ito, Yoichiro pathologist
Jabbari, Bahman neurologist, educator
Jabs, Arthur Dean, Jr., plastic surgeon
Jacobowitz, David Meyer pharmacologist
Jaffe, Elaine Sarkin pathologist
Javitt, Jonathan C. physician, ophthalmologist, health information technologist
Johnson, Joyce Marie psychiatrist, epidemiologist, public health officer
Joy, Robert John Thomas medical history educator
Katz, Stephen Ira dermatologist
Keiser, Harry Robert physician
Kirkham, Perry M. immunologist
Kirschstein, Ruth Lillian physician
†Klebanoff, Mark A. epidemiologist, physician
†Klee, Claude Blenc medical researcher
Kramer, Barnett Sheldon oncologist
Krause, Richard Michael medical scientist, government official, educator, senior researcher
Kupfer, Carl ophthalmologist, science administrator
†Kuznetsov, Vladimir A. biomedical researcher, computational biologist
Lenfant, Claude Jean-Marie physician
†Leon-Sarmiento, Fidias E. neurologist, researcher
Leppert, Phyllis Carolyn obstetrician, gynecologist
†Libutti, Steven Kenneth medical researcher
Linehan, William Marston urologic surgeon, cancer researcher
†Longfellow, David administrator
MacLean, Paul Donald government institute medical research official
†Manolio, Teri A physician
Marini, Ann Marie medical researcher, educator
Masur, Henry internist
Mattison, Donald Roger physician, educator, medical administrator, military officer
McCurdy, Harry Ward otolaryngologist
Metcalfe, Dean Darrel medical research physician
Mills, James Louis medical researcher, pediatric epidemiologist
Minasian, Lori internist, oncologist, educator
†Mullan, Fitzhugh public health physician
Mulshine, James Lawrence oncologist
†Muraro, Paolo A. immunologist, neurologist
Nabel, Elizabeth G. medical researcher, cardiologist
†Nadareishvili, Zurab medical researcher, neurologist
Nagaich, Akhilesh Kumar biomedical researcher
Nelson, Stuart James internist, medical informatician
Neumann, Ronald Daniel nuclear medicine physician, educator
North, A. Frederick physician
†Nutman, Thomas Bruce biomedical research physician
Nyirjesy, Istvan obstetrician, gynecologist
Oldfield, Edward Hudson neurosurgeon, researcher
†Pacher, Pál pharmacologist, educator, researcher
Paul, William Erwin immunologist, researcher
Perlin, Seymour psychiatrist, educator
Piekarz, Richard Lawrence oncologist
Pinn, Vivian W. pathologist, federal agency administrator
Pollard, Harvey B. physician, neuroscientist
Potter, John Francis surgical oncologist, educator
†Quinnan, Gerald Vincent, Jr., medical educator
Quon, Michael James medical scientist, physician
Rabson, Alan Saul physician, educator
Rall, Joseph Edward physician
Rapoport, Judith psychiatrist
Rennert, Owen Murray physician, educator
Reynolds, Herbert Young physician, internist
Rhim, Johng Sik physician, educator, medical researcher
Robbins, Jacob biomedical researcher, endocrinologist
†Robbins, John Bennett medical researcher
Roberts, Doris Emma epidemiologist, consultant, public health nurse
Rogawski, Michael Andrew neurologist, neuroscientist
†Rosenberg, Steven Aaron surgeon, medical researcher
Ross, Donald Morris retired industrial hygienist, consultant
Saffiotti, Umberto pathologist
†SanGiovanni, John Paul ophthalmic epidemiologist
†Shapeero, Lorraine G. physician, educator
Shevach, Ethan Menahem immunologist
Smith, Dale Cary medical historian, educator
Smoller, Bruce Melvyn psychiatrist
†Spong, Catherine Yvonne obstetrician, gynecologist, researcher
Sternberg, Esther May neuroendocrinologist, immunologist, rheumatologist
Straus, Stephen Ezra biomedical researcher
Sturtz, Donald Lee physician, educator, naval officer
†Sunderland, Trey medical researcher, geriatrician

Ursano, Robert Joseph *psychiatrist*
Viehe, Richard B. *medical association administrator*
†Villavicencio, J. Leonel *surgeon, educator*
†Vitiello, Benedetto *psychiatrist, researcher*
Waldmann, Thomas Alexander *medical research scientist, physician*
†Wang, Dai-Yuan *cardiologist*
Wayne, Alan S. *pediatric oncologist, educator*
Wedgwood, Josiah Francis *pediatrician, immunologist, science administrator*
Weinberger, Daniel R. *psychiatrist, neurologist*
Western, Karl August *physician, epidemiologist*
Work, Henry Harcus *physician, educator*
Worth, Melvin H. *surgeon, educator*

Bowie
†Dawodu, Segun Toyin *sports medicine physician, physiatrist*

Chevy Chase
Allison, Adrienne Amelia *voluntary organization administrator*
Alpert, Seymour *anesthesiologist, educator*
†Bargmann, Cornelia *anatomist, educator, biochemist, educator, biophysicist, educator*
Feldman, Bruce Allen *otolaryngologist*
Hamill, John Richard, Jr., *physician*
Hani, Antoine George *psychiatrist, psychoanalyst*
Harlan, William Robert, Jr., *physician, educator, researcher*
†Hersh, Stephen Peter *psychiatrist, psycho-oncologist, educator*
Kullen, Shirley Robinowitz *psychiatric epidemiologist, consultant*
Miller, Franklin G. *bioethicist*
Morgan, Elizabeth *plastic surgeon*
Pilkerton, Arthur Raymond, Jr., *surgeon, educator*
Pogue, John Marshall *physician, editor, researcher*
Posnick, Jeffrey Craig *plastic surgeon*
Romansky, Monroe James *physician, educator*
Rose, John Charles *physician, educator*
†Sanz, Luis E. *gynecologist, educator*
Silver, George Albert *physician, educator*
Tacket, Hall Sanford *retired internist*
Williams, Charles Laval, Jr., *physician, international organization official*

Clinton
Cruz, Wilhelmina Mangahas *critical care physician, educator*

Cockeysville
Fleischmann, Gisela Ebert *retired psychiatrist*

Cockeysville Hunt Valley
Dans, Peter Emanuel *medical educator*
Futcher, Palmer Howard *physician, educator*

College Park
Katz, Ronald Alan *dermatologist*
Resnik, Harvey Lewis Paul *psychiatrist*
Sacks, Charles Bernard *physician, educator*

Columbia
Harrison, Elza Stanley *medical association executive*
Hyman, Lawrence Robert *psychiatrist*
Khurana, Ramesh Kumar *neurologist*
Rey, Alix Charles *psychiatrist*

Crofton
Shah, Natwarlal Bhogilal *physician*

Crownsville
Selvin, Beatrice *retired anesthesiologist*

Darnestown
Cohen, Sanford Irwin *physician, educator*
Gottlieb, Julius Judah *podiatrist*

Denton
Jensen, Christian Edward *family practice physician*

Easton
Danner, David Bigelow *pathologist*
Snow, James Byron, Jr., *physician, research administrator*

Ellicott City
Chen, Hong Yu *pediatrician*

Fort Detrick
Maher, Cornelius Creedon, III, *neurologist, toxicologist, army officer*

Frederick
Anderson, Arthur Osmund *pathologist, immunologist, army officer*
Hanna, Michael George, Jr., *immunologist, pharmaceutical executive*
†Kozlov, Serguei V. *medical researcher, consultant*
†Malone, Robert Wallace *surgeon*

Gaithersburg
Dermody, William Christian *biomedical consultant*
Hegyeli, Ruth Ingeborg Elisabeth Johnsson *pathologist, government official*
†Kinch, Michael S. *cancer researcher*
Liau, Gene *medical educator*

Garrett Park
Lincicome, David Richard *biomedical and animal scientist*

Glen Burnie
Wityk, Joseph John *radiologist*

Greenbelt
Obamogie, Mercy A. *physician*

Hagerstown
Cost, Francis Howard, Jr., *physician*
Strauss, Albert John, Jr., *pediatrician*

Hollywood
Shah, Nayan *internist*

Hyattsville
†Brett, Kate M. *epidemiologist, researcher*
Rose, Deborah *epidemiologist*

Kensington
Blum, Robert Allan *psychiatrist*
Choi, Young Soo *pharmacologist, toxicologist*
Cotlove, Elaine Wolf *psychiatrist, psychoanalyst*
Mirkin, Gabe Baron *allergist, pediatrician, medical writer, educator, radio personality, talk show host*
Szára, Stephen István *pharmacologist, consultant*

Lanham Seabrook
Gokulanathan, Karakat Sankaran *pediatrician, educator*

Laurel
Berkenblit, Scott Ira *orthopaedic surgeon*
Highman, Barbara *dermatologist*

Lutherville
Elma, Bayani Borja *physician*
Frank, Dana Hunt *internist, educator*
Morison, Warwick Lindsay *dermatologist, educator, consultant*
Moses, Howard *neurologist*
Proctor, Leonard Ray *otolaryngologist, educator*

Lutherville Timonium
Dembo, Donald Howard *cardiologist, medical administrator, educator*
Miller, John E. *retired cardiovascular surgeon*
Park, Lee Crandall *psychiatrist*
Pierpont, Ross Z. *former surgeon*
Sternberger, Ludwig Amadeus *neurologist, educator*

Millington
Kingsbury, Robert Coburn *physician, consultant*

North Bethesda
Sontag, James Mitchell *cancer researcher*

North Potomac
Geller, Ronald Gene *biomedical researcher, consultant*

Olney
†Baker, Carl Gwin *research administrator*

Owings Mills
Berman, Wulfred *pediatrician*
Heck, Albert Frank *retired neurologist*

Parkville
Munson, Paul Lewis *pharmacologist*

Perry Point
Miller, Alan Gilmore *psychiatrist*

Potomac
Johnson, W. Taylor *physician*
Waugaman, Richard Merle *psychiatrist, psychoanalyst, educator*

Prince Frederick
Judge, Charles A. *physician, statistician*

Riverdale
Kumar, Shailendra *urologist, educator*

Rockville
Barr, Solomon Efrem *allergist, educator*
Birns, Mark Theodore *physician*
Brown, Martin Howard *physician*
†Chretien, Paul Bernard *oncologist, medical researcher*
†DuPont, Robert Louis *psychiatrist, physician*
Fratantoni, Joseph Charles *medical researcher, hematologist, biotechnology executive*
Gonzalez-Licea, Augustin *pathologist, public health service officer*
Graham, Robert *medical association executive*
Gulya, Aina Julianna *neurotologist, surgeon, educator*
†Gutman, Steven Ifor *pathologist*
Haudenschild, Christian Charles *pathologist, educator*
†Hisada, Michie *physician, epidemiologist*
†Jarugula, Venkateswar Rao *medical researcher*
Johnson, Emery Allen *physician*
Littman, Burt A. *obstetrician-gynecologist*
Lloyd, Douglas Seward *physician, public health administrator*
Masters, Gary Everett *librarian, educator*
†Mofenson, Lynne Meryl *pediatrician*
†Mohan, Aparna Krishna *epidemiologist, physician*
Moritsugu, Kenneth Paul *physician, government official*
Moul, Judd Wendell *urologist, surgeon*
Petrick, Patricia A. *physician, educator*
Przygodzki, Ronald Mieczyslaw *pathologist, researcher*
Robinowitz, Max *pathologist, consultant*
Rodriguez, William Julio *physician*
Senior, John Robert *internist, gastroenterologist, hepatologist, consultant*
Sherman, Linda Ann *infectious disease physician, pathologist, researcher*
Shuren, Jeffrey Eliot *behavioral neurologist, lawyer*
†Skurkovich, Simon *medical scientist*
Tabor, Edward *physician, researcher*
Talwar, Pankaj *physician*
Temple, Robert *physician, federal agency administrator*
Thompson, Susan Diane *physician*

Varricchio, Frederick Elia *pathologist, biochemist*
Veech, Richard Lewis *medical researcher, physician*
Vincent, Michael Paul *plastic surgeon*
Yao, John Sen *physician*

Salisbury
Buchness, Michael Patrick *cardiothoracic surgeon*

Silver Spring
Adams, Diane Loretta *physician*
†Anderson, Sherri L. *medical educator*
Beard, Lillian B. McLean *physician, consultant*
Cruze, Kenneth *retired surgeon*
Eig, Blair Mitchell *pediatrician*
Gaydos, Joel Carl *physician*
Gilbert, Charles Richard Alsop *physician, medical educator*
Grossberg, David Burton *cardiologist*
Heppner, Donald Gray, Jr., *immunology research physician, army officer*
Kaiser, Hans Elmar *pathology educator, researcher*
Kevess-Cohen, Ruth M. *internist, geriatrician*
Levy, William Joel *endocrinologist*
Shaddinger, Dawn Elizabeth *medical researcher*
Waldrop, Francis Neil *physician*
Weinstock, Alan Robert *internist*
White, Robert McKinley, Jr., *oncologist, federal agency administrator*
Williams, James Thomas *physician, educator*
Yanowitz, Edward Stanley *allergist, educator*

Stevenson
Hendler, Nelson Howard *physician, medical clinic director*

Sykesville
O'Connor, William Thomas *retired surgeon*

Takoma Park
Munzer, Alfred *internist*

Timonium
Fitzpatrick, Vincent de Paul, Jr., *retired gynecologist*
Forrester, Alfred Whitfield *psychiatrist, educator*

Towson
Ferrer, Roberto O. *surgeon*
Mc Indoe, Darrell Winfred *retired nuclear medicine physician*
Mordes, Marvin *neurologist*
Spodak, Michael Kenneth *forensic psychiatrist*

Waldorf
Wiggins, Stephen Edward *physician, medical association administrator*

Washington Grove
†Reynolds, Thomas D. *psychiatrist*

Westminster
Wheatley, Charles Henry, III, *education and technology company executive, lawyer*

Wheaton
†Kaliner, Michael Aron *physician, researcher*
White, Martha Vetter *allergy and immunology physician, researcher*

MASSACHUSETTS

Amesbury
Paster, Barrie *family practice physician*

Amherst
Fleischman, Paul Robert *psychiatrist, writer*
Ratner, James Henry *dermatologist*

Andover
Bloom, David Lewis *radiologist*

Arlington
Berkoben, John Perri *physician*
Birk, Lee (Carl Lee Birk) *psychiatrist, educator*

Bedford
Letts, Lindsay Gordon *pharmacologist, educator*
Volicer, Ladislav *physician, educator*

Belmont
Benes, Francine M. *neuroscientist, psychiatrist*
Binder, Sheldon Carl *surgeon*
Coyle, Joseph Thomas *psychiatrist*
de Marneffe, Francis *psychiatrist, hospital administrator*
†Ke, Yong *medical educator, researcher*
Kyomen, Helen H. *psychiatrist*
Onesti, Silvio Joseph *psychiatrist*
Ottenstein, Donald *psychiatrist*
Pope, Harrison Graham, Jr., *psychiatrist, educator*
Sifneos, Peter Emanuel *psychiatrist, educator*
Vuckovic, Alexander *psychiatrist*
†Zhang, Kehong *neuropharmacologist, educator*

Beverly
Chitre, Sharadchandra Raghunandan *physician*
Ledbetter, John Stewart *urologist*

Billerica
Sampson, Robert Carl, Jr., *psychiatrist*

Boston
Abrahm, Janet Lee *hematologist, oncologist, palliative care specialist, educator*
Abu-moustafa, Adel H. *medical educator, dean*
Adams, Douglass Franklin *radiologist, educator, medical ethicist*
Adelstein, S(tanley) James *physician, educator*
Aisenberg, Alan C. *physician, educator, researcher*
Albert, Martin Lawrence *behavioral neurologist*

Alpert, Joel Jacobs *medical educator, pediatrician*
Ampola, Mary G. *pediatrician, geneticist*
Angelis, Michael *surgeon*
†Angelo, E. Joanne *child, adolescent and adult psychiatrist*
Arbeit, Robert David *physician*
Arky, Ronald Alfred *medical educator*
†Armstrong, Elizabeth G. *medical educator*
†Austen, K(arl) Frank *internist, educator*
Austen, W(illiam) Gerald *surgeon, educator*
Avery, Mary Ellen *pediatrician, educator*
Axelrod, Lloyd *endocrinologist, diabetologist, educator*
†Badgaiyan, Rajendra D. *medical educator, researcher*
Bajart, Ann M. *ophthalmologist*
†Barnett, Guy Octo *physician, educator*
Barouch, Dan Hung *physician, scientist*
Bauer, Stuart Barry *urologist*
Baughman, Kenneth Lee *cardiologist, educator*
†Baum, Richard A. *radiologist*
Becker, James Murdoch *surgeon, educator*
Bellows, A. Robert *ophthalmologist, surgeon*
Benacerraf, Baruj *pathologist, educator*
Bern, Murray Morris *hematologist, oncologist*
†Bernhard, William Francis *thoracic and cardiovascular surgeon*
Berson, Eliot Lawrence *ophthalmologist, medical educator*
Bistrian, Bruce Ryan *internist, educator*
Black, Paul Henry *medical educator, researcher*
Black, Peter *surgeon, educator*
Bloch, Kurt Julius *physician*
Bougas, James Andrew *physician, educator, surgeon*
Bousvaros, Athos *pediatric gastroenterologist*
†Brain, Joseph David *biomedical scientist*
Braunwald, Eugene *physician, educator*
Brenner, Barry Morton *physician*
Brown, Robert Stephen *physician, educator, health facility administrator*
Buechler, Elizabeth Jean *obstetrician-gynecologist*
Burke, Louis *gynecologist, educator, researcher*
†Butte, Atul Janardhan *pediatric endocrinologist*
Buxbaum, Robert C(ourtney) *internist*
Calkins, David Ross *physician, medical educator*
Callow, Allan Dana *surgeon*
Cannon, Christopher Paul *cardiologist*
Caplan, Louis Robert *neurology educator*
Carey, Martin Conrad *gastroenterologist, molecular biophysicist, educator, medical geneticist*
Carr, Daniel Barry *anesthesiologist, endocrinologist, medical researcher*
Chakravarti, Arnab *physician, researcher*
†Ciraulo, Domenic Anthony *psychiatrist, educator*
Clouse, Melvin E. *radiologist*
Coffman, Jay Denton *physician, educator*
Cohen, Alan Seymour *internist*
†Cohn, William Ettlinger *cardiologist, thoracic surgeon, product designer*
Collins, Tucker *pathologist, molecular biologist*
Colvin, Robert Barnes *pathologist, researcher*
Creager, Mark Alan *cardiologist*
Crocker, Allen Carrol *pediatrician*
Cua, Christopher Lee *thoracic surgeon*
†Cursiefen, Claus *ophthalmologist, researcher*
†David, John R. *internist, educator*
Delbanco, Thomas Lewis *medical educator, researcher*
DeSanctis, Roman William *cardiologist, educator*
DeSisto, Elizabeth Agnes *medical records specialist*
†Di Carli, Marcelo Fernando *cardiologist*
Dluhy, Robert George *physician*
Dolin, Raphael *medical educator*
Doody, Daniel Patrick *pediatric surgeon*
Doyle, Jennifer *surgical educator, scholar*
†Duff, John Michael *neurosurgeon*
†Dzau, Victor Joseph *physician, scientist, educator*
Earle, Craig Christopher *oncologist, epidemiologist*
Eckstein, Marlene R. *vascular radiologist*
Edelin, Kenneth Carlton *physician*
Egdahl, Richard Harrison *surgeon, medical educator, health science administrator*
Einhorn, Thomas Alfred *orthopaedic surgeon*
Eisenberg, Leon *psychiatrist, educator*
Ellis, F. Henry, Jr., *surgeon, educator*
Epler, Gary Robert *physician, author, educator*
Epstein, Franklin Harold *physician, educator*
Farber, Harrison W. *critical care physician, medical educator*
†Farris, R. Wesley, II, *neurologist*
†Federman, Daniel David *medical educator, educational administrator, endocrinologist*
Fletcher, Robert Hillman *medical educator*
Fletcher, Suzanne Wright *physician, educator*
Folkman, Moses Judah *surgeon, educator*
†Franco, Ramon Arturo *medical educator*
Frank, Markus Hermann *physician, researcher*
†Frederick, Albert R., Jr., *ophthalmologist, surgeon*
Freedberg, A. Stone *physician*
Frei, Emil, III, *physician, medical researcher, medical educator*
Freiman, David Galland *pathologist, educator*
Friedman, Lawrence Samuel *gastroenterologist, educator*
Ganda, Om Prakash *physician, educator*
Gargiulo, Antonio Rosario *reproductive endocrinologist, researcher, clinician*
†Gaughan, Denise Marie *epidemiologist*
Geggel, Robert Leslie *pediatric cardiologist*
Gelfand, Jeffrey Alan *physician, educator*
Gilchrest, Barbara Ann *dermatologist*
Gill, Thomas James, IV, *orthopedic surgeon*
Gillick, Muriel Ruth *physician*
Gimbrone, Michael Anthony, Jr., *research scientist, pathologist, educator*
Glimcher, Melvin Jacob *orthopedic surgeon*
Godleski, John Joseph *pathologist*

Golan, David Eric *biophysicist, pharmacologist, hematologist, medical educator*
Goldberg, Irving Hyman *molecular pharmacology and biochemistry educator*
†Goldberg, Marcia B. *medical educator*
Gottlieb, Leonard Solomon *pathology educator*
Goumnerova, Liliana Christova *physician, neurosurgeon, educator*
Greenberger, Norton Jerald *physician*
Greenblatt, David J. *pharmacologist, educator*
Greiner, Jack Volker *ophthalmologist, physician, surgeon, scientist*
Griswold, Jonathan DeWitt *pediatric anesthesiologist, pharmacology educator*
Grundfast, Kenneth Martin *otolaryngologist*
†Hamblin, Michael R. *biomedical researcher, educator*
Harlow, Edward E., Jr., *oncologist*
Hay, Elizabeth Dexter *embryology researcher, educator*
Healy, Gerald Burke *otolaryngologist*
Hedley-Whyte, E(lizabeth) Tessa *neuropathologist*
Hedley-Whyte, John *anesthesiologist, educator*
Herndon, James Henry *orthopedic surgeon, educator*
Hiatt, Howard H. *physician*
†Hill, Nicholas Snowden *physician, researcher, educator*
Ho, Kalon Kl *internist, researcher*
Hobbs, Nedda Marie *pediatrician*
Howley, Peter Maxwell *pathology educator*
†Hunsaker, Andetta Rotilla *physician, medical educator*
Hunter, David George *physician, researcher*
Hutter, Adolph Matthew, Jr., *cardiologist, educator*
Huvos, Andrew *internist, cardiologist, educator*
Jabre, Anthony *neurosurgeon, educator*
Jabre, Joe F. *neurologist, electromyographer*
Janne d'Othee, Bertrand M. *radiologist, researcher*
Jellinek, Michael Steven *psychiatrist, pediatrician*
Johnson, Michael Lewis *psychiatrist*
Jonas, Richard Andrew *medical educator*
Joyce-Brady, Martin Francis *medical educator, physician, researcher*
Jupiter, Jesse Bernard *orthopedic surgeon*
Kane, Robert Alan *radiologist, researcher*
Kaplan, Marshall Myles *medical educator, researcher, gastroenterologist*
Karasik, David *anatomist, educator, genetic epidemiologist*
†Kassirer, Jerome Paul *medical educator, editor-in-chief*
Kaye, Kenneth Marc *physician, educator, scientist*
Kazemi, Homayoun *physician, medical educator*
Kieff, Elliott Dan *medical educator*
Kitz, Richard John *anesthesiologist, educator*
Klingenstein, R. James *physician*
†Kocher, Mininder Singh *pediaric orthopaedic surgeon, epidemiologist*
Komaroff, Anthony Leader *physician*
Korn, Joseph Howard *physician, educator*
†Krainc, Dimitri *medical educator, researcher*
Krane, Stephen Martin *physician, educator*
Kressel, Herbert Yehude *medical educator*
†Kruch, Aleksandr *retired gynecologist, educator*
†Kruskal, Jonathan Bruce *radiologist, research scientist*
Kulig, John Walter *pediatrician, educator*
†Kupper, Thomas S. *dermatologist, educator*
Laussen, Peter Charles *pediatric cardiac anesthesiologist, intensive care physician*
LeBoff, Meryl Susan *physician, medical educator*
Lee, I-Min *epidemiologist*
†Levine, Deborah *radiologist*
Levinsky, Norman George *physician, educator*
Linfante, Italo *physician, medical educator*
Little, John Bertram *physician, radiobiology educator, researcher*
Livingston, David Morse *biomedical scientist, physician, internist*
Lo Gerfo, Frank William *surgeon*
Loscalzo, Joseph *cardiologist, biochemist*
†Luptak, Ivan *physician, researcher*
Maher, Timothy John *pharmacologist, educator*
†Makrigiorgos, Gerassimos Mike *oncologist*
Mankin, Henry Jay *physician, educator*
Mannick, John Anthony *surgeon*
Manson, JoAnn Elisabeth *endocrinologist*
Marion, Donald William *neurosurgeon*
Martin, Joseph Boyd *neurologist, educator*
Martuza, Robert L. *neurosurgeon*
Mathews-Roth, Micheline Mary *medicine educator, clinical researcher*
McCloskey, Laura Ann *medical educator*
McCormick, Marie Clare *pediatrician, educator*
McDougal, William Scott *urology educator*
Meenan, Robert Francis *rheumatologist, researcher, academician*
Merk, Frederick Bannister *biomedical educator, medical researcher*
Messerle, Judith Rose *medical librarian, public relations director*
Meyer, Jack Edward *radiologist, educator*
Meyerson, Matthew *pathologist, educator, researcher*
Mihm, Martin Charles, Jr., *pathologist, educator*
Milunsky, Aubrey *geneticist, pediatrician, medical educator*
Moellering, Robert Charles, Jr., *internist, educator*
Mongan, James John *physician, hospital administrator*
†Montagne, Michael *pharmacologist, educator*
Montgomery, William Wayne *surgeon*
Morgan, James Philip *pharmacologist, cardiologist, educator*
†Mucci, Lorelei *epidemiologist, researcher*
†Nadelson, Carol Cooperman *psychiatrist, educator*
Naimi, Shapur *cardiologist, educator*
†Nathan, David Gordon *pediatrician, educator*
Oates, Mary Elizabeth *radiologist*
O'Brien, J(ohn) Patrick *psychiatrist, educator*
Oddsson, Lars Ingimar Eugen *biomedical researcher*
†Oettgen, Joerg Peter *cardiologist*
Ogilvy, Christopher Stanley *neurosurgeon, researcher*
Olubodun, Joel Oladapo *medical researcher, physician*
Otis, James A.D. *physician, educator*
Pallotta, Johanna Antonia (Johanna Stephen) *physician, educator, researcher*
Pantanowitz, Liron *pathologist, researcher*
Parrish, John Albert *dermatologist, research administrator*
Paul, Oglesby *cardiologist, educator*
Petersen, Robert Allen *pediatric ophthalmologist*
Philip, Beverly Khnie *anesthesiologist*
Phillips, Russell S. *physician, educator*
†Phipatanakul, Wanda *pediatrician, allergist, immunologist*
Pineda, Roberto, II, *ophthalmologist*
Pochi, Peter Ernest *physician*
Poser, Charles Marcel *neurology educator*
Rabkin, Mitchell Thornton *physician, educator, hospital administrator*
†Rahimi, Nader *physician*
†Raines, Douglas Eric *anesthesiologist*
Ransil, Bernard J(erome) *research physician, methodologist, consultant, educator*
Reid, Lynne McArthur *pathologist*
Relman, Arnold Seymour *physician, educator, editor*
Renner, John Arthur *psychiatrist*
Reppert, Steven Marion *pediatrician, scientist, educator*
Richie, Jerome Paul *surgeon, educator*
Robinson, Malcolm Kenneth *surgeon*
Rockoff, Mark Alan *pediatric anesthesiologist*
†Rosen, Fred Saul *pediatrics educator*
Rosenblatt, Michael *medical researcher, educator*
Roth, Sanford Irwin *pathologist, educator*
Russell, Paul Snowden *surgeon, educator*
†Ryan, Thomas John *academic cardiologis, physician*
Ryser, Hugues Jean-Paul *pharmacologist, medical educator, cell biologist*
Sachs, David Howard *surgery and immunology educator, researcher*
†Sackstein, Robert *hematologist, educator*
Sadeghi-Nejad, Abdollah *pediatrician, educator*
†Sahani, Dushyant V. *radiologist, educator*
Salant, David John *medical educator, nephrologist*
Saper, Clifford Baird *neurobiology and neurology educator*
Schaller, Jane Green *pediatrician*
Schildkraut, Joseph Jacob *psychiatrist, educator*
Schlossman, Stuart Franklin *physician, educator, researcher*
Schlozman, Steven C. *psychiatrist*
†Schnitt, Stuart Jay *pathologist*
†Schroy, Paul Carl, III, *physician*
Schur, Peter Henry *internist*
†Schwerdt, Paul Thomas *cardiologist*
Scott, James Arthur *radiologist, educator*
Seddon, Johanna Margaret *ophthalmologist, epidemiologist*
Seely, Ellen Wells *endocrinologist*
Sege, Robert David *pediatrician*
Seidman, Christine E. *medical educator*
Selkoe, Dennis Jesse *neurologist, researcher, educator*
†Seltzer, Steven Erwin *radiologist, educator*
Shader, Richard Irwin *psychiatrist, pharmacologist, educator*
†Sheikh, Javed *physician, educator*
Sheridan, Robert Leo *surgeon*
Shi, Jialan *pathologist, educator*
Shields, Lawrence Thornton *orthopaedic surgeon, educator*
Shikora, Scott Alan *surgeon*
†Shubrooks, Samuel Joseph, Jr., *cardiologist*
Shucart, William Arthur *neurosurgeon*
†Siegel, Benjamin *pediatrician*
Silen, William *physician, surgery educator*
Simovic, Drasko *neurologist*
†Sledge, Clement Blount *orthopedic surgeon, educator*
†Smetana, Gerald William *internist*
Snydman, David Richard *infectious diseases specialist, educator*
Sober, Arthur Joel *dermatologist, researcher*
Solomon, Caren Grossbard *internist*
Spellman, Mitchell Wright *surgeon, academic administrator*
Sprague, Kellie *hematologist, oncologist*
Stacks, Robert David *pediatrician*
Stair, Thomas Osborne *physician, educator*
Steinberg, Martin H. *hematologist, educator*
Stern, Robert Stuart *dermatologist*
Stossel, Thomas Peter *medical educator, medical researcher, director*
Surman, Owen Stanley *psychiatrist*
Swartz, Morton Norman *medical educator, educator*
Talcott, James Austin *internist, oncologist, educator*
Tang, Yi *radiologist, researcher*
Taubman, Martin Arnold *immunologist, educator*
†Taylor, William C. *physician, medical educator*
Tello, Richard J. *radiologist, researcher*
Tilney, Nicholas Lechmere *surgery educator*
†Tischler, Arthur Steven *pathologist, researcher*
Trichopoulos, Dimitrios Vassilios *epidemiologist, educator*
Trier, Jerry Steven *gastroenterologist, educator*
Urion, David Kimball *pediatric neurologist, researcher, educator*
Vacanti, Joseph Philip *pediatric surgeon, transplant surgeon*
Vachon, Louis *psychiatrist, educator*
Van Marter, Linda Joanne *pediatrician, educator, neonatologist, researcher*
Volpe, Joseph John *pediatric neurologist, educator*
†Warshaw, Andrew Louis *surgeon, researcher*
Warth, James Arthur *physician, researcher*
Weber, Georg Franz *immunologist, cancer researcher*
†Weinberg, Arnold N. *physician, educator*
Weinstein, Robert *hematologist, researcher*
Weiss, Earle Burton *physician*
Weiss, Scott Tillman *internist, research epidemiologist, educator*
Wilson, Peter Wyman *internist, cardiovascular metabolic epidemiologist*
Wilson, Scott Numo *psychiatrist*
Wolf, Philip Alan *neurologist*
†Wyszynski, Diego Federico *epidemiologist, educator*
Young, Lucy H.Y. *physician, retina surgeon*
†Yuan, Junying *medical educator, researcher*
Zaleznik, Abraham *psychoanalyst, management specialist, educator*
†Zambrano, Eduardo Vicente *pathologist, researcher*
Zapol, Warren Myron *anesthesiologist*
Zarins, Bertram *orthopaedic surgeon*
Zervas, Nicholas Themistocles *neurosurgeon*
Zinner, Michael Jeffrey *surgeon, educator*

Boylston
Hanshaw, James Barry *physician, educator*

Brockton
Carlson, Desiree Anice *pathologist*

Brookline
Alarcon, Rogelio Alfonso *physician, researcher*
Basilico, Frederick Calvin *cardiologist*
Bergel, Ernest Walter *psychiatrist, educator*
Boudreau, Francis Helier *obstetrician-gynecologist*
Creasey, David Edward *physician, psychiatrist, educator*
Gurian, Bennett Sheppe *psychiatrist*
Jakab, Irene *psychiatrist*
Jordan, Ruth Ann *physician*
†Lown, Bernard *cardiologist, educator*
Sarfaty, Suzanne *internist and educator*
Schwartz, Bernard *physician*
†Shrier, Lydia Anne *physician*
Tyler, H. Richard *physician, educator*

Burlington
Barrett, David M. *urologist*
†Entrup, Michael Harry *anesthesiologist*
Freidberg, Stephen Roy *neurosurgeon*
†Khettry, Urmila *pathologist*
Moschella, Samuel L. *dermatology educator*
†Nesto, Richard William *cardiologist, researcher*
Oberfield, Richard Alan *oncologist*
Reuter, Karen L. *physician, radiologist*
Schoetz, David John, Jr., *colon and rectal surgeon, educator*

Cambridge
Anderson, William Henry *psychobiologist, educator*
Bizzi, Emilio *neurophysiologist, educator*
Breda, John Alexander *physician, musician*
Brusch, John Lynch *physician, educator, hospital administrator*
†Buchwald, Jed Zachary *environmental health researcher, science history educator*
Coles, Robert *child psychiatrist, educator, author*
Eisen, Herman Nathaniel *immunology researcher, medical educator*
Eisenberg, Carola *psychiatry educator*
Goldstein, Mark Allan *pediatrician, adolescent medicine specialist*
Havens, Leston Laycock *psychiatrist, educator*
†Hirsch, Martin Stanley *physician, researcher, educator*
Kantrowitz, Paul Alan *gastroenterologist*
†Lipsitt, Don Richard *psychiatrist, educator*
London, Irving Myer *physician, educator*
Mathews, Joan Helene *pediatrician*
McCunney, Robert Joseph *physician*
†Monath, Thomas Patrick *physician*
Nathanson, Larry *medical educator, physician*
Pories, Susan Elaine *medical educator*
Quinn, Timothy Robert *dermatopathologist, consultant*
†Rajagopal, Jayaraj *internist, medical educator*
Ris, Howard Clinton, Jr., *nonprofit public policy organization administrator*
Robbins, Stanley Leonard *pathologist, educator*
Shore, Miles Frederick *psychiatrist, educator*
†Smith, Susie Irene *histotechnologist, cytometrist*
Wacker, Warren Ernest Clyde *physician, educator*
Wexler, Donald *psychiatrist, educator*
Wurtman, Richard Jay *physician, educator, inventor*
Yogman, Michael William *pediatrician*

Charlestown
Brown, Robert Horatio *physician, neuromuscular research scientist*
Isselbacher, Kurt Julius *physician*
†Jenike, Michael Andrew *psychiatrist, educator*
Lamont-Havers, Ronald William *physician, research administrator*
Leaf, Alexander *physician, educator*
†Norris, Philip John *medical educator*
†Potts, John Thomas, Jr., *physician, educator*
†Settleman, Jeffrey *medical researcher, medical educator*
Zamecnik, Paul Charles *oncologist, medical research scientist*

Chestnut Hill
Ablon, Steven Luria *psychoanalyst*
Baum, Jules Leonard *ophthalmologist, educator*
Bresnahan, James Francis *retired medical educator*
Dahlben, Salin Abraham *neuropsychiatrist*
Flax, Martin Howard *pathologist, retired educator*
Franklin, Morton Jerome *emergency physician*
†Kaminer, Michael Seth *dermatologist*
Kosasky, Harold Jack *fertility researcher*
Stanbury, John Bruton *physician, educator*
†Teich, Jonathan Marc *emergency medicine physician, internist*
Thier, Samuel Osiah *physician, educator*

Concord
Andrews, Joseph Lyon, Jr., *medical educator, writer, practiconer*
Boger, William Pierce, III, *ophthalmologist*

Danvers
Keenholtz, Steven Laurence *physician*

Dartmouth
Frothingham, Thomas Eliot *pediatrician*
Leclair, Susan Jean *hematologist, clinical laboratory scientist, educator*

Dover
Kim, Ducksoo *radiologist, inventor and educator*

East Boston
Patinkin, Terry Allan *physician*

East Falmouth
Otis, Richard Dickinson *pathologist*

Falmouth
Funkhouser, John Jeremiah *urologist*
Heisler, Kenneth Avery *surgeon*
Sato, Kazuyoshi *pathologist*

Fitchburg
Aclin, Jean Anne *cancer registrar*

Framingham
Capobianco, Anthony G. *physician*
Chiraseveenuprapund, Pat *internist, endocrinologist*
†Kannel, William B. *cardiologist, epidemiologist*
Winston, Eileen Lynn *rheumatologist*

Franklin
Rafal, Keith W.L. *physician*

Gardner
Du Buske, Lawrence M. *immunologist, allergist, rheumotologist*

Gloucester
Anscombe, Roderick John *psychiatrist, educator*
White, Harold Jack *pathologist*

Hadley
Goldwater, Walter Eugene *psychiatrist, musician*

Harwich
Piro, Anthony John *radiologist*

Haverhill
Liguori, Paul Anthony *physician*
MacMillan, Francis Philip *physician*
Rosenbloom, Carl F. *pediatrician*

Hingham
Calnan, Arthur Francis *ophthalmologist*

Hyannis
Chiotellis, Philip Nicos *cardiologist*

Jamaica Plain
Pierce, Chester Middlebrook *retired psychiatrist, educator*
Snider, Gordon Lloyd *physician*

Lenox
Pirani, Conrad Levi *pathologist, educator*

Leominster
Landry, Francis Roderick *medical librarian*

Lexington
Halloran, Katherine Hess *physician, consultant*
†Lacson, Eduardo K., Jr., *nephrologist*
Li, Tongchuan *pharmacologist, researcher*
Pang, Samuel Chow-Ern *reproductive endocrinologist, gynecologist-obstetrician*
Paul, Norman Leo *psychiatrist, educator*

Lincoln
Brandt, John Henry *physician*
Kulka, J(ohannes) Peter *retired physician, pathologist*

Longmeadow
Atamian, Charles *oncologist, surgeon*
Griffin, John Francis *cardiologist*

Lowell
Dubner, Daniel William *pediatrician*
Petakov, Dragan Svetozar *internist, educator*
Wegman, David Howe *health science educator, consultant*

Lynnfield
Yaremchuk, Michael John *plastic surgeon*

Malden
Pirzada, Farouk Ahmad *cardiologist, educator*

Medfield
Woolston-Catlin, Marian *psychiatrist*

Medford
Logan, Bernard J. *obstetrician*
Thacker, Vasant Mukund *obstetrician, gynecologist*

Melrose
Desforges, Jane Fay *medical educator, physician*

Methuen
Shetty, Santosh Kumar *physician*

Milford
Cocchiarella, John Peter *pediatrician*

Monument Beach
Sullivan, Philip G. *retired obstetrician-gynecologist*

Nantucket
Salomon, Lucy *psychiatrist, educator*

Natick
Gottlieb, Michael Norman *internist, educator, health facility administrator*
Schott, John William *psychiatrist*

Needham
Weller, Thomas Huckle *physician, former educator*

Needham Heights
†Hubbell, John Platt *pediatrician, educator*

New Bedford
Shapiro, Gilbert Lawrence *orthopedist*

Newbury
Ablow, Keith Russell *psychiatrist, journalist, author*

Newton
Almozlino, Avraham *neurologist*
Bassuk, Ellen Linda *psychiatrist*
Blacher, Richard Stanley *psychiatrist*
Caplan, Hubert Irwin *medical educator*
†Isaacson, Keith Bryan *gynecologist, medical researcher*
Lisman, Susan R. *anesthesiologist, educator*
Monaco, Anthony Peter *surgery educator, medical institute administrator*
Sasahara, Arthur Asao *cardiologist, educator, researcher*

Newton Centre
Dagi, Linda Rabinowitz *pediatric ophthalmologist*

North Andover
Coleman, Daniel Eugene *physician*
Niccolini, Drew George *gastroenterologist*
Scully, Stephen J. *plastic surgeon*
Wessler, Stanford *physician, educator*

North Dartmouth
Linggood, Rita M. *radiation oncologist*

North Dighton
Cserr, Robert *psychiatrist, physician, hospital administrator*

Northampton
Bloomberg, Sanford *psychiatrist*

Northborough
Fulmer, Hugh Scott *physician, educator*

Norwood
Berliner, Allen Irwin *dermatologist*
Florian, Agustin Max *thoracic and cardiovascular surgeon*

Oxford
Schur, Walter Robert *physician*

Peabody
Lipman, Richard Paul *pediatrician*
Rodman, Elise *physician*

Petersham
Chivian, Eric Seth *psychiatrist, environmental scientist, educator*

Pittsfield
Fanelli, Robert D. *surgeon*
Malkani, Prakash *medical educator, neuroradiologist*

Plymouth
Pieters, Richard Sawyer, Jr., *radiation oncologist, educator*

Pocasset
Terkelsen, Kenneth G. *psychiatrist, hospital administrator*

Provincetown
Dickson, Vivian Franco *biomedical research consultant*

Quincy
Luo, Hong Yuan *biomedical scientist, educator*
Yung, Babington Chun-kuen *radiologist*

Reading
†Hambartsoumian, Eduard *obstetrician, researcher, embryologist*

Rockland
Blethen, Sandra Lee *pediatric endocrinologist*

Roxbury
Berman, Marlene Oscar *neuropsychologist, educator*
Peters, Alan *anatomy educator*

Salem
Reich, Michael Ira *obstetrician/gynecologist*

Scituate
Peters, John Adam *retired pathologist*

Shrewsbury
†Charney, Evan *pediatrician, educator*
De Rosa, Eolo *otolaryngologist*
Magee, Bernard Dale *obstetrician, gynecologist*

Somerville
Allen, Carole Newman *pediatrician*

South Harwich
Rigg, Charles Andrew *pediatrician*

South Wellfleet
Blau, Monte *retired radiology educator*

South Weymouth
Young, Michael Chung-En *allergist, immunologist, pediatrician*

Southborough
Dews, P(eter) B(ooth) *medical scientist, educator*

Springfield
Burkman, Ronald Thomas, Jr., *physician administrator, medical educator*
Coe, Nicholas P.W. *surgeon*
Farkas, Paul Stephen *gastroenterologist*
Frankel, Kenneth Mark *thoracic surgeon*
Friedmann, Paul *surgeon, educator*
Kirkwood, John Robert *neuroradiologist*
Kottamasu, Mohan Rao (K.V.R. Mohan Rao) *physician*
Liptzin, Benjamin *psychiatrist*
Lynn, Morton Daniel *orthopedist*
McGee, William Tobin *intensive care physician*
Petrone, William Francis *physician, microbiologist, corporate executive*
†Sloan, David James *sonographer*
Steingrub, Jay Stanley *critical care physician, educator*

Stockbridge
Shapiro, Edward Robert *psychiatrist, administrator educator psychoanalyst*

Stoneham
Igou, Raymond Alvin, Jr., *orthopedic surgeon*

Swampscott
Brenner, Lawrence *medical librarian, consultant*

Swansea
†Ireland, Linda Ann *internist*

Taunton
Bornstein, Myer Sidney *obstetrician, gynecologist*
Schwartz, Alan Marshall *radiologist*

Vineyard Haven
Jacobs, Gretchen Huntley *psychiatrist*

Waban
Rogoff, Jerome Howard *psychiatrist, psychoanalyst, forensic expert*

Waltham
†Harianawala, Abizer I. *pharmacologist, researcher*
Lackner, James Robert *aerospace medicine educator*
Leach, Robert Ellis *physician, educator*
Mangano, Salvatore Nicholas *surgeon*
Mohanroy, Pradeep *physician*
Padmanabhan, Cape S. *geriatrician*
Schwartz, Joseph Hersh *surgeon, educator*
Smith, Allen Leonard *physician*

Wayland
Chodosh, Sanford *pulmonologist*

Wellesley
Bauman, Margaret Estelle Lang *pediatric neurologist*
Celli, Bartolome Romulo *internist*
Coyne, Mary Downey *biologist, endocrinologist, educator*
Landaw, Stephen Arthur *physician, educator*
Murray, Joseph Edward *retired plastic surgeon*
Pierce, Donald Shelton *retired orthopedic surgeon, educator*
Sexton, John Joseph *oral and maxillofacial surgeon, educator*
Trubow, Marshall David *obstetrician-gynecologist*
Twitchell, Thomas Evans *neurologist, educator*

Wellesley Hills
McAlpine, Frederick Sennett *anesthesiologist*

West Falmouth
Bass, Norman Herbert *physician, scientist, university and hospital administrator, health care executive*
Holz, George G., IV, *medical educator, research scientist*

West Roxbury
Aguilera, Elsa Judith *physiatrist*
Cohen, Carolyn Alta *health educator*
McCully, Kilmer Serjus *pathologist*
†Thatte, Hemant Sadashiv *surgeon, researcher*

West Springfield
Desai, Veena Balvantrai *obstetrician and gynecologist, educator*

Westborough
Appelbaum, Kenneth Lloyd *psychiatrist*
Higano, Norio *retired internist*

Weston
Draskoczy, Paul R. *psychiatrist*
Wells, Lionelle Dudley *psychiatrist, educator*

Westwood
Plimpton, Calvin Hastings *physician, university president*

Williamstown
Stuebner, Erwin August, Jr., *internist*

Winchester
†Baratta, Edmond John *radiochemist, radiation safety officer*
Beck, William Samson *hematologist, educator, biochemist, writer*
†Ericson, William B. *orthopedic hand surgeon*

Winthrop
Lee, James Richard *ophthalmologist, educator*

Woburn
Minkoff, Kenneth Mark *psychiatrist*

Woods Hole
Laster, Leonard *physician, consultant, author*

Worcester
Appelbaum, Paul Stuart *psychiatrist, educator*
Bernhard, Jeffrey David *dermatologist, editor, educator*
Bojar, Robert Michael *cardiothoracic surgeon*
†Daly, Jennifer *physician*
†Dershwitz, Mark *anesthesiologist, researcher*
Drachman, David Alexander *neurologist*
†Gandhi, Pritesh *medical educator*
Goss, Thomas Pixton *orthopaedic surgeon*
Hunter, Richard Edward *retired physician*
Lanza, Robert Paul *medical scientist*
Leppo, Jeffrey Allen *cardiologist*
Licho, Robert *physician, medical educator*
†Litofsky, N. Scott *physician, educator*
†Longcope, Christopher *physician, endocrinology educator*
Ludlum, David Blodgett *pharmacologist, educator*
Nompleggi, Dominic J. *gastroenterologist, medical educator*
Och, Mohamad Rachid *psychiatrist, consultant*
†Selin, Lisa K. *physician*
Smith, Thomas William *neuropathologist*
Smyrnios, Nicholas A. *physician, educator*
Stoff, Jeffrey S. *physician, educator*
†Tonkonogy, Joseph Moses *physician, neuropsychiatrist, researcher*
Yankauer, Alfred *physician, educator*
Yood, Robert A. *rheumatologist*
Zurier, Robert Burton *medical educator, clinical investigator*
Zwerdling, Robert G. *physician*

Yarmouth Port
Gordon, Benjamin Dichter *medical executive, pediatrician*

MICHIGAN

Alma
Sanders, Jack Ford *physician*

Ann Arbor
Abrams, Gerald David *physician, educator*
Ansbacher, Rudi *physician*
†Arbabi, Saman *surgeon, researcher*
Arneson, Wallace Aggergaard, Jr., *surgeon*
Atwater, John Bancroft *physician*
Bacon, George Edgar *pediatrician, educator*
†Bauer, Samuel Thomas *gynecologist, researcher, obstetrician*
†Bergstrom, Terry Joseph *medical educator, physician*
†Biermann, Janet Sybil *orthopaedic surgeon, educator*
Bloom, David Alan *pediatric urology educator*
Bloom, Jane Maginnis *emergency physician*
†Borer, Katarina T. *exercise endocrinologist*
Bowdler, Anthony John *physician, educator*
†Buchman, Steven Richard *plastic surgeon, medical association administrator, director*
†Bude, Ronald Ottomar *radiologist*
Burdi, Alphonse Rocco *anatomist*
Burke, Robert Harry *surgeon, educator*
Carlson, Bruce Martin *anatomist*
Casey, Kenneth Lyman *neurologist*
Cerny, Joseph Charles *urologist, educator*
Chang, Alfred Edward *surgeon*
†Chavey, William E. *physician*
Cho, Kyung Jae *physician, radiologist, educator*
Christensen, A(lbert) Kent *anatomy educator*
Coran, Arnold Gerald *pediatric surgeon*
De La Iglesia, Felix Alberto *pathologist, toxicologist*
†Donabedian, Avedis *physician, educator*
Doyle, Constance Talcott Johnston *physician, educator, medical association administrator*
Dubin, Howard Victor *dermatologist*
Duvernoy, Wolf F.C. *cardiologist*
†Eagle, Kim Allen *cardiologist*
†Faerber, Gary J. *surgeon, educator*
Fajans, Stefan Stanislaus *retired internist*
Feldman, Eva Lucille *neurology educator*
Ferrara, James Lawrence Michael *medical educator, physician, scientist*
Fox, David Alan *rheumatologist, immunologist*
†Franceschi, Renny Theodore *medical educator, dean*
Frueh, Bartley Richard *surgeon*
Gebarski, Stephen S. *neuroradiologist, educator*
Gikas, Paul William *medical educator*
Gilman, Sid *neurologist*
Goldstein, Irwin Joseph *medical research executive*
Greden, John Francis *psychiatrist, educator*
†Greenberg, Harry Seth *neurologist, educator*
Greenfield, Lazar John *surgeon, educator*
Haig, Andrew John *physical medicine and rehabilitation physician, writer*
Hawthorne, Victor Morrison *epidemiologist, educator*
Hensinger, Robert Neil *pediatric orthopaedist*
Hiss, Roland Graham *physician, medical educator*
Hoff, Julian Theodore *physician, educator*
Hollenberg, Paul Frederick *pharmacology educator*
Humes, H(arvey) David *nephrologist, educator*
James, Sherman Athonia *social epidemiologist, educator*
Johnson, Timothy R. B. *obstetrician-gynecologist, educator*
Karam-Hage, Maher A. *psychiatrist, researcher*
Kenyon, George Lommel *pharmaceutical educator, dean*
Kirkpatrick, Garland Penn *pediatrician*
Kuhl, David Edmund *physician, nuclear medicine educator*
†Kuzon, William M., Jr., *plastic surgeon, muscle physiologist*
La Du, Bert Nichols, Jr., *pharmacology educator, physician*
†Langa, Kenneth M. *physician*
†Learned, David Walter *anesthesiologist*
Lichter, Paul Richard *ophthalmology educator*
Lozoff, Betsy *pediatrician*
Margolis, Philip Marcus *psychiatrist, educator*
Martel, William *radiologist, educator*
Maxwell, Donald Robert *pharmacologist*
†Mehta, Rajendra H *cardiologist, researcher*
Modell, Stephen Mark *medical researcher, educator*
Montie, James Edward *urologist, oncologist*
Monto, Arnold Simon *epidemiology educator*
Morgenstern, Lewis B. *medical educator*
Morley, George William *gynecologist*
†Morrison, Sean Joseph *medical researcher*
†Musch, David C. *epidemiologist*
Oliver, William John *pediatrician, educator*
†Oral, Elif Arioglu *endocrinologist, researcher*
Orringer, Mark Burton *surgeon, educator*
Parker, Walter Gee *pediatrician*
Pasyk, Krystyna Anna *dermatologist*
Pitt, Bertram *cardiologist, educator, consultant*
Powsner, Edward Raphael *physician*
Rosenthal, Amnon *pediatric cardiologist*
†Roubidoux, Marilyn A. *radiologist*
Russell, James William *neurologist, neuroscientist, electrophysiologist*
†Sanda, Martin George *urologist*
†Saper, Joel R. *neurologist, educator*
Schottenfeld, David *epidemiologist, educator*
Serwer, Gerald Arthur *medical educator*
Shapiro, Brahm *nuclear medicine physician, endocrinologist*
Sheon, Amy Ruth *biomedical researcher*
†Simpson, Robert Urquhart *medical educator, researcher*
Smith, David John, Jr., *plastic surgeon*
Smith, Donald Cameron *physician, educator*
Strang, Ruth Hancock *pediatric educator, pediatric cardiologist, priest*
Stross, Jeoffrey Knight *physician, educator*
Tandon, Rajiv *psychiatrist, educator*
Terrell, Jeffrey E. *otolaryngologist, researcher, educator*
Thompson, Norman Winslow *surgeon, educator*
Todd, Robert Franklin, III, *oncologist, educator*
†van Golen, Kenneth Louis *medical researcher*
Ward, Peter Allan *pathologist, educator*
Weg, John Gerard *physician*
Wiggins, Roger C. *internist, educator, researcher*
†Wojtys, Edward M. *orthopedic surgeon, sports medicine physician*
Yu, Mei-yu *medical researcher*

Berkley
Hauser, Andrew Max *cardiologist*

Bingham Farms
Farhy, Rodolfo David *internist, cardiologist*
Giles, Conrad Leslie *ophthalmic surgeon*
†Katz, Sidney Franklin *obstetrician, gynecologist*

Birmingham
Edwards, Michael Gerard *physician*

Bloomfield Hills
†Breiner, Sander James *psychiatry educator, psychoanalyst*
Kaufman, Jerome Seymour *retired ophthalmologist*
Klosinski, Deanna Dupree *medical educator, consultant*
Mathog, Robert Henry *otolaryngologist, educator*
Prasad, Niru *physician, television personality*
Rosenzweig, Norman *psychiatry educator administrator*
Stunz, John Henry, Jr., *retired physician*

Chelsea
†Yarows, Steven Allen *internist*

Clarkston
Wydra, Frank Thomas *healthcare executive*

Clinton Township
Brown, Ronald Delano *endocrinologist*
Ho, Robert En Ming *neurosurgeon, educator*

Davison
Tauscher, John Walter *retired pediatrician, emeritus educator*
Weamer, Alan Philip *family practice physician*

Dearborn
Coburn, Ronald Murray *ophthalmic surgeon, researcher*
Fordyce, James George *physician*

Dearborn Heights
Hatem, Ghaleb Fayez *ophthalmologist, hospital administrator*

Detroit
Abella Dominicis, Esteban Martin *hematologist, oncologist, pediatrician*
Aboulafia, Elie David *vascular surgeon*
Amirikia, Hassan *obstetrician, gynecologist*
Arrington, Harold M. *obstetrician*
†Bahrainwala, Abdul Husein *allergist, immunologist*
Balon, Richard *psychiatrist, educator*
†Benninger, Michael Stephen *otolaryngologist*
Bock, Brooks Frederick *emergency physician*
Brooks, Beth Ann *physician*
Coffey, C(harles) Edward *physician*
Cohen, Sanford Ned *pediatrics educator, academic administrator*
†Dhar, Josephine Patricia *medical educator*
Diaz, Fernando Gustavo *neurosurgeon*

Dombrowski, Mitchell Paul *physician, inventor, researcher*
Edwards, Paul Andrew *vitreo-retinal surgeon, ophthalmologist*
†Ehrinpreis, Murray Norman *gastroenterologist, educator*
Eliason, James Frederick *hematology and oncology researcher*
Elkus, Robert Michael *general surgeon*
†Enam, Syed Ather *neurosurgeon, researcher*
Fromm, David *surgeon*
Gardin, Julius Markus *cardiologist, educator*
†Guthikonda, Murali *neurosurgeon*
Hood, Antoinette Foote *dermatologist*
Hurley, Harry James, Jr., *dermatologist, educator*
†Jampel, Robert Steven *ophthalmologist, educator*
Jenkins-Anderson, Barbara Jeanne *pathologist, educator*
Jones, Bruce Allen *pathologist*
Kantrowitz, Adrian *surgeon, educator*
†Kato, Ikuko *epidemiologist*
Kelley, Mark Albert *physician, educator, health care executive*
†Kerin, Nicholas Zeev *cardiologist, researcher*
Kithier, Karel *pathologist, educator*
Kline, Ronald Alvin *vascular surgeon, educator*
Kobernick, Sidney D. *pathologist, educator*
Krull, Edward Alexander *dermatologist*
†Lawson, Noel Seymore *pathologist, consultant*
Li, Xiaoming *pediatrics educator, psychologist*
Lim, Henry Wan-Peng *physician*
†Lisak, Robert Philip *physician, researcher, educator*
Lupulescu, Aurel Peter *medical educator, researcher, physician*
Mahmood, Asim *neurosurgeon*
Maiese, Kenneth *neurologist, neuroscientist*
Marsh, Harold Michael *anesthesiologist*
†Mattingly, Raymond R *pharmacologist, educator*
Miller, Orlando Jack *physician, educator*
Moghissi, Kamran S. *obstetrician, gynecologist, educator*
Newton, Kenneth Kurt *physician, educator, administrator*
†O'Connell, John Bernard, Jr., *medical educator, chairman department of medicine*
Perry, Burton Lars *retired pediatrician*
Peters, William P. *oncologist, science administrator, educator*
Petersen, Steve Alan *orthopaedic surgeon*
Phillips, Eduardo *surgeon, educator*
Porter, Arthur T. *oncologist, educator, medical administrator*
Prasad, Ananda Shiva *medical educator*
†Rajarethinam, Rajaprabhakaran *psychiatrist, educator, researcher*
Segel, Mark Calvin *diagnostic radiologist*
Shields, Anthony Frank *oncologist, hematologist*
Shwayder, Tor Adam *dermatologist, pediatrician, musician*
Silverman, Norman Alan *cardiac surgeon*
Simon, Michael Richard *allergist, immunologist, internist*
Sloan, Andrew Edward *neurosurgeon*
Slovis, Thomas Laurence *radiologist*
Smith, Wilbur Lazar *radiologist, educator*
Sokol, Robert James *obstetrician, gynecologist, educator*
Talpos, Gary B. *surgeon*
†Tobi, Martin *gastroenterologist, researcher*
Tolia, Vasundhara K. *pediatric gastroenterologist, educator*
Treadwell, Marjorie Clarke *medical educator*
Tse, Harley Y. *immunologist, educator*
Vander Heide, Richard Stuart *pathologist, educator, research scientist*
Voudoukis, Ignatios John *internist, cardiologist*
Whitehouse, Fred Waite *endocrinologist, researcher*
Wiener, Joseph *pathologist*

Dexter
Zazove, Philip *family practice physician*

East Lansing
Beckmeyer, Henry Ernest *anesthesiologist, medical educator, pain management specialist*
Brody, Theodore Meyer *pharmacologist, educator*
Davis, Glenn Craig *psychiatrist*
Ebell, Mark Herbert *physician, researcher*
Gottschalk, Alexander *radiologist, diagnostic radiology educator*
Kumar, Ashir *pediatrician, medical educator*
Magen, Myron Shimin *osteopathic physician, educator, university dean*
†Pathak, Dorothy Rybaczyk *epidemiologist, biostatistician*
Rechtien, James Joseph *osteopath, educator*
Reinhart, Mary Ann *medical board executive*
Rosenman, Kenneth D. *medical educator*
Waite, Donald Eugene *medical educator, consultant*
Wang, Donna Hui *investigative medicine director*
†Werner, Arnold *psychiatrist*
Wieting, J. Michael *physician, medical educator*
Willis, Park Weed, III, *cardiologist*

Farmington Hills
Dobritt, Dennis William *physician, researcher, pain management specialist*
Green, Henry Leonard *physician*
Lewis, Barry Kent *cardiologist*
McQuiggan, Mark C. *urologist*
†Sargent, Eric Winslow *otolaryngologist, surgeon*
Simpson, David Allen *osteopath*

Fife Lake
Knecht, Richard Arden *family practitioner*

Flint
Farrehi, Cyrus *cardiologist, educator*
Inoue, Susumu *medical educator*
Levine, Peter Arthur *medical society executive*
†Wiese, David A. *pathologist*

Flushing
Himes, George Elliott *pathologist*

Fort Gratiot
Zimmer, Lawrence Joseph *psychiatrist, internist*

Grand Blanc
Wasfie, Tarik Jawad *surgeon, educator*

Grand Rapids
Bartek, Gordon Luke *radiologist*
Boyce, David Curtis *retired ophthalmologist*
Daniels, Joseph *neuropsychiatrist*
Feenstra, Laurence Henry *physician*
Hinshaw, Mark Waldo *psychiatrist, educator*
Logie, James Wallace *surgeon, retired*
Mazur, David John *psychiatrist, educator*
O'Rourke, Timothy John *physician*
Verdier, David D'Ooge *ophthalmologist, educator*
Vydareny, John Richard *dermatologist*
Wendt, Vernon Earl *internist, cardiologist*
Wilt, Jeffrey Lynn *pulmonary and critical care physician, educator*

Grosse Pointe
Dzul, Paul J. *physician, medical journal editor*
Papaioanou, Helen Antoinette *retired allergist, pediatrician, educator*
Sphire, Raymond Daniel *anesthesiologist, educator*

Grosse Pointe Woods
Sul, Yi Chul *neurologist*

Holland
Zuidema, George Dale *surgeon, educator*

Howell
Yanga, Ismael Duran *surgeon*

Ishpeming
Fitzgerald, Robert Hannon, Jr., *orthopedic surgeon*

Kalamazoo
Butler, Charles Francis *cardiac surgeon*
Fischell, Tim Alexander *cardiologist*
Fisher, George *gerontological educator*
Gladstone, William Sheldon, Jr., *radiologist*
Lavery, J. Patrick *perinatologist*
†Saber, Alan A. *surgeon*
Selzer, Kenneth A. *neurologist, editor*
Taylor, Duncan Paul *research neuropharmacologist*
Weintraub, Jacob Michael *pediatrician*

Kalkaska
Batsakis, John George *pathology educator*

Lake Angelus
Kresge, Bruce Anderson *retired physician*

Lansing
†Fiechtner, Justus John *rheumatologist, consultant*
Neiberg, Alan David *physician*
Sauer, Harold John *physician, educator*
Schott, Cheryl Suzanne *health educator*
Sharif, M. Alan *interventional cardiologist*
Vincent, Frederick Michael, Sr., *neurologist, educator*

Lowell
Gerard, Donald Gordon *physician*

Macomb
DeGiusti, Dominic Lawrence *medical science educator, academic administrator*

Mancelona
Whelan, Joseph L. *neurologist*

Marquette
Chen, Cathleen *physician*
†Mahmood, Tallat *oncologist*

Midland
Snyder, Robert Lee *anesthesiologist*

Milford
Oliveri, Eugene Alfred *gastroenterologist*

Niles
Gibbs, Denis Laurel *radiologist*
Kim, Choong-Man Joseph *radiologist*

Northport
Schultz, Richard Carlton *plastic surgeon*

Northville
Abbasi, Tariq Afzal *psychiatrist, educator*

Oak Park
Kaplan, Randy Kaye *podiatrist*

Okemos
Grimshaw, David Norman *physician, educator*
Hutchinson, Craig Lewis *internist*
Ristow, George Edward *neurologist, educator*

Orchard Lake
Lichtwardt, Harry Edward *physician, surgeon*

Petoskey
Deery, Hugh Gunner, II, *physician*
†Meengs, William Lloyd *cardiologist*

Pleasant Ridge
Krabbenhoft, Kenneth Lester *radiologist, educator*

Pontiac
Silbergleit, Allen *surgeon, researcher, medical educator*

Portage
Chodos, Dale David Jerome *physician, consumer advocate*

Rochester Hills
Badalament, Robert Anthony *urologic oncologist*
Bartunek, James Scott *psychiatrist*

Royal Oak
Al-Sarraf, Muhyi *internist, oncologist*
Bernstein, Jay *pathologist, researcher, educator*
Comstock, Christine Holaday *obstetrician, gynecologist, radiologist, educator*
Dworkin, Howard Jerry *nuclear medicine physician, educator*
LaBan, Myron Miles *physician, administrator*
Malik, Ghaus Muhammad *neurosurgeon*
McCarroll, Kathleen Ann *radiologist, educator*
Proctor, Conrad Arnold *physician*
Ryan, Jack *physician, retired hospital corporation executive*
Shetty, Sugandh Dasu *urological surgeon, researcher*

Saginaw
Ferlinz, Jack *cardiologist, medical educator*
Manning, John Warren, III, *retired surgeon, medical educator*

Saint Clair Shores
Elliott, Luke Alexander *family practice physician*
Field, Stephen Ira *dermatologist, educator*

Southfield
Hammel, Ernest Martin *medical educator, academic administrator*
Malviya, Vinay Kumar *obstetrician-gynecologist*
†Naini, Mansoor Ghazinour *cardiologist*
Newman, Steven E. *neurologist*
O'Hara, John Paul, III, *orthopaedic surgeon*
Perez-Cruet, Mick Jorge *neurological surgeon, educator*
Spitzer, A. Robert *physician, electrical engineer*
Zobl, Eldred Gregory *cardiologist*
†Zubroff, Leonard Saul *surgeon*

Sturgis
Reiff, James Stanley *osteopathic physician, addictions, psychiatric, surgeon*

Taylor
Downham, Thomas Fletcher *dermatologist*

Traverse City
Prusick, Vincent Roger *orthopaedic surgeon*
Supanich, Barbara Ann *family practice physician*
†Tobin, Patrick John *dermatologist*

Trenton
Go, Benedict Anthony *internist*

Troy
†Barton, Stanley L. *ophthalmologist, consultant*
Golusin, Millard R. *obstetrician and gynecologist*
Misra, Dwijen Cristobal *surgeon*
Schafer, Sharon Marie *anesthesiologist*

Utica
Miller, Aileen Etta Martha *medical association administrator, nutritionist*

Warren
Rottman, Michael *physician*
Schock, Martin Irving *oncologist*

West Bloomfield
Hepner, Michael Jules *allergist*
Jones, Lewis Arnold, Jr., *physician, radiologist, consultant*
Joseph, Ramon Rafael *physician, educator*
Sarwer-Foner, Gerald Jacob *physician, educator*
Sawyer, Howard Jerome *physician*
Schechter, Steven Hart *neurologist*
Seidman, Michael David *surgeon, educator*

Woodhaven
Kim, Hyo Sook *anesthesiologist*

Wyandotte
Aguirre, Antonio Azanes, Jr., *physician*

Ypsilanti
Hildebrandt, H(enry) M(ark) *pediatrician*

MINNESOTA

Austin
Rioux, Pierre August *psychiatrist*

Bloomington
†Carpel, Emmett Franklin *ophthalmologist, consultant*

Burnsville
Lakin, James Dennis *allergist, immunologist, director*

Detroit Lakes
†Eginton, Charles Theodore *surgeon, educator*

Duluth
Aufderheide, Arthur Carl *pathologist*
Eckman, Matthew Jay *physiatrist, educator*
Eisenberg, Richard Martin *pharmacology educator*
Hazel, Stewart Jerome *physician*
McKee, David Charles *physician, neurologist*
Sebastian, James Albert *obstetrician, gynecologist, educator*

Edina
Frys, Russell N. *obstetrician-gynecologist*
Justman, Richard Allen *pediatrician*
Sandy, Lewis Gordon *physician, healthcare executive*
Schroeder, Albert John *retired pediatrician*
Tagatz, George Elmo *retired obstetrician, gynecologist, educator*

Wilder, Walter Llewellyn *allergist, immunologist, pediatrician*

Excelsior
Bilka, Paul Joseph *retired physician*

Fridley
Vlodaver, Zeev A. *cardiologist*

Hibbing
Baldwin, Jan Linse *family practice physician*

Lauderdale
Resch, Joseph Anthony *neurologist*

Madelia
Lucek, Donald Walter *surgeon*

Mankato
Huot, Rachel Irene *biomedical educator, research scientist, physician*

Melrose
Hammarsten, James Francis *internist, educator*

Minneapolis
Blackburn, Henry Webster, Jr., *retired physician*
Boudreau, Robert James *nuclear medicine physician, researcher*
Brown, David Mitchell *physician, educator, dean*
†Buchwald, Henry *surgeon, educator, researcher*
Burchell, Howard Bertram *retired physician, educator*
Burton, Charles Victor *physician, surgeon, inventor*
†Bushara, Khalafalla O *neurologist*
Chavers, Blanche Marie *pediatrician, educator, researcher*
†Coetzee, Johannes Christiaan *orthopedic surgeon*
Cohn, Jay N. *cardiologist, educator*
Craig, James Lynn *physician*
†d'Audiffret, Alexandre Christophe *surgeon, researcher, medical educator*
†Domino, Constance Mae *genetics researcher*
Dykstra, Dennis Dale *physiatrist*
Ebeling, Brian Terry *family physician*
Fisch, Robert Otto *medical educator*
Gajl-Peczalska, Kazimiera J. *retired surgical pathologist, pathology educator*
Gerberich, Susan Goodwin *epidemiologist, educator*
Gorlin, Robert James *medical educator, educator*
Gullickson, Glenn, Jr., *physician, educator*
Hanson, Arthur Stuart *physician, consultant*
†Harper, Patricia Nelsen *psychiatrist*
†Hays, Thomas S. *medical educator, medical researcher*
Herzog, Charles A. *cardiologist, researcher*
Hom, David Brian *surgeon*
†Humar, Abhinav *transplant surgeon, clinical researcher*
Jensen, Steven Richard *radiologist, consultant*
Kane, Robert Lewis *public health educator*
†Kashtan, Clifford Elliot *physician*
Kennedy, B(yrl) J(ames) *medicine and oncology educator*
Kletschka, Harold Dale *cardiovascular surgeon, biomedical company executive*
Kump, Warren Lee *retired diagnostic radiologist*
Lake, John Richard *gastroenterologist*
Lentz, Richard David *psychiatrist, educator*
Leon, Arthur Sol *research cardiologist, exercise physiologist*
Leppik, Ilo E. *neurologist, educator*
†LeSage, Mark Gerard *pharmacologist, psychologist*
Levine, Howard Marvin *obstetrician, gynecologist*
Levitt, Seymour Herbert *physician, radiology educator*
Litman, Theodor James *medical educator*
Luepker, Russell Vincent *epidemiology educator*
†Malmquist, Carl Phillip *psychiatrist*
†Mandel, Sheldon Lloyd *dermatologist, educator*
McQuarrie, Donald Gray *surgeon, educator*
Meininger, Eric Thomas *pediatrician, internist*
Najarian, John Sarkis *surgeon, educator*
Nicholas, S. Scott *allergist*
Nuttall, Frank Quentin *physician, researcher*
O'Connor, Patrick J. *family physician, researcher*
Peterson, Douglas Arthur *physician*
Peterson, Phillip Keith *physician, clinical investigator*
Phibbs, Clifford Matthew *surgeon, educator*
Quie, Paul Gerhardt *pediatrician, educator*
Rothenberger, David Albert *surgeon*
Rottenberg, David Allan *neurologist*
Shumway, Sara Jane *cardiothoracic surgeon*
Simon, John Ernest *psychiatrist*
Slocum, Rosemarie *physician services consultant, recruiter*
Staba, Emil John *pharmacognosy and medicinal chemistry educator*
Stenwick, Michael William *retired internist, geriatric medicine consultant*
Sveum, Richard James *allergist*
Swiontkowski, Marc Francis *orthopedist*
Tamzarian, Armin Petrovich *physician*
Thompson, Roby Calvin, Jr., *orthopedic surgeon, educator*
Thompson, Theodore Robert *pediatric educator*
Ulstrom, Robert A. *pediatrician, educator*
†Wang, Yang *cardiology educator, researcher*
Weir, Edward Kenneth *cardiologist, educator*
Wild, John Julian *surgeon, director medical research institute*
Williams, David Neville *physician*

Minnetonka
†Erlandson, Patrick J. *medical association administrator*
Shapiro, Fred Louis *physician, educator*

Olivia
Cosgriff, James Arthur *physician*

Pequot Lakes
Weaver, Arthur Lawrence *retired rheumatologist*

Plymouth
Losasso, Thomas James *anesthesiologist*
Prem, Konald Arthur *physician, educator*

Rochester
†Ackerman, Michael John *medical educator*
Archibald, Reginald Mac Gregor *physician, chemist, educator*
Bartholomew, Lloyd Gibson *physician*
Bastron, James Arthur *retired neurologist*
Beahrs, Oliver Howard *surgeon, educator*
†Beckman, Thomas J. *physician*
†Berry, Daniel John *orthopedist, surgeon*
Bowie, E(dward) J(ohn) Walter *hematologist, researcher*
†Cable, David George *cardiologist, surgeon*
†Charboneau, Joseph William *radiologist, medical educator*
†Charlton, Michael R *physician, researcher*
†Cherry, Kenneth Jerome, Jr., *surgeon*
Chute, Christopher Gregory *medical educator*
Cofield, Robert Hahn *orthopedic surgeon, educator*
Czaja, Albert Joseph *physician, educator*
Danielson, Gordon Kenneth, Jr., *cardiovascular surgeon, educator*
DeRemee, Richard Arthur *physician, educator, researcher*
Deschamps, Claude *thoracic surgeon*
†Douglas, William W. *physician, consultant*
Douglass, Bruce E. *physician*
Dyck, Peter James *neurologist, researcher, educator*
Edwards, William Dean *pathologist*
Engel, Andrew George *neurologist*
Feldt, Robert Hewitt *pediatric cardiologist, educator*
†Fervenza, Fernando C. *nephrologist, educator*
Foote, Robert Leonard *oncologist, educator, researcher*
Fye, W. Bruce, III, *cardiologist*
†Geda, Yonas Endale *neuropsychiatrist, researcher*
Gersh, Bernard J. *cardiologist, researcher, educator*
Gertz, Morie Abraham *physician*
Gharib, Hossein *medical educator*
Gibson, Lawrence Edward *dermatologist*
†Gloviczki, Peter *surgeon*
Gomez, Manuel Rodriguez *physician*
Gorman, Colum Alphonsus *retired endocrinologist*
Gracey, Douglas Robert *physician, physiologist, educator*
Haddy, Francis John *physician, educator*
Hodgson, Jane Elizabeth *obstetrician and gynecologist, consultant*
Hunder, Gene Gerald *physician, educator*
Jaffe, Allan S. *cardiologist, educator*
†Jankowski, Christopher James *anesthesiologist, educator*
Johnson, Charles Daniel *radiologist*
Kyle, Robert Arthur *medical educator, oncologist*
Lanier, William Lovel, Jr., *anesthesiologist, educator*
†Leung, Nelson *physician*
Liebow, Mark *physician*
Lofgren, Karl Adolph *surgeon, educator*
†Loftus, Jr., Edward Vincent *gastroenterologist, writer*
Lucas, Alexander Ralph *child psychiatrist, educator, writer*
Luthra, Harvinder S. *rheumatologist, researcher*
Mackenzie, Ronald Alexander *anesthesiologist*
Malek, Reza Said *urological surgeon*
Malkasian, George Durand, Jr., *physician, educator*
†Malouf, Joseph F. *cardiologist*
Michenfelder, John Donahue *anesthesiology educator*
Midthun, David Eric *physician, consultant*
Moder, Kevin G. *rheumatologist, consultant*
Mrazek, David Allen *pediatric psychiatrist*
Neel, Harry Bryan, III, *surgeon, scientist, educator*
Nelson, Audrey May *physician*
Ohno, Kinji *neurologist, educator*
†Packer, Douglas L. *cardiologist*
Pairolero, Peter Charles *surgeon*
Petersen, Bret T. *gastroenterologist*
Phillips, Sidney Frederick *gastroenterologist, educator*
†Pisansky, Thomas Michael *physician*
Pittelkow, Mark Robert *physician, dermatology educator, researcher*
Podratz, Karl C. *gynecologic surgeon, oncologist, educator*
Puga, Francisco Javier *cardiac surgeon*
Reitemeier, Richard Joseph *physician*
Rhodes, Deborah Jane *internist*
†Rogers, Roy Steele, III, *dermatology educator, dean*
Rosen, Charles Burke *surgeon*
Rosenow, Edward Carl, III, *medical educator*
Ryu, Jay H. *physician, educator, researcher*
Scott, John Paul *medical educator*
Segura, Joseph Weston *urologist, educator*
Siekert, Robert George *neurologist*
†Sim, Franklin H. *orthopedic surgery educator*
Sprung, Juraj *anesthesiologist, educator*
Stegall, Mark D. *surgeon, medical educator*
†Stickler, Gunnar Brynolf *pediatrician*
Swanson, Jerry William *neurologist, educator*
Symmonds, Richard Earl *gynecologist*
Tarvestad, Anthony M. *psychiatrist*
Thompson, Rodney Lee *infectious diseases specialist*
Ward, Louis Emmerson *retired physician*
Wass, C(harles) Thomas *anesthesiologist*
Weinshilboum, Richard M. *pharmacologist, educator, biomedical researcher*
Wells, Lloyd Allan *psychiatrist, educator*
Whisnant, Jack Page *neurologist*
Wiebers, David Owen *physician*
Wood, Michael Bruce *orthopaedic surgeon, researcher, educator*
Woods, John Elmer *plastic surgeon*
Woog, John J. *plastic surgeon*

Saint Cloud
Olson, Barbara Ford *physician*
Rysavy, Richard Ludwig *physician*

Saint Paul
Bender, Jeff Blaine *epidemiologist, veterinarian*
Cavert, Henry Mead *physician, retired educator*
Edwards, Jesse Efrem *physician, educator*
Holter, Arlen Rolf *cardiothoracic surgeon*
†Jaranson, James M. *psychiatrist, public health service officer*
Lamon, Richard Paul *emergency physician, family practice physician*
Larkin, John Edward, Jr., *orthopedic surgeon*
Michael, Alfred Frederick, Jr., *physician, medical educator*
Partington, Michael David *pediatric neurosurgeon*
Stromberg, Bert E. *veterinary medicine educator*
Swaiman, Kenneth Fred *pediatric neurologist, educator*
Titus, Jack L. *pathologist, educator*
Westermeyer, Joseph John *psychiatrist*
Zander, Janet Adele *psychiatrist*

St Paul
Hulbert, Linda Ann *academic librarian*

Virginia
Knabe, George William, Jr., *pathologist, educator*

Waseca
Barr, Leslie Glen *family practice physician*

Wayzata
Muschenheim, Frederick *retired pathologist*

Willmar
Vander Aarde, Stanley Bernard *retired otolaryngologist*

Worthington
Aby, Robert Davis *physician*

MISSISSIPPI

Alcorn State
Sizemore, Robert Carlen *immunologist, educator*

Biloxi
Holman, Charles Milligan *urologist*

Clarksdale
Burnham, Van Robinson, Jr., *general practice physician*

Gautier
Egerton, Charles Pickford *anatomy and physiology educator*

Gulfport
Fooladi, Mike M. *physician, educator*

Jackson
Bloom, Sherman *retired pathologist, educator*
†Burrow, William Hollis, II, *dermatologist*
Campbell, G. Douglas *medical educator*
Corbett, James John *neurologist, neuroophthalmologist*
Cruse, Julius Major, Jr., *pathologist, educator*
Currier, Robert David *neurologist*
Das, Suman Kumar *plastic surgeon, researcher*
Evans, Owen Beverly *neurologist*
Freeland, Alan Edward *orthopedic surgery educator, physician*
Harisdangkul, Valee *physician*
Henderson, Julian Crowder *retired pathologist*
Houston, Gerry Ann *oncologist*
Howard, William Percy *physician*
Kemp, Stephen Frederick *physician*
Kermode, John Cotterill *pharmacology educator, researcher*
Kliesch, William Frank *retired physician*
Lewis, Robert Edwin, Jr., *pathology immunology educator, researcher*
†Mawson, Anthony Richard *epidemiologis, public health educator*
Minocha, Anil *physician, educator, researcher*
Moll, George William *pediatrician, educator*
†Munera, Pedro Antonio *child and adolescent psychiatrist*
Neglen, Nils Peter *surgeon*
Poole, Galen Vincent *surgeon, educator, researcher*
Read, Dale Gilbert *endocrinologist, educator*
†Rhodes, Linda L. *medical transcriptionist, medical assistant*
†Rivlin, Michel E. *gynecologist*
Ross, Ian Beaudoin *neurosurgeon, educator*
Sawyer, Donald E. *physician, urologist*
†Shirley, Aaron *pediatrician*
Sneed, Raphael Corcoran *physiatrist, pediatrician*
Suess, James Francis *retired psychiatry educator*
Thigpen, James Tate *physician, oncology educator*
Walcott, Dexter Winn *allergist*
Williams, Thomas Kennon *retired surgeon*

Laurel
Lacey, Peeler Grayson *diagnostic radiologist*
Lindstrom, Eric Everett *ophthalmologist*

Madison
Saenz, Rebecca Buchanan *family physician*

Meridian
Cook, Donald Eugene *retired orthopedist*

Ocean Springs
Austin, Claude Lidell *retired surgeon*

Pascagoula
Horowitz, Michael Dory *cardiothoracic surgeon*
Meredith, William Robert, Sr., *physician, educator*

Ruleville
Cosue, Lamberto Gutierrez, III, *internist*

Tupelo
Wooldridge, Thomas Dean *nephrologist*

Vicksburg
Hopson, William Briggs, Jr., *surgeon*

Whitfield
Desai, Kirtida D. *medical educator*

MISSOURI

Belton
Blim, Richard Don *retired pediatrician*

Blue Springs
McElroy, Michelle Marie *physician*

Branson
Coscia, Robert Lingua *surgeon, educator*

Cape Girardeau
Lee, David Y.S. *neurologist*

Caruthersville
Puangsuvan, Somporn *surgeon, consultant*

Chesterfield
Flores, Jhonson Eder *anesthesiologist*
Frawley, Thomas Francis *retired physician*

Clayton
Huddleston, Charles B. *surgeon, educator*

Columbia
Aggarwal, Kul *internist, cardiologist, educator*
Allen, William Cecil *physician, educator*
Anderson, Ralph Robert *endocrinology educator*
Barrett, James Thomas *immunologist, educator*
†Bothwell, Marcella Roper *pediatrician, educator, otolaryngologist*
†Braddock, Stephen Robert *pediatrician, educator*
Colwill, Jack Marshall *physician, educator, dean*
Cunningham, Milamari Antoinella *anesthesiologist*
†Dhand, Rajiv *physician*
Eaton, Gary David *physician*
Eggers, George William Nordholtz, Jr., *anesthesiologist, educator*
Frey, Jeffery Paul *internist, geriatrician*
James, Elizabeth Joan Plogsted *pediatrician, educator*
Khojasteh, Ali *medical oncologist, hematologist*
Klachko, David Max *physician, educator*
König, Peter *pediatrician, educator*
Longo, Daniel Robert *health services researcher, medical educator*
Losanoff, Julian Emil *surgeon, educator*
†Loy, Timothy *pathologist*
†Mehr, David Ralph *geriatrician, researcher*
Nolph, Georgia Bower *physician*
Oro, John James *neurosurgeon*
†Perkoff, Gerald Thomas *physician, educator*
Puckett, C. Lin *plastic surgeon, educator*
Silver, Donald *surgeon, educator*
†Swan, Shanna Helen *epidemiologist, researcher*
Tarnove, Lorraine *medical association executive*
Weiss, James Moses Aaron *psychiatrist, educator*
White, Harry Houston *neurologist*
Witten, David Melvin *radiology educator*

Crystal City
†Lourwood, David Lee, Jr., *pharmacotherapist, educator*

Florissant
Owen, Robert Frederick *internist, rheumatologist*
Tanphaichitr, Kongsak *rheumatologist, allergist, immunologist, internist*

Fredericktown
Raksakulthai, Vinai *obstetrician, gynecologist*

Gravois Mills
Dunn, Floyd Emryl *psychiatrist, neurologist, consultant*

Independence
Dorshow-Gordon, Ellen *epidemiologist*

Joplin
Crumpacker, Rex K. *anesthesiologist*
Daus, Arthur Steven *neurological surgeon*
Habermann, James Herbert *retired pathologist*
River, George Lambert *hematologist, oncologist*

Kansas City
Abdou, Nabih I. *physician, educator*
Butler, Merlin Gene *physician, medical geneticist, educator*
Dimond, Edmunds Grey *medical educator*
Dixon, George David *radiologist*
†Fiorella, Russell Michael *pathologist*
Godfrey, William Ashley *ophthalmologist*
Hagan, John Charles, III, *ophthalmologist*
Heymach, George John, III, *physician, educator, health facility administrator, consultant*
Hunzicker, Warren John *research consultant, physician, cardiologist*
Huston, Kent Allen *rheumatologist*
Jonas, Harry S. *medical education consultant*
Lofland, Gary Kenneth *cardiac surgeon*
Long, Edwin Tutt *surgeon*
Lotuaco, Luisa Go *pathologist*
Manimtim, Winston Mendoza *pediatrician, neonatologist*
McCoy, Frederick John *retired plastic surgeon*
McGregor, Douglas Hugh *pathologist, educator*
McKinsey, David Stephen *infectious diseases specialist*
McPhee, Mark Steven *medical educator, physician, gastroenterologist*
Mebust, Winston Keith *surgeon, educator*
Molteni, Agostino *pathology educator*
Poston, Walker Seward, II, *medical educator, researcher*
†Rada, David Charles *dermatologist*
†Sagduyu, Kemal *psychiatrist, educator, researcher*
Sauer, Gordon Chenoweth *retired dermatologist, educator*
Shaw, Gary Yale *otolaryngologist*
Truog, William Edward, III, *pediatrician, educator, researcher*
Van Way, Charles Ward, III, *surgery educator*

Kearney
Waltz, James Richard *physician*

Kirksville
Osborn, Gerald Guy *dean, psychiatrist, educator*
Shumake, James Martin *emergency medicine physician*

Kirkwood
Wood, Floyd Edward, Jr., *pharmacist, consultant*

Lees Summit
Jones, Miles James A. *pathologist, consultant*

Louisiana
Bubenik, Oldrich Venceslas *surgeon, oncologist*

Mexico
†Tillman, Charles Herbert, Jr., *cardiologist*

Nevada
Goldberger, Stephen Henry *otolaryngologist*

North Kansas City
Hellman, Richard *endocrinologist*

Oak Grove
Davis, Jo *naturopath, hypnotherapist*

Saint Charles
Wang, William Weiqi *physician*

Saint Joseph
†Dyer, Gary Alden *dermatologist*

Saint Louis
†Acharya, Jayant Narahari *neurologist, educator*
Albert, Stewart Gary *medical educator, internist, endocrinologist*
Alpers, David Hershel *physician, educator*
Bacon, Bruce Raymond *physician*
Ballinger, Walter Francis *surgeon, educator*
Berg, Leonard *retired neurologist, educator, researcher*
Berland, David I. *psychiatrist, educator*
Bitar, Saad R. *internist*
Black, Kevin John *psychiatrist*
†Blumenthal, Herman Theodore *physician, educator*
Branham, Gregory Harris *facial plastic surgeon*
†Brink, David Scott *clinical pathologist, educator*
Brodeur, Armand Edward *pediatric radiologist*
Cabbabe, Edmond Bechir *plastic and hand surgeon*
Castro, Mario *medical educator, health facility administrator*
Chaplin, Hugh, Jr., *physician, educator*
Chole, Richard Arthur *otolaryngologist, educator*
Cloninger, Claude Robert *psychiatric researcher, educator, genetic epidemiologist*
†Constantino, John Nicholas *medical educator, researcher*
Cross, Dewitte Talmadge, III, *physician, neuroradiologist*
Cryer, Philip Eugene *medical educator, scientist, endocrinologist*
Dewald, Paul Adolph *psychiatrist, educator*
Dodge, Philip Rogers *physician, educator*
Dodson, W(illiam) Edwin *child neurology educator*
Dougherty, Charles Hamilton *pediatrician*
†Dykewicz, Mark Steven *physician*
Evens, Ronald Gene *radiologist, medical center administrator*
Favors, Adolphus C., Jr., *internist*
Feman, Stephen S. *ophthalmologist*
†Ferkol, Thomas William *medical educator, pediatrician*
Fitch, Coy Dean *physician, educator*
Fletcher, James Warren *physician*
Florin, Cynthia *psychiatrist*
Flye, M. Wayne *surgeon, immunologist, educator, writer*
Fonseca, Peter *surgeon*
Gay, William Arthur, Jr., *thoracic surgeon*
Geltman, Edward Mark *cardiologist, educator*
Goebel, Joel Alan *otolaryngologist*
Goldberg, Anne Carol *physician, educator*
Goodenberger, Daniel Marvin *medical educator*
Griffing, George Thomas *medical educator, endocrinologist*
Grossberg, George Thomas *psychiatrist, educator*
Grubb, Robert L., Jr., *neurosurgeon*
Hall, William Kearney *retired dermatologist*
Hanley, Thomas Patrick *obstetrician-gynecologist*
Hanson, Lee Craig *physician*
Heiken, Jay Paul *physician*
Holmes, Nancy Elizabeth *pediatrician*
†Hovsepian, David Minas *radiologist*
†Hruz, Paul W *pediatrician, endocrinologist, research scientist*
Hsu, Chung Yi *neurologist*
Huck, Elizabeth Louise *radiologist*
†Isik, Ugur *neurologist*
Johnston, Marilyn Frances-Meyers *physician, medical educator*
Junker, James A. *radiologist*

†Kaiboriboon, Kitti *neurologist*
Kaminski, Donald Leon *medical educator, surgeon, gastrointestinal physiologist*
Kinsella, Ralph Aloysius, Jr., *physician*
Kipnis, David Morris *physician, educator*
Kolker, Allan Erwin *ophthalmologist*
Kouchoukos, Nicholas Thomas *surgeon*
Lagunoff, David *physician, educator*
†Lasala, John M. *cardiologist, medical educator*
†Le, Thong T. *surgeon*
†Ley, Timothy James *hematologist, molecular biologist*
†Li, Ping *pharmacologist, educator, researcher*
†Loeb, Virgil, Jr., *oncologist, hematologist*
Ludbrook, Philip Albert *cardiologist, clinical researcher, educator*
Majerus, Philip Warren *physician*
Mangelsdorf, Thomas Kelly *psychiatrist, consultant*
Mantovani, John F. *pediatric neurologist*
Martin, Kevin John *nephrologist, educator*
Martin, Wade Hampton, III, *physician, scientist*
McMahon, Robert M. *physician, lawyer*
Mendelson, David Frey *retired neurology educator*
Middelkamp, John Neal *pediatrician, educator*
Mooradian, Arshag Dertad *internist, educator*
Morales-Galarreta, Julio *psychiatrist, child psychoanalyst*
Morley, John Edward *physician*
†Morris, John Carl *neurologist, educator, researcher*
Murphy, George Earl *psychiatrist, educator*
Myerson, Robert J. *radiation oncologist, educator*
Neely, John Gail *otolaryngologist*
North, Carol Sue *psychiatrist, educator*
†Olney, John William *psychiatry educator*
Owens, William Don *anesthesiology educator*
Pan, Yi *neurologist*
Payne, Meredith Jorstad *physician*
Peck, William Arno *physician, educator, university official and dean*
Perez, Carlos A. *radiation oncologist, educator*
Picus, Joel *medical educator*
Post, Stephen Lightner *psychiatrist, psychoanalyst, educator*
†Powers, William John *neurologist*
Premachandra, Bhartur Narasimhaiengar *endocrinology educator, researcher*
Prensky, Arthur Lawrence *pediatric neurologist, educator*
Purkerson, Mabel Louise *physician, physiologist, educator*
Rabun, John S. *forensic psychiatrist*
Radford, Diane Mary *surgeon, surgical oncologist*
Rao, Dabeeru C. *epidemiologist, educator*
Rednam, Krishna Rao Venkata *ophthalmologist*
Reh, Thomas Edward *radiologist, educator*
†Riew, K. Daniel *cervical spine surgeon*
Riner, Ronald Nathan *cardiologist, business consultant*
Robins, Lee Nelken *medical educator*
†Rosenblum, Barry Norton *physician*
Royal, Henry Duval *nuclear medicine physician*
Royce, Robert Killian *retired physician*
†Ryall, Jo-Ellyn M. *psychiatrist*
†Salsich, Gretchen B. *medical researcher, physical therapy educator*
Schonfeld, Gustav *medical educator, researcher, administrator*
Schreiber, James Ralph *obstetrician, researcher*
Schwartz, Alan Leigh *pediatrician, educator*
Shapiro, Larry J. *pediatrician, scientist, educator*
Siegel, Barry Alan *nuclear radiologist*
Singh, Inderjit *nephrologist, internist, medical educator*
Slavin, Raymond Granam *allergist, immunologist*
Smith, Morton Edward *ophthalmology educator, dean*
Smith, Stacey Lee *psychiatrist*
Soper, Nathaniel Jolas *surgeon*
Spector, Gershon Jerry *physician, educator, researcher*
Stenson, William Frederick *gastroenterologist*
Strunk, Robert Charles *physician*
Teitelbaum, Steven Lazarus *pathology educator*
Ternberg, Jessie Lamoin *neurological surgeon*
Tiefenbrunn, Alan James *medical educator*
†Trevathan, Edwin *pediatric neurologist, educator*
Ulett, George Andrew *psychiatrist*
Vedeniapin, Andrei B. *psychiatrist, researcher*
†Vijayan, Anitha *medical educator*
Walentik, Corinne Anne *pediatrician*
Wedner, H. James *physician, researcher*
White, Neil H. *pediatric endocrinologist*
Whyte, Michael Peter *medicine, pediatrics and genetics educator, research director*
Winn, Hung Nguyen *obstetrician, gynecologist, maternal-fetal medicine physician*
Wippold, Franz Joseph, II, *medical educator*
Young, Paul Andrew *anatomist*

Springfield
Baurichter, John Daniel *osteopath*
Geter, Rodney Keith *plastic surgeon*
Hackett, Earl Randolph *neurologist*
Quinn, Rodney David *neurologist*
Stratmann, Henry George *cardiologist*

Town And Country
Levin, Marvin Edgar *physician*

Warrensburg
†Jurkowski, Odin Lech *medical librarian, educator*

Wentzville
†de la Torre, Roger Anibal *surgeon*

MONTANA

Billings
England, John David *neurologist, educator*
Glenn, Guy Charles *pathologist*
Rich, Joseph David *psychiatrist*

Great Falls
Dietrich, Dennis Ward *neurologist*

Helena
Strickler, Jeffrey Harold *pediatrician*

Kalispell
Winkel, R. Dennis *family practice physician*

Missoula
†Beckwith, John Bruce *pediatric pathologist*
Fawcett, Don Wayne *retired anatomist*
Reynolds, William Arthur *retired physician, educator*
Sampson, Ruth Louise *endocrinologist*
Swick, Herbert Morris *medical educator, humanist, neurologist*

Sheridan
Hendrickson, Roman Michael *physician*

Townsend
Lefever, Hollis K. *family practice*

NEBRASKA

Atkinson
Sutherland, John Campbell *pathologist, educator*

Bellevue
Woods, Michael Patrick *obstetrician, educator*

Dakota City
Rodriguez, Manuel Alvarez *pathologist*

Fremont
Keasling, Gerald Frank *obstetrician-gynecologist, educator*

Hastings
Dungan, John Russell, Jr., (Titular Viscount, Dungan of Clare, Hereditary PRince of ERmoy and Arra) *anesthesiologist, health facility administrator*

Kimball
Listopadzki, Dariusz Jaroslaw *internist*

Lincoln
Gard, Joseph Robert *cardiologist*
Hill, Ronald Clair *anesthesiologist*
Michels, Dale E. *physician*
Wilson, Charles Stephen *cardiologist, educator*

Omaha
†Balaji, K.C. *urologist, researcher*
Baltaro, Richard J. *pathologist, medical educator*
Brumback, Roger Alan *neuropathologist, researcher*
Casale, Thomas Bruce *medical educator*
Chan, Wing-Chung *pathologist, educator*
Coccia, Peter F. *physician, pediatric hematologist and oncologist*
Cohen, Samuel Monroe *physician, pathologist, researcher*
Cruz, Abelardo Mer Nilo *physician, geriatrician, internist, rheumatologist, medical educator*
Fayad, Pierre B. *neurologist*
Fleming, William Hare *surgeon*
Frey, Donald Ray *medical educator, administrator*
Fusaro, Ramon Michael *dermatologist, researcher*
†Gao, Xiuhua *medical researcher*
Gendelman, Howard Eliot *biomedical researcher, physician*
Harned, Roger Kent *radiology educator*
Hartman, Herbert Arthur, Jr., *oncologist*
Hellbusch, Leslie Carl *neurosurgeon*
Hodgson, Paul Edmund *surgeon, department chairman*
†Huurman, Walter William *pediatric orthopaedic surgeon, educator*
Imray, Thomas John *radiologist, educator*
Kelly, James Francis, Jr., *retired radiologist*
Kessinger, Margaret Anne *medical educator*
Kobayashi, Roger Hideo *allergy and immunology educator*
Korbitz, Bernard Carl *retired oncologist, hematologist, educator, consultant*
Koszewski, Bohdan Julius *retired internist, medical educator*
Lynch, Thomas Gerald *surgeon, educator*
Mardis, Hal Kennedy *urological surgeon, educator, researcher*
Maurer, Harold Maurice *pediatrician*
Mohiuddin, Syed Maqdoom *cardiologist, educator*
†Mukherjee, Sandeep *gastroenterologist, educator*
Neibel, Oliver Joseph, Jr., *retired medical services executive*
†Norton, Neil S. *anatomist, researcher*
Pearson, Paul Hammond *physician*
Quigley, Herbert Joseph, Jr., *pathologist, educator*
Ramaprasad, Subbaraya *medical educator*
†Recker, Robert R. *medical educator, internist*
Reddy, Ramakrishna L. *physician, pathologist, consultant*
Roffman, Blaine Yale *pathologist*
†Sattar, S. Pirzada *psychiatrist, educator, psychiatrist, researcher*
Sharma, Manoj *health educator, research physician*
Skoog, Donald Paul *retired physician, educator*
Smith, Philip W. *epidemiologist*
Sooriyaarachchi, Gamini Sarathchandra *oncologist, hematologist, educator, researcher*
Truhlsen, Stanley Marshall *retired physician, educator*
Ward, Vernon Graves *internist*

Papillion
Dvorak, Allen Dale *radiologist*

Scottsbluff
Kabalin, John Nicholas *urologist*

NEVADA

Glenbrook
Goldsmith, Harry Sawyer *surgeon, educator*

Henderson
Arumugam, Sivakumar *gastroenterologist*
Roth, Jeffrey Joseph *plastic surgeon*

Las Vegas
Adan, John *consulting interventional cardiologist*
Adashek, Joseph Abraham *obstetrician-gynecologist, educator*
Amirana, M. T. *surgeon*
Bandt, Paul Douglas *physician, neurologist*
†Buzard, Kurt Andre *ophthalmologist*
Carter, Paul Richard *physician*
Cooper, Matthew Marc *cardiothoracic surgeon*
Hanson, Gerald Eugene *oral and maxillofacial surgeon*
Karabachev, Ivan *otolaryngologist*
Kurlinski, John Parker *physician*
Looney, Gerald Lee *medical educator, administrator*
Merkin, Albert Charles *pediatrician, allergist*
Moritz, Timothy Bovie *psychiatrist*
†Mukhopadhyay, Deb Kumar *gastroenterologist, hepatologist*
Mulkey, David Allen *pathologist, educator*
Noback, Richardson Kilbourne *medical educator*
Ogden, Bruce E. *physician, pediatrician*
Seggev, Joram Simon *allergist, clinical immunologist*
Shires, George Thomas *surgeon, educator*
Speck, Eugene Lewis *internist*
Trigiano, Lucien Lewis *physician*
Wax, Arnold *physician*
Zuspan, Frederick Paul *obstetrician, gynecologist, educator*

Reno
Barnet, Robert Joseph *cardiologist, ethicist*
Duan, Dayue *pharmacologist, physiologist*
Edwards, David Allen *internist, educator, researcher*
Forbes, Kenneth Albert Faucher *urological surgeon*
MacKintosh, Frederick Roy *oncologist*
†Small, Elisabeth Chan *psychiatrist, educator*
Zager, Bernard Solomon *physician, consultant*

NEW HAMPSHIRE

Bow
Emery, Paul Emile *psychiatrist*

Concord
Bagan, Merwyn *neurological surgeon*
de Nesnera, Alexander Peter *psychiatrist*
Feder, Robert Elliot *psychiatrist*
Schwartz, Jonathan Ralph *psychiatrist*

Dover
Winkler, Peter Alexander *plastic surgeon*

Durham
Miller, Joseph Morton *internist*

Etna
Ferm, Vergil Harkness *anatomist, embryologist*
Rous, Stephen Norman *urologist, educator*

Exeter
Beeson, Paul Bruce *physician*
Singer, Karl Lawrence *physician, health facility administrator*

Grantham
Figley, Melvin Morgan *radiologist, physician, educator*
Knights, Edwin Munroe *pathologist*

Hampstead
Moore, Raymond Edward *retired physician*

Hanover
Baldwin, John Charles *surgeon, researcher*
Chapman, Robert James *clinical psychiatrist, educator*
Clark, Robin Ervin *public health educator*
†Fiering, Steven *medical educator*
†Koop, Charles Everett *surgeon, educator, former surgeon general*
†Platt, James David *psychiatrist, educator, academic administrator*
Rawnsley, Howard Melody *physician, educator*
Rolett, Ellis Lawrence *medical educator, cardiologist*
Rueckert, Frederic *plastic, reconstructive and hand surgeon*
Zubkoff, Michael *medical educator*

Hooksett
Buchan, Ronald Forbes *internal and preventive medicine physician*

Laconia
Brody, Spencer John *pediatrician*

Lebanon
Bernat, James Lawrence *neurologist, educator*
†Carr, Charles F. *orthopedist*
Clendenning, William Edmund *dermatologist*
Cronenwett, Jack LeMoyne *vascular surgeon educator*
†Fillinger, Mark F. *vascular surgeon, researcher*
Fromm, Hans *gastroenterologist, educator, researcher, hepatologist*
Galton, Valerie Anne *endocrinology educator*
†Gosselin, Benoit Jean *otolaryngologist, facial plastic surgeon, head and neck and reconstructive surgeon*
Kelley, Maurice Leslie, Jr., *gastroenterologist, educator*
McCollum, Robert Wayne *physician, educator*
†Racusin, Robert Jerrold *psychiatry educator*
†Schoolwerth, Anton C. *nephrologist, educator*
Silberfarb, Peter Michael *psychiatrist, educator*
†Simons, Michael *cardiologist*
Smith, Barry David *obstetrician-gynecologist, educator*
van Leeuwen, Dirk Jacob *hepatology educator*
Waugh, Theodore Rogers *orthopedic surgeon*
†Yeager, Mark P. *anesthesiology educator, researcher*

Lee
Young, James Morningstar *physician, naval officer*

Lincoln
Seletz, Jules Mortimor *surgeon*

Littleton
Wilmot, Clare Julia May *surgeon*

Lyme
Cornwell, Gibbons Gray, III, *physician, medical educator, retired*
McIntyre, Oswald Ross *physician*

Manchester
Angoff, Gerald Harvey *cardiologist*
DesRochers, Gerard Camille *surgeon*
Hunt, Sean Emmet *anesthesiologist*
Totten, Mary Anne *internist*
Unger, Gere Nathan *emergency physician, lawyer*

Mirror Lake
Culleton, James Frederick *neurologist*

Nashua
Siroty, William Charles *physician*

New London
Catino, Donald *physician*

North Conway
Phaneuf, Gerald John *retired pathologist*

Portsmouth
Michelsen, W(olfgang) Jost *neurosurgeon, educator, retired*

Tamworth
Colten, Harvey Radin *pediatrician, educator*

West Lebanon
Day, Emerson *physician*

Windham
Levin, Murray Newman *retired surgeon*

NEW JERSEY

Bayonne
Pelosi, Marco Antonio *obstetrician and gynecologist*
Rogow, Louis Michael *oncologist, educator*

Belle Mead
Goodnick, Paul Joel *psychiatrist*

Belleville
Caputo, Wayne James *surgeon, podiatrist*
Sales, Clifford M. *surgeon*

Bernardsville
Dixon, Rosina Berry *physician, pharmaceutical development consultant*
Stahl, Donald Charles *retired orthopedic surgeon*

Bridgewater
Bernson, Marcella S. *psychiatrist*
Hirsch, Paul J. *orthopedist, surgeon, medical executive, educator, editor*
Maynard, Kenneth Irwin *medical educator, researcher*
Stein, Daniel Scott *physician, researcher*

Browns Mills
Cha, Se Do *internist*
De Berardinis, Charles Anthony Joseph *physician*
Lumia, Francis James *internist*

Camden
Ances, I. G(eorge) *obstetrician, gynecologist, educator*
Benson, Gordon D. *gastroenterologist, medical educator, dean*
Camishion, Rudolph Carmen *physician*
Huhn, Richard Dale *physician*
Seidmon, E. James *urologist*
Stahl, Gary Edward *neonatologist*
†Verma, Vijayendra Kishore *internist, cardiologist*

Cape May Court House
†Altman, Brian David *pediatric ophthalmologist*

Cherry Hill
Brachfeld, Jonas *cardiologist, educator*
Goldberg, Jack *hematologist*
Kuchler, Joseph Albert *surgeon*
Margolis, Gerald Joseph *psychiatrist, psychoanalyst*
Olearchyk, Andrew *cardiothoracic surgeon, educator*
Proper, Michael Charles *cardiologist, educator*
Robinson, Mary Jo *pathologist*
Werbitt, Warren *gastroenterologist, educator*

Cliffside Park
Klafter, George *urologist*

PROFESSIONAL INDEX 6415 HEALTHCARE: MEDICINE

Zucker, Howard Alan *pediatric cardiologist, intensivist, anesthesiologist, U.S. deputy assistant secretary for health*

Clifton
Pineda, Albert Anthony *obstetrician, gynecologist, educator*

Demarest
Dornfest, Burton Saul *anatomy educator*

Denville
Husar, Walter Gene *neurologist, neuroscientist, educator*

Dover
Freedman, Pamela Gottesman *gastroenterologist*

East Brunswick
Arno, Joseph Peter *physician, cosmetic surgeon*
†Avendano, Gary Fidel *cardiologist, internist*
Maman, Arie *endocrinologist*
Miller, Andrew David *physician*
†Weiss, Robert Edward *urologist, educator*
Zinkin, Lewis David *physician*

East Hanover
Judge, Rajinder *psychiatrist*
Marks, Peter Wayne *hematologist, oncologist, educator*
O'Byrne, Elizabeth Milikin *pharmacologist, researcher, endocrinologist*
†Wu, Johnny *internist*

East Orange
Wedeen, Richard Peter *physician*

Edgewater
Karol, Cecilia *psychiatrist, psychoanalyst*

Edison
Agarwal, Kishan C. *physician*
Dogra, Vijay Kumar *physician*
Papamitsakis, Nikolaos I.H. *neurologist*

Elizabeth
Berger, Harold Richard *physician*
Cinberg, James Zubow *otolaryngologist, educator*
Millman, Arthur Edward *internist, cardiologist, educator*
Rosenstein, Neil *surgeon, genealogical researcher*
Sananman, Michael Lawrence *neurologist*
Wilchins, Sidney A. *gynecologist*

Englewood
Boyajian, Levon Zakar *psychiatrist, administrator*
Butler, David George *obstetrician, gynecologist*
†Chiorazzi, Mary Lorraine *psychiatrist*
Rosenbaum, David Herbert *neurologist*
Strauss, Raymond Bernard *otolaryngologist*
Wuhl, Charles Michael *psychiatrist*

Englewood Cliffs
Yu, Fei *internist*

Flanders
Huang, Jacob Chen-ya *physician, city official*

Flemington
Rushton, Alan R. *physician, medical historian*

Florham Park
Weisberg, Lynne Willing *psychiatrist, consultant*

Forked River
Novak, Dennis E. *family practice physician*

Fort Lee
Chessler, Richard Kenneth *gastroenterologist, endoscopist*
Goldfischer, Jerome D. *cardiologist*
Li, Tien-Shun *obstetrician, gynecologist, educator*

Franklin Lakes
Ginsberg, Barry Howard *physician, researcher*

Franklin Park
†Jones, Frank A., Jr., *psychiatrist, educator*
Perry, Arthur William *plastic surgeon, educator*

Glen Ridge
Rubin, Roberta Gail *pathologist*
Zbar, Lloyd Irwin Stanley *otolaryngologist, educator*

Gloucester City
Klein, Steven George *osteopathic physician*

Green Brook
†Bokhari, Sabahat *cardiologist*
Hertzberg, Henry *retired radiologist*

Guttenberg
Wright, Jane Cooke *physician, educator, consultant*

Hackensack
De Groote, Robert David *general and vascular surgeon*
Gross, Peter Alan *epidemiologist, researcher*
Haines, Kathleen Ann *physician, educator*
†Masullo, Alfredo Salvatore *dermatologist*
Sperber, Steven Jay *internist*
†Xagoraris, Andreas Ector *pediatric anesthesiologist*

Haddonfield
Capelli, John Placido *nephrologist, educator*

Hamilton
Grace, Michael Judd *immunologist*
Kane, Michael Joel *physician*

Hillsborough
Wang, Xiang *cardiologist, researcher*

Holmdel
Samra, Said Abou *plastic surgeon*

Jersey City
†Kohan, Fereydoon *nuclear medicine physician*
Nicoll, Daniel Jules *internist, insurance company executive*
Shulman, Yale *urologist*
Shusterman, Neil Howard *internist, nephrologist*

Kendall Park
Berger, Richard Stanton *dermatologist*

Kenilworth
†Duffy, Ruth Anne *pharmacologist*
Scott, Mary Celine *pharmacologist*
Staudinger, Heribert Wolfgang *pulmonologist*

Kirkwood Voorhees
Kahn, Marc Leslie *orthopedic surgeon*
Mansukhani, Sunder Hashmatrai *pathology educator*

Lafayette
†Tanis, Jody A. *medical researcher, fire warden*

Lakewood
Wechsler, Harold Herbert *surgeon*

Lawrenceville
Pouleur, Hubert Gustave *cardiologist, consultant*
Rosenthal, Albert Lester *dermatologist, educator*

Livingston
Conde, Miguel A. *hematologist, oncologist*
Duberstein, Joel Lawrence *internist, pulmonologist, educator*
Fernandes, John *physician*
Fisher, Hyman Wendell *physician*
Goldstein, Steven Howard *podiatrist*
Krieger, Abbott Joel *neurosurgeon*
Rickert, Robert Richard *pathologist, educator*
Rokosz, Gregory Joseph *emergency medicine physician, lawyer, educator*
Rommer, James Andrew *physician*
Samojlik, Eugeniusz *medical educator, clinical researcher*
Templeton, Hilda B. *psychiatrist, educator*
†Tillis, Alan Casal *orthopaedic surgeon*
Vlad, Luigina Doroti *endocrinologist*

Long Branch
Fisher, Margaret Catharine *pediatrician, epidemiologist, educator*
Goldberg, Daniel Berney *eye surgeon*
Poch, Herbert Edward *retired pediatrician, educator*
Shagan, Bernard Pellman *endocrinologist, educator*
†Zinterhofer, Louis *pathologist*
Zukaukas, Charles Lawrence *surgeon*

Manalapan
Kelter, Richard John *physician*

Maple Shade
Abidi, S. Manzoor *neurologist*

Maplewood
Shuttleworth, Anne Margaret *psychiatrist*

Margate City
Videll, Jared Steven *cardiologist*

Marlton
Kahn, Sigmund Benham *retired internist and dean*

Medford
Burgess, Samuel Bullock *pathologist, consultant*

Metuchen
Macarin-Mara, Lynn *psychotherapist, consultant*
Slobodien, Howard David *surgeon, educator*

Middletown
Braddom, Randall Lee *physician, medical educator*

Millburn
Heistein, Robert Kenneth *obstetrician and gynecologist*
Kern, Arthur Stephen *physician*
Sostowski, Richard Mark *physician, forensic psychiatrist, psychoanalyst*

Monroe Township
Wallach, Jacques Burton *pathologist, educator*

Montclair
Kaiser, Richard Alan *surgeon*

Moorestown
Cervantes, Luis Augusto *neurosurgeon*

Morris Plains
Elias, Salwa Emil Ghabrial *allergist, immunologist, pediatrician*
Fielding, Stuart *psychopharmacologist*

Morristown
Chevinsky, Aaron Harry *surgeon*
De Rosa, William Thomas *internist, hematologist, oncologist*
Finkel, Marion Judith *physician, pharmaceutical company administrator*
Parr, Grant Van Siclen *surgeon*
Scott, Richard Thomas Thomas, Jr., *reproductive endocrinologist*
†Weisman, Steven Martin *pharmacologist, consultant*

Mount Laurel
Hayken, Gerald Dreux *orthopedic surgeon*

Neptune
Mann, William Joseph, Jr., *gynecologic oncologist*
Rice, Stephen Gary *medical educator, sports medicine physician*
Weber, Charles Alfred, II, *internist, rheumatologist*

New Brunswick
Aisner, Joseph *oncologist, physician*
Bachmann, Gloria Ann *physician, educator*
Bertino, Joseph Rocco *physician, educator*
Chandler, James John *surgeon, educator*
Day-Salvatore, Debra Lynn *medical geneticist*
Ettinger, Lawrence Jay *pediatric hematologist and oncologist, educator*
Gocke, David Joseph *immunology educator, physician, medical scientist*
Gottlieb, Alice Bendix *medical educator*
Graham, Alan Morrison *surgeon*
Greenwald, Alfred Emanuel *retired cosmetic surgeon*
†Grimes, Julia Patrice *physician, researcher*
†Kaufman, Kenneth Roland *psychiatrist, educator*
†Lepore, Frederick Everett *neurologist, educator*
†Lewis, Michael *pediatrician, educator*
†Lowry, Stephen F. *surgeon, educator*
Makhija, Mohan *nuclear medicine physician*
Mandelbaum, David Ezra *pediatric neurologist*
Moreyra, Abel E. *physician, medical educator*
Nosher, John Louis *radiologist*
Nosko, Michael Gerrik *neurosurgeon, educator*
Pinals, Robert Stanton *physician*
Pitchumoni, Capecomorin Sankar *gastroenterologist, educator*
Raska, Karel Frantisek Julian, Jr., *pathologist, virologist, educator*
Rosenberg, Norman *surgeon, educator*
Sage, Jacob I. *neurologist, educator*
Saidi, Parvin *hematologist, medical educator*
Sarode, Satyeswara Krishnappa *physician*
Schaer, Teresa McKinley *internist, geriatrician*
Scully, John Thomas *obstetrician, gynecologist, educator*
Seibold, James Richard *physician, researcher*
†Sigal, Leonard H. *physician*
†Swee, David Ethan *physician*
Trelstad, Robert Laurence *pathology educator, cell biologist*
Upton, Arthur Canfield *experimental pathologist, educator*
Weinstein, Melvin Phillip *physician educator*

Newark
Apuzzio, Joseph J. *obstetrician-gynecologist*
Baker, Herman *medical educator, author*
Baker, Stephen R. *physician*
Bielory, Leonard *allergist, immunologist, medical school administrator*
Chen, Chunguang *cardiologist*
Cherniack, Neil Stanley *physician, medical educator*
Cohen, Stanley *pathologist, educator*
Cook, Stuart Donald *physician, educator*
Donahoo, James Saunders *cardiothoracic surgeon*
Einzig, Stanley *pediatric cardiologist, researcher*
Evans, Hugh E. *pediatrician, educator*
Fu, Shoucheng Joseph *biomedicine educator*
Hamarman, Stephanie *psychiatrist, educator*
Haycock, Christine Elizabeth *retired medical educator, health educator*
Herman, Steven Douglas *cardiothoracic surgeon, educator*
Hobson, Robert Wayne, II, *surgeon*
Iffy, Leslie *medical educator*
Kamalakar, Peri *pediatrician*
Klein, Kenneth Michael *pathologist*
†Lama, Paul J. *surgeon, educator*
Leevy, Carroll Moton *medical educator, hepatology researcher*
Little, Alan Brian *obstetrician, gynecologist, educator*
Materna, Thomas Walter *ophthalmologist*
†Munoz, Eric *surgeon*
†Pletcher, Beth *medical geneticist*
Reichman, Lee Brodersohn *physician*
†Schleifer, Steven J *psychiatrist, educator*
Schwartz, Robert Allen *dermatologist, educator*
Serota, Scott *medical association administrator*
Weiss, Gerson *physician, educator*
Weiss, Stanley H. *physician, epidemiologist, researcher, education educator, consultant, oncologist*
Zarbin, Marco Attilio *ophthalmologist, surgeon, educator*

Newton
Colizza, Wayne Anthony *orthopaedic surgeon*
Johnson, Roland Eric *internist*
Peters, Kurt James *obstetrician, gynecologist*

North Bergen
Kim, Kun-Kil *emergency medicine physician*
Micale, Joseph Nicholas *internist*

North Brunswick
†Cirillo, Vincent J. *medical historian, consultant*

North Plainfield
Weinberger, George Ian *dermatologist*

Nutley
Mostillo, Ralph *medical association administrator*

Oakhurst
Averbach, David Joel *surgeon*

Old Bridge
Brennan, George Gerard *pediatrician*

Orange
Khanna, Yash Kumar *family practice physician, pediatrician*

Paramus
Fakharzadeh, Frederick F. *surgeon*
Hochstein, Martin Alan *endocrinologist*
Kovatis, Paul Evans *orthopedic surgeon, researcher, consultant*
Liva, Edward Louis *eye surgeon*
Rosenstein, Roger G. *hand surgeon*

Park Ridge
Ablin, Richard Joel *immunologist, educator*

Parlin
Flick, Ferdinand Herman *surgeon, prevention medicine physician*
Fuks, Boris Borisovich *immunologist, researcher*

Parsippany
Leviss, Stephen R. *gynecologist*
Peyser, Irving Gerald *surgeon*

Passaic
Haddad, Jamil Raouf *physician*

Paterson
Stewart, Peter J. *general surgery, trauma and critical care physician*

Peapack
Eddey, Gary Erwin *physician, administrator, educator*

Perth Amboy
Kress, Sidney C. *pathologist*

Phillipsburg
Drago, Joseph Rosario *urologist, educator*
Kim, Ih Chin *pediatrician*
Rosenthal, Marvin Bernard *pediatrician, educator*

Piscataway
†Chin, Khew-Voon *medical educator*
Conney, Allan Howard *pharmacologist, researcher*
†Kim, Edward *medical association administrator*
Menza, Matthew A. *psychiatrist*
Rhoads, George Grant *medical epidemiologist*
†Sahota, Amrik *medical researcher, educator, lab administrator*
†Seiden, David *anatomist, educational association administrator*
Suh, Dong-Churl *pharmaceutical economics educator*

Plainfield
Lin, Janet C. *physician*

Point Pleasant Beach
†Motley, John Paul *psychiatrist, consultant*

Princeton
Abrams, Jeffrey Stuart *sports medicine physician, surgeon*
†Bhide, Rajeev S. *medical researcher*
Carver, David Harold *physician, educator*
Clay, Lucius Dubignon, III, *surgeon, educator*
Haynes, William Forby, Jr., *retired internist, cardiologist, educator*
Khawaja, Xavier *biochemical pharmacologist*
McGinnis, James Michael *physician*
Meade, Dale Michael *experimental physicist*
†Notterman, Daniel A. *pediatrician, educator, scientist*
Oppenheimer, Stephen Michael *neurologist, administrator*
Rosen, Arye *microwave, optoelectronics and medicine researcher*
Royds, Robert Bruce *physician*
Scasta, David Lynn *forensic psychiatrist*
Sugerman, Abraham Arthur *psychiatrist, educator*
Szteinbaum, Edward *psychiatrist*
†von der Schmidt, Edward, III, *neurosurgeon, veterinarian*
Wei, Fong *nephrologist*

Randolph
Desai, Gautam T. *physician*

Red Bank
Calabro, Joseph John, III, *physician*
Friedberg, Mark *ophthalmologist*
Macdonald, Donald Arthur, Jr., *physician, surgeon*

Ridgewood
Baddoura, Rashid Joseph *emergency medicine physician*
†Holt, Natalie Frances *physician*
Silverstein, Allen *neurologist, educator*
Sumers, Anne Ricks *ophthalmologist, museum director*

Roseland
Clemente, Celestino *physician, surgeon*
Mashberg, Arthur *medical educator*
Schneider, George *internist, endocrinologist*

Roselle Park
Herzberg, Steven Michael *physician*

Saddle River
Goodman, Jerome David *psychiatrist*

Scotch Plains
Kalischer, Alan Lester *cardiologist*

Short Hills
Chaiken, Bernard Henry *internist, gastroenterologist*
Hurlbut, Terry Allison *pathologist*

Somers Point
Seitman, David Todd *anesthesiologist*

Somerset
De Salva, Salvatore Joseph *retired pharmacologist, toxicologist*
Ilogu, Noel Obiajulu *physician*

Somerville
Fox, Alissa Benimoff *dermatologist*
Fox, James Allen *allergist, immunologist, pediatrician*

South Hackensack
Jacobs, George Braun *neurosurgeon*

South Plainfield
Choi, Soon Chae *orthopaedic surgeon*
Sipski, Mary Leonide *physician, healthcare administrator*

Spring Lake
Harrigan, John Thomas, Jr., *physician, obstetrician-gynecologist*
Talarico, Rudolph Dominic *retired urologist*

Springfield
Kerner, Michael Bernard *gastroenterologist*
Vercesi, Haydée Margarita Chacha *biomedical scientist*
Weisse, Allen Barry *educator, cardiologist, author, historian*
Wosnitzer, Morey *urologist*

Stratford
†McAbee, Gary N. *osteopath, lawyer*
Scali, Victor Joseph *emergency medicine physician*

Summit
Carniol, Paul J. *plastic and reconstructive surgeon, otolaryngologist*
Diamond, Wendi T. *physician*
Malhotra, Harish K. *psychiatrist, educator*
Malhotra, Mahamaya *psychiatrist*
Sheris, Steven Jay *physician*

Teaneck
Ladenheim, Jules Calvin *neurosurgeon*
Scotti, Dennis Joseph *educator, researcher, consultant*
Sweeney, Eugene William *dermatologist*

Tenafly
Altman, Kenneth A(lan) *gastroenterologist, educator*
Grieco, Michael Henry *allergy and infectious diseases physician*

Teterboro
Schwartz, Joyce Gensberg *pathologist*

Titusville
Klincewicz, Stephen Louis *preventive medicine physician*

Toms River
Silvers, Lawrence Wynn *surgeon*

Trenton
Dimasi, Linda Grace *epidemiologist*
Gupta, Rajendra Prasad *physician*
Paul, Sindy Michelle *preventive medicine physician*
Sporn, Aaron Adolph *physician, educator*
Taboada, Javier Gustavo *neurologist*
†Taitsman, James P. *orthopedic surgeon*
Thatsneyakul, Yaovares *physician, consultant*
Tolan, Robert Warren *pediatric infectious disease specialist*
Weinberg, Martin Herbert *retired psychiatrist*
Zanna, Martin Thomas *physician*

Turnersville
DePace, Nicholas Louis *physician*

Union
†Jacobs-Carey, Sheila L. *immunologist*
Silverman, Mitchell S. *endocrinologist/diabetologist*

Upper Montclair
Bluestein, Sanfurd G. *radiologist*

Ventnor City
Mason, James Henry, IV, *retired surgeon*
Zuckerman, Stuart *psychiatrist, forensic examiner, educator*

Vineland
†Clinton, Lawrence Paul *psychiatrist*

Voorhees
Reichman, Joseph Harry *plastic surgeon*

Wall
Monaco, Robert Anthony *radiologist*
O'Neill, James Paul *psychiatrist*

Wayne
Bronstein, Jagoda Ewa *pediatrician*
Gollance, Robert Barnett *ophthalmologist*
Khoury, Hani *surgeon, educator*
†Oriji, Gibson K. *medical educator, medical researcher*
Sgroi, Donald Angelo *obstetrician, gynecologist*
Siepser, Stuart Lewis *cardiologist, internist*

Wenonah
Mishik, Anthony Neal *pediatrician*

West Orange
Brodkin, Roger Harrison *dermatologist, educator*
Casella, Anthony John *cardiologist*
Hill, George James *physician, educator*
Katz, Jeffrey Ivan *urologist*
Langsner, Alan Michael *pediatric cardiologist*
Panagides, John *pharmacologist*
†Roseff, Scott *reproductive endocrinologist*
Spira, Robert Sidney *gastroenterologist*

Westfield
Blum, Richard H. *obstetrician-gynecologist, educator*
Jacobey, John Arthur, III, *surgeon, educator*

Whitehouse Station
Mahmoud, Adel A. *infectious diseases, tropical medicine physician, pharmaceutical executive*

Woodbury
Stambaugh, John Edgar *oncologist, hematologist, pharmacologist, educator*

Wyckoff
Bauer, Theodore James *physician*
Marcus, Linda Susan *dermatologist*
Stahl, Alice Slater *retired psychiatrist*
†Dicpinigaitis, Paul Anthony *orthopaedic surgeon*

NEW MEXICO

Alamogordo
Lindley, Norman Dale *physician*

Albuquerque
Alfidi, Ralph Joseph *radiologist, educator*
†Bailey, Robert A. *child/adolescent psychatrist*
Berman, Stanley Zissman *allergist, immunologist, internist, educator*
Borden, Thomas Allen *urologist, educator*
Bradshaw, Elaine A. *pediatrician*
Cobb, John Candler *medical educator*
†Eldredge, Jonathan DeForest *medical librarian, educator*
Friedman, Herbert Sheldon *urologist*
Haddad, Reem Mariam Edward *physician*
Heffron, Warren A. *medical educator, physician*
Keep, Marcus Floyd *neurosurgeon*
King, Lowell Restell *pediatric urologist*
Knospe, William Herbert *medical educator*
Lee, Roland Robert *radiologist, educator*
Linver, Michael Norman *radiologist*
Logan, Richard *radiologist*
†Mapel, Douglas Wayne *epidemiologist, educator, health facility administrator*
Moneim, Moheb S. *orthopaedic surgeon, educator*
Mora, Federico *neurosurgeon*
Omer, George Elbert, Jr., *orthopaedic surgeon, educator*
Rayburn, William Frazier *obstetrician, gynecologist, educator*
Roth, Paul B. *dean, emergency medicine physician*
Saland, Linda Carol *anatomy educator, neuroscience researcher*
Smith, Anthony Younger *urologist, surgeon*
Smith, Edgar Benton *dermatologist*
Storrs, Bruce Bryson *pediatric neurosurgeon*
Summers, William Koopmans *neuropsychiatrist, researcher*
Turner, Robert Stanley *orthopaedic surgeon, bioethicist*
Uhlenhuth, Eberhard Henry *psychiatrist, educator*
Waitzkin, Howard Bruce *internist, sociologist, educator*
Waxman, Alan Garlett *obstetrician/gynecologist, educator*
Winslow, Walter William *psychiatrist, educator*
Wong, Phillip Allen *osteopathic physician*

Las Cruces
†Blair, Robert Groberg *psychiatrist, educator*
Meltzer, Richard Stuart *cardiologist*
Talamantes, Roberto *developmental pediatrician*

Los Alamos
Smith, Fredrica Emrich *rheumatologist, internist*

Portales
Goodwin, Martin Brune *radiologist*

Rio Rancho
Goss, Jerome Eldon *cardiologist*
Jenkins, James Sherwood, Jr., *pharmacologist*
†Kasirajan, Karthikeshwar *surgeon, researcher*

Rodeo
Scholes, Robert Thornton *physician, research administrator*

Roswell
†Munroe, Shirley Ann *retired hospital association executive, health care consultant*
†Tabrez, Shams S.M. *gastroenterologist*

Ruidoso
Brown, Arlene Meredith *family practice physician, educator*

Santa Fe
†Cohen, Adam J. *plastic surgeon*
Gilmour, Edward Ellis *retired psychiatrist*
Goldstein, Morton Hill *surgeon, educator*
Greer, George Rushton *psychiatrist*
Hoffmann, Louis Gerhard *immunologist, educator*
Kiefer, Helen Chilton *emergency and trauma physician, neurologist*
Kotin, Paul *pathologist*
Schiller, William Richard *surgeon*
Williams, Ralph Chester, Jr., *physician, educator*

Valdez
†Jacobs, Roland William *psychiatrist*

NEW YORK

Albany
Ambros, Robert Andrew *pathologist, educator, writer*
Arseneau, James Charles *physician*
Balsam, Richard Fredric *cardiologist*
Bennett, Edward Virdell, Jr., *surgeon*
Bradley, Wesley Holmes *physician*
Buran, David Runyon *fundraiser*
Catalano, Robert Anthony *ophthalmologist, physician, hospital administrator, writer*
Clark, David Albert *pediatrician, consultant*
Conway de Macario, Everly *immunologist, molecular biologist*
†Dal Col, Richard Herbert *cardiothoracic surgeon*
Davis, Paul Joseph *endocrinologist*
DeFelice, Eugene Anthony *physician, medical educator, author, consultant, magician*
Doyle, Joseph Theobald *physician, educator*
Forrest, George Philip *physician*
Glazer, Joseph A. *medical association administrator*
Hoffmeister, Jana Marie *cardiologist*
Howard, Lyn Jennifer *medical educator*
Jackson, Kenneth William *research scientist, educator*
Kennedy, Debbie A. *plastic surgeon*
Lepow, Martha Lipson *pediatric educator*
Lovely, Thomas John *neurosurgeon, educator*
Macario, Alberto Juan Lorenzo *physician*
MacDowell, Richard T. *surgeon, educator*
Mohler, Edwin Eugene *orthopedic surgeon*
Sills, Stephen Joel *ophthalmologist*
†Spivack, Simon Daniel *physician, scientist, educator*
Swartz, Donald Percy *physician*
Tepper, Clifford *allergist, immunologist, educator*
Timmins, Patrick Farrell, III, *gynecologic oncologist*
Veille, Jean-Claude *maternal-fetal medicine physician, educator*
Verdile, Vincent Paul *dean, emergency physician*

Amagansett
Fleetwood, M. Freile *psychiatrist, educator*

Amherst
Granger, Carl V. *physician, educator*
Roehmholdt, John Michael *urologist, educator*

Amityville
Rubin, Michele S. *radiologist*
Sodaro, Edward Richard *psychiatrist*
Upadhyay, Yogendra Nath *physician, educator*

Armonk
Mellors, Robert Charles *physician, scientist, educator*

Astoria
Sarkissian, Naver Agop *pathologist*

Auburn
Speck, David Dean *ophthalmologist*

Babylon
Epstein, Jeffrey Mark *neurosurgeon*

Bay Shore
†Kirsch, Scott Douglas *family practice physician*
Sampino, Anthony F. *physician, obstetrician and gynecologist*

Bayside
Cortes, Engracio Padilla *oncologist*
Gavencak, John Richard *pediatrician, allergist*
Roth, Joshua S. *obstetrician/gynecologist, educator*

Bayville
Arenberg, Irving Kaufman Karchmer *fund manager, strategist*

Bedford
†Tischler, Gary Lowell *psychiatrist, educator*

Bethpage
De Santis, Mark *osteopathic physician*
Kessler, Richard J. *psychiatrist*
Schneider, Adam Jason *neurologist, neurophysiologist*

Binghamton
Bethje, Robert *retired general surgeon*
Michael, Sandra Dale *medical educator, medical researcher*
Wecker, William A. *preventive medicine physician, neuropsychiatrist*

Briarcliff Manor
Pousada, Lidia *physician*
Weiser, David Joseph *psychiatrist*

Bronx
Bella, Jonathan Noriega *cardiologist*
Bhalodkar, Narendra Chandrakant *cardiologist*
†Bigal, Marcelo E *physician*
Billett, Henny Heisler *hematologist*
Blaufox, Morton Donald *physician, educator, specialist in hypertension*
†Boctor, Fouad Nassif *pathologist, researcher*
Buckley, Peter John *psychiatrist*
†Burgio, Michael *medical researcher*
Buschke, Herman *neurologist*
Butler, Jill Lauren Kraft *internist, educator*
Cohen, Herbert Jesse *physician, educator*
Cohen, Jacob Marc *physician*
Coupey, Susan McGuire *pediatrician, educator*
Das, Ashoke Kumar *internist, consultant*
Dauber, Leonard Gene *oncologist, medical educator*
De Blasio, Maria P. *physician*
Doddi, Seshagiri Rao *psychiatrist*
Dutcher, Janice Jean Phillips *oncologist*
Eder, Howard Abram *physician, education educator*
Fishman, Charles Lawrence *internist*
Fleischer, Norman Samuel *endocrinology administrator, medical educator*
Foreman, Spencer *pulmonary specialist, hospital executive*
Freeman, Leonard Murray *radiologist, nuclear medicine physician, educator*
†Fulop, Milford *physician*
Gerst, Paul Howard *physician*
Gevirtz, Clifford Mark *anesthesiologist*
Gillman, Arthur Emanuel *psychiatrist*
Goldman, Israel David *hematologist, oncologist*
Goldstein, Robert David *plastic surgeon, educator*
Gordon, Garet Mark *cardiologist*
Goudarzi, Behnam Malek *physician*
Greenwald, Edward Samuel *physician*
Gucalp, Rasim Ahmet *oncologist*
Gupta, Sanjeev *physician, researcher*
Hamerman, David Jay *gerontologist, educator*
Heagarty, Margaret Caroline *pediatric physician*
Hirano, Asao *neuropathologist*
Hodgson, W(alter) John (Barry Hodgson) *surgeon*
Jaffé, Ernst Richard *medical educator and administrator*
Janis, Michel *pathology educator*
Kahn, Thomas *medical educator*
†Karkanias, George B. *neurologist, educator*
Karwa, Gattu Lal *urologist*
Kennedy, Gary J. *psychiatrist*
Koss, Leopold G. *physician, pathologist, educator*
Kuhn, Leslie Alvin *cardiologist*
Lieber, Charles Saul *physician, educator*
Macklin, Ruth *bioethics educator*
Nagler, Arnold Leon *pathologist, scientist, educator*
Ofodile, Ferdinand *plastic surgeon*
Okpalanma, Chika *psychiatrist*
Ravikumar, Thanjavur Subramaniam *surgical oncologist*
Reynolds, Benedict Michael *surgeon*
†Reznik, Sandra E. *physician, consultant*
Romney, Seymour Leonard *physician, educator*
Ruben, Robert Joel *physician, educator*
Rubinstein, Arye *pediatrician, microbiologist, educator, immunologist, educator*
Sable, Robert Allen *gastroenterologist*
San Agustin, Mutya *pediatrician*
Scharff, Matthew Daniel *immunologist, cell biologist, educator*
Schaumburg, Herbert Howard *neurology educator*
Shafritz, David Andrew *physician, research scientist*
Shapiro, Nella Irene *surgeon*
Shinnar, Shlomo *child neurologist, educator*
Shirani, Jamshid *internist, cardiologist, researcher*
Siegel, Robert Errol *internist, pulmonologist, educator*
Simon, Sidney *osteopathic physician, educator*
Sohler, Nancy Lynn *epidemiologist*
Sonnenblick, Edmund Hiram *medical educator, cardiologist*
Spitzer, Adrian *pediatrician, medical educator*
Stein, David Kidd *infectious diseases physician, educator*
Stein, Ruth Elizabeth Klein *physician*
Surks, Martin I. *medical educator, endocrinologist*
Tellis, Vivian Anthony *transplant surgeon, administrator*
Trambert, Jonathan Jacob *physician, educator*
Walsh, Christine Ann *pediatric cardiologist*
Walter, Leslie *nephrologist*
†Wertenbaker, Christian *neuro-opthalmologist, writer*
Wiernik, Peter Harris *oncologist, educator*
Williams, Marshall Henry, Jr., *physician, educator*
Younge, Richard George *family physician*
†Zee, Sui *pathologist, educator*
Zonszein, Joel *endocrinologist*

Bronxville
Bertles, John Francis *physician, educator*
†Coffey, Robert J. *neurosurgeon*
DeMartino, Anthony Gabriel *cardiologist, internist*
Levitt, Miriam *pediatrician*

Brooklyn
Abott, Michael Larry *physician*
Ackerman, Jacob Lewis *ophthalmologist*
Alfonso, Antonio Escolar *surgeon*
Amico, Joseph C. *obstetrician, gynecologist*
Avram, Morrell M. *nephrologist, educator, consultant*
†Bakshi, Sanjiv *internist*
Barth, Robert Henry *nephrologist, educator*
Bigajer, Charles *physician, educator*
Biro, Laszlo *dermatologist*
Butler, Brian *podiatric physician*
Chao, Tsai Chung *physician, residency program director*
Charchaflieh, Jean *physician, educator*
Cheung, Chi Pui *internist*
Cohen, Carl I. *psychiatry educator, researcher*
Cohn, Steven Lawrence *internist, medical educator*
†Collins, Ronald Leslie Leopold *physician, neurosurgeon*
Cracco, Roger Quinlan *medical educator, neurologist*
Crum, Albert Byrd *psychiatrist, consultant*
Davidson, Steven J. *emergency physician*
†DeHovitz, Jack Alan *physician, educator, health facility administrator*
Dimant, Jacob *internist*
Edemeka, Udo Edemeka *surgeon*
El Kodsi, Baroukh *gastroenterologist, educator*
Erber, William Franklin *gastroenterologist*
Felman, Yehudi M. *dermatologist*
Fernandes, David Richard *physician*
Finger, Stephen *otolaryngologist*
Friedman, Eli A. *nephrologist, educator*
Furchgott, Robert Francis *pharmacologist, educator*
Goyal, Ravindra Kumar *physician*
†Har-El, Gady *surgeon*
Hollander, Gerald Martin *physician*
Imperato, Pascal James *physician, healthcare administrator, writer, historian*
Jaffe, Eric Allen *physician, educator, researcher*
Jewelewicz, Raphael *obstetrician, gynecologist, educator*

Kaplovitz, Harry Sam *pediatric cardiologist*
Khoury, Nidal Y. *physician*
Kirshenbaum, Richard Irving *public health physician*
Krotowski, Mark H. *physician*
Lash, James *radiologist*
†Leff, Sanford Erwin *cardiologist*
Levy, Norman B. *psychiatrist, educator*
Ligouri, Lorene Delia *obstetrician-gynecologist*
Lombardo, John Wynne *eye surgeon*
†Lowery, Robert Chesley *thoracic surgeon, educator*
Mark, Richard Kushakow *internist*
Mayer, Ira Edward *gastroenterologist*
†Merola, Andrew Angelo *orthopedic surgeon*
Mezey, Andrew Peter *pediatrician, educator*
Miller, Aaron E. *neurologist*
Mirra, Suzanne Samuels *neuropathologist, researcher*
Mittman, Neal *nephrologist, medical educator*
†Moosazadeh, Kioomars *medical educator, researcher*
Norstrand, Iris Fletcher *psychiatrist, neurologist, educator*
Paris Cammer, Barbara Elaine *geriatrician*
Pavlakis, Steven George *medical educator, physician*
Periut, Richard *internist, pulmonologist, intensivist*
Pertschuk, Louis Philip *pathologist, consultant*
Plotz, Charles Mindell *physician, educator*
†Ponnambalam, Ananthasekar *pediatrician, gastroenterologist*
Price, Ely *dermatologist*
Quinones, Jose Ramon, Jr., *obstetrician-gynecologist, educator*
†Rakhmanchik, Emmanuil *gastroenterologist, educator*
Ramaswamy, Prema *pediatrician, cardiologist*
†Ravitz, Leonard J., Jr., *physician, scientist, consultant*
Reich, Nathaniel Edwin *physician, poet, artist, educator*
Reminick, Marshal Scott *intensivist, pulmonologist*
Reyes, Francisco I. *reproductive endocrinologist, researcher*
†Rezkalla, Laurence *internist*
Salwen, Martin J. *pathologist, educator*
Savits, Barry Sorrel *surgeon*
Sawyer, Philip Nicholas *surgeon, educator, health science facility administrator*
Schwarz, Richard Howard *obstetrician, gynecologist, educator*
Seetharaman, Mysore Lakshminarayana *internist*
Shalita, Alan Remi *dermatologist*
Shelov, Steven Patrick *pediatrician, educator*
†Shulman, Abraham *otolaryngology educator, hospital administrator*
Smith, Peter Russell *physician*
Sobin, Allan J. *neurologist*
Spiegel, Allen D. *medical educator, consultant*
Spitalewitz, Samuel *nephrologist*
Sun, Wei Yue *internist*
†Vashist, Sudhir *pediatrician*
Viswanathan, Ramaswamy *physician, educator*
Wagman, Richard Jay *internist, educator*
Weinstock, Judith *obstetrician/gynecologist*
Wolintz, Arthur Harry *physician, neuro-ophthalmologist*
Yogeswaran, Pararajasingam *physician*
Zaman, Mohammad Hamiduz *physician*

Buffalo
Albert, Michael Salvatore *pathologist, medical laboratory executive*
Ambrus, Clara Maria *physician*
Ambrus, Julian L. *physician, medical educator*
†Bandyopadhyay, Arindam *endocrinologist*
Baumler, Robert Albert *cardiologist*
Brody, Harold *neuroanatomist, gerontologist*
Butsch, John Lord *surgeon, educator*
Cohen, Michael E. *physician*
Demmy, Todd Lyle *surgeon*
Dryjski, Maciej Lukasz *vascular surgeon, educator*
Enhorning, Goran *obstetrician, gynecologist, educator*
Flynn, William Joseph, Jr., *surgeon*
Friedman, Irwin *medical and pharmaceutical educator*
†Genco, Robert Joseph *immunologist, periodontist, educator, scientist*
Goldstein, Marion Zucker *psychiatrist-clincian, educator, researcher*
Graham, Saxon (Lloyd Graham) *epidemiology educator*
†Griswold, Kim *physician, researcher*
†Hahn, Theresa *epidemiologist, researcher*
Halbreich, Uriel Morav *psychiatrist, educator*
†Hohn, David *physician*
Hudson, Raymond Anthony *physician*
Kaye, David L. *psychiatrist*
Kipping, Hans F. *dermatologist, educator*
†Krzyzanski, Wojciech *pharmacokineticist, consultant, mathematician*
Kurlan, Marvin Zeft *surgeon, educator*
Lifeso, Robert Murray *surgeon*
†Lippes, Jack *gynecologist, obstetrician, research scientist*
†Lockwood, Alan H. *neurologist, researcher*
Milgrom, Felix *immunologist, educator*
Mindell, Eugene Robert *surgeon, educator*
Mirand, Edwin Albert *medical scientist*
Naughton, John Patrick *cardiologist, educator*
Nolan, James Paul *medical educator, scientist*
Piver, M. Steven *gynecologic oncologist*
Regan, Peter Francis, III, *physician, psychiatry educator*
Richard, Norman Bernard *allergist*
Rosan, Robert Carl *retired physician*
Seller, Robert Herman *cardiologist, family physician*
Shedd, Donald Pomroy *surgeon*
†Sherris, David Allan *surgeon, medical researcher, educator*
Simpson, George True *surgeon, educator*
Stoll, Howard Lester, Jr., *dermatologist*
Torre, Joseph John *endocrinologist*
Trevisan, Maurizio *epidemiologist*
Vladutiu, Adrian O. *physician, educator*
†Welliver, Robert Charles *physician, researcher*
Wieczorek, William Frederick *medical researcher*
Wright, John Robert *pathologist, educator*
†Yang, Li (Luke) Hua *medical educator, researcher*
†Younis, Tallal Hussein *internist, oncologist*

Canaan
Rothenberg, Albert *psychiatrist, educator*

Canandaigua
Wormer, Thomas Andrew *surgeon*

Carmel
Motola, Jay A. *urologist*

Carthage
Ebbels, Bruce Jeffery *physician, health facility administrator*

Cedarhurst
Cohen, Harris L. *diagnostic radiologist, consultant*

Centerport
Fischel, Edward Elliot *physician, educator*

Cheektowaga
Woldman, Sherman *pediatrician*

Chester
Amelar, Richard Daniel *urologist, andrologist*

Chestnut Ridge
Day, Stacey Biswas *physician, educator*

Clifton Park
Blais, Bernard Raymond *ophthalmologist, occupational health physician, educator*
Buhac, Ivo *gastroenterologist*

Clinton
McKee, Francis John *medical association consultant, lawyer*

Cobleskill
Colony, Pamela Cameron *medical researcher, educator*

Cooperstown
Bordley, James, IV, *surgeon*
Franck, Walter Alfred *rheumatologist, medical administrator, educator*
Steinberg, Paul *allergist, immunologist*

Corning
Lin, Min-Chung *obstetrician, gynecologist*

Cortland
Gauss, Karl Frederik *internist, educator, geriatrician*

Cortlandt Manor
Ratnathicam, Wijayan Senthinathan *surgeon*

Croton On Hudson
Werman, David Sanford *psychiatrist, psychoanalyst, educator*

Cutchogue
Cottrell, Thomas Sylvester *pathology educator, university dean*

De Witt
Cohen, Willard *retired cardiologist, intensivist*

Dix Hills
Lee, Won Jay *radiologist*
Lin, Ching-Shen *pathologist*

Dobbs Ferry
Kravath, Richard Elliot *retired pediatrician, educator*
Lavinder, Gale June *medical educator, physical therapist, clinician*
Reddy, Vijaya *emergency physician*

East Aurora
†Carfagna, Vincent O. *physician*

East Berne
Smith, Margery W. *family practice physician*

East Otto
Anderson, Ursula M. *pediatrician*

East Setauket
Adler, Hilton C. *plastic surgeon*
Malbon, Craig Curtis *pharmacology educator, university official*

East Syracuse
Nivarthi, Raju Naga *anesthesiology educator*

Elmhurst
Masci, Joseph Richard *medical educator, physician*
†Toueg, Sam *internist*
Visco, Ferdinand Joseph *cardiologist, educator*

Elmira
Abderhalden, Robert Thomas *internist*
Graham, David Richard *orthopedic surgeon*

Endicott
DeLuca, Paul Michael *retired physician, surgeon*

Far Rockaway
Farron, Robert *physician, family practice*
Madhusoodanan, Subramoniam *psychiatrist, educator*

Farmingdale
Lieberman, Michael Jay *ophthalmologist*

Fayetteville
Chevli, Renate Naren *obstetrician, gynecologist*
Pirodsky, Donald Max *psychiatrist, educator*
Stewart, William A. *medical educator, neurosurgeon*

Fishers Island
Baue, Arthur Edward *surgeon, educator, administrator*

Fishkill
Brocks, Eric *ophthalmologist, surgeon*
Ketcham, Gale Giroux *medical group administrator*
Leopold, Martin Robin *ophthalmologist*

Floral Park
†Mazlen, Roger Geoffrey *physician, clinical pharmacologist, nutritionist*

Flushing
Baik-Han, Won H. *pediatrician, educator, pediatrician, consultant*
Goldberg, Robert Theodore *ophthalmologist, educator*
Hon, John Wingsun *physician*
Karbowitz, Stephen R. *physician*
Kuan, Jackson Hsun *gastroenterologist*
Lorber, Daniel Louis *endocrinologist, educator*
Nussbaum, Michel Ernest *physician*
Pahk, Sang Kee *gastroenterologist*
Person, Philip *biomedical consultant, biochemist, dentist*

Forest Hills
Casson, Ira Richard *neurologist*
Donath, Joseph *physician*
Eden, Alvin Noam *pediatrician, author*
Krikun, Boris Lvovich *neurologist*
Rosman, Lawrence David *endocrinologist*
Samuel, Paul *cardiologist, educator*
Sekler-Katz, Rudolfine *internist, psychiatrist*

Freeport
Burstein, Stephen David *neurosurgeon*
Dimancescu, Mihai D. *neurosurgeon, researcher, educator*

Garden City
Deane, Leland Marc *plastic surgeon*
Good, Larry Irwin *physician, consultant*
Lefland, Renee Rachel *internist*
Madonia, Vincent V. *cardiologist, medical educator*
Wiener, Leo *physician, oncologist*

Garrison
Callahan, Daniel John *biomedical researcher*

Geneva
Dickson, James Edwin, II, *obstetrician, gynecologist*
Givelber, Harry Michael *pathologist*

Glen Cove
Sheehy, John Paul *pediatrician*

Glen Oaks
†Kumra, Sanjiv *psychiatrist*
Siris, Samuel Gidding *psychiatrist*

Glens Falls
Lee, Woong Man *pathologist*
Wurzberger, Bezalel *psychiatrist*
Yovanoff, James *rheumatologist*

Goshen
Roncal, Rogelio *psychiatrist*

Gouverneur
Kuehl, Alexander Edward *physician, health facility administrator, medical educator, writer*

Great Neck
Arlow, Jacob A. *psychiatrist, educator*
Breidbart, Rory Steven *endocrinologist*
Brock, William Alton *pediatric urologist*
Bungarz, William Robert *pediatrician*
Cohen, Herrick Jay *physician*
†Conovitz, Myron William *physician, consultant*
Goldman, Ira Steven *gastroenterologist*
Greenwald, Marc Lehrer *colon and rectal surgeon*
Gross, Lillian *psychiatrist, educator*
Kaplan, Seymour H. *allergist, immunologist, pediatrician*
Kechijian, Paul *dermatologist, educator*
Keller, Alex Jay *plastic and reconstructive surgeon*
Kodsi, Sylvia Rose *ophthalmologist*
Packer, Samuel *ophthalmologist*
Rosenberg, Richard F. *physician, radiologist*
Rothbaum, David *obstetrician-gynecologist*
Shons, Alan Rance *plastic surgeon, surgical oncologist, educator*
Simon, Arthur *pharmacologist, research laboratory executive*
Strauss, Richard Jay *surgeon*
Tepper, Robert Eric *physician*
Weinstock, Gary Alan *internist, allergist*
Wolff, Edward *physician*

Great River
Hayman, Martin Arthur *psychiatrist, educator*

Greenport
Loomis, Earl Alfred, Jr., *psychiatrist*

Guilderland
Gordon, Leonard Victor *retired psychology educator*
Steblay, Raymond William *immunopathologist, researcher*

Hamburg
Calkins, Evan *physician, educator*

Hartsdale
Chait, Maxwell Mani *physician*
Katz, David *gastroenterologist, educator*

Hastings On Hudson
Schorr-Lesnick, Beth *gastroenterologist, internist*

Hawthorne
†Nandedkar, Sanjeev Dattatraya *medical researcher, educator*
Panitz, Lawrence *physician*

Hewlett
Cohen, David Leon *physician*

Hudson
Mustapha, Tamton *gastroenterologist*

Huntington
Alsop, Reese Fell *medical educator*
Bregman, Davis *physician, pain management specialist*
Fritz, Melvin M. *physician*
Goldstein, Ilene Joy *allergist, immunologist*
Joseph, Richard Saul *cardiologist, educator*
Salcedo-Dovi, Hector Eduardo *anatomist, educator, surgeon*
Weinberg, Marc Alan *cardiologist*
Zingale, Robert G. *surgeon*

Ilion
Gay, Douglas MacKenzie *pharmacologist*

Irvington
Ebenstein, Judith Ann *psychiatrist, educator*

Ithaca
Dietert, Rodney Reynolds *immunology and toxicology educator*
Hajek, Ann Elizabeth *insect pathologist*
Whitaker, Susanne Kanis *veterinary medical librarian*

Jackson Heights
Fischbarg, Zulema F. *pediatrician, educator*

Jamaica
Garner, Steven C. *emergency physician*
Grünwald, Hans Wolfgang *internist, hematologist, oncologist*
†Kabir, Mohammed Anowarul *pharmacologist*

Jamestown
Roman, Antonio Regino *cardiologist, internist*

Jamiaca
†Kemeny, M. Margaret *oncologist, hospital administrator, surgeon*

Jericho
Schell, Norman Barnett *physician, consultant*

Johnson City
†Goddard, Bryan Lance *physician, director*

Kenmore
Elibol, Tarik *gastroenterologist, educator*

Kingston
Johnson, Marie-Louise Tully *dermatologist, educator*

Lake Success
Milman, Perry Jay *physician, gastroenterologist*

Lancaster
Batt, Ronald Elmer *gynecologist, scientist, historian*

Larchmont
Rockland, Lawrence Howard *psychiatrist, educator*

Latham
Hardies, Michael John *medical educator, internist*

Laurens
Spoor, John Edward *physician*

Levittown
Levine, Alan Jay *physician*
Montero, Carlos F. *orthopedic surgeon*

Lockport
Carr, Edward Albert, Jr., *medical educator, physician*

Lowville
Becker, Robert Otto *orthopedic surgery educator*
Herrman, John Clinton *surgeon*

Mamaroneck
Coleman, Marshall Donald *psychiatrist, psychoanalyst*
Halpern, Abraham Leon *psychiatrist*
Hoffert, Paul Washington *surgeon*
Rosenthal, Elizabeth Robbins *physician*

Manhasset
Bernstein, David *gastroenterologist*
Boal, Bernard Harvey *cardiologist, educator, author*
Bradley, Thomas Paul *internist*
Chiorazzi, Nicholas *immunologist educator*
†D'Olimpio, James Thomas *oncologist*
Feinberg, Joseph *plastic surgeon*
Fountain, Karen Schueler *physician*
Gauthier, Bernard Gustave *pediatric nephrologist, educator*
Goldberg, Leslie Philip *ophthalmologist*
Krumholz, Burton Alan *obstetrician-gynecologist, educator*

Margulies, Paul *internist, endocrinologist, educator*
Milhorat, Thomas Herrick *neurosurgeon*
†Robeson, William *medical physicist, radiation safety officer*
Rush, Stephen C. *radiation oncologist*
Scherr, Lawrence *physician, educator*
Wadler, Gary I. *physician, consultant*
Wang, Ping *biomedical investigator*
Wecksell, Alan *radiologist*

Manlius
Prior, John Thompson *pathology educator*

Massapequa
Mondschein, Robert H. *surgeon*

Melville
Copperman, Stuart Morton *pediatrician, educator*

Merrick
Gutnik, Zhanna *physician, gastroenterology consultant*

Middletown
Broslovsky, Lewis *physician*
Freifeld, Gerald Sherman *neurosurgeon*

Mineola
†Aloia, John F. *endocrinologist, academic administrator*
Cunha, Burke A. *physician*
Gomolin, Irving Harold *medical educator*
Hines, George Lawrence *surgeon*
Marino, Ronald Vincent *pediatrician, educator*
Saulle, Nunzio *physiatrist*
†Zeldis, Steven Martin *cardiologist*

Monticello
Lauterstein, Joseph *cardiologist*

Mount Kisco
Geissinger-Robertson, Ruth Fabry *retired obstetrician, gynecologist*
Kornhaber, Eugene *psychiatrist*
Mooney, Robert Michael *ophthalmologist*
Schneider, Robert Jay *oncologist*
Stein, Mitchell Brian *physician*
Stillman, Michael Allen *dermatologist*
Wolfson, Robert Allen *physician*

Mount Sinai
Feinberg, Sheldon Norman *pediatrician, educator*

Mount Vernon
Kaufman, Alan *internist, allergist*
Zucker, Arnold Harris *psychiatrist*

Mountainville
Johns, Margaret Bush *neuroendocrinologist, painter, researcher, educator*

Naples
Beal, Myron Clarence *osteopathic physician*

New City
Esser, Aristide Henri *psychiatrist*
Goldstein, Stanley Irving *podiatric surgeon, pharmacist*
Savitz, Martin Harold *neurosurgeon*

New Hampton
Jeyamitra, Devaraj *physician*

New Hartford
Dardano, Anthony Nicholas *obstetrician and gynecologist*
Eidelhoch, Lester Philip *physician, educator, surgeon*

New Hyde Park
Bonagura, Vincent R. *pediatrician, educator, researcher*
Citron, Marc Laurence *oncologist, researcher*
Cohen, Bradley *neurologist*
†Eberhard, Barbara Anne *rheumatologist, researcher*
Gelber, Philip Michael *cardiologist*
Hainline, Brian *neurologist*
Kamler, Kenneth Mark *microsurgeon*
†Lanzkowsky, Philip *physician*
Lih-Brody, Lisa *gastroenterologist*
Lipton, Jeffrey M. *physician*
†Madhok, Ashish Brij *pediatrician, cardiologist*
Mealie, Carl A. *physician, educator*
Moldwin, Robert *physician, urologist*
†Palestro, Christopher J. *physician*
Prisco, Douglas Louis *physician*
†Rai, Kanti Roop *hematologist, oncologist, medical educator*
Romano, Angela *pediatric cardiologist*
Seltzer, Vicki Lynn *obstetrician, gynecologist*
Shah, Manoj Rameshchandra *psychiatrist*
Speiser, Phyllis Witzel *endocrinologist, educator*

New Rochelle
Breindel, David Saul *psychiatrist*
Gable, Carol Brignoli *health economics researcher*
Giges, Burton *psychiatrist, educator, consultant*
Gitler, Bernard *cardiologist and critical care specialist*
Glassman, George Morton *dermatologist*
Hayes, Arthur Hull, Jr., *physician, clinical pharmacology educator, medical school dean, business executive, consultant*
Kleinman, Andrew Young *plastic surgeon*
Levin, Henry Stuart *ophthalmologist*
Lin, Joseph Pen-Tze *retired neuroradiologist*
Lobach, Katherine S. *pediatrician, educator*
Morello, Robert Frank *ophthalmologist*
Perry-Böttinger, Lynne Valencia *interventional cardiologist*
Rovinsky, Joseph Judah *obstetrician, gynecologist*
Shookster, Linda Anne *rheumatologist*
Wolstein, Arthur *podiatrist*

New Windsor
Antony, Ajit Ivan *urologist*
Mandel, Joel Emanuel *orthopedist*
Quintans, Alfredo Sison, Jr., *thoracic and cardiovascular surgeon*

New York
Abramson, Sara Jane *radiologist, educator*
Adler, Karl Paul *medical educator, academic administrator*
†Akfirat, Gokhan Lut *neurologist*
Alderson, Philip Otis *radiologist, educator*
†Allen, Jeffrey C. *pediatric neurologist*
Almeyda, Elizabeth Ann *plastic surgeon*
†Alonso, Daniel R. *medical educator*
Altman, Lawrence Kimball *physician, journalist*
Altman, Roy Peter *pediatric surgeon*
Ames, Richard Pollard *physician, educator, lecturer*
†Angrist, Burton Morris *retired physician, educator*
Antell, Darrick Eugene *plastic surgeon, educator*
Armenakas, Noel Anthony *medical educator*
Aronoff, Michael Stephen *psychiatrist*
Ascherman, Jeffrey Alan *plastic and reconstructive surgeon*
†Ashford, Alfred Robert *internist*
Attia, Alan Lawrence *physician*
Aufses, Arthur H(arold), Jr., *surgeon, medical educator*
Aviv, Jonathan Enoch *otolaryngologist, educator*
Baldwin, David Shepard *physician*
†Baran, David A *cardiologist*
†Barchas, Jack David *psychiatrist, educator*
Barie, Philip Steven *surgeon, educator*
Barker, Barbara Ann *ophthalmologist*
Barondess, Jeremiah Abraham *physician*
Barton, Alice *physician, educator*
Beal, M. Flint *neurologist*
Beaton, Howard L. *surgeon*
Behrens, Myles Michael *neuro-ophthalmologist*
Bellin, Howard Theodore *plastic surgeon*
Berc, Kenneth Myles *psychiatrist*
Berger, Frank Milan *biomedical researcher, scientist, former pharmaceutical company executive*
Berger, Marvin *medical educator*
Bergman, Donald Arthur *endocrinologist*
Bergmann, Steven Robert *medical educator, physician*
Berk, Paul David *physician, scientist, educator*
Bessey, Palmer Quintard *surgeon*
†Beverley, Cordia Luvonne *gastroenterologist*
†Bianco, Fernando J. *urologist, surgeon*
Bickers, David Rinsey *physician, educator*
Bini, Edmund J. *gastroenterologist*
†Birnbaum, Bernard A *radiology educator*
Blitzer, Andrew *otolaryngologist, educator*
Blum, Gerald Myron *psychiatrist*
Bogdonoff, Morton David *physician, educator*
Borer, Jeffrey Stephen *cardiologist*
Brause, Barry David *infectious diseases physician*
Breinin, Goodwin M. *physician*
Brisman, Ronald *clinical neurosurgeon*
Bristow, Cynthia Lynn *immunologist*
Brook, Judith Suzanne *psychiatry and psychology researcher and educator*
Brown, Arthur Edward *physician*
Brown, Jason Walter *neurologist, educator, researcher*
Brown, Robert Stephen, Jr., *physician*
Bruce, Jeffrey Neil *neurosurgeon*
†Brust, John Calvin Morrison *neurology educator*
Burke, Michael Desmond *pathologist, educator*
Butler, Vincent Paul, Jr., *physician, educator*
Butts, Hugh Florenz *physician, psychiatrist, psychoanalyst*
Buxton, Douglas Francisco *ophthalmologist, educator*
†Bye, Michael Robert *pulmonologist, educator*
Bystryn, Jean-Claude *dermatologist, educator*
Caceres, Aileen *physician*
Cahill, Kevin Michael *physician, educator*
†Cammarata, Angelo *surgical oncologist*
Campbell, Magda *child psychiatrist, researcher, educator*
Cancro, Robert *psychiatrist, educator*
Cantor, Richard Ira *physician, corporate health executive*
Caplan, Ronald Mervyn *gynecologist, obstetrician*
Caputo, Thomas Anthony *obstetrician, gynecologist*
Carhuapoma, Juan Ricardo *critical care neurologist, researcher*
Carr, Ronald Edward *ophthalmologist, educator*
†Carucci, John A. *physician*
Casals-Ariet, Jordi *physician*
†Chadburn, Amy *pathologist*
Chahinian, A(ram) Philippe *oncologist*
†Chandrasekhar, Sujana S. *surgeon, otologist/neurotologist*
Chaney, Verne Edward, Jr., *surgeon, foundation executive, educator*
Charney, Jonathan Zachary *neurologist*
Chi, Dennis S. *oncologist, researcher*
Chiu, David Tak Wai *surgeon*
Cholst, Sheldon *psychiatrist, writer*
Chou, Ting-Chao *pharmacology educator*
Chu, Mary Lynn *pediatric neurologist*
Cimino, James Joseph *physician, researcher, educator*
Ciobanu, Niculae *oncologist, researcher*
Cioroiu, Michael Gelu *surgeon*
†Clark, Nancy Ellen *podiatrist*
Clark, Sheryl Diane *physician*
Close, Lanny Garth *otolaryngologist, educator*
Cohen, Elliot L. *urologist, educator*
Cohen, Noel Lee *otolaryngologist, educator*
Cohen, Steven Paul *anesthesiologist, researcher*
Coleman, D. Jackson *ophthalmologist, educator*
Coleman, John William *urologist*
Coleman, Morton *oncologist, hematologist*
Colen, Helen Sass *plastic surgeon*
Coller, Barry Spencer *medicine and pathology educator, hematologist*
†Compte, Maria Emilia *physician, educator, administrator*
Cone, James Elmer *physician*
†Connolly, E. Sander, Jr., *medical educator*
Cooper, Louis Zucker *pediatrician, educator*
Corujo, Marlene *urologic surgeon*
Cosgriff, Stuart Worcester *internist, consultant, medical educator*
Craig, Edward Vincent *orthopaedic surgeon, educator*
†Crawford, Bernard K., Jr., *thoracic surgeon, educator*
Cucin, Robert Louis *plastic surgeon, lawyer*
Cutting, Court Baldwin *plastic surgeon, computer graphics researcher*
Cuttner, Janet *hematologist, educator*
†Dalaveris, Louis *ophthalmologist*
Davis, Kenneth Leon *psychiatrist, pharmacologist, medical educator*
Davis, Leonard *physiatrist*
Davis, Owen Kidder *physician, reproductive endocrinologist*
De Bellis, Robert Henry *physician, medical educator*
Defendi, Vittorio *medical research administrator, pathologist*
Demar, Leon Kenneth *dermatologist*
DeMatteo, Ronald Paul *surgeon*
†Dermksian, George *cardiologist*
Dershaw, D. David *radiologist*
†Desloge, Rosemary Byrne *otolaryngologist, educator*
De Vivo, Darryl Claude *pediatric neurologist*
Dieterich, Douglas Thomas *gastroenterologist, researcher*
Diflo, Thomas *transplant surgeon*
†DiMichele, Donna *medical educator, researcher*
†Disa, Joseph James *plastic surgeon*
Ditkoff, Edward Charles *reproductive endocrinologist*
Dixon, Shirley Lee *emergency physician*
Dohrenwend, Bruce Philip *psychiatric epidemiologist, social psychologist, educator*
Dole, Vincent Paul *medical research executive, educator*
Dolgin, Martin *cardiologist, educator*
Dorfman, Howard David *pathologist, educator*
†Dotan, Z. *medical researcher, urologist*
Downey, John Alexander *physician, educator*
Doyle, Eugenie Fleri *pediatric cardiologist, educator*
Drescher, Jack *psychoanalyst, psychiatrist*
Droller, Michael Jack *urologist*
Drusin, Lewis Martin *physician, educator*
Druss, Richard George *psychiatrist, educator*
†Dubois, Michel *anesthesiologist*
Du Mont, Nicolas *psychiatrist, educator*
†Dunkel, Ira *pediatrician*
Dworetzky, Murray *physician, educator*
Ehlers, Kathryn Hawes (Mrs. James D. Gabler) *physician*
Eidsvold, Gary Mason *physician, public health officer, medical educator*
Elsbach, Peter *physician, medical educator*
English, Joseph Thomas *physician, medical administrator*
Epstein, Seth Paul *immunologist, infectious disease researcher*
Erlenmeyer-Kimling, L. *psychiatrist, researcher*
Evans, Mark Ira *obstetrician, geneticist*
Fahn, Stanley *neurologist, educator*
Farber, Saul Joseph *physician, educator*
Favelukes, Hanne Else *psychiatrist*
†Feig, Stephen Albert *radiologist*
Fein, Oliver T. *physician, medical school dean*
Feinberg, Todd Eliot *physician*
Felderman, Lenora I. *physician*
Feldman, Frieda *physician*
Fennoy, Ilene *pediatrician, endocrinologist*
Field, Steven Philip *medical educator*
Fields, Theodore Robert *physician, rheumatologist*
Fink, Raymond *medical educator*
†Finkel, Jay *psychiatrist*
Fins, Joseph Jack *internist, medical ethicist*
Fischbach, Gerald D. *dean, neurobiology educator*
Fisher, Edward Abraham *cardiologist, educator*
Fisher, Jeffrey David *cardiologist, educator*
Fisher, Laura Lani *physician, medical educator*
Flach, Frederic Francis *psychiatrist*
Flax, Herschel *surgeon*
†Florman, Sander Scott *transplant surgeon*
Foley, Kathleen M. *neurologist, educator, researcher*
Forrest, David Vickers *psychiatrist, educator*
Fortner, Joseph Gerald *surgeon, educator*
Fox, Arthur Charles *physician, educator*
Frankel, Alice Kross *physician, director*
Frantz, Andrew Gibson *endocrinologist, educator, dean*
Freedberg, Irwin Mark *dermatologist*
Freedman, Aaron David *medical educator, former university dean*
Freedman, Alfred Mordecai *psychiatrist, educator*
Freedman, Michael Leonard *geriatrician, educator*
Freeman, Harold Paul *oncologist, educator*
Freiman, Alvin Henry *cardiologist, educator*
Frenkel, Renata *physician*
Fried, Richard Peter *physician*
†Frieden, Thomas R. *public health physician*
†Friedman, Alan Herbert *ophthalmologist*
Friedman, David Bernard *psychiatrist, educator*
Friedman, Emanuel A. *medical educator*
Friedman, Eugene Warren *surgeon*
Friedman, Ira Hugh *surgeon*
Friedman, Richard Alan *psychiatrist*
Frosch, William A. *psychiatry educator, psychoanalyst*
†Frumento, Robert James *anesthesiologist, educator, clinical researcher*
Fuchs, Wayne Scott *medical educator*
Gabrilove, Jacques Lester *physician*
Gadalla, Farida *anesthesiologist*
Galanter, Marc *psychiatrist, educator*
Gebbie, Kristine Moore *health science educator, health official*
Geiger, H. Jack *medical educator*
Gellhorn, Alfred *physician, educator*
Genkins, Gabriel *physician*
Gersony, Welton Mark *physician, pediatric cardiologist, educator*
Gertler, Menard M. *physician, educator*
Giancotti, Filippo Giusto *cell and molecular biologist*
Giardina, Elsa Grace Vonna *cardiologist, educator*
Girardi, Federico Pablo *surgeon, educator*
Glasberg, H(erbert) Mark *psychiatrist, educator*
Glasberg, Scot Bradley *plastic surgeon*
Glassman, Alexander Howard *psychiatrist, researcher*
Glickman, Robert Morris *physician, educator*
Godman, Gabriel Charles *pathology educator*
Gold, Arnold P. *pediatric neurologist*
Goldberg, Harvey Lee *internal medicine*
Golde, David William *physician, educator*
Goldfarb, Alisan Beth *surgeon, educator*
Goldfrank, Lewis Robert *physician*
Goldsmith, Michael Allen *oncologist, educator*
Goldsmith, Stanley Joseph *nuclear medicine physician, educator*
Goldstein, Marc *microsurgeon, urology and reproductive medicine educator, administrator*
Golomb, Frederick Martin *surgeon, educator*
†Gondolesi, Gabriel Eduardo *transplant surgeon*
Gordon, Alan Lee *psychiatrist*
†Gotschlich, Emil Claus *physician*
Gotto, Antonio Marion, Jr., *internist, educator*
Granstein, Richard David *dermatologist*
Grant, Alfred David *orthopaedic surgeon, educator*
Green, Jack Peter *retired pharmacology educator, medical scientist*
Green, Maurice Richard *neuropsychiatrist*
†Greenberg, Henry Morton *physician, educator*
Griffiths, Sylvia Preston *physician, educator*
Gushin, Stephen Ralph *psychiatrist*
Guthrie, Randolph Hobson, Jr., *plastic surgeon, consultant*
Haddad, Heskel Marshall *ophthalmologist, educator*
Hadden, John Winthrop *immunopharmacology educator*
Haight, David Hulen *ophthalmologist*
Halamandaris, Phill Victor *psychiatrist*
Hamburg, David A. *psychiatrist, foundation executive*
Harley, Naomi Hallden *radiation specialist, environmental medicine educator*
Harris, Henry William *physician*
Harris, Matthew Nathan *surgeon, educator*
Harrison, Theodore Joel *otolaryngologist, facial plastic surgeon*
†Haskal, Ziv J. *radiologist, medical educator*
†Hayes, Constance J. *pediatric cardiologist*
Heaney, Mark *internist, oncologist, hematologist*
Heissenbuttel, Robert Holmes *physician*
†Hellenbrand, William E. *physician, cardiologist*
†Hemmings, Hugh Carroll, Jr., *anesthesiologist, pharmacologist, educator*
†Hendin, Herbert *psychiatrist, researcher*
†Hertzig, Margaret E. *psychiatrist*
Hilgartner, Margaret Wehr *retired pediatric hematologist, educator*
Himel, Harvey Norman *medical educator*
Hirsch, Harvey Stuart *psychiatrist*
Hirsch, Jules *physician, scientist*
Hirschhorn, Kurt *pediatrics educator*
Ho, David D. *research physician, virologist*
Hochlerin, Diane *pediatrician, educator*
Hofer, Myron A(rms) *psychiatrist, researcher*
Holland, Jimmie C. *psychiatrist, educator*
Holt, Peter Rolf *physician, educator*
Homayun, Tahira *obstetrician/gynecologist*
†Hopps, Carin Vera *urologist*
Hoskins, Donald W. *medical association administrator*
Housepian, Edgar Minas *neurosurgery educator*
Hu, Dan-Ning *ophthalmologist*
Hugo, Norman Eliot *plastic surgeon, medical educator*
†Hwu, Wen-Jen *physician, oncologist, educator*
Hyman, Bruce Malcolm *ophthalmologist*
Imparato, Anthony Michael *vascular surgeon, medical educator, researcher*
Imperato, Joseph Edward *otolaryngologist*
Imperato-McGinley, Julianne Leonore *endocrinologist, educator*
†Inabnet, William Barlow, III, *surgeon*
Ingram, Douglas Howard *psychoanalyst*
Irie, Philip Shinazo *physician, scientist*
Isay, Richard Alexander *psychiatrist*
†Jacobowitz, Glenn Robert *vascular surgeon*
Jacobs, David Richard *endocrinologist*
Jacobs, Thomas Price *internal medicine educator*
Jafar, Jafar Jewad *neurosurgeon, educator*
Jaffe, Israeli Arron *internist, rheumatologist, educator*
Jarecki, Henry George *physician, financial executive*
Javitt, Norman B. *medical educator, researcher*
†Jay, Harvey H. *dermatologist, educator, researcher*
†Jelinek, Josef Emil *dermatologist*
Johnson, Horton Anton *pathologist*
Jonas, Saran *neurologist, educator*
Jurka, Edith Mila *psychiatrist, researcher*
Kahn, Martin L. *physician, educator*
Kahn, Norman *pharmacology and dentistry educator*
†Kalman, Bernadette *neurologist, researcher*
Kalsner, Stanley *pharmacologist, physiologist, educator*
Kanof, Norman B. *dermatologist*
Kapelman, Barbara Ann *physician, educator*
Kappas, Attallah *physician, medical scientist*
Karasu, T(oksoz) Byram *psychiatry educator*

Katz, Jose *cardiologist, theoretical physicist, educator*
Katz, Lois Anne *internist, nephrologist*
Kauth, Benjamin *podiatry consultant*
Kegeles, Lawrence Steven *psychiatrist, researcher*
Kelly, Patrick Joseph *neurosurgeon, educator*
Kelly, Stephen Euless *ophthalmologist*
Kennish, Arthur *internist, cardiologist*
Khatamee, Masood Ahmad *obstetrician, gynecologist*
†Killip, Thomas *cardiologist*
King, Thomas *physician, physiology educator*
†Kleber, Herbert David *psychiatrist, educator*
Klein, Donald Franklin *psychiatrist, scientist, educator*
Klein, Harvey *physician, educator*
Kleinman, Charles Stephan *physician, medical educator*
Kligfield, Paul David *physician, medicine educator*
Knapp, Albert Bruce *gastroenterologist*
Knapp, Robert Charles *retired obstetrics and gynecology educator*
Koide, Samuel Saburo *biomedical researcher, researcher, physician*
Kolodny, Edwin Hillel *neurologist, geneticist, medical administrator*
Komisar, Arnold *otolaryngologist, educator*
Koopman, Barbara Goldenberg *psychiatrist*
Koplewicz, Harold Samuel *child and adolescent psychiatrist*
†Korelitz, Burton I. *gastroenterologist, educator*
Kosovich, Dushan Radovan *psychiatrist*
Kothbauer, Karl F. *neurosurgeon, researcher*
Kourides, Ione Anne *endocrinologist, researcher, educator*
Kraus, Dennis Harry *surgeon*
Kreek, Mary Jeanne *physician*
Kronzon, Itzhak *physician, educator*
†Kurth, Rebecca Jane *physician*
Lachmann, Elisabeth Amanda *physician*
Lamparello, Patrick John *surgeon, educator*
Landrigan, Philip John *epidemiologist, educator*
†Lang, Enid Asher *psychiatrist*
Langhoff, Erik *physician, educator*
†LaQuaglia, Michael Patrick *pediatric surgeon, neuroblastoma researcher*
Laragh, John Henry *physician, scientist, educator*
†Larson, Steven Mark *physician*
†Laskin, Richard Sheldon *orthopedic surgeon*
Laufer, Ira Jerome *physician*
Laufman, Harold *surgeon, consultant*
Laurence, Jeffrey Conrad *immunologist, educator*
Lawrence, Henry Sherwood *retired physician*
Lawson, William *otolaryngologist, educator*
Lebwohl, Mark Gabriel *dermatologist, educator*
Lee, Tay Bong *surgeon, otolaryngologist*
†Leeman, Cavin P. *psychiatrist*
†Leifer, Edgar *physician, medical educator*
Leitman, Barry Steven *radiologist, educator*
Levitan, Max Fishel *geneticist, anatomy educator*
Levitan, Stephan J. *psychiatrist*
Levy, Albert *family physician*
Lewis, Alfred Baker *psychiatrist*
Lewis, Jonathan Joseph *surgical oncologist, molecular biologist, educator*
Lewy, Robert Max *physician*
Lieberman, James S. *physiatrist, neurologist*
Lin, Pi-Tang *physician*
Lipkin, Martin *physician, scientist*
Lipton, Lester *ophthalmologist, entrepreneur*
Lisman, Richard D. *ophthalmic plastic surgeon*
Liu, Si-kwang *veterinary pathologist*
Lobo, Rogerio A. *obstetrician and gynecologist*
Lockshin, Michael Dan *rheumatologist*
Lodge, Henry Sears *physician*
†Loeb, John Nichols *physician, educator*
Lombardo, Peter Charles *dermatologist*
Loo, Marcus Hsieu-Hong *urologist, physician, educator*
Lopchinsky, Richard Alan *surgeon, educator*
Lubkin, Virginia Leila *ophthalmologist*
Lublin, Fred D. *neurologist, researcher*
†Luloff, Philip *medical doctor, psychiatrist, educator*
Luntz, Maurice Harold *ophthalmologist*
Macken, Daniel Loos *physician, educator*
Macris, Nicholas Theodore *allergist*
Magliato, Henry J. *orthopedic surgeon*
Mahler, Richard Joseph *internist*
†Makari, George Jack *psychiatrist*
Malkin, Stanley Lee *neurologist*
Manger, William Muir *internist, educator*
Marcus, Eric Robert *psychiatrist*
†Marcus, Norman Jay *physician, educator*
Margulis, Alexander Rafailo *physician, educator*
Marin, Deborah B. *psychiatrist, educator*
Mark, Laurence Peter *anesthesiology educator*
†Markowitz, Martin H. *physician*
Marks, Frances *obstetrician-gynecologist, educator*
Marks, Jon Owen *physician*
Marks, Paul Alan *oncologist, cell biologist, educator*
Masterson, James Francis *psychiatrist*
Mayer, Stephan Anthony *neurologist*
McCarty, Maclyn *medical scientist*
McClelland, Shearwood, Jr., *orthopaedic surgeon*
McCormick, Steven A. *pathologist*
Mc Crory, Wallace Willard *pediatrician, educator*
†McDowell, David Michael *psychiatrist, researcher, psychiatrist, educator*
Mc Murtry, James Gilmer, III, *neurosurgeon*
†Megibow, Alec J. *radiologist, educator*
Mellins, Robert B. *pediatrician, educator*
Menche, David Solomon *orthopaedic surgeon*
Mesnikoff, Alvin Murray *psychiatry educator*
Meyers, Paul Andrew *physician, educator*
†Meyers, Philip M. *physician*
Michels, Robert *psychiatrist, educator*
Michelsen, Christopher Bruce Hermann *surgeon*
Mildvan, Donna *infectious diseases physician*
Miller, Sanford Marvin *anesthesiology educator*
Mininberg, David T. *pediatric urology surgeon, educator*
†Mital, Seema *cardiologist, pediatrician, physician*
Mitnick, Hal *rheumatologist*
Mittl, Rainer N. *ophthalmologist*
Mohr, Jay Preston *neurologist, educator*
†Moline, Jacqueline *occupational physician*
Moore, Anne *physician*
†Moses, Jeffrey Warren *cardiologist, educator*
Moss, Melvin Lionel *anatomist, educator*
Moss-Salentijn, Letty (Aleida Moss-Salentijn) *anatomist, educator*
Motzer, Robert John *oncologist, educator*
†Mtui, Estomih Phillip *medical educator*
Muchnick, Richard Stuart *ophthalmologist, educator*
Murphy, Ramon Jeremiah Castroviejo *physician, pediatrician*
Nachman, Ralph Louis *physician, educator*
Nagler, Harris M. *urologic surgeon*
Nahas, Gabriel Georges *pharmacologist, educator, writer*
Naidich, Thomas Paul *neuroradiologist, educator*
†Naka, Yoshifumi *surgeon, researcher*
Neuberg, Hans W. *internist, educator*
Neuspiel, Daniel Robert *pediatrician, epidemiologist*
Neuwirth, Robert Samuel *obstetrician, gynecologist*
Newbold, Herbert Leon, Jr., *psychiatrist, writer*
Newman, Joyce A. *obstetrician/gynecologist*
Newman, Robert Gabriel *physician*
Nguyen, Dung Dang *physician*
Nicholas, James A. *surgeon, consultant, educator*
Nichols, Jeffrey Norman *geriatrician*
Nimer, Stephen *physician, leukemia researcher*
†Nisce, Lourdes *radiologist*
Nixon, Daniel Walker *oncologist, researcher*
Novick, Nelson Lee *dermatologist, internist, writer, consultant, dermatological surgeon*
Ochoa, Manuel, Jr., *oncologist*
Oettgen, Herbert Friedrich *physician*
†Ofri, Danielle *physician*
Okin, Peter Michael *cardiologist*
O'Looney, Patricia Anne *medical program administrator*
Olsson, Carl Alfred *urologist, department chairman*
Ordorica, Steven Anthony *obstetrician, gynecologist, educator*
O'Reilly, Richard John *pediatrician*
Orkin, Louis Richard *physician, educator*
Ort, Paul Joseph *orthopedic surgeon, educator*
Osborn, June Elaine *pediatrician, microbiologist, educator, foundation administrator*
Osborne, Michael Piers *surgeon, researcher, health facility administrator*
Oster, Martin William *oncologist, educator*
Overweg, Norbert Ido Albert *physician*
Oz, Mehmet Cengiz *physician, writer*
Pacella, Bernard Leonardo *psychiatrist*
Palgon, Sheldon *physician*
Pan, Cynthia X. *geriatrician, educator, researcher*
Pardes, Herbert *psychiatrist, educator*
Parness, Ira Allen *pediatric cardiologist*
Pasternak, Gavril William *neurologist, neuropharmacologist*
Patterson, Marc Clayton *pediatric neurologist, researcher, educator*
Pedley, Timothy Asbury, IV, *neurologist, educator, researcher*
Peerschke, Ellinor Irmgard Barbara *hematopathologist, educator*
Pertsemlidis, Demetrius *surgeon, educator*
Phillips, Gerald Baer *internal medicine scientist, educator*
Phoon, Colin Kit-Lun *pediatric cardiologist, medical educator*
†Pierce, Michael Norman *internist*
Pierri, Mary Kathryn Madeline *cardiologist, educator, emergency physician, educator*
†Pierson, Richard Norris, Jr., *medical educator*
Pi-Sunyer, F. Xavier *medical educator, medical investigator*
Plum, Fred *neurologist*
†Pogue, Velvie Anne *nephrologist, educator*
Polenz, Joanna Magda *psychiatrist*
Posner, Jerome Beebe *neurologist, educator*
†Prager, Kenneth M. *pulmonologist, educator*
Present, Daniel H. *physician*
Purcell, Karen Barlar *naturopathic physician, nutritionist, opera singer, speaker*
Quest, Donald O. *neurological surgeon*
Quimby, Fred William *pathology educator, veterinarian*
Quraishi, Nisar Ali *internist*
Rabbani, Farhang *urologic oncologist*
Rabbani, LeRoy Elazar *physician, researcher*
Rabinowitz, Jack Grant *radiologist, educator*
Rainess, Alan Edward *psychiatrist, neurologist, educator*
Ramsay, David Leslie *physician, dermatologist, medical educator*
†Raskin, Keith B. *surgeon*
Raskin, Noel Michael *thoracic surgeon*
Rausen, Aaron Reuben *pediatric hematologist, oncologist*
Raynor, Richard Benjamin *neurosurgeon, educator*
Reader, George G. *retired internal-public health medicine educator*
Redo, S(averio) Frank *surgeon*
Reidenberg, Marcus Milton *physician, educator*
Reiffel, James *cardiologist, educator*
Reiner, Mark Allen *surgeon, educator*
Reisberg, Barry *geropsychiatrist, neuropsychopharmacologist*
Reisner, Milton *psychiatrist, psychoanalyst*
†Renwick, Neil Macdonald *pathologist, researcher*
†Reuter, Victor E. *pathologist, educator*
Rifkind, Arleen B. *physician, researcher*
Ristich, Miodrag *psychiatrist*
Ritch, Robert Harry *ophthalmologist, educator*
†Ritterband, David C. *ophthalmologist, educator*
Rizzo, Frank Albert *physician*
Robertson, Hugh Dunbar *biomedical researcher, consultant*
Rodriguez-Sains, Rene S. *physician, surgeon, educator*
†Roen, Philip Ruben *urologist, surgeon, medical educator*
Rogers, Mark Charles *physician, educator*
Romas, Nicholas Achilles *urologist, educator*
Rosenberg, Victor I. *plastic surgeon, educator*
Rosendorff, Clive *cardiologist*
†Rosenfield, Allan *physician*
†Rosenwaks, Zev *obstetrician, gynecologist, educator, endocrinologist*
†Rovit, Richard Lee *neurological surgeon*
Rowland, Lewis Phillip *neurology educator, editor, clinical investigator*
†Rozentsvit, Inna *neurologist*
Rubin, Albert Louis *physician, educator*
Rubin, Theodore Isaac *psychiatrist, writer*
Rubinstein, Rosalinda *allergist, medical association administrator*
†Ruder, Usha C. *pathologist*
Ruskin, Richard A. *obstetrician-gynecologist*
Sachar, David Bernard *gastroenterologist, medical educator*
Sacks, Jeffrey Howard *psychiatrist, psychoanalyst*
Sadock, Benjamin James *psychiatrist, educator*
Safian, Leroy Scheller *radiologist*
Sager, Clifford J. *psychiatrist, educator*
Salans, Lester Barry *physician, scientist, educator*
Salgo, Peter Lloyd *internist, writer, anesthesiologist*
Sandhu, Harvinder Singh *spinal surgeon, educator*
Saphir, Richard Louis *pediatrician*
Sarno, Martha Taylor *speech and language pathologist, educator*
Saxena, Brij B. *endocrinologist, biochemist, educator*
Sceusa, Nicholas A. *pharmacologist*
Schachter, Edwin Neil *medical educator*
Schaefer, Robert Anthony *internist, gastroenterologist, educator*
Schaefer, Steven David *head and neck surgeon, physiologist*
Schaffner, Bertram Henry *psychiatrist*
Schechter, William Seth *pediatrician, anesthesiologist, educator*
Scheidt, Stephen Slaton *internist, cardiologist*
Schiller, Alan Lewis *physician, educator*
Schlegel, Peter Niles *urologist and educator*
Schley, William Shain *otorhinolaryngologist*
Schneck, Jerome M. *psychiatrist, medical historian, educator*
Schor, Edward Lewis *physician*
Schrag, Peter Edward *physician*
Schuker, Eleanor Sheila *psychiatrist, educator*
Schuster, Carlotta Lief *psychiatrist*
Schwartz, Irving Leon *physician, scientist, educator*
Sclafani, Anthony Paul *plastic surgeon, educator, biomedical researcher*
Sculco, Thomas Peter *surgeon*
Sedlin, Elias David *physician, orthopedic researcher, educator*
Seely, Robert Daniel *physician, medical educator*
†Seidman, Stuart Neil *psychiatrist, researcher*
Selesnick, Samuel Hyman *otolaryngologist*
Sessions, Roy Brumby *otolaryngologist, educator*
Shafer, Stephen Quentin *physician*
Shafir, Michail Kleyner *medical educator, oncologic surgeon*
Shapiro, Theodore *psychiatrist, educator*
Sheinart, Kara Fae *neurologist, educator*
Shepherd, Gillian Mary *physician*
Sherman, Spencer Erwin *ophthalmologist*
Sherr, David Lloyd *radiation oncologist, educator*
Shortliffe, Edward Hance *internist, medical educator, computer scientist*
Siegel, George Lewis *endocrinologist*
Silver, Richard Tobias *physician, educator*
†Silverberg, Nanette Blythe *dermatologist, pediatrician*
Simon, Jane *psychiatrist, educator*
Sitarz, Anneliese Lotte *pediatrics educator, physician*
Skinner, Kristin A. *surgical oncologist*
†Sloan, Nancy L. *epidemiologist*
Smith, Julia A. *internist, oncologist, educator*
Smits, Helen Lida *physician, administrator, educator*
Snyderman, Selma Eleanore *pediatrician, educator*
Soave, Rosemary *internist*
Socarides, Charles William *psychiatrist, psychoanalyst, educator, writer*
Sogani, Pramod Chandra *surgeon, educator*
Solomon, Gail Ellen *physician*
Spaide, Richard Frederick *ophthalmologist*
†Spandorfer, Steven David *internist*
Spencer, Frank Cole *medical educator*
†Spencer, James M. *dermatologist*
Spiegel, Herbert *psychiatrist, educator*
†Spikes, James *psychiatrist, educator*
Springfield, Dempsey Stewart *physician, educator*
Stark, Richard Boies *surgeon, artist*
†Starren, Justin Bruce *medical educator*
Steadman, E. Thomas *gynecologist*
†Steigbigel, Neal H. *medical educator*
Stein, Marvin *psychiatrist, historian*
Stein, Richard Alan *cardiologist, educator*
Steinglass, Peter Joseph *psychiatrist, educator*
Steinherz, Laurel Judith *pediatric cardiologist*
†Stelzer, Paul *cardiac surgeon, educator*
Stenzel, Kurt Hodgson *physician, nephrologist, educator*
Stern, Claudio Daniel *medical educator, embryological researcher*
Stern, Leonard *physician*
Stern, Marvin *psychiatrist, educator*
Sternberg, Stephen Stanley *pathologist, educator*
Stiller, Matthew James *dermatologist*
Stimmel, Barry *cardiologist, internist, educator, university dean*
Stone, Brian A. *urologist, surgeon, educator*
Stoopler, Mark Benjamin *physician*
†Stübgen, Joerg-Patrick *neurologist*
Sulkowicz, Kerry J. *psychiatrist, psychoanalyst, management consultant*
Sullivan, Stephen Gene *psychiatrist, pharmacologist, administrator*
Sun, Tung-Tien *medical science educator*
†Susser, Ezra Saul *psychiatry educator*
Sverdlik, Samuel Simon *physiatrist, physician*
Taha, Assad M. *surgeon*
†Taouli, Bachir *physician, researcher*
Tapper, Michael Leitner *physician*
Tartter, Paul Ian *breast surgeon, educator*
Temple, Donald Edward *medical association executive*
Thomas, Stephen Jay *anesthesiologist*
Thomashow, Byron Martin *pulmonary physician*
Thornton, Yvonne Shirley *physician, author, musician*
†Ting, Windsor *cardiac and thoracic surgeon*
Tolchin, Joan Gubin *psychiatrist, educator*
Tortolani, Anthony John *surgeon, educator*
Tourlitsas, John Constantine *radiologist*
†Tsai, James C. *ophthalmologist, researcher*
Tuhrim, Stanley *physician, neurologist*
Turino, Gerard Michael *physician, medical scientist, educator*
Tzimas, Nicholas Achilles *orthopedic surgeon, educator*
†Ury, Wayne Alan *physician, researcher*
Varriale, Philip *cardiologist*
†Vassalotti, Joseph Alfred *nephrologist, educator*
Vaughan, Edwin Darracott, Jr., *urologist, surgeon*
Verdesca, Arthur Salvatore *internist, corporate medical director*
†Vickers, Andrew Julian *medical researcher*
Vilcek, Jan Tomas *immunologist, medical educator*
†Wadler, Scott *oncology researcher*
Waisman, Jerry *pathologist, educator*
Waksman, Byron Halsted *neuroimmunologist, experimental pathologist, educator, medical association administrator*
Wallace, Joyce Irene Malakoff *internist*
†Wallach, Robert Charles *obstetrician, gynecologist, educator*
Walsh, Joseph Brennan *ophthalmologist*
Wang, Frederick Mark *pediatric ophthalmologist, medical educator*
†Wang, Lu-Hai *medical educator, scientist, researcher*
Waxman, Samuel *oncologist, researcher*
Waye, Jerome D. *internist, gastroenterologist*
†Weiland, Andrew J. *orthopaedic surgeon*
Weinberg, SamueL *pediatric dermatologist*
Weinshenker, Naomi Joyce *clinical psychiatrist, educator, researcher*
Weinstein, I. Bernard *oncologist, geneticist, research administrator*
†Weinstock, David Marc *bone marrow transplantation and infectious diseases physician, researcher*
Weissmann, Gerald *medical educator, researcher, writer, editor*
Welch, Martha Grace *physician, researcher*
Werner, Andrew Joseph *physician, endocrinologist, musicologist*
†West, Alexander Brian *pathologist*
Wharton, Ralph Nathaniel *psychiatrist, educator*
Whelan, Elizabeth Ann Murphy *epidemiologist*
Whitehead, Edgar Douglas *urology educator*
William, Daniel Charles *retired physician*
Winawer, Sidney J. *physician, clinical investigator, educator*
Winick, Myron *educator, physician*
Winters, Robert Wayne *medical educator, pediatrician, healthcare executive*
Wishnick, Marcia Margolis *pediatrician, geneticist, educator*
Wolf, Carl F.W. *physician, biomedical engineer*
Wolff, William I. *surgeon, educator*
†Wolgemuth, Debra J. *obstetrics-gynecology educator*
Wood-Smith, Donald *plastic surgeon*
Worman, Howard Jay *internist, educator*
Yagan, Neda *physician, medical educator*
Yahalom, Joachim *radiologist, educator, oncologist, researcher*
Yeh, Hsu-Chong *radiology educator*
Yin, Beatrice Wei-Tze *medical researcher*
†Yoo Bowne, Helen *otolaryngologist, educator*
Young, Estelle Irene *dermatologist, educator*
Young, Iven S. *physician*
Young, Nicholas *physician*
Yurt, Roger William *surgeon, educator*
Zatlin, Gabriel Stanley *physician*
Zimmerman, Sol Shea *pediatrician*
Zinn, Keith Marshall *ophthalmologist, educator*
Zitrin, Arthur *physician*
Zitsman, Jeffrey Leonard *pediatric surgeon*
Zucker-Franklin, Dorothea *physician, educator*
Zumoff, Barnett *endocrinologist, medical researcher*

Newburgh
Grossman, Stanley Lawrence *surgeon*

Niagara Falls
Sarpel, Suleyman Celalettin *oncologist*

North Tonawanda
Megahed, Mohamed Salah *neurologist, educator*

Northport
Cheng, Edward Hsin-Yi *gastroenterologist, researcher, educator*
Oi, Chieko Munnie *physician*

Oceanside
Behr, Donald Jay *retired internist, cardiologist, educator*

Old Westbury
Chaudhry, Humayun Javaid *physician, medical educator, flight surgeon, writer*

Olean
Broughton, Barry A. *naturopathic physician*
Lewis, Fred Harvey *allergist, immunologist*
Ratanawongsa, Boonlua *ophthalmologist*

Ontario
Loomis, Norman Richard *physician*

Orangeburg
†Citrome, Leslie Lucien *psychiatrist, educator*
Greenberg, William Michael *psychiatrist*
Levine, Jerome *psychiatrist, educator*

Orchard Park
Lee, Richard Vaille *physician, educator*

Ossining
Wolfe, Mary Joan *physician*

Patchogue
Dyckman, Richard Harris *cardiologist*

Pelham
Eaton, Richard Gillette *retired surgeon, educator*

Penn Yan
Strouse, Wayne Steven *physician*

Pittsford
Faloon, William Wassell *physician, educator*

Plainview
Kelemen, John *neurologist, educator*
Krauss, Leo *urologist, educator*
Lieberman, Elliott *urologist*
Mensch, Alan R. *physician, educator*

Plattsburgh
Virostek, Robert Joseph *physician*

Pomona
Landa, George *cardiologist, internist*
Zugibe, Frederick Thomas *retired pathologist*

Port Chester
Marcus, Joel David *pediatrician*

Port Jefferson
Hirschl, Simon *pathologist*

Port Washington
Brownstein, Martin Herbert *dermatopathologist*

Poughkeepsie
†Berlin, Doris Ada *psychiatrist*
Bodack, Mark Peter *physician, medical educator*
†Carino, Aurora Lao *psychiatrist, hospital administrator*
Hansraj, Kenneth Karamchand *surgeon, research scientist*
Murthy, Kurukundi Krishna *neurosurgeon*

Purchase
Frost, Elizabeth Ann McArthur *physician*

Queensbury
De Pan, Harry McCarthy *retired surgeon*

Ravena
Caulfield, Patrick Francis *physician*

Rego Park
Winter, Darius Gerjon *internist*

Rochester
Akiyama, Toshio *cardiologist, educator, researcher*
†Arnold, Georgianne Lee *pediatric geneticist, clinical researcher*
Baum, John *physician*
Benitez, John Griswold *medical toxicologist*
Bennett, John Morrison *hematologist and medical oncologist*
Berg, Robert Lewis *physician, educator*
Bidlack, Jean Marie *pharmacologist, educator, medical researcher*
Bonfiglio, Thomas Albert *pathologist, educator*
Brody, Bernard B. *physician, educator*
Brooks, Walter S. *dermatologist*
Burton, Richard Irving *orthopedist, educator*
Chey, William Yoon *physician*
Cohen, Nicholas *immunologist, educator*
Constine, Louis Sanders, III, *pediatric oncologist, radiation oncologist*
de Papp, Zsolt George *endocrinologist*
†DeWeese, James Arville *surgeon, educator*
Dreyfuss, Eric Martin *allergist*
†Dye, Timothy De Ver *epidemiologist, anthropologist, educator*
Epstein, Ronald M. *family medicine physician, educator*
Frank, Irwin Norman *urologist, educator*
Frazer, John Paul *surgeon*
†Friedman, Susan Marie *geriatrician, educator, medical researcher*
Garroway, Neil Warren *internist, endocrinologist, geriatrician*
Golden, Reynold Stephen *geriatrician, educator*
Goldstein, Marvin Norman *physician*
Griggs, Robert Charles *physician*
Haywood, Anne Mowbray *pediatrics, virology, and biochemistry educator*
Herz, Marvin Ira *physiatrist, educator*
Jozefowicz, Ralph Francis *neurologist*
†Klein, Jonathan David *physician, researcher*
Lanzafame, Raymond Joseph *surgeon, researcher*
Lawrence, Ruth Anderson *pediatrician, clinical toxicologist*
Lichtman, Marshall Albert *medical educator, physician, scientist*
Ling, Frederick S. *cardiology educator*
Lyman, Gary Herbert *epidemiologist, cancer researcher, educator*
Magnussen, Carl Richard *medical educator*
McAnarney, Elizabeth R. *pediatrician, educator*
McDonald, Joseph Valentine *neurosurgeon*
McMeekin, Thomas Owen *dermatologist*
McQuillen, Michael Paul *neurologist, educator, clinical ethicist*
Morgan, William Lionel, Jr., *physician, educator*
Moss, Arthur Jay *physician*
Muechler, Eberhard Karl *physician*
Nazarian, Lawrence Fred *pediatrician*
O'Mara, Robert Edmund George *radiologist, educator*
Ornt, Daniel B. *physician, department chairman*
Panner, Bernard J. *pathologist, educator*
Papadakos, Peter John *critical care physician, educator*
Powers, James Matthew *neuropathologist*
†Quill, Timothy E. *psychiatrist, writer*
Rowley, Peter Templeton *physician, educator*
Schmidt, John Gerhard *neurologist, educator, researcher*
Schrock, Robert D., Jr., *orthopaedic surgeon, educator*
†Schwartz, Seymour Ira *surgeon*
Sherman, Charles Daniel, Jr., *surgeon*
Sloand, James Anthony *physician*
Sparks, Charles Edward *pathologist, educator*
Sparks, Janet Lindsay Dehoff *pathology educator*
Strasser, Alexander L(udwig) *internist*
Toribara, Taft Yutaka *radiation biologist, biophysicist, chemist, toxicologist*
Utell, Mark Jeffrey *medical educator*
Vitullo, B. Benny *pediatrician, neonatologist, educator*
Wheeless, Leon Lum *pathology educator*
Wiley, Jason LaRue, Jr., *neurosurgeon*
Williams, Thomas Franklin *physician, educator*
Wynne, Lyman Carroll *psychiatrist*

Rockaway Park
Guy, Matthew Joel *gastroenterologist, educator*

Rockville Centre
†Donnenfeld, Eric David *ophthalmologist*
Meredith, Gary S. *physician*
Mudgil, Lalta Rani *internist, geriatrician*

Roslyn
Goodman, Kenneth Joel *radiologist*
†Greenberg, Steven M. *physician*
Gulotta, Stephen J. *cardiologist*
Hartman, Nancy Lee *physician*
Lidonnici, Leslie *surgeon*
†Timmermans, Robert *cardiologist*

Roslyn Heights
Rogatz, Peter *physician*
Saravay, Stephen Martin *psychiatrist*

Rye
Barker, Harold Grant *surgeon, educator*
Curtin, Brian Joseph *ophthalmologist*
Hinterbuchner, L. P. *neurologist*
Waltz, Joseph McKendree *neurosurgeon, educator*
Wilmot, Irvin Gorsage *former hospital administrator, educator, consultant*

Rye Brook
Kuntzman, Ronald *pharmacology research executive*

Sagaponack
Eden, John *ophthalmologist*

Salamanca
Patel, Arun Parmanand *physician*

Sands Point
Lear, Erwin *anesthesiologist, educator*

Saranac Lake
Gibbs, Charles Clarence *anesthesiologist*

Scarsdale
Dulit, Everett Paul *psychiatrist, educator*
Edis, Gloria Toby *physician*
Fishbach, Mitchell Harvey *cardiologist*
Jacobs, Theodore Joseph *psychiatrist, educator*
Lipman, Marvin Matthew *medical educator*
Moser, Marvin *physician, educator, author*
Palmer, Trevelyan Edward *physician, thoracic and cardiovascular surgeon*
Perez, Louis Anthony *radiologist*
Schwartz, Kenneth Stuart *surgeon*

Schenectady
Afifi, Alaa Youssef *cardiothoracic surgeon*
Farber, Martin Stuart *rheumatologist*
Schenck, John Frederic *physician*
Skudder, Paul Albert *vascular surgeon*
Zhu, Yudong *medical imaging researcher*

Scotia
de la Rocha, Carlos A. *retired physician*

Selden
Lustik, Boris *pediatrician*

Setauket
Becker, Kenneth H. *physician*
Davenport, Deborah Morgan *obstetrician, gynecologist*

Sleepy Hollow
Chia, David Thien-Shing *internist, gastroenterologist*
Hershman, Jack Ira *urologist*
Mills, Nancy Ellyn *hematologist, oncologist*

Smithtown
Rosen, Bruce Ira *psychiatrist, researcher, educator*
Zippin, Allen Gerald *neurosurgeon*

Somers
Bauman, William Allen *pediatrician, educator, health systems consultant*
Reznick, Steven Michael *orthopedic surgeon, educator*
Rubin, Samuel Harold *physician, consultant*

South Setauket
Solomon, Randall Adam *physician*

Spring Valley
†Liberis, George Nicholas *surgeon*
Rubin, Allan B. *radiologist, consultant*

Staten Island
Bogin, Marc B. *internist, cardiologist*
Bruckstein, Alex Harry *internist, gastroenterologist, geriatrician*
Ferzli, George Salem *surgeon*
Grodman, Richard Stephen *internist, cardiologist*
Jarrett, Mark Paul *rheumatologist, medical administrator*
Lopez Del Castillo, Alfredo *anesthesiologist*
†Margolin, Leon *physician*
Pillari, Vincent Thomas *obstetrician-gynecologist, educator*
Popler, Kenneth *behavioral health services administrator, psychologist*
Saha, Paul Santosh *physician*
Santiamo, Joseph Patrick *geriatrician*
Savino, Michael Anthony *surgeon*
Shiau, John Sou-Cheng *neurosurgeon*
Silverberg, Michael Barry *anesthesiologist*
Stathopoulos, Peter *internist*
Velinov, Milen Todorov *physician, researcher*
†Villanueva, E. Gary *internist, educator*
Winter, Steven *internist, cardiologist*

Stony Brook
Andriola, Mary R. *neurologist, pediatrician*
Bilfinger, Thomas Victor *surgeon, educator*
Carlson, Harold Ernest *endocrinologist, educator*
Cesa, Michael Peter *cardiologist, consultant*
†Chandran, Latha *pediatrician, educator*
Davis, James Norman *neurologist, neurobiology researcher*
Dervan, John Patrick *cardiologist*
Fritts, Harry Washington, Jr., *physician, educator*
Jasiewicz, Ronald Clarence *anesthesiologist, educator*
Jonas, Steven *public health physician, health policy analyst, writer*
Kuchner, Eugene Frederick *neurosurgeon, educator, neuroscientist*
Kvilekval, Kara Helle Victoria *vascular surgeon*
Lane, Dorothy Spiegel *preventive medicine physician*
Liang, Jerome Zhengrong *radiology educator*
†Luft, Benjamin J. *medical educator, health facility administrator*
Meyers, Morton Allen *physician, radiology educator*
Miller, Frederick *pathologist*
†Mirza, Humair *cardiologist, educator*
Priebe, Cedric Joseph, Jr., *pediatric surgeon*
Ricotta, John Joseph *vascular surgeon, educator*
Schoenfeld, Elinor Randi *epidemiologist*
Sokoloff, Leon *pathology educator*
Steigbigel, Roy Theodore *infectious disease physician and scientist, educator*
Steinberg, Amy Wishner *dermatologist*
†Weisbrot, Deborah Marcia *psychiatrist*

Suffern
Bhardwaj, Sushil *medical educator*
Codispoti, Andre John *allergist, immunologist*
Lefkowitz, Louis Hirsch *obstetrician-gynecologist*
Oppenheim, Jeffrey Sable *neurosurgeon*

Syracuse
†Alao, Adekola Olatunji *psychiatrist, educator*
†Alhadheri, Shabib Ali *pediatrician, cardiologist*
†Ashutosh, Kumar *pulmonologist, educator*
Baker, Bruce Edward *orthopedic surgeon, consultant*
Becker, Lorne Arthur *family physician*
Bellanger, Barbara Doris Hoysak *biomedical research technologist*
Bornhurst, Robert Allan *radiologist*
Clausen, Jerry Lee *psychiatrist*
Cohen, William Nathan *radiologist*
Culebras, Antonio *neurologist*
Daly, Robert W. *psychiatrist, medical educator*
†Damron, Timothy Arthur *orthopedic surgeon, researcher*
Geel, Christoph W. *orthopedic trauma surgeon*
Gold, Joseph *medical researcher*
Grant, William Davis *medical educator, dean*
Henry, John Bernard *pathologist, university president*
Horst, Pamela Sue *medical educator, family physician*
Hurwitz, Arthur Andrew *immunologist, educator*
†Kane, Peter Bayard *physician*
†Kaplan, Eugene Alken *psychiatry educator, department chairman*
King, Robert Bainton *neurosurgeon, educator*
†Pato, Carlos Neves *psychiatrist, researcher*
Phillips, Paul Everard *physician, medical educator*
Ramachandran, Tarakad Subramaniam *neurologist, physician*
Rogers, Sherry Anne *physician*
Sagerman, Robert Howard *radiation oncologist*
Sarkar, Siddhartha *pathologist*
Scheinman, Steven Jay *medical educator*
Schiess, William Arnold *health services administrator, geriatrician*
Sheehan, Michael Gerard *allergist*
Streeten, Barbara Wiard *ophthalmologist, medical educator*
Szasz, Thomas Stephen *psychiatrist, educator, writer*
Vardan, Suman *medical educator*
†Welch, Thomas Robert *pediatrician, educator*
Williams, William Joseph *physician, educator*

Tarrytown
†Cocchiarella, Antonio *physician, educator*
Evans, Yonynah Schub (Nina Evans) *child psychiatrist*
Field, Barry Elliot *internist, gastroenterologist*
†Sullivan, Janet Nelson *dermatologist, department chairman, health facility administrator*
Waletzky, Lucy R. *psychiatrist*

Troy
†Bruce, Melody Ann *obstetrician-gynecologist*
Fitzgerald, Edward Francis *epidemiologist, educator*

Tuxedo Park
Regan, Ellen Frances (Mrs. Walston Shepard Brown) *ophthalmologist, educator*
Steinetz, Bernard George, Jr., *endocrinologist*

Upton
Carsten, Arland Leon *radiobiologist, researcher, educator, consultant*
Hamilton, Leonard Derwent *physician, molecular biologist*
Volkow, Nora Dolores *psychiatrist, scientist*
Wang, Gene-Jack *physician, educator, scientist*

Utica
Bowers, Roger Paul *radiologist*
Godecki, Mark Alexander *obstetrician-gynecologist*
Millet, John Bradford *retired surgeon*
Min, Balshik *pathologist*

Valhalla
†Agarwal, Yogesh Kumar *cardiologist, internist*
†Aguero-Rosenfeld, Maria E. *pathologist, microbiologist*
Aronow, Wilbert Solomon *physician, educator*
Cimino, Joseph Anthony *physician, educator*
Del Guercio, Louis Richard Maurice *surgeon, educator, company executive*
†Falvo, Cathey E. *medical educator, director, pediatrician*
Frishman, William Howard *cardiology educator, cardiovascular pharmacologist, gerontologist*
Golombek, Sergio Gustavo *pediatrician, neonatologist, educator*
†Goodman, Alvin Irwin *internist, nephrologist, educator*
†Jayabose, Somasundaram *pediatrician*
†Kibel, Howard David *psychiatrist*
Kline, Susan Anderson *medical school official and dean, internist*
†Lowenfels, Albert Brownold *surgeon, educator*
Madden, Robert Edward *surgeon, educator*
Mallouh, Camille *urologist, medical educator*
†Marks, Stephen J. *neurologist, educator*
McGoldrick, Kathryn Elizabeth *anesthesiologist, educator, writer*
O'Connell, Ralph Anthony *dean, psychiatrist, educator*
†Peterson, Stephen Joseph *internist*
Reed, George Elliott *surgeon, educator, dean*
Safai, Bijan *physician, investigator*
Schwartz, Joel Lawrence *oral pathology educator*
Slim, Michel S. *surgeon, educator, health facility administrator*
Stellman, Steven Dale *epidemiologist*
†Stringel, Gustavo *pediatric surgeon*
†Tiwari, Raj Kumar *medical researcher, educator*
Weinberg, Hubert *plastic surgeon*
Weisburger, John Hans *medical researcher*
Williams, Gary Murray *medical researcher, pathology educator*
Wolf, David Cary *gastroenterologist, medical educator*
Wormser, Gary Paul *epidemiologist, researcher*

Vestal
Grinberg, Raul *internist*

Warsaw
Dy-Ang, Anita C. *pediatrician*

Water Mill
Hagstrom, Jack Walter Carl Kling *retired pathology educator*

Watertown
Garvey, Jeffrey Matthew *medical librarian, educator*

West Haverstraw
Cosman, Felicia *endocrinologist, educator*

West Islip
Doganay, Kazim Levent *physician*
Elkowitz, Sheryl Sue *radiologist*

Westbury
Ente, Gerald *pediatrician*

White Lake
Mendelsohn, Linda Joy *physician*

White Plains
Barland, Peter *rheumatologist, medical educator*
Beran, Samuel Jonathan *plastic surgeon*
Bernard, Robert William *plastic surgeon*
Biers, Martin Henry *physician*
Blass, John Paul *medical educator, physician*
Ciardullo, Robert Carl *plastic surgeon*
Hawkins, Mary E. *ophthalmologist*
†Horowitz, Steven F. *cardiologist*
†Howson, Christopher Paul *medical association administrator, epidemiologist*
Katz, Michael *pediatrician, educator*
Levere, Richard David *internist, educator*
Marano, Anthony Joseph *cardiologist*
Mardirossian, Jonathan *surgeon*
McDowell, Fletcher Hughes *physician, educator*
Monteferrante, Judith Catherine *cardiologist*
Pfeffer, Cynthia Roberta *psychiatrist, educator*
Reiffel, Robert Siskind *plastic surgeon*
Ross, Herbert *physician*

Soley, Robert Lawrence *plastic surgeon*
Straus, Marc Joshua *internist, oncologist, educator, poet*
Turer, Gary Evan *ophthalmologist*
Zevon, Sanford S. *cardiologist, educator*

Williamsville
Burnett, George John *internist*
†Canfield, Cheryl Lucas *epidemiologist*
Hertzog, Robert William *pathologist, consultant, educator*
Ogra, Pearay L. *physician, educator*
Reisman, Robert E. *physician, educator*
Rekate, Albert C. *physician*

Woodbury
Bleicher, Sheldon Joseph *endocrinologist, medical educator*

Woodmere
Kaplan, Joel Howard *psychiatrist*

Woodstock
†Carson, Robert S. *retired medical researcher*

Yonkers
Chumaceiro, Rolando Jose Mendez *family practice physician*
Daman, Harlan Richard *allergist, educator*
Josephberg, Robert Gary *ophthalmologist, consultant, retina and vitreous surgeon*
Mennin, Gerald Stanley *ophthalmologist*
Rosch, Elliott Carl *internist*
†Spagnuolo, Mario *physician*

Yorktown Heights
†Berk, George Ellis *cardiologist*

NORTH CAROLINA

Aberdeen
Jacobson, Peter Lars *neurologist, educator*

Advance
Guth, Caryl Joy *retired anesthesiologist*

Asheboro
Helsabeck, Eric H. *emergency physician*

Asheville
Astler, Vernon Benson *surgeon*
Humphreys, David Harding *plastic surgeon*

Bailey
Brna, Theodore George, Jr., *physician*

Blowing Rock
Littlejohn, Mark Hays *retired radiologist, artist*

Brevard
Finnerty, Frances Martin *medical administrator*

Burlington
Wilson, William Preston *psychiatrist, emeritus educator*

Cary
Kimbrell, Odell Culp, Jr., *internist*

Chapel Hill
Aamoth, Gordon M. *medical association administrator*
†Aris, Robert M *physician, researcher*
Baker, Christopher Cameron *surgeon*
Bernard, Estrada Jefferson, Jr., *neurosurgeon*
Bondurant, Stuart *physician, educational administrator*
Brownlee, Robert Calvin *pediatrician, educator*
Carson, Culley Clyde, III, *urologist, educator*
†Cefalo, Robert Charles *obstetrician, gynecologist*
Coles, William Henry *ophthalmologist, educator*
Collier, Albert M. *pediatric educator, child development center director*
Crews, Fulton Timm *pharmacology educator*
Cromartie, William James *medical educator, researcher*
†Daaleman, Timothy Paul *physician, researcher*
†De Friese, Gordon H. *health services researcher*
De Rosa, Guy Paul *orthopedic surgery educator*
Dogra, Sunil *anesthesiology educator*
Eifrig, David Eric *ophthalmologist, educator*
Farmer, Thomas Wohlsen *neurologist, educator*
Goldsmith, Lowell Alan *medical educator*
Goyer, Robert Andrew *pathology educator*
Graham, John Borden *pathologist, writer, educator*
Greganti, Mac Andrew *physician, medical educator*
Grisham, Joe Wheeler *pathologist, educator*
Hawkins, David Rollo, Sr., *psychiatrist, educator*
Henson, O'Dell Williams, Jr., *anatomy educator*
Hirsch, Philip Francis *pharmacologist, educator*
Hollister, William Gray *psychiatrist*
Houpt, Jeffrey Lyle *dean, psychiatrist, educator*
Howard, James Francis, Jr., *medical educator, neurologist*
†Hulka, Barbara Sorenson *epidemiologist, educator*
Hulka, Jaroslav Fabian *obstetrician, gynecologist*
James, Alton Everette, Jr., *radiologist*
†Lichtman, Steven N. *pediatrician, educator*
†Lieberman, Jeffrey Alan *psychiatrist, educator*
Lohr, Jacob Andrew *physician, pediatrician, educator*
†Lund, Pauline Kay *physiology, pediatrics, nutrition educator*
McMillan, Campbell White *pediatric hematologist*
Miller, C. Arden *physician, educator*
Mitchell, Beverly Shriver *hematologist, oncologist, educator*
†Montgomery, Royce Lee *anatomy educator*
Nebel, William Arthur *obstetrician, gynecologist*
Ontjes, David Ainsworth *medicine and pharmacology educator*
Pagano, Joseph Stephen *physician, researcher, educator*
Palmer, Jeffress Gary *hematologist, educator*
Perkins, Diana Otylia *psychiatrist*
Pillsbury, Harold Crockett, III, *otolaryngologist*
Prange, Arthur Jergen, Jr., *psychiatrist, neurobiologist, educator*
Roberts, Harold Ross *medical educator, hematologist*
Senior, Brent Anthony *otolaryngologist, educator*
Sheldon, George Frank *medical educator*
†Ship, Alan Mitchell *pediatrician, medical association administrator, educator*
Sorenson, James Roger *public health educator*
Spencer, Roger Felix *psychiatrist, psychoanalyst, medical educator*
Stockman, James Anthony, III, *pediatrician*
Sugioka, Kenneth *anesthesiologist educator*
†Thomas, Colin Gordon, Jr., *surgeon, medical educator*
Tilson, Hugh Hanna *epidemiologist*
Tolley, Aubrey Granville *physician, hospital administrator*
†Trejo, JoAnn *medical researcher*
Van Wyk, Judson John *endocrinologist, pediatric educator*
Wheeler, Clayton Eugene, Jr., *dermatologist, educator*
Wilcox, Benson Reid *cardiothoracic surgeon, educator*
Winfield, John Buckner *rheumatologist, educator*

Charlotte
Bell, Don Antonio *neuroradiologist*
Colavita, Paul Gerard *cardiologist, medical educator*
Crowder, Mary Thelma *obstetrician/gynecologist*
Greene, Frederick Leslie *surgeon, educator*
Hall, James Bryan *gynecological oncologist*
Hutcheson, J. Sterling *allergist, immunologist, physician*
Irons, George Vernon, Jr., *cardiologist*
McLanahan, Charles Scott *neurosurgeon*
Nicholson, Henry Hale, Jr., *surgeon*
Raymond, Lawrence William *internist, pulmonary and occupational medicine physician*
Thompson, John Albert, Jr., *dermatologist*
Ullrich, Christopher George *neuroradiologist*
Visser, Valya Elizabeth *physician*

Cornelius
Wortman, William Jerome, Jr., *obstetrician-gynecologist*

Crumpler
Butler, Douglas John *physician*

Durham
†Alexander, Michael Jozef *neurosurgeon, radiologist*
Amos, Dennis B. *immunologist*
Anderson, William Banks, Jr., *ophthalmology educator*
Anlyan, William George *surgeon, university administrator*
Bennett, Peter Brian *researcher, hyperbaric medicine*
Blazer, Dan German, II, *psychiatrist, epidemiologist*
Bollinger, Ralph Randal *surgeon, researcher*
Bossen, Edward Hecht *pathologist*
Bradford, William Dalton *pathologist, educator*
Brodie, Harlow Keith Hammond *psychiatrist, educator, past university president*
Buchanan, Robert Augustus, Jr., *cardiologist*
Buckley, Rebecca Hatcher *physician, educator*
Busse, Ewald William *psychiatrist, educator*
†Butterfield, Marian Isbey *psychiatrist, researcher*
Carter, James Harvey *psychiatrist, educator*
†Cassidy, Frederick *psychiatrist*
†Challa, Pratap *ophthalmologist, researcher*
Christmas, William Anthony *internist, educator*
Cohen, Harvey Jay *physician, educator*
Coleman, Ralph Edward *nuclear medicine physician, educator*
Coppridge, Alton James *urological surgeon*
Dawson, Robert Edward, Sr., *ophthalmologist*
†Edwards, Christopher Levon *medical association administrator*
Epstein, David L. *ophthalmologist, educator*
Falletta, John Matthew *pediatrician, educator*
Foreman, John William *pediatrician, educator*
†Fowler, Vance Garrison, Jr., *internist, educator*
Freemark, Michael Scott *pediatric endocrinologist and educator*
Gaede, Jane Taylor *pathologist, educator*
Giannopoulou, Athina *physician, surgeon*
†Gonzalez-Stawinski, Gonzalo Vincente *surgeon, researcher*
Greenberg, Gary Norman *internist, occupational medicine physician*
Greenfield, Joseph Cholmondeley, Jr., *physician, educator*
Hammond, Charles Bessellieu *obstetrician, gynecologist, educator*
Harmel, Merel Hilber *anesthesiologist, educator*
Harpole, David Harold, Jr., *thoracic surgeon*
Harris, Jerome Sylvan *pediatrician, pediatrics and biochemistry educator*
†Harris, Robert T. *internist*
Hurwitz, Barrie James *neurologist*
Jennings, Robert Burgess *experimental pathologist, medical educator*
Kaprielian, Victoria Susan *medical educator*
Katz, Samuel Lawrence *pediatrician, scientist*
Klitzman, Bruce *physiologist, plastic surgery educator, researcher*
Koepke, John Arthur *hematologist, clinical pathologist*
†Kong, David Franklin *cardiologist, educator*
Krishnan, Krishnaswamy Ranga Rama R. *psychiatry educator*
†Krishnan, Ranga Rama *psychiatrist*
Lack, Leon *pharmacology and biochemistry educator*
Lang, Stephen Norman *orthopedist, surgeon*
Lee, Paul P. *ophthalmologist, educator, consultant, lawyer*
†Lefkowitz, Robert Joseph *physician, educator*
Mark, Daniel Benjamin *cardiologist*
Markert, Mary Louise *pediatrics educator*
Martinez, Maria Dolores *pediatrician*
†Massey, Janice Munn *neurology educator*
McCrory, Michael Elliott *radiologist*
Michener, James Lloyd *medical educator*
Miller, David Edmond *physician*
Murphy, Thomas Miles *pediatrician, educator*
†Newman, Mark Franklin *cardiologist, anesthesiologist*
Oates, Elizabeth Woods *physician, psychiatrist*
†Pappas, Theodore Nick *surgeon, educator*
†Parkerson, George Robert, Jr., *physician, educator*
Pinnell, Sheldon Richard *physician, medical educator, dermatologist*
Pizzo, Salvatore Vincent *pathologist*
Prosnitz, Leonard R. *radiologist*
Radtke, Rodney A. *neurologist*
†Ravin, Carl Eric *radiologist, educator, department chairman*
Robboy, Stanley J. *pathologist, educator*
Sabiston, David Coston, Jr., *surgeon, educator*
Serafin, Donald *plastic surgeon, educator*
Shadduck, Phillip Price *surgeon*
Shelburne, John Daniel *pathologist*
Snyderman, Ralph *medical educator, physician*
Soper, John Tunnicliff *obstetrician-gynecologist, educator*
†Spach, Madison Stockton *cardiologist, educator*
Stead, Eugene Anson, Jr., *physician*
Steffens, David Carl *geriatric psychiatrist*
Stickel, Delford LeFew *retired general surgeon*
Stiles, Gary Lester *cardiologist, molecular pharmacologist, educator*
†Tcheng, James Enlou *physician*
Tedder, Thomas Fletcher *immunology educator, researcher*
†Tendler, David Andrew *internist, educator*
Thompson, William Moreau *radiologist, educator*
Vaslef, Steven Nicholas *surgeon*
Warner, David Samuel *anesthesiologist, educator*
Weiner, Richard David *psychiatrist, researcher*
Wells, Samuel Alonzo, Jr., *surgeon, educator*
Wilkins, Robert Henry *neurosurgeon, editor*
Williams, Redford Brown *medical educator*
Yancy, William Samuel *pediatrician*

Elizabeth City
Lim, Tomas Q., Jr., *physician*

Fairview
Gaffney, Thomas Edward *physician*

Fayetteville
Chipman, Martin *neurologist, educator, retired army officer*
Fietsam, Robert, Jr., *physician*
Hurdle, Thomas Gray *retired urologist*
Lowe, James Edward, Jr., *plastic and reconstructive surgeon*

Four Oaks
Jordan, Lyndon Kirkman *family practice physician*

Gastonia
Cannon, Octavia Manetta *obstetrician-gynecologist*
Prince, George Edward *retired pediatrician*

Greensboro
Cotter, John Burley *ophthalmologist, corneal specialist*
†Ganji, Jagadeesh (Jay) *cardiologist*
Hensel, William Arthur *family physician*
Houston, Frank Matt *dermatologist*
Stevens, Elliott Walker, Jr., *allergist, pulmonologist*
Whalen, Thomas Brian *anesthesiologist*

Greenville
†Babb, Joseph Dolby *physician*
Hoffman, Donald Richard *pathologist, educator*
Lee, Kenneth Stuart *neurosurgeon, educator*
Lehman, John Michael *experimental pathologist-virologist*
Newton, Dale Alan *pediatrician, educator*
Perkin, Ronald Murray *pediatrician, educator*
†Pofahl, Walter Emerson *surgeon*
Pories, Walter Julius *surgeon, educator*
Rose, John David *cardiologist*
Tingelstad, Jon Bunde *retired physician*

Hampstead
Solomon, Robert Douglas *pathology educator*

Hendersonville
†Reinhart, John Belvin *retired child and adolescent psychiatrist, educator*
Roberts, James Allen *urologist*

Hickory
Lefler, Wade Hampton, Jr., *ophthalmologist*

High Point
Bardelas, Jose Antonio *allergist*
Cullom, Joseph William *surgeon*
Draelos, Zoe Diana *dermatologist, consultant*
Kandt, Raymond S. *neurologist*
Williams, Lawrence D. *surgeon*

Hillsborough
Johnston, William Webb *pathologist, educator*
Wallace, Andrew Grover *physician, educator, medical school dean*

Jacksonville
Garrett, Charles Leroy, Jr., *pathologist*

Kinston
Withers, Sydnor Terry, Sr., *retired dermatologist*

Mebane
Langley, Ricky Lee *occupational medicine physician*

Morehead City
Drury, Bradford David *surgeon*

Morganton
Baden, Thomas James *dermatologist*

Mount Airy
Thoppil, Cecil Koshey *pediatrician, consultant, educator*

Murphy
Khan, Rashid Hussain *physician, researcher*

New Bern
Garmise, David Bruce *otolaryngologist, educator*
Lorentzen, James Clifford *radiologist*
Sinning, Mark Alan *thoracic and vascular surgeon*

Newland
Steele, Samuel McDowell *urologist*

Pinehurst
Bussey, George Davis *psychiatrist*

Pisgah Forest
Kempe, Ludwig George *neurological surgeon*

Raeford
Abreu, Sue Hudson *physician, army officer, organizational and healthcare consultant*

Raleigh
Barish, Charles Franklin *internist, gastroenterologist, researcher*
Garrett, Leland Earl *nephrologist, educator*
Hughes, Francis P. *medical organization executive*
†Johnson, Mary Pauline (Polly Johnson) *nursing executive*
Parsons, William Jonathan *cardiologist*
Peacock, Erle Ewart, Jr., *surgeon, lawyer, educator*
Schwarz, Ronald Paul *gastroenterologist*
†Speer, Kevin Paul *surgeon*
Stratas, Nicholas Emanuel *psychiatrist*

Research Triangle Park
Boorman, Gary Alexis *veterinary pathologist*
Dorinsky, Paul Michael *physician, researcher, educator*
†East, Larry Eugene *pharmaceutical researcher, minister*
†Hu, Chuanpu *pharmacologist*
†Hughes, Claude L. *endocrinologist*
Qualls, Charles Wayne, Jr., *research pathologist*
†Roses, Allen David *neurologist, educator*

Roanoke Rapids
†Adiga, Giridhar U. *geriatrician, pharmacologist, researcher, internist*

Rocky Mount
Hendrix, Robert A. *otolaryngologist*

Roxboro
Olds, William Bellamy *physician*

Salisbury
Crowe, John Albert, Jr., *surgeon*

Salter Path
Wiley, Albert Lee, Jr., *physician, engineer, educator*

Southern Pines
Haserick, John Roger *retired dermatologist*
Penick, George Dial *pathologist*

Spencer
Kiser, Glenn Augustus *retired pediatrician, investor*

Statesville
Linnane, James Francis, Jr., *internist, gastroenterologist*

Sylva
Henderson, R(ichard) Winn *physician*

Thomasville
Sprinkle, Robert Lee, Jr., *podiatrist*

Waxhaw
Edwards, Irene Elizabeth (Libby Edwards) *dermatologist, educator, researcher*

Waynesville
McKinney, Alexander Stuart *neurologist, retired*

Whispering Pines
Enlow, Donald Hugh *anatomist, educator, university dean*

Wilmington
Bachman, David *neurologist, pediatric neurologist*
De Maria, Alfred Anthony *neurologist*
Gillen, Howard William *neurologist, medical historian*
Kesler, James L. *ophthalmologist*
†Nakayama, Don K. *surgeon*
Perko, Mike A. *health education and health promotion educator*
Scully, Kevin Slean *orthopaedist, surgeon*
Wilkins, Lucien Sanders *gastroenterologist*

Wilson
Kushner, Michael James *neurologist, consultant, educator*
Ladwig, Harold Allen *neurologist*

Winston Salem
Adler, Michael L. *family physician, educator*
Bell, William Lynn *neurologist, researcher*
†Bencherif, Merouane *medical researcher, business executive*
Bleecker, Eugene R. *internist, educator*
Cheng, Che Ping *cardiologist, researcher, educator*
†Clarkson, Thomas Boston *comparative medicine educator*
Cordell, A(lfred) Robert *cardiothoracic surgeon, educator*
Dean, Richard Henry *surgeon, educator*
Donofrio, Peter Daniel *neurology educator*
Ferree, Carolyn Ruth *radiation oncologist, educator*
Geary, Randolph Lee *vascular surgeon, educator*
Graham, Gloria Flippen *dermatologist*
†Hantgan, Roy Russell *biomedical researcher, educator*
Henrichs, W(alter) Dean *dermatologist*
Hopkins, Judith Owen *oncologist*
†Housman, Tamara Salam *dermatologist*
Howell, Charles Maitland *dermatologist*
†Ibdah, Jamal A. *medical educator*
Ibrahim, Mounir Labib *physician, psychiatrist*
Israel, James Ray *psychiatrist*
James, Francis Marshall, III, *anesthesiologist*
Jorizzo, Joseph L. *dermatology educator*
Kohut, Robert Irwin *otolaryngologist, educator*
†Kritchevsky, Stephen Bennett *epidemiologist, educator*
Levine, Edward A. *surgeon, educator*
†Matlaga, Brian Richard *physician*
Maynard, Charles Douglas *radiologist*
Mueller-Heubach, Eberhard *medical educator*
O'Steen, Wendall Keith *neurobiology and anatomy educator*
Ott, David James *diagnostic radiologist*
Peters, Stephen Paul *medical educator*
†Petrozza, Patricia H. *anesthesiologist*
†Pitovski, Dimitri Zivko *otolaryngologist, educator*
Pittaway, Donald Edward *endocrinology educator, gynecologist*
Podgorny, George *emergency physician*
Rogers, Lee Frank *radiologist*
†St. Clair, Richard W. *medical educator, researcher, health facility administrator*
Schiller, Herbert Miles *pathologist*
Schwartz, Robert Paul *pediatric endocrinologist*
Stein, Barry Edward *medical educator*
Stratta, Robert J. *surgeon*
†Toole, James Francis *medical educator*
Torti, Frank Michael *physician, healthcare administrator*
†Uhl, Henry Stephen Magraw *internist, educator*
Wilson, John Allen *neurosurgeon*
Wolfman, Neil T. *physician*
Yeatts, Robert Patrick *ophthalmologist*
†Zagoria, Ronald Jay *radiologist, educator*

NORTH DAKOTA

Bismarck
Dunnigan, Earl Joseph *nephrologist*
Schwartz, Judy Ellen *cardiothoracic surgeon*

Fargo
Mendez, Alejandro *neurosurgeon*
†Potti, Anil *medical educator*
Scott, David Michael *pharmacy educator*

Grand Forks
Carlson, Edward C. *anatomy educator*
†Lerma, Edgar Villaneuva *nephrologist*
Siegel, Mark Bernard *surgeon*
Sobus, Kerstin MaryLouise *physician, physical therapist*

Williston
Adducci, Joseph Edward *obstetrician, gynecologist*
Naranja, Rogelio Darusin, Sr., *psychiatrist*

OHIO

Akron
Bird, Forrest M. *retired medical inventor*
†Emmett, John Colin *retired inventor, consultant*
Evans, Douglas McCullough *surgeon, educator*
Hopkins, Michael Patrick *gynecologist, oncologist, surgeon*
Milsted, Amy *biomedical educator*
Mubashir, Bashar Ahmad *internist, oncologist, hematologist*
Munetz, Mark Richard *psychiatrist*
Rothmann, Bruce Franklin *pediatric surgeon*
Seiwald, Robert J. *retired inventor*
Spector, Michael Lew *cardiothoracic surgeon*
Timmons, Gerald Dean *pediatric neurologist*

Ashland
Lake-Bruse, Kristy Dean *pharmacologist, toxicologist, researcher, educator*

Athens
Chila, Anthony George *osteopathic educator*

Aurora
†Su, Sunyu *MRI scientist*

Barberton
Buckley, Sheryl Lea *physician, anesthesiologist*

Beachwood
Katzman, Richard A. *cardiologist, internist, consultant*
Moskowitz, Roland Wallace *internist*

Bellefontaine
Graber, Harry Lee *internist*

Bexley
Yashon, David *neurosurgeon, educator*

Brecksville
Ventenilla, Aurora Curamen *psychiatrist*

Brunswick
Kuchynski, Marie *physician*

Bryan
Carrico, Virgil Norman *physician*

Bucyrus
Solt, Robert Lee, Jr., *retired surgeon*

Canton
Gonzalez, Domingo *neurosurgeon*
Howland, Willard J. *radiologist, educator*
Mkparu, Fidelis Okechukwu *cardiologist, educator, consultant*
Nadas, John Adalbert *psychiatrist, educator*
Sicard, Guillermo Rafael *dermatologist*
Starchman, Dale Edward *medical educator*

Chagrin Falls
Lingl, Friedrich Albert *psychiatrist*

Chardon
Dobyns, Brown McIlvaine *surgeon, educator*

Chillicothe
El-Zawahry, M. A. Moneim *epidemiologist, tropical medicine specialist*
Fruth, Beryl Rose *physician*

Cincinnati
Alexander, James Wesley *surgeon, educator*
†Altaye, Mekibib *medical educator, consultant, medical researcher*
Augsburger, James Jay *ophthalmology educator*
Azizkhan, Richard George *pediatric surgeon, educator*
Baughman, Robert Phillip *physician*
Boat, Thomas Frederick *physician, educator, researcher*
Bower, Robert Hewott *surgeon, educator, researcher*
Boyd, Deborah Ann *pediatrician*
Bridenbaugh, Phillip Owen *anesthesiologist, physician*
Buncher, Charles Ralph *epidemiologist, educator*
CaJacob, Daniel Emerson *otolaryngologist*
Carothers, Charles Omsted *retired orthopedic surgeon*
Cavallo, Tito *physician*
†Cecil, Kim Maria *radiologist, educator*
Chatterjee, Malaya *immunologist*
Chatterjee, Sunil Kumar *cancer research scientist*
Chin, Nee Oo Wong *reproductive endocrinologist*
Cole, Theodore John *osteopathic and naturopathic physician*
Collins, Margaret Helen *pathologist*
Cudkowicz, Leon *medical educator*
Datta, Sukdeb *anesthesiologist, pain management specialist*
†De Courten-Myers, Gabrielle Marguerite *neuropathologist*
Dunsker, Stewart B. *physician, neurosurgeon*
†Eckman, Mark H. *physician, educator*
†Estes, Stephen Arthur *dermatologist*
Fenoglio-Preiser, Cecilia Mettler *pathologist, educator*
Fowler, Noble Owen *physician, university administrator*
Freiberg, Richard Albert *orthopaedic surgeon*
†Fukasawa, Kenji *medical researcher*
Gelfand, Michael Joseph *radiology educator*
Gerber, Michael Allen *pediatrician*
Gersin, Keith Steven *surgeon*
Gerson, Myron Craig *cardiologist, researcher*
Gibson, John Phillips *pathologist, toxicologist*
Gluckman, Jack Louis *otolaryngologist, educator, dean*
Greenwalt, Tibor Jack *physician, educator*
Heaton, Charles Lloyd *dermatologist, educator*
Heimlich, Henry J. *physician, surgeon, educator*
Hess, Evelyn Victorine (Mrs. Michael Howett) *medical educator*
†Heubi, James Edward *pediatrician, educator*
†Husseinzadeh, Nader *gynecologist, oncologist*
Ivey, Tom Dexter *cardiac surgeon*
†Kahn, Jessica Annette *pediatrics educator, researcher*
Kereiakes, Dean James *cardiologist*
Khan, Sohaib Ahmed *cancer researcher, molecular cell biology educator*
Kitzmiller, W. John *plastic, reconstructive and hand surgeon, educator*
Knilans, Timothy Kevin *pediatrician*
Kulwin, Dwight Robert *surgeon, educator*
Kuntz, Charles, IV, *neurological surgeon*
Levinson, Joseph E. *physician, emeritus educator*
Loggie, Jennifer Mary Hildreth *medical educator, physician*
Lucas, Stanley Jerome *retired radiologist, physician*
†Luse, Kimberly Ann *radiologic technologist, educator*
Macpherson, Colin R(obertson) *pathologist, educator*
Maltz, Robert *surgeon*
Nasrallah, Henry Ata *psychiatry researcher, educator*
†Nordlund, James John *dermatologist*
Rolfes, Richard James *radiologist*
Rorick, Marvin Horton, III, *physician, neurologist*
Rothenberg, Marc Elliot *pediatrics educator*
Ruddy, Richard M. *physician*
Ryan, Richard J. *emergency medicine physician*
Sacher, Ronald Alan *hematologist*
†Schmidt, James Edward *medical educator, researcher*
Schreiner, Albert William *physician, educator*
Scott, Ralph C. *physician, educator*
†Seiden, Allen Mark *otolaryngologist*
Shani, Hezekiah Gyunda Pyuza *thoracic and cardiovascular surgery*
†Sherman, Kenneth Eliot *medicine educator, researcher*
Shott, Sally Richard *otolaryngologist*
Silberstein, Edward Bernard *nuclear medicine educator, researcher, oncologist*
Spinnato, Joseph Anthony, II, *obstetrician*
Stahl, Donna Laura *surgeon*
Strakowski, Stephen M. *psychiatrist*
†Thomas, Michael A. *endocrinologist, gynecologist*
Thornell, William Clyde *retired physician*
Vilter, Richard William *physician, educator*
†Warshaw, Gregg *geriatrician, educator*
Welsh, George Franklin *plastic surgeon, educator, healthcare consultant*
West, Clark Darwin *pediatric nephrologist, educator*
Williams, Daniel Bryan *obstetrician/gynecologist, educator*
Wilson, James Miller, IV, *cardiovascular surgeon, educator*
Wiot, Jerome Francis *radiologist*
Wood, Robert Emerson *pediatrics educator*
Wright, Creighton Bolter *cardiovascular surgeon, educator*
Yee, Leslie Mitchell *physician executive, educator*
Zuccarello, Mario *neurosurgeon, researcher*

Cleveland
†Abughali, Nazha *pediatrician, consultant*
†Agani, Faton Hilmi *anatomist, educator*
Altose, Murray David *physician, educator*
Awais, George Musa *obstetrician, gynecologist*
Badal, Daniel Walter *psychiatrist, educator*
Baker, Saul Phillip *geriatrician, cardiologist, internist*
Bambakidis, Peter *neurologist, educator*
Barnett, Gene Henry *neurosurgeon*
Bause, George Stephen Loneraven *anesthesiologist*
Berger, Melvin *allergist, immunologist*
Berggren, Jean R. *psychiatrist*
Bethoux, François Andre *physiatrist, researcher*
Bodner, Donald Roger *urologist, medical educator*
Boom, Willem Henry *physician, biomedical researcher*
Bowerfind, Edgar Sihler, Jr., *physician, medical administrator*
Boyd, Arthur Bernette, Jr., *surgeon, clergyman, beverage company executive*
†Brener, Sorin Jakob *physician*
Brody, Robert *dermatologist, educator*
†Brotman, Daniel J. *internist, researcher*
Bruner, William Evans, II, *ophthalmologist, educator, researcher*
Cascorbi, Helmut Freimund *anesthesiologist, educator*
Castele, Theodore John *radiologist*
Chao, Jason *family physician, educator*
†Chukwumerije, Nkemdirim *medical educator*
Cola, Philip Andrew *research administrator*
Cole, Monroe *neurologist, educator*
Cooper, Gregory Scott *epidemiologist, gastroenterologist, educator*
Cowan, Dale Harvey *internist, lawyer*
Daroff, Robert Barry *neurologist, educator*
Davis, Pamela Bowes *pediatric pulmonologist*
Denko, Joanne D. *psychiatrist, writer*
Doershuk, Carl Frederick *physician, pediatrics educator*
Dweik, Raed A. *physician, researcher, educator*
†Eckhout, Jr., Gifford Van *physician*
Eiben, Robert Michael *pediatric neurologist, educator*
Ellis, Lloyd H., Jr., *emergency physician, art historian*
Falcone, Tommaso *reproductive endocrinologist*
†Findling, Robert Lawrence *psychiatrist*
Friedman, Ernest Harvey *physician, psychiatrist*
Griffin, Teresa Beverly *physician*
Hardy, Russell Willis *neurosurgeon*
Harris, John William *hematologist, educator*
Hermann, Robert Ewald *surgeon*
†Hirose, Hitoshi *medical doctor, cardiovascular surgeon*
Holzbach, Raymond Thomas *gastroenterologist, author, educator*
Hoogwerf, Byron James *physician*
Hsi, Eric D. *hematopathologist*
Izant, Robert James, Jr., *pediatric surgeon*
†Jackson, Edgar B., Jr., *medical educator*
†Johnstone, Brian *medical educator*
†Kalahasti, Vidyasagar *cardiologist*
Kass, Lawrence *hematologist, oncologist, hematopathologist*
Korman, Neil J. *dermatologist*
Krishnan, Ravi Venkata *internist*
Lamm, Michael Emanuel *pathologist, immunologist, educator*
Lederman, Michael Marcel *immunologist*
Lefferts, William Geoffrey *physician, educator*
Lenkoski, Leo Douglas *psychiatrist, educator*
Loyke, Hubert Frank *internist, cardiologist*
†Luce, Edward Andrew *plastic surgeon*
Macklis, Roger Milton *physician, educator, researcher*
†McCrae, Keith R. *medical educator, researcher*
McHenry, Martin Christopher *physician, educator*
McQuarrie, Irvine Gray *neurosurgeon, educator*
Medalie, Jack Harvey *physician*
Minai, Omar Ahmad *physician*
Montague, Drogo K. *urologist*
Mossad, Sherif Beniameen *physician*
Neuhauser, Duncan vonBriesen *medical educator*
Novick, Andrew Carl *urologist*
Olness, Karen Norma *pediatrics and international health educator*
Papay, Francis Anthony *plastic surgeon, researcher*
†Pina, Ileana *medical educator*
Pomeranz, Jerome Raphael *dermatopathologist*
Pretlow, Thomas Garrett *physician, pathology educator, researcher*
Raaf, John Hart *surgeon, health facility administrator, educator*
†Rafiroiu, Anca Codruta *medical educator*
Rakita, Louis *cardiologist, educator*
Ransohoff, Richard Milton *neurologist, researcher*
Ratcheson, Robert Allan *neurological surgeon*
†Ratnoff, Oscar Davis *physician, educator*
Resnick, Martin I. *urologist, educator*
Rose, Peter Graham *gynecologic oncologist*
Rothner, Arnold David *pediatric neurologist*
Roulet, Norman Lawrence *psychiatrist, educator*
Ruff, Robert Louis *neurologist, physiology researcher*
Scarpa, Antonio *medicine educator, biomedical scientist*
†Schelling, Jeffrey Robert *biomedical researcher, nephrologist*
Schwartz, Michael Alan *physician*
Seballos, Raul John *internist, medical educator*
Seitz, William Henry, Jr., *surgeon*
Shuck, Jerry Mark *surgeon, educator*
Spano, Kenneth Andrew *surgeon, educator*
Stange, Kurt C. *medical educator*
Stanton-Hicks, Michael D'Arcy *anesthesiologist, pain medicine specialist, educator*
Stavitsky, Abram Benjamin *immunologist, educator*
†Steinmetz, Michael Patrick *physician, neurosurgeon*
Stern, Robert C. *physician, educator*
Strome, Marshall *otolaryngologist, educator*
†Suarez, Jose I. *neurologist, researcher*
†Tetzlaff, John Edwin *physician*
†Topol, Eric Jeffrey *cardiologist, physician, educator*
Utian, Wulf Hessel *gynecologist, endocrinologist*
Walsh, Richard A. *medical educator*
Wang, Fu-Zhang *medical researcher*
†Wang, Kai *cardiologist*
Webster, Leslie Tillotson, Jr., *pharmacologist, educator*
Weiner, George David *medical association executive, researcher*
†Weise, Kathryn L. *pediatrician*
Wiedemann, Herbert Pfeil *physician*
†Willey, Andrea *surgeon, researcher*
Wish, Jay Barry *nephrologist, specialist*
†Wolfman, Alan *medical educator, researcher*
Wolinsky, Emanuel *physician, educator*
Wyllie, Elaine *physician*
Young, Jess Ray *retired internist*
Yue, Cheung Cho *physician*
†Zhang, Amy Yanyun *medical educator*
Zollinger, Robert Milton, Jr., *surgery educator*

Cleveland Heights
Byramjee, Aspi Minoo *surgeon*

Columbus
Barth, Rolf Frederick *pathologist, educator*
†Berntson, Gary Glen *psychiatry, psychology and pediatrics educator*
Beversdorf, David Quentin *neurologist, researcher*
Billings, Charles Edgar *physician*
Bissell, Michael Gilbert *pathologist*
Bloomfield, Clara Derber *oncologist, medical institute administrator*
Boudoulas, Harisios *physician, educator, researcher*
Boué, Daniel Robert *pediatric pathologist, neuropathologist, educator*
Christoforidis, A. John *radiologist, educator*
Clark, Robert Wesley *neurologist*
†Cordle, Christopher T. *immunologist, race boat driver*
Cramblett, Henry Gaylord *pediatrician, virologist, educator*
†Dull, Pamela *physician, educator*
Ellison, Edwin Christopher *physician, surgeon*
†El-Sayed, Osama Mohamed *cardiologist*
Falcone, Robert Edward *surgeon*
Furste, Wesley Leonard, II, *surgeon, educator*
Gahbauer, Reinhard A. *physician*
Haque, Malika Hakim *pediatrician*
†Hertle, Richard William *pediatric ophthalmologist, educator*
Hilliard, Kirk Loveland *osteopathic physician, educator*
Hoffman, Robert Paul *medical educator*
Huheey, Marilyn Jane *ophthalmologist, educator*
Inglis, William Darling *internist, health facility administrator*
Kukielka, Gilbert Leon *physician*
†Ladinsky, Morissa Jean *medical educator, pediatrician*
Lander, Ruth A. *medical group and association administrator*
Leier, Carl Victor *internist, cardiologist*
Lewis, Richard Phelps *physician, educator*
Litvak, Ronald *psychiatrist*
Long, Sarah Elizabeth Brackney *physician*
†Magro, Cynthia Maria *pathologist*
McClung, Hugo Juhling *pediatrician, educator*
Michler, Robert E. *heart surgeon*
Morrow, Grant, III, *medical research director, physician*
Mueller, Charles Frederick *radiologist, educator*
Munson, Robert Sydney *biomedical researcher*
†Nag, Subir K. *radiation oncologist*
Nappi, James Francis *hand surgeon, educator*
Newton, Herbert Bruce *neuro-oncologist*
Newton, William Allen, Jr., *pediatric pathologist*
O'Handley, John G. *physician*
Penn, Gerald Melville *pathologist*
Roseberry, Elizabeth Ann *neonatologist*
Ruberg, Robert Lionel *surgery educator*
Rumberger, John Arthur *cardiologist*
Rund, Douglas Andrew *emergency physician*
St. Pierre, Ronald Leslie *medical and public health educator, university administrator*
Samodelov, Leonid Feodor *anesthesiologist*
Sayers, Martin Peter *pediatric neurosurgeon*
Senhauser, Donald A(lbert) *pathologist, educator*

†Shapiro, Charles Louis *physician*
Sokolov, Howard H. *psychiatrist*
Speicher, Carl Eugene *pathologist*
Stephens, Sheryl Lynne *family practice physician*
†Stoner, Gary David *cancer researcher*
Tsao, Chang Yong *pediatric neurologist*
Tzagournis, Manuel *physician, educator, university administrator*
Vogel, Thomas Timothy *surgeon, health care consultant, lay church worker*
Zhao, Fang Li *medical researcher*

Cuyahoga Falls
Black, Ross R., II, *family physician*

Dayton
Bienenfeld, David Gerald *physician*
Boyle, John Robert *internist*
Carmody, Thomas James *cardiologist*
†Crosby, Lynn A. *orthopaedic surgeon, educator*
Elliott, Daniel Whitacre *surgeon, retired educator*
Gillig, Paulette Marie *psychiatry educator, researcher*
†Heller, Abraham *psychiatrist, educator*
Hitch, David Charles *pediatric surgeon*
†Kay, Jerald *psychiatry educator, researcher*
Lee, Sung Ho *psychiatrist*
Lyman, John Leslie *emergency physician*
Mick, Thomas Charles *radiologist*
Mohler, Stanley Ross *physician, educator*
Monk, Susan Marie *physician, pediatrician*
Nanagas, Maria Teresita Cruz *pediatrician, educator*
Pflum, Barbara Ann *pediatric allergist*
Ruegsegger, Donald Ray, Jr., *radiological physicist, educator*
Weinberg, Sylvan Lee *cardiologist, educator, author, editor*
Wilson, William Campbell McFarland *gastroenterologist*

Defiance
Fout, Larry Roy *physician*

Delaware
Faerber, Abigail Hobbs *physician, farm manager*

Edgerton
Wu, Lawrence Mg Hla Myin *physician*

Euclid Ave
†Simpfendorfer, Conrad Carlos *cardiologist*

Fairview Park
Kothari, Purnima *obstetrician/gynecologist*

Gahanna
Robbins, Darryl Andrew *pediatrician*

Grove City
Kilman, James William *surgeon, educator*

Hamilton
Willke, Thomas John *family physician*

Hilliard
Skillman, Thomas Grant *endocrinology consultant, former educator*

Ironton
†Kadim, Satyanarayana Venkata *cardiologist*

Jefferson
Macklin, Martin Rodbell *psychiatrist*

Kent
Ference-Valenta, Mary Jean *osteopath, health facility administrator*

Lancaster
Woodward, James Kenneth *retired pharmacologist*

Lima
Becker, Dwight Lowell *physician*
Collins, William Thomas *retired pathologist*

Madison
Stafford, Arthur Charles *medical association administrator*

Mansfield
Adair, Charles Valloyd *retired physician*
Capaldo, Guy *obstetrician, gynecologist*
Houston, William Robert Montgomery *ophthalmic surgeon*
Shook, C. David *surgeon*
†Stretanski, Michael F. *neurologist, educator, rehabilitation services professional*

Mason
Beary, John Francis, III, *physician, scientist, pharmaceutical executive*
†Bhatia, Aneeta *cardiac anesthesiologist*
Meyer, Joan Marie *drug researcher*

Massillon
Dishong, Morris William *forensic investigator, nurse*

Medina
Surso, John Michael *physician*

Nelsonville
Davis, Mary W. Allen *medical secretary*

Newark
Pacht, Eric Reed *pulmonary and critical care physician*

North Canton
Di Simone, Robert Nicholas *radiologist, educator*

Norwalk
Gutowicz, Matthew Francis, Jr., *radiologist*
Holman, William Baker *surgeon, coroner*

Novelty
Gutierrez, Yezid *retired pathologist*

Oregon
†Byrne, Paul Adams *pediatrician, educator*

Parma
Lazo, John, Jr., *physician*
Saddleton, Michael John *emergency physician*

Portsmouth
Akhtar, Muhammad I. *neurologist, researcher*

Richfield
Pelagalli, James A. *surgeon*

Rootstown
Blacklow, Robert Stanley *internist, educator*
Brodell, Robert Thomas *internal medicine educator*
Gilchrist, Valerie Jean *medical educator*

Saint Clairsville
†Raymond, Bruce Allen *medical association administrator*

Saint Marys
Dallura, Sal Anthony *physician*

Sandusky
Mahmood, Khalid *physician*

Shaker Heights
†Richardson, Robert Frank, Jr., *neurologist*
White, Eugene A. *retired physician, neuroradiologist*

Springfield
Kurian, Pius *nephrologist, educator*
Wood, Dirk Gregory *surgeon, physician, forensic consultant*

Sylvania
Burkhart, Craig Garrett *dermatologist*

Toledo
Alexander, Kenneth Saul *pharmaceuticals educator*
Barrett, Michael John *anesthesiologist*
Cardwell, Michael Steven *physician, lawyer*
Comerota, Anthony James *vascular surgeon, biomedical researcher*
†Franco-Saenz, Roberto *physician*
†Georgiadis, Gregory Minas *orthopedist, educator*
Goodenday, Lucy Sherman *physician, educator*
Jauregui, Connie Lee *internist*
Jauregui, Luis Ernesto *physician, pharmacologist*
Jhunjhunwala, Jagadish S. *retired urologist*
Kimmel, Sanford Richard *family physician, pediatrician, educator*
Lynn, Christopher Kenneth *internist, educator*
Martin, John Thomas *physician, author, educator*
†Medhkour, Azedine *neurosurgeon, educator*
Mehelas, Thomas James *neuro-ophthalmologist, educator*
Mulrow, Patrick Joseph *medical educator*
Rejent, Marian Magdalen *retired pediatrician*
Shelley, E. Dorinda *dermatologist*
Shelley, Walter Brown *physician, educator*
Zrull, Joel Peter *psychiatry educator*

Troy
Savage, Joseph Scott *physician*
Williams, Craig Foster *osteopathic emergency physician*

WPAFB
Reston, Rocky Russell *anesthesiologist, engineer, educator*

West Chester
Loughman, Barbara Evers *immunologist researcher*

Westerville
Dawdy, W. David *pediatrician*

Westlake
†Nedorost, Susan Todd *dermatologist*
Noveske, Francis Gregory *psychiatrist*
Sheehan, John Patrick *endocrinologist, educator*

Willoughby
Carter, John Robert *physician*
†Combs, Steven Paul *orthopedic surgeon*
Pazirandeh, Mahmood *rheumatologist, consultant*
Thanos, Daniel *retired obstetrician-gynecologist*

Wooster
Kuffner, George Henry *dermatologist, educator*
Lun, Lapman *internist*
Tranovich, Mark *orthopedic surgeon*

Worthington
Winter, Chester Caldwell *physician, surgery educator, historian, writer*

Yellow Springs
Von Gierke, Henning Edgar *biomedical science educator, former government official, researcher*
Webb, Paul *physician, researcher, consultant, educator*

Youngstown
Buckley, John Joseph *obstetrician, gynecologist*
Walton, Ralph Gerald *psychiatrist, educator*

Zanesfield
Tetirick, Jack E. *retired surgeon*

Zanesville
Camma, Albert John *neurosurgeon*
Kopf, George Michael *retired ophthalmologist*
Ray, John Walker *otolaryngologist, educator, broadcast commentator*
Whitacre, Vicki Ann *medical association administrator, retired emergency physician*

OKLAHOMA

Ada
Mynatt, Cecil Ferrell *psychiatrist*

Altus
Rebik, James Michael *otolaryngologist*
Stine, Earle John, Jr., *radiologist*

Blackwell
Ghormley, Luther Wayne *surgeon*

Claremore
Whinery, Michael Albert *physician*

Jenks
Wootan, Gerald Don *osteopathic physician, educator*

Kingfisher
Buswell, Arthur Wilcox *physician, surgeon*

Lawton
Webb, O(rville) Lynn *physician, pharmacologist, educator*

Midwest City
Bogardus, Carl Robert, Jr., *radiologist, educator*

Muskogee
Kent, Bartis Milton *retired physician*

Norman
Berkowitz, Robert Ari *neurobiologist*
Cochran, Gloria Grimes *retired pediatrician*
Dille, John Robert *physician*

Oklahoma City
†Andrews, M. Dewayne *dean, internist, educator*
Bahr, Carman Bloedow *internist*
Blick, Kenneth Edward *clincial chemist, educator*
Bradford, Reagan Howard, Jr., *ophthalmology educator*
Brandt, Edward Newman, Jr., *physician, educator*
Claflin, James Robert *pediatrician, allergist*
Comp, Philip Cinnamon *medical researcher*
Couch, James Russell, Jr., *neurology educator*
Everett, Mark Allen *dermatologist, educator*
Filley, Warren Vernon *allergist, immunologist*
George, James Noel *hematologist, oncologist, educator*
Gilchrist, John Mark *otolaryngologist*
Halverstadt, Donald Bruce *urologist, educator*
Hampton, James Wilburn *hematologist, medical oncologist*
Haywood, B(etty) J(ean) *anesthesiologist*
Hough, Jack Van Doren *otologist*
Jacocks, Mac Alexander *surgeon*
Johnson, Thomas Harold *radiologist*
Kinasewitz, Gary Theodore *medical educator*
Lo, Patrick Punchuk *physician*
Moore, Joanne Iweita *pharmacologist, educator*
Muchmore, John Stephen *endocrinologist*
†Nath, Swapan K. *epidemiologist*
Nour, Bakr M. *surgeon, health facility administrator*
Oehlert, William Herbert, Jr., *cardiologist, administrator, educator*
Pardo, Gabriel *neuro-ophthalmologist, neurologist, researcher*
Parke, David Wilkin, II, *ophthalmologist, educator, healthcare executive*
Perez-Cruet, Jorge *physician, psychopharmacologist, psychophysiologist, psychiatrist, educator, addictionologist, geropsychiatrist*
Pfefferbaum, Betty Jane
†Prodan, Calin Ioan *physician*
Rahhal, Donald K. *obstetrician, gynecologist*
Rix, Robert Alvin, Jr., *retired neurosurgeon*
Rossavik, Ivar Kristian *obstetrician, gynecologist*
†Scofield, Robert Hal *physician, biomedical researcher*
Thadani, Udho *physician, cardiologist*
Tucker, Phebe Mary *psychiatrist, educator*
Turman, Martin Allan *pediatric nephrologist, educator*
Wisdom, Peggy Jean *neurologist*
Wolraich, Mark Lee *pediatrician, educator*
Worsham, Bertrand Ray *psychiatrist*
Zuhdi, Nazih *former surgeon, administrator*

Owasso
Reed, Walter George, Jr., *osteopathic physician*

Stillwater
Cooper, Donald Lee *physician*

Tulsa
Bogomilov, Boris *medical educator*
Brunk, Samuel Frederick *oncologist*
Calvert, Jon Channing *family practice physician*
Coffey, Robert John *pediatrician*
de Leon, Antonio Carmelo, Jr., *internist, cardiologist*
Franken, Joy R. *exercise physiologist*
Friedman, Mark Joel *cardiologist, educator*
Kalbfleisch, John McDowell *cardiologist, educator*
Kramer, John C. *pediatrician*
Liebendorfer, Richard Arthur *internist*
Lindsay, Patricia Mae *physician, medical administrator*
Martin, Edward Thomas *cardiologist, researcher*
McCullough, Robert Dale, II, *osteopath*
Miller, Gerald Cecil *immunologist, laboratory administrator, educator*
Nettles, John Barnwell *obstetrics and gynecology educator*
Nevinny-Stickel, Hans Boris *oncologist*
Okada, Robert Dean *cardiologist*
Perryman, Robert G. *surgeon*
Plunket, Daniel Clark *retired pediatrician*
†Rayborn, M. Yvonne *physician*
Say, Burhan *physician*
Sheehan, William W. *pathologist*
Stearns, Frederic William *dermatologist*
Watson, John Skelly *retired surgeon*

Vinita
Neer, Charles Sumner, II, *orthopedic surgeon, educator*

Weatherford
Pray, Walter Steven *pharmacy educator*
Wolgamott, Gary Dean *medical educator*

OREGON

Ashland
Kirschner, Richard Michael *naturopathic physician, speaker, writer*

Beaverton
†Austin, Glenn *retired pediatrician, medical researcher*

Bend
Brundage, Bruce Howard *cardiologist*

Corvallis
Frey, Bruce E. *radiation oncologist*
Hafner-Eaton, Chris *health services researcher, medical educator, policy analyst*
Steele, Robert Edwin *orthopedic surgeon*

Dundee
Olson, Donald R. *neurosurgeon, consultant*

Eugene
†Christie, Leonard George, Jr., *cardiologist, public health service officer*
†Collis, Dennis K. *orthopedic surgeon*
Flanagan, Latham, Jr., *surgeon*
Johnston, James C. *neurologist, lawyer*
Loescher, Richard Alvin *gastroenterologist*
Roe, Thomas Leroy Willis *pediatrician*
Schroeder, Donald J. *orthopedic surgeon*

Klamath Falls
Bohnen, Robert Frank *hematologist, oncologist, educator*

Medford
Shekhar, Stephen S. *obstetrician, gynecologist*

Milwaukie
Sklovsky, Robert Joel *naturopathic physician, pharmacist, educator*

Newport
Allen, Delmas James *anatomist, educator, university administrator*

Ontario
Tyler, Donald Earl *urologist*

Oregon City
Burke, William Romney *urologist*

Portland
Baker, Diane R.H. *dermatologist*
Bardana, Emil John, Jr., *allergist, immunologist, internist*
Barker, Alan Freund *internist*
†Barkhuizen, Andre *academic rheumatologist*
Barry, John Maynard *urologist*
Bennett, William Michael *internist, nephrologist, educator*
Benson, John Alexander, Jr., *physician, educator*
Berthelsdorf, Siegfried *psychiatrist*
†Biagioli, Frances Emily *physician*
†Blank, Eugene *pediatrician, radiologist, educator*
Burris, Terry Eugene *ophthalmologist, corneal specialist*
Campbell, John Richard *pediatric surgeon*
Cockrell, Janice Louise *pediatric physiatrist*
Connor, William Elliott *physician, educator*
Crawshaw, Ralph *psychiatrist*
Fraunfelder, Frederick Theodore *ophthalmologist, educator*
Glass, Laurel Ellen *gerontologist, developmental biologist, physician, retired educator*
Guderian, Ronald Howard *pathologist*
Hagmeier, Clarence Howard *retired anesthesiologist*
Hansen, Thomas Edward *physician, educator*
Hutchens, Tyra Thornton *physician, educator*
Jacob, Stanley Wallace *surgeon, educator*
Jene, Joanne *anesthesiologist*
Julien, Robert Michael *anesthesiologist, writer*
Kendall, John Walker, Jr., *medical educator, researcher, university dean*
Kohl, Steve *pediatrician, infectious disease physician*
Kohler, Peter Ogden *physician, educator, university president*
MacArthur, Carol Jeanne *pediatric otolaryngology educator*
†Matejuk, Agata *immunologist*
†McFarland, Bentson H. *physician, researcher*
Mozena, John Daniel *podiatrist*
Nesbit, Gary Merlin *neuroradiologist, educator*
Nguyen, Ngan-Lien Thi *internist, surgeon*
Norman, Douglas James *physician*
Osterud, Harold Truman *public health and preventive medicine physician, researcher*
Palmer, Earl A. *ophthalmologist, educator*
Patterson, James Randolph *physician*
†Pentecost, Jeffrey Owen *geriatrician, consultant, physician, researcher*
Prendergast, William John *ophthalmologist*
Richardson, Mark A. *otolaryngologist*

Robertson, Joseph E., Jr., *ophthalmologist, educator*
†Rosenberg, Kenneth David *epidemiologist*
Schmidt, Waldemar Adrian *pathologist, educator*
†Schreiber, Martin Allan *surgeon*
Schwartz, Martin Lerner *physician*
†Scott, John D. *pharmacologist*
†Sells, Clifford Wayne *pediatrician*
†Smith, Dennis B. *neurologist, educator*
†Spackman, Kent Alan *pathologist, educator*
Sutherland, Donald Wood *cardiologist*
Swan, Kenneth Carl *surgeon*
Taylor, Robert Brown *medical educator*
†Tegtmeyer, Kenneth Bren *pediatrician, educator*
†Terry, Mark A. *ophthalmologist, surgeon*
†Tiffany, Natasha Marie *hematologist, researcher, oncologist*
Tolle, Susan W. *internist, educator, educational administrator*
†Ulmer, Todd *orthopedic surgeon*
†Vernon, Jack Allen *otolaryngology educator, laboratory administrator*
†Weleber, Richard Gordon *ophthalmologist, geneticist, medical educator, researcher*
†Zerbe, Kathryn Jane *psychiatrist*
Zerzan, Charles Joseph, Jr., *retired gastroenterologist*
Zimmerman, Gail Marie *medical foundation executive*

Roseburg
Oleskowicz, Jeanette *physician*
Oliphant, Charles Romig *retired physician*

Wilsonville
Bernard, Richard Montgomery *retired physician*
Johnson, Martin Clifton *physician*

PENNSYLVANIA

Abington
Eskin, David J. *cardiologist*
Redmond, John *oncologist*

Allentown
Barrett, Stephen *psychiatrist, educator, consultant*
Gaylor, Donald Hughes *surgeon, educator*
Hess, Leonard Wayne *obstetrician gynecologist, perinatologist*
Khubchandani, Indru Tekchand *colon and rectal surgeon*
Lester, Mark Charles *neurosurgeon*
Maffeo, Alphonse A. *anesthesiologist*
Werhun, Anthony T. *emergency medicine physician, educator*

Allison Park
Hollerman, Charles Edward *retired pediatrician*

Altoona
Fochler, Francis John *surgeon*

Ambridge
Karp, Michael Alan *physician*

Ardmore
Goodrich, Edward Olin *surgeon, educator*

Bakerstown
Beachley, Michael Charles *radiologist*

Bala Cynwyd
Burland, J(ohn) Alexis *psychoanalyst*
Kirschner, Ronald Allen *osteopathic plastic surgeon, otolaryngologist, educator*
Masket, Samuel *medical association administrator*
Tse, Rose Lou *physician, educator*

Bangor
Wolf, Stewart George, Jr., *physician, medical educator*

Beaver
Vasilakis, Alexander *cardiothoracic surgeon*

Bensalem
Lawson-Ndu, Ovunda A. *emergency physician, surgeon*

Bethlehem
Benz, Edward John, Sr., *clinical pathologist*
Chang, Chris C.N. *physician, pediatric surgeon*
Cole, Jack Eli *physician*
Rosenfeld, Joel Charles *surgeon*
Traupman, Arnold Frank *ophthalmologist, educator*

Blairsville
McGaughran, Alan L. *family physician*

Bloomsburg
Avenia, Ronald Joseph *ophthalmologist*

Bradford
Laroche, Roger Renan *psychiatrist*

Bryn Mawr
Bernstein, Guy Thomas *physician, urological surgeon*
Graham, Thomas Hild *neurologist*
Huth, Edward Janavel *physician, editor*
Levitt, Robert E. *gastroenterologist*
McGinnis, David Earl *urologist, educator*
Noone, R. Barrett *plastic surgeon*
Price, Trevor Robert Pryce *psychiatrist, educator*

Butler
Baker, Marvin Palange *cardiologist, internist*

Camp Hill
Brouse, John S. *medical association administrator*
Haidet, Keith R. *radiologist*

Swamidoss, Stephenson *pathologist, health facility administrator*
Tokuhata, George K. *retired medical educator, epidemiologist, consultant*
Yates, James Arthur *plastic surgeon*

Carnegie
Tenicela, Ruben Antialon *anesthesiologist*

Cecil
Keddie, Roland Thomas *physician, hospital administrator, lawyer*

Chester
Schulman, Elliott A. *neurologist, educator, researcher*

Chester Springs
Scheer, R. Scott *physician*

Clifton Heights
Domingo, Orville Harold *surgeon*

Coatesville
Ainslie, George William *psychiatrist, behavioral economist*
Bell, Robert Lloyd *retired neurosurgeon*
Budeir, Mohammed Hassan *surgeon*
†Zarychta, William Alex *emergency physician*

Collegeville
Malinoski, Frank Joseph *general practice physician*
Trott, Edward Ashley *reproductive endocrinologist*
Zhou, Honghui *clinical pharmacokineticist*

Conshohocken
Jacoby, Richard Allen *pathologist, dermatologist*
Johnson, Waine Cecil *dermatologist*

Cranberry Township
Hadidian, Calvin Y. *retired surgeon*
Moore, John Francis *emergency physician*
Walsh, Arthur Campbell *retired psychiatrist*

Danville
Albertini, Robert Elmer *medical executive, physician, consultant*
Bakri, Younes Noaman *surgeon, oncologist, gynecologist*
Bisordi, Joseph Edmund *nephrologist, medical center administrator*
Burns, J. Robert *physician*
Cochran, William John *physician, pediatrician, gastroenterologist, nutritionist, consultant*
Franklin, David Perdue *vascular surgeon, educator*
Makary, Adel Zaki *hematologist*
†Mirza, Mohd Ayoub *internist, researcher*
Pierce, James Clarence *surgeon, educator*
Steele, Glenn Daniel, Jr., *oncologist, healthcare system executive*
Strodel, William Edward *surgeon, medical educator*

Dillsburg
Jackson, George Lyman *retired nuclear medicine physician*

Downingtown
Bahal, Vishal *cardiologist*
Kelly, Edward Aloysius, Jr., *physician*
Newman, Richard August *psychiatrist, educator*

Doylestown
McGarvey, Joseph F. X., Sr., *cardiologist*

Drexel Hill
Malin, Seth Arnold *surgeon, educator*

Dunmore
Sebastianelli, Mario Joseph *internist, nephrologist, health services administrator*

East Berlin
Greer, Robert Bruce, III, *retired orthopedic surgeon, educator*

Easton
Grunberg, Robert Leon Willy *nephrologist, educator*

Elkins Park
Glijansky, Alex *psychiatrist, psychoanalyst*
Siegel, Seymour *retired internist*
Yun, Daniel Duwhan *physician, foundation administrator*

Ephrata
Wolbach, Albert Bogh, Jr., *family practice physician*

Erie
Brunner-Martinez, Kirstin Ellen *pediatrician, psychiatrist*
Haeseler, Carl William *pomology and viticulture educator*
Kish, George Franklin *thoracic and cardiovascular surgeon*
†Long, Richard William *cardiothoracic surgeon*
Mason, Gregg Claude *orthopedic surgeon, researcher*
Michaelides, Doros Nikita *internist, medical educator*
Pett, Stephen Donohoe *cardiovascular surgeon*
Reitz, Mary Ellen *pathologist, health facility administrator*

Fayetteville
Blewitt, George Augustine *physician, consultant*

Flourtown
Brown, Melissa M. *ophthalmologist*

Fort Washington
Pappas, Charles Engelos *plastic surgeon*

Foxburg
Piroch, Joseph Gregory *retired internist, cardiologist*

Franklin
Suk, Jin Hong *pathologist*

Gaines
Beller, Martin Leonard *retired orthopaedic surgeon*

Gettysburg
†Viswanathan, Byravan *retired physician*

Gibsonia
Cauna, Nikolajs *physician, medical educator, scientist*

Gladwyne
Gonick, Paul *retired urologist*
Kaye, Donald *physician, educator*

Glenside
Reiss, George Russell, Jr., *physician*

Greensburg
Catalano, Louis William, Jr., *neurologist*

Hallstead
Remakus, Bernard Leo *physician, medical journalist, author, educator*

Hanover
Howard, Thomas K. *surgeon*
Thomas, Charles Edmund *anesthesiologist, health facility administrator*

Harrisburg
Cadieux, Roger Joseph *physician, mental health care executive*
Chernicoff, David Paul *osteopathic physician, educator*
Jeffries, Richard Haley *physician, broadcasting company executive*
Jones, David John, III, *preventive medicine physician, medical executive*
Logue, James Nicholas *epidemiologist*
Potok, Julian Walter *pathologist*
Rudy, Frank R. *pathologist*
Trautlein, Joseph J. *medical administrator*

Haverford
Aronson, Carl Edward *pharmacology and toxicology educator*
Goppelt, John Walter *physician, psychiatrist*
Rosefsky, Jonathan Benensohn *pediatrician*
Shenkin, Henry Arnold *retired neurosurgeon*

Havertown
Korényi-Both, András Levente *pathologist, educator*

Hazleton
Pascucci, Mary Frances *pathologist*

Hershey
Ballard, James Otis, III, *medical educator, physician*
Berlin, Cheston Milton, Jr., *pediatrician, educator*
Botti, John Joseph *obstetrician-gynecologist*
Burkhart, Keith Karl *emergency medicine physician, medical toxicologist*
Caputo, Gregory Michael *physician, educator*
Davis, Dwight *cardiologist, educator*
Dias, Mark Steven *neurosurgeon*
Domen, Ronald Eugene *physician*
Eyster, Mary Elaine *hematologist, educator*
†Field, John McCabe *medical educator*
Gabbay, Robert Abraham *physician, educator*
Geder, Laszlo *neurologist, educator*
Hammond, James M. *endocrinologist*
†Kees-Folts, Deborah *pediatrician, educator*
Leaman, David Martin *cardiologist, educator*
Leaman, Thomas Leed *medical educator*
Marks, James Garfield, Jr., *dermatologist*
Marshall, Wayne Keith *anesthesiology educator*
McLoughlin, Lucille C. *physician*
Naeye, Richard L. *pathologist, educator*
†Naides, Stanley J. *physician, educator, researcher*
Ouyang, Ann *physician, researcher, educator*
Pierce, William Schuler *cardiac surgeon*
Rohner, Thomas John, Jr., *urologist*
Severs, Walter Bruce *pharmacology educator, researcher*
Tan, Tjiauw-Ling *psychiatrist, educator*
Undar, Akif
Vesell, Elliot Saul *pharmacologist, educator*
Waldhausen, John Anton *retired surgeon, editor*
Wassner, Steven Joel *pediatric nephrologist, educator*
Zelis, Robert Felix *cardiologist, educator*

Hollidaysburg
†Cottle, Harold Ranson *pathologist, laboratory owner*
Mariano, Ana Virginia *retired pathologist*

Huntingdon
Schock, William Wallace *pediatrician*

Huntingdon Valley
Lefton, Harvey Bennett *gastroenterologist, educator, author*

Irwin
Brown, Donald Clyde *surgeon*

Jenkintown
Fisher, Joseph Saul *endocrinologist, consultant*
Greenspan-Margolis, June E. *psychiatrist*
Sadoff, Robert Leslie *psychiatrist, educator*

Johnstown
Green, James Matthew *anesthesiologist*
McNiesh, Lawrence Melvin *radiologist*

Kennett Square
Harrington, Anne Wilson *medical librarian*

King Of Prussia
Sidor, Michael Louis *orthopedic surgeon*

Kingston
Denaro, Anthony Thomas *psychiatrist*

Lancaster
Brod, Roy David *ophthalmologist, educator*
Kendall, Leigh Wakefield *surgeon*
Rung, George W. *physician*

Lansdale
Alpert, Marc H. *surgeon*
Sag, Jerome E. *internist*
Schwartz, Louis Winn *ophthalmologist*

Lemoyne
Klein, Michael Elihu *physician*

Lititz
Mershon, Charles Richard *family physician*

Lower Gwynedd
Pendleton, Robert Grubb *pharmacologist*

Malvern
Berkwits, Leland *physical medicine and rehabilitation physician*
Rucker, Donald W. *emergency physician, educator, consultant*

Mc Murray
Diamond, Daniel Lloyd *surgeon*

Mechanicsburg
Ostdahl, Roger Harold *neurological surgeon*

Media
Cook, Joseph V. *physician*
Kessler, Woodrow Bertram *family practice physician, geriatrician, educator*

Merion Station
Lewis, Paul Le Roy *pathology educator*
Schick, Paul K. *hematologist*

Mill Hall
Greenberg, Michael Richard *family practice physician*

Mohnton
Hildreth, Eugene A. *physician, educator*

Monongahela
Brandon, John Mitchell *physician*
†Yovanof, Silvana *physician*

Mount Gretna
Pakola, Richard Stephen *psychiatrist*

Mount Pleasant
Domit, John *surgeon*

Narberth
Chait, Arnold *retired radiologist*
Comer, Nathan Lawrence *psychiatrist, educator*
Strom, Brian Leslie *internist, educator*

New Hope
Raabe, Gerhard Karl *epidemiologist*

New Tripoli
Hess, Darla Bakersmith *cardiologist, educator*

Newtown
Somers, Anne Ramsay *retired medical educator*

Newtown Square
de Rivas, Carmela Foderaro *psychiatrist, hospital administrator*
Lawrence, Theodore *physician*

Norristown
Becker, Michael Anthony *osteopathic family physician, educator*
Colcher, Robert Ely *surgeon*
Garabedian, Joseph Andre *physician*
Kofsky, Phillip Mark *surgeon*
Tornetta, Frank Joseph *anesthesiologist, educator, consultant*

Oil City
Kumar, Harinath V. *urologist, surgeon*

Olyphant
Batzel, Edward Lee *surgeon*

Orwigsburg
Garloff, Samuel John *psychiatrist*

Paoli
†Glassner, Michael J. *obstetrician, gynecologist*
Lanza, Ralph Andrew *internist*
Scovill, Curtis Neal *physician*

Paradise
Eshleman, Silas Kendrick, III, *retired psychiatrist*

Pennsburg
Shuhler, Phyllis Marie *physician*

Philadelphia
Abrutyn, Elias *infectious diseases physician, administrator*
Ahima, Rexford Sefah *neuroendocrinologist, internist*
Allen, Julian Lewis *medical educator, researcher*
Arce, A. Anthony *psychiatrist, educator*
Asbury, Arthur Knight *neurologist, educator*
Augoustides, John George Themistocles *cardiothoracic anesthesiologist, educator*
Austrian, Robert *physician, educator, department chairman*

PROFESSIONAL INDEX 6425 HEALTHCARE: MEDICINE

†Baltuch, Gordon Hirsh *neurosurgeon*
Barchi, Robert Lawrence *clinical neurologist, neuroscientist, educator*
Barker, Clyde Frederick *surgeon, educator*
Baum, Stanley *radiologist, educator*
Baxt, William Gordon *medical educator*
Bearn, Alexander Gordon *physician, retired pharmaceutical executive*
†Beck, Aaron Temkin *psychiatrist, educator*
Beck, John Robert *pathologist, information scientist*
Bibbo, Marluce *physician, educator*
Bleshman, Michael Henry *radiologist*
Boden, Guenther *endocrinologist*
Bove, Alfred Anthony *medical educator*
Bowman, Marjorie Ann *family practice physician, educator*
Brady, Luther W., Jr., *physician, radiation oncology educator*
Brighton, Carl Theodore *orthopedic surgery educator*
Brodkin, Edward Stuart *psychiatrist, geneticist*
Broennle, A. Michael *anesthesiologist*
Brooks, John Samuel Joseph *pathologist, researcher*
†Brooks-Kayal, Amy R. *pediatrician, researcher, neurologist*
Capizzi, Robert Lawrence *physician*
Cassel, Christine Karen *physician*
Chen, Sow-Yeh *pathology educator*
Clark, Christopher Michael *neurologist, educator, clinic director*
Clarke, John Rodney *surgeon*
†Claudio, Pier Paolo *surgeon, researcher*
Clearfield, Harris Reynold *physician*
Colman, Robert Wolf *physician, medical educator, researcher*
Conn, Rex Boland, Jr., *physician, educator*
Cooper, Edward Sawyer *cardiologist, internist, educator*
Cortner, Jean Alexander *retired physician, educator*
Cotler, Jerome Marvin *orthopaedic surgeon*
Dalinka, Murray Kenneth *radiologist, educator*
D'Angio, Giulio John *radiologist, educator*
Dasgupta, Indranil *physician, educator*
Deforest, Adamadia *pediatric virologist*
DeHoratius, Raphael Joseph *rheumatologist*
Dinoso, Vicente Pescador, Jr., *physician, educator*
DiPalma, Joseph Rupert *pharmacology educator*
Djerassi, Isaac *physician, medical researcher*
Dormans, John Paul *surgeon, educator*
Doty, Richard L. *medical researcher*
Downey, Michael S. *physician, podiatrist*
Duker, Nahum Johanan *pathologist, educator*
Dunkman, W(illiam) Bruce *physician, educator*
Ehrlich, George Edward *rheumatologist, international pharmaceutical consultant*
Eisen, Howard Joel *physician, researcher*
Eisenberg, Burton L. *surgeon*
Eisenberg, Ted Steven *plastic and reconstructive surgeon*
†Emerson, Stephen G. *hematologist, educator, oncologist*
Eskin, Bernard Abraham *obstetrics and gynecology educator, medical researcher*
Esterhai, John Louis, Jr., *surgeon, medical educator*
Feinsmith, Norman *cardiovascular disease physician*
Feldman, Arthur M. *cardiologist*
Feldman, Michael Saul *cardiologist, educator*
Ferniany, Isaac William *health system administrator*
†Ferrari, Victor Alfred *cardiologist*
Fiel, Stanley Bruce *internist, pulmonogist, educator, researcher*
Fisher, Robert *gastroenterologist, health facility administrator*
Fishman, Alfred Paul *physician*
Fraker, Douglas L. *oncologist, endocrinologist, surgeon, educator*
†Frank, Arthur Leonard *physician, educator*
†Frank, Barbara Balis *gastroenterologist, educator*
Frank, Leonard Arnold *physician*
Freese, Andrew *neurosurgeon, educator, scientist*
French, Jacqueline A. *neurologist, educator*
Friedman, Harvey Michael *infectious diseases educator*
Gabrielson, Ira Wilson *physician, educator*
García, Celso-Ramón *obstetrician, gynecologist, educator*
Gardner, Timothy Joseph *surgeon, educator*
Gartland, John Joseph *physician, writer*
†Gelfand, Joel Mitchell *dermatologist, researcher*
Gerner, Edward William *medical educator*
Glick, Jane Mills *biomedical researcher, educator*
Glick, John H. *oncologist, medical educator*
Goldberg, Martin *physician, educator*
Goldstein, Martin Barnet *osteopathic physician, psychiatrist*
Gonzalez-Scarano, Francisco Antonio *neurologist, virologist*
Gozum, Marvin Enriquez *internist*
Graziani, Leonard Joseph *pediatric neurologist, researcher*
Greenspon, Arnold Jack *cardiologist, cardiac electrophysiologist*
Greenstein, Jeffrey Ian *neurologist*
†Grimberg, Adda *pediatrician*
†Grossman, Murray *neurologist*
Gueson, Emerita Torres *obstetrician, gynecologist*
†Gulati, Gene L. *hematologist, educator, consultant*
†Guo, Ping *cancer researcher*
Hallock, James Anthony *pediatrician, health facility administrator*
Hansen-Flaschen, John Hyman *medical educator, researcher*
†hanson, C. William, III, *anesthesiologist, educator*
Hargrove, Walter Clark, III, *cardiothoracic surgeon*
Hasan, Nasir *internist*
Haugaard, Niels *pharmacologist, educator*
Hava, Milos *retired pharmacologist, medical educator*
Heffler, Karen Frankel *ophthalmology educator*
Heitz, James W. *anesthesiologist, internist*
Hernandez, Enrique *gynecologist, educator*
Hillman, Alan L. *internist, educator, researcher*
Holzbaur, Erika L. *medical educator*
Honig, Paul J. *pediatrician, educator*
†Hosalkar, Harish Sadanand *pediatrician, orthopedist, surgeon, consultant*
Ice, Susan M. *psychiatrist*
Jackson, Laird Gray *physician, educator*
Jacobs, Eugene Gardner, Jr., *psychiatrist, psychotherapist, educator*
Jensh, Ronald Paul *anatomist, educator*
Jimbo, Masahito *medical educator*
Jimenez, Sergio A. *internist, science educator, rheumatologist*
Kahn, Sandra J. *anesthesiologist*
†Kaiser, Larry Robert *thoracic surgeon*
Kaji, Hideko *pharmacology educator*
Kang, Yoogoo *anesthesiologist, educator*
†Kashem, M. Abul *medical researcher*
Katz, Julian *gastroenterologist, educator*
Kaufman, Russel Eugene *hematologist, oncologist*
Kaye, Robert *pediatrics educator*
Kazazian, Haig Hagop, Jr., *medical scientist, physician, educator*
Kefalides, Nicholas Alexander *physician, educator*
Kelley, William Nimmons *physician, educator, science administrator, dean*
Kennedy, David William *otolaryngologist, educator*
†Kim, Kwan Eun *nephrologist, educator*
Kimball, Harry Raymond *medical association executive, educator*
Klein-Szanto, Andres J. P. *pathologist*
Kligerman, Morton M. *radiologist*
Klinghoffer, June Florence *physician, educator*
Kolansky, Daniel M. *cardiologist*
†Kolecki, Paul Francis *emergency physician*
Korevaar, Wilhelmina C. *anesthesiologist*
Kosa, Namir Bahjat *physician*
†Kresh, J. Yasha *cardiovascular researcher, educator*
Kurtz, Alfred Bernard *radiologist*
†Kussmaul, William Guy, III, *cardiologist*
Langer, Corey Jay *oncologist*
Le Roux, Peter David *neurosurgeon*
Leventhal, Lawrence Jay *rheumatologist, educator*
Levin, Ronald Mitchell *geriatrician*
Levinson, Arnold Irving *allergist, immunologist*
Levit, Edithe Judith *physician, medical association administrator*
Levitt, Jerry David *medical educator*
Lewis, Frank Russell, Jr., *surgeon*
Li, Weiye *ophthalmologist, biochemist, educator*
Lippa, Carol Frances *neurologist*
†Lipshutz, Laurel Sprung *psychiatrist*
Long, Sarah Sundborg *pediatrician, educator*
Longnecker, David Eugene *anesthesiologist, educator*
Lotke, Paul A. *orthopedic surgeon*
Lubiniecki, Gregory Michael *physician*
Lustig, Robert Allan *radiation oncologist*
Luthra, Veena *psychiatrist*
Ma, Xin-Liang *biomedical researcher, educator*
Madow, Leo *psychiatrist, educator*
Makous, Norman *internist, cardiologist, educator*
Malkowicz, Stanley Bruce *urologist*
Malmud, Leon Samuel *nuclear medicine physician, health facility administrator*
Mancall, Elliott Lee *neurologist, educator*
Manon-Espaillat, Ramon *physician, educator*
Marcotte, Paul John *neurosurgeon, educator*
Margo, Katherine Lane *family physician, educator*
Marino, Ignazio Roberto *transplant surgeon, educator, researcher*
Mastroianni, Luigi, Jr., *physician, educator*
Mayock, Robert Lee *internist*
McClurken, James Bartholomew *surgeon*
Miyamoto, Curtis Trent *medical educator*
†Monos, Dimitrios *medical educator, researcher*
Most-Levin, Carol Lynn *physician, geriatrician*
Movsas, Benjamin *radiation oncologist, researcher*
Mulholland, S. Grant *urologist*
Myers, Allen Richard *rheumatologist*
†Neill, Richard Alan *medical educator, director*
Newberg, Aaron Nelson *physician, pediatrician*
Nimoityn, Philip *cardiologist*
Norris, Charles Morgan *laryngologist, educator*
Nowell, Peter Carey *pathologist, educator*
†O'Brien, Charles P. *psychiatrist, educator*
Olenginski, Jan Anthony *surgeon*
Owens, Gary Mitchell *family physician*
†Pahlavan, Pantea *obstetrician, gynecologist*
Pawlowski, Nicholas Alexander *pediatrician, allergist*
Permut, Stephen Robert *physician, lawyer*
Platsoucas, Chris Dimitrios *immunologist*
Potsic, William Paul *physician, educator*
Pugliese, Maria Alessandra *psychiatrist*
Pyeritz, Reed Edwin *medical geneticist, educator, research director*
Rabinowitz, Howard K. *physician, educator*
†Randall, Peter *plastic surgeon*
Reinecke, Robert Dale *ophthalmologist*
Rickels, Karl *psychiatrist, physician, educator*
†Rickels, Michael Roehrhoff *physician*
Ritchie, Wallace Parks, Jr., *retired surgeon, educator*
Rogers, Fred Baker *medical educator*
Rorke, Lucy Balian *neuropathologist*
Rosen, Rhoda *obstetrician, gynecologist*
Ross, Leonard Lester *anatomist, educator*
Rubin, Emanuel *pathologist, educator*
Rubin, Stephen Curtis *gynecologic oncologist, educator*
†Rudley, Lloyd Dave *psychiatrist*
Russo, Irma Haydee Alvarez de *pathologist*
Rutman, Robert Jesse *bioscience researcher*
Savage, Michael Paul *medicine educator, interventional cardiologist*
Scanlin, Thomas F. *pediatrician, researcher*
Schidlow, Daniel *pediatrician, medical association administrator*
Schimmer, Barry Michael *rheumatologist*
Schless, Guy Lacy *endocrinologist*
Schotland, Donald Lewis *retired medical educator, neurologist*
Schumacher, H(arry) Ralph *internist, rheumatologist, medical educator, researcher*
Schwartz, Gordon Francis *surgeon, educator*
Segal, Bernard Louis *physician, educator*
†Sewell, Catherine Angela *obstetrician, gynecologist*
Shapiro, Sandor Solomon *hematologist*
†Shore, Eric Eugene *internist, consultant, lawyer*
Silberberg, Donald H. *neurologist*
Silberman, Edward Kenneth *physician, educator*
Slap, Joseph William *psychiatrist*
†Slipman, Curtis W. *rehabilitation medicine physician*
Smith, David Stuart *anesthesiology educator, physician*
Sox, Harold Carleton, Jr., *physician, educator, editor*
Spaeth, George Link *physician, ophthalmology educator, writer, educator*
Steinberg, Marvin Edward *orthopaedic surgeon, educator*
Stinnett, James LeBaron *psychiatrist*
Strauss, Jerome Frank, III, *physician, educator*
Stunkard, Albert James *psychiatrist, educator*
Sudak, Howard Stanley *physician, psychiatry educator*
Talerman, Aleksander *pathologist, educator*
†Tasman, William Samuel *ophthalmologist, medical association executive*
Taylor, Susan C. *dermatologist*
Tom, Lawrence Wah-Chan *pediatric otolaryngologist*
Torg, Joseph Steven *orthopaedic surgeon, educator*
Tourtellotte, Charles Dee *physician, educator*
Truant, Allan L. *medical educator, research scientist, health science association administrator*
†Tunkel, Allan Robert *infectious diseases physician, internist, educator*
Tyler, Donald Charles *anesthesiologist*
Unger, Michael *physician, researcher, educator*
†Vaccaro, Alexander R. *orthopedist*
Van Arsdalen, Keith Norman *urologist*
Van Decker, William Arthur *cardiologist*
Varlotta, Laurie *pediatrician, pediatric pulmonologist*
Walinsky, Paul *cardiology educator*
Walker, Manuel Lorenzo *physician*
†Walsh, Peter Newton *physician, researcher*
Wang, Yen *nuclear medicine physician, radiologist*
Webber, John Bentley *orthopedic surgeon*
Wein, Alan Jerome *urologist, educator, researcher*
Weller, Elizabeth Boghossian *child and adolescent psychiatrist*
Werth, Victoria Patricia *dermatologist, educator*
Whitaker, Linton Andin *plastic surgeon*
Wilensky, Robert L. *cardiologist, educator*
Wivel, Nelson Auburn *physician, medical researcher, educator*
Xiao, Ying *medical physicist, researcher, educator*
Yanoff, Myron *ophthalmologist*
Young, Donald Stirling *clinical pathology educator*
Yunginger, John W. *allergist*
Zorowitz, Richard David *physiatrics educator*

Pittsburgh
Adebimpe, Victor Rotimi *psychiatrist*
Adibi, Siamak A. *medical researcher*
Allen, Thomas E. *obstetrician, gynecologist*
Alper, Cuneyt M. *pediatric otolaryngologist*
Bellinger, Mark Frederick *urology educator*
†Busquets, Miguel Antonio *ophthalmologist*
Caritis, Steve Nick *obstetrician, gynecologist, educator*
Chengappa, Roy K. N. *psychiatrist, educator*
Contractor, Farhad M. *diagnostic radiologist, educator*
Cooper, William Marion *physician*
†Craig, Fiona Elizabeth *pathologist*
Cutler, John Charles *physician, educator*
Dameshek, H(arold) Lee *physician*
deGroat, William Chesney *pharmacology educator*
DeKosky, Steven Trent *neurologist*
Detre, Thomas *psychiatrist, educator*
Dixit, Balwant Narayan *pharmacology and toxicology educator*
Doft, Bernard Harvey *ophthalmologist*
Doria, Cataldo *transplant surgeon*
Einhorn, Jerzy *internist, endocrinologist, consultant*
†Fabrega, Horacio, Jr., *psychiatry and anthropology educator*
Finegold, David Neal *medical educator*
Fireman, Philip *pediatrician, allergist, immunologist, medical association executive*
Fisher, Bernard *surgeon, educator*
Fisher, Edwin R. *pathologist*
Fontes, Paulo A. *surgeon, educator*
Frank, Ellen *medical educator, psychiatrist, psychologist, researcher*
Frezza, Ermenegildo Eldo *physician, surgeon*
Friday, Gilbert Anthony, Jr., *pediatrician*
Goldstein, David Meyer *physician*
Gordon, Murray Bruce *endocrinologist*
Hardesty, Lara Ann *radiology educator*
Heckler, Frederick Roger *plastic surgeon*
†Himmelhoch, Jonathan M. *psychiatrist, educator*
Jannetta, Peter Joseph *neurosurgeon, educator*
Janosko, Rudolph E. M. *psychiatrist*
Johnson, Jonas Talmadge *otolaryngologist, educator*
Joyner, Claude Reuben, Jr., *physician, medical educator*
Kalnicki, Shalom *radiologist, educator*
Karol, Meryl Helene *medical educator, researcher*
Khurana, Ramesh Chander *physician, nutritionist, educator*
Kochanek, Patrick Michael *pediatrician, educator*
Kondziolka, Douglas *neurosurgeon*
Korytkowksi, Mary T. *physician*
Krause, Helen Fox *physician, otolaryngologist*
Ku, Andrew *interventional neuroradiologist*
†Kuddus, Ruhul Haque *medical educator*
†Kum-Nji, Philip *pediatrician, educator*
Kupfer, David J. *psychiatry educator*
†Lasorda, David Michael *cardiologist*
Lega, Mark *internist, pulmonologist*
Levine, Arthur Samuel *dean, physician, scientist*
Levine, Macy Irving *physician*
Lewis, Jessica Helen (Mrs. Jack D. Myers) *physician, educator*
†Lotze, Michael T. *immunologist*
Lowery, Willa Dean *obstetrician, gynecologist*
Ludwig, Karl David *psychiatrist*
Lyjak Chorazy, Anna Julia *pediatrician, medical administrator, educator*
MacLeod, Gordon Kenneth *physician, educator*
†Magovern, James Anthony *thoracic surgeon*
Markle, William Howard *family physician, educator*
Mazariegos, George Vincent *pediatric transplant surgeon*
Mehta, Harshad R. *cardiologist*
†Merenstein, Joel Harvey *physician, researcher*
Mitre, Blima Kirmayer *pathologist, educator*
†Moalli, Pamela Ann *surgeon, researcher, obstetrician, gynecologist*
Muder, Robert Richard *physician, epidemiologist*
†Mulsant, Benoit Henri *psychiatry educator, medical researcher*
Myers, Eugene Nicholas *otolaryngologist, otolaryngology educator*
Newcomer, Janet Ann *family physician*
†Paradise, Jack Leon *pediatrician, educator*
†Paterson, David Leslie *epidemiologist*
Pautler, Stanislav *retired anesthesiologist*
Peitzman, Andrew Bertram *surgeon*
Planinsic, Raymond M. *anesthesiologist, educator*
Pollock, Bruce Godfrey *psychiatrist, educator*
Post, James Christopher *pediatric otolaryngologist, molecular geneticist*
Price, Fredric Victor *physician, educator, medical researcher*
Ramalingam, Sakkaraiappan *oncologist*
Rault, Raymond Marcel *nephrologist*
Roche, Karen Ruth *plastic surgeon*
Roth, Loren H. *psychiatrist*
Rubin, Robert Terry *physician, researcher, educator*
Saito, Reisuke *pathologist, researcher*
Sanfilippo, Joseph Salvatore *physician, reproductive endocrinologist, educator*
Serene, Harry E. *surgeon*
Shusterman, Vladimir *medical researcher*
Siker, Ephraim S. *anesthesiologist*
Simmons, Richard L. *surgeon*
Sperling, Mark A. *physician, scientist*
†Stahlfeld, Kurt R *surgeon*
Stanger, Robert Henry *psychiatrist, educator*
Starzl, Thomas Earl *physician, educator*
Suzuki, Jon Byron *medical educator, periodontist, microbiologist*
Swerdlow, Steven Howard *hematopathologist*
Tobon, Hector *gynecologic pathologist, educator*
Troen, Philip *physician, educator*
Urbach, Andrew Harley *pediatrician*
Vagley, Richard Thomas *plastic surgeon*
Vogel, Victor Gerald *medical educator, researcher*
Wald, Arnold *gastroenterologist*
Wald, Niel *public health educator*
†Watters, Edmond Clair *ophthalmologist, educator*
Welch, William Charles *neurosurgeon*
†Wenger, Sharon Louise *pediatrics educator, researcher, cytogeneticist*
Wilberger, James E. *neurosurgeon*
Winnie, Glenna Barbara *pediatric pulmonologist*
Winter, Peter Michael *anesthesiologist, educator*
Zehel, Wendell Evans *surgeon*
Zimmerman, Richard Kent *family physician, preventive medicine specialist*
†Zitelli, Basil J. *pediatrician, educator*

Plymouth Meeting
Nobel, Joel J. *biomedical researcher*

Pottsville
Boran, Robert Paul, Jr., *orthopedic surgeon*

Quakertown
Kulik, Beth A. *physician assistant, educator*

Radnor
Giordano, Antonio *medical educator*
Templeton, John Marks, Jr., *retired pediatric surgeon, foundation executive*

Reading
Brigham, Robert Allan *surgeon, educator*
Brown, Gerard Daniel *neonatologist, pediatrician*
Lusch, Charles Jack *oncologist*

Rochester
Solai, Lalithkumar Kuppusamy *psychiatrist, educator*

Rosemont
Brunt, Manly Yates, Jr., *psychiatrist*

Sayre
Davies, Chris Thomas *plastic and reconstructive surgeon*
Gu, Jeng Yul *radiologist*

Moody, Robert Adams *neurosurgeon*

Schwenksville
De Bias, Dennis Anthony *physician*

Scranton
Rhiew, Francis Changnam *radiologist, physician*

Sellersville
Hollander, Irwin Joel *pathologist, educator*
Rilling, David Carl *surgeon*

Sewickley
Munoz, Alfredo Nectario *emergency medicine physician, pediatrician*
Russell, John Robert *neurosurgeon*

Somerset
Nair, Velupillai Krishnan *cardiologist*

Southampton
Tepper, Richard Edward *infectious disease physician*

Springfield
Arsht, Edwin David *physician*
Sing, Robert Fong *physician*

State College
Wilson, Keith B. *rehabilitation educator*

Sunbury
Hetrick, Theodore Lewis, Jr., *emergency medicine physician*

Swarthmore
Carey, William Bacon *pediatrician, educator*
Katz, Lauren Freidus *psychiatrist*

Thorndale
Hodess, Arthur Bart *cardiologist*

University Park
Yu, Fushun *physiologist, research scientist*

Upland
†Jones, Ancil Arthur *cardiologist*

Upper Darby
Toney, Angela M. *medical administrator and educator*

Vandergrift
Bullard, Ray Elva, Jr., *retired psychiatrist, hospital administrator*

Villanova
Hafkenschiel, Joseph Henry, Jr., *cardiologist, educator*
Urbach, Frederick *physician, educator*

Warren
Bergstein, Jack Marshall *surgeon*

Wayne
Burget, Dean Edwin, Jr., *plastic surgeon*
Lief, Harold Isaiah *psychiatrist*

Waynesboro
Cryer, Theodore Hudson *ophthalmologist, educator*
†Kirk, Daniel Lee *retired physician, consultant*

West Point
Silber, Jeffrey Lee *physician*

West Reading
Carter, Frank Moulton *physician*

Wilkes Barre
Casale, Alfred Stanley *thoracic and cardiovascular surgeon*
Schiowitz, Mark F. *surgeon*

Williamsport
Gouldin, Judith Ann *nuclear medicine physician*
Lattimer, Gary Lee *physician*

Willow Grove
Sirota, Robert Alan *physician, nephrologist*

Wyncote
Leinweber, Bruce Kornblatt *obstetrician, gynecologist, educator*

Wynnewood
Alter, Milton *neurologist, educator*
Brady, John Paul *psychiatrist*
Cander, Leon *retired physician*
Frankl, William Stewart *cardiologist, educator*
Fugaro, Anthony Joseph *anesthesiologist*
Keshgegian, Albert Arakel *pathologist*
†Sell, Christian *biomedical researcher*

Yardley
Fraser, David William *epidemiologist*
Lamonsoff, Norman Charles *psychiatrist*
Lindenbaum, Jeffry Alan *osteopathic family physician, consultant*
Newsom, John Harlan *family physician*
Somma, Beverly Kathleen *medical and marriage educator*

York
Shultz, Suzanne Marie *medical librarian*

RHODE ISLAND

Barrington
Carpenter, Charles Colcock Jones *physician, educator*
Mates, Susan Onthank *physician, medical educator, writer, violinist*
Rosenbloom, Mindy Sharon *psychiatrist*

Block Island
Gasner, Walter Gilbert *retired dermatologist*

Cranston
Migliori, Joseph Louis *physician*
Vavala, Domenic Anthony *medical scientist, educator, retired air force officer*
Yu, Chen *family practice physician*

East Providence
Guggenheim, Frederick Gibson *psychiatry educator*
†Parziale, John R. *physiatrist*

North Providence
Stankiewicz, Andrzej Jerzy *physician, biochemistry educator*

Pawtucket
†Chopra, Pradeep *physician, educator*
Crowley, James Patrick *hematologist, medical educator, immunologist*
Friedman, Joseph Harold *neurologist*
Glicksman, Arvin S(igmund) *radiation oncologist*
Greenblatt, Samuel Harold *neurosurgeon*
Poses, Roy Maurice *physician, educator*

Providence
Amaral, Joseph Ferreira *surgeon*
Aronson, Stanley Maynard *physician, educator*
Besdine, Richard William *medical educator, scientist*
Biron, Christine Anne *medical science educator, researcher*
†Bristow, Lonnie Robert *physician*
Cady, Blake *surgical oncologist*
Calabresi, Paul *oncologist, educator, pharmacologist*
Ceriani, Peter John *medical association administrator*
Davis, Robert Paul *physician, educator*
†DiGiovanni, Christopher William *orthopedic surgeon, orthopedist*
Donahue, John Edward *physician*
Dowben, Robert Morris *physician, scientist*
Easton, J(ohn) Donald *neurologist, educator*
†Elfenbein, Gerald Jay *physician, educator*
Erikson, G(eorge) E(mil) (Erik Erikson) *anatomist, archivist, historian, educator, information specialist*
Gnepp, Douglas Robbin *anatomic pathologist*
Hamolsky, Milton William *physician*
Hennessey, James Vincent *physician, educator*
Jackson, Benjamin Taylor *retired surgeon, educator, medical facility administrator*
Jackson, Ivor *endocrinologist, educator*
†Jenny, Carole *physician, researcher*
Kane, Agnes Brezak *pathologist, educator*
Kitzes, David Louis *cardiologist, educator*
Lewis, David Carleton *medical educator, university center director*
Mayer, Kenneth Hugh *physician*
Merlino, Anthony Frank *orthopedic surgeon*
†Monti, Peter M. *medical educator, researcher*
Oh, William *physician*
Plotz, Richard Douglas *pathologist*
Pueschel, Siegfried M. *pediatrician, educator*
Schiff, Stephen Frank *urologic surgeon*
†Shah, Samir Ashok *gastroenterologist, educator*
Shetty, Taranath *neurologist, educator*
Skowron, Gail *medical educator, researcher*
Thayer, Walter Raymond *internist*
†Tracy, Thomas Francis, Jr., *pediatric surgeon, resarcher, educator*
Vezeridis, Michael Panagiotis *surgeon, educator*
†Weitberg, Alan Barry *physician, researcher*
Williams, Robert Raymond *obstetrician and gynecologist*
Wolston, Jon *psychiatrist*

South Kingstown
Pembrook, Richard Charles *internist, cardiologist*

Wakefield
Fera, Steven Raymond *internist, cardiologist, educator*

Westerly
Bachmann, William Thompson *dermatologist*
Christy, Nicholas Pierson *physician*
Dauphinais, Richard Murray *pathologist*
Gillie, R. Bruce *internist*

Woonsocket
Altongy, Gilbert Joseph *physician*

SOUTH CAROLINA

Aiken
Heyl, Guy Carlisle, Jr., *orthopedic surgeon*
†Nagnur, Shreedhar M. *internist, medical researcher*

Anderson
Abercrombie, Stoney Alton *family physician, educator*
Chipman, Dennis Clarence, Jr., *psychiatrist*
Graham, Tony Randall *anesthesiologist*
†Woodall, Hunter Earl *physician, educator*

Beaufort
Cross, Harold Dick *physician*

Charleston
An, Yuehui Huey *orthopaedic surgeon, educator*
Bell, Norman Howard *physician, endocrinologist, educator*
Bowman, C. Michael *physician*
†Bradley, Scott M. *surgeon*
Brown, Carroll Smith *anesthesiologist*
Carek, Donald J(ohn) *child psychiatry educator*
Carter, James Folger *obstetrician-gynecologist, educator, consultant*
Chambers, Joe Carroll *physician, consultant, educator*
†Chiaramida, Salvatore *cardiologist, educator, health facility administrator*
Daniell, Herman Burch *pharmacologist*
Dobson, Richard Lawrence *dermatologist, educator*
Grush, Owen Charles *psychiatry educator*
Haines, Stephen John *neurological surgeon*
Hoffman, Brenda Joyce *gastroenterology educator*
†Jaffa, Ayad A. *medical educator, medical researcher*
Jaffe, Murray Sherwood *retired surgeon*
Jenrette, Joseph Malphus, III, *radiation oncologist*
Kaplan, Allen P. *physician, educator, researcher*
Key, Janice Dixon *physician, medical educator*
Langdale, Emory Lawrence *retired physician*
Lutz, Myron Howard *obstetrician, gynecologist, surgeon, educator*
Maize, John Christopher *dermatology educator*
Margolius, Harry Stephen *pharmacologist, physician*
Maricq, Hildegard Rand *physician, researcher*
Mayfield, Ronald Keith *endocrinologist, educator*
McCurdy, Layton *medical educator*
Means, Robert Taylor, Jr., *hematologist, educator*
Mohr, Lawrence Charles *physician*
Oldham, John Michael *physician, psychiatrist, educator*
Osguthorpe, John David *otolaryngologist, educator*
Othersen, Henry Biemann, Jr., *pediatric surgeon, physician, educator*
Reuben, Adrian *clinician, researcher, medical educator*
Reves, Joseph Gerald *dean, anesthesiology educator*
Roof, Betty Sams *internist*
Rustin, Rudolph Byrd, III, *surgeon, educator*
Sade, Robert Miles *physician, bioethicist, educator*
†Saul, J. Philip *pediatrician, educator*
Schuman, Stanley Harold *epidemiologist, educator*
Simson, Jo Anne *retired anatomy and cell biology educator, biologist, educator*
†Strange, Charlton Bell, III, *internal medicine educator*
Stuart, Robert Kenneth *internist, oncologist, hematologist, educator*
†Uflacker, Renan *radiologist, researcher*
Underwood, Paul Benjamin *gynecologist, educator*
Waller, John Louis *anesthesiology educator*
†Warrick, Kenneth Ray *dermatologist, cosmetic surgeon*
Willi, Steven Matthew *physician, educator, researcher*
Wilson, Frederick Allen *medical educator, medical center administrator, gastroenterologist*

Chester
†Ryan, John Joseph *physician*

Clemson
Vyavahare, Narendra R. *biomedical researcher, educator*

Columbia
Adcock, David Filmore *radiologist, educator*
Almond, Carl Herman *surgeon, physician, educator*
†Ballington, Don Avell *medical educator*
Brooker, Jeff Zeigler *cardiologist*
Bryan, Charles Stone *internal medicine educator*
†Cuffe, Steven Paul *psychiatrist*
da Silva, Ercio Mario *physician*
Donald, Alexander Grant *psychiatrist, educator*
Flanagan, Clyde Harvey, Jr., *psychiatrist, psychoanalyst, educator*
Gasque, Harrison (Allard Harrison Gasque) *optical supply company executive*
Horger, Edgar Olin, III, *obstetrics and gynecology educator*
Humphries, John O'Neal *physician, educator, university dean*
Hwang, Te-Long *neurologist, educator*
Kennedy, Richard McKinne, III, *anesthesiologist*
Lin, Tu *endocrinologist, educator, researcher, academic administrator*
Long, Robert Glendon *pediatrician*
Metropol, Harry Jack *general and thoracic surgeon*
Rowland, Thomas C., Jr., *obstetrician, gynecologist*
Sheppe, Joseph Andrew *surgeon*
Shmunes, Edward *dermatologist*
Still, Charles Neal *neurologist, consultant*
†Thornhill, Joshua Taylor, IV, *psychiatrist, academic administrator*
†Tripathi, Ramesh Chandra *ophthalmologist, researcher, educator*
Wright, Harry Hercules *psychiatrist*
Zheng, Deyi *physician*

Conway
Delia, Claude William *retired physician, pathologist*
Stanley, Covia LeVance *physician, clergyman*

Florence
Imbeau, Stephen Alan *allergist*

Gaffney
Wheeler, William Earl *general surgeon*

Georgetown
Sprinkle, Ralph Stephen *podiatrist*

Greenville
Bonner, Jack Wilbur, III, *psychiatrist, educator, administrator*
DeLoache, William Redding *pediatrician*
Dreskin, Erving Arthur *pathologist, educator*
Goforth, Augustus Johnson, III, *physician*
Kilgore, Donald Gibson, Jr., *pathologist*
Tenney, William Frank *pediatrician*

Greenwood
Hunton, Richard Edwin *family practice physician*

Greer
Vaught, Richard Loren *urologist*

Hilton Head Island
Birk, Robert Eugene *retired physician, educator*
Bogart, Keith Charles *retired neurologist*
Duvall, Charles Patton *retired internist, oncologist*
Engelman, Karl *physician*
Field, James Bernard *internist, educator*
Hewes, Robert Charles *radiologist*
Humphrey, Edward William *surgeon, medical educator*
Lindner, Joseph, Jr., *physician, medical administrator*
Slachta, Gregory Andrew *urologist*

Inman
Fudenberg, Hugh *neuroimmunologist, educator*

Isle Of Palms
Elliott, Larry Paul *cardiac radiologist, educator*

Lancaster
Wozniak, Robert *physician*

North Augusta
McRee, John Browning, Jr., *physician*

North Charleston
Mintzer, Jacobo E. *physician, researcher*

Orangeburg
Andrews, Fran Wolfe *medical educator*
Hare, Ester Rose *physician*
Smoak, Randolph Duncan, Jr., *surgeon*

Pawleys Island
Gromults, Joseph Michael, Jr., *internist*

Saint Helena Island
Dunn, Adolphus William *orthopedic surgeon*

Seneca
Uden, David Elliott *cardiologist, educator*

Spartanburg
†Lefebvre, John Charles *medical educator, researcher*
Parmley, Richard Turner *pediatric hematologist, oncologist*
Valainis, Gregory Thomas *physician*

Surfside Beach
Favaro, Mary Kaye Asperheim (Mrs. Biagino Philip Favaro) *pediatrician, writer*

West Columbia
Carter, Saralee Lessman *immunologist, microbiologist*
Klutzow, Friedrich Wilhelm *neuropathologist*

SOUTH DAKOTA

Dakota Dunes
Purves, Sherrill J. *retired neurologist*

Huron
Saylor, Howard Leroy, Jr., *retired surgeon*

Sioux Falls
Carpenter, Paul Lynn *cardiologist*
Fenton, Lawrence Jules *pediatric educator*
Flohr, Charles E. *radiologist*
Jaqua, Richard Allen *pathologist*
Rossing, David Robert *internist*
Trujillo, Angelina *endocrinologist*
Vogt, Harry Bruce *physician*
Wegner, Karl Heinrich *physician, educator*
Zawada, Edward Thaddeus, Jr., *physician, educator*

Wagner
Szabo, Andras *internist*

TENNESSEE

Alcoa
Lucas, Melinda Ann *pediatrician, educator*

Bristol
Allerton, Jeffrey Paul *oncologist*

Chattanooga
†Campbell, William O'Neal *retired physician*
Cofer, Joseph Broaddus *surgeon*
Enriquez, Manuel Hipolito *physician*
†Melvin, Terry Ann *physician, director*
Morgan, John Ronald *pediatric cardiologist*
Thow, George Bruce *surgeon*

Cordova
Lieberman, Phillip Louis *allergist, educator*

Crossville
Drabik-Nowak, Renata Anna *internist*

Dunlap
Nelson, Roger Theodore *surgeon*

Fayetteville
Ralston, J. Fred, Jr., *internist*

Franklin
Felch, James Walton *ophthalmologist*

Moessner, Harold Frederic *allergist*
Smolenski, Lisabeth Ann *family practice physician*

Germantown
Hall, Johnnie Cameron *pathologist*
†Kontos, George John, Jr., *surgeon*

Gray
Combs, Stephen Paul *pediatrician, health facility administrator*

Hendersonville
Burt, Alvin Miller, III, *anatomist, cell biologist, educator, writer*

Jackson
Erb, Blair Dillard, Sr., *internist*
Misulis, Karl Edward *physician*
†Patel, Kandarp Bipinchandra *cardiologist*
Swaim, Mark Wendell *hepatologist, molecular biologist, gastroenterologist, educator, photographer*
Taylor, Ronald Fulford *physician*

Jefferson City
Muncy, Estle Pershing *physician*

Johnson City
Coogan, Philip Shields *pathologist*
Cupp, Horace Ballard *surgeon, educator*
Dunkelberger, Brian Herbert *physician*
Hamdy, Ronald Charles *geriatrician*
Hodges, Stanley M. *physician, educator*
Kalin, George Bruno *pathologist, educator*
Kao, Race Li-Chan *medical educator*
Konikiewicz, Leonard Wieslaw *biomedical communications consultant*
Kostrzewa, Richard Michael *pharmacology educator*
Pumariega, Andres Julio *medical educator, researcher*
Rice, Peter J. *pharmacologist, pharmacist*
Shurbaji, M. Salah *pathologist*
Wilson, Jim Lester *physician, medical educator*
Youngberg, George Anthony *pathology educator*

Kingsport
Doty, Robert Douglas, Sr., *retired surgeon*
Grigsby, William P. *surgeon*
Hall, John Richard *surgery educator, researcher*
Mehta, Ashok Vallavdas *pediatric cardiologist*

Knoxville
Acker, Joseph Edington *retired cardiology educator*
Burkhart, John Henry *retired physician*
Conrad, Daniel Edward *physician*
DePersio, Richard John *otolaryngologist, plastic surgeon*
Filston, Howard Church *pediatric surgeon, educator*
†Graber, Glenn C. *medical educator, educational consultant*
Kliefoth, A(rthur) Bernhard, III, *neurosurgeon*
Lett, James Chancey *surgeon, retired*
Schneider, William James *plastic and reconstructive surgeon, chief medical officer*
Shivers, Patricia Bunker Coulson *endocrinologist*
Terry, William Ferrell *pediatrician*
Wise, Edmund Joseph *physician assistant, industrial hygienist*

Maryville
Howard, Cecil Byron *pediatrician*

Memphis
†Anghelescu, Doralina Lucia *anesthesiologist*
Chesney, Russell Wallace *pediatrician*
Cowan, George Sheppard Marshall, Jr., *surgeon, educator, research administrator*
Cox, Clair Edward, II, *urologist, medical educator*
†Crews, Kristine Radomski *pharmacologist*
Dagogo-Jack, Samuel E. *medical educator, physician scientist, endocrinologist*
De Saussure, Richard Laurens, Jr., *retired neurosurgery educator*
†Dickerson, Roland Nelson *pharmacy educator, clinical consultant*
Elliott, Rodney Gorhman *urologist, educator*
Gerald, Barry *radiology educator, neuroradiologist*
Godsey, William Cole *physician*
Green, Joseph Barnet *neurologist, educator*
Heimberg, Murray *pharmacologist, biochemist, physician, educator*
Hughes, Walter Thompson *physician, pediatrics educator*
Kaplan, Robert J. *dermatologist*
Kaste, Sue Creviston *pediatric radiologist, researcher*
Korones, Sheldon Bernarr *physician, educator*
Lazar, Rande Harris *otolaryngologist*
Leal, Gumersindo R. *physician*
Lew, D(ukhee) Betty *physician*
Martin, Daniel C. *surgeon, gynecologist, educator*
Martinez-Hernandez, Antonio *pathology educator*
Mauer, Alvin Marx *physician, medical educator*
Morreim, E. Havvi *medical ethics educator*
Nienhuis, Arthur Wesley *physician, researcher*
Shea, Martin Coyle *physician*
Shochat, Stephen Jay *pediatric surgeon*
Solomon, Solomon Sidney *endocrinologist, pharmacologist, scientist*
Soskel, Norman Terry *physician*
Summitt, Robert Layman, Jr., *obstetrician, gynecologist*
†Talati, Ajay Jayantilal *pediatrician, researcher*
Tonkin, Ina Lynn Dyer *cardiovascular radiologist, educator*
Tutko, Robert Joseph *law enforcement officer, radiology administrator*
Waller, Robert Rex *ophthalmologist, educator, foundation executive*
Wilcox, Harry Hammond *retired medical educator*
Wingate, Robert Lee, Jr., *internist*

Murfreesboro
Coleman, Jack Andrew, Jr., *otolaryngologist*

Nashville
Allen, George Sewell *neurosurgery educator*
Allison, Fred, Jr., *physician, educator*
Averbuch, Mark Stephen *internist*
Baldwin, Harold Scott *pediatrician*
Barnett, Joey Victor *pharmacologist, educator, researcher*
Bates, George William *obstetrician, gynecologist, educator, medical products executive*
Bernard, Louis Joseph *surgeon, educator*
Brill, Aaron Bertrand *nuclear medicine educator*
Brown, Wendy Weinstock *nephrologist, educator*
Burk, Raymond Franklin, Jr., *physician, educator, researcher*
Burnett, Lonnie Sheldon *obstetrics and gynecology educator*
Byrne, Daniel William *biostatistician, educator*
Carroll, Frank Edward *radiologist, researcher*
Clayton, Ellen Wright *medical educator, pediatrician*
Clinton, Mary Ellen *neurologist*
Cotton, Robert Bell *pediatrician, neonatologist, researcher*
DeHart, Roy Lynch *physician, educator*
†Elam, Lloyd Charles *psychiatrist, educator*
Estes, Robert Lewis *ophthalmologist*
†Fazio, Sergio *medical educator, researcher*
†Fields, James Perry *dermatologist, dermatopathologist, allergist*
Finder, Stuart Gregg *medical ethics educator*
Fleischer, Arthur C. *medical educator, radiologist*
Foster, Henry Wendell *medical educator*
Gabbe, Steven Glenn G. *dean, obstetrician, gynecologist, educator*
†George, Alfred L., Jr., *medical educator, researcher*
Graham, Thomas Pegram, Jr., *pediatric cardiologist*
†Griffin, Patti Elaine *medical educator, consultant*
Hamberg, Marcelle Robert *retired urologist*
Jennings, Henry Smith, III, *cardiologist*
Jensen, Roy Andrew *pathologist*
†Kirshner, Howard S *neurologist, medical educator*
Leftwich, Russell Bryant *allergist, immunologist, consultant*
Lynch, John Brown *plastic surgeon, educator*
Marney, Samuel Rowe, Jr., *physician, educator*
Martin, Peter Robert *psychiatrist, pharmacologist*
†May, James M. *medical educator, medical researcher*
McLeod, Alexander Canaday *physician*
†Meltzer, Herbert Yale *psychiatry educator*
Morrow, Jason Drew *medical and pharmacology educator*
Neilson, Eric Grant *physician, educator, health facility administrator*
Oates, John Alexander, III, *medical educator*
O'Day, Denis Michael *ophthalmologist, educator*
O'Neill, James Anthony, Jr., *pediatric surgeon, educator*
Ossoff, Robert Henry *otolaryngological surgeon*
Parker, John Randolph *pathologist, educator*
Partain, Clarence Leon *radiologist, nuclear medicine physician, educator, administrator*
Pinson, Charles Wright *transplant surgeon, educator, hospital administrator*
Propper, Michael Walles *psychiatrist, educator*
Riley, Harris DeWitt, Jr., *pediatrician, medical educator*
†Robert, Pousman Marc *physician, hospital administrator*
†Robertson, Rose Marie *cardiologist, educator*
†Robinson, Nathaniel David, Jr., *physician, consultant*
Robinson, Roscoe Ross *nephrologist, educator*
Roden, Dan Mark *clinical pharmacologist, cardiologist, medical educator*
Ross, Joseph Comer *physician, educator, academic administrator*
†Saposnik, Ira Stephen *physician, historian*
Schwartz, Herbert S. *surgical oncology educator*
Shack, R. Bruce *plastic surgeon*
Smith, Bradley E. *anesthesiologist*
Spengler, Dan Michael *orthopedic surgery educator, researcher, surgeon*
Stahlman, Mildred Thornton *pediatrics and pathology educator, researcher*
Sullivan, James Nelson *physician*
Thornton, Spencer P. *ophthalmologist, educator*
van Eys, Jan *retired pediatrician, educator, administrator*
Van Orden, Lucas S. *psychiatrist*
†Wasserman, David H. *medical educator, researcher*

Oak Ridge
Clapp, Neal Keith *experimental pathologist*
Congdon, Charles C. *pathologist, researcher*
Spray, Paul Ellsworth *retired surgeon*

Shelbyville
Russell, William Lee *surgeon*

Signal Mountain
Swann, Nat Henderson, Jr., *physician*

TEXAS

Abilene
Morgan, Clyde Nathaniel *dermatologist*
Richert, Harvey Miller, II, *ophthalmologist*
Wehmeyer, Donald Lee *hand surgeon*

Amarillo
Biggs, William Curtis *endocrinologist*
†Bohachef, Janet Mae *medical educator*
†Kauffman, Robert Porter *gynecologist, educator*
Laur, William Edward *retired dermatologist*
Marupudi, Sambasiva Rao *surgeon, educator*
Parker, Gerald M. *osteopath, researcher*
†Parker, Lynda Michele *psychiatrist*
Pratt, Donald George *physician*

Aransas Pass
Stehn, Lorraine Strelnick *physician*

Arlington
†Adams, Quentin Mark *neurologist*
Ahmed, M. Basheer *psychiatrist, educator*
de Sousa, Byron N.S. *educator, physician, health and medical consultant*
†Kier, Carlos M. *rheumatologist*
Tingley, Floyd Warren *retired physician*

Austin
Austin, John Riley *surgeon, educator*
Bernstein, Robert *retired physician, state official, former army officer*
DeVere, Ronald *neurologist*
Elequin, Cleto, Jr., *retired physician*
Ersek, Robert Allen *plastic surgeon, inventor*
Eskew, James Robert *otolaryngologist*
Fleeger, David Clark *colon and rectal surgeon*
Freedenberg, Debra *physician, geneticist*
Ivy, John L. *medical educator, researcher*
Mazzetti, Robert F. *real estate manager, retired orthopedic surgeon*
Painter, Theophilus Shickel, Jr., *internist, allergist*
Schleuse, William *retired psychiatrist, psychoanalyst*
†Sutton, Beverly Jewell *psychiatrist*

Baytown
Williams, Drew Davis *surgeon*

Beaumont
Lozano, Jose *nephrologist*
McCord, Michael David *anesthesiologist*
McKenney, Scott Alan *oncologist*

Bedford
Farhat, Georges Antoun *anesthesiologist*

Bellaire
Haywood, Theodore Joseph *physician, educator*
Pokorny, Alex Daniel *psychiatrist*

Bellville
Neely, Robert Allen *retired ophthalmologist*

Big Spring
Reddy, Gaddum Jagan Mohan *surgeon*

Boerne
Wittmer, James Frederick *preventive medicine physician, educator*

Brooks City Base
Balldin, Ulf Ingemar *medical researcher*

Brownsville
Imperial, Henry L. *internist*
Walss, Rodolfo J. *obstetrician-gynecologist, hypnotherapist, artist*

Bryan
Anderson, Frank Gist, Jr., *ophthalmologist, educator*
Dirks, Kenneth Ray *pathologist, medical educator, army officer*

Cleburne
Gates, Steven Leon *physician*

College Station
†Colenda, III, Christopher Columbus *psychiatrist*
Kier, Ann Burnette *pathologist*
Lindner, Luther Edward *pathology educator*
Sampson, Herschel Wayne *anatomy educator*
Tiffany-Castiglioni, Evelyn *biomedical science educator, researcher*

Conroe
Ewing, Joseph Graham *family practice physician*

Corpus Christi
Appel, Truman Frank *surgeon*
Cook, Kenneth Ray *radiologist*
Cox, William Andrew *cardiovascular thoracic surgeon*
Gaylor, James Leroy *biomedical research educator*
Kylstra, Johannes Arnold *physician*
Lim, Alexander Rufasta *neurologist, clinical investigator, clinical neurophysiologist, educator, writer*
Pappas, John Douglas *cardiologist*
Ward, Harold William Cowper *oncologist, educator*

Dallas
Allen, Terry Devereux *urologist, educator*
Bashour, Fouad Anis *cardiology educator*
Beck, Jay M. *gynecologist*
Berbary, Maurice Shehadeh *physician, military officer, hospital administrator, educator*
†Bergstresser, Paul Richard *dermatologist, educator*
Bick, Rodger Lee *hematologist, oncologist, researcher, educator*
†Blomquist, Preston Howard *ophthalmologist*
Blomqvist, Carl Gunnar *cardiologist*
Bolesta, Michael Joseph *orthopedic surgeon*
Bonte, Frederick James *radiology educator, physician*
†Boswell, George Marion, Jr., *orthopedist, health care facility administrator*
Brown, E. Sherwood *psychiatrist*
Caetano, Raul *psychiatrist, educator*
Carman, George Henry *retired physician*
Cavanagh, Harrison Dwight *ophthalmic surgeon, medical educator*
Chason, Jacob (Leon Chason) *retired neuropathologist*
Cheirif, Jorge Berkstein *cardiologist, consultant*
Collins, Robert Howard, Jr., *oncologist*
Coln, C. Dale *pediatric surgeon, educator*
†Cook, William Staton *medical researcher*
Cox, Rody P(owell) *medical educator, internist*
Dees, Tom Moore, II, *internist*
Dewey, Richard B., Jr., *medical educator, administrator*
Eichenwald, Heinz Felix *physician*
Einspruch, Burton Cyril *psychiatrist*
Emmett, Michael *physician, educator*
Ericson, Ruth Ann *retired psychiatrist*
†Feiner, Joel S. *psychiatrist*
Fenves, Andrew Zoltan *nephrologist*
Flatt, Adrian Ede *surgeon*
†Fleckenstein, James Lawrence *radiologist*
Fogwell, Ted E. *obstetrician and gynecologist*
Frenkel, Eugene Phillip *physician*
Friedberg, Errol Clive *pathology educator, researcher*
Gant, Norman Ferrell, Jr., *obstetrician, gynecologist*
Gantt, James Raiford *thoracic surgeon*
Giesecke, Adolph Hartung *anesthesiologist, educator*
Gilman, Alfred Goodman *pharmacologist, educator*
Goldstein, Joseph Leonard *physician, medical educator, molecular genetics scientist*
Grammer, John Colquitte *cardiologist*
Griffeth, Landis King *nuclear medicine physician*
Gross, Gary Neil *allergist, physician*
Guy, L(eona) Ruth *medical educator*
Harper, John Frank *cardiologist*
Harrington, John Norris *ophthalmic plastic and reconstructive surgeon, educator*
Harrington, Marion Ray *ophthalmologist*
†Hilgemann, Donald William *medical educator*
Hinnant, Jerry Herbert *surgeon*
Holman, James *allergist, immunologist*
Homan, Richard Warren *neurologist, academic administrator, medical educator*
Hughes, Waunell McDonald (Mrs. Delbert E. Hughes) *retired psychiatrist*
Hurd, Eric Ray *rheumatologist, internist, educator*
Jessen, Michael Erik *surgeon, educator*
Jester, James Vincent *opthalmology educator*
†Jialal, Ishwarlal *medical educator*
Johnson, Robert Lee, Jr., *physician, educator, researcher*
Joshi, Girish Premji *anesthesiologist, researcher*
Karandikar, Nitin J. *physician, scientist, educator*
Khan, Amanullah *physician*
Kindberg, Shirley Jane *pediatrician*
Kollmeyer, Kenneth Robert *surgeon*
Lakhanpal, Sharad *physician*
Lange, Richard A. *medical educator*
Lewis, Jerry M. *psychiatrist, educator*
Li, Jinping *medical educator, researcher*
Lichliter, Warren Eugene *surgeon, educator*
Lumry, William Raymond *physician, allergist*
Maddrey, Willis Crocker *medical educator, internist, academic administrator, consultant, researcher*
Margolin, Solomon Begelfor *pharmacologist, consultant*
Martin, Jack *physician*
Mc Clelland, Robert Nelson *surgeon, educator*
McCord, Don Lewis *surgeon*
Menter, M(artin) Alan *dermatologist*
Mitchell, Teddy Lee *physician*
Mullins, Charles Brown *physician, academic administrator*
†Murillo, Ricardo Alonso *physician*
New, William Neil *physician, retired naval officer*
Odom, Floyd Clark *surgeon*
Perry, Malcolm Oliver *vascular surgeon*
Phillips, Margaret A. *pharmacology educator*
Pippin, John Joseph *cardiologist*
Race, George Justice *pathology educator*
Roberts, Lynne Jeanine *physician*
†Roberts, William Clifford *medical association administrator*
Rohrich, Rodney James *plastic surgeon, educator*
Romero, Jorge Antonio *neurologist, educator*
Rosenberg, Roger Newman *neurologist, educator*
†Rush, Augustus John *psychiatrist, educator*
Samson, Duke Staples *neurosurgeon*
†Schecter, Arnold Joel *public health educator*
Simon, Theodore Ronald *physician, medical educator*
Skiest, Daniel Jay *medical educator, internist*
Smith, Barry Samuel *physiatrist*
†Sprague, Charles Cameron *medical foundation president*
Stage, Key Hutchinson *urologist*
Stone, Marvin Jules *physician, educator*
†Sutker, William Levin *internist*
Thompson, Jesse Eldon *vascular surgeon*
Trivedi, Madhukar H. *psychiatrist*
Uhr, Jonathan William *immunologist, educator, researcher*
Unger, Roger Harold *physician, scientist*
Wildenthal, C(laud) Kern *physician, educator*
Wilson, Jean Donald *endocrinologist, educator*
Zhou, Xin (Joseph Zhou) *pathologist, medical scientist*
Ziff, Morris *internist, rheumatologist, educator*

El Paso
Copeland, Randolph Leigh *orthopedic surgeon*
Eisner, David George *retired surgeon*
Foley, John Donald *physician*
Gupta, Tej P. *physician*
†Harlass, Frederick E. *obstetrician, gynecologist, perinatologist*
Huchton, Paul Joseph, Jr., *pediatrician*
Jesurun, Carlos Antonio *pediatrician, educator, neonatologist*

†Mulla, Zuber *epidemiologist*
Pazmiño, Patricio Augusto *physician, scientist, consultant*
Taber, David O. *urological surgeon*
Thering, Harlan Robert *plastic surgeon, retired army officer*
Williams, Darryl Marlowe *medical educator*
Zaloznik, Arlene Joyce *oncologist, retired army officer*

Fort Sam Houston
†Givens, Melissa Lousie *emergency physician*
Gordon, Ella Dean *health and nurse educator, women's health and orthopedic nurse*
Hewitson, William Craig *physician, career officer*
†Kragh, John Frederick, Jr., *orthopedist, educator*
†Pak, Hon S. *dermatologist, researcher*

Fort Worth
†Bayona, Manuel *medical educator*
Blanck, Ronald Ray *health science university administrator, internist, military officer*
Bowling, John Robert *osteopathic physician, educator, academic administrator*
†Cottner, Donald *pathologist*
Fleenor, Debra L. *biomedical researcher*
Gillette, Paul Crawford *pediatric cardiologist*
Hahn, Marc B. *dean, anesthesiologist*
Lamensdorf, Hugh *urologist, educator*
Schussler, Irwin *psychiatrist, educator*
Siede, Wolfram *research scientist*
Suba, Steven Antonio *obstetrician, gynecologist*
Thurman, Addison Eugene, Jr., *urologist*
Tobey, Martin Alan *cardiologist*
Willard, Ralph Lawrence *surgery educator, physician, former college president*
Yanni, John Michael *pharmacologist*

Galveston
Angel, Carlos Alberto *pediatric surgeon, urologist*
Bailey, Byron James *otolaryngologist, medical association executive*
Bello-Reuss, Elsa Noemi *physician, educator*
Bernier, George Matthew, Jr., *physician, medical educator, medical school dean*
†Brasier, Allan R. *medical educator*
Bryan, George Thomas *pediatrician, academic administrator*
Burns, Chester Ray *medical history educator*
Calverley, John Robert *physician, educator*
Chen, Lilly Lil-Jing *neurologist, educator*
Chonmaitree, Tasnee *pediatrician, educator, infectious disease specialist*
†Daller, John Alfons *transplant surgeon*
Daniels, Jerry Claude *rheumatologist, educator*
Dawson, Earl Bliss *obstetrics and gynecology educator*
Folse, Dean Sydney *retired pathologist*
Gold, Daniel Howard *ophthalmologist, educator*
Goodwin, Jean McClung *psychiatrist*
†Hudnall, Stanley David *pathology and laboratory medicine educator*
Jacobs, William Fredric *physician*
James, Thomas Naum *cardiologist, educator*
König, Rolf *immunologist, educator*
Levin, William Cohn *hematologist, former university president*
Luthra, Gurinder Kumar *osteopath*
Mayhall, C. Glen *internal medicine educator*
†McKendall, Robert Roland *neurologist, virologist, educator*
Mitch, William Evans *nephrologist*
†Mueller, Rashmi N. *physician, educator*
Norcross-Mehlman, Karyl *neurologist, educator*
†Nusynowitz, Martin Lawrence *nuclear medicine physician*
Pearl, William Richard Emden *pediatric cardiologist*
Saade, George Robert *physician*
Sandstead, Harold Hilton *medical educator*
Shope, Robert Ellis *epidemiology educator*
Smith, David English *physician, educator*
Stout, Landon Clarke, Jr., *pathologist, educator*
Thompson, James Charles *surgeon*
†Vedernikov, Yuri P. *pharmacologist, educator*
White, Robert Brown *medical educator*
Zacharias, Nikolaos Marios *obstetrician/gynecologist*

Garland
Haynsworth, Robert Francis, Jr., *anesthesiologist*
Hockett, Sheri Lynn *radiologist*

Georgetown
Manning, Robert Thomas *physician, educator*
Sawyer, William Dale *physician, educator, university dean, foundation administrator*

Gonzales
Voge, Victoria Mae *occupational medicine physician*

Greenville
†Siles, Fernando M. *child psychiatrist*

Harlingen
Klein, Garner Franklin *cardiologist, internist*

Hockley
Able, Luke William *pediatric surgeon, consultant*

Houston
†Aguilar, Eugenio Alfredo, III, *plastic surgeon*
†Aguilar-Bryan, Lydia *medical educator, medical researcher*
†Ahn, Chul *medical educator*
Alexanian, Raymond *hematologist*
Alford, Bobby Ray *physician, educator, university official*
Allen, Steven Jeffrey *anesthesiologist, educator*
†Amato, Paula *medical educator*
†Arcilla, Juanita R. *physical rehabilitation physician*
†Arens, James F. *anesthesiologist, educator*

Assouad, Mario *internist, nephrologist*
Ayus, Juan Carlos *nephrologist*
Bag, Remzi *nuclear medicine physician, internist, pulmonologist, critical care physician, transplant pulmonologist*
Bailey, Harold Randolph *surgeon*
Ballantyne, Christie Mitchell *medical educator*
Barcenas, Camilo Gustavo *physician*
Barrett, Bernard Morris, Jr., *plastic and reconstructive surgeon*
Baskin, David Stuart *neurosurgeon, educator*
Bast, Robert Clinton, Jr., *medical researcher, medical educator*
†Bedikian, Agop Y. *internist, oncologist, educator*
Bethea, Louise Huffman *allergist*
†Bezold, Louis Irving, III, *pediatrician, cardiologist*
Bodey, Gerald Paul *medical educator, physician*
Bowman, Jeffrey Neil *podiatrist*
Brody, Baruch Alter *medical educator, academic center administrator*
Bruner, Janet M. *neuropathologist*
Bungo, Michael William *physician, educator, science administrator*
Burzynski, Stanislaw Rajmund *internist*
Buster, John Edmond *gynecologist, medical researcher*
Butler, Ian John *neurologist*
†Cabioglu, Neslihan *surgeon*
Carabello, Blase Anthony *cardiology educator*
Cardus, David *physician*
†Castriotta, Richard J. *medical educator, physician*
Catlin, Francis Irving *physician*
Chiou-Tan, Faye *physician, educator*
†Clanton, Thomas Oscar *orthopedic surgeon*
†Clayman, Gary L. *surgeon, educator*
Clifton, Guy L. *neurosurgeon, educator*
†Conrad, Charles A. *neurologist, neuro-oncologist*
Cooley, Denton Arthur *surgeon, educator*
Corriere, Joseph N., Jr., *urologist, educator*
Couch, Robert Barnard *physician, scientist, educator*
Dang, Nam Hoang *medical educator*
†DeBakey, Michael Ellis *cardiovascular surgeon, educator, scientist*
Deter, Russell Lee, II, *obstetrical ultrasonographer*
Drutz, Jan Edwin *pediatrics educator*
DuPont, Herbert Lancashire *medical educator, researcher*
Eisner, Diana *pediatrician*
†Eknoyan, Garabed *medical educator, researcher*
†Ertan, Atilla *medical educator, physician, researcher, health facility administrator*
Esmaeli, BitA *ophthalmologist*
Esteva, Francisco Javier *physician, researcher*
Evans, Harry Launius *pathology educator*
Fan, Leland Lane *pediatrician, educator, medical researcher*
†Feig, Barry W. *surgeon, oncologist*
†Feigon, Judith Tova *ophthalmologist, surgeon, educator*
Ferrendelli, James Anthony *neurologist, educator*
Fischer, Craig Leland *physician*
Fisher, Anna Lee *physician, astronaut*
Fishman, Marvin Allen *pediatrician, neurologist, educator*
Fornage, Bruno Denis *radiologist, educator*
Freireich, Emil J *hematologist, educator*
Fritsch, Derek Adrian *nurse anesthetist*
†Frost, Adaani *internist*
Gabbard, Glen Owens *psychiatrist, psychoanalyst*
Garcia-Gregory, Jorge A. *cardiologist*
Gardezi, Syed A. *medical researcher*
Gigli, Irma *physician, educator, academic administrator*
Gildenberg, Philip Leon *neurosurgeon*
†Gilger, Mark Alan *pediatrician, educator*
†Gilstrap, Larry Cowan *obstetrician gynecologist*
Glassman, Armand Barry *physician, pathologist, scientist, educator, administrator*
Goldman, Stanford Milton *medical educator*
†Gorry, G. Anthony *medical educator, educator*
Graham, David Yates *gastroenterologist*
Grossman, Herbert Barton *urologist, researcher*
Grossman, Robert George *physician, educator*
Guiberteau, Milton J. *radiologist*
Gunn, Albert Edward, Jr., *internist, educator, lawyer, administrator*
Guynn, Robert William *psychiatrist, educator*
†Ha, Chul S *radiation oncologist*
Hall, Robert Joseph *physician, medical educator*
Hamilton, Carlos Robert, Jr., *internist, educator, university official*
Haney, Peter Michael *pediatrics educator*
†Hassoun, Heitham Talal *surgeon, researcher*
Haynie, Thomas Powell, III, *physician*
Herndon, John Wyatt *otolaryngologist*
Herzog, Cynthia Elaine *physician, educator*
Hicks, John Bernard *retired internist*
Ho, Ching *surgeon*
Hortobagyi, Gabriel N. *physician*
Hsu, Katharine Han Kuang *pediatrics educator*
Huang, Jaou-Chen *obstetrician-gynecologist, reproductive endocrinologist*
Jackson, Gilchrist L. *surgeon*
Jankovic, Joseph *neurologist, educator, scientist*
Jemison, Mae Carol *physician, engineer, entrepreneur, philanthropist, educator, former astronaut*
Jhingran, Anuja *oncologist, educator*
Jones, Dan Brigman *ophthalmologist, educator*
Jones, Edith Irby *physician*
Jordon, Robert Earl *physician*
Juneja, Harinder Singh *hematologist*
Kahan, Barry Donald *surgeon, educator*
Kaplan, Alan Leslie *gynecology educator, oncologist*
Katrana, David John *plastic and reconstructive surgeon*
Kaufman, Raymond Henry *physician*
Key, James Everett *ophthalmologist*
Kim, Han-Seob *pathologist*
King, Harry Richard *heart surgeon*

Kirkland, Rebecca Trent *pediatric endocrinologist*
Knight, Jack Vernon *medicine and microbiology educator*
Koch, Douglas Donald *ophthalmologist, educator*
†Koh, Moon-Soo *urologist, researcher*
†Kone, Bruce C. *medical educator, nephrologist*
Kraft, Irvin Alan *psychiatrist*
†Kurzrock, Razelle *internist, educator*
Kutka, Nicholas *nuclear medicine physician*
†Lanza, Frank Leo *gastroenterologist, researcher*
†Layne, Charles Shannon *medical educator*
Leak, Jessie Aronow *anesthesiologist*
Lepow, Ronald S. *podiatrist*
Letsou, George Vasilios *cardiothoracic surgeon*
Li, George *cardiologist*
Low, Morton David *physician, educator, policy consultant*
Lu, Hsin Huang *radiologist, educator*
Macdonald, Eleanor Josephine *epidemiology educator, cancer epidemiology consultant*
Malkoff, Marc David *neurologist*
Marrack, David *pathologist*
Martin, Raymond Anthony *neurologist, educator*
Massin, Edward Krauss *physician*
Max, Ernest *surgeon*
Mayor, Heather Donald *medical educator, molecular biologist*
McKechnie, John Charles *gastroenterologist, educator*
McPherson, Alice Ruth *ophthalmologist, educator*
Mendelsohn, John *oncologist, hematologist, educator*
Merrill, Joseph Melton *medical educator*
Meyer, John Stirling *neurologist, educator*
Milam, John Daniel *pathologist, educator*
Miles, Brian John *urologist*
Miller, Gary Evan *psychiatrist, mental health services administrator*
Miller, Geoffrey *child neurologist*
Miller-Hance, Wanda C. *anesthesiologist*
†Mintz-Hittner, Helen Ann *physician, researcher*
Munk, Zev Moshe *allergist, researcher*
Murad, Ferid *physician*
Murphy, William Alexander, Jr., *diagnostic radiologist, educator*
Padmanabhan, Sivakumar *physician*
Phung, Nguyen Dinh *medical educator*
Portman, Ronald Jay *pediatric nephrologist, researcher*
Powers, William Edward *emergency physician, educator*
Prieto, Victor Gerardo *physician*
Raijman, Isaac *gastroenterologist, endoscopist, educator*
Rao, P. Syamasundar *pediatric cardiologist*
†Rapini, Ronald Peter *dermatology educator*
Rappaport, Norman Harvey *plastic surgeon*
†Rassidakis, George Z *pathologist, researcher*
Ribble, John Charles *medical educator*
Riley, William John *neurologist*
Robb, Geoffrey Lawrence *plastic surgeon*
Rose, Franklin Arthur *plastic surgeon*
Rosenthal, Morris William *pediatrician*
Ross, Michael Wallis *public health educator*
Ross, Patti Jayne *obstetrics and gynecology educator*
Rubenfeld, Sheldon *thyroidologist*
Rudolph, Andrew Henry *dermatologist, educator*
Ruiz, Pedro *psychiatrist*
Samo, Tobias Charles *physician*
Sanderson, Mary Louise *medical association administrator*
†Sargent, John *psychiatrist*
Satitpunwaycha, Pon *surgeon*
Sazama, Kathleen *pathologist, lawyer*
Schachtel, Barbara Harriet Levin *epidemiologist, educator*
Scharold, Mary Louise *psychoanalyst, educator*
Schoolar, Joseph Clayton *psychiatrist, pharmacologist, educator*
†Sdringola-Maranga, Stefano *medical educator, researcher*
Sears, David Alan *medical educator*
Shahjahan, Munir *medical researcher*
†Shan, Kesavan *cardiologist, researcher*
Shearer, William Thomas *pediatrician, educator*
†Sherman, Steven I. *endocrinologist, educator*
Shook, Joan E. *medical educator*
Shulman, Robert Jay *pediatrician, educator, nutritionist*
Simpson, Joe Leigh *obstetrics and gynecology educator*
Singletary, Sonja Eva *surgeon, educator*
Spencer, Dennis D. *medical educator, director*
Spira, Melvin *plastic surgeon*
†Stayer, Stephen A *anesthesiologist*
Stewart, Michael Glenn *medical educator, physician*
Stimson, Paul Gary *pathologist*
Talmage, Edward Arthur *anesthesiologist*
†Tamboli, Pheroze *pathologist*
Teruya, Jun *hematologist, clinical pathologist*
Thomas, Orville C. *retired physician, consultant*
†Torre-Amione, Guillermo *cardiologist, researcher*
Tulloch, Brian Robert *endocrinologist*
Vallbona, Carlos *physician*
Vanderploeg, James M. *preventive medicine physician*
Varma, Datla G.K. *radiologist, researcher*
Walker, William Easton *surgeon, educator, lawyer*
Wall, Matthew J., Jr., *surgeon, scientist*
Watson, David A. *biomedical researcher, educator*
Wheless, James Warren *neurologist*
Wiemer, David Robert *plastic surgeon*
†Wilhelmus, Kirk Robert *ophthalmologist*
Williams, Temple Weatherly, Jr., *internist, educator*
Wolinsky, Jerry Saul *neurology educator*
Wu, Kenneth Kun-Yu *physician, scientist*
†Young, Amy E. *obstetrician, gynecologist, educator*

Zander, Dani S. *pathologist, educator*
Zarin, Jerald Lawrence *pediatrician, physician executive*
Zoghbi, Huda Y. *pediatric neurology and genetics educator*

Humble
Trowbridge, John Parks *physician*

Huntsville
Conwell, Halford Roger *physician*

Hurst
Kotas, Robert Vincent *research physician, educator*

Irving
Kaiser, Fran Elizabeth *endocrinologist, gerontologist*
Meyerson, Lawrence Bernard *physician*

Jacksonville
Wonnacott, James Brian *physician*

Kerrville
Zuber, Randolph Clark *urologist*

Lackland A F B
†Chiou, Andy C. *surgeon*
†Kashyap, Vikram S. *vascular surgeon, military officer*

Lago Vista
Hilton, James Gorton *pharmacologist*

Lake Jackson
Resnick, Harvey *physician*

Laredo
Ali, Ashraf *psychiatrist*

Longview
Frase, Larry Lynn *medical oncologist*

Lubbock
Beck, George Preston *anesthesiologist, educator*
Buesseler, John Aure *ophthalmologist, management consultant*
Illner-Canizaro, Hana *physician, oral surgeon, researcher*
†Joshi, Atul B. *physician*
Kaye, Alan David *anesthesiologist, researcher*
Kurtzman, Neil A. *medical educator*
May, Donald Robert Lee *ophthalmologist, retina and vitreous surgeon, educator, farmer*
Mittemeyer, Bernhard Theodore *urology and surgery educator*
†Prien, Samuel David *medical educator, researcher*
Reid, Ted W. (Ted Warren Reid) *ophthalmology educator*
Schiffer, Randolph Brenton *physician*
Selby, John Horace *surgeon*
†Syapin, Peter John *pharmacologist, research scientist*
Varma, Surendra K. *pediatrician, educator*
Warren, Donald John *retired surgeon, educator*
Way, Barbara Haight *dermatologist*
Woolam, Gerald Lynn *surgeon*

Lufkin
Dean, Odell Joseph, Jr., *urologist, educator*
Perry, Lewis Charles *emergency medicine physician, osteopath*

Magnolia
†Girard, Louis Joseph *ophthalmologist, educator*

Marshall
Sudhivoraseth, Niphon *pediatrician, allergist, immunologist*

Mcallen
Casso, Ramiro Paul *retired family physician, college official*
Ramirez, Mario Efrain *physician*
Robalino, Benjamin David *cardiologist*

Midland
Corwin, James A. *radiation oncologist*

Mineral Wells
Braun, Gustav Milan *facial plastic surgeon, otolaryngologist*

Nacogdoches
Bommanna, Vasudeva M. *allergist, immunologist*

Odessa
Cibley, Laurence Jay *obstetrician, gynecologist*
†McHattie, Thomas John *obstetrician, gynecologist, medical educator*

Pampa
Powell, Dan Clayton *physician*

Pasadena
Cowles, Charles Eugene, Jr., *medical educator*
†Holland, Peter Marc *ophthalmologist*
Shapiro, Edward Muray *dermatologist*
†Stahl, Charlyn Beth *medical educator*

Pearland
Hammond, Raymond William *pharmacotherapy specialist*

Port Lavaca
Cummins, Michelle Marie *otolaryngologist, head and neck surgeon*

Raymondville
Montgomery-Davis, Joseph *osteopathic physician*

Rockport
Johnson, Marilyn *retired obstetrician, gynecologist*

Salado
Wilmer, Harry Aron *psychiatrist, educator*

San Angelo
Anderson, Garry Michael *diagnostic radiologist*
Fischer, Duncan Kinnear *neurosurgeon*

San Antonio
†Ait-Daoud, Nassima *psychiatrist, researcher*
Aust, Joe Bradley *surgeon, educator*
†Bailey, Steven R. *cardiologist, researcher*
Baker, Floyd Wilmer *surgeon, retired army officer*
Beckmann, Charles Henry *cardiologist, educator*
Cepeda, Claudio *psychiatrist*
Chiscano, Alfonso *surgeon*
Cohen, Melvin Lee *pediatrician, psychiatrist, educator*
†Croft, Harry Allen *psychiatrist*
†Currie, Donald M *medical educator*
Di Maio, Vincent Joseph Martin *forensic pathologist*
†Dwyer, Mary Jo *medical librarian*
†Ereshefsky, Larry *psychopharmacologist educator, consultant*
Espino, David V. *geriatrician, family practice physician*
Ferry, Robert Jean, Jr., *pediatric endocrinologist*
Freeman, Theodore Monroe *physician*
Honore, Gerard Marcel *endocrinologist, reproductive endocrinologist*
Horton, Granville Eugene *occupational medicine physician, retired air force officer*
Huff, Robert Whitley *obstetrician, gynecologist, educator*
Jorgensen, James H. *pathologist, educator, microbiologist*
†Kaye, Celia Ilene *pediatrics educator*
†Kolaparthi, VenkataSubbaRao *oncologist*
Koster, Kim Richard *anesthesiologist*
Ledford, Frank Finley, Jr., *surgeon, army officer*
Le Maistre, Charles Aubrey *internist, epidemiologist, educator*
Leon, Robert Leonard *psychiatrist, educator*
Marlin, Arthur Edward *pediatric neurosurgeon, educator*
McFadden, Robert Stetson *hepatologist*
McFee, Arthur Storer *physician*
McGill, Henry Coleman, Jr., *pathologist, educator, researcher*
Mouton, Charles Peter *physician, educator*
Neel, Spurgeon Hart, Jr., *physician, retired army officer*
Ognibene, Andre J(ohn) *physician, army officer, educator*
Park, Myung Kun *medical educator*
Persellin, Robert Harold *physician*
Pestana, Carlos *physician, educator*
†Phillips, William Thomas *nuclear medicine physician, researcher*
†Piest, Kenneth Lee *ophthalmic plastic surgeon, educator*
Polan, Jodie Lea *biomedical researcher*
Pruitt, Basil Arthur, Jr., *surgeon, retired army officer*
†Rainwater, David Luther *biomedical researcher*
Randall, Charles Wilson *gastroenterologist*
Reinker, Kent Alan *orthopedist, surgeon, educator*
Reuter, Stewart Ralston *retired radiologist, lawyer, educator*
Roberts, James Lewis *medical sciences educator*
Schenker, Steven *physician, educator*
Schneider, Frank David *family physician*
Shanklin, Kenneth Dale *plastic and reconstructive surgeon*
Smith, John Marvin, III, *surgeon, educator*
Smith, Reginald Brian Furness *retired anesthesiologist, educator*
Solomon, Diane Hurst *neurologist*
Thomas, John Arlen *pharmacology educator, health science administrator*
Thompson, Robert Knox *surgeon*
Ujioka, Takeshi *endocrinologist*
Verghese, Abraham Cheeran *internist, writer, educator*
Walsh, Nicolas Eugene *rehabilitation medicine physician, educator*
Wilkinson, Tolbert Siener *plastic surgeon*
Wirth, Michael Alan *orthopaedic surgeon*
Wolff, Hugh Lipman *urologist, educator*
Zilveti, Carlos Benjamin *preventive medicine physician, pediatrician*
Zwaan, Johan Thomas *ophthalmologist, educator*

San Marcos
Brender, Jean Diane *epidemiologist, nurse*

Seabrook
Patten, Bernard Michael *neurologist, writer, educator*

Sherman
Essin, Emmett Mohammed, Jr., *obstetrician, gynecologist*
Ibazebo, Ehireme Anthony *physician*

South Padre Island
Adwan, Kenneth Oscar *surgeon*

Temple
Brasher, George Walter *physician, consultant*
Dyck, Walter Peter *gastroenterologist, educator, university official*
Holleman, Vernon Daughty *physician, internist*
Knudsen, Kermit Bruce *physician*
Kuo, Lih *medical educator*
Lynch, Dennis James *plastic surgeon*
Nickel, Allan Eugene *physician, educator*
Rohack, John James *cardiologist*

Texarkana
Harrison, James Wilburn *gynecologist*

Texas City
Korndorffer, William Earl *forensic pathologist*

The Woodlands
Desjardins, Raoul *medical association administrator, financial consultant*
†Zhang, Nan *oncologist, health science association administrator*

Tyler
Hyman, William Jay *internist, oncologist*
Neuenschwander, Pierre Fernand *medical educator*
Pinkenburg, Ronald Joseph *ophthalmologist*

Universal City
Parsa, Brian Bahram *surgeon, military officer*

Waco
Anandaraman, Ramanathan *retired physician*
Bryan, John Joseph *physician*
Dow, David Sontag *retired ophthalmologist*
Reddy, Vemula Shanth *physician*
Richie, Rodney Charles *critical care and pulmonary medicine physician*
Sawyer, Dianne Waddell *obstetrician-gynecologist*
Selke, Oscar O., Jr., *physiatrist, educator*
Slade, Harry Warren *neurological surgeon*

Weatherford
Reitman, Sanford *radiologist*

Webster
Farnam, Jafar *allergist, immunologist, pediatrician*

West
Eisma, Jose A. *physician*

Willis
Rappaport, Martin Paul *internist, nephrologist, educator*

Wimberley
Koeppe, Patsy Poduska *internist, educator*
†Cacayorin, Edwin D. *diagnostic and interventional neuroradiologist*

UTAH

American Fork
†Entezari-Taher, Mohammad *neurologist, researcher*

Hyde Park
Wood, Dennis Allen *pathologist*

Logan
Grover, Scott W *surgeon*
Roberts, Donald Wilson *pathologist, consultant*

Mapleton
Hillyard, Ira William *pharmacologist, educator*

Ogden
Spencer, LaVal Wing *retired physician*

Orem
Butler, Ronald B. *pathologist*
Roberts, Stanley Dwayne *physician, medical educator*

Park City
Carmichael, Paul Louis *ophthalmic surgeon*

Provo
Bott, Jay Cordell *oncologist, hematologist*
Latta, George Haworth, III, *neonatologist*
Merrill, Ray Martell *medical educator, consultant*

Saint George
Gaisford, Walter Dan *surgeon*

Salt Lake City
Adashi, Eli Y. *obstetrician, gynecologist*
Bauer, A(ugust) Robert, Jr., *surgeon, medical educator*
Black, Richard Eugene *pediatric surgeon*
†Blumenthal, Deborah T. *neuro-oncologist*
Brandon, Kathryn Elizabeth Beck *pediatrician*
Burke, John Patrick *internist, educator*
Carey, John Clayton *pediatrician, medical geneticist*
Collett, Camille *family physician*
Davis, Roy Kim *otolaryngologist, health facility administrator*
Fujinami, Robert Shin *neurology educator*
Fults, Daniel Webster, III, *neurosurgeon, educator*
Gleich, Gerald Joseph *immunologist, medical scientist, educator*
Goldstein, Michael L. *neurologist*
Graham, John Wallace *pathologist*
Grosser, Bernard Irving *psychiatry educator*
Hammond, M(ary) Elizabeth Hale *pathologist*
†Jaskowski, Troy D *immunologist, researcher*
Johnson, Dale Gedge *pediatric surgeon*
Kestle, John R.W. *pediatric neurosurgeon, epidemiologist*
Knight, Joseph Adams *pathologist*
Krishna, Kishore Bellamkonda *biomedical researcher, educator*
Layfield, Lester James *pathologist, educator*
Legant, Patricia *internist, oncologist*
†Leiferman, Kristin Marie *physician, educator, science association director*
Lloyd, Ray Dix *health physicist*
Lowry, Michael Roy *physician*
Matsuo, Fumisuke *physician, educator*
†McGee, Zell Allison *epidemiologist, educator*
Middleton, Anthony Wayne, Jr., *urologist, educator*
Moser, Royce, Jr., *physician, medical educator*
Nelson, Russell Marion *surgeon, educator*
Norlin, Charles, Jr., (Chuck Norlin) *pediatrician*
†Parkin, James Lamar *otolaryngologist, educator*
Perkins, Sherrie Lynn *pathologist, educator*
Petersen, Finn Bo *oncologist, educator*
Renzetti, Attilio David, Jr., *physician*
Roberts, William Lewis *clinical pathologist*
Sanchez Alvarado, Alejandro *embryologist, molecular biologist*
Simmons, Rulon Andrus *internist*
†Thomas, David Snow *plastic surgeon*
Walker, Marion Lavelle *neurosurgeon*
Ward, John Robert *physician, educator*

VERMONT

Bradford
†Kaplow, Leonard Samuel *pathologist, educator*

Brattleboro
Agallianos, Dennis Dionysios *psychiatrist*

Burlington
Brown, Kenneth Andrew *cardiologist, educator*
Ciongoli, Alfred Kenneth *neurologist*
Cooper, Sheldon Mark *medical educator, immunology researcher, rheumatologist*
Davis, John Herschel *surgeon, educator, retired*
Krag, Martin Hans *physician, orthopaedist, educator, researcher*
Lidofsky, Steven David *medical educator*
Lucey, Jerold Francis *pediatrician*
†Maugans, Todd Allen *pediatric neurosurgeon*
Morrow, Paul Lowell *forensic pathologist*
†Moses, Peter L. *gastroenterologist, researcher*
Riddick, Daniel Howison *obstetrics and gynecology educator, priest*
Sobel, Burton Elias *physician, educator*
Tampas, John P. *radiologist*
Tranmer, Bruce Ian *neurosurgeon*
Waterman, Gerald Scott *psychiatrist, physician educator*
†Weissgold, David Jay *ophthalmologist, educator*

Colchester
Danielson, Ursel Rehding *psychiatrist*

Dorset
Bamford, Joseph Charles, Jr., *gynecologist, obstetrician, educator, medical missionary, writer*

Jacksonville
Dell, Ralph Bishop *pediatrician, researcher*
Hein, Karen Kramer *pediatrician, epidemiologist*

Norwich
Katz, Arnold Martin *medical educator*

Randolph
Sax, Daniel Saul *neurologist, educator*

Shelburne
Foster, Roger Sherman, Jr., *surgeon, educator, health facility administrator*

South Burlington
Hyman, Neil Hyman *surgeon, educator*
Shinozaki, Tamotsu *retired physician, anesthesiologist*

Stowe
Fagan, William Thomas, Jr., *urologist*

Swanton
Wooding, William Minor *statistics consultant*

Underhill
Danforth, Elliot, Jr., *medical educator*

White River Junction
Friedman, Matthew Joel *psychiatrist, pharmacologist, educator*
Myers, Warren Powers Laird *physician, educator*
†Ogrinc, Gregory Simon *physician, educator*

Winooski
Fenton, Jonathan E. *osteopath*

Woodstock
Killian, Edward James *pediatrician*

VIRGINIA

Afton
McCoy, Sue *surgeon, biochemist*

Alexandria
Akukwe, Chinua *public health physician, health service executive*
Buhain, Wilfrido Javier *medical educator*
Bumgarner, Robert Linville *pathologist, retired military officer*
Chapman, Anthony Bradley *psychiatrist*
Hark, William Henry *medical executive, retired military officer*
Herrera, Clarita *medical association administrator*

Annandale
Lefrak, Edward Arthur *cardiovascular and thoracic surgeon*
Shamburek, Roland Howard *physician*
Simonian, Simon John *surgeon, scientist, educator*
Tavallali, Morad *plastic and reconstructive surgeon*

Arlington
Adams, Hunter (Patch Adams) *internist, health facility administrator*
Dvorak, Josef Cermin *endocrinologist*
Ferraz, Francisco Marconi *neurological surgeon*
Harper, Michael John Kennedy *obstetrics and gynecology educator*
Lundeen, William Bruce *radiologist*
Nguyen-Dinh, Thanh *internist, geriatrician, acupuncturist*
Nirschl, Robert Phillip *orthopedic surgeon*
Shine, Kenneth Irwin *cardiologist, educator*

Charlottesville
Barrett, Eugene Joseph *researcher, medical educator, physician*
Bayliss, E. Virginia *psychiatrist, educator*
Beller, George Allan *medical educator*
†Bruns, David Eugene *medical educator, researcher*
Cantrell, Robert Wendell *otolaryngologist, head and neck surgeon, educator*
Carey, Robert Munson *medical educator, physician*
†Chaidarun, Sushela Songtanin *endocrinologist, researcher*
†Clayton, Anita Louise *psychiatrist, physician*
Conway, Brian Peter *ophthalmologist, educator*
†Corbett, Eugene C., Jr., *medical educator*
Craig, James William *physician, educator, university dean*
†Crosby, Ivan Keith *cardiologist, educator*
Dalton, Claudette Ellis Harloe *anesthesiologist, educator, university official*
Detmer, Don Eugene *health management and policy researcher, medical educator, surgeon*
Durbin, Charles G., Jr., *anesthesiologist, intensivist, educator*
†Elias, W. Jeffrey *neurosurgeon*
Epstein, Robert Marvin *anesthesiologist, educator*
Flickinger, Charles John *anatomist, educator*
Gay, Spencer Bradley *radiologist, educator*
†Gillenwater, Jay Young *urologist, educator*
Greyson, Charles Bruce *psychiatrist*
Gröschel, Dieter Hans Max *physician, educator*
†Hillman, Bruce Jay *radiologist, researcher, consultant, educator*
Hunt, William B. *cardiopulmonary physician*
†Jagger, Janine *epidemiologist*
Jones, Rayford Scott *surgeon, medical educator*
Kassell, Neal Frederic *neurosurgery educator*
Kattwinkel, John *physician, pediatrics educator*
Keats, Theodore Eliot *physician, radiology educator*
†Kelly, Thaddeus Elliott *medical geneticist*
†Kerrigan, D. Casey *physiatrist, educator*
†Kountakis, Stilianos E *surgeon, otolaryngologist*
Lee, Jae Kyun *biomedical researcher, educator*
Mandell, Gerald Lee *physician, medicine educator*
Marshall, John Crook *internal medicine educator, researcher*
Morgan, Raymond F. *plastic surgeon*
Muller, William Henry, Jr., *surgeon, educator*
Nolan, Stanton Peelle *surgeon, educator*
Owen, John Atkinson, Jr., *physician, educator*
Peterson, Kent Wright *physician*
Phillips, Lawrence H., II, *neurologist, educator*
Platts-Mills, Thomas Alexander E. *immunologist, educator, researcher*
Rein, Michael Frank *physician, medical educator*
Rowlingson, John Clyde *anesthesiologist, educator, physician*
Sarembock, Ian Joseph *internist*
Schneider, Edward Martin *retired physician*
Stevenson, Ian *psychiatrist, educator*
Teates, Charles David *radiologist, educator*
Weary, Peyton Edwin *retired medical educator*
Wills, Michael Ralph *medical educator*
†Winther, Birgit *otolaryngologist, researcher*

Chase City
Suslick, Randall Hugh *family practice physician*

Chesapeake
Kovalcik, Paul Jerome *surgeon*
Montag, Thomas William *gynecologic oncologist*
Pugach, Neil Lewis *neurologist*

Christiansburg
Hershey, Jody Henry *public health physician*

Colonial Heights
Chiu, Ming Sung *physician*

Danville
Kovarsky, Joel Severin *rheumatologist, small business owner*

Fairfax
Berger, Robert Martin *urologist*
Binder, Richard Allen *hematologist, oncologist*
Dettinger, Garth Bryant *surgeon, physician, retired air force officer, county health officer*
DuRocher, Frances A. *physician, educator*
Fisher, Linda Alice *physician*
Klayton, Ronald Jay *physician*
Libby, Russell Clark *pediatrician*
†Robert, Nicholas James *hematolgist, oncologist*
Rubinstein, Mark Isaac *physician*
Shapiro, Stephen Robert *cardiologist*
Snyder, Roger Alan *physician, neurologist*
Stage, Thomas Benton *psychiatrist*
Zimmerman, Thomas Fletcher, III, *medical educator, consultant*

Falls Church
Bucur, John Charles *neurological surgeon*
Cooper, James Nelson *medical educator*
Elliott, Virginia F. Harrison *retired anatomist, kinesiologist and educator, investment advisor, publisher, philanthropist*
Evans, Peter Yoshio *ophthalmologist, educator*
Golomb, Herbert Stanley *dermatologist*
Hauda, William Edward, II, *emergency physician*
†Hernandez, Antonio *gynecologist*
Inglefield, Joseph T., Jr., *allergist, immunologist, pediatrician*
Karpick, Ronald John *pulmonologist, internist, geriatrician*
Kurtzke, John Francis, Sr., *neurologist, epidemiologist*
McCullough, William Lawrence *medical readiness consultant*

Scott, Hugh Patrick *physician, naval officer*
Wise, Thomas Nathan *psychiatrist*

Hampton
Brown, Loretta Ann Port *physician, geneticist*

Heathsville
Daniel, John Griffith *physician*

Keswick
Rowe, William Joseph *internist*

Leesburg
Mitchell, Russell Harry *dermatologist*

Lexington
DeSilvey, Dennis Lee *cardiologist, educator, university administrator*

Lynchburg
Cooper, Alan Michael *psychiatrist*
Cunniff, Suzanne *surgical technician*

Manassas
†Gelooo, Nadim Ahmad *cardiologist*

Marion
Armbrister, Douglas Kenley *surgeon*

Mc Lean
Tabrizi, Mehdi Fakher *obstetrician/gynecologist*
Wallace, Robert Bruce *surgeon, retired*
Wright, William Evan *physician*

Mechanicsville
Lordi, William Michael *psychiatrist, child psychiatrist*

Midlothian
Friedel, Robert Oliver *physician*
O'Shanick, Gregory John *physician, medical association administrator*

Monterey
Tabatznik, Bernard *retired physician, educator*

Newport News
Nichols, Allen Bryant *physician, cardiologist*

Norfolk
Andrews, William Cooke *physician*
Archer, Robert Patrick *psychologist, educator*
Counselman, Francis L. *emergency medicine physician, educator*
Evett, Russell Dougherty *internist, educator*
Faulconer, Robert Jamieson *pathologist, educator*
Jenson, Hal Brockbank *physician*
Lester, Richard Garrison *radiologist, educator*
Morrison, Ashton Byrom *pathologist, medical school official*
†Oehninger, Sergio C. *endocrinologist, obstetrician, gynecologist*
Oelberg, David George *neonatologist, educator, researcher*
Rohn, Reuben David *pediatric educator and administrator*
Stallings, Valerie A. *physician, state official*
Valone, James Austin, Jr., *retired surgeon*
Wolcott, Hugh Dixon *obstetrics and gynecology educator*

North Garden
Moses, Hamilton, III, *medical educator, hospital executive, management consultant*

Norton
Vest, Gayle Southworth *obstetrician and gynecologist*
Vest, Steven Lee *gastroenterologist, hepatologist, internist*

Petersburg
Ende, Milton *internist*

Portsmouth
Clare, Frank Brian *neurosurgeon, neurologist*
O'Malley, Timothy Patrick *otolaryngologist*
Yarbrough, Terry Pinckney *physician*

Raven
Joyce, Larry Wayne *physician*

Richlands
Stefanini, Mario *physician, pathologist*

Richmond
Accardo, Pasquale J. *pediatrician, educator*
Ayres, Stephen McClintock *physician, educator*
Balster, Robert Louis *psychopharmacologist*
Bates, Hampton Robert, Jr., *pathologist*
Blumberg, Michael Zangwill *allergist*
Boone, Elwood Bernard, Jr., *physician, urologist*
†Carr, Marcus Eugene, Jr., *internist*
David, Ronald Brian *child neurologist*
DeLorenzo, Robert John *neurologist, molecular neuroscientist*
Dessypris, Emmanuel Nicholas *hematologist-oncologist*
†Doarn, Charles R. *medical educator*
Downs, Robert Woodward, Jr., *endocrinologist, researcher*
Dunn, Leo James *obstetrician, educator, gynecologist, educator*
Franko, Bernard Vincent *pharmacologist, educator*
†Gehr, Lynne Connolly *anesthesiologist*
Graham, Sam Dixon *urologist*
Harris, Louis Selig *pharmacologist, researcher*
Kaplowitz, Lisa Glauser *physician, educator*
Kay, Saul *retired pathologist*
†Kok, Lai Chow *physician, medical educator*
Lawrence, Walter, Jr., *surgeon, educator*
Long, Stephen Paul *anesthesiologist*
Mauck, Henry Page, Jr., *medical and pediatrics educator*
Merrell, Ronald Clifton *surgeon, educator*

Mollen, Edward Leigh *pediatrician, allergist and clinical immunologist*
Neal, Marcus Pinson, Jr., *radiologist, medical educator*
Neifeld, James Paul *surgical oncologist*
†Neufeld, Jacob A. *pediatrician, psychiatrist*
†Osgood, Nancy Jean *college educator, author*
Owen, Duncan Shaw, Jr., *physician, medical educator*
Richardson, David Walthall *cardiologist, educator, consultant*
Sirica, Alphonse Eugene *pathology educator*
Solan, Stuart Miley *physician*
Sugerman, Harvey Jay *surgery educator*
Tunner, William Sams *urological surgeon*
Turner, Elaine S. *allergist, immunologist*
†Vijayaraman, Pugazhendhi *medical educator*
Walton, G. Clifford *family practice physician*
Ward, John Wesley *retired pharmacologist*
Wenzel, Richard Putnam *internist*
Wilkinson, David Stanley *pathologist, consultant, researcher, educator, physician*
Wise, Christopher Murray *internist, rheumatologist*

Roanoke
Hutcheson, Jack Robert *hematologist, medical oncologist*
Kennedy, Stephen Smith *hematologist, oncologist, educator*
†Livingston, Jeffrey Charles *obstetrician, gynecologist*
Vermillion, Robert Lee *obstetrician, gynecologist*

Roseland
Stemmler, Edward Joseph *physician, retired association executive, retired academic dean*
Wood, Maurice *medical educator*

Sterling
Jaffe, Russell Merritt *pathologist, research director*

Suffolk
Carroll, George Joseph *pathologist, educator*

Syria
†Altaffer, Lawrence F., III, *retired physician, artist*

Vienna
Schwartz, Richard Harvey *pediatrician*
Shaver, Timothy Roddy *surgeon*

Virginia Beach
Carlston, John A. *allergist*
McDaniel, David Henry *physician*

White Stone
†Duer, Ellen Ann Dagon *anesthesiologist, general practitioner*

Williamsburg
Connell, Alastair McCrae *physician*
Davis, Richard Bradley *internal medicine, pathology educator, physician*
Jacoby, William Jerome, Jr., *internist, retired military officer*
Maloney, Milford Charles *retired internal medicine educator*
Schwartz, Miles Joseph *cardiologist*
Voorhess, Mary Louise *pediatric endocrinologist*

Winchester
Bechamps, Gerald Joseph *surgeon*
Creasy, Richard Alan *anesthesiologist*
Isenhower, Nelson Nolan *anesthesiologist*
Moore, Richard Carroll, Jr., *family physician*

Wytheville
McConnell, James Joseph *internist*

Yorktown
Ray, Charles Dean *neurosurgeon, spine surgeon, bioengineer, inventor*

WASHINGTON

Auburn
Nazaire, Michel Harry *physician*
†Sata, Lindbergh Saburo *psychiatrist, educator*

Bellevue
Brockenbrough, Edwin Chamberlayne *surgeon*
Hackett, Carol Ann Hedden *physician*
Lipton, Judith Eve *psychiatrist*
Phillips, Zaiga Alksnis *pediatrician*
Shurtleff, David *pediatrician, educator*
†Whatmore, George Bernard *physician, scientist, clinical neurophysiologist*

Bellingham
Harell, George S. *radiologist*
Howe, Warren Billings *physician*
†James, Helen Ann *plastic surgeon*
Shokeir, Marc Omar *pathologist*
Wayne, Marvin Alan *emergency medicine physician*

Bothell
†Lal, Manjari *pharmacologist, researcher*
Weiden, Paul Lincoln *cancer researcher, oncologist, educator*

Bremerton
Lamberg, John David *internist*

Camas
Liem, Annie *pediatrician*

Centralia
Miller, James McCalmont *pediatrician*

Chehalis
Neal-Parker, Shirley Anita *obstetrician and gynecologist*

Clarkston
Chinchinian, Harry *pathologist, educator*

Clyde Hill
Condon, Robert Edward *surgeon, educator, consultant*

Coupeville
Mayhew, Eric George *medical researcher, educator*

Edmonds
Bray, Ronald Eugene *obstetrician/gynecologist*
Crone, Richard Allan *cardiologist, educator*
Yoon, Jay Myoung *oncologist, hematologist, internist*

Ellensburg
Sand, John Halvdan *obstetrician, gynecologist*

Everett
Lee, Anne Marie *endocrinologist*
Smith, Thomas J. *surgeon, educator*

Federal Way
Dorman, Thomas Alfred *internist, orthopaedist*

Gig Harbor
Earley, Laurence Elliott *retired medical educator*

Issaquah
Barchet, Stephen *physician, former naval officer*

Kirkland
Barto, Deborah Ann *physician*
Dunn, Jeffrey Edward *neurologist*

Longview
Sandstrom, Robert Edward *pathologist*

Lynden
Hibbs, Clair M. *retired pathologist*

Mercer Island
Coe, Robert Campbell *retired surgeon*
Elgee, Neil Johnson *retired internist, educator, retired endocrinologist, educator*
Haviland, James West *physician, educator*

Olympia
Hayes, Maxine Delores *physician, pediatrician*
Hildebrand, Alice Grace *physician*
Montgomery, Anne M. *family practice physician, educator, consultant*

Onalaska
Leadbetter, Mark Renton, Jr., *orthopedic surgeon*

Poulsbo
Meyer, Roger Jess Christian *pediatrics educator*
O'Morchoe, Patricia Jean *pathologist, educator*

Pullman
†Robison, Linda M. *epidemiologist, medical researcher*
Sclar, David Alexander *medical policy educator*

Redmond
Turnbull, Lawrence F. *retired anesthesiologist*

Renton
Klaff, Leslie J. *physician, research company executive*

Richland
Bair, William J. *retired radiation biologist*
†Mushen, Robert Linton *ophthalmologist, consultant*
Zirkle, Lewis Greer *orthopedist*

Seabeck
Genuit, David Walter *podiatrist*

Seattle
†Agoff, S. Nicholas *surgical pathologist*
Aigner, B. Robert *neurologist*
Aldea, Gabriel S. *cardiothoracic surgeon, educator*
Ansell, Julian S. *physician, retired urology educator*
Austin, Erik *physician, osteopath*
Austin-Seymour, Mary M. *radiation oncologist*
Blake-Inada, Louis Michael *cardiologist, researcher*
Bornstein, Paul *physician, biochemist*
Bowden, Douglas McHose *neuropsychiatric scientist, educator, research center administrator*
†Casper, Corey *physician, researcher*
Catterall, William A. *pharmacology, neurobiology educator*
†Chatard, Peter Ralph Noel, Jr., *aesthetic plastic surgeon*
†Cheong, Jonathan Cheeyong *medical researcher*
Clarren, Sterling Keith *pediatrician*
Clowes, Alexander Whitehill *surgeon, educator*
†Colquhoun, James S. *physician*
Couser, William Griffith *medical educator, academic administrator, nephrologist*
Dale, David C. *physician, medical educator*
Dawson, Patricia Lucille *surgeon*
Day, Robert Winsor *preventive medicine physician, researcher*
†DeWitt, Dawn E. *medical educator, dean*
Domino, Karen Barbara *anesthesiology educator*
Dunner, David Louis *medical educator*
†Ellis, Georgiana Kehr *internist*
Eschbach, Joseph Wetherill *nephrology educator*
Fall, Gordon Frederick Francis *family physician*
Fine, James Stephen *physician*
†Gardella, Carolyn M *medical researcher, director, medical educator*
Gayle, Helene D. *public health physician*
Geyman, John Payne *physician, educator*
†Giblett, Eloise Rosalie *hematologist, educator*
†Gospe, Sidney Maloch, Jr., *child neurologist*

†Grayston, J. Thomas *medical and public health educator*
Guntheroth, Warren Gaden *pediatrician, educator*
Halar, Eugen Marian *physiatrist, educator*
†Hanel, Douglas Paul *orthopedist, surgeon*
Hazzard, William Russell *geriatrician, educator*
†Heimfeld, Shelly *hematologist, researcher, immunologist, researcher*
Helgerson, Steven Dale *epidemiologist, educator*
Henderson, Maureen McGrath *medical educator*
Holm, Vanja Adele *developmental pediatrician, educator*
Holmes, King Kennard *medical educator*
Hornbein, Thomas Frederic *anesthesiologist*
†Ioannov, George N. *gastroenterologist, researcher*
†Kahn, Steven Emanuel *medical educator*
Kalina, Robert Edward *opthalmologist, educator*
Karl, Helen Weist *pediatric anesthesia and pain management educator, researcher*
Klebanoff, Seymour Joseph *medical educator*
†Kozarek, Richard Anthony *gastroenterologist, educator*
Kraft, George Howard *physician, educator*
Krohn, Kenneth Albert *radiology educator*
Lam, Arthur M. *anesthesiologist, educator*
Larrabee, Wayne Fox, Jr., *facial plastic surgeon*
Likosky, William Harris *neurologist, epidemiologist*
Loeser, John David *neurosurgeon, educator*
Lynn, Anne Marie *anesthesiologist, pediatrician*
Mankoff, David Abraham *nuclear medicine physician*
Martin, George M. *pathologist, gerontologist, educator*
Martin, Thomas R. *medical educator, medical association administrator*
Matsen, Frederick Albert, III, *orthopedic educator*
†McKone, Edward Francis *medical educator*
†Mesiwala, Ali Hakim *neurologist, surgeon*
Modabber, Farrokh *immunologist*
Moore, Daniel Charles *anesthesiologist*
†Nelp, Wil B. *physician, medical educator*
Nelson, James Alonzo *radiologist, educator*
Neppe, Vernon Michael *neuropsychiatrist, psychopharmacologist, forensic specialist, author, educator, playwright*
Nicholls, Stephen Charles *surgeon, educator*
†Oelschlager, Brant Kurt *surgeon, researcher*
Orcutt, James Craig *ophthalmologist*
Pagon, Roberta Anderson *pediatrics educator*
Petersdorf, Robert George *physician, medical educator, academic administrator*
Probstfield, Jeffrey Lynn *cardiology educator, consultant*
Ravenholt, Reimert Thorolf *epidemiologist, researcher*
Risse, Guenter Bernhard *physician, historian, educator*
Rivara, Frederick Peter *pediatrician, educator*
†Routt, Milton Lee (Chip) *orthopedic trauma surgeon, educator*
Rowell, Loring Bernard *medical educator, researcher*
Rutledge, Joe *pathologist, scientist*
Sale, George Edgar *pathologist*
Saneto, Russell Patrick *pediatric neurologist, epileptologist, neurobiologist*
†Schenkman, Kenneth A. *physician, biomedical researcher*
Scott, John Carlyle *retired gynecologist, oncologist*
Shepard, Thomas Hill *physician, educator*
Sherman, Daniel Adam *psychiatrist*
Simkin, Peter Anthony *internist, educator*
Smith, Douglas George *orthopaedic surgeon, educator*
Stenchever, Morton Albert *obstetrician, gynecologist*
Stolov, Walter Charles *physician, rehabilitation educator, physiatrist*
Swanson, August George *physician, retired association executive*
†Teitz, Carol *orthopedist, surgeon, educator*
Thomas, Edward Donnall *physician, researcher*
Tucker, Gary Jay *physician, educator*
†Waldhausen, John Henry Trescher *pediatric surgeon, educator*
†Wessells, Hunter *urologist, researcher*
Winn, H. Richard *surgeon*
Yue, Agnes Kau-Wah *otolaryngologist*
†Zager, Richard A. *medical educator, researcher*
Ziskind, Andrew A. *cardiologist, dean*

Selah
Markin, Karl Edward *obstetrician/gynecologist*

Shoreline
Merendino, K. Alvin *surgical educator*

Spokane
Cohen, Arnold Norman *gastroenterologist*
Gibson, Melvin Roy *pharmacology educator*
Lang, Melanie Sue *physician, oral and maxillofacial surgeon*
Lee, Hi Young *physician, acupuncturist*
Russell, Byron Edward *physical therapy educator*

Tacoma
†Azarow, Kenneth S. *surgeon*
Cuevas, Eduardo Samaniego *internist*
Hori, Kiyoaky *retired anesthesiologist*
Rahe, Richard Henry *psychiatrist, educator*
†Rose, John Creighton *child psychiatrist*
Verhey, Joseph William *psychiatrist, educator*

University Place
Flemming, Stanley Lalit Kumar *family practice physician, mayor, state legislator*
Pliskow, Vita Sari *anesthesiologist*

Vancouver
Perlstein, Abraham Phillip *psychiatrist, educator*
Price, Ernest Howell *retired family practice physician, administrator*

Vashon
Vallarta, Josefina M. *retired child neurologist*

Wenatchee
Knecht, Ben Harrold *surgeon*

WEST VIRGINIA

Beckley
Dinh, Anthony Tung *internist*
Hooper, William Dale *surgeon*

Charleston
Bateman, Mildred Mitchell *retired psychiatrist*
Boland, James Pius *surgeon, educator*
Cochran, Robert Carter *surgical educator*
†Pfister, Alfred Karl *internist, educator*

Clarksburg
Coonley, Craig Joseph *internist, hematologist, oncologist*
de la Pena, Cordell Amado *pathologist*
Sarino, Edgardo Formantes *radiologist, physician*

Elkins
Khatter, Prithipal Singh *radiologist*

Fairmont
Koppel, Donald M(aurice) *internist*

Huntington
Chertow, Bruce S. *endocrinologist*
Cocke, William Marvin, Jr., *plastic surgeon, educator*
Darby, H. Darrel *podiatric surgeon*
Driscoll, Henry Keane *endocrinologist, researcher*
Molina, Rafael Evencio *urologist*
Morabito, Rocco Anthony *urologist*
Mufson, Maurice Albert *physician, educator*
Nerhood, Robert Clarke *obstetrician and gynecologist*
Sebert, Stephen L. *physician*
†Sypher, Blake *medical educator*

Kingwood
Moyers, Sylvia Dean *retired medical record librarian*

Lewisburg
Mazzio-Moore, Joan L. *radiology educator, physician*

Martinsburg
Malin, Howard Gerald *podiatrist*

Morgantown
Albrink, Margaret Joralemon *medical educator*
Bang, Ki Moon *epidemiologist, educator*
Chisholm, Lionel Donald John *ophthalmologist*
Ducatman, Alan Marc *physician*
†Emery, Sanford Emil *orthopedic surgeon*
Fleming, William Wright, Jr., *pharmacology educator*
Glover, Douglas Dennis *obstetrics, gynecology and pharmacology educator*
Hill, Ronald Charles *surgeon, educator*
†Hilloowala, Rumy A. *retired anatomist and anthropologist*
Hogan, Mary Beth *medical educator*
Jabbour, Nabil Milad *ophthalmologist*
†Li, Qingdi Quentin *physician, research scientist, medical educator*
Martin, James Douglas *neurologist*
Voelker, Joseph L. *neurosurgeon*
†Weisse, Martin Edward *pediatrician, educator*

Princeton
Gindin, R. Arthur *retired neurosurgeon*

Ronceverte
Hooper, Anne Dodge *pathologist, educator*

Wheeling
Good, Laurance Frederic *medical foundation administrator*

WISCONSIN

Appleton
Boren, Clark Henry, Jr., *general and vascular surgeon*
Goldsmith, Robin Jean *anesthesiologist*
Luther, Thomas William *retired physician*

Brookfield
Hardman, Harold Francis *pharmacology educator*
Kortebein, Stuart Rowland *orthopedic surgeon*

Cadott
Sanchez, Romulo Manalo *physician*

Drummond
Kingdon, Henry Shannon *retired physician, biochemist, educator, executive*

Fond Du Lac
Treffert, Darold Allen *psychiatrist, author, hospital director*

Fort Atkinson
Anschutz, Harold Fredric, Jr., *family physician*

Green Bay
Anthony, Lewis George *retired internist, cardiologist*
Finesilver, Alan George *rheumatologist*

Hales Corners
Kuwayama, S. Paul *physician, allergist, immunologist*
Lautz, David A. *pediatrician*

Janesville
Gianitsos, Anestis Nicholas *surgeon*

La Crosse
Corser, David Hewson *pediatrician, retired*
Landercasper, Jeffrey *surgeon*
Ross, Arthur J., III, *physician*
Silva, Paul Douglas *reproductive endocrinologist*
Smith, Martin Jay *physician, biomedical research scientist*
Webster, Stephen Burtis *physician, educator*

Lake Geneva
Liebman, Monte Harris *retired psychiatrist*
Petersen, Edward Schmidt *retired physician*

Madison
Albanese, Mark Alan *medical educator*
Albert, Daniel Myron *ophthalmologist, educator*
†Bajad Sunil, Uttamrao *pharmacologist, researcher*
Barry, Terence Patrick *endocrinologist, aquaculturist*
Bass, Paul *pharmacology educator*
Bentz, Michael Lloyd *plastic and reconstructive surgeon*
Blank, Robert Daniel *medical educator*
Brown, Arnold Lanehart, Jr., *pathologist, educator, university dean*
Burgess, Richard Ray *oncology educator, molecular biology researcher, biotechnology consultant*
Cripps, Derek J. *dermatologist, educator*
Dodson, Vernon Nathan *physician, educator*
Fahien, Leonard August *physician, educator*
Faillace, Walter Joseph *medical educator*
Farrell, Philip M. *dean, physician, educator, researcher*
Ford, Charles Nathaniel *otolaryngologist, educator*
Forster, Francis Michael *physician, educator*
†Gern, James E. *physician, researcher*
Glassroth, Jeffrey *physican, medical educator*
Guillery, Rainer Walter *anatomy educator*
Hahn, David Louis *family practice physician, educator*
Hartmann, Henrik Anton *medical educator*
Haughton, Victor Mellet *physician, educator*
†Hecht, Rudolph C. *physician, educator*
†Hirano, Shigeru *surgeon, researcher*
Iskandar, Bermans Jamil *pediatric neurosurgeon*
†January, Craig Taylor *cardiologist, researcher*
Javid, Manucher J. *retired neurosurgery educator*
Jefferson, James Walter *psychiatry educator*
Johnson, Maryl Rae *cardiologist*
Karofsky, Peter Stuart *pediatrician, medical educator*
†Klein, Marjorie Hanson *psychiatry educator*
Laessig, Ronald Harold *preventive medicine and pathology educator, state official*
Lemanske, Robert F., Jr., *allergist, immunologist*
Lindgren, Richard Dan *retired radiologist, healthcare administrator*
MacKinney, Archie Allen, Jr., *physician*
Mahvi, David M. *surgeon, educator*
Maki, Dennis G. *medical educator, researcher, clinician*
Myers, Franklin Lewis, II, *ophthalmologist*
Niederhuber, John Edward *surgical oncologist and molecular immunologist, university educator and administrator*
Nordby, Eugene Jorgen *orthopedic surgeon*
Peters, Henry Augustus *neuropsychiatrist*
Pitot, Henry Clement, III, *pathologist, educator*
Reizner, George Terry *medical educator*
Resnick, Daniel Karel *neurosurgeon, spinal surgeon, medical educator*
Reynolds, Ernest West *retired physician, educator*
Roberts, Leigh Milton *psychiatrist*
Sanchez, Cheryl Pimentel *pediatrician, educator*
Scarborough, John Samuel *pharmacy, medicine and ancient history educator*
Schutta, Henry Szczesny *neurologist, educator*
Selvaggi, Suzanne Marie *pathologist, educator*
Sobkowicz, Hanna Maria *neurology researcher*
Sondel, Paul Mark *pediatric oncologist, educator*
Sonnedecker, Glenn Allen *pharmaceutical historian, pharmaceutical educator*
†Terasawa-Grilley, Ei *medical educator*
†Trier, Todd T. *neurosurgeon*
Walker, Duard Lee *medical educator*
Wenger, Ronald David *surgeon*
Westman, Jack Conrad *child psychiatrist, educator*
Whiffen, James Douglass *surgeon, educator*

Manitowoc
Trader, Joseph Edgar *orthopedic surgeon*

Marinette
†El-Jack, Mohammed S. *urologist*

Marshfield
Bibbo, Christopher *physician*
†Myers, William Osgood *thoracic and cardiovascular surgeon*
Tak, Tahir *cardiologist, researcher*
Vidaillet, Humberto J., Jr., *physician, researcher*
†Yale, Steven Howard *internist*

Menomonee Falls
Fisher, Robert Henri *physician*

Mequon
Cheema, Mohammad Aslam *retired cardiothoracic surgeon, community leader*
Krausen, Anthony Sharnik *plastic surgeon*

Milwaukee
†Agha, Zia *physician, researcher*
Bernstein, Paul Steven *cardiologist*
Campbell, Bruce Hegstad *otolaryngologist, educator*
Carballo, Fernando Anthony *gastroenterologist, hepatologist*
Chan, Carlyle Hung-lun *psychiatrist, educator*
Cohen, Steven Howard *allergist, immunologist, educator*
Cooper, Kristine Marie *internist*
Cooper, Richard Alan *hematologist, college dean, health policy analyst*
Esterly, Nancy Burton *physician*
Feinsilver, Donald Lee *psychiatry educator*
Foldy, Seth Leonard *public health officer, family practice physician*
Goldstein, Paul H(enry) *ophthalmologist, educator*
Gonnering, Russell Stephen *ophthalmic plastic surgeon*
Greaves, William Walter *preventive medicine physician, educator*
†Haasler, George Bruce *cardiothoracic surgeon*
Hur, Su-Ryong *physician, anesthesiologist*
†Kampine, John P. *anesthesiology and physiology educator*
Kidder, Thomas Michael *otolaryngologist*
Kochar, Mahendr Singh *physician, educator, administrator, scientist, writer, consultant*
†Korabic, Edward Walter *medical educator, speech pathology/audiology services professional*
Kovnar, Edward H. *pediatric neurologist, medical educator*
Larson, David Lee *surgeon*
Maiman, Dennis Jay *neurosurgeon*
†Massey, Benson Talmage *gastroenterologist*
Meyer, Jon Keith *psychiatrist, psychoanalyst, educator*
Miller, Edward Carl William *physician*
Moffie, H. Steven *psychiatrist*
†Morris, George L. *neurologist, educator*
Muszynski, Cheryl Ann *neurosurgeon*
Namdari, Bahram *surgeon*
Novak, Joseph Anthony *physician, pathologist*
Oldham, Keith T. *surgeon*
†Pagel, Paul Stanley *anesthesiologist*
Port, Steven Charles *cardiologist, educator*
Rathour, Rajendra Singh *internist*
Schultz, Richard Otto *ophthalmologist, educator*
Shaker, Reza *gastroenterologist, educator*
Shetty, Kaup Rajmohan *endocrinologist, educator*
Shidham, Vinod Baburao *pathologist, cytopathologist, surgical pathologist*
Soergel, Konrad Hermann *physician*
Stokes, Kathleen Sarah *dermatologist, educator*
†Tector, Alfred J. *cardiothoracic surgeon*
Telford, Gordon Laing *surgeon, educator*
Terry, Leon Cass *neurologist, educator*
Wackym, Phillip Ashley *surgeon, researcher, otolaryngologist*
Wagner, Marvin *general and vascular surgeon, educator*
Waltier, David Charles *anesthesiologist, medical researcher*
†Yancey, Kim Bruce *dermatology researcher*
Young, Craig C. *sports medicine physician, educator*

Monroe
Kelly, James Evans *internist*

Oak Creek
Kim, Zaezeung *allergist, immunologist, educator*

Onalaska
Waite, Lawrence Wesley *osteopathic physician, educator*

Oshkosh
Cooper, Janelle Lunette *neurologist, educator*

Plymouth
Sharon, Mark William *family practice physician*

Racine
Stewart, Richard Donald *internist, educator, biographer*

Rhinelander
Agre, James Courtland *physical medicine and rehabilitation*

Stevens Point
†Huncharek, Michael Stephen *oncologist*

Sturgeon Bay
Greaves, Alison Ash *retired physician*

Waukesha
Cahill, Charles Adams, III, *psychiatrist*

Wauwatosa
Hollister, Winston Ned *pathologist*

WYOMING

Casper
Bennion, Scott Desmond *physician*

Cheyenne
Flick, William Fredrick *surgeon*

Jackson
Begelman, Kenneth Marc *cardiovascular surgeon*

Laramie
Kelley, Robert Otis *medical science educator*

Sheridan
Batty, Hugh Kenworthy *physician*

TERRITORIES OF THE UNITED STATES

GUAM

Agana
Espaldon, Ernesto Mercader *plastic surgeon, former senator*

Tamuning
Wresch, Robert Richard *ophthalmologist, medical educator*

NORTHERN MARIANA ISLANDS

Saipan
Khorram, K. David *ophthalmologist*

PUERTO RICO

Carolina
†Agosto, Jose A. *psychiatrist*

Mayaguez
Sahai, Hardeo *medical statistics educator*

San Juan
†Cruz-Korchin, Norma I. *plastic surgeon*
†Del Toro Soto, Jaime *psychiatrist*
Fernandez-Martinez, Jose *physician*
†Grovas, Carlos *orthopedic surgeon*
Lopez-Davila, Liana Esther *radiologist*
†Ortiz, Pedro P *orthopedic surgeon*
Rodriguez, Agustin Antonio *surgeon*
Rodriguez Arroyo, Jesus *gynecologic oncologist*
Rosario-Guardiola, Reinaldo *dermatologist*

Trujillo Alto
†Matos, Brenda Enid *psychiatrist*

VIRGIN ISLANDS

Saint Thomas
Shapiro, Adam Marc *otolaryngologist*

MILITARY ADDRESSES OF THE UNITED STATES

PACIFIC

Apo
Benenson, Michael William *physician, epidemiologist*

Fpo
Rice, James Philip *surgeon*

CANADA

ALBERTA

Calgary
Lederis, Karolis Paul (Karl Lederis) *pharmacologist, educator, researcher*
Leung, Alexander Kwok-Chu *pediatrician*
Smith, Eldon *cardiologist, physiologist, educator*

Edmonton
Gyenes, Gábor *physician, educator*
Miller, Jack David R. *radiologist, physician, educator*

BRITISH COLUMBIA

Vancouver
Baird, Patricia Ann *physician, educator*
Doyle, Patrick John *otolaryngologist, department chairman*
Eaves, Allen Charles Edward *hematologist, medical agency administrator*
Friedman, Sydney M. *anatomy educator, medical researcher*
Hardwick, David Francis *pathologist*
McGeer, Edith Graef *neurological science educator*
Mizgala, Henry F. *physician, consultant, retired medical educator*
Paty, Donald Winston *neurologist, educator*
Roy, Chunilal *psychiatrist*
†Sorensen, Poul Henrik Bredahl *physician, research scientist, pathologist*
Sutter, Morley Carman *medical scientist*
Tingle, Aubrey James *pediatric immunologist, research administrator*

Victoria
D'Orbán, Paul Theodore *psychiatrist*

MANITOBA

Winnipeg
Angel, Aubie *physician, academic administrator*
†Friesen, Henry George *endocrinologist, educator*
Haworth, James Chilton *pediatrics educator*
Israels, Lyonel Garry *hematologist, medical educator*
Naimark, Arnold *medical educator, physiologist, educator*
Persaud, Trivedi Vidhya Nandan *anatomy educator, researcher, consultant*
†Ronald, Allan Ross *internal medicine and medical microbiology educator, researcher*

Ross, Robert Thomas *neurologist, educator*
Schacter, Brent Allan *oncologist, health facility administrator*

NEW BRUNSWICK

Fredericton
†Hanson, Dana W. *dermatologist*

NOVA SCOTIA

Halifax
Casson, Alan Graham *thoracic surgeon, researcher*
Chowdhury, Dhiman *physician, consultant*
Langley, George Ross *medical educator*
Tonks, Robert Stanley *pharmacology and therapeutics educator, former university dean*

Nova Scotia
Collins, John Alfred *retired obstetrician-gynecologist, educator*

ONTARIO

Barry's Bay
Horoszewicz, Juliusz Stanislaw *oncologist, cancer researcher, laboratory administrator*

Cambridge
Brown, Gregory Michael *psychiatrist, educator, researcher*

Hamilton
Basmajian, John Varoujan *medical scientist, educator, physician*
Bienenstock, John *physician, educator*
Roland, Charles Gordon *physician, medical historian, educator*

Kingston
Kaufman, Nathan *pathology educator, physician*
Low, James A. *physician*

London
Amir, Hassan *surgeon, consultant*
Lala, Peeyush Kanti *medical scientist, educator*
Marotta, Joseph Thomas *medical educator*
McMurtry, Robert Y. *medical educator*
McWhinney, Ian Renwick *physician, medical educator*
Strejan, Gill Henric *immunologist, educator*

Manotick
Osmond, Dennis Gordon *medical educator, researcher*

North York Toronto
Turnbull, John Cameron *pharmacist, consultant*

Ottawa
Chance, Graham Wilfrid *retired pediatrician, emeritus educator*
de Bold, Adolfo J. *pathology and physiology educator, research scientist*
Hagen, Paul Beo *physician, medical scientist*
Hurteau, Gilles David *retired obstetrician, gynecologist, educator, dean*
†Jackson, W. Bruce *ophthalmology educator, researcher*
†Langer, Bernard *medical association administrator*
Lavoie, Lionel A. *physician, medical executive*
†McDonald, John *medical association administrator*
†Seely, John F. *physician*
†Vassilyadi, Michael *pediatric neurosurgeon*

Sault Sainte Marie
†Banerjee, Samarendranath *orthopedic surgeon*

Toronto
Alberti, Peter William *otolaryngologist, educator, retired otolaryngologist*
Broder, Irvin *physician, educator*
Bruce, William Robert *physician, educator*
Eisenberg, Howard Edward *physician, psychotherapist, consultant, medical educator, writer*
Farkas, Leslie Gabriel *plastic surgeon*
Kalow, Werner *pharmacologist, toxicologist*
Lindsay, William Kerr *surgeon*
Mc Culloch, Ernest Armstrong *physician, educator*
Nesbitt, Lloyd Ivan *podiatrist*
Ogilvie, Richard Ian *clinical pharmacologist*
Rakoff, Vivian Morris *psychiatrist, writer*
†San, Nguyen Duy *psychiatrist, educator*
Sole, Michael Joseph *cardiologist*
Till, James Edgar *medical educator, researcher*
Turner, Robert Edward *psychiatrist, educator*
Volpé, Robert *endocrinologist, researcher, educator*

QUEBEC

Montpellier
Poirier, Louis Joseph *neurology educator*

Montreal
Beardmore, Harvey Ernest *retired physician, educator*
Becklake, Margaret Rigsby *physician, educator*
†Burgess, John Herbert *physician, educator*
Clermont, Yves Wilfrid *anatomy educator, researcher*
Cruess, Richard Leigh *surgeon, university dean*
Feindel, William Howard Howard *neurosurgeon, consultant*
Freeman, Carolyn Ruth *radiation oncologist*
Genest, Jacques *physician, clinical scientist, administrator*

Gold, Phil *immunologist, educator, researcher*
Goldbloom, Victor Charles
Goltzman, David *endocrinologist, educator, researcher*
Jones, Barbara Ellen *neuroscientist, educator*
Kramer, Michael Stuart *pediatric epidemiologist*
Leblond, Charles Philippe *anatomy educator, researcher*
Mac Lean, Lloyd Douglas *surgeon*
Milic-Emili, Joseph *physician, educator*
Mulder, David S. *cardiovascular surgeon*
Nadeau, Reginald Antoine *medical educator*
Nattel, Stanley *cardiologist, research scientist*
Pasternac, André *cardiologist, educator*
Souhami, Luis *physician, radiation oncology*

Saint-Foy
Dussault, Jean H. *endocrinologist, medical educator*

Verdun
Gauthier, Serge Gaston *neurologist*

SASKATCHEWAN

Saskatoon
Houston, C(larence) Stuart *radiologist, educator*
†Popkin, David Richard *obstetrician, health science administrator*

MEXICO

Mexico City
Murphy, Edward Stack *pathologist*

ARGENTINA

Buenos Aires
Montes, Leopoldo Feliciano *dermatologist, educator*

AUSTRALIA

Nedlands
Oxnard, Charles Ernest *anatomist, anthropologist, human biologist, educator*

Parkville
Azer, Samy Aziz *gastroenterologist, medical educator*
Denton, Derek Ashworth *medical researcher, medical scientist*
Metcalf, Donald *biomedical researcher*

Townsville, Queensland
Ho, Yik Hong *colon and rectal surgeon*

AUSTRIA

Salzburg
Sperl, Wolfgang *pediatrician*

BANGLADESH

Dhaka
Hossain, M. Iqbal *pediatrician, researcher*

BELGIUM

Hornu
Selvais, Philippe Leon *endocrinologist*

BRAZIL

Vitória
Lievore, Ruston *pathologist, consultant*

CHINA

Beijing
Han, Rui *pharmacologist, educator*

Hong Kong
Ng, Chi-Sing *pathologist, consultant*

CROATIA

Zagreb
Solter, Miljenko *endocrinologist, educator*

DENMARK

Copenhagen
Sestoft, Leif *endocrinologist, researcher, educator*

Århus
Mosekilde, Leif *endocrinologist, educator*

ENGLAND

Birmingham
Browne, Roger Michael *oral pathology educator, consultant*

Bristol
Silver, Ian Adair *pathology educator*

Chard
Beer, John Vincent *pathologist, consultant*

Hayes
Hounsfield, Godfrey Newbold *radiation scientist*

Leeds
Gibson, Robert Myles *neurosurgeon, consultant*

London
Johnson, Newell Walter *oral pathologist, physician*
Rutter, Michael Llewellyn *child psychiatry educator*
Stanhope, Richard Graham *pediatric endocrinologist, consultant, pilot*

Preston
Davis, Charles Harvey *neurosurgeon, consultant*

Southampton
Weller, Roy Oliver *neuropathologist*

Teddington
Roberts, Melville Parker *neurosurgeon, neuroanatomist, educator*

FINLAND

Helsinki
Liewendahl, Bo Kristian *clinical pathologist, nuclear physician*

Tampere
Pöntinen, Pekka Juhani *anesthesiologist, consultant*

FRANCE

Montpon
Durca, Eric Marcel *physician for addictions*

Neuilly-sur-Seine
Hewes, Thomas Francis *physician*

Paris
Dausset, Jean *immunologist*
Levy, David Alfred *immunology educator, physician, scientist*

GERMANY

Bremen
Fahle, Manfred *ophthalmology researcher*

Cologne
Karimi-Nejad, Abbas *retired neurosurgeon, educator*
Licht, Christoph *medical professional*

Düren
Rathert, Peter *urologist*

Halle
Schmoll, Hans Joachim *internal medicine, hematology, oncology educator*

Hamburg
Lüdecke, Dieter Konrad *neurosurgeon*

Lübeck
Arnold, Hans Richard *neurosurgeon*

Mannheim
Henn, Fritz Albert *psychiatrist*

Swisttal
Terjung, Birgit *internist, researcher*

Tubingen
Stenzl, Arnulf Karl Marbod *urologist*

Tübingen
Nüsslein-Volhard, Christiane *medical researcher*

Wuppertal
Schubert, Guenther Erich *pathologist*

GREECE

Ioannina
†Theodorou, Daphne J. *radiologist*

HUNGARY

Budapest
Bajtai, Attila *pathologist*
Pentelényi, Thomas John *neurosurgeon*
Szende, Béla *pathologist*

INDIA

Trivandrum
Sambasivan, Mahadeva Iyer *neurosurgeon, consultant*

ISRAEL

Givatayim
Kornel, Ludwig *medical educator, physician, scientist*

Haifa
Mayersdorf, Assa *neurologist*

Petah Tiqwa
Rappaport, Zvi Harry *neurosurgeon*

ITALY

Naples
†de Simone, Giovanni *cardiologist, educator*

Turin
Dianzani, Mario Umberto *pathology educator*

Verona
Bonadonna, Riccardo C. *endocrinologist*

JAPAN

Amagasa ki
Hayakawa, Toru *neurosurgeon*

Gummaken
Okada, Ryozo *educator, clinician and researcher*

Nagoya
Maeda, Kenji *medical educator*

Okayama
Morooka, Hiroshi *neurosurgeon*
Okada, Shigeru *pathology educator*

Okazaki
Ebashi, Setsuro *scientist, educator*

Ota-ku
Sano, Keiji *neurosurgeon, educator*

Saitama
Hozumi, Motoo *medical educator, researcher*

Sapporo
Nakagawa, Koji *endocrinologist, educator*

Tochigi
Honma, Koichi *pathologist, researcher*
Hyodo, Haruo *radiologist, educator*

Tokorozawa
Nakamura, Hiroshi *urology educator*

Tokyo
Fujimoto, Junichiro *pathologist*
Sakuta, Manabu *neurologist, educator*

Wakayama
Ryuzo, Higuchi *medical educator*

Yokohama
Kaneko, Yoshihiro *cardiologist, researcher*

KENYA

Eldoret North Rift
Elias, G.D. Onditi *radiologist, educator*

LEBANON

Beirut
Khatib, Rustom Atfat *gynecologist, researcher, endocrinologist, consultant, economist*

NETHERLANDS

Maastricht
Van Praag, Herman Meir *psychiatrist, educator, researcher*

NEW ZEALAND

Wellington South
Delahunt, Brett *pathologist*

NIGERIA

Ibadan
Grillo, Isaac Adetayo *surgery educator, consultant*

PHILIPPINES

Malate
†Aluquin, Vincent Protacio Roy *pediatric cardiologist*

POLAND

Warsaw
Pluta, Ryszard *neuropathologist, educator*

REPUBLIC OF KOREA

Daegu
Park, Soong-Kook *internist, researcher*

Seoul
Kim, Geun-Eun *surgeon, educator*

Frankel, Jeffrey *neurologist*
Freeman, Maynard Lloyd *nuclear medicine physician, researcher*
Friedman, Arnold Carl *radiologist*
Frishberg, Benjamin M. *neurologist*
Fristoe, Macalyne *speech-language pathologist, psychologist, educator, writer*
Frohman, Larry Philip *neuro-ophthalmologist*
Frost, J. Ormond *otolaryngologist, educator*
Furnas, David William *plastic surgeon, educator*
Gable, Karen Elaine *health science educator*
Gage, Tommy Wilton *retired pharmacologist, dentist, pharmacist, educator*
Gahagan, Thomas Gail *obstetrician, gynecologist*
Galan, Vincent *anesthesiologist*
Galbraith, William Bruce *physician, educator*
Gangarosa, Raymond Eugene *epidemiologist, electrical engineer*
Garcia, Alexander *orthopedic surgeon*
Garcia, Tierry Fernandez *otolaryngologist*
Gardner, John Howland, III, *neurologist*
†Gardner, Renee Vanessa *pediatric hematologist/oncologist, researcher*
†Garg, Sandeep *oncologist*
Garrett, Marshall Lee, Jr., *anesthesiologist, educator*
Gartner, Lawrence Mitchel *pediatrician, medical college educator*
Gathright, John Byron, Jr., *colon and rectal surgeon, educator*
Gaylin, Willard *physician, educator*
Gee, Sharri A. *physician*
Gee, William *surgeon*
Geiger, Albert J., Jr., *radiologist, retired*
Gelb, Alvin Meyer *physician*
Gelpi, Armand Philippe *internist*
Gemell, Nicholas I. *retired radiologist*
Gerard, Gary *neurologist*
Gewitz, Michael Harold *pediatrician*
Gherardi, Gherardo Joseph *pathologist*
Gibson, Milton Eugene *cardiologist*
Gilchrist, Gerald Seymour *pediatric hematologist, oncologist, educator*
Gill, Thomas James, III, *physician, educator*
Gillespie, Gary Don *physician*
Gillett, Richard Clark, Jr., *physician, educator, health facility administrator*
†Ginsburg, Iona Horowitz *psychiatrist*
Glaser, Robert Joy *retired physician, foundation administrator*
Glass, Dorothea Daniels *physiatrist, educator*
Glazer, Barry Michael *anesthesiologist*
†Gleason, Stephen Charles *physician*
†Gleason-Jordan, Irene *pathologist*
Goel, Mahesh Chand *urologist, renal transplant surgeon*
Goffman, Thomas Edward *radiation oncologist, researcher*
Gold, Evan Bruce *ophthalmologist*
Gold, Judith Hammerling *psychiatrist*
Goldberg, Burton David *pathologist, researcher, educator*
Goldberg, Mark Arthur *neurologist*
Goldberg, Michael Ellis *neurologist, neuroscientist*
Golden, Gerald Samuel *retired national medical board executive*
Goldenberg, Marvin Manus *pharmacologist, pharmaceutical developer*
Goldfine, Alan *obstetrician, gynecologist*
Goldstein, Dora Benedict *pharmacologist, educator*
Goldstein, Walter Carl *retired physician*
Gomoll, Allen Warren *cardiovascular pharmacologist*
Goodfellow, Robin Irene *surgeon*
†Goodney, Philip Paul *surgeon, researcher*
Goodwin, Andrew Wirt, II, *radiologist*
Gottfried, Eugene Leslie *physician, educator*
Gould, Howard Richard *retired physician*
Graham, David G. *preventive medicine physician, psychiatrist*
Graham, James Herbert *dermatologist*
Gray, Mary Jane *obstetrician-gynecologist*
Gray, Roland William *pediatrician*
Green, Louis Harry *retired surgeon*
Greenberg, Carolyn Phyllis *anesthesiologist, educator*
Greenberg, Jonathan *neurosurgeon*
Greenberg, Larrie Warren *pediatrician*
Greenberg, Stephen Robert *retired pathology educator*
Greene, Alan Guyer *retired radiologist*
Greene, Donald Richard *dermatologist, educator*
Greene, Laurence Whitridge, Jr., *surgical educator*
Greenfield, Val Shea *ophthalmologist*
Greenstein, Robert *retired radiologist*
Grenitz, Robert *retired obstetrician-gynecologist*
Griffen, Ward O., Jr., *surgeon, educator, medical board executive*
Griffin, John Henry *medical researcher*
Griffith, B(ezaleel) Herold *physician, educator, plastic surgeon*
†Grimes, Katherine Elizabeth *child psychiatrist, researcher*
Grimes, Michael David *podiatrist*
Griner, Paul Francis *physician*
Gross, Ruth Taubenhaus *former pediatrician*
Grossman, Joyce Renee *pediatrician, internist*
Groves, Sheridon Hale *orthopedic surgeon*
Guan, Shangbo G. *physician*
†Guarente, Lenny *medical geneticist, educator*
Gulbrandsen, Patricia Hughes *physician*
†Guo, Daqing *medical researcher*
Gupta, Krishan Lal *physician, medical educator*
†Gutfinger, Dan Eli *cardiologist, surgeon*
Guthrie, James Uhl *retired surgeon*
Guyton, William Lehman, Jr., *retired surgeon*
†Gwyther, Robert Edwin *physician, consultant*
Haft, Gail Klein *pediatrician*
Haggerty, Robert Johns *physician, educator*
Haithcock, William Dana, Jr., *physician*
Hales, Charles Albert *physician, educator*
Halliday, William Ross *retired physician, speleologist, writer*
Hamada, Omar Louis *physician*
Hamdan, Barbara Brunet *preventive medicine physician*
Hamilton, Stanley Ralph *pathologist*
Hanna, Duke Ellsworth *neurological surgeon*
Hansell, John Royer *retired physician*
Hardman, Joel Griffeth *retired pharmacologist*
Harrington, John Tolan *medical educator, dean, physician*
†Harris, Elaine K. *medical consultant*
Harris, John H., Jr., *radiologist*
Harrison, Harold Henry, Sr., *physician, scientist, educator*
Harrison, Saul Isaac *child psychiatrist, medical educator*
Harrop, Daniel Smith, III, *psychiatrist*
Hart, Cecil William Joseph *otolaryngologist, surgeon*
Harvey, Birt *retired pediatrician, educator*
Hassen, Irfan Wadood *physician*
Hatch, Robert *medical educator*
†Hathaway, David Roger *physician, medical educator, scientist*
Hauben, Manfred *physician*
Hawthorne, Douglas D. *medical association administrator*
H'Doubler, Francis Todd, Jr., *surgeon*
†He, Yi *neurosurgeon, researcher*
Healy, Bernadine P. *physician, educator, federal agency administrator, organization executive*
Hecht, Harold Arthur *orchidologist, chiropractor*
Hecker, Gerald Arthur *ophthalmologist, historian*
Heidelberger, Kathleen Patricia *physician*
Heileman, John Phillip *endocrinologist*
Heiner, Douglas Cragun *pediatrician, educator, immunologist, allergist*
†Helfand, Arthur E. *podiatrist*
Hellerstein, David Joel *psychiatrist, writer*
Henderson, Melford J. *epidemiologist, molecular biologist, chemist*
Hendricks, Leonard D. *emergency medicine physician, consultant*
Hennessey, William Joseph *physician*
Henson, Anna Miriam *retired otolaryngologist, retired medical educator*
Heptinstall, Robert Hodgson *physician*
Herrera, Guillermo Antonio *pathologist, educator, researcher*
Higginbotham, Edith Arleane *radiologist, researcher*
Hill, C. Thomas, Jr., *radiologist*
Himes, John Harter *medical researcher, educator*
Hirose, Teruo Terry *surgeon, educator*
†Ho, Matthew R *physician*
Hoadley, John Frank *health policy analyst, educator*
Hoch, Frederic Louis *medical educator*
Hoeprich, Paul Daniel *physician educator*
Hogness, John Rusten *physician, academic administrator*
Holland, Robert Campbell *anatomist, educator*
Hollister, Alan Scudder *clinical pharmacologist, internist*
Holmes, David Richard, Jr., *cardiologist*
Holsgrove, Gareth John *medical association administrator*
Holtzman, Robert Neil Nehemiah *neurosurgeon, neurologist*
Hood, William Boyd, Jr., *cardiologist, educator*
Horner, George Marlin *retired obstetrician-gynecologist*
Horswill, C. Weir *retired obstetrician-gynecologist, photographer*
Hoskins, Iffath Abbasi *obstetrician-gynecologist*
Hoskins, John Howard *urologist, educator*
Hourani, Laurel Lockwood *epidemiologist*
Howard, Terry Thomas *obstetrician, gynecologist*
Howards, Stuart S. *urologist, educator*
Howell, Joel DuBose *internist, educator*
Howell, Julius Ammons *retired plastic surgeon*
Hricak, Hedvig *physician, radiologist*
Huber, Douglas Crawford *pathologist*
Huggins, Charles Edward *obstetrician, gynecologist, educator*
Hunter, Daniel Clyde, Jr., *retired surgeon, educator*
Huntley, Robert Ross *physician, educator*
Hurd, Suzanne Sheldon *retired federal agency health science director*
†Hussain, Aneela Naureen *physician*
Huth, Thomas Joseph *retired surgeon*
†Hutt, Evelyn Ann *geriatrician, researcher*
Hwynn, Julie Huynh *internal medicine physician*
†Ilfeld, Brian Michael *anesthesiologist*
†Ingelfinger, Julie R. *physician, researcher*
†Irish, Thomas Judson *retired plastic surgeon*
Irwin, Peter John *orthopaedic surgeon*
Iserson, Kenneth Victor *emergency medicine educator, bioethicist, author*
†Issa, Amalia Mary *medical educator, researcher*
Iyengar, Ramchandra *retired surgeon*
Izenstark, Joseph Louis *retired radiologist, physician, educator*
Jackman, Jay M. *psychiatrist*
Jackson, Carmault Benjamin, Jr., *physician*
Jackson, David Huntsman *retired cardiologist*
Jacobsen, Brenda *internist, emergency physician*
Jang, Richard Wayson *radiologist, educator*
†Jani, Binoy R. *ophthalmologist, surgeon*
Janicak, Philip Gregory *psychiatry educator, researcher*
Janower, Murray L. *radiologist, consultant*
Janus, Todd Jeffrey *neurologist, medical educator*
†Jensen, Lynn Edward *retired medical association executive, economist*
Jensen, Robert Travis *physician, educator, researcher*
Jewell, Patrick Frank *retired surgeon*
Johnson, Fernly Eldo *surgeon*
Johnson, Leonard Morris *retired pediatric surgeon*
Johnson, Willard Chapin *surgeon, researcher*
Jones, Billy Ernest *dermatology educator*
Jones, Walton Linton *internist, former government official*
†Jordan, Deovina Nasis *administrative nurse*
Joshi, Pratibha C. *immunologist, researcher*
Juskenas, Nellie K. *retired anesthesiologist*
Kader, Fred J. *pediatric neurologist*
Kalil, Nelson *oncologist, researcher*
Kantor, Harvey Sherwin *retired medical educator*
Kao, Simon C. *radiologist, educator*
Kaplan, Gabriela Diana *radiologist*
Karen, Joel S. *plastic surgeon*
Karpinos, Robert Douglas *anesthesiologist*
Kasimis, Basil S. *oncologist*
Katzman, Merle Hershel *retired orthopaedic surgeon*
Kaufman, Stephen Lawrence *radiologist, educator*
Keane, James R. *neurologist*
Keill, Stuart Langdon *psychiatrist*
Keller, Ben Robert, Jr., *gynecologist*
Kelley, Patrick Alan *neurologist, educator*
Kendall, Harry Ovid *internist*
Kerr, Harry Davidson *emergency physician*
Kettelkamp, Donald Benjamin *retired surgeon*
Kettleson, David Noel *retired orthopaedic surgeon, timber manager*
Khachadurian, Avedis *physician*
Khan, Arfa *radiologist, educator*
Kiang, Barbara Norris *scientific research assistant*
Kiesel, Ilmar Otto *retired radiologist*
Kiken, Michael Stephen *obstetrician, gynecologist*
King, Hueston Clark *retired otolaryngologist, educator*
Kinzie, Jeannie Jones *radiation oncologist, nuclear medicine physician*
Kirila, Carol Elizabeth *osteopathic physician, internist*
Kitt, Walter *psychiatrist*
Kivikoski, Asko Ilmari *retired obstetrician, gynecologist*
†Kizer, Jorge R. *cardiologist, epidemiologist*
Klein, Jeffrey Howard *oncologist, internist*
Klitzman, Robert Lloyd *physician, author*
Knapp, Howard Raymond *internist, clinical pharmacologist*
Knecht, Charles Lewis, III, *retired radiologist*
Kniseley, Ralph Marion *pathologist, nuclear medicine physician*
Knobloch, Ferdinand J. *psychiatrist, educator*
†Kohler, Kathryn Alexis *epidemiologist*
Kohrman, Arthur Fisher *pediatrics educator*
Kolansky, Harold *physician, psychiatrist, psychoanalyst*
Kolff, Willem Johan *retired internist, internist, educator*
Korenblit, Pearl *internist*
Kost, Gerald Joseph *biomedical researcher physician*
Kostick, Alexandra *ophthalmologist*
Kough, Robert Hamilton *retired clinical hematologist, consultant*
Kowlessar, Muriel *retired pediatric educator*
Kramer, Elissa Lipcon *nuclear medicine physician, educator*
Kraut, Joel Arthur *ophthalmologist*
Kreb, Robert Joseph, III, *physiatrist*
Kreider, Clement Horst, Jr., *neurosurgeon*
Krizan, Kelly Joe *physician, leather craftsman*
Krop, Stephen *retired pharmacologist*
†Kumar, Sanjaya *epidemiologist, statistician*
Kundel, Harold Louis *radiologist, educator*
Kundu-Raychaudhuri, Smriti Kana *biomedical scientist*
†Kunz, Alexandra Cavitt *physician, anthropologist, researcher*
Kurk, Mitchell *physician*
Kurnick, Nathaniel Bertrand *retired oncologist-hematologist*
Kurotsuchi, Roy Yutaka *obstetrician, gynecologist*
Kushwaha, Sudhir Singh *internist, cardiologist, educator*
†Kydd, William *former medical association administrator*
Kye, Hoon Taik *retired anesthesiologist, educator*
Lai, Eric Pong Shing *family physician, educator*
Land, Allan Stephen *surgeon*
Lang, Ernst Frederick *radiologist*
Larar, Gerald N. *physician, research scientist*
LaRoche, Jane Lawton *emergency physician*
Larson, Richard Smith *pathologist, researcher*
†Larson, Roger Keith *physician, writer*
Lau, Roy Esme *surgeon*
Lauderdale, Vance, Jr., *anesthesiologist*
Laupus, William Edward *physician, educator*
†Lauryssen, Carl *neurosurgeon, director*
Lauterbach, Edward Charles *psychiatric educator*
LaVelle, Arthur *anatomy educator*
Lawless, Michael Rhodes *pediatrics educator*
Lawrence, Christine *physician*
Lawrence, David Long *radiologist*
Layde, Peter Mark *epidemiologist, preventive medicine educator*
LeBeau, Lawrence R. *family practice physician*
Le Cocq, Frank *retired obstetrician/gynecologist*
Lee, David Sack Yee *internist*
Lee, Douglas Ocwah *medical educator*
Lee, Thomas Tehwen *neurosurgeon*
Leibowitz, Leonard D. *retired pediatrician*
Leidy, John William, Jr., *endocrinologist, educator*
Leighton, Leslie Steven *gastroenterologist*
Leman, Craig Billings *surgeon*
Leo, Michael Charles *emergency physician, surgeon, educator*
†Leonetti, John P. *otolaryngologist, surgeon, educator*
†Lesser, Gerson Theodore *medical educator, researcher*
LeVay, Simon *neuroscientist, writer, educator*
†Levenson, Anait S. *cancer researcher, consultant*
Levin, Alan Scott *pathologist, allergist, immunologist, lawyer*
Lewin, Marion Ein *consultant, physician, former medical association administrator*
Lewinsohn, Hilton Cecil *physician*
Li, Zhen *medical researcher*
Lichenstein, Richard *physician, health services administrator*
Lindblom, Laurie Beth *physician*
Linz, Anthony James *osteopathic physician, consultant, educator*
†Lipton, Glenn E. *orthopaedic surgeon*
Loehden, Otto Louis *retired surgeon*
Lohmann, George Young, Jr., *neurosurgeon, hospital executive, international business executive, artist*
Loomis, Salora Dale *psychiatrist*
Loschen, Earl Lee *psychiatrist, educator*
Loube, Samuel Dennis *physician*
Lourenco, Ruy Valentim *physician, educator*
Luchansky, Edward *obstetrician-gynecologist, educator*
Maas, Anthony Ernst *retired pathologist*
Mack, Gaye Ferris *health care educator, flower essence practitioner*
Macleod, Angus *internist*
MacLeod, Gordon C. *surgeon*
Madell, Samuel H. *radiologist*
Madlang, Rodolfo Mojica *retired urologic surgeon*
Maeda, Koichi *pathologist*
Maguire, James Harvey *physician*
Maioriello, Richard Patrick *retired otolaryngologist*
Mair, Douglas Dean *medical educator, consultant*
Maitra, Subir Ranjan *medical educator*
Makhov, Alexander Mikhailovich *medical educator, molecular biology researcher*
Makowski, Edgar Leonard *obstetrician and gynecologist*
Malach, Monte *physician*
Malerstein, Abraham Joseph *psychiatrist, researcher*
Malit, Lee Arnall *physician*
Malone, Richard P. *psychiatrist*
†Mangi, Abeel Abdullah *cardiologist, surgeon*
Mannino, J(oseph) Robert *medical educator*
†Markham, Fred William, Jr., *medical educator*
†Marko, Marlene *psychiatrist*
Markoe, Arnold Michael *radiation oncologist*
Martinez-Maldonado, Manuel *medical service administrator, physician*
Martino, Silvana *osteopath, medical oncologist*
Martone, William James *physician*
Mascola, Richard F. *former medical association administrator*
Massey, Robert Unruh *physician, university dean*
Masters, Joseph Henry *pathologist*
Materson, Richard Stephen *physician, educator*
Mathelier, Amedee C. *obstetrician-gynecologist*
Mathias, Mervin A. *retired surgeon*
Matthews, George Robert *retired radiologist*
Maumus, Craig W(alther) *psychiatrist, consultant*
McCartney, James Robert *psychiatrist*
McCauley, Floyce Reid *psychiatrist*
†McCormick, Kenneth L. *pediatrics educator, researcher*
McCullough, David L. *urologist*
McDonagh, Thomas Joseph *physician*
McDonald, Josh William *surgical pathologist*
McEwen, Bruce S. *neuroendocrinology educator*
†McGuigan, Michael R. *sport science educator*
†McGuirt, William Frederick *otolaryngologist, educator*
McKenzie, Norma DeeAnn *psychiatrist, educator*
McLoud, Theresa Claire *radiologist*
†McNeely, Bonnie L. (K.W. Rowe Jr.) *retired internist and educator*
Meilman, Edward *physician*
Melanson, Susan C. *herbalist*
Mellins, Harry Zachary *radiologist, educator*
Mendels, Joseph *psychiatrist, educator*
Mengel, Charles Edmund *physician, medical educator*
Merenda, Sam John *retired radiologist*
Mereschak, Volmar A. *retired obstetrician-gynecologist*
Merkin, Donald H. *internist*
Meyer, George Wilbur *internist, health facility administrator*
Meyer, Greg Charles *psychiatrist*
Miller, Anthony Bernard *physician, medical researcher*
Miller, Ross Hays *retired neurosurgeon*
Millikan, Clark Harold *physician*
Millman, Arthur Lance *oculoplastic surgeon*
Mills, Jeri *gynecologist*
Milnor, William Robert *physician*
Milstone, Leonard Matthew *physician, educator, researcher*
Mitchell, William Marvin *pathology educator*
Modisher, Melvin Wayne *obstetrician/gynecologist, educator*
Mohaideen, A. Hassan *surgeon, healthcare executive*
Molbegott, Lester Philip *anesthesiologist*
Monif, Gilles R.G. *physician*
†Monninger, Robert Harold George *ophthalmologist, educator*
Montgomery, John Richard *pediatrician, educator*
Moossy, John *neuropathologist, neurologist, consultant*
Moran, Gregory John *emergency medicine physician, educator*
†Morgan, Stanley Charles *plastic and reconstructive surgeon*
Morrison, Karen Margaret *physician*
Morse, Martin A. *plastic surgeon*
Moser, Robert Lawrence *pathologist, health facility administrator*
Mostowycz, Leonidas *radiologist*
Motto, Jerome Arthur *psychiatry educator*
Mountain, Clifton Fletcher *surgeon, educator*
Mueller, Charles Barber *surgeon, educator*
Mulcahy, Gabriel M. *pathologist*
Munger, Bryce Leon *physician, educator*
Munster, Andrew Michael *surgeon, educator*
Murphey, Sheila Ann *infectious diseases physician, educator, researcher*

White, Kerr Lachlan *retired physician, foundation administrator*
White, Richard Thomas *radiologist*
Whitsell, John Crawford, II, *general surgeon*
†Wiecherek, Walter Joseph *internist*
Wilk, Ronald *physician*
Wilkinson, Grant Robert *pharmacology educator*
Williams, John Zigler *anesthesiologist*
Williams, Robert Leon *psychiatrist, neurologist, educator*
Williams, Thomas Lloyd *psychiatrist*
Wilmore, Douglas Wayne *surgeon, educator*
Wilson, Almon Chapman *surgeon, physician, retired naval officer*
Wisoff, Hugh Solomon *neurosurgeon*
Wittmann, Dietmar H. *surgery educator*
Wong, Jeffrey Yun Chung *radiation oncologist, medical researcher*
Wood, Frances Diane *medical secretary, artist*
Worner, Theresa Marie *internist, educator*
Worrell, Richard Vernon *orthopedic surgeon, college dean, dean*
†Xu, Hui *physician*
Yamamoto, Joe *psychiatrist, educator*
Yarchoan, Robert *clinical immunologist, researcher*
Yarington, Charles Thomas, Jr., *surgeon, administrator*
Yielding, K. Lemone *physician*
Yodaiken, Ralph E. *pathologist, occupational medicine physician*
Yollick, Bernard Lawrence *otolaryngologic surgeon*
Yood, Harold Stanley *retired internist*
Youmans, Julian Ray *neurosurgeon, educator*
Youngstrom, Paul Clarence *anesthesiologist*
Yu, Fermin Tong *retired surgeon*
Zabetakis, Paul Michael *nephrologist, educator*
Zaki, Wasfy *physician*
Zapp, John S. *retired medical association administrator*
Zawacki, Bruce Edwin *surgeon, educator, ethicist*
Zhu, Kangmin *epidemiologist*
Ziegler, Robert F. *cardiologist*
Zigun, Benjamin Joshua *psychiatrist, lawyer*
Zimmerman, David Alan *cardiologist*
Zimmerman, Marilyn Claire *surgeon*
Zinner-Kemp, Susan Elizabeth *medical educator*
Zmijewski, Chester Michael *pathology educator*
Zumwalt, Ross Eugene *forensic pathologist, educator*

HUMANITIES: LIBERAL STUDIES

UNITED STATES

ALABAMA

Auburn
Amacher, Richard Earl *literature educator*
Andelson, Robert Vernon *social philosopher, educator*
Flynt, James Wayne *history educator, researcher*
Harrell, David Edwin, Jr., *history educator*
Littleton, Taylor Dowe *humanities educator*
Morrow, Patrick David *English educator*
Noe, Kenneth William *historian, educator*
†Wehrs, Donald Roger *English educator*

Birmingham
Allen, Lee Norcross *historian, educator*
Benditt, Theodore Matthew *humanities educator, educator*
Burden, Cedric Jerome, Sr., *English educator*
Hamilton, Virginia Van der Veer *historian, educator*
Morton, Marilyn Miller *retired genealogy and history educator, lecturer, researcher, travel executive, director*
Tent, James Foster *historian*

Brewton
Reynolds, Harold Mark *language educator*

Camp Hill
Melzer, John T.S. *translator, editor*

Gilbertown
†Ross, Cecil Brandt *literature educator*

Huntsville
Bounds, Sarah Etheline *historian*
Hughes, Kaylene *historian, educator*

Jacksonville
Spector, Daniel Earl *historian, educator*

Lillian
Burnette, Ollen Lawrence, Jr., *historian*

Loachapoka
Schafer, Elizabeth Diane *historian, writer*

Maxwell AFB
Winton, Harold Raymond *historian*

Mobile
Donalson, Malcolm Drew *classics educator*
Gandy, Maurice Edward *English language educator, writer*
Hamner, Eugenie Lambert *English educator*
†Kargleder, Charles Leonard *language educator*
Steadman, John Marcellus, III, *English educator*

Montgomery
Cornett, Lloyd Harvey, Jr., *retired historian*
†Gerard, William Blake *literature educator*

Gribben, Alan *English language educator, research consultant*
Napier, Cameron Mayson Freeman *historic preservationist*
Robinson, Ella Scales *language educator*
Whitt, Mary F. *reading educator, consultant*

New Market
†Kearns, Nancy J. *language educator*

Ramer
Napier, John Hawkins, III, *historian*

Talladega
Jeffers, Trellie Lee James *language educator, dean*

Troy
McPherson, Milton Monroe *history educator*
Mitchell, Norma Taylor *history educator*

Tuscaloosa
†Beito, David Timothy *humanities educator*
Bunker, Matthew D. *humanities educator*
Crowley, John W(illiam) *English language educator*
†Delpar, Helen *historian*
†Freyer, Tony Allan *historian, educator*
Hocutt, Max Oliver *philosophy educator*
†Janiga-Perkins, Constance Gabrielle *language educator*
Lockett, James *history educator*
†Raines, Michael Carl *language educator*
Ruiz-Fornells, Enrique *history and Spanish educator*

Tuskegee Institute
†Olson, Mary *language educator, writer*

ALASKA

Anchorage
Breinig, Jeane M. *English educator, consultant*
†Kim, Taesoo *language educator*
†Kline, Daniel Thomas *English educator*

Fairbanks
†Bird, Roy Kennedy *literature educator, director*
†Cole, Terrence M. *historian, educator*
Corti, Lillian Zell *humanities educator, writer*
Falk, Marvin William *historian, bibliographer*

Juneau
Ruotsala, James Alfred *historian, writer*

ARIZONA

Apache Junction
Bracken, Harry McFarland *philosophy educator*
Ransom, Evelyn Naill *language educator, linguist*

Davis Monthan AFB
Miller, Charles Wallace *historian, environmental geologist, educator*

Flagstaff
Marcus, Karen Melissa *foreign language educator*

Green Valley
Brewington, Arthur William *retired English language educator*

Kingman
Jones, Barbara Christine *educator, linguist, creative arts designer*

Lake Havasu City
Brydon, Ruth Vickery *history educator*

Mesa
†Ohl, John Kennedy *history educator*

Phoenix
Bildhauer, W. Mathias *philosophy educator, real estate broker*
Cristiano, Marilyn Jean *speech communication educator*
Drnjevic, Jonathan Mark *language educator*
Maimon, Elaine Plaskow *English educator, university provost, campus chief executive officer*
Rister, Gene Arnold *humanities educator*
Van Sittert, Barbara C. *retired classics educator, writer*
Zepeda, Guillermo *language educator, speech professional*

Scottsdale
Donaldson, Scott *English language educator, writer*
Land, George A. *philosopher, writer, educator, consultant, speaker*
Mousseux, Renate *language educator*

Sun City
Oppenheimer, Max, Jr., *foreign language educator, consultant*

Surprise
Clark, Lloyd *historian, writer, educator*
Mitsui, James Masao *retired language educator, poet, consultant*
Raat, William Dirk *history educator*

Tempe
Adelson, Roger Dean *history educator, editor, historian*
Bjork, Robert Eric *language professional educator*
Brack, O. M., Jr., *English language educator*
†Doherty, Brian James *musicologist*

†Foster, David William *language educator, humanities educator*
†Garzon, Amalia *Spanish educator, translator*
†Gilfillan, Daniel David *language educator, consultant*
Gruzinska, Aleksandra *language educator*
Iverson, Peter James *historian, educator*
†Lockard, Joseph Franklin *literature educator, writer*
MacKinnon, Stephen R. *Asian studies administrator, educator*
Major, Roy Coleman *language educator*
†Tillman, Hoyt Cleveland *historian, educator, writer*
†Tohe, Laura *English educator*
van Gelderen, Elly *linguistics educator, researcher*
†Wetsel, William David *literature educator*
Wong, Timothy C. *language and literature educator*

Tucson
†Adjarian, Maude Madeleine *literature educator, researcher*
Aiken, Susan Hardy *English language educator*
Birkinbine, John, II, *philatelist*
Boyle, Christopher George *English educator, counselor*
Canfield, John Douglas *English educator, writer, consultant*
Dinnerstein, Leonard *historian, educator*
Gaines, Kendra Holly *English language educator, editorial and writing consultant*
Herrnstadt, Richard Lawrence *American literature educator*
†Ismael, Jenann T. *philosopher, educator*
Kaliher, Michael Dennis *historian, librarian*
Kellogg, Frederick *historian*
Kleese, William Carl *genealogy research consultant, financial services representative*
†Liu, Si *language educator*
†Luprecht, Mark *humanities educator*
†Randall, Lesa B. *humanities educator*
†Schulz, Renate Adele *German studies and second language acquisition educator*
†Sheldon, Richard Neil *retired historian*
Tao, Chia-lin Pao *humanities educator*
†Tinkham, Audrey Evelyn *literature educator*
†Wald-Hopkins, Christine Marie *literature educator*

ARKANSAS

Arkadelphia
Curlin, Jay Russell *English educator*
Graves, John William *historian*

Beebe
Knapp, Stephen John *English educator*

Bella Vista
Fite, Gilbert Courtland *historian, educator, retired*

Conway
†Marshall, Todd Alden *language educator*
Vanderslice, Stephanie M. *humanities educator*
Ziegler, John Alan *historian, political scientist, educator*

Fayetteville
Levine, Daniel Blank *classical studies educator*
Wilkie, Brian Francis *English educator*

Jonesboro
Elkins, Francis Clark *history educator, university official*

Little Rock
Ferguson, John Lewis *state historian*

Malvern
Schultz, Marvin E. *historian, educator*

Mammoth Spring
†Smith, Jo Kay *language educator, school librarian*

Mena
Eddleman, Floyd Eugene *retired English language educator*

Monticello
Babin, Claude Hunter *history educator*

Russellville
Jenkins, Ellen Janet (Jan Jenkins) *historian, history educator*
White, Donna Rae *English educator, writer*

Siloam Springs
†Roby, Warren B. *humanities educator*

State University
†Darwin, John Scott *language educator*
Johnson, Warren *foreign language educator*
Milner, Clyde A., II, *historian*
Schichler, Robert Lawrence *English language educator*

CALIFORNIA

Arcadia
†Samaan, Yvette *language and psychology educator*
Yen, Wen-Hsiung *language and music professional, educator*

Atherton
Bales, Royal Eugene *philosophy educator*

Bakersfield
Kegley, Jacquelyn Ann *philosophy educator*

Beale AFB
Cross, Coy Franklin, II, *historian*

Belvedere Tiburon
FitzGerald, Desmond J. *philosopher, educator*

Berkeley
Alter, Robert Bernard *comparative literature educator, critic*
Anderson, William Scovil *classics educator*
Bloom, Robert *language professional educator*
Booth, Stephen Walter *English language educator*
Costa, Gustavo *Italian studies scholar*
Craig, William *philosopher, educator*
Crews, Frederick Campbell *humanities educator, writer*
Herr, Richard *history educator*
Hodges, Frederick Mansfield *historian*
Karlinsky, Simon *language educator, writer*
Kay, Paul de Young *linguist*
Kerman, Joseph Wilfred *musicologist, critic*
Lichterman, Martin *history educator*
Litwack, Leon Frank *historian, educator*
Long, Anthony Arthur *classics educator*
Mace, Susan Lidgate *comparative literature educator, researcher*
†McWhorter, John Hamilton *linguist, educator*
Middlekauff, Robert Lawrence *history educator, administrator*
Muscatine, Charles *English educator, author*
†Nagler, Michael Nicholas *peace and conflict studies educator*
Rauch, Irmengard *linguist, educator*
Rex, Walter Edwin, III, *humanities educator*
Selz, Peter Howard *art historian, educator*
†Shannon, Thomas Frederic *German language educator*
Sloane, Thomas O. *speech educator*
Tracy, Robert (Robert Edward Tracy) *English language educator, poetry translator*
Wakeman, Frederic Evans, Jr., *historian, educator*
Wilson, W(illiam) Daniel *language professional, educator*
Wolgast, Elizabeth Hankins *philosophy educator*
†Wooll, Frederick *English educator*
Zwerdling, Alex *English educator*

Beverly Hills
Novak, Maximillian Erwin *English language educator*

Cambria
Salaverria, Helena Clara *retired language educator*

Carlsbad
Marx, Michael William *language educator, writer*

Carmel
Chung, Kyung Cho *Korean specialist, educator, writer*

Carrboro
†Ferrán, Jaime M. *language educator*

Carson
†Ferrario, Larry *history and literature educator*

Chico
Shahid-García, María de Lourdes *foreign language educator*

Citrus Heights
Knight, Arthur Winfield *English educator*

Claremont
Ackerman, Gerald Martin *art historian, consultant*
Atlas, Jay David *philosopher, consultant, linguist*
Burns, Richard Dean *history educator, publisher, writer*
Davis, Nathaniel *humanities educator*
Fossum, Robert H(eyerdahl) *retired English literature educator*
Goodrich, Norma Lorre (Mrs. John H. Howard) *French and comparative literature educator*
Kucheman, Clark Arthur *philosophy and religious studies educator*
Lofgren, Charles Augustin *legal and constitutional historian, history educator*
McKirahan, Richard Duncan *classics and philosophy educator*
Moss, Myra Ellen (Myra Moss Rolle) *philosophy educator*
Neumann, Harry *philosophy educator*
Pinney, Thomas Clive *retired English language educator*
Roth, John King *philosopher, educator*
Shimkhada, Deepak *art historian*
Sontag, Frederick Earl *philosophy educator*
Wheeler, Geraldine Hartshorn *historian, essayist*
Woodress, James Leslie, Jr., *English language educator*
Young, Howard Thomas *foreign language educator*

Compton
†Maradiaga Kieffer-Aanonsen, Nora Ludmila *language educator*

Culver City
Clodius, Albert Howard *history educator*

Cupertino
†McCormick, Yumi *language educator, translator*
Tice, Bradley Scott *humanities educator*

Daly City
†Gao, Luji *foreign language educator, columnist*

Davis
†Bernd, Clifford Albrecht *language educator*
†Brody, David *history educator*

†Brower, Daniel Roberts *historian, educator, writer*
†Burnett, Katharine Persis *art historian, educator*
†Druzhnikov, Yuri Ilya *literature educator, writer*
Hayden, John Olin *English literature educator, writer*
Hoffman, Michael Jerome *humanities educator, educator*
Saler, Michael Theodore *history educator*
Tinney, Thomas Milton, Sr., *genealogical research specialist*
Traill, David Angus *classics educator*
Waddington, Raymond Bruce, Jr., *English language educator*
Williamson, Alan Bacher *English literature educator, poet, writer*
Willis, Frank Roy *history educator*

Del Mar
†Johnson, Mary Evans *musicologist, musician*

El Cerrito
Kuo, Ping-chia *historian, educator*

Emeryville
†Reuter, William Charles *historian, educator*

Foster City
†Kellogg, Deren Earl *historian*

Fountain Valley
Le, Vinh Tu *language educator, translator*

Fresno
Bundy-DeSoto, Teresa Mari *language educator, vocalist*
Chang, Sidney H. (Sidney H. Chang) *history educator*
†Garza-Lozano, Nereyda *language educator*
Genini, Ronald Walter *history educator, historian*
Kouymjian, Dickran *art historian, Orientalist, educator*
†Kuhn, Rose Marie *language educator*
†Ng, Franklin C.L. *historian, educator*

Fullerton
Carrithers, Joseph Edward *english composition and literature educator*

Glendale
de Grassi, Leonard *art historian, educator*
Renner, Marguerite *history educator*

Grass Valley
†Gillett, Annette Damron *retired speech and forensics educator*

Hayward
†Gleason, Ken Bell *historian, educator, journalist*
†Hammond, Marian Corleene *retired literature educator*

Hemet
Culverwell, Albert Henry *historian*

Huntington Beach
Peters, Robert L(ouis) *retired English educator, poet, critic*
Winterowd, Walter Ross *English educator*

Irvine
Boyd, Carolyn Patricia *history educator*
Hine, Robert Van Norden, Jr., *historian, educator*
†Kempff, Juergen *language educator*
Key, Mary Ritchie (Mrs. Audley E. Patton) *linguist, writer, educator*
Lillyman, William John *German language educator, academic administrator*
†Rodríguez Ordoñez, Jaime Edmundo *historian, educator*
Sutton, Dana Ferrin *classics educator*

La Jolla
†Esherick, Joseph Wharton *history educator*
Falk, Julia S. *linguist, educator*
†Gutierrez, Ramon A. *history educator*
Kenyon, Karen Beth Smith *literature educator, writer*
Langacker, Ronald Wayne *linguistics educator*
McDonald, Marianne *classicist*
Newmark, Leonard Daniel *linguistics educator*
Olafson, Frederick Arlan *philosophy educator*
Oreskes, Naomi *science historian*
Wright, Andrew *English literature educator*

La Verne
Marcus, Kenneth Hearne *historian, educator*

Laguna Niguel
Teitelbaum, Harry *English educator*

Livermore
Hiskes, Dolores G. *educator*

Long Beach
Lunderville, Gerald Paul *bilingual ESL/social studies educator*
Snider, Clifton Mark *English educator, writer, poet*
Tang, Paul Chi Lung *philosophy educator*

Los Altos
Nivison, David Shepherd *Chinese and philosophy educator*

Los Angeles
Alkon, Paul Kent *English language educator*
Allen, Michael John Bridgman *English educator*
Alpers, Edward Alter *history educator*
†Appleby, Joyce Oldham *historian, educator*
Bahr, Ehrhard *Germanic languages and literature educator*
Bartchy, S(tuart) Scott *history educator, researcher*
Boime, Albert Isaac *art history educator*
Bradshaw, Murray Charles *musicologist, educator*
Burns, Robert Ignatius *historian, educator, clergyman*
Caram, Eve La Salle *English educator, writer*
Cherkin, Adina *interpreter, writer, poet, translator*
Cohen, S(tephen) Marshall *philosophy educator*
Cortinez, Veronica *literature educator*
Crecelius, Daniel Neil *history educator*
Davidson, Herbert Alan *Near Eastern languages and cultures educator*
Del Giudice, Luisa *folklorist, ethnologist, historical institution administrator, educator*
Dobos, Erzsebet *language educator*
Dumitrescu, Domnita *Spanish language educator, researcher*
Dyck, Andrew Roy *philologist, educator*
Fry, Michael Graham *historian, educator*
Greenberg, Douglas Stuart *history educator*
Hadda, Janet Ruth *Yiddish language educator, lay psychoanalyst*
†Heidsieck, Arnold *literature educator*
Hines, Thomas Spight *historian, educator, architecture critic*
Hovannisian, Richard G. *Armenian and Near East history educator*
Hsu, Kylie *language educator, researcher, linguist, educator*
Hundley, Norris Cecil, Jr., *history educator*
†Keenan, Edward L. *linguist, educator, linguist, department chairman*
Kelly, Henry Ansgar *English language educator*
†Klein, Cecelia F. *art historian, educator*
Kolve, V. A. *English literature educator*
†Lagier, Christophe Philippe *language educator*
Laird, David *humanities educator emeritus*
Levine, Philip *classics educator*
Lionnet, Francoise *French and comparative literature educator*
Löfstedt, Bengt Torkel Magnus *classics educator*
Mellor, Ronald John *history educator*
Newhall, Eric Luther *American literature educator*
†Nosco, Peter Erling *humanities educator, consultant*
Poole, Stafford *historian, priest*
Rathbun, John Wilbert *American studies educator*
Rouse, Richard Hunter *historian, educator*
Schaefer, William David *English language educator*
Schutz, John Adolph *historian, educator, former university dean*
Schwartz, Leon *foreign language educator*
See, Carolyn *English language educator, novelist, book critic*
Shideler, Ross Patrick *foreign language and comparative literature educator, writer, translator, poet*
Smith, Bruce R. *English language educator*
Stockwell, Robert Paul *linguist, educator*
†Symcox, Geoffrey Walter *history educator*
Tritle, Lawrence Alan *history educator*
†Troy, Nancy J. *art history educator*
Weber, Eugen *historian, educator, writer*
White, Christopher Todd *language educator*
Wills, John Elliot, Jr., *history educator, writer*
Wohl, Robert *historian, educator*
Wortham, Thomas Richard *English language educator*

Los Gatos
Rogers, Franklin Robert *former language and literature educator, writer, literary critic*

Malibu
Luft, Herbert *history educator, former dean and academic administrator*
Marshall, Donald Glenn *English language and literature educator*

Marina
†Madsen, Roy I., Jr., *language educator*

Menlo Park
Craig, Gordon Alexander *historian, educator*

Merced
Elliott, Gordon Jefferson *retired English language educator*

Mission Viejo
†Brierre, Maud *French and Spanish educator*

Montclair
Haage, Robert Mitchell *retired history educator, organization leader*

Monterey
†Astore, William Joseph *historian, dean*
Franke, Jack Emil *foreign language educator*
†Goldstein, Lynn Meg *language educator*
†Peet, Phyllis Irene *women's studies educator*

Newport Beach
Brown, Giles Tyler *history educator, lecturer*
Mc Culloch, Samuel Clyde *history educator*

Northridge
Chen, Joseph Tao *historian, educator*
†Koistinen, Paul Abraham Carl *historian, educator*

Norwalk
†Pritchard, Gary Paul, Jr., *musicologist, educator*

Oakland
†Berry, Kathleen A. *English language educator*

Oceanside
†Ochoa Carlos, Sergio *language educator*

Orange
†Cumiford, William Lloyd *historian, educator, curator*
†Harran, Marilyn Jean *historian, educator, consultant*
Martin, Mike W. *philosophy educator*
Yeager, Myron Dean *English language educator, business writing consultant*

Oxnard
Hill, Alice Lorraine *history, genealogy and social researcher, educator*

Pacific Palisades
Garwood, Victor Paul *retired speech communication educator, audiology*

Palm Desert
†Kubiak, Andrea Celeste *language educator*

Palm Springs
†Philip, Michel Henri *classicist, writer*

Palmdale
Kilanowski, Dana Marcotte *historian, writer, filmmaker, archaeologist*

Palo Alto
Mommsen, Katharina *retired German language and literature educator*
Walker, Carolyn Peyton *English language educator*
Zwicky, Arnold Melchior, Jr., *linguistics educator*

Pasadena
†Eckford, Wendel *historian, educator*
Elliot, David Clephan *historian, educator*
Kousser, J(oseph) Morgan *history educator*
Mandel, Oscar *literature educator, writer*
†Parr, James Allan *literature professor*

Pebble Beach
†Dallmann, William Charles *speech educator, writer*

Penn Valley
Hodgson, Peter John *author, composer, lecturer*

Piedmont
Putter, Irving *French language educator*

Pittsburg
†Kaiper, Donald Dixon *historian, educator*

Pomona
Cranston, John Welch *historian, educator*
†Evans, William McKee *historian, educator*

Portola Valley
Carnochan, Walter Bliss *retired humanities educator*

Rancho Cucamonga
†Rodriguez, Juan Antonio *literature educator*

Rancho Santa Fe
Ruiz, Ramon Eduardo *history educator*

Richmond
Svoboda, George Jiri *historian, librarian*

Riverside
Elliott, Emory Bernard *English language educator, educational administrator*
Grimm, Reinhold *humanities educator*
Kronenfeld, Judy Zahler *humanities educator, writer*
Ross, Delmer Gerrard *historian, educator*
†Yount, Gwendolyn Audrey *humanities educator*

Rohnert Park
Shinagawa, Larry Hatime *American studies educator*
Wautischer, Helmut *philosophy educator*

Sacramento
†Avendaño, Fausto *language educator, writer*
Carr, Gerald Francis *German educator*
Meindl, Robert James *English language educator*
Reed, Nancy Boyd *English language and elementary education educator*
†Ward, Ruth Ellen *language educator*

Saint Helena
Yates, Donald Alfred *retired literature educator*

San Diego
†Amstadt, Nancy Hollis *retired language educator*
†bar-Lev, Zev *linguist, educator*
Brandes, Raymond Stewart *history educator*
†Cobbs Hoffman, Elizabeth Anne *history educator*
Daley, Arthur Stuart *retired humanities educator*
Darby, Joanne Tyndale (Jaye Darby) *arts and humanities educator*
Davies, Thomas Mockett, Jr., *history educator*
Dunlop, Marianne *retired English as second language educator*
†Ferraro, Joanne M. *humanities educator*
†Genovese, Edgar Nicholas *humanities educator*
González-Trujillo, César Augusto *Chicano studies educator, writer*
Lakritz, Esther *retired English language educator*
Peterson, Richard Hermann *retired history educator*
†Sasaran, Laura Jeanne *humanities educator*
†Scott, Bonnie Kime *English literature educator*
Swank, William George *historian, writer*
Vanderbilt, Kermit *English language educator*
†Wawrytko, Sandra Ann *humanities educator*
†Wilson, Jerry Clark *language educator*

San Francisco
Cherny, Robert Wallace *history educator*
Cohen, Henry *historian, retired educator*
Costa-Zalessow, Natalia *foreign language educator*
Dennehy, Raymond Leo *philosopher, educator*
Hansen, Carol Louise *English language educator*
Henderson, Horace Edward *World War II historian, peace advocate*
†Kelley, Michael Garhart Roosevelt *historian, educator, writer*
Langton, Daniel Joseph *English, writing educator, poet*
Lin, Robert Kwanhwan *language educator, consultant*
Mann, Charles Frederick *language educator, translator, author*
†McGuire, William Albert *humanities educator*
Needleman, Jacob *philosophy educator, writer*
Papakonstantino, Stacy *English language educator*
Satin, Joseph *language professional, university administrator*

San Jose
Gillett, Paula *humanities educator*

San Juan Capistrano
Carlson, Lawrence Arvid *retired English language educator, real estate agent*

San Luis Obispo
Lynch, Joseph James *philosophy educator*

San Marcos
Christman, Albert Bernard *historian*
Tanner, John Douglas, Jr., *history educator, writer*
Yuan, Yuan *English educator, translator*

San Marino
Rolle, Andrew *historian, writer*
†Travis, Albert Hartman *retired ancient language educator*
Zall, Paul Maxwell *retired English language educator, consultant*

San Mateo
Petit, Susan Yount *French and English language educator*

Santa Barbara
Avalle-Arce, Juan Bautista *Spanish language educator*
†Bermúdez, Silvia *literature educator*
Brownlee, Wilson Elliot, Jr., *history educator*
Chafe, Wallace LeSeur *linguist, educator*
Collins, Robert Oakley *history educator*
Crawford, Donald Wesley *philosophy educator, university official*
Del Chiaro, Mario Aldo *art historian, archeologist, etruscologist, educator*
Fingarette, Herbert *philosopher, educator*
†Goldsmith, Melissa Ursula Dawn *musicologist*
Gordon, Helen Heightsman *English language educator, writer, publisher*
Gunn, Giles Buckingham *language educator, religious studies educator, global and international studies educator*
Gutierrez-Jones, Carl Scott *English educator*
Helgerson, Richard *English literature educator*
Hsu, Immanuel Chung Yueh *history educator*
Kuczynski, John-Michael Maxime *humanities educator, writer*
Lindemann, Albert S. *history educator*
McGee, James Sears *historian, educator*
Renehan, Robert Francis Xavier *Greek and Latin educator*
Rose, Mark Allen *humanities educator, educator*
Russell, Jeffrey Burton *historian, educator*
†Sharrer, Harvey L. *language educator*
†Tobin, Ronald William *French language educator*
†Tu, Kuo-ch'ing *literature educator*
Wilkins, Burleigh Taylor *philosophy educator*

Santa Clara
Le, Son Minh *philosophy educator*
Meier, Matthias S(ebastian) *historian*
Mori, Maryellen Toman *language educator, translator, literature educator*
†White, Fred Daniel *literature educator, writer*

Santa Cruz
Beecher, Jonathan French *history educator*
†Jansen, Virginia *art historian, educator*
Lieberman, Fredric *ethnomusicologist, educator, composer*
†Ritscher, Lee A *literature educator*
Stevens, Stanley David *historian, researcher, retired librarian, archivist*
Suckiel, Ellen Kappy *philosophy educator*
†Terdiman, Richard *literature educator*

Santa Monica
Aghabegian, Diana E. Bortnowsky *English language educator, publisher*

Santa Rosa
Aman, Reinhold Albert *philologist, publisher*
Brashear, Charles Ross *English educator, retired, writer*

Saratoga
†deBarling, Ana Maria *language educator*

Sherman Oaks
Howe, Daniel Walker *historian, educator*

Stanford
Anthony, Donald Bruce *humanities educator*
Baker, Keith Michael *history educator*
†Chrissochoidis, Ilias *musicologist*
Dekker, George Gilbert *literature educator, literary scholar, writer*
Dunlop, John Barrett *foreign language educator, research institution scholar*
Duus, Peter *history educator*
Eitner, Lorenz Edwin Alfred *art historian, educator*
†Felstiner, John *literature educator, literary translator*

†Fleishman, Lazar *literature educator*
Fredrickson, George Marsh *history educator*
Gelpi, Albert Joseph *English educator, literary critic*
Greene, Roland *literature educator*
Kennedy, David Michael *historian, educator*
Loftis, John, Jr., (John Clyde Loftis Jr.) *English language educator*
Lohnes, Walter F. W. *German language and literature educator*
Moravcsik, Julius Matthew *philosophy educator*
†Orgel, Stephen Kitay *English language educator*
Perloff, Marjorie Gabrielle *English and comparative literature educator*
†Plebuch, Tobias *musicologist*
Robinson, Paul Arnold *historian, educator, writer*
Sheehan, James John *historian, educator*
†Stansky, Peter David Lyman *historian*
Traugott, Elizabeth Closs *linguist, educator, researcher*

Stinson Beach
†Springer, Mary *humanities educator*

Stockton
†Duffett, Michael Frank *humanities educator, poet*
Ippolito, Christophe *language educator*
Limbaugh, Ronald Hadley *retired history educator, history center director*
†Ward-Lonergan, Jeannene M. *speech educator*

Thousand Oaks
†Reaves, Michaela Crawford *history educator*

Torrance
Anderson, Marilyn Wheeler *English language educator*
†Imbarus, Aura *language educator, consultant*

Tujunga
Daly, Saralyn R. *retired humanities educator, writer*

Ukiah
Lohrli, Anne *retired English language educator, writer*

Vallejo
Brown, Earl Kent *historian, clergyman*
Landauer, Elvie Ann Whitney *humanities educator, writer*

Van Nuys
Ewing, Guin Porter *historian, art collector*
Zucker, Alfred John *English language educator, academic administrator*

Venice
Katz, Brian Philip *language educator, writer*

Wilmington
Burlingame-Smith, June *English language educator, administrator*

Woodland Hills
Siever-Henderson, Patricia *history university educator*

Wrightwood
†LaMay-Abner, Julie Ann *English educator*

Yucaipa
Lardy, Leonard Anthony *English educator*

COLORADO

Boulder
†Bickman, Martin *literature educator, writer*
†Ferme, Valerio Cristiano *language educator*
Gonzalez-del-Valle, Luis Tomas *Spanish language educator*
†Huemer, Michael *philosophy educator*
†Jurafsky, Daniel *linguist*
Menn, Lise *linguistics educator*
Rood, David S. *linguistics educator*
Taylor, Allan Ross *linguist, educator*

Centennial
†Morley, Judy Mattivi *historian, educator, historic site director*

Colorado Springs
Austerman, Donna Lynne *Spanish language educator*
Blackburn, Alexander Lambert *author, English literature educator*
Cramer, Owen Carver *classics educator*
Hallenbeck, Kenneth Luster *retired numismatist*
†Reinitz, Neale Robert *retired literature educator*
Stavig, Mark Luther *English language educator*
Tucker, Frank Hammond *history educator*

Denver
†Castellani, Victor *foreign language and literature educator*
Fasel, Ida *English language educator, writer*
Frederick, Robert Allen *history educator*
†Howard, W. Scott *language educator*
Hughes, J(ohnson) Donald *history educator, editor*
†Johnson, Geraldine Esch *language specialist*
Pfnister, Allan Orel *humanities educator*
Steele, Thomas Joseph *English language educator, writer*
Wetzel, Jodi (Joy Lynn Wetzel) *history and women's studies educator*

Dolores
Kreyche, Gerald Francis *retired philosophy educator*

Durango
Gulliford, Andrew Jellis *historian, photographer*
Smith, Duane Allan *history educator, researcher*

Englewood
Bardsley, Kay *historian, archivist, dance professional*

Erie
Dilly, Marian Jeanette *humanities educator*

Fort Collins
†Cooperman, Matthew B. *language educator*
McComb, David Glendinning *history educator*
Rollin, Bernard Elliot *philosophy educator, consultant on animal ethics*
Sloane, Sarah Jane *English educator*
Tremblay, William Andrew *English language educator, writer*

Golden
Eckley, Wilton Earl, Jr., *humanities educator, educator*
Quirke, Terence Thomas, Jr., *genealogist, retired geologist*

Greeley
†Knott, Alexander Waller *historian, educator*
Worley, Lloyd Douglas *English language educator*

Lakewood
Joy, Carla Marie *history educator*
†Padilla, Francisco S. *language educator*
Woodruff, Kathryn Elaine *English language educator*

Littleton
†Crum, Julie Wade *literature educator*

Palisade
Fay, Abbott Eastman *history educator*

Pueblo
Farwell, Hermon Waldo, Jr., *parliamentarian, educator, former speech communication educator*
Vorpagel, Wilbur Charles *historical consultant*

Sterling
Christian, Roland Carl (Bud Christian) *retired English language and speech communications educator*

U S A F Academy
Newmiller, William Ernest *English educator*

Westminster
†Bocock, Scott Gregory *historian*

CONNECTICUT

Colebrook
McNeill, William Hardy *retired history educator, writer*

Danbury
Aronson, Kristin Janina *philosopher, educator*
Edelstein, David Simeon *historian, educator*
†Roman, Eric *humanities educator*

East Granby
Scanlon, Lawrence Eugene *English language educator*

Enfield
Folmsbee, Patricia Hurley *reading and language arts consultant*

Essex
Hieatt, Allen Kent *language professional, educator*
Hieatt, Constance Bartlett *English language educator*

Fairfield
Eliasoph, Philip *art historian, gallery director*
Levitt, Jesse *retired foreign language educator*
†Mascia, Mark Joseph *language educator*
Newton, Lisa Haenlein *philosopher, educator*

Farmington
†Higgins-Biddle, John Charles *humanities educator, consultant*

Guilford
Colish, Marcia Lillian *history educator*

Hamden
Culler, Arthur Dwight *English language educator*
†McClellan, Edwin *Japanese literature educator*
Mintz, Max M. *historian*
Pelikan, Jaroslav Jan *history educator*
St Aubyn, Frederic Chase *French language educator*

Hartford
Cohn, Jan Kadetsky *American literature and American studies educator*
Decker, Robert Owen *history educator, clergyman*
Gastmann, Albert Lodewijk *retired political science and language educator, writer*
Ogden, Hugh *English literature educator, poet*

Ivoryton
Osborne, John Walter *historian, educator, author*

Killingworth
Sampson, Edward Coolidge *humanities educator*

Manchester
†Salvio, Regina Eugenia *language educator*

Meriden
Chiarenza, Frank John *English language educator*

Middletown
Buel, Richard Van Wyck, Jr., *history educator, writer, editor*
Gillmor, Charles Stewart *history and science educator, researcher*
Heimann-Hast, Sybil Dorothea *language arts and literature educator*
Meyer, Priscilla Ann *Russian language and literature educator*
Miel, Jan *humanities educator*
Pomper, Philip *history educator*
Reed, Joseph Wayne *American studies educator, artist*
Schwarcz, Vera *history educator, poet*
Shapiro, Norman Richard *Romance languages and literatures educator*
Wensinger, Arthur Stevens *language and literature educator, writer*
Winston, Krishna *foreign language professional*

Mystic
Burlingame, Michael Ashton *historian, retired educator*

New Britain
Barnett, Stuart Adrian *English language educator*
Emeagwali, Gloria Thomas *humanities educator*
†Heitner, John A. (Jack Heitner) *English language educator, writer*
Iannone, Abel Pablo *philosophy educator*
Leeds, Barry Howard *English language educator*

New Haven
Bloom, Harold *humanities educator, writer*
Blum, John Morton *historian, educator*
Borroff, Marie *English language educator*
†Brisman, Leslie *English language educator*
Brooks, Peter (Preston) *French and comparative literature educator*
Dupré, Louis *retired philosopher, educator*
Dworski, Sylvia *modern languages educator*
Erlich, Victor *Slavic languages educator*
Frank, Roberta *English language educator*
Freedman, Paul Harris *historian, educator*
Freeman, Joanne Barrie *history educator*
Gilbert, Creighton Eddy *art historian*
Gilman, Todd Seacrist *librarian, scholar, educator, musician*
Goffart, Walter André *history educator*
Gordon, Sarah Herbert *historian*
Greene, Liliane *French language and literature educator, editor*
Hallo, William Wolfgang *Assyriologist*
Harries, Karsten *philosophy educator, researcher*
Hartman, Geoffrey H. *language professional, educator*
†Hernandez-Rodriguez, Rafael *language educator, writer*
Hersey, George Leonard *art history educator, retired*
Hollander, John *humanities educator, poet*
†Holmes, Frederic Lawrence *science historian*
Holquist, James Michael *Russian and comparative literature educator*
Insler, Stanley *philologist, educator*
Kagan, Donald *historian, educator*
Kennedy, Paul Michael *history educator*
Kevles, Daniel Jerome *history educator, writer*
Langer, Lawrence Lee *English educator, writer*
Lord, George deForest *English educator*
MacMullen, Ramsay *retired history educator*
Marcus, Ruth Barcan *philosopher, educator, writer, lecturer*
†Mehring, Christine *art historian*
Ogbaa, Kalu *English literature educator*
Peterson, Linda H. *English language and literature educator*
Pollitt, Jerome Jordan *art history educator*
Prown, Jules David *art historian educator*
†Quaglia, Jordano *language educator, writer*
Rawson, Claude Julien *English educator*
Robinson, Fred Colson *English language educator*
Smith, John Edwin *philosophy educator*
Totman, Conrad Davis *history educator*
Underdown, David Edward *historian, educator*
Wandycz, Piotr Stefan *history educator*
†Weiner, Susan E. *language educator*
Wrightson, Keith Edwin *historian*

New London
Held, Dirk tomDieck *classics educator*
Willauer, George Jacob *English literature educator*

North Haven
Bennett, Harry Louis *history educator*

Old Lyme
Pepe, Joy *art history educator*

Orange
Collier, Christopher *history educator, writer*
Davis, David Brion *historian, educator*

Salisbury
Kilner, Ursula Blanche *genealogist, writer*

Sharon
Chatfield, Judith Spencer *garden historian*

Stamford
Anderson, Susan Leigh *philosophy educator*

Storrs
Gouwens, Kenneth Veld *history educator*
Millikan, Ruth Garrett *philosophy educator*

Storrs Mansfield
Abramson, Arthur Seymour *linguistics educator, researcher*
Brown, Richard David *history educator*
Charters, Ann *biographer, editor, educator*
Coons, Ronald Edward *historian, educator*
Gross, Robert Alan *history educator*
Lederer, Herbert *foreign languages educator*

†Orringer, Nelson Robert *Spanish and comparative literature educator*
Reed, Howard Alexander *historian, educator*
Rosen, William *English language educator*
Shaffer, Jerome Arthur *philosophy educator*

Trumbull
Allen, Richard Stanley (Dick Allen) *English language educator, author*

Warren
Hill, May Brawley *art historian*

Washington
Leab, Daniel Joseph *history educator*

Waterbury
MacLeod, Glen Gary *English language educator*

West Hartford
Camp, J. Holden *history educator*
Collins, Alma Jones *English educator, writer*
†Shea, Thomas F. *literature educator*

West Haven
Glen, Robert Allan *history educator*

Willimantic
Lacey, James Francis *American studies educator*

Windsor
Auten, Arthur Herbert *history educator*

Woodbridge
Ecklund, Constance Cryer *French language educator*

Woodstock
Susla, Jeffrey Jonathan *English language educator*

DELAWARE

Dover
De Roche, Linda Lee *English language educator*
Taylor, Stephen Craig *philosophy educator, researcher, lecturer*

Frederica
†Miller, Mary-Emily *history educator*

Georgetown
Hook, Donald Dwight *humanities educator, writer*
Williams, William Henry *history educator, liberal arts coordinator*

New Castle
Cope, Maurice Erwin *art history educator*

Newark
†Coulet du Gard, Donna M. *language educator*
Day, Robert Androus *English language educator, former library director, editor, publisher*
Halio, Jay Leon *language professional, educator*
Homer, William Innes *art history educator, art expert, author*
Isaacs, Diane Scharfeld *English educator*
Lathrop, Thomas Albert *language educator, educator*
†Panda, Kenneth Bires *English educator*
Schwartz, Norman B. *humanities educator, consultant*
Steiner, Roger Jacob *linguistics educator, writer, researcher*
Tolles, Bryant Franklin, Jr., *history and art history educator*
Venezky, Richard Lawrence *English language educator*
Walker, Jeanne Murray *English educator*
Weintraub, Stanley *arts and humanities educator, writer*
Wolters, Raymond *historian, educator*

Wilmington
Kneavel, Ann Callanan *humanities educator, communications consultant*

DISTRICT OF COLUMBIA

Washington
Albrecht, Kathe Hicks *art historian, visual resources manager*
Bader, William Banks *historian, foundation executive, former corporate executive*
Bedini, Silvio A. *historian, author*
†Beisner, Robert Lee *historian*
Bennett, Betty T. *English literature educator, university dean, writer*
†Bernhardt, Barbara Izabela *language educator, writer*
Billington, James Hadley *historian, librarian*
†Black, Allida Mae *historian, educator, writer, consultant*
Boorstin, Daniel Joseph *historian, lecturer, educator, author, editor*
Broun, Elizabeth *art historian, museum administrator*
Caws, Peter James *philosopher, educator*
†Cheney, Lynne V. *humanities educator, writer*
Cua, Antonio S. *philosopher, educator*
Curran, Robert Emmett *history educator*
Davidson, Dan Eugene *Russian language and area scholar, academic administrator*
Dougherty, Jude Patrick *philosophy educator, dean*
Dudley, William Sheldon *historian*
Duncan, Richard Ray *history educator*
Fain, Cheryl Ann *translator, editor*
†Ferretti, Maddalena F. *humanities educator*
Gibert, Stephen P. *government educator, defense consultant*
Graves-Roman, Patricia Ann *educator, researcher, writer*

PROFESSIONAL INDEX 6439 HUMANITIES: LIBERAL STUDIES

†Hacker, Barton Clyde *historian, writer*
†Hammond, William Michael *historian, educator*
†Hathaway, Robert Morse *historian*
Hawke, Paul Henry *historian*
Heelan, Patrick Aidan *philosophy educator*
†Hershberg, James Gordon *historian, educator*
†Hoak, Michael Shane *historian*
Howland, Nina Davis *historian*
Howland, Richard Hubbard *architectural historian*
Huber, Richard Miller *American studies consultant*
Kalb, Marvin *public policy and government educator*
Kapsch, Robert James *engineering and architectural historian*
Kazin, Michael *history educator, writer*
†Kennedy, Dane Keith *history educator*
Kennedy, Robert Emmet, Jr., *history educator*
Kreidler, Charles W(illiam) *linguist, educator*
Kreinheder, Hazel Fuller *genealogist, historian*
Ladjevardi, Habib *historian*
†Langenbacher, Eric Anton *humanities educator*
†Langer, Erick Detlef *historian, educator*
†Laqueur, Walter *history educator*
Lewis, Victor Bradley *philosopher, educator*
Lichtman, Allan Jay *historian, educator, consultant*
Lightfoot, David William *linguistics educator*
Livingston, Robert Gerald *historian, journalist*
Loesberg, Jonathan *humanities educator*
Long, Pamela Olivia *historian*
Marr, Phebe Ann *historian, educator*
†Mather, Susan M. *humanities educator*
†McAleavey, David *English educator*
McAuliffe, Jane Dammen *religious studies and Islamic studies educator*
†McCartin, Joseph Anthony *historian, educator*
McKelvey, Virginia Maude *language educator*
Miller, Jeanne-Marie Anderson (Mrs. Nathan J. Miller) *English language educator, academic administrator*
†Mujica, Barbara Louise *language educator, writer*
†Ortiz, Ricardo L. *language educator*
†Park, Alice Mary Crandall *genealogist*
Pireddu, Nicoletta *Italian and comparative literature educator*
†Pope, Nancy *historian, curator*
Pritzl, Kurt John *philosophy educator, university dean, priest*
Rand, Harry Zvi *art historian, poet*
Reed, Berenice Anne *art historian, artist, government official*
Reilly, John Marsden *English language educator*
†Richardson, Donna Darlene *historian, consultant, researcher*
†Richardson, Henry Shattuck *philosophy educator*
†Ritchie, Donald A. *historian*
Robb, James Willis *Romance languages educator*
Roberts, Jeanne Addison *retired literature educator*
Rosenblatt, Jason Philip *English language educator*
Rothenberg, Marc *historian*
†Rubin, Andrew N. *literature educator*
Salamon, Linda Bradley *English literature educator*
Schubert, Frank Nicholas *historian*
Scott, Gary Thomas *historian*
Severino, Roberto *foreign language educator, academic administration executive*
Sherman, Nancy *philosophy educator*
Simko, Jan *English, foreign language and literature educator*
Sklarew, Myra *humanities educator, poet*
†Spector, Ronald H. *historian, educator*
Stone, Florence Smith *film festival executive, consultant*
Taylor, Henry Splawn *literature educator, poet, writer*
Thompson, Wayne Wray *historian*
†van Ee, Daun Roell *historian*
Veatch, Robert Marlin *philosophy educator, medical ethics researcher*
†Vining, Margaret Simmons *historian, curator*
Voll, John Obert *history educator*
†Wagstaff, Grayson *musicologist, educator*
†Winkler, David F. *naval historian*
Wippel, John Francis *philosophy educator*
†Wood, Mary Louise *humanities educator*
†Zimand, David Chaim *historian, educator*

FLORIDA

Belleair Bluffs

Alexander, Christina Anamaria *translator, performing company executive*

Beverly Hills

Larsen, Erik *art history educator*

Boca Raton

Collins, Robert Arnold *English language educator*
†Gutting, Gabrielle L. *literature educator, researcher*
McFarland, Thomas *language educator, literature educator*

Bradenton

Bateman, John Jay *classics educator*
†Dickie, George Thomas *philosopher, educator*
Long, Michael Eldon *government and history educator*
Stewart, Priscilla Ann Mabie *art historian, educator*

Brandon

Holladay-Hicks, Sylvia A. *humanities educator*

Coral Gables

†Barentyne-Truluck, Ross *musicologist, educator, voice educator*
†Butterman, Steven Fred *language educator, researcher*
†Saffi, Clinia Mabell *language educator*

Daytona Beach

Carmona, José Antonio *Spanish language educator, English language educator*
†Harrison, William D. *humanities educator*

Englewood

Catterlin, Cindy Lou *English educator*

Fort Lauderdale

Austin, John Norman *classics educator*
†Hennessy, David V. *literature educator*
†Sanderson, Rita Marye *history educator*
van der Veur, Paul W. *humanities educator*

Fort Myers

†Harman, Joyce Elizabeth *humanities educator*
Miner, Thelma Smith *retired American literature educator*

Fort Walton Beach

†Urquhart, Troy Alexander *language educator*

Gainesville

†Balaban, Avraham *literature educator, poet, writer*
Brown, William Samuel, Jr., *communication sciences and disorders educator*
†Calin, William *literature educator*
†Davis, Richard Hunt, Jr., *historian*
Der-Houssikian, Haig *linguistics educator*
†Ginway, Mary Elizabeth *language educator*
†Hartigan, Karelisa Dorothy *classics educator*
†Perrone, Charles A. *humanities educator*
Proctor, Samuel *history educator*
Schmeling, Gareth *classics educator*
Sommerville, Charles John *humanities educator*
Wyatt-Brown, Anne Marbury *linguistics educator*
Wyatt-Brown, Bertram *historian, educator*

Gulfport

Davis, Ann Caldwell *history educator*

Hillsboro Beach

McGarry, Carmen Racine *historian, artist*

Jacksonville

Courtwright, David Todd *history educator, author*
Stanton, Robert John, Jr., *English language educator*

Key Biscayne

Ross, Marilyn J. *English and communications educator*
Zayas-Bazan, Eduardo *foreign language educator*

Lady Lake

Sligh, Gary Lee *English educator*

Lake Worth

Wilson, William J. *English language educator*

Lakeland

†Solberg, Daniel Arnold *language educator*

Madison

McCauley, Barbara Lynne *language educator*

Marathon

Wiecha, Joseph Augustine *linguist, educator*

Melbourne

Jones, Elaine Hancock *humanities educator*

Miami

Johnson-Cousin, Danielle *French literature and cultural studies educator*
†Lifshitz, Felice *historian, educator*
†Llopiz, Jorge Luis *language educator*
†Lorenzo, Guadalupe *language educator, department chairman*
†Mendoza De Arce, Daniel Leonel *retired humanities educator*
Neu, Charles Eric *historian, educator*
Obolensky, Georges *retired humanities educator*
†Rock, Howard B. *humanities educator*
†Ruggiero, Guido *historian, educator*

Milton

Bassett, Chuck *English educator*
Coston, Brenda Maria Bone *language arts educator*

Mount Dora

Anderson, Chester Grant *English educator*

Mulberry

Bowman, Hazel Lois *retired English language educator*

Naples

Griffin, Linda Louise *English language and speech educator*
Kinder, Suzanne Fonay Wemple *historian, educator*

North Port

Seiler, Charlotte Woody *retired educator*

Ocala

†Vazquez, Debra Allen *literature educator*
Zink, David Daniel *retired English educator, writer*

Okeechobee

Egolf, James Edward *history educator, secondary school educator*

Oldsmar

Thompson, Mack Eugene *history educator*

Orlando

†Caldero-Fiqueroa, Ana Jhanilca *language educator*
Ellens, J(ay) Harold *philosopher, educator, psychotherapist, pastor*
Lopez Cruz, Humberto J. *foreign language educator*
Moriarty, Michael Eugene *retired humanities educator*
Pauley, Bruce Frederick *history educator*

Ormond Beach

†Cunsolo, Ronald S. *historian, educator*

Pensacola

Arnold, Barry Raynor *philosophy educator, medical ethicist, minister, counselor*
Diaz, Judy L. *language educator*
Maddock, Lawrence Hill *retired language educator*
McGovern, James Richard *historian*

Port Charlotte

Winters, Stanley B. *history educator, writer, civic activist*

Saint Augustine

Adams, William Roger *historian, consultant*
Keys, Leslee Frances *historic preservation planner*

Saint Petersburg

Reilly, Tracy Lynn *English educator*
Walker, Brigitte Maria *translator, linguistic consultant*

Sarasota

†Benowitz, June Melby *historian, educator*
Doenecke, Justus Drew *history educator*
Jacobson, Jeanne McKee *humanities educator, writer*
Lengyel, Alfonz *art history, archeology and museology educator*
†Snyder, Lee Daniel *historian, educator*
Taplin, Winn Lowell *historian, retired senior intelligence operations officer*

Tallahassee

Bartlett, Richard Adams *American historian, educator*
Davis, Bertram Hylton *retired English educator*
Dorn, Charles Meeker *art education educator*
†Edwards, Leigh Holladay *literature educator*
Golden, Leon *classicist, educator*
†Hadden, Sally *historian, educator*
Halpern, Paul G. *history educator*
Harper, George Mills *English language educator*
Laird, Doris Anne Marley *humanities educator, musician*
†Leushuis, Reinier *language educator*
McGregory, Jerrilyn *English educator*
Mele, Alfred R. *philosophy educator*
†Picart, Caroline Joan (Kay) Santos *philosopher, language educator*
Schlenoff, Zeina Tamer *language educator, literary critic*

Tampa

Anton, John Peter *philosopher, educator*
†Brewer, Priscilla Joan *historian, educator*
Currey, Cecil Barr *history educator*
Kasum, Michael *humanities educator, writer*
Mathews, Richard Barrett *English educator, writer*
Mitchell, Mozella Gordon *English language educator, minister*
Perry, James Frederic *philosophy educator, writer*
Ronson, Bonnie Whaley *literature educator*
Weizmann, Maria Pia *ESL educator*

Titusville

Gadapee, Brett Ronald *English language educator, coach*
†Jackson, Philip Irving *literature educator, writer*

Umatilla

Balandran, Stella Varona *interpreter, lyricist, composer, writer*

Venice

Hooker, Alexander Campbell, Jr., *foreign language educator*

Winter Haven

Small, Norman Morton *speech and humanities educator, theatre producer, director*

Winter Park

Benedict, Dorothy Jones *genealogist, researcher*
Boguslawski, Alexander Prus *Russian studies educator, artist, Internet designer*
†Casey, Roger Neal *English language educator, director, actor, academic administrator*
Mason, Aimee Hunnicutt Romberger *retired philosophy and humanities educator*
Mésavage, Ruth Matilde *language educator*
Seymour, Thaddeus *English educator*
Wilson, Robley Conant, Jr., *English educator, editor, author*

GEORGIA

Americus

Isaacs, Harold *history educator*

Andersonville

Boyles, Frederick Holdren *historian*

Athens

†Balashov, Yuri V. *philosophy educator*
Freer, Coburn *English language educator*
†Gómez-Martinez, José Luis *Spanish language professional, researcher*
Hellerstein, Nina Salant *French literature and language educator*
†Jones, Jimmy Wayne, Jr., *historian, educator*
†Krasnostchekova, Elena Alexander *language educator*
Kretzschmar, William Addison, Jr., *English language educator*
Mamatey, Victor Samuel *history educator*
McGregor, James Harvey Spence *comparative literature educator*
McKnight, Reginald *English educator*
Miller, Ronald Baxter *English language educator, author*
Moore, Margaret Bear *American literature educator*
Moore, Rayburn Sabatzky *American literature educator*
†Spence, Sarah *comparatist educator*

Atlanta

†Bayor, Ronald Howard *history educator*
Benario, Herbert William *classicist, educator*
Blumenthal, Anna Catherine *English educator*
†Burns, Thomas Samuel *history educator*
Chafee, Ingrid Roberta Hoover Coleman *French language educator*
Chow, Rey *literature educator*
Crimmins, Timothy James *history educator*
Davidson, Denise Zara *historian, educator*
†Dobranski, Stephen Bitonti *literature educator*
Evans, Dorinda *art history educator*
†Fine, Laura I *language educator*
Fox-Genovese, Elizabeth Ann Teresa *humanities educator, educator*
†Garard, Charles Justus, Jr., *language educator, writer*
Garrow, David Jeffries *historian, author*
†Hallen, Barry *philosopher, educator*
Hartle, Robert Wyman *retired foreign language and literature educator*
†Judovitz, Dalia *language educator*
†Kallin, Britta *language educator*
Kuntz, Marion Lucile Leathers *classicist, historian, educator*
Luker, Ralph Edlin *history educator*
Manley, Frank *retired English language educator, writer*
†Puszkar, Norbert *classicist, educator*
Rojas, Carlos *Spanish literature educator*
Schaumann, Caroline *language educator*
†Schenbeck, Lawrence *musicologist*

Augusta

†Griswold, Sara Y. *language educator*

Barnesville

†Horn, Jason G. *English educator*

Blue Ridge

Walker, Sarah Harriet *English educator, administrator*

Byron

Morton, Eric *liberal arts educator*

Carrollton

†Steely, Melvin T. *language educator, educator*

Cochran

†Ayres, Brenda Ann *literature educator*
Ricks, John Addison, Jr., *history educator*

College Park

†Payne, Harry Charles *historian, educator*

Dahlonega

†Wiedmann, Sally Nelson *philosophy educator*

Dalton

Hutcheson, John Ambrose, Jr., *history educator*
Mathews, Marsha Anderson *English educator, poet, minister*

Decatur

Dillingham, William Byron *literature educator, author*

Doraville

†Ambrose, Andrew M. *humanities educator*

Dublin

Claxton, Harriett Maroy Jones *retired language educator*

Dunwoody

Duvall, Marjorie L. *English and foreign language educator*

Ellenwood

†Bauman, Mark Keith *historian, educator*

Gainesville

Lorence, James J. *historian, educator*
Strickland, William Bradley *English educator*

Jekyll Island

Jones, William Randolph *history educator*

Macon

Huffman, Joan Brewer *history educator*
†Young-Zook, Monica M. *language educator*

Madison

Aldridge, John Watson *English language educator, author*

Marietta

Rainey, Kenneth Tyler *English language educator*

Milledgeville

Gentry, Marshall Bruce *English educator*

Robins AFB

Head, William Pace *historian, educator*

Rome
†Carper, N. Gordon *historian, educator*

Saint Simons
Spivey, Ted Ray *English educator*

Statesboro
Rodell, Paul Arthur *history educator*
†Suazo-Jaque, Jorge Washington *foreign language educator*

HAWAII

Hilo
Kinney, Jeanne Kawelolani *English studies educator, writer*

Honolulu
Aung-Thwin, Michael Arthur *history educator*
Bender, Byron Wilbur *linguistics educator*
Dyen, Isidore *linguistic scientist, educator*
Fujita, James Hiroshi *history educator*
Hoffmann, Kathryn Ann *humanities educator*
†Kozok, Uli *language educator*
†Ota, Katsuhiro Justin *language educator*
†Papali'i, Aumua Mata'itusi Simanu *language educator*
Peterson, Barbara Ann Bennett *history educator, television personality*
Rapson, Richard L. *history educator*
Rehg, Kenneth Lee *linguistics educator*
†Schweizer, Niklaus R. *German educator*
Seidensticker, Edward George *Japanese language and literature educator*
Stephan, John Jason *historian, educator*
Varley, Herbert Paul *Japanese language and cultural history educator*

Kailua Kona
†Breier, Morton A. *philosopher*

Kaneohe
Nagtalon-Miller, Helen Rosete *humanities educator*

Lihue
†Merritt, Hiroko *linguist, educator*

Pearl City
†Conner, John Wallace *humanities educator*

IDAHO

Boise
Steiner, Stanley F. *literature educator*

Caldwell
†Rember, John V. *literature educator*

Jerome
Ricketts, Virginia Lee *historian, researcher*

Moscow
†Clanton, Orval Gene *historian, educator*
Greever, Janet Groff *history educator*
Harris, Robert Dalton *history educator, researcher, writer*
†Hieronymus, Debra Jean *literature educator*
Lecompte, Janet *historian, writer*

Pocatello
Carter-Cram, Kimberly Kay *French language educator*

Rexburg
†Lima, Amy Williams *linguist, educator*

ILLINOIS

Bloomington
†Brakebill, Tina Stewart *historian, writer*
†Fritzsche, Sonja Rae *humanities educator*
Laurenti, Joseph Luciano *language educator, writer*

Carbondale
Ammon, Harry *history educator*
Chavasse, Philippe *foreign languages educator*
Gilbert, Glenn Gordon *linguistics educator*
Hahn, Lewis Edwin *philosopher, retired educator*
†Hahn, Robert Alan *philosophy educator*
†Lanigan, Richard Leo, Jr., *humanities educator, writer, editor*
†Lawson, Richard Alan *literature educator, photographer*
Molino, Michael Robert *English educator*
†Wiesen, S. Jonathan *historian, educator*

Carterville
†Montaño, Edgar J. *language educator*

Centralia
†Normansell, Steven M. *English language educator*

Champaign
Douglas, George Halsey *writer, educator*
Koenker, Diane P. *history educator*
McGlathery, James Melville *foreign language educator*
O'Neill, John Joseph *speech educator*
Ratner, Lorman Alfred *history educator*
Smith, Ralph Alexander *cultural and educational policy educator*
Spence, Clark Christian *history educator*
Wheeler, Richard Paul *English educator, dean*

Charleston
Irwin, Bonnie D. *English language educator, researcher*
Jones, George Hilton *retired history educator, writer*
†Shirley, Michael Hathorn *historian, educator*

Chicago
Aronson, Howard Isaac *linguist, educator*
Bevington, David Martin *English literature educator*
Biggs, Robert Dale *Near Eastern studies educator*
Booth, Wayne Clayson *English literature and rhetoric educator, author*
Bouson, J. Brooks *English educator*
Brinkman, John Anthony *historian, educator*
Chambers, Richard Leon *retired Turkish language and civilization educator*
Clarke, Jay A. *art historian, curator*
Cohen, Ted *philosophy educator*
Cullen, Charles Thomas *historian, librarian*
De Armas, Frederick Alfred *foreign language educator*
Debus, Allen George *history educator*
Dembowski, Peter Florian *foreign language educator*
Dundzila, Rudra Vilius *language educator, minister*
Edelstein, Teri J. *art history educator, art administrator*
Elshtain, Jean Bethke *social and political ethics educator*
Erlebacher, Albert *history educator*
Fabian, Susan Jean *language educator*
†Farber, Walter T. *assyriologist, educator*
†Friedman, Lester David *humanities educator*
Gannon, Sister Ann Ida *retired philosophy educator, former college administrator*
Gardiner, Judith Kegan *English language and women's studies educator*
Gilbert, Bentley Brinkerhoff *history educator, retired*
Gilfoyle, Timothy Joseph *historian*
†Gilman, Sander Lawrence *German language educator*
†Golb, Norman *historian, writer*
Grant, Robert McQueen *humanities educator*
Gray, Hanna Holborn *history educator*
Gross, Hanns *history educator*
Haley, George *Romance languages educator*
Harris, Neil *historian, educator*
Hellie, Richard *Russian history educator, researcher*
Hillocks, George, Jr., *English educator, researcher, consultant*
Holli, Melvin George *history educator*
Hsia, Sophie S. *language educator*
Ingham, Norman William *Russian literature educator, genealogist*
†Johnston, Mark David *language educator*
†Jordan, Nicole T.N. *historian, educator*
Karanikas, Alexander *English language educator, author, actor*
Keenan, James George *classics educator*
Kolb, Gwin Jackson *language professional, educator*
†Lewis, Russell Lamar *historian, museum administrator*
Liebenow, Franklin Eastburn, Jr., *English literature educator*
Manning, Sylvia *English studies educator*
Meltzer, Sharon Bittenson *English language and humanities educator*
Najita, Tetsuo *history educator*
†Nashat, Guity *historian, education educator, researcher*
†Navia, Bernardo E. *language educator, researcher*
Odishoo, Sarah A. *English language educator*
Orban, Clara Elizabeth *foreign language educator*
Perez, Shabazz *literature educator*
†Perman, Michael *history educator, writer*
†Remini, Robert Vincent *historian*
†Riess, Steven Allan *historian, educator*
Rodgers, Carolyn Marie *literature educator, writer*
Romano-Magner, Patricia R. *English studies educator, researcher*
Rosenheim, Edward Weil *English educator*
Roy, David Tod *Chinese literature educator*
Saller, Richard Paul *classics educator*
Shaughnessy, Edward Louis *Chinese language educator*
Shen, Virginia Shiang-lan *Spanish and Chinese language educator*
†Singleton, Gregory Holmes *historian, educator*
†Sljivic-Simsic, Biljana B. *Slavic and Baltic languages educator*
†Smith, Daniel Scott *history educator, historian*
Sochen, June *history educator*
Tanner, Helen Hornbeck *historian, consultant*
†Tápanes-Inojosa, Adriana *language educator*
Thaden, Edward Carl *history educator*
†Thurner, Arthur W. *historian, educator*
Trumpener, Katie *literature educator*
Vertreace-Doody, Martha Modena *English educator, poet*

DeKalb
†Bentley, John R. *language educator*
†Clymer, Kenton James *history educator*

Deerfield
Priest, Robert J. *intercultural educator*

Dekalb
Baker, William *British literature educator*
Bowers, Jerome David, II, *history educator, consultant*
†Self, Robert Thomas *humanities educator*
†Vande Creek, Drew Evan *historian, educator*

East Peoria
†Chapman, Edgar Leon *literature educator*

Edwardsville
†Ware, Robert Bruce *philosopher, educator*

Elgin
Duffy, John Lewis *retired Latin, English and reading educator*

Evanston
Dean, Dennis Richard *language educator*
†Froula, Christine *English literature educator*
Jones, Dorothy Vincent *diplomatic historian*
†Kalantzis, George *historian, educator*
McCarthy, Thomas Anthony *philosophy educator*
†Paden, William D. *French literature educator*
Sheridan, James Edward *history educator*
†Silvestre, Stephanie *language educator*
Sundquist, Eric John *American studies educator*
Ver Steeg, Clarence Lester *historian, educator*
Well, Irwin *language educator*
Wright, John *classics educator*

Galesburg
Bailey, Stephen *history educator*
Hane, Mikiso *history educator*
†Hellenga, Robert R. *language educator, writer*
McCurry, James Patrick *philosophy and literature educator, poet, artist*

Glen Ellyn
†Fox, Jeffrey Harrison *language educator*
Georgalas, Robert Nicholas *English language educator*

Lake Bluff
Sweetser, Marie-Odile Gauny *retired foreign language educator*

Lake Forest
†Beiriger, Eugene Edward *historian, educator, dean*
†George, David Sanderson *Spanish language educator, writer*
†Le Mahieu, Dan Lloyd *historian, educator*

Macomb
Hallwas, John Edward *English language educator*
†Morelli, Mario Frank *philosophy educator*
†Spencer, Donald Spurgeon *historian, academic administrator*

Mount Vernon
Hall, Sharon Gay *retired language educator, artist*

Normal
Fry, Terry L. *retired English educator*
Hesse, Douglas Dean *English educator*
Lessoff, Alan H. *history educator*
Lord, Timothy Charles *philosophy educator*
Shields, John Charles *American studies and African American studies and literature educator*

Northbrook
Ehrmann, Susanna *foreign language educator, writer, photographer*
Stamper, James M. *retired English language educator*

Oak Park
Pinsky, Ellen Dodge *reading and language educator, education educator*

Orland Park
Capstaff, Genevieve MacKeeby *humanities educator*

Palatine
Herriges, Greg C. *literature educator, writer*
Hull, Elizabeth Anne *retired English language educator*
Keres, Karen Lynne *English language educator*

Peoria
Brill de Ramírez, Susan Berry *English educator*

Rockford
Carlson, Allan Constantine *historian*
Hoshaw, Lloyd *retired historian, educator*
Ward, Douglas Andrew *Spanish and special education educator*

Rolling Meadows
Strongin, Bonnie Lynn *English language educator*

Springfield
Bannister, Dan Wesley *historian, retired*
†Davis, George Cullom *historian*
Temple, Wayne Calhoun *historian, writer*

Urbana
Aldridge, Alfred Owen *English language educator*
Antonsen, Elmer Harold *Germanic languages and linguistics educator*
Arnstein, Walter Leonard *historian, educator*
Baym, Nina *English educator*
Bérubé, Michael *literature educator*
Carringer, Robert *English language and film educator*
Cuno, Kenneth M. *historian, educator*
Guibbory, Achsah *English educator, writer*
Haile, H. G. *German language and literature educator*
Hendrick, George *retired English language educator*
†Hitchins, Keith Arnold *historian, educator*
Hoxie, Frederick Eugene *history educator*
Jacobson, Howard *classics educator*
†Kim, Chin-Woo *linguist, educator*
Lasersohn, Peter Nathan *linguist, educator*
Love, Joseph L. *history educator, former cultural studies center administrator*
McColley, Robert McNair *history educator*
McKay, John Patrick *history educator*
Mortensen, Peter Leslie *English language educator*
Newman, John Kevin *classics educator*
Solberg, Winton Udell *history educator*
†Sousa, Ronald Wayne *foreign language educator*
Spence, Mary Lee *historian, educator*
Talbot, Emile Joseph *French language educator*

Watts, Emily Stipes *English language educator*

Westchester
Masterson, John Patrick *retired English language educator*

Wilmette
Fries, Robert Francis *historian, educator*
†McClure, Julie Anne *literature educator*

INDIANA

Angola
†Zimmerman, James Allen *historian, educator*

Bloomington
Anderson, Judith Helena *English language educator*
Assensoh, Akwasi Bretuo *historian, educator*
Bernhardt-Kabisch, Ernest Karl-Heinz *English and comparative literature educator*
Buelow, George John *musicologist, educator*
†Chaitin, Gilbert D. *humanities educator, researcher*
Choksy, Jamsheed Kairshasp *historian, religious scholar, language professional, humanities educator*
Cohen, William Benjamin *historian, educator*
Dunn, Jon Michael *informatics educator, dean*
†Edgerton, William B. *foreign language educator*
†Eisenberg, Paul David *philosophy educator*
Hanson, Karen *philosopher, educator*
Johnson, Owen Verne *historian, educator*
Johnson, Sidney Malcolm *foreign language educator*
Juergens, George Ivar *history educator*
Knudsen, Laura Georgia *linguist*
†Lloyd, Rosemary *language educator*
Martins, Heitor Miranda *foreign language educator*
Mathiesen, Thomas James *musicology educator*
McCluskey, John Asberry, Jr., *literature educator, writer*
Mickel, Emanuel John *foreign language educator*
†Nordloh, David Joseph *English language educator*
Pletcher, David Mitchell *history educator*
Ransel, David Lorimer *history educator*
Rosenberg, Samuel Nathan *French and Italian language educator*
†Senchuk, Dennis M. *philosopher, educator*
Sinor, Denis *Orientalist, educator*
Valdman, Albert *language and linguistics educator*

Carmel
†Sukapdjo, Wilma Irene *language educator*

Centerville
Wendeln, Darlene Doris *English language educator*

Chesterton
Hayduk, John Matthew *English and journalism educator*

Columbus
Spector, Judith Ann *English educator*

Crawfordsville
Barnes, James John *history educator*
Herzog, Tobey Church *English educator*

East Chicago
Riddle, Jared Matthew *English educator, actor*

Evansville
Drebushenko, David William *philosophy educator*

Fort Wayne
Essig, Erhardt Herbert *English educator*
Fischer, Bernd Jurgen *history educator*
Fox, Linda Chodosh *Spanish language educator*
Scheetz, Sister Mary JoEllen *English language educator*

Greencastle
Dittmer, John Avery *history educator*
Spicer, Harold Otis *retired English language educator, communications educator*
Weiss, Robert Orr *speech educator*

Indianapolis
Baetzhold, Howard George *English language educator*
Beyer, Werner William *retired English educator*
Bodenhamer, David Jackson *historian, educator*
Davis, Kenneth Wayne *English language educator, business communication consultant*
Hanson, Paul Richard *historian, educator*
Houser, Nathan *philosophy educator*
Krasean, Thomas Karl *historian*
†Lantzer, Jason Scott *historian, educator*
Lovejoy, Kim Brian *English educator*
Mason, Thomas Alexander *historian, educator, author*
Plater, William Marmaduke *English language educator, academic administrator*
Rebein, Robert Brian *English studies educator, writer*

Kokomo
†Cameron, Ann M. *language educator*

Muncie
Hayashi, Tetsumaro *retired literature educator, writer, editor*
Hozeski, Bruce William *English language and literature educator*

Newburgh
†Belleau, Leisa A. *English educator*

PROFESSIONAL INDEX 6441 HUMANITIES: LIBERAL STUDIES

Notre Dame
De Santis, Vincent Paul *historian, educator*
Doody, Margaret Anne *English language educator*
†Dubreil, Sebastien *language educator*
Fallon, Stephen Michael *humanities educator*
†Jerez-Farran, Carlos *language educator*
Lanzinger, Klaus *language educator*
Matthias, John Edward *English literature educator*
McInerny, Ralph Matthew *philosophy educator, writer*
McMullin, Ernan Vincent *philosophy educator*
Moevs, Christian Robert *literature educator*
†Moss, Lenny *philosopher, scientist*
Quinn, Philip Lawrence *philosophy educator*
Rosenberg, Charles Michael *art historian, educator*
Tomasula, Steven Anthony *literature educator, writer*

South Bend
Furlong, Patrick J. *historian, educator, university administrator*
Norling, Bernard *retired history educator*
†Scanlan, Margaret *language educator*
van Inwagen, Peter Jan *philosophy educator*
Vasta, Edward *humanities educator*

Terre Haute
Baker, Ronald Lee *English educator*
Brennan, Matthew Cannon *English literature educator, poet*
Carmony, Marvin Dale *linguist, educator*
†Christianson, Gale Edward *historian, educator*
De Marr, Mary Jean *English language educator*
Pickett, William Beatty *history educator*

Valparaiso
†Kavanagh, Frederick Graham *Japanese language educator*
Morgan, David A. *art history educator*
Peters, Howard Nevin *foreign language educator*

Vincennes
Rogers, John Headley *educator*

West Lafayette
†Bache, William B. *retired literature educator, editor, writer*
Bertolet, Rodney Jay *philosophy educator*
Contreni, John Joseph, Jr., *humanities educator, educator*
Cutter, Charles Ross *historian, educator*
†Duran, Angelica Alicia *literature educator*
Mc Bride, William Leon *philosopher, educator*
†Miller, Paul Chamness *language educator*
Mork, Gordon Robert *historian, educator*
Saunders, James Robert *English educator*
†Sundquist, John D. *language educator*
Woodman, Harold David *historian, educator*

Westville
Henning, Teresa Beth *English educator*

IOWA

Ames
†Avalos, Hector Ignacio *language educator*
Courteau, Joanna *foreign language educator*
Cravens, Hamilton *history educator*
St. Germain, Sheryl A. *humanities educator, writer*
Zimmerman, Zora Devrnja *English and folklore educator, university dean*

Avoca
Hardisty, William Lee *English language educator*

Bettendorf
Krein, David Frederick *humanities educator*

Cedar Falls
Clohesy, William Warren *philosopher, educator*
†Maier, Donna Jane-Ellen *history educator*
†Olsen-Dunbar, Jessica Ida *sign language educator*
Wang, Jennie *literature educator*

Cedar Rapids
Berry, Jay Robert, Jr., *English educator*
Heller, Terry L(ynn) *English literature educator, writer*
Lisio, Donald John *historian, educator*

Davenport
†Driscoll, Kerry Sue *language educator*
Kruse, Marylin Lynn *retired foreign language educator*

Decorah
†Christianson, John Robert *historian, educator*
Nelson, Harland Stanley *retired English educator*

Des Moines
McDowell, Frederick Peter Woll *retired English educator*

Dubuque
Arms, Gary D. *English literature educator*
Brimeyer, James Leon *language educator*
†Nadeau, Evelyn *language educator*
Perry, E. Eugene *communication educator*

Grinnell
Irving, Donald C. *English educator*
Kaiser, Daniel Hugh *historian, educator*
Kintner, Philip L. *history educator*
Michaels, Jennifer Tonks *foreign language educator*
Schrift, Alan Douglas *philosophy educator*
Smith, Don Alan *educator*

Iowa City
Addis, Laird Clark, Jr., *philosopher, educator, musician*
Aikin, Judith Popovich *languages educator, academic administrator*
Butchvarov, Panayot Krustev *philosophy educator*
Coolidge, Archibald Cary, Jr., *English language educator, literature researcher*
Ertl, Wolfgang *German language and literature educator*
Folsom, Lowell Edwin *language educator*
Fumerton, Richard Anthony *philosopher, educator*
Gelfand, Lawrence Emerson *historian, educator*
Goldstein, Jonathan Amos *retired ancient history and classics educator*
Green, Peter Morris *classics educator, writer, translator*
Hawley, Ellis Wayne *historian, educator*
Kerber, Linda Kaufman *historian, educator*
Kinsey, Joni Louise *art history educator*
Kowal, Rebekah Jane *American Studies educator*
†Mangum, Teresa Lynn *English literature educator*
Mentzer, Raymond Albert *religious history educator*
†Nash, Jan R. Olive *historian, consultant*
Percas de Ponseti, Helena *foreign language and literature educator*
Raeburn, John Hay *English language educator*
Ringen, Catherine Oleson *linguistics educator*
†Rohrbough, Malcolm Justin *historian, educator*
Scullion, Rosemarie *literature educator*
Solbrig, Ingeborg Hildegard *German literature educator, writer*
Trank, Douglas Monty *rhetoric and speech communications educator*

Lamoni
Wight, Darlene *retired speech educator, emerita educator*

New London
†Wehrle, Robert William *humanities educator*

Pella
†Chia, Ning *history educator*
†Den Adel, Raymond Lee *classics educator*
Ratzlaff, Keith Alan *English educator*

Waterloo
Holub, Jeanne Helen *English language educator*

Waverly
Blair, Rebecca Sue *English educator, lay minister*

KANSAS

Atchison
Homan, Thomasita *English language and literature educator*
Macierowski, Edward Michael *philosopher*

Chanute
Dillard, Dean Innes *English language educator, college official*

Cimarron
Wiseman, susan J. *English educator*

Dighton
Stanley, Ellen May *historian, consultant*

Emporia
Heldrich, Philip Joseph *English educator, academic administrator, writer*

Great Bend
Gunn, Mary Elizabeth *retired English language educator*

Hays
†Duffy, Cheryl Hofstetter *language educator*
Strohkirch, Carolyn Sue *communication educator*

Kansas City
Heflin, Ruth Janelle *English language educator*
†Heller, Jennifer Lynn *developmental studies specialist, consultant*
†Whitehead, Fred *historian, educator, editor*

Lawrence
Alexander, John Thorndike *historian, educator*
†Baron, Frank *language educator*
†Brooks, Karl Boyd *historian*
Casagrande, Peter Joseph *humanities and English educator*
Clowes, Edith W. *language educator, consultant, literature educator, consultant*
†Corbeill, Anthony *classicist, educator*
Debicki, Andrew Peter *foreign language educator*
†Dick, Ernst S. *retired German language educator*
Eldredge, Charles Child, III, *art history educator*
Gunn, James E. *English language educator*
†Johnson, Wallace Stephen, Jr., *Asian languages educator*
†Karcz, Andrzej *literature educator*
†Knittel, Janna Marie *literature educator*
†Kuznesof, Elizabeth Anne *history educator*
Li, Chu-Tsing *art history educator*
†Parker, Stephen Jan *Slavic language and literature educator*
Pasco, Allan Humphrey *literature educator*
Quinn, Dennis B. *English language and literature educator*
Reeves, Patricia Houts (Trish Reeves) *English and humanities educator*
Saul, Norman Eugene *history educator*
†Sax, Benjamin *literature educator*
Schoeck, Richard J(oseph) *English and humanities scholar, poet*

†Tsutsui, William Minoru *historian, educator*
Tuttle, William McCullough, Jr., *history educator*
Woelfel, James Warren *philosophy and humanities educator*
Worth, George John *English literature educator*

Leavenworth
Novak, Michael Paul *English language educator*

Manhattan
Hamscher, Albert Nelson *history educator*
Higham, Robin *historian, editor, publisher*
†Machor, James Lawrence *language educator*
Suleiman, Michael Wadie *humanities educator*

Ottawa
Tyler, Priscilla *retired English language and education educator*

Pittsburg
Franklin, John Thomas Ikeda *English educator*
Meats, Stephen Earl *English educator, editor, writer*

Topeka
Averill, Thomas Fox *writer, educator*

Wichita
Bennett-Kastor, Tina Lynne *linguist, educator*

KENTUCKY

Ashland
St. Clair, Philip Roland *humanities educator, poet*

Bowling Green
Minton, John Dean *historian, educator*
Survant, Joe *English language educator, poet*

Covington
Tenkotte, Paul Allen *history and international studies educator*

Elizabethtown
Cantrell, Douglas Eugene *history educator, author*

Elsmere
†Miller, Jackie Dean, I, *genealogist, historian*

Georgetown
Klotter, James C. *historian, educator*
†Sato, Shigetaka *Japanese language educator*

Highland Heights
†Vitz, Robert Carl *historian, educator*

Lexington
Coffman, Edward McKenzie *history educator*
†Hedlund, Richard Paul *historian, educator, retired historian*
†Hollis, Jessica Lexie *literature educator*
†Nugent, Christopher Donald *history educator*
Shawcross, John Thomas *English educator*
Warth, Robert Douglas *history educator*

Louisville
Ford, Gordon Buell, Jr., *literature educator, writer*
Green, Catherine C. *foreign language educator*
Kearney, Anna Rose *history educator*
Theiss, Gena Lee *genealogist, researcher*

Madisonville
Vander Ploeg, Scott David *literature educator, writer*

Midway
†Smialek, William *musicologist*

Murray
†Waag, C. Michael *foreign language educator*

Owensboro
West, William Robert *history educator*

Richmond
Myers, Marshall Dean *English educator*

Southgate
Glenn, Jerry Hosmer, Jr., *retired language educator*

Williamsburg
Fish, Thomas Edward *English language and literature educator*

Wilmore
Snyder, Howard Albert *educator, author*
†Stratford, Linda Harper *humanities educator*

LOUISIANA

Baton Rouge
Arceneaux, William *historian, educator, association official*
Cooper, William James, Jr., *history educator*
Culbert, David Holbrook *history educator, writer, editor*
Doty, Gresdna Ann *theatre historian, educator*
Hardy, John Edward *English language educator, author*
†Henninger, Katherine *English educator*
Loveland, Anne Carol *history educator*
Olney, James *English language educator*
†Ramirez, Arnulfo Gonzalez *language educator, linguist*
Ricapito, Joseph Virgil (Giuseppe Ricapito) *Spanish, Italian and comparative literature educator*
Sasek, Gloria Burns *English language and literature educator*

†Smith, David Jeddie *American literature educator*
Wheeler, Otis Bullard *retired English educator and university official*
†Younger, Ann Elizabeth *literature educator*

Ethel
Anders, Jane Virginia *genealogist*

Grambling
†Hawthorne, Leroy, Jr., *humanities educator, musician*

Hammond
†Bornier, Evelyne M *language educator*
Broussard, Francis Peter *English educator*
Thorburn, James Alexander *retired humanities educator*

Lafayette
†Laudun, John *literature educator*
Raffel, Burton Nathan *retired educator, poet, writer, translator*

Leesville
Norman, Paralee Frances *English language educator, researcher*

Marksville
Smith, Thomas Sullivan *humanities educator*

Monroe
†Harvey, Gordon Earl *historian, educator, writer*

Natchitoches
Smith, Jeffrey Robert *historian, educator*
Wells, Carol McConnell *genealogist, retired archivist*

New Orleans
Barton, Fredrick Preston *English language educator, administrator*
†Brumfield, William Craft *Slavic studies educator*
Collins, Richard Wayne *English literature educator*
†Frystak, Shannon Lee *historian, researcher*
†García-Castellón, Manuel *literature educator*
†Holditch, William Kenneth *American literature educator*
Kilroy, James Francis *educator*
Luza, Radomir Vaclav *historian, educator*
Martinez, Milton M. *language educator*
Paolini, Gilberto *literature and science educator*
Pindle, Arthur Jackson, Jr., *philosopher, researcher*
Poesch, Jessie Jean *art historian*
Qian, Zhaoming *critic, literature educator*
Reck, Andrew Joseph *philosopher, educator*
Roberts, Louise Nisbet *philosopher, educator*
Schalow, Frank Hickey *philosopher, educator*
Thompson, Annie Laura (Anne) *foreign language educator*
Tucker, Stephen Ray *educator, historian*
Ward, Jerry Washington, Jr., *English language educator*
†Werner, Robin A. *humanities educator*

Pineville
Howell, Thomas *history educator*
Tapley, Philip Allen *language educator, literature educator*

Ruston
Dodge Robbins, Dorothy Ellin *English educator*
Halliburton, Lloyd *Romance philology educator*

Thibodaux
Davis, Albert Joseph *languages and literature educator, novelist, poet*

MAINE

Bar Harbor
Carpenter, William Morton *English educator, writer*

Biddeford
†Rothermel, Dan *humanities educator*

Brunswick
Hodge, James Lee *German language educator*
Martin, Harold Clark *humanities educator*

Bucksport
Ives, Edward Dawson *folklore educator*

Castine
Berleant, Arnold *philosopher*
Hoople, Sally Crosby *retired humanities and communications educator*

Dresden
Turco, Lewis Putnam *English educator*

Lewiston
†Decker, Craig J. *German educator, translator, researcher*

Orono
Hatlen, Burton Norval *English educator*
Rogers, Deborah Dee *English language educator*
Segal, Howard Paul *history educator*

Portland
Louden, Robert Burton *philosopher, educator*
Schwanauer, Francis *philosopher, educator*

Rockport
Goodwin, Doris Helen Kearns *history educator, writer*

Sanford
Allan, Jonathan David *autograph dealer, pop culture historian*

Scarborough
†Hayden, Lisa C. *interpreter, translator, language educator, writer*
Sadik, Marvin Sherwood *art consultant, former museum director*

Waterville
Bassett, Charles Walker *English language educator*
†Moroni, Mario *humanities educator*
Roisman, Hanna Maslovski *classics educator*

MARYLAND

Annapolis
†Beckman, John *literature educator, novelist*
Cooper, Sherod Monroe, Jr., *retired English literature educator*
Lucas, George Ramsdell, Jr., *philosophy educator*
Van De Mark, Brian *historian, educator*

Arnold
Rosen, Susan A. C. *English language educator*

Baltimore
Achinstein, Peter Jacob *philosopher, educator*
Antokol-Meckler, Shirley *humanities educator*
Baldwin, John Wesley *history educator*
†Birt, Robert Earl *philosophy educator, writer*
Cacossa, Anthony Alexander *Romance languages educator*
†Campe, Rüdiger *humanities educator*
Chapelle, Suzanne Ellery Greene *history educator*
Child-Olmsted, Gisèle Alexandra *language educator*
Cohen, Warren I. *history educator*
Cooper, Jerrold Stephen *historian, educator*
Cripps, Thomas Robert *history educator, writer*
DeLuna, D.N. *literary educator*
Forster, Robert *history educator*
†Frey, Ruth Lazetta *historian, educator*
Irwin, John Thomas *humanities educator, educator*
Jeffries, John Worthington *historian, educator*
Johnson, Michael Paul *history educator*
Kessler, Herbert Leon *art historian, educator, university administrator*
†Kitson, John Richard *musicologist*
Knight, Franklin W. *history educator*
Kurth, Lieselotte *foreign language educator*
Lidtke, Vernon LeRoy *history educator*
Peirce, Carol Marshall *English educator*
Ranum, Orest Allen *historian, educator*
†Roller, Matthew Benedict *classics educator*
Russell-Wood, Anthony John R. *history educator*
Schneewind, Jerome Borges *philosophy educator*
Skinner, Daniel Thomas *language educator*
Terborg-Penn, Rosalyn Marian *historian, educator*
Walker, Mack *historian, educator*
Ziff, Larzer *English language educator*

Bel Air
Lu, David John *historian, writer*

Bethesda
Benson, Elizabeth Polk *art specialist*
Duncan, Francis *historian, retired government official*
Gray, James Gordon, Jr., *speech educator*
Highfill, Philip Henry, Jr., *retired language educator*
Theerman, Paul Harold *historian, archivist*
van der Linden, Frank Morris *historian*

Betterton
Kohl, Benjamin Gibbs *historian, educator*

Bowie
Miller, M. Sammye *history educator*
Sterling, Richard Leroy *English and foreign language educator*
Vidal, Pedro Jose *foreign language educator*

Catonsville
Loerke, William Carl *art history educator*

Chevy Chase
†Cline, Ruth Eleanor Harwood *translator*
Fern, Alan Maxwell *art historian, retired museum director*

Cockeysville
Peirce, Brooke *English language educator*

College Park
†Brush, Stephen George *history of science educator*
†De Lorenzo, William E. *foreign language educator*
†Dopp, Bonnie Jo *musicologist, school librarian*
Hallett, Judith Peller *classical studies educator*
†Isaacs, Neil D. *literature educator*
Levinson, Jerrold *humanities educator*
†McCray, William Patrick *historian, writer*
Moses, Claire Goldberg *history and womens studies educator*
†Noll, Franklin Clemens *historian*
Olson, Keith Waldemar *history educator*
Oster, Rose Marie Gunhild *foreign language professional, educator*
Pasch, Alan *philosopher, educator*
†Quintero-Herencia, Juan Carlos *language educator, writer*
Rivers, William Patrick *language policy researcher, consultant*
Rowland, Leslie S. *historian, educator*
†Severn, Stephen Edwin *literature educator*
Spear, Richard Edmund *art history educator*
Struna, Nancy L. *social historian and American studies educator*
Weart, Spencer Richard *historian*
Winton, Calhoun *literature educator*
Yaney, George *history educator*

Columbia
Marshall, Linda Murphy *linguist, government official*

Cumberland
Shreve, Jack *English and Spanish language educator*

Emmitsburg
†Johnson, Curtis Dean *historian, educator*

Frederick
Hein, David *humanities educator*
†Monhollon, Rusty *historian, educator*
Shull, Michael Slade *lecturer, writer, researcher*

Frostburg
Allen, Philip Mark *arts and humanities educator, dean, writer*
Clulee, Nicholas Harkins *history educator*

Glencoe
Weeks, Anne Macleod *English language eductor, education director*

Greenbelt
†Suid, Lawrence H. *historian, writer*

Hyattsville
Bloomfield, Maxwell Herron, III, *history and law educator*
Freedman, Morris *English language educator*
Golden, Marita *English language educator, foundation executive*
Rodgers, Mary Columbro *English educator, academic administrator, writer*

La Plata
Genz, Patricia Ann *English language and literature educator*

Lusby
Eshelman, Ralph Ellsworth *maritime historian, vertebrate paleontologist, cultural resource consultant*

Lutherville Timonium
†Giro, Jorge Antonio *language educator, educator*

Mitchellville
Embree, Ainslie Thomas *history educator*
Heald, Morrell *humanities educator, educator*

Rockville
Brown, David Harry *speech educator*
Cantelon, Philip Louis *historian*
†Durr, Kenneth D. *historian*
Hewlett, Richard Greening *historian*
†Junod, Suzanne White *historian, consultant*
†Kaplan, Lawrence Samuel *historian, educator*
†Kinnane, Adrian *historian*
Pfanz, Harry Willcox *historian*
Soderberg, William Charles *philosophy educator*

Salisbury
†Jennings, Louis Brown *retired humanities educator*
†Jiménez, Carmen Julia *language educator*
†Miller, Timothy Singley *historian, educator, language educator*

Severna Park
Schick, Edgar Brehob *German literature educator*

Silver Spring
Borkovec, Vera Z. *Russian studies educator*
Calinger, Ronald Steve *historian*
Cole, Wayne Stanley *historian, educator*
†Doherty, William Thomas, Jr., *historian, retired educator*
Foster, Victor Lynn *translator*
†Smith, Paul Hubert *retired historian*

Stevenson
North, Percy *art historian, educator*

Takoma Park
Giron, Robert LeRoy *English educator, writer*
Strasser, Susan *historian, researcher, writer*

Towson
Baker, Jean Harvey *history educator*
†Hirschmann, Edwin A. *historian, educator*
†Pineo, Ronn *historian, educator*
†Propst, M. Teresa Carson *historian*
Romero, Patricia Watkins *historian, educator, researcher*

Tracys Landing
Smith, Elbert Benjamin *historian, educator*

University Park
Walker, J. Samuel *historian*

MASSACHUSETTS

Amesbury
Bahre, Jeannette *English language and literature educator, education educator, librarian, educational consultant and tutor*
Labaree, Benjamin Woods *history educator*

Amherst
Baker, Lynne Rudder *philosophy educator*
Bauschinger, Sigrid Elisabeth *German literature educator, researcher*
†Bezucha, Robert Joseph *history educator*
†Clark, Carol Canda *art historian, educator*
†Cohen, Alvin P. *language educator*
Gettier, Edmund Lee, III, *philosophy educator*
Gibson, Walker *retired English language educator, poet, writer*
Greene, Theodore Phinney *historian, educator*
Kinney, Arthur Frederick *literary history educator, writer, editor*
Mauldon, Margaret *translator*
Oates, Stephen Baery *history educator*
Partee, Barbara Hall *linguist, educator*
†Rojas Joo, Juan Armando *language educator, poet*
†Sinha, Manisha *historian, educator*
†Taubman, Jane Andelman *Russian literature educator*
Tawa, Wako *foreign language educator*
Trahan, Elizabeth Welt *retired comparative literature educator*
†Wideman, John Edgar *English literature educator, novelist*
Wier, Dara *poet, English language educator*
Wolff, Robert Paul *philosophy educator*
Wyman, David Sword *historian, educator*

Andover
†Rotundo, E. Anthony *historian, educator*

Auburndale
Lindgren, Charlotte Holt *English language educator*
Winslow, Donald James *retired English educator, archivist*

Belmont
Cavarnos, Constantine Peter *philosopher, writer*
Dohanian, Diran Kavork *art historian, educator*

Boston
Blaisdell, Charmarie Jenkins *historian, educator*
Blakely, Allison *history educator*
Bromsen, Maury Austin *historian, bibliographer, antiquarian bookseller*
†Campbell, Ballard Crooker, Jr., *historian, educator*
Cardona, Rodolfo *Spanish language and literature educator*
Dallek, Robert *history educator*
Daniels, Norman *philosopher, educator*
Florescu, Radu Radu *East European history educator*
Floyd, Juliet Hendricks *philosopher, educator*
Golder, Herbert Alan *classics educator*
†Green, James R. *historian, educator, historian, researcher*
Henry, DeWitt Pawling, II, *creative writing educator, writer, arts administrator*
Hintikka, Jaakko *philosopher, educator*
Jones, Robert Emmet *French language educator, novelist*
Kafker, Frank A. *historian, educator*
Kleiner, Fred Scott *art historian, archaeologist, educator, editor*
†Lazerow, Jama *historian, educator*
Lowry, Bates *art historian, museum director*
Lyons, David Barry *philosophy and law educator*
Mustafa, Shakir *English and Arabic educator*
Neidle, Carol *language educator, researcher*
Ness, Arthur Joseph *musicologist*
†Percy, William Armstrong, III, *historian, educator*
†Perdigao, Lisa Kim *language educator*
Riely, John Cabell *English educator, art historian, consultant*
Rosen, Stanley Howard *humanities educator*
Sanborn, George Freeman, Jr., *genealogist*
Scanlon, Dorothy Therese *history educator*
Tracy, James *history educator, headmaster*
Vasaly, Ann Carol *classical studies educator*
Wermuth, Paul Charles *retired English educator*
Wiseman, James Richard *classicist, archaeologist, educator*

Bridgewater
Hurley, Mike (John Mathias Geretschlaeger) *English language educator*

Brookline
Golden, Herbert Hershel *retired Romance languages educator*
Michopoulos, Aristotle V. *humanities educator, researcher*

Cambridge
Badian, Ernst *history educator*
Bailyn, Bernard *historian, educator*
Biagioli, Mario *history of science educator*
†Blair, Ann *historian*
Bloch, Herbert *classicist, medievalist, historian, educator*
Bolster, Arthur Stanley, Jr., *history educator*
Brustein, Robert Sanford *English language educator, theatre director, author*
Chomsky, (Avram) Noam (Avram Chomsky) *linguistics and philosophy educator*
Clausen, Wendell Vernon *classics educator*
Condry, Ian *humanities educator*
Conley, Tom Clark *literature educator*
Cross, Frank Moore, Jr., *foreign language educator*
†Diop, Samba *language educator*
Dyck, Arthur James *ethicist, educator*
Dyck, Martin *literary theorist, German literature theorist, mathematics historian*
Engell, James Theodore *English educator*
Flier, Michael Stephen *Slavic languages educator*
Fogelson, Robert Michael *history educator, writer, consultant*
Ford, Patrick Kildea *Celtic studies educator*
Gienapp, William Eugene *history educator*
Goldfarb, Warren (David Goldfarb) *philosophy educator*
Graham, Loren Raymond *historian, educator*
Greenblatt, Stephen J. *English language educator*
Guthke, Karl Siegfried *foreign language educator*
Hall, Peter Dobkin *historian, educator*
Hanan, Patrick Dewes *foreign language professional, educator*
Henrichs, Albert Maximinus *classicist, educator*
Huang, Cheng-Teh James *linguistics educator*
†Hutchison, William Robert *history educator*
Iriye, Akira *historian, educator*
Jones, Christopher Prestige *classicist, historian*
Keyser, Samuel Jay *linguistics educator, university official*
†Keyssar, Alexander *historian, educator*
Laiou, Angeliki Evangelos *history educator*
Lunt, Horace Gray *linguist, educator*
MacMaster, Robert Ellsworth *historian, educator*
Maier, Charles Steven *history educator*
Maier, Pauline *history educator*
Malmstad, John Earl *Slavic languages and literatures educator*
Nykrog, Per *French literature educator*
O'Neil, Wayne *linguist, educator*
Ozment, Steven *historian, educator*
†Pesetsky, David Michael *linguist*
Pian, Rulan Chao *musicologist, scholar*
Pipes, Richard *historian, educator*
Rosenberg, Charles Ernest *historian, educator*
†Rosenkrantz, Barbara Gutmann *retired history educator*
Rotberg, Robert Irwin *historian, political economist, educator, editor*
Sevcenko, Ihor *history and literature educator*
Shinagel, Michael *English literature educator*
Simon, Eckehard (Peter) *foreign language educator*
Simons, Thomas W., Jr., *educator*
Singer, Irving *philosophy educator*
Smith, Merritt Roe *history educator*
Sollors, Werner *English language, literature and American studies educator*
Stauffer, John William *cultural historian*
Suleiman, Susan Rubin *romance literature educator, writer*
Tarrant, R(ichard) J(ohn) *classicist, educator*
Thernstrom, Stephan *historian, educator*
Tu, Wei-Ming *historian, philosopher, writer*
Ulrich, Laurel Thatcher *historian, educator*
Vanger, Milton Isadore *history educator*
Vendler, Helen Hennessy *literature educator, poetry critic*
†Ware, Susan W. *historian*
†Weiner, Charles *historian, educator*
Weitzman, Arthur Joshua *English educator*
Wolff, Christoph Johannes *music historian, educator*
†Xiao, Yang *philosopher, educator*
Ziolkowski, Jan Michael *medievalist educator*

Canton
Parker, Virginia Marie *English language educator*

Chestnut Hill
Barth, John Robert *English educator, priest*
Blanchette, Oliva *philosophy educator*
†Bloom, Jonathan M. *humanities educator, writer*
Hachey, Thomas Eugene *British and Irish history educator, consultant*
Reed, James Eldin *consultant, publisher, historian*
†Taylor, E. Dennis *English language educator, editor*
Valette, Rebecca Marianne *Romance languages educator*

Dalton
Fumento, Rocco *retired English and film educator*

Dartmouth
Marlow, James Elliott *English language educator*

Easton
Spicer, Kevin Paul *history educator, priest*

Fall River
Powers, Alan William *literature educator*

Framingham
†Eykman, Christoph W. *language educator*
Horn, Bernard *English language educator, writer, translator*
McCarthy, Desmond Fergus *English literature educator*

Gardner
Cosentino, Patricia Byrne *English educator, poet*

Great Barrington
†Hannoum, Abdelmajid *historian, educator, anthropologist, researcher*

Greenfield
Ruiz, Lillian *English language educator*

Haydenville
Connolly, John Matthew *philosophy educator, administrator*

Holden
Jareckie, Gretchen Kinsman Fillmore *retired English language educator*

Lexington
Cardwell, Guy Adams *retired language educator*
McAleer, John Joseph *English literature educator*
Noether, Emiliana Pasca *historian, educator*
Ryerson, Richard Alan *historian, editor*

Longmeadow
Cobbs, Russell L(ewis) *English language educator*

Lowell
†Aste, Mario Andrea *foreign language educator*
Trounstine, Jean Rollman *humanities educator, writer*

Mattapoisett
Rosenfield, M(anuel) C(harles) *retired history educator, retired coastguard officer*

PROFESSIONAL INDEX 6443 HUMANITIES: LIBERAL STUDIES

Medford
Bedau, Hugo Adam *philosophy educator*
†Ch'en, Li-li *writer, Chinese language, literature and comparative literature educator*
Fyler, John Morgan *English language educator*
Hernandez, Mark Alan *Latin American/Latino literary and cultural studies educator*
Laurent, Pierre-Henri *history educator*
Marcopoulos, George John *history educator*
Ueda, Reed Takashi *historian, educator*
White, Barbara Ehrlich *art history educator*
†Wilson, Jonathan Michael *language educator, writer*

Milton
Frazier, Marie Dunn *speech educator, public relations and human resources specialist*

Milton Village
†Canton, Mamie Ruth *humanities educator*

Natick
†Lewis, Stephanie L. *language educator*

Needham
Bottiglia, William Filbert *humanities educator*
Criscenti, Joseph Thomas *retired history educator*

Newton
Marshall, Robert Lewis *musicologist, educator*
Scheffler, Israel *philosopher, educator*

North Andover
Longsworth, Ellen Louise *art historian, consultant*

North Dartmouth
†Twomey, John Humphrey, Jr., *language educator*
Werly, John McIntyre *historian, educator, retired*
Yoken, Mel B(arton) *French language educator, writer*

North Easton
Wolf-Devine, Celia Curtis *philosophy educator*

Northampton
Elkins, Stanley Maurice *historian, educator*
Ellis, Frank Hale *English literature educator*
Skarda, Patricia Lyn *English literature educator*
Smith, Malcolm Barry Estes *philosophy educator, lawyer*
†Vaget, Hans Rudolf *language professional, educator*
von Klemperer, Klemens *historian, educator*

Norton
Dahl, Curtis *English literature educator*

Onset
Barrs, James Thomas *linguistics educator*

Randolph
Morrissey, Edmond Joseph *classical philologist*

Revere
Paananen, Victor Niles *English educator*

Rockport
Walen, Harry Leonard *historian, lecturer, author*

Sheffield
Baritz, Loren *history educator*

Sherborn
Cushing, Steven *linguist, educator, writer, researcher, consultant*

Shutesbury
Creed, Robert Payson, Sr., *retired literature educator*

South Hadley
Berek, Peter *English educator*
Burns, Michael Thornton *historian, educator, farmer*
Farnham, Anthony Edward *English language educator*
Johnson, Richard August *English language educator*
Mazzocco, Angelo *language educator, cultural historian, linguist*

Springfield
†Bonemery, Anne M. *language educator*
†Geryk, Laura A. *language educator*
Gonzalez De Leon, Fernando *historian, educator*
Habermehl, Lawrence LeRoy *philosophy educator*
Porter, Burton Frederick *philosophy educator, writer, dean*
†Zenor, Jean Ellen *language educator*

Stoughton
Hall, Roger Lee *musicologist, educator, composer*

Truro
Fader, Daniel Nelson *English language educator*

Waltham
Arrom, Silvia Marina *history educator*
Flesch, William B. *English educator*
Goodheart, Eugene *English language educator*
Hale, Jane Alison *French and comparative literature educator*
Hoffman, W. Michael *philosophy educator, administrator*
Jackendoff, Ray Saul *linguistics educator*
†Katchen, Aaron L *historian*
†Putney, Clifford Wallace *historian, educator*
Sarna, Jonathan Daniel *history educator*
Staves, Susan *English educator*

Watertown
†Fein, Michael R. *historian, educator*
Rivers, Wilga Marie *foreign language educator*

Wellesley
Lefkowitz, Mary Rosenthal *Greek literature educator*
†Lloyd-Jones, Sir (Peter) Hugh (Jefferd) *Greek scholar*
Martin, Tony *humanities educator*
†Mistacco, Vicki E. *foreign language educator*

Wellfleet
Mc Feely, William Shield *historian, writer*

West Newton
†Angiolillo, Paul F. *retired language educator*

Weston
Higgins, Sister Therese *English educator, former college president*
†Oates, Mary Josephine *historian, educator*
Vetterling, Mary-Anne *Spanish language and literature educator*

Williamstown
Dalzell, Robert Fenton, Jr., *historian, educator*
Dew, Charles Burgess *historian, educator*
Fuqua, Charles John *retired classics educator*
†Goldstein, Darra Jane *language educator, editor*
Graver, Lawrence Stanley *English language professional*
†Meyers, Peter Alexander *humanities educator, researcher*
Oakley, Francis Christopher *history educator, former college president*
Rudolph, Frederick *history educator*
Stamelman, Richard Howard *French and humanities educator*

Worcester
Billias, George Athan *history educator*
Catto, Bonnie A. *classicist, educator*
Grad, Bonnie Lee *art historian, educator*
Hansen, Peter Holger *history educator, historian*
†Klooster, Willem Wubbo *historian*
Kom, Ambroise *literature educator*
Langevin, Edgar Louis *retired humanities educator*
O'Toole, John Munster *humanities educator*
Vaughan, Alden True *history educator*
Zeugner, John Finn *history educator, writer*

Worthington
†De Mott, Benjamin Haile *educator, author*

MICHIGAN

Adrian
Allego, Donna M. *English educator*
Peeradina, Saleem *English educator, poet*

Albion
Cocks, Geoffrey Campbell *history educator*

Allendale
†Blumreich, Kathleen Marie *language educator*
†Bullock, Kurt Evan *humanities educator*
Cata, Isabelle Marie Gros *foreign language educator*
†Hong, Ran-E *literature educator*

Ann Arbor
Bailey, Richard Weld *English language educator*
Becker, Marvin Burton *historian, educator*
Binetti, Vincenzo Antonio *Italian literature educator*
Blouin, Francis Xavier, Jr., *history educator*
Bornstein, George Jay *literary educator*
†Carson, John *history educator*
Cowen, Roy Chadwell, Jr., *language educator, educator*
Curley, Edwin Munson *philosophy educator*
Dann, John Christie *historian, library director*
Delbanco, Nicholas Franklin *English educator, writer*
Dunnigan, Brian Leigh *military historian, curator*
Eisenberg, Marvin Julius *art history educator*
Eisenstein, Elizabeth Lewisohn *historian, educator*
Ferrell, Robert Hugh *historian, educator*
Feuerwerker, Albert *history educator*
Forsyth, Ilene Haering *art historian*
Garbaty, Thomas Jay *retired English language educator*
Gomez, Luis Oscar *Asian and religious studies educator, clinical psychology educator*
†Goodenough, Elizabeth Noble *literature educator, child advocate*
†Gusain, Lakhan *ancient language educator, researcher*
Hackett, Roger Fleming *history educator*
Izzo, Herbert John *language and linguistics educator, researcher*
†Janko, Richard Charles Murray *humanities educator*
Knott, John Ray, Jr., *language professional, educator*
†Linderman, Gerald Floyd *retired historian*
Lindner, Rudi Paul *historian, educator*
†MacDonald, Michael Patrick *humanities educator*
Mersereau, John, Jr., *Slavic languages and literatures educator*
Munro, Donald Jacques *philosopher, educator*
Orlin, Louis Lawrence *literature and history educator*
Perkins, Barbara M. *English educator, editor*
Perkins, Bradford *history educator*
Potter, David Stone *Greek and Latin educator*
†Prins, Johanna *literature educator*
Pulgram, Ernst *linguist, philologist, Romance and classical linguistics educator, writer*
Railton, Peter Albert *philosophy educator*
Smith, Sidonie *literature educator*
Stolz, Benjamin Armond *foreign language educator*
Tinkle, Theresa L. *language educator*
Trautmann, Thomas Roger *history and anthropology educator*
†Warsi, M. Jahangeer *language educator, researcher*
†Zurier, Rebecca *art history educator*

Benton Harbor
Atwood, Harold Ashley *retired historian*

Big Rapids
Haneline, Douglas Latham *literature educator*
†Kantar, Andrew K. *literature educator*
Mehler, Barry Alan *humanities educator, journalist, consultant*
Sterling, Phillip Duncan *English educator*

Buckley
†Gingerich, Martin Ellsworth *literature educator*

Cedarville
Pittman, Philip McMillan *historian*

Clinton Township
Crawford, Betty Elizabeth *English and computer science educator*

Dearborn
Little, Daniel Eastman *philosophy educator, university program director*
†McMillan, Liana *language educator*
Papazian, Dennis Richard *history educator, political commentator*

Detroit
Abt, Jeffrey *art and art history educator, artist, writer*
†Aronson, Ronald *humanities educator, writer*
Brill, Lesley *literature and film studies educator*
Brunk, Thomas Walter *art historian*
Finkenbine, Roy Eugene *history educator*
†Grusin, Richard Arthur *literature educator, writer*
†Haase, Donald Paul *German language, literature and culture educator*
†Hock, Lisabeth Marie *language educator*
Marotti, Arthur Francis *language educator*
Muller, Herman Joseph *historian, educator*
Small, Melvin *history educator*
†Stivale, Charles Joseph *French language and literature educator*

East Lansing
Anderson, David Daniel *retired humanities educator, writer, editor*
Fisher, Alan Washburn *historian, educator*
Mansour, George P. *Spanish language and literature educator*
Mead, Carl David *retired educator*
Natoli, Joseph *English language educator*
Nelson, James Lindemann *philosophy educator, bioethicist*
Platt, Franklin Dewitt *retired history educator*
Schoenl, William James *history educator*
Stowe, David Ware *history educator, author*
Thomas, Franklin Richard *American studies and language educator, writer*
Whallon, William *humanities educator*

Escanaba
Howard, Alan Charles *retired English language educator*

Farmington
Moehlman, Ruth *historian, writer*

Flushing
Lemke, Laura Ann *language educator, principal*

Grand Rapids
Diephouse, David James *humanities educator, historian*
†Pasquale, Michael David *linguist, educator, linguist, consultant*
†Smith, David I. *German language educator*

Harper Woods
Havrilcsak, Gregory Michael *history educator*

Holland
Huttar, Charles Adolph *retired language educator*
Pannapacker, William Albert, III, *humanities educator*
†Swierenga, Robert *humanities educator, researcher*

Houghton
Whitt, Laurie Anne *philosophy educator*

Huntington Woods
Gutmann, Joseph *art history educator*

Jackson
Feldmann, Judith Gail *language professional, educator*
Kleiner, Elaine Laura *English literature educator*

Jerome
Dillon, Merton Lynn *historian, educator*

Kalamazoo
Blickle, Peter *German language and literature educator, novelist*
Breisach, Ernst A. *historian, educator*
Dybek, Stuart *English educator, writer*
Hilberry, Conrad Arthur *humanities educator, poet*
Jones, Leander Corbin *educator, media specialist*
†Palmitessa, James R. *historian, educator*
Ruoff, Cynthia Osowiec *foreign language educator*
Yoshida, Takashi *historian, researcher*

Livonia
Holtzman, Roberta Lee *French and Spanish language educator*

Marquette
†Brozzo, Shirley A. *language educator*

Midland
Servinski, Sarah Jane (Sarah Jeroue) *language arts educator*

Mount Pleasant
Apter, Ronnie Susan *English educator, translator*
†Kulawik, Krzysztof Andrzej *language educator*
Steffel, Susan Elizabeth *English language and literature educator*

Richmond
†Yaek, Megan Anne *language educator*

Rochester
†Chapman, Sara Eleanor *French historian*

Royal Oak
Akmakjian, Alan Paul *English language, literature and creative writing educator*

Saginaw
Houshiar, Bobbie Kay *language arts educator*

Salem
Riddering, Donald Lee *retired language educator, historian*

Traverse City
†Press, James Gordon *humanities educator*

University Center
Jezierski, John Vincent *historian, educator*

Wayne
Cobbs, Alfred Leon *German language educator*

West Bloomfield
†Stern, Guy *German language and literature educator, writer*
Williamson, Marilyn Lammert *English educator, university administrator*

Ypsilanti
†Cassar, George Harris *historian, educator*
Cere, Ronald Carl *languages educator, consultant, researcher*
†Chamberlain, Kathleen Patricia *humanities educator, writer*
†Coykendall, Abby Lynn *literature educator*
†Thomas, Laurence W. *language educator*
Tucker, William Daniel *English educator*

MINNESOTA

Chaska
†Spargo, Carolyn Marie *language educator, music educator*

Collegeville
Joyce, Robert E. *philosopher, educator*
Tegeder, Vincent George *historian, educator, archivist*

Coon Rapids
Carlson, Linda Marie *language arts educator, consultant*

Duluth
Fetzer, James Henry *philosopher, educator*
Schroeder, Fred Erich Harald *humanities educator*
Tezla, Albert *English educator*

Edina
Clifford, Christine Karen *speech professional, writer*

Elk River
Sandusky, Christine Ann *English language educator*

Fort Ripley
Scott, Ivan Carl *historian, educator*

Mankato
†Janc, John J. *language educator*
†Larsson, Donald Foss *literature educator*

Minneapolis
Bashiri, Iraj *Central Asian studies educator*
Browne, Donald Roger *speech communication educator*
Campbell, Karlyn Kohrs *speech and communication educator*
Clayton, Thomas Swoverland *English educator*
Countryman, James Nelson *English language educator*
Erickson, Gerald Meyer *classical studies educator*
Farah, Caesar Elie *Middle Eastern and Islamic studies educator*
Fergus, Patricia Marguerita *English language educator emeritus, writer, editor*
Firchow, Evelyn Scherabon *German language and literature educator, writer*
Firchow, Peter Edgerly *language professional, educator, author*
Hauch, Valerie Catherine *historian, educator*
†Hirsch, Gordon *British literature educator*
†Jahn, Gary Robert *foreign language educator*
Kohlstedt, Sally Gregory *history educator*
Marling, Karal Ann *art history and social sciences educator, curator*
Miner, Valerie J. *literature educator, writer*
Norberg, Arthur Lawrence, Jr., *historian, physicist educator*
Pazandak, Carol Hendrickson *liberal arts educator*
Phillips, William David *history educator*
Ross, Donald, Jr., *English language educator, university administrator*
Sarles, Harvey B. *humanities educator*

Seidel, Robert Wayne *science historian, educator*
Tracy, James Donald *historian, educator*
Weiss, Gerhard Hans *German language educator*
Wright, William Edward *historian, educator*

Moorhead
Bense, Charles James *English educator*
Buckley, Joan N. *English educator*
Coomber, James Elwood *English language educator*
Glasrud, Clarence Arthur *English educator*
†Totten, Gary *literature educator*
†Virtanen, Beth Louise *literature educator, consultant*

Northfield
Clark, Clifford Edward, Jr., *history educator*
Iseminger, Gary Hudson *philosophy educator*
Mason, Perry Carter *philosophy educator*
McKinsey, Elizabeth *humanities educator, consultant*
Soule, George Alan *literature educator, writer*
Wilkie, Nancy Clausen *classics and archaeology educator*
Yandell, Cathy Marleen *foreign language educator*

Red Wing
†Fritz, Henry Eugene *historian, educator*

Rochester
Erspamer, Peter Roy *humanities educator, writer*
Robbins, Thomas Landau *humanities researcher*

Roseville
Gross, Alan Gerald *rhetoric educator*

Saint Cloud
Braun, Janice Larson *language arts educator*
Hofsommer, Donovan Lowell *history educator*

Saint Paul
Barker-Nunn, Jeanne Beverly *English educator*
†Clemenson, David Lee *philosopher, educator*
Davis, Joy Lee *English language educator*
Glancy, Helen Diane *literature educator*
Mather, Richard Burroughs *retired Chinese language and literature educator*
McDougal, Stuart Yeatman *comparative literature educator, author*
Monson, Dianne Lynn *literacy educator*
†Nielsen, Suzanne Ruth *literature educator, writer*
Stewart, James Brewer *historian, writer, college administrator*
†Weiner, Carl Dorian *historian*
Wright, Michelle Maria *English language educator*

Saint Peter
†Crnkovic, Denis *language educator*

Vadnais Heights
Polakiewicz, Leonard Anthony *foreign language and literature educator*

Waseca
Strand, Melvin LeRoy *English educator*

Winona
†Ni, Ting *historian, educator*
Wilson, Lisa Marie *English educator*

MISSISSIPPI

Bay Saint Louis
Woodward, Ralph Lee, Jr., *historian, educator*

Cleveland
Spencer, William Christopher *English educator*

Clinton
Bigelow, Martha Mitchell *retired historian*

Columbus
†Burger, Michael *humanities educator*
Dunkelberg, Kendall Alan *literature educator, poet*

Goodman
Jones, Rita Ann *retired speech, theater educator*

Gulfport
Swetman, Glenn Robert *English language educator, poet*

Hattiesburg
Barron, Jonathan *language educator*
†O'Brien, Warren Gregory *historian, educator, writer*
†Polk, Noel Earl *English educator*
†Scarborough, William Kauffman *historian, educator*

Jackson
Curtis, Verna Polk *reading educator*
†McLemore-Wheeler, Linda M. *literature educator*

Long Beach
†Smith, James Patterson *humanities educator, consultant*

Magnolia
Coney, Elaine Marie *English and foreign languages educator*

Mississippi State
†Bentley, Gregory W. *literature educator*
Wiltrout, Ann Elizabeth *foreign language educator*

Starkville
†Cheathem, Mark R. *historian, educator*
†Light, George Evans *humanities educator*

Sumrall
Downey, James Cecil *retired music and humanities educator*

University
†Galef, David Adam *British literature educator, writer*
Hall, J(ames) R(obert) *English educator*
Jordan, Winthrop Donaldson *historian, educator*
Kiger, Joseph Charles *history educator*
Landon, Michael de Laval *historian, educator*
†López, Alfred J. *literature educator, writer*

MISSOURI

Branson
Ford, Jean Elizabeth *former English language educator*

Cape Girardeau
Hoffman, Steven James *historian, educator*

Chesterfield
Matros, Larisa Grigoryevna *medical philosophy researcher, writer*

Columbia
Alexander, Thomas Benjamin *history educator*
Anderson, Donald Kennedy, Jr., *English educator*
Bien, Joseph Julius *philosophy educator*
Goodrich, James William *historian, association executive*
Justice, George Lewis *language educator*
†Kvanvig, Jonathan L. *philosophy educator*
Lazzaro-Weis, Carol Marie *foreign languages educator*
Looser, Devoney Kay *English language educator*
Mullen, Edward John, Jr., *Spanish language educator*
Overby, Osmund Rudolf *art historian, educator*
Schwartz, Richard Brenton *English language educator, university dean, writer*
Strickland, Arvarh Eunice *history educator*
Timberlake, Charles Edward *history educator*
Vallentyne, Peter Lloyd *philosophy educator*
Wallach, Barbara Price *classicist, educator*
†Weems, Robert Everett, Jr., *historian, educator*
Zguta, Russell *history educator*

Florissant
Ashhurst, Anna Wayne *foreign language educator*

Jefferson City
†Keitel, Joyce Gillilan *English educator, director*

Joplin
†Karmanova, Tatiana Victorovna *language educator*
Laas, Virginia Jeans *historian, educator*
Merriam, Allen Hayes *speech communication educator*

Kansas City
Benson, Mary Etta *English educator*
Hoffmann, Donald *architectural historian*
LeBeau, Bryan Frank *history educator, author, academic administrator*
Loeb, Jeffrey T. *English language educator*

Kirksville
Davis, Adam Brooke *English educator*
Engber, Cheryl Ann *language educator, linguist*
†Hanley, Mark Young *historian, educator, researcher*
†Reschly, Steven Dale *historian, educator*

Lees Summit
†Parker, Deborah A *language educator, translator*

Marshall
†Wildt, Katherine Ann *literature educator*

Nevada
Campbell, Catherine Ellen *French language educator*

Poplar Bluff
†Rivetti, Andrew Francis *Spanish educator*

Rolla
†Christensen, Lawrence O. *historian, educator*
Malone, Edward Allen *English educator*

Saint Joseph
Chelline, Warren Herman *English educator, clergy member*

Saint Louis
Barmann, Lawrence Francis *history educator, retired*
Blasi, Gerald J. *humanities educator, lawyer*
Brady, Jules Malachi *philosopher, educator, priest*
Burkholder, Mark Alan *historian, educator*
Herbert, Kevin Barry John *classics educator*
†Hulsebosch, Daniel Joseph *historian, educator*
Krukowski, Lucian *philosophy educator, artist*
Madden, Thomas F. *medieval history educator, author*
Mc Namee, Maurice Basil *English language educator*
Perry, Lewis Curtis *historian, educator*
Ruland, Richard Eugene *English and American literature educator, critic, literary historian*
Sale, Merritt *classicist, comparatist, educator*
Schiller, Britt-Marie Christina *philosophy educator*
Schwarz, Egon *humanities and German language educator, writer, literary critic*
Shea, Daniel Bartholomew, Jr., *English language educator, actor*
Ullian, Joseph Silbert *philosophy educator*
van den Berg, Sara Jane *English educator*
Ward, Sylvia A. *reading educator*
Watson, Richard Allan *philosophy educator, writer*
Weixlmann, Joseph Norman, Jr., *English educator, provost*
Wellman, Carl Pierce *philosophy educator*
Witt, Michael John *history educator, priest*

Springfield
Burgess, Ruth Lenora Vassar *speech and language educator*
†Burling, William John *literature educator*
Easley, June Ellen Price *genealogist*
†Giglio, James Nicholas *humanities educator, writer*

Warrensburg
†Foley, William Edward *historian, educator, retired historian*
Robbins, Dorothy Ann *foreign language educator*

Windyville
Blosser, Pamela Elizabeth *metaphysics educator, counselor, minister*

MONTANA

Billings
DeRosier, Arthur Henry, Jr., *historian*
†Gulick, Walter Brooks *philosopher, educator*
†Jensen, Theodore W. *language educator*

Butte
Reardon, Stephen James, Jr., *retired English speech educator*

Kalispell
†Cowan, George D. *literature educator*

Miles City
†Sleight, Garth Hessen *language educator, dean*

Missoula
†Drake, Richard Regis *historian, educator*
Kittredge, William Alfred *humanities educator*
Wigfied-Phillip, Ruth Genivea *genealogist, author, researcher*

NEBRASKA

Lincoln
†Ambrosius, Lloyd Eugene *historian, educator*
Knoll, Robert Edwin *English educator*
Leinieks, Valdis *classicist, educator*
Luebke, Frederick Carl *retired humanities educator*
†Naugle, Ronald Clinton *history educator*
†Olney, Alexander Ian *English educator*
Rawley, James Albert *history educator*
Sawyer, Robert McLaran *history educator*
Stover, John Ford *railroad historian, educator*

Omaha
†Brock, Stephen L. *supervisor international languages, consultant*
Conces, Rory Joseph *philosophy educator*
Horning, Ross Charles, Jr., *historian, educator*
†Maher, Susan N. *language educator*
†Nielsen, Fredrick Henry *historian, educator*
Skau, Michael W. *English educator*

NEVADA

Las Vegas
Adams, Charles Lynford *English language educator*
Hickey, David C. *art historian*
†Tanenhaus, David Spinoza *historian, educator*

Reno
Branch, Michael Paul *humanities educator*
DeMolen, Richard Lee *historian*
Seib, Kenneth Allen *English educator*
Simonian, Lane Peter *history and environmental educator*

Winnemucca
†Bateman, Eric *literature educator*

NEW HAMPSHIRE

Amherst
Perkins, David *English language educator*

Center Sandwich
Folch-Pi, Willa Babcock *romance language educator*

Derry
Holmes, Richard Dale *history consultant*

Durham
†Garcia De La Rasilla, Carmen *language educator*
Hapgood, Robert Derry *English educator*
Lanier, Douglas Mercer *English language and literature educator*
†Linden, Blanche Marie Gemrose *history educator*
Marshall, Grover Edwin *retired French and Italian language educator*
Simic, Charles *English language educator, poet*
Wheeler, Douglas Lanphier *history educator, writer*

Exeter
Knowles, Harvard Vaughan *literature educator*

Freedom
Kucera, Henry *linguistics educator*

Hanover
Bien, Peter Adolph *English language educator, author*
Daniell, Jere Rogers, II, *retired history educator, consultant, public lecturer*
Doney, Willis Frederick *philosophy educator*
Garthwaite, Gene Ralph *historian, educator*
Gert, Bernard *philosopher, educator*
Heffernan, James Anthony Walsh *language and literature educator*
†Higgins, Lynn Anthony *humanities educator, writer*
Kritzman, Lawrence David *humanities educator*
Mansell, Darrel Lee, Jr., *English educator*
Oxenhandler, Neal *language educator, writer*
Russell, Robert Hilton *Romance languages and literature educator*
Scher, Steven Paul *literature educator, educator*
Scherr, Barry Paul *foreign language educator*
Sheldon, Richard Robert *Russian language and literature educator*
Shewmaker, Kenneth Earl *history educator*
Wood, Charles Tuttle *history educator*

Keene
†Crocker, Matthew Hallowell *historian, educator, writer, researcher*
Long, Mark Christopher *English educator*
†Vincent, Charles Paul *humanities educator*

Manchester
†Paradis, Wilfrid H. *retired historian*

Meredith
Heald, Bruce Day *English and music educator, historian*

Mount Sunapee
Marashio, Paul William *humanities educator*

Orford
Beale, Georgia Robison *historian, educator*

Portsmouth
Harter, Hugh Anthony *foreign language educator*

Rumney
Allen, Edward John Bedford *historian, retired educator*

NEW JERSEY

Avon By The Sea
Potter, Emma Josephine Hill *language educator*

Belle Mead
†Brown, Elizabeth Schmeck *fashion historian*

Bergenfield
Hill, George Robert *musicologist, music bibliographer*

Bloomfield
†Conrad, Angela *humanities educator*

Bridgewater
Mc Cormick, Richard Patrick *history educator*

Cape May
Lassner, Franz George *educator*
Turner, Almon Richard *retired art historian, educator*

Cherry Hill
Bond, John Walter *historian*

Clifton
Ressetar, Nancy *foreign language educator*
Stalbaum, Bernardine Ann *English language educator*

Cranford
†Russell, John Joseph *English educator*

Dayton
Adickes, Sandra Elaine *English language educator, writer*

Demarest
Brody, Saul Nathaniel *retired English literature educator*

Edison
Di Pasquale, Emanuel Paul *poet, English language and literature educator*

Ewing
Cole, Robert Carlton *English and journalism educator*

Glassboro
†Coulombe, Joseph Louis *literature educator*
†Wang, Q. Edward *history educator*

Glen Ridge
Coddington, Anne Lillian *retired English literature educator*

Hackensack
Fatemi, Saeid *language educator, writer, researcher*

Hackettstown
†Ripmaster, Terence M. *historian, educator*
Shayner, John Anthony *English language educator, university official*

Hewitt
Mollenkott, Virginia Ramey *English literature and language educator, author, guest lecturer*

Hightstown
Martin, David George *historian, Latin educator, author*

Litwicki, Ellen M. *history educator*
Reiff, Daniel D. *art history educator*

Fresh Meadows
†Duckett, Lila Wheeler *retired language educator, writer*

Garden City
Garner, Richard Keith *classicist, educator*
Jenkins, Kenneth Vincent *literature educator, writer*
†Seyfried, Vincent F. *historian*
Shneidman, J. Lee *historian, educator*

Gardiner
Mabee, Carleton *historian, educator*

Geneseo
Edgar, William John *philosophy educator*
†Gouvernet, Gerard Raoul *language educator*

Geneva
Lee, Steven Peyton *philosophy educator*
Quinby, Lee *humanities educator*

Getzville
Saveth, Edward Norman *history educator*

Glen Cove
Backman, Melvin Abraham *English educator*

Greenvale
†Brier, Robert M *Egyptologist, educator, documentary presenter*
Dircks, Phyllis Toal *English language educator*

Guilderland
Berger, Morris Isaiah *humanities educator*

Hamilton
Blackton, Charles S(tuart) *history educator*
Busch, Briton Cooper *historian, educator*
†Godwin, Joscelyn *humanities educator, writer*
†Jacobs, Jonathan A. *philosopher, educator*
†Khan, Halimur R. *language educator*
Soderberg, Dale LeRoy *English language educator, drama director, producer*
Van Schaack, Eric *art historian, educator*

Hempstead
†Couser, G(riffith) Thomas *literature educator*
McLaren, Joseph *Black literature educator*
†Zapata, Miguel-Angel *language educator, writer*

Herkimer
Martin, Lorraine B. *humanities educator*

Hicksville
Mund, Lorraine G. *English studies educator, writer*

Hillsdale
Parmet, Herbert Samuel *historian, writer*

Hudson
†Lyons, Rosemary *language educator*

Huntington
Dircks, Richard Joseph *English language educator, writer*

Ithaca
Abrams, Meyer Howard *English language educator*
Bailey, Lee Worth *philosophy and religion educator*
Bardaglio, Peter Winthrop *humanities educator*
†Brazell, Karen Woodard *Japanese literature educator*
Colby-Hall, Alice Mary *Romance studies educator*
Culler, Jonathan Dwight *English language educator*
†Dear, Peter Robert *historian, educator*
Eddy, Donald Davis *English language educator*
Fakundiny, Lydia *English language educator*
Groos, Arthur Bernhard, Jr., *German literature and music educator*
Harris, Robert Lee, Jr., *history educator*
Hohendahl, Peter Uwe *German language and literature educator*
Hutcheson, Richard Ervin *philosophy educator, academic administrator*
Kammen, Carol Koyen *historian, educator*
Kammen, Michael *historian, educator*
Koschmann, J. Victor *history educator, academic program director*
Kronik, John William *Romance studies educator*
LaCapra, Dominick Charles *historian, educator*
LaFeber, Walter Frederick *history educator, author*
McConkey, James Rodney *English educator, writer*
†McMillin, Scott *language educator*
Norton, Mary Beth *history educator, writer*
Porte, Joel Miles *English educator*
†Radice, Mark A. *musicologist*
Radzinowicz, Mary Ann *language educator*
Schroeder, Caroline Theresa *humanities educator*
Schwarz, Daniel Roger *English and American literature educator*
Shaw, Harry Edmund *English educator*
Silbey, Joel Henry *history educator*

Jamaica
Ekbatani, Glayol *English as second language educator, program director, writer*
Fay, Thomas A. *philosopher, educator*
George, Marie Ivanka *humanities educator*
Gutierrez, Franklin Abel *Spanish language-Latin America literature educator*
Harmond, Richard Peter *historian, educator*
Kinkley, Jeffrey C. *historian*
†Leet-Brodwin, Leonora *literature educator, writer*
†Millán, Madeline *language educator, translator*
Parmet, Robert David *history educator*
Wintergerst, Ann Charlotte *language educator*

Jericho
Astuto, Philip Louis *retired Spanish educator*

Johnson City
Bernardo, Aldo Sisto *retired foreign language educator*

Kinderhook
†West, Patricia *historian, consultant*

Long Beach
Caplan, Judith Shulamith Langer-Surnamer *genealogist, poet, researcher, editor, educator*

Long Island City
Yin, Kenneth Joseph *language educator*

Loudonville
Fiore, Peter Amadeus *English educator, clergy*

Middle Village
Walter, John Frederick *historical researcher, genealogist*

Monroe
†Charka, Satya Narayana *language educator, dance director*

Monsey
Erickson, Barbara Martha *historian, writer, florist*

Moravia
†Dienhoffer, Margaret Quigley *historian, educator*

Mountainville
Pachner, Joan Helen *art historian, curator*

New Paltz
Fakler, Mary Edith *English educator*
Harris, Kristine *historian, educator*
Hathaway, Richard Dean *retired language educator*
Hauptman, Laurence Marc *history educator*
†Shine, James C. *language educator, lawyer*

New Rochelle
Fitch, Nancy Elizabeth *historian, educator*
†Kraman, Cynthia *language educator*
Schleifer, James Thomas *history educator*

New York
†Aching, Gerard *language educator*
Allentuck, Marcia Epstein *English language and art history educator*
Andreopoulos, George John *history educator, lawyer, political science educator*
†Apter, Emily *language educator*
Arac, Jonathan *English language educator*
Arrillaga, Maria *foreign language educator*
Ashbery, John Lawrence *language educator, poet, playwright, art critic*
Babich, Babette E. *philosophy educator, writer*
Baker, Paul Raymond *history educator*
†Balis, Andrea F. *historian, writer*
†Balmer, Randall *American religion historian*
Becker, Seymour *history educator*
Bender, Thomas *history and humanities educator, writer*
Berghahn, Volker Rolf *history educator*
Bertram, Paul Benjamin *English language educator*
Birns, Nicholas Boe *literature educator, editor*
Bishop, Thomas Walter *French language and literature educator*
Block, Ned *philosopher, educator*
Bonfante, Larissa *classics educator*
Boudreau, A. Allan *historian, writer, educator*
†Boyd, Frances Armstrong *language educator, writer*
Brilliant, Richard *art history educator*
Brinkley, Alan David *historian*
Brooks, Jerome Bernard *English and Afro-American literature educator*
Brown, Jonathan *art historian, fine arts educator*
Brush, Craig Balcombe *retired French language and computer educator*
Bulliet, Richard Williams *history educator, novelist*
Burbank, Jane Richardson *language educator*
Cahn, Steven Mark *philosopher, educator*
Castronovo, David *humanities educator, writer*
Cavallo, Jo Ann *Italian language educator*
Caws, Mary Ann *French language and comparative literature educator, critic*
Cohen, Beth *art historian*
Cohen, Morton Norton *English educator, writer*
Colon, Elsie Flores *American and English literature educator*
Compagnon, Antoine Marcel *French language educator*
Cook, Blanche Wiesen *history educator, journalist*
†Datema, Jessica Venning *humanities educator*
Dawson, Philip *history educator*
Deak, Istvan *historian, educator*
Dearinger, David B. *art historian, curator*
de Menil, Lois Pattison *historian, philanthropist*
†Dickey, Eleanor *humanities educator*
Dore, Anita Wilkes *English language educator*
Dorris, George Edward *historian, educator, editor, author*
Driver, Martha Westcott *English language educator, writer, researcher*
Duberman, Martin *historian, educator*
Ely, Stanley E. *language educator, writer*
Ferrante, Joan Marguerite *language educator, literature educator, writer*
Flinchum, Russell Alan *design historian*
Foner, Eric *historian, educator*
†Force, Pierre Marie *French language and literature educator*
Frank, Elizabeth *English literature, author*
Freedberg, David Adrian *art educator, historian*
†Freedman, (Moses) Maurice *historian, researcher*
Freeman, James Beaumont *philosophy educator*
Frey, Julia Bloch *French language educator, art historian educator*
†Friedman, Sanford *literature educator, writer*
Gay, Peter *history educator, author*
Gerdts, William Henry *art history educator*
Ginter, Valerian Alexius *urban historian, educator*
Gluck, Carol *history educator*
†Graves, Gail Marvel *language educator*
†Greenbaum, Fred *historian, educator*
Gromada, Thaddeus V. *historian, academic administrator*
Harris, Frederick John *foreign language and literature educator*
Harris, Katherine Safford *speech and hearing educator*
Harris, Mary Emma *art historian, landscape designer*
Harris, William Vernon *history educator*
Harvey, David W. *humanities educator*
Harvey, Donald Joseph *history educator*
Heffner, Richard Douglas *historian, educator, communications consultant, television producer*
Held, George *English educator*
†Hendin, Josephine Gattuso *language educator, writer*
Hirschhorn, Bernard *educator, historian, researcher, writer*
Hoeflin, Ronald Kent *philosopher, writer*
†Hornbostel, Paula Rand *art historian*
Howe, Florence *English educator, writer, publisher*
Hunter-Stiebel, Penelope *art historian*
†Izzo, Francesco *musicologist*
Jackson, Kenneth Terry *historian, administrator*
Johnston, Ruth D. *film studies, English literature, and women's studies educator*
†Juchem, Elmar *musicologist, music educator, consultant*
Kaiser, Walter *English language educator*
Karsen, Sonja Petra *retired American-Hispanic literature educator*
†Kaur, Harminder *language educator*
Kerz, Louise *historian*
†Kramer, Lawrence Eliot *musicologist, composer*
Kriegel, Leonard *English language educator*
Krinsky, Carol Herselle *art history educator*
Kroeber, Karl *English language educator*
Lamont, Rosette Clementine *Romance languages educator, theatre journalist, translator*
LaRue, Jan (Pieters) (Adrian LaRue) *musicologist, educator, writer*
Leibowitz, Herbert Akiba *English language educator, author*
Lencek, Rado Ludovik *Slavic languages educator*
Lewyn, Ann Salfeld *retired English as a second language educator*
†Linares, Carlos *language educator, consultant*
†Lodge, Kirsten *language educator*
London, Herbert Ira *humanities educator, institute executive*
Lorch, Maristella De Panizza *medieval and Renaissance scholar, writer*
Low, Anthony *English language educator*
Malefakis, Edward E. *history educator*
Malin, Irving *English literature educator, literary critic*
Marincola, John *classics educator*
†Markowitz, Gerald E. *historian, educator*
Maxwell, Kenneth Robert *historian*
May, Gita *language and literature educator*
Mayerson, Philip *classics educator*
Maynard, John Rogers *English educator*
Maysilles, Elizabeth *speech communication professional, educator*
McClintock, Robert Oliver *history and education educator*
†McLendon, Sally *linguist, educator, anthropologist*
Meisel, Martin *English and comparative literature educator*
Meisel, Perry *English educator*
Menand, Louis *literature educator*
Middendorf, John Harlan *English literature educator*
Middlebrook, Diane Wood *English language educator, writer*
Miller, Nancy K. *literature educator*
Miller, Walter James *English and humanities educator, writer*
Mintz, Samuel Isaiah *English language educator, writer*
Myers, Gerald E. *humanities educator*
†Nash, Stanley Louis *literature educator, religious studies educator*
Olson, Roberta Jeanne Marie *art historian, author, educator, curator*
†Pascucci, Margherita *literature educator*
Paxton, Robert Owen *historian, educator*
Perna, Michael Lewis *language educator*
†Phillips, Louis J. *humanities educator, writer*
†Pissaro, Joachim Stephane Isaac *art historian, educator*
Plottel, Jeanine Parisier *foreign language educator*
Poirier, Richard *literary critic, educator, editor*
Posner, Donald *art historian, educator*
Prettyman, Alfred Emerson *English language and social and behavioral sciences educator, publishing executive*
Quiñones Keber, Eloise *art historian, educator*
Rabassa, Clementine Christos *humanities educator, translator*
†Ragusa, Olga Maria *retired Italian language educator*
†Rainwater van Suntum, Lisa Ann *humanities educator*
Randall, Francis Ballard *historian, educator, writer*
Rass, Rebecca Rivka *writer, English language educator*
Ravitch, Diane Silvers *historian, educator, author, government official*
Raymond, Dorothy Sarnoff *communications consultant, former actress and singer*
Reiman, Donald Henry *English language educator*
Reynolds, Donald Martin *art historian, foundation administrator, educator*
Rheins, Carl Jeffrey
Riback, Estelle Posner *art historian*
Richtman, Jack *French language educator*
†Robertson, Andrew Whitmore *historian*
Roos, Jane Mayo *art history educator*
Rosand, David *art history educator*
Rosenberg, John David *English educator, literary critic*
Rosenblum, Robert *art historian, educator*
Rothman, David J. *history and medical educator*
Rowen, Ruth Halle *musicologist, educator*
Salemi, Joseph Salvatore *classics and humanities educator, poet, writer*
†Saloman, Ora Frishberg *musicologist, educator*
Salvesen, Magda Abercromby *art historian, garden historian*
Sandler, Lucy Freeman *art history educator*
Scharffenberger, Elizabeth Watson *classicist*
Scheindlin, Raymond Paul *Hebrew literature educator, translator*
Schrecker, Ellen Wolf *historian, educator, editor*
†Sedgwick, Eve Kosofsky *literature educator, writer*
Seigel, Jerrold Edward *historian, writer*
Selig, Karl-Ludwig *language and literature educator*
Senie, Harriet F. *art historian*
Serlin, David H. *history educator*
Shea, George William *classicist, educator*
†Shearier, Stephen James *language educator*
Spivak, Gayatri Chakravorty *humanities educator*
Stade, George Gustav *humanities educator*
Steinberg, Leo *art historian, educator*
Steiner, Richard C. *semitic linguist, educator*
Stempleski, Susan *English language professional, writer*
Stephens, Gary Ralph *American literature and journalism educator*
Stern, Fritz Richard *historian, educator*
Stimpson, Catharine Roslyn *English language educator, writer*
†Subirats, Eduardo *language educator*
Tanselle, George Thomas *English language educator, foundation executive*
Taran, Leonardo *classicist, educator*
Travers, Scott Andrew *numismatist*
Tusiani, Joseph *foreign language educator, author*
Ulanov, Alexander *consultant, former literature educator*
Unger, Irwin *historian, educator*
Unger, Peter Kenneth *philosophy educator*
†Waldhorn, Arthur *literature educator, researcher, scriptwriter*
Waley-Cohen, Joanna *humanities educator*
Walker, Robert Harris *historian, writer, editor*
†Walkowitz, Daniel Jay *historian, filmmaker, educator*
Wallenstein, Barry *literature and creative writing educator, poet*
Ward, Aileen *retired humanities educator*
Wasser, Henry *retired American literature and sociology educator*
Weil-Garris Brandt, Kathleen (Kathleen Brandt) *art historian*
Weinberg, H. Barbara *art historian, educator, curator paintings and sculpture*
Wilner, Joshua David *literature educator*
Wixom, William David *art historian, museum administrator, educator*
Wortman, Richard S. *historian, educator*
Yerushalmi, Yosef Hayim *historian, educator*
Yurchenco, Henrietta Weiss *ethnomusicologist, writer*
Zirin, Ronald Andrew *classics educator, psychoanalyst*

Newburgh
Adams, Barbara *English language educator, poet, writer*

Niagara University
Northcutt, Wayne *history educator*
†Sze, Susan *philosopher, educator*

Nyack
Danaher, James P. *philosopher, educator*

Oakdale
Lu, Yuxin *historian, linguist*

Old Westbury
†Jabbour, Georgette N. *linguist, educator*
Navia, Luis E. *philosophy educator, writer*

Olean
†Mazon, Margaret Fausold *language educator*

Oneonta
Malhotra, Ashok Kumar *philosophy educator*
Shrader, Douglas Wall, Jr., *philosophy educator*
Travisano, Thomas Joseph *English language educator*
Wesley, Marilyn Clarke *English language educator*

Oswego
Bishop, Rand *retired humanities educator*
Smiley, Marilynn Jean *musicologist*
†Thurber, Timothy Nels *historian, educator*

Owego
Davis, Joan *English language educator*

Oyster Bay
Gable, John Allen *historian, association executive, educator*

Painted Post
†Kirk, Connie Ann *English educator, writer*

Patchogue
†Kelly, Dorothy Ann *language educator, writer*

Pittsford
French, Henry Pierson, Jr., *historian, educator*

Plattsburgh
†Torres-Padilla, Jose Luis *English educator*

Port Washington
Williams, George Leo *historian, landmark preservationist, educator*

Potsdam
Cross, John William *foreign language educator*
Harder, Kelsie Brown *retired language professional, educator*
†Komara, Edward Michael *musicologist*
Lunt, Lora G. *international education educator, language educator*
†Regan, Marie Carbone *retired language educator*
Serio, John N. *language educator*

Poughkeepsie
Bartlett, Lynn Conant *English literature educator*
Brakas, Jurgis (George) Hoegh *philosopher, educator*
Daniels, Elizabeth Adams *English language educator*
Griffen, Clyde Chesterman *retired history educator*
Hytier, Adrienne Doris *French language educator*
Kelley, David Christopher *philosopher*
Peck, H. Daniel *literature educator, educator*
Sharp, Ronald Alan *English literature educator, dean, author*
Van Norden, Bryan William *Asian studies educator*

Purchase
†Medoff, Rafael *historian, editor*
Redkey, Edwin Storer *history educator*
†Shields, David Brandon *historian, educator*
Waller, Gary Fredric *English language educator, administrator, poet*

Queensbury
Cavaluzzi, Anthony David *English studies educator*

Rensselaer
Semowich, Charles John *art historian, art dealer and appraiser, curator, artist, musician*

Riverdale
Nolte, Claire Elaine *history educator*

Rochester
Bauman, M. Garrett *English educator*
Berman, Milton *history educator*
Chiarenza, Carl *art historian, critic, artist, educator*
†Donaghy, Daniel Delet *literature educator, poet*
Hauser, William Barry *history educator, historian*
Herminghouse, Patricia Anne *foreign language educator*
Hollis, Susan Tower *history educator*
Johnson, Bruce Marvin *English language educator*
Jörgensen, Beth Ellen *Spanish language educator*
Weis, Monica Rosemary *English educator*
Young, Mary Elizabeth *history educator*
Zagorin, Perez *historian, educator*

Rockville Centre
Fitzgerald, Janet Anne *philosophy educator, retired academic administrator*
Gilroy, Jane Hagan *literature educator*

Rome
Zackey, Christopher Albert *mythologist, writer/poet, librarian*

Rush
Smith, Katherine Teresa *history educator*

Sagaponack
Korman, A. Gerd *history, educator, writer*

Saint Bonaventure
†Godet-Calogeras, JeanFrançois *historian, educator*
Wood, Paul William *language educator*

Salem
Nussbaum, Jay *philosophy educator, writer*

Sanborn
Michalak, Janet Carol *reading education educator*

Sayville
Lippman, Sharon Rochelle *art historian, curator, art therapist, writer, artist, filmmaker*

Scarsdale
Graff, Henry Franklin *historian, educator*

Schenectady
†Hartman, Carmen Teresa *language educator*
Jonas, Manfred *historian, educator*
Morris, John Selwyn *philosophy educator, college president emeritus*

Setauket
Simpson, Louis Aston Marantz *English educator, author*

Shirley
Morote, Elsa-Sofia *social sciences educator, business consultant*

Slingerlands
Childs, Rhonda Louise *motivational speaker*
Zacek, Joseph Frederick *history educator, international studies consultant, Central and East European culture and affairs specialist*

Southampton
Brophy, James David, Jr., *humanities educator*

Sparkill
†Lauture, Denize *language educator, writer*
†Sewell, Stacy Kinlock *historian, educator*

Staten Island
Holder, Calvin Beresford *history educator*
†Lawrence, Marilyn Catherine *language educator*
Lombardi, Giancarlo *Italian language educator*
Stearns, Stephen Jerold *history educator, writer*

Stony Brook
Aronoff, Mark H. *linguistics educator, writer, consultant*
†Franco, Charles *language educator*
Goldberg, Homer Beryl *English language educator*
Harris, Alice Carmichael *linguist, educator*
Ihde, Don *philosophy educator, university administrator*
Kuspit, Donald Burton *art historian, art critic, educator*
Levin, Richard Louis *English language educator*
Mignone, Mario B. *Italian studies educator*
†Semmel, Bernard *historian, educator*
†Videb[00e6]k, Bente A. *humanities educator*

Stuyvesant
Tripp, David Enders *numismatist, art historian, cartoonist, author*

Suffern
ommanday, Sue Nancy Shair *English language educator*

Syracuse
Alston, William Payne *philosophy educator*
Denise, Theodore Cullom *philosophy educator*
Field, Daniel *history educator*
†Lambert, Gregg *literature educator*
MacKillop, James John *English language educator, journalist, critic*
Powell, James Matthew *history educator*
†Shires, Linda M. *English educator, writer*
Sternlicht, Sanford *English and theater arts educator, writer*
Tatham, David Frederic *art historian, educator*
Waddy, Patricia A. *architectural history educator*

Troy
Ahlers, Rolf Willi *philosopher, theologian*

Uniondale
Naylor, Natalie *history educator*

Utica
Wagner, Frederick Reese *language professional*

Valhalla
Leone, Stephen Joseph *English language educator, computer technology consultant*

Vestal
Wagar, (Walter) Warren (Walter Wagar) *historian, educator*

Wantagh
†Galvan, Max *humanities educator*

Watertown
†Deidesheimer, Annamaria *English educator*

Williamsburg
†Witherspoon, Maria Bernarda Pena *bilingual educator*

Williamsville
Drew, Fraser Bragg Robert *language educator*
Garton, Charles *classics educator*

Yonkers
Viola, Mary Jo *art history educator*

NORTH CAROLINA

Asheville
Voigt, Ellen *literature educator*

Cary
Mata, Elizabeth Adams *English language educator, land investor*

Chapel Hill
Baron, Samuel Haskell *historian*
Browning, Christopher R. *historian, educator*
Brundage, William Fitzhugh *historian, educator*
†Chang, Kuk Won *humanities educator, researcher*
Davis, Sarah Irwin *retired English language educator*
Debreczeny, Paul *Slavic language educator, writer*
Eaton, Charles Edward *English language educator, author*
†Feinberg, Lawrence Edward *language educator, researcher*
Flora, Joseph M(artin) *English language educator*
Folda, Jaroslav Thayer, III, *art historian*
Grendler, Paul Frederick *history educator*
Handy, Rollo Leroy
†Harris-Lopez, Trudier *language educator, researcher, consultant, writer*
Heninger, Simeon Kahn, Jr., *English language educator*
†Illiano, Antonio *language educator, researcher*
Jones, Houston Gwynne *history educator*

Kohn, Richard H. *historian, educator*
Lee, Sherman Emery *art historian, curator*
Levine, Madeline Geltman *Slavic literatures educator, translator*
Ludington, Townsend *English and American studies educator*
Munsat, Stanley Morris *philosopher, educator*
Nelson, Philip Francis *musicology educator, consultant, choral conductor*
Rabil, Albert, Jr., *humanities educator*
†Sayre-McCord, Geoffrey *philosophy educator*
Schier, Donald Stephen *language educator, educator*
Smith, Sidney Rufus, Jr., *linguist, educator*
Stadter, Philip Austin *classicist, educator*
Stephens, Laurence David, Jr., *linguist, investor, oil industry executive, horse breeder*
Tindall, George Brown *historian, educator*
Williamson, Joel Rudolph *humanities educator*
†YMaisch, William Conrad *language educator*

Charlotte
†Aliaga-Buchenau, Ana-Isabel *humanities educator*
Buchenau, Jurgen *historian*
†Castro, Mary McDermott *language educator*
Gay, William C. *philosophy educator*
Hill, Ruth Foell *language consultant*
†Hopper, Edward Warren *language educator*
Myers, Robert Manson *English educator, author*
Preyer, Norris Watson *history educator*

Concord
†Newman, Sylvia H. *language educator*

Creedmoor
†Husketh, Alma Ormond *language educator*

Cullowhee
Farwell, Harold Frederick, Jr., *English language educator*

Davidson
Cole, Richard Cargill *English language educator*
McMillen, Sally Gregory *history educator*
Williams, Robert Chadwell *history educator*

Durham
Budd, Louis John *English language educator*
Cady, Edwin Harrison *English language educator, author*
Chafe, William Henry *history educator*
Clay, Diskin *classical studies educator*
Colton, Joel *historian, educator*
Davis, Calvin De Armond *historian, educator*
†Fischer, Sibylle Maria *literature educator*
Franklin, John Hope *historian, educator, author*
Golding, Martin Philip *law and philosophy educator*
Guy, David McCutcheon *literature educator*
Holley, Irving Brinton, Jr., *historian, educator*
Jonassaint, Jean *French and Francophone literatures educator*
†Kiss, Elizabeth *philosophy educator*
Lerner, Warren *historian, educator*
Oates, John Francis *classics educator*
†Pfau, Thomas *literature educator*
Preston, Richard Arthur *historian*
Richardson, Lawrence, Jr., *Latin language educator, archeologist*
Roland, Alex Frederick *history educator*
Sanford, David Hawley *philosophy educator*
Scott, Anne Byrd Firor *history educator*
Stewart, Philip Robert *French language educator*
Thompson, James Howard *historian, library administrator*
Thompson, John Herd *history educator*
†Wald, Priscilla B. *language educator*
Williams, George Walton *English educator*
Williams, Jocelyn Jones *reading educator*
Witt, Ronald G. *historian, educator*

Efland
Weinberg, Gerhard Ludwig *history educator*

Elizabeth City
†Lisowski, Joseph Anthony *language educator, poet, writer*
Williams, Rita Carroll *language educator, poet*

Elon
Troxler, Carole Watterson *historian, educator*

Fayetteville
Conley, Raymond Leslie *English language educator*
McMillan, Bettie Barney *English language educator*

Fearrington Village
†Boewe, Charles Ernst *historian, educator*

Franklin
Johnson, Herbert Alan *history and law educator, lawyer, chaplain*

Greensboro
†Almeida, José Agustín *romance languages educator*
Bardolph, Richard *historian, educator*
Benson, Brian Joseph *English language educator, author*
Chappell, Fred Davis *English language educator, poet*
Durham, Carolyn Richardson *foreign language and literature educator*
Penninger, Frieda Elaine *retired English language educator*
Schleunes, Karl A. *history educator*

Greenville
†Ferrell, Henry Clifton, Jr., *historian, educator*
†Kalinowski, Joe *humanities educator, researcher*
†Kopelman, Loretta Mary *philosophy educator*
†Moll, Kevin N. *musicologist, educator*
Runyan, Timothy Jack *historian, educator*

Hendersonville
Harris, James Braxton *retired humanities educator, freelance/self-employed writer*

High Point
McCaslin, Richard Bryan *history educator*

Jacksonville
Fischer, Violeta Pèrez Cubillas *Spanish literature and linguistics educator*
Kimball, Lynn Jerome *historian*

Laurinburg
Alexander, W. M. *philosophy educator*
Bayes, Ronald Homer *English language educator, author*

Mars Hill
†Hinners, R. Gordon *language educator*

Misenheimer
†Edwards, Joyce Perry *language educator*

Murfreesboro
†Moore, Danny Blair *historian, educator*

New Bern
Fegely, Eugene Leroy *retired humanities educator*
†White, James Edward, III, *historian, educator*

Pembroke
Canada, Mark Alan *English educator, researcher*

Pleasant Garden
†Kennett, Lee Boone, Jr., *historian, educator*

Raleigh
†Belk, Leotis S. *language educator*
†Maldonado-DeOliveira, Débora *classicist, researcher*
†McMurry, Linda Ott *retired history educator*
Rhodes, Donald Robert *musicologist, retired electrical engineer*

Salisbury
†Vance, Andrew Anderson, Jr., *humanities educator*

Wilmington
Graham, Otis Livingston, Jr., *history educator*
†Lapaire, Pierre-Jean G. *language educator*
†Veit, Richard Connolly *language educator*

Winston Salem
Barnett, Richard Chambers *historian, educator*
†Borwick, Susan Harden *musicologist, educator*
Gala, Candelas S. *literature educator, language educator*
Hendricks, J(ames) Edwin *historian, educator, consultant, author*
†Margitić, Milorad R. *language educator, researcher*
Oczkowicz, Edyta Katarzyna *English educator*
Shapere, Dudley *philosophy educator*

NORTH DAKOTA

Bismarck
Brudvig, Jon Larsen *history educator*
Newborg, Gerald Gordon *state archives administrator*

Fargo
Anderson, Gerald Dwight *history educator*
Danbom, David Byers *history educator*
Peet, Howard David *English educator, writer*
Peterson, Larry Richard *history educator*

Grand Forks
Caldwell, Mary Ellen *English language educator*
Clingan, Charles Edmund *historian*
Coleman, Joyce Kit *English literature educator, literary historian*

OHIO

Akron
Carley, Michael Jabara *historian, director*
Knepper, George W. *history educator*
McMahon, William Edward *philosophy educator*
†Zangrando, Robert Lewis *historian educator*

Alliance
†Lowe, Kelly Fisher *literature educator*

Ashland
†Schmidt-Rinehart, Barbara Coe *Spanish language educator*

Athens
Alexander, Charles Comer *history educator, writer*
Bleigh, Mildred Allen *genealogist*
Bond, Zinny Sans *linguistics educator*
Borchert, Donald Marvin *philosopher, educator*
Connor, Joan Carol *literature educator*
Crowl, Samuel Renninger *former university dean, english language educator*
†Davidson, Shae Ronald *historian, researcher*
Láscar, Amado José *language educator, writer*
Ping, Charles Jackson *philosophy educator, retired university president*
†Tao, Liang *linguistics educator, researcher*
Whealey, Lois Deimel *humanities scholar*
Whealey, Robert Howard *historian*

Beachwood
Feldman, Donna B. *literature educator*

Berea
†Kennelly, Laura Ballard *writer, educator*

Bluffton
Gundy, Jeffrey Gene *English educator*
†Nisly, L. Lamar *language educator*

Bowling Green
Browne, Ray Broadus *popular culture educator*
Lavezzi, John Charles *art history educator, archaeologist*

Brecksville
Pappas, Effie Vamis *English and business educator, writer, poet, artist*

Chagrin Falls
Rawski, Conrad H(enry) *humanities educator, medievalist*

Cincinnati
Alexander, John Kurt *history educator*
Beaver, Daniel Roy *history educator*
Bleznick, Donald William *Romance languages educator*
Brod, Evelyn Fay *foreign language educator*
Ciani, Alfred Joseph *language professional, associate dean*
†Czarnecki, Kristin E. *humanities educator*
†Finkelstein, Norman *literature educator*
Fujioka-Ito, Noriko *language educator*
Harmon, Patrick *historian, sports commentator*
†Lewis, Gene Dale *historian, educator*
†Lynch, Timothy Patrick *historian, educator*
Muntz, Ernest Gordon *historian, educator*
Schiff, James Andrew *English educator*
Schrier, Arnold *historian, educator*

Cleveland
Anderson, David Gaskill, Jr., *Spanish language educator*
Benseler, David Price *foreign language educator*
†Cummings, Gerardo Tonatiuh *literature educator, researcher*
†Curnow, Kathy *art historian, educator*
†Daley, Margaretmary *language educator, literature educator*
Friedman, Barton Robert *English educator*
Greppin, John Aird Coutts *philologist, editor, educator*
Larson, David Mitchell *English studies educator, writer*
†Ledford, Kenneth Floyd *historian, educator, law educator*
†Levin, Miriam R. *historian, educator*
†Marling, William *literature educator, writer*
McLarty, Colin Slator *philosophy educator*
Miller, Genevieve *retired medical historian*
Pursell, Carroll Wirth *history educator*
Robinson, Alice Helene *English language educator, administrative assistant*
Salomon, Roger Blaine *English language educator*
Taylor, Margaret Wischmeyer *retired language educator*

Cleveland Heights
†Weinbaum, Batya *language educator*

Columbus
Allen, Cameron *genealogist, law educator*
Babcock, Charles Luther *classics educator*
Battersby, James Lyons, Jr., *English language educator*
Beja, Morris *English literature educator*
†Boyle, Kevin Gerard *historian, educator*
†Brooke, John L. *history educator*
Farr, Marcia Elizabeth *English and linguistics educator*
†Farrington, Robert Martin *language educator*
Hahm, David Edgar *classics educator*
Hare, Robert Yates *music history educator*
Hoffmann, Charles Wesley *retired foreign language educator*
Jarvis, Gilbert Andrew *humanities educator, writer*
Kalbouss, George *retired language educator*
†Kasulis, Thomas Patrick *humanities educator*
Kuhn, Albert Joseph *English educator*
†Meier, Samuel Arthur, III, *historian, educator*
Nakayama, Mineharu *Japanese language professional, educator*
Peterson, Gale Eugene *historian*
Rule, John Corwin *history educator*
Scanlan, James Patrick *philosophy and Slavic studies educator*
Silbajoris, Frank Rimvydas *Slavic languages educator*
Stephan, Alexander Friedrich *German language and literature educator*
Turnbull, Robert George *philosopher, educator*

Conneaut
Strawbridge, Mary Elizabeth *English educator*

Dayton
Alexander, Roberta Sue *history educator*
Darst, Betty Jane *historian, educator*
Delgado, Clara S. *English language education specialist*
†Farmer, Linda L. *philosophy educator*
Harden, Oleta Elizabeth *English educator, university administrator*
Haritos, Mary J. *language educator, interpreter*
Martin, Herbert Woodward *English educator, poet*
McWhorter, Stanley Bruce *English educator, researcher*
†Pacernick, Gary B. *literature educator, poet*
Pringle, Mary Beth *English language educator, writer*
Vice, Roy Lee *history educator*

Delaware
†Carpenter, Lynette *language educator*
Lewes, Ulle Erika *English educator*

Dublin
Brooks, Keith *retired speech communication educator*

East Liverpool
Swartz, Patti Capel *literature educator*

Fairborn
Shevin, David A. *English literature educator*

Fremont
Wethington, Norbert Anthony *medieval scholar*

Gambier
†McNair, Glenn Maurice *historian, educator*
†Shutt, Timothy Baker *humanities educator, writer*

Granville
†Knobel, Dale Thomas *history educator, university administrator*
Lisska, Anthony Joseph *humanities educator, philosopher*
Santoni, Ronald Ernest *philosophy educator*
Vogel, Steven Michael *philosopher, educator*

Grove City
Jackson, Steven Donald *English educator*

Hamilton
Womack, Whitney Ayn *English and American literature educator*

Kent
Beer, Barrett Lynn *historian*
†Chism, Rebecca Lynn *language educator*
Hassler, Donald Mackey, II, *English language educator, writer*
Kasten, Wendy Christina *literacy educator, writer, consultant*
Muñoz, Willy Oscar *language educator, researcher*
†Neiderman, Beverly Ann *literature educator*
Reid, S.W. *English educator*
Remley, R. Dirk *English educator, consultant*
Zornow, William Frank *historian, educator*

Kettering
†Fox, Allan B. *literature educator*

Lima
†Lause, Sean Maxim *language educator*
Norton, Holly Louise *English literature educator*

Logan
Conner, Leland Lavon *Indian lorist*

Marietta
Wilbanks, Jan Joseph *retired philosopher*

Mechanicsburg
Schoonover, Amy Jo *English educator, poet*

Newark
†Tebben, Joseph Richard *ancient language educator*

North Canton
†Vazzano, Frank Paul *historian, educator*

Oberlin
†Baumann, Roland M. *historian, archivist, consultant*
Collins, Martha *English language educator, writer*

Oxford
Baird, Jay Warren *historian, educator*
Bauer, Steven Albert *English educator, writer*
Jeep, John Michael *language educator*
Pratt, William Crouch, Jr., *English language educator, writer*
Yamauchi, Edwin Masao *history educator*

Painesville
†McQuaid, Kim *historian, educator, writer*

Saint Clairsville
Fisher, Sandra Irene *English educator*

Sebring
Saffell, John Edgar *retired history educator*

Solon
Gallo, Donald Robert *retired English educator*

Springfield
Hayden, Albert A. *retired historian, educator*
†Sweet, Robert T. *humanities educator*

Steubenville
Fitzgerald, Michael Stuart *history educator, researcher*
†Gerogedes, Kimberly *historian, educator*
†Nodes, Daniel Joseph *humanities educator, researcher*

Strongsville
Blumer, Frederick Elwin *retired philosophy educator*

Tiffin
Davison, Kenneth Edwin *American studies educator, genealogist*
†Moore, Vincent D. *humanities educator, writer*

Toledo
Glaab, Charles Nelson *educator, historian*
Smith, Robert Freeman *history educator*

University Heights
Casciani, Santa *Italian studies educator*
†Goral, Judith Ann *educator*

Warren
†Palmer, Daniel Edward *philosopher*
Yoke, Carl Bernard *English language educator, critic*

West Farmington
Smith, Agnes Monroe *history educator*

Wilmington
Townsend, June H. *foreign language educator*

Wooster
†N'Diaye, Boubacar *humanities educator, researcher*

Wright Patterson Afb
†Underwood, Jeffery Scott *historian, curator*

Yellow Springs
Fogarty, Robert Stephen *historian, educator, editor*
†Wright, Harold P. *language educator*

Youngstown
Bowers, Bege K. *English educator, academic administrator*
Slavin, Morris *historian, educator*

OKLAHOMA

Ada
Daniel, Arlie Verl *speech education educator*

Alva
†Hill, Sharon A. *language educator*
Yates, James Newton *English educator*

Durant
†Flippen, J. Brooks *historian, educator*

Midwest City
Hamilton, Carol Jean *retired English educator, writer, storyteller*

Norman
Brown, Sidney DeVere *history educator*
†Doty, Ralph Edward *classics educator*
Fears, Jesse Rufus *historian, educator, academic dean*
†Genova, Pamela A. *French literature educator*
Gilje, Paul Arn *history educator*
Hengst, Herbert Randall *retired educator*
Leitch, Vincent Barry *literary and cultural studies educator*
Lowitt, Richard *history educator*
Savage, William Woodrow, Jr., *historian, consultant, social sciences educator*
†Yu, Ning *linguist, educator*

Oklahoma City
†Baker, Doug W. *history and humanities educator*
Bowlby, Leymond Ambrose *linguist, translator*
Hall, James Granville, Jr., *history educator*

Stillwater
Agnew, Theodore Lee, Jr., *historian, educator*
Fischer, LeRoy Henry *historian, educator*
Luebke, Neil Robert *philosophy educator*
†Redding, Arthur Francis *language educator*
†Sim, May *humanities educator*
†Smallwood, James Milton *historian, educator*

Tulsa
Buckley, Thomas Hugh *historian, educator*
†Engle, Lars *language educator*
Faingold, Eduardo Daniel *language and linguistics educator, researcher*
†Howland, Jacob *philosopher, educator*

OREGON

Aloha
Gorea, Lucia-Iosefina *English educator, writer, poet*

Ashland
Bornet, Vaughn Davis *former social science educator, research historian*
Levy, Leonard Williams *history educator, author*
†Morris, Daniel Robert *language educator*

Bend
Donohue, Stacey Lee *English language and literature educator*

Clackamas
Etulain, Richard Wayne *historian, educator*

Corvallis
†Campbell, Courtney Scott *humanities educator*

Dayton
McKaughan, Howard Paul *linguistics educator*

Eugene
†Garcia-Pabon, Leonardo *Spanish literature educator, consultant*
Lewis, David Gene *humanities educator*
Li, David Leiwei *English and Asian American studies educator*
†Ojo, Adegboye P. *language educator, translator*
Pascal, C(ecil) Bennett *classics educator*
†Pratt, Scott Lawrence *philosopher, educator*
†Sheets-Johnstone, Maxine *philosophy educator*
†Viles, Andrew Michael *English language educator*
White, David Olds *researcher, former educator*
Wickes, George *English literature educator, writer*

Forest Grove
Boersema, David Brian *philosopher, educator*

Hermiston
Ortiz, James George *educator*

La Grande
Ewing, Marilyn *English educator*

Madras
Ramsey, Jarold William *English language educator, author*

Medford
†Frost, Orcutt William *historian, educator*

Monmouth
†Balke, Frank H. *language educator, director*

Netarts
Hartman-Irwin, Mary Frances *retired language professional*

Pendleton
Grover, Dorys C. *English educator*

Port Orford
Drinnon, Richard *retired history educator*

Portland
†Baillie, James *humanities educator*
Drake, Albert Dee *writer, educator*
†Eakman, Kate J. *history educator*
†Eifler, Mark Anthony *historian, educator*
Faller, Thompson Mason *philosophy educator*
Orloff, Chet *historian*
Sacks, David Harris *historian, humanities educator*
Schmidt, Stanley Eugene *retired speech educator*
†Steele, William Donald *literature educator*
Steinman, Lisa Malinowski *English literature educator, writer*
Vaughan, Thomas James Gregory *historian, writer*

Salem
Dmytryshyn, Basil *historian, educator*

Sutherlin
Rose, Sarah Elizabeth *genealogist, counselor*

Waldport
Harrison, Ruth Feuerborn *retired literature and writing educator*

PENNSYLVANIA

Abington
Knodt, Ellen Andrews *English language educator, writer*

Allentown
Huang, Guiyou *English studies educator, writer*

Annville
†Tezanos-Pinto, Rosa *Hispanic American literature educator*

Ardmore
Gutwirth, Marcel Marc *French literature educator*

Bala Cynwyd
Murphey, Murray Griffin *history educator*

Beaver Falls
Lambert, Lynda Jeanne *humanities and arts educator, artist*

Bethlehem
Beidler, Peter Grant *English educator*
Lindgren, John Ralph *philosophy educator, writer*
Radycki, Diane Josephine *art historian*
Roberts, Leonard Robert *English language educator, poet*
Soderlund, Jean R. *historian, educator, historian, researcher*

Bloomsburg
Yenika-Agbaw, Vivian S. *English studies educator, researcher*

Blue Bell
†Roden, Carol Looney *retired language educator*

Bradford
McCabe, Nancy G. *English educator, writer*

Bryn Mawr
Bolger, Stephen Garrett *English and American studies educator*
Dudden, Arthur Power *historian, educator*
Frank, Edward David, II, *history educator*
Gaisser, Julia Haig *classics educator*
†Jimenez, Carlos *Spanish language educator*
King, Willard Fahrenkamp (Mrs. Edmund Ludwig King) *Spanish language educator*
Krausz, Michael *philosopher, educator*
Lane, Barbara Miller (Barbara Miller-Lane) *humanities educator*
Lang, Mabel Louise *classics educator*
Trout, Charles Hathaway *historian, educator*

Butler
Ledden, Dennis Bruce *literature educator, writer*

California
Schwerdt, Lisa Mary *English language educator*

Carlisle
Fox, Arturo Angel *Spanish language educator*
Shrader, Charles Reginald *historian*

Chambersburg
O'Connor, John Morris, III, *retired philosophy educator*

Coatesville
†Ranft Pollitt, Patricia *retired historian educator*

Doylestown
†Richie, Margaret Bye *architectural historian*

East Stroudsburg
Crackel, Theodore Joseph *historian, consultant*
Donaghay, Marie Martenis *historian, educator*

PROFESSIONAL INDEX 6449 HUMANITIES: LIBERAL STUDIES

Easton
†Upton, Lee *English language educator*

Edinboro
†Hass, Robert Bernard *literature educator*
Jones, Jean Grace *speech educator*

Elizabethtown
Gottfried, Paul Edward *humanities educator, editor*
†Likos Ricci, Patricia Anne *art historian, artist*

Elkins Park
Davidson, Abraham Aba *art historian, educator, photographer*

Erie
Allshouse, Robert Harold *history educator*

Fairfield
Freund, John Richard *former English educator*

Fleetwood
Lindeman, Jack *retired literature educator, poet*

Forty Fort
Meeker, Robert Gardner *English language educator*

Gettysburg
Frassanito, William Allen *historian, consultant, writer*

Greensburg
†Flórez-Estrada, Nancy B. *language educator*

Greenville
†Hall, Mary Theresa *literature educator*

Grove City
Harp, Gillis John *history educator*
Smith, Gary Scott *historian, educator, clergyman*

Gwynedd
Bieber, Konrad Ferdinand *retired language educator*

Gwynedd Valley
†Dern, John Andrew *language educator*
Duclow, Donald Francis *philosophy educator, researcher*
†McGarry, Lisa Coughlin *language educator*

Harrisburg
Boswell, James Aurthur, Jr., *English language educator*
Gibson, Shere Capparella *foreign language educator*
Khanzhina, Helen P. *English educator, translator*

Haverford
Bowman, Frank Paul *retired humanities educator*
Brand, Charles Macy *history educator*
Jorden, Eleanor Harz *linguist, educator*

Havertown
Smith, Phillip Thurmond *historian, educator*

Hermitage
Durek, Dorothy Mary *retired English language educator*

Hershey
Wilson, Philip Kevin *science and medical historian*

Hummelstown
Clouse, Jerry Allan *architectural historian*

Indiana
Cashdollar, Charles David *history educator*
†Rodriguez, Lydia H. *language educator*
Roumm, Phyllis Evelyn Gensbigler *retired literature educator, writer*

Jenkintown
†Frazer, Janet Lynn *historian, educator*

Kittanning
Smits, Ronald Francis *English educator, poet*

Kutztown
Meyer, Susan Moon *speech language pathologist, educator*
Tumbleson, Raymond Dana *English educator*

Lancaster
Binkley, Luther John *philosophy educator*
†Goodling, Kimberly Hall *language educator, consultant*
Joseph, John *history educator*
Rupp, Theodore Hanna *retired French language educator*
Steiner, Robert Lisle *retired language consultant*

Leesport
Jackson, Eric Allen *philatelist*

Levittown
†Zinke, Nancy Carol *humanities educator*

Lewisburg
†Payne, Michael David *English language educator*

Lincoln
†Dade, Lennell R. *humanities educator*

Lock Haven
Congdon, Howard Krebs *philosopher, clergyman, educator*

Lumberville
Fallon, Robert Thomas *English language educator*

Meadville
Helmreich, Jonathan Ernst *history educator*
Katope, Christopher George *English language educator*
Stewart, Anne Williams *historian, writer, researcher*

Media
†Cole, Phyllis Blum *literature educator*
Ginsberg, Robert E. *philosophy educator, editor*
Sorkin, Adam J. *English educator*

Melrose Park
Steinlauf, Michael Charles *historian*

Merion Station
Littell, Marcia Sachs *Holocaust and genocide studies educator*
Ueland, Elizabeth Pritchard *English educator*

Middletown
Johnson, Patricia Ellen *humanities educator*
Richman, Irwin *history educator, author, consultant, lecturer*

Millersville
Craven, Roberta Jill *educator in literature and film*
Miller, Steven Max *humanities educator*

Mont Alto
Russo, Peggy Anne *English language educator*

Nazareth
Haynes, Thomas Morris *philosophy educator*

New Castle
Sands, Christine Louise *English educator*

New Freedom
Sedlak, Valerie Frances *retired English language educator, retired academic administrator*

New Wilmington
†Swerdlow, Milagros Zapata *language educator*

Philadelphia
†Ashvo-Muñoz, Alira *language educator*
Beeman, Richard Roy *historian, educator*
Botwinick, Milton Edward *genealogist, researcher*
†Bowers, Toni M. *literature educator*
Chauhan, Vijay Lakshmi *English educator, writer*
†Crissey, Harrington E., Jr., *English as second language educator*
Davis, Allen Freeman *history educator, author*
de Francesco, John Kenneth *foreign language educator*
†Duclow, Geraldine *historian, theatre and film librarian*
Fusco, Richard *English literature educator*
Hall, Marcia Brown *art historian, educator*
†Hilty, James Walter *historian, educator, media consultant*
Hoenigswald, Henry Max *linguist, author*
†Kallberg, Jeffrey *musicologist*
†Katz, Michael Barry *humanities educator*
Knauer, Georg Nicolaus *classical philologist*
Kusmer, Kenneth Leslie *historian, educator*
Logan, Marie-Rose van Stynvoort *literature educator, editor*
Lowry, Ralph James, Sr., *retired history educator*
Lucid, Robert Francis *English educator*
Means, John Barkley *foreign language educator, association executive*
†Moore, Robin D. *humanities educator*
Morello, Celeste Anne *historian, criminologist*
Moss, Roger William *historian, writer, administrator*
†Peiss, Kathy L. *historian, educator*
Peters, Edward Murray *history educator*
Quann, Joan Louise *French language educator, real estate broker*
Regan, Robert Charles *English language educator*
†Robson, Roy Raymond *historian, educator*
Schiffman, Harold Fosdick *Asian language educator*
Sebold, Russell Perry, III, *Romance languages educator, writer*
†Seneca, Michael Joseph *historian*
†Steinberg, Jonathan *historian*
Steinhardt, Nancy Shatzman *art historian, educator*
Stevens, Rosemary A. *medicine and public health historian*
Weigley, Russell Frank *history educator*
Wiley, Catherine Anne *literature educator*
†Woodside, Lisa Nicole *humanities educator*
Zaller, Robert Michael *history educator*

Philipsburg
†Warg, Ilse-Rose *language educator*

Phoenixville
Lukacs, John Adalbert *historian, retired educator*

Pittsburgh
Andrews, George Reid *historian, educator*
Anthony, Edward Mason *linguistics educator*
Arnett, Ronald Charles *communication educator*
Brignano, Russell Carl *English educator, research specialist*
Buchanan, James Junkin *classics educator*
†Cassaro, James P. *musicologist*
Clack, Jerry *classics educator*
Di Medio, Gregory Lawrence *writer, information systems specialist*
Drescher, Seymour *history educator, writer*
Gale, Robert Lee *retired American literature educator and critic*
Goldstein, Donald Maurice *historian, educator*
†Grunbaum, Adolf *philosophy educator, author*
Harris, Ann Birgitta Sutherland *art historian*
Hicks, Wendell Leon *history educator, publisher, political scientist*
Kiesling, Scott Fabius *linguist, educator*
†Martin, Sean Elliot *literature educator, writer*
McDuffie, Keith A. *literature educator*
Miller, David William *historian, educator*
Paulston, Christina Bratt *linguistics educator*
Petesch, Natalie L. Maines *English language educator, author*
Rawski, Evelyn Sakakida *history educator*
Rescher, Nicholas *philosopher, educator*
Rimer, John Thomas *foreign language educator, academic administrator, writer, translator*
Rosen, Robert Stephen *humanities, theatre arts, TV and English educator*
Seligson, Mitchell A. *Latin American studies educator*
Sheon, Aaron *art historian, educator*
†Spellman, Susan V. *historian*
Tarr, Joel Arthur *history and public policy educator*
Toker, Franklin K. *art history educator, archaeologist, foundation executive*
Udler, Rubin Yakovlevitch *linguist*
Weingartner, Rudolph Herbert *philosophy educator*
Wilkins, Ann Thomas *classics educator*

Reading
†Blessing, Tim H. *historian, educator*
Cinfici, William Frank *historian*

Saint Davids
Cary, Phillip Scott *philosphy educator*

Scranton
Bourcier, Richard Joseph *French language and literature educator*
Dolis, John *English educator*
Domenico, Roy Palmer *history educator*
Homer, Francis Xavier James *history educator*
Kennedy, Lawrence William *historian*
Pang-White, Ann A. *philosophy educator, researcher*
†Reif, Jo Ann *art historian, educator*
†Zaydon, Jemille Ann *English language and communications educator*

Selinsgrove
Fincke, Gary W. *writer, educator*
Kolbert, Jack *foreign language educator, French literature educator, humanities educator*
Whitman, Jeffrey Paul *philosophy educator*

Sharon
†Devey, Richard H. *language educator*

Slippery Rock
Cobb, Larry Russell *ethics educator*
Wilson, Bradley Evans *philosophy educator*
Zinni, Hannah Case *foreign language educator*

South Park
Kuchta, Beatrice L. Esken *English educator*

State College
Goldschmidt, Arthur Eduard, Jr., *history educator, author*
Redford, Donald Bruce *historian, archaeologist*
Robinett, Betty Wallace *linguist, educator*
Schmalstieg, William Riegel *retired Slavic languages educator*
†Strauss, Susan Gayle *linguistics educator*
Swinton, John Ralph *retired language educator, writer*

Swarthmore
Bannister, Robert Corwin, Jr., *historian, educator, retired historian*
Gelzer, David Georg *English educator, missionary*
Kitao, T. Kaori *art history educator*
Lacey, Hugh Matthew *philosophy educator*
†Morgan, Kathryn Lawson *historian, educator*
North, Helen Florence *classicist, educator*
Ostwald, Martin *retired classicist*
†Pagliaro, Harold Emil *English language educator*

Titusville
Hall, Mary Ann *English language educator*
Mulcahy, Richard Patrick *history educator, consultant*

Tunkhannock
Gilmore, Haydn Lewis *English educator*

University Park
†Belz, Julie Anne *language educator*
Brault, Gerard Joseph *French language educator*
Ebitz, David MacKinnon *art historian, educator*
†Fóti, Véronique M. *philosophy educator*
Grosholz, Emily Rolfe *philosophy educator, poet*
Halsey, Martha Taliaferro *Spanish language educator*
†Kadir, Djelal *literature educator, writer, translator, editor*
Lacy, Norris J. *literature educator*
Lima, Robert *Hispanic studies and comparative literature educator*
†Naydan, Michael M. *foreign language educator*
†Nielsen, Aldon Lynn *literature educator*
Rose, Paul Lawrence *history educator*
Spanier, Sandra Whipple *English language educator*
†Story, Julie Ann *English educator*
†Wanner, Adrian J. *literature educator*
†Wheeler, Stephen Michael *classicist*
Williams, Edward Vinson *music history educator*

Upper Burrell
†Franco Gómez, María Angeles *language educator*

Villanova
†Alter, Maria Pospischil *language educator*
Bergquist, James Manning *history educator*
DeLaura, David Joseph *English language educator*
†Durán, Jaime *language educator*
Hunt, John Mortimer, Jr., *classical studies educator*
Salmon, John Hearsey McMillan *historian, educator*

West Chester
Gougher, Ronald Lee *foreign language educator and administrator*
†Hardy, Charles Ashley, III, *historian, educator, film producer*
Hipple, Walter John *English language educator*
†Myrsiades, Kostas Yannis *literature educator*

Wilkes Barre
†Hepp, John Henry, IV, *historian, lawyer*

Wilkes-Barre
†Krawczeniuk, Joseph Volodymyr *humanities educator*

York
Jackson, Renée Bernadette *English language educator*

RHODE ISLAND

East Greenwich
White, Sidney Howard *English educator*

Jamestown
Wright, Harrison Morris *historian, educator*

Kingston
Green, Angel Yvonne *literature educator*
Kim, Yong Choon *philosopher, theologian, educator*
MacLaine, Allan Hugh *English language educator*

Newport
†Grassey, Thomas Brandt *humanities educator*
Haas, William Paul *humanities educator, former college president*

Providence
Bensmaia, Reda *French studies educator, researcher*
†Bewes, Timothy Richard Thomas *language educator*
Boegehold, Alan Lindley *classics educator*
†Bou, Enric *language educator*
Chambers, Timothy Edward *philosopher, educator*
†Donovan, Bruce Elliot *classics educator, university dean*
Enteman, Willard Finley *philosophy educator*
Fornara, Charles William *historian, classicist, educator*
Gerlach, Murney *administrator, educator, historian*
Gill, Mary Louise Glanville *educator of classics and philosophy*
Gleason, Abbott *history educator*
†Gordon-Seifert, Catherine Elizabeth *musicologist, educator*
Gorn, Elliott Jacob *historian, educator, writer*
Kim, Jaegwon *philosophy educator*
Konstan, David *classics and comparative literature educator, researcher*
†Kosmider, Alexia M. *language educator*
Lemons, James Stanley *history educator*
Lesko, Leonard Henry *Egyptologist, educator, publisher*
Monteiro, George *English educator, writer*
Putnam, Michael Courtney Jenkins *classics educator*
Raaflaub, Kurt Arnold *classics educator*
Reid, Margaret Kathleen *literature educator*
Rohr, Donald Gerard *history educator*
Saint-Amand, Pierre Nemours *humanities educator*
Schulz, Juergen *art history educator*
Sosa, Ernest *philosopher, educator*
Terras, Victor *Slavic languages and comparative literature educator*
Trueblood, Alan Stubbs *former modern language educator*
†Vorenberg, Michael *history educator*
Wood, Gordon Stewart *historian, educator*

Smithfield
Litoff, Judy Barrett *history educator*

Wakefield
Coffin, Tristram Potter *retired English educator, writer*

SOUTH CAROLINA

Anderson
†Atang, Christopher *humanities educator*

Beaufort
Flannagan, Roy Catesby, Jr., *English literature educator, editor*

Bluffton
Brown, Dallas Coverdale, Jr., *retired army officer, retired history educator*

Charleston
†Barboza, Sandra Livingston *language educator*
Barrett, Michael Baker *historian, educator*
Lally, Margaret Mates *English educator, poet*
†Thomas, Emory M. *history educator*

Clemson
Grant, H. Roger *history educator*
Morrissey, Lee *literature educator*
Underwood, Richard Allen *English language educator*

Columbia
Ashley, Perry Jonathan *journalism educator*
Baird, Davis W. *philosophy educator*
Briggs, Ward Wright *classics educator*
Bruccoli, Matthew Joseph *English educator, publisher*
Bueno, Otavio Augusto *philosopher, educator*
Edgar, Walter Bellingrath *historian, educator*
Fried, Morris Louis *retired humanities educator*
Geckle, George Leo, III, *retired English language educator*
Howard-Hill, Trevor Howard *English language educator*
†Khushf, George Peter *bioethicist*
Littlefield, Daniel Curtis *historian, educator, researcher*
Long, Eugene Thomas, III, *philosophy educator, administrator*
Meriwether, James Babcock *retired English language educator*
Norman, George Buford, Jr., *foreign language educator*
†Peck, Edward T., Jr., *historian, educator, real estate agent*
†Power, James Tracy *historian*
Scotti, Anthony John, Jr., *historian, educator*
†Smith, Mark Michael *historian, educator*
Sproat, John Gerald *historian, educator*
Synnott, Marcia Graham *history educator*

Conway
Henderson, James David *history educator*
†Rauhut, Nils Christian *philosopher, educator*

Due West
Carlock, John Bruce, Jr., *English educator*

Florence
†Kaufman, Victor Scott *historian, educator*

Greenville
Henderson, Alan Scott *humanities educator*
†Matzko, John Austin *historian*
†McArthur, William Duncan, Jr., *English language educator*

Hilton Head Island
Knox, John, Jr., *philosopher, educator*
Male, Roy Raymond *English language educator*

Lancaster
†Hassell, Darris Anthony *Spanish educator*

Newberry
†O'Shea, Michael Joseph *humanities educator*

North Myrtle Beach
Damerst, William *English and humanities educator*

Orangeburg
†Harrold, Stanley *historian, educator*
Johnson, Alex Claudius *English language educator*
†McIver, Barbara Basore *language educator*

Spartanburg
Deku, Afrikadzata *international, French, English and Afrikan-centric Continental Afrikan scholar, researcher, publisher, writer, educator*
Kay, Charles D. *philosophy educator*
†Wallace, Robin Evan *musicologist, educator*

Spring Island
Hardin, James Neal *German and comparative literature educator, publisher*

SOUTH DAKOTA

Aberdeen
Johnson, Edna Scott *English language educator, volunteer*
†Matta, William B. *language educator*

Brookings
Evans, David Allan *English educator*
†Funchion, Michael F. *historian, educator*
Ryder, Mary Ruth *English language educator*

Rapid City
Van Nuys, Frank *historian, educator*

Sioux Falls
Carlson Aronson, Marilyn A. *English language and education educator*
†Herman, Charles Wendell *history educator*
Huseboe, Arthur Robert *American literature educator*
Olson, Gary Duane *history educator*
Staggers, Kermit LeMoyne, II, *history and political science educator, state legislator, municipal official*
†Zinz, David Albert *humanities educator*

Vermillion
Gasque, Thomas James *retired English educator*
†Haddad, Emily Anne *literature educator*

TENNESSEE

Big Sandy
Chastain, Kenneth Duane *retired foreign language educator*

Chattanooga
†Royer, William A. *language educator*
Steinhoff, Anthony James *European history educator*
†Ward, James Arthur, III, *educator*

Columbia
Curry, Beatrice Chesrown *retired English educator*

Cookeville
Campana, Phillip Joseph *German language educator*

Dayton
Cornelius, Richard Meredith *English language educator*

Fairfield Glade
†Dixon, Fred *retired literature educator*

Jackson
Fant, Gene Clinton, Jr., *English language educator*
McMillin, Barbara Ann *English educator, university dean*

Jefferson City
Baumgardner, James Lewis *history educator*

Johnson City
Drinkard-Hawkshawe, Dorothy Lee *historian, educator, writer*
Schneider, Valerie Lois *speech educator*

Kingsport
†Wolfe, Margaret Ripley *historian, educator, consultant*

Knoxville
Brady, Patrick *French literature educator, novelist*
Cutler, Everette Wayne *history educator*
†Finneran, Richard J. *literature educator*
Fisher, John Hurt *English language educator*
Folks, Cathalin Buhrmann *English language educator*
Hoyng, Peter *humanities educator*
Klein, Milton Martin *history educator*
Moser, Harold Dean *historian*
Reidy, David A. *philosophy educator*
White, Jon Manchip *retired English educator*

Martin
†Alexander, Lynn Mae *English language educator*
†Mohler, Stephen Charles *language educator*
Norton, Dorotha Oliver *speech educator*

Memphis
†Anzaldo-González, Demetrio *literature educator*
†Edwards, Gary Thomas *historian, educator*
Jolly, William Thomas *foreign language educator*
Stagg, Louis Charles *English language and literature educator*
†Tabachnick, Stephen Ely *English literature educator*
Vest, James Murray *foreign language and literature educator*

Murfreesboro
Conard, Rebecca Ann *historian, educator*
†McCash, June Hall *language educator, writer*
†McDaniel, Rhonda Louise *literature educator*
Rupprecht, Nancy Ellen *historian, educator*
†Staples, Amy L.S. *historian, educator*

Nashville
Boorman, Howard Lyon *history educator*
Churchill, Larry Raymond *ethics educator*
Compton, John Joseph *philosophy educator*
Conkin, Paul Keith *history educator*
Cook, Ann Jennalie *English language educator*
Dickerson, Dennis Clark *history educator*
Girgus, Sam B. *English literature educator*
Hassel, Rudolph Christopher *English educator*
Lewis, Lynn C. *English educator, writer*
†Luis, William *language educator*
McCarthy, John Aloysius *language educator, literature educator*
McGinnis, Harrill Coleman *humanities educator*
†Pfanner, Helmut Franz *German language educator*
†Sevin, Dieter Hermann *language and literature professional, educator*
†Todd, Margo *historian, educator*
Voegeli, Victor Jacque *history educator, dean*

Sewanee
Williamson, Samuel Ruthven, Jr., *historian, emeritus university president*

Shiloh
†Allen, Stacy Dale *historian, parks director*

TEXAS

Abilene
Bailey, Fred Arthur *history educator*

Aledo
Worcester, Donald Emmet *history educator, writer*

Alpine
†Nelson, Barbara *literature educator, writer*

Alvin
Crider, Allen Billy *English educator, novelist*

Arlington
†Cohen, Philip Gary *English language educator, dean, academic administrator*
†Green, George N. *historian, educator*
Ignagni, Joseph Anthony *humanities educator, associate dean*
Zurlo, John Anthony *English educator, writer*

Austin
Barkley, Roy Reid *historian, educator, editor, writer*
Bordie, John George *linguistics educator*
Brown, Norman Donald *history educator*
Carleton, Don Edward *history center administrator, educator, writer*
Causey, Robert Louis *philosopher, educator, consultant*
Corredor, Mary B. *language educator, consultant, translator*
Divine, Robert Alexander *history educator*
Dulles, John Watson Foster *history educator*
†Escoto, Luz *language educator*
Farrell, Edmund James *retired English language educator, author*
Freeman, Robert Schofield *musicologist, educator, pianist*
Friedman, Alan Warren *humanities educator*
Gagarin, Michael *literature educator*
Galinsky, Gotthard Karl *classicist, educator*
†Garmong, Robert Allen *philosophy educator*
Garza, Thomas Jesus *language educator*
Graham, Don Ballew *literature educator, writer*
Harms, Robert Thomas *linguist, educator*
Hinojosa-Smith, Roland *language educator, writer*
†Kibler, William Westcott *French language and literature educator*
†Kroll, John Hennig *humanities educator*
La Salle, Peter *English educator, writer*
Lockett, Landon Johnson *former linguistic educator, researcher*
Louis, William Roger *historian*
Mackey, Louis Henry *philosophy educator*
†Meikle, Jeffrey L. *history educator, writer*
†Meyer, Delia Perez *humanities educator*
Middleton, Christopher *Germanic languages and literature educator*
Moag, Rodney Frank *language educator, country music singer*
†Montreuil, Jean-Pierre Y. *language educator*
†Pells, Richard H. *historian, educator*
†Ramon, Emilio *language educator*
Rich, John Martin *humanities educator, researcher*
Seung, Thomas Kaehao *philosophy educator*
†Sole, Carlos A. *language educator*
Staley, Thomas Fabian *language professional, academic administrator*
Sutherland, William Owen Sheppard *English language educator*
Tyler, Ronnie Curtis *historian*
Wadlington, Warwick Paul *English language educator*
Werbow, Stanley Newman *language educator*
Whitbread, Thomas Bacon *English educator, author*
Williams, Diane Elizabeth *architectural historian, photographer*

Beaumont
Hawkins, Emma B. *humanities educator*
Janak, Robert Louis *foreign language educator*

Brownsville
Adams, William Leigh *history educator*
Soldan, Angelika *philosopher, political scientist, educator*

Bryan
Bryant, Keith Lynn, Jr., *history educator*
†Van Ouwerkerk, Anita Harrison *reading educator*

Canyon
†Furnish, Shearle Lee *English and modern languages educator*
Hanson, Trudy L. *speech professional, educator*
†Peddie, Ian A. *language educator*
†Teichmann, Sandra Gail *English educator, writer, playwright, artist*

College Station
Cannon, Garland *linguist, educator*
Christensen, Paul Norman *English educator, writer*
Dethloff, Henry Clay *historian, educator*
†Dunlap, Thomas R. *historian, educator*
Gibson, Claude Louis *English educator*
Harner, James Lowell *English language educator*
Kallendorf, Craig William *English, speech and classical languages educator*
Machann, Clinton John *English educator*
Martin, Carol Jacquelyn *educator, artist*
†Nelson, Claudia B. *literature educator, writer*
Unterberger, Betty Miller *history educator, writer*
†Yang, Lingui *language educator, researcher*

Corpus Christi
Snouffer, Nancy Kendall *English and reading educator*
Wooster, Robert *history educator*

Dallas
†Beard, Kevin E. *language educator*
Cahill, Michael Clark *linguist*
Chawner, Lucia Martha *English educator*
Comini, Alessandra *art historian, educator*
Countryman, Edward Francis *historian, educator*
Crain, John Walter *historian, educator*
Davis, Daisy Sidney *history educator*
Essary, Andrew Charles *philosophy educator, financial analyst*
Hunter, Robert Grams *retired English language educator*
Terry, Marshall Northway, Jr., *English language educator, author*

Denton
Callicott, John Baird *philosopher, educator*
†Chet, Guy *historian, educator*
Kamman, William *historian, educator*
Kesterson, David Bert *English language educator*
†Nik, Ninfa *language educator*
Pettit, Alexander Drummond *English language educator*
Preston, Thomas Ronald *English language educator, researcher*
Snapp, Harry Franklin *historian, educator*
Vaughn, William Preston *historian, educator*
†White, Nora Lizabeth *language educator*

Edinburg
†Haule, James Mark *literature educator*
Helstern, Linda Lizut *language educator, poet*

El Paso
Bailey, Kenneth Kyle *history educator*
Clement-Fouts, Shirley George *educational services executive*
†Dailey, Maceo Crenshaw, Jr., *humanities educator*
†Foster, Helen R. *language educator*
†Müller, Gene Alan *historian, consultant*
Williford, Lex Akers *educator*

Fort Worth
Boller, Paul Franklin, Jr., *retired American history educator, writer*
McWhiney, Grady *history educator*
†Meckna, Michael *musicologist, educator*
Reuter, Frank Theodore *history educator*
Robin, Clara Nell (Claire Robin) *English language educator*
†Wilson, Evelyn M. *literature educator*

Galveston
Ryan, James Gilbert *historian, educator, writer*

Georgetown
Crowley, Weldon Samuel *retired history educator*
Rippy, Frances Marguerite Mayhew *English language educator*
†Saenger, Michael Baird *language educator*

Grand Prairie
Benson, Carol Kay Cantrell *English and Latin educator*

Grapevine
Stack, George Joseph *philosopher, writer*

Harlingen
Martin, Leland Morris (Pappy Martin) *history educator*

Houston
†Belk, Joan Pardue *English educator*
Castañeda, James Agustín *Spanish language educator, university golf coach*
Chance, Jane *English literature educator*
†Coppola, Eileen *philosopher, educator*
de Kanter, Ellen Ann *English and foreign language educator*
Drew, Katherine Fischer *history educator*
Galvani, Christiane Mesch *English as a second language educator, translator*
Gruber, Ira Dempsey *historian, educator*
†Haskell, Thomas Langdon *history educator*
Huston, John Dennis *English educator*
†Hutchinson, Janis Faye *humanities educator, researcher*
Hyman, Harold M. *history educator, consultant*
†Kanellos, Nicolás *foreign language and liberal studies educator, publisher*
Lamb, Sydney MacDonald *linguistics and cognitive science educator*
Leiber, Justin *philosophy educator, writer*
Lowry, Montecue Judson *military historian*
Lutz, Gretchen Kay *English language educator*
Martin, James Kirby *historian, educator*
McEvoy-Jamil, Patricia Ann *English language educator*
Mc Fadden, Joseph Michael *history educator*
†McNamara, Kevin Richard *humanities educator*
Minter, David Lee *English literature educator*
Pasternak, Joanna Murray *humanities educator*
Patten, Robert Lowry *English language educator*
Pryor, William Daniel Lee *humanities educator*
†Rios de Lumbreras, Kristina Marie *language educator*
Sher, George Allen *philosophy educator*
Skura, Meredith Anne *English educator*
Southwell, Samuel Beall *English educator*
Thompson, Ewa M. *foreign language educator*
Tran, Qui-Phiet *English educator*
Urbina, Manuel, II, *legal research historian, history educator*
Vallbona, Rima-Gretel Rothe *foreign language educator, writer*
†Vallejo, Bernardo *linguist, anthropologist, consultant, administrator, writer*
†Winniford, Lee *language educator*
†Woodson, Michael E. *humanities educator*

Huntsville
†Coffey, Joan L. *humanities educator*
Raymond, Kay E(ngelmann) *Spanish language educator, consultant*
†Ruffin, Paul Dean *English language educator*

Irving
Rosemann, Philipp Wolfram *philosopher, educator*
Sommerfeldt, John Robert *historian, educator*

Killeen
Seigman, Deborah Werst *literature educator*

Laredo
Engling, Ezra Samuel *Spanish and literature educator, researcher*

Lubbock
Angstadt, Frances Virginia *language arts and theatre arts educator*
Hurst, Mary Jane *English language educator*
Ketner, Kenneth Laine *philosopher, educator*
†Kuethe, Allan J. *historian, educator*
Pelley, Patricia Marie *Asian history specialist*
Purinton, Marjean D. *English language educator, researcher*
Sears, Edward L. *English language educator, real estate investor*

PROFESSIONAL INDEX 6451 HUMANITIES: LIBERAL STUDIES

Montgomery
Kelsey, Clyde Eastman, Jr., *philosophy and psychology educator*

Nacogdoches
Gaston, Edwin Willmer, Jr., *retired English language educator*

Odessa
Forsyth, Beverly K. *language educator, writer*
Toruño, Rhina M. *Literature educator, researcher, writer*

Paris
Proctor, Richard Owen *historian, public health administrator, army officer*

Ranger
Jones, Roger Walton *English language educator, writer*

Richardson
Redman, Timothy Paul *English language educator, author, chess federation administrator*

Round Top
Lentz, Edwin Lamar *art historian*

Rusk
†McMinn, J. B. *retired philosophy educator, composer*

San Antonio
Behrens, Richard James *language educator*
†Daniel, Marian Phillips *language educator, secondary school educator*
Leighton, Albert Chester *history educator*
†McKinnis, Joanne Jakle *language educator, translator*
†Mendoza, Louis G. *literature educator, researcher*
†Miller, Frank Lubbock (Char), IV, *historian, educator*
Passty, Jeanette Nyda *English language educator, writer*
†Samelson, Rosa Salinas *humanities educator*
Sauer, James Benson *philosopher, educator*
†Smith, Rebecca Lynn *language educator*
von Raffler-Engel, Walburga (Walburga Engel) *linguist, cross-cultural communications specialist, lecturer, writer*
Woodson, Linda Townley *English educator, writer*

San Marcos
Beebe, Susan Jane *English language educator*
†Schuler, Nico Stephan *musicologist*
Wilson, Steven Michael *English educator, poet*

Schertz
†Ringenbach, Paul Thomas *historian, consultant*

Seguin
Moline, Jon Nelson *philosopher, educator, university administrator*

Spicewood
Robbins, Eugene Weldon *genealogist*

Stafford
Rosenkranz, Linda *English educator*

Stephenville
Christopher, Joe Randell *English language educator*

Waco
Collmer, Robert George *English language educator*
†Donnelly, Phillip Johnathan *literature educator*
†Garcia-Corales, Guillermo S. *language educator*
Hunt, Maurice Arthur *English educator, researcher*

Wichita Falls
Bourland, D(elphus) David, Jr., *linguist, educator*
Kindig, Everett William *history educator*

Wylie
†Andrews, Sharon Millicent Parrish *historian, educator*

UTAH

Cedar City
†Mills, James *language educator*

Midway
Hughes, Dean Thomas *English language educator, writer*

Ogden
†Stokes, Jeffery David *Spanish language educator*

Orem
Clark, Bruce Budge *humanities educator, educator*
†Mizell, Karen L. *philosopher, educator*

Paradise
Bremer, Ronald Allan *genealogist, editor*

Provo
Cracroft, Richard Holton *English literature educator*
†Faulconer, James E. *humanities educator*
Forster, Merlin Henry *foreign languages educator, writer, researcher*
†Getmanenko, Nataliya I. *Russian educator, researcher*
Lyon, James Karl *German language educator*
Murphy, John Joseph *English literature educator, critic, editor*
Skinner, Andrew Charles *history educator, religious writer*

Salt Lake City
Arrington, Harriet Ann Horne *historian, biographer, researcher, writer*
Dole, Janice Gail Arnold *literacy educator*
Olsen, Glenn Warren *historian, educator*
Sillars, Malcolm Osgood *communication educator*
Walden, David Michael *historian, writer*

Tremonton
Eakle, Arlene Haslam *genealogist*

West Valley City
†Morales, Nancy Sabrina *translator, consultant*

VERMONT

Barre
Adamski, Gary Matthew *language educator, real estate broker*

Bennington
†Wang, Shunzhu *humanities educator, researcher, translator*

Brattleboro
Fantini, Alvino E. *language educator, humanities educator, consultant*

Burlington
Brandenburg, Richard George *management educator*
Daniels, Robert Vincent *history educator, former state senator*
†Dungy, Kathryn R. *humanities educator*
†Flores, Yolanda *literature educator*
Fogel, Daniel Mark *administrator, English language and American literature educator, author*
Hall, Robert William *philosophy and religion educator*

Middlebury
Jacobs, Travis Beal *historian, educator*
Katz, Michael Ray *Slavic languages educator*
Lamberti, Marjorie *history educator*
Nunley, Charles Arthur *language educator*
Vail, Van Horn *German language educator*

Montpelier
Facos, James Francis *English language educator, author*

New Haven
†Clifford, Deborah Pickman *historian*

Newfane
Reed, John Addison, Jr., *European studies educator*

North Bennington
Feinman, Alvin *retired literature educator, poet*

Norwich
†Carlson, Elizabeth Borden *historian, educator*

Plainfield
Hamlin, Wilfrid Gardiner *retired literature and philosophy educator*

Randolph
Telford, Kenneth Alderman *philosopher, educator, humanities educator*

Shelburne
Weiger, John George *foreign language educator*

Underhill
†Nissenbaum, Stephen Willner *historian*

White River Junction
Madden, Edward Harry *philosopher, educator, retired*

VIRGINIA

Alexandria
†Brent, Julia Deener *language educator*
†Falk, Stanley Lawrence *historian, consultant*
Reuss, Martin Alan *historian*

Annandale
†Brotton, Joyce Dupras *English language educator*
Henretty, Donald Bruce *history educator*
Hutcheon, Wallace Schoonmaker *history educator*

Arlington
Allard, Dean Conrad *historian, retired naval history center director*
Boylan, Michael A. *philosophy educator, writer*
French, Mary B. *educator, editor, photographer, poet and former*
Irizarry, Estelle Diane *foreign language educator, writer, editor*
Strelau, Renate *historical researcher, artist*
Trask, Roger R. *historian*
Wilcox, Shirley Jean Langdon *genealogist*

Ashland
Inge, Milton Thomas *American literature and culture educator, author*

Blacksburg
Baumgartner, Frederic Joseph *history educator*
Doswald, Herman Kenneth *German language educator, academic administrator*
†Fowler, Virginia C. *literature educator*

Bridgewater
Heatwole, John Lawrence *historian, sculptor*

Charlottesville
Abbot, William Wright *history educator*
Arnold, Albert James *foreign language educator*
Battestin, Martin Carey *retired English language educator*
Cano-Ballesta, Juan *Spanish language educator*
Cherno, Melvin *humanities educator*
Coleman, Jonathan Mark *writer, English language educator*
Cushman, Stephen Bigelow *English educator, writer*
Denommé, Robert Thomas *foreign language educator*
Forbes, John Douglas *architectural and economic historian*
Garrett, George Palmer, Jr., *creative writing and English language educator, writer*
Gianniny, Omer Allan, Jr., *retired humanities educator*
Graebner, Norman Arthur *history educator*
†Haberly, David Tristram *language educator*
Hirsch, Eric Donald, Jr., *English language educator, educational reformer*
Humphreys, Paul William *philosophy educator, consultant*
Kellogg, Robert Leland *English language educator*
†Kett, Joseph Francis *historian, educator*
Kraehe, Enno Edward *history educator*
Lang, Cecil Yelverton *English language educator*
Langbaum, Robert Woodrow *English language educator, author*
Leffler, Melvyn P. *history educator*
Levenson, Jacob Clavner *English language educator*
Little, W(illia)m A(lfred) *foreign language educator, researcher*
†Lott, Eric William *literature educator*
Lyons, John David *French, Italian and comparative literature educator*
McGann, Jerome John *English language educator*
Megill, Allan D. *historian*
Midelfort, Hans Christian Erik *history educator*
Mikalson, Jon Dennis *classics educator*
Nohrnberg, James Carson *English language educator*
Oliver, Charles Montgomery *retired English educator*
Perkowski, Jan Louis *language and literature educator*
Peterson, Merrill Daniel *history educator*
†Rini, Joel *language educator*
Rubin, David Lee *humanities educator, publisher*
†Schutte, Anne Jacobson *historian, educator*
Sedgwick, Alexander *historian, educator*
Shaw, Donald Leslie *Spanish language educator*
Spearing, Anthony Colin *English literature educator*
†Stagg, John Charles Anderson *historian*
Stocker, Arthur Frederick *classics educator*
Wright, Charles Penzel, Jr., *English language educator*
Zunz, Olivier Jean *history educator*

Christiansburg
†Fu, I-Ping Phyllis *language educator, researcher*

Covesville
Williams, Patricia Anne *philosopher, writer*

Crozet
†Owen, Sarah-Katharine *language educator*

Danville
Hayes, Jack Irby *historian, educator*

Fairfax
Bailey, Helen McShane *historian*
†Berroa, Rei *literature educator, poet*
Censer, Jack Richard *history educator*
†Foster, John Burt, Jr., *comparative literature educator and researcher*
King, James Cecil *Medievalist, educator*
Lavine, Thelma Zeno *philosophy educator*
†Rubenstein, Richard Edward *humanities educator, writer*
Stearns, Peter Nathaniel *history educator*

Falls Church
†Brown, Lorraine A. *literature educator*

Farmville
Amoss, Benjamin McRae, Jr., *language educator*
Hevener, Fillmer, Jr., *English language educator, writer, portrait artist*

Fort Lee
Sterling, Keir Brooks *historian, educator*

Fredericksburg
Dorman, John Frederick *genealogist*
†Eslinger-Brown, Vanessa Pauline *humanities educator*
†Merrill, Sammy R. *language educator*
†Pitts, Angela L. *humanities educator, researcher*

Front Royal
†Carroll, Warren Hasty *retired historian*

Glen Allen
Hinkle, Douglas Paddock *retired languages educator*
Wright, Sylvia Hoehns *speech professional*

Great Falls
Castro-Klaren, Sara *Latin American literature educator*

Hardyville
White, Gordon Eliot *historian*

Harrisonburg
Alotta, Robert Ignatius *historian, educator, writer*
Culbertson, Charles Randall *historian, writer*
Geary, Robert Francis, Jr., *English educator*
Horst, Samuel Levi *history educator, researcher, writer*
†Hyser, Raymond M. *humanities educator*
Morey, Ann-Janine *English educator*

Hmpden Sydney
†Arieti, James Alexander *classics educator, writer*

Kingstowne
Hixson, Stanley G. *speech, language and computer technology educator*

Lexington
Brooke, George Mercer, Jr., *historian, educator*
Lubin, Timothy Norman Thomas *humanities educator*
Ryan, Halford Ross *speech educator*
Sessions, William Lad *philosophy educator, administrator*
†Warren, James Perrin *language educator*

Lynchburg
†Carey, Charles William, Jr., *historian, educator*
Cornett, Robert Arnold *philosophy educator*
†Partie, David John *language educator*

Manassas
Adamson, Heidi Beth *English educator*

Mc Lean
García-Godoy, Cristián *historian, educator*
Topping, Peter *historian, educator*

McLean
†Kasmeridi, Sofia *translator, researcher*

Newport News
Santoro, Anthony Richard *history educator*

Norfolk
Evans, Rod L. *philosophy educator*
Rutyna, Richard Albert *history educator*

North
Fang, Joong *philosopher, mathematician, educator*

Oakton
†MacCracken, Thomas Gregg *musicologist*

Petersburg
Garrott, Carl Lee *foreign language educator*

Portsmouth
Eaton, James Alonza *humanities educator*
†Paquette, William Arthur *historian, educator*

Radford
†du Plessis, Eric Hollingsworth *literature educator, language educator*

Reston
Coulter-Harris, Deborah Marcella *government analyst*

Richmond
Anderson, Frederick Jarrard *historian*
†Baker, Julie Ann *language educator*
Berry, Boyd McCulloch *English educator*
†Bonfiglio, Thomas Paul *literature and linguistics educator*
Ciulla, Joanne Bridgett *business ethics educator*
Gordon, John L., Jr., *historian, educator*
Hall, James H(errick), Jr., *philosophy educator, writer*
Levit, Héloïse B. (Ginger Levit) *art historian, art dealer, journalist, art consultant, journalist*
Ravaux-Kirkpatrick, Francoise *language professional*
Rilling, John Robert *history educator*
†Urofsky, Melvin Irving *historian, educator, director*
Ward, Harry Merrill *history educator*

Roanoke
Johnson, Julia Mae *literature educator, poet*

Salem
Cartwright, Keith Allen *literature educator*

Staunton
†Metraux, Daniel Alfred *humanities educator*

Sumerduck
McCamy, Sharon Grove *English educator*

Sweet Briar
Grubbs, Judith Evans *classical studies educator*
Piepho, Lee (Edward Lee Piepho) *humanities educator*

Triangle
†Roach, Edward James *historian*

Virginia Beach
Cehelska, Olga M. *musicologist, music therapist*

Williamsburg
Armbrecht, Thomas Jeffrey Dexter *foreign language educator, writer, critic*
Axtell, James Lewis *history educator*
Ball, Donald L. *retired English language educator*
Cell, Gillian Townsend *historian, educator*
Chappell, Miles Linwood, Jr., *art history educator*
Crapol, Edward P. *history educator*
Dowling, John Clarkson *language educator*
Ely, Melvin Patrick *historian, writer, educator*
Esler, Anthony James *historian, novelist, educator*

Hoffman, Ronald *historical institute administrator, educator*
Landen, Robert Geran *retired historian, educator, university administrator*
McGiffert, Michael *retired history educator, editor*
McLane, Henry Earl, Jr., *philosophy educator*
†Nelson, Scott Reynolds *historian*
Nettels, Elsa *English language educator*
Oakley, John Howard *humanities educator*
Tate, Thaddeus W(ilbur), Jr., (Thad Tate) *history educator, historical institute executive, historian*
Wallach, Alan *art historian, educator*

Winchester
†Hofstra, Warren Raymond *historian, educator*
Lewis, John Gibboney *architectural historian*
Meschutt, David Randolph *historian, curator*

Woodbridge
Hoefler, Eric Alexander *language educator*
Hood, Ronald Chalmers, III, *historian, writer*

Yorktown
Romjue, John Lawson *historian, writer*

WASHINGTON

Aberdeen
†Murrell, Gary *historian, educator*

Bellingham
†Gallay, Alan *history educator*
Mache, Ulrich *German language educator*
Murdock, Mary-Elizabeth *history educator*
Whisenhunt, Donald Wayne *history educator*
†Yusa, Michiko *language educator, researcher, philosopher*

Bothell
†Watts, Linda Susan *humanities educator*

Burien
Burgess, Charles Orville *history educator*

Cheney
Smith, Grant William *English language educator, civic fundraiser*
Steiner, Henry-York *English language and literature educator*

Ellensburg
†Gray, Loretta *language educator*

Federal Way
Boling, Joseph Edward *numismatist, retired military officer*

Lake Forest Park
Adams, Hazard Simeon *English educator, writer*

Mercer Island
Dawn, Clarence Ernest *history educator*

Moses Lake
†Riley, Christopher Patrick *humanities educator*

Olympia
Bruce, Robert Vance *historian, educator*

Port Townsend
Kahn, Sy Myron *humanities educator, poet*

Pullman
Burbick, Joan *English educator*
Swan, Susan Linda *history educator*

Richland
†Bauman, Robert Alan *humanities educator, consultant*

Seattle
†Alden, Dauril *historian*
Brandauer, Frederick Paul *Asian language educator*
Bultmann, William Arnold *historian, educator*
Clauss, James Joseph *classics educator*
Coburn, Robert Craig *philosopher, educator*
Coldewey, John Christopher *English literature educator*
Ellison, Herbert Jay *historian, educator*
Fine, Arthur I. *philosopher, educator*
Gerstenberger, Donna Lorine *humanities educator*
†Halmi, Nicholas *language educator*
Harmon, Daniel Patrick *classics educator*
Heer, Nicholas Lawson *Arabist and Islamist educator*
Jones, Edward Louis *historian, educator*
Keyt, David *philosophy and classics educator*
Korg, Jacob *English literature educator*
Levi, Margaret *humanities educator*
Matchett, William H(enry) *English literature educator*
McNamara, Robert James *English language educator, poet*
Newmeyer, Frederick Jaret *linguist, educator*
Nutting, Maureen Murphy *historian, educator*
†Perozo, Jaime J. *humanities educator*
Pressly, Thomas James *history educator*
Pyle, Kenneth Birger *historian, educator*
†Reinert, Otto *language educator*
Snow-Smith, Joanne Inloes *art history educator*
†Stern, Rosella Lee *English educator, writer, director*
VanArsdel, Rosemary Thorstenson *English studies educator*
†Weston, Nathaniel Parker *historian, educator*
Ziadeh, Farhat J. *Middle Eastern studies educator*

Sedro Woolley
Hinckley, Ted C. *historian, educator, writer*

Spokane
Carriker, Robert Charles *history educator*
†Mohrlang, Roger Lloyd *philosopher, educator*
Stackelberg, John Roderick *history educator*

Tacoma
Barnett, Suzanne Wilson *historian, educator*
†Gorbman, Claudia L. *literature educator, researcher*
Jensen, Mark Kevin *foreign language educator*

Walla Walla
Carlsen, James Caldwell *musicologist, educator*
Krieger, William Carl *English language educator*

Yakima
Meshke, George Lewis *drama and humanities educator*

WEST VIRGINIA

Charles Town
Na, Tsung Shun (Terry Na) *Chinese studies educator, writer*

Fairmont
Lach, Peter *humanities educator*
Sanford, Rhonda Lemke *English educator*

Morgantown
Blaydes, Sophia Boyatzies *English language educator*
Bruner, Jeffrey Benham *foreign language educator*
†Conner, Patrick W. *literature educator*
McNerney, Kathleen *literature educator*
Singer, Armand Edwards *foreign language educator*

Reedsville
Williford, Drury Fisher, Jr., *historical researcher, writer, editor*

WISCONSIN

Appleton
Chaney, William Albert *historian, educator*
†Doeringer, Franklin M. *historian, educator*
Goldgar, Bertrand Alvin *literary historian, educator*
Herscher, Susan Kay *English language educator*
Myers, Rex Charles *history educator, retired college dean*

Ashland
†Small, Michele Geslin *English studies and modern languages educator*

Beloit
Gillen, Shawn P. *English language educator, writer*

Chippewa Falls
Schmider, Mary Ellen Heian *American studies educator, academic administrator*

De Pere
†Ellis, Bradford Graham *Spanish language educator, literature educator*

Delafield
Gulgowski, Paul William *German language, social science, and history educator*

Eau Claire
†Nowlan, Robert Andrew *literature educator*
†Pace, Joel Frederic *language educator, researcher*
Sen, Asha *English educator*

Ferryville
Tedeschi, John Alfred *historian, librarian*

Hales Corners
McNally, Vincent Joseph *historian, educator*

Kenosha
Kummings, Donald Dale *English educator*

La Crosse
Judson, John Irving *retired English educator, poet, writer, editor*
Rausch, Joan Mary *art historian*

Madison
Berg, William James *French language educator, writer, translator*
Berghahn, Klaus Leo *German and Jewish studies educator*
Bogue, Allan George *history educator*
†Boyer, Paul Samuel *history educator*
Brembeck, Winston Lamont *retired speech communication educator*
†Bush, Sargent, Jr., *English language educator*
†Card, Claudia Falconer *philosophy educator*
Ciplijauskaite, Birute *humanities educator*
Cronon, William *history educator*
†Dubrow, Heather *English educator*
Frykenberg, Robert Eric *historian, educator*
Hamalainen, Pekka Kalevi *historian, educator*
Hutchison, Jane Campbell *art history educator, researcher*
Klein, Sheldon *computational linguist, educator*
Kleinhenz, Christopher *foreign language educator, researcher*
Knowles, Richard Alan John *English language educator*
Kutler, Stanley Ira *history and law educator, author*
†Loewentsein, David *literature educator*
†Magnan, Sally Sieloff *language educator*
Miernowski, Jan *foreign language educator*
†Murray, Julia Killin *art history educator*
†Noguera, Antonio *language educator*
O'Brien, James Aloysius *foreign language educator*
Powell, Barry Bruce *classicist, educator*
†Radano, Ronald Michael *musicologist, educator*
Rideout, Walter Bates *English educator*
†Scheub, Harold *language educator, literature educator*
†Severson, Shawn Ross *Spanish educator*
Sewell, Richard Herbert *historian, educator*
Singer, Marcus George *philosopher, educator*
Spear, Thomas Turner *history educator*
Vowles, Richard Beckman *literature educator*
Weinbrot, Howard David *English educator*
Wiesenfarth, Joseph John *retired literature educator*

Menasha
†Leahy, Stephen Michael *history educator*

Menomonie
Schuler, Robert Jordan *English educator, writer*

Milwaukee
†Burckel, Nicholas C. *historian, educator, school librarian, dean*
Dale, Scott *Spanish educator*
Gallop, Jane (Jane Anne Gallop) *women's studies educator, writer*
†Jung, Patrick Joseph *humanities educator*
†Lea, Filomena *literature educator, writer*
†Marten, James Alan *historian, educator*
Olson, Frederick Irving *retired history educator*
†Pless, Joel Loren *humanities educator*
†Prucha, Francis Paul *historian, priest*
Rivero, Albert J. *English educator*
Roeming, Robert Frederick *foreign language educator*
Rosenblum, Martin Jack *historian*
Siegel, Kristi Ellen *English educator*
Siegel, Robert Harold *English literature educator, writer*
Swanson, Roy Arthur *classicist, educator*
Theis, Peter George *retired classics educator*
Theoharis, Athan George *history educator*
Ullman, Pierre Lioni *retired Spanish educator*
Waldbaum, Jane Cohn *art history educator*
Weber, Ralph Edward *history educator*

Monona
Brandes, Stuart Dean *historian, educator*

Oshkosh
Grieb, Kenneth Joseph *historian, educator*

Shell Lake
†Hawes, Grace Maxcy *retired archivist, researcher*

Superior
Bischoff, Joan *English educator*
Sutter, Barton E. *literature educator, writer*

Wausau
Veninga, James Frank *humanities educator, editor, author*
Whitney, John Denison *English educator, writer*

West Allis
Aderman, Ralph Merl *language educator*

Whitewater
Ritterbusch, Dale E. *English educator*

WYOMING

Casper
†Durham, Lynda Laurene *language educator*

Cody
Garry, James B. *historian, naturalist, storyteller, writer*
†Price, B. Byron *historian*

Laramie
Chisum, Emmett Dewain *historian, archeologist, researcher*
Nye, Eric William *English language and literature educator*
Roberts, Philip John *history educator, editor*
Williams, Roger Lawrence *historian, educator*

Sheridan
Aguirre-Batty, Mercedes *Spanish and English language and literature educator*
Wajda, Shirley Teresa *historian*

TERRITORIES OF THE UNITED STATES

PUERTO RICO

Ponce
†López-Alvarez, Carmen A. *language educator*

Rio Piedras
†Prosper-Sánchez, Gloria D. *linguist, language educator*

San Juan
Ocasio-Melendez, Marcial Enrique *history educator*

CANADA

ALBERTA

Edmonton
McMaster, Juliet Sylvia *English language educator*

BRITISH COLUMBIA

Burnaby
Buitenhuis, Peter Martinus *language professional, educator*
†Fleming, James Dougal *English educator, writer*
Kitchen, John Martin *historian, educator*

New Westminster
Cogswell, Frederick William *English language educator, poet, editor, publisher*

Sidney
Saddlemyer, Ann (Eleanor Saddlemyer) *educator, critic, theater historian*

Vancouver
Batts, Michael Stanley *German language educator*
Bentley, Thomas Roy *English language educator, writer, consultant, professor emeritus*
Conway, John S. *history educator*
Durrant, Geoffrey Hugh *retired English language educator*
Overmyer, Daniel Lee *Asian studies educator*
Pacheco-Ransanz, Arsenio *Hispanic and Italian studies educator*
Unger, Richard Watson *history educator*

MANITOBA

Winnipeg
Rozumnyj, Jaroslav *literature educator, researcher*

NEW BRUNSWICK

Saint John
Condon, Thomas Joseph *university historian*

NOVA SCOTIA

Halifax
Carrigan, David Owen *history educator*
Gray, James *English literature educator*

ONTARIO

Brampton
Paikeday, Thomas M. *lexicographer and linguistic consultant*

Downsview
Thomas, Clara McCandless *retired English language educator, biographer*

Hamilton
Lee, Alvin A. *literary educator, scholar, author*
McKay, Alexander Gordon *classics educator*

Kingston
Akenson, Donald Harman *historian, educator*
Dick, Susan Marie *English language educator*
Mac Kenzie, Norman Hugh *retired English educator, writer*

London
Collins, Thomas Joseph *English language educator*
Gerber, Douglas Earl *classics educator*
Groden, Michael Lewis *English literature educator*

Nepean
Kallmann, Helmut Max *music historian, retired music librarian*

North York
Adelman, Howard *philosophy educator*

Ottawa
Dray, William Herbert *philosophy educator*
Jaenen, Cornelius John *history educator, consultant*
Staines, David McKenzie *English educator*

Toronto
Blewett, David Lambert *English literature educator*
Dryer, Douglas Poole *retired philosophy educator*
Elkhadem, Saad Eldin Amin *foreign language and literature educator, writer, editor, publisher*
Goetschel, Willi *literary and intellectual historian, philosopher, educator*
Granatstein, Jack Lawrence *history educator*
Herren, Michael Wayne *classical studies educator*
Johnson, Robert Eugene *historian, academic administrator*
Mann, Susan *history educator*
Millgate, Jane *language professional*
Millgate, Michael (Michael Henry Millgate) *retired English educator*
Morey, Carl Reginald *musicologist*
Skvorecky, Josef Vaclav *English literature educator, novelist*
†Webster, Jill Rosemary *historian, educator*
Wevers, John William *retired Semitic languages educator*

Waterloo
Haworth, Lawrence Lindley *philosophy educator*
Suits, Bernard Herbert *philosophy educator*

PRINCE EDWARD ISLAND

Montague
Cregier, Don Mesick *historian, educator, researcher, consultant*

QUEBEC

Montreal
Beugnot, Bernard Andre Henri *French literature educator*
Brown, Peter Gilbert *philosopher, educator, tree farmer*
Duquette, Jean-Pierre *French language and literature educator*
Hoffmann, Peter Conrad Werner *history educator*
Kinsley, William Benton *literature educator, retired*
Morin, Yves-Charles *linguistics educator, researcher*
Ormsby, Eric Linn *educator, researcher, writer*
Silverthorne, Michael James *classics educator*

North Hatley
Jones, Douglas Gordon *retired literature educator*

Sainte-Foy
Murray, Warren James *philosophy educator*

SASKATCHEWAN

Regina
Cleveland, Ray LeRoy *history educator*

MEXICO

Mexico City
Leon-Portilla, Miguel *historian, educator*

Morelia
Warren, J. Benedict *retired history educator*

AUSTRIA

Graz
Weisstein, Ulrich Werner *English literature educator*

Vienna
Steinbruckner, Bruno Friedrich *foreign language educator*

COLOMBIA

Cali
Keppel, Timothy Anderson *humanities educator, writer*

ENGLAND

Eastbourne
Baylen, Joseph Oscar *retired history educator*

Liverpool
Reilly, Thomas *humanities educator*

London
Elson, Sarah Lee *art historian and consultant*
Graubard, Stephen Richards *history educator, editor*
†Martines, Lauro *historian, writer*
Perkin, Harold James *retired social historian, educator*
†Rubin, Patricia Lee *art historian*

Manchester
Briscoe, John *classical languages educator*

Oxford
Carey, John *English language educator, literary critic*
Heilbron, John L. *historian, educator*

Oxfordshire
Rousseau, George Sebastian *humanities educator, historian*

Reading
Ryder, Timothy Thomas *classics educator*

Storrington
Osborne, Stephen J. *philatelist*

FRANCE

Montpellier
Herbert, Catherine Deming *English educator*

Toulouse
Courtés, Joseph Jean-Marie *humanities educator, writer, semiotician*

Vence
Polk, William Roe *historian*

Villeneuve d'Ascq
Allain, Louis *literature educator, scientific advisor*

GERMANY

Düsseldorf
Joppen-Hellwig, Sandra *linguist, researcher*

Hamburg
Ludwig, Walther *classical and neo-Latin studies educator*

Münster
Spevack, Marvin *English educator*

Nuremberg
Doerries, Reinhard René *modern history educator*

Stuttgart
Bettisch, Johann *linguist, researcher*

HONG KONG

Pokfulam
McNaughton, William Frank *translator, educator*

ITALY

Genova
Montanari, Franco *classicist, educator*

Padova
Shea, William Rene *historian, science philosopher, educator*

Pietrasanta Lu
Bugliani, Ann C. *international studies educator*

Verona
Pozzo, Riccardo *philosophy educator*

JAPAN

Bunkyo
Kobayashi, Seiei *English literature educator*

Kanagawa-Ken
Fukatsu, Tanefusa *retired Chinese classics educator*

Kashiwara
Hori, Keiko *English literature educator*

Osaka
†Ishihara, Tsuyoshi *humanities educator*

LEBANON

Beirut
†Nassaar, Christopher Suheil *literature educator, writer*

NEPAL

Kathmandu
†Baker, Ian Archbald *explorer, educator, writer, photographer*

NETHERLANDS

Amsterdam
Kolko, Gabriel *historian, educator*
Verkruijsse, Pieter Jozias *classicist, educator*

NEW ZEALAND

Dunedin
Dominik, William John *classicist, educator*

PORTUGAL

Coimbra
Holm, John Alexander *linguist, educator*

SCOTLAND

Cellardyke
Roff, William Robert *history educator, writer*

Saint Andrews
Dover, Sir Kenneth James *retired Greek scholar*
Lenman, Bruce Philip *historian, educator*

SINGAPORE

Singapore
Reid, Anthony John Stanhope *historian, educator*

SPAIN

Barcelona
†Vidal, Merce *art historian, education educator*

SWEDEN

Lerum
Borei, Sven Hans Emil *translator*

SWITZERLAND

Zurich
Burkert, Walter *Greek language educator, historian*

TAIWAN

Kaohsiung
Sohigian, Diran John *humanities educator*

Taichung
Lu, Shih-Peng *history educator*

THAILAND

Bangkok
†Sammon, William Joseph *historian, consultant*

YEMEN

Aden
†Al-Hamid, Abu-Bakr Muhsin *translator*

ADDRESS UNPUBLISHED

†Abernethy, Sharron Gray *language educator*
†Abruzzo, Margaret Nicola *historian*
Adamson, Michael Robert *history researcher, consultant, educator*
Adler, Raphael *educator emeritus, speech pathologist*
†Agnew, Jennifer Marie *literature educator*
†Allen, Dianna *language educator*
Allmendinger, David Frederick, Jr., *history educator*
†Alvarez, Maria Auxiliadora *language educator, poet, graphics designer*
†Alvarez, René Luis *historian, educator*
Anderson, Jerry Maynard *speech educator, retired*
Angell, Richard Bradshaw *philosophy educator*
Ansbro, John Joseph *philosopher, educator*
†Antliff, Robert Mark *humanities educator*
Appatov, Semyen Iosifovich *historian*
Aptekar, Sheldon I. *speech, theatre, and performing art educator*
Arrathoon, Leigh Adelaide *medievalist, editor, writer, educator*
†Asner, Glen R. *historian*
Attebery, Louie Wayne *English language educator, folklorist*
Aubrey, James Reynolds *English educator*
Babuts, Nicolae *French educator*
Bailey, Charles-James Nice *linguistics educator*
Bailey, David Roy Shackleton *classics educator*
Baker, Ronald James *English language educator, university administrator*
†Bancila, Mihaela *humanities educator*
Basnett, Margaret G. *reading and language arts educator, consultant*
Baxter, Stephen Bartow *retired history educator*
Becker, Lawrence Carlyle *philosopher, educator, writer*
Beecher, Graciela Fernandez *language educator, writer*
Belland, Brian Robert *language educator*
Benario, Janice Martin *retired classics educator*
Benivegna, Vito Nicholas *language educator*
Bercovitch, Sacvan *English language professional, educator*
Berkhofer, Robert Frederick, Jr., *retired history educator*
†Berlin, Edward Alan *musicologist, writer, retired application developer*
†Biles, Gloria C. *historian, educator*
†Binns, Jane Camille *humanities educator*
Blackbourn, David Gordon *history educator*
Blissett, William Frank *English literature educator*
Bok, Sissela *philosopher, writer*
Bolsterli, Margaret Jones *English educator, farmer*
Bolstridge, Alice M. *writer, educator*
†Bombaci, Nancy Margaret *literature educator*
Bonner, Thomas, Jr., *English language educator*
†Bosco, Frederick J. *language and linguistics educator*
Bosmajian, Haig Aram *speech communication educator*
Boyd, William Harland *historian, writer*
Boyd-Brown, Lena Ernestine *history educator, education consultant*
Boyer, Dale Kenneth *English educator*
Brettell, Richard Robson *art historian, museum consultant, educator*
Brewster, Elizabeth Winifred *English language educator, poet, novelist*
Bridges, Leonard Hal *retired history educator, writer*
†Brigham, Judith X. *philosophy educator*
Brody, Jacob Jerome *art history educator*
†Brown, Jennifer N. *humanities educator*
†Brown, Julie Katharine *social historian, photographic historian*
†Bruce, Dickson Davies, Jr., *history educator*
†Brunner, Kathleen Marie *humanities educator*
Bryant, Paul Thompson *English language educator*
Buckner, Sally Beaver *English educator, writer*
Burrill, Kathleen R. F. (Kathleen R. F. Griffin-Burrill) *Turkologist, educator*
Bush, Sarah Lillian *historian*
Bussard, Carmen Adelaide *speech professional*
Buzash, Michael D. *Romance languages educator*
Cachia, Pierre Jacques *Middle East languages and culture educator, researcher*
Caldwell, Louise Phinney *historical researcher, community volunteer*
Cantor, Norman Frank *history educator, writer*
Cappuccio, Richard *language educator*
Carls, Alice Catherine *history educator*
Carmack, Sharon DeBartolo *genealogist, writer*
†Carrasquel-Belandria, Jose Ramon *language educator*
Carrillo, Elisa Anna *history educator, consultant*
Carroll, Rosemary Frances *historian, educator, lawyer*
Cartwright, Talula Elizabeth *writing and leadership educator, consultant*
†Cashman, Tyrone McNally *philosophy educator, consultant*
Cawley, Joseph Douglas *retired reading educator*
Chalfant-Allen, Linda Kay *retired Spanish language educator*
Chambers, Marjorie Bell *historian*
Chandler, Alfred Dupont, Jr., *historian, educator*
Chandra, Pramod *art history educator*
Chess, Sonia Mary *retired language educator*
Chesson, Michael Bedout *history educator*
Childs, Marleta Marie *genealogist, library specialist*
†Cislo, Amy Eisen *language educator*
Clayson, Susan Hollis *art historian, educator*
Clear, Rosemary Elaine *translator, court interpreter, consultant*
Clogan, Paul Maurice *English language and literature educator*
†Coburn, Steven D. *musicologist, educator, musician*
†Cole, Merrill Grant *language educator*
†Colley, Caren R. *language educator*
Condit, Doris Elizabeth *retired historian*
†Connell, Charles R. *language educator*
Cook, Pamela Margaret *French educator*
Cooper, John Milton, Jr., *history educator, author*
†Cornelison, Sally J. *art historian*
†Courtenay, William James *historian, educator*
Courtney, Edward *retired classics educator*
Craig, Herbert Eugene *language educator*
Crimando, Thomas Ignatius *history educator*
†Cummins, Marsha Z. *retired literature educator*
Cunningham, William Francis, Jr., *English language educator, university administrator*
Cuppo Csaki, Luciana *foreign language educator, writer*
Dain, Phyllis *retired library educator, historian*
Darby, Jay Rodney *business and numismatic investment consultant*
†Dattolo, Alphonse A. *language educator*
†Daugherity, Brian James *historian, educator, historian, writer*
Day, James Sanders *history educator*
Defever, Susanna Ethel *English language educator*
Delacampagne, Christian H. *humanities educator*
†Delaty, Simone *retired language educator*
†del Gizzo, Suzanne *language educator*
Demenchonok, Edward Vasilevich *philosopher, linguist, researcher, educator*
Demharter, Cheryl Ann Marie *foreign language educator, former administrator*
Derbyshire, William Wadleigh *language educator, translator*
DeSando, John Anthony *retired humanities educator*
Dias, Kathleen R. *foreign language educator*
Di Paolo, Maria Grazia *language educator, writer*
Dixon, Marc Alan *numismatist, consultant, illustrator*
Djordjevic, Dimitrije *historian, educator*
Doebler, Bettie Anne *language educator, researcher, writer*
†Dornan, Reade Whiting *literature educator, writer*
Dosé, Frederick Philip, Jr., *art historian, art and antiques appraiser, consultant, liquidator*
Driskill, Elita Martin *humanities educator*
†Duhl, Olga Anna *literature educator, researcher*
Dunbar, Maurice Victor *English language educator*
†Dunkley, Larnell, Jr., *literature educator*
Eby, Carl Peter *English educator*
Eby, Cecil DeGrotte *English language educator, writer*
Eckstein, Jerome *philosopher, educator*
Edel, Abraham *philosophy educator*
Edmunds, Lowell (Arthur Lowell Edmunds) *philology educator*
†Egenes, Thomas Arthur *ancient language educator*
†Eidt, Jacob Ivan *language educator*
†Eisner, Sigmund *retired English language educator*
Eledge, Jean Dorothy *French language educator, administrator*
Ellis, John Martin *German literature educator*
†Erickson, Stacy Lynn *literature educator*
Espenlaub, Margo Linn *women's studies educator, writer, artist*
Esterhammer, Angela *literary theorist, educator*
Filler, Susan Melanie *musicologist*
Fisher, Anita Jeanne (Kit Fisher) *language educator*
Flint, John E. *historian, educator*
Foulke, Robert Dana *English educator, travel writer*
†Frazier, DuEwa M. *literature educator, writer*
Friedman, Victor Allen *linguist, educator*
Froberg, Brent Malcolm *classics educator*
Fry, Amelia Roberts *biographer, oral historian*
Gaddis, John Lewis *history educator*
†Garrard, John Gordon *educator*
Gatewood, Willard Badgett, Jr., *retired historian*
Geiselhart, Lorene Annetta *English language educator*
Geist, Kathe Sternbach *art history, cinema and English educator, writer*
Gellinek, Christian Johann *German educator*
Ghymn, Esther Mikyung *English educator, writer*
Gibbs, Carroll Robert *historian, writer*
†Gil Casado, Pablo *Romance languages educator*
Gillespie, Gerald Ernest Paul *comparative literature educator, writer*
Gillett, Mary Caperton *military historian*
Gish, Robert Franklin *English language educator, writer*
†Godwin, Robert Duane *language educator*
Goldstein, Phyllis Ann *art historian, educator*
Gollin, Rita Kaplan *English literature educator*

Graham, Lanier *art historian, curator, cultural planner*
†Grant, Linda Hess *educator*
†Gray, Clarence Jones *foreign language educator, dean emeritus*
Greenberg, Barbara Levenson *literature educator, poet*
Greene, Elinore Aschah *speech and drama professional, writer*
Greene, John Colton *retired history educator*
Greve, Sally Doane *English educator*
†Grindstaff, Mark Joseph *historian*
Grinnell, Helen Dunn *musicologist, arts administrator*
Gromen, Richard John *historian, educator*
Gumpel, Liselotte *retired language educator*
Guo, Sheng Ming *retired history educator*
†Gurnow, Michael Erwin *literature and film educator, art educator*
Gyles, Mary Francis *retired history educator*
Haag, Walter M(onroe), Jr., *philatelist*
Haber, Lynn Becker *English language educator*
†Hall, Kirstina J. *humanities educator*
Hamelin, Marcel *historian, educator*
†Hannon, Patricia *literature educator, writer*
†Hansen, Wells Stevenson *language educator, researcher*
†Hanshe, John *musicologist, writer*
Haring, Ellen Stone (Mrs. E. S. Haring) *philosophy educator*
Harrell, Steven Jeffrey *lexicographer*
Hart, Arthur Alvin *historian, author*
Harth, Erica *French language and comparative literature educator*
Hartman, Marilyn D. *English and Art education educator*
†Haskin, Dayton William *English language educator, researcher*
†Haviland, Kay Lynn (Kade Haviland) *English literature educator*
Haworth, Dale Keith *art history educator, gallery director*
Heller, Janet Ruth *English language, writing and literature educator*
†Henseler, Christine *language educator*
Herbst, Jurgen *history and education educator*
†Hermalyn, Doc *historian, writer*
Hermand, Jost *German language educator*
†High, Jeffrey L. *humanities educator*
Hoart, Gladys Gallagher *English language educator*
Hoffman, Daniel (Daniel Gerard Hoffman) *literature educator, poet*
†Hogan, Katie J. *English educator, women's studies researcher*
†Holloway, Charles Edward *language educator*
Howard, Michael Eliot *historian, educator*
Hsu, Patrick Kuo-Heng *retired languages educator, librarian*
Hudson, Yeager *philosophy educator, minister*
Huffman-Klinkowitz, Julie Ann *genealogist, researcher*
Hughes, Edward Thomas *retired English educator, consultant*
Hughes, Thomas Parke *history educator*
Hunter, J(ames) Paul *English language educator, literary critic, historian*
Huntsinger, Jami L. *English educator*
Hutcheon, Linda Ann *English language educator*
Ivry, Alfred Lyon *history of Jewish and Islamic philosophy educator*
Janney, Kay Print *retired theatre arts educator, theatre director*
Johnson, Clifton Herman *historian, archivist, former research center director*
Johnson, John Prescott *philosophy educator*
Johnson, Mary Elizabeth *retired speech educator*
Johnson, Vernon Eugene *history educator*
†Jones, Marie C. *language educator*
Jones, Peter d'Alroy *historian, writer, retired educator*
†Jorres, Daniel *literature educator*
Kaminsky, Alice Richkin *English language educator*
Kane, Patricia Lanegran *language professional, educator*
Kaplan, Robert B. *linguistics educator, consultant, researcher*
Karlstrom, Paul Johnson *art historian*
Karttunen, Frances Esther *retired linguist, research scientist*
Kaspar, Victoria Ann *school administrator*
Kastor, Frank Sullivan *English language educator*
Katz, Susan Arons *language arts specialist, author, poet*
Kaufman, Janice Horner *foreign language educator, women's and gender studies educator*
Kaufman, Luna Amalia *musicologist*
†Kemmerer, Lisa Ann *humanities educator*
Kerney, Yolonda V. *music historian*
Kessler-Harris, Alice *historian, educator*
†Kim, Marianne Weiss *humanities educator*
Kladiva, Jason Louis *historian, writer*
Kloster, Sherry Ann *language educator*
Knight, Doris Rathbun *retired government and history educator*
Koestenbaum, Wayne *English educator, author*
†Kohler, Sheila M. *humanities educator, writer*
†Kohmstedt, Jeffery John *literature educator, political consultant*
Kolb, Harold Hutchinson, Jr., *English language educator*
Korsgaard, Christine Marion *philosophy educator*
Kowalczyk, David Theodore *English language educator, poet*
†Kralj, Dejan *historian*
Kramer, Dale Vernon *retired English language educator*
Kravitz, Ellen King *musicologist, educator*
†Kuperman, Michael Aron *language educator, writer*
Labor, Earle Gene *English language educator*
LaFemina, Gerry *writing and literature educator*
Lambert, Edythe Rutherford *retired language educator, civic volunteer*
Lamdin, Lois Symons *English educator*
Lederer, Katherine Gay *English language educator*
Lemisch, Jesse *history educator, writer*
Levenback, Karen L. *educator, writer, editor*
Lewis, Douglas *art historian*
Lightburn, Faye Marie *genealogist*
Lindsey, Roberta Lewise *music researcher, historian*
†Lish, Debra Elaine *historian, educator*
Loughran, James Newman *philosophy educator, college administrator*
Lowenthal, Constance *art historian, consultant*
Lukomsky, Vera *musicologist, pianist, music educator*
Lynch, Richard Anthony *philosopher, educator*
†MacGregor, William Bracey *art historian, educator*
MacLaury, Robert E(than) *language educator*
Maehl, William Harvey *historian, educator*
Mahoney, John L. *English literature educator*
Mahoney, Michael Robert Taylor *art historian, educator*
†Manning, Chandra Miller *humanities educator*
Manso, Leira A. *Latin American literature educator, poet*
Mapp, Edward Charles *speech educator*
Marabella, Dawn Marie *ESL educator*
Marchant, JoAnn Reviczky *English language educator, actress*
Marion, Marjorie Anne *English language educator, education consultant*
†Martinez, Efrain *humanities educator, researcher*
†Mason, Matthew E. *humanities educator*
Mastrangelo, Lisa Siobhan *humanities educator*
Mathews, Barbara Jean *genealogist*
†Matuozzi, Robert Norman *historian, archivist*
Mauskopf, Seymour Harold *history educator*
McClure, Evelyn Susan *historian, photographer*
McCormick, John Owen *retired comparative literature educator*
McDermott, Agnes Charlene Senape *philosophy educator*
McDonald, Forrest *historian, educator*
McGann, Lisa B. Napoli *language educator*
†McGarry, Richard Gale *linguist, educator*
†McMurray, David McCain *German studies educator*
McSpadden, Katherine Frances *English language educator*
Meintsma, Peter Evans *history and political science educator*
†Mendelssohn, Michéle *language educator*
†Merrell, James Hart *history educator*
Meyers, Charles Jerome *history educator*
†Millikan, William *labor historian*
Mills, Elizabeth Shown *genealogist, editor, writer*
Miscella, Maria Diana *humanities educator*
Molloy, Sylvia *Latin American literature educator, writer*
†Monaco, Chris *historian, writer, documentary filmmaker*
†Monas, Sidney *retired history educator*
†Moody, Jennifer Joy *language educator, history educator*
†Moore, Cyrus *language educator*
Morgan, Ann Lee *art historian, writer*
Morgan, Edmund Sears *history educator*
Morrill, Penny Chittim *art historian*
Morrison, Robert Reid *retired language educator*
Morrissey, Charles Thomas *historian, educator*
Mosca, Virginia *retired language educator*
†Moshiri, Farnoosh M. *language educator, literature educator*
†Murillo, Marisela *English educator*
Murnion, William Edward *philosopher*
Murphy, Francis *English language educator*
Murphy, Robert James *language educator, consultant*
Nagel, Thomas *philosopher, educator*
Nanay, Bence *philosopher, critic*
†Needham, Jonathan Anton *language educator, poet*
Nehrbass, Richard George *literature educator, writer*
†Nephew, Julia Anne *language educator*
New, Thomas L. *public affairs, consultant*
Newbery, Ilse Sofie Magdalene *German language educator*
†Newman, Georgia A. *literature educator*
†Newman, Marcy Jane Knopf *literature educator, writer*
Nicholas, Lynn Holman *historian, researcher, writer*
Nochman, Lois Wood Kivi (Mrs. Marvin Nochman) *retired educator*
Nostrand, Howard Lee *retired humanities educator*
Novak, Barbara *art history educator*
Nugent, Helen Jean *history educator*
Nugent, Walter Terry King *historian*
†O'Dell, Kimberly Jane *historian, educator*
Ogbar, Jeffrey Ogbonna Green *history educator*
†Ogden, Benjamin *language educator*
Oinas, Felix J. *retired Slavic language educator*
Olson, James Clifton *historian, university president*
Olson, Paul Richard *Spanish literature educator, editor*
†Ornatowski, Cezar Maria *rhetoric and communication educator, consultant*
†Ortolano, Glauco Luiz *language educator, writer*
Osterholm, J(ohn) Roger *humanities educator*
Palmer, Marilyn Joan *English composition educator*
Palter, Robert Monroe *humanities educator*
Panzer, Mary Caroline *historian, museum curator*
Parks, John Gordon *English educator*
Paschoud, François *university educator*
†Patty, William Jordan *historian*
†Perdigó, Luisa Marina *foreign language and literature educator*
Peyser, Joseph Leonard *educator, author, translator, historical researcher*
Pflanze, Otto Paul *history educator*
Pickard, John Benedict *English language educator*
†Picker, John M. *literature educator*
Pickrel, Paul *English educator*
Poindexter, John Michael *language educator, writer*
†Polistena, Joyce Carol *art historian, educator*
Porter, Joseph A. (Joe Ashby Porter) *English language educator, fiction writer*
†Portolano, Marlana *language educator, researcher*
†Pratico, Dominick *historian, educator*
†Pridgen, Rufus Allen *retired literature educator*
Prout, Carl Wesley *retired history educator*
Quint Sehat, Arlene *art history educator, curator, museum administrator*
Rabiola, Samuel Charles *English educator*
†Rackin, Phyllis *English language educator emeritus*
Ranlet, Philip Henry *historian, educator*
†Rann, Robert Kennedy *humanities educator*
Rappaport, Susan Elizabeth *English language educator*
Rebay, Luciano *Italian literature educator, literary critic*
†Reh, Sheila Natkins *humanities educator*
†Reischman, Richard Alan *language educator*
Riasanovsky, Nicholas Valentine *retired historian, educator*
Rich, Lawrence *Spanish language educator*
Richards, David Gleyre *German language educator*
Richardson, Robert Dale, Jr., *English language educator*
Rickard, Ruth David *retired history and political science educator*
Ridge, Martin *historian, educator*
†Rizkallah, Morris Z. *translator*
†Robinson, Harlow Loomis *language educator, historian, educator, writer*
Robinson, Mary Frances *retired French language educator*
†Robles-Cereceres, Oscar Fernando *language educator, researcher, writer*
Rodriguez, Timothy Allen *language educator*
†Rohman, Carrie Lynn *literature educator*
†Rohsenow, John Snowden *linguist, educator*
Rollins, Alfred Brooks, Jr., *historian, educator*
†Romack, Katherine M. *language educator*
Rosenberg, David Alan *military historian, educator*
Rossi, Mary Ann *classicist, research scholar*
Rouman, John Christ *classics educator*
Ruoff, A. LaVonne Brown *English language educator*
†Ryan, Henry Butterfield *historian, consultant*
Ryan, Marleigh Grayer *Japanese language educator*
Saint-Jacques, Bernard *linguistics educator*
Salgado, Susana *Musicologist, researcher, consultant*
Sanborn, Melinde Lutz *genealogist, writer*
Sandford, Virginia Adele *motivational speaker, writer*
†Sandlin, Lisa *literature educator*
†Sanner, Kristin Noelle *language educator*
Sayre, Robert Freeman *English language educator*
Schlagel, Richard H. *philosophy educator*
Schlossman, Beryl Fern *literature educator, writer*
Schmidt, Lawrence Kennedy *philosophy educator*
Schmitz, Dennis Mathew *English language educator*
Schoen, Carol Bronston *retired English language educator*
Schor, Laura Strumingher *historian*
Schwantes, Carlos Arnaldo *history educator, consultant*
†Schweitzer, Christoph Eugen *liberal studies educator*
†Scott, Jane Madeline *language educator*
Scott, Michael Coleman *philosophy educator*
Sellin, Eric *linguist, poet, educator*
†Serdari, Thomai *historian, librarian*
†Serrano, Jorge Luis *language educator*
Sferrazza, Anthony Carl *historian*
†Shaeffer, John Nees *historian, educator*
†Sheehan, P.G. Misty *humanities educator*
Silverman, Kenneth Eugene *English educator, writer*
Singer, Beth J. *philosopher*
Smith, Grover C(leveland) *English language educator*
Smither, Howard Elbert *musicologist, educator*
Smock, Raymond William *historian*
Snyder, William Brandon *linguistics educator*
†Sobrer, Josep Miquel *language educator, writer*
Solis-Klein, Ruth Elizabeth *foreign language educator*
Solomon, Robert Charles *philosopher, educator*
†Solomon-Arnold, Irene Lena *language educator*
Somerville, James Middleton, III, *retired philosophy educator, writer*
Sorrentino, Gilbert *English language educator, novelist, poet*
Starr, Mirabai Paula *philosophy and religious studies educator, writer*
†Steigmann-Gall, Richard Albert *historian, educator*
†Sternbach, Nancy Saporta *language educator, researcher*
†Stewart, Dorothy Mary Hanton *literature educator*
Stoesen, Alexander Rudolph *retired history educator*
Stokes, Sally Ruth Sims *historic preservationist, curator, architectural historian*
Stolarik, M. Mark *history educator*
†Stone, Marilyn *foreign language educator, consultant*
Straulman, Ann Therese *retired English language educator*
Street, John Charles *linguistics educator*
Stringer, Mary Evelyn *art historian, educator*
Strong, Carol Joan *speech professional, researcher*
Struble, John Warthen *music historian, educator*
†Studdard, Melissa Jane *language educator, writer*
Styne, Marlys Marshall *retired English educator*
†Sullivan, Gerald Joseph *Latin and English educator*
Sullivan, Mary Rose *English language educator*
Sutton, Julia *musicologist, dance historian*
Svarlien, Diane Arnson *verse translator, classics educator*
Svrcek, Debbie M. *English educator*
†Sykes, Sam Jones *French educator*
†Tamimi, Maher M. *language educator*
Tayler, Irene *English literature educator*
Teague, Frances Nicol *English language educator*
Tedesco, Paul Herbert *humanities educator*
Thackray, Arnold Wilfrid *historian, foundation executive*
†Thomas, William Griffith, III, *humanities educator, consultant*
†Thomas, Jr., Joseph M. *language educator*
†Thompson, Emily *historian*
†Throne, Stephanie *language educator*
†Tobin, Kathleen Ann *humanities educator*
†Tokumasu, Yukari *language educator*
†Tone, Andrea E. *historian, educator*
Tong, Rosemarie *medical humanities and philosophy educator, consultant and researcher*
Topik, Steven Curtis *historian, educator*
†Torres, Shelby Credle *English educator*
Toulmin, Stephen Edelston *humanities educator*
Trelease, Allen William *historian, educator*
Unger, J. Marshall *linguist, foreign language educator*
Valencia, Margarita *Spanish language educator*
van der Marck, Jan *art historian*
Varacalli, Joseph Anthony *humanities educator, writer*
Vaz, Katherine Anne *language educator*
†Vera Negron, Sandra *literature educator, translator*
Vesper, Ethel Rose *language educator, consultant*
†Wachtel, Shirley Russak *English language educator, writer*
Wagner, Ann Prentice *art historian*
Wagner, Diana Mae *English language educator*
Wait, Eugene Meredith *historian, writer*
Waite, Gerald Phillip *English language educator*
Waller, Martha S. *retired English educator, writer*
Walsh, Roger N. *psychiatry, philosophy and anthropology educator*
†Weber, Heidi Amelia-Anne *historian, educator*
Weddle, Laura Mildred Thomas *retired language educator*
Weisbuch, Robert Alan *English educator*
†Westgate, J. Chris *literature educator*
Wetzel, Heinz *foreign language educator*
Wheeler, Burton M. *literature educator, higher education consultant, college dean*
Whitburn, Merrill Duane *English literature educator*
†White, Charles Sidney John *retired humanities educator*
Whitlow, Stacey Mataxis *English educator, university educator*
†Whittington, Cynthia Denise *English language educator*
Wickliffe, Mary *art historian, artist*
Wiener, Jon *history educator*
Wilder, Alma Ann *English educator, consultant*
Wilkerson, William S. *philosophy educator*
Wirzba, Norman R. *philosophy educator*
Wishnia, Kenneth J.A. *writer, translator, educator*
Wiswall, Dorothy Roller *language educator*
Woodbridge, John Dunning *history and church history educator*
Woodman, Jean Wilson *educator, consultant*
Wright, Beth Segal *art historian, educator*
†Wright, Elizabeth Rebecca *humanities educator*
Wruck, Erich-Oskar *retired foreign language educator, administrator*
Wyatt, Marcia Jean *fine arts educator, administrative assistant*
Yngve, Victor H. *linguist, researcher*
Yolton, John William *philosopher, educator*
†Yomoah, Bruno Kyapuoku *language educator, consultant*
†Youngman, Paul A. *language educator*
Zaferson, William S. *philosophy educator, publisher*
†Zelic, Tomislav *language educator, translator*
†Zimmerman, Lynn Diann *language educator, forensic specialist*
Zimmermann, Thomas Callander Price *retired historian, educator*
†Zubritski, Maria *literature educator, writer*

HUMANITIES: LIBRARIES

UNITED STATES

ALABAMA

Auburn
Havens, Carolyn Clarice *librarian*
Straiton, T(homas) Harmon, Jr., *librarian*

Birmingham
†Beard, Craig Wyeth *librarian*
Clemmons, Nancy Washington *library administrator, educator*

Pueblo
Cress, Cecile Colleen *retired librarian*

Thornton
Sawyer, Michael E. *library director*

Vail
†Wilroy, Jo Ann *librarian*

CONNECTICUT

Avon
†Coburn, Elizabeth Ann *librarian*

Bloomfield
Thorpe, James *humanities researcher*

Cheshire
Walter, Kenneth Gaines *library director*

Chester
Harwood, Eleanor Cash *librarian*

Derby
Augusta, Judith Wood *librarian*

Fairfield
Bryan, Barbara Day *retired librarian*
Dunham, Christopher Scott *librarian*
†King, Ann Stockman *librarian, educator*
Turetsky, Judith *librarian, researcher*

Hamden
Ballard, Terry Lee *librarian, educator*
†Lucas, Doina C. *librarian*

Hartford
Kaimowitz, Jeffrey Hugh *librarian*
Posteraro, Catherine Hammond *librarian, gerontology educator*
Wiggin, Kendall French *state librarian*

Meriden
Trotta, Marcia Marie *librarian, consultant, education educator*

Middletown
Meyers, Arthur Solomon *library director*

Mystic
Rogers, Brian Deane *retired librarian*

New Britain
†Chasse, Emily Schuder *librarian, educator, storyteller*
†Packer, Joan Garrett *librarian*
Tomaiuolo, Nicholas Gregory *librarian, educator*

New Haven
Clarie, Thomas Cashin, II, *librarian*
Martin, Walter Francis, 3rd, *librarian*
Okerson, Ann Shumelda Lillian *librarian*
Oliver-Warren, Mary Elizabeth *retired library science educator*
†Peterson, Sandra Kay *librarian*
†Stahl, Nanette *librarian, theologian*
Stuehrenberg, Paul Frederick *librarian*

Niantic
Deakyne, William John *library director, musician*
†Morrill, Billie Alberta *librarian*

North Canton
†Swibold, Gretchen Ann *librarian, writer*

Simsbury
†Berberich, Patricia Louise *librarian*

Southbury
Rorick, William Calvin *librarian, educator, portrait artist*

Southington
Burkhardt, Dolores Ann *library consultant*

Stamford
Griffith, Katherine Scott *librarian*

West Hartford
Gerjuoy, Herbert George *educator, psychologist, consultant, poet*

Westport
†Schwarz, Shirlee *library consultant*

Wilton
Poundstone, Sally Hill *library director*

DELAWARE

Wilmington
Williams, Richmond Dean *library appraiser, consultant*

DISTRICT OF COLUMBIA

Washington
Akunwafor, Daniel Dominic *librarian, educator*
Basa, Enikö Molnár *librarian*
Carlin, John William *archivist, former governor*
Carlson, Melinda Suzanne *librarian*
Chin, Cecilia Hui-Hsin *librarian*
Converse, Joseph Thomas *archivist, records manager*
Craig, Susan Lyons *library director*
Cylke, Frank Kurt *librarian*
Daffron, MaryEllen *librarian*
Dixson, Diane Elizabeth *acquisitions librarian, tax preparation business owner*
†Doumato, Lamia *librarian, art historian*
†Emperado, Mercedes Lopez *librarian*

Falk, Diane M. *research director, librarian, editor, writer*
Fifer Canby, Susan Melinda *library administrator*
†Fry, Mary Beth *librarian*
Gallup, Jane Harrington *librarian*
Gifford, Prosser *library administrator*
Goldstein, Doris Mueller *librarian, researcher*
Gregory, John Forrest *information technology consultant*
Haley, Roger Kendall *librarian*
Harlem, Susan Lynn *librarian*
†Harness, Gregory C. *Senate librarian*
Hedges, Kamla King *library director*
†Heise, Dorothy Hilbert *librarian, government official*
Heiss, Harry Glen *archivist*
Jackson, Mary Ellen *librarian, consultant*
Kalfatovic, Martin Robert *librarian, writer*
Kiser, Joy Marian *librarian, writer, historian*
Knezo, Genevieve Johanna *science and technology policy researcher*
Lee, Hwa-Wei *librarian, educator, consultant*
Lewis, Robert John Cornelius Koons *university library director, consultant*
†Mann, Thomas *reference librarian*
Mansfield, Jerry Wayne *librarian*
Marcum, Deanna Bowling *library administrator*
Meyer, Margaret Vaughan *librarian, educator*
Missar, Charles Donald *retired librarian*
Moulton, David Aubin *library director*
Peterson, Charles Buckley, III, *librarian, geographer*
Player, Thelma B. *librarian*
Renninger, Mary Karen *librarian*
Robinson, Robert Cribben *librarian, information company executive*
Rovelstad, Mathilde V(erner) *library science educator*
Simpson, Jacqueline Angelia *legal administration*
†Soapes, Thomas F. *archivist*
Thomas, Mary Augusta *library administrator*
Trimble, Kathleen Louise *library director*
Turtell, Neal Timothy *librarian*
Tylenda, Joseph N. *library director*
†Vogelsong, Diana Louise *librarian*
Wasserman, Krystyna Jolanta, *librarian, art historian*
Wattenmaker, Richard Joel *archive director, art scholar*
†Wertz, Virginia Loryma *retired librarian*

FLORIDA

Boca Raton
†Ferrari, Roberto C. *librarian*
†Hermann, Naomi Basel *librarian, interior decorator*
Miller, William *library administrator*
Sarna, Helen Horowitz *retired librarian, educator*

Bradenton
†Ehde, Ava Louise *librarian, educator*

Clearwater
†Glymph, Dianne Tyler *librarian*
Werner, Elizabeth Helen *librarian, language educator*

Coral Gables
†Zavac, Nancy *librarian*

Daytona Beach
†Sigerson, Marjorie Lorraine *librarian*

Deland
Caccamise, Genevra Louise Ball (Mrs. Alfred E. Caccamise) *retired librarian*

Destin
Deel, Frances Quinn *retired librarian*

Fort Lauderdale
Hershenson, Miriam Hannah Ratner *librarian*
Riggs, Donald Eugene *librarian, university official*

Fort Pierce
†Harris, Martha Jane *retired librarian*

Fort Walton Beach
Hill, Carol Koelling *library director*

Gainesville
†Brown, Myra Suzanne *librarian*
Goggin, Margaret Enid (Knox) *librarian, educator*
Primack, Alice Lefler *librarian*
†Stipek, Kathleen *reference librarian*
Willocks, Robert Max *retired librarian*

Gulfport
Bourke, Thomas Anthony *librarian, writer*
Smith, Catherine Louise *library administrator, consultant*

Haines City
Kirk, Sherwood *librarian*

Hernando
Park, Chung Il *retired librarian*

Jacksonville
Farkas, Andrew *library director emeritus, educator, writer*

Jensen Beach
†Lowrie, Jean Elizabeth *librarian, educator*

Lake Worth
Gough, Carolyn Harley *library director*

Lakeland
Reich, David Lee *library director*

Lighthouse Point
Gauthier, Doreen Ann *librarian*

Maitland
Mansson, Joan *librarian, consultant*

Melbourne
Regis, Nina *librarian, educator*

Miami
†Treyz, Joseph Henry *librarian*

Naples
Hainsworth, Melody May *information professional, researcher*
Hall, Beverly Barton *librarian*
Savitzky, Evelyn Robbins *information specialist, librarian*

Oakland Park
Rosenthal, Susan Barbara *retired librarian*

Ocala
Frow, Richard G. *retired librarian*

Orlando
Allison, Anne Marie *retired librarian*
Hodel, Mary Anne *library director*

Oviedo
Hyslop, Gary Lee *retired librarian*

Panama City
Robbins, Dorothy Ann *librarian*

Pensacola
†Bumgardner, Kathryn H. *retired librarian*

Pompano Beach
Bethel, Marilyn Joyce *librarian*

Port Charlotte
Donovan, William Alan *retired librarian*

Saint Petersburg
†Hargrave, Victoria Elizabeth *librarian*
Kent, Allen *library and information sciences educator*

Sanford
†Linsley, Laurie Strickland *information specialist/librarian*

Sarasota
Brandhorst, Wesley Theodore *retired information scientist*
De Gennaro, Richard *retired library director, library advisor*
Hummel, Dana D. Mallett *librarian*
Pike, Nancy M. *librarian*
Retzer, Mary Elizabeth Helm *retired librarian*
†Straight, Elsie Hosking *retired art librarian, sculptor*

Tallahassee
†Fiore, Carole Diane *public library consultant for youth services*
Hunt, Mary Alice *library science educator*
†Jordan, Tracey Alys *librarian*
Mason, Marilyn Gell *library administrator, writer, consultant*
Robbins, Jane Borsch *library science educator, information science educator*
Sapp, Lauren B. *librarian, educator*
Summers, Frank William *retired librarian*
Thompson, Jean Tanner *retired librarian*
Zachert, Martha Jane *retired librarian*

Tampa
Harkness, Mary Lou *librarian*

University Park
†Compain, Rita *librarian*

Venice
Becker, Catherine Hickey Handy *retired librarian*

West Palm Beach
†Davidsson, Robert Iver *librarian*
Terwillegar, Jane Cusack *librarian, educator*

Winter Haven
†Clyne, Rosemarie Blackstone *technical services librarian*

Winter Park
Rogers, Rutherford David *librarian*

Zephyrhills
Martindale, Carla Joy *retired librarian*

GEORGIA

Americus
†Tietjen, Mildred Campbell *librarian, college official*

Athens
Donovan, James M. *librarian, anthropologist*
Potter, William Gray, Jr., *library director*
Rowland, Lucy Minogue *librarian*

Atlanta
Brown, Lorene B(yron) *library educator, educational administrator*
Drake, Miriam Anna *librarian, educator, writer*
Flagg Davis, Vivian Annette *librarian, researcher, public policy consultant*
Lawson, A(bram) Venable *retired librarian*
McDavid, Sara June *librarian*
Roberts, Edward Graham *librarian*
Robison, Carolyn Love *retired librarian*
Thaxton, Mary Lynwood *librarian, researcher*
Wallace, Gladys Baldwin *librarian*

Yates, Ella Gaines *library consultant*

Augusta
Rowland, Arthur Ray *librarian*

Barnesville
†Adams, Cynthia Ann *librarian, media specialist, writing instructor*
†Anderson, Nancy Dixon *librarian*

Brunswick
†Cody, Sara Elizabeth *librarian*

Carrollton
Beard, Charles Edward *library director, consultant*
Goodson, Carol Faye *librarian*

Cleveland
†Edwards, John Carver *retired archivist*

Dalton
Forsee, Joe Brown *library director*
†Jones-Glaze, Barbara Ann *library media specialist*

Decatur
Cravey, Pamela J. *librarian*

Fayetteville
†Neal, Joan Burkes *librarian*

Lithonia
Haller, Hal Martin, Jr., *library director*

Loganville
Wald, Marlena Malmstedt *health science librarian*

Marietta
†Kendall, Susan Gardes *librarian*
Rogers, Gail Elizabeth *library director*

Oxford
McNeill, Mary Kathryn Morgan *librarian*

Rome
Stephens, Michael Thoryne *librarian*

Savannah
†Ball, Ardella Patricia *library media educator*
Dickerson, Lon Richard *library administrator*

Statesboro
Mitchell, Wilfrid Bede *librarian*

Valdosta
Koehler, Wallace *library and information scientist, educator, library and information scientist, researcher*
†Montgomery, Denise Lynne *librarian, researcher*

HAWAII

Aiea
Uyehara, Harry Yoshimi *library educator*

Honolulu
†Geil, Wilma Jean *librarian*
Lee, Pali Jae (Polly Jae Stead Lee) *retired librarian, writer*
Lowell, Virginia Lee *librarian*
Polansky, Patricia Ann *librarian*
Weingand, Darlene Erna *librarian, educator, consultant*

Kahului
†Tolliver, Dorothy *librarian*

Lihue
Stevens, Robert David *librarian, educator*

IDAHO

Boise
Bolles, Charles Avery *librarian*

Buhl
†Spreier, Lois Joanne

Moscow
Force, Ronald Wayne *librarian*

ILLINOIS

Aurora
Christiansen, Raymond Stephan *librarian, educator*

Buffalo
Coss, John Edward *retired archivist*

Carbondale
Bauner, Ruth Elizabeth *library administrator, reference librarian*

Carol Stream
O'Dell, Lynn Marie Luegge (Mrs. Norman D. O'Dell) *librarian*

Cary
McNulty, Diane Rose *library director*

Caseyville
†Stanford, Diana L. *librarian*

Champaign
Rayward, Warden Boyd *librarian, educator*
†Ruan, Lian Jin *library director*

Chicago
Althage, C. Jill *librarian*
Bodi, Sonia Ellen *library director, educator*

College Park
Churchville, Lida Holland *librarian*
Lowell, Howard Parsons *archivist, federal agency administrator*
Wasserman, Paul *library and information science educator*

Columbia
Gruhl, Andrea Morris *librarian*
Klein, Sami Weiner *librarian*

Easton
Bronson, John Orville, Jr., *retired librarian*

Fort Washington
Cross, Rita Faye *librarian, early childhood educator, writer*

Frostburg
†Williams, Pamela S. *librarian*

Greenbelt
Auerbach, Bob Shipley *librarian*
Augustyn, Frederick John, Jr., *librarian*
Hogensen, Margaret Hiner *librarian, consultant*
Moore, Virginia Bradley *librarian*

Kensington
Rather, Lucia Porcher Johnson *library administrator*

Leonardtown
Rudigier, Roberta Lynn *librarian*

Potomac
Broderick, John Caruthers *retired librarian, educator*

Rockville
Henderson, Harriet *librarian*

Salisbury
House, Charletta *librarian*

Silver Spring
Flug, Janice *librarian*
Null, Elisabeth Higgins *librarian, writer*

Solomons
†Heil, Kathleen Ann *librarian*

Takoma Park
von Hake, Margaret Joan *librarian*
†Walton, Charles W. *library director*

Towson
Tull, Willis Clayton, Jr., *librarian*

Upper Marlboro
†Rough, Marianne Christina *librarian, educator*

MASSACHUSETTS

Amesbury
Dowd, Frances Connelly *retired librarian*

Amherst
Bridegam, Willis Edward, Jr., *librarian*
Tenenbaum, Jeffrey Mark *academic librarian*

Auburndale
Tuchman, Maurice Simon *library director*

Boston
Armstrong, Rodney *librarian*
Chen, Ching-chih *information science educator, consultant*
Christopher, Irene *librarian, consultant*
Desnoyers, Megan Floyd *archivist, educator*
†Fisher, Sean Michael *archivist*
Hernon, Peter *library science educator*
†Kominis, Katherine Elizabeth *librarian*
Kowal, Ruth Elizabeth *library administrator*
Maciora, Joseph Gerard Vincent *reference librarian*
Margolis, Bernard Allen *library administrator*
McKain, Joshua Van Kirk *library director*
Peek, Robin Patricia *library and information science educator*
Preece, Barbara G. *librarian*
Trinkaus-Randall, Gregor *librarian, archivist, preservation administrator*
von Fettweis, Yvonne Caché *archivist, historian*
Wendorf, Richard Harold *library director, scholar*
Woodard, Paul Esty *librarian emeritus, nurse*

Brookline
Finkelstein, Norman Henry *librarian*
Wertsman, Vladimir Filip *librarian, information specialist, author, translator*

Cambridge
Bourneuf, Henri Joseph, Jr., *librarian*
Cole, Heather Ellen *librarian*
Flannery, Susan Marie *library administrator*
Gerratt, Bradley Scott *public administrator*
Hamilton, Malcolm Cowan *librarian, editor, indexer, personnel professional*
Horrell, Jeffrey Lanier *library administrator*
Koepp, Donna Pauline Petersen *librarian*
Mullins, James Lee *library administrator*
Riel, Steven Joseph *librarian*
Stoddard, Roger Eliot *librarian*

Carver
Neubauer, Richard A. *library science educator, consultant*

Chestnut Hill
Yavarkovsky, Jerome Harold *library director*

Framingham
Merlini, Sandra Ann *library assistant, writer*

Ipswich
Dyer, Victor Eugene, II, *library administrator*

Leominster
Lambert, Lyn Dee *library media specialist, law librarian*

Lexington
Davis, Barbara M(ae) *librarian*
Freitag, Wolfgang Martin *librarian, educator*
Preve, Roberta Jean *librarian, researcher*

Lowell
†Karr, Ronald Dale *librarian, historian*

Lunenburg
Tallman, Susan Porri *library director*

Marstons Mills
Martin, Susan Katherine *librarian*

Mill River
Jaffe, Katharine Weisman *retired librarian*

Milton
†Jespersen, John Kresten *librarian*

Monson
De Santis, Sylvia *library director*

Natick
Rendell, Kenneth William *rare and historical documents dealer, consultant*

Needham
Mills, Elizabeth Ann *retired librarian*

North Easton
Bundy, Annalee Marshall *library director*

Northampton
Piccinino, Rocco Michael *librarian*

Randolph
Michaud, Charles A. *library director, writer*

Sharon
Roberson, Kip Michael *library director, librarian*

Sheffield
Young, Susan Babson *retired library director*

Shrewsbury
Chang, Isabelle C. *librarian, educator, writer*

Springfield
Stack, May Elizabeth *library director*
Utley, F. Knowlton *library director, educator*

Waltham
Hahn, Bessie King *library administrator, lecturer*

Wellesley
Flynn, Megan Alice *librarian*

Williamstown
Erickson, Peter Brown *librarian, scholar, writer*

Worcester
Dunlap, Ellen S. *library administrator*
McCorison, Marcus Allen *librarian, cultural organization administrator*

MICHIGAN

Albion
Seidl, James C. *librarian*

Allendale
Murray, Diane Elizabeth *librarian*

Ann Arbor
†Allee, Nancy Jane *reference librarian, library administrator*
†Anderson, Patricia Francis *librarian*
Beaubien, Anne Kathleen *librarian*
Bidlack, Russell Eugene *librarian, educator, former dean*
Daub, Peggy Ellen *library administrator*
Dede, Bonnie Aileen *librarian, educator*
Dougherty, Richard Martin *library and information science educator*
Dunlap, Connie *librarian*
†Lin, Mei-Ying *librarian*
†Naeem, Tahira Bryant *librarian*
†Scheffel, Kenneth Paul *archivist*

Auburn Hills
Williams, Calvin *librarian, consultant*

Battle Creek
Lincoln, Margaret *library media specialist*

Detroit
Ashley, Lois A. *retired university reference librarian*
Field, Judith Judy *librarian*
†Krempasky, Frances M. *librarian*
Poremba, David Lee *librarian, writer*
Spyers-Duran, Peter *librarian, educator*

East Lansing
Chapin, Richard Earl *retired librarian*
†Sowards, Steven Wesley *librarian*
Volkening, Thomas Charles *engineering librarian*

Farmington Hills
Papai, Beverly Daffern *library director*

Flint
†Corser, Maureen Slagg *librarian, media specialist*

Flushing
Gordon, Reva Jo *retired librarian*

Grand Rapids
Stewart, Debbie Elaine *librarian, artist*

Grosse Pointe
†Casey, Genevieve M. *librarian, educator*

Holt
Smith, Betty W. *librarian*

Interlochen
Tacke, Eleanor *archivist*

Kalamazoo
Carlson, Andrew Raymond *archivist*
Grotzinger, Laurel Ann *librarian, educator*
Pérez-Stable, Maria Adelaida *librarian*

Lansing
†Johnson, Veronica Ann Wilkerson *information and government services director*

Livonia
Guerriero, Carol Marie *librarian*

Marquette
†Henderson, Roberta Marie *librarian, educator*

Marshall
Garypie, Rudolph Renwick *library director*

Monroe
Carlen, Sister Claudia *librarian, consultant*
†Carmody, Jennifer Lynn *librarian*

Mount Pleasant
Smallwood, Carol *librarian, writer*

Muskegon
†Briggs-Erickson, Carol Ann *librarian*

Okemos
†Brenneise, Harvey Ray *library director*

Owosso
Bentley, Margaret Ann *librarian*
Uptigrove, Kenneth R. *library administrator*

Plymouth
Berry, Charlene Helen *librarian, musician*
deBear, Richard Stephen *library planning consultant*

Port Huron
Miller, Theresa L. *library director*
Wu, Harry Pao-Tung *retired librarian*

Prescott
†Brandau, Christie Pearson *librarian*

Redford
Karpinski, Huberta Elaine *library trustee*

Saint Clair Shores
Woodford, Arthur MacKinnon *library director, historian*

Southfield
Cocozzoli, Gary Richard *library director*

Ypsilanti
†Gordon, Anitra *librarian*

MINNESOTA

Chisago City
Miller, Robert Carl *retired library director*

Collegeville
Haile, Getatchew *retired archivist, educator*

Duluth
Pearce, Donald Joslin *retired librarian*

Hopkins
Young, Margaret Labash *librarian, information consultant, editor*

Mankato
Descy, Don Edmond *library media technology educator, writer, editor*

Minneapolis
Asp, William George *librarian*
Johnson, Donald Clay *librarian, curator*
Johnson, Margaret Ann (Peggy) *library administrator*
Kukla, Edward Richard *rare books & special collections librarian*
Lougee, Wendy Pradt *library director*
†Mabry, Celia Elaine Hales *librarian*
Ostrem, Walter Martin *librarian, educator, consultant*
Shaughnessy, Thomas William *retired librarian*

Morris
†Dean, LeAnn Faye Lindquist *librarian*

Northfield
Hong, Howard Vincent *library administrator, philosophy educator, editor, translator*

Rochester
Homan, J. Michael *library administrator*
Key, Jack Dayton *librarian*
Nienow, Beth Marie *librarian*

Saint Paul
Brudvig, Glenn Lowell *retired library director*
Kane, Lucile M. *retired archivist, historian*
Wagner, Mary Margaret *library and information science educator*

Saint Peter
Haeuser, Michael John *library administrator*

Shakopee
Gouin, Warner Peter *information technology specialist*

Winona
Sullivan, Kathryn Ann *librarian, educator*

Zumbrota
Post, Diana Constance *retired librarian*

MISSISSIPPI

Alcorn State
Yu, May Huang *librarian, educator*

Brookhaven
Ledet, Henry Joseph *librarian*

Calhoun City
Macon, Myra Faye *retired library director*

Columbus
†Nawrocki, Susan Jean *librarian*
†Tousley, Rebecca Perkins *retired librarian*
Wheeley, Nancy Janine *librarian*

Jackson
Smith, Sharman Bridges *former state librarian*

Natchez
†McLemore, Joan Meadows *librarian, consultant*

Ocean Springs
Shaw, Joyce M. *librarian*

Pascagoula
†Smith, Janet *librarian*

Sunflower
Powell, Anice Carpenter *retired librarian*

MISSOURI

Albany
Noble, Cheryl A. *library director*

Bolivar
DeWeese, Eldonna Rose *librarian, editor*

Brentwood
†O'Neill, Kathryn J. *librarian, educator*

Canton
Howe, Sandra Jo *library director*

Chesterfield
Landram, Christina Louella *librarian*

Columbia
Alexander, Martha Sue *retired librarian*
Almony, Robert Allen, Jr., *librarian, businessman*
†Johnson, E. Diane *librarian*

Greenwood
†Zeller, Marilynn Kay *retired librarian*

Hannibal
†Andresen, Julie Ann Dothager *librarian*

Independence
Johnson, Niel Melvin *archivist, historian*

Jefferson City
Parker, Sara Ann *librarian, consultant*

Kansas City
†Bradbury, Daniel Joseph *library administrator*
Miller, William Charles *theological librarian, educator*
Sheldon, Ted Preston *library dean*

Lake Lotawana
Zobrist, Benedict Karl *library director, historian*

Maryville
†Murphy, Kathryn Louise *librarian, educator*

Parkville
Schultis, Gail Ann *library director*

Pleasant Valley
Nelson, Freda Nell Hein *librarian*

Portageville
Dial, Marshall Reece *library director*

Rolla
Stewart, James Andrew *librarian*

Saint Charles
†Reed, Warlene Patricia *retired librarian*

Saint Joseph
Schneider, Julia *library director*

Saint Louis
†Gilchrist, Donna Ann *librarian*
†Guenther, Charles John *librarian, writer*
Heiser, Walter Charles *librarian, priest, educator*
Holt, Glen Edward *library administrator*
Kohnen, Carol Ann *librarian*
Lauenstein, Ann Gail *librarian*
McDonald, Brenda Denise *librarian*
Recklein, Linda Sue *library administrator*
†Reilly, Catherine Herbert *librarian, educator*
Tierney, Catherine Marie *librarian*

Springfield
Busch, Annie *library director*
Pearson, Dana Bart *librarian*

Slawsky, Donna Susan *librarian, singer*
Sullivan, Larry Edward *librarian*
Swartz, Mark Evan *archivist*
Vilchez, Ricardo S. *library supervisor*

Ogdensburg
Franz, David Arthur *library director*

Old Westbury
†Goldstein, Leslie Deborah *library director*

Oneonta
Johnson, Richard David *retired librarian*
†Potter, Janet L. *university librarian, administrator*

Orchard Park
Greenwood, Audrey Gates *retired librarian*

Penfield
†Birkby, Paul Donald *library media specialist, consultant*

Piermont
Brechtel, Unda Jurka *library director*

Plattsburgh
†Ransom, Christina Roxane *librarian*

Port Washington
†Sandy, Catherine Ellen *librarian*

Potsdam
†Hebert, Marianne *librarian*

Poughkeepsie
Van Zanten, Frank Veldhuyzen *retired library system director*

Queens
Hobbs, Helen T.B. *librarian*

Queens Village
Heckman, Lucy T. *librarian*

Rexford
Nitecki, Joseph Zbigniew *librarian*

Richmond Hill
Hamroff, Michael Scott *archives executive*

Rochester
†Buff, Iva Moore *librarian, musicologist*
†Panz, Richard *library director*
Swanton, Susan Irene *retired library director*

Roslyn
†Lehrman, Emily Rosenstein *retired librarian*
†Siahpoosh, Farideh Tamaddon *librarian*

Saratoga Springs
Farley, John Joseph *library science educator emeritus*

Sayville
Edelman, Hendrik *library and information science educator*

Scarborough
Stigall, Phyllis Graham *retired librarian*

Schenectady
Mancuso, J(ohn) James *librarian*

Somers
Lane, David Oliver *retired librarian*

Staten Island
Auh, Yang John *librarian, educational administrator*
Black, Lawrence *librarian*
Mayer, Andrew Mark *librarian, journalist*

Stony Brook
Cook, Jeannine Salvo *library consultant*
Huang, Michael Bailou *librarian*

Syracuse
Abbott, George Lindell *librarian*
Coppola, Elaine Marie *librarian*
Luft, Eric v.d. *librarian, educator*
Stam, David Harry *librarian*

Tuckahoe
†Silk, Eleana S. *librarian*

Tuxedo Park
Friedman, Rodger *antiquarian bookseller, consultant*

Vails Gate
Fife, Betty H. *retired librarian*

Valhalla
Margoshes, Miriam Kagan *information specialist*

Valley Stream
†Eng, Mamie *librarian*

Wellsville
†Jacobs, Mary Sharron *librarian*

West Point
Watson, Georgianna *librarian*

White Plains
Manville, Stewart Roebling *archivist*
Scott-Williams, Wendy Lee *information technology specialist*

Williamsville
Cloudsley, Donald Hugh *library administrator*

NORTH CAROLINA

Asheville
Boyce, Emily Stewart *retired library and information science educator*

Boone
†Wise, Mintron Suzanne *librarian*

Cary
†Larson, Phyllis Shepherd *librarian*

Chapel Hill
Kilgour, Frederick Gridley *librarian, educator*
Moran, Barbara Burns *librarian, educator*
Pruett, James Worrell *librarian, musicologist*
†Strauss, Diane Carol Wheeler *librarian, educator, writer*

Charlotte
Cannon, Robert Eugene *library director*
†Johnston, Elaine Curry *librarian*
Sintz, Edward Francis *librarian*
Welch, Jeanie Maxine *librarian*

Clemmons
†Rawls, Martha Grogan (Molly Rawls) *librarian*

Cove City
Hawkins, Elinor Dixon (Mrs. Carroll Woodard Hawkins) *retired librarian*

Davidson
Jones, Arthur Edwin, Jr., *library administrator, English and American literature educator*
Park, Leland Madison *librarian*

Durham
Canada, Mary Whitfield *retired librarian*

Eden
Williams, Sue Darden *library director*

Elon
Bowman, Randall Hunter *reference and instruction librarian*

Greensboro
Carmichael, James Vinson, Jr., *library and information science educator*
Kovacs, Beatrice *library studies educator*
†Wright, Kieth Carter *librarian, educator*

Greenville
Hadden, Robert Lee *librarian*

Kings Mountain
Turner, Marguerite Rose Cowles *library administrator*

Murfreesboro
Muller, William Albert, III, *library director*

New Bern
Rosen, Wendy Lee *librarian*
White, Rhea Amelia *information scientist, consciousness researcher*

Oxford
†Dorton, Louise *library director*

Pembroke
Sexton, Jean Elizabeth *librarian*

Raleigh
Littleton, Isaac Thomas, III, *retired university library administrator, consultant*
Moore, Thomas Lloyd *librarian*
Russell, Jane Dexter *retired librarian*

Seymour Johnson AFB
Demark, Robin Kay *librarian*

Washington
Timour, John Arnold *retired librarian, medical bibliography and library science educator*

Wilmington
Oakley, Carolyn Cobb *library director, academic administrator*

NORTH DAKOTA

Bismarck
Ott, Doris Ann *librarian*

Mayville
Karaim, Betty June *retired librarian*

OHIO

Ada
Herr, Sharon Marie *librarian*

Akron
Rebenack, John Henry *retired librarian*

Alliance
Clem, Harriet Frances *library director*

Bluffton
Dudley, Durand Stowell *librarian*

Bowerston
Spencer, Dawn Joyce *librarian, educator*

Bowling Green
Singer, Carol Ann *librarian, researcher*

Brecksville
†Tesmer, Nancy Ann Stutler *retired librarian*

Cadiz
Thompson, Sandra Lee *library administrator*

Canton
†Kilcullen, Maureen *librarian, educator*

Cincinnati
†Abate, Anne Katherine *librarian, consultant, educator*
†Bellingham, Roger Gerry *librian, researcher, consultant*
†Bestehorn, Ute Wiltrud *retired librarian*
Bluestein, Barbara Ann *librarian*
Brestel, Mary Beth *librarian*
Everett, Karen Joan *retired librarian, genealogy educator*
Everson, Jean Watkins Dolores *librarian media technical assistant, educator*
Proffitt, Kevin *archivist*
Schutzius, Lucy Jean *retired librarian*
Wellington, Jean Susorney *librarian*
Zafren, Herbert Cecil *librarian, educator*

Cleveland
Abid, Ann B. *art librarian*
Gardner, Richard Kent *retired librarian, educator, consultant*
†Thornton, Glenda Ann *librarian*

Columbus
Branscomb, Lewis Capers, Jr., *librarian, educator*
†Gilmore, Joanne R. *librarian*
†Klotz, Edna May *retired librarian*
†Ludlum, Mary Ellen *librarian*
Meredith, Meri Hill *reference librarian, educator*
†Olson, Carol Ann *librarian*
Olson, Ray Alan *librarian*
Sawyers, Elizabeth Joan *librarian, administrator*
Studer, William Joseph *library educator*

Dayton
Klinck, Cynthia Anne *library director*
†Snively, Ann Wilson *librarian, researcher*
†Wentz, Charlotte Marie *retired librarian*
Wyllie, Stanley Clarke *retired librarian*

Delaware
Schlichting, Catherine Fletcher Nicholson *librarian, educator*

Dublin
Baker, Mary Evelyn *retired librarian*
†Meyer, Betty Jane *former librarian*

East Cleveland
†Linderman, Eric Graham *librarian*

East Palestine
Rohrbaugh, Lisa Anne *librarian*

Eaton
Kendall, Susan Haines *library director*

Elida
†Dicke, Candice Edwards *library educator*

Elmore
Huizenga, Georgiana R. *public library director, storyteller*

Elyria
Bonnell-Mihalis, Pamela Gay *library director*

Fairview Park
Bellamy, John Stark, II, *librarian*

Hubbard
Trucksis, Theresa A. *retired library director*

Hudson
Antonucci, Ron *librarian, editor*

Kenton
Petty, Sue Wright *library director*

Lucasville
†Crotty, Ladonna Deane *librarian*

Lyndhurst
Packer, Diana *retired reference librarian*

Middleburg Heights
Maciuszko, Kathleen Lynn *librarian, educator*

Middletown
Schaefer, Patricia Ann *retired librarian*

Northfield
†Sleeman, Mary (Mrs. John Paul Sleeman) *retired librarian*

Oberlin
English, Ray *library administrator*
Greenberg, Eva Mueller *librarian*

Oxford
Sessions, Judith Ann *librarian, university library dean*

Pemberville
King, Laura Jane *librarian, genealogist*

Pleasant Hill
†Kinney, Virginia Lee *librarian, educator*

Shaker Hts
†Thomas, Rebecca Lynne *librarian, writer*

Steubenville
Hall, Alan Craig *library director*

Tiffin
Hillmer, Margaret Patricia *library director*

Toledo
†Wolter, Virginia Lynn *librarian*

Wickliffe
Fisher, Nancy DeButts *library director*

Wilberforce
Mulhern, Jean Kay *academic library director, consultant*

Wooster
Hickey, Damon Douglas *library director*

Youngstown
Tyson, Edith Slosson *retired librarian, writer*

OKLAHOMA

Hodgen
Brower, Janice Kathleen *library technician*

Midwest City
†McDowell, Cassandra *multi-media specialist*

Norman
Carroll, Frances Laverne *librarian, educator*
Lester, June *library information studies educator*
†Meacham, Mary *science librarian*
Sherman, Mary Angus *public library administrator*
Wilhite, Jeffrey Mark *librarian, educator*

Oklahoma City
Beleu, Steve (Dan Beleu) *librarian*
†Clark, Robert Lloyd, Jr., *librarian*
†King, Barbara Sue *librarian*

Tulsa
Fisk, Francine Joan *librarian*

Welling
Varner, Joyce Ehrhardt *retired librarian*

OREGON

Albany
†White, Diane O'Donnell *retired librarian*

Ashland
Gaulke, Mary Florence *library administrator*

Astoria
Foster, Michael William *librarian*

Beaverton
Pond, Patricia Brown *library science educator, university administrator*

Corvallis
Chau, May Ying *librarian, educator*
Landers, Teresa Price *librarian*
Main, Michael Dee *information developer*

Eugene
Edwards, Ralph M. *librarian*
Hildebrand, Carol Ilene *retired librarian*
Landrum, Frank Woolson *library/media educator*

Pendleton
†Hoeft, Marjorie Claire *librarian*

Portland
†Baughman, Pauline Clara *librarian*
Browne, Joseph Peter *retired librarian*
Eshelman, William Robert *librarian, editor*
Morgan, James Earl *librarian, administrator*

Roseburg
†Cook, Sybilla Avery *school library consultant*

Salem
Kenyon, Carleton Weller *librarian*
Oberg, Larry Reynold *librarian*
Perez, Ernest R. *librarian*
Turnbaugh, Roy Carroll *archivist*

Seaside
Bishop, Virginia Wakeman *retired librarian and humanities educator, small business owner*

Wilsonville
†Humphrey, Lois Ellen *librarian*

PENNSYLVANIA

Allentown
Flautz, Nancy A. *librarian*
Sacks, Patricia Ann *librarian, consultant*
Wagner, Darla L. *librarian*

Altoona
Kinney, Janis Marie *librarian, consultant, storyteller*

Annville
†Paustian, Paul Robert *library director*

Audubon
Tanis, James Robert *library director, history educator, clergyman*

Beaver Falls
Miller, Albert Jay *retired library and information sciences director*

Berwyn
†Langford, Linda Kosmin *library consultant*

Bethlehem
†Collette, Maria D. *librarian*

Bloomsburg
Vann, John Daniel, III, *library consultant, historian*

Brockway
†Emmer, Barbara Louise *librarian, consultant*

Bryn Mawr
Fletcher, Marjorie Amos *librarian*

Butler
†Day, Margaret Ann *research librarian, information specialist*
†Donaldson, Loretta Marie *retired librarian*

Carlisle
McKinzie, James S. *librarian*
†Song, Yongyi *librarian*

Chester
Newell, Katherine Claiborne *librarian*

Clarion
Miller, Andrea Lynn *library science educator*

Corsica
†Elza, Betty Ann *retired librarian*

Cranberry Township
Lorenz, John George *librarian, consultant*

Doylestown
Waite, Frances W. *librarian, professional genealogist*
Wolfinger, Audrey Jane *retired librarian*

Du Bois
Williams, Kathryn Blake *retired librarian*

Glenshaw
Yates, Diane Greiner *librarian*

Greensburg
Duck, Patricia Mary *librarian*

Harrisburg
Emerick, John L. *library director*

Kingsley
McNabb, Corrine Radtke *librarian*

Kutztown
†Mack, Sara Rohrbach *librarian, educator*

Lancaster
Zeager, Lloyd *librarian*

Langhorne
†Black, Dorothy Mary *librarian*
FitzGerald, Dorothy Stickle *librarian*

Lebanon
Bard, Judy Kay *librarian*

Lock Haven
Chang, Shirley Lin (Hsiu-Chu Chang) *librarian, educator*

Mansfield
†Donahue, Martha *librarian, educator, retired*

Mc Murray
Celento, Florence M. *librarian*

Meadville
†Crowe, Virginia Mary *retired librarian*

Monroeville
†Kennedy, Kathy Kay *library director*

New Holland
Fanus, Pauline Rife *librarian*

Oxford
Hostert, Leona Teressa *research librarian*

Philadelphia
Arnold, Lee *library director, archivist*
Azzolina, David Sean *librarian*
Cole, C. Suzanne *librarian*
Gendron, Michèle Marguerite Madeleine *librarian*
Levitt, Martin Lee *library administrator, historian*
†Morman, Edward Terry *librarian, medical historian*
†Pilvin, Barbara Jeanne *librarian*
†Piola, Erika G. *archivist*
†Wright, Barbara Clare *business librarian*

Pittsburgh
Hodge, Patricia Andrea *archivist, consultant*
Josey, E(lonnie) J(Unius) *librarian, educator, former state administrator*
Minnigh, Joel Douglas *library director*
Tancin, Charlotte Ann *librarian*
Ulrich, Lucinda Dykes *librarian*
Willard, Louis Charles *librarian*
Wohleber, Lynne Farr *archivist, librarian*
Yourison, Karola Maria *librarian services professional*

Plymouth
†Castner, Deborah A. *librarian*

Punxsutawney
Dinsmore, Roberta Joan Maier *library director*

Quarryville
†Weston, Janice Leah Colmer *librarian*

Reading
†Wentzel, Judith Ann *librarian*

Scranton
Brandreth, Elizabeth Anne *library director*

Somerset
†Kline, Eva Jane *library services administrator, educator*

Springfield
†Austin, Susan Rebecca *librarian, writer, storyteller*

Topton
Knight, Cheryl DuBois *library director*

University Park
Brockman, William S. *librarian*
Eaton, Nancy Ruth Linton *librarian, university dean*
Joyce, William Leonard *librarian*
†MacEwan, Bonnie *librarian*

Villanova
Olsen, Judith Johnson *reference librarian*

Wayne
Garrison, Guy Grady *librarian, educator*

Wilkes Barre
Mech, Terrence Francis *library director*

Wyomissing
Doherty, Edmond John *retired librarian*

Yardley
Du Bois, Paul Zinkhan *library consultant, book dealer*
Soultoukis, Donna Zoccola *library director*

RHODE ISLAND

Bristol
Deekle, Peter Van *library director*
†McMullen, Susan Taylor *librarian*

Coventry
†Schweinsburg, Jane Duberg *librarian*

Jamestown
Logan, Nancy Allen *library media specialist*

Kingston
Caldwell, Naomi Rachel *library media specialist, educator*
Devin, Robin B. *librarian, anthropologist*
Gilton, Donna Louise *library and information scientist, educator*
†Keefe, Margaret Johnson *librarian*

Middletown
†Ottaviano, Doris Baginski *librarian*

Newport
Schnare, Robert Edey, Jr., *library director, educator*

Providence
Hamerly, Michael T. *librarian, historian*
†Hunt, Cheryl Ruth *librarian*
Kramer, Ilse Elisabeth *rare book bibliographer*

Warwick
Banick, Cheryl R. *librarian*
Charette, Sharon Juliette *library administrator*

SOUTH CAROLINA

Aiken
†Isaacs-Bright, Susan Virginia Kirkpatrick *research librarian, public speaker, advocate*

Beaufort
†Moussatos, Martha Ann Tyree *librarian*

Bluffton
†Cann, Sharon Lee *retired health science librarian*

Charleston
Basler, Thomas G. *librarian, administrator, educator*
†Herbert, Teri Lynn *librarian*

Clemson
Boykin, Joseph Floyd, Jr., *librarian*

Clinton
†Meeks, Mary Janice *librarian*

Columbia
Duggan, Carol Cook *research director*
†Ehrhardt, Margaret Wright *retired librarian*
Griffin, Mary Frances *retired library media consultant*
Helsley, Alexia Jones *archivist*
Johnson, James Bek, Jr., *library director*
†Mazur, Marjorie Akers *retired librarian*
Paulson-Crawford, Carol *conservator, educator*
Rawlinson, Helen Ann *librarian*
Toombs, Kenneth Eldridge *librarian*
Walling, Linda Lucas *librarian, educator*
Warren, Charles David *library administrator*
Willis, Paul Allen *librarian*
Zimmerman, Nancy Picciano *library science educator*

Eastover
†Jones, Shirley Green *librarian*

Hardeeville
Kadar, Karin Patricia *librarian*

Kershaw
Mackey, Margaret Emmie *library media specialist*

Laurens
Cooper, William Copeland *public library director*

Orangeburg
Byers, Keith Thomas *librarian, educator*
Caldwell, Rossie Juanita Brower *retired library service educator*

Rock Hill
Herring, Mark Youngblood *librarian, university dean*

Spartanburg
Anderson, Frank J(ohn) *retired librarian*

Summerville
†O'Brien, Doris J. *librarian*

Walhalla
†Andrus, Susan Joyce *librarian*

SOUTH DAKOTA

Brookings
Graper, Mary Caspers *librarian*
Landau, Elvita Ann *library director*
Marquardt, Steve Robert *library director*

Pierre
Miller, Suzanne Marie *state librarian*

Sioux Falls
Dertien, James LeRoy *librarian*
Thompson, Ronelle Kay Hildebrandt *library director*

TENNESSEE

Chattanooga
Clapp, David Foster *library administrator*

Clarksville
Hester, Bruce Edward *library media specialist, lay worker*

Greeneville
Smith, Myron John, Jr., *librarian, author*

Hendersonville
†Jantz, Cynthia Marie *librarian*

Jonesborough
Kozsuch, Mildred Jeannette *librarian, archivist*

Kingsport
Leonard, Bobbi Bowers Range *educator, librarian*

Knoxville
Albright, Kendra Suzanne *educator*
Cottrell, Jeannette Elizabeth *retired librarian*
†Drumheller, Janet Louise *librarian*
†Earl, Martha Frances *librarian, researcher*
†Felder-Hoehne, Felicia Harris *librarian*
†Matlock, Elizabeth Monger *librarian*

Lawrenceburg
†Pope, Dorothy Mae *librarian*

Lebanon
†Burns, George Franklin *archivist, retired language educator*

Maryville
Tabor, Curtis Harold, Jr., *librarian, minister*

Memphis
Drescher, Judith Altman *library director*
Pourciau, Lester John, Jr., *retired librarian*
†Tipton, Nathan Glen *librarian*
Wallis, Carlton Lamar *librarian*

Murfreesboro
Marshall, John David *retired librarian, author*

Nashville
Gleaves, Edwin Sheffield *librarian*
†Hudgens, Ann Young *librarian, counselor*
†Letson, Ruth Stafford *librarian*
†Lyle, Virginia Reavis *retired archivist, genealogist*
Shockley, Ann Allen *librarian, writer*
Stewart, David Marshall *librarian*
Wilson, Carolyn Taylor *librarian*

Oak Ridge
†Ball, Jacqueline Snyder *librarian, educator*

Paris
McNutt, Gwyn Bellamy *archivist*

Sewanee
Camp, Thomas Edward *retired librarian*
Dunkly, James Warren *theological librarian*
Watson, Gail H. *librarian*

Sparta
Young, Olivia Knowles *retired librarian*

Talbott
†Collins, Fleda Mae *librarian*

TEXAS

Abilene
†Sickbert, Murl Julius, Jr., *music librarian, musicologist*
Specht, Alice Wilson *university libraries dean*
Tucker, John Mark *librarian, educator*

Aledo
Rowe, Sheryl Ann *librarian*

Austin
Billings, Harold Wayne *library director, editor*
†Bingham, Ouita Hyams *librarian*
Covington, Veronica Pro *librarian, educator*
Davis, Donald Gordon, Jr., *librarian, educator, historian*
Fox, Beth Wheeler *library director*

Gracy, David Bergen, II, *archivist, information science educator, writer*
†Howard, Carol Spencer *librarian, journalist*
Jackson, Eugene Bernard *librarian, educator*
Jackson, William Vernon *library science and Latin American studies educator*
Leonhardt, Thomas Wilburn *librarian, library director*
Morrow, Sandra Kay *librarian*
Oram, Robert W. *library administrator*
Payne, John Ross *rare books, archives and photographs appraisal consulting company executive, library science educator*
Rascoe, Paul Stephen *librarian, researcher*
Smith, Dorothy Brand *retired librarian*

Beaumont
Ciallella, Emil Anthony *library director, consultant*

Bellaire
Mote, Marie Therese *reference librarian*

Brownwood
Roby, Annie Beth Brian *librarian*
†Weeks, Patsy Ann Landry *librarian, educator*

Bryan
Ezzell, Catherine *librarian*

Cedar Hill
Hickman, Traphene Parramore *library director, storyteller, library and library building consultant*

Cedar Park
Lam, Pauline Poha *library director*

Channing
Brian, Mary H. *librarian*

Coldspring
Bunch, Robert Craig *librarian*

College Station
†De Petro, Thomas Gerard *librarian, educator*

Corpus Christi
Erwin, Linda McIntosh *librarian, consultant*

Corsicana
Roberts, Nancy Mize *retired librarian, composer, pianist*

Dallas
†Bellavance, Maria Isabel *librarian*
Bockstruck, Lloyd DeWitt *librarian*
Howell, Bradley Sue *librarian*
Ibach, Robert Daniel, Jr., *library director*
†Reed, Kristine Lynn *librarian*
Salazar, Ramiro S. *library administrator*
†Sherrod, Danny Troy *library and information scientist, writer*
Stamelos, Ellen Anne *librarian*
†Turner, Sara Weidner *librarian*
Young, Julia Anne *librarian, elementary education educator*

Denton
Poole, Eva Duraine *librarian*
†Simpson, Carol Mann *librarian, consultant, editor*
†Snapp, Elizabeth *librarian, educator*

El Paso
†Freeman, Mary Anna *librarian*
Gardner, Kerry Ann *librarian*
Strait, Viola Edwina Washington *librarian*

Fort Davis
Gadberry, Vicki Lynn Himes *librarian*

Fort Worth
Allmand, Linda F(aith) *retired library director*
Ard, Harold Jacob *library administrator*
de Tonnancour, Paul Roger Godefroy *library administrator*
Li, Richard T. *retired library director, secondary school educator*
Miller, Carol Lynn *librarian*
Sikes, Mary Taggart *librarian*

Georgetown
Fountain, Joanna Fraser *library consultant, business owner*
Ramsey, Margie *librarian*

Grand Prairie
†Ritterhouse, Kathy Lee *librarian*

Houston
Henington, David Mead *library director*
Hornak, Anna Frances *library administrator*
†Lowman, Sara Allison *library director*
†Porter, Exa Lynn *librarian*
Radoff, Leonard Irving *librarian, consultant*
Russell, John Francis *retired librarian*
Scarbrough, Sara Eunice *librarian, archivist, consultant*
Strommer, Anne Elizabeth Rivard *retired librarian*
Suter, Jon Michael *academic library director, educator*
†Weathers, Barbara Hiller *librarian*
Witmer, John Richard *librarian*

Irving
†Whisennand, Cynthia Simmons *librarian*

Kingsville
†Beach, Regina Lee *librarian*

Longview
†Richardson, Patricia Kay *librarian*

Lubbock
†Good, Stephen Boyd *librarian*

Wood, Richard Courtney *library director, educator*

Lufkin
Harmon, Jacqueline Baas *librarian, infosystems specialist*

Mansfield
Icenhower, Della Maude *retired school librarian*

Marshall
Magrill, Rose Mary *library director*

Mc Camey
Farley, Gail Conley *retired librarian*

McAllen
†Liu, Agnete Mei-cheng *librarian*

Mcallen
McGee, William Howard John *librarian, administrator*

Montgomery
Smith, John Brewster *library administrator*

Odessa
†Dry, Marsha G. *librarian*

Ozona
†York, Sherry White *librarian*

Palestine
Williams, Franklin Cadmus, Jr., *bibliographer*

Round Rock
Ricklefs, Dale Lynne *library director*

San Angelo
Chatfield, Mary Van Abshoven *librarian*
†Kroll, Connie Rae *librarian, information services consultant*

San Antonio
Bowden, Virginia Massey *librarian*
Brewster, Olive Nesbitt *retired librarian*
†Flynn, Norma Jean *librarian*
Frisch, Paul Andrew *librarian*
Gruenbeck, Laurie *librarian*
†Hood, Sandra Dale *librarian*
Jones, Daniel Hare *librarian, consultant*
Kozuch, Julianna Bernadette *librarian, educator*
Lussky, Warren Alfred *librarian, educator, consultant*
†Maroscher, Betty Jean *librarian*
Nance, Betty Love *librarian*
†Odom, Marjorie Mildred Morgan *retired librarian*
Ridder, Linda Gayle *librarian*
†Sylvia, Margaret Joost *librarian*
Wallace, James Oldham *retired librarian*

San Benito
Cavazos, Ana A. *librarian*

Sherman
Hardesty, Larry Lynn *librarian*

Sweetwater
†Taylor, Martha Sue *librarian*

Texas City
Moncla, Carolyn Sue *library director*

Tyler
Albertson, Christopher Adam *librarian*
Green, Douglas Alvin *retired library director*

Van Alstyne
Hazelton, Juanita Louise *librarian*

Weimar
Rocha, Osbelia Maria Juarez *librarian, assistant principal*

UTAH

Orem
Hall, Blaine Hill *retired librarian*

Provo
Jensen, Richard Dennis *librarian*
Smith, Nathan McKay *library and information sciences educator*

Salt Lake City
Buttars, Gerald Anderson *librarian*
Kalana, David Sterling *director of information systems*
Kraus, Peter Leo *librarian, educator*
Mogren, Paul Andrew *librarian*
Owen, Amy *library director*

VERMONT

Johnson
Farara, Joseph Montgomery *library director*

VIRGINIA

Alexandria
Berger, Patricia Wilson *retired librarian*
Brooks, Philip Coolidge, Jr., *archives, museum official*
Cross, Dorothy Abigail *retired librarian*
†Gernand, Bradley Elton *library manager, archivist*
†Gray, Dorothy Louise Allman Pollet *librarian*
O'Brien, Patrick Michael *library administrator*

Amelia Court House
Smith, Adeline Mercer *retired librarian*

Arlington
†Jackson, Nancy Gertrude *retired federal government librarian*

Assawoman
Holley, Pamela Spencer *retired librarian*

Bland
†Newberry, Elizabeth Guthrie *librarian, educator*

Castleton
Hahn, James Maglorie *former librarian, farmer*

Charlottesville
Berkeley, Edmund, Jr., *retired archivist, educator*
Berkeley, Francis Lewis, Jr., *retired archivist*
Frantz, Ray William, Jr., *retired librarian*
Frieden, Charles Leroy *university library administrator*
Stubbs, Kendon Lee *librarian*

Chesapeake
Stillman, Margaret D. *library director*

Danville
†Allmond, Coral Lee *librarian*
†Fountain, Clara Garrett *archivist, librarian*

Dublin
†Cutlip, Susie Saunders *librarian*

Dumfries
Gaudet, Jean Ann *retired librarian, educator*

Falls Church
†Yoshimura, Yoshiko *librarian*

Farmville
Boyer, Calvin James *librarian*

Fort Belvoir
Ramsey, Donna Elaine *librarian*

Franklin
Culpepper, Jo Long *librarian*

Harrisonburg
Gill, Gerald Lawson *librarian*
Swope, Frances Alderson *retired librarian*

Heathsville
†Thompson, Alice Roxana (Ann Thompson) *labor economist*

Hudgins
Story, Martha vanBeuren *retired librarian*

Leesburg
†Fall, Dorothy Eleanor *librarian*

Lexington
Gaines, James Edwin, Jr., *retired librarian*
Krantz, Linda Law *librarian*
†Leach, Maurice Derby, Jr., *librarian, educator*

Newport News
†Boykin, Amy Williams *librarian*

Norfolk
Shaw, Michael Evan *librarian*

Poquoson
Tai, Elizabeth Shi-Jue Lee *library director*

Rapidan
Grimm, Ben Emmet *former library director and consultant*

Richmond
Burner, Clara Miller *librarian*
Gwin, James Ellsworth *librarian*
Treadway, Sandra Gioia *library director*

Roanoke
†Cirasunda, Esther Bond *librarian*

Springfield
†Doran, Doris Jeanne *librarian*

Staunton
†Arnold, Ruth Southgate *librarian*

Stephens City
Stephenson, Richard Walter *librarian, historian, geographer*

Virginia Beach
Sims, Martha J. *library director*

Williamsburg
†Gray, Sarah Virginia *retired librarian*
Moorman, John A. *librarian*

Woodbridge
Andrews, Michael William *librarian, information specialist*

WASHINGTON

Centralia
Meany, Philip Augustus *library director*

Everett
†Dale, Deborah Ann *library technician, poet*

Maple Valley
Willson, David Allen *retired reference librarian, writer*

Olympia
†Beeler, Margery D. *librarian*
Hutchins, Diane Elizabeth Rider *librarian*
Kells, Kari Joy *indexer, librarian*
Zussy, Nancy Louise *librarian*

Port Townsend
Hiatt, Peter *retired librarian studies educator*
†Long, Karen Draut *librarian*
†Wallin, Madge Marie *retired librarian, musician*

Pullman
Chmelir, Lynn Kay *academic librarian*
†Kaag, Cynthia Stewart *library and information scientist, educator, librarian*
Zlatos, Christy *librarian*

Seattle
Blase, Nancy Gross *librarian*
Boylan, Merle Nelson *librarian, educator*
Fidel, Raya *library science educator*
†Greggs, Elizabeth May Bushnell (Mrs. Raymond John Greggs) *retired librarian*
Jacobs, Deborah L. *librarian*
Janes, Joseph W. *library and information science educator*
†Jennerich, Elaine *librarian*
Kruse, Paul Robert *retired librarian, educator*
Pearl, Nancy Linn *librarian*
†Stroup, Elizabeth Faye *librarian*

Sequim
†Lidgate, Doreen Wanda *retired librarian*

Spokane
Bender, Betty Wion *librarian*
†Murray, James Michael *librarian, law librarian, legal educator, lawyer*
Wirt, Michael James *library director*

Tacoma
Crisman, Mary Frances Borden *librarian*

Walla Walla
Yaple, Henry Mack *librarian*

WEST VIRGINIA

Charleston
†Schott, Michael J. *library director*

Glenville
Tubesing, Richard Lee *library director*

Harpers Ferry
†Heriot, Ruthanne *librarian*

Morgantown
Pyles, Rodney Allen *archivist, county official*

Shepherdstown
Elliott, Jean Ann *librarian emeritus*

Weirton
†Fundis, Lois Aleta *librarian*

WISCONSIN

Appleton
Richards, Susan Lynne *library director*

Brillion
Kjelstrup, Cheryl Ann *librarian*

Eau Claire
Tiefel, Virginia May *librarian*

Franklin
Roark, Barbara Ann *librarian*

Horicon
†Bohn, Monica J. *multi-media specialist, educator*

Kenosha
†Kaye, Dina Lynn *librarian*
†Kazell, Doris Lillian *librarian*

Kohler
†Potter, Calvin J. *retired library director*

La Crosse
Polodna, David Lee *library director*

Madison
†Blankenburg, Julie J. *librarian*
Bunge, Charles Albert *library science educator*
†Christensen, Marguerite Alice *librarian*
Kim, Kyung-Sun *library and information scientist, educator*
Korenic, Lynette Marie *librarian*
†Scherdin, Mary Jane Liskovec *librarian, information professional, researcher*

Menomonie
Lueder, Dianne Carol *library director*

Milwaukee
Blasinski, Clare Marie *librarian*
Huston, Kathleen Marie *library administrator*
†Lockett, Sandra Anita Johnson Bokamba *librarian*
Valance, Marsha Jeanne *library director, story teller*

Pine River
†Sallee, Lynn Kant *librarian*

Portage
Jensen, Hans William *library director*

Racine
†MacPhail, Jessica Holman Whitehead *librarian*

Richland Center
Gollata, James Anthony *library director, educator*

River Falls
†Montgomery, Karen E. *library and information scientist*

Thiensville
Roselle, William Charles *librarian*

Wausau
†Eldred, Heather Ann *librarian*

WYOMING

Casper
Cottam, Keith M. *librarian, educator, administrator*

Cheyenne
Boughton, Lesley D. *library director*
Rounds, Linnea Paula *library administrator*

TERRITORIES OF THE UNITED STATES

PUERTO RICO

Carolina
†González Echevarria, Amelia L. *librarian, counselor*

Mayaguez
Rodriguez, Grisell *librarian, educator*

MILITARY ADDRESSES OF THE UNITED STATES

EUROPE

Apo
†Sokolowski, Denise Georgia *librarian, university administrator, educator*
Wakefield, Marie Annette *librarian*

CANADA

ALBERTA

Calgary
MacDonald, Alan Hugh *librarian, university administrator*

Lethbridge
†Rand, Duncan Dawson *librarian, retired*

BRITISH COLUMBIA

North Vancouver
†Ellis, Sarah Elizabeth *librarian*

Vancouver
Aalto, Madeleine *library director*
Piternick, Anne Brearley *librarian, educator*
Rothstein, Samuel *librarian, educator*

Victoria
Richards, Vincent Philip Haslewood *retired librarian*

NOVA SCOTIA

Bedford
Birdsall, William Forest *retired librarian*

Dartmouth
Horrocks, Norman *library and information scientist, educator, editor*

Halifax
Dykstra Lynch, Mary Elizabeth *library and information science educator*

ONTARIO

Guelph
Land, Reginald Brian *library administrator*

Hamilton
†Brackney, William Henry *archivist, historian*

Mississauga
Ryan, Noel *librarian, consultant*

Ottawa
Scott, Marianne Florence *retired librarian, educator*
Sylvestre, Jean Guy *former national librarian*
Wallot, Jean-Pierre *archivist, historian*

Scarborough
Bassnett, Peter James *retired librarian*

Toronto
Bryant, Josephine Harriet *library executive*
Moore, Carole Irene *librarian*
Packer, Katherine Helen *retired library educator*

QUEBEC

Laval
†Adrian, Donna Jean *retired librarian*

Montreal
Large, John Andrew *library and information service educator*
Panneton, Jacques *librarian*

Wilson, C. Daniel, Jr., *library director*
Wilson, Patricia Potter *library science and reading educator, educational and library consultant*
Wingate, Bettye Faye *librarian, educator*
Wolf, Cynthia Tribelhorn *librarian, library educator*
Woodrum, Patricia Ann *librarian*
Woods, Phyllis Michalik *librarian*
Wortman, William Allen *librarian*
Wynar, Bohdan Stephen *librarian, writer, editor*
Zoelle, Andrea Marie *reference librarian*

HUMANITIES: MUSEUMS

UNITED STATES

ALABAMA

Mc Calla
Kes, Vicki Paulette *museum director*

Mobile
Richelson, Paul William *curator*

Montgomery
Johnson, Mark Matthew *museum administrator*

ARIZONA

Flagstaff
Wolf, Arthur Henry *museum administrator*

Phoenix
Ballinger, James K. *art museum executive*

Portal
Zweifel, Richard George *curator*

Tempe
Hoza, Steven Paul *museum curator, consultant, educator, conservator*

Tucson
Daley, Richard Halbert *museum director*
King, James Edward *retired museum director, consultant*

ARKANSAS

Fayetteville
Barlow, Catherine Maurice *curator*

Little Rock
DuBois, Alan Beekman *art museum curator*
Quick, Edward Raymond *museum director, educator, curator*

CALIFORNIA

Berkeley
Baas, Jacquelynn *museum consultant, art historian*
Benedict, Burton *retired museum director, anthropology educator*
†Consey, Kevin Edward *museum administrator*
Day, Lucille Lang *museum administrator, educator, writer*

Bodega Bay
Cohen, Daniel Morris *museum administrator, marine biology researcher*

Caliente
de Fonville, Paul Bliss *monument and library administrator*

Carmel Valley
Wolfe, Maurice Raymond *retired museum director, educator*

Cedar Ridge
Adams, Margaret Bernice *retired museum official*

Costa Mesa
Labbe, Armand Joseph *curator, anthropologist*

La Jolla
Beebe, Mary Livingstone *curator*
Davies, Hugh Marlais *museum director*

Laguna Beach
Solon, Deborah Epstein *curator*

Long Beach
Glenn, Constance White *art museum director, educator, consultant*
Nelson, Harold Bernhard *museum director*

Los Angeles
†Barron, Stephanie *curator*
Byrnes, James Bernard *museum director, consultant*
Hopkins, Henry Tyler *museum director, art educator*
Mulryan, Lenore Hoag *art curator, author*
Powell, James Lawrence *museum director*
Rich, Andrea Louise *museum administrator*
†Strick, Jeremy *curator*
Walsh, John *museum director*

Malibu
Zakian, Michael *museum director*

Mill Valley
†Fuller, Glenn R. *park ranger*

Moraga
Silcox, Frances Eleanor *museum and exhibits planning consultant*

Oakland
Power, Dennis Michael *museum director*

Oxnard
Bacin, Mark Stephen *museum director, retired naval officer*

Pacific Grove
Bailey, Stephen Fairchild *museum director and curator, ornithologist*

Rancho Palos Verdes
Yassin, Robert Alan *museum administrator, curator*

Redding
Peterson, Robyn Gayle *museum curator*

Redlands
Griesemer, Allan David *retired museum director*

San Carlos
Schumacher, Henry Jerold *museum administrator, former career officer, business executive*

San Diego
Hager, Michael W. *museum director*
Petersen, Martin Eugene *curator*

San Francisco
Leviton, Alan Edward *curator*
†O'Neill, Brian *national recreation area administrator*
Parker, Harry S., III, *museum director*
Ross, David A. *art museum director*
Sano, Emily Joy *museum director*

San Marino
Blodgett, Peter John *curator*

Santa Barbara
Karpeles, David *museum director*
Kelm, Bonnie G. *art museum director, educator*

Santa Monica
Gabriel, Jeanette Hanisee *curator, art historian*

Stanford
Seligman, Thomas Knowles *museum administrator*

Stockton
Hepper, Iona Lydia *gallery owner, retired*

Venice
Davis, Kimberly Brooke *art gallery director*

Watsonville
Hernandez, Jo Farb *music director, consultant*

COLORADO

Boulder
Danilov, Victor Joseph *museum management program director, consultant, author, educator*

Colorado Springs
LeMieux, Linda Dailey *museum director*

Cripple Creek
Swanson, Erik Christian *museum director*

Denver
Decatur, Raylene *museum director*
Maytham, Thomas Northrup *art and museum consultant*
Sharp, Lewis I. *museum director*

Fort Collins
†Ketcham, Sally Ann *historic site staff member, consultant*

CONNECTICUT

New Haven
Burger, Richard L. *museum director*
Hickey, Leo J(oseph) *museum curator, educator*
Meyers, Amy *museum director*
Yellis, Kenneth *museum administrator*

New Milford
Stalter, Richard Alan *museum administrator*

North Granby
Riley, Christopher Sibley *museum supervisor*

Pawcatuck
Gualtieri, Joseph Peter *museum director*

Washington
Phillips, Laughlin *art museum chairman emeritus, former magazine editor*

West Hartford
Faude, Wilson Hinsdale *museum director, consultant*

Weston
Daniel, James *curator, business executive, writer, former editor,*
Oliver, Sandra *art dealer, painter*

DELAWARE

Wilmington
Blankenship, Roy *conservator, artist, writer*

DISTRICT OF COLUMBIA

Washington
†Allman, William G. *curator*
Archambault, JoAllyn *museum administrator, anthropologist*
Blair, Thomas Delano *museum administrator*
Bloomfield, Sara J. *museum director*
Bretzfelder, Deborah May *retired museum staff member*
Buhler, Leslie Lynn *museum director*
†Canney, Donald Ladd *museum administrator, historian, writer*
Carr, Carolyn Kinder *deputy director and chief curator*
Coddington, Jonathan A. *curator, research scientist*
Dailey, John Revell *museum administrator, former career officer*
Demetrion, James Thomas *art museum director*
Duckworth, Walter Donald *museum executive, entomologist*
Erwin, Douglas Hamilton *museum director, paleobiologist*
Evelyn, Douglas Everett *museum director*
Fauntleroy, Carma Cecil *arts administration executive*
Fitzhugh, William *curator*
Gates, Jay Rodney *museum director*
Grasselli, Margaret Morgan *curator*
Hand, John Oliver *museum curator*
Hoffmann, Robert Shaw *museum director, educator*
Ketchum, James Roe *curator*
Kornicker, Louis Sampson *museum curator*
Kurin, Richard *museum program director*
Lang, Brian Joseph *museum administrator*
Levy, David Corcos *museum director*
Lowe, Harry *museum director*
Neufeld, Michael John *curator, historian*
Selin, Nina Evvie *philanthropist*
Shapiro, Paul Arnold *museum director*
Shestack, Alan *museum administrator*
†Small, Lawrence M. *museum executive*
Stevenson, Frances Kellogg *museum program director*
Stevenson, Nancy Nelson *museum executive*
Ucko, David Alan *museum consultant*
Weil, Stephen Edward *retired museum official*
West, W. Richard *museum director*
Withuhn, William Lawrence *museum curator, railroad economics and management consultant*
Wolanin, Barbara Ann Boese *art curator, art historian*

FLORIDA

Daytona Beach
Libby, Gary Russell *museum director emeritus, writer*

Gainesville
Dickinson, Joshua Clifton, Jr., *museum director, educator*
†Emery, Kitty Frances *curator, educator*
Willumson, Glenn Gardner *curator, art historian*

Jacksonville
Dundon, Margo Elaine *museum director*
Schlageter, Robert William *museum administrator*

Miami
Morgan, Dahlia *museum director*

Naples
Brown, Alan Marshall, Jr., *art dealer, curator, art appraiser*

Orlando
Morrisey, Marena Grant *art museum administrator*

Palm Beach
Gaudieri, Alexander V. J. *museum director*

Saint Petersburg
Connelly, David O'Brien *art museum administrator, journalist*
†Weaver, F. Louise Beazley *curator, director*

Sarasota
Graham, Douglass of Montrose *museum curator, banker, artist, poet*
Wetenhall, John *museum director*

Tallahassee
Palladino-Craig, Allys *museum director*

GEORGIA

Athens
†Manoguerra, Paul Andrew *curator*

Atlanta
Bevington, Paula Lawton *museum administrator*
Bibb, Daniel Roland *antique painting restorer and conservator*
King, Linda Orr *museum director, consultant*
Przybilla, Carrie Ellen *art curator*
Raney, Jean Puckett *art gallery director, artist*
Vigtel, Gudmund *museum director emeritus*

Columbus
Holcombe, Alfred Robert, Jr., *museum curator*

Roswell
Forbes, John Ripley *museum executive, educator, naturalist*

Savannah
Brandner, Christine Marie *art administrator, artist*

Buxton, Barry Miller *museum director, historical author, educator*

HAWAII

Honolulu
Klobe, Tom *art gallery director*

Mililani
Magee, Donald Edward *retired national park service administrator*

IDAHO

Coeur D Alene
Dahlgren, Dorothy *museum director*

Inkom
Jackson, Allen Keith *retired museum administrator*

ILLINOIS

Bloomington
Bridges, Roger Dean *historical agency administrator*
Koos, Greg *museum director*

Carbondale
Whitlock, John Joseph *museum director*

Chicago
Balzekas, Stanley, Jr., *museum director*
Flynn, John J. *museum curator*
Heltne, Paul Gregory *research scholar*
Kamyszew, Christopher D. *museum curator, executive educator, art consultant*
†Knappenberger, Paul Henry, Jr., *science museum director*
Kubida, Judith Ann *museum administrator*
Mc Carter, John Wilbur, Jr., *museum executive*
Narkiewicz-Laine, Christian K. Gf. *museum director, painter, poet*
Nordland, Gerald *art museum administrator, historian, consultant*
Wood, James Nowell *museum director and executive*

Homewood
MacMaster, Daniel Miller *retired museum official*

Mahomet
Kennedy, Cheryl Lynn *museum director*

Springfield
Hallmark, Donald Parker *museum director, lecturer*
Mc Millan, R(obert) Bruce *museum executive, anthropologist*

INDIANA

Bloomington
Calinescu, Adriana Gabriela *museum curator, art historian*
Gealt, Adelheid Maria *museum director*

Evansville
Streetman, John William, III, *museum official*

Indianapolis
Cilella, Salvatore George, Jr., *museum director*
Gantz, Richard Alan *museum administrator*
Noble, Douglas Ross *museum administrator*
†Tandy, Kisha Renee *curator*

Muncie
Joyaux, Alain Georges *art museum director*

Rochester
Willard, Shirley Ann Ogle *museum director, editor, historian*

IOWA

Cedar Rapids
Pitts, Terence Randolph *museum director, consultant*

West Branch
†Kohan, Carol E. *historical site administrator*

KANSAS

Chanute
Froehlich, Conrad Gerald *museum director, researcher*

Dodge City
Clifton-Smith, Rhonda Darleen *art educator, art center administrator*

Larned
†Linderer, Steve *historic site executive*

Lawrence
Norris, Andrea Spaulding *art museum director*

Manhattan
Walker Schlageck, Kathrine L. *museum educational administrator, educator*

Salina
Douglass, Mary Clement *curator, small business owner*

KENTUCKY

Lexington
Holcomb, Sara Nees *museum director, artist*

Louisville
Becker, Gail Roselyn *museum director*
Bentley, James Robert *association curator, historian, genealogist*
Morrin, Peter Patrick *museum director*

LOUISIANA

New Orleans
Bullard, Edgar John, III, *museum director*
Casellas, Joachim *art gallery executive*
Fagaly, William Arthur *curator*

MAINE

Augusta
Phillips, Joseph Robert *museum director*

Hancock
Silvestro, Clement Mario *museum director, historian*

Kennebunk
Escalet, Frank Diaz *art gallery owner, artist, educator*

MARYLAND

Baltimore
Bolger, Doreen *museum director*
Fiori, Dennis A. *museum director*
Lamp, Frederick John *museum curator*

Clinton
†Whittington, Ralph Edward *curator, librarian*

Friendship
Clagett, Diana Wharton Sinkler *museum docent*

Mitchellville
Marsh, Caryl Amsterdam *museum exhibitions curator, psychologist, advisor*

MASSACHUSETTS

Amherst
Parkhurst, Charles *retired museum director, art historian*

Boston
Cronin, Bonnie Kathryn Lamb *museum director*
Hawley, Anne *museum director*
Howlett, D(onald) Roger *art gallery executive, art historian*
Rogers, Malcolm Austin *museum director, art historian*
Sand, Michael *museum planner, interactive media designer*
Vermeule, Cornelius Clarkson, III, *museum curator*
Wu, Tung *curator, art historian, art educator, artist*

Cambridge
Ellis, David Wertz *retired museum director*
Gaskell, Ivan George Alexander De Wend *art museum curator*
Rexine, John Efstratios, Jr., *museum registrar, artist*
Slive, Seymour *museum director, fine arts educator*
Watson, Rubie *museum director*

Fitchburg
Jareckie, Stephen Barlow *museum curator*

Jamaica Plain
Zahn, Carl Frederick *museum publications director, designer, photographer*

Lexington
Ott, John Harlow *museum administrator*

Lincoln
Capasso, Nicholas John *curator, art historian, public art expert*

Milton
Randall, Lilian Maria Charlotte *museum curator*

Nantucket
Carr, James Revell *museum executive, curator*

Southfield
Melvin, Ronald McKnight *retired museum director*

Springfield
Carvalho, Joseph, III, *museum and library executive*
Muhlberger, Richard Charles *former museum administrator, writer, educator*

Waltham
Arena, Albert A. *museum director*

Watertown
Fairbanks, Jonathan Leo *museum curator*

Wellesley
Crane, Bonnie Loyd *art gallery owner, director, author*
Palmerio, Elvira Castano *art gallery director, art historian*

Williamstown
Conforti, Michael Peter *museum director, art historian*
King, Anthony Gabriel *museum administrator*

Worcester
Welu, James A. *art museum director*

MICHIGAN

Ann Arbor
Bailey, Reeve Maclaren *museum curator*

Chelsea
Sawyer, Charles Henry *art educator, art museum director emeritus*

Dearborn
†Skramstad, Harold Kenneth, Jr., *museum administrator, consultant*

Detroit
Beal, Graham William John *museum director*
Darr, Alan Phipps *curator, historian*
Parrish, Maurice Drue *museum executive*
Peck, Elsie Holmes *curator, art historian, archaeologist*
Peck, William Henry *museum curator, art historian, archaeologist, author, lecturer*

East Lansing
Bandes, Susan Jane *museum director, educator*
Dewhurst, Charles Kurt *museum director, cultural administrator, curator, folklorist, English language educator*

Grand Rapids
Frankforter, Weldon DeLoss *retired museum administrator*

Kalamazoo
†Dietz, Thomas Anthony *curator, educator*
Norris, Richard Patrick *museum director, history educator*

Saginaw
Ondish, Andrea *museum educator*

MINNESOTA

Minneapolis
King, Lyndel Irene Saunders *art museum director*

Saint Paul
†White, William Thomas *curator, historian, educator*

MISSISSIPPI

Natchez
Branyan, Cheryl Munyer *museum administrator, consultant*

MISSOURI

Ballwin
Pallozola, Christine *non-profit administrator*

Florissant
Luebke, Martin Frederick *retired curator*

Kansas City
McKenna, George LaVerne *art museum curator*
Scott, Deborah Emont *curator*
Svadlenak, Jean Hayden *museum consultant*
Youmans, Joyce M. *curator, researcher*

Saint Joseph
Chilcote, Gary M. *museum director, reporter*
Howe, Dean Otis, Jr., *curator, consultant*

Saint Louis
Burke, James Donald *museum administrator*

Springfield
Berger, Jerry Allen *museum director*

MONTANA

Missoula
Brown, Robert Munro *museum director*

NEBRASKA

Boys Town
Lynch, Thomas Joseph *museum and historic house manager*

Chadron
Lecher, Belvadine (Belvadine Reeves) *museum curator*

Crawford
Buecker, Thomas Robert *museum curator*

NEW HAMPSHIRE

Manchester
Stinson, Wesley R. *museum director, archaeologist*

Portsmouth
Nylander, Jane Louise *museum director*

Rindge
Elam, Leslie Albert *retired museum administrator*

NEW JERSEY

Ho Ho Kus
Ciannella, Joeen Moore *museum director*

Holmdel
Smith, Sibley Judson, Jr., *historic site administrator, educator*

Morristown
Miller, Steven H. *museum director*

New Brunswick
Cate, Phillip Dennis *art museum director emeritus*

Newark
Lazar, Lynn *art association administrator, actress*
Reynolds, Valrae *museum curator*

South Orange
Nussbaum Drill, Sheila *gallery director and owner*

Stockton
Leeds, Valerie Ann *curator, art historian, writer*

Wayne
Einreinhofer, Nancy Anne *art gallery director*

NEW MEXICO

Placitas
Smith, Richard Bowen *retired national park superintendent*

Santa Fe
Enyeart, James L. *museum director*
Kennedy, Roger George *museum director, park service executive*
Wilson, Thomas *museum director*

Taos
†Tisdale, Shelby Jo-Anne *museum director, consultant*
Witt, David L. *curator, writer*

NEW YORK

Brooklyn
Ferber, Linda S. *museum curator*
Lehman, Arnold Lester *museum official, art historian*
†Svetvilas, Chanika *museum program coordinator*

Buffalo
Bayles, Jennifer Lucene *museum program director, educator*
Schultz, Douglas George *art museum director*

Cold Spring Harbor
MacKay, Robert Battin *museum director*

Corning
Spillman, Jane Shadel *curator, researcher, writer*
Whitehouse, David Bryn *museum director*

Grand View
Lattes, Jane Flax *museum administrator*

Hamilton
Moynihan, William J. *museum executive*

Huntington
Levinthal, Beth Ellen (Kuby Levinthal) *museum administrator, educator*

Hyde Park
Hunt, Mark Alan *museum director*

Ithaca
Robinson, Franklin Westcott *museum director, art historian*

Jamestown
Reale, Sara Jane *museum education director*

Katonah
Simpson, William Kelly *curator, Egyptologist, educator*

Keene Valley
Lanyon, Wesley Edwin *retired museum curator, ornithologist*

New York
Anderson, Maxwell L. *museum director*
Baragwanath, Albert Kingsmill *curator, writer*
Barnett, Vivian Endicott *curator*
Basquin, Mary Smyth (Kit Basquin) *museum administrator*
Bates, Michael Lawrence *curator*
Bothmer, Dietrich Felix von *museum curator, archaeologist*
Bull, David *fine art conservator*
Carneiro, Robert Leonard *museum curator, anthropologist*
Carpenter, James Michael *curator*
Carr, Claudia *art gallery director, owner, artist*
Cohen, Mildred Thaler *art gallery director*
Cooper, Steve Neil *art gallery owner, photographer*
Cracraft, Joel *curator*
De Ferrari, Gabriella *curator, writer*
de Montebello, Philippe Lannes *museum administrator*
Draper, James David *art museum curator*
Faunce, Sarah Cushing *former museum curator*

Freed, Stanley Arthur *retired museum curator*
Futter, Ellen Victoria *museum administrator*
Glimcher, Arnold B. *art gallery executive*
Gumpert, Lynn *gallery director*
†Gund, Agnes *art museum administrator*
Haskell, Barbara *curator*
†Hawkins, Ashton *museum executive, lawyer*
†Hotchner, Holly *curator, museum director, conservator*
Hoving, Thomas *museum and cultural affairs consultant, author*
Howat, John Keith *retired museum executive*
Jefferson, Kristin Marie *museum director*
Kallir, Jane Katherine *art gallery director, author*
Kardon, Janet *museum director, curator, educator*
†Kendall, Laurel Margarite *curator, anthropologist, educator*
†Kind, Phyllis *art gallery owner*
†Kleeblatt, Norman L. *museum curator*
Kramer, Linda Konheim *curator, art historian*
Krens, Thomas *museum director*
Kuchta, Ronald Andrew *art museum director, magazine editor, curator*
Kujawski, Elizabeth Szancer *art curator, consultant*
Leff, Sandra H. *gallery director, consultant*
Lerner, Martin *museum curator*
Levai, Pierre Alexandre *art gallery executive*
Levine, Louis *museum director, archaeologist*
Lowry, Glenn David *art museum director*
Martin, Mary Anne *art gallery owner*
Mertens, Joan R. *museum curator, art historian*
Messer, Thomas Maria *museum director*
Moore, John Kenneth *curator*
Munhall, Edgar *retired curator, art history educator*
Murdock, Robert Mead *curator*
O'Brien, Catherine Louise *museum administrator*
Oldenburg, Richard Erik *auction house executive*
Pesner, Carole Manishin *art gallery owner*
Platnick, Norman I. *curator, entomologist*
Rosenthal, Nan *curator, educator, author*
Sachs, Samuel, II, *museum director*
Simon, Ronald Charles *curator*
Stiassny, Melanie L.J. *curator*
Sutton, Karen E. *administrator*
Toll, Barbara Elizabeth *art gallery director*
Tyson, Neil DeGrasse *museum director*
Vuilleumier, François *curator, biologist, ornithologist, educator*
Wardropper, Ian Bruce *museum curator, educator*
†Weinberg, Adam D. *museum artistic and program director*
Wright, Gwendolyn *art center director, writer, educator*

Ossining
Cadge, William Fleming *gallery owner, photographer*

Purchase
Gedeon, Lucinda Heyel *museum director*

Rochester
Adams, G. Rollie *museum executive*
Bannon, Anthony Leo *museum director*
Holcomb, Grant, III, *museum director*

Sag Harbor
Cory, David H. *museum administrator, former real esate broker*

Southampton
Lerner, Abram *retired museum director, artist*

Stuyvesant
Tripp, Susan Gerwe *museum director*

Syracuse
Skoler, Celia Rebecca *art gallery director*

Tupper Lake
Welsh, Peter Corbett *museum consultant, historian*

Utica
Schweizer, Paul Douglas *museum director*

Wantagh
Smits, Edward John *museum consultant*

Waterford
Gold, James Paul *museum director*

West Point
Reel, David Mark *museum curator, art historian*

NORTH CAROLINA

Chapel Hill
Bolas, Gerald Douglas *art museum administrator, art history educator*

Durham
Krakauer, Thomas Henry *museum director emeritus*

Kinston
†Duppstadt, Andrew Earl *historic site staff member*

Raleigh
Hansley, Lee *art gallery owner, curator*
Kuhler, Renaldo Gillet *museum official, scientific illustrator*
Wheeler, Lawrence Jefferson *art museum director*

Salisbury
Shalkop, Robert Leroy *retired museum director*

Winston Salem
Rauschenberg, Bradford Lee *museum researcher*
Whittington, Stephen Lunn *museum director*

OHIO

Akron
Kahan, Mitchell Douglas *art museum director*
Tannenbaum, Barbara Lee *curator, art historian*

Athens
†Ahrens, Kent *museum director, art historian*

Cincinnati
Brown, Daniel *art consultant*
Crew, Spencer *museum administrator*
†Desmarais, Charles Joseph *museum director, writer, editor*
Hessler, Gene Joseph *museum curator, retired musician*
Rogers, Millard Foster, Jr., *art museum director emeritus*
Rub, Timothy F. *museum director*
Weston, Phyllis Jean *art gallery director*

Cleves
Tolzmann, Don Heinrich *curator, educator*

Dayton
Meister, Mark Jay *museum director, professional society administrator*
Nyerges, Alexander Lee *museum director*

Kirtland
Johnston, Stanley Howard, Jr., *rare books curator, bibliographer*

Oberlin
Taylor, Gail Richardson *freelance writer, educator, civic worker, lawyer, former university official*

Solon
Ward, William Edward *museum exhibition designer*

University Heights
Cook, Alexander Burns *museum curator, artist, educator*

Youngstown
Ruffer, David Gray *museum director, former college president*

OREGON

Milwaukie
Eichinger, Marilynne Hildegarde *museum administrator*

Portland
Henning, William Thomas *curator*
Jenkins, Donald John *museum administrator*
McKinley, Loren Dhue *museum director*
Taylor, J(ocelyn) Mary *museum administrator, zoologist, educator*

PENNSYLVANIA

Altoona
Moffitt, Charles William *art gallery director*

Camp Hill
McGeary, Clyde Mills *artist, educator, advisor*

Chadds Ford
Duff, James Henry *museum director, environmental administrator*

Erie
Vanco, John L. *art museum director*

Fort Washington
Wint, Dennis Michael *museum director*

Harrisburg
Mahey, John Andrew *retired museum director*

Merion Station
Camp, Kimberly N. *museum administrator, artist*

Philadelphia
Bantel, Linda Mae *former museum curator, consultant*
Carter, John Swain *museum administrator, consultant*
d'Harnoncourt, Anne *museum director, executive*
Reimer, Charles Wilson *curator, consultant*
Shoemaker, Innis Howe *art museum curator*
Turner, Evan Hopkins *retired art museum director*

Pittsburgh
Dawson, Mary Ruth *curator, educator*
DeWalt, Bill *museum director*
King, Elaine A. *curator, art historian, critic*

Reading
Dietrich, Bruce Leinbach *planetarium and museum administrator, astronomer, educator*

Strasburg
Lindsay, George Carroll *former museum director*

Swarthmore
Sawyers, Claire Elyce *arboretum administrator*

University Park
Muhlert, Jan Keene *art museum director*

Villanova
Scott, Robert Montgomery *museum executive, lawyer*

RHODE ISLAND

Newport
MacLeish, Archibald Bruce *museum administrator*

Providence
Fishman, Bernard Philip *museum director*
Hay, Susan Stahr Heller *museum curator*

Saunderstown
Leavitt, Thomas Whittlesey *retired museum director, educator*

SOUTH CAROLINA

Bishopville
Cox, Janson L. *museum administrator*

Charleston
Sloan, Mark Hamilton *art gallery director, educator, author*

Chesnee
†Saunders, J. Farrell *historic site director*

Mount Pleasant
Macdonald, Robert Rigg, Jr., *retired museum director*

Pawleys Island
Noble, Joseph Veach *fine arts administrator*
Tarbox, Gurdon Lucius, Jr., *retired museum executive*

SOUTH DAKOTA

Sioux Falls
Thompson, Harry Floyd, II, *research collections and book publications director*

TENNESSEE

Greeneville
†Corey, Mark *historic site director*

Knoxville
Sickles, Helma-Jane *museum executive*

Memphis
Czestochowski, Joseph Stephen *museum administrator*

Sewanee
Scarbrough, Cleve Knox, Jr., *museum director*

TEXAS

Austin
†Theriot, Edward C. *museum director*

Dallas
Vogel, Donald Stanley *gallery executive, artist*

El Paso
Sipiora, Leonard Paul *retired museum director, art appraiser*

Fort Worth
Auping, Michael G. *curator*

Frisco
Meadows, Patricia Blachly *art curator, civic worker*

Glen Rose
Blankenship, Jenny Mary *museum administrator*

Houston
Bowron, Edgar Peters *art museum curator, administrator*
Latimer, Roy Truett *museum executive*
Lee, Janie C. *curator*
Marzio, Peter Cort *museum director*

Huntsville
Nolan, Patrick Bates *museum director*

Irving
Piqué, Fernando Rafael *international art dealer, artist*

Laredo
Purpura, Peter Joseph *museum curator, exhibition designer*

Odessa
Hewitt, Timothy Martin *museum curator*

San Antonio
Chiego, William J. *museum director*
Endresen, Lisa Castro *curatorial assistant*

UTAH

Salt Lake City
George, Sarah B. *museum director*
Kohler, Dolores Marie *gallery owner*
Oakes, Claudia *museum administrator*

VERMONT

Manchester
Kouwenhoven, Gerrit Wolphertsen *retired museum director*

Montpelier
Dumville, John P. *historic site director*

Shaftsbury
Williams, Robert Joseph *museum director, educator*

VIRGINIA

Alexandria
Lundeberg, Philip Karl Boraas *curator, consultant*

Arlington
Hanle, Paul Arthur *museum administrator*

Charlottesville
†Holmes, Carolyn Coggin *museum director*
Linden, Peppy G. *museum director*

Lexington
Lynn, Michael A. *historic site director*

Lynchburg
Elson, James Martin *retired historic foundation director*

Mount Vernon
Rees, James Conway, IV, *historic site administrator*

Roanoke
Fitzgerald, Mary Eileen *museum program director*

Sterling
Friedheim, Jerry Warden *museum consultant*

Tazewell
Weeks, Ross Leonard, Jr., *museum executive*

Vienna
Damon, Shirley Stockton *art gallery owner*

Virginia Beach
Martin, Roy Butler, Jr., *museum director, retired broker*

Williamsburg
Christison, Muriel Branham *retired art museum director emeritus, fine arts educator*

WASHINGTON

Bellevue
Warren, James Ronald *retired museum director, writer, columnist*

Bellingham
Livesay, Thomas Andrew *museum administrator, lecturer*

Ocean Shores
†Woodwick, Gene L. *museum director*

Redmond
Sobey, Edwin J. C. *museum director, oceanographer, consultant*

Seattle
Bufano, Ralph A. *museum director*
Garfield, Leonard *museum director*
Harrington, LaMar *curator, museum director*
Herman, Lloyd Eldred *curator, consultant, writer*
West, Richard Vincent *art museum director*

Wenatchee
Williams, Keith Roy *museum director*

WISCONSIN

Madison
Garver, Thomas Haskell *curator, art consultant, writer*

Milwaukee
†Green, Edward Anthony *museum director*
Temmer, James Donald *museum director*

WYOMING

Cheyenne
Wilson-McKee, Marie *museum director*

CANADA

ALBERTA

Canmore
Janes, Robert Roy *museum executive, archaeologist, museum consultant*

BRITISH COLUMBIA

Victoria
Finlay, James Campbell *retired museum director*
Segger, Martin Joseph *museum director, art history educator*

NEW BRUNSWICK

Fredericton
Lumsden, Ian Gordon *art gallery director*

NEWFOUNDLAND

Saint John's
Grattan, Patricia Elizabeth *retired art gallery director*

ONTARIO

London
Poole, Nancy Geddes *art gallery curator*

Ottawa
McAvity, John Gillis *museum director, association executive, museologist*

QUEBEC

Montreal
Brisebois, Marcel *museum director*

BELIZE

Cayo
Wulff, Roger LaVern *museum administrator*

FRANCE

Paris
Rosenberg, Pierre Max *museum director*

ADDRESS UNPUBLISHED

Abbott, Rebecca Phillips *museum director, art consultant, photographer*
Armstrong, Thomas Newton, III, *art and garden specialist*
Beach, Milo C. *former art museum director*
Bishop, Budd Harris *retired museum administrator, artist*
Black, Ruth Idella *museum curator*
Booker, Nana Laurel *art gallery owner, consul*
Borrowdale-Cox, Deborah Elizabeth *museum curator*
Brown, Suzanne Wiley *museum director*
Buck, Robert Treat, Jr., *gallery director, former museum director, educator*
Castile, Rand (Jesse Randolph III) *retired museum director*
Cikovsky, Nicolai, Jr., *retired curator, art history educator*
Coke, Frank Van Deren *museum director, photographer*
Combs, Robert Kimbal *museum director*
†Deutschman, Louise Tolliver *curator*
Ebie, William D. *museum director*
Emery, Alan Roy *museum executive*
Fri, Robert Wheeler *retired museum director*
Friedman, Martin *museum director, arts adviser*
Gasteyer, Carlin Evans *museum administrator, museum studies educator*
Glad, Suzanne Lockley *retired museum director*
Graves, Sid Foster, Jr., *retired library and museum director*
Grossman, Cissy *curator, art historian, art exhibit designer, appraiser*
Hartgen, Vincent Andrew *museum director, educator, artist*
Hellmers, Norman Donald *retired historic site director*
Houlihan, Patrick Thomas *museum director*
Jacobowitz, Ellen Sue *museum and temple curator, administrator*
Jacobs, Eleanor *art consultant, retired art administrator*
Kahn, James Steven *retired museum director*
Knowles, Elizabeth Pringle *museum director*
Lane, John Rodger *art museum director*
Lane, Lilly Katherine *museum staff member*
Leal, José Henrique *museum director, marine biologist*
Lusk, Harlan Gilbert *national park superintendent, business executive*
Lutts, Ralph Herbert *scholar, educator, museum administrator*
Matelic, Candace Tangorra *museum studies educator, consultant, museum director*
†McGarvie-Munn, Iain Lachlan *curator, writer, agent*
Mercuri, Joan B. *museum administrator*
Metcalf, William Edwards *educator, museum curator*
Meyer, Ruth Krueger *museum administrator, educator, art historian*
Millard, Charles Warren, III, *museum director, writer*
†Monkman, Betty Claire *curator*
Naeve, Milo Merle *curator, director*
Nasgaard, Roald *museum curator*
†Nickles, Shelley Kaplan *curator, educator*
Pal, Pratapaditya *curator*
Parris, Nina Gumpert *curator, writer, researcher, photographer*
Perrot, Paul Norman *museum director*
Pilgrim, Dianne Hauserman *retired museum director*
Porter, Daniel Reed, III, *museum director*
Powell, Earl Alexander, III, *art museum director*
Prakapas, Eugene Joseph *art gallery director*
†Reisman, Sara Hannah *curator, consultant*
Reuther, Ronald Theodore *museum director*
Robertson, Charles James *museum director emeritus*
Russell, Helen Diane *retired museum curator, educator*
Ryskamp, Charles Andrew *museum executive, educator*
Schneider, Janet M. *arts administrator, curator, painter*

Sennema, David Carl *museum and arts administration consultant*
Shapiro, Michael Edward *museum director*
Shimoda, Jerry Yasutaka *retired national historic park manager*
†Siano, Mary Ann *art gallery director*
Skotheim, Robert Allen *retired college and museum administrator*
Smith, Marjorie Aileen Matthews *museum director*
Steadman, David Wilton *retired museum official*
Stearns, Robert Leland *curator*
Steinhauser, Janice Maureen *arts administrator, educator, artist*
Stewart, Robert Gordon *former museum curator*
Stuart, Joseph Martin *art museum administrator*
Summerfield, John Robert *textile curator*
†Tashev, Kirsten *museum administrator*
Thomas, William Geraint *museum administrator*
†Thyzel, Tim *curator, artist, educator*
Towe, A. Ruth *retired museum director*
Vail, Mary Barbara *publicist*
Vargo, Beth Copeland *curator*
Walker, Roslyn Adele *museum director*
Way, Jacob Edson, III, *museum director*
Whitchurch, Charles Augustus *art gallery owner, humanities educator*
Wieser, Siegfried *planetarium executive director*
Wilson, Karen Lee *museum director*
Wolfe, Townsend Durant, III, *retired art museum director, curator*
Zenev, Irene Louise *museum curator*
Zusy, Catherine *curator*

INDUSTRY: MANUFACTURING
See also **FINANCE: FINANCIAL SERVICES**

UNITED STATES

ALABAMA

Albertville
Rice, Fuhrman D. (Runt Rice) *retired paper company executive*

Andalusia
Taylor, James Marion, II, *automotive wholesale executive*

Birmingham
Bailey, Kelly Frank *occupational health company executive*
Bennett, Joe Claude *pharmaceutical executive*
Campbell, Charles Alton *business executive*
Chrencik, Frank *chemical company executive*
Cohen-DeMarco, Gale Maureen *pharmaceutical executive*
Daniel, Kenneth Rule *former iron and steel manufacturing company executive*
Goldberg, Edward Jay *general contractor*
Hall, Robert Alan *construction company executive*
Harbert, Bill Lebold *retired construction corporation executive*
Holton, J(erry) Thomas *concrete company executive*
†McMahon, John J., Jr., *metal processing company executive*
Neal, Phil Hudson, Jr., *manufacturing company executive*
Sklenar, Herbert Anthony *industrial products manufacturing company executive*
Styslinger, Lee Joseph, Jr., *manufacturing company executive*

Huntsville
†Sapp, A. Eugene, Jr., *former electronics executive*

Montgomery
Taylor, Watson Robbins *construction company executive*

Opelika
Jenkins, Richard Lee *manufacturing company executive*

Tuscaloosa
Fowler, Conrad Murphree *retired manufacturing company executive*

ALASKA

Anchorage
Miller, Kevin Clark *heavy equipment operator, writer*

Big Lake
†DeLoach, Robert Edgar *corporate executive*

Haines
Kaufman, David Graham *construction executive*

Juneau
Smith, Charles Anthony *business executive*

ARIZONA

Carefree
Alexander, Judd Harris *retired paper company executive*
Garr, Carl Robert *manufacturing company executive*

Chandler
Farley, James Newton *manufacturing executive, engineer*

Joyce, Kenneth Thomas *electronics company executive*

Flagstaff
†Motschman, Keith Allen *health products executive*

Gilbert
†Earnhardt, Hal J., III, *automotive executive*

Mesa
DeRosa, Francis Dominic *chemical company executive*
Luth, William Clair *retired research manager*

Paradise Valley
McKennon, Keith Robert *chemical company executive*

Patagonia
Bonner, Herbert Dwight *construction management educator*

Phoenix
Anderson, Milada Filko *manufacturing company executive*
Carter, Ronald Martin, Sr., *pharmaceutical company executive*
Dewane, John Richard *retired manufacturing company executive, consultant, business owner*
Franke, William Augustus *corporate executive*
Giedt, Bruce Alan *paper company executive*
Kitzman, Jerry Matson *pharmaceutical executive*
Klepinger, John William *trailer manufacturing company executive*
Linde, Ronald Keith *corporate executive, private investor*
†McClelland, Norman P. *food products executive*
Stegmayer, Joseph Henry *housing industry executive*
Thompson, Herbert Ernest *tool and die company executive*
Vallee, Roy *electronics company executive*
Van Horssen, Charles Arden *manufacturing executive*
White, Edward Allen *electronics company executive*

Prescott
Parkhurst, Charles Lloyd *electronics company executive*

Scottsdale
Freedman, Stanley Marvin *manufacturing company executive*
Gans, Eugene Howard *cosmetic and pharmaceutical company executive, consultant*
Grenell, James Henry *retired manufacturing company executive*
Hepler, Kenneth Russel *manufacturing executive*
Howard, William Gates, Jr., *electronics company executive*
Jesky, T. J. *pharmaceutical products executive*
Lloyd, Eugene Walter *retired construction company executive*
Rethore, Bernard Gabriel *retired manufacturing and mining company executive*
Walsh, Edward Joseph *toiletries and food company executive*

Sedona
Bell, Robert Matthew *pharmaceutical company consultant*

Surprise
Lazar, Max Seymour *pharmaceutical company executive, retired*

Tucson
Acker, Loren Calvin *medical instrument company executive*
Meeker, Robert Eldon *retired manufacturing company executive*

ARKANSAS

Dardanelle
Prpich, Michael Frank *food company manager*

Fort Smith
Flanders, Donald Hargis *manufacturing company executive*

Hot Springs National Park
Schroeder, Donald Perry *retired food products company executive*

Lakeview
Roe, Richard C. *industry consultant, former home furnishings manufacturing executive*

Little Rock
†Afouna, Mohsen M.I. *pharmaceutical scientist, researcher*
McCoy, Stuart Sherman *manufacturing executive*
Voss, Linda I. *automotive company executive*

North Little Rock
Givens, John Kenneth *manufacturing executive*
Harrison, Angela Eve *manufacturing executive*

Siloam Springs
McMennamy, Roger Neal *automotive executive*

Springdale
Pirozzoli, Heather Jo *food company professional*
Tyson, John H. *food products executive*

CALIFORNIA

Agoura Hills
Currie, Malcolm Roderick *aerospace and automotive executive, scientist*

Alamo
Liggett, Lawrence Melvin *vacuum equipment manufacturing company executive*

Aliso Viejo
Trivelpiece, Craig Evan *computer electronics executive*

Anaheim
Baumgartner, Anton Edward *automotive sales professional*

Aptos
Mechlin, George Francis *electrical manufacturing company executive*

Atherton
Goodman, Sam Richard *electronics company executive*
Hogan, Clarence Lester *retired electronics executive*

Bakersfield
Akers, Tom, Jr., *cotton broker, consultant*
Lundquist, Gene Alan *cotton company executive*
†Thomason, Scott *automobile executive*

Belmont
Endriz, John Guiry *electronics executive, consultant*

Beverly Hills
Colburn, Richard Dunton *business executive*
dePaolis, Potito Umberto *food company executive*
Korn, Lester Bernard *business executive*
Willson, James Douglas *aerospace executive*
Winthrop, John *wines and spirits company executive*

Burbank
Joseff, Joan Castle *manufacturing executive*
Raulinaitis, Pranas Algis *electronics executive, consultant*

Calabasas
Laney, Michael L. *manufacturing executive*

Calistoga
Ogg, Robert Danforth *corporate executive*

Carlsbad
Anderson, Paul Irving *management executive*
Crooke, Stanley Thomas *pharmaceutical company executive*
McNamara, Kevin Michael *floorcovering company executive*
†Turner, Lyle C. *biotechnology company executive*

Carmel
Alich, John Arthur, Jr., *manufacturing executive*

Carmel Valley
Kasson, James Matthews *electronics executive*

Chino
Goodman, Lindsey Alan *furniture manufacturing executive, architect*

Chula Vista
Manary, Richard Deane *manufacturing executive*

City Of Commerce
Johnson, Keith Liddell *chemical company executive*

City Of Industry
Perry, William Joseph *food processing company executive*

Claremont
Forti, William Bell *business executive, inventor*

Colusa
Carter, Jane Foster *agriculture industry executive*

Concord
Thompson, Jeremiah Beiseker *international medical business executive, sinologist*

Corona
†Weisemann, Claus *pharmaceutical executive*

Corona Del Mar
Hochschild, Richard *medical instruments executive, researcher*
Wolf, Karl Everett *aerospace and communications corporation executive*

Coronado
Dalton, Matt *retired foundry executive*
Sack, Edgar Albert *electronics company executive*

Costa Mesa
Alexiou, James *electronics executive*
Brady, John Patrick, Jr., *electronics educator, consultant*
Hazewinkel, Van *manufacturing executive*

Coto De Caza
Bezar, Gilbert Edward *retired aerospace company executive, volunteer*

Cowan Heights
Ruttencutter, Brian Boyle *manufacturing company executive*

Culver City
Leve, Alan Donald *electronic materials manufacturing company owner, executive*

Cupertino
Burg, John Parker *signal processing executive*
Mathias, Leslie Michael *electronic manufacturing company executive*
Sobrato, John A. *construction executive*

Dublin
Mettinger, Karl Lennart *pharmaceutical executive*
Whetten, John D. *food products executive*

El Granada
Tempesta, Michael Steven *pharmaceuticals company executive, chemist*

El Segundo
Eckert, Robert A. *manufacturing company executive*
†Kelble, Jack R. *electronics executive*

Emeryville
Lance, Sean P. *pharmaceutical executive*
Nady, John *electronics company executive*

Encinitas
Bartok, Michelle *cosmetic company executive*

Escalon
Barton, Gerald Lee *farming company executive*

Escondido
Polesetsky, Harold H. *contractor*

Fair Oaks
Chernev, Melvin *retired beverage company executive*

Fallbrook
†Higbee, Donald William *electronics company executive, lawyer*

Fremont
†Huang, Robert *electronics manufacturing executive*
Maurer, Robert Michael *medical company executive*
Rusch, Thomas William *manufacturing executive*

Fullerton
Miller, Arnold *electronics executive*

Gardena
Kanner, Edwin Benjamin *electrical manufacturing company executive*

Greenfield
Munoz, John Joseph *retired transportation company executive*

Hayward
Minzner, Dean Frederick *aviation company executive*

Hesperia
Butcher, Jack Robert (Jack Risin) *manufacturing executive, film producer, actor*

Hillsborough
Keller, John Francis *retired wine company executive, mayor*

Hollywood
Parks, Robert Myers *appliance manufacturing company executive*

Huntington Beach
McGuire, James Charles *aircraft company executive*

Indio
†York, Douglas Arthur *manufacturing and construction company executive*

Irvine
Alspach, Philip Halliday *manufacturing company executive*
Broadhurst, Norman Neil *food products executive*
Cobianchi, Thomas Theodore *engineering and marketing executive, educator*
†Mussey, Joseph Arthur *health and medical product executive*
Pyott, David Edmund Ian *pharmaceutical executive*
Salesky, William Jeffrey *corporate executive*
†Wetterau, Mark S. *food products/distributor executive*

La Jolla
Drake, Hudson Billings *aerospace and electronics company executive*
Elander, Richard Paul *consultant, retired pharmaceutical executive*
Geckler, Richard Delph *metal products company executive, retired*
Holland, Charles Edward *medical products corporate executive*
†Shawver, Laura K. *biotechnology company executive*
Stevens, Paul Irving *manufacturing company executive*

La Puente
†Hitchcock, Frederick E. "Fritz", Jr., *automotive company executive*

Lafayette
Lewis, Sheldon Noah *technology consultant*

Laguna Beach
Wong, Wallace *medical supplies company executive, real estate investor*

Laguna Hills
Rossiter, Bryant William *chemistry consultant*

Laguna Niguel
Nelson, Alfred John *retired pharmaceutical company executive*
†Ricci, Robert Ronald *manufacturing company executive*

Livermore
Bennett, Alan Jerome *electronics executive, physicist*

Livingston
†Carter, Paul *food products executive*
†Fox, Robert August *food company executive*

Lompoc
Bongiorno, James William *electronics company executive*

Long Beach
†Heiser, James S. *manufacturing company executive*

Los Altos
Beer, Clara Louise Johnson *retired electronics executive*

Los Angeles
Adler, Fred Peter *retired electronics company executive*
Ash, Roy Lawrence *business executive*
Atchley, Raymond Deval *technology company executive*
Borneman, John Paul *pharmaceutical executive*
Campion, Robert Thomas *manufacturing company executive*
Hutchins, Joan Morthland *manufacturing executive, farmer*
Irani, Ray R. *oil, gas and chemical company executive*
Karatz, Bruce E. *business executive*
Mager, Artur *retired aerospace company executive, consultant*
Mall, William John, Jr., *aerospace executive, retired Air Force general*
†Marciano, Maurice *apparel executive*
Palevsky, Max *industrialist*
Perkins, William Clinton *company executive*
Ramer, Lawrence Jerome *corporation executive*
Spindler, Paul *corporate executive, consultant*
Tamkin, S. Jerome *business executive, consultant*

Malibu
Dankanyin, Robert John *international business executive*

Mariposa
Sutherland, Gail Russell *retired industrial equipment manufacturing company executive*

Mckinleyville
Thueson, David Orel *pharmaceutical executive, researcher, educator, writer*

Menlo Park
Bremser, George, Jr., *electronics company executive*
Evans, Bob Overton *electronics executive, director*
Kalinske, Thomas J. *education, video game and toy company executive*
Kamin, William Stephen *food company executive, photographer*
Pausa, Clements Edward *electronics company executive*
Saifer, Mark Gary Pierce *pharmaceutical executive*
Taft, David Dakin *chemical executive*
Westcott, Brian John *manufacturing executive*

Mill Valley
Winskill, Robert Wallace *manufacturing executive*

Milpitas
†Cannon, Michael R. *manufacturing executive*
Nishimura, Koichi *former electronics manufacturing company executive*
Roddick, David Bruce *construction company executive*

Mission Viejo
Faley, Robert Lawrence *retired instruments company executive*
Gilbert, Heather Campbell *manufacturing company executive*

Montebello
Meeker, Arlene Dorothy Hallin (Mrs. William Maurice Meeker) *manufacturing company executive*

Montecito
Meghreblian, Robert Vartan *manufacturing executive, physicist*

Monterey
Hanlon, James Allison *confectionery company executive*

Napa
Wahl, Howard Wayne *retired construction company executive, engineer*

Newport Beach
Bennett, Bruce W. *construction company executive, civil engineer*
Jones, Roger Wayne *electronics executive*
Li, Shu *electronics executive*
Mirams, William C. *construction executive*
Wadden, Christopher David *food products executive*

North Hills
†Boeckmann, Herbert F., II, *automotive executive*

Oakland
Koplin, Donald Leroy *health products executive, consumer advocate*
Saunders, Ward Bishop, Jr., *retired aluminum company executive*
Sullivan, G. Craig *household products executive*

Orange
Kaempen, Charles Edward *manufacturing company executive*

Orinda
Graber, William Raymond *pharmaceutical executive*

Oxnard
Kavli, Fred *retired manufacturing executive, retired engineering executive*
Poole, Henry Joe, Jr., *business executive*

Palm Desert
Epstein, Marvin Morris *retired construction company executive*

Palm Springs
†Brain, Jesse *manufacturing executive*

Palo Alto
Balzhiser, Richard Earl *research and development company executive*
Early, James Michael *electronics research consultant*
Goff, Harry Russell *retired manufacturing company executive*
Kincaid, Judith Wells *electronics company executive*
Kung, Frank F. *biotechnology and life sciences investor, venture capitalist*
Staprans, Armand *electronics executive*
Sweitzer, Michael Cook *healthcare product executive*

Palos Verdes Estates
Mackenbach, Frederick W. *welding products manufacturing company executive*

Palos Verdes Peninsula
Grant, Robert Ulysses *retired manufacturing company executive*
Leone, William Charles *retired manufacturing executive*
Thomas, Hayward *manufacturing company executive*
Wilson, Theodore Henry *retired electronics company executive, aerospace engineer*

Pasadena
†Bishop, Robert Calvin *pharmaceutical company executive*
Marlen, James S. *chemical, plastics and building materials manufacturing company executive*
†McNulty, James F. *engineering, construction company executive*
Neal, Philip Mark *diversified manufacturing executive*
Smith, Howard Russell *manufacturing company executive*
Tollenaere, Lawrence Robert *retired industrial products company executive*
†Watson, Noel G. *construction executive*
Weiswasser, Stephen *electronics manufacturing executive*

Playa Del Rey
Mishelevich, David Jacob *medical company executive, consultant*

Pleasanton
Edwards, Traci Van Arsdale *drug company official*
Erbskorn, Amy Gordon *healthcare executive*
†Sundgren, Donald E. *construction executive*

Portola Valley
Purl, O. Thomas *retired electronics company executive*

Prather
Coren, Lance Scott *consulting firm executive*

Rancho Dominguez
Collopy, Christopher Stephen *clothing company executive*
Janura, Jan Arol *apparel manufacturing executive*

Rancho Mirage
Foster, David Ramsey *soap company executive*
Greenbaum, James Richard *liquor distributing company executive, real estate developer*

Rancho Murieta
Irelan, Robert Withers *retired metal products executive*

Rancho Santa Fe
Bestwick, Warren William *retired construction company executive*
Jordan, Charles Morrell *retired automotive designer*
Step, Eugene Lee *retired pharmaceutical company executive*

Redding
†Emmerson, Archie Aldis (Red Emmerson) *sawmill owner*

Redlands
Skomal, Edward Nelson *aerospace company executive, electromagnetic environments consultant*

Redondo Beach
Dockstader, Jack Lee *retired electronics executive*
Kagiwada, Reynold Shigeru *electronics executive*
Ramstein, William Louis *manufacturing company executive*

Redwood City
†Nosler, Peter Cole *construction company executive*

Wang, Chen Chi *electronics company, real estate, finance company, investment services, and international trade executive*

Rescue
Ackerly, Wendy Saunders *construction company executive*

Richmond
†Cohen, Abraham Ezekiel *retired health care company executive*
Dolberg, David Spencer *business executive, marketing professional, lawyer, scientist, molecular biologist*

Riverside
Chamberlain, Willard Thomas *retired metals company executive*
Kummer, Glenn F. *retired manufacturing executive*

Rocklin
Tal, Jacob *electronics executive*

Ross
Nicholson, William Joseph *forest products consultant*

Sacramento
Aldrich, Thomas Albert *former brewing executive, consultant*
Baccigaluppi, Roger John *agricultural company executive*
Geiken, Alan Richard *contractor*
Mack, Edward Gibson *retired business executive*
†Teel, Michael J. *supermarket chain executive*
Venosdel, Daniel Paul *agricultural association administrator*

San Anselmo
Chiaverini, John Edward *construction company executive*

San Carlos
Gutow, Bernard Sidney *packaging manufacturing company executive*

San Clemente
Clark, Earnest Hubert, Jr., *tool company executive*
Halamandaris, Harry *aerospace executive*
†Steinberg, Howard *chemical company executive, consultant*

San Diego
Darmstandler, Harry Max *real estate executive, retired air force officer*
Devine, Brian Kiernan *pet food and supplies company executive*
†Engle, Steven B. *biotechnology company executive*
†Iversen, Leslie Lars *pharmaceutical executive*
†Kranzler, Jay D. *pharmaceutical executive*
†Moos, Walter Hamilton *pharmaceutical company executive*
†Price, Robert E. *manufacturing company executive*
Proehl, Gerald T. *pharmaceutical executive*
Pyatt, Kedar Davis, Jr., *research and development company executive*
Rice, Clare I. *electronics company executive*
†Shen, Larry Z. *pharmaceutical executive, researcher*
Spanos, Alexander Gus *construction company owner, professional sports team owner*
Stevens, William C., Jr., *pharmaceutical executive*
Tidwell, Geoffrey Morgan *medical company executive*

San Francisco
Broadway, Nancy Ruth *landscape design and construction company executive, consultant, model and actress*
Grubb, David H. *construction company executive*
†Haas, Robert Douglas *apparel manufacturing company executive*
Hammergren, John H. *pharmaceutical company executive*
Jewett, George Frederick, Jr., *forest products company executive*
Mahoney, David L. *pharmaceutical wholesale and healthcare management company executive*
Marcus, Robert *aluminum company executive*
†Marineau, Philip Albert *apparel executive*
Merrill, Harvie Martin *manufacturing executive, director*
Seelenfreund, Alan *retired pharmaceutical company executive*
†Tully, Herbert Bullard *chemical manufacturing executive*
Turek, Paul John, III, *construction executive*
Zellerbach, William Joseph *retired paper company executive*

San Jose
Benzing, David Warren *semiconductor equipment company executive*
†Bhattacharjee, Deb *engineering*
Cartwright, Peter *electronics company executive*
Faggin, Federico *electronics executive*
†Fry, John *electronics executive*
Marks, Michael E. *electronics company executive*
Perlegos, George *electronic executive*
Rosendin, Raymond Joseph *electrical contracting company executive*
Sola, Jure *electronics executive*

San Luis Obispo
Sullivan, Thomas James *retired manufacturing company executive*

San Marcos
Page, Leslie Andrew *disinfectant manufacturing company executive*

San Mateo
Halperin, Robert Milton *retired electrical machinery company executive*
Hoops, Alan R. *health care company executive*

Santa Ana
Madden, Thomas A. *automotive parts manufacturing executive*
Murai, Kevin *electronics company executive*
Phanstiel, Howard G. *health care system executive*
Washburn, Lawrence Robert *manufacturing executive*
Yuen, Andy Tak Sing *electronics executive*

Santa Barbara
Barber, Jerry Randel *medical device company executive*
Blasingame, Benjamin Paul *electronics company executive*
Coffin, Dwight Clay *retired grain company executive*
Potter, David Samuel *former automotive company executive*
Prindle, William Roscoe *retired glass company executive*

Santa Clara
Elkus, Richard J., Jr., *electronics company executive*
†Grove, Andrew S. *electronics company executive*
Halla, Brian L. *electronics company executive*

Santa Fe Springs
†Lovatt, Arthur Kingsbury, Jr., *manufacturing company executive*

Santa Monica
Bush, William Glenn *manufacturing company executive, engineer*

Saratoga
Houston, Joseph Brantley, Jr., *optical instrument company executive*
Reagan, Joseph Bernard *retired aerospace executive, management consultant*
†Rollo, F. David *hospital management company executive, health care educator*

Scotts Valley
Nitz, Frederic William *electronics company executive*

Sherman Oaks
Krueger, Kenneth John *nutritionist, educator*

Solana Beach
Arledge, Charles Stone *former aerospace executive, entrepreneur*
Brody, Arthur *industrial executive*
Derbes, Daniel William *manufacturing executive*

Soquel
Goodman, Charles Schaffner, Jr., *food product executive, consultant*

South San Francisco
Hull, Cordell William *business executive*

Sunnyvale
Castor, Jon Stuart *electronics company executive*
Evans, Barton, Jr., *analytical instrument company executive*
†Gutshall, Thomas L. *clinical diagnostics company executive*
†Kempf, Martine *voice control device manufacturing company executive*

Tarzana
Firestone, Morton H. *business management executive*

Thousand Oaks
Nanula, Richard *health products executive*
Sharer, Kevin W. *healthcare products company executive*
Zhao, Sean Zixian *pharmaceutical company executive*

Torrance
Burris, Bill Buchanan, Jr., *automotive marketing executive*

Tustin
Hester, Norman Eric *chemical company technical executive, chemist*

Ukiah
†Newell, Barbara Ann *coatings company executive*

Upland
†Goodman, John M. *construction executive*

Vallejo
Womack, Thomas Houston *manufacturing company executive*

Valley Center
Andersen, Robert *health products, business executive*

Villa Park
Hawe, David Lee *manufacturing consultant, venture capitalist*

Walnut
†Shea, John F. *construction executive, contractor*

Walnut Creek
Hamlin, Kenneth Eldred, Jr., *retired pharmaceutical company executive*
Roath, Stephen D. *retired pharmaceutical company executive*
Shastid, Jon Barton *wine company executive*

Watsonville
Fields, Carl Victor *food company executive*

West Hollywood
Stern, Ruth Szold *business executive, artist*

Westlake Village
†Colburn, Keith W. *electronics executive*
Nichols, Steven *shoe and clothing manufacturing executive*
Weisman, Martin Jerome *retired manufacturing company executive*

Wilmington
Hamai, James Yutaka *business executive*

Woodland Hills
Brown, Michael R. *former defense industry executive*
Gellert, Jay M. *health and medical products executive*
Morishita, Akihiko *trading company executive*

Woodside
Gates, Milo Sedgwick *retired construction company executive*

Yuba City
Sarringar, Michael Ray *manufacturing executive*

COLORADO

Aspen
Hansen, Steven Alan *construction executive*

Boulder
Clark, Melvin Eugene *chemical company executive*
Mancino, John Gregory *software company executive*
Routson, Clell Dennis *manufacturing company executive*

Breckenridge
Ehrhorn, Richard William *electronics company executive*

Broomfield
†Hoover, R. David *packaging company executive*
†Hopper, Terry N. *pharmaceutical executive, consultant, research scientist*

Colorado Springs
†Cimino, Jay *automotive company executive*
†Harris, Patricia Anne *manufacturing executive, physical therapist*
†Knight, Kenneth George *retired aerospace and defense company executive*

Columbine Valley
Plusk, Ronald Frank *manufacturing company executive*

Denver
Alvarado, Linda G. *construction company executive*
Childs, John David *computer hardware and services company executive*
Cooper, Larry S. *carpet industry consultant*
Gates, Charles Cassius *rubber company executive*
Harmsen, Dorothy *food products executive*
Hohner, Kenneth Dwayne *retired fodder company executive*
†Leprino, James G. *food products executive*
Livingston, Johnston Redmond *manufacturing executive*
Malone, Michael William *electronics executive, software engineer*
Marcum, Walter Phillip *manufacturing executive*
†Shaffer, Oren George *former manufacturing company executive*
Shreve, Theodore Norris *construction company executive*

Englewood
Gertz, David Lee *homebuilding company executive*
Mahoney, Gerald Francis *manufacturing company executive*
Reese, Monte Nelson *agricultural association executive*

Fort Collins
Newlin, Douglas Randal *retired lead information engineer*
Watz, Martin Charles *brewery consultant*

Golden
†Coors, Peter Hanson *beverage company executive*
†Coors, William K. *brewery executive*

Greeley
†Morgensen, Jerry Lynn *construction company executive*
†Simons, John S. *food products executive*

Lakewood
Heath, Gary Brian *manufacturing firm executive, engineer*
Rosa, Fredric David *construction company executive*

Littleton
Battilega, John A. *research and development company executive*

Lone Tree
Bauer, Randy Mark *management training firm executive*

Longmont
Breuer, Werner Alfred *retired plastics company executive*

Louisville
Kenney, Belinda Jill Forseman *technology company executive*

Monument
Karasa, Norman Lukas *home builder, developer, geologist*

CONNECTICUT

Bloomfield
Coburn, Richard Joseph *company executive, electrical engineer*

Branford
Chapman, Roger Stevens, Jr., *construction company executive*

Bridgeport
Semple, Cecil Snowdon *retired manufacturing company executive*

Bristol
Barnes, Carlyle Fuller *manufacturing executive*
Barnes, Wallace *manufacturing executive*

Cheshire
Keiser, David Wharton *biotechnology executive*

Danbury
Baker, Leonard Morton *manufacturing company executive*
†Lichtenberger, H(orst) William *chemical company executive*
†Reilley, Dennis H. *chemicals executive*

Darien
Dordelman, William Forsyth *food company executive*
Sprole, Frank Arnott *retired pharmaceutical company executive, lawyer*
Ziegler, William, III, *diversified industry executive*

East Hartford
Cassidy, John Francis, Jr., *industrial technology executive*

Fairfield
Fash, Victoria R. *healthcare company executive*
Harkrader, Milton Keene, Jr., *corporate executive*
Immelt, Jeffrey R. *diversified technology and services company executive*
McLaughlin, John Richardson *electric motor company executive*
Reeves, Edmund Hoffman, III, *food products executive*
Sutphen, Harold Amerman, Jr., *retired paper company executive*

Greenwich
†Cameron, Dort *electronics executive*
Case, Richard Paul *electronics executive*
Dettmer, Robert Gerhart *retired beverage company executive*
Farbish, Alfred B. *waterproofing materials executive*
Kelly, David Austin *investment counselor*
Mango, Wilfred Gilbert, Jr., *real estate and construction company executive*
Moreira-Caunedo, Debra *manufacturing executive*
von der Heyden, Karl Ingolf Mueller *retired manufacturing executive*
Wearly, William Levi *business executive*

Groton
†Bi, Honggang *pharmaceutical executive, researcher*
†Kopchinski, Anita Francine *pharmaceutical executive*

Hartford
Hermann, Robert Jay *manufacturing company engineering executive, consultant*
Raffay, Stephen Joseph *manufacturing company executive*

Madison
Golembeski, Jerome John *wire and cable company executive*

Meriden
Reitz, H(oward) Wesley *construction company executive*

Middlebury
Calarco, Vincent Anthony *specialty chemicals company executive*
Fickenscher, Gerald H. *chemicals company executive*

Naugatuck
Flannery, Joseph Patrick *manufacturing executive, director*

New Canaan
Burns, Ivan Alfred *grocery products and industrial company executive*
Hodgson, Richard *electronics company executive*
Sachs, John Peter *carbon company executive*

New Haven
Birnbaum, Jerome *pharmaceutical executive, consultant*
†Burak, Eric Steven *pharmaceutical researcher*
Hill, Gordon Charles, III, *company executive*

New London
Andrews, Constance Elaine *pharmaceutical executive*

Newtown
†Farrell, Edgar Henry *building components manufacturing executive, lawyer*

North Branford
Mead, Lawrence Myers, Jr., *retired aerospace executive*

Norwalk
Harris, Holton Edwin *plastics machinery manufacturing executive*
†MacInnis, Frank T. *construction company executive, holding company executive*
†Ruggiero, Anthony William *chemical company executive*

Old Lyme
Mangin, Charles-Henri *electronics company executive*

Plainville
Glassman, Gerald Seymour *metal finishing company executive*

Ridgefield
Knortz, Herbert Charles *retired conglomerate company executive*
Levine, Paul Michael *paper industry executive, consultant*
Sadow, Harvey S. *health care company executive*

Riverside
Deering, Allan Brooks *retired soft drink company executive*

Rogers
Kenworthy, Harry William *company executive*

South Kent
Samartini, James Rogers *retired appliance company executive*

Southport
Gryka, George Edwin *chemical company executive*
Wheeler, Wilmot Fitch, Jr., *diversified manufacturing company executive*

Stamford
Allaire, Paul Arthur *office equipment company executive*
Burston, Richard Mervin *business executive*
Caldwell, Philip *retired automobile manufacturing company executive, retired financial services company executive*
Coleman, Ernest Albert *plastics and materials consultant*
†Friedman, Michael *pharmaceutical executive*
Gladstone, Herbert Jack *manufacturing company executive*
Gross, Ronald Martin *forest products executive*
Hollander, Milton Bernard *corporate executive*
Hood, Edward Exum, Jr., *retired electrical manufacturing company executive*
Kingsley, John McCall, Jr., *manufacturing company executive*
Maarbjerg, Mary Penzold *office equipment company executive*
Motroni, Hector John *manufacturing executive*
Munera, Gerard Emmanuel *manufacturing company executive*
Nevans, Roy Norman *food products executive, producer*
†Olson, Richard E. *paper company executive*
†Rand, A. Barry *technology company executive*
†Romeril, Barry D. *office equipment company executive*
†Silver, R. Philip *metal products executive*
Spiegel, Merle Andrea *pharmaceutical company executive*
Thomas, Dennis *paper company executive, former government official*
Williams, Derek, Jr., *pharmaceutical professional*

Thomaston
Mühlanger, Erich *ski manufacturing company executive*

Trumbull
Schmitt, William Howard *cosmetics company executive*

Vernon Rockville
McKeever, Brian Edward *general contractor*

Wallingford
Cohen, Gordon S. *health products executive*
Jia, Weitao *dental products executive, researcher*

Waterbury
Luedke, Frederick Lee *manufacturing company executive*

West Hartford
Clear, Albert F., Jr., *retired hardware manufacturing company executive*
Doran, James Martin *retired food products company executive*

West Haven
Carroll, Joseph Gregory *pharmaceutical company executive*

Westport
Hedge, Arthur Joseph, Jr., *corporate executive*
McKane, David Bennett *business executive*

Wilton
Oberstar, Helen Elizabeth *retired cosmetics company executive*

Windsor
Ferraro, John Francis *business executive, financier*

DELAWARE

Lewes
Nehrling, Arno Herbert, Jr., *retired chemical company executive*

Milford
Konowitz, Herbert Henry *textile company executive*

Montchanin
Olney, Robert C. *diversified products manufacturing executive*

Newark
†Carroll, Charles E. *electronics executive*
†Gore, Robert W. *electronics executive*
Marrs, Barry Lee *executive director*
Molz, Robert Joseph *manufacturing company executive*
Williams, Evelyn Lois *chemical company executive, safety consultant*

Rockland
Rubin, Alan A. *pharmaceutical and biotechnology consultant*

Seaford
Slater, Charles James *construction company executive*

Wilmington
Cason, Roger Lee *retired chemical company executive, educator, consultant*
†Corbo, Vincent J. *textiles executive*
Gibson, Joseph Whitton, Jr., *retired chemical company executive*
Holliday, Charles O., Jr., *chemical company executive*
†Hollingsworth, David Southerland *chemical company executive*
Johns, Emerson Thomas *chemical company executive*
Lassen, John Kai *development company executive*
Lewis, George Withrow *business executive*
Lukach, Carl Andrew *retired chemicals executive*
McCracken, Steven R. *textiles executive*
McLeer, Laureen Dorothy *drug development and pharmaceutical professional*
Rose, Selwyn H. *chemical company executive*
†Tomic, Ernst A. *chemicals executive*
Uffner, Michael S. *automotive executive*
Vary, Eva Maros *retired chemical company executive*
†Wang, Yize Richard *pharmaceutical executive*
Woods, Thomas Stephen *chemicals executive, researcher*
†Woolard, Edgar S., Jr., *chemical company executive*

DISTRICT OF COLUMBIA

Washington
Chambers, Letitia Pearl Caroline *consulting firm executive*
Cook, Richard Kelsey *aerospace industry executive*
†Culp, H. Lawrence *manufacturing executive*
Davis, Lance Alan *research and development executive, metallurgical engineer*
Griffin, Robert Thomas *automotive company executive*
Grossi, Ralph Edward *agricultural conservation organization executive, farmer, rancher*
Halperin, Jerome Arthur *pharmaceutical executive*
Kelly, Marguerite Stehli *fashion executive, consultant*
Misner, Robert David *electronic warfare and magnetic recording consultant, electro-mechanical company executive*
Moore, Robert Madison *food industry executive, lawyer*
Persinger, Del Louis *pharmaceutical company executive*
†Post, Robert Louis *research and development company executive*
Slater, Doris Ernestine Wilke *business executive*
Thompson, Richard Leon *pharmaceutical company executive, lawyer*

FLORIDA

Amelia Island
Adelman, Robert Paul *retired construction company executive, lawyer*
Ash, Frederick Melvin *retired manufacturing company executive*

Anna Maria
Kaiser, Albert Farr *diversified corporation executive*

Boca Raton
Feld, Joseph *construction executive*
Klein, Robert *manufacturing company executive*
O'Donnell, Joseph Michael *electronics executive*
Rabinowitz, Wilbur Melvin *manufacturing executive, consultant*
Wyatt, James Luther *drapery hardware company executive*

Bonita Springs
Rust, William James *retired steel company executive*
Sargent, Charles Lee *manufacturing company executive*

Boynton Beach
Jensen, Reuben Rolland *former automotive company executive*

Bradenton
†Dudley, Perry, Jr., *retired electronics executive*
†Howe, Carroll Victor *construction equipment company executive*
Price, Edgar Hilleary, Jr., *business consultant*

Brooksville
Pylipow, Stanley Ross *retired manufacturing company executive*

Cape Coral
McKinley, James Frank, Jr., *retired manufacturing executive*
Stuart, Robert *container manufacturing executive*

Clearwater
†Kiehl, E. Robert *manufacturing executive, consultant*
Smith, Marion Pafford *avionics company executive, retired*

Coconut Grove
Gorman, Michael Stephen *construction executive*

Coral Gables
Burini, Sonia Montes de Oca *apparel manufacturing and public relations executive*

Deerfield Beach
†Brown, Colin *automotive executive*

Delray Beach
Case, Manning Eugene, Jr., *retired food products executive*
Fitzpatrick, David J. *electronics executive*
Force, Elizabeth Elma *retired pharmaceutical executive, consultant*
Goldenberg, George *retired pharmaceutical company executive*
Himmelright, Robert John, Jr., *rubber company executive*
Jacobson, Herbert Leonard *licensing executive*
Pesses, Marvin *metal products executive, consultant*
Saffer, Alfred *retired chemical company executive*
Smith, John Joseph, Jr., *textile company executive, educator*

Dunedin
Tweedy, Robert Hugh *retired equipment company executive*

Flagler Beach
Stockton, Anderson Berrian *electronics company executive, consultant, genealogist*

Fort Lauderdale
Carney, Dennis Joseph *former steel company executive, consulting company executive*
Jackson, Michael J. *automotive retail company executive*
†Levy, Michael *electronic manufacturing company executive*
†Morse, Edward J. *automotive executive*
Peltzer, Douglas Lea *semiconductor device manufacturing company executive*

Fort Myers
Wendeborn, Richard Donald *retired manufacturing company executive*

Fort Walton Beach
Rogers, Steven Charles *electronics technician*

Hallandale
Glaubinger, Lawrence David *retired manufacturing company executive*

Heathrow
Darbelnet, Robert Louis *automobile association executive*

Hialeah
Engler, Eva Kay *dental and veterinary products company executive*

Hobe Sound
Casey, Edward Paul *manufacturing company executive*
Craig, David Jeoffrey *retired manufacturing company executive*

Homestead
Willner, Eugene Burton *food and liquor company executive*

Indian River Shores
Wiegner, Edward Alex *multi-industry executive*

Jacksonville
Jackson, Julian Ellis *food company executive*
Mahaffy, Telfair *safety scientist*
†Nutter, Wallace Lee *paper manufacturing executive*
Smith, David A. *medical services executive*
Welch, Philip Burland *electronics and office products company executive*

Jupiter
De George, Lawrence Joseph *diversified company executive*
Feinberg, Herbert *apparel and beverage executive*
Garfinkel, Harmon Mark *retired specialty chemicals company executive*
†Wrist, Peter Ellis *retired pulp and paper company executive*

Key Largo
Davidson, Thomas Noel *business executive*

Lakeland
Hatten, William Seward *manufacturing company executive*
Prince, Don David *automotive technician*

Leesburg
Talley, William Giles, Jr., *manufacturing company executive*

Lighthouse Point
Friedrichs, Arthur Martin *manufacturing company executive, retired*

Lutz
Fritzsche, R(obert) Wayne *corporate executive*

Marco Island
Guerrant, David Edward *retired food company executive*
Traher, William George *automotive model maker, retired*

Melbourne
Bush, Norman *research and development executive*

Merritt Island
†Deardoff, R. Bruce *automotive executive*

Miami
Anscher, Bernard *manufacturing executive, investor, management consultant*
Borkan, William Noah *biomedical electronics company executive*
Frigo, James Peter Paul *industrial hardware company executive*
Frost, Philip *pharmaceutical executive, dermatologist*
†Sherman, Beatrice Ettinger *business executive*
Thompson, Allen Joseph *construction executive, civil engineer*
Thornburg, Frederick Fletcher *diversified business executive, lawyer*

Naples
Baldwin, Ralph Belknap *retired manufacturing company executive, astronomer*
Berger, Charles Martin *lawn and garden company executive*
Butler, Frederick George *retired drug company executive*
Dykstra, David Allen *corporate executive*
Gade, Marvin Francis *retired paper company executive*
Laidig, William Rupert *retired paper company executive*
Larson, Wilfred Joseph *chemical company executive*
LaRusso, Anthony Carl *company executive, educator*
Mutz, Oscar Ulysses *manufacturing and distribution executive*
Sharpe, Robert Francis *equipment manufacturing company executive*
Slayton, John Arthur *electric motor manufacturing executive*
Vanderslice, Thomas Aquinas *electronics executive*
von Arx, Dolph William *food products executive*
Whitley, Arthur Francis *retired international manufacturing company executive, engineer, lawyer*
Williams, Edson Poe *retired automotive company executive*

New Port Richey
Lake, Victor Hugo *former manufacturing company executive*
Maysilles, Daniel Bruce *pharmaceutical services executive*
Oosten, Roger Lester *medical manufacturing executive*
Sebring, Marjorie Marie Allison *former home furnishings company executive*

New Smyrna Beach
Skove, Thomas Malcolm *retired manufacturing company financial executive*

Niceville
Litke, Donald Paul *business executive, retired military officer*

North Palm Beach
Hushing, William Collins *retired corporate executive*

North Port
de Silva, John Arthur F. *pharmaceutical executive*

Ocala
Stickeler, Carl Ann Louise *professional parliamentarian*

Ocean Ridge
Grabner, George John *manufacturing executive*

Orlando
Brownlee, Thomas Marshall *manufacturing executive*
Cawthon, Frank H. *retired construction company executive*
Davis, Marvin Arnold *manufacturing company executive*
Pierce, Jerry Earl *business executive*
Rivera, Richard Edwin *restaurant chain executive*
Smyth, Joseph Vincent *manufacturing company executive*
Whitworth, Hall Baker *forest products company executive*

Osprey
Hirons, William Beacom *retired chemical company executive*
Petrik, Gerd *pharmaceutical executive*

Palm Beach
Habicht, Frank Henry *retired industrial executive*
Winkler, Joseph Conrad *former recreational products manufacturing executive*

Palm Beach Gardens
Keppler, William Edmund *multinational company executive*

Staub, W. Arthur *health care products executive*

Palm City
Conklin, George Melville *retired food products executive*
Derrickson, William Borden *manufacturing executive*
Wishart, Ronald Sinclair *retired chemical company executive*

Palm Harbor
Bennett, John Joseph *professional services company executive*
Grace, John Eugene *business forms company executive*

Paxton
Kearns, John William (Bill Kearns) *electronics inventor and executive*

Pinellas Park
Hall, Charles Allen *aerospace and energy consultant*

Plantation
Devol, George Charles, Jr., *manufacturing executive*

Pompano Beach
Fritsch, Billy Dale, Jr., *construction company executive*
Schwartz, Joseph *retired container company executive*

Ponte Vedra Beach
Langford, Dean Ted *lighting and precision materials company executive*

Punta Gorda
Koll, Richard Leroy *retired chemical company executive*

Reddick
Corwin, Joyce Elizabeth Stedman *construction company executive*

Royal Palm Beach
Perez, Jorge Luis *retired manufacturing executive*

Safety Harbor
Dohnal, William Edward *retired steel company executive, consultant, accountant*

Saint Petersburg
Dimas, Marilyn J. *health resources executive*
†Main, Timothy L. *electronics executive*
Mills, William Harold, Jr., *construction company executive*
Naimoli, Vincent Joseph *diversified operating and holding company executive*
Spence, Philip William *manufacturing executive, consultant*

Sarasota
Berkoff, Charles Edward *pharmaceutical executive*
Hoffman, Oscar Allen *retired forest products company executive*
Miranda, Carlos Sa *food products company executive*
Mullane, John Francis *pharmaceutical company executive*
Roth, James Frank *manufacturing company executive, chemist*
Slocum, Donald Hillman *product development executive*
Venit, William Bennett *electrical products company executive, consultant*
West, Bob *pharmaceutical company executive*

South Florida
Hoffman, Randy Michael *automotive executive*

Spring Hill
Martin, Gary J. *retired business executive, mayor*

Stuart
Jaffe, Jeff Hugh *retired food products executive*
Leibson, Irving *retired industrial executive*
McKenna, Sidney F. *retired technical company executive*
Taudien, Edward Paul *retired construction executive*

Summerfield
McNulty, Carell Stewart, Jr., *retired manufacturing company executive, architect*

Sunrise
Bainton, Donald J. *diversified manufacturing company executive*

Tamarac
Auletta, Joan Miglorisi *construction company executive, mortgage and insurance broker*

Tampa
Brown, Troy Anderson, Jr., *retired electrical distributing company executive*
Flom, Edward Leonard *retired steel company executive*
Genter, John Robert *grocery industry executive*
Hyatt, Kenneth E(rnest) *diversified manufacturing executive*
VanButsel, Michael R. *real estate broker, builder and developer*

Tequesta
Peterson, James Robert *retired writing instrument manufacturing executive*
Seal, John S., Jr., *manufacturing company executive*

The Villages
Putnam, Lloyd Alan *retired food products executive, apple specialist*

Valrico
Goldberg, Ron *plastics broker executive*

Venice
Lanford, Luke Dean *retired electronics company executive*

Vero Beach
Allik, Michael *diversified industry executive*
Cartwright, Alton Stuart *electrical manufacturing company executive*
Hughes, George Maxwell Knight *pharmaceutical company executive, retired*
Ingwersen, Martin Lewis *shipyard executive*
Janicki, Robert Stephen *retired pharmaceutical company executive*
MacTaggart, Barry *retired corporate executive*
Reed, Sherman Kennedy *chemical consultant*
Ritterhoff, C(harles) William *retired steel company executive*
Wilcox, Harry Wilbur, Jr., *retired corporate executive*

Village Of Golf
Boer, F. Peter *chemical company executive*

Wesley Chapel
Revelle, Donald Gene *manufacturing and health care company executive, consultant*

West Palm Beach
Jenkins, Ruben Lee *retired chemical company executive, lawyer*
†Roderick, Robert Lee *aerospace executive*
Stern, Harold Peter *business executive*
Vecellio, Leo Arthur, Jr., *construction company executive*

Weston
Staneart, Larry William *technology company marketing executive*

Winter Haven
O'Connor, R. D. *retired health care executive*

Winter Park
Jones, Joseph Wayne *business executive, entrepreneur*
Kincaid, Rodney Lyle *construction company executive*
Kost, Wayne L. *business executive*

GEORGIA

Alpharetta
Brands, James Edwin *medical products executive*
Petersen-Frey, Roland *manufacturing executive*
Thomas, Robert L. *retired manufacturing company executive*

Athens
†Carroll, Archie Benjamin, III, *management educator*
†Eberhart, William Coile *apparel repair specialist, writer*

Atlanta
†Bekkers, John *food products company executive*
Corr, James Vanis *furniture manufacturing executive, investor, lawyer, accountant*
Correll, Alston Dayton, Jr., (Pete Correll) *forest products company executive*
Daft, Douglas N. *food products executive*
Dennison, Stanley Scott *retired forest products company executive, consultant*
Emerson, James Larry *beverage company executive*
†Huff, Danny W. *paper products executive*
†Humphrey, Stephen M. *paperboard company executive*
Johnston, Summerfield K., Jr., *food products executive*
Kline, Lowry F. *food products executive, lawyer*
Liebmann, Seymour W. *construction consultant*
Lubker, John William, II, *manufacturing executive, civil engineer*
Martinez, Ricardo *research and development company executive*
Millikan, James Rolens *cleaning service executive, musician, composer, fitness consultant*
Mitchell, Stephen Milton *manufacturing executive*
Murphy, James Jeffrey *electronics executive*
Prince, Larry L. *automotive parts and supplies company executive*
Reith, Carl Joseph *apparel industry executive*
Rudie, Alan William *pulp and paper research and development educator*
Thorp, Benjamin A., III, *paper manufacturing company executive*
Tilley, Tana Marie *pharamaceutical executive, registered nurse*

Ball Ground
Tucker, Robert Dennard *health care products executive*

Baxley
Reddy, Yenamala Ramachandra *metal processing executive*

Brunswick
Brubaker, Robert Paul *food products executive*
Iannicelli, Joseph *chemical company executive, consultant*

Calhoun
†Lorberbaum, Jeffrey S. *textiles executive*

College Park
Fahy, Nancy Lee *food products marketing executive*

Columbus
†Heard, William T. *automotive executive*
†Leebern, Donald M., Jr., *distilled beverage executive*
Murray, James J. *textiles executive*

Conley
Marcus, James Elbert *manufacturing company executive*

Dalton
†Bouckaert, Carl M. *manufacturing executive*

Duluth
Brody, Aaron Leo *food and packaging consultant*
Hillstead, Richard Averill *product development executive*

Fortson
Schmitt, Ralph George *manufacturing company executive*

Gainesville
Pilgrim, James Rollins *retail furniture company executive*

Hinesville
Baer, William Harold *business executive*

Macon
McFarland, Terry Lynn *construction company executive*

Marietta
Lewis, William Headley, Jr., *manufacturing company executive*
†McGahan, Martin J. *health products executive*
Swanson, William Fredin, III, *manufacturing executive*

Milledgeville
Williamson, John Thomas, Sr., *minerals company executive*

Moultrie
Vereen, William Jerome *uniform manufacturing company executive*

Norcross
Adams, Kenneth Francis *automobile maufacturing company executive*
Rubright, James Alfred *paperboard and packaging company executive*

Oakwood
Smith, David Claiborne *construction company executive*

Rome
Sellers, Jimmie *construction executive*

Roswell
Boley, Dennis Lynn *construction company executive*
Diercks, Chester William, Jr., *capital goods manufacturing company executive*

Savannah
Cartledge, Raymond Eugene *retired paper company executive*
Gillespie, Daniel Curtis, Sr., *retired non-profit company executive, consultant*
Granger, Harvey, Jr., *retired manufacturing company executive*
Peer, George Joseph *metals company executive*
Spitz, Seymour James, Jr., *retired fragrance company executive*
Sprague, William Wallace, Jr., *retired food company executive*

Sea Island
Mc Swiney, James Wilmer *retired pulp and paper manufacturing company executive*

Thomasville
Flowers, Langdon Strong *foods company executive*
†Mc Mullian, Amos Ryals *food company executive*

West Point
Andrews, Gerald Bruce, Sr., *retired textile executive*
Glover, Clifford Clarke *retired construction company executive*

HAWAII

Honolulu
Andrasick, James Stephen *diversified company executive*
Finney, John Edgar, III, *food products executive*
Hughes, Robert Harrison *former agricultural products executive*
Usui, Leslie Raymond *retired clothing executive*

Kaneohe
Vincent, Thomas James *retired manufacturing company executive*

Papaikou
Buyers, John William Amerman *agribusiness and specialty foods company executive*

Princeville
Forth, Kevin Bernard *beverage distributing industry consultant*

IDAHO

Boise
Appleton, Steven R. *electronics executive*
Cleary, Edward William *retired diversified forest products company executive*
Harad, George Jay *manufacturing company executive*
†Hlobik, Lawrence S. *agricultural products executive*
Johnston, Lawrence R. *food products executive*
McClary, James Daly *retired contractor*

Salmon
Snook, Quinton *construction company executive*

ILLINOIS

Abbott Park
†Leiden, Jeffrey Marc *pharmaceutical executive, molecular biologist, cardiologist*
Lussen, John Frederick *pharmaceutical laboratory executive*
Martin, Yvonne Connolly *pharmaceutical company executive*
White, Miles D. *pharmaceutical company executive*

Addison
†Hausner, Karl *health products executive*

Argonne
†Goldman, Arthur Joseph *retired research and development company executive*

Arlington Heights
Church, Herbert Stephen, Jr., *retired construction company executive*
Hughes, John *chemical company executive*
Johnson, Margaret H. *welding company executive*
Li, Norman N. *chemicals executive*

Aurora
Belcher, La Jeune *automotive executive*

Barrington
Furst, Warren Arthur *retired holding company executive*

Bloomingdale
Taylor, Carmen Kaye *apparel company executive*

Broadview
Pang, Joshua Keun-Uk *trade company executive*

Chester
Welge, Donald Edward *food manufacturing executive*

Chicago
Barber, Edward Bruce *medical products executive*
Bellantoni, Maureen Blanchfield *manufacturing and retail executive*
Borenstine, Alvin Jerome *search company executive*
Brake, Cecil Clifford *retired diversified manufacturing executive*
†Bryan, John Henry *food and consumer products company executive*
Bueche, Wendell Francis *agricultural products company executive*
Clarke, Richard Stewart *security company executive*
Cooper, Charles Gilbert *toiletries and cosmetics company executive*
†Cotter, Daniel A. *diversified company executive*
Covalt, Robert Byron *chemicals executive*
Crown, Lester *manufacturing company executive*
†Curran, Raymond M. *paper-based packaging company executive*
Falkof, Melvin Milton *retired food products company executive*
Giesen, Richard Allyn *business executive*
Haas, Howard Green *retired bedding manufacturing company executive*
†Heisley, Michael E., Sr., *manufacturing executive*
Horne, John R. *farm equipment company executive*
Jezuit, Leslie James *manufacturing company executive*
Lockwood, Frank James *manufacturing company executive*
McKee, Keith Earl *manufacturing technology executive*
McMillan, C. Steven *consumer packaged goods company executive*
McQuillen, James Francis *electronics executive*
Moore, Patrick J. *paper company executive*
Murphy, Michael Emmett *retired food company executive*
Nichol, Norman J. *manufacturing executive*
Nichols, John Doane *diversified manufacturing corporation executive*
Parrish, Overton Burgin, Jr., *pharmaceutical corporation executive*
Patel, Homi Burjor *apparel company executive*
†Reum, W. Robert *manufacturing executive*
Rosenberg, Gary Aron *real estate development executive, lawyer*
Singer, Deborah Louise *medical products company executive*
Sippey, Roger Boyd *corporate executive*
Stack, Stephen S. *manufacturing company executive*
Steinfeld, Manfred *furniture manufacturing executive*
†Stone, Alan *container company executive*
Stotler, Edith Ann *retired grain company executive, financial planner*
Wellington, Robert Hall *manufacturing company executive*
Williams, Richard Lucas, III, *electronics company executive, lawyer*
Zeid, Philip L. *metal recycling executive*

Crystal Lake
Althoff, J(ames) L. *construction company executive*
Anderson, Lyle Arthur *retired manufacturing company executive*
†Booth, David Layton *retired chemicals executive*

Decatur
Andreas, G(lenn) Allen, Jr., *agricultural company executive*
Madding, Claudia *agricultural products executive*
Schmalz, Douglas J. *agricultural company executive*
Staley, Henry Mueller *manufacturing company executive*

Deer Park
Buchanan, Richard Kent *electronics company executive*

Deerfield
Graham, William B. *pharmaceutical company executive*
Kraemer, Harry M. Jansen, Jr., *medical products executive*
†Marsh, Miles L. *paper company executive*
†Mason, Earl Leonard *retired food products executive*
Strubel, Richard Perry *company executive*
Zywicki, Robert Albert *electrical distribution company executive*

Dekalb
†Bickner, Bruce *food products executive*
Troyer, Alvah Forrest *agriculture executive, plant breeder*

Des Plaines
Carroll, Barry Joseph *manufacturing and real estate executive*
†Frank, James S. *automotive executive*
Koford, Stuart Keith *electronics executive*

Effingham
Bonutti, Boris Paul *medical company executive*

Elk Grove Village
†Field, Larry *paper company executive*
Nadig, Gerald George *manufacturing executive*

Elmhurst
†Duchossois, Craig *manufacturing executive, heavy*
†Duchossois, Richard Louis *manufacturing executive, racetrack executive*

Evanston
†Butchko, Harriett Hays *food products executive, physician*
Menke, Allen Carl *industrial corporation executive*

Forest Park
Thomas, Alan *candy company executive*

Frankfort
Burhoe, Brian Walter *automotive service executive*

Franklin Park
†Dean, Howard M., Jr., *food company executive*
Simpson, Michael *metals service center executive*

Freeport
†Alldredge, William T. *metal products executive*

Glen Ellyn
Cvengros, Joseph Michael *manufacturing company executive*

Glenview
Blase, Anthony Idomeneus *retired electronics executive, writer, poet*
Farrell, W. James *metal products manufacturing company executive*
Gillis, Marvin Bob *retired chemical executive, consultant*
Hickey, John Thomas *retired electronics company executive*
Ptak, Frank Stanley *manufacturing executive*
Salamoun, Peter V. *retired manufacturing executive*
Smith, Harold B. *manufacturing executive*

Hanover Park
†Renner, Jacqueline Marie *business executive*

Highland Park
Rudo, Milton *retired manufacturing company executive, consultant*

Hoffman Estates
Nicholas, Arthur Soterios *manufacturing company executive*

Indianhead Park
Frisque, Alvin Joseph *retired chemical company executive*

Itasca
†Boler, John M. *manufacturing executive*

Joliet
Schmitz, Edward Henry *retired distribution company executive*

Lake Barrington
Joslin, Robert Scott *pharmaceutical company executive*

Lake Forest
†Buckley, George W. *sporting goods executive*
†Frissora, Mark P. *automotive parts manufacturing company executive*
Hamilton, Peter Bannerman *business executive, lawyer*
Hammar, Lester Everett *health care manufacturing executive, retired*
†Hodgson, Thomas Richard *retired healthcare company executive*
†Keyser, Richard Lee *distribution company executive*
†Larson, Peter N. *company executive*
O'Mara, Thomas Patrick *manufacturing company executive*
†Reyes, M. Judy *food products distribution executive*
Romans, Donald Bishop *corporate executive*

Lake Villa
Anderson, Milton Andrew *chemical executive*

Lanark
Abbott, David Henry *manufacturing company executive*

Libertyville
Baske, C. Alan *manufacturing company executive*
Burrows, Brian William *research and development manufacturing executive*

Lincolnshire
Simes, Stephen Mark *pharmaceutical products executive*
†Wesley, Norman H. *metal products executive*

Lisle
Krehbiel, Frederick August, II, *electronics company executive*

Long Grove
Liuzzi, Robert C. *chemical company executive*

Loves Park
Gloyd, Lawrence Eugene *retired diversified manufacturing company executive*

Mahomet
Bosworth, Douglas LeRoy *international company executive, educator*

Melrose Park
Cernugel, William John *consumer products and special retail executive*
Douglas, Kenneth Jay *food products executive*
Lavin, Bernice E. *cosmetics executive*
Umans, Alvin Robert *manufacturing company executive*
Wechter, Clari Ann *paint manufacturing company executive*

Moline
Becherer, Hans Walter *retired agricultural equipment executive*
Lane, Robert W. *farm equipment manufacturing executive*
Malicki, Gregg Hillard *agricultural equipment manufacturing executive*

Morton Grove
Ernst, Chester Nelson *manufacturing company executive*

Mount Prospect
Nedza, Sandra Louise *manufacturing executive*

Mount Sterling
†Tracy, Patrick F. *food products executive*

Mundelein
Kottayil, Santosh George *pharmaceutical development executive*

Naperville
Katai, Andrew Andras *chemical company executive*
Schaack, Philip Anthony *retired beverage company executive*
†Wake, Richard W. *food products executive*
†Wake, Thomas G. *food products executive*

North Chicago
Dayton, Nick A. *pharmaceutical executive*

Northbrook
Green, David *manufacturing company executive*
Jaeger, Robert Joseph *medical supplies professional*
Sayatovic, Wayne Peter *manufacturing company executive*
Schmidt, Arthur Irwin *steel fabricating company executive*
†Singer, Norman Sol *food products executive, inventor*

Northfield
Carlin, Donald Walter *retired food products executive, consultant*
Hadley, Stanton Thomas *international manufacturing and marketing company executive, lawyer*
Knight, James Atwood *manufacturing executive*
Smeds, Edward William *retired food company executive*
†Sneed, Paula Ann *food products executive*
Stepan, Frank Quinn *chemical company executive*

Oak Brook
†Cantalupo, Jim *food products executive*
Greenberg, Jack M. *food products executive*

Oak Park
Dong, Hanmin *forest products executive*

Orland Park
Gittelman, Marc Jeffrey *manufacturing and financial executive*
Kahn, Jan Edward *manufacturing company executive*

Palatine
Matsushima, Akira Paul *international company executive*

Palos Park
Nelson, Lawrence Evan *business consultant*

Park Ridge
Bales, Edward Wagner *consultant, former manufacturing executive*
Herting, Robert Leslie *pharmaceutical executive*
Markuson, Richard K. *pharmaceutical association executive*
Weber, Philip Joseph *retired manufacturing company executive*

Peoria
Disberger, Dennis Jay *manufacturing executive*
†McPheeters, F. Lynn *manufacturing executive*

Prospect Heights
Byrne, Michael Joseph *manufacturing executive*

Quincy
Walters, Tom Frederick *manufacturing company official*

Rockford
Bippus, David Paul *manufacturing company executive*
Gaylord, Edson I. *manufacturing company executive*
Horst, Bruce Everett *manufacturing company executive*
O'Donnell, William David *retired construction firm executive*

Rolling Meadows
†Cash, Alan Sherwin *electronics assembly specialist*

Rosemont
Isenberg, Howard Lee *manufacturing company executive*
Meinert, John Raymond *investment banker, clothing manufacturing and retailing executive*

Saint Charles
Stone, John McWilliams, Jr., *electronics executive*

Schaumburg
Galvin, Christopher B. *electronics company executive*
†Galvin, Robert W. *electronics executive*

Skokie
†Gupta, Vishal K *pharmaceutical scientist*

Tinley Park
Leeson, Janet Caroline Tollefson *cake specialties company executive*

Union
Perlick, Richard Allan *steel company executive*

Warrenville
Lannert, Robert Cornelius *manufacturing company executive*
Lennes, Gregory *manufacturing and financing company executive*

Waukegan
†Cherry, Peter Ballard *electrical products corporation executive*

Wayne
Brunken, Gerald Walter, Sr., *manufacturing company executive*

Westmont
†Warner, H. Ty *manufacturing executive*

Wheeling
Keats, Glenn Arthur *manufacturing company executive*
Rogers, Richard F. *construction company executive, architect, engineer*

Wilmette
Coughlan, Gary Patrick *pharmaceutical company executive*
Egloff, Fred Robert *manufacturers representative, writer, historian*
†Liberman, Jon C. *business development executive*
Pearlman, Jerry Kent *electronics company executive*

Winnetka
Burt, Robert Norcross *retired diversified manufacturing company executive*
Gavin, James John, Jr., *diversified company executive*
Hartman, Robert S. *retired paper company executive*
Kennedy, George Danner *chemical company executive*
†Puth, John Wells *consulting company executive*
Toll, Daniel Roger *corporate executive, civic leader*
Weldon, Theodore Tefft, Jr., *manufacturing executive*

Woodridge
Stall, Alan David *packaging company executive*

INDIANA

Anderson
Carrell, Terry Eugene *manufacturing company executive*

Brownsburg
Riggs, Anna Claire *metals company executive*

Brownstown
Robertson, Joseph Edmond *grain processing company executive*

Robertson, Richard Robert *grain milling executive*

Butler
Longardner, Craig Theodor *manufacturing executive*

Carmel
Shoup, Charles Samuel, Jr., *chemicals and materials executive*
Walsh, John Charles *metallurgical company executive*

Celestine
†Stout, Robert M. *manufacturing executive*

Chesterton
Brown, Gene W. *steel company executive*

Churubusco
Morgan, Gretna Faye *retired automotive executive*

Columbus
Engelking, Ellen Melinda *pattern company executive, real estate broker, manufacturing company*
†Henderson, James Alan *former engine company executive*
Loughrey, F. Joseph *manufacturing executive*
Miller, Joseph Irwin *automotive manufacturing company executive*

Elkhart
Cerny, Ronald Neal *business executive*
Corson, Thomas Harold *manufacturing company executive*
Holtz, Glenn Edward *band instrument manufacturing executive*
Kloska, Ronald Frank *manufacturing company executive*
Leader, Christopher Robert *manufacturing executive*
Mathias, Margaret Grossman *manufacturing company executive, leasing company executive*
Mischke, Frederick Charles *manufacturing company executive*

Evansville
Koch, Robert Louis, II, *manufacturing company executive, mechanical engineer*
Muehlbauer, James Herman *manufacturing executive*

Fort Wayne
Burns, Thagrus Asher *manufacturing company executive, former life insurance company executive*
Grogg, Terrie Lynn *factory assembler*
Marine, Clyde Lockwood *agricultural business consultant*
†Molfenter, David P. *former electronics executive*
†Rifkin, Leonard *metals company executive*

Franklin
Janis, F. Timothy *technology company executive*

Granger
Miller, Callix Edwin *manufacturing executive, consultant*

Greenfield
Powdrill, Gary Leo *production operations manager*

Indianapolis
†Bindley, William Edward *pharmaceutical executive*
Breier, Alan *pharmaceutical executive*
Bryja, Frank Joseph *food distribution executive*
Carlino, Guy Thomas *consulting company executive*
Dollens, Ronald W. *pharmaceuticals company executive*
†Feldman, Peter Dylan *pharmaceutical executive*
Greer, Charles Eugene *company executive, lawyer*
†Hunt, Robert G. *construction company executive*
Justice, Brady Richmond, Jr., *medical services executive*
Kirkham, James Alvin *manufacturing executive*
Lacy, Andre Balz *industrial executive*
Long, William Allan *retired forest products company executive*
Mc Farland, H. Richard *food company executive*
Risdon, Michael Paul *manufacturing executive*
Salentine, Thomas James *pharmaceutical company executive*
Smith, Donald Archie *religion business executive, consultant*
Smith, K. Clay *machinery transport company executive*
Stewart, Paul Arthur *pharmaceutical company executive*
Taurel, Sidney *pharmaceutical executive*
Tobias, Randall Lee *retired pharmaceutical company executive*
Zapapas, James Richard *pharmaceutical executive*

Lafayette
Meyer, Brud Richard *retired pharmaceutical company executive*

Loogootee
Burcham, Eva Helen (Pat Burcham) *retired electronics technician*

Middlebury
Guequierre, John Phillip *manufacturing executive*

Mishawaka
Altman, Arnold David *business executive*
†Kapson, Jordan *automotive executive*
Rubenstein, Pamela Silver
Silver, Neil Marvin *manufacturing executive*

Muncie
Fisher, John Wesley *manufacturing company executive*
Smith, Van P. *holding company executive*

Munster
Corsiglia, Robert Joseph *electrical construction company executive*
Luerssen, Frank Wonson *retired steel company executive*

Noblesville
Almquist, Donald John *retired electronics company executive*

Portage
Popp, Joseph Bruce *manufacturing executive*

Rosemont
†Reyes, J. Christopher *food products distribution executive*

Valparaiso
Blaschke, Lawrence Raymond *steel manufacturing executive, energy professional*

Washington
Graham, David Bolden *food products executive*

IOWA

Amana
Carroll, Charles A. *manufacturing executive*

Ankeny
†Scott, Beverly Jeanne *contractor, writer*

Birmingham
Goudy, James Joseph Ralph *electronics executive, educator*

Boone
†Beckwith, F. William *food products executive*

Davenport
Bannick, Janice Carol *automotive dealerships executive*
Juckem, Wilfred Philip *manufacturing company executive*

Dubuque
Crahan, Jack Bertsch *retired manufacturing company executive*
McDonald, Robert Delos *manufacturing company executive*
Tully, Thomas Alois *building materials executive, consultant, educator*

Humboldt
Dodgen, John N. *manufacturing executive*

Marshalltown
Foote, Sherrill Lynne *retired manufacturing company technician*

New Hampton
Boge, Arnold Joseph *construction executive, contractor*

Newton
Ward, Dean Morris *appliance manufacturing executive*

Okoboji
Pearson, Gerald Leon *food company executive*

Springville
Nyquist, John Davis *retired radio manufacturing company executive*

Toddville
Hazeltine, Gerald Lester *food products executive*

West Des Moines
Pomerantz, Marvin Alvin *business executive*

KANSAS

Abilene
Britt, Ronald leroy *retired manufacturing company executive*

Hesston
Yost, Lyle Edgar *retired farm equipment manufacturing company executive*

Hutchinson
Dick, Harold Latham *manufacturing executive*

Kansas City
†Baker, Clarence Albert, Sr., *structural steel construction company executive*

Leavenworth
Arneson, George Stephen *manufacturing company executive, management consultant*

Lenexa
Ascher, James John *pharmaceutical executive*
Pierson, John Theodore, Jr., *manufacturer*

Olathe
Kopac, Andrew Joseph *automotive executive*

Salina
Cosco, John Anthony *health care executive, educator, consultant, author*

Shawnee Mission
Gamet, Donald Max *appliance company executive*

Topeka
Plummer, Mary Elizabeth *cosmetologist*

Stroud, Jacqueline Lucille *medical supply company executive*

Wichita
Eby, Martin Keller, Jr., *construction company executive*
Johnson, George Taylor *training and manufacturing company executive*
Koch, Charles de Ganahl *business executive*
†Meyer, Russell William, Jr., *aircraft company executive*
†Nienke, Steven A. *construction company executive*
†Schuster, James Edward *aircraft manufacturing executive*

KENTUCKY

Bellevue
Carpenter, Woodrow Wilson *enamel company executive, ceramic engineer*

Bowling Green
Holland, John Ben *clothing manufacturing company executive*

Covington
†O'Brien, James J. *manufacturing executive*

Erlanger
Cuneo, Dennis Clifford *automotive company executive*

Greenville
Walters, Sue Fox *business executive, accountant*

Lexington
†Chowdhury, Dipak K. *pharmaceutical executive, researcher*

Louisville
Clayton, M. Courtland *engineering, manufacturing sourcing and health wellness and internet technology consultant*
Heiden, Charles Kenneth *retired military officer*
James, Virginia Lynn *contracts executive*
Mountz, Wade *retired health service management executive*
Rapp, Christian Ferree *retired textile home furnishings company executive*
Street, William May *beverage company executive*
Vogel, Werner Paul *retired machine company executive*

Newport
Trauth, David E. *dairy company executive*

Rineyville
Jackson, Charles Wayne *food products executive, former telecommunications industry executive*

LOUISIANA

Baton Rouge
†Bernard, J. M., Jr., *manufacturing executive*
†Turner, Bert S. *construction executive*

Calhoun
Robbins, Marion LeRon *agricultural research/extension executive*

Covington
Napier, William James, Jr., *marine oil and gas construction consultant*

Denham Springs
May, Kenneth Nathaniel *food industry consultant*

Lafayette
Mallet, Alexis, Jr., *construction company executive*

Many
Byles, Robert Valmore *manufacturing company executive*

New Iberia
Grubbs, Conway E. *marine company executive*

New Orleans
Cospolich, James Donald *electrical engineering executive, consultant*
Deasy, William John *construction, marine dredging, engineering and mining company executive*

Slidell
Stroud, Robert Arlen *medical equipment company executive*

MAINE

Andover
Kaltsos, Angelo John *electronics executive, educator, photographer*

Bath
Simone, Gail Elisabeth *manufacturing administrator*

Falmouth
Cabot, Lewis Pickering *manufacturing company executive, art consultant*

Kennebunk
Damon, Edmund Holcombe *retired plastics company executive*

Kennebunkport
Featherman, Bernard *steel company executive*

New Vineyard
Smith, Frederick Orville, II, *wood products manufacturer, retired naval officer*

Portland
Whedon, Ralph Gibbs *manufacturing executive*

Scarborough
Shire, Donald Thomas *retired air products and chemicals executive, lawyer*

South Bristol
Wells, Arthur Stanton *retired manufacturing company executive*

MARYLAND

Annapolis
Hyde, Lawrence Henry, Jr., *industrial company executive*

Baltimore
Deoul, Neal *electronics company executive*
Foster, Lester Anderson, Jr., *retired steel company executive*
Glassgold, Israel Leon *construction company executive, engineer, consultant*
†Glassman, Jon David *research and development company executive*
†Hackerman, Willard *construction services executive*
Legum, Jeffrey Alfred *holding company executive*
†Lucas, Barbara B. *electrical equipment manufacturing executive*
Reeder, Oliver Howard *paint products manufacturing executive*
Rheinstein, Peter Howard *healthcare company executive, consultant, physician, lawyer*
Saba, Walter Pedro *health education communications executive*
Scheeler, Charles *construction company executive*
Strull, Gene *technology consultant, retired electrical manufacturing company executive*

Bethesda
Baird, Charles Fitz *retired mining and metals company executive*
Bregman, Jacob Israel *environmental consulting company executive*
Chin, James Ying *corporate executive*
Spector, Eleanor Ruth *corporation executive*

Bozman
Peterson, H(arry) William *chemicals executive, consultant*

Chevy Chase
Bissinger, Frederick Lewis *retired manufacturing executive, consultant*
Cushen, Walter Edward *contractor, consultant*
Ewing, Frank Marion *lumber company executive, industrial land developer*

Columbia
†Miller, James L. *food products executive*

Easton
Peterson, James Kenneth *manufacturing company executive*

Frederick
†Holl, David Russell *construction executive*

Gaithersburg
Delgado, Dwighd D(ubied) *company executive*

Germantown
Hill-Fessenden, Anne Lynn *multi-faceted food and beverage consultant*

North Potomac
Pergantis, Constantine George *lighting contractor*

Ocean City
Corun, Ronald Lewis *asphalt refining executive*

Owings Mills
Vijayakumar, Rajagopal *filter industry executive*

Potomac
Epstein, Mark Robert *electronics manufacturing executive*
Karson, Emile *international business executive*
Ryan, Frank Thomas *tire company executive*

Rockville
†Correa, Galo A. *construction executive*
Hubert, Barbara Boeklen *pharmaceutical company executive*
Juliana, James Nicholas *ordnance company executive*
Landon, John Campbell *research and development company executive*
Manasse, Henri Richard, Jr., *association executive*
Miller, Kenneth Michael *electronics executive, director*

Saint Michaels
Jones, Raymond Edward, Jr., *brewing executive*
Peck, Charles Edward *retired construction and mortgage executive*

Salisbury
Madden, Heather Ann *aluminum company executive*
†Perdue, James A. *food products executive*

Silver Spring
Coates, Robert Jay *retired electronic scientist, consultant*

Cunningham, Keith Allen *corporate executive, accountant, lawyer, engineer*

Upper Marlboro
Bowles, Liza K. *construction executive*

White Hall
Radigan, Frank Xavier *pharmaceutical company executive*

MASSACHUSETTS

Agawam
Potts, Harold Francis, Jr., *elevator company executive*

Attleboro
Hammerle, Fredric Joseph *technical manufacturing executive*
Stahl, Robert Alan *manufacturing executive, consultant*

Billerica
Kolb, Charles Eugene *research and development company executive*

Blackstone
Tomaszek, Thomas Richard *manufacturing executive*

Boston
†Barnes, Steven W. *diagnostic equipment company executive*
Bodman, Samuel Wright, III, *specialty chemicals and materials company executive*
Chizauskas, Cathleen Jo *manufacturing company executive*
Hoskins, William Keller *pharmaceutical executive, mediator/arbitrator, lawyer*
Leaman, J. Richard, Jr., *paper company executive*
Schorr, Marvin G. *technology company executive*

Burlington
Bright, Willard Mead *manufacturing company executive*
Hall, John Reginald, II, *electronics company executive, retired army officer*
Sproull, Robert Fletcher *research and development company executive*

Cambridge
†Berger, Harvey James *pharmaceutical company executive, physician, educator*
Forney, G(eorge) David, Jr., *retired electronics company executive*
Fox, Irving Harvey *clinical researcher, medical products executive*
Frosch, Robert Alan *retired automobile manufacturing executive, physicist*
Goell, James Emanuel *electronics company executive*
Goldberg, Marc Evan *biotechnology venture capitalist*
Lewis, Henry Rafalsky *manufacturing company executive*
Ryan, Pauline Jen *biomedical company executive*
Scharlack, Ronald Stuart *medical device company executive*
Termeer, Henricus Adrianus *biotechnology company executive*
Thompson, Robert L., Jr., *pharmaceutical executive, lawyer*

Canton
†Fireman, Paul B. *footwear and apparel company executive*

Chatham
McDonell, Horace George, Jr., *instrument company executive*

Chelmsford
Furumoto, Horace Wataru *medical products company executive*

Chelsea
Dickstein, Harvey Leonard *pharmaceutical company executive*
Rabstejnek, George John *photomics executive*

Danvers
Bilow, Howard L. *health care company executive*
Waite, Charles Morrison *food company executive*

Dedham
†Balsamo, Salvatore Anthony *technical and temporary employment companies executive*
DiCamillo, Gary Thomas *manufacturing executive*

Easthampton
Perkins, Homer Guy *manufacturing company executive*

Falmouth
Litschgi, Richard John *computer manufacturing company executive*

Foxboro
Imbault, James Joseph *manufacturing company executive*

Framingham
Deutsch, Marshall E(manuel) *medical products company executive, inventor*
Silverman, Harold Irving *pharmaceutical executive*

Gloucester
Lanzkron, Rolf Wolfgang *manufacturing executive*

Hanson
Norris, John Anthony *health products executive, lawyer, educator*

Haverhill
Bigelow, Peter *electronics executive*

Hingham
Llewellyn, John Schofield, Jr., *former food company executive*

Hopkinton
†Ruettgers, Michael Cadet *electronics executive*
Tucci, Joseph M. *computer software and services executive*

Ipswich
Barth, Elmer Ernest *wire and cable company executive*

Lexington
†Bahcall, Safi R. *pharmaceutical executive*
Baron, Sheldon *research and development company executive*
Berstein, Irving Aaron *biotechnology and medical technology executive*
†Harris, John D., II, *electronics executive*
†Kapples, John W. *electronics executive*
McGirr, David William John *pharmaceutical executive*
†Rhoads, Rebecca R. *electronics executive*
†Shelton, Gregory S. *electronics executive*
Smith, Robert Louis *construction company executive*
†Swanson, William Henry *equipment manufacturing company executive*

Lincoln
Green, David Henry *manufacturing company executive*

Marblehead
Thompson, Michael Laurie *food manufacturing executive*

Marlborough
†Carter, James W. *electronics executive*

Mashpee
Stein, Seymour *electronics scientist*

Medford
Chaturvedi, Pravin R. *pharmaceutical executive*

Middleton
Daniels, William Albert *food products executive*

Natick
Abele, John E. *medical products executive*
Nicholas, Peter M. *medical products executive*

Needham
Cohen, Lewis Cobrain *security products firm executive*
Ingram, George *business executive*

Newton
Chubb, Stephen Darrow *medical corporation executive*
Clarkson, Cheryl Lee *healthcare executive*
†Gerrity, J(ames) Frank, II, *building materials company executive*

North Andover
Jannini, Ralph Humbert, III, *electronics executive*
Patel, Mahendra Rambhai *electronics executive*

North Billerica
Chu, Jeffrey Chuan *business executive, consultant*

Quincy
McClung, J(ames) David *corporate executive, lawyer, academic administrator*

Springfield
†D'Amour, Donald H. *supermarket chain executive*
Gallup, John Gardiner *retired paper company executive*

Sturbridge
Belforte, David Arthur *business executive*

Sudbury
Henderson, Ernest, III, *health care executive*

Taunton
McMullen, John Henry, Jr., *manufacturing company executive, educator*

Tewksbury
†DeMoulas, Telemachus A. *retail grocery company executive*
†Smith, Daniel L. *electronics executive*

Wakefield
Kelley, John Henry *electronics company executive*
†Prabhala, Rao H. *pharmaceutical executive*

Waltham
Ackerman, Robert Wallace *venture management company executive*
Bernstein, Stanley Joseph *manufacturing executive*
†Dekkers, Marijn *electronics executive*
Fiore, Nicholas Francis *special components and materials company executive*
Floyd, John Taylor *electronics executive*

Watertown
Cooper, Marc Lawrence *food products company executive*

Wayland
Gleason III, Charles Richard *dental industry executive, business management consultant*

Wellesley
Gailius, Gilbert Keistutis *manufacturing company executive*
Krieg, Arthur M. *pharmaceutical company executive, internist*

Wellesley Hills
Marcus, William Michael *rubber and vinyl products manufacturing company executive*

West Bridgewater
Wyner, Justin L. *laminating company executive*

Westwood
Kushner, Jeffrey L. *manufacturing company executive*

Wilbraham
Dailey, Franklyn Edward, Jr., *electronic image technology company executive, analyst, consultant*

Williamstown
McGill, Robert Ernest, III, *retired manufacturing company executive*

Winchester
Jackson, Francis Joseph *research and development company executive*

Woburn
Razdan, Raj Kumar *chemicals executive*

Worcester
Nelson, John Martin *corporate executive*

MICHIGAN

Ann Arbor
Caveney, William John *former pharmaceutical company executive, lawyer*
Decker, Raymond Frank *technology transfer executive, metal products executive, scientist*
Herzig, David Jacob *pharmaceutical company executive, consultant*
Penske, Roger S. *manufacturing and transportation executive*
Robertson, David Wayne *pharmaceutical executive*
Winbury, Martin Maurice *pharmaceutical executive, educator*

Auburn Hills
Davidson, William M. *diversified company executive, professional basketball executive*
Farrar, Stephen Prescott *glass products manufacturing executive*
†Fluharty, David Arthur *automotive executive, statistician, consultant*
Gerson, Ralph Joseph *corporate executive*
Hoffman, Frederick William *automotive executive*
Trebing, David Martin *automotive executive*
Weiler, Scott Michael *machine tool manufacturing company executive*

Battle Creek
Gutierrez, Carlos M. *grocery manufacturing company executive*
†Langbo, Arnold Gordon *food company executive*

Benton Harbor
Hopp, Daniel Frederick *manufacturing company executive, lawyer*
Whitwam, David Ray *appliance manufacturing company executive*

Beulah
Edwards, Wallace Winfield *retired automotive company executive*

Birmingham
Foxen, Richard William *manufacturing company executive*
Nicholson, Robert D. *manufacturing executive*
VanDeusen, Bruce Dudley *company executive*

Bloomfield Hills
Frey, Stuart Macklin *automobile manufacturing company executive*
Hagenlocker, Edward E. *retired automobile company executive*
Lapadot, Sonee Spinner *retired automobile manufacturing company official*
Leonard, Michael A. *retired automotive executive*
Maxwell, Jack Erwin *manufacturing company executive*
†O'Brien, Mark J. *real estate/residential construction executive*

Brighton
Crabtree, John David *manufacturing company executive*

Brooklyn
Vischer, Harold Harry *manufacturing company executive*

Burt
Wolverton, Thomas Frank *automotive company supervisor*

Cass City
Althaver, Lambert Ewing *manufacturing company executive*

Dearborn
†Barton, Robert H., III, *automotive executive*
Bixby, Harold Glenn *manufacturing company executive*
Ford, William Clay *automotive company executive, professional sports team executive*
Ford, William Clay, Jr., *automotive executive*
Lundy, J(oseph) Edward *retired automobile company executive*
Mohan Iyengar, Raj *automotive executive, researcher*
†Pestillo, Peter John *automotive executive, lawyer*
Rintamaki, John M. *automotive executive*
†Wagner, Terrance Carl *automotive executive*

Detroit
Dauch, Richard E. *automobile manufacturing company executive*
†DiFeo, Samuel X. *automotive executive*
†Henry, William Lockwood *former food products executive, brewery executive*
Kalman, Andrew *manufacturing company executive*
Kantrowitz, Jean *health products executive*
Levy, Edward Charles, Jr., *manufacturing company executive*
†Rakolta, John, Sr., *construction company executive*
Smith, John Francis, Jr., *automobile company executive*
Wagoner, G. Richard, Jr., *automotive company executive*

Flint
Goodstein, Sanders Abraham *scrap iron company executive*

Franklin
Saulson, Saul S. *chemical company executive*

Fraser
†Winget, Larry J., Sr., *automotive industry executive*

Grand Rapids
Baker, Hollis MacLure *furniture manufacturing company executive*
Dykstra, William Dwight *business executive, consultant*
†Rougier-Chapman, Alwyn Spencer Douglas *furniture manufacturing company executive*
VanderMolen, Robert L. *painting contractor*
†Woodrick, Robert *food products executive*

Grosse Pointe
Wilkinson, Warren Scripps *manufacturing company executive*

Grosse Pointe Farms
Allen, Lee Harrison *industrial consultant, wholesale company executive*
Obolensky, Marilyn Wall (Mrs. Serge Obolensky) *metals company executive*
Valk, Robert Earl *corporate executive*

Grosse Pointe Park
Krebs, William Hoyt *company executive, industrial hygienist*

Harrison Township
McGregor, Theodore Anthony *chemical company executive*

Holland
†Haworth, Gerrard Wendell *office furniture manufacturing company executive*
†Krasa, Robert *manufacturing executive*

Holt
Garrison, Charles Eugene *retired automotive executive*

Jackson
Kelly, Robert Vincent, Jr., *metal company executive*

Kalamazoo
Angelo, Jim *construction company executive*
†Brown, John Wilford *health products executive*
Duchamp, David James *retired pharmaceutical company executive, consultant*
Edmondson, Keith Henry *retired chemical company executive*
Hubbard, William Neill, Jr., *pharmaceutical company executive*
Hudson, Roy Davage *retired pharmaceutical company executive*
Jones, Eugene Gordon *pharmaceutical company executive*
†Markin, David Robert *motor company executive*
Moe, James Burton *pharmaceutical company executive*
†Nye, Jeffrey Scott *pharmaceutical executive, researcher*
Wilson, James Rodney *air equipment company executive*

Lansing
†Stowers, Mark David *chemicals executive*

Madison Heights
Kafarski, Mitchell I. *chemical processing company executive*

Marshall
Davis, Henry Arnold *automotive company executive*

Mason
†Dart, Kenneth *food container manufacturing executive*
Thayer, Bruce Allen *automotive executive, artist*

Midland
Hampton, Leroy *retired chemical company executive*
†Hazleton, Richard A. *chemicals executive*

McCarty, Roger Leland *chemical company official*
Parker, Michael D. *chemicals executive*
Schmidt, William C. *chemical company executive*
Stavropoulos, William S. *chemical executive*

Muskegon
†Blystone, John B. *manufacturing executive*

Northville
Clemens, Michael Terrence *furniture manufacturing representative*

Okemos
Dowley, Joel Edward *manufacturing executive, lawyer*

Plymouth
Vlcek, Donald Joseph, Jr., *food distribution company executive, consultant, business author, executive coach*

Pontiac
Mahone, Barbara Jean *automotive company executive*
Stryker, James William *automotive executive, former military officer*

Port Sanilac
Birdsall, Arthur Anthony *chemical executive*

Rochester
Gouldey, Glenn Charles *manufacturing company executive*
Rossio, Richard Dominic *automobile company executive*

Rose Township
†Fleming, Kathryn Alice *automotive executive*

Royal Oak
Cook, Noel Robert *manufacturing company executive*

Saint Joseph
King, George Raleigh *retired manufacturing executive*

Saranac
†Herbrucks, Stephen *food products executive*

South Haven
Nequist, John Leonard *retired food company executive*

Southfield
†Maibach, Ben C., III, *construction company executive*
Rossiter, Robert E. *interior auto parts manufacturing executive*
†Wisne, Lawrence A. *metal products executive*

Taylor
Manoogian, Richard Alexander *manufacturing company executive*
†Rosowski, Robert Bernard *manufacturing company executive*

Tecumseh
Herrick, Todd W. *manufacturing company executive*

Traverse City
Clous, James M. *electrical equipment company executive, engineer*
†Parsons, John Thoren *corporate executive, inventor*

Troy
Acton, David L(awrence) *automobile company executive*
Battenberg, J. T., III, *automotive company executive*
Buschmann, Siegfried *manufacturing executive*
Corace, Joseph Russell *automotive executive*
Dawes, Alan S. *automotive company executive*
Janak, Peter Harold *automotive company executive*
Martin, Raymond Bruce *plumbing equipment manufacturing company executive*
Serafyn, Alexander Jaroslav *retired automotive executive*
Sharf, Stephan *automotive company executive*
Sloan, Hugh Walter, Jr., *automotive executive*
Yost, Larry D. *automotive executive*

Washington
Gothard, Donald Lee *retired auto company executive*

Williamsburg
Harlan, John Marshall *construction company executive*

Wixom
Sugiyama, Toru Tom *automotive executive*

Zeeland
LaGrand, Kenneth *technology products company executive*

MINNESOTA

Anoka
Sliefert, Paula Rhea *manufacturing company executive*

Austin
†Johnson, Joel W. *food products executive*

Bayport
†Garofalo, Donald R. *window manufacturing executive*

Biwabik
Anderson, Davin Charles *business representative, labor consultant*

Duluth
Whitney, Gwin Richard *brick distribution company executive*

Eagan
Clemens, T. Pat *manufacturing company executive*

Eden Prairie
Cohen, Robert *medical device manufacturing and marketing executive*
Henningsen, Peter, Jr., *diversified industry executive*

Edina
Brown, Charles Eugene *retired electronics company executive*
Prince, Robb Lincoln *manufacturing company executive*
Sampson, John Eugene *consulting company executive*

Excelsior
Carlson, Roger Allan *retired manufacturing executive, accountant*

Fairmont
†Rosen, Thomas J. *food and agricultural products executive*

Inver Grove Heights
Johnson, John D. *grain company executive*

Marshall
†Pippin, M. Lenny *food products executive*
†Schwan, Alfred *food products executive*

Mendota Heights
Frechette, Peter Loren *dental products executive*

Minneapolis
†Collins, Arthur D., Jr., *medical products executive*
Findorff, Robert Lewis *retired air filtration equipment company executive*
George, William Wallace *manufacturing company executive*
Gockel, John Raymond *construction executive*
†Goldberger, Robert D. *food products company executive*
Hale, Roger Loucks *manufacturing company executive*
Jacobs, Irwin Lawrence *diversified corporate executive*
Lehmann, Ernest Karl *consulting company executive, geologist*
†MacMillan, Whitney *food products and import/export company executive*
†McCune, Thomas *construction executive contractor*
†Micek, Ernest S. *former food products executive*
Spoor, William Howard *food company executive*
†Staley, Warren *food products company executive*
Stephenson, Nancy Louise *medical products company professional*
Sullivan, Austin Padraic, Jr., *diversified food company executive*
Van Dyke, William Grant *manufacturing company executive*
Wurtele, Christopher Angus *paint and coatings company executive*

Minnetonka
†Aristidou, Aristos Andrea *bioprocess company executive*
Osterberg, Thomas Karl *construction company executive*

Moorhead
Stenerson, John Gorden *lumber and building materials executive*

Oakdale
Maekawa, Koji Ogura *technology company administrator*

Plymouth
†Friswold, Fred Ravndal *manufacturing executive*
Kahler, Herbert Frederick *diversified business executive*

Rochester
Mayr, James Jerome *fertilizer company executive*
Wood, Michael B. *chief executive officer, president*

Saint Paul
Baukol, Ronald Oliver *company executive*
†Burgstahler, Robert *manufacturing executive*
DeSimone, Livio Diego *retired diversified manufacturing company executive*
Garretson, Donald Everett *retired manufacturing company executive*
Gherty, John E. *food products and agricultural products company executive*
†Johnston, Manley Roderick *research and development company executive, chemist*
Knudson, Mark Bradley *medical corporation executive, venture capitalist*
Lehr, Lewis Wylie *diversified manufacturing company executive*
McNerney, W. James *manufacturing executive*
Miller, Richard Lynn *pharmaceutical scientist*
†Schuman, Allan L. *chemical company executive*
†Vreyens, John Robert *agricultural products executive, educator*

Stillwater
Delaney, John Charles *pharmaceutical company executive*

Wayzata
Blodgett, Frank Caleb *retired food company executive*

Johnson, Sankey Anton *manufacturing company executive*
Luthringshauser, Daniel Rene *manufacturing company executive*
Swanson, Donald Frederick *retired food company executive*

MISSISSIPPI

Hattiesburg
Chain, Bobby Lee *electrical contractor, former mayor*

Jackson
†Johnson, Ronald E. *grocery company executive*
†Julian, Michael *grocery company executive*

Ocean Springs
Furlow, William Lawrence *manufacturing and financial consultant*
Lorenz, Ronald Theodore *manufacturing executive*

MISSOURI

Arnold
†Medart, Mike *manufacturing executive*

Blue Springs
Heller, John L., II, *construction executive*

Carthage
†Jett, Ernest Carroll

Centralia
Everhart, James Gray *retired manufacturing executive*

Chesterfield
Carpenter, Will Dockery *chemical company executive*
King, William Terry *retired manufacturing company executive*
Malvern, Donald *retired aircraft manufacturing company executive*

Clayton
Ball, Kenneth Leon *manufacturing company executive, organizational development consultant*

Fulton
Backer, William Earnest *food products executive*

Granby
Haase, Dixie Carol *retired manufacturing worker, writer*

Hannibal
Coleman, Gloria Jean *chemical manufacturing company professional*

Kansas City
Adams, James Robert *medical organization sales professional*
Bartlett, Paul Dana, Jr., *agribusiness executive*
Berkley, Eugene Bertram (Bert Berkley) *envelope company executive*
†Dunn, Terrence P. *manufacturing executive*
†Hebenstreit, James Bryant *agricultural products executive, bank and venture capital executive*
Johnson, Richard Dean *pharmaceutical consultant, educator*
†Kafoure, Michael D. *food products executive*
†Sullivan, Charles A. *food products executive*
Terry, Robert Brooks *food products executive, lawyer*

Lees Summit
Henley, Joseph Oliver *manufacturing company executive*

Maryland Heights
Toan, Barrett A. *health products executive*

Naylor
Seratt, Rodger Calvin *manufacturing executive*

North Kansas City
Stout, Edward Irvin *medical manufacturing company executive*

Saint Charles
Pundmann, Ed John, Jr., *automotive company executive*

Saint Louis
Abelov, Stephen Lawrence *uniform clothing company executive, consultant*
Adams, Albert Willie, Jr., *lubrication company executive*
Beare, Gene Kerwin *electric company executive*
Bock, Edward John *retired chemical manufacturing company executive*
Browde, Anatole *electronics company executive, consultant*
Brown, JoBeth Goode *food products executive, lawyer*
Busch, August Adolphus, III, *brewery executive*
Choi, Dennis W. *pharmaceutical executive, neurologist, educator*
Cohen, Millard Stuart *diversified manufacturing company executive*
Dill, Charles Anthony *manufacturing and computer company executive*
Farr, David N. *electronics executive*
†Ge, Jisheng *pharmaceutical researcher*
Graff, George Stephen *aerospace company executive*
Gupta, Surendra Kumar *chemical firm executive*
Hirsch, Raymond Robert *chemical company executive, lawyer*
Hogan, Michael Ray *life science executive*
Holman, C. Ray *medical products executive*

Kaestner, John Thomas *beverage company executive*
Keyes, Marion Alvah, IV, *manufacturing company executive*
Knight, Charles Field *electrical equipment manufacturing company executive*
Langness, David Gordon *manufacturing executive*
Leritz, Daniel Raymond *pharmaceutical company executive, consultant*
McCarter, James Philip *biotechnology company executive, researcher*
McDonnell, Sanford Noyes *aircraft company executive*
†McGinnis, W. Patrick *diversified company executive*
McGuinness, Barbara Sue *food products executive*
McKenna, William John *textile products executive*
Monroe, Thomas Edward *industrial corporation executive*
Posgay, Betty Marie *medical equipment company executive, artist*
Reynolds, Robert A., Jr., *electric distributor executive*
Shanahan, Michael Francis *manufacturing executive, former hockey team executive*
†Shapiro, Robert B. *former food products manufacturing executive*
Stearley, Robert Jay *retired packaging company executive*
†Stiritz, William P. *food company executive*
†Stokes, Patrick T. *brewery company executive*
Suter, Albert Edward *manufacturing company executive*
Winter, William Earl *retired beverage company executive*
Zwikelmaier, Kurt E. *pharmaceutical executive*

Sullivan
Penn, Ronald Hulen *manufacturing executive*

MONTANA

Big Sky
Ryan, Raymond D. *retired steel company executive, insurance and marketing firm executive*

Great Falls
†Semenza, Dirk A. *metal fabrication executive*
Sletten, John Robert *construction company executive*

Helena
Warren, Christopher Charles *electronics executive*

Missoula
Washington, Dennis *construction executive*

Stevensville
Derrick, William Dennis *retired physical plant administrator, consultant*

NEBRASKA

Lincoln
Fisher, Calvin David *food manufacturing company executive*
Tavlin, Michael John *manufacturing executive*
Tinstman, Dale Clinton *food products company consultant*

Omaha
Brown, Bob Oliver *retired manufacturing company executive*
†Faith, Marshall E. *grain company executive*
†Linville, Randal L. *agricultural company executive*
Rohde, Bruce C. *food company executive, lawyer*
†Scott, Walter, Jr., *construction company executive*
†Stinson, Kenneth E. *construction company executive*

NEVADA

Boulder City
Fisher, Paul Cary *writing supplies company executive*

Carson City
Burns, Dan W. *manufacturing company executive*

Genoa
Goode, John Martin *manufacturing company executive*

Henderson
Moon, David A. *manufacturing executive*

Hendersonville
Niemeyer, Erin Janice *pharmaceutical sales consultant, journalist, editor*

Incline Village
Strack, Harold Arthur *retired electronics company executive, retired air force officer, planner, analyst, author, musician*
Tedford, Jack Nowlan, III, *construction executive, small business owner*
Yount, George Stuart *paper company executive*

Las Vegas
Albanese, Thomas *food industry executive, consultant*
†Barr, Wallace R. *electronics executive*
Bernard, Thelma Rene *property management professional*

Hirsh, Bernard *supply company executive, consultant*
Jakopec, Carl Thomas *pharmaceutical company executive*
†Jones, Fletcher, Jr., *automotive company executive*
Manley, Edward Harry, Jr., *food products executive*
Opfer, Neil David *construction educator, consultant*
Regazzi, John Henry *retired electronic distributor executive*
Root, Alan Charles *diversified manufacturing company executive*
Strahan, Julia Celestine *electronics company executive*

Reno
Jacobson, Raymond Earl *electronics company entrepreneur and executive*

Sparks
Kramer, Gordon Edward *manufacturing executive*

NEW HAMPSHIRE

Bennington
Verney, Richard Greville *paper company executive*

Grantham
Anderson, Paul Nathaniel, III, (Trip Anderson) *visual communications consultant*

Hampton
Montrone, Paul Michael *scientific instruments company executive*
†Russell, Richard R. *chemicals executive*

Lisbon
Trelfa, Richard Thomas *paper company executive*

Meredith
Hatch, Frederick Tasker *chemicals consultant*

Milford
Morison, John Hopkins *casting manufacturing company executive*

Nashua
Egan, John Frederick *retired electronics executive*
Gregg, Hugh *former cabinet manufacturing company executive, former governor New Hampshire*

New Castle
Rauh, John David *manufacturing company executive*

New London
†Condict, Edgar Rhodes *medical electronics, aviation instrument manufacturing and medical health care executive, inventor, mediator, pastor*

North Hampton
Taylor, Donald *retired manufacturing company executive*
White, Ralph Paul *automotive executive, consultant*

Rochester
Shean, Timothy Joseph *manufacturing company executive*

Winchester
MacKay, Neil Duncan *plastics company executive*

NEW JERSEY

Annandale
Wilson, Terry Douglas *pharmaceutical manager*

Avenel
†Sansone, Paul J. *automotive executive*

Barnegat
Bronkowski, Mark John *textiles executive, real estate agent*

Basking Ridge
Abeles, James David *manufacturing company executive*
Conklin, Donald Ransford *retired pharmaceutical company executive*
Darrow, William Richard *retired pharmaceutical company executive, consultant*
Fotiades, George L. *pharmaceutical executive*
Korn, William David *technology executive*
Munch, Douglas Francis *pharmaceutical and health industry consultant*
Riesenberger, John Richard *pharmaceutical company executive*
Tamarelli, Alan Wayne *venture captial executive*

Bedminster
Shedden, Arthur *pharmaceutical executive, consultant*
Yannuzzi, Elaine Victoria *food and home products executive*

Berkeley Heights
Connell, Grover *food company executive*

Bound Brook
Gould, Donald Everett *retired chemical company executive, consultant*

Bridgeton
Howell, James Burt, III, *retired agricultural products company sales consultant*

Bridgewater
Kennedy, James Andrew *chemical company executive*

Califon
Clarke, Frank Henderson *retired chemical company executive, scientist*

Camden
†Conant, Douglas R. *food products executive*
†Johnson, David Willis *former food products executive*

Cape May
Caruso, Frank S. *pharmaceutical executive*

Clark
Meilan, Celia *food products executive*

Cranbury
Perhach, James Lawrence *pharmaceutical company executive*

Cranford
†Mullen, Edward K. *paper company executive*

Deepwater
Baillie, Joan M. *chemical company official, biology educator*

Denville
Minter, Jerry Burnett *electronic component company executive, engineer*

East Hanover
Bess, Alan L. *pharmaceutical executive, physician*
Dodsworth, Roy W. *pharmaceutical company executive*
Kent, Bruce Jonathan *pharmaceutical executive*
†Martelet, Francois R. *pharmaceutical executive*

East Orange
Loebner, Hugh Gene *manufacturing company executive*

East Rutherford
Glassell, Claes *health products executive*
Mack, James A. *health products executive*

Eatontown
DeGiglio, Michael A. *food products executive*

Edison
Alexander, John Charles *pharmaceutical company executive, physician*
Andreasen, Charles Peter *retired electronics executive*

Elmwood Park
Mitschele, Michael Douglas *concrete and aggregate company executive*

Englewood
Neis, Arnold Hayward *pharmaceutical company executive*
Ostberg, Henry Dean *corporate executive*

Englewood Cliffs
Dash, Barry Harold *pharmaceutical company executive*
†Shoemate, Charles R. *former food company executive*

Fair Haven
McKissock, David Lee *retired manufacturing company executive*

Fairfield
Buchalter, Martin *pharmaceutical medical device company executive*

Fairview
Anton, Harvey *textile company executive*

Fanwood
Butler, William Langdon *manufacturers representative*

Farmingdale
Schluter, Peter Mueller *electronics company executive*

Florham Park
Pollack, Jordan Ellis *pharmaceutical company executive*
Sperber, Martin *pharmaceutical company executive, pharmacist*

Fort Monmouth
Schwering, Felix Karl *electronics engineer, researcher*
Thornton, Clarence Gould *electronics engineering executive*

Franklin Lakes
Castellini, Clateo *retired medical technology company executive*
Friedman, Martin Burton *chemical company executive*

Hainesport
Sylk, Leonard Allen *housing company executive, real estate developer*

Hasbrouck Heights
Watrel, Warren George *pharmaceutical company executive*

Highlands
Hansen, Christian Andreas, Jr., *plastics and chemical company executive*

Hillsborough
Kenyhercz, Thomas Michael *pharmaceutical company executive*

Hillside
†Liu, Rong (Ron) *pharmaceutical executive, researcher*

Hopatcong
Reese, Harry Edwin, Jr., *electronics executive*

Hope
McDonald, John Joseph *electronics executive*

Iselin
†Perry, Barry W. *manufacturing executive*
Smith, Orin Robert *chemical company executive*

Jersey City
†Pietrini, Andrew Gabriel *automotive aftermarket executive*

Kendall Park
Hershenov, Bernard Zion *electronics research and development company executive*

Kenilworth
Gen, Martin *corporate executive*
Hassan, Fred *pharmaceutical executive*

Kinnelon
Klaas, Nicholas Paul *management and technical consultant*

Lawrenceville
Daoust, Donald Roger *pharmaceutical and toiletries company executive, microbiologist*
Yeager, Arthur Leonard *health company executive*

Lebanon
Hakes, Thomas Brion *manufacturing company executive, physician*

Linden
Covino, Charles Peter *chemicals executive*

Little Silver
Brennan, William Joseph *manufacturing company executive*

Livingston
Candido, A. Michael *contracting company executive, real estate manager*

Lyndhurst
Benschip, Gary John *manufacturing company executive*

Madison
Essner, Robert Alan *pharmaceutical executive*
Stafford, John Rogers *pharmaceutical and household products company executive*

Mahwah
Gerstein, David Brown *hardware manufacturing company executive, professional basketball team executive*

Maplewood
Zoss, Abraham Oscar *chemical company executive*

Marlboro
Miller, Duane King *health and beauty care company executive*

Marlton
Gottfried, Benjamin Frank *retired manufacturing executive*
Samek, Edward Lasker *service company executive*

Matawan
Amato, Vincent Vito *business executive*

Medford
Keele, Lyndon Alan *electronics executive*

Montvale
Corrado, Fred *food company executive*

Montville
Willis, Carl Raeburn, Jr., *pharmaceutical executive*

Moorestown
Springer, Douglas Hyde *retired food company executive, lawyer*

Morris Plains
Otani, Mike *optical company executive*

Morristown
Cameron, Nicholas Allen *diversified corporation executive*
Cote, David M. *diversified technology and manufacturing company executive*
DiSerio, Frank Joseph *pharmaceutical company executive, consultant*
Herman, Robert Lewis *cork company executive*
Hittinger, William Charles *electronics company executive*
Huck, John Lloyd *pharmaceutical company executive*
Kirby, Fred Morgan, II, *corporation executive*
Murthy, Andiappan K.S. *technology manager*
†Pokelwaldt, Robert N. *former manufacturing company executive*
†Stranghoener, Larry W. *manufacturing company executive*
Williams, Joseph Dalton *pharmaceutical company executive*

Mountain Lakes
O'Gara, Barbara Ann *soap company executive*

Mountainside
Slabe, James F. *business executive*

Neptune
Karlan, Andrew Warren (Drew Karlan) *pharmaceutical company executive*

New Brunswick
Fine, Roger Seth *pharmaceutical executive, lawyer*
Griffin, Gary Arthur *technological products executive*
Gussin, Robert Zalmon *retired healthcare company executive*
Haines, William Joseph *pharmaceutical company executive*
†Heisen, JoAnn Heffernan *health care company executive*
Larsen, Ralph S(tanley) *retired pharmaceutical company executive*
Lenehan, James T. *pharmaceutical executive*
McGuire, John Lawrence *pharmaceuticals executive*
Mondschein, Lawrence Geoffrey *medical products executive*
Weldon, William C. *pharmaceutical executive*

New Providence
Chatterji, Debajyoti *retired manufacturing company executive, educator*
Longfield, William Herman *health care company executive*
McCaffrey, Robert Henry, Jr., *retired manufacturing company executive*

North Brunswick
Bern, Ronald Lawrence *consulting company executive*
Campbell, Robert Emmett *retired health care products company executive, medical association administrator*
†Ghosh, Alok *pharmaceutical executive*

Northvale
Barna, Richard Allen *lighting company executive, broadcasting executive*
Di Mino, André Anthony *manufacturing executive, consultant*
Mittleberg, Eric Michael *pharmaceutical executive*

Nutley
English, Robert Joseph *electronic corporation executive*

Paramus
Hibler, Robert Bennett *construction executive*
Maclin, Ernest *biomedical diagnostics company executive*

Parsippany
Deones, Jack E. *corporate executive*
Fleisher, Seymour *manufacturing company executive*
Mazur, Leonard L. *pharmaceutical company executive*

Paulsboro
Colacot, Thomas J. *chemicals executive, researcher*

Peapack
Rost, Peter *pharmaceutical company executive*
Rothwell, Timothy Gordon *pharmaceutical company executive*

Piscataway
D'Aloia, G(iambattista) Peter *corporate executive*

Plainfield
Keyko, George John *electronics company executive*

Pompton Plains
Shrem, Charles Joseph *metals corporation executive*

Princeton
Cavanaugh, James Henry *medical corporate executive, former government official*
Cryer, Dennis Robert *pharmaceutical company executive, researcher*
Dovey, Brian Hugh *health care products company executive, venture capitalist*
Goldblatt, Barry Lance *manufacturing executive*
Gregg, John Malcolm Hall *pharmaceutical executive*
Hendrickson, Robert Frederick *pharmaceutical company executive*
Kuebler, Christopher Allen *pharmaceutical executive*
Matray-Devoti, Judith *medical information manager, consultant*
Minton, Dwight Church *manufacturing company executive*
†Mollica, Joseph A. *pharmaceutical executive*
Petrin, Jurij *pharmaceutical company executive*
Sapoff, Meyer *electronics component manufacturer*
Wavle, James Edward, Jr., *pharmaceutical company executive, lawyer*
Wildnauer, Richard Harry *pharmaceutical company executive*

Princeton Junction
Giddings, Clifford Frederick *retired corporate executive*

Rahway
Mandel, Lewis Richard *pharmaceutical company executive*

Ramsey
Sirabian, Stephen James *pharmaceutical executive*

Red Bank
Sgaramella, Peter *chemical products executive, technical consultant*

Ridgefield
Riggs, Rory B. *pharmaceutical executive*

Ridgewood
Healey, Frank Henry *retired research executive*

Riverdale
Fremund, Zdenek Anthony *manufacturing company executive*

Robbinsville
Lu, Ming Qi *pharmaceutical company executive*

Rochelle Park
Schapiro, Jerome Bentley *chemical company executive*

Rockleigh
Shapiro, William *automobile company executive*

Saddle Brook
†Hickey, William V. *manufacturing executive*

Saddle River
†McClelland, William Craig *paper company executive*

Salem
Seabrook, John Martin *retired food products executive, chemical engineer*

Scotch Plains
Abramson, Clarence Allen *pharmaceutical company executive, lawyer*

Secaucus
Liao, Paul Foo-Hung *electronics executive*
†Unanue, Joseph *food products executive*

Skillman
Bolton, Laura Lee *health/medical products executive*

Somerset
Aronson, Louis Vincent, II, *manufacturing executive*
Bardoliwalla, Dinshaw Framroze *chemical executive*
Jones, Andrew William *pharmaceutical executive*

South Hackensack
Cohen, Brett I. *health products executive*

South Orange
Schectman, Stephen Barry *pharmaceuticals company executive*

South Plainfield
Hunsinger, Doyle J. *electronics executive*
Ju, William David *pharmaceutical executive*
Schlossman, Mitchell Lloyd *cosmetics and chemical specialties executive*

Summit
Lindars, Laurence Edward *retired health care products executive*
Pawelec, William John *retired electronics company executive*
Young, Diane Caroline *pharmaceutical executive*
Zachary, Louis George *chemical company consultant*

Teaneck
Feinberg, Robert S. *plastics company executive, marketing professional*
Woerner, Alfred Ira *medical device manufacturer, educator*

Teterboro
Adams, James Mills *retired chemicals executive*

Trenton
Roshon, George Kenneth *manufacturing company executive*

Union
Franklin, William George *manufacturing executive*
Thomas, Ralph H. *manufacturing executive*

Warren
Jackson, John Wyant *medical products executive*

Wayne
†Heyman, Samuel J. *building materials manufacturing company executive*
Jeffrey, Robert George, Jr., *industrial company executive*
Keen, M. Whitney *ink manufacturing company executive*
Stein, Robert Alan *electronics company executive*

West Orange
Eisenberg, R. Neal *restoration company executive*

Westfield
McLean, Vincent Ronald *former manufacturing company financial executive*

Whippany
Golden, John F. *packaging company executive*

Whitehouse Station
Anstice, David W. *pharmaceutical executive*
Bell, Paul R. *pharmaceutical executive*
Clark, Richard T. *pharmaceutical executive*
Frazier, Kenneth C. *pharmaceutical executive*
Gilmartin, Raymond V. *pharmaceutical company executive*
Kelley, Bernard J. *pharmaceutical executive*
Lewent, Judy Carol *pharmaceutical executive*

Yarno, Wendy *pharmaceutical executive*

Woodcliff Lake
Henkel, Herbert Ludwig *manufacturing executive*
Perrella, James Elbert *former manufacturing company executive*

Wyckoff
Brown, James Joseph *manufacturing company executive*

NEW MEXICO

Albuquerque
Friberg, George Joseph *electronics company executive*
Korman, Nathaniel Irving *research and development company executive*

Estancia
Swenka, Arthur John *retired food products executive*

Placitas
†Golleher, George *food company executive*

Rio Rancho
Isenberg, Abraham Charles *shoe manufacturing company executive*

Sandia Park
Wilczynski, Janusz S. *packaging technology executive, retired physicist*

Santa Fe
Odell, John H. *construction executive*

NEW YORK

Albany
Heshmat, Hooshang *manufacturing executive*
Naumann, Hans J. *manufacturing company executive*
Spencer, Keith G. *construction executive*
Standish, John Spencer *textile manufacturing company executive*

Armonk
Sydney, Doris S. *sports touring company executive, interior designer*

Athens
Lew, Roger Alan *manufacturing company executive*

Bangall
Swanson, David Heath *agricultural company executive*

Bath
Ward, Kenneth G. *agricultural products executive*

Bay Shore
Shreve, Sue Ann Gardner *retired health products company administrator*

Bohemia
Hausman, Howard *electronics executive*

Briarcliff Manor
Bingham, J. Peter *electronics research executive*

Bronx
Safyer, Steven M. *chief medical officer*

Brooklyn
Hood, Ernest Alva, Sr., *pharmaceutical company executive*
Karney, Irving Hyman *construction company executive*
Oussani, James John *stapling company executive*
Rutsky, Lester *retired textiles executive, writer*
Zisser, Martin Shepherd *fur apparel manufacturer, investor and trader*

Buffalo
†Rich, Robert E., Jr., *food products company executive*
Starks, Fred William *chemical company executive*

Callicoon
Kurtz, Joel *construction company executive*

Cedarhurst
Cohen, David B. *optical company executive*

Chappaqua
French, Harold Stanley *food company executive*

Clifton Park
Scher, Robert Sander *instrument design company executive*

Cooperstown
Tilton, Webster, Jr., *contractor*

Corning
Behm, Forrest Edwin *glass manufacturing company executive*
Ecklin, Robert Luther *materials company executive*
Houghton, James Richardson *glass manufacturing company executive*

Derby
Goodell, Joseph Edward *manufacturing executive*

East Amherst
Watson, Stewart Charles *construction executive*

East Aurora
Hawk, George Wayne *retired electronics company executive*

East Hampton
Karp, Harvey Lawrence *metal products manufacturing company executive*

East Meadow
Cymbler, Murray Joel *corporate professional*

East Northport
†Kehoe, Thomas J. *food products executive*

Elmsford
Fachnie, H(ugh) Douglas *film manufacturing company official*

Falconer
Ruhlman, Herman C(loyd), Jr., *manufacturing company executive*

Farmingdale
Blum, Melvin *chemical company executive, researcher*

Fayetteville
Pachter, Irwin Jacob *pharmaceutical consultant*

Flushing
Henshel, Harry Bulova *watch manufacturer*

Garden City
Demuth, Nina Lewis *engineering company executive*

Glen Cove
Burnham, Harold Arthur *pharmaceutical company executive, physician*

Great Neck
Arams, Frank Robert *electronics company executive*

Greenvale
†Pall, David B. *manufacturing company executive, chemist*

Hartsdale
Martin, Daniel Richard *pharmaceutical company executive*

Hauppauge
Shalam, John Joseph *car stereo and cellular telephone company executive*

Hicksville
Tucci, Gerald Frank *manufacturing company executive*

Honeoye
Stone, Alan John *manufacturing company executive, real estate executive*

Hoosick Falls
Dodge, Cleveland Earl, Jr., *manufacturing executive, director*

Huntington
Ferares, Kenneth *automobile executive*

Jamestown
Leising, Mary Kathleen *manufacturing executive*
Wellman, Barclay Ormes *furniture company executive*

Lakewood
Anderson, Raymond Quintus *diversified company executive*

Lansing
Gage, George H(enry) *retired high technology company executive*

Latham
Stallman, Donald Lee *corporate executive*

Lewiston
Waters, William Ernest *microelectronics executive*

Liverpool
Morabito, Bruno Paul *machinery manufacturing executive*

Lockport
Schultz, Gerald Alfred (Jerry Schultz) *chemical company executive*
†Steinagle, Martin Gene *contractor, paralegal, poet, writer*

Locust Valley
Schor, Joseph Martin *pharmaceutical executive, biochemist*

Long Island City
DiGiovanni, Eleanor Elma *scaffold installation company executive*

Mamaroneck
Holz, Harold A. *chemical and plastics manufacturing company executive*
Mizrahi, Abraham Mordechay *retired cosmetics and health care company executive, physician*

Manhasset
Keen, Constantine *retired manufacturing company executive*
Lala, Dominick Joseph *manufacturing company executive*

Melville
Kaufman, Stephen P. *former electronics company executive, business educator*
Kissinger, Walter Bernhard *retired automotive test and service equipment manufacturing*

Mount Airy
Woltz, Howard Osler, Jr., *steel and wire products company executive*

Oriental
Sutter, John Richard *manufacturer, investor*

Pine Knoll Shores
Benson, Kenneth Victor *manufacturing company executive, lawyer*

Pinehurst
Nuzzo, Salvatore Joseph *defense/electronics company executive*
O'Neill, John Joseph, Jr., *business consultant, former chemical company executive*

Raleigh
Klein, Verle Wesley *retired corporate executive, retired naval officer*
Prior, William Allen *electronics company executive*
Sloan, O. Temple, Jr., *automotive equipment executive*
Vick, Aaron Conley *contractor, consultant*
Wilson, Donald Hurst, III, *biopharmaceutical industry executive*

Research Triangle Park
Framil, Armando Ramon *business developer*
Key, Karen Letisha *pharmaceutical executive*
Krasny, Harvey Charles *pharmaceutical executive, researcher*

Rockwell
†Daily, James William, III, *manufacturing executive*

Rocky Mount
Stubbs, Will, Jr., *pharmaceutical company manager*

Sanford
Kilmartin, Joseph Francis, Jr., *business executive, consultant*

Shelby
Perry, Stephen Clayton *manufacturing executive*

Statesville
Stelzner, Paul Burke *textile company executive*

Weldon
Barringer, Paul Brandon, II, *lumber company executive*

Wilkesboro
Tillman, Robert L. *home improvement company executive*

Wilmington
Bryden, William Donald, Jr., *retired manufacturing executive, retired military officer*
Thompson, Donald Charles *electronics company executive, former coast guard officer*

Winston Salem
Hanes, Ralph Philip, Jr., *former textiles executive, arts patron, cattle farmer networker*
Maselli, John Anthony *food products company executive*
Schindler, Andrew J. *tobacco company executive*
Sticht, J. Paul *retired food products and tobacco company executive*
Wallace, Roanne *hosiery company executive*

OHIO

Akron
Gibara, Samir G. *tire manufacturing executive*
Glomski, Edward Earl *electronic company executive*
Hackbirth, David William *aluminum company executive*
Kaufman, Donald Leroy *building products executive*
†Keegan, Robert J. *manufacturing executive*
Snider, George Runyon, Jr., *franchising company executive*

Athens
Werner, R(ichard) Budd *retired business executive*

Aurora
Toomey, William Shenberger *retired wire manufacturing company executive*

Beachwood
Weatherhead, Albert John, III, *business executive*

Bellville
Hooker, James Todd *manufacturing executive*

Canton
†Birkholz, Raymond James *metal products manufacturing company executive*
Ewing, David Charles *automobile dealership executive*

Chagrin Falls
Brophy, Jere Hall *manufacturing company executive*
Heckman, Henry Trevennen Shick *steel company executive*

Cincinnati
Ackermann, Russell Albert *manufacturing company executive*
Anderson, Jerry William, Jr., *technical and business consulting executive, educator*
Christensen, Paul Walter, Jr., *gear manufacturing company executive*
Coombe, V. Anderson *retired valve manufacturing company executive*
Fulmer, Michael Clifford *food company administrator*
Kaune, James Edward *ship repair company executive, former naval officer*
Kuhn, John Henry *retired paper industry executive*
Laney, Sandra Eileen *service company executive*
LeCroix, Charles David *research and development company executive, educator*
Leyda, James Perkins *small business consultant, retired pharmaceutical company executive*
Mates, Lawrence A., II, *medical company executive, consultant*
Meinert, Walter *retired chemical company executive, consultant*
Pichler, Joseph Anton *food products executive*
Rishel, James Burton *manufacturing executive, director*
Shepherd, Elsbeth Weichsel *supply chain consultant*
Smale, John Gray *diversified industry executive*
Stern, Joseph Smith, Jr., *former footwear manufacturing company executive*
Thompson, Morley Punshon *textile company executive*

Cleveland
Bradley, J. F., Jr., *retired manufacturing company executive*
Collins, Duane E. *manufacturing executive*
†Connor, Christopher M. *textiles executive*
Cutler, Alexander MacDonald *manufacturing company executive*
Decker, John William *steel company executive*
Gray, James Patrick *business executive, consultant, educator*
Hamilton, William Milton *retired manufacturing executive*
Hardis, Stephen Roger *retired manufacturing company executive*
Ivy, Conway Gayle *paint company executive*
Jameson, J(ames) Larry *chemical company executive*
Kapoor, Vinod Kumar *electrical products executive*
Kay, Albert Joseph *textile executive*
Loop, Floyd D. *health, medical executive*
Luke, Randall Dan *retired tire and rubber company executive, lawyer*
Mac Laren, David Sergeant *manufacturing corporation executive, inventor*
Mandel, Jack N. *manufacturing company executive*
McFadden, John Volney *retired manufacturing company executive*
†Mooney, James P. *chemicals executive*
Nelson, Richard Alan *financial executive*
Parker, Patrick Streeter *manufacturing executive*
Reid, James Sims, Jr., *former automobile parts manufacturer*
Rosenthal, Leighton A. *aviation company executive*
Stone, Harry H. *business executive*
†Tomsich, Robert J. *heavy machinery manufacturing executive*
Unger, Paul A. *packaging and international affairs specialist*
†Washkewicz, Donald E. *manufacturing executive*
Wright, Marshall *retired manufacturing executive, former diplomat*

Columbus
†Anderson, Kerrii B. *construction company executive*
†Campanizzi, Jane *consulting company executive*
Cottingham, Richard Sumner *paper company executive*
Daab-Krzykowski, Andre *pharmaceutical and nutritional manufacturing company administrator*
Halliday, Stephen Mills *manufacturing company executive*
†Kidder, C. Robert *food products executive*
Knilans, Michael Jerome *supermarkets executive*
Lazar, Theodore Aaron *retired manufacturing company executive, lawyer*
Maher, Frank Aloysius *research and development company executive*
McConnell, John Henderson *metal and plastic products manufacturing executive, professional sports team executive*
†Morrison, Craig O. *chemicals executive*
Pfening, Frederic Denver, III, *manufacturing company executive*
†Ricart, Fred *automotive company executive*
Rohrbaugh, Wayne Joseph *chemical company executive*
Solso, Theodore M. *manufacturing executive*
Wigington, Ronald Lee *retired chemical information services executive*
Wolf, J(ohn) Steven *construction executive, land developer*
Yenkin, Bernard Kalman *coatings and resins company executive*

Dayton
†Diggs, Matthew O'Brien, Jr., *air conditioning and refrigeration manufacturing executive*
Duval, Daniel Webster *manufacturing company executive*
Harlan, Norman Ralph *construction executive*
†Hurd, Mark V. *manufacturing executive*
Ladehoff, Leo William *metal products manufacturing executive*
†Mathile, Clayton Lee *pet food company executive*
Nyberg, Lars *former electronics company executive*

Delaware
Eells, William Hastings *retired automobile company executive*
Huml, Donald Scott *manufacturing company executive*

Dublin
†Borror, Douglas G. *construction company executive*
†Clement, Henry Joseph, Jr., *diversified building products executive*
Lamp, Benson J. *tractor company executive*
Miller, Richard J. *wholesale pharmaceutical distribution company executive*
Stratton, James Edward *retired construction educator*

Euclid
Dallos, Joseph *general contractor, remodeler*

Findlay
†Dattilo, Thomas A. *diversified corporation executive*

Garrettsville
Diskin, Michael Edward *plastics industry executive, food service executive*

Gates Mills
Veale, Tinkham, II, *former chemical company executive, engineer*

Grove City
Lok, Silmond Ray *pharmaceutical executive*

Hamilton
Epp, Mary Elizabeth *technologies consultant*

Hilliard
†Brown, Dale *electronics executive*

Holland
D'Anniballe-Holdren, Priscilla Lucille *contracting company executive*

Huber Heights
Panayirci, Sharon Lorraine *textiles executive, design engineer*

Hudson
Galloway, Ethan Charles *technology development executive, former chemicals executive*

Jackson Center
Thompson, Wade Francis Bruce *manufacturing company executive*

Kent
Aro, Ants Gustaf *manufacturing executive*

Lakewood
Cochran, Earl Vernon *retired manufacturing company executive*

Lancaster
Sulick, Robert John *general contractor*

Lima
Pranses, Anthony Louis *retired electric company executive, organization executive*

Lorain
Bado, Kenneth Steve *automotive company administrator*

Mansfield
†Dudley, Kenneth Eugene *manufacturing company executive*
Gorman, James Carvill *pump manufacturing company executive*

Mantua
Ray, James Allen *research consultant*

Mason
Snyder, Barbara Royalty *pharmaceutical executive*
Wilson, Frederic Sandford *pharmaceutical company executive*

Massillon
Snyder, Rachel Ann *manufacturing company specialist*

Maumee
Anderson, Richard Paul *agricultural company executive*

Mayfield Heights
Rankin, Alfred Marshall, Jr., *business executive*

Medina
Smith, Richey *manufacturing executive*
Sullivan, Thomas Christopher *coatings company executive*

Mentor
Callsen, Christian Edward *medical device company executive*

Middleburg Heights
McGinnis, Robert William *electronics company executive*

Milan
Henry, Joseph Patrick *chemical company executive*

New Albany
†Jeffries, Michael S. *apparel executive*

New Bremen
Dicke, James Frederick, II, *manufacturing company executive*

North Ridgeville
Stewart, Arden Ruth *automotive aftermarket manufacturing executive*

Orrville
Kamp, Philip *food products executive*

Painesville
Humphrey, George Magoffin, II, *plastic molding company executive*

Perrysburg
King, John Joseph *manufacturing company executive*

Plain City
Kinman, Gary *company executive*

Randolph
Pecano, Donald Carl *automotive manufacturing executive*

Reynoldsburg
Woodward, Greta Charmaine *construction company executive, rental and investment property manager*

Richfield
Braude, Edwin Simon *manufacturing company executive*

Solon
Rosica, Gabriel Adam *corporate executive, engineer*

Streetsboro
Kearns, Warren Kenneth *business executive*

Sylvania
Lock, Richard William *packaging company executive*

Tipp City
Tighe-Moore, Barbara Jeanne *electronics executive*

Toledo
†Brown, David T. *manufacturing executive*
Lemieux, Joseph Henry *manufacturing company executive*
Romanoff, Milford Martin *building contractor*

Westerville
Lerner, Harold Selwyn *retired apparel executive*
Macfarlane, Alastair Iain Robert *business executive*

Westlake
Hellman, Peter Stuart *technical manufacturing executive*

Wooster
†Basford, James Orlando *container manufacturing company executive*
Price, Ronald James *electrical products company executive*

OKLAHOMA

Bristow
Primeaux, Henry, III, *automotive executive, author, speaker*

Enid
Berry, Robert Bass *construction executive*

Oklahoma City
Turner, Eugene Andrew *manufacturing executive*

Tulsa
Narwold, Lewis Lammers *paper products manufacturer*
Thomas, Robert Eggleston *retired corporate executive*

Wilburton
†Pate, Thomas Lowell *manufacturing executive*

Yukon
Clonts, George Gary *packaging company executive*

OREGON

Ashland
Meese, Celia Edwards *pharmaceutical company executive*

Beaverton
Barnes, Keith Lee *electronics executive*
Knight, Philip H(ampson) *apparel executive*

Eugene
Woolley, Donna Pearl *lumber company executive*

Forest Grove
Jones, Charles J. *wood products manufacturing executive*

Klamath Falls
†Wendt, Richard L. *manufacturing executive*
†Wendt, Roderick C. *manufacturing executive*

Portland
Eberwein, Barton Douglas *construction company executive, consultant*
Flowerree, Robert Edmund *retired forest products company executive*
†Kinnune, William P. *forest products executive*
Leineweber, Peter Anthony *forest products company executive*
Pamplin, Robert Boisseau, Jr., *manufacturing company executive, minister, writer*
Pamplin, Robert Boisseau, Sr., *retired textile manufacturing executive*
Russell, Marjorie Rose *manufacturing company executive*
Steinfeld, Ray, Jr., *food products executive*
Stott, Peter Walter *forest products company executive*

Resnik, David Alan *manufacturing company executive*

SOUTH CAROLINA

Camden
Daniels, John Hancock *agricultural products company executive*

Charleston
Clawson, Harry Quintard Moore *retired business executive*
Geentiens, Gaston Petrus, Jr., *former construction management consultant company executive*
Harding, Enoch, Jr., *clothing executive*
Mahoney, John Joseph *business executive, educator*
Martin, Roblee Boettcher *retired cement manufacturing executive*
Thompson, W(ilmer) Leigh *pharmaceutical company executive, physician, pharmacologist*

Clemson
Petzel, Florence Eloise *textiles educator*

Clinton
Cornelson, George Henry, IV, *retired textile company executive*

Columbia
Robinson, Robert Earl *chemical company executive*
Sumwalt, Robert Llewellyn, Jr., *retired construction company executive*

Denmark
Dolezal, Dale Francis *truck manufacturing company executive*

Fort Mill
†Bowles, Crandall Close *textiles executive*

Greenville
Bauknight, Clarence Brock *consultant*
Klasing, John Christoph *manufacturing executive*
Varin, Roger Robert *textile executive*

Greenwood
†Self, W. M. *textile company executive*

Hilton Head Island
Cunningham, William Henry *retired food products executive*
Harty, James D. *former manufacturing company executive*
Hirsch, Carl Herbert *retired manufacturing company executive*
Lauer, Clinton Dillman *automotive executive*
Lewis, Gene Evans *retired medical equipment company executive*
Love, Richard Emerson *retired equipment manufacturing company executive*
Mersereau, Hiram Stipe *wood products company consultant*
Pritchard, Dalton Harold *retired electronics research engineer*
Rulis, Raymond Joseph *manufacturing company executive, consultant*
Russell, Allen Stevenson *retired aluminum company executive*

Kiawah Island
Zurio, Eugene John *pharmaceutical executive*

Mauldin
†Martin, Sharon D. *automotive executive*

Murrells Inlet
Kelly, Gerald Wayne *chemical coatings company executive*

North Charleston
Zucker, Jerry *chemical manufacturing executive*

Orangeburg
Kent, Harry Ross *construction executive, lay worker*

Rock Hill
Collins, Francis Winfield *chemicals executive*

Simpsonville
†Maguire, D. E. *electronics executive*

Spartanburg
Allen, Robert Watson *retired textile company executive*
Dent, Frederick Baily *former mill executive, former ambassador, former secretary of commerce*
Milliken, Roger *textile company executive*

Townville
Wright, George Cullen *electronics company executive*

SOUTH DAKOTA

Dakota Dunes
†Peterson, Robert L. *meat processing executive*

Sioux Falls
Christensen, David Allen *manufacturing company executive*
Reynolds, Leo Thomas *electronics company executive*
Rosenthal, Joel *manufacturing executive*

TENNESSEE

Bartlett
Huffman, Delton Cleon, Jr., *pharmacy association executive*

Brentwood
Smith, Wayne Thomas *healthcare company executive*

Bristol
Macione, Kyle Pritchett *pharmaceutical company executive, lawyer*

Chattanooga
St. Goar, Herbert *retired food corporation executive*

Collegedale
McKee, Ellsworth R. *food products executive*

Collierville
Duke, Gary James *electronics executive*

Crossville
Lawrence, Ralph Waldo *manufacturing company executive*

Dandridge
Comer, Evan Philip *manufacturing company executive*

Greeneville
Frederick, George Francis *retired manufacturing executive*
Renner, Glenn Delmar *agricultural products executive*

Kingsport
Coover, Harry Wesley *manufacturing company executive*
†Deavenport, Earnest W., Jr., *chemical executive*
†Ferguson, J. Brian *chemicals executive*
Findley, Don Aaron *manufacturing company executive*
Head, William Iverson, Sr., *retired chemical company executive*

Knoxville
Faires, Ross Norbert *manufacturing company executive*
Klingerman, Robert Harvey *manufacturing company executive*
Martin, James Robert *identification company executive*
Stringfield, Hezz, Jr., *contractor, financial consultant*

Lafayette
†Oliver, Barbara Ann *retired apparel executive*

Lookout Mountain
Rymer, S. Bradford, Jr., *retired appliance manufacturing company executive*

Memphis
†Dunavant, William Buchanan, Jr., *textiles executive*
Dunnigan, T. Kevin *electrical and electronics manufacturing company executive*
Karp, Harvey L. *metal products manufacturing executive*
Klyman, Fred Irwin *healthcare executive*
†Levy, Robert Halle *apparel executive, writer*
Mantey, Elmer Martin *food company executive*
†Vargo, Timothy D. *auto part executive*

Nashville
Fitzgerald, Edmund Bacon *electronics industry executive*
Harris, J(acob) George *health care company executive*
Hass, Joseph Monroe *automotive executive*
Hofstead, James Warner *laundry machinery company executive, lawyer*
Livingston, Robert A. *brewing company executive*
†Mizell, Andrew Hooper, III, *concrete company executive*
Wire, William Shidaker, II, *retired apparel and footwear manufacturing company executive*

Oak Ridge
Poutsma, Marvin L. *chemical research administrator*

Smyrna
Lee, Elizabeth Mullins *automotive executive*

Union City
Graham, R(ichard) Newell *soft drink bottling company executive*

TEXAS

Addison
Anderson, Jack Roy *health care company executive*
†Rogers, Richard Raymond *cosmetics company executive*

Alamo
Pritchett, Thomas Ronald *retired metal and chemical company executive*

Allen
Warren, Rita Simpson *manufacturing company executive*

Arlington
Gates, Richard Daniel *retired manufacturing company executive*
Mansen, Steven Robert *manufacturing company executive*
Mc Keen, Chester M., Jr., *retired business executive*

Austin
Culp, Joe C(arl) *electronics executive*
†Maar, Rosina *medical organization executive*

Mason, Franklin Rogers *retired automotive executive*
Rotunda, Joseph Louis *retail and service company executive*
Sullivan, Jerry Stephen *electronics company executive*
Thompson, Larry Flack *nanotechnology and semiconductor process company executive*
Van Buren, William Benjamin, III, *retired pharmaceutical company executive*
Vykukal, Eugene Lawrence *wholesale drug company executive*

Beaumont
Ware, John David *valve and hydrant company executive*

Boerne
Richmond, James Ellis *retired restaurant company executive*

Bryan
Lusas, Edmund William *food processing research executive*

Carrollton
Guy, Marc Duane *assistant city manager*
†Heath, Jinger L. *cosmetics executive*
†Hulbert, Paul William, Jr., *paper, lumber company executive*

College Station
Kainthla, Ramesh Chand *manufacturing company executive*
Palen, Joseph William *chemical process research company executive*

Coppell
†Minyard, Liz *food products executive*

Corpus Christi
Kane, Sam *meat company executive*

Corsicana
McCally, Charles Richard *construction company executive, consultant, mathematician, educator*

Dallas
Barnes, Robert Vertreese, Jr., *masonry contractor executive*
Bartos, Jerry Garland *corporate executive, mechanical engineer*
†Bradford, William Edward *oil field equipment manufacturing company executive*
Bucy, J. Fred, Jr., *retired electronics company executive*
Engles, Gregg L. *food company executive*
†Ethridge, Joseph Alfred *manufacturing executive (heavy)*
†Gafford, Ronald J. *construction executive*
Gifford, Porter William *retired construction materials manufacturing company executive*
Guerin, Dean Patrick *executive*
Hirsch, Laurence Eliot *construction executive, mortgage banker*
Kelley, Michael James *medical services executive, author*
†Korba, Robert W. *manufacturing executive*
Leedom, John Nesbett *distribution company executive, state senator*
Lowe, Jack, Jr., *manufacturing executive*
Margerison, Richard Wayne *diversified industrial company executive*
Murphy, John Joseph *manufacturing company executive*
Pearce, Ronald *retired cosmetic company executive*
Roach, John D. *building products company executive*
Robertson, Beverly Carruth *retired steel company executive*
Rosson, Glenn Richard *building products and furniture company executive*
†Sammons, Elaine D. *corporate executive*
†Schenkel, Pete *food company executive*
†Sherman, Floyd F. *construction executive*
Solomon, William Tarver *general construction company executive*
†Turner, Jim L. *bottler manufacturing executive*
White, Tom Willingham *private investor*
Zumwalt, Richard Dowling *flour mill executive*

Farmers Branch
Armand, Susanne Marie *pharmaceutical products executive*

Fort Mc Kavett
Stokes, Charles Eugene, Jr., *wool merchant, textile executive*

Fort Worth
Curts, Harold Layne *construction executive*
Kemp, Thomas Joseph *retired electronics company executive*
Pearce, Betty McMurray *manufacturing company executive*
†Privitt, Mark B. *construction executive*
Roland, Billy Ray *electronics company executive*
Thornton, Charles Victor *metals executive*
†Williamson, Philip *apparel executive*

Garland
†Heil, Terry W. *defense electronic company executive*
†Keebaugh, Michael D. *electronics executive*

Georgetown
Gerding, Thomas Graham *medical products company executive*

Granbury
Adams, Christopher Steve, Jr., *retired defense electronics corporation executive, former air force officer*

Houston
Austin, Harry Guiden *engineering and construction company executive*

Boren, William Meredith *manufacturing executive*
Cameron, William Duncan *plastics company executive*
Cizik, Robert *manufacturing company executive*
Clyburn, Rose Mary Reed *construction materials company executive*
Cotros, Charles H. *food products company executive*
Goff, Robert Burnside *retired food company executive*
Hafner, Joseph A., Jr., *food company executive*
Hartsfield, Henry Warren, Jr., *electronics executive, retired astronaut*
Hubert, Jean-Luc *chemicals executive*
Huffington, Roy Michael *business executive, former ambassador*
†Hynes, Thomas N. (Toby Hynes) *automotive company executive*
†Kaptopodis, Louis *supermarket chain executive*
Kite, Lewis Donald *pharmaceutical executive*
Klausmeyer, David Michael *scientific instruments manufacturing company executive*
Klotz, David Wayne *executive, civil engineer*
McCleskey, Jerry Michael *retired chemical company executive*
Mehra, Man Mohan *medical products executive, small business owner*
Menscher, Barnet Gary *steel company executive*
Munisteri, Joseph George *construction executive*
Pognonec, Yves Maurice *steel products executive*
Riedel, Alan Ellis *retired manufacturing company executive, lawyer*
†Rock, Douglas Lawrence *manufacturing executive*
Salinas, Martha F. *manufacturing executive*
†Schnieders, Richard J. *food products executive*
†Schumacher, Diane Kosmach *manufacturing executive, lawyer*
†Siess, Charles P., Jr., *manufacturing company executive*
Snowden, Bernice Rives *former construction company executive*
Temple, Robert Winfield *chemical company executive*
Templeton, Robert Earl *engineering and construction company executive*
White, David Alan, Jr., *manufacturing company executive*
Wilson, Carl Weldon, Jr., *construction company executive, civil engineer*
Wnuk, Wade Joseph *manufacturing and service company executive*
Wuensche, Vernon Edgar *construction company executive*

Irving
†Donehower, John W. *retired paper company executive*
†Falk, Thomas J. *paper company executive*
Halbert, David D. *health management services executive*
Pennington, William Lane *manufacturing executive*

League City
Burns, Richard Robert *chemicals executive*

Longview
Mann, Jack Matthewson *bottling company executive*

Lubbock
Hester, Ross Wyatt *retired business forms manufacturing executive*

Mansfield
Siméus, Dumas M. *food products executive*

McKinney
†Schottlaender, Colin *electronics executive*

Montgomery
Steed, Theresa Jean *manufacturing company executive*

Pasadena
Gross, Cynthia Sue *petrochemicals manufacturing executive*
Stephens, Sidney Dee *chemical manufacturing company executive*

Plano
Bain, Travis Whitsett, II, *manufacturing and retail executive*
†Cumming, Marilee *apparel company executive*
Naor, Daniel *food products executive*
†Rochon, John Philip *cosmetics company executive*

Point
Middleton, Ida Lavelle *dairy executive, comptroller*

Richardson
Richards, Frederick Francis, Jr., *manufacturing company executive*
†Schjerven, Robert E. *manufacturing executive*

Richmond
Barratt, Cynthia Louise *pharmaceutical company executive*

Rockwall
Fisher, Gene Jordan *retired chemical company executive*

San Antonio
Bagley, William Evan *application technology specialist*
Cisneros, Henry G. *homebuilding executive, broadcast executive, former federal official*
Cloud, Bruce Benjamin, Sr., *construction company executive*
Lyles, Mark Bradley *advanced technology company executive, dentist*

Williams, Thomas Eugene *pediatric hematologist-oncologist, pharmaceutical executive*
†Zachry, Henry Bartell, Jr., *construction executive*

Santa Fe
Lambert, Willie Lee Bell *mobile equipment company owner, educator*

Seguin
Robinson, Ronald Alan *manufacturing executive*

Sweeny
Griffin, Stanley Ray *machinist*

The Woodlands
Blickwede, Donald Johnson *retired steel company executive*

Tyler
Smith, Howard Thompson *business executive*
Warner, John Andrew *foundry executive*

Zephyr
Lancaster, Carroll Townes, Jr., *business executive*

UTAH

Morgan
Ercanbrack, Gene *food products executive*

Orem
Segelman, Alvin Burton *pharmaceutical executive, researcher, scientist, health science consultant, educator*

Salt Lake City
Anderson, Joseph Andrew, Jr., *retired apparel company executive, retail consultant*
Frank, Thomas *design, construction and management executive*
Hembree, James D. *retired chemical company executive*
†Huntsman, Jon Meade *chemical company executive*
Huntsman, Peter R. *chemicals executive*
Motter, Thomas Franklin *medical products executive*
Norton, Delmar Lynn *candy company executive*
Steiner, Richard Russell *textile & apparel company executive*
Stitley, James Walter, Jr., *food manufacturing executive*

Sandy
†Andriano, Kirk Patrick *pharmaceutical executive*
Clark, Jeffrey Raphiel *research and development company executive*

Vineyard
†Cannon, Joseph A. *steel products company executive, political party official*

VERMONT

Arlington
Nowicki, George Lucian *retired chemical company executive*

Bennington
Killen, Carroll Gorden *electronics company executive*

Brattleboro
Cohen, Richard B. *grocery company executive*

Brownsville
Olderman, Gerald *retired medical device company executive*

North Troy
Spencer, Richard Thomas, III, *healthcare industry executive*

Pittsfield
Wacker, Susan Regina *creative design director*

South Burlington
Pizzagalli, James *construction executive*

South Pomfret
Oatway, Francis Carlyle *corporate executive*

Vergennes
Grant, Edwin Randolph *retail and manufacturing executive*

Windsor
Furnas, Howard Earl *business executive*

VIRGINIA

Alexandria
Crundwell, Duncan James *electronics executive*
Lantz, Phillip Edward *corporate executive, consultant*
Liesemer, Ronald Newell *plastics company executive*
Stempler, Jack Leon *government and aerospace executive*

Arlington
Cocolis, Peter Konstantine *business development executive*
Cox, Henry *research company executive, research engineer*
†Culligan, Thomas M. *electronics executive*
Danjczek, David William *manufacturing company executive*
Gracey, James Steele *corporate director, retired coast guard officer, consultant*
Guirguis, Raouf Albert *health science executive*
†Hollander, Rachelle D.

Howlett, Clifford Theodore, Jr., (Kip Howlett) *chemicals executive*
†Racette, Nancy Kelly *development company executive, consultant*
Weiss, Joel Alexander *environmental and manufacturing executive*
†Woollen, Edmund *electronics executive*

Ashburn
†Cuteri, Frank R., Jr., *automotive executive*

Bassett
Spilman, Robert Henkel *furniture company executive*

Courtland
Minor, Edward Colquitt *paper company executive, lawyer*

Deltaville
Koedel, John Gilbert, Jr., *retired metal products executive*

Dulles
Persavich, Warren Dale *diversified manufacturing company executive*
Steiner, Jeffrey Josef *industrial manufacturing company executive*

Earlysville
Bartoes, Richard Alan *agricultural products executive*

Glen Allen
Fife, William Franklin *retired drug company executive*
Minor, George Gilmer, III, *drug and hospital supply company executive*
Murphey, Robert Stafford *pharmaceutical company executive*
†Stokely, John E. *food distribution executive*

Heathsville
Winkel, Raymond Norman *aerospace industry consultant, avionics manufacturing executive, retired naval officer*

King George
Lund, Rita Pollard *construction executive*

Lynchburg
Denham, Paul Raymond *construction executive*

Manassas
Parrish, Frank Jennings *retired food products executive*

Marion
Grinstead, Paul Lee *materials company official*

Mc Lean
Dempsey, James Raymon *industrial executive*
Levy, Michael Howard *environmental management professional*
†Mars, Forrest E., Jr., *candy company executive*
Mars, Jacqueline Badger *food products executive*
Mars, John Franklin *candy company executive*
†Schar, Dwight C. *construction company executive*

Mechanicsville
Hinkle, Barton Leslie *retired electronics company executive*

Midlothian
Sowder, Donald Dillard *pharmaceutical executive*

Newport News
Banks, Charles Augustus, III, *manufacturing executive*

Nickelsville
Osborne, Kermit Charles, Jr., *contractor, consultant*

Norfolk
Orgel, Vivian August *beauty expert*

Petersburg
Wilson, John Robert, Jr., *pharmaceutical and chemical company executive*

Portsmouth
Mintz, Susan Ashinoff *apparel manufacturing company executive*

Prince George
Dent, Edward Eugene *manufacturing company specialist*

Purcellville
Christ, Thomas Warren *electronics research and development company executive, sociologist*

Reston
†Evan, Bryan J. *electronics executive*
Gorog, William Francis *corporate executive*
Hill, Jim Tom *retired consulting firm executive*
Levner, Louis Jules *contract administrator*
†Picard, Dennis J. *retired electronics company executive*

Richmond
Blumberg, Peter Steven *manufacturing company executive*
Bunzl, Rudolph Hans *retired manufacturing executive*
Gottwald, Floyd Dewey, Jr., *chemical company executive*
Helwig, Arthur Woods *chemical company executive*
O'Keeffe, Charles B. *pharmaceutical executive*
†Pauley, Stanley Frank *manufacturing company executive*

†Sheehan, Jeremiah J. *former metal company executive*
Totten, Arthur Irving, Jr., *retired metals company executive, consultant*

Roanoke
†Castellani, Lawrence P. *automotive company executive*

Smithfield
Luter, Joseph Williamson, III, *meat packing and processing company executive*

Springfield
Franklin, Jude Eric *electronics executive*

Suffolk
Birdsong, George Yancy *manufacturing company executive*
Sorensen, Carl Edward *company executive*

Vienna
de Bearn, Gaston, XIV, *pharmaceutical company executive, consultant*

Virginia Beach
†Hamilton, George Henry, Jr., *energy consultant*

Winchester
Holland, James Tulley *retired plastic products company executive*
Jolly, Bruce Dwight *manufacturing executive*

Yorktown
Gross, Leroy *sugar company executive*

WASHINGTON

Anacortes
Randolph, Carl Lowell *chemical company executive*

Belfair
Hager, Robert Worth *retired aerospace company executive*

Bellevue
Nowik, Dorothy Adam *medical equipment company executive*
Pigott, Mark C. *automotive executive*

Bellingham
†Haggen, Donald E. *food products executive*
Krmpotich, Frank Zvonko *fiberglass company executive, consultant*

Bothell
†Wilds, Daniel O. *health products executive*

Camano Island
Clowes, Garth Anthony *electronics executive, consultant*

Clinton
Holtby, Kenneth Fraser *retired manufacturing executive*

Coupeville
Thom, Richard David *retired aerospace executive*

Federal Way
Miller, William Ray *retired aircraft manufacturing executive*
Rogel, Steven R. *forest products company executive*

Hoquiam
†Lamb, Isabelle Smith *manufacturing company executive*

Issaquah
Massick, James William *heavy equipment manufacturing company executive*
Wainwright, Paul Edward Blech *construction company executive*

Kent
Goo, Abraham Meu Sen *retired aircraft company executive*
Hebeler, Henry Koester *retired aerospace and electronics executive*

Lake Stevens
Durden, Rome L. *aircraft manufacturing company executive*

Lakewood
†Cook, Anne Welsh *lumber company executive*

Longview
Wollenberg, Richard Peter *paper manufacturing company executive*

Manson
Stager, Donald K. *retired construction company executive*

Maple Valley
Brown, Thomas Andrew *retired aircraft/weaponry manufacturing executive*

Medina
Schlotterbeck, Walter Albert *manufacturing company executive, lawyer*

Mercer Island
Gould, Alvin R. *international business executive*

Mill Creek
Stelzer, Gustav R. *retired automotive executive*

Naches
Assink, Nellie Grace *agricultural executive*

Oak Harbor
Daugherty, Kenneth Earl *research company executive, educator*

Redmond
Quinn, Michael Llyn *construction executive*

Renton
Huck, Larry Ralph *manufacturing executive, sales consultant*

Richland
Nolan, John Edward *retired electrical corporation executive*

Seattle
Albrecht, Richard Raymond *retired airplane manufacturing executive, lawyer*
Farrington-Hopf, Susan Kay *plumbing and heating contractor*
†Moseley, Colin *lumber company executive*
Schoenfeld, Walter Edwin *manufacturing company executive*

Spokane
Fosseen, Neal Randolph *business executive, former banker, former mayor*
Siegel, Louis Pendleton *forest products executive*

Tacoma
Hutchings, George Henry *food company executive*

Vancouver
Scott, Gary LeRoy *photographic manufacturing executive, photographer*

WEST VIRGINIA

Charleston
Gardner, Edward Tytus, III, *company executive*

Huntington
deBarbadillo, John Joseph *metallurgist, management executive, metal products executive*

Redmond
†Hylbert, Paul *construction executive*

WISCONSIN

Appleton
Barlow, F(rank) John *mechanical contracting company executive*
Boldt, Oscar Charles *construction company executive*
Grayson, David S. *paper company executive*
Rankin, Arthur David *retired paper company executive*
Spiegelberg, Harry Lester *retired paper products company executive*

Beaver Dam
Shturmakov, Alexander Joseph *automotive industry executive*

Bowler
Maas, Duane Harris *distilling company executive*

Brookfield
Vitek, Richard Kenneth *scientific instrument company executive*

Cedarburg
Schaefer, Gordon Emory *food products executive*

Clintonville
Simpson, Vinson Raleigh *manufacturing company executive*

Eau Claire
†Rasmussen, Earl R *lumber company and home improvement retail executive*

Fall River
Hurst, Jeffrey Paul *agricultural products executive*

Fort Atkinson
Jones, Alan Porter, Jr., *food manufacturing executive*

Grafton
Yarger, James Gregory *chemical company executive*

Green Bay
†Ferguson, Larry P. *food products executive*
†Kress, William F. *manufacturing company executive*
†Kuehne, Carl W. *food products executive*
†Vesta, Richard V. *meat packing company executive*

Ixonia
Peebles, Allene Kay *manufactured housing company executive*

Kohler
†Kohler, Herbert Vollrath, Jr., *diversified manufacturing company executive*

La Crosse
Gelatt, Charles Daniel *manufacturing company executive*

Madison
Klodt, Gerald Joseph *product development executive*
Shain, Irving *retired chemical company executive and university chancellor*

Marathon
Natzke, Paulette Ann *manufacturing executive*

Markesan
Chamberlain, Robert Glenn *retired tool manfacturing executive*

Mequon
Dohmen, Frederick Hoeger *retired wholesale drug company executive*

Milwaukee
Beals, Vaughn Le Roy, Jr., *retired motorcycle manufacturing executive*
Bishop, Charles Joseph *manufacturing company executive*
†Bleustein, Jeffrey L. *automotive executive*
Colbert, Virgis W. *food products executive*
†Davis, Don H., Jr., *multi-industry high-technology company executive*
Hudson, Katherine Mary *manufacturing company executive*
Keyes, James Henry *manufacturing company executive*
Marringa, Jacques Louis *manufacturing company executive*
Martin, Vincent Lionel *manufacturing company executive*
Parker, Charles Walter, Jr., *consultant, retired equipment company executive*
Sterner, Frank Maurice *industrial executive*
Yontz, Kenneth Fredric *medical and chemical company executive*

Neenah
Bergstrom, Dedric Waldemar *retired paper company executive*

Oshkosh
Drebus, Richard William *pharmaceutical company executive*
Zuern, Rosemary Lucile *manufacturing executive, treasurer*

Pleasant Prairie
Morrone, Frank *electronic manufacturing executive*

Racine
Campbell, Edward Joseph *retired machinery company executive*
Konz, Gerald Keith *retired manufacturing company executive*
†Perez, William D. *chemical company executive*
†Rosso, Jean-Pierre *electronics executive*

Sheboygan
Merkel, Daniel A. *dental products company executive*

South Milwaukee
Kitzke, Eugene David *research and development company executive*

Sturtevant
†Johnson, Samuel Curtis *chemical company executive*
†Lawton, Gregory E. *manufacturing executive*

Sussex
Losee, John Frederick, Jr., *manufacturing executive*
Stromberg, Gregory *printing ink company executive*

Waterloo
†Burke, Richard A. *manufacturing executive*

Wisconsin Rapids
Engelhardt, LeRoy A. *retired paper company executive*

WYOMING

Jackson
Furrer, John Rudolf *retired chemicals executive*
Gordon, Stephen Maurice *manufacturing company executive, rancher*

Laramie
†Pope, John Michael *research and development company executive, researcher*

Wilson
Harrell, Samuel Macy *agribusiness executive*

TERRITORIES OF THE UNITED STATES

PUERTO RICO

Dorado
Spector, Michael Joseph *agribusiness executive*

CANADA

ALBERTA

Calgary
Holman, J(ohn) Leonard *retired manufacturing corporation executive*

Edmonton
Stollery, Robert *construction company executive*

BRITISH COLUMBIA

Burnaby
Shen, John Jianyue *fuel cell company executive*

North Vancouver
Gibbs, David George *retired food processing company executive*

Vancouver
Hastings, Paul J. *pharmaceutical executive*

Victoria
Fuller, James Chester Eedy *retired chemical company executive*

MANITOBA

Winnipeg
MacKenzie, George Allan *company executive*

NEW BRUNSWICK

Fredericton
†Grotterod, Knut *retired paper company executive*

NOVA SCOTIA

Halifax
Pincock, Douglas George *electronics company executive*

Stellarton
Sobey, David Frank *food company executive*

ONTARIO

Aurora
Lanthier, Ronald Ross *retired manufacturing company executive*

Burlington
McMulkin, Francis John *retired steel company executive*

Cambridge
Turnbull, Robert Scott *manufacturing company executive*
White, Joseph Charles *manufacturing and retailing company executive*

Don Mills
Hyde, Michael Arthur *chemical company executive*

Hamilton
Hantho, Chuck *retired metal products executive*
Telmer, Frederick Harold *steel products manufacturing executive*

Hanover
Adams, John David Vessot *manufacturing company executive*

Markham
Burns, H(erbert) Michael *corporate director*

Mississauga
Strachan, Graham *pharmaceutical executive*

Mississauga
Kennedy, John W. *health products executive*

Nepean
Chudobiak, Walter James *electronics company executive, electronic engineer*

Newmarket
Walker, Donald J. *automotive systems company executive*

Ottawa
Goodine, Isaac Thomas *development executive, educator*

Sault Sainte Marie
†Dalla-Vicenza, Mario Joseph *steel company executive*

Toronto
Connell, Philip Francis *food industry executive*
Dale, Robert Gordon *business executive*
Detlefsen, Michael E. *food products executive*
Eagles, Stuart Ernest *business executive*
Lennox, R. Ian *health products executive*
Lewitt, Wilfred S. *health products executive*
Macdonald, Donald Stovel *corporate director*
Polistuk, Eugene V. *electronics manufacturing services executive*
Wleugel, John Peter *manufacturing company executive*

QUEBEC

Montreal
Ferguson, Michael John *electronics and communications educator*
Gouin, Serge *corporate executive*
Herling, Michael *steel company executive*
Ivanier, Paul *steel products manufacturing company executive*
Molson, Eric H. *beverage company executive*
Nadeau, Bertin Felix *diversified company executive*
†Plourde, Gerard *company executive*
Redfern, John D. *manufacturing company executive*
Rolland, Lucien Gilbert *paper company executive, director*

Outremont
Larose, Roger *retired pharmaceutical executive, retired dean*

SASKATCHEWAN

Regina
Phillips, Roger *retired steel company executive*

MEXICO

Mexico City
Vargas Legaspi, Juan *manufacturing company executive*

THE BAHAMAS

Nassau
Dingman, Michael David *industrial company executive, international investor*

BELGIUM

Ghent
Hulstaert, Frank *pharmaceutical company executive*

CHINA

Shanghai
Jackson, Robert Keith *manufacturing company executive*

DENMARK

Copenhagen
Drakeman, Lisa N. *biotechnology company executive*

ENGLAND

Ascot Berkshire
Grubman, Wallace Karl *chemical company executive*

Beckenham Kent
Lader, Malcolm Harold *pharmaceutical consultant*

Brentford, Middlesex
Ingram, Robert A. *pharmaceuticals company executive*

London
Goeltz, Richard Karl *distilled spirits and wine company executive*

Milton Keynes
Throdahl, Mark Crandall *medical technology company executive*

Surrey
Vere Hodge, Richard Anthony *pharmaceutical executive, consultant*

Windsor Berkshire
†Ekberg, Jan *retired pharmaceutical company executive*

FINLAND

Espoo
Nuckols, William Marshall *electrical goods manufacturing executive*

Tampere
Malminiemi, Kimmo Heikki *pharmaceutical company executive, researcher*

FRANCE

Nanterre
Payri, Joel *pharmaceutical marketing executive*

Paris
Collomb, Bertrand Pierre *cement company executive*
Lecerf, Olivier Maurice Marie *construction company executive*

GERMANY

Berlin
Meyer-Tischler, Jörg Rudolf Erich *pharmaceutical company executive*
Stock, Günter *pharmaceutical company executive*

Regensburg
Rupprecht, Herbert Harald *pharmaceutical technologist*

Schleusingen-Gethles
Frank, Dieter *retired chemicals executive*

GREECE

Athens
Larounis, George Philip *manufacturing company executive*

Palia Pendeli Athens
Simeon, George Prodrom *healthcare company executive*

JAPAN

Kanagawa-ken
Hoshino, Yoshiro *industrial technology critic*

Tokyo
Maurer, P(aul) Reed *pharmaceutical company executive*
Saba, Shoichi *manufacturing company executive*
Wakumoto, Yoshihiko *electronics company executive, grants executive*

Toyota
Toyoda, Shoichiro *automobile company executive*

JORDAN

Amman
Jalal, Ibrahim Mohammad *pharmaceutical executive*

PHILIPPINES

Laguna
Schellner, Reinhard Anton *business executive*

SOUTH AFRICA

Yaoundé, Cameroon
Provencher-Kambour, Frances *business development advisor*

SPAIN

Madrid
Feltenstein, Harry David, Jr., *chemical executive*

SWEDEN

Stockholm
†Westerberg, Lars *automotive safety systems company executive*

Södertälje
Federsel, Hans-Jürgen *pharmaceutical company executive*

SWITZERLAND

Basel
†Jetzer, Alexandre F. *pharmaceutical executive*

ADDRESS UNPUBLISHED

Aall, Christian Bergengren *software company executive*
Acerra, Michele (Mike Acerra) *engineering and construction company executive*
Adams, Warren Sanford, II, *retired food company executive, lawyer*
Adams, William White *retired manufacturing company executive*
Alford, Becky Dianne *food products executive*
Alig, Frank Douglas Stalnaker *retired construction company executive*
Altschuler, Samuel *retired electronics company executive*
Amadio, Bari Ann *metal fabrication executive, former nurse*
Amstutz, Daniel Gordon *international agriculture industry consultant, former grain dealer, government and intergovernment official*
Anderer, Joseph Henry *textile company executive*
Anderson, Fletcher Neal *chemical executive*
Anderson, Joseph Norman *executive consultant, former food company executive, former college president*
Andersson, Craig Remington *retired chemical company executive*
Andreas, Dwayne Orville *business executive*
Andrews, William Frederick *manufacturing executive*
Angelo, George *pediatric sales representative, lawyer*
†Archibald, Nolan D. *household and industrial products company executive*
Aschauer, Charles Joseph, Jr., *corporate director, former company executive*
Ashraf, Elizabeth Ann *pharmaceutical company executive*
Ashton, Harris John *business executive*
Asmussen, Nils Wirenfeldt *pharmaceutical executive*
Asplin, Edward William *retired packaging company executive*
Atchison, Joseph Edward *pulp and paper industry consultant*
Azarnoff, Daniel Lester *pharmaceutical company consultant*

Banis, Robert Joseph pharmaceutical company executive, educator, publisher
Barber, Marsha company executive
Barca, George Gino winery executive, financial investor
Barron, Charles Elliott retired electronics executive
Barth, David Keck distribution industry consultant
Barton, Glen A. manufacturing company executive
Bass, Robert Olin retired manufacturing executive
Bassin, Gilbert Sheldon manufacturing executive, engineer
Batterden, James Edward retired business executive
Battistelli, Joseph John electronics executive
Batts, Warren Leighton retired diversified industry executive
Bauman, Robert Patten diversified company executive
Bavota, Michael Francis (Michael Ryan) food products executive, freelance writer
†Bayly, George V. manufacturing executive
Beadle, John Grant retired manufacturing company executive
Beck, Albert manufacturing company executive
Beighey, Lawrence Jerome packaging company executive
Bennett, Carrie retired chemical company executive
Bennett, Jay Brett healthcare industry executive
Bennett, Richard Thomas retired manufacturing executive
Beracha, Barry Harris retired food products executive
Bergmann, Donald Gerald pharmaceutical company executive
Bernsen, Harold John manufacturing executive
Bernthal, Harold George healthcare company executive
Berry, Robert Vaughan retired electrical manufacturing company executive
Beutler, Arthur Julius manufacturing company executive
Bevington, E(dmund) Milton electrical machinery manufacturing company executive
Bible, Geoffrey Cyril former tobacco company executive
Bierwirth, John Cocks retired aerospace manufacturing executive
Biggers, William Joseph retired manufacturing company executive
Biggs, Arthur Edward retired chemical manufacturing company executive
Blanchard, Richard Frederick construction executive
Blatt, Lawrence M. pharmaceutical company executive
†Blodgett, Dean Scott product development executive
Blum, Betty Ann footwear company executive
Bocaya, Renato Biso pharmaceutical sales and marketing executive, entrepreneur
Bollenbacher, Herbert Kenneth steel company official
Bos, John Arthur retired aircraft manufacturing executive
Boyer, Robert Allan business executive
†Boyle, R. Emmett metal products executive
Brancato, Leo John manufacturing company executive
Brandinger, Jay Jerome electronics executive
Bratton, William Edward electronics executive, management consultant
†Bridenbaugh, Peter Reese industrial research executive
Brodie, Theodore Hamilton construction company executive
†Bronfman, Edgar Miles, Jr., diversified business executive, producer
Brooker, Robert Elton, Jr., retired manufacturing company executive
Brown, Jerry Milford medical company executive
Bull, Bergen Ira retired equipment manufacturing company executive
Burch, Hamlin Doughty, III, retired sheet metal professional
Butler, Jack Fairchild semiconductors company executive
Buzzelli, James Raymond pharmaceutical company executive
†Calcaterra, Edward Lee construction company executive
Caltrider, Paul Gene pharmaceutical company executive, microbiologist
Calvert, James Francis manufacturing company executive, retired admiral
Campbell, Richard Alden electronics company executive
Candlish, Malcolm manufacturing company executive
Carpenter, Myron Arthur manufacturing company executive
Carver, Juanita Ash plastic company executive
Casey, Gerard William retired food products company executive, lawyer
Cassidy, James Mark construction company executive
Castaldi, David Lawrence healthcare company executive
Castberg, Eileen Sue construction company owner
Champion, Helena Margaret pharmaceutical executive
Chaykin, Robert Leroy manufacturing and marketing executive
Chen, Di electro-optic company executive, consultant
Chihorek, John Paul electronics company executive
Chmielinski, Edward Alexander retired electronics company executive
Cicolani, Angelo George research and development company executive, operating engineer
Closset, Gerard Paul forest products consultant
Clouston, Ross Neal retired food and related products company executive
Coffey, Dennis James performance technology consultant
Cook, Charles William, Jr., manufacturing executive
Cooley, James William retired executive researcher
Cooper, Kenneth Banks business executive, former army officer
Cooper, Norton J. (Sky Cooper) liquor, wine and food company executive
Costello, James Joseph retired electrical manufacturing company executive
Cotting, James Charles manufacturing company executive
Cox, John Francis retired cosmetic company executive
Cox, Wilford Donald retired food company executive
Craft, Edmund Coleman retired automotive parts manufacturing company executive
Crawford, William David office equipment company executive
Crigger, Gary Brant retired manufacturing executive
Cull, Robert Robinette electric products manufacturing company executive
Culwell, Charles Louis retired manufacturing company executive
Curtis, Arnold Bennett retired lumber company executive
Cuthbert, Robert Lowell retired product specialist
Cutter, David Lee pharmaceutical company executive
D'Agostino, Stephen Ignatius bottling company executive
Danziger, Gertrude Seelig metal fabricating executive
Danziger, Glenn Norman former chemical sales company executive
Davis, Darrell L. automotive executive
†DeBruce, Paul agricultural food products company executive
Dempsey, David Allan company official
Denegall, John Palmer, Jr., construction executive
†Deutsche, Kirsten Hansen pharmaceutical company executive
de Vink, Lodewijk J. R. former consumer pharmaceutical products company executive
Diener, Royce corporate director, retired healthcare services company executive
Dillon, Phillip Michael construction company executive
Dinkel, John George automotive executive, consultant
Dohrmann, Russell William manufacturing company executive
Dole, Vincent Paul, III, food products executive
Doran, Charles Edward textile manufacturing executive
Dougherty, Robert Anthony retired manufacturing company executive
Doyle, Irene Elizabeth electronic sales executive, nurse
Dragon, William, Jr., footwear and apparel company executive
Dressler, David Charles retired aerospace company executive
Drew, Walter Harlow retired paper industry executive
†Duhaime, Nina Lee business research and development
Dupps, John Avery, Jr., process machinery company executive
Durr, Robert Joseph construction firm executive, mechanical engineer
Dye, Robert Harris retired manufacturing company executive
Dyer, Natalie Mary health products company executive, physician
Earle, Arthur Percival textile company executive, airport executive
†Eberhardt, H. Alfred retired manufacturing executive, retired mechanical engineer
Eberle, Charles Edward paper and consumer products executive
Eissmann, Walter James consulting company executive
Ellis, Harold Donald auto repair company executive, consultant
Elverum, Gerard William, Jr., retired electronic and diversified company executive
Ely, Paul C., Jr., electronics company executive
Engels, Lawrence Arthur retired metals company executive
Erdeljac, Daniel Joseph retired manufacturing company executive
Fatzinger, James A. S. construction educator, estimator
Fein, Seymour Howard pharmaceutical executive
Finlay, Robert Derek food company executive
†Flaten, Alfred N. retired food and consumer products executive
Fleming, James Stuart, Jr., retired pharmaceutical company manager
Flitcraft, Richard Kirby, II, former chemical company executive
Flynn, Robert James electronic commerce executive
Fogg, Richard Lloyd food products company executive
Ford, Jerry Lee service company executive
Francisco, Wayne automotive executive
†Franklin, Charles E. manufacturing executive
French, Clarence Levi, Jr., retired shipbuilding company executive
Frieling, Gerald Harvey, Jr., specialty steel company executive
Fries, Raymond Sebastian manufacturing company executive
Frisco, Louis Joseph retired materials science company executive, electrical engineer
Fritz, Rene Eugene, Jr., manufacturing executive
Garrison, Paul Cornell retired office products company executive
Garrity, Thomas John pharmaceutical executive
Garruto, John Anthony cosmetics executive
Gates, Martina Marie food products company executive
Gifford, John Irving retired agricultural equipment company executive
Gillin, James pharmaceutical company executive
Goldberg, Lee Winicki furniture company executive
Goodale, Toni Krissel development consultant
Gorman, Joseph Tolle automotive parts manufacturing executive
Gray, Richard Alexander, Jr., retired chemical company executive
Greaser, Constance Udean automotive industry executive
Grieve, Pierson MacDonald retired chemicals executive
Grossman, Jerrold B. pharmaceutical executive
Grove, Richard Charles retired power tool company executive
Guiliano, Francis James office products manufacturing company executive
Gulcher, Robert Harry aircraft company executive
Gurney, Daniel Sexton race car manufacturing company executive, racing team executive
Haas, Frederick Carl retired paper and chemical company executive
Haeberle, William Leroy corporate director, business educator, entrepreneur
†Hake, Ralph F. appliance manufacturing executive
Hakimoglu, Ayhan electronics company executive
Halbrooks, James Richmond (Ricky Halbrooks) sheet metal mechanic
Hamister, Donald Bruce retired electronics company executive
Hammond, Robert Lee retired feed company executive
Harbert, Charles Armon medicinal chemist
Harper, Charles Michel food company executive
Hartmann, George Herman retired manufacturing company executive
Hartwick, Thomas Stanley technical management consultant
Hausman, Arthur Herbert electronics company executive
Hawkins, Ellis Delano manufacturing executive, insurance executive, gaming executive
Hayes, Edwin Junius, Jr., business executive
Hayes, John Patrick retired manufacturing company executive
Heckel, John Louis (Jack Heckel) aerospace company executive
Heilmann, Christian Flemming corporate executive
Heininger, S(amuel) Allen retired chemical company executive
Heller, Ronald Gary manufacturing company executive, lawyer
Henning, George Thomas, Jr., steel company executive
Henze, David Carleton pharmaceutical company executive
Herbert, Gavin Shearer health care products company executive
Herman, Rayna S. pharmaceutical consultant
Hiatt, Arnold shoe manufacturer, importer, retailer
Higman, Sally Lee company executive
†Hill, Katie contractor
Hind, Harry William pharmaceutical company executive
Hirsch, Horst Eberhard business consultant
Hoch, Orion Lindel corporate executive
Hochfeld, William Sidney construction executive, consultant
Honse, Robert W. agricultural company executive
Hook, Jerry B. pharmaceutical consultant
Hornak, Thomas retired electronics company executive
Horovitz, Zola Philip pharmaceutical company executive
Horwitz, David Larry pharmaceuticals company executive, researcher, educator
Hudson, Franklin Donald diversified company executive, consultant
Hudson, William Jeffrey, Jr., manufacturing company executive
†Hughes, David Henry manufacturing company executive
Hulse, Dexter Curtis manufacturing executive
Humphrey, Matthew J. manufacturing specialist
Hurd, Richard Nelson pharmaceutical company executive
Hushen, John Wallace manufacturing company executive
Hutchins, Steven Edward plastics company executive, writer
†Isakson, Peter C. pharmaceutical executive
Isko, Irving D. corporate executive
†Ivanchenko, Lauren Margaret Dowd pharmaceutical executive
Ivester, Melvin Douglas retired beverage company executive
Ix, Robert Edward food company executive
Jackson, Robbi Jo agricultural products company executive, lawyer
Jackson, Robert Howard food company executive, scientist
Jaffe, Marvin Eugene pharmaceutical company executive, neurologist
Johnson, Irving Stanley pharmaceutical company executive, scientist
Johnson, Rogers Bruce retired chemical company executive
†Johnson, Warren Donald retired pharmaceutical executive, former air force officer
Johnstone, John William, Jr., retired chemical company executive
Jones, Christine Massey retired furniture company executive
†Jones, Robert Henry automotive distribution executive
Joyce, William Robert textile machinery company executive
Juhl, Daniel Leo manufacturing and marketing firm executive
Kapcsandy, Louis Endre building construction and manufacturing executive, chemical engineering consultant
†Kaplan, Jerry (S. Jerrold Kaplan) former electronics company executive
Keeler, James Leonard food products company executive
Keith, Brian Thomas automobile executive
Kellgren, George Lars manufacturing company executive
Kelly, Anthony Odrian flooring manufacturing company executive
Kelly, J. Peter steel company executive
Kern, Irving John retired food company executive
Khan, Jamil Akber chemical company executive
Khilnani, Vinod M. manufacturing executive
Kienow, Barry Scott construction executive, architect
†Killhour, William Gherky paper company executive
Killian, William Paul industrial corporate executive
Kimball, Donald Robert retired food company executive
King, Susan Bennett retired glass company executive
Kiselik, Paul Howard manufacturing executive
†Klaehne, Eberhard O W pharmaceutical executive, chemist
Knight, Herbert Borwell manufacturing company executive
Kogan, Richard Jay former pharmaceutical company executive
Krise, Patricia Love automotive industry executive
†Krivai, Galina manufacturing executive
Kronschnabel, Robert James retired manufacturing company executive
Krupp, James Arthur Gustave consultant
Kulik, Rosalyn Franta food company executive, consultant
Kung, Patrick Chung-Shu biotechnology executive
Labrecque, Richard Joseph retired industrial executive
Landon, Robert Gray retired manufacturing company executive
Landsberger, Kurt scientific and medical products executive
Lane, William W. electronics executive
Langer, Dennis Henry pharmaceutical company executive
Langford, Walter Martin retired greeting card and gift wrap manufacturing executive
†Lapinsky, Joseph F. manufacturing company executive
Laskey, Richard Anthony biomedical device executive
Laurenzo, Vincent Dennis industrial management company executive
LeBlanc, Leonard Joseph electronics company executive
Leff, Joseph Norman yarn manufacturing company executive
Lehman, John F., Jr., industrialist
Leonard, Guy Meyers, Jr., international holding company executive
Levaux, Hugh Pierre pharmaceutical executive, consultant
Leveille, Gilbert Antonio food products executive
Lewis, Arthur Dee corporation executive
Lewis, Martin R. paper company executive, consultant
Lewis, Rita Hoffman plastic products manufacturing company executive
Liffers, William Albert retired chemical company executive
Lindsay, James Wiley retired agricultural company executive
Lippincott, Philip Edward retired paper products company executive
Little, Freed Sebastian retired petroleum equipment manufacturing company executive
†Litzenberger, Lesley Margaret textiles executive
Lohman, Gordon Russell retired manufacturing executive
†Long, Larry Dean contractor
†Loredo, Elvira Nieves researcher
Louis-Cotton d'Englesqueville, Francois Pierre automobile company executive
Lowden, John L. retired corporate executive
Lucas, William Ray aerospace consultant
Luke, David Lincoln, III, retired paper company executive
†Lukens, Max L. manufacturing company executive
Lynch, Charles Andrew chemical industry consultant
MacAvoy, Thomas Coleman glass manufacturing executive, educator
Madden, Richard Blaine forest products executive
Malsack, James Thomas retired manufacturing company executive
Manchester, Kenneth Edward electronics executive, consultant
Mangapit, Conrado, Jr., manufacturing company executive
Mangold, John Frederic manufacturing company executive, former naval officer
Marcy, Alvin Newell contractor
Marrington, Bernard Harvey retired automotive company executive
Martin, Albert Charles manufacturing executive, lawyer
Mason, Frank Henry, III, automobile company executive, leasing company executive
Mastin, Wayne Alan strategic planning consultant
Matasovic, Marilyn Estelle business executive

Matteo, Christopher Peter *electronics executive, researcher*
Mattoli, Agostino Marron *international business projects advisor*
Maxwell, Jerome Eugene *corporate executive*
†McClelland, George Duncan *business executive*
†McColman, William Ernest *construction company executive*
†McCracken, Edward R. *electronics executive*
McCurdy, Larry Wayne *automotive parts company executive*
McDonald, William Henry *financial executive*
Mc Donough, Richard Doyle *retired paper company executive*
McGillivray, Donald Dean *seed company executive, agronomist*
†Mehiel, Dennis *paper and packaging company executive*
Merrick, George Boesch *aerospace company executive*
Messmore, David William *construction executive, former psychologist*
Miles, John Frederick *retired manufacturing company executive*
Millard, Charles Phillip *manufacturing company executive*
Miller, Harold Edward *retired manufacturing conglomerate executive, consultant*
†Mills, Charles S. *healthcare supplies and products company executive*
†Miranda, Quirinus Ronnie *research and development company executive*
Miskowski, Lee R. *retired automobile executive*
Moens, David Brian *manufacturing company executive*
†Monighetti, Amy *pharmaceutical executive*
Moore, John Ronald *manufacturing executive*
Moore, Malcolm Frederick *manufacturing executive*
Moore, Vernon Lee *retired food products executive, agriculturist, consultant*
Morelli, Peter Richard *electronic executive*
Morgenstein, William *shoe company executive*
Morris, Albert Jerome *medical company executive*
Morris, G. Ronald *industrial executive*
Mott, Stewart Rawlings *business executive, political activist*
Mudd, Sidney Peter *former beverage company executive*
Mueller, Robert Louis *business executive*
Mukamal, David Samier *sign manufacturing company executive*
Nalin, David Robert *retired pharmaceutical executive*
†Nasser, Jacques *sr. partner, One Equity Partners*
Neff, Jack Kenneth *apparel manufacturing company executive*
Nelson, Glen David *medical products executive, physician*
Nesheim, Robert Olaf *retired food products executive*
†Newport, Patrick Owen *manufacturing executive*
Nine, John Edward *pharmaceutical company executive*
Noe, Elnora (Ellie Noe) *retired chemical company executive*
Nord, Eric Thomas *retired manufacturing executive*
Nordlund, Donald Elmer *manufacturing company executive*
Novak, Alan Lee *retired pharmaceutical company executive*
Oaks, Maurice David *retired pharmaceutical company executive*
O'Donnell, Kevin *retired metal products executive*
Oelman, Robert Schantz *retired manufacturing executive*
Oesterling, Thomas Ovid *retired pharmaceutical company executive*
Ordal, Caspar Reuben *business executive*
Oster, Lewis Henry *manufacturing executive, engineering consultant*
Otstott, Charles Paddock *company executive, retired army officer*
Parker, George *retired pen manufacturing company executive*
Parker, Thomas Lee *business executive*
Peapples, George Alan *retired automotive executive*
Pearce, Paul Francis *retired aerospace electronics company executive*
Peck, Arthur John, Jr., *diversified manufacturing executive, lawyer*
Peck, Daniel Farnum *chemical company executive*
†Perdue, Franklin P. *retired poultry/agricultural products executive*
Peterson, Carl Eric *metals company executive, banker*
Peterson, Robert Austin *manufacturing company executive retired*
Petok, Samuel *retired manufacturing company executive*
Phinizy, Robert Burchall *electronics company executive*
Potts, Gerald Neal *manufacturing company executive*
Powell, Thomas Edward, III, *biological supply company executive, physician*
Preston, Seymour Stotler, III, *manufacturing company executive*
Prevost, Edward James *paint manufacturing executive*
Price, Robert *electronics consultant*
Pruis, John J. *business executive*
Pugliese, Anthony Paul *construction company executive, educator*
Qualls, Robert L. *manufacturing executive, banker, former state official, educator*
Rao, Rama Krishna R. *pharmaceutical company executive*
Rao, Srinath Jayram *electronics professional*
†Ray, Amrit *pharmaceuticals strategist, company executive*
Regan, Paul Jerome, Jr., *manufacturing company executive, consultant*
Regelbrugge, Roger Rafael *steel company executive*
Rhodes, Peter Edward *label company executive*
Richard, Edward H. *manufacturing company executive, former municipal government official*
Richardson, Thomas Andrew *business executive, educator*
Richman, Paul *semiconductor industry executive, educator*
Richman, Peter *electronics executive*
†Riklis, Meshulam *manufacturing and retail executive*
Robbins, Ray C. *manufacturing company executive*
†Roderick, William Carl *construction executive, consultant*
Roesner, Peter Lowell *manufacturing company executive*
Rooke, David Lee *retired chemical company executive*
Roorda, John Francis, Jr., *business consultant*
Rosen, Ana Beatriz *electronics executive*
Rosenberg, Rudy *chemical company executive*
Roudane, Charles *metal and plastic products company executive*
Rubin, Irvin I. *plastics company executive*
Rubinovitz, Samuel *diversified manufacturing company executive*
Rudy, Raymond Bruce, Jr., *retired food company executive*
Rukeyser, Robert James *manufacturing executive*
Rymar, Julian W. *manufacturing company executive*
Sabo, Richard Steven *electrical company executive*
St. John, Bill Dean *diversified equipment and services company executive*
Salathe, John, Jr., *manufacturing company executive*
Saliba, Jacob *manufacturing executive*
Samper, Joseph Phillip *retired photographic products company executive*
Sanders, Wayne R. *paper products manufacturing executive*
Saute, Robert Emile *drug and cosmetic consultant*
†Savin, Ronald Richard *chemical company executive, inventor*
Scheele, Paul Drake *former hospital supply corporate executive*
Schwartz, Charles Phineas, Jr., *financial and business consultant, lawyer*
Schwartz, Samuel *retired chemical company executive, business consultant*
Schwartzberg, Martin M. *chemical company executive*
†Schwier-Williamson, Doris Marie *retired metal products executive*
Serenbetz, Robert *retired manufacturing executive*
†Shapira, David S. *food products/retail grocery executive*
Sharkey, Leonard Arthur *automobile company executive*
†Sharp, William J. *manufacturing company executive*
Shepherd, Mark, Jr., *retired electronics company executive*
Shuster, Robert G. *electronics company executive, consultant*
Siegel, Jack Morton *retired biotechnology company executive*
Silver, George *metal trading and processing company executive*
Simeral, William Goodrich *retired chemical company executive*
Simmons, Marguerite Saffold *pharmaceutical sales professional*
Sissel, George Allen *manufacturing executive, lawyer, engineer*
Slagle, Jacob Winebrenner, Jr., *food products executive, real estate agent*
Smith, Frederick Coe *retired manufacturing executive*
Smith, Goff *industrial equipment manufacturing executive*
Smith, Michael William *construction executive, consultant*
Smith, Rodney *retired electronics executive*
Snyder, Ph.D., Carolyn L. Smith *medical writing director*
†Solloway, C. Robert *retired forest products company executive*
Somers, Louis Robert *retired food company executive*
Sopranos, Orpheus Javaras *manufacturing company executive*
Southerland, S. Duane *manufacturing company executive*
Spliethoff, William Ludwig *chemical company executive*
Starr, Leon *retired chemical research company executive*
Steck, Warren Franklin *retired chemical company executive, biochemist*
Stern, Arthur Paul *electronics company executive*
Stewart, Joseph Turner, Jr., *retired pharmaceutical company executive*
Stewart, Peter Beaufort *retired beverage company executive*
Stivers, William Charles *forest products company executive*
Stoneham, Edward Bryant *technical company executive*
†Stott, Don S. *metal products executive*
Stratton, Robert *retired electronics executive*
Studebaker, Glenn Wayne *steel company executive*
Sudarsky, Jerry M. *industrialist*
Sullivan, Eugene John Joseph *manufacturing company executive*
Sunderman, Deborah Ann *apparel executive, fashion and business educator*
Swanger, Sterling Orville *appliance manufacturing company executive*
Swiff, Kelly *food products executive, civic volunteer, writer*
Szydlowski, Ralph *retired die maker, formability consultant*
Tallett, Elizabeth Edith *biopharmaceutical company executive*
Talley, Robert Morrell *aerospace company executive*
Tannenberg, Dieter E. A. *retired manufacturing company executive*
Taylor, Randall William *quality assurance administrator*
Taylor, Robert Morgan *electronics executive*
Temple, Joseph George, Jr., *retired pharmaceutical executive, retired chemicals executive*
Templin, Kenneth Elwood *paper company executive*
Teplow, Theodore Herzl *retired valve company executive*
Thomas, Tom *retired plastics company executive*
Thompson, Ralph Newell *former chemical corporation executive*
Toupin, Harold Ovid *retired chemical company executive*
†Trice, William Henry *paper company executive*
Trown, Patrick Willoughby *biopharmaceutics company executive*
Tyhach, Richard Joseph *medical products executive, researcher*
Uffelman, Malcolm Rucj *electronics company executive, electrical engineer*
Vajk, Hugo *manufacturing executive*
†Van Himbergen, Thomas *manufacturing company executive*
Van Horn, Rebecca Ann *presentation specialist*
Van Tassel, James Henry *retired electronics executive*
Verderber, Joseph Anthony *capital equipment company executive*
†Verma, Devesh *pharmaceutical executive, researcher*
Vitt, David Aaron *medical manufacturing company executive*
Volkhardt, John Malcolm *food company executive*
†Wardrop, Richard M., Jr., *former steel holding company executive*
Warner, Walter Duke *corporate executive, director*
†Wasserman, Paul S. *corporate development executive*
Wasson, James Walter *aircraft electronics manufacturing company executive*
Watkins, Dean Allen *electronics executive, educator*
Weaver, William Charles *retired industrial executive*
Wechsler, Sergio *automotive executive, consultant*
Weiss, Max Tibor *retired aerospace company executive*
Weitzen, Jeffrey *computer manufacturing company executive*
†Welch, John Francis, Jr., (Jack Welch) *retired electrical manufacturing company executive, management consultant*
Welch, Oliver Wendell *retired pharmaceutical executive*
†Wenstrup, H. Daniel *chemical company executive*
West, Kenneth Irwin *automotive executive*
Wharton, Thomas Williams *medical products executive*
White, Bertram Milton *chemicals executive*
White, Gerald Andrew *retired chemical company executive*
Whitehead, Karl Peter *construction executive, arbitrator, writer*
Wiater, Richard M. *manufacturing executive*
Wiesen, Donald Guy *retired diversified manufacturing company executive*
Wiley, Carl Ross *timber company executive*
Willauer, Whiting Russell *consultant*
†Williams, Carolyn Elizabeth *manufacturing executive*
Witcher, Daniel Dougherty *retired pharmaceutical company executive*
Witt, Hugh Ernest *technology consultant*
Wolff, Brian Richard *metal products executive*
Wollert, Gerald Dale *retired food company executive, investor*
Wolotkiewicz, Marian M. *business executive*
Woods, Christine L. *manufacturing company executive*
Yen, Duen Hsi *corporate executive, physicist*
†Yoh, Harold Lionel, Jr., *retired engineering, construction and management company executive*
Young, James E. *business executive, engineer*
Young, Jay Maitland *healthcare communications consultant*
Young, John Alan *electronics company executive*
Zajac, John *semiconductor equipment company executive*
Zehnder, Frederick John *retired automotive executive*
Zenner, Gretchen Harris *manufacturing executive*
Zimmer, David Lawrence *retired chemical company executive*

INDUSTRY: SERVICE

UNITED STATES

ALABAMA

Auburn
Tullier, Michael Joseph *communications and industrial relations executive*
Zallen, Harold *corporate executive, scientist, former university official*

Birmingham
Etterer, Sepp *industrial relations specialist, consultant, application developer*
Floyd, John Alex, Jr., *marketing executive, editor, horticulturist*
Harris, Aaron *management consultant*
Luckie, Robert Ervin, Jr., *advertising executive*
†Morros, Stephen Vincent *marketing professional, educator*
Parker, John Malcolm *management and financial consultant*
Spahn, James Francis *marketing professional*
Young, Thomas Richard *sales management professional*

Centre
Ellis, Joanne Hammonds *computer consultant*

Gadsden
Grimm, James R. (Ronald Grimm) *multi-industry executive*

Huntsville
Childs, Rand Hampton *data processing executive, consultant*
McIntyre-Ivy, Joan Carol *data processing executive*

Hurtsboro
Bouilliant-Linet, Francis Jacques *global management consultant*

Jacksonville
†Smith, Matthew DuBose *personnel director*

Mobile
Rye, Scott Cairney *advertising executive, author*
Spake, Deborah Foster *marketing professional, educator*

Montgomery
Dillon, Jean Katherine *executive secretary, small business owner*
Hilliard, Lil *sales executive*
†Holifield, Leonard Cleve *security firm executive, educator*
Murkett, Philip Tillotson *human resource executive*
Schloss, Samuel Leopold, Jr., *retired food service executive, consultant*
Smitherman, David Conrad *medical marketing professional*

Ohatchee
Ellis, Bernice Allred *personnel executive*

Pelham
Johnson, Frank William *marketing professional*

Tuskegee Institute
†Madison, Willie Clarence *park administrator*

ALASKA

Anchorage
Brady, Carl Franklin *retired aircraft charter company executive*
†Britton, Emily Maddox *sales executive*
Gottstein, Barnard Jacob *retail and wholesale food company executive, real estate executive*
Parker, Walter Bruce *arctic research specialist, consultant*
Porcaro, Michael Francis *advertising agency executive*
Shively, John Terry *business executive*

Fairbanks
Thompson, Daniel Emerson *vending machine service company executive*

Willow
White, Gwendolyn A. *recreational facility executive*

ARIZONA

Cave Creek
O'Reilly, Thomas Eugene *human resources consultant, retired*

Chandler
Brunello-McCay, Rosanne *sales executive*
Eckstat, Arthur Gene *consultant*
Goyer, Robert Stanton *communication educator*

PROFESSIONAL INDEX 6485 INDUSTRY: SERVICE

Cortaro
Fossland, Joeann Jones *professional speaker, personal coach*

Flagstaff
Bolin, Richard Luddington *industrial development consultant*

Fountain Hills
Lacy, Herman Edgar *management consultant*

Glendale
Baum, Phyllis Gardner *travel management consultant*
†Riales, Ron O. *custodian*
Shimek, John Anton *legal investigation business owner, educator*

Green Valley
Gilliam, Mary *travel executive*
Greenwood, Helen Maxine *retired office manager, executive assistant*
Vanderspek, Peter George *management consultant, writer*

Mesa
Horne, Jeremy *consultant, writer, research executive*
Johnson, Doug *advertising and public relations executive*
Murphy, Edward Francis *executive*

Paradise Valley
Day, Richard Putnam *marketing, strategic planning and employee benefits consultant, arbitrator*
Hazard, Robert Culver, Jr., *hotel executive*

Payson
Brown, James Carrington, III, (Bing Brown) *public relations and communications executive*
Hegarty, Christopher Joseph *management and financial consultant*

Peoria
†Gould, Dorothy Mae *executive secretary, soprano*
Schindler, William Stanley *retired public relations executive, consultant*

Phoenix
Bellus, Ronald Joseph *marketing and communications executive*
Bergamo, Ron *marketing executive*
Denning, Michael Marion *marketing professional, educator*
Drain, Albert Sterling *business management consultant*
Gall, Donald Alan *data processing executive*
Horner, Harry Charles, Jr., *sales executive, theatrical and film consultant*
Hutchinson, Ann *management consultant*
Koffman, Martha Alice *communications and training executive, ergonomist*
LaValle, Jennifer Suzette *marketing communications specialist, consultant*
Lemon, Leslie Gene *retired diversified services company executive*
Meridith, Denise Patricia *business consultant*
Miller, Beatrice Ellen *communications executive*
Murnane, George, III, *business executive*
Newman, Lois Mae *marketing executive*
Shultz, Susan F *executive search and corporate governance executive*
Snell, Richard *holding company executive*
Subach, James Alan *information systems company executive, consultant*

Prescott
Mayol, Richard Thomas *advertising executive, political consultant*
Palmer, Robert Arthur *private investigator*
Stuart, Spencer Raymond *management consultant*

Rio Verde
Scott, Louis Edward *advertising agency executive*

Scottsdale
Baum, Herbert Merrill *consumer products company executive*
Blinder, Martin S. *business consultant, art dealer*
Carter, Carla Cifelli *management consultant*
Comfort, Clifton C. *fraud examiner, management consultant*
Doglione, Arthur George *data processing executive*
Grier, James Edward *hotel company executive, lawyer*
Gwinn, Mary Dolores *business developer, organizational theorist, philosopher, writer, speaker*
Jackson, Donald Frank *organizational development consultant*
Lavenson, Susan Barker *hotel corporate executive, consultant*
La Vista, Frank William *author, educator, speaker*
Lillestol, Jane Brush *development consultant*
MacKinnon, Sally Anne *retired fast food company executive*
Maggard, Woodrow Wilson, Jr., *management consultant*
O'Donnell, William Thomas *management consultant*
Quigley, Jerome Harold *management consultant*
Root, Laura Lee *personal care industry executive*
Rosenfeld, Edward *travel company executive*
Schleifer, Thomas C. *management consultant, author, lecturer*
Schmitz, Shirley Gertrude *marketing and sales executive*
Swanson, Robert Killen *management consultant*
†Van Brunt, Gary T. *consumer products company executive*
Van Weelden, Thomas H. *waste industry company executive*

Sedona
Wolfe, Al *marketing and advertising consultant*

Sun City
Davis, Virginia *trade show producer*

Sun City West
Berkenkamp, Fred Julius *management consultant*
Forti, Lenore Steimle *business consultant*
Stevens, George Richard *business consultant, public policy commentator*

Tempe
Herbert, Christopher Jay *marketing professional, management consultant*
Meehan, Robert Henry *human resources executive, electronics company executive, business educator*
Ortiz, Andrew Flores *management consultant*
Perry, Ronald William *public affairs educator*
Sackton, Frank Joseph *public affairs educator*
Williams, James Eugene *management consultant*
†Yazzie, Aaron Franklin *events laborer*

Tucson
Barton, Stanley Faulkner *management consultant*
Horne, William McHenry *management educator*
Hoyt, Charlee Van Cleve *management executive*
Jones, Frank Wyman *management consultant, mechanical engineer*
Lee, Joyce Ann *computer educator*
Lewis, Wilbur H. *educational management consultant*
Lynn, Linda Brown *business educator*
Reinius, Michele Reed *executive recruiter*
Rose, Hugh *management consultant*
Sankovich, Joseph Bernard *management consultant*
Walker, Ronald Hugh *management consultant*
†Wise, Evan M. *management consultant*

Yuma
Hilgert, Arnie *management and marketing educator*

ARKANSAS

Bentonville
Higham, Paul H. *marketing professional*

Conway
Hatcher, Joe Branch *management consultant*

Fayetteville
Bennett, Sonja Quinn *administrative assistant*
Edmark, David Stanley *communications director*
Webb, Lynne McGovern *communication scholar, consultant*

Fort Smith
Harper, S. Birnie *business brokerage company owner*
Pendergrass, Ewell Dean *communications executive*

Jonesboro
Tims, Robert Austin *data processing official, pilot*

Little Rock
Cox, Frank *advertising executive*
McCaleb, Annette Watts *executive secretary*
Nelson, Rex *communications executive*

Monticello
Webster, Linda Jean *communications educator, media consultant*

Pine Bluff
Long, Edward Arlo *business consultant, retired manufacturing company executive*

CALIFORNIA

Agoura Hills
Gressak, Anthony Raymond, Jr., *sales executive*

Alameda
Billings, Thomas Neal *computer and publishing executive, management consultant, entrepreneur, author, journalist, software designer and inventor*
Potash, Jeremy Warner *public relations executive*

Alamo
Shiffer, James David *retired utility executive, consultant*
Whalen, John Sydney *management consultant*

Alhambra
Knighton, Barbara McLeod *occupational health specialist, risk specialist*

Aliso Viejo
Collazo, Sergio I. *computer company executive*
Harder, Wendy Wetzel *communications executive*
†Hawkins, Gregory J. *consumer products company executive*

Altadena
Dobbins, Maggie Sonne *real estate investment company executive*
Eisen, Glenn Philip *management consultant, teacher*

Anaheim
Kallay, Michael Frank, II, *medical devices company official*
Puzder, Andrew F. *restaurant executive, lawyer*
Sorenson, Sandra Louise *merchandising manager*
Warring, Jerome Thomas *management consultant*

Anaheim Hills
Orlow-Townsend, Dawn Michelle *personal care industry executive*

Arcadia
Talsania, Bharat Himatlal *sales and marketing executive*

Atherton
Baran, Paul *computer executive*
Lowry, Larry Lorn *management consulting company executive*

Avila Beach
McLaren, Archie Campbell, Jr., *marketing executive*

Belvedere Tiburon
Hudnut, David Beecher *retired leasing company executive, lawyer*

Berkeley
Peterson, Roland E. *business management company executive*
†Poulos, Paige M. *public relations executive*
Rippe, Lynn E. *contract administrator*

Beverly Hills
†Berg, Jeffrey Spencer *talent agency executive*
†Bollenbach, Stephen Frasier *hotel executive*
Cantor, Alan Bruce *management consultant, computer software engineer*
Carlson, Gary Lee *public relations executive, director, producer*
David, Clive *event planning executive*
Fickinger, Wayne Joseph *communications executive*
†Hilton, Barron *hotel executive*
Olman, Maryellen *human resources administrator*
Ovitz, Michael S. *communications executive*
Riess, Gordon Sanderson *management consultant*
Shepard, Kathryn Irene *public relations executive*
†Toffel, Alvin Eugene *corporate executive, business and governmental consultant*
Young, Robert Edward *computer company executive*
Zarem, Abe Mordecai *management consulting executive*

Buena Park
McClendon, Irvin Lee, Sr., *office services and computer consultant, writer and editor*

Burbank
†Cook, Richard W. *motion picture company executive*
Frank, Amélie Lorraine *marketing professional*

Camarillo
Cobb, Roy Lampkin, Jr., *retired computer sciences corporation executive*
Cobb, Shirley Ann Dodson *public relations consultant, journalist*

Cambria
Morse, Richard Jay *human resources and organizational development consultant, manufacturers' representative company executive*

Carlsbad
Conway, Daniel Edward *management consultant*
Rodenhausen, John E. *sales executive*
Tompane, Mary Beth *management consultant*
Wilson, Donald Grey *management consultant*

Carmel
Creighton, John Wallis, Jr., *novelist, publisher, former management educator, consultant*
†Evans, Charlotte Mortimer *communications consultant, writer*
Krugman, Stanley Lee *international management consultant*
Lockton, David Ballard *business executive*
Smith, Gordon Paul *management consultant*

Carpinteria
Lovborg, Uffe *diagnostic research company manager*
†Morgan, Alfred Vance *management consulting company executive*

Chatsworth
Henry, Carla L. *advertising executive*
Weisbrod, Ken (Joseph Louis Weisbrod) *marketing professional*

Chico
Hanton, E. Michael *public and personnel relations consultant*

Chino Hills
Burge, Willard, Jr., *software company executive*

Citrus Heights
Osaki, Mark Stephen *writer, development administrator*

Claremont
Berg, Barbara Ann Cowan *corporate workshops consultant, critical incident consultant*

Concord
Travers, Judith Lynnette *human resources executive*

Corona
Lamb, Mildred Shimonishi *retired administrative secretary*

Corona Del Mar
Freeman, Richard Dean *new business start-up service company executive*
†O'Brien, John William, Jr., *investment management company executive, finance educator*
Terrell, A. John *retired university telecommunications director*

Costa Mesa
Florey, Jerry Jay *aerospace and management consultant*
Gimple, W. Thomas *sales executive*

Coyote
Keeshen, Kathleen Kearney *public relations consultant*

Crestline
Douglas, Cindy Holloway *consultant*
Merrill, Steven William *research and development executive*

Culver City
Boonshaft, Hope Judith *public affairs executive*
†Lenk, Edward C. (Toby) *Internet company executive*

Cupertino
Geddes, Barbara Sheryl *communications executive, consultant*

Daly City
Hargrave, Sarah Quesenberry *consulting company executive*

Dana Point
Fabricant, Jill Diane *technology company executive*
Mardian, Robert Charles, Jr., *restaurateur*

Danville
Reed, William Gerald *consulting firm executive*

Davis
†Villarejo, Don *industrial relations specialist, researcher*

Desert Hot Springs
Fulton, Norman Robert *credit manager*

Diamond Bar
White, Joy Mieko *communications executive*

Dublin
Nelson, Elinor S. *human resources consultant, labor arbitrator*

El Cajon
Cole, George Arthur *marketing professional*
Silverberg, Lewis Henry *legal consultant*

El Dorado Hills
Davies, William Ralph *service executive*

El Segundo
Armstrong, Wallace Dowan, Jr., *data processor*
Brown, Lorraine Ann *event coordinator, minister, hypnotist*
Honeycutt, Van B. *computer company executive*
McQuillin, Richard Ross *management consultant*
Olson, Jeanne Innis *technology and technical management executive*

Emeryville
Jobs, Steven Paul *computer company executive*
Smith, Christopher Allen *technology company executive, finance professional*

Encino
Greenberg, Allan *advertising and marketing research consultant*
Laba, Marvin *management consultant*
La Cava, Donald Leon *communications executive*
Saginor, Sidney V. *management consultant*
Semos, William *management consultant, educator, air transportation executive*

Escondido
Daniels, Richard Martin *public relations executive*

Fair Oaks
Maskall, Martha Josephine *web site designer, publisher, health consultant*

Fort Bragg
Galli, Darrell Joseph *management consultant*

Foster City
Lutvak, Mark Allen *computer company executive*

Fountain Valley
Berman, Steven Richard *computer company executive*
Bray, Ronald Lawrence *sales executive*

Fremont
Saraf, Dilip Govind *management consultant*
Tantra, Muljadi *corporate marketing professional*
Tribus, Myron *retired quality counselor, engineer, educator*

Fresno
Ganulin, Judy *public relations professional*

Gardena
Morton, James Carnes, Jr., *automotive company executive*

Glendale
†Altman, Steven *financial consulting company executive*
Misa, Kenneth Franklin *management consultant*

Glendora
Walters, Matthew Paul *recreational facility executive, consultant*

Granada Hills
†O'Connor, Betty Lou *service executive*

Granite Bay
Holtz, Sara *consultant*
†Reisman, Judith Ann Gelernter *media communications executive, educator*

Half Moon Bay
Fennell, Diane Marie *marketing executive, process engineer*
Hinthorn, Micky Terzagian *volunteer, retired*

Hathaway Pines
Williams, Alan Keiser *management consultant*

Hayward
Solé, Pedro *management consultant*

Hemet
†Holley, Robert William *sales executive, minister*

Hillsborough
Kane, Steven Edward *human resources executive*
Westerfield, Putney *management consulting executive*

Huntington Beach
Botsko, Ronald Joseph *business and engineering consultant*
Lopata, Martin Barry *business executive*

Indian Wells
Kelley, John Paul *communications consultant*

Indio
Garra, Raymond Hamilton, II, *marketing executive*

Irvine
Hancock, S. Lee *business executive*
Leets, Peter J. *consulting firm executive*
Maybay, Duane Charles *recycling systems executive*
Paine, David M. *public relations executive*
Pechmann, Cornelia Ann Rachel *marketing professional*
Seller, Gregory Erol *marketing executive, writer, consultant*
West, Robert Lee, Jr., *marketing professional*

Kentfield
Edgar, James Macmillan, Jr., *management consultant*

La Habra
Chase, Cochrane *advertising agency executive*

La Jolla
Bardwick, Judith Marcia *management consultant*
Bryan, John Rodney *management consultant*
Kent, Paula *public relations, marketing and management consultant, lecturer*
Morse, Jack Hatton *management consultant*
Peet, Raymond Edward *consultant*
Reed, James Anthony *hotel and restaurant industry executive and owner, consultant*
Vallbona-Freeman, Marisa Freeman *public relations counselor*

La Puente
Sheridan, Christopher Frederick *human resources executive*

La Quinta
Peden, Lynn Ellen *marketing executive*

Laguna Beach
Arnold, John David *management counselor, catalyst*
Taylor, James Walter *business and management educator*

Laguna Hills
Miller, Eldon Earl *corporate business publications consultant, retired manufacturing company executive*

Laguna Niguel
Greenberg, Lenore *public relations professional*
King, Richard Maurice, Jr., *consultant*
Kursewicz, Lee Z. *marketing consultant*

Lemon Grove
Denning, Eileen Bonar *management consultant*

Livermore
O'Brien, Kevin Charles *business development executive*
Tripodes, James G. *nuclear safety and environmental regulatory affairs professional*

Long Beach
Aldrich, David Lawrence *public relations executive*
†Brown, Roxanne (Jerene Roxanne Brown) *sales executive*
Duffy, Patrick Sean *events producer, real estate consultant*
†Halili, Antonio Marquez *facilities maintenance mechanic*
Sosoka, John Richard *consulting firm executive, engineer*

Los Altos
Esber, Edward Michael, Jr., *software company executive*
Poonja, Mohamed *business reorganization, financial and management consultant*

Los Angeles
Amey, Rae *project management and development consultant*
Bakeman, Carol Ann *travel manager, singer*
Beam, William Washington, III, *data coordinator*
Beamon, Gena R. *human resources specialist*
Beltramo, Michael Norman *management consultant*
Berman, Geoffrey Louis *management company executive*
†Bohle, Sue *public relations executive*
Bremond, Duane Benjamin *marketing professional*
†Burkle, Ronald W. *former food service executive, business investor*
Chang, Edward H. *computer company executive*
†Clow, Lee *advertising agency executive*
†Coget, Jean-Francois Axel Hugues *management researcher*
Conomikes, George Spero *management consultant executive, publisher*
Crosby, Peter Alan *management consultant*
Dallmeyer, Robert Frederick *exhibitions executive*
Doll, Lynne Marie *public relations agency executive*
Engoron, Edward David *food service consultant, television and radio broadcaster*
†Fall, John Robert *management and information technology consultant*
Farrell, Joseph *movie market analyst, producer, entertainment research company executive, writer, sculptor, designer*
Ferry, Richard Michael *executive search firm executive*
Florsheim, Renee Anne *marketing, educator, lawyer*
Frank, Lillian Gorman *human resources executive, psychologist, management consultant*
Geoffrion, Arthur Minot *management scientist*
Georgesco, Victor *printing company executive*
Giffin, Margaret Ethel (Peggy Giffin) *management consultant*
Glen, Paul Michael *management consultant, educator*
Goldstein, Norton Maurice (Goldy Norton) *public relations consultant*
Gottfried, Ira Sidney *management consulting executive*
Hale, Kaycee *research marketing professional*
Hartsough, Gayla Anne Kraetsch *management consultant*
Hill, Bonnie Guiton *company executive*
Hofert, Jack *consulting company executive, lawyer*
Hopkins, Patricia Ann *management consultant*
Humphreys, Robert Lee *advertising executive*
Irving, Jack Howard *technical consultant*
Kline, Richard Stephen *public relations executive*
Knox, Gertie R. *company executive, accountant*
Krueger, Robert William *management consultant*
†Lagasse, Emeril *chef*
Leahy, T. Liam *business development, technology investor*
Levine, Michael *public relations executive, writer, announcer*
Mathias, Alice Irene *business management consultant*
Mracky, Ronald Sydney *marketing and media executive, tourism consultant*
Murray, Alice Pearl *data processing company executive*
Nadler, Gerald *management consultant, educator*
Pearce, Joan DeLap *research company executive*
Popek, Gerald John *computer software company executive, educator*
Rice, Regina Kelly *marketing executive*
Rogers, Ronald *public relations executive*
Schultz, Louis Michael *advertising agency executive*
Shiffman, Leslie Brown *management executive*
Silverman, Bruce Gary *advertising executive*
Simon, Daniel Jack *entertainment executive*
†Sood, Ashish *marketing professional*
Spitzer, Peter George *information systems executive, consultant*
Spivak, Kenin Mathew *executive*
Spofford, Robert Houston *advertising agency executive*
Strawn, Judy C. *public relations professional*
Sylvester, Richard Russell *economist, management executive*
Tardio, Thomas A. *public relations executive*
Tomash, Erwin *retired computer equipment company executive*
Wade, Michael Robert Alexander *marketing specialist*
Zelikow, Howard Monroe *management and financial consultant*

Malibu
Tellem, Susan Mary *public relations executive*

Manhattan Beach
Deutsch, Barry Joseph *consulting and management development company executive*
Di Massa, Ernani Vincenzo, Jr., *broadcast executive, television producer, writer*

Marina Del Rey
Gold, Carol Sapin *international management consultant, speaker*
Uretz, Michael Albert *health and fitness executive*

Menlo Park
Creswell, Donald Creston *business executive*
Fenner, Peter David *communications executive*
†Kvamme, Mark D. *marketing professional*
Middleton, Teresa Muir *Internet company executive, researcher*
Sweeney, Lawrence Earl, Jr., *computer company executive*

Milpitas
Allen, Vicky *sales and marketing professional*
Brown, Michael A. *computer hardware company executive*
Corrigan, Wilfred J. *computer company executive*
†Tufano, Paul *computer company executive*

Mission Viejo
Austin, Berit Synnove *small business owner, central services specialist*
Dillon, Francis Patrick *retired human resources executive, financial, insurance and tax consultant*
McKinney, Monica Lorraine *media/communications company executive, application developer*

Modesto
Cofer, Berdette Henry *public management consulting company executive*

Monrovia
Jemelian, John Nazar *management consultant*

Monte Nido
Brandewie, Richard Anthony *laser and optics consultant*

Moraga
Haag, Carol Ann Gunderson *marketing professional, consultant*

Mountain View
Bennett, Stephen M. *computer company executive*
de Geus, Aart J. *computer software company executive*
Koo, George Ping Shan *business consultant*
Lee, Murlin E. *software company executive*
Miller, Jon Philip *marketing and business development professional, pharmaceutical executive*
†Polese, Kim *software company executive*
Qureishi, A. Salam *computer software and services company executive*

Napa
Brough, Bruce Alvin *public relations and communications executive*

Newbury Park
Lichtenstein, Chase Walter *retired management consultant*
Naulin, John Arthur *entertainment company executive*
Stadler, Katherine Loy *advertising sales executive*

Newport Beach
Gellman, Gloria Gae Seeburger Schick *marketing professional*
Lipson, Melvin Alan *technology and business management consultant*
McCue, Dennis Michael *management consultant*
Monaghan, Anne *public relations consultant*
Shonk, Albert Davenport, Jr., *advertising executive*

Northridge
Garland, G(arfield) Garrett *sales executive, golf professional*

Norwalk
Ori, Jerry Allen *management consultant*

Novato
†Batchelor, Robert Paul *corporate communications specialist, writer*

Oakland
Baldwin, Mark Alan *communications consultant, writer*
Crane, Robert Meredith *health care executive*
†Johnston, Gerald E. *manufacturing company executive*

Oceanside
Peckham, Donald *computer company executive*

Orange
Hurley, Amy Elizabeth *human resources educator*
Kelley, Robert Paul, Jr., *management consultation executive*

Orinda
Woolsey, David Arthur *leasing company executive*

Oroville
Gordon, Daniel Seth *business executive, consultant*

Pacific Palisades
Hagenbuch, Rodney Dale *consulting principal, financial consultant*

Palm Desert
Miller, Donald Ross *management consultant*

Palm Springs
Arnold, Stanley Norman *manufacturing consultant*
Salometo, Peter James Morgan *marketing professional, lawyer*
Scott, Walter, Jr., *business consultant*
Seale, Robert McMillan *office services company executive*
Sheffield, Simone *business executive*
Streeto, Joseph Michael *catering company official*
Underwood, Thomas Woodbrook *communications company executive*

Palo Alto
Allen, Louis Alexander *management consultant*
Barnholt, Edward W. *computer company executive*
†Coughran, William M., Jr., *management consultant, researcher*
Fiorina, Carleton S. (Carly Fiorina) *computer company executive*
Kirk, Carmen Zetler *data processing executive*
Murray, Dave *marketing professional, editor*
Neale-May, Donovan *marketing professional*
†Seethaler, William Charles *international business executive, consultant*
Sullivan, Patrick Henry *management consultant*
Waller, Peter William *public relations executive*

Palos Verdes Estates
Rubenstein, Leonard Samuel *communications executive, ceramist, painter, sculptor, photographer*

Palos Verdes Peninsula
Berg, Kathy Rae *public relations consultant*

Paradise
Bernstein, Elizabeth Ann *retired executive secretary*

Pasadena
Caine, Stephen Howard *data processing executive*
Drutchas, Gerrick Gilbert (Baron Khabarovsky) *investigator*
Kaplan, Gary *executive recruiter*
Koenig, Marie Harriet King *public relations director, fund raising executive*
Nackel, John George *technology executive*
†Pleasants, John *online services company executive*
Stevens, Roy W. *sales and marketing executive*
Watkins, John Francis *management consultant*

Paso Robles
Boxer, Jerome Harvey *computer and management consultant, vintner, accountant*

Petaluma
†Immel, Barbara K. *management consultant*
McKibben, James Denis *marketing and sales executive*

Piedmont
Martin, Hosea L. *public relations and marketing professional*

Playa Del Rey
Weir, Alexander, Jr., *utility consultant, inventor*

Pleasanton
Burd, Steve *food service executive*
Lawson, J(enice) Evelyn *quality assurance professional, pharmacist*
†Payack, Paul JJ *marketing executive*

Portola Valley
Arnold, Maxwell *adveristing executive, writer*

Poway
Waitt, Theodore W. *computer company executive*

Rancho Cucamonga
Deppisch, Paul Vincent *data communications executive*

Rancho Mirage
Abel, Michael L. *marketing executive*

Rancho Santa Fe
Baker, Charles Lynn *management consultant*
Best, Jacob Hilmer, Jr., (Jerry Best Jr.) *retired hotel chain executive*
Gruenwald, George Henry Henry *new products development management consultant, writer*
LaBonté, C(larence) Joseph *financial and marketing executive*
Matthews, Leonard Sarver *advertising and marketing executive*

Redlands
Spee, James Curtis *management consultant, educator*

Redondo Beach
Hollander, Michael Frederic *communications executive*

Redwood City
Bertram, Jack Renard *information systems company executive*
Cook, Paul Maxwell *technology company executive*
Ellison, Lawrence J. *computer company executive*
Johnson, James Harding *advertising executive*
Miller, Anne Kathleen *training company executive, technical marketing consultant*
Stone, Herbert Allen *management consultant*

Richmond
Robles, Eliodoro Gonzales *consulting company executive, educator*

Riverside
†Bargmeyer, Brad D. *communications exectuve, advocate*
O'Reilly, Patrick James *public relations executive*

Rosemead
Rosenblum, Richard Mark *utility executive*

Roseville
Nordman, Oether *security firm executive*

Rutherford
Staglin, Garen Kent *computer service company executive, venture capitalist*

Sacramento
Boekhoudt-Cannon, Gloria Lydia *business education educator*
Briscoe, Agatha Donatto *data processing executive, instructor*

Chandramouli, Srinivasan (Chandra Chandramouli) *management and systems consultant*
Franz, Jennifer Danton *public opinion and marketing researcher*
McElroy, Leo Francis *communications consultant, journalist*
Oseas, Nannette N. *industrial hygienist, toxicologist, educator*
Swatt, Stephen Benton *communications executive, consultant*
Willis, Edward Oliver *management consultant, state official*

Salinas
†Fink, Joseph E. *purchasing agent, finance educator*
†Jeffries, Russell Morden *communications company official*

San Bernardino
Roberts, Katharine Adair *retired bookkeeper*

San Bruno
Mattathil, George Paul *strategic advisor communication technology*

San Carlos
Eby, Michael John *marketing research and technology consultant*

San Clemente
Petrone, Joseph Anthony *business consultant, writer*

San Diego
Berger, Newell James, Jr., *retired security professional*
Comrie, Sandra Melton *human resource executive*
Crisci, Mathew G. *marketing executive, writer*
DiRuscio, Lawrence William *advertising executive*
Evans, John Joseph *management consultant, executive, educator, writer*
Gilbertson, Oswald Irving *marketing executive*
Jacobs, Irwin Mark *communications executive*
Jacobs, Paul E. *communications executive*
Jagoda, Barry Lionel *writer, media adviser, communications consultant*
Jones, Ronald H. *computer information systems executive*
Kilmer, Maurice Douglas *marketing executive*
Kunkel, Scott William *strategic management and entrepreneurship educator*
Larson, Mark Devin *communications executive*
Lundy-Slade, Bettie B. *retired electronics professional*
Mosteller, James Wilbur, III, *data processing executive*
Nelson, Craig Alan *management consultant*
Neumann, Linda Kay *marketing executive*
Partida, Gilbert A. *executive*
†Sasidharan, Vinod *travel and tourism educator, researcher*
Schrock, Donald E. *communications executive*
†Short, Jay Milton *biotechnology company executive*
Taylor, George Allen *advertising agency executive*
Tillinghast, Charles Carpenter, III, *marketing company executive*
Warner, John Hilliard, Jr., *technical services, military and commercial systems and software company executive*
Wertheim, Robert Halley *national security consultant*
Wozniak, Joyce Marie *sales executive*

San Francisco
Adams, Donald Elwin *cultural and organization development administrator, consultant*
Bernstein, Gerald William *management consultant, researcher*
Bierly, Shirley Adelaide *communications executive*
Boehlke, William Fredrick *public relations executive, consultant*
Bondarook, Nina *public relations consultant*
Butenhoff, Susan *public relations executive*
†Calvin, Dorothy Ver Strate *computer company executive*
Colton, Roy Charles *management consultant*
Connelly, Theodore Sample *communications executive*
†Eddington, Thomas L. *human resources consultant*
Falvey, Mary C. *management consultant*
Gordon, Judith *communications consultant, writer*
Hall, Shannon *marketing professional, public relations executive, writer, photographer*
Harlan, Neil Eugene *retired healthcare company executive*
Henderson, Nancy Grace *marketing and technical documentation executive*
Henshaw, Guy Runals *management consultant*
Hernandez, Aileen C(larke) *urban consultant*
†Hill, Thomas Quinton *communication specialist, graphic designer*
Horn, Sabrina *public relations executive*
Hornberger, Deborah Lee *management consultant*
Horne, Grant Nelson *public relations consultant*
Hudson, Patricia Ann Siegel *association management specialist*
†Hynes, Aedhmar *public relations executive*
Jones, J. Gilbert *private investigator*
Jones, Stanton William *management consultant*
Kaufman, Jonathan Allan (Jon Kaufman) *public relations executive*
Kelly, Alan *public relations executive*
Kielarowski, Henry Edward *marketing executive*
Klammer, Joseph Francis *management consultant*
†Kleinknecht, Jochen *management consultant*
†Kurtz, Larry *corporate communications executive*
Landis, Richard Gordon *retired food company executive*
Lee, Ivy, Jr., *public relations consultant*
†Marshall, Scott *advertising agency executive*
Martin-O'Neill, Mary Evelyn *advertising, marketing, business writing, sales training consultant*
†Minor, Halsey *multimedia company executive*
†Muegge, Lyn *advertising executive*
O'Neill, Michael *management educator*
Parker, Diana Lynne *restaurant manager, special events director*
Pollack, Jeffrey Lee *restaurateur*
Riney, Hal Patrick *advertising executive*
Selover, William Charlton *corporate communications and governmental affairs executive*
Solomon, Neal Edward *management consultant, executive recruiter, social theorist, entrepreneur, author*
Sproul, John Allan *retired public utility executive*
Strock, James Martin *management consultant, educator, mediator, writer*
Tonini, Leon Richard *sales professional*
Torme, Margaret Anne *public relations executive, communications consultant*
Wernick, Sandra Margot *advertising and public relations executive*
†Wilbur, Brayton, Jr., *distribution company executive*
Willner, Jay R. *consulting company executive*
†Zaki, Kamran *management consultant*

San Jose
†Adkins, Bryan E. *management consultant, educator*
†Baab, Carlton *advertising executive*
Bingham, H. Raymond *computer software company executive*
Bunn, Charles Nixon *management consultant*
Byers, Charles Frederick *public relations executive, marketing executive*
Chambers, John T. *computer company executive*
Chellam, Kris *data processing executive*
Dean, Burton Victor *management educator*
Guhr, Daniel Johannes *management consultant*
Highlander, Richard William *communications executive*
Hoffman, Lou *public relations executive, educator, writer*
Hutcheson, Jerry Dee *manufacturing company executive*
†Kelly, Michael Lewis *sales executive*
Krolikoski, Stanley Joseph *software company executive*
Monia, Joan
Ricart, Glenn *Internet company executive*
Roberts, Lawrence Gilman *telecommunications company executive*
Roelandts, Willem P. *data processing executive*
Ryland, V. Wallace *business developer*
Scott, Edward William, Jr., *computer software company executive*
Skoll, Jeffrey *Internet company executive*
Vinderschmitt, Bernard V. *data processing executive*
Warnock, John Edward *computer company executive*
Wolak, Edmund L. *engineering administrator*

San Luis Obispo
DuFresne, Armand Frederick *management and engineering consultant*

San Marcos
Barnes, Howard G. *communications executive, film and video producer*

San Mateo
†Aadahl, Jorg *business executive*
Goyan, Jere Edwin *business executive, former university dean*
Helfert, Erich Anton *management consultant, writer, educator*
Jones, Louis Worth *retired management analyst, journalist*
Leong, Carol Jean *electrologist*
Nazzaro, David Alfred *sales executive*
Wiefels, Paul Harold *management consultant*

San Rafael
†Evenhuis, Henk J. *research company executive*
Finkelstein, James Arthur *management consultant*
Howley, Peter Anthony *communications executive*
Sachs, Freeman *retired management consultant, volunteer*
Saunders, Kathryn A. *retired data processing administrator*
Wilson, Ian Holroyde *management consultant, futurist*

San Ramon
†Hossain, Tarique M. *marketing science analyst, educator*
Moore, Justin Edward *data processing executive*

San Ysidro
Ortiz, Antonio Ignacio *public relations executive*

Santa Ana
Boynton, William Lewis *retired electronic manufacturing company official*
LeMaster, Susan M. *marketing executive, writer*
Tanaka, Richard I. *computer products company executive*

Santa Barbara
Adizes, Ichak *management consultant, writer*
Conklin, Hal (Harold Conklin) *public affairs director*
Cooper, Saul *film and TV producer, public relations executive*
Hanley, Kevin Lance *maintenance manager*
Leone, Frank Harrison *health care educator, consultant*
McKee, Kathryn Dian Grant *human resources consultant*
Scheinfeld, James David *travel agency executive*
Schultz, Arthur Warren *communications company executive*

Santa Clara
Barrett, Craig R. *computer company executive*
Benhamou, Eric A. *computer company executive*
Kwong, Donald *contracts administrator, consultant*
Lawrence, Deborah Jean *quality assurance professional*
McNealy, Scott G. *computer company executive*
Morgan, James C. *computer equipment company executive*
†Papadopoulos, Gregory Michael *computer company executive*
Reavis, Liza Anne *semiconductor executive*
Rudolph, Ronald Alvin *human resources specialist*
†Smith, Ronald S. *online retail executive*
Vincent, David Ridgely *management consulting executive*

Santa Fe Springs
Hammond, Judy McLain *business services executive*

Santa Monica
Dargan, John Henry *business executive*
Fenimore, George Wiley *management consultant*
Griffith, Arnold Koons *computer consultant*
Kessler, Robert Allen *data processing executive*
Lempert, Philip *advertising executive, author, television correspondent, columnist*
Patel, Chandra Kumar Naranbhai *communications company executive, educator, researcher, entrepreneur*
†Postaer, Larry *advertising executive*
†Rubin, Gerrold Robert *advertising executive*
Ryan, Jane Frances *corporate communications executive*
Simon, Diane Meyer *environmental services administrator, consultant*
Tennant, John Randall *management advisory company executive*
Williams, Kenneth Scott *entertainment company executive*

Santa Rosa
Cavanagh, John Charles *advertising agency executive*
Howard, Victor *management consultant*
Schudel, Hansjoerg *international business consultant*
Smith, Betty L. *results coach, seminar leader*

Santa Ynez
Krug, Fred Roy *film and television director and producer*
Palola, Harry Joel *international affairs executive, consultant*

Santee
Bourgeois, James Honoré *landscape company executive*
Schenk, Susan Kirkpatrick *nurse educator, consultant, business owner*

Saratoga
Lynch, Milton Terrence *retired advertising agency executive*

Sausalito
Pryor, Lois Marie *management consultant*

Scotts Valley
Crandell, K(enneth) James *management and strategic planning consultant, entrepreneur*
Luczo, Stephen J. *computer equipment company executive*
McClymonds, Jean Ellen *marketing professional*

Sebastopol
Dorr, Daniel Alan *personal and professional development facilitator*
McCarthy, Thomas Edward *retired telecommunications executive*

Sherman Oaks
†Kahn, Mario Santamaria *international marketing executive*
Lindgren, Timothy Joseph *supply company executive*
Winkler, Lee B. *business consultant*

Simi Valley
Ritacco, Patsy Richard *sales executive*

Sonoma
Bow, Stephen Tyler, Jr., *management consultant*

Sonora
Mathias, Betty Jane *communications and community affairs consultant, writer, editor, lecturer*

South Lake Tahoe
Barr, Lois I. *personnel administrator*
Nason, Rochelle *conservation organization administrator*

South Pasadena
Remy, Ray *management and public affairs consultant*

South San Francisco
Lewis, Jason Alvert, Jr., *communications executive*
†Rainey, Gerald Wayne *sales executive*
†Walsh, Gary L. *consumer products company executive*

Stanford
Miller, William Frederick *research company executive, educator, business consultant*
Paté-Cornell, Marie-Elisabeth Lucienne *management and engineering educator*

Stockton
Hoberg, Michael Dean *management analyst, educator*
Jacobs, Marian *advertising agency owner*
Plovnick, Mark Stephen *business educator*

Studio City
Chambers, Clytia Montllor *public relations consultant*
Delnik, Alexander *business development executive, consultant*
Moseley, Chris Rosser *marketing executive*
Richman, Anthony K. *textile rental industry association executive*
Valadez, Rudolph Antonio *security firm executive, consultant, writer, artist*

Sunnyvale
†Andreessen, Marc *communications company executive*
Decker, Susan *Internet company executive*
†Filo, David *Internet company executive*
Gifford, John F. *computer company executive*
Michals, Lee Marie *travel agency administrator*
Patstone, Cheryl *public relations executive*
†Rosensweig, Daniel L. *Internet company executive*
†Semel, Terry S. *Internet company executive*
†Yang, Jerry *Internet company executive*

Sutter Creek
Sanders, Elizabeth Anne Weaver (Betsy Sanders) *management consultant*

Sylmar
Hayes, Cynthia Ann (C.A. Hayes) *administrative assistant, writer*

Tehachapi
Smith-Thompson, Patricia Ann *public relations consultant, educator*

Temecula
Coram, David James *gaming industry professional*

Temple City
Lau, Bobby Wai-Man *marketing professional, investment and financial planner, business startup trainer*

Thousand Oaks
Lark, M. Ann *management consultant, strategic planner, naturalist*
Noonan, Daniel Christopher *consultant*

Torrance
Horwich, Harvey *printer, publisher*
Signorovitch, Dennis J. *communications executive*

Truckee
Sanwick, James Arthur *international executive recruiter, management consultant*

Tujunga
Lathe, Robert Edward *management and financial consultant*

Twentynine Palms
Fultz, Philip Nathaniel *management analyst*

Upland
†Suh, Jung Sook Ky *management consultant, educator*

Vacaville
†Longoria, Steve *security firm executive, consultant*

Valencia
Pocrass, Richard Dale *management consultant*

Vallejo
Crocker, Kenneth Franklin *data processing consultant*

Valley Springs
Vitrac, Jean-Jacques Charles *international business consultant*

Van Nuys
Greenberg, Daniel *electronics rental company executive*
Seymour, Jeffrey Alan *governmental relations consultant*

Venice
Hester, Gail *receptionist, writer*

Ventura
†Tamke, George William *printing/copying company executive*

Victorville
Yochem, Barbara June (Runyan) *sales executive, lecturer*

Villa Park
Britton, Thomas Warren, Jr., *retired management consultant*

Walnut Creek
da Roza, Victoria Cecilia *human resources administrator*
Garlough, William Glenn *marketing executive*
Hammond, Charles Edgar *data processing executive*
Moore, John David *management consultant*
Polgar, Leslie George *venture executive*
Wilkins, Sheila Scanlon *management consultant*

West Covina
†Shanks, Sanford H. *sales executive, writer*

West, Edward Alan *graphics communications executive*

West Hollywood
Einstein, Clifford Jay *advertising executive*
Gates, Lisa *private chef, caterer*
Stern, James Coper *sales executive*

Westlake Village
Murdock, David H. *diversified company executive*
†Pardau, Stuart Lloyd *market research company executive, lawyer, educator*
Smyth, Glen Miller *management consultant*
Troxell, Lucy Davis *management consultant*

Woodland Hills
Ennis, Thomas Michael *management consultant*
†Stahlecker, Barbara Jean *marketing professional, consultant*

Woodside
Arthur, Greer Martin *maritime container leasing firm executive*

COLORADO

Allenspark
†Newman, Dean Gordon *business consultant*

Aspen
Jennings, Richard Milburn *resort developer*

Boulder
Balkin, David Bruce *management consultant, educator*
Burns, Daniel Hobart *management consultant*
†Conway, Robert Edward *corporate executive*
Jerritts, Stephen G. *management consultant*
Marecaux, M. L. *consultant, writer*
Shumick, Diana Lynn *computer executive*

Brighton
Wagner, Samuel Albin Mar *records management executive, educator*

Broomfield
Lybarger, John Steven *human resources development consultant, trainer*

Canon City
Rivera-Reyes, Gladys M. (Gladys Dalton) *retired stenographer, court reporter*

Centennial
Welch, Richard LeRoy *personal improvement company executive*

Colorado Springs
Dunn, David John *human resources executive*
Fagin, Barry Steven *computer science educator, writer*
Ford, James Carlton *human resources executive*
Fortune, James Michael *computer support manager*
Gardner, Donald Gene *management consultant, educator*
Hall, Nechie Tesitor *advertising and public relations executive*
Martz, William B. *management consultant, educator*
Smith, James Micheal *operations executive*

Denver
Blatter, Frank Edward *travel agency executive*
Browne, Spencer Ivan *mortgage company executive, internet executive*
Clinch, Nicholas Bayard, III, *business executive*
Cox, Louis Anthony, Jr., *telecommunications executive*
Dunham, Joan Roberts *administrative assistant*
Hughes, Bradley Richard *business executive*
Johnson, Harold Earl *human resources specialist*
Karsh, Philip Howard *advertising executive*
Kurtz, Maxine *personnel consultant, lawyer*
Lazarus, Steven S. *management consultant, marketing consultant*
Lundy, Barbara Jean *training executive*
Martin, Robert Burton *management and marketing consultant*
Murdock, Pamela Ervilla *travel and advertising company executive*
Murray, James Alan *urban and environmental consultant, investor*
Myhren, Trygve Edward *communications company executive*
Neu, Carl Herbert, Jr., *management consultant*
Pocs, Martin M. *executive search consultant*
Reece, Monique Elizabeth *marketing, advertising and sales consultant*
†Reynolds, Collins James, III, *management consultant*
Shaddock, Paul Franklin, Sr., *human resources executive*
Shadrick, Dorothy Jo *management consultant*
Sundel, Harvey H. *marketing research analyst, consultant*
†Taylor, Julia Fisher *public relations executive*
Williams, Sue M. *corporate communications specialist, writer*

Dumont
Hudson, Miller Newton *public agency manager, consultant*

Durango
Foster, James Henry *advertising and public relations executive*

Edwards
Bryson, Gary Spath *cable television and telephone company executive*

Englewood
Benson, Robert Craig, III, *business consultant*

Cooper, Sharon Marsha *marketing, advertising executive*
Cooper, Steven Jon *healthcare management consultant, educator*
Giesen, John William *advertising executive*
Greenagel, Debra *travel agency executive*
Kuhn, Donald Marshall *marketing professional*
Lake, Stanley James *security consulting company executive, motel chain executive, locksmith*
Neiser, Brent Allen *foundation executive, public affairs and personal finance consultant, speaker*
Shimokubo, Janice Teruko *marketing professional*

Evergreen
Evans, David Lynn *management consultant*

Fort Garland
Moullette, John Brinkley *retired corporate trainer, consultant*

Frederick
Emlen, Warren Metz *computer-related services company owner*

Golden
Fleener, Terry Noel *marketing professional*
Van Dusen, Donna Bayne *communications consultant, educator, researcher*

Grand Junction
Freeman, Neil *accounting and computer consulting firm executive*
Mallory, Elgin Albert *business educator, management consultant, small business owner, school system administrator*

Greeley
Miller, Diane Wilmarth *retired human resources director*

Lakewood
Martinen, John A. *travel company executive*
Walton, Roger Alan *public relations executive, mediator, writer*

Littleton
Fisher, Louis McLane, Jr., *management consultant*
Hopping, William Russell *hospitality industry consultant and appraiser*
Inzano, Karen Lee *advertising agency executive*
Treybig, Edwina Hall *sales executive*

Louisville
†Sontag, Peter Michael *travel management company executive*

Loveland
McKinley, Jeneal Ruth *computer company executive*

Monument
De Francesco, John Blaze, Jr., *public relations consultant, artist, writer*

Niwot
Farrington, Helen Agnes *personnel director*

Pagosa Springs
Howard, Carole Margaret Munroe *retired public relations executive*

Parker
Pastore, Thomas Michael *telecommunications sales executive*

Sedalia
McKee, John Morrison *management consultant*

Sterling
Jones, Laurie Ganong *sales and marketing executive*

Telluride
†Hadley, Paul Burrest, Jr., (Tabbit Hadley) *domestic engineer*

Westminster
Shirai, Scott *communications executive*

CONNECTICUT

Bloomfield
Handel, Morton Emanuel *management consultation executive*

Bridgeport
Gallagher, Joan Frances *business administration educator*
Kantrowitz, Jonathan Daniel *educational publishing and services company executive, lawyer*

Bristol
LaGanga, Donna Brandeis *sales and marketing executive*

Cos Cob
Kucic, Joseph *management consultant, industrial engineer, network engineer, information security specialist*
Murphy, Robert Blair *management consulting company executive*

Darien
Cronk, Leonard *management consultant*
Kobak, James Benedict *management consultant*
Morano, Gerard John *marketing executive*
Rezek, Geoffrey Robert *management consultant*
Welsh, John Francis *retired advertising executive*

East Haddam
Clarke, Cordelia Kay Knight Mazuy *management consultant, artist*
Clarke, Logan, Jr., *management consultant*

East Hampton
Jamieson, Leland *retired career management consultant*

Easton
Berry, Ronald George *marketing professional*

Essex
Thompson, George Lee *consulting and retailing company executive*

Fairfield
Booth, George Keefer *financial service executive*
Dean, George Alden *advertising executive*
Hergenhan, Joyce *public relations executive*
Johnsen, Walter Craig *security firm executive*
Luther, David Byron *management consultant*
McCreight, John A. *management consultant*
Orris-Modugno, Michele Marie *public relations, marketing and advertising consultant*
Whyte, Bruce Lincoln *management executive, marketing professional*

Farmington
†Riley, Deon *human resources specialist, consultant*

Glastonbury
Andrews, Bryant Aylesworth *software company executive*
Pudlo, Frances Theresa *human resources specialist*

Granby
Pfeiffer, Edward Joseph *public relations consultant, photojournalist*

Greens Farms
McManus, John Francis, III, *advertising executive*

Greenwich
Ball, John Fleming *advertising and film production executive*
Bara, Jean Marc *finance and communications executive, artist*
Bollman, Mark Brooks, Jr., *communications executive*
Broadhurst, Austin, Jr., *executive recruiter*
Carmichael, William Daniel *consultant, educator*
Davidson, Thomas Maxwell *international management company executive*
Donley, James Walton *management consultant*
Harrington, Robert Dudley, Jr., *retired printing company executive*
Kestnbaum, Albert S. *advertising executive*
Lewis, Audrey Gersh *financial marketing/public relations consultant*
Lochner, Philip Raymond *retired communications executive, consultant*
Paulson, Paul Joseph *advertising executive*
Perless, Ellen *advertising executive*
Schlafly, Hubert Joseph, Jr., *communications executive*
Srere, Benson M. *communications company executive, consultant*
Whitmore, George Merle, Jr., *management consulting company executive*

Guilford
Mick, Margaret Anne *communications executive*

Hartford
Glasser, Joseph *manufacturing and marketing executive*
Whaley, Charles Henry, IV, *communications company executive*

Kent
Friedman, Frances *public relations executive*

Milford
Olson, Harold Roy *computer company executive*

Monroe
Siegel, Richard Allen *corporate management consultant*

New Canaan
Kamerschen, Robert Jerome *consumer products executive, investor*
Mc Mennamin, George Barry *advertising agency executive*
Means, David Hammond *retired advertising executive*
Ward, Richard Vance, Jr., *management executive*
White, Richard Booth *management consultant*

New Haven
†Rae, Douglas Whiting *management educator*
Singer, Jon Douglas *receptionist, writer*

Newington
Skwirut, John Laurence *computer company executive*

Newtown
Briody, L(aurence) Patrick *journalist, consultant*
Coates, John Peter *technical executive*
Cole, Richard John *marketing executive*
Goodwick, David Lee *advertising executive*

Norfolk
Burrows, John Edward *communications company executive*
O'Malley, Margaret Parlin *marketing administrator*

North Haven
Weaver, Kitra K. *sales and marketing executive*

North Stonington
Neves-Elbaum, Stella Boudrias *design company representative*

Norwalk
Czajkowski-Barrett, Karen Angela *human resources management executive*
Mintz, Lenore Chaice (Lea Mintz) *consultant*
Mundt, Barry Maynard *management consultant*
Nightingale, William Joslyn *management consultant*
Pagano, Michael Pro *advertising executive*
†Weiner, Sandra Joan *computer catalog reseller company executive*
Yeosock, Michael Michael *funeral director, civil engineer*

Old Greenwich
Levine, I. Robert *business executive*

Old Saybrook
Nuhn, Charles Kelsey *advertising executive*
Phillips, William E. *advertising agency executive*

Orange
Beringer, Michael Pennell *public relations executive*
Phillips, Jeannette Veronica *management consultant, gerontologist*

Redding
McClure, Grover Benjamin *management consultant*
Stack, J. William, Jr., *management consultant*
Wetzel, Edward Thomas *business executive*

Ridgefield
Clary, Alexia Barbara *management company executive*
Farrall, George William *marketing executive*
Hancock, Ellen Marie *communications executive*
Lodewick, Philip Hughes *equipment leasing company executive*

Riverside
Geismar, Richard Lee *communications executive*
MacDonald, Gordon Chalmers *management consultant*
McSpadden, Peter Ford *retired advertising agency executive*

Rowayton
Gold, Richard N. *management consultant*

Salisbury
Block, Zenas *management consultant, educator*
Levy, Ira Howard *marketing professional, real estate investor*

Shelton
Coverdale, Watson Shallcross, Jr., *communications company executive*
Mariotti, Margaret *executive secretary*

South Windsor
Famiglietti, Nancy Zima *computer executive*

Southbury
Leonard, John Harry *advertising executive*

Southington
Carrington, Virginia Gail (Vee Carrington) *marketing professional, consultant*

Southport
Savage, Robert Heath *advertising executive*

Stamford
†Braddock, Richard S. *internet company executive*
deKoster, Heinz Adolph *retired technology consultant*
Dell, Warren Frank, II, *management consultant*
Duhov, Benjamin *consulting group executive*
Goodkin, Deborah Gay *mutual funds administrator*
Liebeskind, David *business management consultant, educator*
Miklovic, Daniel Thomas *research executive*
Miller, Wilbur Hobart *business diversification consultant*
Patterson, Denis W. *economic development official*
Pollock, M. Duncan *advertising executive*
Rizzuto, Leandro Peter *consumer products company executive*
Silver, Charles Morton *communications company executive*
Smolyar, Adam J. *business executive*
†Stern, Arlene Helen *human resources specialist*
†Trivisonno, Nicholas Louis *communications company executive, accountant*
Wallfesh, Henry Maurice *business communications company executive, editor, writer*
Wilson, Robert Albert *communications consultant*

Trumbull
London, Michael Jeffrey *public relations executive*

Waterford
Hinkle, Janet *project leader*

West Hartford
Katrichis, Jerome M. *business educator, consultant*

Weston
Murray, Thomas J. *advertising executive*

Westport
Aasen, Lawrence Obert *public relations executive*
Axelson, Linda Rae *event planning specialist*
Blau, Barry *marketing executive, financial investor*

PROFESSIONAL INDEX 6489 INDUSTRY: SERVICE

Gallagher, Michael Robert *consumer products company executive*
Levien, Roger Eli *strategy and innovation consultant*
Schriever, Fred Martin *management consultant, financial investor*

Wethersfield
Franco, Carole Ann *international consultant*
Karwic, Richard A. *management consultant, educator*

Wilton
Bishop, William Wade *advertising executive*
Caravatt, Paul Joseph, Jr., *communications company executive*
Farley, James Parker *retired advertising agency executive*
Flesher, Margaret Covington *communications consultant, writer*
Frank, Robert Allen *advertising executive*
Keenan, James Joseph *organizational consultant, communications educator*
Mitchell, Richard Boyle *security consultant*
Nickel, Albert George *advertising agency executive*
Pethley, Lowell Sherman *retired management consultant*
Schadt, James Phillip *investment and software executive*
Tedesco, Frank Mario *management consultant*
Weiland, Juliette Marie *public relations executive, freelance writer and photographer*

Winsted
Stawicki, Joseph John, Jr., *marketing executive*

Woodbridge
Alvine, Robert *industrialist, entrepreneur*

DELAWARE

Elsmere
Shearin, K. Kay *procurator, legal and humor writer, freelance technical writer*

Milford
Bergmann, William J. *personnel director*

Millsboro
Carter, William Allen *sales executive, insurance company executive*

Newark
†Manrai, Ajay K. *marketing professional, educator*
Nelson, Robert R. *hotel, restaurant and tourism educator*
†Silva, Luis M. *marketing professional*

Wilmington
Dao, Thuy Dinh *nail salon manager*
Douglas, Victoria Jean *marketing professional, communications executive, consultant*
Ehrich, Felix Frederick *technical consultant*
Kjellmark, Eric William, Jr., *management consultant, opera company director*
Shelley, Bernard Franklin *pressure vessel consultant*
Shipley, Samuel Lynn *advertising and public relations executive*

Wyoming
†Bailey, Kay Wood *management consultant*

DISTRICT OF COLUMBIA

Washington
Adams, A. John Bertrand *public affairs consultant*
Alexander, Clifford L., Jr., *management consultant, lawyer, former secretary of army*
Allen, Richard Vincent *international business consultant, policy advisor*
Allnutt, Robert Frederick *management consultant, corporate director*
Alloway, Robert Malcombe *computer consulting executive*
Ansley, Darlene H. *marketing and communications executive*
Barrett, Laurence Irwin *public relations executive, writer*
Bell, Jeanne Viner *public relations counselor*
Berman, Ellen Sue *energy and telecommunications executive, theatre producer*
Boza, Clara Brizeida *marketing and communications executive*
Breul, Jonathan Dutro *consultant*
Butler, Patrick Harold *communications executive*
Carpenter, Bill *public relations executive*
Champlin, Steven M. *management consultant*
Coltman, Edward Jeremiah *communication executive*
Coons, Barbara Lynn *public relations executive, librarian*
Cope, Jeannette Naylor *executive search consultant*
Cornish, Danté Anthony *employee development specialist*
†Corso, John Anthony *management consultant, educator*
Culley-Foster, Anthony Robert *international business consultant*
Dach, Leslie Alan *public relations company executive*
Davis, Rex Darwin *business consultant*
Dawson, Mimi Weyforth *public policy consultant*
Dayton, Deane Kraybill *translation company executive*
Denysyk, Bohdan *international consultant*
Dessaso, Deborah Ann *freelance writer, online communications specialist, consultant*
DeVaul, Diane D. *policy director*
Ducat, Suzanne Basha *television producer, communications specialist*
Dugoff, Howard Jay *business consultant*
Duvall, Henry Franklin, Jr., *public relations executive*
Elder, James Perry *management consultant*
Farber, Donna Sylvie *marketing professional*
Friedman, Steven Eric *communications executive*
Fuller, Edwin Daniel *hotel executive*
Gest, Kathryn Waters *public affairs professional*
Gibbons, Sam Melville *business executive, former congressman*
†Gillespie, Ed *public affairs consultant, political organization executive*
Grant, Carl N. *communications and sales executive*
Griffin, Kelly Ann *public relations executive, consultant*
†Gulino, Denny *communications executive*
Guzda, Henry Peter *industrial relations specialist*
Hager, Susan Kulka *public relations executive*
Hannaford, Peter Dor *public relations executive, writer*
Havlicek, Franklin J. *communications executive*
Herrett, Richard Allison *agricultural research institute administrator*
Hezir, Joseph S. *energy and environmental company executive*
Higgins, James Henry, III, *marketing executive*
Howard, Jack *labor relations consultant*
Howe, Fisher *management consultant, former government official*
Huberman, Benjamin *technology consultant*
Huggins, James Bernard *corporate executive*
Johnson, Thomas Dale *management consultant*
Jordan, Sandra *public relations professional*
Kaludis, George *management consultant, book company executive, educator*
Kelly, James Andrew *policy reseach executive, former government official*
Kimmitt, Joseph Stanley *political consultant*
Kingsley, Mary Lee *marketing professional*
Kleeschulte, Charles A. *communications director*
Kotler, Milton *marketing company executive*
Kraus, Margery *management consultant, communications company executive*
Krueger, Keith Roger *non-profit management executive*
Lambert, Deborah Ketchum *public relations executive*
Lasko, Joel *company executive*
Leibach, Dale William *government relations and public affairs executive*
Levinson, Nanette Segal *international relations educator, administrator*
Lewis, Jordan David *charity organization executive, author, international speaker, educator*
Lisboa-Farrow, Elizabeth Oliver *public and government relations consultant*
†Lowe, Florence Segal *retired public relations executive*
Manatos, Andrew E. *public relations executive*
Mansfield, Edward Patrick, Jr., *advertising executive*
Marriott, John Willard, Jr., *lodging and senior living executive*
Marshall, Maryann Chorba *office administrator*
Martino, Peter Dominic *financial software company executive, real estate developer, real estate broker, federal agency administrator*
Marumoto, William Hideo *management consultant*
McBride, Jonathan Evans *executive search consultant*
McInerney, Joseph Aloysius *hotel executive*
†McLarty, Thomas F., III, (Mack McLarty) *business executive*
McLaughlin, John J. *broadcast executive, television producer, political commentator, journalist*
Mederos, Carolina Luisa *management consultant*
Millian, Kenneth Young *public policy consultant*
Moe, Ronald Chesney *public administration researcher*
Moore, Bob Stahly *communications executive*
Nesbitt, Veronica A. *management executive*
Norman, William Stanley *travel and tourism executive*
O'Brien, Richard Francis *advertising agency association executive*
Palumbo, Benjamin Lewis *public affairs consulting company executive*
Paulson, Gwen O. Gampel *government relations consultant*
Payne, Michael Lee *association management executive*
Pedersen, Wesley Niels M. *public relations and public affairs executive*
Pfeiffer, Leonard, IV, *executive recruiter, consultant*
Pines, Wayne Lloyd *public relations executive*
Posey, Ada Louise *management consultant*
Pyle, Robert Noble *government relations executive*
Rainey, Jean Osgood *public relations executive*
Reed, Travis Dean *public relations executive*
Reingold, Janet Rose *corporate communications specialist*
Rice, Lois Dickson *former computer company executive*
Ridley, Keith Alexander, IV, *funeral director*
Robinson, Elaine *consultant*
Rosebush, James Scott *international management and public affairs consultant, former government official*
Rosenthal, Aaron *management consultant*
Rotunda, Donald Theodore *public relations consultant*
Schriever, Bernard Adolph *management consultant*
Seats, Peggy Chisolm *marketing executive*
†Shaw, William J. *hotel facility executive*
Shear, Natalie Pickus *conference and event management executive*
Sisco, Joseph John *management consultant, corporation director, educator, government official*
Skolfield, Melissa T. *public relations executive, former government official*
Slagle, Larry B. *human resources specialist*
Smith, Nancy Lee *communications official*
Stauffer, Thomas George *retired hotel executive*
Sunderlin, Charles Eugene *consultant*
Swain, Susan Marie *communications executive*
†Swisher, Larry *newspaper executive*
Tanham, George Kilpatrick *retired research company executive*
Tate, Sheila Burke *public relations executive*
Tiefel, William Reginald *hotel company executive*
Timmons, William Evan *corporate executive*
Trowbridge, Alexander Buel, Jr., *business consultant*
Van Allen, Barbara Martz *marketing professional*
Vance, Stephanie *consultant*
Vickery, Raymond Ezekiel, Jr., *international business consultant, lawyer*
Villarreal, June Patricia *sales consultant*
Vondracek, M. Jon *communications executive*
Walcott, John L. *communications executive*
Walker, Savannah T. *retired executive assistant, legislative assistant*
Wallace, Hank *seminar speaker, lawyer*
†Wentsel, Randall Sterling *environmental services administrator*
Wertheim, Mitzi Mallina *technology company executive*
Wheeler, Thomas Edgar *communications technology executive*
Whittlesey, Judith Holloway *public relations executive*
†Wood, Gregory Hirth *communications executive*
Yulish, Charles Barry *public relations executive*
†Zappia, Christopher *marketing professional*

FLORIDA

Arcadia
White, Will Walter, III, *public relations consultant, writer*

Aventura
D'Gabriel, Carlos Leonardo *retired travel executive*

Bascom
Hart, James Whitfield, Jr., *retired corporate public affairs executive, lawyer*

Boca Grande
Dyche, David Bennett, Jr., *retired management consultant*
Winterer, Victoria Thompson *hospitality executive*

Boca Raton
Allen, Barry Morgan *corporate communications consultant*
Breakstone, Robert Albert *consumer products, e-commerce, information technology and consulting executive*
Crossman, William Whittard *retired wire cable and communications executive*
Dorfman, Allen Bernard *international management consultant*
Dunhill, Robert W. *advertising direct mail executive*
Finegold, Ronald *computer services executive*
Kaplan, Judith Helene *company executive*
Katz, Richard Jon *marketing and advertising company executive*
Langbort, Polly *retired advertising executive*
Levin, Marlene *human resources executive, educator*
Monroe, William Lewis *human resources executive*
Rosner, M. Norton *business systems and financial services company executive*
Schechterman, Lawrence *private chef, business consultant*
Turner, Lisa Phillips *human resources executive*
Vissicchio, Andrew John, Jr., *linen service company executive*
Yoder, Patricia Doherty *public relations executive*

Bonita Springs
Ericson, Alvin Charles *marketing professional, consultant*

Boynton Beach
†Ashley, James MacGregor *management consultant*
Charles, Joel *forensic audio and video tape analyst, voice identification consultant*
Schneider, Paul *consultant*
Sondak, Arthur *retired management consultant*

Bradenton
Blanchard, Leonard Albert *educator, consultant, writer*
Doyle, William Jay, II, *business consultant*
Robinson, Hugh R. *retired marketing executive*
Wolf, John Michael *adult education seminar consultant*

Cape Coral
Andert, Darlene (Darlene Andert-Schmidt) *management consultant in corporate governance*
Milaski, John Joseph *business transformation industry consultant*

Casselberry
Lucas, Robert William *human resources consultant, writer*
Pantuso, Vincent Joseph *food service consultant*

Celebration
O'Neal, Kathleen Len *communications executive, writer, management consultant*
Renard, Meredith Anne *marketing and advertising professional*

Clearwater
Brenner, Rena Claudy *communications executive*
Chisholm, William DeWayne *retired contract manager*
Hunt, Peter James *management consultant, statistics educator*
Raymund, Steven A. *computer company executive*
Scarne, John *game company executive*

Cocoa
Davis, Duane Lee *marketing educator*

Coconut Grove
Softness, John *public relations executive*
Taylor, J(ames) Bennett *management consultant*
Turkel, Bruce *advertising executive*

Coral Gables
Bacon, Lydia Leach *human resources professional*
Buchsbaum, Karen Fuson *public relations executive, consultant*
Gould, Taffy *Internet company executive, real estate executive*
Hertz, Arthur Herman *business executive*
Lomonosoff, James Marc *marketing professional*
Nacknouck, James D. *management executive*

Dania
Dozier, Eleanor Cameron *computer company executive, writer*

Davenport
†Vaughn, Rosalyn Mae *human resources specialist*

Daytona Beach
Furstman, Shirley Elsie Daddow *advertising executive*
Schauer, Catharine Guberman *public affairs specialist*

Deerfield Beach
†Moran, James M. *automotive sales executive*

Delray Beach
Charyk, Joseph Vincent *retired satellite telecommunications executive*
Ehrlich, Geraldine Elizabeth *management consultant*
Nelson, Bruce *consumer products company executive*
Nikischer, Frank William, Sr., *retired restaurant owner and operator*
Randall, Priscilla Richmond *travel executive*
Warshaw, Stanley Irving *policy advisor*

Deltona
Zagnoli, Roland Candiano *management and marketing consultant, pharmacist*

Destin
Davis, Christopher Kevin *sales executive*
Ferner, David Charles *non-profit management and development consultant*

Dunedin
Metcalf, Robert John Elmer *industrial consultant*
Samson, Jerome *communications executive, software engineer*

Fernandina Beach
D'Agnese, John Joseph *sanitation, public health and pest management consultant*
Rhodes, Robert Milford *management consultant*

Floral City
Wise, Lawrence George *human resources executive*

Fort Lauderdale
Baruch, Eduard *management consultant*
Cantwell, John Walsh *advertising executive*
Costello, John H., III, *business and marketing executive*
Donaldson, Lisa Miller *city administration*
Fine, Howard Alan *travel industry executive*
Fitch, Mary Killeen *human resources specialist*
†Horowitz, Kenneth A. *communications executive, entrepreneur*
Jotcham, Thomas Denis *marketing communications consultant*
Knight, Kenneth Vincent *leisure company executive, entrepreneur, venture capitalist*
Kobert, Norman Noah *asset management consultant*
Koch, Katherine Rose *communications executive*
Olen, Milton William, Jr., *marketing executive*
Zimmerman, Jordan *marketing professional*

Fort Myers
Antonic, James Paul *international marketing consultant*
Aron, Eve Glicka Serenson *personal care industry executive*
Fulker, Edmund Norman *management consultant*
Goyak, Elizabeth Fairbairn *retired public relations executive*
†Scott, George Alfred *advertising executive, writer*

Fort Pierce
Eisenberg, Susan Mary *retired employment representative*
Locklin, Wilbert Edwin *management consultant*
Thoma, Richard William *chemical safety and waste management consultant*

Gainesville
Siegel, Robert James *communications executive*

Grand Island
Johnson, Tesla Francis *data processing executive, educator*

Hialeah
Grahm, Charles Morton *retired sales executive*

Hobe Sound
Gold, Kenneth R. *computer software consulting executive*

Hollywood
Angstrom, Wayne Raymond *communications executive*
Cowan, Irving *real estate owner, developer*
Ladin, Eugene *communications company executive*
Waganheim, Arthur Brian *marketing executive*

Hutchinson Island
Wanzer, Mary Kathryn *computer company executive, consultant*
Wegman, Harold Hugh *management consultant*

Indian Rocks Beach
Sullivan, Paul William *communications specialist*

Jacksonville
Bodkin, Ruby Pate *corporate executive, real estate broker, educator*
Clark, Mark David *public relations consultant*
†Davis, A. Dano *grocery store chain executive*
Fahner, Harold Thomas *marketing executive*
Jones, Herman Otto, Jr., *corporate professional*
†Lurie, Jay Scott *Internet company executive*
Maxwell, W(ilbur) Richard *retired management consultant*
Motsett, Charles Bourke *sales, marketing and leadership executive*
Rinehart, Harry Elmer *retired sales executive*
Rowland, Allen R. *grocery company executive*
Schramm, Bernard Charles, Jr., *retired advertising agency executive*
Sederbaum, William *marketing executive*
Sterman, Gail K. Mendelson *public relations specialist*

Jacksonville Beach
Hearle, Edward F.R. *retired management consultant*
Saltzman, Irene Cameron *consumer products company executive*

Jupiter
Colucci, Jacqueline Strupp *interpreter, small business administration specialist, sculptor*
Gerson, Irwin Conrad *advertising executive*

Key Biscayne
Duffy, Earl Gavin *hotel executive*
Evans, Peter Kenneth *advertising executive*
Landis, Carolyn Press *corporate executive*

Key Colony Beach
Crenshaw, Patricia Shryack *sales executive, consultant*

Key Largo
Chevins, Anthony Charles *retired advertising agency executive*

Key West
†Braddock, Stephen E. *not-for-profit executive, priest*

Lady Lake
Langevin, Thomas Harvey *higher education consultant*

Lake Suzy
Ogan, Russell Griffith *business executive, retired air force officer*

Lake Worth
Bell, Melvin *management consultant*
Gorman, Marcie Sothern *personal care industry franchise executive*
Saffir, Leonard *public relations executive*

Lakeland
Jackson, Elijah, Jr., *communication executive*
Jenkins, Howard M. *supermarket executive*
Meads, Walter Frederick *communications executive, consultant*
Siedle, Robert Douglas *management consultant*
Waugaman, Richard William *sales executive*
Zucco, Ronda Kay *planning and marketing professional*

Largo
Chambers, Ray Wayne *security and loss control consultant*
†Gould, Glenn Hunting *marketing professional, consultant*
Ray, Roger Buchanan *retired communications executive, lawyer*

Longboat Key
Holcomb, Constance L. *sales and marketing management executive*
†Winfree, Charles Van *management consultant*

Longwood
†Bernabei, Raymond *management consultant*
Faller, Donald E. *marketing and operations executive*
Manjura, Bonnie Doreen *marketing professional, advertising executive, educator*
Walters, Philip Raymond *foundation executive*

Lutz
McNeely, David John *computer programmer*
Miller, Bonnie Sewell *marketing professional, writer*

Maitland
Stephens, Patricia Ann *marketing professional*

Mary Esther
McTyeire, Robert Adams *sound company executive*

Melbourne
Jenkins, Marshall *internet consultant, entrepreneur*
Shaikh, Muzaffar Abid *management science educator*

Melbourne Beach
Harris, Jack Howard, II, *consulting firm executive*

Miami
Adams, William Carryl *public relations educator*
Amos, Betty Giles *restaurant company executive, accountant*
†Arison, Micky *cruise line company executive, sports team executive*
†Blum, Bradley D. *food service executive*
Buehler, Martin *hotel executive*
Carter, Harriet Vanessa *marketing professional, aide*
†Chapple, Michael Joseph *marketing professional, security firm executive*
Cole, Todd Godwin *management consultant transportation*
Collins, Susan Ford *leadership consultant*
Cubas, Jose M(anuel) *advertising agency executive*
Edelcup, Norman Scott *management and financial consultant*
Escalera, Karen Weiner *marketing professional*
Haar, Ana Maria Fernández *advertising and public relations executive*
Herbits, Stephen Edward *strategic consultant*
Hunter, Leland Clair, Jr., *management consultant*
†Lugauer, Steven L. *management consultant*
Mustelier, Alina Olga *travel consultant, music educator*
Neuman, Susan Catherine *public relations and marketing consultant*
Newman, Terrie Lynne *advertising and marketing executive*
Nixon, David Patrick *public relations executive*
Ortiz, Loida A. *communications executive*
Paresky, Linda K. *travel company executive, educator*
Polen-Dorn, Linda Frances *communications executive*
Porter, Charles King *advertising executive*
Sanchez, Fausto H. *advertising agency executive*
Schwartz, Gerald *public relations and fundraising agency executive*
Weiser, Ralph Raphael *business executive*
Weiser, Sherwood Manuel *hotel and corporation executive, lawyer*
Whittington, Robert Wallace *corporate professional*

Miami Beach
†Martinotti, Massimo *advertising executive*
Sharlach, Jeffrey *public relations executive*

Miramar
González Tricoche, Cynthia Marie *human resources specialist*

Naples
Censits, Richard John *retired business executive*
Franco, Anthony M. *public relations executive*
Gilman, John Richard, Jr., *retired management consultant, sculptor*
Hauserman, Jacquita Knight *management consultant*
Kleinrock, Virginia Barry *public relations executive*
Kozitka, Richard Eugene *retired consumer products company executive*
Marshall, Charles *communications company executive*
Mehaffey, John Allen *marketing, newspaper management and advertising executive*
Moore, Mechlin Dongan *communications executive, marketing consultant*
Shields, Bruce Maclean *management consultant*
Sims, William Ronald *advertising executive*

New Port Richey
†Grillo, Robert S. *private investigator, protective services official*

New Smyrna Beach
Satterlee, Peter Hamilton *communications executive, military officer*

North Fort Myers
Fishkind, Lawrence *marketing consultant*
Gray, Carlos Gibson *restaurateur, agricultural products supplier, entertainer, producer*

North Miami
Roslow, Sydney *marketing educator*

North Palm Beach
Spencer, Susan Namm *management consultant*

Ocala
Sostilio, Robert Francis *office equipment marketing consultant*
Sundstrom, Harold Walter *public relations executive*
Toral, Miguel A. *customer service administrator, actor*

Oldsmar
Brunner, George Matthew *management consultant, former business executive*
MacLeod, Donald Martin *corporate professional*

Orange City
Schaeffer, Barbara Hamilton *retired rental leasing company executive, writer*

Orlando
Connolly, Joseph Francis, II, *educational executive, government consultant*
†Ihnat, Michael Anthony *administrative assistant*
†Lee, Joe R. *food service executive*
Morgan, Shirley Ann *information systems lecturer*
Neiman, Norman *aerospace business and marketing executive*
Smetheram, Herbert Edwin *management consultant*
Yesawich, Peter Charles *advertising executive*

Ormond Beach
Stogner, William Louis *pharmaceutical company executive*

Osprey
Cochran, David MacDuffie *management consultant*
Halladay, Laurie Ann *public relations consultant, former franchise executive*

Oviedo
Millstein, Herbert Sydney *management consultant*

Palm Bay
Bigda, Rudolph A. *business and financial consultant*
Kelley, Patricia *marketing representative*

Palm Beach
Flanagan, Joseph Patrick *advertising executive*
Karp, Richard M. *advertising and communication executive*
Rumbough, Stanley Maddox, Jr., *industrialist*
Whiteside, Patricia Lee *fine art antique and personal property appraiser*

Palm Beach Gardens
Druck, Kalman Breschel *public relations counselor*
Mendelson, Richard Donald *former communications company executive*
Van Allen, Veronica Elaine *marketing and public relations professional*

Palmetto
Roehl, Nancy Leary *marketing professional, educator*

Panama City
Dewey, Craig Douglas *operations executive*

Pembroke Pines
Motes, Joseph Mark *cruise and convention promotion company executive*

Pinellas Park
†Mente, Ronald F. *consulting company executive*

Plantation
Bosted, Dorothy Stack *public relations executive*

Pompano Beach
Brands, Robert Franciscus *business executive*
Calevas, Harry Powell *management consultant*
Donnelly, Michael Joseph *management consultant*

Ponte Vedra Beach
Gold, Keith Dean *advertising and design executive*
Leek, Jay Wilbur *management consultant*
Linnen, Thomas Francis *international strategic management consulting firm executive*
Ramsey, William Dale, Jr., *marketing and technology consultant*

Port Charlotte
Reynolds, Helen Elizabeth *management services consultant*

Riverview
Till, Beatriz Maria *international business consultant, translator*

Saint Augustine
Preysz, Louis Robert Fonss, III, *management consultant, educator*
Wiles, Marilyn McCall *communications consultant*

Saint Leo
†Bowden, Randall Glen *marketing and business development administrator*

Saint Lucie West
Hambel, Henry Peter *clinical hypnotherapist, forensic security consultant, educator*

Saint Petersburg
DeLorenzo, David Joseph *retired public relations executive*
Engel, John Jacob *communications executive*
Kubiet, Leo Lawrence *newspaper advertising and marketing executive*
†Sembler, Mel *company executive, ambassador*
Thompson, Dayle Ann *management and accounting systems consultant*

Sanford
Easton, Susan Shearer *organizational development consultant, educator*

Sanibel
Brodbeck, William Jan *marketing consultant, speaker*
Sheldon, Nancy Way *environmental management consultant*

Santa Rosa Beach
Rees, Lane Charles *industrial relations consultant*

Sarasota
Beck, Robert Alfred *hotel administration educator*
Fendrick, Alan Burton *retired advertising executive*
Gittelson, Bernard *public relations consultant, author, lecturer*
Honner Sutherland, B. Joan *advertising executive*
Huff, Russell Joseph *public relations and publishing executive*
Kelly, John Love *public relations executive*
Landis, Edgar David *business consultant*
Lee, Nancy Ranck *management consultant*
Mattran, Donald Albert *management consultant, educator*
Neeley, Delmar George *mediator, pastoral counselor*
Schlegel, John Frederick *management consultant, speaker, trainer*
Shulman, Arthur *communications executive*
Simon, Joseph Patrick *food services executive*
Stickler, Daniel Lee *health care management consultant*

Satellite Beach
Koenig, Harold Paul *management consultant, ecologist, evangelist, writer*

Seffner
†Seaman, Jeffrey *executive*

Stuart
Donohue, Edith M. *human resources specialist, educator*

Sunrise
Sorensen, Allan Chresten *service company executive*

Tallahassee
Cronin, Jerome Joseph, Jr., *marketing educator, consultant*
Morgante, John-Paul *human resources specialist*
Penson, Edward Martin *management consulting company executive*
Slevin, Patrick Jeremiah *media relations consultant*
†Smith, Nevin *company executive*

Tamarac
Page, Earl Michael *management specialist*

Tampa
Ferree, Patricia Ann *case management specialist and trainer*
Greenhalgh, Terry Lamont *marketing executive*
†Hevner, Alan Raymond *educator, consultant*
Highsmith, Jasper Habersham *sales executive*
Johnson, Kenneth LeRoy *airport executive*
Jones, Vaughn Paul *healthcare marketing executive*
Mangiapane, Joseph Arthur *consulting company executive, applied mechanics consultant*
Mathis, Marsha Debra *customer relations manager*
Ortinau, David Joseph *marketing specialist, educator*
†Schneider, Bradley Mark *management consultant*
West, Benjamin B. *advertising executive*

Tarpon Springs
Crismond, Linda Fry *public relations executive*

Tavares
Gross, Paul Allan *health service executive*

Titusville
†Horn, Flora Leola *retired administrative assistant*

Venice
Bluhm, Barbara Jean *communications agency executive*
Christy, Audrey Meyer *public relations consultant*
Harrington, John Vincent *retired communications company executive, engineer, educator*

Vero Beach
Binney, Jan Jarrell *publishing executive*
Fisher, Andrew *management consultant*
Hubner, Robert Wilmore *retired business machines company executive*
Leonsis, Ted *media executive*
McNamara, John J(oseph) *advertising executive, writer*
Menk, Carl William *executive search company executive*
Nesbit, Robert Grover *management consultant*
Nichols, Carl Wheeler *retired advertising agency executive*
Spivak, Alvin A. *retired public relations executive*

Wesley Chapel
Morano, Alison Berke *Internet development consultant*

West Palm Beach
Alimanestianu, Calin *retired hotel consultant*
Darter, Jeffrey Allen *data processing professional*
Lacey, John William Charles *management consultant*
Ronan, William John *management consultant*
Stauderman, Bruce Ford *writer, advertising executive*

Weston
Barnes, William Douglas *advertising executive*
Boyer, Gene T. *management consultant*

Winter Park
†Galperin, Bella L. *management consultant, educator*
Markland, Barbara Carolyn *sales and leasing professional*
Powers, Ronald George *management consultant*

GEORGIA

Alpharetta
Esher, Brian Richard *chief executive officer*
Minner, Thomas O. *marketing executive*
Troop, Paul Melvin *public relations executive, journalist*

Athens
Thomas, Howard Lamar *chef, consultant, writer*

Atlanta
Anderson, Al H., Jr., *communications executive*
†Arnold, Jeffrey *Internet company executive*
Ashley, John Bryan *software executive, management consultant*
†Balloun, James S. *service company executive*
Bennett, Dick *advertising executive*
Beres, Mary Elizabeth *management educator, organizational consultant*
†Betty, Charles Garry *communications executive*
Bradshaw, Rod Eric *personnel consultant*
Brown-Olmstead, Amanda *public relations executive*
Chartier, Kirk Lee Freund *business services executive*
Chasen, Sylvan Herbert *computer applications consultant, investment advisor*
†Christiansen, Bryan *marketing professional, consultant*
†Cohn, Bob *public relations executive*
Cooper, Thomas Luther *retired printing company executive*
Danielson, Gilbert Lawrence *consumer products company executive*
Darden, Claibourne Henry, Jr., *marketing research professional*
Darsey, James Francis *communication educator, author*
Dodson, Daniel, Jr., *advertising executive*
Dodson, Daniel, Sr., *advertising executive*
DuBose, Mary *communication and media professional, educator*
Duffey, Lee *communications company executive*
Dysart, Benjamin Clay, III, *consultant, conservationist, engineer*
Dzvonik, Michael D. *advertising executive*
†Ehrlich, Jeffrey *data processing company executive*
Eubanks, Omer Lafayette *data communications consultant, systems engineer*
Fletcher, Andy *marketing professional*
Fote, Charles T. *computer company executive*
Fuqua, John Brooks *retired consumer products and services company executive*
Goodwin, George Evans *public relations executive*
Greene, Warren *advertising executive*
Harrison, Clifford *chef, small business owner*
Hill, Donald Dee *management consultant, lecturer, writer*
Hoffman, Fred L. *human resources professional*
House, Donald Lee, Sr., *software executive, private investor, management consultant*
Johnson, Jeff *marketing professional*
Kelly, Carol White *company executive*
Kuhn, Brent *advertising executive*
Levy, Rich *advertising executive*
Lnenicka, Wade Sheridan *purchasing official, councilman*
Mahan, James S. *communications company executive*
Malhotra, Naresh Kumar *management educator*
Massey, Charles Knox, Jr., *advertising agency executive*
†McKenzie, Kay Branch *public relations executive*
Mecke, William Moyn *public affairs consultant*
Nardelli, Robert L. *consumer home products executive*
†Oliver, Thomas *hotel executive*
Pucci, Mark Leonard *public relations professional*
Quatrano, Anne *chef, restaurant owner*
Raper, Charles Albert *retired management consultant*
Reda, James Francis *business consultant*
†Robbins, James O. *communications executive*
Ryan, J. Bruce *healthcare management consulting executive*
Soderberg, Bo S. *marketing executive*
Stormont, Richard Mansfield *hotel executive*
Summerlin, Glenn Wood *retired advertising executive*
Tomaszewski, Richard Paul *market representation executive*
Verrill, F. Glenn *advertising executive*
Walker, Betsy Ellen *consulting and systems integration company executive*
White, Ronald Leon *financial management consultant*
Wilding, Diane *marketing, financial and information systems executive*
Yu-Lee, Reginald Tomas *consultant executive*

Augusta
†Dukes, Michael *consumer products company executive*

Carrollton
†Thorn, Stuart Wallace *marketing and financial executive*

Cumming
Copen, Melvyn Robert *management educator, university administrator*
Willadsen, Michael Chris *marketing professional, sales executive*

Dalton
Evans, Thomas Passmore *business and product licensing consultant*

Dawsonville
Jorgensen, Alfred H. *retired data processing executive*

Duluth
Laubscher, Robert James *consumer products company executive*
Watkins, Sydney Lynn *sales executive*

Evans
Welsh, Michael Louis *business executive*

Fairburn
Bobo, Genelle Tant (Nell Bobo) *retired office administrator*

Fayetteville
Hannum, David Lawrence *business consultant, training specialist, educator*

Gainesville
Davis, Connie Waters *public relations and marketing executive*

Griffin
Marshall, Allen Wright, III, *communications executive, financial consultant*

Lavonia
†Masterson Raines, Judith Amanda *marketing executive*

Lawrenceville
Elleby, Gail *management consultant*

Marietta
Ivey, William Hamilton *communications consultant*
Sherrington, Paul William *marketing communications executive*
Smith, Baker Armstrong *management executive, lawyer*
Spann, George William *management consultant*

Mc Rae
Brown, Mary Cathleen *retired executive secretary, poet*

Mineral Bluff
†Smiley, Ralph Neil (Ralph Smylea) *cook*

Mount Berry
Dhir, Krishna Swaroop *business administration educator*

Norcross
Cramer, James Perry *management consultant, architectural firm executive, educator*
†Goodling, Lauri Bohanan *documentation specialist*
Hunter, Douglas Lee *ministry executive, former elevator executive*
†Miller, Tonya Alicia *training and development specialist, management consultant*
Steckerl, Shally A. *executive recruiter*

Oakwood
Jondahl, Terri Elise *importing and distribution company executive*

Oxford
Stamps, George Moreland *communications consultant, facsimile pioneer*

Peachtree City
Arnold, Andrew Allen *management consultant*
Barrell, Dawn Holman *marketing specialist*

Pine Mountain
Callaway, Howard Hollis *business executive*

Roswell
Burgess, John Frank *management consultant, former utility executive, former army officer*
Johnson, Shirley Elaine *management consultant*
Jordan, DuPree, Jr., *management consultant, educator, journalist, publisher, business executive*
Strong-Tidman, Virginia Adele *marketing and advertising executive*

Saint Simons
Dressner, Paul Robert *outside sales and customer service representative*
Riedeburg, Theodore *management consultant, consultant*
Sullivan, Barbara Boyle *management consultant*

Savannah
Lindqvist, Gunnar Jan *management consultant, international trade consultant*
Otter, John Martin, III, *television advertising consultant, retired*
Schafer, Thomas Wilson *advertising agency executive*
Sheehy, Barry Maurice *management consultant*

Smyrna
Moore, Linda Kathleen *personnel agency executive*

HAWAII

Honolulu
Devenot, David Charles *human resource executive*
Dougherty, Raleigh Gordon *manufacturer representative*
†Hartley, Michael J. *online travel executive*
Kashiwa, Russell H. *communication executive*
Kelley, Richard Roy *hotel executive*
Keogh, Richard John *firearms and explosives consultant*
†Klink, Paul Leo *business executive*
Leyden, Michael Joseph, II, (Lei Jie Ming) *international business executive, educator, author*
Miyamoto, Craig Toyoki *public relations executive*

O'Neill, Charles Kelly *marketing executive, former advertising agency executive*
Smales, Fred Benson *corporate executive*
Tatibouet, Andre Stephan *condominium and resort management firm executive*
Yamato, Kei C. *international business consultant*
Yang, David Chie-Hwa *business administration educator*

Kapaau
Ralston, Joanne Smoot *public relations counseling firm executive*

Kihei
Numata, Nobuo *software company executive, consultant, engineer*

Lanai City
Keenan-Abilay, Georgia Ann *service representative*

Waipahu
Look, Pauwilo *creative media developer, architecture marketer*

IDAHO

Bellevue
Pearson, Robert Greenlees *writing services company executive*

Boise
Beaumont, Pamela Jo *marketing professional*
Ewing, Jack *communications executive*
Fiedler, John Amberg *marketing scientist*
Foster, S. Thomas, Jr., *quality management educator, consultant, writer*
Gellert, Edward Bradford *advertising agency executive*
†Lund, Victor L. *retail food company executive*
Sullivan, James Kirk *management consultant*

Idaho Falls
Gregory, Nelson Bruce *retired motel owner, retired naval officer*
†Planchon, Harry Peter, Jr., *research development manager*

Kamiah
Mills, Carol Margaret *business consultant, public relations consultant*

Ketchum
Ziebarth, Robert Charles *management consultant*

Post Falls
Grassi, James Edward *Christian ministry executive director*

ILLINOIS

Abbott Park
Hecker, Lawrence Harris *industrial hygienist*
MacMurray-Schmelter, Kristin Ann *sales and marketing professional*

Addison
Christopher, Doris K. *consumer products company executive*
McDonald, David Eugene *transportation operator*

Aledo
Prosser, Wesley Lewis *advertising and public relations executive*

Algonquin
Larsen, Mark A. *business strategy, executive coach consultant, lawyer*

Alton
Burgess, Robert Ronald *human resources executive*

Aurora
Hopp, Nancy Smith *marketing executive*
Lee, Robert Hugh *management executive*

Bannockburn
†Daube, Lorrie O. *sales executive*

Barrington
Hetzel, William Gelal *executive search consultant*
Mathis, Jack David *advertising executive, consultant*
Murphy, Robert *executive recruiter*
Ross, Frank Howard, III, *management consultant*
Stephens, Norval Blair, Jr., *marketing consultant*
Sweet, Charles Wheeler *retired executive recruiter*

Bartlett
Robinson, Lois Hart *retired public relations executive*

Batavia
Brown, Gerald Curtis *retired army officer, engineering executive*
Mann, Phillip Lynn *data processing company executive*

Belleville
Yarrington, George A. *retired public relations executive, advertising executive, writer*

Bensenville
Kolkey, Eric Samuel *customer service representative*
Mendelsohn, Zehavah Whitney *data processing executive*

Bloomingdale
Flaherty, John Joseph *quality assurance company executive*

Bloomington
Daily, Jean A. *marketing executive, spokesperson*
Walsh, William Joseph *business educator, labor arbitrator*

Broadview
Miczuga, Mark Norbert *dairy official*

Brookfield
Dornhecker, Sandra Lee *human resources executive, consultant*

Buffalo Grove
Samors, Neal *marketing executive*

Burr Ridge
Bottom, Dale Coyle *management consultant*
Zaccone, Suzanne Maria *sales executive*

Calumet City
Kovach, Joseph William *management consultant, psychologist, educator*

Carbondale
Jugenheimer, Donald Wayne *advertising and communications educator, university administrator*
Melcher, Arlyn John *management educator*

Carol Stream
Gale, Neil Jan *Internet company executive, computer scientist, consultant*

Cary
Kruper, John Gerald (Jack Kruper) *sales and marketing executive*

Champaign
Mies, John Charles *internet industry executive*
Moore, Jerry Jay *sales executive, retired archaeologist*

Chicago
Alcantara, Anita Luisa *human resources consultant*
Allen, Belle *management consulting firm executive, communications company executive*
Bacevicius, John Anthony, V, (John Bace) *research executive*
Bailey, Robert, Jr., *advertising executive*
Barry, Richard A. *public relations executive*
Becker, Robert Allen *data processing executive*
Bensinger, Peter Benjamin *consulting firm executive*
Bergstrom, Betty Howard *consulting executive, foundation administrator*
Berman, Cheryl R. *advertising company executive*
Bernatowicz, Frank Allen *management consultant, expert witness*
Beugen, Joan Beth *communications company executive*
Bishop, Mary Oltman *retired advertising executive*
Blumenthal, Joan H. *executive recruiter*
Brandt, William Arthur, Jr., *consulting executive*
Burack, Elmer Howard *management educator*
Cary, Arlene D. *retired hotel company sales executive*
Castorino, Sue *communications executive*
Chipparoni, Guy *communications company executive*
†Chorengel, Bernd *international hotel corporation executive*
Conidi, Daniel Joseph *private investigation agency executive*
Cox, Allan James *management consultant*
†Davis, William L. *publishing company executive*
Deli, Anne Tynion *marketing executive*
Doetsch, Virginia Lamb *former advertising executive, writer*
Donnelley, James Russell *printing company executive*
Echols, M(ary) Evelyn *travel consultant*
Edelman, Daniel Joseph *public relations executive*
Fisher, Eugene *marketing professional*
Fisher, Lawrence Edgar *market research executive, anthropologist*
†FitzSimons, Dennis Joseph *broadcasting executive*
†Fizdale, Richard *advertising agency executive*
Foster, James Reuben *travel company executive*
Frankel, Bernard *advertising executive*
Frazier, Anthany Vincent Earl *addictions, small business, and technology specialist*
Friedlander, Patricia Ann *marketing professional, writer*
Fullmer, Paul *public relations counselor*
†Furcon, John Edward *management and organizational consultant*
Furth, Yvonne *advertising executive*
Gardner, Howard Alan *travel company executive, writer, editor*
Gilbert, David R. *public relations executive*
Glasser, James J. *leasing company executive, retired*
Goldring, Norman Max *advertising executive*
Golin, Alvin *public relations company executive*
Gordon, Howard Lyon *advertising and marketing executive*
Green, RuthAnn *marketing and management consultant*
Haffner, Charles Christian, III, *retired printing company executive*
Hansen, Carl R. *management consultant*
†Hartman, Laura Beth Pincus *management consultant, writer, academic administrator*
†Haupt, Roger A. *advertising executive*
Hayden, Harrold Harrison *information company executive*
Hochhalter, Gordon Ray *advertising communications executive*

Hoey, Rita *public relations executive*
Hofrichter, David Alan *management consultant*
Hollander, Adrian Willoughby *accounting services company executive*
Hollis, Donald Roger *management consultant*
James-Strand, Nancy Leabhard *advertising executive*
Kipper, Barbara Levy *corporate executive*
Kobs, James Fred *direct marketing consultant*
†Koernig, Stephen K. *marketing professional, educator*
Kosinski, Richard Andrew *public relations executive*
Krivkovich, Peter George *advertising executive*
Kuczmarski, Susan Smith *management consulting company executive*
Lambert, Kirsten Schnoor *public relations executive, writer*
Lane, Kenneth Edwin *retired advertising agency executive*
Lerner, Barbara *public policy consultant, researcher, writer*
†Levine, Keith F. *marketing executive*
Lewis, Evelyn *management consultant*
Liebovich, Samuel David *retired steel executive*
Lowry, James Hamilton *management consultant*
Mack, Jim *advertising executive*
Maczulski, Margaret Louise *event marketing professional, meeting manager*
McCallister, Richard Anthony *business consulting company executive*
McConnell, E. Hoy, II, *advertising/public policy executive*
McCullough, Richard Lawrence *advertising agency executive*
Melamed, Leo *global consulting firm executive*
Menendez, Marcelino Eulogio (Marc Menendez) *marketing professional*
Mitchell, Lee Mark *communications executive, investment fund manager, lawyer*
Moster, Mary Clare *public relations executive*
Nelson, Kay Hoyle *retired communication educator*
†Oates, James G. *advertising executive*
O'Shea, Lynne Edeen *management consultant, educator*
Paul, Ronald Neale *management consultant*
Perlman, Kalman Isadore *management consultant, pharmacist*
Pincus, Theodore Henry *public relations executive*
Plank, Betsy (Mrs. Sherman V. Rosenfield) *public relations counsel*
Plotkin, Manuel D. *management consultant, educator, former corporate executive and government official*
Poe, Gertie LaVern *sales executive*
†Posner, Kathy Robin *communications executive*
Pritzker, Thomas Jay *hotel business executive*
Provus, Barbara Lee *executive search consultant*
Rabin, Joseph Harry *marketing research company executive*
Raphaelson, Joel *retired advertising agency executive*
Reid, Daniel James *public relations executive*
Reitman, Jerry Irving *advertising agency executive*
Rich, S. Judith *public relations executive*
Robbins, Henry Zane *public relations and marketing executive*
Rooney, Phillip Bernard *service company executive*
Rosenthal, Albert Jay *advertising agency executive*
Rowe, John W. *utility company executive*
Rozran, Jack Louis *courier service executive*
Schindler, Judi(th) (Judith Kay Schindler) *public relations executive, marketing consultant*
Schneider, Wesley Clair *marketing communications company executive*
Schuh, Anna Marie *human resources professional*
Seals, Theodore Hollis *public relations executive*
Seebert, Kathleen Anne *international sales and marketing executive*
Senior, Richard John Lane *textile rental service executive*
Singer, Emel *staffing industry executive*
Sive, Rebecca Anne *public affairs company executive*
Skala, Gary Dennis *management consultant*
Smith, Scott Clybourn *media company executive*
Stern, Carl William, Jr., *management consultant*
Stith, Mary Beth (Rae) *marketing professional for graphic design*
Stone, James Howard *management consultant*
Strubel, Ella Doyle *advertising and public relations executive*
Struggles, John Edward *management consultant*
Talbot, Pamela *public relations executive*
†Taylor, Collette *public relations executive*
Thompson, Jayne Carr *public relations and communications executive, lawyer*
Thompson, Kenneth Roy *management educator*
Tripp, Marian Barlow Loofe *retired public relations company executive*
Tyson, Kirk W. M. *management consultant*
Vandame, Jean-Marie Richard *management consultant*
Van Den Hende, Fred J(oseph) *human resources executive*
Varchetta, Felix R. *advertising executive*
Weaver, Donna Rae *company executive*
Westcott, Robert Frederick *consultant*
Williams, Mark H. *marketing communications executive*
†Winninghoff, Albert C. M. *advertising company executive*
Wolf, Linda S. *advertising executive*
Wooldridge, Patrice Marie *marketing professional, martial arts and meditation educator*
Zonka, Constance Zipprodt *public relations executive, marketing professional*

Collinsville
Barnum, Mel Bloyce *company executive*

Crete
Langer, Steven *human resources management consultant and industrial psychologist*

Darien
Friedrich, Charles William *corporate executive*

Decatur
Blake, William Henry *credit and public relations consultant*

Deerfield
Eastham, Dennis Michael *advertising executive*
Gater, Chris *advertising executive*
Huff, Gayle Compton *advertising and marketing executive*

Dekalb
Stoia, Dennis Vasile *industrial management educator*

Des Plaines
Cronin, Kathleen Anne *executive search consultant*
†Gochnauer, Richard Wallis *consumer products company executive*
†Santisteban, Joseph Henry *personnel director*

Downers Grove
Beres, Michael John *plant engineer*
Bielefeldt, Catherine C. *sales executive*
Clement, Paul Platts, Jr., *performance technologist, educator*
†Soenen, Michael J. *flower company executive*
Ward, Jonathan P. *service company executive*

Edwardsville
Dietrich, Suzanne Claire *instructional designer, communications consultant*

Elburn
Hansen, H. Jack *management consultant*

Elgin
Rogers, Carleton Carson, Jr., *trade show and convention executive*

Elk Grove Village
Teesdale, Randall Lee *consumer products company executive*

Elmhurst
Choyke, Phyllis May Ford (Mrs. Arthur Davis Choyke Jr.) *management executive, editor, poet*

Evanston
Blair, Virginia Ann *public relations executive*
Gladden, Robert Wiley *corporate executive*
Keith, Thomas Warren, Jr., *marketing executive*
†Neuschel, Robert Percy *management consultant, educator*
Rounds, George R. *executive coach, organization consultant*
Tornabene, Russell C. *communications executive*
Twaddell, Sophia Hantzes *communications executive*

Flossmoor
Crum, James Francis *waste recycling company executive*

Frankfort
Feeney, Kelly Lynn *management consultant*

Freeport
†Galli, Joseph, Jr., *consumer products company executive*

Galesburg
Conway, Lowava Denise *data processing administrator*

Geneseo
Crisp, Sandra Sue *procurement analyst*

Geneva
Carella, J(oseph) Dino *printing company executive*
Montgomery, Joel Robert *communications executive, consultant*
Xagas, Steven George James *diversified employment services firm executive*

Glen Ellyn
†Conti, Paul Louis *management consulting company executive*
Parkhurst, Edwin Wallace, Jr., *healthcare management consultant*
Taylor, Robert Rowe *communications executive, consultant*

Glencoe
Cole, Kathleen Ann *advertising agency executive, retired social worker*
Isaacs, Roger David *public relations executive*
Niefeld, Jaye Sutter *advertising executive*

Glenview
Franklin, Lynne *business communications consultant, writer*
Kaplan, Steven M. *advertising executive*

Groveland
Taylor, Kathy Deanne *marketing executive*

Gurnee
†Schoenfeld, Howard Allen *management consultant, lawyer*

Hanover Park
Carter, Eleanor Elizabeth *business manager*

Hawthorn Woods
Johnson, Samira El-Chehabi *marketing professional*

Highland Park
Axelrod, Leah Joy *tour company executive*
Bakalar, John Stephen *printing and publishing company executive*
Burman, Diane Berger *career management and organization development consultant*
Cohen, Burton David *franchising executive, lawyer*
Harris, Thomas L. *public relations executive*
Herbert, Edward Franklin *public relations executive*

Hinsdale
Carlini, James *management consultant*
Whitney, William Elliot, Jr., *advertising agency executive*

Hoffman Estates
Crook, Stephen Richard *sales and marketing management consultant*
Marino, Nancy A. *marketing professional*
†Martinez, Arthur C. *retail company executive*

Homer Glen
Garr, Daniel Frank *restaurateur*

Hudson
Mills, Lois Jean *company executive, former legislative aide, former education educator*

Itasca
Silver, Marc Laurence *sales and marketing executive*

Joliet
Starner, Barbara Kazmark *marketing, advertising and export sales executive*

Kenilworth
Steingraber, Frederick George *management consultant*

Lake Bluff
Fryburger, Vernon Ray, Jr., *advertising and marketing educator*
Griem, John Michael *management consultant*

Lake Forest
Bradley, Kim Alexandra *sales and marketing specialist*
†Brewer, Paul Huie *advertising executive, artist, portrait painter*
Carter, Donald Patton *advertising executive*
Chieger, Kathryn Jean *recreation company executive*
Crawford, Robert W., Jr., *furniture rental company executive*
Davidson, Richard Alan *data communications company executive*
Fromm, Henry Gordon *retired manufacturing and marketing executive*
Goldstein, Marsha Feder *tour company executive*
Johnson, Richard Darrell *management consultant*
Kenly, Granger Farwell *marketing consultant, college official*
Mitchell, Richard Charles *human resources specialist*
Mohr, Roger John *advertising agency executive*
Rand, Kathy Sue *public relations executive*
†Stecko, Paul T. *packaging company executive*

Lansing
Kaplan, Huette Myra *business educator, training consultant*

Libertyville
Devine, Barbara Armstrong *risk manager*
†Jenniges, Nathaniel John *marketing professional*

Lincolnshire
†Gifford, Dale L. *human resources executive*
Hebda, Lawrence John *data processing executive, consultant*

Lincolnwood
Donovan, John Vincent *consulting company executive*
†Epstein, Ben Irving *management consultant*
Grant, Paul Bernard *industrial relations educator, arbitrator*
Lebedow, Aaron Louis *consulting company executive*

Lisle
Skweres, Thomas W. *advertising executive, writer*
Sohl, Raymond, Jr., *video company executive*

Litchfield
Talley, Hayward Leroy *communications executive*

Marion
†Pearce, Lucinda Jane *management consultant*

Melrose Park
Bernick, Carol Lavin *corporate executive*

Mount Prospect
Gerlitz, Curtis Neal *business executive*
Pulsifer, Edgar Darling *leasing service and sales executive*

Mundelein
Meehan, Jean Marie Ross *human resources, occupational health and safety management consultant*

Naperville
Fritz, Roger Jay *management consultant*
Fuhrer, Larry *management consultant, management educator, finance company executive*
Koch, William Joseph *public relations executive*
Modery, Richard Gillman *marketing and sales executive*
Wallace, Guy William *management consultant*

Niles
Beton, John Allen *communications company executive*
Weisbach, Lou *advertising executive*

North Aurora
Hoover, Lola Mae *retired communications company executive*

Northbrook
Clarey, John Robert *executive search consultant*
Di Spigno, Guy Joseph *international management consultant, industrial psychologist*
†Dordek, Alan Eugene *marketing executive*
Eman Delmar, Evelyn (Evelyn Eman Delmar) *communications executive*
Marshall, Irl Houston, Jr., *franchise consultant*
Moser, Larry Edward *marketing professional*
Ross, Debra Benita *jewelry designer, marketing executive*
Sudbrink, Jane Marie *sales and marketing executive*
Wajer, Ronald Edward *management consultant*

Northfield
Heise, Marilyn Beardsley *public relations company executive*
Sawers, Peter Ritchie *management consultant, educator, retired*

Oak Brook
Camp, Jeffery Mark *Web specialist, military officer*
DeLorey, John Alfred *printing company executive*
Higgens, William John, III, (Trey Higgens) *sales executive*
Nelson, Robert Eddinger *management and development consultant*
†Quinlan, Michael Robert *fast food franchise company executive*
Turner, Fred L. *fast food company executive*

Oak Lawn
Lehman, George Morgan *food sales executive*

Oak Park
Andre, L. Aumund *management consultant*
Burke, Thomas John *communications executive*
Cannon, Patrick Francis *public relations executive*
Devereux, Timothy Edward *advertising executive*

Oakbrook Terrace
†Hegenderfer, Jonita Susan *public relations executive*

Oswego
Weilert, Ronald Lee *data processing executive*

Palatine
Medin, Lowell Ansgard *management executive*
Murphy, Colleen Frances *marketing professional, public relations executive*
Ramunno, Thomas Paul *management consultant*

Park Forest
Orr, Marcia *child development researcher, child care consultant*

Park Ridge
Dickieson, Richard Mark *travel company executive*
Mahaffey, John Christopher *association executive*
†Williams, Sandra Lynn *management consultant*

Peoria
Buchko, Aaron Anthony *management educator*

Prospect Heights
Lynch, William Thomas, Jr., *advertising agency executive*

Quincy
Adams, Beejay (Meredith Elisabeth Jane Adams) *sales executive*

River Forest
Hamper, Robert Joseph *marketing executive*

Riverwoods
Del Tiempo, Sandra Kay *sales executive*

Rockford
Anderson, Max Elliot *television and film production company executive*
†GeRue, Gerald G. *management consultant*
†Lafever, Francis J. *retired sales executive*

Rolling Meadows
Cain, R. Wayne *sales, finance and leasing company executive*

Rosemont
Ames, Sandra Patience *sales executive*
Small, Richard Donald *travel company executive*

Saint Charles
†Benjamin, Lawrence *food service executive*
Frank, Ruby Merinda *employment agency executive*
Griffin, Sheila MB *strategic marketing exceutive*

Schaumburg
Fiore, Colleen Mary *meeting manager*
Hill, Raymond Joseph *packaging company executive*
Stabej, Rudolph John *computer consultant*

Skokie
Gershon, William I. *marketing and communications executive, writer, voiceover actor*
Whalen, Patricia Therese *marketing and public relations educator, consultant*

Springfield
Clark, Thomas Allen *planning and evaluation consultant*
Stroh, Raymond Eugene *retired personnel executive*
Weinhoeft, John Joseph *data processing executive*
Whitaker, Victoria Manuela Katz *publisher, public relations executive, educator, consultant*

Sycamore
Dennis, Peter Ray *environmental corporate executive*

Urbana
Rotzoll, Kim Brewer *advertising and communications educator*

Vernon Hills
Claassen, W(alter) Marshall *employment company executive*
†Edwardson, John Albert *security firm executive*
†Krasny, Michael P. *computer company executive*
Powers, Anthony Richard, Jr., *educational sales professional*

West Dundee
Woltz, Kenneth Allen *consulting executive*

Westchester
Faulkner, Robert Lloyd *advertising executive, graphic designer*

Western Springs
Frommelt, Jeffrey James *management consulting firm executive*
Reggio, Vito Anthony *management consultant*

Wheaton
Brackett, Robert Clark *business valuation specialist*
Long, Charles Franklin *retired corporate communications executive*
Mellott, Robert Vernon *retired advertising executive*

Willowbrook
Foley, Joseph Lawrence *sales executive*
Mathisen-Reid, Rhoda Sharon *international communications consultant*

Winnetka
Hermann, Edward Robert *health engineer, educator, writer, consultant, hygieologist*
Kahn, Paul Frederick *executive search company executive*
Thomas, John Thieme *management consultant*

Wood Dale
Sorensen, Jimmy Louis *management consultant*

Woodstock
Andel, Mark *communications specialist, educator*

INDIANA

Auburn
Kempf, Jane Elmira *marketing executive*

Bloomington
†Hanks, Lawrence Julius, Sr., *management consultant, researcher*
Patterson, James Milton *marketing specialist, educator*

Carmel
Fadely, James Philip *educator, writer*
Mahoney, Margaret Ellis *administrative assistant*

Columbus
Hicks, Gregory Steven *marketing professional*
Szczurek, Thomas Eugene *business executive*
Tucker, Thomas Randall *public relations executive*

Corydon
†Walker, James Harper *retired security firm executive, writer*

Evansville
Zion, Roger Herschel *consulting firm executive, former congressman*

Fort Wayne
Bingi, Prasad *management and marketing educator, consultant*
Coffman, Matthew Thomas *marketing executive, land use planner*
Collins, Linda Lou Powell *manager of contracts*
Schweickart, Jim *advertising executive, broadcast consultant*
Taritas, Karen Joyce *customer service administrator*

Greenwood
Du Bois, William, Jr., *retired public relations professional*
Saint-Pierre, Michael Robert *funeral director, consultant*

Indianapolis
Baker, Marti A(nn) *privacy and compliance consultant*
Barrett, Thomas Joseph *sales executive, computer systems consultant*
Clary, Keith Uhl *retired employee relations executive*
Gilman, Alan B. *restaurant company executive*
Goldstein, Paul Robert *management company executive, consultant*
Harden, Mary Louise *human resources consultant, real estate agent, real estate appraiser*

Kirkpatrick, Robert Hugh *communications executive*
†Liu, Ben Shaw-Ching *marketing professional, educator*
MacDonald, Gary Bruce *communications executive*
May, Linda *delivery business owner*
†Nyhart, Eldon Howard *employee benefits consultant, lawyer*
Quiring, Patti Lee *human resource consulting company executive*
Rati, Robert Dean *data processing executive*
Ruben, Gary A. *marketing and communications consultant*
Santini, Gino *marketing professional*
Sherman, John Judson *public relations executive, writer*
Slaymaker, Gene Arthur *public relations executive*
Smith, Carson Clay *business executive*

Liberty
Pringle, Lewis Gordon *marketing professional, educator*

Michigan City
Pecze, David Emery *marketing professional*
Sherman, Thomas Webster, Jr., *environmental company executive*

Monroeville
Ray, Annette D. *business executive*

Muncie
Barber, Earl Eugene *consulting firm executive*
Kuratko, Donald F. *entrepreneur, educator, consultant*
Norris, Tracy Hopkins *retired public relations executive*

Nappanee
Miller, Philip William *sales executive*

Nashville
Rogers, Frank Andrew *restaurant and hotel executive*

Noblesville
†Bill, Daniel Joseph *executive planning consultant*

Notre Dame
Conlon, Edward J. *management educator*

Santa Claus
Edwards, James Dallas, III, *consulting company executive*

Schererville
Hendricks, Stanley Marshall, II, *executive recruiter, consultant*

South Bend
Anderson, Carolyn Joyce *business development executive*
Brennen, William Elbert *management consultant*

Valparaiso
Schlender, William Elmer *management sciences educator*

Wabash
Scales, Richard Lewis *retired sales representative*

Warsaw
Holbrook, Stephen Eugene *printing executive*

West Lafayette
Fishman, Brian S. *research analyst*
Schendel, Dan Eldon *management consultant, business educator*

IOWA

Ames
Bonomi, Ferne Gater *public relations executive*

Ankeny
Lynn, Robert William *strategic planning consultant*
Rivers, Donald Lee *marketing professional*

Bettendorf
Collins, Kathleen Elizabeth *pharmaceutical company official*

Cedar Falls
†Rawwas, Mohammed Yahya *marketing professional, educator*

Cedar Rapids
Baldwin, Cynthia Ann *industrial hygienist*
Stolte, Larry Gene *marketing executive, former computer and publishing company executive*
Vanderpool, Ward Melvin *management and marketing consultant*
Wiese, Daniel Edward *marketing and communications researcher*

Cherokee
Simonsen, Robert Alan *marketing executive*

Des Moines
Bamford, Carol Marie *marketing executive*

Fairfield
Kelly, Thomas *advertising executive*

George
Symens, Maxine Brinkert Tanner *marketing professional*

Kellogg
Anderson, Dale C. *state agency professional, travel consultant*

Keota
Carmichael, Richard Ardean *marketing professional*

Toddville
Robertson, Florence Winkler *advertising and public relations agency executive*

West Des Moines
Marshall, Russell Frank *consulting company executive*

Williamsburg
Hogan, John Paul *consumer products company executive*

KANSAS

Colby
Baldwin, Irene S. *corporate executive, real estate investor*

Edwardsville
Morgan, Stephen R. *land surveyor*

Hays
†Billinger, Wayne Michael *creative director*

Junction City
Werts, Merrill Harmon *retired management consultant*

Kansas City
†Coker, John Michael *quality assurance professional*
Olofson, Tom William *computer executive*

Lawrence
Burke, Paul E., Jr., *governmental relations consultant*
Mackenzie, Kenneth Donald *management consultant, educator*

Leawood
†Joslin, Janine Elizabeth *preservation consultant*

Lenexa
Ramsey, John Talton *sales executive*

Manhattan
Jackson, William Lawrence (Larry Jackson) *radio station executive*

Mission
Alexander, Anne A. *sales consultant*

Overbrook
Dale, Kenneth Ray *computer executive*

Overland Park
Molz, Philip Jack *management consultant*
Voska, Kathryn Caples *consultant, facilitator*

Salina
Ryan, Stephen Collister *funeral director*

Shawnee Mission
Hanson, Patti Lynn *human resources specialist*
Mealman, Glenn *corporate marketing executive*
Mooney, Justin David *motel executive, consultant*
Putman, Dale Cornelius *management consultant, lawyer*

Topeka
Franklin, Benjamin Barnum *dinner club executive*

Wichita
Herr, Peter Helmut Friederich *sales executive*
Jesseph, Linda *process analyst*
Lerman, Kenneth Barry *marketing professional, consultant*
Menefee, Frederick Lewis *advertising executive*

Winfield
Dolsen, David Horton *mortician*

KENTUCKY

Albany
†Smith, Eugenia Sewell *funeral home executive*

Ashland
Barber, Phillip Robert, III, *communications executive*
Carter, David Edward *communications executive, director*

Bowling Green
†Garrison, Geneva *retired administrative-assistant*

Crestwood
†Snow, Edwin Fawcett *management consultant*

Florence
Gorman, Gayla Marlene Osborne *consumer affairs executive*

Franklin
Herndon, Wallace Eugene, Jr., *human resources manager*

Hopkinsville
Neville, Thomas Lee *food service company executive*

Lexington
Charley, Nancy Jean *communications professional*
†Curlander, Paul Joseph *computer company executive*
Millard, James Kemper *marketing executive*
Miller, Jill Thompson *sales support*

Rogers, Tina Karen Profitt *administrative assistant, writer*

Louisville
Columbus, Shanna S. *advertising executive*
Doran, Vincent Francis *economic development executive*
Fiedler, Hans Karl *network analyst, consultant*
Fullenlove, Carmen Millay (Kit Fullenlove) *public relations executive*
Huber, Lisa Ann Mari Brones *public relations executive*
Lumley, Thomas Dewey *travel professional, real estate investor*
McKinney, Owen Michael *retired security executive, consultant*
Novak, David C. *restaurant company executive*
Peden, Katherine Graham *industrial consultant*
Power, David M. *advertising executive*
Power, Michael L. *advertising executive*
Sutton, John Schuhmann, Jr., *retired purchasing consultant*
†Wagner, James Miller *funeral director*
Wesley, Stephen Burton *training professional*

Pikeville
Justice, Phillip Howard *marketing professional*

Richmond
Whitt, Marcus Calvin *marketing and public relations executive*

LOUISIANA

Baton Rouge
†Callicoatte, Troy D. *loss control consultant*
Crusemann, F(rederick) Ross *advertising agency official*
East, Charles E., Jr., *advertising and public relations executive*
Finney, Clifton Donald *publishing executive*
Kimball, Dorothy Jean *foundation executive*

Hammond
Richardson, Thaddeus Maurice *funeral director*

Lafayette
Sides, Larry Eugene *advertising executive*

Lake Charles
Premeaux, Shane Richard *marketing educator*

Many
Dutton, Frank Elroy *data processing executive, writer*

Metairie
Doody, Barbara Pettett *computer specialist*
Gereighty, Andrea Saunders *polling company executive, poet*
Grimm, John Lloyd *business executive, marketing strategist*
†Morcos, Ann Conti *Internet company executive, writer*

Monroe
Williamson, Stanley G. *management consultant, educator*

New Orleans
Bacot, Marie *management consultant, researcher*
Barden, Janice Kindler *personnel company executive*
Cook, Victor Joseph, Jr., *marketing educator, consultant*
Crumley, Martha Ann *company executive*
†Davis, Pamela Marie *administrative analyst*
†Fertel, Ruth U. *restaurant owner*
†Matthews, Brenda J. *human resources specialist*
†McPhail, Tory *chef*
Menutis, Jamie *training services executive, writer*
†Sonnier, Greg *chef*
Tahir, Mary Elizabeth (Liz Tahir) *marketing professional, consultant, speaker, writer*
Williams, Ronald David *telecommunications executive*

Ruston
Hudnall, Jarrett, Jr., *management and marketing educator*

Shreveport
Wright, Marie Beulah Battey *retired advertising executive*

MAINE

Augusta
Jacobson, James Lamma, Jr., *data processing company executive*
Roberts, Donald Albert *advertising, public relations, marketing and media consultant*

Bar Harbor
Woods, Bryant Prentice *national park ranger*

Brooklin
Schmidt, Klaus Dieter *management consultant, university administrator, marketing and management educator*

Center Lovell
Adams, Herbert Ryan *mediation consultant, retired clergyman, educator, publishing executive*

Ellsworth
Becker, Ray Everett *management consultant*

Falmouth
Kendrick, Peter Murray *communications executive, investor*

Hartland
Larochelle, Richard C. *tanning company executive*

Hollis Center
Kaake, Norman Bradford *quality assurance professional*

Kennebunkport
Entorf, Richard Carl *retired management consultant*

Nobleboro
Birkett, James Davis *management consultant*

Portland
Becker, Seymour *hazardous materials and wastes specialist*
Burgess, Meredith Nancy Strang *advertising agency executive*
Rogers, Richard Mead *food service executive*

South Portland
Fetteroll, Eugene Carl, Jr., *human resources professional*

Sumner
Rudd, David William *management consultant, engineer, consultant*

Westbrook
Lee, Shepard *automobile dealership owner*

Whitefield
Marden, Kenneth Allen *advertising executive*

MARYLAND

Annapolis
†Branand, Claire Diane *advertising executive, writer*
Cann, Nancy Timanus *retail yacht sales executive*
Carman, Anne *management consultant*
Crosby, Ralph Wolf *communications executive*
DiPentima, Renato Anthony *systems executive*
Jefferson, Ralph Harvey *international affairs consultant*
Ross, Thomas Hugh *business consultant, retired military officer*

Baldwin
Decker, James Ludlow *management consultant*

Baltimore
Digges, Edward S(imms) *business management consultant*
Dishon, Cramer Steven *sales executive*
Dodge, Calvert Renaul *education and training executive, author, educator*
Edlund, Timothy Wendell *management educator, consultant, researcher*
Eisner, Henry Wolfgang *advertising agency executive*
†Fried, Herbert Daniel *advertising executive*
Hillman, Sandra Schwartz *public relations executive, marketing professional*
Howes, James Guerdon *communications company executive*
Hug, Richard Ernest *environmental company executive*
Kim, Lillian G. Lee *retired administrative assistant*
Laric, Michael Victor *management and marketing administrator*
Lowenthal, Henry *retired greeting card company executive*
Passano, E. Magruder, Jr., *strategic planning consultant*
Patnode, Gerald Rufus *marketing professional*
Pollard, Shirley *employment training director, community services administrator, consultant*
Roland, Donald Edward *advertising executive*
†Rolland, Donald F. *printing company executive*
Shaper, Christopher Thorne *sales executive*
Talbot, Donald Roy *consulting services executive*
Wolfe, John Thomas *quality assurance professional*

Beltsville
Miller, Ted Robert *policy analyst*
Quirk, Frank Joseph *management consulting company executive*
†Ritz, David M. *photographic retail company executive*
Sickles, Carlton Ralph *employee benefit consultant*

Bethesda
Cody, Thomas Gerald *management consultant, writer*
Cutting, Mary Dorothea *audio and audio-visual communications company executive*
Deane, Leon *retired company executive*
Deutsch, Stanley *consulting company executive, behavioral scientist*
Durek, Thomas Andrew *computer company executive*
Estrin, Melvyn J. *computer products company executive*
Goldschmidt, Peter Graham *physician executive, business development consultant*
Johnson, Eugene Clare *data processing company executive*
McClure, Brooks *management consultant*
Mc Gurn, Barrett *communications executive, writer*
Miller, Judith Wolfe Cohen *consultant*
†Nassetta, Christopher J. *hotel facility executive*
Patterson, Bradley Hawkes *executive*
Robinson, Michael Waring *public relations executive, writer*
Rourke, Bradley Kevin *public affairs executive*
Shellow, Robert *management service company executive, consultant*

Southwick, Paul *retired public relations executive*
†Swartz, Gordon *management consultant*
Terragno, Paul James *information industry executive*
Timenes, Nicolai *policy analyst*
Van Cott, Harold Porter *human factors professional*
†Wool, Jennifer S. *marketing professional*

Bowie
Winegardner, Karen Elizabeth *management consultant*

Bozman
Wyatt, Wilson Watkins, Jr., *management and public relations executive, writer*

Brooklandville
Miller, Paul George *computer company executive*

Cambridge
Spahr, Elizabeth *business executive*

Chesapeake Beach
Felter, Brian Albert *sales executive*

Chestertown
Docksteader, Karen Kemp *marketing professional*
Schreiber, Harry, Jr., *management consultant*

Chevy Chase
Ashe, Aaron Matthew *sales professional*
Baruch, Jordan Jay *management consultant, consultant*
Blaunstein, Phyllis Reid *communications and marketing executive*
Broide, Mace Irwin *retired public affairs consultant*
Greene, Edward Allen *retired public affairs executive*
Greenspoon, Irma Naiman *business executive*
Michaelis, Michael *management and technical consultant*

Cockeysville Hunt Valley
Donaho, John Albert *consultant*
Rallo, James Gilbert *management company executive*
Shepard, George Leo *sales and marketing executive, consultant*
Somerville, Warren Thomas, II, *management consultant*
Whitehurst, William Wilfred, Jr., *management consultant*

College Park
Frank, Howard *systems company executive, dean, educator*

Columbia
Go, Howard Tiang *management consulting firm executive, educator*
Madison, Anne Conway *public relations and marketing professional*
Morice, William Daniel *business and tax counselor*
Singerman, Phillip A. *corporate executive*

Easton
†U'Ren, Marie Rita *travel company executive, pre-school educator*

Elkton
Jasinski-Caldwell, Mary L. *company executive*

Ellicott City
Gleaves, Leon Rogers *marketing and sales executive*
Tucci, Albert William *retired human resources executive, consultant*

Forest Hill
McIntosh, L(orne) William *marketing executive*

Fort Washington
Bradley, Melvin LeRoy *communications company executive*

Frederick
Boyle, Lisa C. *marketing and communications executive*
†Hughes, David Robert *gaming company executive*

Gaithersburg
Carey, John Edward *information services executive*
Flickinger, Harry Harner *organization and business executive, management consultant*
Isbister, James David *pharmaceutical business executive*
†Landel, Michel *food service and management company executive*
Wohl, Ronald H. *management consultant, writing and editorial expert*

Glen Arm
Lotz, George Michael *retired computer graphics executive, graphic designer, photographer*

Greenbelt
Beach, Linda Marie *total quality management professional*
†Fontaine, Kathleen Sturey *human resources specialist*

Gunpowder
Stevens, Jill Winifred *project expediter*

Hagerstown
Jacques, Joseph Howard *human resources professional*

Jessup
Fox, Dawne Marie *safety scientist*

Kensington
Hum, Vance York *technology consulting executive*

Lanham
Fields, Stuart Howard *labor relations specialist*

Lanham Seabrook
Barnes, Margaret Anderson *business consultant*

Leonardtown
Carney, Daniel L. *program and financial management consultant*

Lutherville Timonium
Sackett, Joyce Wilhelmina *hospitality coordinator*

Marydel
Neil, Fred Applestein *public relations executive*

Mitchellville
Akridge, Paul Bai *business consultant*

Mount Airy
†Scott, Leighton Reeves *marketing professional*

Myersville
Patrick, Georgia O'Brien Lakaytis *communications executive*

Oakland
Cavarocchi, Nicholas Guy *public relations executive*

Owings Mills
Perkins, Tammy Jean *title coordinator*

Pocomoke
Hickman, John Norwood *marketing professional*

Potomac
Brashear, Jerry Paul *management consultant*
Brown, Earle Palmer *advertising agency executive*
Fink, Daniel Julien *management consultant*
Foley, Joseph Patrick *public relations executive*
Medin, A. Louis *computer company executive*
Orski, C. Kenneth *consulting company executive, lawyer, publisher*
Owen, Harrison Hollingsworth *management consultant*
Rhode, Alfred Shimon *business consultant, finance educator*
†Shirvinski, Adam John *management consultant*

Reisterstown
Daley, Peter Edmund *business and human resources company executive*

Riverdale
Bernard, Cathy S. *management corporation executive*
Gonzalez Arias, Victor Hugo *management executive*

Rockville
Chaney, Bradford William *educational research consultant*
Hanes, Donald Keith *cooperative communications executive*
MacArthur, Diana Taylor *advanced technology executive*
Smith, Mark Alan *management consultant*
Ward, Neil Anthony *corporate communications specialist*
†Watson, Jerome Roland *marketing professional, researcher*

Salisbury
Newton, Darrell Mottley *communication educator*

Severna Park
Elliott, Kati Marie *communications company official*
†Humphreys Troy, Patricia *communications executive*

Shady Side
†Devine, Donald J. *management and political consultant*

Silver Spring
†Altschul, B J *public relations counselor*
Burke, Margaret Ann *computer and communications company specialist*
Compton, Mary Beatrice Brown (Mrs. Ralph Theodore Compton) *public relations executive, writer*
Cunningham, Keith Allen, II, *computer services company executive*
Fields, Daisy Bresley *human resources specialist, writer*
Hubbell, Katherine Jean *retired marketing professional*
Kenner, Mary Ellen *marketing and communications executive*
Kolodny, Debra Ruth *labor management and non-profit consultant*
†Ledsinger, Charles A. *hotel executive*
Lett, Cynthia Ellen Wein *speaker, trainer, coach*
McCann, Michael F. *industrial hygienist*
Moreno, Donna Marie *communications executive*
Perlmutter, Jerome Herbert *communications specialist*
Raphael, Coleman *business consultant*
Saunders, George Wendell *management consultant, retired government official*
Shih-Carducci, Joan Chia-mo *cooking educator, biochemist, medical technologist, author*

Sparks
Smith, Rodney Russell *operations executive*

Springdale
†Rucker, Michelle Renee *human resources specialist*

Sudlersville
Covington, Donald Kingsley, Jr., *plywood sales executive*

Sykesville
Leizear, Charles William *retired information services executive*

Taneytown
Morrow, Lee *communications executive*

Upper Marlboro
Symlar, Jesse Lee *executive*

Waldorf
Stokely, Mary Curry *marketing specialist*

West Bethesda
Vogelgesang, Sandra Louise *business executive, writer*

West River
Bower, Catherine Downes *communications, management consultant*
Pratt, Katherine Merrick *environmental consulting company executive*

White Hall
Buhite, Thomas Jesse, Sr., *employee benefits consultant*

MASSACHUSETTS

Andover
Hasegawa, Tomohiro *marketing manager*
†Wetherell, David S. *communications executive*

Arlington
Feinleib, Sidney *technology company business executive*

Ayer
Bloom, Edwin John, Jr., *retired human resources consultant*

Bedford
Daltas, Arthur John *management consultant, software services manager*
Wacker-Brawley, Margaret *communications executive*
Webber, Howard Rodney *computer company executive*

Belchertown
Burstein, Michael Clifford *management consultant*
Marsh, Brian Richard *management executive, playwright, educator, clergyman*

Belmont
Bingham, George Walter Chandler *retired sales executive*
Klein, Martin Samuel *management consulting executive*
†Rowe, Richard R. *on-line information and management services company executive*

Beverly
Barger, Richard Wilson *hotel executive*
McMahon, Joyce Arlene *public relations professional*

Bolton
Leighton, Charles Milton *retired specialty consumer products executive*

Boston
Andrews, Kenneth Richmond *business administration educator*
†Arnold, David John *marketing educator, consultant*
Bang, Jens *communications company executive*
Bell, Gregory Knox *management consultant*
Berger, Jerome Morris *communications executive*
†Bertino, Fred *advertising executive*
†Biro, Kathy *advertising executive*
Brodeur, John *public relations executive*
†Bronner, Michael *advertising executive*
Buchin, Stanley Ira *management consultant, finance educator*
Burnham, David Henderson *management consultant*
Carney, Andrea *public relations executive*
Clarke, Terence Michael *public relations and advertising executive*
Coletta, Gerard Charles *management consultant*
Cone, Carol Lynn *public relations executive*
†Connors, Jack, Jr., *advertising executive*
†Connors, John Michael, Jr., *advertising agency executive*
Cutter, Curtis Carly *consulting company executive*
Dowd, Peter Jerome *public relations executive*
†Emerson, Richard B. *marketing company executive*
Eskandarian, Edward *advertising agency executive*
Farrar, Constance Mosher *marketing executive*
Fishbein, Michael Ellis *technical director*
†Gibson, Cathy *administrative assistant*
†Guenther, William H. *management consultant*
Hayes, Andrew Wallace, II, *consumer products company executive*
Hickey, Elizabeth Louise *advertising agency executive*
Hunter, Durant Adams *executive search company executive*
Hurd, J. Nicholas *executive recruiting consultant, former banker*
Judson, Arnold Sidney *management consultant*

PROFESSIONAL INDEX 6495 INDUSTRY: SERVICE

Kaplan, Steven F. *business management executive*
†Kelly, Francis J., III, *global marketing company president and COO*
†Kenny, David *internet professional services executive*
Kilts, James M. *consumer products company executive*
†Lawner, Ron *advertising executive*
†Lawson, Thomas Elsworth *advertising agency executive*
Lazarus, Shelly *advertising executive*
Levy, Stephen Raymond *high technology company executive*
Luongo, C. Paul *public relations executive*
†McGovern, Patrick J. *communications executive*
Michels, William Charles *management consultant*
Pierson, Edward Joseph, Jr., *business executive*
Rimpel, Auguste Eugene, Jr., *management and technical consulting executive*
Rosen, David Michael *public relations administrator, public affairs consultant*
†Roston, Arnold *information specialist, educator, advertising executive, artist, editor*
Saunders, Donald Leslie *hotel owner, real estate investor*
Schneider, Joan *public relations company owner*
Shapiro, Eli *business consultant, educator, economist*
Stybel, Laurence James *business executive*
Tarantino, Louis Gerald *business executive, consultant, lawyer*
Tyszkowski, Robert *business executive*
Van Ranst, Alfred F. *information technology security consultant*
Weber, Larry *public relations executive*
Wu, Guofa Felix *computer company executive*
†Zhu, Guorong *management consultant, researcher*

Brewster
Hillis-Dineen, Madalyn *marketing professional, astrologer, writer*

Brockton
Irving, Robert Churchill *retired quality assurance professional, manufacturing company executive*

Burlington
Coffin, George Jarvis, III, *advertising executive*
McWade, Jessica Christy *marketing professional*

Cambridge
†Adams, Ruth-Anne *chef*
Aspinall, Mara Glickman *marketing and general management professional*
Bloom, Kathryn Ruth *public relations executive*
Brynjolfsson, Erik *management educator, researcher*
Forrester, Jay Wright *management specialist, educator*
†Kim, Jin Gyo *management educator*
Knickrehm, Glenn Allen *management executive*
Malone, Thomas W. *management educator, researcher*
McBride, Robert Albert *training services executive*
Paicopolos, Ernest Michael *public opinion research company executive*
Rowley, Geoffrey Herbert *management consultant*
Shine, Daniel Joseph, Jr., *management consultant*

Centerville
†Shapiro, Harvey *journalist, writer, lyricist*

Chatham
Escalante, Judson Robert *business consultant*

Chelmsford
Fulks, Robert Grady *computer executive*
Sintros, James Lee *management consultant, foundation executive*

Chelsea
†Kaneb, John A. *corporate executive*

Chestnut Hill
Addis, Deborah Jane *management consultant, editor*
Ayas, Karen *management consultant, educator*
Bartunek, Jean Marie *management consultant, educator*
O'Block, Robert Paul *management consultant*

Concord
Eberle, William Denman *international management consultant*
†Farber, Kenneth Lawrence Meyers *management consultant*
Ghosh, Partha S. *management consultant*
Rarich, Anne Lippitt *management and organizational development consultant*
Two Feathers, Morwen *event coordinating company executive*

Danvers
Wilkes, Brent Ames *management consultant*

Dedham
Magner, Jerome Allen *entertainment company executive*
Redstone, Sumner Murray *entertainment company executive, lawyer*

Dennis
Weilbacher, William Manning *advertising and marketing consultant*

Dover
Bonis, Laszlo Joseph *business executive, scientist*
Mehta, Narinder Kumar *marketing executive*
Walker, Laurence Gordon *technology company executive*

Dudley
Boote, Alfred Shepard *marketing researcher, educator*

Duxbury
Albritton, William Hoyle *training and consulting executive, lecturer, writer*

Fall River
Washburn, Stewart Putnam *management consultant*

Falmouth
Nolan, Edmund Francis *management consultant*

Foxboro
Hershman, Judith *advertising executive*

Framingham
Donovan, R. Michael *management consultant*
Hillman, Carol Barbara *communications executive, consultant*
Wulf, Sharon Ann *management consultant*

Gloucester
Hausman, William Ray *fund raising and management consultant*
Littlefield, Paul Damon *retired management consultant*
†Mammola, Dominic *advertising executive*

Groton
Munson, Lawrence Shipley *management consultant*

Harvard
Marolda, Anthony Joseph *management consulting company executive*

Hingham
Harbert, Susan Randall *administrator*

Lancaster
Poduska, John William, Sr., *computer company executive*

Leominster
Lyons, Beryl Barton Anfindsen *sales professional*

Lexington
Betts, Kathleen Vanetta *human resources executive*
Brick, Donald Bernard *software company executive*
Fray, Lionel Louis *management consultant*
Hurd, Philip Justin *executive search consultant*
†Peden, Keith J. *human resources specialist*
†Piano, Phyllis J. *communications executive*
White, Gary Francis *investigation professional*

Littleton
Kulas, Frederick John *computer company executive*

Lynnfield
Solomon, Jerry Lawrence *sports marketing executive, educator*

Malden
Jiang, Yong Ping *research scientist*

Marblehead
Phillips, Peter Lawrence *communications executive*

Marlborough
Aclin, Keith Andrew *technical service executive, educator*

Marstons Mills
Martin, Vincent George *management consultant*

Mashpee
Detschel, Frederick William *management consultant*

Medford
Boisjoly, Russell Paul *international consultant*
Monsma, James Edwin *retired consulting company executive*

Medway
Saenger, Bruce Walter *consulting firm executive*

Melrose
McLennan, Bernice Claire *human resources professional*

Middleboro
Washburn, Stewart Alexander *management consultant*

Milford
Correia, Alberto Abrantes *management executive*

Nantucket
Mercer, Richard Joseph *retired advertising executive, freelance writer*

Natick
Miller, George David *retired military officer, retired not-for-profit developer*

Needham
Grasso, James Anthony *public relations executive, educator*

New Bedford
Anderson, James Linwood *pharmaceutical sales official*

Newton
Kosowsky, David I. *retired biotechnical company executive*

Newton Upper Falls
Pytka, Stephen Milton *office equipment executive*

North Attleboro
Zani, Frederick Caesar *retired corporate consultant*

North Billerica
Carpenter, Elizabeth Jane *communications executive*

North Reading
Day, Ronald Elwin *consulting executive*

Norwell
Case, David Knowlton *management consultant*

Oak Bluffs
†Lamb, Robert *industrial executive*

Osterville
McCarthy, Albert Henry *executive recruiter, consultant*

Palmer
Dupuis, Robert Simeon *sales executive*

Peabody
Arons, Irving J. *technology consultant, writer*
Bierman, George William *technical consulting executive, food technologist*
Finch, Rogers Burton *association management consultant*
†Gordon, Bernard M. *computer company executive*

Pittsfield
†Glazer, Michael L. *consumer products company executive*
Wenner, Gene Charles *arts management executive*

Quincy
Hall, John Raymond, Jr., *fire protection executive*
Levin, Robert Joseph *retail grocery chain store executive*
Young, Richard William *corporate director*

Randolph
†Huntington, Robert Howard *business management executive*

Rockport
Wiberg, Lars Erik *occupational compatibility consultant*

Sheffield
Velmans, Loet Abraham *retired public relations executive*

Sherborn
Hancock, William Frank, Jr., *management consultant*

South Hadley
Colino, Richard Ralph *communications consultant*

Springfield
Ervin, Billy Maxwell *management consultant*
†Vincensi, Avis A. *sales executive, medical educator*

Stoneham
Eaton, Amos Jorge *management consultant*

Stoughton
Adamson, Stephen Charles *retired sales professional*

Stow
Langenwalter, Gary Allan *manufacturing and management consulting company executive*

Sudbury
†Cheema, Zafarullah K. *management consultant*
Kamen, Robert Irwin *research company executive*

Swansea
Holmes, Henry *literary agent, book publicist, writer and editor*

Townsend
Smith, Denise Groleau *data processing professional*

Waban
Rossolimo, Alexander Nicholas *management consultant, business executive, corporate director*

Wakefield
†Brady, Patrick *advertising executive*

Walpole
Coleman, John Joseph *telephone company executive*

Waltham
Buchholz, William James *communications executive, educator*
Colcord, Herbert Nathaniel, III, (Skip Colcord) *corporate communications executive*
Kasputys, Joseph Edward *corporate executive, economist*
O'Hagen, Nicole McCauley *marketing professional*
†Pocock, J. Michael *consumer products company executive*
Schwartz, Steven Mark *marketing executive*

Watertown
Goldstein, Arthur Louis *water purification company executive*

Wayland
Blair, John *consultant*
Caristo-Verrill, Janet Rose *international management consultant*
Harrington, Kay Lorraine *executive secretary*

Wellesley
Anderson, David Langley *management consultant*
Arnold, Peter Gordon *communications consultant*
Mitchell, Donald Wayne *management consultant, investment manager, lawyer, writer*
Tierney, Thomas J. *business management consultant*

Wellesley Hills
†Coco, Samuel Barbin *venture consultant*

West Chatham
Rhinesmith, Stephen Headley *management consultant*

Westborough
Schrager, Mindy Rae *software company professional*

Westford
Endyke, Debra Joan *data communications marketing professional*
Weston, Joan Spencer *editorial and production director, communications executive*
Wing, Carol *marketing professional, writer*

Weston
Stambaugh, Armstrong A., Jr., *restaurant and hotel executive*

Westport
Norcross, Alvin Watt *retired personnel administrator, consultant*

Westwood
Daley, Charles Mike *consumer products company executive*

Williamstown
Driscoll, Genevieve Bosson (Jeanne Bosson Driscoll) *management and organization development consultant*
Sprague, John Louis *management consultant*

Winchester
Ferrera, Arthur Rocco *food distribution company executive*

Winthrop
Brown, Alan Anthony *marketing executive*
Caggiano, Ernest Christopher *funeral director*

Woburn
Mehra, Raman Kumar *aerospace and defense technology executive, automation and control engineering researcher*
Paul, Lois *public relations company executive*

Worcester
Camougis, George *health, safety and environmental consultant*
Candib, Murray A. *business executive, retail management consultant*
Heman, Robert Jerome, Jr., *printing company executive, association executive*

MICHIGAN

Ada
†Brenner, David H. *marketing executive*
†Van Andel, Jay *direct selling company executive*
†Van Andel, Steve Alan *business executive*

Ann Arbor
Agno, John G. *management consultant*
Belcher, Louis David *marketing and operations executive, former mayor*
†Brandon, David A. *food service executive/restaurant manager*
Bryant, Barbara Everitt *academic researcher, market research consultant, former federal agency administrator*
†Flint, H. Howard, II, *printing company executive*
Lindsay, June Campbell McKee *communications executive*
Martin, Claude Raymond, Jr., *marketing consultant, educator*
McGinn, Terence James *business consultant, minister*
Nikoui, Hossein Reza *quality assurance professional*
Oliver, Marguerite Bertoni *food service executive*
Peterson, Julie Ann *media relations executive, consultant*
Sprandel, Dennis Steuart *management consulting company executive*

Big Rapids
Hardy, Victoria Elizabeth *management educator*

Bloomfield Hills
Abel Horowitz, Michelle Susan *advertising executive*
Adams, Charles Francis *advertising and real estate executive*
Berline, James H. *advertising executive, public relations executive*
Bithell, Thomas Charles *human resources and insurance consultant*
Sandy, William Haskell *training and communication systems executive*
Weil, John William *technology management consultant*

Charlotte
Young, Everett J. *management consultant, agricultural economist*

Dearborn
Ahmed, Saleem *management consultant, educator*

Detroit
Dixson, J. B. *communications executive*
Engelhardt, Regina *cosmetologist, artist, small business owner*
McCracken, Caron Francis *computer company executive, consultant*
McCracken, Ina *business executive*
McWhorter, Sharon Louise *business executive, inventor, consultant*
Ponder, Dan *public relations executive*
Rosenau, Pete *public relations executive*
Salter, Linda Lee *security officer*
†Schweitzer, Peter *advertising agency executive*
Spearman-Leach, Anthony Maurice Paul *public policy, communications, marketing and advertising executive*
Werba, Gabriel *public relations consultant*
Zoubareff, Kathy Olga *administrative assistant*

East Lansing
†Diedrich, William Frank *management consultant, speech professional*
†La Ferle, Carrie *advertising executive, educator*
†Torto, Christopher *communications executive*
Wilson, R. Dale *marketing educator, consultant*

Farmington
†Seck, John F., Jr., *communications executive*

Farmington Hills
Bassett, Tina *communications executive*

Ferndale
Gienapp, Helen Fischer *jewelry company owner*

Flushing
Bain, William David *electronics systems technician, writer*

Grand Rapids
Baker, Frank C. (Buzz Baker) *advertising executive*
DeVos, Richard Marvin, Jr., (Dick DeVos) *retired direct sales company executive, sports team executive*
†Gordon, Dan *food service executive*
Kranz, Kenneth Louis *human resources company executive, entrepreneur*
†Messner, James W. *advertising executive*
Purchase-Owens, Francena *human resources specialist, educator*
Sadler, David G(ary) *management executive*
Seyferth, Virginia M. *public relations executive*
Spaulding, Dan *public relations executive*
Zimmerman, John *public relations executive*

Grosse Pointe Farms
†Lada, Warren S. *communications executive*

Grosse Pointe Park
Blevins, William Edward *management consultant*

Grosse Pointe Shores
Caldwell, John Thomas, Jr., *communications executive*

Grosse Pointe Woods
Cusmano, J. Joyce *public relations executive*

Hastings
Jones, Kensinger *advertising executive*

Holland
Mc Gurk, James Henry *consultant company executive*

Kalamazoo
†Gershon, Richard A. *communications educator*
†Kupstas, Corrine Lynn *environmental director, chemical engineer*
Lawrence, William Joseph, Jr., *retired corporate executive*

Kaleva
Lenz, Jeanne Ann *security professional*

Keego Harbor
†Gee, Sharon Lynn *funeral director, educator*

Livonia
Chowdhury, Subir *business executive, author, researcher*
Maibach, Ben C., Jr., *service executive*

Madison Heights
Woodruff, Jane *sales executive*

Marquette
Earle, Mary Margaret *marketing executive*
Pesola, William Ernest *restaurant management executive*

Midland
Maneri, Remo R. *management consultant*

Mount Clemens
Robinson, Earl, Jr., *marketing and economic research executive, transportation executive, business educator, retired air force officer*

Muskegon
Gundy-Reed, Frances Darnell *marketing executive*

Novi
Bricker, Gerald Wayne *marketing executive*
Kinsey, Charles John *industrial auctioneer, consultant, cattle breeder, farmer*

Pontiac
Mitchell, Sheryl Lynn *analyst, educator*

Port Austin
Davis, Frederick Athie *management executive*

Portage
Seely, Robert Eugene *management consultant*

Reed City
Devendorf, Louise Marie *promoter, writer*

Rochester Hills
Pfister, Karl Anton *industrial company executive*

Rockford
Knape, Herbert Fritz *business executive*

Royal Oak
Stanalajczo, Greg Charles *computer and technology company executive*

Saginaw
Scharffe, William Granville *academic administrator, educator*

Saline
Low, Louise Anderson *consulting company executive*

Southfield
Amladi, Prasad Ganesh *management consulting executive, health care consultant, researcher*
Barnett, Marilyn *advertising agency executive*
Caponigro, Jeffrey Ralph *public relations counselor*
Howard, Michael Joseph *communications executive, real estate developer*
†Kalter, Alan *advertising agency executive*
Koch, Albert Acheson *management consultant*
Wagner, Bruce Stanley *marketing professional*

Southgate
Kohn, Julieanne *travel agent*

Troy
Adderley, Terence E. *corporate executive*
Harrison, Christine Delane *company executive*
†Hill, Richard A. *advertising executive*
†Reed, Derryl L. *marketing director*

Walled Lake
Gillespie, J. Martin *sales and distribution company executive*

Warren
Hopp, Anthony James *advertising agency executive*
Miko, Mary V. *personnel director, manufacturing executive*
Wisz, Joseph A., Jr., *management consultant*

Waterford
Land, Robert Donald *business consultant*

West Bloomfield
†Considine, John Joseph *advertising executive*
Lewis, Harold Allen *childcare company executive*

White Cloud
De Haan-Puls, Joyce Elaine *sales account representative, educator*

MINNESOTA

Apple Valley
Kettle, Sally Anne *consulting company executive, educator*

Austin
Budd, Jim *communications manager*

Bloomington
Miller, Kevin Robert *employee benefit consultant*
†Norris, William C. *retired computer systems executive*
Taylor, Susan S. *communications executive*

Brooklyn Park
†Okigwe, JaJa A. *marketing professional, consultant*

Burnsville
Hight, Tim Everett *company executive, consultant*
Ringquist, Lynn Anne *micrographics company executive*

Chaska
Cohen, Cheryl Diane Durda *communications executive*

Duluth
Bailey, Charles William *management consultant, researcher*
Stender, Bruce William *business executive*

Eden Prairie
Carlson, Kenneth George *data processing executive*
Knotek, Robert Frank *management consultant, educator*
Petersen, Maureen Jeanette Miller *management information consultant, former nurse*
†Verdoorn, Sid *food service executive*
Vincelli, Patrick Thomas *human resources specialist*

Edina
Burbank, John Thorn *cleaning industry executive*
Burdick, Lou Brum *public relations executive*
DiGiovanni, Larry Joseph *human resources executive, small business owner*

Polsfuss, Craig Lyle *executive coach and leadership specialist, psychologist, social worker*
Taylor, Scott Maxfield *educator*

Farmington
Wurdeman, Lew Edward *internet consultant*

Hackensack
†Marquart, Petra A. *training consultant*

Hastings
Avent, Sharon L. Hoffman *manufacturing company executive*

Mahtomedi
Brainerd, Richard Charles *human resources executive, consultant, educator*

Mankato
Taylor, Glen A. *printing, direct mail and technology company executive, professional sports team executive*

Maple Grove
McCally, John Frank *healthcare executive, writer*

Minneapolis
Agyenkwah, Kennedy Seth *communications executive*
Anderson, Ron *advertising executive*
†Bonneville, Katherine Ann *human resources specialist, consultant*
Boubelik, Henry Fredrick, Jr., *retired travel company executive*
Courtney, Eugene Whitmal *computer company executive*
†Dunlap, William DeWayne, Jr., *advertising agency executive*
Eickhoff, John R. (Jack Eickhoff) *business executive*
Eisenberg, Jay Lynn *marketing research professional*
Fiedler, Robert Max *management consultant*
Gage, Edwin C., III, (Skip Gage) *travel and marketing services executive*
Harp-Jirschele, Mary *communications executive*
Hunsberger, Roger Moore *web site design company executive, writer, lumber company executive, musician*
Johnson, Lola Norine *retired advertising and public relations executive, educator*
Koutsky, Dean Roger *advertising executive*
McCall, Brian Patrick *industrial relations educator*
†Mouser, Les *advertising executive*
Nelson, Marilyn C. *hotel executive, food service executive, travel services executive, marketing professional*
Perlman, Lawrence *retired business executive, corporate director, consultant*
†Pohlad, Robert C. *consumer products company executive*
Sanger, Stephen W. *consumer products company executive*
Schultz, Louis Edwin *management consultant*
Spong, Douglas K. *public relations executive*
Stage, Brian *hotel executive*
Sullivan, Michael Patrick *food service executive*
Tandon, Rajiv *training company executive*
†Thaivanich, Pattana *marketing professional*
Tracey, Timothy Neal *technology company executive*
Veblen, Thomas Clayton *management consultant*
Wickesberg, Albert Klumb *retired management educator*
Yourzak, Robert Joseph *management consultant, engineer, educator*
Zimmermann, Robert Laurence *marketing professional*
Zoberi, Nadim *management consultant, consultant*

Minnetonka
Christianson, Philip D. *employee benefits executive*
Cross, Bonham E(lwood) *retired newspaper account executive*
Gillies, Donald Richard *marketing and advertising consultant, educator*
Gottier, Richard Chalmers *retired computer company executive*
Kostka, Ronald Wayne *marketing consultant*
Schmidt, Russel Alan, II, *sales executive*

New Brighton
Dobbert, Daniel Joseph *data analyst, researcher, educator*

New Hope
Olson, Clifford Larry *management consultant, entrepreneur*

North Oaks
Blaha, Verle Dennis *golf course executive, electrical engineer*

Northfield
Hangen, William J. *retired business executive*

Pequot Lakes
Gray, Allen (Ernest Bungaard) *radio executive*

Prior Lake
Toren, Brian Keith *futures, multimedia, management consultant*

Rochester
Kinney, Carolyn *executive secretary*
Nevling, Harry Reed *human resources consultant*

Saint Cloud
McIntyre, Vicky Joyce *business owner*

Saint Louis Park
Wikman, Michael Raymond *advertising executive*

Saint Paul
Axelrod, Leonard *court administrator*
Boehnen, David Leo *lawyer*
Davies, Russ *quality assurance professional*
Esposito, Bonnie Lou *marketing professional*
Feinberg, David Erwin *publishing company executive*
Hill, James Stanley *computer consulting company executive*

Sartell
Van Nostrand, Catharine Marie Herr *retired personnel director*

Sauk Rapids
Newman, Donald John *marketing executive*

Savage
Luth, James Curtis *systems consultant*

Stillwater
Cardozo, Richard Nunez *marketing, entrepreneurship and business educator*

Wayzata
Schoen, Charles Judd *service executive*
Waldera, Wayne Eugene *crisis management specialist*

MISSISSIPPI

Biloxi
Culberson, Gary Michael *hotel manager*

Brandon
McCreery, James Allan *retired business services company executive*

Carriere
Woodmansee, Glenn Edward *employee relations executive*

Clinton
Sidgmore, John W. *telecommunications executive*

Columbus
Holt, Robert Ezel *data processing executive*
Labensky, Sarah Ross *culinary educator*

Itta Bena
Hudspeth, Harvey Gresham *history educator*

Jackson
Molpus, Dick H. *management company executive*

Sumrall
Hudson, Mary Kay *executive*

MISSOURI

Belton
Fox, Kevin Christopher *marketing professional*

Berkeley
Campbell, Anita Joyce *computer company executive*

Cape Girardeau
Smallwood, Glenn Walter, Jr., *utility marketing management executive*

Chesterfield
Cooper, Kenneth Carlton *training consultant*
Webster, Ronald D. *communications company executive*

Clayton
Vecchiotti, Robert Anthony *management and organizational consultant*

Columbia
†McKinnon, James Richard *management consultant*

Creve Coeur
Wasserman, Stephen Miles *communications director*

Fenton
†Maritz, W. Stephen *marketing professional, service executive*

Golden City
Howard, Joanne Frances *marketing executive, funeral director, extended care coordinator*

Independence
Booz, Gretchen Arlene *marketing executive*
Burnett, Crystal Blythe *marketing professional*
Evans, Margaret Ann *human resources administrator, business owner*
Grover, Robert Lavern *retired auto worker*

Kansas City
Baker, Ronald Phillip *service company executive*
Belzer, Ellen J. *editor, negotiations and communications consultant*
†Cooper, Corinne *communications consultant, lawyer*
Courson, Marna B.P. *public relations executive*
†Dawson, Elizabeth Ann *marketing professional*
Dillingham, John Allen *marketing professional*
Donovan, Ann Burcham *medical office administrator*
Grossman, Jerome Barnett *retired service firm executive*
†Hall, Donald Joyce, Sr., *greeting card company executive*
†Hall, Donald Joyce, Jr., *consumer products company executive*
Hoffman, Gloria Levy *communications executive*
Kovac, F. Peter *advertising executive*
Krause, Heather Dawn *data processing executive*

PROFESSIONAL INDEX 6497 INDUSTRY: SERVICE

Kuhn, Whitey *advertising executive*
Öhman, Mikael *management consultant*
†O'Shields, Charlie *marketing professional*
Robertson, Leon H. *management consultant, educator*
†Smith, Christopher D. *administrative assistant*
†Solberg, Elizabeth Transou *public relations executive*
†Stowers, James W., III, *data processing executive*
Taylor, Marilyn Levere *management consultant, educator*
Warakomski, Alphonse Walter Joseph, Jr., *sales executive, marketing professional*
Woodson, Stephen William *collection agency executive*

Lake Saint Louis
Dommermuth, William Peter *marketing consultant, educator*

Lees Summit
Aduddle, Larry Steven *marketing and sales executive, consultant*
Duke, Ellen Kay *planned giving administrator*

Olivette
Hollingsworth, Gary Mayes *sales executive, marketing professional*

Parkville
Jacobs, Carl Eugene *printing company official*

Raymore
Mehl, Donald Edward *retired marketing professional*

Rolla
†Bagnall, Lindsay Lomax *human resources specialist*

Saint Charles
Gross, Charles Robert *bank executive, state senator*
Kelly, James Joseph *printing company executive*
Nickisch, Willard Wayne *funeral director*

Saint Louis
Adams, W. Randolph , Jr., *management consultant*
†Bateman, Sharon Louise *public relations executive*
Brickey, Kristin Lynn *healthcare marketing professional*
Davis, Irvin *advertising, public relations, broadcast executive*
Donald, Arnold W. *company executive*
Fosher, Donald Hobart *marketing professional, inventor*
Graham, John Dalby *public relations executive*
Handelman, Alice Samuels *public relations professional, writer*
Hilgert, Raymond Lewis *management and industrial relations educator, consultant, arbitrator*
†Keith, Andrea L. *marketing professional*
Khoury, George Gilbert *printing company executive, baseball association executive*
Lents, Peggy Iglauer *marketing executive*
Peters, Robert James, Sr., *management consultant*
Rosen, Fred *travel company executive*
†Schnuck, Scott C. *grocery store executive*
Sibbald, John Ristow *management consultant*
Stork, Donald Arthur *advertising executive*
Taylor, Andrew C. *rental and leasing company executive*
†Taylor, Jack C. *rental and leasing company executive*
Tyler, William Howard, Jr., *advertising executive, educator*
Vandiver, Donna *public relations executive*
Van Luven, William Robert *management consultant*
Wassell, Loren W. *public affairs professional, writer*
Waterbury, Jackson DeWitt *retired marketing executive*
Weaver, Charles Lyndell, Jr., *institutional and manufacturing facilities administrator, management and marketing systems consultant*
Weldon, Virginia V. *retired corporate executive, physician*
†Wright, Diane *procurement manager*

Springfield
†Denton, D. Keith *management educator*
Kincaid, Paul Kent *public relations professional*
Wang, Guangmiao *business executive, consultant*
Witherspoon, John Thomas *water resources consultant*

Town And Country
Lachenicht-Berkeley, Angela Marie *marketing professional*

Warrenton
Dapron, Elmer Joseph, Jr., *communications executive*

Washington
De Pew, David Philip *advertising executive, consultant, lecturer*

Weston
Murdock, Phelps Dubois, Jr., *marketing consultant, strategic planner*

MONTANA

Belgrade
Aveson, Martha Caralyn *pharmaceutical company executive*

Florence
Egley, Thomas Arthur *computer services executive, accountant*

Great Falls
Paulson-Ehrhardt, Patricia Helen *sales executive*

Helena
Manuel, Vivian *public relations executive*

Missoula
Trask-Tyrell, Nancy *management company executive*

NEBRASKA

Curtis
Khamouna, Mo *communications associate, consultant*

Lincoln
Brownson, E. Ramona Lidstone Brady *retired secretary*

Omaha
Brailey, Susan Louise *quality analyst, educator*
Caggiano, Joseph *advertising executive*
Eggers, James Wesley *executive search consultant*
Frazier, Chet June *advertising agency executive*
Lietzen, John Hervy *human resources executive, health agency volunteer*
Roskens, Ronald William *international business consultant*
†Stanley, Terry Lynn *marketing professional*

NEVADA

Henderson
Bruno, Cathy Eileen *educator, management consultant, former state official*
Cohan, George Sheldon *advertising and public relations executive*
Klink, Karin Elizabeth *medical communications company executive, writer*
Laurich, Lawrence Alvin *company executive*
Roll, Irwin Clifford (Win Roll) *advertising, marketing and publishing executive*

Incline Village
Mitton, Michael Anthony *environmental technology company executive*

Las Vegas
Arce, Phillip William *hotel and casino executive*
Basile, Richard Emanuel *retired management consultant, educator*
Boyle, Carolyn Moore *public relations executive, marketing communications manager*
Collis, Kay Lynn *sales executive*
Crevelt, Dwight Eugene *computer company executive*
Gallagher, Thomas Edmund *hotel executive, lawyer*
Goldstein, Morris *retired entertainment company executive*
Goodwin, Nancy Lee *corporate executive*
Griesche, Robert Price *hospital purchasing executive*
Koon, Ray Harold *management and security consultant*
Landau, Ellis *gaming company executive*
†Lanni, J(oseph) Terrence *hotel corporation executive*
Litman, Brian David *communications executive*
†Loveman, Gary W. *gaming company executive*
Mataseje, Veronica Julia *sales executive*
Pringle, Thomas Hivick *sales executive*
Rowe, Carl Osborn *business consultant*
Shively, Judith Carolyn (Judy Shively) *contract administrator*
Sorrell, Michael E. *consulting company executive*
Springer, Christine Gibbs *management consultant, business owner, educator*
Stark, S. Daniel, Jr., *gaming industry executive*
Thill, John Val *communications professional, writer, consultant*
Welter, William Michael *marketing and advertising executive*

Pahrump
Marsh, Mary Elizabeth Taylor *recreation administrator, dietician, nutritionist*
Parker, Allan Leslie *marketing executive*

Reno
Adams, Kenneth Robert *gaming analyst, writer, consultant, historian*
Dorward, Judith A. *business ordering customer service representative*
Ford, Victoria *retired public relations executive, writer, oral historian*
Howard, Christopher Philip *business consultant*
†Ivan, Francis M. *sales executive, writer*
Johnson, Richard Karl *hospitality company executive*
Munro, Roderick Anthony *business improvement coach*
Sklar, Louise Margaret *computer company executive*

Zephyr Cove
Amico, Charles William *management consultant*

NEW HAMPSHIRE

Bedford
Alderman, Walter Arthur, Jr., *computer company and corporate rescue executive*
Hall, Pamela S. *environmental consulting firm executive*
Steadman, David Rosslyn Ayton *business executive, corporate director*

Center Harbor
Shaw, Robert William, Jr., *management consultant, venture capitalist*

Concord
Mahon, Thomas James *management consultant*
Roberts, George Bernard, Jr., *management and government relations consultant, former state legislator*

Deering
Spitzer, Morton Edward *management consultant*

Enfield
Gamache, Richard Donald *retired business development executive*

Exeter
Harmon, Richard Wingate *management consultant*
Ingram, Lionel Rowan, Jr., *manangement consultant*

Fitzwilliam
Schott, John Robert *international consultant, educator*

Francestown
Risk, Robert Terence *printer, publisher*

Freedom
Stolz, Alan Jay *youth camp executive*

Hampstead
Abdulla, Jennifer Ann *marketing professional, consultant*

Hanover
Quinn, James Brian *business educator*

Jackson
Synnott, William Raymond *retired management consultant*

Keene
Berenson, Paul Stewart *advertising agency executive*

Kingston
Merrill, Lynne Bartlett *public relations executive, advertising executive*

Lee
†Merriman, Chrisann *marketing professional*

Manchester
Bersoux, Henri Robert *management executive*
Bradley, James Harold *public relations consultant*
Colby, George Vincent, III, *logistics executive*
Cusson-Cail, Kathleen *consulting company executive*

Merrimack
†Gallup, Patricia *computer company executive*

Nashua
Hargreaves, David William *communications company executive*
Piper, Linda Ammann *staffing services executive*
Seidel, Carl William *business executive, consultant*

New Castle
Brink, Marion Alice *retired human resources specialist*

New London
Gepfert, Alan Harry *management consultant, business educator, author*
Zuehlke, Richard William *technical communications consultant, writer*

Peterborough
Day, John Sidney *management sciences educator*
Duncan, George *marketing consultant*

Plymouth
†Reed, Laurie Jean *administrative assistant*

Portsmouth
Greene, Douglas Edward *hotel executive*

Rochester
Kramer, Sherri Marcelle *gemologist, jeweler*
†Patel, Piyush *communications executive*

Rye
MacRury, King *management counselor*

Salem
Snierson, Lynne Wendy *communications executive*

Somersworth
Gow, Linda Yvonne Carignan Cherwin *travel executive*

Walpole
Hunter, Barbara Way *public relations consultant*

Waterville Valley
Grimes, Howard Ray *management consultant*

West Lebanon
Lawton, Jacqueline Agnes *retired communications company executive, management consultant*

NEW JERSEY

Allendale
Bisanzo, Mark Thomas *sales executive*

Allenhurst
Hinson, Robert William *advertising executive, consultant*

Asbury Park
Rosenthal, Robert Irwin *consultant*

Atlantic Highlands
Ramsey, Joanne Marie *financial services representative*

Avenel
†Segal, Barry *compnay executive*

Basking Ridge
Buist, Richardson *retired corporate executive, retired banker*
†Horton, Thomas W. *telecommunications executive*
O'Connell, Robert Brendan *public relations and editorial consultant*

Bedminster
Gardner, David John *communications executive, recording engineer*
†Hart, Terry Jonathan *communications executive*

Bergenfield
Janow, Lydia Frances *meeting planner*

Bernardsville
Dixon, Richard Wayne *retired communications company executive*

Bloomfield
Bunin, Jeffrey Howard *management consultant*

Boonton
Bona, Frederick Emil *public relations executive*
Bridges, Beryl Clarke *marketing executive*

Brick
Alpiar, Hal *management and marketing consultant, author*
Pistolakis, Nicholas Stelios *advertising executive*
Roache, Patrick Michael, Jr., *management consultant*
Shortess, Edwin Steevin *marketing consultant*

Bridgewater
Hulse, Robert Douglas *high technology executive*
Sethi, Shyam Sunder *management consultant*
Skidmore, James Albert, Jr., *management, computer technology and engineering services company executive*

Brookside
Fairchild, Samuel Wilson *professional services company executive, former federal agency administrator*

Butler
Ward, Robert Allen, Jr., *advertising executive*

Caldwell
Chatlos, William Edward *management consultant*

Califon
Fouillade, Jean-Paul Eric *management consultant*

Camden
Gans, Samuel Myer *temporary employment service executive*

Carteret
†Neff, Richard B. *consumer products company executive*

Cedar Knolls
Clark, Sharon W. *employee benefits company executive*

Chatham
Lenz, Henry Paul *management consultant*

Cherry Hill
Bashkin, Lloyd Scott *marketing and management consultant*

Chester
Maddalena, Lucille Ann *management consultant*

Clifton
Bronkesh, Annette Cylia *public relations executive*
Burke, Bruce Lowell *consumer products company executive*

Collingswood
Mohrfeld, Richard Gentel *marketing professional*

Convent Station
Tintle, Carmel Joseph *public relations executive*

Cranbury
Roth, Richard C. *marketing executive*

Cranford
Halleck, George Thomas *marketing professional*

Delran
Gilbert, Harry Ephraim, Jr., *retired hotel executive*

Denville
Dudrow, Peter Warren *human resources executive, consultant*

East Hanover
Knight, Frank James *pharmaceutical marketing professional*

East Rutherford
Kempner, Michael W. *public relations executive*
†Kluge, John Werner *broadcasting and advertising executive*

Eatontown
†Rasmussen, Mark William *restaurant owner and chef*

Edison
†Currie, Robert *communications executive*
D'Agostino, Matthew Paul *bakery executive*
Haberman, Louise Shelly *consulting company executive*
Kumar, Krishan *management consultant, company executive*

Elizabeth
Mogensen, Charles Ray, Jr., *food service administrator*

Emerson
Cheslik, Francis Edward *management consultant*
Pavloski, Veronica Theresa *corporate communications specialist*

Englewood
Fay, Toni Georgette *communications executive*

Ewing
D'Antonio, Cynthia Maria *sales and marketing executive*
McCarty, John Albert *advertising and marketing educator, consultant*

Far Hills
Bruett, Karen Diesl *sales and fundraising consultant*
Hambleton, George Blow Elliott *retired management consultant*

Farmingdale
Edwards, Ann Concetta *human resources director*

Florham Park
†Fischer, Pamela Shadel *public relations executive*
Naimark, George Modell *marketing and management consultant*
†Negi, Devendra S. *communications services company administrator*

Fort Lee
Seitel, Fraser Paul *public relations executive*

Franklin Lakes
Williams, Edward David *consulting executive*

Gladstone
Close, Donald Pembroke *management consultant*

Glen Ridge
Agnew, Peter Tomlin *employee benefit consultant*

Green Brook
Bohanan, David John *management consultant*

Hackensack
Carra, Andrew Joseph *advertising executive*

Hackettstown
Van Campen, Stephen Bernard *executive recruiter, consultant*

Haddonfield
Bauer, Raymond Gale *sales professional*

Hamilton
Gideon, Richard Walter *broadcasting management consultant*

Hammonton
Senf, Mary *secretary, artist, writer, poet*

Hampton
Yates, Michael Francis *management consultant*

Hillsborough
Orkin, Neil S. *management consultant, speaker*

Hoboken
Fassoulis, Satiris Galahad *communications company executive*
Leggiere, Philip Guy *publicist, writer, consultant*
†Tardiff, Jill Alexandria *marketing professional, consultant*

Holmdel
Hudson, Wendy Joy *software manager*
Polinsky, Joseph Thomas *recruiting and training consultant*
Vitullo, Anthony Joseph *communications executive*

Iselin
Holcombe, Thomas Charles *technology executive*

Jackson
Hunter, Lynn *sales executive, writer, elementary school educator*

Jersey City
Ascolese, Michael J. *corporate communications executive*
Dupey, Michele Mary *communications specialist*

Lakewood
Woodman, G. Roger *management consultant*

Lavallette
Tesoriero, Philip James *human resource consultant*

Lawrenceville
Adams, Christine Hanson *advertising executive*
Bailey, Lloyd Robert Scott *publishing company executive, editor, historian*
Coleman, Wade Hampton, III, *management consultant, mechanical engineer, former banker*
Cox, Teri P. *public relations executive*
Pohlhaus, John Ernest *international marketing executive, consultant*

Leonia
Pinsdorf, Marion Kathryn *business executive, educator, author*

Liberty Corner
Ganz, Felix *marketing professional*

Lindenwold
Jackson, Yocontalie Ann *entertainment company executive*

Little Silver
Morrison, James Frederick *management consultant*

Livingston
Greenberg, Aaron Rosmarin *public relations executive*
Guerra, Mary Louise *human resources executive*
Sethi, Deepak *leadership development/marketing executive*

Madison
Byrd, Stephen Fred *human resource consultant*
O'Brien, Mary Devon *communications executive, consultant*
Siegel, George Henry *international business development consultant*
Van Cleef, Jabez Lindsay *marketing professional*
Weiner, Lowell B. *corporate communications executive*

Mahwah
Eisner, Susan Pamela *communications executive, management consultant, educator*
Wagner, Susan Jane *sales and marketing consulting company executive*

Manalapan
†Reisman, Joan Ann *executive secretary*

Maplewood
Hamburger, Mary Ann *medical management consultant*
Safian, Gail Robyn *public relations executive*

Margate City
Stoolman, Herbert Leonard *public relations executive*

Marlton
Farnath, Dorothy Whitmyer *recruitment company executive*
Farwell, Nancy Larraine *public relations executive*
Klein, Anne Sceia *public relations executive*
Klein, Gerhart Leopold *public relations executive*
McCullen, Michael John *retired advertising executive*

Matawan
Katz, Irwin *marketing executive*

Mendham
Rosensaft, Lester Jay *management consultant, lawyer, consultant*

Metuchen
Orr, Robert Andrew *management consultant*

Middletown
Heng, Siang Gek *communications executive*

Millburn
Erenburg, Steven Alan *communications executive*

Mine Hill
Nadeau, Michael Joseph *staff assistant*

Monmouth Junction
Lancaster, Barbara Mae *management consulting company executive*

Monroe Township
Cushman, Helen Merle Baker *retired management consultant*
Meshowski, Frank Robert *business consultant*

Montclair
Barnard, Kurt *retail trend/consumer spending forecaster, publisher*
Cannon, David Price *video executive, advertising consultant*
Harvey, Richard Dudley *marketing consultant*

Moorestown
Carson, William Charles *sales and marketing executive*
Delano-Condax, Kate (Kate Delano-Condax Decker) *marketing and public relations executive*

Morganville
West, Earle Huddleston *communications company professional*

Morris Plains
Chamorro, Juan Pablo *financial analyst, business development executive*
Falci, Dennis Michael *sales executive, pharmaceutical executive*
Gulfo, Adele Madelyn *pharmaceutical marketing executive*

Morristown
Cucco, Judith Elene *international marketing professional*
†Edwards, Peter S. *executive management/computer consulting*
Haselmann, John Philip *management consultant*
Largman, Theodore *consultant*
McConnell, John Howard *personnel management consultant, writer*

Musa, John Davis *computer and infosystems executive, software reliability engineering researcher and expert, independent consultant, educator*

Mountainside
Lingle, Kathleen McCall *human resources specialist, consultant, marketing executive, entrepreneur*
Lipton, Bronna Jane *marketing communications executive*

Murray Hill
†D'Amelio, Frank Anthony *communications company executive*

New Brunswick
Andrews, Clinton James *public affairs educator*
Burke, James Edward *consumer products company executive*
†Doorley, John *marketing professional, educator*
Wilson, Robert Nathan *health care company executive*

New Providence
Doescher, William Frederick *communications executive*
Fitzgerald, Kathleen M. *communications company executive*
Russo, Patricia F. *communications executive*

Newark
Fox, Sandra Gail *insurance marketing executive*
Passantino, Benjamin Arthur *business/marketing executive*

North Arlington
Borowski, Jennifer Lucile *corporate administrator*

North Bergen
Latzko, William J. *management consultant*

North Brunswick
Burtnick, Ronald *software consultant, educator*

North Plainfield
Stillwagon, Wesley William *corporate communications professional*

Nutley
Bonagura, Diane Susan *global study manager*

Oldwick
Griggs, Stephen Layng *management consultant*

Paramus
Fader, Seymour Jeremiah *management and engineering consulting company executive*

Park Ridge
Olson, Frank Albert *car rental company executive*

Parsippany
Azzarone, Carol Ann *marketing executive*
Belmonte, Steven Joseph *hotel chain executive*
†Ferguson, Thomas George *retired healthcare advertising agency executive*
Gray, Neil Harold *healthcare marketing executive*
Meyer, Kevin Michael *communication executive*

Paterson
Waitts, James Robert *marketing professional*

Pennington
Bertone, Thomas Lee *management consultant*

Pennsauken
Sygnecki, Christina *sales executive*

Piscataway
Wagner-Westbrook, Bonnie Joan *management professional*

Plainsboro
Devine, Hugh James, Jr., *marketing executive, consultant*
Spiegel, Phyllis *public relations consultant, journalist*

Pleasantville
Andes, Derien Romaric *retired purchasing specialist*

Point Pleasant
Perdunn, Richard Francis *management consultant*

Princeton
Basáñez, Miguel Ebergenyi *opinion pollster, political science educator*
Bishop, James Francis *executive search consulting company executive*
Crespi, Irving *public opinion and market research consultant*
Cullen, Daniel Edward *management consultant*
Davies, Robert Abel, III, *consumer products company executive*
Hillier, James *technology management executive, researcher*
Hollander, Lawrence Jay *marketing executive*
Lincoln, Anna *company executive, foreign languages educator*
Makadok, Stanley *management consultant*
Morris, Mac Glenn *advertising bureau executive*
Narayanan, Vadake K. *management educator, consultant*
O'Neill, Harry William *survey research company executive*
Rogula, James Leroy *consumer products company executive*
Shaub, Marvin Howard *management consultant*
Tomson, Jon Scott *business professional*
†Weidner, Susan Marie *management consultant*

Williams, Brown F *media services company executive*

Randolph
Charm, Joel Barry *consulting consultant executive*
Chen, Kevin S. *corporate executive, consultant, educator*

Red Bank
Reinhart, Peter Sargent *corporate executive, lawyer*

Ridgewood
Sommer, Robert George *public relations executive*
Warner, John Edward *advertising executive*

Ringoes
Tema-Lyn, Laurie *management consultant*

River Edge
Jones, Thomas Owen *computer industry executive*

Rivervale
LaGreca, Thomas Richard *flooring company executive, lawyer*

Rockaway
Gebauer, Kurt Manfred *management executive*

Roseland
Lafer, Fred Seymour *data processing company executive*
Weinbach, Arthur Frederic *computer company executive*

Rumson
Harris, James Ridout *retired communications executive*

Rutherford
Timmins, Michael Joseph *communications services company executive*

Saddle River
O'Connor, Denise Lynn *marketing communications executive*
Roes, Nicholas A. *communications executive*

Scotch Plains
†Johnsen, Karen K. *marketing professional*
†Margiotta, Joseph M. *printing company executive*

Short Hills
Harwood, Jerry *market research executive*
Marlowe, Edward *pharmaceutical company executive*
Schaefer, Charles James, III, *advertising agency executive, consultant*

Skillman
Gauff, Susan Tyrrell *marketing and human resources executive*

Somerset
Austad, Vigdis *computer software company executive*
†Lau, John Tze *computers and communications executive*
Miller, Phyllis Kaden *communications administrator*

Somerville
Dobrinsky, Susan Elizabeth *human resources director*

South Orange
Lapinski, Frances Constance *internet product and marketing management*
Steig, Donald Barry *management consultant*

South Plainfield
Coulter, Barbara Clare *information services company executive*

Spring Lake
Ernst, John Louis *management consultant*
McEntee, Robert Edward *management consultant*

Springfield
Barlow, Mara Lise *public relations executive*

Stanton
Clayton, Raymond Arthur *purchasing executive*

Stone Harbor
Finore Hurd, Diane *marketing executive, publisher*

Summit
Bostwick, Randell A. *retired retail food company executive*
Fuess, Billings Sibley, Jr., *advertising executive*
Pace, Leonard *retired management consultant*
Weinstein, Stephen Brant *communications executive, researcher, writer*

Teaneck
Connola, Donald Pascal, Jr., *management consultant*

Tenafly
Gibbons, Robert Philip *management consultant, director*

Three Bridges
Lawrence, Gerald Graham *management consultant*

Toms River
Kanarkowski, Edward Joseph *data processing company executive*
†Schockaert, Barbara Ann *marketing professional*

Towaco
Gasperini, Elizabeth Carmela (Lisa Gasperini) *marketing consultant, graphic designer*
Huang, Pingsheng *marketing professional, consultant*
Stern, Richard Henry *advertising executive*

Trenton
Barclay, Warren M. *human resources specialist, researcher*

Union
Donovan, Craig Poulenez *public administration educator*

Upper Saddle River
Hurwitz, Mark Henry *sales executive*

Ventnor City
Bolton, Kenneth Albert *management consultant*

Vernon
Farrand, George Nixon, Jr., *marketing professional*

Verona
Greenwald, Robert *public relations executive*

Warren
Blass, Walter Paul *consultant, management educator*
DiPietro, Ralph Anthony *marketing and management consultant, educator*
Kozberg, Ronald Paul *health and human services administrator*

Watchung
Grey, Ruthann E. *communications specialist, management consultant*

Wayne
Donald, Robert Graham *human resources executive*
Mammola, George Charles *business executive*
Sprayberry, Phillip Kent *public relations executive, educator, performing arts association administrator*

West Caldwell
Bentley, Alfred Young, Jr., *information technology and education consultant*
Dixon, Jo-Ann Conte *management consultant*
Page, Frederick West *business consultant*

West Orange
Kyle, Corinne Silverman *management consultant*
Petrokubi, Marilyn *film company executive, researcher, producer*

Westfield
Mazzarese, Michael Louis *executive coach, consultant*

Whiting
Parker, John Osmyn *management consultant*

Woodcliff Lake
Bablin, Mark Edward *security administrator, mortgage consultant*
Morrione, Melchior S. *management consultant, accountant*

Wyckoff
Lavery, Daniel P. *management consultant*

NEW MEXICO

Albuquerque
D'Anza, Lawrence Martin *management consultant*
Deuble, John L., Jr., *environmental science and engineering services consultant*
†Gardner, Lenann McGookey *management consultant*
Giammo, Salvatore Joseph *public relations executive*
Hayo, George Edward *management consultant*
Leach, Richard Maxwell, Jr., (Max Leach Jr.) *corporate professional*
Myers, Carol McClary *retired sales administrator, editor*
Ofte, Donald *retired environmental executive, consultant*
Oppedahl, Phillip Edward *computer company executive*
Ortiz, Kathleen Lucille *travel consultant*
Wellborn, Charles Ivey *science and technology business consultant*

Bosque Farms
Kelly, Brian Matthew *industrial hygienist*

Jemez Springs
Lawrence, Marjorie Diane Long *computer company executive, consultant*

Los Alamos
Kloepper, David Alan *retired management consultant*
Livesay, Valorie Ann *security program analyst*
Petrini, Fabrizio *computer science researcher*

Lovington
Trujillo, Anna *food company administrator, city official*

Moriarty
Haver, Jurgen F. *marketing consultant*

Placitas
Reade, Lewis Pollock *business executive, retired diplomat, engineer*

Roswell
†Cahill, Laurence Roy, Jr., *customer service administrator*

Sandia Park
Greenwell, Ronald Everett *communications executive*

Santa Fe
Brandt, Richard Paul *communications and entertainment company executive*
Icerman, Larry *advanced technology business consultant, research and development administrator*
Mercer, James Lee *management consultant*
Merrin, Seymour *computer marketing company executive*
Miller, Dwight Richard *professional hair care industry executive, cosmetologist, consultant*
Peat, Randall Dean *defense analysis company executive, retired air force officer*
Robinson, Richard Gary *management consultant, accountant*
Taylor, Beverly Lacy *stringed instrument restorer, classical guitarist*

Silver City
Cox, Robert Gene *management consultant*

Tijeras
Keyler, Robert Gordon *material handling company executive*

NEW YORK

Albany
Lustenader, Barbara Diane *human resources specialist*
Mlock, Mary *employee benefits professional*
†Schalit, Robert Edward *advertising executive*

Amherst
Cohen, Herman Nathan *private investigator*
Nickell, Joe Herman *paranormal expert*

Amityville
Brennan, Patrick Thomas *meteorology company executive, meteorologist*

Annandale On Hudson
†Darrow, Emily M. *public relations executive, writer*

Armonk
Bolduc, Ernest Joseph *association management consultant, not-for-profit developer, consultant*
Gerstner, Louis Vincent, Jr., *computer company executive*
Levy, Kenneth James *advertising executive*

Auburn
Chamberlain, Michael Allen *marketing professional, consultant*

Averill Park
Traver, Robert William, Sr., *management consultant, author, lecturer, engineer*

Bainbridge
Compton, John Robinson *retired rake company executive*

Baldwin
Preis, Carl Otto *company executive, mechanical engineer*

Bedford
Husted, William Armstrong *sales executive*
Sarbin, Hershel Benjamin *management consultant, business publisher, lawyer*
Sha, Richard T. *computer company executive*

Bellport
†Hendrie, Elaine *public relations executive*

Bethpage
†Dolan, James *communications executive*
Janczak, Andrew Anthony *executive*
Marrone, Daniel Scott *business, production and quality management educator*

Big Flats
Van Etten, Elwyn Robert *retired marketing specialist*

Binghamton
Yammarino, Francis Joseph *management educator, consultant*

Briarcliff Manor
Driver, Sharon Humphreys *marketing executive*
Read, John Conyers *non-profit management*

Bronx
Aronowitz, Julian *management consultant*
Capodilupo, Jeanne Hatton *public relations executive*
Hudson, Frederick Bernard *management consultant*
Samuels, Leslie Eugene *marketing and management consultant*

Bronxville
Ellinghaus, William Maurice *communications executive*

Brooklyn
Allison, Eric William *management consultant, historic preservationist*
Allison, Mary Ann *consulting company executive, author, speaker*
Aspenberg, Gary Alan *personnel and labor relations professional*
Chandan, Jit S. *management consultant, educator*

Frisch, Ivan Thomas *computer and communications company executive*
Galatianos, Gus A. *computer executive, information systems consultant, real estate developer, educator*
Hendra, Barbara Jane *public relations executive*
Hochberg, Stephen Hugh *retired human resources specialist*
Isaacson, Arline Levine *food association administrator*
Middleton, John Edison *management consultant*
Moehring, Fred Adolf *fastener distribution company executive*
†O'Rourke, John Francis *sales executive*
†Ortega, Maria A. *security firm executive, educator*
†Quamina, Joyce *management consultant*
Reichel, Walter Emil *advertising executive*
Reisler, Helen Barbara *public relations and publicity consultant*
Roche, John Edward *educator, human resources consultant*
Smith, John W(esley), Jr., *data processing executive, consultant*

Buffalo
Fryer, Appleton *publisher, sales executive, lecturer, diplomat*
Goralski, Donald John *public relations executive, counselor*
Halt, James George *advertising executive, graphic designer*
†Levite, Laurence A. *communications executive*
Murphy, Dennis Patrick *hotel business entrepreneur*
Pegels, C. Carl *management science and systems educator*

Central Islip
Hendee, Susan Sykes *culinary and technology educator, consultant*

Cheektowaga
Mruk, Eugene Robert *retired marketing professional, urban planner*

Chester
Mackerodt, Fred *public relations specialist*

Claverack
Barrett, William Gary *advertising and marketing executive*

Commack
Bond, Patricia B. *camping accessories company executive*

Corning
Loose, John W. *sales company executive*

Croton On Hudson
Eswein, Bruce James, II, *human resources executive*
†Plotch, Walter *management consultant, fund raising counselor*

Cutchogue
Gibson, Pamela *business development consultant, audio director*

Delhi
Needham, Nancy Jean *management consultant*

Delmar
Button, Rena Pritsker *public affairs executive*

Dix Hills
Kornhauser, Kenneth Richard *funeral director, executive*

East Hampton
Kinsolving, Charles McIlvaine, Jr., *marketing executive*
Mencher, Stuart Alan *sales and marketing executive*
Rothholz, Peter Lutz *public relations executive*

East Meadow
Bunshaft, Marilyn Janosy *community services specialist*
Fuchs, Jerome Herbert *management consultant*

East Northport
Schlam, Mark Howard *international marketing executive*

Elmira
Paul, Christopher Donald *carpenter, author*

Elmont
Butera, Ann Michele *consulting company executive*

Floral Park
Dudek, Henry Thomas *management consultant*

Flushing
Falk, Joan Frances *public relations executive*

Forest Hills
Dessylas, Ann Atsaves *human resources and office management executive*
Van Westering, James Francis *management consultant, educator*

Fort Drum
Hilferty, Bryan Carey *public relations specialist*

Fredonia
Boltz, James Donald *retired human resources specialist, photographer*
Krohn, Franklin Bernard *marketing specialist, educator*

Frewsburg
Burgeson, Joyce Ann *travel agency official*

Garden City
Conlon, Brian Thomas *promotion executive*
Conlon, Thomas James *marketing executive*
Doucette, Mary-Alyce *computer company executive*
Healy, Margaret Mary *retail marketing executive*

Glen Cove
Carroll, Robert Franklin *communications company executive*

Glen Head
Conway, David Antony *management executive, marketing professional*

Glenwood Landing
Hahn, Joan Marjorie *public relations consultant, marketing consultant*

Great Neck
Friedland, Louis N. *retired communications executive*
Gior, Fino (Serafino Giordano) *electrology company executive*
Goldberg, Melvin Arthur *communications executive*
Means, Rosaline *business executive, business educator*
Stancati, Richard Emanuel *cleaning company and restaurant executive*

Hancock
DeLuca, Ronald *former advertising agency executive, consultant*

Harrison
Wilson, William James *marketing professional*

Hartsdale
Goodman, Stanley Leonard *advertising executive*
Greenawalt, Peggy Freed Tomarkin *advertising executive*

Hastings On Hudson
Cooper, Doris Jean *market research executive*

Haverstraw
Motin, Revell Judith *retired data processing executive*

Hempstead
Charnov, Bruce Hirschl *management educator, chaplain, rabbi*
†Evans, Joel Raymond *marketing educator*
Kruh, Louis *advertising executive, lawyer*
Pell, Arthur Robert *human resources specialist, consultant, author*

Hollis
Greenblatt, Fred Harold *data processing consultant*

Honeoye Falls
Hillabrandt, Larry Lee *service industry executive*
VanAuken, Alan Bradley *management consultant*

Hopewell Junction
Ebersole, Patricia Sue *advertising executive, design educator*

Hurley
Smith, Lewis Motter, Jr., *retired advertising and direct marketing executive*

Islandia
†Kumar, Sanjay *computer company executive*

Islip
Tameling, Gary William *sales executive*

Ithaca
Berry, Michelle Courtney *communication executive, performance artist*
Hedlund, James H. *traffic safety consultant*
Merle, H. Etienne *restaurateur*
Park, Roy Hampton, Jr., *advertising executive*

Jackson Heights
Michaelson, Herbert Bernard *technical communications consultant*

Jamaica
Jawin, Ann Juliano *human resource specialist*
Lyons, Patrick Joseph *management educator*

Jamestown
Elofson, Nancy Meyer *retired office equipment company executive*
†O'Brian, Jonathan D. *recreation director, social sciences educator, language educator, educator*

Jericho
Rosen, Robert Arnold *management company executive, real estate investor*
Seidman, Glenn Elliott *sales and marketing professional*

Kingston
†Harrington, Gerard, III, *marketing and communications executive, business consultant*

Lake Luzerne
Goldstein, Manfred *retired consultant*

Lake Placid
Lussi, Caroline Frances Draper *resort executive*

Lake Success
Rickin, Sheila Anne *personnel professional*

Lakewood
Howlett, Howard Thomas, Jr., *automotive sales consultant*

Lancaster
Neumaier, Gerhard John *environment consulting company executive*

Larchmont
Greenwald, Carol Schiro *professional services marketing research executive*
Plumez, Jean Paul *advertising agency executive, consultant*
Steinberg, Lois Saxelby *marketing executive*
Wielgus, Charles Joseph *information services company executive*

Latham
Schwartz, Robert William *management consultant*

Lewiston
Askins, Nancy Ellen Paulsen *training and organizational development professional*
†Zhou, Zongqing *hospitality and tourism educator*

Lindenhurst
Conklin, Richard Allan *management consultant*

Long Island City
Craig, Elizabeth Coyne *marketing executive*
Schoenberg, David Arthur *business educator*

Loudonville
Burstein, Sharon Ann *corporate communications specialist, designer*

Malverne
Freund, Richard L. *communications company executive, consultant, lawyer*

Mamaroneck
Gorup, Gregory James *marketing executive*

Manlius
Harriff, Suzanna Elizabeth (Bahner) *advertising consultant*
Zlomek, Elizabeth A. *customer service/business processes specialist*

Marcellus
Moser, David John *management consultant*

Melville
†Blechschmidt, Edward Allan *data processing executive*
Krusos, Denis Angelo *communications company executive*
Lieberman, Carol *healthcare marketing communications consultant*
Ponzi Kay, Marylou *human resources specialist*

Merrick
Baron, Theodore *public relations executive*

Middle Island
†Andrews, Gaylen *measurable response public relations expert*
Linick, Andrew S. *direct marketing expert*

Mitchell Field
Reddy, Gerard Anthony *corporate training executive*

Mohegan Lake
Harris-Jones, Yvonne *national trainer, human resources consultant*

Morrisville
Coppola, Joseph Angelo *computer professional, educator*

Mount Kisco
Mann, Richard O. *public relations consulting company executive*
Novak, Gregory *marketing professional*

Mount Vernon
Chagula, Paul Machiya *technology company executive, trade consultant*

New City
Giambalvo, Vincent *management consultant*

New Hyde Park
DeLuca, James Patrick *graphic arts and advertising educator, consultant*

New Paltz
Nyquist, Thomas Eugene *consulting business executive*

New Rochelle
Miller, Rita *personnel consultant, diecasting company executive*

New York
Abernathy, James Logan *public relations executive*
Abramson, Stephanie W. *advertising executive, lawyer*
Achenbaum, Alvin Allen *marketing and management consultant*
Agisim, Philip *advertising and marketing company executive*
Ahrens, Thomas H. *production company executive*
†Aiello, Stephen *public relations executive*
Alafouzo, Antonia *marketing and business strategy professional*
Alexander, Roy *public relations executive, editor, author*
Allen, Alice *communications and marketing executive*
Alschuler, Steven *public relations executive, communications consultant, writer, political consultant*
Althausen, Jack Henry *computer company executive*
Anderson, Arthur Allan *management consultant*
Andolsen, Alan Anthony *management consultant*
Antonuccio, Joseph Albert *management consultant*
Applebaum, Stuart S. *public relations executive*
†Ardai, Charles E. *online services executive*
Arlow, Arnold Jack *advertising agency executive, artist*
Armstrong, C. Michael *communications company executive*
Aronson, Donald Eric *professional services firms consultant, value added tax consultant*
Axelrod, Norman N(athan) *technical planning and technology application consultant*
Bacher, Judith St. George *executive search consultant*
Baker, Stephen *advertising executive, author*
Bancel, Marilyn *fund raising management consultant*
Barnat, Rhonda Katz *public relations executive, writer*
†Barnes, Arthur Roosevelt *advertising executive*
Baron, Sheri *advertising agency executive*
Barrett, Herbert *artists management executive*
Bartlett, Thomas Foster *international management consultant*
Barton, Thomas Heisler *management consultant*
Bartow, Diane Grace *marketing and sales executive*
Baruch, Ralph M. *communications executive*
†Beard, Eugene P. *advertising agency executive*
Becker, Robert A. *advertising executive*
Becker, Susan Kaplan *management and marketing communication consultant, educator*
Beckwith, Rodney Fisk *management consulting firm executive*
Beinecke, William Sperry *corporate executive*
Bell, David Arthur *advertising agency executive*
Bell, Thomas Devereaux, Jr., *communications company executive*
Bellows, Howard Arthur, Jr., *marketing research executive*
Bennett, Barbara Virginia *fashion consultant, concert pianist*
Bennett, James Marvin *consulting company executive*
†Berenson, Robert Leonard *advertising agency executive*
Bergen, John Donald *communications, public affairs executive*
Bernard, David George *retired management consultant*
Bernbach, John Lincoln *corporate strategies and investment executive*
†Bess, Ronald W. *advertising executive*
Biederman, Barron Zachary (Barry Biederman) *advertising agency executive*
Bishop, Susan Katharine *executive search company executive*
Bishopric, Susan Ehrlich *public relations executive*
Blanchard, Ronald Joseph *food service executive*
Bloomgarden, Kathy Finn *public relations executive*
Boice, Craig Kendall *management consultant*
†Borhi, Carol *data processing executive, finance company executive*
†Bostock, Roy Jackson *advertising agency executive*
†Bradstock, John *advertising executive*
Brady, Adelaide Burks *public relations agency executive, giftware catalog executive*
Brenner, Michael Edward *executive search and coaching consultant*
Brooks, Anita Helen *public relations executive*
Brooks, Gary *management consultant*
Brooks, Timothy H. *media executive*
Brown, Arnold *management consultant*
†Brown, Craig *advertising agency executive*
Brown, David Warfield *management educator*
Bruzs, Boris Olgerd *retired management consultant*
†Bungey, Michael *advertising executive*
Burger, Chester *retired management consultant*
Burke, David *corporate chef, executive chef*
Burkhardt, Ronald Robert *advertising executive*
Burson, Harold *public relations executive, director*
Burton, Peggy *advertising and marketing executive*
Byrd, Eva Wilson *communications executive*
Cage, Jack Hays *executive search consultant*
†Capozzi, Lou *public relations executive*
Cappiello, Angela *meeting and marketing manager*
Caress, Robert Seymour *personnel consultant*
†Carey, Thomas Hilton *advertising agency executive*
Carter, Carolyn Houchin *advertising agency executive*
Case, Stephen M. *media and entertainment company executive*
Cavanagh, Richard Edward *research policy organization executive*
Cavior, Warren Joseph *communications executive*
Chajet, Clive *brand and corporate image consultant*
Chandler, Robert Leslie *public relations executive*
Chang, Ling Wei *consulting services executive*
Chapin, Theodore Steinway *entertainment company executive*
Cheney, Richard Eugene *public relations executive, psychoanalyst*
Chesney, Robert Henry *communications/computer/process executive, consultant*
†Chess, William *public relations executive*
Chierchia, Madeline Carmella *management consulting company executive*
Chrisanthopoulos, Peter *advertising executive*
Clarke, Frank William *communication executive*
†Cohen, Brian S. *public relations executive*
Corbin, Herbert Leonard *public relations executive, director*
Cory, Christopher Thayer *communications executive*
Coyne, Nancy Carol *advertising executive*
†Crawford, Bruce Edgar *advertising executive*
Cuddihy, Robert Vincent, Jr., *finance and marketing executive*
Culligan, John William *retired corporate executive*
Dane, Maxwell *former advertising executive*
Daniel, David Ronald *management consultant*
Daum, Julie Hembrock *executive recruiter*
Davidson, Donald William *advertising executive*
DeBow, Jay Howard Camden *public relations executive*
DeBow, Thomas Joseph, Jr., *advertising executive*
Delano, Lester Almy, Jr.,
de Margitay, Gedeon *acquisitions and management consultant*
†Deutsch, Donny *advertising executive*
Dhondt, Steven Thomas *development officer*
Diamond, Harris *corporate communications executive, lawyer*
Dienstag, Eleanor Foa *corporate communications consultant*
†DiMarco, Brian J. *food and beverage consultant*
Dimling, John Arthur *marketing executive*
†DiPiazza, Samuel, Jr., *marketing professional*
†DiSpirito, Rocco *restaurant owner, chef*
Donaldson, John Cecil, Jr., *consumer products company executive*
†Dooner, John Joseph, Jr., *advertising executive*
†Drobis, David R. *public relations company executive*
†Duke, Robin Chandler Tippett *retired public relations executive*
Dunne, Dana Philip C. *management consultant*
Dunne, Diane C. *marketing executive*
Dunst, Laurence David *advertising executive*
†Edelman, Richard Winston *public relations executive*
Edson, Andrew Stephen *public relations executive*
Einach, Charles Donald *advertising and publishing executive*
Eisenhuth, John C. *training professional*
Elkes, Terrence Allen *communications executive*
Elliott, John, Jr., *advertising agency executive*
Emerson, Andi (Mrs. Andi Emerson Weeks) *sales and advertising executive*
Ernst, Kathryn Fitzgerald *management, marketing consulting firm executive, author*
Erosh, William Daniel *advertising executive*
Evans, Alfred Lee, Jr., *advertising executive*
†Exposito, Daisy *advertising executive*
Faber, Neil *advertising executive*
Fabian, Jeanne *entrepreneur, executive recruiter*
Fairbairn, Ursula Farrell *human resources executive*
Falk, Edgar Alan *public relations consulting executive, writer*
Faraone, Teri *public relations executive*
Farinelli, Jean L. *public relations executive*
Faskianos, Irina A. *organization executive*
Feintuch, Henry Philip *public relations executive*
Feldman, Allan Roy *corporate development and marketing executive*
†Feldman, Robert C. *public relations executive*
†Fenwick, Lex *communications executive*
Fernandes, Jeanne Mary *human resource administrator*
Feskoe, Gaffney Jon *management consultant*
Fili-Krushel, Patricia *media company executive*
Fine, Jo Renée *management executive*
Finn, David *public relations company executive, artist*
Finn, Peter *public relations executive*
Fisher, Gary Alan *marketing professional*
Flaherty, Tina Santi *corporate communications executive, writer*
Flaum, Sander Allen *advertising and marketing executive*
†Flay, Bobby *food service executive*
Fleischman, Barbara Greenberg *public relations consultant*
Fletcher, Mary Lee *retired marketing professional*
Fluhr, Howard *consulting firm executive*
Folter, Roland *book historian, rare books company executive, bibliographer*
Foxworth, Jo *advertising agency executive*
†Fudge, Ann Marie *advertising executive*
Gaertner, Stefan *human resources specialist, researcher*
Gardiner, E. Nicholas P. *executive search executive*
Gardner, Ralph David *advertising executive*
†Garfinkel, Lee *advertising agency executive*
Geier, Philip Henry, Jr., *advertising executive*
Geller, Robert James *advertising agency executive*
Geltzer, Sheila Simon *public relations executive*
†Georgescu, Peter Andrew *advertising executive*
Gerard-Sharp, Monica Fleur *communications executive*
Gerberg, Judith Levine *human resource company executive*
†Gilburne, Miles R. *communications executive*
Ginsburg, Sigmund G. *management and executive search consultant*
Girard, Andrea Eaton *communications executive, consultant*
Gitelson, Susan Aurelia *business executive, civic leader*
Glatt, Mitchell Steven *business executive*
Goldschmidt, Charles *advertising agency executive*
Goldsmith, Clifford Henry *former tobacco company executive*
†Goldsmith, Gary L. *advertising executive*
Goldstein, Gary Sanford *executive recruiter*
Goldstein, Henry *philanthropic institutions consultant*
Goldstein, Richard A. *consumer products company executive*
Goldstein, Stuart Zane *public affairs executive*
†Goldstone, Steven F. *consumer products company executive*
Gomez, Francis Dean *corporate executive, former foreign service officer*
Gottlieb, Jerrold Howard *advertising executive*
Greeley, Sean McGovern *sales executive*
Greenberg, Jeffrey W. *professional services company executive*
Greene, Adele S. *management consultant*
Greenland, Leo *advertising executive*
Grefrath, Peter Alan *marketing communications executive*
Griffith, Clark Dexter *risk management professional*
Groberg, James Jay *information sciences company executive*
Grossman, Jack *advertising agency executive*
†Grossman, James A. *public relations executive*
Gumbinner, Paul S. *advertising and executive recruitment agency executive*
†Guskov, Sergey *security firm executive*
Hammond, Lou Rena Charlotte *public relations executive*
Harrison, Judith Anne *human resources executive*
Hart, Karen Ann *advertising executive*
Hatheway, John Harris *advertising agency executive*
Hauser, Joyce Roberta *marketing professional*
†Hearn, David *advertising executive*
Heath, Jeffrey A. *executive recruiter*
Heinzerling, Larry Edward *communications executive*
Heller, Steven Anthony *management consultant*
Hemsing, Josephine Claudia *public relations professional for performing arts*
Henschel, Shirley Myra *licensing agent*
Herbert, Marilynne *public relations executive, freelance photographer*
Herrling, Anthony Carl *public relations executive*
†Hilpert, Dale W. *retail shoe company executive*
Hoog, Thomas W. *public relations executive*
Hooper, Ian (John Derek Glass) *marketing communications executive*
Horvitz, John C. *management consultant*
†Hosokawa, David *advertising executive*
Hudes, Nana Brenda *marketing professional*
Ilson, Bernard *public relations executive*
†Jabbur, Ramzi J. *management consultant*
†Jackson, James Lewis Perdue, II, *entertainment company executive*
Jacoby, Robert Harold *management consulting executive*
Jensen, Dennis Mark *marketing executive*
Johnson, John William, Jr., *executive recruiter*
Jonas, Gilbert *public relations and fund raising executive*
†Jones, Christopher *advertising company executive*
†Josell, Jessica (Jessica Wechsler) *public relations executive*
Josephs, Ray *public relations and advertising executive, writer, international relations consultant*
†Judge, Jerry *business executive*
Just, Gemma Rivoli *retired advertising executive*
†Kaess, Ken *advertising executive*
†Kang, Eliot *advertising executive*
Karalekas, George Steven *advertising agency executive, political consultant*
Karp, Martin Everett *management consultant*
Katz, Marcia *public relations company executive*
Keenan, Michael Edgar *marketing professional*
Kelly, Peter *CEO, president*
Kelmenson, Leo-Arthur *advertising executive*
Kennedy, Daniel John *national and international public relations consultant, communications executive*
Kenny, Roger Michael *executive search consultant, writer*
Kieren, Thomas Henry *management consultant*
Kinser, Richard Edward *management consultant*
Komisarjevsky, Christopher P.A. *public relations executive*
†Kotcher, Raymond Lowell *public relations executive*
Kotuk, Andrea Mikotajuk *public relations executive, writer*
Kraushar, Jonathan Pollack *communications and media consultant*
Kreisberg, Neil Ivan *advertising executive*
Kreston, Martin Howard *advertising, marketing, public relations, and publishing executive*
Krinsky, Robert Daniel *consulting firm executive*
†Krukowski, Jan *communications executive*
†Kuperman, Robert Ian *advertising agency executive*
†Laing, Jennifer *advertising executive*
Lamont, Lee *music management executive*
Land, Irene Stokvis *marketing executive*
Lang, George *restaurateur*
Langton, Cleve Swanson *advertising executive*
Larberg, John Frederick *wine consultant, educator*
Laumont, Philippe Emile *communications executive*
Lazarus, Rochelle Braff *advertising executive*
Leet, Mildred Robbins *corporate executive, consultant*
Leff, Ilene J(afnel) *management consultant, corporate and government executive*
†Lemblé, Patrick *chef*
†Leonardi, Peter M. *marketing professional*
Leslie, John Webster, Jr., (Jack Leslie) *communications company executive*
Leslie, Seymour Marvin *communications executive, director*
Leubert, Alfred Otto Paul *international business consultant, investor*
Levit, Mark Sheldon *advertising executive*
Lewis, Richard Warren *advertising agency executive*
Lilien, Mark Ira *executive*
Lipin, Joan Carol *healthcare executive, consultant*
Lipman, Ira Ackerman *security service company executive*
Lipton, Charles *public relations executive*
Lipton, Joan Elaine *advertising executive*
Lockwood, Helshi *advertising executive*
Loeb, Larry Morris *communications company executive*

Seaford
Spencer, Jean *executive*

Setauket
Palmedo, Philip Franklin *management consulting company executive*

Sherburne
Smith, William Edward *sales executive, telecommunications executive*

Skaneateles
Huxford, J. David *retired sales representative*

Sleepy Hollow
Schmidt, Klaus Franz *advertising executive*

Somers
†Cahill, John T. *consumer products company executive*
Elix, Douglas Thorne *computer company executive*
Faga, Anthony, Jr., *sales operations professional*
Sayers, Ken W(illiam) *writer, consultant and public relations executive, web editor*

Staten Island
Fafian, Joseph, Jr., *management consultant*

Stony Brook
Ohannessian, Harry Haroutune *travel agency executive*

Syosset
Heller, Al *marketing consultant, business journalist*
Irving, Jeffrey Alan *management consultant, educator, lawyer*

Syracuse
Berinstein, William Paul *business executive*
Boghosian, Paula der *computer business consultant*
Mondore, Patricia Anne *health facility administrative assistant, author, composer*
Ramsey, Dan Steven *consultant, business executive*
Russo, Joseph Maria *public affairs executive*

Tallman
Strasser, Joel A. *public relations executive, engineer, executive producer*

Tappan
Fox, Muriel *retired public relations executive*

Tarrytown
Kenney, Dion Patrick *business strategist, entrepreneur*

Thornwood
Bassett, Lawrence C *management consultant*

Tuckahoe
Brecher, Bernd *management consultant*

Valhalla
Campbell, Debra Lynn *marketing and new venture consultant*

Wantagh
Lamb, James P. *advertising executive*

West Nyack
Oppenheim, Robert *beauty industry executive*

Westbury
†McCann, James F. *consumer products company executive*

Westhampton Beach
Maas, Jane Brown *advertising executive*

White Plains
Colwell, Howard Otis *advertising executive*
Crames, Renee Karas *management consultant*
DeMond, Jeffrey Stuart *cable television and telecommunications executive*
Denham, Paul *technology sales and marketing executive*
Lukaszewski, James Edmund *communications executive*
Martin, Thomas Rhodes *communications executive, writer*
Ramlo, Sara B. *computer company executive*
†Salameh, Samer Fadi *communications executive*
†Sternlicht, Barry Stuart *hotel executive*
Sussberg, Milton Joel *marketing professional*

Whitesboro
Bulman, William Patrick *data processing executive*

Williamsville
McAfee, Paul Hindman, III, *marketing professional*
Sobolewski, Timothy Richard *marketing executive*
Stoeckl, Shelley Joan *marketing professional*
Truell, George Foster *management consultant*

Woodbury
Kelly, William Henry *computer company executive, mayor*

Woodhaven
Bolster, Jacqueline Neben (Mrs. John A. Bolster) *communications consultant*

Yonkers
Colabella, George Michael *management, fund raising consultant*
Pickover, Betty Abravanel *retired executive legal secretary, civic volunteer*
Wen, Sheree *computer company executive*

Yorktown Heights
Agerwala, Tilak Krishna Mahesh *computer company executive*
Kessler, Bernard Milton *organizational and human resources development specialist*
Rosenblatt, Stephen Paul *marketing and sales promotion company executive*
Mihailescu, Manuela *marketing executive*

NORTH CAROLINA

Arden
Baker, Kerry Allen *management consultant*

Asheboro
Purvis, Mary Craven *cosmetologist*

Asheville
Mareth, Paul David *multimedia producer*
Summey, Steven Michael *advertising company executive*
Turcot, Marguerite Hogan *innkeeper, medical researcher*
Weimer, William Arthur *computer company executive, consultant*

Beaufort
Burgard, Ralph *cultural and education planner*
Mackenzie, James *fire protection and industrial safety executive*

Boone
Daly, Joseph Patrick *management educator, researcher*
Parker, William Dale *management consultant, political and presidential adviser*

Burlington
Eddins, James William, Jr., *marketing executive*

Canton
Dixon, Shirley Juanita *retired restaurant owner*

Cary
Craig, Harold Kent *mechanical contracting executive, systems analyst*
†Flood, Susan J.A. *marketing strategist*
Goodnight, Jim *computer company executive*
Sail, John *computer company executive*
Taylor, James Francis *marketing professional*
Wait, George William *sales executive*

Chapel Hill
Jerdee, Thomas Harlan *business administration educator, organization psychology researcher and consultant*
Tarascio, Linda Scott *management executive*
Weeks, M. J. *international management consultant*

Charlotte
Burke, Steven Charles *healthcare administration executive*
Butler, Carol King *advertising executive*
Carino, Linda Susan *business consultant*
Cleghorn, John Michael *communications executive*
Eppes, Thomas Evans *advertising executive, public relations executive*
Hudgins, Catherine Harding *business executive*
Kallman, Kathleen Barbara *marketing and business development professional*
Kincaid, Steven Randall *marketing professional*
Lyerly, Elaine Myrick *advertising executive*
†Mickle, Deloris B. *credit manager, artist*
†Moore, Bealer Gwen *transcription company executive*
Ogiri, Dennis Arekpita *educator, political/business management consultant*
Price, Charles R., Jr., *advertising executive*
Rivenbark, Jan Meredith *business consultant*
Wood, Donald Craig *retired marketing professional*

Clayton
Silberman, H. Lee *public relations executive, editorial consultant*

Durham
Amaldoss, Wilfred *marketing educator*
Gunter, Emily Diane *communications executive, marketing professional, real estate developer, author, educator*
Ladd, Marcia Lee *medical equipment and supplies company executive*
Lieberman, Rochelle Phyllis *relocation company executive*
Oakley, Wanda Faye *management consultant, educator*
Otterbourg, Robert Kenneth *public relations consultant, writer*
Squire, Alexander *management consultant*

Edenton
Rossman, Robert Harris *management consultant*

Fayetteville
†Watt, Katherine Ann *administrative assistant*

Gastonia
Eads, Ronald Preston *Christian management consultant*

Goldsboro
Barkley, Monika Johanna *general contracting professional*

Granite Falls
Power, Elizabeth Henry *consultant*

Greensboro
Beahm, Roger *advertising executive*
†Brooks, Darrell Lemont *collections and bad debt manager*
Coyne, William P. *advertising executive*
Dillon, Terri L. *consulting firm executive*
Formo, Brenda Terrell *travel company executive*
Sanders, William Eugene *marketing executive*

Greenville
Finkelday, John Paul *retail sales executive*

Hampstead
Walters, Sherwood George *management consultant, educator*

Harrisburg
Edwards, Larry Cecil *management consultant*

Hickory
†George, Boyd Lee *consumer products company executive*
Speas, Charles Stuart *human resources consultant, entrepreneur*

High Point
Winn, Walter Garnett, Jr., *marketing strategist, advertising executive*

Hillsborough
Eustice, Russell Clifford *consulting company executive, academic director*

Horse Shoe
†Parish, Maryann Kelley *advertising executive*

Kernersville
†Hile, Elizabeth Gwyn *administrative assistant, marketing professional*

Morrisville
†Pucci, Anastasia Conlon *advertising executive*
Wing, Vanette *sales executive, consultant*

New Bern
Naumann, William Carl *consumer products company executive*

North Wilkesboro
Parsons, Irene Adelaide *management consultant*
Pond, Dale C. *company executive*

Pinehurst
Gilmore, Voit *travel executive*
Grantham, Joseph Michael, Jr., *hotel executive, management/marketing consultant*
Mc Dannald, Clyde Elliott, Jr., *management consultation company executive*

Pittsboro
Conley, Patrick *clinic administrator*

Raleigh
Cornish, Thelbert Bernard, Jr., *internet service provider executive*
Daly, Kay R. *public relations professional*
Eberly, Harry Landis *retired communications company executive*
Grubb, Donald Hartman *paper industry company executive*
†Karmanos, Peter, Jr., *computer software company executive, professional sports team executive*
Leak, Robert Edwards *economic development consultant*
Merrell, W. M. *advertising executive*

Research Triangle Park
Clark, Kevin Anthony *marketing executive, communications executive*
Greene, Amy Powers *human resources specialist*

Roxboro
Hollingsworth, Brenda Jackson *employment consultant*

Southern Pines
Owings, Malcolm William *retired management consultant*
Passaro, Paul Charles *business executive*

Supply
Jacobs, Richard Alan *management consultant*
Pollard, Joseph Augustine *advertising and public relations consultant*

Sylva
O'Neal, Moya Frances *management consultant*

Vass
Glassman, Edward *public relations management creativity consultant*

Weaverville
Parsons, Vinson Adair *retired computer software company executive*

Wilmington
Anstatt, Peter Jan *marketing services executive*
Lauria, Rita Marie *media and communications researcher, consultant*
†Maness, Eleanor Palmer *research analyst*

Winston Salem
Cullins, Margaret Carter *customer service administrator, small business owner*
Gunzenhauser, Gerard Ralph, Jr., *management consultant, investor*
Johnston, James Wesley *retired tobacco company executive*
Kaufman, Charlotte S. *communications executive*
Powers, David Murphy *consumer products company executive*

NORTH DAKOTA

Fargo
Tharaldson, Gary Dean *hotel developer and owner*
Wallwork, William Wilson, III, *automobile executive*

Grand Forks
Rolshoven, Ross William *legal investigator, artist*

Mountain
Melsted, Marcella H. *retired administrative assistant, civic worker*

OHIO

Akron
Crawford, Robert John *credit company executive*
Hochschwender, Herman Karl *international consultant*
Jasso, William Gattis *public relations executive*
Sonnecken, Edwin Herbert *management consultant*

Aurora
Ashworth, David J. *management consultant, power company executive*

Avon Lake
Morton, David Ray *sales and marketing executive*

Bay Village
Berger, James Hank *business broker*

Bowling Green
†Sloma, Robert J. *business process consultant*
Varney, Glenn Herbert *management educator*

Bridgeport
Janos, James Donald *security and safety consultant*

Broadview Heights
Sternlieb, Lawrence Jay *marketing professional, writer*

Canton
Thomas, Suzanne Ward *public relations executive, communications educator, radio personality*
Zantopulos, William Theodore *sales representative, small business owner*

Centerville
Corbet, Donald Lee *audio and technology company executive, technical systems educator*

Chagrin Falls
Church, Irene Zaboly *personnel services company executive*
Fisher, Will Stratton *illumination consultant*
Kuby, Barbara Eleanor *personnel director, management consultant*
Stevenson, Thomas Herbert *management consultant, writer, adult education educator*

Chardon
Mihalik, Phyllis Ann *consulting company executive, educator, public speaker*

Chesterland
Spitz, Arnoldt John *international trade professional, consultant*

Chillicothe
Murton, William Norman, II, *telecommunications executive*
Zeigler, Joseph William *surveillance company manager*

Cincinnati
Brown, Dale Patrick *retired advertising executive*
Campbell, Audrey Leigh *communications professional*
Carraher, Charles Jacob, Jr., *professional speaker*
†Charriez, Laston Samuel *marketing professional, director*
Dillon, David Brian *retail grocery executive*
Diltz, Jerry Dwaine *computer science educator, consultant*
Freidheim, Cyrus F., Jr., *management consultant*
†Goodman, Phyllis L. *public relations executive*
Hawkins, Lawrence Charles *management consultant, educator*
Hicks, Irle Raymond *retail food chain executive*
Hutton, Edward Luke *diversified public corporation executive*
Kansal, Achin Suresh *marketing professional, consultant*
Kernan, Jerome Bernard *retired marketing educator, researcher*
Klein, Charles Henle *lithographing company executive*
Kollstedt, Paula Lubke *communications executive, writer*
Lafley, Alan G. *consumer products company executive*
Lange, Scott Leslie *communications company executive, voice professional*
Levine, Aaron *executive*
Liss, Herbert Myron *communications executive*
Lockhart, John Mallery *management consultant*
McNulty, John William *retired public relations executive, automobile company executive*
Moore, John Edward *marketing professional, freelance writer*
Morris, Margaret Elizabeth *marketing professional*
Pancero, Jack Blocher *restaurant executive*
Pender, Richard F. *communications executive, consultant, theater critic*
†Pepper, John Ennis, Jr., *consumer products company executive*
Segal, Richard Arthur, Jr., *advertising agency executive*
Shipley, Tony L(ee) *software company executive*
Stolley, Alexander *advertising executive*
Strauss, James Lester *investment sales executive*
Wasserman, Donald Eugene *human vibration and ergonomics consultant*

Cleveland
Andrica, John Dean *management consultant*
Ballou, Ronald Herman *management educator*
Benghiat, Russell *advertising agency executive*
Byron, Rita Ellen Cooney *travel executive, publisher, real estate agent, civic leader, photojournalist, writer*
Danco, Léon Antoine *management consultant, educator*
Dunbar, Mary Asmundson *communications executive, investor and public relations consultant*
Eaton, Henry Felix *public relations executive*
Fountain, Ronald Glenn *management consultant, finance/marketing executive, management educator*
Hamilton, Nancy Beth *business executive*
Henry, Edward Frank *computer accounting service executive*
Jonovic, Donald J. *management consultant, writer*
Long, Kenneth D. *marketing research administrator*
Mabee, Keith V. *communications/investor relations executive*
Marcus, Donald Howard *advertising executive*
Masek, Jerome Edward *public relations executive*
Nagel, William Lee *management consultant*
Olson, Barry Gay *advertising executive, creative director*
Perkovic, Robert Branko *retired international management consultant*
Pollack, Florence K.Z. *management consultant*
†Pucko, Diane Bowles *public relations executive*
Roop, James John *public relations executive*
Stewart, Jack M. *management consulting firm executive*
Sudow, Thomas Nisan *marketing services company executive, broadcaster, chamber of commerce executive*
Taw, Dudley Joseph *sales executive, director*

Columbus
Alban, Roger Charles *small business consultant*
Barker, Llyle James, Jr., *management consultant, journalism educator*
Bastoky, Bruce Michael *human resources executive*
Burke, Kenneth Andrew *advertising executive*
†Iammartino, Nicholas R. *corporate communications executive*
Kerner, Joseph Frank, Jr., *management consultant, educator*
†Lewicki, Roy James *business educator*
Mann, Lynne Marie *executive administrative assistant*
McClain, Thomas Emerson *communications executive*
McCoy, William Earl, Jr., *economic development training consultant*
Reed, Constance Louise *materials management and purchasing consultant*
Ress, Charles William *management consultant*
Ryan, Robert *consulting company executive*
Sullivan, Ernest Lee *human resources director*
Tipton, Clyde Raymond, Jr., *communications and resources development consultant*
Varga, Steven Carl *human resources professional*
Zambito, John R. *executive search firm executive*

Dayton
Daoud, George Jamil *hotel and motel consultant*
Henley, Terry Lew *computer company executive*
Kegerreis, Robert James *management consultant, marketing educator*
Pasupuleti, Venumadhav *business executive, consultant*
Reading, Anthony John *business executive, accountant*
Riley, David Richard *management consultant, retired military officer*
†Tatar, Jerome F. *business products executive*
Walusis, Eric Michael *product developer, consultant*

Dover
Miller, Mary Katherine *management consultant*

Dublin
Freytag, Donald Ashe *management consultant*
McCauley, William Albert *business executive*
Miller, Charles *business management market research consultant*
Rasheed, Khalid *business executive*
Smith, K(ermit) Wayne *computer company executive*

Elyria
Patton, Thomas James *sales and marketing executive*

Fairfield
Rafalowski, Raymond Victor *printing and publishing executive*

Gahanna
Breen, John Wakefield *personnel services company executive*

Gates Mills
Abbott, James Samuel, III, *marketing executive*
Reitman, Robert Stanley *business consultant, nonprofit agency advisor*

Germantown
Lansaw, Charles Ray *rendering industry executive*

Grove City
Hosler, Elizabeth *management consultant*

Groveport
Reed, Roger Duane *maintenance electrician*

Hilliard
Price, Virginia Ashbaugh *technical service director, workers compensation c*

Holland
Sacksteder, Thomas Michael *corporate executive, entrepreneur, writer*

Independence
Frisman, Roger Lawrence *industrial sales executive*

Jackson
Benson, Steven Clark *management and engineering executive*

Kent
Bissler, Richard Thomas *mortician*

Lancaster
Katlic, John Edward *management consultant*
Phillips, Edward John *consulting firm executive*

Loveland
Dalambakis, Christopher A. *sales executive*
Neidhart, Carol Lynn *pharmaceutical company official*

Mansfield
Crittenden, Sophie Marie *communications executive*
Pesec, David John *data systems executive*

Mantua
Nelson, Hedwig Potok *marketing executive*

Maple Heights
Sargent, Liz Elaine (Elizabeth Sargent) *safety consulting executive*

Marietta
Spisak, John Francis *environmental company executive*

Marion
Fassler, Crystal G. *marketing consultant*

Marysville
Jones-Morton, Pamela *human resources specialist*

Mason
Drees, Stephen Daniel *marketing professional*

Maumee
Konopinski, Virgil James *industrial hygienist, consultant*
Nowak, Patricia Rose *advertising executive*

Mayfield Heights
Newman, Joseph Herzl *advertising consultant*
Rebolj, Joan Kaletta *training and development professional*

Medina
Williams, Paul C(hester) *consultant*

Middletown
Turpin, Richard E. *sales executive*

Napoleon
Frame, Lawrence Milven, Jr., *inventor*

New Albany
Duggan, Thomas Patrick *management consultant*

Newark
†Juodvalkis, Judith L. *human resources specialist*

North Canton
Seltzer, Mitchell Sherman *hotel executive*

Oxford
Yen, David Chi-Chung *management information systems educator*

Perrysburg
Kovacik, Neal Stephen *hotel and restaurant executive*
Loeffler, William Robert *quality productivity delivery specialist, engineering educator*

Powell
†Lee, Robert J. Y. *marketing professional*

Proctorville
Wiley, Jerold Wayne *environmental services executive, retired air force officer*

Saint Clairsville
Stepputtis, Susan Lyn *management consultant, educator*

Salem
Fehr, Kenneth Manbeck *retired computer systems company executive*

Springfield
Henning, William Clifford *cemetery consulting company executive*

Sylvania
Ring, Herbert Everett *management executive*
White, Alan Edward *computer company executive*

Tipp City
Taylor, Robert Homer *quality assurance professional, pilot*

Toledo
Block, Allan James *communications executive*
Cole, Jeffrey Clark *public relations professional*
Paquette, Jack Kenneth *management consultant, writer, historian*

Warren
Westman, Robert Allan *management consultant*

Westerville
Goh, Anthony Li-Shing *marketing professional*

Westlake
†Kuhn, Edwin P. *travel company executive*

Wilberforce
†Venkateswaran, Anuradha *marketing educator*

Worthington
Bender, Bob *advertising executive*
Keller, Kenneth Christen *advertising executive*

Wyoming
Cooley, William Edward *regulatory affairs manager*

Xenia
Nutter, Zoe Dell Lantis *retired public relations executive*

Yellow Springs
Schulsinger, Michael Alan *data processing executive*

Zanesville
†Brown, Eric D. *city planner, consultant, researcher*

OKLAHOMA

Altus
Wilcoxen, Joan Heeren *fitness company executive*

Cleveland
Henry, Kathleen Marie *marketing executive*

Edmond
Keckel, Peter J. *advertising executive*

Lawton
Hooper, Roy B. *lobbyist, consultant*

Monkey Island
Vanatta, Chester B. *retired business executive, educator*

Norman
Whittier, Charles Taylor, Jr., *consulting company executive, educational, management and scientific administrator*

Oklahoma City
Ackerman, Raymond Basil *advertising agency executive*
Binning, Gene Barton *computer company executive*
Blackwell, John Adrian, Jr., *computer company executive*
†Funk, Robert Allen *personnel executive*
Grupe, Robert Charles *corporate training consultant*
LaMotte, Janet Allison *retired management specialist*
McKinnis, Lee Vern *communications executive*

Ringling
†Hammons, Ella *consumer products company executive*

Stillwater
Qu, Hailin *hospitality and tourism professional*

Tulsa
Boyle, Lester Joseph *marketing and broadcast executive*
Crouch, Gary Clinton *financial management company executive, accountant*
Gentry, Bern Leon, Sr., *minority consulting company executive*
Jensen, Joli *communications educator*
Wagner, Ann Louise *management consultant, public relations executive*

OREGON

Albany
Haralson, Linda Jane *communications executive*

Ashland
Hegler, Ellen Marie *business executive, retired educator*

Beaverton
Murray, Jean Rupp *communications executive, writer, speaker*
†Stewart, Kirk T. *public relations executive*

Bend
Wonser, Michael Dean *retired public affairs director, art history educator*

Canby
Flinn, Roberta Jeanne *management, computer applications consultant*

Dayton
†Wright, Beverly June *sales executive*

Eugene
Chambers, Carolyn Silva *communications company executive*
Leeds, Elizabeth Louise *miniature collectibles executive*
Miner, John Burnham *industrial relations educator, writer*

Forest Grove
Carson, William Morris *manpower planning and development advisor*

Jacksonville
Hennion, Reeve Lawrence *communications executive*

Lake Oswego
Edstrom, Pam *public relations executive*
Parrick, Gerald Hathaway *communications and marketing executive*
Waggener, Melissa *public relations executive*

Mcminnville
Naylor-Jackson, Jerry *public relations consultant, retired, entertainer, broadcaster*

Medford
Cole, Richard George *public administrator*
Hildebrandt, Janelle Diner *sales executive*

Pendleton
Bedford, Amy Aldrich *public relations executive*

Portland
Bosch, Samuel Henry *computer company executive*
Conkling, Roger Linton *consultant, business administration educator, retired utility executive*
Day, L. B. *management consultant*
Kupel, Frederick John *business executive*
Linstone, Harold Adrian *management and systems science educator*
Moss, Richard Spencer *communications executive*
Perotto, Gregory Todd *public relations professional*
Smith, Russell Wesley *management and computer applications consultant, organizational development trainer*
Stern, Bruce L. *marketing professional, educator*
Urbanowski, John Richard *lighting systems company official*
†Wieden, Dan G. *advertising executive*

Roseburg
Plunkett, Marvin Wayne *data processing company executive*

Salem
Baker, Edwin Stuart *retired computer consultant*
Benson, Steven Donald *sheet metal research and marketing executive, sheet metal mechanic, programmer, author*
Benton, Jack Mitchell *management consultant*
Milbrath, Mary Merrill Lemke *quality assurance professional*

Shady Cove
Meyers, Sharon May *sales executive*

Tualatin
Hick, Kenneth William *marketing company executive*
Peters, Robert Wayne *direct mail and catalog sales specialist*

PENNSYLVANIA

Altoona
Johnopolos, Stephen Gary *commission outreach representative*

Ardmore
†Lockett-Egan, Marian Workman *advertising executive*

Bala Cynwyd
Straus, Roger Austin *marketing consultant, clinical sociologist*

Bensalem
Gretz, Karl Frederick *training consultant, writer*

Berwyn
Guenther, George Carpenter *travel company executive, retired*

Bethel Park
Willard, John Gerard *consultant, author, lecturer*

Bethlehem
Felix, Patricia Jean *steel company purchasing professional*
†Penny, Roger Pratt *management executive*
†Philpotts, Alvin T. *management consultant*

Blue Bell
Faden, Lee Jeffrey *technical consultant and expert referral company executive*
Nichols, James Lee *advertising executive*
†Tilghman, Christopher Joseph *marketing professional*
Weinbach, Lawrence Allen *computer company executive*

Brentwood
Swanson, Fred A. *retired communications designer, councilman*

Bryn Mawr
Wheeler, Grace R. *retired market researcher*

Buckingham
Altier, William John *management consultant*

Camp Hill
Crist, Christine Myers *consulting executive*

Chadds Ford
Martin, David Warren *management consultant*
Reddish, John Joseph *management consultant*

Chambersburg
Furr, Quint Eugene *marketing executive*
Neilson, Winthrop Cunningham, III, *communications executive, financial communications consultant, photographer*

Coraopolis
Victor, Ronald Joseph, Jr., *banking professional*

Cranberry Twp
Patten, Charles Anthony *management consultant, retired manufacturing company executive, author*

Dallas
Fiegelman, Richard Paul *sales consultant, freelance writer*

Delmont
Thompson, Paul A. *business consultant, performance improvement expert*

East Earl
Jonassen, Gaylord D. *computer company executive, new products and market development*

Emmaus
Zahradnik, Fredric Douglas *publishing executive*

Erie
DeCrease, William Maurice *total quality management consultant*
Egan, Corrine Halperin *management consultant*
Lund, Edwin Harrison *business accounting systems executive*
Ryan, James Thomas *organizational consultant, business owner*

Exton
Duvivier, Jean Fernand *management consultant, consultant*
Mauch, Robert Carl *service industry executive, venture capitalist*

Ford City
Ursiak, David Allen *operations executive, consultant*

Fort Washington
Blumberg, Donald Freed *management consultant*

Gettysburg
Hallberg, Budd Jaye *management consulting firm executive*

Grantville
Sudor, Cynthia Ann *sales and marketing professional*

Greensburg
Boyd, Robert Wright, III, *lamp company executive*

Harrisburg
Elliott, Scott Dean *public relations executive*
Moritz, Milton Edward *security consultant*

Haverford
†Gross, Stanley Carl *marketing consultant*

Havertown
Somach, S. Dennis *communications executive*

Hawley
Dilmore, Joseph Eric *carpenter, poet, writer*

Huntingdon Valley
Vollum, Robert Boone *management consultant*

Indiana
McPherson, Donald Scott *employment relations educator, arbitrator/mediator*
Ruddock, Ellen Sylves *business consultant*

Jamison
Thorne, John Watson, III, *advertising and marketing executive*

Kennett Square
Fish, Robert H. *long term care industry executive*
Hennes, Robert Taft *former management consultant, investment executive*

King Of Prussia
†Angie, Jill Elizabeth *quality assurance professional*
Clauson, Sharyn Ferne *consulting company executive, educator*
Marcus, Stephen Cecil *former printing company executive*
Szabo, Joseph Laszlo *management consultant*

Lafayette Hill
Edwards, JoAnn Louise *human resources executive*

Lancaster
Finger, Robert Roy *marketing executive*
Kelly, Robert Lynn *advertising agency executive*
Taylor, Ann *human resources specialist, educator*

Lemoyne
Powell, Fredrick Charles *business executive*

Lewisburg
Rote, Nelle Fairchild Hefty *business consultant*
Warner-Mills, Susan *organizational and community development consultant*

Lower Burrell
Kinosz, Donald Lee *business process consultant*

Malvern
Brock, Lynmar, Jr., *food service executive*
Herring, Raymond Mark *marketing professional, researcher*

Manns Choice
Braendel, Douglas Arthur *hotel executive*

Mars
McChesney, Charles E. *retired marketing professional*

Mechanicsburg
Moore, Kenneth Lee *executive*
Stone, Thomas Richardson *management consultant*

Media
Garvin, Florence Ward *management consultant*

Middletown
Yucelt, Ugur *marketing professional, educator*

Monroeville
Valentine, Ruthann *counseling company executive*

Montgomeryville
Schmidt, William Max *management consultant, business executive*

Moon Township
Giel, James Arthur, Jr., *employee benefits manager*

Mountainhome
Buttz, Charles William *outdoor advertising executive*

New Hope
Roazzi, Vincent Michael *marketing professional*
Thomsen, Thomas Richard *retired communications company executive*

North Wales
Mann, Elaine Renee *marketing manager*

Nottingham
White, Richard Edmund *marketing executive*

Philadelphia
Adawi, Nadia Sharon *energy cooperative executive*
Barnett, Samuel Treutlen *international company executive*
Barrett, James Edward, Jr., *management consultant*
†Bisaccia-Hanson, Betty *marketing professional, public relations executive*
Bodner, Susan Rachel *marketing and communications executive*
Boyd, Larry Chester *recruitment manager*
Cappelli, Peter H. *human resources educator*
Coulson, Zoe Elizabeth *retired consumer marketing executive*
Di Benedetto, C. Anthony *marketing educator*
Exler, Samuel *retired advertising executive, writer*
Farley, Joseph Michael *human relations executive, editor, publisher*
Feninger, Claude *industry management services company executive*
Finney, Graham Stanley *management consultant*
Fuller, John G.C. *food and drug company executive*
†Greene, Hans *facilities administrator*
Jordan, Clifford Henry *management consultant*
†Mallon, Charles J. *management consultant executive*
Mazzafro, Joseph D. *international adoption agency executive, web designer*
Meyer Weisgerber, Martha Lindsey *account executive*
Oliva, Terence Anthony *marketing educator*
†Pinola, Richard J. *management consultant*
Presser, Janice *business executive*
Roberts, Brian L. *communications executive*
Roberts, Ralph Joel *telecommunications, cable broadcast executive*
Soslow, Arnold *quality consultant*
Stewart, Marvin Lewis *human resources professional*
†Tuan, Kailin *management consultant, educator*
Wiglesworth, Michael Bland *advertising executive*

Phoenixville
Brundage, Russell Archibald *retired data processing executive*

Pittsburgh
Bender, Charles Christian *retail home center executive*
Bonner, Shirley Harrold *business communications educator*
Buchanan, Gloria Jean *sales executive*
Burger, Herbert Francis *advertising agency executive*
Cicero, J. Deborah *management consultant*
Dempsey, Jerry Edward *retired service company executive*
Dieter, Richard Charles *marketing and management professional*
Fisher, James Aiken *industrial marketing consultant*
Genge, William Harrison *advertising executive, writer*
Guinn, Kathleen Anne *human resources specialist*
Horowitz, Don Roy *landscape company executive*
Kolmen, Samuel Norman *retired consultant*
Nath, Raghu *management consultant, educator*
Neel, John Dodd *cemetery executive*
Rathke, Sheila Wells *strategic and marketing consultant*
Reichblum, Audrey Rosenthal *public relations executive, publishing executive*
Richards, Aleta Williams *marketing and quality professional*
Schultheiss, Emily Ekonen *management consultant, writer*
Simmermon, James Everett *credit bureau executive*
Sladack, David Robert *advertising executive*
Tobin, Robert Edwin *regional director*

Plymouth Meeting
Siegal, Jacob J. *management and financial consultant*

Port Royal
Wert, Jonathan Maxwell, II, *management consultant*

Pottstown
Bause, David Francis *printing company professional*
Czuj, Chester Francis, Jr., *food service professional*

Quakertown
Ashcom, John M. *sales executive, general management executive*

Radnor
Marland, Alkis Joseph *rental company executive, computer scientist, educator, financial planner*
Paier, Adolf Arthur *computer software and services company executive*
Thompson, Pamela Padwick *public relations executive*

Reading
Dersh, Rhoda E. *management consultant, business executive*
Hackenberg, Barbara Jean Collar *retired advertising and public relations executive*
Kraras, Gust C. *hotel executive*

Ridley Park
Walls, William Walton, Jr., *management consultant*

Royersford
Rhoads, Michael Dennis *sales executive*

Rydal
Boreen, Henry Isaac *computer company executive*

Saint Davids
McCarthy, Justin Milton *marketing professional*

Scranton
Williams, Holly Thomas *retired business executive*

Shippensburg
Stone, Susan Ridgaway *marketing educator*

Solebury
Gart, Herbert Steven *communications executive, producer*

Southeastern
Amichetti, Dennis Joseph *advertising executive*
Rassbach, Herbert David *marketing executive*

State College
Cao, Guohong *computer science educator*
Subler, Edward Pierre *advertising executive*

Steelton
Zimmerman, Connie Ann *public administrator*

Sunbury
Weis, Robert Freeman *supermarket company executive*

Tannersville
Moore, James Alfred *ski company executive, lawyer*

Temple
Stump, Richard Carl *environmental services administrator, consultant*

Unionville
De Marino, Donald Nicholson *international business executive, former federal agency administrator*

Upper Saint Clair
Anderson, Catherine M. *consulting company executive*

Valley Forge
LaBoon, Lawrence Joseph *human resources specialist, consultant*

Wallingford
Medina, Harold Raymond, III, *marketing executive*

Warrington
O'Hara, Timothy Patrick *marketing professional*
Shaw, Milton Herbert *conglomerate executive*

Washington
Grimm, Donald Lee *executive*

Washington Crossing
Clevenger, Roy Edward *credit and collections manager*

Wayne
Carroll, Robert W. *retired business executive*
Higgs, Jon Scott *computer company executive, researcher*
Meltser, Thomas Avrum *corporate executive*

West Chester
†Briggs, Douglas D. *communications executive*
Dunlop, Edward Arthur *computer company executive*
Hanna, Colin Arthur *county official, management and computer consultant*
Hanson, Diane Charske *management consultant*
Meystel, Michael A. *Internet executive*
Walls, Thomas Francis *professional services administrator*

West Conshohocken
Mullen, Eileen Anne *human resources executive*

Wilkes Barre
Swanek, Susan Ann *quality assurance professional*

Willow Grove
†Asplundh, Christopher B. *tree service company executive*
Schiffman, Louis F. *management consultant*

Woolrich
Himes, Kenneth Alan *retired marketing executive*

Wynnewood
Belinger, Harry Robert *retired business executive*

Wyomissing
Pellecchia, Eve Wassall *management consultant*
Williams-Wennell, Kathi *human resources consultant*

Yardley
Huret, Barry S. *marketing professional, consultant*
Minter, Philip Clayton *retired communications company executive*
Newsom, Carolyn Cardall *management consultant*
Weaver, William Clair, Jr., (Mike Weaver) *human resources development executive*

York
Horn, Russell Eugene, Jr., *business executive*
Livingston, Pamela A. *corporate image and marketing management consultant*
Roetenberg, Aaron David *retail consultant*
Snyder, Jan Louise *administrative aide*

RHODE ISLAND

Barrington
Mihaly, Eugene Bramer *corporate executive, consultant, writer, educator*

East Providence
Furtado-Lavoie, Julia *new business startup consultant, accountant*

Newport
Lowe, Alfred Mifflin, III, *advertising agency executive, writer*

North Kingstown
Kullberg, Gary Walter *advertising agency executive*

Pawtucket
DeWerth, Gordon Henry *management consultant*
Hassenfeld, Alan Geoffrey *consumer products company executive*
O'Neill, John T. *retired toy company executive*
†Verrecchia, Alfred Joseph *consumer products company executive*

Providence
Allio, Robert John *management consultant, educator*
Baar, James A. *public relations and corporate communications executive, author, consultant, internet publisher, software developer*
D'Andrea, Vincent Charles *postal clerk*
†Ostiguy, Stephen W. *human resources specialist*
Pagliarini, John Raymond *public affairs executive*
Roussel, Normand Lucien *advertising executive*
†Whiting, Brian Christopher *hospitality consultant*

Warwick
Lac, Ming Q. *Information technology and electronics executive*
Patchis, Pauline *handwriting expert, consultant*

SOUTH CAROLINA

Bluffton
Reuben, Alvin Bernard *communications and entertainment executive*

Charleston
De Wolff, Louis *management consultant*
Dowell, Richard Patrick *technology company executive*
Osteen, Louis *chef*
Perry, Evelyn Reis *communications company executive*
Waggoner, Robert *chef*

Columbia
Barnum, William Douglas *retired communications company executive*
Chernoff, Marvin *advertising executive*
Grimball, Caroline Gordon *retail sales professional*
Ivester, Joy Godshall *educational administrator*
Quinn, Michael William *public affairs educator*
Silver, Rick *marketing professional*

Darlington
Isgett, John *auto dealership executive*

Greenville
Callahan, Ralph Wilson, Jr., *advertising agency executive*
Fitzgerald, Eugene Francis *management consultant*
Gerretsen, Gilbert Wynand (Gil Gerretsen) *marketing mentor*
Maynard, George Fleming, III, *philanthropic consultant*
Townes, Bobby Joe *travel agency executive*

Hilton Head Island
Estrin, Deborah Perry *human resources executive*
Little, Thomas Mayer *public relations executive*

McKeldin, William Evans *management consultant*
Patton, Joseph Donald, Jr., *management consultant*
Woodrum, Robert Lee *executive search consultant*

Ladys Island
Yates, Linda Snow *financial services marketing executive, real estate*

Lake Wylie
Sanford, James Kenneth *public relations executive*

Laurens
Williams-Tims, Lillie Althea *distribution administrator, genealogist, preservationist, tax specialist*

Mauldin
†Looper-Wilson, Leah Marie *human resources specialist, controller, interior designer*
Wood, Myra Linden Frank *consultant*

Mount Pleasant
Falkowski, Edward J. *executive consultant, business coach*
Hill, Larkin Payne *real estate company data processing executive*

Pawleys Island
Grubb, William Francis Xavier *consumer software executive, marketing executive*
Hannan, Robert Emmet *business development consultant*

Prosperity
Jennings, Wirt Holman, Jr., *retired marketing executive*

Ridgeland
Gardner, James *recreational management executive*

Spartanburg
Mahanes, Michael Wayne *organizational development executive*

Sumter
Gagne, Armand Joseph, Jr., *business administration and computer science educator, consultant*

SOUTH DAKOTA

Rapid City
Johnson, William Jennings *marketing consultant, entrepreneur*

Sioux Falls
Van Pelt, Frances Evelyn *management consultant*

TENNESSEE

Brentwood
LeBlanc, Larry Joseph *management educator*
Martin, William Edwin *business executive, lawyer, government official*

Chattanooga
Meyer, Roger Arnold *management consultant, writer*
Young, Sonia Winer *public relations director, educator*

Cleveland
Rhodes, Arthur Delano *benefits administrator*

Collierville
McKinney, William Douthitt, Jr., *sales and engineering company executive*

Cordova
Romanoff, Stanley M., Jr., *human resource specialist*

Dyersburg
McGrail, Susan King *travel agency executive, accountant*
Scearce, Janna Luebkemann *sales professional*

Gallatin
Bradley, Nolen Eugene, Jr., *personnel executive, educator*
Ellis, Joseph Newlin *retired distribution company executive*

Gatlinburg
Flanagan, Judy *special events professional, entertainment and marketing specialist, professional public speaker*

Germantown
Arendall, Charles Steven *management consultant, educator*
Davis, Tom Ivey, II, *management executive*

Hendersonville
Ambrose, Charles Stuart *sales executive*

Jackson
Freeman, Doris Branch *retired marketing professional*

Knoxville
†Anderson, Charles *printing/publishing company executive*
Cox, Anna Lee *retired administrative assistant*
†Harris, Charles E. *marketing professional*
†Haslam, James A., III, *petroleum sales executive*
Horne, Douglas A. *diversified companies executive*
†Sansom, William B. *consumer products executive*

La Vergne
†Ingram, David B. *entertainment company executive*

Lenoir City
Edwards, C. Karen *consultant company executive*

Madison
Cage, Allie M. *communications executive*
Hadley, John Livingston, V, *management executive, writer*

Maryville
Davis, William Walter *recruiter, trainer*

McKenzie
†Hetrick, William P. *marketing professional, educator*

Memphis
Abston, Dunbar, Jr., *management executive*
Archer, Ward, Jr., *advertising executive*
†Blake, Norman *hotel executive*
Mann, Donald Cameron *record company executive*
†Pulido, Miguel Lazaro *marketing professional*
Williams, Russ *marketing professional*

Nashville
Allbritton, Cliff *personal and organizational consultant*
Brett, John Brendan, Jr., *corporate advertising and public relations executive*
Dobbs, George Albert *funeral director, embalmer*
Evans, Franklin Bachelder *marketing educator emeritus*
Hillenmeyer, Henry Reiling, Jr., *restaurant company executive*
†Ingram, Martha Rivers *company executive*
James, Kay Louise *management consultant, healthcare executive*
†Lawrence, Thomas Patterson *public relations executive*
McNeely, Mark *marketing professional, journalist*
Meredith, Owen Nichols *public relations executive, genealogist*
Moore, William Grover, Jr., *management consultant, former air freight executive, former air force officer*
Murray, Richard Keith *marketing executive*
Shipley Biddy, Shelia *artist management executive*
Van Mol, Louis John, Jr., *public relations executive*

Oak Ridge
Hudson, Sheila Donnette *waste management administrator*
†Reid, Michael David *human resources specialist, consultant*

Pleasant Shade
Blackburn, Bryan David *title abstractor*

Shelbyville
Nelson, Clara Singleton *human resources consultant*

Tullahoma
Gossick, Lee Van *consultant, executive, retired air force officer*

TEXAS

Abilene
Patterson, Coleman E.P. *management educator*
Rogers, Gary Steven *consultant*

Addison
Grote, Dick (Richard Charles Grote) *management consultant, educator, author, radio commentator*

Allen
Battat, Emile A. *management executive*

Amarillo
Stubben, Dolus Jane (D. J. Stubben) *advertising executive*

Arlington
Byas, Teresa Ann Uranga *customer service representative, interior designer*
English, Marlene Cabral *management consultant*
Harris, Vera Evelyn *human resources specialist*
Sawyer, Dolores *motel chain executive*
Sims-Person, LeAnn Michelle *human resources specialist*
Wiig, Karl Martin *knowledge management expert and consultant*

Austin
Barnes, Sally Anderson *human resources consultant, organization effectiveness and employee involvement facilitator*
Casey, James Francis *management consultant*
Curle, Robin Lea *computer software industry executive*
Dabbs Riley, Jeanne Kernodle *retired public relations executive*
Drongowski, Steve *advertising executive*
Hart, Roderick P. *communications educator, researcher, author*
Knapp, Mark Lane *communication educator, consultant*
Laine, Katie Myers *communications consultant, executive coach*
Lenoir, Gloria Cisneros *consultant, educator*
Maguire, Kevin *travel management consultant*
Pate, Jacqueline Hail *retired data processing company executive*
Pearson, Jim Berry, Jr., *human resources specialist*
Rector, Clark Ellsworth *advertising executive*
Robinson, Richard Allen, Jr., *human resources development trainer, consultant*
Smith, Barry Alan *hotel executive, real estate broker*
Sober, Debra Evonne *environmental services administrator*
Sturdevant, Wayne Alan *executive management consultant*
Vande Hey, James Michael *corporate executive, former air force officer*
Vandel, Diana Geis *management consultant*
Walls, Carl Edward, Jr., *food service executive*
York, Candace A. *marketing professional, writer*
†Zrno, John M. *communications executive*

Baytown
Adams-Anderson, Niki Maria *communications company executive*

Bedford
Champney, Raymond Joseph *advertising and marketing executive, consultant*

Bellaire
†Streeter, Kevin D. *management consultant*

Burleson
Buford, Evelyn Claudene Shilling *retired consumer products company executive*

Burnet
Burris, Darrel Gene *retired company executive*

Cedar Hill
Garrett, C. Lynn *researcher, business consultant*

Cleveland
Rice, J. Andrew *management consultant, tree farmer*

College Station
Gunn, Clare Alward *travel consultant, writer, retired educator*
Hise, Richard Todd *marketing professional, educator, consultant*
Sorescu, Alina *marketing professional, educator*

Colleyville
Dodson, George Wayne *computer company executive, consultant*

Coppell
Owen, Cynthia Carol *sales executive*

Corpus Christi
DuVall, Lorraine *recreation center owner*
Stanford, Jane Herring *management consultant and educator, author*

Cypress
†LaCroix, Jeffrey William *management consultant*

Dallas
Alvey, David Lynn *advertising executive, artist, curator, poet*
Bartlett, Richard Chalkley *business executive, writer, conservationist*
Brierley, Harold M. *advertising executive*
Bryant, L. Gerald *management consultant*
Carl, Robert E. *retired marketing company executive*
Dalton, Harry Jirou, Jr., (Jerry Dalton) *public relations executive*
†Davis, John F., III, *travel company executive*
Davis, Rachel Lee Mostert *advertising executive*
Dawson, Edward Joseph *merger and acquisition executive*
Dedman, Robert Henry *sales executive*
Dieste, Tony *marketing professional*
Dillon, Donald Ward *management consultant*
Dozier, David Charles, Jr., *marketing public relations and advertising executive*
Dykeman, Alice Marie *public relations executive*
Ellis, June B. *human resource consultant*
English, Que *public relations executive*
†Frank, Paula Feldman *business executive*
†Govil, Manish Kumar *customer service administrator*
Gray, James Larry *international business executive*
Griffith, Gary Ernest *public affairs executive*
Grimes, David Lynn *communications company executive*
Harkness, R. Kenneth *restaurant chain executive*
Harmel, Warren *marketing professional*
†Hartger, Barbara J. *marketing professional*
Horchow, S(amuel) Roger *marketing consultant*
Ingersoll, Ted Meriam *mail services executive, retired advertising executive*
†Koski, Christine L. *consulting firm executive*
†Kusin, Gary M. *consumer products company executive*
Lane, Alvin Huey, Jr., *management consultant*
Leven, Stephen H. *human resources professional*
Levenson, Stanley Richard *public relations and advertising executive*
†Love, Sammie L. *administrative assistant, writer*
Loveless, Kathy Lynne *client services executive*
Metzner, Richard *advertising executive*
Mong, Robert William, Jr., *media executive*
Murphy, Randall Kent *management consultant*
Newsom, Holly Ann *management consultant*
Nussbaum, Paul A. *retired hospitality executive*
Pace, Carolina Jolliff *communications executive, commercial real estate investor*
Page, Stephen Jeffrey Lawrence *management consulting company executive*
Pearson, Robert Lawrence *executive recruiter*
Perich, Toni Annette *sales executive*
†Rich, Jeffrey A. *computer company executive*
†Richards, Stanford Harvey *advertising agency executive, design studio executive*
Robertson, Jane Ryding *marketing executive*
Rogers, Susan (Sue Rogers) *data processing consultant*
Routman, Daniel Glenn *business development executive, lawyer*
Spiegel, Lawrence Howard *advertising executive*
†Stern, Andrew Milton *public relations executive*
Vanderveld, John, Jr., *international business development specialist*
Von Kennel, Gary Phillip *marketing company executive*
Waters, Rollie O. *management consultant*
Whitt, Robert Ampudia, III, *advertising executive, marketing professional*
Wilber, Robert Edwin *corporate executive*
Wilde, Patrick Joseph *administrator*
Wilson, Catherine Cooper (Kitty Wilson) *communications executive, writer*

Del Rio
Garrett, James William *computer company executive*
Prather, Gerald Luther *management consultant, retired air force officer, judge*

Denton
†Galindo, Rebeca *administrative assistant*

Dripping Springs
Ballard, Mary Melinda *financial communications and investment banking firm executive, consumer advocate*
Nicholas, Nickie Lee *retired industrial hygienist*

Duncanville
Jenkins, Tony Dean *salesman*

Edinburg
†Martínez-López, Carmen Leonor *management consultant, educator*

El Paso
Deerman, Ruth Gillett *sales professional, flying instructor*
Potter, Wylie Shattuck *marketing professional*
Roberts, Ernst Edward *marketing consultant*

Fort Worth
Appel, Bernard Sidney *marketing consultant, former electronic company executive*
Bradshaw, James Edward (Jim Bradshaw) *consultant*
Davis, Carol Lyn *administrative assistant*
Faulkner, Karl Max *photography director*
Genett-Schrader, Ann G. *public relations executive*
Holman, Karen Marie Anderson *purchasing agent*
†Jones, Terrell B. *travel company executive*
Livengood, Charlotte Louise *employee development specialist*
Shannon, Larry Redding *public relations executive*
Staffel, Edward Ross, Jr., *executive, consultant*
Williams, Emma *management executive*

Fredericksburg
Arnold, George Lawrence *retired advertising company executive*
Benedict, Mark J *government analyst, marketing executive, lawyer, real estate investment consultant*

Frisco
Migdol, Marvin Jacob *public relations and marketing executive, consultant*

Garland
Basham, Lloyd Moman *manufacturing service company executive*
Jaksa, David Michael *wireless network company official*
Odom, Judy *software company executive*

Greenville
Brown, Harley Mitchell *retired computer company executive, writer*

Heath
Hargrave, Robert Warren *retired hair styling salon chain executive*

Highland Village
Lawrence, William Clarence *business executive, lawyer, mediator, politician*
Richardson, K. Scott *sales executive*

Houston
Adams, C. Lee *marketing executive*
Baysal, Edip *executive*
Blackburn, Sadie Gwin Allen *executive*
Burnett, Clarence Aubrey (Rusty Burnett) *personnel services company executive*
Burnett, Susan Walk *personnel service company owner*
Carlberg, W. Charles *advertising executive*
Crystal, Jonathan Andrew *executive recruiter*
Flato, William Roeder, Jr., *software development company executive*
Gilbert, Harold Stanley *retired warehousing company executive*
Goings, Austin Nelson *sales executive*
Helland, George Archibald, Jr., *management consultant, manufacturing executive, former government official*
Holmes, Roscette Yvonne Lewis *organizational development and training consultant*
Ifft, Lewis George, III, *company administrator*
Jeanneret, Paul Richard *management consultant*
Keating, Tim *chef*
Keller, Robert Bounds *marketing professional, consultant, inventor*
Kors, R. Paul *search company executive*
Krueger, Artur W. G. *international business consultant*
Lampl, Lee Ann *internet marketing professional*
Larkin, William Vincent, Jr., *company executive*
†Leth, Steven A. *management consultant*

Levy, Robert Edward *management consultant*
†Mampre, Virginia Elizabeth *communications executive*
Margotta, Maurice Howard, Jr., *management consultant*
Mayo, Carolyn *marketing professional, public relations executive*
McCollam, Marion Andrus *consulting firm executive, educator*
McKim, Paul Arthur *management consultant, retired petroleum executive*
†Morabito, Philip A. *public relations executive*
Morrison, Scott David *management consultant*
Mulholland, Jane E. *management consultant*
Myers, James Clark *advertising and public relations executive*
O'Brient, David Warren *sales executive, consultant*
O'Laughlin, Francis Michael, III, *management consultant*
Olstead, Christopher Eric *consulting executive, talent manager*
Palmer, James Edward *public relations executive*
Ribble, Anne Hoerner *communications executive*
Rieke, Ronald Alfred *computer company executive*
Roberts, Paul *chef*
Saunders, William Arthur *management consultant*
Sill, Gerald de Schrenck *hotel executive*
Smith, Claire *chef*
Solymosy, Edmond Sigmond Albert *international marketing executive, retired army officer*
Sperber, Matthew Arnold *direct marketing company executive*
Springer, Wayne Gilbert *computer company executive*
Vollmer, Helen *public relations executive*
Willmann, Donnie Glenn *safety executive*
Woods, Stephanie Elise *computer company executive, entrepreneur*
Yuen, Benson Bolden *airline management consultant, software executive*

Humble
Gruman, Robert Richard *energy management consultant*

Huntsville
Smyth, Joseph Philip *travel industry executive*
Sower, Victor Edmund *management educator*
Stowe, Charles Robinson Beecher *management consultant, educator, lawyer*

Hurst
Bishara, Amin Tawadros *management and consulting firm executive, technical services executive*

Irving
Dinicola, Robert *consumer products company executive*
Gibson, Colvin Donald *human resources specialist*
Gretzinger, Ralph Edwin, III, *management consultant*
Nugent, John Hilliard *communications executive*
†Rose, Rachel *marketing professional*
†Vamanan, Mayur *advisory consultant*
Wicks, William Withington *retired public relations executive*

Junction
Evans, Jo Burt *communications executive, rancher*

Kerrville
Cremer, Richard Eldon *marketing professional*

Kingwood
†Chamoun-Nicolas, Habib *business development consultant*
Hawk, Phillip Michael *service corporation executive*
Wigglesworth, David Cunningham *business and management consultant*

Laredo
†Kohl, John Preston *management educator*

Lewisville
Tucker, Phyllis Anita *sales representative, guidance counselor*

Lubbock
Davis, Alvin G. *company executive*
Fontenot, Andrea Dean *communications executive*
Lawson, Melanie Kay *management administrator, early childhood consultant*

Mineola
Rosene, Ralph Walfred *consulting company executive*

Pasadena
McClay, Harvey Curtis *data processing executive*

Penitas
Loomis, Robert Arthur *retired sales executive*

Plano
Collumb, Peter John *communications company executive*
Dougherty, F(rancis) Kelly *data processing executive*
Grogan, Timothy James *business executive, golf professional*
Hahn, Cathy Ann Clifford *sales executive*
†Heller, Jeffrey M. *data systems executive*
Scott, Terry Lee *communications company executive*
Smith, Jerralyn Renée *marketing professional, consultant*

Port Arthur
†Munoz, Andrea Lee *human resources specialist*

Port Lavaca
Boyd, Ann Fisher *office administrator*

Richardson
Armstrong, Robert Stevenson, Jr., *sales executive*
Chlamtac, Imrich *computer company executive, educator*
Fahrlander, Henry William, Jr., *management consultant*
Madden, Marie Frances *marketing professional*
Sperrin, Graham Frederick *marketing professional*
Witherspoon, William Tom *company executive*

Rockwall
Bush, Larry Don *communications company administrator*
Wiorkowski, Gabrielle Kay *database consultant*

Round Rock
Dell, Michael S. *computer company executive*
†Hudson, Michel Colette *consultant*
Regan, James Richard, Jr., *computer company executive*
Wahl, William Bryan *marketing professional, real estate officer*

San Angelo
Coe, Robert Stanford *retired management educator*

San Antonio
Best, Thomas L. *trainer, consultant*
Bromley, Ernest W. *communications executive*
Butt, Charles Clarence *food service executive*
†Ellis, James D. *communications executive, corporate lawyer*
Garcia, Henry Frank *supply management and project management consultant and trainer*
Labenz-Hough, Marlene *dispute resolution professional*
Montemayor, Carlos Rene *advertising agency executive*
Schonhoff, Robert Lee *marketing and advertising executive*
Shirley, Graham Edward *management executive*
Whitesell, Stephen Ernest *parks and recreation director*

San Marcos
Moore, Patsy Sites *food service consultant*

Southlake
Elliott, Dennis Dawson *communications executive*
Sorge, Karen Lee *commercial printing company executive, consultant*

Spring
†Ciancimino, Joseph Andrew *data processing executive*
Cooley, Andrew Lyman *corporation executive, former army officer*
Maxfield, Mary Constance *management consultant*

Spring Branch
Barban, Arnold Melvin *advertising educator*

Stafford
Sanchelli, Charles Raymond (Chuck Sanchelli) *tennis company executive*

Stephenville
McMahan, Barbara Jean *administrative assistant*

Stonewall
Bendele, Nichole A. *public relations executive, writer*

Sugar Land
Michaels, Alan J. *safety and occupational health executive*
Preng, David Edward *management consultant*

The Woodlands
Glenn, Gerald Marvin *marketing, engineering and construction executive*
Jack, Nancy Rayford *supplemental resource company executive, consultant*
Jones, Susan Chafin *management consultant*
King, Carl Edward *employee screening executive*

Trophy Club
Caffee, Virginia Maureen *executive assistant*
Holley, Cyrus Helmer *management consulting service executive*

Tyler
Ellis, John David *data processing executive*
Resnik, Linda Ilene *marketing and information executive, publisher, consultant, writer*

Victoria
Logan, Mary Calkin *development and public relations consultant*

Waco
Meyer, Paul James *communications company executive*

Willis
Snider, Robert Larry *management consultant*

UTAH

Heber City
McLean, Hugh Angus *management consultant*

Logan
Callister, Ronda *management and human resources educator*

Murray
†Garrity, June H. *communications director, executive secretary*

Orem
Morey, Robert Hardy *communications executive*
Sawyer, Thomas Edgar *management consultant*

Park City
Milner, Harold William *hotel executive*

Provo
Bartlett, Leonard Lee *retired communications educator, retired advertising agency executive*
Herrera, Shirley Mae *personnel and security executive*

Salt Lake City
†Davis, Gene *public relations professional, state legislator*
Davis, Loyd Evan *defense industry marketing professional*
Elkins, Glen Ray *retired service company executive*
Hutcherson, Christopher Alfred *marketing, recruiting and educational fundraising executive*
†Williams, J. Richard *service executive, real estate executive*

Sandy
Skidmore, Joyce Thorum *public relations and communication executive*
York, Theodore Robert *retired consulting company executive*

VERMONT

Burlington
Fillmore, Mary Dingee *management consultant*
Heffernan, Patricia Conner *management consultant*

East Wallingford
Graf, Marjorie Beck *sales and marketing executive*

Lower Waterford
Burnham, Patricia White *consultant, advocate, writer, business executive*

Lyndonville
Toborg, Alfred *history educator*

Middlebury
Benoit, Philip Grosvenor *communications executive, educator, writer*

Montpelier
Fitzhugh, William Wyvill, Jr., *printing company executive*

Newfane
Farber, Lillian *retired photography equipment company executive*

Stowe
Fiddler Nichols, Barbara Dillow *sales and marketing professional*

Waitsfield
Hiscock, Richard Carson *marine safety investigator*
Parrish, Thomas Kirkpatrick, III, *marketing consultant*

Woodstock
Hoyt, Coleman Williams *postal consultant*
Matlins, Stuart M. *management consultant, publisher*

VIRGINIA

Abingdon
Ramos-Cano, Hazel Balatero *caterer, chef, innkeeper, restauranteur, entrepreneur*
Smith, Jack C. *supermarket executive*

Alexandria
Ancell, Robert Manning *leadership organization executive*
Ashford, John Edward *communications executive*
Borden, Enid A. *public relations executive*
Courtney, William Harrison *business executive*
Davis, Ruth Margaret (Mrs. Benjamin Franklin Lohr) *technology management executive*
Del Fosse, Claude Marie *aerospace software executive*
Devantier, Paul W. *communications executive, broadcaster, administrator*
Flater, Morris Eugene *executive, lawyer*
Foster, Robert Francis *communications executive*
Frommer, Lawrence Julian *retired travel company executive*
Harris, David Ford *management consultant, retired government official*
James, Carol Lee *communications executive*
Laurent, Lawrence Bell *communications executive, former journalist*
McMillan, Charles William *consulting company executive*
†Moran, Donald Will *consulting company executive*
Morris, Robert Crane *management training executive*
Nelson, David Leonard *process management systems company executive*
Newton, Hugh C. *public relations executive*
Nodeen, Janey Price *company executive*
†Pitzer, Jack Todd *purchasing agent, consultant, purchasing agent, educator*
Rogers, Paul A'Court *management consulting executive*
Schlachtmeyer, Albert Stephen *management consultant*
Simmons, Richard De Lacey *mass media executive*
Starr, James Edward *logistics management executive*
Stone, Ann E.W. *direct marketing company executive*
Trent, Darrell M. *academic and corporate executive*
Walker, William Woodard, Jr., *management consultant, telecommunications technology*
Widner, Ralph Randolph *retired civic executive*

Annandale
Gioconda, Thomas F. *management consultant, retired military officer*
Greinke, Everett Donald *corporate executive, international programs consultant*
Jarvis, Elbert, II, (Jay Jarvis) *employee benefits specialist*
Khim, Jay Wook *high technology systems integration executive*

Arlington
Beaty, James Thomas *retired buyer*
Erwin, Frank William *personnel research and publishing executive*
Feeley, Karen Adler *training services executive, consultant*
Fosdick, Cora Prifold (Cora Prifold Beebe) *management consultant*
Gallagher, Anne Porter *business executive*
Gianturco, Delio E. *management consultant, educator, author*
Johnson, Rosemary Wrucke *personnel management specialist*
Kamensky, John Michael *management consultant*
Kanter, L. Erick *public relations executive*
Luchok, Joseph Alan *communications executive, consultant*
McGinn, Daniel G. *public relations executive*
Metz, Craig Huseman *business executive*
Morris, John Woodland, II, *businessman, former army officer*
Newburger, Beth Weinstein *medical telecommunications company executive*
Plevyak, Thomas Joseph *communications executive*
Potvin, William Tracey *management consultant*
Samburg, A. Gene *security company executive*
Shaker, William Haygood *marketing professional, public policy reformer*
Verburg, Edwin Arnold *management consultant*
Zorthian, Barry *communications executive*

Basye
James, Louis Meredith *personnel executive*

Blacksburg
Weaver, Pamela Ann *hospitality research professional*

Burgess
Burch, Michael Ira *public relations executive, former government official*

Burke
†Smith, Pearl Richardson *management consultant*

Chantilly
Anderson, Maynard Carlyle *national and international security executive*
Gavin, Mary Ellen *consultant*
Lalley, Frank Edward *computer company executive*
Nathan, Richard Arnold *technology company executive*
Sullivan, Penelope Dietz *computer software development company executive*
Wallace, Renee Michelle *corporate executive*
Watkins, Felix Scott *printing company executive*

Charlottesville
Bly-Monnen, April M. *quality assurance professional*
Brown, Holmes *public affairs executive*
Cohen, Helen Herz *camp owner, director*
Colley, John Leonard, Jr., *educator, author, management consultant*
Haigh, Robert William *business administration educator*
MacIlwaine, Mary Jarratt *public relations executive*
Wolcott, John Winthrop, III, *retired corporate executive*

Dunn Loring
Blankinship, Henry Massie *management consultant*

Fairfax
Baker, Daniel Richard *computer company executive, consultant*
Byam, M(arie) Elizabeth *data processing management consultant*
Gaddy, Dale *executive*
Gross, Patrick Walter *business executive, management consultant*
†Kieffer, Jarold Alan *publications company executive, writer*
McCormick, Robert Junior *company executive, former government official*
Saverot, Pierre-Michel *nuclear waste management company executive*
†Welles, Judith *public affairs executive*
Witek, James Eugene *retired public relations executive*

Falls Church
Bingman, Charles Franklin *public administration executive and educator*
Cain, David Lee *corporate executive*
Miller, Mary Jeannette *office management specialist*
Nashman, Alvin Eli *computer company executive*
Orkand, Donald Saul *management consultant*

Farmville
Adrian, Mitchell *management consultant, educator*

Cleveland
DeKarske, Steven Ronald *purchasing agent*

Darien
Miller, Malcolm Henry *manufacturing sales executive, real estate developer*

Dodgeville
Eisenberg, Lee B. *communications executive, author*

Eau Claire
Leary, Robin Janell *administrative secretary, county government official*

Edgerton
Douglas, Susan *data processing specialist, consultant*

Elkhorn
O'Brien, Francis Joseph *internet company executive*

Fond Du Lac
†Ingle, Sud Ranganath *management consultant*

Fox Point
King, Frederic *health services management executive, educator*

Glendale
Foran, David John *public relations consultant*

Grafton
Schneider, Carol Ann *staffing services company executive*

Green Bay
†Bush, Robert G. *food service executive*
†Meng, John C. *food service executive*

Hales Corners
Keesler, Rachael Gay *management professional*

Hayward
Peterson, Louis Robert *retired consumer products company executive*

Hudson
Kathan, Debra *personnel director, educator*

Janesville
Butters, John Patrick *educator, tour director*
Roth, Sarah Eve *occupational safety professional*

Jefferson
Morgan, Gaylin F. *public relations consultant*
Myers, Gary *public relations executive*

Kewaunee
Allen, Gerald Campbell Forrest *management consulting company owner*

La Crosse
Anderson, Gwyn C. *computer company executive, computer consultant*
†Ross, William Henry *human resources specialist, educator*

Lake Geneva
Weed, Edward Reilly *marketing executive*

Madison
Henderson, Arvis Burl *data processing executive, biochemist*
Knapstein, Michael *advertising executive*
Kuzuhara, Loren Wyatt *management consultant, educator*
Odom, John Yancy *human resources specialist, writer*
Rux, Paul Philip *management consultant, educator*
Stites, Susan Kay *writer, human resources consultant*

Menomonee Falls
Bujanovich, William Matthew *marketing professional*

Menomonie
†Brey, Eric Trent *hospitality and tourism educator*

Mequon
Diesem, John Lawrence *business executive*
Elias, Paul S. *marketing executive*

Middleton
Cotherman, Audrey Mathews *management and policy consultant, administrator*
Lee, Leslie Warren *marketing executive, public speaker*

Milwaukee
Arbit, Bruce *direct marketing executive, consultant*
†Clayton, Rebecca D. *customer service administrator*
Colbert, Virgis William *brewery company executive*
Cole, John Dewey *management consultant*
†Constable, John *advertising executive*
Davis, Thomas William *computer company executive*
Hunter, Victor Lee *marketing executive, consultant*
Huss, William Lee *computer analyst*
Joerres, Jeffrey A. *staffing company executive*
Joseph, Jules K. *retired public relations executive*
Kerr, Dorothy Marie Burmeister *marketing executive, consultant*
†Laughlin, Steven L. *advertising executive*
Mahler, Stephanie Irene *retired administrative manager*
Manning, Kenneth Paul *technologies company executive*
Paul, Mary *human resources professional*

Peck, Curtiss S. *organization development consultant, author, educator*
†Quadracci, Thomas A. *printing company executive*
Randall, William Seymour *leasing company executive*
Roozen, Mary Louise *public relations executive*
†Sayles, Ronald Lyle *computer executive*
Shapiro, Robert Donald *management advisor on strategy and acquisitions/divestitures*
Shiely, John Stephen *company executive, lawyer*
Walthers, Bruce Julius *hobby industry executive*

Oshkosh
Siepmann, James Patrick *research company executive, retired physician*

Plymouth
Gentine, Lee Michael *marketing professional*

Racine
Klein, Gabriella Sonja *retired communications executive*

Sheboygan
†Schoemer, Jack Robert (John Robert Schoemer) *human resources specialist, director*

Thiensville
Dickow, James Fred *management consultant*

Two Rivers
Heller, Mark *communications executive*

Waterford
Karraker, Louis Rendleman *retired corporate executive*

Wausau
Wadzinski, Mary Beth *administrative assistant*

Wauwatosa
Wright, Isaac Wilson, Jr., *quality assurance professional*

Weyauwega
Hanneman, Elaine Esther *salesperson*

Wisconsin Rapids
Knuteson, Miles Gene *advertising executive*

WYOMING

Fort Laramie
†Mack, James A. *parks director*

Sheridan
Taylor, Judith Ann *marketing and sales executive*

Wilson
Fritz, Jack Wayne *communications and marketing company executive*

TERRITORIES OF THE UNITED STATES

PUERTO RICO

Caparra
†Cuevas-Santiago, Nelly *collections and bad debt manager*

VIRGIN ISLANDS

Saint Croix
King, Robert Howard *marketing professional*

Saint Thomas
O'Bryan, James A. *communications specialist, political organization administrator*

MILITARY ADDRESSES OF THE UNITED STATES

EUROPE

Apo
Simpson, Sandra Kay *logistics management specialist*

CANADA

ALBERTA

Calgary
Hume, James Borden *corporate professional, foundation executive*
Manz, Calvin Kim *technology sector entrepreneur*

Edmonton
McKenna, Patrick James *management consultant*

BRITISH COLUMBIA

Vancouver
Campbell, Bruce Alan *corporate and executive coach*
†Chu, Allen Yum-Ching *automation company executive, systems consultant*
Collins, Mary *management consultant, former Canadian legislator*

Cormier, Jean G. *communications company executive*
Frey, Gerrard Rupert (Gary Frey) *management consultant, consultant*
Saywell, William George Gabriel *business development and management consultant*

Victoria
Nuttall, Richard Norris *management consultant, physician*

West Vancouver
Rae, Barbara Joyce *former employee placement company executive*

MANITOBA

Winnipeg
Asper, Leonard *communications executive*

NEWFOUNDLAND

Saint John's
Rowe, Allan Duncan *company executive*

NOVA SCOTIA

Halifax
Gratwick, John *management consulting executive, writer, consultant*
Thompson, William Grant *management executive*

North Sydney
†Nickerson, Jerry Edgar Alan *business executive*

Victoria Beach
Fisher, James W., Jr., *management consultant*

ONTARIO

Brampton
Plastina, Frank *communications executive*
†Roth, John Andrew *internet communications executive*

Freelton
Sonnenberg, Hardy *data processing company research and development executive, engineer*

Gloucester
Boisvert, Laurier Joseph *communications executive*

Grampton
Dunn, Frank A. *communications executive*

Halton Hills
McCoubrey, R. James *advertising and broadcast executive*

Kanata
Butcher, Paul *communications executive*
Smith, Don *communications executive*

Markham
Ho, Kwok Yuen *data processing executive*

Mississauga
Farrell, Craig *hotel executive*
Melnyk, Eugene N. *private investigator*
Thibault, J(oseph) Laurent *service company executive*

Niagara-on-the Lake
Nielsen-Jones, Ian Richard *lottery and gaming executive, business operations consultant*

North York
Denham, Frederick Ronald *management consultant*

Ottawa
Courtois, Bernard Andre *communications executive*
Dawson, Peter Henry *telecommunications components executive*
Ouellet, André *business executive*
Sharp, Mitchell William *advisor to prime minister*

Saint Catharines
Bergevin, V. Réal *customer relationship management executive*

Toronto
Bandeen, Robert Angus *management consultant*
Carder, Paul Charles *retired advertising executive*
Conway, Heather *communications executive*
Curlook, Walter *management consultant*
Fatt, William R. *hospitality company executive*
Fierheller, George Alfred *corporate director*
Gregor, Tibor Philip *retired management consultant*
Jacob, Ellis *entertainment company executive*
Nesbitt, Mark *management consultant*
Rogers, Edward Samuel *communications company executive*
Seiersen, Nicholas Steen *management consultant*
Sharp, Isadore *hotel facility executive*
Thase, Gunter Hermann *marketing executive*
Viner, Peter *communications executive*
Wilson, Michael Holcombe *investment banker, former Canadian government official*

QUEBEC

Eastman
Emond, Lionel Joseph *management consultant*

Leclercville
Morin, Pierre Jean *retired management consultant*

Montreal
Audet, Henri *retired communications executive*
Beauregard, Luc *public relations executive*
Neveu, Jean *printing company executive*
Sirois, Charles *communications executive*
Tournier, Jean-Pierre *consultant company executive*
Wood, Dennis *communications executive*

Mount Royal
Chauvette, Claude R. *building materials company administrator*
Glezos, Matthews *consumer products and services company executive*

Saint-Faustin-Lac-Carre
Des Marais, Pierre, II, *communications holding company executive*

Oakville
Jelinek, John Joseph *public relations executive*

Richmond
Cordoba, Mike *food service executive*

MEXICO

Guanajuato
Cardno, Donald Barry *retired personnel director*

Mexico City
Nicholas, Ronald Wayde *business consultant*

Mexico DF
Ceniceros, Maciel Hector Alfonso *business systems executive, consultant*

Monterrey
Amores, Jose E. *cultural director*

ARGENTINA

Buenos Aires
Farias Bouvier, Nestor *consulting company executive*

AUSTRALIA

Armidale
Cooksey, Ray Wagner *human resource management educator*

Killara
Lesser, Steven John *organizational development consultant*

Melbourne
Bellin, Howard *management consultant company executive*

North Sydney
Scott, Brian Walter *management consultant*

Saint Lucia
Edwards, Sir Llewellyn Roy *company executive*

AUSTRIA

Vienna
Dee, James Phillip *human resources consultant*
†Sindelka, Josef *postal service and telecommunications administrator*

BARBADOS

Christ Church
Waithe, Mary Rebecca *personnel director, dance instructor*

BELGIUM

Brussels
Everard, Eric *company administrator*
Rossi, Pierre Marie *consultancy company executive*

Leuven
Huypens, Jozef Maria Alfons *communication consultant*

CHINA

Beijing
†Yizhong, Li *business executive*

DENMARK

Aarhus
Herborg-Nielsen, Thorkild *retired business educator*
Hjalager, Anne-Mette *management consultant*

Copenhagen
Jiménez-Beltran, Domingo *executive*

Hoersholm
Sørensen, Erik *international company executive*

Odense
Keldmann, Erik Christian Vilhelm *innovation company executive*

Soro
Ersgaard, Ole Kristian *marketing and management consultant, business developer*

EGYPT

Cairo
Fahmy, Ibrahim Mounir *hotel executive*

ENGLAND

Berkshire
Perry, Sir Michael (Sir Michael Sydney Perry) *industrialist*

Canterbury
Holwell, Peter *management consultant*
Lynch, Edward Philip *management consultant*

Chelmsford
Hayes, Eric James *consulting company executive*

Durham
Miller, Susan Janet *business educator, researcher*

Hatfield
Payton, Roger Louis *consultant*

High Holborn
Russo, Anthony Joseph *public relations professional*

Letchworth
Everitt-Newton, Katherine Evelyn *international management consultant*

Lincolnshire
Axcell, Douglas Norman *business consultant, minister*

London
†Davis, Ian *management consulting firm executive*
†Dyson, Tim *public relations executive*
Habgood, Anthony John *corporate executive*
Hallissey, Michael *strategic consultant*
Hanson, Lord (Lord James Edward Hanson) *industrialist*
Hayward-Williams, Carolyn Rose *management and technology consultant*
Larsson, Per Olof *management consultant*
Leaf, Robert Stephen *public relations executive*
Nelson, Walter Henry *communications consultant, author*
Nordberg, Donald *communications executive*
Pinner, Stephen John *management consultant*
Rubin, James P. *international affairs analyst, public affairs administrator*
Taylor, John Michael *research director*

Middlesex
Walji, Jabir Mohamed *strategic consultant*

Reigate
Baker, Martin William *management consultant*

Stroud
Robinson, John Beckwith *development management consultant*

Surrey
Weston, Sir John (Sir Philip John Weston) *company non-executive director, retired diplomat*

FINLAND

Tampere
Lehtinen, Seppo Ilmari *retired management consultant, educator*

Turku
Suotmaa, Juha Olavi *training manager, journalist, lecturer*

FRANCE

Boulogne
de Tilly, Charles-Edouard *sales professional*

Chambéry
Starcher, George William *management consultant*

Paris
Courtaud, Bernard Jean-Jacques *human resource consulting company executive*
Danon, Laurence Miriel *business executive*
Marcus, Claude *advertising executive*
Rouvillois, Philippe *research and development executive*
†Unwin, Geoff *consulting company executive*

Suresnes
de Pouzilhac, Alain Duplessis *advertising executive*

GERMANY

Düsseldorf
†Schulz, Ekkehard *business executive*
†Simson, Wilhelm *company executive*

Essen
†Albrecht, Theo *business executive*

Frankfurt
Neukirchen, Kajo *industry executive*

Hamburg
Brogan, John Andrew, III, *capital management company executive*

Munich
Miller, Gerald Milton, II, *management consultant*

Neu Isenburg
†Hoare-Temple, Piers Howard *building maintenance executive*

Obertshausen
†Albrecht, Karl *automotive and household plastic parts executive*

Otterfing
Carregal-Ferreira, Jorge *software company executive*

GREECE

Athens
Logothetis, Nickolas *management consultant, researcher, educator*

HONG KONG

Central Hong Kong
†Hanrahan, Paul Thaddeus *marketing executive*

Taipo
Fung, Richard Lap Chung *business executive*

INDONESIA

Jakarta
Slamet, Yohan Robertus *communications executive*

ISRAEL

Givatayim
Findler, Hans Josef *retired business executive*

Holon
Morris, David Joseph *communications systems consultant, educator*

Rehovot
Zipori-Beckenstein, Pninit *business administration educator, researcher*

ITALY

Iseo (Brescia)
Cavagna, Antonino Fortunato *management consultant*

Milan
Barbanti, Paolo *management consultant*

Palermo
Mendola, Louis André Mantegna *business consultant marketing and advertising, historian*

Rome
Flood, Gregory Charles *human resources management specialist*

JAPAN

TK

Shinagawa-Ku
†Ando, Kunitake *consumer products company executive*

Choyoda-ku
†Sakoda, Futoshi *executive*

Kanagawa
Yanagawa, Tsutomu *technology transfer company engineer*

Nagoya
†Takeyama, Eizo *company executive*

Tokyo
Akaike, Masami *communications technology educator*
†Hakoshima, Shin-ichi *business executive*
Miura, Akio *quality assurance management professional*
Osawa, Paula Mariani *trading company executive*

Tsukuba-shi
Kobayashi, Susumu *computer company executive*

NETHERLANDS

Anstelveen
†Reilly, Paul C. *consulting company executive*

Leerdam
†Blom, Frans Leendert *quality assurance professional*

Leiden
Dornbush, K. Terry *former ambassador, consulting company executive, educator*

NORWAY

Oslo
Heyerdahl, Jens P. *business executive*

Sandvika
Kriger, Mark Phillip *management education educator, consultant, writer*

PERU

Lima
Arrarte, Eduardo R. *travel agency executive*

PHILIPPINES

Makati City
Locsin, Enrique Lopez *company executive*

Quezon City
Go, Josiah Lim *business executive, educator*

REPUBLIC OF KOREA

Seoul
Jang, Song-Hyon *management consultant*

SCOTLAND

Edinburgh
Napuk, Kerry F. *management executive*

Fife
Scott, Adam *jurist, educator, clergyman*

SOUTH AFRICA

Halfway House
Cleary, Sean Michael *executive*

SPAIN

Madrid
Muniain, Javier P. *computer software company executive, theoretical physicist, researcher*

SWEDEN

Göteborg
†Johansson, Lennart Valdemar *Swedish industrialist*

Nykoping
Hakansson, Kjell Georg *business consultant*

Stockholm
Gyll, John Sören *company executive*
Johnson, Antonia Axson *corporate executive*
Persson, Ivar Lennart *military program director*
Stare, Peter Knut Johan *human resource consultant*
Stubert, Harald Gunnar *management consultant*

SWITZERLAND

Grancia
Mantegazza, Sergio *executive*

Prilly
†Domeniconi, Reto *business executive*

ADDRESS UNPUBLISHED

Abarbanel, Judith Edna *marketing executive*
Abbey, Richard Lawrence *human resources specialist*
Abraham, Nathan Samuel *advertising agency and public relations executive, marketing professional*
Adamson, James B. *business executive*
Adkinson, Brian Lee *manufacturing company executive*
†Aggarwal, Lalit K. *company executive, educator*
Albert, Margaret Cook *communications executive*
†Allen, Bennie Carnel *employee relations specialist*
Allen, Paul G. *computer company executive, professional sports team executive*
†Allmon, Michael W, Sr., *sales executive*
Amatangelo, Nicholas S. *retired financial printing and document management services exetuive*
Amparado, Keith D. *communications company executive*
Anderegg, Karen Klok *business executive*
Anderson, Mark Robert *data processing executive, biochemist*
Anderson, Warren Lee, II, *marketing professional*
Andringa, Michael Robert *management consultant*
†Angelis, Victoria Saris *restaurant manager, consultant*
Appell, Louise Sophia *consulting company executive*
†Arnheim, Louise A *marketing professional*
Asensi, Gustavo *advertising executive, filmmaker*
Assunto, Richard Anthony *human resources specialist*
Aurilia, Christine Marie *administrative assistant*
Bagby, John R. *management consultant*
Bailey, Steven Scott *operations research analyst*
Bainbridge, Dona Bardelli *international marketing executive*
Balick, Kenneth D. *international business executive*
Ballard, Marion Scattergood *software development professional*
Bamberger, Gerald Francis *plastics marketing consultant*
Bannister, Candida Cleve *data processing executive*
Barad, Jill Elikann *family products company executive*
Barca, Kathleen *marketing executive*
Barger, William James *management consultant, educator*
Barnes, Wesley Edward *energy and environmental executive*
Barnett, Elizabeth Hale *organizational consultant*
Barrett, Paulette Singer *public relations executive*
Barron, Peggy Pennisi *management consultant*
Barsuk, Sidney Alan *management consultant, educator*
Bartlett, Arthur Eugene *food service executive*
Bartlett, David *management consultant*
Barto, Rebecca Lynn *business analyst*
Battle, Emery Alford, Jr., *sales executive*
Bauer, Barbara Ann *marketing consultant*
Baysinger, Stephen Michael *quality assurance professional*
Beasley, Barbara Starin *sales executive, marketing professional*
Beatty, Wilbur C. *contract management executive*
Beck, Timothy Daniel *human resources specialist, consultant*
Beeber, Marshall Lawrence *sales executive*
Bell, Jacqueline Michelle *marketing professional, public relations executive*
Bell, Regina Jean *corporate consulting company executive*
Bell, Theodore Augustus *advertising executive*
Benjamin, Laura J. *management consultant, speech professional*
Bennett, Saul *public relations agency executive*
Benney, Douglas Mabley *direct marketing executive, consultant*
Bergelt, Philip Robert, Jr., *printer, antiques dealer*
Berger, Frank Stanley *management executive*
Berman, Robert S. *marketing consultant*
Berman-Hammer, Susan *public relations executive*
Berra, Robert Louis *human resources consultant*
Berzas, Elizabeth Ann *marketing professional, public relations executive*
Bey, Joan S. *retired public information specialist, writer*
Birk, John R. *management consultant*
Bisconti, Ann Stouffer *public opinion research company executive*
Bissell, Brent John *advertising and direct marketing executive*
†Blacker, Harriet *public relations executive*
Blaine, Davis Robert *investment banker, valuation consultant executive*
Blake, John Edward *retired car rental company executive*
Blatz, Linda Jeanne *management professional*
Boatwright, Charlotte Jeanne *marketing professional, public relations executive*
Bodine, Larry *marketing consultant*
Boldosser, Randy Richard *communications company executive*
Boobyer, Don J. *computer operator, bookkeeper*
Boone, Earle Marion *business executive*
Borges, William, III, *management consultant*
Botkin, Monty Lane *computer company executive*
Bower, Shelley Ann *business management consultant*
Bowers, Patricia Newsome *communications executive*
Bowes, Henry Edward *retired communications executive*
†Bowling, Kelly K *management consultant*
†Bramucci, Raymond L. *employment and training executive*
Brannick, Ellen Marie *retired management consultant*
Brashears, Sumner *funeral director*
Brecht, Sally Ann *quality assurance executive*
Brennan, Donna Lesley *public relations company executive*
Brennen, Stephen Alfred *international business consultant*
Britt, Rebecca Fae *communications executive*
Broderson, Thelma Sylvia *marketing professional*
Brody, Martin *food service company executive*
Brown, Sylvia *public relations executive, advertising executive*
Brown, W. Michael *publishing company executive*
Browne, Ann April *purchasing manager*
Bucciero, Joseph Mario, Jr., *executive consultant*
Buck, Linda Dee *executive recruiting company executive*
Buckholtz, Thomas Joel *computer and telecommunications executive*
Bugbee, Joan Barthelme *retired corporate communications executive*
Buras-Elsen, Brenda Allynn *retired public affairs executive*
Burgdoerfer, Jerry J. *marketing and distribution executive*
Burge, John Wesley, Jr., *management consultant, consultant*
Burgess, Michael H. *management consultant*
Burnham, J. V. *retired sales executive*

Burton, Robert Gene *printing and publishing executive*
Butler, Robert Thomas *retired advertising executive*
Butts, Carol Henderson *human resources specialist, consultant*
Caine, Raymond William, Jr., *retired public relations executive*
†Caldwell, Cicely *human resources specialist, consultant*
Caldwell, Judy Carol *advertising executive, public relations executive, consultant, writer, designer*
Cameron, Daniel Forrest *communications executive*
Camp, Alethea Taylor *executive and organizational design consultant*
Campbell, William *research analyst, educator, artist*
Camper, John Saxton *public relations and marketing executive*
†Capanoli, Brian Mario *sales executive*
Cappello, Eve *speaker, trainer, author*
Carpenter-Mason, Beverly Nadine *quality assurance professional, medical/surgical nurse*
Carrol, Nora *educational/communication company executive, artist*
Carter, Jaine M(arie) *human resources specialist, director*
†Carter, Karen D. *management professional*
Cartwright, Phillip August *management consultant*
Casadesus, Penelope Ann *advertising executive, film producer*
Cecil, Alex Thomson *travel executive*
Chacon, Michael Ernest *computer company executive*
Chamberlain, William Edwin, Jr., *management consultant*
Chaput, Eugene Michael *advertising executive*
Charles, Lyn Ellen *marketing executive, commercial artist, photograph*
Chaseman, Joel *communications consultant*
Cheek, Arthur Lee *administrative professional*
Cheser, Raymond Norris, III, *healthcare company executive*
†Chill, Myrtle N. *advertising copywriter, promoter*
Chin, Janet Sau-Ying *data processing executive, consultant*
Chlebowski, John Francis, Jr., *business executive*
Choueifati, Antoine (Tony Choueifati) *computer company executive*
†Christian, Lori Coffelt *marketing professional*
Christopher, Richard Scott *public relations and advertising executive, editor*
Ciccarelli, Chick *marketing professional*
Citron, Richard Ira *management consultant*
Cittone, Henry Aron *hotel and restaurant management educator*
Clemmons, Evelyn Yvonne *administrative assistant*
Cliff, Karissa *consumer researcher, recruiter*
Cobb, John Cecil, Jr., (Jack Cobb) *communications specialist and executive*
Cochetti, Roger James *international communications and internet company executive*
Coenson, Barbara *marketing and sales professional*
Cohn, Robin Jean *crisis management executive, author*
Coin, Sheila Regan *organization and management development consultant*
Coleman, Claire Kohn *public relations executive*
Collins, Frank Charles, Jr., *industrial and service quality specialist*
†Collins, Richard Stratton (Dick Collins) *retired public relations executive*
Cone, Frances McFadden *data processing consultant*
Connell, Carol Matheson *corporate strategist, consultant*
Connell, Shirley Hudgins *public relations professional*
†Cook, Jane Hampton *communications executive, consultant*
Cook, Norma Baker *consulting company executive*
Cooper, James Robert, III, *computer software company executive, mobile communications consultant*
Cooper, Janis Campbell *retired public relations executive*
Cooper, Patricia Gorman *management consultant*
Corbett, Michael Arthur, Jr., *business management consultant*
Corle, Frederic William, II, *marketing professional*
Cornett, Cathy G. Turner *consulting company executive, artist*
Cortese, Richard Anthony *computer company executive*
Cotter, Lawrence Raffety *management consultant*
†Coven, Alysa Louise *advertising/marketing professional*
Covington, Marsha Elaine *communications consultant*
†Crall, Aaron H. *restaurant company executive, artist*
Crawford, William Walsh *retired consumer products company executive*
Criswell, Kimberly Ann *executive coach, communications consultant, performing artist*
Croce, Robert J. *corporate government relations executive*
Croft, Kathryn Delaine *business executive, consultant*
†Crowe, James Quell *communications executive*
Cruse, Denton W. *marketing and advertising executive, consultant*
Cruver, Suzanne Lee *communications executive, writer*
Curry, Carlton E. *corporate executive, city councilman*
†Cutler, Norman Barry *funeral service executive*
Dababneh, Awwad J. *human factors specialist, ergonomist, consultant*
Daghlian, John Edward *advertising agency executive*
Dakin, Karl Jonathan *new product developer*
Dangoor, David Ezra Ramsi *consumer goods company executive*
D'Arcy, Jan Therese *communications executive*
Darien, Steven Martin *management consulting company executive*
Dasburg, John Harold *restaurant executive*
†Dattner, Benjamin *management consultant*
DaVerne, Steven Richard *advertising director, artist, illustrator, behavior analyst*
†Davis, Heather Lynne *communications officer*
†Dawson, Leslie Naryne *quality assurance professional*
Deacon, David Emmerson *business executive*
Decker, Gilbert Felton *consultant*
Deloatch, Cheryl Lee *communications company executive*
Demmitt, Joyce Miller *management consultant*
De Sofi, Oliver Julius *data processing executive*
de Urioste, George Adolfo *software company executive*
DeVaney, Carol Susan *management consultant*
DeVore, Kimberly K. *business executive*
deWilde, David Michael *management consultant, former executive search consultant, financial services executive, lawyer*
Dewing, Henry Woods, Sr., *telecommunications executive*
†Dharamsi, Shamez Shiraz *marketing professional, consultant*
Diamond, Susan Zee *management consultant*
Dickinson, Victoria Ann *visual arts administrator*
DiDomenico, Mauro, Jr., *communication executive*
Diehl, Stephen Anthony *human resources consultant*
Dirks, Leslie Chant *communications and electronics company executive*
Dirvin, Gerald Vincent *retired consumer products company executive*
Doan, Mary Frances *advertising executive*
Dodson, Donald Mills *retired restaurant executive*
Doherty, Evelyn Marie *data processing consultant*
Dolgow, Allan Bentley *management consultant*
Dolich, Andrew Bruce *sports marketing executive*
Doll, Patricia Marie *marketing and public relations advertising consultant*
Dolman, John Phillips, Jr., (Tim Dolman) *communications company executive*
D'Onofrio, Mary Ann *medical transcription company executive*
Dorn, Natalie Reid *consultant*
Dorn, Norman Philip *management consulting firm executive*
Doud, Wallace C. *retired information systems executive*
Douglass, Betty Jean *retired executive secretary*
Douty, Lucy Evelyn *sales and marketing executive*
Dow, Peter Anthony *advertising agency executive*
Dowie, Ian James *management consultant*
Droullard, Steven Maurice *jewelry company executive*
Dudley, Craig James *retired executive recruiter*
Dudley, Elizabeth Hymer *retired security executive, community volunteer*
Duffy, Martin Edward *management consultant, economist*
Duke, William Edward *public affairs executive*
†Dunn Kelly, Ruth Emma *management consultant*
Dunsky, Menahem *retired advertising agency executive, communications consultant, painter*
Durbetaki, N. John *software company executive*
Dwan, Dennis Edwin *broadcast executive, photographer*
East, Janette Diane *marketing consultant*
Easton, Charles Clement, Jr., *corporate executive*
Ecton, Donna R. *business executive*
Eddy, David Maxon *health policy and management administrator*
Effner, Marsha Gay *retired employee development officer*
Eggleston, G(eorge) Dudley *management consultant, publisher*
Elkind, Mort William *business consultant*
Ellig, Bruce Robert *personnel director*
Ellis, Steven George *public relations/corporate communication executive*
Emerling, Carol G(reenbaum) *consultant*
Emerson, Daniel Everett *retired communications company executive*
Engels, Thomas Joseph *sales executive*
Erb, Richard Louis Lundin *resort and hotel executive*
Erzinger, Dennis Eugene, Sr., *factory automation executive*
Evans, Victor Miles *retired funeral home, cemetery company executive*
Everett, Elbert Kyle *marketing executive, consultant*
Faletra, Robert *technology company executive*
Faron, Fay Cheryl *private investigator, writer*
Farrell, William Edgar *sales executive, infosystems specialist, management consultant*
Fay, Conner Martindale *retired business executive*
Feagles, Gerald Franklin *marketing executive*
Feinberg, Glenda Joyce *restaurant chain executive*
Feiner, Ava Sophia *public affairs and management consultant, economist*
Feller, Robert William Andrew *baseball team public relations executive, retired baseball player*
Fernández, Alberto Antonio *security professional*
Fertig-Dykes, Susan Beatrice *communications executive, human resources professional, community and civil society facilitator*
Field, Ellen *marketing professional*
Fila, Joseph Duncan *marketing and sales executive, public relations executive, real estate broker, investor*
Finkelstein, Seymour *business consultant*
Fischer, Angela Brown *business executive, civic volunteer*
Fischer, Russell Leonard *public relations executive*
Fisher, Fenimore *business development consultant*
†Fitzgerald, Walter George *marketing consulting company executive*
Flagg, Norman Lee *retired advertising executive*
Fleisher, Gary Mitchell *employment industry and management consulting executive*
†Fleming, Cecil *business executive*
†Foote, William Chapin *business executive*
Ford, E(mma) Jane *public relations executive*
Ford, Kay Louise *innovation consulting executive*
Forester, Jean Martha Brouillette *innkeeper, retired librarian, educator*
†Foronda, Barbara Elaine *professional organizer, writer*
Fox, Gretchen Hovemeyer *freelance editor, genealogical consultant*
Fox-Clarkson, Anne C. *computer company executive*
Francis, Philip Hamilton *management consultant*
Franke, John Charles *retired human resources executive*
Frappia, Linda Ann *management executive*
Frear, Jon S. *pet services company executive*
Fredman, Mimi Ungar Coppersmith *advertising and publishing executive*
Fricks, Ernest Eugene *management consultant*
Friedman, Marla Lee *marketing professional*
Galbraith, Nanette Elaine Gerks *forensic and management sciences company executive*
Gallert, Barbara Lynn *communications executive*
Gamble, Mary G(race) *marketing and organizational development professional*
Gambrell, Luck Flanders *corporate executive*
Garahan, Peter Thomas *software company executive*
Gardner, Meredith Lee *communication consultant*
†Gauthier, Abbie Gail *administrative assistant, writer*
Gaw, James Richard *corporate executive*
Gendell, Gerald Stanleigh *retired public affairs executive*
†George, William Douglas, Jr., *retired consumer products company executive*
Gerlach, Douglas Eldon *financial writer, Internet developer*
†Giddings, Helen *personnel management executive*
Gilbert, Rebecca J. *marketing executive*
Gilford, Leon *business executive and consultant*
Gillice, Sondra Jupin (Mrs. Gardner Russell Brown) *sales and marketing executive*
Gillinson, Andrew Stuart *marketing communications executive*
Glacel, Barbara Pate *management consultant*
Glass, Kenneth Edward *management consultant*
Glatzer, Robert Anthony *marketing and sales executive*
Gleba, Beth Ann (Beth Ann Coleman) *communications executive*
Gluys, Charles Byron *retired marketing management consultant*
Goldberg, Victor Joel *retired data processing company executive*
Goldfarb, Muriel Bernice *marketing and advertising consultant*
Goldin, Ian Andrew *executive*
Goldman, Alfred Emmanuel *marketing research consultant*
Goldman, Joseph Elias *retired advertising executive*
†Goldsmith, Jeff Charles *management consultant*
Goll, Stephen E. *telecommuncations executive*
Gordon-Love, Sharel E. *consumer products company executive, writer*
Gorsline, Stephen Paul *security specialist*
Goss, Martha Clark *consulting company executive*
Gottlieb, Alan Merril *advertising, fundraising and broadcasting executive, writer*
Goulimis, Janet Theresa *human resources professional*
Grace, Jason Roy *advertising agency executive*
Grace, Marcia Bell *advertising executive*
Green, Howard Alan *management consultant, educator*
Greene, Alvin *service company executive, management consultant*
Greenhut, Deborah Schneider *management consultant*
Griesbauer, Michele Elaine *newspaper official*
Grindal, Mary Ann *former sales professional*
Grody, Mark Stephen *public relations executive*
Gross, Laura Ann *marketing and communications professional, acupuncturist, herbalist*
Gross, Leslie Pamela *sales executive, consultant*
Gross, Rosalie-Ethelyn *secretary*
Growick, Philip *advertising executive*
Gruenfeld, Kevin E. *marketing professional, researcher*
Gschwind, Donald *management and engineering consultant*
Guarno, Peter Gary *consumer products company executive*
Guerra, Armando J. *corporate professional*
Gugel, Craig Thomas *advertising and strategic research executive*
Gumpert, Gustav *public relations executive*
Gunderson, Ted Lee *security consultant*
Gurwitch, Arnold Andrew *communications executive*
Haegele, John Ernest *business executive*
Hagel, John, III, *management consultant*
Hairston, James Christopher *food service distribution executive*
Hall, Hansel Crimiel *communications executive*
Haller, Robert Terrence *marketing, advertising and public relations consultant*
Hamilton, Judith Hall *computer company executive*
Hamilton, Thomas Michael *marketing executive*
Hamlin, Sonya B. *communications specialist*
Hamm, Vernon Louis, Jr., *management and financial consultant*
Hanes, Darlene Marie *marketing professional*
Hansen, Leland Joe *communications executive*
Hargadon, Bernard Joseph, Jr., *retired consumer goods company executive*
Harlan, Kathleen Troy (Kay Harlan) *management consultant*
Harlan, Raymond Carter *retired communication executive, writer, educator*
Harold, Tom *advertising executive*
†Harr, Lucy Loraine *public relations executive*
Harris, David Philip *crisis management executive*
Harris, Denise Michelle *advertising account executive*
Harris, Louis *public opinion analyst, columnist*
Harris, Paul Smith *human resources professional*
Harris, Robert Norman *advertising and communications educator*
Harris, William John *retired management holding company executive, consultant*
Harrison, Alonzo *construction company executive*
Hartsock, Linda Sue *educational and management association executive*
Hausman, Harriet Seceley *administrator*
†Haver-Allen, Ann *communications director*
Hayes, Janet Gray *retired business manager, former mayor*
Hazard, Christopher Wedvik *international business executive*
Heath, Ross Bradley *consulting company executive*
Heisler, Elwood Douglas *hotel executive*
Heller, Arthur *advertising agency executive*
Helm, Lewis Marshall *public affairs executive*
Hendrickson, William George *business executive*
†Hendron, Michael G. *management consultant*
Henry, Philip Lawrence *marketing professional*
Henselmeier, Sandra Nadine *retired training and development consulting firm executive*
Herbert, Carol Sellers *farming executive, lawyer*
Hersher, Richard Donald *management consultant*
Herzog, John Lanfield *public policy, advertising and public relations executive*
Hess, Sidney Wayne *management consultant, educator*
Heuer, Margaret B. *retired microcomputer laboratory coordinator*
Hickerson, Glenn Lindsey *leasing company executive*
Hickman, Terrie Taylor *administrator*
Hildebrandt, Frederick Dean, Jr., *management consultant*
Hill, Patricia Francine *information services executive*
Hirahara, Patti *public relations executive*
†Hoar, Frederick M. *public relations executive*
Hochreiter, John Allen *computer company owner, firefighter*
Hochschild, Carroll Shepherd *computer company and medical equipment executive, educator*
Hock, Morton *entertainment advertising executive*
Hodgen, Maurice Denzil *management consultant, retired education educator*
Hoffman, Darnay Robert *management consultant*
†Holand, Pamela Krisida *professional organizer*
Holcepl, James Robert *sales professional*
Holcomb, Rita *landscaper*
Holland, Henry Norman *marketing and management consultant*
Hollis, Robbie Smagula *marketing communications executive*
Holt, Carolyn Marie *youth employment and training specialist, secondary school educator*
Holzman, D. Keith *management consultant, record company executive, producer, arts consultant*
Honkanen, Jari Olavi *telecommunications company executive*
Hoopes, Townsend Walter *retired management consultant, retired federal agency administrator*
Hope, Thomas Walker *marketing professional*
Hornby, Kenneth Peter *office technology executive*
Hosea, Julia Hiller *communications executive, paralegal*
Houghtaling, Pamela Ann *technology marketing professional, writer*
†Houston, Stanley Dunsmore *retired public relations executive*
Hudson, Stanton Harold, Jr., *public relations executive, educator, academic administrator*
†Hughes, Lorraine Williams *credit counselor, housing specialist*
†Hull, Ronald R. *human resources specialist*
Humbach, Miriam Jane *marketing and financial professional*
Humphrey, Doris Davenport *publishing company executive, consultant, educator*
Hunt, Martha *sales executive, researcher*
Hunt, Martin Kyle *corporate strategist*
Huppe, Alex *public relations executive*
Hurley, William Joseph *business executive*
Huyler, Jean Wiley *communications executive, consultant*
Ichaporia, Pallan R. *pharmaceutical marketing executive*
Imlah, MaryPat *sales, advertising and marketing executive*
Infante-Ogbac, Daisy Inocentes *sales executive, marketing executive, real estate broker*
Infosino, Iara Ciurria *management consultant*
Intrater, Cheryl Watson Waylor *career management consultant*
Irvine, William Burriss *management consultant*
Irwin, Byron *management executive*

Rubin, Martin N. *meeting planner, consultant*
Ruggles, Rudy Lamont, Jr., *international security advisor*
Russell, Carol Ann *personnel service company executive*
Rydholm, Ralph Williams *advertising agency executive*
Rypczyk, Candice Leigh *employee relations executive*
Sacks, Temi J. *public relations executive*
Salem, Susanne Frances *consulting executive*
Saligman, Harvey *retired consumer products and services company executive*
Saliola, Frances *retired corporate administrator*
Sanders, John Kenneth *marketing communications executive*
Saucier, Guylaine *corporate director*
Sauerhaft, Stan *public relations executive, consultant*
†Saul, Bradley Scott *communications, advertising and entertainment executive*
Scaglione, Cecil Frank *marketing executive, publisher*
Sceiford, Mary Elizabeth *retired public television administrator*
Schaeffer, Robert Allen *strategic communications consultant, educator, writer*
Scheidecker, Jane *management consultant, academic administrator*
Schmid, Andrew Michael, Jr., *advertising executive*
Schmutz, Charles Reid *university foundation executive*
Schonberg, Alan Robert *management recruiting executive*
Schreckinger, Sy Edward *advertising executive, consultant*
Schropfer, David Waldron *pharmaceutical executive, educator, consultant*
†Schubert, Helen Celia *public relations executive*
Schult, Dain Leslie *broadcast executive, consultant*
Schulz, Michael John *fire and explosion analyst, consultant*
Schulz, Raymond Alexander *medical marketing professional, consultant*
Schur, Maxine Rose *travel essayist, children's author*
Schwartz, Stephen Blair *retired information industry executive*
Scutt, Cheryl Lynn *marketing communications executive*
Sease, Gene Elwood *public relations company executive*
Seelig, Gerard Leo *management consultant*
Seemann, Rosalie Mary *international business and foreign policy association executive*
Semsekwa, Amir A.M.T. Juma *management executive*
Severino, Elizabeth Forrest *consulting company executive, animal communicator and spiritual healer*
Shafran, Hank *public relations executive*
Shain, Kenneth Stephen *software company executive, author, industrialist*
Shalhoup, Judy Lynn *marketing communications executive*
Shapiro, Mark *advertising executive*
Shaw, Jack Allen *communications company executive*
Sheehan, Robert James, II, *management and market research consultant*
Sheeline, Paul Cushing *hotel executive*
Shei, Juliana Chiang *international technology manager*
Shelton, Robert Warren *marketing executive*
Sherman, Francis George Harry *advertising agency executive*
Shikuma, Eugene Yujin *travel agency executive*
Sibilla, Suzanne Rose *training and organizational development consultant*
Sidebottom, William George *communications executive*
Sidnam, Alan Northcote *retired advertising executive, venture capitalist*
Siegel, Herbert Bernard *management consultant*
Simari, Nanci Joan *herbalist*
Simpson, Andrea Lynn *communications executive*
Sincoff, Michael Z. *human resources and marketing professional*
Singer, David Michael *marketing and public relations company executive*
Singleton-Wood, Allan James *communications executive*
Sklansky, David Bruce *gambling expert, writer*
Slee, Vergil N. *healthcare informatics executive, physician, author*
Smiley, Ronald Michael *communications executive*
Smith, Brian *business consultant, educator*
Smith, Sydney David *data processing executive*
Smith, Thomas Winston *cotton marketing executive, retired*
†Smith-Hilliker, Renée Anne *executive secretary*
Smyth, Cornelius Edmonston *retired hotel executive*
Snedden, James Douglas *retired health service management consultant*
Snyder, John Millard *travel company executive, educator*
Sollender, Joel David *management consultant, financial executive*
Soloway, Jay Stephen *consulting firm executive*
Sommers, William Paul *management consultant, research and development institute executive*
†Sorgi, Deborah B(ernadette) *educational software company executive*
Souveroff, Vernon William, Jr., *business executive*
Speakes, Larry Melvin *public relations executive, writer*
†Spears, Donald Edward *management consultant*
Speer, Richard John *security consultant*
Spellman, Douglas Toby *advertising executive*
Spirn, Michele Sobel *communications professional, writer*
Spivak, Joan Carol *healthcare communications specialist*
Sproat, Kezia Vanmeter *communications executive, writer*
Srere, Linda Jean *former advertising executive*
Sroge, Maxwell Harold *marketing consultant, publishing executive*
†Stambaugh, Michele Williams *development consultant*
†Stark, Diana *public relations and promotion executive*
Starkweather, Frederick Thomas *retired data processing executive*
Steele, Frank Richard *retired consumer products company executive*
Stengel, Ronald Francis *management consultant*
Stenitzer, George Ignatius *corporate communications executive*
Stepanski, Anthony Francis, Jr., *computer software company executive*
Stephenson, Toni Edwards *publisher, investment management executive, communications executive*
Stern, S(eesa) Beatrice *executive secretary, registered nurse*
Stevens, Berton Louis, Jr., *data processing manager*
Stevenson, Robert B. *software company executive, application developer*
Stewart, Arthur Irving, III, (Art Stewart) *management consultant*
Stewart, Miriam *utilization review nurse*
Stillman, Richard Joseph *retired army officer, consultant, publisher writer*
Stocklin, Alma Katherine *retired public relations consultant*
Stoorza Gill, Gail *corporate professional*
Strength, Janis Grace *management executive, educator*
Strenski, James B. *retired communications executive*
Stults, Walter Black *management consultant, former trade organization executive*
Sturges, John Siebrand *management consultant*
Sullivan, John Louis, Jr., *retired search company executive*
Sullivan, Nell Inklebarger *retired administrative official, counselor*
Sutlin, Vivian *advertising executive*
†Swenson, Douglas *management consultant*
Szabo, Yurika Lin *marketing executive, advertising executive*
Szybicki, Edmund *executive*
Taplett, Lloyd Melvin *human resources management consultant*
Tarar, Afzal M. *management consultant*
Tarr, Curtis W. *business executive*
†Taylor, Michelle Y. *human resources consultant*
Temerlin, Liener *advertising agency executive*
†Temsamani, Driss *marketing professional*
Tenney, Frank Putnam *marketing executive*
Terry, Kay Adell *marketing executive*
Terry, Richard Frank *data transcriber*
Tesarek, Dennis George *retired business consultant, writer, educator*
Tew, E. James, Jr., *management services company executive*
Thatcher, Gayle Marie *sales executive*
Thomas, Joe Carroll *retired human resources director*
Thompson, Craig Snover *corporate communications executive*
Thompson, Richard Stephen *management consultant*
Thongsak, Vajeeprasee Thomas *business planning executive*
Thrall, Richard Cameron, Jr., *broadcasting executive*
Thurner, Agnes H. *retired executive secretary*
Tipton, Gary Lee *retired services company executive*
Tocci, Neil Michael *marketing and corporate communications executive, educator*
Todd, Edward William *marketing professional*
Toevs, Alden Louis *management consultant, researcher*
Togerson, John Dennis *computer software company executive, retired*
Tooley, Charles Frederick *communications executive, consultant*
Treasure-Terrell, Suzanne Marie *marketing and sales professional, writer, poet, lyricist*
Trembley, Paul Gerard *communications executive, announcer*
Triolo, Peter *advertising agency executive, marketing educator, consultant*
Triplett, Arlene Ann *management consultant*
Tritter, Richard Paul *strategic planning, safety and risk management consulting executive*
†Trucksess, H.A., III, *company executive*
Tuft, Mary Ann *executive search firm executive*
Turks, Hildegard Maria (Hildegard Maria Chronis) *retired security investigator, writer*
Turner, William Cochrane *international management consultant*
Turner, Zita Renee *collections and bad debt manager*
Turney, Denise *human resources specialist, writer*
†Turpin-Thomas, Cindi Lee *communications executive, writer*
Tuttle, William G(ilbert) T(ownsend), Jr., *research executive*
Tytler, Linda Jean *communications and public affairs executive, retired state legislator*
Udowitz, Robert Howard *public relations executive*
Ulosevich, Steven Nils *social scientist, management consultant, educator, trainer*
Utheza, Herve Jean Louis *communications executive*
Uvena, Frank John *retired printing company executive, lawyer*
Vallerand, Philippe Georges *sales executive*
Van Dine, Alan Charles *advertising agency executive, writer*
Van Houten, Elizabeth Ann *corporate communications executive, painter*
Vogel, William Dickerman *financial services executive*
Wadley, M. Richard *consumer products executive*
Wagner, Leana Moree *computer executive, graphic designer, fine artist*
†Wall, Carolyn Raimondi *communications executive*
Walser, Clarke L. *management consultant*
Walsh, William Albert *management consultant, former naval officer*
†Walton, Kami Sue *public relations executive*
†Watts, Karen Southall *management consultant*
Weathersby, George Byron *business executive*
Webb, Doris McIntosh *human resources specialist*
Webb, William Timothy *mobile communications professional*
Weismantel, Gregory Nelson *management consultant and software executive*
Weispfenning, John Thomas *communications educator, consultant*
Wells, Victor Hugh, Jr., *retired advertising agency executive*
Wentz, Jeffrey Lee *information systems executive*
Weppelman, Roger Michael *retired regulatory compliance officer*
Werkman, Rosemarie Anne *former public relations professional, civic worker*
Weston, Saundra Olivia (Saundra Laidlaw) *quality assurance professional, minister*
†Weyl, Tom F. *advertising executive*
Wheaton, Alice Alshuler *administrative assistant*
Whelan, James Robert *communications executive, international trade and investment consultant, author, educator, mining executive*
Whitaker, Shirley Ann *telecommunications company marketing executive*
White, Bonnie Yvonne *management consultant, retired educator*
White, Erskine Norman, Jr., *management company executive*
Wice, Durand Copple *security officer*
Wicks, David O., Jr., *communications executive*
Wiginton, Jay Spencer *sales executive*
Wilds, Karen R. *housing authority executive*
Williams, Alfred Blythe *management consultant, educator*
Williams, Earle Carter *retired professional services company executive*
Williams, Harry Edward *retired management consultant*
Williams, John Charles, II, *data processing executive*
Williams, Louis Clair, Jr., *public relations executive*
Willig, Karl Victor *computer firm executive*
†Wilson-Stewart, Marilyn Lucille *retired human resources director*
Wimpress, Gordon Duncan, Jr., *corporate consultant, foundation executive*
Winsor, David John *cost consultant*
†Winter, Nancy Fitz *media and public relations executive*
Wise, Susan Tamsberg *management and communications consultant, speaker*
Wolf, William Martin *computer company executive, consultant*
†Womack, Nora Lynn *marketing professional*
Worth, Gary James *communications executive*
†Wu, Xinglu *retired, writer*
Wyatt, Robert Saunders *executive search consultant*
Xu, Chen-Wei *data processing executive*
Yadrick, Robert Martin *occupational analyst*
Yaeger, Therese Francis *management professional*
Yakich, David Eli *international sales executive*
Yetto, John Henry *company executive*
Yocam, Delbert Wayne *retired software products company executive*
Young, Elizabeth Bell *consultant*
Youst, David Bennett *career development educator*
Zanes, George William *management, marketing, human resources consultant*
Zeien, Alfred M. *former consumer products company executive*
Zeller, Joseph Paul *advertising executive*
Zinnen, Robert Oliver *general management executive*
Zuckerman, Martin Harvey *personnel director*

INDUSTRY: TRADE

UNITED STATES

ALABAMA

Birmingham
Blair, Ludie Mae Riley *retired furniture company executive*
George, Frank Wade *small business owner, antiquarian book dealer*
Martin, R. Brad *retail executive*
Pizitz, Richard Alan *retail and real estate group executive*

Cullman
Freeman, Chester Willie *small business owner*

Dothan
Rabon, Ronald Ray *retail jewelry store chain executive*

Mobile
Jones, Joseph Seymour *small business owner, poet*

Montrose
†Haynie, Betty Jo Gillmore *personal property appraiser, antiques dealer*

Tuscaloosa
Blackburn, John Leslie *small business owner*

ALASKA

Anchorage
Schnell, Roger Thomas *business owner, retired state official and career officer*

Salcha
Alsip, Cheryl Ann *small business owner*

ARIZONA

Chandler
†Basha, Edward N., Jr., *grocery chain owner*

Glendale
Lack, Larry Henry *small business owner*

Sun City
Thompson, Betty Jane *small business owner*

Tempe
LaFaro, Angelo John *small business owner*

ARKANSAS

Bentonville
†Glass, David D. *department store company executive, professional baseball team executive*
Scott, Harold Lee, Jr., *retail executive*
Walton, S. Robson *discount department store chain executive*

Hot Springs National Park
Tanenbaum, Bernard Jerome, Jr., *corporate executive*

Little Rock
Dillard, William, II, *department store chain executive*
†Swepston, Gene Fain *small business owner*

CALIFORNIA

Beverly Hills
Rainey, Ronald Paul *artist manager*
Schwartz, Stephan Andrew *entrepreneur, writer*

Bodega Bay
†Freeman, Donna Cook *small business owner*

Brisbane
Orban, Kurt *foreign trade company executive*

Burbank
Wise, Woodrow Wilson, Jr., *retired small business owner*

Cathedral City
Jackman, Robert Alan *retail executive*

Colton
†Brown, Jack H. *supermarket company executive*

Downieville
Forbes, Cynthia Ann *small business owner, marketing educator*

Emeryville
Weaver, Velather Edwards *small business owner*

Fair Oaks
Church, Bryan P. *business owner, educator*

Fairfax
Delaney, Marion Patricia *retail executive*

Fremont
Buswell, Debra Sue *small business owner, programmer, analyst*
Lane, Eric Jay *retail executive*

Fresno
Winslow, Norman Eldon *business executive*

Garden Grove
Virgo, Muriel Agnes *swimming school owner*

Glendale
Hughes, B. Wayne *retail executive*

Hat Creek
Shepard, David Haspel *film restoration specialist*

Indian Wells
Biagi, Richard Charles *retail executive, real estate consultant*

Irvine
Teta, Todd Nicholas *technology consultant, real estate developer*

Janesville
Lathrop, Lawrence Erwin, Jr., *retired business owner, retired state forest ranger*

La Jolla
Moon, Mona McTaggart *speaker, trainer, consultant, educator*

Laguna Beach
Pelton, Virginia Lue *small business owner*

Lake Forest
Prior, Michelle *antiques dealer, caterer*

Lancaster
Dalrymple, Marilyn Anita *small business owner, photographer*

Lockeford
Walker, Nancy Anne *antiques importer*

Long Beach
†Altman, Mimi Angster *business owner*
Hart, Peggy I. *small business owner*

Los Angeles
Hawley, Philip Metschan *retired retail executive, consultant*
Roeder, Richard Kenneth *business owner, lawyer*
Sinay, Joseph *retail executive*
Williams, Theodore Earle *retired industrial distribution company executive*

Los Osos
Just, Faye Jordan *antique restoration company executive*

Millbrae
Chow, Eileen Siu-Ha *computer retailing, investment company executive*

Modesto
†Piccinini, Robert M. *grocery store chain executive*

Newark
†Balmuth, Michael A. *retail executive*

Newport Coast
Pavony, William H. *retail executive, consultant*

Northridge
Orenstein, Michael (Ian Orenstein) *philatelic dealer, columnist*

Oakland
Michael, Gary G. *retired retail supermarket and drug chain executive, university administrator*

Oceanside
Bell, Sharon Kaye *small business owner*

Orange
†Underwood, Vernon O., Jr., *grocery stores executive*

Orinda
Somerset, Harold Richard *retail executive*

Pacific Palisades
Diehl, Richard Kurth *retail business consultant*

Palm Desert
Vander Naald Egenes, Joan Elizabeth *business owner, educator*

Palos Verdes Peninsula
Slayden, James Bragdon *retired department store executive*

Pasadena
Olson, Diana Craft *image and etiquette consultant*

Redlands
Sagmeister, Edward Frank *retired military officer, business owner*

Riverside
Anderson, Jolene Slover *small business owner, publishing executive, consultant*

San Diego
Ross-Serakos, Vonia P.
Saito, Frank Kiyoji *import and export firm executive*

San Francisco
Draper, William Henry, III, *import/export company executive*
†Fisher, Donald G. *casual apparel chain stores executive*
Folkman, David H. *retail, wholesale and consumer products consultant*
†Man, Yvonne *maritime company executive*
Nicolaï, Judithe *international business executive*
†Pressler, Paul S. *retail executive*
Ullman, Myron Edward, III, *retail executive*

Simi Valley
Vigdor, James Scott *distribution executive*

Skyforest
Wagner, Cheri J. *business owner*

Sonoma
Weinberger, Lilla Gilbrech *bookseller*

Torrance
Jarc, Frank Robert *retail executive*

Upland
Graw, LeRoy Harry *purchasing and contract management company executive*

Ventura
Anderson, William *retail company executive, business education educator*

Walnut Creek
†Bryant, Warren F. *retail executive*
Long, Robert Merrill *retail drug company executive*

West Sacramento
†Coyne, William J. *retail executive*
†Solomon, Russell M. *retail products executive*

†Teel, James E. *supermarket and drug store retail executive*
†Teel, Joyce Raley *supermarket and drugstore retail executive*

Westminster
†Nguyen, Duoc Tan *small business owner*

COLORADO

Arvada
†Glodava, Mila Garcia *entrepreneur, educator, consultant*

Aurora
Onyeuku, Alfred Eme *small business owner, consultant*

Boulder
Meyer, Andrea Peroutka *small business owner*

Colorado Springs
Noyes, Richard Hall *bookseller*

Delta
Lowell, Lauretta Jane *craftsperson, poet*

Denver
Cashman, Michael Richard *small business owner*
Maul, Carol Elaine *small business owner*
Nelson, LeAnn Lindbeck *small business owner*
Newberry, Elizabeth Carter *greenhouse and floral company owner*
Oakes, Terry Louis *retail clothing store executive*

Lafayette
†Lutton, Cheri *small business owner, researcher*

Loveland
Rodman, Alpine C. *arts and crafts company executive, photographer*
Rodman, Sue A. *wholesale company executive, artist, writer*

CONNECTICUT

Avon
Kling, Phradie (Phradie Kling Gold) *small business owner, educator*

Cheshire
Bozzuto, Michael Adam *wholesale grocery company executive*

Enfield
Squires, William Allen *distribution company executive*

Fairfield
Wexler, Herbert Ira *retail company executive*

Glastonbury
Hilton, John David *business owner, infosystems specialist*

Greenwich
Rudy, Kathleen Vermeulen *small business owner*

New London
Johnson, Diana Atwood *business owner, innkeeper*

Norwalk
Bennett, Carl *retired discount department store executive*
†York, Jerome B. *computer retail executive*

Rocky Hill
†Ettore, Joseph R. *discount department store chain executive*

Shelton
Pagliaro, Frank Carl, Jr., *collection agency executive, city official*

Stamford
†Gilman, Kenneth B. *retail executive*
Hollinger, Morton *business owner*

West Haven
Mendez, Angela M. *small business owner*

DELAWARE

Rehoboth Beach
Piklo, Charlene Lorraine *retail management executive*

DISTRICT OF COLUMBIA

Washington
Carr, Marie Pinak *book distribution company executive*
Chalkley, Jacqueline Ann *retail company executive*
Hocker, John Robert *technical operations executive*
Kimmitt, Robert Michael *executive, banker, diplomat, lawyer*
McGraw, Lavinia Morgan *retired retail company executive*
Pelavin, Diane Christine *small business owner*
†Sinha, Phulgenda *small business owner*
Steitz, Philip Wakeford *research corporation owner*
Tetelman, Alice Fran *small business owner*
†Wides, Louise D. *small business owner, consultant*
Wurtzel, Alan Leon *retail company executive*

FLORIDA

Aventura
Katzenstein, Thea *retail executive, jewelry designer*

Boca Raton
†Ricciardi, Salvatore *wholesale distribution executive*

Boynton Beach
†Mark, Audra *small business owner, educator*

Bradenton
Beall, Robert Matthews, II, *retail chain executive*
Rutstein, Stanley Harold *apparel retailing company executive*

Brandon
Pomeroy, Wyman Burdette *business owner, consultant*

Casselberry
†Homayssi, Ruby Lee *small business owner*

Clearwater
Hoornstra, Edward H. *retail company executive*
Maxwell, Richard Anthony *retail executive*
Pathak, Sunit Rawly *business owner, consultant, journalist*
Turley, Stewart *retired retail company executive*

Englewood
Heintz, Mary Ethel *business owner*

Fort Lauderdale
Kropp, Stacy Anne *small business owner*
Loos, John Thompson *business owner*

Fort Myers
Colgate, Doris Eleanor *sailing school owner and administrator*
Moore, Spencer Roneal *retired business owner, accounts receivable funder*
Ranney, Mary Elizabeth *business executive*

Fort Myers Beach
Tatarian, Mary Linda *retailer, real estate broker*

Gainesville
Hollien, Patricia Ann *small business owner, scientist*
McClellan, Richard Augustus *small business owner*
Silas, Nancy *small business owner*

Highland Beach
Frager, Albert S. *retired retail food company executive*

Jacksonville
Constantini, JoAnn M. *small business owner, consultant*
†Lazaran, Frank *retail executive*
Tolford, Frank Stefan *bookstore executive*

Key West
Murphy, S(usan) (Jane Murphy) *small business owner*

Lakeland
†Jenkins, Charles H., Jr., *retail company executive*
Luther, George Albert *truck brokerage executive*

Longboat Key
Goldsmith, Jack Landman *former retail company executive*

Merritt Island
Smith, David Edward *business executive, aerospace engineer, aerospace scientist*

Miami
Becker, Isidore A. *business executive*
†Chaplin, Harvey *wine and liquor wholesale executive*
†Ferrari, Leonardo *small business owner*
Milgrim, Franklin Marshall *merchant*
Newlin, Kimrey Dayton *international trade consultant, political consultant, personal computer analyst*
Risi, Louis James, Jr., *business executive*

Miramar
Catalano, Carl Philip *small business owner*

Naples
McCarthy, Joseph Harold *consultant, former retail food company executive*
White, Warren Wurtele *retired retailing executive*

Orlando
Ruffier, Joan Dial *small business owner, accountant*

Palm Bay
Galin, Tad, Sr., *home business owner*

Palm Beach
Black, Leonard Julius *retail store consultant*

Panama City
Adams, Logan G. *small business owner*

Parrish
Corey, Kay Janis *business owner, designer, nurse*

Plant City
†Oom, Rita K. *small business owner, consultant*

Saint Augustine
Bishop, Claire DeArment *small business owner, former librarian*

Saint Petersburg
†Despanza-Sprenger, Lynette Charlie *small business owner*
†McEwen, Aila Erman *small business owner*
†Nunn, Margaret Baker *owner boutique*

Sarasota
Meyer, B. Fred *small business executive, home designer and builder, product designer*

Sunrise
Delgado, Orlando *import company executive*

Tampa
Davis, Blondell Gilliam *business manager, evangelist, artist, author, poet*

West Melbourne
Fetner, Suzanne *small business owner*

Winter Haven
Cody, Mark Edward *small business owner, martial arts instructor*

Winter Park
Kindlund, Newton Carlton *retail executive*

GEORGIA

Alpharetta
Greene, Melinda Jean *retail maintenance analyst*
Watts, William David *corporate executive, business owner*

Appling
Jones, Nancy Steed *small business owner*

Athens
Brown, Jane Martin Thornton *educational administrator*

Atlanta
†Andrews, Charles *wholesale distribution executive*
†Davis, Jay M. *wholesale distribution executive*
Marcus, Bernard *retired retail executive*

Cartersville
Benham, Lelia *small business owner, social and political activist*

Centerville
Deane, Karen Peklo *retail executive*

Cumming
†Pruitt-Streetman, Shirley Irene *small business owner*

Dalton
†Saul, Julian *retail executive*

Decatur
Murray, Raymond Lee *retired clothing designer, writer*

Dunwoody
†Maddox, Jerry Aven *Retired Catalog Management Executive*

Lawrenceville
Parr, Sandra Hardy *small business owner*

Macon
†Davis, Anita Yvonne *small business owner, writer*

Marietta
Short-Mayfield, Patricia Ahlene *business owner*

Norcross
Braden, Victoria Jane *small business owner*

Social Circle
Penland, John Thomas *retired import and export and development companies executive*

Statesboro
Bacon, Martha Brantley *small business owner*

Townsend
Hicks, Virginia Hobson *bookstore owner, educator*

Valdosta
Halter, H(enry) James, Jr., (Diamond Jim Halter) *retail executive*

Vidalia
Fortner, Billie Jean *small business owner*

HAWAII

Honolulu
Lee, Candie Ching Wah *retail executive*

Kailua Kona
Luizzi, Ronald *wholesale distribution executive*

IDAHO

Boise
†Long, William D. *grocery store executive*

ILLINOIS

Bensenville
Leach, Donald Paul *small business owner*

Burr Ridge
Jones, Shirley Joyce *small business owner, fashion designer*

Chicago
Christianson, Stanley David *corporate executive*
Dobrick, Jo-Anne *retail executive, environmentalist, consultant*
Dowling, Doris Anderson *business owner, educator, consultant*
Gall, Betty Bluebaum *office services company executive*
†Lycardi, Joan C. *small business owner, artist*
Tomaino, Joseph Carmine *former retail executive, former postal inspector*
Vrablik, Edward Robert *import/export company executive*
Vyn, Kathleen A. *small business owner*
Will, Jon Nicholson *small business owner, financial consultant*

Decatur
Bradshaw, Billy Dean *retired retail executive*

Deerfield
Bernauer, David W. *retail company executive*

Glen Ellyn
Baloun, John Charles *wholesale grocery company executive, retired*

Glencoe
Nebenzahl, Kenneth *rare book and map dealer, author*

Glenview
†Letham, Dennis J. *wholesale company executive*

Gurnee
Hedrick, Geary Dean *small business owner*

Hoffman Estates
Lacy, Alan Jasper *retail executive*

Lincolnshire
†Knopik, Robert *retail executive, consultant*

Lisle
Bradna, Joanne Justice *manufacturer's representative*

Marion
Yeager, Twynette *antiques and gift shop owner, retired educator*

Morton Grove
McKenna, Andrew James *paper distribution and printing company executive, baseball club executive*

Oak Brook
†Hodnik, David F. *retail company executive*

Palatine
†Cesario, Robert Charles *franchise executive, consultant*

River Grove
†Traut, Christopher D. *educational materials distribution executive*

Saint Charles
†LaHood, Julie Ann *small business owner*
Liska, Margaret Naylor *retired small business owner*

Skokie
Van Gelder, Marc Christiaan *retail executive*

Steger
Carpenter, Kenneth Russell *international trading executive*

Wheeling
Ochsner, Othon Henry, II, *importer, restaurant critic*
Schulman, Alan Michael *small business owner*

Wilmette
Mc Nitt, Willard Charles *business executive*
Williams, Emory *former retail company executive, banker*

Winnetka
Person, Paula (Mrs. P. Barry Person) *social skills organization executive, entrepreneur*

INDIANA

Bloomington
†Stephens, Jay Martin *business owner*

Elkhart
Drexler, Rudy Matthew, Jr., *professional law enforcement dog trainer*

Evansville
Blesch, K(athy) Suzann *small business owner*

Fort Wayne
Cast, Anita Hursh *small business owner*
Cummings, William Robert, Jr., *business executive*
Curtis, Douglas Homer *small business owner*

Griffith
Spires, Roberta Lynn *small business owner*

Indianapolis
†La Crosse, James *retail executive*
Norwalk, Kelli Curran *retail executive, entrepreneur*
Pyle, R. Michael *wholesale distribution executive, educator*
Seneff, Smiley Howard *business owner*

Jasper
Newman, Leonard Jay *retail jewel merchant, gemologist*

Sandborn
Hartsburg, Judith Catherine *small business owner*

IOWA

Cedar Falls
Sweet, Cynthia Rae *small business owner*

Cedar Rapids
Baldwin, George Koehler *retired retail executive*

Davenport
†Sievert, Mary Elizabeth *small business owner, retired secondary school educator*

Marshalltown
Shawstad, Raymond Vernon *retired business owner, computer specialist*

Orange City
Korver, Gerry R(ozeboom) *business executive*

Sioux City
Bagley, Hughes Anderson, Sr., *retail executive, consultant*

West Des Moines
†Pearson, Ronald Dale *retail food stores corporation executive*

KANSAS

Kansas City
Baska, James Louis *wholesale grocery company executive*
Carolan, Douglas *wholesale company executive*

Osawatomie
Jimenez, Bettie Eileen *retired small business owner*

Overland Park
Douglas, Shirley Lorene *small business owner, councilwoman*

Shawnee Mission
†Moeller, Laura Lee *former retail executive, library consultant*

Wichita
Moore, Peggy Sue *corporation executive*

KENTUCKY

Bowling Green
†Gipson, Jim *wholesale distribution executive*

Lancaster
Arnold, Cecil Benjamin *former small business owner*

Lexington
Johnson, Lizabeth Lettie *small business owner, insurance agent*

Louisville
Smith, Donald Ray *magazine dealer*

Middleburg
†Kleffman, Ken *small business owner, rancher*

Winchester
Book, John Kenneth (Kenny Book) *retail store owner*

LOUISIANA

Abbeville
†Cao, (Francis) Khang Van *small business owner, poet*

Houma
Rhodes, Gene Paul *small business owner*

Lafayette
Zuschlag, Richard Emery *small business owner*

New Orleans
†Sheridan, Patrick G. *import/export company executive*

MAINE

Bridgton
Dunbar, Shirley Eugenia-Doris *small business owner, author, lecturer*

Freeport
†Gorman, Leon A. *mail order company executive*
Sidar, Thomas Wilson *retail executive*

Portland
†Farrington, Hugh G. *wholesale food and retail drug company executive*
Massaua, John Roger *retail executive*

Sedgwick
Donnell, William Ray *small business owner, communications executive*

MARYLAND

Baltimore
Cain, Marcena Jean Beesley *retail executive*
Dorenfeld, Alan Steven *fundraising executive*
Richburg, Shirley *business owner, operator*
Schilling, Franklin Charles, Jr., *retail management professional*

Stein, Bernard Alvin *business consultant*
Wions, Steven Paul *small business owner*

Cockeysville Hunt Valley
Connor, Geoffrey Warren *wine merchant, wine writer*

Ellicott City
Huey, J(oseph) Wistar, III, *import/export executive*

Forest Hill
Klein, Shirley Snyderman *retail executive*

Potomac
Shapiro, Richard Gerald *retired department store executive, consultant*

Riva
Barto, Bradley Edward *small business owner, educator*

Rockville
Kamerow, Norman Warren *business owner, financial services executive*

Severna Park
Wilmot, Elizabeth C. *business owner*

MASSACHUSETTS

Auburndale
Fowler, Frederick Victor, Jr., *import company executive*

Boston
Rosenberg, Manuel *retail company executive*

Cambridge
Lazarus, Maurice *retired retail executive*

Canton
†Bentas, Lily Haseotes *retail executive*
Palihnich, Nicholas Joseph, Jr., *retail executive*

Cotuit
Thibideau, Regina *retail executive, social worker*

Framingham
English, Edmond *retail company executive*
Sargent, Ronald L. *retail office and business products executive*

Hadley
Zion, Ellen C. *small business owner*

Holyoke
Radner, Sidney Hollis *retired rug company executive*

Medfield
McQuillen, Jeremiah Joseph *distribution executive*

Natick
†Wedge, Michael T. *wholesale distribution executive*
†Zarkin, Herbert J. *retail company executive*

Needham
DerMarderosian, Diran Robert *rug cleaning company executive*

Newburyport
Lessard, Arnold Fred *international business executive*

Orleans
York, Elizabeth Jane *innkeeper*

Plympton
O'Connell, Philip Edward *retired retail business owner*

Somerville
†Franklin, David *small business owner, researcher*

MICHIGAN

Ann Arbor
†Josefowicz, Gregory P. *retail executive*

Bad Axe
Sullivan, James Gerald *business owner, postal letter carrier*

Battle Creek
Hazel, James R. C., Jr., *small business owner, volunteer*

Bloomfield Hills
Robinson, Jack Albert *retail drug stores executive*

Detroit
Childress-Brown, Nazarene *small business owner, writer*
Washington, Lantz H. *small business owner*

Grand Rapids
DeLapa, Judith Anne *business owner*
†Meijer, Douglas *retail company executive*
†Meijer, Hank *retail company executive*
Morin, William Raymond *bookstore chain executive*
†Sturken, Craig *retail executive*

Midland
Huntress, Betty Ann *retired small business owner, retired elementary school educator*

Muskegon
†McKitrick, James Thomas *retired retail executive*

Naubinway
Beaudoin, Robert Lawrence *small business owner*

Portage
†Dobler, Janis Dolores *small business owner*

Royal Oak
Corwin, Vera-Anne Versfelt *small business owner, consultant*

Southfield
Bledsoe, Laurita *small business owner, publisher*
Portnoy, Lynn Ann *fashion retailer*
Primo, Joan Erwina *retail and real estate consulting business owner*

Troy
†Day, Julian C. *retail executive*
Strome, Stephen *distribution company executive*

MINNESOTA

Eden Prairie
Anderson, Bradbury H. *retail executive*
†Knous, Pamela K. *wholesale distribution executive*
†Noddle, Jeffrey *retail and food distribution executive*
Schulze, Richard M. *retail electronics company executive*

Edina
Emmerich, Karol Denise *foundation executive, daylily hybridizer, former retail executive*
Froemming, Herbert Dean *retired retail executive*

Excelsior
Beeler, Donald Daryl *retired retail executive*

Grand Rapids
Crane, Faye *small business owner*

Hibbing
Freeman, Linda Marie *consultant and technical writing company executive*

Minneapolis
†Erickson, Ronald A. *retail executive*
Mammel, Russell Norman *retired food distribution company executive*
Paulu, Frances Brown *international center administrator*
Reichgott Junge, Ember D. *small business owner, former state senator, lawyer, writer, broadcast analyst, radio personality*
†Trestman, Frank D. *distribution company executive, director*
Ulrich, Robert J. *retail executive*

Saint Paul
Nash, Nicholas David *retailing executive*
Siefken, Mark W. *small business owner*

Waite Park
Bauer, Edward Alphonse *electrical contractor*

Walker
Collins, Thomas William *caterer, consultant*

West Saint Paul
†Sittard, Herman Joseph *public relations executive, editor, retired*

MISSOURI

Aurora
Goodman, N. Jane *small business owner, legal analyst*

Bolivar
Ryneveld, Edna Lynn Copeland *small business owner, healthcare educator*

Charleston
Cassell, Lucille Richardson *small business owner*

Creve Coeur
Kemper, Christina *small business owner, respiratory therapist, elementary educator*

Cuba
Work, Bruce Van Syoc *business consultant*

Eureka
Zimmers, Vivian Eleanor *development and administrative consultant*

Franklin
Becker, Barbara Ann Stulac (Bobbie Becker) *small business owner*

Independence
†Wagner, Linda S. *small business owner*

Kansas City
Truitt, Kenneth Ray *owner*

Kingsville
†Stimac, John Anthony *small business owner, poet, cartoonist*

Lebanon
Louderback, Kevin Wayne *business owner*

Maryland Heights
Marcus, John *wholesale distribution executive*

O Fallon
Wood, Leslie Ann *retail administrator*

Overland
Clark, Maxine *retail executive*

Saint Louis
Bridgewater, Bernard Adolphus, Jr., *retired footwear company executive, consultant*
Edison, Bernard Alan *retired retail apparel company executive*
Hendricks, Flora Ann *small business owner, social worker, special education educator*
†Hinshaw, Juanita *electric distributor executive*
Kahn, Eugene S. *department store chain executive*
Newman, Andrew Edison *restaurant executive*
†Rudd, Susan *retail executive*
†Schnuck, Craig D. *grocery store company executive*
Upbin, Hal Jay *consumer products executive*

St. Louis
†Novak, Camille *small business owner, consultant*

MONTANA

Helena
Brown, Jan Whitney *small business owner*

NEBRASKA

Lincoln
Rawley, Ann Keyser *small business owner, picture framer*
Steffen/Heikes, Maxine Lynn *small business owner*

NEVADA

Las Vegas
Halpin, Thomas S. *military antiques dealer*
Marcovitz, Leonard Edward *retail executive*

NEW HAMPSHIRE

Manchester
Poloian, Lynda Gamans *retailing educator*

New Castle
Friese, George Ralph *retail executive*

New London
Thoma, Kurt Michael *business owner*

Rochester
Coviello, Robert Frank *retail executive*

Warner
Face, Wayne Bruce *small business owner*

NEW JERSEY

Bridgeton
†Fisher, Douglas Howard *retail executive*

Carteret
†Scott, Eileen Rose *retail executive*

Colts Neck
†Mauro, Anthony Peter *small business owner*

East Orange
Teetsell, Janice Marie Newman *business owner, lawyer*

Elizabeth
Gellert, George Geza *food importing company executive*

Freehold
Foster, Eric Harold, Jr., *retail executive*

Hoboken
Aronovich, Ilya *small business owner*
Schultz, Kenneth Carl *antiques dealer*

Livingston
†Piscopo, Phil *wholesale distribution executive*

Montclair
Lang, William Charles *financial executive*

Neptune
†Harran, Susan R. *small business owner, writer*

North Bergen
†Slatner, Thomas Allen *bookseller*

Paramus
Eyler, John H., Jr., *retail toy and game company executive*
†Goldstein, Michael *retail executive*

Paterson
Papageorgis, Jack *small business owner*

Pennington
Donnelly, Gerard Kevin *marketing and retail executive*

Princeton
†Bergman, Victoria Besterman *small business owner, consultant*
Cohen, Isaac Louis (Ike Cohen) *small business owner*
Hochschwender, Karl Albert *international trade and government relations consultant*
Simmons, Warren Hathaway, Jr., *retired retail executive*

Seaside Park
Tweed, John Louis *consultant, association executive, lecturer, small business owner*

South River
Fontaine, Bernard Leo, Jr., *small business owner*

Verona
Brightman, Robert Lloyd *importer, textile company executive, consultant*

Vineland
Middleton, Denise *restaurant owner, real estate agent, educator*

NEW MEXICO

Albuquerque
Phillips, Larry Duane *gemologist, appraiser*

Elephant Butte
Anton, Carol J. *small business owner, writer*

Santa Fe
†Caplan, Jessica Marie *small business owner, artist*

Tijeras
Sholtis, Joseph Arnold, Jr., *business owner, nuclear and aerospace engineer, consultant*

NEW YORK

Appleton
Singer, Thomas Kenyon *international business consultant, orchardist*

Bellport
Regalmuto, Nancy Marie *small business owner, psychic consultant, therapist*

Bergen
Woodworth, Beth Elaine *business owner*

Binghamton
Bochnovich, John Andrew *small business owner*
Florance, Douglas Allan *wholesale distributor*

Bronx
Downs, Peter Campbell *small business owner*
Kramer, Eleanor *retired real estate broker, tax practitioner, financial consultant*
†Lyons, Maxine Evadney *small business owner, poet*

Brooklyn
†Cochran, Addie Mae *small business owner, writer*
Fuerst, Adolph *consultant*
†Magliocco, John *wholesale distribution executive*
Zelin, Jerome *retired retail executive*

Buffalo
Cozzi, Ronald Lee *antiquarian book seller, rare book appraiser*

Chateaugay
Kanzler, Kathleen Patricia *kennel owner*

Cheektowaga
†Landahl, Steven A. *small business owner, writer*

Dewitt
Grady, Brenda Jayne *small business owner, business consultant, instructor*

Franklin Square
Ciuffo, Anthony Frank *small business owner*

Jamaica
Capellan, Angel *small business executive*

Katonah
Levine, Pamela Gail *business owner*

Larchmont
†Moody, Kathryn Currier *small business owner*

Lewiston
Simonson, Lee J. *small business owner*

New York
Abrahamsen, Abel *wholesale and retail import company executive*
Anchlia, Than Mal *wholesale distribution executive*
Brown, Andreas Le *book store and art gallery executive*
Campagnolo, Ann-Casey *retail executive*
Caputo, Lucio *trade company executive*
Catsimatidis, John Andreas *retail chain executive, airline executive*
Chung, Chia Mou (Charles Chung) *former Oriental art business owner*
Doherty, Karen Ann *import company executive*
Donohue, Margaret Anne *retail company executive*
Drexler, Millard S. *retail executive*
†Farah, Roger *retail company executive*
Finkelstein, Edward Sydney *department store executive*
Ho, Weifan Lee *merchandise executive*
Isogai, Masaharu *international business consultant, former women's apparel executive*
†Kettaneh, Anthony C. *small business owner, consultant*
†Lundgren, Terry J. *retail executive*
Matthews, Norman Stuart *department store executive*
Michelson, Gertrude Geraldine *retired retail company executive*
Mondlin, Marvin *retail executive, antiquarian book dealer*
Quint, Ira *retail executive*
†Riggio, Stephen *book store chain executive*
Rostenberg, Leona *rare book dealer, writer*
Sadove, Stephen Irving *retail executive*

Schiller, Justin Galland *antiquarian bookseller, researcher, editor*
Schlussel, Joseph Lazar *diamond dealer, publisher*
†Serra, Matthew D. *retail executive*
Sorensen, Jane Forester *small business owner, consultant*
†Stanton, Ronald P. *export company executive*
Stern, Madeleine Bettina *rare books dealer, author*
Strauss, Edward Robert *carpet company executive*
Tendler, David *international trade company executive*
Vander Heyden, Marsha Ann *business owner*
Washburn, Joan Thomas *business owner, art gallery director*

Ossining
Getts, Nino *studio owner*

Port Washington
Goldschein, Steven M. *computer retail executive*

Purchase
Wilson, Sherri Diane *shopping center official*

Red Hook
Rovigo, Connie Brigitta *jewelry and fine arts retailer*

Rochester
McCurdy, Gilbert Geier *retired retailer*

Ronkonkoma
†Nussdorf, Glenn *distribution executive*

Rye
Francis, Charles Gordon *business executive, writer*

Sag Harbor
Barry, Nada Davies *retail business owner*

Sands Point
Cohen, Ida Bogin (Mrs. Savin Cohen) *import and export executive*

Skaneateles
†Filkins, Susan Esther *small business owner*

Tannersville
Byrne, Patricia Curran *small business owner*
Kline, Linda *employment consultant*

West Islip
†Carpenter, Angie M. *county legislator, small business owner, editor*

NORTH CAROLINA

Asheville
Keleher, Michael Cassat *cabinet maker*

Brevard
Pulliam, Steve Cameron *business executive*

Charlotte
†Belk, John Montgomery *retail company executive*
Gambrell, Sarah Belk *retail executive*
Graham, Sylvia Angelenia *wholesale distributor, retail buyer*
†Levine, Howard R. *retail executive*

Fayetteville
†Shaffer, Denny Richard *small business owner*

Greensboro
Kiser, Mose, III, *small business owner*

Hendersonville
Heltman, Robert Fairchild *distribution executive*

High Point
†Payne-Raymond, Howard *small business owner*

Kitty Hawk
Pratt, Alice Ford *small business owner, music educator*

Lexington
Brammer, T. Hawk *small business owner*

Raleigh
Tracy, John Michael *small business owner, composer*

Rocky Mount
†Wordsworth, Jerry L. *wholesale distribution executive*

Shelby
Rogers, Robert Hamer *small business executive*

Spindale
Howard, Elizabeth Ann Blanton *courier service executive*

Wilson
†Atkinson, Ann Lennette *mortician*

NORTH DAKOTA

Fargo
†McWilliams, Carey Scott *small business owner, writer*

OHIO

Beachwood
†Fufuka, Natika Njeri Yaa *business executive*

Bellevue
Davenport, Thomas Herbert *small business owner*

Bexley
Unverferth, Barbara Patten *small business owner*

Chesterland
Aster, Ruth Marie Rhydderch *business owner*

Cincinnati
Hodge, Robert Joseph *retail executive*
Roth, Roger Douglas *small business owner*
Zimmerman, James M. *retail company executive*

Cleveland
Crosby, Fred McClellan *retail home and office furnishings executive*
Spisak-Siemientkowski, Sara Louise *small business owner, apparel executive*

Columbus
LaHowchic, Nicholas John *retail specialty company executive*
†Potter, Michael J. *retail stores executive*
Schlesinger, Leonard Arthur *retail executive*
†Schottenstein, Jay L. *retail executive*
Wexner, Leslie Herbert *retail executive*

Dayton
Jenefsky, Jack *wholesale company executive*
†Petrick, Joseph Anthony *small business owner, management consultant, educator*

Dublin
Walter, Robert D. *wholesale pharmaceutical distribution executive*

Fairlawn
Brubaker, Karen Sue *small business owner*

Galion
Butterfield, James T. *small business owner*

Helena
Moss, Clifton Michael *factory laborer, small business owner*

Hudson
Duchon, Roseann Marie *business owner, consultant*

Middletown
Kay, Patricia Kremer *business owner*

Milford
Conover, Nellie Coburn *retail furniture company executive*

Newark
Black, Boyd Carson *small business owner*

Peninsula
Ludwig, Richard Joseph *small business owner*

Pickerington
Callander, Kay Eileen Paisley *business owner, retired education educator, writer*

Shaker Heights
†Feuer, Michael *office products superstore executive*

Warren
Thompson, Eric Thomas *retail executive*

West Jefferson
Puckett, Helen Louise *retired tax consulting company executive*

Youngstown
Catoline-Ackerman, Pauline Dessie *small business owner*
Gottron, Francis Robert, III, *small business owner*

OKLAHOMA

McAlester
Kirby, Odell *retired small business owner, retired newswriter, writer*

Oklahoma City
Hansen, Mark S. *food marketing and distribution company executive*
Williams, Richard Donald *retired wholesale food company executive*

OREGON

Ashland
Chamberlain, Kent Clair *business owner, poet*

Bend
Nosler, Robert Amos *sports company executive*

Burns
†Timms, Eugene Dale *wholesale business owner, state senator*

Eugene
Gillespie, Penny Hannig *business owner*

Myrtle Creek
Shirtcliff, John Delzell *business owner, oil jobber*

Oregon City
Harrison, Thomas Samuel, IV, *small business owner*

Portland
Greenstein, Merle Edward *import and export company executive*

†Tomjack, T.J. *wholesale distribution executive*

Salem
Robertson, Marian Ella (Marian Ella Hall) *small business owner, handwriting analyst*

PENNSYLVANIA

Allison Park
Rust, S. Murray, III, *builder, real estate developer*

Altoona
Kaufman, Harry *retail executive*
†Sheetz, Stanton R. *grocery retail executive*

Berwyn
Fry, Clarence Herbert *retired retail executive*

Blue Bell
Drye, William James, Jr., *business owner*

Bristol
†Boneparth, Peter *retail executive*

Camp Hill
Miller, Robert G. *drug store chain company executive*

Chester Springs
†Donovan, Sean William *small business owner, writer*

Eighty Four
Hardy, Joseph A., Sr., *wholesale distribution executive*

Erie
Hagen, Thomas Bailey *business owner, former state official, retired insurance company executive*

Fleetwood
Lewis, Dana Kenneth *human services/communications consultant, author*

Glenside
Frudakis, Rosalie *small business owner*

Hawley
Kanzer, Larry *small business owner, food service director*

Lebanon
Ondrusek, David Francis *discount store chain executive*

Media
†Wood, Richard D., Jr., *retail executive*

Reading
†Boscov, Albert *retail executive*

Roaring Spring
Smith, Larry Dennis *paper mill stores executive*

Shamokin Dam
Matter, Harry H. *retired wholesale business executive and vice president, reflexologist*

Sharon
Rosenblum, Harold Arthur *grocery distribution executive*

Shiremanstown
Nesbit, William Terry *small business owner, consultant*

Stroudsburg
Wormack, Karen Elise *small business owner, poet*

Valencia
Richards, David Christopher *small business owner, organist*

Villanova
Vander Veer, Suzanne *aupair business executive*

Washington
Erdner, Jon W. *small business owner, securities trader*

Williamsport
Largen, Joseph *retailer, furniture manufacturer, book wholesaler*

Wormleysburg
Grass, Alexander *retail company executive*

Yardley
Desai, Cawas Jal *business executive*

York
Hake, Theodore Lowell *auction house owner*

RHODE ISLAND

Block Island
Connolly, Violette M. *small business owner*

Woonsocket
Ryan, Thomas M. *drug store chain executive*

SOUTH CAROLINA

Anderson
Caperton, Richard Walton *photographer, automobile repair company executive, educator, consultant*

Columbia
Clark, David Randolph *food distributor*

Lexington
†Kennedy, Sandra Elaine *small business owner*

Yemassee
Olendorf, William Carr, Jr., *small business owner*

TENNESSEE

Chattanooga
Gould, Mary Christa *small business owner*

Collierville
Hays, Louise Stovall *retail fashion executive*

Goodlettsville
†Shaffer, Donald S. *retail executive*

Johnson City
Sell, Joan Isobel *mobile home company owner*

Knoxville
†French, Christy Tillery *small business owner*
Harris, Charles Edgar *retired wholesale distribution company executive*
Jenkins, Frances Owens *retired small business owner*
Walker, W. Jack *retired small business owner*

Lafayette
Crowder, Bonnie Walton *small business owner, composer*

Memphis
†Odland, Steve *retail executive*
Schaefgen, Philip P. *business owner, insurance agent, real estate broker, consultant, certified public accountant*
Wright Carrier, J. T. *business owner*

Nashville
Reid, Donna Joyce *small business owner*
†Turner, Cal, Jr., *discount stores executive*
Zibart, Michael Alan *wholesale book company executive*

TEXAS

Amarillo
Marmaduke, John H. *retail executive*

Argyle
Merritt, Joe Frank *industrial supply executive*

Arlington
Satterlee, Warren Sanford, II. *retail management professional*

Athens
Geddie, Thomas Edwin *retired small business owner*

Baytown
†Martinez, Jerry *import/export agent*

Beaumont
Alter, Nelson Tobias *jewelry retailer and wholesaler*
Alter, Shirley Jacobs *jewelry store owner*

Bellaire
Teas, John Frederick *small business owner*

Brenham
†Lubbock, Mildred Marcelle (Midge Lubbock) *former small business owner*

Bryan
Smith, Elouise Beard *restaurant owner*

Carthage
Cooke, Walta Pippen *automobile dealership owner*

Corpus Christi
Finley, George Alvin, III, *wholesale executive*

Dallas
Augur, Marilyn Hussman *distribution executive*
Callahan, Rickey Don *business owner*
†Compton, Harold F. *retail executive*
†Glazer, Bennett J. *wholesale distribution executive*
†Oesterreicher, James E. *former department stores executive*
Stone, Donald James *retired retail executive*
†Tansky, Burton *department store executive*

El Paso
Arnett, Rita Ann *small business owner, consultant*
Deckert, Myrna Jean *small business owner, consultant*
Miller, Deane Guynes *salon and cosmetic studio owner*

Elmendorf
Teague, Mary Elizabeth *small business owner*

Fort Worth
Michero, William Henderson *retired retail trade executive*
Roach, John Vinson, II, *retail company executive*
Roberts, Leonard H. *retail executive*
Thompson, Carson R. *retail and manufacturing company executive*

Gainesville
†Brooks, Jerry Robert *small business owner*

Hitchcock
Shaffer, Richard Paul *business owner, retired career military officer*

Horseshoe Bay
Simpson, H. Richard (Dick Simpson) *retailer*

Houston
†Barricklo, Jack Nelson *small business owner*
†Blount, Darlene *small business owner, consultant*
Castillo, Josephine *small business owner, educator*
Gaucher, Jane Heyck *retail executive*
†Levit, Max *wholesale distribution executive, food service executive*
†Levit, Milton *grocery supply company executive*
Nesbitt, DeEtte DuPree *small business owner, investor*
Texas, Sam Fayad *small business owner, political activist*
Wagner, Charlene Brook *publishing consultant*
Wike, D. Elaine *business executive*
Williams, Robert Lyle *corporate executive, consultant*
Woodhouse, John Frederick *food distribution company executive*

Kemp
Skinner, John Vernon *retail credit executive*

Kingwood
Spartz, Alice Anne Lenore *retired retail executive*

Lago Vista
Hughes, James Baker, Jr., *retail executive, consultant*

Lewisville
†Willmott, Peter Sherman *retail executive*

Longview
McKinley, Jimmie Joe *business executive*
Sonnier, David Joseph *wholesale distributing executive*

Lubbock
Willingham, Mary Maxine *fashion retailer*

Mc Kinney
Fairman, Jarrett Sylvester *retail company executive*

Odessa
Brumelle, Kenneth Coy *retail store owner*

Plano
Neppl, Walter Joseph *retired retail store executive*
Questrom, Allen I. *retail executive*
Samford, Karen Elaine *small business owner, consultant*

Round Mountain
McReynolds, Mary Maureen *small business owner*

San Antonio
Keck, Judith Marie Burke *business owner, retired career officer*
†Lopez, M. Edward *small business owner*

Seabrook
Spears, James Grady *small business owner*

Sulphur Springs
†McKenzie, Michael K. *wholesale company executive*

Terrell
Wolfe, Tracey Dianne *distributing company executive*

Tyler
†Brookshire, Bruce G. *retail grocery store executive*
†Edwards, D. M. *retail, wholesale distribution and commercial real estate investment executive*

Waxahachie
Johnson, Ronald Kay *retail company executive*

Wimberley
Ellis, John *small business owner*

UTAH

Park City
†Archer, Lucy Ann *small business owner, librarian*

VERMONT

Colchester
Lawton, Lorilee Ann *fire sprinkler contractor company owner, accountant*

Putney
Loring, Honey *small business owner*

VIRGINIA

Alexandria
Elkins, Dan *small business owner, educator*

Arlington
Scarborough, Robert Henry, Jr., *enterpreneur*

Bristow
Schrock, Simon *retail executive*

Burke
†Austin, Sandra J. *small business owner*

Chantilly
†Tobin, Robert G. *supermarket chain executive*

Charlottesville
Lupton, Mary Hosmer *retired small business owner*

Fairfax
Pugh, Arthur James (Jay Pugh) *retired department store executive, consultant*

Mc Lean
Landfield, James Seymour *small business owner*
Vandemark, Robert Goodyear *retired retail company executive*

Merrifield
†Rodriguez, Leopoldo *wholesale distribution executive*

Nellysford
†Pfaltz, Katharine *small business owner, writer*

Norfolk
DeVenny, Lillian Nickell *trophy company executive*

Occoquan
Nemecek, Albert Duncan, Jr., *retail company executive, investment banker, management consultant*

Onley
Schonfeld, Walter Tibor *retired jewelry importer, writer*

Purcellville
Sharples, Winston Singleton *automobile importer and distributor*

Richmond
†Casini, Jane Sloan *wholesale distribution executive*
Gilinsky, Stanley Ellis *department store executive*
Luo, Shawn Haisheng *retail company executive*
McCollough, W. Alan *electronics retail executive*

Salem
Brand, Edward Cabell *retail executive*

Staunton
Hammaker, Paul M. *retail executive, business educator, author*

Upperville
†Powell Gebhard, Joy Lee (Bok Sin Lee) *small business owner, importer*

Vienna
Edwards, Phillip Milton *retired import-export company executive*
Gardner, Joel Sylvanus *tempest products company executive*

Williamsburg
Cauthen, Charles Edward, Jr., *retail executive, business consultant*

WASHINGTON

Buckley
Christensen, Doris Ann *antique dealer, researcher, writer*

Duvall
†Weiss, William Hans *small business owner*

Ellensburg
Shults, Mary J. *retail store owner*

Issaquah
†Galanti, Richard A. *wholesale business executive*
Sinegal, James D. *wholesale distribution executive*

Monroe
Kirwan, Katharyn Grace (Mrs. Gerald Bourke Kirwan Jr.) *retail executive*

Nordland
Denniston, Martha Kent *business owner, author*

Seattle
Bridge, Herbert Marvin *jewelry executive*
Fix, Wilbur James *department store executive*
Leale, Olivia Mason *import marketing company executive*
Nordstrom, Blake W. *retail executive*
Scroggie, Wayne Lee *trade and computing consultant*
Smith, Mara A. *small business owner, artist*
Stearns, Susan Tracey *lighting design company executive, lawyer*
†Stewart, Thomas J. *wholesale distribution executive*

Sedro Woolley
Peterson, Carol Powell *restaurant owner*

Spokane
†Chamberlain, Barbara Kaye *small business owner, communications executive*
Leighton, Jack Richard *small business owner, former educator*
†Sines, Randy Dwain *business executive*

Yakima
Newland, Ruth Laura *small business owner*

WEST VIRGINIA

Martinsburg
Ayers, Anne Louise *small business owner, consultant, counselor*

WISCONSIN

Beloit
†Hendricks, Kenneth *wholesale distribution executive*

Bowler
Bartholomaus, Brett William *small business owner*

Eau Claire
Helland, Mark Duane *small business owner*
Menard, John R., Jr., *home improvement retail executive*

Green Bay
†Duncan, Sam K. *retail executive*

Hurley
Nicholls, Thomas Maurice *business owner*

Menomonee Falls
†Mansell, Kevin B. *retail executive*
Montgomery, R. Lawrence *department store chain executive*

Milwaukee
Papas, George Nick *bakery company executive*
Wucherer, Ruth Marie *business owner*

Pewaukee
†Mariano, Robert A. *retail executive*

Warrens
Potter, June Anita *small business owner*

Wausau
Builer, Dorothy Marion *business owner*

WYOMING

Jackson
Law, Clarene Alta *innkeeper, state legislator*

CANADA

ALBERTA

Calgary
Slater, Gary *retail executive*

MANITOBA

Winnipeg
Cohen, Albert Diamond *retail executive*

ONTARIO

Aurora
Stronach, Belinda *retail executive*

Niagara-on-the-Lake
Ryan, James Franklin *retail executive*

QUEBEC

Montreal
Toutant, Sylvain *retail executive*

MEXICO

Mexico City
†Burgos, Hector Hugo *trading company executive*
Kim, Earnest Jae-Hyun *import and export company executive*

BRAZIL

Sao Paolo
†Rawl, Arthur Julian (Lord of Cursons) *retail executive, accountant, consultant, author*

CHINA

Shanghai
†Chueh, Chun Fei *import/export company executive*

ENGLAND

London
Williams-Jones, Michael Robert *media company executive*

GERMANY

Cologne
Hempleman, Warwick *small business owner*

JAPAN

Osaka
Takada, Fujio *jewelry store owner*

SWEDEN

Stockholm
Stachowiak, Dennis Kenneth *trading company executive*

ADDRESS UNPUBLISHED

Alexakos, Frances Marie *counselor, business owner, psychology educator, researcher, producer, editor*
Aved, Barry *retail executive, consultant*
Baker, Edward Kevin *retail executive*
Barrett, Judith Ann *salon owner*
Beavers, Karen Marjorie *small business owner*
Bice, Michael David *retail and wholesale executive, marketing consultant, insurance consultant*
Binder, Madeline Dotti *retail executive*
†Bird, Patricia Coleen *business owner*
Blum, Gerald Henry *department store executive*
Brabec, Rosemary Jean *retail executive*
Bradshaw, John Robert Covington, III, *internet service company executive*
Brodsky, Robert Jay *wholesale executive*
Burris, Lauren Bayleran *business owner*
Busch, Joyce Ida *small business owner*
Campbell, Edward Clinton *small business owner, violin maker*
Castro, Teresa Jacira *small business owner*
Cavnar, Margaret Mary (Peggy Cavnar) *business executive, former state legislator, nurse, consultant*
Chevalier, Paul Edward *retired retail executive, lawyer*
Clark, Sue Janet *business owner*
†Clayton, Eddie J. *small business owner, writer*
Colgate, Stephen *small business owner*
Conaway, Charles C. *former retail company executive*
Cope, Kenneth Wayne *chain store executive*
†Corcoran, Philip E. *wholesale distribution executive*
Cox, Joy Dean *business executive*
†Crowley, Jerome Joseph, Jr., *retired retail executive*
Cuba, Nan Brindley *small business owner, writer*
Davis, Suzy *information center owner*
Day, John Denton *retired company executive, cattle and horse rancher, breeder, trainer, wrangler, actor, educator*
DeVivo, Ange *former small business owner*
†Dominick, Kathleen Marilyn *small business owner, consultant*
Douglass, Susan Daniel *retired consultant*
Dozier, Gloria Anne Clifton *retired buyer*
Dusenbury, Ruth Cole *business owner*
Dwight, Harvey Alpheus *retired small business owner*
Dworin, Micki (Maxine Dworin) *automobile dealership executive*
Dyer, Arlene Thelma *retail company owner*
Eddy, Melissa Jane *small business owner*
Edwards, Patrick Ross *former retail company executive, lawyer, management consultant*
Ellis, Patricia Weathers *small business owner, retired electronic technician*
†Englander, Tom *business owner*
†Eyring, Maxine Louise *small business owner, esthetician*
Farr, Ivanne Estelle *small business owner, consultant, artist, sculptor*
Fehr, Gregory Paris *marketing and distribution company executive*
Feuer, Marshall Zev *import/export company executive*
Fields, Douglas Philip *building supply wholesale company executive*
Fields, Leo *former jewelry company executive, investor*
Finnigan, Robert Emmet *retired small business owner*
†Fortgang, Charles *wholesale distribution executive*
Franzetti, Lillian Angelina *former automobile dealership owner*
Fulrath, Andrew Wesley *retired small business owner*
Galvao, Louis Alberto *import and export corporation executive, consultant*
Gamroth, Arthur Paul *small business owner*
Gardner, Gwendolyn Smith *retail executive*
Geoffroy, Charles Henry *retired business executive*
German, Monica Ann *small business owner*
Goldberg, Nancy G. *business owner, community volunteer*
Goldman, Gerald Hillis *beverage distribution company executive*
Goldner, Sheldon Herbert *export-import company executive*
Goldstein, Alfred George *retail and consumer products executive*
Goldstein, Norman Ray *international trading company executive, consultant*
Goodman, Gail Busman *small business owner*
Gray, Deborah Mary *wine importer*
Haas, Edward Lee *business executive, consultant*
†Hall, Floyd *retired retail executive*
Harrop, Diane Glaser *shop owner, mayor, writer, consultant*
Hedman, Janice Lee *business executive*
Hirsch, Larry Joseph *retired retail executive, lawyer*
Holmquist, Jeffery R. *retail executive*
Holzer, Barbara Coursey *innkeeper, minister, writer, educator*
Howell, William Robert *retail company executive*
Hunt, Jerry Macon, Sr., *retail executive*
Imershein, William Leonard *trimmings company executive, retired*
†Johnson, Dolores Estelle *shop owner, retired*
†Jorndt, Louis Daniel *former retail drug store chain executive*

Knutson, Georgianna (Geegee Knutson) *retired small business owner*
Kogut, John Anthony *retail/wholesale executive*
Kopack, Pamela Lee (Pamela Lee MacMinn) *business services executive*
†Kurz, Alan Scott *retired small business owner*
Kwasnick, Paul Jack *retail executive*
Lape, Michael John *small business owner*
Larrimore, Randall Walter *retired wholesale company executive*
Lehrer, Merrill Clark *retail sales consultant*
Lipsey, Joseph, Jr., *water bottling company executive, retail and wholesale corporation executive*
†Love, Margaret Marks *business owner*
Marcus, Lee Evan *small business owner, consultant, accountant*
Marshall, George Dwire *retired supermarket chain executive*
Martini, Robert Edward *wholesale pharmaceutical and medical supplies company executive*
†Masten, Jacqueline Gwendolyn *small business owner*
Meek, Forrest Burns *retired trading company executive*
Mench, John William *retail store executive, electrical engineer*
Metz, Steven William *small business owner*
Meyer, Lasker Marcel *retail executive*
Molinari, Ana Maria *salon owner*
Moy, Audrey *retired retail buyer*
Napoleon, Donald Paul *retail executive*
Nicholas, Lawrence Bruce *advisory company executive*
Nishimura, Joseph Yo *retired retail executive, accountant*
O'Donnell Rich, Dorothy Juanita *small business owner*
Oppman, John Christopher *small business owner*
Orem, Cassandra Elizabeth (Sandra Orem) *small business owner, educator, holistic health consultant and practitioner*
Orton, Patricia Osborn *marina owner, real estate investor*
Paterson, Robert E. *trading stamp company executive*
Pearl, B. Michael *business owner*
†Pham, Lara Bach-Vien *small business owner*
Ramsey, Lucie Avra *small business owner, consultant*
Ransome, Ernest Leslie, III, *retail company executive*
Raskin, Michael A. *retail company executive*
Raymond, Ural Wayne *retired retail executive*
Rizel, Paul Jonas *small business owner*
Rodbell, Clyde Armand *retired distribution executive*
Rohner, Bonnie-Jean *small business owner, computer consultant*
Rosen, Eden Ruth *promoter, public advocate, merchandiser, consultant, writer*
Ruland, Mildred Ardelia *retail executive, retail buyer*
Runge, Donald Edward *food wholesale company executive*
Salinger, Ruth Angier *international trade company executive, environmental administrator*
Samson, Alvin *former distributing company executive, consultant*
Scott, Sylvia Jane *small business owner*
Segal, Robert S. *retail executive*
Sewell, Phyllis Shapiro *retail chain executive*
Sharp, Richard L. *retail company executive*
Shaw, Richard Melvin *gemologist, gold company executive*
Slater, Kristie *small business owner*
Snellen, Deborah Sue *training consulting company executive*
Snodgrass, Lynn *small business owner, former state legislator*
Spitzer, Matthew Lawrence *retired retail store executive*
†Stemberg, Thomas George *retail office supply store executive*
Stettner, Jerald W. *retail drugs stores executive*
Thayer, Martha Ann *small business owner*
Tielke, James Clemens *retail and manufacturing management consultant*
†Topolewski-Green, Mary Jo Therese *small business owner*
Trutter, John Thomas *consulting company executive*
†Turner, Natalie A. *retired small business owner, consultant*
Vandenburg, Kathy Helen *small business owner, career coach, resume writer*
Vernon, Carl Atlee, Jr., *retired wholesale food distributor executive*
Waddle, John Frederick *former retail chain executive*
Werries, E. Dean *food distribution company executive*
White, Bruce Emerson, Jr., *graphic design executive*
Wien, Stuart Lewis *retired supermarket chain executive*
Williams, Leona Rae *small business owner, consultant*
Winter, Richard Samuel, Jr., *computer training company owner, writer*
†Wolff, Dennis C. *farm owner*
Wylie, Pamela Jane *writer, producer, consultant, small business owner*
Zamansky, Jeffrey Ira *small business owner*

Zodl, Joseph Arthur *international trade executive, consultant*

INDUSTRY: TRANSPORTATION

UNITED STATES

ALABAMA

Abbeville
Anderson, Ruth T. *retired air traffic controller*

Athens
Ruf, Donnie Lee *delivery service provider, fashion model, clothing designer*

Birmingham
Haworth, Michael Elliott, Jr., *aerospace company executive*

Fort Rucker
Koach, Stephen Francis *flight instructor, retired army officer*

Gulf Shores
Wallace, John Loys *aviation services executive*

Huntsville
Heidish, Louise Oridge-Schwallie *transportation specialist, marketing professional*

Meridianville
Oberhausen, Joyce Ann Wynn *aircraft company executive, artist*

Remlap
Mathews, Clayton Jerome *trucking executive*

ALASKA

Anchorage
Sullivan, George Murray *transportation consultant, former mayor*
Williams, Eleanor Joyce *retired government air traffic control specialist*

ARIZONA

Phoenix
Krietor, David *airport authority executive*

Prescott
Waldock, William David *aeronautical science and aviation safety educator*

Sun City West
Hartzog, Ira Barnes *aviation executive*

Tucson
Mercker, Mary Alice *aviation school administrator*

ARKANSAS

Bella Vista
Pogue, William Reid *former astronaut, foundation executive, business and aerospace consultant*

Fort Smith
Young, Robert A., III, *freight systems executive*

Huntsville
Carr, Gerald Paul *former astronaut, retired business executive, former marine officer*

Lowell
†Hunt, J. B. *transportation executive*

Pine Bluff
Seawell, William Thomas *former airline executive*

CALIFORNIA

Anaheim
Linhart, Eddie Gene *aerospace executive*

Blue Jay
Gourley, James Walter, III, *airport executive*

Camarillo
McConnel, Richard Appleton *aerospace company official*

Edwards
Brand, Vance Devoe *astronaut*
Smolka, James William *aerospace research pilot*

Fremont
Smith, Bernald Stephen *retired airline pilot, aviation consultant*

Gilroy
Borton, George Robert *retired airline captain*

Hermosa Beach
Kokalj, James Edward *retired aerospace administrator*

Irvine
†Lorimer, Mark W. *transportation company executive*

La Mesa
Hansen, Grant Lewis *retired aerospace and information systems executive*

Long Beach
Anderson, Gerald Verne *retired aerospace company executive*
Myers, John Wescott *aviation executive*

Los Angeles
†Bruce, William A. *airport executive*
Gasich, Welko Elton *retired aerospace executive, management consultant*
Kennard, Lydia H. *airport terminal executive*
Kresa, Kent *aerospace executive*
†Park, Sam-Koo *transportation executive*
†Sugar, Ronald D. *aerospace executive*
Welborne, John Howard *railway company executive, lawyer*

Los Osos
Moore, Walter Dengel *rapid transit system professional*

Malibu
Ensign, Richard Papworth *transportation executive*

Menlo Park
O'Brien, Raymond Francis *transportation executive*

Montecito
Coln, William Alexander, III, *retired pilot*

Newbury Park
Lindsey, Joanne M. *flight attendant, poet*

Oakland
†Crowley, Thomas B., Jr., *water transportation executive*
Haskell, Arthur Jacob *retired steamship company executive*

Palo Alto
Kott, Joseph *transportation executive, consultant, educator*
†Moffitt, Donald Eugene *transportation company executive*

Palos Verdes Peninsula
Slusser, Robert Wyman *aerospace company executive*

Pasadena
Hemann, Raymond Glenn *research company executive*

Pleasanton
†Wu, Jia Hao *transportation executive, researcher, consultant*

Ramona
Hoffman, Wayne Melvin *retired airline official*

Richmond
Shladover, Steven Elliot *transportation research professional*

Riverside
†Bielucke, Edward Anthony, III, *transportation executive, writer*

Rolling Hills Estates
Rechtin, Eberhardt *retired aerospace executive, retired educator*

Sacramento
†Hall, Terry L. *aerospace executive*

San Diego
Reading, James Edward *transportation executive*

San Francisco
Anschutz, Philip F. *transportation executive, communications executive*
Brice, Charles Steven *airline executive*
Martin, John L. *airport executive*

San Luis Obispo
Williams, David Alexander *retired chief pilot*

San Mateo
Trabitz, Eugene Leonard *aerospace company executive*

Santa Ana
Dean, William Evans *aerospace industry executive*

Santa Maria
Moss, Elizabeth Lucille (Betty Moss) *transportation company executive*

Sherman Oaks
Caren, Robert Poston *aerospace company executive*

Temecula
Steiling, Daniel Paul *retired railroad conductor, writer, geographer*

Tulare
Avila, John Santos *agricultural pilot*

COLORADO

Broomfield
Bobrick, Steven Aaron *transportation executive*

Colorado Springs
Pickett, David Franklin, Jr., *technology company executive*

Denver
Baumgartner, Bruce *airport terminal executive*
†Davis, Jerry Ray *retired railroad company executive*
†McMorris, Jerry *transportation company executive, sports team executive*
Meurlin, Keith W. *airport manager*
†Pahs, Stephen Walter *pilot, real estate broker*

Golden
Lindsay, Nathan James *space systems consultant, retired military officer*

Littleton
Kleinknecht, Kenneth Samuel *retired aerospace company executive, former federal space agency official*
Strang, Sandra Lee *airline official*

Trinidad
Potter, William Bartlett *business executive*

CONNECTICUT

Clinton
Zack, Steven Jeffrey *master automotive instructor*

Essex
Lyon, Rick (Richard Woodward) *water transportation professional, poet*

Greenwich
Roitsch, Paul Albert *pilot*

Hartford
David, George Alfred Lawrence *aerospace transportation executive*

Newington
Leeds, Robin Leigh *transportation executive*

Stamford
Barker, James Rex *water transportation executive, director*
Tregurtha, Paul Richard *marine transportation company executive*

DELAWARE

Dagsboro
Lally, Richard Francis *aviation security consultant, former association executive, former government official*

DISTRICT OF COLUMBIA

Washington
Altschul, Alfred Samuel *airline executive*
†Boehler, Gabriel D. *aerospace company executive, educator*
Donohue, Thomas Joseph *transportation association executive*
Donovan, George Joseph *industry executive, consultant*
Schulz, William Henry *transportation executive*
Yingst, Bambi *transportation executive*

FLORIDA

Boca Raton
Garelick, Martin *retired transportation executive*

Coral Gables
Higginbottom, Samuel Logan *retired aerospace company executive*

Daytona Beach
†Miller, Sanford *car rental company executive*

Estero
Barney, Charles Richard *retired transportation executive*

Fort Lauderdale
Scanlon, George Patrick *transportation services executive, accountant*
Sherry, William F. *airport executive*

Jacksonville
Hamilton, Susan Owens *transportation company executive, lawyer*
Kilbourne, Krystal Hewett *retired rail transportation executive*
Maier, William Ernst, Jr., *railroad executive*
†Ward, Michael J. *rail transportation executive*

Largo
Manty, Brian Alan *high technology company executive*

Miami
†Burns, M. Anthony *transportation services company executive*
Dellapa, Gary J. *aviation consultant*
Gittens, Angela *airport executive*
Krissel, Susan Hinkle *transportation company executive*
San Pedro, Ofelia *transportation services executive, energy planner*
†Swienton, Gregory T. *transportation company executive*
Williams, Eric Joseph *transportation executive*

Naples
Johnson, Walter L. *transportation company executive*
Myers, Robert Jay *retired aerospace company executive*

Orlando
Davis, H. Alan *retired airline captain, consultant*
Pearlman, Louis Jay *aviation and entertainment company executive*
Van den Berg, Egerton *airport executive*

Palm Beach Gardens
Colussy, Dan Alfred *aviation executive*

Palm Harbor
Morgan, Albert George Leonard *retired airline pilot, writer*

Ponte Vedra Beach
Fiorentino, Thomas Martin *transportation executive, lawyer*
Hamilton, William Berry, Jr., *retired shipping company executive*
Spence, Richard Dee *former railroad executive*

Royal Palm Beach
Zucker, Leonard Charles *trucking executive, rabbi*

Sanibel
Hasselman, Richard B. *retired transportation company executive*

Stuart
Logan, Henry Vincent *transportation executive, consultant*

Tallahassee
Thagard, Norman E. *astronaut, physician, engineer, educator*

Tampa
Miller, Louis E. *airport terminal executive, accountant*

Weeki Wachee
Luffsey, Walter Stith *air transportation executive, consultant*

GEORGIA

Alpharetta
Chatlen, Stanley Lee *logistics executive*

Atlanta
Decosta, Benjamin *airport executive*
Eskew, Michael L. *package distribution company executive*
Kelly, James P. *delivery service executive*
Mullin, Leo Francis *airline executive*

Newnan
McBroom, Thomas William, Sr., *aviation consultant*

Roswell
Dolan, Dennis Joseph *airline pilot, lawyer*

HAWAII

Honolulu
Pfeiffer, Robert John *business executive*
Wilson, Charles Robert *port captain, harbor master*

Mountain View
Peterson, Gerald Joseph *aerospace executive, consultant*

IDAHO

Boise
Ilett, Frank, Jr., *trucking company executive, educator*

Filer
Conder, Jimmie Lee *commercial pilot, farmer*

Idaho Falls
Thorsen, James Hugh *retired aviation director, retired airport manager*

ILLINOIS

AMF Ohare
†Guyette, James M. *airline executive*
Kalcevic, Timothy Francis *airline pilot, educator*

Arlington Heights
Hudson, Ronald Morgan *aviation planner*

Broadview
Christopher, Alexander George *transportation company executive*

Champaign
Winstanley, Derek *water resource executive*

Chicago
al-Chalabi, Suhail Abdul-Jabbar *transportation executive*
Barriger, John Walker, IV, *transportation executive*
†Burkhardt, Edward Arnold *railway executive*
Fischbach, Charles Peter *railway executive consultant, lawyer, arbitrator, mediator*
Heineman, Ben Walter *corporation executive*
†Loney, Mary Rose *airport administrator*
Nord, Henry J. *transportation executive*
Reed, John Shedd *former railway executive*
Tilton, Glenn F. *air transportation executive*

Hanover Park
Manton, William Jeffrey *operating engineer, fleet consultant*

Lake Barrington
†Worrell, Sharyn Dianne *retired flight attendant*

Lansing
Ansary, Hanson Jaber *transportation and telecommunications executive*

Lombard
†Yeager, Phillip Charles *transportation company exeucutive*

Mount Vernon
Nicholson, Gerald Lee *airport administrator*

Naperville
†Gannon, Jeffrey P. *trucking/relocation services executive*

Oak Brook
Duerinck, Louis T. *retired railroad executive, attorney*

Park Ridge
Carr, Gilbert Randle *retired railroad executive*

Warrenville
†Ustian, Daniel C. *trucking executive*

Westmont
†Kelley, Brian P. *transportation executive*

INDIANA

Griffith
Luetschwager, Mary Susan *transportation company professional*

Noblesville
Morrison, Joseph Young *transportation consultant*

IOWA

Fort Dodge
Smith, William G. *transportation executive*

KANSAS

Overland Park
†Martin, William F. *retired transportation executive*

Topeka
Uhler, William Grant, IV, *transportation executive*

KENTUCKY

Franklin
Clark, James Benton *railroad industry consultant, former executive*

Louisville
Christopher, Ray Louis *pilot, journalist, author*
†DeLong, James Clifford *air transportation executive*
Hayes, William Meredith *pilot, retired career officer*

LOUISIANA

Kenner
Williams, Roy *airport terminal executive*

New Orleans
Amoss, W. James, Jr., *shipping company executive*
†Delery, Ferdinand Joseph, III, *aerospace transportation executive*
Johnson, Peter Forbes *transportation executive, business owner*

West Monroe
Howard, Alton Johnathan *publishing company executive*

MAINE

Nobleboro
Fisher, Allan Campbell *retired railway executive*

Rockland
Ziegelaar, Bob W. *transportation executive*

MARYLAND

Annapolis
Moellering, John Henry *aviation maintenance company executive*

Baltimore
Steele, George Peabody *retired marine transportation executive*

Bethesda
Coffman, Vance D. *aerospace company executive*
Coleman, Joseph Michael *truck lease and logistics consultant*
O'Neill, Malcolm R. *aerospace executive*

Centreville
Comfort, Paul William *county administrator, lawyer, writer*

Chevy Chase
Farrell, Joseph Michael *steamship company executive*

Columbia
Gottfeld, Gunther Max *retired urban mass transit official, consultant*

Gibson Island
Forster, William Hull *aerospace executive*

Glenn Dale
Pierson, Kenneth Lantz *motor carrier safety consultant*

Rockville
Fthenakis, Emanuel John *diversified aerospace company executive*
Porter, John Robert, Jr., *space technology company executive, geochemist*

MASSACHUSETTS

Boston
Doherty, Robert Francis, Jr., *aerospace and defense industry professional*
Klotz, Charles Rodger *shipping company and investment company executive*

Brookline
Frankel, Ernst Gabriel *shipping and aviation business executive, educator*

Cambridge
John, Richard Rodda *transportation executive*
Widnall, Sheila Evans *aeronautical educator, former secretary of the airforce, former university official*

Chatham
Bohman, Raynard Frederick, Jr., *transportation consultant, professional association administrator*

Concord
Smith, Eric Parkman *retired railroad executive*

Cotuit
Ballou, Kenneth Walter *retired business executive, university dean*

East Boston
†Coy, Craig P. *airport terminal executive*

Lexington
Burnham, Daniel Patrick *aerospace transportation executive*

Marlborough
Birstein, Seymour Joseph *aerospace company executive*
Brower, David Charles *transportation executive*

Methuen
Mason, Phillip Howard *aircraft company executive, retired army officer*

North Billerica
†Mellon, Timothy *transportation executive*

Stow
Shrader, William Whitney *radar consulting scientist*

Wilmington
Buckley, Robert Paul *aerospace company executive*

Woods Hole
Raskin, Fred Charles *transportation and utility holding company executive*

MICHIGAN

Allen Park
Boulos, Edward Nashed *transportation specialist*

Ann Arbor
Drake, John Warren *aviation consultant*

Athens
Kilgore, Marchon June *transportation company executive, genealogist*

Detroit
Robinson, Lester W. *airport executive*

Grand Rapids
Auwers, Stanley John *motor carrier executive*

Northville
Curley, Juanita Dale *pilot, writer*

Rapid City
Overbeck, Gene Edward *retired airline executive, lawyer*

MINNESOTA

Duluth
Hartley, Alan Haselton *lexicographer, stevedoring administrator*

Eden Prairie
†Wiehoff, John P. *trucking executive*

Minneapolis
†Anderson, Tim *airport terminal executive*
Hamiel, Jeff *airport executive*
Harper, Donald Victor *retired transportation and logistics educator*
Nyrop, Donald William *airline executive*
Olson, James Richard *retired transportation company executive*

Rosemount
†Wise, Mark Edward *aircraft maintenance technician, musician*

Saint Paul
Anderson, Richard H. *air transportation executive*
†Checchi, Alfred A. *airline company executive*
Engle, Donald Edward *retired railway executive, lawyer*

Warba
Currie, Earl James *transportation executive*

MISSISSIPPI

Pascagoula
Dur, Philip Alphonse *defense aerospace executive, retired naval officer*

Pass Christian
Clark, John Walter, Jr., *shipping company executive*

MISSOURI

Blue Springs
Reed, Tony Norman *aviation company executive*

Bridgeton
Delaney, Robert Vernon *logistics and transportation executive*

Fenton
Baer, Robert J. *transportation company executive*
†McClure, Richard P. *transportation executive*

Kansas City
Baisden, Eleanor Marguerite *retired airline compensation executive, consultant*
Widmar, Russell C. *airport executive*

Lambert Airport
Griggs, Leonard LeRoy, Jr., *airport executive*

Saint Louis
†Compton, William F. *air transportation executive*

Tecumseh
Davis, Michael Chase *retired aerospace industry executive, retired military officer*

Warrensburg
Horine, John William *aviation educator*

NEBRASKA

Omaha
Davidson, Richard K. *railroad company executive*

NEVADA

Lake Tahoe
†Sprague, Billy Michael *aerospace transportation executive*

Las Vegas
Walker, Randall H. *air transportation executive*

Yerington
Burrowes, Robert Arthur *transportation consultant, travel-tour operator*

NEW HAMPSHIRE

Dover
Nelson, Michael Underhill *association executive*

Hancock
Baddour, Anne Bridge *pilot*

NEW JERSEY

Alpine
Vandersteel, William *transportation executive*

Cherry Hill
Holfeld, Donald Rae *railroad consultant*

Edison
Mahadeshwar, Sanjay Sakharam *marine consultant*

Flemington
Kettler, Carl Frederick *airline executive*

Lincroft
Botti, Olenio T. *retired transporation executive, writer*

Margate City
Karsten, Philip *air traffic control automation system designer*

Martinsville
Weiss, Allan Joseph *transport company executive, lawyer*

Morristown
Olcott, John Whiting *aviation executive*

Mount Laurel
Batory, Ronald Louis *rail transportation executive*
Buchan, Alan Bradley *rail transportation executive, consultant*

Newark
Baer, Susan M. *airport executive*
†Goldman, Lois M. *transportation planner*

North Bergen
Pohan, Armand *transportation executive, professional hockey club executive, lawyer*

Raritan
Alatzas, George *delivery service company executive*

Roseland
Sugahara, Byron Masahiko *transportation company executive*

Union
White, Robert Leslie Gordon, Jr., *aerospace company executive*

Wharton
Krosser, Howard S. *aerospace company executive*

NEW MEXICO

Albuquerque
†Masefield, Oliver Leslie Peter *aerospace transportation executive, aerospace engineer*
Weh, Allen Edward *aviation executive*

Kirtland Afb
†Huybrechts, Steven Marc *space system technologist*

Santa Fe
Swartz, William John *retired transportation resources company executive*

NEW YORK

Albany
Joyce, William George, Jr., *transportation executive*

Babylon
Collis, Charles *aircraft company executive*

Carmel
Shen, Chia Theng *former steamship company executive, religious institute official*

Centerport
Trotta, Ric Charles *aerospace company executive, consultant*

Cooperstown
Rich, Walter George *railroad transportation executive*

Flushing
†Kroeppel, Warren *airport terminal executive*

Garden City
Campbell, James R. *transportation executive*

Great Neck
Pollack, Paul Robert *airline service company executive*

Huntington
Jackson, Richard Montgomery *former airline executive*

Jamaica
Feldman, Arlene Butler *aviation industry executive*
†Graser, Alfred J. *airport terminal executive, director*
Mc Kinnon, Clinton Dan *aerospace transportation executive*
†Seliga, Charles G. *airport administrator*

Jamestown
Walker, Timothy Craig *transportation executive*

Kingston
McGuire, Thomas Peter *show boat captain, secondary school educator*

Massena
†Edwards, Keith B. *airport administrator*

New York
Apostolakis, James John *shipping company executive, pharmaceutical executive*
†Cosbey, Ted *water transportation executive*
Danaher, Frank Erwin *transportation technologist*
Evans, James Hurlburt *retired transportation and natural resources executive*
Evans, Mary Johnston *corporate director*
Gilliam, Paula Hutter *transportation company executive*
Hyman, Morton Peter *shipping company executive*
Johnsen, Niels Winchester *ocean shipping company executive*
Sinagra, Jack G. *air transportation executive*
Thayer, Russell, III, *airlines executive*
Wright, Joseph Robert, Jr., *corporate executive*

Peekskill
Harte, Andrew Dennis *transportation company executive, travel agent*

Syracuse
Everett, Charles Roosevelt, Jr., *airport executive*

NORTH CAROLINA

Chapel Hill
Waller, Patricia Fossum *transportation executive, researcher, psychologist*

Charlotte
Murray, Peter William *airline executive, educator, college administrator*

Cherryville
Mayhew, Kenneth Edwin, Jr., *transportation company executive*

Kannapolis
Thigpen, Alton Hill *motor transportation company executive*

New Bern
Klein, Donald Louis *retired air transportation executive*

Winston Salem
Berrier, J. Alan *transportation executive, entrepreneur*

NORTH DAKOTA

Grand Forks
Skroch, Larry Eugene *railway conductor*

OHIO

Akron
Hundley, Larry Willis *aerospace company executive*

Cincinnati
Holscher, Robert F. *airport terminal executive*
Trotta, Vincent John *transportation executive*

Cleveland
†Enty, Richard McDougald *rail transportation administrator*

Columbus
Howell, Connie Sue *state transportation dispatcher*
Mason, Raymond E., Jr., *distributing company executive*

Painesville
Luhta, Caroline Naumann *airport manager, flight educator*

Piqua
Disbrow, Michael Ray *aerospace supplier company executive*

Rocky River
Shively, Daniel Jerome *retired transportation executive*

Vermilion
Smith, Al, Jr., *air traffic controller, retired*

Xenia
Bigelow, Daniel James *aerospace executive*

OKLAHOMA

Grove
Trippensee, Gary Alan *aerospace executive, retired*

Tulsa
Eaton, Leonard James, Jr., *aerospace executive*
Munro, Michael Donald *air transportation executive, retired military officer*

OREGON

Medford
Rogers, Gardner Spencer *railroad company executive*

Oakland
Smelt, Ronald *retired air transportation executive*

Portland
Corich, Christopher Blaze *airport planner*
†Lewis, Kenneth *shipping executive*
Wyatt, Bill *airport executive*

West Linn
Brockley, John P. *airport terminal executive*

PENNSYLVANIA

Allentown
Doughty, George Franklin *airport administrator*

Bristol
Shenefelt, Arthur B. *transportation executive, consultant*

Clarion
Canaday, Doris Charlene *retired traffic representative*

Conshohocken
Cunningham, James Gerald, Jr., *transportation company executive*

Essington
†Piasecki, Frank Nicholas *aircraft corporation executive, aeronautics engineer*

New Oxford
Frock, J. Daniel *transportation executive, retired manufacturing company executive*

Philadelphia
Terry, John Joseph *transportation investor*

Pittsburgh
Charochak, Dale Michael *airport executive*

Reading
Young, Richard Robert *logistics and transportation educator*

Trout Run
McKissick, Michael Landon *transportation consultant*

York
Grossman, Robert Allen *transportation executive*
Rebert, Jephrey Lee *transportation planner, musician*

RHODE ISLAND

Providence
Campbell, Lewis B. *aerospace technology executive*

SOUTH CAROLINA

Columbia
Conrad, Paul Ernest *transportation consultant*

Greer
Taylor, Carter W. *aviation educator, consultant, lecturer*

SOUTH DAKOTA

Rapid City
Prodan, John *aviation executive*

Sioux Falls
Smith, Murray Thomas *transportation company executive*

TENNESSEE

Chattanooga
Quinn, Patrick *tranportation executive*

Memphis
†Adams, John C. *transportation executive*
Cox, Larry D. *airport executive*
Graf, Alan B., Jr., *transportation executive*
Smith, Frederick Wallace *delivery service executive*

Morristown
Johnson, Evelyn Bryan *airport terminal executive*

Nashville
†Ingram, Orrin Henry, II, *transportation executive*

TEXAS

Colleyville
Roth, Robert William *technology specialist*

DFW Airport
Hinkle, Minerva Hernandez *airport terminal executive*

Dallas
Arpey, Gerard J. *air transportation executive*
Fegan, Jeffrey P. *airport executive*
†Kelleher, Herbert David *airline executive, lawyer*
Kolli, Sai *airline executive, educator*
†Parker, James Francis *lawyer*
†Risley, Tom *aerospace transportation executive*

Dickinson
Bush, Robert Thomas *shipping company executive*

Euless
Tunnell, Clida Diane *air transportation specialist*

Fort Worth
Baker, Robert Woodward *airline executive*
†Krebs, Robert Duncan *rail transportation company executive*
Rose, Matthew K. *rail transportation executive*
Shoemaker, Sandra Kaye *aerospace executive*
†Silverberg, Kalman Gans *rail transportation executive*

Fredericksburg
Scannell, William Edward *aerospace company executive, consultant, psychologist*

Georgetown
Aadnesen, Christopher *rail transportation executive, consultant*

Harlingen
Farris, Robert Gene *transportation company executive*

Houston
Archambault, Lee Joseph *astronaut*
Ashby, Jeffrey S. *astronaut*
Baker, Michael A. *astronaut*
Barry, Allan Ronald *ship pilot, corporate executive*
Bethune, Gordon *airline executive*
Bloomfield, Michael J. *astronaut*
Bowersox, Kenneth D. *astronaut*
Brandenstein, Daniel Charles *astronaut, retired naval officer*
Burbank, Daniel C. *astronaut*
Bursch, Daniel W. *astronaut*
Cabana, Robert D. *astronaut*
Carey, Duane Gene (Digger) *astronaut*

Chang-Diaz, Franklin R. *astronaut*
Cockrell, Kenneth D. *astronaut*
Creamer, Timothy J. *astronaut*
Curbeam, Robert L., Jr., *astronaut*
Currie, Nancy Jane *astronaut*
Doi, Takao *astronaut*
Fincke, Edward Michael (Mike) *astronaut*
Foale, C. Michael *astronaut*
Foreman, Michael J. *astronaut*
Forrester, Patrick G. *astronaut*
Frick, Stephen N. *astronaut*
Fuglesong, Christer *astronaut*
Hadfield, Chris A. *astronaut*
Herrington, John B. *astronaut, military officer*
Higginbotham, Joan E. *astronaut*
Hobaugh, Charles O. *astronaut*
Ivins, Marcia S. *astronaut*
Jett, Brent W. *astronaut, military officer*
Kelly, Mark E. *astronaut*
Kilrain, Susan *astronaut*
Kregel, Kevin R. *astronaut*
Lopez-Alegria, Michael Eladio *astronaut*
Lu, Edward Tsang *astronaut*
Morin, Lee Miller Emile *astronaut*
Myers, A. Maurice *transportation executive*
Noriega, Carlos I. *astronaut*
O'Connor, Bryan D. *astronaut*
Pailes, William *astronaut*
Parazynski, Scott E. *astronaut*
Pawelczyk, James A. *astronaut, educator*
Payton, Gary E. *astronaut*
Peterkin, George Alexander, Jr., *marine transportation company executive*
Poindexter, Alan *astronaut*
Pontes, Marcos C. *astronaut*
Precourt, Charles J. *astronaut, retired military officer*
Pudwill Gorie, Dominic L. *astronaut*
Ross, Jerry L. *astronaut*
Shriver, Loren J. *astronaut*
Smith, Gordon Eugene *pilot*
Sturckow, Frederick W. (Rick) *astronaut*
Tani, Daniel M. *astronaut*
Tanner, Joseph Richard *astronaut*
Thirsk, Robert Brent *astronaut*
Thomas, Andrew S.W. *astronaut*
Thomas, Donald A. *astronaut*
Tryggvason, Bjarni V. *astronaut*
Vacar, Richard M. *airport executive*
Voss, James S. *astronaut*
Voss, Janice E. *astronaut*
Walker, Charles D. *astronaut*
Walz, Carl E. *astronaut*
Wetherbee, James D. *astronaut*
Wilcutt, Terence W. *astronaut*
Williams, David R. *astronaut*
Williams, Jeffrey N. *astronaut*
Williams, Sunita L. *astronaut*
Wombwell, John Futrell *air transportation executive*
Young, John Watts *astronaut*
Zamka, George D. *astronaut*

Irving
Plaskett, Thomas George *transportation company executive, corporate director*

Lindale
Carter, Thomas Smith, Jr., *retired rail transportation executive*

Roanoke
Steward, Jerry Wayne *air transportation executive, consultant*

San Antonio
Hedrick, John O. *transportation executive*

Sheppard AFB
Seigars, Brian A. *air traffic controller*

Thorndale
Fish, Howard Math *aerospace industry executive*

UTAH

Bountiful
Clement, Walter Hough *retired railroad executive*

Dugway
Eshom-Oviatt, Corina May *air transportation executive*

North Salt Lake
Bouley, Joseph Richard *pilot*

Orem
Snow, Marlon O. *trucking executive, state agency administrator*

VERMONT

Middlebury
Bergesen, Robert Nelson *transportation consultant*

South Burlington
†Hamilton, John J., Jr., *airport executive*

VIRGINIA

Arlington
Beyer, Barbara Lynn *aviation consultant*
†Gangwal, Rakesh *airline executive*
Harrington, George Fred *aviation consultant*
Langstaff, David Hamilton *aerospace industry executive*
Mainwaring, Thomas Lloyd *management consultant, former motor freight company executive*
†Siegel, David N. *air transportation executive*

Stevens, Robert J. *former aerospace transportation executive*
Stokes, B. R. *retired transportation consultant*
Sweeney, Randall W. *aerospace transportation executive*
Wolf, Stephen M. *airline executive*

Catlett
Broderick, Anthony James *air transportation executive*

Chesterfield
Congdon, John Rhodes *transportation executive*

Dulles
Miller, Donald Eugene *aerospace executive*

Fairfax
†Harrison, Robert Allen *retired aerospace transportation executive*

Fairfax Station
Starry, Donn Albert *former aerospace company executive, former army officer*

Falls Church
Tether, Anthony John *aerospace executive*

Gainesville
Levell, Edward, Jr., *retired aiport executive*

Hampton
†Daniels, Cindy Lou *space agency executive*

Manassas
Kinsler, Bruce Whitney *air traffic controller, aerospace engineer*

Mc Lean
Dewar, James McEwen *marketing, aerospace and defense executive, developing nations consultant*

Norfolk
Goode, David Ronald *transportation company executive*
McKinnon, Arnold Borden *retired transportation company executive*
Tobias, Stephen C. *rail transportation executive*

Poquoson
Holloway, Paul Fayette *retired aerospace executive*

Reston
Crawford, Lawrence Robert *aviation and aerospace consultant*
Harris, Paul Lynwood *retired aerospace transportation executive*
Kreyling, Edward George, Jr., *railroad executive*

Richmond
Watkins, Hays Thomas *retired railroad executive*

Sterling
Baskir, Geoffrey Scott *airport planner*
†Thompson, David Walker *astronautics company executive*

Vienna
Rogers, Raymond Jesse *retired federal railroad associate administrator*

Williamsburg
Spitzer, Cary Redford *avionics consultant, electrical engineer*

WASHINGTON

Bainbridge Island
Cioc, Charles Gregory

Issaquah
Southern, Valerie *transportation consultant*

Kent
Bangsund, Edward Lee *former aerospace company executive, consultant*

Kirkland
Clarkson, Lawrence William *air transportation executive*

Seattle
Brown, Janiece Alfreida *pilot*
Cline, Robert Stanley *retired air freight company executive*
Condit, Philip Murray *aerospace executive, engineer*
Donaway, Carl D. *messenger service executive*
Grinstein, Gerald *transportation executive*
†Kelley, John F. *airline executive*
Lindsey, Gina Marie *airport executive*
Schmidt, Peter Gustav *shipbuilding industry executive*
Strombom, Cathy Jean *transportation planner, consultant*
Thornton, Dean Dickson *retired airplane company executive*

Spanaway
Loete, Steven Donald *pilot*

Vashon
Mantle, Peter John *aerospace executive, consultant*

WISCONSIN

Appleton
Petinga, Charles Michael *transportation executive*

Green Bay
†Lofgren, Christopher B. *trucking executive*
†Schneider, Donald J. *trucking company executive*

Oshkosh
Schoenrock, Tracy Allen *airline pilot, aviation consultant*

Tomah
Johnson, Linda Arlene *petroleum and flatbed semi-freight transporter*

WYOMING

Worland
Woods, Lawrence Milton *airline company executive*

CANADA

ALBERTA

Calgary
McCaig, Jeffrey James *transportation company executive*

Edmonton
Marcotte, Brian *transportation executive*

NOVA SCOTIA

Halifax
Oldfield, Karen *transportation executive*
Renouf, Harold Augustus *business consultant, retired*

ONTARIO

Brampton
Savoie, Leonard Norman *transportation company executive*

Mississauga
Tobias, Kal *transportation executive*

Ottawa
Duncan, Mark *air transportation executive*
O'Donnell, Scott Richard *aviation administrator*

QUEBEC

Montreal
Tellier, Paul M. *railroad transportation executive*

Sain -Sauveur
Hanigan, Lawrence *retired railway executive*

Saint-Anne-Des-Lacs
Rochette, Louis *retired shipowner and shipbuilder*

MEXICO

Mexico City
†Martens, Ernesto *air, aerospace transportation executive*

AUSTRALIA

Springfield
Spalvins, Janis Gunars *steamship company executive*

BELGIUM

Brussels
McCullough, Ross A., Jr., *delivery service executive*

DENMARK

Vedbaek
Nordqvist, Erik Askbo *shipping company executive*

ENGLAND

Harmondsworth
Marshall, Lord Colin (Lord Marshall of Knightsbridge) *airline executive*

London
†Bland, Sir Christopher (Francis Buchan Bland) *freight company executive*
Kallakis, Achilleas Michalis S. *shipping company executive*

ITALY

Augusta
Bella, Giovanni *shipping agent*

Genoa
Cosulich, Paolo Ulisse *shipping company executive, consultant*

SWITZERLAND

Geneva
Aaronson, Robert Jay *aviation executive*

ADDRESS UNPUBLISHED

Adolph, Kathryn Ann *passenger service employee*
Ames, Donald Paul *retired aerospace company executive, researcher*
Barber, Theodore Francis *aircraft mechanics professional*
Blanchard, David Lawrence *aerospace executive, real estate developer, management consultant*
Bodden, Jane Ellen *retired airline reservations manager*
Brazier, Don Roland *retired railroad executive*
Brown, Donald Douglas *transportation company executive, retired air force officer, consultant*
Brown, Robert E. *retired transportation executive*
Brunson, Burlie Allen *aerospace transportation executive*
Burton, Raymond Charles, Jr., *retired transportation company executive*
Butterfield, Alexander Porter *former business executive, government official*
Carty, Donald J. *former airline company executive*
†Collins, Eileen Marie *astronaut*
Cook, Stephen Champlin *retired shipping company executive*
Cooper, John Byrne, Jr., *airline pilot*
Crowder, Richard Morgan *pilot*
Culbertson, Philip Edgar, Sr., *aerospace company executive, consultant*
Dansby, Ronnie *transportation executive*
Deets, Dwain Aaron *retired aerospace technology executive*
Dely, Steven *aerospace company executive*
†Diaz, Alphonso Vincent *aerospace executive*
Felix, Cheryl A. *air transportation executive*
Ferreira, Jo Ann Jeanette Chanoux *time-definite transportation industry executive*
Ferrell, David Stanley *aerospace company executive*
Foss, Charles R. *contracting officer*
Gitner, Gerald L. *air transportation executive, investment banker*
Glover, Lisa Marie *transportation consultant*
Goldstein, Bernard *transportation and casino gaming company executive*
Graebner, James Herbert *transportation executive*
Gray, Richard Arden *retired transportation executive*
Greenblatt, Maurice Theodore *transportation executive*
Hails, Robert Emmet *aerospace consultant, business executive, former air force officer*
†Hard, Brian *truck leasing company executive*
Hawkins, Willis Moore *aerospace and astronautical consultant*
Hedrick, Larry Willis *retired airport executive*
Heitz, Edward Fred *freight traffic consultant*
†Hidalgo, Miguel *transportation company executive*
Johnson, Gregory Carl *pilot, astronaut, career officer*
Keenan, Anthony Lee *trucking company executive*
King, Edward William *retired transportation executive*
Kondas, Nicholas Frank *retired shipping company executive*
Krause, Kurth Werner *aerospace executive*
Latino, Mark Vincent *rapid transit executive*
†La Vista, Jaqueline Gable *air transportation executive*
Lesko, Harry Joseph *transportation company executive*
†Lette, Daniel Ivan *pilot*
Lewis, Andrew Lindsay, Jr., (Drew Lewis) *former transportation and natural resources executive*
Lewis, Martin Edward *shipping company executive, foreign government concessionary*
Marshall, Charles Noble *rail transportation executive*
Masiello, Rocco Joseph *airlines and aerospace manufacturing executive*
Mast, Stewart Dale *retired airport manager*
†Matthews, L. White, III, *railroad executive*
McCarthy, Paul Fenton *aerospace executive, former naval officer*
†Melton, Augustus Allen, Jr., *retired airport executive*
Musgrave, Story *astronaut, surgeon, pilot, physiologist, educator*
Orsbon, Benjamin Thomas *transportation planner*
Quade, Marshall Ross *transportation planner*
Quesnel, Gregory L. *transportation company executive*
Recanati, Elias Isaac *retired shipping company executive*
Regalado, Raul L. *airport executive*
Reitz, Douglas John Frank *airline captain, computer consultant*
Renda, Dominic Phillip *airline executive*
Rivkind, Perry Abbot *federal railroad agency administrator*
Rose, Carol Ann *retired air transportation executive*
Rose, James Turner *aerospace consultant*
Rosenberger, Timothy Joseph *transportation planning consultant*
Ruegg, Donald George *retired railway company executive*
Saleh, Brian Behrooz *aerospace executive*
Savitz, Maxine Lazarus *aerospace company executive*
Schaefer, C. Barry *railroad executive, lawyer, investment banker*
†Seymour, Joseph John *air transportation executive*
Shockley, Edward Julian *retired aerospace company executive*
Snowden, Lawrence Fontaine *retired aircraft company executive, retired marine corps general officer*
Stromquist, Kenneth James, Jr., *pilot, retired military officer*
Swanson, Ralph William *aerospace executive, consultant, engineer*
Valine, Delmar Edmond, Sr., *corporate executive*
van Hoften, James Dougal Adrianus *business executive, former astronaut*
Vejvoda, Edward *aerospace company executive*
Voss, Omer Gerald *truck company executive*
Walker, Garland Wayne *aircraft inspector*
Wallace, F. Blake *aerospace executive, mechanical engineer*
Washburn, Donald Arthur *business executive, private investor*

INDUSTRY: UTILITIES, ENERGY, RESOURCES

UNITED STATES

ALABAMA

Birmingham
Franklin, H. Allen *electric company executive*
Hutchins, William Bruce, III, *utility company executive*

Foley
St. John, Henry Sewell, Jr., *utility company executive*

Shoal Creek
Ahearn, John Francis, Jr., *retired oil and gas company executive*

ALASKA

Fairbanks
Beistline, Earl Hoover *mining consultant*

ARIZONA

Phoenix
De Michele, O. Mark *utility company executive*
Huffman, Edgar Joseph *oil company executive*

Prescott
†Bennett, Kenneth R. *oil company executive, state legislator*

Scottsdale
†Birkelbach, Albert Ottmar *retired oil company executive*
Bullerdick, Kim H. *petroleum executive*

Sedona
Dansby, John Walter *retired oil company executive*

Sun City
Black, Robert Frederick *former oil company executive*

Sun City West
O'Brien, Gerald James *utilities executive*

Tucson
Heller, Frederick *retired mining company executive*
Jamison, Harrison Clyde *oil company executive, retired*
Peeler, Stuart Thorne *petroleum industry executive and independent oil operator*
Peters, Charles William *research and development company manager*

ARKANSAS

El Dorado
†Deming, Claiborne P. *oil industry executive*
Watkins, Jerry West *retired oil company executive, lawyer*

Hot Springs National Park
Counts, Mary Lou *retired telephone company executive*

Little Rock
Ford, Joe Thomas *telephone company executive, former state senator*

CALIFORNIA

Anaheim
Fenton, Donald Mason *retired oil company executive*
†Stegemeier, Richard Joseph *oil company executive*

Beverly Hills
Levingston, John Colville Bowring *telecommunications executive*

Carmel
Aurner, Robert Ray, II, *oil company, auto diagnostic, restaurant franchise and company development executive*
Hamilton, Lyman Critchfield, Jr., *telecommunications industry executive*

Carmichael
Crabbe, John Crozier *telecommunications consultant*

Danville
Levine, Michael *telecommunications industry executive, consultant*

El Segundo
Williamson, Charles R. *energy company executive*

Elk Grove
Romano, Sheila June *telecommunications industry executive, artist, writer*

Folsom
Regan, William Joseph, Jr., *energy company executive*

Hillsborough
Quigley, Philip J. *retired telecommunications industry executive*

Irvine
Shirilau, Mark Steven *utilities executive*

La Jolla
Rinaker, Samuel Mayo, Jr., *retired utilities executive*
Trujillo, Solomon D. *telecommunications executive*

Los Angeles
Chazen, Stephen I. *oil company executive*
Van Horne, R. Richard *oil company executive*
Voelte, Donald R. *energy company executive*

Los Gatos
Koomen, Cornelis Jan *telecommunications and electronics executive*

Manteca
Talmage, Kenneth Kellogg *business executive*

Marina Del Rey
Carter, Janice Joene *telecommunications executive*

Mill Valley
Premo, Paul Mark *oil company executive*

Mission Viejo
Dergarabedian, Paul *energy and environmental company executive*

Monterey Park
Montag, David Moses *telecommunications industry executive*

Napa
Savage, Michael John Kirkness *oil company and arts management executive*

Newport Coast
Swan, Peer Alden *public utility executive*

Oakland
Morris, Ronald Lew *oil and gas company executive*

Pacific Palisades
Klein, Joseph Mark *retired mining company executive*
Middleton, James Arthur *oil and gas company executive*
Mulryan, Henry Trist *mineral company executive, consultant*

Palo Alto
Glauthier, T. J. *non-profit executive*

Palos Verdes Peninsula
Christie, Hans Frederick *retired utility company subsidiaries executive, consultant*

Pasadena
White-Thomson, Ian leonard *retired mining executive*

Petaluma
Frederickson, Arman Frederick *minerals and petroleum company executive*

Piedmont
Willrich, Mason *energy industry executive*

Riverside
Pratt, John Jackson *property manager, retired telephone installer*

Rosemead
Bryson, John E. *utilities company executive*

Sacramento
†Madden, Kenneth Robert *mining executive*

San Diego
Baum, Stephen L. *utilities company executive*
Cota, John Francis *utility executive*
Gray-Bussard, Dolly H. *energy company executive*

San Francisco
†Bonney, John Dennis *retired oil company executive*
Flittie, Clifford Gilliland *retired petroleum company executive*
†Glynn, Robert D., Jr., *electric power and gas industry executive*
O'Reilly, David J. *oil company executive*
†Watson, John S. *oil company executive*
Williams, Neville *international solar energy corporation executive*
Woertz, Patricia A. *petroleum industry executive*

San Jose
Foy, Robert W(illard) *utilities executive*
Malis, Andrew Gary *telecommunications company executive*
Quon, Malcolm Yee *defence systems company executive*

San Rafael
Latno, Arthur Clement, Jr., *telephone company executive*

Santa Barbara
Mahoney, Tim J. *utility company executive*
Mc Duffie, Malcolm *oil company executive*

South Pasadena
Finnell, Michael Hartman *corporate executive*

Stanford
Brinegar, Claude Stout *retired oil company executive*

Templeton
Gandsey, Louis John *petroleum and environmental consultant*

Van Nuys
Farman, Richard Donald *energy company executive*
Fisher, Earl Monty *utilities executive*

COLORADO

Boulder
Hill, Melvin James *oil company executive*

Colorado Springs
King, Peter Joseph, Jr., *retired gas company executive*

Denver
Anderson, Donald H. *gas industry executive*
Cambre, Ronald C. *mining executive*
Danos, Robert McClure *retired oil company executive*
Hall, Larry Dean *energy company executive, lawyer*
Macey, William Blackmore *oil company executive*
†Mohebbi, Afshin *telecommunications industry executive*
Norman, John Edward *petroleum landman*
Notebaert, Richard C. *telecommunications industry executive*
Owens, Marvin Franklin, Jr., *oil company executive*
Trueblood, Harry Albert, Jr., *oil company executive*
Vickery, Robert Bruce *oil industry executive, consultant*

Durango
Thurston, William Richardson *oil and gas industry executive, geologist*

Englewood
†Malone, John C. *telecommunications executive*

Evergreen
McEldowney, Roland Conant *gold mining company executive, photographer*

Golden
†Manion, Randolph Thomas *energy executive, consumer products company executive*
Matthews, Thomas Michael *former energy company executive*

Lakewood
Coakley, William Thomas *retired utilities executive*

Littleton
Fryt, Monte Stanislaus *petroleum company executive, speaker, advisor*
VanderLinden, Camilla Denice Dunn *telecommunications industry manager*
Vostiar, John *retired telecommunications industry executive*

Loveland
Bierbaum, J. Armin *petroleum company executive, consultant*

CONNECTICUT

Bridgeport
Silvestri, Robert *electric company executive*

Darien
Kutz, Kenneth John *retired mining executive*

East Hartford
Venkatesh, Prasana Krishnamurthi *oil industry executive, researcher*

Fairfield
†Trotter, Lloyd G. *electric power industry executive*

Greenwich
Alonzo, Martin Vincent *mining and aluminum company executive, investor, financial consultant*
Bennett, Jack Franklin *oil company executive*
DeCrane, Alfred Charles, Jr., *petroleum company executive*
Nelson, Don Harris *gas and oil industry executive*
Schmidt, Herman J. *former oil company executive*

Tell, William Kirn, Jr., *retired oil company executive, lawyer*

Guilford
Morgan, Leon Alford *retired utility executive*

Madison
Evans, Evan *petroleum executive*
Kay, Herbert *retired natural resources company executive*

New Canaan
Bartlett, Dede Thompson *communications consultant*
Hedley, Robert Peveril *retired petroleum and chemical company executive*
McIvor, Donald Kenneth *retired petroleum company executive*

Old Greenwich
Hittle, Richard Howard *corporate executive, international affairs consultant*

Southport
Damson, Barrie Morton *oil and gas exploration company executive*

Stamford
Bijur, Peter I. *retired petroleum company executive*
Gardiner, Hobart Clive *petroleum company executive*
Jacobson, Ishier *retired utility executive*
Mc Kinley, John Key *retired oil company executive*

West Haven
Bowerman, Richard Henry *utility company executive, lawyer*

Westport
Nedom, H. Arthur *petroleum consultant*

DELAWARE

Newark
Connelly, Donald Preston *retired electric and gas utility company executive*

Wilmington
Cosgrove, Howard Edward, Jr., *utility executive*

DISTRICT OF COLUMBIA

Washington
Bradshaw, Richard Eugene *government relations, energy and environment consultant*
Buchan, Douglas Charles *petroleum company executive, government official*
Deland, Michael Reeves *energy executive*
†Derrick, John Martin, Jr., *electric company executive*
Friedman, Gregory H. *energy administrator*
Hedlund, Charles John *oil company executive, conservationist*
McCollam, William, Jr., *utility company executive*
McGee, Robert Merrill *oil company executive*
Modiano, Albert Louis *gas, oil industry executive*
Nelson, Larry Dean *telecommunications and computer systems company executive, consultant*
Paige, Hilliard Wegner *corporate director, consultant*
†Sterling, Christopher H. *telecommunications educator*
Thompson, William Reid *public utility executive, lawyer*
Wraase, Dennis Richard *utilities company executive, accountant*

FLORIDA

Belleair Beach
Ayers, Richard Wayne *electrical company official, writer, journalist*

Boca Grande
McInnes, Donald Gordon *railroad executive*

Boca Raton
Gralla, Eugene *natural gas company executive*

Bradenton
Watkins, William, Jr., *electric power industry executive*

Deerfield Beach
Laser, Charles, Jr., *oil company executive*

Eustis
Welch, Jerry *oil company executive*

Fort Lauderdale
Sklar, Alexander *electric company executive*

Jacksonville
Francis, James Delbert *oil company executive*
Milbrath, Robert Henry *retired petroleum executive*

Juno Beach
†Broadhead, James Lowell *electrical power industry executive*

Key West
Evans, John Derby *telecommunications company executive*

Largo
Dolan, John E. *consultant, retired utility executive*

Loader, Jay Gordon *retired utility company executive*

Longwood
Cirello, John *utility and engineering company executive*

Marco Island
Meyer, Jon Howard *utility executive, consultant*

Naples
Johnson, Kenneth Oscar *oil company executive*
Johnson, Zane Quentin *retired petroleum company executive*
Marino, William Francis *telecommunications industry executive, consultant*
Rowe, Jack Field *retired electric utility executive*

North Palm Beach
Hay, Lewis, III, *utilities company executive*

Orlando
Houser, Ruth G. *financial executive*

Palm Beach
Donnell, John Randolph *retired petroleum executive*

Palm Beach Gardens
Harnett, Joseph Durham *oil company executive*

Palm Coast
Farrell, Joseph Christopher *retired mining executive, services executive*

Ponte Vedra Beach
Green, Norman Kenneth *retired oil industry executive, former naval officer*
Wood, Quentin Eugene *oil company executive*

Saint Petersburg
Fleming, William Sloan *energy executive, computer company executive*

Sun City Center
McGrath, John Francis *utility executive*

Tallahassee
Laughlin, William Eugene *retired electric power industry executive*

Tampa
Leavengood, Victor Price *telephone company executive*

Venice
Torrey, Richard Frank *utility executive*

West Palm Beach
Kiely, Dan Ray *telecommunications and banking consultant*
Smith, Betsy Keiser *telecommunications company executive*

Winter Park
Spake, Ned Bernarr *energy company executive*

GEORGIA

Alpharetta
Adams, Rex M. *telecommunications executive*

Atlanta
Ackerman, F. Duane *telecommunication industry executive*
†Bolch, Carl Edward, Jr., *petroleum company executive, lawyer*
Chilton, Horace Thomas *pipeline company executive*
†Dahlberg, Alfred William *electric company executive*
†Duques, Ric *information services executive*
Frost, Norman Cooper *retired telephone company executive*
Fuller, S(heri) Marce *energy executive*
Griffin, Clayton Houstoun *retired power company engineer, lecturer*
Owen, Steven Keith *utility executive*
Ramsey, Ira Clayton *retired pipeline company executive*

Dalton
Bundros, Thomas Anthony *utilities executive*

Gainesville
Leet, Richard Hale *oil company executive*

High Shoals
Bracewell, Gaynor Lee *hydro electric plant owner, developer*

Savannah
Gilbert, John B. *retired electric and power company official*

Snellville
Keyes, David Taylor *telecommunications company administrator*

Social Circle
O'Connor, Patricia Eryl *telecommunications consultant*

HAWAII

Honolulu
Williams, Carl Harwell *utilities executive*

Waikoloa
Calvert, Delbert William *energy executive*

IDAHO

Coeur D Alene
Griffith, William Alexander *former mining company executive*

Idaho Falls
Newman, Stanley Ray *oil refining company executive*

Mountain Home
Hiddleston, Ronal Eugene *mining executive*

ILLINOIS

Argonne
Ban, Stephen Dennis *gas industry executive*

Barrington Hills
Perry, I. Chet *petroleum company executive*

Chicago
Brooker, Thomas Kimball *oil company executive*
†Carlson, LeRoy Theodore, Jr., *telecommunications industry executive*
Dunn, Christopher Joseph *telecommunications industry executive*
Morrow, Richard Martin *retired oil company executive*
Rowe, John William *utility executive*
†Strobel, Pamela B. *energy executive*

Decatur
Womeldorff, Porter John *utilities executive*

Flossmoor
Pierce, Shelby Crawford *management and oil industry consultant*

Geneva
Pershing, Robert George *telecommunications company executive*

Hinsdale
Brandt, John Ashworth *fuel company executive*

Naperville
Burken, Ruth Marie *utility company executive*

Oak Brook
†Barnholt, Brandon K. *gas station/convenience store executive*

Orland Park
English, Floyd Leroy *telecommunications company executive*

Peoria
DuBois, Mark Benjamin *former utilities executive, educator*

River Forest
Batlivala, Robert Bomi D. *oil company executive, economics educator*

INDIANA

Brownsburg
Diasio, Richard Leonard *power transmission executive, sports facility executive, race car manufacturer executive*

Columbus
Able, Warren Walter *natural resource company executive, physician*

Frankfort
Stonehill, Lloyd Herschel *gas company executive, mechanical engineer*

Greensburg
Schilling, Don Russell *electric utility executive*

Highland
Purcell, James Francis *former utility executive, consultant*

Indianapolis
Griffiths, David Neal *utility executive*
Husted, Ralph Waldo *former utility executive*
Krueger, Betty Jane *telecommunications company executive*
Todd, Zane Grey *retired utilities executive*

Lawrenceburg
Dautel, Charles Shreve *retired mining company executive*

Merrillville
Neale, Gary Lee *utilities executive*

IOWA

Des Moines
†Abel, Gregory E. *utility company executive*
†Sokol, David L. *energy services provider company executive*

Lidderdale
Hagemann, Dolores Ann *water company official*

KANSAS

Eskridge
Taylor, Russell Benton *mining executive*

Overland Park
†Forsee, Gary D. *telecommunications industry executive*

Pittsburg
Nettels, George Edward, Jr., *retired mining executive*

Shawnee Mission
Esrey, William Todd *telecommunications company executive*

Topeka
Spencer, William Edwin *telephone company executive, engineer*

Wichita
Cadman, Wilson Kennedy *retired utility company executive*
Varner, Sterling Verl *retired oil company executive*

KENTUCKY

Ashland
†Tepper, Scott M. *mining executive*
Weaver, Carlton Davis *retired oil industry executive*
†Yancey, Robert Earl, Jr., *retired oil company executive*

Covington
†Brothers, John Alfred *retired oil company executive*
Quin, Joseph Marvin *oil company executive*

Crescent Springs
Chellgren, Paul Wilbur *industrial company executive*

Glasgow
Duvo, Mechelle Louise *oil company executive, consultant*

Louisville
†Hale, Roger W. *utilities company executive*
Ronald, Peter *utility executive*
Royer, Robert Lewis *retired utility company executive*

Paducah
Starkey, Russell Bruce, Jr., *energy executive*

LOUISIANA

Lafayette
Gaubert, Ronald Joseph *gas and oil industry executive, management consultant, real estate broker*

Monroe
Fouts, James Fremont *mining company executive*

New Orleans
Bachmann, Richard Arthur *oil company executive*
Leonard, J. Wayne *energy company executive*
Lind, Thomas Otto *barge transportation company executive*
†Lupberger, Edwin Adolph *retired utility executive*
Murrish, Charles Howard *oil and gas exploration company executive, geologist*

Shreveport
Zadeck, Donald Julian *oil and gas exploration company executive*

Springfield
Carron, Ronald Joseph *electric power industry professional*

MAINE

Augusta
Weil, Gordon Lee *energy executive, publishing executive*

Surry
Kilgore, John Edward, Jr., *former petroleum company executive*

Yarmouth
Haynes, Peter Lancaster *retired utility executive*

MARYLAND

Annapolis
Ellis, George Fitzallen, Jr., *retired energy services company executive*
Marienthal, George *telecommunications company executive*

Baltimore
Ihrie, Robert *oil, gas and real estate company executive*
†Owsley, Thomas L. *oil industry executive*
†Poindexter, Christian Herndon *utility company executive*

Bethesda
Ikle, Doris Margret *energy executive*
McMurphy, Michael Allen *energy company executive, lawyer*
Olmsted, Jerauld Lockwood *telephone company executive*

Boyds
†Love, Dana Francis Ignatius *telecommunications industry executive*

Ellicott City
Perry, Nancy Trotter *former telecommunications company executive*

Glen Arm
Jackson, Theodore Marshall *retired oil company executive*

Hagerstown
†Evanson, Paul John *utilities executive*
Noia, Alan James *utility company executive*

Hughesville
Hilwig, Joseph Michael *electric company director*
Tudor, Thomas Rae *electric power industry executive*

Lutherville Timonium
Bevis, Robert E. *retired oil company executive*

Silver Spring
Jacobs, George *broadcast engineering consulting company executive*
Russo, Anthony Sebastian *telecommunications industry executive*

MASSACHUSETTS

Boston
†Kennedy, Joseph Patrick, II, *utilities executive, former congressman*

Cambridge
Rodgers, Gilbert M. *energy executive*

Centerville
Anderson, Gerald Edwin *utilities executive*
Scherer, Harold Nicholas, Jr., *electric utility company executive, engineer*

Chelsea
†Kaneb, Gary R. *oil industry executive*

Danvers
Dolan, John Ralph *retired corporation executive*

Harwich Port
Staszesky, Francis Myron *independent energy consultant*

Melrose
Brown, Ronald Osborne *telecommunications and computer systems consultant*

Needham
Cogswell, John Heyland *retired telecommunications executive, financial consultant*
Rafferty, James Paul *telecommunications executive*

Waltham
†Slifka, Alfred A. *oil corporation executive*

Wayland
Wald, Fritz Veit *solar energy corporation executive*

West Springfield
Morris, Michael G. *utilities executive*

Westborough
Bok, Joan Toland *utility executive*

MICHIGAN

Dearborn
†Fryling, Victor J. *energy company executive*
Webb, Thomas J. *utilities executive*
Whipple, Kenneth *utilities executive*

Detroit
Earley, Anthony Francis, Jr., *utilities company executive, lawyer*

Fraser
Cattaneo, Michael S. *heating and cooling company executive*

Grosse Pointe
Smith, Stanton Kinnie, Jr., *utility executive*

Saint Clair Shores
Glancy, Alfred Robinson, III, *retired public utility company executive*

Shelby Township
Fillbrook, Thomas George *telephone company executive*

MINNESOTA

Eden Prairie
Emison, James Wade *petroleum company executive*

Fergus Falls
MacFarlane, John Charles *utility company executive*

Minneapolis
Brunetti, Wayne H. *utility company executive*
†Brunetti, Wayne Henry *utilities executive*

Saint Paul
Robertson, Jerry Earl *retired manufacturing company executive*

MISSISSIPPI

Clinton
†Roberts, Bert C., Jr., *telecommunications company executive*

Jackson
†Lampton, Leslie B., Sr., *oil industry executive*

MISSOURI

Clayton
†Novelly, Paul Anthony *petrochemical and refining company executive*

Kansas City
Baker, John Russell *utilities executive*
Green, Robert K. *energy executive*
Potter, George William, Jr., *mining executive*

Lebanon
Beavers, Roy Lackey *retired utility executive, essayist, activist*

Saint Louis
Engelhardt, Irl F. *coal company executive*
†Mueller, Charles William *electric utility executive*
O'Malley, Thomas D. *petroleum industry executive*
Quenon, Robert Hagerty *retired mining consultant and holding company executive*
†Vogel, Carl E. *telecommunications industry executive*

Springfield
Jura, James J. *electric utility executive*

MONTANA

Bigfork
Shennum, Robert Herman *retired telephone company executive*

Billings
Nance, Robert Lewis *oil company executive*

Butte
Burke, John James *utility executive*
Mc Elwain, Joseph Arthur *retired power company executive*

Missoula
Brumit, Lawrence Edward, III, *oil field service company executive*

NEBRASKA

Hastings
Creigh, Thomas, Jr., *utility executive*

Omaha
†Hawks, Howard L. *energy executive*

NEVADA

Henderson
Trimble, Thomas James *retired utility company executive, lawyer*

Las Vegas
Grace, John William *electrical company executive*
Laub, William Murray *retired utility executive*

Reno
Busig, Rick Harold *mining executive*
Gundersen, Wayne Campbell *management consultant, oil and gas consultant*
†Higgins, Walter M., III, *electric power industry executive*

Winnemucca
Hesse, Martha O. *natural gas company executive*

NEW HAMPSHIRE

Loudon
Tomajczyk, S(tephen) F(rancis) *communications company executive, author*

Portsmouth
Powers, Henry Martin, Jr., *oil industry executive*
Tillinghast, John Avery *utilities executive*

NEW JERSEY

Basking Ridge
Collis, Sidney Robert *retired telephone company executive*
Matthews, Craig Gerard *energy company executive*
Peterson, Donald K. *telecommunications executive*

Bedminster
†Dorman, David W. *telecommunications industry executive*

Chatham
Sundberg, Carl-Erik Wilhelm *telecommunications executive, researcher*

Edison
†Francis, Peter T. *gas industry executive, oil industry executive*

Fort Lee
Schiessler, Robert Walter *retired chemical and oil company executive*

Glen Ridge
McGovern, Thomas Aquinas *retired utility executive*

Holmdel
Sullivan, Timothy Patrick *telecommunications company executive*

Lincroft
Tessem, Steven E. *energy executive*

Maplewood
†Joel, Amos Edward, Jr., *telecommunications consultant*

Monroe Township
Avery, James Stephen *oil company executive*

Morristown
Hafer, Frederick Douglass *utility executive*
†McMahon, Kevin J. *telecommunications industry executive*

Mount Laurel
Rabbe, David Ellsworth *oil company executive*

Newark
Ferland, E. James *electric power industry executive*

Nutley
Mallard, Stephen Anthony *retired utility company executive*

Peapack
Walsh, Philip Cornelius *retired mining executive*

Piscataway
Kelly, Robert Emmett *telecommunications company administrator*

Princeton
Farley, Edward Raymond, Jr., *mining and manufacturing company executive*
McCullough, John Price *retired oil company executive*

Princeton Junction
Kangovi, Sach *telecommunications industry executive*

Red Bank
Chynoweth, Alan Gerald *retired telecommunications research executive, consultant*

South Plainfield
Burke, Jacqueline Yvonne *telecommunications executive*

Summit
Pollak, Henry Otto *retired utility research executive, educator*

Union
Lewandowski, Andrew Anthony *utilities executive, consultant*

Watchung
Cohen, Melvin Irwin *retired communications systems and technology executive*

Westfield
Specht, Gordon Dean *retired petroleum executive*

Whippany
Bi, Qi *telecommunications industry executive*

Wrightstown
Drechsel, Edward Russell, Jr., *retired utility company executive*

NEW MEXICO

Corrales
Sageser, Kendall Wayne *mineral exploration executive*

Farmington
Macaluso, Frank Augustus *oil company executive, banker*

Hobbs
Garey, Donald Lee *pipeline and oil company executive*

Roswell
Anderson, Donald Bernard *oil company executive*
Robinson, Mark Leighton *oil company executive, petroleum geologist, horse farm owner*

Santa Fe
Pickrell, Thomas Richard *retired oil company executive*

Tijeras
Ellison, Luther Frederick *oil company executive*

NEW YORK

Albany
von Schack, Wesley W. *energy services company executive*

Armonk
Engel, Joel Stanley *telecommunications executive*

Binghamton
Carrigg, James A. *retired utility company executive*

Blauvelt
Gillespie, John Fagan *mining executive*

Brooklyn
Bisbee, Joyce Evelyn *utility company manager*
Catell, Robert Barry *gas utility executive*

Buffalo
Ackerman, Philip Charles *utilities executive, lawyer*

Fresh Meadows
Jackson, Rhonda *telecommunications professional, poet*

Greenvale
Cordaro, Matthew Charles *energy and utility executive, educator*

Irvington
Carey, Edward John *utility executive*

Jericho
†Fitteron, John Joseph *gas industry executive, real estate company executive*

New York
Alpert, Warren *oil company executive, philanthropist*
Baird, Dugald Euan *global technology services company executive*
Belknap, Norton *petroleum company consultant*
Brown, Edward James, Sr., *utility executive*
Case, Hadley *oil company executive*
Delaney, Robert Vincent *former gas company executive, economic development consultant*
Douglas, Paul Wolff *retired mining executive*
Freilich, Joan Sherman *utilities executive*
Gelfand, Neal *oil company executive*
Hess, John B. *oil industry executive*
†Lee, Charles Robert *telecommunications company executive*
Luce, Charles Franklin *former utilities executive, lawyer*
†Lyons, John Matthew *telecommunications executive, broadcasting executive*
McGrath, Eugene R. *utility company executive*
Morse, Edward Lewis *petroleum industry executive*
Mossavar-Rahmani, Bijan *oil and gas company executive*
Osborne, Richard de Jongh *mining and metals company executive*
†Salerno, Frederic V. *telecommunications company executive*
Seidenberg, Ivan G. *telecommunications company executive*
Silverman, Henry Richard *diversified business executive, lawyer*
Warner, Rawleigh, Jr., *oil company executive*

Rye
Lawi, David Steven *energy, oil and gas, entertainment, agriservice and thermoplastic resins industries executive, merchant banker*

Schenectady
Robb, Walter Lee *retired electric company executive, management company executive*

Syosset
Vermylen, Paul Anthony, Jr., *oil company executive*

Syracuse
Davis, William E. *utility executive*

Wappingers Falls
Nolan, John Thomas, Jr., *retired oil industry administrator*

West Harrison
Brazell, James Ervin *oil company executive, lawyer*

White Plains
Underweiser, Irwin Philip *mining executive, lawyer*

NORTH CAROLINA

Asheboro
Croom, John Henry, III, *utility company executive*

Black Mountain
Cody, Hiram Sedgwick, Jr., *retired telephone company executive*

Cary
Buckler, Sheldon A. *technology company executive*

Charlotte
Ervine, Timothy DuWayne *utilities executive*
Grigg, William Humphrey *utility executive*
Osborne, Richard Jay *electric utility company executive*
Priory, Richard Baldwin *electric power industry executive*

Durham
Fassett, John D. *retired utility executive, consultant*

Hendersonville
Haynes, John Mabin *retired utilities executive*

Raleigh
Cavanaugh, William, III, *electric utility company executive*
†Clapp, Allen Linville *electric supply and communications utility consultant, mediator/arbitrator*
Johnson, William Dean *power company executive*
Smith, Sherwood Hubbard, Jr., *retired electric utilities company executive*

Southern Shores
Kegel, William George *mining company executive*

NORTH DAKOTA

Stanton
Grannis, Joseph M. *power plant operator*

OHIO

Akron
Spetrino, Russell John *retired utility company executive, lawyer*

Bannock
†Gentile, Anthony *coal company executive*

Bexley
Maloney, Gerald P. *retired utilities executive*

Canton
Stage, Richard Lee *consultant, retired utilities executive*

Cincinnati
Ehrnschwender, Arthur Robert *former utility company executive*
Leahy, Kevin Sean *energy company strategist*
†Randolph, Jackson Harold *utility company executive*
Rogers, James Eugene *electric and gas utility executive*
Victor, William Weir *retired telephone company executive, consultant*

Cleveland
Bray, Pierce *business consultant*
Ginn, Robert Martin *retired utility company executive*
Kuehn, Richard Arthur *telecommunications consultant*
Miller, John Robert *oil industry executive*

Columbus
Draper, E(rnest) Linn, Jr., *electric utility executive*
†Richard, Oliver, III, (Rick Richard) *energy company executive*
Vassell, Gregory S. *electric utility consultant*

Findlay
Yammine, Riad Nassif *retired oil company executive*

Painesville
Smith, William Robert *utility company executive*

Perrysburg
Williamson, John Pritchard *utility executive*

Springfield
Weatherby, Donald Alan *telecommunications industry executive, writer*

Sterling
†Stetz, Ernest James *retired building and power consultant*

Westerville
Feck, Luke Matthew *retired utility executive*

Westlake
Connelly, John James *retired oil company technical specialist*

OKLAHOMA

Bartlesville
†Allen, W. Wayne *retired oil industry executive*
Cox, Glenn Andrew, Jr., *petroleum company executive*
Mulva, James Joseph *oil company executive*
Silas, Cecil Jesse *retired petroleum company executive*

Enid
Ward, Llewellyn Orcutt, III, *oil company executive*

Grove
Winters, J(ohn) Otis *retired oil industry consultant*

Jennings
Nixon, Arlie James *gas and oil company executive*

Oklahoma City
Campbell, David Gwynne *petroleum executive, geologist*
Cleary, William B. *oil industry executive*
†Corbett, Luke R. *energy executive*
Cummings, Sean Spencer *oil and gas industry executive*
†Gustafson, William Gene *oil industry executive*
†Harlan, Ross Edgar *retired utility company executive, writer, lecturer, consultant*
Kirkpatrick, John Elson *retired oil company executive, retired naval reserve officer*
†Nichols, J. Larry *energy company executive, lawyer*
Peace, H. W., II, *oil company executive*
Reich, Richard Allen *energy company executive*
Wortham, James Mason, Sr., *gas supply company official*

Ponca City
†Fraenkel, Dan *oil industry executive, researcher*
Leonard, Samuel Wallace *oil company and bank executive*

Seminole
Moran, Melvin Robert *oil industry executive*

Tulsa
Bailey, Keith E. *petroleum pipeline company executive*
Berlin, Steven Ritt *oil company executive*
Braumiller, Allen Spooner *oil and gas exploration company executive, geologist*
†Cadieux, Chester *gas industry executive*
Dotson, George Stephen *drilling company executive*
Horkey, William Richard *retired diversified oil company executive*
Ingram, Charles Clark, Jr., *energy company executive*
†Jones, Geoffrey Kyle *telecommunications industry executive*
King, Peter Cotterill *former utilities executive*
Kronfeld, Edwin *natural gas company executive*
Kyle, David L. *gas industry executive*
†Malcolm, Steven J. *petroleum pipeline company executive*
Repasky, Mark Edward *oil and gas company executive*

OREGON

Portland
Bacon, Vicky Lee *lighting services executive*
Frisbee, Don Calvin *retired utilities executive*

Salem
†Heine, Steven Robert *telecommunications industry executive, poet, writer*

PENNSYLVANIA

Allentown
Gadomski, Robert Eugene *chemical and industrial gas company executive*
Hecht, William F. *electric power industry executive*
Wagner, Harold A. *industrial gas and chemical company executive*
Walton, David P. *utility company executive*

Allison Park
Sullivan, Neil Maxwell *oil and gas company executive*

Bryn Mawr
Braha, Thomas I. *business executive*

Coraopolis
Koepfinger, Joseph Leo *retired utilities executive*
†Marshall, David D. *electric utilities executive*

Doylestown
Haeussler, Charles Louis, II, *oil company executive*

Gladwyne
Patten, Lanny Ray *industrial gas industry executive*

Glenmoore
Moulton, Frank Ray, Jr., *retired oil company executive*

Haverford
Olson, Robert Edward *coal mining executive*

Johnstown
Simmons, Elroy, Jr., *retired utility executive*

King Of Prussia
Greenberg, Lon Richard *energy company executive, lawyer*

Maple Glen
Jacobson, Bonnie Brown *energy consulting company executive, statistician, writer, researcher*

Philadelphia
Calman, Robert Frederick *mining executive*
Drosdick, John Girard *oil company executive*
†McNeill, Corbin Asahel, Jr., *utility executive*

Pittsburgh
Bartley, Burnett Graham, Jr., *oil company and manufacturing executive*
†Corcoran, Thomas A. *metals and mining company executive*
†Davidson, George A., Jr., *retired utility company executive*
Stirewalt, John Newman *coal company executive*
Wagner, Florence Zeleznik *telecommunications executive*

Presto
Moeller, Audrey Carolyn *retired energy company executive, corporate secretary*

Radnor
Castle, Joseph Lanktree, II, *energy company executive, consultant*

Wayne
Lefevre, Thomas Vernon *retired utility company executive, lawyer*

West Sunbury
Stewart, Mark Thomas *gas industry executive*

SOUTH CAROLINA

Columbia
†Timmerman, William B. *utilities company financial executive*

Hilton Head Island
Simpson, John Wistar *energy consultant, former manufacturing company executive*

Johns Island
Behnke, Wallace Blanchard, Jr., *consultant, engineer, retired utility executive*

Kiawah Island
Reed, Rex Raymond *retired telephone company executive*

Murrells Inlet
Justice, Franklin Pierce, Jr., *oil company executive*

Myrtle Beach
Atkinson, Harold Witherspoon *utilities consultant, real estate broker*

SOUTH DAKOTA

Rapid City
Lien, Bruce Hawkins *minerals and oil company executive*

TENNESSEE

Brentwood
Goodwin, William Dean *consulting company executive*

Knoxville
Bates, Benjamin Johnson *telecommunications educator, researcher*

Nashville
†Adams, Kenneth Stanley, Jr., (Bud Adams) *energy company executive, football executive*

TEXAS

Addison
†Murray, Patrick M. *oilfield service company executive*
Pryor, Richard Walter *telecommunications executive, retired air force officer*

Austin
Deisler, Paul Frederick, Jr., *retired oil company executive*
Franklin, Robert Drury *oil company executive, lawyer*
Gibson, Jerry Leigh *oil company executive*
Haas, Joseph Marshall *petroleum consultant*

Beaumont
Smith, Floyd Rodenback *retired utilities executive*

Breckenridge
Reaugh, O(rland) H. *oil industry executive*

Conroe
Mitchell, Robert James *petroleum company executive*

Corpus Christi
Benner, Richard Walter *oil company executive, geologist, engineer*
Haas, Paul Raymond *petroleum company executive*
Norman, Wyatt Thomas, III, *landman, consultant*
Paulson, Bernard Arthur *oil company executive, consultant*

Crane
Crawford, Judy Carol *energy services company executive*

Cypress
Day, Robert Michael *oil company executive*

Dallas
Biegler, David W. *energy executive*
Brachman, Malcolm K. *oil company executive*
†Brooks, Edgar R. (Dick Brooks) *utility company executive*
Carson, Virginia Hill *oil and gas executive*
†Farrington, Jerry S. *utility holding company executive*
Fielder, Charles Robert *oil industry executive*
Goss, James Walter *oil company executive*
Gratton, Patrick John Francis *oil company executive*
†Hunt, Ray L. *petroleum company executive*
Jones, Everett Riley, Jr., *oil company executive*
Lesar, David J. *oil industry executive*
†Mitchell, A. Joe, Jr., *telecommunications industry executive*
Moneypenny, Edward William *business executive*
Moore, Christopher Robertson Kinley *energy industry consultant*
Nevins, William J. *oil and gas brokerage executive, consultant*
Nye, Erle Allen *electric power industry executive, lawyer*
Patton, Bob J. *oil industry executive*
Perry, George Wilson *oil and gas company executive*
Plummer, Paul James *energy executive*
Robinson, Edgar Allen *retired oil company executive*
Sizer, Phillip Spelman *consultant, retired oil field services executive*
Slawter, John David, Jr., *oil company and manufacturing executive*
Smith, R. J., Jr., *oil company executive*

Flower Mound
Cox, David Leon *telecommunications company executive*

Fort Worth
Armiger, Gene Gibbon *telecommunications executive, consultant*
Boschetti, Philip J. *oil company executive*
Hudson, Edward Randall, Jr., *gas, oil industry executive*
Hyde, Clarence Brodie, II, *oil company executive*

Fredericksburg
Malec, William Frank *utilities company executive*

Frisco
Mackenzie, John *retired oil industry executive*

Horseshoe Bay
Jorden, James Roy *oil company engineering executive, consultant*

Houston
Armstrong, Greg L. *oil company executive*
Barracano, Henry Ralph *retired oil company executive, consultant*
Barrow, Thomas Davies *oil and mining company executive*
Bartling, Phyllis McGinness *oil company executive*
Blanton, Jack Sawtelle *oil company executive*
Bonneville, Richard Briggs *retired petroleum exploration and production executive*
Bookout, John Frank, Jr., *oil company executive*
Bowen, William Jackson *retired gas company executive*
Bryan, James Lee *oil field service company executive*
†Bryan, J(ames) P(erry), Jr., *energy company executive*
†Bulmahn, T. Paul *oil and gas company executive*
Campbell, Carl David *oil industry executive*
Capps, Ethan LeRoy *oil company executive*
Carameros, George Demitrius, Jr., *natural gas company executive*
Carter, John Boyd, Jr., *oil operator, bank executive*
Cazalot, Clarence P., Jr., *oil industry executive*
Chalmers, David B. *petroleum executive*
Cox, Frank D. (Buddy Cox) *oil company executive, exploration consultant*
Danburg, Jerome Samuel *oil company executive*
Davis, Leon *oil company executive*
DeVault, John Lee *oil company executive, geophysicist*
Dice, Bruce Burton *exploration company executive*
Dienstbier, Dan *gas and oil company executive*
†Dorey, Louis J. *gas industry executive, lawyer*
Dreyer, Alec Gilbert *independent power producer*
Drury, Leonard Leroy *retired oil company executive*
†Duncan, Dan L. *gas company executive*
Dunham, Archie Wallace *petroleum and chemical products company executive*
Edens, Donald Keith *oil company executive*
Foster, Joe B. *oil company executive*
Frost, John Elliott *minerals company executive*
Fulwiler, Robert Neal *oil company executive*
Garrison, David Lacey, Jr., *oil company executive*
Goodman, Herbert Irwin *petroleum company executive*
†Goodman, Joe Read *utilities executive*
†Gries, Michael F. *industrial maintenance industry executive*
Hoglund, Forrest Eugene *petroleum company executive, retired*
Irwin, John Robert *oil and gas drilling executive*
Johnson, Wayne D. *gas industry executive*
†Kelly, Robert Corby *energy executive, writer*
Kerr, Baine Perkins *oil company executive*
Kirkland, John David *oil and gas company executive, lawyer*
Kuntz, Hal Goggan *petroleum exploration company executive*
Letbetter, R. Steve *energy company executive*
Loveland, Eugene Franklin *petroleum executive*
Luigs, Charles Russell *retired gas and oil drilling industry executive*
Mathis, James Forrest *retired petroleum company executive*
†Morgan, William V. *oil and gas pipeline and storage executive*
Myers, Franklin *oil industry executive*
Nanz, Robert Hamilton *petroleum consultant*
Nestvold, Elwood Olaf *oil and gas industry consultant*
Nyberg, Donald Arvid *oil company executive*
†Reynolds, John Terrence *oil industry executive*
Roff, J(ohn) Hugh, Jr., *energy company executive*
Rose, Robert Ernest *gas & oil drilling industry executive*
†Rossler, Willis Kenneth, Jr., *petroleum company executive*
†Russell, Donald Glenn *oil company executive*
Saizan, Paula Theresa *oil company executive*
Scott, John McGregor *oil and gas industry executive, real estate investor*
Segner, Edmund Peter, III, *natural gas company executive*
†Shackouls, Bobby S. *oil and gas industry executive*
†Smith, Dan F. *oil company executive*
Smith, David Kingman *retired oil company executive, consultant*
†Soliman, Sam *gas, oil and chemical industry executive, investment company executive*
Van Dyke, Gene *oil company executive*
†Watson, Chuck *energy and communications industry executive*
†Wiley, Michael E. *oil industry executive*
Williams, Robert Henry *oil company executive*
†Williamson, Bruce A. *oil industry executive*
Wilson, Edward Converse, Jr., *oil and natural gas production company executive*

Ingram
Hughes, David Michael *oil service company executive, rancher*

Irving
Crowley, L. C. *telecommunications company executive*
†Humphreys, Donald D. *oil company executive*
Longwell, Harry *oil company executive*
Lutz, Matthew Charles *oil company executive, geologist*

†Nottingham, Jeffrey E *energy executive*

Kemah
Cofran, George Lee *telecommunication consultant*

Kerrville
O'Shields, Richard Lee *retired natural gas company executive*

Kingwood
Delap, J. Q., Jr., *gas company executive*

Mc Kinney
Dickinson, Richard Raymond *retired oil company executive*

Midland
Grover, Rosalind Redfern *oil and gas company executive*

Missouri City
†Tchamengo, Mathias Ngoufi *energy executive, mathematician*

Montgomery
Falkingham, Donald Herbert *oil company executive*

Pasadena
Burt, Billy George *oil company professional*

Pearsall
†Galloway, Gale Lee *oil and gas executive, rancher*

Plano
Satz, Jeffrey S. *telecommunications industry executive, consultant*
Schuh, Frank Joseph *drilling engineering company executive, consultant*

Port Aransas
Swetnam, Monte Newton *petroleum exploration executive*

Pottsboro
Hanning, Gary William *utility executive, water company executive, consultant*

Richardson
Jones, Malinda Thiessen *telecommunications company executive*
Killam, Jill Minervini *oil and gas company executive*
McDaniel, Dolan Kenneth *oil exploration service company executive*

Salado
Parks, Lloyd Lee *oil company executive*

San Antonio
†Gaulin, Jean *gas industry executive*
Greehey, William Eugene *energy company executive*
†Hemminghaus, Roger Roy *energy company executive, chemical engineer*
Klaerner, Curtis Maurice *former oil company executive*
McCoy, Reagan Scott *oil company executive, lawyer*
Shipman, Ross Lovelace *petroleum executive*
West, Robert Van Osdell, Jr., *retired petroleum executive*
Whitacre, Edward E., Jr., *telecommunications executive*

Sealy
Young, Milton Earl *retired petroleum company executive*

The Woodlands
†Allison, Robert James, Jr., *oil and gas company executive*
Manson, Lewis Auman *energy research executive*
Sharman, Richard Lee *telecommunications executive, consultant*

UTAH

Ogden
†Adams, J. Phillip *oil industry executive*

Park City
Edwards, Howard Lee *retired petroleum company executive, lawyer*

Salt Lake City
†Holding, R(obert) E(arl) *oil company executive*

VERMONT

Barnard
Larson, John Hyde *retired utilities executive*

North Clarendon
Freed, Walter Everett *petroleum company executive, state representative*

VIRGINIA

Alexandria
Hirsch, Robert Louis *energy executive*
Smith, Jeffrey Greenwood *industry executive, retired army officer*

Annandale
Hanrahan, Margaret Villar (Peggi Hanrahan) *oil company executive*
Willner, Larry Elliott *telecommunications company executive, consultant*

Arlington
Bakke, Dennis W. *energy company executive*
Eppink, Jeffrey Francis *energy and environment consultant*

Fairfax
†O'Leary, Robert J. *oil industry executive*

Lexington
Tyree, Lewis, Jr., *retired compressed gas company executive, inventor, technical consultant*

Lynchburg
†Gale, J. Darren *nuclear energy industry executive*
Womack, Edgar Allen, Jr., *energy executive*

Reston
Cerf, Vinton Gray *telecommunications company executive*

Richmond
Capps, Thomas Edward *utilities company executive, lawyer*
†Cross, John Robert *retired telecommunications industry executive, travel consultant*
†Kellett, Janet *telecommunications industry executive, educator*

Springfield
Bentz, Edward Joseph, Jr., *energy, environment and transportation management consulting firm executive*

Sterling
Oller, William Maxwell *retired energy company executive, retired naval officer*

Suffolk
Hines, Angus Irving, Jr., *petroleum marketing executive*

WASHINGTON

Anacortes
Hoffmann, Manfred Walter *consulting company executive*

Bellevue
Groten, Barnet *energy company executive*

Republic
Ferguson, Robert Bruce *minerals company executive*

Richland
Wright, Malcolm Sturtevant *nuclear energy industry executive, retired military officer*

Seattle
Beighle, Douglas Paul *aerospace industry executive, retired*

Sequim
Beaton, Roy Howard *retired nuclear industry executive*

Spokane
Eliassen, Jon Eric *retired utility company executive*
Ely, Gary G. *utilities company executive*

WEST VIRGINIA

Bluefield
Reid, William James *mining executive*

Charleston
Bennett, Robert Menzies *retired gas pipeline company executive*

WISCONSIN

La Crosse
Rude, Brian David *utilities company executive*

Madison
Barr, James, III, *telecommunications company executive*
Davis, Erroll Brown, Jr., *utility executive*

Milwaukee
†Abdoo, Richard A. *utilities company executive*
Goetsch, John Hubert *consultant and retired utility company executive*

Stone Lake
Voss, William Charles *retired oil company executive*

Wauwatosa
Kostecke, B. William *utilities executive*

WYOMING

Casper
Stroock, Thomas Frank *oil and gas company executive*

Riverton
Bebout, Eli Daniel *oil executive*

TERRITORIES OF THE UNITED STATES

VIRGIN ISLANDS

Saint Thomas
Prior, Cornelius Bernard, Jr., *utilities company executive, financial consultant*

CANADA

ALBERTA

Calgary
Anderson, J.C. *oil and gas exploration company executive, rancher*
Faithfull, Timothy William *petroleum industry executive*
George, Richard Lee *oil industry executive*
Haskayne, Richard Francis *retired utility company executive*
Horton, William Russell *retired utility company executive*
Maier, Gerald James *corporate executive*
McKinnon, F(rancis) A(rthur) Richard *utility executive*
Morgan, Gwyn *oil and gas executive*
O'Brien, David Peter *business executive*
Pick, Michael Claude *international exploration consultant*
Pourbaix, Alexander *energy executive*
Seaman, Daryl Kenneth *oil company executive*
Southern, Nancy C. *utilities executive*
Southern, Ronald D. *diversified corporation executive*
Swartout, Hank B. *oil and gas industry executive*
Travis, Vance Kenneth *petroleum business executive*
Wagner, Norman Ernest *corporate education executive*

Red Deer
Donald, Jack C. *corporate executive*

BRITISH COLUMBIA

Vancouver
Keevil, Norman B. *mining executive*

MANITOBA

Saint Andrews
Lang, Otto *industry executive, former Canadian cabinet minister*

Winnipeg
Burns, James William *business executive*

NOVA SCOTIA

Halifax
Mann, David *energy and services company executive*

ONTARIO

Brockville
Spalding, James Stuart *retired telecommunications company executive*

North York
Blundell, William Richard Charles *retired electric company executive*

Toronto
Clitheroe, Eleanor *utilities executive*
Hickson, Robin Julian *mining company executive*
Hyland, Geoffrey Fyfe *energy service company executive*
Martin, Robert William *corporate director*
Munk, Peter *mining executive*
Osler, Gordon Peter *retired utility company executive*
†Peterson, Robert B. *petroleum company executive*
Wilson, Lynton Ronald *retired telecommunications company executive*

QUEBEC

Montreal
Caillé, André *public service company executive*
Cyr, J. V. Raymond *telecommunications industry executive*
†Engen, D(onald) Travis *diversified telecommunications company executive*

ENGLAND

London
Gillam, Sir Patrick *oil company executive, banker*
Greener, Anthony *telecommunications industry executive*
Hill, Gregory Paul *oil company executive*
McIntyre, Norman F. *petroleum industry executive*

JAPAN

Yokohama
Ito, Noboru *electric power industry executive*

NETHERLANDS

The Hague
Van Wachem, Lodewijk Christiaan *petroleum company executive*

ADDRESS UNPUBLISHED

Addy, Frederick Seale *retired oil company executive*
Akel, Ollie James *oil company executive*
Anderson, Robert Orville *oil and gas company executive*
†Andras, Oscar Sidney *oil company executive*
Arlidge, John Walter *retired utility company executive*
Arnold, William Howard *retired nuclear fuel executive*
Arthur, John Morrison *retired utility executive*
Ataie, Ata Jennati *oil products marketing executive*
Barham, Charles Dewey, Jr., *electric utility executive, lawyer*
Barrack, William Sample, Jr., *petroleum company executive*
Baumgartner, John H. *refining and petroleum products company executive*
Berry, William Willis *retired utility executive*
Bishop, Carol *oil company executive*
Blodgett, Omer William *electric company design consultant*
Bowlin, Michael Ray *retired oil company executive*
Browne, (Edmund) John Phillip *oil company executive*
Bruce, James Edmund *retired utility company executive*
Bumbery, Joseph Lawrence *diversified telecommunications company executive*
Capellas, Michael D. *telecommunications industry executive*
†Catacosinos, William James *utility company executive*
Chelle, Robert Frederick *entrepreneurial leadership educator*
Chen, George Chi-Ming *energy company executive*
Clemons, Julie Payne *telephone company manager*
Coffin, Bertha Louise *telephone company executive*
Cole, Reginald David *water treatment executive*
Conger, Harry Milton *mining company executive*
Cookson, Albert Ernest *telephone and telegraph company executive*
Counsil, William Glenn *electric utility executive*
Curtis, Edward Joseph, Jr., *gas industry executive, management consultant*
Dickey, Joseph William *utility executive, engineer*
DiCorcia, Edward Thomas *retired oil industry executive*
Di Giovanni, Anthony *retired coal mining company executive*
Dragoumis, Paul *electric utility company executive*
Driscoll, Garrett Bates *retired telecommunications executive*
Eltringham, Thomas James Gyger *telecommunications professional*
Engibous, Thomas James *electronics company executive*
Ewing, Wayne Turner *coal company executive*
Fagin, David Kyle *natural resources executive*
Finger, Harold B. *consultant*
Fitzgeorge, Harold James *former oil and gas company executive*
Flickinger, Joe Arden *telecommunications educator*
Ford, Judith Ann Tudor *retired natural gas distribution company executive*
†Fox, James R. *telecommunications technician*
Gabel, Ronald Glen *telecommunications executive*
Garberding, Larry Gilbert *retired utilities companies executive*
Gardner, Richard Hartwell *retired oil industry executive*
Gerard, Roy Dupuy *oil company executive, retired*
Gottschalk, Charles M. *international energy consultant*
Green, Richard Calvin, Jr., *electric power and gas industry executive*
Greer, Carl Crawford *petroleum company executive*
Gurian, Mal *telecommunications executive*
Hall, Milton Reese *retired oil company executive*
Hamilton, Allan Corning *retired oil company executive*
Hammer, Harold Harlan *oil company financial executive*
Hampton, Rex Herbert *former mining executive, director*
Hancock, John Coulter *telecommunications company executive*
Harris, Howard Hunter *oil company executive*
Heiney, John Weitzel *former utility executive*
Herron, Edwin Hunter, Jr., *energy consultant*
Hines, Andrew Hampton, Jr., *utilities executive*
Hogg, Karen Sue *telecommunications and information systems executive*
†Howard, James Joseph, III, *utility company executive*
Howard, Stephen Wrigley *telecommunications executive*
Huffman, James Thomas William *oil exploration company executive*
Hurst, Leland Lyle *natural gas company executive*
Jackson, Robert William *utility company executive, retired*
†Johnson, Curtis Lildon *drilling engineer*
Judge, Rosemary Ann *oil company executive*
†Kaculi, Xhemal T. *oil industry executive, researcher*

Kebblish, John Basil *retired coal company executive, consultant*
Kettel, Edward Joseph *oil company executive, retired*
†Kholodnyi, Valery Alexandrovich *energy executive, researcher*
King, William Collins *oil company executive*
Kinzer, James Raymond *retired pipeline company executive*
Kirkby, Maurice Anthony *oil company executive*
Kuehn, Ronald L., Jr., *natural resources company executive*
Kush, Charles Andrew, III, *telecommunications executive, internet entrepreneur*
Land, Kenneth Dean *test and balance agency executive, building commission agent, energy and environmental consultant*
Leva, James Robert *retired electric utility company executive*
Lewis, Floyd Wallace *former electric utility executive*
Lilly, Edward Guerrant, Jr., *retired utility company executive*
Long, Alfred B. *former oil company executive, consultant*
Lortie, John William *solar research company executive*
Losse, John William, Jr., *mining company executive*
Maher, Patrick Joseph *retired utility company executive*
Markle, Roger A(llan) *retired oil company executive*
Mayo, John Sullivan *telecommunications company executive*
Mc Carthy, Walter John, Jr., *retired utility executive*
McCormick, William Thomas, Jr., *electric and gas company executive*
McCready, Kenneth Frank *former electric utility executive*
McSweeny, William Francis *petroleum company executive, author*
Mickelson, H(erald) Fred *electric utility executive*
Montgomery, Roy Delbert *retired gas utility company executive*
Monty, Charles Embert *utility company executive*
Morrell, Gene Paul *liquid terminal company executive, consultant*
Morrow, George Lester *retired oil and gas executive*
Munsey, Virdell Everard, Jr., *retired utility executive*
Murray, Allen Edward *deceased oil company executive*
Nicholson, Leland Ross *retired utilities company executive, energy consultant*
Nurenberg, David *retired oil company executive*
O'Connor, James John *retired utility company executive*
O'Hare, James Raymond *energy company executive*
Ormasa, John *retired utility executive, lawyer*
Osterhoff, James Marvin *retired telecommunications company executive*
Pack, Allen S. *retired coal company executive*
Peckham, Donald Eugene *retired utilities company executive*
Perry, Kenneth Walter *retired integrated oil company executive*
Pierce, Lisa Margaret *telecommunications executive, product and market development manager, lecturer*
Portal, Gilbert Marcel Adrien *oil company executive*
Quillen, Lloyd Douglas *oil and gas executive*
Raymond, Lee R. *oil company executive*
Rendu, Jean-Michel Marie *mining executive*
Roe, Thomas Coombe *former utility company executive*
Rogers, Justin Towner, Jr., *retired utility company executive*
St. Clair, Thomas McBryar *mining and manufacturing company executive*
Samuels, John Stockwell, III, *mining company executive, financier*
Sanders, Charles Franklin *management and engineering consultant*
Schenck, Jack Lee *retired electric utility executive*
Schenker, Leo *retired utility company executive*
Scoates, Wesley Marvin *mining company executive*
†Scott, Donahue *energy executive*
Scott, Isadore Meyer *former energy company executive*
Shattuck, Mayo Adams, III, *integrated utility executive*
†Shoup, Andrew James, Jr., *retired oil company executive*
Shultz, Delray Franklin (Lucky Shultz) *business and management consultant, coach*
Smith, Paul Vergon, Jr., *corporate executive, retired oil company executive*
†Sticker, Harry *telecommunications industry executive*
Stratman, Joseph Lee *retired petroleum refining company executive, consultant, chemical engineer*
Taylor, Leslie George *mining executive, finance company executive*
Thomas, Kenneth Glyndwr *mining executive*
Thompson, Jack Edward *mining company executive*
Thorn, Terence Hastings *international energy industry executive*
Threet, Jack Curtis *oil company executive*
Townsend, Thomas Perkins *former mining company executive*
Tucker, H. Richard *oil company executive*
Tuer, David A. *petroleum industry executive*
Turner, Thomas Marshall *telecommunications executive, consultant*
†Vincent, Bruce Havird *oil and gas company executive*
Watson, George W. *energy executive*

Weaver, William Schildecker *retired electric power industry executive*
Wessner, Deborah Marie *telecommunications executive, information systems consultant*
Wheeler, John Charles *telecommunications professional*
Wickstrom, Jon Alan *telecommunications executive, consultant*
Wilson, Walter Clinton *retired gas industry executive*
Wise, William Allen *energy company executive*
Witte, Merlin Michael *oil company executive*
Wood, Willis Bowne, Jr., *retired utilities executive*
Wright, Mae A. *engineering, communications and nuclear waste management specialist*
Wright, Randolph Earle *retired petroleum company executive*

INFORMATION TECHNOLOGY
See also SCIENCE: MATHEMATICS AND COMPUTER SCIENCE

UNITED STATES

ALABAMA

Florence
†Foote, Avon Edward *web developer/producer, communications educator*

Huntsville
Giroir, Michael James *software analyst*
Preston, Robert Kevin *software quality engineer*

Wilsonville
Copeland, David A. *software engineer*

ARIZONA

Phoenix
†Murray, Vincent Smith *network technician, historian*

Scottsdale
Stott, Brian *software company executive, consultant*

Surprise
Jackson, Randy *information technology executive*

Tempe
†Crown, Eric J. *information systems executive*
Shoemaker, Scott David *network consultant, educator*

Tucson
Donoghue, John Charles *software management consultant*
Fredericksen, Dick Hartman *retired computer programmer*
Karson, Catherine June *database administrator*

CALIFORNIA

Burbank
Ha, Chong Wan *information technology executive*

Burlingame
†Muller, Richard Forrest *information technology executive*

Calabasas
Sloan, Michael Dana *information systems specialist*

Campbell
Kendall, Burton Nathaniel *software designer*
Mizer, Richard Anthony *technology company executive*

Cupertino
Haskell, Barry Geoffry *computer company researcher*

Cypress
Cao, Dac-Buu *software engineer*

Danville
Bergsten, James Robert *computer technology architect*

Del Mar
Fricke, Martin Paul *science company executive*

Emeryville
†Nenov, Ivo P. *mathematical and software researcher*

Escondido
Huang, Kun Lien *software engineer, scientist*

Foster City
Barnett, David Hughes *software engineer, computer systems architect*

Fremont
†Puri, Umesh Chandra *application developer*
Sarkar, Arindam *information technology executive*
†Tang, John *network technician, information scientist, educator*

Glen Ellen
Hurlbert, Roger William *information service industry executive*

Granada Hills
Shoemaker, Harold Lloyd *infosystem specialist*

Half Moon Bay
Melvin, Jay Wayne *computer programmer*

Harbor City
Lee, Grace Tze *information services company executive*

Highland
Lee, Robert Erich *information technology consultant*

Irvine
Godfrey, Raymond Michael *information systems educator*
Smith, Vincent C. *information technology executive*
von Tilsit, Heidemarie *information management specialist*

La Mesa
Tansey, Lisa Rebecca *database administrator, dancer, masseuse, musician*

Long Beach
Loganbill, G. Bruce *logopedic pathologist*

Los Alamitos
Weinberger, Frank *information management consultant*

Los Angeles
†Brooks, Robert Eugene *decision support software designer*
Hwang, John Dzen *information systems educator*
Rodriguez, Edward John *educational software developer*

Lynwood
†Legesse, Solomon *technology executive*

Malibu
Jeffrey, Francis *software developer, forecaster*

Martinez
Tong, Siu Wing *computer programmer*

Menlo Park
Zdeblick, Mark James *information technology executive*

Milpitas
Treichel, Helmuth W.A. *technology executive*

Nipomo
Schindler, Keith William *software engineer*

Oakland
Wills, John Arthur *computer programmer, analyst*

Palo Alto
Dong, Xuzhu *information technology manager*
Fried, Louis Lester *information technology and management consultant*
Karlsson, Magnus *computer engineer/scientist, researcher*
Mahmood, Aamer *computer system architect*
Mayo, Robert N. *computer science researcher*

Pleasanton
June, David Harold *information technology specialist*

Poway
Turner, David G. *information technology executive*

Rancho Palos Verdes
Savage, Terry Richard *information systems executive*

Redwood City
†Hagart-Alexander, Claud *software engineer*
Rohde, James Vincent *software systems company executive*

Sacramento
Doyel, Cindy Marie *information systems specialist*

San Diego
†Backes, Jack Abraham *application developer*
Goldstein, Mark Kingston Levin *information technology executive, researcher*
†Kronewitter, Frank Dell *software engineer, researcher*
†Kubilus, Norbert John *information technology executive*
Mercurio, Philip Joseph *computer programmer/analyst*
Pottenger, Mark McClelland *computer programmer*
Tom, Lawrence *technology executive*
Wadlington, W. M. *retired commodity futures trader and financial engineer*

San Francisco
Gaposchkin, Peter John Arthur *programmer analyst, physicist*
Keeney, Ralph Lyons *decision and risk analyst, educator*
Maloney, James John *network administrator*
Oppel, Andrew John *computer systems consultant*
Penn, Lee *information technology consultant, journalist*
†Ryan, Dennis *information technology executive*
Tow, Bruce Lincoln *computer software architect, consultant*

San Jose
Donald, Helen Louise *software engineer*
Halloran, Mike *software company executive, music publishing executive*
†Trung (Danny), Dang Van *systems administrator*
Whitman, Meg (Margaret C. Whitman) *internet company executive*

San Mateo
†Brzozowsky, Keith William *software consultant*

San Ramon
Schofield, James Roy *computer programmer*

Santa Ana
Foster, Kent B. *information technology executive*

Santa Barbara
Adler, William F. *technology business development consultant*
Boehm, Eric Hartzell *information management executive*

Santa Clara
Chen, Deanford Frederick *software engineer*
Hall, William Spencer *software engineer*

Santa Cruz
†Lindquist, Claude S. *technical consultant and executive, educator, researcher*

Scotts Valley
Janssen, James Robert *consulting software engineer*

South San Francisco
Salerno, Philip Adams *information systems specialist*

Thousand Oaks
Knight, Jeffrey Richard *information technology specialist*

Tracy
†Harris, Kathleen Renee *information technology supervisor, fashion designer*

Tustin
†Wang, Feng Kevin *application developer, computer company executive*

Walnut Creek
Arnold, William Thomas *software developer, chemist*
Rose, Joan L. *computer security specialist*

Westlake Village
Gibson, John Robert *software engineer*

COLORADO

Arvada
Tingley, Walter Watson *computer systems manager*

Colorado Springs
Heffron, Michael Edward *software engineer, computer scientist*
Thor, Paul Viets *computer science educator*

Denver
Hamrick, Joseph Eugene, Jr., *information services specialist*
Hoffer, Philip Craig *information technology manager, consultant*
†Thompson, Joseph Paul *retired systems administrator*

Englewood
Barth, David Victor *computer systems designer, consultant*

Fraser
Hibbs, John David *software executive, engineer, business owner*

Littleton
Bradley, James Alexander *software engineer, researcher*

Louisville
Maddock, Jerome Torrence *information services specialist*

Thornton
Siska, Robert John *softwre engineer*

CONNECTICUT

Enfield
Oliver, Bruce Lawrence *information systems specialist, educator*

Mashantucket
Yale, John Paul *computer systems developer*

New Britain
Margiotta, Mary-Lou Ann *software engineer*

Tolland
Butterworth, Michael *computer programmer*

Westport
Frese, Edward Scheer, Jr., *information technology executive, consultant*

DELAWARE

Bear
Longfellow, Charles Alfred *information officer*

Newark
Godwin, Ralph Edward *retired computer operator*

DISTRICT OF COLUMBIA

Washington
Belak, Michael James *information systems executive*
†Day, Melvin Sherman *information and telecommunications company executive*
Esfandiary, Dara Sadigh *information technology executive*
Fu, Zhiwei *information technology manager, consultant*
Hungate, Joseph Irvin, III, *information technology executive*
McConnell, Bruce William *information technology executive*
Nguyen, Alex Thinh *internet company executive, aerospace engineer, consultant*
Rausch, Howard *information service executive*
Rose, George Andrew *software developer, information systems specialist*
Vaughan, Kenneth Edward
†Withrow, Frank B *education technical consultant*

FLORIDA

Alachua
Neubauer, Hugo Duane, Jr., *computer network engineer*

Boca Raton
Kewley, Sharon Lynn *systems analyst, consultant*

Cape Canaveral
Field, Thomas Harold *software design engineer*

Coral Springs
Sanders, Marc Andrew *computer technical consultant*

Fort Pierce
Hurley, William Joseph *retired information systems executive*

Jacksonville
Chambers, Jack Allen *educator*
Crawford, Maria Lynn *technical support analyst*

Lutz
Learn, Doris Lynn *application developer*

Melbourne
Hughes, Edwin Lawson *retired information technology executive*

Orlando
Andrew, Brian J. *information technology company executive*
†Steward, Sherry *information technology executive, educator*

Palm Bay
Herro, John Joseph *software specialist*

Saint Petersburg
Metzger, Kathleen Ann *computer systems specialist*

Tallahassee
Leavell, Michael Ray *computer programmer, analyst*
Mason, Robert McSpadden *technology management educator, consultant*

Tampa
†Gill, Thomas Grandon *information technology executive, educator*
Wyman, Richard Thomas *information services consultant*

Venice
Kleinlein, Kathy Lynn *training and development executive*

West Palm Beach
Eager, William Earl *information systems corporation executive*

GEORGIA

Alpharetta
Derr, Bruce Woods *information technology executive*
Desai, Hiren D. *software engineer*
Salay, Cindy Rolston *systems engineer, registered nurse*

Atlanta
Coady, William Francis *information technology executive, consultant*
Goldfarb, Eric Daniel *information technology executive, computer industry analyst*
†Kochengin, Sergey Alexandrovich *information technology consultant*
†Rink, Christopher Lee *information technology consultant, photographer*

Dublin
Watt, Dwight, Jr. (Arthur Dwight Watt Jr.) *computer programming and microcomputer specialist*

Duluth
Manley, Lance Filson *data processing consultant*

Mableton
Boyle, Robert Daniel *information technology executive*

Marietta
Guentner, Gail Marie *software engineer*
†Watson, Michael Jeffrey *information technology manager*

Savannah
Palanca, Terilyn *software industry analyst*

HAWAII

Honolulu
Bossert, Philip Joseph *information systems executive*
Sekine, Deborah Keiko *systems analyst, programmer*

Kihei
Wright, Thomas Parker *application developer*

IDAHO

Nampa
Coon, Daren Ross *public administrator*

ILLINOIS

Champaign
†Pegg, Edward T. *webmaster, mathematician, consultant*
Veasey, Byron Keith *information systems consultant*

Chicago
Balasa, Florin *software engineer, mathematician*
Bariff, Martin Louis *information systems educator, consultant*
Buckley, Joseph Paul, III, *polygraph specialist*
Costin, J(oseph) Laurence, Jr., *information services executive*
Cox, Clifford Ernest *information systems consulting executive, former school administrator*
Dwyer, Dennis D. *information technology executive*
Kaplan, Jonathan Harris *healthcare business transformation and information technology specialist*
†Krawczyk, Eva *information systems analyst, educator*
†Stark, Henry *technology educator*

Crystal Lake
Halperin, Richard George *information technology executive*

Dunlap
St John, Ronald *retired strategic planning professional, writer, educator*

Evanston
Atkin, Lawrence Ronald *computer software engineer*
Fisher, Andrew Taylor *computer software developer*

Libertyville
Shen, Xiaohui *application developer, researcher*

Northfield
Pratt, Murray Lester *collaborative commerce specialist*

Oak Brook
†Marcus, Carol A. *information technology manager*

Rockford
Duck, Vaughn Michael *software company executive*

Schaumburg
†Sikora, Sheryl L. *application developer*

Skokie
Seeder, Richard Owen *infosystems specialist*

Vernon Hills
†Halitsky, Steve *application developer, researcher*

Woodridge
Puthenpurakal, Joseph Mathew *information technology executive*

INDIANA

Bloomington
Glass, Robert L. *software engineering educator*
Henson, Jane Elizabeth *information management professional, adult educati*

Gary
Knapp, Judith Ann *computer information systems educator*

Indianapolis
†Lowe, Mary Katherine *technology company executive, writer*
Villars, Jill Annette *webmaster*

Spencer
Young, Frederic Hisgin *information systems executive, data processing consultant*

IOWA

Ankeny
Creswell, Dorothy Anne *computer consultant*

Cedar Falls
Kashef, Ali Ebrahim *industrial technology educator*

Cedar Rapids
Richardson, Robert Edward *data processing analyst*

Davenport
†Graham, Sally Jo *information technology executive, marketing professional*

Pella
†Johnson, Mark J *computer science educator*

KANSAS

Manhattan
Streeter, John Willis *information systems manager*

Overland Park
Leonard, Markus Dayle *software systems engineer*

KENTUCKY

Louisville
†McWane, Mark Paul *technology consultant*

LOUISIANA

New Orleans
†Ferrari, Daniel Joseph *business development manager*

MAINE

Portland
Frank, William Fielding *computer systems design executive, consultant*

MARYLAND

Baltimore
†Narvaez, Bernice Williams *software developer, consultant*
Park, Mary Woodfill *information consultant*

Bethesda
Poulos, Stephen Paul *information systems specialist*

Clarksburg
Gellineau, Antonio Cortes *system software specialist*

Cockeysville Hunt Valley
Elkin, Lois Shanman *business systems company executive*

Columbia
Fox, Barry Howard *software engineer*

Gaithersburg
Hoferek, Mary Judith *information systems specialist, educator*
Kemmerer, Sharon Jean *computer systems analyst*

Germantown
Wade, Suzanne *project manager*

Hanover
†Chiarella, Donald Joseph Gray *information systems specialist, educator*

Hyattsville
†Asongu, Januarius Jingwa *information technology executive*
Bender, Howard Jeffrey *software engineering consultant*

Lanham
†Hardin, David Jesse *application developer*

Millersville
Schulmeyer, G(eorge) Gordon *information systems executive, consultant*

Montgomery Village
Hewitt, Emmett Clyde, III, *software acquisition executive*

Odenton
Mucha, John Frank *information systems professional*

Riverdale
†Williams, Lisa Monique *information technology executive*

Rockville
Basinger, William Daniel *computer programmer*
Nevin, Joseph Francis *computer systems engineer*

Suitland
Doe, Patricia Louise *information technology executive*

MASSACHUSETTS

Acton
†Neale, John Jorgensen *research and development manager*

Beverly
Smith, Derek Armand *information technology executive*

Boston
Stallman, Richard Matthew *software developer*
White, Jan Tuttle (Mrs. Benjamin Winthrop White) *information technology executive*

Cambridge
Cooper, Mary Campbell *information services executive*
O'Donnell, Patrick Alan *software development scientist*
Sterbenz, James Philip Guenther *computer network scientist*
Toomer, Cynthia Yvonne *information systems administrator*

Chicopee
Pace, Eston A. *systems administrator*

Duxbury
Zachmann, William Francis *computer and communications industry market research company executive*

Gloucester
Knupp, Ralph *information technology executive*

Hudson
Chen, I-Yu *computer software executive*

Littleton
Lau, Joanna T. *information technology executive*

Needham
†Wang, Samuel James *information technology executive*

North Chelmsford
Aramini, Michael Joseph *software engineer*

Sudbury
McCree, Paul William, Jr., *systems design and engineering company executive*

Waltham
O'Donnell, Teresa Hohol *application developer, electrical engineer*
Thamhain, Hans Jurgen *information technology manager, researcher*

Westford
Selesky, Donald Bryant *software developer*

MICHIGAN

Ann Arbor
Krieg, Martha Fessler *software engineer*

Auburn Hills
Mukundan, Gopalan *technology specialist*

Brighton
Rice, Gary D. *software engineer, consultant*

Detroit
†Stern, Myles Steven *information technology educator, consultant*

Grand Rapids
Becker, Robert Joseph *database consultant, computer science specialist, database software developer and educator*

Kalamazoo
Targowski, Andrew Stanislaw *computer information educator, consultant*

Warren
Bley, Ann *program analyst, business manager*

MINNESOTA

Caledonia
Eppelheimer, Linda Louise *software educator*

Edina
Stryk, Robert Anthony *retired software engineer*

Elk River
McClure, Alvin Bruce *technical consultant*

Excelsior
Henke, Janice Carine *educational software developer and marketer*

Lakeville
Anderson, Erik W.L. *web designer*

Maple Grove
Prins, LaVonne Kay *programmer analyst*

Maplewood
†Veal, Ruffin, III, *information technology executive, county official*

Minneapolis
Krause, Timothy Gilbert *web site manager*
†Zhdanov, Dmitry *information technology executive, educator, financial consultant*

New Brighton
Schwartz, Joan Lam *computer graphics consultant, writer, artist*

Saint Paul
Adusumalli, Prasad (Venkata) *software engineer, engineering executive*
Jasthi, Siva Rama Krishna *software professional, consultant*

MISSISSIPPI

University
Roach, David Giles *information technology executive*

MISSOURI

Canton
Ellis, James Ira *network technician*

Hazelwood
Burleski, Joseph Anthony, Jr., *information technology executive*

Kansas City
Han, Yijie *information technology educator*

Saint Louis
†Condoor, Sridhar S. *information technology educator*
Elliott, Susan Spoehrer *information technology executive*
Heck, Debra Upchurch *information technology, procurement professional*
Ottinger, Maurice Armand *software engineer, educator*

Trenton
Myntti, Jon Nicholas *software engineer*

NEBRASKA

Lincoln
Revesz, Peter Z. *computer science educator*

Omaha
Ben-Yaacov, Gideon *computer systems designer*

NEVADA

Las Vegas
Marcella, Joseph *information system administrator*

North Las Vegas
Folden, Norman C. (Skip Folden) *information systems executive, consultant*

Reno
Ragavan, Anpalaki Jeyabalasinkham *software developer, researcher*

NEW HAMPSHIRE

Franconia
Schaffer, David Edwin *retired management systems executive*

Merrimack
Wolf, Robert Farkas *systems and avionics company executive, environmental planning consultant*

Nashua
Meagher, Robert Michael *software engineer*
Smith, Thomas Raymond, III, *software engineer*

Plymouth
Drexel, Peter George *computer science educator*

Weare
White, Karen Ruth Jones *information systems executive*

NEW JERSEY

Atlantic City
†Irwin, Germaine *information technology executive*

Berlin
Flacco, Elaine Germano *computer programmer*

Cherry Hill
Schelm, Roger Leonard *information systems specialist*

Cinnaminson
Kauffmann, Robert Fredrick *software engineer*

East Hanover
Cohen, Lori *computer software developer*

East Orange
†Chandan, Kamlesh C. *information technology executive, researcher*

Edison
Chakrapani, J(ayatheertha) *information technologist*

Hackettstown
Fremon, Richard C. *retired infosystems specialist*

Iselin
Beardsley, Jacob Edward *retired computer software company executive*

Liberty Corner
†Cipriano, Michael Rocco *information technology consultant*

Livingston
Burns, Edward Charles *infosystems specialist*

Middletown
Jaros, Robert James *information technology executive*

Morristown
Bockian, James Bernard *computer systems executive, writer*

Mount Laurel
Li, Pearl Nei-Chien Chu *technology company executive*

Murray Hill
†Ritchie, Dennis M. *software engineer*

Newark
Gopalakrishnan, Shanthi *technology educator*
Nash, Alicia *computer programmer, physicist*

Parsippany
Visocki, Nancy Gayle *information services consultant*

Piscataway
Kenney, Mary R. *software engineer*
†Kiddie, Thomas James *application developer, educator*

Plainsboro
Yam, Aileen Lynette *programmer*

Princeton
Kelble, William Francis *information services editor*

Smithville
Bergeron, Robert Francis, Jr., (Terry Bergeron) *software engineer*

Somerset
†Lee, Thai Theresa *information technology executive*

South Orange
Long, Philip Lee *information systems executive*
Williams, Veronica Ann *marketing and business consultant*

Sparta
Guida, Pat *information broker, literature chemist*

Wayne
Chludzinski, Christopher James *information systems professional, consultant*

Woodbridge
†Myerson, Paul Andrew *software company executive, management consultant*

NEW MEXICO

Albuquerque
Orman, John Leo *software engineer, writer*

Las Cruces
Kilmer, Neal Harold *software engineer*

NEW YORK

Albany
Hsia, Franklin Wen-Hai *computer programmer, systems analyst, consultant*
Klaas, Ottmar *software engineer*

Armonk
Dajnowicz, Jan *software and hardware designer, researcher*
Harreld, James Bruce *information technology executive*

Ballston Lake
McCann, Chris (Christian David McCann) *software engineer, educator*

Brooklyn
Davis, William Terry *software engineer, technology manager*
Doucette, David Robert *computer systems company executive*
†Fowler, John Dale, Jr., *biotechnology executive*

Buffalo
Haarmeyer, David Alan *computer programmer/analyst, educator*
Overton, Nicole Yolanda *program analyst*

Cazenovia
Carlson, William Clifford *retired defense company executive, retired naval officer*

Dundee
Pfendt, Henry George *retired information systems executive, management consultant*

Forest Hills
Guthy, George Edward *retired information systems executive*
Mindin, Vladimir Yudovich *information systems specialist, chemist, educator*

Glen Wild
Kaszas, William Joseph *technology educator*

Hicksville
Yen, Henry Chin-Yuan *computer systems programmer, software engineer, consulting company executive*

Jamaica
Chropufka, Mark A. *information management specialist, poet*
†Washington, William Thomas *technical manager, educator*

Johnstown
Prestopnik, Richard John *electronics and computer educator*

Lancaster
†Gainey, Ernest J., III, *internet security specialist*

Liverpool
Harris, Dana Bound *software company executive*

Maspeth
Heppa, Douglas Van *computer specialist*

Melville
Provenzano, Dominic *information specialist*

New City
Teplitzky, Philip Herman *information technology executive*

New York
Adams, Jeffrey Alan *web producer, writer*
Baker, Michelle Lynn *software designer*
Chang, Mona Mei-Hsuan *computer programmer, analyst*
Garvin, Andrew Paul *information company executive, author, consultant*
Gilmore, Jennifer A.W. *computer specialist, educator*
Green-Dorsey, Jean Audrey *information technology executive*
Haddock, Robert Lynn *information services entrepreneur, writer, inventor*
Hauben, Jay Robert *computer technician, writer, editor*
Hedbring, Charles *computer consultant, writer*
Herbert, Marc Louis *software engineer*
Hopple, Richard Van Tromp, Jr., *internet media executive*
Jones, Gwenyth Ellen *publishing information systems/technology executive*
Karlin, Muriel Schlosberg *information technology manager, consultant*
Koufaris, Marios *information technology educator*
†Livshiz, Boris *software engineer*
Mehlman, Lon Douglas *information technology specialist, investment banker, venture capitalist*
Morris, Stephen Burritt *marketing information executive*
†O'Connor, Kevin *computer programing executive*
Powell, Timothy Wood *information executive, consultant*
Sawyer, Deborah Christine *information services company executive*
Shionoiri, Hideo *computer technologist*
Stein, Jacob *computer programmer, analyst*
Svinkelstin, Abraham Joshua *information technology executive*
Waite, David Allen *software development executive*
Wyn-Jones, Alun (William Wyn-Jones) *software developer, mathematician*

Olean
Stevens, Edward Ira *information systems educator*

Owego
Zendle, Howard Mark *software development researcher*

Pearl River
Galante, Joseph Anthony, Jr., *computer programmer*
Wang, John Xiaowu *software company executive*

Pittsford
†Kalnitz, Paul Richard *software developer*
Saini, Vasant Durgadas *computer software company executive*

Poughkeepsie
Guski, Richard Henry *software engineer*

Rochester
Adiletta, Debra Jean Olson *business analyst consultant*
Fowler, Robert Archibald *infosystems company executive*
LaSpagnoletta, Benjamin Joseph *infosystems specialist*

Schenectady
Lommel, James M. *information technology manager*

Somers
Sanford, Linda S. *information technology executive*

Stony Brook
Dorojevets, Mikhail *application developer, educator*

Syracuse
Gartner, Joseph Charles *business systems administrator*
Hollander, Howard Robert *software engineering executive*

Troy
†Demertzoglou, Pindaro Epaminonda *systems administrator, education educator*
Jahng, Jungjoo *information technology educator*

Utica
Brooks, Sarah *software developer, consultant, educator*

White Plains
Palmisano, Samuel J. *information technology executive*
Tealdi, Javier Hernan *computer/network support specialist*
Winterton, Joseph Henry *computer software executive*

NORTH CAROLINA

Cary
Berryman, Patricia Lord *software engineer*
Goodnight, James H. *software company executive*
Sall, John *information technology executive*

Chapel Hill
Hill, Robert Folwell, Jr., *information systems specialist*
Jepsen, Thomas Charles *information technology professional, technology historian*
Smith, Janet Sue *systems specialist*

Edenton
Flynn, Patrick *designer, programmer, consultant*

OHIO

Akron
Powell, Robert Eugene *computer operator*

Cincinnati
Fairobent, Douglas Kevin *computer programmer*
Lajoie, Richard John, Jr., *information technology executive*

Cleveland
Lowry, Dennis Martin *information technology executive*

Columbus
Brown, Rowland Chauncey Widrig *information systems, strategic planning and ethics consultant*
Taylor, Celianna Isley *information systems specialist*
Zapp, David Edwin *infosystems specialist, investment consultant*

Dayton
Lamb, Rebecca Ann *software engineer, educator*
Siefert, David Michael *information technology executive, manufacturing executive*

Dublin
Spies, Phyllis Bova *information services company executive*

Hamilton
Fein, Thomas Paul *software support specialist*

Marion
Rowe, Lisa Dawn *computer programmer/analyst, computer consultant*

Mayfield
Cukrowicz, Kevin Francis *information technology manager, military officer*

North Olmsted
Galysh, Robert Alan *information technology manager*

Pickerington
Blackman, Edwin Jackson *software engineer*

Toledo
Cummings, Erwin Karl *information technology executive*

Twinsburg
Sugar, Robert Joseph *software engineer, physicist*

Upper Sandusky
Baker, Harrison Scott *computer consultant*

Westerville
†Topping, Elizabeth Ann *production manager, graphics designer, historian*

Westlake
Whitehouse, John Harlan, Jr., *systems software consultant, diagnostician*

Worthington
Trevor, Alexander Bruen *technology consultant*

OKLAHOMA

Ada
Baker, Judith Ann *retired computer technician*

Bartlesville
Norfleet, Scott Alan *software engineer*

Jones
Jones, Jeffery Lynn *software engineer*

Mustang
Laurent, J(erry) Suzanna *technical communications specialist*

Tulsa
†Davis, Lourie Irene Bell *computer education and information systems specialist*

OREGON

Banks
Fleming, Kathleen Gail *retired computer operations specialist*

Beaverton
Guers, Christian Alain *information systems specialist*
Hebert, Carol Ann *software engineer*

Corvallis
Wechsler, Susan Linda *research and development software manager*

Hillsboro
Fischer, Avraham *software engineer*

Portland
McCullough-Dieter, Carol Mae *database administrator*

PENNSYLVANIA

Blue Bell
Young, Charles Randall *software and marketing professional*

Canonsburg
Mukherjee, Siddhartha *application developer*

Cashtown
Saliu, Ion *software developer, computer programmer*

Clarks Summit
†Weiss, Tammy Lee *information technology manager*
Yadouga, Michelle Marianne *computer operator*

Exton
Fu, Don Hongbin *software engineer*

Gladwyne
Stick, Alyce Cushing *systems administrator, consultant*

King Of Prussia
Swank, Annette Marie *software designer*

Mechanicsburg
Bitner, Jerri Lynne *information technology professional, consultant*

Palmyra
Singer, William Harry *interactive multimedia architect, software engineer, expert systems designer, consultant, entrepreneur, ceramic artist*

Philadelphia
Brown, Ronald Rea *software engineer, artist*
Condon, J. Emmett *information technology executive*
Walker, Allen Lyon *logistics analyst*

Pittsburgh
Levine, David Lawrence *software engineer*
Mead, Nancy Rose *software engineer*
Smith, Dennis Bruce *software engineer*
†Tropeck, Kevin D. *information technology manager, writer*
†Yaskolko, Sergey *application developer*

Red Hill
DiMarco, Thomas William *software engineer*

Swarthmore
Kaufman, John Robert *marketing and information management consultant*

University Park
†Park, Jonghun *science and technology educator*

Upper Darby
†Horwitz, Seth *information technology executive*

RHODE ISLAND

West Greenwich
†Duggan, John David, Jr., *computer technician*

SOUTH CAROLINA

Chapin
Pettit, James Robert *computer programmer*

Columbia
Duggan, Kevin *information technology professional*

Lancaster
Carter, Richard Bonner *application developer*

TENNESSEE

Cordova
Hamilton, David John *information technology administrator*

Memphis
†Yankaway, Jerel Jerome *application developer*

TEXAS

Arlington
Gilbert, Susan Lynn *software engineer*

Austin
Cooper, William Wager *business educator*
Craparo, John S. *information technology executive*
Huber, John Charles *information technology executive, director*
Shaw, James *information technology specialist*
Winegar, Albert Lee *computer systems company executive*

Carrollton
Conrad, Philip Jefferson *software development engineer*

Cleburne
†Black, Alvin M. *application developer*

Dallas
†Daly, David Michael *information technology executive*
Gensheimer, Elizabeth Lucille *software specialist*
†Kruse, Ann Gray *computer programmer*
Matelan, Mathew Nicholas *software engineer*
Schweitzer, Loren Marcus *computer programmer*
Sidhu, Sanjiv *information technology executive*

Fort Hood
†Anderson, Nanci Louise *computer analyst*

Fort Worth
Hodgkins, W. Grant *supply chain improvements manager, consultant*

Grand Prairie
Thomas, Michael S. *software engineer*

Houston
†Flanders, Melanie G. *information architect*
Kramm, Deborah Ann *information technology executive*
Parker, Norman Neil, Jr., *software systems analyst, mathematics educator*
Schein, Daniel *webmaster, photographer*

Katy
Poland, Sydney Wade *software designer*

Lakeway
Gans, Dennis Joseph *information technology manager, financial analyst*

Lampasas
Stephens, Billie Lowell *information assurance manager*

Nevada
Dillard, Ronda Lenser *software engineer*

Plano
Benn, Douglas Frank *information technology and computer science executive*
James, Michael Thames *information technology executive, consultant*

Richardson
†Zeng, Guoping *application developer, researcher, education educator*

Round Rock
†Anandan, Santhosh *application developer*

San Antonio
Gardner, Raymond Alan *webmaster, writer*
Grubb, Robert Lynn *computer system designer*

Southlake
Cuomo, Andrew *information technology executive*
Jackson, Jeffery M. *information technology executive*

Stafford
Forbes, Sharon Elizabeth *software engineer*

The Woodlands
Lewis, Daniel Edward *information technology executive*

Wichita Falls
Passos, Nelson Luiz *computer science educator*

UTAH

Logan
Kadis, Jonathan Brynn *information technology executive*

Provo
Allen, Paul B. *information technology executive*
Herring, Mike *information technology executive*
Kitto, Franklin Curtis *computer systems specialist*
Moon, David C. *information technology executive*
Stockham, Tom *information technology executive*
Thayne, Daren *information technology executive*

VERMONT

South Burlington
Crouse, Roger Leslie *information technology executive*

VIRGINIA

Alexandria
Bragg, Lincoln Ellsworth *application developer*
†Callaghan, John William, Jr., *information technology manager, retired military officer*
Cooper, Roger Merlin *information technology executive, federal government official, school administrator*
Ivanetich, Richard John *information technology executive*

Arlington
Gault, Jeffrey Wayne *information technology executive*
Wu, Michael Ming-Kun *software engineer*

Fairfax
Gentle, James Edward *computer software executive*
Golden, John Joseph, Jr., *information systems executive*
Palmer, James Daniel *information technology educator*
Sage, Andrew Patrick, Jr., *systems engineer, management educator*
Truong, Long Khanh *software consultant*

Falls Church
McCue, David J. *information systems specialist, entrepreneur*
Rice, Rick Blackburn *computer programmer, systems analyst*

Herndon
Ras-Work, Andenet T. *software company executive*

Leesburg
†Navarro-Ramirez, Daniel *application developer*

Manassas
Heishman, Ricci Lynn *information technology educator*

Reston
Davy, William Allen *account executive*

Richmond
†Holmes Martin, Norma Anne *electronic and computer consultant, web site designer, writer*

Springfield
Lautzenheiser, Marvin Wendell *computer software engineer*
Quick, Danny Richard *computer systems engineer*

Vienna
Shelby, Ronald Van Dorn *information technology executive*

WASHINGTON

Bellevue
†Tian, Hongqi *application developer, researcher*

Connell
Wells, Roger Stanley *software engineer*

Federal Way
Rawsthorne, Daniel Andrew *software engineering executive*

Issaquah
Tripp, Leonard Lee *software engineer*

Olympia
Icenogle, Ronald Dean *software engineer, writer, physical chemist*

Redmond
Allchin, Jim *information technology executive*
Arbogast, Brian *information technology executive*
Ayala, Orlando *information technology executive*
Bach, Robert J. *information technology executive*
Belluzzo, Rick *information technology executive*
Black, Deborah *information technology executive*
Blakeley-Perez, Jose Alfredo *software architect*
Boggs, Scott *information technology executive*
Brass, Dick *information technology executive*
Brummel, Lisa *information technology executive*
Burgman, Doug *information technology executive*
Button, Tom *information technology executive*
Cabrera, Luis Felipe *software architect*
Christensen, Juha *information technology executive*
Cole, David *information technology executive*
DelBene, Kurt *information technology executive*
DeVaan, Jon *information technology executive*
Devenuti, Richard R. *information technology executive*
Elliot, Gerri *information technology executive*
Emerson, Richard P. *information technology executive*
Fade, Richard *information technology executive*
Flessner, Paul *information technology executive*
Gates, Bill (William Henry Gates III) *software company executive*
George, Grant *information technology executive*
Hebert, Kathleen *information technology executive*
Judah, Norman *information technology executive*
Kaplan, Richard *information technology executive*
Koch, Mitchell *information technology executive*
Kolomiets, Alexei *computer programmer*
Kong, Kenneth Sehkiang *software testing engineer*
Lane, James F. *software engineer*
Levin, Lewis *information technology executive*
Moore, Lori *information technology executive*
Muglia, Bob *information technology executive*
Mundie, Craig *information technology executive*
Nadella, Satya *information technology executive*
Norman, Bill *information technology executive*
Parthasarathy, Sanjay *information technology executive*
Pathe, Peter *information technology executive*
Poole, Will *information technology executive*
Raikes, Jeff *information technology executive*
Rashid, Richard F. *information technology executive*
Rawding, Michael *information technology executive*
Rudder, Eric *information technology executive*
Shaw, Kendrick Matthew *software engineer*
Short, Robert *information technology executive*
Sinneck, Michael *information technology executive*
Sinofsky, Steven *information technology executive*
Smith, Bradford Lee *information technology executive*
Somasegar, Sivarama Kichenane *information technology executive*
Sparks, Lindsay *information technology executive*
Stockdale, Russell *information technology executive*

Toutonghi, Michael *information technology executive*
Valentine, Brian *information technology executive*
Vaskevitch, David *information technology executive*
Veghte, Bill *information technology executive*
Vigil, Henry P. *information technology executive*
Waldman, Ben *information technology executive*
†Zhu, Min *application developer, researcher*

Seattle
Gates, Theodore Allan, Jr., *database administrator*
Tesler, Lawrence Gordon *technology company executive*

Snoqualmie
Nelson, Walter William *computer programmer, consultant*

Vancouver
Middlewood, Martin Eugene *technical communications specialist, writer, consultant*

Woodinville
Lanter, Sean Keith *software engineer*

WEST VIRGINIA

Martinsburg
†Day, Michael Gordon *information technology executive, educator*

WISCONSIN

Appleton
Hess, Sharon Marie *computer programmer*

Cambridge
Vance, Leslie Edwin *information technology educator*

Jackson
†Kasica, George Raymond *computer technician, consultant, emergency medical technician*

Madison
Cravens, Stanley H. *software development manager*
Michel, Sharon Lee *systems and information technology director*

Milwaukee
Kraut, Joanne Lenora *computer programmer, analyst*

WYOMING

Casper
Davis, Lois Ann *computer specialist, educator*

Cheyenne
Southworth, Rod Brand *retired computer science educator*

Jackson
Herrick, Gregory Evans *technology corporation executive*

CANADA

ALBERTA

Edmonton
Muzyka, Ray *application developer*
Zeschuk, Greg *application developer*

NOVA SCOTIA

Halifax
LeValliant, Debbie *information technology executive*

ONTARIO

Ottawa
Burney, Derek *information technology executive*

Waterloo
Balsillie, Jim *information technology executive*
Lazaridis, Mike *information technology executive*

QUEBEC

Laval
Savoie, Paul-André *information technology executive*

MEXICO

Mexico City
Guzman-Arenas, Adolfo *computer science researcher, electronics engineer*

BELGIUM

Vergnes, Bernard *information technology executive*

ENGLAND

Macclesfield
Graham, Dorothy Ruth *software engineering consultant*

FRANCE

Paris
Courtois, Jean-Philippe *information technology executive*

JAPAN

Kyoto
Ohno, Yutaka *information sciences educator*

Tokyo
Harada, Norio *software engineer, researcher, educator*

PORTUGAL

Armacão de Pêra
Litzenboerger, Wolfgang *software engineering executive, industrial consultant*

SWITZERLAND

Arth
Stanek, Bruno L. *software developer, author, commentator*

ADDRESS UNPUBLISHED

†Alexander, Nancy A. *information technology manager, consultant*
Ancheta, Caesar Paul *software developer*
Andriole, Stephen John *information systems executive*
Aouriri, Chedley *software engineer, computer science educator*
†Archangelsky, Dmitry A *application developer, researcher*
Asokan, Unisa *information professional*
Bao, Lichun *application developer, educator*
Bartle, Richard Allan *computer games designer*
Behnke, Doleen *computer and environmental specialist, consultant*
Bennett, Robert LeRoy *computer software development company executive*
Bergstrom, Richard William Houlder, Sr., *information technology executive*
Bluitt, Karen *information technology executive*
†Book, Kevin *information technology executive, consultant*
Borenstein, Nathaniel Solomon *computer programmer, inventor, educator*
Boyd, Kenneth R. *application and web programmer, mathematician*
Brown, Michael *information technology executive*
Brown, Richard Harris *information technology executive*
Burroughs, Pamela Gayle *information systems specialist*
Castle, James Cameron *information systems executive*
Cheng, Alexander Lihdar *information technology executive*
†Cherin, Stephen J. *computer programmer, management consultant*
Cibbarelli, Pamela Ruth *information executive*
Coullard, Chad *information systems specialist*
Csaszar, Peter *software engineer*
Davidson-Kennedy, Doris Ann *information technology executive, real estate broker*
Dellagnena, Gail Lynn *computer programmer analyst, consultant*
Eggleston, Claud Hunt, III, *company executive, venture capitalist*
Erickson, Garwood Elliott *computer consulting company executive, entrepreneur*
Etheridge, Diana Carol *internet business executive*
Eyerman, David John *software engineer*
Feder, Adam Barry *software engineer*
†Ferk, Franc *information technology executive*
Fuller, Pamela Dorr *software engineer*
†Fulp, Errin *computer science educator*
†George, Stephan (Steve) Anthony *web site designer*
Goggin, John R. *software quality engineer*
Green, Thornton George *software engineer*
Greene Lloyd, Nancy Ellen *retired infosystems specialist, physicist*
Grundlehner, Conrad Ernest *information company executive, economic consultant*
Gurspan, Mitchell Scott *technology architect, author*
Hill, Judith Swigost *business analyst, information systems engineer*
Hochstein, Eric Cameron *software executive*
Holmes, Richard Albert *software engineer, consultant*
Hooper, Gerry Don *retired information systems specialist, consultant*
Hosmer, Hilary Holden *computer systems educator*
†Hunter, Allison Marie *web site designer*
†Hunter, Kenneth M. *business information systems educator*
Hutchens, Nicki Jean *software developer*
Jaw, Andrew Chung-Shiang *software analyst*
Jones, Carleton Shaw *information systems company executive, lawyer*
Jordan, Michael Hugh *information technology executive*
Kalmanson, Jennifer Dawn *systems engineer, physicist*
Kelley, Mary Elizabeth (Mary LaGrone) *information technology executive*
†Khlabystova, Milena *web programmer, educator*
Killian, Jane Carolyn Crawley *computer consultant*
Kiser, M.L. *computer programmer, freelance artist, writer, poet*
Knight, Thomas Jefferson, Jr., *technology consultant, trainer*
Krieger, Robert Alan *software engineer*
Kurfehs, Joseph Morris *information security executive*
LaRocco, Elizabeth Anne *management information systems professional*
Laufman, Harrington Butler *systems programmer*
†Lester, Shane Michael *information technology executive, educator*
†Leven, Linda *application developer, writer, actor, model, artist*
Levy, Leslie Ann *application developer*
Lin, Linda I-li *computer consultant, trainer*
Mahmoud, Ahmed Mohamed *information technology executive*
Mansour, Stephen Malik *software developer, mathematician*
Marchetti, Reesa *web manager, editor*
Maruoka, Jo Ann Elizabeth *retired information systems manager*
McGervey, Teresa Ann *technical information specialist*
Mills, Kevin Lee *information technology researcher*
Minshall, Greg *computer programmer*
Morgan, M. Jane *computer systems consultant*
Morrison, Martin *computer systems analyst*
Mosher, Sue A. *computer consultant*
†Mueller, Gary Alfred *software engineer*
Nason, Dolores Irene *computer company executive, social services administrator, eucharistic minister*
†Negandhi, Manoj Mahendra *technology consultant*
Nicols, Angela C. *software engineer, computer consultant*
†Novak, Jon *information technology executive*
†Pace, Kary Dwight *web programmer*
Paris, Steven Mark *application developer*
†Pelton, Walter Eugene *information technology executive, mathematician, physicist*
†Pick, Daniel Maynard *application developer, researcher*
Pierce, Charles Earl *software engineer, entrepreneur*
Potts, Ronald Clyde *computer programmer, analyst*
Rankin, Jason Richard *knowledge manager*
Reece, David Bryson *information systems administrator*
†Repa, Scott J. *production manager*
Roberts, Bruce Dan *application developer, department chairman*
Roberts, Marie Dyer *retired computer systems specialist*
†Rosario, Elaine M. *systems administrator*
Rose, Brita May *web site designer, writer, peace activist*
Rudnick, Ben *software professional, retail automotive executive*
Ruth, Edward Keith *information systems specialist, management consultant*
Salwin, Arthur Elliott *software engineer*
†Schmidt, Eric (Emerson) *information technology executive*
Schneider, Sharon M. *systems administrator, information technologist*
Schoen, Howard Franklin *computer programmer, analyst*
†Schramm, Geoffrey Saunders *webmaster*
†Scott, Karen Elizabeth *information technology assistant*
†Sharapov, Ilya A. *application developer*
†Shepherd, Dan W. *information technology manager*
Sherwood, Kenneth Wesley *retired information technology executive*
Simmons, Scott Martin *information specialist*
Snow, Claude Henry, Jr., *information services executive, consultant*
Spence, Dianna Jeannene *software engineer, educator*
Spoehel, Ronald Ross *information technology executive*
Steinberg, Stephen Arthur *information technology executive, consultant*
Stentz, Steven Thomas *writer, researcher, project consultant*
†Stern, Bo *software engineer*
Tarjan, Robert Wegg *retired information services executive, part-time math teacher*
Thompson, John W. *information technology executive*
Thompson, Joyce Lurine *retired information systems specialist*
†Thompson, Kenneth *software engineer*
Toirac, S(eth) Thomas *software engineering executive, consultant*
†Valiev, Souleiman *software engineer*
Vaszily, Brian William *writer*
†Vaughn, John *information technology manager, consultant*
Wikarski, Nancy Susan *information technology consultant*
Williams, David Keith *technical trainer*
†Wolfgang, Hugh Edwin *application developer*
Woodside, George Robert *computer software developer*
Wright, Max *information processing executive, consultant, youth leadership corporate training executive*
Zehring, Karen *information executive*
Zheng, Lisa Liqing *computer consultant*
Zimov, Bruce Steven *software engineer*

INTERNET *See* INFORMATION TECHNOLOGY

LAW: JUDICIAL ADMINISTRATION

UNITED STATES

ALABAMA

Albertville
Johnson, Clark Everette, Jr., *judge*

Anniston
Harwell, Edwin Whitley *judge*

Ashland
Ingram, Kenneth Frank *retired state supreme court justice*

Birmingham
Acker, William Marsh, Jr., *federal judge*
Bennett, Thomas B. *federal judge*
Blackburn, Sharon Lovelace *federal judge*
Guin, Junius Foy, Jr., *federal judge*
Pointer, Sam Clyde, Jr., *retired federal judge, lawyer*
Privett, Caryl Penney *judge*

Florence
Tease, James Edward *judge*

Gadsden
Sledge, James Scott *judge*

Mobile
Butler, Charles Randolph, Jr., *federal judge*
†Cox, Emmett Ripley *judge*
Mahoney, Margaret A. *federal judge*
Milling, Bert William, Jr., *magistrate judge*

Montgomery
Black, Robert Coleman *judge, lawyer*
Carnes, Edward E. *federal judge*
De Ment, Ira *judge*
Dubina, Joel Fredrick *federal judge*
Godbold, John Cooper *judge*
Harwood, Robert Bernard, Jr., *state supreme court justice*
Hobbs, Truman McGill *federal judge*
Hooper, Perry Ollie *retired state supreme court judge*
Houston, James Gorman, Jr., *state supreme court justice*
Lyons, Champ, Jr., *state supreme court justice*
Maddox, Alva Hugh *retired state supreme court justice*
Moore, Roy S. *state supreme court chief justice*
Steele, Rodney Redfearn *judge*
Woodall, Thomas A. *state supreme court justice*

Tuscaloosa
England, John Henry, Jr., *judge*

Wetumpka
Bush, John B. *circuit judge*

ALASKA

Anchorage
Branson, Albert Harold (Harry Branson) *judge, educator*
Eastaugh, Robert L. *state supreme court justice*
Fabe, Dana Anderson *state supreme court chief justice*
Singleton, James Keith *federal judge*
von der Heydt, James Arnold *federal judge*

Fairbanks
Kleinfeld, Andrew J. *federal judge*

Juneau
Carpeneti, Walter L. *judge*

ARIZONA

Bisbee
Holland, Robert Dale *retired judge*

Green Valley
McDonough, Russell Charles *retired state supreme court justice*

Mesa
Hicks, Bethany Gribben *judge, commissioner, lawyer*

Phoenix
Anderson, Lawrence Ohaco *magistrate judge, lawyer*
Berch, Rebecca White *state supreme court justice, lawyer*
Broomfield, Robert Cameron *federal judge*
Canby, William Cameron, Jr., *judge*
Carroll, Earl Hamblin *federal judge*
Gaines, Francis Pendleton, III, *judge*
Jones, Charles E. *chief justice supreme court*
Martone, Frederick J. *judge*
McClennen, Crane *judge*
McGregor, Ruth Van Roekel *state supreme court justice*
Myers, Robert David *judge*
Rosenblatt, Paul Gerhardt *judge*
Ryan, Michael D. *state supreme court justice*
Schroeder, Mary Murphy *federal judge*
Silver, Roslyn O. *federal judge*
Silverman, Barry G. *federal judge*
Strand, Roger Gordon *federal judge*
Weisenburger, Theodore Maurice *retired judge, poet, educator, writer*
Winthrop, Lawrence Fredrick *judge*

Tucson
Brammer, J. William, Jr., *judge, lawyer*
Browning, William Docker *federal judge*
Lacagnina, Michael Anthony *judge*
Roll, John McCarthy *judge*
Zlaket, Thomas Andrew *attorney, former state supreme court chief justice*

ARKANSAS

Batesville
Harkey, John Norman *judge*

Conway
Hays, Steele *retired state supreme court judge*

El Dorado
Barnes, Harry Francis *federal judge*

Fayetteville
Hendren, Jimm Larry *federal judge*
Smith, Lavenski R. (Vence Smith) *federal judge*
Waters, H. Franklin *federal judge*

Little Rock
Arnold, Morris Sheppard *judge*
Arnold, Richard Sheppard *federal judge*
Arnold, W. H. (Dub Arnold) *state supreme court chief justice*
Corbin, Donald L. *state supreme court justice*
Glaze, Thomas A. *state supreme court justice*
†Roaf, Andree Layton *judge*
Stroud, John Fred, Jr., *judge*
Thornton, Ray *state supreme court justice, former congressman*
Wright, Susan Webber *judge*

CALIFORNIA

Alameda
Bartalini, C. Richard *judge*

Burbank
Schacter, David Martin *judge*

Chatsworth
Schwab, Howard Joel *judge*

Fort Bragg
Lehan, Jonathan Michael *judge*

Fresno
Coyle, Robert Everett *federal judge*
Wanger, Oliver Winston *federal judge*

Glendale
Early, Alexander Rieman, III, *judge*

Irvine
Curtis, Jesse William, Jr., *retired federal judge*

Long Beach
Tucker, Marcus Othello *judge*

Los Angeles
Alarcon, Arthur Lawrence *federal judge*
Armstrong, Orville *judge*
Bufford, Samuel Lawrence *federal judge*
Chavez, Victor Edwin *judge*
Collins, Audrey B. *judge*
Curry, Daniel Arthur *judge*
Donovan, Thomas B. *judge*
Fleming, Macklin *judge, author*
Highberger, William Foster *lawyer*
†Ito, Lance Allan *judge*
†Johnson, Earl, Jr., *judge, author*
Kelleher, Robert Joseph *judge*
Mohr, Anthony James *judge*
Mosk, Richard Mitchell *judge*
Pfaelzer, Mariana R. *federal judge*
Rafeedie, Edward *senior federal judge*
Takasugi, Robert Mitsuhiro *federal judge*
Tevrizian, Dickran M., Jr., *judge*
Yager, Thomas C. *retired judge*

Mendocino
Masterson, William A. *retired judge*

Newport Beach
Glass, Geoffrey Theodore *judge*

Oakland
Newsome, Randall Jackson *judge*
Wilken, Claudia *judge*

Pacific Palisades
Anwyl-Davies, Marcus John *judge, arbitrator*

Pasadena
Boochever, Robert *judge*
Fernandez, Ferdinand Francis *federal judge*
Fisher, Raymond Corley *judge*
Goodwin, Alfred Theodore *federal judge*
Hall, Cynthia Holcomb *federal judge*
Johnson, Barbara Jean *retired judge, lawyer*
Kozinski, Alex *federal judge*
Nelson, Dorothy Wright (Mrs. James F. Nelson) *federal judge*
Paez, Richard A. *federal judge*
Rymer, Pamela Ann *federal judge*
Tashima, Atsushi Wallace *federal judge*

Riverside
†Holmes, Dallas Scott *judge, educator*

Timlin, Robert J. *judge*

Sacramento
Kolkey, Daniel Miles *judge*
Levi, David F. *federal judge*
Moulds, John F. *federal judge*
Russell, David E. *judge*
Van Camp, Brian Ralph *judge*

San Diego
Aaron, Cynthia G. *judge*
Adler, Louise DeCarl *judge*
Bowie, Peter Wentworth *judge, educator*
Brewster, Rudi Milton *judge*
Burns, Larry Alan *judge*
Gonzalez, Irma Elsa *federal judge*
†Harutunian, Albert T(heodore), III, *judge*
Lewis, Gerald Jorgensen *judge*
McKeown, Mary Margaret *federal judge*
Rhoades, John Skylstead, Sr., *federal judge*
Thompson, David Renwick *federal judge*
Thompson, Gordon, Jr., *federal judge*
Turrentine, Howard Boyd *federal judge*
Wallace, J. Clifford *federal judge*

San Francisco
Baxter, Marvin Ray *state supreme court justice*
Berzon, Marsha S. *federal judge*
†Breall, Susan *judge*
Brown, Janice Rogers *state supreme court justice*
Browning, James Robert *federal judge*
Bybee, Jay Scott *judge, federal agency administrator*
†Callahan, Consuelo Maria *federal judge*
Chin, Ming *state supreme court justice*
Conti, Samuel *federal judge*
Fletcher, William A. *federal judge, law educator*
George, Ronald M. *state supreme court chief justice*
Graber, Susan P. *federal judge*
Haerle, Paul Raymond *judge*
Jarvis, Donald Bertram *judge*
Kennard, Joyce L. *judge*
Low, Harry William *judge*
Moreno, Carlos R. *state supreme court justice*
Noonan, John T., Jr., *judge, law educator*
Robertson, Armand James, II, *judge*
Schwarzer, William W *federal judge*
Sneed, Joseph Tyree, III, *federal judge*
Walker, Vaughn R. *federal judge*
Wardlaw, Kim A.M. *federal judge*
Werdegar, Kathryn Mickle *state supreme court justice*
Zimmerman, Bernard *judge*

San Jose
Fogel, Jeremy Don *judge*
†Maloney, Patrick Raymond *retired judge*
Stewart, Melinda Jane *judge*

San Marino
Mortimer, Wendell Reed, Jr., *judge*

Santa Ana
Barr, James Norman *federal judge*
Ferguson, Warren John *judge*
Stotler, Alicemarie Huber *judge*

Santa Barbara
Aldisert, Ruggero John *judge*

Santa Monica
Vega, Benjamin Urbizo *retired judge, television producer*

Sonoma
Herron, Ellen Patricia *retired judge*

South Lake Tahoe
Kingsbury, Suzanne Nelson *judge, educator*

Studio City
Gold, Arnold Henry *judge*
Horowitz, David Allen *retired judge, mediator, arbitrator*

Woodland Hills
Lax, Kathleen Thompson *judge*
Mund, Geraldine *judge*
Pregerson, Harry *federal judge*

Yosemite National Park
Best, Hollis Garber *judge*

COLORADO

Denver
Abram, Donald Eugene *retired federal judge*
Coats, Nathan B. *state supreme court justice*
Ebel, David M. *federal judge*
Felter, Edwin Lester, Jr., *judge*
Hobbs, Gregory James, Jr., *state supreme court justice*
Kane, John Lawrence, Jr., *judge*
Keithley, Roger Lee *judge*
Kirshbaum, Howard M. *retired judge, arbiter*
Kourlis, Rebecca Love *state supreme court justice*
Lucero, Carlos *federal judge*
Martinez, Alex J. *state supreme court justice*
†Mc Connell, Michael W. *judge, law educator*
McWilliams, Robert Hugh *federal judge*
Miller, Walker David *judge*
Mullarkey, Mary J. *state supreme court chief justice*
Nottingham, Edward Willis, Jr., *federal judge*
Porfilio, John Carbone *federal judge*
Rovira, Luis Dario *state supreme court justice*
Satter, Raymond Nathan *judge*
Swihart, Steven Taylor *judge*
†Tymkovich, Timothy *federal judge*

Englewood
Coffman, Penelope Dalton *judge*

Erickson, William Hurt *retired state supreme court justice*

Fort Collins
Gandy, H. Conway *retired judge, state official*

Golden
Rodgers, Frederic Barker *judge*

Leadville
Watson, Jack Crozier *retired state supreme court justice*

CONNECTICUT

Bridgeport
Eginton, Warren William *federal judge*

Danbury
Cutsumpas, Lloyd *judge*
Upson, Thomas Fisher *judge, former state senator, lawyer*
Yamin, Dianne Elizabeth *judge*

Deep River
†Spallone, Jeanne Field *retired state judge*

Hartford
Bieluch, William Charles *judge*
Borden, David M. *state supreme court justice*
Chatigny, Robert Neil *judge*
Craig, Joyce Krutick *judge*
Droney, Christopher F. *judge*
Katz, Joette *state supreme court justice*
Killian, Robert Kenneth, Jr., *judge, lawyer*
Martinez, Donna F. *federal judge*
Newman, Jon O. *federal judge*
Norcott, Flemming L., Jr., *state supreme court justice*
Peters, Ellen Ash *judge, trial referee, retired state supreme court justice*
Schaller, Barry R. *judge*
Shea, David Michael *state supreme court justice*
Squatrito, Dominic J. *judge*
Thompson, Alvin W. *judge*
Wright, Douglass Brownell *retired judge, lawyer*

New Britain
Meskill, Thomas J. *federal judge*

New Haven
Berdon, Robert Irwin *judge trial referee, retired state supreme court justice*
Burns, Ellen Bree *federal judge*
Cabranes, José Alberto *judge*
Calabresi, Guido *judge, law educator*
Walker, John Mercer, Jr., *federal judge*
†Winter, Ralph Karl, Jr., *federal judge*

New London
Santaniello, Angelo Gary *retired state supreme court justice*

Stamford
Callahan, Robert Jeremiah *retired judge, mediator*

Vernon Rockville
Purnell, Oliver James, III, *judge*

Waterbury
Goettel, Gerard Louis *federal judge*
McDonald, Francis Michael *judge trial referee, retired state supreme court justice*

DELAWARE

Georgetown
Holland, Randy James *state supreme court justice*

Wilmington
Ambro, Thomas L. *federal judge*
Balick, Helen Shaffer *retired judge*
Berger, Carolyn *state supreme court justice*
Latchum, James Levin *federal judge*
Roth, Jane Richards *federal judge*
Schwartz, Murray Merle *federal judge*
Stapleton, Walter King *federal judge*
Veasey, Eugene Norman *state supreme court chief justice*

DISTRICT OF COLUMBIA

Washington
Archer, Glenn LeRoy, Jr., *federal judge*
Bartnoff, Judith *judge*
Baskir, Lawrence M. *chief judge*
Bayly, John Henry, Jr., *judge*
Beghe, Renato *federal judge*
Belson, James Anthony *judge*
Berkley, Burton *federal judge*
†Breyer, Stephen Gerald *United States supreme court justice*
Bryson, William Curtis *federal judge*
Burnett, Arthur Louis, Sr., *judge*
Chabot, Herbert L. *judge*
Chiechi, Carolyn Phyllis *federal judge*
†Clevenger, Raymond Charles, III, *federal judge*
Cohen, Mary Ann *judge*
Cowen, Wilson *judge*
Crawford, Susan Jean *federal judge*
Dawson, Howard Athalone, Jr., *federal judge*
Edwards, Harry T. *judge*
Effron, Andrew S. *federal judge*
Farley, John Joseph, III, *federal judge*
Ferren, John Maxwell *judge*
Foley, Maurice Brian *federal judge*
Friedman, Daniel Mortimer *federal judge*
Gajarsa, Arthur J. *circuit court judge*
Gale, Joseph H. *federal judge*
†Gallagher, George R. *retired judge*
Garland, Merrick Brian *federal judge*
Gerber, Joel *federal judge*
Gibson, Reginald Walker *federal judge*
Ginsburg, Douglas Howard *federal judge*
Ginsburg, Ruth Bader *United States supreme court justice*
Glickman, Stephen *state supreme court justice*
Gonzales, Alberto R. *federal official, former state supreme court justice, former secretary of state*
Goodrich, George Herbert *judge*
Green, Joyce Hens *federal judge*
Henderson, Karen LeCraft *federal judge*
Hewitt, Emily Clark *judge, minister*
Ivers, Donald Louis *judge*
Jackson, Thomas Penfield *federal judge*
Jacobs, Julian I. *federal judge*
Johnson, Norma Holloway *federal judge*
Kennedy, Anthony McLeod *United States supreme court justice*
Kern, John Worth, III, *judge*
Kessler, Gladys *federal judge*
†King, Warren R. *judge*
Kline, Norman Douglas *federal judge*
Kramer, Kenneth Bentley *federal judge, former congressman*
Laro, David *judge*
†Leon, Richard J. *federal judge*
Liberty, Arthur Andrew *judge*
Lourie, Alan David *federal judge*
Mack, Julia Cooper *retired judge*
Margolis, Lawrence Stanley *federal judge*
Marvel, L. Paige *federal judge*
Mayer, Haldane Robert *federal chief judge*
Mencher, Bruce Stephan *judge*
Merow, James F. *federal judge*
Michel, Paul Redmond *federal judge*
Miller, Christine Odell Cook *judge*
Newman, Pauline *judge*
Oberdorfer, Louis F. *federal judge*
O'Connor, Sandra Day *United States supreme court justice*
Plager, S. Jay *judge*
Prost, Sharon *federal judge*
Rader, Randall Ray *federal judge*
Randolph, A(rthur) Raymond *federal judge*
Rehnquist, William Hubbs *United States supreme court chief justice*
†Roberts, John Glover, Jr., *federal judge*
Robertson, James *judge*
Rogers, Judith W. *federal judge*
Ruiz, Vanessa *judge*
Ruwe, Robert P. *federal judge*
Scalia, Antonin *judge*
Schall, Alvin Anthony *federal judge*
Schwelb, Frank Ernest *appellate judge*
Sentelle, David Bryan *federal judge*
Simpson, Charles Reagan *retired judge*
Smith, Loren Allan *federal judge*
Smith, Roy Philip *judge*
Steadman, John Montague *appellate court judge*
Steinberg, Jonathan Robert *judge*
Stevens, John Paul *judge*
Sullivan, Eugene Raymond *federal judge*
Swift, Stephen Jensen *federal judge*
Sypolt, Diane Gilbert *federal judge*
Tatel, David Stephen *federal judge*
Terry, John Alfred *state supreme court judge*
Thomas, Clarence *United States supreme court justice*
Thornton, Michael B. *federal judge*
Turner, James Thomas *judge*
Wagner, Annice McBryde *judge*
Wagner, Curtis Lee, Jr., *judge*
Wald, Patricia McGowan *retired federal judge*
†Walton, Reggie Barnett *judge*
Wells, Thomas B. *federal judge*
Williams, Stephen Fain *federal judge*
Yoder, Ronnie A. *judge*

FLORIDA

Boca Raton
Bernstein, Edwin S. *judge*

Clearwater
Peters, Robert Timothy *judge*

Daytona Beach
Palmer, William D. *judge*

Deland
Rouse, Robert Kelly, Jr., *judge*
Sanders, Edwin Perry Bartley *judge*

Destin
Robinson, Wilkes Coleman *retired federal judge*

Fort Lauderdale
Dimitrouleas, William Peter *judge*
Gonzalez, Jose Alejandro, Jr., *federal judge*
Ray, Raymond B. *federal judge*
Seltzer, Barry S. *federal judge*
Zloch, William J. *federal judge*

Fort Myers
Schoonover, Jack Ronald *retired judge*
Shafer, Robert Tinsley, Jr., *judge*

Jacksonville
Black, Susan Harrell *judge*
Hill, James Clinkscales *federal judge*
Melton, Howell Webster, Sr., *federal judge*
Schlesinger, Harvey Erwin *judge*
Tjoflat, Gerald Bard *federal judge*

Longboat Key
Morse, Marvin Henry *retired judge*

Merritt Island
Johnson, Clarence Traylor, Jr., *state judge*

Miami
Bandstra, Ted E. *federal judge*
Barkett, Rosemary *circuit judge*
Brown, Stephen Thomas *judge*
Cristol, A. Jay *federal judge*
Davis, Edward Bertrand *retired federal judge, lawyer*
Freeman, Gill Sherryl *judge*
Friedman, Ronald Michael *judge*
Graham, Donald Lynn *federal judge*
Highsmith, Shelby *federal judge*
Karlan, Sandy Ellen *judge*
King, James Lawrence *federal judge*
Marcus, Stanley *federal judge*
Rosinek, Jeffrey *judge*
†Seitz, Patricia Ann *judge*
Shevin, Robert Lewis
Siegel, Paul *judge*
Wilson, Thomas Strong, Jr., (Tam Wilson) *judge*

North Palm Beach
Siegendorf, Arden M. *judge*

Orlando
Glazebrook, James Grinstead *judge*
Thorpe, Janet Claire *judge*
Young, George Cressler *federal judge*

Panama City
Smith, Larry Glenn *retired state judge*

Saint Petersburg
Chipman, Marion Walter *retired judge*
Grube, Karl Bertram *judge*
Roney, Paul H(itch) *federal judge*

Tallahassee
Anstead, Harry Lee *state supreme court justice*
Grimes, Stephen Henry *retired state supreme court justice*
McCord, Guyte Pierce, Jr., *retired judge*
Pariente, Barbara J. *state supreme court justice*
Webster, Peter David *judge*
Wells, Charles Talley *state supreme court justice*

Tampa
Baynes, Thomas Edward, Jr., *judge, lawyer, educator*
Dail, Joseph Garner, Jr., *judge*
Glenn, Paul M. *federal judge*
Kovachevich, Elizabeth Anne *judge*
Wilson, Charles Reginald *federal judge*

Viera
†Rainwater, Tonya B. *judge*

West Palm Beach
Ryskamp, Kenneth Lee *federal judge*
Wroble, Arthur Gerard *judge*

GEORGIA

Atlanta
Benham, Robert *state supreme court justice*
Birch, Stanley Francis, Jr., *federal judge*
Carley, George H. *judge*
Carnes, Julie Elizabeth *judge*
Deane, Richard Hunter, Jr., *lawyer, former federal judge*
Edmondson, James Larry *federal judge*
Feldman, Joel Martin *magistrate judge*
Fletcher, Norman S. *state supreme court justice*
Hines, Preston Harris *state supreme court justice*
Hull, Frank Mays *federal judge*
Hunstein, Carol *state supreme court justice*
Kravitch, Phyllis A. *federal judge*
Moore, Thelma Wyatt *judge*
O'Kelley, William Clark *federal judge*
Sears, Leah J. *state supreme court justice*
Thompson, Hugh P. *state supreme court justice*
Ward, Horace Taliaferro *federal judge*

Augusta
Barfield, W. Leon *federal judge*
Bowen, Dudley Hollingsworth, Jr., *federal judge*

Cleveland
Barrett, David Eugene *judge*

Columbus
Laney, John Thomas, III, *federal judge*

Evans
Allard, David Henry *judge*

Hazlehurst
Wilkes, E.M., III, *judge*

Lawrenceville
Reeves, Gene *judge*

Macon
Anderson, Robert Lanier, III, *judge*
Hershner, Robert Franklin, Jr., *judge*
Owens, Wilbur Dawson, Jr., *federal judge*
Phillips, J(ohn) Taylor *judge*

Marietta
Smith, George Thornewell *retired state supreme court justice*

Newnan
Drake, W. Homer, Jr., *federal judge*

Rome
Murphy, Harold Loyd *federal judge*

Savannah
Moore, William Theodore, Jr., *judge*

Sylvania
Jenkins, Michael Grady *judge*

HAWAII

Honolulu
Acoba, Simeon Rivera, Jr., *state supreme court justice, educator*
Choy, Herbert Young Cho *federal judge*

Clifton, Richard Randall *judge*
Gillmor, Helen *federal judge*
Heen, Walter Meheula *retired judge, former political party executive*
Levinson, Steven Henry *state supreme court justice*
Moon, Ronald T. Y. *state supreme court chief justice*
Nakayama, Paula Aiko *state supreme court justice*

IDAHO

Boise
Eismann, Daniel T. *state supreme court justice*
Lodge, Edward James *federal judge*
McDevitt, Charles Francis *retired state supreme court justice, lawyer*
Nelson, Thomas G. *federal judge*
Pappas, Jim D. *federal bankruptcy judge*
Silak, Cathy R. *former state supreme court justice*
Trott, Stephen Spangler *federal judge, musician*
Winmill, B. Lynn *judge*

Idaho Falls
Shindurling, Jon J. *judge*

Twin Falls
†Hohnhorst, John Charles *judge*

ILLINOIS

Barrington
Wynn, Thomas Joseph *judge, educator*

Belleville
Ferguson, John Marshall *retired federal judge*

Benton
Foreman, James Louis *retired judge*
Gilbert, J. Phil *federal judge*

Chicago
Alesia, James H(enry) *judge*
Ashman, Martin C. *federal judge*
Aspen, Marvin Edward *federal judge*
Bauer, William Joseph *federal judge*
Bucklo, Elaine Edwards *United States district court judge*
†Cousins, William, Jr., *retired judge*
Cudahy, Richard D. *judge*
Denlow, Morton *federal magistrate judge*
Easterbrook, Frank Hoover *federal judge*
Fairchild, Thomas E. *federal judge*
Fitzgerald, Thomas Robert *judge*
Flaum, Joel Martin *judge*
Funderburk, Raymond *judge*
Gottschall, Joan B. *judge*
Hart, William Thomas *federal judge*
Johnson, Glenn Thompson *judge*
Keys, Arlander *federal judge*
Kowalski, Thaddeus Lawrence *retired judge*
Leighton, George Neves *retired federal judge*
Leinenweber, Harry D. *federal judge*
†Markey, Howard Thomas *retired law educator, former federal judge*
Moran, James Byron *federal judge*
Morrissey, George Michael *judge*
Nordberg, John Albert *federal judge*
Pallmeyer, Rebecca Ruth *judge*
Posner, Richard Allen *federal judge*
Rovner, Ilana Kara Diamond *federal judge*
Schmetterer, Jack Baer *federal judge*
Sonderby, Susan Pierson *federal judge*
Squires, John Henry *judge*
Williams, Ann Claire *federal judge*

Danville
Garman, Rita B. *judge*

Downers Grove
McGarr, Frank James *retired federal judge, dispute resolution consultant*

Edwardsville
Crowder, Barbara Lynn *judge*

Glenview
†Tristano, Sandra *circuit court judge*

Hennepin
Bumgarner, James McNabb *judge*

Homewood
Dietch, Henry Xerxes *judge*

Maple Park
Nickels, John L. *retired state supreme court justice*

Northbrook
Leikin, Mitchell *retired judge*

Peoria
Heiple, James Dee *retired state supreme court justice*
Mihm, Michael Martin *federal judge*

Pontiac
Glennon, Charles Edward *retired judge, lawyer*

Rockford
Reinhard, Philip G. *federal judge*

Rolling Meadows
Roti, Thomas David *judge*

Springfield
Evans, Charles H. *federal judge*
Miller, Benjamin K. *retired state supreme court justice*
Mills, Richard Henry *federal judge*
Wood, Harlington, Jr., *federal judge*

Waukegan
Brady, Terrence Joseph *judge*

Wheaton
Leston, Patrick John *judge*

Wilmette
Bowman, George Arthur, Jr.,

INDIANA

Boonville
Aylsworth, Robert Reed *lawyer*
Campbell, Edward Adolph *judge, electrical engineer*

Evansville
Capshaw, Tommie Dean *judge*

Fort Wayne
Cosbey, Roger B. *federal magistrate judge*
Lee, William Charles *judge*

Hammond
Rodovich, Andrew Paul *magistrate*

Indianapolis
Barker, Sarah Evans *judge*
Boehm, Theodore Reed *judge*
Dickson, Brent E(llis) *state supreme court justice*
Dillin, S. Hugh *federal judge*
Fisher, Thomas Graham *judge*
Foster, Kennard P. *magistrate judge*
Givan, Richard Martin *retired state supreme court justice*
Hamilton, David F. *judge*
McKinney, Larry J. *federal judge*
Metz, Anthony J., III, *federal judge*
Rucker, Robert D. *state supreme court justice*
Shepard, Randall Terry *state supreme court chief justice*
Shields, V. Sue *federal magistrate judge*

Kokomo
Stein, Eleanor Bankoff *judge*

Lafayette
Kanne, Michael Stephen *federal judge*

Lagrange
Brown, George E. *judge, educator*

South Bend
Brueseke, Harold Edward *magistrate*
Manion, Daniel Anthony *federal judge*
Ripple, Kenneth Francis *federal judge*
Rodibaugh, Robert Kurtz *retired judge*
Sharp, Allen *federal judge*

IOWA

Algona
Andreasen, James Hallis *retired state supreme court judge*

Cedar Rapids
Hansen, David Rasmussen *federal judge*
Mc Manus, Edward Joseph *federal judge*
Melloy, Michael J. *federal judge*

Chariton
Stuart, William Corwin *judge*

Council Bluffs
Peterson, Richard William *retired judge, lawyer*

Des Moines
Bremer, Celeste F. *judge*
Carter, James H. *judge*
†Colloton, Steven M. *judge*
Fagg, George Gardner *federal judge*
Harris, K. David *senior state supreme court justice*
Larson, Jerry Leroy *state supreme court justice*
Lavorato, Louis A. *state supreme court chief justice*
McGiverin, Arthur A. *former state supreme court chief justice*
Streit, Michael J. *state supreme court justice*
Ternus, Marsha K. *state supreme court justice*
Vietor, Harold Duane *federal judge*
Walters, Ross A. *federal judge*
Wolle, Charles Robert *judge*

Osceola
Reynoldson, Walter Ward *retired judge, lawyer*

Sioux City
O'Brien, Donald Eugene *federal judge*

KANSAS

Colby
Ress, Richard Joseph *judge*

Kansas City
Lungstrum, John W. *federal judge*
Rushfelt, Gerald Lloyd *magistrate judge*
VanBebber, George Thomas *federal judge*
Vratil, Kathryn Hoefer *federal judge*
Waxse, David John *judge*

Lawrence
Briscoe, Mary Beck *federal judge*
Six, Fred N. *retired state supreme court justice*

Newton
Walker, Richard Bruce *judge*

Olathe
Leben, Steve *judge*

Topeka
Allegrucci, Donald Lee *state supreme court justice*
Cox, Joseph Lawrence *judge*
Crow, Sam Alfred *judge*
Davis, Robert Edward *state supreme court justice*
Larson, Edward *state supreme court justice*
Marquardt, Christel Elisabeth *judge*
McFarland, Kay Eleanor *state supreme court chief justice*
Rogers, Richard Dean *federal judge*

Wichita
Brown, Wesley Ernest *federal judge*

KENTUCKY

Bowling Green
Huddleston, Joseph Russell *judge*

Elizabethtown
Cooper, William S. *state supreme court justice*

Frankfort
Johnstone, Martin E. *state supreme court justice*
Lambert, Joseph Earl *state supreme court chief justice*
Wintersheimer, Donald Carl *state supreme court justice*

Hopkinsville
†Adams, James G., Jr., *judge, lawyer*

Lexington
Coffman, Jennifer Burcham *federal judge*
Forester, Karl S. *chief district court judge*
Keller, James *state supreme court justice*
Varellas, Sandra Motte *judge*

London
Siler, Eugene Edward, Jr., *federal judge*

Louisville
Boggs, Danny Julian *judge*
Martin, Boyce Ficklen, Jr., *federal judge*

Murray
Buckingham, David Cowan *judge*

Newport
Wehr, William James *judge*

Paducah
Graves, John William *state supreme court justice*
King, W. David *magistrate judge*

Prestonsburg
Stumbo, Janet Lynn *state supreme court justice*

Wickliffe
Shadoan, William Lewis *judge*

LOUISIANA

Alexandria
†Little, F. A., Jr., *judge*

Baton Rouge
Cole, Luther Francis *former state supreme court associate justice*
Parker, John Victor *federal judge*
Polozola, Frank Joseph *federal judge*
Riedlinger, Stephen C. *federal judge*

Lafayette
Davis, William Eugene *judge*
Duhe, John Malcolm, Jr., *federal judge*

Lake Charles
Trimble, James T., Jr., *federal judge*

Marksville
Spruill, Kerry Lyndon *judge*

Metairie
Schwartz, Charles, Jr., *federal judge*

New Orleans
Beer, Peter Hill *federal judge*
Brown, Jerry A. *federal bankruptcy judge*
Calogero, Pascal Frank, Jr., *judge*
Clement, Edith Brown *federal judge*
Dennis, James Leon *judge*
Duplantier, Adrian Guy *federal judge*
Duval, Stanwood Richardson, Jr., *judge*
Johnson, Bernette J. *state supreme court justice*
Kimball, Catherine D. *state supreme court justice*
Knoll, Jeannette Theriot *state supreme court justice*
Traylor, Chet D. *state supreme court justice*
Victory, Jeffrey Paul *state supreme court justice*
Weimer, John L. *state supreme court justice*
Wiener, Jacques Loeb, Jr., *judge*

Ponchatoula
Kuhn, James E. *judge*

Shreveport
Payne, Roy Steven *judge*
Shemwell, Robert H. *federal judge*
Stagg, Tom *federal judge*
Stewart, Carl E. *federal judge*

MAINE

Auburn
Clifford, Robert William *state supreme court justice*

Augusta
Calkins, Susan W. *state supreme court justice*

Dana, Howard H., Jr., *state supreme court justice*

Bath
Field, Joseph Hooper *judge*

Portland
Alexander, Donald G. *state supreme court justice*
Bradford, Carl O. *judge*
Carter, Gene *judge*
Coffin, Frank Morey *judge*
Glassman, Caroline Duby *state supreme court justice*
Hornby, David Brock *federal judge*
Lipez, Kermit V. *federal judge, former state supreme court judge*
McKusick, Vincent Lee *former state supreme court chief justice, lawyer, arbitrator, mediator*
Wathen, Daniel Everett *former state supreme court chief justice*

Rockland
Collins, Samuel W., Jr., *judge*

MARYLAND

Accokeek
Beddow, Richard Harold *judge*

Annapolis
Battaglia, Lynne Ann *judge*
Cathell, Dale Roberts *judge*
Eldridge, John Cole *judge*

Baltimore
Bell, Robert M. *state supreme court justice*
Black, Walter Evan, Jr., *federal judge*
Bredar, James Kelleher *judge*
†Davis, Andre Maurice *judge, educator*
Derby, Ernest Stephen *federal judge*
Gauvey, Susan Kathryn *judge*
Harvey, Alexander, II, *federal judge*
Legg, Benson Everett *federal judge*
Motz, Diana Gribbon *federal judge*
Motz, John Frederick *federal judge*
Niemeyer, Paul Victor *federal judge*
Northrop, Edward Skottowe *federal judge*
Quarles, William Daniel, Jr., *judge*
Rodowsky, Lawrence Francis *retired state judge*
Smalkin, Frederic N. *federal judge*

Bethesda
Harris, Stanley S. *retired judge, arbitrator, mediator*
Nejelski, Paul Arthur *retired judge, freelance writer*

Cambridge
Ames, George Robert, Jr., *judge*

Greenbelt
Messitte, Peter Jo *judge*

Rockville
Megan, Thomas Ignatius *retired judge*

Upper Marlboro
Chasanow, Howard Stuart *retired judge, mediator*
†Krauser, Sherrie L. *judge*

MASSACHUSETTS

Boston
Boudin, Michael *federal judge*
Bowler, Marianne Bianca *judge*
Bownes, Hugh Henry *judge*
Campbell, Levin Hicks *judge*
Collings, Robert Biddlecombe *judge*
Connolly, Thomas Edward *judge*
Cowin, Judith A. *state supreme court judge*
Dreben, Raya Spiegel *judge*
Fishman, Kenneth Jay *judge*
Greaney, John M. *state supreme court justice*
Hillman, William Chernick *federal bankruptcy judge, educator*
Ireland, Roderick L. *state supreme court justice*
Keeton, Robert Ernest *federal judge*
Kenner, Carol J. *federal bankruptcy judge*
Lasker, Morris E. *judge*
Lindsay, Reginald Carl *judge*
Lynch, Sandra Lea *federal judge*
Marshall, Margaret Hilary *state supreme court chief justice*
Saris, Patti Barbara *federal judge*
Skinner, Walter Jay *federal judge*
Spina, Francis X. *state supreme court judge*
Stahl, Norman H. *judge*
Stearns, Richard Gaylore *judge*
Tauro, Joseph Louis *federal judge*
Torruella, Juan R. *federal judge*
Woodlock, Douglas Preston *judge*
Young, William Glover *federal judge*
Zobel, Rya Weickert *federal judge*

Cambridge
Boorstein, Beverly Weinger *judge*
Kaplan, Benjamin *judge*

Harwich Port
Smith, Ralph Wesley, Jr., *retired federal judge*

Longmeadow
Keady, George Cregan, Jr., *judge*

Springfield
Crampton, Rebekah Jean *judge, educator*
Freedman, Frank Harlan *federal judge*
Neiman, Kenneth Paul *judge*
Ponsor, Michael Adrian *federal judge*

Washington
Sacco, Rudolph Augustine *retired judge*

Worcester
Gorton, Nathaniel M. *federal judge*

MICHIGAN

Ann Arbor
Guy, Ralph B., Jr., *federal judge*
Pepe, Steven Douglas *federal magistrate judge*

Birmingham
Kaufman, Ira Gladstone *judge*

Detroit
Callahan, J(ohn) William (Bill Callahan) *judge*
Corrigan, Maura Denise *judge*
Duggan, Patrick James *federal judge*
Edmunds, Nancy Garlock *federal judge*
Feikens, John *federal judge*
Friedman, Bernard Alvin *federal judge*
Keith, Damon Jerome *federal judge*
Komives, Paul J. *federal judge*
Levin, Charles Leonard *state supreme court justice*
†Millender, Beatrice Pennie *magistrate judge*
O'Meara, John Corbett *federal judge*
Rosen, Gerald Ellis *federal judge*
Ryan, James Leo *federal judge*
Taylor, Anna Diggs *judge*
Teranes, Paul S. *county judge, mediator*
Woods, George Edward *judge*

Glen Arbor
Newblatt, Stewart Albert *federal judge*

Grand Rapids
Bell, Robert Holmes *district judge*
Brenneman, Hugh Warren, Jr., *judge*
Miles, Wendell A. *federal judge*
Quist, Gordon Jay *federal judge*
Scoville, Joseph Giacomo *federal magistrate, judge*

Haslett
Hollenshead, Robert Earl *retired judge*

Kalamazoo
Enslen, Richard Alan *federal judge*

Kentwood
Kelly, William Garrett *judge*

Lansing
Cavanagh, Michael Francis *state supreme court justice*
Harrison, Michael Gregory *judge*
McKeague, David William *judge*
Owens, Donald Stanley *judge*
Spence, Howard Tee Devon *judge, arbitrator, lawyer, consultant, insurance executive, government official*
Suhrheinrich, Richard Fred *federal judge*
Taylor, Clifford Woodworth *state supreme court justice*

Montague
Hillman, Douglas Woodruff *retired judge*

Pontiac
Andrews, Steven Nicholas *judge*

Port Huron
Keyes, Allen E. *retired judge*

Saginaw
†Jackson, Darnell *judge*
McGraw, Patrick John *judge*

Saint Clair Shores
Hausner, John Herman *judge*
Ryan, Harold Martin *judge*

Southfield
Graves, Ray Reynolds *retired judge*

Traverse City
Weaver, Elizabeth A. *state supreme court justice*

MINNESOTA

Albert Lea
Sturtz, William Rosenberg *retired judge*

Duluth
Heaney, Gerald William *federal judge*

Eden Prairie
Arthur, Lindsay Grier *retired judge, author, editor*

Lake Elmo
Tomljanovich, Esther M. *state supreme court justice*

Minneapolis
Alton, Ann Leslie *judge, lawyer, educator*
Amdahl, Douglas Kenneth *retired state supreme court justice*
Davis, Michael J. *judge*
Doty, David Singleton *federal judge*
Lebedoff, Jonathan Galanter *federal judge*
Loken, James Burton *federal judge*
Montgomery, Ann D. *federal judge, educator*
Murphy, Diana E. *federal judge*
Noel, Franklin Linwood *judge*
Rosenbaum, James Michael *judge*

Minnetonka
Rogers, James Devitt *judge*

Saint Cloud
Nierengarten, Roger Joseph *judge*

Saint Paul
Alsop, Donald Douglas *federal judge*

Anderson, Paul Holden *state supreme court justice*
Kyle, Richard House *federal judge*
Lay, Donald Pomeroy *federal judge*
Mason, John Milton (Jack Mason) *judge*
Renner, Robert George *federal judge*
Stringer, Edward Charles *judge, lawyer*
Willis, Bruce Donald *judge*

MISSISSIPPI

Aberdeen
Davidson, Glen Harris *federal judge*
Houston, David Winston *federal judge*

Biloxi
Roper, John Marlin, Sr., *federal magistrate judge*
Senter, Lyonel Thomas, Jr., *federal judge*

Gulfport
Russell, Dan M., Jr., *federal judge*

Jackson
Barksdale, Rhesa Hawkins *federal judge*
Diaz, Oliver E., Jr., *state supreme court justice*
Easley, Charles D., Jr., *state supreme court justice*
Graves, James E. *state supreme court justice, educator*
Jolly, E. Grady *federal judge*
Lee, Tom Stewart *judge*
McRae, Charles R. (Chuck McCrae) *state supreme court justice*
Pittman, Edwin Lloyd *state supreme court chief justice*
Smith, James W., Jr., *state supreme court justice*
Sugg, Robert Perkins *former state supreme court justice*

Natchez
Bramlette, David C., III, *federal judge*

Oxford
†Mills, Michael Paul *judge*

MISSOURI

Benton
†Heckemeyer, Anthony Joseph *circuit court judge*

Cape Girardeau
Blanton, Lewis M. *federal judge*

Hannibal
Reinhard, James Richard *retired judge*

Jefferson City
Benton, W. Duane *judge*
Blackmar, Charles Blakey *state supreme court justice*
Covington, Ann K. *former state supreme court justice*
Knox, William Arthur *judge*
Price, William Ray, Jr., *state supreme court judge*
Stith, Laura Denvir *state supreme court justice*
Teitelman, Richard B. *state supreme court justice*
White, Ronnie L. *state supreme court justice*
Wolff, Michael A. *state supreme court judge*

Kansas City
Bowman, Pasco Middleton, II, *judge*
Gaitan, Fernando J., Jr., *federal judge*
Gibson, John Robert *federal judge*
Laughrey, Nanette Kay *judge, federal*
Sachs, Howard F(rederic) *federal judge*
Ulrich, Robert Gene *judge*
Wright, Scott Olin *federal judge*

Saint Charles
Karll, Jo Ann *state administrative law judge, lawyer*

Saint Louis
†Burger, Joan M. *judge*
Filippine, Edward Louis *federal judge*
Gaertner, Gary M., Sr., *judge*
Hamilton, Jean Constance *judge*
Limbaugh, Stephen Nathaniel *federal judge*
McMillian, Theodore *federal judge*
Medler, Mary Ann L. *federal judge*
Noce, David D. *federal magistrate judge*
Ohmer, Steven Russell *judge*
Seiler, James Elmer *judge*

Springfield
Holstein, John Charles *former state supreme court judge*

West Plains
Dunlap, David Houston *judge*

MONTANA

Billings
Fagg, Russell *judge, lawyer*
Thomas, Sidney R. *federal judge*

Butte
Krueger, Kurt Donn *district court judge*

Hamilton
Langton, Jeffrey H. *judge*

Helena
Cotter, Patricia O'Brien *state supreme court justice*
Gray, Karla Marie *state supreme court chief justice*
Leaphart, W. William *state supreme court justice*
Nelson, James C *state supreme court justice*
Regnier, James *state supreme court justice*

Rice, Jim *state supreme court justice*

Polson
Turnage, Jean Allen *retired state supreme court chief justice*

NEBRASKA

Lincoln
Beam, Clarence Arlen *judge*
Connolly, William M. *state supreme court justice*
Gerrard, John M. *state supreme court justice*
Hastings, William Charles *retired state supreme court chief justice*
Hendry, John *state supreme court justice*
Kopf, Richard G. *federal judge*
McCormack, Michael *state supreme court justice*
Piester, David L(ee) *magistrate judge*
Urbom, Warren Keith *federal judge*
Wright, John F. *judge*

Omaha
Grant, John Thomas *retired state supreme court justice*
Riley, William Jay *federal judge*
Shanahan, Thomas M. *judge*
Strom, Lyle Elmer *judge*

NEVADA

Carson City
Maupin, A. William *state supreme court justice*
Rose, Robert E(dgar) *state supreme court justice*

Las Vegas
Becker, Nancy Anne *state supreme court justice*
Bell, Stewart Lynn *judge*
Johnston, Robert Jake *federal magistrate judge*
Mahan, James Cameron *judge*
Pro, Philip Martin *judge*
Rawlinson, Johnnie Blakeney *federal judge*

Reno
Brunetti, Melvin T. *federal judge*
Hagen, David Warner *judge*
Hug, Procter Ralph, Jr., *federal judge*
McKibben, Howard D. *federal judge*
McQuaid, Robert A., Jr., *federal judge*
Reed, Edward Cornelius, Jr., *federal judge*

NEW HAMPSHIRE

Concord
Brock, David Allen *state supreme court chief justice*
Broderick, John T., Jr., *state supreme court justice*
DiClerico, Joseph Anthony, Jr., *federal judge*
Duggan, James E., Jr., *state supreme court justice*
†Howard, Jeffrey R. *judge*
McAuliffe, Steven James *federal judge*
Muirhead, James Russell *federal judge*
Nadeau, Joseph P. *state supreme court justice*

Rochester
†Jones, Franklin Charles *judge*

NEW JERSEY

Atlantic City
Knight, Edward R. *judge, lawyer, educator, psychologist*

Camden
Brotman, Stanley Seymour *federal judge*
Irenas, Joseph Eron *judge, director*
Laskin, Lee B. *judge, lawyer, state senator*
Simandle, Jerome B. *federal judge*

Egg Harbor Township
Lashman, Shelley Bortin *retired judge*

Flemington
Verniero, Peter G. *state supreme court justice*

Freehold
Fisher, Clarkson Sherman, Jr., *judge*
Newman, James Michael *judge, lawyer*

Hackensack
Cipollone, Anthony Dominic *judge, educator*
Kestin, Howard H. *judge*
Stein, Gary S. *retired judge, lawyer*

Millburn
Kuttner, Bernard A. *retired judge*

Morristown
Hansbury, Stephan Charles *judge*
LaVecchia, Jaynee *state supreme court justice*
Speer, John Kirby *judge*

Newark
Ackerman, Harold A. *federal judge*
Alito, Samuel Anthony, Jr., *federal judge*
Barry, Maryanne Trump *federal judge*
Bissell, John W. *federal judge*
Debevoise, Dickinson Richards *federal judge*
Fuentes, Julio M. *federal judge*
Garth, Leonard I. *judge*
Greenaway, Joseph Anthony, Jr., *judge*
Lechner, Alfred James, Jr., *judge*

Oceanport
†D'Amico, John, Jr., *judge*

Somerville
Yurasko, Frank Noel *judge*

Trenton
Cooper, Mary Little *federal judge, former banking commissioner*
Cowen, Robert E. *federal judge*
Gindin, William Howard *judge*
Greenberg, Morton Ira *federal judge*
Hughes, John J. *federal judge, educator*
Long, Virginia *state supreme court justice*
Poritz, Deborah T. *state supreme court chief justice, former attorney general*
Thompson, Anne Elise *federal judge*
†Wallace, John E. *judge*
Zazzali, James R. *state supreme court associate justice*

Warren
Coleman, James H., Jr., *former state supreme court justice*

NEW MEXICO

Albuquerque
Black, Bruce D. *judge*
Conway, John E. *federal judge*
Dal Santo, Diane *writer, retired judge*
Franchini, Gene Edward *state supreme court justice*
Hansen, Curtis LeRoy *federal judge*
Hartz, Harris L. *federal judge*
Parker, James Aubrey *federal judge*

Paterson
Rothstadt, Garry Sigmund *judge*

Roswell
Baldock, Bobby Ray *judge*

Santa Fe
Kelly, Paul Joseph, Jr., *judge*
Maes, Petra Jimenez *state supreme court justice*
Minzner, Pamela Burgy *state supreme court justice*
Serna, Patricio *state supreme court justice*

Silver City
Hodges, Norman *retired district judge*

NEW YORK

Albany
Graffeo, Victoria A. *state appeals court judge*
Kaye, Judith Smith *state court chief justice*
Meader, John Daniel *judge*
Miner, Roger Jeffrey *judge*
†Read, Susan Phillips *judge*

Binghamton
Regenbogen, Adam *judge*

Bronx
Engoron, Arthur Fredericks *judge*
Massaro, Dominic Robert *judge, public official, writer*
Sonberg, Michael Robert *judge*

Brooklyn
Ambrosio, Michael Angelo *judge*
Amon, Carol Bagley *federal judge*
Bramwell, Henry *federal judge*
Garaufis, Nicholas G. *district court judge*
Harkavy, Ira Baer *Supreme Court justice*
Korman, Edward R. *federal judge*
Levy, Robert Morris *judge*
Pohorelsky, Viktor Vaclav *federal magistrate judge*
Reichbach, Gustin Lewis *state supreme court justice*
Ryan, Leonard Eames *judge*
Sifton, Charles Proctor *federal judge*
Solomon, Martin M. *judge*
Trager, David G. *federal judge*
Weinstein, Jack Bertrand *federal judge*

Buffalo
Bucki, Carl Leo *judge*
Elfvin, John Thomas *federal judge*
Foschio, Leslie George *judge*
Schroeder, Harold Kenneth, Jr., *U.S. magistrate judge*
Skretny, William Marion *federal judge*

Catskill
Lalor, Daniel Kevin *judge*

Central Islip
Bernstein, Stan *federal bankruptcy judge*
Boyle, E. Thomas *federal magistrate judge*
Cyganowski, Melanie L. *bankruptcy judge*
Eisenberg, Dorothy *federal judge*
Platt, Thomas Collier, Jr., *federal judge*
Seybert, Joanna *federal judge*
Spatt, Arthur Donald *federal judge*

Delhi
†Becker, Carl Frederick *judge*

Garden City
Harwood, Stanley *retired judge, lawyer*

Jamaica
Grayshaw, James Raymond *judge*

Kingston
Bradley, Vincent Gerard *judge*

Long Beach
Shechtman, Harry *retired judge, law educator*

New York
Aquilino, Thomas Joseph, Jr., *federal judge, law educator*
Baer, Harold, Jr., *judge*
Berman, Richard Miles *judge*
Blinder, Albert Allan *judge*

Buchwald, Naomi Reice *judge*
Carman, Gregory Wright *federal judge*
Cedarbaum, Miriam Goldman *federal judge*
Ciparick, Carmen Beauchamp *judge*
Feinberg, Wilfred *judge*
Francis, James Clark, IV, *judge*
Freedman, Helen E. *justice*
Gerber, Robert Evan *judge*
Griesa, Thomas Poole *federal judge*
Gropper, Allan Louis *bankruptcy judge*
Haight, Charles Sherman, Jr., *federal judge*
Jacobs, Dennis *federal judge*
Kaplan, Lewis A. *judge*
Katzmann, Robert Allen *judge*
Kearse, Amalya Lyle *federal judge*
Keenan, John Fontaine *judge*
Knapp, Whitman *federal judge*
Koeltl, John George *judge*
Leisure, Peter Keeton *federal judge*
Leval, Pierre Nelson *federal judge*
McLaughlin, Joseph Michael *federal judge, law educator*
Motley, Constance Baker (Mrs. Joel Wilson Motley) *federal judge, former city official*
Musgrave, R. Kenton *federal judge*
Nelson, Barbara Anne *judge*
Owen, Richard *federal judge*
Patterson, Robert Porter, Jr., *federal judge*
Peck, Andrew Jay *federal judge*
Pogue, Donald Carl *federal judge*
Pollack, Milton *federal judge*
Pooler, Rosemary S. *federal judge*
Preska, Loretta A. *federal judge*
Raggi, Reena *circuit judge*
Rakoff, Jed Saul *federal judge, author*
Sack, Robert David *judge, educator*
Sklar, Stanley Lawrence *judge*
Smith, George Bundy *state court justice*
Sotomayor, Sonia *judge*
Sprizzo, John Emilio *judge*
Straub, Chester John *judge*
Titone, Vito Joseph *former state court justice*
Tsoucalas, Nicholas *federal judge*
†Wesley, Richard C. *judge*
Williams, Milton Lawrence *judge, educator*

Port Washington
Jones, Farrell *retired judge*

Poughkeepsie
Dolan, Thomas Joseph *judge*
Rosenblatt, Albert Martin *state appeals court judge*
Sproat, Christine A. *judge*

Rochester
Kehoe, L. Paul *state judge*
†Larimer, David George *federal judge*
Siragusa, Charles J. *judge*
Van Graafeiland, Ellsworth Alfred *federal judge*

Rome
Simons, Richard Duncan *lawyer, retired judge*

Sag Harbor
Pierce, Lawrence Warren *retired federal judge*

Schenectady
Levine, Howard Arnold *judge*

Smallwood
Golden, Elliott *judge*

Syracuse
McCurn, Neal Peters *federal judge*
Munson, Howard G. *federal judge*
Scullin, Frederick James, Jr., *federal judge*
Wells, Peter Nathaniel *judge, lawyer*

Utica
Cardamone, Richard J. *judge*
Hurd, David Norman *federal judge*

Webster
Witmer, G. Robert *retired state supreme court justice*

White Plains
Conner, William Curtis *judge*
Ellerby, James Edward, Jr., *judge*
Hardin, Adlai Stevenson, Jr., *judge*
Nastasi, Aldo A. *judge*
Parker, Barrington D., Jr., *federal judge, lawyer*
West, Joseph King *judge*

NORTH CAROLINA

Asheville
Thornburg, Lacy Herman *federal judge*

Charlotte
Campbell, Hugh Brown, Jr., *judge*
Horn, Carl, III, *federal judge*
Mullen, Graham C. *federal judge*

Greensboro
Bullock, Frank William, Jr., *federal judge*
Frye, Henry E. *retired state supreme court chief justice*
Stocks, William L. *federal judge*

Monroe
Taylor, Susan Chandler *state judge*

Raleigh
Brown, James Joseph *judge*
†Duncan, Allyson K. *judge*
Eagles, Sidney Smith, Jr., *judge*
Martin, Mark D. *state supreme court justice*
Orr, Robert F. *judge*
Small, Alden Thomas *judge*

Wilson
Leonard, J. Rich *federal judge, educator*

Winston Salem
Beaty, James Arthur, Jr., *federal judge*
Eliason, Russell Allen *judge*
†Ross, Thomas Warren, Sr., *judge*

NORTH DAKOTA

Bismarck
Sandstrom, Dale Vernon *state supreme court justice*
VandeWalle, Gerald Wayne *state supreme court chief justice*
Van Sickle, Bruce Marion *federal judge*

Fargo
Bright, Myron H. *federal judge*
Bye, Kermit Edward *federal judge, lawyer*
Hill, William A(lexander) *judge*
Magill, Frank John *federal judge*

OHIO

Akron
Bell, Samuel H. *federal judge, educator*

Bowling Green
†Baird, James Abington *retired judge*
†Mayberry, Alan Reed *judge*

Cincinnati
Beckwith, Sandra Shank *judge*
Black, Robert L., Jr., *retired judge*
Clay, Eric L. *federal judge*
†Cook, Deborah L. *judge, former state supreme court justice*
Dlott, Susan Judy *judge, lawyer*
Hopkins, Jeffrey P. *federal judge*
Jones, Nathaniel Raphael *retired federal judge*
Karam, Ernest *chief magistrate*
Kennedy, Cornelia Groefsema *federal judge*
Nelson, David Aldrich *judge*
†Nelson, Frederick Dickson *judge*
Painter, Mark Philip *judge*
Perlman, Burton *judge*
†Rogers, John Marshall *judge, law educator*
Spiegel, S. Arthur *federal judge*

Circleville
Ammer, William *retired judge*
†Long, Jan Michael *judge*

Cleveland
Burke, Lillian Walker *retired judge*
Gaughan, Patricia Anne *judge*
Kilbane, Anne L. *judge*
Krupansky, Robert Bazil *federal judge*
Manos, John M. *federal judge*
Markus, Richard M. *judge, mediator*
Matia, Paul Ramon *federal judge*
Moore, Karen Nelson *judge*
Morgenstern-Clarren, Pat *federal judge*
Oliver, Solomon, Jr., *judge*
Wells, Lesley *judge*

Columbus
Caldwell, Charles M. *federal judge*
Calhoun, Donald Eugene, Jr., *federal judge*
†Cole, Ransey Guy, Jr., *federal judge*
Douglas, Andrew *retired state supreme court justice*
Holschuh, John David *federal judge*
King, Norah McCann *federal judge*
Mc Cormac, John Waverly *judge*
Moyer, Thomas J. *state supreme court chief justice*
Norris, Alan Eugene *federal judge*
O'Connor, Maureen *judge*
Pfeifer, Paul E. *state supreme court justice*
Resnick, Alice Robie *judge*
Sargus, Edmund A., Jr., *judge*
Sellers, Barbara Jackson *federal judge*
Smith, George Curtis *judge*
Sweeney, Asher William *state supreme court justice*
Sweeney, Francis E. *state supreme court justice*

Dayton
Anderson, Charles Austin *judge*
Clark, William Alfred *federal judge*
Knapp, James Ian Keith *judge*
Merz, Michael *federal judge*
Petzold, John Paul *judge*

Kettering
Porter, Walter Arthur *retired judge*

Lisbon
Dailey, Coleen Hall *magistrate, lawyer*

Lucasville
Reno, Ottie Wayne *former judge*

Marion
Rogers, Richard Michael *judge*

Medina
Batchelder, Alice M. *federal judge*

Sandusky
Stacey, James Allen *retired judge*

Toledo
Potter, John William *federal judge*

Warren
Nader, Robert Alexander *judge, lawyer*

Xenia
†Wolaver, Stephen Arthur *judge, lawyer*

Youngstown
Bodoh, William T. *federal judge*

OKLAHOMA

Atoka
Gabbard, Douglas, II, (James Gabbard) *judge*

Guthrie
Brooks, Larry Roger *judge*

Lawton
Moore, Roy Dean *retired judge*

Norman
Trimble, Preston Albert *retired judge*

Oklahoma City
Alley, Wayne Edward *federal judge, retired army officer*
Bohanon, Luther L. *federal judge*
Hargrave, Rudolph *state supreme court chief justice*
Henry, Robert Harlan *federal judge, former attorney general*
Hodges, Ralph B. *state supreme court justice*
Holloway, William Judson, Jr., *federal judge*
Lavender, Robert Eugene *state supreme court justice*
Leonard, Timothy Dwight *judge*
Lumpkin, Gary leonard *judge*
Miles-La Grange, Vicki *judge*
Opala, Marian P(eter) *state supreme court justice*
Russell, David L. *federal judge*
Summers, Hardy *state supreme court justice*
TeSelle, John *retired judge*
Thompson, Ralph Gordon *federal judge*
Watt, Joseph Michael *state supreme court chief justice*
West, Lee Roy *federal judge*

Purcell
Mantooth, John Albert *judge*

Tulsa
Brett, Thomas Rutherford *federal judge*
Brightmire, Paul William *retired judge*
Cook, Harold Dale *federal judge*
Eagan, Claire Veronica *district court judge*
Frizzell, Gregory Kent K. *judge*
Goodman, Jerry L(ynn) *judge*
Holmes, Sven Erik *federal judge, educator*
Kern, Terry C. *judge*
Seymour, Stephanie Kulp *federal judge*
Taylor, Joe Clinton *judge*

OREGON

Portland
Beatty, John Cabeen, Jr., *judge*
†Buttler, John Howland *retired judge, retired arbitrator*
Dunn, Randall L. *federal judge*
Fisher, Ann Lewis *judge*
Frye, Helen Jackson *federal judge*
Jones, Robert Edward *federal judge*
King, Garr Michael *federal judge*
Leavy, Edward *federal judge*
Marsh, Malcolm F. *federal judge*
O'Scannlain, Diarmuid Fionntain *federal judge*
Panner, Owen M. *federal judge*
Roth, Phillip Joseph *retired judge*
Skopil, Otto Richard, Jr., *federal judge*
Stewart, Janice Mae *judge*
Sullivan, Donal D. *federal bankruptcy judge*
†Tanzer, Jacob *retired judge*
Unis, Richard L. *judge*
Van Hoomissen, George Albert *state supreme court justice*

Salem
Balmer, Thomas Ancil *state supreme court justice*
Carson, Wallace Preston, Jr., *judge*
De Muniz, Paul J. *state supreme court justice*
Durham, Robert Donald, Jr., *state supreme court justice*
Linde, Hans Arthur *state supreme court justice*
Peterson, Edwin J. *retired judge, mediator, law educator*
Riggs, R. William *judge*

Sweet Home
Miller, Keith Allen *judge, lawyer*

PENNSYLVANIA

Allentown
Platt, William Henry *judge*

Allison Park
Craig, David W. *judge, author*

Bala Cynwyd
Beck, Phyllis Whitman *judge*

Doylestown
Rubenstein, Alan Morris *county judge*

Easton
Van Antwerpen, Franklin Stuart *federal judge*

Erie
Mencer, Glenn Everell *federal judge*
Nygaard, Richard Lowell *federal judge*

Harrisburg
Rambo, Sylvia H. *federal judge*

Johnstown
Smith, D. Brooks *federal judge*

Newtown Square
Scholl, David Allen *former federal judge, lawyer*

Philadelphia
Angell, M(ary) Faith *federal magistrate judge*
Bartle, Harvey, III, *federal judge*
Bechtle, Louis Charles *lawyer, retired federal judge*
Becker, Edward Roy *judge*
Buckwalter, Ronald Lawrence *federal judge*
Chertoff, Michael *judge*
Dalzell, Stewart *federal judge*
Fullam, John P. *federal judge*
Green, Clifford Scott *federal judge*
Joyner, J(ames) Curtis *judge*
Kelly, Robert F. *federal judge*
McKee, Theodore A. *federal judge*
Newcomer, Clarence Charles *federal judge*
Nigro, Russell M. *state supreme court justice*
O'Neill, Thomas Newman, Jr., *federal judge*
Pollak, Louis Heilprin *judge, educator*
Reed, Lowell A., Jr., *federal judge*
Rendell, Marjorie O. *federal judge*
Robreno, Eduardo C. *federal judge*
Rueter, Thomas James *federal judge*
Rufe, Cynthia Marie *judge*
Savage, Timothy Joseph *judge*
Scirica, Anthony Joseph *federal judge*
Sloviter, Dolores Korman *federal judge*
Weiner, Charles R. *federal judge*
Yohn, William H(endricks), Jr., *federal judge*

Pittsburgh
Cohill, Maurice Blanchard, Jr., *federal judge*
†Colville, Robert E. *judge*
Conti, Joy Flowers *judge*
Cosetti, Joseph Louis *federal judge*
Diamond, Gustave *federal judge*
Fitzgerald, Judith Klaswick *federal judge*
Flaherty, John Paul, Jr., *judge*
Lally-Green, Maureen Ellen *superior court judge, law educator*
Lee, Donald John *federal judge*
McCullough, M. Bruce *judge*
Ross, Eunice Latshaw *judge*
Sensenich, Ila Jeanne *judge*
Skwaryk, Robert Francis *judge*
Standish, William Lloyd *judge*
Weis, Joseph Francis, Jr., *federal judge*
Ziegler, Donald Emil *federal judge*

Scranton
Blewitt, Thomas Michael *federal magistrate judge*
Conaboy, Richard Paul *federal judge*
Harhut, Chet *judge*
Nealon, William Joseph, Jr., *federal judge*
O'Malley, Carlon Martin *judge*
Vanaskie, Thomas Ignatius *judge*

Uniontown
Franks, William J. *judge*

Washington
Mc Cune, Barron Patterson *retired federal judge*

West Conshohocken
Newman, Sandra Schultz *state supreme court justice*

Wilkes Barre
Rosenn, Max *federal judge*
Schwartz, Roger Alan *judge*

Williamsport
McClure, James Focht, Jr., *federal judge*
Muir, Malcolm *federal judge*

RHODE ISLAND

Providence
Goldberg, Maureen McKenna *state supreme court justice*
Hagopian, Jacob *federal judge*
†Keough, Joseph Aloysios *judge*
Lagueux, Ronald Rene *federal judge*
Lisi, Mary M. *federal judge*
Ragosta, Vincent A.F. *judge*
Selya, Bruce Marshall *federal judge*
Weisberger, Joseph Robert *retired judge*
Williams, Frank J. *judge, historian, writer*

SOUTH CAROLINA

Camden
Chapman, Robert Foster *judge*
Jacobs, Rolly Warren *judge*

Charleston
Hawkins, Falcon Black, Jr., *federal judge*
Young, Roger M. *judge*

Columbia
Bristow, Walter James, Jr., *retired judge*
Burnett, E. C., III, *state supreme court justice*
Hamilton, Clyde Henry *judge*
†Kosko, George Carter *judge*
†Shedd, Dennis W. *federal judge*
Toal, Jean Hoefer *state supreme court chief justice*

Greenville
Traxler, William Byrd, Jr., *federal judge*
Wilkins, William Walter *federal judge*

Greenwood
Moore, James E. *state supreme court justice*

Marion
Waller, John Henry, Jr., *state supreme court justice*

Myrtle Beach
Harwell, David Walker *retired state supreme court chief justice*

Orangeburg
Finney, Ernest Adolphus, Jr., *retired state supreme court chief justice*

SOUTH DAKOTA

Deadwood
Johns, Timothy Robert *judge*

Pierre
Gilbertson, David *state supreme court justice*
Konenkamp, John K. *state supreme court justice*
Miller, Robert Arthur *former state supreme court chief justice*
Sabers, Richard Wayne *state supreme court justice*
Zinter, Steven L. *state supreme court justice*

Sioux Falls
Piersol, Lawrence L. *federal judge*
Severson, Glen Arthur *circuit court judge*
Wollman, Roger Leland *federal judge*

TENNESSEE

Chattanooga
Barker, William M. *state supreme court justice*
Edgar, R(obert) Allan *federal judge*
Franks, Herschel Pickens *judge*
Powers, John Y. *federal judge*

Jackson
Boswell, G(eorge) Harvey *federal judge*
Breen, John Daniel *federal judge*
Todd, James Dale *federal judge*

Johnson City
Kiener, John Leslie *judge*

Kingsport
McLellan, John Sidney, III, *judge*

Knoxville
Anderson, Edward Riley *state supreme court justice*
Jordan, Robert Leon *judge*
Murrian, Robert Phillip *retired state judge, educator*
Phillips, Thomas Wade *judge, lawyer*

Memphis
Gibbons, Julia Smith *federal judge*
Gilman, Ronald Lee *judge*
McRae, Robert Malcolm, Jr., *federal judge*
Vescovo, Diane Kirkland *federal judge*

Nashville
Birch, Adolpho A., Jr., *state supreme court justice*
Brown, Joe Blackburn *judge*
Daughtrey, Martha Craig *federal judge*
Drowota, Frank F., III, *state supreme court chief justice*
Echols, Robert L. *federal judge*
Merritt, Gilbert Stroud *federal judge*
Nixon, John Trice *judge*
Trauger, Aleta Arthur *judge*
Wiseman, Thomas Anderton, Jr., *federal judge*

Newport
Porter, James Kenneth *retired judge*

Signal Mountain
Cooper, Robert Elbert *state supreme court justice*

TEXAS

Amarillo
Johnson, Philip Wayne *judge*
Robinson, Mary Lou *federal judge*

Arlington
Wright, James Edward *judge*

Austin
Benavides, Fortunato Pedro (Pete Benavides) *federal judge*
Coronado, Santiago Sybert (Jim Coronado) *judge*
Garwood, William Lockhart *judge*
Greenhill, Joe Robert *former chief justice state supreme court, lawyer*
Hecht, Nathan Lincoln *state supreme court justice*
Hudspeth, Harry Lee *federal judge*
Jefferson, Wallace B. *state supreme court justice*
Johnson, Cheryl Ann *judge*
†Meyers, Lawrence Edward *state judge*
Miller, Charles E. (Chuck Miller) *judge*
Nowlin, James Robertson *federal judge*
O'Neill, Harriet *state supreme court justice*
Owen, Priscilla Richman *state supreme court justice*
Perkins, Robert Anton *judge*
Phillips, Thomas Royall *judge*
Pope, Andrew Jackson, Jr., (Jack Pope) *retired judge*
Ray, Cread L., Jr., *retired state supreme court justice*
Reavley, Thomas Morrow *federal judge*
Sparks, Sam *federal judge*
Williams, Mary Pearl *judge*

Beaumont
Burgess, Don R. *judge*
Cobb, Howell *federal judge*

Bellaire
†Martin, John Randolph *judge*

Brownsville
Garza, Reynaldo G. *federal judge*

Bryan
Smith, Steven Lee *judge*

Corpus Christi
Head, Hayden Wilson, Jr., *judge*

Jack, Janis Graham *judge*

Dallas
Abramson, Harold Calvin *federal bankruptcy judge*
Higginbotham, Patrick Errol *federal judge*
Lewis, Marilea Whatley *judge*
Price, Robert Eben *judge*
Robertson, Ted Zanderson *judge*
Sanders, Harold Barefoot, Jr., *judge*

Edinburg
Hinojosa, Federico Gustavo, Jr., *judge*

El Paso
Briones, David *judge*

Fort Worth
McBryde, John Henry *federal judge*
Tillman, Massie Monroe *mediator, arbitrator, art gallery owner, retired federal judge*

Galveston
Froeschner, John R. *federal judge*

Houston
Atlas, Nancy Friedman *judge*
Blackmon, Willie Edward Boney *judge, military officer*
Bue, Carl Olaf, Jr., *retired federal judge*
DeMoss, Harold Raymond, Jr., *federal judge*
Gilmore, Vanessa D. *federal judge*
Hanks, George Carol, Jr., *state judge*
Hittner, David *federal judge*
Hoyt, Kenneth M. *federal judge*
Hughes, Lynn Nettleton *federal judge*
Jones, Edith Hollan *federal judge*
King, Carolyn Dineen *federal judge*
Lake, Sim *federal judge*
Rosenthal, Lee H. *federal judge*
Schwarz, Paul Winston *judge*
Smith, Jerry Edwin *federal judge*
Sondock, Ruby Kless *retired judge*
York, James Martin *judge*

Kaufman
Tygrett, Howard Volney, Jr., *judge, lawyer*

Lockhart
McCormick, Michael Jerry *retired judge*

Longview
Martin, William Clifford, III, *judge*

Mcallen
Hinojosa, Ricardo H. *federal judge*

Midland
Furgeson, William Royal *federal judge*
†Morrow, William Clarence *judge, lawyer, mediator*

New Braunfels
Zipp, Ronald Duane *judge, priest, real estate broker*

Pampa
Cain, Donald Ezell *judge*

Richmond
Elliott, Brady Gifford *judge*

San Antonio
Duncan, Sarah Baker *judge*
Garza, Emilio M(iller) *federal judge*
Hardberger, Phillip Duane *judge, lawyer, journalist*
King, Ronald Baker *federal judge*
†Prado, Edward Charles *federal judge*

Sherman
Brown, Paul Neeley *federal judge*

Temple
Clawson, James F., Jr., *judge, mediator, arbitrator*
Skelton, Byron George *former federal judge*

Tyler
Guthrie, Judith K. *federal judge*
McKee, Harry W. *federal judge*
Parker, Robert M. *federal judge*
Steger, William Merritt *federal judge*

Victoria
Rainey, John David *federal judge*

UTAH

Provo
Schofield, Anthony Wayne *judge*

Salt Lake City
Anderson, Stephen Hale *federal judge*
Clark, Glen Edward *judge*
Durham, Christine Meaders *state supreme court chief justice*
Durrant, Matthew B. *state supreme court justice*
Greene, John Thomas *judge*
Jenkins, Bruce Sterling *federal judge*
McKay, Monroe Gunn *federal judge*
Murphy, Michael R. *federal judge*
Rigtrup, Kenneth *state judge, arbitrator, mediator*
Sam, David *federal judge*

VERMONT

Brattleboro
†Murtha, J. Garvan *federal judge*
Oakes, James L. *federal judge*

Hyde Park
Fitzpatrick, Philip J. *probate judge, retired lawyer*

Montpelier
Dooley, John Augustine, III, *state supreme court justice*
Gibson, Ernest Willard, III, *retired state supreme court justice*
Johnson, Denise Reinka *state supreme court justice*

Waterbury Center
Amestoy, Jeffrey Lee *state supreme court chief justice*

Woodstock
Billings, Franklin Swift, Jr., *federal judge*

VIRGINIA

Abingdon
Jones, James Parker *federal judge*
Widener, Hiram Emory, Jr., *judge*
Williams, Glen Morgan *federal judge*

Alexandria
Bostetter, Martin V. B., Jr., *bankruptcy court judge*
Luttig, J. Michael *federal judge*

Charlottesville
Crigler, B. Waugh *US magistrate judge*
Hogshire, Edward Leigh *judge*
Wilkinson, James Harvie, III, *federal judge*

Chesterfield
Davis, Bonnie Christell *judge*

Covington
Stephenson, Roscoe Bolar, Jr., *state supreme court justice*

Fairfax
Stitt, David Tillman *judge*
Williams, Marcus Doyle *judge*

Falls Church
Barton, Robert Leroy, Jr., *judge, educator*
Cooper, Jean Saralee *judge*

Fredericksburg
Brown, Harold Eugene *retired magistrate*

King George
Revercomb, Horace Austin, III, *judge*

Lynchburg
Burnette, Ralph Edwin, Jr., *judge*
†Harris, Dale Hutter *judge, lecturer*
Moon, Norman K. *judge*

Manassas
Van Broekhoven, Rollin Adrian *federal judge*

Mc Lean
Anthony, Joan Caton *administrative judge*

Norfolk
Adams, David Huntington *judge*
Bonney, Hal James, Jr., *federal judge*
Clarke, J. Calvitt, Jr., *federal judge*
Jackson, Raymond A. *federal judge*
Miller, Tommy Eugene *federal judge*
Morgan, Henry Coke, Jr., *judge*
Prince, William Taliaferro *retired federal judge*

Richmond
Bickerstaff, Patsy Anne *judge, writer, poet*
Carrico, Harry Lee *retired judge*
Compton, Asbury Christian *state supreme court justice*
Gregory, Roger Lee *federal judge*
Hassell, Leroy Rountree, Sr., *state supreme court chief justice*
Kinser, Cynthia D. *state supreme court justice*
Lacy, Elizabeth Bermingham *state supreme court justice*
Lemons, Donald W. *state supreme court justice*
Poff, Richard Harding *retired state supreme court justice*
Tice, Douglas Oscar, Jr., *federal bankruptcy judge*
Williams, Karen Johnson *federal judge*
Williams, Richard Leroy *federal judge*

Roanoke
Turk, James Clinton *federal judge*

Salem
Koontz, Lawrence L., Jr., *state supreme court justice*
Pearson, Henry Clyde *retired judge*

Virginia Beach
Keenan, Barbara Milano *judge*

WASHINGTON

Bellevue
Andersen, James A. *retired state supreme court justice*

Ephrata
Fitterer, Richard Clarence *judge*

Everett
Bowden, George Newton *judge*

Mercer Island
†Noe, James Alva *retired judge*

Olympia
Alexander, Gerry L. *state supreme court chief justice*
Bridge, Bobbe J. *state supreme court justice*
Guy, Richard P. *retired state supreme court justice*
Ireland, Faith *state supreme court justice*
Johnson, Charles William *state supreme court justice*
Madsen, Barbara A *state supreme court justice*
Sanders, Richard Browning *judge*
Smith, Charles Z. *retired state supreme court justice*

Seattle
Beezer, Robert Renaut *federal judge*
Bladen, Edwin Mark *lawyer, judge*
Dimmick, Carolyn Reaber *federal judge*
Farris, Jerome Edward *judge*
Fletcher, Betty Binns *judge*
Gibson, John Eric *judge*
Gould, Ronald Murray *federal judge*
Mc Govern, Walter T. *federal judge*
Rothstein, Barbara Jacobs *federal judge*
Tallman, Richard C. *federal judge, lawyer*
Weinberg, John Lee *federal judge*
Wright, Eugene Allen *federal judge*
Zilly, Thomas Samuel *federal judge*

Spokane
Imbrogno, Cynthia *magistrate judge*
Murphy, James Michael *retired judge, mediator, arbitrator*
Van Sickle, Frederick L. *federal judge*
Whaley, Robert Hamilton *judge*

Tacoma
Arnold, J. Kelley *U.S. magistrate judge*
Bryan, Robert J. *federal judge*

Tukwila
Talmadge, Philip Albert *former state supreme court justice, former state senator*

Vancouver
Harris, Robert L(ee) *judge*

Yakima
Boyd, Lauri Louise *lawyer, judge*
McDonald, Alan Angus *federal judge*
Suko, Lonny Ray *judge*

WEST VIRGINIA

Charleston
Albright, Joseph P. *state supreme court justice*
Brewer, Lewis Gordon *judge, lawyer, educator*
Davis, Robin Jean *state supreme court justice*
Haden, Charles Harold, II, *federal judge*
King, Robert Bruce *federal judge*
Marland, Melissa Kaye *judge*
Maynard, Elliott *state supreme court justice*
McGraw, Warren Randolph *state supreme court justice*
Michael, M. Blane *federal judge*
Stanley, Mary Elizabeth *judge*
Starcher, Larry Victor *state supreme court chief justice*
Wilson, Robert Bryan *judge*

Elkins
Maxwell, Robert Earl *federal judge*

Martinsburg
Wilkes, Christopher Comas *judge*

Wheeling
†Recht, Arthur *former state supreme court justice*

WISCONSIN

Appleton
Froehlich, Harold Vernon *judge, former congressman*

Madison
Abrahamson, Shirley Schlanger *state supreme court chief justice*
Bablitch, William A. *state supreme court justice*
Bartell, Angela Gina Baldi *judge*
Bradley, Ann Walsh *state supreme court justice*
Crocker, Stephen L. *federal magistrate judge*
Deininger, David George *judge*
†Foust, Charles William *judge*
Heffernan, Nathan Stewart *retired state supreme court chief justice*
Martin, Robert David *judge, educator*
Shabaz, John C. *judge*
Sykes, Diane S. *state supreme court justice*
Wilcox, Jon P. *state supreme court justice*

Milwaukee
Adelman, Lynn *federal judge*
Evans, Terence Thomas *federal judge*
Goodstein, Aaron E. *federal magistrate judge*
Shapiro, James Edward *judge*
Stadtmueller, Joseph Peter *federal judge*

WYOMING

Cheyenne
Brimmer, Clarence Addison *federal judge*
Brorby, Wade *federal judge*
Golden, T. Michael *state supreme court justice*
Hill, William U. *state supreme court chief justice*
Kite, Marilyn S. *state supreme court justice, lawyer*
Lehman, Larry L. *state supreme court justice*
O'Brien, Terrence Leo *federal judge*
Voigt, Barton R. *state supreme court justice*

Cody
Patrick, H. Hunter *judge*

Yellowstone National Park
Cole, Stephen E. *magistrate judge*

TERRITORIES OF THE UNITED STATES

GUAM

Hagatna
†Maraman, Katherine Ann *judge*

PUERTO RICO

San Juan
Acosta, Raymond Luis *federal judge*
Andreu-Garcia, Jose Antonio *territory supreme court chief justice*
Casellas, Salvador E. *judge*
Castellanos, Jesus Antonio *U.S. magistrate judge*
†Dominguez, Daniel R. *judge*
Fusté, José Antonio *federal judge*
Fuster, Jaime B. *supreme court justice*
Hernandez-Denton, Federico *supreme court justice*
Merly, Miriam Naveira *state supreme court justice*
Rebollo-Lopez, Francisco *state supreme court justice*
Rivera Perez, Efrain E. *state supreme court justice*

VIRGIN ISLANDS

Charlotte Amalie
Barnard, Geoffrey W. *magistrate judge*

Christiansted
Finch, Raymond Lawrence *chief judge*
Resnick, Jeffrey Lance *federal magistrate judge*

St Croix
Moore, Thomas Kail *magistrate district court judge*

CANADA

ALBERTA

Edmonton
Fraser, Catherine Anne *Canadian chief justice*
Stevenson, William Alexander *retired justice of Supreme Court of Canada*

BRITISH COLUMBIA

Vancouver
de Weerdt, Mark Murray *retired judge*
Lysyk, Kenneth Martin *judge*

NEW BRUNSWICK

Fredericton
Strange, Henry Hazen *judge*

Westfield
Logan, Rodman Emmason *retired jurist*

NOVA SCOTIA

Halifax
Glube, Constance Rachelle *Canadian chief justice*

ONTARIO

Bracebridge
Evans, John David Daniel *judge*

Ottawa
Décary, Robert *judge*
Gonthier, Charles Doherty *Canadian supreme court justice*
Heald, Darrel Verner *retired Canadian federal judge*
Lamer, Antonio *retired Canadian supreme court chief justice*
MacKay, William Andrew *judge*
Major, John Charles *judge*
Margeson, Theodore Earl *judge*
McLachlin, Beverley *Canadian supreme court chief justice*
Strayer, Barry Lee *federal judge*

Toronto
Boland, Janet Lang *judge*
Harris, Sydney Malcolm *retired judge*
McMurtry, R. Roy *chief justice*

QUEBEC

Montreal
Bisson, Claude *retired chief justice of Quebec*
Gold, Alan B. *former Canadian chief justice*
Rothman, Melvin L. *judge*

Quebec
L'Heureux-Dubé, Claire *judge*

SASKATCHEWAN

Regina
Bayda, Edward Dmytro *judge*

NETHERLANDS

The Hague
Aldrich, George Hoover *judge, arbitrator*
Allison, Richard Clark *judge*

ADDRESS UNPUBLISHED

Abbott, Bob *state supreme court justice*
Albritton, William Harold, III, *federal judge*
Altenbernd, Chris W. *judge*
Amundson, Robert A. *state supreme court justice*
Austin, John DeLong *judge*
Baca, Joseph Francis *retired judge*
Barrett, James Emmett *retired judge*
Bauer, Fred L. *judge, lawyer, accountant, arbitration*
Beisner, Ralph Andrew *judge*
Bellacosa, Joseph W. *retired state supreme court justice*
Bertelsman, William Odis *federal judge*
†Blake, Stanford *judge, lawyer*
Boren, Roger W. *judge*
Brackett, Colquitt Prater, Jr., *judge, lawyer*
Brown, Michael John *retired judge*
Brown, Robert Laidlaw *state supreme court justice*
Buckley, James Lane *retired judge*
Butterfield, G. K., Jr., *former state supreme court justice*
Callow, Keith McLean *judge*
Callow, William Grant *retired judge*
Campbell, John M. *judge*
Campbell, Todd J. *judge*
Campbell, Vincent Bernard *judge, lawyer*
Castagna, William John *federal judge*
Ceci, Louis J. *former state supreme court justice*
Clark, Thomas Alonzo *retired federal judge*
Cochran, George Moffett *retired judge*
Coffey, John Louis *judge*
Cohn, Avern Levin *district judge*
Colaianni, Joseph Vincent *judge*
Compton, Allen T. *retired state supreme court justice*
Cook, Julian Abele, Jr., *federal judge*
Cyr, Conrad Keefe *federal judge*
Dacey, Kathleen Ryan *judge*
Daugherty, Frederick Alvin *federal judge*
Davis, Marguerite Herr *judge*
Day, Roland Bernard *retired chief justice state supreme court*
Dela Cruz, Jose Santos *retired state supreme court justice*
Eaton, Joe Oscar *federal judge*
Engel, Albert Joseph *retired federal judge*
Enoch, Craig Trively *state supreme court justice*
Epstein, Judith Ann *judge*
Fahrnbruch, Dale E. *retired state supreme court justice*
Fay, Peter Thorp *judge*
†Fecteau, Francis Roger *judge*
Fisk, Merlin Edgar *judge*
Flynn, Peter Anthony *judge*
Foster, Robert Lawson *retired judge, deacon*
Freeman, Charles E. *state supreme court justice*
Gardner, Anne Lancaster *judge*
Garibaldi, Marie Louise *former state supreme court justice*
Gillette, W. Michael *state supreme court justice*
Goetz, Clarence Edward *retired judge, retired chief magistrate judge*
Goldstein, Debra Holly *judge*
Gorence, Patricia Josetta *judge*
†Grant, Isabella Horton *retired judge*
Griffin, Robert Paul *former United States senator, state supreme court justice*
Hamblen, Lapsley Walker, Jr., *judge*
Hankinson, Deborah G. *former state supreme court justice*
Harding, Major Best *former state supreme court chief justice*
†Harris, Darlene *judge, lawyer, county legislator*
Harrison, Moses W., II, *state supreme court chief justice*
Hawkins, Michael Daly *federal judge*
Hayek, Carolyn Jean *retired judge*
Hellerstein, Alvin Kenneth *judge*
Hightower, Jack English *former state supreme court justice, congressman*
Hodge, Verne Antonio *retired chief judge*
Hogan, Thomas Francis *federal judge*
Howard, Alex T., Jr., *federal judge*
Howe, Richard Cuddy *state supreme court justice*
Hunt, William E., Sr., *retired state supreme court justice*
Hunter, Elmo Bolton *federal judge*
Joiner, Charles Wycliffe *judge*
Jones, Phyllis Gene *judge*
Kauger, Yvonne *state supreme court justice*
Kenworthy, William Eugene *judge*
Kilbride, Thomas L. *judge*
Krupansky, Blanche *retired judge*
Latham, Joseph William *judge*
Laycraft, James Herbert *retired judge*
Lee, Dan M. *retired state supreme court chief justice*
Leeson, Susan M. *former state supreme court judge*
Lemmon, Harry Thomas *retired state supreme court justice*
Linn, Richard *federal judge*
Lively, Pierce *federal judge*
Lockett, Tyler Charles *retired state supreme court justice*
Magnuson, Paul Arthur *federal judge*
Marcus, Walter F., Jr., *retired state supreme court justice*

Matthews, Warren Wayne *state supreme court justice*
McClure, Ann Crawford *judge, lawyer*
McCown, Hale *retired judge*
McGuire, Robert C. *retired federal bankruptcy judge*
McKee, Roger Curtis *retired federal judge*
Metzner, Charles Miller *federal judge*
Moeller, James *retired state supreme court justice*
Moore, Stephen Edward *judge*
Murray, Florence Kerins *retired state supreme court justice*
Mydland, Gordon James *judge*
Nangle, John Francis *federal judge*
Nesbit, Phyllis Schneider *judge*
Neuman, Linda Kinney *retired state supreme court justice*
Newbern, William David *retired state supreme court justice*
Newman, Theodore Roosevelt, Jr., *judge*
O'Connor, Michol *judge*
Papadakos, Nicholas Peter *retired state supreme court justice*
Payne, Mary Libby *retired judge*
†Pokras, Sheila Frances *retired judge*
Porter, James Morris *retired judge*
Prager, David *retired state supreme court chief justice*
Prather, Lenore Loving *former state supreme court chief justice*
Pusateri, James Anthony *judge*
Quillen, William Tatem *retired judge, lawyer, educator*
†Ra'anan, Michael Yehuda *judge*
Rabin, Gilbert *judge, lawyer*
Raffalli, Henri Christian *retired commissioner and administrative law judge, educator, criminologist*
Ramil, Mario R. *retired state supreme court justice*
Reinhardt, Stephen Roy *federal judge*
Rice, Walter Herbert *federal judge*
Ross, Donald Roe *federal judge*
Russon, Leonard H. *state supreme court justice*
†Schade, George August, Jr., *judge*
Schroeder, Gerald Frank *state supreme court vice chief justice*
Schultz, Louis William *retired judge*
Senechal, Alice R. *judge, lawyer*
Shaw, Leander Jerry, Jr., *retired state supreme court justice*
Sheedy, Patrick Thomas *judge*
Shubb, William Barnet *judge*
Silberman, Laurence Hirsch *federal judge*
Simms, Robert D. *former state supreme court justice*
Sinclair, Virgil Lee, Jr., *judge, writer*
Sognier, John Woodward *retired judge*
Souter, David Hackett *United States supreme court justice*
Stahl, Madonna *retired judge*
Staker, Robert Jackson *judge*
Stamos, John James *judge*
Stanton, Louis Lee *federal judge*
Sweet, Robert Workman *federal judge*
Tacha, Deanell Reece *federal judge*
Trout, Linda Copple *state supreme court chief justice*
Utter, Robert French *retired judge*
Waldon, Alton Ronald, Jr., *judge*
Walsh, Joseph Thomas *state supreme court justice*
Wellford, Harry Walker *retired federal judge*
†White, Helene Nita *federal judge*
White, Renee Allyn *judge*
Wicker, Thomas Carey, Jr., *retired judge*
Williams, Spencer Mortimer *federal judge*
Wood, Diane Pamela *judge*
Young, C. Clifton *former state supreme court justice*
Zappala, Stephen A. *state supreme court justice*
Zobel, Hiller Bellin *retired judge, writer*

LAW: LAW PRACTICE AND ADMINISTRATION

UNITED STATES

ALABAMA

Andalusia
Fuller, William Sidney *lawyer*
†Lanier, Grady Oliver, III, *lawyer*

Anniston
Comfort, Kenneth A. *court official*
Klinefelter, James Louis *lawyer*

Auburn
Samford, Thomas Drake, III, *lawyer*

Bay Minette
Granade, Fred King *lawyer*

Birmingham
Albritton, William Harold, IV, *lawyer*
Avant, Grady, Jr., *lawyer*
Baker, David Remember *lawyer*
Balch, Samuel Eason *lawyer*
Bird, John Commons *arbitrator, educator*
Blan, Ollie Lionel, Jr., *retired lawyer*
Boardman, Mark Seymour *lawyer*
Brooke, William Wade *business executive, lawyer*
Brown, Ephraim Taylor, Jr., *lawyer*
Brown, Stephen Edward *lawyer*
†Carmody, Richard Patrick *lawyer*
Carruthers, Thomas Neely *lawyer*
Christ, Chris Steve *lawyer*

†Christian, Thomas William *lawyer*
Cicio, Anthony Lee *lawyer*
Cole, Charles DuBose, II, *law educator*
Coleman, Brittin Turner *lawyer*
Coleman, John James, III, *lawyer, educator*
Cook, Ralph D. *lawyer, retired state supreme court justice*
Cooper, Jerome A. *lawyer*
Cooper, N. Lee *lawyer*
Cullen, William Zachary *lawyer*
Davis, Julian Mason, Jr., *lawyer*
†Denaburg, Charles L(eon) *lawyer*
Denson, William Frank, III, *lawyer*
†Dobbs, Carney H. *retired lawyer, retired insurance company executive*
†Donahue, Timothy Patrick *lawyer*
Farley, Joseph McConnell *lawyer*
†Ferguson, Harold Laverne, Jr., *lawyer*
Foster, Arthur Key, Jr., *retired lawyer*
Friend, Edward Malcolm, III, *lawyer, educator*
Furman, Howard *mediator, arbitrator, lawyer*
†Gale, Fournier Joseph, III, *lawyer*
Gamble, Joseph Graham, Jr., *lawyer*
Garner, Robert Edward Lee *lawyer*
Givhan, Robert Marcus *lawyer*
†Haskell, Wyatt Rushton *lawyer*
Hinton, James Forrest, Jr., *lawyer*
Howell, William Ashley, III, *lawyer*
Jackson, Keith *law educator*
Kracke, Robert Russell *lawyer*
Lacy, Alexander Shelton *lawyer*
†Langum, David John *law educator, historian*
Logan, J. Patrick *lawyer*
Long, Thad Gladden *lawyer*
Martin, Arthur Lee, Jr., *lawyer*
Mc Millan, George Duncan Hastie, Jr., *lawyer, former state official*
McWhorter, Hobart Amory, Jr., *lawyer*
Mills, William Hayes *lawyer*
Molen, John Klauminzer *lawyer*
†Nelson, Leonard John, III, *lawyer, educator*
Nettles, Bert Sheffield *lawyer*
Newton, Alexander Worthy *lawyer*
Norris, Robert Wheeler *military officer*
North, James Little *lawyer*
Palmer, Robert Leslie *lawyer*
Redden, Lawrence Drew *lawyer*
Rogers, Ernest Mabry *lawyer*
Rotch, James E. *lawyer*
Rountree, Asa *lawyer*
Sansbury, Michael Todd *lawyer*
Selfe, Edward Milton *lawyer*
†Shanks, William Ennis, Jr., *lawyer*
†Smith, Carol Ann *lawyer*
Stabler, Lewis Vastine, Jr., *lawyer*
†Stewart, Donald W. *lawyer*
Stewart, Joseph Grier *lawyer*
Theibert, Richard Wilder *lawyer, educator*
Thompson, Charles Amos *lawyer*
†Trimmier, Charles Stephen, Jr., *lawyer*
Vinson, Laurence Duncan, Jr., *lawyer*
Weeks, Arthur Andrew *lawyer, law educator*
†Whiteside, David Powers, Jr., *lawyer*
Wilson, James Charles, Jr., *lawyer*
†Wright, Allison Marshall *lawyer*
Wrinkle, John Newton *lawyer*
†Wyatt, Charles Herbert, Jr., *lawyer*

Clanton
Jackson, John Hollis, Jr., *lawyer*

Cullman
Poston, Beverly Paschal *lawyer*

Dadeville
Adair, Charles Robert, Jr., *lawyer*

Decatur
Belser, Howard McGriff, Jr., *lawyer*
Caddell, John A. *lawyer*

Demopolis
Dinning, Woodford Wyndham, Jr., *lawyer*
Lloyd, Hugh Adams *lawyer*

Dothan
†Huskey, Dow Thobern *lawyer*

Eufaula
Twitchell, E(rvin) Eugene *lawyer*

Florence
Schuessler, Cindy Sandlin *lawyer, judge*

Foley
Leatherbury, Gregory Luce, Jr., *lawyer*

Gadsden
Cornett, Bradley Williams *lawyer*

Huntsville
Baxter, James Thomas, III, *lawyer*
†Durnya, Louis Richard *lawyer*
Gabig, Jerome S., Jr., *lawyer*
Huckaby, Gary Carlton *lawyer*
Richardson, Patrick William *lawyer*
†Vargo, Robert Frank *lawyer*

Mobile
Armbrecht, William Henry, III, *retired lawyer*
Braswell, Louis Erskine *lawyer*
Brock, Glen Porter, Jr., *lawyer*
Coley, F(ranklin) Luke, Jr., *lawyer*
Finkbohner, George Wheeler, Jr., *lawyer*
Graddick, Charles Allen *lawyer*
Harris, Benjamin Harte, Jr., *lawyer*
Helmsing, Frederick George *lawyer*
Holland, Lyman Faith, Jr., *lawyer*
Holmes, Broox Garrett *lawyer*
Johnston, Neil Chunn *lawyer*
†Meigs, Walter Ralph *lawyer, dry dock and shipbuilding company executive*
†Moore, Richard Wayne *prosecutor*
Murchison, David Roderick *lawyer*
Peebles, E(mory) B(ush), III, *lawyer*
†Pennington, Al *lawyer*
Philips, Abe L., Jr., *lawyer*

PROFESSIONAL INDEX 6537 LAW: LAW PRACTICE AND ADMINISTRATION

Roedder, William Chapman, Jr., *lawyer*
†Tidwell, William C., III, *lawyer*
Vulevich, Edward, Jr., *prosecutor*
Waldrop, Norman Erskine, Jr., *lawyer*

Montgomery
Byars, Walter Ryland, Jr., *lawyer*
†Carter, Gordon Thomas *lawyer*
†Dees, Morris Seligman, Jr., *lawyer*
Ely, Robert Eugene *lawyer, author, educator*
Hamner, Reginald Turner *lawyer*
Hester, Douglas Benjamin *lawyer, federal official*
†Honey, William Chipman *lawyer, educator*
Kloess, Lawrence Herman, Jr., *retired lawyer*
Laurie, Robin Garrett *lawyer*
Lawson, Thomas Seay, Jr., *lawyer*
Leslie, Henry Arthur *lawyer, retired banker*
Lewis, Joseph Brady (Jay Lewis) *lawyer*
McFadden, Frank Hampton *lawyer, business executive, former judge*
Nachman, Merton Roland, Jr., *lawyer*
Prestwood, Alvin Tennyson *lawyer*
Salmon, Joseph Thaddeus *lawyer*
Smith, Maury Drane *lawyer*
†Stakely, Charles Averett *lawyer*
Volz, Charles Harvie, Jr., *lawyer*
Wood, James Jerry *lawyer*

Moulton
Dutton, Mark Anthony *lawyer*

Northport
Allen, Randy Lee *lawyer*

Opelika
†Hand, Benny Charles, Jr., *lawyer, judge*
Samford, Yetta Glenn, Jr., *lawyer, director*

Orange Beach
Adams, Daniel Fenton *law educator*
Loveless, Ralph Peyton *lawyer*

Owens Cross Roads
Williams, Lowell Craig *lawyer, employee relations executive*

Sheffield
Hamby, Gene Malcolm, Jr., *lawyer*

Tuscaloosa
Cook, Camille Wright *retired law educator*
†Filler, Daniel M. *law educator*
†Hoff, Timothy *law educator, priest*
†Hubbard, Perry *lawyer, educator*
Williams, Roger Courtland *lawyer*

Tuscumbia
†Munsey, Stanley Edward *lawyer*

Woodstock
†Downs, Bernard Boozer, Jr., *lawyer*

ALASKA

Anchorage
†Allingham, Lynn Marie *lawyer*
Anderson, Kathleen Gay *mediator, hearing officer, arbitrator, trainer*
†Bankston, William Marcus *lawyer*
Bond, Marc Douglas *lawyer*
Breckberg, Robert Lee *lawyer*
†Brown, Harold MacVane *lawyer*
Butler, Rex Lamont *lawyer*
Cantor, James Elliot *lawyer*
De Lisio, Stephen Scott *lawyer, director, pastor*
Dickson, Robert Jay *lawyer*
Ealy, Jonathan Bruce *lawyer*
Ebell, C(ecil) Walter *lawyer*
†Feldman, Jeffrey Marc *lawyer*
Flynn, Charles P. *lawyer*
Fortier, Samuel John *lawyer*
Hughes, Mary Katherine *lawyer*
Jones, Thomas Brooks *lawyer, educator*
Metzger, Yale Hyder *lawyer, educator*
Nosek, Francis John *lawyer, diplomat*
†Oesting, David W. *lawyer*
Owens, Robert Patrick *lawyer*
†Pfiffner, Frank Albert *lawyer*
†Richmond, Robert Lawrence *lawyer*
Roberts, John Derham *lawyer*
Ross, Wayne Anthony *lawyer*
†Sneed, Spencer Craig *lawyer*
†Walther, Dale Jay *lawyer*
Weinig, Richard Arthur *lawyer*
†Willard-Jones, Donna C. *lawyer*
Wohlforth, Eric Evans *lawyer*

Bethel
Cooke, Christopher Robert *former state judge, lawyer*
McMahon, Craig Roger *lawyer*

Fairbanks
Schendel, William Burnett *lawyer*

Juneau
†Eastaugh, Frederick Orlebar *lawyer*
Kolkhorst, Kathryn Mackay *lawyer*
Sonneman, Joseph Abram *lawyer, researcher, mediator, photographer*
†Tangen, Jon Paul *lawyer*

Kodiak
Jamin, Matthew Daniel *lawyer, magistrate judge*
Ott, Andrew Eduard *lawyer*

Nondalton
Gay, Sarah Elizabeth *lawyer*

ARIZONA

Eloy
O'Leary, Thomas Michael *lawyer*

Flagstaff
Cowser, Danny Lee *lawyer, mental health specialist*
Gliege, John Gerhardt *lawyer*
Lacey, Henry Bernard *lawyer*
Stoops, Daniel J. *lawyer*

Kingman
Basinger, Richard Lee *lawyer*

Mesa
Gunderson, Brent Merrill *lawyer*

Paradise Valley
North, Gerald David William *lawyer*
Tubman, William Charles *lawyer*

Peoria
Engelhardt, Thomas Francis *lawyer, consultant*

Phoenix
Allen, Robert Eugene Barton *lawyer*
Alsentzer, William James, Jr., *lawyer*
†Andersen, Ronald Meredith *lawyer*
†Avilez, Victoria Marie *lawyer*
Bain, C. Randall *lawyer*
Baker, William Dunlap *lawyer*
Bakker, Thomas Gordon *lawyer*
Barclay, Steven Calder *lawyer*
Begam, Robert George *lawyer*
†Beshears, Robert Gene *lawyer*
Bivens, Donald Wayne *lawyer, judge*
Blanchard, Charles Alan *lawyer, former state senator*
Bodney, David Jeremy *lawyer*
†Bouma, John Jacob *lawyer*
†Brewer, Stephanie L. *lawyer*
Burke, Timothy John *lawyer*
Case, David Leon *lawyer*
Chanen, Steven Robert *lawyer*
Chenal, Thomas Kevin *lawyer*
Coghill, William Thomas, Jr., *retired lawyer*
Cohen, Jon Stephan *lawyer*
Cole, George Thomas *lawyer*
Coleman, George Joseph, III, (Jay Coleman) *lawyer*
†Comus, Louis Francis, Jr., *lawyer*
Condo, James Robert *lawyer*
Conrad, John Regis *lawyer, engineering executive, consultant*
Cooledge, Richard Calvin *lawyer*
Coppersmith, Sam *lawyer*
Crockett, Clyll Webb *lawyer*
Cunningham, James Patrick *lawyer*
†Cure, Carol Campbell *lawyer*
Curzon, Thomas Henry *lawyer*
Davies, David George *lawyer, educator*
†Dawson, John Joseph *lawyer*
Derouin, James Gilbert *lawyer*
Dinner, Janice Marie *lawyer*
Dunipace, Ian Douglas *lawyer*
Ehmann, Anthony Valentine *lawyer*
Esahak, George Michael *lawyer*
Everett, James Joseph *lawyer*
Feinstein, Allen Lewis *lawyer*
Flickinger, Don Jacob *patent agent*
Florence, Henry John *lawyer*
Gaffney, Donald Lee *lawyer*
Galbut, Martin Richard *lawyer*
†Gallagher, Michael L. *lawyer*
Gerber, Rudolph Joseph *lawyer, educator*
Gilbert, Donald Roy *lawyer*
Gladner, Marc Stefan *lawyer*
Gomez, David Frederick *lawyer*
†Grant, Merwin Darwin *lawyer*
Griller, Gordon Moore *court administrator*
Halpern, Barry David *lawyer*
†Hammond, Larry Austin *lawyer*
Harris, Ray Kendall *lawyer*
Harrison, Mark Isaac *lawyer*
Hay, John Leonard *lawyer*
Hayden, William Robert *lawyer*
Henderson, James Forney *lawyer*
Hicks, William Albert, III, *lawyer*
Hienton, James Robert *lawyer*
Hiller, Neil Howard *lawyer*
†Hirsch, Steven A. *lawyer*
Hoecker, Thomas Ralph *lawyer*
Howard, William Matthew *arbitrator, writer, lawyer*
Huntwork, James Roden *lawyer*
Inman, William Peter *lawyer*
Jacobson, Edward (Julian Edward Jacobson) *lawyer*
†Jacques, Raoul Thomas *lawyer*
James, Charles E., Jr., *lawyer*
Jirauch, Charles W. *lawyer*
Johnston, Logan Truax, III, *lawyer*
†Kasarjian, Levon, Jr., *lawyer*
†Klahr, Gary Peter *retired lawyer*
Klausner, Jack Daniel *lawyer*
†Klein, R. Kent *lawyer*
Knoller, Guy David *lawyer*
Koester, Berthold Karl *lawyer, law educator, retired honorary German consul*
Kurn, Neal *lawyer*
Lawrence, Steven Thomas *lawyer*
†Leshner, Stephen I. *lawyer*
†Levetown, Robert Alexander *lawyer*
Lubin, Stanley *lawyer*
†Lyons, George Harris *lawyer*
Martori, Joseph Peter *lawyer*
Mc Clennen, Louis *lawyer, educator*
†McCormick, Kathryn Ellen *prosecutor*
McRae, Hamilton Eugene, III, *lawyer*
Merritt, Nancy-Jo *lawyer*
Meschkow, Jordan M. *lawyer*
Meyers, Howard Craig *lawyer*
Olsen, Alfred Jon *lawyer*
Olson, Kevin Lory *lawyer*
O'Steen, Van *lawyer*
Petitti, Michael Joseph, Jr., *lawyer*
†Phillips, James Harold *lawyer*
Pidgeon, Steven D. *lawyer*
Pietzsch, Michael Edward *lawyer*
Platt, Warren E. *lawyer*
Plattner, Richard Serber *lawyer*
Pogson, Stephen Walter *lawyer*
Preston, Bruce Marshall *lawyer, educator*
Price, Charles Steven *lawyer*
Rathwell, Peter John *lawyer*
Refo, Patricia Lee *lawyer*
†Riikola, Michael Edward *lawyer*
Rivera, Jose de Jesus *lawyer*
Rose, David L. *lawyer*
†Rose, Scott A. *lawyer*
Rosen, Sidney Marvin *lawyer*
Rudolph, Gilbert Lawrence *lawyer*
Ryan, D. Jay *lawyer*
Savage, Stephen Michael *lawyer*
†Schneider, Elizabeth Kelley *law librarian*
Sherk, Kenneth John *lawyer*
Silverman, Alan Henry *lawyer*
†Smith, Susan Kimsey *lawyer*
Song Ong, Roxanne Kay *lawyer, judge*
†Spencer, Roger Keith *lawyer*
†Squire, Bruce M. *lawyer*
†Sterns, Patricia Margaret *lawyer, consultant*
Storey, Lee A. *lawyer*
Storey, Norman C. *lawyer*
Swartz, Melvin Jay *lawyer, writer*
†Tennen, Leslie Irwin *lawyer, consultant, inventor*
Theobald, Scott M. *lawyer*
Thompson, Joel Erik *lawyer*
Thompson, Terence William *lawyer*
Thumma, Samuel Anderson *lawyer*
Tomback, Jay Loren *lawyer*
Torrens, Daniel *lawyer*
Udall, Calvin Hunt *lawyer*
Ulrich, Paul Graham *lawyer, writer, editor*
Walker, Richard K. *lawyer*
Wall, Donald Arthur *lawyer*
Wheeler, Steven M. *lawyer*
Whisler, James Steven *lawyer, mining and manufacturing executive*
Williams, Quinn Patrick *lawyer*
†Wirken, Charles William *lawyer*
Wolf, G. Van Velsor, Jr., *lawyer*

Prescott
Goodman, Mark N. *lawyer*
Gose, Richard Vernie *lawyer*
Madden, Paul Robert *lawyer, director*
†Perry, John Richard, Jr., *lawyer, mediator*

Rio Rico
Ryan, John Duncan *lawyer*

Scottsdale
Amrozowicz, Paul Douglas *lawyer, electrical engineer*
Berry, Charles Richard *lawyer*
†Case, Stephen Shevlin *lawyer*
Handy, Robert Maxwell *lawyer*
Hutchison, Stanley Philip *retired lawyer*
Jorden, Douglas Allen *lawyer, zoning hearing officer*
Krupp, Clarence William *lawyer, personnel and hospital administrator*
Lindgren, D(erbin) Kenneth, Jr., *retired lawyer*
Lowry, Edward Francis, Jr., *lawyer*
Marks, Merton Eleazer *lawyer, international arbitrator, mediator, consultant*
†Overgaard, Cordell Jersild *lawyer, business executive*
†Whittington, Thomas Lee *lawyer*

Sun City
Hauer, James Albert *lawyer*
Keesling, Karen Ruth *lawyer*
Treece, James Lyle *lawyer*

Sun City West
Vision, Blanche Stein *retired judge*

Surprise
Fennelly, Jane Corey *lawyer*
Lowe, Robert Charles *lawyer, banker*

Tempe
Bender, Paul *lawyer, educator*
Bucklin, Leonard Herbert *lawyer*
†Ching, Anthony Bartholomew *lawyer, educator, consultant*
†Furnish, Dale Beck *lawyer, educator*
Jones, Owen Donald *law educator*
Matheson, Alan Adams *law educator*
Moya, Patrick Robert *lawyer*
Schatzki, George *law educator*
Shimpock, Kathy Elizabeth *lawyer, writer*
†Sigler, Mary Elizabeth *law educator*
Spritzer, Ralph Simon *lawyer, educator*

Tucson
Bainton, Denise Marlene *lawyer*
Betteridge, Frances Carpenter *retired lawyer, mediator*
Blackman, Jeffrey William *lawyer*
Cope, Thom K. *lawyer*
Corey, Barry Martin *lawyer*
D'Antonio, James Joseph *lawyer*
Dobbs, Dan Byron *lawyer, educator*
†Dyer, James Harrison *lawyer*
Eckhardt, August Gottlieb *retired law educator*
Esposito, Joseph Louis *lawyer*
†Falbaum, Bertram Seymour *law educator, investigator*
Feldman, Stanley George *lawyer*
Fortman, Marvin *law educator, consultant*
Froman, Sandra Sue *lawyer*
Gantz, David Alfred *lawyer, university official*
Gonzales, Richard Joseph *lawyer*
Heaphy, John Merrill *lawyer*
Hirsh, Robert Joel *lawyer*
Hyams, Harold *lawyer*
†Isaak, G. Eugene *lawyer*
Jurkowitz, Daniel S. *lawyer, prosecutor, judge*
Kaucher, James William *lawyer*
Kimble, William Earl *lawyer*
Kitchen, Charles William *lawyer*
Kozolchyk, Boris *law educator, consultant*
Lesher, Stephen Harrison *lawyer*
Mc Donald, John Richard *lawyer*
†McDonough, Lawrence *lawyer*
McNamara, Patrick Robert *lawyer*
Meehan, Michael Joseph *lawyer*
Morrow, James Franklin *lawyer*
Pace, Thomas M. *lawyer*
Robinson, Bernard Leo *retired lawyer*
Ruth, Henry Swartley *retired lawyer*
†Samet, Dee-Dee *lawyer*
Schorr, S. L. *lawyer*
†Simmons, Sarah R. *lawyer*
Staubitz, Arthur Frederick *lawyer, healthcare products company executive*
Strong, John William *lawyer, educator*
Tindall, Robert Emmett *lawyer, educator*

Yuma
Hossler, David Joseph *lawyer, law educator*
Hunt, Gerald Wallace *lawyer*

ARKANSAS

Apo
Gordon, Carey Nathaniel *lawyer, federal agency administrator*

Bentonville
†Hyde, Thomas D. *lawyer*

Cherokee Village
Burke, Richard Kitchens *lawyer, educator*

Conway
Johnson, James Douglas (Jim Johnson) *lawyer*

Crossett
Hubbell, Billy James *lawyer*

El Dorado
†Wynne, William Joseph *lawyer*

Fayetteville
Bassett, Woodson William, Jr., *lawyer*
Epley, Lewis Everett, Jr., *lawyer*
Kester, Charles Melvin *lawyer*
†Nance, Cynthia Eleanor *law educator*
Pearson, Charles Thomas, Jr., *lawyer, director*
†Pettus, E. Lamar *lawyer*
Poore, Shannon Leigh *lawyer*
†Rhoads, Robert K. *lawyer, retail executive*

Fort Smith
†Karr, Charles *lawyer*

Harrison
Pinson, Jerry D. *lawyer*

Helena
Roscopf, Charles Buford *lawyer*

Jonesboro
†Deacon, John C. *lawyer*
Womack, Tom D. *lawyer*

Little Rock
Anderson, Philip Sidney *lawyer*
Bohannon, Charles Tad *lawyer*
Campbell, George Emerson *lawyer*
†Carpenter, Thomas Milton *lawyer*
Casey, Paula Jean *former prosecutor*
†Catlett, S. Graham *lawyer*
Cross, J. Bruce *lawyer*
Dillahunty, Wilbur Harris *lawyer*
Drummond, Winslow *lawyer*
Fogleman, John Albert *lawyer, retired judge*
Frank, Ben William *lawyer, administrator*
Griffin, William Mell, III, *lawyer*
Gunter, Russell Allen *lawyer*
Haley, John Harvey *lawyer*
†Hargis, David Michael *lawyer*
Haught, William Dixon *lawyer, writer*
†Hearne, Mary *retired legal secretary, artist*
†Heuer, Sam Tate *lawyer*
Jennings, Alston *lawyer*
Jones, Stephen Witsell *lawyer*
†Light, Robert Vann *lawyer*
Lipe, Linda Bon *lawyer*
Mackey, Diane Stoakes *lawyer*
Marshall, William Taylor *lawyer*
May, Ronald Alan *lawyer*
†Miller, Peter Alexander *lawyer*
Murphey, Arthur Gage, Jr., *law educator*
Nelson, Edward Sheffield *lawyer, former utility company executive*
†Scott, Isaac Alexander, Jr., *lawyer*
Sherman, William Farrar *lawyer, former state legislator*
†Simpson, James Marlon, Jr., *lawyer*
Smith, Anne Orsi *lawyer*
Stockburger, Jean Dawson *lawyer*
Thomas, Thorp *lawyer*
Witherspoon, Carolyn Brack *lawyer*
Wright, Robert Ross, III, *law educator*

Malvern
Dodd, Jerry Lee *lawyer*

Marion
Fogleman, John Nelson *lawyer*

Marked Tree
†Everett, Mike *lawyer*

Mena
Thrailkill, Daniel B. *lawyer*

Monticello
Ball, William Kenneth *lawyer*

Morrilton
†Denniston, Jeannie L. *lawyer*

Mountain Home
†Strother, Lane Howard *lawyer*

Newport
Thaxton, Marvin Dell *lawyer*

North Little Rock
Patty, Claibourne Watkins, Jr., *lawyer*

Pine Bluff
Jones, John Harris *lawyer*
Ramsay, Louis Lafayette, Jr., *lawyer, banker*
Strode, Joseph Arlin *lawyer*

Searcy
Hughes, Teresa Lee *lawyer, educator*
†Hughes, Thomas Morgan, III, *lawyer*

Warren
Claycomb, Hugh Murray *lawyer, author*

West Memphis
†Fogleman, Julian Barton *lawyer*

CALIFORNIA

Alameda
Stonehouse, James Adam *lawyer*

Alamo
Fleisher, Steven M. *lawyer*
Madden, Palmer Brown *lawyer*
†Thiessen, Brian David *lawyer*

Altadena
Montgomery, Cranston Parker *retired lawyer*

Anaheim Hills
Searle, Peter J. *lawyer*

Antioch
Richards, Gerald Thomas *lawyer, consultant, educator, writer*

Aptos
†Kehoe, Dennis Joseph *lawyer*

Arcadia
Gelber, Louise C(arp) *lawyer*
Mc Cormack, Francis Xavier *lawyer, former oil company executive*
†Morris, Gary Wayne *lawyer*

Atherton
Ferris, Robert Albert *lawyer, venture capitalist*

Bakersfield
Barmann, Bernard Charles, Sr., *lawyer*
Farr, G(ardner) Neil *retired lawyer*
Kind, Kenneth Wayne *lawyer, real estate broker*
Martin, George Francis *lawyer*

Belvedere Tiburon
†Allan, Walter Robert *lawyer*
Bremer, William Richard *lawyer*
Buell, Edward Rick, II, *lawyer*
Widman, Gary Lee *lawyer, former government official*

Berkeley
†Barnes, Thomas G. *law educator*
Barton, Babette B. *lawyer, educator*
Berring, Robert Charles, Jr., *law educator, law librarian, former dean*
Buxbaum, Richard M. *law educator, lawyer*
Choper, Jesse Herbert *law educator, university dean*
†Edelman, Lauren B. *law educator, sociologist, educator*
Eisenberg, Melvin A. *law educator*
Feeley, Malcolm McCollum *law educator, political scientist*
Frickey, Philip Paul *law educator*
Halbach, Edward Christian, Jr., *law educator, educator*
Haley, George Patrick *lawyer*
Kadish, Sanford Harold *law educator*
†Mason, Mary Ann *college program director, lawyer, computer consultant*
McNulty, John Kent *lawyer, educator*
Messinger, Sheldon L(eopold) *law educator*
Mishkin, Paul J. *lawyer, educator*
Moran, Rachel *lawyer, educator*
Ogg, Wilson Reid *lawyer, judge, poet, lyricist, curator, publisher, educator, philosopher, social scientist, parapsychologist*
†Pakter, Walter Jay *legal scholar and educator, aviation lawyer*
Post, Robert Charles *law educator*
Pyle, Walter K. *lawyer*
Rappaport, Stuart Ramon *lawyer*
†Reidhaar, Donald Laverne *lawyer*
Ross, Julia *lawyer*
Scheiber, Harry N. *law educator*
†Sorensen, Linda *lawyer*
Sparks, John Edward *lawyer*
†Weisselberg, Charles D. *law educator*
Woodhouse, Thomas Edwin *lawyer*
Zimring, Franklin E. *law educator, lawyer*

Beverly Hills
Amado, Honey Kessler *lawyer*
Anderson, Kenneth Allen *lawyer, hotel executive*
Bear, Jeffrey Lewis *lawyer*
Brickwood, Susan Callaghan *lawyer*
Brown, Hermione Kopp *lawyer*
Burns, Marvin Gerald *lawyer*
†Chanin, Jeffrey *lawyer*
Hogan, Steven L. *lawyer*
†Horowitz, Stephen Paul *lawyer*
Horwin, Leonard *retired lawyer*
Jaffe, F. Filmore *lawyer, retired judge*
Kite, Richard Lloyd *lawyer, real estate development company executive*
Ramer, Bruce M. *lawyer*
Rosky, Burton Seymour *lawyer*
Russell, Irwin Emanuel *lawyer*
Schaefer, Susan G. *lawyer*
†Schiff, Gunther Hans *lawyer*
†Sherwood, Arthur Lawrence *lawyer*

Shire, Harold Raymond *law educator, writer, scientist*
Sobelle, Richard E. *lawyer*
†Thompson, Richard Dickson *lawyer*
†Warren, Steve *lawyer*

Big Bear Lake
Prewoznik, Jerome Frank *lawyer*

Bonita
†Kline, Paul Conley *lawyer*

Burbank
Ajalat, Sol Peter *lawyer*
Braverman, Alan N. *lawyer*
†Lee, Paulette Wang *lawyer*
†Nevis, Tillam *lawyer*

Burlingame
Cotchett, Joseph Winters *lawyer, author*
Denten, Christopher Peter *lawyer*
Ocheltree, Richard Lawrence *lawyer, retired forest products company executive*

Calabasas
Grimwade, Richard Llewellyn *lawyer*
Tennen, Ken *lawyer*

California City
Friedl, Rick *lawyer, former academic administrator*

Calimesa
†McNulty, James Francis, Jr., *lawyer, industrial designer*

Camarillo
Lingl, James Peter *lawyer*

Cambria
Stotter, James, II, *lawyer, legal consultant*

Campbell
Beizer, Lance Kurt *lawyer*

Canoga Park
†Adams, Anne Claire *lawyer*

Carlsbad
Duringer, David Robert *lawyer*

Carmel
Robinson, John Minor *lawyer, retired business executive*

Carmichael
Halpenny, Diana Doris *lawyer*

Cathedral City
Paul, Vivian *lawyer*

Cerritos
Sarno, Maria Erlinda *lawyer, scientist*

Chatsworth
Klein, Jeffrey S. *lawyer, media executive*

Chico
Fuller, David Ralph *lawyer*
Lenzi, Albert James, Jr., *lawyer*

Chino
Determan, John David *lawyer*

Chino Hills
Pearson, April Virginia *lawyer*

Chula Vista
Santee, Dale William *lawyer, air force officer*

City Of Industry
Churchill, James Allen *lawyer*

Claremont
Ansell, Edward Orin *lawyer*
Ferguson, Cleve Robert *lawyer, educator*
Gray, Paul Bryan *lawyer, historian, arbitrator*

Coalinga
Frame, Ted Ronald *lawyer*

Concord
†Schwartz, Eric *lawyer*

Copperopolis
†Wooster, Kelly C. *lawyer*

Corona
Everett Nollkamper, Pamela Irene *legal management company executive, educator*

Coronado
†Adelson, Benedict James *retired lawyer*
Betts, Barbara Lang *lawyer, rancher, realtor*
†Heisner, John Richard *lawyer*
Plumb, Robert Thompson, II, *lawyer*

Costa Mesa
Anderson, Jon David *lawyer*
†Angell, Susan L. *lawyer*
Caldwell, Courtney Lynn *lawyer, real estate consultant*
†Connally, Michael W. *lawyer*
Currie, Robert Emil *lawyer*
Daniels, James Walter *lawyer*
Frieden, Clifford E. *lawyer*
Guilford, Andrew John *lawyer*
Hay, Howard Clinton *lawyer*
Jones, H(arold) Gilbert, Jr., *lawyer*
†Kramer, Kenneth Scott *lawyer*
†Marshall, Ellen Ruth *lawyer*
†Phelps, Aaron K(ay) *lawyer*
†Rose, I. Nelson *lawyer, educator*
Schaaf, Douglas Allan *lawyer*
Tanner, R. Marshall *lawyer*
Tennyson, Peter Joseph *lawyer*

Cotati
Robertson, William Abbott *arbitrator, mediator, lawyer*

Cupertino
Jelinch, Frank Anthony *lawyer*
Simon, Nancy Ruth *lawyer*
Svalya, Phillip Gordon *lawyer*

Cypress
Olschwang, Alan Paul *lawyer*

Danville
Candland, D. Stuart *lawyer*
†Raines, Richard Clifton *lawyer*

Darwin
Palazzo, Robert Paul *lawyer, accountant*

Davis
Bartosic, Florian *law educator, lawyer, arbitrator*
Bruch, Carol Sophie *lawyer, educator*
Chander, Anupam *lawyer*
Feeney, Floyd Fulton *legal educator*
Imwinkelried, Edward John *law educator*
Johnson, Kevin Raymond *law educator*
†Shimomura, Floyd Dudley *lawyer, educator*
Wydick, Richard Crews *lawyer, educator*

Del Mar
Seitman, John Michael *lawyer, arbitrator, mediator*

Downey
Duzey, Robert Lindsey *lawyer*
Schauf, Carolyn Jane *lawyer*
Tompkins, Dwight Edward *lawyer*

Downieville
Allen, Lawrence Richard *prosecutor*

East Palo Alto
Bates, William, III, *lawyer*
Furbush, David Malcolm *lawyer*

El Cajon
Graf, Sheryl Susan *lawyer*

El Centro
†Sutherland, Lowell Francis *lawyer*

El Cerrito
Garbarino, Joseph William *labor arbitrator, economics and business educator*

El Segundo
Gambaro, Ernest Umberto *lawyer, consultant, engineer*
†Hunter, Larry Dean *lawyer*
Muhlbach, Robert Arthur *lawyer*
†Pearce, Harry Jonathan *lawyer*
†Schimmenti, John Joseph *lawyer*
†Willis, Judy Ann *lawyer*
†Zucker, David Clark *lawyer*

Emeryville
†Blackburn, Robert Parker *lawyer*
Howe, Drayton Ford, Jr., *lawyer*
†Ostrach, Michael Sherwood *lawyer, business executive*

Encinitas
Forrester, Kevin Kreg *lawyer*
Nemeth, Valerie Ann *lawyer*
Wigmore, John Grant *lawyer*
Williams, Michael Edward *lawyer*

Encino
Levine, Thomas Jeffrey Pello *lawyer*
Smith, Selma Moidel *lawyer, composer*
†Weissman, I. Donald *lawyer*

Escondido
Godone-Maresca, Lillian *lawyer*
Mayer, James Hock *mediator, lawyer*

Eureka
†Clark, Dwight William *lawyer*

Fallbrook
Sorbello, Joseph Charles *retired lawyer*

Folsom
†Goodwin, James Jeffries *lawyer*

Foothill Ranch
Weiss, Sherman David *lawyer, consultant*

Foster City
†Jeffrey, John Orval *lawyer*
Lonnquist, George Eric *lawyer*

Fremont
Cummings, John Patrick *lawyer*
Kitta, John Noah *lawyer*

Fresno
Ewell, A. Ben, Jr., *lawyer, businessman*
Howe, Ronald Evans *lawyer, minister, small business owner*
Jamison, Daniel Oliver *lawyer*
Lambe, James Patrick *lawyer*
McGregor, John Joseph *lawyer*
Renberg, Michael Loren *lawyer*

Fullerton
†Ackerman, Richard Charles *lawyer, state legislator*
†Bush, William Merritt *lawyer*
Goldstein, Edward David *lawyer, former glass company executive*
Moerbeek, Stanley Leonard *lawyer*
Roberts, Mark Scott *lawyer*
†Smiley, Stanley Robert *lawyer*
Steinmeyer, Robert Jay *lawyer*
†Talmo, Ronald Victor *lawyer, law educator*

Glendale
†Davidson, Suzanne Mouron *lawyer*
†Fluharty, Jesse Ernest *lawyer*
Green, Norman Harry *lawyer*
Hoffman, Donald M. *lawyer*
Kazanjian, Phillip Carl *lawyer*
MacDonald, Kirk Stewart *lawyer*
Martinetti, Ronald Anthony *lawyer*
Polley, Terry Lee *lawyer*
Scott, A. Timothy *lawyer, business executive*
Toscano, Oscar Ernesto *lawyer*
†Young, George Walter *lawyer*

Gold River
Andrew, John Henry *lawyer, retail corporation executive, author*

Granada Hills
†Weitkamp, Fredrick John *lawyer*

Grass Valley
Bell, Joseph James *lawyer*
Hawkins, Richard Michael *lawyer*

Greenbrae
Bonapart, Alan David *lawyer*

Half Moon Bay
Lambert, Frederick William *lawyer, educator*

Hayward
Smith, John Kerwin *lawyer*
Stern, Ralph David *lawyer*

Hollywood
Gould, Julian Saul *lawyer*

Huntington Beach
Armstrong, Alan Leigh *lawyer*
Cook, Debbie *lawyer, councilman*
Jensen, Dennis Lowell *lawyer*
Nikas, Richard John *lawyer*

Imperial Beach
Merkin, William Leslie *retired lawyer*

Indian Wells
Criste, Virginia Spiegel *lawyer*
†Weinberg, Steven Jay *lawyer*

Indio
De Salva, Christopher Joseph *lawyer, consultant*

Inverness
†Ciani, Judith Elaine *retired lawyer*

Irvine
Bastiaanse, Gerard C. *lawyer*
Beard, Ronald Stratton *lawyer*
Black, William Rea *lawyer*
Clark, Karen Heath *lawyer*
Farrell, Teresa Joanning *lawyer*
†Goldstock, Barry Philip *lawyer*
Hensley, William Michael *lawyer*
Hilker, Walter Robert, Jr., *lawyer*
Hurst, Charles Wilson *lawyer*
Knobbe, Louis Joseph *lawyer, educator*
†Martens, Don Walter *lawyer*
Petrasich, John Moris *lawyer*
†Ristau, Kenneth Eugene, Jr., *lawyer*
†Shirley, Robert Bryce *lawyer*
Specter, Richard Bruce *lawyer*
Stone, Samuel Beckner *lawyer*
†Wertheim, Jay Philip *lawyer*
White, Alyssa Milman *lawyer, educator*
Wintrode, Ralph Charles *lawyer*

La Canada
Baker, Althea Ross *court hearing officer, lawyer, mediator, arbitrator, educator*

La Canada Flintridge
Costello, Francis William *lawyer*
Wallace, James Wendell *lawyer*

La Habra
†Hyslop, Richard Stewart *law educator*

La Jolla
Kirchheimer, Arthur E(dward) *lawyer, business executive*
Peterson, Paul Ames *lawyer, educator*
Shannahan, William Paul *lawyer*
Wilkins, Floyd, Jr., *retired lawyer, consultant*
†Wilson, Bonnie Jean *lawyer, educator, investor*
†ZoBell, Karl *lawyer*

La Palma
Kreeger, Margaret Ryan *lawyer*

Lafayette
Davies, Paul Lewis, Jr., *retired lawyer*
Michelsen, Diane *lawyer*

Laguna Hills
Beck, Gregory Michael *lawyer*
†Mathews, Stanton Terry *lawyer*
Reinglass, Michelle Annette *lawyer*
†Tuohey, Conrad Gravier *lawyer*

Laguna Niguel
McEvers, Duff Steven *lawyer*

Lake Forest
Ballard, Ronald Michael *lawyer, political consultant*

Lancaster
Bianchi, David Wayne *lawyer*

Larkspur
†Burke, Robert Thomas *lawyer*
Greenberg, Myron Silver *lawyer*
Ratner, David Louis *retired law educator*
†Saxe, Steven Louis *lawyer*

Monterey Park
†Singer-Frankes, Deborah *lawyer*

Morgan Hill
Foster, John Robert *lawyer*

Morro Bay
†Merzon, James Bert *lawyer*

Mountain View
†Bull, Howard Livingston *lawyer*
Pasahow, Lynn H(arold) *lawyer*
†Radlo, Edward John *lawyer, mathematician*

Napa
Kuntz, Charles Powers *lawyer*
Meyers, David W. *lawyer, writer, educator*
Snow, Tower Charles, Jr., *lawyer*

Newport Beach
Adams, William Gillette *lawyer*
Allen, Russell G. *lawyer*
Baskin, Scott David *lawyer*
†Brown, Ernest Christopher *lawyer, engineer*
Calcagnie, Kevin Frank *lawyer*
Cano, Kristin Maria *lawyer*
Carman, Ernest Day *lawyer*
Carmichael, David Richard *lawyer*
Cordova, Ron *lawyer*
Cranford, Steven L. *lawyer*
†Harlan, Nancy Margaret *lawyer*
Jeffers, Michael Bogue *lawyer*
Johnson, Thomas Webber, Jr., *lawyer*
Jones, Sheldon Atwell *lawyer*
†Lawless, William Burns *lawyer, retired judge, academic administrator*
Mallory, Frank Linus *lawyer*
Mandel, Maurice, II, *lawyer, educator, mediator*
†Matsen, Jeffrey Robert *lawyer*
Millar, Richard William, Jr., *lawyer*
Mortensen, Arvid LeGrande *lawyer*
†Otto, James Daniel *lawyer*
Pepe, Stephen Phillip *lawyer*
Phillips, Layn R. *lawyer*
Schiff, Laurie *lawyer*
Schilling, John Russell *lawyer, retail executive*
Schnapp, Roger Herbert *lawyer, consultant*
Schumacher, Stephen Joseph *lawyer, educator*
Wagner, John Leo *lawyer, former magistrate judge*
Weissbard, Samuel Held *lawyer*
Wentworth, Theodore Sumner *lawyer*
Wolf, Alan Steven *lawyer*

North Fork
Flanagan, James Henry, Jr., *lawyer, writer, business educator*

North Hollywood
Kreger, Melvin Joseph *lawyer*
Winogradsky, Steven *lawyer*
Zimring, Stuart David *lawyer*

Novato
Lewin, Werner Siegfried, Jr., *lawyer*

Oak Park
Schulner, Keith Alan *lawyer, business owner*
Vinson, William Theodore *lawyer, diversified corporation executive*

Oakland
Allen, Jeffrey Michael *lawyer*
†Anderson, Doris Elaine *lawyer*
†Bacon, Robert Dale *lawyer*
Bewley, Peter David *lawyer*
Bjork, Robert David, Jr., *lawyer*
Bryant, Arthur H. *lawyer*
†Buckley, Mike Clifford *lawyer*
Deming, Willis Riley *lawyer*
Drexel, Baron Jerome *lawyer*
†Johnson, Kenneth F. *lawyer*
Leslie, Robert Lorne *lawyer*
Lomhoff, Peter George *lawyer*
Loving, Deborah June Pierre *lawyer, real estate broker*
McCarthy, Steven Michael *lawyer*
†Miller, Kirk Edward *lawyer, health foundation executive*
Miller, Thomas Robbins *lawyer, publisher*
†Nelson, Luella Eline *lawyer*
O'Dwyer, Thomas Stephen *lawyer*
Quinby, William Albert *lawyer, mediator, arbitrator*
†Reese, Charles Woodrow, Jr., *lawyer*
Roster, Michael *lawyer*
†Rutherford, Constance Mary *lawyer*
Skaff, Andrew Joseph *lawyer, public utilities, energy and transportation executive*
Stromme, Gary L. *law librarian*
Sutcliffe, Eric *lawyer*
†Washington, Kaye *lawyer*
Webster, William Hodges *lawyer*
†West, Natalie Elsa *lawyer*
Wood, James Michael *lawyer*

Oceanside
†Doucette, Jodi Leazott *lawyer*

Ontario
Dunn, Donald Jack *law librarian, law educator, dean, lawyer*
Ogbogu, Cecilia Ify *lawyer*
Perri, Audrey Ann *lawyer*
Seagull, Helen Ann *paralegal, educator, writer, public relations consultant, medical assistant*

Orange
Avdeef, Thomas *lawyer*
Batchelor, James Kent *lawyer*
Bennett, William Perry *lawyer*
†Doti, Frank John *law educator, consultant*
†Sanders, Gary Wayne *lawyer*
†Weissberg-Ortiz, Judith Lee *lawyer*

Orinda
†Casey, Kathleen Heirich *lawyer, educator*
Hetland, John Robert *lawyer, educator*
Sohnen, Harvey *lawyer*

Oxnard
Gerber, David A. *lawyer*

Pacific Palisades
Cale, Charles Griffin *lawyer, private investor*
Dean, Ronald Glenn *lawyer*
Dickson, Robert Lee *lawyer*
Flattery, Thomas Long *lawyer, legal administrator*
Horowitz, Edward Jay *lawyer*
†Jones, Edgar Allan, Jr., *law educator, arbitrator, lawyer*
Lagle, John Franklin *lawyer*
†Mendel, Dennis D. *lawyer*
Sevilla, Stanley *lawyer*
Share, Richard Hudson *lawyer*
Verrone, Patric Miller *lawyer, writer*

Palm Desert
Goldberg, Martin Stanford *retired lawyer*
†Pierno, Anthony Robert *lawyer*
†Wheeler, William Chamberlain, Jr., *association administrator, lawyer*

Palm Springs
Diodosio, Charles Joseph *lawyer*
Dupree, Stanley M. *lawyer*
FitzGerald, John Edward, III, *lawyer*
†Harris, Michael David *lawyer*

Palmdale
Finch, Susan Chloë *mediator, educator*

Palo Alto
†Baron, Frederick David *lawyer*
†Baum, Brandon *lawyer, law educator*
Bebb, Richard S. *lawyer*
†Benton, Lee F. *lawyer*
Bradley, Donald Edward *lawyer*
Casillas, Mark *lawyer*
Climan, Richard Elliot *lawyer*
Cohen, Nancy Mahoney *lawyer*
†Cunningham, Brian C. *lawyer, corporate executive*
Dwyer, John Charles *lawyer*
Gaither, James C. *lawyer*
†Hinckley, Robert Craig *lawyer*
†Jackson, Cynthia L. *lawyer*
†Johnston, Alan Cope *lawyer*
Klay, Anna Nettie *lawyer*
†Lacovara, Michael *lawyer*
Laurie, Ronald Sheldon *lawyer*
Massey, Henry P., Jr., *lawyer*
Miller, Michael Patiky *lawyer*
†Mosher, Roger L. *lawyer*
Nopar, Alan Scott *lawyer*
Nordlund, Donald Craig *lawyer*
Nycum, Susan Hubbell *lawyer*
†O'Brien, Bradford Carl *lawyer*
†O'Brien, Christina Maria *lawyer*
O'Rourke, C. Larry *lawyer*
Patterson, Robert Edward *lawyer*
Phair, Joseph Baschon *lawyer*
†Rinsky, Arthur C. *lawyer*
Simon, James Lowell *lawyer*
Smith, Glenn A. *lawyer*
†Spanner, Robert Alan *lawyer*
†Steer, Reginald David *lawyer*
Tanner, Douglas Alan *lawyer*
Tiffany, Joseph Raymond, II, *lawyer*
†Trumbull, Terry ALan *energy and environmental consultant, lawyer*
Van Atta, David Murray *lawyer*
Wheeler, Raymond Louis *lawyer*

Palos Verdes Estates
Blackman, Lee L. *lawyer*
DeLuce, Richard David *lawyer*
Toftness, Cecil Gillman *lawyer, consultant*

Paramount
Hall, Howard Harry *lawyer*

Pasadena
Armour, George Porter *lawyer*
Ashley-Farrand, Margalo *lawyer, mediator, private judge*
Brenner, Anita Susan *lawyer*
Bunt Smith, Helen Marguerite *lawyer*
Call, Merlin Wendell *lawyer*
Calleton, Theodore Edward *lawyer, educator*
D'Angelo, Robert William *lawyer*
Davis, Edmond Ray *lawyer*
Epstein, Bruce Howard *lawyer*
Haight, James Theron *lawyer, corporate executive*
Hunt, Gordon *lawyer*
Koelzer, George Joseph *lawyer*
Logan, Francis Dummer *retired lawyer*
†Mosher, Sally Ekenberg *lawyer, musician*
Mueth, Joseph Edward *lawyer*
Myers, R(alph) Chandler *lawyer*
†Stolzberg, Michael Meyer *lawyer*
Tanner, Dee Boshard *retired lawyer*
†Taylor, John David *lawyer*
Wyatt, Joseph Lucian, Jr., *lawyer, writer*
Yohalem, Harry Morton *lawyer*
Zuetel, Kenneth Roy, Jr., *lawyer*

Paso Robles
Knecht, James Herbert *lawyer*

Pebble Beach
Robinson, William Adams *lawyer*

Petaluma
Castagnola, George Joseph, Jr., *lawyer, mediator, secondary education educator*

Pittsburg
†Williscroft-Barcus, Beverly Ruth *lawyer*

Placentia
Evans, Winthrop Shattuck *retired lawyer*

Placerville
†Winkler, Jack Richmond *lawyer, writer*

Pleasant Hill
Gearheart, Mark Edwin *lawyer*
Otis, Roy James *lawyer*

Pleasanton
Fine, Marjorie Lynn *lawyer*
Hearey, Elizabeth Berle *lawyer*
MacDonald, Peter David *lawyer*
Opperwall, Stephen Gabriel *lawyer*
Scott, G. Judson, Jr., *lawyer*
Staley, John Fredric *lawyer*

Plymouth
Andreason, John Christian *lawyer*

Point Richmond
Edgington, John Arthur *lawyer*

Pomona
Palmer, Robert Alan *lawyer, educator*
†Partritz, Joan Elizabeth *lawyer, educator*
Young, Norman Gregory *law educator, lawyer*

Portola Valley
Cooper, John Joseph *lawyer*

Rancho Mirage
Leydorf, Frederick Leroy *lawyer*
Reuben, Don Harold *lawyer*

Rancho Palos Verdes
Swank, Damon Raynard *lawyer*

Rancho Santa Fe
Peterson, Nad A. *retired lawyer*

Rancho Santa Margarita
Curtis, John Joseph *lawyer*

Redondo Beach
Mercant, Jon Jeffry *lawyer, educator, musician*

Redwood City
Bell, Frank Ouray, Jr., *lawyer*
Coddington, Clinton Hays *lawyer*
Mandel, Martin Louis *lawyer*
Millard, Richard Steven *lawyer*
Tight, Dexter Corwin *lawyer*
Wilhelm, Robert Oscar *lawyer, civil engineer, developer*

Rialto
Davis, David Earl *lawyer*

Richmond
Jenkins, Everett Wilbur, Jr., *lawyer, author, historian*
Kirk-Duggan, Michael Allan *retired law, economics and computer sciences educator*

Ridgecrest
Long, Andre Edwin *law educator, lawyer*

Riverside
†Bergman, Daniel Charles *county official, lawyer, environmental manager*
Darling, Scott Edward *lawyer*
†Lear, William H. *lawyer*
Marlatt, Michael James *lawyer*
Sklar, Wilford Nathaniel *retired lawyer, real estate broker*

Rolling Hills
Rumbaugh, Charles Earl *arbitrator, mediator, educator, lawyer, speaker, judge*

Rosemead
†Danner, Bryant Craig *lawyer*

Sacramento
Arkin, Michael Barry *lawyer, arbitrator, writer*
†Barilla, Frank (Rocky Barilla) *lawyer, consultant, educator*
Bell, Wayne S. *lawyer, state agency official*
Birney, Philip Ripley *lawyer*
†Blake, D. Steven *lawyer*
Bobrow, Susan Lukin *lawyer*
†Bowen, Debra Lynn *lawyer, state legislator*
Brazier, John Richard *lawyer, physician*
Brewer, Roy Edward *lawyer*
Brookman, Anthony Raymond *lawyer*
Burton, Randall James *lawyer*
Carrel, Marc Louis *lawyer, public affairs consultant*
Day, James McAdam, Jr., *lawyer*
Foster, Douglas Taylor *lawyer, investor*
Friedman, Morton Lee *lawyer*
Giguiere, Michele Louise *lawyer*
†Goode, Barry Paul *lawyer*
Houpt, James Edward *lawyer*
Janigian, Bruce Jasper *lawyer, educator*
Keiner, Christian Mark *lawyer*
Landsberg, Brian Keith *law educator*
Malloy, Michael Patrick *law educator, consultant*
†McGrath, William Arthur *arbitrator, mediator*
Mueller, Virginia Schwartz *lawyer*
Radford, R. S. *lawyer, law educator*
Rich, Ben Arthur *lawyer, educator*
Robbins, Stephen J. M. *lawyer*
Rodriguez, Miquel *prosecutor*
Root, Gerald Edward *legal administrator*
†Scott, Windie Olivia *lawyer*
†Severaid, Ronald Harold *lawyer*
Taylor, Walter Wallace *retired lawyer*
Twiss, Robert Manning *prosecutor*
Ubaldi, Michael Vincent *lawyer*
†Ueda, Kara Kimiko *lawyer*
Wile, Philip Hodges *law educator*
Willis, Dawn Louise *legal assistant, small business owner*
Wishek, Michael Bradley *lawyer*

Saint Helena
Marvin, Monica Louise Wolf *lawyer*

Salinas
Bolles, Donald Scott *lawyer*

San Anselmo
Murphy, Barry Ames *lawyer*
Truett, Harold Joseph, III, (Tim Truett) *lawyer*

San Bernardino
Eskin, Barry Sanford *court investigator*
Fullerton, Robert Victor *lawyer*
Prince, Timothy Peter *lawyer*

San Carlos
Lee, John Jin *lawyer*
†Mitchell, Sally E. *lawyer, city official, former mayor*

San Clemente
Fisher, Myron R. *lawyer*
Geyser, Lynne M. *lawyer, writer*

San Diego
†Barton, Thomas Donald *lawyer, educator*
†Bayer, Richard Stewart *lawyer*
†Bird, Charles Albert *lawyer*
Bleiler, Charles Arthur *lawyer*
†Boggs, William S. *lawyer*
†Boyle, Michael Fabian *lawyer*
Brierton, Cheryl Lynn *lawyer*
Brooks, John White *lawyer*
Brown, LaMar Bevan *lawyer*
Buzunis, Constantine Dino *lawyer*
Christensen, Charles Brophy *lawyer*
†Claus, Laurence Paul *law educator*
Cogan, Mary Jo Gleber *lawyer*
Copeland, Robert Glenn *lawyer*
Damoose, George Lynn *lawyer*
Dawe, James Robert *lawyer*
Dershem, Larry Douglas *lawyer, author*
†Dorne, David J. *lawyer*
Dostart, Paul Joseph *lawyer, investor and director*
Dyer, Charles Richard *law librarian, law educator*
†Edwards, James Richard *lawyer*
Eigner, William Whitling *lawyer*
Estep, Arthur Lee *lawyer*
Fauchier, Dan R(ay) *mediator, arbitrator, educator, construction management consultant,*
Fellmeth, Robert Charles *law educator*
†Foerster, Barrett Jonathan *lawyer*
†Friedman, Gary E. *lawyer*
†German, G. Michael *lawyer*
Gold, Steven Bruce *lawyer*
Guinn, Stanley Willis *lawyer*
Hansotte, Louis Bernard *retired lawyer*
†Heidrich, Robert Wesley *lawyer*
†Herring, Charles David *lawyer, educator*
†Higgs, Craig DeWitt *lawyer*
Hofflund, Paul *lawyer*
Iredale, Eugene Gerald *lawyer*
Klinedinst, John David *lawyer*
Kremer, Matthew Markus *lawyer, mediator, judge pro tem*
†Kuntz, William Richard, Jr., *lawyer*
Lathrop, Mitchell Lee *lawyer*
LeBeau, Charles Paul *lawyer*
†Longstreth, Robert Christy *lawyer*
Lowenstam, Susan Guggenheim *lawyer*
†Lustbader, Philip Lawrence *lawyer, stock brokerage executive*
Margolis, Anita Joy *lawyer*
McClellan, Craig Rene *lawyer*
McDermott, Thomas John, Jr., *lawyer*
McGinnis, Robert E. *lawyer*
†McVey, Lane Leroy *lawyer*
†Mebane, Julie Shaffer *lawyer*
Miller, William Charles *lawyer*
Mittermiller, James Joseph *lawyer*
Morris, Grant Harold *law educator*
Morris, Sandra Joan *lawyer*
Mulcahy, Robert Joseph *lawyer*
O'Malley, James Terence *lawyer*
Payne, Margaret Anne *lawyer*
Peters, Richard *lawyer*
Petix, Stephen Vincent *lawyer*
†Potter-Hill, Lynne Ann *lawyer*
Preston, David Raymond *lawyer*
Pugh, Richard Crawford *lawyer*
†Reed, T. Michael *lawyer*
Reif, Louis Raymond *lawyer, utilities executive*
†Riley, Kirk Holden *lawyer*
Roseman, Charles Sanford *lawyer*
Ross, Terry D. *lawyer*
†Roth-Douquet, Kathryn Gaie *lawyer*
Samuelson, Derrick William *lawyer*
Sceper, Duane Harold *lawyer*
†Schoville, Dennis A(rnold) *lawyer*
Schwartz, Jeffrey Scott *lawyer*
†Seidenwurm, Richard Lewis *lawyer*
Shapiro, Philip Alan *lawyer*
†Shaw, Richard Allan *lawyer*
Shearer, William Kennedy *lawyer, publisher*
Shelton, Dorothy Diehl Rees *lawyer*
Shippey, Sandra Lee *lawyer*
Smith, Steven Ray *law educator*
Snaid, Leon Jeffrey *lawyer*
Snyder, David Richard *lawyer*
Sterrett, James Kelley, II, *lawyer*
Stock, Lauri Jane *lawyer*
†Sullivan, Patrick James *lawyer*
Sullivan, William Francis *lawyer*
Tragen, Irving Glenne *consultant*
†Underwood, Anthony Paul *lawyer*
Valliant, James Stevens *lawyer*
Weaver, Michael James *lawyer*
Young, David Bradley *lawyer*

San Francisco
†Abbott, Barry Alexander *lawyer*
†Alderman, William Fields *lawyer*
Alexander, Mary Elsie *lawyer*
Alexander, Robert C. *lawyer*
†Alexis, Geraldine M. *lawyer*
Allen, Paul Alfred *lawyer, educator*
Anderson, Edward Virgil *lawyer*
Arbuthnot, Robert Murray *lawyer*

Armour, Maya Lynne *lawyer*
Baker, Cameron *lawyer*
†Baker, Steven Wright *lawyer*
Barbagelata, Robert Dominic *lawyer*
Bauch, Thomas Jay *financial/investment advisor, lawyer, educator, former apparel company executive*
†Baxter, Ralph H., Jr., *lawyer*
Berns, Philip Allan *lawyer*
Bleich, Jeffrey Laurence *lawyer, law educator*
Bondoc, Rommel *lawyer*
Borowsky, Philip *lawyer*
Borson, Daniel Benjamin *lawyer, educator, physiologist, researcher*
†Bostwick, James Stephen *lawyer*
Bothwell, Anthony Peirson Xavier, Sr., *lawyer, educator*
Boutin, Peter Rucker *lawyer*
†Boven, Douglas George *lawyer*
†Boyd, William Elkins *lawyer*
†Brick, Ann Veta *lawyer*
Bridges, Robert Lysle *retired lawyer*
Briscoe, John *lawyer*
Brown, Donald Wesley *lawyer*
Bruen, James A. *lawyer*
Burden, James Ewers *lawyer*
Burns, Brian Patrick *lawyer, business executive*
Byrne, Robert William *lawyer*
†Callan, Terrence A. *lawyer*
Campbell, Scott Robert *lawyer, former food company executive*
Carley, Donald Martin *lawyer*
Carter, John Douglas *lawyer*
†Caspersen, R(alph) Frederick *lawyer*
Cheatham, Robert William *lawyer*
†Cohler, Charles B. *lawyer*
Cohn, Nathan *lawyer*
Coleman, Thomas Young *lawyer*
Coombe, George William, Jr., *lawyer, retired banker*
Corcoran, Maureen Elizabeth *lawyer*
Crawford, Roy Edgington, III, *lawyer*
Crist, Paul Grant *lawyer*
Davis, Roger Lewis *lawyer*
Deane, Elaine *lawyer*
†Dell, Robert Michael *lawyer*
DeMuro, Paul Robert *lawyer*
Diekmann, Gilmore Frederick, Jr., *lawyer*
Donovan, Charles Stephen *lawyer*
Dryden, Robert Eugene *lawyer*
†Duffy, Jan *law educator, lawyer*
Dunne, Kevin Joseph *lawyer*
Dworkin, Michael Leonard *lawyer*
Edwards, Robin Morse *lawyer*
†Endsley, Meredith Nelson *lawyer*
Evers, William Dohrmann *lawyer*
Fastiff, Wesley J. *lawyer*
Feller, Lloyd Harris *lawyer*
Fergus, Gary Scott *lawyer*
Finberg, James Michael *lawyer*
Finck, Kevin William *lawyer*
†Fisher, Kathleen V. *lawyer*
†Fledderman, Harry L. *lawyer*
Fogel, Paul David *lawyer*
Folberg, Harold Jay *lawyer, mediator, educator, university dean*
Forsythe, Janet Winifred *lawyer*
Foster, David Scott *lawyer*
Freeman, Tom M. *lawyer*
Freud, Nicholas S. *lawyer*
Friedman, K. Bruce *lawyer*
Friese, Robert Charles *lawyer*
Frohlich, Jack T. *lawyer, computer educator, consultant*
Furth, Frederick Paul *lawyer*
Garvey, Joanne Marie *lawyer*
Gelhaus, Robert Joseph *lawyer, publisher*
†Getto, Ernest John *lawyer*
Glazer, Jack Henry *lawyer*
†Gowdy, Franklin Brockway *lawyer*
Gresham, Zane Oliver *lawyer*
Guggenhime, Richard Johnson *lawyer*
†Haas, Raymond P. *lawyer*
Haas, Richard *lawyer*
Hall, Paul J. *lawyer*
Hammond, George Charles *lawyer*
Heilbron, David M(ichael) *lawyer*
†Henke, Dan *law educator*
Henson, Ray David *law educator, consultant*
Hilton, Stanley Goumas *lawyer, educator, writer*
Hinman, Harvey DeForest *lawyer*
†Hisert, George A. *lawyer*
Hockett, Christopher Burch *lawyer*
Hofmann, John Richard, Jr., *retired lawyer*
Holden, Frederick Douglass, Jr., *lawyer*
Homer, Barry Wayne *lawyer*
Howard, Carl *lawyer*
Hudner, Philip *lawyer, rancher*
†Hudson, Mark Woodbridge *lawyer*
†Hunter, William Dennis *lawyer*
†Hurabiell, John Philip, Sr., *lawyer*
Innes, Kenneth Frederick, III, *lawyer*
James, David Lee *lawyer, international advisor, author*
Johns, Richard Seth Ellis *lawyer*
†Johnson, Gardiner *lawyer*
Kasanin, Mark Owen *lawyer*
Kelly, J. Michael *lawyer*
Kern, John McDougall *lawyer*
Kimport, David Lloyd *lawyer*
Klott, David Lee *lawyer*
Knapp, Charles Lincoln *law educator*
Knebel, Jack Gillen *lawyer*
†Knutzen, Martha Lorraine *lawyer*
Koeppel, John A. *lawyer*
Kuhl, Paul Beach *lawyer*
Ladar, Jerrold Morton *lawyer*
Lane, Fielding H. *lawyer*
Larson, John William *lawyer*
Lasky, Moses *lawyer*
Latta, Thomas Albert *lawyer*
La Vine, Robert L. *lawyer*
Leshy, John David *lawyer, legal educator, government official*
Libbin, Anne Edna *lawyer*
Livsey, Robert Callister *lawyer*
†Lopes, James Louis *lawyer*
Lynch, Timothy Jeremiah-Mahoney *lawyer, educator, theologian, realtor, writer*
MacGowan, Eugenia *lawyer*
†Mack, John Oscar *lawyer*
Maier, Peter Klaus *lawyer, business executive*
Mann, Bruce Alan *lawyer, investment banker*
Manning, Jerome Alan *retired lawyer*
Marcus, Richard Leon *lawyer, educator*
†Marshall, Raymond Charles *lawyer*
Martel, John Sheldon *lawyer, writer*
†Martin, Stephen James *retired lawyer*
Mattes, Martin Anthony *lawyer*
†McDevitt, Ray Edward *lawyer*
McElhinny, Harold John *lawyer*
McGuckin, John Hugh, Jr., *lawyer*
†McKenzie, John F. *lawyer*
Mc Laughlin, Jerome Michael *lawyer, shipping company executive*
McNally, Thomas Charles, III, *lawyer*
†Meyerson, Ivan D. *lawyer, holding company executive*
†Miles, Donald F. *lawyer*
Miller, William Napier Cripps *lawyer*
†Millner, Dianne Maxine *lawyer*
Millstein, David J. *lawyer*
Minnick, Malcolm David *lawyer*
Mitchell, Bruce Tyson *lawyer*
Moore, Scott Michael *lawyer*
Morrissey, John Carroll, Sr., *lawyer*
†Murphy, Arthur John, Jr., *lawyer*
†Murray, Kathleen Anne *lawyer*
†Musfelt, Duane Clark *lawyer*
Musser, Sandra G. *retired lawyer*
†Nelson, Paul Douglas *lawyer*
†Norris, Cynthia Ann *lawyer*
Odgers, Richard William *lawyer*
Offer, Stuart Jay *lawyer*
Olson, Robert Howard *lawyer*
Olson, Walter Gilbert *lawyer*
Palmer, Venrice Romito *lawyer, educator*
Parker, Harold Allen *lawyer, real estate executive*
Patula, Rodney Richard *lawyer*
Penskar, Mark Howard *lawyer*
Petty, George Oliver *lawyer*
†Phillips, Richard Myron *lawyer, educator*
Poole, Edward G. *attorney*
Poole, Gordon Leicester *lawyer*
Popofsky, Melvin Laurence *lawyer*
Ragan, Charles Ransom *lawyer*
Raven, Robert Dunbar *lawyer*
†Rea, John Martin *lawyer, state official*
Reding, John Anthony *lawyer*
Reese, John Robert *lawyer*
Rembe, Toni *lawyer, director*
Renfrew, Charles Byron *lawyer*
†Rice, Denis Timlin *lawyer*
Richards, Norman Blanchard *lawyer*
Richardson, Daniel Ralph *lawyer*
†Rogan, Richard A. *lawyer*
Rosch, John Thomas *lawyer*
†Rose, Jordan Payman *lawyer*
Rosen, Joshua Nathan *lawyer*
Rosen, Sanford Jay *lawyer*
Rossmann, Antonio *lawyer, educator*
†Rowland, John Arthur *lawyer*
Rubin, Michael *lawyer*
†Russoniello, Joseph Pascal *lawyer*
Salomon, Darrell Joseph *lawyer*
Savage, Mark Randall *lawyer*
Scarlett, Randall H. *lawyer*
†Schochet, Harvey S. *lawyer*
†Schon, Steven Eliot *lawyer*
Seabolt, Richard L. *lawyer*
Seavey, William Arthur *lawyer, vintner*
Seegal, John Franklin *lawyer*
†Seneker, Carl James, II, (Kim Seneker) *lawyer*
Shapiro, Gary John *lawyer*
Sharp, Stefanie Teresa *lawyer*
Shenk, George H. *lawyer*
†Sherman, Martin Peter *lawyer*
†Shiffman, Michael A. *lawyer*
Singer, Allen Morris *lawyer*
†Siniscalco, Gary Richard *lawyer*
Small, Marshall Lee *lawyer*
Smegal, Thomas Frank, Jr., *lawyer*
Smith, Kerry Clark *lawyer*
Smith, Robert Michael *lawyer, mediator, arbitrator*
Soberon, Presentacion Zablan *state bar administrator*
Sparks, Thomas E., Jr., *lawyer*
†Spiegel, Hart Hunter *retired lawyer*
Staring, Graydon Shaw *lawyer*
Stotter, Lawrence Henry *lawyer*
Stromberg, Ross Ernest *lawyer*
Stroup, Stanley Stephenson *lawyer, educator*
Sugarman, Myron George *lawyer*
Sullivan, Robert Edward *lawyer*
Sutton, John Paul *lawyer*
Taylor, William James (Zak Taylor) *lawyer*
†Thomas, William Scott *lawyer*
Thompson, Robert Charles *lawyer*
†Thornton, Charles Victor *lawyer*
Tobin, James Michael *lawyer*
†Tonsing, Michael John *lawyer*
Trautman, William Ellsworth *lawyer*
Traynor, John Michael *lawyer*
†Truong, D. Hiep *lawyer*
†Tuthill, James Peirce *lawyer*
Utrecht, Paul F. *lawyer*
Veaco, Kristina *lawyer*
Venning, Robert Stanley *lawyer*
Walcher, Alan Ernest *lawyer*
Walker, Ralph Clifford *lawyer*
Walker, Walter Herbert, III, *lawyer, writer*
Walsh, Francis Richard *law educator, lawyer, arbitrator*
†Walsh, Joseph Richard *lawyer, bank executive*
Wang, William Kai-Sheng *law educator*
Warmer, Richard Craig *lawyer*
Weber, Arnold I. *lawyer*
Weiner, Jody Carl *lawyer, author, producer*
†Welborn, Caryl Bartelman *lawyer*
Whelan, John William *law educator*
Whitehead, David Barry *lawyer*
Wild, Nelson Hopkins *lawyer*
Wilson, John Pasley *law educator*
Wingate, C. Keith *law educator*
Wolf, Carl *lawyer*
Wood, Robert Warren *lawyer*
†Woods, James Robert *lawyer*
†Worthington, Bruce R. *lawyer*
Wyle, Frederick S. *lawyer*
Young, Bryant Llewellyn *lawyer, business executive*
Young, Douglas Rea *lawyer*
Ziegler, R. W., Jr., *lawyer, consultant*
Ziering, William Mark *lawyer*

San Gabriel

†Garcia, Bonifacio Bonny *lawyer*

San Jose

Bohn, Robert Herbert *lawyer*
†Cory, Charles Johnson *lawyer*
Cummins, Charles Fitch, Jr., *lawyer*
Doan, Gerald Xuyen Van *lawyer*
†Fowler, John Wellington *lawyer*
Gallo, Joan Rosenberg *lawyer*
Gonzales, Daniel S. *lawyer*
†Gregg, Richard *lawyer*
Hernández, Fernando Vargas *lawyer*
Jorgensen, Norman Eric *lawyer*
Katzman, Irwin *lawyer*
Katzman, Richard Alan *lawyer, arbitrator*
Kennedy, George Wendell *prosecutor*
†Kepner, Anne Jones *lawyer*
Kraw, George Martin *lawyer, essayist*
McManis, James *lawyer*
Mitchell, David Walker *lawyer*
†Morgan, Robert Hall *lawyer*
†Naegele, Joseph Loyola, Sr., *lawyer*
Narayan, Beverly Elaine *lawyer*
†Roush, George Edgar *lawyer*
Sauers, William Dale *lawyer, playwright*
Stein, John C. *lawyer*
Stutzman, Thomas Chase, Sr., *lawyer*
Terry, Michael Joseph *legal process supervisor, court trainer*
Thomson, Hugh Talbert *lawyer*
Towery, James E. *lawyer*
Yates-Carter, Lynne *lawyer*

San Juan Capistrano

Graves, Patrick Lee *lawyer*
Suzuki, Yasuhiko *retired law educator*

San Luis Obispo

Dorsi, Stephen Nathan *lawyer*

San Marcos

Berry, Dawn Bradley *writer, lawyer, jeweler*

San Marino

Cranston, Howard Stephen *lawyer, management consultant*
Galbraith, James Marshall *lawyer, business executive*
Tomich, Lillian *lawyer*

San Mateo

Bhatnagar, Mary Elizabeth *lawyer*
†Dummer, William L *lawyer, writer*
Grill, Lawrence J. *lawyer, accountant, corporate/banking executive*
Kane, Robert Francis *lawyer, former ambassador, consultant*
Kenney, William Fitzgerald *lawyer*
Monaco, Daniel Joseph *lawyer*
†O'Reilly, Terence John *lawyer*
Slabach, Stephen Hall *lawyer*
†Tormey, James Roland, Jr., *lawyer*

San Rafael

Chilvers, Robert Merritt *lawyer*
Drexler, Kenneth *lawyer*
Duke, George F. *lawyer*
Fairbairn, Sydney Elise *lawyer*
Freitas, David Prince *lawyer*
†Kathrein, Reed Richard *lawyer*
Roth, Hadden Wing *lawyer*

San Ramon

Freed, Kenneth Alan *lawyer*
†Welch, Thomas Andrew *retired lawyer, arbitrator*

Sanger

Chynoweth, W. Edward *retired lawyer, farmer*

Santa Ana

†Anderson, James E., Jr., *lawyer*
†Andres, Eugen Charles *lawyer*
Capizzi, Michael Robert *prosecutor*
Dillard, John Martin *lawyer, pilot*
Fay-Schmidt, Patricia Ann *paralegal*
Harley, Robison Dooling, Jr., *lawyer, educator*
Ingalsbe, William James *lawyer*
†Mei, Tom Y. K. *lawyer*
Patt, Herbert Jacob *lawyer*
Storer, Maryruth *law librarian*
Toledano, James *lawyer*

Santa Barbara

Ah-Tye, Kirk Thomas *lawyer*
Bauer, Marvin Agather *lawyer*
†Dickey, Denise Ann *lawyer, arbitrator*
Egenolf, Robert F. *lawyer*
Elliott, Warren G. *lawyer*
†Howell, Weldon U., Jr., *lawyer*
Israel, Barry John *lawyer*
†McCollum, Susan Hill *lawyer*
McEwen, Willard Winfield, Jr., *lawyer, judge*
Metzinger, Timothy Edward *lawyer*
Perloff, Jean Marcosson *lawyer*
Reed, Frank Fremont, II, *retired lawyer*
Stirling, Clark Tillman *lawyer*
Sulzbach, Christi Rocovich *lawyer*

Santa Clara

Alexander, George Jonathon *law educator, former dean*
Blawie, James Louis *law educator*
†Dunlap, F. Thomas, Jr., *lawyer, electronics company executive*
†Hood, Mary Dullea *law librarian*
Ludgus, Nancy Lucke *lawyer*
Weller, Douglas LaFontaine *patent lawyer*

Santa Cruz

†Costello, Donald Fredric *lawyer*
Schalk, Robert Partridge *lawyer*
Seligmann, William Robert *lawyer, author*

Santa Maria

Kelly, Quentin Patrick *lawyer*

Santa Monica

Boltz, Gerald Edmund *lawyer*
Bower, Allan Maxwell *lawyer*
†Carlson, Jeffery John *lawyer*
Cooper, Jay Leslie *lawyer*
Costello, Edward J., Jr., *arbitrator, mediator, lawyer*
†Custer, Barbara Ann *lawyer*
Genego, William Joseph *lawyer*
Hinerfeld, Robert Elliot *lawyer*
Hirsch, Richard Gary *lawyer*
Hofer, Stephen Robert *lawyer*
†Jones, William Allen *lawyer, entertainment company executive*
†Kaplowitz, Karen (Jill) *lawyer, business consultant*
†Kinney, James Howard *lawyer*
Kirkland, John C. *lawyer*
†Kranzdorf, Jeffrey Paul *lawyer, recording company executive, television producer*
†Levin, Marvin Eugene *lawyer*
Loo, Thomas S. *lawyer*
McMillan, M. Sean *lawyer*
†McNally, Susan Fowler *lawyer*
Morgan, Kermit Johnson *lawyer*
Muller, Edward Robert *lawyer*
Pizzulli, Francis Cosmo Joseph *lawyer, bioethicist*
Preble, Laurence George *lawyer*
Ringler, Jerome Lawrence *lawyer*
Risman, Michael *lawyer, business executive, securities company executive, real estate developer*
†Roberts, Virgil Patrick *lawyer, business executive*
†Schlei, Norbert Anthony *lawyer*
†Stone, Arnold Joseph *lawyer*

Santa Rosa

Adams, Delphine Szyndrowski *lawyer*
Clement, Clayton Emerson *lawyer*
Courteau, Girard Robert *retired prosecutor*
†Gack, Kenneth David *lawyer*
O'Connor, Paul Daniel *lawyer*

Sausalito

Berkman, William Roger *lawyer, army reserve officer*
†Gordon, Robert Eugene *lawyer*

Seal Beach

†Hennen, Thomas Waldo *lawyer*
Weitzman, Marc Herschel *lawyer*

Seaside

Weingarten, Saul Myer *lawyer*

Sebastopol

Hillberg, Marylou Elin *lawyer*

Selma

†Janian, Paulette *lawyer*

Sherman Oaks

Crump, Gerald Franklin *retired lawyer*
Feldman, Phillip *lawyer*
Joyce, Stephen Michael *lawyer*
Levin, Evanne Lynn *lawyer*

Sonoma

Obninsky, Victor Peter *lawyer*

Stanford

Barton, John Hays *law educator*
Cohen, William *law educator*
Donohue, John Joseph *law educator*
Franklin, Marc Adam *law educator*
Friedman, Lawrence M. *law educator*
Goldstein, Paul *lawyer, educator*
†Gould, William Benjamin, IV, *lawyer, educator, federal agency administrator*
Mann, J. Keith *retired law educator, arbitrator*
Scott, Kenneth Eugene *lawyer, educator*
Sofaer, Abraham David *lawyer, educator, judge, consultant*

Stevenson Ranch

†Bovasso, Louis Joseph *lawyer*

Stockton

Blewett, Robert Noall *lawyer*

Studio City

Miller, Charles Maurice *lawyer*
Withers, Arlene Falk *mediator*

Sunnyvale

McReynolds, Stephen Paul *lawyer*
†Schiefelbein, Lester Willis, Jr., *lawyer*
Thornton, D. Whitney, II, *lawyer*
Wehde, Albert Edward *lawyer*
Zahrt, William Dietrich, II, *lawyer*

Tahoe City

Hirshon, Jack Thomas *lawyer*

Tarzana

Gentile, Joseph F. *lawyer, educator*

Thousand Oaks

Geiser, Thomas Christopher *lawyer*
Trover, Ellen Lloyd *lawyer*

Toluca Lake
Runquist, Lisa A. *lawyer*

Torrance
Bryan, Sharon Ann *lawyer*
†Donovan, Dennis Francis *lawyer*
Kaufman, Sanford Paul *lawyer*
Kohan, Betsy Burns *lawyer*
Matsunaga, Geoffrey Dean *lawyer*
Moore, Christopher M. *lawyer*
Petillon, Lee Ritchey *lawyer*
†Ward, Anthony John *lawyer*

Tracy
Hay, Dennis Lee *lawyer*

Tustin
Kraft, Henry Robert *lawyer*
Madory, Richard Eugene *lawyer*

Ukiah
†Sager, Madeline Dean *lawyer*

Vallejo
†Smith, Frank Leonard, III, *lawyer*

Van Nuys
Arabian, Armand *arbitrator, mediator, lawyer*
Mikesell, Richard Lyon *lawyer, financial counselor*

Venice
Schanes, Christine *lawyer*

Ventura
Bray, Laurack Doyle *lawyer*
Gartner, Harold Henry, III, *lawyer*
Kump, Kary Ronald *lawyer*

Visalia
†Atkins, Thomas Jay *lawyer, missionary and pastor*
Crowe, Daniel Walston *lawyer*
Crowe, John T. *lawyer*
Hart, Timothy Ray *lawyer, dean*
Higgins, John Stuart, Jr., *lawyer*

Walnut
McKee, Catherine Lynch *law educator, lawyer*

Walnut Creek
Anderson, Robert Leroy *lawyer*
Baker, Roy Gordon, Jr., *lawyer*
†Bicksler, Diana Guido *lawyer*
Burnison, Boyd Edward *lawyer*
Curtin, Daniel Joseph, Jr., *lawyer*
De Benedictis, Dario *lawyer, arbitrator, mediator*
Derby, Steven Leo *lawyer*
Everson, Martin Joseph *lawyer*
†Gardner, Trudi York *lawyer, insurance company executive*
Ginsburg, Gerald J. *lawyer, business executive*
Hanschen, Peter Walter *lawyer*
Horner, Clifford R. *lawyer*
†Lederman, Henry David *lawyer*
Ogilby, Barry Ray *lawyer*
Pagter, Carl Richard *lawyer*
Pinkerton, Albert Duane, II, *lawyer*
Rainey, William Joel *lawyer*
Skaggs, Sanford Merle *lawyer*
†Van Voorhis, Thomas *lawyer*
Willson, Prentiss, Jr., *lawyer*

West Covina
†Ebiner, Robert Maurice *lawyer*
McHale, Edward Robertson *retired lawyer*

West Hollywood
†Lyon, John David *lawyer, computer products company executive*

Westlake Village
Chuman, Frank Fujio *lawyer*
†Levinson, Christopher Gregory *legal administrator*
†Sullivan, Mark Francis *lawyer*

Windsor
Greiner, Robert Philip *lawyer, real estate broker*

Woodland
Melton, Barry *lawyer, musician*

Woodland Hills
Barrett, Robert Matthew *law educator, lawyer*
†Even, Randolph M. *lawyer*
Glick, Earl A. *retired lawyer*
Johnson-Champ, Debra Sue *lawyer, educator, writer, artist*
Kaufman, Albert I. *lawyer*
Koep, Richard Michael *lawyer*
Lin, Lawrence Shuh Liang *lawyer*
†Rolin, Christopher E(rnest) *lawyer*
Weinman, Glenn Alan *lawyer*

COLORADO

Alamosa
Garcia, Castelar Medardo *lawyer*

Arvada
Carney, TJ *lawyer*
†Peck, Kenneth E. *lawyer*

Aspen
Peirce, Frederick Fairbanks *lawyer*

Aurora
†Hampton, Clyde Robert *lawyer, educator*
Katz, Michael Jeffery *lawyer*
Khanna, Kishanlal K. *lawyer, educator*
Seybert, Janet Rose *lawyer, military officer*
Staelin, Earl Hudson *lawyer*
Stauffer, Scott William *lawyer, accountant*

Avon
†Marks, Richard Samuel *lawyer, real estate development executive*

Basalt
Shipp, Dan Shackelford *lawyer*

Boulder
Anuta, Karl Frederick *lawyer*
Bellac, Patricia Sharman *lawyer*
Bintliff, Barbara Ann *law librarian, educator*
Cope, Joseph Adams *lawyer*
†Danielson, Luke Jeffries *lawyer*
Deaktor, Darryl Barnett *lawyer*
DuVivier, Katharine Keyes *lawyer, educator*
Echohawk, John Ernest *lawyer*
Fenster, Herbert Lawrence *lawyer*
Fiflis, Ted James *lawyer, educator*
Flowers, William Harold, Jr., *lawyer*
†Getches, David Harding *law educator, state environmental executive, lawyer*
†Halpern, Alexander *lawyer*
Kerr, Baine Perkins, Jr., *lawyer, writer*
LaVelle, Betty Sullivan Dougherty *legal professional*
Manka, Ronald Eugene *lawyer*
Moses, Raphael Jacob *lawyer*
†Nagel, Robert Forder *legal educator, lawyer*
†O'Connor, Heidi Roberts *federal appellate lawyer*
Peterson, Courtland Harry *law educator*
Porzak, Glenn E. *lawyer*
Purvis, John Anderson *lawyer, educator*
†Waggoner, Michael James *law educator*
†Wittemyer, John *lawyer*

Breckenridge
Fromm, Jeffery Bernard *lawyer*

Broomfield
Jonsen, Eric Richard *lawyer*

Canon City
McDermott, John Arthur *lawyer*

Carbondale
Wohl, Kenneth Allan *lawyer*

Centennial
Carlton, Diane Michele *lawyer*
McClung, Merle Steven *lawyer*

Cherry Hills Village
Kerwin, Mary Ann Collins *lawyer*

Colorado Springs
Adams, Deborah Rowland *lawyer*
Buell, Bruce Temple *lawyer*
Cross, Thomas Robert *lawyer*
†Donley, Jerry Alan *lawyer*
Evans, Paul Vernon *lawyer*
Everson, Steven Lee *lawyer, real estate executive*
Fisher, Robert Scott *lawyer*
Gaddis, Larry Roy *lawyer*
Gefreh, Paul Thomas *lawyer*
Gregory, Margaret Ellen *lawyer*
Keene, Kenneth Paul *lawyer*
Kendall, Phillip Alan *lawyer*
Kubida, William Joseph *lawyer*
†Lohman, Richard Verne *lawyer*
MacDougall, Malcolm Edward *lawyer*
McCready, Guy Michael *lawyer*
Palermo, Norman Anthony *lawyer*
Purvis, Randall W. B. *lawyer*
Rhodes, Eric Foster *employee relations consultant, writer*
†Rouss, Ruth *lawyer*
†Rowan, Ronald Thomas *lawyer*
Slivka, Michael Andrew *lawyer*
†Swanson, Victoria Clare Heldman *lawyer*
Walker, Jonathan Lee *lawyer*
Wheeler, Stephen Frederick *legal administration*

Crested Butte
Renfrow, Jay Royce *lawyer*

Delta
†Schottelkotte, Michael Roger *lawyer, judge*

Denver
Aisenberg, Bennett S. *lawyer*
†Aschkinasi, David Jay *lawyer*
Atlass, Theodore Bruce *lawyer, educator*
Austin, H(arry) Gregory *lawyer*
Bader, Gerald Louis, Jr., *lawyer*
Bain, Donald Knight *lawyer*
Belitz, Paul Edward *lawyer*
Benson, Robert Eugene *lawyer*
Benton, Auburn Edgar *lawyer*
Blair, Andrew Lane, Jr., *lawyer, educator*
Blitz, Stephen M. *lawyer*
†Braverman, Janis Ann Breggin *lawyer*
Breeskin, Michael Wayne *lawyer*
Brega, Charles Franklin *lawyer*
Breitenstein, Peter Frederic *lawyer*
Bronstein, Robert *retired lawyer*
†Brown, James Elliott *lawyer*
Burford, Anne McGill *lawyer*
Burkhardt, Donald Malcolm *retired lawyer*
Butler, David *lawyer*
Byrne, Thomas J. *lawyer*
Cain, Douglas Mylchreest *lawyer*
Callison, James William *lawyer*
Campbell, Leonard M. *lawyer*
Campbell, William J. *lawyer*
Carr, James Francis *lawyer*
Carrigan, Jim R. *arbitrator, mediator, retired judge*
†Carson, William Scott *lawyer*
†Cassidy, Samuel H. *lawyer, lieutenant governor, state legislator, humanities educator*
Cheroutes, Michael Louis *lawyer*
†Cohen, Jeffrey *lawyer*
Cooper, Paul Douglas *lawyer*
Cope, Thomas Field *lawyer*
†Copeland, Eugene Leroy *lawyer, writer*
Cox, William Vaughan *lawyer*
Crow, Nancy Rebecca *lawyer*
Daily, Richard W. *lawyer*
Dauer, Edward Arnold *law educator*
Dean, James Benwell *lawyer*
Deikman, Eugene Lawrence *lawyer*
DeLaney, Herbert Wade, Jr., *lawyer*
DeMuth, Alan Cornelius *lawyer*
Dolan, Brian Thomas *lawyer*
Dorr, Robert Charles *lawyer*
Dowdle, Patrick Dennis *lawyer*
†Dunham, Stephen Sampson *lawyer*
†Eberle, Donald Cramer *lawyer, governmental relations consultant*
†Ebert, Darlene Marie *lawyer*
†Eckstein, John Alan *lawyer*
Edwards, Daniel Walden *lawyer*
Eklund, Carl Andrew *lawyer*
†Estes, Mark Ernest *law librarian*
†Fanganello, Joseph Michael *lawyer*
Faxon, Thomas Baker *retired lawyer*
Finn, John Stephen *lawyer*
Fortune, Lowell *lawyer*
Freeman, Deborah Lynn *lawyer*
Friedberg, Alan Charles *lawyer*
Gehres, James *retired lawyer*
George, Russell Lloyd *lawyer, former state legislator*
†Gilbert, Alan Jay *lawyer, educator*
Goldberg, Gregory Eban *lawyer*
†Grant, Patrick Alexander *lawyer, association administrator*
Green, Jersey Michael-Lee *lawyer*
Grimshaw, Thomas Tollin *lawyer*
Grissom, Garth Clyde *lawyer, director*
Gustus, Stacey A. *legal secretary*
Hamel, Fred Meade *lawyer*
Harris, Dale Ray *lawyer*
†Hartley, James Edward *lawyer*
†Hautzinger, James Edward *lawyer*
†Hawley, Robert Cross *lawyer*
Heiserman, Robert Gifford *lawyer*
Hendrix, Lynn Parker *lawyer*
Hensen, Stephen Jerome *lawyer*
Hilbert, Otto Karl, II, *lawyer*
Hill, Robert F. *lawyer*
Hoagland, Donald Wright *lawyer*
Hoffman, Daniel Steven *lawyer, law educator*
†Holder, Holly Irene *lawyer*
Holme, Richard Phillips *lawyer*
Hopfenbeck, George Martin, Jr., *lawyer*
Hopkins, Donald J. *lawyer*
†Houtsma, Peter C. *lawyer*
†Husband, John Michael *lawyer*
Imig, William Graff *lawyer, lobbyist*
Irwin, R. Robert *lawyer*
†Jablonski, James Arthur *lawyer*
Jacobs, Paul Alan *lawyer*
†Johnson, Philip Edward *lawyer*
Jones, Richard Michael *lawyer*
Kahn, Benjamin Alexander *lawyer*
†Kahn, Edwin Sam *lawyer*
†Kanan, Gregory Brian *lawyer*
Kaplan, Marc J. *lawyer*
Keatinge, Robert Reed *lawyer*
Keller, Glen Elven, Jr., *lawyer*
Kintzele, John Alfred *lawyer*
†Krendl, Cathy Stricklin *lawyer*
Law, John Manning *retired lawyer*
Lerman, Eileen R. *lawyer*
†Levis, William Herst *lawyer*
London, David L. *lawyer*
Long, Martin Edward *lawyer*
Low, Andrew M. *lawyer*
Low, John Wayland *lawyer*
†Lutz, John Shafroth *lawyer*
†Major, Alice Jean *lawyer*
Malatesta, Mary Anne *lawyer*
Marquess, Lawrence Wade *lawyer*
Martin, Dallas Rea *lawyer*
Martz, Clyde Ollen *lawyer, educator*
Mauro, Richard Frank *lawyer, investment manager*
McCabe, John L. *lawyer*
McConnell, Michael Theodore *lawyer*
McDowell, Karen Ann *lawyer*
McIntosh, Carolyn Leigh *lawyer*
McLain, William Allen *lawyer*
McManus, Richard Griswold, Jr., *lawyer*
McMichael, Donald Earl *lawyer*
Merker, Steven Joseph *lawyer*
†Merrick, Glenn Warren *lawyer*
Miller, Gale Timothy *lawyer*
Miller, J. Kent *lawyer, educator*
Miller, Robert Nolen *lawyer*
†Mitchem, Allen P. *lawyer*
†Mitchem, James E. *lawyer*
Moore, Steven Woodrow *lawyer*
Moye, John Edward *lawyer*
Murane, William Edward *lawyer*
Nanda, Ved Prakash *law educator, university official*
Nelson, John Gustaf *lawyer*
Nelson, L. Bruce *lawyer*
Newcom, Jennings Jay *lawyer*
Nier, Harry Kaufman *lawyer*
O'Keefe, Edward Franklin *lawyer*
Olsen, M. Kent *lawyer, educator*
Otten, Arthur Edward, Jr., *lawyer, corporate executive*
†Oxman, Stephen Eliot *lawyer*
Palmer, David Gilbert *lawyer*
†Pascoe, Donald Monte *lawyer*
Potter, Gary Thomas *lawyer*
†Pratt, Kevin Burton *lawyer*
†Prichard, Vincent Marvin *lawyer*
Prochnow, James R. *lawyer*
Puckett, Paul Walter *lawyer*
Quiat, Gerald M. *lawyer*
Quiat, Marshall *lawyer*
Ray, Bruce David *lawyer, writer*
Rench, Stephen Charles *lawyer*
Rich, Robert Stephen *lawyer*
†Rigg, John Brownlee, Jr., *lawyer*
Rockwood, Linda Lee *lawyer*
Roesler, John Bruce *lawyer*
Roy, Arthur Putnam *lawyer*
Ruppert, John Lawrence *lawyer*
Sarney, Saul Richard *lawyer*
†Sattler, Bruce Weimer *lawyer*
Sayre, John Marshall *lawyer, former government official*
Schmidt, L(ail) William, Jr., *lawyer*
Seawell, Donald Ray *lawyer, publisher, arts center executive, producer*
†Shea, Kevin Michael *lawyer*
†Shepherd, John Frederic *lawyer*
Skok, Paul Joseph *lawyer*
†Slavin, Howard Leslie *lawyer, real estate broker, law educator, judge*
†Solano, Henry L. *lawyer*
Starrs, Elizabeth Anne *lawyer*
†Steefel, David Simon *lawyer*
†Strenski, Robert Francis *lawyer*
Thomasch, Roger Paul *lawyer*
Timmins, Edward Patrick *lawyer*
Tisdale, Douglas Michael *lawyer*
Ulrich, Theodore Albert *lawyer*
van Westrum, Anthony *lawyer, arbitrator, mediator*
†Von Wald, Richard B. *lawyer*
Walsh, John Francis *lawyer*
Weinstein, David Akers *lawyer*
†Welch, Carol Mae *lawyer*
Wheeler, Malcolm Edward *lawyer, educator*
Wilcox, Martha Anne *lawyer*
†Williams, Andrea Irene *arbitrator, mediator, consultant*
Williams, Michael Anthony *lawyer*
Wohlgenant, Richard Glen *lawyer, director*
Wollins, David Hart *lawyer*
Woodward, Lester Ray *lawyer*
Wunnicke, Brooke *lawyer*
Yegge, Robert Bernard *law educator, dean*

Durango
Burnham, Bryson Paine *retired lawyer*
Sherman, Lester Ivan Jerry *retired lawyer*

Englewood
†Coffee, Melvin Arnold *retired lawyer*
†Deutsch, Harvey Elliot *lawyer*
†Epstein, Joseph Marc *lawyer*
Figa, Phillip Sam *lawyer*
†Karstaedt, Arthur R., III, *lawyer*
Lidstone, Herrick Kenley, Jr., *lawyer*
Shannon, Malcolm Lloyd, Jr., *lawyer, educator*
Simmons, David Norman *lawyer*
Spencer, Margaret Gilliam *lawyer*
Steinhauser, John William *retired lawyer*
Wagner, David James *lawyer*

Fort Collins
Downey, Arthur Harold, Jr., *lawyer, mediator*
Gast, Richard Shaeffer *lawyer*
Gilmore, Timothy Jonathan *paralegal*
Hjelmfelt, David Charles *lawyer*
†Johnson, Donald Edward, Jr., *lawyer*
Redder, Thomas Joseph *lawyer, judge, legislator, federal administrator, biotech executive*
Rogers, Garth Winfield *lawyer*

Fort Morgan
Higinbotham, Jacquelyn Joan *lawyer*

Frisco
Helmer, David Alan *lawyer*
McElyea, Monica Sergent *lawyer*

Glenwood Springs
Karp, Sander Neil *lawyer*

Golden
Carney, Deborah Leah Turner *lawyer*
Eiberger, Carl Frederick *lawyer*
Hughes, Marcia Marie *lawyer, consultant, motivational speaker*
Kopel, David Benjamin *lawyer*
†Outerbridge, Cheryl *lawyer*
†Phillipson, Donald E. *lawyer*
Snead, Kathleen Marie *lawyer*

Grand Junction
†Casebolt, James Stanton *lawyer*
†Griff, Harry *lawyer*
†Lachance, Paul Arthur *legal educator, consultant*

Greeley
Houtchens, Barnard *retired lawyer*

Greenwood Village
†Aspinwall, David Charles *lawyer, insurance company executive*
Dymond, Lewis Wandell *lawyer, mediator, educator*
†Fierst, Bruce Philip *lawyer*
Gallegos, Larry Duayne *lawyer*
Karr, David Dean *lawyer*
Nixon, Scott Sherman *lawyer*
Poe, Robert Alan *lawyer*
Ramsey, John Arthur *lawyer*
†Unruh, Kurt D. *lawyer, consultant*

Highlands Ranch
Hagen, Glenn W. *lawyer*
Mierzwa, Joseph William *lawyer, legal communications consultant*

Lakewood
Brant, John Getty *lawyer*
Guyton, Samuel Percy *retired lawyer*
Isely, Henry Philip *association executive, integrative engineer, writer, educator*
Jacobson, Dennis John *lawyer*
McElwee, Dennis John *lawyer, former pharmaceutical company executive*
Scott, Peter Bryan *lawyer*
Thome, Dennis Wesley *lawyer*
Wilson, James Robert *lawyer*
†Yuthas, George Anthony *lawyer*

Leadville
Bellhouse, Carol *lawyer*

Littleton
Carleno, Harry Eugene *lawyer*

Cypser, Darlene Ann *lawyer, movie producer*
Meyer, Milton Edward, Jr., *lawyer, artist*
Mielke, Donald Earl *lawyer, lobbyist*
Robinson, Warren A. (Rip Robinson) *lawyer*
Truhlar, Doris Broaddus *lawyer*
Unkelbach, L. Cary *lawyer*

Lone Tree
Spelts, Richard John *lawyer*

Longmont
†Bisgard, Eileen Bernice Reid *lawyer*
†Flanders, Laurence Burdette, Jr., *retired lawyer*

Louisville
†Kenney, Alan Adams *lawyer*
Raymond, Dorothy Gill *lawyer*

Montrose
†Overholser, John W. *lawyer*

Morrison
Bowen, Peter Geoffrey *arbitrator, business educator*

Parker
Greenberg, Morton Paul *lawyer, consultant, life settlement broker*

Placerville
Reagan, Harry Edwin, III, *lawyer*

Pueblo
Farley, Thomas T. *lawyer*
Humes, James Calhoun *lawyer, communications consultant, writer, educator*
Kogovsek, Daniel Charles *lawyer*
O'Conner, Loretta Rae *lawyer*

Rocky Ford
†Mendenhall, Harry Barton *lawyer*

Sedalia
Ewing, Mary *lawyer*
†Ewing, Robert Craig *lawyer, educator*

Thornton
Sherk, George William *lawyer*

Westcliffe
†Snyder, Paul *lawyer*

Westminster
†Gaither, John Francis, Jr., *lawyer*

CONNECTICUT

Avon
Godbout, Arthur Richard, Jr., *lawyer*
†Widing, Carol Scharfe *lawyer*

Bloomfield
Kelly, John Michael *lawyer*
†Messemer, Glenn Matthew *lawyer*

Bridgeport
†Goldberger, Robert R. *lawyer*
†Graham, Kenneth Albert *lawyer*
†Kern, Irving J. *lawyer*
Schrandt, Curtis Leon *lawyer, securities analyst, financial advisor*
†Schwartz, Lawrence B. *lawyer, accountant, banker*
†Sheldon, Robert Ryel *lawyer*
Zeldes, Jacob Dean *lawyer*

Brookfield
Lewis, Edwin Leonard, III, *lawyer*
Secola, Joseph Paul *lawyer*

Brooklyn
Dune, Steve Charles *retired lawyer*

Canaan
Capecelatro, Mark John *lawyer*

Colchester
Broder, Joseph Arnold *lawyer*

Danbury
Chaifetz, David Harvey *lawyer*
Keenan, Linda Lee *paralegal*
†Stichnoth, John A. *corporate lawyer*

Danielson
Jungeberg, Thomas Donald *lawyer*

Darien
Beach, Stephen Holbrook *lawyer*
Brown, James Shelly *lawyer*
Dale, Erwin Randolph *lawyer, author*
Himmelreich, David Baker *lawyer*
Prince, Kenneth Stephen *lawyer*
Swiggart, Carolyn Clay *lawyer*

Derby
McEvoy, Sharlene Ann *law educator*

Enfield
Berger, Robert Bertram *lawyer*

Fairfield
Caruso, Daniel F. *lawyer, judge, former state legislator*
Denniston, Brackett Badger, III, *lawyer*
†Heineman, Benjamin Walter, Jr., *lawyer*
Huth, William Edward *lawyer*
Osis, Daiga Guntra *lawyer*

Farmington
†Grafstein, Joel M. *lawyer*
Harvey, Elton Bartlett, III, *lawyer*
Mandell, Joel *lawyer*
Wiechmann, Eric Watt *lawyer*

Glastonbury
Rintoul, David Skinner *lawyer*
†Stephan, George Peter *lawyer, international business consultant*

Greenwich
Bam, Foster *lawyer*
Bentley, Peter *lawyer*
Berk, Alan S. *law firm executive*
Brandrup, Douglas Warren *lawyer*
Cantor, Samuel C. *lawyer, company executive*
Cantwell, Robert *lawyer*
Coleman, Joel Clifford *lawyer*
Dederick, Ronald Osburn *lawyer*
Forrow, Brian Derek *lawyer, corporation executive*
†Hurwich, Robert Allan *lawyer, multimedia, manufacturing and services company executive*
Lowenstein, Peter David *lawyer*
Lynch, William Redington *lawyer*
McDonald, Paul Kimball *lawyer, investment executive*
Mendenhall, John Ryan *retired lawyer, transportation executive*
More, Douglas McLochlan *lawyer*
Nimetz, Matthew *investment company executive*
Pascarella, Henry William *lawyer*
†Putman, Linda Murray *lawyer*
Schoonmaker, Samuel Vail, III, *lawyer*
Selby, Leland Clay *lawyer*
Storms, Clifford Beekman *lawyer*

Groton
†Cocheo, John Frank *lawyer*
†Stuart, Peter Fred *lawyer*

Hamden
Bershtein, Herman Sammy *lawyer*
†Eisner, Lawrence Brand *lawyer, real estate developer*
Greenblatt, Morton Harold *retired assistant attorney general*
Margulies, Martin B. *lawyer, educator*
Stankewich, Paul Joseph *lawyer*

Hartford
Alfano, Charles Thomas, Sr., *lawyer*
Anthony, J(ulian) Danford, Jr., *lawyer*
Appel, Robert Eugene *lawyer, educator*
†Baldini, Laura Flynn *lawyer*
†Bartolini, James Daniel *lawyer*
Bennett, Jessie F. *lawyer*
Berall, Frank Stewart *lawyer*
Blumberg, Phillip Irvin *law educator*
Bonee, John Leon, III, *lawyer*
†Buck, Gurdon Hall *lawyer, urban planner*
Cain, George Harvey *lawyer, business executive*
Cantor, Donald Jerome *lawyer*
†Caspar, George J., III, *lawyer*
Coyle, Michael Lee *lawyer*
Cullina, William Michael *lawyer*
Davis, Andrew Neil *lawyer, educator*
Del Negro, John Thomas *lawyer*
Dempsey, Edward Joseph *lawyer*
Dennis, Anthony James *lawyer*
Donnell, Brian James *lawyer*
Fain, Joel Maurice *lawyer*
Flaschen, Evan Daniel *lawyer*
Godfrey, Robert Douglas *lawyer*
Harrison, Thomas Flatley *lawyer*
Johnson, Dwight Alan *lawyer*
Kennedy, Jack Stanners *lawyer*
Knickerbocker, Robert Platt, Jr., *lawyer*
Korzenik, Armand Alexander *lawyer*
Leonhardt, Clifton Andrew *lawyer, public official*
Lloyd, Alex *lawyer*
†Lloyd, James Hendrie, III, *lawyer*
Lotstein, James Irving *lawyer*
Lyon, James Burroughs *lawyer*
Margulies, Beth Zeldes *assistant attorney general*
†McCracken, Gregory William *lawyer*
Merriam, Dwight Haines *lawyer, land use planner*
Metzler, Robert J., II, *lawyer*
Middlebrook, Stephen Beach *lawyer*
Miller, Jeffrey Clark *lawyer*
Milliken, Charles Buckland *lawyer*
†Morawetz, Thomas H. *law educator*
†Morrison, Francis Henry *lawyer*
Nimirowski, Ramona Furphy *legal administrator*
Nolan, John Blanchard *lawyer*
Orth, Paul William *retired lawyer*
Packard, Stephen Michael *lawyer*
†Paul, Jeremy Ralph *law educator*
Pepe, Louis Robert *lawyer, educator*
Pinney, Sidney Dillingham, Jr., *lawyer*
Richter, Donald Paul *lawyer*
Ryan, David Thomas *lawyer*
Schroth, Peter W(illiam) *lawyer, management and law educator*
See, Edmund M. *lawyer*
Shaw, L. Edward, Jr., *lawyer*
Smyth, Gerard A. *lawyer, administrator*
Sorokin, Ethel Silver *lawyer*
Space, Theodore Maxwell *lawyer*
Speziale, John Albert *lawyer*
Stravalle-Schmidt, Ann Roberta *lawyer*
Sylvester, Kathryn Rose *lawyer*
Tancredi, James J. *lawyer*
Tanski, James Michael *lawyer*
Taylor, Allan Bert *lawyer*
Thomas, Calvert *lawyer*
Voigt, Richard *lawyer*
Webster, Arthur Edward *lawyer*
†Weinberger, Steven *lawyer, educator*
Wilson-Coker, Patricia Anne *lawyer, social service administrator, educator*
Wolin, Neal Steven *lawyer*
Wolman, Martin *lawyer*
Young, Roland Frederic, III, *lawyer*

Lakeville
Cook, Charles David *international lawyer, arbitrator, consultant*
Jones, Ronald David *lawyer*

†Rout, Robert Howard *lawyer*

Litchfield
Fiederowicz, Walter Michael *lawyer*

Madison
Clendenen, William Herbert, Jr., *lawyer*

Manchester
Horwitz, Melvin *lawyer, physician*

Meriden
Lowry, Houston Putnam *lawyer*

Middlefield
†Lang, Edward Gerald *lawyer*

Milford
Berchem, Robert Lee, Sr., *lawyer*

Monroe
Hyman, Andrew Theodore *patent lawyer, physicist*
†Oliver, Milton McKinnon *lawyer, German translator, patent database searcher*

Mystic
Antipas, Constantine George *lawyer, civil engineer*
†Valentine, Garrison Norton *lawyer*

New Britain
Pearl, Helen Zalkan *lawyer*

New Canaan
Baker, George Walter *lawyer*
Steinmetz, Richard Bird, Jr., *lawyer*
Vasta, Vincent Joseph, Jr., *lawyer*

New Haven
Birnbaum, Irwin Morton *lawyer*
Burt, Robert Amsterdam *lawyer, educator*
Clark, Elias *law educator*
†Coan, Richard Morton *lawyer*
Cohen, Morris Leo *retired law librarian and educator*
Days, Drew S., III, *lawyer, law educator*
De Lio, Anthony Peter *lawyer*
†Donnelly, Robert L. *lawyer, corporation executive*
Duke, Steven Barry *law educator*
Ellickson, Robert Chester *law educator*
Freed, Daniel Josef *law educator*
Gastwirth, Donald Edward *lawyer, literary agent*
Geisler, Thomas Milton, Jr., *lawyer*
Gewirtz, Paul D. *lawyer, legal educator*
Gildea, Brian Michael *lawyer*
†Goetsch, Charles Carnahan *lawyer, legal historian*
Goldstein, Abraham Samuel *lawyer, educator*
Greenfield, James Robert *lawyer*
†Holt, Philetus Havens, IV, *lawyer, consultant*
Johnstone, Quintin *law educator, writer*
Knag, Paul Everett *lawyer*
Langbein, John Harriss *lawyer, educator*
Priest, George L. *law educator*
Reiner, Leona Hudak *consultant, attorney*
Reisman, William M. *lawyer, educator*
Robinson, Dorothy K. *lawyer*
Rose-Ackerman, Susan *law and political economy educator*
Schloss, Irving Steven *lawyer*
Skalka, Douglas Scott *lawyer*
†Sobol, Alan J. *lawyer*
Wiznia, Carolann Kamens *lawyer*

New London
Asselin, John Thomas *lawyer*
Dupont, Ralph Paul *lawyer, educator*
Johnstone, Philip MacLaren *lawyer*
Kalkstein, Joshua Adam *lawyer*
Reardon, Robert Ignatius, Jr., *lawyer*

New Milford
Edmondson, John Richard *lawyer, pharmaceutical manufacturing company executive*

Norfolk
Jessup, Philip Caryl, Jr.,

North Haven
Gradoville, Robert Thomas *lawyer*

North Stonington
Svengalis, Kendall Frayne *law librarian, educator, publishing executive*

Norwalk
†Cammaker, Sheldon Ira *lawyer*
Lang, Jules *lawyer*
Raikes, Charles FitzGerald *retired lawyer*

Norwich
Anderson, Carl Dennis *lawyer*
Masters, Barbara J. *lawyer*

Old Lyme
Crandall, Oliver Perry *lawyer, poet*

Plainville
Anderson, William Carl *lawyer*
†Zagorsky, Peter Joseph *lawyer*

Redding
Gooch, Anthony Cushing *lawyer*
Russell, Allan David *lawyer*

Ridgefield
†Bracken, Nanette Beattie *lawyer*
Fricke, Richard John *lawyer*
Sherman, Harold *lawyer*

Rocky Hill
†Lissy, David H. *corporate lawyer*

Roxbury
Friedman, John Maxwell, Jr., *lawyer*
Knutson, David Harry *retired lawyer, banker*

Shelton
Asija, S(atya) Pal *lawyer*
†Ryan, William Joseph, Jr., *lawyer*

Simsbury
Main, Philip David *lawyer, probate judge*

South Windsor
Gerlt, Wayne Christopher *lawyer*

Southbury
Auerbach, Ernest Sigmund *lawyer, company executive, writer*

Southport
Pickerstein, Harold James *lawyer*
Sanetti, Stephen Louis *lawyer*
†Williams, Michael Peter Anthony *lawyer*

Stamford
Barreca, Christopher Anthony *lawyer*
†Benedict, Peter Behrends *lawyer*
Bobrow, Henry Bernard *lawyer*
Bowen, Patrick Harvey *lawyer, consultant*
†Critelli, Michael J. *lawyer, manufacturing executive*
Daniels, Daniel Lloyd *lawyer*
Della Rocco, Kenneth Anthony *lawyer*
Gold, Steven Michael *lawyer*
†Hubschman, Henry A. *lawyer*
†Jensen, Frode, III, *lawyer*
Kweskin, Edward Michael *lawyer*
Lalli, Michael Anthony *lawyer*
†Lieberman, Steven Paul *lawyer*
†Ligelis, Gregory John *lawyer*
Margolis, Emanuel *lawyer, educator*
McDonald, Cassandra Burns *lawyer*
McGrath, Richard *lawyer*
Merritt, William Alfred, Jr., *lawyer, telecommunications company executive*
†Mirsky, Ellis Richard *lawyer*
Nichols, Ralph Arthur *lawyer*
Perle, Eugene Gabriel *lawyer*
†Rohrer, Dean Cougill *lawyer*
Rose, Richard Loomis *lawyer*
Sarner, Richard Alan *lawyer*
Shanman, James Alan *lawyer*
Skidd, Thomas Patrick, Jr., *lawyer*
Stapleton, James Francis *lawyer*
†Swerdloff, David Alan *lawyer*
Teitell, Conrad Laurence *lawyer, author*
Willkie, Wendell Lewis, II, *lawyer*
Yonkman, Fredrick Albers *lawyer, management consultant*

Stonington
Van Rees, Cornelius S. *lawyer*

Storrs Mansfield
Tucker, Edwin Wallace *law educator*

Stratford
Kossl, Thomas Leonard *lawyer*
O'Rourke, James Louis *lawyer*

Torrington
Leard, David Carl *lawyer*
Wall, Robert Anthony, Jr., *lawyer*

Trumbull
Czajkowski, Frank Henry *lawyer*
Williams, Ronald Doherty *lawyer*

Wallingford
Galligan, Matthew G. *lawyer*

Washington
Fishman, Mitchell Steven *lawyer*

Waterbury
Dost, Mark W. *lawyer*
Marano, Richard Michael *lawyer*

West Hartford
Dowling, Vincent John *retired lawyer*
Elliot, Ralph Gregory *lawyer*
Nereberg, Eliot Joel *lawyer*
Storm, Robert Warren *lawyer*
Swerdloff, Ileen Pollock *lawyer*
Swerdloff, Mark Harris *lawyer*

Westbrook
†Vogell, Connie *paralegal*

Weston
Aibel, Howard J. *lawyer, arbitrator, mediator*
Cohen, Fred Howard *lawyer, investment company executive*
Murray, Stephen James *lawyer*
Strauss, Ellen Louise Feldman *lawyer*

Westport
†Amschler, James Ralph *lawyer, relocation company executive*
Barton, James Miller *lawyer, international business consultant*
Carr, Cynthia *lawyer*
Cramer, Allan P. *lawyer*
Daw, Harold John *lawyer, director*
Dimes, Edwin Kinsley *lawyer*
Grodd, Leslie Eric *lawyer*
†Kanaga, Lawrence Wesley *lawyer*
Kosakow, James Matthew *lawyer*
Lindskog, David Richard *lawyer*
Paul, Roland Arthur *lawyer*
Razzano, Pasquale Angelo *lawyer*
Saxl, Richard Hildreth *lawyer*
Sheiman, Ronald Lee *lawyer*
Spitzer, Vlad Gerard *lawyer*

Wethersfield
Terk, Glenn Thomas *lawyer*

Willimantic
†Schiller, Howard Barry lawyer

Wilton
Adams, Thomas Tilley lawyer
Duke, Robert Dominick lawyer
Healy, James Casey lawyer
Silverman, Melvin J. lawyer

Windsor
Lerman, Kenneth B. lawyer

DELAWARE

Dover
†Babiarz, Francis Stanley lawyer
Ennis, Bruce Clifford lawyer
†McNulty, Mark Andrew lawyer, state official
Steele, Myron Thomas lawyer
Stone, F. L. Peter lawyer
Twilley, Joshua Marion lawyer

Greenville
Long, Linda Ann lawyer

New Castle
Curran, Barbara Sanson lawyer

Newark
Elson, Charles Myer law educator
McCann, Richard Stephen lawyer
†Welsh, Paul Patrick retired lawyer

Wilmington
Bader, John Merwin lawyer
Baumann, Julian Henry, Jr., lawyer
†Biondi, O. Francis lawyer
Bissell, Rolin Plumb lawyer
Carey, John Patrick, III, lawyer
†Carey, Robert George lawyer
Carpenter, Edmund Nelson, II, retired lawyer
†Ciconte, Edward Thomas lawyer
Cooch, Edward W(ebb), Jr., lawyer
†Cottrell, Paul (William Cottrell) lawyer, educator
†Coulter, Chad W. lawyer, insurance company executive
†Davis, James Francis lawyer
Devine, Donn lawyer, genealogist, former city official
DiLiberto, Richard Anthony, Jr., lawyer
Dinnage, James David lawyer
†Elzufon, John A. lawyer
Erisman, James A. lawyer
Flame, Andrew Jay lawyer
Fullerton, Stuart Latimer corporate lawyer
†Gamble, Donald Geoffrey Bidmead lawyer
Gilliam, James H., Jr., lawyer, private investor, consultant
Goldman, Michael David lawyer
†Gordon, William Edmund, Jr., lawyer
Green, James Samuel lawyer
Grossman, Jerome Kent lawyer, accountant
Hannon, Leo Francis retired lawyer, educator
†Hatch, Denison Hurlbut, Jr., lawyer
Herdeg, John Andrew lawyer
Jewell, George Benson lawyer, educator, minister
Jolles, Janet K. Pilling lawyer
†Julian, J. R. lawyer
Katzenstein, Robert John lawyer
†Kelleher, Daniel Francis lawyer
Kimmel, Morton Richard lawyer
Kirk, Richard Dillon lawyer
Kirkpatrick, Andrew Booth, Jr., lawyer
Klayman, Barry Martin lawyer
Kristol, Daniel Marvin lawyer
†Lynn, James Torrence, III, lawyer
Magee, Thomas Hugh lawyer
Malik, John Stephen lawyer
†MaloneyHuss, Mary M. lawyer
Martin, William Joseph, III, lawyer
Meitner, Pamela lawyer, educator
Mekler, Arlen B. lawyer, chemist
Melnik, Selinda A. lawyer
†Ott, William Griffith law educator, writer
†Parsons, Donald Francis lawyer
Pazuniak, George lawyer
†Petrilli, Michelle Leslie lawyer
Rodgers, Stephen John lawyer, physician, consultant
Rothschild, Steven James lawyer
Salinger, Frank Max lawyer
Semple, James William lawyer
†Sheridan, John Robert lawyer
†Sullivan, Lawrence Matthew lawyer
Waisanen, Christine M. lawyer, writer
Ward, Rodman, Jr., lawyer, director
†Whitney, Douglas Edgar, Sr., lawyer
Wier, Richard Royal, Jr., lawyer

DISTRICT OF COLUMBIA

Washington
Aaronson, David Ernest law educator, lawyer
Abbott, Alden Francis lawyer, government official, educator
Abeles, Charles Calvert retired lawyer
Acheson, David Campion lawyer, author, policy analyst
†Ackerson, Nels J(ohn) lawyer
†Adams, John Jillson lawyer
Adams, Roger C. lawyer
†Adelman, Roger Mark lawyer, educator
Adler, Howard, Jr., lawyer
Adler, Howard Bruce lawyer
†Adler, Robert Martin lawyer
†Agrast, Mark David lawyer
Ain, Sanford King lawyer
Aisenberg, Irwin Morton lawyer
Alexander, Clifford Joseph lawyer
Alexander, Donald Crichton lawyer
Allan, Richmond Frederick lawyer
†Allard, Nicholas W. lawyer
Allen, William Hayes lawyer, educator
†Alvarez, Scott G. lawyer
Anderson, Frederick Randolph, Jr., lawyer, law educator
Andrew, Joseph Jerald lawyer
Andrews, Mark Joseph lawyer
†Anthony, Stephen Pierce lawyer
Apperson, Bernard James lawyer
Apple, James Glenn lawyer, educator
†Argiropoulos, Kathleen O'Neill lawyer
†Aron, Mark G. lawyer, transportation executive
Arthur, Andrew Reiser lawyer
Ashton, Richard M. federal lawyer
†Asmuth, Gretchen law librarian, records manager
†Attridge, Daniel F. lawyer
Atwood, James R. lawyer
Augustini, Michael Charles lawyer
Avil, Richard Daniel, Jr., lawyer
†Axelrad, Jeffrey lawyer
Axelrod, Jonathan Gans lawyer
Ayer, Donald Belton lawyer
Babby, Lon S. lawyer
†Bachman, Kenneth Leroy, Jr., lawyer
Bachrach, Eve Elizabeth lawyer
Baer, William J. lawyer
Ball, Markham (Robert Ball) lawyer, arbitrator, educator
Banzhaf, John F., III, legal association administrator, lawyer
Baran, Jan Witold lawyer, educator
†Barcella, Ernest Lawrence, Jr., lawyer
Bardin, David J. lawyer
Barnes, Donald Michael lawyer
Barnes, Mark James lawyer
Barnett, Robert Bruce lawyer, educator
Barr, Michael Blanton lawyer
†Barrie, John Paul lawyer, educator
Barron, Jerome Aure law educator
Bartlett, John Laurence lawyer
Bartlett, Michael John lawyer
Basseches, Robert Treinis lawyer
Batla, Raymond John, Jr., lawyer
Bauleke, Howard Paul lawyer
†Baum, Alissa L. lawyer
Bebchick, Leonard Norman lawyer
Beckwith, Edward Jay lawyer
†Bednar, Richard John lawyer, law educator
Beisner, John Herbert lawyer
Beizer, Robert A. lawyer
†Bell, Robert Brooks lawyer
Bell, Stephen Robert lawyer
Beller, Herbert N. lawyer
Bellinger, Edgar Thomson lawyer
Bellinger, John Bellinger, III, lawyer, government official
Bello, Judith Hippler lawyer
Belman, Murray Joel lawyer
Bennett, Alexander Elliot lawyer
Beresford, Douglas Lincoln lawyer
Bergner, Jane Cohen lawyer
Berl, Joseph M. lawyer
Berman, Marshall Fox lawyer
Bernabei, Lynne Ann lawyer
Berner, Frederic George, Jr., lawyer
Bernstein, Mitchell Harris lawyer
†Berz, David Richard lawyer
Besozzi, Paul Charles lawyer
Best, Judah lawyer
Betts, Kirk Howard lawyer
†Bickwit, Leonard, Jr., lawyer
Biddle, Timothy Maurice lawyer
Bierman, James Norman lawyer
Bingaman, Anne K. lawyer
Birnbaum, S. Elizabeth lawyer
Birnkrant, Henry Joseph lawyer
†Bishop, James Dodson lawyer, mediator
Bixler, John Mourer lawyer
Black, Stephen Franklin lawyer
Blair, David Belmont lawyer
Blair, Robert Allen business executive, lawyer
Blair, William McCormick, Jr., lawyer
Blake, Jonathan Dewey lawyer
Blazek-White, Doris lawyer
Bleakley, Peter Kimberley lawyer
Bleicher, Samuel Abram lawyer, government official
Bliss, Donald Tiffany, Jr., lawyer
Bloch, Richard Isaac labor arbitrator
Bloch, Stuart Marshall lawyer
Blumenfeld, Jeffrey lawyer, educator
Blumer, Dennis Hull lawyer, academic administrator
Bodansky, Robert Lee lawyer
Bodner, John, Jr., lawyer
Boehm, Steven Bruce lawyer
Bogard, Lawrence Joseph lawyer
Boger, William Hanna lawyer
Boggs, George Trenholm lawyer
Boggs, Judith Susan lawyer, health policy expert
Boggs, Thomas Hale, Jr., lawyer, director
Boland, Christopher Thomas, II, lawyer
Bolton, John Robert lawyer, government official
Bonvillian, William Boone lawyer
Born, Brooksley Elizabeth lawyer
†Borod, Donald Lee lawyer
Borsari, George Robert, Jr., lawyer, broadcaster
Boskey, Bennett lawyer
Boss, Lenard Barrett lawyer
†Bowie, Darren A. legal adviser
Boyd, Alan Martin lawyer, legal administrator
Boyd, Stephen Mather arbitrator, mediator, lawyer
†Boykin, Hamilton Haight lawyer
Bradlow, Daniel David law educator
†Brady, Richard Alan lawyer
Brame, Joseph Robert, III, lawyer
†Branch, Ronald Drewitt lawyer
†Braverman, Burt Alan lawyer
†Bredhoff, Elliot lawyer
Bregman, Arthur Randolph lawyer, educator
Brenner, Janet Maybin Walker lawyer
Brewster, Christopher Ralph lawyer
Brick, Barrett Lee lawyer
Briggs, Alan Leonard lawyer
Brinkmann, Robert Joseph lawyer
Brockway, David Hunt lawyer
Bromm, Susan Elizabeth lawyer, government official
†Bromwich, Michael Ray lawyer
Bronstein, Alvin J. lawyer
Brown, Charles Freeman, II, lawyer
Brown, David Nelson lawyer
Brown, Donald Arthur lawyer
Brown, George Leslie legislative affairs and business development consultant, former manufacturing company executive, former lieutenant governor
Brown, Preston lawyer
†Brown, Richard L. lawyer
Brown, Thomas Philip, III, lawyer
Browne, Richard Cullen lawyer
Bruce, E(stel) Edward lawyer
†Brunenkant, Jon Lodwick lawyer
Brunsvold, Brian Garrett lawyer, educator
Brustein, Michael Labe lawyer
Buc, Nancy Lillian lawyer
Bucholtz, Harold Ronald lawyer
Buckley, Jeremiah Stephen lawyer
Buckley, John Joseph, Jr., lawyer
†Bucklin, Donald Thomas lawyer
†Buffon, Charles Edward lawyer
Burack, Michael Leonard lawyer
Burchfield, Bobby Roy lawyer
Burchill, William Roberts, Jr., lawyer
Burka, Robert Alan lawyer
Burns, Stephen Gilbert lawyer
Burt, Jeffrey Amsterdam lawyer
Busby, David lawyer
Buscemi, Peter lawyer
Butler, Michael Francis lawyer
Calamaro, Raymond Stuart lawyer
Calderwood, James Albert lawyer
Cameron, Duncan Hume lawyer
Camp, John Clayton lawyer
Campbell, James Sargent lawyer
Canfield, Edward Francis lawyer, business executive
†Cannady, Teresa Lynn lawyer
†Cantor, Richard Alan lawyer
Caplin, Mortimer Maxwell lawyer, educator
†Carey, Hugh L. lawyer, former governor
Carey, Sarah Collins lawyer
Carlson, Amy L. lawyer
Carneal, George Upshur lawyer
Carney, Robert Thomas lawyer
†Carome, Patrick Joseph lawyer
†Carpenter, Russell H., Jr., lawyer
Carpenter, Sheila Jane lawyer
Carr, Lawrence Edward, Jr., lawyer
Carroll, J. Speed lawyer, financial executive
Carrow, Milton Michael law educator
Carter, Barry Edward lawyer, educator, administrator
Carter, William Joseph lawyer
Casey, Bernard J. lawyer
†Cash, Roderick William, Jr., lawyer
Cashen, Henry Christopher, II, lawyer, former government official
Casserly, James Lund lawyer
Cassidy, Robert Charles, Jr., lawyer
Chabot, Elliot Charles lawyer
Chameides, Steven B. lawyer
†Chandler, James Phillip law educator
Chanin, Michael Henry lawyer
Chanin, Robert Howard lawyer
Chapoton, John Edgar lawyer, government official
Chopko, Mark E. lawyer
Christaldi, Brian lawyer
Christian, Betty Jo lawyer
Christian, Ernest Silsbee, Jr., lawyer
Cicconi, James William lawyer
Clagett, Brice McAdoo lawyer, writer
Clark, LeRoy D. legal educator, lawyer
Close, David Palmer lawyer
Cobb, Calvin Hayes, Jr., lawyer
Cobbs, Nicholas Hammer lawyer
Coerper, Milo George lawyer, priest
Coffield, Shirley Ann lawyer, educator
Cohen, Edward Barth lawyer
Cohen, Louis Richard lawyer
†Cohen, Nelson Craig lawyer
Cohen, Sheldon Stanley lawyer
Cohn, Sherman Louis lawyer, educator
Cole, John Pope, Jr., lawyer
Cole, Robert Theodore lawyer
Coleman, William Thaddeus, Jr., lawyer
Collins, Daniel Francis lawyer
†Collins, John Timothy lawyer
Collinson, Dale Stanley lawyer
Colson, Earl Morton lawyer, educator
†Columbus, R. Timothy lawyer
Comstock, Robert Francis lawyer
†Connelly, Warren E. lawyer
Cook, Harry Clayton, Jr., lawyer
Cook, Michael Harry lawyer
Cooper, Alan Samuel lawyer, educator
Cooper, Clement Theodore lawyer
†Cooper, Richard Melvyn lawyer
Cooter, Dale A. lawyer
Cope, John R(obert) lawyer
Cortese, Alfred William, Jr., lawyer, consultant
Cox, Kenneth Allen lawyer, communications consultant
Craft, Robert Homan, Jr., lawyer
Craig, Gregory Bestor lawyer, government official
Crosby, William Duncan, Jr., lawyer
†Crowell, Eldon Hubbard lawyer
Cruden, John Charles lawyer
Crumlish, Joseph Dougherty lawyer
†Crump, John lawyer
Crump, Ronald Cordell lawyer
†Culvahouse, Arthur Boggess, Jr., lawyer
Cummings, Frank lawyer
Cummins, Howard Wallace lawyer
Cutler, Lloyd Norton lawyer
Cymrot, Mark Alan lawyer
Cys, Richard L. lawyer
Czarra, Edgar F., Jr., lawyer
Daddario, Emilio Quincy retired lawyer
Dalley, George Albert lawyer, consultant
Dam, Kenneth W. lawyer, law educator, federal agency administrator
Danas, Andrew Michael lawyer
Daniels, Diana M. lawyer
†Da Ponte, John Joseph, Jr., lawyer
Davidow, Joel lawyer
Davidson, Daniel Ira lawyer
Davidson, Daniel Morton lawyer
Davidson, Tom William lawyer
Davies, Charles R. lawyer
Davison, Calvin retired lawyer
†Day, James MacDonald lawyer, educator
†deKieffer, Donald Eulette lawyer
†DeLeon, Patrick Henry lawyer
de Leon, Sylvia A. lawyer
Dembling, Paul Gerald lawyer, former government official
Denger, Michael Louis lawyer
Denison, Mary Boney lawyer
Denny, Judith Ann retired lawyer
Deso, Robert Edward, Jr., lawyer
†Determan, Sara-Ann lawyer
Devall, James Lee lawyer
Dewey-Balzhiser, Anne Elizabeth Marie lawyer
Dicello, Francis P. lawyer
Diercks, Walter Elmer lawyer
Dinan, Donald Robert lawyer
Dinerstein, Robert David lawyer
Dinh, Viet D. law educator
Disenhaus, Helen Elizabeth lawyer
Disheroon, Fred Russell lawyer
Docter, Charles Alfred lawyer, former state legislator
Dolan, Michael William lawyer
†Dole, Robert J. lawyer, former senator
Donegan, Charles Edward lawyer, educator
Donohoe, Charles Richard general patent counsel
Doolittle, Jesse William, Jr., lawyer
Dorsen, David M(ilton) lawyer
†Douglas, John Woolman lawyer
Dowley, Joseph Kyran lawyer, member congressional staff
Downey, Arthur Thomas, III, lawyer
Downs, Clark Evans lawyer
Dreisbach, Daniel Livingstone lawyer, educator
Drinan, Robert Frederick lawyer, former congressman, educator, clergyman
Dunn, Herbert Irvin lawyer
Dunner, Donald Robert lawyer
Durney, Michael Cavalier lawyer
Durnil, Gordon Kay lawyer, diplomat, arbitrator, political party official
†Dutton, Frederick Gary lawyer
Dye, Alan Page lawyer
Dye, Stuart S. lawyer
Dyk, Timothy Belcher federal judge, educator
†Eastment, Thomas James lawyer
Easton, John Jay, Jr., lawyer
Edelman, Alan Irwin lawyer
Edelman, Marian Wright (Mrs. Peter B. Edelman) lawyer
Edson, Charles Louis lawyer, educator
Efros, Ellen Ann lawyer
Ehrenhaft, Peter David lawyer
Eisenberg, Meyer lawyer
Elcano, Mary S. lawyer
†Eldridge, William Butler lawyer
El-Fishawy, Saad Samuel lawyer
Ellicott, John LeMoyne lawyer
Ellis, Courtenay lawyer
Elmer, Brian Christian lawyer
Elrod, Eugene Richard lawyer
Emery, Nancy Beth lawyer
Enzel, David Howard lawyer
Epstein, Gary Marvin lawyer
Epstein, Lionel Charles lawyer
Epstien, Jay Alan lawyer
†Ertel, Ruth Robinson lawyer, government official
†Ervin, Susan Chadwick lawyer
Esslinger, John Thomas lawyer
†Evans, Donald Charles, Jr., lawyer
Evans, Robert David legal association executive
Everett, Ralph Bernard lawyer
Ewing, Ky Pepper, Jr., lawyer
Fahrenkopf, Frank Joseph, Jr., lawyer
Fairbanks, Richard Monroe, III, lawyer, former ambassador at large
Faley, R(ichard) Scott lawyer
Fanone, Joseph Anthony lawyer
Farabow, Ford Franklin, Jr., lawyer
Faron, Robert Steven lawyer
†Fawell, Reed Marquette, III, lawyer
Fedders, John Michael lawyer
†Feder, David L. lawyer
Feffer, Gerald Alan lawyer
Feinberg, Kenneth Roy lawyer, law educator
Feinstein, Nathan B. lawyer
Feldhaus, Stephen Martin lawyer
Feldman, Clarice Rochelle lawyer
Feldman, Mark B. lawyer
Feldman, Roger David lawyer
†Fels, Nicholas Wolff lawyer
Ferrand, Louis George lawyer
Ferrara, Ralph C. lawyer
†Fex, Cecilia lawyer
Fielding, Fred Fisher lawyer
†Fienberg, Linda Doris lawyer
Fingham, Richard Frank lawyer
Finkel, Eugene Jay lawyer
†Finston, Susan Kling lawyer
Firestone, Charles Morton lawyer, educator
Fishburne, Benjamin P., III, lawyer
Fisher, Benjamin Chatburn lawyer
Fitzpatrick, James Franklin lawyer
Flannery, Ellen Joanne lawyer
Fleischaker, Marc L. lawyer
Flowe, Benjamin Hugh, Jr., lawyer
†Flowe, Carol Connor lawyer
Fogarty, John Patrick Cody lawyer
Forester, John Gordon, Jr., lawyer
Forrest, Herbert Emerson lawyer
Foster, C(harles) Allen lawyer
†Foster, Mark Wingate lawyer
Fowler, J. Edward lawyer
Fowler, Tillie Kidd lawyer
†Fox, Hamilton Phillips, III, lawyer
†Fox, Paul Walter lawyer
Frank, David Lewis lawyer

Pate, Michael Lynn *lawyer*
†Patterson, Eliza *lawyer*
†Patton, Frances Anne *lawyer*
Paul, William McCann *lawyer*
†Payton, John *lawyer*
Pearlman, Ronald Alan *lawyer, educator*
Pearlstein, Paul Davis *lawyer*
Peck, Robert Stephen *lawyer, educator*
Pedersen, William Francis *lawyer*
Peet, Richard Clayton *lawyer, consultant*
Perlik, William R. *lawyer*
Perlman, Matthew Saul *lawyer*
Peters, Frederick Whitten *lawyer*
Peterson, Charles Hayes *lawyer*
†Petito, Christopher Salvatore *lawyer*
Petrash, Jeffrey Michael *lawyer*
Pfeiffer, Margaret Kolodny *lawyer*
Pfeiffer, Steven Bernard *lawyer*
Phemister, Thomas Alexander *lawyer*
†Philion, Norman Joseph, III, *lawyer*
Phillips, Carter Glasgow *lawyer*
Pickering, John Harold *lawyer*
Pittman, Lisa *lawyer*
Pittman, Steuart Lansing *lawyer*
Plaine, Daniel J. *lawyer*
Plaine, Lloyd Leva *lawyer*
Platt, Laurence Eric *lawyer*
Platt, Roger *lawyer, lobbyist*
Pluta, Tom *lawyer*
Podberesky, Samuel *lawyer*
Poe, Luke Harvey, Jr., *lawyer*
Pogue, L(loyd) Welch *lawyer*
Policy, Vincent Mark *lawyer*
Pollak, Stephen John *lawyer*
†Polon, Ira H. *lawyer*
Poneman, Daniel Bruce *lawyer*
Postol, Lawrence Philip *lawyer*
†Potenza, Joseph Michael *lawyer*
Potter, Trevor Alexander McClurg *lawyer*
Potts, Ramsay Douglas *lawyer, aviator*
Potts, Stephen Deaderick *lawyer*
Povich, David *lawyer*
Powers, Richard Edward, Jr., *lawyer*
Preston, Richard McKim *lawyer*
Prettyman, Elijah Barrett, Jr., *lawyer*
Price, Daniel Martin *lawyer*
†Price, Donald Douglas *lawyer*
Price, Griffith Baley, Jr., *lawyer*
Price, Joseph Hubbard *lawyer*
Pulley, Lewis Carl *lawyer*
Pusey, William Anderson *lawyer*
Quale, John Carter *lawyer*
Quarles, James Linwood, III, *lawyer*
Quarles, Randal Keith *lawyer, federal official, bank executive*
Quarterman, Cynthia Louise *lawyer*
Quint, Arnold Harris *lawyer*
Quintiere, Gary Gandolfo *lawyer*
Rabecs, Robert Nicholas *lawyer*
Rabekoff, Elise Jane *lawyer*
Racicot, Marc F. *lawyer, former governor*
Rademaker, Stephen Geoffrey *lawyer*
Rafferty, James Gerard *lawyer*
Raimo, Bernard (Bernie Raimo) *lawyer*
†Rauh, Carl Stephen *lawyer*
Raul, Alan Charles *lawyer*
†Reade, Claire Elizabeth *lawyer*
Reid, Inez Smith *lawyer, educator*
Rein, Bert Walter *lawyer*
Repper, George Robert *lawyer*
Resor, Stanley Rogers *lawyer*
Rezneck, Daniel Albert *lawyer*
Rhyne, Sidney White *lawyer*
Rice, Paul Jackson *lawyer, educator*
†Richards, Femi Soyinka *lawyer*
Richards, Suzanne V. *lawyer*
Richmond, David Walker *lawyer*
Richmond, Marilyn Susan *lawyer*
†Rider, James Lincoln *lawyer*
Rieser, Joseph A., Jr., *lawyer*
Rill, James Franklin *lawyer*
†Rissetto, Harry A. *lawyer*
Ritter, Jeffrey Blake *lawyer, consultant*
Rivers, Richard Robinson *lawyer*
Rizzo, James Gerard *lawyer*
Robbins, Robert Bernard *lawyer*
†Roberts, Edward Thomas *lawyer*
Roberts, James Harold, III, *lawyer*
Robinson, Davis Rowland *lawyer*
†Robinson, Stephanie *tax lawyer*
†Roccograndi, Anthony Joseph *lawyer*
Rockefeller, Edwin Shaffer *lawyer*
Rocque, Vincent Joseph *lawyer*
Rodemeyer, Michael Leonard, Jr., *lawyer*
Rogers, Paul Grant *lawyer, former congressman*
Rogers, William Dill *lawyer*
Rogovin, John A. *lawyer*
Rohner, Ralph John *lawyer, educator, university dean*
Roll, David Lee *lawyer*
Romeo, Peter John *lawyer*
Rooney, Kevin Davitt *lawyer*
Rose, Jonathan Chapman *lawyer*
Rosenberg, Ruth Helen Borsuk *lawyer*
Rosenblatt, Peter Ronald *lawyer, former ambassador*
Rosenbloom, David Harry *political science and law educator*
Rosenbloom, H. David *lawyer*
Rosenkrantz, Steven Jay *lawyer*
Rosenthal, Douglas Eurico *lawyer, author*
Rosenthal, Ilene Goldstein *lawyer*
Rosenthal, Steven Siegmund *lawyer*
Ross, Douglas *lawyer*
Ross, Stanford G. *lawyer, government official*
Rossotti, Barbara Jill Margulies *lawyer*
†Rothberg, Loretta Sue *lawyer*
†Rothenberg, Gilbert Steven *lawyer, law educator*
Rowden, Marcus Aubrey *lawyer, former government official*
Rowe, Richard Holmes *lawyer*
Rubin, Kenneth Allen *lawyer*
Ruddy, Frank *lawyer, former ambassador*
Rule, Charles Frederick (Rick Rule) *lawyer*
Rusch, Jonathan Jay *lawyer*
Russell, Michael James *lawyer*
Russin, Jonathan *lawyer, consultant*
Russo, Roy R. *lawyer*
Rutstein, David W. *lawyer, food products executive*
Ruttenberg, Charles Byron *lawyer*
Ruttinger, George David *lawyer*
†Rutzick, Mark Charles *lawyer*
Ryan, Frederick Joseph, Jr., *lawyer, retired federal official, broadcast executive*
†Ryan, Joseph *lawyer*
Ryerson, Paul Sommer *lawyer*
Sacher, Steven Jay *lawyer*
†Sackler, Arthur Brian *lawyer*
†Safir, Peter Oliver *lawyer*
Sagalkin, Sanford *lawyer*
St. Amand, Janet G. *government relations lawyer*
Salem, George Richard *lawyer*
Salgado, Elizabeth M. R. *lawyer*
†Salsbury, Michael H. *lawyer*
Saltzburg, Stephen Allan *law educator, consultant*
Samuelson, Kenneth Lee *lawyer*
Sanford, Bruce William *lawyer*
Santos, Leonard Ernest *lawyer*
†Sargentich, Thomas Oliver *law educator, researcher*
†Schaffner, Joan Elsa *law educator*
Schafrick, Frederick Craig *lawyer*
†Scheige, Steven Sheldon *lawyer*
Scheman, L. Ronald *lawyer, professional society administrator*
Schiffer, Lois Jane *lawyer*
Schmeltzer, Edward *lawyer*
Schmidt, Edward Craig *lawyer*
Schmidt, Richard Marten, Jr., *lawyer*
Schmidt, William Arthur, Jr., *lawyer*
†Schneebaum, Steven Marc *lawyer*
Schneider, Matthew Roger *lawyer*
Schor, Laurence *lawyer*
Schropp, James Howard *lawyer*
Schwaab, Richard Lewis *lawyer, educator*
Schwartz, Daniel C. *lawyer*
Schwartz, Gregory John *lawyer, business and investments transactions specialist*
Schwartz, Herman *law educator*
Schwartz, Victor Elliot *lawyer, educator*
Schwebel, Stephen Myron *mediator*
†Sclafani, Frances Ann *lawyer, federal agency executive*
Scott, Betsy Sue *lawyer*
Scott, Thomas Jefferson, Jr., *lawyer, electrical engineer*
Sears, John Patrick *lawyer*
Sears, Mary Helen *lawyer*
†Seeger, Edwin Howard *lawyer*
Shaffer, David James *lawyer*
Shanmugam, Kannon Kumar *lawyer*
Shelley, Herbert Carl *lawyer*
Sherman, Gerald Howard *lawyer, educator*
Sherman, Jonathan Henry *lawyer*
Sherman, Lawrence Jay *lawyer*
†Shieber, William J. *lawyer*
Shriver, Robert Sargent, Jr., *lawyer*
Shulman, Stephen Neal *lawyer*
†Shuman, Mark Patrick *lawyer, economist*
Siebert, Thomas L. *lawyer, diplomat*
Siegel, Michael Eric *judicial center official*
Siegel, Richard David *lawyer, former government official*
†Siekman, Thomas Clement *lawyer*
Silver, Harry R. *lawyer*
†Simons, Barbara M. *lawyer*
Simons, Lawrence Brook *lawyer*
Simpson, John M. *lawyer*
Singer, Daniel Morris *lawyer*
Singleton, Harry Michael *lawyer*
†Skinner, William Polk *lawyer*
†Slater, Valerie A. *lawyer*
Sloame, Stuart C. *lawyer*
†Smith, Brian William *lawyer, former government official*
Smith, Daniel Clifford *lawyer*
†Smith, Duncan Campbell, III, *lawyer*
Smith, Dwight Chichester, III, *lawyer*
Smith, Emory Clark *lawyer, financial advisor*
†Smith, Turner Taliaferro, Jr., *lawyer*
Smoot, Oliver Reed, Jr., *lawyer, trade association administrator*
Smyth, Paul Burton *lawyer*
Sohn, Louis Bruno *lawyer, educator*
†Sokal, Allen Marcel *lawyer*
†Solomon, Frederic *lawyer*
†Solomon, Lewis David *law educator*
Solomon, Rodney Jeff *lawyer*
Solomons, Mark Elliott *lawyer, art dealer, entrepreneur*
Sonde, Theodore Irwin *lawyer*
Spaeder, Roger Campbell *lawyer*
Spaeth, Steven Michael *lawyer*
Spector, Phillip Louis *lawyer*
Spencer, George Henry *lawyer*
†Stanley, Keith Eugene *lawyer*
Starrs, James Edward *law and forensics educator, consultant*
†Statland, Edward Morris *lawyer*
Stauffer, Ronald Eugene *lawyer*
Stayin, Randolph John *lawyer*
Stein, Daniel Alan *public interest lawyer*
Steiner, David Miller *lawyer*
†Steinwurtzel, Richard A. *lawyer*
Stern, Gerald Mann *lawyer*
Stern, Samuel Alan *lawyer*
Sterrett, Samuel Black *lawyer, former judge*
Stevens, Herbert Francis *lawyer, law educator*
Stevens, Paul Schott *lawyer*
Stewart, David Pentland *lawyer, educator*
†Stock, Stuart Chase *lawyer*
†Stoll, Richard G(iles) *lawyer*
Stone, Donald Raymond *lawyer*
Straser, Richard Alan *lawyer*
Strauss, Stanley Robert *lawyer*
Streb, Paul Gerard *arbitrator*
Stromberg, Clifford Douglas *lawyer*
Stromberg, Jean Wilbur Gleason *lawyer*
Strong, Carter *lawyer*
Stuart, Pamela Bruce *lawyer*
Stucky, Jean Seibert *lawyer*
Stucky, Scott Wallace *lawyer*
Sullivan, Brendan V., Jr., *lawyer*
Sullivan, David Bryan *lawyer*
Sullivan, Timothy *lawyer*
Summers, Janis Lee *lawyer*
Sundermeyer, Michael S. *lawyer*
Swankin, David Arnold *lawyer, consumer advocate*
†Swendiman, Alan Robert *lawyer*
Tabackman, Steven Carl *lawyer*
Tallent, Stephen Edison *lawyer*
Tannenwald, Peter *lawyer*
Tauber, Mark J. *lawyer*
†Taurman, John David *lawyer*
Taylor, James, Jr., *lawyer*
Taylor, Ralph Arthur, Jr., *lawyer*
Taylor, Richard Powell *lawyer*
Teague, Randal Cornell, Sr., *lawyer*
Teichler, Stephen Lin *lawyer*
Temko, Stanley Leonard *lawyer*
Tetzlaff, Charles Robert *lawyer*
Theroux, Eugene *lawyer*
Thomas, Ritchie Tucker *lawyer*
Thornburgh, Dick (Richard L. Thornburgh) *lawyer, former United Nations official, former United States attorney general, former governor*
†Thornton, Leslie *lawyer*
Tigar, Michael Edward *law educator*
Tirana, Bardyl Rifat *lawyer*
Tomlinson, Margaret Lynch *lawyer*
Tompert, James Emil *lawyer*
Tompkins, Joseph Buford, Jr., *lawyer*
Topelius, Kathleen Ellis *lawyer*
†Topol, Allan Jerry *lawyer*
Townsend, John Michael *lawyer*
Trager, Michael David *lawyer*
†Trencher, William Mannes *lawyer*
Trimble, Sandra Ellingson *lawyer*
Trinder, Rachel Bandele *lawyer*
†Trooboff, Peter Dennis *lawyer*
Troyer, Thomas Alfred *lawyer*
Tufaro, Richard Chase *lawyer*
Tulumello, Andrew Santo *lawyer*
Tung, Ko-Yung *lawyer*
Tuohey, Mark Henry, III, *lawyer*
Turnage, Fred Douglas *lawyer*
Tushnet, Mark Victor *law educator*
Tyler, Peggy Lynne Bailey *lawyer*
Tyner, Lee Reichelderfer *lawyer*
Uehlein, E(dward) Carl, Jr., *lawyer*
Unger, Laura S. *lawyer, commissioner*
Unger, Peter Van Buren *lawyer*
Vacketta, Carl Lee *lawyer, educator*
Vakerics, Thomas Vincent *lawyer*
Valentine, Debra A. *attorney*
Valentine, Steven Richards *lawyer*
†Vanderstar, John *lawyer*
Vanderver, Timothy Arthur, Jr., *lawyer*
Vardaman, John Wesley *lawyer*
†Vaughn, Robert Gene *law educator*
Verner, James Melton *lawyer*
Verrill, Charles Owen, Jr., *lawyer*
Vickery, Ann Morgan *lawyer*
Vieth, Gifford Duane *lawyer*
Villa, John Kazar *lawyer*
Vince, Clinton Andrew *lawyer*
Violante, Joseph Anthony *lawyer*
Waits, John A. *lawyer*
Waldron, Jonathan Kent *lawyer*
Wallace, Don, Jr., *law educator*
Wallace, James Harold, Jr., *lawyer*
Walsh, Michael J. *lawyer*
†Ward, Erica Anne *lawyer, educator*
†Wasserstrom, Ellen *lawyer*
Waters, Jennifer Nash *lawyer*
Waz, Joseph Walter, Jr., *government relations consultant, author*
Weadon, Donald Alford, Jr., *lawyer*
Webber, Richard John *lawyer*
Webster, William Hedgcock *lawyer*
Wedgwood, Ruth *law educator, international affairs expert*
Wegener, Mark Douglas *lawyer*
Weidenfeld, Edward Lee *lawyer*
Weiland, Paul S. *lawyer*
Weimer, Douglas Reid *lawyer*
Weiner, Kenneth Brian *lawyer*
Weinman, Howard Mark *lawyer*
Weinmann, Eric *retired lawyer*
Weinstein, Martin James *lawyer*
Weisgall, Jonathan Michael *lawyer*
Weiss, Arnold Hans
Weiss, Edith Brown *law educator*
Weiss, Mark Anschel *lawyer*
Weiss, Stephen J. *lawyer*
Weissman, William R. *lawyer*
Wellen, Robert Howard *lawyer*
Wenner, Charles Roderick *lawyer*
West, Gail Berry *lawyer*
†West, Joseph D. *lawyer*
Whitaker, A(lbert) Duncan *lawyer*
White, Lee Calvin *lawyer*
†White-Mahaffey, Virginia Louise *lawyer*
Whiting, Richard Albert *lawyer*
Whitley, Joe Dally *lawyer*
Wilchins, Howard Martin *lawyer*
Wilder, Roland Percival, Jr., *lawyer*
†Wilderotter, James Arthur *lawyer*
Wiley, Richard Emerson *lawyer*
Williams, Julie Lloyd *lawyer*
Williams, Karen Hastie *lawyer*
†Williams, Thomas Raymond *lawyer*
†Willmeth, Roger Earl *lawyer*
Wilmarth, Arthur Edward, Jr. *law educator*
Wilner, Thomas Bernard *lawyer*
Wilson, Michael Moureau *lawyer, physician*
Wine, L. Mark *lawyer*
Winston, Judith Ann *lawyer*
Winter, Douglas K. *lawyer, writer*
Wintrol, John Patrick *lawyer*
Wiseman, Alan M(itchell) *lawyer*
Wiss, Marcia A. *lawyer*
†Wolf, Christopher *lawyer*
†Wolf, William B., Jr., *lawyer*
†Wolff, Alan William *lawyer*
Wolff, Elroy Harris *lawyer*
†Wolff, Paul Martin *lawyer*
Woodall, Samuel Roy, Jr., *lawyer*
†Woodworth, Ramsey Lloyd *lawyer*
Work, Charles Robert *lawyer*
Worsley, James Randolph, Jr., *lawyer*
Worthy, Kenneth Martin *retired lawyer*
Worthy, Patricia Morris *law educator, lawyer*
Wray, Robert *lawyer*
Wu, Frank H. *law educator, journalist*
Wyss, John Benedict *lawyer*
Yablon, Jeffery Lee *lawyer*
Yambrusic, Edward Slavko *lawyer, consultant*
†Yannucci, Thomas David *lawyer*
Zane, Phillip Craig *lawyer*
Zax, Leonard A. *lawyer*
Zimmer, Michael J. *lawyer*
†Zimmer, Richard Alan *educational association administrator,lawyer, former congressman*
Zimmerman, Edwin Morton *lawyer*
Zipp, Joel Frederick *lawyer*
Zollar, Carolyn Catherine *lawyer*
Zuckman, Harvey Lyle *law educator*
†Zwick, Kenneth Lowell *lawyer, director*

Washington Naval Yard
Allahut, Louis *lawyer*

Wasington
†Cinquegrana, Americo Ralph *lawyer*

FLORIDA

Alachua
Gaines, Weaver Henderson *lawyer*

Altamonte Springs
Diefenbach, Dale Alan *retired law librarian*
†Fisher, James Craig *lawyer*
Gunewardene, Roshani Mala *lawyer*
†Heindl, Phares Matthews *lawyer*
Hoogland, Robert Frederics *lawyer*

Apopka
Seward, Jeffrey James *lawyer, protective services official, educator, administrator*

Arcadia
Cherry, Paul Stephen *lawyer*
†McGavic, Mitzie W. *court clerk*

Atlantic Beach
Bruno, Lisa *law librarian*

Aventura
Kaplan, Daniel *lawyer*

Bartow
Artigliere, Ralph *lawyer, educator, judge*
Cury, Bruce Paul *lawyer, magistrate, law educator*

Bascom
Brooten, Kenneth Edward, Jr., *retired lawyer, rancher, author, chief counsel United States Congress*

Bay Harbor Islands
Ryce, Donald Theodore *lawyer*

Boca Grande
Brock, Mitchell *lawyer*

Boca Raton
Arent, Albert Ezra *retired lawyer*
Beber, Robert H. *lawyer, financial services executive*
Buckstein, Mark Aaron *lawyer, mediator, educator*
Camilleri, Michael *lawyer, educator*
Erdman, Joseph *lawyer*
Fier, Elihu *lawyer, educator*
†Garlick, Michael *lawyer*
Godofsky, Stanley *lawyer*
Golis, Paul Robert *lawyer*
†Jacobs, Joseph James *lawyer, communications company executive*
Kassner, Herbert Seymore *lawyer*
†Kenwood, Joel David *lawyer*
Kitzes, William Fredric *lawyer, safety analyst, consultant*
Klein, Peter William *lawyer, corporate officer, investment company executive*
Kornberg, Joel Barry *lawyer, emergency physician*
McNair, Russell Arthur, Jr., *lawyer*
Reinstein, Joel *lawyer*
†Sax, Spencer Meridith *lawyer*
†Siegel, Lisa Beth *lawyer, accountant*
Silver, Barry Morris *lawyer*
Turner, Hugh Joseph, Jr., *lawyer*
Wallach, Steven Ernst *lawyer, pilot*
Wichinsky, Glenn Ellis *lawyer*
Willis, John Alexander *lawyer*

Bonita Springs
Dignan, Thomas Gregory, Jr., *lawyer*
Olander, Ray Gunnar *retired lawyer*

Boynton Beach
Babler, Wayne E. *lawyer, retired telephone company executive*
†Dembicer, Edwin Herbert *retired lawyer*
Hermann, Philip J. *lawyer*

Bradenton
Brenner, Frank *lawyer*
Clements, Allen, Jr., *retired lawyer*
LaForest, Lana Jean *lawyer*
Lopacki, Edward Joseph, Jr., *lawyer*
Thomas, Ella Cooper *lawyer*

Brandon
Curry, Clifton Conrad, Jr., *lawyer*
England, Lynne Lipton *lawyer, speech pathologist, audiologist*
Tittsworth, Clayton (Clayton Magness Tittsworth) *lawyer*

PROFESSIONAL INDEX 6547 LAW: LAW PRACTICE AND ADMINISTRATION

Brooksville
†Brown, James Milton *law educator*

Bushnell
Hagin, T. Richard *lawyer*

Cape Coral
†Driscoll, Dawn-Marie *lawyer*

Clearwater
Bairstow, Frances Kanevsky *arbitrator, mediator, educator*
Coleman, Jeffrey Peters *lawyer*
†Dougall-Sides, Leslie K. *lawyer*
†Falkner, William Carroll *lawyer*
Free, E. LeBron *lawyer, mediator*
Hogan, Elwood *lawyer*
Rogers, H. Dennis *lawyer*
Sandefer, G(eorge) Larry *lawyer*
Swope, Scott Paul *lawyer*
Tragos, George Euripedes *lawyer*
Weidemeyer, Carleton Lloyd *lawyer*
Zschau, Julius James *lawyer*

Cocoa
†Pound, Frank R., Jr., *lawyer*

Cocoa Beach
Burch, William Mark, II, *retired lawyer*
Church, Glenn J. *lawyer*

Coconut Grove
Arboleya, Carlos Joaquin *lawyer, broker*
Denaro, Gregory *lawyer*
Freeman, Lewis Bernard *forensic accountant, lawyer*
McAmis, Edwin Earl *lawyer*

Coral Gables
†Anthony, Andrew John *lawyer*
Bolton, David *lawyer, educator*
Cano, Mario Stephen *lawyer*
Dady, Robert Edward *lawyer*
David, George A. *lawyer*
Ely, John Hart *lawyer, university dean*
†Felder-Rodriguez, Monica Lee *lawyer*
Fletcher, Paul Gerald *lawyer*
Fournaris, Theodore James *lawyer*
Friedman, Marvin Ross *lawyer*
Gustafson, Anne-Lise Dirks *lawyer, foreign consul*
Haggard, William Andrew *lawyer*
Hoffman, Carl H. *lawyer*
Kearns, John W. *lawyer*
Manning, Elliott *lawyer, educator*
†Moreno, Fernando *lawyer, educator*
Moss, Ambler Holmes, Jr., *lawyer, former ambassador*
O'Donnell, Anthony Joseph, Jr., *lawyer, educator*
Paul, Robert *lawyer*
Pettigrew, Richard A. *lawyer*
†Regalado, Eloisa *lawyer*
Rust, Robert Warren *retired lawyer*
†Sacasas, Rene *lawyer*
Simpson, Russell Gordon *lawyer, former mayor, not-for-profit developer, consultant*
†Sugarman, Robert Alan *lawyer*

Coral Springs
Polin, Alan Jay *lawyer*
Wise, Steven M. *lawyer, author*

Davie
†Richmond, Michael Lloyd *lawyer, educator*

Daytona Beach
Barker, Robert Osborne (Bob Barker) *educator, mediator*
Neitzke, Eric Karl *lawyer*
Watts, C. Allen *lawyer*

Deerfield Beach
Buck, Thomas Randolph *retired lawyer, financial services executive*
Lenoff, Michele Malka *lawyer*

Delray Beach
Armstrong, Jack Gilliland *lawyer*
Larry, R. Heath *lawyer, director*
Reichart, Stuart Richard *lawyer*
Silberman, Charlotte Schatzberg *retired lawyer, artist*

Edgewater
Dunagan, Walter Benton *lawyer, educator*

Floral City
Williams, Nelson Garrett *retired lawyer, mediator*

Fort Lauderdale
†Adams, Daniel Lee *lawyer*
Adams, S. Charles *lawyer, speaker, writer, financial consultant, radio and television commentator*
†Ballot, Alissa E. *lawyer*
Barnard, George Smith *lawyer, former federal agency official*
Bogenschutz, J. David *lawyer*
Bunnell, George Eli *lawyer*
Bustamante, Nestor *lawyer*
†Cane, Marilyn Blumberg *lawyer, educator*
Clubb, Bruce Edwin *retired lawyer*
†Cole, James Otis *lawyer*
†Denman, James Burton *lawyer*
Di Giulian, Bruno L. *lawyer*
Dressler, Robert A. *lawyer*
Dutko, Michael Edward *lawyer*
Fischer, Carey Michael *lawyer*
Gardner, Russell Menese *lawyer*
Golden, E(dward) Scott *lawyer*
†Goldsten, Robert Emanuel *lawyer, investor*
Gude, Nancy Carlson *lawyer*
Haliczer, James Solomon *lawyer*
Harbaugh, Joseph Delbert *legal educator, consultant*
Hargrove, John Russell *lawyer*
Harris, Jeffrey Mark *lawyer, educator*
Heath, Thomas Clark *lawyer*
Hess, George Franklin, II, *lawyer*
Hester, Julia A. *lawyer*
Hirsch, Jeffrey Allan *lawyer*
Hoines, David Alan *lawyer*
James, Gordon, III, *lawyer*
Jarvis, Robert Mark *law educator*
Katz, Thomas Owen *lawyer*
King, Robert Lee *lawyer*
Kreizinger, Loreen I. *lawyer, nurse*
Kubler, Frank Lawrence *lawyer*
†Levitt, Preston Curtis *lawyer*
Lundt, Eric L. *lawyer*
Meeks, William Herman, III, *lawyer*
Moss, Stephen B. *lawyer*
†Oltman, John Harold *patent lawyer*
Richmond, Gail Levin *law educator*
Roselli, Richard Joseph *lawyer*
Ruback, Alan Steven *lawyer*
†Russell, Terrence Joseph *lawyer*
Sanders, Dale R. *lawyer*
Schneider, Laz Levkoff *lawyer*
Schreiber, Alan Hickman *lawyer*
Sherman, Richard Allen, Sr., *lawyer*
†Spellacy, John Frederick *lawyer*
Stankee, Glen Allen *lawyer*
†Stinson, Steven Arthur *lawyer*
Strickland, Wilton L. *lawyer*
†Tacher, Robert Frederick *lawyer*
†Toothaker-Walker, Stephanie Jean *lawyer*
†Weissman, Jeffrey Mark *lawyer*
Wich, Donald Anthony, Jr., *lawyer*

Fort Myers
Clarkson, Julian Derieux *lawyer*
Colasurd, Richard Michael *lawyer*
Dalton, Anne *lawyer*
Finman, Sheldon Eliot *lawyer, mediator*
Harrison, Simon M. *mediator, lawyer, arbitrator*
Kiernan, Edwin A., Jr., *lawyer, corporation executive*
Medvecky, Robert Stephen *lawyer*
Morse, John Harleigh *lawyer, director*
Peterson, Rodney Delos *mediator, forensic economist*
†Terry, T(aylor) Rankin, Jr., *lawyer*

Ft Myers
†O'Donnell, Bernard Joseph, Jr., *lawyer*

Gainesville
Criser, Marshall M. *lawyer, retired university president*
DeThomasis, Craig Constantine *lawyer, educator*
†Gordon, Michael Wallace *law educator*
†Hiers, Richard Hyde *lawyer, educator, writer*
Huszar, Arlene Celia *lawyer, mediator*
Israel, Jerold Harvey *law educator*
†Jones, Clifford Alan *lawyer*
Kaimowitz, Gabe Hillel *lawyer*
Kurrus, Thomas William *lawyer*
Maurer, Virginia Gallaher *law educator*
†McCoy, Francis Tyrone *law educator*
†McMahon, Martin James, Jr., *law educator, consultant*
Rosenblatt, Howard Marshall *lawyer, financial professional*
Smith, David Thornton *lawyer, educator*
†Taylor, Grace Elizabeth Woodall (Betty Taylor) *law educator, law library administrator*
Van Alstyne, W. Scott, Jr., *lawyer, educator*
Weyrauch, Walter Otto *law educator*
White, Jill Carolyn *lawyer*

Gulf Breeze
Burr, Timothy Fuller *lawyer*
Jester, William David *lawyer*

Gulfport
Allen, John Thomas, Jr., *lawyer*

Haines City
†Mc Dougall, Dugald Stewart *retired lawyer*

Highland Beach
Haight, Carol Barbara *lawyer*

Hobe Sound
Buetens, Eric D. *lawyer*
Markoe, Frank, Jr., *lawyer, business and hospital executive*
Matheson, William Lyon *lawyer*

Hollywood
Colbert, Dia Teresa *legal assistant*
Engel, Tala *lawyer*
†Hollander, Bruce Lee *lawyer, business executive*
Korthals, Candace Durbin *lawyer*
†Phillips, Gary Stephen *lawyer*
†Rogovin, Lawrence H. *lawyer*
Zebersky, Edward Herbert *lawyer*

Indialantic
†Rosenberg, Priscilla Elliott *lawyer*

Indian Harbor Beach
Tasker, Molly Jean *lawyer*

Jacksonville
Ball, Haywood Moreland *lawyer*
Beytagh, Francis Xavier, Jr., *law educator*
Boyer, Tyrie Alvis *lawyer*
Braddock, Donald Layton *lawyer, accountant, real estate broker, investor*
Bradford, Dana Gibson, II, *lawyer*
Bridgman, Mary Wood *lawyer*
Bryan, Joseph Shepard, Jr., *lawyer*
Bullock, Bruce Stanley *lawyer*
Burnett, Mary Parham *lawyer, airline captain*
Callender, John Francis *lawyer*
Christian, Gary Irvin *lawyer*
†Coffman, Daniel Ray, Jr., *lawyer*
Coker, Howard Coleman *lawyer*
Commander, Charles Edward *lawyer, real estate consultant*
Cooke, Alexander Hamilton *lawyer*
Cramer, Jeffrey Allen *lawyer*
Farmer, Guy Otto, II, *lawyer*
Gabel, George DeSaussure, Jr., *lawyer*
Glocker, Theodore William *lawyer, accountant*
Grogan, Michael Kevin *lawyer, negotiator*
Hair, Mattox S. *mediator, arbitrator, former judge, lawyer*
Halverson, Steven Thomas *lawyer, construction executive*
Hodge, James Edward *lawyer*
Hollon, John O(aks) *lawyer*
Houser, John Edward *lawyer*
†Kaunitz, Karen Rose Koppel *retired lawyer*
†Kelso, Linda Yayoi *lawyer*
Kent, John Bradford *lawyer*
Korn, Michael Jeffrey *lawyer*
Lee, Lewis Swift *lawyer*
Legler, Mitchell Wooten *lawyer*
Link, Robert James *lawyer, educator*
McBurney, Charles Walker, Jr., *lawyer*
McWilliams, John Lawrence, III, *lawyer*
Moseley, James Francis *lawyer*
O'Neal, Michael Scott, Sr., *lawyer*
Pillans, Charles Palmer, III, *lawyer*
Posgay, Matthew Nichols *lawyer*
Reed, Ronald Ernst *lawyer*
Rinaman, James Curtis, Jr., *lawyer*
†Rumrell, Richard Gary *lawyer*
†Schupp, Robert Warren *law educator*
Thomas, Archibald Johns, III, *lawyer*
Thrasher, John *lawyer, former state legislator*
Wallis, Donald Wills *lawyer*
White, Edward Alfred *lawyer*

Jasper
McCormick, John Hoyle *lawyer*

Jensen Beach
McHale, Michael John *lawyer*
Stuart, Harold Cutliff *lawyer, business executive*

Juno Beach
Clark, David William *lawyer, councilman*

Jupiter
del Russo, Alessandra Luini *retired law educator*

Key Biscayne
†Pearson, John Edward *lawyer*

Key Largo
Mattson, James Stewart *lawyer, environmental scientist, educator*

Key West
Brihammar, B. Niklas *lawyer*
Davila, Gregory David *lawyer*
Eden, Nathan E. *lawyer*
MacDougall, Peter *lawyer*
Smith, Wayne LaRue *lawyer, consultant*

Lake Buena Vista
Schmudde, Lee Gene *corporate lawyer*

Lake Placid
Roberts, William B. *lawyer, business executive*

Lake Wales
Adams, Paul Winfrey *lawyer, business executive*
Wales, Gwynne Huntington *retired lawyer*

Lake Worth
Kreidler, Frank Allan *lawyer*
Rose, Norman *retired lawyer, retired accountant*

Lakeland
Harris, Christy Franklin *lawyer*
Kittleson, Henry Marshall *lawyer*
Knowlton, Kevin Charles *lawyer*
Koren, Edward Franz *lawyer*
†Wendel, John Fredric *lawyer, professional sports consultant*

Largo
Christ, Earle L. *lawyer*
†Fedor, Allan John *lawyer*
†Hafling, Marilyn Elizabeth *lawyer*
Trevena, John Harry *lawyer*

Lecanto
Corsi, Philip Donald *lawyer*
Fischer, Theodore David *retired lawyer*

Leesburg
Austin, Robert Eugene, Jr., *lawyer*
Fechtel, Vincent John *legal administrator*

Live Oak
Peters, Lee Ira, Jr., *public defender*

Longboat Key
Freeman, Richard Merrell *lawyer, corporate director*

Longwood
Cordes, Alexander Charles *lawyer*
Tomasulo, Virginia Merrills *retired lawyer*

Lutz
Hayes, Timothy George *lawyer, consultant*

Maitland
Bailey, Michael Keith *lawyer*
†Rajtar, Steven Allen *lawyer*
†Trees, Philip Hugh *lawyer*

Marco Island
†Arnold, James Leonard *lawyer*

Melbourne
Cacciatore, S. Sammy *lawyer*
Cacciatore, Sammy Michel *lawyer*
†Dixon, Richard Dean *lawyer, educator*
Gougelman, Paul Reina *lawyer*
Kaner, Cem *lawyer, computer software consultant, educator*
†Stack, Charles Rickman *lawyer*
Trachtman, Jerry H. *lawyer*

Miami
†Akar, Virginia Maya *lawyer*
Amber, Laurie Kaufman *lawyer*
†Anderson, Terence James *law educator*
Arteaga, Harold Augustine *lawyer*
Astigarraga, Jose I(gnacio) *lawyer*
†Baena, Scott Louis *lawyer*
Baker, Thomas Eugene *law educator*
Baumberger, Charles Henry *lawyer*
Beasley, Joseph Wayne *lawyer*
Beckham, Walter Hull, Jr., *lawyer, educator*
Berman, Bruce Judson *lawyer*
Black, Roy *lawyer*
Blumberg, Edward Robert *lawyer*
Bronis, Stephen Jay *lawyer*
Burnett, Henry *lawyer*
Burton, Richard Jay *lawyer*
Cardenas, Alberto R. *lawyer*
Carnesoltas, Ana-Maria *lawyer*
Chabrow, Penn Benjamin *lawyer*
Clarke, Mercer Kaye *lawyer*
†Coffey, Kendall Brindley *lawyer*
Cohen, Jeffrey Michael *lawyer*
†Connor, Terence Gregory *lawyer*
†Culmo, Elisabeth M. *lawyer*
Curtis, Karen Haynes *lawyer*
†David, Christopher Mark *lawyer*
†Diaz, Benito Humberto *lawyer*
Dienstag, Cynthia Jill *lawyer*
Eaton, Joel Douglas *lawyer*
Elliot, Cameron Robert *lawyer*
Evans, Thomas William *lawyer*
Feinsmith, Paul Lowell *lawyer*
Ferrell, Milton Morgan, Jr., *lawyer*
Fishman, Lewis Warren *lawyer, educator*
Fontes, J. Mario F., Jr., *lawyer*
Friedman, Richard Nathan *lawyer*
Garrett, Richard G. *lawyer*
†Gelb, George Edward *lawyer*
†Gitlitz, Stuart Hal *lawyer*
Glickman, Fred Elliott *lawyer*
†Glinn, Franklyn Barry *lawyer*
Godofsky, Lawrence *lawyer*
†Golden, Donald Alan *lawyer*
Gragg, Karl Lawrence *lawyer*
Greenberg, Stewart Gary *lawyer*
Greenleaf, Walter Franklin *lawyer*
Greer, Alan Graham *lawyer*
Grossman, Robert Louis *lawyer*
Hajek, Robert J., Sr., *lawyer, real estate broker, commodities broker, nursing home owner*
†Hall, Adam Stuart *lawyer*
Hall, Andrew Clifford *lawyer*
Hall, Miles Lewis, Jr., *lawyer*
Halsey, Douglas Martin *lawyer*
Hartz, Steven Edward Marshall *lawyer, educator*
Hauser, Helen Ann *lawyer, consultant*
Hector, Louis Julius *lawyer*
Hickey, John Heyward (Jack Hickey) *lawyer*
Hirsch, Milton *lawyer*
Hoffman, Larry J. *lawyer*
Hollander, Frank *lawyer*
Houlihan, Gerald John *lawyer*
Hudson, Robert Franklin, Jr., *lawyer*
Imperato, Joseph John *lawyer, composer*
Jacobson, Bernard *lawyer*
Johnston, Philip Connelly *lawyer*
Katz, Lawrence Sheldon *lawyer*
Klock, Joseph Peter, Jr., *lawyer*
Korchin, Judith Miriam *lawyer*
Kritzer, Glenn Bruce *lawyer*
†Kuker, Alan Michael *lawyer*
Kurzban, Ira Jay *lawyer*
Lampen, Richard Jay *lawyer, investment banker*
Lancaster, Kenneth G. *lawyer*
Landy, Burton Aaron *lawyer*
†Lazenby, Robert Alfred *lawyer*
Leslie, Richard McLaughlin *lawyer, educator*
Levine, Robert Jeffrey *lawyer*
Lipcon, Charles Roy *lawyer*
†Lipoff, Norman Harold *lawyer*
Long, Maxine Master *lawyer*
Louis, Paul Adolph *lawyer*
Maher, Stephen Trivett *lawyer, educator*
†Maniatty, Philip Ward *lawyer*
†Marin, Ana Maria *lawyer*
Matthews, Douglas Eugene *lawyer, educator, consultant*
McCain, David B. *lawyer*
McKenna, Peter Dennis *lawyer*
Mehta, Eileen Rose *lawyer*
†Mendoza, Enid Duany *lawyer*
†Miller, James M. *lawyer*
Miller, Raymond Vincent, Jr., *lawyer*
†Miller Udell, Bronwyn *lawyer*
†Milstein, Richard Craig *lawyer*
Morton, Richard *lawyer, financial consultant*
Mudd, John Philip *lawyer*
Mullins, Edward M. *lawyer*
Murai, Rene Vicente *lawyer*
Murphy, Timothy James *lawyer*
Nachwalter, Michael *lawyer*
Nuernberg, William R(ichard) *lawyer*
O'Connor, Kathleen Mary *lawyer*
O'Meara, Vicki A. *lawyer*
Osman, Edith Gabriella *lawyer*
†Palahach, Michael *lawyer*
Payne, R.W., Jr., *lawyer*
†Peltz, Robert Dwight *lawyer*
Pena, Guillermo Enrique *lawyer*
Podhurst, Aaron Samuel *lawyer*
Poston, Rebekah Jane *lawyer*
Pratt, John Patrick *lawyer*
Pruna, Laura Maria *lawyer*
Quentel, Albert Drew *lawyer*
Quirantes, Albert M. *lawyer*
†Richman, Gerald F. *lawyer*
†Robinson, Thomas Adair *law educator, consultant*
†Roman, Ronald Peter *lawyer*
Ronzetti, Thomas A. Tucker *lawyer, law educator*
†Rosen, Michael James *lawyer*
Rothman, David Bill *lawyer*
Ruffner, Charles Louis *lawyer*

Sacher, Barton Stuart *lawyer*
†Samole, Myron Michael *lawyer, management consultant*
Santoro, Thomas Mead *lawyer*
Sargent, Joanne Elaine *lawyer*
†Schiffrin, Michael Edward *lawyer*
Schuette, Charles A. *lawyer*
†Schwartz, Bruce S. *lawyer*
Sharpstein, Richard Alan *lawyer*
Silber, Norman Jules *lawyer*
Simmons, Sherwin Palmer *lawyer*
Skolnick, S. Harold *lawyer*
Stansell, Leland Edwin, Jr., *lawyer, mediator, educator*
Stein, Allan Mark *lawyer*
†Steinberg, Marty *lawyer*
†Stieglitz, Albert Blackwell *lawyer*
Stokes, Paul Mason *lawyer*
†Stuever, Fred Ray *lawyer*
Thornton, John William, Sr., *lawyer*
Touby, Kathleen Anita *lawyer*
Vento, M. Thérèse *lawyer*
Walton, Rodney Earl *lawyer*
Wasson, Roy D. *lawyer*
Weiner, Lawrence *lawyer*
Weinger, Steven Murray *lawyer*
Weinstein, Alan Edward *lawyer*
Weinstein, Andrew H. *lawyer*
†Welbaum, R(ome) Earl *lawyer*
†Whisenand, James Dudley *lawyer*
Wiseheart, Malcolm Boyd, Jr., *lawyer*
Wright, Robert Thomas, Jr., *lawyer*
†Zamora, Antonio Rafael *lawyer*

Miami Beach
Arbuz, Joseph Robert *lawyer*
Brodie, Ronald *lawyer, author*
Zukernick, Harry *lawyer*

Miami Gardens
Ersek, Gregory Joseph Mark *lawyer, business administrator*

Miami Lakes
Dominik, Jack Edward *lawyer*

Miramar Beach
†Sayre, George Edward *retired lawyer*

Naples
Anderson, John Thomas *lawyer*
Berning, Randall Karl *lawyer, consultant, educator, publisher*
Blumenthal, Ronnie *lawyer*
Bruce, Jackson Martin, Jr., *lawyer*
Buckley, Frederick Jean *lawyer*
Budd, David Glenn *lawyer*
Cimino, Richard Dennis *lawyer*
Crehan, Joseph Edward *lawyer*
Doub, William Offutt *lawyer*
Doyle, Robert Eugene, Jr., *lawyer*
Ericson, Roger Delwin *lawyer, forest resource company executive*
Fultz, Robert Edward *lawyer*
†Irvin, Robert Julian *lawyer*
McCaffrey, Judith Elizabeth *lawyer*
†McDonnell, Michael R. N. *lawyer*
McSwiney, Charles Ronald *lawyer*
Norton, Elizabeth Wychgel *lawyer*
Petersen, David L. *lawyer*
Putzell, Edwin Joseph, Jr., *lawyer, mayor*
Rigor, Bradley Glenn *lawyer*
Schauer, Wilbert Edward, Jr., *lawyer, manufacturing company executive*
Smith, Numa Lamar, Jr., *lawyer*
†Spanton, William Floyd *lawyer, consultant*
†Steinhouse, Carl Lewis *lawyer*
Stevens, William Kenneth *lawyer*
Strauss, Jerome Manfred *lawyer, banker*
Werder, Horst Heinrich *lawyer*
†Westman, Carl Edward *lawyer*

New Port Richey
Focht, Theodore Harold *lawyer, educator*

North Miami
Dellagloria, John Castle *city attorney, educator*

North Miami Beach
Slewett, Robert David *lawyer*
Zipkin, Sheldon Lee *lawyer, educator*

North Palm Beach
Coyle, Dennis Patrick *lawyer*
Daniels, Bruce Joel *lawyer*
Stauder, Michael H. *lawyer*

Ocala
†Hatch, John D. *lawyer*
Spivey, Stephen Dale *lawyer*

Okeechobee
Selmi, William, Jr., *lawyer*

Oldsmar
Hirschman, Sherman Joseph *lawyer, accountant, educator*

Opa Locka
Light, Alfred Robert *lawyer, political scientist, educator*

Orlando
†Abbott, Charles Warren *lawyer*
Ahlers, Glen-Peter, Sr., *law library director, educator, consultant*
Blackford, Robert Newton *lawyer, director*
Blackwell, Bruce Beuford *lawyer*
Boyles, William Archer *lawyer*
†Capouano, Albert D. *lawyer*
Chong, Stephen Chu Ling *lawyer*
Christiansen, Patrick T. *lawyer*
Conti, Louis Thomas Moore *lawyer*
†Cunningham, James Owen *lawyer*
Davidson, Richard Dodge *lawyer*
deBeaubien, Hugo H. *lawyer*
Dempsey, Bernard Hayden, Jr., *lawyer*
Eagan, William Leon *lawyer*
Fildes, Richard James *lawyer*
†Frey, Louis, Jr., *lawyer, federal and state government official*
Gold, I. Randall *lawyer*
Griffin, Harmon Terrell *lawyer*
Handley, Leon Hunter *lawyer*
Harris, Gordon H. *lawyer*
Hartley, Carl William, Jr., *lawyer*
Hendry, Robert Ryon *lawyer*
Henry, William Oscar Eugene *lawyer*
†Hill, Brian Donovan *lawyer*
Hille, Robert John *lawyer, trust officer*
Hurt, Jennings Laverne, III, *lawyer*
Ioppolo, Frank S., Jr., *lawyer*
Jontz, Jeffry Robert *lawyer*
†Kantor, Hal Halperin *lawyer*
Kehoe, Terrence Edward *lawyer*
Leonhardt, Frederick Wayne *lawyer*
†Lubet, Marc Leslie *lawyer*
Metz, Larry Edward *lawyer*
Mock, Frank Mackenzie *lawyer*
Morgan, Mary Ann *lawyer*
†Motes, Carl Dalton *lawyer*
†Murrell, Robert George *lawyer*
Nadeau, Robert Bertrand, Jr., *lawyer*
Nants, Bruce Arlington *lawyer*
†Neff, A. Guy *lawyer*
Peterson, David Eugene *lawyer*
†Pierce, John Gerald (Jerry Pierce) *lawyer*
Reed, John Alton *lawyer*
Russ, James Matthias *lawyer*
Salzman, Gary Scott *lawyer*
Sheaffer, William Jay *lawyer*
Sims, Roger W. *lawyer*
Skambis, Christopher Charles, Jr., *lawyer*
Snively, Stephen Wayne *lawyer*
Spoonhour, James Michael *lawyer*
Subin, Eli Harold *lawyer*
†Swann, Richard Rockwell *lawyer, banker*
†Weiss, Christopher John *lawyer*
†Williamson, Michael George *lawyer*
Wilson, William Berry *lawyer*
Yates, Leighton Delevan, Jr., *lawyer*

Palatka
Baldwin, Allen Adail *lawyer, writer*

Palm Bay
Howard, Marilyn Hoey *lawyer*

Palm Beach
Adler, Frederick Richard *lawyer, financier*
Canary, Nancy Halliday *lawyer*
Crawford, Sandra Kay *lawyer*
†Cummings, William Roger *international tax consultant, property management executive*
Devins, Robert Sylvester *retired lawyer*
Graubard, Seymour *lawyer*
Hastings, Lawrence Vaeth *lawyer, physician, educator*
Rauch, George Washington *lawyer, director*

Palm Beach Gardens
Auerbach, Paul Ira *lawyer*
†Blum, Irving Ronald *lawyer*
Pumphrey, Gerald Robert *lawyer*
†Scott, Alan Fulton, Jr., *lawyer*
†Seidman, Jennifer L. *lawyer*
Telepas, George Peter *retired lawyer*

Palm Coast
Duncan, Donald William *lawyer*
Patz, Edward Frank *retired lawyer*

Palm Harbor
†Baker, Gary Hugh *lawyer*
Rezanka, Thomas W. *lawyer*
Summers-Powell, Alan *lawyer*

Panama City
Allan, Sher L. *lawyer, mediator*

Parkland
†Masanoff, Michael David *lawyer*

Pass A Grille Beach
Garnett, Stanley Iredale, II, *lawyer, utility company executive*

Pensacola
Bozeman, Frank Carmack *lawyer*
Echsner, Stephen Herre *lawyer*
Gaines, Robert Pendleton *retired lawyer*
Geeker, Nicholas Peter *lawyer, judge*
George, Katie *lawyer*
Jespersen, Robert Randolph *legal consultant*
Levin, Fredric Gerson *lawyer*
Moulton, Wilbur Wright, Jr., *lawyer*
Soloway, Daniel Mark *lawyer*
Windham, John Franklin *lawyer, educator*
†Woodward, David Luther *lawyer, consultant*

Pineland
Donlon, William James *retired lawyer*

Plant City
Buchman, Kenneth William *lawyer*
Sparkman, Steven Leonard *lawyer*

Plantation
Crespi, Ted *lawyer*
Sperry, Martin Jay *lawyer*
Stone, Marc J. *lawyer*

Pompano Beach
Hasenauer, Judith Anne *lawyer*
Kory, Marianne Greene *lawyer*
Meloy, Sybil Piskur *retired lawyer*
Saunders, James Dalton *lawyer*
†Service, John Gregory *law educator*
Shulmister, M(orris) Ross *lawyer*
Szilassy, Sandor *retired lawyer, library director, educator*

Ponte Vedra Beach
Horty, John Francis *lawyer*
Kuhn, Bowie K. *lawyer, former professional baseball commissioner, consultant*

Port Charlotte
Levin, Allen Jay *lawyer*

Port Saint Lucie
Lambert, George Robert *lawyer, realtor*

Saint Augustine
Ansbacher, Sidney Franklyn *lawyer*
Poole, Sharon Alexandra *lawyer*

Saint Petersburg
Battaglia, Anthony Sylvester *lawyer*
Battaglia, Brian Peter *lawyer*
†Bernstein, Howard Mark *lawyer*
†Boydstun, Charles Bryant, Jr., *lawyer*
Carrere, Charles Scott *law educator, judge*
Escarraz, Enrique, III, *lawyer*
Georges, Richard Martin *lawyer, educator*
Glass, Roy Leonard *lawyer*
Harrell, Roy G., Jr., *lawyer*
Hudkins, John W. *lawyer*
Jacob, Bruce Robert *law educator*
†Keane, Michael J. *lawyer*
Kiefner, John Robert, Jr., *lawyer, educator*
Lang, Joseph Hagedorn *lawyer*
Mann, Sam Henry, Jr., *lawyer*
Moody, Lizabeth Ann *law educator*
Ross, Howard Philip *lawyer*
Scott, Kathryn Fenderson *lawyer*
†Swygert, Michael I(rven) *legal educator*
Wadley, W(illiam) Thomas *lawyer*
†Wein, Stephen Joshua *lawyer*

Saint Petersburg Beach
†Gagan, James Ephriam *lawyer*

Sarasota
Christopher, William Garth *lawyer*
Clarke, Garvey Elliott *lawyer*
Close, Michael John *lawyer*
Conetta, Tami Foley *lawyer*
Ehrlich, Bernard Herbert *lawyer, association executive*
Fetterman, James Charles *lawyer*
†Foreman, Michael Loren *lawyer*
Garland, Richard Roger *lawyer*
Gladding, Nicholas C. *lawyer*
Greenfield, Robert Kauffman *retired lawyer*
Heitler, George *lawyer*
Herb, F(rank) Steven *lawyer*
Hull, J(ames) Richard *retired lawyer, business executive*
Kimbrough, Robert Averyt *lawyer*
Partoyan, Garo Arakel *lawyer*
Phillips, Elvin Willis *lawyer*
Raimi, Burton Louis *lawyer*
Rossi, William Matthew *lawyer*
Summonte, Joseph F., Jr., *lawyer*
Wadsworth, Dyer Seymour *retired lawyer*
Wagner von Igelgrund, Wenceslas Joseph *law educator*
†Wolfe, Richard Barry Michael *retired lawyer*

Sebring
†McCollum, James Fountain *lawyer*
Trombley, Michael Jerome *lawyer*
Weimer, Peter Dwight *retired mediator, lawyer, corporate executive*

Shalimar
Chesser, David Michael *lawyer*

South Miami
†Keedy, Christian David *lawyer*

Stuart
McManus, F. Shields *lawyer*

Sun City Center
Fuller, Samuel Ashby *retired lawyer, mining company executive*
†L'Ecuyer, Eleanor Creed *lawyer, retired career officer*

Tallahassee
Aurell, John Karl *lawyer*
Boyd, Joseph Arthur, Jr., *lawyer*
Carson, Leonard Allen *lawyer*
†Conners, Patricia A. *lawyer*
Cummings, Frederic Alan *lawyer*
Curtin, Lawrence N. *lawyer*
Davis, William Howard *lawyer*
DeFoor, J. Allison, II, *lawyer*
Downie, Robert Collins, II, *lawyer*
Ervin, Robert Marvin *lawyer*
Fonvielle, Charles David *lawyer*
France, Belinda Takach *lawyer, business owner*
Gary, Thomas *lawyer*
†Gievers, Karen A. *lawyer*
Griffith, Elwin Jabez *lawyer, university administrator*
Herskovitz, S(am) Marc *lawyer*
Holcomb, Lyle Donald, Jr., *retired lawyer*
†Kerns, David Vincent *lawyer*
†Larson, Sharon D. *lawyer, human resources specialist*
Mang, Douglas Arthur *lawyer*
Manley, Walter Wilson, II, *lawyer, business educator*
Marshall, Marilyn Josephine *lawyer*
†Masterson, Stephen Michael *lawyer*
†McHugh, William F. *legal educator*
Miller, Gregory R. *lawyer*
†Miller, Morris Henry *lawyer*
Minnick, Bruce Alexander *lawyer*
Morphonios, Dean B. *lawyer*
Phipps, Benjamin Kimball, II, *lawyer*
Reid, Robert C. *lawyer*
Schroeder, Edwin Maher *law educator*
Sheffield, Frank Elwyn *lawyer*
†Sprowls, Paul Alan *lawyer*
†Stinson, Donna Holshouser *lawyer*
Teson, Fernando Roberto *law educator, consultant*
Thiele, Herbert William Albert *lawyer*
Varn, Wilfred Claude *lawyer*
Whitney, Enoch Jonathan *lawyer*
Zaiser, Kent Ames *lawyer*

Tamarac
Fischler, Shirley Balter *retired lawyer*

Tampa
Adkins, Edward Cleland *lawyer*
†Aitken, Thomas Dean *lawyer*
†Albritton, Arthur Dallas *lawyer*
Alley, John-Edward *lawyer*
†Alpert, Jonathan Louis *lawyer*
Anton, David *lawyer*
Barkin, Marvin E. *lawyer*
†Barton, Bernard Alan, Jr., *lawyer*
Berkowitz, Herbert Mattis *lawyer*
Blacklidge, Raymond Mark *lawyer*
Blue, James Monroe *lawyer*
†Bowen, Paul Henry, Jr., *lawyer*
Buell, Mark Paul *lawyer*
Butler, Paul Bascomb, Jr., *lawyer*
Campbell, Richard Bruce *lawyer*
Corcoran, Clement Timothy, III, *lawyer*
Cunningham, Anthony Willard *lawyer*
Davis, Kirk Stuart *lawyer*
Davis, Richard Earl *lawyer*
DeVaney, Donna Brookes *lawyer*
Doliner, Nathaniel Lee *lawyer*
Donovan, Brian Joseph *lawyer*
Ellwanger, Thomas John *lawyer*
†Emerton, Robert Walter, III, *lawyer*
†Fantauzzi, Anthony Joseph, III, *lawyer*
†Feegel, John Richard *pathologist*
Fraley, F. Ronald *lawyer*
†Fuller, Diana Lynn *lawyer*
Gardner, J. Stephen *lawyer*
Gilbert, Leonard Harold *lawyer*
†Gilbert, Richard Allen *lawyer*
Givens, Stann William *lawyer*
Gordon, Jeffrey (Jack Gordon) *lawyer*
Grammig, Robert James *lawyer*
Hardy, Paul Duane *lawyer*
Heyck, Joseph Giraud, Jr., *lawyer*
Humphries, J. Bob *lawyer*
Huneycutt, Alice Ruth *lawyer*
Janney, Oliver James *lawyer, plastics and semiconductor company executive*
Jirotka, George M. *lawyer*
Jones, John Arthur *lawyer*
Kelly, Thomas Paine, Jr., *lawyer*
Knopik, Christopher Scott *lawyer*
Koehler, Martha-Kaye *lawyer*
Lamb, Bruce Douglas *lawyer*
Lane, Robin *lawyer*
Lau, Mary Applegate *lawyer, arbitrator, mediator*
Levine, Jack Anton *lawyer*
Litschgi, A. Byrne *lawyer*
MacDonald, Thomas Cook, Jr., *lawyer, mediator*
Mandelbaum, Samuel Robert *lawyer*
Martin, Gary Wayne *lawyer*
McAdams, John Pope *lawyer*
†McDevitt, Sheila Marie *lawyer, energy company executive*
McKay, Richard James *lawyer*
†Murray, John Michael *lawyer*
Neumaier, Mark Adam *lawyer*
Oehler, Richard Dale *lawyer*
Olson, John Karl *lawyer*
O'Neill, Albert Clarence, Jr., *lawyer*
Patrick, Victor Phillip *lawyer*
Pellett, Jon Michael *lawyer*
Petrila, John Philip *health law educator*
Rardon, Larry L. *lawyer*
Real, Catherine Williams *lawyer*
Roberson, Bruce Heerdt *lawyer*
Robinson, John William, IV, *lawyer*
Rosenkranz, Stanley William *lawyer*
†Rydberg, Marsha Griffin *lawyer*
Schwenke, Roger Dean *lawyer*
†Somers, Clifford Louis *lawyer*
Stagg, Clyde Lawrence *lawyer*
Stallings, Norman (Charles Norman Stallings) *lawyer*
Steele, Rebecca Harrison *lawyer, educator*
Stigall, Scott Owen *lawyer*
Stiles, Mary Ann *lawyer, author, lobbyist*
Tanzer, Jed Samuel *lawyer, financial consultant*
Taub, Theodore Calvin *lawyer*
Teblum, Gary Ira *lawyer*
†Thomas, Gregg Darrow *lawyer*
Thomas, Wayne Lee *lawyer*
Tirella, David Theodore *lawyer*
†Vento, John Sebastian *lawyer*
Vessel, Robert Leslie *lawyer*
Wagner, Frederick William (Bill Wagner) *lawyer*
Waller, Edward Martin, Jr., *lawyer*
Watson, Roberta Casper *lawyer*
†Weaver, Ronald Lee *lawyer*
Whatley, Jacqueline Beltram *lawyer*

Tequesta
Kay, Richard Broughton *lawyer*

Venice
Brott, Irving Deerin, Jr., *lawyer, judge*
Miller, Allan John *lawyer*

Vero Beach
Case, Douglas Manning *lawyer*
Goff, Michael Harper *retired lawyer*
†Gordon, William Stout *lawyer*
Kenrich, John Lewis *retired lawyer*
†O'Haire, Michael *lawyer*
Parlin, Charles C., Jr., *retired lawyer*

Wellington
Beck, Jan Scott *lawyer*

West Palm Beach
Austin, Scott Raymond *lawyer*
Baker, Bernard Robert, II, *lawyer*
†Barnett, Charles Dawson *lawyer*
Beall, Kenneth Sutter, Jr., *lawyer*
Beasley, James W., Jr., *lawyer*

†Carres, Louis George *lawyer*
Chopin, L. Frank *lawyer*
Chopin, Susan Gardiner *lawyer*
Conrad, Bette Anne Kester *lawyer, writer, minister*
Damico, Paul Anthony *lawyer, educator*
Dunkum, Betty Lee *lawyer*
†Dytrych, Denise Distel *lawyer*
Eyler, Bonnie *lawyer*
Finley, Chandler R. *lawyer*
Gildan, Phillip Clarke *lawyer*
†Grogan, Robert Harris *lawyer*
†Henry, Thornton Montagu *lawyer*
Hill, Thomas William, Jr., *lawyer, educator*
Hoch, Rand *lawyer, mediator*
Koffler, Warren William *lawyer*
Kornspan, Susan Felischner *lawyer*
Lampert, Michael Allen *lawyer*
†Lane, Matthew Jay *lawyer*
Layman, David Michael *lawyer*
Montgomery, Robert Morel, Jr., *lawyer*
Moore, George Crawford Jackson *lawyer*
Mrachek, Lorin Louis *lawyer*
Norton, William Alan *lawyer*
Orlovsky, Donald Albert *lawyer*
Penalta, C. Richard *prosecutor*
Reid, Justus Webb *lawyer*
†Roberts, George Preston, Jr., (Rusty Roberts) *lawyer*
Sklar, William Paul *lawyer, educator*
Smith, David Shiverick *lawyer, former ambassador*
Spillias, Kenneth George *lawyer*
Tabernilla, Armando Alejandro *lawyer*
Weitzman, Linda Sue *lawyer*
Zeller, Ronald John *lawyer*

Weston
Kniskern, Joseph Warren *lawyer*

Winter Haven
Dyal, Lucius Mahlon, Jr., *lawyer*

Winter Park
†Ackert, T(errence) W(illiam) *lawyer*
†Builder, J. Lindsay, Jr., *lawyer*
†Godbold, Gene Hamilton *lawyer*
Hadley, Ralph Vincent, III, *lawyer*
Heinle, Richard Alan *lawyer*
Johnson, Kraig Nelson *lawyer, mediator*
Wagner, Lynn Edward *lawyer*

GEORGIA

Albany
†Moorhead, William David, III, *lawyer, corporate executive*

Alpharetta
Boynton, Frederick George *lawyer*

Athens
Barrow, John J. *lawyer*
Beaird, James Ralph *law educator, dean*
Carlson, Ronald Lee *lawyer, educator*
†Chaffin, Verner Franklin *lawyer, educator*
Davis, Claude-Leonard *lawyer, university official*
Ellington, Charles Ronald *lawyer, educator*
†Heald, Paul Justin *law educator, writer*
Hellerstein, Walter *lawyer*
Houser, Ronald Edward *lawyer, mediator*
Huszagh, Fredrick Wickett *lawyer, educator, information management company executive*
†Kurtz, Paul Michael *law educator*
Larson, Edward John *law educator, lawyer, historian*
Puckett, Elizabeth Ann *law librarian, law educator*
Sachs, Margaret V. *law educator*

Atlanta
†Abernathy, Thomas Edwards, IV, *lawyer*
Abrams, Harold Eugene *lawyer*
Albert, Ross Alan *lawyer*
†Aldridge, John *lawyer*
†Alexander, Kent B. *lawyer*
Alexander, Miles Jordan *lawyer*
†Anderson, Peter Joseph *lawyer*
†Attridge, Richard Byron *lawyer*
Bankoff, Joseph R. *lawyer*
†Banks, Linda T. *legal assistant, massage therapist*
Barker, Clayton Robert, III, *lawyer*
Barkoff, Rupert Mitchell *lawyer*
†Bassett, Peter Q. *lawyer*
Bates, Beverly Bailey *lawyer*
Batson, Richard Neal *lawyer*
Baum, Stanley M. *lawyer*
†Beckham, Walter Hull, III, *lawyer*
Bennett, Jay D. *lawyer*
Billington, Barry E. *lawyer*
Bird, Wendell Raleigh *lawyer*
†Bisbee, David George *lawyer*
Blackburn, William Stanley *lawyer*
Blackstock, Jerry B. *lawyer*
†Blank, A(ndrew) Russell *lawyer*
Bloodworth, A(lbert) W(illiam) Franklin *lawyer*
Bonds, John Wilfred, Jr., *lawyer*
Bondurant, Emmet Jopling, II, *lawyer*
Booth, Gordon Dean, Jr., *lawyer*
†Bradley, Phillip Alden *lawyer*
Bramlett, Jeffrey Owen *lawyer*
†Branch, Thomas Broughton, III, *lawyer*
Bratton, James Henry, Jr., *lawyer*
Brown, John Robert *lawyer*
Byrne, Granville Bland, III, *lawyer*
Cadenhead, Alfred Paul *lawyer*
Calhoun, Scott Douglas *lawyer*
Calvert, Matthew James *lawyer*
Campbell, Charles Edward *lawyer*
Capron, John M. *lawyer*
Cargill, Robert Mason *lawyer*
†Carpenter, David Allan *lawyer*
†Carson, Christopher Leonard *lawyer*
Cavallini, Donna Francesca *law librarian*
Cavin, Kristine Smith *lawyer*
Chalker, Ronald Franklin *lawyer, educator*
Chilivis, Nickolas Peter *lawyer*
Chisholm, Tommy *lawyer, utility company executive*
Churchill, Joseph Lacy *lawyer*
Clarke, Thomas Hal *lawyer*
†Cobb, Charles Kenche *lawyer, real estate broker*
Cohen, Ezra Harry *lawyer*
Cohen, George Leon *lawyer*
Cohen, N. Jerold *lawyer*
Collins, Donnell Jawan *lawyer*
Collins, Steven M. *lawyer*
Cooper, Lawrence Allen *lawyer*
†Cooper, William Lewis *research librarian, lawyer, consultant*
†Coxe, Tench Charles *lawyer*
Croft, Terrence Lee *lawyer*
Cutshaw, Kenneth Andrew *lawyer*
Davies, Caleb, IV, *lawyer*
Davis, E(dward) Marcus *lawyer*
Davis, Frank Tradewell, Jr., *lawyer*
Denny, Richard Alden, Jr., *retired lawyer*
Despriet, John G. *lawyer*
Dobbs, C. Edward *lawyer, educator*
Doyle, Michael Anthony *lawyer*
Driver, Walter W., Jr., *lawyer*
Drucker, Michael Stuart *lawyer*
Duffey, William Simon, Jr., *lawyer*
Durrett, James Frazer, Jr., *retired lawyer*
Eckl, William Wray *lawyer*
†Edge, J(ulian) Dexter, Jr., *lawyer*
Edwards, Stephen Allen *lawyer*
Egan, Michael Joseph *retired lawyer, state legislator*
Epstein, David Gustav *lawyer*
Farnham, Clayton Henson *lawyer*
Fellows, Henry David, Jr., *lawyer*
Felton, Jule Wimberly, Jr., *lawyer*
Fleming, Julian Denver, Jr., *lawyer*
Forbes, Theodore McCoy, Jr., *arbitrator, mediator, retired lawyer*
Foreman, Edward Rawson *retired lawyer*
Franklin, Charles Scothern *lawyer*
Frenzel, James Charles *lawyer*
Gambrell, David Henry *lawyer*
Gannon, Mark Stephen *lawyer*
Ganz, Charles David *lawyer*
†Genberg, Ira *lawyer*
Girth, Marjorie Louisa *lawyer, educator*
Glaser, Arthur Henry *lawyer, mediator*
Goldstein, Elliott *lawyer, director*
Gonzalez-Pita, J. Alberto *lawyer*
Grady, Kevin E. *lawyer*
Grant, Walter Matthews *lawyer, corporate executive*
†Groton, James Purnell *lawyer, arbitrator*
Haas, George Aaron *lawyer*
Hanson, Avarita Laurel *lawyer*
Harkey, Robert Shelton *lawyer*
Harness, William Walter *lawyer*
†Hasson, James Keith, Jr., *lawyer, law educator*
Hawks, Barrett Kingsbury *lawyer*
Heady, Eugene Joseph *lawyer*
Hendricks, Nathan VanMeter, III, *lawyer*
Henwood, William Scott *lawyer*
Hinchey, John William *lawyer*
Hoff, Gerhardt Michael *lawyer, insurance company executive*
Hoffman, Michael William *lawyer, accountant*
Hopkins, John David *lawyer*
Howard, Harry Clay *lawyer*
Howell, Arthur *lawyer*
Hunter, Forrest Walker *lawyer*
†Ide, Roy William, III, *lawyer*
Isaf, Fred Thomas *lawyer*
Izard, John *lawyer*
Janney, Donald Wayne *lawyer*
†Jeffries, McChesney Hill, Jr., *lawyer*
Jenkins, Albert Felton, Jr., *lawyer*
Jones, Evan Wier *lawyer*
Jones, Frank Cater *retired lawyer*
†Jones, Glower Whitehead *lawyer*
Katz, Joel Abraham *lawyer, music consultant*
Kaufman, Mark David *lawyer*
†Kelley, James Francis *lawyer*
†Kelley, Jeffrey Wendell *lawyer*
Kessler, Richard Paul, Jr., *lawyer*
Killingsworth, Vernon Scott *technology lawyer*
Killorin, Robert Ware *lawyer*
Kinkopf, Neil Joesph *law educator*
Kinzer, William Luther *lawyer*
†Kirby, Peter Cornelius *lawyer, policy analyst*
Kitchens, Joyce Ellen *lawyer*
Kitchens, William H. *lawyer*
Klamon, Lawrence Paine *lawyer*
Kneisel, Edmund M. *lawyer*
Knowles, Marjorie Fine *lawyer, educator, dean*
Koplan, Andrew Bennet *lawyer*
Lackland, Theodore Howard *lawyer*
Lamon, Harry Vincent, Jr., *lawyer, director*
Landau, Michael B. *law educator, musician, writer*
Landon, James Henry *lawyer*
Lanier, George H. *lawyer*
Leach, James Glover *lawyer*
†Lee, William Clement, III, *lawyer*
Leibel, Steven K. *lawyer*
Leonard, David Morse *lawyer*
Lester, Charles Turner, Jr., *lawyer*
†Levy, Bertram Louis *lawyer*
Linder, Harvey Ronald *lawyer, arbitrator, mediator*
Linkous, William Joseph, Jr., *lawyer*
Lipshutz, Robert Jerome *lawyer, former government official*
Liss, Matthew M. *lawyer*
†Longhi, Patrick George *lawyer, educator*
†Lore, Stephen Melvin *lawyer*
Lower, Robert Cassel *lawyer, educator*
†Maines, James Allen *lawyer*
Manley, David Bott, III, *lawyer*
†Manning, Clarence Bond *lawyer*
†Marianes, William Byron *lawyer*
Marshall, John Treutlen *lawyer, educator*
Marshall, Thomas Oliver, Jr., *lawyer*
Marvin, Charles Arthur *law educator*
McAlpin, Kirk Martin *lawyer*
McCloud, Robert Olmsted, Jr., *lawyer*
†McGill, John Gardner *lawyer*
McNeill, Thomas Ray *lawyer*
McVey, Walter Lewis *lawyer, educator*
†Meyer, William Lorne *lawyer*
Miller, Janise Luevenia Monica *lawyer*
Mobley, John Homer, II, *lawyer*
†Moderow, Joseph Robert *lawyer, package distribution company executive*
Moeling, Walter Goos, IV, *lawyer*
Mull, Gale W. *lawyer*
Muller, William Manning *corporate lawyer*
Murphy, Richard Patrick *lawyer*
Myers, Johnnie Dumas *law educator*
†Oakley, Mary Ann Bryant *lawyer*
Ordover, Abraham Philip *lawyer, mediator*
Ortiz, Jay Richard Gentry *lawyer*
Owen, Robert Hubert *lawyer, former real estate broker*
Paquin, Jeffrey Dean *lawyer*
†Parker, Wilmer, III, *lawyer, educator*
Patrick, Deval Laurdine *lawyer*
†Patterson, William Robert *retired lawyer*
Persons, W. Ray *lawyer, educator*
Phillips, Barry *lawyer*
Piassick, Joel Bernard *lawyer*
Pike, Larry Samuel *lawyer*
Pilcher, James Brownie *lawyer*
Pless, Laurance Davidson *lawyer*
†Poe, H. Sadler *lawyer*
†Powell, Douglas Richard *lawyer*
Prince, David Cannon *lawyer*
Pryor, Shepherd Green, III, *lawyer*
Raby, Kenneth Alan *lawyer, retired army officer*
†Rajan, Anandhi *lawyer*
†Raskin, Daniel Ellis *lawyer*
Rattray, James Bailey *lawyer*
Reed, Glen Alfred *lawyer*
†Remar, Robert Boyle *lawyer*
Rhodes, Thomas Willard *lawyer*
Ridley, Clarence Haverty *lawyer*
†Robinson, Willie Edward *lawyer*
Rogers, C. B. *lawyer*
†Rumsey, D(avid) Lake, Jr., *lawyer*
Salo, Ann Sexton Distler *lawyer*
Savell, Edward Lupo *lawyer*
Schroder, Jack Spalding, Jr., *lawyer*
Schroeder, Eric Peter *lawyer*
Schulte, Jeffrey Lewis *lawyer*
Shapiro, George Howard *retired lawyer*
Sibley, Horace Holden *lawyer*
Sibley, James Malcolm *retired lawyer*
Smith, Alexander Wyly, Jr., *lawyer*
Smith, Jeffrey Michael *lawyer*
Smith, Sidney Oslin, Jr., *lawyer*
†Smith, Walton Napier *lawyer*
Spalten, David Elliot *lawyer*
Stallings, Ronald Denis *lawyer*
Stephenson, Mason Williams *lawyer*
Stine, J(ames) Larry *lawyer*
†Stokes, James Sewell *lawyer*
Strauss, Robert David *lawyer*
Sullivan, Terrance Charles *lawyer*
Sweeney, Neal James *lawyer*
Swift, Frank Meador *lawyer*
†Tanenbaum, Allan Jay *lawyer*
Tanner, W(alter) Rhett *lawyer*
Taylor, George Kimbrough, Jr., *lawyer*
Taylor, Roger Dale *lawyer*
†Thomas, James Joseph, II, *lawyer*
†Thrower, Randolph William *lawyer*
Varner, Chilton Davis *lawyer*
Veal, Rex R. *lawyer*
Wakefield, Stephen Alan *lawyer*
Walsh, W. Terence *lawyer*
Weathersby, James Roy *lawyer*
†Webb, J. David *lawyer*
Weber, Gerald Richard *legal association administrator, educator*
Wellon, Robert G. *lawyer*
Williams, Joel Cash *lawyer*
Williams, Neil, Jr., *lawyer*
Williamson, James Robert, Jr., *lawyer*
Wilson, James Hargrove, Jr., *lawyer*
Winkler, Allen Warren *lawyer, educator*
†Wood, L. Lin, Jr., *lawyer*
Worley, David *lawyer*
†Wright, Frederick Lewis, II, *lawyer*
Wright, Peter Meldrim *lawyer*
Young, Michael Anthony *lawyer*
†Young, Robert George *lawyer*
Zabka, Sven Paul *lawyer*
Zink, Charles Talbott *lawyer*

Augusta
Cooney, William J. *lawyer*
†Dickert, Neal Workman *lawyer*
Lee, Lansing Burrows, Jr., *lawyer, corporate executive*
†Miller, Alfred Montague *lawyer*
†Wheale, Duncan Douglas *lawyer*
Woods, Gerald Wayne *lawyer*

Brunswick
†McLemore, Gilbert Carmichael, Jr., *lawyer*

Canton
Hasty, William Grady, Jr., *lawyer*

Carrollton
Tisinger, David Harvey *lawyer*

College Park
Stokes, Arch *lawyer, writer*

Columbus
Brinkley, Jack Thomas *lawyer, former congressman*
Harp, John Anderson *lawyer*
Johnson, Walter Frank, Jr., *lawyer*
McGlamry, Max Reginald *lawyer*
Page, William Marion *lawyer*
†Patrick, James Duvall, Jr., *lawyer*
Poydasheff, Robert Stephen *lawyer*

Conyers
†Snapp, William Dorsey *lawyer*

Cordele
†Christy, Gary Christopher *lawyer*

Decatur
†Baker, Herman Dupree *lawyer*
Cooper, James Russell *retired law educator*
Guest, Abbi Taylor *lawyer, judge, educator*
†Keyes, Gwendolyn Rebecca *lawyer, educator*
Murphy, Deborah Jane *lawyer*

Doraville
Gerstein, Joe Willie *lawyer*

Douglas
Sims, Rebecca Littleton *lawyer*

Dublin
Greene, Jule Blounte *lawyer*

Duluth
Sloan, Donnie Robert, Jr., *lawyer*

Dunwoody
Callison, James W. *former lawyer, consultant, airline executive*

Eastman
†Wiggins, James L. *lawyer*

Fayetteville
†Fox, Patrick Joseph *lawyer*

Gainesville
Gilliam, Steven Philip, Sr., *lawyer*
Hester, Francis Bartow, III, (Frank Hester) *lawyer*
Schuder, Raymond Francis *lawyer*

Hamilton
Byrd, Gary Ellis *lawyer*
Chewning, Martha Frances MacMillan *lawyer*

Hinesville
Turner, Dwayne Curtis *lawyer*

Jasper
Marger, Edwin *lawyer*

Kennesaw
†Raines, Susan Summers *mediator, educator*

Kingsland
†Ossick, John Joseph, Jr., *lawyer*

Lawrenceville
Henson, Gene Ethridge *retired legal administrator*

Leesburg
†Myers, David Wayne *legal assistant*

Macon
†Brown, Stephen Phillip *judge*
Cole, John Prince *lawyer, university official*
†Dodson, Carr Glover *lawyer, director*
Ennis, Edgar William, Jr., *lawyer*
Hutto, Richard Jay *lawyer*
Robinson, W. Lee *lawyer*
Scarbary, Otis Lee *lawyer*
†Snow, Cubbedge, Jr., *lawyer*

Madison
DuBose, Charles Wilson *lawyer*

Marietta
Ahlstrom, Michael Joseph *lawyer*
Bentley, Fred Douglas, Sr., *lawyer*
Clay, Charles Commander (Chuck Clay) *lawyer, state senator*
Ingram, George Conley *lawyer, judge*
†Lurie, Jeanne Flora *lawyer*
McManus, Constance *lawyer*
Orr, John Traylor, Jr., *lawyer*

Mcdonough
Crumbley, R. Alex *lawyer*

Metter
Doremus, Ogden *lawyer*

Milledgeville
†Bradley, Wayne Bernard *lawyer*
Buice, Bonnie Carl *lawyer, priest*

Newnan
Franklin, Bruce Walter *lawyer*
Moore, Marianna Gay *law librarian, consultant*

Norcross
Hahn, Stanley Robert, Jr., *lawyer, financial executive*

Ocilla
†Pujadas, Thomas Edward *lawyer*

Rome
Brinson, Robert Maddox *lawyer*
†McCrory, Aldous Desmond *lawyer*

Roswell
Baker, Anita Diane *lawyer*
Birmingham, Richard Gregory *lawyer*
†Broome, Barry Dean *lawyer, estate and financial planning consultant*
England, John Melvin *lawyer, clergyman*
Mimms, Thomas Bowman, Jr., *lawyer*
Roland, Raymond William *lawyer, mediator, arbitrator*

Saint Marys
†Smith, Charles Courtland, Jr., *lawyer, state legislator*

Saint Simons Island
Thau, William Albert, Jr., *lawyer*

Savannah
Bowman, Catherine McKenzie *lawyer*
Dickey, David Herschel *lawyer, accountant*
†Forbes, Morton Gerald *lawyer*
†Friedman, Julian Richard *lawyer*
Gannam, Michael Joseph *lawyer*
Painter, Paul Wain, Jr., *lawyer*
Rawson, William Robert *lawyer, retired manufacturing company executive*
Stillwell, Walter Brooks, III, *lawyer*

Sea Island
Revoile, Charles Patrick *lawyer*

Sky Valley
Wilkinson, Albert Mims, Jr., *lawyer*

Smyrna
Seigler, Michael Edward *lawyer, librarian*

Snellville
Giallanza, Charles Philip *lawyer*

Statesboro
Stone, Ralph Kenny *lawyer*

Stone Mountain
†Le, Chi-Dinh *law educator, writer*
Minter, Kendall Arthur *lawyer*

Swainsboro
†Cadle, Jerry Neal *lawyer*

Tifton
†Fitzgerald, Anthony Patrick *criminal justice educator*

Tiger
Corry, Robert Emmett *lawyer*

Tucker
Armstrong, Edwin Alan *lawyer*
Wheeler, Edd Dudley *lawyer*

Valdosta
Bright, Joseph Converse *lawyer*
Cork, Robert Lander *lawyer*
Dodd, Roger J. *lawyer*
Edwards, Edith Martha *lawyer*
Sinnott, John Patrick *lawyer, educator*
Steinberg, Teresa Sherwood *paralegal, legal administrator*

Watkinsville
Wright, Robert Joseph *lawyer*

Zebulon
Watson, Forrest Albert, Jr., *lawyer, bank executive*

HAWAII

Hanalei
Bunyan, S. Wyanne *arbitrator, mediator, realtor*

Honolulu
Adams, Jo-Ann Marie *lawyer*
Adaniya, Kevin Seisho *lawyer*
Akinaka, Asa Masayoshi *lawyer*
Archer, Richard Joseph *lawyer*
Bloede, Victor Carl *lawyer, academic executive*
Boas, Frank *retired lawyer*
Bourgoin, David L. *lawyer, real estate broker, trade broker, educator, video/television producer*
Bunn, Robert Burgess *lawyer*
Callies, David Lee *lawyer, educator*
Campbell, Naomi Sylvia *lawyer*
Carson, Ellen Godbey *lawyer*
Case, James Hebard *lawyer*
Cassiday, Benjamin Buckles, III, *lawyer*
Char, Vernon Fook Leong *lawyer*
†Chung, Steven Kamsein *lawyer*
†Coates, Bradley Allen *lawyer*
Crumpton, Charles Whitmarsh *lawyer*
Dang, Marvin S. C. *lawyer*
Deaver, Phillip Lester *lawyer*
Devens, Paul *lawyer*
†Dodd, William Horace *lawyer*
†Duffy, James Earl, Jr., *lawyer*
Edmunds, John Sanford *lawyer*
†Faust, Anne Sonia *lawyer*
†Fujiyama, Wallace Sachio *lawyer*
Fukumoto, Leslie Satsuki *lawyer*
Gay, E(mil) Laurence *lawyer*
Gelber, Don Jeffrey *lawyer*
†Geshell, Richard Steven *lawyer*
Godbey, Robert Carson *lawyer*
Grande, Thomas Robert *lawyer*
†Hazlett, Mark A. *lawyer*
Heller, Ronald Ian *lawyer*
Hipp, Kenneth Byron *lawyer*
Hirai, Craig Kazuo *lawyer*
†Hite, Robert Griffith *lawyer*
Ichinose, Susan M. *lawyer*
Iijima, Chris K. *law educator*
Ingersoll, Richard King *lawyer*
Iwai, Wilfred Kiyoshi *lawyer*
†Kane, Joelle K.K.S. *lawyer*
Katayama, Robert Nobuichi *lawyer*
Kawachika, James Akio *lawyer*
†Kuniyuki, Ken Takaharu *lawyer*
Kupchak, Kenneth Roy *lawyer*
†Lacy, John R. *lawyer*
Lau, Eugene Wing Iu *lawyer*
†Lee, Patricia Y. *lawyer*
Lilly, Michael Alexander *lawyer, writer*
Lombardi, Dennis M. *lawyer*
Ma, Alan Wai-Chuen *lawyer*
†Marks, Michael J. *lawyer, corporate executive*
†Marrack, Alexander Case *lawyer*
Mau-Shimizu, Patricia Ann *lawyer*
McShane, Rosemary *lawyer*
Miller, Clifford Joel *lawyer*
Miller, Richard Sherwin *law educator*
Miyasaki, Shuichi *lawyer*
Moore, Ernest Carroll, III, *lawyer*
Moroney, Michael John *lawyer*
†Morse, Jack Craig *lawyer*
Nakata, Gary Kenji *lawyer*
†Okinaga, Carrie Kiyono *lawyer*
Okinaga, Lawrence Shoji *lawyer*
†Okuma-Sepe, Cheryl *lawyer*
Oldenburg, Ronald Troy *lawyer*
O'Neill, Ralph James *lawyer*
†Plum, William J. *lawyer*
†Portnoy, Jeffrey Steven *lawyer*
Potts, Dennis Walker *lawyer*
Quinn, William Francis *lawyer, director*
†Reber, David James *lawyer*
Reinke, Stefan Michael *lawyer*
Rohrer, Reed Beaver *lawyer*
†Rolls, John Marland, Jr., *lawyer*
Sato, Glenn Kenji *lawyer*
Schnack, Harold Clifford *retired lawyer*
Stacey, Richard Wayne *lawyer*
Sumida, Kevin P.H. *lawyer*
Suzuki, Norman Hitoshi *lawyer*
Taylor, Carroll Stribling *lawyer*
†Thielen, Cynthia Henry *lawyer, state legislator*
Turbin, Richard *lawyer*
Umebayashi, Clyde Satoru *lawyer*
†Van Dyke, Jon Markham Markham *law educator*
Wong, Alfred Mun Kong *lawyer*
Wong, James Thomas *lawyer*
Woo, Vernon Ying-Tsai *lawyer, real estate developer, judge*

Kailua
Webb, Charles Robert *lawyer, police officer*

Kailua Kona
Zola, Michael S. *lawyer*

Kaneohe
Donahoe, Peter Aloysius *lawyer*
†Huber, Thomas P. *lawyer*
Shulman, Corinne Edwards Lewis *mediator*

Kapolei
†Zabanal, Eduardo Olegario *lawyer*

Kihei
Burns, Richard Gordon *retired lawyer, writer, consultant*

Kilauea
Polli, Robert Paul *lawyer*

Kula
Maloney, Michael Patrick *lawyer, mediator, arbitrator*
Richardson, Robert Allen *retired lawyer, educator*
Rohlfing, Frederick William *lawyer, political consultant, retired judge*

Paia
Richman, Joel Eser *lawyer, mediator, arbitrator*

Wailuku
Kinaka, William Tatsuo *lawyer*

IDAHO

Boise
Burke, Cameron S. *legal administration*
Derr, Allen R. *lawyer*
†Erickson, Robert Stanley *lawyer*
Geston, Mark Symington *lawyer*
Hoagland, Samuel Albert *lawyer, pharmacist*
Leroy, David Henry *lawyer, state and federal official*
Lombardi, David Richard *lawyer*
†Luker, Lynn Michael *lawyer*
†Mauk, William Lloyd *lawyer*
†McGown, John, Jr., *lawyer*
Meyer, Christopher Hawkins *lawyer*
Minnich, Diane Kay *legal association administrator*
Noack, Harold Quincy, Jr., *lawyer*
Park, William Anthony (Tony Park) *lawyer*
Schild, Raymond Douglas *lawyer*
Shurtliff, Marvin Karl *lawyer*
†Storti, Philip Craig *lawyer*
†Thomas, Eugene C. *lawyer*
†VanHole, William Remi *lawyer*
Whittier, Monte Ray *lawyer*

Caldwell
Kerrick, David Ellsworth *lawyer*

Coeur D Alene
Garbrecht, Louis *lawyer*

Driggs
Cantwell, William Patterson *lawyer*

Eagle
Richardson, Betty H. *lawyer, former prosecutor*

Fort Hall
†Hall, Clyde Matthew *lawyer, advocate*

Hailey
Hogue, Terry Glynn *lawyer*
Youngblood, Deborah Sue *lawyer, speech pathology/audiology services professional*

Idaho Falls
Avery, John Orval *lawyer*
†St. Clair, John Gilbert *lawyer*

Kamiah
Mills, Lawrence *lawyer, business and transportation consultant*

Ketchum
†Holland, Robert James *retired lawyer*

Lewiston
Tait, John Reid *lawyer*

Moscow
Bielenberg, Leonard Herman *lawyer*
Greene, Timothy Geddes *lawyer*
Vincenti, Sheldon Arnold *law educator, lawyer*

Pocatello
Nye, W. Marcus W. *lawyer*

Twin Falls
Berry, L. Clyel *lawyer*
†Fassett, Stephanie A. *lawyer*
Hansen, John Joseph *lawyer*
†Sudweeks, Jay Dean *lawyer*

ILLINOIS

Abbott Park
Brock, Charles Marquis *lawyer*

Alton
Hoagland, Karl King, Jr., *lawyer*

Anna
†Plesko, Jeffrey Michael *lawyer*

Argonne
Tanzman, Edward Alan *lawyer*

Arlington Heights
Giampietro, Wayne Bruce *lawyer*
Tucker, Bowen Hayward *lawyer*

Aurora
Camic, David Edward *lawyer*
Dreyer, John Edward *lawyer*
McCleary, Scott Fitzgerald *lawyer*

Barrington
Lee, William Marshall *lawyer*
Wyatt, James Frank, Jr., *lawyer*

Belleville
Bauman, John Duane *lawyer*
Boyle, Richard Edward *lawyer*
†Gossage, Roza *lawyer, educator*
Heiligenstein, Christian Enric *lawyer*
Hess, Frederick J. *lawyer*
Mathis, Patrick Bischof *lawyer*
Neville, James Edward *lawyer*
†Parham, James Robert *lawyer*
Ripplinger, George Raymond, Jr., *lawyer*

Bloomington
Bragg, Michael Ellis *lawyer, insurance company executive*
Eckols, Thomas Aud *lawyer, educator*
Kelly, Timothy William *lawyer*
†McHugh, Donald P. *lawyer*
Wozniak, Debra Gail *lawyer*

Bourbonnais
Engels, Patricia Louise *lawyer*

Burr Ridge
Brennan, James Joseph *lawyer, banking and financial services executive*

Calumet City
†Scullion, Annette Murphy *lawyer, educator*
Scullion, Kevin Peter *lawyer*

Carbondale
Clemons, John Robert *lawyer*
†Lee, Mark Richard *lawyer, educator*
Matthews, Elizabeth Woodfin *law librarian, law educator*
Schroeder, William Arthur *law educator*
†Wesley, Howard Barry *lawyer*

Carrollton
Strickland, Hugh Alfred *lawyer*

Carthage
Glidden, John Redmond *lawyer*

Champaign
†Boyle, Francis Anthony *law educator*
Cribbet, John Edward *law educator, former university chancellor*
†Gunsalus, Carolyn Kristina *law educator, consultant*
Harden, Richard Russell *lawyer*
Jacobsen, Magdalena Gretchen *former mediator, former federal agency executive*
Kindt, John Warren *lawyer, educator, consultant*
Krause, Harry Dieter *law educator*
Maggs, Peter Blount *lawyer, educator*
Mamer, Stuart Mies *lawyer*
Mc Cord, John Harrison *lawyer, educator*
Meyer, David Douglas *lawyer, educator*
Miller, Harold Arthur *lawyer*
Nowak, John E. *law educator*
Rawles, Edward Hugh *lawyer*

Charleston
Gano, Kenneth Redman, Jr., *lawyer*

Chatham
†Post, Alan Richard *lawyer*

Chicago
Abrams, Lee Norman *lawyer*
Abt, Ralph Edwin *lawyer*
Acker, Ann *lawyer*
Acker, Frederick George *lawyer*
Ackerman, David Paul *lawyer*
†Adducci, James Dominick *lawyer*
Adelman, Stanley Joseph *lawyer*
Adelman, Steven Herbert *lawyer*
Alexander, Ian Robert *lawyer*
Allen, Ronald Jay *law educator*
Allen, Thomas Draper *lawyer*
Altman, Louis *lawyer, author, educator*
†Amend, James Michael *lawyer*
Anderson, J. Trent *lawyer*
Anderson, Kimball Richard *lawyer*
Anderson, Paul Stewart *lawyer*
†Anderson, William Cornelius, III, *lawyer*
Angst, Gerald L. *lawyer*
Anthony, Michael Francis *lawyer*
Antonio, Douglas John *lawyer*
Anvaripour, M. A. *lawyer*
Appel, Nina Schick *law educator, dean*
†Archer, James G. *lawyer*
Armstrong, Edwin Richard *lawyer, publisher, editor*
Aronson, Virginia L. *lawyer*
Athas, Gus James *lawyer*
Auerbach, Marshall Jay *lawyer*
Avery, Robert Dean *lawyer*
Badel, Julie *lawyer*
Baer, John Richard Frederick *lawyer*
Bailey, Robert Short *lawyer*
Baird, Douglas Gordon *law educator, dean*
Baker, Bruce Jay *lawyer*
Baker, James Edward Sproul *retired lawyer*
Baker, Pamela *lawyer*
Baldwin, Shaun McParland *lawyer*
†Bandes, Susan Anne *lawyer*
Banoff, Sheldon Irwin *lawyer*
Banta, Don Arthur *retired lawyer*
†Barack, Peter Joseph *lawyer, educator*
†Bardgett, John E. *lawyer*
Barker, William Thomas *lawyer*
Barr, John Robert *retired lawyer*
†Barrett, Roger Watson *lawyer*
†Barron, Harold Sheldon *lawyer*
Barron, Howard Robert *lawyer*
Baruch, Hurd *lawyer*
Bashwiner, Steven Lacelle *lawyer*
Baugher, Peter V. *lawyer*
†Beatty, William Glenn *lawyer*
†Beck, Philip S. *lawyer*
Beem, Jack Darrel *lawyer*
Bellah, Kenneth David *lawyer*
†Bellows, Laurel Gordon *lawyer*
Bennett, Robert William *law educator*
Berens, Mark Harry *lawyer*
Berenzweig, Jack Charles *lawyer*
Berger, Robert Michael *lawyer*
Berghoff, Paul Henry *lawyer*
Bernardini, Charles *lawyer, former alderman*
Berner, Robert Lee, Jr., *lawyer*
†Bernick, David M. *lawyer*
Berning, Larry D. *lawyer*
†Bernstein, Charles Bernard *lawyer*
Berolzheimer, Karl *lawyer*
†Berry, Richard Morgan *lawyer*
Biebel, Paul Philip, Jr., *lawyer*
†Bienen, Leigh Buchanan *lawyer*
Bierig, Jack R. *lawyer, educator*
Bitner, John Howard *lawyer*
Bixby, Frank Lyman *lawyer*
Blatt, Richard Lee *lawyer*
Block, Neal Jay *lawyer*
†Bloom, Christopher Arthur *lawyer*
Blount, Michael Eugene *lawyer*
Blume, Paul Chiappe *lawyer*
Bobbitt, Ronald Albert *lawyer*
Bodenstein, Ira *lawyer*
Boehnen, Daniel A. *lawyer*
†Boies, Wilber H. *lawyer*
Boocock, Stephen William *lawyer*
†Boodell, Thomas Joseph, Jr., *lawyer*
Bowe, William J(ohn) *lawyer*
†Bowen, Stephen Stewart *lawyer*
†Bowman, Phillip Boynton *lawyer*
Bramnik, Robert Paul *lawyer*
†Braun, Frederick B. *lawyer*
Bresnahan, Arthur Stephen *lawyer*
Brezina, David Charles *lawyer, educator*
Brice, Roger Thomas *lawyer*
Bridgman, Thomas Francis *retired lawyer*
†Brittain, Max Gordon, Jr., *lawyer*
Brizzolara, Charles Anthony *lawyer, director*
Brown, Alan Crawford *lawyer*
Brown, Donald James, Jr., *lawyer*
Brown, Gregory K. *lawyer*
Brown, Steven Spencer *lawyer*
Bulger, Brian Wegg *lawyer*
Burdelik, Thomas L. *lawyer*
Burgdoerfer, Jerry *lawyer*
Burke, John Michael *lawyer*
Burke, Thomas Joseph, Jr., *lawyer*
†Burns, Terrence Michael *lawyer*
Busey, Roxane C. *lawyer*
Bussman, Donald Herbert *lawyer*
Carlin, Dennis J. *lawyer*
Carlson, Walter Carl *lawyer*
Carren, Jeffrey P. *lawyer*
Carroll, William Kenneth *law educator, psychologist, theologian*
Cass, Robert Michael *lawyer, consultant*
Cassel, Douglass Watts, Jr., *lawyer, educator, journalist*
Chandler, Kent, Jr., *lawyer*
Cheely, Daniel Joseph *lawyer*
Chefitz, Joel Gerald *lawyer*
†Chemers, Robert Marc *lawyer*
Cherney, James Alan *lawyer*
†Cherry, Daniel Ronald *lawyer*
†Chester, Mark Vincent *lawyer*
Chestnut, John William *lawyer*
Chiles, Stephen Michael *lawyer*
Cicero, Frank, Jr., *lawyer*
Clemens, Richard Glenn *lawyer*
†Clifford, Robert A. *lawyer*
Clinton, Edward Xavier *lawyer*
Closen, Michael Lee *law educator*
Cohen, Melanie Rovner *lawyer*
†Cohen, Stephen Bruce *lawyer*
†Collen, John *lawyer*
Collen, Sheldon Orrin *lawyer*
Conklin, Thomas William *lawyer*
Connelly, Mary Jo *lawyer*
Conway, Michael Maurice *lawyer*
†Cooley, John Wayne *lawyer*
Copeland, Edward Jerome *lawyer*
†Corwin, Sherman Phillip *lawyer*

†Costello, John William *lawyer*
Coulson, William Roy *lawyer*
Crane, Mark *lawyer*
Craven, George W. *lawyer*
Crawford, Dewey Byers *lawyer*
Cremin, Susan Elizabeth *lawyer*
Crisham, Thomas Michael *lawyer*
Crossan, John Robert *lawyer*
Csar, Michael F. *lawyer*
Cunningham, Robert James *lawyer*
Cunningham, Thomas Justin *lawyer*
Cusack, John Thomas *lawyer*
Custer, Charles Francis *lawyer*
†Daley, Susan Jean *lawyer*
Daniels, John Draper *lawyer*
Davis, Muller *lawyer*
Davis, Scott Jonathan *lawyer*
†Decker, John Francis *lawyer, educator*
Decker, Richard Knore *lawyer*
Deitrick, William Edgar *lawyer*
Delp, Wilbur Charles, Jr., *lawyer*
D'Esposito, Julian C., Jr., *lawyer*
Despres, Leon Mathis *lawyer, former city official*
†DeVries, James Howard *lawyer*
DeWolfe, John Chauncey, Jr., *lawyer*
†De Yoe, David P. *lawyer*
†Dinkes, William *lawyer*
Ditkowsky, Kenneth K. *lawyer*
†Dixon, Stewart Strawn *lawyer, consultant*
Docksey, John Ross *lawyer*
Dockterman, Michael *lawyer*
†Domanskis, Alexander Rimas *lawyer*
†Dombrow, Anthony Eric *lawyer*
Donlevy, John Dearden *lawyer*
Donner, Ted A. *lawyer*
Donohoe, Jerome Francis *lawyer*
Downing, Robert Allan *lawyer*
Doyle, John Robert *lawyer*
Drumke, Michael William *lawyer*
Drymalski, Raymond Hibner *lawyer, banker*
†Dubbs, John William, III, *lawyer*
DuCanto, Joseph Nunzio *lawyer, educator*
Duncan, John Patrick Cavanaugh *lawyer*
Dunn, Edwin Rydell *lawyer*
Durchslag, Stephen P. *lawyer*
†Dutterer, Dennis Alton *lawyer*
Dykstra, Paul Hopkins *lawyer*
Early, Bert Hylton *lawyer, consultant*
Edelman, Alvin *lawyer*
Egan, Kevin James *lawyer*
Eggert, Russell Raymond *lawyer*
†Eglit, Howard Charles *educator, lawyer, arbitrator*
Eimer, Nathan Philip *lawyer*
Ekdahl, Jon Nels *lawyer, association executive*
Elden, Gary Michael *lawyer*
Ellwood, Scott *lawyer*
Elson, Alex *lawyer, educator, arbitrator*
†Emerson, Carter Whitney *lawyer*
English, John Dwight *lawyer*
Erens, Jay Allan *lawyer*
Esrick, Jerald Paul *lawyer*
Even, Francis Alphonse *lawyer*
Fahey, Hallie Joan Miller *lawyer*
Farber, Bernard John *lawyer*
Fazio, Peter Victor, Jr., *lawyer*
†Feagley, Michael Rowe *lawyer*
†Feinberg, Gary H. *lawyer, retail company executive*
Feinstein, Fred Ira *lawyer*
†Feldman, Scott Milton *lawyer*
Fellows, Jerry Kenneth *lawyer*
Felsenthal, Steven Altus *lawyer, educator*
Ferencz, Robert Arnold *lawyer*
Ferrini, James Thomas *lawyer*
Field, Robert Edward *lawyer*
†Fifield, Sean C. *lawyer*
Fina, Paul Joseph *lawyer*
Finke, Robert Forge *lawyer*
†Fishman, Robert Michael *lawyer*
Fitch, Morgan Lewis, Jr., *intellectual property lawyer*
Fitzpatrick, Christine Morris *legal administrator, former television executive*
†Flannery, John Francis *lawyer*
Flaxman, Kenneth N. *lawyer*
†Ford, Diane *lawyer*
Formeller, Daniel Richard *lawyer*
Fort, Jeffrey C. *lawyer*
Foudree, Bruce William *lawyer*
†Fox, Kathy Pinkstaff *lawyer*
Fox, Paul T. *lawyer*
Franch, Richard Thomas *lawyer*
†Franczek, James Clement, Jr., *lawyer*
Franklin, Richard Mark *lawyer*
†Franks, Jack Darrow *lawyer*
Frazen, Mitchell Hale *lawyer*
†Freeborn, Michael D. *lawyer*
†Freehling, Paul Edward *lawyer*
Freeman, Lee Allen, Jr., *lawyer*
Freeman, Louis S. *lawyer*
†Freeman, Richard Lyons *lawyer*
†Freerksen, Gregory Nathan *lawyer*
Friedman, Lawrence Milton *lawyer*
Friedman, Roselyn L. *lawyer, mediator*
†Frisch, Sidney, Jr., *lawyer, real estate developer*
Fross, Roger Raymond *lawyer*
Fuller, Perry Lucian *lawyer*
Furlane, Mark Elliott *lawyer*
†Gaggini, John Edmund *lawyer*
†Gagliardo, Joseph M(ichael) *lawyer*
Gallanis, Kathryn Ann *prosecutor*
Garber, Samuel B. *lawyer, business/turnaround management consultant*
Garth, Bryant Geoffrey *law educator, foundation executive*
George, John Martin, Jr., *lawyer*
Geraldson, Raymond I., Jr., *lawyer*
†Gerber, David Joseph *legal educator, lawyer*
†Gerber, Lawrence *lawyer*
†Gerdy, Harry *lawyer*
Geren, Gerald S. *lawyer*
Gerlits, Francis Joseph *lawyer*
Gerske, Janet Fay *lawyer*
Gerstein, Mark Douglas *lawyer*
Gerstman, George Henry *lawyer*
Gertz, Theodore Gerson *lawyer*
†Getzoff, William Morey *lawyer*
Gibbons, William John *lawyer*
Gilbert, Howard N(orman) *lawyer, director*
Gilford, Steven Ross *lawyer*
Gladden, James Walter, Jr., *lawyer*
†Glick, Paul Mitchell *lawyer, educator*
Glieberman, Herbert Allen *lawyer*
†Godfrey, Richard Cartier *lawyer*
Golan, Stephen Leonard *lawyer*
Goldblatt, Stanford Jay *lawyer*
Golden, Bruce Paul *lawyer*
Goldman, Louis Budwig *lawyer*
Goldschmidt, Lynn Harvey *lawyer*
Goodman, Ann Paton *lawyer*
Goodman, Gary Alan *lawyer*
Gordon, James S. *lawyer, director*
Gottlieb, Gidon Alain Guy *law educator*
Gralen, Donald John *lawyer*
Grant, Robert Nathan *lawyer*
Greenfield, Michael C. *lawyer*
Greenspan, Jeffrey Dov *lawyer*
†Gregg, Jon Mann *lawyer*
Griffith, Donald Kendall *lawyer*
Grossberg, David Alan *lawyer*
†Guilfoyle, Robert Thomas *retired lawyer*
Guthman, Jack *lawyer*
Hahn, Frederic Louis *lawyer*
Halloran, Michael John *lawyer*
†Hamblet, Michael Jon *lawyer, city official, former state official*
Hammesfahr, Robert Winter *lawyer*
Hannah, Wayne Robertson, Jr., *lawyer*
Hannay, William Mouat, III, *lawyer*
Hanson, Ronald William *lawyer*
Hardgrove, James Alan *lawyer*
†Harper, Steven James *lawyer*
Harrington, Carol A. *lawyer*
Harrington, James Timothy *lawyer*
Harris, Donald Ray *lawyer*
Harrold, Bernard *lawyer*
Harvey, Elizabeth Schroer *lawyer*
Haskins, Charles Gregory, Jr., *lawyer*
Hayes, David John Arthur, Jr., *legal association executive*
†Hayes, John Daniel *lawyer*
Hayward, Thomas Zander, Jr., *lawyer*
Head, Patrick James *lawyer*
Heatwole, Mark M. *lawyer*
Heinz, William Denby *lawyer*
Heisler, Quentin George, Jr., *lawyer*
Helman, Robert Alan *lawyer*
Helmholz, R(ichard) H(enry) *law educator*
Henning, Joel Frank *lawyer, author, publisher, consultant*
Henry, Brian Thomas *lawyer*
Henry, Frederick Edward *lawyer*
Henry, Kenneth Alan *lawyer*
†Henry, Robert John *lawyer*
†Herald, J. Patrick *lawyer*
Herbert, William Carlisle *lawyer*
Herman, Sidney N. *lawyer*
†Herpe, David A. *lawyer*
Herzog, Fred F. *law educator*
Hess, Sidney J., Jr., *lawyer*
†Hesse, Carolyn Sue *lawyer*
†Hickey, John Thomas, Jr., *lawyer*
Hickman, Frederic W. *lawyer*
Hilliard, David Craig *lawyer, educator*
Hodes, Scott *lawyer*
Hofer, Roy Ellis *lawyer*
Hoff, John Scott *lawyer*
Hoffa, Thomas Edward *lawyer*
Hoffman, Richard Bruce *lawyer*
Hoffman, Valerie Jane *lawyer*
Hogan, Kenneth James *lawyer*
Holleb, Marshall Maynard *lawyer*
Hollins, Mitchell Leslie *lawyer*
†Homburger, Thomas Charles *lawyer*
Horwich, Allan *lawyer*
Hoskins, Richard Jerold *lawyer*
Howe, Jonathan Thomas *lawyer*
†Howell, R(obert) Thomas, Jr., *lawyer, former food company executive*
†Howlett, Michael Joseph, Jr., *lawyer, educator*
Howser, Richard Glen *lawyer*
Hubbard, Elizabeth Louise *lawyer*
Hummel, Gregory William *lawyer*
Hunt, Lawrence Halley, Jr., *lawyer*
Hunter, James Galbraith, Jr., *lawyer*
Hurwitz, Joel Michael *lawyer*
†Hutchinson, Dennis James *law educator*
Hyman, Michael Bruce *lawyer*
Iwan, Lori E. *lawyer*
Jacobson, Marian Slutz *lawyer*
Jacobson, Richard Joseph *lawyer*
Jaconetty, Thomas Anthony *lawyer*
Jahns, Jeffrey *lawyer*
Janger, Richard Kenneth *lawyer*
Joern, Charles Edward, Jr., *lawyer*
†Johnson, Elmer William *lawyer*
†Johnson, Garrett Bruce *lawyer*
Johnson, Gary Thomas *lawyer*
Johnson, Lael Frederic *lawyer*
Johnson, Richard Fred *lawyer*
Johnson, Tige Christopher *lawyer*
Joseph, Robert Thomas *lawyer*
Junewicz, James J. *lawyer*
Kallick, David A. *lawyer*
Kamin, Chester Thomas *lawyer*
Kaminsky, Richard Alan *lawyer*
†Kaplan, Howard Gordon *lawyer*
Kaplan, Jared *lawyer*
Kaplan, Sidney Mountbatten *lawyer*
Karu, Gilda M(all) *lawyer, federal agency administrator*
†Kato, Yvonne Marie *lawyer*
†Katz, Avrum Sidney *lawyer*
Katz, Harold Ambrose *lawyer, former state legislator*
Katz, Stuart Charles *lawyer, jazz musician*
Kaufman, Andrew Michael *lawyer*
Kawitt, Alan *lawyer*
Kelly, Charles Arthur *lawyer*
Kenney, Frank Deming *lawyer*
Kikoler, Stephen Philip *lawyer*
Kim, Michael Charles *lawyer*
King, Sharon Louise *lawyer*
Kins, Juris *lawyer*
Kipperman, Lawrence I. *lawyer*
Kirkland, John Leonard *lawyer*
†Kirkpatrick, John Everett *lawyer*
Kissel, Richard John *lawyer*
Kite, Steven B. *lawyer*
†Kleczek, David A. *lawyer*
Klein, Robert Marshall *lawyer*
Klenk, James Andrew *lawyer*
Knight, Christopher Nichols *lawyer*
Kohn, Shalom L. *lawyer*
Kohn, William Irwin *lawyer*
Kolek, Robert Edward *lawyer*
Kolmin, Kenneth Guy *lawyer*
Kozak, John W. *lawyer*
Kravitt, Jason Harris Paperno *lawyer*
Kriss, Robert J. *lawyer*
Kroll, Barry Lewis *lawyer*
†Krueger, Herbert William *lawyer*
†Kuhlman, Richard Sherwin *lawyer*
Kunkle, William Joseph *lawyer*
†Ladd, Jeffrey Raymond *lawyer*
†Lagarde, Christine *lawyer*
Laidlaw, Andrew R. *lawyer*
†Landan, Henry Sinclair *business consultant*
Landes, William M. *law educator*
Landow-Esser, Janine Marise *lawyer*
Landsberg, Jill Warren *lawyer, educator, arbitrator*
†Landsman, Stephen A. *lawyer*
†Lane, Ronald Alan *lawyer*
Laner, Richard Warren *lawyer*
Lang, Gordon, Jr., *retired lawyer*
Lapin, Andrew William *lawyer*
Latimer, Kenneth Alan *lawyer*
Lefkow, Michael Francis *lawyer*
Levenfeld, Milton Arthur *lawyer*
Levi, John G. *lawyer*
Levin, Charles Edward *lawyer*
Levin, Jack S. *lawyer*
†Levy, David Henry *lawyer*
Leyhane, Francis John, III, *lawyer*
†Lidaka, Maris V. *lawyer*
†Lieberman, Richard Elliot *lawyer*
Linklater, William Joseph *lawyer*
Lippe, Melvin Karl *lawyer*
Lipton, Lois Jean *lawyer*
†Lipton, Richard M. *lawyer*
Litwin, Burton Howard *lawyer*
†Lloyd, Robert Allen *lawyer*
Lochbihler, Frederick Vincent *lawyer*
Lockwood, Gary Lee *lawyer*
Looman, James R. *lawyer*
Lorch, Kenneth F. *lawyer*
†Lorentzen, John Carol *lawyer*
Lubin, Donald G. *lawyer*
Lundergan, Barbara Keough *lawyer*
†Luscombe, George A. II *lawyer*
Lutter, Paul Allen *lawyer*
Lyerla, Bradford Peter *lawyer*
Lynch, John James *lawyer*
Lynch, John Peter *lawyer*
MacCarthy, Terence Francis *lawyer*
†Mack, John Melvin *lawyer*
Maher, David Willard *lawyer*
†Maher, Francesca Marciniak *lawyer, air transportation executive*
Malinowski, Arthur Anthony *lawyer, labor arbitrator*
Malkin, Cary Jay *lawyer*
†Mancoff, Neal Alan *lawyer*
Mandel, Reid Alan *lawyer*
Mandler, Thomas Yale *lawyer*
Mansfield, Karen Lee *lawyer*
Manzo, Edward David *patent lawyer*
†Margolin, Stephen M. *lawyer*
Marick, Michael Miron *lawyer*
Marshall, John David *lawyer*
Martin, Alan Joseph *lawyer*
Martin, Arthur Mead *lawyer*
Marwedel, Warren John *lawyer*
Mason, Richard J. *lawyer*
Mattson, Stephen Joseph *lawyer*
†Matushek, Edward J., III, *lawyer*
Mayer, Frank D., Jr., *lawyer*
McCaleb, Malcolm, Jr., *lawyer*
McClure, James Julius, Jr., *lawyer, former city official*
McCombs, Mark James *lawyer*
McCracken, Thomas James, Jr., *lawyer*
McCrohon, Craig *lawyer*
McCue, Judith W. *lawyer*
McDermott, John H(enry) *lawyer*
McDermott, Robert B. *lawyer*
†McDonald, Thomas Alexander *lawyer*
McDonough, John Michael *lawyer*
†McErlean, Charles Flavian, Jr., *lawyer*
†McGahey, John Patrick *lawyer*
†McGonegle, Timothy Joseph *lawyer*
McKenzie, Robert Ernest *lawyer*
†McLaren, Richard Wellington, Jr., *lawyer*
McLaughlin, T. Mark *lawyer*
McLees, John Alan *lawyer*
†McMahon, Thomas Michael *lawyer*
†McMenamin, John Robert *lawyer*
McVisk, William Kilburn *lawyer*
McWhirter, Bruce J. *retired lawyer*
Mehlman, Mark Franklin *lawyer*
Melton, David Reuben *lawyer*
Meltzer, Bernard David *law educator*
Meltzer, Robert Craig *lawyer, educator*
Meyer, John Albert *lawyer*
Michaels, Richard Edward *lawyer*
Michalak, Edward Francis *lawyer*
Michod, Charles Louis, Jr., *lawyer*
Mikva, Abner Joseph *lawyer, retired federal judge*
Miller, Edward Boone *lawyer*
Miller, John Leed *lawyer*
Miller, Paul J. *lawyer*
†Miller, Ronald Stuart *lawyer*
Miller, Stephen Ralph *lawyer*
†Millichap, Paul Anthony *lawyer*
Millner, Robert B. *lawyer*
Minichello, Dennis *lawyer*
Minow, Newton Norman *lawyer, educator*
Molins, Marcel J. *lawyer*
Mollet, Chris John *lawyer*
Molo, Steven Francis *lawyer*
†Mone, Peter John *lawyer*
Montgomery, William Adam *lawyer*
Morrison, Portia Owen *lawyer*
†Morrow, John E. *lawyer*
Morsch, Thomas Harvey *lawyer*
†Muchin, Allan B. *lawyer*
Mullen, J. Thomas *lawyer*
Mullen, Michael T. *lawyer*
Muller, Kurt Alexander *lawyer*
Mumford, Manly Whitman *lawyer*
Murdock, Charles William *lawyer, educator*
Murray, Daniel Charles *trial lawyer*
Murray, Daniel Richard *lawyer*
Murtaugh, Christopher David *lawyer*
Myers, Lonn William *lawyer*
Napleton, Robert Joseph *lawyer*
†Nash, Gordon Bernard, Jr., *lawyer*
Nechin, Herbert Benjamin *lawyer*
Neumeier, Matthew Michael *lawyer, educator*
†Nicolaides, Mary *lawyer*
Niehoff, Philip John *lawyer*
Niro, Cheryl *lawyer*
Nitikman, Franklin W. *lawyer*
Nord, Robert Eamor *lawyer*
Notz, John Kranz, Jr., *arbitrator and mediator, retired lawyer*
Nowacki, James Nelson *lawyer*
Nugent, Lori S. *lawyer*
Nussbaum, Bernard J. *lawyer*
O'Brien, James Phillip *lawyer*
O'Brien, Patrick William *lawyer*
Oesterle, Eric Adam *lawyer*
O'Hagan, James Joseph *lawyer*
†O'Keefe, Kevin Michael *lawyer*
O'Leary, Daniel Vincent, Jr., *lawyer*
Olian, Robert Martin *lawyer*
O'Malley, John Daniel *law educator, banker*
O'Meara, John Francis *lawyer*
Orin, Stuart I. *lawyer*
O'Toole, William George *lawyer*
Overgaard, Mitchell Jersild *lawyer*
Overton, George Washington *lawyer*
Pallasch, B. Michael *lawyer, director*
Palmer, John Bernard, III, *lawyer*
Palmer, Robert Towne *lawyer, banker*
Panich, Danuta Bembenista *lawyer*
Parkhurst, Todd Sheldon *lawyer*
Parson, Jason A. *lawyer*
Partridge, Mark Van Buren *lawyer, educator, writer*
†Parzen, Stanley Julius *lawyer*
Pascal, Roger *lawyer*
†Patner, Marshall *lawyer*
Pavalon, Eugene Irving *lawyer*
†Pavela, D. Jean *lawyer, law association administrator*
Pelton, Russell Meredith, Jr., *lawyer*
Perlberg, Jules Martin *lawyer*
Perrin, James Kirk *lawyer*
Petersen, Donald Sondergaard *lawyer*
Petersen, William Otto *lawyer*
†Peterson, Donald George *lawyer*
†Peterson, Ronald Roger *lawyer*
Pimentel, Julio Gumeresindo *lawyer, accountant*
†Pirok, Edward Warren *lawyer, consultant*
Pitt, George *lawyer, investment banker*
Polaski, Anne Spencer *lawyer*
Pollock, Earl Edward *lawyer*
†Pope, Michael Arthur *lawyer*
†Power, Joseph Aloysius, Jr., *lawyer*
Presser, Stephen Bruce *lawyer, educator*
†Price, Charles T. *lawyer*
Price, Paul L. *lawyer*
Prior, Gary L. *lawyer*
Pritikin, James B. *lawyer*
Prochnow, Douglas Lee *lawyer*
Prochnow, Herbert Victor, Jr., *retired lawyer*
†Quinlan, William Joseph, Jr., *lawyer, director*
Rankin, James Winton *lawyer*
Ratner, Gerald *lawyer*
†Rauner, Vincent Joseph *lawyer, electronics company executive, retired*
†Redman, Clarence Owen *lawyer*
Reed, Keith Allen *lawyer*
Reich, Allan J. *lawyer*
Reicin, Ronald Ian *lawyer*
Reiter, Michael A. *lawyer, educator*
Relias, John Alexis *lawyer*
Resnick, Donald Ira *lawyer*
Reum, James Michael *lawyer*
Rhind, James Thomas *lawyer*
†Richman, John Marshall *retired lawyer, business executive*
Richmond, James Glidden *lawyer*
Richter, Tobin Marais *lawyer*
Rieger, Mitchell Sheridan *lawyer*
Rissman, Burton Richard *lawyer*
Rizowy, Carlos Guillermo *lawyer, educator, political analyst*
Rizzo, Ronald Stephen *lawyer*
Roberts, John Charles *law educator*
†Rogowski, Walter S. *lawyer*
Rohrman, Douglass Frederick *lawyer*
Rooney, Matthew A. *lawyer*
Roper, Harry Joseph *lawyer*
Ropski, Gary Melchior *lawyer*
†Rosenberg, H. James *lawyer*
Rosenbloom, Lewis Stanley *lawyer*
Rowe, Diane Elizabeth *law clerk*
Rubin, E(rwin) Leonard *lawyer*
†Rudnick, Paul David *lawyer*
Rudo, Saul E. *tax lawyer*
Ruiz, Michele Ilene *lawyer*
Rundio, Louis Michael, Jr., *lawyer*
Russell, Paul Frederick *lawyer*
Rutkoff, Alan Stuart *lawyer*
†Ruttenberg, Harold Seymour *lawyer*
Ruxin, Paul Theodore *lawyer*
†Ryder, David R. *lawyer*
†Ryken, Robert Leslie *lawyer*
†Samuels, Lawrence Robert *lawyer*
Sanders, Richard Henry *lawyer*
Saunders, George Lawton, Jr., *lawyer*
Saunders, Terry Rose *lawyer*
†Sawyier, Michael Tod *lawyer, director*

Schaffner, Howard Sheldon *lawyer*
Schar, Stephen L. *lawyer*
†Scheller, Arthur Martin, Jr., *law educator*
Schiller, Donald Charles *lawyer*
Schilt, Margaret Anne *lawyer*
Schimberg, A(rmand) Bruce *retired lawyer*
Schink, James Harvey *lawyer*
Schneider, Dan W. *lawyer, consultant*
†Schneider, Robert Jerome *lawyer*
Schoonhoven, Ray James *retired lawyer*
Schoumacher, Bruce Herbert *lawyer*
Schreck, Robert A., Jr., *lawyer*
†Schriver, John T., III, *lawyer*
†Schulman, Jerry Allen *lawyer*
Schulte, Stephen Charles *lawyer*
Schulz, Keith Donald *corporate lawyer, writer*
†Schuman, William Paul *lawyer*
Schupp, Anastasia Luka *retired lawyer*
†Schur, Gerald *lawyer*
†Schwab, Stephen Wayne *lawyer*
Schwartz, Donald Lee *lawyer*
†Schwartz, Stuart Randall *lawyer*
Scogland, William Lee *lawyer*
†Scudder, Theodore Townsend, III, *lawyer*
†Senderowitz, Stephen Jay *lawyer*
†Sennet, Charles Joseph *lawyer*
Serritella, James Anthony *lawyer*
Serritella, William David *lawyer*
Serwer, Alan Michael *lawyer*
Sfikas, Peter Michael *lawyer, educator*
†Shaman, Jeffrey M. *law educator*
Shapiro, Harold David *lawyer, educator*
Shapiro, Stephen Michael *lawyer*
Shapo, Marshall Schambelan *lawyer, educator*
†Sheppard, Berton Scott *lawyer*
†Sherman, Ian Matthew *lawyer*
Shields, Thomas Charles *lawyer*
Shindler, Donald A. *lawyer*
Shoenberger, Allen Edward *law educator*
Shurtz, Steven Park *lawyer*
Siegel, Howard Jerome *lawyer*
Silberman, Alan Harvey *lawyer*
Silets, Harvey Marvin *lawyer*
Simon, John Bern *lawyer*
Simon, Seymour *lawyer, former state supreme court justice*
Siske, Roger Charles *lawyer*
Sklarsky, Charles B. *lawyer*
†Slutzky, Lorence Harley *lawyer*
Smart, Allen Rich, II, *lawyer*
†Smedinghoff, Thomas J. *lawyer*
Smith, Arthur B., Jr., *lawyer*
Smith, Gordon Howell *lawyer*
†Smith, Herman Eugene *retired lawyer*
Smith, James Barry *lawyer*
Smith, Ronald Charles *lawyer, educator*
Smith, Tefft Weldon *lawyer*
Snider, Lawrence K. *lawyer*
†Snyderman, Perry James *lawyer*
Solovy, Jerold Sherwin *lawyer*
Spain, Richard Colby *lawyer*
Spector, David M. *lawyer*
Spellmire, George W. *lawyer*
Sproger, Charles Edmund *retired lawyer*
Sprowl, Charles Riggs *lawyer*
Stack, Paul Francis *lawyer*
†Staley, Charles Ralls *lawyer*
†Stanhaus, James Steven *lawyer*
Starkman, Gary Lee *lawyer*
†Stassen, John Henry *lawyer*
†Stavins, Richard Lee *lawyer*
Steinberg, Morton M. *lawyer*
Steinman, Joan Ellen *law educator*
Sternstein, Allan J. *lawyer*
Stevenson, Adlai Ewing, III, *lawyer, former senator*
†Stiegel, Michael A. *lawyer*
Stillman, Nina Gidden *lawyer*
Stone, Geoffrey Richard *law educator, lawyer*
†Streff, William Albert, Jr., *lawyer*
†Strom, Michael A. *lawyer*
Sullivan, Barry *lawyer*
Sullivan, Marcia Waite *lawyer*
Sullivan, Thomas Patrick *lawyer*
†Sumners, Pamela Lauren *lawyer*
Sussman, Arthur Melvin *law educator, foundation administrator*
Sweeney, James Raymond *lawyer*
Swibel, Steven Warren *lawyer*
Sykes, Alan O'Neil *lawyer, educator*
Tabin, Julius *patent lawyer, physicist*
Tarun, Robert Walter *lawyer*
Tenenbaum, J. Samuel *lawyer*
Tetzlaff, Theodore R. *lawyer*
Theis, William Harold *lawyer, educator*
Theobald, Edward Robert *lawyer*
Thies, Richard Brian *lawyer*
Thomas, Frederick Bradley *lawyer*
Thomas, Stephen Paul *lawyer*
†Thompson, David F. *lawyer*
Thompson, James Robert, Jr., *lawyer, former governor*
†Thompson, Michael *lawyer*
Thomson, George Ronald *lawyer, educator*
Tinaglia, Michael Lee *lawyer*
Tobin, Craig Daniel *lawyer*
Tobin, Thomas F. *lawyer*
†Toohey, James Kevin *lawyer*
Toriani, Denise Maria *legal administrator*
Trapp, James McCreery *lawyer*
†Treston, Sherry S. *lawyer*
Trienens, Howard Joseph *lawyer*
Trost, Eileen Bannon *lawyer*
Tryban, Esther Elizabeth *lawyer*
†Turow, Scott F. *lawyer, writer*
Ungaretti, Richard Anthony *lawyer*
Van Demark, Ruth Elaine *lawyer*
Van Tine, Matthew Eric *lawyer*
Ventrelli, Anita Marie *lawyer*
†Veverka, Donald John *lawyer*
Vojcanin, Sava Alexander *lawyer*
Von Mandel, Michael Jacques *lawyer*
Vree, Roger Allen *lawyer*
Wade, Edwin Lee *author, lawyer*
Wahlen, Edwin Alfred *lawyer*
Wander, Herbert Stanton *lawyer*
Wanke, Ronald Lee *lawyer*
Weaver, Timothy Allan *lawyer*
Webster, David Macpherson *lawyer*
†Weigle, Maurice S. *lawyer*
Weinkopf, Friedrich J. *lawyer*
Weissman, Michael Lewis *lawyer*
Weldon-Linne, Madeleine Marie *lawyer*
Wexler, Richard Lewis *lawyer*
Whalen, Wayne W. *lawyer*
White, Linda Diane *lawyer*
Wiggins, Charles Henry, Jr., *lawyer*
Wilcox, Mark Dean *lawyer*
Wildman, Max Edward *lawyer, director*
Wilson, Clarence Sylvester, Jr., *lawyer, educator*
Wilson, Roger Goodwin *lawyer*
Wise, William Jerrard *lawyer*
Witcoff, Sheldon William *lawyer*
Witt, Alan Michael *lawyer, accountant*
Wolf, Charles Benno *lawyer*
Wright, Judith Margaret *law librarian, educator, dean*
Wright, Richard W. *lawyer, law educator*
Zabel, Sheldon Alter *lawyer, law educator*
Zemm, Sandra Phyllis *lawyer*
Zenner, Sheldon Toby *lawyer*
†Zolno, Mark S. *lawyer*

Chicago Heights
Cifelli, John Louis *lawyer*

Collinsville
Freeman, David Ralph *lawyer*
†Tognarelli, Richard Lee *lawyer*

Crete
†Teykl, James Stephen *lawyer*

Crystal Lake
Bishop, James Francis *lawyer*
Franz, William Mansur *lawyer*
Shank, William O. *lawyer*
Thoms, Jeannine Aumond *lawyer*

Danville
†Hubbard, Fred Leonhardt *lawyer*
†Young, William Allen *lawyer*

DeKalb
Davidson, Kenneth Lawrence *lawyer, educator*

Decatur
Dunn, John Francis *lawyer, state representative*
Smith, David James *corporate lawyer*

Deer Park
Vanderpoel, James Robert *lawyer*

Deerfield
Birmingham, William Joseph *lawyer*
Dawson, Suzanne Stockus *lawyer*
†Kaplan, Alan Michael *lawyer*
†Lane, William Edward *lawyer, inventor*
†Oettinger, Julian Alan *lawyer, pharmacy company executive*
Scott, Theodore R. *lawyer*
Vollen, Robert Jay *lawyer*

Dekalb
Schneider, Daniel Max *law educator*
Tucker, Watson Billopp *lawyer*
Witmer, John Harper, Jr., *lawyer*

Des Plaines
Brodl, Raymond Frank *lawyer, former lumber company executive*
Kotelman, Laura Mary *lawyer*

Downers Grove
†Mason, Peter Ian *lawyer*
†Myers, Daniel N. *lawyer, association executive*
Siedlecki, Nancy Therese *lawyer, funeral director*

East Alton
Clark, Mark Jeffrey *paralegal, researcher*
†Delaney, John Martin, Jr., *lawyer*

East Moline
Silliman, Richard George *retired lawyer, retired farm machinery company executive*

Edwardsville
Carlson, Jon Gordon *lawyer*
Gorman, James Edward *lawyer*
Hunsaker, Richard Kendall *lawyer*
Rikli, Donald Carl *lawyer*
†Schum, Randolph Edgar *lawyer*

Elgin
†Akemann, David R. *lawyer*
Carbary, Jonathan Leigh *lawyer*
†Juergensmeyer, John Eli *lawyer*
Moltz, Martin Paul *lawyer*
Roeser, Ronald O. *lawyer, consultant*

Elmwood Park
Spina, Anthony Ferdinand *lawyer*

Eureka
†Harrod, Daniel Mark *lawyer*

Evanston
†Creamer, Robert Allan *lawyer*
DeWolfe, Ruthanne K.S. *lawyer, psychologist, accountant*
Morrison, John Horton *lawyer*
Reilly, Francis X. *lawyer, consultant*
†Rosic, George Steve *lawyer*
Salem, Richard Allen *mediator*
Schulte, Bruce John *lawyer*
Wine-Banks, Jill Susan *lawyer*
Witwer, Samuel Weiler, Jr., *lawyer*

Flossmoor
Gevers, Marcia Bonita *lawyer, lecturer, mediator, consultant*

Freeport
†Eden, Robert Elwood *lawyer*

Geneva
†Landmeier, Allen Lee *lawyer*

Genoa
Cromley, Jon Lowell *lawyer*

Gillespie
†Verticchio, Rick *lawyer*

Glen Ellyn
Conti, Lee Ann *lawyer*
Hudson, Dennis Lee *lawyer, retired government official, arbitrator, educator*
†O'Connell, Daniel James *lawyer*
Sandrok, Richard William *lawyer*
Ulrich, Werner *patent lawyer*

Glenview
†Baetz, W. Timothy *lawyer*
Berkman, Michael G. *lawyer, chemical consultant*
Knox, James Edwin *lawyer*
Marmet, Gottlieb John *lawyer*

Gurnee
Southern, Robert Allen *lawyer*

Hazel Crest
†Gurion, Henry Baruch *lawyer*

Highland Park
Karol, Nathaniel H. *lawyer, consultant*
Nelson, Richard David *lawyer*
Ruder, David Sturtevant *lawyer, educator, government official*
Schindel, Donald Marvin *retired lawyer*
†Schlifke, James Steven *lawyer*

Hinsdale
Avgeris, George Nicholas *lawyer*
Diamant, William *lawyer*
Farrug, Eugene Joseph, Sr., *retired lawyer*
†Walker, Daniel, Jr., *lawyer*
†Wise, Nancy Joan *lawyer*

Hoffman Estates
†Williams, Richard Nesbitt *lawyer, educator*

Hoopeston
Manion, Paul Thomas *lawyer*

Jacksonville
†Kuster, Larry Donald *lawyer*

Joliet
Lenard, George Dean *lawyer*

Kankakee
Marek, James Dennis *lawyer*

Kenilworth
Feng, Paul Yen-Hsiung *lawyer, chemist*
McKittrick, William Wood *lawyer*
Milnikel, Robert Saxon *lawyer*
†Weaver, Clifford Lee *retired lawyer, winery owner*

La Grange
Kerr, Alexander Duncan, Jr., *lawyer*

La Salle
†McClintock, Thomas Lee *lawyer*

Lafox
Seils, William George *lawyer*

Lake Bluff
Burns, Kenneth Jones, Jr., *lawyer, consultant*
†Kennedy, John Foran *retired lawyer*

Lake Forest
†Covington, George Morse *lawyer*
Emerson, William Harry *lawyer, retired, oil company executive*
Francois, William Armand *lawyer*
Galatz, Henry Francis *lawyer*
†Niemann, William Lovekamp *lawyer*
Palmer, Ann Therese Darin *lawyer*
Sikorovsky, Eugene Frank *retired lawyer*

Lake Zurich
†Scott, John Joseph *lawyer*

Lansing
Hill, Philip *retired lawyer*

Libertyville
DeSanto, James John *lawyer*
†Fato, Gildo E. *lawyer, chemical engineer*
Rallo, Douglas *lawyer*

Lincolnshire
Bartlett, Robert William *lawyer*
Para, Gerard Albert *lawyer, real estate broker, consultant*

Lincolnwood
Kagan, Andrew Besdin *lawyer, educator*
Zaremski, Miles Jay *lawyer*

Lisle
Butt, Edward Thomas, Jr., *lawyer*

Lombard
†Goodman, Elliott I(rvin) *retired lawyer*
O'Shea, Patrick Joseph *lawyer, electrical engineer*

Long Grove
Obert, Paul Richard *lawyer, manufacturing company executive*

Marengo
Franks, Herbert Hoover *lawyer*

Mattoon
Horsley, Jack Everett *lawyer, writer*

Mokena
Sangmeister, George Edward *lawyer, consultant, former congressman*

Moline
Cleaver, William Lehn *lawyer*
Morrison, Deborah Jean *lawyer*
†Schwiebert, Mark William *lawyer, mayor*

Monticello
Tracy, William Francis, II, *lawyer*

Morris
†Rooks, John Newton *lawyer*

Mount Vernon
Harvey, Morris Lane *lawyer*

Murphysboro
McCann, Maurice Joseph *lawyer*

Naperville
Fawell, Harris W. *lawyer, former congressman*
Fenech, Joseph Charles *lawyer*
Larson, Mark Edward, Jr., *lawyer, educator, financial advisor*
Levy, Steven B. *lawyer*
Nortell, Bruce *lawyer*
Shaw, Michael Allan *lawyer, mail order company executive*
Tibble, Douglas Clair *lawyer*

Normal
Bender, Paul Edward *lawyer*
Rochelle, Victor Cleanthus *lawyer*
Spears, Larry Jonell *lawyer*

North Chicago
de Lasa, José M. *lawyer*

Northbrook
†Abbey, G(eorge) Marshall *lawyer, former health care company executive, general counsel*
Bohlender, Hugh Darrow *lawyer*
Clark, David Keith *lawyer, real estate developer*
Dilling, Kirkpatrick Wallwick *lawyer*
†Fox, Michael Edward *lawyer*
Irons, Spencer Ernest *lawyer*
Lapin, Harvey I. *lawyer*
McGinn, Mary J. *lawyer, insurance company executive*
Rosemarin, Carey Stephen *lawyer*
Rotchford, Patricia Kathleen *lawyer, mediator*
Sernett, Richard Patrick *lawyer*
Stewart, Charles Leslie *lawyer*
Wallace, Harry Leland *lawyer*

Northfield
Giza, David Alan *lawyer*

Oak Brook
†Barnes, Karen Kay *lawyer*
Bennett, Margaret Airola *lawyer*
Congalton, Susan Tichenor *lawyer*
La Petina, Gary Michael *lawyer*
Marchetti, Marilyn H. *lawyer*
†Miller, Ralph William, Jr., *lawyer*
Mlsna, Kathryn Kimura *lawyer*
O'Brien, Walter Joseph, II, *lawyer*
Oldfield, E. Lawrence *lawyer*
†Ras, Robert A. *lawyer*

Oak Forest
†Narko, Medard Martin *lawyer*

Oak Lawn
Tucker, Berry Kenneth *lawyer*

Oak Park
Schubert, Blake H. *lawyer, investor*
Sengpiehl, Paul Marvin *lawyer, former state official*

Oakbrook Terrace
Hicks, James Thomas *lawyer, physician*
LaForte, George Francis, Jr., *lawyer*
Weiland, Mark Bradley *corporate lawyer*
Willis, Douglas Alan *lawyer*

Oswego
May, Frank Brendan, Jr., *lawyer*

Palatine
†Cannon, Benjamin Winton *lawyer, business executive*
†Hildebrandt, Sharrie L. *legal technology educator, paralegal*
Victor, Michael Gary *lawyer, physician*
†Wardell, John Watson *lawyer*
†Zamarin, Ronald George *lawyer*

Palos Heights
Taylor, Joseph Henry *lawyer*

Paris
Bell, Allen Andrew, Jr., *lawyer*

Park Forest
Goodrich, John Bernard *lawyer, consultant*

Park Ridge
†Devience, Alex, Jr., *law educator*
†Franklin, Randy Wayne *lawyer*
Hegarty, Mary Frances *lawyer*
LaRue, Paul Hubert *retired lawyer*
†Nagel, Karen Annette Elizabeth *lawyer, editor*
Naker, Mary Leslie *legal firm executive*
Schmidt, Wayne Walter *law association executive*
†Zimmermann, John Joseph *lawyer*

Peoria
Allen, Lyle Wallace *lawyer*
Bertschy, Timothy L. *lawyer*

PROFESSIONAL INDEX 6553 LAW: LAW PRACTICE AND ADMINISTRATION

Chenevert, Donald James, Jr., *lawyer*
Coletta, Ralph John *retired lawyer*
†Elias, John Samuel *lawyer*
Ferrari, Gary John *lawyer*
Higgs, David Lawrence *lawyer*
O'Brien, Daniel Robert *lawyer*
†Parsons, Richard Hugo *lawyer*
Prusak, Maximilian Michael *lawyer*
†Sinn, David Randall *lawyer*
Strodel, Robert Carl *lawyer*
†Swain, W. Timothy *lawyer*
†Traicoff, Sandra M. *lawyer*
Winget, Walter Winfield *lawyer*

Pinckneyville
Johnson, Don Edwin *lawyer*

Prospect Heights
Leopold, Mark F. *lawyer*

Quincy
†Rapp, James Anthony *lawyer, author*

River Forest
Li, Tze-chung *lawyer, educator*
Marcello, Frank F. *lawyer, educator, writer*

Riverside
Kubiczky, Stephen Ralph *lawyer*

Riverwoods
Ford, Michael W. *lawyer*

Rock Island
VanDerGinst, Dennis Allen *lawyer*
Wallace, Franklin Sherwood *lawyer, director*

Rockford
Fredrickson, Robert Alan *lawyer*
Johnson, Thomas Stuart *lawyer*
†Knight, William D., Jr., *lawyer*
Mateer, Don M. *lawyer*
Reno, Roger *lawyer*

Rolling Meadows
Sullivan, Michael D. *lawyer*

Roselle
Bassitt, Janet Louise *lawyer*

Schaumburg
Frano, Andrew Joseph *lawyer, civil engineer*
†Lawson, A. Peter *lawyer*

Schiller Park
Congalton, Christopher William *lawyer*

Skokie
†Bauer, Michael *lawyer*
†Denkewalter, Kim Richard *lawyer*
Gopman, Howard Z. *lawyer*
†Gotkin, Michael Stanley *lawyer, director*
Kahn, Bert L. *lawyer*
Plotnick, Paul William *lawyer*
†Sachs, Irving Joseph *lawyer, accountant, pension consultant*

South Holland
Bell, Jason Cameron *lawyer*
†Wolf, Wayne Lowell *criminal justice educator, researcher*

Springfield
Bergschneider, David Philip *legal administrator*
Cullen, Mark Kenneth *lawyer*
Darby, Karen Sue *legal education administrator*
Feldman, Howard William *lawyer*
Immke, Keith Henry *lawyer*
Kerr, Gary Enrico *lawyer, educator*
†Londrigan, James Thomas *lawyer*
Malany, Le Grand Lynn *lawyer, engineer, bank executive*
†Mathewson, Mark Stuart *lawyer, editor*
†Mool, Deanna S. *lawyer*
Morse, Saul Julian *lawyer*
Reed, Robert Phillip *lawyer*
Rominger, M. Kyle *lawyer*
Rowe, Max L. *lawyer, corporate executive, management and political consultant, writer, judge*
Van Meter, Abram DeBois *lawyer, retired banker*

Sycamore
Smith, Peter Thomas *lawyer*

Taylorville
Austin, Daniel William *lawyer*

Tinley Park
Chin, Davis *lawyer*
Kenny, Mary Alice *lawyer, law librarian*

Toledo
Prather, William C., III, *lawyer, writer*

Urbana
Balbach, Stanley Byron *lawyer*
Fitz-Gerald, Roger Miller *lawyer*
†Thies, Richard Leon *lawyer, director*
†Uchtmann, Donald Louis *lawyer, law educator*
†Webber, Carl Maddra *lawyer*

Warrenville
Gordon, Robert M. *lawyer*
Johnson, Douglas Wells *lawyer*

Waterloo
Coffee, Richard Jerome, II, *lawyer*

Waukegan
Bairstow, Richard Raymond *retired lawyer*
Hall, Albert L. *retired lawyer*
†Hartman, Marshall J. *lawyer*
†Henrick, Michael Francis *lawyer*
Leibowitz, David Perry *lawyer*

Westchester
Castellano, Christine Marie *lawyer*
Matuga, Edward Anthony *lawyer*

Western Springs
Hanson, Heidi Elizabeth *lawyer*
Mudd, Anne Chestney *mediator, law educator, real estate broker*
Rhoads, Paul Kelly *lawyer*
Shannon, Peter Michael, Jr., *lawyer*
†Young, Robert Bruce *lawyer*

Wheaton
Cunningham, William Francis *lawyer*
Didzerekis, Paul Patrick *lawyer*
†Dudgeon, Thomas Carl *judge*
†Field, Harold Gregory *lawyer*
†Mirabile, Thomas Keith *lawyer*
Pollock, Bradley Neil *lawyer*
Stein, Lawrence A. *lawyer*

Wheeling
†Janich, Daniel Nicholas *lawyer*
Kulinsky, Lois *lawyer*

Willowbrook
Walton, Stanley Anthony, III, *lawyer*

Wilmette
Atkinson, Jeff John Frederick *law educator, lawyer, writer*
Browder, William Bayard *corporation executive, lawyer*
Frick, Robert Hathaway *retired lawyer*
†Geller, William Alan *criminal justice researcher, police and public safety consultant*
Gilbert, Howard Earl *lawyer*
Griffith, James D. *retired lawyer*
Lieberman, Eugene *lawyer*

Winnetka
Crowe, Robert William *lawyer, mediator*
Davis, Britton Anthony *retired lawyer*
†Fawcett, Dwight Winter *retired lawyer*
Greenblatt, Ray Harris *lawyer*
Hales, Daniel B. *lawyer*
Krucks, William Norman *lawyer*
Ryan, Robert Jeffers *lawyer*
Sutter, William Paul *lawyer*

Winthrop Harbor
Getz, James Edward *legal association administrator*

Woodridge
Erickson, Diane Quinn *lawyer, artist, small business owner*

Woodstock
Ackley, Robert O. *lawyer*

INDIANA

Anderson
Woodruff, Randall Lee *lawyer*

Beech Grove
Brown, Richard Lawrence *lawyer*

Bloomington
Aman, Alfred Charles, Jr., *law educator*
Cate, Fred Harrison *law educator, lawyer*
Dilts, Jon Paul *law educator*
Franklin, Frederick Russell *retired legal association executive*
†Grodner, Geoffrey Mitchell *lawyer*
Like, Lance D. *lawyer*
†Mallor, Andrew C. *lawyer*
Mann, Robert David *lawyer*
Shreve, Gene Russell *law educator*
Tackitt, Sylvan Wright *lawyer*

Boonville
†Neff, Mark Edward *lawyer*

Carmel
Bruess, Charles Edward *lawyer*
Stein, Richard Paul *lawyer*
Wilson, Randolph Preston *lawyer, businessman*

Columbus
Crump, Francis Jefferson, III, *lawyer*
Harrison, Patrick Woods *lawyer*
†Perkins Senn, Karon Elaine *lawyer*
†Zaharako, Lew Daleure *lawyer*

Danville
Baldwin, Jeffrey Kenton *lawyer, educator*

Decatur
Spady, Margaret Vidya *lawyer, nurse*

Elkhart
Gassere, Eugene Arthur *lawyer, business executive*
Treckelo, Richard M. *lawyer*
Wicks, Charles Carter *lawyer*

Evansville
Baugh, Jerry Phelps *lawyer*
Berger, Charles Lee *lawyer*
Bodkin, Robert Thomas *lawyer*
Clouse, John Daniel *lawyer*
Harrison, Joseph Heavrin *lawyer*
†Hayes, Philip Harold *lawyer*
Miller, Daniel Raymond *prosecutor*
Wallace, Keith M. *lawyer*

Fort Wayne
†Cain, Tim J. *lawyer*
Fink, Thomas Michael *lawyer*
Gehring, Ronald Kent *lawyer*
Kauffman, Kent David *law educator*
Lawson, Jack Wayne *lawyer*
Lebamoff, Ivan Argire *lawyer*
†Pope, Mark Andrew *lawyer, university administrator*
Shoaff, Thomas Mitchell *lawyer*
Young, Randy William *lawyer*

Fowler
Weist, William Bernard *lawyer*

Frankfort
Appleton, Alan B. *lawyer*

Franklin
Hamner, Lance Dalton *prosecutor*
†Loveall, George Michael *lawyer*

Gary
†Boscia, James Dominic *lawyer*
Hall, John Henry *lawyer, historian, educator*
Lewis, Robert Lee *lawyer*

Greenfield
Dobbins, Caryl Dean *lawyer*

Greenwood
Bekes, Gregory E. *lawyer*
Van Valer, Joe Ned *lawyer, land developer*

Hammond
Diamond, Eugene Christopher *lawyer, hospital administrator*
†Manges, Jill D. *lawyer, nurse*

Highland
Fine, William Irwin *lawyer*
†Goodman, Samuel J. *lawyer*

Hobart
Longer, William John *lawyer*

Indianapolis
Albright, Terrill D. *lawyer*
Allen, David James *lawyer*
†Ancel, Jerald Irwin *lawyer*
Badger, David Harry *lawyer*
Barrett, David Olan *lawyer*
Beckwith, Lewis Daniel *lawyer*
†Belknap, Jerry P. *lawyer*
†Bennett, Maxine Taylor *lawyer*
†Betley, Leonard John *lawyer*
Blythe, James David, II, *lawyer*
Boldt, Michael Herbert *lawyer*
Born, Samuel Roydon, II, *lawyer*
Boyko, Ihor Nestor *lawyer*
Bush, Robert Bradford *corporate lawyer*
Caress, Timothy Charles *lawyer*
Carlberg, James Edwin *lawyer*
Carney, Joseph Buckingham *lawyer*
Carr, David J. *lawyer*
Choplin, John M., II, *lawyer*
Cline, Lance Douglas *lawyer*
Cole, Elsa Kircher *lawyer*
Cole, Roland Jay *lawyer*
†Coons, Stephen Merle *lawyer*
Culp, Charles William *lawyer*
†De Haan, Karen L. *lawyer, accountant*
Dorocke, Lawrence Francis *lawyer*
Downs, Thomas K. *lawyer*
Dutton, Clarence Benjamin *retired lawyer*
†Elberger, Ronald Edward *lawyer*
†Emhardt, Charles David *lawyer*
†Evans, Daniel Fraley, Jr., *lawyer*
Ewbank, Thomas Peters *lawyer, retired banker*
†Fisher, James R. *lawyer*
FitzGibbon, Daniel Harvey *lawyer*
†Frank, Sarah Myers *lawyer*
Fruehwald, Kristin G. *lawyer*
Funk, David Albert *retired law educator*
Gilliland, John Campbell, II, *lawyer*
†Greenberg, Harold *legal educator*
†Hackman, Marvin Lawrence *lawyer*
†Hays, Thomas Clyde *lawyer*
Hendrickson, Thomas Atherton *lawyer*
Hetzner, Marc A. *lawyer*
Hiner, Leslie Davis *lawyer, consultant*
Holt, John Manly *retired corporate lawyer*
Holtzlander, Stephanie Franco *lawyer*
Horn, Brenda Sue *lawyer*
Hovde, F. Boyd *lawyer*
Jegen, Lawrence A., III, *law educator*
Johnston, Joanne Spitznagel *lawyer, writing consultant*
Johnstone, Robert Philip *lawyer*
Johnting, Wendell *law librarian*
†Kahlenbeck, Howard, Jr., *lawyer*
†Kappes, Philip Spangler *lawyer*
†Kashani, Hamid Reza *lawyer, computer consultant*
Kautzman, John Fredrick *lawyer*
Kemper, James Dee *lawyer*
†Kendall, Rebecca O. *lawyer, pharmaceutical company executive*
Kerr, William Andrew *lawyer, educator*
King, J. Bradley *lawyer*
Kirk, Carol *lawyer*
Klaper, Martin Jay *lawyer*
Kleiman, David Harold *lawyer*
Knauer, James A. *lawyer*
Knebel, Donald Earl *lawyer*
Koch, Edna Mae *lawyer, nurse*
Koeller, Robert Marion *lawyer, director*
Lee, Stephen W. *lawyer*
Lofton, Thomas Milton *lawyer*
Lowe, Louis Robert, Jr., *lawyer*
†Maine, Michael Roland *lawyer*
McCarthy, Kevin Bart *lawyer*
†McKeon, Thomas Joseph *lawyer*
McKinney, Dennis Keith *lawyer*
McTurnan, Lee Bowes *lawyer*
†Merrill, William H., Jr., *lawyer, corporate professional*
Miller, David Anthony *lawyer*
Miller, David W. *lawyer*
Moffatt, Michael Alan *lawyer*
†Neff, Robert Matthew *lawyer, financial services executive*
Nolan, Alan Tucker *retired lawyer, labor arbitrator, writer*
Padgett, Gregory Lee *lawyer*
Paul, Stephen Howard *lawyer*
Pennamped, Bruce Michael *lawyer*
†Petersen, James L. *lawyer*
Reese, Jason Ruskin *lawyer*
Render, John Clifford *lawyer*
Reynolds, Robert Hugh *lawyer*
†Reynolds, William Carl *law editor*
Ritz, Stephen Mark *lawyer*
†Roberts, Patricia Susan *lawyer*
Roberts, William Everett *lawyer*
Russell, David Williams *lawyer*
†Rusthoven, Peter James *lawyer*
Ryder, Henry C(lay) *lawyer*
Scaletta, Phillip Ralph, III, *lawyer*
Schlegel, Fred Eugene *lawyer*
Schreckengast, William Owen *lawyer*
†Schwarz, James Harold *lawyer*
Scism, Daniel Reed *lawyer*
†Shadley, Sue Ann *lawyer*
Shideler, Shirley Ann Williams *lawyer*
Shula, Robert Joseph *lawyer*
Stayton, Thomas George *lawyer*
Steger, Evan Evans, III, *retired lawyer*
Stieff, John Joseph *legislative lawyer, educator*
†Strain, James Arthur *lawyer*
Sutherland, Donald Gray *retired lawyer*
†Tabler, Susan Beidler *lawyer*
Talesnick, Stanley *lawyer*
Taylor, Jay Gordon *lawyer*
Townsend, Earl C., Jr., *lawyer, writer*
Tuchman, Steven Leslie *lawyer, consul*
Vandivier, Blair Robert *lawyer*
†Walker, Ross Paul *lawyer*
Wallace, Edna Marie *paralegal*
Wampler, Lloyd Charles *retired lawyer*
Wampler, Robert Joseph *lawyer*
Warren, Bradford Lloyd *lawyer*
Wellnitz, Craig Otto *lawyer, English language educator*
Whale, Arthur Richard *retired lawyer*
White, James Patrick *law educator*
Wishard, Gordon Davis *lawyer*
Wood, William Jerome *lawyer*
Yerkeson, Douglas Alan *lawyer*
†Yosha, Louis Buddy *lawyer*

Jeffersonville
Hoehn, Elmer Louis *lawyer, state and federal agency administrator, educator, consultant*

Kokomo
Bayliff, Edgar W. *lawyer*
Maugans, John Conrad *lawyer*

La Porte
†Drayton, V. Michael *lawyer, educator*

Lafayette
Benton, Anthony Stuart *lawyer*
Bumbleburg, Joseph Theodore *lawyer*
Gerde, Carlyle Noyes (Cy Gerde) *lawyer*
†Hart, Russell Holiday *retired lawyer*
Layden, Charles Max *lawyer*
Layden, Lynn McVey *lawyer*
†Pennell, Stephen Richard *lawyer*

Lagrange
Glick, Cynthia Susan *lawyer*

Lawrenceburg
Ewan, William Kenneth *lawyer*

Lebanon
Donaldson, John Weber *lawyer*

Merrillville
Brenman, Stephen Morris *lawyer*
Gioia, Daniel August *lawyer*
Manous, Peter J. *lawyer*

Monticello
†Guy, John Martin *lawyer*

Mount Vernon
Bach, Steve Crawford *lawyer*
Baier, Elizabeth Domsic *lawyer*

Muncie
Dennis, Ralph Emerson, Jr., *lawyer*
Kelly, Eric Damian *lawyer, educator*
†Reed, Samuel Lee *lawyer*
†Smith, Gregory Butler *lawyer*

Munster
Amber, Douglas George *lawyer*

Newburgh
†Dewey, Dennis James *lawyer*

Notre Dame
Gunn, Alan *law educator*

Sandborn
Gregg, John Richard *lawyer*

Seymour
Pardieck, Roger Lee *lawyer*

Shelbyville
Harrold, Dennis Edward *lawyer*
Lisher, James Richard *lawyer*

South Bend
Bonini, James *federal court official*
Carey, John Leo *lawyer*
Carrington, Michael Davis *criminal justice administrator, educator, consultant*
†Casey, Robert Fitzgerald *lawyer, educator*
Ford, George Burt *lawyer*
Kalamaros, Philip E. *lawyer*
†Palmer, Robert Joseph *lawyer*
Reinke, William John *lawyer*
Seall, Stephen Albert *lawyer*
Shaffer, Thomas Lindsay *lawyer, educator*
Vogel, Nelson J., Jr., *lawyer*
Wilson, William Leigh *lawyer, educator*

Terre Haute
Bitzegaio, Harold James *retired lawyer*
†Bopp, James, Jr., *lawyer*
Coleson, Richard Eugene *lawyer, minister*
Kesler, John A. *lawyer, land developer*

Valparaiso
Conison, Jay *lawyer*
Koeppen, Raymond Bradley *lawyer*
†Persyn, Mary Geraldine *law librarian, law educator*

Vincennes
Emison, Ewing Rabb, Jr., *lawyer*
†Smith, Bruce Arthur *lawyer*

Warsaw
Walmer, James L. *lawyer*

West Lafayette
Scaletta, Phillip Jasper *lawyer, educator*

Zionsville
†Bradley, Charles Harvey *lawyer*

IOWA

Albia
†Pabst, Alfred Mark *lawyer*

Algona
Lipps, Thomas W. *lawyer*

Ames
Kaufmann, Jeffrey Baer *business educator, lawyer*

Burlington
Hoth, Steven Sergey *lawyer, educator*

Carroll
Comito, Frank Joseph *lawyer*

Cedar Rapids
Albright, Justin W. *retired lawyer*
†Gray, William Oxley *retired lawyer*
Harms, Allan L. *patent lawyer*
Nazette, Richard Follett *lawyer*
Riley, Tom Joseph *lawyer*
Wilson, Robert Foster *lawyer*

Charles City
Mc Cartney, Ralph Farnham *lawyer*

Clinton
†Frey, A. John, Jr., *lawyer*

Council Bluffs
†Jennings, Dean Thomas *lawyer*
†Pechacek, Frank Warren, Jr., *lawyer*

Davenport
Bush, Michael Kevin *lawyer*
Dettmann, David Allen *lawyer*
Lane, Gary Matthew *lawyer*
Le Grand, Clay *lawyer, former state justice*
Shaw, Donald Hardy *lawyer*

Des Moines
Begleiter, Martin David *law educator, consultant*
Begleiter, Ronni Frankel *lawyer*
Bennett, Edward James *lawyer*
Brown, Paul Edmondson *lawyer*
Burns, Bernard John, III, *public defender*
†Calkins, Richard M. *lawyer*
Campbell, Bruce Irving *lawyer*
Claypool, David L. *lawyer*
Conlin, Roxanne Barton *lawyer*
Cortese, Joseph Samuel, II, *lawyer*
Duckworth, Marvin E. *lawyer, educator*
Edwards, John Duncan *law educator, librarian*
Finley, Kerry A. *lawyer*
Fisher, Thomas George, Jr., *lawyer*
Fisher, Thomas George *lawyer, retired media company executive*
Flaherty, Daniel Lee *prosecutor*
Flynn, Scott D. *lawyer*
Foxhoven, Jerry Ray *lawyer*
Frederici, C. Carleton *lawyer*
†Graves, Bruce *lawyer, director*
Graziano, Craig Frank *lawyer*
Grefe, Rolland Eugene *lawyer*
Hansell, Edgar Frank *lawyer*
Harris, Charles Elmer *lawyer*
Hill, Luther Lyons, Jr., *lawyer*
Hockenberg, Harlan David *lawyer*
Jensen, Dick Leroy *lawyer*
Koehn, William James *lawyer*
†Luchtel, Keith Edward *lawyer*
Murray, William Michael (Mike Murray) *lawyer*
Norris, Glenn L. *lawyer*
†Nowadzky, Roger Alan *lawyer, lobbyist*
Peddicord, Roland Dale *lawyer*
Phipps, David Lee *lawyer*
Power, Joseph Edward *lawyer*
†Seitzinger, Edward Francis *lawyer*
Shors, John D. *lawyer*
Simpson, Lyle Lee *lawyer*
†Stoffregen, Philip Eugene *lawyer*
Stork, Frank James *lawyer*
Tipton, Sheila Kay *lawyer*
Wilcox, Gregory B. *lawyer*
†Zumbach, Steven Elmer *lawyer*

Dubuque
Ernst, Daniel Pearson *lawyer*
Hammer, David Lindley *lawyer, writer*

Fort Madison
Sallen, David Urban *lawyer*

Garner
†Hovda, Theodore James *lawyer*

Greenfield
†Howe, Jay Edwin *lawyer*

Grundy Center
†Kliebenstein, Don *lawyer*

Hull
De Koster, John G. *lawyer*

Indianola
Ouderkirk, Mason James *lawyer*

Iowa City
†Bezanson, Randall Peter *law educator*
Bonfield, Arthur Earl *lawyer, educator*
Downer, Robert Nelson *lawyer*
Hayek, John William *lawyer*
Hobart, Thomas D. *lawyer*
Kurtz, Sheldon Francis *lawyer, educator*
Spies, Leon Fred *lawyer*
†Stensvaag, John-Mark *legal educator, lawyer*
Tomkovicz, James Joseph *law educator*
Wing, Adrien Katherine *law educator*

Keokuk
Hoffman, James Paul *lawyer, hypnotist*

Marshalltown
Brennecke, Allen Eugene *lawyer*
Brooks, Patrick William *lawyer*

Mason City
Heiny, James Ray *lawyer*
Winston, Harold Ronald *lawyer*

Muscatine
Coulter, Charles Roy *lawyer*
Lande, Roger Lee *lawyer*
Nepple, James Anthony *lawyer*

Nevada
Countryman, Dayton Wendell *lawyer*

Newton
†Caldwell, Gilbert Raymond, III, *lawyer*

Ottumwa
Krafka, Mary Baird *lawyer*

Parkersburg
Lawler, Thomas Albert *lawyer*

Sioux City
†Gerhart, Steven George *lawyer*
Giles, William Jefferson, III, *lawyer*
Madsen, George Frank *lawyer*
Mayne, Wiley Edward *lawyer*
Peterson, Delaine Charles *lawyer, bank executive*
†Poulson, Jeffrey Lee *lawyer*

Wapello
Hicklin, Edwin Anderson *lawyer*

Waterloo
Molinaro-Blonigan, Mary Robin *lawyer*

West Des Moines
†Brown, John Lewis *lawyer*
Cutler, Charles Edward *lawyer*
†McEnroe, Michael Louis *lawyer*

Winfield
Carty, John Wesley *lawyer*

KANSAS

Concordia
†Brewer, Dana *lawyer, educator*

Emporia
†Meierhoff, Gayle Patrice *lawyer, accountant*

Fort Scott
Short, Forrest Edwin *lawyer*

Garden City
†Loyd, Ward Eugene *lawyer, state legislator*
†Pierce, Ricklin Ray *lawyer*

Gardner
Webb, William Duncan *lawyer, mediator*

Hays
Zerr, Dean A. *legal assistant, retired nurse practitioner*

Hutchinson
Chalfant, William Young *lawyer, author, historian*
Hayes, John Francis *lawyer*
Swearer, William Brooks *lawyer*

Iola
Toland, Clyde William *lawyer*
Toland, John Robert *lawyer*

Junction City
†Davis, Victor Allen, Jr., *executive magistrate*

Kansas City
O'Neill, Thomas Tyrone *lawyer*

Lawrence
Casad, Robert Clair *legal educator*
Karlin, Calvin Joseph *lawyer*
†Levin, Murray Scott *law educator, arbitrator, mediator*
Nordling, Bernard Erick *lawyer*
Smith, Glee Sidney, Jr., *lawyer*
Turnbull, H. Rutherford, III, *law educator, lawyer*

Leawood
Bohm, Jack Nelson *retired lawyer*
Johnston, Jocelyn Stanwell *paralegal*

Lincoln
†Crangle, Robert D. *lawyer, management consultant, entrepreneur, manufacturing executive*
Marshall, Susan *lawyer*

Olathe
Haskin, J. Michael *lawyer*
†High, William Fray *lawyer*
Norton, Jay Lewis *lawyer, recording company executive*
Scott, Robert Gene *lawyer*

Overland Park
Abele, Robert Christopher *lawyer*
Ayers, Jeffrey David *lawyer*
†Barnett, James Monroe *lawyer*
Branham, Melanie J. *lawyer*
Callahan, Michael Thomas *lawyer, writer, arbitrator, construction executive, consultant*
Devlin, James Richard *lawyer*
Keplinger, Bruce (Donald Keplinger) *lawyer*
Klamann, John Michael *lawyer*
Krauss, Carl F. *lawyer*
†Ruse, Steven Douglas *lawyer*
Sampson, William Roth *lawyer*
Smith, Daniel Lynn *lawyer*
Smith, Jill Galbreath *lawyer*
Spaeth, Nicholas John *lawyer, former state attorney general*
†Steinkamp, Robert Theodore *lawyer*
†Willard, James Robert *retired lawyer*
Woods, Richard Dale *lawyer*

Pittsburg
†Short, Timothy Allen *lawyer*

Prairie Village
Sharp, Rex Arthur *lawyer*
Stanton, Roger D. *lawyer*

Pratt
†Stull, Gordon Bruce *lawyer*

Salina
†Neustrom, Patrik William *lawyer*
Owens, William Dean *lawyer*

Shawnee Mission
†Adkins, David Jay *lawyer*
Badgerow, John Nicholas *lawyer*
Bond, Richard Lee *lawyer, state senator*
Gaar, Norman Edward *lawyer, former state senator*
Gastl, Eugene Francis *lawyer*
Helder, Jan Pleasant, Jr., *lawyer*
†Johntz, John Hoffman, Jr., *lawyer*
Nulton, William Clements *retired lawyer*
Smith, Edwin Dudley *lawyer*
Snyder, Willard Breidenthal *lawyer*
Sparks, Billy Schley *lawyer*
Starrett, Frederick Kent *lawyer*

Syracuse
Gale, Robert Harrison, Jr., *lawyer*

Topeka
Concannon, James M. *law educator, university dean*
Dimmitt, Lawrence Andrew *retired lawyer, law educator*
Elrod, Linda Diane Henry *lawyer, educator*
Hamilton, John Richard *lawyer*
†Haney, Thomas Dwight *lawyer, educator*
Hejtmanek, Danton Charles *lawyer*
†Horttor, Donald J. *lawyer*
Keefer, J(ames) Michael *lawyer*
†Ochs, Robert Duane *lawyer*
†Sabatini, Frank Carmine *lawyer, bank executive*
†Schroer, Gene Eldon *lawyer*
†Snyder, Brock Robert *lawyer*
Wright, James C. *lawyer*

Ulysses
†Hathaway, Gary Ray *lawyer*

Wamego
Lang, John Ernest *lawyer*

Wichita
Ayres, Ted Dean *lawyer, academic counsel*
Badger, Ronald Kay *lawyer*
†Coombs, Eugene G. *lawyer*
Depew, Spencer Long *lawyer*
Docking, Thomas Robert *lawyer, former state lieutenant governor*
†Foote, Richard Van *lawyer*
†Guy, James Matheus *lawyer, realtor*
†Hund, Edward Joseph *lawyer*
†Johnson, Kevin Blaine *lawyer, educator*
†Kellogg, Darrell Dean *lawyer*
Kennedy, Joseph Winston *lawyer*
Kinch, E. L. Lee *lawyer*
Peare, Dan C. *lawyer*
Randels, Ed L. *lawyer*
†Ratner, Payne Harry, Jr., *lawyer*
Sorensen, Harvey R. *lawyer*
Steele, Thomas Lee *lawyer*
Stephenson, Richard Ismert *lawyer*
Thompson, Lee (Morris Thompson) *lawyer*
†Van Fleet, G. Nelson *financial executive*
Winkler, Dana John *lawyer*
†Woolf, John Paul *lawyer*

Winfield
Andreas, Warren Dale *lawyer*
Krusor, Mark William *lawyer*

KENTUCKY

Bowling Green
†Parker, William Jerry *lawyer*
Rudloff, William Joseph *lawyer*
Sparks, David Thomas *lawyer*
Wilcher, Larry K. *lawyer*

Covington
†Davidson, David Edgar *lawyer*
†Kerr, Thomas Robert *lawyer*
†Stepner, Donald Leon *lawyer*
Wolnitzek, Stephen Dale *lawyer*

Crestwood
Ray, Ronald Dudley *lawyer*

Florence
Frohlich, Anthony William *lawyer, master commissioner*
Monohan, Edward Sheehan, IV, *lawyer*

Fort Campbell
Ruth, Bryce Clinton, Jr., *lawyer*

Fort Thomas
Whalen, Paul Lewellin *lawyer, educator, mediator*

Frankfort
Carroll, Julian Morton *lawyer, former governor*
Chadwick, Robert *lawyer, judge*
†Congleton, Conley Cole, III, *lawyer*
Gillig, John Stephenson *lawyer*
†Miller, Carl Theodore *lawyer*
Palmore, John Stanley, Jr., *retired lawyer*
Ryan, Perry T. *assistant attorney general, author*

Glasgow
†Baker, Walter Arnold *lawyer*
Gardner, Woodford Lloyd, Jr., *lawyer*

Greenville
†Yonts, Larry Brent *lawyer*

Harlan
Ford, Mark L. *lawyer*

Harrods Creek
Keeney, Steven Harris *lawyer*

Highland Heights
†Dieffenbach, Charles Maxwell *emeritus law educator, lawyer*
Rini, Alice Gertrude *law educator, lawyer, nursing educator*

Lebanon
Higdon, Frederick Alonzo *lawyer, accountant*

Lexington
Bagby, Glen Stovall *lawyer*
Basconi, Pamela Bray *lawyer*
Beshear, Steven Lynn *lawyer*
†Breathitt, Edward Thompson, Jr., *lawyer, railroad executive, former governor*
Bryson, Arthur Joseph *lawyer*
Cox, Walter Clay Jr. *lawyer, real estate broker*
Curtz, Chauncey S.R. *lawyer, real estate company executive*
Ecabert, Peter Leo *lawyer, accountant*
†Elliott, Robert Lloyd *lawyer*
Fink, Joseph Leslie, III, *law educator*
Fryman, Virgil Thomas, Jr., *lawyer*
†Garmer, William Robert *lawyer*
Goldman, Alvin Lee *lawyer, educator, arbitrator*
Goldman, Elisabeth Paris *lawyer*
Henry, Kevin Gudgel *lawyer*
Hickey, John King *lawyer, career officer*
†Irtz, Frederick G., II, *lawyer*
†Lester, Roy David *lawyer*
†Levy, Charlotte Lois *law librarian, educator, consultant, lawyer*
Lewis, Thomas Proctor *law educator*
Masterton, Lucinda Cronin *lawyer*
†McKinstry, Taft Avent *lawyer*
Michael, Douglas Charles *law educator*
Miller, Harry B(enjamin) *lawyer*
Newberry, James Henry, Jr., *lawyer*
Turley, Robert Joe *lawyer*
†Underwood, Richard Harvey *law educator*
Vimont, Richard Elgin *lawyer*

London
Jensen, Thomas Lee *lawyer*
Keller, John Warren *lawyer*

Louisville
Ament, Mark Steven *lawyer*
Ardery, Philip Pendleton *lawyer*
Ballantine, John Tilden *lawyer*
†Bardenwerper, William Burr *lawyer*
Barr, James Houston, III, *lawyer*
Benfield, Ann Kolb *lawyer*
Blaine, Steven Robert *lawyer*
Buckaway, William Allen, Jr., *lawyer*
Chauvin, Leonard Stanley, Jr., *lawyer*
Cohen, Edwin Louis *lawyer*
Conner, Stewart Edmund *lawyer*
Cowan, Frederic Joseph *lawyer*
†Cutler, Irwin Herbert *lawyer*
Davidson, Gordon Byron *lawyer*
Dudley, George Ellsworth *lawyer*
†Duffy, Martin Patrick *lawyer*
†Eades, Ronald Wayne *law educator*
†Early, Stephen Barry *lawyer*
Ely, Hiram, III, *lawyer*
†Ethridge, Larry Clayton *lawyer*
Faller, Rhoda *lawyer*
Fenton, Thomas Conner *lawyer*
Ferguson, Jo McCown *lawyer*
Fowler, Michael Ross *law and politics educator*
Fuchs, Olivia Anne Morris *lawyer*
Gilman, Sheldon Glenn *lawyer*
†Gorman, Chris *lawyer*
Gowin, Richard Bryan *lawyer*
Guethlein, William O. *lawyer*
Hallenberg, Robert Lewis *lawyer*
Hopson, Edwin Sharp *lawyer*
†Jewell, Franklin P. *lawyer*
Karageorge, Thomas George *lawyer*
Klotter, John Charles *retired legal educator*
†Lanier, Philip M. *lawyer*
Lavelle, Charles Joseph *lawyer*
Lay, Norvie Lee *law educator*

Lyndrup, Peggy B. *lawyer*
Maggiolo, Allison Joseph *lawyer*
Manly, Samuel *lawyer*
Mellen, Francis Joseph, Jr., *lawyer*
Morgan-White, Stephanie Lynn *lawyer*
†Northern, Richard *lawyer*
Osborn, John Simcoe, Jr., *lawyer*
Palmer, Larry Isaac *lawyer, educator*
†Partin, C. Fred *lawyer*
Pedley, Lawrence Lindsay *lawyer*
Pelfrey, D. Patton *lawyer*
Pettyjohn, Shirley Ellis *lawyer, real estate executive*
Reed, John Squires, II, *lawyer*
Rose, Charles Alexander *lawyer*
Rothstein, Mark Alan *health law and bioethics educator*
Runyon, Keith Leslie *lawyer, newspaper editor*
Shaikun, Michael Gary *lawyer*
†Silverthorn, Robert Sterner, Jr., *lawyer*
Skees, William Leonard, Jr., *lawyer*
Smith, R(obert) Michael *lawyer*
Talbott, Ben Johnson, Jr., *lawyer*
†Tannon, Jay Middleton *lawyer*
Valenti, Michael A. *lawyer*
Vincenti, Michael Baxter *lawyer*
†Vish, Donald H. *lawyer*
Welsh, Sir Alfred John *lawyer, international advisor*
Wren, Harold Gwyn *arbitrator, lawyer, legal educator*

Munfordville
Lang, George Edward *lawyer*

Newport
Siverd, Robert Joseph *lawyer*

Owensboro
Miller, James Monroe *lawyer*

Paducah
Treece, Randy Lionel *lawyer*

Paintsville
Massengale, Roger Lee *lawyer*

Pineville
Lawson, Susan Coleman *lawyer*

Prospect
Aberson, Leslie Donald *lawyer*

Richmond
†Weldon, C. Michael *lawyer*

Shepherdsville
Givhan, Thomas Bartram *lawyer*

Somerset
†Prather, John Gideon *lawyer*
Prather, John Gideon, Jr., *lawyer*

LOUISIANA

Alexandria
Gist, Howard Battle, Jr., *lawyer*

Baton Rouge
Anderson, Lawrence Robert, Jr., *lawyer*
Blackman, John Calhoun, IV, *lawyer*
Boren, James Edgar *lawyer*
Byrd, Warren Edgar, II, *lawyer*
†Decuir, Winston G., Sr., *lawyer*
Fenet, Robert Wickliffe *lawyer*
†Hymel, L(ezin) J(oseph) *lawyer, former prosecutor*
Johnson, Joseph Clayton, Jr., *lawyer*
Landry, Frances Leggio *lawyer*
Leonard, Paul Haralson *retired lawyer*
Pugh, George Willard *law educator*
†Pyle, Susan H. *legal association official*
Richards, Marta Alison *lawyer*
†Rubin, Michael Harry *lawyer, educator*
Schroeder, Leila Obier *retired law educator*
†Stracener, Carol Elizabeth *lawyer*
Taylor, John McKowen *lawyer*
Unglesby, Lewis O. *lawyer*
Walsh, Milton O'Neal *lawyer*
Wittenbrink, Jeffrey Scott *lawyer*

Bunkie
McKay, Dan Boies, Jr., *lawyer*

Cheneyville
†Ewin, Gordon Overton *retired lawyer, farmer*

Covington
†Looney, James Holland *lawyer*
Paddison, David Robert *lawyer*
Rice, Winston Edward *lawyer*
Thornton, Lucie Elizabeth *lawyer*

Cut Off
†Cheramie, Carlton Joseph *lawyer, business consultant*

Franklin
McClelland, James Ray *lawyer*

Hammond
Ross, Kenneth L. *lawyer*

Jefferson
Conino, Joseph Aloysius *lawyer*

Jennings
Miller, Ruth Loyd *lawyer, author*

Kenner
Valvo, Barbara-Ann *lawyer, surgeon*

La Place
Cicet, Donald James *lawyer*

Lafayette
†Angers, Winston Thomas *lawyer*
Breaux, Paul Joseph *lawyer, pharmacist*
Cloutier, Monique Legendre *lawyer*
Davidson, James Joseph, III, *lawyer*
Durio, William Henry *lawyer*
†Foster, David Smith *mediator, arbitrator, private adjudicator*
Goforth, William H. *lawyer*
Judice, Marc Wayne *lawyer*
Mansfield, James Norman, III, *lawyer*
Morgan, Glenn L. *lawyer*
Myers, Stephen Hawley *lawyer*
Saloom, Kaliste Joseph, Jr., *lawyer, retired judge*
Skinner, Michael David *lawyer, political organization administrator*

Lake Charles
†Nieset, James Robert *lawyer*
Parkerson, Hardy Martell *lawyer*
Sanchez, Walter Marshall *lawyer*
Shaddock, William Edward, Jr., *lawyer*
Veron, J. Michael *lawyer, writer*

Leesville
Smith, Simeon Christie, III, *lawyer, judge*
Smith, Simeon Christie, IV, *lawyer*

Mandeville
Christian, John Catlett, Jr., *lawyer*
Cressy, David Sarrat *lawyer*
Olivier, Jason (Jason Thomas Olivier) *lawyer*

Marksville
Riddle, Charles Addison, III, *district attorney, former state legislator*

Metairie
Album, Jerald Lewis *lawyer*
Derbes, Albert Joseph, III, *lawyer, accountant*
†Dinwiddie, Bruce Wayland *lawyer*
Ford, Robert David *lawyer*
Gauthier, Celeste Anne *lawyer*
Hardy, Ashton Richard *lawyer*
Haygood, John Warren *retired lawyer*
Nuzum, Robert Weston *lawyer*
Weaver, Marshall Gueringer *lawyer*

Minden
†Johnson, James McDade *lawyer*

Monroe
Curry, Robert Lee, III, *lawyer*
Sartor, Daniel Ryan, Jr., *lawyer*

Morgan City
†Ramsey, Robert Scott, Jr., *lawyer*

New Orleans
†Abaunza, Donald Richard *lawyer*
†Abbott, Hirschel Theron, Jr., *lawyer*
Abbott, Lawrence E. *lawyer*
†Acomb, Robert Bailey, Jr., *lawyer, educator*
Alsobrook, Henry Bernis, Jr., *lawyer*
†Angelico, Dennis Michael *lawyer*
†Ates, J. Robert *lawyer*
Babst, James A. *lawyer*
Barham, Mack Elwin *lawyer, educator*
Barnett, William Michael *lawyer*
†Baroni, Barry Joseph *law educator, mediator, arbitrator*
Barry, Francis Julian, Jr., *lawyer*
Beahm, Franklin D. *lawyer*
Beck, William Harold, Jr., *lawyer*
Benjamin, Edward Bernard, Jr., *lawyer*
†Berkett, Marian Mayer *lawyer*
Bieck, Robert Barton, Jr., *lawyer*
†Bordes, Jane S. *lawyer*
Bronfin, Fred *lawyer*
Butcher, Bruce Cameron *lawyer*
Butler, Peter Joseph *lawyer*
Cheatwood, Roy Clifton *lawyer*
Childress, Steven Alan *law educator*
Claverie, Philip deVilliers *lawyer*
Coleman, James Julian, Jr., *lawyer, industrialist, real estate executive*
Coleman, James Julian *lawyer*
Combe, John Clifford, Jr., *lawyer*
Correro, Anthony James, III, *lawyer*
Crusto, Mitchell Ferdinand *lawyer, educator, consultant*
†Danner, William Bekurs *lawyer*
†Darden, Marshall Taylor *lawyer*
David, Robert Jefferson *lawyer*
Denegre, George *lawyer*
†Desue, Christine L. *lawyer*
Duggins, David Dryden *lawyer*
Eustis, Richmond Minor *lawyer*
Fagan, George Davidson *lawyer*
†Fendler, Sherman Gene *lawyer*
Fierke, Thomas Garner *lawyer*
Force, Robert *law educator*
Forman, William Harper, Jr., *lawyer*
Friedman, Joel William *law educator*
†Gandy, Kim Allison *lawyer*
†Gay, Esmond Phelps *lawyer*
†Getten, Thomas Frank *lawyer*
†Goins, Richard Anthony *lawyer, educator*
Grant, Arthur Gordon, Jr., *lawyer, educator*
Healy, George William, III, *lawyer, mediator*
Hearin, Robert Matlock, Jr., *lawyer*
Hearn, Sharon Sklamba *lawyer*
†Hoffman, Donald Alfred *lawyer*
Hollis, Charles Hatfield *lawyer*
Johnson, Patrick, Jr., *lawyer*
Jones, Philip Kirkpatrick, Jr., *lawyer*
Judell, Harold Benn *lawyer*
†Kern, Clifford Harold, Jr., *retired lawyer*
Kupperman, Stephen Henry *lawyer*
Lemann, Thomas Berthelot *lawyer*
Lindquist, Donald August *lawyer*
Lombardo Trostorff, Danielle Maria *lawyer, educator*
Lovett, William Anthony *law and economics educator*
Lowe, Robert Charles *lawyer*
†Malone, Ernest Roland, Jr., *lawyer*

†Manard, Robert Lynn, III, *lawyer*
Marcus, Bernard *lawyer, consultant*
Masinter, Paul James *lawyer*
McDaniel, Donald Hamilton *lawyer*
†McGlone, Michael Anthony *lawyer*
McMillan, Lee Richards, II, *lawyer*
Mintz, Albert *lawyer*
Molony, Michael Janssens, Jr., *lawyer, arbitrator, mediator*
Morris, Edith Henderson *lawyer*
†Mote, Clyde A *lawyer*
†Murchison, Henry Dillon *lawyer, director*
Nehrbass, Seth Martin *patent lawyer*
†Orrill, R. Ray, Jr., *lawyer, director*
†Osakwe, Christopher *lawyer, educator*
Ostendorf, Lance Stephen *entertainment/artist personal manager, lawyer, investor, financial consultant and planner*
Palmer, Vernon Valentine *law educator*
Pearce, John Y. *lawyer*
Perlis, Sharon A. *lawyer*
Ponoroff, Lawrence *law educator, legal consultant*
†Reed, John Wilson *lawyer*
†Riess, George Febiger *lawyer, educator*
Rodriguez, Antonio Jose *lawyer*
Rosen, Charles, II, *lawyer*
Rosen, William Warren *lawyer*
Roux, Kermit Louis, III, *lawyer*
†Sessions, Cicero Columbus *retired lawyer*
†Sher, Leopold Zangwill *lawyer*
†Shields, Lloyd Noble *lawyer, educator*
Simon, H(uey) Paul *lawyer*
Sinnott, John William *lawyer*
Sinor, Howard Earl, Jr., *lawyer*
Snyder, Charles Aubrey *lawyer*
†Sommers, William John, Jr., *lawyer*
Stapp, Dan Ernest *retired lawyer, utility executive*
Steinberg, Sylvan Julian *lawyer*
†Stetter, Roger Alan *lawyer*
†Sutterfield, James Ray *lawyer*
Thomas, Joseph Winand *lawyer*
†Title, Peter Stephen *lawyer*
Vance, Robert Patrick *lawyer*
Vaudry, J. William, Jr., *lawyer*
Villavaso, Stephen Donald *lawyer, urban planner*
Wax, George Louis *lawyer*
Wedig, Regina Scotto *lawyer*
Weinmann, John Giffen *lawyer, diplomat*
Weiss, Kenneth Andrew *lawyer, law educator*
Willems, Constance Charles *lawyer*
Wolfe, Richard Peel *lawyer*

Shreveport
†Allen, Marguerite E. *legal association administrator*
Arceneaux, M(artin) Thomas *lawyer*
Bryant, J(ames) Bruce *lawyer*
Carmody, Arthur Roderick, Jr., *lawyer, director*
†Chastain, Merritt Banning, Jr., *lawyer*
Clark, James E. *lawyer*
Cox, John Thomas, Jr., *lawyer*
Halliburton, John Robert *lawyer*
Hardtner, Quintin Theodore, III, *lawyer*
Hetherwick, Gilbert Lewis *lawyer*
Perlman, Jerald Lee *lawyer*
Politz, Nyle Anthony *lawyer*
Ramey, Cecil Edward, Jr., *lawyer*
Smith, Brian David *lawyer, educator*
Woodman, Walter James *lawyer*

Slidell
Shamis, Edward Anthony, Jr., *lawyer*
Singletary, Alvin D. *lawyer*

Thibodaux
Clement, Leslie Joseph, Jr., *lawyer*

Winnfield
†Simmons, Kermit Mixon *lawyer*

MAINE

Auburn
†Abbott, Charles Henry *lawyer*

Augusta
Wake, Robert Alan *lawyer*

Bangor
Gilbert, Charles E., III, *lawyer*
Gould, Edward Ward *lawyer*

Bass Harbor
Ervin, Spencer *lawyer*

Bath
†Watson, Thomas Riley *lawyer, state legislator*

Brewer
Ebitz, Elizabeth Kelly *lawyer*

Brunswick
Lamothe, Arthur J. *lawyer*
Owen, H. Martyn *lawyer*

Castine
Wiswall, Frank Lawrence, Jr., *lawyer, educator*

Falmouth
†Curran, Richard Emery, Jr., *lawyer*

Farmington
Holman, Joseph Frederick *retired lawyer*

Houlton
†Sylvester, Torrey Alden *lawyer*

Old Orchard Beach
Fowler, Daniel L.T. *legal services executive*

Orrs Island
Nelson, Robert Louis *lawyer*

Portland
Coggeshall, Bruce Amsden *lawyer*
†Courtney, Ann M. *lawyer*
Culley, Peter William *lawyer*
†Friedrich, Craig William *lawyer*
Graffam, Ward Irving *lawyer*
Hansel, Gregory Paul *lawyer*
†Harvey, Charles Albert, Jr., *lawyer*
Hunt, David Evans *lawyer*
Ingalls, Everett Palmer, III, *lawyer*
†Keenan, James Francis *lawyer*
Lancaster, Ralph Ivan, Jr., *lawyer*
LeBlanc, Richard Philip *lawyer*
Lehman, Kenneth William *lawyer*
†Martin, Joel Clark *lawyer*
McHold, Sharon Lawrence *lawyer, mediator*
†Neagle, Christopher Scott *lawyer*
Rundlett, Ellsworth Turner, III, *lawyer*
Smith, William Charles *lawyer*
Stauffer, Eric P. *lawyer*
White, Jeffrey Munroe *lawyer*
Whiting, Stephen Clyde *lawyer*
Zarr, Melvyn *lawyer, law educator*

Raymond
Coughlan, Patrick Campbell *lawyer, mediator*

Tenants Harbor
Bates, John Cecil, Jr., *lawyer*

Wells
Carleton, Joseph George, Jr., *lawyer, state legislator*

York
Berlew, Frank Kingston *lawyer*
†Redfield, Sarah Erlick *law educator*

MARYLAND

Abingdon
Wolf, Martin Eugene *lawyer, educator*

Annapolis
Burns, B. Darren *lawyer*
Conwell, John Fredrick *lawyer*
†Dembrow, Dana Lee *lawyer*
†Duckett, Warren Bird, Jr., *lawyer*
Duncan, Charles Tignor *lawyer*
Evans, William Davidson, Jr., *lawyer*
†Jones, Sylvanus Benson *adjudicator, consultant, lawyer*
†Klein, Robert Dale *lawyer*
Levitan, Laurence *lawyer, former state senator*
Lillard, John Franklin, III, *lawyer*
Lucas, Steven Mitchell *lawyer*
†Michaelson, Benjamin, Jr., *lawyer, director*
Perkins, Roger Allan *lawyer*
†Ruth, John Nicholas *lawyer, insurance company executive*

Ashton
Whelan, Roger Michael *lawyer, educator*

Baltimore
†Aisenstark, Avery *lawyer, educator*
Archibald, James Kenway *lawyer*
Arnick, John Stephen *lawyer, legislator*
Baker, William Parr *lawyer*
Bartlett, James Wilson, III, *lawyer*
Berlage, Jan Ingham *lawyer*
Blakeslee, Wesley Daniel *lawyer, consultant*
Blanton, Edward Lee, Jr., *lawyer*
†Bogen, David Skillen *law educator*
Bowen, Lowell Reed *lawyer*
Bruner, William Gwathmey, III, *lawyer*
Burch, Francis Boucher, Jr., *lawyer*
Carbine, James Edmond *lawyer*
Carey, Anthony Morris *lawyer*
Chaplin, Peggy Louie *lawyer*
Chiu, Hungdah *lawyer, legal educator*
Chriss, Timothy D.A. *lawyer*
†Civiletti, Benjamin R. *lawyer, former United States attorney general*
Coleman, Louis Kress *prosecutor*
Cook, Bryson Leitch *lawyer*
†Coppel, Lawrence David *lawyer*
Crowe, Thomas Leonard *lawyer*
Curran, Robert Bruce *lawyer*
†Dempsey, Andrew Francis, Jr., *lawyer*
De Shields-Minnis, Tarra Ramit *lawyer*
Devan, Deborah Hunt *lawyer*
†Dilloff, Neil Joel *lawyer*
Dopkin, Mark Dregant *lawyer*
Dubé, Lawrence Edward, Jr., *lawyer*
Ellin, Marvin *lawyer*
Engel, Paul Bernard *lawyer*
Evans, Nolly Seymour *lawyer*
Eveleth, Janet Stidman *law association administrator*
Fax, Charles Samuel *lawyer*
Ferguson, Robert L., Jr., *lawyer*
Ferro, Elizabeth Krams *lawyer*
Fisher, Morton Poe, Jr., *lawyer*
Friedman, Barry Howard *lawyer, physician*
Gately, Mark Donohue *lawyer*
Gilbert, Blaine Louis *lawyer*
Goldman, Brian Arthur *lawyer, accountant*
Golomb, George Edwin *lawyer*
Gray, Frank Truan *lawyer*
Gray, Oscar Shalom *lawyer*
Hafets, Richard Jay *lawyer*
Haines, Thomas W. W. *lawyer*
Hanks, James Judge, Jr., *lawyer*
Hansen, Christopher Agnew *lawyer*
Hendler, Michael G. *lawyer*
Herschman, Jeffrey D. *lawyer*
Himeles, Martin Stanley, Jr., *lawyer*
Hirsh, Theodore William *lawyer*
Hochberg, Bayard Zabdial *lawyer*
Honemann, Daniel Henry *lawyer*
Howell, Harley Thomas *lawyer*
Hubbard, Herbert Hendrix *lawyer*
†Isacoff, Richard Irwin *lawyer*
Johnston, Edward Allan *lawyer*

Johnston, George W. *lawyer*
Jones, John Martin, Jr., *lawyer*
Kandel, Nelson Robert *lawyer*
Katz, Laurence M. *legal educator*
Katz, Lawrence Edward *lawyer*
Kramer, Paul R. *lawyer*
Kuryk, David Neal *lawyer*
†Lasson, Kenneth *law educator, author, lawyer*
Levin, Edward Jesse *lawyer*
Levine, Richard E. *lawyer*
Liebmann, George W(illiam) *lawyer*
Lohr, Walter George, Jr., *lawyer*
†Loker, F(rank) Ford, Jr., *lawyer*
Lundy, Audie Lee, Jr., *lawyer*
MacColl, J. A. *lawyer*
McClung, A(lexander) Keith, Jr., *retired lawyer*
†McLain, Lynn *law educator*
McPherson, Donald Paxton, III, *lawyer*
McWilliams, John Michael *lawyer*
Meiselman, Alyson *lawyer, mediator/arbitrator*
Melvin, Norman Cecil *lawyer*
Miller, Decatur Howard *lawyer*
Mitchell, Hugh Allen, Jr., *lawyer*
Mogol, Alan Jay *lawyer*
Moser, M(artin) Peter *lawyer*
†Onyemaechi, Pauline *lawyer*
Orman, Leonard Arnold *lawyer*
Pappas, George Frank *lawyer*
Plant, Albin MacDonough *lawyer*
Plummer, Risque Wilson *retired lawyer*
Pokempner, Joseph Kres *lawyer*
Pollak, Joanne E. *lawyer*
Pollak, Mark *lawyer*
Powell, Roger Norman *lawyer*
†Pretl, Michael Albert *lawyer*
Radding, Andrew *lawyer*
†Rafferty, William Bernard *lawyer*
Reno, Russell Ronald, Jr., *lawyer*
†Rettberg, Charles Clayland, Jr., *lawyer*
Reynolds, William Leroy *lawyer, educator*
Robinson, Zelig *lawyer*
Rosenthal, William J. *lawyer*
†Russell, Thomas Edgie, III, *lawyer, construction materials company executive*
Schochor, Jonathan *lawyer, educator*
Schwinn, Steven David *lawyer, mediator*
Scriggins, Larry Palmer *lawyer, director*
Sfekas, Stephen James *lawyer, educator*
†Shannonhouse, Royal Graham, III, *lawyer, educator*
Shapiro, Harry Dean *lawyer*
Short, Alexander Campbell *lawyer*
Snyder, Mark Allen *lawyer*
Speed, Leslie Bokee *lawyer*
Stalfort, John Arthur *lawyer*
Stewart, C(ornelius) Van Leuven *lawyer*
†Stiller, Shale David *lawyer, educator*
†Strachan, Nell B. *lawyer*
†Sturman, Philip *lawyer*
Summers, Thomas Carey *lawyer*
Sykes, Melvin Julius *lawyer*
†Trotter, Richard *law educator, arbitrator*
†Uehlinger, Gerard Paul *lawyer*
Walker, Irving Edward *lawyer*
Wasserman, Richard Leo *lawyer*
Whitman, Marland Hamilton, Jr., *lawyer*
Wilson, Thomas Matthew, III, *lawyer*
Winn, James Julius, Jr., *lawyer*
Wolf, Cyd Beth *lawyer, entrepreneur*
Zinkham, W. Robert *lawyer*

Bel Air
Miller, Max Dunham, Jr., *lawyer*
Wilson, Christian Burhenn *lawyer*

Bethesda
Abrams, Stanley David *lawyer*
Baird, Bruce Allen *lawyer*
†Ballman, B. George *lawyer*
Bauersfeld, Carl Frederick *lawyer*
Beatty, Richard Scrivener *retired lawyer*
Burton, Charles Henning *lawyer*
Calvert, Gordon Lee *retired legal association executive*
†Cohen, Jay Loring *lawyer*
Damico, Nicholas Peter *lawyer*
†Daniels, Michael Paul *retired lawyer*
Deckelbaum, Nelson *lawyer*
Dennin, Joseph Francis *lawyer, former government official*
Dickstein, Sidney *lawyer*
Eisen, Eric Anshel *lawyer*
English, William deShay *lawyer, director*
Eule, Norman Louis *lawyer*
Feuerstein, Donald Martin *lawyer*
†Franklin, William Jay *lawyer*
†Frosh, Brian Esten *lawyer, state senator*
Goodwin, Robert Cronin *lawyer*
Gottlieb, Jonathan W. *lawyer*
Hagberg, Viola Wilgus *lawyer*
Himelfarb, Stephen Roy *lawyer*
†Keplinger, Michael Scott *lawyer*
Mannix, Charles Raymond *law educator*
†Menaker, Frank H., Jr., *lawyer*
Moss, Stephen Edward *lawyer*
Nelson, William Eugene *lawyer*
Pankopf, Arthur, Jr., *lawyer*
Pipkin, James Harold, Jr., *lawyer*
Rivkin, Steven Robert *lawyer*
Robertson, Paul Joseph *lawyer, educator*
Rosenberg, Mark Louis *lawyer*
Rosengren, Paul Gregory *lawyer*
Ross, William Warfield *lawyer*
Schifter, Richard *lawyer*
†Schimel, Richard E. *lawyer*
Schoem, Alan Howard *lawyer*
Silver, David *lawyer*
†Tanenbaum, Richard Hugh *lawyer*
Toomey, Thomas Murray *lawyer*
Weinberger, Alan David *lawyer, corporate executive*

Bowie
McCarthy, Kevin John *lawyer*

Brookeville
Johns, Warren LeRoi *lawyer*

Burtonsville
Covington, Marlow Stanley *retired lawyer*

Cabin John
†Capo, Rafael V. *lawyer*

Cambridge
Jenkins, Robert Rowe *lawyer*

Catonsville
Zumbrun, Alvin John Thomas *law and criminology educator*

Chestertown
Mowell, George Mitchell *lawyer*

Chevy Chase
†Atkinson, Janet E. *lawyer*
Bruder, George Frederick *lawyer*
Chase, Nicholas Joseph *lawyer, educator*
Gildenhorn, Joseph Bernard *lawyer, businessman, former diplomat*
†Goldman, Janis Meresman *lawyer, law firm executive*
Harr, Karl Gottlieb, Jr., *retired lawyer*
Ketcham, Orman Weston *lawyer, former judge*
Klain, Ronald Alan *lawyer*
Mackall, Laidler Bowie *lawyer*
Meyerson, Christopher Cortlandt *lawyer*
†Murphy, Brian Charles *lawyer*
Ragland, Robert Allen *lawyer*
†Schwartzman, Robin Berman *lawyer*
Toy, Charles David *lawyer*
Weiss, Harlan Lee *lawyer*

Clinton
Hill, Keith Maurice *editor*

Cockeysville
Barnes, Peter *retired lawyer*

Cockeysville Hunt Valley
Edgett, William Maloy *lawyer, labor arbitrator*

College Park
Feinstein, Frederick Lee *lawyer*
†Gobbel, Luther Russell *lawyer*
Neal, Edward Garrison *lawyer*
†Pavela, Gary Michael *legal educator, administrator*
†Rosen, Steven *lawyer*

Columbia
Closson, Walter Franklin *child support prosecutor*
†Maseritz, Guy B. *lawyer*
†Siegel, David Burton *lawyer*
Ulman, Louis Jay *lawyer*

Crofton
Doherty, Daniel Joseph, III, *lawyer*

Crownsville
Irish, Leon Eugene *lawyer, educator, non-profit organization executive*

Derwood
Wong, Richard Lee *lawyer*

Easton
Ikenberry, Henry Cephas, Jr., *lawyer*
Maffitt, James Strawbridge *lawyer*

Elkton
†Scott, Doris Petersen *lawyer*

Ellicott City
Pairo, Preston Abercrombie, Jr., *lawyer*

Fort Washington
Alexander, Gary R. *lawyer, state legislator, lobbyist*

Frederick
Hogan, Ilona Modly *lawyer*
Sica, John *lawyer*

Gaithersburg
McDowell, Donna Schultz *lawyer, educator*
Sherer, Samuel Ayers *lawyer, urban planning consultant*

Glyndon
Renbaum, Barry Jeffrey *lawyer*

Greenbelt
Billingsley, Lance W. *lawyer*
Brugger, George Albert *lawyer*
Greenwald, Andrew Eric *lawyer*
Jackley, Michael Dano *lawyer*
Jascourt, Hugh D. *lawyer, arbitrator, mediator*

Hagerstown
Berkson, Jacob Benjamin *lawyer, author, conservationist*
†Gilbert, Howard William, Jr., *lawyer*

Hanover
Classen, Henry Ward *lawyer, educator*

Hyattsville
Levy, David Lawrence *lawyer, legal association administrator, advocate*
†Matty, Robert Jay *lawyer*
Rummel, Edgar Ferrand *retired lawyer*
Spiegel, Robert Alan *lawyer*

Kensington
Dauster, William Gary *lawyer, economist*
†Groner, Isaac Nathan *lawyer*
Mathias, Joseph Marshall *lawyer, judge*

Leonardtown
Lacer, Alfred Antonio *lawyer, educator*

Linthicum
†Burns, Michael William *lawyer former state legislator*

Lutherville
Freeland, Charles *lawyer, accountant*
Mc Kenney, Walter Gibbs, Jr., *lawyer, publishing company executive*

New Market
Gabriel, Eberhard John *lawyer*

North Potomac
†Keane, James Ignatius *lawyer, consultant*
Lehman, Leonard *retired lawyer, consultant*

Owings
Parrett, Sherman O. *lawyer*

Owings Mills
Granat, Richard Stuart *lawyer, educator*

Oxon Hill
†Fields, Richard Lawrence *lawyer, consultant*

Parkville
Hill, Milton King, Jr., *retired lawyer*

Pasadena
Asti, Alison Louise *lawyer*

Patuxent River
Fitzhugh, David Michael *lawyer*

Pocomoke City
†Porter, James Harry, Jr., *lawyer*

Potomac
Feldman, Myer *lawyer*
Hall, William Darlington *lawyer*
Meyer, Lawrence George *lawyer*
Mullenbach, Linda Herman *lawyer*
Parker, Ellis Jackson, III, *lawyer, broadcaster*
Peter, Phillips Smith *lawyer*
Powell, Robert Dominick *lawyer*
†Redding, Robert Ellsworth *lawyer*
Troffkin, Howard Julian *lawyer, diversified company executive*

Prince Frederick
†Reynolds, Christopher John *lawyer*

Rockville
Armstrong, Kenneth *lawyer*
Avery, Bruce Edward *lawyer*
Barkley, Brian Evan *lawyer, political consultant*
Barron, Myra Hymovich *lawyer*
Berryman, Richard Byron *lawyer*
Cheston, Sheila Carol *lawyer*
Cromwell, James Julian *lawyer*
Daisley, William Prescott *lawyer*
De Jong, David Samuel *lawyer, educator*
Doyle, Thomas Edward *lawyer, educator*
Frye, Roland Mushat, Jr., *lawyer*
†Gordon, Michael Robert *lawyer, state legislator*
Kadish, Richard L. *lawyer*
Karp, Ronald Alvin *lawyer*
Katz, Steven Martin *lawyer, accountant*
Kerxton, Alan Smith *lawyer*
Kessel, John Philip *lawyer*
Michael, Robert Roy *lawyer*
Molitor, Graham Thomas Tate *lawyer*
Patrick, Philip Howard *lawyer*
†Rachanow, Gerald Marvin *lawyer, pharmacist*
Roberts, Christopher Chalmers *lawyer*
†Smith, David Robinson *lawyer*
†Thompson, James Lee *lawyer*
Titus, Roger Warren *lawyer*
Tomar, Richard Thomas *lawyer*
Van Grack, Steven *lawyer*
Zaphiriou, George Aristotle *lawyer, educator*

Ruxton
Lewis, Alexander Ingersoll, III, *lawyer*

Saint Michaels
Brown, Omer Forrest, II, *lawyer*

Salisbury
Clarke, Wm. A. Lee, III, *lawyer*

Severna Park
Lilly, John Richard, II, *lawyer*

Showell
Grech, Christopher Alan *lawyer, consultant*

Silver Spring
Craig, Paul Max, Jr., *retired lawyer*
†Ehrenkranz, Gil *lawyer*
Germain, Regina *lawyer*
Gold, George Myron *lawyer, editor, writer, consultant*
Hannan, Myles *lawyer, banker*
Katz, Jonathan L. *lawyer*
Kramer, Gerson Balfour *lawyer*
Lederer, Max Donald, Jr., *lawyer*
Weissenborn, Anne Adkins *lawyer*
†Wheeler, Anne Marie *lawyer*

Takoma Park
Dunn, John Benjamin *lawyer*

Towson
Campion, Renée *lawyer*
Carney, Bradford George Yost *lawyer, educator*
Lutz, Randall Matthew *lawyer*
†Maher Arcodia, Patricia *lawyer*
Miller, Herbert H. *lawyer*
†Morrow, Thomas Campbell *lawyer*
Proctor, Kenneth Donald *lawyer*
Putzel, Constance Kellner *lawyer*

Upper Marlboro
†Brennan, William Collins, Jr., *lawyer*
†Morrison, Anne Deinlein *law librarian*
†Vaughan, James Joseph Michael *lawyer*

Wallace, Sean Daniel *lawyer, judge*

Waldorf
†Bolden, Melvin Wilberforce, Jr., *lawyer*

West Bethesda
†Scully, Roger Tehan, II, *lawyer*

Westminster
Dulany, William Bevard *lawyer*
Preston, Charles Michael *lawyer*
Staples, Lyle Newton *lawyer*

Wheaton
Johnson, Laurence F(leming) *lawyer*
Kirchman, Eric Hans *lawyer*

MASSACHUSETTS

Acton
McCadden, Joseph A. *lawyer*

Amesbury
Swartz, Mark Lee *lawyer*

Amherst
Howland, Richard Moulton *retired lawyer*
Katsh, M. Ethan *law educator*
Mazor, Lester Jay *law educator*

Andover
†McDaniel, Paul R. *law educator, lawyer*

Arlington
†Bowen, Steven Holmes *lawyer*

Ashfield
Pepyne, Edward Walter *lawyer, psychologist, former educator*

Auburndale
Bernard, Michael Mark *lawyer, city planning consultant*

Barnstable
†Mycock, Frederick Charles *lawyer*
†Perry, Blair Lane *lawyer*

Bedford
Nason, Leonard Yoshimoto *lawyer, writer, publisher*
†Paglierani, Ronald Joseph *lawyer*

Belmont
Greer, Gordon Bruce *retired lawyer, writer*
Simpson, Russell Avington *retired law firm administrator*
†Zito, Frank R. *lawyer, accountant*

Boston
Abbott, William Saunders *lawyer*
Abraham, Nicholas Albert *lawyer, real estate developer*
Abrams, Roger Ian *law educator, arbitrator*
†Albrecht, Peter Leffingwell *lawyer*
Aresty, Jeffrey M. *lawyer*
Auerbach, Joseph *lawyer, educator, retired*
Ayoub, Paul Joseph *lawyer*
Bae, Frank S. H. *law educator, law library administrator*
Bangs, Will Johnston *lawyer*
†Barber, Robert Cushman *lawyer*
Beard, Charles Julian *lawyer*
Benjamin, William Chase *lawyer*
Bernhard, Alexander Alfred *lawyer*
Berry, Janis Marie *lawyer*
Bines, Harvey Ernest *lawyer, educator, writer*
Bloch, Donald Martin *lawyer*
†Bloom, Howard Martin *lawyer*
Blumenreich, Gene Arnold *lawyer*
Bodoff, Joseph Samuel Uberman *lawyer*
Bohnen, Michael J. *lawyer*
Bok, John Fairfield *lawyer*
Bornheimer, Allen Millard *lawyer*
Boumil, Marcia Mobilia *legal educator, mediator, writer, lawyer*
Brody, Richard Eric *lawyer*
Brountas, Paul Peter *lawyer*
Brown, Matthew *lawyer*
Brown, Michael Robert *lawyer*
Buchanan, Robert McLeod *lawyer*
Burleigh, Lewis Albert *lawyer*
Burns, Thomas David *lawyer*
Burr, Francis Hardon *lawyer*
Caccese, Michael Stephen *lawyer*
Campbell, Richard P. *lawyer*
Carpenter, Robert Brent *lawyer*
Carr, Stephen W. *lawyer*
Carter, T(homas) Barton *law educator*
Casby, Robert William *lawyer*
Casner, Truman Snell *lawyer*
Clendenen, Patrick Thomas *lawyer*
Clymer, John Howard *lawyer*
Cogan, John Francis, Jr., *lawyer*
Cohn, Andrew Howard *lawyer*
Connors, Donald Louis *lawyer, land use planner*
†Coolidge, Francis Lowell *lawyer*
Craver, James Bernard *lawyer*
Cronin, Philip Mark *lawyer*
Curley, Robert Ambrose, Jr., *lawyer*
Daley, Paul Patrick *lawyer*
†Dando, A. Jeffrey *lawyer, consultant*
†Davis, Christopher Patrick *lawyer*
Davis, Joshua Malcolm *lawyer, educator*
Daynard, Richard Alan *law educator*
Delaney, John White *lawyer*
Del Bono, Irene Lillian (Irene Stone Guild Del Bono) *lawyer*
DeRensis, Paul *lawyer*
de Rham, Casimir, Jr., *lawyer*
†Deutsch, Stephen B. *lawyer*
Dillon, James Joseph *lawyer*
Dineen, John K. *lawyer*
Donahue, Charlotte Mary *lawyer*
Drachman, Allan Warren *lawyer, arbitrator*
Edwards, Richard Lansing *lawyer*

Marks, Scott Charles *lawyer*
Moran, Philip David *lawyer*
†Shachok, Mary Ellen *lawyer*
Wasserman, Stephen Alan *lawyer*
†Witt, Carol A. *lawyer*

Shrewsbury
†Kapelner, David Israel *lawyer, educator*

South Hamilton
Campbell, Diana Butt *lawyer*

South Orleans
†Wherry, Edward John, Jr., *lawyer*

Springfield
Bock, Robert Leroy *law educator*
Burke, Michael Henry *lawyer*
†Burstein, Merwyn Jerome *lawyer*
Dibble, Francis Daniel, Jr., *lawyer*
†Fein, Sherman Edward *lawyer, psychologist*
Fialky, Gary Lewis *lawyer*
Gelinas, Robert Albert *lawyer*
Goldstein, Anne Brenda *law educator*
Maidman, Stephen Paul *lawyer*
McCarthy, Charles Francis, Jr., *lawyer*
†Miles, Judith Ellen *lawyer, educator*
Miller, J(ohn) Wesley, III, *lawyer*
Nicolai, Paul Peter *lawyer*
Oldershaw, Louis Frederick *lawyer*
Santopietro, Albert Robert *lawyer*
†Sheils, James Bernard *lawyer*
Susse, Sandra Slone *lawyer*
Weiss, Ronald Phillip *lawyer*

Stoughton
Gabovitch, Steven Alan *lawyer, accountant*
George, Arthur Charles *lawyer*
Schepps, Victoria Hayward *lawyer*

Truro
Friedman, Edward David *lawyer, arbitrator*

Wakefield
†Courtenay, Lisa A. *paralegal, foundation administrator*
Lucas, Robert Frank *lawyer*

Waltham
Barnes-Brown, Peter Newton *lawyer*
†Dickie, Robert Benjamin *lawyer, consultant, educator*

Watertown
Kaloosdian, Robert Aram *lawyer*
†Karaian, Norma Maksoodian *lawyer*

Wayland
Norris, Melvin *lawyer*

Wellesley
Giroux, Eugene Xavier *lawyer*
Goglia, Charles A., Jr., *lawyer*
Marx, Peter A. *lawyer*
Silberman, Robert A. S. *lawyer*

West Chatham
Rowley, Glenn Harry *lawyer*

West Falmouth
Carlson, David Bret *lawyer*

West Springfield
Ely, John P. *lawyer*

Weston
†Bateman, Thomas Robert *lawyer*
†Freeman, Florence Eleanor *lawyer*
Lashman, L. Edward *arbitrator, mediator, consultant*
Schwartz, Edward Lester *retired lawyer*
Thomas, Roger Meriwether *lawyer*

Winchester
Bigelow, Robert P. *lawyer, arbitrator, mediator, journalist*

Winthrop
Brown, Patricia Irene *retired law librarian, lawyer*

Woburn
†Kuelthau, Paul Stauffer *lawyer*
†Lovins, Nelson Preston *lawyer*
Murray, Philip Edmund, Jr., *lawyer*

Worcester
Baldiga, Joseph Hilding *lawyer*
Balko, George Anthony, III, *lawyer, educator*
†Bernstein, William Elliott *lawyer*
Cowan, Fairman Chaffee *lawyer*
Donnelly, James Corcoran, Jr., *lawyer*
Felper, David Michael *lawyer*
Lougee, David Louis *lawyer*
Moschos, Demitrios Mina *lawyer*
Moschos, Michael Christos *lawyer*
Silver, Marvin S. *lawyer*
Storey, Harry Stephens *lawyer*

Yarmouth Port
Paquin, Thomas Christopher *lawyer*

MICHIGAN

Ada
Mc Callum, Charles Edward *lawyer*

Alpena
Hunter, Mark John *lawyer, photographer*

Ann Arbor
Allen, Layman Edward *law educator, research scientist*
Anderson, Austin Gothard *lawyer, university administrator*
Britton, Clarold Lawrence *lawyer, consultant*
Browder, Olin Lorraine *legal educator*
Buesser, Anthony Carpenter *lawyer*
Cooper, Edward Hayes *lawyer, educator*
DeVine, Edmond Francis *lawyer*
Dew, Thomas Edward *lawyer*
Dobranski, Bernard *law educator*
Eggertsen, John Hale *lawyer*
Ellmann, Douglas Stanley *lawyer*
†Frankena, Karl Roelofs *lawyer*
†Garcia, Elisa Dolores *lawyer*
Goethel, Stephen B. *lawyer*
Hertz, Dawn Leslie *lawyer*
†Howse, Robert Lloyd *law educator, consultant*
Joscelyn, Kent B(uckley) *lawyer*
Kahn, Douglas Allen *legal educator*
Kamisar, Yale *lawyer, educator*
Keppelman, Nancy *lawyer*
Krier, James Edward *law educator, writer*
Krislov, Marvin *lawyer, educator*
Lempert, Richard Owen *lawyer, educator*
†MacKinnon, Catharine Alice *lawyer, law educator, legal scholar, writer*
Muraski, Anthony Augustus *lawyer*
Niehoff, Leonard Marvin *lawyer*
†O'Brien, Darlene Anne *lawyer*
Reed, John Wesley *lawyer, educator*
Ryan, Marianne Elizabeth *lawyer*
Schneider, Carl Edward *law educator*
Siedel, George John, III, *law educator*
Vining, Joseph (George Joseph Vining) *law educator*
White, James Boyd *law educator*
Widmayer, Warren J. *lawyer*

Auburn Hills
†Huss, Allan Michael *lawyer*
O'Brien, William J., III, *lawyer*

Bay City
Greve, Guy Robert *lawyer*

Beverly Hills
Hertzberg, David Gordon *retired lawyer*

Bingham Farms
Banas, C(hristine) Leslie *lawyer*
Burstein, Richard Joel *lawyer*
Goren, Steven Eliot *lawyer*
Lebow, Michael Jeffrey *lawyer*

Birmingham
Elsman, James Leonard, Jr., *lawyer*
Harms, Steven Alan *lawyer*
Kienbaum, Thomas Gerd *lawyer*
Podolsky, Arnold Mark *lawyer, physician*
Robinson, Marietta S. *lawyer*
Schaefer, John Frederick *lawyer, educator*
Sweeney, Thomas Frederick *lawyer*
†Thorpe, Norman Ralph *lawyer, automobile company executive, retired air force officer*
Wells, Steven Wayne *lawyer*
Zacharski, Dennis Edward *lawyer*

Bloomfield Hills
Baker, Robert Edward *lawyer, retired financial corporation executive*
Berlow, Robert Alan *lawyer*
†Birnkrant, Sherwin Maurice *lawyer*
Brodhead, William McNulty *lawyer, former congressman*
Charla, Leonard Francis *lawyer*
Clippert, Charles Frederick *lawyer*
Cranmer, Thomas William *lawyer*
Cunningham, Gary H. *lawyer*
Dawson, Stephen Everette *lawyer*
Deron, Edward Michael *lawyer*
Gold, Edward David *lawyer*
Googasian, George Ara *lawyer*
Gornbein, Henry Seidel *lawyer*
Gotthelf, Beth *lawyer*
Janover, Robert H. *lawyer*
Kasischke, Louis Walter *lawyer*
Kirk, John MacGregor *lawyer*
Klein, Coleman Eugene *lawyer*
†Lamping, William Jay *lawyer*
Ledwidge, Patrick Joseph *lawyer*
LoPrete, James Hugh *lawyer*
Martin, J(oseph) Patrick *lawyer*
McCuen, John Francis, Jr., *lawyer*
McDonald, Patrick Allen *lawyer, arbitrator, educator*
†McGarry, Alexander Banting *lawyer*
Meyer, George Herbert *lawyer*
Morganroth, Fred *lawyer*
Mucha, John, III, *lawyer*
Nern, Christopher Carl *lawyer*
Norris, John Hart *lawyer, director*
Pappas, Edward Harvey *lawyer*
Rader, Ralph Terrance *lawyer*
Simon, Evelyn *lawyer*
Snyder, George Edward *lawyer*
Solomon, Mark Raymond *lawyer, educator*
Sommerfeld, David William *lawyer, educator*
Stewart, Michael B. *lawyer, mechanical and aerospace engineer*
†Tallerico, Thomas Joseph *lawyer*
Victor, Richard Steven *lawyer*
Williams, J. Bryan *lawyer*
Williams, Walter Joseph *lawyer*
Yamin, Joseph Francis *lawyer, counselor*

Center Line
Litch, John Michael *lawyer*

Charlevoix
Telgenhof, Allen Ray *lawyer*

Clarkston
†Bullard, Rockwood Wilde, III, *lawyer*

Dearborn
Demorest, Mark Stuart *lawyer*
Kahn, Mark Leo *arbitrator, educator*
Kershner, Rodger A. *corporate lawyer*
Taub, Robert Allan *lawyer*

Decatur
Kinney, Gregory Hoppes *lawyer*

Detroit
†Adams, James Charles *lawyer*
Andreoff, Christopher Andon *lawyer*
Babcock, Charles Witten, Jr., *lawyer*
†Barr, Charles Joseph Gore *lawyer*
Brady, Edmund Matthew, Jr., *lawyer*
Brand, George Edward, Jr., *lawyer*
Brustad, Orin Daniel *lawyer*
Candler, James Nall, Jr., *lawyer*
Charfoos, Lawrence Selig *lawyer*
Christian, Terry Clifton *lawyer*
Cohan, Leon Sumner *lawyer, retired electric company executive*
Cohen, Norton Jacob *lawyer*
Collier, James Warren *lawyer*
Connor, Laurence Davis *lawyer, director*
Cothorn, John Arthur *lawyer*
Darlow, Julia Donovan *lawyer*
†Deason, Herold McClure *lawyer*
Devaney, Dennis Martin *lawyer, educator*
Draper, James Wilson *lawyer*
Dunn, William Bradley *lawyer*
†Entenman, John Alfred *lawyer*
†Everingham, James Theodore *lawyer*
†Faison, W. Mack *lawyer*
Fellrath, Richard Frederic *lawyer*
†Felt, Julia Kay *lawyer*
†Fromm, Frederick Andrew, Jr., *lawyer*
Glotta, Ronald Delon *lawyer*
†Gottschalk, Thomas A. *lawyer*
†Gunderson, Michael Arthur *lawyer*
Gushee, Richard Bordley *lawyer*
Hampton, Verne Churchill, II, *lawyer*
†Harbour, Nancy Caine *lawyer*
†Harris, Patricia Skalny *lawyer*
Jacobs, John Patrick *lawyer*
Johnson, Cynthia L(e) M(ae) *lawyer*
†Krsul, John Aloysius, Jr., *lawyer*
Kuehn, George E. *lawyer, former beverage company executive*
†Labadie, Dwight Daniel *lawyer*
Lamborn, LeRoy Leslie *law educator*
Lawrence, John Kidder *lawyer*
Leuchtman, Stephen Nathan *lawyer*
Lewand, F. Thomas *lawyer*
Lockman, Stuart M. *lawyer*
Longhofer, Ronald Stephen *lawyer*
Mamat, Frank Trustick *lawyer*
Maurer, David Leo *lawyer*
McKim, Samuel John, III, *lawyer*
Mengel, Christopher Emile *lawyer, educator*
Miller, George DeWitt, Jr., *lawyer*
Mitseff, Carl *lawyer*
†Motlagh, Cyrus K. *law educator*
Myers, Rodman Nathaniel *lawyer*
Nadeau, Steven C. *lawyer*
Nemeth, Patricia Marie *lawyer*
Nix, Robert Royal, II, *lawyer*
Norris, Megan Pinney *lawyer*
Parker, Ross Gail *lawyer*
Peters, John Douglas *lawyer, artist*
Rasmussen, Douglas John *lawyer*
Richardson, Ralph Herman *lawyer*
Rogers, Hon Paulletto *researcher, writer*
†Rohm, Benita Jill *lawyer*
Rohr, Richard David *lawyer*
Rozof, Phyllis Claire *lawyer*
Saxton, William Marvin *lawyer*
Scholler, Thomas Peter *lawyer, accountant*
Schwartz, Alan E. *lawyer, director*
Scott, John Edward Smith *lawyer*
Sedler, Robert Allen *law educator*
Semple, Lloyd Ashby *lawyer*
Shaevsky, Mark *lawyer*
Shannon, Margaret Anne *lawyer*
Shapiro, Michael Bruce *lawyer*
†Shulman, Margaret Alex Rabinovich *lawyer, musician*
†Smith, James Albert *lawyer*
Sparrow, Herbert George, III, *lawyer, educator*
†Spencer, William Thomas *lawyer*
†Sullivan, Thomas Michael *lawyer*
†Tarnacki, Duane L. *lawyer*
Thelen, Bruce Cyril *lawyer*
†Thomas, Russell Joseph, Jr., *lawyer*
Thoms, David Moore *lawyer*
Thurber, Peter Palms *lawyer*
†Tickner, Ellen Mindy *lawyer*
Timm, Roger K. *lawyer*
Torpey, Scott Raymond *lawyer*
Valade, Alan Michael *lawyer*
Volz, William Harry *law educator, administrator*
†Ward, George Edward *lawyer, law educator*
Wise, John Augustus *lawyer, director*
Wittlinger, Timothy David *lawyer*
†Wyrick, Jermaine Albert *lawyer*
†Zalman, Marvin *law educator*

Dexter
Millman, Jode Susan *lawyer, writer*

East Lansing
Bassett, Debra Lyn *lawyer, educator*
Bitensky, Susan Helen *law educator*
Johnson, Clark Cumings *lawyer, educator*
Joseph, Raymond *lawyer*
Lashbrooke, Elvin Carroll, Jr., *law educator, consultant*
†Revelos, Constantine Nicholas *law educator, writer*
†Stenzel, Paulette Lynn *business law educator, lawyer*
†Vincent, Adrian Roger *lawyer*
Wilkinson, William Sherwood *lawyer*

Eastpointe
Schultz, Kathleen Stefani *lawyer*

Farmington
†Harms, Donald C. *lawyer*
McFarland, Robert Edwin *lawyer*

Farmington Hills
†Cooper, Douglas Kenneth *lawyer*
Fenton, Robert Leonard *lawyer, literary agent, movie producer, writer*
Fershtman, Julie Ilene *lawyer*
Foley, Thomas John *lawyer*
Hampton, William Peck *lawyer*
Kippert, Robert John, Jr., *lawyer*
Meyer, Philip Gilbert *lawyer*
†Moore, Roy F. *lawyer*
Taravella, Christopher Anthony *lawyer*

Fenton
Hildner, Phillips Brooks, II, *lawyer*

Flint
†Busch, Arthur Allen *lawyer, educator*
Cooley, Richard Eugene *lawyer*
†Gernstein, Stanley B. *lawyer*
Hart, Clifford Harvey *lawyer*
Henneke, Edward George *lawyer*
Powers, Edward Herbert *lawyer*

Fort Gratiot
Carson, Robert William *lawyer*

Frankfort
Gerberding, Miles Carston *lawyer*

Franklin
†Hogan, Kempf *lawyer*

Fremont
†Price, Russell Eugene *lawyer*

Gaylord
Topp, Susan Hlywa *lawyer*

Grand Blanc
Jakeway, Edwin William *lawyer*

Grand Rapids
Barnes, Thomas John *lawyer*
Blackwell, Thomas Francis *lawyer*
Bradshaw, Conrad Allan *lawyer*
†Cameron, John Gray, Jr., *lawyer*
Curtin, Timothy John *lawyer*
Davis, Henry Barnard, Jr., *lawyer*
Davis, Mark Murray *lawyer*
†Dodge, David A. *lawyer*
†Halliday, William James, Jr., *lawyer*
†Harris, Richard W. *law educator, lawyer*
Khorey, David Eugene *lawyer*
Litton, Randall Gale *lawyer*
Mears, Patrick Edward *lawyer*
†Neckers, Bruce Warren *lawyer*
†Pylman, Norman Herbert, II, *lawyer*
Rinck, James Richard *lawyer*
†Rynbrandt, Kevin Abraham *lawyer*
Spies, Frank Stadler *lawyer*
Sytsma, Fredric A. *lawyer*
Titley, Larry J. *lawyer*
†VanderLaan, Robert D. *lawyer*
Van Haren, W(illiam) Michael *lawyer*
Van't Hof, William Keith *lawyer*

Grosse Pointe
†Behringer, Samuel Joseph, Jr., *lawyer*
Cobau, John Reed *lawyer*
Goss, James William *lawyer*

Grosse Pointe Farms
Axe, John Randolph *lawyer, financial executive*
Brucker, Wilber Marion *retired lawyer*

Grosse Pointe Park
Centner, Charles William *lawyer, educator*
McIntyre, Anita Grace Jordan *lawyer*
Mogk, John Edward *law educator, association executive, consultant*

Grosse Pointe Woods
Pytell, Robert Henry *retired lawyer, former judge*

Hamtramck
†Kaczmarek, Carla *lawyer*

Harbor Springs
Smith, Wayne Richard *lawyer*
Turner, Lester Nathan *lawyer, international trade consultant*

Hickory Corners
Bristol, Norman *lawyer, arbitrator, former food company executive*

Highland
Bullard, Willis Clare, Jr., *lawyer*

Holland
Murphy, Max Ray *lawyer*
†Waltz, Jon Richard *lawyer, educator, author*

Howell
†Parker, Robert Ernser *lawyer*

Huntington Woods
†Maxwell, Brenda J. *lawyer*

Inkster
†Bullock, Steven Carl *lawyer*

Irons
Getty, Gerald Winkler *lawyer*

Jackson
Brunner, James Edwin *lawyer*
†Firestone, Richard Bartlett *lawyer*
Jacobs, Wendell Early, Jr., *lawyer*

Jenison
Kruse, Pamela Jean *lawyer*

Kalamazoo
Bauckham, John Henry *lawyer*
Bus, Roger Jay *lawyer*
†Cinabro, Robert Henry *lawyer*
Durham, Sidney Down *lawyer*
Enslen, Pamela Chapman *lawyer*
†Freeberg, Edward Ronald *lawyer*
Gordon, Edgar George *retired lawyer*
Hatch, Hazen van den Berg *lawyer*

†Lantz, William Charles *lawyer*
Larson, Bruce Robert *lawyer, educator*
Orwoll, Gregg S. K. *lawyer*
Somsen, Henry Northrop *retired lawyer*

Rosemount
†Tesch, Tamara Dianne *lawyer*

Saint Cloud
Hughes, Kevin John *lawyer*
Seifert, Luke Michael *lawyer*

Saint Joseph
Olheiser, Mary David *lawyer, educator*

Saint Louis Park
Nightingale, Tracy Irene *lawyer*
†Seaburg, Jean *lawyer*

Saint Paul
Allison, John Robert *lawyer*
Awsumb, Robert Ardin *lawyer*
†Bastian, Gary Warren *judge*
†Black, Bert *state administrator, lawyer*
Carruthers, Philip Charles *lawyer, public official*
Cassidy, Edward Q. *lawyer*
†Cobb, Elizabeth H. *lawyer*
Daly, Joseph Leo *law educator*
Degnan, John Michael *lawyer*
†Dietz, Charlton Henry *lawyer*
Duckstad, Jon Robert *lawyer, educator*
Failinger, Marie Anita *law educator, editor*
†Fisk, Martin H. *lawyer*
Galvin, Michael John, Jr., *lawyer*
Geis, Jerome Arthur *lawyer, legal educator*
†Hansen, Eric Peter *lawyer*
Hansen, Robyn L. *lawyer*
Harris, Ruth Jensen *lawyer*
Jacobs, Stephen Louis *lawyer*
Johnson, Paul Oren *lawyer*
Jones, C. Paul *lawyer, educator*
Karasov, Phyllis *lawyer*
Kirwin, Kenneth Francis *law educator*
†Knapp, John Anthony *lawyer*
Larson, David Allen *law educator*
Lebedoff, Randy Miller *lawyer*
Leighton, Robert Joseph *lawyer*
†LeVander, Bernhard Wilhelm *retired lawyer*
LeVander, Harold Powrie, Jr., *lawyer*
Maclin, Alan Hall *lawyer*
†McNeely, John J. *lawyer*
†Meyer, Theodore James *lawyer*
Noonan, James C. *lawyer, mediator, arbitrator*
†O'Leary, Daniel Brian *lawyer, educator*
Rebane, John T. *lawyer*
†Rothman, Mitchell Lewis *lawyer, educator*
†Sarazin, Mary Eileen *lawyer*
Seymour, McNeil Vernam *lawyer*
†Sheahan, Michael John *lawyer*
†Spencer, David James *lawyer*
†Tourek, Steven Charles *lawyer*
Trojack, John Edward *lawyer*
Winthrop, Sherman *lawyer*
†Woutat, Paul Gustav *lawyer*
†Yucel, Edgar Kent *lawyer, consultant*

South Saint Paul
†Pugh, Thomas Wilfred *lawyer*

St Paul
Dayton, Charles Kelly *lawyer*
†Norton, John William *lawyer, mediator*

Stillwater
†Hutchinson, Michael Clark *lawyer*

Wayzata
†Alton, Howard Robert, Jr., *lawyer, real estate and food company executive*
Johnson, Eugene Laurence *lawyer*
Reutiman, Robert William, Jr., *lawyer*

Winona
Borman, John *trial lawyer, arbitrator, mediator*
Brosnahan, Roger Paul *lawyer*

MISSISSIPPI

Batesville
Cook, William Leslie, Jr., *lawyer*

Bay Saint Louis
Bernstein, Joseph *lawyer*

Biloxi
†Dornan, Donald C., Jr., *lawyer*
O'Barr, Bobby Gene, Sr., *lawyer*

Clarksdale
†Connell, Edward Peacock, Sr., *lawyer*

Cleveland
Alexander, William Brooks *lawyer, former state senator*

Diamondhead
Reddien, Charles Henry, II, *lawyer, corporate executive, consultant*

Gloster
Davis, Cynthia D'Ascenzo *lawyer*

Greenville
Martin, Andrew Ayers *lawyer, physician, educator*

Greenwood
Deaton, Charles Milton *lawyer*

Grenada
Hill, Clyde Vernon, Jr., *prosecutor*

Gulfport
Allen, Harry Roger *lawyer*
Desmond, Susan Fahey *lawyer*
†Owen, Joe Sam *lawyer*

Hattiesburg
Adelman, Michael Schwartz *lawyer*
†Boatner, Jerra *legal assistant*

Hernando
Brown, William A. *lawyer, mediator, arbitrator*

Jackson
Black, D(eWitt) Carl(isle), Jr., *lawyer*
Burch, Donald Victor *lawyer*
Chatham, Lloyd Reeve *lawyer*
†Clark, David Wright *lawyer*
Corlew, John Gordon *lawyer*
†Currie, Edward Jones, Jr., *lawyer*
†Edds, Stephen Charles *lawyer*
Eicher, Donald E., III, *lawyer*
†Goodman, William Flournoy, III, *lawyer*
Grant, Russell Porter, Jr., *lawyer, petroleum land man*
†Hafter, Jerome Charles *lawyer*
Hammond, Frank Jefferson, III, *lawyer*
†Harkins, Patrick Nicholas, III, *lawyer*
†Hauberg, Robert Engelbrecht, Jr., *lawyer*
Henegan, John C(lark) *lawyer*
Hewes, George Poindexter, III, *lawyer*
Hosemann, C. Delbert, Jr., *lawyer*
Howell, Joel Walter, III, *lawyer*
Hughes, Byron William *lawyer, oil exploration company executive*
Johnson, Mark Wayne *lawyer*
Langford, James Jerry *lawyer*
Martinez, Eduardo Vidal *lawyer*
Moize, Jerry Dee *lawyer, government official*
†O'Mara, James Wright *lawyer*
Ray, H. M. *lawyer*
†Scanlon, Pat H. *lawyer*
Shinn, Clinton Wesley *lawyer*
†Travis, Jay A., III, *lawyer*
†Walker, John Leonard *lawyer*
West, Carol Catherine *law educator*
†Wilson, L(eonard) H(enry) *lawyer*
Wilson, William Roberts, Jr., (Bob Wilson) *lawyer, apparel executive*
Wise, Robert Powell *lawyer*

Kiln
†Thissell, Charles William *lawyer*

Madison
Obert, Keith David *lawyer*

Mccomb
Starrett, Keith *lawyer*

Meridian
†Primeaux, Lawrence *lawyer*

Ocean Springs
†Denham, Earl Lamar *lawyer*
Luckey, Alwyn Hall *lawyer*

Olive Branch
†Carnall, George Hursey, II, *lawyer, business executive*

Oxford
Lewis, Ronald Wayne *lawyer*
Rayburn, S. T. *lawyer*

Pascagoula
Hunter, John Leslie *lawyer*

Raymond
Moss, Jack Gibson *lawyer*

Ridgeland
Boackle, K F. *lawyer, writer, real estate broker*

Southaven
†Taylor, Ronald Louis *lawyer*

Starkville
Yoste, Charles Todd *lawyer*

Tupelo
Bush, Fred Marshall, Jr., *lawyer*
†Clayton, Claude F., Jr., *lawyer*

University
Howorth, David Bishop *lawyer*

MISSOURI

Ballwin
†Banton, Stephen Chandler *lawyer*

Cape Girardeau
Lowes, Albert Charles *lawyer*
McManaman, Kenneth Charles *lawyer*
†O'Loughlin, John Patrick *lawyer*

Carthage
Weissenberger, Harry George *lawyer*

Cassville
†Melton, Emory Leon *lawyer, state legislator, publisher*

Chesterfield
Coffin, Richard Keith *lawyer*
Denneen, John Paul *lawyer*
†Hier, Marshall David *lawyer*
Pollihan, Thomas Henry *lawyer*
Ross, Richard Lee *retired lawyer*
†Stalnaker, Tim *lawyer*

Clayton
Fluhr, Steven Solomon *lawyer*
Komen, Leonard *lawyer*
Mohrman, Henry J(oe), Jr., *lawyer, investment manager*
†Radloff, Stuart Jay *lawyer*
Schwartz, Theodore Frank *lawyer*
†Tremayne, Eric Flory *lawyer*

Columbia
†Arnet, William Francis *lawyer*
Bunn, Ronald Freeze *lawyer, academic administrator*
Crepeau, Dewey Lee *lawyer, educator*
Harter, Philip J. *lawyer, educator*
Mays, William Gay, II, *lawyer, real estate developer*
Moore, Mitchell Jay *lawyer, law educator*
Parrigin, Elizabeth Ellington *lawyer*
Peth, Howard Allen *lawyer, educator*
Phillips, Walter Ray *lawyer, educator*
Schwabe, John Bennett, II, *lawyer*
†Turley, J. William *lawyer*
Welliver, Warren Dee *lawyer, retired state supreme court justice*
Westbrook, James Edwin *lawyer, educator*
Whitman, Dale Alan *lawyer, law educator*

Cuba
Lange, C. William *lawyer, educator*

Fenton
Stolar, Henry Samuel *lawyer*

Florissant
Boyle, Patrick Otto *lawyer*

Hannibal
Welch, Joseph Daniel *lawyer*

Hermann
Puchta, Randolph E. *lawyer*

Hillsboro
Howald, John William *lawyer*

Independence
Cady, Elwyn Loomis, Jr., *medico legal consultant, educator*
Farrington, Buford Lee *lawyer*
Lashley, Curtis Dale *lawyer*
†Rice, Guy Garner *lawyer*
Smith, R(onald) Scott *lawyer*
Watkins, Susan Gail *lawyer*

Jackson
Waldron, Kenneth Lynn *lawyer*

Jefferson City
Bartlett, Alex *lawyer*
Deutsch, James Bernard *lawyer*
Easley, Glenn Edward *lawyer*
Martin, Cathleen A. *lawyer*
Pritchett, Michael Eugene Cook *lawyer*
†Riner, James William *lawyer*
Tettlebaum, Harvey M. *lawyer*

Joplin
Scott, Robert Haywood, Jr., *lawyer*

Kansas City
Anderson, Christopher James *lawyer*
Bartunek, Robert R(ichard), Jr., *lawyer*
Bates, William Hubert *lawyer*
†Beck, William G. *lawyer*
Becker, Thomas Bain *lawyer*
Beckerman, Dale Lee *lawyer*
Beckett, Theodore Charles *lawyer*
Beihl, Frederick *lawyer*
†Berkowitz, Lawrence M. *lawyer*
Bevan, Robert Lewis *lawyer*
†Blackwood, George Dean, Jr., *lawyer*
Boggs, James Dotson *lawyer*
Bradshaw, Jean Paul, II, *lawyer*
Brake, Timothy L. *lawyer*
Brous, Thomas Richard *lawyer*
Canfield, Robert Cleo *lawyer*
Clarke, Milton Charles *lawyer*
†Clegg, Karen Kohler *lawyer*
Cobb, Kenneth Alan *lawyer*
Cowden, John William *lawyer*
Crawford, Howard Allen *lawyer*
Cross, William Dennis *lawyer*
Davis, John Charles *lawyer*
Deacy, Thomas Edward, Jr., *lawyer*
†Delaney, Michael Francis *lawyer*
†Dietrich, William Gale *lawyer, real estate developer, consultant*
Dolson, Edward M. *lawyer*
Egan, Charles Joseph, Jr., *lawyer, greeting card company executive*
Eldridge, Truman Kermit, Jr., *lawyer*
†English, Mark Gregory *lawyer*
Fershee, Susan Joyce *lawyer*
Foster, Mark Stephen *lawyer*
Frantze, David Wayne *lawyer*
†Freilich, Robert H. *lawyer, educator*
Frisbie, Charles *lawyer*
Gaines, Robert Darryl *lawyer, food services executive*
Gardner, Brian E. *lawyer*
†Gilmore, Webb Reilly *lawyer*
Gorman, Gerald Warner *lawyer*
Graham, Harold Steven *lawyer*
†Gusewelle, Anne Elizabeth *lawyer*
Handley, Gerald Matthew *lawyer, educator*
Healy, Michael Patrick *lawyer*
Herman, Robert Stephen *lawyer*
†Hill, Stephen L., Jr., *lawyer, former prosecutor*
Hindman, Larrie C. *lawyer*
†Howes, Brian Thomas *lawyer*
Hubbell, Ernest *lawyer*
Johnson, Leonard James *lawyer*
Johnson, Mark Eugene *lawyer*
†Johnston, John Steven *lawyer*
Joyce, Michael Patrick *lawyer*
Kaplan, Harvey L. *lawyer*
Kilroy, John Muir *lawyer*
Kilroy, William Terrence *lawyer*
King, Richard Allen *lawyer*
Kitchin, John Joseph *lawyer*
Koelling, Thomas Winsor *lawyer*
Langworthy, Robert Burton *lawyer*
Laue, Brant Mitchell *lawyer*
†Levine, Bernard Benton *lawyer*
Lindsey, David Hosford *lawyer*
Lolli, Don R(ay) *lawyer*
Lombardi, Cornelius Ennis, Jr., *lawyer*
Lotven, Howard Lee *lawyer*
Matheny, Edward Taylor, Jr., *lawyer*
McKinney, Janet Kay *law librarian*
McManus, James William *lawyer*
†Miller, George Spencer *lawyer*
Milton, Chad Earl *lawyer*
Minnick, David Michael *lawyer*
Moore, Stephen James *lawyer*
Mordy, James Calvin *lawyer*
Newsom, James Thomas *lawyer*
Norton, John Hise *lawyer*
Palmer, Dennis Dale *lawyer*
Parrette, Leslie Jackson *lawyer*
Pelofsky, Joel *lawyer*
Pemberton, Bradley Powell *lawyer*
Plax, Karen Ann *lawyer*
Popper, Robert *law educator, former dean*
Price, James Tucker *lawyer*
†Proctor, George Edwin, Jr., *lawyer*
†Reardon, Michael Edward *lawyer*
Redmond, Christopher John *lawyer*
Sader, Neil Steven *lawyer*
Sands, Darry Gene *lawyer*
Satterlee, Terry Jean *lawyer*
Scarritt, Richard Winn *lawyer*
†Sears, Kelley Dean *lawyer*
Seigfreid, James Thomas *lawyer*
Setzler, Edward Allan *lawyer*
†Shapiro, Alvin Dale *lawyer*
Shaw, John W. *lawyer*
Shay, David Eugene *lawyer*
†Sherman, Joseph Allen, Jr., *lawyer*
Shughart, Donald Louis *lawyer*
Spalty, Edward Robert *lawyer*
Sparks, Stephen Stone *lawyer*
Spencer, Richard Henry *lawyer*
Suter, Carol J. *non-profit organization executive, lawyer*
†Taff, Earl Wayne *lawyer*
Todd, Stephen Max *lawyer*
Toll, Perry Mark *lawyer, educator*
Tyler, John Edward, III, *lawyer*
Van Dyke, Thomas Wesley *lawyer*
Vering, John Albert *lawyer*
Viani, James Laurence *lawyer*
White, Jerusha Lynn *lawyer*
†Whittaker, Judith Ann Cameron *lawyer*
Willy, Thomas Ralph *lawyer*
Wirken, James Charles *lawyer*
Wrobley, Ralph Gene *lawyer*
Wyrsch, James Robert *lawyer, educator, author*

Keytesville
Wheeler, James Julian *lawyer*

Lake Saint Louis
Callahan, Robert John, Jr., *lawyer, arbitrator*

Lamar
Geddie, Rowland Hill, III, *lawyer*

Lees Summit
Walsh, Thomas Joseph *lawyer*

Liberty
Sayles, Cathy A. *lawyer*

Manchester
Forsman, Alpheus Edwin *lawyer*

Marshall
Peterson, William Allen *lawyer*

Maryland Heights
Cooper, Richard Alan *lawyer*
Stevens, Julie Ann *lawyer*

Mexico
Hagan, Ann P. *lawyer*

Rock Port
Mulvania, Walter Lowell *lawyer*

Rolla
Hickle, William Earl *lawyer, judge*
†Thomas, William Herman, Jr., *lawyer*

Saint Ann
Johnson, Harold Gene *lawyer*

Saint Charles
Dorsey, Mary Elizabeth *lawyer*
Dorsey, Richard Peter, III, *lawyer, former state legislator*
Ritter, Robert Thornton *lawyer*

Saint Joseph
Davis, Lance Barrow *lawyer, municipal judge*
Kranitz, Theodore Mitchell *lawyer*
Taylor, Michael Leslie *lawyer*

Saint Louis
Appleton, R. O., Jr., *lawyer*
Arnold, Fred English *lawyer*
Arnold, John Fox *lawyer*
Atwood, Hollye Stolz *lawyer*
Aylward, Ronald Lee *lawyer*
Babington, Charles Martin, III, *lawyer*
Baldwin, Edwin Steedman *lawyer*
Banks, Eric Kendall *lawyer*
Barken, Bernard Allen *lawyer*
Baum, Gordon Lee *lawyer, non-profit organization administrator*
Becker, David Mandel *law educator, author, consultant*
Behrens, Brian Charles *lawyer, associate*
Berendt, Robert Tryon *lawyer*
Berger, John Torrey, Jr., *lawyer*
Blanke, Richard Brian *lawyer*
Boggs, Beth Clemens *lawyer*
Breece, Robert William, Jr., *lawyer*
Brickey, Kathleen Fitzgerald *law educator*
Brickler, John Weise *lawyer*
Brown, Paul Sherman *lawyer*
Brownlee, Robert Hammel *lawyer*

Bruning, Anthony Steven *lawyer*
Bryan, Henry C(lark), Jr., *retired lawyer*
Buckley, Eugene Kenyon *lawyer*
Burke, Thomas Michael *lawyer*
Burton, Earl Gillespie, III, *lawyer*
†Carius, Jeffrey Rapp *lawyer*
Carlson, Mary Susan *lawyer*
Carp, Larry *lawyer*
Carr, Gary Thomas *lawyer*
Clear, John Michael *lawyer*
Conran, Joseph Palmer *lawyer*
Cornfeld, Dave Louis *lawyer*
†Crowe, Robert Alan *lawyer*
Cullen, James D. *lawyer*
DeWoskin, Alan Ellis *lawyer*
Dorwart, Donald Bruce *lawyer*
†Dougherty, Alfred Franklin, Jr., *lawyer*
Dowd, Edward L., Jr., *lawyer, former prosecutor*
Duesenberg, Richard William *lawyer*
Elbert, Charles Steiner *lawyer*
Elliott, Howard, Jr., *lawyer, gas distribution
   company executive*
†Ellis, Dorsey Daniel, Jr., *lawyer, educator*
†Erbs, Thomas J. *lawyer, arbitrator*
Erlinger, James H., III, *lawyer*
†Erwin, James Walter *lawyer*
Evans, Lawrence E. *lawyer, educator*
Falk, William James *lawyer*
Feder, Gary Harold *lawyer*
Floyd, Walter Leo *lawyer*
Fogle, James Lee *lawyer*
Gerard, Jules Bernard *law educator*
Gianoulakis, John Louis *lawyer*
Gilhousen, Brent James *lawyer*
Gillis, John Lamb, Jr., *lawyer*
Godiner, Donald Leonard *lawyer*
Goebel, John J. *lawyer, director*
Goldenhersh, Robert Stanley *lawyer*
Goldstein, Steven *lawyer*
Goodman, Harold S. *lawyer*
Graham, Robert Clare, III, *lawyer*
Gray, Charles Elmer *lawyer, rancher, investor*
†Grebel, Lawrence Bovard *lawyer*
Green, Dennis Joseph *lawyer*
Greenley, Beverly Jane *lawyer, educator*
Guerri, William Grant *lawyer*
†Gunn, Michael Peter *lawyer*
Haar, Robert Theodore *lawyer*
Hansen, Charles *lawyer*
Harris, Whitney Robson *lawyer, educator,
   military officer, philanthropist*
†Hays, Ruth *lawyer*
†Hiles, Bradley Stephen *lawyer*
Hunt, Jeffrey Brian *lawyer*
Inkley, John James, Jr., *lawyer*
†Jaudes, Richard Edward *lawyer*
Johnson, E. Perry *lawyer*
†Johnson, William Ashton *retired lawyer*
†Keating, Michael Joseph *lawyer*
Keller, Juan Dane *lawyer*
Klobasa, John Anthony *lawyer*
†Kohn, Alan Charles *lawyer*
Kolker, Scott Lee *lawyer*
Kortenhof, Joseph Michael *lawyer, educator*
Kramer, Donald Burton *lawyer*
Kuhlmann, Fred Mark *lawyer, business executive*
Lamming, John Harold *lawyer*
Lane, Frank Joseph, Jr., *lawyer*
Lause, Michael Francis *lawyer*
Lebowitz, Albert *lawyer, writer*
Leontsinis, George John *lawyer*
Lieberman, Edward Jay *lawyer*
Lowenhaupt, Charles Abraham *lawyer*
Lowther, Thomas Edward *lawyer*
Luberda, George Joseph *lawyer, educator*
Lucchesi, Lionel Louis *lawyer*
Lucy, Robert Meredith *lawyer*
Mandelstamm, Jerome Robert *lawyer*
Marks, Murry Aaron *lawyer*
†Martin, Carla A. *lawyer, veterinarian*
†Massey, Raymond Lee *lawyer*
McCarter, Charles Chase *lawyer*
McDaniel, James Edwin *lawyer*
McKinnis, Michael B. *lawyer*
Meehan, John Justin *lawyer*
Meisel, George Vincent *lawyer*
Merrill, Charles Eugene *lawyer*
Metcalfe, Walter Lee, Jr., *lawyer*
Meyer, John Strauch, Jr., *lawyer*
†Michener, John Athol *lawyer*
Michenfelder, Albert A. *lawyer*
†Miller, Dwight Whittemore *lawyer*
Mohan, John J. *lawyer*
Moore, McPherson Dorsett *lawyer*
Mulligan, Michael Dennis *lawyer*
Needham, Carol Ann *lawyer, educator*
Neville, James Morton *retired lawyer, consumer
   products executive*
Newman, Charles A. *lawyer*
Newman, Joan Meskiel *lawyer*
Noel, Edwin Lawrence *lawyer*
O'Keefe, Michael Daniel *lawyer*
Olson, Robert Grant *lawyer*
Palans, Lloyd Alex *lawyer*
†Paule, Donald Wayne *lawyer*
Peper, Christian Baird *lawyer*
Perotti, Rose Norma *lawyer*
†Phoenix, G. Keith *lawyer*
Pickle, Robert Douglas *lawyer, footwear industry
   executive*
Pleban, Sarah Shelledy *lawyer*
Poscover, Maury B. *lawyer*
Pruellage, John Kenneth *lawyer*
†Rabbitt, Daniel Thomas, Jr., *lawyer*
Reeg, Kurtis Bradford *lawyer*
Rice, Canice Timothy, Jr., *lawyer*
†Rice, Charles Marcus, II, *lawyer*
Riddle, Veryl Lee *lawyer*
Ritter, Robert Forcier *lawyer*
Ritterskamp, Douglas Dolvin *lawyer*
†Rose, Albert Schoenburg *lawyer, educator*
Rubenstein, Jerome Max *lawyer*
Sale, Llewellyn, III, *lawyer*
Sant, John Talbot *lawyer*
Schoene, Kathleen Snyder *lawyer*
Schramm, Paul Howard *lawyer*

Searls, Eileen Haughey *retired lawyer, librarian,
   educator*
Sestric, Anthony James *lawyer*
Shalowitz, Howard A. *lawyer*
Sherby, Kathleen Reilly *lawyer*
†Siegel, Cordell *lawyer*
Smith, Arthur Lee *lawyer*
Sneeringer, Stephen Geddes *lawyer*
Sobol, Lawrence Raymond *lawyer*
†Stewart, Allan Forbes *lawyer*
†Sugg, Reed Waller *lawyer*
Suhre, Walter Anthony, Jr., *retired lawyer and
   brewery executive*
Sullivan, Edward Lawrence *lawyer*
Switzer, Frederick Michael, III, *lawyer,
   arbitrator, mediator*
Teasdale, Kenneth Fulbright *lawyer*
Tierney, Michael Edward *lawyer*
†Turcotte, John Arthur, Jr., *lawyer*
Tutt, Louise Thompson *lawyer*
Virtel, James John *lawyer*
†Wall, Catherine Wynne *lawyer*
Walsh, Joseph Leo, III, *lawyer*
Walsh, Thomas Charles *lawyer*
Watters, Richard Donald *lawyer*
Webb Anderson, JoAnn Marie *lawyer,
   community advocate*
Weiss, Charles Andrew *lawyer*
Welch, David William *lawyer*
Will, Robert John *lawyer*
Williams, Theodore Joseph, Jr., *lawyer*
Wilson, Margaret Bush *lawyer*
†Withers, W. Wayne *lawyer*
Woodruff, Bruce Emery *lawyer*
Young, Marvin Oscar *lawyer*

Salem
†Hall, Glenn Allen *lawyer, state representative*

Sedalia
Gardner, R. Scott *lawyer*

Springfield
Arneson, James Herman *lawyer*
Baxter-Smith, Gregory John *lawyer*
Carlson, Thomas Joseph *real estate developer,
   lawyer, mayor*
Crites, Richard Don *lawyer*
FitzGerald, Kevin Michael *lawyer, mediator*
Groce, Steven Fred *lawyer*
Hedrick, Peggy Shepherd *lawyer*
Hulston, John Kenton *lawyer, director*
Lowther, Gerald Halbert *lawyer*
†McCurry, Bruce *lawyer*
McDonald, William Henry *lawyer*
McGinnis, M. Sean *lawyer*
†Powell, William Don *lawyer*
Roberts, Patrick Kent *lawyer*
†Sherwood, Devon Fredrick *lawyer*
Starnes, James Wright *lawyer*

Stockton
†Hammons, Brian Kent *lawyer, business executive*

Troy
Beck, James David *lawyer*

Union
Schmelz, Brenda Lea *legal assistant*

MONTANA

Billings
Aldrich, Richard Kingsley *lawyer*
†Baugh, Gary Todd *lawyer*
Beiswanger, Gary Lee *lawyer*
Cromley, Brent Reed *lawyer, state senator*
Haughey, James McCrea *lawyer, artist*
†Jones, James Leonard *lawyer*
Malee, Thomas Michael *lawyer*
†Mitchell, Laura Ann *lawyer*
Sites, James Philip *lawyer, consultant*
Toole, Bruce Ryan *retired lawyer*
Towe, Thomas Edward *lawyer*

Bozeman
Conover, Richard Corrill *lawyer*
Frohnmayer, John Edward *lawyer, legal scholar,
   ethicist, writer*
†Harris, Christopher Kirk *lawyer*
Nelson, Steven Dwayne *lawyer*
Wylie, Paul Richter, Jr., *lawyer*

Butte
McCarthy, Bernard Francis *lawyer*

Cameron
Van Doren, Emerson Barclay *mediator*

Columbia Falls
Chisholm, Dean D. *lawyer*

Great Falls
†Blewett, Alexander, III, *lawyer*
Doherty, Steve *lawyer, former state legislator*
George, Michael Joseph *lawyer*
†Gray, Orville *lawyer*
†Hartelius, Channing Julius *lawyer*
Speer, John Elmer *paralegal, reporter, counselor*

Havre
Moog, Mary Ann Pimley *lawyer*

Helena
Gersovitz, Jeremy *lawyer*
†Grant, John Halloran *lawyer*
Meadows, Judith Adams *law librarian, educator*

Kalispell
Nardi, Stephen J. *lawyer*

Livingston
Jovick, Robert L. *lawyer*

Missoula
Bowman, Jean Louise *lawyer, civic worker*

George, Alexander Andrew *lawyer*
†Molloy, Donald William *lawyer*
Morales, Julio K. *lawyer*
Vannatta, Shane Anthony *lawyer*

Ronan
Grainey, Philip J. *lawyer*

Whitehall
Bernard, Donald Ray *law educator, international
   business counselor*

NEBRASKA

Bellevue
†Schroeder, Van Ace *lawyer*

Columbus
Schumacher, Paul Maynard *lawyer*

Crete
Panec, William Joseph *lawyer*

Fremont
Line, William Gunderson *lawyer*

Grand Island
†Ahlschwede, Earl David *lawyer*
†Cuypers, Charles James *lawyer*
Piccolo, Gerard Anthony *lawyer*

Hildreth
Jelkin, John Lamoine *lawyer*

Holdrege
Klein, Michael Clarence *lawyer*

Kearney
Voigt, Steven Russell *lawyer*

Lincoln
Alexis, Carl Odman *lawyer, earth scientist*
Atwood, Raymond Percival, Jr., *lawyer*
Bancroft, Webb Ernest *lawyer*
Blake, William George *lawyer*
Brohman, Mark Allen *lawyer, biologist*
Colleran, Kevin *lawyer*
†Frobom, LeAnn Larson *lawyer*
†Gardner, Martin Ralph *law educator*
Guthery, John M. *lawyer*
†Harnsberger, Richard Stephen *law educator*
Hewitt, James Watt *retired lawyer*
Johnson, Douglas Blaikie *lawyer*
†Johnson, Warren Charles *retired lawyer*
Leiter, Richard Allen *law librarian, law educator*
Lichty, Warren Dewey, Jr., *lawyer*
Lyons, William Harry *law educator*
McClain, Richard Douglas *lawyer*
Ogle, Robbin Sue *criminal justice educator*
†Rembolt, James Earl *lawyer*
Rowe, David Winfield *lawyer*
†Smith, Richard Wendell *lawyer*
†Thrasher, Louis Michael *lawyer*
Zink, Walter Earl, II, *lawyer*

Norfolk
†Domina, David Alan *lawyer*

North Platte
†Baumann, Larry R(oger) *lawyer*

Omaha
Achelpohl, Steven Edward *lawyer, political
   organization administrator*
Barmettler, Joseph John *lawyer*
Barrett, Frank Joseph *lawyer, former insurance
   company executive*
Brownrigg, John Clinton *lawyer*
Burke, Thomas Raymond *lawyer*
Caporale, D. Nick *lawyer*
Dolan, James Vincent *lawyer*
Ellsworth, John David *lawyer*
Frank, Julie Ann *lawyer*
†Fuller, Diana Clare *lawyer*
Gleason, James Mullaney *lawyer, insurance
   executive*
Hamann, Deryl Frederick *lawyer, bank executive*
Jenkins, Melvin Lemuel *lawyer*
Jensen, Sam *lawyer*
†Kozlik, Michael David *lawyer*
†Kreifels, Frank Anthony *lawyer, corporate
   executive*
Krutter, Forrest Nathan *lawyer*
†LaPuzza, Paul James *lawyer*
Lee, Dennis Patrick *lawyer, judge*
†Mangrum, Richard Collin *law educator*
†McCusker, Thomas J. *corporate lawyer,
   insurance company executive*
†Miller, Roger James *lawyer*
Minter, Gregory Byron *lawyer, educator*
Monaghan, Thomas Justin *former prosecutor*
Moylan, James Harold *lawyer*
Niemann, Nicholas Kent *lawyer*
†O'Connor, Robert Edward, Jr., *lawyer*
†O'Hara, Michael James *law educator, researcher*
Pollak, Oliver Burt *lawyer, educator*
Runge, Patrick Richard *lawyer*
†Schrempp, Warren C. *lawyer*
Schropp, Tobin *lawyer*
Stenberg, Donald B. *lawyer*
von Bernuth, Carl W. *lawyer, diversified
   corporation executive*
Vosburg, Bruce David *lawyer*

Papillion
†Rice, John Edward *lawyer*

NEVADA

Carson City
Ross, Donald Henry *lawyer*

Elko
Puccinelli, Andrew James *lawyer*

Las Vegas
Arum, Robert *lawyer, sports events promoter*
†Ashleman, Ivan Reno, II, *health care executive,
   lawyer*
Brown, Joseph Wentling *lawyer*
Bryan, Richard H. *lawyer, educator, former
   senator*
Buckley, Michael Edward *lawyer*
Curran, William P. *lawyer*
Ecker, Howard *lawyer*
Faiss, Robert Dean *lawyer*
Galatz, Neil Gilbert *lawyer*
†Galliher, Keith Edwin, Jr., *lawyer*
†Goldberg, Aubrey *lawyer*
Goodwin, John Robert *lawyer, law educator,
   author*
Gray, Patricia Joyce *legal administration*
Greene, Addison Kent *lawyer, accountant*
†Hagendorf, Stanley *lawyer, writer*
Hilbrecht, Norman Ty *lawyer*
Hill, Judith Deegan *lawyer*
†Kravitz, Martin Jay *lawyer*
Lovell, Carl Erwin, Jr., *lawyer*
Lucas, Craig John *lawyer*
†Miller, Robert Joseph *lawyer, former governor*
†Nasky, H(arold) Gregory *lawyer*
O'Connell, John F. *lawyer, retired law educator*
†Padgett, Anne *lawyer*
Rodefer, Jeffrey Robert *lawyer, prosecutor*
Schreiber, David M. *lawyer, judge*
Singer, Michael Howard *lawyer*
Sklar, Alan Curtis *lawyer*
Solomon, Jack Avrum, Jr., *lawyer, automotive
   distributor, art dealer*
Wilson, Joseph Morris, III, *lawyer*

Reno
†Barkley, Thierry Vincent *lawyer*
†Bible, Paul Alfred *lawyer*
†Chaires, Robert Harold, Jr., *law educator*
Chubb, Janet L. *lawyer*
Dunn, Larry K. *lawyer*
Fletcher, Douglas Charles *lawyer*
†Guild, Clark Joseph, Jr., *lawyer*
Hibbs, Loyal Robert *lawyer*
Manson, Gary Lyle *lawyer*
†Pagni, Albert Frank *lawyer*
Putney, Mark William *lawyer, utility executive*
†Robison, Kent Richard *lawyer*
Ryan, Robert Collins *lawyer*
†Stumpf, Felix Franklin *law educator*
Whitbeck, Jill Karla *lawyer*

Sparks
†Sage, Larry Guy *lawyer*

Sun Valley
Mumm, Christopher Eric *lawyer, county
   government official*

NEW HAMPSHIRE

Concord
Chamberlain, Douglas Reginald *lawyer*
Garvey, John Burwell *lawyer*
†Harrison, Keith Michaele *law educator*
McDonald, Joseph F., III, *lawyer*
McLaughlin, Philip T. *lawyer, former state
   attorney general*
†Potter, Fred Leon *lawyer, insurance company
   executive, consultant*
†Rapp, Elaine *paralegal*
Rath, Thomas David *lawyer, former state
   attorney general*
Richardson, Gary Burleigh *lawyer*
Rines, Robert Harvey *lawyer, inventor, educator,
   composer*
†Smith, Gregory Hayes *lawyer*
Topham, Lee Evans *lawyer*

Dover
Catalfo, Alfred, Jr., (Alfio Catalfo) *lawyer*

East Sullivan
Hoffman, John Ernest, Jr., *retired lawyer*

Exeter
DeMitchell, Terri Ann *law educator*
Donahue, Michael Joseph *lawyer*
Vogelman, Lawrence Allen *law educator, lawyer*

Gorham
Cote, Thomas Jacques *lawyer*

Grantham
Goss, Richard Henry *lawyer*

Hanover
Gardner, Peter Jaglom *lawyer, publisher*
Harvey, Nicholas D. N., Jr., *lawyer*
Lundquist, Weyman Ivan *lawyer*

Hollis
Lumbard, Eliot Howland *lawyer, educator*
Merritt, Thomas Butler *lawyer*

Hooksett
Rogers, David John *lawyer*

Keene
Bell, Ernest Lorne, III, *retired lawyer*
Gardner, Eric Raymond *lawyer*

Laconia
†Martin, Willard Gordon, Jr., *lawyer*
†Mitchell, Walter Louis, III, *lawyer*

Lebanon
†Baker, William Arnold *lawyer*

Lyme
Carmichael, Donald Scott *lawyer, business
   executive*

Manchester
†Brown, Stanley Melvin *lawyer*
Bussiere, Emile R. *lawyer*
Goodwin, Rolf Ervine *lawyer*
†Hutchins, Peter Edward *lawyer*
†Middleton, Jack Baer *lawyer*
Monson, John Rudolph *lawyer*
Nixon, David L. *lawyer*
†Peltonen, John Ernest *lawyer*
Richards, Thomas H. *lawyer, arbitrator*
Rubin, Jeffrey Mark *lawyer, insurance company executive*
†Thornton, Edward Robert, Jr., *lawyer*
Zachos, Kimon Stephen *lawyer*

Nashua
Hanson, Arnold Philip *retired lawyer*
Raudonis, Valerie Christine *lawyer*

New Durham
Uttal, Susan *legal administrator*

New London
Baldwin, William Howard *lawyer, retired foundation executive*
Merwin, John David *retired lawyer, former governor*
Plant, David William *lawyer*

Newport
Work, Michael Jay *lawyer*

Orford
Martin, Allen *retired lawyer*

Plainfield
Brown, Judith Olans *lawyer, educator*

Plymouth
Deachman, Ross Varick *lawyer*

Portsmouth
†Abelson, Elias *lawyer*
Beckett, William Henry Miller *lawyer*
DeGrandpre, Charles Allyson *lawyer*
Doleac, Charles Bartholomew *lawyer*
†Harman, Terrie *lawyer*
McGee, John Paul, Jr., *lawyer*
†Shaines, Robert Arthur *lawyer*
Tober, Stephen Lloyd *lawyer*
Volk, Kenneth Hohne *lawyer*
Watson, Thomas Roger *lawyer*

Rochester
Hall, Fred William, Jr., *lawyer*

Seabrook
Ganz, Mary Keohan *lawyer*

Warner
†Coolidge, Daniel Scott *lawyer*

West Lebanon
Isaacs, Robert Charles *retired lawyer*

Wolfeboro
†Mertens, Edward Joseph, II, *lawyer*
†Walker, George William *lawyer*

NEW JERSEY

Allendale
Rosenblum, Edward G. *lawyer*

Asbury Park
†Darnell, Alan Mark *lawyer*
†Rosenbloom, Norma Frisch *lawyer*

Atlantic City
Jacobson, Carole Renee *lawyer, educator*
†Paarz, Robert Emil *lawyer*

Atlantic Highlands
†Marshall, Anthony Parr *retired lawyer*

Barnegat Light
Gibbs, Frederick Winfield *lawyer, communications company executive*

Barrington
Guice, Stephen Wayne *lawyer*

Basking Ridge
†DeBois, James Adolphus *lawyer*
†Jones, William Johnson *lawyer*
†O'Carroll, Anita Louise *lawyer*

Bay Head
†Kellogg, James Crane *lawyer*

Belle Mead
Gladstone, Robert Albert *lawyer*

Bloomfield
Lordi, Katherine Mary *lawyer*
Weisert, Kent Albert Frederick *lawyer*

Boonton
Bucco, Anthony Mark *lawyer*
Massler, Howard Arnold *lawyer, corporate executive*
Walzer, James Harvey *lawyer, author*

Brick
Tivenan, Charles Patrick *lawyer*

Bridgewater
Conroy, Robert John *lawyer*
Dahling, Gerald Vernon *lawyer*
Linett, David *lawyer*
Schoppmann, Michael Joseph *lawyer*

Budd Lake
Webb, John Gibbon, III, *lawyer*

Caldwell
Castano, Gregory Joseph *lawyer*

Camden
Farmer, James A., II, *lawyer*
†Furey, John J. *lawyer*
†Patterson, Dennis Michael *lawyer, educator*
Pomorski, Stanislaw *lawyer, educator*
†Robinson, Paul Harper *lawyer, educator*

Cape May Court House
Fineberg, Robert Alan *lawyer*

Chatham
Jacobs, Andrew Robert *lawyer*
Zegas, Alan Lee *lawyer*

Cherry Hill
Adler, John Herbert *lawyer, state legislator*
Feldman, Arnold H. *lawyer*
Garrigle, William Aloysius *lawyer*
Jozwiak, Steven Jay *lawyer*
†Liebman, Emmanuel *lawyer*
Myers, Daniel William, II, *lawyer*
Polansky, Steven Jay *lawyer*
Rabil, Mitchell Joseph *lawyer*
Rose, Joel Alan *legal consultant*
†Roth, Kenneth David *lawyer*
Shapiro, Richard Allen *lawyer*
Spielberg, Joshua Morris *lawyer*
Tomar, William *lawyer*
Weinstein, Steven *lawyer*

Chester
Pfaffenroth, Peter Albert *lawyer*

Clark
Farina, Mario G. *lawyer*

Cliffside Park
Diktas, Christos James *lawyer*

Clifton
Feinstein, Miles Roger *lawyer*
Lieb, L. Robert *lawyer*
Malamud, Alexander *lawyer, consultant*
†Mohammed, Sohail *lawyer, consultant*
Palma, Nicholas James *lawyer*

Collingswood
Martin, Burchard V. *lawyer*

Cranbury
†Bronner, William Roche *lawyer*
Gupta, Rajat Kumar *lawyer, accountant*
Iatesta, John Michael *lawyer*

Cranford
De Luca, Thomas George *lawyer*
†Messing, Sara Virginia Drick *lawyer*

East Brunswick
Applebaum, Charles *lawyer*

East Hanover
Kayser, Kenneth Wayne *lawyer*

Edgewater
Virelli, Louis James, Jr., *lawyer*

Edison
†Behr, Omri M. *lawyer*
Fink, Edward Murray *lawyer, educator*
O'Brien, John Graham *lawyer*
†Vercammen, Kenneth Albert *lawyer, prosecutor*

Elizabeth
Budanitsky, Sander *lawyer*
Kabak, Douglas Thomas *lawyer*

Elmwood Park
Mangano, Louis *lawyer*

Englewood
†Gelber, Linda Cecile *lawyer, banker*
†Milstein, Edward Philip *lawyer*

Englewood Cliffs
Heller, Hanes Ayres *lawyer*
Masi, John Roger *lawyer*

Fair Lawn
Delloff, Stefan T. *lawyer*

Fairfield
†Connell, William Terrence *lawyer, judge*

Fanwood
†Mitzner, Michael Jay *lawyer*

Far Hills
Corash, Richard *lawyer*

Flemington
†Lenagh, Thomas Hugh *lawyer, financial advisor*
Michels, Kevin Howard *lawyer*
Miller, Louis H. *lawyer*
Nielsen, Lynn Carol *lawyer, educational consultant*
†Wolfson, William Steven *lawyer*

Florham Park
Chase, Eric Lewis *lawyer*
Hardin, William Downer *retired lawyer*
Kandravy, John *lawyer*
Laulicht, Murray Jack *lawyer*
LeVine, Walter Daniel *lawyer, accountant*
Nittoly, Paul Gerard *lawyer*
O'Connell, Daniel F. *lawyer*
Pantel, Glenn Steven *lawyer*
Reid, Charles Adams, III, *lawyer*

Fort Lee
Cox, Melvin Monroe *lawyer*

Franklin Lakes
Hector, Bruce John *lawyer*

Freehold
Lijoi, Peter Bruno *lawyer*

Garfield
Herpst, Robert Dix *lawyer, optics and materials technology executive*

Garwood
Maher, Gary Laurence *lawyer*

Glen Rock
Britcher, E. Drew *lawyer*
Markey, Brian Michael *lawyer*

Greenwich
Lane, Mark *lawyer, educator, writer*

Hackensack
Caminiti, Donald Angelo *lawyer*
Croland, Barry I. *lawyer*
Curtis, Robert Kern *lawyer, physics educator*
D'Alessandro, Dianne Marie *public defender*
Duus, Gordon Cochran *lawyer*
Fede, Andrew Thomas *lawyer, educator*
Gerlanc, Glenn Marc *lawyer*
Greenberg, Steven Morey *lawyer*
†Horan, John Donohoe *lawyer*
†Kiel, Paul Edward *lawyer*
Mullin, Patrick Allen *lawyer*
Pollinger, William Joshua *lawyer*
†Robinson, Sandra Ann *lawyer*
Steinbach, Harold I. *lawyer*
†Strull, James Richard *lawyer*
Vort, Robert A. *lawyer*

Hackettstown
†Kobert, Joel A. *lawyer*
Mulligan, Elinor Patterson *lawyer*

Haddon Heights
Cipparone, Rocco C., Jr., *lawyer*

Haddonfield
Andres, Kenneth G., Jr., *lawyer*
Chiulli, E. Antoinette *lawyer*
Ewan, David E. *lawyer*
Fuoco, Philip Stephen *lawyer*
†Graziano, Ronald Anthony *lawyer*
Heuisler, Charles William *lawyer*
Iavicoli, Mario Anthony *lawyer*
Mitchell, Matthew Kyle *lawyer*
†Smith, Carol J. *legal secretary, medical transcriptionist*

Hamilton
Haushalter, Harry *lawyer*

Hammonton
Woolson, Charles E., Jr., *lawyer*

Haworth
Albrecht, William Kenneth *lawyer*

Hillsborough
Ames, Marc L. *lawyer*

Hillsdale
Hodinar, Michael *lawyer, publishing company executive*

Ho Ho Kus
Bryan, Thomas Lynn *lawyer, educator*
†Somerwitz, Herbert Saul *lawyer*

Hoboken
Sommers, George R. *lawyer*

Holmdel
Suhr, J. Nicholas *lawyer*

Iselin
Dornbusch, Arthur A., II, *lawyer*
Goodman, Barry S. *lawyer*
Walker, Linda Lee *lawyer*

Jersey City
†Amadeo, Natial Salvatore *lawyer*
D'Alessandro, Daniel Anthony *lawyer, educator*
Frisch, Harry David *lawyer, consultant, investment company executive*
Guarini, Frank Joseph *lawyer, real estate developer*
McFadden, Rosemary Theresa *lawyer, financial services executive*
Nevins, Arthur Gerard, Jr., *lawyer*
Russo, Gregory Thomas *lawyer*
Signorile, Vincent Anthony *lawyer*
†Wind, Jack Jay *lawyer*

Kearny
Brady, Lawrence Peter *lawyer*

Kendall Park
Fisch, Joseph *lawyer*

Kenilworth
Hoffman, John Fletcher *lawyer*

Keyport
Colmant, Andrew Robert *lawyer*

Lebanon
Johnstone, Irvine Blakeley, III, *lawyer*

Liberty Corner
†Apruzzese, Vincent John *lawyer*
Feldman, Elda Beylerian *lawyer*
McDermott, Frank Xavier *lawyer, lobbyist*
†Thompson, T. Jay *lawyer*

Linden
Littman, David Bernard *lawyer*

Little Falls
Draper, Daniel Clay *retired lawyer*

Little Silver
Schmidt, Daniel Edward, IV, *lawyer, commercial arbitrator*

Livingston
Klein, Peter Martin *lawyer, retired transportation company executive*
Rinsky, Joel Charles *lawyer*
Rosenberg, Paul I. *lawyer*
†Sukoneck, Ira David *lawyer*

Lyndhurst
†Fallon, Francis E(dward) *lawyer, corporation executive*
†McNamara, Patrick James *lawyer*

Madison
†Guigon, John V. *corporate lawyer*
†McGrath, Joseph Patrick *lawyer*

Manalapan
Stone, Fred Michael *lawyer*

Mc Afee
Fogel, Richard *lawyer, educator*

Mendham
Tramutola, Joseph Louis *lawyer, educator*

Metuchen
Eugene, John *lawyer*
Frizell, David J. *lawyer*

Middletown
†Friedman, Richard Lloyd *lawyer*

Millburn
Diamond, Richard S. *lawyer*
Grosman, Alan M. *lawyer*

Milltown
†Haws, Robert John *lawyer*

Montclair
Brown, Geraldine Reed *lawyer, consulting executive*
†Brown, Ronald Wellington *lawyer, educator, consultant, business executive, entrepreneur*
Conrad, David Williams *lawyer*
Gutman, Richard Martin *lawyer*
Pransky, Joan E. *lawyer, community organizer*
Ward, Roger Coursen *lawyer*

Montville
Buzak, Edward Joseph *lawyer*

Moorestown
Kearney, John Francis, III, *lawyer*
Slemmer, Carl Weber, Jr., *retired lawyer*

Morristown
Aspero, Benedict Vincent *lawyer*
†Barba, Julius William *lawyer*
Bartkus, Robert Edward *lawyer*
Berkley, Peter Lee *lawyer*
Bernstein, Jan Lenore *lawyer*
Bromberg, Myron James *lawyer*
†Bryant, George McEwan *lawyer*
†Capezza, Michelle *lawyer*
Clark, Grant Lawrence *corporate lawyer*
Doyle, David Perrie *lawyer*
Fishman, Richard Glenn *lawyer, accountant*
Fletcher, Michael S. *lawyer*
Geppert, John Gustave, Jr., *lawyer*
Gillen, James Robert *lawyer, insurance company executive*
Herzberg, Peter Jay *lawyer*
Huettner, Richard Alfred *lawyer*
Humick, Thomas Charles Campbell *lawyer*
Hyland, William Francis *lawyer*
Korf, Gene Robert *lawyer*
Kreindler, Peter Michael *lawyer*
O'Grady, Dennis Joseph *lawyer*
Pollock, Stewart Glasson *lawyer, former state supreme court justice*
Rose, Robert Gordon *lawyer*
Rosenthal, Meyer L(ouis) *lawyer*
Sherman, Sandra Brown *lawyer*
Stanton, Patrick Michael *lawyer*
Whitmer, Frederick Lee *lawyer*

Mount Holly
Mintz, Jeffry Alan *lawyer, mediator, consultant*

Mountain Lakes
Daniel, Royal Thomas, III, *lawyer, engineer, accountant*

Mountainside
Helander, Robert Charles *lawyer*
†Weiseman, Jac Burton *lawyer*

New Brunswick
†Biribauer, Richard Frank *lawyer*
Miller, Arthur Harold *lawyer*
Scott, David Rodick *lawyer, legal educator*
†Shirtz, Joseph Frank *lawyer, consultant*
†Yorke, Marianne *lawyer, real estate executive*

New Providence
Bernstein, Nadia J. *lawyer*
Chobot, John Charles *lawyer*
Cooper, R. John, III, *lawyer*
Hurley, Lawrence Joseph *lawyer*
†Maxeiner, James Randolph *lawyer*
McCarthy, G. Daniel *lawyer*

New Vernon
Kushen, Allan Stanford *retired lawyer*

Newark
Askin, Frank *law educator*
†Autin, Diana Marie Therese Katherine *lawyer, educator*
Bizub, Johanna Catherine *law librarian*
Brenner, John Finn *lawyer*
†Brescher, John B., Jr., *lawyer*

Cahn, Jeffrey Barton *lawyer*
†Cohen, Carol I. *lawyer*
Costenbader, Charles Michael *lawyer*
Creenan, Katherine Heras *lawyer*
Cummis, Clive Sanford *lawyer*
Day, Edward Francis, Jr., *lawyer*
Dee, Francis X. *lawyer*
Defeis, Elizabeth Frances *law educator, lawyer*
Del Tufo, Robert J. *lawyer, former US attorney, former state attorney general*
Deutsch, Stuart Lewis *law educator*
Eittreim, Richard MacNutt *lawyer*
English, Nicholas Conover *lawyer*
Fox, Jeanne Marie *lawyer*
Freilich, Irvin Mayer *lawyer*
Garde, John Charles *lawyer*
Greenberg, Stephen Michael *lawyer, business executive*
Haring, Eugene Miller *lawyer*
Harrison, Roslyn Siman *lawyer*
†Hill, Richard Warren *lawyer*
Karp, Donald Mathew *lawyer, banker*
Knee, Stephen H. *lawyer*
Kott, David Russell *lawyer*
Kuller, Jonathan Mark *lawyer*
Levine, Benjamin *lawyer*
Liftin, John M. *lawyer*
Liftin, John Matthew *lawyer*
Lowenkron, Ruth *lawyer*
†McGuire, William B(enedict) *lawyer*
McKinney, John Adams, Jr., *lawyer*
†Medvin, Alan York *lawyer*
Miller, Richard Allan *lawyer*
Muscato, Andrew *lawyer*
Neuer, Philip David *lawyer, real estate consultant*
O'Connor Quinn, Deirdre *lawyer*
Paul, James Caverly Newlin *law educator, retired dean*
Pollock, Jeffrey M. *lawyer*
Rak, Lorraine Karen *lawyer*
†Raveson, Louis Sheppard *lawyer, educator*
Reich, Laurence *lawyer*
Reilly, William Thomas *lawyer*
Robertson, William Withers *lawyer*
†Scally, John Joseph, Jr., *lawyer*
†Schachter, Paul *lawyer*
Siegal, Joel Davis *lawyer*
Simmons, Peter *law and urban planning educator*
Slavitt, Ben J. *lawyer*
Tischman, Michael Bernard *lawyer*
Vajtay, Stephen Michael, Jr., *lawyer*
Wachenfeld, William Thomas *lawyer, foundation executive*
†Wayne, Robert Andrew *lawyer*
Wyer, James Ingersoll *lawyer*
Zuckerman, Herbert Lawrence *lawyer*

Newton
Cox, William Martin *lawyer, educator*

North Plainfield
Dowling, Joan E. *lawyer*

Oakhurst
Defino, Joseph Francis *lawyer*

Oakland
Goldenberg, Eva J. *lawyer*

Ocean
Weisberg, Adam Jon *lawyer*

Ocean City
Boardman, Harold Frederick, Jr., *lawyer, retired corporate executive*

Old Bridge
Downs, Thomas Edward, IV, *lawyer*

Oradell
Blakeslee, Edward Eaton *lawyer, insurance executive*
†Mavroudis, John M. *lawyer*

Paramus
†Gilbert, Stephen Alan *lawyer, organization executive*
Levy, Joseph *lawyer*

Parsippany
Kallmann, Stanley Walter *lawyer*
Prague, Ronald Jay *lawyer*

Passaic
Mussano, Theodore Anthony *court services supervisor*

Pennington
Gorrin, Eugene *lawyer*
Kozlowski, Thomas Joseph, Jr., *lawyer, trust company executive*

Piscataway
Smith, Bob *lawyer, state senator, educator*

Pitman
Cloues, Edward Blanchard, II, *lawyer*

Point Pleasant Beach
Herr, Philip Michael *lawyer, accountant*

Pompton Plains
Ludemann, Cathie Jane *lawyer*

Princeton
Ackourey, Peter Paul *lawyer*
Alford, Duncan Earl *lawyer*
Anderson, Ellis Bernard *retired lawyer, pharmaceutical company executive*
Atkins, Thomas Herman *lawyer*
Beidler, Marsha Wolf *lawyer*
Benesch, Katherine *lawyer*
Bergman, Edward Jonathan *lawyer, educator*
Duquette, David Joseph, Jr., *lawyer, investor*
†Durst, Robert Joseph, II, *lawyer*
Greenman, Jane Friedlieb *lawyer, human resources specialist*
Grossman, Allen Neil *lawyer*
Hill, James Scott *lawyer*
Katz, Stanley Nider *law history educator*
Katzenbach, Nicholas deBelleville *lawyer*
†Kirstein, Philip Lawrence *lawyer, investment company executive*
Lewin, Ross Allen *lawyer*
Picco, Steven Joseph *lawyer*
Plevy, Arthur L. *lawyer*
†Rose, Edith Sprung *retired lawyer*
Sutphin, William Taylor *lawyer*
Ufford, Charles Wilbur, Jr., *lawyer*
Wong, Linda *lawyer*
Wood, Joshua Warren, III, *lawyer, foundation executive*

Princeton Junction
DiSciullo, Alan Michael *lawyer*

Ramsey
†Weber, Walter Winfield, Jr., *lawyer, director*

Red Bank
Anderson, James Francis *lawyer*
Michaelson, Peter Lee *lawyer*
Warshaw, Michael Thomas *lawyer*

Ridgewood
†Conneen, James Thomas *lawyer, management consultant*
Harris, Micalyn Shafer *lawyer, educator, arbitrator, mediator*
Seigel, Jan Kearney *lawyer*

River Edge
Spiegel, Edna Z. *lawyer*
†Sullivan, Eugene John *lawyer*

Rockaway
Bruno, Anthony D. *lawyer*
†Cowan, Alvin Randall *lawyer*

Roseland
Bennett, John K. *lawyer*
†Besser, Albert Gordon *lawyer*
Chapman, Philip Lawrence *lawyer*
Danzis, Colin Michael *lawyer*
Eakeley, Douglas Scott *lawyer*
†Kayne, Michele S. *lawyer*
Kenny, George James *lawyer*
†Levithan, Allen B. *lawyer*
Lowenstein, Alan Victor *lawyer*
†Ploscowe, Stephen Allen *lawyer*
†Positan, Wayne John *lawyer*
Smith, Dennis Jay *lawyer*
Smith, Wendy Hope *lawyer*
Stern, Herbert Jay *lawyer*
Tarino, Gary Edward *lawyer*
Vanderbilt, Arthur T., II, *lawyer*
†Wovsaniker, Alan *lawyer, educator*

Saddle Brook
Knopf, Barry Abraham *lawyer, educator*
Pearlman, Peter Steven *lawyer*

Salem
Petrin, Helen Fite *lawyer, consultant, mediator*

Sayreville
Corman, Randy *lawyer*

Scotch Plains
Hayes, Lewis Mifflin, Jr., *lawyer*
Klock, John Henry *lawyer*
†Kraus, Robert H. *lawyer*
Shaw, Alan *lawyer, corporate executive*

Secaucus
Bruckner, Willa Cohen *lawyer*
Fitzpatrick, Harold Francis *lawyer*
†Goldstein, Ira J. *lawyer*
Holt, Michael Bartholomew *lawyer*

Sewell
Crouse, Farrell R. *lawyer*
Fichera, Lewis Carmen *lawyer*

Ship Bottom
Shackleton, Richard James *lawyer, director*

Short Hills
Fast, Kenneth H. *lawyer*
Hazlehurst, Robert Purviance, Jr., *lawyer*
Kaye, Marc Mendell *lawyer*
Marshall, John Patrick *lawyer*
Schirmeister, Charles F. *retired lawyer*
Siegfried, David Charles *retired lawyer*

Sicklerville
†Corbisiero Love, Angela M. *lawyer*

Skillman
Altman, Jane R. *lawyer*

Somers Point
Baylinson, Christopher Michael *lawyer*

Somerset
Green, Jeffrey C. *lawyer*

Somerville
Fleischman, Joseph Jacob *lawyer*
†Fuerst, Steven Bernard *lawyer*
Gross, Carol Ann *lawyer*
†Hutcheon, Peter David *lawyer*
Laskey, James Howard *lawyer*
†Lieberman, Marvin Samuel *lawyer*
†O'Brian, Harold Samuel *lawyer*

South Amboy
†McDonnell, William John *lawyer*

South Orange
Delo, Ellen Sanderson *lawyer*

Sparta
McMeen, Elmer Ellsworth, III, *retired lawyer, guitarist*

Springfield
Grayson Kurzweil, Bette Rita *lawyer*
Mytelka, Arnold Krieger *lawyer*
†Yudes, James Peyton *lawyer*

Stone Harbor
Taylor, Robert Lee *lawyer, former judge*

Summit
Caming, H. W. William *lawyer, consultant*
†Cooper, John Weeks *lawyer*
†Katz, Michael Albert *lawyer*
Kenyon, Edward Tipton *lawyer*
Macioce, Frank Michael *lawyer, financial services company executive*
Mele, Gregg Charles *lawyer*
†Pfaltz, Hugo Menzel, Jr., *lawyer*
†Saffer, Judith Mack *lawyer*
Woller, James Alan *lawyer*

Tenafly
Badr, Gamal Moursi *legal consultant*
†Spike, Michele Kahn *lawyer*

Toms River
Berman, Michael Barry *lawyer*
Coratti, John Edward *judicial clerk*
Leone, Stephan Robert *lawyer*

Trenton
Caldwell, Wesley Stuart, III, *lawyer, lobbyist*
Deltuvia, John Joseph, Jr., *systems and procedural analyst*
Doherty, Robert Christopher *lawyer*
Frost, Barry Warren *lawyer*
†Isele, William Paul *lawyer*
Jones, Dale Edwin *public defender*
Kirschner, Philip *lawyer*
Levin, Susan Bass *lawyer*
Metzger, John Mackay *lawyer*
Mroz, Richard S. *lawyer*
Sterns, Joel Henry *lawyer*

Union
Bottitta, Joseph Anthony *lawyer*
Greenstein, Richard Henry *lawyer*
Rosenberg, A. Irving *lawyer*

Union City
Rondon, Edania Cecilia *lawyer*
†Stier, Edwin H. *lawyer*

Vauxhall
Ross, Mark Samuel *lawyer, educator, funeral director, writer*

Verona
Hock, Frederick Wyeth *lawyer*

Vineland
O'Neill, Joseph Dean *lawyer*

Voorhees
†Suflas, Steven William *lawyer*

Wall
Nucciarone, A. Patrick *lawyer*

Warren
Bernstein, Eric Martin *lawyer*
DiFrancesco, Donald T. *lawyer*
Gargano, Francine Ann *lawyer*
Jacobson, Gary Steven *lawyer*
Kraus, Steven Gary *lawyer*

West Orange
Gordon, Harrison J. *lawyer*
Jordan, Leo John *lawyer*
Richmond, Harold Nicholas *lawyer*
Samson, David *lawyer*

Westfield
Bobis, Daniel Harold *lawyer*
†Dughi, Louis John, Jr., *lawyer*
Gutterman, Alan J. *lawyer*
Hrycak, Michael Paul *lawyer*
†Stewart, Robert Campbell *lawyer*

Westmont
Lario, Frank M., Jr., *lawyer, judge*
Martin, Burchard Samuel *lawyer*

Westwood
McGuirl, Robert Joseph *lawyer*

Whippany
Meola, Janice Grace *lawyer*

Willingboro
Tarver, Margaret Leggett *lawyer, forensic scientist*

Woodbridge
†Babineau, Anne Serzan *lawyer*
†Barcan, Stephen Emanuel *lawyer*
Buchsbaum, Peter A. *lawyer*
Golden, Daniel Lewis *lawyer*
Goldenberg, Steven Saul *lawyer*
Harris, Brett Rosenberg *lawyer*
Hoberman, Stuart A. *lawyer*
Lepelstat, Martin L. *lawyer*
Schaff, Michael Frederick *lawyer*
†Sterling, Harold G. *lawyer, real estate developer, bank executive*

Woodbury
Adler, Lewis Gerard *lawyer*
Celano, Peter J., Jr., *lawyer*

Woodcliff Lake
Clemen, John Douglas *lawyer*
Nachtigal, Patricia *lawyer*
Phillips, John C. *lawyer*
†Pollack, Jane Susan *lawyer*

Wyckoff
Spizziri, John Anthony *lawyer*

NEW MEXICO

Albuquerque
Aurbach, Robert Michael *lawyer, consultant, photographer*
Ausherman, Larry Price *lawyer*
†Bardacke, Paul Gregory *lawyer, former attorney general*
Beach, Arthur O'Neal *lawyer*
Bova, Vincent Arthur, Jr., *lawyer, consultant, photographer*
Cargo, David Francis *lawyer*
Caruso, Mark John *lawyer*
Chavez, Martin Joseph *lawyer, mayor*
Colbert, Kathryn Hendon *lawyer*
Cooper, Steven Mark *law educator, writer*
Dorr, Roderick A. *lawyer*
Farmer, Terry D(wayne) *lawyer*
Fitzgerald, James Paul *lawyer*
Gorman, Robert Dennis *lawyer*
Haltom, B(illy) Reid *lawyer*
Hart, Frederick Michael *law educator*
†Hauhart, Robert Charles *lawyer, educator*
Keleher, Michael Lawrence *lawyer*
Long, Stephen Carrel Mike *lawyer*
Lopez, Floyd William *lawyer*
†Lopez, Martin, III, *lawyer*
†Melton, Robert Earl *lawyer*
Messersmith, Lanny Dee *lawyer*
Moise, Steven Kahn *lawyer, rancher, merchant banker*
Mueller, Diane Mayne *lawyer*
Payne, Lucy Ann Salsbury *law librarian, educator, lawyer*
Ramo, Roberta Cooper *lawyer*
Rivera, Rhonda Rae *lawyer, labor artibrator*
†Robb, John Donald, Jr., *lawyer*
†Roberts, Randal William *lawyer*
Roehl, Jerrald J. *lawyer*
Schuler, Alison Kay *lawyer*
Sisk, Daniel Arthur *lawyer*
Slade, Lynn *lawyer*
†Stetson, Catherine Baker *lawyer, lobbyist*
†Thornton, J. Duke *lawyer*
†Tinnin, Robert Priest, Jr., *lawyer*
Word, Terry Mullins *lawyer*

Carlsbad
Byers, Matthew T(odd) *lawyer, educator*

Chama
McElhaney, James Willson *lawyer, educator, author, trial consultant*

Clovis
Skarda, Lynell Griffith *lawyer, banker*

Deming
Sherman, Frederick Hood *lawyer*

Farmington
Gurley, Curtis Raymond *lawyer*
Moeller, Floyd Douglas *lawyer*
Morgan, Jack M. *lawyer*
†Strother, Robin Dale *lawyer*
†Titus, Victor Allen *lawyer*
†Tully, Richard T. C. *lawyer, petroleum landman*

Hobbs
Stout, Lowell *lawyer*

Las Cruces
†Jay, William Walton *lawyer*
Lindley, Jearl Ray *lawyer*
Lutz, William Lan *lawyer*
Sandenaw, Thomas Arthur, Jr., *lawyer*
Winfree, Latham Thomas *law educator*

Los Alamos
Herr, Bruce *lawyer*

Placitas
Schoen, Stevan Jay *lawyer*

Roswell
Bassett, John Walden, Jr., *lawyer*
Kraft, Richard Lee *lawyer*
Olson, Richard Earl *lawyer, state legislator*

Ruidoso
†Dutton, Dominic Edward *lawyer*

Santa Fe
†Aarons, Stephen D. *lawyer*
Abeles, Richard Alan *lawyer*
Bienvenu, John Charles *lawyer*
†Brannen, Jeffrey Richard *lawyer*
Burton, John Paul (Jack Burton) *lawyer*
Carpenter, Richard Norris *retired lawyer*
Casey, Patrick Anthony *lawyer*
Coffield, Conrad Eugene *lawyer*
Cunningham, David Fratt *lawyer*
Dodds, Robert James, III, *lawyer*
Farber, Steven Glenn *lawyer*
†Garber, Bruce Samuel *lawyer*
George, W. Peyton *lawyer*
Hickey, John Miller *lawyer*
Johnson, Reverdy *lawyer*
Justice, Jack Burton *retired lawyer, writer*
McClaugherty, Joe L. *lawyer, educator*
†Mills, Thomas C.H. *lawyer*
Moll, Deborah Adelaide *lawyer*
Noland, Charles Donald *lawyer, educator*
Schwarz, Michael *lawyer*
†Singleton, Sarah Michael *lawyer*
Weckesser, Susan Oneacre *lawyer*
†Wertheim, Jerry *lawyer*
†Wolford, Richard Howard *lawyer*
Zorie, Stephanie Marie *lawyer*

Seneca
Monroe, Kendyl Kurth *retired lawyer*

Silver City
Foy, Thomas Paul *lawyer, retired state legislator, retired banker*

Socorro
†Smith, Leslie Clark *lawyer*

Taos
†Boles, David LaVelle *lawyer*

NEW YORK

Albany
Alessi, Robert Joseph *lawyer, pharmacist, real estate developer*
Barsamian, J(ohn) Albert *lawyer, judge, educator, criminologist, arbitrator*
Doherty, Glen Patrick *lawyer*
†Engel, David Anthony *lawyer*
†Fein, Scott Norris *lawyer*
Fernandez, Hermes A., III, *lawyer*
Gosdeck, Thomas Joseph *lawyer*
Hanna, John, Jr., *lawyer, educator, arbitrator, mediator*
Hoffman, Nancy E. *lawyer*
Koff, Howard Michael *lawyer*
†Kornstein, Michael Allen *lawyer*
Lansing, Mark Daniel *lawyer*
Lefkowitz, Jerome *lawyer*
Mishler, Mark Sean *lawyer*
Powers, John Kieran *lawyer*
Pozner, Louis-Jack *lawyer*
Provorny, Frederick Alan *lawyer, educator*
†Regal, Evan Charles *lawyer*
Ruggeri, Robert Edward *lawyer*
Ruzow, Daniel Arthur *lawyer*
Scott, William Proctor, III, *lawyer*
Selchick, Jeffrey Mark *arbitrator, judge*
Stanton, Victoria Mead *lawyer*

Amagansett
Frankl, Kenneth Richard *retired lawyer*

Amherst
Jones, E. Thomas *lawyer*
Murray, William Michael *lawyer*

Andover
†Hutter, Robert Grant *lawyer*

Ardsley
†Glauberman, Melvin L. *lawyer*

Ardsley On Hudson
Stein, Milton Michael *lawyer*

Armonk
Moskowitz, Stuart Stanley *lawyer*
†Moss, Eric Harold *lawyer*
Quinn, James W. *lawyer*
Wolff, Kurt Jakob *lawyer, director*

Atlantic Beach
Lore, Martin Maxwell *lawyer*

Babylon
Garvey, Jane Roberts *lawyer*
Hennelly, Edmund Paul *lawyer, oil company executive*

Ballston Spa
Brown, Ifigenia Theodore *lawyer*

Bayside
Bernstein, Barry S. *lawyer*

Bedford
Atkins, Ronald Raymond *lawyer*

Bellerose
Bearak, Corey B(ecker) *lawyer*

Bethpage
Lemle, Robert Spencer *lawyer*

Binghamton
Anderson, Warren Mattice *lawyer*
Axtell, Clayton Morgan, Jr., *lawyer*
Beck, Stephanie G. *lawyer*
Chivers, James Leeds *lawyer*
Gates, Gregory Ansel *lawyer*
Gerhart, Eugene Clifton *lawyer*
Gouldin, David Millen *lawyer*
Kramer, Philip Joseph *lawyer*
Peckham, Eugene Eliot *surogate judge, lawyer*
Price, Paul Marnell *lawyer*
†Thompson, Carlton Frederick *lawyer*

Bridgehampton
Cummings, Richard M. *law educator, consultant, writer*

Bronx
Balka, Sigmund Ronell *lawyer*
Cornfield, Melvin *lawyer, university institute director*
Kennedy, David J. *lawyer*
Kostelny, Albert Joseph, Jr., *lawyer*
Margid, Leonard *lawyer*
†Weil, Gary Ronald *lawyer*

Bronxville
Cutler, Kenneth Burnett *lawyer, investment company executive*
Falvey, Patrick Joseph *lawyer*
Fuller, David Otis, Jr., *lawyer*
Garber, Robert Edward *lawyer, insurance company executive*
Hagendorn, William H. *lawyer*

Brooklyn
Barabash, Claire *lawyer, special education administrator, psychologist*
†Bohm, Joel Lawrence *lawyer*
Cohen, Gary *lawyer*
†Diamond, Murray J. *lawyer*
†Dorf, Robert Clay *lawyer*
Eibel, Andrew H. *lawyer*
Henderson, Janice Elizabeth *law librarian*
Herzog, Lester Barry *lawyer, educator*
Jacobson, Barry Stephen *lawyer, judge*
†Johnson, Donald Raymond *lawyer*
Kamins, Barry Michael *lawyer*
Karmel, Roberta Segal *lawyer, educator*
Kirberger, Elizabeth *lawyer, consultant*
Kramer, Meyer *lawyer, editor, clergyman*
McDermott, Frank Clark *lawyer*
Miles, Gavin Wentworth *lawyer*
Nuccio, Paul Vincent *lawyer*
Onken, George Marcellus *retired lawyer*
†Pannizzo, Frank J. *general counsel*
Raskind, Leo Joseph *law educator*
†Reich, Edward Stuart *lawyer*
†Roth, Pamela Susan *lawyer*
†Rubenstein, Allen Ira *lawyer*
Solan, Lawrence Michael *lawyer*
†Steinberg, Jerome Leonard *lawyer*
Stone, Dianne St. Christine *legal aid society executive*
†Tsismenakis, Georgia *lawyer, tax accountant*
Twersky, Jonathan *lawyer*

Buffalo
Bailey, Thomas Charles *lawyer*
†Barber, Janice Ann *lawyer*
Barney, Thomas McNamee *lawyer*
†Brock, David George *lawyer*
Brown, Jerrold Stanley *lawyer*
Brydges, Thomas Eugene *lawyer*
Day, Donald Sheldon *lawyer*
†De Marie, Anthony Joseph *lawyer*
Feuerstein, Alan Ricky *lawyer*
†Fine, Robert Paul *lawyer*
Fisher, Cheryl Smith *lawyer*
Freedman, Maryann Saccomando *lawyer*
Friedman, Scott Edward *lawyer, author, business consultant*
Gardner, Arnold Burton *lawyer*
Gardner, Sue Shaffer *lawyer*
Glanville, Robert Edward *lawyer*
†Goldberg, Neil A. *lawyer*
Goldstein, Brian Alan *lawyer, physician*
Goldstein, Bruce A. *lawyer*
†Gorman, Gerald Patrick *lawyer*
Grasser, George Robert *lawyer, real estate consultant*
Greene, Robert Michael *lawyer*
†Greenspon, Burton Edward *lawyer*
Halpern, Ralph Lawrence *lawyer*
Hayes, J. Michael *lawyer*
Headrick, Thomas Edward *lawyer, educator*
Heilman, Pamela Davis *lawyer*
Herdzik, Arthur Alan *lawyer*
†Jacobs, Charles P. *lawyer*
Jasen, Matthew Joseph *lawyer, state justice*
†Kotaska, Gary F. *lawyer*
Kristoff, Karl W. *lawyer*
Manning, Kenneth Alan *lawyer*
McElvein, Thomas Irving, Jr., *lawyer*
Miller, Charles Louis, II, *consultant*
Mucci, Gary Louis *lawyer*
Newman, Stephen Michael *lawyer*
O'Donnell, Denise Ellen *lawyer*
Odza, Randall M. *lawyer*
O'Loughlin, Sandra S. *lawyer*
Oppenheimer, Randolph Carl *lawyer*
Pajak, David Joseph *lawyer, consultant*
†Parker, Michelle *lawyer*
Pearson, Paul David *lawyer, mediator*
†Rachlin, Lauren David *lawyer*
Runfola, Ross Thomas *lawyer, educator, writer, journalist, poet*
Salisbury, Eugene W. *lawyer, justice*
†Schoenborn, Daniel Leonard *lawyer*
†Schreck, Robert J. *lawyer*
†Segalla, Thomas Francis *lawyer*
Sherwood, Arthur Morley *lawyer*
†Swart, Michael *lawyer*
Szanyi, Kevin Andrew *lawyer*
†Tanous, James Joseph *lawyer*
Toohey, Philip S. *lawyer*
Wisbaum, Wayne David *lawyer*

Camillus
Endieveri, Anthony Frank *lawyer*

Canaan
Grant Bruce, Darlene Camille *lawyer*
Pennell, William Brooke *lawyer*

Cape Vincent
Stiefel, Linda Shields *lawyer*

Carle Place
Seiden, Steven Jay *lawyer*

Carmel
Grossman, Victor G. *lawyer*
Laporte, Cloyd, Jr., *lawyer, retired manufacturing executive*
Lowe, E(dwin) Nobles *lawyer*

Cazenovia
Shattuck, George Clement *retired lawyer*

Cedarhurst
†Klein, Irwin Grant *lawyer*
Taubenfeld, Harry Samuel *lawyer*

Chappaqua
Castrataro, Barbara Ann *lawyer*
Pollet, Susan L. *lawyer*

Chestnut Ridge
Burns, Richard Owen *lawyer*

Chittenango
Baum, Peter Alan *lawyer*

Clifton Park
Healy, Joseph Robert *lawyer*
Hilts, Earl T. *lawyer, government official, educator*

Cold Spring Harbor
Walton, Robert Prentiss *lawyer*

Commack
†Braun, Robert Alan *lawyer*
Somer, Stanley Jerome *lawyer*
Steindler, Walter G. *retired lawyer*

Corning
Hauselt, Denise Ann *lawyer*
Ughetta, William Casper *lawyer, manufacturing company executive*

Cortland
†Taylor, Leland Baridon *lawyer*

Cortlandt Manor
†Buhler, Gregory Wallace *lawyer*
Galella, Joseph Peter *lawyer*

Croton On Hudson
†Hoffman, Paul Shafer *lawyer*

Crugers
Walther, Zerita Esperance *paralegal*

Dansville
Vogel, John Walter *lawyer*

Deer Park
†Rolla, Mario F. *lawyer*

Delhi
†Hartmann, James M. *lawyer*

Delmar
Cavanaugh, John Joseph, Jr., *lawyer*
Everett, James, Jr., *lawyer*
†Netter, Miriam Maccoby *lawyer*

Depew
Saleh, David John *lawyer*

Dix Hills
†Tucker, Robert Henry *lawyer*

Dobbs Ferry
†Barnett, Richard Earl *lawyer, distributing company executive*
Griesar, William Howard *lawyer*
Juettner, Diana D'Amico *lawyer, educator*
Maiocchi, Christine *lawyer*
†McGrath, John Joseph *law educator*

Douglaston
Walsh, Sean M. *lawyer, audio-video computer forensics consultant*

Dunkirk
Woodbury, Robert Charles *lawyer*

East Hampton
Ehren, Charles Alexander, Jr., *lawyer, educator*
Twomey, Thomas A., Jr., *lawyer, educator*

East Meadow
Adler, Ira Jay *lawyer*
Bergman, Bruce J. *lawyer*
Hyman, Montague Allan *lawyer, educator*

East Northport
Juliano, John Louis *lawyer*
Ryesky, Kenneth H. *lawyer*

Elma
Markello, Jeffrey Philip *lawyer*

Elmira
†Stone, Kathleen Gale *law educator*

Elmsford
†Neustadt, Paul *lawyer*
†Parker, James K. *corporate lawyer*

Fairport
Young, Thomas Paul *lawyer*

Farmingdale
Firetog, Theodore Warren *lawyer*

Fayetteville
†Gingold, Neil Marshall *lawyer*

Floral Park
Chatoff, Michael Alan *lawyer*

Flushing
Deerson, Adele Shapiro *lawyer, educator*
Farago, John Michael *law educator, hearing officer, consultant*
†Giaimo, Joseph Octavius *lawyer*
Plotnik, Katya Michele *lawyer*
Schwartz, Estar Alma *lawyer*
†Seibel, Robert Franklin *law educator*
†Zalesne, Deborah *law educator*

Forest Hills
Addabbo, Dominic Lucian *lawyer*
Grant, Susan Irene *lawyer*
Rivers, Theodore John *paralegal, educator*

Forestville
Adams, Lee Towne *lawyer*

Franklin Square
Vanora, Jerome Patrick *lawyer*

Freeport
Berg, Alan *lawyer, arbitrator*

Fresh Meadows
Greenberg, Robert Jay *law educator*

Garden City
Caputo, Kathryn Mary *paralegal*
Carnesi, Kenneth Brian *lawyer*
Cohen, Harvey *lawyer*
Cook, George Valentine *lawyer, consultant*
DaSilva, Willard H. *lawyer, educator*
†Dent, Thomas Augustine *lawyer*
DiMascio, John Philip *lawyer*
Ehrlich, Jerome Harry *lawyer*
Fischoff, Gary Charles *lawyer*
Fishberg, Gerard *lawyer*
Friedenberg, Gary Howard *lawyer*
†Ginsberg, Eugene Stanley *lawyer, arbitrator, mediator*
Haskel, Jules J. *lawyer*
†Jones, Lawrence Tunnicliffe *lawyer*
Kaplan, Joel Stuart *lawyer*
Lioz, Lawrence Stephen *lawyer, accountant*
Minicucci, Richard Francis *lawyer, former hospital administrator*
Ostrow, Michael Jay *lawyer*
†Sawyer, James *lawyer*
†Schupbach, Arthur Christopher *lawyer*
Tomao, Peter Joseph *lawyer*

Geneseo
Macko, John *lawyer, farmer*

Geneva
Brind, David Hutchison *lawyer, judge*

Glen Cove
Lewis, Felice Flanery *lawyer, educator*
Mills, Charles Gardner *lawyer*
Rathkopf, Daren Anthony *lawyer*

Glen Head
Savinetti, Louis Gerard *lawyer*

Glens Falls
Baker, Carl TenEyck *lawyer*
Bartlett, Richard James *lawyer*
†Cullum, James Edward *lawyer*
†Firth, Peter Alan *lawyer*
†Lebowitz, Jack Richard *lawyer*
McMillen, Robert Stewart *lawyer*
†Meyer, Martin Arthur *lawyer*
Pontiff, Paul E. *lawyer*

Gouverneur
Leader, Robert John *lawyer*

Great Neck
Kimm, Michael S. *lawyer*
Lowenbraun, Solomon Mortimer *lawyer*
Rockowitz, Noah Ezra *lawyer*
Salzman, Stanley P. *lawyer*
Wachsman, Harvey Frederick *lawyer, neurosurgeon*
Wershals, Paul Leonard *lawyer*
Wimpfheimer, Steven *lawyer*

Greenvale
Halper, Emanuel B(arry) *real estate lawyer, developer, consultant, author*

Hamburg
Hargesheimer, Elbert, III, *lawyer*

Hancock
Sienko, Leonard Edward, Jr., *lawyer*

Harrison
Hertz, Natalie Zucker *retired lawyer*
Kolbrener, Jonathan *lawyer*
†Strone, Michael Jonathan *lawyer*

Hartsdale
†Bowie, April Dene't *lawyer, arbitrator*
Kroll, Arthur Herbert *educator, consultant*

Hastings On Hudson
Thornlow, Carolyn *law firm administrator, consultant*

Hawthorne
Jacobs, Jeffrey Lee *lawyer, education network company executive*
Traub, Richard Kenneth *lawyer*

Hempstead
†Diamond, David Arthur *law educator*
Furey, James Michael *lawyer*
Mahon, Malachy Thomas, Sr., *lawyer, educator*
Resnick, Alan Neal *law educator, lawyer*

Hicksville
Giuffré, John Joseph *lawyer*

Hillsdale
Lunde, Asbjorn Rudolph *lawyer*

Hollis
Singh, Harbachan *solicitor, barrister*

Hornell
Pulos, William Whitaker *lawyer*

Houghton
Brautigam, David Clyde *lawyer, judge*

Hudson
Agata, Burton C. *law educator, lawyer*
Davis, Deborah Lynn *lawyer*
Howard, Andrew Baker *lawyer*

Huntington
Brettschneider, Rita Roberta Fischman *lawyer*
German, June Resnick *lawyer*
Glickstein, Howard Alan *law educator*
Hochberg, Ronald Mark *lawyer*
†Jordan, Daniel Patrick, Jr., *law librarian*
Levitan, Katherine D. *lawyer*
Liput, Andrew Lawrence *lawyer, educator*
Morris, Jeffrey Brandon *law educator*
Munson, Nancy K. *lawyer*

Robinson, Kenneth Patrick lawyer, electronics company executive
Tucker, William P. lawyer, writer

Irvington
Bonomi, John Gurnee retired lawyer

Islandia
Buckley, Terrence Patrick lawyer
Pruzansky, Joshua Murdock lawyer

Ithaca
Barcelo, John James, III, law educator
Barney, John Charles lawyer
Basefsky, Stuart Mark law librarian, library and information scientist, journalist
Gold, Michael Evan law educator
Hammond, Jane Laura retired law librarian, lawyer
Hay, George Alan law and economics educator
Macey, Jonathan R. law educator
Martin, Peter William lawyer, educator
Roberts, E. F. lawyer, educator
Rossi, Faust F. lawyer, educator
†Summers, Robert Samuel lawyer, author, educator
Thoron, Gray lawyer, educator
Yale-Loehr, Stephen William lawyer, editor

Jackson Heights
†Goldblum, A. Paul lawyer

Jamaica
Angione, Howard Francis lawyer, editor
Brown, Kenneth Lloyd lawyer
Clauss, Wayne Francis court clerk
Hall, Michael disability processing specialist
†Shapiro, Irving lawyer
Tschinkel, Andrew Joseph, Jr., law librarian

Jamesport
Cardinale, Philip John lawyer, educator

Jamestown
Beckstrom, Charles G. lawyer
Idzik, Martin Francis lawyer

Jamesville
DeCrow, Karen lawyer, author, lecturer

Jericho
Blau, Harvey Ronald lawyer
Corso, Frank Mitchell lawyer
Hecht, Donald Stuart lawyer
Kurtzberg, Howard lawyer
Rehbock, Richard Alexander lawyer
Schatkin, Andrew James lawyer
†Semel, Martin Ira lawyer

Keeseville
Turetsky, Aaron lawyer

Kew Gardens
†Adler, David Neil lawyer
Ford, Bernadette K. lawyer
Nizin, Leslie Stephen lawyer
Reichel, Aaron Israel lawyer, rabbi, editor
†Sparrow, Robert E. lawyer

Kingston
Ellison, Patricia Lee lawyer

Lake George
Hayes, Norman Robert, Jr., lawyer

Lake Sucess
†Epstein, Joel Donald lawyer

Lancaster
Walsh, J(ohn) B(ronson) lawyer

Larchmont
Berridge, George Bradford retired lawyer
Bloom, Lee Hurley lawyer, public affairs consultant, retired household products manufacturing executive
Davis, Wendell, Jr., lawyer
Gaffney, Mark William lawyer
McSherry, William John, Jr., lawyer, consultant
Pelton, Russell Gilbert retired lawyer
†Ungar, Lawrence Beryl lawyer
White, Thomas Edward lawyer

Latham
Brearton, James Joseph lawyer
Conway, Robert George, Jr., lawyer
Piedmont, Richard Stuart lawyer

Lawrence
Goldstein, Irwin Melvin lawyer

Lockport
Brodsky, Felice Adrienne lawyer
Penney, Charles Rand lawyer, civic worker, world traveler

Long Beach
Levine, Samuel Milton lawyer, retired judge, mediator, arbitrator
Solomon, Robert H. lawyer

Long Island City
Alimaras, Gus lawyer
Della-Giustina, Jo-Ann Subotin lawyer
Mathers, Allen Stanley judge, arbitrator, consultant
Wanderman, Susan Mae lawyer

Lynbrook
Korth, Jay Thomas lawyer

Mahopac
Sequeira, Manuel Alexandre, Jr., lawyer

Malone
Grue, Thomas Andrew lawyer

Malverne
Benigno, Thomas Daniel lawyer

Manchester
†Gillis, Joan legal administrative assistant

Manhasset
Benewitz, Maurice Charles labor arbitrator, educator
Gastwirth, Stuart Lawrence lawyer
Wachtler, Sol law educator, retired judge, arbitration corporation executive, writer

Manlius
Mathewson, George Atterbury lawyer

Massapequa
Van Gorder, John Frederic lawyer

Melville
†Cahn, Richard Caleb lawyer
D'Angelo-Mayer, Ida lawyer
Fine, Barry Kenneth lawyer
Klatell, Robert Edward lawyer, electronics company executive
Lane, Arthur Alan lawyer
McMillan, Robert Ralph lawyer
Schoenfeld, Michael P. lawyer

Middletown
Kossar, Ronald Steven lawyer

Mineola
†Albicocco, Santa lawyer, county official
Bartlett, Clifford Adams, Jr., lawyer
Bartol, Ernest Thomas lawyer
†Cohen, Stanley Dale lawyer
Daniels, John Hill lawyer
Fowler, David Thomas lawyer
Klein, Arnold Spencer lawyer
Kunken, Kenneth James lawyer
Levin, A. Thomas lawyer
Lynn, Robert Patrick, Jr., lawyer
Meyer, Bernard Stern lawyer, former judge
Millman, Bruce Russell lawyer
Monaghan, Peter Gerard lawyer
Nogee, Jeffrey Laurence lawyer
Paterson, Basil Alexander lawyer
Pogrebin, Bertrand B. lawyer
Rubine, Robert Samuel lawyer
Sandback, William Arthur lawyer
†Santemma, Jon Noel lawyer
Schaffer, David Irving lawyer
†Shaheen Alesi, Barbara lawyer
Smolev, Terence Elliot lawyer, educator
†Spizz, Harvey Warren lawyer
Tankoos, Sandra Maxine court reporting services executive
†Tannenbaum, Bernard lawyer
†Weinstock, Benjamin lawyer

Mohegan Lake
Stokes, Ron lawyer

Montauk
Kahn, Richard Dreyfus lawyer

Mount Kisco
Curran, Maurice Francis lawyer
Goodhue, Mary Brier lawyer, former state senator
Harris, Isaac Ron lawyer
†Icahn, Carl C. arbitrator, options specialist, corporation executive

Mount Sinai
†Gillin, Donna Lynn lawyer

Mount Vernon
†Davison, Irwin Stuart lawyer

Nassau
Moldoff, William Morris retired lawyer

Neponsit
Re, Edward Domenic law educator, retired federal judge

New City
Abel, Steven L. lawyer, mediator
Fenster, Robert David lawyer
Marcus, Robert Bruce lawyer

New Hartford
Chapin, Mary Q. television personality, arbitrator, mediator, writer, performing artist
McKennan, John T. lawyer

New Hyde Park
Jensen, Richard Currie lawyer
Offner, Eric Delmonte lawyer
Rose, Elihu Isaac lawyer

New Rochelle
Blotner, Norman David lawyer, real estate broker, corporate executive
†Ferencz, Benjamin Berell lawyer
Gunning, Francis Patrick lawyer, insurance association executive
Herman, William Charles lawyer
Lurie, Alvin David lawyer
Stevens, Roger Ross lawyer

New York
†Abelle, Patsy Caples lawyer
Abrams, Robert lawyer, former state attorney general
†Adair, Wendell Hinton, Jr., lawyer
†Adams, Daniel Nelson lawyer
Adams, George Bell lawyer
†Adams, Robert Brereton lawyer
Aidinoff, M(erton) Bernard retired lawyer
Ajhar, Marsha G. lawyer
Aksen, Gerald arbitrator, lawyer, educator
Albert, Garett J. lawyer
†Alcott, Mark Howard lawyer
Alden, Steven Michael lawyer
Alessandroni, Venan Joseph lawyer
Allen, Leon Arthur, Jr., lawyer
Alter, Eleanor Breitel lawyer
Altieri, Peter Louis lawyer
Amdur, Martin Bennett lawyer
Amhowitz, Harris J. lawyer, educator
Amsterdam, Anthony Guy law educator
Amsterdam, Mark Lemle lawyer
Andersen, Richard Esten lawyer
Andresen, Malcolm lawyer
Andrews, Gordon Clark lawyer
Andrus, Roger Douglas lawyer
Annenberg, Norman lawyer
Anthoine, Robert lawyer, educator
Appel, Albert M. lawyer
Appelbaum, Ann Harriet lawyer
†Appleman, Jolene W. patent lawyer
Arenson, Gregory K. lawyer
Arkin, Stanley S. lawyer
Arlen, Jennifer Hall law educator
Arouh, Jeffrey Alan lawyer
Arquit, Kevin James lawyer
Ashton, Robert W. lawyer, foundation administrator
Atkins, Peter Allan lawyer
†Augustine, Cynthia H. lawyer
†Axinn, Stephen Mark lawyer
Bach, Thomas Handford lawyer, investor
Bachelder, Joseph Elmer, III, lawyer
Backman, Gerald Stephen lawyer
Badertscher, David Glen law librarian, consultant
†Baechtold, Robert Louis lawyer
Bagger, Richard Hartvig lawyer
Bahler, Gary M. lawyer
†Bahlke, Conrad George lawyer
Bainton, J(ohn) Joseph lawyer
Baity, John Cooley lawyer
Baker, Stuart David lawyer
†Ballon, Charles lawyer
Bamberger, Michael Albert lawyer
Bancroft, Alexander Clerihew lawyer
Bancroft, Margaret Armstrong lawyer
Bankston, Archie Moore lawyer
Barandes, Robert lawyer
Barasch, Clarence Sylvan lawyer
Barasch, Mal Livingston lawyer
Barist, Jeffrey lawyer
Barnard, Robert N. lawyer
Barnett, Gary lawyer
†Barr, William Pelham lawyer, former attorney general of United States
†Barrett, Edward Mitchell lawyer
†Barrett, Jane lawyer
Barry, David Earl lawyer
Barry, Desmond Thomas, Jr., lawyer
Barth, Mark Harold lawyer
Barthold, Walter lawyer
Bartlett, Joseph Warren lawyer
†Bartlett, Linda Gail lawyer
Bason, George R., Jr., lawyer
Bassen, Ned Henry lawyer
†Basta, Paul M. lawyer
†Bauer, George A., III, lawyer
Baumgardner, John Ellwood, Jr., lawyer
Baumgarten, Paul Anthony retired lawyer
Baumgarten, Sidney lawyer, company executive
Baumrin, Bernard Stefan Herbert lawyer, educator
Bazerman, Steven Howard lawyer
Bear, Larry Alan lawyer, educator
Beck, Andrew James lawyer
Beckman, Michael lawyer
Beekman, William Bedloe lawyer
Beerbower, Cynthia Gibson lawyer
Beerbower, John Edwin lawyer
Begley, Louis lawyer, writer
Behr, Alan Andrew lawyer, writer, photographer
Bell, Derrick Albert law educator, author, lecturer
Bell, Jonathan Robert lawyer
†Beller, Gary A. lawyer, insurance company executive
Bender, John Charles lawyer
Benedict, James Nelson lawyer
Benenson, Mark Keith lawyer
Benjamin, Jeff lawyer, pharmaceutical executive
Benkard, James W. B. lawyer
Bennett, Scott Lawrence lawyer
Beranbaum, John A. lawyer
†Berg, Gale Diane lawyer
Bergan, Edmund Paul, Jr., lawyer
Berger, George lawyer
Bergman, Robert Ira laywer
Bergtraum, Howard Michael lawyer
Berkowsky, Peter Arthur lawyer, retired military officer
Berland, Sanford Neil lawyer
Berman, Keith solicitor, lawyer
Bernard, Richard Phillip lawyer
Bernstein, Daniel Lewis lawyer
Bernstein, David William lawyer
†Bernstein, Donald Scott lawyer
Beshar, Peter Justus lawyer
Beshar, Robert Peter lawyer
Bezanson, Thomas Edward lawyer
Bialkin, Kenneth Jules lawyer, director
Bialo, Kenneth Marc lawyer
Bicks, David Peter lawyer
Bidwell, James Truman, Jr., lawyer
Bigelow, Robert Wilson trial lawyer
†Bingham, A. Walker, III, lawyer
Birnbaum, Edward Lester lawyer
Birnbaum, Julian R. lawyer
Birnbaum, Sheila L. lawyer, educator
†Bivona, John Vincent lawyer
Black, Barbara Aronstein legal history educator
Black, James Isaac, III, lawyer
Black, Louis Engleman lawyer
Blackman, Kenneth Robert lawyer
Blair, James Newell lawyer
†Blasi, Vincent A. lawyer, educator
Block, William Kenneth lawyer
Bluestone, Andrew Lavoott lawyer
Blumberg, Gerald lawyer
Blume, Lawrence Dayton lawyer
Blumkin, Linda Ruth lawyer
Bockstein, Herbert lawyer
Boddie, Reginald Alonzo lawyer
Bodovitz, James Philip lawyer
Boehner, Leonard Bruce lawyer
†Boggio, Miriam Altagracia lawyer
Booth, Edgar Hirsch lawyer
Booth, Mitchell B. lawyer
†Borchard, William Marshall lawyer
†Borenstein, Eugene Reed lawyer
Borisoff, Richard Stuart lawyer
Boros, Jerome S. lawyer
Borsody, Robert Peter lawyer
†Borstein, Leon Baer lawyer
Bosses, Stevan J. lawyer
Bowden, William P., Jr., lawyer, banker
Boxer, Leonard lawyer
Boynton, James Stephen lawyer
Bradley, E. Michael lawyer
Braid, Frederick Donald lawyer
Brand, Irving lawyer
†Braslow, Dean Gerald lawyer
Braun, Jeffrey Louis lawyer
Brauner, David A. lawyer
Brecker, Jeffrey Ross lawyer, educator
Breglio, John F. lawyer
Breinin, Bartley James lawyer
Bressler, Bernard lawyer
Brewer, William Dane lawyer
†Brilliant, Andrew Prince lawyer
Bring, Murray H. retired lawyer
Broadwater, Douglas Dwight lawyer
†Brock, Charles Lawrence lawyer, business executive
Broder, Douglas Fisher lawyer
Brodsky, David Michael lawyer
Brodsky, Samuel lawyer
Bromberger, Allen Richard legal association administrator
Brome, Thomas Reed lawyer
Bronstein, Richard J. lawyer
Brooks, Lorimer Page patent lawyer
†Brossman, Mark Edward lawyer
Broude, Richard Frederick lawyer, educator
Browdy, Joseph Eugene lawyer
Brown, Charles D. lawyer
†Brown, James Sylvester, Jr., lawyer
Brown, Meredith M. lawyer
Brown, Paul M. lawyer
Brown, Peter Megargee lawyer, writer, lecturer
Brown, Ralph Sawyer, Jr., retired lawyer, business executive
Browne, Jeffrey Francis lawyer
Brownwood, David Owen lawyer
Brumm, James Earl lawyer, trading company executive
Brundige, Robert William, Jr., lawyer
Bryan, Barry Richard lawyer
Buchman, M. Abraham lawyer
Buchwald, Don David lawyer
†Buckley, Susan lawyer
Buckman, James Edward lawyer
Budd, Thomas Witbeck lawyer
Burak, H(oward) Paul lawyer
†Burgman, Dierdre Ann lawyer
Burgweger, Francis Joseph Dewes, Jr., lawyer
†Burrows, Kenneth David lawyer
Burrows, Michael Donald lawyer
Bursky, Herman Aaron lawyer
†Burstein, Neil Alan lawyer
†Bushnell, George Edward, III, lawyer
Butler, Samuel Coles lawyer, director
Butler, William Joseph lawyer, educator
Buttenwieser, Lawrence Benjamin lawyer
Butterklee, Neil Howard lawyer
Butterman, Jay Ronald lawyer
†Byrnes, Richard James lawyer
†Cable, Paul Andrew lawyer
Caginalp, Aydin S. lawyer
Cameron, Nina Rao lawyer, government official
Cannell, John Redferne lawyer
Canoni, John David lawyer
†Cantor, Louis lawyer
†Cantor, Melvyn Leon retired lawyer
†Carden, Constance law educator, lawyer
Cardozo, Benjamin Mordecai lawyer
Carling, Francis lawyer, mediator
Carlson, Theodore Joshua lawyer, retired utility company executive
Carter, James Hal, Jr., lawyer
Carter, Zachary W. lawyer
Cashman, Gideon lawyer
Castel, P. Kevin lawyer
Caulfield, Jerome Joseph lawyer
Cayea, Donald Joseph lawyer
Caytas, Ivo George lawyer
†Celedonia, Baila Handelman lawyer
Chaitman, Helen Davis lawyer
Champion, Sara Stewart lawyer
Chan, Lai Lee lawyer
Chapnick, David B. lawyer
Chappell, John Charles lawyer
Chasey, Jacqueline lawyer
Chazen, Hartley James lawyer
Chen, Wesley lawyer
Chiang, Yung Frank law educator
Chiarchiaro, Frank John lawyer
Chilstrom, Robert Meade lawyer
Chin, Sylvia Fung lawyer
Cho, Tai Yong lawyer
Christensen, Henry, III, lawyer
Christy, Arthur Hill lawyer
Chromow, Sheri P. lawyer
†Cirillo, Richard Allan lawyer
Clapman, Peter Carlyle lawyer, insurance company executive
Clark, Carolyn Cochran lawyer
Clark, Celia Rue lawyer
†Clark, Jonathan Montgomery lawyer
Clark, Merrell Edward, Jr., lawyer
Clary, Richard Wayland lawyer
Cliff, Walter Conway lawyer
Cogan, Sarah Edwards lawyer
Cohen, Edmund Stephen lawyer
Cohen, Edward Herschel lawyer
Cohen, Henry Rodgin lawyer
Cohen, Howard Marvin lawyer
†Cohen, Marcy Sharon lawyer

†Peskin, Stephan Haskel *lawyer*
Peterson, Charles Gordon *retired lawyer*
Pettibone, Peter John *lawyer*
Phillips, Anthony Francis *lawyer*
Phillips, Barnet, IV, *lawyer*
†Pidot, Whitney Dean *lawyer*
Pierce, Morton Allen *lawyer*
†Piliero, Robert Donald *lawyer*
Pinczower, Kenneth Ephraim *lawyer*
†Pinover, Eugene Alfred *lawyer*
†Pisano, Vincent James *lawyer*
†Plevan, Kenneth A. *lawyer*
Plotkin, Loren H. *lawyer*
Polevoy, Nancy Tally *lawyer, social worker, genealogist*
Pollack, Stanley P. *lawyer*
Pollak, Martin Marshall *lawyer, training company executive*
†Pollan, Stephen Michael *lawyer, personal finance expert, speaker, author*
†Posen, Richard L. *lawyer*
Posen, Susan Orzack *lawyer*
Posner, Louis Joseph *lawyer, accountant*
Poulson, Richard Jasper Metcalfe *lawyer*
Powell, James Henry *lawyer*
Price, Robert *lawyer, media executive, investment banker*
Primps, William Guthrie *lawyer*
†Probstein, Jon Michael *lawyer*
Prochnow, Thomas Herbert *lawyer*
†Profusek, Robert Alan *lawyer*
Prutzman, Lewis Donald *lawyer*
Puleo, Frank Charles *lawyer*
†Purtell, Lawrence Robert *lawyer*
Quale, Andrew Christopher, Jr., *lawyer*
†Quinlan, Guy Christian *lawyer*
Quinn, Francis F. *lawyer*
†Quinn, Linda Catherine *lawyer*
Quinn, Yvonne Susan *lawyer*
Raab, Sheldon *lawyer, director*
Rabb, Bruce *lawyer*
Rabb, Harriet Schaffer *university administrator, government official, lawyer, educator*
Rabin, Jack *lawyer*
†Rabinowitz, Daniel Lawrence *lawyer, director*
Radin, Sam *lawyer, estate planner*
†Rado, Peter Thomas *lawyer*
Radon, Jenik Richard *lawyer*
†Radway, Robert J. *lawyer, consultant, educator*
Rahm, David Alan *lawyer*
Rahm, Susan Berkman *lawyer*
Ralli, Constantine Pandia *lawyer*
†Rand, Deborah *lawyer*
Rand, Harry Israel *lawyer*
Rand, William *lawyer, former state justice*
Rankin, Clyde Evan, III, *lawyer*
Rapoport, Bernard Robert *lawyer*
Rappaport, Charles Owen *lawyer*
Rappaport, Linda Ellen *lawyer*
Raylesberg, Alan Ira *lawyer*
Redlich, Norman *lawyer, educator*
†Redpath, John S(loneker), Jr., *lawyer, publishing company executive*
†Reibstein, Richard Jay *lawyer*
Reich, Larry Sam *lawyer*
Reid, Edward Snover, III, *lawyer*
Reid, John Phillip *law educator*
Reilly, Conor Desmond *lawyer*
Reilly, Edward Arthur *lawyer*
†Reilly, John A. *lawyer*
†Reiner, John Paul *lawyer*
†Reiniger, Douglas Haigh *lawyer*
Reinthaler, Richard Walter *lawyer*
Reiss, Steven Alan *lawyer, law educator*
†Renehan, John Boyle *lawyer*
†Resnicow, Norman Jakob *lawyer*
Reverdin, Bernard J. *lawyer*
Reynard, Muriel Joyce *lawyer*
Rice, Donald Sands *lawyer, entrepreneuer*
Rice, Joseph Lee, III, *lawyer*
Rich, R(obert) Bruce *lawyer*
Richards, David Alan *lawyer*
Richey, Kent Ramon *lawyer*
Richman, Martin Franklin *lawyer*
Rifkind, Robert S(inger) *lawyer*
Rigolosi, Elaine La Monica *lawyer, educator, consultant*
Rikon, Michael *lawyer*
Riley, Scott C. *lawyer*
Ringel, Dean *lawyer*
Ringer, James Milton *lawyer*
Ritter, Ann L. *lawyer*
Rivera, Walter *lawyer*
Roberts, Burton Bennett *lawyer, retired judge*
Roberts, Sidney I. *lawyer*
†Roberts, Thomas Raymond *lawyer*
Robertson, Edwin David *lawyer*
Robertson, Mark Allen *lawyer*
Robinson, Barbara Paul *lawyer*
Robinson, Irwin Jay *lawyer*
†Robinson, Marvin Stuart *lawyer*
Rocklen, Kathy Hellenbrand *lawyer*
†Rockwell, William Hearne *lawyer*
†Rodman, Lawrence Bernard *lawyer*
Rodman, Leroy Eli *lawyer*
Rodriguez, Vincent Angel *lawyer, director*
†Rogers, Laurence Steven *lawyer*
Rogers, Theodore Otto, Jr., *lawyer*
Rogoff, Jeffrey Scott *lawyer*
Rohrbach, Heidi A. *lawyer*
Rolfe, Ronald Stuart *lawyer*
Romans, John Niebrugge *lawyer*
Romney, Richard Bruce *lawyer*
Rooney, Paul C., Jr., *lawyer, retired*
Rootenberg, Sharyn Michele *lawyer*
Rosen, Richard Lewis *lawyer, real estate developer*
Rosenberg, Alan Stewart *lawyer*
†Rosenberg, David *lawyer*
Rosenberg, Gary Marc *lawyer*
†Rosenberg, Gerald Alan *lawyer*
Rosenberg, Jerome Roy *lawyer, accountant*
Rosenberg, Marc Steven *lawyer*
Rosenblum, William F., Jr., *lawyer*
Rosenfeld, Arthur H. *lawyer, publisher*
Rosenfeld, Steven B. *lawyer*
Rosensaft, Menachem Zwi *lawyer, writer, foundation administrator, advocate*
Rosenzweig, Charles Leonard *lawyer*
†Rosenzweig, Theodore B. *lawyer*
†Rosner, Jonathan Levi *lawyer*
†Rosow, Malcolm Bertram *lawyer*
Rosow, Stuart L. *lawyer*
†Ross, Gerald Elliott *lawyer*
Ross, Matthew *lawyer*
†Ross, Michael Aaron *lawyer*
Rossen, Jordan *lawyer*
Rostow, Charles Nicholas *lawyer, educator*
†Roth, Eric M. *lawyer*
Roth, Judith Shulman *lawyer*
Roth, Paul Norman *lawyer*
Roth, Richard Alan *lawyer*
Rothberg, Glenda Fay Morris *lawyer*
Rothenberg, Michael Andrew *lawyer, not-for-profit administrator*
Rothman, Bernard *lawyer*
Rothman, Dennis Michael *lawyer*
Rothman, Henry Isaac *lawyer*
Rover, Edward Frank *lawyer*
Rovine, Arthur William *lawyer*
Rubenstein, Joshua Seth *lawyer*
Rubin, Herbert *lawyer*
Rubin, Richard Allan *lawyer*
†Rubin, Stephen Wayne *lawyer*
Rubinstein, Frederic Armand *lawyer*
Rudoff, Sheldon *lawyer*
Ruebhausen, Oscar Melick *retired lawyer*
Ruegger, Philip T., III, *lawyer*
†Rusmisel, Stephen R. *lawyer*
Russo, Thomas Anthony *lawyer*
†Ryan, Thomas Patrick *lawyer*
Sabel, Bradley Kent *lawyer*
Sachs, David *lawyer*
†Sacks, Ira Stephen *lawyer*
Saft, Stuart Mark *lawyer*
Sahid, Joseph Robert *lawyer*
†Salomon, Philippe M. *lawyer*
Salter, Kevin Thornton *lawyer*
†Salup, Stephen *lawyer, educator*
Salvan, Sherwood Allen *lawyer*
Samuels, Leslie B. *lawyer*
Sandler, Ross *law educator*
Sanford, Eric *lawyer*
Sanseverino, Raymond Anthony *lawyer*
Sassoon, Andre Gabriel *lawyer*
Satine, Barry Roy *lawyer*
Saufer, Isaac Aaron *lawyer*
Saunders, Mark A. *lawyer*
Saunders, Paul Christopher *lawyer*
Savitt, Susan Schenkel *lawyer*
Savrin, Louis *lawyer*
†Scala, James Robert *lawyer*
Schaab, Arnold J. *lawyer*
Schachter, Oscar *lawyer, educator, arbitrator*
Schaffer, Seth Andrew *lawyer*
Schapiro, Donald *lawyer*
Schechter, Howard *lawyer*
†Scheck, Barry C. *legal association administrator, educator*
Scheiman, Eugene R. *lawyer*
Scheler, Brad Eric *lawyer*
Scher, Irving *lawyer*
†Scher, Stanley Jules *lawyer*
Scherzer, Mark P. *lawyer*
†Schiff, Kenneth Edmund *lawyer*
†Schlain, Barbara Ellen *lawyer*
Schlesinger, Sanford Joel *lawyer*
†Schlosser, Karin A. *lawyer*
Schmertz, Eric Joseph *lawyer, educator*
Schmidt, Charles Edward *lawyer*
Schmidt, Joseph W. *lawyer*
Schmitt, John Patrick *lawyer*
Schmolka, Leo Louis *law educator*
Schneider, Howard *lawyer*
Schneider, Willys Hope *lawyer*
Schneiderman, Irwin *lawyer*
†Schnurman, Alan Joseph *lawyer*
†Schoemen, Michael E. *lawyer*
Schorr, Brian Lewis *lawyer, business executive*
Schreiber, Paul Solomon *lawyer*
Schreyer, Leslie John *lawyer*
Schroeder, Edmund R. *lawyer*
Schueller, Thomas George *lawyer*
Schulhofer, Stephen Joseph *law educator, consultant*
†Schumacher, Harry Richard *lawyer*
Schwab, Harold Lee *lawyer*
†Schwab, Jeffrey A. *lawyer*
Schwab, Terrance W. *lawyer*
Schwartz, Barry Fredric *lawyer, diversified holding company executive*
Schwartz, Herbert Frederick *lawyer*
Schwartz, Marvin *lawyer*
Schwartz, Renee Gerstler *lawyer*
†Schwartz, Stephen Jay *lawyer*
Schwartz, William *lawyer, educator*
†Schwed, Peter Gregory *lawyer*
Schwind, Michael Angelo *law educator*
†Seay, J. David *lawyer, educator*
Sederbaum, Arthur David *lawyer*
Segall, Harold Abraham *lawyer*
Seidel, Selvyn *lawyer, educator*
Seidler, B(ernard) Alan *lawyer*
Seifert, Thomas Lloyd *lawyer*
Seiff, Eric A. *lawyer*
Seigel, Stuart Evan *lawyer*
Seligman, Delice *lawyer*
Seligman, Frederick *lawyer*
Seltzer, Richard C. *lawyer*
Selver, Paul Darryl *lawyer*
Semaya, Francine Levitt *lawyer*
Senzel, Martin Lee *lawyer*
Serbaroli, Francis J. *lawyer, educator, writer*
Serchuk, Ivan *lawyer*
†Serota, Irving *lawyer*
†Serota, James Ian *lawyer*
Serota, Susan Perlstadt *lawyer, educator*
Setrakian, Berge *lawyer*
Seward, George Chester *lawyer*
Seymour, Everett Hedden, Jr., *lawyer*
Shackman, Beverly Anne *lawyer*
Shaffer, Donald *lawyer*
†Shainwald, Sybil *lawyer*
†Shandell, Richard Elliot *lawyer*
Shapiro, Aleena Rieger *lawyer*
Shapiro, Isaac *lawyer*
Shapiro, Stanley K. *lawyer*
†Sharpe, Robert Francis, Jr., *lawyer*
Shaw, Melvin Robert *lawyer*
Shea, Edward Emmett *lawyer, educator, author*
Shea, James William *lawyer*
Shechtman, Ronald H. *lawyer*
†Sheehan, Robert C. *lawyer*
Sheikh, Kemal A. *lawyer*
Shen, Michael *lawyer*
†Shenker, Joseph C. *lawyer*
Shepard, Robert M. *lawyer, investment banker, engineer*
Shepherd, John Michael *lawyer*
Shientag, Florence Perlow *lawyer*
Shipper, David W. *lawyer*
Shorter, James Russell, Jr., *lawyer*
Shoss, Cynthia Renée *lawyer*
Shyer, John D. *lawyer*
Sidamon-Eristoff, Constantine *lawyer*
Siegel, Edward M. *lawyer*
Siegel, Jeffrey Norton *lawyer*
Siegel, Stanley *lawyer, educator*
Siffert, John Sand *lawyer, educator, writer*
Sigmond, Carol Ann *lawyer*
Silberberg, Richard Howard *lawyer*
Silkenat, James Robert *lawyer*
Siller, Stephen I. *lawyer*
Silverberg, Jay Lloyd *lawyer*
Silverberg, Michael Joel *lawyer*
Silverman, Arthur Charles *lawyer*
†Silverman, Jennifer D. *lawyer*
†Silverman, Leon *lawyer*
Silverman, Moses *lawyer*
Simmons, Peter Lawrence *lawyer*
Simon, Michael Scott *lawyer*
Simone, Joseph R. *lawyer*
Simons, Albert, III, *lawyer*
Sinsheimer, Warren Jack *lawyer*
Siskind, Arthur *lawyer, director*
Siskind, Donald Henry *lawyer*
Skigen, Patricia Sue *lawyer*
Skolnick, Jerome H. *law educator*
†Slade, Jeffrey Christopher *lawyer*
†Sladkus, Harvey Ira *lawyer*
†Slater, Alice Joan *lawyer*
Small, Jonathan Andrew *lawyer*
Smalley, David Vincent *lawyer*
Smith, Bradley Youle *lawyer*
Smith, Edward Paul, Jr., *lawyer*
†Smith, Edwin Lloyd *lawyer*
Smith, Morton Alan *lawyer*
†Smith, Robert Blakeman *lawyer*
Smith, Robert Everett *lawyer*
†Smith, Robert Sherlock *lawyer, educator*
Smith, Vincent Milton *lawyer, designer, Feng Shui lecturer, consultant, writer*
Smoak, Evan L. *lawyer*
Snow, Charles *lawyer*
†Sobel, Gerald *lawyer*
†Solomon, Stephen L. *lawyer*
Sorkin, David James *lawyer*
Sorkin, Laurence Truman *lawyer*
Sovern, Michael Ira *law educator*
Soyster, Margaret Blair *lawyer*
Spanbock, Maurice Samuel *lawyer*
Spatt, Robert Edward *lawyer*
Spear, Harvey M. *lawyer*
Spelfogel, Evan J. *lawyer, educator*
Sperling, Allan George *lawyer*
Spero, C. Michael *lawyer*
Spiegel, Jerrold Bruce *lawyer*
Spillane, Dennis Kevin *lawyer*
†Spivack, Edith Irene *lawyer*
†Spivak, Leonard A. *lawyer*
Squire, Walter Charles *lawyer*
†Staffaroni, Robert J. *lawyer*
†Stamm, Charles H. *lawyer*
Starer, Brian Douglas *lawyer*
†Stark, Richard Alvin *lawyer*
†Stark, Robert J. *lawyer*
Stathis, Nicholas John *lawyer*
†Stebbings, Robert Yeo *lawyer, partner*
†Steigman, Ernest R. *lawyer*
Stein, Stephen William *lawyer*
Steinberg, Howard Eli *lawyer, diversified financial services company executive*
Stephenson, Alan Clements *lawyer*
Stern, Peter R. *lawyer*
Sternman, Joel W. *lawyer*
Steuer, Richard Marc *lawyer*
Stever, Donald Winfred *lawyer*
Stewart, Richard Burleson *law educator*
†Steyer, Hume Richmond *lawyer*
†Stimmel, Todd Richard *lawyer, business executive*
Stoll, Neal Richard *lawyer*
Stone, David Philip *lawyer*
Stone, Merrill Brent *lawyer*
†Stratakis, Christ *lawyer*
Stratton, Walter Love *lawyer*
Strauss, Gary Joseph *lawyer*
†Streicker, Richard Daniel *lawyer, record company executive*
Strickon, Harvey Alan *lawyer*
Stringer, Ronald E. *lawyer, educator*
†Strock, Marcus *lawyer*
Strom, Milton Gary *lawyer*
Strossen, Nadine *law educator, human rights activist*
†Strum, Jay Gerson *lawyer*
Struve, Guy Miller *lawyer*
Stuart, Alice Melissa *lawyer*
Sugarman, Irwin J. *lawyer*
Sugarman, Robert Gary *lawyer*
Sun, Jeffrey C. *legal educator*
Sussman, Alexander Ralph *lawyer*
Sutter, Laurence Brener *lawyer*
Swain, Laura Taylor *judge*
†Swardenski, Jay Gordon *lawyer*
Sweeney, Thomas Joseph, Jr., *lawyer*
Swire, James Bennett *lawyer*
Szabo, Elizabeth MaryAnn *lawyer*
†Tallackson, Jeffrey Stephen *lawyer*
Tancredi, Laurence Richard *law and psychiatry educator, physician*
†Tanenbaum, Gerald Stephen *lawyer*
†Tanenbaum, Jeffrey L. *lawyer*
Tarnoff, Jerome *lawyer*
Taylor, Job, III, *lawyer*
†Taylor, John Chestnut, III, *lawyer*
Taylor, Richard Trelore *retired lawyer*
†Taylor, Willard B. *lawyer*
†Tehan, John Bashir *lawyer*
Teich, Howard Bernard *lawyer, activist, public affairs specialist*
Teiman, Richard B. *lawyer*
Teplen, Philip H. *lawyer*
Terry, Frederick Arthur, Jr., *lawyer*
†Terry, James Joseph, Jr., *lawyer*
Testa, Michael Harold *lawyer*
Thackeray, Jonathan E. *lawyer*
Thalacker, Arbie Robert *lawyer, director*
Thaler, Craig H. *lawyer*
†Thomas, Jeremiah Lindsay, III, *lawyer*
Thomas, Robert Morton, Jr., *lawyer*
Thomas, Roger Warren *lawyer*
Thompson, Katherine Genevieve *lawyer*
Thompson, Loran Tyson *lawyer*
†Thompson, Marttie Louis *lawyer*
Thoyer, Judith Reinhardt *lawyer*
†Tighe, Maria Theresa *project manager*
Tillinghast, David Rollhaus *lawyer*
†Toback, Arthur Malcolm *lawyer*
Todd, Ronald Gary *lawyer*
Tract, Marc Mitchell *lawyer*
Tracy, Janet Ruth *legal educator, librarian*
Tramontine, John Orlando *retired lawyer*
Traube, Victoria Gilbert *lawyer*
Treadway, James Curran Erik Corbett *lawyer, investment company executive, former government official*
Treanor, William Michael *law educator*
†Tricarico, Joseph Archangelo *lawyer*
Tritter, Daniel F. *lawyer, writer*
Trott, Dennis C(harles) *lawyer*
Tulchin, David Bruce *lawyer*
Turner, E. Deane *lawyer*
Ulrey, Prescott David *lawyer*
Underberg, Mark Alan *lawyer*
Uram, Gerald Robert *lawyer*
Urowsky, Richard J. *lawyer*
Vachss, Andrew Henry *lawyer, author, juvenile justice and child abuse consultant*
Van Gundy, Gregory Frank *lawyer*
Vanni, Robert John *lawyer*
Varet, Michael A. *lawyer*
Vassallo, Edward E. *lawyer*
Vassallo, John A. *lawyer*
†Vassil, John Charles *lawyer*
Vega, Matias Alfonso *lawyer*
Vernon, Darryl Mitchell *lawyer*
Versfelt, David Scott *lawyer*
†Victor, A. Paul *lawyer*
Viener, John D. *lawyer*
Vig, Vernon Edward *lawyer*
Viktora, Richard Emil *lawyer*
Vitkowsky, Vincent Joseph *lawyer*
†Vladeck, Judith Pomarlen *lawyer*
Vogel, Howard Stanley *lawyer*
von Mehren, Robert Brandt *lawyer, retired*
Wachtel, Norman Jay *lawyer*
Wailand, George *lawyer*
Wainwright, Carroll Livingston, Jr., *lawyer*
Waks, Jay Warren *lawyer*
Wald, Bernard Joseph *lawyer*
Waldman, Seymour Morton *lawyer*
†Walinsky, Adam *lawyer, foundation administrator*
†Walker, John Lockwood *lawyer*
Wallace, Nora Ann *lawyer*
Wallace, Walter C. *lawyer, government official*
Wallach, Eric Jean *lawyer*
†Wallach, Evan Jonathan *judge, international law educator*
Wallance, Gregory J. *lawyer*
†Wallman, Lester *lawyer*
Walpin, Gerald *lawyer*
Wang, Albert Huai-En *lawyer*
Warden, John L. *lawyer*
Warren, William Bradford *lawyer*
†Warwick, Kathleen Ann *corporate lawyer*
Washburn, David Thacher *lawyer*
Waterman, William, Jr., *lawyer*
Watson, Kipp Elliott *lawyer*
Watson, Solomon Brown, IV, *lawyer, business executive*
†Wattman, Malcolm Peter *lawyer*
Watts, David Eide *lawyer*
Weiksner, Sandra S. *lawyer*
Weinberg, Herschel Mayer *lawyer*
†Weinberg, Jeffrey J. *lawyer*
Weinberg, Steven Lewis *lawyer*
Weinberger, Harold Paul *lawyer*
Weiner, Andrew Jay *lawyer*
Weiner, Earl David *lawyer*
Weiner, Stephen Arthur *lawyer*
Weinrich, Johnathan Edward *lawyer*
Weinschel, Alan Jay *lawyer*
Weinstein, Ruth Joseph *lawyer*
Weinstock, Leonard *lawyer*
Weir, Peter Frank *lawyer*
Weisbrod, Carl *lawyer, public official*
Weiser, Martin Jay *lawyer*
Weiss, Jonathan Arthur *lawyer*
Weiss, Lawrence N. *lawyer*
Weld, Jonathan Minot *lawyer*
Welikson, Jeffrey Alan *lawyer*
Wellington, Harry Hillel *lawyer, educator*
†Wells, Andrew Norman *lawyer*
Welt, Philip Stanley *lawyer, consultant*
Wender, Ira Tensard *lawyer*
Werner, Robert L. *lawyer, consultant*
Wesely, Edwin Joseph *lawyer*
†West, Stephen Kingsbury *lawyer, director*
Wexelbaum, Michael *lawyer*
Whelchel, Betty Anne *lawyer*
White, Harry Edward, Jr., *lawyer*
White, John Patrick *lawyer*
†White, Katherine Patricia *lawyer*
White, Mary Jo *lawyer*

Whitman, Charles S., III, *lawyer*
Whoriskey, Robert Donald *lawyer*
Wilcox, John Caven *lawyer, corporate consultant*
†Wildes, Leon *lawyer, educator*
†Wilensky, Saul *lawyer*
Wilkinson, John Hart *lawyer*
Williamson, Douglas Franklin, Jr., *lawyer*
†Williamson, Walter *lawyer*
Willinger, Lowell David *lawyer*
Willis, William Ervin *lawyer*
Wilson, Paul Holliday, Jr., *lawyer*
Wimpfheimer, Michael Clark *lawyer*
Windels, Paul, Jr., *lawyer*
†Winfield, Richard Neill *lawyer*
Wing, John Russell *lawyer*
Winger, Ralph O. *lawyer*
Winslade, Thomas Edwin *lawyer*
Winterer, Philip Steele *lawyer*
Wise, Aaron Noah *lawyer*
†Wiseman, Michael Martin *lawyer*
†Wishingrad, Jay Marc *lawyer*
Witherwax, Charles Halsey *lawyer, arbitrator, mediator*
Witkin, Eric Douglas *lawyer*
Witmeyer, John Jacob, III, *lawyer*
†Wolf, Diane R. *law consultant*
Wolf, Gary Wickert *lawyer*
Wolfe, James Ronald *lawyer*
Wolff, Jesse David *lawyer*
Wolkoff, Eugene Arnold *lawyer*
Wolson, Craig Alan *lawyer*
†Wood, David Clarence *lawyer*
Worenklein, Jacob Joshua *lawyer*
Wray, Cecil, Jr., *lawyer*
Wulf, Melvin Lawrence *lawyer*
Wyckoff, E. Lisk, Jr., *lawyer*
Yamin, Michael Geoffrey *lawyer*
†Yeager, Dennis Randall *lawyer*
Yelenick, Mary Therese *lawyer*
Yerman, Fredric Warren *lawyer*
Yodowitz, Edward Jay *lawyer*
Young, Alice *lawyer*
Young, John Edward *lawyer*
Youngwood, Alfred Donald *lawyer*
Zaitzeff, Roger Michael *lawyer*
Zammit, Joseph Paul *lawyer*
Zaslowsky, David Paul *lawyer*
Zauderer, Mark Carl *lawyer*
Zedrosser, Joseph John *lawyer*
Zeligson, Sheryl *lawyer*
†Zeller, Paul William *lawyer*
Zerin, Steven David *lawyer*
†Ziegler, Henry Steinway *lawyer*
Ziegler, John Augustus, Jr., *lawyer*
Zifchak, William C. *lawyer*
Zimmett, Mark Paul *lawyer, educator*
Zirinsky, Bruce R. *lawyer*
†Zissu, Roger L. *lawyer*
Zivin, Norman H. *lawyer*
Zoeller, Donald J. *lawyer*
Zoogman, Nicholas Jay *lawyer*
Zornow, David M. *lawyer*
Zucker, Howard *lawyer*
†Zuckerman, Joseph *lawyer*
†Zuckerman, Paul Herbert *lawyer*
Zukerman, Michael *lawyer*

Newark
†Reid, James Edward *lawyer*

Newburgh
†Zeisel, Laura *lawyer, educator*

Niagara Falls
Berrigan, Patrick Joseph *lawyer*
Levine, David Ethan *lawyer*

Nyack
†Cane, Barbara Haak *lawyer*
Cember, M. Nathan *lawyer, speaker*

Old Chatham
†Severs, Charles A., III, *lawyer*

Oneida
Matthews, William D(oty) *lawyer, consumer products manufacturing company executive*
†Rudnick, Marvin Jack *lawyer*

Orangeburg
Rivet, Diana Wittmer *lawyer, developer*

Orchard Park
Sullivan, Mortimer Allen, Jr., *lawyer*

Ossining
Daly, William Joseph *lawyer*

Oswego
Greene, Stephen Craig *lawyer*

Oyster Bay
Bernstein, Jacob *lawyer*
Ott, Gilbert Russell, Jr., *lawyer*
Robinson, Edward T., III, *lawyer*

Patchogue
†Cartier, Rudolph Henri, Jr., *lawyer, legal educator*
Esteve, Edward V. *lawyer*

Pearl River
Meyer, Irwin Stephan *lawyer, accountant*

Perry
Kelly, Michael Joseph *lawyer*

Pittsford
Braunsdorf, Paul Raymond *lawyer*
George, Richard Neill *retired lawyer*
Hampson, Thomas Meredith *lawyer*
†Hartman, James Matthew *lawyer*
Scutt, Robert Carl *lawyer*
Snyder, Donald Edward *corporate executive*
Stonehill, Eric *lawyer*
Turri, Joseph A. *lawyer*
Willett, Thomas Edward *lawyer*

Pleasantville
Ahrensfeld, Thomas Frederick *lawyer*
†Campriello, Christina Matthews *lawyer, librarian*

Pomona
Fisch, Edith L. *lawyer*

Port Chester
Levin, Jeffrey L. *lawyer*
Messina, JoAnn L. *court administrator*

Port Jefferson
Hindin, Seymour *lawyer*

Port Washington
Feldman, Jay Newman *lawyer, telecommunications executive*
Forman, James Douglas *lawyer*
Ullman, Leo Solomon *lawyer*

Poughkeepsie
†Adin, Richard H(enry) *lawyer, editor, publisher*
Dietz, Robert Barron *lawyer*
Doherty, John Francis *criminal justice educator*
†Kenny, Philip William *lawyer*
Kranis, Michael David *lawyer, judge*
LaRose, Keith Vernon *lawyer*
O'Neil, D. James *lawyer*
Ostertag, Robert Louis *lawyer*
Shatz, Phillip *lawyer, banker, insurance executive*
Taphorn, Joseph Bernard *lawyer*
Wallace, Herbert Norman *lawyer*

Purchase
†Andrews, David Ralph *lawyer*
Gioffre, Bruno Joseph *lawyer*
Kelly, Edmund Joseph *lawyer, investment banker*
†Lyons, Gary George *lawyer*
†McKenna, Matthew Morgan *lawyer*
Pauley, Matthew Alfred *law educator*
Wallach, Ira David *lawyer, business executive*

Queensbury
Sleight, Virginia Mae *lawyer*

Rhinebeck
Melley, Steven Michael *lawyer*

Riverhead
Kelley, Christopher Donald *lawyer*

Rochester
Blyth, John E. *lawyer, educator*
Buckley, Michael Francis *lawyer*
Clement, Thomas Earl *retired lawyer*
Clifford, Eugene Thomas *lawyer*
Colby, William Michael *lawyer*
Corcoran, Christopher Holmes *lawyer*
†Dolin, Lonny H. *lawyer*
Doyle, Justin P. *lawyer*
†Evans, Eric Alan *lawyer*
Goldman, Joel J. *retired lawyer*
Gootnick, Margery Fischbein *lawyer*
Gross, Bryon William *lawyer*
†Hallenbeck, Alfred M. *lawyer*
Harris, Wayne Manley *lawyer*
Heyman, Sidney *lawyer, educator*
Jacobson, Peter A. *lawyer*
†Kelly, Mary Kathleen *lawyer, researcher*
Kraus, Sherry Stokes *lawyer*
Kurland, Harold Arthur *lawyer*
Law, Michael R. *lawyer*
Lundback, Staffan Bengt Gunnar *lawyer*
Lustig, Douglas James *lawyer*
†Madden, Neal D. *lawyer*
†Mayka, Stephen Paul *lawyer*
McCrory, John Brooks *retired lawyer*
Moore, James Conklin *lawyer*
Morris, James E. *lawyer, judge, educator*
Morrison, Patrice B. *lawyer*
Palermo, Anthony Robert *lawyer*
Paley, Gerald Larry *lawyer*
†Payment, Kenneth Arnold *lawyer*
†Rosenbaum, Richard Merrill *lawyer*
Rosner, Leonard Allen *lawyer*
Schumacher, Jon Lee *lawyer*
Servis, William George *lawyer*
Smith, Jules Louis *lawyer*
Speranza, Paul Samuel, Jr., *lawyer*
Stewart, Sue S. *lawyer*
Swett, Albert Hersey *retired lawyer, business executive, consultant*
Twietmeyer, Don Henry *lawyer*
†Vick, Paul Ashton *lawyer*
†Vigdor, Justin Leonard *lawyer*
Waite, Stephen Holden *lawyer*
†Whitaker, Benjamin Palmer, Jr., *lawyer*
†Wild, Robert Warren *lawyer*
Witmer, George Robert, Jr., *lawyer*

Rome
Griffith, Emlyn Irving *lawyer*

Roslyn
Zeitlan, Marilyn Labb *lawyer*

Rye
Dixon, Paul Edward *lawyer, metal products and manufacturing company executive*

Rye Brook
Eck, Robert Joseph *lawyer*

Salamanca
Brady, Thomas Carl *lawyer*

Sands Point
Busner, Philip H. *retired lawyer*
Hoynes, Louis LeNoir, Jr., *lawyer*

Saratoga Springs
†Willig, William Paul *lawyer*

Scarsdale
†Angel, Dennis *lawyer*
Beuchert, Edward William *lawyer*
Callaghan, Georgann Mary *lawyer*

†Ellis, James Henry *lawyer, management consultant*
Gerber, Roger Alan *lawyer, business consultant*
Hoffman, Richard M. *lawyer*
Kanter, Carl Irwin *retired lawyer*
King, Robert Lucien *lawyer*
Korzenik, Sidney S. *lawyer*
†Liegl, Joseph Leslie *lawyer*
Macchia, Vincent Michael *lawyer*
O'Brien, Edward Ignatius *private investor, corporation director*
Perko, Kenneth Albert, Jr., *lawyer, art dealer*
Sheehan, Larry John *lawyer*

Schenectady
Grace, Ellen Maria *attorney*
Levine, Sanford Harold *lawyer*
Mueller, Philip Winfield *lawyer*
Taub, Eli Irwin *arbitrator, mediator, lawyer*
Yablon, Jay Russell *lawyer*

Scottsville
Williams, Henry Ward, Jr., *lawyer, writer*

Seagate
Levitt, Sidney Bernard *lawyer*

Sherrill
Campanie, Samuel John *lawyer*

Skaneateles
Weiss, Rhett Louis *business executive, lawyer*

Smithtown
†Brooks, Sondra *lawyer*
Dowis, Lenore *lawyer*
Goodman, Richard Shalem *lawyer, orthopedic surgeon*
†Holland, Marvin Arthur *lawyer, educator*
Spellman, Thomas Joseph, Jr., *lawyer*

Somers
Lemke, Judith A. *lawyer*
†McGuire, Pamela Cottam *lawyer*

South Richmond Hill
Scheich, John F. *lawyer*

Southampton
Lopez, David *lawyer*

Spring Valley
†Barr, Harvey Stephen *lawyer*

Staten Island
†Fusco, John Anthony *lawyer*
Howard, Davis Jonathan *lawyer, educator, writer*
Humphries, Edward Francis *lawyer*
Klingle, Philip Anthony *law librarian*
Landron, Michel John *lawyer*
Marra, Ralph Peter *lawyer*
Miller, Claire Cody *lawyer, mediator*
Neuberger, Jerome M. *lawyer*

Stony Point
Diederich, Michael David, Jr., *lawyer*

Suffern
Stack, Daniel *lawyer, financial consultant*

Syosset
Bermas, Stephen *lawyer*

Syracuse
Ackerman, Kenneth Edward *lawyer, educator*
Barclay, H(ugh) Douglas *lawyer, former state senator*
Bodow, Wayne R. *lawyer*
Bogart, William Harry *lawyer*
Bradley, Roger William *lawyer*
Brickwedde, Richard James *lawyer*
†Bullock, Stephen C. *lawyer*
Burstein, Alan Stuart *lawyer*
Burstyn, Harold Lewis *lawyer*
Cirando, John Anthony *lawyer*
DiLorenzo, Louis Patrick *lawyer*
Dove, Jeffrey Austin *lawyer*
Fiske, Jordan Jay *lawyer, retired prosecutor*
Fitzpatrick, James David *lawyer*
Gaal, John *lawyer*
Gerber, Edward F. *lawyer, educator*
Gilman, Karen Frenzel *legal assistant*
Greene, Arthur M. *lawyer*
†Grizanti, Anthony J. *lawyer*
Hancock, Stewart F., Jr., *law educator, judge*
Hayes, David Michael *lawyer*
†Heath, Joseph John *lawyer*
Herzog, Peter Emilius *retired legal educator*
Hole, Richard Douglas *lawyer*
Hubbard, Peter Lawrence *lawyer*
†King, Bernard T. *lawyer*
Kopp, Robert Walter *lawyer*
Kram, Richard Corey *lawyer*
†Michaels, Beverly Ann *lawyer*
†O'Connor, Michael E. *lawyer*
Paquette, Steven A. *lawyer*
†Pellow, David Matthew *lawyer*
Rivette, Francis Robert *lawyer*
†Rosenthal, Alan *lawyer*
†Rothman, Robert Pierson *lawyer*
†Shulman, Barry Martin *lawyer*
†Simmons, Doreen Anne *lawyer*
†Simmons, Harvey Owen, III, *lawyer*
†Sparkes, James Edward *lawyer*
Traylor, Robert Arthur *lawyer*
Wladis, Mark Neil *lawyer*
Zimmerman, Aaron Mark *lawyer*
Zimmerman, Golda *lawyer, educator*

Tarrytown
†Mach, Joseph David *lawyer*

Ticonderoga
Howe, Edwin A(lberts), Jr., *lawyer*

Troy
†Beeler, Patricia *court administrator*

Burch, Mary Seelye Quinn *law librarian, consultant*
Finkel, Sanford Norman *lawyer*
Frost, Jerome Kenneth *lawyer*
Jones, E. Stewart, Jr., *lawyer*
Marinstein, Elliott Fred *lawyer*

Tupper Lake
Johnson, David Wesley *lawyer*

Uniondale
Beck, Leland S. *lawyer*
†Bennett, James Davison *lawyer*
Cassidy, David Michael *lawyer*
Eilen, Howard Scott *lawyer, mediator*
†Good, Douglas Jay *lawyer*
Gracin, Hank *lawyer*
†Kessler, Lawrence W. *law educator, lawyer*
Kestenbaum, Harold Lee *lawyer*
Pratt, George Cheney *law educator, retired federal judge*

Utica
Brennan, John Joseph *lawyer, legal administrator*

Valatie
Benamati, Dennis Charles *librarian, editor, consultant*

Valley Stream
Blakeman, Royal Edwin *lawyer*
Levine, Marilyn Markovich *lawyer, arbitrator*

Vestal
McGuire, John Thomas *lawyer, educator*

Walden
Gubits, David Barry *lawyer*

Wappingers Falls
Haynes, Paul R. *lawyer*

Waterford
Glavin, A. Rita Chandellier (Mrs. James Henry Glavin III) *lawyer*
Glavin, James Henry, III, *lawyer*

Watertown
Marsh, Leonard Roy *lawyer*
Militello, Samuel Philip *lawyer*

Watkins Glen
Argetsinger, Cameron R. *lawyer*

West Babylon
†Weinreb, Michael Leonard *lawyer*

Westbury
Boes, Lawrence William *lawyer*
†Ciovacco, Robert John *lawyer*
Dwyer, Diane Marie *lawyer, judge*
†Whiteman, Robert Gordon *lawyer*

White Plains
Alin, Robert David *lawyer*
†Bavero, Ronald Joseph *lawyer, legal educator*
Berlin, Alan Daniel *lawyer, international energy and legal consultant*
†Berman, Henry Stephen *lawyer*
†Blank, Philip Bernardini *lawyer, educator*
Bodnar, Peter O. *lawyer*
Carey, John *lawyer, judge*
Carlucci, Joseph P. *lawyer*
D'Aloise, Lawrence T., Jr., *lawyer*
Danziger, Joel Bernard *lawyer*
†Doernberg, Donald Lane *law educator*
Doyle, Dennis T. *lawyer*
Feder, Robert *lawyer*
†Fleming, Robert Burke *law educator, lawyer*
Gjertsen, O. Gerard *lawyer*
Greenspan, Leon Joseph *lawyer*
Greenspan, Michael Evan *lawyer*
†Guida, Toni M. *lawyer*
Halpern, Philip Morgan *lawyer*
Jacobson, Sandra W. *lawyer*
Keane, Thomas J. *lawyer*
Klein, Paul E. *lawyer*
Kurzman, Robert Graham *lawyer, educator*
Levine, Steven Jon *lawyer*
Longo, Ronald Anthony *lawyer*
†Madden, M. Stuart *lawyer*
Maffeo, Vincent Anthony *lawyer, executive*
Munneke, Gary Arthur *law educator, consultant*
Payson, Martin F. *lawyer*
†Pitegoff, Thomas Michael *lawyer*
†Robinson, Nicholas Adams *lawyer, educator*
Rosenberg, Michael *lawyer*
Ryan, Robert Davis *lawyer*
†Scheinkman, Alan David *lawyer, legal educator*
Silverberg, Steven Mark *lawyer*
Sloan, F(rank) Blaine *law educator*
Taft, Nathaniel Belmont *lawyer*
Topol, Robin April Levitt *lawyer*

Williamsville
Ross, Christopher T.W. *lawyer*

Wolcott
Bartlett, Cody Blake *lawyer, educator*

Woodbury
Mangia, Angelo James *lawyer*

Woodmere
Jeffries, Seymour Barnard *lawyer*
Raab, Ira Jerry *lawyer, judge*

Yonkers
Connors, James Patrick *lawyer*

NORTH CAROLINA

Arden
Seagle, J. Harold *lawyer*

Asheboro
Burton, Bernard Ottway *lawyer*

Asheville
Bissette, Winston Louis, Jr., *lawyer, mayor*
Chidnese, Patrick N. *retired lawyer*
Cogburn, Max Oliver *lawyer*
Davis, Roy Walton, Jr., *lawyer*
Dillard, John Robert *lawyer*
Frue, William Calhoun *lawyer*
Gantt, Charles David *lawyer*
Hamilton, Jackson Douglas *lawyer*
Howell, George Washington *lawyer, consultant*
Hyde, Herbert Lee *lawyer*
Johnston, John Devereaux, Jr., *law educator, retired*
Lavelle, Brian Francis David *lawyer*
Lawrence, Betty Tenn *lawyer*
Leake, Larry Bruce *lawyer*
Sharpe, Keith Yount *retired lawyer*
†Starnes, Oscar Edwin, Jr., *lawyer*
Wilson, Thomas Douglas, Jr., *lawyer*

Beaufort
†Tilghman, Carl Lewis *lawyer*

Black Mountain
Le Van, Nolan Gerald *lawyer, consultant*

Buies Creek
Davis, Ferd Leary, Jr., *law educator, lawyer, consultant*
Whichard, Willis Padgett *law educator, retired state supreme court justice*

Burlington
Slayton, John Howard *lawyer, trust company executive*

Carthage
†Lapping, Sherwod Foster *lawyer*

Cary
†Brooks, David Victor *lawyer*
Montgomery, Charles Harvey *lawyer*
Reinhard, Steven Ira *lawyer*
Taylor, Marvin Edward, Jr., *lawyer*

Chapel Hill
Boyarsky, Saul *lawyer, forensic urologist, physiologist, educator*
Broun, Kenneth Stanley *lawyer, educator*
Brower, David John *lawyer, urban planner, educator*
Campbell, William Aubrey *law educator*
Crassweller, Robert Doell *retired lawyer, writer*
Crohn, Max Henry, Jr., *lawyer*
Daye, Charles Edward *law educator*
†Dellinger, Anne Maxwell *law educator*
Freedman, Irving Melvin *lawyer*
Gressman, Eugene *lawyer*
Hardin, Paul, III, *law educator*
Haskell, Paul Gershon *retired law educator*
Herman-Giddens, Gregory *lawyer*
Hultquist, Steven John *lawyer*
Lawrence, David Michael *lawyer, educator*
Lilley, Albert Frederick *retired lawyer*
Loeb, Ben Fohl, Jr., *lawyer, educator*
†Mann, Richard Allan *law educator*
†Sechriest, Mary Pauline *lawyer*
Wegner, Judith Welch *law educator, former dean*

Charlotte
Ayscue, Edwin Osborne, Jr., *lawyer*
Bell, Paul Buckner *lawyer*
†Belthoff, Richard Charles, Jr., *lawyer*
Bernstein, Mark R. *retired lawyer*
†Blackburn, Richard Wallace *lawyer*
†Brackett, Martin Luther, Jr., *lawyer*
Bragg, Ellis Meredith, Jr., *lawyer*
Buchan, Jonathan Edward, Jr., *lawyer*
Buckley, Charles Robinson, III, *lawyer*
†Calloway, Mark T. *lawyer, former prosecutor*
†Cannon, Thomas Roberts *lawyer*
Chambers, Julius LeVonne *lawyer*
Chesson, Calvin White *lawyer, educator*
†Connette, Edward Grant, III, *lawyer*
†Cowell, Marion Aubrey, Jr., *lawyer*
Dagenhart, Larry Jones *lawyer*
†Dunn, Jackson Thomas, Jr., *lawyer, legal educator*
Durham, J(oseph) Porter, Jr., *lawyer, educator*
Edwards, Mark Brownlow *lawyer*
Hanna, George Verner, III, *lawyer*
†Harris, Charles Marcus *lawyer*
Linker, Raymond Otho, Jr., *lawyer*
Loughridge, John Halsted, Jr., *lawyer*
McBryde, Neill Gregory *lawyer*
†McClure, M. DeVondria *lawyer*
†Miller, John Randolph *lawyer*
Monge, Jay Parry *lawyer*
Newitt, John Garwood, Jr., *lawyer*
†Orsbon, Richard Anthony *lawyer*
Penn, Philip Julian *lawyer*
†Polking, Paul J. *lawyer*
Preston, James Young *lawyer*
†Pruden, James Norfleet, III, *lawyer*
†Raper, William Cranford *lawyer*
Sink, Robert C. *lawyer*
Taylor, David Brooke *lawyer, banker*
Thigpen, Richard Elton, Jr., *lawyer*
Thompson, Sydnor, Jr., (Charles William Sydnor Thompson Jr.) *lawyer, mediator, arbitrator*
Van Allen, William Kent *lawyer*
Van Alstyne, Vance Brownell *arbitration management consultant*
Vinroot, Richard Allen *lawyer, mayor*
Waggoner, William Johnson *lawyer*
Wagner, Kenneth Lynn *lawyer*
Walker, Clarence Wesley *lawyer*
Whelpley, David B., Jr., *lawyer*
Wood, William McBrayer *lawyer*
Woolard, William Leon *lawyer, electrical distributing company executive*
Youngs, Jennifer Ann *lawyer*
Zeller, Michael Eugene *lawyer*

Cherokee
Martin, Harry Corpening *lawyer, retired state supreme court justice*

Cherryville
Huffstetler, Palmer Eugene *lawyer*

Cullowhee
Wilson, LeVon Edward *law educator, lawyer*

Dunn
†Pope, Patrick Harris *lawyer, business executive*

Durham
†Admay, Catherine Adcock *law lecturer, researcher*
Bartlett, Katharine Tiffany *law educator*
Carpenter, Charles Francis *lawyer*
Carrington, Paul DeWitt *lawyer, educator*
Christie, George Custis *lawyer, educator, author*
Cox, James D. *law educator*
Fisher, Stewart Wayne *lawyer*
Havighurst, Clark Canfield *law educator*
Holder, Angela Roddey *lawyer, educator*
Horowitz, Donald Leonard *lawyer, educator, researcher, political scientist, arbitrator*
†Lewis, David Olin *lawyer, educator*
Markham, Charles Buchanan *retired lawyer*
Maxwell, Richard Callender *lawyer, educator*
†McCusker, Paul Donald *lawyer, educator*
McMahon, John Alexander *law educator*
Mosteller, Robert P. *law educator*
Priest, Peter H. *lawyer*
Robertson, Horace Bascomb, Jr., *retired law educator*
Rowe, Thomas Dudley, Jr., *law educator*
Schwarcz, Steven Lance *law educator, lawyer*
Shimm, Melvin Gerald *law educator*
†Thompson, Sharon Andrea *lawyer*
Wicker, R. David, Jr., *lawyer*

Eden
†Doss, Marion Kenneth *lawyer*

Elkin
Gillespie, James Davis *lawyer*

Fairview
Rhynedance, Harold Dexter, Jr., *lawyer, consultant*

Fayetteville
†Rand, Anthony Eden *lawyer*
Ruppe, Arthur Maxwell *lawyer*
Townsend, William Jackson *lawyer*

Gastonia
Stott, Grady Bernell *lawyer*

Greensboro
Capone, Lucien, III, *lawyer*
Davis, Herbert Owen *lawyer*
Floyd, Jack William *lawyer*
Galloway, Hunter Henderson, III, *lawyer, small business owner*
Glover, Durant Murrell *lawyer*
Gumbiner, Kenneth Jay *lawyer*
Harrington, Ellis Jackson, Jr., *lawyer*
Hunter, Bynum Merritt *lawyer*
Koonce, Neil Wright *lawyer*
†Lloyd, Robert Blackwell, Jr., *lawyer*
Melvin, Charles Edward, Jr., *lawyer*
Oakley, Joel Neese *lawyer*
†St. George, Nicholas James *lawyer, manufactured housing company executive*
Schell, Braxton *lawyer*
Smith, Lanty L(loyd) *lawyer, business executive*
Swan, George Steven *law educator*
Turner, James Reginald *lawyer*

Greenville
†Stevens, David Boyette *law educator*

Hertford
Cole, Janice McKenzie *former prosecutor*

Hickory
Smith, Young Merritt, Jr., *lawyer*

High Point
McAllister, Kenneth Wayne *lawyer*
Sheahan, Robert Emmett *lawyer, consultant*

Jacksonville
†Taylor, Vaughan Edward *lawyer, educator*

Jamestown
Schmitt, William Allen *lawyer*

Kinston
Braswell, Edwin Maurice, Jr., *lawyer*
†Jones, Paul Lawrence *lawyer*

Kitty Hawk
Tucker, Don Eugene *retired lawyer*

Lake Junaluska
Garrett, William Walton *retired law educator*

Leland
Barnhardt, Zeb Elonzo, Jr., *lawyer*

Lenoir
Flaherty, David Thomas, Jr., *lawyer*

Marion
Burgin, Charles Edward *lawyer*

Murphy
Bata, Rudolph Andrew, Jr., *lawyer*

New Bern
Davis, James Lee *lawyer*
†Flowers, Kent Gordon, Jr., *lawyer*
Overholt, Hugh Robert *lawyer, retired army officer*

Newton
Cutchin, John Franks *lawyer*

Raleigh
Blackburn, James B., III, *lawyer*
Byrd, Stephen Timothy *lawyer*
Carlton, Alfred Pershing, Jr., *lawyer*
Carter, Jean Gordon *lawyer*
†Currin, Samuel Thomas *lawyer, former judge*
Dannelly, William David *lawyer*
†Darrow, Mary J. *federal lawyer*
Davis, Egbert Lawrence, III, *lawyer*
Davis, Thomas Hill, Jr., *lawyer*
Dixon, Wright Tracy, Jr., *retired lawyer*
Edwards, Charles Archibald *lawyer*
Ellis, Lester Neal, Jr., *lawyer*
Ellis, Richard W. *lawyer*
Glass, Fred Stephen *lawyer*
Graham, William Edgar, Jr., *lawyer, retired utility company executive*
Graham, William Thomas *lawyer*
Hall, John Thomas *lawyer, educator*
Harazin, William Dennis *lawyer*
†Hargrove, Wade Hampton *lawyer*
Hensey, Charles McKinnon *retired lawyer*
†Hoon, Peggy Ellen *lawyer, librarian*
Huggard, John Parker *lawyer*
†Hunt, James Baxter, Jr., *lawyer, retired governor*
Hunter, Richard Samford, Jr., *lawyer*
†Jernigan, John Lee *lawyer*
†Jordan, John Richard, Jr., *lawyer*
Joyner, Walton Kitchin *lawyer*
Kapp, Michael Keith *lawyer*
Kurz, Mary Elizabeth *lawyer*
†Little, James David *lawyer*
Maupin, Armistead Jones *lawyer*
Mitchell, Burley Bayard, Jr., *lawyer*
Neely, Charles B., Jr., *lawyer*
†Palmer, William Ralph *retired lawyer*
Pinnix, John Lawrence *lawyer*
Powell, Durwood Royce *lawyer*
Ragsdale, George Robinson *lawyer*
Roach, Wesley Linville *lawyer, insurance executive*
Simpson, Steven Drexell *lawyer*
Suhr, Paul Augustine *lawyer*
†Taylor, Raymond Mason *lawyer, former government official, educator*
Trott, William Macnider *lawyer*
Wetsch, Laura Johnson *lawyer*
Wicker, Dennis A. *lawyer*

Research Triangle Park
Diosegy, Arlene Jayne *lawyer, consultant*

Rocky Mount
Zipf, Robert Eugene, Jr., *legal medicine consultant, pathologist*

Roxboro
†Mitchell, P. Susan *lawyer*

Salisbury
†Blanton, Mary Rutherford *lawyer, educator*

Sanford
Raisig, Paul Jones, Jr., *lawyer*

Smithfield
Schulz, Bradley Nicholas *lawyer*

Southern Pines
Caliri, David Joseph *retired lawyer, insurance agent*

Tabor City
Jorgensen, Ralph Gubler *lawyer, accountant*

Tarboro
Hopkins, Grover Prevatte *lawyer*
O'Malley, Susan Marie *lawyer*

Thomasville
†Reynolds, Mark Floyd, II, *lawyer, management and labor consultant*

Tryon
McDermott, Renée R(assler) *lawyer*

Wilkesboro
Gray, William Campbell *lawyer*
†Hellrung, Stephen Andrew *lawyer*

Wilmington
†Jones, Lucian Cox *lawyer*
McCauley, Cleyburn Lycurgus *lawyer*
Medlock, Donald Larson *lawyer*

Winston Salem
Adams, Alfred Gray *lawyer*
†Alexander, Charles Jackson, II, *lawyer*
Barnhill, Henry Grady, Jr., *lawyer*
†Blynn, Guy Marc *lawyer*
†Brett, Anthony H. *lawyer*
†Comerford, Walter Thompson, Jr., *lawyer*
Dahl, Tyrus Vance, Jr., *lawyer*
Davis, Linwood Layfield *lawyer*
Foy, Herbert Miles, III, *lawyer, educator*
Gitter, Allan Reinhold *lawyer*
Greason, Murray Crossley, Jr., *lawyer*
Gunter, Michael Donwell *lawyer*
Herring, Jerone Carson *lawyer, bank executive*
Holton, Walter Clinton, Jr., *lawyer*
Leonard, R. Michael *lawyer*
†Logan, David Andrew *lawyer, educator*
Maready, William Frank *lawyer*
Osborn, Malcolm Everett *lawyer*
†Porter, Leon Eugene, Jr., *lawyer*
Ray, Michael Edwin *lawyer*
Robinson, Edward Norwood *lawyer*
†Roemer, Henry Conrad, Jr., *lawyer*
†Ross, Charles Thomas *lawyer*
Sandridge, William Pendleton, Jr., *lawyer*
Steele, Thomas McKnight *law educator*
†Strayhorn, Ralph Nichols, Jr., *lawyer*
†Tate, David Kirk *lawyer*
Thrift, Ashley Ormand *lawyer*
†Vaughn, Robert Candler, II, *lawyer*
Walker, George Kontz *law educator*
Wells, Dewey Wallace *lawyer*
Womble, William Fletcher *lawyer*

NORTH DAKOTA

Bismarck
Klemin, Lawrence R. *lawyer*
Murry, Charles Emerson *lawyer, official*
Nelson, Keithe Eugene *state court administrator, lawyer*
Snyder, Robert John *lawyer*

Dickinson
Ficek, Vince H. *lawyer*
Greenwood, Dann Edward *lawyer*
Greenwood, Mark Lawrence *lawyer*
†Herauf, William Anton *lawyer*

Fargo
Amlund, Curtis Arthur *law educator*
†Unhjem, Michael Bruce *lawyer*

Grand Forks
Anderson, Damon Ernest *lawyer*
Cilz, Douglas Arthur *lawyer*
Clapp, Richard Allen *lawyer*
Hand, James Stanley *lawyer*
Vogel, Robert *retired lawyer, educator*
Widdel, John Earl, Jr., *lawyer*

Jamestown
†Ottmar, Timothy Jon *lawyer, municipal judge*

Mandan
Bair, Bruce B. *lawyer*

Minot
Armstrong, Phillip Dale *lawyer*
†Backes, Orlin William *lawyer*

Oakes
McLean, Stephen M. *lawyer*

West Fargo
Martin, Bradley L *legal consultant, composer*

OHIO

Ada
†Fenton, Howard Nathan, III, *lawyer, educator*
Streib, Victor Lee *dean*
†Veltri, Stephen Charles *lawyer, educator*

Akron
†Aynes, Richard L(ee) *law educator*
Bonsky, Jack Alan *lawyer*
†Cherpas, Christopher Theodore *lawyer*
Chrisant, Rosemarie Kathryn *law library administrator*
Fisher, James Lee *lawyer*
Flannery, Harry Audley *lawyer*
Glinsek, Gerald John *lawyer*
Harvie, Crawford Thomas *lawyer*
Holloway, Donald Phillip *lawyer*
Kreek, Louis Francis, Jr., *lawyer*
Lammert, Thomas Edward *lawyer*
Lee, Brant Thomas *lawyer, federal official, educator*
Lombardi, Frederick McKean *lawyer*
Richert, Paul *law educator*
†Rooney, George Willard *lawyer*
Rupert, Scott Hendricks *lawyer*
Schrader, Alfred Eugene *lawyer*
†Stark, Michael Lee *lawyer*
Tipping, Harry A. *lawyer*
Trotter, Thomas Robert *lawyer*
†Wolfe, John Leslie *lawyer*

Athens
†Bridgewater, Erle Henry *lawyer*
Gall, Robert Jay *lawyer*
Hedges, Richard Houston *lawyer, epidemiologist*
Lavelle, William Ambrose *lawyer, judge*
†Yanity, Joseph Blair, Jr., *lawyer*

Aurora
Berry, Dean Lester *lawyer*

Barnesville
Jefferis, Paul Bruce *lawyer*

Batavia
Pattison, George Edgar *lawyer*

Bay Village
Kapp, C. Terrence *lawyer*

Beachwood
Lewis, Cherie Sue *lawyer, English language and journalism educator*
†Pinkas, Robert Paul *lawyer, venture capitalist*

Beavercreek
Richardson, Arthur Wilhelm *lawyer*

Bryan
†Gretick, Anthony Louis *lawyer, judge*

Bucyrus
Neff, Robert Clark, Sr., *lawyer*

Canfield
Beck, James Hayes *lawyer*
Hill, Thomas Allen *lawyer*

Canton
†Barnhart, Gene *lawyer*
Davis, Richard E. *lawyer*
†Herbert, David Lee *lawyer, author*
Huryn, Christopher Michael *lawyer*
Mokodean, Michael John *lawyer, accountant*
†Plakas, Leonidas Evangelos *lawyer*

†Sandrock, Scott Paul *lawyer*
†Tzangas, George John *lawyer*

Celina
†Lammers, Thomas Dean *lawyer, educator*
†Myers, Daniel *lawyer*

Centerville
Giffen, Daniel Harris *lawyer, educator*

Chagrin Falls
†Blattner, Robert A. *lawyer*
Calfee, William Lewis *lawyer*
Freedman, Howard Joel *lawyer*

Chillicothe
Boulger, William Charles *lawyer*

Cincinnati
Adams, Edmund John *lawyer*
Anderson, James Milton *lawyer*
Anderson, William Hopple *lawyer*
Anthony, Thomas Dale *lawyer*
Bahlman, William Thorne, Jr., *retired lawyer*
Bibus, Thomas William *lawyer*
Black, Stephen L. *lawyer*
†Broderick, Dennis John *lawyer, retail company executive*
Bromberg, Robert Sheldon *lawyer*
†Bruvold, Kathleen Parker *lawyer*
†Buechner, Robert William *lawyer, educator*
Burke, Timothy Michael *lawyer, educator*
†Calico, Paul B. *lawyer*
†Carlson, Jennie Peaslack *lawyer*
Carr, George Francis, Jr., *lawyer*
†Carroll, James Joseph *lawyer*
Chesley, Stanley Morris *lawyer*
Christenson, Gordon A. *law educator*
Cioffi, Michael Lawrence *lawyer*
Cissell, James Charles *lawyer*
Cobey, John Geoffrey *lawyer, consultant*
Cohen, Edward *lawyer*
Corwin, Melanie S. *lawyer*
Craig, L. Clifford *lawyer*
Davis, Robert Lawrence *lawyer*
Dehner, Joseph Julnes *lawyer*
DeLong, Deborah *lawyer*
†Diller, Edward Dietrich *lawyer*
Dornette, W(illiam) Stuart *lawyer, educator*
†Eaton, Janet Ruth *lawyer*
†Evans, James E. *lawyer*
Faller, Susan Grogan *lawyer*
Ferrell, Susan R. *lawyer*
Finan, Richard H.
Fink, Jerold Albert *lawyer*
Flanagan, John Anthony *lawyer, educator*
Freedman, William Mark *lawyer, educator*
Friedman, Penny *lawyer*
Gettler, Benjamin *lawyer, manufacturing company executive*
Goodman, Stanley *lawyer*
Greenberg, Gerald Stephen *lawyer*
Halpert, Douglas Joshua *lawyer*
Hardy, William Robinson *lawyer*
Harris, Irving *lawyer*
†Harris, Jerald David *lawyer*
†Heldman, James Gardner *lawyer*
†Heldman, Paul W. *lawyer, grocery store company executive*
Henderson, Stephen Paul *lawyer*
Hermanies, John Hans *retired lawyer*
Hill, Thomas Clark *lawyer*
Hoffheimer, Daniel Joseph *lawyer*
Holschuh, John David, Jr., *lawyer*
Hust, Bruce Kevin *lawyer*
†Johnson, James J. *lawyer*
Kelley, John Joseph, Jr., *lawyer*
Kelley, Rebecca Crouse (Rebecca Ann Kelley) *lawyer, academic administrator, not-for-profit fundraiser*
Kiel, Frederick Orin *lawyer*
Kordons, Uldis *lawyer*
†Krass, Marc Stern *lawyer*
Lawrence, James Kaufman Lebensburger *lawyer*
Lesick, John Richard *lawyer, consultant, retired lawyer*
Levin, Debbe Ann *lawyer*
Lindberg, Charles David *lawyer*
†Lloyd, David Livingstone, Jr., *lawyer*
Lugbill, Ann *lawyer*
Lutz, James Gurney *lawyer*
Manley, Robert Edward *lawyer, economist*
Mann, David Scott *lawyer*
Markesbery, Maria Saba *lawyer*
†Marks, Edward G. *lawyer*
Maxwell, Robert Wallace, II, *lawyer*
McClain, William Andrew *lawyer*
McDowell, John Eugene *lawyer*
Mc Henry, Powell *lawyer*
Meranus, Leonard Stanley *lawyer*
†Meyer, Charles Mulvihill *lawyer*
Meyers, Karen Diane *lawyer, educator, corporate officer*
†Meyers, Pamela Sue *lawyer*
†Miller, Gail Franklin *lawyer*
Naylor, Paul Donald *lawyer*
Nechemias, Stephen Murray *lawyer*
Neltner, Michael Martin *lawyer*
Neumark, Michael Harry *lawyer*
†Nippert, Alfred Kuno, Jr., *lawyer*
Olson, Robert Wyrick *lawyer*
†O'Reilly, James Thomas *lawyer, educator, author*
†Owens, Robert Emmett, Jr., *lawyer*
Parker, R. Joseph *lawyer*
Petrie, Bruce Inglis *lawyer*
Phillips, T. Stephen *lawyer*
Porter, Robert Carl, Jr., *lawyer*
†Ralston, James Allen *lawyer*
Reichert, David *lawyer*
Rich, Robert Edward *lawyer*
Rose, Donald McGregor *retired lawyer*
Rubin, Robert Samuel *lawyer*
Scacchetti, David J. *lawyer*
Schuck, Thomas Robert *lawyer, farmer*
Shea, Joseph William, III, *lawyer*
Shore, Thomas Spencer, Jr., *retired lawyer*
Silbersack, Mark Louis *lawyer*
Smith, Sheila Marie *lawyer*
Stanton, Jeanne Frances *retired lawyer*
†Stith, John Stephen *lawyer*
Strauss, William Victor *lawyer*
Swigert, James Mack *lawyer*
Tobias, Charles Harrison, Jr., *lawyer*
Tobias, Paul Henry *lawyer*
†Townsend, Robert J. *lawyer*
Tranter, Terence Michael *lawyer*
†Trauth, Joseph Louis, Jr., *lawyer*
Vander Laan, Mark Alan *lawyer*
Vogel, Cedric Wakelee *lawyer*
Wales, Ross Elliot *lawyer*
†Watts, Barbara Gayle *law academic administrator*
Weeks, Steven Wiley *lawyer*
Whitaker, Glenn Virgil *lawyer*
Woodside, Frank C., III, *lawyer, educator, physician*
Zavatsky, Michael Joseph *lawyer*
Zealey, Sharon Janine *lawyer*

Cleveland
Adamo, Kenneth R. *lawyer*
†Adams, Albert T. *lawyer*
Alcox, Patrick Joseph *lawyer*
Andrews, Oakley V. *lawyer*
Ashmus, Keith Allen *lawyer*
Austin, Arthur Donald, II, *lawyer, educator*
Bacon, Brett Kermit *lawyer*
Bates, Walter Alan *former lawyer*
Baughman, R(obert) Patrick *lawyer*
Berger, Sanford Jason *lawyer, securities dealer, real estate broker*
Berick, James Herschel *lawyer*
Besse, Ralph Moore *retired lawyer*
Billington, Glenn Earle *lawyer*
Birne, Kenneth Andrew *lawyer*
†Bixenstine, Kim Fenton *lawyer*
Blackford, Jason Collier *lawyer*
†Bloch, Marc Joel *lawyer*
Boukis, Kenneth *lawyer*
Boyko, Christopher Allan *lawyer, judge*
Braverman, Herbert Leslie *lawyer*
Bravo, Kenneth Allan *lawyer*
Brennan, Maureen *lawyer*
Brown, Bruce Andrew *lawyer*
Brown, Harry M. *lawyer, consultant*
Brown, Seymour R. *lawyer, director*
Brucken, Robert Matthew *lawyer*
†Brunn, Thomas Leo, Sr., *lawyer*
Burchmore, David Wegner *lawyer*
Burge, David Alan *patent lawyer, writer*
Burke, Kathleen B. *lawyer*
Cairns, James Donald *lawyer*
Calfee, John Beverly *retired lawyer*
Callahan, Thomas James *lawyer*
Clarke, Charles Fenton *lawyer*
†Climer, James Alan *lawyer*
Collin, Thomas James *lawyer*
Condeni, Joseph Anthony *lawyer*
†Conner, William Herbert *lawyer*
Coquillette, William Hollis *lawyer*
Crehore, Charles Aaron *lawyer*
†Cudak, Gail Linda *lawyer*
Currivan, John Daniel *lawyer*
Cyphert, Michael A. *lawyer*
†Dampeer, John Lyell *retired lawyer*
†Dauscher, Raymond G. *lawyer*
†Diamant, Michael Harlan *lawyer*
†DiVenere, Anthony Joseph *lawyer*
Doris, Alan S(anford) *lawyer*
Drinko, John Deaver *lawyer*
Duncan, Ed Eugene *lawyer*
†Dunn, George J. *lawyer, oil company executive*
Duvin, Robert Phillip *lawyer*
†Ensign, Gregory Moore *lawyer*
Ernst, Christopher Mark *lawyer*
†Eyre, Paul P. *lawyer*
Fabens, Andrew Lawrie, III, *lawyer*
Falsgraf, William Wendell *lawyer*
Fay, Regan Joseph *lawyer*
†Feliciano, José Celso *lawyer*
Felty, Kriss Delbert *lawyer*
Fisher, Thomas Edward *lawyer*
Fletcher, Robert *retired lawyer, horologist*
†Foote, Richard Charles *lawyer*
†Freimuth, Marc William *lawyer*
Friedman, Avery S. *lawyer*
Friedman, Harold Edward *lawyer*
Gippin, Robert Malcolm *lawyer*
Glaser, Robert Edward *lawyer*
Goins, Frances Floriano *lawyer*
Gold, Gerald Seymour *lawyer*
Goldberg, James R. *lawyer*
Goldfarb, Bernard Sanford *lawyer*
Goler, Michael David *lawyer*
Gray, R. Benton *lawyer*
Groetzinger, Jon, Jr., *lawyer, consumer products executive*
Grossman, Theodore Martin *lawyer*
Haiman, Irwin Sanford *lawyer*
Hardy, Michael Lynn *lawyer*
Henes, Samuel Ernst *lawyer*
Hochman, Kenneth George *lawyer*
Hoerner, Robert Jack *lawyer*
†Hoffman, Mark Leslie *lawyer, film maker*
Hollington, Richard Rings, Jr., *lawyer*
Horvitz, Michael John *lawyer*
Jacobs, Leslie William *lawyer*
Jaffe, Donald Nolan *lawyer*
James, Ronald J. *lawyer*
Janke, Ronald Robert *lawyer*
Jeffers, John William *lawyer*
†Jensen, Erik Michael *law educator*
Jorgenson, Mary Ann *lawyer*
†Karp, Marvin Louis *lawyer*
Katcher, Richard *lawyer*
Katz, Lewis Robert *law educator*
†Katz, Mark David *lawyer*
Kelly, Dennis Michael *lawyer*
Kilbane, Thomas Stanton *lawyer*
†Kirner, Paul Timothy *lawyer*
Kola, Arthur Anthony *lawyer*
†Kondzer, Thomas Allen *lawyer*
†Kopit, Alan Stuart *lawyer*
Kraemer, Lisa Russert *lawyer*
Kramer, Eugene Leo *lawyer*
Krawczak, Kenneth Francis *lawyer*
†Kundtz, John Andrew *lawyer*
Kurit, Neil *lawyer*
LaFond, Thomas Joseph *lawyer*
Lawniczak, James Michael *lawyer*
†Lazzaro, S. Robert E. *lawyer*
Lease, Robert K. *lawyer*
Leavitt, Jeffrey Stuart *lawyer*
Leiken, Earl Murray *lawyer*
Lewis, John Bruce *lawyer*
Lewis, John Francis *lawyer*
Lewis, Robert Lawrence *lawyer, educator*
Lowe, James Allison *lawyer, educator*
Markey, Robert Guy *lawyer*
Marting, Michael G. *lawyer*
Mason, Thomas Albert *lawyer*
McAndrews, James Patrick *lawyer*
Mc Cartan, Patrick Francis *lawyer*
McCarthy, Mark Francis *lawyer*
McLaughlin, Patrick Michael *lawyer*
Mehlman, Maxwell Jonathan *law educator*
†Meyer, G. Christopher *lawyer*
†Millisor, Kenneth Ray *lawyer*
Millstone, David Jeffrey *lawyer*
Monihan, Mary Elizabeth *lawyer*
Moore, Kenneth Cameron *lawyer*
†Morgenstern, Conrad J. *lawyer*
†Nave, Michele Garrick *lawyer*
†Neff, Owen Calvin *lawyer*
Newman, John M., Jr., *lawyer*
Norman, Forrest Alonzo *lawyer*
Ollinger, W. James *lawyer, director*
Osborne, Frank R. *lawyer, educator, lecturer*
Pace, Stanley Dan *lawyer*
Pallam, John James *lawyer*
Pearlman, Samuel Segel *lawyer, educator*
†Perris, Terrence George *lawyer*
Podboy, Alvin Michael, Jr., *law library director, lawyer*
Presti, Geralyn Marie *lawyer*
Preston, Robert Bruce *retired lawyer*
Putka, Andrew Charles *lawyer*
Rains, M. Neal *lawyer*
Rapp, Robert Neil *lawyer*
Reppert, Richard Levi *lawyer*
Rosenbaum, Jacob I. *lawyer*
Ruf, H(arold) William, Jr., *retired lawyer, corporation executive*
Sanislo, Paul Steve *lawyer*
Sawyer, Raymond Terry *lawyer, consultant, theater producer*
†Schatz, William Bonsall *lawyer*
Schiller, James Joseph *lawyer*
Shapiro, Fred David *lawyer*
Sharpe, Calvin William *law educator, arbitrator*
†Shore, Michael Allan *lawyer, accountant*
†Shumaker, Roger Lee *lawyer*
Sicherman, Marvin Allen *lawyer*
Skulina, Thomas Raymond *lawyer*
Slinger, Michael Jeffery *law library director*
Sogg, Wilton Sherman *lawyer*
Solomon, Randall Lee *lawyer*
Spero, Keith Erwin *lawyer, educator*
†Spurgeon, Roberta Kaye *lawyer*
Stanley, Hugh Monroe, Jr., *lawyer*
Steindler, Howard Allen *lawyer*
Stevens, Thomas Charles *lawyer*
Stovsky, Michael David *lawyer*
Strauch, John L. *lawyer*
†Strauss, David J. *lawyer*
Striefsky, Linda A(nn) *lawyer*
Strimbu, Victor, Jr., *lawyer*
Stuhan, Richard George *lawyer*
†Stuhldreher, George William *lawyer*
Swartzbaugh, Marc L. *lawyer*
Sweeney, Emily Margaret *prosecutor*
Szaller, James Francis *lawyer*
Taft, Seth Chase *retired lawyer*
†Thimmig, Diana M. *lawyer*
Toohey, Brian Frederick *lawyer*
Toomajian, William Martin *lawyer*
†Turoff, Jack Newton *lawyer*
Utrata, Carl Ignatius *corporate counsel, corporate executive*
†Vance, Victoria Lynne *lawyer*
von Mehren, George M. *lawyer*
Waldeck, John Walter, Jr., *lawyer*
Wallach, Mark Irwin *lawyer*
Watson, Richard Thomas *lawyer*
†Weaver, Robin Geoffrey *lawyer, educator*
Weber, Robert Carl *lawyer*
Weiler, Jeffry Louis *lawyer*
†Weisman, Fred *lawyer*
Weiss, Leon Alan *lawyer*
†Werber, Stephen Jay *lawyer, educator*
Whitney, Richard Buckner *lawyer*
Willenbrink, Rose Ann *lawyer*
Withers, Carl Raymond *lawyer*
Young, James Edward *lawyer*
Zambie, Allan John *lawyer*

Cleveland Heights
Gutfeld, Norman E. *lawyer*

Columbus
Adams, John Marshall *lawyer*
†Allen, Richard Lee, Jr., *lawyer*
Anderson, Jon Mac *lawyer, educator*
Aukland, Duncan Dayton *lawyer*
Bailey, Daniel Allen *lawyer*
Balthaser, James Harvey *lawyer*
Barnes, Wallace Ray *retired lawyer*
†Barrett, Phillip Heston *lawyer, director*
Belton, John Thomas *lawyer*
†Bennett, Robert Thomas *lawyer, professional athletics manager*
†Bloomfield, David Solomon *lawyer, educator*
Booker, James Douglas *retired lawyer, government official*
Bridgman, G(eorge) Ross *lawyer*
Brinkman, Dale Thomas *lawyer*
Brooks, Richard Dickinson *lawyer*
Brown, Herbert Russell *lawyer, writer*
Brubaker, Robert Loring *lawyer*
Buchenroth, Stephen Richard *lawyer*
Carnahan, John Anderson *lawyer*
†Carpenter, Michael H. *lawyer*
Casey, John Frederick *lawyer*
Chappelear, Stephen Eric *lawyer*
Chavers, Dane Carroll *lawyer*
Chester, John Jonas *lawyer, educator*
†Cunningham, Guy Henry, III, *lawyer*
Cvetanovich, Dan L. *lawyer*
D'Aurora, Jack *lawyer*
DeRousie, Charles Stuart *lawyer*
Di Lorenzo, John Florio, Jr., *retired lawyer (corporate)*
Diroll, David John *lawyer*
†Dowd, Andrew Joseph *lawyer, utility company executive*
Draper, Gerald Linden *lawyer*
Drexel, Ray Phillips *lawyer*
Dunlay, Catherine Telles *lawyer*
Eblin, Robert L. *lawyer*
†Eichenberger, Jerry Alan *lawyer*
Emens, J. Richard *lawyer*
Fahey, Richard Paul *lawyer*
Fay, Frank Allen *lawyer*
Fay, Terrence Michael *lawyer*
†Feheley, Lawrence Francis *lawyer*
Ferguson, Gerald Paul *lawyer*
†Fisher, Fredrick Lee *lawyer*
Fisher, Lloyd Edison, Jr., *lawyer*
Frasier, Ralph Kennedy *lawyer, banker*
Frye, Richard Arthur *lawyer*
†Gall, John R. *lawyer*
†Gerling, Joseph Anthony *lawyer*
Gittes, Frederick M. *lawyer*
Goulder, Diane Kessler *lawyer*
Greek, Darold I. *lawyer*
Gross, James Howard *lawyer*
Hardymon, David Wayne *lawyer*
†Hatler, Patricia Ruth *lawyer*
Haught, Jack Gregg *lawyer*
Hill, Kathleen Blickenstaff *lawyer, mental health nurse, nursing educator*
Hollenbaugh, H(enry) Ritchey *lawyer*
Hutson, Jeffrey Woodward *lawyer*
†Jenkins, George L. *lawyer, entrepreneur*
Johnson, Mark Alan *lawyer*
Kasouf, Joseph Chickery *lawyer, consultant*
†Kemp, Daniel Warren *lawyer*
Ketcham, Richard Scott *lawyer*
Kilgore, Terry Lee *lawyer*
†King, G. Roger *lawyer*
†King, James R. *lawyer*
Kuehnle, Kenton Lee *lawyer*
Kurtz, Charles Jewett, III, *lawyer*
La Cour, Louis Bernard *lawyer*
Larzelere, Kathy Lynn Heckler *paralegal*
Lehman, Harry Jac *lawyer*
Liggett, Luther LeRoy, Jr., *lawyer*
Long, Thomas Leslie *lawyer*
Maloon, Jeffrey Lee *lawyer*
Mann, William Craig *lawyer*
Markus, Kent Richard *lawyer*
Maynard, Robert Howell *retired lawyer*
McConnaughey, George Carlton, Jr., *retired lawyer*
McCutchan, Gordon Eugene *retired lawyer, insurance company executive*
McDermott, Kevin R. *lawyer*
McKenna, Alvin James *lawyer*
McMahon, John Patrick *lawyer*
Miller, Michael Stratton *lawyer*
Miller, Terry Morrow *lawyer*
Minor, Robert Allen *lawyer*
Mirman, Joel Harvey *lawyer*
Moloney, Thomas E. *lawyer*
†Mone, Robert Paul *lawyer*
Morgan, Dennis Richard *lawyer*
Moul, William Charles *lawyer*
Nelson, Janice Eileen *paralegal, artist*
Oman, Richard Heer *lawyer*
Petricoff, M. Howard *lawyer, educator*
Phillips, James Edgar *lawyer*
†Pittner, Nicholas Andrew *lawyer*
Pressley, Fred G., Jr., *lawyer*
Quigley, John Bernard *law educator*
Radnor, Alan T. *lawyer*
Ramey, Denny L. *bar association executive director*
Reasoner, Willis Irl, III, *lawyer*
Ring, Victoria Alexandra *paralegal, notary*
Robins, Ronald Albert, Jr., *lawyer*
Robinson, Barry R. *lawyer*
Robinson, Randal D. *lawyer*
Robol, Richard Thomas *lawyer*
Rose, Michael Dean *lawyer, educator*
†Rowland, Ronald Lee *lawyer*
Ryan, Joseph W., Jr., *lawyer*
†Sawyer, Theodore D(aniel) *lawyer*
Schrag, Edward A., Jr., *lawyer*
†Schwartz, Robert S. *lawyer*
†Selcer, David Mark *lawyer*
†Shayne, Stanley H. *lawyer*
Sidman, Robert John *lawyer*
†Sites, Richard Loren *lawyer, educator*
†Stanton, Elizabeth McCool *lawyer*
Stern, Geoffrey *lawyer, disciplinary counsel*
Stinehart, Roger Ray *lawyer*
†Stover, Stephan Wallace *lawyer, state agency administrator*
Taft, Sheldon Ashley *lawyer*
Taggart, Thomas Michael *lawyer*
Tait, Robert E. *lawyer*
Tarpy, Thomas Michael *lawyer*
Taylor, Joel Sanford *retired lawyer*
Thomas, Duke Winston *lawyer*
Todd, William Michael *lawyer*
Turano, David A. *lawyer*
Tyack, Thomas Michael *lawyer*
Vorys, Arthur Isaiah *lawyer*
Warner, Charles Collins *lawyer*
Whipps, Edward Franklin *lawyer*
Wightman, Alec *lawyer*
Willcox, Roderick Harrison *lawyer*
Wiseman, Randolph Carson *lawyer*
Wolper, Beatrice Emens *lawyer*
Yeazel, Keith Arthur *lawyer*

Cuyahoga Falls
Jones, John Frank *retired lawyer*

Dayton
Blaschak, Thomas R. *lawyer*
†Bridgman, Susan R. *tax lawyer*
Burick, Lawrence T. *lawyer*
Carver, Todd B. *corporate lawyer, law professor*
Chema, Susan Russell *lawyer*
Conway, Mark Allyn *lawyer*
Deutsch, David M. *lawyer*
†Farquhar, Robert Nichols *lawyer*
Faruki, Charles Joseph *lawyer*
Goelz, Robert Dean *lawyer*
Hadley, Robert James *lawyer*
Heyman, Ralph Edmond *lawyer*
Holz, Michael Harold *lawyer*
Jenks, Thomas Edward *lawyer*
Johnson, C. Terry *lawyer*
Kinlin, Donald James *lawyer*
†Kloppenberg, Lisa A. *law educator*
†Koeller, Lynn Garver *public defender*
Krebs, Leo Francis *lawyer*
Lockhart, Gregory Gordon *prosecutor*
Macklin, Crofford Johnson, Jr., *lawyer*
†Nauman, Joseph George *lawyer*
Owens, Mark Ernest *lawyer, legal administrator*
Posey, Terry Wayne *lawyer*
†Rambo, James Edmondson *lawyer*
Randall, Vernellia *lawyer, nurse, educator*
Rapp, Gerald Duane *lawyer, manufacturing company executive*
Roberts, Brian Michael *lawyer*
Rogers, Richard Hunter *lawyer, business executive*
Saul, Irving Isaac *lawyer*
Schneble, Alfred William, III, *lawyer*
Taronji, Jaime, Jr., *lawyer*
Tweel, Donna Shank *lawyer*
†Vaughn, Noel Wyandt *lawyer*
Watts, Steven Richard *lawyer*

Dublin
Coco, Mark Steven *lawyer*
†Farrell, Clifford Michael *lawyer*
Inzetta, Mark Stephen *lawyer*
†Lane, James Edward *retired lawyer, consultant*
Maloon, Jerry L. *trial lawyer, physician, medico legal consultant*
Sheffer, Brent Alan *lawyer*
Tenuta, Luigia *lawyer*

Eaton
Thomas, James William *lawyer*

Fairborn
Mayer, Michael A. *lawyer, educator*
Miles, David R. *lawyer*

Findlay
Jetton, Girard Reuel, Jr., *lawyer, retired oil company executive*
Kentris, George Lawrence *lawyer*
Kline, James Edward *lawyer*
Rakestraw, Gregory Allen *lawyer*

Fremont
Albrechta, Joseph Francis *lawyer*

Gambier
Leech, Charles Russell, Jr., *lawyer*

Garfield Heights
Demer, Margaret Elizabeth *lawyer*

Geneva
Epstein, Sherry Stein *lawyer*

Hamilton
Bressler, H.J. *lawyer, judge*
†Olivas, Adolf *lawyer, mayor*

Hartville
†McPherson, James Willis, Jr., *retired lawyer*

Hillsboro
†Coss, Rocky Alan *lawyer*

Howard
Lee, William Johnson *lawyer*

Hudson
Elliott, Frances Carano *lawyer, educator*

Independence
Schwallie, Daniel Phillip *legal consultant*

Ironton
†Allen, Craig Adams *lawyer, director*
Collier, James Bruce *lawyer*

Jackson
Lewis, Richard M. *lawyer*

Jefferson
Geary, Michael Philip *lawyer*
Lemire, Jerome Albert *lawyer, geologist*

Kent
†Boczek, Boleslaw Adam *retired law educator*
Nome, William Andreas *lawyer*

Kenton
Tudor, John Martin *lawyer, educator*

Kettering
Eubank, David Lynn *lawyer, consultant*

Lakewood
Baxter, Howard H. *retired lawyer*
†Fortunato, Christopher R. *lawyer*

Lancaster
Libert, Donald Joseph *lawyer*

Lebanon
Baldwin, James Edward *lawyer, city administrator*

Lima
Jacobs, Ann Elizabeth *lawyer*
Robenalt, John Alton *lawyer*

Logan
Kernen, Will *lawyer*

Lorain
†Mumford, Beverly Jean *paralegal*
†Wiersma, David Charles *lawyer*

Mansfield
Wolf, Marcus Alan *lawyer*

Marietta
Fields, William Albert *lawyer*
Huck, Daniel N. *lawyer, educator*

Marion
Slagle, James William *lawyer*

Massillon
†Beane, Frank Llewellyn *lawyer*
Netzly, Dwight H. *lawyer*

Maumee
Marsh, Benjamin Franklin *lawyer*
McBride, Beverly Jean *lawyer*
Tuschman, James Marshall *lawyer*
Zouhary, Kathleen Maher *lawyer*

Mechanicsburg
Saxbe, William Bart *lawyer, former government official*

Medina
Ballard, John Stuart *retired educator, former mayor, former lawyer*

Mentor
Driggs, Charles Mulford *lawyer*
†McCarter, William Kent *lawyer*

Miamisburg
Andreozzi, Louis Joseph *lawyer*
Byrd, James Everett *lawyer*

Middletown
†Bailey, William Rufus *lawyer, corporation executive*
Rathman, William Ernest *retired lawyer, minister*

Milford Center
McDonald, Alan Thomas *lawyer*

Minerva
Martin, Robert Dale *lawyer*

Mount Vernon
Turner, Harry Edward *lawyer*

Newark
†Gordon, L(eland) James *lawyer*
Hite, David L. *lawyer*
Hostetter, James William *lawyer*
Mantonya, John Butcher *lawyer*
Meyer, Christopher Richard *lawyer*
Reidy, Thomas Anthony *lawyer*

North Canton
Dettinger, Warren Walter *lawyer*

North Olmsted
Dorchak, Thomas J. *lawyer*
Ruben, Alan Miles *law educator*

Norwalk
Fresch, Marie Beth *court reporting company executive*

Oxford
Brown, Edward Maurice *retired lawyer, business executive*

Painesville
†Aveni, Anthony Joseph *lawyer, educator*
Campbell, Margaret Susan *defender*

Pepper Pike
†Schnell, Carlton Bryce *lawyer*

Portsmouth
Crowder, Marjorie Briggs *lawyer*
Gerlach, Franklin Theodore *lawyer*
†Grimshaw, Lynn Alan *lawyer*
Horr, William Henry *retired lawyer*

Ravenna
Giulitto, Paula Christine *lawyer*

Richwood
Hoffman, Scott Lee *lawyer*

Rocky River
Grady, Francis Xavier *lawyer*

Saint Clairsville
Hanlon, Lodge L. *lawyer, insurance agency executive, accountant*

Saint Marys
Kemp, Barrett George *lawyer*

Salem
Bowman, Scott McMahan *lawyer*
Slack, Mark Robert *lawyer*

Seaman
Young, Vernon Lewis *lawyer*

Shaker Heights
Band, Jordan Clifford *lawyer*
†Barz, Patricia *lawyer*
Donnem, Roland William *retired lawyer, real estate owner, developer*
Ekelman, Daniel Louis *lawyer*
Messinger, Donald Hathaway *lawyer*

Ondrey Gruber, William Michael *lawyer*

Springboro
†Sharts, John Edwin, III, *lawyer*

Springfield
Browne, William Bitner *lawyer*
Harkins, Daniel Conger *lawyer*
†Lagos, James Harry *lawyer*
Wilt, Valerie Rae *lawyer*

Sylvania
†Callahan, John Joseph *lawyer*

Tiffin
Huth, Lester Charles *lawyer*

Toledo
†Allotta, Joseph John *lawyer*
Anspach, Robert Michael *lawyer*
Baker, Richard Southworth *lawyer*
Boggs, Ralph Stuart *retired lawyer*
Brown, Charles Earl *lawyer*
Calcamuggio, Larry Glenn *lawyer*
Dalrymple, Thomas Lawrence *retired lawyer*
Dane, Stephen Mark *lawyer*
Doner, Gary William *lawyer*
Edwards, Richard Walton, Jr., *law educator*
†Friedman, Howard Martin *law educator*
Gottlieb, Arnold Neal *lawyer*
Jackson, Reginald Sherman, Jr., *lawyer, educator*
La Rue, Carl Forman *lawyer*
O'Connell, Maurice Daniel *lawyer*
Pletz, Thomas Gregory *lawyer*
St. Clair, Donald David *lawyer*
Spitzer, John Brumback *lawyer*
†Ward, David A. *corporate lawyer*
Webb, Thomas Irwin, Jr., *lawyer, director*
†White, Kenneth James *lawyer*
Wicklund, David Wayne *lawyer*
†Witherell, Dennis Patrick *lawyer*

Troy
Bazler, Frank Ellis *retired lawyer*

Twinsburg
†Kramer, Timothy Eugene *lawyer*

Wadsworth
†McIlvaine, James Ross *lawyer*
†Paul, Dennis Edward *lawyer*

Warren
Letson, William Normand *lawyer*
Rossi, Anthony Gerald *lawyer*
Swauger, Terry Allen *lawyer*
†Woodall, W. Dallas *lawyer*

Wellston
Oths, Joseph Anthony *lawyer*

West Union
Schlueter, James William *lawyer*

Westerville
†Bell, Albert Leo *retired lawyer*
Lancione, Bernard Gabe *lawyer*
Westervelt, Charles Ephraim, Jr., *lawyer*
†Young, Sheldon Mike *lawyer, author*

Westlake
Donahue, Charles Bertrand, II, *lawyer*
Kolick, Daniel Joseph *lawyer*

Wickliffe
Kidder, Fred Dockstater *lawyer*

Willard
†Thornton, Robert Floyd *lawyer*

Willoughby
†Cruikshank, David Earl *lawyer*

Wilmington
Schutt, Walter Eugene *lawyer*

Wooster
Haught, Sharon Kay *lawyer*
†Johnston, John Clifford, Jr., *lawyer*
Kennedy, Charles Allen *lawyer*
†Moore, Arthur William *retired lawyer*

Worthington
Albert, Robert Hamilton *lawyer*
Juhola, Michael Duane *lawyer*

Xenia
Chappars, Timothy Stephen *lawyer*

Youngstown
Ausnehmer, John Edward *lawyer*
Briach, George Gary *lawyer, consultant*
Carlin, Clair Myron *lawyer*
†Giannini, Matthew Carlo *lawyer, educator*
Jeren, John Anthony, Jr., *lawyer*
Nadler, Myron Jay *lawyer, director*
†Newman, Christopher John *lawyer*
Roth, Daniel Benjamin *lawyer, business executive*
Rupeka, Robert W. *court administrator*

Zanesville
Micheli, Frank James *lawyer*

OKLAHOMA

Alva
Mitchell, Allan Edwin *lawyer*

Antlers
Stamper, Joe Allen *lawyer*

Bartlesville
Koch, Robert Charles *lawyer, community activist*
Roff, Alan Lee *lawyer, consultant*

Broken Arrow
†Jones, Ronald Lee *lawyer, writer*
Stewart, Murray Baker *retired lawyer*

Chandler
Swanson, Robert Lee *lawyer*

Claremore
†Burrage, Billy Michael *lawyer, retired judge*

Duncan
†Rodgers, Ricardo Juan (Rick Rodgers) *lawyer*

Edmond
Conner, Leslie Lynn, Jr., *lawyer*
Lester, Andrew William *lawyer*
Loving, Susan Brimer *lawyer, former state official*

El Reno
McCurdy, Gary Dean *district judge, educator*

Enid
Jones, Stephen *lawyer*
McNaughton, Alexander Bryant *lawyer*

Eufaula
†Dawson, Cindy Marie *lawyer*

Guthrie
†Davis, Frank Wayne *lawyer*

Guymon
Wood, Donald Euriah *lawyer*

Kingfisher
Baker, Thomas Edward *lawyer, accountant*

Lawton
†Ashton, Mark Alfred *lawyer*

Mcalester
Cornish, Richard Pool *lawyer*

Muskogee
Frix, Paige Lane *lawyer, accountant*
Gallant, Jeffrey Andrew *lawyer*
Robinson, Adelbert Carl *lawyer, judge*
Williams, Betty Outhier *lawyer*

Norman
Hastie, John Douglas *lawyer*
McFall, Sara Weer *lawyer*
†Petersen, Catherine Holland *lawyer*
†Sweeney, Everett John *lawyer*
Talley, Richard Bates *lawyer*

Oklahoma City
Allen, Robert Dee *lawyer*
Barth, J. Edward *lawyer, shareholder*
Beech, Johnny Gale *lawyer*
†Beveridge, Norwood Pierson *law educator*
Boston, William Clayton *lawyer*
†Bridges, Annita Marie *lawyer*
Christiansen, Mark D. *lawyer*
†Coats, Andrew Montgomery *lawyer, former mayor, dean*
Court, Leonard *lawyer, educator*
Cunningham, Stanley Lloyd *lawyer*
Davenport, Gerald Bruce *lawyer*
Decker, Michael Lynn *lawyer, judge*
Durand, Jack Raymond *retired lawyer*
Elder, James Carl *lawyer*
†Epperson, Kraettli Quynton *lawyer, educator*
†Fenton, Elliott Clayton *lawyer*
Ferguson, Steven Edward *lawyer*
†Fuller, G. M. *lawyer*
Hanna, Terry Ross *lawyer, small business owner*
Hemry, Jerome Eldon *lawyer*
Kallstrom, James David *lawyer*
Kline, David Adam *lawyer, educator, writer*
Kline, Timothy Deal *lawyer*
Legg, William Jefferson *lawyer*
Margo, Robert Cravens *lawyer*
Mather, Stephanie June *lawyer*
†McMillin, James Craig *lawyer*
Moler, Edward Harold *lawyer*
Necco, Alexander David *lawyer, educator*
†Nelon, Robert Dale *lawyer*
Nesbitt, Charles Rudolph *lawyer, energy consultant*
Pain, Betsy M. *lawyer*
Paliotta, Armand *lawyer*
Parrott, Nancy Sharon *lawyer*
Paul, William George *lawyer*
Rockett, D. Joe *lawyer, director*
Ross, William Jarboe *lawyer, director*
Roth, James Anthony *lawyer*
†Ryan, Patrick M. *lawyer*
Schuster, E. Elaine *lawyer*
Schwabe, George Blaine, III, *lawyer*
Stanley, Brian Jordan *lawyer*
Steinhorn, Irwin Harry *lawyer, educator, corporate executive*
†Stewart, Robert D., Jr., *lawyer*
Stringer, L.E. (Dean Stringer) *retired lawyer*
Tompkins, Raymond Edgar *lawyer*
Towery, Curtis Kent *lawyer*
Tuck-Richmond, Doletta Sue *prosecutor*
†Wallace, Thomas Andrew *lawyer*
Walsh, Lawrence Edward *lawyer*
†Willey, Benjamin Tucker, Jr., *lawyer*
Wilson, Julia Ann Yother *lawyer*
Woods, Harry Arthur, II, *lawyer*
†Zeaman, Christian Michael *lawyer, writer*
Zevnik-Sawatzky, Donna Dee *retired litigation coordinator*

Ponca City
Northcutt, Clarence Dewey *lawyer*
Raley, John W., Jr., *lawyer*

Pryor
Stinson, Marion Dennis *lawyer, land use planner, judge*

Sapulpa
Gardner, Dale Ray *lawyer*

Seminole
Elsener, G. Dale *lawyer*

Stillwater
Fischer, Richard Samuel *lawyer*
†Frye, Edward Moses *law educator*

Tinker AFB
Livingston, Douglas Mark *lawyer*

Tulsa
Abrahamson, A. Craig *lawyer*
Anderson, William Carl *lawyer*
Arrington, John Leslie, Jr., *lawyer*
Ballard, Elizabeth Ann *lawyer*
Balman, Steven K. *lawyer*
Belsky, Martin Henry *law educator, lawyer*
Biolchini, Robert Fredrick *lawyer*
Bires, Dennis Eugene *legal educator*
Bowles, Margo La Joy *lawyer*
†Bowman, David Wesley *lawyer*
Brewster, Clark Otto *lawyer*
†Brune, Kenneth Leonard *lawyer*
Bryant, Hubert Hale *lawyer*
Chandler, Ronald Jay *lawyer*
Clark, Gary Carl *lawyer*
Clark, Joseph Francis, Jr., *lawyer*
Cooper, Richard Casey *lawyer*
Coulter, Jean Walpole *lawyer*
Crawford, B. *lawyer*
Dexter, Deirdre O'Neil Elizabeth *lawyer*
Draughon, Scott Wilson *lawyer, social worker, educator*
†Eagleton, Edward John *lawyer*
Eldridge, Richard Mark *lawyer*
Engel, David Wayne *lawyer, federal official*
Farrell, John L., Jr., *lawyer, business executive*
†Ferguson, Dallas Eugene *lawyer*
†Finkelman, Paul *law educator*
†Frey, Martin Alan *lawyer, educator*
Gaberino, John Anthony, Jr., *lawyer*
Gotwals, Charles Place, Jr., *lawyer*
Hatfield, Jack Kenton *lawyer, accountant*
Haynie, Tony Wayne *lawyer*
Herrold, David Henry *lawyer*
Howard, Gene Claude *retired lawyer, retired state senator*
Huffman, Robert Allen, Jr., *lawyer*
†Hughes, William Earle *lawyer*
Imel, John Michael *lawyer*
Johnson, Cornelius Raymond *assistant city attorney*
Kihle, Donald Arthur *lawyer*
Kincaid, James Lewis *lawyer*
Luthey, Graydon Dean, Jr., *lawyer, educator*
Matthies, Mary Constance T. *lawyer*
Moffett, J. Denny *lawyer*
Nemec, Michael Lee *lawyer*
Nigh, Robert Russell, Jr., *lawyer*
Orlowski, D. Faith *lawyer*
Raynolds, William F., II, *lawyer*
Riggs, M. David *lawyer, rancher*
Slicker, Frederick Kent *lawyer*
†Sneed, James Lynde *lawyer*
†Spiegelberg, Frank David *lawyer*
Steltzlen, Janelle Hicks *lawyer*
Stockwell, Lance *law educator*
Strecker, David Eugene *lawyer*
†Thompson, Anne *court administrator*

Vinita
Curnutte, Mark William *lawyer*
Johnston, Oscar Black, III, *lawyer*

Yukon
Hixson, Wendell Mark *lawyer*

OREGON

Ashland
†Uherbelau, Judy *lawyer, state legislator*

Astoria
Haskell, Donald McMillan *lawyer*

Bend
Achterman, Gail Louise *lawyer*

Brookings
Maxwell, William Stirling *retired lawyer*

Canby
Drummond, Gerard Kasper *lawyer, retired minerals company executive*

Cannon Beach
Hillestad, Charles Andrew *lawyer*

Central Point
Richardson, Dennis Michael *lawyer, educator*

Coos Bay
†McClellan, Janet Elaine *law educator*

Coquille
Lounsbury, Steven Richard *lawyer*

Eugene
Aldave, Barbara Bader *law educator, lawyer*
Castle, Grace Eleanor *legal investigator*
Clark, Chapin DeWitt *law educator*
DuPriest, Douglas Millhollen *lawyer*
Etter, Orval
Kirkpatrick, Laird Clifford *law educator*
Mumford, William Porter, II, *retired lawyer*
†Ryer, Charles Wilfred *lawyer, court administrator*
Sahlstrom, E(lmer) Bernard *retired lawyer*
Scoles, Eugene Francis *law educator, lawyer*
Thompson, Edward P. *lawyer*

Florence
Clark, David Lewis *lawyer*

Grants Pass
Day, Gregory Thomas *lawyer*

Hillsboro
†Uffelman, John Edward *lawyer*

La Grande
Joseph, Steven Jay *lawyer*

Lake Oswego
Byczynski, Edward Frank *lawyer, financial executive*
Kuntz, Joel Dubois *lawyer*
†Lyons, Allen Ward *lawyer, educator*
†Nelson, Thomas Howard *lawyer*
Rasmussen, Richard Robert *lawyer*

Lincoln City
Arant, Eugene Wesley *lawyer*
Elliott, Scott *lawyer, seminarian*

Medford
Deatherage, William Vernon *lawyer*
O'Connor, Karl William (Goodyear Johnson) *lawyer*

Newport
Greco, Guy Benjamin *lawyer*

Pendleton
†Rew, Lawrence Boyd *lawyer*

Portland
Abrams, Marc *lawyer, state political party executive*
Abravanel, Allan Ray *lawyer*
Anderson, Herbert Hatfield *lawyer, farmer*
Anderson, Mark Alexander *lawyer*
†Anfuso, Victor L'Episcopo *lawyer, business consultant*
Arthur, Michael Elbert *lawyer, financial advisor*
Bauman, Frank Anthony *lawyer*
Bernstine, Daniel O'Neal *law educator, university president*
Birmingham, Patrick Michael *lawyer*
Blitz, Charles Akin *lawyer*
†Boly, Jeffrey Elwyn *retired lawyer*
Brenneman, Delbert Jay *lawyer*
†Brownstein, Richard Joseph *lawyer*
†Burt, Robert Gene *lawyer, educator*
Byrne, Gregory William *lawyer*
Cable, John Franklin *lawyer*
Canaday, Richard A. *lawyer*
†Cooney, Thomas Emmett *lawyer*
†Cooper, Nancy M. *lawyer*
Crowell, John B., Jr., *lawyer, former government official*
†Dailey, Dianne K. *lawyer*
DeChaine, Dean Dennis *lawyer*
Deering, Thomas Phillips *retired lawyer*
†Dennison-Leonard, Sarah *lawyer*
Dotten, Michael Chester *lawyer*
†DuBoff, Leonard David *lawyer*
Duden, Paul Russell *lawyer, managing partner*
†Ellis, Barnes Humphreys *lawyer*
English, Stephen Francis *lawyer*
Epstein, Edward Louis *lawyer*
Fedde, G(abriel) Bernhard *retired lawyer*
Feuerstein, Howard M. *lawyer*
Firestone, Gary *lawyer*
†Flaherty, Thomas Joseph *lawyer*
Foley, Ridgway Knight, Jr., *lawyer, writer*
Franzke, Richard Albert *lawyer*
†Froebe, Gerald Allen *lawyer*
Fulsher, Allan Arthur *lawyer*
Funk, William F. *lawyer, educator*
†Glasgow, Robert Efrom *lawyer*
Greene, Herbert Bruce *lawyer, investor*
Grossmann, Ronald Stanyer *lawyer*
Hanna, Harry Mitchell *lawyer*
†Harnden, Edwin A. *lawyer*
Harrell, Gary Paul *lawyer*
Hart, John Edward *lawyer*
Helmer, M(artha) Christie *lawyer*
Hergenhan, Kenneth William *lawyer*
Hinkle, Charles Frederick *lawyer, clergyman, educator*
Hirshon, Robert Edward *lawyer*
Holman, Donald Reid *retired lawyer*
†Houser, Douglas Guy *lawyer*
†Huffman, James Lloyd *law educator*
Hurd, Paul Gemmill *lawyer*
†Jarvis, Peter R. *lawyer*
Johnson, Mark Andrew *lawyer*
†Johnston, David Frederick *lawyer*
†Jolles, Bernard *lawyer*
Josephson, Richard Carl *lawyer*
Kennedy, Jack Leland *lawyer*
Kester, Randall Blair *lawyer*
Klarquist, Kenneth Stevens, Jr., *lawyer*
Krahmer, Donald Leroy, Jr., *lawyer*
Lezak, Sidney Irving *lawyer, mediator*
†Livingston, Louis Bayer *lawyer*
†Love, Linda C. *lawyer*
Love, William Edward *lawyer*
†Lusky, John Anderson *lawyer*
Maloney, Robert E., Jr., *lawyer*
Martson, William Frederick, Jr., *lawyer*
Matarazzo, Harris Starr *lawyer*
Mc Bride, Thomas Frederick *lawyer, former university dean, government official*
†Menashe, Albert Alan *lawyer*
Meyer, Paul Richard *lawyer*
Miller, William Richey, Jr., *lawyer*
†Moulun, Renee *lawyer*
Mowe, Gregory Robert *lawyer*
Noonan, William Donald *lawyer, physician*
†Nunn, Robert Warne *lawyer*
O'Brien, Kathleen *lawyer*
†O'Neill, Phoebe Joan *retired lawyer*
†Purcell, John F. *lawyer*
Richardson, Campbell *retired lawyer*
Richter, Peter Christian *lawyer*
†Rieke, Forrest Neill *lawyer*
†Rosen, Steven O. *lawyer*
Rosenbaum, Lois Omenn *lawyer*
Sand, Thomas Charles *lawyer*
Savage, John William *lawyer*
Schuster, Philip Frederick, II, *lawyer, writer, law educator*
†Scott, Lewis Kelly *lawyer*
†Seymour, Steven Wayne *lawyer*
Shorr, Scott Alden *lawyer*
Simpson, Robert Glenn *lawyer*
Smith, Douglas Dean *lawyer*
†Smith, Lester V., Jr., *lawyer, educator*
Sokol, Larry Nides *lawyer, educator*
†Spencer, John Richard *lawyer, business executive*
†Stephens, Donald L., Jr., *lawyer*
Stewart, Milton Roy *lawyer*
Stone, Richard James *lawyer*
Strader, Timothy Richards *lawyer*
Sullivan, Edward Joseph *lawyer, educator*
Swanson, Leslie Martin, Jr., *lawyer*
Tremaine, H. Stewart *retired lawyer*
Van Valkenburg, Edgar Walter *lawyer*
†Waggoner, James Clyde *lawyer*
Weaver, Delbert Allen *lawyer*
Westwood, James Nicholson *lawyer*
Whinston, Arthur Lewis *lawyer*
White, Douglas James, Jr., *lawyer*
Williams, Sharon A. *lawyer*
Wilson, Owen Meredith, Jr., *lawyer*
Wood, Marcus Andrew *lawyer*
Wyse, William Walker *lawyer, real estate executive*
Zalutsky, Morton Herman *lawyer*

Salem
Bailey, Henry John, III, *retired lawyer, educator*
Breen, Richard F., Jr., *law librarian, lawyer, educator*
†Feibleman, Gilbert Bruce *lawyer*
Gangle, Sandra Smith *arbitrator, mediator*
Mannix, Kevin Leese *lawyer, political organization executive*
Nafziger, James Albert Richmond *lawyer, educator*
Nicholson, Bradley James *lawyer*
†Robertson, Joseph David *lawyer*
Roy, Matthew Lansing *lawyer*
Swaim, Michael E. *lawyer, former mayor*

Tigard
Lowry, David Burton *lawyer*

Wilsonville
Yacob, Yosef *lawyer, economist*

PENNSYLVANIA

Abington
Budman, Alan David *lawyer, law educator*

Aliquippa
†Palmieri, John Anthony *lawyer*

Allentown
Altemose, Mark Kenneth *lawyer*
Brown, Robert Wayne *lawyer*
Fox, James Hoppes *retired lawyer*
Holt, Leon Conrad, Jr., *lawyer, business executive*
Nagel, Edward McCaul *lawyer, former utilities executive*
Noonan, Charles Thomas *lawyer*
†Scherline, Jay Alan *lawyer, educator*
†Somach, Richard Brent *lawyer*

Allison Park
Herrington, John David, III, *lawyer, director*
Ries, William Campbell *lawyer*

Altoona
†Loveless, Patricia Claire *law educator*
Serbin, Richard Martin *lawyer*

Ardmore
†Bocchino, Anthony J. *law educator, consultant*
Butterworth, David Gardner *lawyer*
Narin, Stephen B. *lawyer*

Bala Cynwyd
Aris, John Lynnwood *lawyer*
Cades, Stewart Russell *lawyer, communications company executive*
Chovanes, Eugene *lawyer*
Garrity, Vincent Francis, Jr., *lawyer*
Glusman, David H. *litigation support consultant*
Kane-Vanni, Patricia Ruth *lawyer, paleontology educator*
Manko, Joseph Martin, Sr., *lawyer*
Odell, Herbert *lawyer*
Schwartz, Jeffrey Byron *lawyer*
Wiener, Thomas Eli *lawyer*

Bellefonte
Arnold, J. Karen *lawyer*

Berwyn
Markle, John, Jr., *lawyer*
Watters, Edward McLain, III, *lawyer*
Wood, Thomas E. *lawyer*

Bethlehem
Graham, William Henry *lawyer*
†Hemphill, Meredith, Jr., *retired lawyer*
Spry, Donald Francis, II, *lawyer*

Blue Bell
Elliott, John Michael *lawyer*
Swansen, Samuel Theodore *lawyer*

Boyertown
†Boyd, Craig Stephen *lawyer*

Bradford
Hauser, Christopher George *lawyer*

Brookville
Smith, Sharon Louise *lawyer, consultant*

Bryn Mawr
Frick, Benjamin Charles *lawyer*
Hankin, Mitchell Robert *lawyer*
†Henry, Ronald George *lawyer, consultant*
†Jackson, Millard Irving, Jr., *lawyer*
Phillips, Stephen S. *lawyer*
†Stahl, Roy Howard *lawyer*

Camp Hill
Mackin, Charles Philip, Jr., *lawyer*

Carlisle
Turo, Ron *lawyer*

Center Valley
Smillie, Douglas James *lawyer*

Chadds Ford
Cohen, Felix Asher *lawyer*

Clarks Summit
Beemer, John Barry *lawyer*

Conshohocken
Bramson, Robert Sherman *lawyer*

Doylestown
Bolla, William Joseph *lawyer*
†Earnheart, Frank Jones *lawyer*
Elliott, Richard Howard *lawyer*
Hall, Peter C. *lawyer, defender*
Karsch, Jay Harris *lawyer*
†Mellon, Thomas Edward, Jr., *lawyer*

Drexel Hill
McDonnell, Michael T., Jr., *lawyer*

East Stroudsburg
Jacobson, Gilbert H. *lawyer, director*

Easton
Brown, Robert Carroll *lawyer*
Molino, Mildred A. *lawyer*
Noel, Nicholas, III, *lawyer*
Stitt, Thomas Paul, Sr., *lawyer*

Elkins Park
Schneider, Carl William *lawyer*
Shmukler, Stanford *lawyer*

Erie
Adair, Evan Edward *lawyer*
Bernard, Bruce William *lawyer*
†Yeager, Kathleen M. *court administrator*
Zamboldi, Richard Henry *lawyer*

Etters
†Steps, Barbara Jill *lawyer*

Exton
Ashton, Mark Randolph *lawyer*
Hedges, Donald Walton *lawyer*

Fort Washington
Moulton, Hugh Geoffrey *lawyer, retired business executive*

Gibsonia
†Benson, Stuart Wells, III, *lawyer*

Gladwyne
Acton, David *lawyer*
Booth, Harold Waverly *lawyer, finance and investment company executive*

Glenside
Mermelstein, Jules Joshua *lawyer, township commissioner*

Greensburg
Gounley, Dennis Joseph *lawyer*
Heubel, William Bernard *lawyer, international contract consultant*

Grove City
McBride, Milford Lawrence, Jr., *lawyer*

Harrisburg
Burcat, Joel Robin *lawyer*
†Cicconi, Christopher M. *lawyer*
Cline, Andrew Haley *lawyer*
Diehm, James Warren *lawyer, educator*
Downey, Brian Patrick *lawyer*
†Feinour, John Stephen *lawyer*
Frye, Mary Catherine *prosecutor*
†Gornish, Gerald *lawyer*
Hafer, Joseph Page *lawyer*
Hanson, Robert DeLolle *lawyer*
Howett, John Charles, Jr., *lawyer*
Kane, Yvette *lawyer, federal judge*
Kelly, Robert Edward, Jr., *lawyer*
Klein, Michael D. *lawyer*
Kury, Franklin Leo *lawyer*
Lee, Seung Jai *lawyer, legal administrator*
Lighty, Fredrick W. *lawyer*
Long, Robert Howard, Jr., *lawyer*
Miller, Leslie Anne *lawyer*
†Murren, Philip Joseph *lawyer*
Preski, Brian Joseph *lawyer*
Reiley, Robert *lawyer, educator*
Schore, Niles *lawyer*
Selkowitz, Larry Bryan *lawyer*
Sheldon, J. Michael *lawyer, educator*
†Skelly, Joseph Gordon *lawyer*
Stefanon, Anthony *lawyer*
Sullivan, John Cornelius, Jr., *lawyer*
Teplitz, Robert Forman *lawyer*
Van Zile, Philip Taylor, III, *lawyer, educator*
Warshaw, Allen Charles *lawyer*
West, James Joseph *lawyer*

Hatboro
John, Robert McClintock *lawyer*

Haverford
Stiller, Jennifer Anne *lawyer*
Stroud, James Stanley *retired lawyer*

Havertown
Besser, Amy Helene *lawyer*

Hazleton
†Pedri, Charles Raymond *lawyer*

Hershey
†Reese, Robert M. *corporate lawyer*
†Simmons, Bryan John *lawyer*

Hollidaysburg
†Evey, Merle Kenton *lawyer*

Honey Brook
DePaul, Anthony Kenneth *lawyer*

Horsham
Best, Franklin Luther, Jr., *lawyer*
Coker, Caroline Tiffany *lawyer*

Huntingdon Valley
Forman, Howard Irving *lawyer, former government official*
Kaufman, David Joseph *lawyer*

Indiana
Barbor, John Howard *lawyer*
Bell, Paul Anthony, II, *lawyer*

Jenkintown
Dickstein, Joan Borteck *arbitrator, conflict management consultant*

Jersey Shore
Flayhart, Martin Albert *lawyer*

Johnstown
Glosser, William Louis *lawyer*
Kaharick, Jerome John *lawyer*
Kaminsky, Ira Samuel *lawyer*

Jones Mills
Fish, Paul Waring *lawyer*

Kennett Square
†Bainbridge, John Seaman *retired law school administrator, law educator, lawyer*
Partnoy, Ronald Allen *lawyer*
†Temple, L. Peter *lawyer*

King Of Prussia
Boles, Donald Michael *lawyer*
DeMaria, Joseph Carminus *lawyer*
Gadsden, Christopher Henry *lawyer, educator*
Schneider, Pam Horvitz *lawyer*

Kingston
Meyer, Martin Jay *lawyer*
†Shaffer, Charles Alan *lawyer*

Lake Harmony
Polansky, Larry Paul *court administrator, consultant*

Lancaster
Eaby, Christian Earl *lawyer, small business owner*
†Gray, Kathleen Ann *lawyer*
Nast, Dianne Martha *lawyer*
Pyfer, John Frederick, Jr., *lawyer*
Roda, Joseph Francis *lawyer*
Whare, Wanda Snyder *lawyer*
Zimmerman, D(onald) Patrick *lawyer*

Langhorne
Hillje, Barbara Brown *lawyer*
†Killough, Stephen Pinckney *lawyer, director*

Lansdale
Sultanik, Jeffrey Ted *lawyer*

Lansdowne
Kyriazis, Arthur John (Athanasios Ioannis Kyriazis) *lawyer, biotechnologist*

Lehigh Valley
†McGonagle, John Joseph, Jr., *lawyer*

Lemoyne
Stewart, Richard Williams *lawyer*

Lewisburg
†Knight, Louise Osborn *lawyer*

Lock Haven
Snowiss, Alvin L. *lawyer*

Malvern
Cameron, John Clifford *lawyer, health science facility administrator*
†Doerr, John Maxwell *lawyer*
†May, Judy Royer *lawyer*

Marietta
Shumaker, Harold Dennis *lawyer*

Mc Keesport
Kessler, Steven Fisher *lawyer*

Mc Murray
Brzustowicz, John Cinq-Mars *lawyer*

Meadville
Shafer, Raymond Philip *lawyer, business executive*

Media
Berman, Bernard Mayer *lawyer*
Blake, David Gordon *lawyer*
†Cramp, John Franklin *lawyer*
D'Amico, Andrew J. *lawyer*
DiOrio, Robert Michael *lawyer, public official*
†Durham, James W. *lawyer*
Emerson, Sterling Jonathan *lawyer*
Ewing, Robert Clark *lawyer*
Firkser, Robert Michael *lawyer*
Lipton, Robert Stephen *lawyer*
†List, Anthony Francis *lawyer*
Malloy, Michael Joseph *lawyer*
†McNitt, David Garver *lawyer*
†Mulligan, John Thomas *lawyer*
Tomlinson, Herbert Weston *lawyer*

Mendenhall
Reinert, Norbert Frederick *patent lawyer, retired chemical company executive*

Mercer
Kochems, Robert Gregory *lawyer*

Middletown
Pannebaker, James Boyd *lawyer*

Monroeville
Baum, Alan Stuart *lawyer*

Mont Alto
Achampong, Francis Kofi *law educator, consultant*

Moon Township
Alstadt, Lynn Jeffery *lawyer*

Morrisville
Dobin, Edward I. *lawyer*
Heefner, William Frederick *lawyer*
†Hershenson, Gerald Martin *lawyer*

Mount Gretna
Warshaw, Roberta Sue *lawyer, financial specialist*

Mount Pleasant
Johnson, Michael A. *lawyer*

Narberth
†Rovner, David Patrick Ryan *lawyer*

New Buffalo
Cramer, John McNaight *lawyer*

New Castle
Kelly, Lawrence M. *lawyer*
Mangino, Matthew Thomas *lawyer*
†Mojock, David Theodore *lawyer*

New Cumberland
Yakowicz, Vincent X. *lawyer, consultant*

New Kensington
†Wallace, Henry Jared, Jr., *lawyer*

Newtown
Flum, Joseph *lawyer*
Godwin, Robert Anthony *lawyer*
Kardos, Mel D. *lawyer, educator*
Renninger, John Snowden *lawyer*

Newtown Square
Bower, Ward Alan *management consultant, lawyer*
†Crowley, James Michael *lawyer*

Norristown
Aman, George Matthias, III, *lawyer*
Andrews, Cheri D. *lawyer*
Britt, Earl Thomas *lawyer*
Cowperthwait, Lindley Murray *lawyer*
†Gold-Bikin, Lynne Z. *lawyer*
†Gowen, Thomas Leo, Jr., *lawyer*
Gregg, John Pennypacker *lawyer*
Milner, Kenneth Paul *lawyer*
Rees, Thomas Dynevor *lawyer*
Rounick, Jack A. *lawyer, company executive*
†Sosnov, Amy W(iener) *lawyer*

North Wales
†Brady, George Charles, III, *lawyer*

Orefield
†Dimmich, Jeffrey Robert *lawyer*

Paoli
Griffith, Edward *lawyer*

Philadelphia
Aaron, Kenneth Ellyot *lawyer*
†Abraham, Richard Paul *lawyer*
Abramowitz, Robert Leslie *lawyer*
Adamany, David Walter *law and political science educator*
Adams, Arlin Marvin *lawyer, arbitrator, mediator, retired judge*
Agran, Raymond Daniel *lawyer*
†Allen-Castellitto, Anita LaFrance *law educator*
Anders, Jerrold P. *lawyer*
Aronstein, Martin Joseph *law educator, lawyer*
Auten, David Charles *lawyer*
Baccini, Laurance Ellis *lawyer*
Bachman, Arthur *lawyer*
Barrett, John J(ames), Jr., *lawyer*
†Battis, David Gregory *lawyer*
†Beam, Robert Charles *lawyer*
Beasley, James Edwin *lawyer*
Berenato, Mark Anthony *lawyer, insurance executive*
Berger, David *lawyer*
Berger, Harold *lawyer, electrical engineer*
†Berger, Lawrence Howard *lawyer*
Berkley, Emily Carolan *lawyer*
Berkman, Richard Lyle *lawyer*
Bernard, John Marley *lawyer, educator*
Bershad, Jack R. *retired lawyer*
Bildersee, Robert Alan *lawyer*
Binder, David Franklin *lawyer, author*
Black, Allen Decatur *lawyer*
Blumstein, Edward *lawyer*
Boggia, Eugene Stephen *lawyer*
Bogutz, Jerome Edwin *lawyer, educator*
Bonovitz, Sheldon M. *lawyer*
Boss, Amelia Helen *law educator, lawyer*
†Bradshaw, William Elbert *lawyer*
Bressler, Barry E. *lawyer*
†Brier, Bonnie Susan *lawyer*
Brown, Stephen D. *lawyer*
Brown, William Hill, III, *lawyer*
Browne, Stanhope Stryker *lawyer*
Buccino, Ernest John, Jr., *lawyer*
Burbank, Stephen Bradner *law educator*
Cabot, Stephen Jay *lawyer*
Caldwell, John Warwick *lawyer*
Calvert, Jay H., Jr., *lawyer*
Cannon, John, III, *lawyer*
Caravasos, NiaLena *lawyer*
Carnecchia, Baldo M., Jr., *lawyer*
†Carson, Timothy Joseph *lawyer*
Casper, Charles B. *lawyer*
Cherken, Harry Sarkis, Jr., *lawyer*
Cheston, George Morris *lawyer*
Chimples, George *lawyer*
Clark, John Arthur *lawyer*
Clark, William H., Jr., *lawyer*
Coleman, Robert J. *lawyer*
Colli, Bart Joseph *lawyer*
Collings, Robert L. *lawyer*
Comisky, Hope A. *lawyer*
Connor, Joseph Patrick, III, *lawyer*
Cooney, J(ohn) Gordon, Jr., *lawyer*
Cox, Roger Frazier *lawyer*
Coyne, Charles Cole *lawyer*
Cramer, Harold *lawyer*
†Craven, Charles Warren *lawyer*
Cross, Milton H. *lawyer*
Czech, Paul Andrew *lawyer*
Dabrowski, Doris Jane *lawyer*
Damsgaard, Kell Marsh *lawyer*
Davidson, Stuart West *lawyer*
Davis, Alan Jay *lawyer*
†Davis, C. VanLeer, III, *lawyer*
Davis, Howard Jeffrey *lawyer*
DeBunda, Salvatore Michael *lawyer*
†DeFusco Ochal, Mary Theresa *lawyer*
Del Raso, Joseph Vincent *lawyer*
Devlin, John Gerard *lawyer, author*
Diaz, Nelson *lawyer*
Dichter, Mark S. *lawyer*
Dilks, Park Bankert, Jr., *lawyer*
Donner, Henry Jay *lawyer*
Donohue, James J. *lawyer*
Donohue, John Patrick *lawyer*
Doran, William Michael *lawyer*
Dorfman, John Charles *lawyer*
Drake, William Frank, Jr., *lawyer*
Dubin, Leonard *lawyer*
Dubin, Stephen Victor *lawyer*
Durant, Marc *lawyer*
Dworetzky, Joseph Anthony *lawyer, city official*
†Elliott, Homer Lee *lawyer*
Epstein, Alan Bruce *lawyer*
Esser, Carl Eric *lawyer*
Everett, Carl Bell *lawyer*
†Ewald, William Bragg, III, *law educator, philosopher, educator*
Fader, Henry Conrad *lawyer*
Fala, Herman C. *lawyer*
†Farley, Barbara L. *lawyer*
Feirson, Steven B. *lawyer*
Fickler, Arlene *lawyer*
Fiebach, H. Robert *lawyer*
†Fine, Lawrence B. *lawyer*
Finkelstein, Joseph Simon *lawyer*
Fitts, Michael Andrew *law educator, dean*
Flanagan, Joseph Patrick, Jr., *lawyer*
†Fox, Reeder Rodman *lawyer*
†Frank, George Andrew *lawyer*
Frank, Harvey *lawyer, author*
Freedman, Robert Louis *lawyer*
†Fritton, Karl Andrew *lawyer*
Gadon, Steven Franklin *lawyer*
Garcia, Rudolph *lawyer*
Genkin, Barry Howard *lawyer*
†Girard-diCarlo, David Franklin *lawyer*
†Gittis, Howard *lawyer*
Glazer, Ronald Barry *lawyer*
†Goldberg, Joseph *lawyer*
Goldberg, Marvin Allen *lawyer, business consultant*
Goldberg, Richard Robert *lawyer*
Goldman, Gary Craig *lawyer*
Goldman, Jerry Stephen *lawyer*
Goldsmith, Howard Michael *lawyer*
Goldstein, William Marks *lawyer*
Goodman, Stephen Murry *lawyer*
Gough, John Francis *lawyer*
†Granoff, Gail Patricia *lawyer*
Grant, M. Duncan *lawyer*
†Gratke, Fred Edward *lawyer*
Greenfield, Bruce Harold *lawyer, banker*
†Griffin, Deborah S. *lawyer*
Grove, David Lavan *lawyer*
Haley, Vincent Peter *lawyer*
†Hangley, William Thomas *lawyer*
Hanselmann, Fredrick Charles *lawyer*
Harkins, John Graham, Jr., *lawyer*
Harmelin, Stephen Joseph *lawyer*
†Harvey, Gregory Merrill *lawyer*
Haviland, Bancroft Dawley *lawyer*
Heintz, Paul Capron *lawyer*
Heinzen, Bernard George *lawyer*
Henrich, William Joseph, Jr., *lawyer*
†Herman, Charles Jacob *lawyer*
Hess, H. Ober *lawyer, director*
†Hickok, D. Alicia *lawyer*
Hoffman, Alan Jay *lawyer*
Horn, Robert F. *lawyer*
†Horn Epstein, Phyllis Lynn *lawyer*
Hottensen, Margaret M. *lawyer*
†Howard, William Herbert *lawyer*
Hoyle, Lawrence Truman, Jr., *lawyer*
Hunter, James Austen, Jr., *lawyer*
Ivey, Stephen David *lawyer*
Jellinek, Miles Andrew *lawyer*
Jones, Robert Jeffries *lawyer*
Kahn, James Robert *lawyer*
Kaier, Edward John *lawyer*
Kaiser, Linda Susan *lawyer*
†Kanter, Seymour *lawyer*
Kaplan, Arthur Mitchell *lawyer*
†Kaplan, Jerome *lawyer, accountant*
Keene, John Clark *lawyer, educator*
†Kelley, George Lawrence, Jr., *lawyer*
Kempin, Frederick Gustav, Jr., *lawyer, educator*
Kessler, Alan Craig *lawyer*
Klasko, Herbert Ronald *lawyer, law educator, writer*
Klein, Howard Bruce *lawyer, law educator*
Kolsby, Herbert F. *lawyer, educator*
Kopp, Charles Gilbert *lawyer*
Kormes, John Winston *lawyer*
†Kramer, Gilda Lea *lawyer*
Krzyzanowski, Richard L. *lawyer, corporate executive*
†LaCheen, Stephen Robert *lawyer*
Lawn, Timothy Regis *lawyer*
Ledwith, John Francis *lawyer*
Leonard, Thomas *lawyer*
Levin, Murray Simon *lawyer*
Lewis, John Hardy, Jr., *lawyer*
Libonati, Michael Ernest *law educator, writer*
Lichtenstein, Robert Jay *lawyer*
†Lillie, Charisse Ranielle *lawyer, educator*
Lipman, Frederick D. *lawyer, author, educator*
Lombard, John James, Jr., *lawyer, writer*
Loveless, George Group *retired lawyer*
Lowery, William Herbert *lawyer*
†Lucey, John David, Jr., *lawyer*
†MacDonald, John Alexander *lawyer*
Madva, Stephen Alan *lawyer*
Magargee, W(illiam) Scott, III, *lawyer*
Magaziner, Fred Thomas *lawyer*
Mann, Theodore R. *lawyer*
Mannino, Edward Francis *lawyer, educator*
†Marino, Donald C. *lawyer*
Mason, Theodore W. *lawyer*
Mathes, Stephen Jon *lawyer*
Mattoon, Peter Mills *lawyer*
Maxey, David Walker *lawyer*
†McAneny, Eileen S. *lawyer*
McCarron, Jeffrey Baldwin *lawyer*
†McGurk, Eugene David, Jr., *lawyer*
McHugh, James Joseph *lawyer*
McKeever, John Eugene *lawyer*
†McMenamin, Richard F. *lawyer*
McQuiston, Robert Earl *lawyer*
Meigs, John Forsyth *lawyer*
Messa, Joseph Louis, Jr., *lawyer*
Meyers, Howard L. *lawyer*
Milbourne, Walter Robertson *lawyer*
Miller, Henry Franklin *lawyer*
Milone, Francis Michael *lawyer*
Mirabello, Francis Joseph *lawyer*
†Morris, Roland *lawyer*
†Moses, Bonnie Smith *lawyer, educator*
Moss, Arthur Henshey *lawyer*
Mullinix, Edward Wingate *lawyer*
†Mulvey, W. Michael *lawyer*
Murphy, William Patrick *lawyer, editor, writer*
†Newman, George Henry *lawyer*
Nofer, George Hancock *lawyer*
O'Brien, William Jerome, II, *lawyer*
O'Connor, Joseph A., Jr., *lawyer*
Ominsky, Andrew Michael *lawyer*
Ominsky, Harris *lawyer*
O'Reilly, Timothy Patrick *lawyer*
Ossip, Michael J. *lawyer*
Oswald, Stanton S. *lawyer*
Pagliaro, James Domenic *lawyer*
Palmer, Richard Ware *lawyer*
Panek, Edward Stanley, Jr., *lawyer*
†Panzer, Mitchell Emanuel *lawyer*
Parry, William DeWitt *lawyer*
Pasek, Jeffrey Ivan *lawyer*
Patton, Peter Mark *lawyer*
Pauciulo, John William *lawyer*
†Perry, David *lawyer, insurance executive, real estate consultant*
†Pillai, K. G. Jan *law educator, lawyer*
Pollack, Michael *lawyer*
Porrata-Doria, Rafael Alfonso *law educator*
Posner, Edward Martin *lawyer*
Poul, Franklin *lawyer*
Powell, Walter Hecht *labor arbitrator*
Presser, Stefan *lawyer, educator*
†Prewitt, David Edward *lawyer*
Price, Robert Stanley *lawyer*
Promislo, Daniel *lawyer*
Putney, Paul William *lawyer*
Rabinowitz, Samuel Nathan *lawyer*
Rachofsky, David J. *lawyer*
Rackow, Julian Paul *lawyer*
Rainone, Michael Carmine *lawyer*
Rainville, Christina *lawyer*
Ramsey, Natalie D. *lawyer*
Raymond, Fred Douglas, III, *lawyer*
†Real, Frank Joseph, Jr., *lawyer, accountant*
†Reath, Henry (Thompson) *lawyer*
Reich, Abraham Charles *lawyer*
Reisman, Jason Eric *lawyer*
Reiss, John Barlow *lawyer*
Reiter, Joseph Henry *lawyer, retired judge*
Reitz, Curtis Randall *lawyer, educator*
Resnick, Stephanie *lawyer*
Rhoads, Nancy Glenn *lawyer*
Rhodes, Alice Graham *lawyer*
Roberts, Carl Geoffrey *lawyer*
Root, Stanley William, Jr., *lawyer, retired*
Rosenbleeth, Richard M. *lawyer*
Rosenbloom, Sanford M. *lawyer*
Rosenstein, James Alfred *lawyer, mediator, negotiation facilitator*
Ross, Daniel R. *lawyer*
†Ross, Murray Louis *lawyer, business executive*
Samuel, Ralph David *lawyer*
†Sartorius, Peter S. *lawyer*
Satinsky, Barnett *lawyer*
Schaub, Harry Carl *lawyer*
Scher, Howard Dennis *lawyer*
Schneider, Richard Graham *lawyer*
Schoener, George Francis, Jr., *lawyer*
Schorling, William Harrison *lawyer*
Schwartz, Robert M. *lawyer*
Segal, Robert Martin *lawyer*
Shapiro, Raymond L. *lawyer*
Sheils, Denis Francis *lawyer*

Shestack, Jerome Joseph *lawyer*
Shiekman, Laurence Zeid *lawyer*
Siddiqui, Shahram Mohammad *lawyer*
Siegel, Bernard Louis *lawyer*
Sigmond, Richard Brian *lawyer*
Simkanich, John Joseph *lawyer, engineer*
†Sloane, Richard *lawyer*
†Smith, John Francis, III, *lawyer*
Solano, Carl Anthony *lawyer*
†Sonnenfeld, Marc Jay *lawyer*
†Sorokin, Sharon L. *lawyer*
Spaeth, Edmund Benjamin, Jr., *retired lawyer, retired law educator, former judge*
†Spector, Martin Wolf *lawyer, business executive*
Speyer, Debra Gail *lawyer*
Spolan, Harmon Samuel *lawyer*
Steinberg, Robert Philip *lawyer*
Stern, Joan Naomi *lawyer*
Stevens, Mark Alan *lawyer, environmental engineer*
Stewart, Robert Forrest, Jr., *lawyer*
Strasbaugh, Wayne Ralph *lawyer*
Strazzella, James Anthony *law educator, lawyer*
Strickler, Matthew M. *lawyer*
†Stroebel, John Stephen *lawyer*
Stuntebeck, Clinton A. *lawyer*
Subak, John Thomas *lawyer*
Summers, Clyde Wilson *law educator*
Temin, Michael Lehman *lawyer*
Thomas, Lowell Shumway, Jr., *lawyer*
Tiger, Ira Paul *lawyer*
Tractenberg, Craig R. *lawyer*
Vaira, Peter Francis *lawyer*
†Voluck, Jeffrey M. *lawyer*
Warner, Theodore Kugler, Jr., *lawyer*
Weil, Jeffrey George *lawyer*
Wert, Robert Clifton *lawyer*
Whinston, Stephen Alan *lawyer*
Whiteside, William Anthony, Jr., *retired lawyer*
†Whitman, Jules Isidoré *lawyer*
†Wiener, Ronald Martin *lawyer*
Wild, Richard P. *lawyer*
Wittels, Barnaby Caesar *lawyer, writer*
Wolf, Robert B. *lawyer*
Wolff, Deborah H(orowitz) *lawyer*
Wright, Minturn Tatum, III, *lawyer*
Wrobleski, Jeanne Pauline *lawyer*
Young, Andrew Brodbeck *lawyer*

Pipersville
Sigety, Charles Edward *lawyer, family business consultant*

Pittsburgh
Aaron, Marcus, II, *lawyer*
Aderson, Sanford M. *lawyer*
Artz, John Curtis *lawyer*
Baldauf, Kent Edward *lawyer*
†Barrett, Karen Moore *lawyer*
Basinski, Anthony Joseph *lawyer*
Bleier, Michael E. *lawyer*
Blenko, Walter John, Jr., *lawyer*
Bonessa, Dennis R. *lawyer*
Boswell, William Paret *lawyer*
Breault, Theodore E(dward) *lawyer*
Brown, David Ronald *lawyer*
Brown, Ronald James *lawyer, consultant*
Candris, Laura A. *lawyer*
Chaban, Lawrence Richard *lawyer*
Chase, Norma *lawyer*
Cheever, George Martin *lawyer*
Chipman, Debra Decker *paralegal*
†Chute, Alan Dale *lawyer*
Cohen, Henry C. *lawyer*
Cohen, Robert (Robert Avram Cohen) *lawyer*
Colen, Frederick Haas *lawyer*
Coney, Aims C., Jr., *lawyer, labor-management negotiator*
Conlon, Raymond Joseph *lawyer*
Connors, Eugene Kenneth *lawyer, educator*
Cooper, Thomas Louis *lawyer*
Corbett, Thomas Wingett, Jr., *lawyer*
Cowan, Barton Zalman *lawyer*
†Crayne, Larry Randolph *lawyer*
Daniel, Robert Michael *lawyer*
Davenport, Ronald Ross, Jr., *lawyer*
Davis, Lewis U., Jr., *lawyer*
DeForest, Walter Pattison, III, *lawyer*
Demmler, John Henry *retired lawyer*
Donnelly, Thomas Joseph *lawyer, director*
Doty, Robert Walter *lawyer*
Ehrenwerth, David Harry *lawyer*
Evans, Bruce Dwight *lawyer*
†Feldstein, Jay Harris *lawyer*
†Flanagan, Joanna Scarlata *lawyer*
Flatley, Lawrence Edward *lawyer*
Flinn, Michael James *lawyer*
Fort, James Tomlinson *lawyer*
†Frank, Frederick Newman *lawyer*
Frank, Ronald William *lawyer, financier*
Geeseman, Robert George *lawyer*
Gold, Harold Arthur *lawyer*
Goldberg, Mark Joel *lawyer*
Hardie, James Hiller *lawyer*
Hartman, Ronald G. *lawyer*
†Harty, James Quinn *lawyer*
Hellman, Arthur David *law educator, consultant*
Helmrich, Joel Marc *lawyer*
†Herchenroether, Peter Young *lawyer*
Hershey, Dale *lawyer, educator*
Hershey, Nathan *lawyer, educator*
Hess, Emerson Garfield *lawyer*
Hill, John Howard *lawyer*
†Hitt, Leo N. *lawyer, educator*
Hollinshead, Earl Darnell, Jr., *lawyer*
Hornak, Mark Raymond *lawyer*
Hull, John Daniel, IV, *lawyer*
Hurnyak, Christina Kaiser *lawyer*
Irvine, Peter Bennington *clergyman*
Isabella, Mary Margaret *lawyer*
Johnson, Barbara Elizabeth *lawyer*
Johnson, Robert Alan *lawyer*
Jones, Craig Ward *lawyer*
Kearns, John J., III, *lawyer*
Kenrick, Charles William *lawyer*
Ketter, David Lee *lawyer*
King, Paul Martin *lawyer*

Klett, Edwin L. *lawyer*
Krebs, Robert Alan *lawyer*
†Lashay, Jill Maria *lawyer*
Lerach, Richard Fleming *lawyer*
Letwin, Jeffrey William *lawyer*
Litman, Roslyn Margolis *lawyer, educator*
†Lovett, Robert G. *lawyer*
†Lucchino, Frank Joseph *lawyer, county official*
Lynch, Victor K. *lawyer*
†Lyncheski, John E. *lawyer*
MacBeth, Lynn Ellen *lawyer*
Mahood, James Edward *lawyer*
†Marsico, Leonard Joseph *lawyer*
McCartney, Robert Charles *retired lawyer*
McGinley, John Regis, Jr., *lawyer*
McGough, Walter Thomas, Jr., *lawyer*
McLaughlin, John Sherman *lawyer*
Meisel, Alan *law educator*
Meyers, Jerry Ivan *lawyer*
Miller, David A. *lawyer*
Mulvihill, Keithley D. *lawyer*
Murdoch, David Armot *lawyer*
†Nasri, William Zaki *legal educator, copyright consultant*
Nordenberg, Mark Alan *law educator, academic administrator*
Norris, James Harold *lawyer*
Ober, Russell John, Jr., *lawyer*
O'Connor, Edward Gearing *lawyer*
Olson, Stephen M(ichael) *lawyer*
Orsatti, Ernest Benjamin *lawyer*
†Parker, James Lee *lawyer*
†Perry, John F. *lawyer*
Perry, Jon Robert *lawyer*
Pfaff, Robert James *lawyer*
Phillips, Larry Edward *lawyer*
Plowman, Jack Wesley *lawyer*
Pollack, David L. *lawyer*
†Post, Peter David *lawyer*
Powderly, William H., III, *lawyer*
Prosperi, Louis Anthony *lawyer*
Randolph, Robert DeWitt *lawyer*
Reed, W. Franklin *lawyer*
Restivo, James John, Jr., *lawyer*
†Richards, Robert Byam *lawyer*
Ritchey, Patrick William *lawyer*
Rosen, Richard David *lawyer*
Rosenberger, Bryan David *lawyer*
†Saunders, Martin Johnston *lawyer*
Scheinholtz, Leonard Louis *lawyer*
Schwendeman, Paul William *lawyer*
Segal, Frederick Leslie *lawyer*
Sell, William Edward *law educator*
†Seymour, Donald Edward *lawyer*
†Shane, Peter Milo *law educator*
Sherry, John Sebastian *lawyer*
Shuman, Joseph Duff *lawyer*
Silverman, Arnold Barry *lawyer*
†Singer, Paul Meyer *lawyer*
†Smith, James Ignatius, III, *bar association executive*
Sokol, Stephen M. *lawyer*
†Specter, Howard Alan *lawyer*
†Springer, Eric Winston *lawyer, director*
Strader, James David *lawyer*
Stroyd, Arthur Heister *lawyer*
Sutton, William Dwight *lawyer*
Sweeney, Clayton Anthony *lawyer, business executive*
Symons, Edward Leonard, Jr., *investment adviser*
Tarasi, Louis Michael, Jr., *lawyer*
Thompson, Thomas Martin *lawyer*
Thurman, Andrew Edward *lawyer*
Tully, Bernard Michael *lawyer*
†Tungate, David E. *lawyer, educator*
Turner, Harry Woodruff *lawyer*
†Ubinger, John W., Jr., *lawyer*
Ulven, Mark Edward *lawyer*
†Ummer, James Walter *lawyer*
Van Kirk, Thomas L. *lawyer*
Vater, Charles J. *lawyer*
Veeder, Peter Greig *lawyer*
von Waldow, Arnd N. *lawyer*
Ward, Thomas Jerome *lawyer*
†Weil, Andrew L. *lawyer*
†Wiley, S. Donald *lawyer, food products executive*
Wilkinson, James Allan *lawyer, healthcare executive*
†Wiltse, James Burdick *lawyer*
†Winter, Nelson Warren *lawyer*
Yorsz, Stanley *lawyer*
Zangrilli, Albert Joseph, Jr., *lawyer*
Zittrain, Lester Eugene *lawyer*

Plymouth
Musto, Joseph John *lawyer*

Plymouth Meeting
Kranzdorf, Norman M(elvin) *lawyer, real estate executive*

Pottsville
Tamulonis, Frank Louis, Jr., *lawyer*

Reading
†Linton, Jack Arthur *lawyer*
†Page, Clemson North, Jr., *lawyer*
†Roland, John Wanner *lawyer*
Rothermel, Daniel Krott *lawyer, holding company executive*

Ridley Park
Clark, John H., Jr., *lawyer*

Saint Davids
Donnella, Michael Andre *lawyer, pharmaceutical company executive*

Scranton
Burke, Henry Patrick *lawyer*
Cimini, Joseph Fedele *law educator, lawyer, former magistrate*
Friedrichs, David O. *legal educator*
Haggerty, James Joseph *lawyer*
Howley, James McAndrew *lawyer*
Wilson, Charles Frank *lawyer, law educator*

Selinsgrove
Davis, Richard Owen *lawyer*

Sewickley
†Mance, Jack Michael *retired lawyer, insurance company executive*

Sharon
Dill, William Allen *lawyer*
Kosmowski, Audra Michele *lawyer*

Shiremanstown
Gould, Thomas Denton *lawyer*

Solebury
Cross, Robert William *lawyer, venture capital executive*
Valentine, H. Jeffrey *legal association executive*

Somerset
Barkman, Jon Albert *lawyer*

Spring House
Rosoff, William A. *lawyer, executive*

Springfield
Maclay, Donald Merle *retired lawyer*

State College
Loviscky, Douglas Charles *tax lawyer*
Nollau, Lee Gordon *lawyer*

Stroudsburg
†Upright, Kirby Grant *lawyer*

Sunbury
Fernsler, John Paul *lawyer*
Saylor, Charles Horace *lawyer, judge*

Swarthmore
Elman, Gerry Jay *lawyer*
Ullman, Roger Roland *lawyer, realtor*

Trevose
McEvilly, James Patrick, Jr., *lawyer*

Uniontown
†Coldren, Ira Burdette, Jr., *lawyer*
†Davis, James Thomas *lawyer*

Valley Forge
Bovaird, Brendan Peter *lawyer*
Corchin, Mark Alan *lawyer*
†Walters, Bette Jean *lawyer*

Villanova
Bersoff, Donald Neil *lawyer, psychologist*
Maule, James Edward *law educator, lawyer*
Mulroney, Michael *lawyer, law educator, graduate program director*
Zearfoss, Herbert Keyser *lawyer*

Warren
Ristau, Mark Moody *lawyer, petroleum consultant*

Washington
Allison, Jonathan *retired lawyer*
Lerner, William C. *lawyer*
Posner, David S. *lawyer*
Richman, Stephen I. *lawyer*
Schwarz, Frederick A.O., Jr., *lawyer*

Washington Crossing
†Sloca, Steven Lane *lawyer*

Wayne
Dixon, E. A., Jr., *lawyer*
Wilson, Bruce Brighton *retired transportation executive, lawyer*

Waynesboro
Maxwell, LeRoy Stevenson *retired lawyer*

West Chester
Ewing, Joseph Neff, Jr., *retired lawyer*
Osborn, John Edward *lawyer, pharmaceutical and biotechnology industry executive, former government official, writer*

West Conshohocken
Teillon, Louis Pierre, Jr., *lawyer*

West Mifflin
Kemp, Kathleen Nagy *lawyer*

Wexford
Micale, Frank Jude *lawyer*

Wilkes Barre
Roth, Eugene *lawyer*
Ufberg, Murray *lawyer*

Williamsport
Ertel, Allen Edward *lawyer, former congressman*
Knecht, William L. *lawyer*

Willow Grove
Glassmoyer, Thomas Parvin *lawyer*

Womelsdorf
Worley, Jane Ludwig *lawyer*

Wormleysburg
Cherewka, Michael *lawyer*

Wynnewood
†Stapleton, Larrick B. *lawyer*

Wyomissing
Turner, David Eldridge *lawyer*

Yardley
Hamberg, Gilbert Lee *lawyer*

York
†Hoffmeyer, William Frederick *lawyer, educator*

RHODE ISLAND

Barrington
Soutter, Thomas Douglas *retired lawyer*

Bristol
Bogus, Carl Thomas *law educator*
Clark, Esther Frances *law educator*
Kent, Robert Brydon *law educator*

Cranston
Coletti, John Anthony *lawyer, furniture and realty company executive*
Factor, Alfred *lawyer*
Ioanes, Joyce *lawyer, social worker*
†Simonian, John S. *lawyer*

East Greenwich
Dence, Edward William, Jr., *lawyer, banker*

Jamestown
Parks, Albert Lauriston *lawyer*

Little Compton
Caron, Wilfred Rene *retired lawyer*

Newport
McConnell, David Kelso *lawyer*
Scheck, Frank Foetisch *retired lawyer*

North Providence
Lombardi, Valentino Dennis *lawyer*

Pawtucket
†Hendel, Maurice William *lawyer, consultant*
Kranseler, Lawrence Michael *lawyer*

Portsmouth
Levie, Howard S(idney) *lawyer, educator, writer*

Providence
Berkelhammer, Robert Bruce *lawyer*
Carlotti, Stephen Jon *lawyer*
†Conley, Patrick T. *lawyer*
Courage, Thomas Roberts *lawyer*
Curran, Joseph Patrick *lawyer*
Demopulos, Harold William *lawyer*
Farrell, Margaret Dawson *lawyer*
Field, Noel Macdonald, Jr., *lawyer*
Fogarty, Edward Michael *lawyer*
Furness, Peter John *lawyer*
Gale, Edwin John *judge*
Gasbarro, Pasco, Jr., *lawyer*
Hastings, Edwin H(amilton) *lawyer*
Johnson, Vahe Duncan *lawyer*
Jones, Lauren Evans *lawyer*
Kean, John Vaughan *retired lawyer*
Kersh, DeWitte Talmadge, Jr., *lawyer*
Kraemer, Michael Frederick *lawyer*
Licht, Richard A. *lawyer*
Long, Beverly Glenn *retired lawyer*
Long, Nicholas Trott *lawyer*
McAndrew, Thomas Joseph *lawyer*
McCann, Gail Elizabeth *lawyer*
McElroy, Michael Robert *lawyer*
McIntyre, Jerry L. *lawyer*
†McMahon, John Joseph *lawyer*
Medeiros, Matthew Francis *lawyer*
Olsen, Hans Peter *lawyer*
†Prentiss, Richard Daniel *lawyer*
Ratcliffe, J. Richard *lawyer*
Reilly, Charles James *lawyer, educator, accountant*
Robinson, William Philip, III, *lawyer*
Salter, Lester Herbert *lawyer*
†Salvadore, Guido Richard *lawyer*
Sherman, Deming Eliot *lawyer*
†Silver, Paul Allen *lawyer*
Smith, Robert Ellis *lawyer, journalist*
Staples, Richard Farnsworth *lawyer*
†Tobin, Bentley *lawyer*
Tramonti, John, Jr., *lawyer*
Walker, Howard Ernest *lawyer*

Scituate
Gorham, Bradford *lawyer*

Wakefield
Hart, Kenneth Nelson *lawyer*
Rothschild, Donald Phillip *lawyer, arbitrator*

Warwick
Knowles, Charles Timothy *lawyer, state legislator, military officer, educator*
†Penza, Joseph Fulvio, Jr., *lawyer*
†Riffkin, Mitchell Sanford *lawyer*

West Warwick
Bottella, Tammy Ann *lawyer*
Pollock, Bruce Gerald *lawyer*

Woonsocket
Koutsogiane, Phillip Charles *lawyer*
†Lankowsky, Zenon P. *lawyer*
†Roszkowski, Joseph John *lawyer*

SOUTH CAROLINA

Aiken
Alan, Matthew W. A. *lawyer*
Amabile, John Louis *lawyer*
Marine, Andrew Craig *lawyer*
Pearce, Richard Lee *lawyer*
Rudnick, Irene Krugman *lawyer, former state legislator, educator*

Beaufort
Harvey, William Brantley, Jr., *lawyer, former lieutenant governor*

Bishopville
†Jennings, Jacob Hill *lawyer, director*

Charleston
Branham, C. Michael *lawyer*

Cannon, Hugh *lawyer*
Farr, Charles Sims *lawyer*
Freer, Robert Elliott, Jr., *lawyer*
Good, Joseph Cole, Jr., *lawyer*
Groves, Stephen Peterson, Sr., *lawyer*
Helms, William Collier, III, *lawyer*
†Hughston, Thomas Leslie, Jr., *lawyer*
Kahn, Ellis Irvin *lawyer*
Patrick, Charles William, Jr., *lawyer*
Robinson, Neil Cibley, Jr., *lawyer*
Spitz, Hugo Max *retired lawyer*

Clemson
Cox, Headley Morris, Jr., *lawyer, educator*

Columbia
Arvay, Nancy Joan *lawyer*
Babcock, Keith Moss *lawyer*
Bernstein, Barry Joel *lawyer*
Blanton, Hoover Clarence *lawyer*
Buchanan, William Jennings *lawyer, judge*
Carpenter, Charles Elford, Jr., *lawyer*
Cooper, Robert Gordon *lawyer*
†Cotty, William Frank (Bill Cotty) *lawyer, state legislator*
†Cross, Joseph Russell, Jr., *law librarian*
Crystal, Nathan Maxwell *law educator, consultant*
Day, Richard Earl *lawyer, educator*
†Felix, Robert Louis *law educator*
Finkel, Gerald Michael *lawyer*
Gibbes, William Holman *lawyer*
†Gray, Elizabeth Van Doren *lawyer*
†Halford, Raymond Gaines *lawyer*
Handel, Richard Craig *lawyer*
Harpootlian, Richard Ara *lawyer*
Jones, Hartwell Kelley, Jr., *lawyer*
†Land, John Calhoun, III, *lawyer, state legislator*
Lester, Ken Harrison *lawyer*
Leventis, George Chris *lawyer*
†Lewis, Ernest Crosby *lawyer*
Mack, Francis Marion *lawyer, engineer*
Matthews, Steve Allen *lawyer*
McCullough, Ralph Clayton, II, *lawyer, educator*
McLeod, Walton James *lawyer, state legislator*
McQuillan, Barbara Glatz *paralegal*
Morrison, Stephen George *lawyer*
Nexsen, Julian Jacobs *lawyer*
†Oswald, Billy Robertson *lawyer*
†Painter, Samuel Franklin *lawyer*
Pansegrau, Phaedra Renée *lawyer*
†Pollard, William Albert *lawyer*
Rouse, LeGrand Ariail, II, *retired lawyer, educator*
Schwarz, Fred *lawyer, ophthalmic plastic surgeon*
Sheftman, Howard Stephen *lawyer*
Strom, J. Preston, Jr., *lawyer*
Strong, Franklin Wallace, Jr., *lawyer*
Swerling, Jack Bruce *lawyer*
Tate, Harold Simmons, Jr., *lawyer*
†Todd, Albert Creswell, III, *lawyer*
Wilson, Karen Wilkerson *paralegal*
Yarborough, Clinton Joseph *lawyer*
Young, Robert *lawyer*

Conway
Martin, Gregory Keith *lawyer, mayor*
Suggs, Michael Edward *lawyer*

Georgetown
Moore, Albert Cunningham *lawyer, insurance company executive*

Greenville
Christophillis, Constantine S. *lawyer*
†Coates, William Alexander *lawyer*
Cowan, John Joseph *retired lawyer*
Dobson, Robert Albertus, III, *lawyer, executive, volunteer*
Edwards, Harry LaFoy *lawyer*
Ferguson, Donald Littlefield *lawyer*
Foulke, Edwin Gerhart, Jr., *lawyer*
Horton, James Wright *retired lawyer*
†Hutson, Melvin Robert *lawyer*
†Lynch, J. Timothy *lawyer*
†Massey, Raymond David *lawyer*
Mauldin, John Inglis *public defender*
McKinney, Ronald W. *lawyer*
Phillips, Joseph Brantley, Jr., *lawyer*
Riley, Richard Wilson *lawyer, federal official*
Todd, John Dickerson, Jr., *retired lawyer*
Walters, Johnnie McKeiver *lawyer*
Wyche, Cyril Thomas *lawyer*
Wyche, Madison Baker, III, *lawyer*

Greenwood
Nexsen, Julian Jacobs, Jr., *lawyer*

Hemingway
†Chandler, William Henry *lawyer*

Hilton Head Island
Becker, Karl Martin *lawyer*
Berry, Loren Curtis *retired lawyer, consultant*
†Donohoe, James Day *lawyer*
Finn, Chester Evans *retired lawyer*
Hagoort, Thomas Henry *lawyer*
McKay, John Judson, Jr., *lawyer*
Rose, William Shepard, Jr., *lawyer*
†West, John Carl *lawyer, former ambassador, former governor*

Irmo
Brown, Leonard Ashleigh (Smokey), Jr., *lawyer*

Johns Island
†Carter, Mary Andrews *paralegal*

Kiawah Island
Coyle, Martin Adolphus, Jr., *lawyer, consultant*
Neuman, Robert Henry *lawyer*

Langley
Bell, Robert Morrall *lawyer*

Mount Pleasant
McConnell, John William, Jr., *lawyer*

Myrtle Beach
Breen, David Hart *lawyer*
†Rice, Hugh Thompson, Jr., *tax lawyer*

Newberry
†Partridge, William Franklin, Jr., *lawyer*

North Charleston
Laddaga, Lawrence Alexander *lawyer*

Pacolet
Dineen, Joseph Lawrence *legal compliance professional, consultant*

Rock Hill
Hardin, James Carlisle, III, *lawyer, educator*

Salem
Everett, C(harles) Curtis *retired lawyer*

Spartanburg
Anthony, Kenneth C., Jr., *lawyer*
†Smith, William Douglas *lawyer*
Wise, Steven Lanier *lawyer, clergyman*

Sumter
Kolb, Wade S., Jr., *lawyer*

Walterboro
†Cone, George Wallis *lawyer*

West Columbia
Jedziniak, Lee Peter *lawyer, educator, insurance company officer*

SOUTH DAKOTA

Britton
Farrar, Frank Leroy *lawyer, former governor*

Fort Pierre
†Poches, Charles, Jr., *lawyer*

Gregory
†Johnson, Charles Rick *lawyer*

Pierre
†Eichstadt, Craig Martin *lawyer*
Fulton, Neil *lawyer*
†Gerdes, David Alan *lawyer*
Johnson, Julie Marie *lawyer, lobbyist, judge*
†Thompson, Charles Murray *lawyer*

Rapid City
Foye, Thomas Harold *lawyer*
Hagg, Rexford A. *lawyer, former state legislatorr*
Lebrun, Gene N. *lawyer*
Olson, James Warren *lawyer*
†Shultz, Donald Richard *lawyer*
†Stuck, Haven Laurence *lawyer*
Thatcher, Anna Marie *lawyer, law educator*

Sioux Falls
Haas, Joseph Alan *court administrator, lawyer*
Hattervig, Karen Ann *lawyer*
†Hayes, Robert E. *lawyer*
†Howard, Cynthia *lawyer, county official*
Johnson, Richard Arlo *lawyer*
†Johnson, Thomas Jerald *lawyer*
†Luce, Michael Leigh *lawyer*
Marshall, Mark F. *lawyer*

Spearfish
Hood, Earl James *lawyer, state legislator*

Vermillion
†Davidson, John Henry *legal educator*

Yankton
Heubaum, William Lincoln *retired lawyer*

TENNESSEE

Athens
†Higgins, Kenneth Dyke *lawyer*

Brentwood
Mc Creary, James Franklin *lawyer, mediator*
Provine, John Calhoun *retired lawyer*
Schreiber, Kurt Gilbert *lawyer*

Chattanooga
Akers, Samuel Lee *lawyer*
†Bowen, Maurice Richard, Jr., *lawyer, director*
Bryan, Rosemarie Luise *lawyer*
Campbell, Paul, III, *lawyer*
Cooper, Gary Allan *lawyer*
†Gearhiser, Charles Josef *lawyer*
Hays, Melissa Padgett *lawyer*
Helton, Thomas Oswald *lawyer*
†Jessup, William Eugene *lawyer*
Moore, Hugh Jacob, Jr., *lawyer*
†Morris, Buckner Stuart *lawyer*
†Proctor, John Franklin *lawyer*
Ragan, Charles Oliver, Jr., *lawyer*
Vital, Patricia Best *lawyer*
Walker, Robert Kirk *lawyer*
†Williams, Rosemary Helen *paralegal*

Clarksville
Love, Michael Joseph *lawyer*

Collierville
Springfield, James Francis *retired lawyer, banker*

Cookeville
Acuff, John Edgar *lawyer*
Day, David Owen *lawyer*
Qualls, Steven Daniel *lawyer*

Cordova
†Swan, Michael Robert *lawyer*

Crossville
Marlow, James Allen *lawyer*

Fayetteville
Dickey, John Harwell *lawyer*

Germantown
†Richards, Janet Leach *lawyer, educator*
Waddell, Phillip Dean *lawyer*

Hendersonville
McCaleb, Joe Wallace *lawyer*

Humboldt
†Boyte, George Griffin *lawyer*

Johnson City
†Culp, James David *lawyer, educator*
Epps, James Haws, III, *lawyer*
King, Robert Lewis *lawyer*
†McArdle, Erin Dougherty *lawyer*

Kingsport
Boyd, Lon Vernon *lawyer, alderman*
†Collings, Kay P. *legal office administrator*
Pierce, Phylis Mise *lawyer*
†Tweed, Douglas Steven *lawyer*

Knoxville
Bly, Robert Maurice *lawyer*
Creekmore, David Dickason *lawyer, educator*
Cremins, William Carroll *lawyer*
†Davies, Thomas Young, III, *lawyer, law educator*
Dillard, W. Thomas *lawyer*
Giordano, Lawrence Francis *lawyer*
Hagood, Lewis Russell *lawyer*
Howard, Lewis Spilman *lawyer*
Johnson, Steven Boyd *lawyer*
Lloyd, Francis Leon, Jr., *lawyer*
†Lucas, John Allen *lawyer*
McCall, Jack Humphreys, Jr., *lawyer*
Oberman, Steven *lawyer*
†Ogden, Harry Peoples *lawyer*
Phillips, Jerry Juan *law educator*
Rayson, Edwin Hope *lawyer*
†Ritchie, Albert *lawyer*
Roach, Jon Gilbert *lawyer*
Routh, John William *lawyer*
†Smartt, John Madison *lawyer*
†Swanson, Charles Walter *lawyer*
Wheeler, John Watson *lawyer*
White, Edward Gibson, II, *lawyer*
Worthington, Carole Yard Lynch *lawyer*

Lebanon
Blackstock, James Fielding *lawyer*
Hibbett, Robert Neland *lawyer*
†Rochelle, Robert Thomas *lawyer, former state legislator*

Martin
Ogg, Elton Jerald, Jr., *educator, academic administrator*

Mc Ewen
Williams, John Lee *lawyer*

Memphis
Allen, Newton Perkins *lawyer*
Bland, James Theodore, Jr., *lawyer*
Broadhurst, Jerome Anthony *lawyer*
Carr, Oscar Clark, III, *lawyer*
Chafetz, Samuel David *lawyer*
†Chambliss, Prince Caesar, Jr., *lawyer*
Clark, Ross Bert, II, *lawyer*
†Coffman, Claude T. *law educator, lawyer*
Cook, August Joseph *lawyer, accountant*
†Glassman, Richard *lawyer*
Harvey, Albert C. *lawyer*
†Holmes, Jenanne Nelson *lawyer*
Jackson, Thomas Francis, III, *lawyer*
†Kahn, Bruce Meyer *lawyer*
†Kuhn, Brian Lawrence *lawyer*
Lait, Hayden David *lawyer*
Ledbetter, Paul Mark *lawyer, writer*
Manire, James McDonnell *lawyer*
†Masterson, Kenneth Rhodes *lawyer*
Matthews, Paul Aaron *lawyer*
McLean, Robert Alexander *lawyer*
Monypeny, David Murray *lawyer*
Moore, Dwight Terry *lawyer*
†Moriarty, Herbert Bernard, Jr., *lawyer*
†Noel, Randall Deane *lawyer*
Patton, Charles Henry *lawyer, educator*
†Raines, Jim Neal *lawyer*
Rawlins, Donald Ray *lawyer*
Rice, George Lawrence, III, (Larry Rice) *lawyer*
Schuler, Walter E. *lawyer*
Scroggs, Larry Kenneth *lawyer, state legislator*
Sossaman, William Lynwood *lawyer*
Tate, Stonewall Shepherd *lawyer*
†Taylor, Jerry F(rancis) *lawyer*
Terry, Joseph Ray, Jr., *lawyer*
Walsh, Thomas James, Jr., *lawyer*
Webb, Kathleen Rochford *lawyer*
Williams, J. Maxwell *lawyer, arbitrator and mediator*
†Winchester, Richard Lee, Jr., *lawyer*

Murfreesboro
†Heffington, Jack Grisham *lawyer, banker, insurance company executive, horse breeder*

Nashville
Barrett, George Edward *lawyer*
Bass, James Orin *lawyer*
Belton, Robert *law educator*
Bloch, Frank Samuel *law educator*
Blumstein, James Franklin *law educator, lawyer, consultant*
†Bohn, Cynthia Jane *lawyer*
Bostick, Charles Dent *retired lawyer, educator*
Bramlett, Paul Kent *lawyer*
†Bruce, William Roland *lawyer*
Carr, Davis Haden *lawyer*
Cecelic, Jerone Charles *lawyer*
†Charney, Jonathan Isa *law educator, lawyer*
Cheek, James Howe, III, *lawyer, educator*
Cobb, Stephen A. *lawyer*
†Cohen, Stephen Ira *lawyer, state legislator*
Conner, Lewis Homer, Jr., *lawyer*
Cooney, Charles Hayes *lawyer*
†Crutchfield, William Ward *lawyer, state legislator*
Day, John Arthur *lawyer*
Edwards, Samuel Hollis *lawyer, urban/regional planner*
Eisen, Steven Jeffrey *lawyer*
†Ely, James Wallace, Jr., *law educator*
Gannon, John Sexton *lawyer, management consultant, arbitrator, mediator*
Gillmor, John Edward *lawyer*
Hardin, Hal D. *lawyer, judge, federal official*
Hart, Richard Banner *lawyer*
†Hirt, Janet Rose *law educator, law librarian*
Kelley, James Russell *lawyer*
†Lawless, Thomas William *lawyer*
†Leathers, Ramsey Barthell *lawyer*
Ledyard, Robins Heard *lawyer*
†Little, Hampton Stennis, Jr., *lawyer, educator*
Lowell, Roland M. *lawyer*
†Lyon, Philip K(irkland) *lawyer*
Maier, Harold Geistweit *law educator, lawyer*
May, Joseph Leserman (Jack May) *lawyer*
Mayden, Barbara Mendel *lawyer*
Parker, Mary Ann *lawyer*
†Patterson, Robert Shepherd *lawyer*
Penny, William Lewis *lawyer*
Petrey, R. Claybourne, Jr., *lawyer*
†Rush, Stephen Kenneth *lawyer*
†Sanders, James F. *lawyer*
†Sims, Wilson *lawyer*
Soderquist, Larry Dean *law educator, lawyer, consultant, writer*
†Steele, Robert Michael *lawyer*
†Stevens, Amy W. *lawyer*
Thomas, Randall Stuart *lawyer, educator*
†Thomas, Robert Paige *lawyer*
Torrey, Claudia Olivia *lawyer*
Tudor, Bynum Ellsworth, III, *lawyer*
Tuke, Robert Dudley *lawyer, educator*
†Walkup, John Knox *lawyer*
Waterhouse, Rachel L. *lawyer*
Winstead, George Alvis *law librarian, biochemist, educator, consultant*
†Woods, Larry David *lawyer, educator*
Yarbrough, Edward Meacham *lawyer*
Yoo, Christopher S. *law educator*
Youngblood, Elaine Michele *lawyer*
Yuspeh, Alan Ralph *lawyer, healthcare company executive*

Newport
Bell, John Alton *lawyer, judge*
Bunnell, John Blake *lawyer*
†Campbell, Roy Timothy, Jr., *lawyer*

Oak Ridge
†Wilkinson, Robert Warren *lawyer*

Parsons
†Townsend, Edwin Clay *lawyer*

Powell
Hyman, Roger David *lawyer*

Rogersville
Skelton, Mark Albert *lawyer*

Sevierville
Waters, John B. *lawyer*

Signal Mountain
Anderson, Charles Hill *lawyer*

Soddy Daisy
Leitner, Paul Revere *lawyer*

Springfield
Richter, Lisa Sherrill *lawyer*
Wilks, Larry Dean *lawyer*

Trenton
Harrell, Limmie Lee, Jr., *lawyer*
†Malone, Gayle *lawyer, consultant*

Waverly
†Peeler, William James *lawyer*

TEXAS

Abilene
Boone, Billy Warren *lawyer, judge*
Boone, Celia Trimble *lawyer*
Robinson, Vianei Lopez *lawyer*
Sartain, James Edward *lawyer*
†Stevenson-Williams, Deydra *court administrator*
Suttle, Stephen Hungate *lawyer*
Wilson, Stanley Patterson *retired lawyer*

Addison
Hranitzky, Rachel Robyn *lawyer*
†Kneipper, Richard Keith *lawyer*
Lawson, Gary B. *lawyer*
†Lynch, Jeffrey Scott *lawyer*
Parr, Richard Arnold, II, *lawyer*
†Pommerening, Edwin Carlton *lawyer*

Amarillo
†Cross, Janis Alexander *lawyer*
Madden, Wales Hendrix, Jr., *lawyer*
McDougall, Gerald Duane *lawyer*
Smithee, John True *lawyer, state legislator*
Woods, John William *retired lawyer*

Arlington
Dowdy, John Vernard, Jr., *lawyer, educator, arbitrator, mediator*
Rosenberry, William Kenneth *lawyer, educator*

Austin
Allday, Martin Lewis *lawyer*
Allison, James Purney *lawyer*

Euless
Paran, Mark Lloyd *retired lawyer*

Farmersville
Seward, Richard Bevin *lawyer*

Flower Mound
Hunt, David Ford *lawyer*
Maddocks, Robert Allen *lawyer, manufacturing company executive*

Fort Worth
Berenson, William Keith *lawyer*
Brown, C. Harold *lawyer*
Brown, Richard Lee *lawyer, director*
Carr, Thomas Eldridge *lawyer*
Chalk, John Allen, Sr., *lawyer*
Chappell, David Franklin *lawyer*
Collins, Whitfield James *lawyer*
Crumley, John Walter *lawyer*
Curry, Donald Robert *lawyer, oil company executive*
Dean, Beale *lawyer*
†Dent, Edward Dwain *lawyer*
Dickson, Victor Paul *lawyer*
Elliott, Frank Wallace *lawyer, educator*
Fanous, Nikki Hobert *lawyer*
Harcrow, E. Earl *lawyer*
Hart, John Clifton *lawyer*
Hayes, Larry B. *lawyer*
†Ingram, Denny Ouzts, Jr., *lawyer, educator*
Kelly, Dee J. *lawyer*
Kelly, Raymond Boone, III, *lawyer*
†Larimore, Tom L. *lawyer*
Mack, Theodore *lawyer*
McConnell, Michael Arthur *lawyer*
†Miller, Stewart Ransom *lawyer*
Minton, Jerry Davis *lawyer, consultant, retired banker*
†Moros, Nicholas Peter *railroad executive, lawyer*
Munn, Cecil Edwin *lawyer*
†Paddock, Michael Buckley *lawyer*
Phillips, Robert James, Jr., *lawyer, corporate executive*
Quinn, Francis Xavier *arbitrator, mediator, author, lecturer*
Sharpe, James Shelby *lawyer*
Simon, Roger Frank *law educator*
Streck, Frederick Louis, III, *lawyer*
Tillman, Karen Sue *lawyer*
†Wagner, Andrew Porter *lawyer*
Wallach, David Michael *lawyer*
Watson, Robert Francis *lawyer*
Weekley, Frederick Clay, Jr., *lawyer*
West, Robert Grady *lawyer*

Friendswood
Youngdahl, Jay Thomas *lawyer*

Galveston
Caldwell, Garnett Ernest *lawyer*
Kilgore, Jeffrey Harper *lawyer*
Neves, Kerry Lane *lawyer*
O'Toole, Austin Martin *lawyer*
Vie, George William, III, *lawyer*

Garland
Irby, Holt *lawyer*
Morgan, Hicks Bernard *lawyer, treasurer*

Georgetown
Bryce, William Delf *lawyer*

Graham
†Richie, Boyd Lynn *lawyer*

Grapevine
Franks, Jon Michael *lawyer, mediator*

Hallettsville
Baber, Wilbur H., Jr., *lawyer*

Harlingen
Johnson, Orrin Wendell *lawyer*
Pope, William L. *lawyer, judge*

Heath
Kolodey, Fred James *lawyer*

Horseshoe Bay
†Welch, Robert Morrow, Jr., *lawyer*

Houston
Addison, Linda Leuchter *lawyer, writer*
†Alderman, Richard Mark *legal educator, lawyer, television and radio commentator*
Allender, John Roland *lawyer*
Amandes, Christopher Bruce *lawyer*
Amann, Leslie Kiefer *lawyer, educator*
†Amaon, Gary P. *lawyer*
Amdur, Arthur R. *lawyer*
†Anani, Tarig *lawyer*
Anderson, Doris Ehlinger *lawyer*
Anderson, Eric Severin *lawyer*
Anderson, Thomas Dunaway *retired lawyer*
†Atkins, Bruce Alexander *lawyer*
Atlas, Scott Jerome *lawyer*
†Ballanfant, Richard Burton *lawyer*
Bargfrede, James Allen *lawyer*
Barnett, Edward William *lawyer*
Barton, Sarah Muriel *lawyer*
Bech, Douglas York *lawyer, resort executive*
Beirne, Martin Douglas *lawyer*
Bellatti, Lawrence Lee *lawyer*
Berg, David Howard *lawyer*
Berger, Barry Stuart *lawyer*
†Berner, Arthur Samuel *lawyer*
Bilger, Bruce R. *lawyer*
†Bistline, F. Walter, Jr., *lawyer, photographer*
Blackshear, A. T., Jr., *lawyer*
Bland, John Lloyd *lawyer*
Bliss, Ronald Glenn *lawyer*
Block, Nelson R(ichard) *lawyer*
Bluestein, Edwin A., Jr., *lawyer*
Bradie, Peter Richard *lawyer, engineer*
†Brady, Norman Conrad *lawyer, corporate executive*
Brann, Richard Roland *lawyer*
Bridges, David Manning *lawyer*
Brinson, Gay Creswell, Jr., *retired lawyer*
Brown, David Hurst *lawyer, partner*
†Brown, William Alley *lawyer*
Brunson, John Soles *lawyer, investor*
Buckingham, Edwin John, III, *lawyer*
Burch, Voris Reagan *retired lawyer, mediator, arbitrator*
Burg, Brent Lawrence *lawyer*
Burton, Joseph Randolph *lawyer*
Busby, Justin Brett *lawyer*
Bux, William John *lawyer*
Caddy, Michael Douglas *lawyer*
Caldwell, Rodney Kent *lawyer*
†Callahan, Gerald William *lawyer, oil company executive*
Campbell, Bert Louis *lawyer, mediator, arbitrator*
†Campos, Elizabeth Balli *lawyer*
Carr, Edward A. *lawyer*
†Carroll, James Vincent, III, *lawyer*
Carstarphen, Edward Morgan, III, *lawyer*
Carter, John Francis, II, *lawyer*
Carter, John Loyd *lawyer*
†Caudill, William Howard *lawyer*
Chandler, George Francis, III, *lawyer, naval architect*
Clarke, Robert Logan *lawyer*
Cline, Vivian Melinda *lawyer*
Clore, Lawrence Hubert *lawyer*
Coghlan, Kelly Jack *lawyer*
†Coleman, Francis J., Jr., *lawyer*
Conlon, Michael William *lawyer*
†Connelly, George William *lawyer*
Cook, B. Thomas *lawyer*
Cook, Eugene Augustus *lawyer*
Cooney, James Patrick *lawyer*
†Cooper, Thomas Randolph *lawyer*
Cox, James Talley *lawyer*
Craig, Robert Mark, III, *lawyer, educator*
†Crain, Alan Rau, Jr., *lawyer*
Crinion, Gregory Paul *lawyer*
†Crocker, Samuel Sackett *lawyer*
†Crowl, Rodney Keith *lawyer*
†Cunningham, Tom Alan *lawyer*
Curry, Alton Frank *lawyer*
Davis, Martha Algenita Scott *lawyer*
Davis, Stephen Drake *lawyer*
DeMent, James Alderson, Jr., *lawyer*
Devlin, Francis James *lawyer*
Diaz-Arrastia, George Ravelo *lawyer*
†Dilg, Joseph Carl *lawyer*
†Dillard, Stephen C. *lawyer*
Dinkins, Carol Eggert *lawyer*
Disher, David Alan *lawyer, consultant*
†Driscoll, Michael Hardee *lawyer*
†Dula, Arthur McKee, III, *lawyer*
Dunlop, Fred Hurston *lawyer*
Durham, William Andrew *lawyer*
Dworsky, Clara Weiner *lawyer, former merchandise brokerage executive*
Dykes, Osborne Jefferson, III, *lawyer*
Eastin, Keith E. *lawyer*
Edwards, Blaine Douglass *lawyer*
Eiland, Gary Wayne *lawyer*
†Ellis, David Dale *lawyer*
Engerrand, Kenneth G. *lawyer, law educator*
Essmyer, Michael Martin *lawyer*
Eubank, J. Thomas *lawyer*
Farenthold, Frances Tarlton *lawyer*
†Farley, Jan Edwin *lawyer*
Farnsworth, T. Brooke *lawyer*
Fason, Rita Miller *lawyer*
Finch, Michael Paul *lawyer*
Fladung, Richard Denis *lawyer*
Fleming, George Matthews *lawyer*
Forlano, Frederick Peter *lawyer*
Foster, Charles Crawford *lawyer, educator*
Frost, Charles Estes, Jr., *lawyer*
Fullenweider, Donn Charles *lawyer*
Gates, Stephen Frye *lawyer, oil industry executive*
Gayle, Gibson, Jr., *lawyer*
Gibson, Rex Hilton *lawyer*
†Gillmore, Kathleen Cory *lawyer*
†Gissel, L. Henry, Jr., *lawyer*
†Goldberg, Charles Ned *lawyer*
Goldman, Nathan Carliner *lawyer, educator*
†Gomez, Lynne Marie *lawyer*
Gover, Alan Shore *lawyer*
Grace, James Martin, Jr., *lawyer*
Graving, Richard John *law educator*
†Grossberg, Marc Elias *lawyer*
†Guest, Floyd Emory, Jr., *lawyer*
†Gunter, Joseph Clifford, III, *lawyer*
Gutheinz, Joseph Richard, Jr., *lawyer, former politician, investigative consultant, retired army officer and NASA official, educator, author*
Hall, Charles Washington *lawyer*
Hamel, Lee *lawyer*
Harper, Alfred John, II, *lawyer*
Harrington, Bruce Michael *lawyer, investor*
Harris, Warren Wayne *lawyer*
†Hartrick, Janice Kay *lawyer*
†Harvin, David Tarleton *lawyer*
Hawash, Michael Andrew *lawyer*
Heinrich, Randall Wayne *lawyer*
Heinrich, Timothy John *lawyer*
Hinton, Paula Weems *lawyer*
Holloway, Gordon Arthur *lawyer*
Hollyfield, John Scoggins *lawyer*
Holstead, John Burnham *retired lawyer*
Hope, Henry Welcker *lawyer*
Hoyt, Mont Powell *lawyer*
Hu, Daniel David *lawyer*
†Hudson, Franklin *lawyer, real estate developer*
Hudspeth, Chalmers Mac *lawyer, educator*
†Hurd, John R. *lawyer*
†Irvin, Michael P. *lawyer*
Jansen, Donald Orville *lawyer*
Jensen, William Powell *lawyer, educator*
Jeske, Charles Matthew *lawyer*
Jewell, George Hiram *lawyer*
Jones, Frank Griffith *lawyer*
Jordan, Charles Milton *lawyer*
†Kaplan, Lee Landa *lawyer*
Kay, Joel Phillip *lawyer*
Keen, Brenda Denniston *lawyer*
†Keiter, Aaron *lawyer*
Kelly, Hugh Rice *retired lawyer, retired energy executive*
†Kelso, R. Randall *law educator*
Kemp, Roland Connor *lawyer*
†Kendall, Frank Russell, Sr., *lawyer*
†Kennedy, John Edward *lawyer*
Ketchand, Robert Lee *lawyer*
Kirk, John Robert, Jr., *lawyer*
Kline, Allen Haber, Jr., *lawyer*
Koenig, Rodney Curtis *lawyer, rancher*
†Kolb, John E. *lawyer*
Kratochvil, L(ouis) Glen *lawyer*
Krebs, Arno William, Jr., *lawyer*
†Kruse, Charles Thomas *lawyer*
†Kruse, Layne E. *lawyer*
†Kurz, Thomas Patrick *lawyer*
LaBoon, Robert Bruce *lawyer*
†Lacey, David Morgan *lawyer, school administrator*
†LaFuze, William L. *lawyer*
Lake, Kathleen Cooper *lawyer*
Larkin, Lee Roy *retired lawyer*
†Linden, William M. *lawyer*
Lopez, David Tiburcio *lawyer, educator, arbitrator, mediator*
Lynch, John Edward, Jr., *lawyer*
Marlow, Orval Lee, II, *lawyer*
†Maroney, James Francis, III, *lawyer*
Marston, Edgar Jean, III, *lawyer*
Martin, Jay Griffith *lawyer*
Martin, Paul Edward *lawyer*
Massad, Stephen Albert *lawyer*
Masters, Claude Bivin *lawyer*
McClure, Daniel M. *lawyer*
†McDade, Thomas Rambaut *lawyer, rancher*
McDaniel, Jarrel Dave *lawyer*
†McDonald, Donald C. *lawyer*
McFall, Donald Beury *lawyer*
†McQuarrie, Claude Monroe, III, *lawyer*
Meek, Susan Bieber *lawyer, physician, mediator, consultant*
Michael, Charles Joseph *lawyer*
†Michaels, Kevin Richard *lawyer*
Moehlman, Michael Scott *lawyer*
Moncure, John Lewis *lawyer*
†Montague, H. Dixon *lawyer*
†Montesinos, Marlene C. *lawyer, mediator, arbitrator*
Morgan, Richard Greer *lawyer*
Moroney, Linda L.S. (Muffie) *lawyer, educator*
Morris, Carloss (William Morris) *lawyer, insurance company executive*
Murphy, Ewell Edward, Jr., *lawyer*
Nacol, Mae *lawyer*
Nations, Howard Lynn *lawyer*
†Neslage, John Edward *lawyer*
Ney, Judy Larson *lawyer, sociology educator*
Nolen, Roy Lemuel *retired lawyer*
†Norman, Kenneth Glen *lawyer*
†Nunnally, Knox Dillon *lawyer*
O'Brien, Eva Fromm *lawyer*
Oldham, Darius Dudley *lawyer*
Oldham, J. Thomas *lawyer, educator*
†Osterberg, Edward Charles, Jr., *lawyer*
†Paden, Lyman R. *lawyer*
Paul, Thomas Daniel *lawyer*
Paulsen, James Walter *law educator*
Pesikoff, Bette Schein *lawyer*
Pettiette, Alison Yvonne *lawyer*
Pitts, Gary Benjamin *lawyer*
Plaeger, Frederick Joseph, II, *lawyer*
Poitevent, Edward Butts, II, *lawyer*
†Porter, Thomas William, III, *lawyer*
Pravel, Bernarr Roe *lawyer*
Prestridge, Pamela Adair *lawyer*
†Pritchard, William Winther *lawyer, drilling company executive*
Pugsley, Frank Burruss *lawyer*
†Raley, John Wesley, III, *lawyer*
Ray, Hugh Massey, Jr., *lawyer*
Reasoner, Barrett Hodges *lawyer*
Reasoner, Harry Max *lawyer*
†Redden, Joe Winston, Jr., *lawyer*
Reinbolt, Donna McNulty *lawyer*
Richter, Dawn Slater *lawyer*
†Roberson, Clifford Eugene *law educator, lawyer*
Robertson, James Woolsey *lawyer*
Rogers, Arthur Hamilton, III, *lawyer*
Rowland, Robert Alexander, III, *lawyer*
Rozzell, Scott Ellis *lawyer*
Ryan, Thomas William *lawyer*
Ryan, Vince *lawyer*
Salch, Steven Charles *lawyer, mediator, arbitrator*
Sales, James Bohus *lawyer*
Sapp, Walter William *lawyer, energy company executive*
Saunders, Charles Albert *lawyer*
Schechter, Arthur Louis *lawyer*
†Scholin, Margo S. *lawyer*
†Scholl, Stephen Gerrard *lawyer*
Schwartz, Charles Walter *lawyer*
Schwartzel, Charles Boone *lawyer*
Scott, Ronald *lawyer*
†Seale, Robert Arthur, Jr., *lawyer*
†Segal, Steven E. *lawyer*
†Sellingsloh, John S. *lawyer*
Shaddock, Carroll Sidney *lawyer*
†Shannon, Joel Ingram *lawyer*
Shead, William C. *lawyer*
†Sheppard, Ben H., Jr., *lawyer*
†Sherman, Robert Taylor, Jr., *lawyer*
†Shouse, August Edward *lawyer*
Shurn, Peter Joseph, III, *lawyer*
†Silva, Eugene Joseph *lawyer*
Simmons, Stephen Judson *lawyer*
Sing, William Bender *lawyer*
†Slaydon, Kathleen Amelia *lawyer*
†Smith, Alison Leigh *lawyer*
†Smith, Walter John *lawyer*
Sonfield, Robert Leon, Jr., *lawyer*
Sorrels, Randall Owen *lawyer*
Spalding, Andrew Freeman *lawyer*
Staine, Ross (Ross Donan Allison Staine Jr.) *lawyer*
†Stephens, R(obert) Gary *lawyer*
Stewart, Pamela L. *lawyer*
Still, Charles Henry, Sr., *lawyer*
†Stradley, William Jackson *lawyer*
Streng, William Paul *lawyer, educator*
Susman, Morton Lee *lawyer*
Susman, Stephen Daily *lawyer*
Sydow, Michael David *lawyer*
Szalkowski, Charles Conrad *lawyer*
†Tabak, Morris *lawyer*
†Tartt, Blake *lawyer*
Tavormina, John William *lawyer*
†Thurmond, Gerald Pittman *lawyer*
†Toedt, D(ell) C(harles), III, *lawyer*
Touchy, Deborah K.P. *lawyer, accountant*
Tripp, Karen Bryant *lawyer*
Van Fleet, George Allan *lawyer*
†Van Winkle, Danny L. *lawyer*
Varner, David Eugene *lawyer*
Vickery, Edward Downtain *lawyer*
Wall, Kenneth E., Jr., *lawyer*
Wallis, Olney Gray *lawyer*
Walton, Dan Gibson *lawyer*
Watson, John Allen *lawyer*
Webb, Jack M. *lawyer*
Weber, Fredric Alan *lawyer*
†Weiner, Sanford Alan *lawyer*
†Weller, Philip Douglas *lawyer*
†Wells, Benjamin Gladney *lawyer*
†Welsh, H. Ronald *lawyer*
Westby, Timothy Scott *lawyer, researcher*
†Wharton, Thomas H(eard), Jr., *lawyer*
Wheelan, R(ichelieu) E(dward) *lawyer*
†Wiese, Larry Clevenger *lawyer*
Wilde, Carlton D. *lawyer, director*
Wilde, William Key *lawyer*
†Wilfong, Hugh C., II, *lawyer*
†Williams, Marjorie L. *retired lawyer*
Williamson, Peter David *lawyer*
†Wood, Judson Robert *lawyer*
Worthington, William Albert, III, *lawyer*
Woung-Chapman, Marguerite Natalie *lawyer*
Wray, Thomas Jefferson *lawyer*
Yetter, R. Paul *lawyer*
Yokubaitis, Roger T. *lawyer*
Zeigler, Ann dePender *lawyer*

Humble
†Gaffney, Richard Cook *lawyer*
†Pickle, George Edward *lawyer*

Huntsville
†Peck, Leonard Warren, Jr., *lawyer*

Hurst
Leach, Terry Ray *lawyer, judge*

Irving
†Beach, Charles Addison *lawyer*
French, Colin Val *lawyer*
Lockyer, Charles Warren, Jr., *corporate executive*
†Matthews, Charles W. *lawyer*

Jacksonville
Brewer, Brett *lawyer*

Kerrville
Parmley, Robert James *lawyer, consultant*

Kilgore
Rorschach, Richard Gordon *lawyer*

Killeen
Roberts, Burk Austin *lawyer*

Lamesa
Saleh, John *lawyer*

Lancaster
†Sewell, Cameron Dee *lawyer*

Liberty
Wheat, John Nixon *lawyer*

Lindale
Jackson, Gary Dean *lawyer*

Lockhart
†Shomette, Donna M. Dixson *paralegal*

Longview
†Harrison, Guy Newell *lawyer*
Welge, Jack Herman, Jr., *lawyer*

Lubbock
Crowson, James Lawrence *lawyer, financial company executive, academic administrator*
Davis, Jimmy Frank *assistant attorney general*
†Nelson, Jack Odell, Jr., *lawyer*
Purdom, Thomas James *lawyer*
Skillern, Frank Fletcher *law educator*

Mason
Johnson, Rufus Winfield *lawyer*

Mc Kinney
†Dowdy, William Clarence, Jr., *retired lawyer*
Roessler, P. Dee *lawyer, mediator, former judge, educator*

Mcallen
Carrera, Victor Manuel *lawyer*
Connors, Joseph Aloysius, III, *lawyer*
†Mills, William Michael *lawyer*
†Thaddeus, Aloysius Peter, Jr., *lawyer*

Midland
Estes, Andrew Harper *lawyer*
Frost, Wayne N. *lawyer*
Taylor, Nicholas C. *lawyer, state agency administrator, energy executive*
Truitt, Robert Ralph, Jr., *lawyer*

Mineola
Bruce, Robert Denton *lawyer*

Missouri City
Hodges, Jot Holiver, Jr., *retired lawyer, business executive*

New Braunfels
Benfield, Marion Wilson, Jr., *law educator*
†Reimer, Bill Monroe *lawyer*

Odessa
Hendrick, Benard Calvin, VII, *lawyer*

Orange
Dugas, Louis, Jr., *lawyer*

Paris
Standifer, Rick M. *lawyer*

Pasadena
Harrison, Brooks Talton *law firm official*

Plainview
Lafont, William Harold *lawyer, farmer*

Plano
Blachly, Jack Lee *lawyer*
†Friedlander, D. Gilbert *lawyer*
Hemingway, Richard William *law educator*
Levine, Harold *lawyer*
†Lotter, Charles Robert *corporate lawyer, retail company legal executive*
†Shaddock, William Charles *lawyer*

Pottsboro
Thomas, Ann Van Wynen *law educator*

Richardson
Austin, Ann Sheree *lawyer*
Conkel, Robert Dale *lawyer, pension consultant*
DeBusk, Manuel Conrad *lawyer, business executive*
Douglas, John Paul *lawyer*
Martin, Richard Kelley *lawyer*
Olson, Dennis Oliver *lawyer*
Sowers, Wesley Hoyt *lawyer, management consultant*

Rockport
Benningfield, Carol Ann *lawyer*
Porter, Charles Raleigh, Jr., *retired lawyer*

Rockwall
Bruce, Dana Glenn *lawyer*
Holt, Charles William, Jr., *lawyer, mediator*

Rowlett
Lyon, Robert Charles *lawyer*

San Angelo
†McLaughlin, John Mark *lawyer*
Sutton, John Ewing *lawyer*

San Antonio
†Allison, Stephen Philip *lawyer*
Armstrong, William Tucker, III, *lawyer*
Barton, James Cary *lawyer*
†Bayern, Arthur Herbert *lawyer*
Becker, Douglas Wesley *lawyer*
†Bettac, Robert Edward *lawyer*
Biery, Evelyn Hudson *lawyer*
†Brennan, James Patrick, Sr., *lawyer, insurance company executive*
Countryman, Thomas Arthur *lawyer*
†de la Garza, Luis Adolfo *lawyer*
Durbin, Richard Louis, Jr., *lawyer*
Eyster, Charles Richard *lawyer, oil and gas exploration executive*
†Ferguson, Charles Alan *lawyer*
Frigerio, Charles Straith *lawyer*
Goldsmith, Richard Elsinger *lawyer*
Guess, James David *lawyer*
Hardy, Harvey Louchard *retired lawyer*
Higdon, James Noel *lawyer*
†Hohman, A. J., Jr., *lawyer*
Javore, Gary William *lawyer*
Johnson, Anne Stuckly *retired lawyer*
†Johnson, Vincent Robert *law educator, educator*
Juárez, José Roberto, Jr., *law educator*
†Kelfer, Marvin Gerald (Jerry Kelfer) *lawyer*
†Koppenheffer, Julie B. *lawyer*
Labay, Eugene Benedict *lawyer*
Liesenfeld, Vincent Joseph *lawyer*
Lutter, Charles William, Jr., *lawyer*
Maloney, Marynell *lawyer*
†Millet, John Porath *lawyer*
Morrow, Carol Lynn *lawyer*
Moynihan, John Bignell *retired lawyer*
†Myers, J(oseph) Michael *lawyer*
†Netemeyer, Margaret *lawyer*
Oliva, Suzanne Dapra *lawyer, accountant*
†Oppenheimer, Jesse Halff *lawyer*
Patrick, Dane Herman *lawyer*
Pfeiffer, Philip J. *lawyer*
Putman, Michael (James Michael Putman) *lawyer*
Raign, Michael Stephen *lawyer*
Reams, Bernard Dinsmore, Jr., *lawyer, educator*
Rodriguez, Xavier *lawyer*
Ross, James Ulric *lawyer, accountant, educator*
†Ruttenberg, Frank Z. *lawyer*
Sakai, Peter A. *lawyer*
Schlueter, David Arnold *law educator*
†Schmutz, John Francis *lawyer*
Schuk, Linda Lee *legal assistant, business educator*
Spears, Sally *lawyer*
Steen, John Thomas, Jr., *lawyer*
Valadez, Robert Allen *lawyer*
†Vazquez, Gilbert Falcon *lawyer*
Veitch, Thomas Harold *lawyer*
Wachsmuth, Robert William *lawyer*
Wallis, Ben Alton, Jr., *lawyer*
Welmaker, Forrest Nolan *lawyer*
Williamson, Deborah Daywood *lawyer*
†Wolf, Michael Jay *lawyer*

San Marcos
†Parkin-Speer, Diane *English law educator*

San Saba
†Hamilton, Elwin Lomax *lawyer*

Seabrook
†Winchell, Michael George *lawyer*

Sherman
Freels, Jesse Saunders, Jr., *lawyer*

Spring
Farley, Andrew Newell *lawyer, consultant*
Hendricks, Randal Arlan *lawyer*

Stephenville
Batson, David Warren *lawyer*

Sterling City
†Durham, Drew Taylor *lawyer*

Sugar Land
Aldrich, Lovell W(eld) *lawyer*
†Greer, Raymond White *lawyer*
Hitchcock, Bion Earl *lawyer*

Temple
†Clements, Jamie Hager *lawyer*
Cuba, Benjamin James *lawyer, mediator*
†Pickle, Jerry Richard *lawyer*

Texarkana
Poff, Franklin Albright, Jr., *lawyer*

The Woodlands
Hagerman, John David *lawyer*
Schlacks, Stephen Mark *lawyer, educator*
Turek, Douglas D. *lawyer*

Tyler
Alworth, Charles Wesley *lawyer, engineer*
Ellis, Donald Lee *lawyer*
Hadden, Arthur Roby *lawyer*
Lake, David Alan *investments lawyer*
Patterson, Donald Ross *lawyer, educator*

Waco
†Cherry, David Earl *lawyer*
†Crook, Betty Ross *lawyer*
Hall, Donald Orell *lawyer, rancher*
Mackenzie, Charles Alfred *lawyer*
Morrison, Michael Dean *lawyer, law educator*
Page, Jack Randall *lawyer*
Smith, Cullen *lawyer*
Villarreal, Fernando Marin *lawyer*

Weslaco
Pomerantz, Jerald Michael *lawyer*

Wharton
Roades, John Leslie *lawyer*

Wichita Falls
Altman, William Kean *lawyer*
Goff, Robert William, Jr., *lawyer*
†Wesbrooks, Perry *lawyer, consultant*

Wimberley
Brinsmade, Lyon Louis *retired lawyer*

Yoakum
Kvinta, Charles J. *lawyer*

UTAH

Logan
Honaker, Jimmie Joe *lawyer, ecologist*

Manti
Petersen, Benton Lauritz *paralegal*

Midvale
Dahl, Everett E. *lawyer*

Ogden
Kaufman, Steven Michael *lawyer*
Mecham, Glenn Jefferson *lawyer, mayor*
Sullivan, Kevin Patrick *lawyer*
Warner, Frank Shrake *lawyer*

Orem
Michell, Auriel Ibn *lawyer, writer*

Park City
Schiesswohl, Cynthia Rae Schlegel *lawyer*

Pork City
Kelly, John Patrick *lawyer*

Provo
Abbott, Charles Favour *lawyer*
Brown, Joseph William *retired patent agent*

Saint George
Gallian, Russell Joseph *lawyer*
Terry, Gary A. *lawyer, former trade association executive*

Salt Lake City
Adams, Joseph Keith *lawyer*
Anderson, Craig W. *lawyer*
Atkin, Gary Eugene *lawyer*
Barton, Paul J. *lawyer*
Barusch, Lawrence Roos *lawyer*
Baucom, Sidney George *lawyer*
Berman, Daniel Lewis *lawyer*
†Bigler, Glade S. *lawyer*
†Bushnell, Daniel S. *lawyer*
Callister, Louis Henry, Jr., *lawyer*
†Christensen, Harold Graham *lawyer*
Christensen, Patricia Anne Watkins *lawyer*
Christensen, Ray Richards *lawyer*
Clark, Scott H. *lawyer*
Colessides, Nick John *lawyer*
Cornaby, Kay Sterling *lawyer, former state senator*
†Corporon, Mary Caroline *lawyer*

Curtis, LeGrand R., Jr., *lawyer*
Gardiner, Lester Raymond, Jr., *lawyer*
Gessel, David Clyde *lawyer, consultant*
†Gordon, Robert *utility company executive, lawyer*
Heaton, Jon C. *lawyer*
Holbrook, Donald Benson *lawyer*
Holbrook, James Russell *law educator*
Holtkamp, James Arnold *lawyer, educator*
Hunter, M(ilton) Reed, Jr., *lawyer*
Jensen, Dallin W. *lawyer*
Jeppesen, Alan Karl *lawyer*
Jones, Ken Paul *lawyer*
†Kennard, Raeburn Gleason *lawyer*
†Kimball, Spencer Levan *lawyer, educator*
Kirkham, John Spencer *lawyer, director*
Lambert, Dale John *lawyer*
Lochhead, Robert Bruce *lawyer*
Mabey, Ralph R. *lawyer*
Manning, Brent V. *lawyer*
McConkie, Oscar Walter *lawyer*
McIntosh, Terrie Tuckett *lawyer*
Mooney, Jerome Henri *lawyer*
Moore, James R. *lawyer*
Nielsen, Greg Ross *lawyer*
Nydegger, Rick D. *lawyer*
Ockey, Ronald J. *lawyer*
Rasmussen, Thomas Val, Jr., *lawyer, small business owner*
†Roberts, Jack Earl *lawyer, ski resort operator, wood products company executive, real estate developer*
Schwendiman, Stephen Glenn *lawyer*
Scofield, David Willson *lawyer*
Shea, Patrick A. *lawyer, educator*
Sine, Wesley Franklin *lawyer*
†Smith, Janet Hugie *lawyer*
Spurgeon, Edward Dutcher *law educator, foundation administrator*
†Teitelbaum, Lee E. *law educator, former dean*
Thompson, Neil Daniel *legal and genealogical researcher, retired lawyer*
†Verhaaren, Harold Carl *lawyer*
West, Stephen Allan *lawyer*
†Workman, H(arley) Ross *patent lawyer*
Zimmer, Markus Bernhard *federal court administrator*

South Jordan
Larson, Bryan A. *lawyer*

Spanish Fork
Ashworth, Brent Ferrin *lawyer*

Vernal
Judd, Dennis L. *lawyer*

VERMONT

Barre
†Koch, Thomas Frederick *lawyer*
Togut, Torin Dana *lawyer*

Bellows Falls
†Massucco, Lawrence Raymond *lawyer*

Brattleboro
McCarty, William Michael, Jr., *lawyer*
Reid, David G. *lawyer*

Burlington
Blackwood, Eileen Morris *lawyer*
Dinse, John Merrell *lawyer*
†Frank, Joseph Elihu *lawyer*
†Leddy, John Thomas *lawyer*
†Lisman, Bernard *lawyer*
McMahon, Dennis C. *lawyer, writer*
†Miller, Elizabeth H. *lawyer, educator*
†Morrow, Emily Rubenstein *lawyer, estate planner*
†Rendall, Donald James, Jr., *lawyer*
Shattuck, Gary G. *lawyer*
Wick, Hilton Addison *lawyer*

Castleton
Stafford, Robert Theodore *lawyer, former senator*

Chester
†Holme, John Charles, Jr., *lawyer*

Colchester
†Garcia, Luis Cesareo *lawyer*
Salmon, Thomas Paul *lawyer, academic administrator*

Concord
Norsworthy, Elizabeth Krassovsky *lawyer*

Essex Junction
Walsh, Robert Anthony *lawyer*

Montpelier
Appel, Robert Joseph *lawyer*
Diamond, M. Jerome *lawyer, former state official*
Guild, Alden *retired lawyer*
Malley, J. Wallace, Jr., *lawyer*
Putter, David Seth *lawyer*

Norwich
†Chase, Jonathon B. *law educator*

Proctor
Keyser, Frank Ray, Jr., *lawyer, former governor*

Rutland
Bloomer, William John *lawyer*
†Cleary, David Laurence *lawyer*
Dardeck, Stephen A. *lawyer*
Facey, John Abbott, III, *lawyer*
Faignant, John Paul *lawyer, educator*
Taylor, A. Jeffry *lawyer*

Shelburne
Canfield, Andrew Trotter *lawyer, writer*

South Burlington
Adams, Charles Jairus *lawyer*

South Royalton
Wroth, L(awrence) Kinvin *lawyer, educator*

Stowe
Anderson, Rudolph J., Jr., *lawyer*
Whiteman, Joseph David *retired lawyer, manufacturing company executive*

Waitsfield
Raphael, Albert Ash, Jr., *lawyer*

Windsor
†Porto, Brian L. *lawyer, writer*

Woodstock
Dagger, William Carson *lawyer*

VIRGINIA

Abingdon
Conway, Berry Leslie, II, *lawyer*
McElroy, Howard Chowning *lawyer*
Shortridge, Judy Beth *lawyer*
Shortridge, Michael L. *lawyer*
Taylor, Janet Droke *legal secretary*

Alexandria
Abell, Richard Bender (Richard Lon Welch) *lawyer, federal judicial official*
Beach, Barbara Purse *lawyer*
Bjornson, Christopher Raymond *lawyer*
Buechner, Jack W(illiam) *lawyer, government affairs consultant, educational association administrator*
Burch, John Thomas, Jr., *lawyer*
Burgess, David *lawyer*
†Bussewitz, Roy Jon *lawyer, pharmacist*
Dennison, Donald Lee *lawyer*
†DiMuro, Bernard Joseph *lawyer*
Duffett, Benton Samuel, Jr., *lawyer*
Dunham, Frank Willard *lawyer*
Elston, Michael James *lawyer, educator*
Franklin, Jeanne F. *lawyer*
Georges, Peter John *lawyer*
Goodman, Sherri Wasserman *lawyer*
Goolrick, Robert Mason *lawyer*
Hathaway, Fred William *lawyer*
Hawkins, Edward J. *retired lawyer*
Higgins, Mary Celeste *lawyer, researcher*
Holcomb, Richard Dennis *lawyer*
Huckabee, Harlow Maxwell *lawyer, writer*
Hussey, Ward MacLean *lawyer, former government official*
Hutzelman, Martha Louise *lawyer*
†Kaplan, Richard Alan *government official*
Kinzler, Peter *lawyer*
Kiyonaga, John Cady *lawyer*
Kopp, Eugene Paul *lawyer*
Kotlarchuk, Ihor O. E. *lawyer*
Lauderdale, Katherine Sue *lawyer*
Levine, Steven Mark *lawyer*
Maloof, Farahe Paul *lawyer*
McClure, Roger John *lawyer*
McDowell, Charles Eager *lawyer, retired military officer*
O'Hara, John Patrick *lawyer, accountant*
O'Leary, Brian Michael *lawyer*
Paturis, E(mmanuel) Michael *lawyer*
Pyle, Howard *lawyer, consultant*
†Rosenthal, Edward Scott *lawyer*
Schultz, Franklin M. *retired lawyer*
Schweikart, Debora Ellen Ellen *lawyer*
Sczudlo, Walter Joseph *lawyer*
†Siegel, Kenneth Eric *lawyer*
†Smith, Kevin Hopkins *lawyer*
Straub, Peter Thornton *lawyer*
Sturtevant, Brereton *retired lawyer, former government official*
Swift, Stephen Christopher *lawyer*
Swinburn, Charles *lawyer*
Van Cleve, Ruth Gill *retired lawyer, government official*
Von Drehle, Ramon Arnold *lawyer*
Walkup, Charlotte Lloyd *lawyer*
Walkup, Homer Allen *lawyer, writer*
Wendel, Charles Allen *lawyer*
Wieder, Bruce Terrill *lawyer, electrical engineer*
Williams, John Edward *lawyer*
Winzer, P.J. *lawyer*

Annandale
†Armstrong, Henry Jere *judge, lawyer*
Hovis, Robert Houston, III, *lawyer*

Arlington
†Alper, Joanne Fogel *lawyer*
Anthony, Robert Armstrong *lawyer, educator*
Barry, Lance Leonard *judge*
Brenner, Edgar H. *law administrator*
Carbaugh, John Edward, Jr., *lawyer*
†Cohen, Sheldon Irwin *lawyer*
Cragin, Charles Langmaid *lawyer*
Dalglish, Lucy Ann *lawyer, organization executive*
Dobeck, Robert Bradley *lawyer*
Doyle, Gerard Francis *lawyer*
Drayton, William *social entrepreneur, lawyer, management consultant*
Fowler, David Lucas *corporate lawyer*
Garnett, Griffin Taylor *lawyer, writer*
†Glazier, Jonathan Hemenway *lawyer*
Goldman, William Scott *lawyer*
Green, Richard Alan *lawyer*
Hansen, Kenneth D. *lawyer, ophthalmologist*
Hansen, Orval *lawyer, former congressman, think tank executive*
Johnson, Charles Owen *retired lawyer*
†Kelly, John James *lawyer*
Korman, James William *lawyer*
Krauss, Michael Ian *law educator*
Kuelbs, John Thomas *lawyer*
Landry, Walter Joseph *lawyer*

Levinson, Lawrence Edward *lawyer, corporation executive*
Litman, Richard Curtis *lawyer*
Malone, William Grady *retired lawyer*
Mastromarco, Dan Ralph *lawyer, consultant*
Mathis, Mark Jay *lawyer*
McDermott, Francis Owen *retired lawyer*
Monroe, Carl Dean, III, *lawyer*
Morris, Roy Leslie *lawyer, electrical engineer, venture capitalist*
Mossinghoff, Gerald Joseph *lawyer*
Muchow, David John *lawyer, business executive*
Parker, Jeffrey Scott *law educator*
†Polak, Carol Schrier *lawyer*
Pomeranz, Morton *lawyer, educator*
Rotunda, Ronald Daniel *law educator, consultant*
Swenson, Diane Kay *lawyer*
Walker, Woodrow Wilson *retired lawyer, cattle and timber farmer, real estate investor*
†Weinberg, Robert Lester *lawyer, law educator*
Welty, Charles Douglas *lawyer*

Blacksburg
Jensen, Walter Edward *lawyer, educator*

Blackstone
Allen, Jeffrey Rodgers *lawyer*

Bristol
Alan, Sondra Kirschner *lawyer*

Burke
Hipfel, Steven J. *lawyer*
†Lingo, Robert S(amuel) *lawyer*

Charlottesville
†Abraham, Kenneth Samuel *law educator*
Alford, Neill Herbert, Jr., *retired law educator*
Bonnie, Richard Jeffrey *law educator, lawyer*
Cannon, Jonathan Z. *lawyer, educator*
Chandler, Lawrence Bradford, Jr., *lawyer*
Cohen, Edwin Samuel *lawyer, educator*
Dooley, Michael P. *law educator*
†Dunn, William Wyly *corporate lawyer*
Groiss, Fred George *lawyer*
Henderson, Stanley Dale *lawyer, educator*
Hodous, Robert Power *lawyer*
Howard, Arthur Ellsworth Dick *law educator*
Kitch, Edmund Wells *lawyer, educator, private investor*
Kudravetz, David Waller *lawyer*
Landess, Fred Stone *lawyer*
Martin, David Alan *law educator*
McKay, John Douglas *lawyer*
Meador, Daniel John *law educator*
Menefee, Samuel Pyeatt *lawyer, anthropologist*
†Merrill, Richard Austin *lawyer*
Middleditch, Leigh Benjamin, Jr., *lawyer, educator*
Monahan, John T. *law educator, psychologist*
Moore, John Norton *lawyer, diplomat, educator*
Musselman, Robert Metcalfe *lawyer*
O'Connell, Jeffrey *law educator*
Robinette, Christopher John *lawyer*
Slaughter, Edward Ratliff, Jr., *lawyer*
Stroud, Robert Edward *lawyer*
Turner, Robert Foster *law educator, former government official, writer*
Wadlington, Walter James *law educator*
Wenger, Larry Bruce *law librarian, law educator*
White, George Edward *law educator, lawyer*
White, Thomas Raeburn, III, *law educator, consultant*
Whitehead, John Wayne *law educator, organization administrator, author*
Wilson, Lester Arnauld, III, *lawyer*
†Wyatt, Deborah Chasen *lawyer*

Chesapeake
Brown, John Wayne *lawyer*
Jones, John Lou *arbitrator, retired railroad executive*
Mastronardi, Corinne Marie *lawyer*

Chester
Connelly, Colin Charles *lawyer*
Gray, Charles Robert *lawyer*

Culpeper
Dulaney, Richard Alvin *lawyer*

Danville
Conway, French Hoge *lawyer*
Goodman, Lewis Elton, Jr., *lawyer*
Martin, James Chandler *lawyer*
Regan, Michael Patrick *lawyer*
Talbott, Frank, III, *lawyer*

Disputanta
†Will, Joseph Henry Michael *lawyer, retired military officer*

Dunn Loring
Melton, Michael Eric *lawyer, engineer*

Earlysville
Grattan, George Gilmer, IV, *lawyer*

Edinburg
Cohen, Lewis Isaac *lawyer*

Fairfax
Abrams, Sheri *lawyer*
Anderson, David Lawrence *lawyer*
Appler, Thomas L. *lawyer*
Arnold, William McCauley *lawyer*
Arntson, Peter Andrew *lawyer*
Baird, Charles Bruce *lawyer, consultant*
Becker, James Richard *lawyer*
†Brown, Gary Wayne *lawyer*
Callahan, Timothy J. *lawyer, investment advisor*
Downey, Richard Lawrence *lawyer*
Dwornik, Frances Pierson *lawyer*
Folk, Thomas Robert *lawyer*
Frieden, Jonathan David *lawyer*
Hopson, Everett George *retired lawyer*
Mackall, Henry Clinton *lawyer*

†Rust, John Howson, Jr., *lawyer, state legislator*
Sanderson, Douglas Jay *lawyer*
†Saul, Ira Stephen *lawyer*
†Schwartz, Philip *lawyer*
Scott, Robert William *mediator, lawyer, educator, consultant*

Fairfax Station
Bishop, Alfred Chilton, Jr., *lawyer*
Carver, George Allen, Jr., *retired lawyer*

Falls Church
Brady, Rupert Joseph *lawyer*
Chabraja, Nicholas D.
Christman, Bruce Lee *lawyer*
Diamond, Robert Michael *lawyer*
Elderkin, Helaine Grace *lawyer*
Field, David Ellis *lawyer*
Golden, Wilson *lawyer*
†Hartshorn, Roland DeWitt *lawyer*
Honigberg, Carol Crossman *lawyer*
Jennings, Thomas Parks *lawyer*
Kirk, Dennis Dean *lawyer*
†Lynn, Edward E. *corporate executive, lawyer*
†Meserve, Richard Andrew *lawyer*
Nunes, Morris A. *lawyer*
Padilla, David Joseph *lawyer, diplomat*
Perkins, Jack Edwin *lawyer*
†Robey, Daniel Lance *lawyer*
Schmidt, Paul Wickham *lawyer*
Thomas, William Griffith *lawyer*
Ward, Joe Henry, Jr., *retired lawyer*
Wood, John Martin *lawyer*

Fort Eustis
†Smail, Laurence Mitchell *lawyer, educator*

Franklin
Cobb, G. Elliott, Jr., *lawyer*

Fredericksburg
Allen, Edward Lefebvre *lawyer*
Billingsley, Robert Thaine *lawyer*
Scriven, Wayne Marcus *lawyer*

Front Royal
·Napier, Ronald Lewis *lawyer*

Galax
Kapp, John Paul *lawyer, physician, educator*

Glen Allen
Batzli, Terrence Raymond *lawyer*
†Settlage, Steven Paul *lawyer*

Gloucester
Hicks, C. Flippo *lawyer*

Great Falls
Anikeeff, Anthony Hotchkiss *lawyer*
Neidich, George Arthur *lawyer*
Preston, Charles George *lawyer*
Rath, Francis Steven *lawyer*

Halifax
Greenbacker, John Everett *retired lawyer and naval officer*

Hampton
McNider, James Small, III, *lawyer*
Nelson, Wallace Jay *patent attorney*

Hayes
Casson, Richard Frederick *lawyer, travel bureau executive*

Haymarket
Frank, Jacob *lawyer*

Heathsville
McKerns, Charles Joseph *lawyer*

Herndon
†Geldon, Fred Wolman *lawyer*
Wilkin, William Edmund *lawyer*

Hot Springs
†Deeds, Robert Creigh *lawyer, state legislator*

Irvington
†Ward, Richard Alvord *retired lawyer*

Ivy
Wilcox, Harvey John *lawyer*

Lebanon
Compton, Carnis Eugene *lawyer*

Leesburg
Jacob, Walter Charles *lawyer*
†Price, Stephen Conwell *lawyer*

Lexington
Jost, Timothy Stoltzfus *law educator*
Kirgis, Frederic Lee *law educator*
Krotoszynski, Ronald James, Jr., *law educator*
Sundby, Scott Edwin *law educator*
Wiant, Sarah Kirsten *law library administrator, educator*

Locust Grove
Grante, Jullian Irving *criminal justice consultant*

Lynchburg
Angel, James Joseph *lawyer*
†Davidson, Frank Gassaway, III, *lawyer*
Healy, Joseph Francis, Jr., *lawyer, retired air transportation executive*
Packert, G(ayla) Beth *retired lawyer*

Manakin Sabot
Bright, Craig Bartley *lawyer*

Manassas
Foote, John Holland *lawyer*

Martinsville
Frith, Douglas Kyle *retired lawyer*
†Smith, James Randolph, Jr., *lawyer*

Mc Lean
Alexander, Fred Calvin, Jr., *lawyer*
Andrews, Minerva Wilson *retired lawyer*
Aucutt, Ronald David *lawyer*
†Baker, Keith Leon *lawyer*
Bardack, Paul Roitman *lawyer, consultant*
Brady, Phillip Donley *lawyer*
†Brown, Frank Eugene, Jr., *lawyer*
Brown, Thomas Cartmel, Jr., *lawyer*
Byrnes, William Joseph *lawyer*
Chapple, Thomas Leslie *lawyer*
Church, Randolph Warner, Jr., *lawyer*
Corson, J. Jay, IV, *lawyer*
†Daniels, Michael Alan *lawyer*
†Dunn, James Edward, Jr., *corporate consultant, lawyer*
Fritz, Thomas Vincent *business executive*
Gammon, James Alan *lawyer*
Head, James Philip *lawyer*
Herge, J. Curtis *lawyer*
Hicks, C. Thomas, III, *lawyer*
Hoffmann, Martin Richard *lawyer*
Ingersoll, William Boley *lawyer, real estate developer*
Kennedy, Cornelius Bryant *retired lawyer*
Kondracki, Edward John *lawyer*
†Kruchko, John Gregory *lawyer*
Lazar, Dale Steven *lawyer*
LeSourd, Nancy Susan Oliver *lawyer, writer*
Marino, Michael Frank, III, *lawyer*
McCorkindale, Douglas Hamilton *lawyer, publishing company executive*
Molineaux, Charles Borromeo *lawyer, arbitrator, columnist, poet*
Morris, James Malachy *lawyer*
Murphy, Thomas Patrick *lawyer*
Neel, Samuel Ellison *lawyer*
O'Brien, Francis Anthony *retired lawyer*
Olsen, Robert Eric *lawyer, educator, writer*
Olson, William Jeffrey *lawyer*
Redmond, Robert *lawyer, educator*
Shapiro, Nelson Hirsh *lawyer*
Sherzer, Harvey Gerald *lawyer*
Sparks, Robert Ronold, Jr., *lawyer*
Stephens, William Theodore *lawyer, business executive*
Stump, John Sutton *retired lawyer*
Susko, Carol Lynne *lawyer, accountant*
Tansill, Frederick Joseph *lawyer*
Townsend, Christopher Gordon *lawyer*
Van Lare, Wendell John *lawyer*
†Wall, Barbara Wartelle *lawyer*
†Walter, Michael Joseph *lawyer*

Middleburg
Beddall, Thomas Henry *lawyer*

Midlothian
†Hall, Franklin Perkins *lawyer, banker, state official*
†Nelson, Margaret Rose *lawyer, legal educator*
Shands, William Ridley, Jr., *lawyer*
Tuttle, Roger Lewis *lawyer, educator*

Mount Vernon
Spiegel, H. Jay *lawyer*

Nellysford
Sims, John Rogers, Jr., *lawyer*

Newport News
†Clarkson, Stephen Batchelder *lawyer*
Cuthrell, Carl Edward *lawyer, educator, clergyman*
Hatten, Robert Randolph *lawyer*
Kamp, Arthur Joseph, Jr., *lawyer*
Martin, Terrence Keech *lawyer, city councilor*
Saunders, Bryan Leslie *lawyer*
Segall, James Arnold *lawyer*
Thro, William Eugene *lawyer, university administrator*

Norfolk
Baird, Edward Rouzie, Jr., *lawyer*
Bishop, Bruce Taylor *lawyer*
Clark, Morton Hutchinson *lawyer*
†Corrigan, James Joseph, II, *retired lawyer*
Cranford, Page Deronde *lawyer*
Crenshaw, Francis Nelson *retired lawyer*
Davis, Terry Hunter, Jr., *lawyer*
Drescher, John Webb *lawyer*
†Glasser, Michael A. *lawyer*
†Johnson, Thomas G., Jr., *lawyer*
Knight, Montgomery, Jr., *lawyer*
†Land, Charles Edwards *lawyer*
†Lawrence, Joe Gray, Jr., *lawyer*
†Mayo, Alex T., Jr., *lawyer*
Miller, Joseph Aaron *lawyer, musician*
Parker, Richard Wilson *lawyer, rail transportation executive*
†Parsons, Rymn James *lawyer*
Pearson, John Yeardley, Jr., *lawyer*
Rashkind, Alan Brody *lawyer*
Rephan, Jack *lawyer*
Russell, C. Edward, Jr., *lawyer*
Ryan, John M. *lawyer*
Shannon, John Sanford *lawyer, retired railway executive*
†Smith, Richard Muldrow *lawyer*
Ventker, David Neil *lawyer*
†Ware, Guilford Dudley *lawyer*
Zahn, Richard William, Jr., *lawyer*

Norton
Jessee, Roy Mark *lawyer*

Oakton
†Cutchin, James McKenney, IV, *lawyer, engineer*
Duesenberg, Robert H. *retired lawyer*
Randolph, Christopher Craven *lawyer*
Vernava, Anthony Michael *lawyer*

Petersburg
Baskervill, Charles Thornton *lawyer*

Everitt, Alice Lubin *labor arbitrator*
Rosenstock, Louis Anthony, III, *lawyer*
Spero, Morton Bertram *retired lawyer*
†White, William Earle *lawyer*

Portsmouth
Brennan, John William *lawyer, real estate broker*
†Lavin, Barbara Hofheins *lawyer*
Moody, Willard James, Sr., *lawyer*
Porter, J. Ridgely, III, *lawyer*

Providence Forge
Richardson, William Winfree, III, *lawyer*

Pulaski
McCarthy, Thomas James, Jr., *lawyer*

Radford
Davis, Richard Waters *lawyer*
Turk, James Clinton, Jr., *lawyer*

Reston
Bredehoft, Elaine Charlson *lawyer*
Lowell, Bret *lawyer*
Maitland, Guy Edison Clay *lawyer*
Mendelsohn, Stuart *lawyer, elected official*
Platt, Leslie A. *lawyer*
Rau, Lee Arthur *lawyer*
Scharff, Joseph Laurent *lawyer*
Toole, John Harper *lawyer*
Walton, Edmund Lewis, Jr., *lawyer*

Richmond
Addison, David Dunham *lawyer*
Aghdami, Farhad *lawyer*
Allen, Wilbur Coleman *lawyer*
Anderson, Patricia Coulter *paralegal*
†Anutta, Lucile Jamison *lawyer*
†Bagley, Philip Joseph, III, *lawyer*
Baliles, Gerald L. *lawyer, former governor*
Belcher, Dennis Irl *lawyer*
Bing, Richard McPhail *lawyer*
Booker, Lewis Thomas *lawyer*
†Boone, David Eason *lawyer*
Brasfield, Evans Booker *lawyer*
†Broadbent, Peter Edwin, Jr., *lawyer*
Brockenbrough, Henry Watkins *lawyer*
Brooks, Robert Franklin, Sr., *lawyer*
Buffenstein, Allan S. *lawyer*
Buford, Robert Pegram *lawyer*
Burke, John K(irkland), Jr., *lawyer*
Burrus, Robert Lewis, Jr., *lawyer*
†Burtch, Jack Willard, Jr., *lawyer*
Butler, Donald K. *lawyer*
Cantor, Irvin Victor *lawyer*
Canup, James W.C. *lawyer*
Carrell, Daniel Allan *lawyer*
Carter, Joseph Carlyle, Jr., *lawyer*
Catlett, Richard H., Jr., *retired lawyer*
Clinard, Robert Noel *lawyer*
Cohn, David Stephen *lawyer*
Cutchins, Clifford Armstrong, IV, *lawyer*
Dabney, H. Slayton, Jr., *lawyer*
†DeCamps, Charles Michael *lawyer*
Denny, Collins, III, *lawyer*
Dotson, Donald L. *lawyer*
Dray, Mark S. *lawyer*
Edmonds, Thomas Andrew *legal association administrator*
Ellis, Andrew Jackson, Jr., *lawyer*
Elmore, Edward Whitehead *lawyer*
Flippen, Edward L. *lawyer*
†Freeman, George Clemon, Jr., *lawyer*
Gary, Richard David *lawyer*
Goodpasture, Philip Henry *lawyer*
†Goolsby, Allen Cunningham, III, *lawyer*
Graves, H. Brice *retired lawyer*
Hackney, Virginia Howitz *lawyer*
Hall, Stephen Charles *lawyer*
Hettrick, George Harrison *lawyer*
Horsley, Waller Holladay *lawyer*
Howell, George Cook, III, *lawyer*
Kearfott, Joseph Conrad *lawyer*
†King, William H., Jr., *lawyer*
†Landin, David Craig *lawyer*
Ledbetter, David Oscar *lawyer*
Levit, Jay J(oseph) *lawyer*
McClard, Jack Edward *lawyer*
McFarlane, Walter Alexander *lawyer, educator*
Merhige, Robert Reynold, Jr., *lawyer*
†Mezzullo, Louis Albert *lawyer*
Milme, Patrick Joseph *retired lawyer*
Minardi, Richard A., Jr., *lawyer*
Moore, Thurston Roach *lawyer*
Musick, Robert Lawrence, Jr., *lawyer*
Nagle, David Edward *lawyer, columnist*
Pasco, Hansell Merrill *retired lawyer*
†Patterson, Robert Hobson, Jr., *lawyer*
†Pearsall, John Wesley *lawyer*
Phillips, James Dixon *mediator, consultant, educator*
Pinckney, Charles Cotesworth *lawyer*
Pope, Robert Dean *lawyer*
Powell, Lewis Franklin, III, *lawyer*
Rainey, Gordon Fryer, Jr., *lawyer*
Reed, Austin F. *lawyer*
Rigsby, Linda Flory *lawyer*
Robinson, John Victor *lawyer*
†Robinson, Thomas Hart *lawyer, educator*
Rolfe, Robert Martin *lawyer*
†Rowe, William L. S. *lawyer*
Rucker, Douglas Pendleton, Jr., *lawyer*
Rudlin, David Alan *lawyer*
Ryland, Walter H. *lawyer*
Sharer, John Daniel *lawyer*
†Shields, William Gilbert *lawyer*
Slater, Thomas Glascock, Jr., *lawyer*
Slaughter, Alexander Hoke *lawyer*
†Smith, Julious Perry, Jr., *lawyer*
Smith, R. Gordon *lawyer*
Smolla, Rodney Alan *lawyer, educator, dean*
Spahn, Gary Joseph *lawyer*
†Sper, Jane *lawyer*
Starke, Harold E., Jr., *lawyer*
†Street, Walter Scott, III, *lawyer*
Strickland, William Jesse *lawyer*
Thomas, John Charles *lawyer, former state supreme court justice*

Thompson, Paul Michael *lawyer*
†Totten, Randolph Fowler *lawyer*
Troy, Anthony Francis *lawyer*
Urelius, Shawn Renea *lawyer*
†Waddell, William Robert *lawyer*
Walsh, James Hamilton *lawyer*
Walsh, William Arthur, Jr., *lawyer*
Warthen, Harry Justice, III, *lawyer*
†Wellford, Hill B., Jr., *lawyer*
White, Hugh Vernon, Jr., *lawyer*
Whitlock, Julie Marie *lawyer*
†Williamson, Thomas W., Jr., *lawyer*
Witt, Walter Francis, Jr., *lawyer*
Wright, Wiley Reed, Jr., *lawyer, retired judge, mediator*

Roanoke
Barnhill, David Stan *lawyer*
Bates, Harold Martin *lawyer*
Butler, Manley Caldwell *retired lawyer*
Densmore, Douglas Warren *lawyer*
Effel, Laura *lawyer*
†Farnham, David Alexander *lawyer*
Fishwick, John Palmer *retired lawyer, retired railroad executive*
Glenn, Robert Eastwood *lawyer*
Harris, Bayard Easter *lawyer*
†Harrison, David George *lawyer*
Hylton, Myles Talbert *lawyer*
Jennings, James Wilson, Jr., *lawyer*
Lemon, William Jacob *lawyer*
†Marshall, Heman Alexander, III, *lawyer*
Mundy, Gardner Marshall *lawyer*
Reese, Joan Carol *mediator, consultant, coach*
†Steele, Anita Martin (Margaret Anne Martin) *law librarian, legal educator*
Woodrum, Clifton A., III, *lawyer, state legislator*

Salem
†Griffith, H(oward) Morgan *lawyer*

Schley
McVey, Henry Hanna, III, *retired lawyer*

Spotsylvania
Manthei, Richard Dale *retired lawyer, health care company executive*

Springfield
Chappell, Milton Leroy *lawyer*
Costello, Daniel Brian *lawyer, consultant*
†Eley, Randall Robbi *lawyer*
Englert, Roy Theodore *lawyer*
LaJeunesse, Raymond John, Jr., *lawyer*
Long, Clarence Dickinson, III, *lawyer*
†Townsend, Joachim Rudiger (Jack Townsend) *lawyer*

Sterling
Clegg, Roger Burton *lawyer*

Suffolk
Young, Hubert Howell, Jr., *lawyer, real estate investor and developer*

Tazewell
†Mullins, Roger Wayne *lawyer*

Tysons Corner
Hogue, Dale Curtis, Sr., *lawyer*

Vienna
Bonacquist, Harold Frank, Jr., *lawyer*
†Gavin, Donald Glenn
Hagberg, Chris Eric *lawyer*
Johnson, Richard Clark *lawyer*
Lublinski, Michael *lawyer*
Maiwurm, James John *lawyer*
†Price, Ilene Rosenberg *lawyer*
Razzano, Frank Charles *lawyer*
†Schuyler, Marilynn L. *lawyer, mediator, government administrator*
Settle, Eric Lawrence *lawyer*
Stearns, Frank Warren *lawyer*
†Stockstill, Charles James *lawyer, engineer*
Titus, Bruce Earl *lawyer*
Whitaker, Thomas Patrick *lawyer*

Virginia Beach
Blachman, Michael Joel *lawyer*
Buzard, David Andrew *lawyer*
Clark, Donald H. *lawyer*
Frantz, Thomas Richard *lawyer*
Hajek, Francis Paul *lawyer*
Harrell, Charles Lydon, Jr., *lawyer*
Hernandez, Michael Vincent *law educator*
Pickett, Owen B. *lawyer, congressman*
Savage, Toy Dixon, Jr., *lawyer*
Schon, Alan Wallace *lawyer, actor*
Spitzli, Donald Hawkes, Jr., *lawyer*
Swope, Richard McAllister *retired lawyer*

Warrenton
†Brooke, Edward William *lawyer, former senator*
Howard, Blair Duncan *lawyer*

Waterford
Harris, Caspa, Jr., *lawyer, educator, association administrator*

White Stone
Ames, John Lewis *lawyer*

Williamsburg
Burdette, Robert Bruce *retired lawyer*
Church, Dale Walker *lawyer*
†Dewhirst, John Ward *lawyer*
Geddy, Vernon Meredith, Jr., *lawyer*
†Graham, David Browning *lawyer*
Lund, Wendell Luther *retired lawyer*
Marcus, Paul *law educator*
Margolin, Robert Jeremy *lawyer*
†Merritt, James Edward *lawyer*
Sullivan, Timothy Jackson *law educator, academic administrator*
Whyte, James Primrose, Jr., *former law educator*

Winchester
†Tisinger, Billy Joe *lawyer*

Wise
Kennedy, J. Jack, Jr., *court administrator, lawyer*

Woodstock
Walton, Morgan Lauck, III, *lawyer*

Wytheville
Baird, Thomas Bryan, Jr., *retired lawyer*

WASHINGTON

Bainbridge Island
†Morisset, Mason Dale *lawyer*
Otorowski, Christopher Lee *lawyer*

Bellevue
Cowan, Douglas Leo *lawyer*
Hand, Bruce George *lawyer*
Hannah, Lawrence Burlison *lawyer*
Landau, Felix *lawyer*
McCutcheon, James Edward, III, *lawyer*
†Medved, Robert Allen *lawyer*
Neate, Robert Edward *lawyer*
Parker, Omar Sigmund, Jr., *lawyer*
Sebris, Robert, Jr., *lawyer*
Sweeney, David Brian *lawyer*
†Tee, Virginia *lawyer*
Tyndall, Jay Mark *lawyer*
†Yarington, Barbara J. *lawyer*
†Zackey, Jonathan Thomas *lawyer*

Bellingham
Anderson, David Bowen *lawyer*
Buri, Philip James *lawyer*
Packer, Mark Barry *lawyer, financial consultant, foundation official*
Pritchett, Russell William *lawyer, educator*
Raas, Daniel Alan *lawyer*

Bremerton
Cunningham, Gary Allen *lawyer*

Centralia
Bates, Charles Walter *lawyer, human resources executive, politician*
Buzzard, Steven Ray *lawyer*

Edmonds
Crump, David Lee *lawyer*
Hall, Michael Wayne *lawyer, judge*

Everett
Dewell, Julian C. *lawyer*
Fitzpatrick, Thomas Mark *lawyer*
Mestel, Mark David *lawyer*

Federal Way
Nance, John Joseph *lawyer, writer, air safety analyst, broadcaster, consultant*

Friday Harbor
Gonser, Thomas Howard *lawyer, former bar association executive*

Gig Harbor
Thompson, Ronald Edward *lawyer*

Hoquiam
Kahler, Ray William *lawyer*
Kessler, Keith Leon *lawyer*

Issaquah
†Benoliel, Joel *lawyer*
Moch, Robert Gaston *retired lawyer*
Oles, Stuart Gregory *lawyer*
Sterling, Michael Erwin *lawyer*

Kennewick
Hames, William Lester *lawyer*

Keyport
Treacy, Gerald Bernard, Jr., *lawyer*

Kirkland
Dorkin, Frederic Eugene *lawyer*

Lynnwood
Wolff, Joel Henry *lawyer, human factors engineer*

Mercer Island
†Halverson, Lowell Klark *lawyer*

Montesano
Stewart, James Malcolm *lawyer*

Mount Vernon
Moser, C. Thomas *lawyer*

Newcastle
Erxleben, William Charles *lawyer, consultant*

Olympia
Hayward, Allen William *government lawyer*
Miller, Allen Terry, Jr., *lawyer*
†Reynolds, Dennis Dean *lawyer*
Roe, Charles Barnett *lawyer*
Walker, Francis Joseph *lawyer*
Welsh, John Beresford, Jr., *retired lawyer*
Wilson, Wesley M. *retired lawyer, writer*

Port Angeles
Gay, Carl Lloyd *lawyer*

Redmond
†Neukom, William H. *lawyer*
Waldbaum, Alan G. *lawyer*

Renton
Swanson, Arthur Dean *lawyer*

Richland
Norris, Kenneth Michael *lawyer*

Sammamish
†Waitt, Robert Kenneth *lawyer*

Seattle
†Alsdorf, Robert Hermann *lawyer*
†Anderson, Gene S. *lawyer*
Anderson, Peter MacArthur *lawyer*
Andrews, J. David *lawyer*
Aramburu, John Richard *lawyer*
Bagshaw, Bradley Holmes *lawyer*
Bateman, Heidi S. *lawyer*
Birmingham, Richard Joseph *lawyer*
Black, W. L. Rivers, III, *lawyer*
†Blair, M. Wayne *lawyer*
Blom, Daniel Charles *lawyer, investor*
†Blumenfeld, Charles Raban *lawyer*
Boeder, Thomas L. *lawyer*
Boman, Marc Allen *lawyer*
†Bridge, Jonathan Joseph *lawyer, retail executive*
Bringman, Joseph Edward *lawyer*
Burke, William Thomas *law educator, lawyer*
†Burns, Robert William *lawyer*
Cavanaugh, Michael Everett *lawyer, arbitrator, mediator*
Char, Patricia Helen *lawyer*
Claflin, Arthur Cary *lawyer*
Clinton, Richard M. *lawyer*
†Comfort, Robert Dennis *lawyer*
Cornell, Kenneth Lee *lawyer*
Corning, Nicholas F. *lawyer*
Creim, Jerry Alan *lawyer*
†Cross, Bruce Michael *lawyer*
†Cumbow, Robert Charles *lawyer, writer, educator*
Cutler, Philip Edgerton *lawyer*
Dalton, Thomas George *paralegal, social worker, legal consultant*
Davis, John MacDougall *lawyer*
†Davison, Audrey M. *lawyer, consultant*
†DeVore, Paul Cameron *lawyer*
Diamond, Josef *lawyer*
Dolan, Andrew Kevin *lawyer*
Easter, Scott Beyer *lawyer*
Ellis, James Reed *retired lawyer*
Ferrer, Rafael Douglas Paul *lawyer*
†Fitzpatrick, Joan Marie *law educator*
Free, Robert Alan *lawyer*
Freeman, Antoinette Rosefeldt *lawyer*
†Gerrard, Keith *lawyer*
†Gibbs, Nancy Patricia *lawyer*
Giles, Robert Edward, Jr., *lawyer*
†Ginsberg, Phillip H(enry) *lawyer*
Gittinger, D. Wayne *lawyer*
†Glover, Karen E. *lawyer*
†Goeltz, Thomas A. *lawyer*
Gonick, Peter B. *lawyer*
Gores, Thomas C. *lawyer*
Gorton, Slade *attorney, former senator*
Gottlieb, Daniel Seth *lawyer*
Graham, Stephen Michael *lawyer*
Gray, Marvin Lee, Jr., *lawyer*
Greenan, Thomas J. *lawyer*
†Greenfield, Ester Frances *lawyer*
Haman, Raymond William *lawyer*
Hansen, Wayne W. *lawyer*
Hazelton, Penny Ann *law librarian, educator*
Hecht, Irene Margret *lawyer*
†Hermsen, James R. *lawyer*
Hilpert, Edward Theodore, Jr., *lawyer*
Hough, Mark Mason *lawyer*
Huston, John Charles *law educator*
Hutcheson, Mark Andrew *lawyer*
Isaki, Lucy Power Slyngstad *lawyer*
†Jaffe, Robert Stanley *lawyer*
Johnson, Bruce Edward Humble *lawyer*
Judson, C(harles) James (Jim Judson) *lawyer*
Kane, Alan Henry *lawyer*
Kaplan, Barry Martin *lawyer*
Keegan, John E. *lawyer*
Kilbane, Thomas M. *lawyer*
Kinsey, Ronald C., Jr., *lawyer*
Klein, Otto George, III, *lawyer*
Koehler, Reginald Stafford, III, *lawyer*
Kuhrau, Edward W. *lawyer*
Leed, Roger Melvin *lawyer*
†Leen, David Arthur *lawyer*
Leitzell, Terry Lee *lawyer*
†Lemly, Thomas Adger *lawyer*
†Levy, Barbara Jo *lawyer, personal life coach*
Loftus, Thomas Daniel *lawyer*
Lundgren, Gail M. *lawyer*
†Lundin, John W. *lawyer, urban planner*
Maleng, Norm *prosecutor*
†Malkin, Michelle Lynn *lawyer*
Malone, Thomas William *lawyer*
Marshall, David Stanley *lawyer*
Mastroianni, Anna Catherine *law educator*
McCann, Richard Eugene *retired lawyer*
McConaughy, Bennet Alan *lawyer*
McCune, Philip Spear *lawyer*
McKay, John *lawyer*
McKay, Michael Dennis *lawyer*
McKinstry, Ronald E. *lawyer*
†McLaughlin, Thomas Jeffrey *lawyer*
Mines, Michael *lawyer*
†Mitchell, Robert Bertelson, Jr., *lawyer*
†Moren, Charles Verner *lawyer, judge*
Mucklestone, Peter John *lawyer*
Murray, Michael Kent *lawyer*
Mussehl, Robert Clarence *lawyer*
Needle, Jeffrey Lowell *lawyer*
Niemi, Janice *retired lawyer, former state legislator*
Novotny, Patricia Susan *lawyer, educator*
†Nye, Daniel Alan *lawyer, consultant*
Oehler, Richard William *lawyer*
Olsen, Harold Fremont *lawyer*
Olver, Michael Lynn *lawyer*
Palmer, Douglas S., Jr., *lawyer*
†Parks, Gerald Thomas, Jr., *lawyer, business executive*
Parks, Patricia Jean *lawyer*
Paul, Thomas Frank *lawyer*
†Perisho, Russell L. *lawyer*
Peterson, Jan Eric *lawyer*
Petrie, Gregory Steven *lawyer*
Prentke, Richard Ottesen *lawyer*
Price, John Richard *lawyer, law educator*
†Pritchard, Llewelyn G. *lawyer*
Redman, Eric *lawyer*
†Riley, Stewart Patrick *lawyer*
Ritter, Daniel Benjamin *lawyer*
†Riviera, Daniel John *lawyer*
Rosen, Jon Howard *lawyer*
Rummage, Stephen Michael *lawyer*
Russell, Robie George *lawyer*
†Sandler, Michael David *lawyer*
Sandman, Irvin W(illis) *lawyer*
Sausser, Gail Dianne *lawyer*
Sayre, Matt Melvin Mathias *lawyer*
Schneidler, Jon Gordon *lawyer*
Schwartz, Irwin H. *lawyer*
Scott, Brian David *lawyer*
†Simburg, Melvyn Jay *lawyer*
†Smith, James Alexander, Jr., *lawyer*
Soltys, John Joseph *lawyer*
Spitzer, Hugh D. *lawyer*
Squires, William Randolph, III, *lawyer*
Starr, Isidore *law educator*
†Steel, John Murray *lawyer*
Stoebuck, William Brees *law educator*
†Stokke, Diane Rees *lawyer*
†Sullivan, Daniel Frederick *lawyer*
Sussman, Neil A. *lawyer*
†Tausend, Fredric Cutner *lawyer, dean*
Tessier, Dennis Medward *paralegal, lecturer, legal advisor, consultant, cartoonist*
Thomas, Elizabeth *lawyer*
Thorson, Lee A. *lawyer*
†Tomlinson, John Randolph *lawyer*
Tousley, Russell Frederick *lawyer*
Treiger, Irwin Louis *lawyer*
Tucker, Kathryn Louise *lawyer, educator*
†Tune, James Fulcher *lawyer*
Van Kampen, Al *lawyer*
Vogel, David Seth *lawyer*
Vreeland, Victoria Lynn *lawyer*
Wagoner, David Everett *lawyer*
†Waldman, Bart Jay *lawyer*
Wayne, Robert Jonathan *lawyer, educator*
Wechsler, Mary Heyrman *lawyer*
†White, Rick *lawyer, former congressman*
White, Thomas S. *lawyer*
Whitehead, James Fred, III, *lawyer*
Whitson, Lish *lawyer*
Williams, J. Vernon *retired lawyer*
Wilson, Richard Randolph *lawyer*
†Yalowitz, Kenneth Gregg *lawyer*

Snohomish
Renkens, Madeline A. *lawyer*

Spokane
Anderson, Robert Edward *lawyer*
†Clements, Theodore *lawyer, law educator, dean*
Connolly, K. Thomas *lawyer*
Esposito, Joseph Anthony *lawyer*
Eymann, Richard Charles *lawyer*
Grovdahl, Steven Noel *court commissioner*
Harbaugh, Daniel Paul *lawyer*
Koegen, Roy Jerome *lawyer*
†Kovacevich, Robert Eugene *lawyer*
†Leipham, Jay Edward *lawyer*
Michaelsen, Howard Kenneth *lawyer*
Pontarolo, Michael Joseph *lawyer*
†Powers, Mark Gregory *consultant, lawyer*
†Scanlon, Robert Charles *lawyer*
†Schuchart, Frederick Mark *lawyer*

Tacoma
†Barline, John *lawyer*
Beale, Robert Lyndon *lawyer*
†Carlisle, Dale L. *lawyer*
Condon, David Bruce *lawyer*
Holt, William E. *lawyer*
Hostnik, Charles Rivoire *lawyer*
†Kram, Peter *lawyer*
Krueger, James A. *lawyer*
†Lowenberg, Timothy Joseph *lawyer*
Malanca, Albert Robert *lawyer, mediator*
Miller, Judson Frederick *lawyer, former military officer*
†Waldo, James Chandler *lawyer*
Wang, Arthur Ching-li *administrative law judge, law educator*

Tumwater
Edmondson, Frank Kelley, Jr., *lawyer, legal administrator*

Vashon
Canavor, Frederick Charles, Jr., *lawyer*

Walla Walla
Hayner, Herman Henry *lawyer*
Mitchell, Michael Sherman *lawyer*

Yakima
Larson, Paul Martin *lawyer*

WEST VIRGINIA

Beckley
Kennedy, David Tinsley *retired lawyer, labor arbitrator*

Bluefield
Evans, Wayne Lewis *lawyer*
Kantor, Isaac Norris *lawyer*

Charleston
Bell, Harry Fullerton, Jr., *lawyer*
†Berthold, Robert Vernon, Jr., *lawyer*
Brenneman Harrah, Sandra *lawyer*
Brown, James Knight *lawyer*
†Callaghan, Dan O. *lawyer*
†Chaney, Vincent Verlando
Davis, James Hornor, III, *lawyer*
Dissen, James Hardiman *lawyer*
George, Larry Wayne *lawyer*

†Heath, Mark E. *lawyer*
†Kopelman, Larry Gordon *lawyer*
†Lane, Charlotte *lawyer*
McClaugherty, John Lewis *lawyer*
†Neely, Richard *lawyer*
O'Connor, Otis Leslie *lawyer, director*
†Price, Brian Alton *lawyer*
†Robinson, E. Glenn *lawyer*
†Rowe, Larry Linwell *lawyer*
†Slack, John Mark, III, *lawyer*
†Teare, John Richard, Jr., *lawyer*
Victorson, Michael Bruce *lawyer*
Zak, Robert Joseph *lawyer*

Fairmont
Stanton, George Patrick, Jr., *lawyer*

Fairview
Bunner, William Keck *lawyer*

Huntington
Bagley, Charles Frank, III, *lawyer*
McGuire, James Grant *lawyer*

Lewisburg
Ford, Richard Edmond *lawyer*

Logan
Hrutkay, Lidella Wilson *lawyer, state legislator*

Martinsburg
Hill, Philip Bonner *lawyer*
Martin, Clarence Eugene, III, *lawyer*

Morgantown
Cleckley, Franklin D. *law educator*
Fisher, John Welton, II, *law educator, magistrate judge, university official*
†Fusco, Andrew G. *lawyer*
Morris, William Otis, Jr., *lawyer, educator, writer*
Ringer, Darrell Wayne (Dan Ringer) *lawyer*

Parkersburg
Keltner, Robert Earl *lawyer, researcher, business executive*
†Richardson, William Berkley *lawyer*

Wellsburg
Viderman, Linda Jean *paralegal, corporate executive*

Wheeling
Gardill, James Clark *lawyer*
Gompers, Joseph Alan *lawyer*
Wilmoth, William David *lawyer*

WISCONSIN

Appleton
†Chudacoff, Bruce Michael *lawyer*
Lonergan, Kevin *lawyer*
Murray, John Daniel *lawyer*
†Siddall, Michael Sheridan *lawyer*
Thenell, Heather Jo *lawyer*

Beloit
†Blakely, Robert George *lawyer*

Brookfield
Benson, Scott Michael *lawyer*

Chippewa Falls
Hunt, Heather M. *lawyer*

Colby
Nikolay, Frank Lawrence *lawyer*

Cross Plains
Moretti, Jay Donald *lawyer*

Deerfield
Pappas, David Christopher *lawyer*

Delafield
McClure, Thomas James *lawyer*

Eagle River
Kulzick, Ken Stafford *retired lawyer, travel writer*

Eau Claire
Frank, John LeRoy *lawyer, government executive, educator*
†Stark, Lisa Kay *lawyer*

Elcho
†Hatfield, Deborah L. *lawyer*

Elkhorn
Sweet, Lowell Elwin *lawyer, writer*

Evansville
Connors, William Edward *lawyer*

Fond Du Lac
†English, Dale Lowell *circuit court judge*

Germantown
Ehlinger, Ralph Jerome *lawyer*

Glendale
†Hill, John Glenwood, Jr., *university counsel, lawyer*

Green Bay
†Schober, Thomas Leonard *lawyer*

Hales Corners
Case, Karen Ann *lawyer*

Hayward
Ueland, Sigurd, Jr., *retired lawyer*

Janesville
Steil, George Kenneth, Sr., *lawyer*

Williams, Mary Beth *lawyer*

Kenosha
Clarke, Alan William *lawyer*
†Higgins, John Patrick *lawyer, mediator, educator, lobbyist*
†Richter, David Jerome *lawyer*
†Rose, Terry William *lawyer*

La Crosse
Klos, Jerome John *lawyer, director*
Nix, Edmund Alfred *lawyer*
Sleik, Thomas Scott *lawyer*

Lake Geneva
Braden, Berwyn Bartow *lawyer*
McCormack, Joanne Marie *lawyer*

Little Chute
Cornett, Paul Michael, Sr., *lawyer*

Madison
Anderson, Michael Steven *lawyer*
Baldwin, Gordon Brewster *law educator, lawyer*
Baldwin, Janice Murphy *lawyer*
Barnhill, Charles Joseph, Jr., *lawyer*
Barnick, Helen *retired judicial clerk*
Bartell, Jeffrey Bruce *lawyer*
Blanchard, Brian Wheatley *lawyer*
Bochert, Linda H. *lawyer*
Boucher, Joseph W(illiam) *lawyer, accountant, educator, writer*
Boyer, Dennis Lee *lawyer, lobbyist, writer*
Braden, Betty Jane *legal association administrator*
Bremer, Howard Walter *lawyer, consultant*
Brewster, Francis Anthony *lawyer*
Bugge, Lawrence John *lawyer, educator*
†Chandler, Richard Gates *lawyer*
Croake, Paul Allen *lawyer*
Cronin, Kevin Brian *lawyer*
Curry, Robert Lee *lawyer*
†Doran, Kenneth John *lawyer*
†Ehlke, Bruce Frederic *lawyer*
†Everard, Gerald Wilfred *lawyer, trust company executive*
Field, Henry Augustus, Jr., *lawyer*
Fleischli, George Robert *lawyer*
Hanson, David James *lawyer*
Helstad, Orrin L. *lawyer, legal educator*
Hempe, A. Henry *lawyer, state agency official*
Heymann, S. Richard *lawyer*
Hildebrand, Daniel Walter *lawyer*
Hofeldt, John W. *lawyer*
Jones, James Edward, Jr., *retired law educator*
†Kennedy, Debora A. *lawyer*
Kuehling, Robert Warren *lawyer, accountant*
Langer, Richard J. *lawyer*
Linstroth, Tod Brian *lawyer*
†Long, Theodore James *lawyer*
†Mebane, David Cummins *lawyer*
Melli, Marygold Shire *law educator*
Michaelis, Karen Lauree *law educator*
†Mitby, John Chester *lawyer*
†Mowris, Gerald William *lawyer*
†Pernitz, Scott Gregory *lawyer*
Petershack, Richard Eugene *lawyer*
Pitzner, Richard William *lawyer*
Prange, Roy Leonard, Jr., *lawyer*
Provis, Timothy Alan *lawyer*
Ragatz, Thomas George *lawyer*
Rankin, Gene Raymond *lawyer*
Roberson, Linda *lawyer*
Schmid, John Henry, Jr., *lawyer*
Schooler, Steven James *lawyer*
†Steingass, Susan R. *lawyer*
Stoddard, Glenn McDonald *lawyer*
Temkin, Harvey L. *lawyer*
†Thomas, Gloria *lawyer, nurse, state program administrator*
Van Ryzin, Gary James *lawyer, accountant*
Vaughan, Michael Richard *lawyer*
Wagner, Burton Allan *lawyer*
Walsh, David Graves *lawyer*
Wood, Tracey Ann *lawyer*

Mc Farland
†Abbott, William Anthony *lawyer*

Menomonee Falls
†Hurt, Michael Carter *lawyer*

Mequon
†Burroughs, Charles Edward *lawyer*
†Rapkin, Stephanie Gayle *lawyer, educator*

Middleton
Berman, Ronald Charles *lawyer, accountant*

Milwaukee
Abraham, William John, Jr., *lawyer*
†Ariker, Shanti Alice *lawyer*
Babler, Wayne E., Jr., *lawyer*
†Ballman, Patricia Kling *lawyer*
Bannen, John Thomas *lawyer*
Barnes, Paul McClung *lawyer*
Beightol, Scott Christopher *lawyer*
Berkoff, Marshall Richard *lawyer*
Biehl, Michael Melvin *lawyer, author*
Biller, Joel Wilson *lawyer, former foreign service officer*
Blain, Peter Charles *lawyer*
Bliss, Richard Jon *lawyer*
†Bolger, T(homas) Michael *lawyer*
Bratt, Herbert Sidney *lawyer*
Bremer, John M. *lawyer*
Bruce, Peter Wayne *lawyer, insurance company executive*
Busch, John Arthur *lawyer*
Calise, William Joseph, Jr., *lawyer*
Cannon, David Joseph *lawyer*
Casey, John Alexander *lawyer*
Casper, Richard Henry *lawyer*
Christiansen, Keith Allan *lawyer*
Clark, James Richard *lawyer*
Connolly, Gerald Edward *lawyer*
Cutler, Richard W. *lawyer*

Daily, Frank J(erome) *lawyer*
Dallman, Robert Edward *lawyer*
Dencker, Lester J. *lawyer*
Donahue, John Edward *lawyer*
Duback, Steven Rahr *lawyer*
Ericson, James Donald *lawyer, insurance executive*
Fitzgerald, Kevin Gerard *lawyer*
Florsheim, Richard Steven *lawyer*
Frautschi, Timothy Clark *lawyer*
Friedman, James Dennis *lawyer*
Gaines, Irving David *lawyer*
Galanis, John William *lawyer*
Gallagher, Richard Sidney *lawyer*
Gefke, Henry Jerome *lawyer*
Gemignani, Joseph Adolph *lawyer*
Ghiardi, James Domenic *lawyer, educator*
Giese, Heiner *lawyer, real estate investor*
Gimbel, Franklyn M. *lawyer*
Goodkind, Conrad George *lawyer*
Graber, Richard William *lawyer, political organization worker*
Grenig, Jay Edward *law educator*
Haberman, F. William *lawyer*
Habush, Robert Lee *lawyer*
Harrington, John Timothy *retired lawyer*
Hase, David John *lawyer*
†Hatch, Michael Ward *lawyer*
Hoefle, Paul Ryan *lawyer*
Hoffman, Nathaniel A. *lawyer*
Holz, Harry George *lawyer*
Iding, Allan Earl *lawyer*
†Israel, Scott Michael *lawyer*
†Johnson, James N. *lawyer*
Jost, Lawrence John *lawyer*
Kessler, Joan F. *lawyer*
Kircher, John Joseph *law educator*
†Knight, George B. *lawyer*
Kringel, Jerome Howard *lawyer*
Krueger, Raymond Robert *lawyer*
Kubale, Bernard Stephen *lawyer*
Kurtz, Harvey A. *lawyer*
LaBudde, Roy Christian *lawyer*
Levit, William Harold, Jr., *lawyer*
Levy, Alan M. *lawyer*
Lueders, Wayne Richard *lawyer*
MacGregor, David Lee *lawyer*
MacIver, John Kenneth *lawyer*
Margolis, Marvin Allen *lawyer*
Martin, Quinn William *lawyer*
Maynard, John Ralph *lawyer*
McGaffey, Jere D. *lawyer*
McSweeney, Maurice J. (Marc McSweeney) *lawyer*
Medved, Paul Stanley *lawyer*
Meldman, Clifford Kay *lawyer*
Meldman, Robert Edward *lawyer*
Melin, Robert Arthur *lawyer*
Michelstetter, Stanley Hubert *lawyer*
Mulcahy, Robert William *lawyer*
Nelson, Randy Scott *lawyer*
Nelson, Roy Hugh, Jr., *lawyer, mediator, arbitrator*
Olivieri, José Alberto *lawyer*
O'Shaughnessy, James Patrick *lawyer*
†Patzke, John Charles *lawyer*
Peckerman, Bruce Martin *lawyer*
Peltin, Sherwin Carl *lawyer*
†Pettit, Roger Lee *lawyer*
Phillips, Thomas John *lawyer*
Pindyck, Bruce Eben *lawyer, corporate executive*
Powell, Edmund William *lawyer*
Reardon, Timothy P. *lawyer*
Richman, Stephen Erik *lawyer*
Rieselbach, Allen Newman *lawyer*
Rintelman, Donald Brian *lawyer*
Roge, Bret Alan *lawyer*
Ryan, Patrick Michael *lawyer*
Sanfilippo, Jon Walter *lawyer, commissioner*
Schnur, Robert Arnold *lawyer*
Scrivner, Thomas William *lawyer*
†Shapiro, Robyn Sue *lawyer, educator*
Shriner, Thomas L., Jr., *lawyer*
Skipper, Walter John *lawyer*
Slavik, Donald Harlan *lawyer*
Smith, David Bruce *lawyer*
†Somers, Kristina Elizabeth *lawyer*
†Sostarich, Mark Edward *lawyer*
Stephens, Marla Jean *lawyer*
Sturm, William Charles *lawyer*
Surridge, Stephen Zehring *lawyer, writer*
Terschan, Frank Robert *lawyer*
Titley, Robert L. *lawyer*
Trecek, Timothy Scott *lawyer*
Walmer, Edwin Fitch *lawyer*
Whyte, George Kenneth, Jr., *lawyer*
Wiley, Edwin Packard *retired lawyer*
Will, Trevor Jonathan *lawyer*
Williams, Clay Rule *lawyer*
Winsten, Saul Nathan *lawyer*
Wynn, Stanford Alan *lawyer*

Minocqua
†Lund, John Richard *lawyer, director*

Monroe
Kittelsen, Rodney Olin *lawyer*

Mosinee
Hartz, Luetta Bertha *legal secretary*
Schira, Diana Rae *lawyer*

New Berlin
Schober, Thomas Gregory *lawyer*

Oak Creek
Giblin, Louis *lawyer*

Oshkosh
Curtis, George Warren *lawyer*
†Kelly, John Martin *lawyer*
Wilde, William Richard *lawyer*
Zierdt, Alyson Kathleen *lawyer*

Pepin
Seymour, Mary Frances *lawyer*

Pewaukee
Engel, John Charles *lawyer, lobbyist*

Platteville
†Van Buren, David Paul *criminal justice educator*

Port Washington
Check, Melvin Anthony *lawyer*

Racine
Coates, Glenn Richard *lawyer*
Crawford, Timothy Patrick *lawyer, accountant*
Du Rocher, James Howard *lawyer*
Dye, William Ellsworth *lawyer*
Gasiorkiewicz, Eugene Anthony *lawyer*
Mekeel, Steven Leyon *lawyer*
Rudebusch, Alice Ann *lawyer*
†Schoone, Adrian Paul *lawyer*
†Stutt, John Barry *lawyer*

Rhinelander
†McEldowney, Todd Richard *lawyer*
Reese, Kirk David *lawyer*
Saari, John William, Jr., *lawyer*

Ripon
Prissel, Barbara Ann *paralegal, law educator*

Stevens Point
Hamlar, Portia Yvonne Trenholm *lawyer, writer, educator*

Stoughton
†Wetzel, Volker Knoppke *law educator*

Sturgeon Bay
Korb, Joan *lawyer*

Sturtevant
†Brandes, Jo Anne *lawyer*

Sun Prairie
Berkenstadt, James Allan *lawyer*
Eustice, Francis Joseph *lawyer*

Waukesha
Bohren, Michael Oscar *lawyer*
†Davis, J. Mac *lawyer, state judge*
†Jastroch, Leonard Andrew *lawyer*
Macy, John Patrick *lawyer*

Wausau
†Dietrich, Dean Richard *lawyer*
†Drengler, William Allan John *lawyer*
Gray, Robert Joseph *lawyer*
†Grischke, Alan Edward *lawyer*
†Kammer, Robert Arthur, Jr., *lawyer*
Orr, San Watterson, Jr., *lawyer*

Wauwatosa
†Alexander, Robert Gardner *lawyer*
Bonneson, Paul Garland *lawyer*

WYOMING

Buffalo
†Kirven, Timothy J. *lawyer*

Casper
†Benson, Kimberly Dawn *paralegal*
†Burke, Daniel Martin *lawyer*
Combs, W(illiam) Henry, III, *lawyer*
Durham, Harry Blaine, III, *lawyer*
Gray, Jan Charles *lawyer, business owner*
Hjelmstad, William David *lawyer*
Lowe, Robert Stanley *lawyer*
†McCall, Donn Jay *lawyer*
†Reese, Thomas Frank *lawyer*

Cheyenne
†Bailey, Henry Franklin, Jr., *lawyer*
Carlson, Kathleen Bussart *law librarian*
†Carmichael, David H. *lawyer*
Dyekman, Gregory Chris *lawyer*
Freudenthal, Steven Franklin *lawyer, political organization chairman*
Hanes, John Grier *lawyer, state legislator*
McKinley, John Clark *lawyer*
†Palma, Jack D. *lawyer*
Scorsine, John Magnus *lawyer*

Cody
†Johnson, Wallace Harold *lawyer*
Stradley, Richard Lee *lawyer*

Jackson
Schuster, Robert Parks *lawyer*
Shockey, Gary Lee *lawyer*
Spence, Gerald Leonard *lawyer, writer*

Laramie
Kinney, Lisa Frances *lawyer*
†Selig, Joel Louis *lawyer, educator*
Smith, Thomas Shore *lawyer*

Riverton
Girard, Nettabell *lawyer*

Rock Springs
†Tyler, Marvin Lee *lawyer, educator*

Sheridan
Lonabaugh, Ellsworth Eugene *retired lawyer*

Wheatland
Hunkins, Raymond Breedlove *lawyer, rancher*
Jones, Eric E. *lawyer*

Worland
Sweeny, Wendy Press *lawyer*

TERRITORIES OF THE UNITED STATES

GUAM

Hagatna
Black, Frederick A.
†Troutman, Charles Henry, III, *lawyer*

NORTHERN MARIANA ISLANDS

Saipan
Soll, Herbert D. *lawyer*

PUERTO RICO

Old San Juan
Weinstein-Bacal, Stuart Allen *lawyer, educator*

San Juan
Irizarry-Yunque, Carlos Juan *lawyer, educator*
†Martinez-Munoz, Hector *lawyer*
Pierluisi, Pedro R. *lawyer*
Ramos, Carlos E. *law educator*
Rodriguez-Diaz, Juan E. *lawyer*

VIRGIN ISLANDS

Charlotte Amalie
Bolt, Thomas Alvin Waldrep *lawyer*
Feuerzeig, Henry Louis *lawyer*

Christiansted
Franks, William Woolery *lawyer*

St Thomas
Caffee, Lorren Dale *lawyer*
Kleinfeld, Denis Alan *lawyer*

MILITARY ADDRESSES OF THE UNITED STATES

EUROPE

Apo
Frame, Nancy Davis *lawyer*
Kammerer, Kelly Christian *lawyer*

Fpo
Blazewick, Robert B. *lawyer, educator, military officer*

CANADA

ALBERTA

Calgary
†Boettger, Roy Dennis *barrister, solicitor*
Hughes, Margaret Eileen *law educator, former dean*
†Iverach, Robert John *lawyer*
Lougheed, Peter *lawyer, former Canadian premier*

Edmonton
†Kennedy, John William *lawyer*
Patrick, Lynn Allen *lawyer, corporate governance and land development*
†Singleton, John Robinson *lawyer*

BRITISH COLUMBIA

Burnaby
Switlo, Janice Georgina Alice E. *barrister, solicitor, mediator, negotiator, legal and business consultant, strategist*

Sooke
Howard, John Lindsay *lawyer, forest industry company executive*

Vancouver
Bonner, Robert William *lawyer, director*
†Giles, Jack Michael *lawyer*
Head, Ivan Leigh *law educator*
†Ladner, Thomas E. *lawyer*
McEachern, Allan *lawyer*
Penikett, Antony David John *negotiator, writer, politician*
Peterson, Leslie Raymond *barrister*

Victoria
†MacIsaac, Ronald Francis *lawyer*

MANITOBA

Winnipeg
Anderson, David Trevor *law educator*
Edwards, Clifford Henry Coad *law educator*
Schnoor, Jeffrey Arnold *lawyer*

NEW BRUNSWICK

Moncton
McKenna, Frank Joseph *lawyer*

Rothesay
Fairweather, Robert Gordon Lee *lawyer*

NOVA SCOTIA

Halifax
Dexter, Robert Paul *lawyer*
Mingo, James William Edgar *lawyer*

ONTARIO

Harrow
†Kurtz, James P. *administrative law judge*

Oakville
†O'Reilly, Denis *aluminum company executive, lawyer*

Ottawa
Beaudoin, Gérald A(rmand) *lawyer, educator, senator*
d'Aquino, Thomas *lawyer, entrepreneur, educator, strategist, council chief executive*
Iacobucci, Frank *lawyer, educator, jurist*
Tassé, Roger *lawyer, former Canadian government official*
Urie, John James *lawyer, retired Canadian federal judge*

Toronto
Arthurs, Harry William *legal educator, former university president*
†Beaugrand, Kenneth Louis *lawyer, business executive*
Bristow, David Ian *lawyer*
Chester, Robert Simon George *lawyer*
Cowan, Charles Gibbs *lawyer, corporate executive*
Davis, William Grenville *lawyer, former Canadian government official*
Dickens, Bernard Morris *law educator*
Dubin, Charles Leonard *lawyer*
Elliott, Roy Fraser *lawyer, holding and management company executive*
Farquharson, Gordon MacKay *lawyer, director*
Herbst, Renate Diane *lawyer*
McKeown, William Philip *lawyer*
Peterson, David Robert *lawyer, former Canadian government official*

Unionville
Gulden, Simon *lawyer, investment/real estate development executive, business and legal consultant*

QUEBEC

Chicoutimi
Cain, Michael Haney *lawyer*

Ile Perrot
Lalonde, Marc *lawyer, former Canadian government official*

Montreal
Cobbett, Stuart Hanson *lawyer*
Jeanniot, Michel Andre *lawyer*
Kaufman, Donna S. *lawyer*
Lacoste, Paul *lawyer, educator, university official*
Popovici, Adrian *law educator*
Pound, Richard William Duncan *lawyer, accountant*
Robb, James Alexander *lawyer*
†Scraire, Jean-Claude *lawyer, investment management executive*
Tremblay, Andre Gabriel *lawyer*
Vennat, Michel *lawyer, bank executive*

Quebec
LeMay, Jacques *lawyer*
Verge, Pierre *legal educator*

Sainte-Foy
Normand, Robert *retired lawyer*

Sillery
Dinan, Robert Michael *lawyer*

Westmount
Fortier, L. Yves *barrister*

SASKATCHEWAN

Regina
MacKay, Harold Hugh *lawyer*

Saskatoon
Ish, Daniel Russell *law educator, academic administrator*

Ottawa
†Easter, Arnold Wayne *solicitor*

Whale Cove
Rodnunsky, Sidney *lawyer, educator*

MEXICO

Cuauhtemoc
†Aleman, José Vicente Aguinaco *legal administrator*

BANGLADESH

Kushtia
Latifur Rahaman, Rasul Boaksh *legal profession executive*

BELGIUM

Brussels
Barnum, John Wallace *lawyer*
Bustin, George Leo *lawyer*
Liebman, Howard Mark *lawyer*
Staab, Diane D. *lawyer*

BELIZE

Belize City
Brown, Sir George Noel *chief justice*

BRAZIL

Brasília
†Pertenece, Jose Paulo Sepulveda *legal administrator*

DENMARK

Copenhagen
Elmer, Michael Bendik *legal administrator*

Odense
Lauritsen, Kaj Torben *lawyer, former association executive*

ENGLAND

Bedfordshire
Montgomery, John Warwick *law educator, theologian*

Beverley
Edles, Gary Joel *lawyer*

London
Bergman, Mark Steven *lawyer*
†Carrow, Robert Duane *lawyer, barrister*
Cole, Richard A. *retired lawyer*
Fabricant, Arthur E. *lawyer, corporate executive*
†Glass, Douglas B. *lawyer*
Glazer, Barry David *lawyer*
Haubold, Samuel Allen *lawyer*
Hicks, J. Portis *lawyer*
Hudson, Manley O., Jr., *lawyer*
Mandly, Charles Robert, Jr., *lawyer*
McDonald, Joel Matthews *lawyer*
Morrison, William David *lawyer*
Northrip, Robert Earl *lawyer*
Phocas, George John *international lawyer, business executive*
Quillen, Cecil Dyer, III, *lawyer*
Rolle, Martha Collins (Martha Traudt Collins) *lawyer*
†Stern, Stephen Jeffrey *lawyer*
Stevens, Robert Bocking *lawyer, educator*
Thomas, Allen Lloyd *lawyer, private investor*
†Zonana, Victor *lawyer, educator*

Luton Bedfordshire
Ndikum, Philip Forsang *barrister*

Wiltshire
Sherwin, James Terry *lawyer*

FINLAND

Helsinki
Juhani, Erma *lawyer, former stock exchange executive*

FRANCE

Paris
Baum, Axel Helmuth *lawyer*
Bedjaoui, M. Mohammed *former judge International Court of Justice*
Landers, Steven E. *lawyer*
Ramette, Vincent Alfred *legal information specialist*
Reeves, Van Kirk *lawyer*
Régnier, Marc Charles *lawyer, corporate executive*
Salans, Carl Fredric *lawyer*

GERMANY

Frankfurt
Simitis, Spiros *legal educator*

Göttingen
Starck, Christian Walter *jurist*

Karlsruhe
†Geib, Karlmann *legal administrator*

GRENADA

Saint George's
Helgerson, John Walter *lawyer*

HONG KONG

Hong Kong
Choo, Yeow Ming *lawyer*
O'Brien, Timothy James *lawyer*
Scown, Michael John *lawyer*

INDONESIA

Jakarta
Hsi, Edward Yang *lawyer, industrialist, medical venture capitalist, political advisor*

IRELAND

Dublin
Calvani, Terry *lawyer*

ISRAEL

Jerusalem
Rosenne, Meir *lawyer, government agency administrator*

Ramat-Gan
Aron, Roberto *lawyer, writer, educator*

Tel Aviv
Gross, Joseph H. *lawyer, educator*

ITALY

Rome
McGurn, William Barrett, III, *lawyer*

JAPAN

Hachioji
Kojima, Takeshi *law educator, arbitrator, writer*

Minato-Ku Tokyo
Ishizuka, Nobuhisa *lawyer*

Sanda City Hyogo-ken
Brown, Sylvia G. *law educator*

Tokyo
†Gustafson, Albert Katsuaki *lawyer, engineer*
Nakamura, Hideo *law educator*
Shirai, Shun *law educator, lawyer*

LUXEMBOURG

Brussels
Lenz, Carl Otto *European advocate general*

Kirchberg
Leger, Philippe *legal administrator*

NETHERLANDS

Amsterdam
Liem, Edwin T.H. *lawyer*

The Hague
Brower, Charles Nelson *lawyer, judge*
Buergenthal, Thomas *international judge, educator*
Fleischhauer, Carl-August *judge of international court of justice*
Higgins, Dame Rosalyn *judge of international court of justice*
Jiuyong, Shi *judge*
Kooijmans, Pieter Hendrik *judge International Court of Justice*
Koroma, Abdul G. *judge of international court of justice*
†Martens, S.K. *legal administrator, retired*
Parra-Aranguren, Gonzalo *judge International Court of Justice*
Rezek, Francisco *judge, former supreme court justice, educator*

Utrecht
Packer, Corinne Angéline Agnés *human rights law consultant*

NORWAY

Oslo
Fitzpatrick, Whitfield Westfeldt *lawyer*
Fleischer, Carl August *law educator, consultant*

PERU

Lima
Lee, Henry *lawyer*

PHILIPPINES

Manila
Sumida, Gerald Aquinas *lawyer*

POLAND

Cracow
Kasper, Horst Manfred *lawyer*

PORTUGAL

Funchal
Mayda, Jaro *lawyer, educator, writer, consultant*

SAUDI ARABIA

Riyadh
Taylor, Frederick William, Jr., (Fritz Taylor) *lawyer*

SCOTLAND

Edinburgh
Macneil, Ian Roderick *lawyer, educator*

SOUTH AFRICA

Johannesburg
Tager, Louise Arlene *high court advocate*

Waterkloof
Aiello, James Andrew *lawyer*

SPAIN

Madrid
Delgado Barrio, Francisco Javier *president supreme court of Spain*
Herrero Rodriguez de Miñon, Miguel *former Spanish member of parliament, lawyer, international legal consultant*

SWEDEN

Lidingö
Crapon de Caprona, Count Noël François Marie *lawyer, retired United Nations official, historian*

Malmö
Akesson, Anders Gustav *lawyer*

SWITZERLAND

Chambesy
Javits, Eric Moses *lawyer, diplomat*

Chateau d'Oex
Berman, Joshua Mordecai *lawyer, manufacturing company executive*

Fribourg
Gurley, Franklin Louis *lawyer, military historian*

Geneva
Capron, Alexander Morgan *lawyer, educator, philosopher*

Lausanne
†Muller, Peter-Alexander *legal administration executive*

TANZANIA

Arusha
Rapp, Stephen John *international prosecutor*

VENEZUELA

Caracas
†Andrade, Juan Carlos *lawyer*

ADDRESS UNPUBLISHED

Abrahams, Samuel *writer, retired lawyer*
†Abramson, Elliott Myron *law educator, researcher*
Adams, David Gray *lawyer*
Adams, Frances Grant, II, *lawyer*
Adams, Thomas Lynch, Jr., *lawyer*
Agraz, Francisco Javier, Sr., *lawyer, public affairs representative*
Aikman, Albert Edward *lawyer*
Alberger, William Relph *lawyer, government official*
Albin, Barry G. *lawyer, rabbi, energetic healer*
Alfred, Stephen Jay *retired lawyer*
Allen, William *lawyer*
Alpern, Andrew *lawyer, architect, historian*
Altman, Barbara Jean Friedman *lawyer*
Amberg, Stanley Louis *lawyer*
Anderson, Alan Stewert *lawyer*
Anderson, Geoffrey Allen *retired lawyer*
Anderson, John Bayard *lawyer, educator, former congressman*
Anderson, Jon Eric *lawyer*
Anderson, Keith *retired lawyer, retired banker*
†Anderson, Suellen *lawyer*
Ansley, Shepard Bryan *lawyer*
Antolin, Stanislav *patent lawyer*
†Apodaca, Patrick Vincent *lawyer*
†Archer, Dennis Wayne *lawyer, former mayor*
Areen, Judith Carol *law educator, university dean*
†Arkin, L. Jules *lawyer*
Arnold, Craig Anthony (Tony Arnold) *law educator*
Arnold, Jerome Gilbert *lawyer*
†Ascher, Richard Alan *lawyer*
Ashe, Bernard Flemming *arbitrator, educator, lawyer*
Asmar, Laila Michelle *lawyer*
Atchison, Rodney Raymond *retired lawyer, arbitrator*
Atkins, Robert Alan *lawyer*
†Attaway, Fritz Edward Edward *lawyer*

†Atterbury, Robert Rennie, III, *retired lawyer*
Avery, James Thomas, III, *lawyer, management consultant*
Babb, Frank Edward *lawyer, executive*
Bagley, William Thompson *lawyer*
Bain, William Donald, Jr., *lawyer, chemical company executive*
Baker, Donald *lawyer, director*
Baker, James A. *lawyer, former state supreme court justice*
Baker, William Thompson, Jr., *lawyer*
Bakken, Gordon Morris *law educator*
Bakkensen, John Reser *lawyer*
Bales, John Foster, III, *retired lawyer*
Ball, James Herington *retired lawyer*
Bandy, Jack D. *lawyer*
†Barlow, William Kyle *lawyer, state legislator*
†Barnett, Randy Evan *law educator*
Barton, Ellen Louise *lawyer, educator, consultant*
†Bartz, David John *lawyer*
†Basiszta, Martin Winston *lawyer*
Bates, Charles Turner *lawyer, educator*
Baum, Stanley David *lawyer*
†Bean, Bruce Winfield *lawyer*
Beattie, Charles Robert, III, *lawyer*
†Beattie, Donald Gilbert *lawyer*
Beauzay, Victor H(ilton) *lawyer*
Beck, Stuart Edwin *lawyer*
Beldock, Myron *lawyer*
Bell, Haney Hardy, III, *lawyer*
Belleville, Philip Frederick *lawyer*
Bennett, Steven Alan *lawyer*
†Beresin, Marta Ilene *lawyer*
Bergan, William Luke *lawyer*
Berger, Marc Joseph *lawyer*
Beringer, William Ernst *mediator, arbitrator, lawyer*
Berle, Peter Adolf Augustus *lawyer, media director*
Bernstein, George L. *lawyer, accountant*
Bernstein, Merton Clay *law educator, lawyer, arbitrator*
Berrey, Robert Forrest *lawyer*
Berry, Robert Worth *lawyer, educator, retired army officer*
Bersin, Alan Douglas *lawyer, school system administrator*
Bertram, Manya M. *retired lawyer*
Besing, Ray Gilbert *lawyer, writer, lecturer*
Bettenhausen, Matthew Robert *lawyer*
Beukema, John Frederick *lawyer*
Biehl, Kathy Anne *author, lawyer*
†Bierce, William B. *lawyer*
Bierstedt, Peter Richard *lawyer, entertainment industry consultant*
Billauer, Barbara Pfeffer *lawyer, educator*
Birmingham, Thomas F. *lawyer, former state legislator*
†Blake, John Freeman *financial lawyer*
Blatt, Harold Geller *lawyer*
Blazzard, Norse Novar *lawyer*
Bleveans, John *lawyer*
Blevins, Jeffrey Alexander *lawyer*
Block, Dennis Jeffrey *lawyer*
Block, Richard Raphael *lawyer, arbitrator*
Bloom, Charles Joseph *lawyer*
Bloomer, Harold Franklin, Jr., *retired lawyer*
Bloomfield, David Charles *lawyer, educator, public and not-for-profit executive*
Blow, George *lawyer*
†Blumenthal, William *lawyer*
Boesel, Milton Charles, Jr., *lawyer, business executive*
Boho, Dan L. *lawyer*
Bonham, John Dwight *retired lawyer*
Bonham-Yeaman, Doria *retired law educator*
Booher, Alice Ann *lawyer*
Boone, Harold Thomas *retired lawyer*
Boone, Richard Winston, Sr., *lawyer*
†Booth, Robert Ward *lawyer*
Borenstein, Milton Conrad *lawyer, manufacturing company executive*
Bork, Robert Heron *lawyer, author, educator, former federal judge*
Borowitz, Albert Ira *lawyer, author*
†Bossio, Salvatore *lawyer*
Bost, Thomas Glen *lawyer, educator*
†Bostrom, Robert Everett *lawyer*
Bouvier, Marshall Andre *lawyer*
Bower, Jean Ramsay *lawyer, writer*
Boyd, Thomas Marshall *lawyer*
Bradford, Barbara Reed *lawyer*
Bradley, Amelia Jane *lawyer*
Brafford, William Charles *lawyer*
Branagan, James Joseph *lawyer*
Bransdorfer, Stephen Christie *lawyer*
†Branstetter, Cecil Dewey, Sr., *lawyer*
Brantz, George Murray *retired lawyer*
Brashear, William Ronald *lawyer, writer*
Brauer, Rhonda Lyn *lawyer*
Braun, Jerome Irwin *lawyer*
†Brechbill, Susan Reynolds *lawyer, educator*
Bredehoft, Michael Roger *lawyer, mediator*
Brehl, James William *lawyer*
Brewer, Edward Cage, III, *law educator*
†Brigham, Henry Day, Jr., *retired lawyer*
Brink, Richard Edward *lawyer*
Brodhead, David Crawmer *lawyer*
Bronner, James Russell *retired lawyer*
Broughton, Phillip Charles *lawyer, director*
Brown, Charles Dodgson *lawyer*
Brown, J. E. (Buster Brown) *lawyer, consultant*
Brown, Peter Ogden *lawyer*
Brumbaugh, John Moore *lawyer*
†Buccella, William Victor *lawyer*
Buchanan, William H., Jr., *retired lawyer, venture capitalist*
Buchbinder, Darrell Bruce *lawyer*
Buchmann, Alan Paul *lawyer*
Buechel, William Benjamin *lawyer*
†Buehler, John Wilson *lawyer*
Burgess, Hayden Fern (Poka Laenni) *lawyer*
Burkey, Lee Melville *lawyer*
†Burrows, Maile Leilani *court clerk*
Butler, James Robertson, Jr., *lawyer*
Buttrey, Donald Wayne *lawyer*
Cacciatore, Ronald Keith *lawyer*

†Califano, Joseph Anthony, Jr., *lawyer, public health policy educator, writer*
Cambrice, Robert Louis *lawyer*
Campbell, Frederick Hollister *retired lawyer, historian*
Campbell, John William *prosecutor*
Campion, Thomas Francis *lawyer*
†Canady, Charles Terrence *lawyer, former congressman*
Capps, James Leigh, II, *lawyer, reserve military career officer*
Cardinali, Albert John *lawyer*
†Caretti, Richard Louis *lawyer*
Carey, Eleanor Mackey *lawyer, financial consultant*
Carmack, Mildred Jean *retired lawyer*
†Carrol, Robert Kelton *lawyer*
Carroll, Joseph J(ohn) *lawyer*
Carten, Francis Noel *lawyer*
Carter, Jeanne Wilmot *lawyer, publisher*
Casella, Peter F(iore) *patent and licensing executive*
Casey, Robert Reisch *lawyer*
Casselman, William E., II, *lawyer*
Cassidy, John Harold *lawyer*
Castel, Jean Gabriel *lawyer*
Castro, Raul Hector *lawyer, former ambassador, former governor*
Catuzzi, J(erome) P(rimo), Jr., *lawyer*
Cazalas, Mary Rebecca Williams *lawyer, nurse*
Chamberlin, Michael Meade *lawyer*
Charles, Robert Bruce *lawyer*
Chasnoff, Jules *retired lawyer*
Chave, Carolyn Margaret *arbitrator, retired lawyer*
Cheek, Michael Carroll *lawyer*
Cherovsky, Erwin Louis *lawyer, writer*
Choukas-Bradley, James Richard *lawyer*
†Christensen, Karen Kay *lawyer*
Cifarelli, Thomas Abitabile *lawyer*
Citron, Beatrice Sally *law librarian, lawyer, educator*
†Clabaugh, Elmer Eugene, Jr., *retired lawyer*
Clark, Anja Maria *lawyer*
†Clark, Beverly Ann *lawyer*
Clark, Donald Otis *lawyer*
Clarke, Edward Owen, Jr., *lawyer*
†Cling, B. J. *lawyer, psychologist*
Clow, Timothy James *lawyer*
Cobb, Miles Alan *retired lawyer*
Cohen, Gail Ehrlich *lawyer, banker*
Cohen, Sandon Lee *lawyer*
Coleman, Richard William *retired lawyer*
Coleman, Robert Lee *retired lawyer*
Collins, Theodore John *lawyer*
Colman, Richard Thomas *retired lawyer*
Colodny, Edwin Irving *lawyer, retired air transportation executive*
Cologne, Gordon Bennett *lawyer*
Colsky, Andrew Evan *lawyer, mediator, arbitrator*
Colton, Sterling Don *lawyer, business executive, missionary*
†Comisky, Ian Michael *lawyer*
Condra, Allen Lee *lawyer, state official*
†Conine, Gary Bainard *lawyer, educator*
†Conlon, Cynthia Kelly *lawyer, educator*
Connell, William D. *lawyer*
Connelly, Sharon Rudolph *lawyer*
†Cook, Donald Charles *lawyer*
Cook, Quentin LaMar *lawyer, healthcare executive, church leader*
†Cook, S. Alan *lawyer, accountant*
Cooke, William L. *lawyer*
Cooper, Hal Dean *lawyer*
Coplin, Mark David *lawyer*
†Corle, James Thomas *lawyer*
Corlett, Edward Stanley, III, *retired lawyer*
Coughlan, Kenneth L. *lawyer*
Coviello, Frank Joseph *lawyer*
Cox, Chapman Beecher *lawyer, corporate executive*
Cox, Marshall *lawyer*
Craig, Vicki Rene *lawyer*
†Crain, J. Lester, Jr., *corporate lawyer*
Cramer, Mark Clifton *lawyer*
Crawford, Carol Tallman *law educator*
Crawford, Muriel Laura *lawyer, author, educator*
Cremins, James Smyth *political party official, lawyer*
Crocker, Saone Baron *lawyer*
Cronson, Robert Granville *lawyer*
†Crook, Donald Martin *lawyer*
Crowe, James Joseph *lawyer*
Crown, Nancy Elizabeth *lawyer*
†Cunningham, Alice Welt *lawyer, legal educator*
Curtin, Jeanne B. *lawyer*
†Dandridge, LeNor *paralegal*
Danser, Bonita Kay *legal administrator, consultant*
†Datiles, J. Michelle *legal researcher*
Davidson, Barry Rodney *lawyer*
†D'Avignon, Roy Joseph *lawyer*
†Davis, Clarence Clinton, Jr., *lawyer*
Davis, Donald Glenn *lawyer*
Davis, Earon Scott *environmental health law consultant, lawyer*
Davis, Frederick Benjamin *retired law educator*
Davis, Roger Edwin *lawyer, retired discount chain executive*
Davis, Wanda Rose *lawyer*
Dean, Michael M. *lawyer*
Dees, C. Stanley *lawyer*
DeLaFuente, Charles *lawyer, educator, journalist*
Denaro, Charles Thomas *lawyer*
DiBattiste, Carol A. *lawyer*
Dickerman, John Melvin *lawyer*
Diehl, Deborah Hilda *lawyer*
Dietel, James Edwin *lawyer, consultant*
DiFronzo, Michael A. *lawyer, accountant*
Dillon, Clifford Brien *retired lawyer*
Dimitry, Theodore George *retired lawyer*
†Dissen, Walter Charles *lawyer*
†Dixon, John Morris, Jr., *lawyer*
†Dixon, Steven Bedford *lawyer*
Dodds, Lawrence Donald *lawyer*
Dokurno, Anthony David *lawyer*

Dolan, John F. *lawyer*
†Dolan, Peter Brown *lawyer*
Dolce, Julia Wagner *lawyer*
Dolph, Wilbert Emery *lawyer*
Dondanville, John Wallace *lawyer*
Donnally, Robert Andrew *lawyer*
Dow, William French, III, *lawyer*
Dowben, Carla Lurie *lawyer, educator*
Drabkin, Murray *lawyer*
†Drost, Marianne *lawyer*
Dubuc, Carroll Edward *lawyer*
Dulles, Frederick Hendrik *lawyer*
DuMontier, Clarissa Williams *lawyer*
†Dunau, Anastasia Thannhauser *retired administrative law judge*
Dunfee, Thomas Wylie *law educator*
Dunn, Robert Lawrence *lawyer*
Dunn, Warren Howard *retired lawyer, brewery executive*
†Dunst, Isabel Paula *lawyer*
Durfield, Timothy Richard *legal assistant*
Durgom-Powers, Jane Ellyn *lawyer*
†Eaken, Bruce Webb, Jr., *lawyer*
Easterling, Charles Armo *lawyer*
Eaton, Larry Ralph *lawyer*
Eder, Elaine AnnMarie *lawyer*
†Edwards, Christine Annette *retired lawyer, securities firm executive*
†Edwards, James Malone *lawyer*
Edwards, Jerome *lawyer*
Edwards, Priscilla Ann *paralegal, business owner*
Edwards, Richard Alan *retired lawyer*
Edwards, William Thomas, Jr., *lawyer, consultant*
Eichhorn, Frederick Foltz, Jr., *retired lawyer*
Elbery, Kathleen Marie *lawyer, accountant, cartoonist*
Ellenberger, Jack Stuart *law librarian*
Elliott, James Ward *lawyer*
Ellis, Carolyn Terry *lawyer*
Elster, J. Robert *lawyer*
Embry, Stephen Creston *lawyer*
Engelhardt, John Hugo *lawyer, banker*
†English, Gregory Bruce *lawyer*
Erlebacher, Arlene Cernik *retired lawyer*
Erlenborn, John Neal *lawyer, educator, former congressman*
†Esposito, Mark Mario *lawyer*
Estes, Carl Lewis, II, *lawyer*
Etra, Lionel *lawyer*
Ettinger, Joseph Alan *lawyer*
Eustis, Albert Anthony *lawyer, diversified industry corporate executive*
Everdell, William *retired lawyer*
Faber, Michael Warren *lawyer*
Fanwick, Ernest *lawyer*
†Fappiano, Tara C. *lawyer*
Farley, Barbara Suzanne *lawyer*
Farmakides, John Basil *lawyer*
Farmer, Cornelia Griffin *lawyer, consultant, hearings official*
†Feazell, Thomas Lee *lawyer, business executive*
Feierstein, Mark Errol *retired lawyer*
Fekete, George Otto *judge, lawyer, pharmacist*
Fellers, Rhonda Gay *lawyer*
Fellman, Gerry Louis *lawyer, arbitrator*
†Fenwick, Lynda Beck *lawyer, writer*
Ferguson, Bradford Lee *lawyer*
Ferraro, Geraldine Anne *lawyer, former congresswoman*
Field, Arthur Norman *lawyer*
Finelsen, Libbi June *lawyer*
Fink, Norman Stiles *lawyer, educational administrator, fundraising consultant*
†Fino, Teresa Cristina *legal secretary, business owner*
Fiorito, Edward Gerald *lawyer*
Fischer, David Jon *lawyer*
†Fishback, David Simon *lawyer*
Fiss, Owen M. *law educator, educator*
†Flanary, Donald Herbert, Jr., *lawyer*
Fleischman, Herman Israel *lawyer*
Flick, John Edmond *lawyer*
†Flynn, Michael *lawyer*
Ford, Ashley Lloyd *lawyer, retired consumer products company executive*
Forry, John Ingram *retired lawyer*
Forster, Clifford *lawyer*
†Fort, Denise Douglas *law educator, former state official*
Foster, Judith Christine *lawyer, writer*
†Foster, Lloyd Bennett *lawyer, musician*
Fowler, Donald Raymond *retired lawyer, educator*
Fowler, Flora Daun *retired lawyer*
Fox, Eleanor Mae Cohen *lawyer, educator, writer*
Fraidin, Stephen *lawyer*
Frankel, James Burton *retired lawyer*
Franklin, Michael Harold *arbitrator, lawyer, consultant*
Frawley, Michael Keith *lawyer*
Freed, Evan Phillip *lawyer*
Freedman, Monroe Henry *lawyer, educator, columnist*
French, Daniel J. *former prosecutor*
†Freund, Samuel J. *lawyer*
Fried, Charles *law educator*
†Friedlander, James Stuart *lawyer*
Friedman, Paul Richard *lawyer*
Frost, Sterling Newell *arbitrator, mediator, management consultant*
Fryburger, Lawrence Bruce *lawyer, mediator, writer*
Futter, Victor *lawyer*
Gaberman, Harry *retired lawyer*
†Gaines, Cherie Adelaide *lawyer*
†Galbraith, Allan Lee *lawyer*
Gamble, E. James *lawyer, accountant*
†Garcia, Sara Kruger *lawyer*
Gaul, Stuart Crawford *lawyer*
Gaunt, Janet Lois *arbitrator, mediator*
Gee, Robert Neil *law librarian*
Geloso-Barone, Rosalia A. *lawyer*
George, Joyce Jackson *lawyer, judge emeritus*
Gersch, Charles Frant *lawyer*

†Neugarten, Jerrold Lee *lawyer*
Newman, Carol L. *lawyer*
Newman, Mary Lynn Canmann *lawyer*
Nguyen, Paul Dung Quoc *lawyer*
Noddings, Sarah Ellen *lawyer*
Nolen, William Giles *lawyer, accountant*
Norman, Albert George, Jr., *lawyer*
Nugent, Shane Vincent *lawyer*
†Nussbaum, Peter David *lawyer*
Oates, Carl Everette *lawyer, director*
†Ober, Richard Francis, Jr., *lawyer, banker*
O'Brien, Charles H. *lawyer, retired state supreme court chief justice*
O'Brien, J. Willard *lawyer, educator*
†O'Bryon, Maureen *lawyer*
O'Connell, Philip Raymond *retired lawyer, paper company executive*
O'Connor, Edward Vincent, Jr., *lawyer*
O'Dell, Joan Elizabeth *lawyer, mediator, business executive, educator*
†Olson, Carol Duane *lawyer*
†O'Mara, William Michael *lawyer*
†O'Neal, Mike Elkins *university business executive, lawyer*
Orlebeke, William Ronald *retired lawyer, writer*
Orloff, Neil *lawyer, artist*
†Ostergaard, Joni Hammersla *lawyer*
Otis, Lee Liberman *lawyer, educator*
Padilla, James Earl *lawyer*
Pagano, Eugene Salvatore Rooney *lawyer*
Painton, Russell Elliott *lawyer, mechanical engineer*
Pal, Prabir Kumar (Sunny Pal) *law firm counselor*
†Palizzi, Anthony N. *retired lawyer, retail corporation executive*
Pallot, Joseph Wedeles *lawyer*
†Parker, Robert Marc *lawyer, insurance executive*
Parkison, James Max *trial court administrator, educator*
Parks, Jane deLoach *retired law librarian, legal assistant*
Parr, Royse Milton *retired lawyer, writer*
Partridge, Bruce James *lawyer, educator, writer*
Pascale, Daniel Richard *lawyer*
Paul, Eve W. *retired lawyer*
Paul, Richard Wright *lawyer*
Paulus, Norma Jean Petersen *lawyer*
Pawlik, James David *lawyer, historian*
Pear, Charles E., Jr., *lawyer*
Peccarelli, Anthony Marando *lawyer*
Penzer, Mark *lawyer, editor, corporate trainer, former publisher*
†Perkins, Dosite Hugh, Jr., *retired lawyer*
Perkins, James Wood *lawyer*
Perlman, Richard Brian *lawyer*
Perlstein, William James *lawyer*
Perrin, Michael Warren *lawyer*
†Perritt, Henry Hardy, Jr., *law educator*
Perry, George Williamson *lawyer*
Peshkin, Samuel David *lawyer*
Peters, R. Jonathan *lawyer, manufacturing company executive*
Peterson, Howard Cooper *lawyer, accountant*
Phillips, Dorothy Kay *lawyer*
Phillips, Florence Tsu *lawyer, choreographer, dance educator*
Phillips, Leo Harold, Jr., *lawyer*
Pianko, Theodore A. *lawyer*
†Pickard, Terry Roy *lawyer*
†Pietrzak, Alfred Robert *lawyer*
Piga, Stephen Mulry *retired lawyer*
Pitcher, Griffith Fontaine *lawyer*
†Plaza, Eva M. *lawyer*
Pogue, Richard Welch *lawyer*
Poliakoff, Gary A. *lawyer, educator*
Pollard, Henry *mediator, arbitrator*
Polsky, Howard David *lawyer*
Porter, Michael Pell *lawyer*
Portnoy, Sara S. *lawyer*
Post, Ruth-Ellen *lawyer, educator*
Potter, Tanya Jean *lawyer*
Powers, Elizabeth Whitmel *lawyer*
Pratt, Robert Windsor *lawyer*
Prem, F. Herbert, Jr., *lawyer*
Price, Alfred Lee *lawyer, mining company executive*
Prince, Andrew Steven *lawyer, former government official*
†Prinz, Kristie Dawn *lawyer*
Prugh, George Shipley *lawyer*
Purtle, John Ingram *lawyer, former state supreme court justice*
Pusateri, Lawrence Xavier *lawyer*
Pustilnik, David Daniel *lawyer*
Putney, Wainscott Walker *lawyer*
Quay, Thomas Emery *lawyer*
†Quayle, Marilyn Tucker *lawyer, wife of former vice president of United States*
Quigley, Leonard Vincent *lawyer*
Quillen, Cecil Dyer, Jr., *lawyer, consultant*
Quinlan, J(oseph) Michael *lawyer*
Rabkin, Peggy Ann *retired lawyer*
Randall, Ronald Ray *lawyer*
†Randolph, Kenneth E. *retired lawyer*
†Ratti, Ricardo Allen *lawyer*
Raubicheck, Charles Joseph *lawyer, educator*
Rawls, Frank Macklin *lawyer*
Rawls, John D. *lawyer*
Raymond, David Walker *lawyer*
Reath, George, Jr., *lawyer, mediator, arbitrator*
Reber, Joseph E. *lawyer*
Redleaf, Diane Lynn *lawyer*
Redmond, Patricia Ann *lawyer*
Reeder, Robert Harry *retired lawyer*
Regenstreif, Herbert *lawyer*
Rehmus, Charles Martin *law educator, arbitrator*
Reiche, Frank Perley *lawyer, former federal commissioner*
Reid, Joan Evangeline *lawyer, stockbroker*
Reidenberg, Joel R. *law educator*
Reis, Harold F. *lawyer*
†Reiss, Jerome *retired lawyer*
Reister, Ruth Alkema *lawyer, business executive*
Reiter, Glenn Mitchell *lawyer*
†Reith, Daniel I. *retired lawyer*
Reminger, Richard Thomas *lawyer, artist*
Reveal, Ernest Ira, III, *retired lawyer*
Reynolds, William Bradford *lawyer*
Rhee, Albert *lawyer, author*
†Ribaudo, Ronald Salvatore *lawyer*
Rich, Michael Joseph *lawyer*
Richardson, John Carroll *lawyer, tax legislative consultant*
Richeson, Hugh Anthony, Jr., *lawyer*
†Richman, Stephen Charles *lawyer*
Ricks, Joycia Camilla *complaints manager, lawyer*
Ring, Renee Etheline *lawyer*
Rivera, Oscar R. *lawyer, corporate executive*
Rivers, Kenneth Jay *retired judicial administrator, consultant*
†Rochlin, Paul R. *lawyer*
Rodenburg, Clifton Glenn *lawyer*
Rodriguez, Vivian N. *lawyer, accountant*
Roe, Mark J. *law educator*
†Roethe, James Norton *lawyer*
Rohrer, George John *retired lawyer*
Rombach, Louis Herman *lawyer, chemist*
Rosen, Martin Jack *lawyer*
Rosenberg, Gabriel Joseph *legal consultant, physician*
†Rosenberg, Sheli Zysman *lawyer, financial management executive*
Rosenhouse, Howard *retired lawyer*
Rosenn, Harold *lawyer*
†Rosner, Seth *lawyer, educator*
Ross, Catherine Jane *lawyer, social policy analyst*
Ross, Robert A. *lawyer*
Roth, Michael *lawyer*
Rothman, Howard Joel *lawyer*
Rowe, Audrey *paralegal*
†Royal, Carl Andrew *lawyer*
Rubenfeld, Stanley Irwin *lawyer, director, mediator, arbitrator*
†Rubinkowski, Conrad Sigmund *lawyer, film critic*
†Rubinstein, Esta *paralegal*
Rudolph, Wallace Morton *law educator*
Ruff, Edward Joseph *retired lawyer*
Ruhm, Thomas Francis *retired lawyer, investor*
Sabino, William *lawyer, consultant*
Sack, Edward J. *retired lawyer*
Sagawa, Shirley Sachi *lawyer*
†Sage, Albert Liston, III, *lawyer, educator*
St. Claire, Frank Arthur *lawyer*
†St. John, Donald J. *lawyer*
Saliterman, Richard Arlen *lawyer*
†Saltzman, Michael I. *lawyer, educator, author*
Sampson, David Synnott *lawyer*
Samuels, Janet Lee *lawyer*
Santman, Leon Duane *lawyer, former federal government executive*
Sapp, John Raymond *lawyer*
Satorius, Daniel Mark *lawyer, film producer, television producer*
Sauder, Virginia Lynne Heisey *paralegal*
Saunders, Lonna Jeanne *lawyer, newscaster, talk show host*
Sax, Joseph Lawrence *lawyer, educator*
Schacht, Ronald Stuart *lawyer*
Schaefer, William Goerman *lawyer*
Schaudies, Jesse P., Jr., *business executive*
†Schlegel, Dick Reeves *lawyer, judge*
†Schley, Michael Dodson *lawyer*
Schlueter, Linda Lee *law educator*
Schmidt, Kathleen Marie *lawyer*
Schmoll, Harry F., Jr., *lawyer, educator*
Schmults, Edward Charles *lawyer, corporate and philanthropic administrator*
†Schoenwald, Maurice Louis *retired lawyer*
†Schollander, Wendell, III, *lawyer*
Schrag, Philip Gordon *law educator*
Schram, Ronald Byard *lawyer*
†Schrier, Morris M. *consultant*
Schroeder, Edward james *lawyer*
Schuck, Peter Horner *lawyer, educator*
Schultz, Dennis Bernard *lawyer*
Schulz, Lawrence A. *lawyer*
Schwab, Eileen Caulfield *lawyer, educator*
Schwartz, Arthur Jay *lawyer*
Seaver, Robert Leslie *retired law educator*
Segel, Karen Lynn Joseph *lawyer, taxation specialist*
Seidman, Ellen Shapiro *lawyer, government official*
Seifert, Stephen Wayne *lawyer, performing arts executive*
†Sercarz, Maurice Henri *lawyer*
Sexton, David Farrington *lawyer, investment banking executive*
Shaffer, Richard James *lawyer, former manufacturing company executive*
Shaffert, Kurt *retired lawyer, chemical engineer*
Shambaugh, Stephen Ward *lawyer*
Shapiro, Edwin Stanley *lawyer, judge*
†Shapiro, Howard Alan *retired lawyer*
Shapiro, Sander Wolf *retired lawyer*
Sharett, Alan Richard *lawyer, environmental and disability litigator, mediator and arbitrator, law educator*
Shattuck, Cathie Ann *lawyer, former government official*
Sheldon, Terry Edwin *lawyer, business consultant, advisor*
†Sheriff, Seymour *retired lawyer*
†Sherling, Fred W. *lawyer*
Shook, Ann Jones *lawyer*
Shuman, Samuel Irving *lawyer, law educator*
Sides, Jack Davis, Jr., *lawyer*
Siegan, Bernard Herbert *lawyer, educator*
Siegel, Sarah Ann *lawyer*
Siemer, Deanne Clemence *lawyer*
Siemon, Joyce Marilyn *lawyer, writer*
†Silberman, Curt C. *lawyer*
Silver, Carol Ruth *lawyer*
Silverberg, Mark Victor *lawyer, educator*
Simmons, Raymond Hedelius *lawyer*
Simon, Robert G. *lawyer*
†Simonsen, Gregory Mark *lawyer*
†Simonton, Robert Bennet *lawyer*
Siporin, Sheldon *lawyer, consultant*
Siu, Wang-Ngai *solicitor*
Skolnik, Barnet David *retired lawyer*
Slavitt, David Walton *retired lawyer*
Sliger, Herbert Jacquemin, Jr., *lawyer*
†Slive, Steven Howard *lawyer*
Slonaker, Norman Dale *lawyer*
†Slough, Major Carl *lawyer*
Small, Daniel Priestley *lawyer, educator*
Smith, Carole Dianne *retired lawyer, editor, writer, product developer*
Smith, Deirdre O'Meara *lawyer*
Smith, Edward Reaugh *retired lawyer, retired funeral home executive*
Smith, George Patrick, II, *lawyer, educator*
†Smith, H(arold) Lawrence *lawyer*
Smith, James A. *lawyer*
Smith, Jeanette Elizabeth *lawyer*
Smith, Joy Karen Turnheim *lawyer*
Smith, Lauren Ashley *lawyer, journalist, clergyman, physicist*
Smith, Maura Abeln *lawyer*
Smith, Ronald Ehlbert *lawyer, educator, pastor, public speaker, writer, motivator, real estate developer*
†Smith, Walter Ernest *lawyer*
Smouse, H(ervey) Russell *lawyer*
Soble, Mark Richard *lawyer*
†Solberg, Thomas Allan *lawyer*
Solkoff, Jerome Ira *lawyer, consultant, lecturer*
Spanninger, Beth Anne *lawyer*
Speaker, Susan Jane *lawyer*
Speers, Roland Root, II, *lawyer*
†Spicer, S(amuel) Gary *lawyer, writer*
Spiegel, Jayson Leslie *lawyer, organization executive*
Spitzberg, Irving Joseph, Jr., *lawyer*
Sprecher, Drexel Andreas *retired lawyer, writer*
†Springer, Paul David *lawyer, motion picture company executive*
Sprung, Arnold *lawyer*
Squires, Katherine Landey *lawyer*
Stack, Beatriz de Greiff *lawyer*
Stanisci, Thomas William *lawyer*
†Starr, Kenneth Winston *lawyer*
†Steer, Richard Lane *lawyer*
†Steinberg, Mark Robert *lawyer*
Stern, John Jules *lawyer*
Stillman, Elinor Hadley *retired lawyer*
†Stinchfield, John Edward *lawyer*
Stoiber, Carlton Ray *nuclear law consultant, retired federal official*
Stone, Andrew Grover *lawyer*
Stone, Edward Herman *lawyer*
Stream, Arnold Crager *lawyer, writer*
Streicher, James Franklin *lawyer*
Strutin, Kennard Regan *lawyer, educator, legal information consultant*
Subin, Florence *retired lawyer*
Sulton, Anne Thomas *lawyer, criminologist*
†Sulzbach, Deborah *law librarian*
Surles, Richard Hurlbut, Jr., *retired law librarian*
Surratt, John Richard *lawyer*
Sussman, Howard S(ivin) *lawyer*
Swacker, Frank Warren *lawyer*
Swann, Barbara *lawyer*
Sweeney, Deidre Ann *lawyer*
†Swift, Aubrey Earl *lawyer, petroleum engineer*
Sydnor, Edgar Starke *lawyer*
Szuch, Clyde Andrew *lawyer*
†Tachna, Ruth C. *retired lawyer*
Taliaferro, Henry Beauford, Jr., *retired lawyer*
Tamen, Harriet *lawyer*
Tanaka, J(eannie) E. *lawyer*
Tanenbaum, Jay Harvey *lawyer*
Tanner, Eric Benson *lawyer*
Tapley, James Leroy *retired lawyer, railway corporation executive*
†Tasker, Joseph *lawyer, educator*
Tatgenhorst, Robert (Charles Tatgenhorst) *lawyer, educator*
Taub, Nadine *law educator*
Tavrow, Richard Lawrence *lawyer, corporate executive*
Taylor, Jill Olsen *lawyer, artist*
Taylor, Richard James *lawyer*
Termini, Roseann Bridget *law educator*
Terp, Thomas Thomsen *lawyer*
Terrell, G. Irvin *lawyer*
†Theberge, Norman Bartlett *educator, lawyer*
Thiele, Howard Nellis, Jr., *lawyer*
Thomajan, Robert *lawyer, management consultant*
Thoman, Henry Nixon *lawyer*
Thomas, Franklin Augustine *lawyer, consultant*
Thorne, William Albert *retired lawyer*
†Tierney, Kevin Joseph *lawyer, arbitrator, mediator*
Tingle, James O'Malley *retired lawyer*
†Tisci, Michael Anthony *lawyer*
Toensing, Victoria *lawyer*
Tolentino, Casimiro Urbano *lawyer*
†Toomey, Richard Andrew, Jr., *lawyer*
Torgerson, Larry Keith *lawyer*
Torkildson, Raymond Maynard *lawyer*
†Townsend, Peter Lee *lawyer*
Treacy, Vincent Edward *lawyer*
Trieweiler, Terry Nicholas *lawyer, former state supreme court justice*
Trimble, William Cattell, Jr., *retired lawyer*
Trotta, Frank P., Jr., *lawyer*
Troutwine, Gayle Leone *lawyer*
†Tucker, William E. *lawyer, consultant*
Turen, Barbara Ellen *lawyer*
Turner, George Mason *lawyer*
Twardy, Stanley Albert, Jr., *lawyer*
Tyson, David Richard *former lawyer, political party official*
†Vaden, Frank Samuel, III, *lawyer, engineer*
Vallianos, Carole Wagner *lawyer*
Valois, Robert Arthur *lawyer*
Vamos, Florence M. *lawyer*
van Gestel, Allan *judge*
Van Vleet, William Benjamin *retired lawyer, life insurance company executive*
†Vigil, David Charles *lawyer*
Vila, Adis Maria *lawyer, academic administrator*
Vinar, Benjamin *lawyer*
von Sauers, Joseph F. *lawyer*
Voorhees, James Dayton, Jr., *lawyer*
Wagner, Arthur Ward, Jr., *lawyer*
†Wagner, Thomas Joseph *lawyer, insurance company executive*
†Wald, Michael H. *lawyer, educator*
Walder, Noeleen Gwynaeth *lawyer*
Walker, Craig Michael *lawyer*
†Walker, Jordan Clyde, Sr., *lawyer, real estate executive*
Walker, Mark A. *lawyer*
†Walker, Richard Henry *lawyer*
†Walker, Shonn Wayne *lawyer*
†Wallack, Rina Evelyn *lawyer*
Wallin, James Peter *lawyer*
Walner, Robert Joel *lawyer*
Wang, George K.F. *international lawyer*
Warren, Mark Edward *lawyer*
Watson, John Michael *lawyer*
Waxman, Seth Paul *lawyer*
Webster, Robert Kenly *lawyer*
Weeks, Tresi Lea *lawyer*
Weil, Peter Henry *lawyer*
Weiland, Charles Hankes *lawyer*
Weinmann, Richard Adrian *lawyer, arbitrator*
†Weinstein, Arthur Gary *lawyer*
Weisberg, David Charles *lawyer*
Weisman, Paul Howard *lawyer*
†Weiss, Alvin *lawyer*
Weldon, Jeffrey Alan *lawyer*
Weller, Keith Austin *lawyer, corporate officer*
†Wells, Hugh Neal, IV, *lawyer*
Wessel, Peter *lawyer*
Wessling, Robert Bruce *retired lawyer*
†Weston, Michael C. *retired lawyer*
†Westphal, Marjorie Lord *lawyer*
Wetherill, Eikins *lawyer, stock exchange executive*
Wheeler, R(ichard) Kenneth *lawyer, educator*
Whelan, Stephen Thomas, Jr., *lawyer*
White, John Joseph, III, *lawyer*
White, Kendred Alan *lawyer*
White, William Nelson *lawyer*
†Whitehorn, Jo-Ann H. *lawyer*
Whitehouse, Sheldon *lawyer, former state attorney general*
†Whitworth, J. Bryan, Jr., *former oil company executive, lawyer*
Wiehl, Lis W. *law educator*
†Wiggins, Sharon I. *legal assistant*
Wigler, Andrew Jeffrey *lawyer*
Wilburn, Mary Nelson *retired lawyer, translator, poet*
Wildhack, William August, Jr., *lawyer*
Wiley, Richard Arthur *lawyer*
†Wilkins, Jerry L. *lawyer, clergyman*
Williams, William John, Jr., *lawyer*
Williamson, Edwin Dargan *lawyer, former federal official*
Wilson, Hugh Steven *lawyer*
Wilson, Paul W., Jr., *lawyer, entrepreneur*
Wilson, Rhys Thaddeus *lawyer*
Wilson, Virgil James, III, *lawyer*
Winkelman, Johnny Martin *lawyer, real estate development consultant and Indian gaming consultant*
Winslow, F(rancis) Dana *judge, former record company owner*
Winslow, John Franklin *lawyer*
Winslow, Julian Dallas *retired lawyer, historian, writer*
Wirtz, William Willard *lawyer*
Wise, Sandra Casber *lawyer*
Wittig, Raymond Shaffer *lawyer, information technology manager, consultant*
Woessner, Warren Dexter *lawyer*
†Wohlschlaeger, Frederick George *lawyer*
Wolfson, Michael George *lawyer*
Wong-Diaz, Francisco Raimundo *lawyer, educator*
Wood, Robert Charles *lawyer, real estate developer*
Wooldridge, William Charles *lawyer*
Woolsey, John Munro, Jr., *retired lawyer*
Worthington, Daniel Glen *lawyer, educator*
†Wright, Brian Richard *lawyer, banker*
Wright, Robert Payton *lawyer*
Wriston, Kathryn Dineen *lawyer, business executive*
Wruble, Bernhardt Karp *lawyer*
Wunderlich, Howard Jeffrey *lawyer*
Wunsch, Kathryn Sutherland *retired lawyer*
Wyatt, Robert Lee, IV, *lawyer*
Wyshak, Lillian Worthing *lawyer*
Yarbro, Alan David *lawyer*
Yeager, Mark Leonard *lawyer*
Young, John Hardin *lawyer, corporate executive*
Yurchuck, Roger Alexander *retired lawyer*
Zagorin, Janet Susan *legal firm administrator, marketing professional*
Zarro, Janice Anne *lawyer*
†Zerger, Kirsten Louise *mediator, lawyer*
Ziegler, William Alexander *lawyer*

Zillman, Donald Norman *law educator, university official*
Zimmerman, Jean *lawyer*
Zohn, Martin Steven *lawyer*

MEDICINE *See* HEALTHCARE: MEDICINE

MILITARY

UNITED STATES

ALABAMA

Alexander City
Shuler, Ellie Givan, Jr., *retired military officer, military museum administrator*

Auburn
Tolbert, Clinton Jame *army officer, machinist*

Birmingham
Davis, Gwendolyn Louise *air force officer, English educator*

Enterprise
Parker, Ellis D. *retired career officer, aviation executive*

Foley
Kingston, George Willis *retired naval officer, small business owner*

Fort Rucker
†Jones, Anthony Ray *military career officer*

Huntsville
Gawronski, Elizabeth Ann *retired army officer*
Urias, John M. *military officer, government agency administrator*
Watts, William Park *naval officer*
Williamson, Donald Ray *retired career Army officer*

Maxwell AFB
†MacGhee, David F. *military officer*
†Timmerman, Thomas J. *military planner, operations analyst*

Montgomery
Boston, Hollis Buford, Jr., *retired military officer*
Fry, Donna Marie *military officer, educator*

Ozark
Hennies, Clyde Albert (Lou Hennies) *military officer, state official, military academy administrator*

Redstone Arsenal
†Parlier, Greg H. *military officer, engineer*

Union Grove
Roberts, Lynn Novak *government employee*

ALASKA

Anchorage
Erving, Claude Moore, Jr., *career officer, pilot*
Gamble, Patrick K. *retired military officer, rail transportation executive*

ARIZONA

Davis Monthan AFB
†Barksdale, Barry W. *career officer*
†Foglesong, Robert H. *lieutenant general United States Air Force*
Woods, Sharhonda Michele *military officer*

Green Valley
Bennett, Bradley Frederick *retired military officer, science association director*

Phoenix
Beltrán, Anthony Natalicio *non-commissioned officer, deacon*
Lawlis, Patricia Kite *air force officer, computer consultant*
Melner, Sinclair Lewis *retired military officer*

Prescott
Schaeffer, Reiner Horst *military officer, foreign language professional*

Scottsdale
Coffinger, Maralin Katharyne *retired career officer, consultant*

Sierra Vista
Smith, Donna Nadine *army noncommissioned officer*

Tucson
†Ensign, John D. *retired military officer*
Wickham, John Adams, Jr., *retired army officer*

Yuma
Hudson, John Irvin *retired career officer*

ARKANSAS

Blytheville
Slowik, Richard Andrew *air force officer*

Mountain Home
Baker, Robert Leon *naval medical officer*

CALIFORNIA

Anaheim
O'Berry, Carl Gerald *former career officer, electrical engineer*

Arroyo Grande
Oseguera, Palma Marie *retired career officer*

Bonita
Curtis, Richard Earl *former naval officer, former company executive, business consultant*

Camp Pendleton
Prato, Kimberly *public affairs officer*

Carlsbad
Kauderer, Bernard Marvin *retired naval officer, consultant*

Carmichael
McHugh, James Joseph *retired naval officer, retired associate dean*

Chula Vista
Briggs, Franklin Henry *retired naval officer*
Worthington, George Rhodes *retired naval officer*

Coronado
Butcher, Bobby Gene *retired military officer*

El Segundo
Harper, David Taylor *civilian military employee*

Escondido
Briggs, Edward Samuel *naval officer*
Dotto, Peter Attilius *retired marine corps officer, defense consultant*

Folsom
Jefferds, William John *military advisor*

Fort Irwin
†Webster, William G., Jr., *army officer*

Healdsburg
Eade, George James *retired air force officer, research executive, defense consultant*

Long Beach
Higginson, John *retired career officer*
VavRosky, Mark James *career officer, educator*

Los Alamitos
Dunne, Donald Redmond *military officer*

Los Altos Hills
Wheeler, Frank Knowles Blasdell *retired military officer, business consultant*

Monterey
Hoivik, Thomas Harry *military educator, international consultant*
Matthews, David Fort *career officer*
Schrady, David Alan *civilian military employee, educator*

Napa
Smith, Robert Bruce *former security consultant, retired career officer*

Oxnard
Kirschbaum, Alan Ira *air force officer, systems integration specialist*

Palo Alto
Parker, James Wesley *former career naval officer, investment company executive*

Pebble Beach
Mauz, Henry Herrward, Jr., *retired naval officer*

Riverside
Czekanski, James P. *military officer*

San Diego
Contreras, Thomas J., Jr., *career officer*
†Everett, Hobart Ray, Jr., *engineer, naval officer, consultant, researcher*
Koenig, Harold Martin *former United States Navy surgeon general*

San Francisco
†Gifford, Fereuza *retired military officer*

San Marcos
†Jones, William Henry *retired military officer*

Santa Barbara
Conley, Philip James, Jr., *retired air force officer*

Santa Maria
Everhart, Leon Eugene *retired career officer*
Roadarmel, Stanley Bruce *civilian military employee*

Santa Rosa
Andriano-Moore, Richard Count *retired military officer, secondary school educator, elementary school educator*
Bowen, James Thomas *career officer*

Seal Beach
Mirick, Robert Allen *military officer*

Seaside
Gales, Samuel Joel *retired civilian military employee, counselor*

Stockton
Anderson, Vincent Paul *military officer*

Travis AFB
†Kelly, Christopher A. *brigadier general United States air force*

Vandenberg Afb
Hamel, Michael A. *career officer*

Windsor
Sparks, Bennett Sher *retired military officer*

COLORADO

Cheyenne Mountain AFB
Bradley, John A. *military officer*

Colorado Springs
Bowen, Clotilde Marion Dent *retired career officer, psychiatrist*
Delph, Kathleen Anne *foundation administrator, development director*
†Drennan, Jerry M. *career officer*
Geraci, Richard V. *military officer, government agency administrator*
Kelley, Douglas Eaton *military officer*
†Klodnicki, Richard Henry *military officer, systems analyst*
Meyerrose, Dale William *career officer*
Partridge, William J. *military officer, government agency administrator*
Skora, Wayne Philip *retired air force officer*

Denver
Avrit, Richard Calvin *defense consultant, career officer*
Charlip, Ralph Blair *military officer, health facility administrator*
Dugan, Michael Joseph *former career officer, health agency executive*

Durango
Fogleman, Ronald Robert *retired air force officer, consultant*

Falcon AFB
†Dylewski, Gary R. *retired career officer*

Fort Collins
Roberts, Archibald Edward *retired career officer, writer*

Henderson
Thompson, Robert Frank, Jr., *career officer*

Monument
Breckner, William John, Jr., *retired air force officer, corporate executive, consultant*
Caine, Philip David *retired military officer, author*

Peterson AFB
†Dekok, Roger Gregory *career officer*

U S A F Academy
†Dallager, John R. *career officer*
Krise, Thomas Warren *military officer, English language educator*

Woodland Park
Stewart, Robert Lee *retired career officer, astronaut*

CONNECTICUT

Niantic
Hunt, Francis Howard *retired navy laboratory official*

DELAWARE

Wilmington
†Krulak, Charles Chandler *marine officer*

DISTRICT OF COLUMBIA

Bolling AFB
†Dendinger, William J. *career officer, chaplain*

Fort Mcnair
†Chilcoat, Richard Allen *army officer, university president*

Pentagon
Adams, Ronald Emerson *army officer, federal agency administrator*

Washington
†Aboul-Enein, Youssef H. *military officer*
†Adams, Patrick O. *career officer*
Albright, Joseph William *army officer*
†Barrett, Thomas J. *military officer*
†Barry, John L. *military officer*
Bath, Ronald J. *military officer*
Bedard, Emil R. *career officer*
Bowman, Frank Lee (Skip Bowman) *admiral and director naval nuclear propulsion*
†Brown, Richard E., III, *military officer*
Bussy, Carvel de *retired military officer, educator*
†Campbell, William H. *career officer*
†Cannon, Charles Curtis, Jr., *military career officer*
†Casey, George W. *military career officer*
†Clark, Vernon E. *chief of US Naval Operations*
†Clem, Ralph S. *career officer*
†Collins, Thomas Hansen *coast guard officer*
Crawford, Hunt Dorn, Jr., *retired military officer, educator, diplomat*
Davis, Harley Cleo *retired career officer*
Dils, Robert M. *military officer*
†Dodgen, Larry J. *career officer*
Engel, Richard L. *career officer*
England, Gordon R. *civilian military employee*

†Fogelsong, Robert H. *military officer*
Frizzelle, Charles Delano, Jr., *military officer, educator*
Fuhrman, Russell L. *career officer*
Gibson, Christopher Patrick *military career officer*
†Gibson, Emmitt E. *career officer*
†Gill, Clair F. *military career officer*
Goodpaster, Andrew Jackson *retired army officer*
Gordon, John A. *career officer*
Greenert, Jonathan W. *career officer*
†Hagee, Michael W. *commandant of the US Marine Corps*
Helmly, James R. *military officer*
Hobbins, William T. *career officer*
Hooper, John David *coast guard officer*
†Huffman, Walter B. *army officer*
†Hunter, Milton *army officer*
Huston, John Wilson *air force officer, historian*
†Johnson, Hansford Tillman *civilian military employee*
Jumper, John Phillip *chief of staff US Air Force*
†Kellogg, Joseph K., Jr., *military career officer*
†Kelly, Rodney P. *career officer*
Kostelnik, Michael Charles *retired air force major general*
†Kudlacz, Michael S. *career officer*
Leaf, Howard Westley *retired air force officer, military official*
Lietzau, William Kendall *career officer, lawyer*
Loren, Donald Patrick *naval officer*
†Malcolm, Mark Alan *military analyst*
Marchand, Michael J. *military officer*
†Maude, Timothy J. *career officer*
†McElwee, Jerry W. *military career officer*
McGinn, Dennis Vincent *career officer*
†McGrath, Kevin Michael *military analyst, civilian military employee, researcher*
Metcalf, Howard *military officer*
†Metz, Thomas Fredric *military career officer*
†Metzger, James W. *military officer*
†Montero, Mario F., Jr., *military career officer*
†Moorhead, Glen W., III, *career officer*
Nutting, Wallace Hall *army officer*
Odom, William Eldridge *army officer, educator*
†Ohle, David H. *military career officer*
†Pace, Peter *military officer*
†Pamerleau, Susan L. *career officer*
†Pellegrino, Stephen Charles *civilian military employee*
Petrie, John Noel *career officer*
Pionk, Jerome Lee *government official, association administrator*
Plewes, Thomas Jeffrey *military officer*
Rives, Jack L. *military officer*
Robison, Victor James, Jr., *retired military officer*
Romeo, Ross Victor *army officer*
Romig, Thomas J. *military officer*
†Schmitt, John K. *army officer*
†Schoomaker, Peter J. *military officer*
†Schwartz, Norton A. *military officer*
†Scott, Bruce K. *army officer*
†Scott, Terry D. *military officer*
Scowcroft, Brent *retired air force officer, government official*
†Shea, Donald William *military officer*
†Sherrard, James E., III, *career officer*
Shipway, John Francis *career officer, retired*
Simmons, Edwin Howard *marine corps officer, historian*
†Sinn, Jerry L. *army officer*
†Stewart, Joseph D. *merchant marine officer*
Swarthworth, Sharon T. *military officer*
†Thompson, John C. *military career officer*
†Tilley, Jack L. *military officer*
†Totushek, John B. *military officer, federal agency administrator*
Tyler, Cecilia Kay *career officer*
Van Winkle, Hans A. *military officer*
†von Kaenel, Howard J. *army officer*
Weaver, Christopher E. *naval officer*
†Wehrle, Joseph H., Jr., *military officer*
Williamson, William Simpson *military science educator*

FLORIDA

Brandon
Hirohata, Derek Kazuyoshi *air force officer, lawyer*

Destin
Stansberry, James Wesley *air force officer*

Fernandina Beach
Rogers, Robert Burnett *naval officer*

Fort Myers
McDonough, Joseph Corbett *former army officer, aviation consultant*

Haines City
Clement, Robert William *retired air force officer*

Jacksonville
Carlson, Raymond Howard *retired military officer, prosecutor*
Delaney, Kevin Francis *retired naval officer, consulting firm executive*
Lestage, Daniel Barfield *retired naval officer, physician*
Surrency, Gary Lawrence *military officer, counselor, writer*

Kissimmee
Dean, James Wendell *military officer, nurse*

Lake Forest
Ross, Jimmy Douglas *retired military officer*

Longwood
Smyth, Joseph Patrick *retired naval officer, physician*

Lutz
Bedke, Ernest Alford *retired air force officer*

Macdill AFB
†Cofer, Jonathan H. *career officer*

Melbourne
Hodges, Carroll Broadus *retired army officer*
Laposata, Joseph Samuel *army officer*
Simokaitis, Frank Joseph *air force officer, lawyer*

Melbourne Beach
Scanlon, Charles Francis *retired army officer, defense consultant, writer, publisher*

Naples
Delano, Victor *retired naval officer*
Slaff, Allan Paul *naval officer, university administrator, educator, entrepeneur*

Nokomis
Albano, Anthony William *retired career officer, secondary school educator*

Orlando
†Bond, William L. *career officer*
Bundy, David John *civilian military employee*
†Geis, John P. *military career officer*

Oviedo
Parker, Harry Lee *retired army officer, counselor*

Palm Beach Gardens
Giordano, Andrew Anthony *retired naval officer*
Horton, Edward Carl *retired military officer, public administrator*

Panama City
†Cox, Ron Dean *non-commissioned officer, educator, psychologist*

Pensacola
†Diggs, Yonna Darlene *civilian military employee*

Riverview
Cyril, Todd Alexander *military officer*

Sarasota
Cooper, William Ewing, Jr., *retired army officer*
Gauch, Eugene William, Jr., *retired air force officer*
Harvey, Donald Phillips *retired naval officer*
Heiser, Rolland Valentine *former army officer, foundation executive*
†McLain, John Howard *retired military officer*

Tallahassee
Davis, Larry Michael *air force officer, healthcare manager, consultant*
†Ervin, Charles Phifer, Jr., *retired military officer, education educator*

Tampa
†Abizaid, John P. *career officer*
Jackson, Dennis Kent *military career officer*
Matheny, Charles Woodburn, Jr., *former army officer, civil engineer, city official*
†Sandstrom, James E. *military career officer*

Tyndall AFB
Arnold, Larry Keith *major general United States Air Force*

Valrico
Dillard, Nancy Rose *naval officer*

West Palm Beach
Thomashow, Steven Roy *military officer, intelligence officer*

GEORGIA

Athens
Yarvis, Jeffrey Scott *military officer, social worker*

Atlanta
Harrison, George Brooks *research engineer, retired career officer*
McGuinn, Michael Edward, III, *retired army officer*

Columbus
Downie, Richard Duncan *military officer, government agency administrator*

Conyers
Closs, James William *retired non-commissioned officer, financial analyst, educator*

Duluth
Holutiak-Hallick, Stephen Peter, Jr., *retired army officer, businessman, educator*

Fayetteville
Adams, Michael Keith *retired military officer*

Forest Park
†Fisher, George Alexander, Jr., *lieutenant general United States Army*
†Grace-Crum, Phyllis Venetia *military officer*
†Riggs, John M. *army officer*

Fort Benning
Livingston, Joyce Torbic *civilian military employee*

Fort Gordon
†Griffin, Robert F. *military career officer*

Fort Mcpherson
Crowder, Henry Alvin *military officer*
†Edwards, Warren Chappelle *military career officer*
†Hendrix, John Walter *lieutenant general United States Army*
Piacentini, Nicholas A., Jr., *military officer*

Williamson, Kenneth N. *civilian military employee*
Yingling, John A. *military officer*

Greensboro
Watts, Ronald Lester *retired military officer*

Jonesboro
Galvin, John Rogers *educator, retired army officer*

Kathleen
Uzzell-Baggett, Karon Lynette *career officer*

Marietta
Bankers, James *military officer*

Peachtree City
Eichelberger, Charles Bell *retired career officer*
Yeosock, John John *army officer*

Robins AFB
Batbie, John J., Jr., *military officer*
Whaley, Wallace W. *military officer*

Robins Afb
†Haines, Dennis G. *military officer*

Warner Robins
Nugteren, Cornelius *air force officer*

HAWAII

Camp H M Smith
Hailston, Earl B. *career officer*
Hollingsworth, Bobby G. *career officer*

Hickam AFB
Polk, Steven R. *military officer*

Honolulu
Hays, Ronald Jackson *career officer*
†Ishihara, Bryan K. *operations research analyst*

Kaneohe
Pimper, Elizabeth Marie *naval officer*

Kaneohe Bay
†Bogdan, Wojciech *military officer*

ILLINOIS

Chicago
Bajek, Frank Michael *retired army officer, financial consultant*

Hoffman Estates
Pagonis, William Gus *retired army general*

Mattoon
Phipps, John Randolph *retired army officer*

O Fallon
Voellger, Gary A. *business consulting executive, retired air force officer*

Rockford
Borling, John Lorin *military officer*

Springfield
Herriford, Robert Levi, Sr., *army officer*

Taylor Ridge
†Potthast, David Raymond *retired military officer, secondary school educator*

INDIANA

Indianapolis
Poel, Robert Walter *air force officer, physician*

Valparaiso
†MacGregor, Matt J. *military officer*

KANSAS

Fort Leavenworth
†Berlin, Robert Harry *military studies educator*
Schneider, James Joseph *military theory educator, consultant*

Fort Riley
McFarren, Freddy E. *military career officer*

KENTUCKY

Fort Campbell
†Clark, Robert T. *career officer*

Fort Knox
†Gaddis, Evan R. *army officer*

LOUISIANA

Bossier City
Bond, William Jennings, Jr., *retired air force officer, scholar, educator*

Marrero
Kenyon, Robert Wayne *career officer*

New Orleans
Bald, Ronald James *military officer*
†McCarthy, Dennis M. *military officer*
†Steele, Toney Chapman *military officer, poet*

MAINE

Bath
Dillon, Francis Richard *retired air force officer*

Orrington
Snyder, Arnold Lee, Jr., *retired air force officer, research director*

MARYLAND

Aberdeen Proving Ground
†Doesburg, John C. *military career officer*

Adelphi
Kendrick, Kerry *military officer*

Annapolis
Finerty, Martin Joseph, Jr., *military officer, researcher, association management executive*
Katz, Douglas Jeffrey *retired naval officer, consultant*
- †Strother, Thomas W. *military officer, educator*
Trost, Carlisle Albert Herman *retired naval officer*
Whitford, Dennis James *naval officer, meteorologist, oceanographer*

Arnold
Williams, James Arthur *retired army officer, information systems company executive*

Baltimore
†Michitsch, John F. *career officer*
†Scales, Robert H., Jr., *retired army officer*

Bethesda
Balsam, Marion Joyce *retired naval officer, pediatrician*
Daniel, Charles Dwelle, Jr., *consultant, retired army officer*
Hauck, Frederick Hamilton *retired naval officer, astronaut, business executive*
Less, Anthony Albert *retired naval officer*
Martin, Kathleen L. *military officer, hospital administrator*
†Merchant, P. Glenn *military officer, physician*
Owen, Thomas Barron *retired naval officer, space company executive*
Schmidt, Raymond Paul *naval career officer, historian, government official*
Sizemore, R. Tom, III, *military officer, hospital administrator*
Wishart, Leonard Plumer, III, *army officer*
Zimble, James Allen *naval officer, physician*

Burtonsville
Hudson, McKinley *army officer, retired zoo deputy director*

Fort George G Meade
†Hayden, Michael V. *career officer, federal agency administrator*

Germantown
Schlaikjer, Stephen Allan *foreign service officer*

Hagerstown
Blickenstaff, Danny Jay *retired civilian military employee*

Lutherville Timonium
Sagerholm, James Alvin *retired naval officer*

Middletown
Young, Wayne Stevens *military officer, human resources administrator*

Patuxent River
Dyer, Joseph Wendell *career officer*

Potomac Falls
Mc Mullen, Thomas Henry *retired air force officer*

Severn
Nobles, Danny Gene *army officer*

Silver Spring
Brog, David *consultant, former air force officer*
†Fryauff, David J. *military officer, research scientist, microbiologist*
Oberst, Richard B. *military officer, hospital administrator*

Solomons
Dorsey, James Francis, Jr., *naval officer*

Trappe
Anderson, Andrew Herbert *retired army officer*

MASSACHUSETTS

Boston
Donahue, Conrad James *career naval officer, educator*

Cambridge
†Hutchison, William Edward, Jr., *military officer, aerospace engineer*
Thornton, Wayne Allen *naval officer, engineer, political scientist*

Hanscom AFB
†Kenne, Leslie F. *military officer*

Lexington
Trainor, Bernard Edmund *retired military officer*

Natick
†Mangual, Jesus A. *army officer*

North Oxford
Carney, Roger Francis Xavier *retired army officer*

Osterville
Schwarztrauber, Sayre Archie *former naval officer, maritime consultant*

MINNESOTA

Edina
Shadley, Robert D. *retired army officer*

MISSISSIPPI

Keesler AFB
Locker, Dan Lewis *career officer*
†Pelak, Andrew J., Jr., *military officer*

Pass Christian
McCardell, James Elton *retired naval officer*

MISSOURI

Belton
†Shodean, Lisa Diane *military officer*

Chesterfield
Willis, Frank Edward *retired air force officer*

Florissant
Reese, Alferd George *retired army civilian logistics specialist*

Fort Leonard Wood
†Flowers, Robert B. *military career officer*
†Ryder, Donald J. *military career officer*

Imperial
McGraw, Bryan Kelly *military officer*

Poplar Bluff
Young, William Webb *military officer, poet*

Saint Louis
Strevey, Tracy Elmer, Jr., *army officer, surgeon, physician executive*

NEBRASKA

Offutt A F B
Gooch, Stanford Rondall *Air Force Operations research analyst*
†Hinson, Robert C. *career officer*
Mies, Richard W. *career officer*

NEVADA

Henderson
Creech, Wilbur Lyman *retired career officer*

Nellis AFB
†Johnston, Lawrence D. *career officer*

NEW HAMPSHIRE

Center Ossipee
Sargent, Douglas Robert *air force officer, engineer*

NEW JERSEY

Fort Monmouth
Flanigan, Richard Joseph *retired career officer, company executive*

Marlton
Lindholm, Lori Ann *naval officer*

Moorestown
Apperson, Jack Alfonso *retired army officer, business executive*

Princeton
Unruh, Howard K., Jr., *military officer, university administrator*

South Orange
Collins, John W., Jr., *retired military officer, technologist, educator*

NEW MEXICO

Albuquerque
Flournoy, John Charles, Sr., *civilian military employee, retired military officer*
Lucchetti, Lynn L. *career officer*

Belen
Smith, Helen Elizabeth *retired career officer*

Cedar Crest
Sheppard, Jack W. *retired career officer*

Kirtland Afb
†Gideon, Francis C., Jr., *career officer*

Santa Fe
Kiley, Leo Austin *retired military officer, nuclear energy industry executive*
Sumner, Gordon, Jr., *retired military officer*

NEW YORK

Fort Drum
†Miller, Thomas G. *career officer*

Hamburg
Markulis, Henryk John *career military officer*

New York
Dresser, Noreen Dean O'Hara *civilian army official, artist*

Oneonta
†Desjarlais, Georgia Kathrine *retired military officer*

Orient
Hanson, Thor *retired health agency executive and naval officer*

Rome
Ferens, Daniel Vincent *civilian military employee*

Spring Valley
Steinberg, Milton *civilian military employee*

West Point
†Boettner, Daisie Dawson *military officer, mechanical engineering educator*
†Bozeman, Laura Beth *military officer, educator*
†Schweitzer, Steven John *military officer*
†Zinsser, Nathaniel Wadsworth *civilian military employee, director*

Westbury
McGrath, Edward Gerard *retired military officer, journalist*

NORTH CAROLINA

Chapel Hill
Linville, Ray Pate *educational administrator, analyst, editor, writer*

Fort Bragg
†Boykin, William G. *career officer*
†Brown, Bryan D. *career officer*
†McNeill, Dan K. *military career officer*
†Ryneska, John Joseph *military career officer*

Matthews
Hixson, Nathan Hanks *retired military officer*

Pinehurst
Carroll, Kent Jean *retired naval officer*

Research Triangle Park
Sculley, Patrick David *retired army officer, science honor society director*

Spring Hope
Hildreth, James Robert *retired air force officer*

Swansboro
Juhl, Harold Alexander *retired career officer, construction executive*

OHIO

Cincinnati
†Griffin, Robert H. *career officer*
Smittle, Nelson Dean *military analyst, artist*

Cleveland
Adams, Gene Autry *retired military officer*

Dayton
Heil, Michael Lloyd *military officer, academic administrator*

Enon
Whitlock, David C. *retired military officer*

Fairborn
†Moore, Margaret Anne *retired civilian military employee*
Nowak, John Michael *retired air force officer, company executive*

Tiffin
Einsel, David William, Jr., *retired army officer and consultant*

Wright Patterson Afb
Kelley, Joseph E. *career officer*
Maguire, Frank Edward *retired non-commissioned military officer*
Nielsen, Paul Douglas *Air Force officer, engineering manager*
†Paul, Richard R. *military officer*
Szucs, Andrew Eric *program manager*

OKLAHOMA

Edmond
†Hopwood, Howard Hoppy Perry *military officer*

Oklahoma City
Blount, James Robert *military career officer*
†Reimer, Dennis J. *career military officer*
Siewert, Edgar Allen *retired military non-commissioned officer*

Tinker AFB
Goodman, Ernest Monroe *military officer*
†Johnson, Charles L., II, *military officer*

Vance AFB
Sandstrom, Dirk William *air force officer, hospital administrator*

PENNSYLVANIA

Bethlehem
Rokke, Ervin Jerome *college president*

Camp Hill
Pearsall, Gregory Howard *naval officer, real estate executive*

Gettysburg
Coughenour, Kavin Luther *career officer, military historian*

Johnstown
Samples, Jerry Wayne *military officer, educator*

King Of Prussia
Gallis, John Nicholas *retired military officer, executive leadership training consultant*

Mechanicsburg
Derr, William James *retired non-commissioned officer*
Kinney, Linford Nelson *retired army officer*

Philadelphia
†Dobbs, Stanley *military officer, information quality engineer*
Retz, William Andrew *retired naval officer*

Wayne
Long, Peter Avard Chipman *retired rear admiral United States Navy*

RHODE ISLAND

Newport
†Carpenter, Stanley Dean MacDonald *military officer, educator*

Portsmouth
Bergstrom, Albion Andrew *military officer, educator*

SOUTH CAROLINA

Anderson
Vallo, Victor William, Jr. *military officer, music educator*

Bluffton
Pendley, William Tyler *naval officer, international relations educator*

Charleston
Grinalds, John Southy *military officer, academic administrator*
Watts, Claudius Elmer, III, *retired military officer*

Columbia
Badders, Rebecca Susanne *military officer, educator, writer*

Fort Jackson
†Brinsfield, John Wesley *military officer, educator*

Hilton Head Island
Brown, Arthur Edmon, Jr., *retired army officer*

Newberry
Lander, James Albert *retired military officer, comptroller*

Seneca
Clausen, Hugh Joseph *retired army officer*

Shaw A F B
†Cameron, Hugh C. *career officer*

Sumter
Kellum, Donald Arthur *military officer*

Wedgefield
McLaurin, Hugh McFaddin, III, *military officer, historian consultant*

York
Blackwell, Paul Eugene, Sr., *army officer*

SOUTH DAKOTA

Rapid City
Sykora, Harold James *military officer*

TENNESSEE

Knoxville
†Bounds, Jordan T. *military officer*

Memphis
West, Christopher Eugene *military officer*

TEXAS

Austin
Meigs, Montgomery Cunningham, Jr., *retired military officer, educator*

Belton
Harrison, Benjamin Leslie *retired army officer*
Shoemaker, Robert Morin *retired army officer, county government official*

Bullard
Morley, William George *retired military officer, educator*

College Station

Carlton, Paul Kendall, Jr., *physician, retired air force officer*
†Schunicht, Shannon Anthony *retired army officer, politician*

Fort Sam Houston
†DeWitt, Ralph Ogden, Jr., *military career history*
Moloff, Alan Lawrence *military officer, physician*
†Peake, James Benjamin *military career officer*
†Williams, Pat L. *military officer*

Fort Worth
Lichtman, David Michael *military officer, health care administrator, orthopedist, educator*
Tanzi, David E. *military officer*

Garland
Stimpson, Ritchie Ples *retired military officer*

Georgetown
Graham, Charles Passmore *retired army officer*
Weyrauch, Paul Turney *retired army officer, retired principal*

Harker Heights
Hughes, William Foster *career officer, surgeon, obstetrician, gynecologist*

Houston
Tucker, Hillary Albert *retired intelligence officer, writer*
Turner, Max Allen *career officer, chemical engineer*

Kelly A F B
†Bielowicz, Paul L. *career officer*
†Elliott, Carol C. *career officer*

Killeen
Campbell, Troy David *officer*

Lackland A F B
†Dremsa, Theresa Lynn *military officer, researcher*
†Farage, Michael N. *career officer*
†Mabry, Earl W. *military officer*

Midlothian
Sibley, James Scarborough *career officer*

Plano
Edmonds, Albert J. *career officer*

Randolph A F B
†Lamontagne, Donald A. *career officer*
†Welser, William, III, *military officer*

San Antonio
Clarke, Mary Elizabeth *retired career officer*
Detro, John Fitzgerald *military officer*
Hill, William Victor, II, *retired army officer, secondary school educator*
†Kelling, George Horton *retired military officer*
Kline, John William *retired air force officer, management consultant*
Marsh, Nelson Leroy *military officer*
Massaro, James C. *military officer, government agency administrator*
Murdock, Robert McClellan *air force officer*
Reneau, Marvin Bryan *military officer, business educator*

San Marcos
Bullock, Jerry McKee *retired military officer, consultant, educator*

Sheppard AFB
†Cook, Sharla J. *career officer*

The Woodlands
Jones, Lincoln, III, *army officer*

Universal City
Sargeant, Stephen T. *military officer*

UTAH

Highland
Baum, Kerry Robert *retired military officer, director*

Hill Air Force Base
Bergren, Scott C. *career officer*
†Roellig, Richard H. *career officer*

Salt Lake City
†Hemingway, Donald William *military officer, lawyer, educator*
McFerren, Carl Davis, II, *retired military officer, risk management consultant*

VERMONT

Burlington
Cram, Reginald Maurice *retired air force officer*

VIRGINIA

Alexandria
Adams, Ranald Trevor, Jr., *retired air force officer*
†Bexfield, James Nelson *military analyst*
Bowman, Richard Carl *defense consultant, retired air force officer*
Briggs, Fergus Paul *retired military officer, federal government official*
Brown, Frederic Joseph *army officer*
Burke, Kelly Howard *former air force officer, business executive, investor*
Curtin, Gary Lee *air force officer*
DeLuca, Anthony J. *civilian military employee*

Dunn, Bernard Daniel *former naval officer, consultant*
Falter, Vincent Eugene *retired army officer, consultant*
Fedorochko, William, Jr., *retired army officer, defense policy analyst*
†Garrett, Thomas W. *career officer*
†Gatanas, Harry D. *career officer*
†Gust, David R. *military career officer*
†Jackson, Gary Lee *military analyst*
Kroesen, Frederick James *retired army officer, consultant*
Larson, Charles Robert *naval officer*
Lyons, James Aloysius, Jr., *naval officer*
McNair, Carl Herbert, Jr., *army officer, aeronautical engineer*
Seely, James Michael *defense consultant, retired naval officer, small business owner*
†Smith, Larry G. *career military officer*
Sulick, Joseph Edward, Sr., *information technology professional*
†Whelden, Craig B. *army officer*
†Wooten, Ralph G. *career officer*

Arlington
Bosch, Brian James *retired military officer*
Carr, Kenneth Monroe *naval officer*
Coady, Philip James, Jr., *retired naval officer*
†Costello, John *military officer*
Cosumano, Joseph *military officer, government agency administrator*
†Davis, Russell C. *career officer*
DeFilippi, George *retired air force officer*
Dietrick, Kevin M. *military officer*
Dubin, Henry C. *civilian military employee*
Forrester, Eugene Priest *former army officer, management marketing consultant*
Graves, Ernest, Jr., *retired army officer, engineer*
†Gunhus, Gaylord T. *military career officer*
†James, Daniel, III, *military officer*
Kem, Richard Samuel *retired army officer*
Lisanby, James Walker *retired naval officer*
†Lupia, Eugene A. *military officer*
Miller, Kenneth Gregory *retired air force officer*
Putnam, George W., Jr., *retired army officer*
Rees, Raymond F. *military officer*
Rogers, Alan Victor *former career officer*
†Schultz, Roger C. *career officer*
Singstock, David John *military officer*
†Weaver, Paul A., Jr., *career officer*
Wilcox, John Gregor *military analyst*

Ashburn
Tice, Raphael Dean *army officer*
Weyman, Steven Aloysius *military officer, retired*

Buena Vista
Tichenor, James Robert, III, *retired military officer*

Burke
O'Connor, Edward Cornelius *army officer*

Chantilly
†Crawford, Tommy F. *career officer*
Saunders, Norman Thomas *consultant*
Watkiss, Eric John *naval officer*

Chesapeake
Martin, Glenn Michael *military officer*
Picotte, Leonard Francis *naval officer*
Powers, Robert Lawrence *civilian military employee*
Rendin, Robert Winter *emergency planner*

Dahlgren
Cryer, John *military officer, government agency administrator*
Steiner, Alan P. *military officer, government agency administrator*

Dulles
†Moore, William F. *military officer*

Fairfax
Johnson, Wallace *retired army officer*
Rosenkranz, Robert Bernard *military officer*
Tobin, Paul Edward, Jr., *naval officer*

Fairfax Station
Baer, Robert Jacob *retired army officer*
Thompson, Jonathan Sims *army officer*

Falls Church
†Cain, Eddie *army officer*
Gray, D'Wayne *retired marine corps officer*
†Hill, Mack C. *career officer*
Layman, Lawrence *naval officer*
Randolph, Leonard McElroy, Jr., *career officer*

Fort Belvoir
†Anderson, Frank J., Jr., *career officer*
†Foley, David W. *career officer*
†Noonan, Robert W., Jr., *career officer*
O'Reilly, Kenneth William *military officer*
St. John, Adrian, II, *retired army officer*

Fort Lee
†Courter, Robert J., Jr., *air force officer*
†Solomon, Billy K. *army officer*

Fort Monroe
†Abrams, John N. *army officer*

Fort Myer
Hart, Herbert Michael *military officer*

Herndon
Glacel, Robert Allan *retired military career officer*
Montgomery, Hugh Everett, Jr., *civilian military executive*

Lancaster
Rowden, William Henry *naval officer*

Langley AFB
†Bigum, Randall K. *career officer*
†Perryman, Gerald F., Jr., *career officer*

Lynchburg
Snead, George Murrell, Jr., *army officer, scientist, consultant*

Manassas
†Bottorff, Gerald L. *retired military officer, foundation administrator*

Mc Lean
Cowhill, William Joseph *retired naval officer, consultant*
Molino, Thomas Michael *retired military officer*
Oren, John Birdsell *retired coast guard officer*
Yarborough, William Glenn, Jr., *military officer, forest farmer, defense and international business executive*

Merrifield
Earner, William Anthony, Jr., *naval officer*

Millboro
Minetree, James Lawrence, III, *retired military officer, educator*

Mount Jackson
Sylvester, George Howard *retired air force officer*

Nokesville
Jaynes, Robert Henry, Jr., *retired military officer*

Norfolk
†Berndt, Martin R. *career officer*
Burnette, Thomas N. *career officer*
†Cash, Dean W. *military career officer*
†Kernan, William Frank *career officer*
Klain, David Richard *naval officer*
Konetzni, Albert H., Jr., *career officer*
Kubic, Charles Richard *naval officer*
†Marr, Richard C. *military officer*
Train, Harry Depue, II, *retired naval officer*

Oakton
Frost, S. David *retired naval officer*

Quantico
Harrington, Jeffrey Michael *military officer*
†Howard, Patrick Gene *marine corps officer*
Sanftleben, Kurt Allen *career officer*

Reston
Brown, James Robert *retired air force officer*
Miller, John Edward *army officer, technology executive, educational administrator*
Naylon, Michael Edward *retired army officer*
Wilkinson, Edward Anderson, Jr., *retired naval officer, business executive*

Richmond
Dilworth, Robert Lexow *career military officer, educator*

Rosslyn
McCarthy, Michael James *military intelligence officer*

Spotsylvania
Orsini, Eric Andrew *army official*

Springfield
Roberts, Paul Franklin, II, *financial executive*
Watts, Helena Roselle *military analyst*

Stafford
Haddock, Raymond Earl *career officer*

Vienna
Chamberlin, Edward Robert *career officer, educator*
Chandler, Hubert Thomas *former army officer*
Jenkins, Robert Gordon *retired air force officer, technology executive, government executive*
Webb, William Loyd, Jr., *army officer*

White Stone
Wroth, James Melvin *retired military officer*

Woodbridge
†Messerschmidt, William Harclerode *retired army noncommissioned officer, percussionist*

WASHINGTON

Anacortes
Higgins, Robert (Robert Walter Higgins) *career officer, physician*

Fort Lewis
†Smith, Zannie O. *career officer*

Lynnwood
Jenes, Theodore George, Jr., *retired career officer*

Oak Harbor
†Applehans, Denver Lee *military officer*

WYOMING

Fe Warren Afb
†Neary, Thomas H. *career officer*

MILITARY ADDRESSES OF THE UNITED STATES

ATLANTIC

Fpo
Green, Kevin Patrick *career officer*

EUROPE

Apo
†Baptiste, Thomas L. *career officer*
†Begert, William J. *lieutenant general United States Air Force*
†Corley, John D. W. *military officer*
Ralston, Joseph W. *career officer*

Fpo
Holmes, Michael L. *career officer*

PACIFIC

Apo
Dunkle, Keith Allen *military officer*
†Dunn, Michael M. *military officer*
†Herrin, Mark Malachi *military officer*
†Hester, Paul V. *career officer*
Mangum, Ronald Scott *army officer*
Moseley, William Earl *career officer*
†Pearson, Teressa M. *military officer*

Fpo
Stone, David M. *career officer*

CANADA

ONTARIO

Bracebridge
MacKenzie, Lewis Wharton *military officer*

Ottawa
de Chastelain, A(lfred) John G(ardyne) D(rummond) *Canadian army officer, diplomat*
Henault, R. R. *military officer*

Stittsville
Tellier, Henri *retired Canadian military officer*

Winnipeg
†Hodgkins, William F. *career officer*

CHINA

Beijing
†Prueher, Joseph W. *military officer*

INDONESIA

Jakarta
Callison, Charles Stuart *retired foreign service officer, development economist*

ADDRESS UNPUBLISHED

Adams, Michael John *retired air force non-commissioned officer*
Aldridge, Donald O'Neal *military officer*
Anderson, Edgar Ratcliffe, Jr., *career officer, hospital administrator, physician*
Anderson, William Robert *career naval officer*
Astriab, Steven Michael *army officer*
Austin, Robert Clarke *naval officer*
Barber, James Alden *navy officer, educator*
Baril, Maurice *career officer*
†Barnidge, Leroy, Jr., *military officer*
Bartrem, Duane Harvey *retired military officer, designer, building consultant*
Bauman, Richard Arnold *coast guard officer*
Baxter, Duby Yvonne *government official*
†Bell, Burwell Baxter, III, *general United States Army*
Benedict, John Anthony, II, *army officer*
Blackwell, Thomas George *military police officer*
Blanchard, George Samuel *retired army officer*
Block, Emil Nathaniel, Jr., *retired air force officer*
Boardman, Elizabeth Drake *naval reserve officer*
Bonomo, Joseph Ralph *naval officer*
†Boutelle, Steven W. *army officer*
†Buckley, Edward T., Jr., *career officer*
Buker, Robert Hutchinson, Sr., *army officer, thoracic surgeon*
Campbell, Brian Scott *army officer*
†Campbell, James L. *military career officer*
Carlile, Christopher Blake *military officer, pilot*
Chelberg, Robert Douglas *army officer*
†Chicky, Jon Edward, Jr., *military officer*
†Clark, Wesley K. *retired military officer*
†Cody, Richard A. *army officer*
Coolidge, Charles H., Jr., *career officer*
Cooper, William Thomas *retired air force officer, writer, educator*
†Crown, John S. *military officer, statistician, consultant*
†Curran, John Mark *military career officer*
Davis, Dempsie Augustus *former air force officer, educator, financial advisor*
Davis, Henry Jefferson, Jr., *former naval officer*
Davis, Steven Michael *air force officer, test pilot*
†Dewey, Colin David *merchant seaman*
†Donald, James E. *career officer*
Dozier, James Lee *former army officer*
Eberhart, Ralph E. *career officer*
†Ellis, Edward R. *career officer*
Ellis, James O., Jr., *military officer*
Ellis, Larry R. *military officer*
Ertwine, Dean R. *retired military officer*
†Evans, Jack *city official*
†Fallon, William J. *career officer*
†Fargo, Thomas Boulton *career officer*
Farmer, Kenneth, Jr., *military officer*
Foote, Evelyn Patricia *retired military officer*
Fowler, Stephen Eugene *retired military officer, human resources executive*
Franks, Tommy Ray *retired army officer*
†Gallinger, Robert Arthur *retired military officer, writer*
†Galloway, William Rodney *military officer*
Gardner, Emerson N., Jr., *military officer*
†Garner, Jay Montgomery *former career officer*
†Gerras, Stephen Joseph *military officer, psychologist*
†Giambastiani, Edmund P., Jr., *military officer, federal agency administrator*
†Goslin, Thomas B. *career officer*
Gray, David Lawrence *retired air force officer*
Grebb, Michael D. *military officer, systems analyst*
†Grechanik, Jeffrey *military officer*
†Greeley, Jennifer Ann *military officer, educator*
Gunn, Lee Fredric *career officer*
Guthrie, Wallace Nessler, Jr., *naval officer*
Hagee, Jesko Michael *naval officer*
Hagenbeck, Franklin Lee *military officer*
Hale, Todd Benjamin *military officer, electrical engineer*
†Handy, John W. *career officer*
Harper, Henry H. *retired military officer*
Harris, Marcelite Jordan *retired career officer*
†Hayes, Bernard M. *military officer, researcher*
†Heckman, Gary Walter *military career officer*
Henry, Charles Howard *non-commissioned officer*
Henry, Gary Norman *air force officer, astronautical engineer*
†Hessert, Wilfred O. *military officer*
†Hill, James T. *career officer*
†Holland, Charles R. *military officer*
Hoover, John Elwood *former military officer, consultant, author, speaker on US military history*
Hostettler, Stephen John *naval officer*
†Ivany, Robert Rudolph *military officer, historian*
Johnson, Silas R., Jr., *consultant, retired air force officer*
Jones, David Charles *retired air force officer, former chairman Joint Chiefs of Staff*
†Jones, James L., Jr., *military officer*
Juskowiak, Terry Eugene *career military officer*
Kane, Robert Barry *career officer*
Kather, Gerhard *retired federal administrator*
†Keane, John Michael *career officer*
†Kearns, Michael Shawn *career officer*
Keene-Burgess, Ruth Frances *military official*
Kelley, Larry Dale *retired army officer*
Kennedy, William F. *army reserve technician*
†Kern, Paul John *army officer*
†Kerrick, Donald L. *career officer*
Kerwin, Walter Thomas, Jr., *career officer, consultant*
King, Charolette Elaine *retired administrative officer*
King, Chris Allen *military officer*
Kojac, Jeffrey Stanley *military officer*
Kutyna, Donald Joseph *air force officer*
Lautenbacher, Conrad Charles, Jr., *naval officer, management consultant, federal government executive*
†Lee, Paul M., Jr., *military officer*
Lindquist, Michael Adrian *career military officer*
Lyons, John W(inship) *retired government official, chemist, consultant*
Manganaro, Francis Ferdinand *naval officer*
Marlow, Edward A. *former army officer*
Maroyka, Eric Martin *military officer, pharmacist*
Martin, James Victor, Jr., *foreign service officer, writer*
Mc Fadden, George Linus *retired army officer*
McLean, Craig Elliott *retired non-commissioned officer*
Minners, Howard Alyn *physician, research administrator*
Moore, William Leroy, Jr., *career officer, physician*
Morgan, Thomas Rowland *retired marine corps officer*
Mullen, William Joseph, III, *military analyst, retired career officer*
Nabors, Robert L. *military officer*
Nelson, Ben, Jr., *retired air force officer*
Newcomb, Robert Carl *retired naval officer, real estate broker*
Ninos, Nicholas Peter *retired career officer, physician*
†Nyland, William L. *military officer*
Oerding, James Bryan *military educator*
†Oestreicher, Edward G. *military officer*
Olson, Phillip Roger *naval officer*
Palmer, Dave Richard *retired military officer, academic administrator*
Parent, Rodolphe Jean *Canadian air force officer, pilot*
Peay, J.H. Binford, III, *retired army officer*
Penny, Brent Anthony *career officer*
Pirie, Robert Burns, Jr., *defense analyst*
Prendergast, Kenneth Lee Michael, Jr., *career officer*
Price, Robert Ira *coast guard officer*
†Radzik, Albin F. *military analyst, consultant*
Randolph, Jacqueline Geneva *military officer, writer, small business owner*
Reason, J. Paul *naval officer*
†Rhoades, M. Stephen *career officer*
Rigdon, David Tedrick *air force officer, geneticist, director*
†Riley, James Clifford *military career officer*
Riley, Robert Shean *Colonel, United States Army, retired, writer, publisher*
Robinson, David Brooks *retired naval officer*
Robinson, Ronald Gene *military contract negotiator, educator*
Roche, James G. *civilian military employee*
Rogers, Bernard William *military officer*
Rondeau, Ann E. *career officer*
Rubenstein, David Aaron *military officer, health care administrator*
Russillo, Alfred George *retired military officer, military officer, educator*
Sanderson, James Richard *naval officer, planning and investment company consultant*
Scholes, Edison Earl *army officer*
Schumacher, William Jacob *retired army officer*
Shalikashvili, John Malchase *retired military career officer*
Shapiro, Sumner *retired naval officer, business executive*
Shaw, John Frederick *retired naval officer*
†Shinseki, Eric Ken *former chief of staff United States Army*
†Shoaf, Frank Joseph *military officer*
Silliman, John Parks, Jr., *national guard officer, engineering consultant*
Smith, Loretta Mae *civilian military officer*
†Smith, Stuart Douglas *military officer, minister*
Smoker, Roy Ellis *retired military officer*
Springer, Robert Dale *retired air force officer, consultant, lecturer*
Taylor, James L. *naval officer*
Taylor, Wesley Bayard, Jr., *retired army officer*
†Tillman, Shirley *retired military officer*
†Tivnan, Brian Francis *military officer, researcher*
Tregurtha, James David *retired career Navy officer, engineer*
Truckenbrodt, Yolanda Bernabe *retired air force officer, consultant*
†Trybula, David *military officer, economist*
Tuttle, Jerry Owen *retired naval officer, business executive*
Vessey, John William, Jr., *army officer*
Vincent, Hal Wellman *marine corps officer, investor*
Walden, Joseph Lawrence *career officer*
†Wallace, Stewart S. *career military officer*
Weiss, Donald A. *naval officer*
†Weller, Grant Thomas *military officer, historian*
Wetekam, Donald J. *career officer*
Wheeler, Albin Gray *army officer, educator, retail executive*
†Wilcox, Brian James *military analyst*
Wilson, Dwight Liston *former military officer, investment advisor*
Wilson, Frances C. *career military officer*
Wilson, Lawrence Woodrow *retired air force officer, family physician*
†Zais, Mitchell M. *career military officer*
Zuick, Ernest Ronald, Jr., *career officer, advertising executive*

REAL ESTATE

UNITED STATES

ALABAMA

Anniston
Umling, David Arthur *urban planner*

Arab
Hammond, Ralph Charles *real estate executive*

Hayden
Standridge, Jean *real estate executive, real estate broker*

Montgomery
Cassels, Martha Beasley *realtor, developer*

Orange Beach
Gordon, Beth N. *real estate appraiser*

Tuscaloosa
McFarland, James William *real estate development company executive*

ALASKA

Anchorage
Behrend, Donald Fraser *environmental educator, university administrator*
Kelly, Maxine Ann *retired property developer*
Rentschler, Carl Thomas *real estate executive, consultant*

Girdwood
Trautner, John James *real estate executive*

Wrangell
†Clarke, Laurence B. *retired real estate broker, writer*

ARIZONA

Bullhead City
†Jones, Vernon Quentin *surveyor*

Camp Verde
Bell, Daniel Carroll *realtor, community association, ranch and land manager*

Cottonwood
Gorriaz, Mary Alice *real estate broker*

Mesa
McCollum, Alvin August *consultant, real estate company executive*

Peoria
Morrison, Manley Glenn *real estate investor, former army officer*

Phoenix
Clements, John Robert *real estate professional*
Lewis, Orme, Jr., *real estate company executive, land use adviser*
Sertich, Kelli Ann *land use planner*

Prescott
Anderson, Walter Lee *environmental educator, artist, photographer*
Martinez, Anthony Joseph *real estate appraiser*

Scottsdale
Leonard, George Edmund *real estate, bank, high tech and consulting executive*

Sedona
Copeland, Suzanne Johnson *real estate executive*

Sun City
Meade, Kenneth John *realty company owner, broker*

Tempe
Jungbluth, Kirk E.

Tucson
Best, Gary Thorman *commercial real estate broker*
Bodinson, Holt *conservationist*
Jaffe, Steven Alan *real estate investor and management executive*
Jones, John Stanley *urban development executive*
Lanham, Sandra *conservationist*
Lehrling, Terry James *real estate broker*
Longan, George Baker, III, *real estate company executive*
Masque, Maria L. *urban planner*
Swihart, H. Gregg *real estate company executive*
Tang, Esther Don *development consultant, retired social worker*

West Sedona
Lane, Margaret Anna Smith *real estate property manager, real estate developer*

ARKANSAS

Bella Vista
Cooper, John Alfred, Jr., *community development company executive*

Hot Springs National Park
Craft, Kay Stark *real estate company executive*

Magnolia
Juniker, Anthony Michael *economic developer, consultant*

Pine Bluff
Holmes, Claire Coleman *real estate broker*

CALIFORNIA

Aliso Viejo
Dascenzi, Hazel Marie *real estate broker*

Arcadia
Freedman, Gregg *real estate appraisal company executive*

Berkeley
Grimes, Ruth Elaine *city planner*
Wachs, Martin *urban planning educator, author, consultant*
Worrell, Ernst *energy and environmental analyst, researcher*

Beverly Hills
Bergman, Nancy Palm *real estate investment company executive*
Glazer, Guilford *real estate developer*
Seeger, Melinda Wayne *realtor*
†Shapell, Nathan *financial and real estate executive*
Tamkin, Curtis Sloane *real estate development company executive*
Victor, Robert Eugene *real estate corporation executive, lawyer*

Big Sur
Cross, Robert Louis *realtor, land use planner, writer, landscape architect, appraiser*

Campbell
Nicholson, Joseph Bruce *real estate developer*

Corona Del Mar
Eaton, Barry David *retired city planner*

Coronado
Stames, William Alexander *realtor, cost management executive*

Costa Mesa
Cohen, Stanley *commercial real estate developer*

Cupertino
Berg, Karl *real estate company executive*

Cypress
Osgood, Frank William *urban and economic planner, writer*

Fair Oaks
Papa, Michael Joseph *real estate broker*
Yarrigle, Charlene Sandra Shuey *realtor, investment advisor*

Fontana
Atkinson, Donald D., Sr., *real estate broker*

Fountain Valley
Smith, Marie Edmonds *real estate agent, property manager*

Glendale
†Gedjeyan, Hovannes John *real estate broker*

Goleta
Jammalamadaka, Vijaya Lakshmi *environmental specialist*

Granite Bay
Kemper, Dorla Dean Eaton (Dorla Dean Eaton) *real estate broker*

Grass Valley
Lunde, Karen Tamm *real estate broker*
Ozanich, Charles George *real estate broker*

Hermosa Beach
Williams, Jack Jeff *realtor, retired executive administrator*

Huntington Beach
Jackle, Karen Dee *real estate company executive*
†Myles, Margaret Jean *real estate appraiser*

Irvine
Chronley, James Andrew *real estate executive*
Stack, Geoffrey Lawrence *real estate developer*

La Jolla
Anthony, Harry Antoniades *city planner, architect, educator*
Foley, L(ewis) Michael *real estate executive*
Ripley, Stuart McKinnon *real estate consultant*

La Mirada
Lewis, Frederick Thomas *property manager*

Lafayette
Peters, Ray John *surveyor*

Laguna Beach
Hanauer, Joe Franklin *real estate executive*

Laguna Niguel
York, James Orison *real estate executive*

Long Beach
†Davies, Grace Lucille *real estate broker, educator*
McClune, Michael Marlyn *real estate executive*
McGann, John Milton *real estate executive*
Rosenberg, Jill *realtor, civic leader*

Los Angeles
Gilchrist, Richard Irwin *real estate developer*
Kay, Kenneth Jeffrey *real estate company executive*
Levy, Alan David *real estate executive*
Linsk, Michael Stephen *real estate executive*
Loukaitou-Sideris, Anastasia *urban planner, educator, urban planner, consultant*
Miller, Gary Douglas *business tax reform consultant, former aerospace company executive*
Rundel, Philip Wilson *environmentalist, consultant, science educator*
Swartz, Roslyn Holt *real estate executive*

Lynwood
Dove, Donald Augustine *city planner, educator*

Manhattan Beach
Schoenfeld, Lawrence Jon *real estate developer, asset lender*

Mission Viejo
Harris, Ruby Lee *real estate agent*

Moraga
Gerold, Charles McAdow *real estate broker*

Newport Beach
Fawcett, John Scott *real estate developer*
Kenney, William John, Jr., *real estate development executive*
Matteucci, Dominick Vincent *real estate developer*
Mink, Maxine Mock *real estate company executive*
Webb, H. Lawrence *real estate executive*

Oakland
Arazi, Lorri Rosenberg *real estate broker*
Miller, Connie Joy *assistant real estate officer, broker*
†Ostrander, Willis Frederick *real estate appraiser*

Oceanside
Munson, Lucille Marguerite (Mrs. Arthur E. Munson) *real estate broker*

Ontario
Ariss, David William, Sr., *real estate developer, consultant*

Palm Springs
Coffey, Nancy Ann *real estate broker*

Palmdale
Anderson, R(obert) Gregg *real estate company executive*

Palo Alto
Moore, Cassandra Chrones *real estate broker and policy analyst*
Wong, Y(ing) Wood *real estate investment company executive, real estate development company executive, venture capital investment company executive*

Pasadena
Crowley, John Crane *real estate developer*
Kathol, Anthony Louis *real estate executive*

Penn Valley
Nix, Barbara Lois *real estate broker*

Piedmont
†Weil, Arthur J. *real estate broker, poet*

Placentia
†Ambrose, Henry Bartlett *real estate broker, writer*

Rancho Mirage
Masotti, Louis Henry *real estate educator, consultant*

Rancho Santa Fe
Dieffenbach, Otto Weaver, III, *real estate company executive*

Redondo Beach
Abernethy, Robert John *real estate developer*

Riverside
Oakes, Judy Dianne *real estate broker*

Rolling Hills Estates
Allbee, Sandra Moll *real estate broker*

Sacramento
Oliva, Stephen Edward *resource conservationist, lawyer*

San Bernardino
Willis, Harold Wendt, Sr., *real estate developer*

San Diego
Davis, James McCoy *retired real estate executive*
Davis, John Warren *real estate broker*
Mc Comic, Robert Barry *real estate development company executive, lawyer*

San Francisco
Bracken, Thomas Robert James *real estate investment executive*
Freund, Fredric S. *real estate broker, property manager*
McIntyre, Robert Wheeler *retired conservation organization executive*
Shorenstein, Walter Herbert *commercial real estate development company executive*

San Jose
Rothblatt, Donald Noah *urban and regional planner, educator*

San Marcos
DeMarco, Ralph John *real estate developer*
Wingert, Hannelore Christiane *real estate agent, chemical company executive*

San Mateo
Knight, Alexa Davey *real estate company executive, real estate broker*

Santa Ana
Danoff-Kraus, Pamela Sue *real estate developer*

Santa Cruz
Dilbeck, Charles Stevens, Jr., *real estate company executive*
Hersley, Dennis Charles *environmentalist, software systems consultant*

Santa Monica
Rodrigues, William Patrick, Jr., *city planner*

Santa Rosa
Rabinowitsh, Steve *urban planner educator, city council member*

Spring Valley
†Roberts, Carolyn June *real estate broker*

Twain Harte
Kinsinger, Robert Earl *property company executive, educational consultant*

Upland
Lewis, Goldy Sarah *real estate developer, corporation executive*

Visalia
Nevin, David Wright *real estate broker, mortgage broker*

Vista
Cavanaugh, Kenneth Clinton *retired housing consultant*

West Hills
Struhl, Stanley Frederick *real estate developer*

Woodland Hills
Katz, Cleo *real estate educator*

Yorba Linda
Vilardi, Agnes Francine *real estate broker*

COLORADO

Aspen
Clauson, F.L. Stan, Jr., *city planner, consultant*

Aurora
Wessler, Mary Hraha *real estate company executive*

Boulder
Stepanek, Joseph Edward *industrial development consultant*

Colorado Springs
Bowers, Zella Zane *real estate broker*
Christensen, C. Lewis *real estate developer*

Commerce City
Hayes, James Anthony *city planner, business owner*

Denver
†Waits, Frankie A. *real estate broker*

Englewood
Moran, Gregory Allan *real estate developer*

Fort Collins
Driscoll, Richard Stark *retired land evaluation and land use planner*
Frink, Eugene Hudson, Jr., *business and real estate consultant*
Jensen, Margaret *real estate broker*
Sprague, Amaris Jeanne *real estate broker*

Golden
Ellsworth, Joseph Cordon *real estate executive, lawyer*

Littleton
Grant, Newell M. *real estate investment manager*

Louisville
Schonbrun, Michael K. *real estate developer, director*

Monument
Boggs, Steven Eugene *real estate broker, lawyer*

Pueblo
Heizer, Ida Ann *retired real estate broker*

Vail
Kelton, Arthur Marvin, Jr., *real estate developer*

Woody Creek
Jenkins, Robert Berryman *real estate developer*

CONNECTICUT

Bethel
Kurfehs, Harold Charles *real estate executive*

Bridgeport
Dexter, Gregory Warren *real estate and financial investor*
Schwartz, James Peter *real estate broker*

Danbury
Anderson, Alan Reinold *real estate executive, communications consultant*

Greenwich
Badman, John, III, *real estate developer, architect*
Griggs, Nina M. *realtor*
Urstadt, Charles J. *real estate executive*

New Haven
Alexander, Bruce Donald *real estate executive, educator*
Harrison, Henry Starin *real estate educator, entrepreneur*

Norwalk
Brooks, Torrey Dexter *real estate executive*
Sinclair, David Macowan *marine surveyor*

Old Greenwich
Parris, Sally Nye *real estate agent*

Plymouth
Hall, William Smith, Jr., *land surveyor*

Stamford
Koproski, Alexander Robert *real estate executive*
Ried, Tessa *environmentalist*

Waterbury
Ogrodnik, Lana Kathleen *real estate broker*

DELAWARE

Dover
Coyle, Kevin Francis *planner*
Taylor, Suzonne Berry Stewart *real estate broker*

Lewes
Little, R. Donald *real estate entrepreneur*

Newark
Byrne, John Michael *energy and environmental policy educator, researcher*

Rockland
Burdick, Kim Rogers *historic preservation consultant*

Wilmington
Falk, Lloyd Leopold *water pollution control consultant*
Maley, Patricia Ann *preservation planner*

DISTRICT OF COLUMBIA

Washington
Anlian, Steven James *urban planner, consultant*
Blackwelder, Brent Francis *environmentalist*
Carr, Thomas A. *real estate company executive*
Gelburd, Diane Elizabeth *conservationist*
Guruswamy, Dharmithran *urban planner*
Herbert, John David *urban planner*
Janes, William Sargent *real estate corporation executive*
John, Frank Herbert, Jr., *real estate appraiser, real estate investor, health products executive*
Meyer, Alden Merrill *environmental association executive*
Soule, Jeffrey Lyn *urban planner, consultant*

Stollman, Israel *city planner*
Stone, Roger David *environmentalist*
Train, Russell Errol *environmentalist*
Wallace Douglas, Jean *conservationist*
Wheeler, Douglas Paul *conservationist, government official, lawyer*
Wilder, James Edward *resident manager*

FLORIDA

Arcadia
Schmidt, Harold Eugene *real estate company executive*

Boca Raton
Innes-Brown, Georgette Meyer *real estate broker, insurance broker*
Konrad, Agnes Crossman *retired real estate agent, retired educator*
Langfield, Raymond Lee *real estate developer*
Párkányi, Marie Hřebíček *real estate broker*

Bradenton
†Becker, Nancy S. *retired real estate broker, retired shop owner*
Frederick, Nancy Ackerman *real estate broker*

Cedar Key
Starnes, Earl Maxwell *urban and regional planner, architect*

Celebration
Crabtree, Valleri Jayne *real estate executive, lawyer*

Coral Gables
Meyers, Stuart Irwin *real estate developer*
Stover, James Howard *retired real estate executive*

Dade City
Currier, Douglas Gilfillan, II, *urban planner*

Deland
Caccamise, Alfred Edward *real estate executive*

Fort Lauderdale
Craib, Kenneth Bryden *resource development executive, physicist, economist*
Markos, Chris *retired real estate company executive*
Moraitis, Karen Karl *real estate broker*
Taylor, Ralph Orien, Jr., *real estate developer, investor*

Fort Myers
Beever, Lisa Britt-Dodd *transportation and environmental planner, researcher*
Courtney, James Edmond *real estate developer*
Jenkins-Owen, Sharon *land use planner*
†Van Vleck, Pamela Kay *real estate company officer*
Wassersug, Stephen Robert *environmental consultant*

Fort Walton Beach
Cooke, Fred Charles *real estate broker*

Gainesville
Nozzi, Dom *urban planner*
York, Vermelle Cardwell *real estate broker and developer*

Hollywood
Burton, John Jacob *retired real estate company executive appraiser*

Jacksonville
Aleschus, Justine Lawrence *retired real estate broker*
Clarkson, Charles Andrew *real estate investment executive*
Lovett, Radford Dow *marine terminal real estate and investment company executive*
Pearce, Jennifer Sue *real estate appraiser*
Stern, Steven Alan *sports development owner*

Jupiter
Mutters, David Ray *real estate broker*

Lake Worth
Shepherd, Charles Clinton *real estate executive*

Lantana
Weeks, Charles, Jr., *real estate executive, retired publishing company executive*

Lecanto
Dixon, Charles Sim *urban planner*

Longboat Key
Jeglie, Jill A. *urban planner*

Longwood
Gasperoni, Emil, Sr., *realtor, developer*

Lutz
Corbitt, Doris Orene *retired real estate agent, dietician*

Maitland
Vallee, Judith Delaney *environmentalist, writer, fundraiser*

Melbourne
Glindeman, Henry Peter, Jr., *real estate developer*
Michalski, Thomas Joseph *city planner, developer*

Miami
Bregman, Michael Evan *urban planner*
Glogower, Michael Howard *public housing senior functional specialist*
Miller, Stuart A. *real estate executive, lawyer*

Nestor Castellano, Brenda Diana *real estate company executive*
Raffel, Leroy B. *real estate development company executive*
Salvaneschi, Luigi *real estate and development executive, business educator*
Segal, Simon *real estate executive, finance company executive*
†Strudler, Robert Jacob *real estate development executive*
West, Macdonald *real estate executive*

Naples
Dorio, Martin Matthew, Jr., *real estate company executive, investor*
Llewellyn, Leonard Frank *real estate broker, investment company executive*
Noe, Samuel VanArsdale, Jr., *retired urban planning educator*
Stastny, John Anton *real estate executive*

Niceville
Rasmussen, Robert Dee *retired real estate appraiser*

North Miami
Markson, Daniel Ben *real estate developer, consultant, syndicator*

Ocala
Booth, Jane Schuele *real estate company executive, real estate broker*

Ocean Ridge
Mueller, Gerry *realtor, investor, former internet executive*

Orlando
Watson, Barry Lee *real estate and mortgage broker, investor, contractor, builder, developer*

Palm Beach
Bagby, Martha L. Green *real estate holding company executive, writer, publishing executive*
Coudert, Dale Hokin *real estate executive, marketing consultant*
Dillard, Rodney Jefferson *real estate executive*
Klotsche, Charles Martin *real estate development company executive, photographer, writer, financial columnist*

Palm Beach Gardens
†Bragdon, Clifford Richardson *city planner, educator*

Palm Coast
Barnes, Judith Ann *real estate executive*

Panama City
Navon, Robert *real estate investor, former book publisher*

Parkland
Landman, Deborah Tracy *real estate company executive, fitness trainer, small business owner*

Pensacola
Brooks, Joseph Franklin *real estate executive*

Plantation
†Weiss, David I. *land developer, business executive, lawyer*

Ponte Vedra Beach
Berry, Clare Gebert *real estate broker*

Port Charlotte
Wall, Edward Millard *environmental consulting executive*

Riviera Beach
Totten, Gloria Jean (Dolly Totten) *real estate executive, financial consultant*

Saint Petersburg
Hurley, John Kenneth *real estate and merchant banking executive*
Rummel, Harold Edwin *real estate development and retail sales executive*
Smyth, Walter G. *real estate broker*

Saint Petersburg Beach
Hurley, Frank Thomas, Jr., *realtor*

Sarasota
Blomgren, Bruce Holmes *real estate developer, marina developer, consultant*
Byron, E. Lee *real estate broker*
Gidel, Robert Hugh *real estate investor*
†Reichert, Robert Joseph *real estate appraiser*
Scheitlin, Constance Joy *real estate broker, accountant*

Sebring
Sherrick, Daniel Noah *real estate broker*

Tallahassee
Lisenby, Dorrece Edenfield *realtor*
Morgan, Constance Louise *real estate executive*
Tookes, James Nelson *real estate investment company executive*

Tampa
Kanstoroom, David Arnold *real estate developer, entrepreneur*
Purcell, Henry, III, *real estate developer*
Smith, Barbara Jean *real estate broker*
Stair, Wilson Alfred, Jr., *urban planner, landscape architect*

Valrico
Parrado, Peter Joseph *real estate executive*
Tirelli, Maria Del Carmen S. *retired realtor*

Vero Beach
Freeman, Donald Wilford *real estate developer, horse breeder*

West Palm Beach
Lutey, Joyce Louise *real estate broker*

Winter Park
Strawn, Frances Freeland *real estate executive*

GEORGIA

Alpharetta
Charania, Barkat *real estate consultant*
Weitz, John Jerome, Jr., *city planner*

Athens
Melton, Wayne Charles *real estate executive*
Meyer, Gail Barry *retired real estate broker*

Atlanta
Comstock, Robert Donald, Jr., *real estate executive*
Cupp, Robert Erhard *land use planner, golf course architect*
Curtis, Philip Kerry *real estate developer, real estate company executive*
Glover, John Trapnell *real estate executive*
†McKissick, Todd Gaillard *real estate company executive*
Ossewaarde, Anne Winkler *real estate developer*
Raines, Tim D. *real estate corporation executive*
Simpson, Allan Boyd *real estate company executive*
†Stringer, George Clarke *real estate company executive, construction management advisor*
Wieland, John *real estate executive*
Winchester, Jesse Gregory *commercial real estate company executive*
Wolbrink, James Francis *real estate investor*

Bainbridge
King, Steven C. *real estate agent, retired research scientist*

Columbus
Bailey, Herta Luise *real estate broker*

Cumming
French, James Thomas *real estate broker*

Flovilla
†Lamb, Deryle Jean *preservationist*

Folkston
Crumbley, Esther Helen Kendrick *realtor, former councilwoman, retired secondary education educator*

Macon
Jones, John Ellis *real estate broker*

Marietta
Ballard, Judy Thomas *real estate broker*
Cline, Robert Thomas *retired land developer*
†Shapiro, Abra Blair *real estate company executive*

Newnan
Barron, Lindsey Hand *real estate broker*
Barron, Thomas Willis *real estate broker*

Peachtree City
Clark, James Kermit, Jr., *real estate executive*

Sautee Nacoochee
Richardson, James Sommerfield *real estate company executive*

Stockbridge
Hughes, Woodrow Milton *real estate broker*

Stone Mountain
†Malone, Embry *property manager, advocate*

Toccoa
Maypole, John Floyd *real estate holding company executive*

Tucker
Roberts, Thomas Heym *city and regional planner, consultant*

HAWAII

Honolulu
Adcock, Betty-Lee *real estate company executive, real estate broker*
Baker, Helen Doyle Peil *realtor*
Chiu, Margaret Chi Yuan Liu *retired real estate broker*
Graham, Donald Houston, Jr., *real estate developer*
Kwok, Reginald Yin-Wang *urban planning and development educator, architect*
Lighter, Eric Aaron *real estate and law enforcement software developer, consultant*
Xie, Shang-Ping *environmental studies educator*

Kapolei
Wong, Edwina A. Lee *real estate broker*

Koloa
Cobb, Rowena Noelani Blake *real estate broker*

Mililani
Olsen, Harris Leland *writer, novelist, educator, retired real estate and international business executive, diplomat*

IDAHO

Idaho Falls
†Thorsen, Nancy Dain *real estate broker*

Troy
Hepler, Merlin Judson, Jr., *real estate broker*

ILLINOIS

Aurora
Stephens, Steve Arnold *real estate broker*

Barrington
Fowler, Susan Michele *real estate broker, entrepreneur*

Champaign
Guttenberg, Albert Ziskind *planning educator*

Chicago
Benson, Sara Elizabeth *real estate broker, real estate appraiser*
Bohn, Charlotte Galitz *retired real estate executive*
†Bucksbaum, Matthew *real estate investment trust company executive*
Bynoe, Peter Charles Bernard *real estate developer, lawyer*
Daley, Vincent Raymond, Jr., *real estate company executive, consultant*
Daly, Patrick F. *real estate executive, architect*
Darchun, Lino Auksutis *real estate professional*
Eubanks-Pope, Sharon G. *real estate company executive, entrepreneur*
Field, Karen Ann (Karen Ann Schaffner) *real estate broker*
Foerster, James Fredrick *urban planning educator, university administrator*
Galowich, Ronald Howard *real estate investment executive, venture capitalist*
Glaze, Robert Howe *real estate executive*
Good, Sheldon Fred *realtor*
Hayes, Jacqueline Crement *real estate broker*
Klebba, Raymond Allen *property manager*
Lapidus, Dennis *real estate developer*
Metz, Adam S. *real estate executive*
Pappas, Philip James *real estate company executive*
Reilly, Robert Frederick *valuation consultant*
†Reschke, Michael W. *real estate executive*
Rubenstein, Eric Davis *real estate executive*
Schwab, James Charles *urban planner*
Scott, Stuart L. *real estate company executive*
Shapiro, Nicholas John *real estate executive*
Skoien, Gary *real estate company executive*
Strobeck, Charles LeRoy *real estate executive*
Totlis, Gust John *retired title insurance company executive*
Travis, Dempsey Jerome *author, real estate executive and developer*
Wirtz, William Wadsworth *real estate executive, professional sports team executive*
Wood Prince, William Norman *investments and real estate professional*

Dundee
Ulakovich, Ronald Stephen *real estate developer*

Edwardsville
Wentz, Charles Alvin, Jr., *environmentalist, chemical engineer*

Galena
Schwerdtfeger, Carl Richard *real estate executive*

Glen Carbon
Ottwein, Merrill William George *real estate company executive, veterinarian*

Highland Park
Stein, Paula Jean Anne Barton *hotel real estate executive, broker*

Hinsdale
Nibeck, Susan Nelson *real estate sales agent*

Inverness
Regopoulos, Efstathios A. *real estate developer, consultant*

Lake Zurich
Schultz, Carl Herbert *real estate management and development company executive*

Libertyville
†Ritson, Scott Campbell *real estate management and development consultant*

Long Grove
Van Der Bosch, Susan Hartnett *real estate broker*

Naperville
†Harvard, Rita Grace *real estate agent, volunteer*

Northbrook
Levy, Arnold S(tuart) *real estate company executive*

Northfield
Kleinman, Burton Howard *real estate investor*

Oak Brook
Fichter, David Harry *conservationist, environmentalist*

INDIANA

Bloomington
Oswalt, Aria Lucinda *real estate broker*

Evansville
Matthews, C(harles) David *real estate appraiser, consultant*

Fort Wayne
Hirschy, Gordon Harold *real estate broker, auctioneer*

Werling, Donn Paul *environmental educator*

Greenwood
Tomlin, Jeanne Brannon *real estate broker, small business owner*

Indianapolis
Borns, Robert Aaron *real estate developer*
†Crosser, Richard H. *real estate company executive*
†Jewett, John Rhodes *real estate executive*
Mullen, Thomas Edgar *real estate consultant*
Simon, Melvin *real estate developer, professional basketball executive*
Sokolov, Richard Saul *real estate company executive*

Jeffersonville
†McMichael, Jeane Casey *real estate company executive, educator*
Reisert, Charles Edward, Jr., *real estate executive*

Kokomo
Wilson, Paul Wayne *retired real estate developer*

Lafayette
Shook, James Creighton *real estate executive*

Newburgh
Tierney, Gordon Paul *real estate broker, genealogist*

Terre Haute
Perry, Eston Lee *real estate and equipment leasing company executive*

IOWA

Ames
†Wendell, Barbara Taylor *retired real estate agent*

Cedar Rapids
Baermann, Donna Lee Roth *real estate property executive, retired insurance analyst*
Knepper, Eugene Arthur *realtor*

Osage
Kolbet, Kevin Michael *real estate company executive*

Spencer
Lemke, Alan James *environmental specialist*

KANSAS

Overland Park
McChesney, Samuel Parker, III, *real estate executive*

Stilwell
Roeseler, Wolfgang Guenther Joachim *city planner*

Topeka
Barnett, Mary Lorene *real estate manager*

KENTUCKY

Bowling Green
Stewart, Harold Sanford *real estate investment and supply executive*

Covington
Fleischer-Rieveschl, Ellen Lee *real estate agent*

Danville
Crouch, Betty Louise *real estate broker*

Fort Mitchell
Weiskittel, Ralph Joseph *real estate broker*

Glasgow
Wyatt, Elnoria *real estate broker*

Lexington
Gable, Robert Elledy *real estate investment company executive*

Louisville
Gott, Marjorie Eda Crosby *conservationist, former educator*

Winchester
†Cantrell, Georgia Ann *realtor*

LOUISIANA

Baton Rouge
Mohr, Jeffrey Michael *real estate and insurance executive*
†Skillman, Ernest Edward, Jr., *real estate sales and management executive*

Covington
Maurin, James E. *real estate executive*

Monroe
Guy, William Achilles, Jr., (Rod Guy Jr.) *urban planner, economic development consultant*

New Orleans
Bell, Bryan *real estate and oil investment executive, educator*
Jones, Glenn Earle *property management executive*

Shreveport
Robinson, Edna Earle *real estate company executive*

MAINE

Bangor
Foster, Walter Herbert, Jr., *real estate company executive*

Gardiner
Gosline, Norman Abbot *real estate appraiser, consultant*

Lincolnville
Williams, Robert Luther *city planning consultant*

Port Clyde
Duarte, Patricia M. *real estate and insurance broker*

MARYLAND

Annapolis
†Wright, David Lawrence *realtor, real estate broker*

Baltimore
DeVito, Mathias Joseph *retired real estate executive*
Henson, Daniel P., III, *real estate developer*
Rosen, Michael Howard *real estate executive*

Bethesda
†Clark, A. James *real estate company executive*
Gilreath, Jerry Hollandsworth *retired community planner*
Kibbe, James William *real estate broker*
Sams, James Farid *real estate development company executive*

Burtonsville
Kammeyer, Sonia Margaretha *real estate agent*

Cambridge
Miller, Robert Edvin *environmental education specialist, researcher, industrial hygienist*

Chevy Chase
†Lee, Edward Brooke, Jr., *real estate executive, fund raiser*

Columbia
Hilderbrandt, Donald Franklin, II, *urban designer, landscape architect, artist*
McCuan, William Patrick *real estate company executive*
Millspaugh, Martin Laurence *real estate developer, urban development consultant*

Frederick
Whelihan, Alan Stuart *real estate developer, automotive executive*

Potomac
Noonan, Patrick Francis *conservation executive*

Reisterstown
Bart, Polly Turner *real estate developer*

Rockville
†Brewer-Pecson, Dorothy Wynne *environmentalist*
Furman, Robert Ralph *real estate developer*

Salisbury
Nutter, David George *urban planner*

Silver Spring
†Laughlin, Naomi Myers *realtor*
†McCray, Lora *real estate developer*
Youla, Sandra Lynn *land use planner, consultant*

Takoma Park
Urciolo, John Raphael, II, *real estate developer, real estate and finance educator*

MASSACHUSETTS

Amherst
Bentley, Richard Norcross *regional planner, writer, educator*
Larson, Joseph Stanley *environmentalist, educator, researcher*

Arlington
Van Orman, Jeanne *planning consultant*

Ayer
Holmes, Jean Louise *real estate investor, Holocaust scholar, educator*

Boston
Beal, Robert Lawrence *real estate executive*
Collins, Harris Edwin *real estate appraiser*
Holland, James R. *real estate corporation executive*
Lovejoy, George Montgomery, Jr., *real estate company executive*
Lundgren, Richard John *real estate executive, city planner, preservationist*
Roberts, Sandra Brown *realty company executive*
Thibedeau, Richard Herbert *environmental planner, administrator*
Thomas, Carol Louise Joseph *community planning company executive*

Brockton
Compton, William Thomas *real estate investor*

Cambridge
†Axelrod, Emily H. *urban planner*
de Marneffe, Barbara Rowe *historic preservationist*
Fleming, Ronald Lee *urban designer, arts administrator, preservation planner, environmental educator*
Ross, Matthew Alan *real estate company executive*

Spunt, Shepard Armin *real estate executive, management and financial consultant*
Susskind, Lawrence Elliott *urban and environmental planner, educator, public dispute mediator*
van Houtum, Diana Chang *real estate executive and developer*
Vigier, François Claude Denis *city planning educator*
Wood, Richard Robinson *real estate executive*

East Bridgewater
Farrell, Sharon Elaine *retired real estate broker*

East Orleans
Thomsen, Charles Hakon *real estate company executive*

Fairhaven
Hotchkiss, Henry Washington *real estate broker and financial consultant*

Falmouth
Milkman, Marianne Friedenthal *retired city planner*

Gloucester
Sallah, Majeed (Jim Sallah) *real estate developer*

Lexington
Frieden, Bernard Joel *urban studies educator*
Linkov, Igor *conservationist, consultant*

Longmeadow
Louargand, Marc Andrew *real estate executive, financial consultant*

Medford
Comeau, Lorene Anita Emerson *real estate developer*

Newton
Havens, Candace Jean *planning consultant*
Nahigian, Robert John *real estate development broker*

Rockport
Johnson, Janet Lou *real estate company executive, writer*

Waltham
Nelson, Arthur Hunt *real estate management development company executive*

Whitinsville
†O'Connell, Roberta M. *realtor*

Winchester
Blackham, Ann Rosemary (Mrs. J. W. Blackham) *realtor*

Woburn
Cummings, William Stanley *real estate company executive*

MICHIGAN

Ann Arbor
Clark, Thomas B., Sr., *real estate broker*
Surovell, Edward David *real estate company executive*

Bellaire
Keller, Theodore G., Jr., *investment property owner and manager*

Clarkston
Ylvisaker, John Richard *real estate developer, consultant*

East Lansing
Anderton, James Franklin, IV, *real estate development executive*
Strauss, Eric James *urban planning educator, lawyer, consultant*

Farmington Hills
Beron, Gail Laskey *real estate analyst, appraiser, consultant*

Grosse Ile
Smith, Veronica Latta *real estate corporation officer*

Grosse Pointe Farms
Dunlap, Connie Sue Zimmerman *real estate professional*

Grosse Pointe Shores
LaHood, Mary Anne *real estate investor*

Houghton
Utt, Glenn S., Jr., *motel investor, former biotech and pharmaceutical industry company executive*

Livonia
Borin, Jeffrey Nathan *real estate developer*

Milan
Patton, Lisa Darlene *urban planner*

Portage
Maury, Nancy Jane (Nancy Jane Gooch) *realtor, mortgage company executive*

Saginaw
Cline, Thomas William *real estate leasing company executive, management consultant*

White Lake
Clyburn, Luther Linn *real estate broker, appraiser, ship captain*

MINNESOTA

Aitkin
Morton, Craig Richard *real estate investor*

Duluth
Bowman, Roger Manwaring *real estate executive*

Mankato
Nickerson, Ronald George *recreation and parks educator*

Minneapolis
Boelter, Philip Floyd *real estate company officer, mortgage company executive*
Bolan, Richard Stuart *urban planner, educator, researcher*
Fine, Bob *lawyer, real estate developer*
Fine, William Irwin *real estate developer*
Kreiser, Frank David *real estate executive*
Lucas, Margaret Exner *housing developer*
Stuebner, James Cloyd *real estate developer, contractor*
Vergin, Timothy Lynn *commercial real estate appraiser, broker, investor*
Walker, Walter Willard *real estate and investments executive*

North Oaks
McDonald, Malcolm Willis *retired real estate company executive*

Saint Peter
Turnbull, Charles Vincent *retired real estate broker*

MISSISSIPPI

Clarksdale
Magdovitz, Lawrence Maynard *real estate executive, lawyer*

Meridian
Church, George Millord *retired real estate company executive*

MISSOURI

Ash Grove
Johnson, Iver Christian *valuation company executive*

Bucklin
Payne, Flora Fern *real estate broker*

Chesterfield
Morley, Harry Thomas, Jr., *real estate executive*

Columbia
Northway, Wanda I. *real estate company executive*

Gray Summit
Desloge, Christopher Davis, Sr., *real estate and merchant banking executive*

Holden
Martin, Laurabelle *real estate and farm land owner and manager*

Independence
Francis, Mary Frances Van Dyke *real estate executive, editor*

Ironton
Sebastian, Phylis Sue (Ingram) *real estate broker, art appraiser*

Kansas City
Shutz, Byron Christopher *real estate executive*

Saint Joseph
Rachow, Sharon Dianne *realtor*

Saint Louis
Hundelt, Craig Thomas *realtor, engineering executive*
Koehler, Harry George *real estate executive*
Lang, Danny Robert *planning consultant*
Marking, T(heodore) Joseph, Jr., *transportation and urban planner*
Meissner, Edwin Benjamin, Jr., *retired real estate broker*

Springfield
Aull, Elizabeth Berryman *real estate development executive*

Town And Country
Kaegel, Ray Martin *real estate and insurance broker*

MONTANA

Great Falls
Stevens, George Alexander *real estate broker*

Havre
Coffman, Barbara LeAnn *environmentalist*

Sidney
Beagle, John Gordon *real estate broker*

NEBRASKA

Lincoln
Vestal, Lowell Alan *real estate manager*

Madison
Wozniak, Richard Michael, Sr., *retired city and regional planner*

Omaha
Gallagher, Paula Marie *real estate appraiser*
Neal, Bonnie Jean *real estate agent*

NEVADA

Carson City
Empey, Gene F. *real estate executive*
Evangelatos, Gregory Gerasimos *city planner*

Las Vegas
Broughton, James Walter *real estate development executive, consultant*
†Hale, Marsha Bentley *writer, real estate rehabilitator, song writer, mannequin historian*
Lee, Theodore Bo *real estate developer*
Pulliam, Francine Sarno *real estate broker, real estate developer*

Reno
Coleman, James Scott *environmental research executive*
Davenport, Janet Lee *real estate agent, small business owner*

NEW HAMPSHIRE

Concord
Speltz, Michael John *land protection specialist*

Hinsdale
†Smith, Edwin O. *real estate executive, state legislator*

NEW JERSEY

Atlantic Highlands
Hawley, Joseph B. *property management executive, educator*

Barnegat
†Ackerman, Donald Robert *retired surveyor, retired real estate agent*

Bedminster
Hudacsko, Dennis Wayne

Bloomfield
Moese, Mark Douglas *environmental consultant*

Bound Brook
Chandler, Marguerite Nella *real estate corporation executive*

Bridgeport
Walters, Charles Joseph *real estate developer*

Chatham
Lax, Philip *land developer, space planner*

Cherry Hill
Copsetta, Norman George *real estate executive*

Englewood Cliffs
Books, Roberta Paula *real estate finance executive*

Flemington
Salamon, Renay *real estate broker*

Green Brook
Elias, Donald Francis *environmental consultant*

Hackensack
Gingras, Paul Joseph *real estate management company executive*

Haworth
Strum, Brian J. *real estate executive*

Hazlet
Fisher, David Bruce *land development executive*

Jersey City
Russell, Helen Ross *environmental consultant, author*

Livingston
Marlow, Ian Michael *real estate company executive*

Medford
Brown, Annie Marie Vedel *real estate broker*

Princeton
Broad, Barbara Prentice *retired real estate agent*

Randolph
Femminella, Charles Joseph, Jr., *real estate appraiser, tax assessor, broker*

Rutherford
Stein, Seena Deborah *real estate executive*

Sea Girt
Cleary, Martin Joseph *real estate company executive*

Skillman
Pariso, Jean Brunner *retired real estate agent*

Somerset
DiMeglio, Nicolas Joseph *real estate broker, small business owner*

Somerville
McCracken, Anthony Vekony, Sr., *land use planner, environmental scientist*

South Orange
Thonet, John A. *environmental planning and engineering consultant*

Summit
†Clynes, Carolann Elizabeth *realtor*

Upper Saddle River
Marron, Darlene Lorraine *real estate development executive, financial and marketing consultant*

Woodcliff Lake
Kallet, Harriet Feldman *real estate broker*

NEW MEXICO

Albuquerque
†Davis, Betty Bourbonia *real estate investment executive*
Godfrey, Richard George *real estate appraiser, consultant*
Kinney, Carol Naus Roberts *real estate broker*
Navarro, Janyte Janine *real estate executive*
Stahl, Jack Leland *real estate company executive*

Cerrillos
Briggs, Barbara Jean Holmes *real estate developer*

Mora
†Hanks, Eugene Ralph *land developer, rancher, forester, retired military officer, investor*

Santa Fe
Perkins, Linda Gillespie *real estate executive*

NEW YORK

Albany
Kiang, Walter T. *environmentalist, state official*
Morris, Margretta Elizabeth *conservationist*

Auburn
Long, Michael Howard *urban planner, landscape architect*

Baldwinsville
Hansen, Beverly Anne *environmental policy educator*

Binghamton
Hudak, Michael John *environmentalist, writer, photographer*

Brewster
Killackey, Dorothy Helen *real estate professional, former educator*

Bronx
Robinson, John Gwilym *conservationist*

Brooklyn
Bubaris, Gus John *real estate analyst*
Ferretti, Jeffrey John *real estate broker, mortgage broker*
Hill, Isabel Thigpen *urban planner, filmmaker*
Markgraf, Rosemarie *real estate broker*
Stuckey, James P. *real estate company executive*

Cairo
Heck, Karl Thomas *community development planner*

Canaan
Belknap, Michael H. P. *real estate developer*

Central Islip
McGowan, Harold *real estate developer, investor, scientist, author, philanthropist*

Clifton Park
Miller, Robert Carl *real estate developer*

Clifton Springs
DeRuyter, Marilyn *real estate broker*

Cold Spring
Miller, Timothy Earl *planning company executive*

Cooperstown
Huntington, Robert Graham *environmental business consultant*

Delmar
Matuszek, John Michael, Jr., *environmental scientist, educator, consultant*

Douglaston
Balbi, Kenneth Emilio *environmental specialist, researcher*

Dundee
Miller, Ronald K. *real estate broker, educator*

East Durham
Farren, Carol Elese *facility management consultant*

Elizabethtown
†Houseal, Brian L. *conservationist*

Elmsford
Raymond, George Marc *city planner, educator*

Goshen
Ward, William Francis, Jr., *real estate investment banker*

Great Neck
Rosenthal, Gladys M. *real estate appraiser*

Huntington
†Petersen, Patricia J. *real estate company executive*

Irvington
Trent, Bertram James *real estate executive*

Jericho
Axinn, Donald Everett *real estate investor and developer, poet, writer*

Larchmont
Levi, James Harry *real estate executive, investment banker*

Mohegan Lake
Charney, Lena London *property manager, poet*

Mount Vernon
Rossini, Joseph *contracting and development corporate executive*

New Hyde Park
Cooper, Milton *real estate investment trust executive*

New York
Benenson, Edward Hartley *realty company executive*
†Betts, Roland W. *real estate developer*
†Boxer, Jason T. *title company executive*
Brooks, Peter Stuyvesant *real estate consultant*
†Clancy, John Patrick *real estate company executive*
Cohen, Irving Elias *real estate executive*
†Cuneo, Jack Alfred *real estate investment executive*
Felner, Richard M. *real estate consultant, lawyer*
Fox-Freund, Barbara Susan *real estate company executive*
Garfield, Leslie Jerome *real estate executive*
Gochberg, Thomas *real estate investor, financial executive*
Goddess, Lynn Barbara *commercial real estate broker*
Goldenberg, Charles Lawrence *real estate company executive*
Grau, Marcy Beinish *real estate broker, former investment banker*
Greene, Elizabeth Ivory *real estate company official*
Hemmerdinger, H. Dale *real estate executive*
Hernstadt, Judith Filenbaum *city planner, real estate executive, broadcasting executive*
Hirschfeld, Elie *real estate developer*
Host, Stig *real estate company executive, oil company executive*
Howell, William Page *real estate company executive*
Hutton, Ernest Watson, Jr., *urban designer, city planner*
Kalikow, Peter Stephen *real estate developer, former newspaper owner, publisher*
†Kane, Marilyn *real estate company executive*
†Kendall Levine, Judy *real estate broker, interior designer, writer*
Lavori, Nora *real estate executive, lawyer*
Macy, Steven C. *real estate investor*
Marder, John G. *real estate investor, marketing consultant, corporate director, bison rancher*
Marshall, Alton Garwood *real estate counselor*
Nimetz, Gloria Lorch *real estate broker, photographer*
Nolan, Christopher Aloysius, III, *real estate developer, architect*
Perry-Widney, Marilyn (Marilyn Perry) *international finance and real estate executive, television producer*
Petz, Edwin V. *real estate executive, lawyer*
Rose, Daniel *real estate company executive, consultant*
Rose, Elihu *real estate executive*
Ruben, Lawrence *real estate developer, building company executive, lawyer*
Schlang, David *real estate executive, lawyer*
Scott, Stanley DeForest *real estate executive, former lithography company executive*
Smith, Andrew Alfred, Jr., *urban planner*
Stein, Ellen Gail *executive manager*
Stroer, Rosemary Ann *real estate broker*
Thomas, Violeta de los Angeles *real estate broker*
†Tishman, John L. *realty and construction company executive*
†Toote, Gloria E. A. *real estate developer, lawyer, columnist*
Warsawer, Harold Newton *real estate appraiser and consultant*
†Weiss, Donald S. *real estate developer*
Wolf, Peter Michael *investment manager, writer*
Zacharias, Thomas Elling *real estate executive*

Pawling
Wood, Christopher L.J. *real estate executive*

Rochester
Walker, Michael Charles, Sr., *retirement services executive*

Rye
Feinberg, Norman Maurice *real estate company executive*

Scarsdale
†Lawyer, William Grove *conservationist*

Stony Brook
Koppelman, Lee Edward *regional planner, educator*

Syracuse
De Long, Jacob Edward *real estate broker*
Whaley, Ross Samuel *environmentalist, educator*

Watertown
Evans, Lance Michael *real estate board executive*

West Seneca
†Wirth, Sandra Lee *real estate company owner*

White Plains
McCarthy, John Robert *real estate firm officer*

NORTH CAROLINA

Ararat
Marsh, Joseph Virgil *real estate broker, investment advisor*

Asheville
Cragnolin, Karen Zambella *real estate developer, lawyer*

Chapel Hill
Weiss, Shirley F. *urban and regional planner, economist, educator*

Charlotte
Cox, Linda Smoak *real estate broker*
Morrison, Robert Haywood *real estate developer*
Wiggins, Nancy Bowen *real estate broker, market research consultant*

Conover
Williams, Randolph Stuart *urban planner*

Fayetteville
Kendrick, Mark Cleveland *real estate executive*

Murphy
Pezzella, Jerry James, Jr., *investment and real estate executive*

Raleigh
Willer, Edward Herman *real estate broker*

Statesville
Redman, William Walter, Jr., *realtor*

Winston Salem
Doggett, Aubrey Clayton, Jr., *real estate executive, consultant*

NORTH DAKOTA

Bismarck
Christianson, James D. *real estate developer*
Clairmont, William Edward *real estate developer*

OHIO

Amelia
Hayden, John W. *real estate company executive*

Beachwood
†Wolstein, Scott Alan *real estate company executive*

Cincinnati
Dunigan, Dennis Wayne *real estate executive*
Edelman, David Joel *urban planning executive*
Levine, Steven Alan *real estate appraiser, association executive*
Randman, Barry I. *real estate developer*
Schuler, Robert Leo *appraiser, consultant*

Cleveland
Gould, Bonnie M(arincic) *realtor*
Maier, Howard Robert *urban planner, government agency administrator*

Columbus
Coopersmith, Jeffrey Alan *real estate developer*
Pyatt, Leo Anthony *retired real estate broker*
Voss, Jerrold Richard *city planner, educator, university official*

Dayton
†Stout, Donald Everett *real estate developer, environmental preservationist*
Wertz, Kenneth Dean *real estate executive*

Dublin
†Kramb, Amy Lynn *environmentalist*

Findlay
Williams, Kathy Margene *real estate broker*

Gates Mills
Schanfarber, Richard Carl *real estate broker*

Granville
Kerens, Steven Robert *real estate executive*

Hebron
Slater, Wanda Marie Worth *property manager*

Hudson
Stec, John Zygmunt *real estate executive*

Mentor
Krone, Norman Bernard *commercial real estate developer, lawyer*

Parma
Verba, Betty Lou *real estate executive, investor*

Pataskala
Honnold, Kathryn S. *real estate agent*

Salem
Barcey, Harold Edward Dean (Hal Barcey) *real estate counselor*

Shaker Heights
Solganik, Marvin *real estate executive*
Winter, John Alexander *realtor, real estate appraiser*

Shelby
Phelan, Martha Armstrong *realtor*

Toledo
Batt, Nick *property and investment executive*
†Sabra, Ponn Mahayosnand *realtor*

Westerville
McCurdy, Kurt Basquin *real estate corporation officer*

Wilmington
Evans, Elizabeth Ann West *retired realtor*

Worthington
Winston, Janet Margaret *real estate agent, civic volunteer*

Youngstown
Camacci, Michael A. *commercial real estate broker, development consultant*

OKLAHOMA

Norman
Zelby, Rachel *realtor*

Oklahoma City
Bradford, Dennis Doyle *real estate broker, developer*

Tulsa
Henderson, James Ronald *industrial real estate developer*
Matthews, Dane Dikeman *urban planner*

Warr Acres
Phillips, Richard Carey *real estate executive*

OREGON

Burns
Christensen, Denise Danyel *real estate broker*

Gladstone
Beals, Herbert Kyle *community planner, historian, consultant*

Portland
Cogan, Arnold M. *planning consultant*
Dickinson, Janet Mae Webster *relocation consulting executive*
Lavigne, Peter Marshall *environmentalist, lawyer, educator*
Lilly, Elizabeth Giles *mobile park executive*
Standring, James Douglas *real estate developer*

Salem
Derfler, Eugene L. *real estate agent, former state legislator*

Springfield
Davis, George Donald *executive land use policy consultant*
Jennison, Brian (Lester) *environmental specialist*

PENNSYLVANIA

Allentown
Saab, Deanne Keltum *real estate appraiser, real estate broker*

Ardmore
Waetzman, Larry Samuel *planning company executive*

Blue Bell
Deschaine, Barbara Ralph *retired real estate broker*

Chadds Ford
Moore, Bruce E. *real estate company executive*

Doylestown
Long, Ronald Alex *real estate and financial consultant, lawyer, educator*

Elkins Park
Havir, Bryan Thomas *urban planner*

Erie
Gottschalk, Frank Klaus *real estate company executive*

Indiana
Masilela, Calvin Onias *land use planner, educator*

Lansdale
†Gaskins-Dainis, Ina R. *retired real estate agent*

Malvern
Stainback, John Philip *public/private finance and development executive*

Meadville
Cable, Mabel Elizabeth *urban planner, artist*

New Castle
Craig, Stephen John *urban planner*

Philadelphia
Bacon, Edmund Norwood *city planner*
Birch, Eugenie Ladner *urban planning educator*
Gowa, Andrew *real estate investor, lawyer*
Lipkin, Edward B. *real estate developer*
Mellman, Leonard *real estate investor and advisor*
Peck, Robert McCracken *naturalist, science historian, writer*
Pew, Robert Anderson *retired real estate and equipment leasing corporation officer*
Plumer, Alvin H. (Bud) *realtor*

Pittsburgh
Novick, Ivan Jay *real estate executive*

Sarraf, Roberta Jean *planning consultant*
Sokoloff, Terri Ann *real estate broker*

Southeastern
Zlotolow-Stambler, Ernest *real estate executive, architectural executive*

Springfield
Reeves, Thomas A. *naturalist*

Washington Crossing
Hauf, John George *real estate broker*

West Chester
Eddy, Heath Robert *urban planner*
Knuth Fischer, Cynthia Strout *environmental consultant*

Willow Grove
Moore, Norma Jean *real estate broker*

York
Moul, Marlin Eugene *real estate broker*

RHODE ISLAND

Foster
Sawyer, Mildred Clementina *retired real estate agent*

Providence
Bonin, Paul Joseph *real estate and banking executive*
Hitt, Mary Frances Lyster *environmentalist, deacon*

Wakefield
†Morrison, Fred Beverly *real estate consultant*

Warwick
Palumbo, Edward Paul *real estate appraiser, writer*

SOUTH CAROLINA

Beaufort
Chambers, Henry Carroll *realty broker*

Charleston
Limehouse, Harry Bancroft, Jr., *real estate developer, transportation consultant*

Columbia
Sloan, Saundra Jennings *real estate company executive*

Easley
Spearman, Patsy Cordle *real estate broker*

Greenville
Crawford, William David *real estate broker, consultant*
Shockley, Milton M., Jr., *real estate brokerage executive*
Simmons, David Jeffrey *real estate executive*

Hilton Head Island
Gruchacz, Robert S. *real estate executive*

Spartanburg
Gray, Gwen Cash *real estate broker*

Summerville
Christie, Joseph Francis *city planner*

SOUTH DAKOTA

Rapid City
Hamilton, Douglas Warren *real estate executive*

Sioux Falls
Kilian, Thomas Randolph *rural economic developer, consultant*
†Wilkes, Jeffrey Blaine *real estate appraiser*

TENNESSEE

Brentwood
Raskin, Edwin Berner *real estate executive*

Bristol
Hardin, Gerald Larson *city planner and community developer, educator*

Harrogate
†Daniel, Barbara Ann *realtor, advertising executive*

Kingsport
Bailey, William Henry *real estate appraiser*

Memphis
Haizlip, Henry Hardin, Jr., *real estate consultant, former banker*

Nashville
Anderson, Janice Linn *real estate brokerage professional, paralegal*
Beck, Robert Beryl *real estate executive*

Powell
Cossé, R. Paul *realty company executive*

TEXAS

Addison
Kimbler, Larry Bernard *real estate executive, accountant*

Austin
Barbara, Paul Frank *chemistry educator*
Stoll, William Hermann *real estate company executive*

Brenham
Moorman, Robert Lawson *real estate appraiser and broker*

Bryan
Jackson, Thomas O. *real estate appraiser, urban planner*

Calvert
Alemán, Marthanne Payne *environmental planner, consultant*

Conroe
Judge, Dolores Barbara *real estate broker*

Coppell
†Sellers, James Justin *real estate analyst, consultant*

Dallas
Doran, Mark Richard *real estate financial executive*
†Dowdle, Jeff *real estate broker*
†Marlow, Patricia Bair Bond *realtor*
Moss, Robert Williams *real estate developer*
†Perot, H. Ross, Jr., *real estate developer, former sports team executive*
Stuart, Spencer Raymond, Jr., *real estate development company executive*
Yeslow, Rosemarie *real estate professional*

El Paso
Keller, Robert M. *real estate broker*
Lyle, James Arthur *real estate broker*

Fort Worth
Kronick, Norman Marks *real estate developer, investor, philanthropist*

Galveston
McLeod, E. Douglas *real estate developer, lawyer*

Granbury
Almy, Earle Vaughn, Jr., (Buddy Almy) *real estate executive*

Hillsboro
McClendon, Fred Vernon *real estate professional, business consultant, equine and realty appraiser, financial consultant*

Houston
Barrere, Jamie Newton *real estate executive*
Goldsmith, Billy Joe *real estate broker, rancher*
Harris, Lyttleton Tazwell, IV, *property management-investment company executive*
Henry, Randolph Marshall *investments executive, real estate broker*
Johnson, Craig M. *real estate development executive*
Kollaer, Jim C. *real estate executive, architect*
Lanier, Robert C. (Bob Lanier) *real estate owner, developer, former mayor*
Lehrer, Kenneth Eugene *economic consultant*
Sadowski, Chester Philip, Jr., *real estate executive*
†Waltrip, Robert L. *environmentalist*

Lubbock
Wall, Betty Jane *real estate consultant*

Mico
Shockey, Thomas Edward *real estate executive, engineer*

Plano
Wilke, Chet *real estate broker*

Port Aransas
Turner, Elizabeth Adams Noble (Betty Turner) *real estate company executive*

Rowlett
Efrussy, Alan Maurice *urban planner*

San Antonio
†Condos, Barbara Seale *real estate broker, developer, investor*
Cottingham, Stephen Kent *real estate development executive, researcher, minister, educator*
Williamson, Fletcher Phillips *real estate broker*

Seguin
Patton, Orin Clyde *real estate executive, retired military officer*

Wichita Falls
†Hoffman, Thomas Paul *realtor, educator*

UTAH

Garden City
Campbell, Jane Turner *retired realtor, retired secondary school educator*

Midvale
Teerlink, J(oseph) Leland *real estate developer*

Ogden
Webber, John Robert *real estate broker, musician, educator*

VERMONT

Burlington
Van Raalte, Barbara G. *retired realtor*

Colchester
Sweeny, Arthur, III, *realtor*

Groton
Shields, Margaret Agnes *land surveyors association executive*

Middlebury
†Jenks-Jay, Nan *environmentalist educator*

VIRGINIA

Abingdon
Humphreys, Lois H. *realtor*

Alexandria
Borum, Olin Henry *realtor, former government official*
Campagna, Dianna Gwin *real estate broker*
Michael, Ann Dozier Marino *real estate broker*

Bristow
Mac Donald, Margaret Clark *retired real estate agent*

Charlottesville
Greenwood, Virginia Maxine McLeod *real estate executive, broker*
Meeks, Debra *realtor*

Dumfries
Thrall, Eileen Fowler *real estate broker, government staff official*

Haymarket
Crafton-Masterson, Adrienne *real estate company executive*

Herndon
Duceman, Mark Eugene *planner*

Lansdowne
Fujishiro, Katakazu Kenneth *retired urban/regional planner, engineer*

Mc Lean
Alberts, Henry Celler *real estate company executive*
McLean, Robert, III, *real estate company executive*
Nobil, James Howard, Jr., *real estate investor, developer, consultant, broker*
Talbot, Martha Hayne *conservationist, biologist*

Nellysford
McWane, Joyce Hobbs *title company executive*

Newport News
Goldberg, Ivan Baer *real estate executive*
Goldberg, Stanley Irwin *real estate company executive*

Oakton
Brauer, Gwendolyn Gail *real estate broker*

Palmyra
Mulckhuyse, Jacob John *retired energy conservation consultant*

Reston
Van Putten, Mark *environmentalist*

Richmond
†Girone, Joan Christine Cruse *realtor, former county official*
Tuck, Grayson Edwin *real estate agent, former natural gas transmission executive*

Virginia Beach
†Divaris, Michael B. *real estate development company*
Gallagher, Vicki Smith *real estate agent*
Pefley, Charles Saunders *real estate broker*

WASHINGTON

Federal Way
McMichael, J(ack) Richard *real estate developer*

Friday Harbor
Padve, Martha Bertonneau *urban planning and arts consultant, fundraiser*

Marysville
Wright, Donna Marie *real estate company executive*

Oakville
†Magnus, Lennea D. *community development planner*

Redmond
Doman, Margaret Horn *government policy and process consultant, civic official*

Rollingbay
Morris, Donald Charles *real estate company executive*

Seattle
Dillard, Marilyn Dianne *property manager*
Ecklund, Ralph Earl *property manager*
Eskelin, John Thurston *city planner*
Sander, Susan Berry *environmental planning engineering corporation executive*
Sasaki, Tsutomu (Tom Sasaki) *real estate company executive, international trading company executive, consultant*
Wesley, Virginia Anne *real estate property manager*

Sequim
Jackson, Patrick Joseph *real estate company officer*

WEST VIRGINIA

Weirton
Diniaco, Gus G. *real estate appraiser*

WISCONSIN

Beaver Dam
Butterbrodt, John Ervin *real estate executive*
Manthe, Cora De Munck *real estate company executive*

Lake Mills
Lazaris, Pamela Adriane *community planning and development consultant*

Madison
Mullins, Jerome Joseph *real estate developer, consulting engineer*
Ring, Gerald J. *real estate developer, insurance executive*
Vandell, Kerry Dean *real estate and urban economics educator*

Milwaukee
Glazer, Gerald Sherwin *real estate broker*
Gondek, Mary Jane (Mary Jane Suchorski) *property manager*
Machulak, Edward Leon *real estate, mining and advertising company executive*

Pewaukee
Jasiorkowski, Robert Lee *real estate broker, computer consultant*

River Falls
Brown, Kevin James *researcher, consultant*

Wauwatosa
Franke, Brent Douglas *real estate/insurance executive*

CANADA

ALBERTA

Calgary
McEwen, Alexander Campbell *cadastral studies educator, former Canadian government official, land administration consultant*
Milavsky, Harold Phillip *real estate executive*

NOVA SCOTIA

Stellarton
Sobey, Donald Creighton Rae *real estate developer*

ONTARIO

Etobicoke
McIntyre, John George Wallace *real estate development and management consultant*

Newmarket
Wood, Neil Roderick *real estate development company executive*

Ottawa
Gordon, Steve *real estate executive*

Toronto
Arnell, Gordon Edwin *real estate development company executive*
Braithwaite, J. Lorne *real estate executive*
Carrothers, Gerald Arthur Patrick *environmental and city planning educator*
Dimma, William Andrew *real estate executive*

QUEBEC

Montreal
Gabbour, Iskandar *city and regional planning educator*

MEXICO

Garza Garcia
Gustafson, Eric William *real estate investor, wildlife habitat conservationist*

BULGARIA

Sofia
Exerowa, Dotchi Russeva *chemist, researcher*

CHINA

Hong Kong
†Kee, Lee Shau *real estate developer*

ENGLAND

London
Hall, Sir Peter Geoffrey *urban and regional planning educator*

GERMANY

Frankfurt
Hauck, Michael Georg *real estate company executive*

MONACO

Monte Carlo
Lovett, Laurence Dow *retired real estate and steamship executive*

SPAIN

Adeje
Grindley, Bruce Alan *real estate agency executive*

ADDRESS UNPUBLISHED

Allen, Linda Graves *real estate agent*
†Anderson, Amy Lee *realtor*
Andrews, Adelaide *real estate company executive*
Aulbach, George Louis *retired real estate company executive*
Austin, Grant William *real estate appraiser*
Baiman, Gail *real estate broker*
Barrett, Linda L. *real estate consultant*
Bartolini, Bruce Anthony *real estate executive*
Beal, Merrill David *conservationist, museum director*
Bergau, Frank Conrad *real estate, commercial and investment properties executive*
Berliner, Ruth Shirley *real estate company executive*
Bernhardt, Arthur Dieter *building industry executive and consultant*
†Berry, Mary Pat *real estate developer, consultant*
Bland, Eveline Mae *real estate broker, musician, music instructor*
Boeshe, Barbara Louise *real estate executive*
Branca, Frank Joseph *realtor, retired police officer*
Brock, Eric John *urban planner, historian, consultant*
Broek, Howard Windolph *real estate executive*
Brooks, Michael Paul *urban planning educator*
Browning, Vivian Berniece *land developer*
Carter, Judith Rockwell *real estate broker*
Chase, J. Vincent *shopping center executive, justice of the peace*
Chesler, Doris Adelle *real estate professional*
Clark, Philip Hart *retired urban and regional planner*
Cohen, Stanley Alvin *land use planner*
Corey, Kenneth Edward *urban planning and geography educator, researcher*
Corkran, Virginia B. *retired realtor*
Crawford, Susan Alice *realtor, artist*
Dahlberg, Burton Francis *real estate corporation executive*
Dasso, Jerome Joseph *real estate educator*
Davis, Mary Byrd *conservationist, researcher*
DeBock, Ronald Gene *real estate company executive*
Dickey, Robert Marvin (Rick Dickey) *property manager*
Economou-Pease, Bessie Carasoulas *city planner, consultant*
Edwards, Kathleen *real estate broker, former educator*
Elkin, Norman *urban planner*
Ellett, Alan Sidney *real estate development company executive*
Ellis, William Ben *environmental educator, retired utility executive*
Engels, Beatrice Ann *retired real estate company executive, poet, artist*
Estrin, Richard William *real estate broker, retired newspaper editor*
†Fetterly, Lynn Lawrence *real estate broker, developer*
Fino, Marie Georgette Keck *retired real estate broker*
Fischer, Michael Ludwig *environmental executive*
Fischer, Zoe Ann *real estate and property marketing company executive, consultant*
Fisk, Ian T. *economic development consultant, publishing executive*
Fournier, Walter Frank *real estate executive*
Fredericks, Patricia Ann *real estate executive*
Garling, Carol Elizabeth *real estate executive and developer*
Gasper, Ruth Eileen *real estate executive*
Gayle, Margot *preservationist, writer*
Gellman, Isaiah *environmental consultant*
Gilbert, Frederick E. *development planner, Africanist, consultant*
Godwin, Ralph Lee, Jr., *real estate executive*
Goldspiel, Arnold Nelson *real estate executive*
Goodman, Daniel Solomon *real estate broker, consultant*
Greenberg, Judith Ann *real estate developer*
Gutstein, Carol Feinhandler *realtor*
Hakala, Karen Louise *retired real estate administrator*
†Hedrich, Cleda Pollard *real estate broker, writer*
Holleb, Doris B. *urban planner, economist*
Hufschmidt, Maynard Michael *resources planning educator*
Hughes, Kenneth Martin *planner*
Johnson, Kay Durbahn *real estate manager, consultant*
Karakey, Sherry JoAnne *real estate company executive, interior designer*
Kremer, Honor Frances (Noreen Kremer) *real estate broker, small business owner*
Lamy, M(ary) Rebecca *consultant, land developer, government official*

†Law, Beth *environmental protection specialist*
Ledford, Janet Marie Smalley *real estate appraiser, consultant*
Lehman, Joan Alice *real estate executive*
Levine, Michael Joseph *economic development executive*
MacNeill, James William *international environment consultant*
Maguire, Robert Francis, III, *real estate investor*
Maier, Robert Henry *real estate executive*
Manakos, Froso P. *real estate executive*
Mann, Clarence Charles *real estate company official*
Maxwell, James L. *non-profit management executive*
McGowan, Keith Richard *environmental planner*
McManus, Joseph Warn *urban planner, architect*
McNeil, Edward Warren *real estate company executive*
Mercurio, Renard Michael *real estate corporation executive*
Meyer, Daniel Kramer *real estate executive*
Michalak, Craig Lance *real estate executive, consultant*
Miller, Esther Scobie Powers *appraiser, water colorist, gallery owner*
Mohamed, Joseph, Sr., *real estate broker, farmer*
Nederveld, Ruth Elizabeth *retired real estate executive*
O'Leary, Timothy Michael *real estate corporation officer*
Painter, Diana Jean *urban designer, artist, architectural historian*
Peck, Edwin Russell *retired real estate management executive*
†Pence, Jean Virginia *retired real estate broker*
†Pinnock, Monica D. *realtor, minister*
Potter, J. Stewart *property manager*
Powell, Kathleen Lynch *lawyer, real estate executive*
†Rassman, Joel H. *real estate company executive, accountant*
Ridloff, Richard *real estate investment advisor, lawyer, consultant*
Riss, Robert Bailey *real estate investor*
Rohe, William Michael *urban planning educator*
Rosenfeld, Mark Kenneth *real estate developer*
Ross, Beverley Long *real estate broker*
Roths, Beverly Owen *environmentalist*
Schneider, Rita Joyce *property management company executive, real estate broker, mortgage broker*
†Smith, Mary Louise *real estate broker*
Snook, Paul *real estate company executive*
Toshach, Clarice Oversby *real estate developer, former computer executive*
Trask, John Maurice, Jr., *property owner*
Trump, Donald John *real estate developer*
Voell, Richard Allen *retired private investor*
Walker, Helen Smith *retired real estate broker*
Wallace, Robert Carlson *real estate investor*
Weinberg, Paul Jay *real estate company officer*
Weiss, Scott Alan *commercial real estate consultant*
Welles, Virginia Chrisman *land use planner*
†Wheeler, Stephen Maxwell *urban planner, consultant*
†Williams, Phyllis Cutforth *retired realtor*
Wisehart, Arthur McKee *property management executive, lawyer*
Woods, Sandra Kay *real estate executive*

RELIGION

UNITED STATES

ALABAMA

Andalusia
Patterson, Edwin *minister*

Birmingham
Bains, David Ralph *religious studies educator*
†Bray, Gerald Lewis *minister, educator*
†Foley, David E. *bishop*
Hull, William Edward *theology educator*
Morrison, Gregg Scott *theology educator, college administrator*
Roby, Jasper *bishop*
Savage, Laura L. *ministry consultant, author, speaker*
†Scales, William Clinton, Sr., *minister, small business owner*
Zahl, Paul Francis Matthew *dean*

Camden
Lewis, Robert Henry *lay worker*

Cordova
Anthony, Yancey Lamar *minister*

Cullman
Lott, Roger Richard Stanley *priest*

Decatur
Cummins, David Loyal *mission director*

Greensboro
Massey, James Earl *clergyman, educator*

Mobile
Lipscomb, Oscar Hugh *archbishop*
†Taylor, Cecil Ray *religious studies educator, minister*
Zoghby, James Francis *priest*

Oneonta
Turner, Jeff Neal *minister*

Union Grove
Drew, Thomas Paul *chaplain*

ALASKA

Anchorage
†Charles, George P. *religious studies educator*
Fleming, Carolyn Elizabeth *religious organization administrator, interior designer*

ARIZONA

Duncan
Ouzts, Eugene Thomas *minister, secondary education educator*

Green Valley
Pike, George Harold, Jr., *religious organization executive, clergyman*

Hereford
†Seeland, Arthur David *bishop, psychotherapist*

Phoenix
†Kuzma, George Martin *retired bishop*

Scottsdale
Coutts, Lawrence Robert *publisher*
Kaufman, Jeffrey Allen *publisher*
Kilgore, L(eRoy) Wilson *minister*
Sapp, Donald Gene *retired minister*

Sun City
Hamilton, Ronald Ray *minister*
Lapsley, James Norvell, Jr., *minister, pastoral theology educator*
Randall, Claire *church executive*

Sun City West
Schmitz, Charles Edison *evangelist*

Tempe
Wentz, Richard Eugene *religious studies educator*

Tucson
Perret, Gary William *priest, educator*
†Wright, J. Edward *theology studies educator*

ARKANSAS

El Dorado
Lee, Vernon Roy *minister*

Gillett
Copley, Stephen Jean *minister*

Greenbrier
Reed, James David *retired minister, social worker*

Hot Springs Village
†Smith, Preston *minister*

Marion
Hughes, Michael Randolph *evangelist*

Russellville
†Morrow, Hubert W. *retired minister, retired theology studies educator, writer, educator*

Searcy
†Allen, Jimmy R. *religious studies educator*

Siloam Springs
Lewis, Cecil Dwain *minister*

Subiaco
†Pirrera, Aaron Charles *priest, headmaster*

CALIFORNIA

Acton
Butman, Harry Raymond *clergyman, writer*

Altadena
Willans, Jean Stone *bishop, religious organization executive*
Willans, Richard James *bishop, religious organization executive*

Angwin
Maxwell, Donald Malcolm *clergyman, religious educator*

Azusa
†Vest, R. Lamar *church administrator*

Bakersfield
†Frazier, Jo Frances *religious organization administrator*
Zarra, Ernest Joseph, III, *educator, researcher*

Berkeley
Gelpi, Donald Louis *theology studies educator*
Mudge, Lewis Seymour *theologian, educator, university dean*
Welch, Claude (Claude Raymond Welch) *theology educator*

Big Sur
†Wong, Joseph H. *religious organization administrator, theology studies educator*

Burbank
Bower, Richard James *minister*

Camarillo
†Ford, Paul Francis *theology studies educator, musician*

Canoga Park
Dickey, Gary Alan *minister*

Castro Valley
Morrison, Glenn Leslie *minister*

Claremont
†Genung, Dan Baldwin *minister, writer*
Reynolds, Margaret Ann *minister, educator*
Sanders, James Alvin *minister, religious studies educator*
Tengbom, Luverne Charles *retired religion educator*

Clovis
†Smith, William Clarke *clergyman*

Concord
Jones, Gerald Edward *religion educator*

Costa Mesa
Williams, William Corey *theology educator, consultant*

Del Mar
Randall, Chandler Corydon *church rector*

Duarte
†Buckley, Cornelius Michael *priest, educator, chaplain*
Driskill, James Lawrence *minister*
Probst, John Elwin *chaplain, minister*

El Cerrito
†Maxwell, John E. *priest, educator*

El Segundo
Rozman, James D. *military chaplain*

El Sobrante
White, Nelson Henry *writer, publisher, realtor*

Elk Grove
Vang, Timothy Teng *religious organization administrator*

Escondido
†Baugh, Steven Michael *theology studies educator*
Linzey, Verna May *minister, writer*

Etna
Auxentios, *clergyman*

Fountain Valley
Einstein, Stephen Jan *rabbi*

Fresno
Steinbock, John Thomas *bishop*
Xiong, Tousu Saydangnmvang *minister*

Garden Grove
†Schuller, Robert Harold *minister, writer*

Happy Camp
Black, Barbara Ann *publisher*

Irvine
Rachlis, Arnold Israel *rabbi, religion educator*
Regener, Connie Sue *minister, religious commentator*
Reisman, Richard S. *publisher*

La Jolla
Freedman, David Noel *religious studies educator*
Waddy, Lawrence Heber *religious writer*

La Mirada
†Rhee, Victor Sung-yul *theology studies educator, minister*

Laguna Hills
Wheatley, Melvin Ernest, Jr., *retired bishop*

Livermore
Christopher, Steven Lee *religious studies educator*

Loma Linda
†Lewis, Victor Wayne, I, *minister*

Long Beach
Lowentrout, Peter Murray *religious studies educator*

Los Alamitos
Booth, John Nicholls *minister, writer, photographer*

Los Angeles
Arzube, Juan Alfredo *bishop*
Berenbaum, Michael Gary *theology educator*
Borsch, Frederick Houk *bishop*
Boyd, Malcolm *minister, writer*
Breuer, Stephen Ernest *religious organization administrator*
†Chedid, John G. *retired bishop*
Crossley, John Parshley, Jr., *religous studies educator, researcher, consultant*
Daya Mata, Sri (Faye Wright) *clergywoman*
Fitzgerald, Tikhon (Lee R. H. Fitzgerald) *bishop*
Freehling, Allen Isaac *rabbi*
Hudson, Christopher John *publisher*
Knight, Henry L. *minister*
Mahony, Roger Michael *archbishop*
Mc Pherson, Rolf Kennedy *clergyman, religious organization administrator*
Milligan, Sister Mary *theology educator, religious consultant*
O'Connor, Kevin Thomas *religious organization administrator*
†Ogilvie, Lloyd John *clergyman*
Raymond, Wilfred J. *priest, educator*
Williams, Ronald Dean *minister, religious organization administrator*

Los Gatos
Frugoli, Anthony Francis *priest, educator*

Malibu
†Flynn, Carl Frederick *religious studies educator*

Mill Valley
Crews, William Odell, Jr., *religious organization administrator*

Modesto
Blair, Jimmy *minister, educator*

Monterey Park
Szeto, Paul (Cheuk-Ching Szeto) *religious mission executive*

Mountain View
Ching, Andy Kwok-yee *minister*

Newhall
†Halstead, Thomas A. *theology studies educator*

Oakland
Jakubowsky, Frank Raymond *religious writer*
Patten, Bebe Harrison *minister, chancellor*

Orange
Brown, Tod David *bishop*
Mc Farland, Norman Francis *bishop*

Palm Desert
Cedar, Paul Arnold *church executive, minister*
Dugan, Robert Perry, Jr., *retired minister, religious organization administrator*
Ponder, Catherine *clergywoman, author*
Stenhouse, Everett Ray *clergy administrator*

Palm Springs
Jones, Milton Wakefield *publisher*
Rupracht, William George *chaplain*

Palo Alto
Forbes, Alfred Dean *religious studies researcher*

Palos Verdes Peninsula
Cubillos, Robert Hernan *church administrator, philosophy educator*

Pasadena
Shuster, Marguerite *minister, educator*

Petaluma
Stubblefield, Jerry Mason *religious educator, minister*

Pittsburg
Schmalenberger, Jerry Lew *pastor, religious studies educator*

Pixley
†Golden, Raymond Lee *retired theology studies educator, retired minister*

Portola Valley
Garsh, Thomas Burton *publisher*

Redding
Nicholas, David Robert *minister, college president*

Reedley
Dick, Henry Henry *minister*

Richmond
Kirk-Duggan, Cheryl Ann *religious studies educator*

Sacramento
Cole, Glen David *minister*
Quinn, Francis A. *bishop*

San Bernardino
Burgess, Mary Alice (Mary Alice Wickizer) *publisher*

San Diego
Bauer, Judy Marie *minister*
†Brom, Robert H. *bishop*
Cabrera, Quincy Rodolfo *minister, educator*
Downing, David Charles *retired minister*
Fleischmann, Paul *religious organization administrator, minister*
Hunt, Barnabas John *priest, religious organization administrator*
Jenson, Ronald Allen *religious executive, educator*
Plovanich, Patricia Ann *theologian, educator*

San Francisco
Brickner, David *religious organization administrator, consultant*
DuBose, Francis Marquis *clergyman*
†Forsberg, C. Robert *retired minister, editor*
Godfrey, Donal Charles *priest*
Grohe, Linda Squires *dean*
Kelly, James Anthony *priest*
Kendall, Robert Daniel *priest, theology educator*
†Levada, William Joseph *archbishop*
Reed, Robert Daniel *publisher*
Rosen, Moishe *religious organization founder*
Sawyer, Frank Denzil *clergyman*

San Jose
Es-Haq, Fereidoun *minister, marriage and family therapist*

San Juan Bautista
Fort, Robert Bradley *minister*

San Juan Capistrano
†Ogden, Maurice B. *retired minister, writer*

San Rafael
Trepp, Leo *rabbi*

Santa Barbara
†Albanese, Catherine *religious studies educator*
Campbell, Robert Charles *minister, theology educator*
†Friedland, Roger *religious studies educator, writer*

Gillquist, Peter Edward *church organization executive*
†O'Jack, Justin *religious studies educator, researcher*

Santa Clara
†Tollini, Frederick Paul *priest, theater educator*

Santa Monica
Renetzky, Alvin *publisher*

Santa Rosa
Walsh, Daniel Francis *bishop*

Santee
Morris, Henry Madison, III, *minister, speaker, writer, consultant*

Solana Beach
Friedman, Maurice Stanley *religious educator*

Sonora
Chandler, E(dwin) Russell *clergyman, writer*
Jones, Georgia Ann *publisher*

Stockton
Mathre, Lawrence Gerhard *minister, federal agency administrator*

Temple City
Perkins, Floyd Jerry *retired theology educator*

Thousand Oaks
Hudson, Barbara *religious writer, actor*

Tulare
Cooke, William Robert *minister, mayor*

Turlock
Stensether, John Eldon *minister*

Union City
Velarde, Heide Marie *publisher, writer, lyricist*

Upland
Jordan, Charles Wesley *retired bishop*

Vallejo
McGowan, Thomas Randolph *retired religious organization executive*

Walnut Creek
Davis, Ron Lee *clergyman, author*

West Hollywood
Perry, Troy D. *clergyman, religious organization administrator*

Whittier
†Price, Joseph Llewellyn *religious educator*

Yucaipa
Horn, Paul Ervin *minister*

COLORADO

Arvada
†Howard, Barry Christopher *minister*
Pettit, Claud Martin *religious organization administrator*

Aurora
Nichols, Clyde Richard *clergyman, company executive*
Stifel, Frederick Benton *pastor, biochemist, nutritionist*

Buena Vista
Goddard, Hazel Bryan *religious organization administrator*

Canon City
Williamson, Edward Henry *chaplain, army officer*

Colorado Springs
†Eyman, Roger Allen *minister*
Freeman, J. P. Ladyhawk *vicar, underwater exploration, security and transportation executive, educator, fashion model, legislative advocate*
†Hanifen, Richard Charles *retired bishop*
†Harmon, Jeanne Ann *writer*
†Johnson, Henry Fred *clergy*
Loux, Gordon Dale *company executive*
Pickle, Joseph Wesley, Jr., *religious studies educator*

Denver
Bramwell, Bevil Robert *theology studies educator, priest*
Brownlee, Judith Marilyn *priestess, psychotherapist, psychic*
†Chaput, Charles J. *archbishop*
Lewallen, Elinor Kirby *religious organization executive, lay church worker*
Meeks, Mark Anthony *minister*
Sheeran, Michael John Leo *priest, college administrator*

Dillon
Follett, Robert John Richard *publisher*

Fort Collins
Chorpenning, H. R., III, *minister*
Rolston, Holmes, III, *theologian, educator, philosopher*

Greeley
Van Gorp, Gary Wayne *clergyman*

Lafayette
Short, Ray Everett *minister, sociology educator emeritus, author, lecturer*

Lakewood
Barger, Louise Baldwin *religious organization administrator*
Hickman, Ruth Virginia *Bible educator*

Littleton
Estep, John Hayes *religious organization administrator, clergyman*

Northglenn
Winter, William Paul, Jr., *ministry director*

Westcliffe
Jones, Daniel Edwin, Jr., *bishop*

Wheat Ridge
Wilcox, Mary Marks *retired Christian education consultant, educator*

CONNECTICUT

Bethany
Childs, Brevard Springs *religious educator*

Bridgeport
Black, Hillel Moses *publisher*
Byrd, Charles Everett *clergyman*
Lori, William E. *bishop*

East Hartford
Henry, Paul Eugene, Jr., *minister*
Scholsky, Martin Joseph *priest*

Greenwich
Johnson, Herbert Michael *publisher*
Moore, John Plunkett Dennis *publisher*

Hamden
Dittes, James Edward *psychology of religion educator*
Forman, Charles William *religious studies educator*

Hartford
†Cronin, Daniel Anthony *archbishop*
†Markham, Ian Stephen *theology studies educator, dean*
Winter, Miriam Therese (Gloria Frances Winter) *nun, religious education educator*

Kent
White, Roger Bradley *priest*

Lyme
Bessie, Simon Michael *publisher*

Middletown
Crites, Stephen Decatur *religion educator*
†Hoffmann, Leonard A *church administrator, director*
†McAlister, Elizabeth *religious studies educator*
Rockwood, Irving E., Jr., *publisher*

Monroe
Davis, Bobby J. *pastor, family therapist*

New Haven
†Bhayro, Siam *religious studies educator*
Malherbe, Abraham Johannes, VI, *religion educator, writer*
Meeks, Wayne A. *religious studies educator*
Weinstein, Stanley *Buddhist studies educator*
Wilson, Robert Rutherford *religious studies educator*

Newtown
Wismar, Gregory Just *minister*

North Haven
Hudson, Richard L. *retired educator, clergyman*

Norwich
Cote, Michael Richard *bishop*
Hart, Daniel Anthony *bishop*

Plantsville
Roy, Ralph Lord *clergyman*

Ridgefield
Davie, Malcolm Henderson *city official*

Shelton
Wham, William Neil *publisher*

Southbury
†Normann, Margaret Ella *deacon, educator*

Stamford
†Lennick, Robert Brent *rabbi*

Torrington
Drobena, Thomas John *minister, educator*

Trumbull
†Linck, Joseph Charles *priest*

Westport
Davis, Joel *publisher*

Wilton
Steinfeld, Thomas Albert *publisher*

Woodstock Valley
Allaby, Stanley Reynolds *clergyman*

DELAWARE

Dover
Deuble, Lottie Edwards *lay worker*

Wilmington
Gewirtz, Leonard Benjamin *rabbi*
Linderman, Jeanne Herron *priest*
†Saltarelli, Michael A. *priest*

DISTRICT OF COLUMBIA

Washington
Allen, William Jere *minister*
Apostolos-Cappadona, Diane Pan *religion and art educator*
Baxter, Nathan Dwight *dean*
Beltz, William Albert *publisher*
Burke, John *priest*
Cole, Basil B. *priest, religious studies educator*
Di Lella, Alexander Anthony *biblical studies educator*
Donders, Joseph Gerard *priest*
Dunn, James Milton *religious organization administrator*
Dunton, James Raynor *publisher*
Farrelly, Mark John *retired theologian, priest*
Fay, William Patrick *church administrator*
Fitzmyer, Joseph Augustine *theology educator, priest*
Godsey, John Drew *minister, theology educator emeritus*
Hayden, John Carleton *priest, history educator*
Hickey, James Aloysius Cardinal *emeritus archbishop*
Hug, James Edwin *religious organization executive*
†Irwin, Paul Garfield *minister, social services executive*
Kane, Annette Pieslak *religious organization executive*
Maldonado, F. César *priest, educator*
Marshall, Ann Louise *pastoral counselor*
McCarrick, Theodore Edgar Cardinal *archbishop*
†McCrabb, Donald Raymond *pastoral field educator*
†Moore, Matthew David *religious studies educator*
Novak, Michael (Michael John Novak) *religion educator, author, editor*
O'Brien, Edwin Frederick *archbishop*
Payne, Steven Lawrence *priest*
Pitts, Tyrone S. *reverend*
Rabinowitz, Stanley Samuel *rabbi*
Romig, Edgar Dutcher *clergyman*
Roque, Francis Xavier *auxiliary bishop*
Ross, Robinette Davis *publisher*
Rowson, Richard Cavanagh *publisher*
Saperstein, Marc Eli *theology studies educator, rabbi*
Sokolowski, Robert S. *priest, educator*
†Sullivan, John Fox *publisher*
Trisco, Robert Frederick *church historian, educator*
Wiseman, James Anthony *theology studies educator*
Wogaman, John Philip *retired minister*

FLORIDA

Boca Raton
Agler, Richard Dean *rabbi*
Eisenberg, Robin Ledgin *religious education administrator*
Laine, Iris Ruth *minister, public relations/advertising executive*
Singer, Merle Elliot *rabbi*

Boynton Beach
Gill, Milton Randall *minister, artist*

Carrollwood
O'Keefe, Fredrick Rea *bishop, consultant, educator, writer*

Coral Gables
Fitzgerald, John Thomas, Jr., *religious studies educator*
†Omer-Sherman, Ranen E *religious studies educator, researcher*

Crawfordville
†Brumby, James Remley, III, (Knox Brumby) *retired priest*

Daytona Beach
Bronson, Oswald Perry, Sr., *religious organization administrator, clergyman*

Delray Beach
Wells, Mary Elizabeth Thompson *minister*

Fort Lauderdale
Beatty, Robert Clinton *religious studies educator*
Eynon, Steven Scott *minister*

Fort Myers
Griffin, Jerry J. *chaplain*
Massa, Conrad Harry *religious studies educator*

Holiday
Swatos, William Henry, Jr., *priest, sociologist*

Hollywood
Fell, Frederick Victor *publisher*

Holmes Beach
Evanofski, Bernard Peter *Roman Catholic priest*

Jacksonville
†Gaston, Joseph *minister, educator*
Holliday, Patricia Ruth McKenzie *evangelist*
†Mueller, Cherone *religious organization administrator, writer, minister*
Taylor, Robert M. *minister*
Zbiegien, M. Andrea *chaplain, religious education educator, consultant, educational administrator*

Lakeland
Willoughby, Robert Earl *minister, writer*

Longwood
Dalles, John Allan *minister*

Melbourne
Krieger, Robert Edward *publisher.*

Miami
†Gray, Frances Boone *minister*
†Northup, Lesley Armstrong *religious studies educator, priest*
Patterson, Rickey Lee *clergyman*
Weeks, Marta Joan *retired priest*
†Wenski, Thomas Gerard *bishop*

Miami Beach
Lehrman, Irving *rabbi*

Miami Shores
†Favalora, John Clement *bishop*

Milton
Melvin, Hiram Joseph *religious organization administrator, minister*

Naples
Salt, Alfred Lewis *priest*

Ocala
Kofink, Wayne Alan *minister*

Orange Park
Bartholomew, John Niles *retired church administrator*

Orlando
O'Farrell, Mark Theodore *religious organization administrator*

Pace
Stoudenmire, William Ward *minister*

Palm Beach Gardens
McCall, Duke Kimbrough *clergyman*

Palm Harbor
Fischer, John Jules *clergy member, theology educator, writer*

Penney Farms
†Muilenburg, John Powell *minister*

Pensacola
Cox, Amie C. *publisher*
†Mountcastle, William Wallace, Jr., *philosophy and religion educator*
†Ricard, John H. *bishop, educator*

Pompano Beach
Corsello, Lily Joann *minister, counselor, educator*

Saint Augustine
McCarty, Doran Chester *religious organization administrator*
Rice, David Preston *minister, educator*

Sarasota
Hackl, Alphons J. *publisher*
Hilt, Thomas Harry *minister*
Jones, Tracey Kirk, Jr., *minister, educator*
Larsen, Lawrence Bernard, Jr., *priest, pastoral psychotherapist*
McFarlin, Diane Hooten *publisher*

Sunrise
Thompson, Yaakov *rabbi*

Tallahassee
McBride, Donna Jannean *publisher*

Tarpon Springs
Pittman, Roy Clinton, Jr., *neurosurgeon, lawyer, theologian, philosopher*

Titusville
†Rodney, Gifford Michael *minister, writer*

Venice
†Nevins, John J. *bishop*

Vero Beach
Beran, Denis Carl *publisher*

West Palm Beach
Johnson, Martin Allen *publisher*
Nelms, Lewis Caldwell *minister*
Nolan, Richard Thomas *clergyman, educator*
Westman, Steven Ronald *rabbi*

Winter Haven
Lindsey, Jane Willann *minister*

Yalaha
Searcy, Dorothy James *missionary*

GEORGIA

Albany
†Revills, Isaiah *minister*

Alpharetta
†McCullar, Michael D. *pastor*

Americus
Gonzalez, George G. *priest, pastor*

Athens
†Spears, Louise Elizabeth *minister, secondary school educator*

Atlanta
Coleman, David Michael *religious organization executive*
†Donoghue, John Francis *archbishop*
Holladay, Carl R. *New Testament educator*
†Patton, Laurie Louise *religious studies educator, writer*
Skillrud, Harold Clayton *minister, retired bishop*

Melbourne (continued)
Stanley, Ronnie L., Jr., *theology educator, college dean, clergyman*
Westerhoff, John Henry, III, *clergyman, theologian, educator*

Augusta
MacLeod, James L. *minister, finance company executive, art gallery owner*

Conyers
Telnack, Methodius Richard *priest, monk, craftsman*

Dacula
Murphree, Harold T. *retired minister*

Dahlonega
Newman, Thomas Daniel *minister, school administrator*

Decatur
Gary, Julia Thomas *retired minister*
Hagood, Thomas Richard, Jr., *minister, publisher*
Hale, Cynthia Lynette *religious organization administrator*
Morris, Robert Renly *minister, clinical pastoral education supervisor*

Ellenwood
Pack, Bobigene *minister, writer*

Jonesboro
Dawson, Lewis Edward *minister, retired military officer*

Lagrange
†Cook, John Granger *religious studies educator, philosopher, educator*

Lawrenceville
Gericke, Paul William *minister, educator*

Macon
Franklin, Roosevelt *minister*
Staton, Cecil Pope, Jr., *religious and academic publisher, educator*

Metter
Guido, Michael Anthony *evangelist*

Norcross
Granger, Philip Richard *minister*

Riverdale
Waters, John W. *minister, educator*

Savannah
†Boland, John Kevin *bishop*
Webb, James Calvin *minister*

Stone Mountain
†Adair, James Robert Jr., Jr., *religious studies educator*
†Burklin, Frederick O. *minister, educator*

Sylvania
Martin, Charles Wade *pastor*

Valdosta
Robertson, Dale Wayne *minister*

Woodstock
Collins, David Browning *religious institution administrator*

HAWAII

Honolulu
Merrifield, Donald Paul *hispanic ministries coordinator*

Kihei
†Palusky, Alice *missionary, educator*

Pearl City
Scott, David Irvin *minister*

Waianae
Hiapo, Patricia Kamaka *lay worker*

IDAHO

Boise
Lawrence, Ralph A. *minister*

Jerome
Feiss, Hugh Bernard *priest, religious educator*

Nampa
Bowers, Curtis Ray, Jr., *chaplain*

Priest River
Booker, Bruce Robert *rabbi*

ILLINOIS

Addieville
Utke, Robert Ahrens *minister*

Bartlett
Robinson, Jack Fay *clergyman*

Belleville
†Gregory, Wilton D. *bishop*
Kramer, Andrew Joseph *clergyman*
Studer, Louis *priest, religious organization administrator*
Wittenbrink, Boniface Leo *priest*

Bensenville
Matera, Richard Ernest *retired minister*

Buffalo Grove
Dimond, Robert Edward *publisher*

Calumet City
†De Loera, David F. *religious studies educator*

Carol Stream
Myra, Harold Lawrence *publisher*

Chicago
Almen, Lowell Gordon *church official*
†Anderson, Philip Vernon *retired pastor*
Barbour, Claude Marie *minister, educator*
Baumhart, Raymond Charles *Roman Catholic church administrator*
Betz, Hans Dieter *theology educator*
Bevans, Stephen Bennett *priest, educator*
Black, Robert Durward *ecumenical television producer*
Browning, Don Spencer *religious educator*
†Bumbaugh, David Edward *religious studies educator, minister*
†Butler, Colette M. *minister*
Chriszt, Dennis Francis *priest*
Doniger, Wendy *history of religions educator*
George, Francis *archbishop*
James, Marie Moody *clergywoman, musician, vocal music educator*
Jegen, Sister Carol Frances *religion educator*
†Kobler, John F. *priest, researcher*
Lathon, Sheraine *clergyman*
†Lotocky, Innocent Hilarius *bishop*
Marshall, Cody *bishop*
Martin, Dennis Dale *religious studies educator*
McDonald, Theresa Beatrice Pierce (Mrs. Ollie McDonald) *church official, minister*
McGinn, Bernard John *religious educator*
Overbeck, Thomas Jerome *university liturgist, consultant*
†Poethig, Eunice Blanchard *clergywoman*
Rodriguez, David Gonzalez, Jr., *priest, art and religion educator*
Shafer, Eric Christopher *minister*
Simon, Mordecai *religious association administrator, clergyman*
Snyder, Graydon F. *religion educator*
Szarek, Gene *religious studies educator*
Walter, Charles Sebastian *Roman Catholic priest*
Whelan, Winifred Olwyn *theology studies educator*
Williamson, Thomas Michael *pastor, civil servant*
†Wilson, George Edward *religious organization administrator, minister*
Yu, Anthony C. *religion and literature educator*

Darien
Russell, John Fintan *theology educator, editor*

Decatur
†Mittal, Sushil *religious studies educator*

Deerfield
Becker, Gerald Arthur *publisher*
Larsen, David Leonard *retired religion educator*
†Lunde, Jonathan M. *religious studies educator*
Schnabel, Eckhard Johannes *theologian, educator*

Elk Grove Village
Stein, David Timothy *minister*

Flossmoor
Santos, Andrew J., III, *priest*

Fulton
Bomgarden, Stanley Ralph *minister*

Glenview
Braun, Eunice Hockspeier *religious order executive, author, lecturer*

Highland Park
Cohodes, Eli Aaron *publisher*
Einisman, Myron Sachar *publisher*

Itasca
Constant, Anita Aurelia *publisher*

Joliet
†Imesch, Joseph Leopold *bishop*
Kaffer, Roger Louis *bishop*

Kenilworth
Bowen, Gilbert Willard *minister*

Libertyville
Schroeder, W(illiam) Widick *religion educator*

Lincoln
Wilson, Robert Allen *religion educator*

Lisle
†Lorenz, Matthias E. *priest, consultant*

Loves Park
†Schlub, Teresa Rae *minister*

Moline
Johnson, Mary Lou *lay worker, educator*

Naperville
Landwehr, Arthur John *minister*

Niles
Grace, John Joseph *retired priest*

Oak Lawn
Wright, Steven Randall *minister*

Oak Park
Cary, William Sterling *retired church executive*
Gambro, John M. *priest, secondary school educator*
Gerson, Gary Stanford *rabbi*
Thomas, Malayilmelathethil *minister, English language educator*

Saint Michaels
Berlin, Donald Robert *rabbi*

Silver Spring
Beach, Bert Beverly *clergyman*
†Cathey, Mary Ellen Jackson *religious studies educator*
†Chery, Reginald *minister*
Herbers, Tod Arthur *publisher*
Hunt, Mary Elizabeth *religious studies educator*
Marvin, John George *clergyman, church organization executive*
O'Meara, Noel P. *priest, religious organization administrator*
†Paulsen, Jan *clergyman, church administrator*
Thompson, George Ralph *church administrator*

MASSACHUSETTS

Amherst
Wilcox, Bruce Gordon *publisher*
Wills, David Wood *minister, educator*

Auburn
Bachelder, Robert Stephen *minister*

Berlin
Lohr, Harold Russell *retired bishop*

Boston
Bard, Terry Ross *rabbi, psychologist, educator*
†Harris, Virginia Sydness *religious studies educator*
Katz, Steven Theodore *religious studies educator*
Kessler, Diane Cooksey *religious organization administrator, minister*
Kopaczynski, Germain *priest*
Korff, Y. A. *grand rabbi*
Mason, Herbert Warren, Jr., *religion and history educator, author*
Polak, Joseph A. *rabbi, judge*
Rouner, Leroy Stephens *religious studies educator, philosophy educator*
Shaw, M. Thomas, III, *bishop*
Williams, Rhys *minister*
Worthley, Harold Field *minister, educator*

Brockton
Lightford, Melvin *minister*

Brookline
†Samra, Nicholas James *bishop*
†Skeete, Helen Watkins *minister, counselor*

Cambridge
†Aitken, Ellen Bradshaw *religious studies educator*
Clifford, Richard John *religious studies educator*
Das, Lama Surya *theology studies educator*
Edington, Mark David Wheeler *clergyman, educational administrator*
Fiorenza, Francis P. *religion educator*
†Gomes, Peter John *clergyman, educator*
Graham, William Albert *religion educator, history educator*
Horn, Henry Eyster *retired minister*
Kaufman, Gordon Dester *theology educator*
Koester, Helmut Heinrich *theologian, educator*
Picardi, Gerard A. *publisher*
Schuessler Fiorenza, Elisabeth *theology educator*
Williams, Preston Noah *theology educator*

Chelsea
†Barclay, Peter Roy *minister, counselor*

Chestnut Hill
Helmick, Raymond Glen *priest, educator*
Mc Innes, William Charles *priest, academic administrator*
Schatkin, Margaret Amy *theology educator*

Dedham
Janson, Barbara Jean *publisher*

Dorchester
†Boles, John P. *bishop*

Haverhill
Korinow, Ira Lee *rabbi*

Lexington
Jaffe, Howard Lawrence *rabbi*

Ludlow
Tetherly, Jonathan Collieson *chaplain, educator*

Mashpee
Payne, Paula Marie *minister*

Medford
O'Leary, David Michael *priest, educator*

Methuen
McNaughton, William John *retired bishop*

New Bedford
Kellaway, Richard Allen *minister, art association administrator, coordinator*

Newton
Sullivan, Francis Alfred *priest, educator*
Tannenwald, Leslie Keiter *rabbi, justice of peace, educational administrator, chaplain*

Northampton
Derr, Thomas Sieger *religion educator*
Donfried, Karl Paul *minister, theology educator*

Plainfield
Reynolds, Frank Everett *religious studies educator*

Randolph
Whitaker, Arthur Luther *retired minister, psychologist*

South Boston
Clancy, Richard Francis *priest*

South Hamilton
†Ciampa, Roy Emilius *religious studies educator*

Sudbury
Deutsch, Judith *clergywoman*

Waltham
Delaney, Mary Anne *retired theology studies educator*
Reisman, Bernard *theology educator*

Watertown
Regan, Thomas Joseph *priest, educator*

Wellesley
†Hobbs, Edward Craig *religious studies educator*

Weston
Barry, William Anthony *priest, writer*
Oelgeschlager, Guenther Karl *publisher*

Westwood
Bier, Louis Henry Gustav *minister*

Williamstown
Eusden, John Dykstra *theology educator, minister*

Worcester
Beaulieu, Peter Raymond *priest*
†Clark, William Anthony *religious studies educator*
Covino, Paul Francis Xavier *religious executive, college chaplain, consultant*
Parsons, Edwin Spencer *clergyman, educator*
Reilly, Daniel Patrick *bishop*
Scanlon, Peter Joseph *priest*
Uhl, Christopher Martin *lawyer*

MICHIGAN

Ann Arbor
†Phifer, Kenneth W. *minister*

Berrien Springs
†Moskala, Jiri *religious studies educator*

Bloomfield Hills
Syme, Daniel Bailey *rabbi, institution executive*

Burton
Meissner, Suzanne Banks *pastoral associate*

Clarkston
Keough, James Gillman, Jr., *minister*

Dearborn
Hess, Margaret Johnston *religious writer, educator*

Detroit
†Anderson, Moses B. *bishop*
Boyea, Earl Alfred *bishop*
Dister, John E. *religious organization administrator*
†Fastiggi, Robert L. *religious studies educator*
†Maida, Adam Joseph Cardinal *archbishop*
Mc Gehee, H(arry) Coleman, Jr., *bishop*
Silverman, Mark *publisher*
†Trapp, Daniel John *priest*
Vigneron, Allen Henry *theology educator, rector, auxiliary bishop*

Farmington
Penberthy, Stanley Josiah, Jr., *publisher*
Wine, Sherwin Theodore *rabbi*

Farmington Hills
Plaut, Jonathan Victor *rabbi*

Flint
†Bonner, Darlene E. *minister, writer*

Gaylord
†Cooney, Patrick Ronald *bishop*

Grand Rapids
Barnes, Rosemary Lois *minister*
Beals, Paul Archer *religious studies educator*
DeVries, Robert K. *religious book publisher*
Schwanda, Tom *religious studies educator*

Hastings
Wright, Stephen Nathan *religious organization administrator*

Holland
Cook, James Ivan *clergyman, religion educator*
Van Voorst, Robert E. *theology educator, minister*

Jackson
Popp, Nathaniel *archbishop*

Johannesburg
Kropf, Richard William *priest, theologian*

Kalamazoo
Badra, Robert George *theology studies educator, humanities educator*

Livonia
Gepford, William George *minister*
Haggard, Joan Claire *church musician, piano instructor, accompanist, adjudicator*

Marquette
Burt, John Harris *bishop*

Midland
Clarkson, William Morris *children's pastor*

Northville
Davis, Lawrence Edward *church official*

Port Huron
Hoffacker, Charles Edward *minister, writer*

Portage
Lee, Edward L. *retired bishop*

Rochester Hills
†Stevenson, Gregory Matthew *religious studies educator*

Roscommon
Mainprize, Donald Charles *minister, writer*

Southfield
Ibrahim, Ibrahim N. *bishop*
Willingham, Edward Bacon, Jr., *ecumenical minister, administrator*

Spring Arbor
Thompson, Stanley B. *church administrator*

Taylor
†Drutchas, Geoffrey Gilbert *minister, historian, writer*

Whitehall
Sirotko, Theodore Francis *priest, retired military officer*

Ypsilanti
O'Connor, Bernard Joseph *priest*

MINNESOTA

Alexandria
Hultstrand, Donald Maynard *bishop*

Austin
Alcorn, Wallace Arthur *minister, writer*
Morgan, Robert Ashton *minister, ethics and world religions educator*

Bloomington
Brokke, Catherine Juliet *mission executive*
McDill, Thomas Allison *minister*

Collegeville
†Rolfson, Helen C. *theology studies educator, translator*
†Wolfe, Regina Wentzel *religious studies educator*

Cottage Grove
Hudnut, Robert Kilborne *clergyman, author*

Crookston
†Balke, Victor H. *bishop*

Edina
Brown, Laurence David *retired bishop*
Putnam, Frederick Warren, Jr., *bishop*

Ely
Swenson, L. Anne *publisher*

Excelsior
Fenske, Jerald Allan *minister*
Parker, Robert Chauncey Humphrey *clergyman, publishing executive, psychic*

Fergus Falls
Overgaard, Robert Milton *retired religious organization administrator*

Inver Grove Heights
Koenig, Robert August *clergyman, educator*

Lake Elmo
Schultz, Clarence John *minister*

Mankato
Orvick, George Myron *church denomination executive, minister*
†Purscell, Keith William *minister*

Maple Grove
†Alexander, Donald L. *theologian, educator, minister*

Minneapolis
†Battle, Willa Lee Grant *clergywoman, educational administrator*
Bormaster, Lisa Kay *publisher*
Dyrud, Amos Oliver *minister, educator*
Graham, William Franklin (William Franklin Graham) *evangelist*
Hamel, William John *church administrator, minister*
Klemp, Harold *minister, writer*
Miller, William Alvin *clergyman, author, lecturer*
Moraczewski, Robert Leo *publisher*
Soderquist, Ronald Bruce *minister, ministry consultant*

Moorhead
Jacobson, Arland Dean *religion educator*

Northfield
Crouter, Richard Earl *religion educator*
Swanson, Stephen Olney *minister, retired English educator*

Oakdale
Be Vier, William A. *religious studies educator*

Rosemount
Aadland, Thomas Vernon *minister*

Roseville
McMillan, Mary Bigelow *retired minister, volunteer*

Saint Paul
†Caneday, Ardel Bruce *religious studies educator, writer*
†Flynn, Harry Joseph *bishop*
†Haemig, Mary Jane *religious studies educator*
Hopper, David Henry *religion educator*
Jaberg, Eugene Carl *theology educator, administrator*
Mullin, James Albert *executive*

Woodbury
Woodruff, Ellen Louise *chaplain*

MISSISSIPPI

Biloxi
Howze, Joseph Lawson Edward *retired bishop*

Clinton
Hensley, John Clark *religious organization administrator, minister*

Florence
Anding, Robert Eugene *retired religion educator, minister*

Hattiesburg
Wood, Forrest E., Jr., *philosophy and religion educator*

Indianola
Matthews, David *clergyman*

Jackson
Duncan, Jennings Ligon, III, *minister*
Gordon, Granville Hollis *church official*
Gray, Duncan Montgomery, Jr., *retired bishop*
Larsen, Samuel Harry *minister, educator*
McKnight, William Edwin *minister*
Yates, Steven Bradley *publisher*

Minter City
Mitchell, Patsy Malier *religious school founder and administrator*

MISSOURI

Ballwin
Ackerson, Charles Stanley *minister, social worker*

Bridgeton
Asma, Lawrence Francis *priest*

Cameron
Rose-Heim, William Bentley *minister, mediator, business owner, entrepreneur*

Charleston
Wallhausen, Mildred Carolyn *publisher*

Dittmer
Miller, Bertin *priest, social administrator*

Excelsior Springs
Mitchell, Earl Wesley *clergyman*

Fayette
Davis, H(umphrey) Denny *publisher*
Keeling, Joe Keith *religion educator, college official and dean*

Florissant
Stormer, John Anthony *minister emeritus, author, publisher*

Hazelwood
Rose, Joseph Hugh *clergyman*
Urshan, Nathaniel Andrew *minister, church administrator*

Highlandville
Pruter, Karl Hugo *bishop*

Independence
Bryan, Kay Marie *minister*
Lindgren, A(lan) Bruce *church administrator*
Tyree, Alan Dean *clergyman*

Jefferson City
King, Robert Henry *minister, church denomination executive, former educator*

Joplin
Butler, Paul Thurman *retired religious studies educator*
Minor, Ronald Ray *minister*
Wilson, Aaron Martin *religious studies educator, college executive*

Kansas City
Adams, Charles Geoffrey *minister, educator*
Cunningham, Paul George *minister*
Diehl, James Harvey *church administrator*
Friedlander, Edward Robert *pathologist*
Gray, Helen Theresa Gott *religion editor*
Hebenstreit, Jean Estill Stark *religion educator, practitioner*
Juarez, Martin *priest*
Knight, John Allan *clergyman, philosophy and religion educator*
Mazza, Biagio *religious studies educator*
Petosa, Jason Joseph *publisher*
Rowden, A(lphro) J(ohn) *minister*
†Wilder, Terry L. *religious studies educator*

Laddonia
Scheffler, Lewis Francis *pastor, educator, research scientist*

Lees Summit
Demetreon, Daiboune Elayne *minister*
†Lord, Heaven *theology studies educator, consultant, minister*

North Kansas City
Conner, Leonard Wayne *association administrator, layworker*

Ozark
†Thornton, Andrew John *minister*

Perryville
Shelby, Charles Francis *priest, not-for-profit fundraiser*

Poplar Bluff
Black, Ronnie Delane *religious organization administrator, mayor*
Carr, Charles Louis *retired religious organization administrator*
Duncan, Leland Ray *retired mission administrator*

Raymore
Miller, William Lee, Jr., *minister*

Saint Louis
Brungs, Robert Anthony *theology educator, institute director*
DaCorte, Allan Francis *priest, financial consultant and advisor*
Mahsman, David Lawrence *religious publications editor*
McClain, Curtis Keith, Jr., *religious studies educator, minister*
Merrell, James Lee *religious editor, clergyman*
Naumann, Joseph F. *bishop*
†O'Keefe, Martin D. *priest, theology studies educator*
Poellot, Luther *minister*
†Shreckhise, Robert Lynn *minister, theology studies educator*
†Weber, Gloria Richie *retired minister, retired state legislator*
Wiley, Gregory Robert *publisher*
Wilke, LeRoy *church administrator*

Springfield
†Baird, Robert Dean *mission director*
Gillming, Kenneth *church administrator*
†Haltom, Michael Fred *religious studies educator, military officer*
Trask, Thomas Edward *religious organization administrator*
White, John Lee *theology studies educator*

MONTANA

Helena
Hart, John William *theology and ecology educator*
†Holmes, Robert M. *minister, counselor, educator*
Jones, Charles Irving *bishop*

Kalispell
†Vickers, Lee Louise *minister*

Terry
Bruno, Peter Jackson *pastor, counselor, consultant*

NEBRASKA

Grand Island
Mc Namara, Lawrence J. *bishop*
Zichek, Melvin Eddie *retired clergyman, educator*

Hastings
McCarthy, David Bruce *minister*

Lincoln
†Bruskewitz, Fabian W. *bishop*
Wiersbe, Warren Wendell *clergyman, author, lecturer*

Omaha
†Curtiss, Elden F. *bishop*
Harmless, J. William *theologian, educator*
Russell, Martin John *minister*
Zuerlein, Damian Joseph *priest*

Seward
Etzold, Herman Albert *clergyman, theology educator*

NEVADA

Las Vegas
Bishop, Leo Kenneth *clergyman, educator*

Reno
Apassa, Cyril Omo-Osagie *clergyman, educator*
Chrystal, William George *minister*
Savoy, Douglas Eugene *bishop, religious studies educator, explorer, writer*
†Straling, Phillip Francis *bishop*
Walrath, Harry Rienzi *retired minister*
Weld, Roger Bowen *religious organization administrator*

NEW HAMPSHIRE

Center Sandwich
Booty, John Everitt *emeritus educator*

Hanover
Green, Ronald Michael *ethics and religious studies educator*
Hemphill, Margaret Ayars *priest, artist*

Hollis
Litchfield, Barbara Mae Smith *clergywoman*

Jaffrey
Van Ness, Patricia Wood *religious studies educator, consultant, author*

Loudon
Moore, Beatrice *religious organization administrator*

Manchester
Christian, Francis Joseph *bishop*
Kuehne, Dale Stanway *minister, political science educator*
McCormack, John Brendan *bishop*
Reynolds, Gregory Edward *minister*

North Hampton
†Osenton, Thomas George *publisher*

Warner
Bodine, John Jermain *pastor*

West Chesterfield
Garinger, Louis Daniel *religion educator*

NEW JERSEY

Caldwell
Campbell, Sister Maura *religious studies and philosophy educator*
†Orians, Thomas Wayne *priest*

Chatham
Marconi, Dominic Anthony *retired bishop*

Clinton
†Moore, Alma Donst *writer, lyricist*

Cranbury
Yoseloff, Thomas *publisher*

Denville
Tartaglia, Richard V. *priest*

Eatontown
Priesand, Sally Jane *rabbi*

Edison
†Roskoski, John *religious studies educator, coach*

Englewood
Chandrankunnel, Mathew Michael *priest, educator*
Saliba, Philip E. *archbishop*

Flemington
Jaffe, Evan *rabbi*

Freehold
Jawidzik, Edward Mark *priest*
Medley, Alex Roy *executive minister*

Hightstown
Hull, Gretchen Gaebelein *lay worker, writer, lecturer*

Jersey City
Ashley, Willard Walden C., Sr., *minister*
Burns, Hugh L. *priest, writer*
†Katz, Colleen *publisher*

Lakewood
Levovitz, Pesach Zechariah *rabbi*

Little Falls
Glasser, Lynn Schreiber *publisher*

Madison
†Ariarajah, S. Wesley *educator, former clergyman, church administrator*
†Farias, Joseph G. *priest, consultant*
Yrigoyen, Charles, Jr., *church denomination executive*

Mahwah
Padovano, Anthony Thomas *theologian, educator*

Marlton
Clemens, David Allen *minister*

Medford
Hogan, Thomas Harlan *publisher*

Middletown
Klincewicz, John Gregory *deacon, mathematician*

Montclair
Ewers, Paul Joseph *priest*
Leggett, Paul Arthur *minister*

Morris Plains
Spong, John Shelby *retired bishop*

Mount Laurel
†Ruggiano, Cheryl Anna *minister, insurance agent*

Neptune
Collins, Robert T. *publisher*
Manuel, Sandra Lorraine *minister*

New Brunswick
Bowden, Henry Warner *religion educator*
Johnson, James Turner *theology studies educator*

Newark
Curley, Augustine James Francis *priest, educator*
Howard, M(oses) William, Jr., *minister*
Johnson, Evelyn *minister, educator*

Newfield
Hartman, Jeffrey Edward *pastor*

Northvale
Aronson, Jason *publisher*

Ocean Grove
Anderson, James Frederick *clergyman*

Paterson
Paulhus, Thomas A. *educator*

Point Pleasant
Marjanczyk, Joseph Anicetus *priest*

Pomona
Constantelos, Demetrios John *priest, educator*

Pompton Plains
Scroggs, Robin Jerome *theology educator*

Princeton
Allen, Diogenes *clergyman, philosophy educator*
Armstrong, Richard Stoll *minister, educator, writer, poet*
Belshaw, George Phelps Mellick *bishop*
†Griffith, Ruth Marie *religious studies educator*
Metzger, Bruce Manning *clergyman, educator*
Miller, Patrick Dwight, Jr., *religion educator, minister*
Olson, Dennis Thorald *religion educator*
West, Charles Converse *theologian, educator*

Ridgewood
Kiernan, Richard Francis *publisher*

Rochelle Park
Brandt, Robert Barry *lay worker*

Rutherford
Gerety, Peter Leo *archbishop*

Sayreville
Tedesco, Richard Albert *minister*

South Orange
Fleming, Edward J. *priest, educator*
†Frizzell, Lawrence Edward *religious studies educator, priest*

Summit
May, Ernest Max *charitable organization official*

Teaneck
Meno, John Peter *chorepiscopus*

Toms River
Donaldson, Marcia Jean *lay worker*

Trenton
Old, Hughes Oliphant *research theologian, clergyman*

Union
Korbman, Meyer Hyman *rabbi, public school administrator*

Union City
Younan, Joseph *bishop*

Watchung
Miller, John Ronald *minister*

West Milford
Stelpstra, William John *minister*

West Orange
Guthrie, William Anthony *minister*

West Paterson
†Pataki, Andrew *bishop*

Westville
Doughty, A. Glenn *minister*

NEW MEXICO

Moriarty
†Moonwalker, Tu *minister, counselor*

Portales
Overton, Edwin Dean *campus minister, educator*

Springer
Dear, John *priest*

NEW YORK

Adams Center
Hood, Thomas Gregory *minister*

Albany
Bowen, Mary Lu *ecumenical administrator*

Angola
Green, Gerard Leo *priest, educator*

Baldwin Place
Kurian, George Thomas *publisher*

Bedford
Hughart, Thomas Arthur *minister*

Brainard
Isaksen, Robert L. *retired bishop*

Bronx
†Berman, Wesley R. *minister, retired social worker*
†Canavan, Francis *priest, educator*
Dulles, Avery *cardinal, theologian*
Hennessy, Thomas Christopher *clergyman, educator, retired university dean*
Hunt, George William *priest, magazine editor*
Kirmse, Sister Anne-Marie Rose *nun, educator, researcher*
McShane, Joseph Michael *priest, theology studies educator*
Motte, Sister Mary Margaret *missionary*
Parker, Everett Carlton *clergyman*

Ruffing, Janet Kathryn *spirituality educator*

Brooklyn
Al-Hafeez, Humza *minister, editor*
†Ben-Menachem, David *religious studies educator*
Bowers, John Carl *minister, lawyer*
†Catanello, Ignatius Anthony *bishop*
DiMarzio, Nicholas Anthony *bishop*
Gagliardi, Mario Carmelo *priest*
Garrison, Maurice Allen Martin *missionary, minister*
Goldstein, Niles Elliot *rabbi, author*
Huneke, John George *minister*
Pasciuto, Joseph Doria *priest*
Scult, Mel *Judaic studies educator, researcher*

Cambridge
Kriss, Gary W(ayne) *Episcopal priest*

Candor
†Trinidad, William J. *pastor*

Canton
O'Connor, Daniel William *retired religious studies and classical languages educator*

Centerport
McQueeney, Henry Martin, Sr., *publisher*
Stevens, Martin Brian *publisher*

Chautauqua
Mackenzie, John Anderson Ross *historian, educator*

Clyde
Searle, Robert Ferguson *minister*

Corning
Davis, Francis Raymond *priest*

Coxsackie
†Moyna, John Lawrence *priest*

Douglaston
Valero, René Arnold *clergyman*

East Aurora
Hayes, Bonaventure Francis *priest*

Elma
Virkler, Mark William *religious educator*

Elmira
Singletary, Caglar Juan *minister*

Far Rockaway
Kelly, George Anthony *clergyman, author, educator*

Glen Cove
Costa, Thomas Charles *priest*

Glen Head
Huber, Don Lawrence *publisher*

Grand Island
Backus, Kevin Michael *minister*
Hefner, Judith Ann *priest, counselor*

Hawthorne
Scheffler, Eckart Arthur *publisher*

Hollis
Stephens, B. Consuela *minister, consultant*

Huntington
Massa, James *priest, theology studies educator*

Jamaica
Cush, John Patrick *priest, theology studies educator*
Flanagan, Patrick Sean Liam *priest*
†Primeaux, Patrick *priest, religious studies educator*

Kingston
Tsirpanlis, Constantine N. *theology, philosophy, classics and history educator*

Larchmont
Rainier, Robert Paul *publisher, consultant*

Lindenhurst
Hamilton, Daniel Stephen *clergyman*

Mechanicville
Rhodes, Alan Charles *minister*

Middle Village
Kolatch, Alfred Jacob *publisher*

Millbrook
†Lindsley, James Elliott *minister, writer*

Mount Vernon
Moore, W. Darin *minister*

Narrowsburg
†Jones, Thomas Peter *priest*

New York
Anderson, Fred Richard *minister, writer*
Baranski, Joan Sullivan *publisher*
Begell, William *publisher*
†Bergtraum, Henry M. *minister*
Bradsell, Kenneth Raymond *minister*
Bretton-Granatoor, Gary Martin *rabbi*
Chanes, Jerome Alan *non-profit organization administrator, public affairs analyst*
Church, Frank Forrester *minister, author, columnist*
Ciangio, Sister Donna Lenore *religious organization administrator*
Cone, James Hal *theologian, educator, author*
†Demetrios, *archbishop*
Doherty, Thomas *publisher*

Driver, Tom Faw *theologian, writer, justice/peace advocate, photographer*
Forbes, Christopher (Kip Forbes) *publisher*
Forbes, Timothy Carter *publisher*
Friedman, Herbert A. *rabbi, educator, fund raising executive*
Friedman, J. Roger *publisher*
Gage, Robert Clifford *minister*
Geer, John Farr *retired religious organization administrator*
Germano, William Paul *publisher*
Giniger, Kenneth Seeman *publisher*
Ginsberg, Hersh Meier *rabbi, religious organization executive*
Griswold, Frank Tracy, III, *bishop*
Habecker, Eugene Brubaker *religious association executive*
Harvey, O.S.F.S., John F *priest, theologian, educator*
Hertzberg, Arthur *rabbi, educator*
Hirsch, Roseann Conte *publisher*
Holmes, Miriam H. *publisher*
Kraemer, David C. *theology educator*
Laurus, (Laurus Skurla) *archbishop*
†Leonard, Richard Davis *minister*
Mann, Anthony *minister, dean*
Mattila, Daniel E. *priest, social worker*
McGeady, Sister Mary Rose *religious organization administrator, psychologist*
Meyer, Sheldon *publisher*
Mironovich, Alex *publisher*
†Molho, Emanuel *publisher*
Murdoch, (Keith) Rupert *publisher*
Ochs, Carol Rebecca *theologian, philosophy and religion educator*
O'Keefe, Vincent Thomas *clergyman, educational administrator*
Oshin, Diane *publisher*
†Paro, Jeff *publisher*
Platzner, Linda *publisher*
Powers, Edward Alton *minister, educator*
Rabinowitz, Mayer Elya *rabbi, educator*
Reidy, Carolyn Kroll *publisher*
Rosenberg, Ellen Y. *religious association administrator*
Ross, Norman Alan *publisher*
Roth, Sol *rabbi*
Rusch, William Graham *religious organization administrator*
Schiffrin, Andre *publisher*
Schorsch, Ismar *clergyman, Jewish history educator*
Shillady, William Scott *minister*
Shriver, Donald Woods, Jr., *theology educator*
Siegel, Morton Kallos *religious organization administrator, educational administrator*
Simpson, Mary Michael *priest, psychotherapist*
Stock, Ben *religious organization consultant*
Stolper, Pinchas Aryeh *religious organization executive, rabbi*
Talley, Truman Macdonald *publisher*
Tannenbaum, Bernice Salpeter *national religious organization executive*
Thurman, Robert *philosophy, religious studies educator*
Truesdell, Walter George *minister, librarian*
Tucker, Alan David *publisher*
Twiname, John Dean *minister, human services administrator*
Ware, Alberta *minister, educator*
†Waxenberg, Alan M. *publisher*
Welsh, Donald Emory *publisher*
Whiteman, Douglas E. *publisher*
Wiener, Marvin S. *rabbi, editor, executive*
Wolnek, Stephen S. *church administrator*
†Yoffie, Erich H. *church administrator*
Yu, Andrew *minister*
Zanetti, Richard Joseph *publisher*
Zeldin, Richard Packer *publisher*

Newport
Wilson, Eldon Ray *minister*

Niagara Falls
†Douglas, Frances Sonia *minister*

Niskayuna
Nichols, Albert Myron *retired minister*

Nyack
Mann, Kenneth Walker *retired minister, psychologist*
Poston, Larry Allan *religious studies educator*

Pawling
Peale, Ruth Stafford (Mrs. Norman Vincent Peale) *religious leader*

Pleasantville
Hundersmarck, Lawrence F. *theology studies educator*

Poughkeepsie
Glasse, John Howell *retired philosophy and theology educator*
Harmelink, Herman, III, *clergyman, author, educator, ecumenist*

Purchase
Jones, James Edwards, Sr., *religion educator*

Rochester
Cauthen, Kenneth *theological educator*
†Clark, Matthew Harvey *bishop*
†Elliott, Ralph H. *educator*
Gripe, Alan Gordon *minister*
Lacey, Dorothy Ellen *theology studies educator, religious organization administrator*
Santos, Wilma *missionary*
Webster, Gordon Visscher, Jr., *minister*

Rockville Centre
Batule, Robert John *priest, writer*

Scarsdale
Goodwin, Everett Carlton *minister*

Johnson, William Alexander *clergyman, philosophy educator*

Setauket
Gard, Richard Abbott *religious institute executive, educator*

Speculator
Kelly, Paul John *priest*

Spencertown
Lieber, Charles Donald *publisher*

Syosset
†Theodosius, *retired leader of the Orthodox Church in America*

Syracuse
Costello, Thomas Joseph *bishop*
Harrison, Frank J. *retired bishop*
Lang, James Patrick *priest*
†Moynihan, James M. *bishop*
Schiess, Betty Bone *priest*
†Watts, James Washington *religion educator*
Wiggins, James Bryan *religion educator*

Tarrytown
Winings, Kathy *religion educator*

Troy
Phelan, Thomas *clergyman, academic administrator, educator*

Unionville
Kemnitz, Thomas Milton *publisher*

West Shokan
Mackey, Jeffrey Allen *priest*

Westbury
De Pauw, Gommar Albert *priest, educator*

Williamsville
Jones, Robert Alfred *retired clergyman*

Yonkers
Donovan, Agnes M. *nun*
Gunner, Murray *religious organization administrator*
Mazzella, Anthony J. *minister, psychotherapist, musician*

Youngstown
Lamb, Charles F. *educator, retired minister*

NORTH CAROLINA

Asheville
Rogers, Garry Lee *minister, medical technician*
Sims, Bennett Jones *minister, educator*

Belmont
†Baumstein, Paschal M. *priest*

Boiling Springs
Arnold, Ernest Woodrow *minister*

Cary
Taylor, David Wyatt Aiken *retired clergyman*
Vandergriff, Kenneth Lynn *minister*

Cashiers
Henson, Phillip Rickman *religious organization administrator, minister*

Chapel Hill
Dixon, John Wesley, Jr., *retired religion and art educator*

Charlotte
Curlin, William G. *bishop*
Freeman, Sidney Lee *minister, educator*
†Gregory, Jeannette T. *publisher, writer*
Helton, Max Edward *minister, consultant, religious organization executive*
Oliver, John William Posegate *minister*
Reeves, John Craig *religious studies educator*
Ross, David Edmond *church official*
Walker, Jewett Lynius *clergyman, church official*

Concord
Robinson, Harold Oscar *clergyman, educator*

Durham
Dorn, Louis Otto *retired minister, consultant*
Efird, James Michael *theology educator*
McClain, Gregory David *minister*
Meyers, Eric Mark *religion educator*
Smith, Harmon Lee, Jr., *clergyman, moral theology educator*
†Steinmetz, David Curtis *religious studies educator*

Fairview
Eck, David Wilson *minister*

Fletcher
†Tolbert, Gary J. *minister*

Greensboro
Clark, Lawrence James *minister*
Dziordz, Walter Michael *priest*
Schnatterly, Michael Dean *priest*

Greenville
Jackson, Bobby Rand *minister*

Hendersonville
Trexler, Edgar Ray *minister, editor*

Hickory
McDaniel, Michael Conway Dixon *bishop, retired theology educator*

High Point
Boger, Richard Edwin, Jr., *minister*

Hudson
Dellinger, Charles Wade *minister*

Lake Junaluska
Tullis, Edward Lewis *retired bishop*

Monroe
Kyle, John Emery *mission executive*

Raleigh
Buchanan, Ray Allen *clergyman*
Lolley, William Randall *minister*
Vigen, James Bruce *minister, theologian*

Reidsville
Hart, Richard Wesley *religious organization administrator, pastor*

Rocky Mount
†Dickens, Alice McKnight *minister*

Rutherfordton
Conley, Katherine Logan *religious studies educator*

Salisbury
Terry, Roger Harold *minister, musician, composer, author, editor*

Southport
Harrelson, Walter Joseph *minister, religion educator emeritus*

Trenton
Dillahunty, George Robert *minister*

Wake Forest
†Patterson, Paige *church administrator, former seminary president*

Wallace
Johnson, James Wilson *pastor*

Waynesville
Hale, Joseph Rice *church organization executive*

Weaverville
Edwards, Otis Carl, Jr., *theology educator*

Wilmington
Conser, Walter Hurley, Jr., *religion and philosophy educator*
Stokes, John Lemacks, II, *clergyman, retired university official*

Wilson
Wood, Gerald David *religious organization administrator*

Winston Salem
Beach, Franklin Darrel *minister*
Capps, Richard Henry *retired minister*
Ludolf, Marilyn Marie Keaton *lay worker*
†Mendez, John *minister*
Rights, Graham Henry *retired minister*
Spach, Jule Christian *church executive*
Winn, Albert Curry *clergyman*

NORTH DAKOTA

Fargo
Aquila, Samuel Joseph *bishop*
Foss, Richard John *bishop*
Sullivan, James Stephen *retired bishop*

OHIO

Ashland
†deSilva, David Arthur *theology studies educator*
†Hawk, L. Daniel *minister, religious studies educator*
Watson, JoAnn Ford *theology educator*

Athens
†Morgans, Bob D. *minister*

Beavercreek
Bennett, Anna Dell *minister, religion educator, retired elementary school educator*

Canton
Mann, John Martin *minister*
Watson, Duane Frederick *religious studies educator*

Cincinnati
Adams, Mendle Eugene *minister*
Anderson, Joan Balyeat *religion educator, minister*
Harrington, Jeremy Thomas *priest, publishing executive*
Levy, Ralph David *theology educator*
Maher, Terry Marina *religious organization administrator*
Pilarczyk, Daniel Edward *archbishop*
Sallquist, Gary Ardin *minister, non-profit executive*
†Thatcher, Tom *religious studies educator*
Zola, Gary Phillip *rabbi, historian, religious educational administrator*

Clayton
Stutzman, L. Lee *pastor*

Cleveland
Abrams, Sylvia Fleck *religious studies educator*
†Battle, Hilary Howard *minister, educator*
Borchert, Catherine Glennan *minister*
Buhrow, William Carl *religious organization administrator*
Cohen, Armond E. *rabbi*
Knull, Erhard *minister*
†Pilla, Anthony Michael *bishop*

Columbus
Darling, George Curtis *minister, administrator*
Donovan, Dennis Dale *priest*
†Thomas, M. Carolyn *theology studies educator*
Watson, John Allan *clergyman*

Dayton
Leigh, Gloria Lorraine *retired religious studies educator*

Delaware
Lattimore, Vergel Lyronne *minister, educator, counselor*

Euclid
Obloy, Leonard Gerard *priest*

Fairlawn
France, Dorothy Daniel *minister*

Findlay
Fry, Charles George *theologian, educator*
Resseguie, James Lynn *theology educator*
Wilkin, Richard Edwin *clergyman, religious organization executive*

Granville
Woodyard, David Oliver *religious studies educator, clergy member*

Greentown
†Pipes, Randy Paul *minister, church administrator*

Hartville
†Hazlett, George Alvin *minister, mediator*

Ironton
Cremeans, James L. *minister*

Kettering
†Nuzzi, Ronald James *priest, educator*

Lakeside
Mead, Millard Wilmer *retired minister*

Lakewood
Sherry, Paul Henry *minister, religious organization administrator*

London
Hughes, Clyde Matthew *religious denomination executive*

Loveland
Grimmet, Alex J. *clergyman, school administrator, elementary and secondary education educator*

Lyons
†Myers, John William *minister, poet, editor, publisher*

Mansfield
†Whitmer, Eugene Roger *minister, retired secondary school educator*

Miamisburg
†Brewster, Charles Edward *writer, engineer*

Oberlin
Zinn, Grover Alfonso, Jr., *religion educator*

Sebring
Doty, James Edward *pastor, psychologist*

Sidney
Lawrence, Wayne Allen *publisher*

Steubenville
Scanlan, Michael *priest, academic administrator*
Sheldon, Gilbert Ignatius *clergyman*

Struthers
Sugden, Richard Lee *pastor*

Tiffin
†Kill, Sister Marietta *nun, music educator*

Waterville
Yeager, Robert Julius *priest, financial consultant*

Waverly
Hays, Richard Secrest *minister*

Westerville
Schultz, Arthur LeRoy *clergyman, educator*

Wickliffe
Pevec, Anthony Edward *bishop*

Wintersville
George, Gary Mark *pastor, church administrator*

Worthington
Browning, Robert Lynn *educator, clergyman*

OKLAHOMA

Bartlesville
Sweem, Billy Don *minister*

Bethany
Leggett, James Daniel *bishop*

Oklahoma City
†Beltran, Eusebius Joseph *archbishop*
Clayton, Lawrence Otto *minister, writer, educator, alcohol and drug counselor*
Hampton, Carol McDonald *priest, educator, historian*

Jones, Charles Edwin *historian, bibliographer, chaplain*
†Ridley, Betty Ann *religious educator, church worker*
Sheldon, Eli Howard *minister*
Taylor-White-Grigsby, Queen Delores *minister, consultant*

Shawnee
Wilks, Thomas Milton *religious studies educator, minister*

Tahlequah
†Roberts, James David *pastor, construction executive*
Snyder, Travis Carroll *evangelist*

Texhoma
Jackson, Paul Howard *minister*

Tulsa
Cox, William Jackson *retired bishop*
Gottschalk, Sister Mary Therese *nun, hospital administrator*
†Grizzle, Trevor Lloyd *religious studies educator, minister*
Osborn, La Donna Carol *clergywoman*
Rex, Lonnie Royce *religious organization administrator*
Roberts, Oral (Granville Oral Roberts) *clergyman*
†Sotak, John Joseph *priest, educator*

Vinita
Wright, Jo Anne *Episcopal priest*

OREGON

Beaverton
Mitchell, Bettie Phaenon *religious organization administrator*

Corvallis
Dennis, John Davison *minister*
McCarthy, William Robert *minister*

Eugene
Sanders, Jack Thomas *religious studies educator*

Keizer
Null, Paul Bryan *minister*

Philomath
Stensvad, Allan Maurice *minister*

Portland
†Becker, Matthew Lee *religious studies educator, minister*
†Bryant, Carmen Julia *missionary, educator*
Langrock, Karl Frederick *former academic administrator*
Richards, Herbert East *minister emeritus, commentator*
Riddle, Earl Waldo *retired church official, small business owner*

Salem
Muntz, J(ohn) Richard *clergyman*

Turner
Ratzlaff, Ruben Menno *religion educator, minister*

PENNSYLVANIA

Akron
Livingston, Margery Elsie *missionary, clinical psychologist*

Allentown
†Cullen, Edward Peter *bishop*
Revak, Francis Charles *priest, educator*

Bensalem
Warkulwiz, Victor Philip *priest, physicist, educator*

Bethel Park
Bevan, Norman Edward *religious organization executive*

Bethlehem
Steffen, Lloyd Howard *minister, religion educator*
†Weissler, Chava (Lenore) *religious studies educator*

Beyer
Cornell, William Harvey *clergyman*

Bradford
Cox, J. Arthur *minister*

Camp Hill
Johnston, Thomas McElree, Jr., *retired church administrator*

Center Valley
†Dailey, Thomas F. *religious studies educator, director*

Chambersburg
Fleming, Steven Robert *minister*
Reber, Calvin Henry *theological studies educator, minister*

Clarion
Grejda, Gail Fulton *dean*

Clinton
Talbot, Mary Lee *minister*

Coatesville
Green, Norman Marston, Jr., *minister*

Cranberry Township
Tiller, Olive Marie *retired church worker*

Drexel Hill
Thompson, William David *minister, homiletics educator*

Elizabethtown
Brown, Dale Weaver *clergyman, theologian, educator*
Johnson, Clarence Ray *minister*

Ephrata
Young, David Samuel *minister*

Erie
Murphy, Michael Joseph *retired bishop*
Rowley, Robert Deane, Jr., *bishop*
†Trautman, Donald W. *bishop*

Exeter
Henderson, Robb Alan *minister*

Frederick
Mellon, Bradley Floyd *pastor, religion educator*

Glenside
Kalkwarf, Leonard V. *minister*
†McCartney, Dan G. *theology studies educator, musician*

Gwynedd
LeFevre, Perry Deyo *minister, theology educator*

Harrisburg
Chambers, Clarice Lorraine *clergy, educational consultant*
†Dattilo, Nicholas C. *bishop*

Hatfield
Taylor, Alan Charles *chaplain, counselor, researcher*

Haverford
Kee, Howard Clark *religion educator*

Havertown
Koenig, Robert Emil *clergyman*

Herminie
Taylor, John Calvin *missionary, dentist*

Huntingdon
Durnbaugh, Donald Floyd *church history educator, researcher*

Immaculata
Hickey, Gregory J. *priest, academic administrator*

Jim Thorpe
Umbehocker, Kenneth Sheldon *priest*

Johnstown
Miloro, Protopresbter Frank *church official, religious studies educator*
Nicholas, (Richard G. Smisko) *bishop*
Smisko, Nicholas Richard *bishop, educator*

Kutztown
Johnson, Nils, Jr., *minister*

Lancaster
Glick, Garland Wayne *retired theological seminary president*

Lewisburg
Jump, Chester Jackson, Jr., *clergyman, church official*

Lititz
Haines, Ronald H. *retired bishop*
Martin, Harold Sheaffer *minister, educator*

Malvern
Brighton, Ruth Louise *lay worker, educator*

Meadville
Durlesser, James Arthur *clergyman, writer, lecturer*

Mendenhall
Lee, Virginia Diane *lay worker*

Mifflinburg
Bayly, Thomas Glen *minister, publisher religious material*

Philadelphia
Bartlett, Allen Lyman, Jr., *retired bishop*
Bracey, Cookie Frances Lee *minister*
Burch, Francis Floyd *clergyman*
Butz, Geneva Mae *pastor*
Darling, Pamela Ann Wood *writer, editor, speaker, religious consultant*
Maher, E. J. *retired priest*
Marple, Dorothy Jane *retired church executive*
Oh, Michael Young-Suk *PhD student & researcher, minister & theological seminary president*
†Poythress, Vern Sheridan *religion educator, minister*
†Rigali, Justin F. *archbishop*
Ryken, Philip Graham *minister, theologian, writer*
†Sulyk, Stephen *retired archbishop*
Wengert, Timothy *church history educator, clergyman*

Pittsburgh
Bashore, George Willis *retired bishop*
Brauner, Ronald Allan *religion educator*
†Burgess, John Paul *minister, religion educator*
Collins, Rose Ann *minister*
Drabiska, Frank John *priest, parochial school educator*
Holder, Gerald D., Jr., *dean*

Koedel, Robert Craig *minister, historian, educator*
Maximos, Metropolitan (Maximos Demetrios Aghiorgoussis) *bishop, metropolitan*
McCoid, Donald James *bishop*
Mc Dowell, John B. *bishop*
Mina, John Louis (Ivan Minea) *religious studies educator, archivist*
Myers, William Richard *minister, educator*
Schaub, Marilyn McNamara *religion educator*
Shaffer, Terry George *pastor*
†Slusser, Michael *theology studies educator, department chairman, priest*
†Zeolla, Kim Anne *minister*

Quarryville
Harris, Robert Laird *minister, theology educator emeritus*

Rebersburg
Kuhns, Nancy Evelyn *minister*

Rochester
Garlathy, Frank Bryan *minister*

Rydal
Black, Thomas Donald *retired religious organization administrator*

Saint Peters
†Detterline, Milton E., Jr., *minister*

Scranton
De Celles, Charles Edouard *theologian, educator*
†Dougherty, John Martin *bishop*
Timlin, James Clifford *bishop*

Souderton
Lapp, James Merrill *clergyman, marriage and family therapist*

Sunbury
Ely, Donald J(ean) *clergyman, secondary school educator*

Swarthmore
Frost, Jerry William *religion and history educator, library administrator*

Tylersport
Raub, Donald Wilmer *minister, author*

Valley Forge
†Wright-Riggins, Aidsand F., III, *religious organization executive*

Villanova
Eigo, Francis Augustine *theology studies educator*

Wayne
Rabii, Patricia Berg *church administrator*

Waynesburg
Visser, Richard Edgar *minister*

West Chester
Palmer, Donald Curtis *retired interdenominational missionary society executive*

Williamsport
Cox, Albert Edward *retired pastor*
Rauhut, John Frederick *pastor*

Wynnewood
McNally, Michael James *priest*
Prior, Joseph Gerard *priest, educator*
Russell, Horace Orlando *theology studies educator*
Sider, Ronald J. *theology educator, author*
Wachs, Saul Philip *Jewish education educator*

RHODE ISLAND

Johnston
†Spina, Douglas John *priest, educator*

Lincoln
Barlow, August Ralph, Jr., *minister*

Middletown
Demy, Timothy James *military chaplain*

Providence
Frerichs, Ernest Sunley *religious studies educator*
†Mulvee, Robert Edward *bishop*
Olyan, Saul Mitchell *religious studies educator*
Taylor, Richard Henry *minister*

Woonsocket
St. Godard, Edward G. *Roman Catholic priest*

SOUTH CAROLINA

Anderson
Sustar, T. David *religious organization administrator*
Wisler, Darla Lee *pastor*

Chapin
Branham, Mack Carison, Jr., *retired theological seminary educator, minister*

Charleston
Donehue, John Douglas *interdenominational ministries executive*
Salmon, Edward Lloyd, Jr., *bishop*

Columbia
†Adams, John Hurst *bishop*

Jones, Donald Lee *religious studies educator*

Florence
Baroody, Albert Joseph, Jr., *pastoral counselor*

Greenville
Bell, Robert Daniel *religious studies educator*

Leesville
Crumley, James Robert, Jr., *retired clergyman*

Spartanburg
Bullard, John Moore *religion educator, church musician*
†Norrell, Thomas H. *minister, educator*

Summerville
Holler, Adlai Cornwell, Jr., *minister*

Taylors
Smith, Morton Howison *religious organization administrator, educator*
Vaughn, John Carroll *minister, educator*

White Rock
Aull, James Stroud *retired bishop*

Winnsboro
McCants, Clyde Taft *retired clergyman*

SOUTH DAKOTA

Freeman
Roussos, Stephen Bernard *minister*

Philip
†Grossenburg, John Anthony *minister*

Sioux Falls
Carlson, Robert James *bishop*
Cowles, Ronald Eugene *church administrator*

Watertown
Witcher, Gary Royal *minister, educator*

TENNESSEE

Antioch
Worthington, Melvin Leroy *minister, writer*

Brentwood
Stephens, Shirley Lynne *writer, editor*

Bristol
Hill, Kenneth Clyde *clergyman*

Chattanooga
†Haden, Benjamin *minister, retired publishing executive, broadcast executive*
Harman, William P. *religious studies educator*
Maloney, J. Patrick *minister, educator, seminary administrator*
Mohney, Nell Webb *religion educator, speaker, author*
Ragon, Robert Ronald *clergyman*

Clarksville
Reaves, Barry Reco *minister*

Cleveland
Taylor, William Al *church administrator*

Cookeville
Adkisson, Randall Lynn *minister*

Eads
Ratzlaff, David Edward *minister*

Franklin
Young, William Edgar *religious organization official*

Germantown
Allison, Beverly Gray *seminary president, evangelism educator*
Floyd, John David *theology educator, minister*

Hermitage
Chambers, Curtis Allen *clergyman, church communications executive*

Jackson
Maynard, Terrell Dennis *minister*

Johnson City
Freeman, Wendell Lee *minister*
Phillips, Dorothy Alease *lay church worker, educator, freelance writer*

Knoxville
†Bridges, Carl Branson *religious studies educator*
Prince, Matthew Sperry *religious organization executive*
Stooksbury, William Claude *minister*

La Follette
Eads, Ora Wilbert *clergyman, church official*

Lebanon
Criscoe, Arthur Hugh *religious organization administrator, educator*

Loudon
Hallstrand, Sarah Laymon *denomination executive*
Jones, Robert Gean *religion educator*

Madison
Spillers, James Andrew *Bible and history educator, minister*

Memphis
Magrill, Joe Richard, Jr., *religious organization administrator, minister*

†McKenzie, Steven L. *theology studies educator, writer*
†Steib, James Terry *bishop*
Todd, Virgil Holcomb *clergyman, religion educator*
†Walker, Randolph Meade *minister*

Murfreesboro
Walker, David Ellis, Jr., *educator, minister, consultant*

Nashville
†Chapman, Morris Hines *denominational executive*
Hall, Richard Clyde, Jr., *retired religious educational administrator*
Kmiec, Edward Urban *bishop*
Land, Richard Dale *minister, religious organization administrator*
†Moss, Carl Michael *minister, religious studies educator*
Pursell, Cleo Wilburn *church official*
†TeSelle, Eugene Arthur, Jr., *religion educator*

Nolensville
†Lessard, Lisa Kathleen Hamlin *spiritual counselor*

Pegram
Barnes, Craig Martin *minister*

Sewanee
Hughes, Robert Davis, III, *theology studies educator*
†Lytle, Guy Fitch, III, *priest, educator, dean*

Signal Mountain
Hall, Thor *religion educator*

Waynesboro
Owen, Timothy Andrew *minister*

TEXAS

Abilene
Baird, Larry Don *minister, nurse*

Alice
Tetlie, Harold *priest*

Amarillo
DeVaughn, Michael Richard *minister, administrator*
Klein, Jerry Lee, Sr., *religion educator, minister*

Arlington
Lingerfelt, B. Eugene, Jr., *minister*

Austin
†Alanís, Javier Rolando *theologian, religious studies educator*
Bernard, David Kane *minister, writer, editor*
Hitchcock, Joanna *publisher*
†Jinkins, Wm. Michael *theology studies educator*
†Ricker, George M. *minister, educator*
Wahlberg, Philip Lawrence *former bishop*
Worthing, Carol Marie *minister*

Brownsville
Fitzpatrick, John J. *bishop*
Pena, Raymundo Joseph *bishop*

Canyon Lake
Reinhardt, Linda Kay *minister*

Christoval
Mueller, James H. *priest*

Cleburne
Bushor, Mark Eldon *pastor, writer, consultant*

Dallas
Austin-Thorn, Cynthia Kay *religious organization administrator, poet*
Blue, J(ohn) Ronald *evangelical mission executive*
Carnes, Joseph Sydney *clergyman*
Daves, Don Michael *minister*
†Esqueda, Octavio Javier *religious studies educator*
†Galante, Joseph A. *bishop*
†Grahmann, Charles V. *bishop*
Gross, Harriet P. Marcus *religious studies and writing educator*
Harrell, Roy Harrison, Jr., *minister*
Kirby, James Edmund, Jr., *theology educator*
Lang, James Devore, Jr., *ministry executive*
Lee, Allan Wren *clergyman*
†Lovin, Robin Warren *clergy member, educator*
Lumpkin, Vicki G. *minister*
Oden, William Bryant *bishop, educator*
Pauley, Shirley Stewart *religious organization executive*
Pinson, William Meredith, Jr., *pastor, writer, administrator*
Rieger, Joerg *theology studies educator*
Valentine, Foy Dan *clergyman*
Wiles, Charles Preston *minister*
†Wood, Charles Monroe *theology educator*

Deer Park
Deutsch, Lawrence Ira *minister*

Fort Worth
Blaising, Craig Alan *religious studies educator*
Garrett, James Leo, Jr., *theology educator*
Gilbert, James Cayce *minister*
Huey, F. B., Jr., *minister, theology educator*
†Pierce, Timothy Michael *religious studies educator*
Rogers, Charles Ray *minister, religious organization administrator*
Teegarden, Kenneth Leroy *clergyman*
Toulouse, Mark Gene *religion educator*
Yaites, LilliAnn *minister*

Granbury
Faith, James Albert, Jr., *minister*

Grand Prairie
†Fickling, Karl Frederick *church consultant, educator*

Houston
Arnold, James Phillip *religious studies educator, history educator*
Barrett, Michael Joseph *priest*
Beard, Dennis Alton *pastor*
Ellis, Walter Leon *minister*
†Fiorenza, Joseph A. *bishop*
†Hasten, Ralph Gerald *minister, protective services official*
Joyce, James Daniel *clergyman*
Karff, Samuel Egal *rabbi*
Lahart, Daniel Kenneth *priest, educational administrator*
†Lickteig, Bernard Fabian *retired priest, retired parochial school educator*
†Mattox, Ethel Odessa *writer*
Nelson, John Robert *theology educator, clergyman*
Nielsen, Niels Christian, Jr., *theology educator*
Prokurat, Michael *theology studies educator, minister*
Stephens, Carson Wade *minister*
Strieder, Leon F. *priest, theology studies educator*

Jacksonville
Blaylock, James Carl *clergyman, librarian*

Keene
†Willis, Lloyd Allan *religious studies educator*

Kerrville
Lawson, Carole Jean *religious educator, author, poet*
Williams, William Henry, II, *publisher*

Kingwood
Barkley, Bronson Lee *minister*

Liberty
Hughes, Paul Anthony *minister, musician, songwriter, author, publisher*

Lubbock
Blevins, Stanley Nance *minister, educator*
†McKay-Wilkinson, Julie Ann *minister, marriage and family therapist*
Neyland, Malcolm *priest, curator*

Odessa
Pugh, Jessie Truman *minister*

Plano
Miller, Ken Leroy *religious studies educator, consultant, writer*

Richardson
Conrad, Flavius Leslie, Jr., *retired minister*
Lowe, J. Allen *minister*
Williams, James Francis, Jr., *religious organization administrator*

Sabinal
Soos, Richard Anthony *pastor*

San Antonio
Fecher, Vincent John *priest*
†Jones, Oscar Calvin *minister, dean*
Leies, John Alex *theology educator, clergyman*
Mc Allister, Gerald Nicholas *retired bishop, clergyman*
†Rankin, John Karl *retired minister, retired theology studies educator*

Schulenburg
Clark, I. E. *publisher*

Southlake
Linzey, James Franklin *minister, military officer, vocalist*

Spring
Hunt, T(homas) W(ebb) *retired religion educator*

Temple
Beyer, Richard J. *priest, writer*

Terrell
Landon, Michael Lee *religious studies educator*

The Woodlands
Machle, Edward Johnstone *theology educator, retired*
Sudbury, John Dean *religious foundation executive, petroleum chemist*

Tyler
Corrada del Rio, Alvaro *bishop*

Victoria
†Fellhauer, David E. *bishop*

Waco
Flanders, Henry Jackson, Jr., *religious studies educator*
Lewis, Martha Nell *Christian educator, minister, expressive arts therapist*
Talbert, Charles Harold *religion educator*

Waxahachie
†Tschoepe, Thomas *retired bishop*

UTAH

Ogden
Harrington, Mary Evelina Paulson (Polly Harrington) *religious journalist, writer, educator*

Salt Lake City
Bateman, Merrill Joseph *church administrator*
†Eyring, Henry Bennion *bishop*
†Haight, David B. *religious organization administrator*
Hinckley, Gordon B. *religious organization administrator*
†Holland, Jeffrey R. *religious organization administrator*
Maxwell, Neal A. *religious organization administrator*
Monson, Thomas Spencer *religious organization administrator, former publishing company executive*
†Niederauer, George H. *bishop*
†Packer, Boyd K. *church official*
†Perry, L. Tom *religious organization administrator, merchant*
†Scott, Richard G. *religious organization administrator*
Smith, Eldred Gee *church leader*
†Wirthlin, Joseph B. *religious organization administrator*

VERMONT

Brattleboro
†Hawkes, Mary Newgeon *minister, educator, retired*

Burlington
Angell, Kenneth Anthony *bishop*

Middlebury
Ferm, Robert Livingston *religion educator*

Newport
Guerrette, Richard Hector *priest, psychotherapist, management consultant, writer*

Newport Center
MacKellar, James Marsh *minister*

Northfield
Wick, William Shinn *clergyman, chaplain*

Pawlet
Buechner, Carl Frederick *minister, author*

Quechee
Wood, R. Stewart, Jr., *retired bishop*

White River Junction
Rutter, Frances Tompson *publisher*

Wolcott
Fisher, Neal Floyd *religious organization administrator*

VIRGINIA

Alexandria
Handal, Ephrem I. (Ihsan Handal) *theology studies educator, deacon*
Lewis, Lloyd Alexander *priest, educator*

Amissville
Coutu, Charles Arthur *deacon*

Arlington
Terzian, Grace Paine *publisher*

Ashland
†Tuell, Steven Shawn *religious studies educator, minister*

Big Island
Durham, John I. *retired religious studies educator*

Blacksburg
Grover, Norman LaMotte *theologian, philosopher*

Chantilly
Chrzanowski, Leye Jeannette *publisher*

Charlottesville
Childress, James Franklin *theology and medical educator*
Finley, Robert Van Eaton *minister*
Scott, Nathan Alexander, Jr., *minister, literary critic, religious educator*
Unsworth, Richard Preston *minister, educator, school administrator*

Chesapeake
Stafford, Kenneth Victor, Sr., *minister*

Emory
Kellogg, Frederic Richard *religious studies educator*

Falls Church
†Bankson, Marjory *religious association administrator*
Benton, Nicholas Frederick *publisher*
†Lotz, Denton *minister, church official*

Fincastle
Cummings, Kevin Bryan *minister*

Floyd
Cosby, John Canada *retired lay worker*

Fredericksburg
Bailey, Amos Purnell *clergyman, syndicated columnist, author*

Front Royal
Andes, Larry Dale *minister*

Harrisonburg
Augsburger, Aaron Donald *clergyman*
Burkholder, Owen Eugene *religious organization administrator*

King George
Agnew, Christopher Mack *minister, historian*

Lexington
Hodges, Louis Wendell *religion educator*

Lynchburg
†Brindle, Wayne Allan *religious studies educator*
Falwell, Jerry L. *minister*

Lyndhurst
Dieter, Melvin Easterday *retired minister, educator*

Martinsville
Plonk, William McGuire *retired minister*
Shackleford, William Alton, Sr., *minister*

Mc Lean
Topping, Eva Catafygiotu *writer, lecturer, educator*

Mechanicsville
Gerrish, Brian Albert *theologian, educator*

Midlothian
Hanes-Stevens, LaVerne E. *minister, social services administrator*

Mineral
Speer, Jack Atkeson *publisher*

Palmyra
Brown, Nan Marie *clergywoman*

Radford
McNeil, Ramsey English *religious studies educator*

Richmond
Aigner, Emily Burke *Christian lay minister*
Barton, Jonathan Miller *clergyman*
Dombalis, Constantine Nicholas *minister, writer*
Fisher, Edgar Jacob, Jr., *religious organization administrator*
†Hicks, Douglas A. *religious studies educator, minister*
Lee, Peter James *bishop*
Moore, John Sterling, Jr., *retired minister*
Rogers, Isabel Wood *retired theological educator*
Wooten, Joan Hedrich *minister*

Roanoke
Easterling, Eddie Jean *publisher*
MacLean, Iain Stewart *minister, educator*

Staunton
Kopp, George Philip, Jr., *minister*

Sterling
Piper, Thomas Samuel *minister, consultant*

Vienna
Burr, Ronald Edwin *publisher*

Virginia Beach
Christy, Larry Todd *publisher*
Synan, Harold Vinson *minister, university dean*
Williams, J(ohn) Rodman *theologian, educator, clergyman*

Williamsburg
Holmes, David Lynn *religion educator*

Winchester
Herzfeld, Garson *rabbi*
Kohl, Harold *missionary, educator*

Woodberry Forest
Campbell, Dennis Marion *educator, university administrator, theologian*

Wytheville
Starks, Charles Wiley *minister*

Yorktown
Ivy, Richard F. *retired minister*
Wood, James Edward, Jr., *religion educator, author*

WASHINGTON

Arlington
Kell, Lyle Nicholas *retired minister, retired real estate broker*

Bellevue
Berkley, James Donald *clergyman*

Bothell
Wirt, Sherwood Eliot *minister, writer*

Chehalis
Detrick, Donald Howard *minister*

Des Moines
†Andrews, William F. *minister*
Tuell, Jack Marvin *retired bishop*

Fairfield
Adams, Glen Cameron *publisher*

Moses Lake
Sanderson, Holladay Worth *priest*

Prosser
Cooper, Lynn Dale *retired minister, retired navy chaplain*

Seattle
Burrows, Elizabeth MacDonald *religious organization executive, educator*
Fluke, Lyla Schram (Mrs. John M. Fluke Sr.) *publisher*
†Moe-Lobeda, Cynthia Diane *theology studies educator*
Robb, John Wesley *religion educator*
Szeto, Hung *publisher*

Spokane
†Edwards, James Robert *religious educator*
Lee, Richard Francis James *evangelical clergyman, media consultant, lawyer*
Polley, Harvey Lee *retired missionary, math and science educator*

Tacoma
Peterson, Thomas Charles *minister, pastoral counselor and therapist*
Reigstad, Ruth Elaine *lay worker, retired physical therapy consultant*
Wiegman, Eugene William *minister, former college administrator*

Toppenish
Warren, Larry Michael *clergyman*

University Place
Seiber, Richard Allan *retired minister*

Vancouver
Congdon, Roger Douglass *theology educator, minister*

Walla Walla
†Palmer, James F. *minister*

WEST VIRGINIA

Beckley
Rehbein, Edward Andrew *minister, geologist, consultant*

Charleston
Ives, Samuel Clifton *minister*
Leasor, Jane *religion and philosophy educator, musician*
Scott, Olof Henderson, Jr., *priest*

Fairmont
Stevens, Earl Patrick *minister*

Fayetteville
†Seay-Bell, Margaretta *pastoral counselor*

Hinton
Glaser, Robert Harvey, Sr., *retired pastor*

Maysel
†Paxton, James R. *minister*

Morgantown
Cayton, Mary Evelyn *minister*

Paden City
Ezharath, Joseph *pastor*

Wheeling
†Keppel, John H. *minister*
†Thurston, Bonnie Bowman *religion educator, minister*

WISCONSIN

Appleton
Abitz, James H. *religious organization executive*

Bayfield
Wilhelm, Sister Phyllis *religious studies educator, director*

Eau Claire
Kirby, H(arry) Scott *priest*

Green Bay
Banks, Robert J. *bishop*
Geisendorfer, James Vernon *religious writer, researcher*

Iola
Mishler, Clifford Leslie *publisher*

Lake Geneva
Slocum, Robert Boak

Madison
†Cohen, Charles Lloyd *history and religious studies educator*
Fitchen, Allen Nelson *publisher*
Fox, Michael Vass *Hebrew educator*
Little, George Daniel *clergyman*
Thomas, J. Mark *sociology educator, research fellow, minister*

Manitowoc
Klingeisen, Richard Herman *priest*

Middleton
McDermott, Molly *lay minister*

Milwaukee
Blumberg, Sherry Helene *Jewish education educator*
Healy, Cletus S. J. *priest*
Hirsch, June Schaut *priest*
Huebner, Sister Rosemarita *nun, art educator*
†Misner, Paul *theology educator*
Radde, Dale Lee *religious organization administrator, deacon, editor, pastor*
Robertson, Michael Swing *minister*
Stubbe, Ray William *minister, writer*
Weakland, Rembert G. *retired archbishop*

Mukwonago
Scarvie, Walter Bernard *clergyman*

Nashotah
Munday, Robert Stevenson *priest, academic administrator*

Oshkosh
Barwig, Regis Norbert James *priest*

Rice Lake
Alho, Sister Bonnie Kathleen *pastoral associate*

Sturgeon Bay
Van Duyse, Francis Donald (Fritz Van) *publisher*

Webster
Punch, William Anthony (Nicholas Punch) *priest*

Wisconsin Rapids
Parker, Arnold John *minister*

WYOMING

Cheyenne
†Hart, Joseph H. *bishop emeritus*

Worland
Foster, William Silas, Jr., *minister*

TERRITORIES OF THE UNITED STATES

AMERICAN SAMOA

Pago Pago
Weitzel, John Quinn *bishop*

FEDERATED STATES OF MICRONESIA

Chuuk
Samo, Amando *bishop*

Pohnpei
Hezel, Francis Xavier *clergy member, educator*

GUAM

Agana
Apuron, Anthony Sablan *archbishop*

PUERTO RICO

San Juan
Aponte Martinez, Luis Cardinal *archbishop emeritus*
Gonzalez, Roberto O. *bishop*

CANADA

ALBERTA

Edmonton
Mac Neil, Joseph Neil *archbishop*
Rahfeldt, Daryl Gene *minister*

BRITISH COLUMBIA

Prince George
Kerr, Nancy Karolyn *pastor, mental health consultant*

Richmond
Plomp, Teunis (Tony Plomp) *minister*

Victoria
Hollis, Reginald *archbishop*

MANITOBA

Churchill
Rouleau, Reynald *bishop*

NEWFOUNDLAND

Corner Brook
Payne, Sidney Stewart *retired archbishop*

NOVA SCOTIA

Little Bras d'Or
LeForte, John Stewart Archibald *retreat house manager*

ONTARIO

Brampton
Bastian, Donald Noel *retired bishop*

Cambridge
MacBain, William Halley *minister, theology educator, seminary chancellor*

Kingston
Read, Allan Alexander *minister*

Kitchener
Winger, Roger Elson *retired church administrator*

London
Hooper, Wayne Nelson *clergy member*

Ottawa
Macklem, Michael Kirkpatrick *publisher*
Ryan, William Francis *priest*
Squire, Anne Marguerite *religious leader*

Peterborough
Kristensen, John *church organization administrator*

Pickering
Irwin, John Wesley *publisher*

Sault Sainte Marie
Ferris, Ronald Curry *bishop*

Scarborough
†Mikloshazy, Attila *bishop*

Toronto
Finlay, Terence Edward *archbishop*
Harris, Nicholas George *publisher*
Jay, Charles Douglas *religion educator, college administrator, clergyman*
McWilliam, Joanne Elizabeth *retired religion educator*
Novak, David *Judaic studies educator, rabbi*
O'Mara, John Aloysius *retired bishop*
Plaut, Wolf Gunther *minister, author*

Waterloo
Van Seters, John *biblical literature educator, retired*

Windsor
La Rocque, Eugene Philippe *bishop emeritus*

QUEBEC

Beauharnois
Lebel, Robert *bishop*

Chicoutimi
Couture, Jean Guy *bishop*

Hull
Ebacher, Roger *archbishop*

Montreal
Hutchison, Andrew Sandford *archbishop*
Robillard, Edmond *priest*
Turcotte, Jean-Claude Cardinal *archbishop*

Outremont
Derderian, Hovnan *church official*

Quebec
Stavert, Alexander Bruce *bishop*

Rimouski
Blanchet, Bertrand *archbishop*

Rouyn
Hamelin, Jean-Guy *bishop*

Westmount
Coolidge, Robert Tytus *deacon, historian, educator*

SASKATCHEWAN

Saskatoon
Jacobson, Sverre Theodore *retired minister*

MEXICO

Aguascalientes
Godinez Flores, Ramon *bishop*

Guadalajara
†Sandoval Iñiguez, Juan Cardinal *archbishop*

Mexico City
†Rivera Carrera, Norberto Cardinal *archbishop*

San Nicolas
†Suarez Rivera, Adolfo Antonio Cardinal *retired archbishop*

THE BAHAMAS

Nassau
†Harrison, Johnnie Sheppard *religious organization administrator*

BELGIUM

Brussels
Jadot, Jean Lambert Octave *clergyman*

BRAZIL

Rio de Janeiro
Sales, Eugenio de Araujo Cardinal *emeritus archbishop*

CHILE

Talca
McNamee, Sister Catherine *educator*

ENGLAND

London
Hornyak, Eugene Augustine *bishop*

Oxford
Gulbrandsen, Natalie Webber *religious association administrator*
Ker, Ian Turnbull *priest, scholar*

Tunbridge Wells
Howden, Frank Newton *Episcopal priest, humanities educator*

FRANCE

Vanves
Dubs, Patrick Christian *publisher*

IRAN

Tehran
Mardinkha, Khnania, IV, *church administrator*

ITALY

Rome
Baum, William Wakefield Cardinal *archbishop emeritus*
Billy, Dennis Joseph *priest*
†Gagnon, Edouard Cardinal *ecclesiastic*
Kolvenbach, Peter Hans *priest, religious order superior*

Vatican City
Foley, John Patrick *archbishop*
Stafford, James Francis *cardinal*
Szoka, Edmund Casimir Cardinal *archbishop*

JAPAN

Kyoto
Zikmund, Barbara Brown *minister, church history educator*

Nagoya
Seland, John Joseph *priest, educator*

KENYA

Nairobi
†Kim, Caleb Chul-Soo *theology studies educator, minister*

SOUTH AFRICA

Cape Town
Tutu, Desmond Mpilo *archbishop emeritus*

SRI LANKA

Battilacoa
Miller, Benjamin Henry *priest, human rights advocate*

VATICAN CITY

Citta del Vaticano
†Stafford, J. Francis Cardinal *archbishop*

Vatican City
John Paul, His Holiness Pope, II, (Karol Jozef Wojtyla) *bishop of Rome*

ADDRESS UNPUBLISHED

†Abrahamson, Karen K. *theologian, editor*
†Aitken, Robert Baker *religious studies educator, writer*
Allison, Andrew Marvin *church administrator*
Ambrozic, Aloysius Cardinal (His Eminence Aloysius Cardinal Ambrozic) *cardinal*
Anderman, David E. *minister*
Anderson, John Firth *church administrator, librarian*
Armstrong, (Arthur) James (Arthur Armstrong) *educator, consultant, lecturer, writer*
Baehr, Theodore *religious organization administrator, communications executive*
Banks, Deirdre Margaret *retired church organization administrator*
†Barber, John Joseph *minister, writer*
†Barbey, Adélaïde *publisher*
Barker, Verlyn Lloyd *retired minister, educator*
Barré, Lloyd Milton *retired religion educator, researcher, writer*
Bayne, David Cowan *priest, legal scholar, law educator*
Bechtol, Larry Owen *pastor*
Beldon, Sanford T. *publisher*
Bender, Ross Thomas *minister*
Bersin, Ruth Hargrave *priest, social services administrator*
Bevilacqua, Anthony Joseph Cardinal *archbishop emeritus*
Bodey, Richard Allen *minister, educator*
Bordy, Bill (William James Bordy) *publisher*
Born, Ethel Wolfe *religious writer*
†Bosco, Anthony Gerard *bishop*
Bothwell, John Charles *retired archbishop*

Broadwater, James E. *publisher*
Brooks, Babert Vincent *publisher*
Buckley, Michael J. *theology educator*
Cacciavillan, Agostino *cardinal*
Capon, Edwin Gould *church organization administrator, clergyman*
Castle, Howard Blaine *retired religious organization administrator*
Cenkner, William *religion educator, academic administrator*
Chewning, Richard Carter *retired religious business ethics educator*
Clement, John Edward Strausz *retired minister, retired religious organization administrator*
Clymer, Wayne Kenton *bishop*
Cobb, John Boswell, Jr., *clergyman, educator*
Cole, Clifford Adair *clergyman*
†Collins, Joda Lee *minister*
Corbett, Gordon Leroy *minister*
Crabtree, Davida Foy *minister*
†Craddock, Elaine *religious studies educator*
Culverhouse, Cecil Griffith *minister*
Derickson, Stanley Lewis *minister, writer*
Dipko, Thomas Earl *retired minister, national church executive*
Dornette, Ralph Meredith *religious organization administrator, educator, minister*
Douglass, Jane Dempsey *theology educator*
†Dubay, Thomas E. *priest, writer*
Dudick, Michael Joseph *retired bishop*
Duecker, Robert Sheldon *retired bishop*
Egan, Edward M. *cardinal*
Ely, Laurence Driggs, III, *theoretical Christian astrologer*
Emerson, R. Clark *priest, business administrator*
English-Anderson, San Dei *minister*
Epp, Eldon Jay *religion educator*
Epps, William David *priest*
Ewing, Elisabeth Anne Rooney *priest*
Ewing, James E. *priest*
Fant, Clyde Edward, Jr., *religion educator*
Farley, Benjamin Wirt *religious studies educator, writer*
Fazio, Evelyn M. *publisher*
Ferguson, Whitworth, III, *pastor*
Finnegan, Sara Anne (Sara Lycett) *publisher*
Fisher, Robert Bruce *priest*
Forst, Marion Francis *bishop*
Frankson-Kendrick, Sarah Jane *publisher*
Fricklas, Anita Alper *retired religious organization administrator*
Frost, Linda Gail *clergyman, hospital chaplain*
Fry, Hedy *member of parliament*
Fry, Malcolm Craig *retired clergyman*
Fullmer, Lee Wayne *retired minister*
Gandolfo, Lucian John *minister, federal official*
Gemignani, Michael Caesar *clergyman, retired educator*
Gerstner, Jonathan Neil *religious studies educator*
†Goloversic, Mary Cecelia *writer*
Gralla, Milton *publisher*
Grant, Leonard Tydings *clergyman*
Gregory, Myra May *religious organization administrator, educator*
Gretser, George Westfall *publisher*
Griffin, James Anthony *bishop*
†Guccione, Robert Charles Josep *publisher*
Guerrera, Vittorio *priest*
Gutmann, Reinhart Bruno *clergyman, social worker*
Hagelstein, Robert Philip *publisher*
Haines, Lee Mark, Jr., *religious denomination administrator*
Hambidge, Douglas Walter *archbishop*
Hammond, Charles Ainley *clergyman*
Harman, Robert John *retired religious organization administrator*
Harris, Rogers Sanders *bishop*
Haryono, Ignatius Wibisono *writer*
Hernandez, Ramon Robert *retired clergyman and librarian*
Hill, Paul Mark *clergyman*
Hofford, James Loveday *Christian evangelist, columnist, poet*
Holle, Reginald Henry *retired bishop*
Holleman, John L. *priest*
Holleman, Sandy Lee *religious organization administrator*
Hoops, William James *clergyman*
†Hughes, Edward T. *retired bishop*
Hummel, Gene Maywood *retired bishop*
Huras, William David *retired bishop*
Hurley, Francis T. *retired archbishop*
Huron, Roderick Eugene *minister, writer*
Hurst, Kenneth Thurston *publisher*
†Jarrell, Charles Michael *bishop*
Jiler, William Laurence *publisher*
Johnson, Gordon Gilbert *religion educator, minister*
Johnson, Jennie *chaplain, social worker*
Jones, William Augustus, Jr., *retired bishop*
Joslin, David Bruce *bishop*
Kari, Daven Michael *religious studies educator*
Keeler, William H. *archbishop*
Kelley, Edward Allen *publisher*
Kellogg, David *publisher*
Kempski, Ralph Aloisius *bishop*
King, Sandra L. *writer*
Korom, Frank Joseph *religion educator*
†Krause, Edward Charles *priest, educator*
†Krein, Suzanne Ruth *writer*
Kucera, Daniel William *retired bishop*
Landes, George Miller *biblical studies educator*
Lansdale, H. Parker *minister, historian, non-profit administrator*
†Law, Bernard Francis Cardinal *retired archbishop*
Leavy, Herbert Theodore *publisher*
Levy, Valery *publisher*
Light, Arthur Heath *bishop*
Lindstrom, Donald Fredrick, Jr., *priest, consultant*
Loew, Brenda *publisher*
Lohmuller, Martin Nicholas *bishop*
Loppnow, Milo Alvin *clergyman, former church official*
Lucas, Bert Albert *pastor, social services administrator, consultant*
Luetkehoelter, Gottlieb Werner (Lee Luetkehoelter) *retired bishop, clergyman*
Lugenbeel, Edward Elmer *publisher*
†Maginnis, Robert P. *bishop*
Mali, Paul *publisher, retired management educator*
Mann, Daniel *religious organization worker*
†Marti, Gerardo *minister, sociologist, educator*
†Martino, Joseph F. *bishop*
McClellan, Larry Allen *educator, writer, minister*
McClinton, Wendell C. *religious organization administrator*
†McClurg, Patricia A. *minister*
†McCoy, Gordon R. *minister*
McDermott, Lucinda Mary *ecumenical minister, teacher, philosopher, poet, author, psychologist*
McKelway, Alexander Jeffrey *religion studies educator*
McKinley, Ellen Bacon *priest*
†Mc Kinney, Joseph Crescent *retired bishop*
McMaster, Belle Miller *religious organization administrator*
McQuilkin, John Robertson *religion educator, academic administrator, writer*
Meade, Kenneth Albert *retired minister*
Melczek, Dale J. *bishop*
Melvin, Billy Alfred *clergyman*
Melzer, Barbara Evelyn *minister*
Milhouse, Paul William *bishop*
Miller, Mary Hotchkiss *lay worker*
Miller, Vernon Dallace *minister*
Mischke, Carl Herbert *retired religious association executive*
Moffett, Samuel Hugh *retired educator, minister*
Muckerman, Norman James *priest, writer*
Mulder, Edwin George *retired minister, church official*
Mullan, Donald William *archbishop*
Murray, Pius Charles William *priest, librarian, educator*
Nance, David W. *minister*
Netterville, George Bronson *retired minister*
†Nieva, Constantino S. *priest, researcher*
Norgren, William Andrew *retired religious denomination administrator*
Nottingham, William Jesse *retired church mission executive, minister*
Nunn, Charles Burgess *religious organization executive*
Nwokoye, Patrick Ikechukwu *priest, researcher*
Nycklemoe, Glenn Winston *bishop*
Nygren, Malcolm Ernest *minister*
Oestmann, Irma Emma *minister*
Ofstedal, Paul Estrem *retired clergy member*
†O'Malley, J. Steven *theology studies educator, minister*
Ortiz, Angel Vicente *church administrator*
Osborne, James Alfred *religious organization administrator*
Ostaszewski, Alyce Vitella *religion educator*
Osvath, Ludovic Lajos *minister*
Palms, Roger Curtis *educator, editor, clergyman*
†Peace, John T. *religious studies educator*
Peck, Paul Lachlan *minister*
Post, Avery Denison *retired church official*
Poteat, James Donald *retired diaconal minister, retired military officer*
Powell, Charles William *former minister, personal and professional development coach*
†Powell, Donald David *religious studies educator*
Preus, David Walter *bishop, minister*
Probasco, Calvin Henry Charles *clergyman, college administrator*
Ramos, Miguel Willie *priest, educator*
Reamer, Shirley Jean *minister*
Reed, Thomas Lee, II, *minister, social worker, educator*
Reho, James Hughes *religious studies educator*
Reynolds, Lewis Dayton *pastor*
Righter, Walter Cameron *bishop*
Ritchings, Frances Anne *priest*
Roesch, Joseph Gerard *priest, theology studies educator*
Ruof, Richard Alan *minister*
Rupe, Meredith *minister*
Ryk, Mary A. *retired chaplain, poet*
Salatka, Charles Alexander *retired archbishop*
Sanfilippo, Mary Helena *nun*
Scharlemann, Robert Paul *religious studies educator, clergyman*
Schmiel, David Gerhard *clergyman, religious education administrator*
Schmitt, Howard Stanley *minister*
Schuelke, John Paul *religious organization administrator*
Seale, James Millard *retired religious organization administrator, clergyman*
Shotwell, Malcolm Green *retired minister*
†Sider, Harvey Ray *retired minister*
Singletary, Patricia Ann *minister*
Sit, Hong Chan *minister*
Sloyan, Gerard Stephen *religious studies educator, priest*
Smith, Ann Hamill *retired religion educator*
Smith, D(aisy) Mullett *publisher*
Snyder, Robert Carl *retired minister*
Solano, Julio Rafael *priest, educator*
†Sonsino, Rifat *retired rabbi*
Spake, Kluane *minister, writer*
Sparks, William Sheral *retired seminary librarian*
Sprenger, Ernest Henry *pastor, translator*
†Steffee, Nina Dean *publisher*
Stendahl, Krister *retired bishop*
Stines, Fred, Jr., *publisher*
Sullivan, James Lenox *clergyman*
†Swayd, Samy *religious studies educator*
Taylor, Lewis Jerome, Jr., *priest*
Taylor, Thomas Fuller *religious society administrator*
Thompson, Eugene Mayne *retired minister*
Thompson, Richard Lloyd *retired pastor*
Thottupuram, Kurian Cherian *priest, college director, educator*
Tillman, William Morris, Jr., *theology educator*
Traylor, William Robert *publisher*
†Troxel, Ronald Lewis *religious studies educator*
Vachon, Louis-Albert Cardinal *archbishop*
Van Dyck, Nicholas Booraem *minister, foundation official*
Vasko, Peter Theodore Frederick *priest*
†Vlazny, John George *bishop*
Von Gonten, Kevin Paul *priest, liturgist, theologian*
Waltz, Alan Kent *clergyman, denominational executive*
Wantland, William Charles *retired bishop, lawyer*
†Washington-Cretter, Brian E. *minister, sheet metal assembler, riveter*
Weinhauer, William Gillette *retired bishop*
†Weinkauf, Mary Louise Stanley *clergywoman*
White, James Floyd *theology educator*
White, Lerrill James *clinical pastoral educator*
Williams, Ervin Eugene *religious organization administrator*
†Williams, Michael James *theology studies educator, associate pastor*
Wills, Charles Francis *former church executive, retired career officer*
Wilson, Lois M. *minister*
†Wilson, Warren Samuel *clergyman, bishop*
†Winslow, David Allen *chaplain, retired naval officer*
Wisehart, Mary Ruth *retired religious organization executive*
Wold, Margaret Barth *religion educator, author*
Wooten, Cecil Aaron *retired religious organization administrator*
Ziegler, Earl Keller *minister*
Zirbes, Mary Kenneth *retired minister*

SCIENCE: LIFE SCIENCE

UNITED STATES

ALABAMA

Auburn
Ball, Donald Maury *agronomist, consultant*
Dobson, F. Stephen *ecologist*
Zhang, Daowei *forest economist, researcher, educator*

Birmingham
Ball, Laurence Andrew *microbiologist, educator, researcher*
Davenport, Horace Willard *physiologist, science educator*
Elgavish, Ada *molecular and cellular biologist*
Finley, Sara Crews *medical geneticist, educator*
Haddox, Jeffrey Lynn *vision scientist*
Marchase, Richard Banfield *cell biologist, educator*
Mueller, Robin Sue *biology educator*
Page, John Gardner *research administrator, scientist*
†Peti-Peterdi, Janos *physiologist*
Shoemaker, Richard L. *retired physiologist*

Daphne
Nelson, David Herman *biologist, educator, researcher*

Decatur
O'Brien, Richard Alan *research scientist*

Huntsville
†Bearden, Thomas Eugene *research scientist, researcher*
Gillani, Noor Velshi *atmospheric scientist, researcher, educator*

Mobile
French, Elizabeth Irene *biology educator, violinist*
†Parker, James Courtney *physiologist, researcher*

Montgomery
Aleinikov, Andrei Grigoryevich *science administrator, researcher, consultant*
†Griffin, Broderick DeVond *science educator, political consultant*
Sass, Neil Leslie *toxicologist*

Talladega
†Schwinghamer, Mary Denise *veterinarian*

Tuskegee Institute
Ahl, Alwynelle Self *zoology, ecology and veterinary medical executive*

ALASKA

Anchorage
Davies, Garry *biology educator*
†Maki, Alan Walter *biologist, environmental scientist*
Nielsen, Jennifer Lee *molecular ecologist, researcher*

Fairbanks
†Bowyer, R. Terry *science educator*
Kessel, Brina *ornithologist, educator, researcher*
†Schamel, Douglas L. *science educator, researcher*

Gustavus
Burgess, Marilyn K. *science educator*

Juneau
Shepard, Beatrice L. *retired microbiologist, historian*
†Smith, Winston Paul *wildlife scientist, forest service*

Soldotna
Franzmann, Albert Wilhelm *wildlife veterinarian, consultant*

ARIZONA

Bisbee
Behney, Charles Augustus, Jr., *veterinarian*
Milton, John P. *ecologist, educator, author, photographer*

Flagstaff
Cortner, Hanna Joan *research scientist, educator*
Hammond, Howard David *retired botanist, editor*
Phillips, Arthur Morton, III, *botanist, consultant*
Price, Peter Wilfrid *ecology educator, researcher*
Putnam, William Lowell *science association administrator*

Glendale
Collins, Richard Francis *microbiologist, educator*

Mesa
†Tudor-Locke, Catrine Elizabeth *research scientist, educator, research scientist, consultant*

Phoenix
Bolin, Vernon Spencer *microbiologist, consultant*
†DelParigi, Angelo *research scientist*
Kimball, Bruce Arnold *soil scientist*
Revie, Jean E. *science educator*

Prescott
†Fleischner, Thomas Lowe *conservation biologist, educator*
†Sloan, Marjorie Hawkins *science educator, retired advertising executive*
Welna, Jerome Sheldon *agriculturist, consultant*

Scottsdale
†Northey, William Thomas *microbiologist, educator*

Surprise
Steffan, Wallace Allan *entomologist, educator, museum director*
Veigel, Jon Michael *science administrator*

Taylor
Kerr, Barbara Prosser *research scientist, educator*

Tempe
Amin, Omar Mohamed *parasitologist*
†Lohr, Dennis E. *research scientist, education educator*
†Velupillai Mani, Ramesh *research scientist*

Tucson
Acker, Robert Flint *microbiologist*
Besselsen, David Guy *veterinary pathologist, researcher*
Brusca, Richard Charles *biologist, researcher, educator*
Childs, Richard Francis *retired scientist, educator*
Erickson, Eric Herman, Jr., *entomologist, scientist*
Erickson, Robert Porter *genetics researcher, educator, clinician*
Fritts, Harold Clark *dendrochronology educator, researcher*
Gerba, Charles Peter *microbiologist, educator*
Green, Robert Scott *biotechnology company executive*
Hildebrand, John G(rant) *neurobiologist, educator*
Hull, Herbert Mitchell *plant physiologist, researcher*
Jeter, Wayburn Stewart *retired microbiology educator, microbiologist*
Kaszniak, Alfred Wayne *neuropsychologist*
McCormick, Floyd Guy, Jr., *agricultural educator, college administrator*
†Mendelson, Neil H. *microbial geneticist, educator*
Metcalfe, Darrel Seymour *agronomist, educator*
Neuman, Shlomo P. *hydrology educator*
Shannon, Robert Rennie *optical sciences center administrator, educator*
†Strausfeld, Nicholas James *neurobiology and evolutionary biology researcher, educator*
Winfree, Arthur Taylor *biologist, educator*
Yocum, Harrison Gerald *horticulturist, botanist, educator, researcher*

Wikieup
Brattstrom, Bayard Holmes *biology educator*

ARKANSAS

Bella Vista
Musacchia, X(avier) J(oseph) *physiology and biophysics educator*

Cherokee Village
Hollingsworth, John Alexander *retired science and mathematics educator, writer, consultant*

Fayetteville
Brown, Connell Jean *retired animal science educator*
Morris, Justin Roy *food scientist, consultant, enologist, research director, science administrator*
Musick, Gerald Joe *retired entomology educator*
Riggs, Robert Dale *plant pathology and nematology educator, researcher*

Steele, Kenneth Franklin, Jr., *science educator, director*

Jefferson
Casciano, Daniel Anthony *biologist, educator*
Hotchkiss, Charlotte Evans *veterinarian, researcher*

Little Rock
Hinson, Jack Allsbrook *research toxicologist, educator*
†Jacobi, Sandra E. *molecular biologist, researcher*
Logan, Michael J. *veterinary epidemiology officer*
†Machaca, Khaled *cell biologist, educator*
McSwain, Byrdie Engle *laboratory scientist, immunohemotologist*
†Price, Peter Michael *molecular biology researcher, educator*
Tucker, Gary Edward *botanist, wetland scientist, ecologist*
Wight, Patricia Anne *neuroscience educator*
Zhang, Xuming *microbiology educator*

Monticello
Ficklin, Robert Lee *soil scientist, research scientist*

CALIFORNIA

Alameda
Luther, John Stafford *biology educator, consultant*

Albany
Schwimmer, Sigmund *food enzymologist*

Anaheim
Lawton, Michael James *entomologist, pest management specialist*

Atherton
Starr, Chauncey *research institute executive*

Berkeley
Anderson, John Richard *entomologist, educator*
Baldwin, Bruce Gregg *botany educator, researcher*
Barrett, Reginald Haughton *biology educator, wildlife management educator*
Bern, Howard Alan *science educator, research biologist*
Brenner, Sydney *molecular biologist, researcher*
Burnside, Mary Beth *biology educator, researcher*
Casida, John Edward *entomology educator*
Chandler, David *scientist, educator*
Dickinson, Michael *physiologist*
Freeling, Michael Richard *genetics educator, researcher*
Getz, Wayne Marcus *biomathematician, researcher, educator*
Hazen, Terry Clyde *microbial ecologist, educator*
Levine, Mark David *science administrator, director*
Levine, Michael Steven *science educator*
Lidicker, William Zander, Jr., *zoologist, educator*
Martin, G. Steven *biochemist, educator*
Quinn, Nigel William Trevelyan *scientist, engineer*
†Rudin, Norah *forensic DNA consultant, science writer*
Schachman, Howard Kapnek *molecular biologist, educator*
Spear, Robert Clinton *environmental health educator, consultant*
†Sposito, Garrison *soil scientist, educator, reseacher*
†Stross, Fred Helmut *research scientist*
Teeguarden, Dennis Earl *forest economist, educator*
Wake, David Burton *biology educator*
Wake, Marvalee Hendricks *biology educator*
Willhite, Calvin Campbell *toxicologist*
Wood, David Lee *entomologist, educator*

Beverly Hills
Darko, Denis F. *research scientist, educator, physician*
Smith, Marilyn Noeltner *retired science educator*

Bodega Bay
Clegg, James Standish *physiologist, biochemist, educator*
Cohen, Anne Carolyn Constant *biologist*
Hand, Cadet Hammond, Jr., *marine biologist, educator*

Carlsbad
Hale, David Fredrick *biotechnologist*
Pernasetti, Flavia Mercer *molecular biologist*

Carmel
Epel, David *biologist, educator*
Pasten, Laura Jean *veterinarian*

Chico
Cooke, Ron Charles *science educator*
Ediger, Robert Ike *botanist, educator*

Claremont
Purves, William Kirkwood *biologist, educator*

Copperopolis
†Ezell, Wayland L. *biologist, educator*

Coronado
Foster, Brian Duane *biologist, consultant*

Cupertino
Cheeseman, Douglas Taylor, Jr., *wildlife tour executive, photographer, educator*

Davis
Allard, Robert Wayne *geneticist, educator*
Ardans, Alexander Andrew *veterinarian, laboratory director, educator*
Barbour, Michael G(eorge) *botany educator, ecological consultant*
Baskin, Ronald Joseph *cell biologist, physiologist, biophysicist educator, dean*
Cliver, Dean Otis *microbiologist, educator*
Colvin, Harry Walter, Jr., *physiology educator*
Epstein, Emanuel *plant physiologist*
Ernst, Ralph Ambrose *poultry specialist*
Freedland, Richard Allan *retired biologist, educator*
Gifford, Ernest Milton *biologist, educator*
Hastings, Alan *environmental biology educator*
Hess, Charles Edward *environmental horticulture educator*
Hope, Hakon *research scientist*
Horwitz, Barbara Ann *physiologist, educator, consultant*
Hristova, Krassimira Radoykova *microbiologist, researcher*
Jones, Edward George *neuroscience professor*
Kado, Clarence Isao *molecular biologist*
Kester, Dale Emmert *pomologist, educator*
Klasing, Susan Allen *environmental toxicologist*
Kofranek, Anton Miles *floriculturist, educator*
†Korvatska, Elena *biologist, educator*
Laidlaw, Harry Hyde, Jr., *entomology educator*
Meyer, Margaret Eleanor *microbiologist, educator*
Moyle, Peter Briggs *fisheries and biology educator*
Murphy, Terence Martin *biology educator*
Qualset, Calvin O. *plant genetics and agronomy educator*
Rhode, Edward Albert *veterinary medicine educator, veterinary cardiologist*
Rost, Thomas Lowell *plant biology educator*
Savageau, Michael Antonio *science educator, engineering educator*
Schoener, Thomas William *zoology educator, researcher*
Sillman, Arnold Joel *physiologist, educator*
Steffey, Eugene Paul *veterinary medicine educator*
Stewart, James Ian *agricultural water scientist, cropping system developer, consultant*
Watt, Kenneth Edmund Ferguson *zoology educator*
Williams, William Arnold *agronomy educator*

Del Mar
Farquhar, Marilyn Gist *cell biology and pathology educator*

Duarte
Vaughn, James English, Jr., *neurobiologist*

Emeryville
Choi, Doo-Sup *molecular biologist*

Fallbrook
Loeber, Thomas Stanton *retired biologist*

Foster City
Ladunga, Istvan (Steve Ladunga) *computational molecular biologist*

Fremont
Li, Fuhe *research scientist, science administrator*
Mah, Tina Lily *science administrator*
White, Raymond Leslie *geneticist*

Fullerton
Jones, Claris Eugene, Jr., *botanist, educator*

Garden Grove
Gandhi, Manish P. *microbiologist*

Gardena
Hu, Steve Seng-Chiu *scientific research company executive, academic administrator*

Hayward
†Deshpande, Deepa Suhas *research scientist*

Healdsburg
Vedros, Neylan Anthony *microbiologist, educator*

Hollywood
Stepanov, Sergei Valentinovich *consultant, researcher*

Hopland
Jones, Milton Bennion *retired agronomist, educator*

Irvine
Ayala, Francisco José *geneticist, educator*
Demetrescu, Mihai Constantin *research scientist, educator, computer company executive*
Lenhoff, Howard Maer *biological sciences educator, academic administrator, activist*
Silverman, Paul Hyman *science administrator, former university official*
†Suarez-Villa, Luis *innovation and technological change, economic and social development, regional analysis educator*

Kelseyville
Sandmeyer, E. E. *toxicologist, consultant*

Kensington
Stent, Gunther Siegmund *molecular biologist, educator*

La Jolla
Alvariño De Leira, Angeles (Angeles Alvariño) *biologist, oceanographer*
Bloom, Floyd Elliott *physician, research scientist*
Brooks, Charles Lee, III, *computational biophysicist, educator*
†Degryse, Bernard *cell biologist*
Guillemin, Roger C. L. *physiologist*
Haxo, Francis Theodore *marine biologist*
Helinski, Donald Raymond *biologist, educator*
Hughes, Gordon F. *research scientist, electrical engineer*
Hunter, Tony (Anthony Rex Hunter) *molecular biologist, educator*
Ideker, Trey *computational biologist, molecular biologist*
Lewin, Ralph Arnold *biologist*
Pollok, Brian Andrew *biotechnology company executive*
Richman, Douglas Daniel *medical virologist, educator, internist*
West, John Burnard *physiologist, physician, educator*
Wilkie, Donald Walter *biologist, aquarium museum director*
Youngstedt, Shawn Douglas *research scientist*

La Verne
Jones, Jay H. *biology and biochemistry educator*
Neher, Robert Trostle *biology educator*

Laguna Niguel
Coleman, Roger Dixon *bacteriologist*

Lake Arrowhead
Asher, James Edward *forestry consultant, engineer, arborist, forensic expert*

Livermore
Balasubramanian, Krishnan *research scientist, educator*

Loma Linda
Aloia, Roland Craig *scientist, administrator, educator*
Fechter, Laurence David *toxicology educator, researcher*
†Fodor, Istvan *molecular biologist, researcher*
Longo, Lawrence Daniel *physiologist, obstetrician-gynecologist*
†Schwab, Ernest Roe, III *physiology educator, researcher*

Long Beach
Schubel, Jerry Robert *marine science educator, scientist, university dean*
Swatek, Frank Edward *microbiology educator*
†Tai, Kwok-Keung *biologist, researcher*

Los Alamitos
Aberman, Harold Mark *veterinarian*

Los Altos
King, Chi-Yu *research scientist*

Los Angeles
Alkana, Ronald Lee *neuroscientist*
Bailey, Julia Nancy *geneticist*
Baker, Robert Frank *molecular biologist, educator*
Bharitkar, Sunil Ganpat *research scientist, technology specialist*
Birren, James Emmett *university research center executive*
Bok, Dean *cell biologist, educator*
Bottjer, David John *earth scientist, biologist, educator*
Collias, Nicholas Elias *zoology educator, ornithologist*
Craft, Cheryl Mae *neurobiologist, anatomist, researcher*
Davies, Kelvin James Anthony *research scientist, educator, consultant, author*
†Diamond, Jared Mason *biologist*
Dragan, Feodor Feodorovich *research scientist*
Eisenberg, David Samuel *molecular biologist, educator*
†Fabunan, Ruben G *research scientist*
Finegold, Sydney Martin *microbiology educator*
Fu, Qianjie *research scientist*
Gilman, John Joseph *research scientist*
Gordon, Malcolm Stephen *biology educator*
Grinnell, Alan Dale *neurobiologist, educator, researcher*
Haglund, Thomas Roy *research biologist, consultant, educator*
†Heaney, Anthony Patrick *research scientist*
Horwitz, Marcus Aaron *microbiologist, immunologist*
†Hui, Eric Ka-Wai *virologist, researcher*
Kadner, Carl George *biology educator emeritus*
Kast, W. Martin *microbiology and immunology educator*
†Khawli, Leslie Albert *research scientist, educator*
†Ljubimov, Alexander V. *molecular biologist, cell biologist, researcher*
Lu, John Kuew-Hsiung *physiology educator, endocrinologist*
McClure, William Owen *biologist*
McGowen, Gerald Ellis *biologist*
Melnick, Michael *geneticist, educator*
Mohr, John Luther *biologist, environmental consultant*
Phinney, Bernard O. *research scientist, educator*
Slavkin, Harold Charles *biologist*
Sonnenschein, Ralph Robert *physiologist*
Szego, Clara Marian *cell biologist, educator*
Taylor, Charles Ellett *biologist, educator*
Villablanca, Jaime Rolando *medical neuroscientist, educator*
Xiao, Guishan *research scientist*
Xue, Yongkang *science educator*
Yang, Yang *science educator*
†Yuan, Huidong *molecular biologist*

Los Gatos
Mahmoudi, Massoud

Los Osos
Law, Orley Thomas *retired neuroscientist, educator, consultant, poet*

Malibu
Hunt, Valerie Virginia *electrophysiologist, educator*

Martinez
Thomas, Walter Dill, Jr., *retired forest pathologist, consultant*

Menlo Park
Crane, Hewitt David *science advisor*
Jorgensen, Paul J. *research company executive*

Merced
Olsen, David Magnor *chemistry and astronomy educator*

Mi Wuk Village
Rainey, Barbara Ann *sensory evaluation consultant*

Modesto
Hardage, Darwin "Dar" Henry *animal technologist*
Moe, Andrew Irving *veterinarian*

Moffett Field
Friedmann, E(merich) Imre *biologist, educator*
Kittel, Peter *research scientist*
Salerno, Louis J. *research scientist*

Monrovia
Kimnach, Myron William *botanist, horticulturist*

Monterey
Rowe, Neil Charles *science educator*

Moraga
Brown, James Edward *retired research scientist*

Napa
Moore, Bonnie Lou *biology educator, consultant*

Nevada City
Whitsel, Richard Harry *biologist, entomologist*

Oakland
Collins, James Francis *toxicologist*
Earle, Sylvia Alice *research biologist, oceanographer*
†Elkin, Lynne Osman *science historian, educator*
Granoff, Dan Martin *research scientist*
Hemmerich, Stefan *biomedical scientist, biotechnologist*
Jedrzejas, Mark J. *microbiologist, researcher*
†Spencer, Carol Lynn *biologist, educator*
Willson, Clyde D. *biologist, educator*

Palm Desert
Olson, Phillip David LeRoy *agriculturist, chemist*
Sausman, Karen *zoological park administrator*

Palmdale
Smith, Maureen McBride *laboratory administrator*

Palo Alto
Anderson, Charles Arthur *former research institute administrator*
Botstein, David *geneticist, educator*
Briggs, Winslow Russell *plant biologist, educator*
Eggers, Alfred John, Jr., *research corporation executive*
Gerety, Robert John *microbiologist, pharmaceutical company executive, pediatrician, vaccinologist*
Johnson, Noble Marshall *research scientist*
†Omana-Zapata, Imelda *research scientist*
†Pake, George Edward *research executive, physicist*
Sanders, William John *research scientist*
Sharma, Bhavender Paul *biotechnologist*
†Tsien, Richard Winyu *biology educator*
Yu, Jiun-Der *mechanics researcher*

Pasadena
†Abelson, John Norman *biology educator*
Beer, Reinhard *atmospheric scientist*
Bertani, Lillian Elizabeth Teegarden *biologist, researcher, educator*
†Choi-Yim, Haein *research scientist*
Davidson, Eric Harris *molecular and developmental biologist, educator*
Hussein, Ziad A. *electromagnetics scientist, researcher*
Lewis, Edward B. *biology educator*
Meyerowitz, Elliot Martin *biologist, educator*
Njoku, Eni Gerald *research scientist*
Owen, Ray David *biology educator*
Scott, David Clinton *research scientist*
†Sterling, Thomas L. *research scientist, educator*
Tappan, Janice Ruth Vogel *animal behavior researcher*
Varshavsky, Alexander Jacob *molecular biologist*
Yazami, Rachid *research scientist, consultant, editor*

Pebble Beach
Sanford-Hugus, Barbara *geneticist, consultant*

Pleasanton
Choy, Clement Kin-Man *research scientist*

Pomona
Keating, Eugene Kneeland *animal scientist, educator*

Redwood City
Neville, Roy Gerald *scientist, chemical management and environmental consultant*

Richmond
Beall, Frank Carroll *science director and educator*
Dixon, Thelma Dunnebacke *research scientist*
Forghani-Abkenari, Bagher *virologist, researcher*

Ridgecrest
†Paik, Sun Hye *cell biologist, research scientist*

Riverside

Bartnicki-Garcia, Salomon *microbiologist, educator*
Embleton, Tom William *horticultural science educator*
Erwin, Donald Carroll *plant pathology educator*
Goldberg, Sabine Ruth *soil scientist*
Hall, Anthony Elmitt *crop ecologist*
Martins-Green, Manuela *cell biologist*
Page, Albert Lee *soil science educator, researcher*
Sherman, Irwin William *biological sciences educator*
Spencer, William Franklin, Sr., *soil scientist, researcher*
Van Gundy, Seymour Dean *nematologist, plant pathologist, educator*
Zentmyer, George Aubrey *plant pathology educator*

Sacramento

Booze, Thomas Franklin *toxicologist*
†Brittan, Martin R. *biologist, educator*
Edwards, Michael Steven Brent
Hackney, Robert Ward *plant pathologist, nematologist, parasitologist, molecular geneticist, commercial arbitrator*
†Loewy, Erich H. *bioethicist*
Rosenberg, Dan Yale *retired plant pathologist*

Salinas

Lewellen, Robert Thomas *research geneticist*

San Bernardino

Mian, Lal Shah *entomologist, educator*

San Diego

Bartus, Raymond Thomas *neuroscientist, pharmaceutical executive, writer*
Bernstein, Sanford Irwin *biology educator*
Crick, Francis Harry Compton *science educator, researcher*
Dulbecco, Renato *biologist, educator*
Eckhart, Walter *molecular biologist, educator*
†Elliott, Graham *science educator*
Georgakakos, Konstantine Peter *research hydrologist*
Hayes, Claude Quinten Christopher *research scientist, inventor*
Heinemann, Stephen F. *molecular neurobiologist educator*
Kadous, Tamer Adel *research scientist*
†Kassel, Daniel Brian *biotechnologist, researcher*
McGraw, Donald Jesse *biologist, science historian, writer*
Myers, Douglas George *zoological society administrator*
Olevsky, Eugene A. *research scientist, educator*
Panetta, Joseph Daniel *biotechnology executive*
Risser, Arthur Crane, Jr., *zoo administrator*
Sejnowski, Terrence Joseph *science educator*
Thomas, Charles Allen, Jr., *molecular biologist, educator*
Vause, Edwin Hamilton *research foundation administrator*
Weinrich, James Donald *psychobiologist, internet consultant*
Yamazaki, Shinji *research scientist*
Zyskind, Judith Weaver *molecular biology educator, entrepreneur*

San Francisco

Barchas, Eric G. *veterinarian*
Blackburn, Elizabeth Helen *molecular biologist*
Block, Jon E. *clinical trials consultant*
†Borchardt, Kenneth Andrew *microbiology consultant, educator*
†Daadi, Marcel M. *neuroscientist, researcher*
†Dallman, Mary F. *physiologist, science educator*
†Elbeik, Tarek Ali *research scientist*
Furst, Arthur *toxicologist, educator*
Ganong, William F(rancis) *physiologist, physician*
Heyneman, Donald *parasitology and tropical medicine educator*
Horton, Jonathan Charles *neuroscientist, neuro-ophthalmologist*
La Farge, Timothy *retired plant geneticist*
Lyon, David William *research executive*
Márquez-Magaña, Leticia Maria *biology educator*
Nichols, Richard Alan *ecologist*
Ralston, Henry James, III, *neurobiologist, anatomist, educator*
†Vyas, Girish Narmadashankar *virologist, immunohematologist*
Waterhouse, Richard Valentine *retired science educator, consultant*
Wickramasekera, Ian Edward *psychophysiologist, psychology educator*
Yamamoto, Keith Robert *molecular biologist, educator*

San Jose

Khalfin, Igor B. *research scientist*
Mailachalam, Babu *research scientist*
Panescu, Dorin *biomedical scientist*
Zaro, Brad A. *research company executive, biologist*

San Juan Capistrano

White, Beverly Jane *cytogeneticist*

San Luis Obispo

Piirto, Douglas Donald *forester, educator, academic administrator*
Waldo, Anna Lee *retired science educator, writer*

San Marino

Benzer, Seymour *neuroscience educator*

Santa Barbara

Badash, Lawrence *science history educator*
Christman, Arthur Castner, Jr., *scientific advisor*
†Gibor, Aharon *biologist, educator*
Kryter, Karl David *retired research scientist*

Schneider, Edward Lee *botanic garden administrator*
Tucker, Shirley Lois Cotter *botany educator, researcher*

Santa Clara

Janis, Michael Jon *molecular biologist, entrepreneur*

Santa Cruz

Beevers, Harry *biologist, educator*
Griggs, Gary Bruce *science administrator, oceanographer, geologist, educator*
Langenheim, Jean Harmon *biology educator*

Santa Monica

Augenstein, Bruno W. *research scientist, researcher*
Honour, Lynda Charmaine *research scientist, educator, psychotherapist*

Santa Rosa

Schafer, John Francis *retired plant pathologist*

Santee

Morris, John David *research institute administrator, geology educator*

Saratoga

Greenleaf, John Edward *research physiologist*

South San Francisco

Goodman, Corey Scott *neurobiology educator, researcher, biotechnology company executive*

Stanford

†Belichenko, Pavel Vasilievich *neuroscientist, researcher*
Campbell, Allan McCulloch *bacteriology educator*
Cohen, Stanley Norman *geneticist, educator*
†Companys, Yosem Eduardo *research scientist*
Cox, David R. *geneticist, educator*
Djerassi, Carl *writer, retired chemistry educator*
Ehrlich, Anne Howland *research biologist*
Ehrlich, Paul Ralph *biology educator*
Elliott, David Duncan, III, *science research company executive*
Francke, Uta *medical geneticist, genetics researcher, educator*
Hanawalt, Philip Courtland *biology educator, researcher*
Matin, A. *microbiology educator, consultant*
†Nayak, Nihar Ranjan *reproductive physiologist*
†Ngo, Khiem Viet *research scientist*
Shapiro, Lucille *molecular biology educator*
Shooter, Eric Manvers *neurobiology educator, consultant*
†Wandell, Brian A. *neuroscientist, educator*
Yanofsky, Charles *biology educator*

Stockton

Jongeward, Gregg Duane *biology educator, researcher*
Magness, Rhonda Ann *microbiologist*
McNeal, Dale William, Jr., *biological sciences educator*

Temecula

Spjut, Richard Wayne *botanist, consultant*

Terra Bella

Gletne, Jeffrey Scott *forester*

The Sea Ranch

Hayflick, Leonard *microbiologist, cell biologist, gerontologist, educator, writer*

Thousand Oaks

Malmuth, Norman David *research scientist, program manager*

Tulare

Vickrey, Herta M. *microbiologist*

Turlock

†Tereshchenko, Alexander Pavlovich *research scientist, educator*

Valencia

Fogel, Jennifer Lynn *technical associate, researcher*

Vista

Hofmann, Frieder Karl *biotechnologist, consultant*

Walnut

Smith, Harry Mendell, Jr., *science educator*

Walnut Creek

Seaborg, David Michael *evolutionary biologist*

Westminster

Allen, Merrill James *marine biologist*

Woodland

Squires, Richard Felt *research scientist*

Woodland Hills

Fox, Stuart Ira *physiologist*

COLORADO

Aspen

Pullen, Margaret I. *genetics physicist*

Aurora

Dooley, J. Gordon *food scientist*
†Sun, Juan *biologist, immunologist*
Zuschlag, Nancy Hansen *environmental and nature resources educator*

Boulder

Armstrong, David Michael *biology educator*

Breed, Michael Dallam *environmental, population, organismic biology educator*
Byerly, Radford, Jr., *science policy official*
Clifford, Steven Francis *science research director*
De Fries, John Clarence *behavioral genetics educator, researcher*
Meier, Mark Frederick *research scientist, glaciologist, educator*
Mitchell, Joan LaVerne *research scientist*
Murino, Clifford John *atmospheric and oceanic research institute executive*
Prescott, David Marshall *biology educator*
Rast, Mark Peter *research scientist*
Robba, William A. *research scientist, consultant*
Staehelin, Lucas Andrew *cell biology educator*

Carbondale

Cowgill, Ursula Moser *biologist, educator, environmental consultant*

Colorado Springs

Bybee, Rodger Wayne *science education administrator*
Cameron, Paul Drummond *research facility administrator*
Comes, Robert George *research scientist*
Herron, Sherry Shelton *biology educator*
Mattoon, James Richard *biology educator*
Tindall, Jon W. *research scientist*
West, Ralph Leland *veterinarian*
Wilcox, Michael John *vision systems researcher, medical educator*

Denver

Anderson, Larry *science educator*
†Burgoon, Mark P. *science educator*
Curran-Everett, Douglas C. *scientist, educator, physiologist*
Ehret, Josephine Mary *microbiologist, researcher*
Freiheit, Clayton Fredric *zoo director*
†Heppler, Robin Lee *science administrator*
Holmes, Randall Kent *microbiology educator, physician, university administrator*
Koul, Hari Krishen *research scientist, rights activist*
LaMendola, Walter Franklin *technology educator, business executive*
Puck, Theodore Thomas *geneticist, biophysicist, educator*
Richardson, Elizabeth Hall *retired ecologist*

Fort Collins

†Bartels, Randy A. *science educator, researcher*
†Delgado, Jorge A. *soil scientist*
Follett, Ronald Francis *soil scientist*
Halvorson, Ardell David *soil scientist, researcher*
Keim, Wayne Franklin *retired genetics educator, plant geneticist*
Knopf, Fritz L. *biologist*
Lumb, William Valjean *veterinarian*
Mader, Douglas Paul *research administrator*
Mortvedt, John Jacob *soil scientist, researcher*
Ogg, James Elvis *microbiologist, educator*
Peterson, Gary Andrew *agronomics researcher*
Phemister, Robert David *veterinary medical educator*
Seidel, George Elias, Jr., *animal scientist, educator*
Shands, Henry Lee *plant geneticist, administrator*
Smith, Dwight Raymond *ecology and wildlife educator, writer*
Smith, Ralph Earl *virologist*
Stoaks, Ralph Duval *biotechnologist, consultant*
Terauds, Juris *retired science educator, research scientist*

Highlands Ranch

Brierley, James Alan *biohydrometallurgy consultant*

Lakewood

Bettinghaus, Erwin Paul *research scientist*
Soeth, James Richard *forester*

Littleton

Vail, Charles Daniel *veterinarian, consultant*

Longmont

Dierks, Richard Ernest *veterinarian, educational administrator*

Northglenn

†Hemlock, Roberta Leigh *veterinary technician*

Silver Cliff

Weber, Kent *wildlife organization administrator*

CONNECTICUT

Branford

Gordon, John Charles *forestry educator*

Canaan

†Mercer, John Charles *veterinary technician, pharmacy technician*

Darien

Burchenal, Joan Riley *science educator*

East Glastonbury

Smith, David Clark *research scientist*

Farmington

†Banya, Santonino Ku'Caya *science educator*
Bronner, Felix *physiologist, biophysicist, educator, painter*
Klobutcher, Lawrence Anthony *molecular biologist, educator*
Rothfield, Lawrence I. *microbiology educator*

Groton

Huang, Liang Hsiung *microbiologist*
†Smock, Steven Lee *cell biologist, molecular biologist*

Tassinari, Melissa Sherman *toxicologist*

Hamden

†Bulger, Carrie Ann *science educator*
Delehant, Raymond Leonard *botanist, educator*
Richardson, Dennis James *biologist, educator*
Smith, David Martyn *forestry educator*

Hartford

Wolf, Barry *genetics, pediatric educator*

Madison

Kilbourne, Edwin Dennis *virologist, educator*

Middletown

Zito, Christopher Richard *molecular biologist, biochemist*

Milford

Calabrese, Anthony *marine biologist*
Turko, Alexander Anthony *biology educator, hypnotherapist*

Naugatuck

Davis, Robert Glenn *research scientist*

New Haven

Altman, Sidney *biology educator*
Anderson, John Frederick *science administrator, entomologist, researcher*
Aronson, Peter Samuel *medical scientist, physiology educator*
Brown, Thomas Huntington *neuroscientist*
Brunson, Kenneth Wayne *cancer biologist*
Chandler, William Knox *physiologist*
†Ciuparu, Dragos Mihael *research scientist, educator*
Cohen, Lawrence Baruch *neurobiologist, educator*
Galston, Arthur William *biology educator*
†Goldman-Rakic, Patricia Shoer *neuroscience educator*
Graedel, Thomas Eldon *industrial ecology educator, researcher*
Hoffman, Joseph Frederick *physiology educator*
†Jarvin, Linda *research scientist*
Park, Jeffrey John *science educator*
Pollard, Thomas Dean *cell biologist, educator*
Rakic, Pasko *neuroscientist, educator*
Redmond, Donald Eugene, Jr., *neuroscientist, educator*
Stolwijk, Jan Adrianus Jozef *physiologist, biophysicist*
Summers, William Cofield *science educator*
†Udier-Blagovic, Marina *science educator, researcher*
Waggoner, Paul Edward *agricultural scientist*
Wagner, Günter Paul *biologist, educator*
†Wall, Joyce Elizabeth Maria *neuroscientist, educator*
Warren, Graham Barry *cell biology educator*

Old Greenwich

†DeOrchis, Frankie Juanita *forester, writer*

Ridgefield

†Pargellis, Christopher Allen *biologist, researcher*

Southport

Hill, David Lawrence *research corporation executive*

Storrs

†Leadbetter, Edward Renton *microbiologist, educator*

Storrs Mansfield

Kotula, Anthony William *retired research food scientist*
Laufer, Hans *developmental biologist, educator*
Marcus, Philip Irving *virology educator, researcher*
Slater, James Alexander *entomologist, educator*
Tian, Xiuchun *research scientist*

West Haven

†Bryant, Matthew Scott *research scientist*

West Simsbury

Morest, Donald Kent *neuroscientist, educator*

Westport

Altman, Lawrence Gene *biologist, educator*

Woodbury

Whelan, William Paul *retired research scientist*

DELAWARE

Dover

Broderick, Cyril Emery, Sr., *plant physiologist, educator*

Greenville

Schroeder, Herman Elbert *scientific consultant*

Hockessin

Mills, George Alexander *retired science administrator*

Newark

Campbell, Linzy Leon *molecular biology researcher, educator*
†DeLorme, Michael *toxicologist, researcher*
Harik, Vasyl Michael *research scientist*
Shapiro, Allan David *plant biology educator*
Sparks, Donald Lewis *soil chemistry educator*
Yan, Xiao-Hai *science center director, educator*

Wilmington

DeCherney, George Stephen *research scientist, research facility administrator, pharmaceutical executive*
Eleuterio, Marianne Kingsbury *retired genetics educator*

Hartzell, Charles R. *research administrator, biochemist, cell biologist*
Katz, Manfred *research scientist, consultant*
†Sarich, Troy C. *science association director*
†Van Dyk, Tina Kangas *microbiologist, researcher*
Waritz, Richard Stefan *toxicologist, researcher*

DISTRICT OF COLUMBIA

Washington
Abernathy, Charles Owen *toxicologist*
Abrams, Cynthia F. Katlin *nutrition scientist, educator*
Affronti, Lewis Francis, Sr., *microbiologist, educator*
Ampy, Franklin Roosevelt *zoologist, educator*
Apple, Martin Allen *science executive, scientist, educator*
Batdorf, Lynn Robert *horticulturist*
Beehler, Bruce McPherson *research zoologist, ornithologist, conservationist*
Berg, Patricia Elene *molecular biologist*
Bernthal, Frederick Michael *association executive*
Briscuso, Raymond J. *biotechnologist*
Brown, Lester Russell *research institute executive*
†Burbelo, Peter Denis *molecular cell biologist*
Carhart, Homer W(alter) *retired research scientist*
†Chamot, Dennis *research organization executive*
Coleman, Bernell *physiologist, educator*
†Colglazier, E. William *science academy administrator, physicist*
Collette, Bruce Baden *ichthyologist*
Cook-Deegan, Robert Mullan *science and health policy analyst, physician*
Corell, Robert Walden *science administrator, educator*
Crum, John Kistler *chemical society director*
Davis, Donald Ray *entomologist*
Davis, Randy Lee *soil scientist*
DeGiovanni-Donnelly, Rosalie Frances *biology researcher, educator*
Elias, Thomas Sam *botanist, author*
Feldbaum, Carl *biotechnologist*
Feulner, Edwin John, Jr., *research foundation executive*
Gunter, Christie D. *geneticist*
Hammonds, Timothy Merrill *association executive, economist*
Harding, Fann *health scientist, administrator*
Harter, Donald Harry *neurologist, medical educator*
Hazen, Robert Miller *research scientist, writer*
Heinze, John Edward *microbiologist, industrial researcher/developer*
Henkin, Robert Irwin *neurobiologist, internal medicine, nutrition and neurology educator, scientific products company executive, taste and smell disease physician*
†Highton, Richard Taylor *biologist, educator*
Hope, William Duane *zoologist, curator*
Huntress, Wesley Theodore, Jr., *scientist*
Kapetanakos, Christos Anastasios *science administrator, physics educator*
Kass, Leon Richard *science educator*
Kennedy, Eugene Richard *microbiologist, university dean*
Kramer, Jay Harlan *physiologist, researcher, educator*
Lacher, Thomas Edward, Jr., *tropical ecologist*
†Mauery, D. Richard *research scientist*
Meyers, Wayne Marvin *microbiologist*
†Miller, Alan Stanley *ecology center administrator, law educator*
Nabholz, Joseph Vincent *biologist, ecologist*
Nightingale, Elena Ottolenghi *geneticist, physician, administrator*
Pannu, Sardul Singh *science educator, researcher*
Pellmar, Terry C. *neurophysiologist, researcher*
Porter, Leah LeEarle *biological researcher, industry executive*
Pyke, Thomas Nicholas, Jr., *government science and engineering administrator*
Ridenour, Amy Moritz *research center administrator*
Riley, Terry Zene *biologist, researcher*
Schad, Theodore MacNeeve *science research administrator, civil engineer, consultant*
Schram, Susan Gale *agriculturist, consultant*
Simpson, Michael Marcial *science specialist, consultant*
Soloway, Rose Ann Gould *clinical toxicologist*
Southerland, Derrick Theodore *microbiologist*
Tidball, M. Elizabeth Peters *physiologist, educator, research director*
Todhunter, John Anthony *toxicologist, consultant*
Torrey, Barbara Boyle *research council administrator*
†Wallace, William Charles *science educator, neurobiologist*
Wasshausen, Dieter Carl *systematic botanist*
West, Robert MacLellan *science educator, consultant*
Wilkinson, Ronald Sterne *science administrator, environmentalist, historian*
Wong, Lee-Jun Chang *human geneticist*

FLORIDA

Boca Raton
Furman, Mark Evan *human performance scientist*
Lee, Xiaoyang *scientist*
Samuels, William Mason *physiology association executive*

Boynton Beach
†Yudell, Barbara R. *science educator, writer*

Bradenton
Maynard, Donald Nelson *horticulturist, educator*

Rechcigl, Jack Edward *soil and environmental sciences educator*
Schuster, David J. *entomologist, researcher*

Brandon
†Jurch, George R., Jr., *retired science educator*
Urka, Martin C. *soil scientist, retired*

Clearwater
Bramante, Pietro Ottavio *physiology educator, retired pathology specialist*

Cocoa
†Dhere, Neelkanth G *research scientist*

Coral Gables
Lucà-Moretti, Maurizio *research scientist, nutrition researcher*

Coral Springs
Bolene, Rosalie Steele (Margaret Bolene) *bacteriologist, civic worker*

Daytona Beach
Duma, Richard Joseph *microbiologist, physician, pathologist, researcher, educator*
Scott, John Brooks *retired research institute executive*

Delray Beach
Chavin, Walter *biological science educator and researcher*

Destin
†Giadrosich, Donald Louis *research scientist, retired electrical engineer*

Fort Lauderdale
Fitzpatrick, George E. *research scientist, educator*
Tsai, James H. *entomologist, educator*

Fort Pierce
Calvert, David Victor *soil science educator*
Herman, Richard J. *marine life administrator*
Rice, Mary Esther *biologist*

Gainesville
Besch, Emerson Louis *physiology educator, past academic administrator*
Bihorac, Azra *research scientist*
Burridge, Michael John *veterinarian, educator, research director*
Cantliffe, Daniel James *horticulture educator*
Clemmons, Roger Mayeda *veterinarian, educator*
Conrad, Joseph Henry *animal nutrition educator*
Dilcher, David Leonard *paleobotany educator, research scholar*
Drummond, Willa Hendricks *physiology and medical educator*
Drury, Kenneth Clayton *biological scientist*
†Dunn, William A., Jr., *cell biologist, educator*
Green, Eleanor Myers *veterinarian, educator*
Grobman, Hulda Gross (Mrs. Arnold B. Grobman) *retired health sciences educator*
Gutekunst, Richard Ralph *microbiology educator*
Hall, David Walter *botanist, consultant*
Hoy, Marjorie Ann *entomology educator*
Jaeger, Marc Julius *physiology educator, researcher*
Jones, David Alwyn *geneticist, botany educator*
Jones, Richard Lamar *entomology educator*
†Li, Qin-Bao *biological scientist, laboratory manager*
Mead, Frank Waldreth *taxonomic entomologist*
Nguyen, Ru *entomologist*
Nicoletti, Paul Lee *retired veterinarian, educator*
Oberlander, Herbert *retired physiologist*
Popenoe, Hugh Llywelyn *soils educator*
Purcifull, Dan Elwood *plant virologist, educator*
Quesenberry, Kenneth Hays *agronomy educator*
Schelske, Claire L. *limnologist, educator*
Schmidt-Nielsen, Bodil Mimi (Mrs. Roger G. Chagnon) *physiologist, educator*
Seale, James Lawrence, Jr., *agricultural economics educator, international trade researcher*
Stern, William Louis *botanist, educator*
Teixeira, Arthur Alves *food engineer, educator, consultant*
Vierck, Charles John, Jr., *neuroscience educator, scientist*
Wilcox, Charles Julian *geneticist, educator*
†Yamamoto, Janet Kazuko *science educator*
Yarmola, Elena Georgiyevna *research scientist*

Gulf Breeze
Menzer, Robert Everett *toxicologist, educator*

Hobe Sound
Hand, Peter James *neurobiologist, educator*

Hollywood
Matasa, Claude George *researcher, science administrator, educator*
†Rosenthal, Phyllis Karen *toxicologist, clinical chemist*

Holmes Beach
Anderson, Herbert G. *marine biologist, researcher*

Homestead
Dong, Quan *ecologist, educator*
Roberts, Larry Spurgeon *biological sciences educator, zoologist*

Jacksonville
Bodkin, Lawrence Edward *research development company executive, gemologist, inventor, writer*
†Claborn, David Merrell *entomologist*
Loucks, Terry Lee *writer, retired biosystems executive*
Younkin, Steven G. *neuroscientist*

Key Biscayne
Grey, Jerry *science educator*

Lake Alfred
Kender, Walter John *horticulturist, educator*

Lake Placid
Bohlen, Patrick Joseph *ecologist, researcher*

Lakeland
†Manners, Malcolm M. *horticulturist, educator*

Margate
Franks, Allen P. *research institute executive, educator*

Melbourne
Helmstetter, Charles Edward *microbiologist*
Storrs, Eleanor Emerett *research institute consultant*

Miami
†Buchwald, Peter Sandor *research scientist*
Colwin, Arthur Lentz *biologist, educator*
Hackman, John Clement *neuropharmacology educator, neurophysiologist*
†Ling, Jian *research scientist, consultant*
Muench, Karl Hugo *clinical geneticist*
†Myrberg, Arthur August, Jr., *marine biological sciences educator*
†Przybylski-Pol, Alexander *biotechnologist*
Tucker, Gail Susan *biology science educator*

Naples
Dacey, George Clement *retired laboratory administrator, consultant*

Orlando
†Dubey, Vinod Shanker *microbiologist, biochemist, researcher*
Walters, Linda Jane *marine biologist, educator, researcher*

Palm City
Boss, Manley Leon *plant physiologist*

Palm Coast
Bullard, Ervin Trowbridge *horticulturist*

Pensacola
†Temme, Leonard A. *research scientist*

Punta Gorda
Beever, James William, III, *biologist*

Ramrod Key
Clark, John Russell *marine biologist*

Ruskin
Briscoe, Anne M. *retired scientist, educator*

Saint Augustine
Flemister, Launcelot Johnson *physiologist, educator*

Saint Petersburg
Byrd, Isaac Burlin *fishery biologist, fisheries administrator*
Mueller, O. Thomas *molecular geneticist, pediatrics educator*

Sarasota
Clark, Eugenie *zoologist, educator*
Eichholz, Alexander A. *physiology researcher, consultant*
Jarzen, David MacArthur *research scientist*
†Lowman, Margaret D. *botanist*
Mahadevan, Kumar *marine laboratory director, researcher*
Rinker, H. Bruce *ecologist*
Seibert, Russell Jacob *botanist, research associate*

Stuart
Robinson, Michael Hill *retired zoological park director, biologist*

Sun City Center
Rubin, Robert Jay *toxicologist*

Tallahassee
Long, Michael Christian *forester*
Muchovej, James John *botanist, plant pathologist, educator*

Tampa
†Beach, Kevin Scott *marine biologist, educator*
Germroth, Peter *biologist, educator*
†Hayes, James Donald *pharmaceutical research scientist*
Hickman, Hugh V. *science educator, researcher*
Jove, Richard *molecular biologist*
†Ketcham, Beverly Lynn *biologist, educator*
Lim, Daniel Van *microbiology educator*
†Willing, Alison Elizabeth *neuroscientist*
Wu, Jie *molecular biologist, educator*

Vero Beach
Grobman, Arnold Brams *retired biology educator and academic administrator*

West Palm Beach
Chen, Zhikang (Ken Chen) *remote sensing scientist*
†VanArman, Peggy Ellen Gilbert *biology educator*

Winter Park
Fluno, John Arthur *entomologist, consultant*

GEORGIA

Alpharetta
Balows, Albert *microbiologist, educator*
Rettig, Terry *veterinarian, wildlife consultant*

Athens
Agosin, Moises Kankolsky *zoology educator*
Albersheim, Peter *biology educator*
Alberts, James Joseph *scientist, researcher*
Atwater, Mary Monroe *science educator*
Avise, John Charles *geneticist, educator*
Baile, Clifton A. *biologist, researcher*
Giles, Norman Henry *educator, geneticist*
Kim, Seock-Ho *educator*
†Mauricio, Rodney *ecological geneticist, educator*
†Meyers, Joseph Michael *biologist, researcher*
Payne, William Jackson *microbiologist, educator*
Plummer, Gayther L(ynn) *ecologist, climatologist, researcher*
†Ritter, Hope Thomas, Jr., *cell biologist, educator*
Tyler, David Earl *veterinary medical educator*

Atlanta
Benitez, Jorge Antonio *microbiology educator*
†Black, Carolyn Morris *microbiologist, educator, science administrator*
†Cantalupo, Claudio *neuroscientist, researcher*
Carey, Gerald John, Jr., *retired research institute director emeritus, former air force officer*
Chernoff, Yury Olegovich *biologist, educator*
Circeo, Louis Joseph, Jr., *research scientist, civil engineer*
Clifton, David Samuel , Jr., *research executive, economist*
Compans, Richard W. *microbiology educator*
†Danner, Dean Jay *geneticist*
†Eisen, Arri *biologist, educator*
Fowler, Bruce Andrew *toxicologist, researcher*
†Gorman, Susan E. *toxicologist, consultant*
Gyamfi, Phyllis *research scientist, researcher*
Jeffery, Geoffrey Marron *medical parasitologist*
Jiang, Baoming *scientist*
McGowan, John Edward, Jr., *clinical epidemiology educator, microbiologist, infectious diseases specialist*
†McQueen, David Vincent *research scientist*
†Pearce, Bradley Dixon *neuroscientist, pharmacologist*
†Pillay, Allan *microbiologist*
Pratt, Harry Davis *retired entomologist*
†Shur, Barry David *cell biologist, researcher*
Spitznagel, John Keith *microbiologist, immunologist, physician*
Steg, Leo *research and development executive*
†Stojiljkovic, Igor *microbiologist, researcher*
Traynelis, Stephen Francis *neuroscientist, educator*

Augusta
Baker, Carleton Harold *physiology educator*
Barnes, Vernon Anthony *research scientist*
†Bieberich, Erhard *biologist*
Kutlar, Ferdane *genetics educator, researcher*
Yu, Robert Kuan-jen *biochemistry educator*

Baldwin
Smith, John Andrew *veterinarian*

Bowden
†Sulzer, Alexander Jackson *retired research microbiologist, educator*

Columbus
Gore, James Arnold *biology educator, aquatic ecologist, hydrologist*
Riggsby, Ernest Duward *science educator, educational development executive*
Zuiderveen, Jeffrey Alan *biology educator, toxicology consultant, aquatic toxicologist*

Dahlonega
Pandres, Dave, Jr., *science educator, researcher*

Decatur
Cavallaro, Joseph John *retired microbiologist*

Duluth
Johnston, William David *biotechnology executive*

Dunwoody
La Motte, Louis Cossitt, Jr., *medical scientist, consultant*

Griffin
Doyle, Michael Patrick *microbiologist, educator, director*
Duncan, Ronny Rush *agriculturist, turf researcher, consultant*
Shuman, Larry Myers *soil chemist*

Macon
Adkison, Linda Russell *geneticist, consultant*
Carson, Juanita Elaine *biologist, educator*
Volpe, Erminio Peter *biologist, educator*

Milledgeville
McGinnis, Michael Boyd *chemistry educator*

Norcross
Dibb, David Walter *research association administrator*
†McDonald, James *science foundation executive*
Wagner, Robert Earl *retired agronomist*

Saint Simons
Donahoo, William Patrick *science administrator, consultant, science administrator, educator*

Savannah
Eaves, George Newton *lecturer, consultant, research administrator*

Tifton
†Burton, Glenn Willard *geneticist*

HAWAII

Ewa Beach
Chock, Alvin Keali'i *retired botanist*

Hawaii National Park
Camp, Richard J. *ecologist, statistician, researcher*

Hilo
Follett, Peter Arnold *entomologist, researcher*
Ko, Wen-hsiung *plant pathology educator*

Honolulu
Blanchard, Robert J. *neuroscientist*
Carson, Hampton Lawrence *geneticist, educator*
Kamemoto, Fred Isamu *retired zoologist*
Kanenaka, Rebecca Yae *microbiologist*
Li, PingAn *neurobiologist, educator*
Mandel, Morton *molecular biologist*
Nigg, Claudio Renato *science educator*
Sagawa, Yoneo *horticulturist, educator*
Teramura, Alan Hiroshi *science educator*

Kalaheo
Cox, Paul Alan *ethnobotanist, educator*

Ocean View
Baglow, David Richard *marine facility administrator*

Tripler Army Medical Center
Garshnek, Victoria *physiologist, research educator*
Uyehara, Catherine Fay Takako (Catherine Yamauchi) *physiologist, educator, pharmacologist*

IDAHO

Idaho Falls
†Buongiorno, Jacopo *research scientist*

Moscow
Moffitt, Christine M. *biologist, educator*
Roberts, Lorin Watson *botanist, educator*

Pocatello
McCune, Mary Joan Huxley *microbiology educator*

Post Falls
Brede, Andrew Douglas *research director, plant breeder*

Twin Falls
Burton, Lawrence DeVere *agriculturist, educator*

ILLINOIS

Abbott Park
Frazier, Douglas Byron *health care consultant*
Nardelli, Christy Ann *research scientist*

Argonne
Metz, William Clinton *science facility administrator*
Schriesheim, Alan *research administrator*

Aurora
Goebel, Edwin M. *microbiology educator, school administrator*

Bensenville
†Brekke, Stewart Ernest *retired chemistry and physics educator*

Berwyn
Parker, Alan John *veterinary neurologist, educator, researcher*

Bridgeview
Parmer, Dan Gerald *veterinarian*

Brookfield
Rabb, George Bernard *zoologist, conservationist*

Buffalo Grove
†Rivtis, Arkady *science educator, consultant*

Burr Ridge
Rosenberg, Robert Brinkmann *technology organization executive*

Carbondale
Burr, Brooks Milo *zoology educator*
Klubek, Brian Paul *science educator, researcher*

Champaign
Batzli, George Oliver *ecology educator*
Levin, Geoffrey Arthur *botanist*
Novak, Robert J. *science educator*
Ridlen, Samuel Franklin *agriculture educator*
Sanderson, Glen Charles *science director*
Stout, Glenn Emanuel *retired science administrator*

Chicago
Allampallam, Krishnan *biotechnology consultant*
Beattie, Ted Arthur *zoological gardens and aquarium administrator*
Bell, Kevin J. *zoological park administrator*
Betts, Richard Russell *science educator*
†Catchpole, Hubert Ralph *physiologist*
Chakrabarty, Ananda Mohan *microbiologist*
De, Devasmita *research aquarist*
†DeCoursey, Thomas Eric *physiologist, educator*
Desjardins, Claude *physiologist, dean*
Drantz, Veronica Ellen *science educator and consultant*
Ernest, J. Terry *ocular physiologist, educator*
Feder, Martin Elliott *biology researcher and educator*
Fisher, Lester Emil *zoo administrator*
Fukui, Yoshio *biology educator*
Gassman, Merrill Loren *biologist, educator*
Greenberg, Bernard *entomologist, educator*
Haselkorn, Robert *virology educator*
Kocka, Frank Edward *microbiologist*
Kopec, John William *research scientist*
Kordylewski, Leszek *cell biologist, forensic scientist*
†Lindquist, Susan Lee *biology and microbiology educator*
Mahowald, Anthony Peter *geneticist, developmental biologist, educator*
†Maniotis, Andrew James *cell biologist, researcher*
Mateles, Richard Isaac *biotechnologist*
McClintock, Martha K. *biologist, educator*
Mullins, Obera *retired microbiologist*
Murphy, Ricardo *biophysicist, plant physiologist*
†Norris, James Carlton *toxicologist*
Park, Thomas Joseph *biology researcher, educator*
Pavlova, Sylvia I. *microbiologist, researcher*
†Peeples, Mark Edward *virology researcher, educator*
Pick, Ruth *research scientist, physician, educator*
Rasenick, Mark Mitchell *neuroscientist*
†Rebbaa, Abdelhadi *research scientist*
Ritter, Mary Catherine *research scientist, educator*
Roizman, Bernard *virologist, educator*
Rothman-Denes, Lucia Beatriz *biology educator*
Seiden, Lewis S. *neuroscientist*
Shirbroun, Richard Elmer *veterinarian, cattleman*
Shott, Susan *medical biostatistician, educator*
Solaro, Ross John *physiologist, biophysicist*
Storb, Ursula Beate *molecular genetics and cell biology educator*
Straus, Lorna Puttkammer *biology educator*
Tarnow, Fredric Herman *science educator*
Thompson, Steven *zoological park administrator*
Tuchman, Nancy Crandall *biology educator, aquatic ecology researcher*
†Wehrmacher, William Henry *physiology educator, clinical cardiologist*

Danville
Craig, Hurshel Eugene *agronomist*

Dekalb
King, Kenneth Paul *science educator*
Vary, Patricia Susan *biologist, educator, retired geneticist*
Zar, Jerrold H(oward) *biologist, statistician*

Elmhurst
†Bahariev, Dimitar B. *plant pathologist*

Evanston
Dallos, Peter John *neurobiologist, educator*
Lewis, Frederick D. *science educator*
†Mason, Thomas Oliver *materials science and engineering educator, researcher*
Novales, Ronald Richards *zoologist, educator*
Ruggero, Mario Alfredo *physiologist, educator*
Takahashi, Joseph S. *neuroscientist, educator*
Wu, Tai Te *biological sciences and engineering educator*

Glendale Heights
Pimental, Patricia Ann *neuropsychologist, consulting company executive, author*

Glenview
Kinigakis, Panagiotis *research scientist, engineer, inventor, author*
Zheng, Zuoxing *food microbiologist*

Harvey
Liem, Khian Kioe *medical entomologist*

Hinsdale
Pawley, Ray Lynn *zoological park consultant, real estate developer*

Homewood
Pumper, Robert William *microbiologist, educator*

Lake Bluff
Braendle, Donald Harold *geneticist, researcher*

Libertyville
Beach, Robert Mark *biologist*

Lisle
Davis, Gregory Thomas *marine surveyor*
Smith, Jared Russell William *research executive, research scientist, consultant, poet*
Ware, George Henry *botanist*

Lombard
Velardo, Joseph Thomas *molecular biology and endocrinology educator*

Macomb
Anderson, Richard Vernon *ecology educator, researcher*
Barclay, Martha Jane *science educator, research scientist*
Ribbens, Eric *plant ecologist, educator*

Maywood
Cera, Lee Marie *veterinarian*

Monticello
†Gucker, Douglas *agronomist, consultant*

Normal
†Brown, Lauren Evans *zoologist, researcher, zoologist, educator*
Smith, Robert Lee *agriculturalist*

North Chicago
Albach, Richard Allen *microbiology educator*
†Katdare, Ashok V. *science administrator*
†Sladek, Celia Davis *neuroscientist, educator*

Northbrook
King, Robert Charles *biologist, educator*
†Storhoff, James Justin *scientist*

Oak Brook
Ding, Jianchi *embryologist, researcher*

River Grove
Gardner, Sandi B. *biology educator*

Rock Island
Dziadyk, Bohdan *botany and ecology educator*

Romeoville
Vander Vliet, Valerie Jeanne *biology educator*

Savoy
Sinclair, James Burton *retired plant pathology educator, consultant*

Schaumburg
Eickelmann, Nancy Sue *research scientist*

Skokie
Bell, Rosonald Renae *toxicologist*

Springfield
Munyer, Edward A. *zoologist, museum administrator*
†Reichensperger, Joel David *neuroscientist*

Urbana
†Allain, Jean Paul *research scientist*
Banwart, Wayne Lee *agronomy, environmental science educator*
Buetow, Dennis Edward *physiologist, educator*
Burger, Ambrose William *agronomy educator*
Chow, Poo *wood technologist, scientist*
Crang, Richard Francis Earl *plant and cell biologist, research center administrator*
Cronan, Jr., John Emerson *microbiologist*
Dziuk, Philip John *animal scientist educator*
Feng, Albert *science educator, researcher*
Frazzetta, Thomas Henry *evolutionary biologist, functional morphologist, educator*
Friedman, Stanley *insect physiologist, educator*
Garrigus, Upson Stanley *animal science and international agriculture educator*
†Ge, Pinghua *research scientist*
Greenough, William Tallant *psychobiologist, educator*
Heath, James Edward *physiology educator, retired*
Heichel, Gary Harold *crop sciences educator*
Hoeft, Robert Gene *agriculture educator*
Hoffmeister, Donald Frederick *zoologist, educator*
Holt, Donald A. *agronomist, consultant, retired academic administrator*
Hymowitz, Theodore *plant geneticist, educator*
Mc Glamery, Marshal Dean *crop scientist, weed science educator*
Meyer, Richard Charles *microbiologist, educator*
Nanney, David Ledbetter *genetics educator*
Rebeiz, Constantin A. *plant physiology educator, laboratory director*
Ridgway, Marcella Davies *veterinarian*
Seigler, David Stanley *botanist, chemist, educator*
Waldbauer, Gilbert Peter *entomologist, educator*
Whitt, Gregory Sidney *evolution educator*
Wolfe, Ralph Stoner *microbiology educator*

Westchester
Webb, Emily *retired plant morphologist*

INDIANA

Bloomington
Clevenger, Sarah *botanist, computer consultant*
Gest, Howard *microbiologist, educator*
Hammel, Harold Theodore *physiology and biophysics educator, researcher*
Heiser, Charles Bixler, Jr., *botany educator*
Hites, Ronald Atlee *environmental science educator, chemist*
†Nagendra, Harini *ecologist, researcher*
Nolan, Val, Jr., *biologist, lawyer*
Rebec, George Vincent *neuroscience researcher, educator, administrator*
Ruesink, Albert William *biologist, plant sciences educator*
Weinberg, Eugene David *microbiologist, educator*

Carmel
†Branstutter, Joseph Wayne *research scientist*
†Scott, Judson Richard *arborist, consultant*

Chesterton
Wiemann, Marion Russell, Jr., (Baron of Camster) *biologist*

Evansville
Brenneman, James Alden *biology educator*

Fishers
†Bigatti, Silvia Marcela *science educator*

Greenfield
Myerholtz, Ralph W., Jr., *retired chemical company executive, chemist, researcher*

Hammond
Gealt, Michael A. *environmental microbiologist, educator*

Hobart
Seeley, Mark *agronomist*

Indianapolis
Borst, Philip Craig *veterinarian, councilman*
Christian, Joe Clark *medical genetics researcher, educator*
†Damush, Teresa Marie *research scientist*
Heiman, Mark Louis *research scientist*
Johnson, Gerald, III, *cardiovascular physiologist, researcher*
Lahiri, Debomoy Kumar *molecular neurobiologist, educator*
Ochs, Sidney *neurophysiology educator*
Rhoades, Rodney Allen *physiologist, educator*
Thomas, Jerry Arthur *soil scientist*

Kokomo
Roales, Robert R. *natural science educator*

Lafayette
Achgill, Ralph Kenneth *retired research scientist*
Harris, Donald Wayne *research scientist*

Lanesville
Cleveland, Peggy Rose Richey *cytotechnologist*

Muncie
Amschler, Denise H. *health science educator*
Hendrix, Jon Richard *biology educator*
Henzlik, Raymond Eugene *zoophysiologist, educator*
Mertens, Thomas Robert *biology educator*
Volk, Christian J. *microbiologist, research scientist*
Wise, Charles Davidson *science educator*

Notre Dame
Jensen, Richard Jorg *biology educator*
Lafield, Karen Woodrow *science educator, demographer*
Pollard, Morris *microbiologist, educator*

South Bend
†House, Harold Von *science educator, consultant*

Terre Haute
Dusanic, Donald Gabriel *parasitology educator, microbiologist*

West Lafayette
Albright, Jack Lawrence *animal science and veterinary educator*
Amstutz, Harold Emerson *veterinarian, educator*
†Cassers, Daniel Lee *forester, educator*
Diekman, Mark A. *animal science educator*
†Duerstock, Bradley S. *neurobiologist, researcher*
Edwards, Charles Richard *entomology and pest management educator*
†Hess, Dale Eshleman *geneticist, educator*
Hoxie, Robert Prynne *retired entomologist*
Hunt, Michael O'Leary *wood science and engineering educator*
Johannsen, Chris Jakob *agronomist, educator, administrator*
†Latch, Emily Latch *geneticist*
Le Master, Dennis Clyde *natural resource economics and policy educator*
Lofgren, Donna Lee *geneticist*
Mason, Sally Kay Frost *biology educator, provost*
McFee, William Warren *soil scientist*
Nelson, Philip Edwin *food scientist, educator*
Ohm, Herbert Willis *agronomy educator*
Schreiber, Marvin Mandel *agronomist, educator*
Stob, Martin *physiology educator*
White, Joe Lloyd *soil scientist, educator*

IOWA

Ames
Anderson, Lloyd Lee *animal science educator*
Beran, George Wesley *veterinary microbiology educator*
Berger, P(hilip) Jeffrey *animal science educator, quantitative geneticist*
Ghoshal, Nani Gopal *veterinarian, educator*
Greve, John Henry *veterinary parasitologist, educator*
Hallauer, Arnel Roy *geneticist*
Hatfield, Jerry Lee *plant physiologist, biometeorologist*
Hoffman, Mark Peter *animal scientist*
Imsande, John David *geneticist, researcher, educator*
Johnson, Lawrence Alan *cereal technologist, educator, administrator*
Karlen, Douglas Lawrence *soil scientist*
Kelly, James Michael *plant and soil scientist*
Lee, Seong-Jae *researcher*
Mengeling, William Lloyd *retired veterinarian, virologist*
Mertins, James Walter *entomologist*
†Moon, Harley William *veterinarian*
Moore, Kenneth James *agronomy educator, scientist*
O'Berry, Phillip Aaron *veterinarian*
Richt, Juergen Albrecht *veterinarian*
Ross, Richard Francis *veterinarian, microbiologist, educator, dean*
Seaton, Vaughn Allen *retired veterinary pathology educator*
†Stalheim, Ole Henry V. *veterinarian, educator*
Thompson, Louis Milton *agronomy educator, scientist*
Voss, Regis Dale *agronomist, educator*
Willham, Richard Lewis *animal science educator*

Des Moines
Rosen, Matthew Stephen *botanist, consultant*

Grinnell
Campbell, David George *ecologist, researcher, author*
Walker, Waldo Sylvester *biology educator, academic administrator*

Iowa City
Cruden, Robert William *botany educator*
Hausler, William John, Jr., *microbiologist, educator, public health laboratory administrator*
†Hell, Johannes Wilhelm *neuroscientist, researcher*
Husted, Russell Forest *research scientist*
Kessel, Richard Glen *zoology educator*

Reynolds, David G(eorge) *retired physiologist, educator*
Tang, Jun *research scientist, educator*
Wunder, Charles C(ooper) *physiology and biophysics educator, gravitational biologist*

Johnston
Arvidson, Robert Benjamin, Jr., *geneticist, consultant*
Berry, James Alan *plant pathologist, research scientist*
Duvick, Donald Nelson *plant breeder*

KANSAS

Emporia
Sundberg, Marshall David *biology educator*

Hays
Coyne, Patrick Ivan *physiological ecologist*
Michaud, J.P. *entomologist, researcher*

Kansas City
Behbehani, Abbas M. *clinical virologist, educator*
Greenwald, Gilbert Saul *physiologist*
Karrer, Rathe Stevens *psychophysiologist*
Samson, Frederick Eugene, Jr., *neuroscientist, educator*

Lawrence
Armitage, Kenneth Barclay *biology educator, ecologist*
Bovee, Eugene Cleveland *protozoologist, emeritus educator*
Byers, George William *retired entomology educator*
Johnston, Richard Fourness *biologist, educator*
Lichtwardt, Robert William *mycologist*
Michener, Charles Duncan *entomologist, educator, researcher*
Shankel, Delbert Merrill *microbiology and biology educator*

Manhattan
Erickson, Howard Hugh *veterinarian, physiology educator*
†Haub, Mark D. *exercise physiologist*
Kaufman, Donald Wayne *research ecologist*
Kirkham, M. B. *plant physiologist, educator*
Mengel, David Bruce *agronomy and soil science educator*
Posler, Gerry Lynn *agronomist, educator*

Neosho Falls
Bader, Robert Smith *biology, zoology educator and researcher*

Parsons
Lomas, Lyle Wayne *agricultural research administrator, educator*

Shawnee Mission
Goetz, Kenneth Lee *cardiovascular physiologist, research consultant, writer*

Sterling
Beechan, Curtis Michael *science educator*

Topeka
Mara, John Lawrence *retired veterinarian, consultant*

Wichita
Schneegurt, Mark Allen *microbiologist, researcher*

KENTUCKY

Bowling Green
Ahmed, S. Basheer *research company executive, educator*

Cynthiana
Bandurski, Bruce Lord *retired ecological and environmental scientist*

Lexington
Abu Kwaik, Yousef A. *microbiologist, educator, research scientist*
Barnhart, Charles Elmer *animal sciences educator*
Frye, Wilbur Wayne *retired soil science educator, researcher, administrator*
Goodman, Norman Loyal *microbiologist, educator*
†Hopper, Kevin R. *biologist*
Humphries, Asa Alan, Jr., *biologist, educator, dean*
†Jackson, Carney Brand *veterinarian*
†Lodder, Robert A. *science educator*
Love, Harold Gibson *agricultural economics educator*
†Lutz, Martha Victoria Rosett *entomologist*
Mitchell, George Ernest, Jr., *animal scientist, educator*
Rangnekar, Vivek Mangesh *molecular biologist, researcher*
†Sekulic, Dusan P. *science educator, researcher*
Timoney, Peter Joseph *veterinarian, virologist, educator, consultant*
†Wekstein, David Robert *physiology educator, researcher*

Louisville
†Lominadze, David *physiologist, researcher*

Murray
Keller, Randal Joseph *toxicology educator*

Prestonsburg
Pridham, Thomas Grenville *retired research microbiologist*

Richmond
Branson, Branley Allan *biology educator*

LOUISIANA

Baton Rouge
Besch, Everett Dickman *veterinarian, university dean and educator emeritus*
Burns, Paul Yoder *forester, educator*
Chapman, Russell Leonard *botany educator*
Hansel, William *biology educator*
Head, Jonathan Frederick *cell biologist*
Liuzzo, Joseph Anthony *food science educator*
Murai, Norimoto *plant molecular biologist, educator*
Patrick, William Hardy, Jr., *wetland biogeochemist, educator, laboratory director*

Chauvin
Sammarco, Paul William *ecologist, researcher*

Eunice
Al-Dujaili, Jameel Sadeq *microbiology educator, researcher*

Lake Charles
Hinton, Juliana Guillory *biologist, educator*

Metairie
Westerman, Albert Barry *marine surveyor and consultant*

New Orleans
Beard, Elizabeth Letitia *physiologist, educator*
Fingerman, Milton *biologist, educator*
†Geng, Chuan-Dong *research scientist*
Ivens, Mary Sue *microbiologist, mycologist*
Kahn, Marc Jeffrey *science educator*
Levitzky, Michael Gordon *physiology educator, researcher*
Lingle, Sarah Elizabeth *research scientist*
†Martinson, Robert J. *biologist, writer*
Mitchell, Kenneth D. *physiologist, medical educator*
Navar, Luis Gabriel *physiology educator, researcher*
Pedersen, Pedie *physiology educator*
†Rajasekaran, Kanniah *agricultural biotechnologist, researcher*
Superneau, Duane William *geneticist, physician*
Welden, Arthur Luna *biology educator*

Shreveport
Bradley, Ronald James *neuroscientist*
†Feelisch, Martin *research scientist, consultant*
Jamison, Richard Melvin *virologist, educator*
Whitlock, Laura Alice *research scientist*

MAINE

Bangor
Knight, Fred Barrows *forester, entomologist, educator*

Bar Harbor
Leiter, Edward Henry *cell biologist*
Paigen, Kenneth *geneticist, science administrator*
Shultz, Leonard Donald *research scientist*
†Todd, Sean Kevin *science educator*

Brunswick
Guay, David Adalbert *biology educator*

Damariscotta
Fuller, Melvin Stuart *botany educator*

Harpswell
Bird, Henry Lonsdale *biologist, priest*

Mount Desert
Crawford, Richard Bradway *biologist, biochemist, educator*

Orono
Chute, Harold LeRoy *veterinary pathologist, former chemical company executive*
Ellis, William Grenville, Jr., *marine biologist, educator*

Waterville
Fleming, James Rodger *science historian, educator*

MARYLAND

Aberdeen Proving Ground
Evans, Edward Spencer, Jr., *entomologist*
Stuebing, Edward Willis *research scientist*

Annapolis
Anderson, William Carl *association executive, environmental engineer, consultant*

Baltimore
Abel, Francis Lee *physiology educator*
Aranovich, Gregory *chemical engineering educator, researcher*
†Bhardwaj, Anish *neuroscientist, medical educator*
Bohr, Vilhelm Alfred *laboratory chief*
Brady, Joseph Vincent *behavioral biologist, educator*
Brown, Donald David *biology educator*
Clark, Patricia *molecular biologist*
DeTolla, Louis James *research scientist and veterinarian*
Fenton, Matthew John *immunologist, molecular biologist*
Gall, Joseph Grafton *biologist, researcher, educator*
Gallo, Robert Charles C. *research scientist*
Goldberg, Alan Marvin *toxicologist, educator*
Grollman, Sigmund Sidney *physiology educator*
Habermann, Helen Margaret *plant physiologist, educator*
Hansen, Barbara Caleen *physiologist, science educator*
Isaacs, John T. *research scientist*
Jabs, Ethylin Wang *human genetics physician, scientist, educator*
Jones, Lynne Christine Heilenman *orthopaedic surgery educator*
†Kinsman, Stephen L. *research scientist*
†Kirsch, Thorsten *cell biologist, educator*
Littlefield, John Walley *geneticist, cell biologist, pediatrician*
Massof, Robert William *neuroscientist, educator*
McKusick, Victor Almon *geneticist, educator, physician*
†Permutt, Solbert *physiologist, physician*
Platt, Austin P. *retired science educator*
Roberts, Randolph Wilson *health and science educator*
Seydoux, Geraldine *molecular biologist*
Suskind, Sigmund Richard *microbiology educator*
Trpis, Milan *vector biologist, scientist, educator*
†Zangen, Abraham *neuroscience researcher, consultant*

Beltsville
Adams, Jean Ruth *entomologist, researcher*
Baligar, Virupax C. *research soil scientist*
Chitwood, David Joseph *zoologist, researcher*
Hackett, Kevin James *insect pathologist*
Schneider, Edwin Kahn *research scientist*

Bethesda
Adler, Henry Joseph *research scientist*
Bennink, Jack Richard *microbiologist, researcher*
Borgaonkar, Digamber Shankarrao *cytogeneticist, educator*
Brady, Roscoe Owen *neurogeneticist, educator*
†Burg, Maurice Benjamin *physiologist, internist*
Candotti, Fabio *geneticist*
†Caruccio, Lorraine G. *research scientist*
Chan, Wai-Yee *geneticist, educator*
Collins, Francis S. *medical research scientist*
Condliffe, Peter George *research scientist*
Dorr, Ann Pierce *science educator*
Dwyer, Dennis Michael *microbiologist*
Frank, Martin *physiology educator, health scientist, association executive*
Fraumeni, Joseph Francis, Jr., *scientific researcher, medical educator, physician, military officer*
†Galperin, Michael Y. *microbiologist*
Gartland, William Joseph, Jr., *research institute administrator*
†Gershengorn, Marvin C *research scientist, director*
Gruber, Jack *virologist, cancer research program administrator, medical researcher*
Guttman, Helene Nathan *biomedical research consultant, transpersonal counselor, regression therapist*
Hancock, Charles Cavanaugh, Jr., *scientific association administrator*
Hausman, Steven Jack *health science administrator*
Jackson, Michael John *retired physiologist, association executive*
Jordan, Elke *molecular biologist, government medical research institute executive*
Kallioniemi, Olli Pekka *geneticist, researcher*
†Ketha, Venkata Krishna Mohan *microbiologist, researcher*
†Lai, Zhennan *research scientist*
Lorber, Mortimer *retired physiology educator*
Mattson, Janet Marie *contracting officer, microbiologist*
Miller, Louis Howard *biologist, researcher*
Monjan, Andrew Arthur *health science administrator*
Moss, Bernard *virologist, researcher*
†Muraro, Paolo Antonio *research scientist*
Myers, Lawrence Stanley, Jr., *radiation biologist*
Nash, Howard Allen *geneticist, researcher*
Ochej, Helen Wanda *biologist, researcher, information scientist*
Pakaluk, Debra Lorraine Behm *science educator, community service coordinator*
Petralia, Ronald Sebastian *entomologist, neurobiologist*
Purcell, Robert Harry *virologist, researcher*
Raben, Nina *molecular biologist, biochemist*
Robinson, David Mason *cell physiologist*
Robison, Wilbur Gerald, Jr., *research biologist*
†Rosner, Judah L. *molecular biologist, geneticist*
Ryan, Kevin William *virologist, researcher, science educator, clinical research administrator*
Salmoiraghi, Gian Carlo *physiologist, educator*
†Schneider, Julie Ann *geneticist*
Sewell, Rodney Milton *biologist*
Shulman, Lawrence Edward *biomedical research administrator, rheumatologist*
Sokoloff, Louis *physiologist, neurochemist*
Ungerleider, Leslie G. *neuroscientist*
Webster, Henry de Forest *neuroscientist*
†Wexler, Philip *toxicologist*
Wurtz, Robert Henry *neuroscientist*
Yamada, Kenneth Manao *cell biologist*
Zierdt, Charles Henry *microbiologist*

Chevy Chase
Choppin, Purnell Whittington *research administrator, virology researcher, educator*
Van Akkeren, Lorraine Sue *research assistant*

Clarksburg
Gonano, J. Roland *technology research and development manager*

College Park
Cooper, Chester Lawrence *research administrator*
Diener, Theodor Otto *plant pathologist, researcher*
†Fagan, William F. *ecologist*
Fanning, Delvin Seymour *soil science educator*
†Izaurralde, Roberto César *science educator, researcher*
Jeffery, William Richard *developmental biology educator, researcher*
†Lea-Cox, John Derek *plant physiologist*
Miller, Raymond Jarvis *agronomy educator*
Stark, Francis C(io), Jr., *horticulturist, educator*
Tamboli, Prabhakar *agriculturist, educator*
Weil, Raymond Richard *soil scientist*
Weiner, Ronald Martin *microbiology and cell biology educator, research scientist*

Columbia
Ernest, Michael Vance, Sr., *research chemist*
Keeton, Morris Teuton *research scholar*
Nie, Guojun *research scientist*

Derwood
Kusterer, Thomas *project administrator*
†Vaughn, Steven D. *veterinary administrator*

Edgewater
Kushlan, James A. *biologist, research administrator, author, educator*
Staines, Charles L. *entomologist, researcher*

Frederick
Boyd, Ann Lewis *biology educator*
Knisely, Ralph Franklin *retired microbiologist*
Rossio, Jeffrey L. *biologist, educator*

Gaithersburg
Aiuto, Russell *science education consultant*
Barker, Peter Eugene *biologist, researcher*
Baum, Howard Richard *research scientist*
Johnson, Virgil Evans, Jr., *research scientist*
†Leader, Shelah Gilbert *research scientist*
†Mummaneni, Padmaja *research scientist, educator*

Garrett Park
Baldwin, Calvin Benham, Jr., *retired medical research administrator*

Germantown
Gong, Yu *molecular biologist*
Iqbal, Zafar *biochemist, neurochemist*
Norcross, Marvin Augustus *veterinarian, retired government agency official*

Greenbelt
Comiso, Josefino Cacas *research scientist*
Dantzler, Andrew Alan *science administrator*
†Middleton, Elizabeth McPhee *research scientist*
Thomas, Lindsey Kay, Jr., *research ecology biologist, educator, consultant*

Kensington
Jackson, William David *research executive*

Lanham
†Kumako, Kuami Mawunyo *agricultural scientist*

Laurel
Rorie, Conrad Jonathan *scientist, naval officer*
Sathyamoorthy, Venugopal *research biologist*

Libertytown
Lindblad, Richard Arthur *retired health services administrator, drug abuse epidemiologist*

Monkton
Mountcastle, Vernon Benjamin *neurophysiologist*

North Bethesda
Anderson, Owen Raymond *scientific and educational organization executive*

Odenton
Evans, William Lee *biologist, educator*

Potomac
Brewer, Nathan Ronald *veterinarian, consultant*
†Khachaturian, Zaven Setrak *neuroscientist*

Princess Anne
Joshi, Jagmohan *agronomist, consultant*

Rockville
Bayne, Kathryn Ann Louise *veterinarian*
Beer, Janusz Zygmunt *radiation and photo biologist, scientist*
Benz, Daniel Arthur *animal scientist*
Bush, Donna *forensic toxicologist*
Clancy, Carolyn *science foundation director, researcher, educator*
Cowan, William Maxwell *neurobiologist*
Crawford, Lester Mills , Jr., *veterinarian*
Gluckstein, Fritz Paul *veterinarian, biomedical information specialist*
Henricson, Beth Ellen *microbiologist*
Hill, Tabitha Kimberly *science educator*
Kafka, Marian Stern *neuroscientist*
MacGregor, James Thomas *toxicologist*
Mertz, Walter *retired government research executive*
Pospisil, George Curtis *human research educator*
Rosen, Saul Woolf *research scientist, health facility administrator*
Shah, Vinod Purushottam *research scientist*
Sundlof, Stephen Frederick *veterinary administrator*
Venter, J. Craig *science foundation director*

Saint Michaels
Ferraro, Linda Ann *veterinarian*

Salisbury
Moultrie, Fred *geneticist, researcher*
Tasker, John Baker *veterinary medical educator, college dean*

Silver Spring
Brandt, Carl David *research virologist*
Erk, Frank Chris *biologist, educator*

Kant, Gloria Jean *retired neuroscientist, researcher*
†Lindler, Luther Edgar *microbiologist, researcher*

Suitland
Vandiver, Pamela Bowren *research scientist*

West River
Howl, Joanne Healey *veterinarian, writer*

MASSACHUSETTS

Amherst
Margulis, Lynn (Lynn Alexander) *biologist, educator*
Palmer, John Derry *physiology educator*
Palser, Barbara F. *botany researcher, retired educator*
†Webley, Wilmore Christopher *microbiologist, researcher*
Zimmermann, Robert A. *molecular biologist, educator*

Andover
Strohmeier, Gregg Robert *research scientist*

Bedford
Griffin, Donald R(edfield) *zoology educator*

Beverly
McReynolds, Larry Austin *molecular biologist*
Roberts, Richard John *molecular biologist, consultant, research director*

Boston
†Altshuler, David Matthew *geneticist, endocrinologist*
†Broitman, Selwyn Arthur *microbiologist, educator*
†Cai, Tianxi *science educator*
Carradini, Lawrence *comparative biologist, science administrator*
Chattopadhyay, Naibedya *physiologist, educator, researcher*
Cohen, Jonathan Brewer *molecular neurobiologist, biochemist*
Demidov, Vadim V. *biotechnologist, writer*
†Elahi, Dariush *physiologist, researcher*
Essex, Myron Elmer *microbiology and virology educator*
Essig, Alvin *physiology educator*
†Evgenov, Oleg V. *medical scientist*
Foote, Warren Edgar *neuroscientist, psychologist, educator*
†García-Cardeña, Guillermo *cell biologist, researcher*
†Gilmore, Thomas David *biologist*
Hubel, David Hunter *physiologist, science educator*
Kahn, Carl Ronald *research laboratory administrator*
†Kravitz, Edward Arthur *neuroscientist*
Krolewski, Bozena K. *molecular biologist, researcher, cell biologist*
†Kwan, Paul W. *science educator*
†Lane, Harlan *science educator, researcher*
Leeman, Susan Epstein *neuroscientist, educator*
Lehar, Steven M. *research scientist*
Lewis, Kim *microbiologist*
†McKnight, Christopher James *science educator*
†Myers, Richard Hepworth *medical geneticist, educator*
†Rajadhyaksha, Milind Madhav *research scientist*
Ratner, Marcia *research scientist*
Shatz, Carla J. *biology educator*
†Shinn-Cunningham, Barbara Gail *auditory neuroscientist, electrical engineer*
Sidman, Richard Leon *neuroscientist, educator*
Smith, Donald Edward Harold *research animal specialist*
Sonenshein, Abraham Lincoln *microbiology educator*
Streilein, J. Wayne *research scientist*
Thorn, Frank *vision scientist, educator, researcher*
Tosteson, Daniel Charles *physiologist, medical school dean emeritus*
Turner, Raymond Edward *science educator, researcher, administrator*
†Xiao, Zhi-Xiong Jim *science educator, educator*

Brookline
Rosner, Anthony Leopold *research director, biochemist*

Cambridge
Arkhipova, Irina R. *biologist*
Barnett, David Philip *horticulturist*
Beckwith, Jonathan Roger *geneticist*
Bogorad, Lawrence *biologist, educator*
Dowling, John Elliott *biology educator*
Forman, Richard T. T. *ecology educator*
Fox, Maurice Sanford *molecular biologist, educator*
Gilbert, Walter *molecular biologist, educator*
Goldberg, Ray Allan *agriculturist, educator*
Hastings, John Woodland *biologist, educator*
Hopkins, Nancy H. *biology educator*
Horvitz, Howard Robert *biology educator, researcher*
Hubbard, Ruth *biology educator*
Hynes, Richard Olding *biology researcher, educator*
†Ivanov, Eugene *geneticist, researcher*
Knoll, Andrew Herbert T. *biology educator*
Levi, Herbert Walter *biologist, educator*
Ma, Hai-Fei *research scientist*
Magasanik, Boris *microbiology educator*
Marcus, Richard Sargon *research scientist*
Mayr, Ernst *retired zoologist, philosopher*
Melton, Douglas A. *molecular and cell biology educator*
Mickelson, Claudia Ann *biosafety officer, scientist*
Montana, Enrico Sakai *research scientist*
Pardue, Mary-Lou *biology educator*
Pero, Janice *molecular biologist*
Prinn, Ronald G. *atmospheric science educator*
Rich, Alexander *molecular biologist, educator*
†Rogers, Stephen G. *biotechnologist*
Sharp, Phillip Allen *biologist, educator*
Tannenbaum, Steven Robert *toxicologist, chemist*
Tonegawa, Susumu *biology educator*
Torriani-Gorini, Annamaria *microbiologist, educator*
Villa-Komaroff, Lydia *molecular biologist, educator, university official*
Vincent, James Louis *biotechnology company executive*
Wilson, Edward Osborne *biologist, educator, writer*
Winkler, Gunther *biotechnology executive, drug development expert*
†Wogan, Gerald Norman *toxicology educator*
†Wurtman, Judith Joy *research scientist*

Charlestown
Moskowitz, Michael Arthur *neuroscientist, neurologist*
†Puglielli, Luigi *research scientist*

Chestnut Hill
Ting, Yu-chen *science educator, researcher*

Concord
Huxley, Hugh Esmor *molecular biologist, educator*

Danvers
Kocur, Sean Edward *toxicologist*

Falmouth
Milkman, Roger Dawson *genetics educator, molecular evolution researcher*
Pearce, Jack Bodell *marine biologist, educator*

Framingham
†Beckwitt, Richard David *biology educator, researcher*
Goldman, Ralph Frederick *research physiologist, educator*
†Jiang, Canwen *genetic scientist, researcher*

Holliston
Prosser, Robert Arthur *retired research scientist*

Hopkinton
Sen, Asok C. *research scientist*

Hull
†Tanzi, Rudolph Emile *neuroscientist*

Jamaica Plain
†Parris, Thomas Martin *research scientist, consultant*

Lexington
Drouilhet, Paul Raymond, Jr., *science laboratory director, electrical engineer*
Fillios, Louis Charles *retired science educator*
Gibbs, Martin *biologist, educator*
Melngailis, Ivars *solid state researcher*
Peet, Norton Paul *science administrator*

Lincoln
Payne, Roger Searle *zoology researcher and administrator, conservationist*

Lowell
Coleman, Robert Marshall *biology educator*

Ludlow
Roberge, Lawrence Francis *neuroscientist, biotechnology consultant, writer, bioethicist, educator*

Natick
Sahatjian, Ronald Alexander *science foundation executive*

New Bedford
Buff, Eugene *geneticist, researcher*

North Grafton
Schwartz, Anthony *veterinary surgeon, educator*
†Singh, Inderpal *research scientist, veterinarian*

Norwood
Pence, Robert Dudley *biomedical research administrator, hospital administrator*

Roxbury
†Hamilton, James Arthur *biomedical researcher, biophysics educator*
Resnick, Oscar *neuroscientist*

Sharon
Zhang, Ying Hua *research scientist*

Shrewsbury
†Baguisi, Alexander *embryologist*

Somerville
†Bykanov, Alexander N. *research scientist*

South Hadley
Bledzki, Leszek Andrzej *limnologist, researcher*
Kaltenbach, Jane Couffer *zoology educator*

Southborough
Madras, Bertha Kalifon *neuroscientist, educator, consultant*

Southfield
†Mathews, Rita White *retired research scientist, educator*

Sudbury
Richards, James Carlton *microbiologist, business executive*

Waltham
Galinat, Walton Clarence *research scientist*

Wellesley Hills
Nicodemus, Christopher Farley *biotechnology educator, physician, researcher*

West Falmouth
Vaccaro, Ralph Francis *marine biologist*

Westborough
Lampi, Rauno Andrew *food and science engineer*
Nichols, Guy Warren *retired institute executive, utilities executive*

Weston
Marshall, Jean McElroy *physiologist*

Winchester
Harrison, Bettina Hall *retired biology educator*

Woburn
†Vogeli, Bernhard *research scientist*

Woods Hole
Colinvaux, Paul A. *research scientist, writer*
Houghton, Richard Arnold *research ecologist*
Inoué, Shinya *microscopy and cell biology scientist, educator*
Loewenstein, Werner Randolph *physiologist, biophysicist, educator*
Woodwell, George Masters *ecology research director, lecturer*

Worcester
Bagshaw, Joseph Charles *molecular biologist, educator*
Engle, Linda Jane *molecular biologist*
†Harnois, Marion C. *toxicologist, consultant*
He, Jiang *medical scientist*
Kennedy, Linda Mann *neuroscience educator, researcher*
Leach, Michael William *research pathologist*
Mendenhall, Harlan Vincent *research surgeon*
Witman, George Bodo, III, *cell biologist, researcher*

MICHIGAN

Albion
Stowell, Ewell Addison *botany educator, forestry consultant*

Ann Arbor
Beeton, Alfred Merle *laboratory director, limnologist, biologist, educator, environmentalist*
†Brideau, Roger J. *microbiologist, researcher*
Britton, Laurence George *research scientist*
Clewell, Don B. *microbial geneticist, educator*
Cochran, Kenneth William *toxicologist*
Dawson, William Ryan *zoology educator*
Drach, John Charles *scientist, educator*
†Edwards, Paul N. *science educator*
Fancher, Paul Strimple *research scientist*
Gelehrter, Thomas David *medical and genetics educator, physician*
Hartung, Rolf *environmental toxicology educator, researcher, consultant*
Hawkins, Joseph Elmer, Jr., *retired acoustic physiologist, medical educator*
He, Tianyuan *molecular biologist*
Horowitz, Samuel Boris *biomedical researcher, educational consultant*
Kaufman, Peter Bishop *biological sciences educator*
Kerppola, Tom Klaus William *research scientist, educator*
Kostyo, Jack Lawrence *physiology educator*
Kothary, Piyush C. *research scientist*
†Ling, Song *research scientist*
†Ma, Bing *research scientist*
Moore, Thomas Edwin *biology educator, museum director*
†Moran, John Vincent *geneticist, molecular biologist, researcher*
Neidhardt, Frederick Carl *microbiologist, educator*
Park, Euisu *research scientist*
Petty, Elizabeth Marie *geneticist*
†Petty, Howard Raymond *cell biology educator*
†Rathcke, Beverly Jean *biologist, educator*
Richardson, Rudy James *toxicology and neurosciences educator*
†Rowley, Larry Lee *research scientist, educator*
†Sarabandi, Kamal *science administrator*
Shappirio, David Gordon *biologist, educator*
Sloat, Barbara Furin *cell biologist, educator*
Stoermer, Eugene Filmore *biologist, educator*
Stoltenberg, Scott Frank *research scientist*
Weatherbee, Ellen Gene Elliott *botanist, educator*
Whitehouse, Frank, Jr., *microbiologist, educator*
Williams, John Andrew *physiology educator, consultant*
†Withey, Jeffrey Howard *molecular biologist, researcher*
Xie, Jingping *microbiologist, pediatrician*

Bay City
Nicholson, William Noel *clinical neuropsychologist*

Brooklyn
Freeman, Fred Wesley *forester, educator*

Detroit
Bhalla, Deepak Kumar *cell biologist, toxicologist, educator*
†Boinpally, Ramesh Rao *research scientist, pharmacist, educator*
Edwards, Brian Francis Peregrine *science educator*
†Hudson, Alan Paul *microbiologist, educator, research scientist*
†Jammalamadaka, Papa Rao *molecular biologist*
†Joiner, Michael Charles *radiation biologist, researcher*
Krawetz, Stephen Andrew *molecular medicine and genetics scientist*
Lerner, Stephen Alexander *microbiologist, physician, educator*
Novak, Raymond Francis *environmental health/toxicology research institute director, pharmacology educator*
Phillis, John Whitfield *physiologist, educator*
†Rahman, Km Wahidur *research scientist*
Smiecinski-Salkowski, Alicia *genetic counselor*
†Soltanian-Zadeh, Hamid *research scientist, educator*
†Van Dyke, Daniel L. *geneticist*
†Wheater, Michelle Kurpakus *biologist, educator*

East Lansing
Bromley, Stephen C. *zoology educator*
Bukovac, Martin John *horticulturist, educator*
Buskirk, Daniel D. *animal scientist, educator*
Dennis, Frank George, Jr., *retired horticulture educator*
Fromm, Paul Oliver *physiology educator*
Gerhardt, Philipp *microbiologist, educator*
Hackel, Emanuel *science educator*
Johnson, John Irwin, Jr., *neuroscientist*
Kende, Hans Janos *plant physiology educator*
Lenski, Richard Eimer *evolutionary biologist, educator*
McMeekin, Dorothy *botany, plant pathology educator*
Nelson, Ronald Harvey *animal science educator, researcher*
Patterson, Maria Jevitz *microbiology-pediatric infectious disease educator*
Petrides, George Athan *ecologist, educator*
Root-Bernstein, Robert Scott *biologist, educator*
†Thomashow, Michael F. *microbiologist, educator*

Edwardsburg
Floyd, Alton David *cell biologist, consultant*

Erie
Mohsen, Zohair Husein *entomologist, research scientist*

Grand Rapids
Carlotti, Ronald John *food scientist*
Petkus, Alan Francis *microbiologist*
Vande Woude, George Franklin *molecular biologist, cancer researcher*

Gregory
Banks, Peter Morgan *physics educator, investor, business consultant*

Hickory Corners
Lauff, George Howard *biologist*

Kalamazoo
†Buchanan, Lewis Victor *research scientist*
Kujawski, Daniel *science educator*
Marshall, Vincent de Paul *industrial microbiologist, researcher*
†Teagarden, Dirk Lowell *research scientist*

Lansing
†Nsofor, Leslie Monagolum *food scientist, researcher*

Ludington
Denner, Melvin Walter *retired life sciences educator*

Marquette
Riipi, Linda Ruth *biology educator*

Midland
Bus, James Stanley *toxicologist*
Davidson, John Hunter *agriculturist*

Mount Pleasant
Novitski, Charles Edward *biology educator*

Okemos
King, John Arthur *zoologist, educator*

Pleasant Ridge
Rizzo, Donald Charles *biology educator*

Portage
Elliott, George Algimon *pathologist, toxicologist, veterinarian*

Rochester
Lindemann, Charles Benard *cell biologist, researcher*
†Lu, Lunjin *science educator*

Rochester Hills
Unakar, Nalin Jayantilal *biological sciences educator*

Royal Oak
Kagan, Ron *zoological park administrator*

Sanford
Wilmot, Thomas Ray *medical entomologist, educator*

Spring Arbor
Buratovich, Michael Anthony *geneticist*

University Center
Pelzer, Charles Francis *human molecular geneticist, biologist, educator, research scientist*

Warren
Cheng, Yang-Tse *research scientist, materials scientist, physicist*

Ypsilanti
Caswell, Herbert Hall, Jr., *retired biology educator*

MINNESOTA

Chaska
Kwak, Seung-Keon *research scientist*

Detroit Lakes
Johansson, John Thomas *retired science educator*

Duluth
Heller, Lois Jane *physiologist, educator, researcher*
Johnson, Arthur Gilbert *microbiology educator*
Whitmyer, Robert Wayne *soil scientist, consultant, researcher*

Mapleton
John, Hugo Herman *natural resources educator*

Marcell
Aldrich, Richard John *agronomist, educator*

Minneapolis
Dworkin, Martin *microbiologist, educator*
†Engebretson, Mark Jerome *science educator, researcher*
Gorham, Eville *ecologist, biogeochemist*
Gudmundson, Barbara Rohrke *ecologist*
†Guillaume, Germaine Cornelissen *chronobiologist, researcher*
Haase, Ashley Thomson *microbiology educator, researcher*
Huang, Victor Tsangmin *food scientist, researcher*
†Lazarevic, Aleksandar *research scientist*
Lee, Hon Cheung *physiology educator*
Magee, Paul Terry *geneticist and molecular biologist, educator*
†Opitz, Donald L *science educator*
Polunovsky, Vitaly Alex *cell biologist*
Serstock, Doris Shay *retired microbiologist, educator, civic worker*
Sinha, Akhouri A. *research scientist, educator*
Symosek, Peter Frank *research scientist*
Wagenaar, Alexander Clarence *educator*
Watson, Dennis Wallace *microbiology educator, scientist*

Moorhead
Gee, Robert LeRoy *agriculturist, dairy farmer*

Plymouth
†Kodali, Dharma Rao *research scientist*

Prior Lake
Tufte, Obert Norman *retired research executive*

Rochester
Bajzer, Željko *scientist, educator*
Croghan, Gary Alan *cancer research scientist, physician*
Frestedt, Joy Louise *science administrator*
†Guo, ZengKui *research scientist*
†Harris, Peter C. *molecular biologist, educator*
Maher, L. James, III, *molecular biologist*
Shepherd, John Thompson *physiologist*

Roseville
Marten, Gordon Cornelius *research agronomist, educator, federal agency administrator*
Ucko, Franz *research scientist, consultant, writer*

Saint Joseph
Kirick, Daniel John *agronomist*

Saint Paul
Barnwell, Franklin Hershel *zoology educator*
Cheng, H(wei) H(sien) *soil scientist, agronomic and environmental science educator*
Davis, Margaret Bryan *paleoecology researcher, educator*
Dee, Scott Allen *veterinarian, researcher*
Diesch, Stanley La Verne *veterinarian, educator*
Ek, Alan Ryan *forester, educator*
Feeney, Daniel Arthur *veterinary radiologist*
Johnson, Kenneth Harvey *veterinary pathologist*
Kommedahl, Thor *plant pathology educator*
Leonard, Kurt John *plant pathologist, retired university program director*
McKinnell, Robert Gilmore *retired zoology, genetics and cell biology educator*
McNiel, Elizabeth Ann *veterinarian, educator*
†Mesce, Karen Anne *neurobiologist, educator*
Munson, Robert Dean *agronomist, soil scientist, consultant*
Newman, Raymond Melvin *biologist, educator*
Phillips, Ronald Lewis *plant geneticist, educator*
Pomeroy, Benjamin Sherwood *veterinary medicine educator*
Radcliffe, Edward Bruce *entomologist*
Roy, Robert Russell *toxicologist*
†Shmulsky, Rubin *forester, educator*
Wendt, Hans W. *life scientist*
Wilson, Michael John *biologist, educator*

MISSISSIPPI

Biloxi
McCaughan, Della Marie *retired science educator*

Hattiesburg
Thames, Shelby Freland *science educator, academic administrator*

Jackson
McDaniel, Larry Scott *microbiology and surgery educator*
Mosley, Jessie Bryant *retired science educator*

Lorman
Ezekwe, Michael Obi *animal science educator*
Panicker, Girish Kumar *agricultural scientist, consultant*

Mississippi State
Jenkins, Johnie Norton *research geneticist, research administrator*
Reddy, Kambham Raja *plant physiology educator*

Oxford
Duke, Stephen Oscar *physiologist, researcher, educator*
†Rego, Cesar *science educator, researcher*

Stoneville
†Hamel, Paul Bernard *ornithologist, researcher*
Ranney, Carleton David *plant pathology researcher, administrator*
Wilson, Alphus Dan *plant pathologist, researcher*

University
Keiser, Edmund Davis, Jr., *biologist, educator*

MISSOURI

Ballwin
Sidoti, Daniel R. *food technologist*

Bridgeton
Hemming, Bruce Clark *microbiologist*

Canton
Glover, Albert Downing *retired veterinarian*

Cape Girardeau
Miles, Donald Orval *clinical microbiologist*

Chesterfield
†Doshi, Parul D. *research scientist*
Graham, Donald James *food technologist*
Williams, Luther Steward *research scientist*

Columbia
Blevins, Dale Glenn *agronomy educator*
Brown, Olen Ray *medical microbiology and toxicology expert witness, researcher, educator, consultant, writer*
David, John Dewood *biology educator*
Davis, James O(thello) *physiology educator*
Ezashi, Toshihiko *molecular biologist*
Finkelstein, Richard Alan *retired microbiology educator, consultant*
Ignoffo, Carlo Michael *insect pathologist-virologist*
Mitchell, Roger Lowry *retired agronomy educator*
Morehouse, Lawrence Glen *veterinarian, educator*
Munson, Richard Howard *horticulturist*
Nelson, C. Jerry *agronomy educator*
Poehlmann, Carl John *agronomist, researcher*
†Roberts, R. Michael *animal scientist, biochemist, educator*
Vogt, Albert Ralph *forester, educator, program director*
Yanders, Armon Frederick *biological sciences educator, research administrator*
Youmans, William Barton *physiologist*

Eureka
Lindsey, Susan Lyndaker *zoologist*
Sexton, Owen James *vertebrate ecology educator, conservationist*

Fayette
†Enochs, M. Rebecca *science educator*

Greenwood
Klaus, Suzanne Lynne *horticulturist, production specialist*

Jefferson City
Giroir, Louis Eric *toxicologist*
Reidinger, Russell Frederick, Jr., *fish and wildlife scientist*

Kansas City
†Ellies, Debra L *biologist*
†Gist, Richard Michael *research scientist*
Hagsten, Ib *animal scientist, livestock consultant*
Peters, Ralph Irwin, Jr., *biology educator, researcher*
†Reichard, Larry A. *biologist, educator*
Sauer, Brian *molecular geneticist, researcher*

Kirksville
Peterson, Donald Fred *physiologist, educator*

Rolla
†Suzuki, Toshio *research scientist*

Saint Charles
Radke, Rodney Owen *agricultural research executive, consultant*

Saint Louis
Agrawal, Harish Chandra *neurobiologist, researcher, educator*
Allen, Garland Edward *biology educator, science historian*
Bourne, Carol Elizabeth Mulligan *biology educator, phycologist*
Carvalho, John Joseph, IV, *molecular geneticist, philosopher of science*
Croat, Thomas Bernard *botanical curator*
Curran, Michael Walter *management scientist*
Curtiss, Roy, III, *biology educator*
†Deng, Fan *research scientist*
†Goodenough, Ursula Wiltshire *cell biologist, researcher, educator*
†Grant, Hugh *biotechnology company executive*
Green, Maurice *molecular biologist, virologist, educator*
Gutsche, Henry William *retired scientist, writer*
Hawkins, Peggy Anne *veterinarian*
Hoessle, Charles Herman *zoo director*
Holland, Mark Robert *research scientist*

†Lala, Deepak S *research scientist*
Laskowski, Leonard Francis, Jr., *microbiologist*
†Rowland, Douglas John *research scientist*
†Saleem, Kadharbatcha S *neurobiologist, research scientist*
Schlesinger, Milton J. *virology educator, researcher*
Sutter, Jane Elizabeth *science educator, writer, conservationist*
Templeton, Alan Robert *biology educator*
†Weck, Margaret A. *science educator, educator*
Wyrwich, Kathleen W. *health research educator*
Zardini, Elsa Matilde *botanist, educator*
Zhu, Xin Liang *molecular biologist, researcher*

Springfield
Mathis, Alicia *biologist*
Steffen, Alan Leslie *entomologist*

Wentzville
†Garrett, Dwayne Everett *veterinary clinic executive*

West Plains
Wilcoxson, Roy Dell *plant pathology educator and researcher*

Windyville
Condron, Barbara O'Guinn *metaphysics educator, school administrator, publisher*

MONTANA

Alzada
Ericsson, Ronald James *applied biology executive*

Bozeman
†Goodrich, John M. *conservation ecologist*
Patten, Duncan Theunissen *ecologist educator*
Todd, Kenneth S., Jr., *parasitologist, educator*

Hamilton
Hadlow, William *retired veterinarian, pathologist*

Havre
Clouse, Vickie Rae *biologist, paleontologist, educator*

Missoula
†Langner, Heiko Walter *soil scientist, chemist*

Polson
Stanford, Jack Arthur *biological station administrator*

Red Lodge
Kauffman, Marvin Earl *geoscience consultant*

Saint Regis
Arney, James Douglas *forestry biometrics consultant*

NEBRASKA

Gering
Weihing, John Lawson *plant pathologist, state senator*

Lincoln
Adams, Charles Henry *retired animal scientist, educator*
Freidline, Charles *science educator*
Genoways, Hugh Howard *systematic biologist, educator*
Hanway, Donald Grant *retired agronomist, educator*
†Keeler, Kathleen Howard *biological sciences educator, ecologist*
†Li, Weixing *research scientist, educator*
Massengale, Martin Andrew *agronomist, university president*
Sander, Donald Henry *soil scientist, researcher*
Taylor, Stephen Lloyd *food toxicologist, educator, food scientist*
†Van Etten, James *plant pathologist, educator*

Omaha
Badeer, Henry Sarkis *physiology educator*
†Bandi, Nagesh *research scientist*
Carson, Steven Douglas *science educator, biomedical researcher*
†Nawaz, Zafar *biology educator, researcher*
Nizami, Iftikhar Riaz *research scientist*

Scottsbluff
†Schnell, Judy Kay *biology educator, division chair*

NEVADA

Carson City
†Krivan, Howard Calvin *microbiologist*

Fallon
Isidoro, Edith Annette *horticulturist*

Las Vegas
Alexander, John Bradfield *scientist, retired army officer*
Capanna, Albert Howard *neurosurgeon, neuroscientist, lawyer*

Minden
Petchenev, Alex *scientist*

North Las Vegas
Blizard, Susan Kennedy *biology educator*

Reno
Bohmont, Dale Wendell *agricultural consultant*
†Deyde, Varough Mohamed *microbiologist, researcher*

Gifford, Gerald Frederic *retired science educator*
Smith, Aaron *retired research director, clinical psychologist*

NEW HAMPSHIRE

Center Harbor
Smith, William Hulse *forestry and environmental studies educator*

Concord
Hartman, Sally P. *toxicologist*

Durham
Golinski, Jan Victor *history of science educator*
Pistole, Thomas Gordon *microbiology educator, researcher*
Shigo, Alex Lloyd *biologist, educator, publishing executive*

Hanover
Gilbert, John Jouett *aquatic ecologist, educator*
Spiegel, Evelyn Sclufer *biology educator, researcher*
Spiegel, Melvin *retired biology educator*
Tomlinson, George Herbert *retired industrial company research executive*

Lebanon
Munck, Allan Ulf *physiologist, educator*
Ou, Lo-Chang *physiology educator*

Lyme
Swan, Henry *forester, consultant*

Sanbornton
Weiant, Elizabeth Abbott *retired biology educator*

Silver Lake
Pallone, Adrian Joseph *research scientist*

NEW JERSEY

Bridgewater
Rebmann, Nina Sophie *research scientist*
Yang, Ruikang *research scientist*

Caldwell
†Choi, Sook C. *physiologist, educator*

Camden
Martin, Joseph Vinson *neurobiologist, educator*

Clifton
Yau, Edward Tintai *toxicologist, pharmacologist*

Cranbury
Izrailev, Sergei *research scientist*
Salles, Fernando Javier *molecular biologist, biotechnologist*

Cranford
Jenssen, Warren Donald *microbiologist, consultant*

Dayton
†Guo, Mintong *pharmaceutical scientist*

East Brunswick
Dombrowski, Anne Wesseling *retired microbiologist, researcher*

East Hanover
Foley, James Edward *scientist, pharmaceutical company executive*
Nemecek, Georgina Marie *molecular pharmacologist*

East Rutherford
Shalyt, Eugene *chemical researcher*

Edison
Menoutis, James Vassillios *research scientist*

Flemington
Wiedl-Kramer, Sheila Colleen *biologist*

Highlands
Psuty, Norbert Phillip *marine sciences educator*

Hoboken
Abel, Robert Berger *science administrator*
Panikov, Nicolai Sergeyevich *microbiologist, researcher*
Yevick, George Johannus *scientist*

Holmdel
Zhang, Xuemei *reliability scientist*

Hopatcong
Oken, Robert *neuroscientist, researcher, consultant*

Jersey City
Singer, Howard Jack *biology educator*

Kinnelon
Richardson, Joseph Blancet *retired science educator, educational consultant*

Lakewood
Witman, Edward Paul *philosophy educator*

Lebanon
Frascella, Daniel William, Jr., *scientist*

Madison
Demain, Arnold Lester *microbiologist, educator*

Mahwah
†Johnson, Roger *science educator*

Marlton
Sidelsky, Patricia Loney *science educator*

Montclair
Chinard, Francis Pierre *physiologist, physician, consultant*

Morristown
Garrett, Mark William *research engineer*
Rusch, George Michael *toxicology and risk assessment director*

Mount Arlington
Cohen, Irving David *science administrator*

New Brunswick
Day, Peter Rodney *geneticist, educator*
Ehrenfeld, David William *biology educator, writer*
Funk, Cyril Reed, Jr., *agronomist, educator*
Grassle, Judith Payne *marine biology educator*
Lachance, Paul Albert *food science educator, clergyman*
Maramorosch, Karl *virologist, educator*
Montville, Thomas Joseph *food microbiologist, educator*
Pramer, David *microbiologist, educator, research administrator*
Tedrow, John Charles Fremont *soils educator*
Vayda, Andrew P. *human ecology and anthropology educator*
Wang, Yanxin *research scientist*

New Providence
Ogawa, Seiji *research scientist, biophysicist*

Newark
Ledeen, Robert Wagner *neurochemist, educator*
Qiu, Zeyuan *researcher, educator*
Thomas, Andrew Philip *physiologist*
†Vatner, Stephen F. *physiologist, researcher, research scientist*

Northvale
†Kota, Venkata Rangaiah *research scientist, researcher*

Nutley
Dennin, Robert Aloysius, Jr., *pharmaceutical research scientist*

Piscataway
Denhardt, David Tilton *molecular and cell biology educator*
Ebright, Richard High *molecular biologist*
Egger, M. David *neurobiology educator*
Gaffar, Abdul *research scientist, administrator*
†Rothkopf, Michael H. *science educator, researcher*
Sit, Ping-Fai *research scientist*
†van Frankenhuijsen, Machiel *science educator*
Wang, Tsuey Tang *science educator, venture capitalist*
†Zhao, Dandan *molecular biologist, biomedical researcher*

Plainfield
Frost, David *former biology educator, medical editor, consultant*

Pomona
Jahangir, Z(ulfiquar) M(uhammed) G(olam) Sarwar *molecular biologist, educator*

Port Norris
Canzonier, Walter Jude *shellfish aquaculturist*

Princeton
Altmann, Stuart Allen *biologist, educator*
Ballou, Janice Donelon *research director*
†Bassler, Bonnie *molecular biologist*
Drakeman, Donald Lee *biotechnology company executive, lawyer*
Enquist, Lynn William *molecular biologist*
Gould, James L. *biology educator*
Grigger, Jane Elizabeth *earth science educator, photographer*
Jacobs, William Paul *botanist, educator*
†Krishnan, Mahesh *research scientist*
†Marshall, Carol Joyce *clinical project director*
Merrill, Leland Gilbert, Jr., *retired environmental science educator*
Steinberg, Malcolm Saul *biologist, educator*
Wieschaus, Eric F. *molecular biologist, educator*
Witkin, Evelyn Maisel *retired geneticist*

Rahway
Strack, Alison Merwin *neurobiologist*

Randolph
†Johannessen, Janet A. *science educator*

Red Bank
Fred, Rogers Murray, III, *veterinary oncologist*

Shrewsbury
Westerman, Liane Marie *research scientist executive*

Somerset
Murray, Bertram George, Jr., *biology educator*
Trivedi, Harsh Mahendra *technical associate, educator, writer*

Stanton
Kille, John William, Jr., *toxicology and biomedical product consultant*

Teaneck
Rojas Wahl, Roy Uwe *research scientist*

Teterboro
Gambino, S(alvatore) Raymond *medical laboratory executive, educator*

Toms River
Kudryasheva, Alexandra A. *microbiologist, radiobiologist, biotechnologist, educator*
Okusanya, Olubukanla Tejumola *ecologist*

Trenton
Roy, Herbert Clarence *research scientist*

Union
Rosenthal, Judith Wolder *biological sciences educator*

Upper Montclair
Thiruvathukal, John V. *science educator, consultant, writer*

West Trenton
†Tessler, Steven *ecologist, data processing executive*

Westfield
Brown, Shirley Mark *retired science administrator*

Wyckoff
Cropper, Susan Peggy *veterinarian*

NEW MEXICO

Albuquerque
†Bear, David George
†Cheng, Yung Sung *research scientist*
Danley, J. Mark *biologist, educator, actor*
Fisher, Don Carlton *toxicologist*
Henderson, Rogene Faulkner *toxicologist, researcher*
Hsi, David Ching Heng *plant pathologist and geneticist, educator*
Mauderly, Joe Lloyd *pulmonary toxicologist*
Muggenburg, Bruce Al *veterinary physiologist*

Alto
Thrasher, Jack Dwayne *toxicologist, researcher, consultant*

Capitan
Reimann, Bernhard Erwin Ferdinand *retired biologist*

Cedar Crest
Rypka, Eugene Weston *microbiologist*

Las Cruces
†Cooch, F. Graham *ecologist, educator, ecologist, researcher*
McElyea, Ulysses, Jr., *veterinarian*
Schemnitz, Sanford David *wildlife biology educator*
Tonn, Robert James *retired entomologist*

Los Alamos
Browne, John Charles *physics researcher, former national research laboratory executive*
Canavan, Gregory H. *science educator*
Gregg, Charles Thornton *research company executive*
Wallace, Terry Charles, Sr., *retired technical administrator, researcher*

Santa Fe
Guthrie, Catherine S. (Catherine S. Nicholson-Guthrie) *research scientist*
Harding, Marie *ecological executive, artist*
Phipps, Claude Raymond *research scientist*
Smith, Philip Meek *science policy consultant, writer*
Wagner, Robert Philip *geneticist, educator*
†Whalen, William J. *retired physiologist*

Shiprock
Billy, Bahe *soil scientist, educator*

NEW YORK

Albany
Able, Kenneth Paul *biology educator*
Burger, Harold Alan *virologist*
D'Elia, Christopher Francis *marine biologist, educator*
Eadon, George A. *scientist, administrator, educator*
Fayo, Anthony Thomas *research scientist*
Hong, Chia-Swee *research scientist*
†Lnenicka, Gregory Allen *biologist, educator*
MacColl, Robert *research scientist, biomedical educator*
Mizejewski, Gerald Jude *research scientist*
Mongin, Alexander Anatolievich *neuroscientist, educator*
†Rieder, Conly LeRoy *cell biologist, consultant*
Stevens, Roy W. *microbiologist, researcher*
Stewart, Margaret McBride *biology educator, researcher*

Amherst
†Edsberg, Laura E. *research scientist, consultant*
†Jin, Jin Yan *science educator*

Annandale
†Cutler, Robert W. *biologist, educator*

Annandale On Hudson
Ferguson, John Barclay *biology educator*

Bronx
Adinolfi, Marion Darlyne *research scientist*
Bennett, Michael Vander Laan *neuroscience educator*
Conway, William Gaylord *zoologist, zoo director, conservationist*
Delprete, Piero Giuseppe *botanist, curator, educator*
Fidock, David Armand *microbiology educator*
Font, Cecilio Rafael *biology educator, physician*
†Johnson, Anne Bradstreet *research physician, educator*
Mukherjee, Asit Baran *geneticist, educator*
Schaller, George Beals *zoologist*
Scheuer, James *physician, educator, researcher*
Szilagyi, George *microbiologist, physician*
†Waelsch, Salome Gluecksohn *geneticist, educator*

Bronxville
Hutchison, Dorris Jeannette *retired microbiologist, educator*

Brooklyn
Altura, Bella T. *physiologist, educator*
Altura, Burton Myron *physiologist, educator*
Bernd, Paulette Sally *anatomy and cell biology educator*
†Bornstein, Sandra *science educator*
Carswell, Lois Malakoff *botanical gardens executive, consultant*
Djordjevic, Bozidar *radiation biologist*
Gabriel, Mordecai Lionel *biologist, educator*
Jacobson, Leslie Sari *biologist, educator*
Kramer, Allan Franklin, II, *researcher, botanical garden official*
Lipson, Steven Mark *clinical virologist, microbiologist, educator*
List, Bobye Goodman *science foundation director*
Oley, Nancy H. *psychobiologist, educator*
Patan, Sybill Petra *research scientist*
Schiffman, Gerald *microbiologist, educator*
Skyler, Marc Norman *biology educator*
Tiedge, Henri *neuroscientist, educator, researcher*
Vassalle, Mario *physiologist*
†Wasserman, Aaron O. *biologist, educator*
Zuk, Judith *botanic garden administrator*

Buffalo
Berezney, Ronald *molecular biologist*
†Cummings, K. Michael *research scientist*
Duax, William Leo *biological researcher*
†Egilmez, Nejat K. *science educator*
†Kirby, Amy Elizabeth *microbiologist, researcher*
†Matsui, Sei-ichi *geneticist*
Still, Ivan Henry *research scientist*
†Sun, Qi-Hong *cell biologist, immunologist*
Tomasi, Thomas B. *cell biologist, administrator*
Wen, Sihai *research engineer, materials scientist*
Zawicki, Joseph Leo *science educator*

Burnt Hills
DeVries, Robert Charles *scientist, researcher, consultant*

Canandaigua
†Handa, Y. Paul *research scientist, engineering executive*

Cheektowaga
Keem, Michael Dennis *veterinarian*

Cobleskill
Ingels, Jack Edward *horticulture educator*

Cold Spring Harbor
†Grodzicker, Terri I. *research scientist, educator, academic administrator*
Honey, Sangeet *molecular biologist, research scientist*
Watson, James Dewey *molecular biologist, educator*

Conklin
Fisher, Dale Dunbar *animal scientist, dairy nutritionist*

Cooperstown
Harman, Willard Nelson *malacologist, educator*

Corning
†Pindel, David Lee *biologist, educator*

Depew
Koch, Ronald Peter *retired biologist*

Dobbs Ferry
†Minorsky, Peter Vladimir *plant physiologist*

Dunkirk
Strauser, Jeffrey Arthur *biologist, educator*

East Aurora
†Sand, Seaward Alwyn *geneticist, researcher*

East Hampton
Murbach, David Paul *horticulturist*

Elmhurst
Kekatos, Deppie-Tinny Z. *microbiologist, researcher, lab technologist*

Fairport
Chari, Krishnan *research scientist*

Farmingdale
Mencarelli, Victor Aristide *microbiologist*

Flushing
Commoner, Barry *biologist, educator*
Kranepool, Harry Anthony *science educator*

Fredonia
Benton, Allen Haydon *biology educator*
†Brown, William Douglas *biology educator*

Garden City
Podwall, Kathryn Stanley *biology educator*

Germantown
Geistfeld, James Gordon *veterinarian*

Great Neck
Puttlitz, Donald Herbert *medical microbiologist*

Hamilton
Belanger, Kenneth Douglas *cell and molecular biologist, educator*

Hawthorne
†Chojnicki, Eric Walter Theodore *molecular geneticist*
Darzynkiewicz, Zbigniew D. *research scientist*

Hempstead
Hastings, Harold Morris *science educator*

Homer
Gustafson, John Alfred *biology educator*

Ithaca
Alexander, Martin *environmental toxicologist, consultant*
Ballantyne, Joseph M. *science educator, program administrator, researcher*
Blackler, Antonie William Charles *biologist*
Chiang, Huai Chang *entomologist, educator*
Davies, Peter John *plant physiology educator, researcher*
Earle, Elizabeth Deutsch *biology educator*
Eisner, Thomas *biologist, educator*
Fick, Gary Warren *agronomy educator, forage crops researcher*
Foote, Robert Hutchinson *animal physiology educator*
Fox, Francis Henry *retired veterinarian*
Ghiorse, William Cushing *microbiology educator, editor*
Gillett, James Warren *ecotoxicology educator*
Grunes, David Leon *research soil scientist, educator, editor*
Hairston, Nelson George, Jr., *ecologist, educator*
†Hotchkiss, Joseph Henry *toxicologist, educator*
Jagendorf, André Tridon *plant physiologist*
Kallfelz, Francis A. *veterinary medicine educator*
Kennedy, Wilbert Keith, Sr., *agronomy educator, retired university official*
Kingsbury, John Merriam *botanist, educator*
Korf, Richard Paul *mycology educator*
Kramer, John Paul *entomologist, educator*
†Krivoshein, Arcadius V. *research scientist*
Lengemann, Frederick William *physiology educator, scientist*
Mai, William Frederick *plant nematologist, educator*
Mortlock, Robert Paul *microbiologist, educator*
†Nasrallah, June *plant pathologist, department chairman*
Novak, Joseph Donald *science educator, knowledge studies specialist*
Pimentel, David *ecologist, educator*
Poppensiek, George Charles *veterinary scientist, educator*
Schlafer, Donald Hughes *veterinary pathologist*
Seeley, John George *horticulture educator*
Walcott, Charles *neurobiology and behavior educator*
Wasserman, Robert Harold *biology educator*
Welch, Ross Maynard *plant physiologist, researcher, educator*
†Wiedmann, Martin *microbiologist, educator, environmental scientist, veterinarian*

Levittown
Stalter, Richard B. *biology educator, researcher*

Loudonville
†LaRow, Edward J. *biologist, educator*

Macedon
McGee, Dennis Emmett *research technologist*

Mahopac
Fliss, Albert Edward, Jr., *molecular biologist*

Manhasset
Bialer, Martin George *geneticist*

Manorville
Esp, Barbara Ann Lorraine *educational researcher, educator*

Melville
Doering, Charles Henry *research scientist, educator, editor, publisher*
Goldstein, Mindy Sue *biologist*

Millbrook
Jones, Clive Gareth *ecologist, researcher*
Likens, Gene Elden *biology and ecology educator, administrator*

Neponsit
†Nicastri, Ann G. *science educator*

New Hyde Park
Isenberg, Henry David *microbiology educator*

New Paltz
Ho, Hon Hing *biology educator*

New Rochelle
Beardsley, Robert Eugene *microbiologist, educator*

New York
Anderson, O(rvil) Roger *biology educator, marine biology and protozoology researcher*
Auer, Manfred Stefan *structural biologist, biochemist*
Ben-Hur, Ehud *research scientist, researcher*
Bernheimer, Alan Weyl *microbiologist*
Bhattacharya, Satyajit *research scientist*
Blobel, Günter *cell biologist, educator*
Bock, Walter Joseph *zoology educator*
Botkin, Daniel Benjamin *biologist, environmental scientist, writer*
Bucolo, Gail Ann *biotechnologist*
†Caesar, Godfrey Wrensford *biologist, educator*
Catanzaro, Daniel Frank *molecular biologist, educator*

PROFESSIONAL INDEX 6615 SCIENCE: LIFE SCIENCE

Chaganti, Raju S. *geneticist, educator, researcher*
Cherksey, Bruce David *physiology educator*
Chua, Nam-Hai *plant molecular biologist, educator*
Cohen, David Harris *neurobiology educator, university official*
Cohen, Joel Ephraim *biologist, educator, demographer*
Cranefield, Paul Frederic *physiology educator, physician, scientist*
Dales, Samuel *microbiologist, virologist, educator*
Dandashi, S. Alexander *operations research scientist, consultant, corporate & government advisor*
Davis, Jessica G. *clinical geneticist, pediatrician*
Desnick, Robert John *human geneticist*
Despommier, Dickson Donald *microbiology educator, parasitologist, researcher*
†DiLandro, Anthony Charles *science educator, funeral director*
†Dottin, Robert P. *biologist, educator*
Feldman, Samuel Mitchell *neuroscientist, educator*
Frost, Darrel Richmond *biologist, administrator*
Georgakopoulos, Anastasios *molecular biology*
†Giampietro, Philip Francis *clinical geneticist, pediatrics educator*
Greengard, Paul *neuroscientist*
Hiller, Jacob Moses *research scientist*
Hirschhorn, Rochelle *genetics educator*
Hudspeth, Albert James *biomedical researcher, educator*
Johnson, Jeffrey Grant *research scientist, psychology educator*
Kandel, Eric Richard *neuroscience educator*
Kelly, Thomas Jesse, Jr., *molecular biologist*
Leaman, Leonard S., Jr., *science educator*
Lederberg, Joshua *geneticist, educator*
Levandowsky, Michael *marine biologist*
Llinás, Rodolfo Riascos *medical educator, researcher*
Maas, Werner Karl *microbiology educator*
†MacNamara, Brian Scott *veterinarian, law educator*
Mei, Dolores Marie *research administrator*
Mombaerts, Peter *biology educator*
Moroz, Pavel Emanuel *research scientist*
Morse, Stephen Scott *virologist, immunologist, epidemiologist*
†Moy, Richard L. *virologist*
†Naini, Ali *molecular geneticist, research scientist*
†Nathanielsz, Peter William *physiologist*
Osgood, Richard Magee, Jr., *applied physics educator, electrical engineering educator, research administrator, educator*
†Palhan, Vikas Bavi *molecular biologist, researcher*
Penalver, Angelica Maria *research scientist*
Pergolizzi, Robert George *molecular biologist, educator*
Pietruski, John Michael, Jr., *biotechnology company executive, pharmaceuticals executive*
Pollack, Robert Elliot *biologist, educator, author*
Rapa Rafaniello, Helen Marie *forensic scientist*
Ribary, Urs *neuroscientist, researcher, educator*
Rozen, Jerome George, Jr., *research entomologist, museum curator and research administrator*
Rybin, Vitalyi Olegovich *research scientist*
Sabatini, David Domingo *cell biologist, biochemist*
Sastry, Srin *scientist, researcher, educator*
†Saunders, Sylvia Christie *biologist, educator*
†Schacher, Samuel *neurobiologist, educator*
†Seyedi, Nahid *physiologist, researcher*
Sheetz, Michael Patrick *cell biology educator*
Shelanski, Michael L. *cell biologist, educator*
Silverstein, Samuel Charles *cellular biology and physiology educator, researcher*
†Stirling, Alexandra Lucero *science administrator*
Stotzky, Guenther *microbiologist, educator*
Stutman, Leonard Jay *research scientist, cardiologist*
Sultzer, Barnet Martin *microbiology and immunology researcher*
†Tang, Youmin *research scientist*
Telang, Nitin T. *cancer biologist, educator*
Tierno, Philip Mario, Jr., *microbiologist, educator, researcher*
Tietjen, John Henry *retired biology and oceanography educator*
Trager, William *biology educator*
†Wegesin, Domonick J. *neuroscientist, educator*
Wharton, Danny Carroll *zoo biologist*
Wiesel, Torsten Nils *neurobiologist, educator*
Windhager, Erich Ernst *physiologist, educator*
Young, Michael Warren *geneticist, educator*
Zinder, Norton David *genetics educator, university dean*

Orangeburg
†Ginsberg, Stephen D *neuroscientist*
Yuan, Aidong (David Yuan) *cell biologist, researcher*

Owego
Kemp, Eugene Thomas *retired veterinarian*

Palisades
†Huang, Huei-Ping *research scientist*
Miller, Roberta Balstad *science administrator*

Palmyra
Hill, Cynthia Maressa *ecological planner, environmental scientist*

Patchogue
Gibbons, Edward Francis *psychobiologist*

Pearl River
†Almoazen, Hassan *research scientist*
Barik, Sudhakar *microbiologist, research scientist*
Bigelis, Ramunas *research scientist*
Chen, Guodong *scientist, enzymologist, biochemical engineer*
Forgacs, Joseph *mycotoxicologist*
Yamashita, Ayako *research scientist*

Pittsford
Coleman, Paul David *neurobiology researcher, educator*
Thorndike, Elizabeth *educator*

Purchase
Ehrman, Lee *geneticist, educator*

Rego Park
Iosebashvili, Alexander *research scientist, educator*

Rensselaer
Perez, Ana Veronica *developmental biology researcher*

Riverhead
Daughtrey, Margery L. *plant pathologist*
Kent, Robert John *marine biologist*

Rochester
Chang, Chawnshang *science educator, laboratory administrator*
Chang, Jack Che-Man *imaging materials and media administrator*
Clarkson, Thomas William *toxicologist, educator*
Doty, Robert William *neurophysiologist, educator*
Frisina, Robert Dana *sensory neuroscientist, educator*
†Lawton, Kathy G. *biology educator*
Madaras, Marcel Bradut *research scientist*
Morrow, Paul Edward *toxicology educator*
Muchmore, William Breuleux *zoologist, educator*
Rodgers, Suzanne Hooker *ergonomics consultant, physiologist*
†Stark, Egon *microbiologist, educator*
†Weiss, Bernard *toxicology educator*

Rockville Centre
†Koechel, Loretta *science educator*

Saranac Lake
†Smiley, Stephen Todd *research scientist*

Schenectady
Mayes, Brian A. *toxicologist*

Southold
Callis, Jerry Jackson *veterinarian*

Stanfordville
Tetor, David R. *agriculturist, consultant*

Stone Ridge
Terpening, Donald Lester *science educator, medical technologist*

Stony Brook
†Akella, Umasundari Srivenkata *research scholar*
Chen, Dongqing *medical image processing researcher*
Lennarz, William Joseph *research biologist, educator*
Levinton, Jeffrey S. *biology educator, oceanographer*
Rohlf, F. James *biometrician, educator*
Semyonov, Oleg G. *research scientist*

Suffern
Menon, Gopinathan Kunnariath *scientist, researcher*

Syracuse
Dunham, Philip Bigelow *biology educator, physiologist*
†Turner, Christopher Edward *cell biology educator*
Verrillo, Ronald Thomas *neuroscience educator, researcher*
†Weiskirch, Larry M *science educator*

Troy
Berg, Daniel *science and technology educator*
Ehrlich, Henry Lutz *biology educator*
†Lvov, Yuri Victorovich *science educator*
Ross, Sydney *science educator, researcher*
Rumyantsev, Sergey L. *research scientist, educator*
Watson, E Bruce *science educator*

Tuxedo Park
Lippmann, Morton *environmental health science researcher*

Upton
Liu, Yangang *atmospheric scientist*

Utica
Antzelevitch, Charles *research center executive*
†Dumaine, Robert *research scientist, educator*

Valhalla
Chung, Fung-Lung *cancer research scientist*
Kleinman, Wayne Alan *research scientist*
Wolin, Michael Stuart *physiology educator*

Waterford
Wang, Yi-Feng *polymer scientist, consultant*

Webster
Chow, Tsu Sen *research scientist*

White Plains
Peyton, Donald Leon *retired standards association executive*
Smith, Gerard Peter *neuroscientist*

Yorktown Heights
Wynne, James *research scientist*

NORTH CAROLINA

Asheboro
Jones, David M. *zoological park administrator*

Asheville
Parresol, Bernard Ross *research biometrician, statistician*

Brevard
Glesener, Robert Richard *biologist, educator, biologist, researcher*
Lewert, Robert Murdoch *microbiologist, educator*

Cary
†Acharya, Prathima S. *research scientist*

Chapel Hill
Andrews, Richard Nigel Lyon *public policy educator, environmental studies administrator*
Farber, Rosann Alexander *geneticist, educator*
†Feduccia, J. Alan *biologist, educator*
Judd, Burke Haycock *geneticist*
†LaMantia, Anthony-Samuel *developmental neurobiologist, educator*
Lundblad, Roger Lauren *biotechnology consultant*
Simmons, Otto DeBruhl, III, *microbiologist, researcher*
Smithies, Oliver *geneticist, educator*
†Straley, Joseph Ward *retired molecular spectrascopist, retired science educator*
Stumpf, Walter Erich *cell biology educator, researcher*
Warren, Donald William *physiology educator, dentistry educator*
Weiss, Charles Manuel *environmental biologist*
Wetzel, Robert George *botany educator*

Davidson
Ramirez, Julio Jesus *neuroscientist*

Durham
Blum, Jacob Joseph *physiologist, educator*
Gillham, Nicholas Wright *geneticist, educator*
†Gitler, Daniel *neurobiologist, researcher*
†Glibert, John H. *research scientist*
Keene, Jack Donald *molecular genetics and microbiology educator*
Malling, Heinrich Valdemar *geneticist*
Merrick, Bruce Alex *research scientist*
Moore, John Wilson *neurophysiologist, educator*
†Mushak, Paul *toxicologist, consultant*
†Nadadur, Srikanth S *molecular biologist*
Naylor, Aubrey Willard *botany educator*
Nicklas, Robert Bruce *cell biologist, educator*
Raetz, Christian R. H. *biochemistry educator*
Richardson, Stephen Giles *biotechnology company executive*
Rose, Jed Eugene *research scientist*
Rouse, Doris Jane *physiologist, research administrator*
Schmidt-Nielsen, Knut *physiologist, educator*
†Wesseling, John F. *neuroscientist*

Gastonia
Flynn, Duane James *entomologist*

Greensboro
Aldridge, David William *biologist, educator*
†Cowett, Everett R *retired agronomist*
Gdanitz, Robert J. *research scientist, educator*
O'Brien, William John *ecology researcher*
Rowan, William Boyd *parasitologist, writer*

Greenville
†Huo, Shouquan *research scientist, educator*
Meggs, William Joel *toxicologist, internist, emergency physician, educator*
Summers, Kyle *biologist, educator*

Hendersonville
Brittain, James Edward *science and technology educator, researcher*

Kitty Hawk
Sjoerdsma, Albert *research institute executive*

Little Switzerland
Gross, Samson Richard *geneticist, biochemist, educator*

New Bern
Ash, William James *geneticist, educator*

Pittsboro
Giess, Edward August *crystal growth scientist*

Raleigh
Aronson, Arthur Lawrence *retired veterinarian, toxicologist, educator, pharmacologist*
Barefoot, Aldos Cortez, Jr., *forester, educator*
Benson, D(avid) Michael *plant pathologist*
Branch, Stacy *veterinarian, educator*
Chang, Hou-min *science educator, researcher*
Cook, Maurice Gayle *soil science educator, consultant*
Cooper, Arthur Wells *ecologist, educator*
Dunphy, Edward James *crop science extension specialist*
Gardner, Donald E. *toxicologist, consultant*
Gordon, Morris Aaron *medical mycologist, microbiologist*
Hardin, James W. *botanist, herbarium curator, educator*
Hassan, Hosni Moustafa *microbiologist, biochemist, toxicologist and food scientist, educator*
Havlin, John Leroy *soil scientist, educator*
Hodgson, Ernest *toxicology educator*
Humenik, Frank *science educator, consultant*
Kelman, Arthur *plant pathologist, educator*
Kuznetsov, Andrey Valer'evich *science educator*
Lytle, Charles Franklin *biology educator*
Malindzak, George Steve, Jr., *cardiopulmonary physiology, toxicologist, biomedical engineer*
Moreland, Donald Edwin *plant physiologist*
Scandalios, John George *geneticist, educator*
Stuber, Charles William *genetics educator, researcher*
†Sun, Ge *research scientist, educator*
†Wentworth, Thomas Ralph *ecologist*
Zeng, Zhao-Bang *geneticist, educator*

Research Triangle Park
de Serres, Frederick Joseph *genetic toxicologist*
†Dryga, Sergey Alexander *biotechnologist*
†Geron, Christopher Douglas *ecologist, environmental scientist, researcher*
†Melnick, Ronald L. *toxicologist, researcher*
Mumford, Stephen Douglas *research scientist*

Richfield
Shaver, William Adam *forester*

Washington
Heck, Henry D'Arcy *retired toxicologist, consultant*

Wilmington
Bolen, Eric George *biology educator*
Roer, Robert David *physiologist, educator*
Watanabe, Wade Osamu *marine biologist*
†Webster, William David *biologist, educator*

Winston Salem
Cheng, Heng-Jie *physician scientist*
†Ganz, Charles *laboratory executive*
Gmeiner, William Henry *science educator*
Laxminarayana, Dama *geneticist, researcher, educator*
†Mizel, Steven B. *microbiologist, educator*
Rautaharju, Pentti Matti *research scientist, educator*
Seckar, Joel Andreas *toxicologist, chemist*

NORTH DAKOTA

Bismarck
Carlisle, Ronald Dwight *nursery owner*

Fargo
†Johansen, Robert Henny *horticulturist, geneticist*
Schmidt, Claude Henri *retired research administrator*

Jamestown
Cox, Robert Ripley, Jr., *wildlfe research biologist*

Minot
Morgan, Rose Marie *retired biology educator*

OHIO

Ada
Keiser, Terry Dean *biologist, educator*

Akron
†Chung, Benjamin T. F. *science educator*
†Dick, John Stewart, Jr., *rheologist, consultant*
Millman, Irving *microbiologist, educator, retired inventor*

Archbold
Bergman, Jerry Rae *science educator*

Ashland
Rueger, Daniel Scott *horticulture educator*

Athens
Ungar, Irwin Allan *botany educator*
Xu, Li *science educator*

Avon Lake
Zurcher, Vickie Lee *geneticist*

Bowling Green
Clark, Eloise Elizabeth *biologist, educator*
Heckman, Carol A. *biology educator*

Canton
Bernstein, Penny L. *biologist, educator*

Cincinnati
†Erway, Lawrence Clifton, Jr., *biologist, educator*
Etges, Frank Joseph *parasitology educator*
Grinshpun, Sergey A. *science educator, science administrator*
Horseman, Nelson Douglas *molecular and cellular physiology educator*
McDaniels, Audrey Evelyn *microbiologist*
†Melnyk, Lisa Jo *research scientist*
†Monaco, John J. *molecular genetics research educator*
Saal, Howard Max *clinical geneticist, pediatrician, educator*
Schaefer, Dale W. *science educator*
Schaefer, Frank William, III, *microbiologist, researcher*
†Schultz, Jo El Jean *research scientist, educator*
Sperelakis, Nicholas, Sr., *physiology and biophysics educator, researcher*
Sunagawa, Masanori *physiologist, researcher*

Cleveland
Blackwell, John *science educator*
†Buck, Matthias *science educator*
Dell'Osso, Louis Frank *neuroscience educator*
†Jacobs, Michael Roy *microbiologist, researcher*
†Kehres, David George *microbiologist, researcher*
Malhotra, Indu *research scientist, researcher*
Miyoshi, Kazuhisa *senior research scientist*
Perry, George *neuroscientist, educator*
Stepien, Carol Ann *molecular geneticist, fisheries educator*
Suri, Jasjit S. *research scientist*
Taylor, Steve Henry *zoologist*
van den Bogert, Antonie Johannes *biomechanics researcher, consultant*

†Zigmond, Richard Eric *neuroscientist, researcher*

Columbus
†Abraham, Brian M. *research scientist*
Capen, Charles Chabert *veterinary pathology educator*
Cheesman, Kerry Lee *education educator, researcher*
Chou, Richard Chunwah *neuroscientist, internist*
Disinger, John Franklin *natural resources educator*
Fawcett, Sherwood Luther *research laboratory executive*
Fry, Donald Lewis *physiologist, educator*
Glaser, Ronald *microbiology educator, scientist*
Kapral, Frank Albert *medical microbiology and immunology educator*
Melling, Jack *biotechnologist, director*
Modisette, Laura Jessen *information designer*
Needham, Glen Ray *entomology and acarology educator, researcher*
Peterle, Tony John *zoologist, educator*
Pieper, Heinz Paul *physiology educator*
†Piggrem, Gary Wayne *science educator, writer*
Reeve, John Newton *molecular biology and microbiology educator*
†Robinson, David Milton *microbiologist*
Roth, Robert Earl *environmental educator*
Snyder, Susan Leach *science educator, writer*
Stansbery, David Honor *ecologist*
Triplehorn, Charles A. *entomology educator, insects curator*
von Recum, Andreas F. *veterinarian, bioengineer*
Warmbrod, James Robert *agriculture educator, university administrator*
Wood, Jackie Dale *physiologist, educator, researcher*
Yohn, David Stewart *virologist, science administrator*
Zartman, David Lester *animal sciences educator, researcher*

Dayton
Chen, Chenggang *research scientist*
Isaacson, Milton Stanley (Jim Isaacson) *research and development company executive, engineer*
Trivedi, Hitesh K. *research scientist*

Delaware
Fry, Anne Evans *zoology educator*
†Iverson, Louis Robert *research ecologist*

Fairborn
Byczkowski, Janusz Zbigniew *toxicologist*

Galloway
†Ghosh, Sanjib Kumar *retired science educator, consultant*

Granville
Haubrich, Robert Rice *biology educator*

Kent
Cooperrider, Tom S. *botanist, educator*
Dutta, Hiran Moyee *biologist, educator*
†House-Soremekun, Bessie *political science educator*
†Seed, Alexander John *science educator*

Oberlin
Cleeton, David Lawrence *economist, educational administrator*
†Luck, Dennis Noel *biologist, educator, researcher*

Oxford
Eshbaugh, W(illiam) Hardy *botanist, educator*

Portsmouth
†Burns, Eugene Hugh, Jr., *biology educator*

Rootstown
Jamison, James Mark *cell biologist*

Shaker Heights
†Wohlever, Linda L. *mathematician and science educator*

Springfield
Hobbs, Horton Holcombe, III, *biology educator*
Ryu, Kyoo-Hai Lee *physiologist*

Strongsville
†Eley, Richard Robert *science educator*

Toledo
Chakraborty, Joana *physiology educator, research center administrator*

Wooster
Ferree, David Curtis *horticultural researcher*
Grewal, Parwinder S. *biologist, educator*
Lafever, Howard Nelson *plant breeder, geneticist, educator*
†Saif, Linda J. *animal scientist*

OKLAHOMA

Durant
Ludrick, Brad Burton *science educator*
Rice, Stanley Arthur *biology educator*

Edmond
Caire, William *biologist, educator*

Newcastle
Mudroch, Kimberly Ann *veterinarian*

Norman
Carpenter, Charles Congden *zoologist, educator*
†Hui, Dafeng *ecologist, statistician*
Hutchison, Victor Hobbs *biologist, educator*
Wang, Han *developmental biologist*

Ochelata
Hitzman, Donald Oliver *microbiologist*

Oklahoma City
Branch, John Curtis *biology educator, lawyer*
†Cunningham, Madeleine White *microbiologist, immunologist*
†Flournoy, Dayl Jean *clinical microbiologist, educator*
Friedberg, Wallace *biologist, researcher*
Li, Shibo *medical genetics educator*

Pawhuska
Strahm, Samuel Edward *veterinarian*

Ponca City
Wann, Laymond Doyle *retired petroleum research scientist*

Sand Springs
Quinn, Art Jay *veterinarian, retired educator*

Stillwater
Campbell, John Roy *animal science educator, academic administrator*
Confer, Anthony Wayne *veterinary pathologist, educator*
Ewing, Sidney Alton *veterinary medical educator, parasitologist*
Gilliland, Stanley Eugene *dairy-food microbiology educator*
Grischkowsky, Daniel Richard *research scientist, educator*
Langwig, John Edward *retired wood science educator*
†Lynch, Thomas Bernard *science educator*

Tulsa
Korstad, John Edward *biology educator*

OREGON

Ashland
Christianson, Roger Gordon *biology educator*

Beaverton
Liu, Kevin H. *research scientist, software architect*

Corvallis
Castellano, Michael Angelo *research forester*
Castle, Emery Neal *agricultural and resource economist, educator*
Chambers, Kenton Lee *botany educator*
Frakes, Rodney Vance *plant geneticist, educator*
†Haig, Susan *ecologist, educator*
Morita, Richard Yukio *microbiology and oceanography educator*
Rose, Robert William, Jr., (Robin Rose) *forest regeneration scientist, educator*
Rygiewicz, Paul Thaddeus *plant ecologist*
Sun, Osbert Jianxin *ecophysiologist, researcher*
Westwood, Melvin Neil *horticulturist, pomologist*
Young, J. Lowell *soil chemist, biologist*

Eugene
Holzapfel, Christina Marie *biologist*
Matthews, Brian W. *molecular biology educator*

Hillsboro
Matlock, John Hudson *science administrator, materials engineer*

Pendleton
Klepper, Elizabeth Lee *physiologist*

Phoenix
Blackman, David Lee *research scientist*

Portland
Bhagwan, Sudhir *computer industry and research executive, consultant*
Gillette, Richard Gareth *neurophysiology educator, researcher*
Hagenstein, William David *forester, consultant*
Harary, Keith *research scientist, writer, science journalist*
Haynes, Richard Walter *research scientist*
Kolmes, Steven Albert *biologist, educator*
Machida, Curtis A. *research molecular neurobiologist, educator*
†Mark, Gregory Paul *neuroscientist, educator*
†Talerico, Karen Amann *science educator, consultant*

Salem
Erickson, Ray Charles *retired wildlife biologist*

Talent
MacMillen, Richard Edward *biological sciences educator, researcher*

Yachats
Gerdemann, James Wessel *plant pathologist, educator*

PENNSYLVANIA

Abington
Hand, Christopher Michael *cancer research scientist, medical consultant, therapeutic medical physicist, educator*

Allentown
Oplinger, Carl Spadt *biology educator*

Ambler
Crowell, Richard Lane *microbiologist, educator*

Andalusia
Ewalt, Jacquelyn Marie *biologist*

Apollo
Burks, Brian Scott *veterinarian*

Bala Cynwyd
Corliss, John Ozro *zoology educator*

Bethlehem
Lloyd, Thomas Blair *research scientist, consultant*

Broomall
†Lentini, Eugene Anthony *retired physiologist, consultant*

Bryn Mawr
Hung, Paul Porwen *biotechnologist, educator, consultant*

Collegeville
Merchenthaler, Istvan Jozsef *neuroscientist, morphologist*
Shao, Dalei *molecular biologist, researcher*

Cresson
McCool, Deborah Joyclyn *science educator*

Devon
Porter, Roger John *medical research administrator, neurologist, pharmacologist*

Doylestown
Mishler, John Milton (Yochanan Menashsheh ben Shaul) *natural sciences educator, administrator, artist*

Drexel Hill
Breslin, Elizabeth Walker *biological scientist, biomedical consultant*

Easton
Fried, Bernard *parasitologist, biology educator*

Edinboro
Miller, G(erson) H(arry) *research institute director, mathematician, computer scientist, chemist*
Thomas, Paul Milton *retired science educator*

Elizabethtown
†Coren, Jonathon Silow *science educator, researcher*

Elizabethville
Romberger, John Albert *scientist, historian*

Exton
†Hidalgo, Ismael J. *pharmaceutical scientist*
†Meegalla, Sanath *research scientist*
Molloy, Christopher John *molecular and cellular pharmacologist*

Gladwyne
Allen, Theresa Ohotnicky *neurobiologist, consultant*

Haverford
Erickson, Ralph O. *botany educator*

Hershey
Lang, Carol Max *veterinarian, educator*
†Norgren, Ralph *neuroscientist*

Holland
Umbreit, Wayne William *bacteriologist, educator*

Holtwood
Liebman, Shirley Anne *analytical research scientist*

Indiana
†Hunter, Herbert M. *science educator*

Kennett Square
Fussell, Catharine Pugh *biological researcher*
†Poppenga, Robert H. *veterinary toxicology educator*
Whitlock, Robert H. *veterinarian, educator*

Lansdale
Elliott, Arthur Y. *microbiologist, administrator*
†Holloway, M(ary) Katharine *research scientist, chemist*

Lewisburg
Candland, Douglas Keith *educator*
Sojka, Gary Allan *biologist, educator, university official*

Media
Black, Robert Corl *biology educator*
Brobeck, John Raymond *physiology educator*

Mercersburg
Gift, Gerald Brenton *biology educator*

Murrysville
Lain, David Cornelius *health scientist, researcher*

Narberth
Nathanson, Neal *virologist, epidemiologist, educator*

Oreland
Maerker, Gerhard *food science consultant*

Philadelphia
†Adler, Martin William *neuropharmacologist*
Anderson, Christopher Jon
†Assoian, Richard Kenneth *molecular biologist, educator*
Balliet, Arthur Gerald *molecular biologist, researcher*
Beilstein, Henry Richard *microbiologist, educator*
Brinster, Ralph Lawrence *biologist, educator*
†Cashmore, Anthony *biologist, educator*
Coss, Ronald Allen *radiation biologist, cell biologist*
†Davatzikos, Ph.D., Christos *research scientist, educator*
DiBerardino, Marie Antoinette *developmental biologist, educator*
†Eberwine, James *molecular biologist, educator*
Eisenstein, Toby K. *microbiology educator*
Fenik, Victor Borisovich *neurobiologist, researcher*
Furth, John Jacob *molecular biologist, pathologist, educator*
Giger, Urs *veterinarian*
Hammond, Benjamin Franklin *microbiologist, educator*
Harvey, Colin Edwin *veterinary medicine educator*
Havas, Helga Francis *microbiologist, immunologist*
Hoskins, Alexander L. (Pete Hoskins) *zoological park administrator*
Hua, Xianxin *cell and cancer biology educator*
Huang, Wenlin *scientist, researcher*
†Jaynes, James B. *geneticist, educator*
Kaji, Akira *microbiology scientist, educator*
Koprowski, Hilary *microbiologist, educator*
†Krymskaya, Vera P. *science educator*
Lambertsen, Christian James *environmental physiologist, physician, educator*
†Lelkes, Peter Istvan *cellular and molecular tissue engineer*
†Linebarger, Marcia C. *psycholinguistics researcher*
Meyer, Paul William *arboretum director, horticulturist*
†Naidu, Jaideep Taragula *science educator, researcher*
Newberg, Andrew B. *neuroscientist*
Patrick, Ruth (Mrs. Ruth Hodge Van Dusen) *limnologist, diatom taxonomist, educator*
Pepe, Frank A. *cell and developmental biology educator*
Perry, Robert Palese *molecular biologist, educator*
Rosenbloom, Joel *molecular biologist, educator*
Salzberg, Brian Matthew *neuroscience and physiology educator*
Sanger, Joseph William *cell biologist*
Saunders, James C. *neuroscientist, educator*
Schwartz, Arthur Gerald *microbiology educator*
Silvers, Willys Kent *geneticist*
Soffer, Martin Harvey *environmentalist, city planner*
Thomson, Keith Stewart *biologist, author*
Van Dongen, Hans Philemon Anna *research scientist, educator*
Young, Robert Crabill *medical researcher, science facility administrator, internist*

Pipersville
Erickson, Edward Leonard *biotechnology company executive, administrator*

Pitcairn
Rose, Robert Didier *neurophysiologist*

Pittsburgh
Cruz, Robyn Flaum *research scientist, clinician*
Dekay, Michael L. *decision science educator*
Edmonds, Mary Patricia *biological sciences educator*
Ehrlich, Garth David *molecular biologist*
Feingold, David Sidney *microbiology educator*
Fletcher, Ronald Darling *microbiologist educator*
Goldschmidt, Yadin Y *science educator*
Goldstein, Gerald *research scientist*
Harrold, Ronald Thomas *research scientist*
Kamboh, M. Ilyas *geneticist*
Kiger, Robert William *botanist, science historian, educator*
LaJohn, Lawrence Anthony *research scientist*
Marazita, Mary Louise *genetics researcher*
Moore, Robert Yates *neuroscience educator*
Murphy, Robert Francis *biology educator and researcher*
Partanen, Carl Richard *biology educator*
Shu, Peter H.C. *research scientist*
†Wang, Huamin *research scientist*
Youngner, Julius Stuart *microbiologist, educator*
Zhang, Yingze *molecular biologist*

Scranton
Clymer, Jay Phaon, III, *science educator*
Tarutis, William John, Jr., *ecology educator, wetlands scientist*

Slippery Rock
Chmielewski, Jerry George *botanist, educator*

State College
Hettche, L. Raymond *research director*
†Madjid, A. Hamid *retired science educator*

Swarthmore
Gilbert, Scott Frederick *biologist, educator, author*

University Park
Bollag, Jean-Marc *soil biochemistry educator, consultant*
Buskirk, Elsworth Robert *physiologist, educator*
Buss, Edward George *geneticist*
Demirci, Ali *microbiological and food engineer*
†Duiker, Sjoerd Willem *soil scientist, educator*
†Eser, Semih *science educator, consultant, researcher*
Fedoroff, Nina Vsevolod *research scientist, consultant, educator*
Fowler, H(oratio) Seymour *retired science educator*
Hagen, Daniel Russell *physiologist, educator*
Ma, Hong *plant molecular biologist, educator*
McPheron, Bruce Alan *entomologist*
Stern, Robert Morris *gastrointestinal psychophysiology researcher, psychology educator*
Stinson, Richard Floyd *retired horticulturist, educator*
†Yu, Wenhua *science educator*

PROFESSIONAL INDEX 6617 SCIENCE: LIFE SCIENCE

Zatsiorsky, Vladimir Moiseevich (Michailovich) *biomechanics educator, researcher*

Wallingford
Severdia, Anthony George *chemistry researcher*

Wayne
Krutsick, Robert Stanley *retired science center executive*
Thelen, Edmund *research executive*

West Chester
Flood, Dorothy Garnett *neuroscientist*
Perkins, Brenda Elizabeth *veterinarian*

West Mifflin
Clayton, John Charles *scientist, researcher*

West Point
Hilleman, Maurice Ralph *virus research scientist*
Manning, Barton Harley *neuroscientist*
†Schaffner, Carolyn Marie *research administrator, biologist*
Weekley, Leslie Bruce *veterinarian, pharmacologist*

Wilkes Barre
Hayes, Wilbur Frank *retired biology educator*
Ogren, Robert Edward *biologist, educator*

Wynnewood
Prendergast, George C. *cancer biologist, researcher*
Rubin, Leonard Sidney *physiologist, educator, researcher*

RHODE ISLAND

Cranston
Mruk, Charles Karzimer *agronomist*

Kingston
Goos, Roger Delmon *mycologist*
Harrison, Robert William *zoologist, educator*
†Markin, Karen Mary *research scientist, journalist*
Shaikh, Zahir Ahmad *toxicologist, educator*

Newport
Koch, Robert Michael *research scientist, consultant, educator*

North Scituate
Dupree, Thomas Andrew *forester, state official*

Providence
Chen, Qian *cell biologist, developmental biologist*
Dickersin, Kay *researcher, educator*
Lederberg, Seymour Samuel *molecular biologist, educator*
Nunes-Düby, Simone Edith *molecular biology researcher*
†Takao, Motoharu *physiologist*
Wood, Craig Breckinridge *paleobiologist, natural science educator*
Zavada, Michael Stephen *plant science educator*

SOUTH CAROLINA

Anderson
†Rhoe, Wilhelmina Robinson *retired science educator*

Charleston
†Forsythe, Dennis M. *biology educator*
†Huang, Peng *science educator*
†Ogretmen, Besim *science educator, molecular biologist, researcher*
Ray, Swapan Kumar *molecular biologist*
†Yu, Shan Ping *neuroscientist, educator*

Clemson
Straka, Thomas James *forester, educator*

Columbia
Corey, David Thomas *invertebrate zoology specialist*
†Fox, Alvin None *bacteriology educator, researcher*
Hughes, Austin Leland *biological sciences educator*
†Vidal, Jose *science educator*
Watabe, Norimitsu *biology and marine science educator*

Easley
Spearman, David Hagood *veterinarian*

Greenville
Cureton, Claudette Hazel Chapman *biology educator*

Greenwood
†Collins, Julianne Shea *research scientist*

Hilton Head Island
Adams, William Hensley *ecologist, educator*
Lefer, Allan Mark *physiologist*

Orangeburg
Kalapathy, Uruthira Pasupathy *food scientist, researcher*

Prosperity
Long, William McMurray *physiology educator*

Spartanburg
Leonard, Walter Raymond *retired biology educator*

SOUTH DAKOTA

Pierre
†Repsys, Andrew J. *aquatic biologist, limnologist, water quality specialist, environmental biologist*

Rapid City
Rogers, Deborah S. *human biology educator, writer*

Sioux Falls
Smit, Paula Francine *research scientist*

Volga
Moldenhauer, William Calvin *soil scientist*

TENNESSEE

Clinton
Tyndall, Richard Lawrence *microbiologist, researcher*

Cookeville
Forest, Herman Silva *biology educator*

Gatlinburg
Cave, Kent R. *national park ranger*

Johnson City
Rasch, Ellen Myrberg *cell biology educator*

Knoxville
Anderson, Ilse Janell *clinical geneticist*
Carroll, Roger Clinton *medical biology educator*
Chen, James Pai-fun *biology educator, researcher*
Creasia, Donald Anthony *toxicologist, researcher*
Holton, Raymond William *botanist, educator*
Joseph, Timothy Wacht *writer*
Mazur, Peter *cell physiologist, cryobiologist*
†McCarthy, John F. *science educator*
Mc Hargue, Carl Jack *research laboratory administrator*

Maryville
Hall, Marion Trufant *botany educator, arboretum director*

Memphis
Chung, King-Thom *microbiologist, educator*
Freeman, Bob A. *retired microbiology educator, retired dean*
†Hofmann, Polly A. *physiologist, science educator*
Howe, Martha Morgan *microbiologist, educator*
†Luo, Rensheng *structural biologist, researcher*
Pfeffer, Lawrence Marc *cell biologist*
†Raghow, Sharan Dhaliwal *scientist, educator*
Van Middlesworth, Lester *physiology, biophysics and medicine educator*
†Wise, George Urban *botanic garden administrator, horticulturist, entomologist*

Nashville
Auerbach, Stanley Irving *ecologist, environmental scientist, educator*
†Casagrande, Vivien Alice *neuroscientist, researcher*
Fischer, Charlotte Froese *researcher, educator*
Orgebin-Crist, Marie-Claire *biology educator*
Phillips, John A(tlas), III, *geneticist, educator*
†Shneyder, Artyom V. *science educator, researcher*

Oak Ridge
Gu, Baohua *soil scientist, chemist*
†Phillips, Debra Helen *soil scientist, researcher*
Xu, Ying *computational biologist*

Sewanee
Hawkins, Travis Montgomery, Sr., *horticulturist, landscape consultant*
McGlothlin, Karen Leah *science educator*
Yeatman, Harry Clay *biologist, educator*

Smithville
†Vaughn, Eulalia Cobb *retired science educator, mathematician*

TEXAS

Abilene
†Hernandez, Patricia B. *biologist, educator*

Amarillo
Chisum, Matthew Eual *research scientist, laboratory administrator*

Arlington
Smatresk, Neal Joseph *physiologist, biology educator, science education consultant*

Austin
Arkeen, Solomon Jae *forensic counselor*
Biesele, John Julius *biologist, educator*
†Boggiano, Michael Humberto *geneticist, small business owner*
Breunig, Robert Glass *botanical facility administrator*
Delco, Exalton A., Jr., *retired biology educator*
Drummond Borg, Lesley Margaret *clinical geneticist*
Grant, Verne Edwin *biology educator*
Jacobson, Antone Gardner *zoology educator*
Lukenbill, Willis Bernard
†Olsen, Christopher Mark *research scientist*
Patterson, Donald Eugene *research scientist*
†Sarkar, Sahotra *biologist, philosophy educator*
Sutton, Harry Eldon *geneticist, educator*
Thornton, Joseph Scott *research institute executive, materials scientist*
Walker, James Roy *microbiologist*

Bandera
Bartley, William Call *science administrator*

Bogata
†Marris, Roy O. *agriculturist, consultant*

Bryan
Milford, Murray Hudson *retired soil science educator*

Bushland
Unger, Paul Walter *retired soil scientist*

Canyon
Burton, Robert Clyde *science educator*
Stewart, B(obby) A(lton) *soil scientist, educator*

Cedar Park
Albin, Leslie Owens *biology educator*

Cibolo
Newsom, Melvin Max *retired research company executive*

College Station
Armstrong, Robert Beall *physiologist, educator*
Beaver, Bonnie Veryle *veterinarian, educator*
Black, Samuel Harold *microbiology and immunology educator*
Borlaug, Norman Ernest *agricultural scientist*
Bridges, Charles Hubert *veterinarian, educator*
Brown, Robert Dale *wildlife science educator, department head*
Dees, William Leslie *veterinary medicine educator*
Drees, Bastiaan Meijer *entomologist*
Hall, Timothy Couzens *biology educator, consultant*
Kohel, Russell James *geneticist*
McCallum, Roderick Eugene *dean, microbiologist*
McCrady, James David *veterinarian, educator*
Neill, William Harold, Jr., *biological science educator and researcher*
†Nobles, Maria Morgun *soil scientist, researcher*
Rosberg, David William *plant sciences educator*
†Song, Joon Jin *research scientist, educator*
Turner, Nancy Delane *nutritionist, educator, researcher*
Wilding, Lawrence Paul *retired pedology educator, soil science consultant*
†Wu, Xiaoqiang *molecular biologist, researcher*

Corpus Christi
Berkebile, Charles Alan *geology educator, hydrogeology researcher*
Schake, Lowell Martin *animal science educator*

Corsicana
Carroll, Ray Dean, Sr., *veterinarian*

Dallas
Brown, Michael Stuart *geneticist, educator, administrator*
Goel, Ajay *molecular biologist, researcher*
Herbert, Brittney-Shea *cancer biologist*
Reinert, James A. *entomology educator*
Sinton, Christopher Michael *neurophysiologist, educator*
†Suppes, Trisha *neuroscientist*
Vitetta, Ellen Shapiro *microbiologist educator, immunologist*

Denton
†Crawford, Gladys Pauline *microbiologist, educator*
†Kennedy, James H. *biologist, educator*
†Marshall, David Douglas *science educator*
Schwalm, Fritz Ekkehardt *biology educator*
Ver Duin, D'Arlene K. *research scientist*

Desoto
Ball, Millicent Joan (Penny Ball) *science educator, consultant*

Diboll
Fisher, Richard Forrest *research scientist, department chairman*

El Paso
Conway, John Bell *health educator, university dean*
Johnson, Jerry Douglas *biology educator*

Fort Sam Houston
Convertino, Victor Anthony *physiologist, educator, research scientist, civil servant*

Fort Worth
Koger, David Gordon *science administrator*
Lowseth, Lisa Anne *veterinarian*
Manning, Walter Scott, Jr., *veterinarian*

Galveston
Budelmann, Bernd Ulrich *zoologist, educator*
Frederickson, Christopher John *neuroscientist*
†Gu, Yanping *neuroscientist, researcher*
Horning, Markus *marine biologist, educator*
†Mossberg, Kurt A. *science educator*
Prakash, Satya *biology educator*
Santschi, Peter Hans *marine sciences educator*
Willis, William Darrell, Jr., *neurophysiologist, educator*
Würsig, Bernd Gerhard *marine biology educator*
Zimmerman, Roger Joseph *fishery biologist*

Georgetown
Girvin, Eb Carl *biology educator*

Hempstead
Propst, Catherine Lamb *biotechnology company executive*

Houston
Brown, Jack Harold Upton *physiologist, biomedical engineer, academic administrator*
†Burau, Keith Dean *science educator, researcher*
Butel, Janet Susan *research scientist, virology educator*
†Chen, Jinling *science administrator*
Chiao, Paul J. *molecular biologist, educator*
†Chiappetta, Eugene Louis *science educator*
DeBakey, Lois *science communications educator, writer, editor*
DeBakey, Selma *science communications educator, writer, editor, lecturer*
Dronamraju, Krishna Rao *geneticist*
Durham, Susan K. *research scientist*
†Etkin, Laurence D. *geneticist, educator*
Fox, George Edward *molecular biology educator*
Glasser, Adrian *physiologist, researcher, scientist*
Goldstein, Margaret Ann *biologist*
†Gorbunova, Vera *biologist*
Heilman, William Joseph *research scientist, consultant*
Jurtshuk, Peter, Jr., *microbiologist, educator*
Kellaway, Peter *neurophysiologist, researcher*
Konisky, Jordan *microbiology educator*
Lake, James Ronald *behavioral neuroscience researcher*
Louderback, Truman Eugene *environmental project manager*
Mouchaty, Suzette Kay *biologist*
Nelson, David Loren *geneticist, educator*
Ramsey, Kathleen Sommer *toxicologist*
Roman, Gregg William *geneticist, researcher*
†Ruvolo, Peter *molecular biologist*
Sass, Ronald Lewis *biology and chemistry educator*
Schultz, Stanley George *physiologist, educator*
Seaton, Alberta Jones *biologist, educator, consultant*
Steele, James Harlan *former public health veterinarian, educator*
Weng, Han-Rong *neuroscientist, researcher*
White, Ronald Joseph *life and biomedical scientist, physiology educator*
Xu, Xiaochun *biologist, researcher*
Zhang, Chunlong *environmental educator*
Zhou, Juhua *molecular biologist*

Hunt
Price, Donald Albert *veterinarian, consultant*

Irving
Fukui, George Masaaki *microbiology consultant*

Lackland A F B
Burghardt, Walter Francis, Jr., *veterinarian*

Lubbock
Hentges, David John *microbiology educator*
†Hice, Christine Lorraine *research scientist*
Jackson, Raymond Carl *cytogeneticist*
Skoog, Gerald Duane *science educator*
Wendt, Charles William *soil physicist, educator*

Mcallen
†Villarino, Mario Alberto *veterinarian, researcher*

Pearland
Shurtleff, Malcolm C. *plant pathologist, consultant, educator, extension specialist*

Plano
MacAlpine, Michelle Lewis *neuroscientist*

Richardson
Gray, Donald Melvin *molecular and cell biology educator*
Wood, Joseph George *neurobiologist, educator*

San Antonio
Burch, James Leo *science research institute executive*
Corrigan, Helen González *retired cytologist*
†Duggirala, Ravindranath *geneticist, researcher*
†Firulli, Anthony B. *physiologist, educator*
Gates, Mahlon Eugene *applied research executive, former government official, former army officer*
†Hale, William Grant *veterinarian, educator*
†Hamill, Frank Alexander *biologist, researcher*
Irving, George Washington, III, *veterinarian, research director, small business executive*
†Kittle, Joseph S. *science administrator, consultant*
Martinez, Joe Louis, Jr., *neurobiologist, educator*
Masoro, Edward Joseph, Jr., *physiology educator*
McComas, David John *science administrator, space physicist*
McIntosh, Dennis Keith *veterinarian, consultant*
†Webb, James Taylor *physiologist, pilot*
†Zoghby, Jeriad Marcus *lead quantitative analyst, consultant*

San Marcos
McLean, Robert James Cameron *microbiologist, educator*

Stephenville
Simpson, Charles Edmond *crop science educator*

The Woodlands
Bala, Sriram *research scientist*

Uvalde
Ramsey, Frank Allen *veterinarian, retired army officer*

Vernon
Slosser, Jeffrey Eric *research entomologist*

Waco
Hartberg, Warren Keith *biologist, educator*
Hillis, William Daniel *biology educator*
†Lee, Myeongwoo *molecular biologist, cell biologist*
Wivagg, Daniel Edwin *biology educator, editor*

Warda
Kunze, George William *retired soil scientist*

Wharton
Walker, Douglas Baynard *science educator*

UTAH

Ephraim
Blauer, A. Clyde *microbiologist, educator, botanist*

Genola
†Newcomb, Helene E *retired research scientist*

Logan
†McNeal, Lyle Glen *science educator, rancher, consultant*
Rasmussen, Harry Paul *horticulture and landscape educator*
Sidwell, Robert William *virologist, educator*

Orem
Crookston, R. Kent *agronomy educator*

Providence
Vest, Hyrum Grant, Jr., *retired horticultural sciences educator*

Provo
Baumann, Richard William *science educator, consultant*
Blake, George Rowland *soil science educator, water resources research administrator*
†Harper, Kimball Taylor *ecologist, educator*
McArthur, Eldon Durant *geneticist, researcher*
Smith, H(oward) Duane *zoology educator*
Woodbury, Dixon John *physiologist, educator, research scientist*

Salt Lake City
†Anigbogu, Angela Ngozi *research scientist*
Capecchi, Mario Renato *geneticist, educator*
†Emerson, Sharon B. *biology researcher and educator*
Gesteland, Raymond F. *geneticist*
Lasater, Eric Martin *neurobiologist*
McGill, Lawrence David *veterinary pathologist*
Salisbury, Frank Boyer *plant physiologist, educator, author*

Springville
†Bybee, Paul Joseph *zoologist, educator*

VERMONT

Brattleboro
Ames, Adelbert, III, *neurophysiologist, educator*

Burlington
†Bousquet, Daniel William *forester, educator*
Hendley, Edith Di Pasquale *physiology and neuroscience educator*
†Kindstedt, Paul Stephen *food science educator*

Charlotte
Melby, Edward Carlos, Jr., *veterinarian*

Greensboro
Hill, Lewis Reuben *horticulturist, nursery owner, author*

Morrisville
Lechevalier, Hubert Arthur *microbiology educator*
Lechevalier, Mary Pfeil *retired microbiologist, educator*

Norwich
Naumann, Robert Bruno Alexander *chemistry and physics educator*

Rutland
Hebert, Lynn David *science and computer educator, writer*

Shoreham
Lynch, Peter *biology educator*

Waterbury
†Travis, Randall Howard *retired physiologist, retired endocrinologist*

VIRGINIA

Alexandria
Woolley, Mary Elizabeth *research administrator*

Amissville
Hunter, Beverly Claire *research scientist, educator*

Arlington
Alam, Shawn *biologist*
†Blanchard, David Joseph *research scientist*
Cheney, David Warren *science and technology policy analyst, executive*
Colwell, Rita Rossi *microbiologist, molecular biologist, federal agency administrator, medical educator*
Czech, Brian Martin *biologist, economist*
Goldberg, Lawrence Spencer *science foundation engineering administrator, physicist*
Haq, Bilal Ul *national science foundation program director, researcher*
Harris, William James, Jr., *research administrator, educator*
Held, Joe Roger *veterinarian, epidemiologist*
Jewell, Susan Diane *wildlife biologist, writer*
Junker, Bobby Ray *research and development executive, physicist*
†Morse, Larry Eugene *botanist, conservationist*
O'Neill, Brian *research organization administrator*
Tolbert, Margaret Ellen Mayo *science foundation administrator*

Big Stone Gap
Ogbonnaya, Chuks Alfred *entomologist, agronomist, environmentalist*

Blacksburg
Burkhart, Harold Eugene *forestry educator*
Cowles, Joe Richard *biology educator*
Gwazdauskas, Francis Charles *animal science educator, dairy scientist*
Hallerman, Eric Michael *geneticist, educator*
†Kabir, Firoz *wood technologist, researcher*
Youngs, Robert Leland *forestry educator*

Burke
Zelasko, Nancy Faber *research scientist educator*

Charlottesville
Garrett, Reginald Hooker *biology educator, researcher*
Perez-Reyes, Edward *molecular physiologist*
Somlyo, Andrew Paul *physiology, biophysics and cardiology educator*
Tuttle, Jeremy Ballou *neurobiologist*
Wright, Theodore Robert Fairbank *biologist, educator*

Dulles
Elias, Antonio L. *science administrator*

Fairfax
Barreto, Ernest *science educator, researcher*
Geller, Harold Arthur *earth and space sciences executive, educator*
Peters, Esther Caroline *aquatic toxicologist, pathobiologist, consultant*
†Soyfer, Valery Nikolayevich *geneticist, biophysicist*

Falls Church
Hart, C(harles) W(illard), Jr., *zoologist, curator*
Severin, Scott Robert *veterinarian, army officer*
Shah, Syed-Waqar *science educator*
Simpson, John Arol *retired government executive, physicist*

Front Royal
Douglas, J(ocelyn) Fielding *toxicologist, consultant*

Hampton
Gatski, Thomas Bernard *research scientist*

Harrisonburg
Wubah, Daniel Asua *microbiologist, educator, dean*

Haymarket
Katz, Alan Charles *toxicologist*

Keswick
Rafajko, Robert Richard *medical research company executive*

Leesburg
Mokhtarzadeh, Ahmad Agha *agronomist, consultant*

Manakin Sabot
†Bayliss, John Temple *retired science educator, retired energy executive*
Henson, Kristin L. *veterinary pathologist*

Manassas
Isbister, Jenefir Diane Wilkinson *microbiologist, researcher, educator, consultant*

Mc Lean
Cardwell, Thomas Augusta, III, *research scientist, retired career officer, executive*
Krugman, Stanley Liebert *science administrator, geneticist*
Layson, William McIntyre *retired research consulting company executive*
Talbot, Lee Merriam *ecologist, educator, association executive*

Midlothian
Wang, Buqian *materials research scientist*

Newport News
†Harris, Charles George *research scientist, consultant*

Norfolk
†Colberg-Ochs, Sheri Renee *physiologist, educator*

Richmond
Gregory, Jean Winfrey *ecologist, educator*
†Marciano-Cabral, Francine M. *microbiology and immunology educator, protozoologist*

Roanoke
Woods, Walter Ralph *retired agricultural scientist, administrator*

Staunton
Cook, Clarence Edgar *research facility scientist*

Wallops Island
Habeger, Steven Richard *science administrator*

Williamsburg
Griffith, Melvin Eugene *entomologist, public health official*
Guastaferro, Angelo *science administrator, consultant*
Terman, C. Richard *science educator*

Wise
†Jansen, Kevin P. *biology educator*

WASHINGTON

Edmonds
Paul, Ronald Stanley *research institute executive*

Friday Harbor
Brookbank, John W(arren) *retired microbiology educator*
Kozloff, Eugene Nicholas *zoologist, educator, author*

Kennewick
Cobb, William Thompson *environmental and agricultural consultant*

Mountlake Terrace
Cannon, Christine Anne *veterinarian*

Olympia
†Heilenday, Frank Tod *science educator*
Raphael, Martin George *research wildlife biologist*

Prosser
Proebsting, Edward Louis, Jr., *retired research horticulturist*

Pullman
Henson, James Bond *veterinary pathologist*
Hosick, Howard Lawrence *cell biology educator, academic administrator*
†Yurgel, Svetlana N. *microbiologist, researcher*

Redmond
Kelman, Bruce Jerry *toxicologist, consultant*

Richland
Chikalla, Thomas David *retired science facility administrator*
Harris, Robert Vail, Jr., *research scientist, information scientist*
Lin, Yuehe *research scientist*
Thevuthasan, Theva Suntharampillai *research scientist*

Seattle
†Andersen, Marin (Robyn) *research scientist*
†Aprikyan, Andranik Goorgen *molecular biologist, biomedical researcher*
Bassingthwaighte, James Bucklin *physiologist, educator, medical researcher*
Boersma, P. Dee *marine biologist, educator*
Brownstein, Barbara Lavin *geneticist, educator, university official*
†Calvin, William Howard *neurophysiologist*
Evans, Charles Albert *microbiology educator*
Hartwell, Leland Harrison *geneticist, educator*
Hille, Bertil *physiology educator*
†Hohmann, John G. *neurobiologist*
Hood, Leroy Edward *molecular biologist, educator*
Karr, James Richard *ecologist, educator, research director*
Kirby, Ronald Eugene *fish and wildlife research administrator*
Klausner, Richard D. *cell biologist, researcher*
Kruckeberg, Arthur Rice *botanist, educator*
†Montine, Thomas Jude *neuropathologist, researcher*
Motulsky, Arno Gunther *geneticist, physician, educator*
Olstad, Roger Gale *science educator*
Orians, Gordon Howell *biology educator*
†Ranganathan, Rajesh *neuroscientist, researcher*
Schiffrin, Milton Julius *physiologist*
†Schlosser, Ann E. *science educator*
Smith, Orville Auverne *physiology educator*
†Tews, Leonard L. *retired science educator, poet*
Tukey, Harold Bradford, Jr., *horticulture educator*
Utter, Fred M *science educator, researcher*
Wooster, Warren S(criver) *marine science educator*
Wott, John Arthur *arboretum and botanical garden executive, horticulture educator*

Sequim
Pearson, Walter Howard *marine biologist, researcher*

Silverdale
Tozer, William Evans *entomologist, educator*

Spokane
Richard, Gerald Lawrence *retired soil scientist*

Walla Walla
Gallinat, Michael Paul *fisheries biologist*

Wenatchee
Elfving, Don C. *horticulturist, educator*
Schrader, Lawrence Edwin *plant physiologist, educator*

WEST VIRGINIA

Buckhannon
†McCormick, Rodger John *biologist, educator, minister*

Charleston
Bhasin, Madan Mohan *research scientist*
Gillespie, William Harry *forestry executive, geology educator*

Clarksburg
Walmsley, James Naylor *hydroponic farming executive*

Falling Waters
Schellhaas, Linda Jean *toxicologist, consultant*

Kearneysville
Biggs, Alan Richard *plant pathologist, educator*
Wilson, Charles Lindsay *research scientist*

Morgantown
Cochrane, Robert Lowe *biologist*
Gladfelter, Wilbert Eugene *physiology educator*
Nath, Joginder *genetics and biology educator, researcher*
Shuck, L. Zane *research scientist*

Vienna
Wells, Gordon Lee *science educator*

WISCONSIN

Cottage Grove
Lund, Daryl Bert *food science educator*

Kenosha
†Li, Zhaohui *science educator*

Land O Lakes
Jaroski-Graf, Jill Ann *biology educator, writer, dental hygienist*

Madison
Barnes, Robert F *agronomist*
Beyer-Mears, Annette *physiologist*
Bisgard, Gerald Edwin *biosciences educator, researcher*
Brock, Thomas Dale *microbiology educator*
Burkholder, Wendell Eugene *retired entomology educator, researcher*
Crow, James Franklin *retired genetics educator*
†De Foliart, Gene Ray *retired entomologist, educator*
Easterday, Bernard Carlyle *veterinary medicine educator*
Greaser, Marion Lewis *science educator*
Greenspan, Daniel S. *molecular biologist, educator*
Hagedorn, Donald James *phytopathologist, educator, agricultural consultant*
Hall, David Charles *retired zoo director, veterinarian*
Hopen, Herbert John *horticulture educator*
Iltis, Hugh Hellmut *plant taxonomist-evolutionist, educator*
Jeanne, Robert Lawrence *entomologist, educator*
Kaesberg, Paul Joseph *virology researcher*
Keesey, Richard E. *retired behavioral neuroscience educator*
Kemnitz, Joseph William *physiologist, researcher*
Lillesand, Thomas Martin *remote sensing educator*
†Mandrekar, Michelle Nelson *research scientist*
Marrett, Cora B.
Mertz, Janet Elaine *molecular biology researcher, educator, consultant*
Newcomb, Eldon Henry *retired botany educator*
Nishikida, Koichi *research scientist*
†Peercy, Paul Stuart *laboratory director, physics researcher*
Pella, Milton Orville *retired science educator*
Reynolds, Ronald *research scientist, educator*
Ris, Hans *zoologist, educator*
Rueckert, Roland Rudyard *retired virologist, educator*
Sharkey, Thomas David *educator, botanist*
†Sun, Dandan *neuroscientist, researcher*
Sunde, Milton Lester *retired poultry science educator*
Susman, Millard *geneticist, educator*
Szybalski, Waclaw *geneticist, educator*
Welker, Wallace Irving *neurophysiologist, educator*
†Zhu, Xinsheng *physiologist, biochemist*

Mequon
Arnholt, Philip J. *biologist, educator*

Milwaukee
Barboi, Alexandru Cezar *neuroscientist, researcher*
Boese, Gil Karyle *cultural organization executive*
Hutz, Reinhold Josef *physiologist, educator*
Ignacio, Reinere John Dy *research scientist*
Rhead, William James *biochemical geneticist*
†Schaefer, Jame *science educator*
†Stowe, David F *physiologist*

Oconomowoc
Luedke, Patricia Georgianne *microbiologist*

Shawano
†Heikes, Keith *science administrator*

Sheboygan
Strysick, Michael Otto *terrestrial ecologist, physicist, microbiologist*

WYOMING

Cheyenne
Schuman, Gerald Eugene *soil scientist, researcher*

Green River
Logan, Howard G. *retired science and technology educator*

Laramie
Lewis, Randolph Vance *molecular biologist, researcher*
McDonnel Smedts, Anna Christina *biologist*
Villemez, Clarence Louis *biologist, educator*
†Weatherford, Lawrence *science educator, consultant*

Saratoga
Collamer, Sonja Mae Soreide *retired veterinary facility administrator*

Yellowstone National Park
Whipple, Jennifer Jean *botanist*

TERRITORIES OF THE UNITED STATES

GUAM

Mangilao
†Lobban, Christopher Simon *science educator*
Tsuda, Roy Toshio *marine biologist, educator*

PUERTO RICO

Aguadilla
Gómez-Jiménez, Carlos *science educator, microbiologist, geneticist*

San Juan
†Candelas, Graciela C. *biologist, educator*
†Hillyer, George V. *microbiologist, educator, medical researcher*

CANADA

ALBERTA

Calgary
Jones, Geoffrey Melvill *physiology research educator*
Yoon, Ji-Won *virology, immunology and diabetes educator, research administrator*

Edmonton
Christian, Ralph Gordon *agricultural research and animal health consultant*
Cossins, Edwin Albert *biology educator, academic administrator*

Lethbridge
Cho, Hyun Ju *retired veterinary research scientist*

BRITISH COLUMBIA

Bamfield
Druehl, Louis Dix *biology educator*

Burnaby
Borden, John Harvey *entomologist, educator*

Sidney
Bigelow, Margaret Elizabeth Barr (M.E. Barr) *mycology educator*
Kendrick, William Bryce *biology educator, writer, publisher, consultant*
Mann, Cedric Robert *retired institute administrator, oceanographer*

Vancouver
Campbell, Jack James Ramsay *microbiology educator*
Hoar, William Stewart *zoologist, educator*
Jones, David Robert *zoology educator*
Lindsey, Casimir Charles *zoologist, educator*
Maclachlan, Gordon Alistair *biology educator, researcher*
Mc Lean, Donald Millis *microbiology, pathology educator, physician*
Newman, Murray Arthur *aquarium administrator*
Phillips, Anthony George *neurobiology educator*
Phillips, John Edward *zoologist, educator*
Rennie, Paul Steven *research scientist*
Shaw, Michael *biologist, educator*
Wellington, William George *entomologist, ecologist, educator*

Victoria
Turpin, David Howard *biologist, educator*

West Vancouver
Donaldson, Edward Mossop *research scientist, aquaculture consultant*

MANITOBA

Winnipeg
†Alfa, Michelle Josephine *microbiologist, educator*
Suzuki, Isamu *microbiology educator, researcher*

NEW BRUNSWICK

Moncton
Hanson, John Mark *ecologist, researcher*

NEWFOUNDLAND

Saint John's
Davis, Charles Carroll *aquatic biologist, educator*

NOVA SCOTIA

Dartmouth
Mann, Kenneth Henry *marine ecologist*

Halifax
Hall, Brian Keith *biology educator, author, scientist*

ONTARIO

Bowmanville
Evans, Essi H. *research scientist*

Deep River
Newcombe, Howard Borden *biologist, consultant*

Downsview
Forer, Arthur H. *biology educator, researcher, editor*

Greely
Lister, Earle Edward *animal science consultant*

Guelph
Beveridge, Terrance James *microbiology educator, researcher*
Bewley, John Derek *botany researcher, educator*
Jorgensen, Erik *forest pathologist, educator, consultant*
Kasha, Kenneth John *agriculturist, educator*
Oaks, B. Ann *retired plant physiologist, educator*

Kingston
Leggett, William C. *biology educator, academic administrator*
Smallman, Beverley N. *biology educator*
Wyatt, Gerard Robert *biology educator, researcher*

London
Locke, Michael *zoology educator*

North York
Davey, Kenneth George *biologist, university official*
Regan, David *brain researcher, psychology and biology educator*
Wyatt, Philip Richard *geneticist, physician, researcher*

Ottawa
Baum, Bernard Rene *research scientist*
Beare-Rogers, Joyce Louise *former research executive*
†Bernstein, Alan *research scientist, federal agency administrator*
Bhartia, Prakash *defense research management executive, researcher, educator*
Fallis, Albert Murray *microbiology educator*
Francis, Charles MacKenzie *wildlife biologist*
Hughes, Stanley John *mycologist*
Perry, Malcolm Blythe *biologist, researcher*
Sells, Bruce Howard *biomedical sciences educator*
Storey, Kenneth Bruce *biology educator*

Peterborough
Hutchinson, Thomas Cuthbert *ecology and environmental educator*

Scarborough
White, Calvin John *zoo executive, financial manager, zoological association executive*

Stittsville
MacLeod, Robert Angus *microbiology educator, researcher*

Toronto
Carlen, Peter Louis *neuroscientist educator, science administrator*
Kerr, David Wylie *natural resource company executive*
Liversage, Richard Albert *cell biologist, educator*
MacLennan, David Herman *research scientist, educator*
Moens, Peter B. *biology researcher and educator*
Stadelman, William Ralph *chemical institution executive*
Tobe, Stephen Solomon *zoology educator*
Zhuo, Min *neurobiology educator*

Vineland Station
Errampalli, Deena *molecular plant pathologist, researcher*

Waterloo
Hynes, Hugh Bernard Noel *biologist, educator*
Warner, Barry Gregory *ecologist, educator*

QUEBEC

Laval
Pavilanis, Vytautas *microbiology educator, physician*
Talbot, Pierre Joseph *microbiologist, researcher*

Montreal
Carroll, Robert Lynn *biology educator, vertebrate paleontologist, museum curator*
Chang, Thomas Ming Swi *medical scientist, biotechnologist*
Dansereau, Pierre *retired ecologist*
Diksic, Mirko *research scientist, educator*
Gibbs, Sarah Preble *biologist, educator*
Jolicoeur, Paul *molecular biologist*

Quebec
Cote, Steeve D. *biologist*
Potvin, Pierre *physiologist, educator*
Trudel, Marc J. *botanist, educator*

Sainte-Anne-de-Bellevue
Grant, William Frederick *geneticist, educator*

Sherbrooke
Bourget, Edwin Robert *marine ecologist, educator*

SASKATCHEWAN

Regina
Davis, Gordon Richard Fuerst *retired biologist, translator*

Saskatoon
Babiuk, Lorne Alan *virologist, immunologist, research administrator*
Huang, Pan Ming *soil science educator*
Kartha, Kutty Krishnan *plant pathologist*
Khachatourians, George (Gharadaghi) *microbiologist, educator*
Shokeir, Mohamed Hassan Kamel *medical geneticist, educator*

MEXICO

Mexico City
Cabrera-Jimenez, Jorge Alberto *scientific researcher*

AUSTRALIA

Randwick
Hall, Peter Francis *physiologist*

Southport
Buckley, Ralf Christopher *research scientist*

BELGIUM

Antwerp
Snyders, Dirk Johan *electrophysiologist, biophysicist, educator*

Ghent
Deforce, Dieter Lucïen Daniël *research scientist, educator*

Leuven
Novoa de Armas, Hector *scientific researcher*

Oost-Vlaanderen
Stroobandt, Dirk Rudy *research scientist, educator*

CHINA

Shanghai
Xu, Bin *research scientist*

COSTA RICA

San José
Bien, Amos *ecologist*

CROATIA

Zagreb
Štambuk, Nikola *research scientist*

CZECH REPUBLIC

Kromeriz
Benada, Jaroslav *research scientist, consultant*

Prague
Bubeník, Jan *cancer researcher, biology educator*

ENGLAND

Cambridge
Huxley, Sir Andrew (Sir Andrew Fielding Huxley) *physiologist, educator*
Klug, Aaron *molecular biologist*
Sanger, Frederick *retired molecular biologist*

Kent
Pecorino, Lauren Teresa *biologist*

Kent Cranbrook
Hattersley-Smith, Geoffrey Francis *retired government research scientist*

Leeds
Phillips, Oliver *tropical forest ecologist*

London
Morris, Desmond (John) *zoologist, author, artist*

Oxford
Gowans, Sir James Learmonth *science administrator, immunologist*
May, Robert McCredie *biology educator*

South Mimms
Stacey, Glyn Nigel *cell biologist*

ESTONIA

Tartu
Bichevin, Victor Vasily *research scientist*

FINLAND

Helsinki
Kurvonen, Timo Lauri *research scientist*
Tuomi, Tapani Mika *research scientist*

FRANCE

Gif-sur-Yvette
Duplessy, Jean Claude *research scientist*

Mulhouse
Mondadori, Cesare *neurobiologist, researcher*

Noisy le Grand
Le Quéré, Jean François Marie *scientific instrumentation researcher*

Orsay
Fiszer-Szafarz, Berta (Berta Safars) *research scientist, researcher*

Paris
Jacob, François *biologist, educator*
Kourilsky, François Michel *research scientist*
Montagnier, Luc Antoine *virologist*
Raharinaivo, André Léon *research executive, educator*

GERMANY

Cologne
Tüllner, Horst-Ulrich *research scientist, science administrator*

Friedrichshafen
Duerr, Johannes Klaus *research scientist*

Muenchen
Schneider, Christian Claus *veterinarian, researcher, investment company executive*

Rostock
†Liddle, Brantley Thomas *research scientist*

Stuttgart
von Klitzing, Klaus *research facility administrator, physicist*

U'haching
Ruge, Michael Helmuth *research scientist, consultant, mathematician*

Würzburg
Hölldobler, Berthold Karl *zoologist, educator*

HONG KONG

Hong Kong
Tsui, Lap-Chee *molecular genetics educator*

Kowloon
Kung, Shain-dow *molecular biologist, academic administrator*
Randall, David John *physiologist, zoologist, educator*

HUNGARY

Budapest
Tetenyi, Pal Gabor *research scientist, former national agency official*

INDIA

Bangalore
Nagpurwala, Quamber Husain *scientist*

New Delhi
Narain, Prem *agricultural scientist, educator, researcher*
Srivastava, Radhey Shyam *scientist, researcher*

Ranchi
Srivastava, Vishnu Chandra *agronomy educator*

IRELAND

Carlow
Cunningham, Patrick Colm *research scientist, science administrator*

ISRAEL

Karkur
Hillel, Daniel *soil physics and hydrology educator, researcher, consultant*

Rehovot
Sachs, Leo *geneticist, educator*

Rosh-Pina
Gophen, Moshe *research scientist*

ITALY

Naples
Tarro, Giulio *virologist*

Rome
Levi-Montalcini, Rita *neurobiologist, researcher*

San Donato
Bellussi, Giuseppe Carlo *research manager*

JAPAN

Mitaka
Okamura, Hideki *research scientist, physicist*

Tokyo
Arai, Toshihiko *retired microbiology and immunology educator*
Ishii, Akira *medical parasitologist, malariologist, allergologist*

NEW ZEALAND

Palmerston North
Krone, Cheryl A. *research scientist, consultant*

NORWAY

Kjeller
Maeland, Arnulf Julius *research scientist*

Stavanger
Farmen, Ragne Kristin Bentsen *molecular biologist, researcher*

POLAND

Cracow
Tadeusiewicz, Ryszard *scientist, biomedical engineer, educator*

Warsaw
Koscielak, Jerzy *scientist, science administrator*

RUSSIA

Moscow
Gusev, Yeugeniy Mikhailovich *research scientist*

SCOTLAND

Gullane
Collins, Jeffrey Hamilton *research facility administrator, electrical engineering educator*

SOUTH AFRICA

Scottsville
Savage, Michael John *agrometeorologist, researcher, educator*

SPAIN

Madrid
†Sanchez-Cespedes, Montserrat *molecular biologist, researcher*

SWEDEN

Uppsala
Carr, Andrew *zoologist*

SWITZERLAND

Basel
Arber, Werner *microbiologist*
Gehring, Walter Jakob *biology and genetics educator*

Zurich
Wüthrich, Kurt *molecular biologist, biophysical chemist, educator*

TAIWAN

Taichung
Wilson, Thomas Woodrow, III, *research scientist, consultant*

UKRAINE

Truskavets
Popovych Ihor, L'vovych *physician, researcher*

ADDRESS UNPUBLISHED

Abedin, Sultanal *research phytotaxonomist*
Ahearne, John Francis *scientific research administrator, researcher*
Ahlquist, Paul Gerald *molecular biology researcher, educator*
Ahrens, Franklin Alfred *veterinary pharmacology educator*
†Aikens, Martha Brunette *national park service administrator*
Alexander, Edward Russell *retired disease research administrator, educator*
†Alfinito, Peter Daniel *neuroscientist*
Allen, Lew, Jr., *laboratory executive, former air force officer*
†Al-Ramadan, Saeed Y. *veterinarian, researcher*
Andrews, Richard Vincent *physiologist, educator*
Andrey, Ladislav George *scientist*
Arnott, Howard Joseph *biology educator, university dean*
Asato, Yukio *molecular geneticist, educator*
Atkin, J Myron *science educator*
Baldwin, C. Andrea, Jr., *retired science educator*
Bandyopadhyay, Ram Shyamal *molecular biologist, researcher*
†Banerjee, Kalyani *science educator, researcher*
Bansil, Arun *research scientist*
Barabino, William Albert *science and technology researcher, inventor*
†Barch, Davis R. *neuroscientist, application developer*
Barlow, John Sutton *neurophysiologist, electroencephalographer, lexicographer*
Barnard, Donald Roy *medical and veterinary entomologist*
Barnes-Kempton, Isabel Janet *microbiology educator, college dean*
Barrett, Izadore *retired fisheries research administrator*
Barron, Almen L. *microbiologist, department chairman*
Becherer, Richard Joseph *science administrator, physicist*
Beggs, William H. *microbiologist, researcher*
Bernard, Richard Lawson *geneticist, retired*
Bers, Donald Martin *physiology educator*
†Bertram, Melissa C. *agricultural research scientist*
Bick, Katherine Livingstone *neurobiologist, international liaison, consultant*
Bidwell, Roger Grafton Shelford *biologist, educator*
Bishop, William Peter *science administrator, management consultant*
Blum, Samuel *retired research scientist*
Bonner, John Tyler *biology educator*
†Boyette, Lisa Wynn *retired research scientist*
†Boyle, Tatiana Gennadievna *research scientist*
Brar, Gurdarshan Singh *soil scientist, researcher*
Bremner, John McColl *agronomy and biochemistry educator*
Brill, Winston Jonas *microbiologist, educator, research director, publisher and management consultant*
Brock, Mary Anne *research investigator, consultant*
†Brown, Jeannette Elizabeth *retired science educator*
†Browne, Frederick Douglas *physiologist, educator*
Bryant, Donald Ashley *molecular biologist*
Bucknum, Michael John *research scientist, crystallographer, educator*
Bula, Raymond J. *agronomist*
Bullock, Theodore Holmes *biologist, educator*
Burkes, Lionel Seaton *science educator, writer, researcher*
Burns, Denver P. *forestry research administrator*
Burnside, Orvin Charles *agronomy educator, researcher*
Caldwell, Elwood Fleming *food scientist, educator*
†Calvert, Peter Deane *neuroscientist, medical educator*
Cameron, Roy Eugene *scientist*
†Chai, Xin-Sheng *research scientist*
†Champey, Elaine *science and technology research coordinator*
Champlin, William Glen *clinical microbiologist-immunologist*
Chapman, Kenneth Maynard *science administrator*
Chen, Chong *research scientist*
Chung-Welch, Nancy Yuen Ming *biologist*
Clayton, David A(lvin) *biology educator*
Cockerham, Lorris G. *radiation toxicologist*
Cole, Jerome Foster *research company executive*
†Coleman, Nicholas Vass *microbiologist*
Collins, Angelo *science educator, educator*
Conover, Lloyd Hillyard *retired pharmaceutical research scientist and executive*
Cooney, Joseph J. *microbiologist, educator*
Coyle, Marie Bridget *retired microbiology educator, laboratory director*
Creech, John Lewis *retired scientist, consultant*
Cross, Harold Zane *agronomist, educator*
D'Alesandro, Philip Anthony *parasitologist, immunologist, retired educator*
Damon, Edward George *retired biologist*
Dayton, Kathleen G. *clinical research coordinator*
Decker, Walter Johns *toxicologist*
†Delmarre, David *formulation scientist*
Detweiler, David Kenneth *veterinary physiologist, educator*
†Dudley, Richard George *fisheries and natural resources consultant*
Dugan, Patrick Raymond *microbiologist, university dean*
Durham, Thena Monts *microbiologist, researcher, management executive*
Edwards, Charles *neuroscientist, educator*
Ellner, Paul Daniel *clinical microbiologist*
Elson, Hannah Friedman *biologist, researcher*
Eno, Amos Stewart *natural resource foundation administrator*
Eugster, Albrecht Konrad *veterinarian, laboratory director, emeritus*
Evans, Charles Wayne, II, *biologist, researcher*
Fan, Hung Y. *virology educator, consultant*
Fang, Mark (Yanchu Fang) *geneticist*
Farah, Kimberly Sue *chemistry educator, researcher*
Farkas, Daniel Frederick *food science and technology educator*
Feldman, Jack L. *neurobiology educator*
†Filvaroff, Ellen H. *research scientist*
Flemming, David Paul *biologist*
Fogel, Esther Marian (Esther Marian Roseig) *veterinary researcher*
Foglesong, Paul David *molecular biology and microbiology educator*
Fox, Michael Wilson *veterinarian, bioethicist, animal behaviorist*
Foy, Charles Daley *retired soil scientist*
Freeman, Arthur *veterinarian, retired association administrator*
†Fuller, Stephen W. *science educator*
†Gabor-Hotchkiss, Magda *research scientist, librarian*
Gage, Patrick (Leonard Patrick Gage) *biotech/pharmaceutical consultant*
Galison, Peter Louis *history of science educator*
†Gao, Haiyan *science educator*
Garruto, Ralph Michael *research anthropologist, educator, biologist, neuroscientist*
Gay, William Ingalls *veterinarian, health science administrator*
†Gerhardt, Fritz *ecologist, educator, researcher*
Gill, William Robert *soil scientist*
Gimenez, Daniel *soil scientist, educator*
Glick, J. Leslie *bio and information technology entrepreneur*
Goldstein, Barry Bruce *biologist, food company executive, lawyer*
Goodwin, Richard Hale *botany educator*
Gordis, Enoch *retired science administrator, internist*
Gorin, Abbye Alexander *electronics researcher*
Grand, Cindy *foundation director*
Green, Bennett Donald *biotechnologist*
Greenman, David Lewis *retired physiologist and toxicologist*
Hall, Barry G. *evolutionary biologist*
Hamdy, Mostafa Kamal *microbiologist, educator*
Hamilton, William Howard *laboratory executive*
†Han, Qiwen *research scientist*
Hauptmann, Randal Mark *biotechnologist*
Hayakawa, Kan-Ichi *retired food science educator*
†Heindl, Jason Eugene *research scientist*
Heinicke, Ralph Martin *consultant*
Helgeson, John Paul *plant physiologist, researcher*
Hendricks, Gilbert L., III, *neuroendocrine immune physiologist, researcher*
Herz, Michael Joseph *marine environmental scientist*
Hildebrand, Verna Lee *human ecology educator*
Hinerfeld, Lee Ann *veterinarian*
Holmes, Francis William *plant pathologist, educator*
Howard-Peebles, Patricia N. *clinical cytogeneticist*
Howells, John Gwilym *medical scientist*
Iacono, James Michael *research center administrator, nutrition educator*
Idouraine, Ahmed *nutritionist, food chemist, tissue culture engineer*
†Irby, Rosalyn Bryson *molecular biologist, researcher*
Izlar, Robert Lee *forester*
†Jaworski, Ernest G. *retired biotechnologist*
Johnson, Heidi Smith *science educator, educator*
Kalidindi, Surya Raju *science educator*
Kamrin, Michael Arnold *toxicology educator*
Kapitonov, Vladimir V. *molecular biologist*
Karp, Gerald Charles *biologist, educator, writer*
Karr, Gerald Lee *agricultural economist, state senator*
Kassal, Robert James *polymer research scientist*
Katz, Anne Harris *biologist, educator, writer, aviator*
†Kayo, Ide *research scientist*
Kennedy, Charles *retired neuroscientist, retired medical educator*
Kerr, Janet Spence *physiologist, pharmacologist*
†Khatsenko, Oleg Gennady *research scientist*
Kim, Charles Wesley *microbiology educator*
King, Richard Eugene *soil scientist, educator*
Kirsteuer, Ernst Karl Eberhart *biologist, curator*
†Kitchen, Chester *toxicologist, forensic specialist*
Kittleson, Mark Douglas *veterinary cardiologist, veterinary medicine educator*
†Klopatek, Jeffrey Matthew *ecology educator*
Knapik, Joseph John *research physiologist*
†Ko, Lan *molecular biologist, researcher*
Koller, Loren D. *veterinary medicine educator*
†Konar, Nandini *research scientist*
Kornguth, Steven Edward *biologist*
Kurtz, Myra Berman *microbiologist*
†Lake, James A. *molecular biology educator*
Lambert, Richard Bowles, Jr., *festival administrator*
Langdale, Noah Noel, Jr., *research educator, former university president*
†Larsson, Hans Peter *science educator*
Latham, James Richard *research scientist*
Layne, James Nathaniel *vertebrate biologist*
Leath, Kenneth Thomas *research plant pathologist, educator, agricultural consultant*
†Leder, Philip *geneticist, educator*
Leventhal, Ruth *retired parasitology educator, university official*
Li, Qing'an *scientist, researcher*
†Link-Plante, Julia A. *horticulturist, entomologist, writer*
Lockwood, John LeBaron *plant pathologist, educator*
Lundgren, Regina Ellen (Regina Scott) *research scientist*
Lynch, Harry James *retired biologist*
Lynch, John Thomas *retired science foundation administrator, physicist*
Magee, John Francis *research company executive*
†Malhotra, Gouri Gupchup *research scientist*
Martino, Joseph Paul *research scientist, researcher*
Maslansky, Carol Jeanne *toxicologist*
Maunder, Addison Bruce *agronomic research company executive*
McCann, Peter Paul *biology researcher, educator*
McClellan, Roger Orville *toxicologist*
†McKeever, Kenneth Harrington *veterinarian, educator*
McShefferty, John *retired research company executive, consultant*
†Melnikova, Vladislava Olegovna *photobiologist*
Menn, Julius Joel *scientist*
Metzler, Ruth Horton *genealogical educator*
Miller, Patrick William *research administrator, educator*
†Miller, Susan M. *science educator, researcher*
Mitchell, John Laurin Amos *biological science educator*
†Mitchell, Margaret Yvonne *forester*
†Modugno, Francesmary *research scientist*
Moerschel, David Jonathan *biologist*
Molnar, Stephen Paul *research scientist*
Monzingo, Agnes Yvonne *veterinary technician*
Moore, J Strother *science educator, researcher*
Moss, Thomas Henry *science association administrator*
Mudavanhu, Blessing *research scientist*
Mumford, Russell Eugene *biologist, educator, writer*
Murarka, Shyam Prasad *science and engineering educator, administrator*
Murray, Joseph James, Jr., *zoologist*
†Nelson-Le Gall, Sharon A. *science educator, researcher*
Nesmelova, Irina Vladislavovna *research scientist, physicist*
Newell, William Keith *neurobiological researcher*
Nikaido, Hiroshi *microbiologist*
†Nucifora, Giuseppina *molecular biologist, researcher*
O'Brien, Inge Frances Rapstine *research scientist, geological and geophysical consultant*
Oswald, Robert Bernard *science administrator, nuclear engineer*
Owens, Vivian Ann *plant science educator, researcher*
Paganelli, Charles Victor *physiologist, educator*
Palade, George Emil *biologist, educator*
†Paule, Wendelin J. *cell biologist, educator*
Peaslee, Margaret Mae Hermanek *zoology educator*
Pedersen, Michael *research scientist*
†Penfold, Linda Margaret *reproductive physiologist, researcher*
Peter, Richard Ector *zoology educator*
†Peters, Linda Marie Leitch *research scientist, educator*
Pettit, Ghery DeWitt *retired veterinary medicine educator*
†Phogat, Sanjay Kumar *molecular virologist, researcher*
Pielou, Evelyn C. *biologist*
Pinter, Gabriel George *physiology educator*
Pitelka, Louis Frank *ecologist*
Plotkin, Stanley Alan *medical virologist*
†Polley, Richard Donald *microbiologist, polymer chemist*
Popenoe, John *horticultural consultant, retired botanical garden administrator*
Prazak, Bessmarie Lillian *science educator*
Raisys, Vidmantas A. *toxicology educator, clinical chemist*
†Randall, Lorrie Boullion *science educator*
Reid, Janet Warner *biologist consultant*
Repik, Aleksandr Vladimirovich *molecular biologist*
Roeller, Herbert Alfred *biology and medical scientist, educator*
Rogers, Jack David *plant pathologist, educator*
†Rooney, Thomas Paul *ecologist*
Rose, Michael Robertson *evolutionary biology educator, consultant*
†Rosenbaum, Manuel *retired microbiologist, retired systems analyst*
Ross, Jeffrey Alan *research biologist*
Rothman, Frank George *biology educator, biochemical genetics researcher*
Rothman, Robert *science educator*
Russell, Liane Brauch *retired geneticist*
Saalfeld, Fred Erich *science educator, researcher*
Salthe, Stanley Norman *retired theoretical biology educator*
Samuels, Linda S. *science administrator*
Sattler, Rolf *retired plant morphologist, educator*
Schaechter, Moselio *microbiology educator*
†Scherer, James R. *research scientist*
†Schlub, Robert Louis *plant pathologist, educator*
Shahied, Ishak I. *science educator*
Simpson, Frederick James *retired research administrator*
Sjostrand, Fritiof Stig *biologist, educator*
Smith, Hamilton Othanel *molecular biologist, educator*
Snow, Joel Alan *research director*
Sokal, Robert Reuven *biology educator, author*
Soper, James Herbert *botanist, curator*
Southwick, Charles Henry *zoologist, educator*
Sponsler, George Curtis, III, *research administrator, lawyer*
Stadtländer, Christian Thomas Karl-Heinz *microbiologist, researcher*
Stavroulakis, Anthea Merrie *biology educator*
Steinberg, Marshall *retired toxicologist*
Stickle, David Walter *microbiologist*
Stickney, Robert Roy *fisheries educator*
Stokes, Samuel Newton *environmental conservationist*
Stone, John Floyd *soil physics researcher and educator*
Stroud, Richard Hamilton *aquatic biologist, scientist, consultant*
Stump, John Edward *veterinary anatomy educator, ethologist*
Sugintas, Nora Maria *veterinarian, scientist, medical company executive, performing arts dancer, photographer*
Sullivan, Harry Truman *research scientist*
Suthers, Hannah Louise Bonsey *biologist*
Talmage, David Wilson *microbiology and medical educator, physician, former university administrator*
Tandler, Bernard *cell biology educator*
Taylor, Murry Allan *retired forester*
Taylor, Roy Lewis *botanist, educator*
†Taylor, Welton Ivan *microbiologist, consultant, food scientist*
Teng, Shuye *research scientist*
Thomas, Teresa Ann *microbiologist, educator*
Thompson, Thomas Daniel *biology and chemistry educator*
†Tian, Lianfang *research scientist*
Tigges, Michael Gerard *veterinarian, government medical officer*
†Topolski, Catherine *science educator*
†Tsay, Andy A. *science educator*
Ullman, Edwin Fisher *biotechnology consultant*

Van Arsdel, Eugene Parr *tree pathologist, meteorologist*
†Vankat, John Lyman *science educator, researcher*
Vaughan, John Charles, III, *horticultural products executive*
†Velmurugan, Soundarapandian *microbiologist, researcher*
†Verma, Geeta K. *science educator*
Wang, Wei *research scientist*
†Wasserman, Gerald Steward *psychobiology educator*
Watson, Cheryl S. *cell and molecular biology educator, researcher*
Weber, Lavern John *retired marine science administrator, educator*
Weck, Edward Alexander *molecular biologist, biochemist*
Wei, Qingyi *cancer research educator*
†Welsch, Michael Andrew *exercise physiologist, researcher*
Wiatr, Christopher Louis *microbiologist*
Wilkinson, Stanley Ralph *retired agronomist*
Willson, Mary Frances *ecology researcher, educator*
Wolf, Larry Louis *biology educator*
Wooten, Frank Thomas *retired research facility executive*
Wu, Andy Ting *research scientist*
†Xiang, Mengqing *molecular biologist*
Yang, Xiangzhong *research scientist, administrator, educator*
†Yates, Karen E. *research scientist*
Young, Jerry Wesley *retired animal nutrition educator*
Young, Judith Anne *animal conservationist*
†Yu, Jun *biologist*
Yunis, Jorge Jose *anatomy, pathology, and microbiology educator*
Zak, John Michael *retired agronomy educator*
†Zaretzky-Jones, Franca Rebecca *microbiologist, researcher*
Zhang, Hongtao *research scientist*
†Zhang, Zhe George *science educator, operations research specialist*
Zhang, Zhongjian *research scientist*
Zhao, Guang-Quan *developmental reproductive biologist, researcher*
†Zhao, Liying *science educator, researcher*
Zhu, Yong *research scientist*
Zwislocki, Jozef John *neuroscience educator, researcher*

SCIENCE: MATHEMATICS AND COMPUTER SCIENCE *See also* INFORMATION TECHNOLOGY

UNITED STATES

ALABAMA

Athens
Hodson, Roy Goode, Jr., *retired logistician*

Auburn
Govil, Narendra Kumar *mathematics educator*
†Jenda, Overtoun Malandula *mathematician, educator, mathematician, researcher, dean*

Birmingham
Jones, Warren Thomas *computer science educator*
Peeples, William Dewey, Jr., *mathematics educator*
†Reilly, Kevin Denis *computer scientist, educator*
Whigham, Mark Anthony *computer scientist*

Florence
Johnson, Johnny Ray *mathematics educator*

Huntsville
Freas, George Wilson, II, *computer consultant*
†McAuley, Van Alfon *aerospace mathematician*
Pruitt, Alice Fay *mathematician, engineer*
†Tolbert, Timothy Ray *systems analyst, military officer*

Mobile
McCleery, Winston Theodore *computer consulting company executive*

Montgomery
†Kim, Ki Hang *mathematician*

Pelham
Turner, Malcolm Elijah *biomathematician, educator*

Tuscaloosa
†Mysore, Shrikanth Bhaskar *operations research specialist*

ALASKA

Anchorage
Mann, Lester Perry *mathematics educator*
Marx, Donald Lee *statistician, educator*

Juneau
†Blitz, Brian G. *mathematician, educator*

ARIZONA

Fort Huachuca
Clark, Brian Thomas *mathematical statistician, operations research analyst*

Fountain Hills
Israel, Robert Allan *statistician*

Gilbert
Stith, Joseph *computer infosystems specialist, author*

Glendale
†Strom, April Dawn *mathematician, educator*

Mesa
Berger, James Charles *computer consultant and systems educator*
Estabrook, Brooke Kendell *instructional technologist*

Phoenix
Doto, Irene Louise *statistician*
†Pillalamarri, Seshasayi *computer scientist and engineer, researcher*

Scottsdale
Drake, Albert Estern *retired statistics educator, farming administrator*
McCabe, Mary Williamson *computer systems analyst*

Sierra Vista
Sizemore, Nicky Lee *computer scientist*

Tempe
Bristol, Stanley David *mathematician, educator*
Golshani, Forouzan *computer science and engineering educator*
†Razdan, Anshuman *computer scientist, researcher*
Smith, Harvey Alvin *mathematics educator, consultant*
Yau, Stephen Sik-sang *computer science and engineering educator, computer scientist, researcher*

Tucson
Alexander, Edward Harrison *mathematician, educator*
Veaner, Allen Barnet *information science educator*
Willoughby, Stephen Schuyler *mathematics educator*
Yang, Tao *information science educator, researcher*
†Zakharov, Vladimir E. *mathematician, researcher*

ARKANSAS

Arkadelphia
†Coventry, Debra Ann *mathematician, educator*
†Worth, Fred *mathematician, educator*

Batesville
Carius, Robert Wilhelm *mathematics and science educator, retired naval officer*

Conway
McDermott, Cecil Wade *mathematics educator, educational program director*
Spatz, Kenneth Chris(topher), Jr., *statistics educator*

Fort Smith
Smith-Leins, Terri L. *mathematics educator*

Little Rock
†Chiang, Chia-Chu *computer scientist, educator*
Townsend, James Willis *computer scientist*
†Yarberry, Lonnie Stephen *information scientist, director*

Magnolia
Avard, Joseph L. *mathematician, educator*

Pine Bluff
†Lakew, Dejenie Alemayehu *mathematics educator*

Russellville
†Finan, Marcel Bassil *mathematics educator, researcher*

State University
Miao, Jie *mathematics educator*

CALIFORNIA

Altadena
Fairbanks, Mary Kathleen *computer scientist, researcher*

Arcadia
†Seitz, Charles Lewis *computer scientist and engineer*

Azusa
Sambasivam, Samuel E. *computer science and mathematics educator*

Bakersfield
†Fiedler, Joseph Robert *mathematician, educator*

Berkeley
Arveson, William Barnes *mathematics educator*
†Bajcsy, Ruzena Kucerova *computer science educator*
Bakalov, Bojko Nentchev *mathematician*
Bergman, George Mark *mathematician, educator*
Bickel, Peter John *statistician, educator*
Budaev, Bair V. *mathematician, researcher*
†Chern, Shiing-Shen *mathematics educator*
Chorin, Alexandre Joel *mathematician, educator*
Cooper, Michael David *information systems educator*
Cooper, William Secord *information science educator*
Eisenbud, David *mathematics educator*
Freedman, David Amiel *statistics educator, consultant*
Graham, Susan Lois *computer science educator, consultant*
Henkin, Leon Albert *mathematician, educator*
Hyman, Edward Jay *forensic psychologist, cognitive and information scientist, consultant, educator, television news commentator*
Kaplansky, Irving *mathematician, educator, research institute director*
Karp, Richard Manning *computer sciences educator*
Lehmann, Erich Leo *statistics educator*
Osserman, Robert *mathematician, educator, writer*
Pham, Quang Xuan *statistics educator*
Séquin, Carlo H. *computer science educator*
†Shaffer, Juliet Popper *statistics educator*
†Sim, Alexander *computer scientist, researcher*
Smith, Alan Jay *computer science educator, consultant*
Tarter, Michael Ernest *biostatistician, educator*
Vojta, Paul Alan *mathematics educator*
Wahl, Bernt Rainer *mathematician, writer, application developer*
Wehausen, John Vrooman *mathematician, educator*
Wolf, Joseph Albert *mathematician, educator*
Yu, Bin *statistician, educator*

Brea
Painchaud, Phillip Andre *metrologist*

Carlsbad
Halberg, Charles John August, Jr., *mathematics educator*

Carson
Kowalski, Kazimierz *computer science educator, researcher*
Suchenek, Marek Andrzej *computer science educator*
Toh, Chai *information science educator*

Chatsworth
Ulin, Samuel Alexander *computer systems developer*

Claremont
Coleman, Courtney Stafford *mathematician, educator*
Cooke, Kenneth Lloyd *mathematician, educator*
Grabiner, Sandy *mathematics educator*
Henriksen, Melvin *mathematician, educator*
Myhre, Janet *mathematician, educator*
†Shahriari, Shahriar *mathematics educator*

Concord
Fuld, Fred, III, *computer consultant, financial consultant*

Costa Mesa
Demille, Dianne Lynne *mathematics educator, administrator*

Davis
†Fannjiang, Albert *mathematician, educator*
Mulase, Motohico *mathematics educator*
Olsson, Ronald Arthur *computer science educator*
Walters, Richard Francis *computer science educator*
Wegelin, Jacob Andreas *statistician*

Downey
Stormes, John Max *instructional systems developer*

El Cerrito
Stenmark, Jean Kerr *mathematics educator*

Elk Grove
McDavid, Douglas Warren *executive research consultant*

Encino
Hein, Jennifer Loomis *information technology consultant*

Escondido
Ziegler, James Russell *computer consultant*

Foothill Ranch
Sperling, Scott Edward *software consultant, Bible expositor*

Fresno
Michael, James Daniel *computer scientist*

Fullerton
Lupash, Lawrence Ovidiu *computer analyst, researcher*

Hayward
Duncan, Doris Gottschalk *information systems educator*
†Roby, Tom *mathematician, educator*
Sabharwal, Ranjit Singh *mathematician*

Hillsborough
Komissarchik, Edward *computer scientist*

Irvine
Abu-Mostafa, Ayman Said *computer consultant*
Hoffman, Donald David *cognitive and computer science educator*
†Kaneda, Masayoshi *mathematics educator, researcher*
Kobsa, Alfred *computer scientist, educator*
†Lafky, Deborah Beranek Palser *information scientist, researcher*
Lathrop, Richard Harold *computer science educator*
Li, Peter Wai-Kwong *mathematics educator*
Saari, Donald Gene *mathematician, economist*

La Canada
Sanchez, Victor David *computer scientist, educator*

La Canada Flintridge
†Leko, Gabrielle M. *mathematician, educator*

La Jolla
†Bunch, James Raymond *mathematician, educator*
Burgin, George Hans *computer scientist, educator*
Buss, Samuel Rudolph Rudolph *mathematics educator, researcher*
Graham, Ronald Lewis *mathematician*
Halkin, Hubert *mathematics educator, research mathematician*
Harvey, A. Raymond *mathematician, educator*
†Majumdar, Amitava *computer scientist, educator, nuclear engineer*
Martin, James John, Jr., *retired consulting research firm executive, systems analyst*
†Micciancio, Daniele *computer scientist*
Rosen, Judah Ben *computer scientist*
Rosenblatt, Murray *mathematics educator*
Terras, Audrey Anne *mathematics educator*
Wulbert, Daniel Eliot *mathematician, educator*
Zyroff, Ellen Slotoroff *information scientist, classicist, educator*

Livermore
Fodor, Imola Katalin *mathematician, researcher*
Haga, Enoch John *computer educator, author*
†Zhu, Xinhai *computer scientist*

Long Beach
Dawson, Dixie Tuttle *mathematics consultant*
Gittleman, Arthur Paul *computer science and engineering educator*
Schroeder, Arnold Leon *mathematics educator*
Wollmer, Richard Dietrich *statistics and operations research educator*

Los Angeles
Arbib, Michael Anthony *neuroscientist, educator, computer scientist*
Bekey, George Albert *computer scientist, educator, engineer*
Boehm, Barry William *computer science educator*
Bowers, David Paul *operations analyst*
†Brown, Robert Freeman *mathematics educator*
Burgin, Mark Semjonovich *mathematician, computer scientist, philosopher*
†Chacko, George Kuttickal *systems science educator, consultant*
Dabrowska, Dorota Maria *statistician, educator*
Delaney, Matthew Sylvester *mathematics educator, academic administrator*
Estrin, Gerald *computer scientist, engineering educator, academic administrator*
Golomb, Solomon Wolf *mathematician, electrical engineer, educator, university official*
Gordon, Basil *mathematics educator*
Greenberger, Martin *biotechnologist, information scientist, educator*
Holt, James Franklin *retired numerical analyst, scientific programmer analyst*
Jacobsen, Laren *programmer, analyst*
Jones, Gerald Paul *software educator*
Kalaba, Robert Edwin *applied mathematician*
†Kolesnik, Grigori *mathematician, educator, mathematician, researcher*
Pearl, Judea *computer scientist, educator*
Petak, William John *systems management educator*
Port, Sidney Charles *mathematician, educator*
†Verona, Andrei *mathematician, educator*
Waterman, Michael Spencer *mathematics educator, biology educator*
†Woods, Shirley *mathematics educator, writer*
†Ziane, Mohammed Boulanouar *mathematician, educator*

Los Gatos
Rissanen, Jorma Johannes *computer scientist*

Malibu
Stalzer, Mark Anthony *computer scientist, technical director*

Marina Del Rey
†Neuman, Clifford *computer scientist, educator*
Touch, Joseph Dean *computer scientist, educator*

Menlo Park
Bourne, Charles Percy *information scientist, educator*
†Exuzides, Alex *statistician, researcher*
Mulgaonkar, Prasanna G. *computer scientist*
Neumann, Peter Gabriel *computer scientist*

Moffett Field
Biswas, Rupak *computer scientist*
†Havelund, Klaus *computer scientist*

Monterey
Denning, Peter James *computer scientist, engineer*
Schneidewind, Norman Floyd *computer scientist, educator*

Moss Landing
Lange, Lester Henry *mathematics educator*

Mountain View
Clancey, William John *computer scientist, researcher*
Crawford, Walt *systems analyst*
†Gluhovsky, Ilya *statistician, researcher*

Newark
Nemenman, Mark Yefim *mathematics and computers educator, consultant*

Oakland
†Givant, Steven Roger *mathematician, computer scientist, educator*

Jackson, M. Leigh *analyst programmer, fine art photographer, graphic designer*
Lepowsky, William Leonard *mathematics and statistics educator*
Lowndes, David Alan *retired programmer analyst, application developer*
Lubliner, Irving *mathematics educator, consultant*
Zelmanowitz, Julius Martin *mathematics educator, university administrator*

Orange
Smith, John LeRoy *mathematician, educator*

Oxnard
Hayashi, Alan T. *mathematics educator*
†Neilson, Jane Scott *mathematics educator*

Palo Alto
Efird, Jimmy Thomas *statistician*
Keller, Arthur Michael *computer science researcher*

Paradise
Barr, Donald Roy *statistics and operations research educator, statistician*

Pasadena
†Borodin, Alexei *mathematician*
Braverman, Amy Joan *statistician, researcher*
Franklin, Joel Nicholas *mathematician, educator*
Fu, Li Min *biomedical and computer science educator*
Gref, Lynn G. *mathematician*
†Koon, Wang-Sang *mathematician, researcher*
Reimer, Jennifer Ann *computer scientist*
Saffman, Philip G. *mathematician, educator*

Pomona
†Agvanian, Youri *mathematician, educator, physicist*
Bernau, Simon John *mathematics educator*
†Kim, Hoon *statistician, educator*

Portola Valley
Kuo, Franklin F. *computer scientist, electrical engineer*

Redondo Beach
Sillman, George Douglas *computer programmer analyst*
Woike, Lynne Ann *computer scientist*

Redwood Shores
Chaudhry, Nauman Ahmed *computer scientist*

Riverside
Ratliff, Louis Jackson, Jr., *mathematics educator*
†Schaible, Siegfried *mathematician, educator*
†Wilson, Jason *mathematician, educator*

Roseville
Reichmann, Péter Iván *mathematician*

Sacramento
Kho, James Wang *computer scientist*
†Norman, Ben Eric *mathematician, educator*

San Diego
†Fellows, Christohper Charles *information scientist*
Garrison, Betty Bernhardt *retired mathematics educator*
Hales, Alfred Washington *mathematics educator, consultant*
Legrand, Shawn Pierre *computer systems programmer*
Loper, Warren Edward *computer scientist*
†McLeod, Douglas Bailey *mathematician, educator*
Mestechkin, Mikhail Markovich *math physicist*
Rubin, Stuart Harvey *computer science educator, researcher*
Tsybakov, Boris Solomon *information theory and communication networks researcher, educator*
Van Tassel, Lowell Thomas *mathematics educator*
†Velo, Ani Piro *mathematician, educator*
Willerding, Margaret Frances *mathematician, educator*

San Francisco
Backus, John *computer scientist*
Cruse, Allan Baird *mathematician, computer scientist, educator*
DePrimo, Gaetano Manfred
†Fendel, Dan *mathematician, educator*
†Kao, John Sterling *mathematician, educator*
Leung, Kason Kai Ching *computer specialist*
Low, Arnold Kinman *systems executive*
†Lu, Ying *statistician, educator*
Shvidler, Mark Joseph *mathematician*

San Gabriel
Kettemborough, Clifford Russell *computer scientist, consultant, manager*

San Jose
Evans, Donald Foster *quality engineer, computer consultant*
Shah, Girish Popatlal *information technology consultant*
Togasaki, Shinobu *computer scientist*

San Luis Obispo
Itnyre, Jacqueline Harriet *systems analyst*

San Marino
Lashley, Virginia Stephenson Hughes *retired computer science educator*

San Rafael
Barker, Celeste Arlette *computer scientist*

Santa Barbara
Johnsen, Eugene Carlyle *mathematician and educator*
Marcus, Marvin *mathematician, educator*
Minc, Henryk *mathematics educator*
Newman, Morris *mathematician, educator*
Simons, Stephen *mathematics educator, researcher*

Santa Clara
†Farris, Frank A. *mathematician, educator, editor*
Halmos, Paul Richard *mathematician, educator*
Klosinski, Leonard Frank *mathematics educator*
†Ross, Peter *mathematician, educator*
Smith, Stephen Allen *mathematician, educator*

Santa Cruz
Huskey, Harry Douglas *information and computer science educator*
Levinson, Robert Arlen *computer science educator, consultant*
Miller, Ethan *computer science educator*

Santa Monica
Chow, Brian Gee-Yin *policy analyst, researcher*
Ware, Willis Howard *computer scientist*

Santee
Peters, Raymond Eugene *computer systems company executive*

Saratoga
Park, Joseph Chul Hui *computer scientist*

Stanford
Anderson, Theodore Wilbur *statistics educator*
Brown, Byron William, Jr., *biostatistician, educator*
Dantzig, George Bernard *applied mathematics educator*
†Eliashberg, Yakov *mathematician, educator*
Feigenbaum, Edward Albert *computer science educator*
Karlin, Samuel *mathematics educator, researcher*
Keller, Joseph Bishop *mathematician, educator*
Knuth, Donald Ervin *computer sciences educator*
McCarthy, John *computer scientist, educator*
Moses, Lincoln E. *statistician, educator*
Musen, Mark Alan *computer science educator, physician*
†Olkin, Ingram *mathematician, educator*
Ornstein, Donald Samuel *mathematician, educator*
Schoen, Richard Melvin *mathematics educator, researcher*
Ullman, Jeffrey David *computer scientist, educator*

Sunnyvale
Frank, Jeremy D. *computer scientist*

Temecula
†May, Brian Thomas *mathematician, educator*

Thousand Oaks
Sladek, Lyle Virgil *mathematician, educator*
Urban, Gary Ross *computer and information processing consultant*

Torrance
†Kerstiens, Gene J. *mathemagenician, consultant*

Tustin
Re Velle, Jack B(oyer) *statistician, consultant*

Ukiah
†Speed, Cynthia Agnes *retired mathematics educator*

West Covina
†Jee, James Rodney *statistician*

Westlake Village
Anastasi, Richard Joseph *computer software consultant*
Munson, John Backus *computer systems consultant, retired computer engineering company executive*

Woodland Hills
Stratton, Gregory Alexander *computer specialist, administrator, mayor*

Yucaipa
†Ramirez, Stephen John *mathematician, educator*

COLORADO

Boulder
Beylkin, Gregory *mathematician*
Glover, Fred William *artificial intelligence and optimization research director, educator*
Monarchi, David Edward *management scientist, information scientist, educator*
Mycielski, Jan *mathematician, educator*
Uhrik, Carl Thomas *computer scientist, educator*

Colorado Springs
Simmons, George Finlay *mathematics educator*

Denver
†Cosgrove, Gregory Patrick *information scientist*
†Im, Kun Shin *information scientist, educator*
Knyazev, Andrew *mathematician, consultant*
Koh, Eunmee *mathematician, educator, consultant*
Lee, Hyunyoung *computer scientist, educator*
Mendez, Celestino Galo *mathematics educator*
†Moreno, Abel *computer scientist, educator, director*
†Talman, Louis A. *mathematician*

Fort Collins
Brockwell, Peter John *statistics educator*
†Loy, Ivan *mathematician, educator*
Mielke, Paul William, Jr., *statistician, consultant*

Grand Junction
Bornmann, Lewis Joseph *computer scientist*

Littleton
Riley, Mary Jane *computer scientist*

Loveland
Geisendorfer, Nancy Kay *mathematics educator*

Winter Park
†Newberry, Hal D. *operations specialist*

Woodland Park
Olson, Warren Kinley *operations research analyst, engineer, physicist*
Trench, William Frederick *mathematician, educator*

CONNECTICUT

Cheshire
Tufte, Edward Rolf *writer, publisher, statistics educator*

Danbury
Wright, Marie Anne *management information systems educator*

Fairfield
Eigel, Edwin George, Jr., *mathematics educator, retired university president*
Shaffer, Dorothy Browne *retired mathematician, educator*
†Weiss, Joan Wyzkoski *mathematics educator*

Hartford
†Hoim, Terje *mathematician, educator*
Swyers, Donald G. *information scientist*
Younessi, Houman *computer science educator*

Manchester
Szymonik, Peter Ted *information scientist, consultant, systems analyst*

Middletown
Comfort, William Wistar *mathematics educator*
Hager, Anthony Wood *mathematics educator*
Reid, James Dolan *mathematics educator, researcher*

New Britain
†O'Connell, Brian Michael *computer scientist, educator*

New Haven
†Coifman, Ronald R. *mathematician, educator*
†Cole, First Dana *computer scientist, educator*
Howe, Roger Evans *mathematician, educator*
Mandelbrot, Benoit B. *mathematician, scientist, educator*
Margulis, Gregory A. *mathematics educator, researcher*
†Martinsson, Per-Gunnar Johan *mathematician, mechanical engineer*
Massey, William S. *mathematician, educator*
Mostow, George Daniel *mathematics educator*
†Orszag, Steven Alan *applied mathematician, educator*
†Peralta, Rene Caupolican *cryptologist, educator*
Seligman, George Benham *mathematics educator*

Stamford
Fiorino, Anthony Saverio (Tony Eitan) *research analyst*
Frank, Laura Jean *computer scientist*
Mersereau, Stephen Crocker *electronic commerce executive*
Popelyukhin, Aleksey *mathematician, educator, actuary, researcher*

Storrs Mansfield
†Abikoff, William *mathematician, educator*

Trumbull
Wigsten, Paul Bradley, Jr., *computer and financial consultant*

Wallingford
†Odeshoo, Linda *biostatistician, mathematician, educator*

Waterbury
Rosa, Domenico *mathematics educator*

West Hartford
Welna, Cecilia *mathematics educator*

West Haven
†Song, James Xin *statistician, consultant*

Willimantic
Koirala, Hari Prasad *mathematics educator*

Wilton
Brown, James Thompson, Jr., *computer information scientist, logistics specialist*

DELAWARE

Newark
Chester, Daniel Leon *computer scientist, educator, consultant*
Colton, David Lem *mathematician, educator*
Stark, Robert Martin *mathematician, civil engineer, educator*

Wilmington
Shevchuck, Harry *retired image systems consultant*
Smeck, William H. *computer scientist*

DISTRICT OF COLUMBIA

Washington
†Baran, Christine *systems analyst*
†Barbehenn, Elizabeth *research analyst*
Basu, Sudeshna *mathematician, educator, researcher*
Chen, Li *computer scientist, software engineer*
Chiazze, Leonard, Jr., *biostatistician, epidemiologist, educator*
Cohen, Michael Paul *statistician*
†Coleman, Charles David *statistician, demographer*
Coles, Bertha Sharon Giles *visual information specialist*
Fisher, Gordon McCracken *program analyst*
†Gillman, Daniel W. *information scientist*
Goldfield, Edwin David *statistician*
Goldhaber, Jacob Kopel *retired mathematician, educator*
Gray, Mary Wheat *statistician, lawyer*
Hedges, Harry George *computer scientist, educator*
†Hogan, Howard *statistician, educator*
Kahlow, Barbara Fenvessy *statistician*
Kotz, Samuel *statistician, educator, translator, editor*
Lutterodt, Clement H. *mathematician, educator*
†MacDonald, Purificacion O. *statistician, researcher*
Mahmoud, Hosam M. *statistics educator, academic administrator*
Mann, Charles Roy *statistician*
†McCulley, Helen Marie *mathematician*
Miller, Judith Rosalind *mathematician, educator*
†Nolan, John Patrick *mathematician, educator*
Przytycki, Jozef Henryk *mathematician, educator*
†Rassam, Ghassan Noel *information scientist*
Ryan, David Alan *computer specialist*
Saworotnow, Parfeny Pavlovich *mathematician, educator*
Shaw, William Frederick *statistician*
†Singpurwalla, Nozer Darabsha *statistician, engineer, educator*
Viehe, Karl William *mathematics educator, lawyer, investment banker*
†Wooten, Russell *operations research specialist*
Wulf, William Allan *computer information scientist, educator, federal agency administrator*
Yasnoff, William Alan *computer scientist, preventive medicine physician*

FLORIDA

Bonita Springs
Powell, Robert Ellis *mathematics educator, college dean*

Casselberry
†Sen, Pranab Kumar *statistics educator*

Clearwater
Stein, Roger Richard *microcomputer specialist, educator*

Clewiston
Griffith, Lonzo, Jr., *technology specialist, educator, farmer*

Coral Gables
Green, Willie Harold *mathematician, physicist*
Howard, Bernard Eufinger *mathematics and computer science educator*

Daytona Beach
Pagan Ortiz, Alex Omar *computer systems analyst, educator*
†Seenith, Sivasundaram *mathematician, educator*

Delray Beach
Beckman, Frank Samuel *computer science educator, researcher*
Hegstrom, William Jean *mathematics educator*
Mavrides, Gregory *computer scientist, psychoanalyst, computer engineer, computer company executive*

Dunedin
†Gurr, Jim R. *statistician*
Klingbiel, Paul Herman *retired information science consultant*

Fort Lauderdale
Littman, Marlyn Kemper *information scientist, educator*

Gainesville
†Bona, Miklos *mathematician, educator*
Cenzer, Douglas Alfred *mathematician, educator*
Dinculeanu, Nicolae *mathematician, educator*
Emch, Gerard Gustav *mathematics and physics educator*
Weinrich, Brian Erwin *mathematician, computer scientist*
Zapletal, Jindrich *mathematician*

Highland Beach
Schor, Stanley Sidney *mathematical sciences educator*

Jacksonville
Cole, Linda Sue *grant program planner, computer software professional*
Robinson, Christine Marie *mathematics educator*
Shoup, James Raymond *computer systems consultant*

Lake Mary
Aparicio, Julio L. *systems analyst*

Largo
Camara, Vincent Antonin Reginald *mathematician, educator, statistician, researcher*

Melbourne
Lakshmikantham, Vangipuram *mathematics educator*
Trotter, Shirley Ann *retired computer specialist*

Wilson, Sal *computer systems analyst, business executive*

Grinnell
Adelberg, Arnold Melvin *mathematics educator, researcher*
†Chamberland, Marc A. *mathematician, educator*
Ferguson, Pamela Anderson *mathematics educator, educational administrator*

Iowa City
Broffitt, James Drake *professor statistics and actuarial science*
†Fuller, Kent Ralph *mathematician, educator*
Hogg, Robert Vincent, Jr., *mathematical statistician, educator*
Jorgensen, Palle Erik Tikob E T *mathematician, educator*
Robertson, Timothy Joel *statistician, educator*

Mason City
†Attleson, Adriana Lee *mathematics educator*

Storm Lake
McDaniel, Timothy Elton *mathematics, statistics and business educator*

Stratford
†Tollefson Conard, Margot Helena *statistician*

KANSAS

Arkansas City
†Nichols, Gregory A. *mathematician, educator*

Lawrence
Himmelberg, Charles John, III, *mathematics educator, researcher*
Price, Griffith Baley *mathematician, educator*
†Van Vleck, Fred Scott *mathematician, educator, researcher*
Wallace, Victor Lew *computer science educator*

Lenexa
Gressel, Gary Lee *computer scientist*

Manhattan
Higgins, James Jacob *statistics educator*
Lin, Zongzhu *mathematician, educator*

Shawnee Mission
Flora, Jairus Dale, Jr., *statistician*

Topeka
Charlwood, Kevin Edward *mathematician, educator*

Wichita
Acker, Andrew French, III, *mathematics educator, researcher*
Chopra, Dharam Vir *statistician, educator*
Palmer, Ada Margaret *systems analyst, consultant*

KENTUCKY

Lexington
Klapper, Andrew *computer scientist, educator*
Wasilkowski, Grzegorz W. *computer scientist*

Louisville
Brantley, William Albert *information architect, consultant*
Greaver, Joanne Hutchins *mathematics educator, author*
Hoye, Robert Earl *systems science educator*
Mosier, Jo Ann *mathematics educator*
Noble, Stephen Lloyd *information scientist*

Morehead
Chatham, Richard Douglas *mathematics educator*
Mann, James Darwin *mathematics educator*

Murray
†Fister, Katherine Renee *mathematician, educator*

Richmond
King, Amy Cathryne Patterson *retired, mathematics educator, researcher*

Somerset
†Angevine, Roger Lee *mathematician, educator*

Wilmore
†Lee, Duk-Hyung *mathematician, educator*

LOUISIANA

Baton Rouge
Dasbach, Oliver T. *mathematician, educator*
Oxley, James Grieve *mathematics educator*

Hammond
†Cannon, G. Alan *mathematician, educator*

Lafayette
†Cain, Judith Sharp *mathematics consultant*
Christov, Christo Ivanov *mathematician, educator*
†Hongthong, Siriporn *mathematician, educator*

New Orleans
Birtel, Frank Thomas *mathematician, philosopher, educator*
Dauns, John *mathematician, educator*
Harvey, John Grover *mathematics educator*
Mislove, Michael William *mathematics educator, theoretical computer scientist*
†Thomson, Jessica Lee *biostatistician, educator, consultant, researcher*
†Yang, DaGang *mathematician, educator*

Ruston
Dai, Weizhong *applied mathematician, educator*

Shreveport
†Brandl, Mary-Katherine *mathematics educator*

MAINE

Brunswick
Tucker, Allen Brown, Jr., *computer science educator*

Orono
†Bradley, David Michael *mathematician, educator*

Palermo
Anderson, Alfred Oliver *mathematician, consultant*

Yarmouth
Grover, Mark Donald *computer scientist*

MARYLAND

Adamstown
Tidball, Charles Stanley *computer scientist, educator*

Adelphi
Kirwan, William English, II, *mathematics educator, university official, academic administrator*

Annapolis
†Crawford, Carol Gloria *mathematician, educator*
Konkowski, Deborah Ann *mathematics educator*

Baltimore
Arsham, Hossein *operations research analyst*
Bausell, R. Barker, Jr., *research methodology educator*
Boardman, John Michael *mathematician, educator*
Choudhury, Dipa *mathematician, educator*
Kosaraju, S. Rao *computer science educator, researcher*
Masson, Gerald M. *computer science educator*
Potra, Florian Alexander *mathematics educator*
†Rosenberg, Edwin Harold *systems analyst*
Semiatin, Charles Paul *computer science consultant*
Sherman, Alan Theodore *computer science educator*
Shiffman, Bernard *mathematician, educator*
Wierman, John Charles *mathematician, educator*

Bethesda
Altschul, Stephen Frank *mathematician*
Chartrand, Robert Lee *information scientist*
†Coady, Sean Arthur *statistician*
†Di Marino, Michael E. *biostatistician*
Humphrey, Susanne Marguerite *information scientist*
Lillard, Mark Hill, III, *computer consulting executive, former air force officer*
Lipkin, Bernice Sacks *computer science educator*
Moriyama, Iwao Milton *statistician, consultant*
Moshman, Jack *statistical consultant*
Navarro, Joseph Anthony *statistician, consultant*
Schulman, Jacque-Lynne Amann *information scientist*
Smith, Kent Ashton *scientific and technical information executive*
†Zheng, Gang *mathematician, statistician, researcher*

Catonsville
Forgionne, Guisseppi Antonio *information scientis, educator*

College Park
Antman, Stuart Sheldon *mathematician, educator*
Edgeman, Rick Lee *statistics educator, consultant*
†Freidlin, Mark Iosif *mathematician, educator*
†Grillakis, Manoussos *mathematician, educator*
Lucas, Henry Cameron, Jr., *information systems educator, writer, consultant*
Maddulapalli, Kumar Anil *information scientist*
Miller, Raymond Edward *computer science educator*
Minker, Jack *computer scientist, educator*
Olver, Frank William John *research mathematician*
Rosenfeld, Azriel *computer science educator, consultant*
Shneiderman, Ben Abraham *computer science educator, writer*
Swistak, Piotr Tomasz *mathematician, sociologist*
White, Marilyn Domas *information science educator*
Yorke, James Alan *chaos mathematician*
Zelkowitz, Marvin Victor *computer science educator*

Columbia
Gregorie, Corazon Arzalem *operations supervisor*

Eldersburg
Spohn, William Gideon, Jr., *mathematician, musician*

Fort George G Meade
Schmitt, Robert Lee *computer scientist*

Fort Washington
Wilcox, Richard Hoag *information scientist*

Gaithersburg
†Boisvert, Ronald Fernand *computer scientist*
Carasso, Alfred Sam *mathematician*

Gilsinn, David Edmund *mathematician, researcher*
Rosenblatt, Joan Raup *mathematical statistician*
Zhang, Nien Fan *statistician*

Garrett Park
McDowell, Eugene Charles *systems analyst, bioethicist*

Hanover
Alger, James Arthur *computer consultant*

Hunt Valley
Igusa, Jun-Ichi *mathematician, educator*

Hyattsville
Embody, Daniel Robert *biometrician*
†Gonzalez, Joe Fred, Jr., *mathematical statistician, educator*
†Shimizu, Iris M. *statistician, consultant*

Kensington
Lisle, Martha Oglesby *retired mathematics educator*

Lexington Park
†Jackameit, Kevin Charles *information scientist*

Linthicum Heights
Tietz, Dietmar Juergen *computer Web engineer, scientist*

Madison
Hoffman, Kenneth Myron *mathematician, educator*

Potomac
Crowson, Henry Lawrence *mathematician, educator*
Frieder, Gideon *computer science and engineering educator*
Medin, Julia Adele *mathematics educator, researcher*

Rockville
†Ashby, Florence Helen *mathematics educator*
Kalton, Graham *survey statistician*
Pennello, Gene Anthony *statistician*
†Tracy, LaRee Ann *statistician, medical researcher*

Salisbury
†Ennels, Edward Charles *mathematician, educator*

Silver Spring
†Gold, Karen F. *operations research specialist, educator*
Hetzel, Alice M. *statistician, researcher*
Hoch, Peggy Marie *computer scientist*
Sammet, Jean E. *computer scientist*
Sirken, Monroe Gilbert *statistician*
Weiss, Leonard *mathematician, consultant*

Simpsonville
Bluher, Gregory *computer scientist, mathematician*

Sparks
Riley, Sarah Anne *information scientist*

Towson
†Coughlin, James Patrick *mathematician, educator*
Lazar, Jonathan Kumin *computer scientist, educator*
Shah, Shirish Kalyanbhai *computer science, chemistry and environmental science educator*
Shirley, Lawrence Hoyt *mathematician, educator*
Zimmerman, Jay James *mathematics educator*

Washington
†Bevan, William Charles *systems analyst*

MASSACHUSETTS

Acton
Smith, Raoul Normand *computer science educator*

Amherst
†Hayes, David Ryan *mathematics educator*
Rager, John Ewing, III, *computer science educator*
Velleman, Daniel Jon *mathematics educator*

Andover
†Lang, Corbin F. *mathematician, educator*

Arlington
Nahigian, Russell Ara *mathematician*

Bedford
Mahler, Philip Henry *mathematics educator*

Belmont
Magidson, Jay *statistician*
Reynolds, William Francis *mathematics educator*

Billerica
Guivens, Norman Roy, Jr., *mathematician, engineer*

Boston
Berkey, Dennis D. *mathematics educator*
D'Agostino, Ralph Benedict *mathematician, statistician, educator, consultant*
Falb, Peter Lawrence *mathematician, educator, investment company executive*
Gilmore, Maurice Eugene *mathematics educator*
†Granoff, Barry *mathematician, educator*
Kon, Mark Andrew *mathematics educator*
Moseby, LeBaron Clarence, Jr., *mathematics and computer science educator*
†Nam, Byung-Ho *statistician, educator*
Nyberg, Stanley Eric *cognitive scientist*
Previato, Emma *mathematics educator*

†Ramoni, Marco F. *computer scientist*
†Roché, Catherine Konold *software engineer*
Schoenfeld, David Alan *statistician, educator*
Schribman, Shelley Iris *database engineer, consultant*
Sclaroff, Stan *computer science educator*
†Tsaoussidis, Vassilis *computer scientist, educator*
Warga, Jack *mathematician, educator*
Zelen, Marvin *statistics educator*

Brookline
Belenky, Alexander Solomonovich *mathematician, consultant, researcher*

Cambridge
Bartee, Thomas Creson *computer scientist, educator*
Chernoff, Herman *statistics educator*
Dennis, Jack Bonnell *computer scientist, educator*
Dudley, Richard Mansfield *mathematician, educator*
Funes, Pablo Jose *computer science researcher*
†Gleason, Andrew Mattei *retired mathematician, educator*
Greenspan, Harvey Philip *applied mathematician, educator*
Grosz, Barbara Jean *computer science educator*
Helgason, Sigurdur *mathematician, educator*
†Hoaglin, David Caster *statistician, researcher*
Kac, Victor G. *mathematician, educator*
Kazhdan, David *mathematician, educator*
Light, Richard Jay *statistician, education educator*
Lynch, Nancy Ann *computer scientist, educator*
Mack, Robert Whiting *computer consultant*
Mackey, George Whitelaw *mathematician, educator*
†Mazur, Barry Charles *mathematician*
Meng, Xiao-Li *statistician*
Moses, Joel *computer scientist, educator*
Mosteller, Frederick *mathematical statistician, educator*
Oettinger, Anthony Gervin *mathematician, educator*
Orlin, James Berger *mathematician, management scientist, educator*
Roberts, Edward Baer *technology management educator*
Rockart, John Fralick *information systems researcher*
Rubin, Donald Bruce *statistician, educator, research company executive*
Singer, Isadore Manuel *mathematician, educator*
Stanley, Richard P. *mathematics educator*
Strang, William Gilbert *mathematician, educator*
Toomre, Alar *applied mathematician, theoretical astronomer*
†Vadhan, Salil Pravin *computer scientist, educator*
Valiant, Leslie Gabriel *computer scientist, educator*
†Yau, Shing-Tung *mathematics educator*

Chelmsford
Barlas, Julie Sandall *computer scientist, former librarian*

Dartmouth
Mikolajczak, Boleslaw *computer science educator, researcher, consultant*

Dennis
Loveland, Donald William *retired computer science educator*

Duxbury
Thrasher, Dianne Elizabeth *mathematics educator, computer consultant*

East Falmouth
Forte, Margaret Layman *mathematics educator*

Essex
Lane, Evelyn Procter Conant *computer operator*

Framingham
Feldman, Susan Eleanor *technology analyst*
Lavin, Philip Todd *biostatistician executive*
Mabrouk, Sarah Lou *mathematician, educator*
Yonda, Alfred William *mathematician*

Franklin
Roxin, Emilio Oscar *mathematics educator*

Greenfield
Robinson, John Alan *logic and computer science educator*

Hopkinton
Black, David Lionel *computer scientist*

Hudson
Champine, George A. *computer scientist*

Lexington
Cho, John Yungdo Nagamichi *atmospheric research scientist*
†Kelly, Kevin A. *mathematician, educator*
Taft, S. Tucker *computer scientist*

Lincoln
LeGates, John Crews Boulton *information scientist*

Medford
Cowen, Lenore Jennifer *mathematician, educator, computer scientist*
Jacob, Robert Joseph Kassel *computer scientist, educator*
†Kaul, Anton *mathematician, educator*

Natick
†Evans, John Clifford *statistician*

Newton Centre
Williamson, Susan *mathematician, educator*

North Andover
†Hull, Thomas Clinton *mathmatics educator*

North Dartmouth
†Hegedus, Stephen John *mathematician, educator, researcher*

Scituate
†Ekstrom, John Edward *mathematician, educator*

Shrewsbury
†Fondurulia, Julie A. *computer scientist*
Garabedian, Charles, Jr., *mathematician, educator*

Sudbury
Woldman, Evelyn Jandorf *computer information specialist, educator*

Waltham
Brown, Edgar Henry, Jr., *mathematician, educator*

Watertown
†Stoddard, Anne Maher *biostatistician, researcher, educator*

Wayland
Stanvick, David J. *information scientist*

Wellesley Hills
†Kurzweil, Raymond C. *computer scientist, entrepreneur*

Westfield
Buckmore, Alvah Clarence, Jr., *computer scientist, ballistician*

Westford
Haramundanis, Katherine Leonora *information scientist, writer, astronomer*

Weston
Berwick, Robert Cregar *computer science educator*

Westport Point
Fanning, William Henry, Jr., *computer specialist*

Westwood
Smith, Denis Joseph *mathematics educator*

Winchester
Dalton, Robert Edgar *mathematician, computer scientist*

Worcester
Kotzen, Marshall Jason *mathematics educator*
Lurie, Konstantin Anatoly *mathematician, educator*
Malone, Joseph James *mathematics educator, researcher*

MICHIGAN

Ann Arbor
Bartle, Robert Gardner *retired mathematics educator*
†Becker, Mark Paul Paul *statistics and sociology educator, consultant*
Beutler, Frederick Joseph *information scientist*
Blass, Andreas Raphael *mathematics educator*
Brown, Morton B. *biostatistics educator*
Conway, Lynn *computer scientist, electrical engineer, educator*
Gehring, Frederick William *mathematician, educator*
Hadjiiski, Lubomir Mintchev *computer scientist, researcher*
Hill, Bruce Marvin *statistician, scientist, educator*
Leabo, Dick A. *retired statistics educator*
Lewis, Donald John *mathematics educator*
McPherson, Michael Robert *information scientist, university director*
Wilde, Alan Conrad *mathematician*

Auburn Hills
Neumann, Charles Henry *mathematician, educator*

Belleville
Meyer, Thomas J. *mathematics educator*

Bellevue
Hamel, Louis Reginald *systems analysis consultant*

Big Rapids
†Siddikov, Bakhodirzhon *mathematician, educator*
†Tymes, Nathaniel, Jr., *statistician, educator*

Bloomfield Hills
Graff, Robert Alan *computer consultant*
Greenwood, Frank *information scientist, educator*
Nuss, Shirley Ann *computer coordinator, educator*

Dearborn
Brown, James Ward *mathematician, educator, author*

Detroit
Dwyer, John M. *mathematician, statistician, computer scientist*
Gunasekera, Thilak Wijenayaka *mathematician, educator*
Morrison, Gary Ray *instructional technology educator, researcher*
Rajlich, Vaclav Thomas *computer science educator, researcher, consultant*
Schreiber, Bertram Manuel *mathematics*

Spansky, Robert Alan *computer systems analyst, retired*

East Lansing
Hilbert, Virginia Lois *computer consultant and training executive*
Li, Tien-Yien *mathematics educator*
McCarthy, John David *mathematician, educator*
Moran, Daniel Austin *mathematician, educator*
Stapleton, James Hall *statistician, educator*
Weng, John Juyang *computer science educator, researcher*

Farmington
Ginsberg, Myron *computer scientist*

Farmington Hills
Karniotis, Stephen Paul *computer scientist*

Flint
McCartin, Brian James *mathematician, educator*

Ironwood
†Hopkins, Larry Michael *mathematics and computer science educator*

Kalamazoo
†Yang, Li *computer scientist, educator*

Livonia
Schwartz, Randy Ken *mathematics educator*

Melvindale
Saenz, Gilbert *computer programmer and analyst, poet*

Mount Pleasant
Lee, Carl *statistician, educator*
Lenker, Susan S. *mathematician, educator, consultant*

Northville
Hansen, Jean Marie *math and computer educator*

Novi
Chow, Chi-Ming *retired mathematics educator*

Plymouth
Lou, Zheng (David) *technical specialist*

Pontiac
Jack, Dixie Lynn *software consultant, social worker*

Saline
Cornell, Richard Garth *biostatistics educator*

Southfield
†Bindschadler, David E. *mathematician, department chairman, application developer*
Findlay, Annette Marie *information systems executive*

Troy
†Zetu, Dan *statistician, educator*

Warren
Johnson, Leonard Gustave *research mathematician, consultant*
†Xia, George Z. *statistician, educator*

West Bloomfield
Miller, Nancy Ellen *computer consultant*

Ypsilanti
Farah, Badie Naiem *computer information systems educator, consultant*
Janardan, Konanur Gundappasetty *mathematics and statistics educator*
Warner, Jo F. *mathematics educator*

MINNESOTA

Bloomington
†Jensen, Richard Allen *mathematician, educator*

Golden Valley
Savitt, Steven Lee *computer scientist*

Mankato
Hopkins, Layne Victor *computer science educator*

Minneapolis
Adlis, Susan Annette *biostatistician*
Aris, Rutherford *applied mathematician, educator*
†Arnold, Douglas Norman *mathematician*
Bingham, Christopher *statistics educator*
Brasket, Curt Justin *systems analyst, chess player*
†Coult, Nicholas Ashton *mathematician, educator*
Garfield, Joan Barbara *statistics educator*
Lipovetsky, Stan (Stanislav Lipovetsky) *statistician, mathematician*
†Mangen, David Joseph *statistician, researcher*
Markus, Lawrence *retired mathematics educator*
Miller, Willard, Jr., *mathematics educator*
Pour-El, Marian Boykan *mathematician, educator*
Serrin, James Burton *mathematics educator*
Warner, William Hamer *applied mathematician*

Moorhead
Heuer, Gerald Arthur *mathematician, educator*

Moose Lake
DeVillion, Kevin John *computer systems administrator, consultant*

Northfield
Appleyard, David Frank *mathematics and computer science educator*
†Dobrow, Robert Paul *statistician, educator*
Steen, Lynn Arthur *mathematician, educator*

Princeton
Buntrock, Robert Edward *information consultant, organic chemist*

Rochester
Grosset, Jessica Ariane *computer analyst*

Roseville
Kane, George Francis *systems analyst*

Saint Charles
Van Norman, Willis Roger *computer systems researcher*

Saint Cloud
Olagunju, Amos Omotayo *computer science educator, consultant*

Saint Paul
†Geisser, Seymour *statistics educator*

Shakopee
Qiu, Peihua *statistician, educator, statistician, researcher*

Winona
†Pascual, Felino Garcia *mathematician, educator*

MISSISSIPPI

Alcorn
†Hawkins, Sidney Taylor *mathematician, educator*

Long Beach
Miller, James Edward *computer scientist, educator*

Mississippi State
Aktosun, Tuncay *mathematical physics educator*
†Dobson, Edward Tauscher *mathematician*
†Qian, Chuanxi *mathematics educator*

MISSOURI

Columbia
Basu, Asit Prakas *statistician*
Beem, John Kelly *mathematician, educator*
†Casazza, Peter George *mathematician, educator*
Schrader, Keith William *mathematician*
Shang, Yi *computer scientist, educator*
Sun, Ron *computer scientist, cognitive scientist*

Concordia
Bockelman, Melvin F. *retired computer scientist, writer*

Ferguson
†Pescarino, Richard Angelo *mathematician, educator*

Hillsboro
†Meyers, Beverly Anne *mathematician, educator*
Stinson, Stanley Thomas *project manager*

Independence
Peake, Candice K. Loper *data processing professional*

Joplin
†Cassens, Patrick *mathematician, educator*

Kansas City
†Menning, Melissa Christine *mathematics educator*
Noe, James Kirby *computer consultant*
Van Dyne, Michele Miley *information engineer*

Maryville
†Sadek, Jawad *mathematics educator*

O Fallon
Raeuchle, John Steven *software engineer*

Rolla
Grimm, Louis John *mathematician, educator*
Le, Vy K. *mathematician, educator*
Madria, Sanjay *computer scientist, educator*
Zobrist, George Winston *computer scientist, educator*

Saint Louis
Baernstein, Albert, II, *mathematician, educator*
Boothby, William Munger *mathematics educator*
Cawns, Albert Edward *computer systems consultant*
Chakraborty, Uday Kumar *computer scientist, educator*
Freese, Raymond William *mathematics educator*
Haskins, James Leslie *mathematics educator*
Pollack, Seymour Victor *computer science educator*
Pope, Mark L. *counseling psychologist, educator*
Thompson, Mary Roberta *computer consultant*
Wilson, Edward Nathan *mathematician, educator*

Springfield
Robertson, Ruth Ann *systems analyst, engineer*

Trenton
Pushkarsky, Louis Paul *retired mathematics educator*

MONTANA

Billings
Chen, Yenn-Kunn Oliver *mathematician, educator*

Bozeman
Barrett, Louis C. *mathematician, educator*
†Pernarowski, Mark *mathematician, educator*

Missoula
†Wilson, Jane A. *mathematician, educator*

NEBRASKA

Kearney
Fredrickson, Scott Alfred *instructional technology educator, consultant*

Lincoln
†Harris, Bernard *statistician, mathematician, educator*

Omaha
†Jiang, Hong *information scientist*
Wilhelmi, Cynthia Joy *information technology professional, consultant*

NEVADA

Ely
Daniels, Frank Emmett *mathematician, educator*

Incline Village
Bixby, Robert Eugene *computer, mathematics educator*

Las Vegas
Blattner, Meera McCuaig *computer science educator*
Lima, Donald Roger *retired computer programmer*
Matovina, Jim *mathematician, educator*

Reno
Kleinfeld, Erwin *mathematician, educator*
Kozubowski, Tomasz J. *mathematics and statistics educator, researcher*

Yerington
Price, Thomas Munro *computer consultant*

NEW HAMPSHIRE

Broad Brook
Johnston, Robert Everett *information management executive*

Durham
Appel, Kenneth I. *mathematician, educator*

Hanover
Baumgartner, James Earl *mathematics educator*
Kurtz, Thomas Eugene *mathematics educator*
Lamperti, John Williams *mathematician, educator*
†Stemkoski, Lee John *mathematician*

Peterborough
Mason, Robert Marion *mathematician, musician*

NEW JERSEY

Berlin
†Sabato, Mary Louise *mathematician, educator*

Chatham
Frommer, Ann *systems analyst*
White, Benjamin Steven *mathematician, researcher*

Clifton
Minkoff, John *applied mathematics, signal processing, and engineering educator*

Cresskill
Jurasek, John Paul *mathematics educator, counselor*

East Hanover
†Georgieva, Anna Vladimirova *mathematician*

Edison
Doherty, Patricia Ann *computer systems analyst*
†Miniere, Michael Anthony *mathematician, educator*

Elizabeth
†Daley, Todd Maurice *mathematics educator*

Englewood Cliffs
Wernick, Edward Raymond *computer company executive*

Florham Park
Goguen, Healfdene Hrothgar *computer scientist, consultant*
Rabinovich, Michael *computer scientist*
Shor, Peter W. *mathematician, researcher*

Fort Monmouth
Leciston, David John *computer scientist*

Highlands
Dann, Emily *mathematics educator*

Hoboken
†Lenci, Marco *mathematician, educator*

Jersey City
Poiani, Eileen Louise *mathematics educator, college administrator, higher education planner*

Kenilworth
†Abreu, Paula Cristina *statistician, researcher*

Lakewood
Houle, Joseph E. *mathematics educator*

Lodi
†Armington, Thomas C. *mathematician, educator*

Madison
Van Wyk, Christopher John *computer science educator*

Maplewood
Slepian, David *mathematician, communications engineer*

Matawan
†Campbell, Earl Duncan *computer consultant*
Rivera-Dominguez, Alberto *mathematics educator, mechanical engineer*

Middletown
†Kogan, Yaakov *mathematician, researcher*
Orost, Joseph Martin *computer scientist*

Morristown
Reiley, T. Phillip *consultant*

Mount Laurel
†Huttner, Louise Ann *mathematician, educator*

Murray Hill
Weiss, Alan Arthur *mathematician, researcher*

Neshanic Station
Muckenhoupt, Benjamin *retired mathematics educator*

New Brunswick
Allender, Eric Warren *computer science educator*
†Bahri, Abbas *mathematician, educator*
†Jagerman, David Lewis *mathematician*
†Kruskal, Martin David *mathematical physicist, astrophysicist*
Kulikowski, Casimir Alexander *computer science and engineering educator*
Saracevic, Tefko *information science educator*
Scanlon, Jane Cronin *mathematics educator*
Strawderman, William E. *statistics educator*
†Weibel, Charles Alexander *mathematician*

New Providence
Freund, Roland Wilhelm *mathematician*

Newark
†Barannyk, Lyudmyla Leonidivna *mathematician, educator, researcher*
Blackmore, Denis Louis *mathematics educator, researcher*
†Kappraff, Jay Marvin *mathematics educator*
Miura, Robert Mitsuru *mathematician, researcher, educator*
†Nakayama, Marvin K. *computer scientist, educator*
†Shih, Frank Yeong-Chyang *computer scientist, researcher*

North Arlington
Benedetto, Lorraine Ann *computer scientist*

Oradell
Tong, Hing *mathematician, educator*

Piscataway
Lepowsky, James *mathematician, educator*
Osofsky, Barbara Langer *mathematician, educator*
Taft, Earl Jay *mathematics educator*
Wu, Tsong-Ho *operations researcher*

Pomona
†Iyer, Renganathan Ganesan *mathematician*

Princeton
Chazelle, Bernard *computer science educator*
Deligne, Pierre René *mathematician*
Gear, Charles William *computer scientist*
Griffiths, Phillip A. *mathematician, academic administrator*
Gunning, Robert Clifford *mathematician, educator*
Haberman, Shelby Joel *statistician, educator*
†Khutoryansky, Naum M. *mathematician, educator*
Kohn, Joseph John *mathematician, educator*
Langlands, Robert Phelan *mathematician, educator*
Lee, Ruby Bei-Loh *multimedia and computer systems architect*
Levin, Simon Asher *mathematician, ecologist, educator*
Lipschutz-Yevick, Miriam Amalie *mathematician*
MacPherson, Robert Duncan *mathematician, educator*
Mihram, George Arthur *mathematician*
Nash, John Forbes, Jr., *research mathematician*
†Seymour, Paul Douglas *mathematician, educator*
†Sinharay, Sandip *statistician, researcher*
Tinker, Michael *technical researcher*

Princeton Junction
†Wu, Huan-ter *statistician*

Ridgefield Park
Litwinowicz, Anthony *information specialist, researcher*

Rivervale
Posamentier, Alfred Steven *mathematics educator, university administrator*

Rockaway
Spencer, Carol Anne *computer systems analyst*

Short Hills
†Ng, Jennifer *statistician*

Somerset
Becker, Phyllis *systems analyst*

Teaneck
Zwass, Vladimir *information systems educator*

Tinton Falls
†Westerman, H. Robert *systems analyst*

Union
†Emanouilidis, Emanuel V. *computer scientist, educator*

Weehawken
†Metallo, Frances Rosebell *mathematics educator*

West Orange
†Ko, Chia-Wen *biostatistician, researcher*
†Sharon, Jay H. *systems analyst*

Westwood
Badalamenti, Anthony Francis *mathematician, researcher*

Whippany
Rajkumar, Ajay *computer scientist, consultant*

Willingboro
Ingerman, Peter Zilahy *systems analyst, consultant*

Yardville
Zweig, Steven Frederick *statistician*

NEW MEXICO

Albuquerque
Bell, Stoughton *computer scientist, mathematician, educator*
Christensen, Ronald *statistician, educator*
†Huzurbazar, Aparna V. *statistician*
Ihde, Mary Katherine *retired mathematics educator*
Ingham, Kenneth LeRoy, III, *systems programmer, consultant*
Krostag, Diane Theresa Michaels *clinical informatics analyst*

Farmington
Doig, Beverly Irene *retired systems specialist*

Gallup
Smarandache, Florentin *mathematics researcher, writer*

Las Cruces
Adams, J. Mack *computer science educator*
Bustamante, Donald D. *information systems administrator, consultant*

Los Lunas
†Robinson, Mary Reid *mathematics educator*

Santa Fe
Kellner, Richard George *mathematician, computer scientist*

NEW YORK

Albany
†Craigue, Leslie J. *systems analyst*
Murray, Neil Vincent *computer science educator*
Rosenkrantz, Daniel J. *computer science educator*
Wilson, Brian Eugene *computer scientist*

Alfred
Torpey, Robin Lee *information scientist, educator*

Amherst
†Lawvere, Francis William *mathematician, educator*

Annandale On Hudson
Thomas, Sarah Rebecca *computer science educator*

Aurora
Shilepsky, Arnold Charles *mathematics educator, computer consultant*

Binghamton
Beck, Matthias *mathematician, educator*
Geer, James Francis *mathematics educator*
Hilton, Peter John *mathematician, educator*
Klir, George Jiri *systems science educator*
Zaslavsky, Thomas *mathematics educator*
Zhang, Zhongfei *computer science educator, researcher, consultant*

Bluff Point
Fitch, Linda Bauman *educator*

Brockport
Michaels, John G. *mathematics educator*

Bronx
Farley, Rosemary Carroll *mathematics and computer science educator*
†Fitting, Melvin Chris *computer scientist, educator*
Koranyi, Adam *mathematics educator*
Rose, Israel Harold *mathematics educator*
Seltzer, William *statistician, social researcher, former international organization director*

Bronxville
Ventriglia, Anthony Emilo *mathematics educator*

Brooklyn
Hilsenrath, Joel Alan *computer scientist, entreprenuer*
†Lieberman, Burton Barnet *mathematics educator*
Lutwak, Erwin *mathematician, educator*
Menil, Violeta Cruz *mathematician, educator, mathematician, consultant*
†Paliogiannis, Fotios Constantine *mathematician, educator*
Pennisten, John William *computer scientist, linguist, actuary*
Weill, Georges Gustave *mathematics educator*

Brookville
Berresford, Geoffrey Case *mathematics educator*

Buffalo
Bross, Irwin Dudley Jackson *biostatistician*
Coburn, Lewis Alan *mathematics educator*
Goodberry, Diane Jean (Diane Oberkircher) *mathematics educator, tax accountant*
Halavais, Alexander Michael Campbell *information scientist, educator*
Hauptman, Herbert Aaron *mathematician, educator, researcher*
He, Xin *computer scientist, educator*
Ho, Alex Wing-keung *statistician*
Huard, James Gerald *mathematician, educator*
Penniman, W. David *information scientist, educator, consultant*
Priore, Roger L. *biostatistics educator, consultant*
Seitz, Mary Lee *mathematics educator*
Shapiro, Stuart Charles *computer scientist, educator*
Wiesenberg, Russel John *statistician*

Corning
Neubauer, Dean Veral *statistician*

Dix Hills
Blumstein, Reneé J. *research and statistical consultant*
Guram, Gurpal Singh *mathematician, educator*

Endwell
Thesier, Leslie Ann Eisen *computer programmer, mathematician*

Flushing
†Kao, Hui-Sheng *mathematics educator*
Mendelson, Elliott *mathematician, educator*

Forest Hills
Gebaide, Stephen Elliot *retired mathematics and computer science educator*

Geneseo
†Haddad, Caroline N. *mathematics educator, researcher*
†Lin, Rong *computer scientist, educator*

Great Neck
Schussheim, Joan Lana *mathematics educator*

Hamburg
O'Day, John Ignatius *retired computer science educator*

Hamilton
Tucker, Thomas William *mathematics professor*

Hawthorne
†Banikazemi, Mohammad *computer scientist, researcher*
Chen, Shyh-Kwei *computer scientist, researcher*
†Dan, Asit *computer scientist, research scientist*

Hempstead
†Greenwell, Raymond N. *mathematician, educator, writer*

Hicksville
O'Connor, Ann Ruth *information systems educator*

Ithaca
Conway, Richard Walter *computer scientist, educator*
Dynkin, Eugene B. *mathematics educator*
Earle, Clifford John, Jr., *mathematician*
Elber, Ron *computer science educator*
Hartmanis, Juris *computer scientist, educator*
Hopcroft, John Edward *computer scientist*
Morgenstern, Matthew *computer scientist*
Nerode, Anil *mathematician, educator*
Shore, Richard Arnold *mathematics educator*
†Taimina, Daina *mathematician, educator*
†Todd, Michael Jeremy *mathematician, educator, researcher*
Trotter, Leslie Earl *operations research educator, consultant*

Kenmore
Kenny, John Edward *computer analyst*

Kingston
Shaffer, Sheila Weekes *mathematics educator*

Liverpool
Allen, David Charles *computer science educator*

Long Island City
Rothenhaus, Robert Charles *mathematics educator*

Massapequa
Batt, Alyse Schwartz *technical officer*

New Paltz
Li, Keqin *computer scientist, educator*

New York
†Agwu, Nkechi Madonna *mathematics educator*
†Anderson, Dennis *computer scientist information technology educator*
Aschoff, Lawrence Michael (Mick Aschoff) *computer information scientist*
Banino, Christopher C. *information technology administrator*
†Barquero, Pedro Benjamin *mathematician, researcher*
†Chachanidze-Margolin, Lia Leon *mathematician, educator, physicist, researcher*
Chichilnisky, Graciela *mathematician, economist, writer, educator, writer*
Christ, Lily Esther Shih *mathematics educator*
Derman, Cyrus *mathematical statistician*
Dobelis, Miervaldis Christian *systems designer*
Edwards, Harold Mortimer *mathematics educator*
Feiner, Steven Keith *computer science educator, consultant, lecturer*
Finch, Lawrence Nelson, II, *computer scientist, consultant*
Frankel, Martin Richard *statistician, educator, consultant*
Gardella, Francis John *mathematics educator*
†Garritano, Joseph A. *information scientist*
†Gomory, Ralph Edward *mathematician, manufacturing company executive, foundation executive*
Gross, Jonathan Light *computer scientist, mathematician, educator*
Habib, Ibrahim Wahby *computer networks engineer, educator, consultant*
Hauben, Ronda Joan *researcher, writer, scholar*
†Katti, Shriniwas K. *retired statistician, consultant*
Kavalerchik, Boris Yakovlevich *information technology developer, researcher*
Kurnow, Ernest *statistician, educator*
Lax, Peter David *mathematician, educator*
Lipan, Howard Kenneth *information and technology consultant*
†Lo, Shaw-Hwa *statistician, educator*
McMillan, Marilyn Ayres *information systems scientist, university official*
Morawetz, Cathleen Synge *mathematician*
†Moskowitz, Martin A. *mathematician, educator*
Moyne, John Abel *computer scientist, linguist, educator*
Negoita, Constantin Virgil *computer scientist, educator*
Nirenberg, Louis *mathematician, educator*
†Paik, Myunghee Cho *statistician, educator*
†Peshansky, Alexandre *computer specialist*
†Pierre, Dwight Anthony *mathematician, educator*
†Preiss, Mitchell Paul *mathematics educator*
Sarkar, Indra Neil *medical informatician*
Saul, Mark E. *mathematics educator, consultant*
Schank, Roger Carl *computer science and psychology educator*
Sellers, Peter Hoadley *mathematician, educator*
Sohmer, Bernard *mathematics educator, administrator*
Taylor, Jean Ellen *mathematics researcher and educator*
†Teixeira, Klement *mathematician, educator*
Traub, J(oseph) F(rederick) *computer scientist, educator*
Vosburg, Suzanne K. *research scientist*
Werschulz, Arthur Gustav *computer and information sciences educator*
Widlund, Olof Bertil *computer science educator*

New York Mills
Blank, William Russell *mathematics educator*

Nyack
McMahon, Donald J. *statistician, consultant*

Orangeburg
†Lin, Shang Ping *statistician, researcher*

Pittsford
Hollingsworth, Jack Waring *mathematics and computer science educator*

Poughkeepsie
†Basener, Richard Francis Joseph *mathematician, application developer*

Rhinebeck
Hellerman, Leo *retired computer scientist and mathematician*
Scherr, Allan Lee *computer scientist, executive, consultant*

Riverdale
†Bencsáth, Katalin A. *mathematician*

Rochester
Angel, Allen Robert *mathematics educator, author, consultant*
†Hall, William Jackson *statistician, educator*
Jackson, J. Edward *retired statistician*
McNamara, Timothy James *mathematics educator*
Oakes, David *statistician*
Raimi, Ralph Alexis *mathematics educator*
Simon, William *biomathematician, educator*
Wolf, Walter Alan *computer science educator*
†Zhao, Hongwei *biostatistician*

Sleepy Hollow
Maun, Mary Ellen *computer consultant*

Southampton
Melter, Robert Alan *mathematics educator, researcher*

Staten Island
Shullich, Robert Harlan *systems analyst*
†Uttaro, Thomas Edward *information officer, statistician*

Stillwater
†O'Connor, Abigail Elizabeth *mathematician, educator, science educator*

Stony Brook
Anderson, Michael Thomas *mathematics researcher, educator*
Chen, John J. *biostatistician, educator*
Dolezal, Vaclav Jan *retired mathematician, educator*
Glimm, James Gilbert *mathematician, educator*
Laspina, Peter Joseph *computer resource educator*
Lawson, H(erbert) Blaine, Jr., *mathematician, educator*

Michelsohn, Marie-Louise *mathematician, educator*
Tewarson, Reginald Prabhakar *retired mathematics educator, consultant*
Tucker, Alan Curtiss *mathematics educator*
Yang, Yuanyuan *computer science and electrical engineer, educator*

Syracuse
Basta, Carlo R. *information systems specialist, consultant*
Graver, Jack Edward *mathematics educator*
Hansen, Per Brinch *computer scientist, researcher*
†Hsu, Lifang *statistician, department chairman*
Pardee, Otway O'Meara *computer science educator*
Romeu, Jorge Luis *mathematics educator, writer*
Sheehe, Paul Robert *statistician, educator, biologist*
Tanner, Jane *mathematics educator*

Troy
Chi, Benjamin E. *computer network executive*
Szymanski, Boleslaw Karol *computer scientist, educator, entrepreneur*

Wallkill
Bittner, Ronald Joseph *computer systems analyst, magician*

West Hempstead
Guggenheimer, Heinrich Walter *mathematician, educator*

Westbury
Sandler, Gerald Howard *computer science educator, company executive*

White Plains
Chen, Shuang *computer science professional*
†Heo, Moonseong *statistician, researcher*
Machover, Carl *computer graphics consultant*

Williamsville
Berner, Robert Frank *managerial statistics educator, administrator*
Brown, Stephen Ira *philosophy educator*

Yonkers
Goon, Gilbert *software consultant*

Yorktown Heights
Auslander, Marc Alan *computer scientist*
d'Heurle, François Max *research scientist, engineering executive*
Hoffman, Alan Jerome *mathematician, educator*
†Lei, Hui *computer scientist*
Puri, Ruchir *operations research specialist*
Rigoutsos, Isidore *computer scientist*
Saon, George A. *computer scientist, researcher*
Verma, Dinesh Chandra *computer science researcher, writer*
Winograd, Shmuel *mathematician*

NORTH CAROLINA

Archdale
†O'Hara, Karen Ann *mathematician, educator*

Asheville
Codd, Richard Trent, Jr., *computer scientist, educator*

Cape Carteret
Mullikin, Thomas Wilson *mathematics educator*

Chapel Hill
†Assani, Idris *mathematician, educator*
Brooks, Frederick Phillips, Jr., *computer scientist, educator*
Brown, Keith John *computer applications analyst*
Coulter, Elizabeth Jackson *biostatistician, educator*

Charlotte
Dai, Xingde *mathematics educator*
Kawczak, Janusz *mathematician, educator*
Ras, Zbigniew Wieslaw *computer science educator*

Cullowhee
Willis, Ralph Houston *mathematics educator*

Davidson
Swallow, John *mathematician, educator*

Durham
Lavery, John Edward *mathematician*
Reif, John Henry *computer science educator*
Rose, Donald James *computer science educator*

Elizabeth City
†Manglik, Vinod Prakash *statistician, consultant, educator*

Fort Bragg
†Swain, Jeffery Alvin *systems analyst*

Greensboro
Blanchet-Sadri, Francine *mathematician, educator*
Kurepa, Alexandra *mathematics educator*

Raleigh
†Bakalov, Bojko *mathematician*
Chou, Wushow *computer scientist, educator*
Fabrizio, Louis Michael *educator*
Ghosh, Sujit Kumar *statistics educator, researcher*
†Jing, Naihuan N. *mathematician*
Nelson, Larry A. *statistics educator, consultant*
†Weir, Bruce Spencer *statistician, educator, geneticist*

Research Triangle Park
†Krishen, Alok *biostatistician*

Salisbury
†Sullivan, Sharon Lee *mathematician, educator*

Southport
Johnston, Dennis Roy *computer systems integrator*

Statesville
Schinck, Amelie G. *mathematician, educator*

West Jefferson
Merrion, Arthur Benjamin *mathematics educator, tree farmer*

NORTH DAKOTA

Fargo
†Coykendall, James B. *mathematician*

OHIO

Ada
Boyadzhiev, Khristo Nonev *mathematician, educator, researcher*

Akron
Wortham, James Calvin *retired mathematics educator*

Athens
Arhangel'skii, Alexander Vladimirovich *mathematician, researcher*
Wen, Shih-Liang *mathematics educator*

Berea
Little, Richard Allen *mathematics and computer science educator*

Bowling Green
Newman, Elsie Louise *mathematics educator*

Brookpark
Cotton, Barbara Jean *systems analyst*

Canton
†Kasturiarachi, Aloysius Bathi *mathematician, educator, mathematician, researcher*

Cincinnati
†Dumas, H. Scott *mathematician*
Flick, Thomas Michael *mathematics educator, educational administrator*
†Groetsch, Charles William *mathematics educator*
Semon, Warren Lloyd *retired computer sciences educator*
Succop, Paul Allan *biostatistics educator, consultant*
Wilsey, Philip Arthur *computer science educator*

Cleveland
Cirincione, Ross Joseph *mathematician, educator*
Clark, Robert Arthur *mathematician, educator*
Flynn, James O'Donnell *statistician, educator*
Goffman, William *mathematician, educator*
Lyytinen, Kalle Juhani *computer scientist, educator*
Robinson, Stewart Marshall *mathematician, educator*
Szarek, Stanislaw Jerzy *mathematics educator*
Waren, Allan David *computer information scientist, educator*
Woycyznski, Wojbor Andrzej *mathematician, educator*

Columbus
Chandrasekaran, Balakrishnan *computer and information science educator*
Dull, Clifford John *religious groups analyst*
Friedman, Avner *mathematician, educator*
†Kang, Soon-Yi *mathematician, educator*
Kindig, Fred Eugene Eugene *statistics educator, arbitrator*
†Minor, Darrell P. *mathematician, educator*
†Morris, Theodore Allan *information scientist, educator*
Muller, Mervin Edgar *computer scientist, statistician, educator*
†Nandor, Mark J. *mathematician, educator*
†Wang, Deliang *computer scientist, educator*
Zweben, Stuart Harvey *information scientist, educator*

Dayton
Chung, Soon Myoung *computer scientist, educator*
Garcia, Oscar Nicolas *computer science educator*
Khalimsky, Efim *mathematics and computer science educator*
Mandrell, Gene Douglas *retired management consultant*
Rucker, Richard S. *information systems executive*
Staker, Robert Dale *cost analyst, computer scientist, biologist, educator*
†Tian, Mei *mathematician, educator*

Granville
Bonar, Daniel Donald *mathematics educator*

Grove City
Kimethu, Susan Wanja *computer specialist, database manager*

Hamilton
†Pollack, Frederic S. *mathematician, educator*

Kent
†Bansal, Arvind Kumar *computer scientist, educator*
Kluth, Frederick John *computer consultant, artist*
†Reed, Beverly Marie *mathematician, educator*
Varga, Richard Steven *mathematics educator*

Kirtland
†Armstrong, William Allen *mathematician, educator, textbook writer*

Lakeside Marblehead
Garrow, Robert Joseph, Jr., *mathematician, educator*

Loveland
Paul, Jerome L. *mathematician, educator*

Mansfield
Gregory, Thomas Bradford *mathematics educator*

Miamisburg
Irizarry, Francisco Armando *information systems executive, lawyer*

Newark
Gartner, Daniel Lee *computer information executive*

Oxford
Moore, Frank William *computer science educator, pianist*

Shaker Heights
Switzer, Brian Carl *strategic information systems designer*

Stow
Hollis, William Frederick *information scientist*

Vermilion
Vance, Elbridge Putnam *mathematics educator*

Wilberforce
Hargraves, William Frederick, II, *mathematics and computer science educator*

Wooster
†Geiser, Robert Neil *computer scientist*
Hales, Raleigh Stanton, Jr., *mathematics educator, academic administrator*
†Pierce, Pamela Bitler *mathematics educator*

Youngstown
†Smotzer, Thomas David *mathematician*
Yozwiak, Bernard James *retired mathematics educator and academic administrator*

OKLAHOMA

Alva
†Marlin, Benjamin Arthur *mathematician, researcher, computer scientist, educator*

Edmond
Loman, Mary LaVerne *retired mathematics educator*

Norman
Bethel, Joann D. *computer programmer, analyst*
Kim, Changwook *computer science educator*
Lakshmivarahan, Sivaramakrishnan *computer science educator*
Provine, Lorraine *retired mathematics educator*

Oklahoma City
Philipp, Anita Marie *computer sciences educator*
Tang, Irving Che-hong *mathematician, educator*

Stillwater
†Gunzenhauser, Michael Gerard *mathematician, educator*
†Payton, Mark Edward *statistician, educator*

Tahlequah
†Diamantopoulos, John C.D. *mathematician, educator*

Tulsa
†Dimiceli, Vincent Edward *mathematician, educator*
†Lang, Andrew Stuart Ian Donald *mathematician, consultant*
†Sowell, Debra Ann Olson *mathematician, educator, academic administrator*

OREGON

Beaverton
Davis, Stanford Melvin *engineering executive, internet consultant*
Thompson, Greg Alan *computer sciences consulting executive*

Corvallis
Parks, Harold Raymond *mathematician, educator*
†Qu, Annie *statistician, educator*
Shiue, Wen-Tsong *electrical and computer scientist, educator*
Tenca, Alexandre Ferreira *computer scientist, electrical engineer*

Eugene
Andrews, Fred Charles *mathematics educator*
Curtis, Charles W. *mathematician, writer*
†Isenberg, James Allen *mathematics and physics researcher, educator*
Kennevan, Walter James *computer science educator*
Tresham, Aaron Keith *mathematician*

Forest Grove
†Boardman, Michael *mathematician, educator*

Hillsboro
Daim, Tugrul Unsal *technology management specialist, educator*
Pixley, Carl Preston *mathematician*

Oregon City
†Baratto, Stefan *mathematics educator*

Portland
Ahuja, Jagdish Chand *mathematics educator*
†Daescu, Dacian N. *mathematics educator*
Hall, Howard Pickering *engineering and mathematics educator*
Lambert, Richard William *mathematics educator*

Salem
Struble, George Waring *computer science educator*

Sherwood
Forcier, Richard Charles *information technology educator, computer applications consultant*

Tualatin
Brown, Robert Wallace *retired mathematics educator*

PENNSYLVANIA

Abington
Ayoub, Ayoub Barsoum *mathematician, educator*

Allentown
Russell, Alan Harold *computer specialist, educator*

Aston
DiMarco, David *mathematician, educator*

Bethlehem
Bieri, Barbara Normile *systems analyst, consultant*
Ghosh, Bhaskar Kumar *statistics educator, researcher*
Rivlin, Ronald Samuel *mathematics educator emeritus*
Schattschneider, Doris Jean *mathematics educator*
Schiesser, William E. *mathematician, researcher*

Blue Bell
Halas, Cynthia Ann *business information specialist*

Bradford
†Slimick, John Charles *computer science educator*

Bridgeville
Allen, David Woodroffe *computer scientist*

Bryn Mawr
Ackoff, Russell Lincoln *systems sciences educator*
Goldstine, Herman Heine *mathematician, association executive*

Center Valley
†Wisniewski, Daniel Patrick *mathematics educator*

Clarion
Carbone, Rose Elaine *mathematics educator*

Coatesville
Burton, Mary Louise Himes *computer specialist*

Coraopolis
Skovira, Robert Joseph *information scientist, educator*

Doylestown
†Wachtel, Howard K. *mathematics, educator*

Easton
Traldi, Lorenzo *mathematician, educator*

Fort Washington
†Chao, Georgia *biostatistician*

Hershey
King, Carolyn Marie *mathematics educator*

Indiana
†Shim, Leem Seop *computer scinetist, educator, researcher*

Johnstown
†Ferencak, Michael Neill *mathematician, educator*

Kennett Square
†Whitlock, Herbert Ian *systems analyst*

King Of Prussia
†Yan, Ying *statistician, researcher*

Marion Center
Bomboy, John David *mathematics educator*

Meadville
Cable, Charles Allen *mathematician*

Mechanicsburg
Harper, Diane Marie *retired communications retailer*
Nattress, Debra Lynn *computer systems analyst*

Monroeville
Bowlden, Henry James *computer science consultant*

Philadelphia
Banerji, Ranan Bihari *mathematics and computer science educator*
Collons, Rodger Duane *decision sciences educator*
†Conrad, Bruce Phillips *mathematics educator*
Cowles, Roger E. *computer consultant*
de Cani, John Stapley *statistician, educator*
†Fernholz, Luisa Turrin *statistician, educator*

Freyd, Peter John *mathematician, computer scientist, educator*
Garfield, Eugene *information scientist, author, publisher*
Iglewicz, Boris *statistician, educator*
Kadison, Richard Vincent *mathematician, educator*
Knopp, Marvin Isadore *mathematics educator*
Manas, Gerald Bennett *systems analyst, consultant, information technology manager*
Mode, Charles J. *mathematician, educator*
Porter, Gerald Joseph *mathematician, educator*
†Ratcliffe, Sarah Jane *biostatistician*
Roth, Marilyn Dorothy *information scientist*
Scedrov, Andre *mathematics and computer science researcher, educator*
Shatz, Stephen Sidney *mathematician, educator*
Smith, Woollcott *statistician, educator*
†Szyld, Daniel Benjamin *mathematician, educator*
Warner, Frank Wilson, III, *mathematics educator*
Zietz, Stanley *mathematics educator*

Phoenixville
Koenig, Michael Edward Davison *information science educator*

Pittsburgh
Balas, Egon *applied mathematician, educator*
†Bocea, Marian *mathematician*
Carbo, Toni (Toni Carbo Bearman) *information scientist, educator*
Chrysanthis, Panos Kypros *computer science educator, researcher*
Dannenberg, Roger Berry *computer scientist*
Druzdzel, Marek Jozef *researcher and educator*
Duncan, George Thomas *statistician, educator*
Fienberg, Stephen Elliott *statistician*
Gurtin, Morton Edward *mathematics educator*
†Houck, Patricia Rose *statistician, researcher*
†Joshi, James Bikram Dhoj *information scientist, educator*
Kadane, Joseph B. *statistics educator*
†Kemerer, Chris F. *information scientist, educator*
Lehoczky, John Paul *statistics educator*
†Moiseev, Igor Valentinovich *information scientist*
†Noll, Walter *mathematics educator*
Schäffer, Juan Jorge *mathematics educator*
Shaw, Mary M. *computer science educator*
Zamboni, Beth Ann *statistician, educator*

Reading
Rochowicz, John Anthony, Jr., *mathematician, mathematics and physics educator*

Rydal
Bacon, George Hughes, Jr., *retired systems analyst*

Schnecksville
†Schillow, Ned William *mathematics educator*

Swarthmore
Kelemen, Charles F. *computer science educator*

Tobyhanna
Lapidus, Arnold *mathematician, educator*

Trevose
Satz, Ronald Wayne *systems engineer, consultant*

University Park
Andrews, George Eyre *mathematics educator*
Antle, Charles Edward *statistics educator*
Barlow, Jesse Louis *computer scientist, educator*
Wang, James Ze *computer scientist, educator*
†Waterhouse, William Charles *mathematics educator*

Vandergrift
Kulick, Richard John *computer scientist, researcher*

Villanova
Beck, Robert Edward *computer scientist, educator*
Norton, Douglas Evatt *mathematician, educator*
Scheffler, Barbara Jane *statistician, business executive*

Wallingford
Morrison, Donald Franklin *statistician, educator*

Washington
Forrest, Robert Gilliland *mathematics educator*

Willow Grove
†Levin, Joshua Zev *computer scientist, consultant*

RHODE ISLAND

Kingston
†Beauregard, Raymond A. *mathematician, educator*

Providence
Beckmann, Martin Joseph *retired economics educator*
Dafermos, Constantine Michael *applied mathematics educator*
Davis, Philip J. *mathematician*
Ewing, John Harwood *mathematics educator*
Fleming, Wendell Helms *mathematician, educator*
Freiberger, Walter Frederick *mathematics educator, actuarial science consultant, educator*
Gottschalk, Walter Helbig *mathematician, educator*
Hesthaven, Jan Sickmann *mathematician, educator*
Intrator, Orna *statistician, educator, health services researcher*
Kushner, Harold Joseph *mathematics educator*
Savage, John Edmund *computer science educator, researcher*
Shu, Chi-Wang *mathematics educator, researcher*
Silverman, Joseph Hillel *mathematics educator*

SOUTH CAROLINA

Aiken
Li, Rao *mathematician, computer scientist*

Charleston
†Agrest, Emmanuil M. *mathematician, physicist, educator*
Chen, Mei-Qin *mathematics educator*
Huang, Peng *statistician*
Tilley, Barbara *statistician, consultant*

Clemson
†Brawley, Joel Vincent *mathematician, educator*
†Kostreva, Michael Martin *mathematics educator*

Columbia
Eastman, Caroline Merriam *computer science and engineering educator*

Johns Island
Richbart, Carolyn Mae *mathematics educator*

Mount Pleasant
Lupo, David Emory *computer scientist*

Orangeburg
†Bozinovski, Stevo *computer science educator, researcher*
Champy, William, Jr., *mathematician, educator, researcher, scientist, writer, biologist, chemist, inventor, physicist*
†Viswanath, Guttalu Ramachandra Rao *mathematics educator, consultant, researcher*

Pendleton
†Marshall, Gerald Lee *mathematician, educator*

Spartanburg
Codespoti, Daniel Joseph *computer science educator*
Hilton, Theodore Craig *computer scientist, Internet company executive*

Sullivans Island
Robb, Nathaniel Heyward, Jr., *retired remote sensing company executive*

Summerville
Diamond, Michael Shawn *science and math educator, computer consultant*

SOUTH DAKOTA

Aberdeen
Markanda, Raj Kumar *mathematics educator*

Vermillion
†Lio, Yuhlong *mathematician, educator*

TENNESSEE

Brownsville
Kalin, Robert *retired mathematics educator*

Chattanooga
†Banasiak, Mayme Kay Hampton *mathematician, educator*
Johnson, Joseph Erle *mathematician*
†Kennedy, Daniel *mathematics educator*

Collegedale
†Moore, Robert Crumley *mathematician, educator*

Cookeville
†Ramaswamy, Srini *computer science educator, software consultant*

Johnson City
Pumariega, JoAnne Buttacavoli *mathematics educator*

Knoxville
Anderson, David Fenimore *mathematics educator*
Dongarra, Jack *mathematician, educator*
Lenhart, Suzanne Marie *mathematician, educator*
†Schaefer, Philip William *mathematics educator, researcher*

Martin
Petty, James Alan *mathematics educator, consultant*

Memphis
Franklin, Stanley Phillip *computer scientist, cognitive scientist, mathematician, educator*
Goldstein, Jerome Arthur *mathematics educator*
Schelp, Richard Herbert *mathematics educator*

Murfreesboro
†Bloomer, Lisa A. *mathematician, educator*

Nashville
Beauchamp, John Jones *mathematician, educator*
†Cooil, Bruce Kimo *mathematical statistician, statistics educator*
Dupont, William Dudley *biostatistician, educator*
Fischer, Patrick Carl *computer scientist, retired educator*
Jonsson, Bjarni *mathematician, educator*
McCowan, Otis Blakely *mathematics educator*
†Pinter, Mike *mathematician, educator*
Williams, Marsha Rhea *computer scientist, educator, researcher, consultant*

Oak Ridge
†Hartley, Dean S., III, *operations research specialist*
Raridon, Richard Jay *computer specialist*

TEXAS

Abilene
Retzer, Kenneth Albert *mathematics educator, entrepreneur*

Arlington
Corduneanu, Constantin C. *mathematician, educator*
Greenspan, Donald *mathematician, educator*
Han, Chien-Pai *statistics educator*
†Kojouharov, Hristo Venelinov *mathematician, educator, mathematician, researcher*
Simon, Hank *information science executive*

Austin
Clark, Charles T(aliferro) *retired business statistics educator*
Crane, Gary Wade *mathematician, physicist*
Garner, Harvey Louis *computer scientist, consultant, electrical engineering educator*
Gillman, Leonard *mathematician, educator*
Jones, William Richard *database administrator*
Lam, Simon Shin-Sing *computer science educator*
Moyers, Robert Charles *systems analyst, state official, microcomputer consultant, government systems developer*
Novak, Gordon S., Jr., *computer scientist, educator*
Seifoullaev, Roustam Kafar *mathematician, programmer*
†Sun, Shuyu *mathematician, chemical engineer, petroleum engineer*
Turney, James Edward *computer scientist*
Williamson, Hugh Jackson *statistician*
Worden, Sue Janine *engineer, scientist*

Beaumont
Chiou, Paul C.J. *statistician, educator*

Brownsville
†Yi, Taeil *mathematician, educator*
†Zdansky, Janice Cecelia *mathematician*

Center
Morris, William Lewis *mathematician*

College Station
Ewing, Richard Edward *mathematics, chemical and petroleum engineering educator*
Parzen, Emanuel *statistical scientist*
†Thomadakis, Michael Evaggelos *computer scientist, educator, computer scientist, researcher*
†Zheng, Qi *statistician, biomathematician*

Cypress
Burghduff, John Brian *mathematics educator*

Dallas
†Ajaev, Vladimir S. *mathematician, educator*
Barr, Richard Stuart *computer science and management science educator*
Chen, Zhangxin John *mathematics educator*
†Humpreys, Natalia Alexandra *mathematician*
Szczesniak, Raymond Albin *systems analyst, researcher*

Denton
Mauldin, Richard Daniel *mathematics educator*
Renka, Robert Joseph *computer science educator, consultant*
Swigger, Kathleen Mary *computer science educator*

Edinburg
†Wu, Xiaodong *computer science educator*

El Paso
Foged, Leslie Owen *mathematician, educator*
Tchoshanov, Mourat Ashirovich *mathematician, educator*
†Youngman, Daryl Ray, Jr., *operations research specialist*

Fort Hood
†Scott, Karen Lou *systems analyst*

Fort Worth
†Browning, Tyson R. *operations research specialist*
Doran, Robert Stuart *mathematician, educator*
†Mohamed, Riad A. *operations research specialist, educator*
Sullenberger, Ara Broocks *mathematics educator*

Galveston
†Robertson, Paul Francis *mathematician, educator*

Houston
†Baker, Denise R. *technical computer educator, consultant*
Freeman, Marjorie Schaefer *mathematician, educator*
Gardner, Everette Shaw, Jr., *information sciences educator, consultant, author*
Glowinski, Roland *mathematics educator*
Golubitsky, Martin Aaron *mathematician, educator*
Hempel, John P. *mathematics educator*
Hoang, Hung Manh *technology advisor*
†Ionascu, Ileana *mathematician, educator*
Johnson, Olin Glynn *computer science educator*
†Kakadiaris, Ioannis *computer science educator*
Liles, Clifton Roy *software designer*
†Ma, Jingjing *mathematician*
†Malley, Wendi Sheree *statistician, researcher*
Miller, Charles Rickie *thermal and fluid systems analyst, engineering manager*
Riedi, Rudolf Hermann *mathematics researcher*
Scott, David Warren *statistics educator*
†Stacks, Thistle N. *mathematician, educator*
Tong, Louis Lik-Fu *information scientist*
Wang, Chao-Cheng *mathematician, engineer*
Woo, Walter *computer systems consultant*
Wright, Clark Phillips *computer systems specialist*

Irving
Anderson, Michael Curtis *computer industry analyst*
Conger, Sue Ann *computer information systems educator*

Kingsville
Cecil, David Rolf *mathematician, educator*
Morey, Philip Stockton, Jr., *mathematics educator*
Schreur, Barbara *computer science educator*

Laredo
Mendiola, Anna Maria G. *mathematics educator*

Lewisville
Ferguson, R. Neil *computer systems consultant*

Lubbock
Conover, William Jay *statistics educator*
†Neusel, Mara Dicle *mathematician, educator*

Manor
Young, William David *computer scientist*

McKinney
†Easttom, Chuck *computer scientist, educator*

Mesquite
Sepulvado, Joseph Michael *computer information scientist*

New Caney
Hayes, Ann Carson *computer services executive*

Odessa
Nickel, James Alvin *mathematician, educator, consultant*

Richardson
†Constantinescu, Tiberiu *mathematician*

Round Rock
Khalid, Humayun *computer scientist, consultant*

San Antonio
Cao, Weiming *mathematician, educator*
Estep, Myrna Lynne *systems analyst, philosophy educator*
†Grosu, Daniel *computer scientist*
Hall, Douglas Lee *computer science educator*
†Le, Dung *mathmatics educator, researcher*

San Marcos
†Keller, Thomas Michael *mathematician, educator*

Temple
Rajab, Mohammad Hasan *biostatistician, educator*

Tyler
†Bailey, Nan Hutchins *mathematician, educator*
Kulkarni, Arun Digambar *computer science educator*

Waco
Henderson, Johnny *mathematician, educator*
Odell, Patrick Lowry *mathematics educator*
Rolf, Howard Leroy *mathematician, educator*
Walbesser, Henry Herman *computer science educator*

Whitehouse
Cavanaugh, Charles Davis *computer scientist, educator*

UTAH

Logan
†Beasley, LeRoy B. *mathematics educator*

Murray
Purdie, Tonya Marie Thomas *school registrar*

Orem
Moore, Hal G. *mathematician, educator*

Provo
Hansen, James Vernon *computer science, information systems educator*
Ivie, Evan Leon *computer science educator*
Jarvis, Tyler J. *mathematician*
†Rencher, Alvin C. *statistician, educator*

Salt Lake City
Horn, Susan Dadakis *statistics educator*
†Johnson, Christopher Ray *medicine, computer science, mathematics, and bioengineering educator*
Tsodikov, Alexander David *biostatistician, educator*

VERMONT

Burlington
†Aleong, John *statistician, educator*
Bernard, Ronald Allan *computer performance analyst*
Haugh, Larry Douglas *statistics educator*
Tourin, Peter Tanny *computer scientist, educator*

Middlebury
†Olinick, Michael *mathematician, educator*

North Bennington
Adler, Irving *mathematician*

Randolph Center
Calter, Paul Arthur *mathematician, educator, writer*

Reading
Barnes, John Gilbert Presslie *computer language designer*

FRANCE

Avignon
De Mori, Renato *computer science educator, researcher*

Paris
Serre, Jean-Pierre *mathematician, scholar*
†Tuckwell, Henry Clavering *mathematician, researcher*
Yuechiming, Roger Yue Yuen Shing *mathematics educator*

GERMANY

Bremen
Wells, Raymond O'Neil, Jr., *mathematics educator, researcher*

Schwerte
Rosenberg, Alex *mathematician, educator*

HUNGARY

Szeged
†Nyúl, László G. *mathematician, educator, researcher*

JAPAN

Ichihara
Kuma, Hisao *information systems educator*

Nara
Kasami, Tadao *information science educator*

Sapporo
Asari, Eikichi *information sciences educator, researcher*

Tokyo
Eto, Hajime *information scientist, educator*

LEBANON

Beirut
†Habre, Samer S *mathematician, educator*

SCOTLAND

Edinburgh
Atiyah, Sir Michael Francis *mathematician*

SWITZERLAND

Zurich
†Kalman, Rudolf Emil *research mathematician, system scientist*

ADDRESS UNPUBLISHED

Aaron, Bud *systems analyst*
Afelbil, Martin *statistician, researcher*
Altheide, Phyllis Sage *computer scientist, software engineer*
Amgott, Steven Mitchell *mathematics educator*
†Anderson, Jacqueline Annette *computer specialist*
Arden, Bruce Wesley *retired computer scientist, retired engineering educator*
Arian, Eyal *mathematician*
Bailar, Barbara Ann *statistician, researcher*
†Belinsky, Rachel *mathematician, educator*
Berkovitz, Leonard David *mathematician, educator*
Berra, P. Bruce *computer educator*
Binkley, Timothy *computer graphics educator*
Booty, Michael Richard *mathematician educator*
Botway, Lloyd Frederick *computer scientist, consultant*
Bowlby, Richard Eric *retired computer systems analyst*
Brooks, Mark Hunter *information technology project administrator*
Browder, Felix Earl *mathematician, educator*
Brown, Alton Raymond *mathematician, researcher*
Cabrera, Joao B.D. *information scientist*
Cameron, Kirk MacGregor Drummond *statistician*
†Campbell, Russell Bruce *mathematics educator*
†Campbell, Sharon Milligan *mathematician, educator*
Case, Colleen Mae *computer graphics educator*
†Chance, Beth L. *statistician, educator, statistician, researcher*
Chen, Tar Timothy *biostatistician*
†Chen, Xia *mathematician, educator*
Chiu, Chichia *mathematician, educator*
Combs, Roy James, Jr., *analyst, researcher*
†Conn, Richard Lee *computer scientist, educator*
Corbett, James Joseph *retired computer programmer*
Corbett, Lenora Meade *mathematician, community college educator*
Covin, Carol Louise *computer consultant*
†Crawford, Jennifer *mathematician, secondary school educator*
Croog, Roslyn Zeporah *chief systems engineer*
Czajko, Jakub *computer scientist, researcher, mathematician, physics researcher*
Dar, Huma Bashir *computer scientist, researcher, educator, South Asianist*
de Champeaux de Laboulaye, Dennis *computer scientist*
DiBenedetto, Emmanuele *molecular physiology, biophysicist, writer*
†Donahue, Rafe Michael *statistician*
Downey, Deborah Ann *systems specialist*
Dunlop, Dorothy D. *statistician*
Dunn, Neil F. *retired computer science educator*
Earl, Boyd L. *mathematician*
Efros, Leonid *computer software scientist and developer*
Eklof, Paul C. *mathematician, educator*
Elam, Fred Eldon *retired career army officer*
Elliott, David LeRoy *mathematician, educator, engineering educator*
†Farid, Farid O. *mathematics educator*
Fedorowicz, Jane *information systems educator*
†Feng, Bao Qi (Pao Chi) (Edward) *mathematician, educator*
Ferguson, James Clarke *mathematician, algorithmist*
Fisher, Gordon McCrea *mathematician, educator*
†Flores, Alfinio *mathematician, educator*
†Fraser, Ailana Margaret *mathematician, educator*
Freitag, Harlow *retired computer scientist and corporate executive*
Friedman, Sanford Howard *information scientist*
Garland, Howard *mathematician, educator*
†Ge, Xianping *computer scientist*
Gelenbe, Sami Erol *computer scientist, educator*
Gelfand, Israel Moseevich *mathematician, biologist*
†George, Joey F. *computer science educator*
†Gera, Ralucca Mihaela *mathematician, educator*
Gerson, Donald Jerome *computer scientist, consultant*
Gibson, Beatrice Ann *retired systems analyst, artist*
†Gilchrest, Yadira Vellon *computer scientist*
Gilford, Dorothy Morrow *statistician, researcher*
Gnanadesikan, Ramanathan *retired statistics educator, researcher*
Goldberg, Samuel *retired mathematician, foundation officer*
Goldman, Benjamin Allen *statistician, writer*
†Golubeva, Anna *mathematician, application developer*
†Gorenstein, Samuel *retired mathematician, educator*
Gosciewski, Robert Louis *logistician*
Graham, Kirsten Rae *computer scientist, educator*
Graham, Parker Lee, II, *information executive*
†Grasserbauer, Doris *computer scientist, educator*
Greever, Margaret Quarles *retired mathematics educator*
Grenander, Ulf *mathematics educator*
†Guan, Zhuang-Dan Daniel *mathematician, educator*
Halberstam, Heini *mathematics educator*
Hamblen, John Wesley *computer scientist, genealogist*
†Hanley, Jodi Ann *mathematician, educator*
†Hanson, Richard Joseph *computer scientist, consultant*
Harris, Theodore Edward *mathematician, educator*
†Heller, George Glen *retired computer scientist, educator*
†Henle, James Marston *mathematician, educator*
Hildebrand, Francis Begnaud *mathematics educator*
Hinton, Norman Wayne *retired information services executive*
Holland, Burt S. *statistics educator, consultant*
Holland, Michael James *computer services administrator*
†Holland, Richard A. *statistician*
Hornback, Joseph Hope *mathematics educator*
House, Stephen Eugene *information systems consultant*
Hunte, Beryl Eleanor *mathematics educator, consultant*
Husain, Taqdir *mathematics educator*
Iberall, Althea Ruth *computer scientist, playwright*
†Ilk, Ozlem *statistics educator, researcher*
Jabine, Thomas Boyd *statistical consultant*
†Jetley, Karun *systems analyst, consultant*
†Jiang, Tao *mathematician, educator*
Johnson, Carolyn A. *retired computer specialist*
Johnson, Kevin Rogers *analyst, journalist*
Jones, Anita Katherine *computer scientist, educator*
Juberg, Richard Kent
Kadota, Takashi Theodore *mathematician, electrical engineer*
Karnaugh, Maurice *computer scientist, educator*
Katzper, Meyer *analyst*
Keating, Regina G. *computer analyst consultant*
†Kelly, Daniel Thomas *statistician*
Kirshbaum, Jon Alan *information systems consultant, retired educational administrator*
Kister, James Milton *retired mathematician, educator*
Klein, Heinz Karl *information systems researcher*
Kobayashi, Ikuo *information systems engineer*
Krantz, Steven George *mathematics educator, writer*
Kushner, Todd Roger *computer scientist, software engineer*
Kvitko, Arkady *mathematician, researcher*
Lamm, Harriet A. *mathematics educator*
Lampson, Butler Wright *computer scientist*
†Landau, Susan *computer scientist*
Lane, Adelaide Irene *computer systems specialist, researcher*
Lange, Frederick Edward, Jr., *computer information systems architect*
Larson, Janice Talley *computer science programmer*
†Lea, Bih-Ru *computer science educator*
Lee, Dong Hoon *mathematician, educator*
Lerner, Vladimir Semion *computer scientist, educator*
Levine, Maita Faye *mathematics educator*
Li, Bao Qin *mathematics educator, researcher*
†Li, Xiaojie *statistician, consultant*
†Littlejohn, Lance L. *mathematics educator*
Liu, Xiaoqing Frank *computer scientist, educator*
†Liu, Yong *computer scientist, researcher*
Loguinov, Dmitri *computer scientist, educator*
Low, Emmet Francis, Jr., *mathematics educator*
Lynch, Robert Emmett *mathematics educator*
†MacLane, Saunders *mathematician, educator*
†Magerlein, James M. *operations research specialist*
Mahoney, Linda Kay *mathematics educator*
Main, Myrna Joan *retired mathematics educator*
Maisel, Herbert *computer science educator*
Mangan, Patricia Ann Pritchett *statistician*
Manika, John Francis *computer systems educator, computer information systems analyst*
†Markham, Thomas Lowell *mathematics educator*
†Massad, Jordan Elias *mathematician*
Mathieu, Michele Suzanne *computer scientist, consultant*
Matsushita, Marimi *educator, mathematician*
Medrek, Joseph *computer operator*
†Mell, William Eric *mathematician*
†Meza, Jane L. *biostatistician, educator*
Miller, Allen Richard *retired mathematician*
Mints, Grigori Efroim *mathematics specialist*
Moore-Freeman, Karen Celyn *analyst, director*
Morrison, Ann Hess *information technology specialist*
†Moulton, John D. *mathematician*
Moyers, Ernest Everett S. *retired computer research scientist*
Mumick, Inderpal Singh *computer scientist, engineer*
Nah, Fiona Fui-Hoon *information technology educator, researcher*
†Nanda, Seema *mathematician, educator, entrepreneur*
Nation, David Arthur *retired computer scientist, sculptor*
Natsuyama, Harriet Hatsune Kagiwada *mathematician, educator*
†Neller, Todd W. *computer science educator*
†Ng, Kam Chuen *mathematician*
†Nguyen, Dong *computer scientist, researcher*
Noh, Jun-yong *computer scientist, researcher*
Norton, Robert Michael *mathematician, educator, statistician*
Nuzzo, Anthony Gerald *services executive*
Olshen, Richard A. *statistician, educator*
Padberg, Harriet Ann *mathematics educator*
Pasles, Paul C. *mathematician, educator*
Patterson, Patricia Lynn *applied mathematician, physicist, inventor*
Pattison, Jon Allen *computer scientist, consultant*
Paul, Vera Maxine *mathematics educator*
Pendleton, Joan Marie *microprocessor designer*
Perko, Walter Kim *pilot, computer engineer, songwriter, poet*
Pickle, Linda Williams *biostatistician*
Pollock, Karen Anne *computer analyst*
Rall, Louis Baker *mathematician, educator, consultant*
Ramalingam, Ganesan *computer scientist*
†Ratnasingam, Pauline *information scientist, educator*
Reese, Edward James, Jr., *computer scientist*
†Reese, Michael *mathematics educator*
Richgels, Glen William *mathematics educator*
†Riffenburgh, Robert Harry *biostatistician, researcher*
Ritter, Jack Charles *mathematician, computer graphics designer*
Robold, Alice Ilene *retired mathematician, educator*
†Rochette, Alexandre C. *computer scientist*
†Romano, Nicholas Charles *information scientist, educator*
†Roop, Mitchell A. *information scientist*
†Sa, Ping *statistician, educator*
Schmidt, Rodney Albert *computer science educator, retired*
†Schneider, Chris Allan *mathematician, educator, statistician, educator*
Schneider, Edgar Rolf Gottfried *retired mathematician, application developer, writer*
Seidman, Stephen Benjamin *dean, computer science educator*
Sexton, Mary Ann *information systems professional, music educator, pastoral musician*
Shaffer, Judy Ann *educator, data processing professional*
Shier, Gloria Bulan *mathematics educator*
Sills, Richard Reynolds *scientist, educator*
†Singer-Cohen, Karen Beth *mathematician, educator*
†Skoda, Mary E. *mathematician, educator*
Sloane, Neil James Alexander *mathematician, researcher*
Smith, Kathleen Ann *mathematics educator*
†Soifer, Jed Joshua *mathematics and science educator*
Sowa, Artur *mathematician, researcher*
Spangler, Richard Carl *mathematics educator*
Spinrad, Robert Joseph *computer scientist*
Stanard, Christopher Leon *statistician*
Stewart-Pérez, Renice Ann *technology writer, internal systems professional*
Stuart, Sandra Joyce *computer information scientist*
Suchyta, Casimir John, III, *computer analyst, researcher*
†Sullivan, Keith Montgomery *operations research specialist*
†Sung, Myong-Hee *mathematician, researcher*
Suppes, Patrick *philosophy, statistics, psychology educator and education*
Suthaharan, Shanmugathasan *computer science educator, researcher*
†Szarvas, Tibor Ferenc *mathematician, educator*
†Talebi, Norollah *mathematics educator, researcher*
Tan, Hui Qian *computer science and civil engineering educator*
†Temam, Roger M. *mathematician, educator*
†Theoret, Julie Marie *mathematician, educator*
Thomas, Tarquin Craig *computer scientist, writer*
Tishkevich, Frances Mary *mathematics educator*
Tobiassen, Barbara Sue *systems analyst consultant, educator, Peace Corps volunteer*
†Troy, William C. *mathematician, educator*
Tyrl, Paul *mathematics educator, researcher, consultant*
Ullman, Nelly Szabo *statistician, educator*
†Van Ness, Stephen A. *systems analyst, writer*
Vasily, John Timothy *information systems executive, state government official*
†Vrenios, Alexander *computer software systems developer*
†Wadleigh, Kevin Richard *mathematician*
Wagner, Ellyn S(anti) *mathematics educator*
Waller, Ray Albert *statistician*
†Walls, Ray *computer science educator*
Wetsch, John Robert *information systems specialist*
†Wiens, Brian *statistician*
Wilkins, J. Ernest, Jr., *mathematician, educator*
†Wilmer, Archie, III, *mathematician, educator*
Winder, Robert Owen *mathematician, computer engineer, geophysicist*
Wolfram, David Anthony *computer scientist*
Wozniak, Stephen Gary *computer scientist*
Wren, Stephen Corey *mathematician, inventor*
Wu, Margaret Anne *computer scientist, educator*
Yackel, James William *mathematician, academic administrator*
†Yang, Zejiang *statistician, educator*
†Yao, Yongwei *mathematician, researcher*
Yntema, Mary Katherine *retired mathematics educator*
Young, Sharon Laree *mathematics educator*
†Yunus, Ilya Aleksandrovich *mathematician, computer scientist, software engineer*
Zeilberger, Doron *researcher, mathematics educator*
†Zenkov, Dmitry *mathematician, educator*
†Zhang, Yao *statistician*
Zierler, Neal *retired mathematician*
Zuo, Yijun *statistician, educator*

SCIENCE: PHYSICAL SCIENCE

UNITED STATES

ALABAMA

Auburn
Neely, William Charles *chemistry educator, consultant, research scientist*
†Samoylova, Tatiana I *biochemist, researcher*
Vodyanoy, Vitaly Jacob *biophysicist, educator*

Auburn University
†Chen, An-Ban *physicist, educator*

Birmingham
Elgavish, Gabriel Andreas *physical biochemistry educator*
Krishna, N(epalli) Rama *biochemist*
Miyagawa, Ichiro *physicist*
Moran, Mary Shanks *hydrogeologist*
Robinson, Edward Lee *retired physics educator, consultant*
Vyazovkin, Sergey *chemist, educator*

Dothan
Mocker, Hans Walter *physicist*

Enterprise
Stagliano, James Joseph *physical science educator, scientist*

Gordo
McKnight, William Baldwin *physics educator*

Huntsville
Allan, Barry David *research chemist, government official*
Bowden, Charles Malcolm *research physicist, educator*
Brandon, Walter Wiley, Jr., *retired physicist, retired aerospace engineer*
Campbell, Jonathan Wesley *astrophysicist, aerospace engineer*
Cornatzer, William Eugene *retired biochemistry educator*
Costes, Nicholas Constantine *aerospace technologist, university educator, retired government official*
Decher, Rudolf *physicist, researcher*
Dobson, Christopher Calvin *physicist*
†Liu, Jiwen *research scientist*
London, John Rutherford, III, *aerospace program administrator*
Miller, Walter Edward *physical scientist, researcher*
Norman, Ralph Louis *physicist, consultant*
Parnell, Thomas Alfred *physicist*
Smith, Robert Earl *space scientist*
Stuhlinger, Ernst *physicist*
Vaughan, William Walton *atmospheric scientist*
Wright, John Collins *retired chemistry educator*

Mobile
†Harpen, Michael Dennis *physicist, educator*

Montgomery
Tan, Boen Hie *analytical biochemist, biomedical scientist*

PROFESSIONAL INDEX 6631 SCIENCE: PHYSICAL SCIENCE

Normal
†Edwards, Matthew E. *physicist, educator*

Tuscaloosa
Cava, Michael Patrick *chemist, educator*
LaMoreaux, Philip Elmer *geologist, hydrogeologist, consultant*
Mancini, Ernest Anthony *geologist, educator, researcher*
Oltz, Donald Frederick *research mineral resources executive*
Vincent, John Bertram *chemist, educator*

ALASKA

Anchorage
Ennis, William Lee *physics educator*
Keffer, Maria Jean *environmental auditor*
Patrick, Leslie Dayle *hydrologist*
Sells, Colin David *meteorologist*

Fairbanks
Duffy, Lawrence Kevin *biochemist, educator*
Fathauer, Theodore Frederick *meteorologist*
Lingle, Craig Stanley *glaciologist, educator*
Roederer, Juan Gualterio *physics educator*
Wackerbauer, Renate Anna *physicist*
Weller, Gunter Ernst *geophysics educator*

ARIZONA

Flagstaff
Barlow, Nadine Gail *planetary geoscientist*
Shoemaker, Carolyn Spellman *planetary astronomer*
Young, Robert Donald *physicist, educator*

Green Valley
Bates, Charles Carpenter *oceanographer*
Dingle, Albert Nelson *meteorology educator*

Litchfield Park
McKeighen, Ronald Eugene *physicist*

Mesa
Dorland, Elizabeth M. *chemistry educator*

Peoria
Dapples, Edward Charles *retired geologist, educator*
Lichtenberg, Larry Ray *chemist, consultant, researcher*
McMahon, Maribeth Lovette *physicist*

Phoenix
Everett, Paul Marvin *physicist*
O'Neal, Steven G. *chemist, educator*
†Spraggins, Robert Lee *organic chemist, research scientist*

Scottsdale
Hockmuth, Joseph Frank *physicist, psychotherapist*
Kinsinger, Jack Burl *chemist, educator*

Tempe
Bauer, Ernst Georg *physicist, educator*
Black, Kristine Mary *physicist*
Blankenship, Robert Eugene *biochemistry educator*
Buseck, Peter R. *geochemistry educator*
Chamberlin, Ralph Vary *physicist, educator*
Cowley, John Maxwell *physics educator*
Glick, Milton Don *chemist, university administrator*
Goronkin, Herbert *physicist*
Juvet, Richard Spalding, Jr., *chemistry educator*
McKelvy, Michael John *materials chemist, research scientist*
Moore, Carleton Bryant *geochemistry educator*
Pettit, George Robert *cancer researcher*
Smith, David John *physicist, educator*
Starrfield, Sumner Grosby *astrophysics educator, researcher*
†Theodore, David *research scientist*
Vandenberg, Edwin James *chemist, educator*
Winicov, Ilga Butelis *biochemist, educator*

Tucson
Angel, James Roger Prior *astronomer*
Barrett, Bruce Richard *physics educator*
Basford, Robert Eugene *retired biochemistry educator, researcher*
†Biddulph, Dana Lee *research scientist*
Bloembergen, Nicolaas *physicist, educator*
Broadfoot, Albert Lyle *physicist*
Cameron, Alastair Graham Walter *astrophysicist, educator*
Crawford, David L. *astronomer*
Dave, Romeel *astronomer, educator, researcher*
Davis, Stanley Nelson *hydrologist, educator*
Dessler, Alexander Jack *astrophysicist, educator*
De Young, David Spencer *astrophysicist, educator*
Dunn, Floyd *biophysics and biomedical engeering educator*
Fink, James Brewster *geophysicist, consultant*
Girardeau, Marvin Denham *physics educator*
Gruhl, James *energy scientist, artist*
Gutsche, Carl David *chemistry educator*
Harrison, Edward Robert *physicist, educator, science administrator*
Hay, Richard Le Roy *geology educator*
Haynes, Caleb Vance, Jr., *geology and archaeology educator*
Hays, James Fred *geologist, educator*
Hill, Henry Allen *physicist, educator*
Hubbard, William Bogel *planetary sciences educator*
Hunten, Donald Mount *planetary scientist, educator*
Jackson, Kenneth Arthur *physicist, researcher*
Jefferies, John Trevor *astrophysicist, observatory administrator*
Kamilli, Robert Joseph *geologist*
Kennicutt, Robert Charles, Jr., *astronomer*
Kim, Jeong-Kyun *metallurgist, researcher*
Lamb, Willis Eugene, Jr., *physicist, educator*
Law, John Harold *biochemistry educator*
Lunine, Jonathan Irving *astronomer, educator*
Macleod, Hugh Angus McIntosh *optical science educator, physicist, consultant*
Magee, Wayne Edward *biochemistry educator, researcher*
Marcialis, Robert Louis *planetary astronomer*
Morrison, Roger Barron *geologist*
Neugebauer, Marcia *physicist, administrator*
Nordman, Olli *research scientist*
†Pacholczyk, Andrzej Grzegorz *astrophysicist*
Parmenter, Robert Haley *physics educator*
Prewitt, Charles Thompson *geochemist*
Roemer, Elizabeth *astronomer, educator*
Sewell, Charles Robertson *geologist, exploration company executive, investor*
Siegler, Nicholas *astrophysicist*
†Stein, Daniel L. *physicist, educator*
Swalin, Richard Arthur *scientist, company executive*
Tifft, William Grant *astronomer, educator*
Wang, Wei *chemist, researcher*
Wehinger, Peter Augustus *astronomer, educator*
†Whitaker, Ewen Adair *retired astronomer*
Willis, Clifford Leon *geologist*
Wolff, Sidney Carne *astronomer, observatory administrator*
Zheng, Zhiping *chemistry educator*

ARKANSAS

Bella Vista
Johnson, A(lyn) William *chemistry educator, writer, researcher, consultant*
†Sautter, Chester Arthur *physicist, educator*

Fayetteville
Lacy, Claud Harold Sandberg *astronomer, educator*
†Shaw, Colin G. *physicist, researcher, mathematics educator*
Wilkins, Charles L. *chemist, educator*

Little Rock
†Basnakian, Alexei G. *biochemist, researcher*
Braithwaite, Wilfred John *physics educator*
Darsey, Jerome Anthony (Jerry Darsey) *chemistry educator, consultant*
†Rollefson, Aimar Andre *physicist, department chairman*

Marianna
Carroll, Stephen Douglas *chemist, researcher*

Pine Bluff
Perschbacher, Peter Wesley *environmental scientist, educator*
Walker, Richard Brian *chemistry educator*

CALIFORNIA

Alameda
Liu, Zenghe *research scientist*

Albany
Eastwood, DeLyle *chemist*

Alhambra
†Im, Jaemo *research scientist*

Altadena
Mkryan, Sonya *geophysicist, educator, research scientist*

Apple Valley
Mays, George Walter, Jr., *educational technology educator, consultant, tutor*

Arcata
†Lamberson, Roland H. *environmental scientist, educator, mathematician*
Zoellner, Robert William *chemistry educator*

Atascadero
Ogier, Walter Thomas *retired physics educator*

Atherton
Coleman, Robert Griffin *geology educator*
Gill, Stephen Paschall *retired physicist, mathematician*
Levinthal, Elliott Charles *physicist, educator*

Auburn
Hess, Patrick Henry *chemist, researcher*

Azusa
Kostoulas, Ioannis Georgiou *physicist*

Bayside
Cocks, George Gosson *retired chemical microscopy educator*

Bellflower
Martin, Melissa Carol *radiological physicist*

Berkeley
Attwood, David Thomas *physicist, educator*
†Baldocchi, Dennis David *micrometeorologist*
Barnett, R(alph) Michael *theoretical physicist, educational agency administrator*
Bartlett, Neil *chemist, emeritus educator*
Bergman, Robert George *chemist, educator*
Bolt, Bruce Alan *seismologist*
Bragg, Robert Henry *physicist, educator*
Carmichael, Ian Stuart Edward *geologist, educator*
Cerny, Joseph, III, *chemistry educator, scientific laboratory administrator, university dean and official*
Chamberlain, Owen *nuclear physicist*
Chamberlin, Michael John *biochemistry educator*
Chew, Geoffrey Foucar *physicist*
Clarke, John *physics educator*
Diamond, Richard Martin *nuclear chemist*
†Dietrich, William E. *geophysicist, educator*
Fleming, Graham Richard *chemistry educator*
Fowler, Thomas Kenneth *physicist*
Fréchet, Jean Marie Joseph *chemistry educator*
Gaillard, Mary Katharine *physics educator*
Glaser, Donald Arthur *physicist*
Goldhaber, Gerson *physicist, educator*
Hahn, Erwin Louis *physicist, educator*
Haller, Eugene Ernest *materials scientist, educator*
Heathcock, Clayton Howell *chemistry educator, researcher*
Hoffman, Darleane Christian *chemistry educator*
Jackson, J(ohn) David *physicist, educator*
Johnston, Harold S(ledge) *chemistry educator*
Kerth, Leroy T. *physics educator*
Klinman, Judith Pollock *biochemist, educator*
Koshland, Daniel Edward, Jr., *biochemist, educator*
Langridge, Robert *scientist, educator*
Leopold, Luna Bergere *geology educator*
Lester, William Alexander, Jr., *chemist, educator*
Linn, Stuart Michael *biochemist, educator*
Lipps, Jere Henry *paleontology educator*
Lu, Adolph *physicist, researcher*
Ma, Chung-Pei Michelle *astronomer, educator*
Marletta, Michael A. *biochemistry educator, researcher, protein chemist*
McKee, Christopher Fulton *physicist, educator, astronomer, educator*
Merchant, Carolyn *environmental history educator*
Miller, William Hughes *theoretical chemist, educator*
Pavlath, Attila Endre *research chemist*
Perez-Mendez, Victor *physics educator*
Perry, Dale Lynn *chemist*
Phillips, Norman Edgar *chemistry educator*
†Price, Lynn Kauffman *environmental scientist*
Rasmussen, John Oscar *nuclear research scientist*
Raymond, Kenneth Norman *chemistry educator, research chemist*
†Richardson, John David *physicist*
Ritchie, Robert Oliver *materials science educator*
Shen, Yuen-Ron *physics educator*
Shugart, Howard Alan *physicist, educator*
Somorjai, Gabor Arpad *chemist, educator*
†Spieler, Helmuth *physicist*
Steiner, Herbert Max *physics educator*
Strauss, Herbert Leopold *chemistry educator*
Streitwieser, Andrew, Jr., *chemistry educator*
†Tanner, Lee E. *retired materials scientist, photographer, writer, curator*
Thompson, Anthony Wayne *metallurgist, educator, consultant*
†Tjian, Robert Tse Nan *biochemistry educator, biology researcher, virology researcher*
Townes, Charles Hard *physics educator*
Trilling, George Henry *physicist, educator*
Valentine, James William *paleobiology educator, writer*
Weber, Eicke Richard *physicist*
Wurtele, Morton Gaither *meteorologist, educator*

Brea
Shen, Gene Giin-Yuan *organic chemist*

Burbank
Razouk, Rashad Elias *retired chemistry educator*

Burlingame
Hubbard, Gregory Scott *physicist*

California City
Paiva, Clifford Anthony *physicist, consultant*

Camarillo
Leerabhandh, Marjorie Bravo *chemist, educator*

Canyon Lake
Schilling, Frederick Augustus, Jr., *geologist, consultant*

Carlsbad
Lu, Taijin *physical chemist, researcher*
Smith, Warren James *optical scientist, consultant, lecturer*

Carmel
†Jung, Glenn Harold *retired oceanographer educator, researcher*
Vagnini, Livio Lee *chemist, forensic consultant*

Carpinteria
Fisher, John Crocker *physicist*

Castaic
†Holmes, Dale Arthur *optics scientist*

China Lake
Bennett, Jean Louise McPherson *physicist, research scientist*

Chino
Koestel, Mark Alfred *geologist, photographer*

Chula Vista
Smith, Peggy O'Doniel *physicist, educator*
Wolk, Martin *physicist, electronics engineer*

City Of Industry
Ji, Qing *chemist, researcher*

Claremont
Helliwell, Thomas McCaffree *physicist, educator*
Oxtoby, David William *college president, chemistry educator*

Concord
Hearst, John Eugene *chemistry educator, researcher, consultant*

Corona
Garrett, Thomas Monroe *chemist*

Corona Del Mar
Britten, Roy John *biophysicist*

Costa Mesa
Lattanzio, Stephen Paul *astronomy educator*
Medina-Puerta, Antonio *research scientist*

Crescent City
Carter, Neville Louis *geophysicist, educator*

Culver City
Tang, Yin Sheng *physicist*

Dana Point
Parker, John Marchbank *consulting geologist*

Davis
Burri, Betty Jane *research chemist*
Cahill, Thomas Andrew *physicist, educator*
Conn, Eric Edward *plant biochemist*
Day, Howard Wilman *geology educator*
†Duan, Ren-Guan *materials scientist*
Jungerman, John Albert *physics educator*
Lagunas-Solar, Manuel Claudio *research radiochemist*
Mukherjee, Amiya K. *metallurgy and materials science educator*
Nash, Charles Presley *chemistry educator*
Painter, Ruth Robbins *retired environmental biochemist*
Shackelford, James Floyd *materials science educator, researcher*
Stumpf, Paul Karl *biochemistry educator emeritus*
Troy, Frederic Arthur, II, *medical biochemistry educator*
Turcotte, Donald Lawson *geophysical sciences educator*
Volman, David Herschel *chemistry educator*
Wooten, Frederick (Oliver Wooten) *applied science educator*

Duarte
Kabingue, Ken *biochemist*
Yoshida, Akira *biochemist*

El Cerrito
Alpen, Edward Lewis *biophysicist, educator*
Coyner, Eugene Casper *chemist, consultant, economist*
†Koenig, James Bennett *geologist, consultant*
Koths, Kirston Edward *biochemist*
Siri, William E. *physicist, consultant*
Templeton, David Henry, Jr., *chemist, educator*

Emeryville
Gombocz, Erich Alfred *biochemist*
Masri, Merle Sid *biochemist, consultant*

Encinitas
Goldberg, Edward Davidow *geochemist, educator*
Payne, James Richard *environmental chemist*

Encino
Hawthorne, Marion Frederick *chemistry educator*
Phelps, Michael Edward *biophysics educator*
Thorpe, Gary Stephen *chemistry educator*

Escondido
Tomomatsu, Hideo *chemist*

Flintridge
Pickering, William Hayward *research scientist*

Foster City
Hotz, Henry Palmer *retired physicist*
Zaidi, Iqbal Mehdi *biochemist, scientist*

Fountain Valley
Davis, Jeremy Matthew *chemist*

Fresno
Kauffman, George Bernard *chemistry educator*

Fullerton
Fearn, Heidi *physicist, educator*
Shapiro, Mark Howard *physicist, educator, academic dean, consultant*
Wan, Julia Chang *retired science educator*

Glen Ellen
Berkland, James Omer *geologist*

Glendale
†Kazarian, Poghos F. *physicist, researcher, educator*

Grass Valley
Bennison, Allan Parnell *geological consultant*

Hayward
Yeliseev, Alexei Arkadievich *biochemist, researcher*

Hemet
†Berger, Lev Isaac *physicist, educator*

Hollister
Smith, George Larry *analytical and environmental chemist*
Spencer, Douglas Lloyd *chemist, manufacturing executive*

Inglewood
Lewis, Roy Roosevelt *physicist*

Irvine
Aswad, Dana William *biochemist, educator*
Bander, Myron *physics educator, university dean*
Bradshaw, Ralph Alden *biochemistry educator*
†Choi, Bernard *laser scientist, researcher*
Clark, Bruce Robert *geologist, consultant*
Dzyaloshinskii, Igor Ekhielievich *physicist*

Manasson, Vladimir Alexandrovich *physicist*
Maradudin, Alexei A. *physics educator*
McLaughlin, Calvin Sturgis *biochemistry educator*
Nalcioglu, Orhan *physics educator, radiological sciences educator*
Nowick, Arthur Stanley *metallurgy and materials science educator*
Overman, Larry Eugene *chemistry educator*
Phalen, Robert Franklynn *environmental scientist*
Qin, Suofu *biochemist*
Rowland, Frank Sherwood *chemistry educator*
Rynn, Nathan *physics educator, consultant*
†Shen, Ba-Zhong *research scientist*
Tumakov, Vladimir Leonidovich *physicist, researcher*
Wallis, Richard Fisher *physicist, educator*
†Warble, Charles Edward *materials scientist*
White, Stephen Halley *biophysicist, educator*
Zhu, Peter Chaoquan *chemist*

Kensington
Appelman, Evan Hugh *retired chemist*
Connick, Robert Elwell *retired chemistry educator*

La Canada Flintridge
Baines, Kevin Hays *planetary scientist, astronomer*

La Jolla
Andre, Michael Paul *physicist, educator*
Arnold, James Richard *chemist, educator*
Asmus, John Fredrich *physicist*
Backus, George Edward *theoretical geophysicist*
Berger, Wolfgang H. *oceanographer, marine geologist*
Boger, Dale L. *chemistry educator*
Buckingham, Michael John *oceanography educator*
Burbidge, E. Margaret *astronomer, educator*
Case, Kenneth Myron *physics educator*
†Cometto-Muñiz, Jorge Enrique *biochemist, researcher*
†Cordova, Armando *chemist*
Cox, Charles Shipley *oceanography researcher, educator*
Cunningham, Bruce Arthur *biochemist, educator*
Driscoll, Charles Frederick *physics educator*
Edelman, Gerald Maurice *biochemist, neuroscientist, educator*
†Ely, Kathryn R. *crystallographer*
Fisher, Frederick Hendrick *oceanographer emeritus*
Fisher, Robert Lloyd *retired geologist, retired oceanographer*
Fokin, Valery Valerievich *chemistry educator, researcher*
Geiduschek, E(rnest) Peter *biophysics and molecular biology educator*
Itano, Harvey Akio *biochemistry educator*
Kadonaga, James Takuro *biochemist*
Kitada, Shinichi *biochemist*
Kolodner, Richard David *biochemist, educator, geneticist*
Lal, Devendra *nuclear geophysics educator*
Lauer, James Lothar *physicist, educator*
†Lindenberg, Katja *chemistry educator*
McCammon, James Andrew *chemistry educator*
McIlwain, Carl Edwin *physicist*
†Munk, Walter Heinrich *geophysics educator*
O'Neil, Thomas Michael *physicist, educator*
Patton, Stuart *biochemist, educator*
Ride, Sally Kristen *physics educator, scientist, former astronaut*
Rosenbluth, Marshall Nicholas *physicist*
Schimmel, Paul Reinhard *biochemist, biophysicist, educator*
Sham, Lu Jeu *physics educator*
Sharpless, K. Barry *chemist, educator*
Shor, George G., Jr., *geophysicist, oceanographic administrator, engineer*
Shuler, Kurt Egon *chemist, educator*
Somerville, Richard Chapin James *atmospheric scientist, educator*
Spiess, Fred Noel *oceanographer, educator*
Stone, William Ross *research and development company executive, physicist*
Taur, Yuan *physicist, researcher*
Tietz, Norbert Wolfgang *clinical chemistry educator, administrator*
Tsien, Roger Yonchien *chemist, cell biologist*
Vale, Wylie W. *biochemist*
Van Lint, Victor Anton Jacobus *physicist*
Verma, Inder M. *biochemist*
Watson, Kenneth Marshall *physics educator*
Wolynes, Peter Guy *chemistry researcher, educator*
York, Herbert Frank *physics educator, government official*

La Verne
†Gabelich, Christopher James *environment specialist, researcher*
Hwang, Cordelia Jong *chemist*

Laguna Beach
Benford, Gregory Albert *physicist, writer*
Castro, Charles Edward *chemist, consultant*

Laguna Woods
Batdorf, Samuel B(urbridge) *physicist*

Lancaster
Kiersch, George Alfred *geological consultant, retired educator*

Livermore
Alder, Berni Julian *physicist, researcher*
Cook, Robert Crossland *research chemist*
Deleray, Arthur Loyd *chemist, educator*
Ellsaesser, Hugh Walter *retired atmospheric scientist*
†Ezzedine, Souheil M. *physicist, researcher*
Futch, Archer Hamner *retired physicist*
Glenzer, Siegfried Heinz *physicist, educator, researcher*
Holzrichter, John F. *physicist*
Hooper, Edwin Bickford *physicist*
Kidder, Ray Edward *physicist, consultant*
Kirkwood, Robert Keith *applied physicist*
†Lambert, Michael Allen *physicist*
Lau, Albert Man-Fai *physicist*
Leith, Cecil Eldon, Jr., *retired physicist*
Nuckolls, John Hopkins *physicist, researcher*
Schock, Robert Norman *geophysicist*
Shotts, Wayne J. *nuclear scientist, federal agency administrator*
Spiller, Eberhard Adolf *physicist, researcher*
Tarter, Curtis Bruce *physicist, science administrator*

Loma Linda
Slattery, Charles Wilbur *biochemistry educator*
Wilcox, Ronald Bruce *biochemistry educator, researcher*

Long Beach
Bauer, Roger Duane *chemistry educator, science consultant*
Hu, Chi Yu *physicist, educator*
†Li, Lijuan *chemistry educator*
McAbee, Douglas DeWitt *biochemistry educator, researcher*
McGaughey, Charles Gilbert *retired research biochemist*

Los Altos
Hahn, Harold Thomas *physical chemist, chemical engineer*
Vickers, Roger Spencer *physicist, environmental mapping director*

Los Altos Hills
Dyal, Palmer *retired physicist*

Los Angeles
Adamson, Arthur Wilson *chemistry educator*
Allerton, Samuel Ellsworth *biochemist*
Anderson, W. French *biochemist, physician*
Benson, Sidney William *chemistry researcher*
Bhaumik, Mani Lal *physicist*
Billig, Franklin Anthony *chemist*
Boyer, Paul D. *biochemist, educator*
Byers, Nina *physics educator*
Campbell, Kenneth Eugene, Jr., *vertebrate paleontologist, ornithologist*
Carter, Emily Ann *physical chemist, researcher, educator*
Chapman, Orville Lamar *chemist, educator*
Coleman, Charles Clyde *physicist, educator*
Coleman, Paul Jerome, Jr., *physicist, educator*
Cornwall, John Michael *physics educator, consultant, researcher*
Coroniti, Ferdinand Vincent *physics educator, consultant*
Dows, David Alan *chemistry educator*
Dunn, Arnold Samuel *biochemistry educator*
Dunn, Bruce Sidney *materials science educator*
Fischer, Alfred George *geology educator*
Foote, Christopher Spencer *chemist, educator*
Fulco, Armand John *biochemist*
Ganas, Perry Spiros *physicist*
Ghez, Andrea Mia *astronomy and physics educator*
Ghil, Michael *atmospheric scientist, geophysicist*
Hall, Clarence Albert, Jr., *geologist, educator*
Houk, Kendall Newcomb *chemistry educator*
Igo, George Jerome *physics educator*
Jaffe, Sigmund *chemist, educator*
Jordan, Thomas Hillman *geophysicist, educator*
Kaplan, Isaac Raymond *chemistry educator, corporate executive*
Knopoff, Leon *geophysics educator*
Kobe, Lan *medical physicist*
Koga, Rokutaro (Rocky Koga) *physicist*
Levine, Raphael David *chemistry educator*
Maki, Kazumi *physicist, educator*
Markland, Francis Swaby, Jr., *biochemist, educator*
McLean, Ian Small *astronomer, physics educator*
†McWilliams, James C. *earth sciences educator*
†Neelin, J. David *meteorologist, educator*
Neufeld, Elizabeth Fondal *biochemist, educator*
†Nimni, Marcel Ephraim *biochemistry educator*
Olah, George Andrew *chemist*
Paulson, Donald Robert *chemistry educator*
Reiss, Howard *chemistry educator*
Roberts, Sidney *biological chemist*
Rubin, Alan Edward *meteorite researcher, science popularizer*
Scott, Robert Lane *chemist, educator*
Shrivastava, Prakash N. *medical physicist, educator*
Shvetsov, Alexander Anatolievich *biochemist, researcher*
Smith, Emil L. *biochemist, consultant*
Smith, William Ray *retired biophysicist, retired engineer*
†Smolentsev, Sergey Yurievich *physics educator, researcher*
Stanton, Robert James, Jr., *geologist, educator*
Stellwagen, Robert Harwood *biochemistry educator*
Thorne, Richard Mansergh *physicist, educator*
Trimble, Stanley Wayne *hydrology and geography educator*
Ufimtsev, Pyotr Yakovlevich *physicist, electrical engineer, educator*
Vilesov, Andrey Fedorovitch *research physical chemist*
Whitten, Charles Alexander, Jr., *physics educator*
Woodruff, Fay *paleoceanographer, geological researcher*
Wudl, Fred *chemistry educator*
Yanai, Michio *atmospheric scientist*
Yang, Henry S. (Hong Yang) *metallurgist, materials engineer*

Los Gatos
Foy, Wade Hampton *research scientist*

Los Osos
Topp, Alphonso Axel, Jr., *environmental scientist, consultant*

Malibu
Liu, David Shiao-Kung *physical scientist*
Mataré, Herbert F. *physicist, consultant*
Pepper, David M. *physicist, educator, writer, inventor*

Marina
Shane, William Whitney *astronomer*

McKinleyville
†Peithman, Roscoe Edward *physicist, educator*

Menlo Park
†Allison, Anthony Clifford *research scientist, consultant*
Boyarski, Adam Michael *physicist*
Bukry, John David *geologist*
Coward, David Hand *physicist, researcher*
†Drell, Sidney David *physicist, educator*
Dusel-Bacon, Cynthia *geologist, researcher*
Funkhouser, Lawrence William *retired geologist*
Herrmannsfeldt, William Bernard *physicist*
Holzer, Thomas Lequear *geologist*
Kuwabara, James Shigeru *research hydrologist*
Lachenbruch, Arthur Herold *geophysicist, researcher*
†McGarr, Arthur Francis *geophysicist*
Penzias, Arno Allan *astrophysicist, technology consultant, research scientist, information systems specialist*
Richter, Burton *physicist*
Taylor, Richard Edward *physicist, educator*
Tokheim, Robert Edward *physicist*

Modesto
Morrison, Robert Lee *physical scientist*

Moffett Field
†Caldwell, William Frank *aerospace project manager, mechanical engineer*
Lissauer, Jack Jonathan *astronomy educator*
†Whiting, Ellis Eugene *retired research scientist*

Mokelumne Hill
Testa, Stephen Michael *geologist, consultant*

Monrovia
Andary, Thomas Joseph *biochemist, researcher*

Montecito
Wheelon, Albert Dewell *physicist*

Monterey
Collins, Curtis Allan *oceanographer*
Le, Ly Ngoc (Le Ngoc Ly) *environmental physicist, educator, research scientist*
Rago, Thomas Ashton *physical oceanographer*
Shull, Harrison *chemist, educator*

Morgan Hill
Kuster, Robert Kenneth *former scientist*

Moss Landing
Brewer, Peter George *ocean geochemist*
Coale, Kenneth Hamilton *biogeochemist, educator*

Mountain View
Popovici, Alexander Mihai *geophysicist, business executive*
Salama, Farid *astrophycicist, spectroscopist, research scientist*

Murrieta
Lake, Bruce Meno *applied physicist*

Newport Beach
†Kolyer, John McNaughton *materials specialist, chemist*

Northridge
Smathers, James Burton *medical physicist, educator*
Stampke, Stuart Reh *physicist, researcher*

Novato
Hanahan, Donald James *biochemist, educator*

Oakland
Ames, Bruce N(athan) *biochemist, molecular biologist*
Brust, David *physicist*
Carwell, Hattie Virginia *health physicist*
†Finkle, Bernard J *biochemist, researcher*
Harpster, Robert Eugene *engineering geologist*
Keeports, David Dale *physical science educator*
Linford, Rulon Kesler *physicist, engineer*
Meyer, Carl Beat *chemical consultant, mediator, arbitrator, lawyer*
Steele, Richard Donald *researcher, linguist, physicist*
Wong, Ivan Gynmun *seismologist*

Orange
Korb, Lawrence John *metallurgist*
Salenius, Sylvia Marja *environmental planner*
Talbott, George Robert *physicist, mathematician, educator*

Orinda
Baker, Don Robert *chemist, inventor, writer*
Heftmann, Erich *biochemist*

Oroville
Sincoff, Steven Lawrence *chemistry educator*

Pacific Palisades
Gregor, Eduard *laser physicist, consultant*

Palo Alto
Andersen, Torben Brender *optical researcher, astronomer, software engineer*
Cohen, Karl Paley *nuclear energy consultant*
Cutler, Leonard Samuel *physicist*
†Dabbagh, Karim *research scientist*
Eng, Lawrence Fook *biochemistry educator, neurochemist*
Ernst, Wallace Gary *geology educator*
Flory, Curt Alan *research physicist*
Gabashvili, Irene *biophysicist*
Gliner, Erast Boris *theoretical physicist*
Huberman, Bernardo A *physicist*
Loewenstein, Walter Bernard *nuclear power technologist*
Perl, Martin Lewis *physicist, educator, chemical engineer*
Saxena, Arjun Nath *physicist*
Schulz, Michael *physicist*
Skoog, Douglas Arvid *retired chemistry educator, writer*
Taimuty, Samuel Isaac *physicist*
†Tucker, Brian *seismologist*
Varney, Robert Nathan *retired physicist, researcher*

Palos Verdes Estates
Joshi, Satish Devdas *organic chemist*
Paulikas, George Algis *retired physicist*

Paradise
Wilder, James D. *geology and mining administrator*

Pasadena
Albee, Arden Leroy *geologist, educator*
Allen, Clarence Roderic *geologist, educator*
Anderson, Don Lynn *geophysicist*
Barnes, Charles Andrew *physicist, educator*
Bejczy, Antal Károly *research scientist, research facility administrator*
Blandford, Roger David *astronomy educator*
Boehm, Felix Hans *physicist, educator*
†Breen, David Edward *physicist, researcher*
Chahine, Moustafa Toufic *atmospheric scientist*
Chan, Sunney Ignatius *chemist, educator*
†Cooray, Asantha Roshan *astrophysicist, researcher*
Culick, Fred Ellsworth Clow *physics and engineering educator*
Dervan, Peter Brendan *chemistry educator*
Dressler, Alan Michael *astronomer*
Duxbury, Thomas Carl *planetary scientist*
Ellis, Richard Salisbury *astronomer, educator*
Ferber, Robert Rudolf *physics researcher, educator, science administrator*
Frautschi, Steven Clark *physicist, educator*
Friedl, Randall Raymond *environmental scientist*
Fu, Lee-Lueng *oceanographer*
Fultz, Brent Thomas *materials scientist, educator, researcher*
†Goldreich, Peter Martin *astrophysics and planetary physics educator*
Goodstein, David Louis *physics educator*
Gray, Harry Barkus *chemistry educator*
Grubbs, Robert Howard *chemistry educator*
Gurnis, Michael Christopher *geological sciences educator*
Heindl, Clifford Joseph *physicist, researcher*
Hitlin, David George *physicist, educator*
Ingersoll, Andrew Perry *planetary science educator*
Janssen, Michael Allen *astronomer*
Jastrow, Robert *physicist, educator*
†Jun, Insoo *nuclear scientist, researcher*
†Kahle, Anne B. *geophysicist*
Koonin, Steven Elliot *physicist, educator, academic administrator*
Kuppermann, Aron *physical chemist, educator*
Leonard, Nelson Jordan *chemistry educator*
Lewis, Nathan Saul *chemistry educator*
Liepmann, Hans Wolfgang *physicist, educator*
Marcus, Rudolph Arthur *chemist*
Mc Koy, Basil Vincent Charles *theoretical chemist, educator*
†Parilis, Edward S. *physicist, researcher, consultant*
Politzer, Hugh David *physicist, educator*
Roberts, John D. *chemist, educator*
Sackmann, Inge-Juliana *astrophysicist*
Sanders, Gary Hilton *physicist*
Sargent, Wallace Leslie William *astronomer, educator*
Schmidt, Maarten *astronomy educator*
Sekanina, Zdenek *astronomer*
Sharp, Robert Phillip *geology educator*
†Silver, Leon Theodore *geologist, educator*
†Stoltz, Brian Mark *chemist, educator*
Stone, Edward C. *physicist, educator*
Thorne, Kip Stephen *physicist, educator*
Tombrello, Thomas Anthony, Jr., *physics educator, consultant*
Vogt, Rochus Eugen *physicist, educator*
Wasserburg, Gerald Joseph *geology and geophysics educator*
Webster, Christopher R. *chemist, physicist, research scientist*
†Wennberg, Paul *chemist*
Yau, Kevin Kam-ching *astronomer*
Yeomans, Donald Keith *astronomer*
Yorke, Harold W. *astrophysicist*
Zewail, Ahmed Hassan *chemistry and physics educator, editor, consultant*

Pleasanton
Bjorkholm, John Ernst *retired physicist*
Denavit, Jacques *retired physicist*
Stallings, Charles Henry *retired physicist*

Point Mugu
Fisk, Charles John *meteorologist, researcher, consultant*

Pomona
Aurilia, Antonio *physicist, educator*
Bidlack, Wayne Ross *nutritional biochemist, toxicologist, food scientist*

Rancho Palos Verdes
Smirnov, Alexei Vladimirovich *research scientist, consultant*

Rancho Santa Fe
Creutz, Edward Chester *physicist, museum consultant*

PROFESSIONAL INDEX 6633 SCIENCE: PHYSICAL SCIENCE

Redondo Beach
Barter, James Duncan *physicist*
Contescu, Cristian Ion *chemist, researcher*
Foster, John Stuart, Jr., *physicist, former defense industry executive*
Mulvey, Gerald John *meteorologist*

Redwood City
Nacht, Sergio *biochemist*

Richmond
Birman, Alexander *physicist, researcher*
Ward, Carl Edward *research chemist*

Ridgecrest
Bennett, Harold Earl *physicist, optics researcher*

Riverside
Green, Harry Western, II, *geology-geophysics educator*
Korotkov, Alexander N. *physicist, educator, researcher*
Rabenstein, Dallas Leroy *chemistry educator*
Wild, Robert Lee *physics educator*
Zaera, Francisco *chemistry educator, consultant*
Zank, Gary Paul *phyicist*

Rohnert Park
Tenn, Joseph Simon *physics and astronomy educator*
Trowbridge, Dale Brian *educator*

Sacramento
Dedrick, Kent Gentry *retired physicist, researcher*
†Peterson, Roy Martin, Jr., *environmental scientist*

Salinas
Mercurio, Edward Peter *natural science educator*

San Carlos
Dafforn, Geoffrey Alan *biochemist*
Taniere, Romain Andre *pharmaceutical company scientist*

San Clemente
Wolfram, Thomas *physicist, educator*

San Diego
Bussard, Robert William *physicist*
Cantor, Charles Robert *biochemistry educator*
Carsola, Alfred James *oceanographer, geologist, educator*
Cobble, James Wikle *chemistry educator*
†Crute, James John *biochemist, researcher*
Gastil, Russell Gordon *geologist, educator*
Gillespie, George Hubert *physicist*
†Haener, Juan A. *physicist*
Kovacic, Peter *chemistry educator*
Kraus, Pansy Daegling *gemology consultant, editor, writer*
L'Annunziata, Michael Frank *chemist, consultant*
Lao, Lang Li *nuclear fusion research physicist*
Lapota, David *oceanographer, marine biologist*
Mohan, Chandra *research biochemistry educator*
Morgan, Mark Quenten *astrophysics educator*
Murakami, Masanori *physicist*
Pecsok, Robert Louis *chemist, educator*
Pincus, Howard J. *geologist, engineer, educator*
†Prado, Pablo Jose *physicist, researcher*
†Ren, Steven Shijun *chemist*
†Robbins, Eleanora Iberall *biogeologist, researcher*
Shneour, Elie Alexis *biophysicist, researcher, historian*
Springer, Wayne Richard *healthcare system official, research biochemist*
Stetson, Robert Francis *retired metallurgist*
†Stewart, Morgan Elizabeth *research scientist*
Turcu, Ion Cristian Edmond *physicist*

San Francisco
Batterman, Boris William *physicist, educator, academic director*
Burlingame, Alma Lyman *chemist, educator*
Cassman, Marvin *biochemist*
Cluff, Lloyd Sterling *earthquake geologist*
Dickinson, Wade *physicist, oil and gas company executive, educator*
Dill, Kenneth Austin *pharmaceutical chemistry educator*
†Goldstein, David Baird *energy program director, physicist*
Grodsky, Gerold Morton *biochemistry educator*
Highsmith, Stefan *biochemistry educator*
James, Thomas Larry *chemistry educator*
Kelly, Regis Baker *biochemistry educator, biophysics educator*
Mandra, York T. *geology educator*
Marshall, Grayson William, Jr., *biomaterials scientist, health sciences educator*
Marzke, Ronald Oscar *physics and astronomy educator*
Nguyen, Ann Cac Khue *pharmaceutical and medicinal chemist*
Tilinin, Igor Stanislavovich *physicist, educator*

San Jose
Castellano, Joseph Anthony *retired chemist, management consulting firm executive*
Eigler, Donald Mark *physicist*
Finkelstein, Jerome *physicist, educator*
Forster, Julian *physicist, consultant*
Gruber, John Balsbaugh *physics educator, university administrator*
Hoyt, Roger Franklin *physicist*
Luo, Qingzheng *physics researcher*
Neptune, John Addison *chemistry educator, consultant*
Nimmagadda, Rao Rajagopala *materials scientist, researcher*
Parkin, Stuart Stephen Papworth *materials scientist*
Pitts, William Clarence *physicist*
Winters, Harold Franklin *physicist*

San Luis Obispo
Grismore, Roger *physics educator, researcher*
Hafemeister, David Walter *physicist*

San Mateo
Haisch, Bernard Michael *astronomer, researcher*
Holmes, John Richard *physicist, educator*

San Pedro
Plutchak, Noel Bernard *meteorologist, consultant*
Simmons, William *physicist, retired aerospace research executive*

San Rafael
Pomerantz, Martin Arthur *astronomer, educator*

San Ramon
Su, George Shenghui (Sheng-Hui Su) *chemist, medical researcher, educator*

Santa Ana
†Kropp, William Rudolph *physicist*

Santa Barbara
Ahlers, Guenter *physicist, educator*
Crowell, John C(hambers) *geology educator, researcher*
Dunne, Thomas *geology educator*
Gossard, Arthur Charles *physicist, researcher*
Heeger, Alan Jay *physicist, educator*
Hubbard, Arthur Thornton *chemistry educator, electro-surface chemist*
Kennedy, John Harvey *chemistry educator*
Kohn, Walter *educator, physicist*
Langer, James Stephen *physicist, educator*
Luyendyk, Bruce Peter *geophysicist, educator, institution administrator*
Macdonald, Ken Craig *geophysicist*
Martzen, Philip D. *physicist, software developer*
Meinel, Aden Baker *optics scientist*
Pilgeram, Laurence Oscar *biochemist*
Polívka, Jiří *physicist*
Slater, Paul Bernard *physicist*
Tilton, George Robert *geochemistry educator*
Veigele, William John *physicist*
White, Robert Stephen *physics educator*
Wilson, Leslie *biochemist, cell biologist, biology educator*
Yankwich, Peter Ewald *chemistry educator*

Santa Clara
Gozani, Tsahi *nuclear physicist*
Lau, John Hon Shing *electronics scientist*
Lee, Chan-Yun *physicist, process engineer, educator*
Tang, Xianmin *physicist, researcher*

Santa Cruz
Brown, George Stephen *physics educator*
Bunnett, Joseph Frederick *chemist, educator*
Epps, Harland Warren *astronomy educator, optical design consultant*
Faber, Sandra Moore *astronomer, educator*
Fan, Guangwei *seismologist*
Flatté, Stanley Martin *physicist, educator*
Goldbeck, Robert Arthur, Jr., *physical chemist*
Hill, Terrell Leslie *chemist, biophysicist*
Lay, Thorne *geosciences educator*
Osterbrock, Donald E(dward) *astronomy educator*
Sands, Matthew Linzee *physicist, educator*
Williams, Quentin Christopher *geophysicist, educator*
Wipke, W. Todd *chemistry educator*
Wu, Ru-Shan *geophysicist*

Santa Maria
Ellis, Emory Leon *former biochemist*

Santa Monica
Intriligator, Devrie Shapiro *physicist*
Park, Edward Cahill, Jr., *retired physicist*
Shipbaugh, Calvin LeRoy *physicist*

Santa Rosa
Yatsenko, Nikolai Afanasyevich *physics researcher, educator*

Solana Beach
Agnew, Harold Melvin *physicist*

South Pasadena
†Li, Songtao *research scientist*

South San Francisco
Zhong, Min *chemist*

Stanford
Allen, Matthew Arnold *physicist*
†Alter, Orly *theoretical physicist, geneticist*
Baldwin, Robert Lesh *biochemist, educator*
Batygin, Yuri Konstantinovich *accelerator physicist*
Berg, Paul *biochemist, educator*
Bienenstock, Arthur Irwin *physicist, educator, federal official*
Brauman, John I. *chemist, educator*
Brunger, Axel Thomas *biophysicist, researcher, educator*
Bube, Richard Howard *materials scientist, educator*
Byer, Robert Louis *applied physics educator, university dean*
Chao, Alexander Wu *physicist, educator*
Collman, James Paddock *chemistry educator*
Fayer, Michael David *chemist, educator*
Fetter, Alexander Lees *theoretical physicist, educator*
†Flinn, Paul Anthony *materials scientist*
Harbaugh, John Warvelle *geologist, educator*
Harrison, Walter Ashley *physicist, educator*
Herring, William Conyers *physicist, emeritus educator*
Kornberg, Arthur *biochemist, educator*
Kovach, Robert Louis *geophysics educator*
Laughlin, Robert B. *physics educator*
Lehman, I(srael) Robert *biochemist, educator*
Little, William Arthur *physicist, educator*
†Matson, Pamela Anne *environmental scientist, science educator*
McConnell, Harden Marsden *biophysical chemistry researcher, chemistry educator*
†Moerner, William Esco *physical chemist*
†Mukerji, Tapan *geophysicist, researcher*
Osheroff, Douglas Dean *educator, physicist, researcher*
Ross, John *physical chemist, educator*
Schneider, Stephen Henry *climatologist, environmental policy analyst, researcher*
Spicer, William Edward, III, *physicist, educator, engineer*
Taube, Henry *chemistry educator*
Thompson, George Albert *geophysics educator*
Trost, Barry Martin *chemist, educator*
Vailionis, Arturas *physicist*
Wagoner, Robert Vernon *astrophysicist, educator*
Walt, Martin *physicist, consulting educator*
Wang, Suwen *physicist, consultant*
Zare, Richard Neil *chemistry educator*

Sunnyvale
Chang, William Zhi-Ming *physicist, researcher*
Holmes, Richard Brooks *mathematical physicist*
O'Handley, Douglas Alexander *astronomer*
Thissell, James Dennis *physicist*

Tarzana
Meyers, Robert Allen *chemist, publisher*

Toluca Lake
Litwack, Gerald *biochemistry researcher, educator, administrator*

Torrance
Lieberman, Robert Arthur *physicist*
Parfenov, Alexander Vsevolodovitch *physicist, researcher*
Rogers, Howard H. *retired chemist*

Tustin
Clauson, Gary Lewis *chemist*

Upland
Innes, William B. *chemist, consultant*

Vacaville
Engle, Susan Ann *chemist*

Valencia
Levy, Ezra Cesar *aerospace scientist, real estate broker*

Vandenberg AFB
Miller, David Allen *air force officer*

Walnut Creek
Wu, Tse Cheng *research chemist*

Woodland Hills
Monteau, Norman Keith *gemologist*

Woodside
Ashley, Holt *aerospace scientist, educator*
Klein, August Stone *retired physicist*

Yorba Linda
Loeblich, Helen Nina Tappan *paleontologist, educator*

COLORADO

Arvada
Brown, Mark Steven *medical physicist*
Yang, In Che *hydrologist, researcher*

Aurora
Grace, William Pershing *petroleum geologist, real estate developer*

Boulder
Albritton, Daniel Lee *atmospheric scientist*
Alldredge, Leroy Romney *retired geophysicist*
Bartlett, David Farnham *physics educator*
Begelman, Mitchell Craig *astrophysicist, educator, writer*
Chappell, Charles Franklin *meteorologist, consultant*
Conti, Peter Selby *astronomy educator*
Cornell, Eric Allin *physics educator*
Cristol, Stanley Jerome *chemistry educator*
Fleming, Rex James *meteorologist*
Garstang, Roy Henry *astrophysicist, educator*
Grabowski, Wojciech W. *physicist, researcher*
Hermann, Allen Max *physics educator*
Herring, Jackson Rea *physicist*
Hogg, David Clarence *physicist*
Joselyn, Jo Ann *space scientist*
Kapteyn, Henry Cornelius *physics and engineering educator*
Kellogg, William Welch *meteorologist, researcher*
King, Edward Louis *retired chemistry educator*
Kisslinger, Carl *geophysicist, educator*
Koch, Tad Harbison *chemistry educator, researcher*
Lally, Vincent Edward *atmospheric scientist*
LeMone, Margaret Anne *atmospheric scientist*
Lineberger, William Carl *chemistry educator*
Low, Boon Chye *physicist*
MacDonald, Alexander Edward *meteorologist*
Mahanthappa, Kalyana Thipperudraiah *physicist, educator*
Mahlman, Jerry David *research meteorologist*
Malde, Harold Edwin *retired federal government geologist*
McCray, Richard Alan *astrophysicist, educator*
Miller, Harold William *nuclear geochemist*
Ostashev, Vladimir E. *physicist, researcher*
Pankove, Jacques Isaac *physicist, researcher*
†Pierpont, Cortlandt *chemist, educator*
Randa, James Paul *physicist, electrical engineer*
Ridley, Brian Ward *physics educator, researcher*
Robinson, Peter *retired paleontology educator, consultant*
Roellig, Leonard Oscar *physics educator*
Schneider, Nicholas McCord *planetary scientist, educator, textbook author*
Schnell, Russell Clifford *atmospheric scientist, researcher*
†Serreze, Mark Clifford *environmental scientist, researcher*
†Smith, Joel B. *environmental scientist, consultant*
Snell, Esmond Emerson *biochemist*
Snow, Theodore Peck *astrophysics educator*
Tatarskii, Valerian Il'Ich *physics researcher*
Tolbert, Bert Mills *biochemist, educator*
Trenberth, Kevin Edward *atmospheric scientist*
Truce, William Everett *chemist, educator*
Washington, Warren Morton *meteorologist*
Wieman, Carl E. *physics educator*
†Ye, Jun *physicist, researcher*
Zhao, Cong Long *physicist*

Brighton
Rinkenberger, Richard Krug *physical scientist, geologist, consultant*

Centennial
Sherlin, Jerry Michael *retired hydro meteorological technician*

Colorado Springs
Corry, Charles Elmo *geophysicist, consultant*
Hoffman, John Raleigh *physicist*
Rogers, Steven Ray *physicist*
Schwartz, Donald *chemistry educator*
Stahl, Philip Anthony *physics educator*

Denver
†Babayev, Djangir Ali Ikram *physicist, researcher*
†Bouzide, Abderrahim *chemist, researcher*
†Bufe, Charles Glenn *geophysicist, researcher*
Chappell, Willard Ray *physics educator, environmental scientist*
Cobban, William Aubrey *paleontologist*
Eaton, Gareth Richard *chemistry educator, university dean*
Fails, Thomas Glenn *geologist*
Hetzel, Fredrick William *biophysicist, educator*
Iona, Mario *retired physics educator*
†Jibson, Randall Wade *geologist*
Johnson, Walter Earl *geophysicist*
Klipping, Robert Samuel *geophysicist*
Landon, Susan Melinda *petroleum geologist*
Mullineaux, Donal Ray *geologist*
Neumann, Herschel *physics educator*
Sadun, Alberto Carlo *astrophysicist, educator*
Shawe, Daniel Reeves *geologist*
Smith, Dwight Morrell *chemistry educator*
Weihaupt, John George *geosciences educator, scientist, university administrator*

Dillon
Roder, Hans Martin *retired physicist, consultant*

Englewood
Gabel, Connie *chemist, educator*
Strauss, Eric L. *retired materials scientist*

Evergreen
Haun, John Daniel *petroleum geologist, educator*
Heyl, Allen Van, Jr., *geologist*

Fort Collins
Bernstein, Elliot Roy *chemistry educator*
Fixman, Marshall *chemist, educator*
Ladanyi, Branka Maria *chemist, educator*
Meyers, Albert Irving *emeritus chemistry educator*
Mosier, Arvin Ray *chemist, researcher*
Patton, Carl Elliott *physics educator*
Schumm, Stanley Alfred *geologist, educator*
Vonder Haar, Thomas H. *meteorology educator*
Woolhiser, David Arthur *hydrologist*

Golden
†Contreras, Miguel Alberto *materials scientist, researcher*
Hamilton, Warren Bell *geologist, researcher, geophysicist, educator*
Hu, Jian *physicist, researcher*
Krauss, George *metallurgist*
†Speer, John Gordon *metallurgist, educator, materials scientist, educator*
†Stoffel, Thomas *research scientist*
Trefny, John Ulric *college president*
Wei, Su-Huai *physicist, researcher*
Weimer, Robert Jay *geology educator, energy consultant, civic leader*
Zhong, Dalong *materials scientist, consultant*

Grand Junction
Duray, John Robert *physicist*
Rutz, Richard Frederick *physicist, researcher*

Highlands Ranch
Krinsky, Fredda S. *clinical chemist, consultant*

Lafayette
McNeill, William *environmental scientist*

Lakewood
†Goolsby, Donald Allton *water resources scientist*
Hansen, Richard Olaf *geophysicist, educator*
Quinn, John Michael *physicist, geophysicist*

Littleton
Harney, Patricia Rae *enviromental technical supervisor*
Paull, Richard Allen *geologist, educator*

Ridgway
Lathrop, Kaye Don *nuclear scientist, educator*

CONNECTICUT

Bethany
Bergen, Robert Ludlum, Jr., *retired materials scientist*

Bethel
Cheh, Huk Yuk *electrochemist, battery company executive*
Schetky, Laurence McDonald *metallurgist, researcher*

Bloomfield
Ivey, Elizabeth S. *retired physicist, educator*

Branford
DeSimone, Robert Walter *medicinal chemist, educator*

Bridgeport
Ettre, Leslie Stephen *chemist*
†Reed, Charles Eli *retired chemist, chemical engineer*

Clinton
†Panayotov, Christo Angelov *research scientist, consultant*

Coventry
Ferguson, Ronald Max *chemistry educator, researcher*

Danbury
†Joyce, William H. *chemist*
†Pastor, Stephen Daniel *chemistry educator, researcher*

East Hartford
Danko, Gene Andrew *materials scientist*

Farmington
Goodson, Richard Carle, Jr., *chemist, consultant*
Osborn, Mary Jane Merten *biochemist, educator*
Slepchenko, Boris Moyseyevich *mathematical physicist, educator*
Spencer, Richard Paul *biochemist, educator, physician*

Groton
Colgan, Stephen Thomson *analytical chemist*
Kavarnos, George James *research chemist*
Swindell, Archie Calhoun, Jr., *research biochemist, statistician*
†Wallach, Morton L. *scientist*

Guilford
Handschumacher, Robert Edmund *biochemistry educator*

Ledyard
Chiang, Albert Chinfa *polymer chemist*

Manchester
Galasso, Francis Salvatore *materials scientist*

Middletown
Fry, Albert Joseph *chemistry educator*

Naugatuck
Stott, Paul Edwin *chemist, research manager*

New Britain
Baskerville, Charles Alexander *geologist, educator*
Dimmick, Charles William *geology educator*

New Haven
Adair, Robert Kemp *physicist, educator*
†Baltay, Charles *physicist, educator*
Berson, Jerome Abraham *chemistry educator*
Bromley, David Allan *physicist, engineer, educator*
Casten, Richard Francis *physicist*
Chertow, Marian Ruth *industrial ecologist, educator*
Chupka, William Andrew *chemical physicist, educator*
Halvorsen, Per Helge *medical physicist, educator*
Herzenberg, Arvid *physicist, educator*
Klein, Martin Jesse *physicist, educator, science historian*
†Marchesi, Vincent T. *biochemist, educator*
Moore, Peter Bartlett *biochemist, educator*
Reed, Mark Arthur *educator, researcher*
Richards, Frederic Middlebrook *biochemist, educator*
Shulman, Robert Gerson *biophysics educator*
Skinner, Helen Catherine Wild *biomineralogist*
Slayman, Clifford Leroy *biophysicist, educator*
Sofia, Sabatino *astronomy educator*
†Steitz, Joan Argetsinger *biochemistry educator*
Tully, John Charles *research chemical physicist*
Turekian, Karl Karekin *geochemistry educator*
Wolf, Werner Paul *physicist, educator*
Zamfir, Nicolae Victor *physicist, researcher*
Zeller, Michael Edward *physicist, educator*

New London
Thompson, Douglas Marshall *geomorphologist, educator*

New Milford
Fabricand, Burton Paul *physicist, educator*

Ridgefield
†Matteo, Martha R. *biochemist*
Sen, Pabitra N. *physicist, researcher*
Wang, Yuwen *chemist, researcher*

Rocky Hill
Chu, Hsien-Kun *chemist, researcher*

Sandy Hook
†Hopkins, Homer Thawley *chemist, researcher, retired chemist*

Shelton
Zeller, Claude *physicist, researcher*

Southbury
Morehead, Frederick Ferguson *retired physical chemist*

Stamford
Chang, Ted T. *chemist*
Courter, Jeanne Lynn *materials scientist*

Stonington
Mantz, Arlan W. *physics educator*

Storrs Mansfield
Azaroff, Leonid Vladimirovitch *physics educator*
Bartram, Ralph Herbert *physicist*
Devereux, Owen Francis *metallurgy educator*
Hahn, Yukap *physics educator, researcher*
Klemens, Paul Gustav *physicist, educator*
Marcus, Harris Leon *materials science educator*
Stwalley, William Calvin *physics and chemistry educator*
Suib, Steven Lawrence *chemist*

Tolland
Feller, Winthrop Bruce *physicist*

Wallingford
Poindexter, Graham S. *chemist*
†Romine, Jeffrey Lee *chemist*

Washington
Strojny, Norman *analytical chemist*

Waterford
Johnson, Gary William *environmental scientist, consultant*

West Hartford
Markham, Claire Agnes (M. Clare Markham) *retired chemistry educator, consultant*

West Haven
Onton, Ann Louise Reuther *chemist*

Westport
Smith, Peter Wolfgang *physicist, artist*

Willington
Chao, Yong-Sheng *physicist*

Woodbury
Skinner, Brian John *geologist, educator*

DELAWARE

Dover
Wasfi, Sadiq Hassan *chemistry educator*

New Castle
Bellenger, George Collier, Jr., *physics educator*
†Fairchild, Edward Harold *chemist, researcher*

Newark
Böer, Karl Wolfgang *physicist, educator*
Burmeister, John Luther *chemistry educator, consultant*
Esrey, Elizabeth Gove Goodier *chemist, biologist*
Evans, Dennis Hyde *chemist, educator*
Gorski, Robert Alexander *chemist, consultant*
Murray, Richard Bennett *physics educator*
Ness, Norman Frederick *astrophysicist, educator, administrator*
Shipman, Harry Longfellow *astrophysicist, educator*
Theopold, Klaus Hellmut *chemistry educator*
Trofimenko, Swiatoslaw *chemist, researcher, consultant*
Vassiliou, Eustathios *chemist, consultant*
Wei, Tie-Quan *biochemist*

Seaford
Norton, Lilburn Lafayette *chemist, consultant*

Wilmington
Crittenden, Eugene Dwight, Jr., *chemical company executive*
Fletcher, Jeffrey Edward *editor, medical writer*
Jezl, Barbara Ann *retired chemist, automation consultant*
Kissa, Erik *retired chemist, consultant*
Kwolek, Stephanie Louise *chemist, researcher*
Marcali, Jean Gregory *chemist, retired*
†McCoy, Verl Eugene, Jr., *physical chemist, consultant*
†Memeger, Wesley, Jr., *retired chemist, painter*
Moore, Carl Gordon *chemist, educator*
Parshall, George William *chemist, researcher*
Smook, Malcolm Andrew *chemist, chemical company executive*

DISTRICT OF COLUMBIA

Washington
Abelson, Philip Hauge *physicist*
†Adelman, Clifford *research analyst*
†Andreadis, Tim D. *physicist, researcher*
Beall, James Howard *physicist, educator, public policy analysis*
Beck, Richard Thomas *scientific facility administrator*
Berendzen, Richard *astronomer, educator, author*
Brown, Louis *physicist, researcher*
Campbell, Bruce *geologist*
Cheetham, Alan Herbert *paleontologist*
Clarke, Robert Reside *biochemist, researcher*
†Cross, Freddie Lee *research scientist*
Crumbling, Deana Marie *environmental scientist*
†Dastoor, Minoo *biochemist*
Davidson, Eugene Abraham *biochemist, university administrator*
Domning, Daryl Paul *paleontologist, educator*
Donohue, Joyce Morrissey *biochemist, toxicologist, nutritionist, educator*
Dutro, John Thomas, Jr., *geologist, paleontologist*
†Eghbal, Morad *geologist, lawyer*
El Khadem, Hassan Saad *chemistry educator, researcher*
Esfandiary, Mary S. *physical scientist, operations consultant*
Feigelson, Boris N. *physical chemist, researcher, materials scientist*
Fogleman, Guy Carroll *physicist, mathematician, educator*
Friedberg, Felix *biochemist, educator*
Galloway, Eilene Marie *space and astronautics consultant*
Giacconi, Riccardo *astrophysicist, educator*
Goff, James Franklin *physicist, consultant*
Goldstein, Allan Leonard *biochemist, educator*
Hallgren, Richard Edwin *meteorologist*
Handel, Mark David *atmospheric scientist*
Hart, Katherine Marie *environmental scientist*
Harwit, Martin Otto *astrophysicist, writer, educator, museum director*
Heineman, Heinz *chemist*
Heinemann, Heinz *chemist, educator, researcher, consultant*
Higgins, Peter Thomas *technology consultant*
Holland, Christie Anna *biochemist, virologist*
Holloway, John Thomas *physicist, consultant*
Howard, Russell Alfred *astrophysicist, researcher*
Imam, M. Ashraf *materials scientist, educator*
Johnson, Charles Minor *physicist*
Johnston, Kenneth John *astronomer, scientific director naval observatory*
Karle, Isabella L. *chemist*
Karle, Jerome *physicist, researcher*
Kimble, Melinda Louise *environmental administrator*
Klein, Philipp Hillel *electronic materials consultant*
Larson, Paul Melvin *physics researcher*
†Lash, Jonathan *non-profit environment/development executive*
Ledley, Robert Steven *biophysicist*
Lee, Yuen San *chemist*
Lehman, Donald Richard *physicist, educator, academic administrator*
Lehmberg, Robert Henry *research physicist*
Logsdon, John Mortimer, III, *aerospace analyst, educator*
†Loyevsky, Mark Michael *biochemist, researcher*
Lozansky, Edward Dmitry *physicist, author, consultant*
Mahmood, M. F. *research scientist, educator*
Mandula, Jeffrey Ellis *physicist*
Meijer, Paul Herman Ernst *educator, physicist*
Morehouse, David Frank *geologist*
Oliver, William Albert, Jr., *paleontologist, researcher*
Oran, Elaine Surick *physicist, engineer*
Orbach, Raymond Lee *physicist, educator*
Pardavi-Horvath, Martha Maria *physicist, educator*
Pascu, Dan *astronomer*
Pojeta, John, Jr., *geologist, researcher*
Pope, Michael Thor *chemistry educator*
Press, Frank *geophysicist*
Roper, Odean S. *environmentalist, researcher*
Rosenberg, Jerome David *physicist*
Ross, Malcolm *minerals consultant*
Sáenz, Albert William *theoretical physicist, researcher, consultant*
Sayre, Edward Vale *chemist*
Schachter, Myron Marvin *retired research chemist, engineer*
Schierow, Linda-Jo *environmental policy analyst*
†Schwartzman, David William *chemist, educator*
Shamim, Mah Talat *chemist*
Shanny, Ramy *physicist*
Shuler, James Mannie *health physicist*
Siegel, Frederic Richard *geology educator*
Singer, Maxine Frank *retired biochemist, scientific institute executive*
†Singh, Daljhit *science and technology conuselor, chemical engineer and technology educator*
Solomon, Sean Carl *geophysicist, lab administrator*
Spencer, John Howard *radio astronomer*
Spilhaus, Athelstan Frederick, Jr., *oceanographer, association executive*
Spinrad, Richard William *oceanographer, researcher*
Stanley, Jean-Daniel *geological oceanographer*
Steadman, Stephen Geoffrey *physicist*
Uberall, Herbert Michael Stefan *physicist, educator*
Vertes, Akos *chemist, educator*
†Wende, Charles David *aerospace scientist*
Wetherill, George West *geophysicist, planetary scientist*
White, Robert Mayer *meteorologist*
†Willard, Matthew Ashe *materials scientist, researcher*
Yochelson, Ellis L9eon) *paleontologist*
Yoder, Hatten Schuyler, Jr., *petrologist*
Youtcheff, John Sheldon *physicist*

FLORIDA

Alachua
Schneider, Richard T(heodore) *optics research executive, engineer*

Boca Raton
Resnick, Robert *physicist, educator*
Rosenkranz, Herbert S. *public health educator*
Ross, Fred Michael *organic chemist*
Weissbach, Herbert *biochemist, researcher*
Wiesenfeld, John Richard *chemistry educator*

Bonita Springs
Brown, Theodore Lawrence *chemistry educator*

Boynton Beach
Balis, Moses Earl *biochemist, educator*

Bradenton
Charlton, Gordon Randolph *physicist*
Compton, Charles Daniel *chemistry educator*
Engelhard, Arthur William *research scientist, consultant*

Cape Coral
West, John Merle *retired physicist, nuclear consultant*

Cocoa
McCluney, Ross (William Ross McCluney) *research physicist, education educator*
Muradov, Nazim Ziraddin *chemist, researcher*

Coral Gables
Criss, Cecil M. *chemistry educator*
Einspruch, Norman Gerald *physicist, engineering educator*
Glaser, Luis *biochemistry educator*
Leblanc, Roger Maurice *chemistry educator*
Van Vliet, Carolyne Marina *physicist, educator*

Dade City
Burdick, Glenn Arthur *physicist, engineering educator*

Daytona Beach
Swanson, Gerald Carl *chemistry educator*

Delray Beach
Solon, Leonard R(aymond) *retired physicist, educator, consultant*
Zarwyn, Berthold *physical scientist*

Fort Myers
Herriott, Donald Richard *optical physicist*
Horecker, Bernard Leonard *retired biochemistry educator*
Missimer, Thomas Michael *geologist*

Fort Pierce
†Fuchs, Eran *oceanographer, researcher*

Gainesville
Butler, George Bergen *chemistry educator*
†Cabrera-Trujillo, Remigio *research scientist*
Cousins, Robert John *nutritional biochemist, educator*
Davis, George Kelso *nutrition biochemist, educator*
Fan, Z. Hugh *chemist, biomedical engineer*
Hanrahan, Robert Joseph *chemist, educator*
Hanson, Harold Palmer *physicist, government official, editor, academic administrator*
Holloway, Paul Howard *materials science educator*
Katritzky, Alan Roy *chemistry educator, consultant*
†Mareci, Thomas Harold *biophysicist, educator*
Micha, David Allan *chemistry and physics educator*
Mitselmakher, Guenakh *physics educator, researcher*
Ohrn, Nils Yngve *chemistry and physics educator*
Perry, Vernon G. *research scientist, educator*
Sabin, John Rogers *physics educator*
†Sigmund, Wolfgang M. *materials scientist, educator*
Singley, John Edward, Jr., *retired environmental scientist, consultant*
Sisler, Harry Hall *chemist, educator*
Stavrev, Krassimir K. *chemist, researcher*
Stehli, Francis Greenough *geologist, educator*
Trickey, Samuel Baldwin *physics educator, researcher, university administrator*
†Tsao, Jennie Ching-I *research scientist, educator*
Yost, Richard Alan *chemistry educator*

Gonzalez
Plischke, Le Moyne Wilfred *research chemist*

Hialeah Gardens
Tuninskaya, Galina M. *chemist, consultant*

Jacksonville
Beattie, Donald A. *energy scientist, consultant*

Jupiter
Jacobson, Jerry Irving *biophysicist, theoretical physicist*

Key West
Trammell, Herbert Eugene *physicist, laboratory executive*

Lakeland
McFarlin, Richard Francis *retired industrial chemist, researcher*

Longboat Key
Stapleton, Harvey James *physics educator*

Lutz
Koff, Fred William *retired research chemist*

Melbourne
Babich, Michael Wayne *chemistry educator, educational administrator*
Burckhalter, Joseph Harold *chemistry educator*
Nelson, Gordon Leigh *chemist, educator*

Miami
Blanco, Luciano-Nilo *physicist*
†Freire, Jose A. *physicist, writer*
†Hirschberg, Joseph Gustav *educator, physicist*
†Kowalska, Maria Teresa *research scientist, educator*
†Li, Qi *research scientist, consultant*
Mares-Guia, Marcos Luiz *biochemist, consultant*
Mooers, Christopher Northrup Kennard *physical oceanographer, educator*
†Nakashima, Tadayoshi *retired biochemist, researcher*
Ostlund, H. Gote *atmospheric and marine scientist, educator*
†Perez-Stable, Carlos *research scientist*
Woessner, Jacob Frederick, Jr., *biochemistry educator*

Mount Dora
Foote, Nathan Maxted *retired physical science educator*

Mulberry
Baumann, Arthur Nicholas *chemist, consultant*

Naples
Leitner, Alfred *mathematical physicist, educator, educational film producer*
Marcuvitz, Nathan *electrophysics educator*

Ocala
Fredericks, William John *chemistry educator*

Orange Park
Walsh, Gregory Sheehan *optical systems professional*

Orlando
Baker, Peter Mitchell *laser scientist, educator, science administrator*
Blue, Joseph Edward *physicist*
Llewellyn, Ralph Alvin *physics educator*
†Mujat, Mircea *optics scientist*
†Phanstiel, Otto *chemistry educator, consultant*
Schulte, Alfons Friedrich *physicist, educator*
†Stegeman, George I. *physicist, educator*
Ting, Robert Yen-ying *physicist*

Ormond Beach
Kanfer, Julian Norman *biochemist, educator*

Palatka
Ouyang, Ying *environmental scientist, educator*

Palm Beach Gardens
Bonifazi, Stephen *chemist*
Levitt, George *retired chemist*

Palm Harbor
†Bradley, Richard *chemist, consultant*

Panama City
Rackers, Thomas William *physicist, researcher*
Shugart, Cecil Glenn *retired physics educator*

Pensacola
Steinhoff, Raymond O(akley) *consulting geologist*

Rockledge
Deitch, D. Gregory *meteorologist*

Saint Petersburg
Hansel, Paul George *physicist, consultant*
†Hsu, Tsong Han *chemist, researcher*
Rydstrom, Carlton Lionel *chemist, chemicals consultant*

Sanford
Dickison, Alexander Kane *physical science educator*

Sarasota
Kerker, Milton *chemistry educator*
Myerson, Albert Leon *physical chemist*
Pierce, Richard Harry *oceanographer*

Tallahassee
Caspar, Donald L.D. *biophysics and structural biology educator*
Choppin, Gregory Robert *chemistry educator*
†Gleeson, Thomas Alexander *retired meteorologist*
Han, Ke *materials scientist, metallurgy consultant*
Herndon, Roy Clifford *physicist*
Kemper, Kirby Wayne *physics educator*
Kromhout, Robert Andrew *educator*
Loper, David Eric *geophysics educator, mathematics educator*
Mandelkern, Leo *biophysics and chemistry educator*
Manousakis, Efstratios *physicist, educator*
Marshall, Alan George *chemistry and biochemistry educator*
Moulton, Grace Charbonnet *physics educator*
Pfeffer, Richard Lawrence *meteorology and geophysics educator*
†Plendl, Hans S. *retired physicist, editor*
Rikvold, Per Arne *physics researcher and educator*
Robson, Donald *physics educator*
Saha, Bidhan Chandra *physicist, educator*
Schrieffer, John Robert *physics educator, science administrator*
†Wahl, Horst Dieter *physicist, researcher, educator*
Zou, Xiaolei *meteorologist, educator*

Tampa
Johnson, Anthony O'Leary (Andy Johnson) *meteorologist, consultant*
†Martin, Dean Frederick *chemist, educator*
Szonntagh, Eugene L. *chemical engineer, chemist, hygienist, educator, archaeometrist, musicologist, organist, historian*
†Zhu, Yiliang *research scientist, educator*

Venice
Feldmann, Edward George *pharmaceutical chemist, pharmacologist*

West Palm Beach
Iqbal, Tariq *physics educator, researcher*
Witt, Gerhardt Meyer *hydrogeologist*

GEORGIA

Alpharetta
Hung, William Mo-Wei *chemist*

Athens
Black, Clanton Candler, Jr., *biochemistry educator, researcher*
Chu, Chung Kwang *medicinal chemistry educator*
Johnson, Michael Kenneth *chemistry educator*
†Loux, Nicholas Thomas *chemist, researcher*
Pelletier, S. William *chemistry educator*
Schaefer, Henry Frederick, III, *chemistry educator*
†Sophianopoulos, Judy Ann *environmental scientist*
Yamaguchi, Yukio *chemistry research scientist*
Yen, William Mao-Shung *physicist, consultant*

Atlanta
Allison, Stuart Anthony *chemistry educator, researcher*
Banerjee, Sujit *environmental scientist, educator*
Bosah, Francis N. *molecular biochemist, educator*
Cramer, Howard Ross *geologist, environmental consultant*
Dickinson, Robert Earl *atmospheric scientist, educator*
Finkelstein, David Ritz *physicist, educator, consultant*
Fox, Ronald Forrest *physics educator*
Gimmestad, Gary Gene *physicist, researcher*
Hardcastle, Kenneth Irvin *crystallographer, researcher*
Harmer, Don Stutler *physicist, educator, nuclear engineer*
Iacobucci, Guillermo Arturo *chemist*
Johnson, Ronald Carl *chemistry educator*
Kahn, Bernd *radiochemist, educator*
Lin, Ming-Chang *physical chemistry educator, researcher*
Long, Leland Timothy *geophysicist educator, seismologist*
†Mallena, Sirish *chemist, researcher*
Massey, Walter Eugene *physicist, science foundation administrator*
Msezane, Alfred Zakele *physics educator*
Prilutsky, Boris Isaakovich *biophysicist*
†Snyder, Robert Lyman *materials scientist, educator*
Strekowski, Lucjan *chemistry educator*
Valk, Henry Snowden *physicist, educator*
Wong, Ching-Ping *chemist, materials scientist, engineer, educator*

Douglasville
Campbell, Bruce Henry *chemist*

Duluth
Bridges, Alan Lynn *physicist, computer scientist, systems software engineer*
†Gereben, Istvan Bela *retired oceanographer, retired acoustical engineer*

Hull
Melton, Charles Estel *retired physicist, educator*

Lithonia
Baxter, Gene Francis *chemical researcher, consultant*

Marietta
Berryhill, Henry Lee, Jr., *geologist, researcher*
Sink, John Davis *scientist, clergy member*

Norcross
Smith, David Carr *organic chemist*

Peachtree City
Roobol, Norman Richard *industrial coatings consultant, educator*

Riverdale
Awachie, Peter Ifeacho Anazoba *chemistry educator, research chemist*

Savannah
Sanders, James Grady *biogeochemist*
Simonaitis, Richard Ambrose *chemist*
Walter, Paul Hermann Lawrence *chemistry educator*
Windom, Herbert Lynn *oceanographer, environmental scientist*

Statesboro
Mobley, Cleon Marion, Jr., (Chip Mobley) *physics educator, real estate developer*

Stone Mountain
Reichert, Leo Edmund, Jr., *biochemist, endocrinologist*

HAWAII

Hawaii National Park
Swanson, Donald Alan *geologist*

Hilo
†Jarvi, Susan I. *research scientist, educator*

Honolulu
Brantley, Lee Reed *chemistry educator*
Chen, Yi-Leng *meteorologist, educator*
Ekern, Paul C. *retired meteorologist*
Hawke, Bernard Ray *planetary scientist*
Herbig, George Howard *astronomer, educator*
Hey, Richard Noble *marine geophysicist*
Ihrig, Judson La Moure *chemist*
Jensen, Craig Martin *chemistry educator*
Keil, Klaus *geology educator, consultant*
Khan, Mohammad Asad *geophysicist, educator, former energy minister and senator of Pakistan*
Mader, Charles Lavern *chemist*
Ogburn, Hugh Bell *chemical engineer, consultant*
Raleigh, Cecil Baring *geophysicist*
Rosendal, Hans Erik *meteorologist*
†Wills-Toro, Luis Alberto *physicist, mathematician*
Zinin, Pavel V. *physicist*

Kihei
Borchers, Robert Reece *physicist and administrator*

Waikoloa
Morris, Victor Franklin, Jr., *retired meteorology educator*

IDAHO

Boise
Bai, Bin *physicist, researcher*
†Johnson, Howard Earl *chemist, educator*
†Punnoose, Alex *physics educator*

Idaho Falls
†Hurley, David Howard *physicist*
Schrader, Bradley *physicist*

Mc Call
Hamilton, Charles Howard *metallurgy educator*

Moscow
Machleidt, Ruprecht *physicist*
Miller, Maynard Malcolm *geologist, educator, research institute director, explorer, legislator*
Renfrew, Malcolm MacKenzie *chemist, educator*
Shreeve, Jean'ne Marie *chemist, educator*
Stumpf, Bernhard Josef *physicist, educator*

Pocatello
Gesell, Thomas Frederick *physicist, educator*

Twin Falls
Tarter, James Gordon *chemistry educator*

ILLINOIS

Abbott Park
†Abad-Zapatero, Celerino *crystallographer, researcher*
Jeng, Tzyy-Wen *biochemist, researcher*

Argonne
†Ahmad, Irshad *physicist, nuclear chemist*
Derrick, Malcolm *physicist*
Katz, Joseph Jacob *retired chemist, educator*
Lawson, Robert Davis *theoretical nuclear physicist*
†Lienert, Ulrich *physicist*
†Perlow, Gilbert J(erome) *editor*
Peshkin, Murray *physicist*
Sabau, Carmen Sybile *chemist*
Steindler, Martin Joseph *chemist*
Teng, Lee Chang-Li *researcher in accelerator and beam physics*

Arlington Heights
Lewin, Seymour Zalman *chemistry educator, consultant*
Smith, Norman Obed *physical chemist, educator*

Aurora
Shevchenko, Sergey Markovich *organic chemist*

Batavia
Balbekov, Valeri I. *physicist, researcher*
Bardeen, William Allan *research physicist*
Chrisman, Bruce Lowell *physicist, administrator*
Fischler, Mark Steven *physicist*
Jonckheere, Alan Mathew *physicist*
Lach, Joseph Theodore *physicist*
Quigg, Chris *physicist*
Raja, Rajendran *physicist*
†Tollestrup, Alvin Virgil *physicist*
†Yeh, Gong Ping (G.P.) *physicist*

Carbondale
Henneberger, Walter Carl *retired physicist*

Champaign
Buschbach, Thomas Charles *geologist, consultant*
Cartwright, Keros *hydrogeologist, researcher*
Gross, David Lee *geologist*
Hager, Lowell Paul *biochemistry educator*
Herzog, Beverly Leah *hydrogeologist*
Hwang, Hue-Hwa *geochemist*
Krug, Edward Charles *environmental scientist*
Panno, Samuel Vincent *geochemist*
Slichter, Charles Pence *physicist, educator*
Wolfram, Stephen *physicist, computer company executive*

Chicago
†Batra, Inder P. *physics educator, researcher*
Beckers, Jacques Maurice *astrophysicist*
Berry, Richard Stephen *chemist*
†Bezkorovainy, Anatoly *medical educator, biochemist*
†Blumberg, Avrom Aaron *physical chemistry educator*
Chambers, Donald Arthur *biochemistry and molecular medicine educator*
†Chen, Chin-Tu *medical physics educator*
Clayton, Robert Norman *chemist, educator*
Cronin, James Watson *physicist, educator*
Erber, Thomas *physics educator*
Freed, Karl Frederick *chemistry educator*
Freund, Peter G.O. *physicist, educator*
†Giger, Maryellen Lissak *medical physicist*
Gislason, Eric Arni *chemistry educator*
Goldwasser, Eugene *biochemist, educator*
Gomer, Robert *chemistry educator*
Halpern, Jack *chemist, educator*
Harvey, Ronald Gilbert *research chemist*
Herzenberg, Caroline Stuart Littlejohn *physicist*
Hildebrand, Roger Henry *astrophysicist, physicist*
Iqbal, Zafar Mohd *cancer researcher, biochemist, pharmacologist, toxicologist, consultant, molecular biologist*
†Kadanoff, Leo Philip *physicist, educator*
†Keiderling, Timothy Allen *chemistry educator, researcher*
Kleppa, Ole J. *chemistry educator*
Kouvel, James Spyros *physicist, educator*
Krawetz, Arthur Altshuler *chemist, science administrator*
Lehman, Dennis Dale *chemistry educator*
Levy, Donald Harris *chemistry educator*
Liao, Shutsung *biochemist, oncologist*
Makinen, Marvin William *biophysicist, educator*
Mintzer, David *physics educator*
Nagel, Sidney Robert *physics educator*
Nambu, Yoichiro *physics educator*
Oehme, Reinhard *physicist, educator*
Oka, Takeshi *physicist, chemist, astronomer, educator*
Olsen, Edward John *geologist, educator, curator*
Palmer, Patrick Edward *radio astronomer, educator*
Parra, Ruben Dario *chemist, educator*
Platzman, George William *geophysicist, educator*
Reiffel, Leonard *physicist, medical physicist, scientific consultant*
Robbins, Kenneth Carl *biochemist*
Rosner, Jonathan Lincoln *physicist, educator*
Rosner, Robert *astrophysicist, educator*
Sager, William Frederick *retired chemistry educator*
Schillinger, Edwin Joseph *physics educator*
Schlossman, Mark Loren *physicist, physics educator*
Schug, Kenneth Robert *chemistry educator*
Sills, Thomas W. *physical science educator*
Steiner, Donald Frederick *biochemist, physician, educator*
Stroscio, Michael Anthony *physicist, educator*
Trenary, Michael *chemist, educator*
Truran, James Wellington, Jr., *astrophysicist, educator*
Turner, Michael Stanley *astrophysics educator*
Winston, Roland *physicist, educator*
York, Donald Gilbert *astronomy educator, researcher*

Deerfield
Guttman, Arnold R. *chemist, educator*

Dekalb
Kimball, Clyde William *physicist, educator*
Rossing, Thomas D. *physics educator*

Downers Grove
†Feinstein, Robert Norman *retired biochemist*
Shen, Sin-Yan *physicist, conductor, acoustics specialist, music director*

Elk Grove Village
Jan, Chwu-Ching Hwang *environmental chemistry consultant*

Elmhurst
Betinis, Emanuel James *physics and mathematics educator*

Evanston
Allred, Albert Louis *chemistry educator*
†Fu, Lei *materials scientist, research scientist*
Genkin, Gennady *physicist*
Ibers, James Arthur *chemist, educator*
Lambert, Joseph Buckley *chemistry educator*
†Margoliash, Emanuel *biochemist, educator*
Meshii, Masahiro *materials science educator*
Moore, C. Bradley *chemistry educator*
Oakes, Robert James *physics educator*
Okal, Emile Andre *geophysicist, educator*
Olson, Gregory Bruce *materials science and engineering educator, academic director*
Patashinski, Alexander Z. *physicist, materials science consultant*
Pople, Sir John Anthony *chemistry educator*
Sachtler, Wolfgang Max Hugo *chemistry educator*
Schluter, Robert Arvel *physicist*
Seidman, David N(athaniel) *materials science and engineering educator*
Shriver, Duward Felix *chemistry educator, researcher, consultant*
Silverman, Richard Bruce *chemist, biochemist, educator*
Spears, Kenneth George *chemistry educator*
Taam, Ronald Everett *physics and astronomy educator*
Walter, Robert Irving *chemistry educator, chemist*
Weertman, Johannes *materials science educator*
Weertman, Julia Randall *materials science and engineering educator*
Wessels, Bruce W. *materials scientist, educator*

Glen Ellyn
Mooring, F. Paul *physics editor*

Glencoe
Surgi, Marion Rene *chemist*

Glenview
Rorig, Kurt Joachim *chemist, research director*

Hinsdale
Kaminsky, Manfred Stephan *physicist*

Homer Glen
Bhatti, Neeloo *environmental scientist*

Homewood
Parker, Eugene Newman *retired physicist, educator*

Joliet
Foster, Raymond Orville *physics educator, priest*

Kinsman
†Kotamarthi, V. Rao *meteorologist*

Lake Bluff
Vander Voort, George Frederic *metallurgist*

Lake Forest
Crovetti, Aldo Joseph *retired chemist, consultant*
Weston, Arthur Walter *chemist, scientific and business executive*

Lemont
Williams, Jack Marvin *research chemist*
†Zapol, Peter *research scientist*

Lisle
Staab, Thomas Eugene *chemist*

Lombard
McCoy, Jeanie Shearer *analytical chemist, consultant*

Maywood
†Bermes, Edward William, Jr., *biochemist, educator*
Schultz, Richard Michael *biochemistry educator, researcher*

Mount Carmel
Fornoff, Frank J(unior) *retired chemistry educator, consultant*

Naperville
Arzoumanidis, Gregory G. *chemist*
Kaduk, James Albert *crystallographer*
Rosenmann, Daniel *physicist, educator*
Sellers, Gregory Jude *physicist*
Sherren, Anne Terry *chemistry educator*

Normal
Throckmorton, Peter Eugene *retired organic chemist, consultant*

North Chicago
Kemp, Robert Grant *biochemist, educator*
†Ku, Yi-Yin *organic chemist*
Loga, Sanda *physicist, educator*

Northbrook
Colton, Frank Benjamin *retired chemist*

Northfield
Shabica, Charles Wright *geologist, earth science educator*

Oak Park
Fanta, Paul Edward *chemist, educator*

Palos Hills
Vasiliauskas, Edmund *chemistry educator*

Peoria
Chamberlain, Joseph Miles *astronomer, educator*
Cunningham, Raymond Leo *retired research chemist*
†Fanta, George Frederick *chemist, researcher*
Nielsen, Harald Christian *retired chemist, researcher*
†Reith, Maarten Edward A. *neurochemist*
Saha, Badal Chandra *biochemist*

Philo
Wood, Susanne Griffiths *environmental chemist, microbiologist*

Rock Island
Anderson, Richard Charles *geology educator*
Sundelius, Harold W. *geology educator*

Rockford
Walhout, Justine Simon *chemistry educator*
Yu, Fu-Li *biochemistry educator, cancer researcher*

Skokie
†Hamer, Martin *retired chemist*

Springfield
Gallina, Charles Onofrio *nuclear scientist*

Urbana
Beak, Peter Andrew *chemistry educator*
Birnbaum, Howard Kent *materials science educator*
Crofts, Antony Richard *biochemistry and biophysics educator*
†Dikanov, Sergei A. *physicist, researcher*
†Ehrlich, Gert *science educator, researcher*
Forbes, Richard Mather *biochemistry educator*
Fujiwara, Mitsuko *chemist, researcher, chemist, educator*
Ginsberg, Donald Maurice *physicist, educator*
Goldwasser, Edwin Leo *physicist*
Govindjee, *biophysics, biochemistry, and biology educator*
Greene, Laura Helen *physicist*
Gruebele, Martin *chemistry, physics, and biophysics educator*
Iben, Icko, Jr., *astrophysicist, educator*
Jonas, Jiri *chemist, educator*
†Kelleher, Neil L. *chemist, educator*
Kieffer, Susan Werner *geologist, educator, real estate developer, consultant*
Kirkpatrick, R(obert) James *geology educator*
Klein, Miles Vincent *physics educator*
Kushner, Mark Jay *physics and engineering educator*
Lauterbur, Paul C(hristian) *chemistry educator*
Lazarus, David *physicist, educator*
Makri, Nancy *chemistry educator*
Mapother, Dillon Edward *physicist, university official*
Odintsov, Boris Mikhailovich *physicist, researcher*
Rowland, Theodore Justin *physicist, educator*
Salamon, Myron Ben *physicist, educator, dean*
Satterthwaite, Cameron B. *physics educator*
†Scheeline, Alexander *chemistry educator*
Simon, Jack Aaron *geologist, former state official*
Snyder, Lewis Emil *astrophysicist, educator*
Suslick, Kenneth Sanders *chemistry educator*
Switzer, Robert Lee *biochemistry educator*
†Ting, Mingfang *geophysicist, educator*
†Webbink, Ronald Frederick *astrophysicist, educator*

Urbana-Champaign
Jarrell, Wesley Michael *environmental scientist, educator*

Wilmette
Klotz, Irving Myron *chemist, educator*
Rocek, Jan *chemist, educator*

Worth
Ammeraal, Robert Neal *biochemist*

INDIANA

Bloomington
†Bronstein, Lyudmila M. *chemist*
Davidson, Ernest Roy *chemist, educator*
Easton, Susan Dawn *biochemist, educator*
Edmondson, Frank Kelley *retired astronomer*
†Glazier, James Alexander *biophysicist, researcher*
Grimmond, C. Susan B. *atmospheric scientist, educator*
Hattin, Donald Edward *geologist, educator*
Hendry, Archibald Wagstaff *physics educator*
Huffman, John Curtis *chemist*
Letsinger, Robert Lewis *chemistry educator*
Peters, Dennis Gail *chemist*
Pollock, Robert Elwood *nuclear scientist*
Putnam, Frank William *biochemistry and immunology educator*
Schaich, William L. *physics educator*
Smith, Ronald Thomas *environmental scientist*

Brazil
Blackwell, Dale Bascom *physicist*

Chesterton
Crewe, Albert Victor *physicist, artist, business executive*

Elkhart
Free, Helen Mae *chemist, consultant*

Evansville
Ellis, Joe Mike *reclamation scientist*
McGinness, James D. *chemist*

Fort Branch
Hillenbrand, Gary F. *chemist, educator*

Fort Wayne
Kmety-Stevenson, Carmen Ramona *physicist*
Stevenson, Kenneth Lee *chemist, educator*

Indianapolis
Aprison, Morris Herman *biochemist, experimental and theoretical neurobiologist, emeritus educator*
†Boschmann, Erwin *chemistry educator*
†Boyd, Donald Bradford *chemist*
Bulloff, Jack John *physical chemist, consultant*
Hermann, Robert Bell *physical chemist, consultant*
Mirsky, Arthur *geologist, educator*
Wong, David T. *biochemist, researcher*
Zheng, Qi-Huang *chemist, educator*

Lafayette
Brewster, James Henry *retired chemistry educator*
Brown, Herbert Charles *chemistry educator*
Feuer, Henry *retired chemist*
Loeffler, Frank Joseph *physicist, educator*
Porile, Norbert Thomas *chemistry educator*
Whistler, Roy Lester *chemist, educator, industrialist*

Madison
Tatera, James Frank *chemist, process analysis specialist*

Mishawaka
Braunsdorf, James Allen *physics educator*

Mount Vernon
Sabnis, Ram Wasudeo *research chemist*

Muncie
Harris, Joseph McAllister *retired chemist*

Notre Dame
†Burns, Peter Carman *geologist, educator*
Chipman, Daniel Myron *chemist, researcher, educator*
Helquist, Paul M. *chemistry educator, researcher*
Huber, Paul William *biochemistry educator, researcher*
Meisel, Dan *chemist*
Mobashery, Shahriar *chemist*
Mukasyan, Alexander Sergeevich *scientist*
Scheidt, W. Robert *chemistry educator, researcher*
Schuler, Robert Hugo *chemist, educator*
Shephard, William Danks *physicist, educator*
Tripathi, Gorakh Nath Ram *physical chemist*
Trozzolo, Anthony Marion *chemistry educator*

South Bend
†Winkler, Erhard M. *geologist, educator, consultant*

Terre Haute
Guthrie, Frank Albert *chemistry educator*

West Lafayette
Adelman, Steven Allen *theoretical physical chemist, chemistry educator*
Amy, Jonathan Weekes *scientist, educator*
Barnes, Virgil Everett, II, *physics educator*
Cramer, William Anthony *biochemistry and biophysics researcher, educator*
Diamond, Sidney *chemist, educator*
Hanks, Alan R. *chemistry educator*
Judd, William Robert *engineering geologist, educator*

Laskowski, Michael, Jr., *chemist, educator*
Lipschutz, Michael Elazar *chemistry educator, consultant, researcher*
Margerum, Dale William *chemistry educator*
McMillin, David Robert *chemistry educator*
Morrison, Harry *chemistry educator, university dean*
Overhauser, Albert Warner *physicist*
Rossmann, Michael George *biochemist, educator*

IOWA

Ames
Armstrong, Daniel Wayne *chemist, educator*
Barnes, Richard George *physicist, educator*
†Barton, Thomas Jackson *chemistry educator*
Biner, Bulent Suleyman *materials scientist, educator*
Bowen, George Hamilton, Jr., *astrophysicist, educator*
Caldwell, Wallace Caughey *physicist, engineer*
Clem, John Richard *physicist, educator*
Fritz, James Sherwood *chemist, educator*
Gschneidner, Karl Albert, Jr., *metallurgist, educator, editor, consultant*
Horowitz, Jack *biochemistry educator*
Jacobson, Robert Andrew *chemistry educator*
Smith, John Francis *materials science educator*
Snyder, John Evan *physicist*
Thiel, Patricia Ann *chemistry educator*
Yeung, Edward Szeshing *chemist*

Cedar Falls
†Koob, Robert Duane *chemistry educator, educational administrator*

Davenport
Mitchell, Robert Carl *physicist, educator*

Des Moines
Bartschat, Klaus Richard Wilhelm *physics educator*

Dubuque
Churchill, Thomas John *broadcast meteorologist*

Iowa City
Baker, Richard Graves *geology educator, palynologist*
Burton, Donald Joseph *chemistry educator*
Campbell, Kevin Peter *physiology and biophysics educator, researcher*
Donelson, John Everett *biochemistry educator, molecular biologist*
Hansen, Peter Jacob *chemistry educator*
Koch, Donald LeRoy *retired geologist, state agency administrator*
Linhardt, Robert John J *medicinal chemistry educator*
Montgomery, Rex *biochemist, educator*
Plapp, Bryce Vernon *biochemistry educator*
Tallent, William Hugh *chemist, research administrator*

Le Mars
Rebstock, Theodore Lynn *chemist, educator, retired research scientist*

North Liberty
Glenister, Brian Frederick *geologist, educator*

Spirit Lake
Brett, George Wendell *retired geologist, philatelist*

West Des Moines
Lynch, David William *physicist, retired educator*

KANSAS

Atchison
Lane, Elizabeth Ann *genealogist, researcher*
Mani, Ramaswamy *chemist, researcher*

Hays
Wiese, Thomas John *biochemistry educator*

Kansas City
Noelken, Milton Edward *biochemistry educator, researcher*

Lawrence
Ammar, Raymond George *physicist, educator*
Angino, Ernest Edward *retired geology and engineering educator*
Brady, Lawrence Lee *geologist*
Dreschhoff, Gisela Auguste Marie *physicist, educator*
Enos, Paul *geologist, educator*
Gerhard, Lee Clarence *geologist, educator*
Harmony, Marlin Dale *chemistry educator*
Landgrebe, John Allan *chemistry educator*
Merriam, Daniel F(rancis) *geologist*
Mitscher, Lester Allen *chemist, educator*

Lebanon
Colwell, John Edwin *retired aerospace scientist*

Manhattan
Jiang, Hongxing *physics educator, researcher*
†Koodali, Ranjit Thazhathaveetil *chemist, researcher*
Setser, Donald Wayne *chemistry educator*

North Newton
Quiring, Frank Stanley *chemist, educator*

Overland Park
Ostby, Frederick Paul, Jr., *meteorologist, retired government official , science administrator*

Pittsburg
Foresman, James Buckey *geologist, geochemist, industrial hygienist*

Topeka
Barton, Janice Sweeny *chemistry educator*

Wichita
Alexander, David Robert *astronomer, educator*
Andrew, Kenneth L. *research physicist, physics educator*
Cowdery, Robert Douglas *consulting geologist*
†D'Souza, Francis *chemistry educator*
†Seneviratne, Waruna Prasanna *research scientist*

KENTUCKY

Bowling Green
Slocum, Donald Warren *chemist*

Florence
Lawson, Harry Wilbur *chemist, consultant, writer*
Redding, Rogers Walker *physics educator, university official*

Lexington
Brown, William Randall *geology educator*
DeLong, Lance Eric *physics educator, researcher*
Ettensohn, Frank Robert *geologist, educator*
Hamilton-Kemp, Thomas Rogers *organic chemist, educator*
Haney, Donald Clay *geologist*
Kern, Bernard Donald *retired educator, physicist*
Lodder, Robert Andrew *chemistry and pharmaceutics educator*
†Penn, Lynn Sharon *materials scientist, educator*

Louisville
Belanger, William Joseph *chemist, polymer applications consultant*
Cohn, David V(alor) *biochemist, educator*
†Glenn, Furman Eugene *industrial chemist*
Prough, Russell Allen *biochemistry educator, university official*
Taylor, Kenneth Grant *chemistry educator*

Sturgis
Thornsberry, Willis Lee, Jr., *chemist*

Vancleve
†Murphree, Quincy Carl *physicist, educator*

LOUISIANA

Baton Rouge
Gonzalez, Gabriela Ines *physics educator*
Guo, Dong-Sheng *physicist*
Kaiser, Mark John *research scientist, science educator*
Mc Glynn, Sean Patrick *physical chemist, educator*
O'Connell, Robert Francis *physics educator*
Sen Gupta, Barun Kumar *geology educator, researcher*
Stockbauer, Roger Lewis *physicist, educator*
Traynham, James Gibson *chemist, educator*
Van Lopik, Jack Richard *geologist, educator*

Covington
Vercellotti, John Raymond *research chemist*

Kenner
deMonsabert, Winston Russel *chemist, consultant*

Metairie
†Arthur, Jett Clinton *retired chemist*
Hartman, James Austin *retired geologist*
Horkowitz, Sylvester Peter *chemist*

Monroe
Zander, Arlen Ray *retired physics educator*

Natchitoches
Keller, Nadya Clark *retired biochemistry educator, researcher*

New Orleans
Allen, Gary Curtiss *geology educator*
Benerito, Ruth Rogan (Mrs. Frank H. Benerito) *chemist*
Bertoniere, Noelie Rita *research chemist*
Perdew, John Paul *physics educator, condensed matter and density functional theorist*
Prockop, Darwin Johnson *biochemist, physician*
Rosensteel, George Thomas *physics educator, nuclear physicist*
Roskoski, Robert, Jr., *biochemist, educator, author*
Seab, Charles Gregory *astrophysicist, educator*

Shreveport
Goorley, John Theodore *consulting chemist*
Kolomytkin, Oleg *biophysicist, consultant*

Slidell
Breeding, J. Ernest, Jr., (Sunny Breeding) *physicist, travel consultant, photographer, web master, webmaster*
Fishman, Louis *physicist, educator*
White, Elmer *physicist, researcher*

MAINE

Belfast
Porter, Bernard Harden *consulting physicist, author, publisher*

Brunswick
Nagle, Jeffrey Karl *chemist, educator*

Friendship
Owen, Wadsworth *oceanographer, consultant*

Jonesport
Komp, Richard Joseph *solar scientist*

Kittery
McNally, James Henry *physicist, defense consultant*

Orono
Borns, Harold William, Jr., *geologist, educator*
Norton, Stephen Allen *geological sciences educator*

Portland
Bohan, Thomas Lynch *physicist, lawyer*

Presque Isle
Knopp, Michael A. *chemist, educator*

Seal Cove
Young, David Michael *biochemistry and molecular biology educator, physician*

Stoneham
Meka, Gail Jean *chemist, consultant*

MARYLAND

Aberdeen
de Rosset, William S. *physicist*

Aberdeen Proving Ground
Carrieri, Arthur Helmut *physicist, researcher*
Miziolek, Andrzej Wladyslaw *research physicist*
Sliney, David Hammond *medical physicist*
Smith, John Richard *analytical chemist*
Steger, Ralph James *chemist*

Adelphi
Brandt, Howard Edward *physicist*
Chang, Sam Shifeng *meteorologist*
Gaunaurd, Guillermo C. *physicist, engineer, researcher*
†Smith, Doran Dakota *physicist*
Whalin, Robert W. *physicist*

Annapolis
Behrens, James William *physicist, administrator, author*
Bontoyan, Warren Roberts *chemist, state laboratories administrator*
Brunk, William Edward *astronomer*
Clotworthy, John Harris *oceanographic consultant*
Hammer, Jacob Myer *physicist, consultant*
Wolf, Alfred A. *physicist, educator*

Baltimore
Allen, Ronald John *astrophysics educator, researcher*
Chen, Shiyi *physicist, educator*
Deutsch, Robert William *physicist*
Eichhorn, Gunther Louis *chemist, researcher*
†Fu, Jie *biopolymer scientist, educator*
Fulton, Thomas *theoretical physicist, educator*
Green, Robert Edward, Jr., *physicist, educator*
†Guiles, Ronald Davis *biochemist, educator*
Haig, Frank Rawle *physics educator, clergyman*
Hauser, Michael George *astrophysicist*
Helm, Donald Cairney *hydrogeologist, engineer, educator*
Herstein, Louis Arthur, III, *physicist*
Judd, Brian Raymond *physicist, educator*
†Kriss, Gerard Anthony *astronomer*
Krolik, Julian Henry *astrophysicist, educator*
Krueger, Arlin James *physicist*
Lane, Malcolm Daniel *biological chemistry educator*
Lee, Yung-Keun *physicist, educator*
Margon, Bruce Henry *astrophysicist, educator*
Marsh, Bruce David *geologist, educator*
†McQuade, Kevin J. *research scientist, physical therapist*
Moos, H. Warren *physicist, astronomer, educator, administrator*
Nickon, Alex *chemist, educator*
Norman, Colin Arthur *astrophysics educator*
Posner, Gary Herbert *chemist, educator*
Rasera, Robert L. *physics educator*
†Rose, George David *biophysics educator*
Roseman, Saul *biochemist, educator*
Roth, George Stanley *biochemist, researcher, physiologist*
Shamoo, Adil Elias *biochemist, biophysicist, educator*
Silverstone, Harris J. *chemistry educator*
Stanley, Steven Mitchell *paleobiologist, educator*
Steiner, Robert Frank *biochemist*
Ts'o, Paul On-Pong *biophysical chemist, educator*
Westerhout, Gart *retired astronomer*

Bel Air
Cash, LaVerne (Cynthia Cash) *physicist*
Stuempfle, Arthur Karl *physical scientist*

Beltsville
Johnson, Phyllis Elaine *chemist, researcher*

Berlin
Passwater, Richard Albert *biochemist, author*

Bethesda
Ahmad, Imad Aldean *astronomer, educator, consultant*
Azaryan, Anahit Vazgenovna *biochemist, researcher*
Backus, Robert Coburn *biophysical chemist*
Berger, Robert Lewis *retired biophysicist, researcher*
Dunn, Bonnie Brill *chemist*
Ehrenstein, Gerald *retired biophysicist*
Fales, Henry Marshall *chemist*
Gilfrich, John Valentine *retired chemist*
Giovanelli, John *research chemist*
Huebner, John Stephen *geologist*
Murayama, Makio *biochemist*
†Ramchandani, Vijay Arjun *research scientist*
Revesz, Akos George *physicist*

Rice, Jerry Mercer *biochemist, consultant*
Rice, Kenner Cralle *medicinal chemist*
Roberts, David Duncan *biochemist*
Snitch, Thomas Harold *science educator, consultant*
Stadtman, Earl Reece *biochemist, researcher*
Tabor, Herbert *biochemist*
Trus, Benes Louis *structural chemist*
Vaughan, Martha *biochemist, educator*
Wente, Van Arthur *consultant, retired government official*
Wiese, Wolfgang Lothar *physicist, researcher*
Witkop, Bernhard *chemist*
Zoon, Kathryn Christine *biochemist*

Cabin John
Oertel, Goetz Kuno Heinrich *physicist, professional science administrator*
Shropshire, Walter, Jr., *biophysicist emeritus, pastor*
Townsend, John William, Jr., *physicist, retired federal aerospace agency executive*

Cambridge
Koch-Eilers, Evamaria Wysk *oceanographer, researcher*

Camp Springs
Le Comte, Douglas Munzer *meteorologist*
Wagner, Andrew James *meteorologist, elder, educator*
Weinreb, Michael Philip *physicist*

Chevy Chase
Cech, Thomas Robert *chemistry and biochemistry educator*
Hudson, Ralph P. *physicist*
Mielke, James Edward *geochemist*
Promisel, Nathan E. *materials scientist, metallurgical engineer*
Sinclair, Rolf Malcolm *retired physicist*

College Park
Anisimov, Mikhail A. *physicist, educator, research scientist*
Coffey, Timothy *physicist*
DeFries, Ruth S. *earth system scientist, researcher*
DeSilva, Alan W. *physics educator, researcher*
Dusold, Laurence Richard *chemist, computer specialist*
Fenselau, Catherine Clarke *chemistry educator*
Fisher, Michael Ellis *mathematical physicist, chemist*
Gluckstern, Robert Leonard *physics educator*
Griem, Hans Rudolf *physicist, educator*
Griffin, James Joseph *physics educator*
Grim, Samuel Oram *chemistry educator*
Helz, George Rudolph *chemistry educator, research center director*
Kundu, Mukul Ranjan *physics and astronomy educator*
Li, Zhanqing *meteorologist, educator*
Lubkin, Gloria Becker *physicist*
Mc Donald, Frank Bethune *physicist*
McIlrath, Thomas *physicist, educator*
Misner, Charles William *physics educator*
Moore, John Hays *chemistry educator*
Murphy, Thomas James *physicist, educator*
Nusinovich, Gregory Semeon *physicist, researcher*
Rabin, Herbert *physicist, university official*
Rasmusson, Eugene Martin *meteorology researcher*
Redish, Edward Frederick *physicist, educator*
Rosenberg, Norman Jack *agricultural meteorologist, educator*
Silverman, Joseph *chemistry educator, scientist*
Skuja, Andris *physics educator*
Stith, James Herman *physics educator*
Sundaresan, P. Ramnathan *research chemist, consultant*
Walters, William Ben *chemistry educator*
Zen, E-an *research geologist, educator*
Zhang, Da-lin D. *meteorologist, educator*

Columbia
Bareis, Donna Lynn *biochemist, pharmacologist*
†Das, Naresh Chandra *research scientist*
Fisher, Dale John *chemist, instrumentation and medical diagnostic device investigator*
†Fritz, Steven L *physicist*
Khare, Mohan *chemist, researcher*

Crofton
Kniffen, Donald Avery *astrophysicist, educator, researcher*

Darnestown
Hoffer, James Brian *physicist, consultant*

Dayton
Fischell, Robert Ellentuch *physicist*

Elkridge
Morgan, Gary Lorin *biophysicist, inventor, researcher*

Elkton
Xu, Ping *chemist*

Fort Washington
Omoike, Isaac Irabor *chemist, publishing executive, writer*

Frederick
Garver, Robert Vernon *research physicist*

Gaithersburg
Adams, James Michael *nuclear physicist*
†Bendersky, Leonid A. *metallurgist, researcher*
Cahn, John Werner *metallurgist, educator*
Caplin, Jerrold Leon *health physicist*
Caswell, Randall Smith *physicist*
Celotta, Robert James *physicist*
Chang, Ren Fang *physicist, researcher*
Colle, Ronald *research chemist*

DiMarzio, Edmund Armand *physicist*
Hamer, Walter Jay *chemical consultant, science writer*
Hancock, Diane Kerr *research chemist*
Harman, George Gibson *physicist, consultant*
Hsu, Stephen Ming *materials scientist, chemical engineer*
Hubbell, John Howard *radiation physicist*
Jacox, Marilyn Esther *chemist*
Karam, Lisa Robert *research chemist*
†Lynn, Jeffrey Whidden *research physicist, educator*
McLaughlin, William Lowndes *physicist, researcher*
Phillips, William Daniel *physicist*
Pierce, Daniel Thornton *physicist*
Ruckman, Mark Warren *physicist*
Sengers, Johanna M. H. Levelt *thermophysicist*
Taketomi, Susamu *physicist, researcher*
Taylor, Barry Norman *physicist*
Tesk, John Aloysius *materials scientist*
†Werner, Samuel Alfred *physics and astronomy educator*
Wu, Yung C. *retired chemist*

Garrett Park
Melville, Robert Seaman *chemist*

Germantown
Foulke, Judith Diane *health physicist*
Laufer, Allan Henry *chemist*
Varma, Matesh N. *materials scientist, director*

Glen Arm
Larrabee, Martin Glover *biophysics educator*

Greenbelt
†Cohen, Steven Charles *geophysicist*
†Eplee, Robert Eugene *geophysicist*
Fixsen, Dale J. *physicist*
Hendley, Coit Taylor, III, *chemistry educator*
Hollis, Jan Michael *astrophysicist, scientific computer analyst*
Maran, Stephen Paul *astronomer*
Mather, John Cromwell *astrophysicist*
Moskalenko, Igor Vladimirovich *physicist, astrophysicist*
Mumma, Michael Jon *physicist, researcher*
Ormes, Jonathan Fairfield *astrophysicist, science administrator, researcher*
Parkinson, Claire L. *climatologist*
†Shirron, Peter John *physicist*
Simpson, Joanne Malkus *meteorologist*
Stief, Louis John *chemist*
†Tao, Wei-Kuo *meteorologist, researcher*
Wiscombe, Warren Jackman *research scientist*
Wood, H(oward) John, III, *astrophysicist, astronomer*

Havre De Grace
Russell, William Alexander, Jr., *environmental scientist*

Huntingtown
Faust, William Roscoe *physicist*

Lanham
Degnan, John James, III, *physicist*

Laurel
Babin, Steven Michael *atmospheric scientist, researcher*
Guo, Yanping *physicist*
Kossiakoff, Alexander *chemist, researcher*
Lui, Anthony Tat Yin *physicist*
Maurer, Richard Hornsby *physicist*
Peri, Joseph Silvio Julius *physicist, mathematician*

Linthicum Heights
†Stein, David Eric *physicist, defense analyst*

Mechanicsville
Henderson, Madeline Mary (Berry Henderson) *chemist, researcher, consultant*

Monrovia
McCurdy, John Dennis *biochemist, toxicologist*

Montgomery Village
Kushner, Lawrence Maurice *physical chemist, consultant*
Murray, Peter *metallurgist, manufacturing company executive*
Robinson, Henry Ward *meteorologist*

Morningside
McClain, Edward Fifer, Jr., *retired physicist*

North Bethesda
Shapiro, Maurice Mandel *nuclear astrophysicist*

Parkton
Fitzgerald, Edwin Roger *physicist, educator*

Parkville
Jensen, Arthur Seigfried *consulting engineering physicist*

Pasadena
Young, Russell Dawson *physics consultant*

Potomac
Casella, Russell Carl *physicist*

Princess Anne
†Gupta, Gian Chand *environmental scientist*

Reisterstown
Tannenbaum, Harvey *defense technology consultant*

Rockville
Buchanan, John Donald *retired health physicist, radiochemist*
Edinger, Stanley Evan *clinical chemist*

†Ermolaeva, Maria D. *bioinformatician, researcher*
Farahani, Mahnaz *chemist, scientist*
Finlayson, John Sylvester *biochemist*
Georgiev, Goshko Atanasov *agrometeorologist, researcher*
Jamieson, Graham A. *biochemist, organization official*
Kruger, Jerome *materials science educator, consultant*
Landry, Robert Joseph *physicist*
Rao, Potarazu Krishna *environmental consultant*
Sansalone, William Robert *biochemistry educator, researcher*
Schindler, Albert Isadore *physicist, educator*
†Shojaei, Amir Hossein *pharmaceutical scientist*
†Vermeulen, Roel *research scientist*
Wallenmeyer, William Anton *retired physicist*
Wang, Chung Shan *physicist*
Yang, Liqiu *physicist*
†Yu, Mei-ying Wong *chemist, researcher*

Salisbury
Mulligan, Joseph Francis *physicist, science historian, educator*
Rotariu, George Julian *retired physical chemist, consultant*

Sandy Spring
Kanarowski, Stanley Martin *chemist, chemical engineer, government official*

Severna Park
Lesikar, James Daniel, II, *physicist, engineer*

Silver Spring
†Anderson, Richard McDonald *hydrologist, engineer*
Ehrlich, Charles David *physicist*
Gray, Allan P. *chemist, health and environmental consultant*
Scheer, Milton David *chemical physicist*
Whitmore, Frank Clifford, Jr., *geologist*
Wilson, William Stanley *oceanographer*
Young, Jay Alfred *chemical safety and health consultant, writer, editor*

Suitland
Rao, Desiraju Bhavanarayana *meteorologist, oceanographer, educator*
Scofield, Roderick Arthur *meteorologist, researcher, educator*

Temple Hills
Strauss, Simon Wolf *chemist, materials scientist*

Walkersville
Huiberts, Pieter J. *development chemist*

Wheaton
Ma, Qingli *environmental hydrologist*

MASSACHUSETTS

Acton
Conoby, Joseph Francis *chemist*

Agawam
Kantor, Simon William *chemistry educator*

Amherst
Archer, Ronald Dean *chemist, educator*
Bernstein, Herbert Joseph *physicist, consultant, educator*
Byron, Frederick William, Jr., *physicist, educator, university vice chancellor*
David, Donald J. *chemist, researcher*
Fink, Richard David *chemist, educator*
†Goldstein, Joseph Irwin *materials scientist, educator*
Hallock, Robert Bruce *physics educator*
MacKnight, William John *chemist, educator*
Peterson, Gerald Alvin *physics educator*
Rabin, Monroe Stephen Zane *physicist*
Romer, Robert Horton *physicist, educator*
Scott, David Knight *physicist, university administrator*
Stein, Richard Stephen *chemistry educator*

Arlington
Leonardos, Gregory *chemist, odor consultant, educator*
Vaughn, Thomas Joseph *earth science educator, administrator*

Ayer
Desper, Clyde Richard *retired polymer scientist*

Bedford
Klyosov, Anatole Alex *biochemist, researcher*

Belmont
Neumeyer, John Leopold *research company administrator, chemistry educator*

Beverly
†Rose, Peter Henry *nuclear physicist*

Billerica
Kardauskas, Michael John *materials scientist, consultant*
†Luong, Nam Thoai *biochemist, researcher*
Miller, Dawn Marie *meteorologist*
†Wang, Meng-Jiao *research scientist*

Boston
Anselme, Jean-Pierre Louis Marie *chemist*
Brecher, Kenneth *astrophysicist, educator*
Brownell, Gordon Lee *physicist, educator*
Chakrabarti, Supriya *space astrophysicist*
Clarke, John Terrel *astrophysicist*
Cohen, Robert Sonné *physicist, philosopher, educator*
De Rocco, Andrew Gabriel *physicist, educator*
Edmonds, Dean Stockett, Jr., *physicist, educator, director*

El-Baz, Farouk *science administrator, educator*
†Ghabbour, Elham A. *research scientist, educator*
Guertin, Robert Powell *physics educator, university dean*
Horne, Ralph Albert *environmental chemist*
Kennedy, Eugene Patrick *biochemist, educator*
Koch, Magaly *geologist, researcher*
Kornberg, Sir Hans Leo *biochemist, educator*
Laursen, Richard Allan *chemistry educator*
Le Quesne, Philip William *chemistry educator, researcher*
Levitin, Lev Berovich *research scientist, educator*
Malenka, Bertram Julian *physicist, educator*
Miliora, Maria Teresa *chemist, psychotherapist, psychoanalyst, educator*
Pardee, Arthur Beck *biochemist, educator*
Small, Donald MacFarland *biophysics educator, gastroenterologist*
Stanley, H(arry) Eugene *physicist, educator*
Staples, Mark Andrew *biochemist*
Steinmetz, Michael *biochemist*
Stollar, Bernard David *biochemist, educator*
Torchilin, Vladimir Petrovich *biochemist, researcher*
Wang, Jian *physical chemist, researcher*

Bourne
Fantozzi, Peggy Ryone *geologist, environmental planner*

Brookfield
Anderson, Theodore Robert *physicist*

Brookline
Tuchman, Avraham *physicist, researcher*

Byfield
Yesair, David Wayne *biochemist*

Cambridge
Alberty, Robert Arnold *chemistry educator*
†An, Shuwang *chemist, researcher*
†Arkani-Hamed, Nima *physicist*
Auld, David Stuart *biochemist, educator*
Barger, James Edwin *physicist*
Biemann, Klaus *chemistry educator*
Blout, Elkan Rogers *biological chemistry educator, university dean*
Bradt, Hale Van Dorn *physicist, x-ray astronomer, educator*
Branscomb, Lewis McAdory *physicist, researcher*
Brooks, Harvey *physics educator*
Burchfiel, Burrell Clark *geology educator*
Canizares, Claude Roger *astrophysicist, educator*
Ceyer, Sylvia T. *chemistry educator*
Clark, George Whipple *physics educator*
Cohn, Daniel Ross *physicist*
Coleman, Sidney Richard *physicist, educator*
Corey, Elias James *chemistry educator*
Dalgarno, Alexander *astronomy educator*
Dame, Thomas Michael *radio astronomer*
Eagar, Thomas Waddy *metallurgist, educator*
Ehntholt, Daniel James *chemist*
Ehrenfried, George *photographic physicist, educator*
Ehrenreich, Henry *physicist, educator*
Evans, David A(lbert) *chemistry educator*
Evans, James Brian *geophysics educator*
Feld, Michael Stephen *physics educator*
Foner, Simon *research physicist*
French, Anthony Philip *physicist, educator*
Frey, Frederick August *geochemistry researcher, educator*
Friedman, Jerome Isaac *physics educator, researcher*
Garrelick, Joel Marc *acoustical scientist, consultant*
Geller, Margaret Joan *astrophysicist, educator*
Gingerich, Owen Jay *astronomer, educator*
Goldstone, Jeffrey *physicist, educator*
Gordon, Roy Gerald *chemistry educator*
Greene, Frederick D., II, *chemistry educator*
Grindlay, Jonathan Ellis *astrophysics educator*
Grove, Timothy Lynn *geology educator*
Guth, Alan Harvey *physicist, educator*
Halperin, Bertrand Israel *physics educator*
Hau, Lene *physicist, optics scientist*
†Hau, Lene Vestergaard *physicist, educator*
Herschbach, Dudley Robert *chemistry educator*
Holton, Gerald *physicist, science historian*
Horwitz, Paul *physicist*
Houtchens, Robert Austin, Jr., *biochemist*
Hu, Haijun *atmospheric scientist, electrical engineer*
Huang, Kerson *physics educator*
Huchra, John Peter *astronomer, educator*
Jackiw, Roman *physicist, educator*
Jaffe, Arthur Michael *physicist, mathematician, educator*
Joss, Paul Christopher *astrophysicist, atmospheric physicist, educator*
Kamentsky, Louis Aaron *biophysicist*
Kandimalla, Ekambareswara Rao *molecular medicinal chemist*
Kerman, Arthur Kent *physicist, educator*
Ketterle, Wolfgang *physics educator*
Khorana, Har Gobind *professor, chemist*
King, Ronold Wyeth Percival *physics educator*
Kistiakowsky, Vera *physics researcher, educator*
Klemperer, William *chemistry educator*
†Lermusiaux, Pierre F.J. *oceanographer, engineer*
†Lewin, Walter H.G. *physicist*
Lindzen, Richard Siegmund *meteorologist, educator*
Lippard, Stephen James *chemist, educator*
Lipscomb, William Nunn, Jr., *physical chemistry educator*
Livingston, James Duane *physicist, educator*
Lomon, Earle Leonard *physicist, educator, consultant*
Low, Francis Eugene *physics educator*
Lyon, Richard Harold *physicist educator,*
Marsden, Brian Geoffrey *astronomer*
Martin, Paul Cecil *physicist, educator*
Marvin, Ursula Bailey *retired geologist*
Milner, Richard Gerard *physicist*
Molina, Mario Jose *physical chemist, educator*
Moran, James Michael, Jr., *astronomer, educator*
Nelson, David Robert *physics educator*
Newell, Reginald Edward *physics educator*
Odinecs, Aleksandrs *biochemist*
Olbert, Stanislaw *physicist*
Oppenheim, Irwin *chemical physicist, educator*
Paul, William *physicist, educator*
Petaev, Mikhail Ivanovich *geologist, researcher*
Petersen, Ulrich *geology educator*
Pettengill, Gordon H(emenway) *physicist, educator*
Ramsey, Norman F. *physicist, educator*
Redwine, Robert Page *physicist, educator*
Roedder, Edwin Woods *geologist*
Rose, Robert Michael *materials science and engineering educator*
Ross, Caroline Anne *materials science educator*
Rubin, Lawrence Gilbert *physicist, laboratory manager*
Sagar, Ambuj D. *environmental and technology policy professional*
Salzmann, George Stephen *biochemist, priest*
†Schechter, Paul *physicist, educator*
Schild, Rudolph Ernst *astronomer, educator*
Schrock, Richard Royce *chemistry educator*
Seyferth, Dietmar *chemist, educator*
Shapiro, Irwin Ira *physicist, educator*
Silbey, Robert James *chemistry educator, researcher, consultant*
Solomon, Arthur Kaskel *biophysics educator*
Spaepen, Frans August *applied physics researcher, educator*
Stark, Antony Albert *astronomer*
Steinfeld, Jeffrey Irwin *chemistry educator, consultant, writer*
Strandberg, Malcom Woodrow Pershing *physicist*
Thaddeus, Patrick *physicist, educator*
Ting, Samuel Chao Chung *physicist, educator*
Tinkham, Michael *physicist, educator*
Verdine, Gregory Lawrence *chemist, educator*
Vessot, Robert Frederick Charles *physicist, researcher*
Waugh, John Stewart *chemist, educator*
†Weill, Peter D. *research scientist*
Weinberg, Robert Allan *biochemist, educator*
Westheimer, Frank Henry *chemist, educator*
Whipple, Fred Lawrence *astronomer*
Whitesides, George McClelland *chemistry educator*
Wilson, Robert Woodrow *radio astronomer*
Wood, John Armstead *planetary scientist, geological sciences educator*
†Xie, Xiaoliang Sunney *chemist, educator*

Charlestown
Cheng, Leo Ling *biophysicist, researcher*

Chelmsford
Kirkpatrick, Francis H(ubbard) *biophysicist, intellectual property practitioner, consultant*

Chestnut Hill
Fourkas, John T. *chemistry educator*

Concord
MacNichol, Edward Ford, Jr., *biophysicist, educator, consultant*

Cotuit
Miller, Robert Charles *retired physicist*

East Longmeadow
Skutnik, Bolesh J. *optics scientist, lay worker, lawyer*

East Orleans
Romey, William Dowden *geologist, educator*

Fall River
Guillemette, Mark Edgar *textile technologist*

Falmouth
†Adelman, William J., Jr., *biophysicist*
Goody, Richard Mead *geophysicist*

Framingham
Dawicki, Doloretta Diane *analytical chemist, research biochemist, educator*

Franklin
Shastry, Shambhu Kadhambiny *scientist, engineering executive, consultant*

Gloucester
Socolow, Arthur Abraham *geologist*

Hanscom AFB
Mailloux, Robert Joseph *physicist*

Haverhill
DeSchuytner, Edward Alphonse *biochemist, educator*

Hopkinton
Haller, William Paul *analytical chemist, robotics and automation specialist*

Lexington
Buchanan, John Machlin *biochemistry educator*
Dionne, Gerald Francis *research physicist, educator, consultant*
Nash, Leonard Kollender *chemistry educator*
Silverman, Sam Mendel *physicist, lawyer*
†Wang, Chi Hua *chemist, education educator*
Williamson, Richard Cardinal *physicist*

Lexington
Steiner, John William *retired biophysicist*

Lowell
Kannenberg, Lloyd Chambers *physicist, educator*
Kegel, Gunter Heinrich Reinhard *physics educator, researcher*
Wakim, Fahd George *physicist, educator*

Marblehead
Cohen, Merrill *chemist*

Medford
Cavallaro, Mary Caroline *retired physics educator*
Chaisson, Eric Joseph *astrophysicist, science administrator, educator*
Gunther, Leon *physicist, educator*
Mc Carthy, Kathryn A. *physicist*
Schneps, Jack *physics educator*

Medway
†Arthur, Wallace *physicist, educator*

Natick
Haden, Billy Harper *research biochemist*
Kennedy, Dallas Clarence, II, *physicist, educator, writer*

Needham
Holt, Stephen S. *astrophysicist*

Newton
Aronow, Saul *radiological physicist, consultant*
Dunlap, William Crawford *physicist*
Heyn, Arno Harry Albert *retired chemistry educator*
Jeanloz, Roger William *biochemist, educator*
Lichtin, Norman Nahum *chemistry educator*
Penezina, Oksana P. *biochemist*

North Andover
†Shenai-Khatkhate, Deodatta Vinayak *chemical researcher*

North Dartmouth
Dowd, John Peter *physics educator*
Sauro, Joseph Pio *physics educator*

Northampton
Fleck, George Morrison *chemistry educator*

Orleans
Avery, William Hinckley *physicist, chemist*

Pittsfield
Wheelock, Kenneth Steven *chemist*

Randolph
Manos, Sarantos John *physics educator*

Roxbury
Simons, Elizabeth R(eiman) *biochemist, educator*

Salem
Brown, Walter Redvers John *physicist*

Shrewsbury
Nixon, Eugene Ray *chemist, educator*

South Dartmouth
Mellberg, Leonard Evert *physicist*

South Hadley
Campbell, Mary Kathryn *chemistry educator*
Leal, Joseph Rogers *chemist*

Springfield
Smist, Julianne Marie *chemist, educator*

Waltham
De Rosier, David John *biophysicist, educator*
Deser, Stanley *physicist, educator*
Epstein, Irving Robert *chemistry educator*
Foxman, Bruce Mayer *chemist, educator*
Lees, Marjorie Berman *biochemist, neuroscientist*
Petsko, Gregory Anthony *chemistry and biochemistry scientist educator*
Workman, Jerome James, Jr., *chemist*

Watertown
Lin, Juchui Ray (Ju-Chui Lin) *polymer scientist*

Wayland
Brynjolfsson, Ari *nuclear physicist*
Clark, Melville, Jr., *physicist, electrical engineer*

Wellesley
Charpie, Robert Alan *physicist, researcher*

Wenham
Herrmann, Robert Lawrence *biochemist, educator*

Westborough
Trubko, Sergey Vladimir *optical designer, scientist*

Westford
†Fennelly, Paul F. *chemist*
Salah, Joseph Elias *research scientist, educator*

Weston
Lin, Alice Lee Lan *physicist, researcher, educator*
Schloemann, Ernst Fritz (Rudolf August) *physicist, engineer*
Wang, Chia Ping *physicist, educator*

Williamstown
Markgraf, J(ohn) Hodge *chemist, educator*
Park, David Allen *physicist, educator*
Pasachoff, Jay Myron *astronomer, educator*
Wobus, Reinhard Arthur *geologist, educator*

Winchendon
Scanio, Charles John Vincent *chemist, consultant*

Winchester
Milburn, Richard Henry *physics educator*

Woods Hole
Berggren, William Alfred *geologist, research micropaleontologist, educator*
Cohen, Seymour Stanley *biochemist, educator*
†Fenwick, Judith L. *oceanographer, researcher*
Gagosian, Robert B. *chemist, educator*
Payne, Richard Earl *physical oceanographer*
Steele, John Hyslop *marine scientist, oceanographic institute administrator*
Uchupi, Elazar *geologist, researcher*
Von Herzen, Richard Pierre *research scientist, consultant*

Worcester
Pavlik, James William *chemistry educator*
†Saha, Deepak *metallurgist, researcher*
Zarbis-Papastoitsis, Grigoris *biochemist*

Yarmouth Port
Darby, Joseph Branch, Jr., *retired metallurgist, government official*
LeBaron, Francis Newton *biochemistry educator*

MICHIGAN

Albion
Green, David William *chemist, educator*
Taylor, Lawrence Dow *geologist, educator*

Ann Arbor
Agranoff, Bernard William *biochemist, educator*
Akerlof, Carl William *physics educator*
Aller, Margo Friedel *astronomer*
Ashe, Arthur James, III, *chemistry educator*
Atreya, Sushil Kumar *planetary-space science educator, astrophysicist*
Bartell, Lawrence Sims *chemist, educator*
Clarke, Roy *physicist, educator*
Coward, James Kenderdine *chemist*
Crane, Horace Richard *physicist, educator*
Crippen, Gordon Marvin *chemist*
Dekker, Eugene Earl *biochemistry educator*
†Dixon, Jack Edward *biological chemistry educator, consultant*
Donahue, Thomas Michael *physics educator*
Drake, Richard Paul *physicist, educator*
Duff, Michael James *physicist*
Farrand, William Richard *geology educator*
Fisk, Lennard Ayres *physicist, educator*
Freese, Katherine *physicist, educator*
Haddock, Fred(erick) T(heodore), Jr., *astronomer, educator*
Hagel, William Carl *metallurgical consultant*
Jones, Lawrence William *retired educator, physicist*
Kesler, Stephen Edward *economic geology educator*
Krimm, Samuel *physicist, educator*
Krisch, Alan David *physics educator*
Longone, Daniel Thomas *chemistry educator emeritus*
†Ludwig, Martha *biochemist, educator*
Matthews, Rowena Green *biological chemistry educator*
Mazzeo, Anthony R. *chemist*
Neal, Homer Alfred *physics educator, researcher, university administrator*
Nordman, Christer Eric *chemistry educator*
Nriagu, Jerome Okon *environmental geochemist*
Parkinson, William Charles *physicist, educator*
Pollack, Henry Nathan *geophysics educator*
†Raffel, David M. *medical physicist*
†Ransom, Richard Frederick *biochemist*
Robertson, Richard Earl *physical chemist, educator*
Roe, Byron Paul *physics educator*
Roush, William R. *chemistry educator*
Schacht, Jochen Heinrich *biochemistry educator*
Steel, Duncan Gregory *physics educator*
†Sun, Kai *materials scientist, research scientist*
van der Pluijm, Bernardus Adrianus (Ben van der Pluijm) *geologist, educator*
Van der Voo, Rob *geophysicist*
Veltman, Martinus J.G. *retired physics educator*
Wharton, John James, Jr., *research physicist*
Zhang, Youxue *geology educator*

Battle Creek
†Gates, Jeffrey Ralph *research scientist, epidemiologist*

Belleville
†Wilson, David James *chemistry researcher, educator*

Big Rapids
Mathison, Ian William *chemistry educator, academic dean*

Birmingham
Smith, George Wolfram *physicist, educator*

Dearborn
Ball, James Charles *biochemist, researcher, herpetologist*
†Crosbie, Gary Mark *research scientist, artist*

Detroit
Bowen, David R. *science and technology educator, consultant*
Drescher, Dennis George *biochemist, researcher*
Frade, Peter Daniel *chemist, educator, administrator*
Gupta, Suraj Narayan *physicist, educator*
Johnson, Carl Randolph *chemist, educator*
Kirschner, Stanley *chemist*
Oliver, John Preston *chemistry educator, academic administrator*
Orton, Colin George *medical physicist*
Svoboda, Mary Beth *health physicist, environmental science educator*
Yin, Fang-Fang *medical physicist, educator*

East Lansing
Abolins, Maris Arvids *physics researcher and educator*
Austin, Sam M. *physics educator*
Benenson, Walter *nuclear physics educator*
Blosser, Henry Gabriel *physicist*

PROFESSIONAL INDEX 6639 SCIENCE: PHYSICAL SCIENCE

Burnett, Jean Bullard (Mrs. James R. Burnett) *biochemist, educator*
Case, Eldon Darrel *materials science educator*
Cross, Aureal Theophilus *geology and botany educator*
D'Itri, Frank Michael *environmental research chemist*
Dugan, LeRoy *chemist, educator*
Dye, James Louis *chemistry educator*
Gelbke, Claus-Konrad *nuclear physics educator*
Harrison, Michael Jay *physicist, educator*
†Mertzimekis, Theodore *nuclear physicist, researcher*
Mohanty, Amar K. *polymer scientist, educator, researcher*
Preiss, Jack *biochemistry educator*
Stein, Robert Foster *astrophysicist, educator*
Summitt, Robert (William Summitt) *chemist, educator*

Farmington Hills
Chapman, Gilbert Bryant *physicist*
Theodore, Ares Nicholas *research chemist*

Highland
Brown, Ray Kent *biochemist, physician, educator*

Hillsdale
†Baron, Lee Ann *chemist, educator*

Holland
Inghram, Mark Gordon *physicist, educator*
Williams, Donald Howard *chemist, educator, chemist, consultant*

Kalamazoo
Chateauneuf, John Edward *chemistry educator, researcher*
Chou, Kuo-Chen *biophysical chemist*
Greenfield, John Charles *bio-organic chemist*
Jones, Randall Marvin *chemist*

Leland
Small, Hamish *chemist*

Madison Heights
Koshy, Vettithara Cherian *chemistry educator, technical director and formulator*

Maple City
Ryant, Charles Joseph, Jr., *environment executive*

Midland
Chao, Marshall *chemist*
Dorman, Linneaus Cuthbert *retired chemist*
Dreyfuss, Patricia *retired chemist, researcher*
Leng, Marguerite Lambert
Nowak, Robert Michael *chemist*
So, Ying-Hung *chemistry researcher*

Mount Pleasant
Dietrich, Richard Vincent *geologist, educator*
Fornari, Marco *physicist*

Northville
Bohm, Henry Victor *physicist*

Rochester
Ovshinsky, Stanford Robert *physicist, inventor, energy executive, information company executive*

Rochester Hills
Fritzsche, Hellmut *physics educator*

Romulus
Yussouff, Mohammed *retired physicist, educator*

Saginaw
Wierzbicki, Jacek Gabriel *physicist, researcher*

Saint Joseph
Akber, Syed Farooq *medical physicist*

Sears
†McCullough, Willard G. *retired biochemist*

Shelby Township
Heremans, Joseph Pierre *physicist*

Southfield
Ben, Manuel *chemist*

Three Rivers
Boyer, Nicodemus Elijah *chemist, consultant*

Warren
Deak, Charles Karol *chemist*
†Dunker, Alan Melvin *physical chemist, researcher*
Herbst, Jan Francis *physicist, researcher*
†Yang, Jihui *research scientist*

West Bloomfield
Harwood, Julius J. *metallurgist, educator*

Wyandotte
Aslam, Syed *chemist, research*

Ypsilanti
Barnes, James Milton *physics and astronomy educator*

MINNESOTA

Apple Valley
Brown, Francis William *chemist, consultant*

Austin
Holman, Ralph Theodore *biochemistry and nutrition educator*
Schmid, Harald Heinrich Otto *biochemistry educator, academic director*

Bloomington
†Bekrenev, Anatoliy *physicist*
Pust, Ladislav *physicist, researcher*

Duluth
Rapp, George Robert (Rip Rapp) *geology and archeology educator*
Zhdankin, Viktor Vladimirovich *chemistry educator*

Lake Elmo
Vivona, Daniel Nicholas *chemist*

Minneapolis
Ackerman, Eugene *biophysics educator*
Berg, Stanton Oneal *firearms and ballistics consultant*
†Cornelissen, Germaine *physicist, educator*
Goldman, Allen Marshall *physics educator*
Halley, James Woods *physics educator*
Hamermesh, Morton *physicist, educator*
Hogenkamp, Henricus Petrus Cornelis *biochemistry researcher, biochemistry educator*
†Isakovic, Abdel *physicist, researcher*
Johnson, Robert Glenn *geology and geophysics educator*
†Kaiser, Daniel Robert *research scientist*
Kruse, Paul Walters, Jr., *physicist, consultant*
Kuhi, Leonard Vello *astronomer, university administrator*
Marshak, Marvin Lloyd *physicist, educator*
Portoghese, Philip Salvatore *medicinal chemist, educator*
Rubens, Sidney Michel *physicist, technical advisor*
Truhlar, Donald Gene *chemist, educator*
Usacheva, Marina Nikolaevna *photochemist, researcher*
Wood, Wellington Gibson, III, *biochemistry educator*

Moorhead
Strong, Judith Ann *chemist, educator*

Northfield
Casper, Barry Michael *physics educator*
Cederberg, James *physics educator*
†Fick, Herbert J. *chemist, consultant*
Henrickson, Eiler Leonard *retired geologist, educator*

Plymouth
Bonne, Ulrich *chemical physicist*

Rochester
Bhattacharyya, Kalyan Kumar *scientist, biomedical engineer*
Vetter, Richard James *health physicist*

Saint Paul
Altenberger, Andrzej Ryszard *physical chemist, chemistry educator*
Newmark, Richard Alan *chemist*
Perry, James Alfred *environmental scientist, consultant, science educator, director*
Prager, Stephen *chemistry educator*
Schwartz, A(lbert) Truman *chemistry educator*
†Sheshukov, Aleksey Y. *hydrologist, researcher*
Thompson, Mary Eileen *chemistry educator*
Walton, Matt Savage *retired geologist, educator*

Waseca
Capriglione, Ralph Raymond *geologist, educator*

Wayzata
Furda, Ivan *chemist, consultant*

White Bear Lake
Holmen, Reynold Algott Emanuel *chemist*

MISSISSIPPI

Bay Saint Louis
Hurlburt, Harley Ernest *ocean modeling and prediction scientist*
Lewando, Alfred Gerard, Jr., *oceanographer*
†Liu, Cheng-Chien *oceanographer, researcher*
Rondeau, Clement Robert *petroleum geologist*

Clinton
Mather, Bryant *consultant*

Hattiesburg
Bedenbaugh, Angela Lea Owen *chemistry educator, researcher*
Urban, Marek W. *chemistry, polymers and coatings educator*

Jackson
Smith, Edgar Eugene *biochemist, university administrator*

Olive Branch
†Farr, Walter Evans *chemist, chemical engineer*

Picayune
Lowrie, Allen *geologist, oceanographer*

Stennis Space Center
†Chin-Bing, Stanley Arthur *physicist, educator*
Fleischer, Peter *research geologist, oceanographer, educator*
Jacobs, Gregg Arthur *oceanographer, researcher*
Kamenkovich, Vladimir Moiseevich *oceanographer, educator*

University
Breazeale, Mack Alfred *physics educator*

MISSOURI

Ballwin
Sabacky, Jerome (Jerry Sabacky) *retired research chemist*

Cape Girardeau
Hathaway, Ruth Ann *chemist*

Chesterfield
Fujiwara, Hideji *chemist, researcher*
Kurz, James Eckhardt *retired chemist*

Clinton
Kelsay, David Roland *chemist*

Columbia
†Abbitt, Robbyn Jo Forry *geographic information systems specialist*
Bauman, John E., Jr., *chemistry educator*
Decker, Wayne Leroy *meteorologist, educator*
Ethington, Raymond Lindsay *geology educator, researcher*
Sun, Albert Yung-Kwang *biochemistry and neurochemistry educator*
Weisman, Gary Andrew *biochemist*
Wixom, Robert Llewellyn *biochemistry educator*

Creve Coeur
Bockserman, Robert Julian *chemist*

Ferguson
Chubb, Charles Ray *physicist, researcher*

Kansas City
Cheng, Kuang Lu *chemist, educator*
Ching, Wai Yim *physics educator, researcher*
Durig, James Robert *chemistry educator*
Hasan, Syed Eqbal *environmental geologist, educator*
Kloth, Carolyn *meteorologist*
Lott, Peter F. *chemist*
Parizek, Eldon Joseph *geologist, educator, dean*
Rost, William Joseph *chemist*
Wilkinson, Ralph Russell *biochemistry educator, toxicologist*
Wrobel, Jerzy Michal *physicist, educator*

Kirksville
Festa, Roger Reginald *chemist, educator*

Lees Summit
Hubbard, Harold Mead *environmental scientist, consultant*

Maryland Heights
Chinn, Rex Arlyn *chemist*

Rolla
Adawi, Ibrahim Hasan *physics educator*
Alexander, Ralph William, Jr., *physics educator*
Gregg, Jay Mason *geology educator*
Mc Farland, Robert Harold *physicist, educator*
Oboh-Ikuenobe, Francisca Emiede *geologist, educator, researcher*
Sotiriou-Leventis, Chariklia *chemist, educator, researcher*
†Trueblood, Max Blair *physicist, educator*

Saint Louis
Agarwal, Ramesh Kumar *aeronautical scientist, researcher, educator*
Bender, Carl Martin *physics educator, consultant*
Burgess, James Harland *physics educator, researcher*
Frieden, Carl *biochemist, educator*
Friedlander, Michael Wulf *physicist, educator*
Gokel, George William *organic chemist, educator*
Handel, Peter H. *physics educator*
Hawkins, Pamela Leigh Huffman *biochemist*
Huynh, Quang Khai *biochemist*
Israel, Martin Henry *astrophysicist, educator, academic administrator*
†Knowles, William S. *retired chemist*
Macias, Edward S. *chemistry educator, university official and dean*
Marshall, Garland Ross *biochemist, biophysicist, medical educator*
Miller, James Gegan *research scientist, physics educator*
Murray, Robert Wallace *chemistry educator*
Purdy, James Aaron *medical physics educator*
Rodriguez, José Luis *biochemist*
†Schilling, James Stanford *physicist, educator*
Sorensen, Keld *biochemist*
Walker, Robert Mowbray *physicist, educator*
Weisenfeld, Robert Beller *chemist, researcher*
Welch, Michael John *chemistry educator, researcher*
Wrighton, Mark Stephen *chemistry educator*

Springfield
Thompson, Clifton C. *retired chemistry educator, university administrator*
Toste, Anthony Paim *chemistry educator, researcher*

MONTANA

Bozeman
†Drobizhev, Mikhail Anatolievich *physicist*
Horner, John Robert *paleontologist, researcher*

Columbia Falls
Spade, George Lawrence (George Shenker) *scientist*

Dayton
Volborth, Alexis von *geochemist, geological engineering educator*

Kalispell
Freiberg, Robert Jerry *laser physicist, engineer, technology administrator, consultant*

Livingston
Wright, Richard Kirk *physicist, materials researcher, consultant*

Missoula
†DeGraw, Joseph Irving, Jr., *chemist, consultant*
Osterheld, R(obert) Keith *chemistry educator*

Monarch
†Baker, David Warren *earth scientist*

NEBRASKA

Kearney
Wubbels, Gene Gerald *chemistry educator*

Lincoln
Brakke, Myron Kendall *retired research chemist, educator*
De Silva, Handunnetti Sakuntala V. *physicist*
Jones, Lee Bennett *chemist, educator, university official*
Kaplan, Sanford Sandy *geologist*
†Spreitzer, Robert Joseph *biochemist, educator*
Treves, Samuel Blain *geologist, educator*
Yoder, Bruce Alan *chemist*

Omaha
Bergt, Gregory Paul *chemist, consultant*
†Lockridge, Oksana *biochemist, educator, researcher*
Watt, Dean Day *retired biochemistry educator*
Zepf, Thomas Herman *physics educator, researcher*

NEVADA

Boulder City
Huntoon, Peter Wesley *geoscience consultant*

Carson City
Crawford, John Edward *geologist, scientist*

Henderson
Holloway, Robert Wester *radiochemist*
Trivelpiece, Alvin William *physicist, educator, consultant*

Las Vegas
Broca, Laurent Antoine *aerospace scientist*
Kielhorn, Richard Werner *chemist*
Nacht, Steve Jerry *geologist*
Nicol, Malcolm F. *physical chemistry educator*

Reno
Kantsyrev, Victor Leonidovich *physicist*
Price, Jonathan G. *geologist*
Sladek, Ronald John *physics educator*
Stockwell, William Ross *atmospheric chemist*
Taranik, James Vladimir *geologist, educator*

Sparks
Bonham, Harold Florian *research geologist, consultant*

NEW HAMPSHIRE

Durham
Tischler, Herbert *geologist, educator*

Freedom
Keith, Barry Harold *environmental scientist*

Grantham
Grimley, Robert Thomas *chemistry educator*

Hanover
Bel Bruno, Joseph James *chemistry educator*
†Curphey, Thomas John *chemist, researcher*
Feng, Xiahong *geochemist, educator*
Montgomery, David Campbell *physicist, educator*
†Perovich, Donald Kole *geophysicist*
†Spencer, Thomas A. *chemist, educator*
Stockmayer, Walter H(ugo) *chemistry educator*
Sturge, Michael Dudley *physicist, educator*
Wegner, Gary Alan *astronomer*

Merrimack
Hosker, Donald *materials research technician*

Salem
Simmons, Marvin Gene *geophysics educator*

NEW JERSEY

Annandale
Baugh, Lisa Saunders (Lisa Saunders Boffa) *research chemist*
Gorbaty, Martin Leo *chemist, researcher*
Johnston, John Eric *chemist*

Basking Ridge
Morgan, Samuel P(ope) *physicist, applied mathematician*

Belleville
†Asiaie, Reza *research scientist*
Berenfeld, Mark M. *chemist*

Berkeley Heights
Geusic, Joseph Edward Edward *physicist*
Mac Rae, Alfred Urquhart *physicist, electrical engineer*

Bogota
Condon, Francis Edward *retired chemistry educator*

Bridgewater
†Chapel, Sunny *research scientist*
Holder, Neville Lewis *chemist*

Budd Lake
Khazen, Aleksandr Moiseyevich *physicist*

Caldwell
†Surmatis, Joseph D. *retired chemist*

Camden
Beck, David Paul *biochemist*

Cherry Hill
Hill, Connie Ray, Jr., *physicist*

Cliffside Park
†Ginos, James Zissis *retired research chemist*

Columbia
Timcenko, Lydia Teodora *biochemist, chemist*

Demarest
Ruderman, Warren *chemist*

East Brunswick
Wagman, Gerald Howard *retired biochemist*

East Hanover
Edelson, Edward Harold *research chemist*

Edison
†Lee, Willy Weisheng *chemist, researcher*

Egg Harbor Township
Li, Huasheng *scientist*

Elizabeth
Arnold, Kristin Anne *chemist*

Far Hills
McCall, David Warren *retired chemistry research director, consultant*

Freehold
Kwon, Joon Taek *retired chemistry researcher*

Hamilton
Barclay, Robert, Jr., *chemist*

Highland Park
Brudner, Harvey Jerome *physicist*
Feigenbaum, Abraham Samuel *nutritional biochemist*

Hightstown
Shoemaker, Frank Crawford *physicist, educator*

Hillsborough
Smagorinsky, Joseph *meteorologist*

Hoboken
Attygalle, Athula Buddhagosha *chemist, researcher*
Schmidt, George *physicist, educator*

Holmdel
†Curtis, Thomas H. *physicist*
Gordon, James Power *optics scientist*
Kaminow, Ivan Paul *physicist*
Mollenauer, Linn Frederick *physicist*

Jackson
†Arminas, Scott Arnold *chemist, poet, writer*

Jersey City
Hozer, Leszek *materials scientist, engineer*
Koster, Emlyn Howard *geologist, educator*
Nakhla, Atif Mounir *scientist, biochemist*

Kenilworth
Baroudy, Bahige Mourad *biochemist, researcher*
Evans, Charlie Anderson *chemist*
†Korfmacher, Walter Averill *chemist, researcher*
Pramanik, Birendra Nath *research executive*

Lakewood
Karol, Frederick John *industrial chemist*

Lambertville
Beyea, Jan Edgar *physicist*

Lawrenceville
Brill, Michael Henry *physicist, vision scientist, editor*
Sheats, John Eugene *chemistry educator*

Leonia
†Kurtz, Anthony David *physicist*

Livingston
†Green, Richard *research scientist, consultant*

Madison
†Carter, Ashley Hale *physicist, educator*

Mahwah
Yeh, Lun-Shu Ray *electrochemist*

Manahawkin
Logan, Ralph Andre *physicist*

Manasquan
Pond, Thomas Alexander *physics educator, university official*

Maplewood
Johnson, Dewey, Jr., *retired biochemist*
Tatyrek, Alfred Frank *consultant, materials and environmental engineer, analytical and research chemist*

Mendham
Dombrowski, Robert Theodore *materials scientist and information architect*
Lunt, Harry Edward *metallurgist, consultant*

Middletown
†Iannone, Patrick Paul *optics scientist, researcher*
Lundgren, Carl William, Jr., *physicist*

Millington
Glockmann, Walter Friedrich *physicist, consultant*

Milltown
Sacharow, Stanley *chemist, consultant, writer*

Montclair
Kowalski, Stephen Wesley *retired chemistry educator*

Montvale
Litchfield, John Edward *chemist*

Morris Plains
Capellos, Chris Spiridon *chemist*

Morristown
Golecki, Ilan *physicist, researcher, educator*
Hernandez, Marissa *physicist*

Mountainside
Vice, Susan F. *medicinal chemist*

Murray Hill
Kozhevnikov, Michael Boris *physicist, researcher*

Neptune
Aguiar, Adam Martin *chemist, educator*

New Brunswick
Fisher, Hans *nutritional biochemistry educator*
Liao, Mei-June *biopharmaceutical company executive*
Pandey, Ramesh Chandra *chemist, executive*
Rona, Peter Arnold *oceanographer, researcher, educator*
Rosen, Robert Thomas *analytical and food chemist*
Strauss, Ulrich Paul *chemist, educator*

New Providence
Helfand, Eugene *chemist*
Lanzerotti, Louis John *physicist*
Laskowski, Edward John *chemist*
Sivco, Deborah Lee *research materials scientist*
White, Alice Elizabeth *physicist, researcher*

Newark
†Arrigo, Cindy Jo *biochemist, researcher*
Mitra, Somenath Sam *environmental scientist, educator*
Spruch, Grace Marmor *physics educator*
Waelde, Lawrence Richard *chemist*

North Plainfield
Thomas, Lewis *physicist, researcher*

Nutley
†Hung, Frank Chien-Hsin *chemist, researcher*
Kong, Norman *chemist*
Liu, Chao-Min *biochemist, biotechnologist, researcher*

Oldwick
Sinfelt, John Henry *chemist*
†Van Doren, Shaun Clark *chemist*

Paulsboro
†Langley, Michael Lee *chemist*

Piscataway
†Alexe, Gabriela *research scientist*
Champe, Pamela Chambers *biochemistry educator, writer*
Choe, Yun Hwang *chemist, educator*
Cohen, Morrel Herman *physicist, biologist, educator*
Goldman, Alan Stuart *chemistry educator*
Idol, James Daniel, Jr., *chemist, educator, inventor, consultant*
Kissin, Yury Viktor *chemist, geochemist*
†Kotliar, B. Gabriel *physics educator*
Leath, Paul Larry *physicist, educator, former university official*
Lebowitz, Joel Louis *mathematical physicist, educator*
Lindenfeld, Peter *physics educator*
Manowitz, Paul *biochemist, researcher, educator*
Polefka, Thomas Gregory *biochemist*
Robbins, Allen Bishop *physics educator*
Robinson, David Alton *climatologist, geography educator*
Shatkin, Aaron Jeffrey *biochemistry educator*
Snitzer, Elias *physicist*
Witz, Gisela *scientist, educator*
Yacowitz, Harold *biochemist, nutritionist*

Point Pleasant
Berkman, Samuel *materials scientist*

Pomona
†Paul, Edward *chemistry educator*
Sharon, Yitzhak Yaakov *physicist, educator*

Port Murray
Kunzler, John Eugene *physicist*

Princeton
Adler, Stephen Louis *physicist*
†Arunasalam, Vickramasingam (Willie) *retired physicist*
†Bahcall, John Norris *astrophysicist*
Bonini, William Emory *geophysics educator*
Brinkman, William Frank *physicist, research executive*
†Chando, Theodore John *research scientist*
Christman, Edward Arthur *physicist*
Davidson, Ronald Crosby *physicist, educator*
Dyson, Freeman John *physicist, educator*
Finn, Frances Mary *biochemistry researcher*
Fisch, Nathaniel Joseph *physicist*
Fitch, Val Logsdon *physics educator*
Florey, Klaus Georg *chemist, pharmaceutical consultant*
†Gaudi, Bernard Scott *astronomer, researcher*
Grisham, Larry Richard *physicist, consultant*
Groves, John Taylor, III, *chemist, educator*
Hawryluk, Richard Janusz *physicist*
Hill, Kenneth Wayne *physicist*
Hopfield, John Joseph *biophysicist, educator*
Hulse, Russell Alan *physicist*
Hut, Piet *astrophysics educator*
Jenkins, Edward Beynon *research astronomer*
Kauzmann, Walter Joseph *chemistry educator*
Kyin, Saw William *chemist, consultant*
†Lewandowski, Jerome L. *physicist*
Lieb, Elliott Hershel *physicist, mathematician, educator*
Long, Frank Wesley, Jr., *chemist*
Manabe, Syukuro *climatologist*
McClure, Donald Stuart *physical chemist, educator*
Ondetti, Miguel Angel *chemist, consultant*
Oppenheimer, Michael *physicist*
Ostriker, Jeremiah Paul *astrophysicist*
Potasek, Mary Joyce *physicist, researcher*
Ramaprasad, Kackadasam Raghavachar *physical chemist*
Royce, Barrie Saunders Hart *physicist, educator*
Rutherford, Paul Harding *physicist*
†Sabb, Annmarie Louise *chemist, researcher*
Seman, Charles Jacob *research meteorologist*
Smith, Arthur John Stewart *physicist, educator*
Spiro, Thomas George *chemistry educator*
†Srolovitz, David J. *materials scientist*
Sterzer, Fred *research physicist*
Stillinger, Frank Henry *chemist, educator*
Tang, Chao *physicist*
Taylor, Joseph Hooton, Jr., *radio astronomer*
Torquato, Salvatore *materials science and chemistry educator*
Tremaine, Scott Duncan *astrophysicist*
Van Houten, Franklyn Bosworth *geologist, educator*
Wheeler, John Archibald *physicist*
Wightman, Arthur Strong *physicist, educator*
Wilkinson, David Todd *physics educator*
†Zhou, Jikou *materials scientist, researcher*
Zung, Jonathan Bruce *chemist*

Princeton Junction
Eckler, Paul Eugene *chemist*

Rahway
Garcia, Maria Luisa *biochemist, researcher*
Kaczorowski, Gregory John *biochemist, researcher, science administrator*

Somerville
Dammel, Ralph Rainer *chemist, researcher*

South Hackensack
Stier, Roger Edwin *chemist, researcher*

South Plainfield
Chu, Sung Nee George *materials scientist*

Springfield
Panish, Morton B. *retired physical chemist*

Stirling
Walsh, Peter Joseph *physics educator*

Summit
Burbank, Robinson Derry *crystallographer*
Phillips, James Charles *physicist, educator*
Rosensweig, Ronald Ellis *scientist consultant*
Vandenberg, Joka Maria *physicist, researcher*

Teaneck
Fajans, Jack *physics educator*
Nagy, Christa Fiedler *biochemist*

Teterboro
Contois, John Henry *clinical chemist, researcher*

Tinton Falls
Eiselt, Michael Herbert *optics scientist*

Trenton
Parsa, Bahman *nuclear chemist*

Union
Zois, Constantine Nicholas Athanasios *meteorology educator*

Wayne
†Kardan, Mahmoud *chemist, educator*

West Caldwell
Piel, Emil J. *retired science and engineering educator*

Westfield
Bartok, William *environmental technologies consultant*

Woodbury
†Nace, Donald M. *retired chemist*

NEW MEXICO

Albuquerque
Beckel, Charles Leroy *physicist, educator*
Chronister, Richard Davis *physicist*
Eliseev, Petr Georgievich *physicist, researcher*
Gander, John Edward *biochemistry educator*
Garland, James Wilson, Jr., *retired physics educator*
Harrison, Charles Wagner, Jr., *applied physicist*
Jagnow, David Henry *petroleum geologist*
Johnson, Ralph Theodore, Jr., *physicist*
Leeper, Ramon Joe *physicist*
Loftfield, Robert Berner *biochemistry educator*
Papyrin, Anatolii Nikiforovich *physicist, researcher*
Pryor, Richard J. *physicist, researcher*
†Renschler, Clifford L. *chemist*
†Taylor, Douglas John *materials scientist, researcher, materials engineer*
Torres, Barbara Wood *technical services professional*
Vianco, Paul Thomas *metallurgist*
Weissman, Suzanne Heisler *analytical chemist*
†Westwood, Albert Ronald Clifton *materials scientist, researcher*

Carlsbad
Paviet-Hartmann, Patricia *chemist, researcher*
Xiong, Yongliang *geochemist*

Kirtland Afb
Alejandro, Steven B. *physicist*
Degnan, James Henry *physicist*
Paxton, Alan Hugh *physicist*

Las Cruces
Coker, Cheryl Ann *kinesiologist*
†Giordano, Thomas H. *chemist, educator*
Richardson, Albert Edward *chemistry educator, consultant, researcher*

Los Alamos
Beck, Charles Milburn, II, *analytical chemist*
Becker, Stephen A. *physicist, designer*
Brown, Lowell Severt *physicist, educator*
Butko, Vladimir Yuryevich *physicist, researcher*
Caramana, Edward J. *physicist*
†Clausen, Bjørn *materials scientist, researcher*
Cucchiara, Alfred Louis *health physicist*
†Duan, Yixiang *research scientist, chemist*
Engelhardt, Albert George *physicist*
Gibson, Benjamin Franklin *physicist*
Grilly, Edward Rogers *physicist*
Hansen, Glen Arthur *scientist, researcher*
Höchbauer, Tobias Franz Wolfgang *physicist, researcher*
Johnson, Mikkel Borlaug *physicist*
Judd, O'Dean P. *physicist*
Keepin, George Robert, Jr., *physicist*
King, Jerry Wayne *research chemist*
Kubas, Gregory Joseph *research chemist*
Lu, Ningping *environmental chemist*
†Lyman, John L. *chemist, researcher*
Makaruk, Hanna Ewa *theoretical physicist*
†Maloy, Stuart *materials scientist, engineer*
†Masunov, Artem *theoretical chemist, researcher*
Mead, William Charles *physicist*
†Michael, Martin Nieto *theoretical physicist*
Michaudon, André Francisque *physicist*
Mihalas, Dimitri Manuel *astrophysicist, educator*
Mitchell, Terence Edward *materials scientist*
Morales, Reynaldo *physicist*
Nix, James Rayford *nuclear physicist, consultant*
Press, William Henry *astrophysicist, computer scientist*
Rosen, Louis *physicist*
Selden, Robert Wentworth *physicist, science advisor*
Sharp, David Howland *physicist*
Sickafus, Kurt Edward *materials scientist, researcher*
Silver, Gary L. *chemist*
Smith, James Lawrence *research physicist*
Snell, Charles Murrell *physicist, astrophysicist*
Terrell, James (Nelson James Terrell) *physicist*
†Venhaus, Thomas J. *physicist*
†Vesselinov, Velimir Valentinov *hydrogeologist, researcher*
Wahl, Arthur Charles *retired chemistry educator*
†Wallstrom, Timothy C. *physicist*
Wienke, Bruce R. *physicist, consultant*
Williams, Joel Mann *polymer material scientist*
WoldeGabriel, Giday *research geologist*
†Zhang, Dongxiao *research scientist*

Los Lunas
Seiler, Fritz Arnold *physicist*

Placitas
Long, Timothy Scott *chemist, consultant*

Santa Fe
Allen, John Polk *environmental scientist*
Cowan, George Arthur *chemist, bank executive, director*
Fisher, Philip Chapin *physicist*
Fisher, Robert Alan *laser physicist*
Gell-Mann, Murray *theoretical physicist, educator*
Giovanielli, Damon Vincent *physicist, consulting company executive*
Jones, Walter Harrison *chemist, educator*
Leibowitz, Jack Richard *physicist, educator*
†Lynn, John Eric *nuclear physics research consultant*
†Mason, Allen Smith *atmospheric chemist*
Montgomery, Michael Davis *physics/astrophysics company executive, consultant , real estate company executive*
Romanowski, Thomas Andrew *physics educator*
†Sayre, William O. *geologist, educator*
†Stalker, James Raghi *meteorologist, environmental services administrator*
White, David Hywel *physics educator*
Whitten, David George *chemistry educator*

Santa Teresa
Rogash, Joseph Alan *meteorologist, educator*

Socorro
Broadhead, Ronald Frigon *petroleum geologist, geology educator*
†Phillips, Fred Melville *hydrology educator*

Sunspot
Keil, Stephen Lesley *astrophysicist*

Tesuque
Bundy, Wayne M. *retired geologist, consultant*

NEW YORK

Albany
Fakundiny, Robert Harry *geologist, educator, consultant*
Galivan, John Henry *biochemist, educator, public health officer, research administrator*
†Iyer, Seema *chemist*
Kim, Jai Soo *physics educator*

MacDonald, Carolyn Ann *physicist, educator*
Schneider, Allan Stanford *biochemistry, neuroscience and pharmacology educator, biomedical research scientist*
Willis, John Patrick *chemist*
Yalcintas, M. Güven *medical physicist*

Alfred
Boehlert, Carl Joseph *materials scientist, educator*
Pye, Lenwood David *materials science educator, researcher, consultant*
Wang, Xingwu *physics educator*

Alfred Station
Condrate, Robert Adam, Sr., *spectroscopy educator*

Amherst
Ismail, Abu Zafar Mohamed *physics educator, researcher, consultant*

Ballston Spa
Westbrook, Jack Hall *metallurgist, consultant*

Big Flats
Keck, Donald Bruce *physicist*

Binghamton
Coates, Donald Robert *geology educator, scientist*
Eisch, John Joseph *chemist, educator, writer, consultant*
Nelson, Charles A. *physicist, educator*
†Sadik, Omowunmi A. *electrochemist, educator*
Whittingham, M(ichael) Stanley *chemist*

Brewster
Blyakhman, Yefim Moisei *chemist, researcher*

Bronx
†Khrapunov, Sergei *biophysicist*
Murthy, Vadiraja Venkatesa *biochemist, researcher, educator*
Shamos, Morris Herbert *physicist educator*
Siddons, Sarah Mae *chemist*
Thysen, Benjamin *biochemist, health science facility administrator, researcher*
Yalow, Rosalyn Sussman *biophysicist*

Brookhaven
Kouts, Herbert John Cecil *retired physicist*

Brooklyn
Armenakas, Anthony Emmanuel *aerospace educator*
Castleman, Louis Samuel *metallurgist, educator*
Charton, Marvin *chemist, educator*
Choudhury, Deo Chand *physicist, educator*
Eirich, Frederick Roland *chemist, educator*
Fleyshman, Bentsion *physicist, researcher, retired mathematician*
Franco, Victor *theoretical physics educator*
Friedman, Gerald Manfred *geologist, educator*
Izmailov, Alexander F. *physicist, mathematician, researcher*
Jivetin, Alexander *geophysicist, educator*
Karan, Hiroko Ito *organic chemistry educator*
Krieger, Joseph Bernard *physicist, physics educator*
Mashkevich, Stefan Vladimirovich *physicist, researcher, computer scientist*
Mook, Sarah *retired chemist*
Morawetz, Herbert *chemistry educator*
Pearce, Eli M. *chemistry educator, administrator*
Rokhvarger, Anatoly Efim *materials science and ceramic technology scientist*
Sarutto, Anne MArie Rita *research scientist*
†Shcherbakova, Estella *chemist, mathematician, educator*
Tamir, Theodor *electrophysics researcher, educator*
Wolf, Edward Lincoln *physics educator*
Wolfe, Allan *physicist*

Brooktondale
Eberhard, Anatol *retired chemistry educator*

Buffalo
Amborski, Leonard Edward *chemist*
Anbar, Michael *biophysics educator*
Baier, Robert Edward *chemist, educator*
Bardos, Thomas Joseph *chemist, educator*
Coppens, Philip *chemist*
†Hu, Ke *medicinal chemist, pharmacologist*
Jain, Piyare Lal *physics educator*
Patel, Mulchand Shambhubhai *biochemist, researcher*
Rashba, Emmanuel Iosif *physicist, educator*
Reitan, Paul Hartman *geologist, educator*
†Tenne, Dirk *research scientist*
Treanor, Charles Edward *scientist*
Tritsch, George Leopold *biochemist, educator, retired biomedical researcher*
Wang, Jui Hsin *biochemistry educator*

Canandaigua
Lowther, Frank Eugene *research physicist*

Chappaqua
Weinberger, Robert *analytical chemist*

Chateaugay
Holt, Peter Robert Bacon *geophysicist*

Chestnut Ridge
Huntoon, Robert Brian *chemist, food industry consultant*

Clarence
†Xing, Weibing *research scientist*

Clinton
Ring, James Walter *physics educator*

Cooperstown
Peters, Theodore, Jr., *research biochemist, consultant*

Coram
Dudnikov, Vadim G. *physicist, researcher*

Corning
Miller, Roger Allen *physicist*
Sala, Martin Andrew *biophysicist, inventor*
†Stookey, Stanley Donald *chemist*
†Visovsky, Nick John *research scientist*
Williams, Jimmie Lewis *research chemist*

Dunkirk
Huels, Steven Mark *physicist, mathematician, astronomer*

East Hampton
Garrett, Charles Geoffrey Blythe *physicist, consultant*

Elmira
Stephens, Lawrence James *chemistry educator, program director*

Endwell
Albrecht, William Melvin *research chemist, consultant*

Fairport
Lawrynowicz, Witold J. *chemist, writer*

Farmingdale
Nolan, Peter John *physics educator*

Flushing
†Engel, Robert *chemist, educator, dean*
Finks, Robert Melvin *paleontologist, educator*
†Genack, Azriel Z. *physicist, educator*
†Gizis, Evangelos John *biochemist*
Goldman, Norman Lewis *chemistry educator*
Speidel, David Harold *geology educator*

Fredonia
Berkley, John L. *geology educator, meteoriticist*

Freeport
Pullman, Maynard Edward *biochemist*

Geneva
†Roelofs, Wendell Lee *biochemistry educator, consultant*

Great Neck
Rutkin, Philip *chemist*

Guilderland
Siggins, James E. *chemist*

Hannacroix
Schwebler, Stephen *retired chemist*

Hempstead
†Stauber, Michael C. *physicist, consultant*

Horseheads
Josbeno, Larry Joseph *physics educator*

Irvington
Devons, Samuel *educator, physicist*
Elbaum, Marek *electro-optical sciences executive, researcher*

Ithaca
Ashcroft, Neil William *physics educator, researcher*
Bassett, William Akers *geologist, educator, retired*
Bauer, Simon Harvey *chemistry educator*
Bauman, Dale Elton *nutritional biochemistry educator*
Berkelman, Karl *physics educator*
Bethe, Hans Albrecht *physicist, educator*
Burns, Joseph Arthur *planetary science educator*
Carpenter, Barry Keith *chemistry educator, researcher*
Crittenden, James Arthur *physicist*
Fay, Robert Clinton *chemist, educator*
Fitchen, Douglas Beach *physicist, educator*
†Flanagan, Eanna Eamonn *physicist*
Freed, Jack Herschel *chemist, educator*
†Ginsparg, Paul *physicist*
Gold, Thomas *astronomer, educator*
Goldsmith, Paul Felix *physics and astronomy educator*
Hart, Edward Walter *physicist*
Hess, George Paul *biochemist, educator*
Hoffmann, Roald *chemist, educator*
Holcomb, Donald Frank *physicist, academic administrator*
Kinoshita, Toichiro *physicist*
Lee, David Morris *physics educator*
Lepage, Gerard Peter *physics educator*
Liboff, Richard Lawrence *physicist, educator*
Lumley, John Leask *physicist, educator*
McLafferty, Fred Warren *chemist, educator*
McMurry, John Edward *chemistry educator*
Meinwald, Jerrold *chemist, educator*
Mermin, N. David *physicist, educator, writer*
Oliver, Jack Ertle *geophysicist, educator*
Renwick, J. Alan *chemist, ecologist*
Richardson, Robert Coleman *physics educator, researcher*
Salpeter, Edwin Ernest *physical sciences educator*
Scheraga, Harold Abraham *physical chemistry educator*
Slate, Floyd Owen *chemist, materials scientist, civil engineer, educator, researcher*
Smilgies, Detlef-Matthias Friedrich *physicist*
Terzian, Yervant *astronomy and astrophysics educator*
†Teukolsky, Saul *physicist, educator*
Thomas, J. Earl *retired physicist*
York, James Wesley, Jr., *theoretical physicist, educator*

Jamaica
Greenberg, Jacob *biochemist, educator, consultant*

Lengyel, István *chemist, educator*
Sun, Siao Fang *chemistry educator*

Larchmont
Guttenplan, Joseph B. *biochemist, educator*

Latham
Lvovsky, Yuri *physicist, applied superconductivity engineer*

Lewiston
Dexter, Theodore Henry *chemist*

Mamaroneck
Mazzola, Claude Joseph *physicist, small business owner*

Manhasset
Callaway, David James Edward *physicist, protein chemist, bioinformaticist, expedition mountaineer*
Kingsley, Peter Bernard *physics researcher*
Spetsieris, Phoebe George *physicist, scientific software engineer, researcher*

Manlius
Brophy, Mary O'Reilly *environmental scientist*
Martonosi, Anthony Nicholas *biochemistry educator, researcher*

Maryland
Miller, J(ames) Robert *chemistry educator*

Melville
Damadian, Raymond Vahan *biophysicist*
Pelle, Edward Gerard *biochemist*

Millbrook
Cole, Jonathan Jay *aquatic scientist, researcher*

New Hyde Park
Klein, Bernard *clinical chemist*

New Paltz
Lavallee, David Kenneth *chemistry educator, researcher*

New Rochelle
Margolin, Harold *metallurgical educator*

New York
Allison, Michael David *space scientist, astronomy educator*
Amols, Howard Ira *medical physicist*
Baker, William Oliver *retired research chemist*
Bederson, Benjamin *physicist, educator*
Bell, Susan Koelle *paleontologist*
Berne, Bruce J. *chemistry educator*
Borowitz, Sidney *retired physics educator*
Boskey, Adele Ludin *biochemistry educator, researcher*
Breslow, Esther May Greenberg *biochemistry educator, researcher*
Breslow, Ronald Charles *chemist*
Campbell, George, Jr., *physicist, administrator*
Cheng, Chuen Yan *biochemist, educator*
Chevray, Rene *physics educator*
Cohen, Ezechiel Godert David *physicist, educator*
Courant, Ernest David *physicist, educator*
Cross, George Alan Martin *biochemistry educator, researcher*
Cummins, Herman Zachary *physicist*
de Duve, Christian René *chemist, educator*
Demler, Frederick Russel *minerals economist, commodities broker*
Edelman, Isidore Samuel *biochemist and medical educator*
Eisenthal, Kenneth B. *physical chemistry educator*
Erlanger, Bernard Ferdinand *biochemist, educator*
Ferrier, Joseph John *atmospheric physicist*
Fox, Jack Jay *chemist, educator*
Fraenkel, George Kessler *chemistry educator*
Goulianos, Konstantin *physics educator*
†Greene, Nathanael Wade *environmental scientist*
†Haines, Thomas Henry *biochemist, educator, biochemist, researcher*
Harris, Cyril Manton *physicist, engineering and architecture educator, consulting acoustical engineer*
Hassan, Sergio Alejandro *physicist, biophysicist, researcher*
Hershkowitz, Allen J. *waste management specialist, researcher*
Hoffert, Martin Irving *applied science educator*
Hoffman, Linda M. *chemist, educator*
Huang, Limin *chemist, researcher*
Kaku, Michio *theoretical nuclear physicist, educator*
Kantor, Frederick William *physicist*
†Katsoyannis, Panayotis George *biochemist, educator*
Katz, Thomas J. *chemistry educator*
Khuri, Nicola Najib *physicist, educator*
Koplik, Joel *physicist, educator*
Krasna, Alvin Isaac *biochemist, educator*
†Krauskopf, John *research scientist, educator*
Kuo, John Tsungfen *geophysicist, educator, researcher*
Lieberman, Seymour *biochemist, educator*
Liu, Charles *astrophysicist*
Lubell, Michael Stephen *physicist, researcher, physics educator*
Marshall, Thomas Carlisle *applied physics educator*
McKay, Kenneth Gardiner *physicist, electronics company executive*
McNelis, Edward Joseph *chemistry educator*
Merrifield, Robert Bruce *biochemist, educator*
Middleton, David *physicist, applied mathematician, educator*
Nakanishi, Koji *chemistry educator, research institute administrator*
Navratil, Gerald Anton *physicist, educator*

Newell, Norman Dennis *paleontologist, geologist, museum curator, educator*
†Nickoloff, Edward Lee *radiology physicist*
Norell, Mark Allen *paleontology educator*
Oppenheimer, Ben R. *research scientist*
Oreskes, Irwin *biochemistry educator*
Parkin, Gerard Francis Ralph *chemistry educator, researcher*
Pechukas, Philip *chemistry educator*
Percus, Jerome Kenneth *physicist, educator*
Peskin, Charles *physicist, educator*
Pinczuk, Aron *physicist*
†Pokotilov, Andriy *physicist*
Rechkoblit, Olga A. *biochemist, researcher*
Rhodes, Yorke E(dward) *organic chemist, educator*
Robinson, Enders Anthony *geophysicist, educator, writer*
Roeder, Robert Gayle *biochemist, educator*
Sarachik, Myriam Paula Morgenstein *physics educator*
Schwartz, Melvin *physics educator, laboratory administrator*
†Scott, Willard Herman *meteorologist, newscaster*
Shalit, Hanoch *imaging scientist, executive*
Simon, Eric Jacob *neurochemist, educator*
Soter, Steven *research scientist*
Stork, Gilbert *chemistry educator, investigator*
Störmer, Horst Ludwig *physicist*
Stroke, Hinko Henry *physicist, educator*
Turro, Nicholas John *chemistry educator*
Watanabe, Yoichi *medical physicist, researcher*
Werthamer, Nathan Richard *physicist*

Niagara Falls
Bharadwaj, Prem Datta *physics educator*
Knowles, Richard Norris *chemist*

Niskayuna
†Edelheit, Lewis S. *research physicist*
†Hancu, Ileana *research scientist*
Kambour, Roger Peabody *retired polymer physical chemist, researcher*
Katz, Samuel *geophysics educator*
†Kebbede, Anteneh *materials scientist, researcher*
Lafferty, James Martin *retired physicist*
White, Frederick Andrew *physics educator, physicist*

Northport
Allocca, John Anthony *medical research scientist*

Oneonta
Hickey, Francis Roger *physicist, educator*
Horner, Carl Matthew *chemistry educator*
Merilan, Michael Preston *astrophysicist, educator, dean*

Oswego
Silveira, Augustine, Jr., *chemistry educator*

Palisades
Cane, Mark Alan *oceanography and climate researcher*
†Goddard, Lisa *meteorologist*
Hayes, Dennis Edward *geophysicist, educator*
Kellogg, Herbert Humphrey *metallurgist, educator*
Mason, Simon James *climatologist*
Richards, Paul Granston *geophysics educator, seismologist*

Patchogue
Marr, Robert Bruce *physicist, educator*

Pearl River
†Barringer, William Charles *retired chemist*
†Doedée, Marijo *chemist*
†Gorovits, Boris *analytical biochemist*

Peru
Dawson, James Clifford *environmental science educator, geologist*

Pittsford
Goldstein, David Arthur *biophysicist, educator*

Pomona
Gletsos, Constantine *chemist*

Potsdam
Fendler, Janos Hugo *chemistry educator*
Hopke, Philip Karl *chemical engineering educator, atmospheric scientist*
Islam, Muhammad Azadul *physicist, educator, researcher*
Mackay, Raymond Arthur *chemist*
Matijevic, Egon *chemistry educator*
Privman, Vladimir *physics educator*
Vaska, Lauri *chemist, retired educator*

Poughkeepsie
Beck, Curt Werner *chemist, educator*
Deiters, Sister Joan Adele *psychoanalyst, nun, chemistry educator*
Lang, William Warner *physicist*
Pliskin, William Aaron *physicist*

Ridge
Blume, Martin *physicist*

Rochester
†Basavappa, Ravi *biophysical scientist, educator*
Bigelow, Nicholas Pierre *physicist, educator*
Boeckman, Robert Kenneth, Jr., *chemistry educator, organic chemistry researcher*
Cain, B(urton) Edward *chemistry educator*
Conwell, Esther Marly *physicist, researcher*
Duarte, Francisco Javier *physicist, researcher*
Elder, Fred Kingsley, Jr., *physicist, educator*
Farrar, James Martin *chemistry educator*
Ferbel, Thomas *physics educator, physicist*
Gates, Marshall DeMotte, Jr., *chemistry educator*
Hilf, Russell *biochemist, educator*
Kampmeier, Jack August Carlos *chemist, educator*
Kende, Andrew Steven *chemist, educator*

Kingslake, Rudolf *retired optical designer*
Knauer, James Philip *physicist*
Knox, Robert Seiple *physicist, educator*
†Li, James Chen Min *materials science educator*
Luckey, George William *research chemist*
Makous, Walter Leon *visual scientist, educator*
Mercer, Kermit Ray *biophysicist*
Salamone, Joseph Charles *polymer chemistry educator*
†Saunders, William Hundley, Jr., *retired chemist, educator*
Sherman, Fred *biochemist, educator*
Thomas, John Howard *astrophysicist, engineer, educator*
Thorndike, Edward Harmon *physicist*
Weiss, David Steven *chemist*

Ronkonkoma
Chue, Randy Shek-Ming *aerospace scientist*

Roslyn
Stein, Theodore Anthony *biochemist, educator*

Rouses Point
Weierstall, Richard Paul *retired pharmaceutical chemist*

Saint James
Bigeleisen, Jacob *chemist, educator*

Scarborough
Wittcoff, Harold Aaron *chemist*

Scarsdale
Porosoff, Harold *chemist, research and development director*

Schenectady
Alpher, Ralph Asher *physicist, educator*
Fleischer, Robert Louis *physics educator*
Frost, Robert Edwin *chemistry educator*
Luborsky, Fred Everett *research physicist*
Philip, A. G. Davis *astronomer, editor, educator*
Smith, Lowell Scott *physicist*

Sherburne
Dodd, Jack Gordon, Jr., *physicist, educator*

South Setauket
Friedlander, Gerhart *nuclear chemist*

Southampton
Roth, Howard *chemist, engineer, consultant*

Southold
Bachrach, Howard L. *biochemist*

Spencerport
Vizy, Kalman Nicholas *research physicist, educator*

Staten Island
Yang, Song-Yu *research biochemist*

Stony Brook
Alexander, John Macmillan, Jr., *chemistry educator*
Bokuniewicz, Henry Joseph *oceanography educator*
Bonner, Francis Truesdale *chemist, educator, university dean*
Brown, Gerald Edward *physicist, educator*
Chen, JiuHua *physicist, geophysicist, educator*
Geller, Marvin Alan *meteorology educator, researcher*
Kahn, Peter B. *physics educator*
Kirz, Janos *physicist*
Ojima, Iwao *chemistry educator*
†Peterson, Deane Millar *astronomer, educator*
Swanson, Robert Lawrence *oceanographer, academic program administrator*
Wurster, Charles Frederick *environmental scientist, educator*
Yang, Chen Ning *physicist*

Syosset
†Lief, Eugene Paul *physicist*

Syracuse
Baldwin, John Edwin *chemistry educator*
Burgess, John H. *ergonomist, consultant*
Conan, Robert James, Jr., *chemistry educator, consultant*
Honig, Arnold *physics educator, researcher*
Levy, H. Richard *biochemistry educator*
Muller, Ernest H. *geology educator*
Prucha, John James *geologist, educator*
Robinson, Joseph Edward *geology educator, consulting petroleum geologist*
Sage, Martin Lee *chemistry educator*
Smith, Kenneth Judson, Jr., *chemist, theoretician, educator*
†Stone, Sheldon L. *physicist, educator*

Tarrytown
O'Brien, Anne Therese *chemist*

Troy
Ferris, James Peter *chemist, educator*
Giaever, Ivar *physicist*
Krause, Sonja *chemistry educator*
Levinger, Joseph Solomon *physicist, educator*
Medicus, Heinrich Adolf *physicist, educator*
Sperber, Daniel *physicist*
Wang, Kegang *physicist, materials scientist*

Upton
Bond, Peter Danford *physicist*
Chaudhari, Praveen *materials physicist*
†Goldhaber, Maurice *physicist, researcher*
Harbottle, Garman *chemist*
Hendrie, Joseph Mallam *physicist, nuclear engineer, government official*
†Lin, Mow S. *chemist*
†Lindenbaum, S(eymour) J(oseph) *physicist*
Lowenstein, Derek Irving *physicist*
Meinhold, Charles Boyd *health physicist*
†Petrovic, Cedomir *research scientist*
Rau, Ralph Ronald *retired physicist*
Ruggiero, Alessandro G. *physicist, researcher*
Setlow, Jane Kellock *biophysicist*
Setlow, Richard Burton *biophysicist, researcher*
†Sheehy, Brian *physicist*
Sutin, Norman *chemistry educator, scientist*
Tannenbaum, Michael J(ay) *physicist*
Zarcone, Michael Joseph *experimental physicist, consultant*

Utica
Iodice, Arthur Alfonso *biochemist*

Valhalla
Zhong, Yuanzhen *research chemist*

Victor
Szalapski, Robert Francis *theoretical physicist*

Wappingers Falls
McCamy, Calvin Samuel *optics scientist*

Webster
†Meyer, Robert J. *physicist*
†Zhang, Shengliang *materials scientist, physicist*

Wellsville
Van Tyne, Arthur Morris *geologist*

West Point
†Leupold, Herbert August *physicist*

White Plains
Flanigen, Edith Marie *materials scientist, consultant*
†Surpris, Joseph W. *research scientist*

Yorktown Heights
Dimitrakopoulos, Christos Dimitrios *materials scientist*
Fowler, Alan Bicksler *retired physicist*
†Kang, Sung Kwon *materials scientist, researcher*
Keyes, Robert W. *physicist, researcher*
Lang, Norton David *physicist*
Mooney, Patricia May *physicist*
Ning, Tak Hung *physicist, microelectronic technologist*
Wu, Chai Wah *research scientist*

NORTH CAROLINA

Apex
Shendrikar, Arun Dhondopant *environmental scientist, chemist*

Asheville
Easterling, David Royer *climatologist*
Haggard, William Henry *meteorologist*
Kessler, Donald Joe *research scientist, physicist, consultant*

Cary
Kung, Pang-Jen *materials scientist, electrical engineer*

Chapel Hill
Bursey, Maurice M. *chemistry educator*
Davis, Morris Schuyler *astronomer*
Dokholyan, Nikolay Vasilyevich *physicist*
Eliel, Ernest Ludwig *chemist, educator*
Forman, Donald T. *biochemist, educator*
Frampton, Paul Howard *physics researcher, educator*
†Hallfors, Denise Dion *research scientist, researcher*
Irene, Eugene Arthur *physical chemistry and materials science educator, researcher*
Kim, Chong Soong *aerosol science and inhalation technology researcher*
Lee, Kuo-Hsiung *medicinal chemistry educator*
Ligett, Waldo Buford *chemist*
Macdonald, James Ross *physicist, educator*
Merzbacher, Eugen *physicist, educator*
Mitchell, Earl Nelson *physicist, educator*
Murray, Royce Wilton *chemistry educator*
Parr, Robert Ghormley *chemistry educator*
Pedersen, Lee G. *chemistry educator*
Rogers, John James William *geology educator*
†Roth, Barbara *chemist, educator*
Shelton, Robert Neal *physics educator, researcher*
Slifkin, Lawrence Myer *physics educator*
†Tsui, Frank *physicist, educator*
Wolfenden, Richard Vance *biochemistry educator*

Charlotte
Mueller, Werner Heinrich *chemical company executive*
Roels, Oswald Albert *oceanographer, educator, business executive*

Duck
Majewski, Theodore Eugene *chemist*

Durham
Chao, James Lee *chemist, educator*
Chesnut, Donald Blair *retired chemistry educator*
Cocks, Franklin Hadley *materials scientist*
Fridovich, Irwin *biochemistry educator*
Goshaw, Alfred T. *physicist, educator*
Hammes, Gordon G. *chemistry educator*
Hobbs, Marcus Edwin *chemistry educator*
Jaszczak, Ronald Jack *physicist, researcher, consultant*
Joklik, Wolfgang Karl *biochemist, virologist, educator*
†Khismatullin, Damir Borisovich *physicist, mathematician*
†Lutes, Christopher Charles *environmental scientist, consultant*
Meyer, Horst *physics educator*
Pearsall, George Wilbur *materials scientist, mechanical engineer, educator, consultant*
Perkins, Ronald Dee *geologist, educator*
Peterson, Max Rupert, Jr., *chemist, researcher*
Roberson, Nathan Russell *physicist, educator*
Sedor, Frank A. *chemist*
Smith, Peter *chemist, educator, consultant*
Walker, William D. *physicist, educator, researcher*
Walter, Richard Lawrence *physicist, educator*
†Whiddon, Curtis Scott *medical physicist*
Yoshizumi, Terry Takatoshi *medical physicist*
†Zhirnov, Victor *physicist, researcher*

Elizabeth City
Choudhury, Abdul Latif *physics educator*

Greensboro
Clark, Clifton Bob *physicist*
Dyakonov, Alexander J. *physical chemist, researcher*
Williams, Irving Laurence *physics educator*

Hendersonville
Halm, James Maurice *retired chemist, poet*
Kratz, Howard Russel *physicist, researcher*
Saby, John Sanford *physicist, consultant*

Linwood
Barnes, Melver Raymond *retired chemist*

New Hill
Weber, Michael Howard *senior nuclear control operator*

Pinehurst
Huizenga, John Robert *nuclear chemist, educator*

Pittsboro
Quinn, Jarus William *physicist, former association executive*

Raleigh
Arya, Satya Pal *meteorology educator*
Aspnes, David Erik *physicist, educator*
Bernholc, Jerzy *physicist, educator*
†Cuculo, John A. *chemist, educator*
Cuomo, Jerome John *materials scientist*
Deihl, Susan Galyen *historic preservationist*
†Khaledi, Morteza G *chemistry educator*
Kim, Ilki *physicist*
Mitchell, Gary Earl *physicist, educator*
Owens, Tyler Benjamin *chemist*
Senzel, Alan Joseph *analytical chemistry consultant, music critic*
Sheng, Quan *chemist, management consultant*
Swaisgood, Harold Everett *biochemist, educator*
Whangbo, Myung Hwan *chemistry educator*
Whitten, Jerry Lynn *chemistry educator*

Research Triangle Park
Copeland, William Chenery *biochemist*
Fisher, Robert Perry *health effects scientist*
†Pouliot, George A. *physical scientist, researcher*
Selkirk, James Kirkwood *biochemist, researcher*

Salisbury
Hlavay, Jay Alan *financial analyst*

Stella
Quin, Louis DuBose *chemist, educator*

Tryon
Mellberg, James Richard *dental research chemist*

Washington
†Blackwell, F. Oris *environmental scientist, educator*

Wilmington
Bissette, Samuel Delk *astronomer, artist, financial executive*

Winston Salem
Cunningham, Carol Clem *biochemistry educator, researcher*
Dobbins, James Talmage, Jr., *analytical chemist, researcher*
Mokrasch, Lewis Carl *neurochemist, educator*
Rodgman, Alan *chemist, consultant*

NORTH DAKOTA

Fargo
†Tallman, Dennis Earl *chemistry educator, research scientist*

Grand Forks
Hardersen, Paul Scott *planetary scientist*
Jacobs, Francis Albin *biochemist, educator*
Nordlie, Robert Conrad *biochemistry educator*
Thomasson, Kathryn Ambler *chemistry educator, biophysical researcher*

OHIO

Akron
Eby, Ronald K. *polymer science educator, researcher*
Gent, Alan Neville *physicist, educator*
Kennedy, Joseph Paul *chemist, researcher*
Piirma, Irja *chemist, educator*
†Xu, Shucheng *chemistry educator, researcher*

Beachwood
Saiakhov, Roustem Damirovich *chemist, consultant*

Beavercreek
Gupta, Vijay Kumar *chemistry educator*
Ruh, Robert *materials scientist*

Bowling Green
Neckers, Douglas Carlyle *chemistry educator*

Burbank
Koucky, Frank Louis *geology educator, archeogeology researcher*

Centerburg
Reynolds, Don William *geologist*

Chardon
Uscheek, David Petrovich *retired chemist*

Chillicothe
Johnson, Mark Alan *biochemist*

Cincinnati
†Bender, Daniel F. *chemist, education educator*
Briskin, Madeleine *paleo-oceanographer, paleoclimatologist, micropaleontologist*
Francis, Marion David *consulting chemist*
Goodman, Bernard *physics educator*
Jensen, Elwood Vernon *biochemist*
Kawahara, Fred Katsumi *research chemist*
Kupper, Philip Lloyd *chemist*
Meal, Larie *chemistry educator, researcher, consultant*
Merchant, Mylon Eugene *physicist, engineer*
Mukerjee, Debdas *environmental health scientist, educator*
Relyea, Carl Miller *retired hydrologist*
Robertson, Jerald Lee *physicist*
Rockwell, R(onald) James, Jr., *laser and electro-optics consultant*
Stimson, Evelyn Marie Reinheimer *chemist*
Tancous, Jean Jacobs *chemist*
†Urbansky, Edward Todd *research chemist*
Varma, Rajender Singh *organic chemist*
Witten, Louis *physics educator*
Zhou, Taili *metallurgist*

Circleville
†England, Richard Jay *retired chemist*

Cleveland
Bidelman, William Pendry *astronomer, educator*
Brown, Robert William *physics educator, physicist*
Carey, Paul Richard *biophysicist*
Chamis, Christos Constantinos *aerospace scientist, educator*
†DeGuire, Mark Robert *materials scientist, educator*
Deissler, Robert George *fluid dynamicist, researcher*
Dowell, Michael Brendan *chemist*
Hanson, Richard Winfield *biochemist, educator*
Jenkins, Thomas Llewellyn *physics educator*
Klopman, Gilles *chemistry educator*
Kowalski, Kenneth Lawrence *physicist, educator*
Krieger, Irvin Mitchell *chemistry educator, consultant*
Landau, Bernard Robert *biochemistry educator, physician*
Lando, Jerome Burton *macromolecular science educator*
Leventis, Nicholas *chemist, research scientist*
Liu, Jingzhi *biophysicist, neuroscientist*
Matisoff, Gerald *geology educator*
Mawardi, Osman Kamel *plasma physicist*
Rogers, Charles Edwin *physical chemistry educator*
Schuele, Donald Edward *physics educator*
†Simha, Robert *chemistry educator, researcher*
Slobozhanin, Lev Arkadievich *fluid mechanics researcher*
†Zhang, Nengli *thermophysics scientist*
Zhu, Dongming *materials scientist*

Cleveland Heights
Collins, Sunniva Refsnes *metallurgist*

Columbus
Adelson, Edward *physicist, musician*
Behrman, Edward Joseph *biochemistry educator*
Bergstrom, Stig Magnus *geology educator*
Boyd, Richard Nelson *physics educator*
Chisholm, Malcolm Harold *chemistry educator*
†Chiu, Ing-Ming *biochemistry educator*
Corbato, Charles Edward *geology educator*
Cornwell, David George *biochemist, educator*
Daehn, Glenn Steven *materials scientist*
De Lucia, Frank Charles *physicist, educator*
Elliot, David Hawksley *geologist, educator*
†Faulkner, Lynn LeRoy *research scientist*
Faure, Gunter *geology educator*
Firestone, Richard Francis *chemistry educator*
Foland, Kenneth A. *geological sciences educator*
Goodridge, Alan Gardner *research biochemist, educator*
Gordon, Sydney Michael *research chemist*
Heinz, Ulrich Walter *theoretical physics educator*
Herbst, Eric *physicist, astronomer, chemist*
†Li, Wenxia *materials scientist, materials engineer, researcher*
Ling, Ta-Yung *physicist*
Marzluf, George Austin *biochemistry educator*
Mayer, Victor James *geologist, educator*
Meites, Samuel *clinical chemist, educator*
Milford, Frederick John *retired research company executive*
Miller, Terry Alan *chemistry educator*
Newsom, Gerald Higley *astronomy educator*
Preobrazhensky, Alexander Anatoliyevich *biochemist*
Reibel, Kurt *physicist, educator*
Relle, Ferenc Matyas *chemist*
†Schumacher, Douglass William *physicist*
Soloway, Albert Herman *medicinal chemist*
Voss, Anne Coble *nutritional biochemist*
Wali, Mohan Kishen *environmental science and natural resources educator*
Wilkins, John Warren *physics educator*
Wojcicki, Andrew Adalbert *chemist, educator*

Copley
Hayasi, Nisiki *physicist, applied mathematician, business executive, inventor*

PROFESSIONAL INDEX 6643 SCIENCE: PHYSICAL SCIENCE

Dayton
Battino, Rubin *chemistry educator, retired*
Dushkina, Natalia Mitkova *physicist, researcher*
Emrick, Donald Day *chemist, consultant*
Gregor, Clunie Bryan *geology educator*
Huang, Mei Qing *physics educator, researcher*
Janning, John Louis *research scientist, consultant*
Nielsen, Philip Edward *physicist, research manager*
Weathington, Billy Christopher *analytical chemist*

Fairborn
Kingston, David L. *retired physicist*

Hamilton
Cantrell, Joseph Sires *chemistry educator*

Harrison
Jones, Hobert W. *health physics and radiochemistry consultant*

Kent
Myers, R(alph) Thomas *chemist, educator*
Tuan, Debbie Fu-Tai *chemistry educator*

Liberty Township
Conditt, Margaret Karen *research scientist, policy analyst*

Mansfield
Gibson, David Mark *biochemist, educator*

Marietta
Jache, Albert William *retired chemistry educator, scientist*
Putnam, Robert Ervin *chemist, consultant*

Middletown
Marine, Susan Sonchik *analytical chemist, educator*

Milford
†Vester, John William *biochemist, retired medical educator*

New Albany
Williams, James Case *metallurgist*

Norwalk
Germann, Richard P(aul) *consultant, pharmaceutical company chemist, executive*

Oberlin
Carlton, Terry Scott *chemist, educator*
Simonson, Bruce Miller *geologist, educator*
†Singer, Leonard S. *chemist, research scientist, consultant*
Warner, Robert Edson *physics educator*
Weinstock, Robert *physics educator*

Oxford
Gordon, Gilbert *chemist, educator*
Macklin, Philip Alan *physics educator*
Yang, Kewu *chemist*

Painesville
Dietrich, Joseph Jacob *retired chemist, research executive*
Pyne, William Joseph *chemist*

Sheffield Village
Herdendorf, Charles Edward, III, *oceanographer, limnologist, consultant*

Toledo
Averill, Bruce Alan *chemistry educator*
Ivanov, Alexander V. *biochemist, researcher*
†Miroshnichenko, Anatoly S. *astronomer, researcher*

Walton Hills
†Elliott, Stanley B. *chemist, researcher*

Warren
Blaih, Salah Moustafa *chemist, pharmacist, educator*
Zimmerman, Doris Lucile *chemist*

Warrensville Heights
Jain, Nemi Chand *chemist, coating scientist, educator*

Waverly
Manuta, David Mark *research chemist, consultant*

West Chester
Mack, Mark Philip *chemical company executive*

Westerville
Markham, Richard Lawrence *chemist*

Wickliffe
Dunn, Horton, Jr., *organic chemist*
Kornbrekke, Ralph Erik *colloid chemist*

Wright Patterson Afb
Garscadden, Alan *physicist*

Yellow Springs
Spokane, Robert Bruce *biophysical chemist*

Youngstown
Zitto, Richard Joseph *physics educator*

OKLAHOMA

Ada
Stafford, Donald Gene *chemistry educator*

Bartlesville
Dwiggins, Claudius William, Jr., *chemist*
Eastman, Alan Dan *chemist*
Hogan, John Paul *chemistry researcher, consultant*
Meier, Paul Frederick *chemist, chemical engineer*

Durant
Wright, John Ricken *chemist, educator*

Fort Towson
Pike, Thomas Harrison *plant chemist*

Norman
Atkinson, Gordon *chemistry educator*
Bluestein, Howard Bruce *meteorology educator*
†Cheng, Deping *chemist, researcher*
Cowan, John James *physicist, educator, astronomer, educator*
Davies-Jones, Robert Peter *meteorologist*
Deming, David *geologist, educator*
Eilts, Michael Dean *research meteorologist, manager*
Fogel, Norman *retired chemistry educator*
Kessler, Edwin *meteorology educator, consultant*
Lamb, Peter James *meteorology educator, researcher, consultant*
Magarian, Robert Armen *medicinal chemist, researcher, educator , author, inventor*
Mankin, Charles John *geology educator*
Pigott, John Dowling *geologist, geophysicist, geochemist, educator, consultant*
Shapiro, Alan Meyer *meteorology educator, researcher*
Shiau, Bor-Jier (Ben Shiau) *environmental scientist, researcher*

Nowata
Osborn, Ann George *retired chemist*

Oklahoma City
Alaupovic, Petar *biochemist, educator*
England, Gary Alan *television meteorologist*
Johnson, B(ruce) Connor *biochemist, educator, consultant*
Matsumoto, Hiroyuki *biochemistry educator, researcher*
Troutman, George William *geologist, petroleum geological advisor*
Van De Steeg, Garet Edward *chemical consultant, environmental consultant*
Weigel, Paul Henry *biochemistry educator, researcher, consultant*
Zhu, Hua *biochemist, researcher*

Ponca City
†Linder, Donald E. *retired environmental scientist, rancher*

Skiatook
Harwell, Kenneth E. *chemist, researcher, consultant*

Stillwater
Berlin, Kenneth Darrell Darrell *chemistry educator, consultant, researcher*
Sherman, Robert Lee, Jr., *chemist, educator*
Zhang, Minquan *chemistry educator*

Tulsa
Anderson, David Walter *physics educator, consultant*
Blais, Roger Nathaniel *physics educator*
Busch, Daniel Adolph *geologist, educator*
Horn, Myron Kay *consulting petroleum geologist, author, educator*
Smothers, William Edgar, Jr., *geophysical exploration company executive*

OREGON

Ashland
Addicott, Warren Oliver *retired geologist, educator*
Grover, James Robb *chemist, editor*

Beaverton
Eisner, Alvin *optics scientist*

Bend
Gustafson, Lewis Allan *retired geologist*

Chiloquin
Siemens, Richard Ernest *retired metallurgy administrator, researcher*

Corvallis
Boedtker, Olaf A. *physicist*
Dalrymple, Gary Brent *research geologist*
Drake, Charles Whitney *physicist*
McKinney, William Mark *retired geology educator*
Moore, George W(illiam) *geologist*
Seyb, Leslie Philip *chemist, researcher*
Shoemaker, Clara Brink *retired chemistry researcher*
Simoneit, Bernd Rolf Tatsuo *geochemistry educator*
Sleight, Arthur William *chemist, educator*
Van Holde, Kensal Edward *biochemistry educator*
Yeats, Robert Sheppard *geologist, educator*

Dallas
White, Donald Harvey *physics educator emeritus*

Eugene
Crasemann, Bernd *physicist, educator*
Csonka, Paul L. *theoretical physicist, educator*
Donnelly, Russell James *physicist, educator*
Griffith, Osbie Hayes *chemistry educator*
Maurer, Robert Distler *retired industrial physicist*
Mazo, Robert Marc *chemistry educator, retired*
Retallack, Gregory John *geologist, educator*
Schellman, John A. *chemistry educator*
von Hippel, Peter Hans *chemistry educator, molecular biology researcher*
Youngquist, Walter Lewellyn *consulting geologist*

Otter Rock
†Kassner, Michael Ernest *materials science educator, researcher*

Portland
Abel, William Edward *applied physicist, consultant*
Claycomb, Cecil Keith *biochemist, educator*
Griffiths, David *physicist, educator*
Hammond, George Simms *chemist, consultant*
Lincoln, Sandra Eleanor *chemistry educator*
Pearson, David Petri *chemist*
Weeks, Wilford Frank *retired geophysics educator, glaciologist*

Salem
Gillette, P. Roger *physicist, systems engineer*

PENNSYLVANIA

Alcoa Center
Ray, Siba Prasad *materials scientist, ceramics scientist*

Allentown
Goldey, James Mearns *retired physicist*
Orphanides, Gus George *licensing executive*
†Pinschmidt, Robert Krantz, Jr., *chemist, researcher*

Ambler
†Veber, Daniel Frank *chemist, researcher*

Ardmore
Stanley, Edward Alexander *geologist, forensic scientist, technical and academic administrator*

Berwyn
Devlin, Thomas McKeown *biochemist, educator*

Bethlehem
Heindel, Ned Duane *chemistry educator*
Herman, Richard Gerald *research chemist, consultant, educator*
Hertzberg, Richard Warren *materials science and engineering educator, researcher*
Kanofsky, Alvin Sheldon *physics educator*
Lyman, Charles Edson *materials scientist, educator*
Smyth, Donald Morgan *chemical educator, researcher*
Yu, Zicheng *paleoclimatologist*

Blue Bell
Wilson, H(arold) Fred(erick) *chemist, research scientist*

Bryn Mawr
Crawford, Maria Luisa Buse *geology educator*
Francl, Michelle *chemist, educator*
Mallory, Frank Bryant *chemistry educator*

Camp Hill
Zook, Merlin Wayne *meteorologist, educator*

Carlisle
Laws, Kenneth L. *physics educator, author*
Long, Howard Charles *physics educator emeritus*

Chester Springs
Siegel, Richard Charles *biochemist*

Danville
†Chan, Yiumo *biochemist*
Maier, Vincent Baines *radiation physicist*

Doylestown
Brink, Frank, Jr., *biophysicist, former educator*

Elkins Park
Prince, Morton Bronenberg *physicist*
Zelac, Ronald Edward *physicist*

Feasterville
Dickstein, Jack *chemist*

Fleetwood
Maurer, Gernant Elmer *metallurgical executive, consultant*

Fort Washington
Chen, Jen-Chi *polymer chemist*
Creech, Hugh John *chemist, researcher*
Wuchter, Richard B. *retired research scientist, real estate agent*

Gettysburg
Fortnum, Donald H *chemistry educator, retired*

Gladwyne
Fenichel, Richard Lee *retired biochemist*

Gouldsboro
Nass, Leonard Ira *chemist, consultant*

Harrisburg
Mowery, J. Ronald *geologist, physicist, educator*

Hazleton
Miller, David Emanuel *physics educator, researcher*

Hershey
King, Steven Harold *health physicist*

Huntingdon
Trexler, John Peter *retired geology educator, researcher*

Huntingdon Valley
Godfrey, John Carl *medicinal chemist*

Irwin
†Biancheria, Amilcare *environmental scientist, consultant*

Johnstown
Brice, William Riley *geology educator, planetary science educator*

Kennett Square
Lippincott, Sarah Lee *astronomer, graphologist*
Wilson, Armin *chemist, retired*

King Of Prussia
McFarland, Andrew George *analytical chemist, researcher*

Lancaster
Kirsch, Stephen Augustine *retired geology educator*

Lehman
†Felty, Wayne Lee *chemist, educator*

Lincoln University
†Getaneh, Misganaw *physicist, educator*
Williams, Willie, Jr., *physicist, educator*

Malvern
Fisher, Sallie Ann *chemist*

Mc Murray
Mortimer, James Winslow *analytical chemist*

Media
Voltz, Sterling Ernest *physical chemist, researcher*

Middletown
Dodge, Clifford Howle *geologist*

Monroeville
Parker, James Roger *chemist*

Mount Joy
Lodde, Gordon Maynard *health physics consultant*

New Holland
Papadakis, Emmanuel Philippos *physicist, consultant*

New Hope
Lee, Robert William *organic chemist*

Newtown
Long, Harry (On-Yuen Eng) *chemist, science and technology executive, consultant*

Noxen
†Wood, Thomas G. *chemist, educator*

Oakdale
Wang, Chuan-Bao *chemist, research scientist*

Philadelphia
Ajzenberg-Selove, Fay *physicist, educator*
Burstein, Elias *physicist, educator*
†Chance, Britton *biophysics and physical chemistry educator emeritus*
Chapman, John Donald *research biophysicist*
Childress, Scott Julius *medicinal chemist*
Cohn, Mildred *biochemist, educator*
Dalton, David Robert *chemistry educator*
Davis, Raymond, Jr., *physical chemistry researcher*
Dutton, P(eter) Leslie *biochemist, educator*
Farren, Ann Louise *chemist, information scientist, educator*
Fitts, Donald Dennis *chemist, educator*
Glusker, Jenny Pickworth *chemist*
Gogotsi, Yury *materials science educator*
Halpern, Paul Harold *physicist*
Hameka, Hendrik Frederik *chemist, educator*
Havas, Peter *physicist, educator*
†Heiney, Paul A. *chemist, educator*
Hossain, Murshed *physicist, researcher*
Intemann, Robert Louis *physics educator, researcher*
Kachur, Alexander Victor *chemist*
Klein, Abraham *physics educator, researcher*
†Ko, Frank K. *materials scientist, educator*
Kricka, Larry J. *chemistry educator*
Kritchevsky, David *biochemist, educator*
Langacker, Paul George *physics educator*
Levitt, Israel Monroe *retired astronomer*
Li, Lin *physicist, biophysicist*
MacDiarmid, Alan Graham *metallurgist, educator*
Malamud, Daniel *biochemistry educator*
Maurer, Paul Herbert *biochemist, educator*
Narangajavana, Kanthaka *mass spectrometrist*
†Nath, Amar *chemist, educator*
Noordergraaf, Abraham *biophysics educator*
†Orlovskaya, Nina *materials scientist*
Saiz, Leonor *physicist, researcher*
Scandura, Joseph Michael *cognitive scientist, software engineer*
Takashima, Shiro *biophysics educator*
Thoman, Charles James *chemistry educator*
Vitek, Vaclav *materials scientist*
Wales, Walter D. *physicist, educator*
Wickstrom, Eric *biophysical chemist, educator*
†Wroblewski, Krzysztof *chemist, educator*

Pittsburgh
Berry, Guy Curtis *polymer science educator, researcher*
Biondi, Manfred Anthony *physicist, educator*
Bothner-By, Aksel Arnold *chemist, horseman*
Carr, Walter James, Jr., *research physicist, consultant*
Cassidy, William Arthur *geology and planetary science educator*
Choyke, Wolfgang Justus *physicist*
Cohen, Bernard Leonard *physicist, educator*
Coltman, John Wesley *physicist*
Curran, Dennis Patrick *chemist, educator*

Deerfield, David Wiley, II, *chemist*
Dormish, Jeffrey Frank *chemist*
Emmerich, Werner Sigmund *physicist, educator*
Feller, Robert Livingston *chemist, art conservation scientist*
Fetkovich, John G. *physics educator*
Gerjuoy, Edward *physicist, lawyer*
Itkin, Ivan *nuclear scientist, applied mathematician*
Jen-Jacobson, Linda *biochemist, educator*
†Klein-Seetharaman, Judith *biochemist*
Kumta, Prashant Nagesh *materials science educator, engineering educator, consultant*
Laughlin, David Eugene *materials science educator, metallurgical consultant*
Leney, George Willard *retired consulting engineer*
Lu, Songwei *materials scientist*
Lyberatos, Andreas *physicist, researcher*
Marra, Kacey G. *research scientist, educator*
Maśka, Rudolf *retired chemist, finance executive*
Massalski, Thaddeus Bronislaw *materials scientist, educator*
Matyjaszewski, Krzysztof *chemist, educator*
Morse, Lewis David *microencapsulation polymer chemist, consultant*
Nagle, John Frederick *physicist*
†Nanda, Ajaya Kumar *chemist, educator*
Page, Lorne Albert *physicist, educator*
Plazek, Donald John *materials science educator*
Rosenberg, Jerome Laib *chemist, educator*
†Ruddy, Francis (Frank) Henry *nuclear physicist*
Sashin, Donald *pet physicist, radiological physicist, educator*
Sekerka, Robert Floyd *physics educator, scientist*
Shapiro, Zalman Mordecai *chemist, consultant*
White, Robert Marshall *physicist, government official, educator*
Yates, John Thomas, Jr., *chemistry educator, research director*
Yoldas, Bulent Erturk *materials scientist, educator*
Young, Hugh David *physics educator, writer, organist*
Yushmanov, Victor Evgenievich *biophysicist, researcher*

Rosemount
Berliner, Ernst *chemistry educator*

Saint Marys
†Sorg, David Joseph *materials physicist*

Scranton
Baumann, Christopher Anthony *chemist, educator*

Spring House
Hann, William Mathis *chemist, researcher*
Rieck, Albert Charles *chemist*

State College
Garrett, Steven Lurie *physicist*
†German, Randall Michael *materials engineering educator, consultant*
Ginoza, William *former biophysics educator*
Henisch, Heinz Kurt *retired physics educator*
†Roy, Della Martin *materials science educator, researcher*
Schmalz, Robert Fowler *geology educator*

Swarthmore
Bilaniuk, Oleksa Myron *physicist, educator*
Pasternack, Robert Francis *chemistry educator*

Towanda
†Singh Gaur, Raj Pal *research scientist*

University Park
Allcock, Harry R. *chemistry educator*
Barnes, Hubert Lloyd *geochemistry educator*
†Benkovic, Stephen James *chemist*
Blackadar, Alfred Kimball *meteorologist, educator*
Cahir, John Joseph *meteorologist, educational administrator*
Castleman, Albert Welford, Jr., *physical chemist, educator*
Coleman, Michael Murray *polymer science educator*
Collins, John Clements *physicist, educator*
Dutton, John Altnow *meteorologist, educator*
Hammes-Schiffer, Sharon *chemist, educator*
Hosler, Charles Luther, Jr., *meteorologist, educator*
Howell, Benjamin Franklin, Jr., *geophysicist, educator*
Jackman, Lloyd Miles *chemistry educator*
Kasting, James Fraser *research meteorologist, physicist*
Liu, Zi-Kui *materials science and engineering educator*
Ma, Xiaoliang *research scientist*
Mahan, Gerald Dennis *physics educator, researcher*
†Ross, A. Catharine *biochemist, educator*
Roy, Rustum *interdisciplinary educator, materials researcher*
Semouchkina, Elena *physicist, researcher*
†Sokol, Paul E. *physicist, educator, physicist, researcher*
Song, Chunshan *chemist, chemical engineer, educator*
White, William Blaine *geochemist, educator*
Winograd, Nicholas *chemist*

Valley Forge
Erb, Doretta Louise Barker *polymer scientist*
Erb, Robert Allan *physical scientist*

Villanova
Edwards, John Ralph *retired chemist, educator*
Phares, Alain Joseph *physicist, educator*

Wayne
†Kauffman, Joel Mervin *chemistry educator, researcher, consultant*

†Lockyer, Nigel S *physicist*

Waynesburg
†Maguire, Mildred May *chemistry educator, magnetic resonance researcher*

West Point
†Hartman, George David *chemist, director*
†Lindsley, Craig William *physicist, researcher*

Wyndmoor
Farrell, Harold Maron, Jr., *chemist*
Fishman, Marshall Lewis *chemist*
Irwin, Peter Lloyd *biochemist, microbiologist*
Liu, Lin Shu *biomaterials scientist*
†Marmer, William N. *chemist, researcher*
Pfeffer, Philip Elliot *biophysicist*

Wynnewood
Rosen, Gerald Harris *physicist, consultant, educator*

Yardley
Grossman, Irving Gross *retired geologist*
Yee, David *chemist, technology analyst*

RHODE ISLAND

East Greenwich
Carlson, Shawn Eric *physicist*

Kingston
Nixon, Scott West *oceanography science educator*
†Parang, Keykavous *chemist, educator*
Wen, Yuming *research scientist*

Narragansett
Pilson, Michael Edward Quinton *oceanography educator*

Providence
Avery, Donald Hills *metallurgist, educator, ethnographer*
Briant, Clyde Leonard *metallurgist, educator*
Carpenter, Gene Blakely *crystallography and chemistry educator*
Cooper, Leon N. *physicist, educator*
Cooper, Reid Franklin *geoscience and materials science educator*
Dahlberg, Albert Edward *biochemistry educator*
Elbaum, Charles *physicist, educator, researcher*
Gerritsen, Hendrik Jurjen *physics educator, researcher*
Greene, Edward Forbes *chemistry educator*
Head, James W., III, *geological sciences educator*
Houghton, Anthony *physics educator, research scientist*
Lanou, Robert Eugene, Jr., *physicist, educator*
Levin, Frank S. *physicist, educator*
Pieters, Carle McGetchin *geology educator, planetary scientist, researcher*
Stratt, Richard Mark *chemistry researcher, educator*
Tauc, Jan *physics educator*
Widgoff, Mildred *physicist, educator*

Wakefield
Moore, George Emerson, Jr., *geologist, educator*

West Kingston
Storm, Carlyle Bell *chemist*

Westerly
Hindle, Marguerita Cecelia *textile chemist, consultant*

SOUTH CAROLINA

Aiken
Dickson, Paul Wesley, Jr., *physicist*

Charleston
Delli Colli, Humbert Thomas *chemist, product development specialist*

Clemson
Beyerlein, Adolph Louis *retired chemist, educator*
Clayton, Donald Delbert *astrophysicist, nuclear physicist, educator*
Davies, Brian Ewart *environmental sciences educator*
†Hickman, James J. *research scientist, educator*
Krause, Lois Ruth Breur *chemistry educator*

Columbia
Edge, Ronald Dovaston *physics educator*
Farber, Emmanuel *pathology and biochemistry educator*
Garde, Anand Madhav *materials scientist*
†Hansen, William Frank *hydrologist*
Nagpal, Madan Lal *biochemist, educator, researcher*
Profeta, Salvatore, Jr., *chemist*
Secor, Donald Terry, Jr., *geologist, educator*
Shafer, John Milton *hydrologist, consultant, software developer*

Easley
McLaughlin, Bruce Duane *materials scientist*

Florence
Havens, Timothy John *physicist*

Hilton Head Island
Carpenter, William G. *chemist, consultant*

Johns Island
Norton, Norman James *retired exploration geologist, educator*

Mount Pleasant
Thordarson, William *retired hydrogeologist*

Orangeburg
†Bullard-Dillard, Rebecca *biochemist, educator*

Pendleton
Spain, James Dorris, Jr., *biochemist, educator*

Spartanburg
Kuhn, Hans Heinrich *retired chemist*

SOUTH DAKOTA

Brookings
Duffey, George Henry *physics educator*

Hermosa
Schirber, James Emmanuel *retired physicist*

Rapid City
Squillace, Paul J *hydrologist, researcher*

Sioux Falls
Viste, Arlen Ellard *chemistry educator*

Spearfish
Erickson, Richard Ames *physicist, emeritus educator*

TENNESSEE

Clinton
Hutchens, Gail R. *chemist*

Cookeville
Kumar, Krishna *retired physics educator*

Fayetteville
Wolfhard, Hans Georg *research scientist*

Greenback
Weeks, Robert Andrew *materials science researcher, educator*

Johnson City
Kasmai, Hamid Saleh *chemistry educator, researcher, consultant*

Kingsport
Germinario, Louis Thomas *materials scientist*
Gose, William Christopher *retired chemist*

Knoxville
Alexeff, Igor *physicist, electrical engineer, educator emeritus*
Dahotre, Narendra Bapurao *materials scientist, researcher, educator*
†Dixon, John Emit *health physics specialist*
Gentry, Robert Vance *physicist, researcher, writer*
†Ghosh, Narendra Nath *research scientist*
Renshaw, Amanda Frances *retired physicist, nuclear engineer*
Schweitzer, George Keene *chemistry educator*
Williams, Thomas Ffrancon *chemist, educator*
Wunderlich, Bernhard *physical chemistry educator*

Memphis
Crane, Laura Jane *research chemist*
Desiderio, Dominic Morse, Jr., *chemistry and neurochemistry educator*
Fain, John Nicholas *biochemistry educator*
†Ferreira, Antonio Mario *chemist, educator*
Jernigan, Howard Maxwell, Jr., *biochemistry educator, researcher*
Lasslo, Andrew *medicinal chemist, educator*

Morristown
Culvern, Julian Brewer *retired chemist, educator*

Murfreesboro
MacDougall, Preston John *chemistry educator*

Nashville
Bayuzick, Robert J. *materials scientist, educator*
Boutaud, Olivier Gilles *biochemistry research educator*
Chytil, Frank *biochemist*
Cunningham, Leon William *biochemist, educator*
Dettbarn, Wolf-Dietrich *neurochemist, pharmacologist, educator*
Feldman, Leonard Cecil *physicist*
Fort, Tomlinson *chemist, chemical engineering educator*
Hall, Douglas Scott *astronomy educator*
Heiser, Arnold Melvin *astronomer*
Hercules, David Michael *chemistry educator, consultant*
Kono, Tetsuro *biochemist, physiologist, educator*
Lukehart, Charles Martin *chemistry educator*
Ramayya, Akunuri V. *physics educator*
Roos, Charles Edwin *physicist*
Silberman, Enrique *physics researcher and administrator*
Surowiec, Andrew Julius *biophysicist, researcher*
Wert, James Junior *materials scientist, educator*

Oak Ridge
Borie, Bernard Simon, Jr., *retired physicist, educator*
†Byun, Thak-Sang *research scientist, educator*
Carlsmith, Roger Snedden *chemistry and energy conservation researcher*
Dai, Sheng *chemist, materials scientist*
Dickens, Justin Kirk *nuclear physicist*
Gifford, Franklin Andrew, Jr., *meteorologist, consultant*
Hartman, Frederick Cooper *biochemist, researcher*
Horak, James Albert *materials scientist, nuclear engineer, educator*
Hu, Zhiyu *research scientist, educator*

Jang, Young-Il *research scientist, consultant*
Klueh, Ronald Lloyd *metallurgist*
Krause, Manfred Otto *physicist*
Larson, Bennett Charles *solid state physicist, researcher*
†Lindberg, Steven Eric *geochemist*
Maienschein, Fred *retired physicist*
Manly, William Donald *metallurgist*
†Mei, Viung Chung (Vince G. Mei) *research scientist, mechanical engineer*
Plasil, Franz *physicist*
Postma, Herman *physicist, consultant*
†Protopopescu, Vladimir Alexandru *research scientist, educator*
†Wang, Jian-Guang *engineering physicist*
Watson, Evelyn Egner *radiation scientist*
Weinberg, Alvin Martin *physicist*
Yoo, Man Hyong *materials scientist*
Young, Jack Phillip *chemist*
Zucker, Alexander *physicist, administrator*

Signal Mountain
Howe, Lyman Harold, III, *chemist, researcher*

TEXAS

Arlington
Cuntz, Manfred *astrophysicist, researcher, educator*
Damuth, John Erwin *marine geologist*
Kirk, Wiley Price, Jr., *physics and electrical engineering educator*
Pomerantz, Martin *chemistry educator, researcher*
Shanmugam, Ganapathy *geologist, researcher*
Smith, Charles Isaac *geology educator*
†Willoughby, Sarah-Margaret C. *chemist, educator, chemical engineer, consultant*

Austin
Ancker-Johnson, Betsy *physicist, engineer, retired automotive company executive*
Bard, Allen Joseph *chemist, educator*
Bengtson, Roger Dean *physicist, department chairman*
Bersuker, Isaac Borukhovich *chemistry researcher, educator*
Boggs, James Ernest *chemistry educator*
Carballo, Juan-Antonio *research scientist*
Clark, Roy Thomas, Jr., *chemistry educator, administrator*
DeWitt-Morette, Cécile *physicist*
Duncombe, Raynor Lockwood *astronomer*
Erskine, James Lorenzo *physics educator*
Fisher, William Lawrence *geologist, educator*
Folk, Robert Louis *geologist, educator*
†Folkers, Karl August *chemistry educator*
†Fomel, Sergey *geophysicist*
Fonken, Gerhard Joseph *retired chemistry educator, academic administrator*
Gentle, Kenneth William *physicist*
Griffy, Thomas Alan *physics educator*
†Ibison, Michael *physicist, researcher*
Kimmel, Troy Max, Jr., *meteorologist*
Mark, Hans Michael *physicist, government official*
Maxwell, Arthur Eugene *oceanographer, marine geophysicist, educator*
†Mear, Charles Eugene *geologist, consultant*
†Mooney, John Bradford, Jr., *oceanographer, engineer, consultant*
†Pachon, Julian Enrique *research scientist, consultant*
Phillips, Joseph Daniel *geophysicist, oceanographer*
Posey, Daniel Earl *analytical chemist*
Reed, Lester James *biochemist, educator*
†Roy, Indrajit Ghosh *geophysicist, educator*
†Ruez, Dennis R. *geology educator*
Stewart, Kent Kallam *analytical biochemistry educator*
Swinney, Harry Leonard *physics educator*
Tatham, Robert Haines *geophysicist, educator*
Trafton, Laurence Munro *astronomer, researcher*
Udagawa, Takeshi *physicist, educator*
Wheeler, John Craig *astrophysicist, writer*
White, John Michael *chemistry educator*
Williams, Calvit Herndon *environmental chemist*
Willson, C. Grant *chemistry educator, engineering educator*
Ziegler, Daniel Martin *chemistry educator*

Baytown
†Botto, Robert Irving *analytical chemist, antique dealer*
Kolb, Rainer *chemist*

Beaumont
Bahrim, Cristian *physicist, educator*

College Station
Arnowitt, Richard Lewis *physics educator, researcher*
Berg, Robert Raymond *geologist, educator*
Conway, Dwight Colbur *chemistry educator*
Cotton, Frank Albert *chemist*
Eaton, Gordon Pryor *geologist, consultant*
Fackler, John Paul, Jr., *chemistry educator*
Fitzpatrick, Paul Frederick *biochemistry educator*
Goodman, David Wayne *research chemist, educator*
Hardy, John Christopher *physicist, educator*
Holcombe, Troy Leon *marine geologist*
Laane, Jaan *chemistry educator*
McIntyre, John Armin *physics educator*
McIntyre, Peter Mastin *physicist, educator*
†Mohamed, Ahmed A. *chemist, researcher*
Nachman, Ronald James *research chemist*
Natowitz, Joseph B. *chemistry educator, research administrator*
O'Connor, Rod *chemist, consultant, inventor*
Prescott, John Mack *biochemist, retired university administrator*
Reid, Robert Osborne *oceanographer*
Scott, Alastair Ian *chemistry educator*
Stewart, Robert Henry *oceanographer, educator*

Trache, Andreea Apostol *physicist*
Trache, Livius-Marian *physicist, research scientist, educator*
Wild, James Robert *biochemistry and genetics educator*
Zhu, Jianting *hydrologist*

Conroe
Nachman, Joseph Frank *metallurgical consultant*

Dallas
Brooks, James Elwood *geologist, educator*
Estabrook, Ronald Winfield *chemistry educator*
Frank, Steven Neil *chemist*
Gibbs, James Alanson *geologist*
Marshall, John Harris, Jr., *geologist, oil company executive*
Maxey, Susan Marie *geology department head*
Ries, Edward Richard *petroleum geologist, consultant*
†Rutter, Jared *biochemist*
Sharp, William Wheeler *geologist*
Tsyganov, Edward N. *physicist, educator*
Wheeler, Edward Norwood *chemical consultant*
†Willis, Monte Shaw *research scientist*
Woolley, Bryan (Lowell Bryan Woolley) *author, journalist*

Denton
Chang, Yongbin *physicist*
Saleh, Farida Yousry *chemistry educator*
†Smith, H. Morgan *environmental scientist, educator*

Edinburg
Hannan, Mohammad A. *physicist, educator*
Mahmood, Akhtar Hasan *physicist, educator, researcher*

Fort Worth
Bailey, James Stephen *scientist*
Caldwell, Billy Ray *geologist*
Quarles, Carroll Adair, Jr., *physicist, educator*
Reinecke, Manfred G. *chemistry educator*
Webb, Theodore Stratton, Jr., *aerospace scientist, consultant*

Freeport
Marks, Maurice J. *chemist*

Fulshear
Martin, Alden Jeffrey *petrophysicist, geologist*

Galveston
Bonchev, Danail Georgiev *chemist, educator*
Gorenstein, David G. *chemistry and biochemistry educator*
Kurosky, Alexander *biochemist, educator*
Mc Adoo, David John *neurochemist*
†Peerce, Brian E *biochemist, education educator*
Schoenbucher, Bruce *health physicist*
Yang, Xianbin *chemist, researcher*

Houston
Abbey, George W. S. *space center executive*
Ahmad, Salahuddin *nuclear scientist*
Anderson, Richard Carl *geophysical exploration company executive*
Askew, William Earl *chemist, educator*
Baker, Stephen Denio *physics educator*
Bering, Edgar Andrew, III, *physicist, educator*
Black, David Charles *astrophysicist*
Bonner, Billy Edward *physics educator*
Bott, Simon Gregory *chemistry educator, researcher*
Brooks, Philip Russell *chemistry educator, researcher*
Brotzen, Franz Richard *materials science educator*
Burke, Kevin Charles Antony *geologist*
Chu, Paul Ching-Wu *physicist, educator*
Chu, Wei-Kan *physicist, educator*
Curl, Robert Floyd, Jr., *chemistry educator*
Freeman, John Clinton *meteorologist, oceanographer*
†Geilikman, Mikhail Boris *research scientist, educator*
Gibson, Everett Kay, Jr., *space scientist, geochemist*
Goloby, George William, Jr., *environmental scientist, editor, ornithologist, aviculturist*
Hackerman, Norman *chemist, academic administrator*
Halbouty, Michel Thomas *geologist, petroleum engineer, petroleum operator*
Hussain, Moinuddin Syed *geologist, reservoir engineer, consultant*
†Ibbott, Geoffrey Stephen *physicist*
Jeevarajan, Judith A. *chemist*
Kasi, Leela Peshkar *pharmaceutical chemist*
Keenmon, Kendall A. *geologist, consultant, writer*
†Khabashesku, Valery N. *chemist, educator*
Kinsey, James Lloyd *chemist, educator*
Kit, Saul *biochemist, educator*
Kochi, Jay Kazuo *chemist, educator*
†Kosterev, Anatoliy A. *research scientist*
Kouri, Donald Jack *chemist, educator*
Lane, Neal Francis *physics educator, former government official*
Langford, Roland Everett *environmental scientist, safety engineer, writer*
Lewis, Edward Sheldon *chemistry educator*
Liang, Edison Parktak *astrophysicist, educator, researcher*
Lu, Bao-Yuan *biochemist, researcher*
Margrave, John Lee *chemist, educator, university administrator*
Matthews, Kathleen Shive *biochemistry educator*
McCleary, Henry Glen *geophysicist*
Mendelson, Robert Allen *polymer scientist, rheologist*
Mu, Yaoming *physicist, researcher*
†Nemphos, Speros P. *chemist, consultant*
Nordlander, Peter Jan Arne *physics educator, researcher*
Pusey, Walter Carroll, III, *geologist, consultant*
Reso, Anthony *geologist, educator, earth resources economist*
Rong, Shu *materials scientist, researcher*
Rudolph, Frederick Byron *biochemistry educator*
Scuseria, Gustavo Enrique *theoretical chemist*
Sercombe, William John *geologist*
Sisson, Virginia Baker *geology educator*
Skolnick, Malcolm Harris *biophysics researcher, educator, lawyer, mediator, biotechnology executive*
Smalley, Richard Errett *chemistry and physics educator, researcher*
Soileau, Kerry Michael *aerospace technologist, researcher*
Starkschall, George *medical physicist*
Talwani, Manik *geophysicist, educator*
Vant-Hull, Lorin L. *physics educator, consultant*
Vilas, Faith *aerospace scientist*
Wakil, Salih Jawad *biochemistry educator*
Wei, Ying *chemist*
Weinstein, Roy *physics educator, researcher*
Weisman, R(obert) Bruce *physical chemist, educator*
†Wensel, Theodore G. *biochemist, educator*
Wilson, Thomas Leon *physicist, researcher*

Humble
Brinkley, Charles Alexander *geologist*

Hurst
Benge, Raymond Doyle, Jr., *astronomy educator*

Irving
Hendrickson, Constance Marie McRight *chemist, consultant*
Holdar, Robert Martin *chemist*

Kerrville
Shaw, Alan Bosworth *geologist, paleontologist*
†Sparks, Don Bertrand *retired geophysicist*

Lubbock
Adamcik, Joe Alfred *retired chemistry educator, retired attorney*
Everse, Johannes *biochemist, researcher*
Laing, Malcolm Brian *geologist, consultant*
Spallholz, Julian Ernest *biochemistry educator, consultant*
†Viatchenko-Karpinski, Serge *biophysicist, researcher*

Midland
Berner, Leo De Witte, Jr., *retired oceanographer*
Osborne, Willie Carroll *petroleum geologist, consultant*

Nacogdoches
†Zhang, Zhizhen *chemist*

New Braunfels
Wilson, James Lee *retired geology educator, consultant*

Pasadena
Root, M. Belinda *chemist*

Plano
Kellogg, James Warner *aerospace management consultant*

Richardson
Johnson, Francis Severin *physicist*
†Manton, William Inwood *geologist, educator*
Rutford, Robert Hoxie *geologist, educator*

Round Rock
Hill, David Wayne *geologist*

Rowlett
Patterson, Edward Palmer *retired physical scientist*

San Antonio
Bachrach, Steven Maurice *chemistry educator*
Budalur, Thyagarajan Subbanarayan *chemistry educator*
Burton, Russell Rohan *aerospace scientist, researcher*
†Cragnolino, Gustavo Adolfo *research scientist*
Denny, John Bernard *biochemist, educator*
Gladstone, George Randall *planetary scientist*
Hammond, Weldon Woolf, Jr., *hydrogeologist*
Lyle, Robert Edward *chemist*
Markwell, Dick R(obert) *retired chemist*
Masters, Bettie Sue Siler *biochemist, educator*
Pensado, Osvaldo *research scientist*
Rafelson, Max Emanuel, Jr., *biochemist, medical school administrator*
Sablik, Martin John *research physicist*
Synek, Miroslav *physicist, chemist, world affairs independent consultant, researcher*
Tsin, Andrew Tsang Cheung *cell biology and biochemistry researcher*

Southlake
Herrmann, Debra McGuire *chemist, educator*

Sugar Land
Downs, Hartley H., III, *chemist*
Huston, Daniel Cliff *geophysicist*
Mamedov, Edouard Akhmed *chemist, researcher*
Ren, Hong-Wen *physicist, materials scientist*

The Woodlands
Westmoreland, Thomas Delbert, Jr., *chemist*

Uvalde
Graham, Robert Albert *research physicist*

Vernon
Roberson, Mark Allen *physicist, educator*

Waco
Cleaver, Gerald Bryan *physicist, researcher*
†Hassell, Clinton Alton *chemist, educator*
Pedrotti, Leno Stephano *physics educator*
Ward, Bennie Franklin Leon *physics educator*

UTAH

American Fork
Zhou, Bing-Nan *chemist, educator*

Brigham City
Fife, Dennis Jensen *chemistry educator, air force officer*
Hepworth, John Leonard *chemist, researcher*

Dugway
Phan, Richard Man *chemist*

Hildale
Wall, Lloyd L. *geological engineer*

Holladay
O'Halloran, Thomas Alphonsus, Jr., *physicist, educator*

Logan
Aust, Steven Douglas *biochemistry, biotechnology and toxicology educator*
Schunk, Robert Walter *space physics research administrator*

North Logan
Sunderland, Norman Ray (Norm Sunderland) *health physicist, nuclear engineer educator*

Provo
Cheney, Brigham Vernon *physical chemist, consultant, retired physical chemist*
Hall, Howard Tracy *chemist*

Saint George
Ponder, Herman *geologist*

Salt Lake City
Anspaugh, Lynn Richard *research biophysicist*
Armentrout, Peter Bruce *chemistry educator*
Bryson, Melvin Joseph *retired biochemist*
Dick, Bertram Gale, Jr., *physics educator*
Efros, Alexei L. *physics educator, researcher*
Foltz, Rodger Lowell *chemistry educator, mass spectroscopist*
Gondolo, Paolo *physicist*
Gortatowski, Melvin Jerome *retired chemist*
Kenison, Lynn T. *chemist*
Olson, Ferron Allred *metallurgist, educator*
Parry, Robert Walter *chemistry educator*
Picard, M(eredith) Dane *geologist*
Velick, Sidney Frederick *research biochemist, educator*
Zhdanov, Michael Semenovich *geophysicist, educator*

VERMONT

Burlington
Nyborg, Wesley Lemars *physics educator*
†Weed, Lawrence L. *biochemist*

Middlebury
Winkler, Paul Frank, Jr., *astrophysicist, educator*

Shelburne
White, William North *chemistry educator*

Thetford
Hoagland, Mahlon *biochemist, educator*

VIRGINIA

Alexandria
Biberman, Lucien Morton *physicist, researcher*
Brenner, Alfred Ephraim *physicist*
Campbell, Francis James *retired chemist*
Carter, William Harold, Sr., *physicist, researcher, electrical engineer*
†Kaplan, David Jeremy *research scientist, consultant*
Krebs, Martha *physicist, federal science agency administrator*
Masterson, Kleber Sanlin, Jr., *physicist*
Milling, Marcus Eugene, Sr., *geologist*
Muir, Warren Roger *chemist, executive*
O'Connor, Thomas Edward *petroleum geologist, management consultant*
Ray, Terrill Wylie *physical scientist*
Romney, Carl F. *seismologist*
Toulmin, Priestley *retired geologist*
Zook, Theresa Fuetterer *gemologist, consultant*

Annandale
Matuszko, Anthony Joseph *research chemist, administrator*

Arlington
Cavanaugh, Margaret Anne *chemist*
Chubb, Talbot Albert *physicist*
Debney, George C. *mathematical physicist*
Dickman, Robert Laurence *physicist, researcher*
Dorman, Craig Emery *oceanographer, academic administrator*
Ensminger, Luther Glenn *chemist, consultant*
†Frederick, William George DeMott *defense company executive, consultant*
Kostoff, Ronald Neil *aerospace scientist*
†Lean, Judith *physicist, researcher*
Leinen, Margaret Sandra *oceanographic researcher*
Matthews, Allan Freeman *geologist*
Ordway, Frederick Ira, III, *educator, consultant, researcher, writer*
Reynolds, Peter James *physicist*
†Schwartz, Lyle Howard *materials scientist, science administrator*
Swanberg, Neil Ralph *scientist, educator*
Weber, Alfons *physicist*
Whitcomb, James Hall *geophysicist, foundation administrator*
†Yoder, James A. *oceanographer, educator*
Zirkind, Ralph *physicist, educator*

Ashburn
Bennett, Lawrence Herman *physicist*

Big Stone Gap
Harris, William Stacy *physics educator*

Blacksburg
Graybeal, Jack Daniel *chemist, educator*
Täuber, Uwe Claus *physicist*

Charlottesville
Biltonen, Rodney Lincoln *biochemistry and pharmacology educator*
Bloomfield, Louis Aub *physicist, educator*
Brill, Arthur Sylvan *biophysics educator*
Chevalier, Roger Alan *astronomy educator, consultant*
Fredrick, Laurence William *astronomer, educator*
Gaskin, Felicia *biochemist, educator*
Good, Richard Standish *geologist*
†Goyne, Christopher Paul *aerospace scientist, educator*
Grimes, Russell Newell *chemistry educator, inorganic chemist*
Hornberger, George Milton *environmental science educator*
Kellermann, Kenneth Irwin *astrophysicist, scientist*
Kerr, Anthony Robert *scientist*
Kuhlmann-Wilsdorf, Doris *materials scientist, educator*
Martin, Robert Bruce *chemistry educator*
Meem, James Lawrence, Jr., *nuclear scientist*
Pate, Brooks *chemist*
Roberts, Morton Spitz *astronomer*
Sarazin, Craig Leigh *astronomer, educator*
Shen, Tsung Ying *medicinal chemistry educator*
Song, Xiaotong *physicist, educator*
Sundberg, Richard Jay *chemistry educator*
Vanden Bout, Paul Adrian *astronomer, physicist, educator*

Clifton
Brooks, Matthew Wayne *agrichemical regulatory chemist, consultant*

Dahlgren
Bressler, Barry Lee *theoretical physicist, systems analyst*
Holt, William Henry *physicist, researcher*
Walters, Robert Ancil *physicist, mathematician*

Dumfries
Meyer, Howard Robert, Jr., *research scientist*

Fairfax
Morowitz, Harold Joseph *biophysicist, educator*
Stalick, Wayne M. *chemistry educator, law firm consultant*
†Xing, Guang-Qian *aerospace scientist*

Falls Church
Akkara, Joseph Augustine *chemist, educator*
Benson, William Edward (Barnes) *geologist*
Spindel, William *retired chemist, consultant*

Farmville
Moon, William Arthur, Jr., *petroleum geologist, consultant*

Floyd
Clemens, Donald Faull *chemistry educator*

Fredericksburg
†Nikolić, Nikola *physics educator*

Gainesville
Steger, Edward Herman *chemist*

Hampden Sydney
Joyner, Weyland Thomas *physicist, educator, business consultant*

Hampton
Axenson, Theresa J. *physicist*
Elmustafa, Abdelmageed Ahmed *senior research scientist*
Houbolt, John Cornelius *physicist*
Jin, Zhonghai *physicist*
Tripathi, Ram Kishore *physicist, researcher*
†Yamakov, Vesselin Ivanov *aerospace scientist, researcher*

Harrisonburg
Baker, George Harold, III, *physicist*

Herndon
Crossfield, Albert Scott *aeronautical science consultant, pilot*
†Drew, Lawrence James *geologist, statistician*

Lexington
Spencer, Edgar Winston *geology educator*

Lynchburg
McClenon, John Raymond *retired chemistry educator*
Morgan, Evan *retired chemist*

Mc Lean
Carter, William Walton *physicist, researcher*
Doyle, Frederick Joseph *retired government research scientist*
Freund, Henry Philip *physicist*
Hoffman, Ronald Bruce *biophysicist, life scientist, consultant*
Theon, John Speridon *meteorologist, researcher*
Williams, Thomas Blake *natural resources consultant, educator*

McLean
†Kitchens, Clarence Wesley, Jr., *technology administrator*

Midlothian
†Cruse, Robert Ridgely *retired research chemist*

Monroe
†Pettus, William G. *retired nuclear scientist, research scientist*

Naval Base
†Barton, Laura Ann *aerospace experimental psychologist, consultant, researcher*

Newport News
Krafft, Geoffrey Arthur *physicist*

Norfolk
Noginov, Mikhail A. *physicist, researcher, educator*

Petersburg
Brown, Jack D(elbert) *chemist, researcher*
Stronach, Carey Elliott *physicist, educator*

Philomont
Conte, Joseph John, II, *meteorologist, management consultant*

Reston
Groat, Charles George *geologist, science administrator*
Kramish, Arnold *physicist, historian, author*
Menzie, William David, II, *geologist, educator*
Peck, Dallas Lynn *retired geologist*

Richmond
†Danilkovitch, Alla *research scientist*
Fenn, John Bennett *chemist, educator*
Lilly, Arnys Clifton, Jr., *physicist*
†Safo, Martin K. *research scientist, educator*
†Su, Lianyong *research scientist*
Tiedemann, Albert William, Jr., *retired chemist*
White, Morris Fred, Jr., *physicist*

Salem
Fisher, Charles Harold *chemistry educator, researcher*

Sandston
†Zhao, Wei (Wayne) *materials scientist, researcher*

Toano
Carlson, David Emil *physicist, researcher*

Vienna
†Bhide, Manohar Gopal *nuclear scientist, educator*
Wiesnet, Donald Richard *retired hydrologist*

Williamsburg
DeFotis, Gary Constantine *chemical physicist, educator*
Dunning, Kenneth Laverne *research physicist*
Goodwin, Bruce Kesseli *retired geology educator, researcher*
Starnes, William Herbert, Jr., *chemist, educator*

Winchester
Ludwig, George Harry *physicist, electrical engineer*

Woodbridge
Trussell, Charlie Ward *physicist*

WASHINGTON

Bellevue
Benveniste, Jacob *retired physicist*
Watson, Mathew D. *optical scientist*

Bellingham
Cox, David Jackson *biochemistry educator*

Bothell
Alvi, Khisal Ahmed *chemist*

Eastsound
Fowles, George Richard *physicist, educator*

Ellensburg
Hickey, Robert James, III, *geologist, geographer, educator*
Rosell, Sharon Lynn *physics and chemistry educator, researcher*

Everett
Brown, Frederick Calvin *physicist, educator*

Federal Way
Ma, Zhenkui *remote sensing applications scientist, consultant*

Friday Harbor
Agosta, William Carleton *chemist, educator*

Kirkland
Jin, Doo Jung *geophysicist, educator, researcher*

Lakewood
Harding, Karen Elaine *chemistry educator*

Lopez Island
Whetten, John Theodore *geologist, researcher*

Lynden
Harshman, Dale Richard *physicist*

Lynnwood
Olsen, Kenneth Harold *geophysicist, astrophysicist*

Manchester
Fearon, Lee Charles *chemist*

Oak Harbor
Crampton, George Harris *neuroscientist, retired army officer*

Olympia
Bloomquist, Rodney Gordon *geologist*
Yake, William Ellsworth *environmental scientist, writer, poet*

Pullman
Banas, Emil Mike *physicist, educator*
†Franz, Eldon Henry *environmental scientist, educator, ecologist*
Hipps, Kerry W(ayne) *chemistry educator, research scientist*
Ryan, Clarence Augustine, Jr., *biochemistry educator*
†Satterlee, James D. *chemist, educator*

Redmond
Borgs, Christian H. *mathematical physicist*

Richland
Adam, William James *nuclear scientist*
Bevelacqua, Joseph John *physicist, researcher*
Bratvold, Thomas Erik *physicist*
Bush, Spencer Harrison *metallurgist, consultant*
Elderkin, Charles Edwin *retired meteorologist*
†Exarhos, Gregory James *physical chemist, research scientist*
Fruchter, Jonathan Sewell *research scientist, geochemist*
†Hrma, Pavel *materials scientist, educator*
Jacobsen, Gerald Bernhardt *biochemist*
Moore, Emmett Burris, Jr., *physical chemist, educator*
Napier, Bruce Alan *physicist*
Onishi, Yasuo *environmental researcher*
Sundaram, Shanmugavelayutham Kamakshi *materials scientist, consultant*

Seattle
Andersen, Niels Hjorth *chemistry educator, biophysics researcher, consultant*
Banse, Karl *retired oceanography educator*
Baum, William Alvin *astronomer, educator*
Bernard, Eddie Nolan *oceanographer*
Bichsel, Hans *physicist, consultant, researcher*
Borden, Weston Thatcher *chemistry educator*
Brown, Craig William *physical chemist*
Brown, Robert Alan *atmospheric science educator, research scientist*
Christian, Gary Dale *chemistry educator*
Clark, Kenneth Courtright *retired physics and geophysics educator*
Conway, Howard *geophysicist, educator*
Creager, Joe Scott *geology and oceanography educator*
†Dale, Beverly A. *biochemist, researcher*
Dalton, Larry Raymond *chemistry educator, researcher, consultant*
Dehmelt, Hans Georg *physicist, educator*
Erdmann, Joachim Christian *physicist*
Evans, Bernard William *geologist, educator*
Farwell, George Wells *retired physicist*
Fischer, Edmond Henri *biochemistry educator*
Fischer, Fred Walter *physicist, engineer, educator*
Floss, Heinz G. *chemistry educator, scientist*
Gerhart, James Basil *physics educator*
Gordon, Milton Paul *biochemist, educator*
Gouterman, Martin Paul *chemistry educator*
Halver, John Emil *nutritional biochemist*
Heath, George Ross *oceanographer*
Henley, Ernest Mark *physics educator, university dean emeritus*
Hermann, Albert Joseph *oceanographer*
Hodge, Paul William *astronomer, educator*
Ingalls, Robert Lynn *physicist, educator*
Kells, Lyman F. *research scientist*
King, Ivan Robert *astronomy educator*
Kovchegov, Yuri V. *physicist, educator*
Krebs, Edwin Gerhard *biochemistry educator*
Kwiram, Alvin L. *physical chemistry educator, university official*
Lord, Jere Johns *retired physics educator*
Lubatti, Henry Joseph *physicist, educator*
Malins, Donald Clive *biochemistry, researcher*
Pocker, Yeshayau *chemistry, biochemistry educator*
Porter, Stephen Cummings *geologist, educator*
Rabinovitch, Benton Seymour *chemist, educator emeritus*
Reed, Ronald Keith *oceanographer, researcher*
Reinhardt, William Parker *chemical physicist, educator*
Stern, Edward Abraham *physics educator*
Thouless, David James *retired physicist, educator*
Turecek, Frantisek *chemistry educator*
Walsh, Kenneth Andrew *biochemist*
Weitkamp, William George *retired nuclear physicist*
Wilets, Lawrence *physics educator*
Yuan, Chun *physicist, educator*

Silverdale
Walske, M(ax) Carl, Jr., *physicist*

Spokane
Crosby, Glenn Arthur *chemistry educator*

Tacoma
Wolf, Frederick George *environmental scientist, administrator*

Vancouver
Cohen, Norm *chemist*
Iverson, Richard Matthew *earth scientist*
Valanis, Kirk Christian *theoretical mechanics researcher, educator*

West Richland
Ryan, Jack Lewis *chemist, researcher, consultant, educator*

WEST VIRGINIA

Charleston
Galya, Thomas Andrew *geologist*

Keyser
Falkowski, Theresa Gae *chemistry educator*

Morgantown
Beattie, Diana Scott *biochemistry educator*
Seehra, Mohindar Singh *physics educator, researcher*

WISCONSIN

Appleton
†Lokensgard, Jerrold Paul *chemist, educator, organic chemist*

Cudahy
Shen, Gangshu *metallurgist*

Eau Claire
†Whitfield, Scott Burwick *physics educator*

Green Bay
Pearson, Carol Ann *chemistry educator, science resource manager*

Kenosha
Ramesh, Kalahasti Subrahmanyam *materials scientist*

La Crosse
Rozelle, Lee Theodore *physical chemist, researcher*

Lake Geneva
Dobray, Alan Michael *theoretical physicist, research scientist*

Madison
Adler, Julius *biochemist, biologist, educator*
Anderson, Louis Wilmer, Jr., *physicist, educator*
Balantekin, Akif Baha *physicist, educator*
Barger, Vernon Duane *physicist, educator*
Beinert, Helmut *biochemist*
Bentley, Charles Raymond *geophysics educator*
Botez, Dan *physicist*
Burris, Robert Harza *biochemist, educator*
Callen, James Donald *plasma physicist, nuclear engineer*
Cassinelli, Joseph Patrick *astronomy educator*
Christensen, Nikolas Ivan *geophysicist, educator*
Churchwell, Edward Bruce *astronomer, educator*
Clay, Clarence Samuel *acoustical oceanographer*
Cleland, W(illiam) Wallace *biochemistry educator*
Code, Arthur Dodd *astrophysics educator*
Connors, Kenneth Antonio *retired chemistry educator*
Craddock, Campbell (John Campbell Craddock) *geologist, educator*
Curtiss, Charles Francis *chemist, educator*
DeWerd, Larry Albert *medical physicist, educator*
Dott, Robert Henry, Jr., *geologist, educator*
Ediger, Mark D. *chemistry educator*
Evenson, Merle Armin *chemist, educator*
Farrar, Thomas C. *chemist, educator*
Fennema, Owen Richard *food chemistry educator*
Frey, Perry A. *biochemistry educator*
Gorski, Jack *biochemistry educator*
Hamers, Robert J. *chemistry educator, researcher*
Hedden, Gregory Dexter *environmental science educator, consultant*
Himpsel, Franz Josef *physicist, educator*
Hokin, Lowell Edward *biochemist, educator*
Houghton, David Drew *meteorologist, educator*
Kiessling, Laura Lee *chemist, researcher*
Lagally, Max Gunter *physics educator*
Lardy, Henry A(rnold) *biochemistry educator*
Lawler, James Edward *physics educator*
Lee, Peter *materials scientist*
Maher, Louis James, Jr., *geologist, educator*
Morton, Stephen Dana *chemist, consultant*
Mukerjee, Pasupati *chemistry educator*
Perlman, Katherine Lenard (Kato Lenard) *organic chemist*
Pray, Lloyd Charles *geologist, educator*
Rich, Daniel Hulbert *chemistry educator*
Savage, Blair deWillis *astronomer, educator*
Sazhin, Sergey Victorovich *electrochemist, researcher*
Scherer, Victor Richard *physicist, computer specialist, consultant, musician*
Sih, Charles John *pharmaceutical chemistry educator*
Skinner, James Lauriston *chemist, educator*
†Stump, Kurt Edward *research scientist*
Suttie, John Weston *biochemist*
†Symon, Keith Randolph *physics educator, consultant*
†Tomé, Wolfgang Axel *physicist, researcher, educator*
Trubetskoy, Vladimir Sergeevich *polymer chemist*
Vaughan, Worth Edward *chemistry educator*
Wakker, Bart P. *astronomer*
Zhu, Junyong *research scientist*
Zimmerman, Howard Elliot *chemist, educator*

Milwaukee
Bader, Alfred Robert *chemist*
Baker, John Edward *cardiac biochemist, educator*
Burch, Thaddeus Joseph, Jr., *physics educator, clergyman*
Buss, Daniel Frank *environmental scientist*
Greenler, Robert George *physics educator, researcher*
Griffith, Owen Wendell *biochemistry educator*
Haworth, Daniel Thomas *chemistry educator*
Hendee, William Richard *medical physics educator, university official, radiologist*
Holme, Thomas A. *chemistry educator, researcher*
†Hsieh, Jiang *research scientist*
Karkheck, John Peter *physics educator, researcher*
Saldin, Dilano Kerzaman *physicist, educator*
†Schrader, David M. *physicist, researcher, writer*
†Sosnovsky, George *chemist, educator*
Wilkie, Charles A. *chemistry educator*

Neenah
Wang, James Hongxue *polymer scientist*

Oregon
†Draeger, Norman Arthur *physical chemist, research and development company executive*
Roselle, Paul Lucas *material scientist*

Oshkosh
†Utke, Allen R(ay) *chemist, educator*

Racine
Isenberg, Norbert *chemist, educator*
Langenegger, Armin *radiation physicist*

Schofield
Adams, James William *former chemist*

Washington Island
Raup, David Malcolm *paleontology educator*

Waukesha
†Kocharian, Armen *physicist*

Williams Bay
Hobbs, Lewis Mankin *astronomer*

WYOMING

Big Horn
Schultz, Harry Pershing *chemistry researcher, retired educator*

Casper
Cvancara, Alan Milton *geologist, educator*
Ptasynski, Harry *geologist, oil producer*
Wold, John Schiller *geologist, former congressman*

Laramie
†Frost, Carol D. *geology educator*
Hausel, William Dan *economic geologist, martial artist, public speaker, writer, artist*
Meyer, Edmond Gerald *energy and natural resources educator, resources scientist, entrepreneur, former chemistry educator, university administrator*
Robertson, Raymond Eliot *research chemist*

Story
†Bredehoeft, John Dallas *geologist*

TERRITORIES OF THE UNITED STATES

PUERTO RICO

Angeles
Avila, Carlos Alberto *physics researcher, inventor*

Mayaguez
†Meléndez, Enrique *chemist, educator*

Vega Alta
Matos, Cruz Alfonso *environmental consultant*

CANADA

ALBERTA

Calgary
Campbell, Finley Alexander *geologist, consultant*
Mossop, Grant Dilworth *geologist, researcher*
Walker, Roger Geoffrey *geology educator, consultant*

Drumheller
Currie, Philip John *research paleontologist, museum curator*

Edmonton
Gough, Denis Ian *geophysics educator*
Harris, Walter Edgar *chemistry educator*
Kay, Cyril Max *biochemist, educator*
Kratochvil, Byron George *chemistry educator, researcher*
Rutter, Nathaniel Westlund *geologist, educator*
Stelck, Charles Richard *geology educator*

BRITISH COLUMBIA

Burnaby
Wainwright, David Stanley *intellectual property professional*

Lions Bay
Bartholomew, Gilbert Alfred *retired physicist*

Sidney
Petrie, William *physicist, researcher*
van den Bergh, Sidney *astronomer*

Vancouver
Bloom, Myer *physicist, educator*
Brunstein, John David *biochemist, researcher*
Hardy, Walter Newbold *physics educator, researcher*
Ozier, Irving *physicist, educator*
Pickard, George Lawson *physics educator*
Pincock, Richard Earl *chemistry educator*

TAIWAN

Taipei

Lee, Yuan Tseh *chemistry educator*

ADDRESS UNPUBLISHED

†Abdaladze, Merabi *physicist*
Adams, Daniel Otis *chemist*
Aftel, Mandy *perfumer*
Ahmad, Moghisuddin *research chemist*
†Ahuja, Satinder *chemist, consultant*
Akasofu, Syun-Ichi *geophysicist, educator*
Alexander, Thomas G. *chemist, researcher*
Alexandratos, Spiro Dionisios *chemistry educator, dean*
Anders, Edward *chemist, educator*
Andersen, Hans Christian *chemistry educator*
†Andersen, Roy Stuart *physicist*
Anderson, Philip Warren *physicist, educator*
†Antar, Ghassan Youssef *research scientist*
Arenstein, Walter Alan *environmental scientist*
Armstrong, Donald *biochemistry, pathophysiology educator*
Arnett, Edward McCollin *chemistry educator, researcher*
Atkins, Ernest Eugene *chemist, retired*
Atlas, David *meteorologist, research scientist*
Baker, Daniel Neil *physicist*
Baldwin, George Curriden *physicist, educator*
Ball, Lawrence *retired physical scientist*
Bandeen, William Reid *retired meteorologist*
Barr, John Baldwin *chemist, research scientist*
Bartzatt, Ronald Lee *research biochemist, consultant*
Bassford, Lynn Foster *physicist, engineer*
Bauer, Henry Hermann *chemistry and science educator*
Baur, Werner Heinz *mineralogist, educator*
Behl, Wishvender Kumar *research chemist*
Behrendt, John Charles *geophysicist researcher, writer*
†Belluomini, Wendy *microprocessor design researcher*
Benjamin, Arlin James *physicist*
Bennett, William Ralph, Jr., *physicist, educator*
Bernfeld, Peter Harry William *retired biochemist*
†Bernstein, Bruce S. *chemist, consultant*
Bersin, Richard Lewis *physicist, plasma process technologist*
Berthold, John William, III, *physicist*
Biederman, Edwin Williams, Jr., *retired petroleum geologist*
Bigelow, Charles Cross *retired biochemist, retired university administrator*
Bikales, Norbert M. *chemist, science administrator*
Birgeneau, Robert Joseph *physicist, educator*
Blander, Milton *chemist*
Bodanszky, Miklos *chemist, educator*
Bondar, Richard Jay Laurent *biochemist*
†Bowers, Larry Donald *chemistry and pathology educator*
Boyer, Herbert Wayne *retired biochemist*
Boyes, Stephen Richard *hydrogeologic consultant*
Bradbeer, Clive *biochemistry and microbiology educator, research scientist*
Braden, Charles Hosea *physicist, university administrator*
†Braun, Artur *physicist*
†Braun, Daniel *physicist, researcher*
Breakiron, Lee Allen *astronomer*
Bretthauer, Erich Walter *chemist, educator*
Brown, Barbara S. *environmental scientist*
Brown, Rhonda Rochelle *chemist, health facility administrator, lawyer*
Bunyan, Ellen Lackey Spotz *retired chemist*
Callahan, Thomas Jay *petroleum engineer, geologist, consultant*
Calvert, Jack George *atmospheric chemist, educator*
Cane, David E. *chemistry educator*
Capasso, Federico *physicist*
Cardman, Lawrence Santo *physics educator, research administrator*
Carroll, Harvey Franklin *chemistry and nutrition educator*
Cathou, Renata Egone *chemist, consultant*
†Chadsey, Harold A. *astronomer*
Chang, Clarence Dayton *retired chemist*
Chemla, Daniel S. *physics educator*
†Chen, Yen-Chu *physicist*
†Cheng, Baolian *physicist*
†Chiu, Bella Chao *astrophysicist, writer*
Chow, Jimmy Tai-Nin *chemist*
Christoffersen, Ralph Earl *chemist, researcher*
Chu, Benjamin Thomas Peng-Nien *chemistry educator*
Chu, Steven *physics educator*
Church, Eugene Lent *physicist, consulting scientist*
Clarke, George Alton *chemist, academic administrator, retired*
Clark-Simpson, Carolyn A. *aerospace technologist, life scientist*
Clayton-Townsend, JoAnn *aerospace analyst*
Cohen, Philip *retired hydrogeologist*
Cohen, Stanley *biochemistry educator*
Collins, George William, II, *astrophysics educator, writer*
Colwell, Joshua Edwards *astronomer, researcher*
Compton, W. Dale *physicist, researcher, engineer*
Conerly-Perks, Erlene Brinson *retired chemist*
†Coop, Andrew *chemist, educator*
Cooper, Austin Morris *chemist, chemical engineer, consultant, researcher*
Cox, James Carl, Jr., *chemist, researcher, lexicographer, consultant*
Craven, Stephen M. *retired research chemist*
Critoph, Eugene *retired physicist, nuclear research company executive*
Crutzen, Paul Josef *research meteorologist, chemist*
Cuatrecasas, Pedro Martin *research biochemist, pharmaceutical executive*
Dale, Wesley John *chemistry educator*
†Dalitsch, Walter William *aerospace medicine specialist*
Danes, Zdenko Frankenberger *physicist, consultant*
Daniels, James Maurice *retired physicist*
Daniels, William Burton *retired physicist, educator*
Dash, Sanford Mark *aerospace scientist*
Daves, Glenn Doyle, Jr., *science educator, chemist, researcher*
Day, Richard Allen *chemistry educator*
Deisenhofer, Johann *biochemistry educator, researcher*
†DeJesus, Onofre T *chemist*
De Loach, Bernard Collins, Jr., *retired physicist*
Denton, Medona Bonner *research chemistry educator*
Deryuga, Vyacheslav O. *nuclear physicist, computer scientist, consultant*
Detert, Miriam Anne *chemical analyst*
Dickinson, William Richard *retired geologist*
Dickman, Robert S. *aerospace consultant, retired career officer*
Diehl, Harry Alfred *chemist, genealogist*
Ding, Michael S. *physical scientist*
Dixon, Gordon Henry *biochemist, educator*
Donath, Fred Arthur *geologist, geophysicist*
Doorish, John Francis *physicist, mathematician, educator*
Dorfman, Benjamin Fridel *physicist*
†Dossena, Tiziano Thomas *environmental scientist*
Doumani, George Alexander *earth and environmental scientist*
Dow, Garnett McCormick *geoscientist*
Dubin, Daniel Herschel Eli *physicist, educator*
†Ducoste, Joel J. *research scientist, educator*
Easterbrook, Eliot Knights *chemist*
Ebisuzaki, Yukiko *retired chemistry educator*
Eck, Robert Edwin *physicist*
†Edwards, Helen Thom *physicist*
†Einhorn, Martin B. *physics educator*
Elliott, Brig (Chip) *network scientist*
English, Bruce Vaughan *environmental consultant*
Esquivel, Agerico Liwag *retired research physicist*
Ewen, H.I. *physicist*
Feldmann, Frank Neil *chemistry educator*
†Fey, Willard *global environmental researcher, educator*
Fioto, George Anthony *chemist*
Flor, Loy Lorenz *retired chemist, corrosion engineer, consultant*
Flynn, George William *chemistry educator, researcher*
Ford, Kenneth William *physicist*
†Fossuo Talom, Patrick *research scientist*
Fox, John David *educator, physicist*
Fradkin, David Milton *physicist, educator*
Franz, John E. *bio-organic chemist, researcher*
Franz, Judy R. *physics educator*
Friedlander, Charles Douglas (Chuck Friedlander) *space consultant*
†Funck, Dennis Light *chemist, researcher*
†Fung, Bing Man *chemistry educator*
Gardner, Wilford Robert *physicist, educator*
Garwood, William Everett *chemist researcher*
†Gedevanishvili, Shalva *materials scientist, researcher*
Gelboin, Harry Victor *biochemistry educator, researcher*
Geller, Seymour *retired educator, researcher*
†Gerstein, Mark Bender *biophysicist, bioinformatician*
Gervay, Joseph Edmund *chemist, researcher, retired research scientist*
Getting, Ivan Alexander *physicist, former aerospace company executive*
Gilinsky, Victor *physicist*
Glashow, Sheldon Lee *physicist, educator*
Glesk, Ivan *physicist, educator, researcher*
Goldberger, Marvin Leonard *physicist, educator*
Golden, David Edward *physicist*
Goldstein, Irving Solomon *chemistry educator, consultant*
Gordon, William Edwin *physicist, engineer, educator, university official*
†Gotthelf, Eric *astrophysicist, research scientist*
Grady, Lee Timothy *pharmaceutical chemist*
Grayeski, Mary Lynn *chemist, consultant*
Greaves, William Webster *chemist, patent analyst, community liaison*
Griesé, John William, III, *astronomer, educator, mental health advocate*
Grimes, James Gordon *geologist*
Gummel, Hermann Karl *retired physicist, laboratory administrator*
Gunter, William Dayle, Jr., *physicist, consultant*
Guo, Xiaofeng *physicist*
Gutsch, William Anthony, Jr., *astronomer*
Hagemier, Herman Frederick *chemist*
Hakkila, Eero Arnold *retired nuclear safeguards technology chemist*
Hall, Frederick Keith *chemist*
Hall, Grace Rosalie *physicist, educator, writer*
Halpern, Alvin Michael *retired physicist, educator, consultant*
Hardaway, Robert Morris, III, *retired physician, educator, retired army officer*
Hardy, Ralph W. F. *biochemist, biotechnology executive*
Haslett, Jared Wooddell *physicist, educator*
Hassan, Sayed Mohammed *analytical chemist*
Hatcher, Herbert John *biochemist, microbiologist*
Heeschen, David Sutphin *astronomer, educator*
†Heilman, David Michael *scientist, military officer*
Heller, Adam *chemist, researcher*
Hereford, Frank Loucks, Jr., *physicist, educator*
Herzfeld, Charles Maria *physicist, educator*
Hinkley, Everett David, Jr., *physicist, business executive*
Ho, Chih-Ming *physicist, educator*
Ho, John Wing-Shing *biochemistry educator, researcher*
Hoeg, Donald Francis *chemist, consultant, former research and development executive*
Hoffleit, Ellen Dorrit *astronomer*
Hogen-Esch, Thieo E. *chemistry educator*
Holbrow, Charles Howard *physicist, educator*
Holeman, George Robert *health physicist, consultant*
Holmes, Jerry Dell *retired chemist*
Horton, Robert Carlton *geologist*
†Hosang, Robert Michael *research scientist*
Howard, Robert Franklin *observatory administrator, astronomer*
Hubbard, Stevan Ralph *biophysicist, educator*
Huie, Robert Elliott *research chemist*
Ignatiev, Alex *physics researcher*
Ingle, James Chesney, Jr., *geology educator*
Inlow, Rush Osborne *chemist*
Jarmie, Nelson *physicist, consultant*
John, Sarah *physicist*
Johnson, Arthur William, Jr., *retired planetarium executive*
Johnson, Charles Leslie *aerospace physicist, consultant*
Johnson, David Wilfred, Jr., *ceramic scientist, researcher*
Johnston, Pauline Kay *chemist*
†Johnstone, Carol Joanne *physicist*
Jones, Roger Alan *chemistry educator, researcher, consultant*
Jones, Thornton Keith *research chemist*
Jordan, Robert Reed *geologist, educator*
Jordan, Thomas Fredrick *physics educator*
Jung, Hilda Ziifle *retired physicist*
Kasprzak, Lucian Alexander *physicist, researcher, technical manager*
Kastner, Marc Aaron *physics educator*
†Kelsey, Donald Ross *chemist*
Kennefick, Christine Marie *materials scientist*
Kerr, Donald MacLean, Jr., *physicist*
Kerwin, Larkin *retired physics educator*
†Kim, Yeong K. *polymer composite process specialist, researcher*
Klema, Ernest Donald *nuclear physicist, educator*
Klute, Allan Aloys *physicist, economist*
Knight, Patricia Marie *medical device researcher, consultant*
Knudsen, William Claire *geophysicist, researcher*
†Koppolu, Ajoy P.K. *research scientist, chemical engineer*
Korn, Jessica Susan *research scientist, educator*
Kraichnan, Robert Harry *physicist, consultant*
Kravitz, Rubin *chemist*
Kropschot, Richard Henry *retired physicist, science laboratory administrato*
Kukla, Maija Meijer *research scientist, educator*
Kumar, Kaplesh *materials scientist*
Kustin, Kenneth *chemist*
Lacerenza, Joseph Charles *research scientist*
†Lam, Cuong Kim *research scientist*
Langerak, Esley Oren *retired research chemist*
Laporte, Leo Frederic *earth sciences educator, paleontologist*
†Laszlo, Pierre *chemistry educator*
Le, Yvonne Diemvan *chemist*
Leachtenauer, Jon Clark *optical scientist*
LeBlond, Paul Henri *oceanographer, educator*
Lederman, Leon Max *physicist, educator*
Ledley, Tamara Shapiro *earth system scientist, climatologist*
Lehmann, (A) Spencer *retired chemist, retired chemical engineer*
Leston, Gerd *research chemist, retired*
†Leung, Mary Ann Elizabeth *chemist*
Leus McFarlen, Patricia Cheryl *water chemist*
Levenson, Marc David *optics and lasers specialist, scientist, editor*
Levi, Barbara Goss *physicist, editor*
Lightman, Alan Paige *writer, physicist, educator*
Lippincott, James Lippincott *biochemistry and biological sciences educator*
Lo, Shui-yin *physicist*
Loach, Paul Allen *biochemist, biophysicist, educator*
Loftin, Richard Bowen *physics and computer science educator, researcher*
Lornitzo, Frank *retired chemist*
Los, Marinus *retired agrochemical researcher*
Lukacs, Michael Edward *electro-optics researcher*
†Lundy, Richard Alan *physicist, consultant*
Lurix, Paul Leslie, Jr., *chemist*
Maddin, Robert *metallurgist educator*
Maglich, Bogdan Castle *physicist*
†Makarov, Oleg P. *physicist, educator*
Maling, George Croswell, Jr., *physicist*
†Maltsev, Nikolai Elyseevich *research scientist*
†March, Jacqueline Front *retired chemist*
Marcuse, Dietrich *retired physicist*
Marinetti, Guido V. *biochemistry educator*
†Mashnik, Stepan G. *physicist*
Mauzy, Michael Philip *environmental consultant, chemical engineer*
Mayo, Dana Walker *chemistry educator*
McCormick, Donald Bruce *retired biochemist, educator*
McManus, James William *chemist, researcher*
McTague, John Paul *materials scientist, educator, chemist, researcher*
Melvin, Peter Joseph *astrophysicist, educator*
Mendelson, Sol *physical science educator, consultant*
†Metz, Werner Adam *physicist*
Miller, Herman Lunden *retired physicist*
Miller, Phillip Edward *environmental scientist*
Mil'shtein, Samson *semiconductor physicist*
†Mishin, Yuri *materials scientist, educator*
Mislow, Kurt Martin *chemist, educator*
†Moeck, Peter *crystallographer, materials scientist*
†Morton, Roger R.A. *research scientist*
†Mukerjee, Shaibal *environmental scientist*
Mullis, Kary Banks *biochemist*
Munson, Ronald Alfred *retired chemist*
†Mutsuddi, Mousumi *research scientist*
Nagys, Elizabeth Ann *environmental issues educator*
Nalwa, Hari Singh *materials scientist, polymer chemist*
Nemec, Josef *retired organic chemist, researcher*
Neumark, Gertrude Fanny *materials science educator*
Nevill, William Albert *chemistry educator*
Newton, Roger Gerhard *educator, physicist*
†Ng, Edward W. *aerospace scientist*
Ni, Luqun *research scientist*
Nirenberg, Marshall Warren *biochemist*
Nobles, Laurence Hewit *retired geology educator*
Ogliaruso, Michael Anthony *retired chemist, educator, actor*
Olsen, Clifford Wayne *retired physical chemist, consultant*
Oort, Abraham Hans *meteorologist, researcher, educator*
†Orr, J. Richie *physicist*
Orttung, William Herbert *chemistry educator*
†Pall-Pallant, Teri *paleontologist, inventor, behavioral scientist, design engineer, advertising agency executive*
Palmer, Larry George *chemist*
Palmer, Ricky Samuel *physicist*
Panofsky, Wolfgang Kurt Hermann *physicist, educator*
†Parr, Albert Clarence *physicist*
Patchett, Arthur Allan *medicinal chemist, pharmaceutical executive*
Pautler, Maria Christine Sadusky *environmental scientist*
Pearson, Ralph Gottfrid *chemistry educator*
Peiris, Suhithi Mahesica *research chemist*
†Peng, Weiqun *physicist, research scientist*
Petersen, Arne Joaquin *chemist*
Phillips, Julia Mae *physicist*
Platau, Gerard Oscar *chemist, consultant*
Plerou, Vasiliki *physicist*
Pocock, Frederick James *environmental scientist, engineer, consultant*
Portis, Alan Mark *physicist, educator*
†Poss, Andrew Joseph *chemist, writer*
Pound, Robert Vivian *physics educator*
Pradzynski, Andrzej Henryk *chemist*
†Pretka, John E. *retired chemist*
Price, Clifford Warren *retired metallurgist, researcher*
Price, Paul Buford *physicist, educator*
Proctor, Richard J. *geologist, consultant*
Pursey, Derek Lindsay *physics educator*
Pytte, Agnar *physicist, former university president*
†Qi, Zhigang *materials scientist, chemist*
Qutub, Musa Yacub *hydrogeologist, educator, consultant*
Rabó, Jule Anthony *chemical researcher, consultant*
Rayzman, Viktor Lazarevich *metallurgist, consultant*
Reeb, Sue Ellen *biochemist*
Reichmanis, Elsa *chemist*
Rhyne, James Jennings *condensed matter physicist*
Rice, Stuart Alan *chemist, educator*
Richards, Paul Linford *physics educator, researcher*
Richardson, Charles Clifton *biochemist, educator*
Richardson, Jasper Edgar *nuclear physicist*
Richart, Douglas Stephen *retired chemist*
Rider, Paul Edward *physicist, educator*
Roberts, Thomas George *retired physicist*
Robertson, John Archibald Law *nuclear scientist*
Rodgers, Robert Aubrey *physicist*
Rokke, Douglas Lind *physicist, educator*
Rose, Marian Henrietta *physics researcher*
Rose, William Kenneth *astronomy educator*
†Rosenberg, Eli Ira *physicist, educator*
Rosenblum, Stephen Saul *chemist, researcher*
Rosenkilde, Carl Edward *physicist*
Ross, Alberta Barkley *retired chemist*
Roychoudhuri, Chandrasekhar *physicist*
Rubin, Vera Cooper *astronomer, researcher*
Ruedenberg, Klaus *theoretical chemist, educator*
†Rybczyk, Joseph Anthony *physicist, researcher, writer*
Satinover, Jeffrey B. *physicist, psychiatrist, writer*
Sayre, David *retired physicist*
Schmidt, Ruth A(nna) M(arie) *geologist*
Scholz, Christopher Henry *geophysicist, writer*
Schonhorn, Harold *chemist, researcher*
Schutz, Donald Frank *geochemist, environmental corporate executive*
Schwartz, Shirley E. *chemist, researcher*
Scott, T. Gordon *chemistry and math educator, writer*
Setters, Paula Louise Henderson *physics educator*
Shapiro, Jacob *physicist, educator*
†Sharmasarkar, Shankar *chemist, educator*
Sharon, Timothy Michael *physicist*
Sheinin, Rose *biochemist, educator*
Shirley, David Arthur *chemistry educator, science administrator*
†Simpson, Gerald D *retired research scientist, consultant, educator*
Singer, Jeffrey Michael *organic analytical chemist*
Singer, S(iegfried) Fred *geophysicist, educator*
Slade, Paul Graham *physicist*
Smith, Charles Haddon *geoscientist, consultant*
Smither-Kopperl, Margaret Lydia *research scientist*
Sobolev, Alexandre Andreevich *physicist*
†Solomon, Susan *chemist, scientist*
Speier, John Leo, Jr., *retired chemist*
Spejewski, Eugene Henry *physicist, educator*
Spencer, David Anthony *geologist, researcher*
Squibb, Samuel Dexter *chemistry educator*
Srinivasan, Rangaswamy *chemical physicist*
Stevenson, Paul Michael *physics educator, researcher*
Straus, Leon Stephan *physicist*
Strouth, Baron Howard Steven *geologist, mining engineer*
Stubbs, Gerald *biochemist, educator*

Sullivan, Nicholas G. science educator, speleologist
†Sultan, Cornel research scientist, consultant
Sumrall, Linda geophysicist
†Sun, Zuo research scientist, consultant
Sundaresan, Mosur Kalyanaraman physics educator
Sunderman, Duane Neuman chemist, research institute executive
Swezey, Christopher Stephen geologist
Symchowicz, Samson retired biochemist
†Takesue, Renee Kimiyo research geologist
Taylor, Kathleen (Christine Taylor) physical chemist, researcher
Tedford, Charles Franklin biophysicist
Ter-Mikirtychev, Valerii Vartanovich physicist, researcher
Tilley, David Ronald physicist, educator
Tipler, Frank Jennings, III, physicist
†Toppel, Bert Jack retired physicist
Tuul, Johannes physics educator, researcher
Upgren, Arthur Reinhold, Jr., astronomer, educator, writer
Urry, Grant Wayne retired chemistry educator
Van Dalen, Gordon John physicist, educator
van der Meer, Simon physicist
Vanderwalker, Diane Mary materials scientist
Vanier, Jacques physicist
Van Riper, Kenneth Alan astrophysicist and researcher
†Veach, Allen Marshall research physicist
†Venkatu, Doulatabad A. retired metallurgist
Veronis, George geophysicist, educator
Vilenchik, Michael Marc biophysicist, oncologist
Villforth, John Carl health physicist
Vinet, Luc physicist
Vo, Nghia Van materials scientist, electrical engineer
Vook, Frederick Ludwig physicist, consultant
Voorhees, Kent Jay chemist
†Wadi Ramahi, Shada Jamal physicist, researcher
Wahl, Floyd Michael geologist
Wald, Francine Joy Weintraub (Mrs. Bernard J. Wald) physicist, academic administrator
Wall, Frederick Theodore retired chemistry educator
Wallace, Jane House retired geologist
Wallace, Robert Earl geologist
Wattenberg, Albert physicist, educator
Weinberg, Steven physics educator
Weisburger, Elizabeth Kreiser retired chemist, editor
†Weisel, Clifford Paul environmental health educator
Weisz, Paul B(urg) physicist
Wellner, Marcel Nahum physics educator, researcher
Wells, Robert Hartley chemistry professional
Wheeler, John Oliver geologist
White, William Charles physicist
Wiener, Russell Warren environmental scientist, researcher
Wilson, Kenneth Geddes physics research administrator
Winterling, George Alfred meteorologist, broadcaster
Wolff, Manfred Ernst medicinal chemist, pharmaceutical company executive
Wolff, Peter Adalbert physicist, educator
†Wong, Kuok-Shoong Daniel research scientist
Woo, Jonathan C. G. chemist, portfolio manager, management consultant
Wood, Joan retired chemist
Woodruff, Truman O(wen) physicist, emeritus educator
Wright, William Wynn chemist
Wroblowa, Halina Stefania electrochemist
Wyrtki, Klaus oceanography educator
†Xu, J.M. (Jimmy) physicist, educator, engineer
Yates, David John C. chemist, researcher
Yavorsky, James Anthony chemist, educator
Yu, David U.L. physicist, researcher
†Zaffaroni, Alejandro C. biochemist, medical research company executive
Zakim, David biochemist
Zaleski, Jan Franciszek biochemist
†Zhang, Yue research scientist
†Zheng, Zhiyin research scientist, consultant
Zhou, Huanchun chemist, administrator
Zhou, Jinyuan physicist, educator
Zimm, Bruno Hasbrouck physical chemistry educator

SOCIAL SCIENCE

UNITED STATES

ALABAMA

Auburn
Jardine, Murray Donald political science educator
Seroka, James Henry social sciences educator, university administrator
Whitten, David Owen economics educator

Birmingham
Bradley, Laurence Alan psychologist
Martin, Roy Clayton clinical neuropsychologist
Mishra, Digambar political science educator
Morrisey, Michael A. health economics educator
Nunn, Grady Harrison political science educator emeritus
†Schwebel, David Charles psychologist, educator
Taub, Edward psychology researcher

Collinsville
Beasley, Mary Catherine home economics educator, administrator, researcher

Dothan
Wright, Burton sociologist

Duncanville
Prescott, Perry Don psychology educator, counselor

Evergreen
†Ausby, Kenneth Lavon criminologist

Hartselle
Slate, Joe Hutson psychologist, educator

Huntsville
Traylor, Orba Forest economist, lawyer, educator

Jacksonville
Dunaway, Carolyn Bennett retired sociology educator
†Jackson, Harvey Hardaway, III, history educator, columnist

Livingston
Wenger, Jay Lamar psychology educator

Maplesville
Nichols, J Hugh economic development consultant

Mobile
Agapos, Michael Angelo economics educator
Sawyer, Ana Maria Ramirez clinical psychologist
Suess, James Francis clinical psychologist
Vitulli, William Francis psychology educator, retired

Montevallo
McChesney, Robert Michael, Sr., educator

Montgomery
Mathew, Tom economics educator
Wendzel, Robert Leroy political science educator

Normal
Jarrett, Alfred A. social policy analyst

Pell City
Passey, George Edward psychology educator

Tuscaloosa
Baklanoff, Eric Nicholas economist, educator
Bindon, James Robert anthropology educator
Cramer, Dale Lewis retired economics educator
Fish, Mary Martha economics educator

ALASKA

Anchorage
Fisher, Margaret Eleanor psychologist, lawyer, arbitrator, mediator, educator
Gier, Karan Hancock psychologist
†Ippolito, Maria F. psychologist, educator
Obermeyer, Theresa Nangle sociology educator
Suddock, Frances Suter Thorson grief educator, writer
†Wood, Darryl Scott criminologist, educator

Fairbanks
McBeath, Gerald Alan political science educator, researcher
Simon, James Johnson Koffroth anthropologist

ARIZONA

Flagstaff
†Cothran, Dan Allen political scientist, educator
McDonald, Craydon Dean psychologist
Pavlik, William Bruce psychologist, educator
†Schlosberg, David political scientist, educator
Smith, Zachary Alden political science and public administration educator

Fort Defiance
Livingston, Alfred James archaeologist, consultant

Gilbert
Metcalf, Virgil Alonzo economics educator

Glendale
Mathis, F. John economist, educator

Green Valley
Leege, David Calhoun political scientist, educator

Nogales
†Robertson, Leon S retired sociologist, retired social sciences educator

Phoenix
Bostwick, Todd William city archaeologist
†Downey, Janet Marion anthropologist, educator
Lyon, William James sociology educator
McCarthy, M. Juliann school psychologist
†Shaffer, Dennis Michael psychology educator
Wolf, Irna Lynn psychologist

Prescott
Huard, Donald V. psychologist, educator
Lorant, John Herman retired economist, health policy analyst

Sacaton
Stephenson, Larry Kirk stategic planner, management, geography educator

Scottsdale
Braun, Stephen Hughes psychologist
Dean, Leslie Alan (Cap Dean) economist, consultant
†Roberts, Joan Ila psychologist, educator

Sierra Vista
Lutes, Todd Oakley political science educator

Sun City West
Nordin, John Algot economist, educator

Sun Lakes
Cantor, David Jules economist

Tempe
Alisky, Marvin Howard political science educator
†Dagger, Richard Keith political science and philosphy educator
Gordon, Leonard retired sociology educator
Guinouard, Donald Edgar psychologist
Haygood, Robert Collins industrial psychologist, educator, consultant
Johanson, Donald Carl physical anthropologist
Knox, Robert Lee educator
Lounsbury, John Frederick geographer, educator
McCormack, Brian Jerome political science educator
Pasqualetti, Martin J. geography educator
Simon, Sheldon Weiss political science educator
Strom, Robert Duane psychologist, educator
Uttal, William R(eichenstein) psychology and engineering educator, research scientist
Weigend, Guido Gustav geographer, educator

Tucson
Axinn, George Harold rural sociology educator
†Batterbury, Simon Peregrine John geographer, educator
Bechtel, Robert Bernard social sciences educator, consultant
Bedford, Felice L. psychologist, educator
Billings, Richard Bruce economics educator, consultant
Birkby, Walter Hudson forensic anthropologist, consultant
†Breiger, Ronald Louis social sciences educator
Brewer, David L. sociologist
Chaves, Mark Alan sociologist, educator
Clarke, James Weston political science educator, writer
Done, Robert Stacy educator, consultant
Fontana, Bernard Lee retired anthropologist, writer, consultant
Gibbs, David N(eil) history and political science educator
Hartley, Roger Edward political science educator
Ingram, Helen Moyer political science educator
†Kay, Margarita anthropologist, consultant, nurse
Marshall, Robert Herman economics educator
Mishler, William, II, political science educator
Peterson, V. Spike political science educator
Reitan, Ralph Meldahl clinical neuropsychologist, former educator
Smith, David Wayne psychologist, educator
Snyder, Richard Gerald research scientist, administrator, educator, consultant
Soren, David archaeologist, educator, writer
Stini, William Arthur anthropologist, educator
Stubblefield, Thomas Mason agricultural economist, educator
Taylor, Lester Dean economics educator, consultant
Thompson, Raymond Harris retired anthropologist, educator
Underwood, Jane Hainline Hammons anthropologist, educator
Volgy, Thomas John political science educator, organization official
Wahlke, John Charles political science educator

West Sedona
Eggert, Robert John, Sr., economist

Yuma
†Anderson, Stacey Ann school psychologist
†Mangan, Peter A. psychologist, educator
†McCarthy, Sherri Nevada psychologist, educator, educational consultant
Norton, Dunbar Sutton economic developer

ARKANSAS

Fayetteville
Mc Gimsey, Charles Robert, III, anthropologist

Fort Smith
Clark, Susan Glasson economics educator

Hot Springs National Park
Plummer, Jack Moore psychologist

Little Rock
Briscoe, David Lloyd academic sociologist, educator
Kaza, Greg John economist, educator
Ledbetter, Calvin Reville, Jr., (Cal Ledbetter) political science educator, university dean, former legislator

Mountain Home
†Hatcher, Milton Wright psychologist, educator

Pine Bluff
Engle, Carole Ruth aquaculture economics educator
Tai, Chong-Soo Stephen political scientist, educator

Siloam Springs
Oliver, Gary Jackson psychologist, educator

State University
Crawford, Jerry Lee economics educator
Power, Mary Susan political scientist, educator

CALIFORNIA

Alameda
Dahlquist, John Paul economics educator

Anaheim
Strudwick, Ivan H. archaeologist
Torbat, Akbar Esfahani investment advisor, economics educator, researcher

Apple Valley
Fisher, Weston Joseph economist

Arcata
Bowker, Lee Harrington sociologist, educator, writer
Emenhiser, JeDon Allen political science educator, academic administrator
Meyer, John Mark political scientist, educator

Atherton
Alexander, Theron behavioral scientist, psychologist, writer

Bakersfield
Myren, Richard Albert criminal justice consultant
Singer, George Milton clinical psychologist

Barstow
Nyborg, Kenneth Wayne retired social sciences educator, small business owner

Benicia
Nelson, Elmer Kingsholm, Jr., educator, writer, mediator, consultant

Berkeley
Akerlof, George Arthur economics educator
Alhadeff, David Albert economics educator
Auerbach, Alan Jeffrey economist, educator
†Baumrind, Diana research psychologist
Bellah, Robert Neelly sociologist, educator
†Berck, Peter agricultural economics educator
Bevir, William Mark political science educator
Brandes, Stanley Howard anthropology educator, writer
Breslauer, George William political science educator
Canfield, Judy S. psychologist
Cheit, Earl Frank economist, educator
Cole, Robert E. sociologist, educator
Colson, Elizabeth Florence anthropologist
Deck, Richard Allen political scientist, consultant, writer, human rights activist
Foster, George McClelland, Jr., anthropologist, educator
Freedman, Mervin Burton psychologist, educator
Gilbert, Richard Joseph economics educator
†Hermalin, Benjamin E. economics educator
†Hout, Michael sociologist, educator
Howell, Francis Clark paleo-anthropologist
Hu, Teh-wei economics educator
Jensen, Arthur Robert psychology educator
Judge, George Garrett economics educator
Kessler, Seymour clinical psychologist, consultant
Kirch, Patrick Vinton anthropology educator, archaeologist
Lambert, Nadine Murphy psychologist, educator
Landau, Martin political science educator
Lee, Ronald Demos demographer, economist, educator
Letiche, John Marion economist, educator
Lyons, Richard Kent economics educator
Maisel, Sherman Joseph economist, educator
Marquard, Steven Sandel economist, financial consultant
Maslach, Christina psychology educator
Mayer, Thomas economics educator
McFadden, Daniel Little economist, educator
†McKown, Clark Atwater psychologist
Muir, William Ker, Jr., political science educator
Nader, Laura anthropology educator
Norgaard, Richard Bruce economist, educator, consultant
†Norris, Carl William psychologist
†O'Brien, Kevin Joseph political scientist, educator
Quigley, John Michael economist, educator
Ranney, Austin (Joseph Ranney) political science educator
Rausser, Gordon C(lyde) agricultural and resource economics educator
Reich, Michael economics educator
Roland, Gerard economics educator
Rosenzweig, Mark Richard psychology educator
†Scheper-Hughes, Nancy Marie anthropologist, writer, education educator
Smolensky, Eugene economics educator
†Starn, Randolph history educator
Stewart, Patricia Rhodes former clinical psychologist, researcher
†Stimson, Shannon Colleen political scientist, educator
Sulloway, Frank Jones psychologist, historian
Swope, Alan Joseph psychologist, educator
Ulman, Lloyd retired social sciences educator
Williamson, Oliver Eaton economics and law educator
Wolfinger, Raymond Edwin political science educator

Beverly Hills
Blakeley, Linda psychologist, speaker
Reiner, Margot Ellen political scientist, educator
Yaryan, Ruby Bell psychologist

Bonita
Deane, Debbe psychologist, journalist, editor, consultant

Brentwood
Baker, Paul Thornell anthropology educator

Burlingame
Schwantes, Robert Sidney international relations executive

Carlsbad
Somit, Albert political educator

Carmichael
Hellmuth, William Frederick, Jr., *economics educator*

Carpinteria
Schmidhauser, John Richard *political science educator*
Wheeler, John Harvey *political scientist, writer*

Carson
†Moore, Jerry D. *anthropologist, educator*
Palmer, Beverly Blazey *psychologist, educator*

Chico
Brislain, Judy Ann *psychologist*
†Loker, William Meverell *anthropologist, educator*
McNall, Scott Grant *sociologist, educator, academic administrator*
†Schmidt, Diane Ellen *political scientist*
†Spear, Paul Stanley *psychology educator, musician*
Thomas, Stafford Tutt *political scientist, educator*

Chula Vista
McGowan, Charlotte Acord *anthropologist*

Claremont
Albaum, Jean Stirling *psychologist, educator*
Bjork, Gordon Carl *economist, educator*
†Csikszentmihalyi, Mihaly *psychology educator*
Lasswell, Marcia Lee *psychologist, educator*
Leeb, Charles Samuel *clinical psychologist*
Likens, James Dean *economics educator*
†Phelps, Orme Wheelock *economics educator emeritus*
Pitney, John Joseph, Jr., *political science educator*
Rossum, Ralph Arthur *political science educator*
Smith, Gary Nance *economics educator*
Wents, Doris Roberta *psychologist*

Compton
Drew, Sharon Lee *sociologist*

Corona Del Mar
Hinderaker, Ivan *political science educator*

Culver City
Friedland, David L. *industrial and organizational psychologist*
Maltzman, Irving Myron *psychology educator*

Davis
Cohen, Lawrence Edward *sociology educator, criminologist*
Cook, Roberta Lynn *agricultural economist, educator*
Ennis, Michael Patrick *psychologist, educator*
Goldstone, Jack Andrew *sociologist*
Groth, Alexander Jacob *political science educator*
Mason, William A(lvin) *psychologist, educator, researcher*
McHenry, Henry Malcolm *anthropologist, educator*
Musolf, Lloyd Daryl *political science educator, institute administrator*
Owings, Donald Henry *psychology educator*
Rodolfa, Emil Raymond *psychologist*
Rothchild, Donald Sylvester *political science educator*
Simonton, Dean Keith *psychology educator*
Skinner, G(eorge) William *anthropologist, educator*
Smith, Michael Peter *social science educator, researcher*
Spindler, George Dearborn *anthropologist, educator, writer, editor*
Sumner, Daniel Alan *economist, educator*
Tuma, Elias H. *economist, educator*

Del Mar
Boynton, Robert Merrill *retired psychology educator*

Encino
Nicolosi, Joseph *psychologist, writer, researcher*

Escondido
Damsbo, Ann Marie *psychologist*
Niehoff, Arthur Herman *anthropologist, writer*

Fairfield
Stevenson, James D(onald), Jr., *psychologist, counselor*

Fallbrook
Bryant, Don Estes *economist, scientist*

Foster City
Thomlinson, Ralph *demographer, educator*

Fremont
Feinberg, Richard Alan *clinical psychologist*
Nguyen, Sam (Van Nguyen) *economist, researcher*

Fresno
Dackawich, S. John *sociology educator*
Joseph, James William *political analyst*
O'Brien, John Conway *economist, educator, writer*
O'Connor, Kevin John *psychologist, educator*
van der Elst, Dirk Hendrik *cultural anthropologist, educator*

Fullerton
de Rios, Marlene Dobkin *medical anthropologist, educator*
†Elliott-Scheinberg, Wendy *history educator, genealogist*
Fleissig, Adrian R. *economics educator, consultant*
Hershey, Gerald Lee *psychologist, educator*
Kaisch, Kenneth Burton *psychologist, priest*

Glendale
Hadley, Paul Ervin *international relations educator*
Shahshahani, Ahmad *economics educator*

Glendora
Condiff, David Wesley *clinical psychologist*

Goleta
Frech, Harry Edward, III, *economics educator, consultant*
Zuk, Gerald Harvey *psychologist, consultant*

Granada Hills
Aller, Wayne Kendall *psychology educator, researcher, computer education company executive, property manager*

Granite Bay
Hartmann, Frederick Howard *political science educator emeritus*

Guerneville
†Mannino, J. Davis *psychologist, educator, author*

Hayward
Jun, Jong Sup *public administration educator*
Reevy-Manning, Gretchen Maria *psychology educator*

Healdsburg
Glad, Joan Bourne *retired clinical psychologist, educator*

Hemet
Levine, Elaine Prado *school psychologist, musician, artist*

Hermosa Beach
Wickwire, Patricia Joanne Nellor *psychologist, educator*

Highland
Miller, R. Warburton *psychologist, citrus farmer*

Hollywood
Fisher, Joel Marshall *political scientist, legal consultant, educator*
†Nyirenda, Vukani Gaskell *social sciences educator*

Huntington Beach
Martin, Wilfred Wesley Finny *psychologist, property owner and manager*

Inglewood
Kierulff, Stephen Charles *psychologist*

Irvine
Antonelli, G. Aldo *logic and philosophy of science educator*
Bean, Frank D(awson) *sociology and demography educator*
Bernal, Victoria *anthropologist, educator*
†Braunstein, Myron Lee *psychology educator*
Burton, Michael Ladd *anthropology educator*
Danziger, James Norris *political science educator*
DeSipio, Louis *political science educator*
†Ferguson, James *anthropologist, educator*
Freeman, Linton Clarke *sociology educator*
Gehricke, Jean-Guido *psychologist, researcher*
Greenberger, Ellen *psychologist, educator*
Huff, C(larence) Ronald *public policy and criminology educator*
†Lave, Charles Arthur *economics educator*
London, Ray William *consultant, mediator, arbitrator, researcher*
Luce, R(obert) Duncan *psychology educator*
Margolis, Julius *economist, educator*
Monroe, Kristen Renwick *political scientist, educator*
Schonfeld, William Rost *political science educator, researcher*
†Skyrms, Brian *social science educator*
Small, Kenneth Alan *economics educator*
Sperling, George *cognitive scientist, educator*
Treas, Judith Kay *sociology educator*
White, Douglas Richie *anthropology educator*

Kensington
Kolenda, Pauline M. *anthropology educator, researcher*

Kenwood
Podboy, John Watts *clinical, forensic psychologist*

La Habra
Lundberg, Lois Ann *political consultant, property manager executive*

La Jolla
Attiyeh, Richard Eugene *economics educator*
Cain, William Stanley *experimental psychologist, educator, researcher*
†Carson, Richard Taylor, Jr., *economics educator*
Coburn, Marjorie Foster *psychologist, educator*
Cowhey, Peter Francis *international relations educator, consultant*
†Crawford, Vincent Paul *economist, educator*
†Fantino, Edmund *psychology educator*
Farson, Richard Evans *psychologist*
Granger, Clive William John *economist, educator*
Harris, Philip Robert *management and space psychologist*
†Lambrou, Peter Thomas *psychologist*
Lane, Sylvia *economist, educator*
Machina, Mark Joseph *economist*
†Madsen, Richard Paul *sociology educator, writer*
Mandler, George *psychologist, educator*
Mandler, Jean Matter *psychologist, educator*
Phillips, David P. *sociologist, educator*
Pratt, George Janes, Jr., *psychologist, author*
†Sobel, Joel Kenneth *economist*
Spiro, Melford Elliot *anthropology educator*

Starr, Ross Marc *economist, educator*
Timmermann, Allan Gilling *economics educator*
Weiner, Ferne *psychologist*
White, Halbert Lynn, Jr., *economist, educator, consultant*
White, Michelle Jo *economics educator*

La Mirada
†Lingenfelter, Judith Elaine *social sciences educator*
Pike, Patricia Louise *psychology educator*

La Verne
Gelm, Richard Joseph *political scientist, educator*

Laguna Beach
Bent, Alan Edward *political science educator, administrator*
Dale, Leon Andrew *economist, educator*

Laguna Niguel
Freeland, Darryl Creighton *psychologist, educator*

Lake Arrowhead
Beckman, James Wallace Bim *economist, marketing executive, educator*

Lancaster
Ellsworth, Richard German *psychologist*

Larkspur
Saxton, Lloyd *psychologist, writer*

Long Beach
Fiebert, Martin Stephen *psychology educator, psychologist*
Kenigsberg, Martin Ira *psychologist*
†Lazarowitz, Arlene *social sciences educator*
†Quam-Wickham, Nancy Lynn *history educator*
Stevens, Tom Granville *psychologist, educator*

Los Altos
Carr, Jacquelyn B. *psychologist, educator*
Haines, Richard Foster *retired psychologist*

Los Angeles
Acosta, Frank Xavier *psychologist, educator*
†Albright, Julie Marie *sociologist, educator*
Allen, William Richard *retired economist*
Alvarez, Rodolfo *sociology educator, consultant*
Anawalt, Patricia Rieff *anthropologist, researcher*
Arnold, Jeanne Eloise *anthropologist, educator*
Bailey, Kenneth D. *sociology educator*
Bennett, Charles Franklin, Jr., *biogeographer, educator*
Browner, Carole Helen *anthropologist, educator*
Brubaker, William Rogers *sociology educator*
Burns, Marcelline *psychologist, researcher*
†Chambers, Mortimer Hardin, Jr., *retired history educator*
Champagne, Duane Willard *sociology educator*
Cheeseboro, Margrit *economics educator*
Clark, Burton Robert *sociologist, educator*
Clark, William Arthur V. *geographer, demographer*
Coombs, Robert Holman *behavioral scientist, medical educator, therapist, writer*
†Cosgrove, Denis Edmund *geographer, writer*
Currie, Janet M. *economics educator*
Dafter, Roger E. *psychologist*
†Darby, Michael Rucker *economist, educator*
Dawson, Adam *private investigator*
Dekmejian, Richard Hrair *political science educator*
Demsetz, Harold *economist, educator*
Edgerton, Robert Breckenridge *anthropologist, educator*
Ellickson, Bryan Carl *economics educator*
Forness, Steven Robert *educational psychologist*
†Frank, Gelya *anthropologist, educator*
Friedland, Lilli *psychologist, consultant*
Goldberg, Herb *psychologist, educator*
Goldschmidt, Walter Rochs *anthropologist, educator*
†Goldstein, Michael Saul *sociologist*
Greenberg, Ira Arthur *psychologist*
Griffiths, Barbara Lorraine *psychologist, marriage-family therapist, writer*
Harberger, Arnold Carl *economist, educator*
Hirsch, Werner Zvi *economist, educator*
†Hoskins, Janet Alison *anthropologist, film producer*
Intriligator, Michael David *economist, educator*
Kandal, Terry R. *sociology educator, consultant*
Klein, Benjamin *economics educator, consultant*
La Force, James Clayburn, Jr., *economist, educator*
Lapatin, Kenneth D.S. *archaeologist, art historian*
Leijonhufvud, Axel Stig Bengt *economics educator*
Lesser, Ian O. *foreign affairs expert*
Lowenthal, Abraham Frederic *international relations educator*
MacLeod, William Bentley *economics and law educator*
Maida, Carl Albert *anthropologist*
Malamuth, Neil Moshe *psychology and communication educator*
Maquet, Jacques Jerome Pierre *anthropologist, writer*
†Martinez, Dai'Quiriya S. *social studies educator*
Michael, William Burton *psychologist, educator*
Miller, Eric *neuropsychologist*
†Monkkonen, Eric H. *social sciences educator*
Montoya, Velma *economist, policy consultant*
Morgner, Aurelius *economist, educator*
Nelson, Howard Joseph *geographer, educator*
Nilles, John Mathias (Jack Nilles) *futurist*
Nixon, John Harmon *retired economist*
Noel, Hans Christopher *political scientist*
Odell, John Stephen *political scientist*
Orme, Antony Ronald *geography educator*
†Powell, Wonda A. *social studies educator, writer*

Raven, Bertram H(erbert) *psychology educator*
Renteln, Alison Dundes *political science educator*
†Roy, William Glenn *sociology educator*
Sandler, Todd Michael *economist, educator, political scientist, educator*
Sapra, Sunil K. *economics educator*
Sears, David O'Keefe *psychology educator*
Seeman, Melvin *sociologist, educator*
Shieh, John Ting-chung *economics educator*
Shneidman, Edwin S. *psychologist, educator, thanatologist, suicidologist*
Sklar, Richard Lawrence *political science educator*
Squire, Molly Ann *organizational psychologist*
Strack, Stephen Naylor *psychologist*
Thompson, Earl Albert *economics educator*
Thompson, Richard Frederick *psychologist, neuroscientist, educator*
Totten, George Oakley, III, *political science educator*
Turner, Ralph Herbert *sociologist, educator*
Watson, Sharon Gitin *psychologist, executive*
Wittrock, Merlin Carl *educational psychologist*
Wong, James Bok *economist, engineer, technologist*
Wong-McDonald, Ana *psychologist*
Zeitlin, Maurice *sociology educator, writer*
Zucker, Lynne Goodman *sociology educator, consultant*

Los Gatos
Lee, Alfred Theodore *research psychologist*

Madera
Glynn, James A. *sociology educator, author*

Malibu
Lloyd, Robert Baldwin *political science educator*
Monsma, Stephen Vos *political scientist, educator*
Smith, David Matthew *economist, educator*

Mendocino
†Bilas, Richard A. *economist*

Menlo Park
Clair, Theodore Nat *educational psychologist*
Keeley, Michael Clark *economist*
Lindzey, Gardner *psychologist, educator*
†Tiet, Quyen Q. *clinical psychologist, researcher*
Vane, Sylvia Brakke *anthropologist, publisher, cultural resource management company executive, writer*

Mill Valley
Harner, Michael James *anthropologist, educator, author*

Modesto
Berry, John Charles *clinical psychologist, educational administrator*

Moffett Field
†Bernhard, Roberta *research psychologist*
Cohen, Malcolm Martin *psychologist, researcher*

Monrovia
†Miller, Karen *clinical psychologist, neuropsychologist*

Monteca
Hoffmann, James Vernon, Jr., *social studies educator, writer*

Monterey
Boger, Dan Calvin *statistical and economic consultant, educator*
Caldwell, Joni *psychology and women's studies educator, small business owner*
Mehrabian, Albert *psychology educator, author, researcher*
Reese, William Albert, III, *psychologist, clinical neuropsychologist*

Moraga
Meisch, Lynn Ann *anthropologist, educator*

Newport Beach
Becker, Juliette *psychologist, marriage and family therapist*
Lawson, Thomas Cheney *fraud examiner*
Whittemore, Paul Baxter *psychologist*

Northridge
Harwick, Betty Corinne Burns *sociology educator*
Mitchell, Rie Rogers *psychologist, counselor, educator*
Reagan, Janet Thompson *psychologist, educator*

Novato
Bugental, James Frederick Thomas *retired psychologist, educator*

Oakland
Anderson, Robert Thomas *anthropologist, researcher, physician*
Delmain, Fred *industrial psychologist*
De Vos, George Alphonse *psychologist, anthropologist*
Farrell, Kenneth Royden *economist*
Nebelkopf, Ethan *psychologist*
Neeley, Beverly Evon *sociologist, consultant*
Potter, Beverly Ann *management psychologist, consultant, publisher*
Vaux, Henry James, Jr., *economics educator*

Oceanside
Hertweck, E. Romayne *psychology educator*

Orange
Blaser, Arthur Weston *political science educator, writer*
Booth, Donald Richard *economist, educator*

Orinda
Amoroso, Richard Louis *cosmologist, educator*

Pacific Palisades
Hoffenberg, Marvin *retired political science educator, consultant*
Katz, George Gershon *psychologist*
Longaker, Richard Pancoast *political science educator emeritus*

Palo Alto
Beutler, Larry Edward *psychology educator*
Brown, H. William *urban economist, private banker*
Calvin, Allen David *psychologist, educator*
†Castro, Cynthia M *clinical psychologist, researcher*
Flanagan, Robert Joseph *economics educator*
Hahn, Gordon Martin *political scientist, writer*
Hammett, Benjamin Cowles *psychologist*
Moos, Rudolf H. *psychologist, researcher*
Rosaldo, Renato Ignacio, Jr., *cultural anthropology educator*
Scitovsky, Anne Aickelin *economist, researcher*
Tart, Charles Theodore *psychologist, educator*

Palos Verdes Estates
Loether, Herman John *sociologist, educator*

Pasadena
Bjorck, Jeffrey Paul *psychology educator, clinical psychologist*
Davis, Lance Edwin *economics educator*
Grether, David Maclay *economics educator*
Horner, Althea Jane *psychologist*
Ledyard, John Odell *economics educator, consultant*
Scudder, Thayer *anthropologist, educator*

Paso Robles
Rocha, Marilyn Eva *retired clinical psychologist*

Placentia
Gobar, Alfred Julian *retired economic consultant, educator*

Pleasant Hill
Richard, Robert Carter *psychologist*

Pomona
Garrity, Rodman Fox *psychologist, educator*
McClelland, Harold Franklin *economics educator*
Singer-Chang, Gail Leslie *social sciences educator, dean*

Portola Valley
Ward, Robert Edward *retired political science educator and university administrator*

Rancho Mirage
Lacey, John Irving *psychologist, physiologist, educator*

Rancho Santa Margarita
Aguilera, Donna Conant *psychologist, researcher*

Redding
Drake, Patricia Evelyn *psychologist*

Redondo Beach
Naples, Caesar Joseph *law and public policy educator, lawyer, consultant*

Riverside
Adrian, Charles Raymond *political science educator*
Carpenter, Mark Warren *social sciences educator*
Griffin, Keith Broadwell *economics educator*
Petrinovich, Lewis Franklin *psychology educator*
Rosenthal, Robert *psychology educator*
Taylor, R. Ervin, Jr., *archaeologist*
Turk, Austin Theodore *sociology educator*

Rohnert Park
†Brassington, Glenn Sidney *psychologist, educator*
Byrne, Noel Thomas *sociologist, educator*
Criswell, Eleanor Camp *psychologist*
Ochoa, Eduardo Martin *economics educator*
Phillips, Peter Martin *sociologist, educator, media researcher*
†Rosin, R. Thomas *anthropologist, educator*

Rolling Hills Estates
Castor, Wilbur Wright *futurist, writer, consultant, playwright, actor*

Sacramento
†Behrman, Bruce Ward *social sciences educator*
Bennett, Lawrence Allen *psychologist, criminal justice researcher*
Boylan, Richard John *psychologist, psychotherapist, researcher, anthropologist, educator*
Bruce, Thomas Edward *psychology educator, thanatologist*
Gibson, Patrice Vandegrift *anthropologist, educator*
Harris, Wilson *psychiatrist, research scientist*
†Kawamoto, Walter *family life educator, consultant*
Majesty, Melvin Sidney *psychologist, consultant*
Newland, Chester Albert *public administration educator*
Post, August Alan *economist, artist*
Sherwood, Robert Petersen *retired sociology educator*
Wassmer, Robert William *economics educator*
†Yang, Yung Y. *economics educator, consultant*

San Bernardino
†Fenelon, James V. *sociologist, educator, poet, advocate*
Maul, Terry Lee *psychologist, educator*
Turpin, Joseph Ovila *counselor, educator*

San Carlos
Hoffman, Paul Jerome *psychologist, statistician*

San Diego
Bales, Robert Freed *social psychologist, educator*
†Besada, Hany Gamil *international affairs administrator, researcher*
Blade, Melinda Kim *archaeologist, educator, researcher*
Callahan, LeeAnn Lucille *psychologist*
Edwards, Darrel *psychologist*
Emerick, Robert Earl *sociologist, educator*
†Gamble, Lynn Hunter *anthropologist, educator*
Gazell, James Albert *public administration educator*
Getis, Arthur *geography educator*
Grossbard-Shechtman, Amyra *economist, educator, researcher*
Hamilton, James Douglas *economics educator*
†Heer, David Macalpine *sociology educator*
Hoston, Germaine Annette *political science educator*
Kiesler, Charles Adolphus *psychologist, academic administrator*
Lewis, Shirley Jeane *psychotherapist, educator*
Madhavan, Murugappa Chettiar *economics educator, international consultant*
McKeown, Michael Eugene *psychologist, consultant*
Nagao, Norris Sadato *educator, consultant*
†Ojeda, Norma *social sciences educator, researcher*
Pryde, Philip Rust *retired geography educator*
†Shedroff, Sharon D. *psychologist, researcher, anthropologist, consultant*
Stoessinger, John George *political science educator*
Storer, Norman William *sociologist, educator*
Sutton, L. Paul *criminal justice educator*
Trembley, Mark Michel *geographer, educator*
†Van Kirk, Jaye Frances *psychology educator*
Vaughn, Billy Eldridge *psychology educator, publisher*
Weeks, John Robert *geographer, sociology educator*

San Francisco
Adler, Nancy Elinor *psychologist, educator*
Butz, Otto William *political science educator*
Chou, Erwin C. *economist*
Cirese, Robert Charles *economist, real estate investment counselor*
Elias, Robert Alan *political science educator*
Estes, Carroll Lynn *sociologist, educator*
Fox, Patrick John *sociology educator*
Gemello, John Michael *economics educator, consultant, academic administrator*
Hawthorne, Mark R. *investigator, educator*
Hudson, Darril *political scientist, educator*
Kalicki, Jan H. *economist, political scientist*
Kloos, Helmut *geographer*
Krippner, Stanley Curtis *psychologist*
†Liu, Samuel T. *economist, consultant*
†Luft, Harold S. *health economist*
Marston, Michael *urban economist, asset management executive*
†Mattimore, Patrick *social sciences educator*
†Porter, Dorothy Elizabeth *history educator*
Rather, Lee *psychologist, educator*
Rice, Dorothy Pechman (Mrs. John Donald Rice) *medical economist*
Rubin, Seth Isaiah *psychologist*
†Rudebusch, Glenn D. *economist*
Schneider, Kirk J. *psychologist, writer*
Sedway, Lynn Massel *real estate economist*
Smith, Robert Charles *political science educator, researcher*
Soh, Chunghee Sarah *anthropology educator*
†van den Daele, Leland Douglas *psychology educator, psychological measurement company executive*
Warner, Rollin Miles, Jr., *economics educator, real estate broker*
Woo, Chi-Keung *energy economist, consultant*

San Gabriel
Chan, Daniel Siu-Kwong *psychologist*

San Jose
Cedolini, Anthony John *psychologist*
McDowell, Jennifer *sociologist, composer, playwright, publisher*
Van Selst, Mark G(ordon) A(egid) *psychology educator, researcher*
Voth, Alden H. *political science educator*

San Luis Obispo
Culbertson, James Thomas *psychologist*
Fairbanks II, William Louis *anthropologist, educator*
Geringer, John Michael *economist, educator*

San Rafael
Hanson, Rick *psychologist*
†Hoyt, Michael F. *psychologist, writer*
Tosti, Donald Thomas *psychologist, consultant*

Santa Barbara
Aigner, Dennis John *economics educator, consultant*
†Baker, Gordon Edward *political science educator*
Bohn, Henning *economist, educator*
Comanor, William S. *economist, educator*
Davidson, Roger H(arry) *political scientist, educator*
Erasmus, Charles John *anthropologist, educator*
Ford, Anabel *research anthropologist, archaeologist*
Gravitz, Herbert L. *clinical psychologist, writer*
Jochim, Michael Allan *archaeologist*
Kelliher, Richard James *psychologist*
Kendler, Howard H(arvard) *psychologist, educator*
Mack, Judith Cole Schrim *political scientist, educator*

Mayer, Richard Edwin *psychology educator*
†Pointer, Richard Wayne *history educator*
Robinson, William I. *sociologist, journalist*
Scheff, Thomas Joel *sociologist, educator*
Sengupta, Jati Kumar *economics educator*
Sherman, Alan Robert *psychologist, educator*
Steigerwald, Douglas Gardiner *economics educator*

Santa Clara
Field, Alexander James *economics educator*
Plante, Thomas Gerard *psychologist*

Santa Cruz
Bridgeman, Bruce *psychobiology educator*
Chinn, Menzie David *economics educator*
Crosby, Faye Jacqueline *psychology educator, author*
Crow, Ben *sociologist, educator*
†Males, Michael Arnold *sociologist, educator, writer, consultant*
Pettigrew, Thomas Fraser *social psychologist, educator*
Roby, Pamela Ann *sociology educator*
Smith, M(ahlon) Brewster *psychologist, educator*
Tharp, Roland George *psychology, education educator*

Santa Monica
Dreyfus, Edward A. *psychologist*
Falender-Zohn, Carol Ann *psychologist*
Russell, Marlou *psychologist*
Smith, James Patrick *economist*
Veit, Clairice Gene Tipton *measurement psychologist*
Wolf, Charles, Jr., *economist, educator*
Zimmerman, Bill *political consultant*

Saratoga
Baratta-Lorton, Robert *economics educator*
Levy, Ruth J. *clinical psychologist, consultant*
Thelin, Peter Carl *economist, educator*

Sausalito
Klingensmith, Arthur Paul *industrial and organizational psychologist, consultant*

Seaside
†Mendoza, Ruben G. *anthropologist, educator, archaeologist*

Sherman Oaks
Gross, Sharon Ruth *forensic psychologist, researcher*
Weinstein, Charles David *psychologist*

Soledad
Zika, Bill *psychologist*

Somerset
Carr, Les *psychologist, educator*

Somis
Premack, David *psychologist*

Sonora
Clarke, Paula Katherine *anthropology educator, sociology educator*

Stanford
†Amemiya, Takeshi *economist, statistician*
Anderson, Martin Carl *economist*
Arrow, Kenneth Joseph *economist, educator*
Bandura, Albert *psychologist, educator*
Befu, Harumi *anthropology educator*
Brody, Richard Alan *political science educator, researcher*
†Bueno de Mesquita, Bruce James *political science educator*
Bunzel, John Harvey *political science educator, researcher*
Carlsmith, James Merrill *psychologist, educator*
Damon, William Van Buren *developmental psychologist, educator, writer*
Enthoven, Alain Charles *economist, educator*
Friedman, Milton *economist, educator*
Fuchs, Victor Robert *economist, educator*
Gage, Nathaniel Lees *psychologist, educator*
George, Alexander Lawrence *political scientist, educator*
Hall, Robert Ernest *economics educator*
Hickman, Bert George, Jr., *economist, educator*
Howell, James Edwin *economist, educator*
Huntington, Hillard Griswold *economist*
Inkeles, Alex *sociology educator*
Johnston, Bruce Foster *economics educator*
†Klein, Richard G. *anthropologist, educator*
Krumboltz, John Dwight *psychologist, educator*
Kurz, Mordecai *economics educator*
Laitin, David Dennis *political science educator*
Lau, Lawrence Juen-Yee *economics educator, consultant*
Lazear, Edward Paul *economics and labor relations educator, researcher*
Lewis, John Wilson *political science educator*
Maccoby, Eleanor Emmons *psychology educator*
March, James Gardner *social scientist, educator*
Mc Lure, Charles E., Jr., *economist, consultant*
Noll, Roger Gordon *economist, educator*
†Padilla, Amado M. *psychologist, adult education educator*
Ricardo-Campbell, Rita *economist, educator*
Roberts, Donald John *economics and business educator, consultant*
†Scott, W. Richard *sociologist, educator, retired sociologist*
Scott, W(illiam) Richard *sociology educator*
Van Horne, James Carter *economist, educator*
Zimbardo, Philip George *psychologist, educator, writer*

Stockton
Werner, Roger Harry *archaeologist*

Studio City
Howard, Stephen James *clinical psychologist*

Sylmar
Yguado, Alex Rocco *economics educator*

Thousand Oaks
Uellendahl, Gail Elizabeth *psychologist*
Woolley, J(onathan) Michael *health economist, economic consultant*

Trabuco Canyon
Addy, Jo Alison Phears *economist*

Turlock
Ahlem, Lloyd Harold *psychologist*

Van Nuys
Solomon, Rhonda Hope *school and educational psychologist*

Ventura
Bowles, Walter Donald *economist, educator*
Lipinski, Barbara Janina *psychologist, psychotherapist, educator, writer*
Naurath, David Allison *engineering psychologist, researcher*

Victorville
Dilliard, Maxine K. *retired school psychologist*

Visalia
Daniels, Madeline Marie *forensic psychologist, educator, author*

Walnut Creek
Keith, Bruce Edgar *political analyst, genealogist*

Weed
Ryan, Daberath *chemistry educator*

Woodland Hills
Holland, Kathleen *political science educator*
Nierenberg, Norman *urban land economist, retired state official*
Pohl, John Martin DeLand *archaeologist*

COLORADO

Arvada
Yamamoto, Kaoru *retired psychology and education educator*

Aspen
Manosevitz, Martin *psychologist*

Boulder
Adler, Patricia Ann *sociologist, educator*
Beer, Francis Anthony *political science educator*
Borysenko, Joan *psychologist, biologist*
Bourne, Lyle Eugene, Jr., *psychology educator*
Greenberg, Edward Seymour *political science educator, writer*
Healy, Alice Fenvessy *psychology educator, researcher*
Jessor, Richard *psychologist, educator*
Kilmer, Eve Ann *psychologist*
Kintsch, Walter *psychology educator, director*
Menken, Jane Ava *demographer, educator*
†Owen-Riesch, Anna Lou *economics and history educator*
†Shankman, Paul Andrew *anthropologist, educator*
Walker, Deward Edgar, Jr., *anthropologist, educator*
White, Gilbert F(owler) *geographer, educator*
Zax, Jeffrey Stephen *economist, educator*

Broomfield
†Hoffman, Marilyn Kay *psychologist*

Castle Rock
Gehlmann, Sheila Cathleen *psychologist, research analyst*

Centennial
Milliken, John Gordon *research economist*

Clifton
Hall, L. Michael *psychologist, writer*

Colorado Springs
Adams, Tucker Hart *economic research company executive*
Brooks, Glenn Ellis *political science educator, educational administrator*
Standing Bear, Zugguelgeres Galafach *criminologist, forensic scientist, educator*

Denver
Adelman, Jonathan Reuben *political science educator, consultant*
†Britz, John Dominic, II, *political scientist, consultant*
Conger, John Janeway *psychologist, educator*
Laird, Frank N. *political science educator*
Lefly, Dianne Louise *research psychologist*
Mendelsohn, Harold *sociologist, educator*
Moeller, Richard Robert *political science educator*
Moody, Eric John *psychologist, researcher*
Nelson, Sarah Milledge *archaeology educator*
Purcell, Kenneth *psychology educator, university dean*
Snyder, Charles Royce *sociologist, educator*
Zimet, Carl Norman *psychologist, educator*

Durango
Zeller, Christopher Lee *archaeologist, preservationist*

Englewood
Bayes, Marjorie Andress *psychologist*
Haupenthal, Laura Ann *clinical psychologist*

Estes Park
Moore, Omar Khayyam *experimental sociologist*

Fort Collins
Bennett, Jacqueline Beekman *school psychologist*
Bennett, Thomas LeRoy, Jr., *clinical neuropsychology educator*
Eitzen, David Stanley *sociologist, educator*
Held, Royer Burnell *economics educator*
Marvel, M. Kim *psychologist, researcher*
†Moorcroft, William Herbert *retired bio-psychologist, educator, researcher*
Ozawa, Terutomo *economics educator, consultant*
Suinn, Richard Michael *psychologist*
Weiler, Stephan *economist, educator*

Golden
Moore, Michal Charles *land economist, educator*
Petrick, Alfred, Jr., *mineral economics educator, consultant*
Wellisch, William Jeremiah *social psychology educator*

Grand Junction
Bacon, Phillip *geographer, author, consultant*

Greeley
Kelsey, Michael Loyal *geography educator*
Moore, Melanie *sociology educator*
†Woody, William Douglas *social sciences educator, researcher*

Greenwood Village
Hendrick, Hal Wilmans *human factors educator*

Lafayette
Conrad, Kelley Allen *industrial and organizational psychologist*

Lakewood
Kulkarni, Kishore Ganesh *economics educator, consultant*
Lipson, Jonathan Mark *psychologist*
O'Brien, Kathleen Ann *economist*

Littleton
Cabell, Elizabeth Arlisse *psychologist*
Lohman, Loretta Cecelia *social scientist, consultant*

Nederland
Sutton, Philip D(ietrich) *psychologist, educator*

Pine
Jones, David Milton *economist, educator*

Pueblo
†Keller, Robert L. *sociologist, educator*
Kulkosky, Paul Joseph *psychology educator*
Mo, Suchoon *psychology educator*
Vega, Jose Guadalupe *neuropsychologist, clinical professional*

Silverthorne
Nobe, Kenneth Charles *international agricultural and water resource economics consultant*

CONNECTICUT

Barkhamsted
†Stokes, Susan *political science educator*

Bloomfield
Scheuch, Richard *economist, educator*

Branford
Frase, Lawrence Thomas *psychologist, science administrator*
Glick, Marion Shepherd *psychology, educator*

Bridgeport
†Gerber, Frances Joyce *early childhood educator*
†Maloney, Maureen Murphy *social sciences educator*
Salzman, Beverly E. *behavioral and social sciences educator, consultant*

Chester
Feldmann, Shirley Clark *psychology educator*

Cornwall Bridge
Leich, John Foster *political scientist, European languages educator*

Danbury
Kuther, Tara L. *psychology educator*
Tolor, Alexander *psychologist, educator*

East Hartford
Banas, Richard Frederick *geographer*

Fairfield
Kleine, Herman *economist*
Timmermann, Sandra *educational gerontologist, communication specialist*

Greenwich
Clark, Harry Warren *public policy consultant*

Guilford
Chatt, Allen Barrett *psychologist, neuroscientist*

Hamden
Pisani, Lawrence Frank *sociology educator*

Hartford
Behuniak, Peter *psychometrician, educational psychologist, educational consultant*
Curran, Ward Schenk *economist, educator*
Giannaros, Demetrios Spiros *economist, educator, politician*
Gunderson, Gerald Axel *economics educator, administrator*
Naples, Nancy A. *sociology and women's studies educator*
Robison, Julie Thompson *gerontologist, educator*

Higganum
de Brigard, Emilie *anthropologist, consultant*

Mansfield
Katz, Leonard *psychology educator*

Middlebury
Phillips, Walter Mills, III, *psychologist, educator*

Middletown
Barber, William Joseph *educator, economist*
Blume, Ginger (Elaine Blume) *psychologist*
Cline, John Carroll *clinical psychologist*
Miller, Richard Alan *economist, educator*
Scheibe, Karl Edward *psychology educator*
Wasch, William Karl *gerontologist, contractor*
Yohe, Gary Wynn *economics educator*

Milford
Haigh, Charles *criminal justice educator*
Taylor, Charles Henry *psychoanalyst, educator*

Naugatuck
Suscovich, David J. *neuropsychologist, marriage and family therapist*

New Britain
†Foster, Walton Brown *political science educator*
Mitrano, John R. *sociology educator*

New Canaan
Marcus, Edward *economist, educator*
Thomas, Marianne Gregory *school psychologist*

New Haven
Bell, Wendell *sociologist, educator, futurist*
Blatt, Sidney Jules *psychology educator and investigator, psychoanalyst*
Brainard, William Crittenden *economist, educator, university official*
Brantl, Sister Charlesmarie *economics educator*
Brownell, Kelly David *psychologist, educator*
Coe, Michael Douglas *anthropologist, educator*
Conklin, Harold Colyer *anthropologist, educator*
Crakes, Gary Michael *economics educator*
†Dudley, Kathryn Marie *anthropology and American studies educator*
Ember, Carol R. *anthropology educator, author*
Ember, Melvin Lawrence *anthropologist, educator*
Erikson, Kai *sociologist, educator*
Evenson, Robert Eugene *economist, educator*
Hoge, Michael Alan *psychologist*
†Jackson, Shirley Ann *sociology educator*
†Kaufman, Alan Stephen *psychologist, educator*
Kazdin, Alan E. *psychology educator*
LaPalombara, Joseph *political science and industrial management educator*
MacAvoy, Paul Webster *economics, management educator, university dean*
Marks, Lawrence Edward *psychologist, educator*
†Marmor, Theodore Richard *political science and public management educator*
Mayhew, David Raymond *political science educator*
McGuire, William James *social psychology educator*
†Mindell, Constance *social studies educator*
†Mostaghimi, Mehdi *economist, educator*
†Nelson, Alondra R. *social sciences educator*
Peck, Merton Joseph *economist, educator*
Phillips, Peter Charles Bonest *economist, educator, researcher*
Pospisil, Leopold Jaroslav *anthropology and law educator*
Ranis, Gustav *economist, educator*
Reynolds, Lloyd George *economist, educator*
Rouse, Irving *anthropologist, emeritus educator*
Russett, Bruce Martin *political science educator*
Scarf, Herbert Eli *economics educator*
Schultz, T. Paul *economics educator*
†Shahar, Golan *psychologist, researcher, psychotherapist*
Shapiro, Ian *political science educator*
Shubik, Martin *economics educator*
†Sternberg, Robert Jeffrey *psychology educator, researcher*
Stevens, Joseph Charles *psychology educator*
Sutterlin, James Smyrl *political science educator, researcher*
Wallerstein, Immanuel *sociologist*
Westerfield, Holt Bradford *political scientist, educator*
Yeager, Catherine Anne *research psychologist*
†Zigler, Edward Frank *psychologist, educator*

New London
Winter, Jerry Alan *sociology educator*

New Milford
Tower, Roni Beth *psychologist*

North Grosvenordale
Murphy, Kathleen Jane *psychologist, educator*

North Haven
Dahl, Robert Alan *political science educator*
Mahl, George Franklin *psychoanalyst, psychologist, educator*

Old Lyme
Johnson, James Myron *psychologist, educator*

Putnam
†Osgood-Lemay, Sheri *child protective investigator, psychologist*

Ridgefield
Stoddard, William Bert, Jr., *economist*

Sharon
Mesniaeff, Gregory *economist, securities analyst*

South Windsor
Saakvitne, Karen Winslow *psychologist*

Southbury
Atwood, Edward Charles *economist, educator*

Stamford
Grossman, Sanford Jay *economics educator*
Robins, Robert Sidwar *political science educator, administrator*
Teeters, Nancy Hays *economist, director*

Storrs
†Langlois, Richard Normand *economist, educator*

Storrs Mansfield
Britner, Preston Arthur, IV, *developmental psychologist, educator*
Dewar, Robert Earl, Jr., *anthropologist, educator*
Dussart, Francoise *anthropologist, educator*
Miller, Thomas William *psychologist*
Reiter, Howard Lee *political scientist, educator*
Sazama, Gerald Walter *economist, educator*

Voluntown
Thevenet, Patricia Confrey *social studies educator*

Waterbury
†Jacobs, Timothy Lester *sociologist, educator, genealogist*

West Hartford
Farnen, Russell Francis *political scientist, educator*
Panik, Michael Joseph *economics educator*

Westport
Losen, Stuart Melvin *clinical psychologist*

Willimantic
Danforth, Jeffrey Scott *psychologist, educator*
Mann, Prem Singh *economics educator*
†Nilsson, Andrew Thorpe *social sciences educator*

DELAWARE

Camden Wyoming
Porterfield, Craig Allen *psychologist, consultant*

Dover
Hoff, Samuel Boyer *political science educator*

Lewes
Chapman, Janet Carter Goodrich (Mrs. John William Chapman) *economist, educator*

Millsboro
Tennov, Dorothy *psychologist*

Newark
Abrams, Burton A. *economics educator*
Bilinsky, Yaroslav *political scientist*
Brams, Marvin Robert *economist, mental health counselor, interfaith minister*
Bunkše, Edmunds Valdemārs *geographer, educator, consultant*
DiRenzo, Gordon James *sociologist, psychologist, educator*
†Garland, Howard *psychology educator*
Graham, Frances Keesler (Mrs. David Tredway Graham) *psychologist, educator*
Gulick, Walter Lawrence *psychologist, former college president*
Koford, Kenneth John *economics educator*
Mangone, Gerard J. *international and maritime law educator*
Palley, Marian Lief *political science educator, author*
Raffel, Jeffrey Allen *urban affairs educator*
Tannian, Francis Xavier *economist, educator*
†Wilgen, Julie Mapes *family studies educator*
Zuckerman, Marvin *psychologist*

Wilmington
Kneavel, Thomas Charles, Jr., *psychologist, educator*

DISTRICT OF COLUMBIA

Washington
Aaron, Henry Jacob *economics educator*
Abler, Ronald Francis *geography educator*
Agee, Eve *anthropologist*
Alagappa, Muthiah *international politics researcher*
Albanese, Jay Samuel *criminologist, educator*
Allen, Catherine Jean *anthropologist, educator*
An, Mark Yuying *economist*
Arend, Anthony Clark *international relations educator*
†Arias, Omar S. *economist*
Aschheim, Joseph *economist, educator*
Ashbrook, Arthur Garwood, Jr., *economist, educator*
Åslund, Anders *economist*
†Axtell, Robert Lea *economist*
Ayittey, George Billy Nii *economics educator, consultant, researcher*
Baer, Michael Alan *political scientist, educator*
†Baker, Pauline Halpern *political scientist, policy analyst*
Bartlett, Bruce Reeves *economist, columnist*
Barton, Jean Marie *psychologist, educator*
Becker, Mary Louise *political scientist*
Belinfante, Alexander Erik Ernst *economist, statistician*
Bergmann, Barbara Rose *economics educator*
Besen, Stanley Martin *economist*
Bhattacharya, Rina *economist*
Blair, Margaret Mendenhall *research economist, consultant, law educator*
Bloch, Farrell Edward *economist, writer*
Bluth, B. J. (Elizabeth Jean Catherine Bluth) *sociologist, aerospace technologist*
Bolino, August Constantino *economics educator*

Boughton, James Murray *economist*
Brimmer, Andrew Felton *economic and financial consultant*
Broad, Robin *political economist, educator, researcher*
Bruck, Nicholas *economist, educator*
Brzezinski, Zbigniew *political science educator, author*
Buckberg, Albert *retired economist*
†Buist, Henry *economist*
Burtless, Gary Thomas *economist, consultant*
Calder, Kent Eyring *political science educator, diplomat*
Caldwell, Willard E. *psychologist, educator*
†Canagarajah, R. Sudharshan *economist*
Carliner, Michael Simon *economist, association executive*
Carpenter, Ted Galen *political scientist*
†Carro, Cecilia *political scientist, researcher*
†Chang, Won *economist*
Checchi, Vincent Victor *economist*
Chollet, Deborah *economist, educator*
Choudhury, Raj Deo *business development manager*
Cline, William Richard *economist, educator*
†Cole, Daniel Gerard *geographer, information scientist, cartographer*
Collins, Eileen Louise *economist*
Corbet, Richard Hugh *trade policy specialist, writer*
†Cordella, Tito *economist*
Craig, John Tucker *economist, consultant*
Crocker, William Henry *ethnologist, researcher*
Crowe, William James, Jr., *educator, international consultant*
Danziger, Raphael *political scientist, researcher*
†Davis, Shelton Harold *sociologist, educator*
†Day, Lincoln Hubert *demographer, educator*
Dillon, Wilton Sterling *anthropologist, foundation administrator*
Dizard, Wilson Paul, Jr., *international affairs consultant, educator*
Downs, Anthony *urban economist, real estate consultant*
Eads, George Curtis *economic consultant*
†Eberstadt, Nicholas Nash *social sciences educator, researcher*
Ehrenreich, Robert Marc *archaeologist, materials scientist, museum administrator*
†English, Richard Allyn *sociologist, social work educator*
†Ericsson, Neil R. *economist, consultant*
Ershler, William Baldwin *biogerontologist, educator*
Etzioni, Amitai *sociologist, educator*
Fajors, Nique *policy advisor*
Farrow, Robert Scott *economist, educator*
Faux, Jeff (Geoffrey Peter Faux) *economist, writer*
Feshbach, Murray *demographer, educator*
Feuer, Marvin C. *political scientist, educator*
Fisher, Sylvia Kay *psychologist, researcher, consultant*
Flattau, Pamela Ebert *research psychologist, consultant*
Fowler, Raymond Dalton *psychologist, educator*
Franco, Robert *economist*
Frank, Isaiah *economist, educator*
Fratzscher, Oliver *economist*
†Froehle, Bryan Thomas *sociologist, director*
†Fukuyama, Francis *political scientist, educator*
Gallo, Anthony Ernest *playwright, economist*
Gelos, R. Gaston *economist*
Gernert, Jeffrey Jared *clinical psychologist*
Gillingham, Robert Fenton *economist, consultant*
Godson, Roy Simon *political scientist, think tank executive*
Gonzalez-Hermosillo, Brenda *economist, researcher*
Goode, Richard Benjamin *economist, educator*
†Goodman, William Charles *economist, playwright*
Gordon, Lincoln *political economist*
Grapin, Jacqueline G. *economist*
Gravelle, Jane Gibson *economist*
Greenberg, Milton *political scientist, educator*
Gubser, Peter Anton *political scientist, writer, educator*
†Haaga, John Gregory *demographer*
Hall, George Robert *economist*
Halperin, Morton H. *political scientist*
Harper, Robert Allan *retired consulting psychologist*
Harrison, Glennon Joseph *economist*
Hawkins, Monica Spann *environmental health scientist*
Helms, Robert Brake *economist, research director*
Heravi, Mehdi *economist*
Hess, Stephen *political scientist, author*
Hollerbach, Paula Elizabeth *demographer, researcher*
Honohan, Patrick *economist*
Hudson, Michael Craig *political science educator*
Hufbauer, Gary Clyde *lawyer*
Hughes, Kent Higgon *economist*
Jacobson, Allen Howard *economist*
Jaspersen, Frederick Zarr *economist*
Jimenez, Emmanuel *economist*
Johnson, Robert Henry *political science educator*
Jones, William Bowdoin *political scientist, retired diplomat, lawyer*
Joyner, Christopher Clayton *international relations educator*
Juan-Ramon, V. Hugo *economist*
†Kandil, Magda ElSayed *economist*
Kane, Michael Barry *social science research executive*
Kazmierczak, Matthew *economist, researcher*
Kemp, Geoffrey Thomas Howard *international affairs specialist*
Kendrick, John Whitefield *economist, educator, consultant*
Kennedy, Muriel *psychologist, consultant, educator*
†Kenny, Charles James *economist, researcher*

†Kilpatrick, Henry Edward *economist, educator*
Kirkpatrick, Jeane Duane Jordan *political scientist, government official*
Korologos, Tom Chris *government affairs consultant, former federal official*
Krueger, Anne O. *economist*
Krulfeld, Ruth Marilyn *anthropologist, educator*
Kuh, Charlotte Virginia *economist*
Kybal, Elba Gómez del Rey *economist, non-profit organization executive*
Laden, Ben Ellis *economist, writer*
Lardy, Nicholas Richard *economist, educator*
LeoGrande, William Mark *political science educator, writer*
Lerman, Allen H. *economist*
Liebenson, Herbert *economist, trade association executive*
Lieber, Robert James *political science educator, writer*
Littig, Lawrence William *psychologist, educator*
Lopez Calix, Jose Roberto *economist*
Madian, Alan Leonard *economist, management consultant*
Makalou, Oumar *economic advisor*
Manchester, Paul Brunson *economist*
Mann, Thomas Edward *political scientist*
Marcuss, Rosemary Daly *economist*
Martin, William J. *economist*
Martinez, Herminia S. *economist, banker*
Maudlin, Robert V. *economics and government affairs consultant*
McGinnies, Elliott Morse *psychologist, educator*
Meggers, Betty J(ane) *anthropologist, researcher*
Melanson, Richard Allen *political science educator*
Mellor, John Williams *economist, policy consultant firm executive*
Mendis, Patrick *economist, geographer, educator*
Metz, Helen Chapin *retired Middle East analyst*
Millar, James Robert *economist, educator, university official*
Miller, David Christopher *psychologist, researcher*
Miller, James Clifford, III, *economist*
Miller, Margery Silberman *psychologist, speech pathologist, medical educator and administrator*
†Mistral, Jacques *economist*
Moon, Marilyn Lee *economist*
Morgan, Bruce Ray *international consultant*
Morris, Cynthia Taft *economics educator*
Muldrow, Tressie Wright *psychologist*
†Muller, Steven *international studies educator, academic administrator*
Nagorski, Zygmunt *political scientist, writer*
Nakhleh, Emile A. *political science educator*
Nash, John Davidson, Jr., *economist*
Nelsen, Hart Michael *sociologist, educator*
Nelson, Candice Jean *political science educator*
Newman, Monroe *retired economist, educator*
Niskanen, William Arthur, Jr., *economist, think-tank executive*
Noland, Marcus *economist, educator*
O'Connor, Karen *political science educator, researcher, writer*
O'Dell, Michael James *social sciences specialist*
Ooms, Van Doorn *economist*
Orszag, Jonathan Marc *economist, consultant*
Orszag, Peter Richard *economist*
Ortner, Donald J. *biological anthropologist, educator*
Oweiss, Ibrahim Mohamed *economist, educator*
Ozer, Martha Ross *psychologist, counselor*
Pasternack, Robert Harry *school psychologist*
Pasurka, Jr., Carl A. *economist*
†Patterson, James E. *agricultural economist, speech professional*
Penner, Rudolph Gerhard *economist, educator*
Perry, George Lewis *research economist, consultant*
Phillips, Karen Borlaug *economist, railroad industry executive*
Phillips, Susan Meredith *financial economist, university administrator*
Pickenpaugh, Thomas Edward *archaeologist, anthropologist*
Popkin, Joel *economic consulting company executive*
Prestowitz, Clyde Vincent *economist, researcher*
Quintanilla-Villanueva, Rosalinda *economist*
Randall, Robert L(ee) *ecological economist*
Raslear, Thomas Gregory *psychologist*
†Ravallion, Martin *economist*
Ravenal, Earl Cedric *international relations educator, author*
Reich, Bernard *political science educator*
Reich, Otto Juan *political analyst, business consultant*
Reingold, David Ami *sociologist, educator*
Relyea, Harold Clarence *political scientist*
Roberts, Markley *economist, educator*
Roberts, Walter Ronald *political science educator, former government official*
†Rodriguez, Rita Maria *economist*
Roett, Riordan *political science educator, consultant*
Rosenau, James Nathan *political scientist, author*
Rosenberg, Joel Barry *government economist*
Ruser, John William *economist*
Ryn, Claes Gösta *political science educator, author, research institute administrator*
Sacher, Seth Barry *economist*
†Sawhill, Isabel Van Devanter *economist*
Scheffman, David Theodore *economist, management educator, consultant*
Schildhaus, Sam *political scientist, researcher*
Schley, Wayne Arthur *political consultant*
†Schmukler, Sergio L. *economist*
†Scholl, Kathleen Kay *economist*
†Shambaugh, David Leigh *political scientist, educator, writer*
Shroder, Mark Davis *economist*
Sibley, Lynn M. *anthropologist, educator*
Silverman, Lester Paul *economist, energy industry consultant*
Simes, Dimitri Konstantin *international affairs expert and educator*
Sloboda, Brian William *economist*
Smith, Bruce David *archaeologist*
Snyder, Jed C. *foreign affairs specialist*
Solomon, Elinor Harris *economics educator*
Solomon, Richard Harvey *political scientist*
Steinberg, David Isaac *economic development consultant, educator*
Stelzer, Irwin Mark *economist*
Stent, Angela E. *political scientist, educator, director*
†Stephenson, Sherry Madeline *economist*
Sterner, Michael Edmund *international affairs consultant*
Stewart, John Todd *economist, consultant*
Stone, Russell A. *sociology educator*
Stover, Mark Edward *economist*
Sunley, Emil McKee *economist*
Sweeney, Richard James *economics educator*
Toder, Eric Jay *economist*
Turner, John Andrew *economist*
†Valenzuela, Arturo Arms *political science educator, writer, consultant*
Voll, Sarah Potts *economic consultant*
Wahlbeck, Paul J. *political science educator, lawyer*
Wasserman, Gary B. *political scientist, writer, consultant*
Weintraub, Sidney *economist, educator*
Weiss, David Alan *international trade consultant*
Weiss, Randall Dunn *economist*
White, John Kenneth *politics educator*
†White, Roger Stuart *economist*
Whitehurst, Grover Jay *psychologist and educator*
†Wicks, Elliot Kundert *health economist*
Wilensky, Gail Roggin *economist, researcher*
†Williamson, Dean Victor *economist*
Williamson, John *economist*
Willner, Ann Ruth *political scientist, educator*
Willner, Dorothy *anthropologist, educator*
Wilson, Ewen Maclellan *economist*
Wolf, Alfred Clarence *retired economist*
Wolf, Patrick John *political science educator*
Wood, Bernard Anthony *anthropology educator*
Yellen, John Edward *archaeologist*
Zakheim, Dov Solomon *economist, government official*
Zhang, Zhiwei, Sr., *research scientist*

FLORIDA

Anna Maria
Romans, John Thomas *retired economics educator*

Bal Harbour
Bond, Alma Halbert *psychoanalyst, author*

Boca Raton
†Early, John D. *anthropologist, educator*
Latané, Bibb *social psychologist*
Schlager, Maynard M(orton) *psychologist, consultant*
Tata, Robert Joseph *retired geographer, educator*

Boynton Beach
Mittel, John J. *economist, corporate executive*

Bradenton
Ellman, Norman Kenneth *psychologist, psychoanalyst*

Brandon
Mussenden, Gerald *psychologist*

Clearwater
Bernsdorff, Oliver Thomas *social sciences educator*
Peterson, James Robert *engineering psychologist*

Cocoa
McLendon, Dorothy *school psychologist*

Coral Gables
Schwartztol, Holly Wechsler *psychologist*

Davie
Morris, Joseph Raymond *business and economics educator*

Daytona
†Wilson, Neva June *psychologist, educator*

Deland
Wood, Richard Harvey, Jr., *economics educator*

Delray Beach
Levinson, Harry *psychologist, educator*

Dunedin
†O'Dea, J. David *psychologist, educator*

Dunnellon
Dixon, W(illiam) Robert *retired educational psychology educator*

Estero
Routh, Donald K(ent) *psychology educator*

Fort Lauderdale
Azrin, Nathan Harold *psychologist, educator*
Bartelstone, Rona Sue *gerontologist*
Collins, Ronald William *psychologist, educator*
Levant, Ronald F. *psychologist, educator*
Maxwell, Sara Elizabeth *psychologist, educator, speech pathologist, director*
Pellet, Pedro Fernando *economist, educator, consultant*

Fort Myers
Smith, Paul Frederick *economist, former educator*

Gainesville
†Albarracín, Dolores *psychologist, educator*
Ardelt, Monika *sociologist, educator*
Bernard, H. Russell *anthropologist, educator, scientific editor*
Carr, Glenna Dodson *retired economics educator*
Conway, M. Margaret *political science educator, consultant*
Dewsbury, Donald Allen *historian of psychology, comparative psychologist*
Doty, Leilani *geriatric neuropsychologist, administrator*
Frazer, William Johnson, Jr., *economics educator*
Hornberger, Robert Howard *psychologist*
Milanich, Jerald Thomas *archaeologist, museum curator*
Mills, Teheran L. (Terry Mills) *sociology educator*
Moore, John Hartwell *anthropology educator, consultant*
Parker, Karen F. *sociology educator*
Severy, Lawrence James *psychologist, educator*
†Shih, Chuan-kang *anthropologist*
Stansbury, James Patrick *anthropologist, researcher*
Teitelbaum, Philip *psychologist*
Thiele, Leslie Paul *political science educator*
von Mering, Otto Oswald *anthropology educator*
Wagner, Eric Armin *sociology educator*
Wass, Hannelore Lina *educational psychology educator*
White, Susie Mae *school psychologist*

Hollywood
Foreman, Edwin Francis *economist, real estate broker*
Sundel, Martin *psychologist, educator, management consultant*
Valdes, Jacqueline Chehebar *psychologist, consultant, researcher*

Jacksonville
Brady, James Joseph *economics educator*
Ejimofor, Cornelius Ogu *political scientist, educator*
†Godfrey, John Munro *economic consultant*
Libby, Ronald Theodore *political science educator, consultant, researcher*
Urbina, Susana Patricia *psychology educator, consultant*

Juno Beach
Penn, Sherry Eve *communication psychologist, educator*

Lakeland
Ratliff, Charles Edward, Jr., *economics educator*

Largo
Ellis, Susan Gottenberg *psychologist*

Longboat Key
Albee, George Wilson *psychology educator*

Maitland
Blackburn, John Oliver *economist, consultant*
Leli, Dano Anthony *neuropsychologist, educator*
Von Hilsheimer, George Edwin, III, *neuropsychologist*

Melbourne
Tepperman, Barbara-Dawn A. *clinical psychologist, marriage/family therapist*

Miami
Armstrong, Floyd Daniel *pediatric psychologist*
Averch, Harvey Allan *economist, educator, academic administrator*
Bieley, Peggy M. *economist*
†Bravo, Irene Maria *psychologist, educator*
Field, Julia Allen *activist, strategist, poet*
Finley, Gordon Ellis *psychology educator*
Humphries, Joan Ropes *psychologist, educator*
Huysman, Arlene Weiss *psychologist, educator, writer*
Kanet, Roger Edward *political science educator*
†Koncsol, Stephen Wayne *psychologist, educator*
Nissen, Bruce Allen *labor studies educator*
Rosenbaum, Allan *public administration educator, academic administrator, international governance advisor*
Rosenberg, Mark B. *political science educator, university official*
Russell, Elbert Winslow *neuropsychologist*
Salazar-Carrillo, Jorge *economics educator*

Orlando
Lanier, Drew Noble *political science educator*
†Renk, Kimberly Dawn *social sciences educator*

Ormond Beach
Boyle, Susan Jean Higle *social studies educator*

Palm Bay
Seifer, Ronald Leslie *psychologist*

Palm Beach
Amling, Frederick *economist, educator, investment advisor*

Palm City
†Whichello, Carol *political scientist, educator, writer*

Palm Coast
Brumback, Gary Bruce *industrial and organizational psychologist*

Palm Harbor
Padberg, Daniel Ivan *agricultural economics educator, researcher*

Panama City
Roberts, Paul Craig, III, *economics educator, author, columnist*

Pensacola
Davis, Wesley D. *psychologist, educator*
DeMaria, Michael Brant *psychologist*
Kernstock, Elwyn Nicholas *political science educator, author*
Killian, Lewis Martin *sociology educator*
Long, H. Owen *retired economics educator, fiction writer*
†Philen, Robert Carleton *anthropologist, educator*

Plantation
Michael, Diann Dee *psychologist, educator*

Pompano Beach
Pigott, Melissa Ann *social psychologist*

Ponte Vedra Beach
Moore, David Graham *sociologist, educator*
Wu, Hsiu Kwang *economist, educator*

Port Charlotte
Von Holden, Martin Harvey *psychologist*

Port Saint Lucie
Augelli, John Pat *geographer, educator , writer, consulant, rancher*

Roseland
Canterbury-Counts, W. Douglas *psychologist*

Saint Augustine
Henderson, Hazel *writer, lecturer*

Saint Petersburg
Baker, Victoria Jean *anthropology educator*
Hua, Shiping *political science educator*
Meyers, Allan D. *archaeologist*
Smith, Sarah Jeanne *gerontologist*
Stewart, Sheila Kay *anthropologist, archaeologist*

Sanibel
Crown, David Allan *criminologist, educator*

Sarasota
Campbell, Michael Harry *psychologist, academic administrator*
Coufoudakis, Van *political science educator*
Cramer, Stanley Howard *psychology educator, author*
Elmendorf-Landgraf, Mary Lindsay *retired anthropologist*
Gordon, Sanford Daniel *economics educator*
Hamberg, Daniel *economist, educator*
Masters, John Christopher *psychologist, educator, writer*
†Ruva, Christine Lorraine *psychologist, educator*
Serrie, Hendrick *retired anthropology and international business educator*

Sparr
Tovi, Murray *futurist, research scientist*

Stuart
Dimbath, Merle F. *economic consultant, business educator*

Summerland Key
Muth, John Fraser *economics educator*

Sun City Center
Hall, John Fry *psychologist, educator*
Leonard, William Norris *economist, educator*

Tallahassee
Benson, Bruce Lowell *economics educator*
Canterbery, E. Ray *economics educator*
Cobbe, James Hamilton *economics educator*
Cockrell, Wilburn Allen *archaeologist*
Ericsson, Karl Anders *cognitive psychologist, educator, researcher*
Guy, Mary Ellen Johnston *political science educator*
Holcombe, Randall Gregory *economics educator*
†Isaac, Larry W. *sociologist, educator*
Johnson, Benjamin F., VI, *economist, consultant*
Laird, William Everette, Jr., *economics educator, administrator*
Macesich, George *econmomics professor*
Moore, Kurt Richard *anthropologist, fundraiser, investor*
Nam, Charles Benjamin *demographer, sociologist, educator*
†Roady, Elston Edward (Steve) *political scientist, educator*
Serow, William John *economics educator*
Standley-Burt, Nancy Vilma *psychologist, educator, retired*
Thompson, Gregory Lee *social sciences educator*

Tampa
Allen, Tammy D. *psychologist*
†Brady, Kathleen Deming *psychologist, occupational therapist, educator*
Clark, Michael Earl *psychologist*
DeSalvo, Joseph Salvatore *economics educator, researcher*
Ernst, Roger *international studies educator, consultant*
Heide, Kathleen Margaret *criminology educator, psychotherapist*
Kimmel, Ellen Bishop *psychologist, educator*
MacManus, Susan Ann *political science educator, researcher*
Paulson, Robert I. *social work educator*
Piper, John Richard *political science educator*
Tykot, Robert Howard *social sciences educator, archaeologist*
Vanden, Harry Edwin *political science educator*
Weiner, Irving Bernard *psychologist*

Tequesta
Swets, John Arthur *psychologist, researcher*

Valkaria
Kinney, Marcelle Anne *economist, consultant*

Venice
Gooding, Charles Thomas *psychology educator, retired college provost*

Vero Beach
Liggett, Malcolm Hugh *labor economist, educator*

West Palm Beach
Dye, Thomas Roy *political science educator*
†Gold, Bela *economist, educator*
McCluskey, Neil Gerard *gerontologist, educator, literary agent*

GEORGIA

Albany
†Michaels, Anne E. *psychologist, educator*
Stallworth, Charles Derotha, Jr., *psychologist*

Athens
Allsbrook, Ogden Olmstead, Jr., *retired economics educator*
Bertsch, Gary Kenneth *political scientist, educator*
Clute, Robert Eugene *political and social science educator*
†Crepaz, Markus Michael Leopold *political scientist, educator*
Dagley, John C. *psychologist*
Dorfman, Jeffrey H. *economist, educator*
Dunn, Delmer Delano *political science educator*
†Fincher, Cameron Lane *psychology educator*
Garbin, Albeno Patrick *sociology educator*
Hermanowicz, Joseph Craig *sociologist, educator*
Kamerschen, David Roy *economist, educator*
McNulty, Thomas L. *sociology educator*
Nichols, William Curtis *psychologist, family therapist, consultant*
O'Toole, Laurence Joseph *political science educator, researcher*
Rosen, Sidney *psychologist*
Tesser, Abraham *social psychologist*
Turner, Steven Cornell *agricultural economics educator*

Atlanta
†Aiken, Verndy Fred *economist*
Bahl, Roy Winford *economist, educator, consultant*
Baker, Lauren Alexis *psychology educator, aerial performer*
Banks, Bettie Sheppard *psychologist*
Brown, Courtney *political science educator, research institute administrator*
†Chiang, Tze I. *economist, researcher, economist, consultant*
Curran, Christopher *economics educator*
†Downs, William Murray *political scientist, educator, researcher*
Endicott, John Edgar *international relations educator*
Ferriss, Abbott Lamoyne *sociology educator emeritus*
Fox, Mary Frank *sociology educator and researcher*
Garland, LaRetta Matthews *nursing educator*
Kennedy, Robert *international affairs educator*
Knapp, Charles Boynton *economist, educator, university president*
L'Abate, Luciano *psychologist*
Levy, Daniel *economics educator*
†Littrell, Jill *social sciences educator*
†Marder, Elissa *psychologist, educator*
Muth, Richard Ferris *economics educator*
†Neumann, Mary Louise Spink *anthropologist, researcher*
†Nielsen, Tjai Michael *psychologist, consultant, researcher*
Paredes, James Anthony *anthropologist, educator*
Payne, Maxwell Carr, Jr., *retired psychology educator*
†Reese, Cynthia Dene *psychologist, educator, quality assurance professional, risk management consultant*
Remington, Thomas Frederick *political science educator*
Rothbaum, Barbara Olasov *psychologist, educator*
Rubin, Paul Harold *economist*
Snarey, John Robert *psychologist, researcher, educator*
Stephan, Paula Elizabeth *economics educator, university official*
Stewart, Barbara Dunbar *insurance consultant*
Thursby, Jerry Gilbert *economics educator, consultant*
Thursby, Marie Currie *economics educator*
Tillman, Mary Norman *urban affairs consultant*
Vaughn, Michael S. *criminal justice educator*
Wald, Michael Leonard *economist*
Weiss, Jay M(ichael) *psychologist, educator*

Augusta
†Davis, Catherine Lucy *psychologist, medical researcher*
†Watkins, Ralph Craig *social sciences educator*

Barnesville
Terry, Pamela Mays *psychology educator*

Carrollton
Aanstoos, Christopher Michael *psychology educator*
†Cao, Li *social studies educator, educator*
Clark, Janet Eileen *political scientist, educator*
Purk, Janice Kay *sociology and gerontology educator*
Stone, Sandra Smith *sociologist, researcher*

College Park
Atkinson, Bruce Earl *clinical psychologist, christian counselor*

Columbus
Kerr, Allen Stewart *retired psychologist*
McFarland, Samuel P., Jr., *psychologist*

Dacula
Daniel, Raymond *economist*

Dahlonega
Friedman, Barry David *political scientist, educator*
Pippert, John Marvin *sociology educator*

Decatur
†Beran, Michael James *research psychologist, primatologist*
Bockwitz, Cynthia Lee *psychologist, psychology and women's studies educator*
Denny, Dallas *psychological examiner*
†Lucius, Randall H. *psychologist*

Demorest
Vance, Cynthia Lynn *psychology educator*

Dublin
Alexander, Judith Elaine *psychologist*

Dunwoody
Chacholiades, Miltiades *economics educator*

East Point
Rogers, Rhonwyn Voncelle *therapist, psychology educator*

Evans
Zachert, Virginia *psychologist, educator*

Fort Valley
Chandras, Kananur V. *psychology educator*

Franklin Springs
†Bobic, Michael P. *political scientist, educator*

Kennesaw
Frank, Mary Lou Bryant *psychologist, educator*
Karcher, Barbara Correnti *sociologist, educator*
†La Rosa, Agatino *geographer, educator*
†Li, Chien-pin *political scientist, educator*
Shock, David Robert *political science educator*

Lawrenceville
Carter, Dale William *psychologist*
†Dickerson, Claudia Thompson *psychologist*
Reuter, Helen Hyde *psychologist*

Lilburn
Neumann, Thomas William *archaeologist*

Macon
Andrews, Charles Haynes *economics educator*
Craig, Kern William *political science educator*
Lewis, Sandra Combs *research psychologist, writer*
Murdoch, Bernard Constantine *psychology educator*

Marietta
Dudley, Gary Edward *clinical psychologist*

Milledgeville
Isaac, Walter Lon *psychology educator*
Peterson, Dave Leonard *psychologist*

Mountain City
Kennedy, Robinette *anthropologist, researcher*

Oxford
Cody, William Bermond *political science educator*

Ringgold
Hayes Gladson, Laura Joanna *psychologist*

Rome
Granrose, Cherlyn Sue *psychology educator, researcher*
Johnson, Alberta Clark *psychology educator*

Roswell
Klein, John Jacob *retired economist*

Statesboro
Henry, Nicholas Llewellyn *public administration educator*
†Pino, Nathan Willett *criminologist, educator, sociologist*

Stockbridge
Grimes, Richard Allen *economics educator*

Stone Mountain
Havick, John J. *political science educator*
†Roth, Edie Cowan *psychologist*

Suwanee
Swanson, David H(enry) *consultant, retired economist, educator*

Toccoa Falls
†Allison Jr., Norman E. *anthropologist, educator*

HAWAII

Hilo
Dixon, Paul William *psychology educator*
VanderVoort, Debra Jean *counseling psychology educator, school psychologist*

Holualoa
Scarr, Sandra Wood *psychology educator, researcher*

Honolulu
Bitterman, Morton Edward *psychologist, educator*
Brislin, Richard Walter *psychology educator*
Cho, Lee-Jay *social scientist, demographer*
†Finney, Ben Rudolph *anthropologist, educator*
Flannelly, Kevin J. *psychologist, research analyst*
Fullmer, Daniel Warren *former psychologist, educator*
Hatfield, Elaine Catherine *psychology educator*
Ishikawa-Fullmer, Janet Satomi *psychologist, educator*
Jordan, Amos Azariah, Jr., *foreign affairs educator, retired army officer*
Kennedy, Reneau Charlene Ufford *forensic psychologist, consultant*
Kumar, Raj *psychologist, hypnotherapist*
La Croix, Sumner Jonathan *economics educator*
Laney, Leroy Olan *economist, banker, educator*
Leung, PingSun *agricultural economist*
Mark, Shelley Muin *economist, educator, government official*
†Marsella, Anthony Joseph *psychologist, educator*
Nordyke, Eleanor Cole *population researcher, public health nurse*
Ogawa, Dennis Masaaki *American studies educator*
Paige, Glenn Durland *political scientist, educator*
Riggs, Fred Warren *political science educator*
Shay, Roshani Cari *political science educator*
†Spencer, James H. *social sciences educator, consultant*
Stamper, Ewa Szumotalska *psychologist*
†Steinemann, Namji Kim *social studies educator*
Suh, Dae-Sook *political science educator*
Yang, Guobin *sociologist, sinologist*

Kahului
Shaw, Virginia Ruth *clinical psychologist*

Wahiawa
Kiyota, Heide Pauline *clinical psychologist*

IDAHO

Boise
†Clump, Michael A. *psychologist, educator*
Overgaard, Willard Michele *retired political scientist, jurisprudent*

Moscow
Ghazanfar, Shaikh Mohammed *economics educator, researcher, author*
†Isik, Murat *agricultural economist, researcher*

Pocatello
Piland, Neill Finnes *health services economist, researcher*

Post Falls
†Deatherage, Edward L. *psychologist*

Sandpoint
†Glock, Charles Young *sociologist, writer*

Troy
†de Rocher, Denise D. *social sciences educator*

Twin Falls
Wright, Frances Jane *educational psychologist*

ILLINOIS

Arlington Heights
Griffin, Jean Latz *political strategist, writer*
Lewin, Pearl Goldman *psychologist*
Tongue, William Walter *economics and business consultant, educator emeritus*

Aurora
Strassberg, Barbara Ann *sociology educator, researcher*

Barrington
Chung, Joseph Sang-hoon *economics educator*

Barrington Hills
Wood, Andrée Robitaille *archaeologist, researcher*

Carbondale
†Benford, Robert Dee *sociology educator, editor*
†Hill, Jonathan David *anthropology researcher, educator, editor*
Johnson, Elmer Hubert *sociologist, researcher in criminology*
†Karau, Steven James *social psychologist, researcher*
Melone, Albert P. *political science educator, writer, researcher, consultant*
Trescott, Paul Barton *educator*

Champaign
Ahadi, Stephan Ahad *psychologist, psychometrician*
Arnould, Richard Julius *economist, educator, consultant*
Brueckner, Jan Keith *economics educator*
Davis, James Henry *retired psychology educator*
Diener, Edward Francis *psychologist, researcher*
Due, John Fitzgerald *economist, educator emeritus*
Dulany, Donelson Edwin, Jr., *psychology educator*
Eriksen, Charles Walter *psychologist, educator*
Farmer, Helen Sweeney *psychology educator*
Ferber, Marianne Abeles *economics educator*
Gold, Paul Ernest *psychology educator, behavioral neuroscience educator*
Grinols, Earl Leroy, III, *economist, educator*
Humphreys, Lloyd Girton *research psychologist, educator*
†Luo, Xiaowei *sociologist, educator*
†Scott, Anna Marie Porter Wall *sociology educator*
Seppala, Juha Ilmari *economist, educator*
Sprenkle, Case Middleton *economist, educator*
Triandis, Harry Charalambos *psychology educator*

Charleston
Canivez, Gary Lynn *psychologist, educator*
Havey, J. Michael *psychologist, educator*

Chicago
Aliber, Robert Z. *economist, educator*
Allen, Danielle *political scientist, educator*
Baum, Bernard Helmut *sociologist, educator*
Becker, Gary Stanley *economist, educator*
Bidwell, Charles Edward *sociologist, educator*
†Birchenall, Javier Arturo *economist, researcher*
Block, Richard L. *sociologist, criminologist, educator*
Boyer, John William *history educator, dean*
Cacioppo, John Terrance *psychology educator, researcher*
Cain, Louis Perkins, III, *economist, educator*
Carlton, Dennis William *economics educator*
Carnes, Bruce Alfred *gerontologist, researcher*
Coase, Ronald Harry *economist, educator*
Cohler, Bertram Joseph *social sciences educator, clinical psychologist*
Cropsey, Joseph *political science educator*
Cruthird, Robert Lee *sociology educator*
Drezner, Daniel William *political scientist, educator*
Dust, Margaret Cecile *psychology educator*
†Fernandez, James *anthropology educator*
Fogel, Robert William *economist, educator, historian*
Freeman, Leslie Gordon *anthropologist, educator*
Freeman, Susan Tax *anthropologist, educator, culinary historian*
Friedrich, Paul *anthropologist , linguist, poet*
Gardiner, John Andrew *political science educator*
Gavrilov, Leonid A. *gerontologist*
Genetski, Robert James *economist*
†Geyer, Michael *history educator*
Gibson, McGuire *archaeologist, educator*
Ginsburg, Norton Sydney *retired geographer*
Gittins, Anthony J. *theology studies educator*
Gould, John Philip *economist, educator*
Grampp, William Dyer *economist, educator*
Grossman, Lisa Robbin *clinical psychologist, lawyer*
†Haboub, Wael Joumaa *political scientist, educator*
Hansen, John Mark *political scientist*
Harris, Chauncy Dennison *geographer, educator*
Hebel, Doris A. *astrologer*
Heckman, James Joseph *economist, econometrician, educator*
Higinbotham, Harlow Niles *economist*
†Hollis-Sawyer, Lisa Ann *psychologist, gerontologist, researcher*
Huyck, Margaret Hellie *psychology educator*
Johnson, Janet Helen *Egyptology educator*
Kaplan, Morton A. *political science and philosophy educator*
Kaye, Richard William *labor economist*
Kennedy, Eugene Cullen *psychology educator, writer*
Kopf, David Heath *economic consultant*
Lamont, Owen Austin *economist*
Larson, Allan Louis *political scientist, educator, lay church worker*
Laumann, Edward Otto *sociology educator*
Levine, Donald Nathan *sociologist, educator*
Lippman, Jessica G. *clinical psychologist, educator*
Lipson, Charles Henry *political scientist, educator*
Liu, Ben-chieh *economist*
Lucas, Robert Emerson, Jr., *economist, educator*
†Luhrmann, Tanya Marie *anthropology educator, writer*
McNeill, G. David *psycholinguist, educator*
Mikesell, Marvin Wray *geography educator*
Miller, Oscar *economics educator*
Mondschean, Thomas Smith *economics educator*
Moretti, Robert James *psychologist, educator*
Morewitz, Stephen John *behavioral scientist, consultant, educator*
Morris, Norval *criminologist, educator*
†Mufson, Elliott J. *psychologist, director, neurologist, educator*
Mugnaini, Enrico *neuroscience educator*
Myerson, Roger Bruce *economist, game theorist, educator*
Nicholas, Ralph Wallace W. *anthropologist, educator*
Peltzman, Sam *economics educator*
Pugh, Roderick Wellington *psychologist, educator*
Rieger, Pearl Beverly *psychoeducational diagnostician, consultant*
Rogalski, Carol Jean *clinical psychologist, educator*
Rosen, Ellen Freda *psychologist, educator*
Rosen, George *economist, educator*
Rosenblum, Victor Gregory *political science and law educator*
Rowan, Thomas Bernard, III, *political science educator*
Sah, Raaj *economist, advisor, educator*
Sanders, Jacquelyn Seevak *psychologist, educator*
†Shevell, Steven King *psychology educator*
Simons, Helen *school psychologist, psychotherapist, educator*
Simpson, Dick Weldon *political science educator*
Sladen, Bernard Jacob *psychologist*
Smith, Raymond Thomas *anthropology educator*
Smith, Stan Vladimir *economist, financial service company executive*
Stein, Howard *economics educator*
Stocking, George Ward, Jr., *anthropology educator*
Stolzenberg, Ross Mark *sociology educator*
Stover, Leon (Eugene Stover) *anthropology educator, writer, critic*
Sweeney, John Adrian *clinical psychologist*
†Tatom, John Anthony *economist*
Taub, Richard Paul *social sciences educator*
Telser, Lester Greenspan *educator, economist*

Thomas, Joseph Erumappettical *psychologist*
†Thompson, John H. *social science executive*
Upshaw, Harry Stephan *psychology educator*
Walberg, Herbert John *psychologist, educator, consultant*
Zagar, Robert John *psychologist, researcher*
Zellner, Arnold *economics and statistics educator*

Darien
Klassek, Christine Paulette *behavioral scientist*

DeKalb
†Frisch, Morton Jerome *political scientist, educator*
†Luo, Wei *social sciences educator*
†Shimizu, Hidetada *psychologist, educator*
†Slotsve, George Aaron *economist, educator, consultant*

Deerfield
Halpin, Mary Elizabeth *psychologist*

Dekalb
Rembusch, Joseph John *psychologist, management consulting company executive*
Skeels, Jack William *economics educator, consultant*

Downers Grove
Feeney, Don Joseph, Jr., *psychologist*

East Alton
Boger, Gena Cecile *school psychologist*

Edwardsville
Browne, Dallas *anthropology educator*
†Butki, Brian David *psychologist, educator*
Ferguson, Eva Dreikurs *psychologist, educator, researcher, author*
Lin, Steven An-Yhi *economics educator, consultant*

Evanston
Bienen, Henry Samuel *political science educator, university executive*
Braeutigam, Ronald Ray *economics educator*
†Canes-Wrone, Brandice *political scientist, educator*
Fine, Gary Alan *sociology educator*
Gordon, Robert James *economics educator*
†Hunter, Albert Dale *sociology educator, poet*
Hurter, Arthur Patrick *economist, educator*
Irons, William George *anthropology educator*
†Koenigsberg, Judy Z. Nulman *clinical psychologist*
Matzkin, Rosa Liliana *economics educator*
Mills, Edwin Smith *economics educator*
Mortensen, Dale Thomas *economics educator*
Moskos, Charles C. *sociology educator*
Reiter, Stanley *economist, educator*
Senn, Peter Richard *economist, consultant*
Shanas, Ethel *sociology educator*
Spier, Kathryn Elizabeth *economist, educator*
†Sweet, Jerry James *clinical psychologist*
†Weisbrod, Burton Allen *economist, educator*

Glen Carbon
†Pogatshnik, Lee Wolfram *psychologist, educator*

Glen Ellyn
Frateschi, Lawrence Jan *economist, statistician, educator*

Harrisburg
†Lees, Matthew Thomas *political scientist, educator*

Hinsdale
Dederick, Robert Gogan *economist*

Homewood
Lyttle, Christopher Sherman *medical sociologist*

Huntley
Saporta, Jack *psychologist, educator*

Joliet
Holmgren, Myron Roger *social sciences educator*

Macomb
Radosh, Mary *sociology educator*
Tang, Shengming *sociology educator*
Walzer, Norman Charles *economics educator*

Maryville
Stark, Patricia Ann *psychologist*

Milford
†Beall, Pamela Honn *therapist, radio talks-show host, writer*

Moline
†LeBlanc, Bruce David *sociologist*
Morgan, Rebecca Susan *psychologist*

Morton Grove
Farber, Isadore E. *psychologist, educator*

Naperville
Cowlishaw, Mary Lou *government educator*
Kelley, Karl Neal *psychology educator*

Normal
Bjorklund, Diane Louise *sociology educator*
Skibo, James M. *anthropologist, educator*

Olympia Fields
Sprinkel, Beryl Wayne *economist, consultant*

Orland Park
Antia, Kersey H. *industrial and clinical psychologist, consultant*
Natvig, Connie Bea *clinical psychologist*

Palos Heights
Breems, Bradley G. *sociologist, educator*

Peoria
Curtis, R. Craig *political science educator*

Rockford
Clodius, Robert LeRoy *economist, educator*
Mc Nelly, Frederick Wright, Jr., *psychologist*

Saint Charles
Osowiec, Darlene Ann *clinical psychologist, educator, consultant*

Schaumburg
Burroughs, Susan Marie *industrial and organizational psychologist, educator*

Skokie
Yogev, Sara *psychologist*

Springfield
Jacobson, Doranne *photographer*
Mooney, Christopher Zimmer *political science educator*
Phillips, John Robert *political scientist, educator*
Reyman, Jonathan Eric *archaeologist, anthropologist, researcher*
Wehrle, Leroy Snyder *economist, educator*

Urbana
Baer, Werner *economist, educator*
Bruner, Edward M. *anthropology educator*
Carmen, Ira Harris *political scientist, educator*
†Due, Jean Margaret *agricultural economist, educator*
Gabriel, Michael *psychology educator*
Giertz, J. Fred *economics educator*
Giles, Eugene *anthropology educator*
Gove, Samuel Kimball *political science educator*
Kolodziej, Edward Albert *political scientist, educator*
Nettl, Bruno *anthropology and musicology educator*
†Pahre, Robert *social sciences educator*
Resek, Robert William *economist*
Rich, Robert F. *law and political science educator*
Schmidt, Stephen Christopher *agricultural economist, educator*
Wirt, Frederick Marshall *retired political scientist, educator*
Yu, George Tzuchiao *political science educator*

Wheaton
Allen, Henry Lee *sociology educator, consultant*
Nieves, Alvaro Lezcano *sociology educator*

Wilmette
Schloss, Nathan *retired economist*
Walker, Ronald Edward *psychologist, educator*

Winnetka
Krueger, Deborah A. Blake *school psychologist, consultant*

INDIANA

Bloomington
†Agranoff, Robert *political scientist, educator*
Alex-Assensoh, Yvette Marie *political scientist*
Baye, Michael Roy *economics educator*
†Becker, Robert Allen *economist, educator*
Caldwell, Lynton Keith *social scientist, educator*
Conrad, Geoffrey Wentworth *archaeologist, educator*
Dinsmoor, James Arthur *psychology educator*
†Estell, David B. *psychologist, educator*
Estes, William Kaye *psychologist, educator*
†Gieryn, Thomas Fredrick *sociologist, educator*
Guth, Sherman Leon (S. Lee Guth) *psychologist, educator*
Mikesell, John L. *economics educator*
Moran, Emilio Federico *anthropology and ecology educator*
Ostrom, Vincent A(lfred) *political science educator*
Patrick, John Joseph *social sciences educator*
Peebles, Christopher Spalding *anthropologist, dean, academic administrator*
Risinger, C. Frederick *social studies educator*
†St. John, Edward P. *social sciences educator*
Saunders, W(arren) Phillip, Jr., *economics educator, consultant, author*
Smith, Frederick Robert, Jr., *social studies educator, educator*
Spulber, Nicolas *economics educator emeritus*
Stryker, Sheldon *sociologist, educator*
Timberlake, William David *psychology educator*
†Toth, Nicholas Patrick *anthropologist, educator, archaeologist*
von Furstenberg, George Michael *economics educator, researcher*
Wicker, Elmus Rogers *economics educator*

Carmel
Rychlak, Joseph Frank *psychology educator, theoretician*

Columbus
Hackett, John Thomas *retired economist*
Williams, Robert Joseph *behavioral health services executive, psychologist*

Crown Point
Kristevski, Alex C. *clinical psychologist*

Evansville
Milner, Wesley Tyre *political science educator*
Tonso, William Rae *retired sociology educator, freelance writer*

Franklin
Launey, George Volney, III, *economics educator*

Gary
†Hoyert, Mark Sudlow *psychology educator*

Granger
Craypo, Charles *labor economics educator*

Greenwood
†Waldkoetter, Raymond Oliver *psychologist, consultant*

Hanover
Calkins, Ralph Nelson *economics educator*
†Crone, James Alan *sociologist, educator*

Indianapolis
†Fastenau, Philip S. *neuropsychologist, educator*
†Featherstonaugh, Henry Gordon *psychologist, health facility administrator*
Krauss, John Landers *public policy, urban affairs consultant, mediator, arbitrator*
Mason, David Stewart *political science educator*
†Namjoshi, Madhav *economist, educator*
†Sachs, Stephen Mark *political scientist, consultant*
Spechler, Martin Charles *economist*

Kokomo
†Wysong, Earl Edward *sociologist, educator*

Lafayette
Dzhafarov, Ehtibar N. *mathematical psychologist*
Hardin, Lowell Stewart *retired economics educator*
Schönemann, Peter Hans *psychology educator*
Schweickert, Richard Justus *psychologist, educator*

Madison
Rawson, Harve E. *psychologist, writer*

Marion
†Boivin, Michael J. *psychologist, educator, psychologist, researcher*

Muncie
Bogg, Richard Allan *sociologist, educator*
Cheng, Chu Yuan *economics educator*
Meyer, Fred Albert, Jr., *political science educator*
Sinclair, Brian Robert *psychologist, architect, educator*
Swartz, B(enjamin) K(insell), Jr., *archaeologist, educator*

Noblesville
Hart, Stuart Newton *psychologist, educator*

Notre Dame
Arnold, Peri Ethan *political scientist*
Bartell, Ernest *economist, educator, priest*
Despres, Leo Arthur *sociology and anthropology educator, academic administrator*
Dowty, Alan Kent *political scientist, educator*
Ghilarducci, M. Teresa *economist, educator*
Mainwaring, Scott Patterson *political scientist, educator*
†Mark, Nelson C. *economist*
McElroy, Jerome Lathrop *economics educator*
Mirowski, Philip Edward *economics educator*
Moore, Kenneth E. *anthropologist, educator, writer*
Sent, Esther-Mirjam *economics educator*
Swartz, Thomas R. *economist, educator*
Valenzuela, Julio Samuel *sociologist, educator*
Weigert, Andrew Joseph *sociology educator*
†Welch, Michael R. *sociologist, educator*

Richmond
Veramallay, Ashton Isardatt *economist, educator*

Ridgeville
Church, Jay Kay *psychologist, educator*

Salem
Karkut, Richard Theodore *clinical psychologist*

South Bend
Torstrick, Rebecca Lee *anthropologist, educator*

Terre Haute
†Kukral, Michael Andrew *geographer, educator*

Trafalgar
†Montgomery, Steven Charles *psychologist, minister*

West Lafayette
Cicirelli, Victor George *psychologist*
Connor, John Murray *agricultural economics educator*
Farris, Paul Leonard *agricultural economist*
Gruen, Gerald Elmer *psychologist, educator*
Horwich, George *economist, educator*
Jagacinski, Carolyn Mary *psychology educator*
Kadiyala, Koteswara Rao *econometrics educator*
†Kelly, Janice R. *psychologist, educator*
Knudsen, Dean DeWayne *sociology educator*
†Kovenock, Daniel J. *economist, educator*
Martin, Marshall Allen *agricultural economist*
Patrick, George Frederick *agricultural economics educator*
Perrucci, Robert *sociologist, educator*
Swensen, Clifford Henrik, Jr., *psychologist, educator*
Theen, Rolf Heinz-Wilhelm *political science educator*
Watts, Michael Wayne *economist*
Wegener, Duane T. *social psychology educator*
Weidenaar, Dennis Jay *economics educator*
Weinstein, Michael Alan *political science educator*

IOWA

Ames
Ahmann, John Stanley *psychologist, educator*
Bhattacharya, Joydeep *economics educator*
Fox, Karl August *economist, eco-behavioral scientist*
Gradwohl, David Mayer *anthropology educator*
Harl, Neil Eugene *economist, lawyer, educator*
Klonglan, Gerald Edward *sociology educator*
†Martin, Peter *psychology educator*
Meyer, Charles William *economics educator*
Orazem, Peter Francis *economics educator*
Quirmbach, Herman Charles *economics educator*
†Tesfatsion, Leigh S. *economics educator, consultant*
†Whiteford, Michael Bonneville *anthropology educator*

Cedar Falls
Gilgen, Albert Rudolph *psychologist, educator*

Cedar Rapids
Patton, James Edward *school psychologist*

Clive
Miller, Kenneth Edward *sociologist, educator*

Coggon
Hammer, Robert Eugene *psychologist*

Coralville
Lueder, Barbara Ann *school psychologist*

Des Moines
Beeman, David Gerard *psychologist*
Demorest, Allan Frederick *retired psychologist*
Sanders, Arthur *political scientist, educator*
Sinay, Tony *economist, educator*

Dubuque
Jorgensen, Gerald Thomas *psychologist, educator, lawyer*

Fayette
Barker, Richard Alexander *organizational psychologist*

Grinnell
Moyer, H. Wayne *political science educator*

Iowa City
Albrecht, William Price *economist, educator, government official*
Barkan, Joel David *political science educator, consultant*
Block, Robert I. *psychologist, researcher, educator*
Forsythe, Robert Elliott *economics educator*
Geweke, John Frederick *economics educator*
Hudson, John Boswell *sociologist, educator*
Kim, Chong Lim *political science educator*
Loewenberg, Gerhard *political science educator*
Nathan, Peter E. *psychologist, educator*
Pogue, Thomas Franklin *economics educator, consultant*
Shannon, Lyle William *sociology educator*
Siebert, Calvin D. *economist, educator*
Skinstad, Anne Helene *psychologist, researcher*
Suls, Jerry M. *psychologist, educator*
Wasserman, Edward Arnold *psychology educator*

Knoxville
Joslyn, Wallace Danforth *retired psychologist*

Le Mars
†Embree, Robert Arthur *retired psychologist, minister*

Nevada
Bivens, Gordon Ellsworth *economist, educator*

Oskaloosa
Porter, David Lindsey *history and political science educator, author*

Pella
Baker-Roelofs, Mina Marie *retired home economist, educator*
Racheter, Donald Paul *political science educator*

Sioux City
Hatfield, Susan Williams *school psychologist*

West Des Moines
Thompson, Gerald Everett *economics educator*

KANSAS

Andover
Ahmad, Ayaz *economist*

Atchison
Misceo, Giovanni Francesco *psychology educator*

Dodge City
Ryan, Michael Timothy *sociology educator*

Emporia
Kaplan, David Marshall *psychologist, educator*

Great Bend
†Bealer, Richard T. *social sciences educator*

Kansas City
Penick, Elizabeth C. *psychologist*
Twillman, Robert Keith *psychologist*

Larned
Cerullo, Rudy Michael, II, *psychology, theology educator, minister*

Lawrence
Antonio, Robert John *sociology educator*
Barnett, William Arnold *economics educator*
Dean, Bartholomew Crispin *anthropology educator*
†Finger, Michael Steven *psychologist, educator, statistician, consultant*

Heller, Francis H(oward) *law and political science educator emeritus*
Multon, Karen Diane *psychologist, educator*
†Rosenbloom, Joshua Levi *economist, educator*
Shaffer, Harry George *economics educator*
†Snyder, Charles Richard *psychologist, educator*

Manhattan
Babcock, Michael Ward *economics educator*
Barnett, Mark A. *psychology educator*
Featherstone, Allen Merril *economics educator*
Hoyt, Kenneth Boyd *educational psychology educator*
Middendorf, Gerad D. *sociology educator*
Nafziger, Estel Wayne *economics educator*
Phares, E. Jerry *psychology educator*
Richter, William Louis *social sciences educator*
Thomas, Lloyd Brewster *economics educator*
Wallis, Robert Ray *psychologist*

McPherson
†Midgley, Bryan Duaine *behavioral science educator*

Ottawa
Brady, Gordon Leonard, Jr., *economist*

Overland Park
Burger, Henry G. *vocabulary scientist, anthropologist, publisher*
FitzGerald, Thomas Joe *psychologist*

Pittsburg
Behlar, Patricia Ann *political science educator*

Prairie Village
Lyon, Joanne B. *psychologist*

Saint John
Robinson, Alexander Jacob *clinical psychologist*

Shawnee Mission
Gaar, Marilyn Audrey Wiegraffe *political scientist, educator, property manager*
Gensheimer, Cynthia Francis *economics educator*

Topeka
Cann, Steven J. *political science educator*
MacDonald, Pamelyn Marie *psychology educator*
Spohn, Herbert Emil *psychologist*

Wichita
Ericson, David Frank *political scientist, educator*
Kahn, Melvin A. *political science educator*

Winfield
Schul, Bill Dean *psychological administrator, author*

KENTUCKY

Bowling Green
Cangemi, Joseph Peter *psychologist, consultant, educator*
Cravens, Raymond Lewis *retired political science educator*
Wassom, John Clark *economics educator*

Campbellsville
†Chowning, John E. *political scientist, educator, minister*

Corbin
Doby, John Thomas *social psychologist*

Covington
Giesbrecht, Martin Gerhard *retired economics educator, clarinetist*
Littleton, Nan Elizabeth Feldkamp *psychologist, educator*

Eddyville
Cooley-Parker, Sheila Leanne *psychologist, consultant, educator*

Flemingsburg
Story, Joseph C. *economist, consultant*

Fort Mitchell
Euskirchen, George John *business administration and economics educator*

Georgetown
†Caza, Brian Patrick *political scientist, educator*

Highland Heights
†Burkholder, Jo Ellen *anthropologist, educator*
Donnelly, Sharlotte K. B. Neely *anthropology educator, author*

Independence
Hopgood, James F. *anthropologist, educator*

Lexington
Gallagher, Eugene Bennett *sociologist, medical educator*
Hall, Harry H. *agricultural economics educator*
Hochstrasser, Donald Lee *cultural anthropologist, community health and public administrator*
Hultman, Charles William *economics educator*
Stempel, John Dallas *international studies educator*
Stilwell, William Earle, III, *psychology educator, retired military officer*
Straus, Robert *behavioral sciences educator*
Wildasin, David E(arl) *economics educator*
Worell, Judith P. *psychologist, educator*
Zentall, Thomas R. *psychologist, educator*

Louisville
Edgell, Stephen Edward *psychology educator, statistical consultant*
Garfinkel, Herbert *political science educator, university official*
Gregg, Gary L., II, *political science educator*

Meyer, Peter Bert *economist, urban policy educator*
†Stanton, M(orris) Duncan *psychologist, researcher, dean*
Titzl, Mary Trueheart *social work educator, consultant*
†Ziegler, Charles Edward *political science educator, department chairman*

Morehead
Miller, Green Russell *economist, educator*

Murray
Milkman, Martin Irving *economics educator*

Pikeville
Cade, Nancy Jean *history and political science educator*

Prestonsburg
†Mc Aninch, Robert Danford *philosophy and government affairs educator*

Richmond
Engle, Fred Allen, Jr., *economics educator, author*

Versailles
Stober, William John, II, *economics educator*

LOUISIANA

Alexandria
†Thevenot, Maude Travis *retired home economist*

Baton Rouge
Beard, Thomas Rex *economics educator*
Cramer, Gail Latimer *economist*
Daniel, Ross Preston, III, *economist, educator*
Riopelle, Arthur Jean *psychologist*

Bossier City
Holt, Edwin Joseph *psychology educator*

Hammond
Durand, Charles Eric *psychologist, educator*

Lafayette
Dur, Philip Francis *political scientist, educator, retired foreign service officer*
Falcon, Chuck Tilton *psychologist, writer*
MacNair, Wilmer Everett *sociologist, educator, minister*

Lake Charles
Middleton, George, Jr., *clinical child psychologist*
†Weeber, Stan C. *sociologist, educator*

Metairie
Falco, Maria Josephine *political scientist, academic administrator*
Wood, Jonathan Stuart *economist, educator*

Monroe
Fouts, Elizabeth Browne *psychologist, metals company executive*

New Orleans
Andrews, E. Wyllys *archaeologist, educator*
Balée, William L. *anthropology educator*
Boudreaux, Kenneth Justin *economics and finance educator, consultant*
Brazier, Mary Margaret *psychology educator, researcher*
Bricker, Harvey Miller *anthropology educator*
Bricker, Victoria Reifler *anthropology educator*
Freudenberger, Herman *retired economics educator*
Jacobsen, Thomas Warren *retired archaeologist, educator, freelance journalist*
Langston, Thomas Samuel *political science educator*
Lee, Silas, III, *sociologist, public opinion research consultant*
Moely, Barbara E. *psychology researcher, educator*
Olson, Richard David *psychology educator*
O'Neal, Edgar Carl *psychology educator*
Paradise, Louis Vincent *educational psychology educator, university official*
Prins, Brandon Christopher *political scientist, educator*

Oakdale
†Bellah, Lisa Danielle *psychologist, educator*

Pineville
Thrasher, Fay C. *clinical psychologist*

Ruston
Sale, Tom S., III, *financial economist*

Shreveport
Joiner, Gary Dillard *cartographer, history educator, author*
Pederson, William David *political scientist, educator*
Staats, Thomas Elwyn *neuropsychologist*

MAINE

Augusta
Nickerson, John Mitchell *political science educator*

Bangor
Ward, Debora Elliott *psychologist*

Bath
Stoudt, Howard Webster *biological anthropologist, human factors specialist, consultant*

Brunswick
Crandall, Elizabeth Walbert *home economics educator*
Fitzgerald, John Michael *economist, educator*
Fuchs, Alfred Herman Herman *psychologist, educator*
Morgan, Richard Ernest *political scientist, educator*
Riley, Matilda White (Mrs. John W. Riley Jr.) *sociologist*
†Yarbrough, Jean Mary *political science educator*

Falmouth
McCoy, Carol P. *psychologist, training executive*
Pierce, Philip Sargent *clinical psychologist*

Farmington
Melcher, James Patrick *political scientist, educator*

Hallowell
MacLean, Neil V. *forensic psychologist*

Kittery Point
Howells, William White *anthropology educator*

Lewiston
Dennison, Gerard Francis *economic analyst*
Kessler, Mark Allen *political scientist, educator*
Murray, Michael Peter *economist, educator*

Little Deer Isle
Mills, David Harlow *psychologist, association executive*

Orono
Barkan, Steven Edward *sociology educator*
Boyle, Kevin John *economics educator, consultant*
Cohn, Steven Frederick *sociology educator, consultant*
Devino, William Stanley *economist, educator*
Goldstone, Sanford *psychology educator*
Martindale, Colin Eugene *psychology educator, author*
Munson, Henry Lee, Jr., *anthropologist, educator*
†See, Scott William *history educator*
†Teisl, Mario F. *economics educator, researcher*

Portland
†O'Brien, John Matthew *psychologist, educator*

Sanford
Will, Jerrie Ann *psychologist*

Sidney
Tietenberg, Thomas *economist, department chairman*

Surry
Pickett, Betty Horenstein *psychologist*

Waterville
Gemery, Henry Albert *economics educator*
Gilkes, Cheryl Louise Townsend *sociologist, educator, minister*

Wells
†Lahar, Cindy J. *psychologist, educator*

MARYLAND

Annapolis
Frantzich, Stephen Edward *political science educator*
Gurr, Ted Robert *political science educator, author*
†Yee, Cordell D.K. *cartographer, educator*

Arnold
Smith, Robert Gillen *retired political science consultant*

Baltimore
Albert, Ira Bernard *social sciences educator*
Alonso, Diane Lindwarm *cognitive psychologist*
†Anderson, Gerard Fenton *economist, university program administrator*
Barnow, Burt S. *economist*
Bass, Scott Arthur *community psychologist, gerontologist, educator*
Bellack, Alan Scott *clinical psychologist*
Bright, Margaret *sociologist*
Bucher, Richard David *sociology educator*
†Carroll, Christopher Dixon *economics educator*
Catania, A(nthony) Charles *psychology educator*
Christ, Carl Finley *economist, educator*
Cooper, Joseph *political scientist, educator*
Davis, Carole Joan *psychologist, consultant*
Dietze, Gottfried *political science educator*
Entwisle, Doris Roberts *sociology educator*
Feldstein, Stanley *psychologist*
†Fogel, Joshua *psychologist, researcher*
Freeland, Mark Sydnes *economist*
Ginsberg, Benjamin *political science educator*
Goldfarb, Marsha Geier *economics educator, health services researcher*
Green, Bert Franklin, Jr., *psychologist*
Groenheim, Henri Arnold *psychologist, consultant*
Grossman, Joel B(arry) *political science educator*
Howard, J. Woodford, Jr., *political science educator*
Hula, Kevin William *political scientist, educator*
Jamison, Kay *psychologist*
Karni, Edi *economics educator*
LaVeist, Thomas Alexis *sociologist*
Maccini, Louis John *economic educator*
Melick, Clifford Francis *sociologist, researcher*
Mintz, Sidney Wilfred *anthropologist*
Money, John William *psychologist, educator*
Peake, Charles Franklin *economist, educator*
Pelizzo, Riccardo *political scientist*

†Pincus, Fred Leonard *sociology educator*
†Puglisi, Mary Joanna *psychologist*
Radin, Beryl Avis *public administration and policy educator*
Rose, Hugh *retired economics educator*
Salamon, Lester Milton *political science educator*
†Short, John Rennie *geographer, educator*
Sinnott, Jan Marie Dynda *psychologist*
†Soeken, Karen Lynne *research methods educator, researcher*
Stanley, Julian Cecil, Jr., *psychology educator*
Takacs, Wendy Emery *economics educator*
Wolman, M. Gordon *geography educator*
Young, Hobart Peyton *economist, mathematician, educator*

Bel Air
†Downes, Lilli M. *sociologist, social psychologist*
Faunce, William Dale *clinical psychologist, researcher, consultant*

Beltsville
Loeb, Marcia Joan *retired research psychologist*

Bethesda
Banik, Sambhu Nath *psychologist*
†Cleary, Robert Edward *government and public affairs educator*
De Vries, Barend Arie *economist, educator*
de Vries, Margaret Garritsen *economist*
Dommen, Arthur John *agricultural economist, historian*
Duncan, Constance Catharine *psychologist, educator, researcher*
Fischetti, Michael *public administration educator, arbitrator*
Galston, William Arthur *political scientist, educator*
Gschwindt de Gyor, Peter George, Sr., *economist*
Guadagno, Mary Ann Noecker *social scientist, consultant*
Haugan, Gertrude M. *clinical psychologist*
Holland, Robert Carl *economist*
Hutchinson, David Michael *economist*
Hyson, Charles David *economist, consultant*
Jamison, Dean Tecumseh *economist*
Knox, Sarah Stuart *psychophysiologist, researcher*
†Krantz, David S. *medical psychology educator, researcher*
Lamb, Michael E. *psychology researcher*
Lystad, Mary Hanemann (Mrs. Robert Lystad) *sociologist, author*
Mirsky, Allan Franklin *psychologist, researcher*
†Orr, Larry L. *economist*
Reiser, Brian Sydney *economist, statistician*
Reynolds, Robert Joel *economist, consultant*
Ruttenberg, Ruth A. *economist*
Schooler, Carmi *psychologist, sociologist, researcher*
Skolnik, Jonathan *economist*
Solomon, Robert *economist*
Striner, Herbert Edward *economics educator*
Sumberg, Theodore A. *retired economist*
Taylor, William Jesse, Jr., *international studies educator, research corporation president*
Timmer, Charles Peter *agricultural and development economist*
Wechsler, Andrew Robert *international economic consultant*
Youker, Robert Bliss *economist, consultant*

Bowie
Newhouse, Quentin, Jr., *social psychologist, educator, researcher*
Yager, Joseph Arthur, Jr., *economist*

Charlotte Hall
Brown, Ira Hugo *psychologist, educator*

Chestertown
†Littlefield, Lauren Montenegro *psychologist, educator*
McCall, Davy Henderson *economics educator, consultant*
Wendel, Richard Frederick *economist, educator, consultant*

Chevy Chase
Alexander, Arthur Jacob *economist*
Charen, Solomon *psychologist*
Cody, Peter Malcolm *economist, development, management consultant*
Emery, Robert Firestone *economist, educator*
Froomkin, Joseph *economic consultant*
Lewis, Gwendolyn Lorita *sociologist, policy analyst*
Linowes, David Francis *political economist, educator, corporate executive*
Norwood, Bernard *economist*
Norwood, Janet Lippe *economist*
Opper, Barbara Negri *financial economist*
Sapin, Burton Malcolm *political science educator, foreign policy analyst*
Teitel, Simon *economist, educator*

College Park
Brown, Richard Harvey *sociology, cultural studies and communications scholar, educator*
Chavas, Jean-Paul *economist, educator*
Elkin, Stephen Lloyd *political science educator*
†Ernstein, Julie H. *archaeologist, educator, researcher*
Gaylin, Ned L. *psychology educator*
Goode, B. Erich *sociologist, educator, retired criminologist*
†Helms, Janet Elteser *psychology educator, consultant, researcher*
Just, Richard Eugene *agricultural and resource economics educator consultant*
Lichtenberg, Erik Russell *economics educator*
Lyon, Andrew Bennet *economics educator*
Marshall, Monty Glenn *political research scientist, consultant*
Nembhard, Jessica Gitt Gordon *economist*
Nerlove, Marc Leon *economics educator*

Olson, Charles Eric *economist*
Panagariya, Arvind *economics educator*
Piper, Don Courtney *political science educator*
Presser, Harriet Betty *sociology educator*
Presser, Stanley *sociology educator*
Quester, George Herman *political science educator*
Schelling, Thomas Crombie *economist, educator*
Schneider, Benjamin *psychology educator*
Schwedler, Jillian Marie *political science educator*
Segal, David Robert *sociology educator*
Sigall, Harold Fred *psychology educator*
Sorenson, Georgia Lynn Jones *political scientist, educator*
Terchek, Ronald John *political science educator*
Tismaneanu, Vladimir *political science educator, researcher*
Zantek, Paul Francis *management scientist, educator*

Columbia
Bell, James Edward *psychologist, educator*
May, John Raymond *clinical psychologist*

Cumberland
Heckert, Paul Charles *sociologist, educator*

Davidsonville
Blaxall, Martha Ossoff *economist*

Ellicott City
Webster, Sharon B. *economist*

Emmitsburg
Zarnowski, C(hester) Frank *economics educator*

Fort Washington
McCafferty, James Arthur *sociologist*

Frederick
Cable, Dana Gerard *psychologist*

Frostburg
†Sigerstad, Thomas Daniel *psychologist, educator*

Gaithersburg
Ross, Sherman *psychologist, educator*

Hagerstown
†Ward, Spring Tina *history and political science educator*

Hereford
Flemmer, David Duane *clinical psychologist*

Hyattsville
McClain, George Nelson *economist, lawyer*

Jefferson
Dybell, Elizabeth Anne Sledden *clinical psychologist*

Kensington
Aborn, Murray *social scientist, researcher*
Gerra, Martin J(erome), Jr., *economist, educator*

La Plata
†Bryant, Maria Isabel *social sciences educator*

Lanham Seabrook
Corrothers, Helen Gladys *criminal justice official*

Lexington Park
Donely, George Anthony Thomas, III, *economist, consultant*

Lutherville
Chait, Andrea Melinda *school psychologist*
Eisenberg, Joseph Martin *psychologist, consultant*

Lutherville Timonium
Muuss, Rolf Eduard *retired psychologist, author*

Mc Henry
Kelly, Robert William *economist*

Mechanicsville
Rands, Robert Lawrence *archaeologist*

Mitchellville
Blasier, Cole *political scientist, educator*
Henle, Peter *retired economic consultant, arbitrator*

Odenton
Reich, Merrill Drury *intelligence consultant, writer*

Potomac
Jones, Sidney Lewis *economist, researcher, educator*
†Kling, William *economist, retired foreign service officer*
Oh, John Kie-Chiang *political science educator, university official*
Reichley, A. James *political scientist*
Rotberg, Iris Comens *social scientist*
Vadus, Gloria A. *scientific document examiner*
Walker, Charls Edward *economist, consultant*
Weiss, Michael David *mathematician, mathematical economist*
Wonnacott, Paul *economics educator*
†Young, Lih Ying H. *economist, consultant*

Rockville
Cohen-Mansfield, Jiska *psychologist, educator, researcher*
Feingold, S. Norman *psychologist*
Kurzman, Harold Philip *transportation economist, consultant*
†Mehrabi, Shah M. *economist, educator*
Niewiaroski, Trudi Osmers (Gertrude Niewiaroski) *social studies educator*
Wilson, James J. *public administration consultant*

Royal Oak
Israel, Lesley Lowe *political scientist, consultant*

Saint Marys City
Stabile, Donald Robert *economics educator, academic administrator*

Salisbury
Wu, Ying *economics educator, researcher*

Silver Spring
Ahmad, Mirza Muzaffar *economic advisor*
Alexander, Herbert E. *political scientist*
Ascher, Bernard *economist*
Blankenheimer, Bernard *economics consultant*
Burcroff, Richard Tomkinson, II, *economist*
Glickman, Albert Seymour *psychologist, educator*
Hsueh, Chun-tu *political scientist, historian, foundation executive*
†Katz, Pearl *anthropoligist, public health analyst*
†Mohr, Christina *retired economist*
Oswald, Rudolph A. *economist*
†Park, Sangkyun *economist*
Rayburn, Carole Ann (Mary Aida Rayburn) *psychologist, researcher, writer, consultant*
Rivera-Sinclair, Elsa *psychologist, consultant, researcher*
Wang, Kung-Lee *economics consultant*

Temple Hills
Day, Mary Jane Thomas *cartographer*
Smith, Irving *gerontologist*

Westminster
†Medina, Janet Gail *school psychologist, educator*

MASSACHUSETTS

Acton
Evans, Robert, Jr., *economics educator*

Agawam
†Sylvester, John Andrew *social studies educator*

Amherst
Alfange, Dean, Jr., *political science educator*
Averill, James Reed *psychology educator*
Benson, Lucy Wilson *political and diplomatic consultant*
Berger, Seymour Maurice *social psychologist*
†Blass, Elliott M. *psychologist, educator*
†Cole, John Wallace *retired anthropologist, researcher, educator, consultant*
Demerath, Nicholas Jay, III, *sociology educator*
†Haas, Peter M. *political science educator*
Halpern, Joel Martin *anthropologist, photographer*
Klare, Michael Thomas *social science educator, program director*
Mc Donagh, Edward Charles *sociologist, university administrator*
Mills, Patricia Jagentowicz *political philosophy educator, writer*
Misra, Joya *sociology and public policy educator*
†Oppenheim, Felix E. *political science educator*
Rossi, Alice S. *sociology educator, author*
Strickland, Bonnie Ruth *psychologist, educator*
Taubman, William Chase *political science educator*
Whitbourne, Susan Krauss *psychology educator*
Woodbury, Richard Benjamin *anthropologist, educator*

Andover
Arce, Pedro L. *economic development executive, banker*

Babson Park
Jones, Kent Albert *economist, educator*

Bedford
†Carey, Kathleen *economist*

Belmont
Feldstein, Kathleen Foley *economist, consultant*
Heyman, Gene Morris *research psychologist, educator*
†Kargman, Marie Witkin *marriage counselor, consultant*
Killgore, William Dale (Scott), Jr., *neuropsychologist*
Levendusky, Philip George *psychologist, education administrator*
Ronningstam, Elsa Frideborg *psychologist, educator*

Berkley
Murtagh, Michael Paul *psychologist*

Beverly
Arnold, Gordon B. *social science educator*

Boston
Barfield, Thomas Jefferson, III, *anthropology educator, consultant*
Berger, Harvey Robert *psychologist*
†Buckley, Todd Charles *psychologist*
Bustin, Edouard Jean *political scientist, educator*
†Connor, Walter Downing *political scientist, educator, researcher*
Dentler, Robert Arnold *sociologist, educator*
Ellis, Randall Poor *economist, educator*
†Ellison, Marcia A. *anthropologist, researcher*
Gamst, Frederick Charles *social anthropologist*
Garrett, Gerald R. *sociology educator, criminologist, consultant*
Gleason, Jean Berko *psychology educator*
Hammond, Norman David Curle *archaeology educator, researcher*
Hofmann, Stefan Georg *psychologist, researcher*
Kerr, William Robert *economist, consultant*
†Larsen, Ulla Margrethe *demographer educator, consultant*
†Leffert, James Steven *psychologist*

†Maki, Dean Michael *economist*
Manning, Peter Kirby *sociologist educator*
Martin, Cathie Jo *political scientist, educator*
Mason, Emanuel Joel *psychology educator*
Mayers, David *political science and history educator*
†McGuire, Thomas G. *economist, educator, mental health services professional, researcher*
McIntyre, Mildred Jean *clinical psychologist, writer, neuroscientist*
Merton, Robert C. *economist, educator*
Miller, Bradley Adam *economist*
Murphy, Evelyn Frances *economist*
Newhouse, Joseph Paul *economist, educator*
Nolan, Cathal J. *historian*
Norman, Dennis Keith *psychologist, educator*
Palmer, David Scott *political scientist, educator*
Plotkin, Irving H(erman) *economist, consultant*
Ra'anan, Uri (Heinz Felix Frischwasser) *international politics educator*
Rossell, Christine Hamilton *political science educator*
Roth, Alvin Eliot *economics educator*
†Russell, John Malcolm *archaeologist, educator*
Salinger, Michael Alvin *economist, educator*
Sanders, Irwin Taylor *sociology educator*
Schachter, Gustav *economics educator*
Schmidt, Vivien Ann *political scientist, educator*
Strahler, Alan H. *geography educator, author, researcher*
Terkla, David Gabriel *economics educator*
Watanabe, Paul Yashihiko *political scientist, educator*
Woerner, Frederick Frank *international relations educator*
Yeager, Peter Cleary *sociologist, educator*

Braintree
Salloway, Josephine Plovnick *psychologist, marriage and family therapist, mental health counselor, psychology educator, college counselor*

Brockton
O'Brien, John Steininger *clinical psychologist*
O'Farrell, Timothy James *psychologist, educator*

Brookline
Buchin, Jacqueline Chase *clinical psychologist*
†Cottle, Thomas Joseph *sociologist*
Cromwell, Adelaide M. *sociology educator*
Kanin, Doris May *political scientist, consultant*

Burlington
Harding, Wayne Michael *sociologist, researcher*

Cambridge
Abt, Clark C. *social scientist, executive, engineer, publisher, educator*
Alt, James Edward *political science educator*
Altman, Micah *social scientist, researcher*
Appley, Mortimer Herbert *psychologist, university president emeritus*
†Bailyn, Lotte *psychology and management educator*
Bator, Francis Michel *economist, educator*
Berndt, Ernst Rudolf *economist, educator*
Blackmer, Donald Laurence Morton *political scientist*
Borjas, George J(esus) *economics educator*
Brown, Edgar Cary *retired economics educator*
Campbell, John Young *economics educator*
Caves, Richard Earl *economist, educator*
Champion, Hale (Charles Hale Champion) *political science educator, former public official*
Cooper, Richard Newell *economist, educator*
Dominguez, Jorge Ignacio *government educator*
Drago-Severson, Eleanor Elizabeth E. *developmental psychologist, educator, researcher*
Dunlop, John Thomas *economics educator, former secretary of labor*
†Dynarski, Susan Marie *social studies educator*
Eckaus, Richard Samuel *economist, educator*
Ellwood, David Tabor *public policy educator*
Feldstein, Martin Stuart *economist, educator*
Fisher, Franklin Marvin *economist*
Friedman, Benjamin Morton *economics educator*
Galbraith, John Kenneth *retired economist*
Gardner, Howard Earl *writer*
†George, Kenneth Martin *anthropology educator*
Goldin, Claudia Dale *economics educator*
Goldman, Marshall Irwin *economist, educator*
Hanser, Philip *econometrician*
†Hausman, Jerry Allen *economics educator, consultant*
†Hersch, Joni *economist, educator*
Hoffmann, Inge Schneier *psychologist, educator*
Holzman, Philip Seidman *psychologist, educator*
Ingbar, Mary Lee *economist*
Jacoby, Henry Donnan *economist, educator*
Jencks, Christopher Sandys *public policy educator*
Johnson, Willard Raymond *political science educator, consultant*
Jorgenson, Dale Weldeau *economist, educator*
Joskow, Paul Lewis *economist, educator*
Juma, Calestous *international development educator*
Kagan, Jerome *psychologist, educator*
Katz, Lawrence Francis *economics educator*
Kaysen, Carl *economics educator*
Kelman, Herbert Chanoch *psychology educator*
Keniston, Kenneth *psychologist, educator*
Kennedy, Stephen Dandridge *economist, researcher*
Keyfitz, Nathan *sociologist, demographer, educator*
Kleinman, Arthur Michael *medical anthropologist, psychiatrist, educator*
Lamberg-Karlovsky, Clifford Charles *anthropologist, archaeologist*
Langer, Ellen Jane *psychologist, educator, writer*
LeVine, Robert Alan *anthropology educator, researcher*

Lieberson, Stanley *sociologist, educator*
Linsky, Marty *public policy educator, consultant*
Maass, Arthur *political science and environmental studies educator*
Maher, Brendan Arnold *psychology educator, editor*
Meyer, John Robert *economist, educator*
Moore, Mark Harrison *criminal justice and public policy educator*
Neustadt, Richard Elliott *political scientist, educator*
Perkins, Dwight Heald *economics educator*
Pfaltzgraff, Robert Louis, Jr., *political scientist, educator*
Pinker, Steven A. *cognitive scientist, educator*
Poterba, James Michael *economist, educator*
Pye, Lucian Wilmot *political science educator*
Rathjens, George William *political scientist, educator*
Rogoff, Kenneth Saul *economics educator*
Rosovsky, Henry *economist, educator*
Ruggie, John Gerard *political science educator, diplomat*
Samuelson, Paul Anthony *economist, educator*
Sapolsky, Harvey Morton *political scientist, educator*
Schneider, Franz *psychology researcher*
Skolnikoff, Eugene B. *political science educator*
Solow, Robert Merton *economist, educator*
Temin, Peter *economist, educator*
Thompson, Dennis Frank *political science and ethics educator, consultant*
Verba, Sidney *political scientist, educator*
Viscusi, W(illiam) G. Kip *economics educator*
Vogel, Ezra F. *sociology educator*
Vogt, Evon Zartman, Jr., *anthropologist, writer*
Westerlund, Elaine M. *psychologist, educator*
Willie, Charles Vert *sociology educator*
Wilson, William Julius *sociologist, educator*
†Yip, Winnie *health economics educator*
Zeckhauser, Richard Jay *economist, educator*
Zeidenstein, George *population educator*
Zhang, Hui *research political scientist*
Zinberg, Dorothy Shore *science policy educator*

Charlestown
Lasko, Natasha B. *psychologist*

Chestnut Hill
Baum, Christopher Frederick *economics educator, consultant*
Carfora, John Michael *economics educator, academic administrator*
Siegel, Richard Allen *economist*
Smith, David Horton *social sciences educator*
Williamson, John Butler *sociology educator*
Wolfe, Alan *political science educator, writer*

Concord
Codere, Helen Frances *anthropologist, educator, university dean*

Dorchester
†Berg, John Conrad *political science educator*
Johnson, Crystal Elaine *psychologist, community activist, poet, writer, educator*

Fitchburg
Spero, Joshua Benjamin *political scientist, educator*

Framingham
West, Doe *bioethicist, social justice activist, researcher*

Gloucester
McCarl, Henry Newton *economics and geology consultant, venture capitalist*

Groton
Huguenin, Nancy Hoffman *behavioral psychologist*

Haverhill
Heineman, William A. *political scientist, educator*

Haydenville
Shallcross, Doris Jane *creative behavioral educator*

Ipswich
Jennings, Frederic Beach, Jr., *economist, saltwater flyfishing guide*

Lexington
Bernardi, John Lawrence, Jr., *economic historian, educator, consultant*
Collins, Allan Meakin *cognitive scientist, psychologist, educator*
Gutheim, Allen Herman *economist*
Horowitz, Morris A. *retired economics educator*
Jordan, Judith Victoria *clinical psychologist, educator*
Papanek, Gustav Fritz *economist, educator*
†Ronchi, Donald M. *psychologist, educator*
Shapiro, Marian Kaplun *psychologist*
Washburn, Barbara Polk *cartographer, researcher, explorer*

Lincoln
Barrett, Beatrice Helene *psychologist*

Lowell
†Berkowitz, William R. *psychologist, writer, consultant*
Galizzi, Monica *economics educator*
Kunzendorf, Robert Godfrey *psychologist, educator, researcher*

Medford
Conklin, John Evan *sociology educator*
DeBold, Joseph Francis *psychology educator*
Elkind, David *psychology educator*
Goodwin, Neva R. *economist*
Miczek, Klaus Alexander *psychology educator*

Melrose
Henken, Bernard Samuel *clinical psychologist, speech pathologist*

Middleboro
Green, Michael Jeffrey *retired psychologist, consultant, administrator*

Montague
Kohler, Heinz *economics educator*

Nantucket
Sangree, Walter Hinchman *social anthropologist, educator*

Natick
Banderet, Louis Eugene *psychologist*
Bensel, Carolyn Kirkbride *psychologist*
Johnson, Richard Frederick *psychologist, researcher, educator*

Needham
Boulding, Elise Marie *sociologist, educator*
Glaser, Daniel *sociologist, educator*

New Bedford
Speser, Phyllis Leah *social scientist, consultant*

New Town
Carton, Lonnie Caming *educational psychologist*

Newton
Holbik, Karel *economics educator*

Newton Center
Adams, F. Gerard *economist, educator*
†Cousineau, Madeleine *sociologist, educator*

Newton Highlands
Fanger, Mark *psychologist, psychotherapist, consultant*

North Adams
Sabot, Richard Henry *economics educator, researcher, investor, entrepreneur*

North Andover
Martin, Curtis Harmon *political science educator*

North Dartmouth
Barrow, Clyde Wayne *political scientist, educator*
Magrass, Yale Robert *sociology educator, writer*

North Eastham
Hallowell, Burton Crosby *economist, educator*

Northampton
Lehmann, Phyllis Williams *archaeologist, educator*
Rose, Peter Isaac *sociologist, writer*
†Zimbalist, Andrew S. *economist, educator*

Norwood
Luiselli, James Kenneth *psychologist*

Orleans
Rappaport, Margaret M.W.E. *psychologist, physician, author, pilot, consultant*

Plainfield
Nash, June Caprice *anthropology educator*

Quincy
Spangler, Arthur Stephenson, Jr., *psychologist*

Raynham
Kaplan, Kenneth Barry *psychologist*

Rockport
Harries, James Theodore *psychologist*

Salem
Goss, Laurence Edward, Jr., *geographer, educator*
Higgins, Gina O'Connell *psychologist, writer*
†Levy, Richard J. *political scientist, educator*

Shelburne Falls
Collard, Roberta R. *emeritus educator, researcher*

Sherborn
Anderson, James Everett *economics educator*

Shrewsbury
†Lucas, Sandra J. *psychologist*

Siasconset
Emerson, Alice Frey *political scientist, educator emerita*

Somerville
Meagher, Robert Francis *international economic law consultant*

South Hadley
†Townsley, Eleanor Rose *sociologist, educator*
†Wartenberg, Thomas Eliot *social sciences educator, writer*

South Natick
Cantor, Pamela Corliss *psychologist*

Springfield
Agonafer, Mulugeta Gabriel *political scientist, educator*
Napolitan, Joseph *political consultant*

Truro
Kelley, Maryellen R. *economist, management consultant*

Vineyard Haven
Hoffman, Michael Linsay *economist*

Waltham
Cecchetti, Stephen Giovanni *economics educator*
Domar, Alice Diane *psychologist, educator*
Flynn, Patricia Marie *economics educator*
McCulloch, Rachel *economics researcher, educator*
†Morgan, Claudia Ann *social scientist*
†Saler, Benson *retired anthropologist*
Sekuler, Robert William *psychologist, educator*
†Shepard, Donald Sloane *public policy research educator*
Thomas, Janet Marie *economics educator*
Unger, Rhoda Kesler *psychology educator*

Wellesley
Bishop, Robert Lyle *economist, educator*
Eilts, Hermann Frederick *international relations educator, former diplomat*
Giddon, Donald B(ernard) *psychologist, educator*
Miller, Linda B. *political scientist*
Morant, Ricardo Bernardino *psychology educator*
Paarlberg, Robert L. *political science educator*
Rollins, Judith Ann *sociologist, educator, researcher, writer*
Stettner, Edward A. *political science educator*

West Newton
Cox, Donald C. *economics educator*

Westborough
Staffier, Pamela Moorman *psychologist*
Tobias, Lester Lee *psychological consultant*

Weston
Kraft, Gerald *economist*

Williamstown
Bolton, Roger Edwin *economist, educator*
†Brown, Michael F. *anthropologist, educator*
Bruton, Henry Jackson *educator, economist*
Cramer, Phebe *psychologist*
Fuller, Renee Nuni *psychologist, educational publisher*
Kassin, Saul *psychology educator*
†Nolan, James Lawry, Jr., *sociologist*
Sheahan, John Bernard *economist, educator*
Solomon, Paul Robert *neuropsychologist, educator*
Varese, Federico *political science educator*

Woods Hole
Jin, Di *economist*

Worcester
Dyer-Cole, Pauline *school psychologist, educator*
†Fisher, William Henry *sociologist, researcher, educator*
Mathisen, Howard *psychologist, minister*
McDowell, David Jamison *clinical psychologist*
Radzicki, Michael Joseph *economist*
Ross, Robert Jon Sanford *sociology educator*
Thomas, Ward John *political science educator*
Turner, Billie Lee, II, *geography educator*
Upshur, Carole Christofk *psychologist, educator*
Wapner, Seymour *psychologist, educator, administrator*
†Wilkes, John M. *social sciences educator*

MICHIGAN

Adrian
Weathers, Milledge Wright *retired economics educator*

Allendale
†Murphy, Kimmarie A. *anthropologist, educator*
†Raney, David Alan *history educator*

Ann Arbor
Apperson, Jean *psychologist*
Arlinghaus, Sandra Judith Lach *mathematical geographer, educator*
Bachman, Jerald Graybill *psychologist, researcher*
†Bao, Shuming *economist, researcher*
Behling, Charles Frederick *psychology educator*
Berent, Stanley *psychologist, educator, researcher, consultant*
Bishop, Elizabeth Shreve *psychologist*
Brace, C. Loring *anthropologist, educator*
Cohen, Malcolm Stuart *economist, business executive*
Converse, Philip Ernest *social science educator*
Courant, Paul Noah *economist, educator, academic administrator*
Dominguez, Kathryn Mary *educator*
Eron, Leonard David *psychology educator*
Freedman, Ronald *sociology educator*
Frey, William H. *demographer, educator*
Fusfeld, Daniel Roland *economist*
Garn, Stanley Marion *physical anthropologist, educator*
Gomberg, Edith S. Lisansky *psychologist, educator*
Gone, Joseph Patrick *psychologist, educator*
Hagen, John William *psychology educator*
†Himle, Joseph Alan *social sciences educator*
House, James Stephen *sociological social psychologist, educator*
Howrey, Eugene Philip *economics educator, consultant*
Inglehart, Ronald Franklin *political science educator*
Jackson, James Sidney *psychology educator*
Johnston, Lloyd Douglas *social scientist*
†Kahn, Robert L(ouis) *psychologist, educator*
Kingdon, John Wells *political science educator*
Kmenta, Jan *economics educator*
Kornblum, Sylvan *psychologist*
Mackie-Mason, Jeffrey King *economics and information technology educator*
Manis, Melvin *psychologist, educator*
Markovits, Andrei Steven *political science educator*
Mc Cracken, Paul Winston *retired economist, business educator*
McKeachie, Wilbert James *psychologist, educator*
Mitchell, Edward John *economist, retired educator*
Mizruchi, Mark Sheldon *sociology and business administration educator*
Moholy-Nagy, Hattula *archaeologist*
†Mueggler, Erik *anthropologist, educator*
Nisbett, Richard Eugene *psychology educator*
Parsons, Jeffrey Robinson *anthropologist, educator*
Pedley, John Griffiths *archaeologist, educator*
Pierce, Roy *political science educator*
Price, Richard Henry *psychologist, educator*
†Quintyn, Conrad Bezekiah *anthropologist, educator*
Saxonhouse, Gary Roger *economics educator, consultant*
Shapiro, Matthew David *economist, educator*
Singer, Eleanor *sociologist, editor*
Singer, J. David *political science educator*
Stafford, Frank P. *economist, educator*
Stafford, Frank Peter, Jr., *economics educator, consultant*
Steiner, Peter Otto *economics educator, dean*
Thornton, Arland *sociologist, educator*
Wellman, Henry M. *psychology educator*
Whitman, Marina Von Neumann *economist, educator*
Williams, Melvin Donald *anthropologist, educator*
Woronoff, Israel *former psychology educator*
Zucker, Robert A(lpert) *psychologist*

Auburn Hills
Etefia, Florence Victoria *school psychologist*

Battle Creek
Andert, Jeffrey Norman *clinical psychologist*

Big Rapids
Karafa, Joseph A. *psychology educator, consultant*
†Roy, Donald H. *political scientist, educator*

Bloomfield Hills
Belavek, Debra Louise *school psychologist*
Sugrue, Dennis Patrick *clinical psychologist*

Clifford
Staples, Lynne Livingston Mills *retired psychologist, educator, consultant*

Detroit
Alexander, Sheldon *psychology educator*
Cantoni, Louis Joseph *psychologist, poet, sculptor*
Ferguson, Tamara *clinical sociologist*
Fleming, George Robert *psychologist*
†Foreman, Kelly Marie *anthropologist, music educator*
Goodman, Allen Charles *economist, educator*
†Ketterer, Mark William *psychologist, research scientist*
†MacDonald, Douglas Andrew *psychologist, educator*
Marx, Thomas George *economist*
McArthur, Steven Francis *psychologist, educator*
Stack, Steven John, Jr., *criminal justice educator*
Trix, Frances *linguistic anthropologist, consultant*

Duluth
Bower, John Richard Fenn *archaeologist, educator*

East Lansing
Abeles, Norman *psychologist, educator*
Abramson, Paul Robert *political scientist, educator*
Allen, Bruce Templeton *economics educator*
Allen, William Barclay *political scientist, consultant, writer*
Baillie, Richard Thomas *economist, educator*
Barlowe, Raleigh *economist, educator*
Busch, Lawrence Michael *sociologist, researcher*
†Crewe, Nancy Moe *psychologist and educator*
Dow, Steven Benjamin *social studies educator*
Finifter, Ada Weintraub *political scientist, educator*
Gass, Gertrude Zemon *psychologist, researcher*
Ilgen, Daniel Richard *psychology educator*
Kalof, Linda Henry *sociologist, educator*
Koo, Anthony Ying Chang *economist, educator*
Kreinin, Mordecha Eliahu *economics educator*
Ladenson, Mark Lawrence *economist, educator*
Liedholm, Carl Edward *economics educator*
Manderscheid, Lester Vincent *agricultural economics educator*
McKinley, Camille Dombrowski *psychologist*
Menchik, Paul Leonard *economist, educator*
Obst, Norman Philip *economist, educator*
Press, Charles *retired political science educator*
Robbins, Lawrence Harry *anthropologist, educator*
Rubner, Michael *international relations educator, university administrator*
Stieber, Jack *economist, educator, labor arbitrator*
Strassmann, W. Paul *economics educator*
Talhelm, Daniel Roderick *economics consulting firm executive, educator*
Useem, Ruth Hill *sociology educator*
Winder, Clarence Leland *psychologist, educator*
Woodbury, Stephen Abbott *economics educator*

Flint
Rozycki, Paul Andrew *political science educator*

Gaylord
Backlund, James David *psychology educator*

Grand Blanc
Reddy, Nallapu Narayan *economics educator*

Grand Haven
Parmelee, Walker Michael *psychologist*

Grand Rapids
Jansma, Theodore John, Jr., *psychologist*
Kooistra, William Henry *clinical psychologist*
MacDonald, David Richard *industrial psychologist*
Tiemstra, John Peter *economics educator*
Yamazaki, Makoto *economics educator*

Grosse Pointe Farms
Kerns, Gertrude Yvonne *psychologist*

Harbor Springs
Ketcham, Warren Andrew *psychologist, educator*

Hillsdale
Wolfram, Gary Lee *economics educator, consultant*

Holland
Claar, Victor Vyron *economics educator*
Holmes, Jack Edward *political science educator*

Howell
Rohrabacher, Janet Hammond *geneologist, archivist*

Kalamazoo
†DeChano, Lisa M *geographer, educator*
Mc Allister, Lester Belden *economics educator*
Sichel, Werner *economics educator*

Lansing
Ballbach, Philip Thornton *political consultant, investor*
†Geckil, Ilhan Kubilay *economist, consultant*

Livonia
Levitt, Leon *business administration educator*
Woods, Edythe B. *psychology educator*

Marquette
Swaine, Howard Ralph *economist, educator, consultant*

Mount Pleasant
Browne, William P. *political science educator*
Dunbar, Gary Leo *psychology educator*

Niles
Hamburg, Roger Phillip *retired political science and public affairs educator*

Northport
Thomas, Philip Stanley *economist, educator*

Novi
Sobczak, Judy Marie *clinical psychologist*

Okemos
Berkman, Claire Fleet *psychologist*
Solo, Robert Alexander *economist, educator*

Port Huron
Moss, Carl Arthur *psychologist*

Rochester
†Kubicek, Paul J. *political scientist, educator*
Nesbary, Dale K. *social sciences educator*

Rochester Hills
Minton, Henry Lee *psychology educator*

Saint Clair Shores
Neal-Vittiglio, Cynthia Karen *clinical psychologist*

Saline
Hansen, Janice Elizabeth *psychologist*

Sault Sainte Marie
Johnson, Gary Robert *political scientist*

Southfield
Birdsong, Emil Ardell *clinical psychologist*
Gregory, Karl Dwight *economist, educator, consultant*
Thimotheose, Kadakampallil George *psychologist*
Weiner, Karen Colby (Karen Lynn Colby) *psychologist, lawyer*

Sterling Heights
Campbell, Terence Warren *forensic psychologist*

University Center
†Dykhuizen, C. Jeffrey *child development psychologist, educator*
Hill, Alan Gordon *sociologist, educator*
Hoerneman, Calvin A., Jr., *economics educator*

Ypsilanti
Bishop, J. Joe *social studies educator*
Friedman, Monroe *psychologist, educator*
Weinstein, Jay A. *social science educator, researcher*

MINNESOTA

Collegeville
Raverty, Thomas Donald (Aaron Raverty) *anthropologist, monk*

Duluth
Hoffman, Richard George *psychologist*
Stoddard, Patricia Florence Coulter *retired psychologist*

Eden Prairie
DeMann, Michael Marcus *psychologist*

Edina
Gottesman, Irving Isadore *psychology educator*

†Rosenblum, Ava F. *sociologist, educator*

Forest Lake
Marchese, Ronald Thomas *ancient history and archaeology educator*

Mankato
Friend, Donald Agar *geographer, geomorphologist, educator*
Slocum, Fred *political scientist, educator*

Minneapolis
Adams, John Stephen *geography educator*
Bancroft, Ann E. *polar explorer*
Bouchard, Thomas Joseph, Jr., *psychology educator, researcher*
Chipman, John Somerset *economist, educator*
Erickson, W(alter) Bruce *business and economics educator, entrepreneur*
Frank, Kerry Dean *psychology educator, consultant*
Gudeman, Stephen Frederick *anthropology educator*
Holmes, Thomas J. *economist, educator*
Holt, Robert Theodore *political scientist, dean, educator*
†Hurwicz, Leonid *economist, educator*
Johnson, Badri Nahvi *sociology educator, real estate business owner*
Johnson, David Wolcott *psychologist, educator*
Knoke, David Harmon *sociology educator*
Kudrle, Robert Thomas *economist, educator*
Lewis, Stephen Richmond, Jr., *economist, educator, academic administrator*
†McConnell, Scott Rushton *educational psychology educator*
Mohring, Herbert *economics educator*
Nightingale, Edmund Joseph *clinical psychologist, educator*
Ostrom, Don *political science educator*
Porter, Philip Wayland *geography educator*
Prescott, Edward C. *economist, educator*
Reiss, Ira Leonard *retired sociology educator, writer*
Rogers, William Cecil *political science educator, consultant*
Savelsberg, Joachim Josef *sociologist, educator*
Schreiner, John Christian *economics consultant, software publisher*
Schwartzberg, Joseph Emanuel *geographer, educator*
Scoville, James Griffin *economics educator*
Shively, William Phillips *political scientist, educator*
†Skovholt, Thomas Meyer *psychology educator*
†Sroufe, Lawrence Alan *child psychologist, educator*
Strommen, Merton Peter *research psychologist, clergyman*
Ward, David Allen *sociology educator*
Ysseldyke, James Edward *psychology educator, dean*

Minnetonka
Humphrey, Sandra McLeod *psychologist*

Moorhead
Noblitt, Harding Coolidge *political scientist, educator*
Trainor, John Felix *retired economics educator*

Morris
Demos, Vasilikie Polytimy *sociology educator*
†Joo, Seung-Ho *political scientist, educator*

Northfield
Clark, William Hartley *political science educator*

Rochester
Taylor, Jeffrey Lee *political science educator, author*

Saint Cloud
Frank, Stephen Ira *political science educator*
†Leppman, Elizabeth Jane *geographer, educator*
Prout, Robert Stephen *higher education consultant, law enforcement consultant*
Tripp, Luke Samuel *educator*
†Ward, Edward Anthony *economist, educator*

Saint Louis Park
Schlutter, Lois Cochrane *psychologist*

Saint Paul
†Alvi, Shahid Anwar *sociology educator*
Bengston, David Neil *economist, educator*
Dahl, Reynold Paul *applied economics educator*
D'Aurora, James Joseph *psychologist, consultant*
Eidman, Vernon Roy *agricultural economist, educator*
Harris, Duchess *social sciences educator*
Jessup, Paul Frederick *financial economist, educator*
Mabry, Paul Davis *psychobiologist, educator, researcher*
Malecki, Edward Stanley, Jr., *political science educator*
Raup, Philip Martin *retired agricultural economics educator*
Rosenblatt, Paul Conrad *family educator*
Rossmann, Jack Eugene *psychology educator*
Ruttan, Vernon Wesley *agricultural economist*
Schultz, David A. *political science educator, editor, writer, lawyer*
Swenson, Tami Charlotte *research analyst*
Zimmerman, Larry John *anthropologist, educator*

Saint Peter
Leitch, Richard *political science educator*
Mc Rostie, Clair Neil *economics educator*

Winona
Holm, Joy Alice *psychology educator, goldsmith, artist, art educator*

MISSISSIPPI

Biloxi
Cox, Albert Harrington, Jr., *economist*
Crumbaugh, James Charles *psychologist*

Forest
Park, James Wallace *economics educator*

Hattiesburg
Burrus, John N(ewell) *sociology educator*
Davis, Charles Raymond *political scientist, educator*
†Schweinle, Amy *psychologist, educator*
Waltman, Jerold Lloyd *political scientist, educator*

Mississippi State
Clynch, Edward John *political science educator, researcher*
Wall, Diane Eve *political science educator*
†Watson, Thomas Steuart *psychologist, educator*

Natchez
Dunnell, Robert Chester *archaeologist, educator*

Oxford
Roberts, Michael Dean *psychologist*

Ridgeland
O'Neill, Paul John *retired psychology educator*

Tupelo
Witty, Thomas Ezekiel, III, *psychologist, researcher*

MISSOURI

Bolivar
Brown, Autry *psychology educator, clergyman*
Hood, Michael Lee *psychologist, clinical researcher, educator*

Chesterfield
Falk, Barbara Marie *psychologist*

Columbia
Bank, Barbara J. *sociology educator*
Benson, Jerry Kenneth *sociologist*
Biddle, Bruce Jesse *social psychologist, educator*
Eastman, Harold Dwight *retired social studies educator, journalist*
Geary, David Cyril *psychology educator*
†Good, Glenn Edward *psychologist, educator*
†Gubrium, Jaber F. *sociology educator*
†Lambert, Michael Canute *psychologist, educator*
Lo, Clarence Y. H. *sociology educator, writer*
LoPiccolo, Joseph *psychologist, educator, author*
Ratti, Ronald Andrew *economics educator*
Rowlett, Ralph Morgan *archaeologist, educator*
Salter, Christopher Lord *geography educator*
Yarwood, Dean Lesley *political science educator*

Fayette
Hirsch, Michael Lee *mayor*
McIntosh, William David *mathematics educator emeritus*

Fulton
Jefferson, Kurt Wayne *political science educator*

Grandview
Justesen, Don Robert *psychologist*

Half Way
Graves, Jerrell Loren *demographic studies researcher*

Hollister
Herron, Gayle Ann *forensic psychologist, mental health consultant, psychotherapist, health facility administrator, columnist*

Kansas City
Bell, Stephanie *economics educator*
Coveney, Raymond Martin, Jr., *educator*
Eddy, William Bahret *psychology educator, university dean*
Fecht, Daniel R. *psychologist, actor*
Graham, Charles *research psychologist*
Lubin, Bernard *psychologist, educator*
†Nagle, Jean Susan Karabacz *sociologist, psychologist*
Roosa, Jan Bertorotta *clinical psychologist*
†Wynkoop, Mary Ann *American studies educator*

Kirksville
Maglio, Christopher John *psychologist, educator*
Nnadozie, Emmanuel *economist, educator*

Kirkwood
Mosby, Robert J. *psychologist*

Lees Summit
Rethemeyer, Robert John *social studies educator*

Maryville
Kharadia, Virabhai Chelabhai *economist, educator, researcher*

Raytown
Smith, Robert Francis *psychologist, consultant*

Saint Clair
Gullet, Leon Estle *retired cartographer*

Saint Joseph
Boor, Myron Vernon *psychologist, educator*
Hamzaee, Reza Gholi *economics educator*

Saint Louis
Beck, Lois Grant *anthropologist, educator, author*
Berliant, Marcus Craig *economist*
Browman, David L(udvig) *archaeologist*

Drucker, Mark Lewis *public administration educator, consultant*
Entessar, Tahmineh *political scientist, educator*
Epstein, Lee Joan *political science educator*
Felix, David *retired economics educator, consultant*
Greenbaum, Stuart I. *economist, educator*
Gruenberg, Gladys Walleman *economics educator, arbitrator*
Kling, Merle *political scientist, university official*
Laster, Atlas, Jr., *psychologist*
Leven, Charles Louis *economics educator*
Le Vine, Victor Theodore *political science educator*
Lindsey, Linda Lee *sociology educator*
†McMahon, Judith Wantland *psychologist, educator*
Miller, Gary J. *political economist*
North, Douglass Cecil *economist, educator*
O'Connell, Daniel Craig *psychology educator*
†Patterson, Miles Lawrence *psychology educator*
†Polgar, Michael F. *sociology educator, researcher*
Rosenzweig, Saul *psychologist, educator, administrator*
Salisbury, Robert Holt *political science educator*
Schmid, Frank Andreas *economist*
Smith, Richard Jay *anthropologist, orthodontist, educator*
Storandt, Martha *psychologist*
Thompson, Vetta Lynn Sanders *psychologist, educator*
Virgo, John Michael *economist, researcher, educator*
†Voss, K. Dirk *social sciences educator, researcher*
Watson, Patty Jo *anthropology educator*
Weidenbaum, Murray Lew *economist, educator*
Welch, Patrick James *economics educator, author, consultant*
Witherspoon, William *investment economist*

Springfield
†Rutherford, Ken Robin *political scientist, educator*
Stone, Allan David *economics educator*
Van Cleave, William Robert *international relations educator*

Urbana
†Frey, Lucille Pauline *social studies educator, consultant*

MONTANA

Bozeman
Duffié, Mary Katharine *anthropologist, researcher, educator*
Gray, Philip Howard *former psychologist, writer*

Helena
†Lowney, Jeremiah *sociologist, educator, priest*
Seiler, Karen Peake *organizational psychologist*

Kalispell
Gallagher, Tonya Marie *family support specialist*

Missoula
Grieves, Forest Leslie *political science educator*
Lopach, James Joseph *political science educator*
Power, Thomas Michael *economist, educator*

NEBRASKA

Alliance
Haefele, Edwin Theodore *political theorist, consultant*

Chadron
†Hinesley, Gail Ann *social sciences educator*

Grand Island
Buettner, Anne Yu Ramona Wing-mui *psychologist*

Harrison
Knudson, Ruthann *environmental consultant*

Hastings
Wigert, Lee Roy *psychology educator*

Kearney
Harrold, Francis Bernard, Jr., *anthropology educator*

Lincoln
Auld, James S. *educational psychologist*
†Bodvarsson, Orn Bodvar *economist, educator*
Deegan, Mary Jo *sociology educator*
MacPhee, Craig Robert *economist, educator*
McCutcheon, Allan Lee *sociology educator*
Ottoson, Howard Warren *agricultural economist, former university administrator*
Parker, Keith Dwight *sociology educator*
Peterson, Wallace Carroll, Sr., *economics educator*
Riefler, Roger Frank *economics educator*
Rohren, Brenda Marie Anderson *therapist, educator*
Stoddard, Robert H. *geography educator*

Omaha
Allen, Robert Francis *economist, educator*
†Bartle, John R. *social sciences educator*
†Clark, Terry Dee *political scientist, educator*
†Dilly, Barbara Jane *anthropologist, educator*
†Johnson, Lerlean Newsome *sociologist*
Justice, Bob Joe *corporate development executive*
North, Terry Claire *clinical psychologist*

NEVADA

Carson City
Loftis, Rebecca Hope *psychologist*

East Ely
Alderman, Minnis Amelia *psychologist, educator, small business owner*

Incline Village
Jones, Robert Alonzo *economist*

Las Vegas
Bowers, Michael Wayne *political science educator, writer*
Epstein, William Maurice *social work educator*
Goldstein, Steven Edward *psychologist*
Goodall, Leonard Edwin *public administration educator*
†Gottschalk, Simon *sociologist, educator*
†Jelen, Ted G. *political scientist*
Meiner, Sue Ellen Thompson *gerontologist, nurse practitioner, nursing educator and researcher, legal nurse consultant*
Mortillaro, Louis Francis *psychologist*
Weeks, Gerald *psychology educator*

Reno
Cargill, Thomas Frank *economist, educator*
Chapman, Samuel Greeley *political science educator, criminologist*
Cummings, Nicholas Andrew *psychologist*
†Fruzzetti, Alan E. *psychologist, educator*
Leland, Joy Hanson *anthropologist, alcohol research specialist*
Lemire, David Stephen *school psychologist, educator*
Solso, Robert L. *psychology educator*
Weinberg, Leonard Burton *political scientist*

Zephyr Cove
Hudzinski, Leonard Gerard *social sciences educator, researcher*

NEW HAMPSHIRE

Bedford
Collins, Diana Josephine *psychologist*

Dover
Charos, Evangelos Nikolaou *economics educator*

Durham
†Boy, Angelo V. *psychology educator*
DeVries, Willem *philosophy educator*
†Gumprecht, Blake *geographer*
Kendall-Tackett, Kathleen Ann *researcher, health psychologist*
Palmer, Stuart Hunter *sociology educator*
†Scharff, Robert Caesar *social sciences educator, writer, humanities educator*
Woodward, Robert Simpson, IV, *economics educator*

Francestown
Foster, Margery Somers *economics educator*

Hanover
Baldwin, William Lee *economics educator*
Blanchflower, David Graham *economics educator*
Bower, Richard Stuart *economist, educator*
Campbell, Colin Dearborn *economist, educator*
Clement, Meredith Owen *economist, educator*
Demko, George Joseph *geographer*
Dunlop, David Wallace *economist, educator*
†Endicott, Kirk Michael *anthropologist, educator*
Fischel, William Alan *economics educator*
Hall, Raymond *sociology educator*
Kleck, Robert Eldon *psychology educator*
Lyons, Gene Martin *political scientist, educator*
Masters, Roger Davis *government and neurotoxicology educator*
†Petitto, Laura-Ann *social sciences educator*
Riggs, Lorrin Andrews *psychologist, educator*
Rutter, Jeremy Bentham *archaeologist, educator*
Starzinger, Vincent Evans *political science educator*
Welsch, Robert Louis *anthropologist, curator*

Henniker
Braiterman, Thea Gilda *economics educator, state legislator, selectman*

Hooksett
Clamp, Christina A. *sociology educator*

Keene
†Alvarez, Kristin Jones *geographer, educator*
Baldwin, Peter Arthur *psychologist, educator, author, minister*

Lebanon
Emery, Virginia Olga Beattie *psychologist, researcher*

Londonderry
Jacobs, Edward Harold *psychologist*

North Hampton
Dodge, Peter *retired sociology educator*

Portsmouth
Cole-McCrea, Candace *social sciences educator*

Rindge
Costa, Kelli Ann *anthropologist, educator, archaeologist*

Rochester
Diamond, David Roger *psychologist*

Salem
Silverman, Cathy Alice *anthropologist, researcher*

NEW JERSEY

Bayonne
Masella, Robert Thomas *political science and geography educator, funeral service*

Belmar
De Santo, Donald James *psychologist, educational administrator*

Blackwood
Busky, Donald Frank *political science educator*

Camden
†Goertzel, Ted George *sociologist, educator*
Harrison, Russell Sage *political science educator, consultant*
Van Til, Jon *sociology educator*
Worrall, John Dennis *economics educator, consultant, writer*
Yamada, Tetsuji *health economist, educator*

Cranbury
Hawver, Dennis A. *psychological consultant*

Denville
Breed, Ria *anthropologist*

Deptford
Kelly, Barbara Sue *psychologist*

Dover
Seadler, Stephen Edward *social scientist*

East Brunswick
Einhorn, Carl Murray *psychologist*

East Orange
Wolff, Derish Michael *economist, company executive*

Eatontown
Sager, Lawrence Cooper *psychologist*

Edison
Barcun, Seymour *economics educator*

Englewood Cliffs
Farrell, Patricia Ann *psychologist, educator, writer*

Ewing
Robboy, Howard Alan *sociologist, educator*

Florham Park
Brodkin, Adele Ruth Meyer *psychologist*

Fort Lee
Kofman, Mikhail *economist, engineering executive*

Fort Monmouth
Anderson, Bergie Wayne *human factors psychologist*

Gillette
Pfafflin, Sheila Murphy *psychologist*

Hackensack
†Abdelrazek, Rawan *economist*
†Schwartz, Mildred Anne *retired sociologist*

Hasbrouck Heights
Perham, Roy Gates, III, *industrial psychologist*

Highland Park
Like, Russel C. *economist, consultant, writer*
Smith, Neil *geography educator*

Jackson
Leveson, Irving Frederick *economist*
Turner, Pamela *psychologist*

Jersey City
Hordon, Harris Eugene *economics educator*

Lakewood
†Levine, Stephen M. *psychologist, educator*

Lawrenceville
Grannatt, Milton Henderson, III, *economist*
Plaut, Thomas F.A. *psychologist*

Livingston
Friedman, Merton Hirsch *retired psychologist, educator*

Lodi
†Guillory, Ann Verrett *psychologist, educator*

Lyndhurst
Bunda, Stephen Myron *political advisor, counselor, lawyer, classical philosopher*

Madison
Reader, Jonathan Whittier *sociology educator, consultant*

Mahwah
Frundt, Henry John *sociologist, educator*

Medford
Klugman, Peter Jay *psychologist, consultant*

Mendham
Haldopoulos, Martha A. *psychologist*

Milltown
Sacharow, Beverly *gerontologist*

Mine Hill
Robertiello, Gina Marie *criminal justice educator*

Mountain Lakes
†Loomis, Rebecca C. *psychology educator*

New Brunswick
Alexander, Robert Jackson *economist, educator*
Aronoff, Myron Joel *anthropologist, educator, political scientist, educator*
Dutta, Manoranjan *economics educator*
Glasser, Paul Harold *sociologist, educator, social worker, university administrator*
Glickman, Norman Jay *economist, urban policy analyst*
Killingsworth, Mark R. *economics educator, consultant*
Louis, Barbara R. *psychologist, educator, consultant*
Mechanic, David *social sciences educator*
Midlarsky, Manus Issachar *political scientist, educator*
†Nordstrom, Karl Fredrik *geographer, educator*
Pallone, Nathaniel John *psychologist, educator*
Reock, Ernest C., Jr., *retired government services educator, academic director*
†Rockoff, Hugh Touff *economist, educator*
Rosenberg, Seymour *psychologist, educator*
Russell, Louise Bennett *economist, educator*
†Shapiro, Warren *anthropologist, educator*
Swanson, Norman Rasmus *social sciences educator*
Tiger, Lionel *social scientist, anthropology consultant*
Toby, Jackson *sociologist, educator*

New Providence
Roth, Robert Howard *psychologist*

Newark
Adler, Freda Schaffer (Mrs. G. O. W. Mueller) *criminologist, educator*
Carroll, John Douglas *mathematical and statistical psychologist*
Cheng, Mei-Fang *psychobiology educator, neuroethology researcher*
Ferguson, Yale Hicks *political science educator*
Hiltz, Starr Roxanne *sociologist, educator, computer scientist, writer, lecturer, consultant*
Pagán, Gilberto, Jr., *clinical psychologist*
Schoonmaker, L. Craig *political organization executive*

Oakland
†Guller, Irving Bernard *forensic, clinical psychologist, consultant*

Paramus
†Perkins-Munn, Tiffany Sabrena *psychologist, researcher*

Parsippany
Rappaport, Alan Fred *clinical psychologist*

Piscataway
Alderfer, Clayton Paul *organizational consultant, educator, writer, administrator*
Cherniss, Cary *psychologist, educator*
†Hudson, Judith Anne *developmental psychologist, researcher*
Julesz, Bela *experimental psychologist, educator, electrical engineer*
†Kilianski, Stephen *psychologist, educator*
Mitchell, James Kenneth *geography educator*
Peterson, Donald Robert *psychologist, educator, university administrator*
Sass, Louis Arnorsson *psychology educator*
Schwebel, Milton *psychologist, educator*
Stein, Arlene J. *sociology educator, writer*
Waxman, Chaim I. *sociology educator, researcher*
†West, Mark Otto *psychology educator*
White, Helene R. *sociologist, educator*

Port Elizabeth
Ficcaglia, Leslie M. *psychologist, portrait artist*

Princeton
Barlow, Walter Greenwood *public opinion analyst, management consultant*
†Berinsky, Adam Jeremiah *political scientist, educator*
Blackman, Sue Anne Batey *economics researcher*
Bogan, Elizabeth Chapin *economist, educator*
Bogucki, Peter Ignatius *archaeologist*
Bradford, David Frantz *economist*
Chow, Gregory Chi-Chong *economist, educator*
Coffey, Joseph Irving *international affairs educator*
Cook, Michael Allan *social sciences educator*
Cooper, Joel *psychology educator*
Deneen, Patrick John *political scientist, educator*
Doig, Jameson Wallace *political science educator*
Ekstrom, Ruth Burt *psychologist*
Elliott-Moskwa, Elaine Sally *psychologist, researcher*
Fried, Eleanor Reingold *psychologist, educator*
Geertz, Clifford James *anthropology educator*
George, Robert Peter *political philosopher, lawyer*
Gilpin, Robert George, Jr., *political science educator*
Glucksberg, Sam *psychology educator*
Gordenker, Leon *political sciences educator*
Greenstein, Fred Irwin *political science educator*
Gross, Charles Gordon *psychology educator, neuroscientist*
Hirschman, Albert Otto *political economist, educator*
Hitz, Frederick Porter *public and international affairs educator*
Johnson-Laird, Philip Nicholas *psychologist*
†Kahneman, Daniel *psychology educator*
Kateb, George Anthony *political science educator*
Kenen, Peter Bain *economist, educator*
Kuenne, Robert Eugene *economics educator*
Malkiel, Burton Gordon *economist, educator*
Manning, Winton Howard *psychologist, educational administrator*
Maskin, Eric Stark *economics educator*
Miller, George Armitage *psychologist, educator*
Parry, Scott Brink *psychologist*
Reinhardt, Uwe Ernst *economist, educator*
Rosenthal, Howard Lewis *political science educator*
Rozman, Gilbert Friedell *sociologist, educator*
Scheinkman, José Alexandre *economics educator*
Shear, Ione Mylonas *archaeologist*
Shear, Theodore Leslie, Jr., *archaeologist, educator*
†Shimer, Robert J. *economist, educator*
Sims, Watson Shadrack *research executive, journalist*
Spence, Donald Pond *psychologist, psychoanalyst*
†Starr, Paul Elliot *sociologist, writer, editor, educator*
Stricker, Lawrence J. *psychologist*
†Tienda, Marta *demographer, educator*
†Tucker, Joshua Aaron *political scientist*
Walzer, Michael *political science educator*
Westoff, Charles Francis *demographer, educator*
†Whittington, Keith Edward *political scientist, educator*
Willig, Robert Daniel *economics educator*
Willingham, Warren Willcox *psychologist, testing service executive*
Wrong, Dennis Hume *sociologist, educator*

Red Bank
McWhinney, Madeline H. (Mrs. John Denny Dale) *economist, director*

Saddle River
Lasser, Gail Maria *psychologist, educator*

Scotch Plains
Hallard, Wayne Bruce *retired economist*

Somerset
Dahbany, Avivah *psychologist, educator*
Lichtig, Leo Kenneth *health economist*

South Orange
Marbach, Joseph R. *political scientist, educator*
Steiner, Gloria Litwin *psychologist*

Springfield
Shilling, A. Gary *economic consultant, investment advisor*

Summit
Hall, Pamela Elizabeth *psychologist*

Sussex
MacMurren, Harold Henry, Jr., *psychologist, lawyer*

Teaneck
Browne, Robert Span *economist, researcher*
Brudner, Helen Gross *social sciences educator*
Cassimatis, Peter John *economics educator*
Gibbs, Margaret Smith *psycholgy educator*
Westin, Alan Furman *political science educator*

Tenafly
Blank, Marion Sue *psychologist, educator*

Tinton Falls
Butler, Nancy Taylor *gender equity specialist, program director*

Titusville
Bhattacharjya, Ashoke Sanjoy *economist, researcher*

Trenton
McGowan, Joan Yuhas *development researcher*
Nayerahmadi, Habib *psychologist*

Union
Kim, Youn-Suk Ernest *economist, educator*
Sigmon, Scott B. *psychologist*

Verona
Aronow, Edward *psychologist, educator*

Wayne
Principe, Michael Luis *political science educator*
Salny, Abbie Feinstein *psychologist*
Sheffield, Carole Jean *political science educator*

Westwood
Fabrikant, Craig Steven *psychologist*

Woodbine
†White, Robert Jeffrey *psychologist*

NEW MEXICO

Albuquerque
Baker, Arnold Barry *economist*
Baker, Chester Bird *agricultural economics educator*
Basso, Keith Hamilton *cultural anthropologist, linguist, educator*
Davidge, K. Genevieve *clinical social worker*
DeWitt, Mary Therese *forensic anthropologist, archaeologist*
Harris, Fred R. *political scientist, educator, retired senator*
Heady, Ferrel *retired political science educator*
May, Philip Alan *sociology educator*
†Raish, Carol Brooks *anthropologist, archaeologist*
Schwerin, Karl Henry *anthropology educator, researcher*
Slesnick, Natasha *psychologist, researcher*
Straus, Lawrence Guy *anthropology educator, editor-in-chief*
Stuart, David Edward *anthropologist, writer, educator*
Wynne, Louis *psychologist*

Bayard
Lopez, Linda Carol *social sciences educator*

Corrales
Adams, James Frederick *psychologist, educational administrator*

El Prado
Young, Jon Nathan *archeologist*

Kirtland Afb
Tritten, James John *national security educator*

Las Cruces
Libbin, James David *agricultural economics educator*
Roscoe, Stanley Nelson *psychologist, aeronautical engineer*
Trafimow, David A. *psychology educator*
Ward, James D. *government educator, writer*

Las Vegas
Riley, Carroll Lavern *anthropology educator*

Los Alamos
Chomko, Stephen Alexander *archaeologist*
Masse, William Bruce *archaeologist*
Thompson, Lois Jean Heidke Ore *psychologist*

Nageezi
Moore, Roger Albert, Jr., *archaeologist*

Santa Fe
Anderson, Darrell Edward *psychologist, educator*
Clinard, Marshall Barron *sociologist, educator*
Kingman, Elizabeth Yelm *anthropologist*
Noble, Merrill Emmett *retired psychology educator, psychologist*
Schaafsma, Polly Dix *archaeologist, researcher*
Williams, Stephen *anthropologist, educator*

NEW YORK

Albany
Alba, Richard Denis *sociologist, educator*
Batt, H. William *political scientist*
Cruz, José Edgardo *political science educator*
Fortune, Anne E. *social worker, educator*
Ley, Ronald *psychologist, educator*
Moore, Gwen Lova *social sciences educator*
Nathan, Richard P(erle) *political scientist, educator*
Nesler, Mitchell Scott *psychology researcher*
Sattinger, Michael Jack *economics educator, researcher*
Smith, Michael Ernest *archaeologist, educator*
Teevan, Richard Collier *psychology educator*
Thompson, Frank Joseph *political science educator*
Zimmerman, Joseph Francis *political scientist, educator*

Alfred
Greil, Arthur Lawrence *sociology educator*

Amherst
Aurbach, Herbert Alexander *sociology educator*

Amityville
Studer, Patricia S. *psychologist*

Annandale On Hudson
Papadimitriou, Dimitri Basil *economist, college administrator*

Armonk
Grove, David Lawrence *economist, director*

Averill Park
Haines, Walter Wells *retired economics educator*

Bayside
Cohen, Daniel *psychologist, educator*

Bellport
Moeller, Mary Ella *retired home economist, educator, radio commentator*

Binghamton
†Gates, Leslie Carlisle *sociology educator*
Henderson, Daniel Joseph *economist*
Isaacson, Robert Lee *psychology educator, researcher*
James, Gary Douglas *biological anthropologist, educator, researcher*
Levis, Donald James *psychologist, educator*
Polachek, Solomon William *economist, educator*
†Ziemski, Connie Marie *social studies educator*

Brockport
Flanagan, Timothy James *criminal justice educator, university official*

Bronx
†Basu, Parantap *economist, educator*
Bauman, Laurie Julia *sociologist, researcher*
Burton, Leslie Anne *psychologist*
Chang, Mabel Li *economist, educator*
De La Cancela, Victor *psychologist*
Fishman, Joshua Aaron *sociolinguist, educator*
Hooker, Olivia J. *psychologist, educator*
Jankowski, Jeffery J. *developmental psychology educator*
Kelly, Mary Susan *psychologist, educator*
Myers, Jr., George Joseph Stephen *historical archaeologist, researcher*
Navran, Leslie *retired clinical psychologist*
Procidano, Mary Elizabeth *psychologist, educator*

Bronxville
Mills, Nicolaus *American studies educator, writer*
Moudud, Jamee K. *economist, economics educator, researcher*

Brooklyn
Bajwa, Shazia *sociologist*

Bloom, Howard Kenneth *paleopsychologist, writer*
Boloker, Rose L. *school psychologist*
Donovan, Dennis Joseph *addictionologist*
Frantzve, Jerri Lyn *psychologist, educator, consultant*
Gielen, Uwe Peter *psychology educator*
†Ginsburg, Helen *economics educator*
Gogate, Lakshmi J. *psychologist, researcher*
Isacoff, Mark *psychologist*
James, Milton Garnet *economist*
Jean-Louis, Girardin *psychologist, educator, researcher*
Kaplan, Mitchell Alan *sociologist, researcher*
†Kreisler, Rochelle *psychologist*
Nye, William Roger *psychologist*
Reinisch, June Machover *psychologist, educator*
Rothenberg, Mira Kowarski *clinical psychologist and psychotherapist*
Sciabarra, Chris Matthew *political scientist*
Solomon, Nathan Andrew *clinical psychologist*
Somers, Marion *gerontologist, family counselor*
Szenberg, Michael *economics educator, editor, consultant*
Torz, Richard J. *economics and finance educator*
Varma, Ranbir *economics educator*
Weinstein, Marie Pastore *psychologist*
Wolin, Doris Diamond *psychologist*

Brookville
†Kusukawa, Akira *demographer, educator*

Buffalo
Boot, John C.G. *economist, educator*
†Buddie, Amy M. *psychologist, researcher*
Butler, Arthur D. *retired economics educator*
Capaldi, Elizabeth Ann Deutsch *psychological sciences educator*
Delaney, Tim *sociologist, educator*
Ehrlich, Isaac *economist, educator, economist, department chairman*
Floss, Frederick George *economics and finance educator, consultant*
Franz, Laurence W(erner) *economics educator, college official*
Gort, Michael *economics educator*
Hetzner, Donald Raymund *social studies educator, forensic social scientist*
†Holmes, James M. *social studies educator, educator*
Hurwitz, Mark S. *political scientist, educator, lawyer*
Lamb, Charles Moody *political scientist, educator*
Levy, Kenneth Jay *psychology educator, academic administrator*
†Otterbein, Keith F. *anthropologist, educator*
†Sankoh, Joseph S. *political scientist, educator*
Tedlock, Barbara Helen *anthropologist, educator, academic administrator*
Weisstein, Naomi *neuroscientist, psychology educator, writer*

Canton
Perry, Richard John *anthropology educator*
†Thornton, Thomas *anthropologist, educator*

Clayton
Schmidt, Karl M., Jr., *political science educator*

Clinton
Raybeck, Douglas *anthropologist, educator*
†Stevens, Mitchell L. *sociologist, educator*

Commack
Nilson, Patricia *clinical psychologist*

Conesus
Dadrian, Vahakn Norair *sociology educator*

Cooperstown
†Fenton, William Nelson *anthropologist, anthropology educator emeritus*

Cortland
Haines, Herbert H. *sociology educator*
Young, Anderson Briggs *recreation educator, administrator*

Cortlandt Manor
Genis, Alice Singer *psychologist*

De Witt
Pearl, Harvey *rehabilitation psychologist*

Delhi
Van Brunt, Arthur Hoffman (Peter) *economist, educator*

Delmar
Mancuso, James Carmin *psychologist, educator*

Dix Hills
Pugliese, Paul Jones *cartographer*

Dobbs Ferry
†Culhane, Hind Rassam *psychologist, educator, film historian*
Kraetzer, Mary C. *sociologist, educator, consultant*
†Perelle, Ira B. *psychologist, educator*
Sutton, Francis Xavier *social scientist, consultant*

Dunkirk
Rushboldt, Raymond Jude *political science educator*

East Aurora
Speller, Kerstin G. Rinta *psychologist*

East Meadow
Albert, Gerald *clinical psychologist*

Fairport
Fisher, Jerid Martin *neuropsychologist*

Feura Bush
Byrne, Donn Erwin *psychologist, educator*

Fishkill
Stein, Paula Nancy *psychologist, educator*

Flushing
Amsterdam, David Erik *school psychologist*
Angrilli, Albert *psychology educator*
†Gregersen, Edgar Alstrup *anthropologist, educator, linguist, writer, researcher*
Hacker, Andrew *political science educator*
Krasner, Michael Alan *political science educator*
Lakah, Jacqueline Rabbat *political scientist, consultant*
Li, Hongzhi *Falun Dafa founder, author*
Min, Pyong Gap *sociologist, researcher*
†Pellitteri, John Steven *psychologist, therapist, educator*
Psomiades, Harry John *political science educator*
Smith, Charles William *social sciences educator, sociologist*

Forest Hills
†Bertolini, Joseph Clifford *political scientist, educator*
Moskowitz, Arnold X. *economist, strategist, educator*

Fredonia
Klonsky, Bruce Gary *educator*

Garden City
Mascia, Joseph Serafino *banking, economics and finance educator*
Ohrenstein, Roman Abraham *economics educator, economist, rabbi*
Steil, Janice M. *social psychology educator*

Garrison
Murray, Thomas Henry *bioethics educator, writer*

Geneseo
Battersby, Harold Ronald *retired anthropologist, archaeologist, linguist*
Olczak, Paul Vincent *psychology educator*

Geneva
†Curl, Layton Seth *psychologist, consultant, educator*
†D'Amico, Francine J. *political scientist, educator*

Gilboa
Petroff, John *economics educator, software company executive*

Great Neck
†Aronson, Margaret Rupp *school psychologist*
Christie, George Nicholas *economist, consultant*
Hamovitch, William *university official*
Joskow, Jules *economic research company executive*
Minkoff, Jack *economics educator, retired*

Greenport
Watts, Harold Wesley *economist, educator*

Greenvale
Zwicker, Charles *economist, educator, accountant, consultant*

Hamilton
Blum, Lester *educator*
Haines, Michael Robert *economist, educator*
Johnston, Michael (William Johnston) *political science educator, university administrator*

Hampton Bays
Baker, Donald Gene *social sciences educator*

Hempstead
Block, Jules Richard *retired psychologist, educator, university official*
Krauze, Tadeusz Karol *sociologist, educator*
Levinthal, Charles Frederick *psychologist, psychology educator, writer*
Wattel, Harold Louis *economics educator*

Hewlett
Salamon, Michael Jacob *psychologist, health care and psychology educator, media consultant*

Howes Cave
†Becker, Mary Druke *anthropologist, researcher*

Huletts Landing
Kapusinski, Albert Thomas *economist, educator*

Ithaca
Ascher, Robert *anthropologist, educator, archaeologist, educator, film producer*
†Assie-Lumumba, N'Dri T. *Africana studies educator*
Beneria, Lourdes *economist, educator*
Bensel, Richard Franklin *political science educator*
Briggs, Vernon Mason, Jr., *economics educator*
Chapman, Lewis Duane *economist*
Darlington, Richard Benjamin *psychology educator*
Easley, David *economics educator*
Ehrenberg, Ronald Gordon *economist, educator*
Fireside, Harvey Francis *political scientist, educator*
Forker, Olan Dean *agricultural economics educator*
†Heckathorn, Douglas D. *sociologist, educator, epidemiologist*
Isard, Walter *economics educator*
Jarrow, Robert Alan *economics and finance educator, consultant*
Kahn, Alfred Edward *economist, educator, government official*
Kennedy, Kenneth Adrian Raine *biological anthropologist, forensic anthropologist*
LaDue, Eddy Lorain *economist, educator*
Lowi, Theodore J(ay) *political science educator*
Lyons, Thomas Patrick *economics educator*
Pelto, Gretel H. *nutritional anthropologist, educator*
Rosen, Bernard Carl *sociologist, social psychologist, educator*
†Santiago-Irizarry, Vilma Iris *anthropologist, educator, lawyer*
Shell, Karl *economist*
Smith, Robert John *anthropology educator*
Stycos, Joseph Mayone *retired demographer, educator*
Thorbecke, Erik *economics educator*
Tomek, William Goodrich *agricultural economist*
Waldman, Michael *economist, educator*

Jamaica
†Biafora, Frank A. *sociologist, educator, dean*
Clark, Charles Michael Andres *economics educator*
Divale, William T.
†Gesualdi, Louis J. *social sciences educator*
Lees, Francis *economics educator*

Jamestown
Victor, Jeffrey Spencer *retired sociology educator*

Katonah
Wenglowski, Gary Martin *economist*

Keuka Park
†Sorenson, E. Richard *anthropologist*

Kings Point
†Greenwald, Richard Alan *history educator*

Larchmont
Siegel, Nathaniel Harold *sociology educator*

Levittown
†Elliott, Franklyn *psychologist*
Juszczak, Nicholas Mauro *psychology educator*

Liberty
†Green, Harold Martin *social science writer*

Liverpool
Egan, Marsha Christine *school psychologist*

Mamaroneck
Carty, Mary Ellen *psychologist*
†Scheidlinger, Saul *psychologist*

Manhasset
†Fisch, Gene S. *psychologist, researcher, statistician*
Pam, Eleanor *behavorial sciences educator*

Massapequa
Bogorad, Barbara Ellen *psychologist*

Mexico
Sade, Donald Stone *anthropology educator*

Middletown
Schwartz, Robert Marc *psychology educator*

Millbrook
Flexner, Kurt Fisher *economist, educator*

Mount Kisco
Schwarz, Wolfgang *psychologist*

Mount Vernon
Cammarosano, Joseph Raphael *economist, educator*

Nanuet
†Spielman, Lisa Anne *psychologist, researcher, statistician, consultant*

New City
Frawley-O'Dea, Mary Gail *clinical psychologist, psychoanalyst, educator*
Harari, Zaraleya Kurzweil *psychologist, psychotherapist*
Spalding, Mary Branch *psychologist, psychotherapist*
Wechman, Robert Joseph *economist, educator*

New Paltz
†Neuman, Joel H. *psychologist, educator*
Schnell, George Adam *geographer, educator*
Smiley, Albert Keith *economist, resort executive*

New Rochelle
Berlage, Gai Ingham *sociologist, educator*
Golub, Sharon Bramson *psychologist, educator*
Grimes, Tresmaine Judith Rubain *psychology educator*

New York
†Alfonso, Vincent C *psychology educator*
Andersen, Marianne Singer *clinical psychologist*
Andersen, Susan Marie *educator, researcher, clinician, policy advisor*
Andreassi, John Lawrence *psychologist, educator*
Angelo, Larian *economist*
Anspach, Ernst *economist, lawyer*
Arther, Richard Oberlin *polygraphist, educator*
Baldwin, David Allen *political science educator*
Bardach, Joan Lucile *clinical psychologist*
†Barker, Michael *social scientist*
†Barrish, Carol Lampert *psychologist*
Barron, Susan *clinical psychologist*
†Bartolini, Leonardo *economist*
†Belot, Gordon *philosophy*
Betts, Richard Kevin *political science educator*
Bird, Sharlene *clinical psychologist*
Blakely, Edward James *economics educator*
Blechner, Mark Jacob *psychologist, educator*
Bogart, Leo *sociologist*
Bonnett, Thomas W. *political scientist, writer*
Boodey, Cecil Webster, Jr., *political science educator*
Boorstein, Laurence *economist, educator*
Bowen, William Gordon *economist, educator, foundation administrator*
Bowers, Patricia Eleanor Fritz *economist*
Braham, Randolph Lewis *political science educator*
Brams, Steven John *political scientist, educator, game theorist*
Brooks-Gunn, Jeanne *psychologist*
†Buchholz, Ester Schaler Schaler *psychologist*
Buck, Louise Zierdt *psychologist*
Butler, Robert Neil *gerontologist, psychiatrist, writer, educator*
Caraley, Demetrios James *political scientist, educator, writer*
Carey, Alida Livingston *political scientist, writer, reporter*
Chadwick, Bruce Percy *political scientist, consultant*
Chamberlain, Mariam Kenosian *economist*
Chamberlain, Neil Cornelius Wolverton *economist, emeritus educator*
Chandrasekar, Krishnamurti *economics educator*
Charney, Craig Russell *pollster, political scientist*
Chelstrom, Marilyn Ann *political education consultant*
Clamar, Aphrodite J. *psychologist*
†Clark, Wilder Crawford *medical psychologist*
†Clarke, Lewis Ryland *history educator*
Cochrane, James Louis *economist*
Cohen, Michael *psychologist*
Cohen, Stephen Frand *political scientist, historian, educator, author, broadcaster*
Cole, Ann Harriet *psychologist, communications consultant*
†Cole, Jonathan Richard *sociologist, academic administrator*
Comitas, Lambros *anthropologist, educator*
Connelly, Joan Breton *archaeologist*
†Creed, Gerald W. *anthropologist, educator, researcher*
Dalton, Dennis Gilmore *political science educator*
del Cerro, Gerardo *sociologist, researcher*
deMause, Lloyd *psychohistorian*
†Demeny, Paul George *demographer, researcher*
Denoon, David Baugh Holden *economist, educator, consultant*
Denton, Michael John *research economist, energy risk expert, financial engineer, finance company executive*
†DeWind, Josh *social science researcher*
Domowitz, Ian *economics educator*
Dowling, Edward Thomas *economics educator*
Duke, Anthony Drexel *sociologist, educator, philanthropist*
Edinger, Lewis Joachim *political science educator*
Edwards, Franklin R. *economist, educator, consultant*
Edwards, Linda Nasif *economics educator*
Eisenstein, Hester *sociology educator*
Elinson, Jack *sociology educator*
Ellis, Albert *clinical psychologist, educator, author*
Engler, Robert *political science educator, author*
Esaki, Howard Yuji *economist*
Fancher, Edwin Crawford *psychologist, educator*
Felgran, Steven David *economist, educator*
Finger, Seymour Maxwell *political science educator, former ambassador*
Fox, Richard Gabriel *anthropologist, educator*
Franklin, Julian Harold *political science educator*
Freidenbergs, Ingrid *psychologist*
Freund, William Curt *economist, educator*
Frost, Ellen Elizabeth *psychologist*
Gale, Douglas Maxwell *economics educator*
Gans, Herbert J. *sociologist, educator*
Gediman, Helen K. *psychologist*
Gerber, Gwendolyn Loretta *psychologist, educator*
Gianaris, Nicholas Vasil *economics educator*
Glass, David Carter *psychology educator*
Glickman, Michael Richard *social studies educator*
Gluck, Andrew Lee *vocational economic analyst, counselor, philosopher*
Goldberger, Leo *psychologist, educator*
Goss, Mary E. Weber *sociology educator*
Greene, Kay C. *psychologist, author*
†Gross, Alan Ellis *psychologist, educator, researcher, mediator, consultant*
Gross, Feliks *writer*
Grossman, Michael *economics educator*
Gullo, Stephen Pernice *psychologist, corporate executive*
Habachy, Suzan Salwa Saba *development economist, non profit administrator*
Halper, Thomas *political science educator*
Hamilton, Linda Helen *clinical psychologist*
Hammer, Emanuel Frederick *clinical psychologist, psychoanalyst*
Hannigan, Pamela S. *economist, educator*
Harari, Carmi *clinical psychologist, psychoanalyst*
Harbeson, John Willis *political science educator*
†Harkavy-Friedman, Jill Martine *psychologist*
Heal, Geoffrey Martin *economics and business educator*
†Heilbroner, Robert Louis *economist, writer*
Heilbrun, James *economist, educator*
†Henshaw, Stanley K. *sociologist researcher, consultant*
Herman, Barry Martin *international economist*
Heyde, Martha Bennett (Mrs. Ernest R. Heyde) *psychologist*
Heydebrand, Wolf Von *sociology educator*
Higgins, E. Tory *psychology educator, research scientist*
Hoffman, Martin Leon *psychology educator*
Holloway, Ralph Leslie *anthropology educator*
Hormats, Robert David *investment banker*
Hoxter, Curtis Joseph *international economic adviser, public relations and public affairs counselor*
Ivanovitch, Michael S. *economist*

Jacoby, Jacob *consumer psychology educator*
Jasso, Guillermina *sociologist, educator*
Jervis, Robert *political science educator*
Jiha, Jacques *economist*
Jonas, Ruth Haber *psychologist*
Kandel, Denise Bystryn *sociologist*
Kaplan, Lawrence Jay *economist, educator*
Kappagoda, Samantha *economist, editor*
Karl, Kurt Erskine *economist*
Kasinitz, Philip *sociologist, educator*
Kavaler-Adler, Susan *clinical psychologist*
Kavesh, Robert A. *economist, educator*
Kazemi, Farhad *political scientist, educator*
Klebaner, Benjamin Joseph *economics educator*
Koss, Richard Allen, Jr., *economist*
Kothera, Lynne Maxine *clinical psychologist*
Krauss, Herbert Harris *psychologist*
†Kuriloff, Emily Anne *psychologist, educator*
Kurzweil, Edith *sociology educator, editor*
Kvint, Vladimir Lev *economist, educator, mining engineer*
Laderman, Carol C. *anthropologist, educator*
Laibman, David *economist, educator*
Lazarcik, Gregor *educator, financial research company executive, economist*
Leahey, Miles Carey *economist*
Lefkowitz, Joel M. *psychologist, educator*
Lehman, Edward William *sociology educator, researcher*
Lentner, Howard Henry *political scientist*
Lew, Jacob *public administration educator*
Lichtblau, John H. *economist*
Lipsey, Robert Edward *economist, educator*
Magee-Egan, Pauline Cecilia *psychology and management educator*
Maldonado-Bear, Rita Marinita *economist, educator*
Marlin, John Tepper *economist, writer, consultant*
Martin, Linda Gaye *demographer, economist*
Marty, Alvin Leonard *economist, educator*
†Mattli, Walter *political scientist, educator*
Mc Cullough, J. Lee *industrial psychologist*
Mead, Lawrence Myers, III, *political science educator*
†Mendelsohn, Susan Lynn *psychologist, researcher*
Meyer-Bahlburg, Heino F.L. *psychologist, educator*
Miller, Lisa Friedman *psychology educator*
Mincer, Jacob *economics educator*
Molz, Redmond Kathleen *public administration educator*
Muller, Charlotte Feldman *economist, educator*
Mundell, Robert Alexander *economist, educator*
Murphy, Austin de la Salle *economist, educator, banker*
Nadiri, M. Ishaq *economics educator, researcher, lecturer, consultant*
Nakamura, James I. *economics educator*
†Natarajan, Mangai *criminal justice educator*
Netzer, Dick *economics educator*
Ollman, Bertell *social sciences educator*
O'Neill, June Ellenoff *economist*
†Panagopoulos, Costas *political scientist, educator*
Papalia, Diane Ellen *human development educator*
Patrick, Hugh Talbot *economist, educator*
Pawliczko, Ann Maria *demographer*
Peck, Fred Neil *economist, educator*
Perey, Arnold *anthropologist, educator*
Persell, Caroline Hodges *sociologist, educator, author, researcher, consultant*
†Petchesky, Rosalind Pollack *political scientist, educator, social sciences educator*
Phelps, Edmund Strother *economics educator*
Piven, Frances Fox *political scientist, educator*
Prager, Jonas *economics educator, consultant*
Pye, Gordon Bruce *economist*
Quackenbush, Margery Clouser *psychoanalyst, administrator*
Radner, Roy *economist, educator, researcher*
Rao, Sethuramiah Lakshminarayana *demographer, United Nations official*
Reich, Stephen *psychologist*
Rieber, Robert W. *psychology educator, linguistics educator*
Riss, Eric *psychologist*
Rivlin, Benjamin *political science educator*
Robinson, Daniel N. *psychology and philosophy educator*
Rosenthal, Gert *economist*
Ross, Jeffrey Allan *political scientist, educator*
†Sachs, Jeffrey David *economist, educator*
Sands, Harry *psychologist, health administrator, researcher*
Sarnoff, Irving *retired psychology educator, author*
Sbaity-Kassem, Fatima Hasan *political economist, researcher*
Scanlon, Rosemary *economist*
Scelsa, Joseph Vincent *sociologist, educator, university executive*
Schilling, Warner Roller *political scientist, educator*
Schneider, Greta *economist, speaker, author, security consultant*
†Schneier, Edward Vincent *political science educator*
Schotter, Andrew Roye *economics educator, consultant*
Schupbach, Rosa Lechner *retired economist*
Schwab, George David *social science educator, author*
Schwartz, Anna Jacobson *economic historian*
Schwartzman, David *economist, educator*
Scott, Nancy Ellen *psychologist*
Sheldon, Eleanor Harriet Bernert *sociologist, writer*
Sherry, George Leon *political science educator*
Silver, Morris *economist, educator*
Simon, Jacqueline Albert *political scientist, journalist*
Small, George LeRoy *geographer, educator*
Smithson, Charles Wayne *economist, consultant*
Solecki, R. Stefan *anthropologist, educator*
Soulé, Charles Raymond, Jr., *psychologist*
Stewart, Ruth Ann *political scientist, educator*
Stiefel, Leanna *economics educator, education researcher*
Stiglitz, Joseph Eugene *economist, educator*
Suraci, Patrick Joseph *clinical psychologist*
Sylla, Richard Eugene *economics educator*
Tallmer, Margot Sallop *psychologist, psychoanalyst, gerontologist*
Taylor, Lance Jerome *economics educator*
Tekiner, Deniz Halil *sociologist, writer*
Terris, Lillian Dick *psychologist, association executive*
Tester, Leonard Wayne *psychology educator*
Tien, Charles P. *political scientist, educator*
Todaro, Michael Paul *economics educator, consultant*
Velayo, Richard Soriano *psychologist, educator, researcher*
†Walker, Gina Luria *social sciences educator, department chairman*
Walter, Ingo *economics educator*
Wang, N(ian) T(Zu) *economist, educator*
Weiss, Samuel Abraham *psychologist, psychoanalyst*
Wellisz, Stanislaw *economics educator*
White, Lawrence J. *economics educator*
Wolff, Edward Nathan *economist, educator*
Zarnowitz, Victor *economist, educator*
Zawistowski, Stephen Louis *psychologist, educator*
†Zolberg, Vera Lenchner *sociology educator*

Newburgh
Fallon, Rae Mary *psychology educator, early childhood consultant*

Niagara University
Osberg, Timothy Michael *psychologist, educator, researcher*
Whitney, Stewart Bowman *social psychology educator and program director*

Niskayuna
Wright, Theodore Paul, Jr., *political science educator*

North Woodmere
Aviles, Alice Alers *psychologist*

Oakdale
Cunha, Carlos Alberto *political scientist, educator*

Old Westbury
Ozelli, Tunch *economics educator, consultant*

Oneonta
Malone, Laurence Joseph *economics educator, writer*

Oswego
Gordon, Norman Botnick *psychology educator*

Oyster Bay
Trevor, Bronson *economist*

Plattsburgh
Beach, Charles Randall *economic developer*
Bethlen, Francis R. *emeritus business and economics educator, food distribution engineering specialist*
†Rumney, Thomas Arthur *geographer, educator*

Pleasant Valley
Marshall, Natalie Junemann *economics educator*

Pleasantville
†Katen, Joan Alice *political scientist, educator*

Port Washington
Goh, David Shuh-Jen *psychology educator*

Potsdam
†Atesoglu, H. Sonmez *economist, educator*
Hanson, David Justin *sociology educator, researcher*
Wickman, Peter M. *sociologist, educator*

Poughkeepsie
de Leeuw, Frank *economist*
Johnson, M(aurice) Glen *political science educator*
Johnson-Lans, Shirley B. *economist, educator*
†Mantz, Jeffrey William *anthropologist, educator*
†Moon, Seungsook *sociologist, educator*
Shapiro, Ronald Gary *psychologist*

Purchase
Foner, Nancy *anthropologist, educator*
Ryan, Edward W. *economics educator*
†Waclawski, Janine *psychologist, educator*

Queens
†Singh, Ronald *social sciences educator, researcher*

Rensselaer
Stull, Scott D. *archaeologist*

Rochester
Batabyal, Amitrajeet Amarnath *economics educator*
Bluhm, William Theodore *political scientist, educator*
Deci, Edward Lewis *psychologist, educator*
DuBrin, Andrew John *behavioral sciences, management educator, writer*
Fenno, Richard Francis, Jr., *political scientist, educator*
Hopkins, Thomas Duvall *economics educator*
Johnston, Frank C. *psychologist*
Jones, Ronald Winthrop *economics educator*
Landsburg, Steven Elliot *economics and mathematics educator*
Laties, Victor Gregory *psychology educator*
Levy, Harold David *psycholinguist*
Long, John Broaddus, Jr., *economist, educator*
†McHugh, Ernestine Louise *anthropologist, educator*
Mc Kenzie, Lionel Wilfred *economist, educator*
Niemi, Richard Gene *political science educator*
Oi, Walter Yasuo *economics educator*
Plosser, Charles Irving *economist, educator*
Regenstreif, S(amuel) Peter *political scientist, educator*
†Renner, Michael John *biological psychologist, educator*
Steamer, Robert Julius *political science educator*
†Stone, Randall Warren *political scientist, educator*
Vernarelli, Michael Joseph *economics educator, consultant*
†Wolkoff, Michael J. *economist, department chairman*
Zax, Melvin *psychologist, educator*

Rockville Centre
Lewittes, Don Jordan *clinical psychologist*

Roslyn
†Kinghorn, Carol Ann *school psychologist*

Rye Brook
Aquino, Joseph Mario *clinical psychologist*

Scarborough
Parks, Robert Henry *consulting economist, educator*

Scarsdale
Cohen, Irwin *economist*
Wesely, Yolanda Thereza *retired sociologist, marketing professional, researcher*
Wolfzahn, Annabelle Forsmith *psychologist*

Schenectady
Board, Joseph Breckinridge, Jr., *political scientist, educator*
†Sharlet, Robert *political science educator, researcher*

Shoreham
Ciborowski, Paul John *counseling psychology educator*

Slingerlands
Bragle, George W. *criminal justice educator*
Lahiri, Kajal *economics educator*

Smithtown
Fritzhand, Irvin Dick *psychologist*

Staten Island
Hu, Shaohua *political scientist*
Meltzer, Yale Leon *economist, educator*
Roig, Miguel *psychology educator*

Stony Brook
Goodman, Norman *sociologist, researcher*
Grim, Patrick Neal *philosopher, logician, educator*
Heyman, Richard E. *psychology educator*
†Judex, Stefan *psychologist, educator*
Jyringi, Darlene M. *gerontologist*
Katkin, Edward Samuel *psychology educator*
Moll, Ute Martha *pathologist, medical researcher*
Neuberger, Egon *economics educator*
Schneider, Mark *political science educator*
Segal, Jeffrey A. *political scientist, educator*
Stolzberg, Mark Elliott *psychologist*
Stone, Elizabeth Cecilia *anthropology educator*
Tanur, Judith Mark *sociologist, educator*
Travis, Martin Bice *political scientist, educator*

Suffern
Lieberman, Charles *economist*

Syracuse
Birkhead, Guthrie Sweeney, Jr., *political scientist, university dean*
†Black, Dan A. *economist*
Bloom, Max Robert *economics educator, consultant*
Braungart, Margaret Mitchell *psychology and bioethics educator*
Braungart, Richard Gottfried *sociology and international relations educator*
Fiske, Sandra Rappaport *psychologist, educator*
Frohock, Fred Manuel *political science educator*
Griffith, Daniel Alva *geography educator*
Hevern, Vincent William *psychologist, priest*
Kriesberg, Louis *sociologist, educator*
Mazur, Allan Carl *sociologist, engineer, educator*
Meinig, Donald William *geography educator*
†Mizruchi, Ephraim Harold *sociologist, educator*
Monmonier, Mark *geographer, graphics educator, essayist*
†Reeher, Grant Davis *social sciences educator, writer*
Schwartz, Richard Derecktor *sociologist, educator*
Sprafkin, Robert Peter *psychologist, educator*
Wadley, Susan Snow *anthropologist*
Zito, George Vincent *sociologist, sociology educator*

Tarrytown
Lawry, John D. *psychologist, educator*
Weiner, Max *educational psychology educator*

Tonawanda
Cavanaugh, David K. *clinical psychologist*

Troy
Athanasiou, Robert Byron *physician, psychologist*
Brazil, Harold Edmund *political science educator*
Schechter, Stephen L. *political scientist*

Wappingers Falls
Sucich, Diana Catherine *school psychologist, counselor*

Warwick
Kaminsky, Anatol *educator, writer*

Webster
Scherer, Marcia Joslyn *psychologist, researcher, educator*

West Point
Niccoli, Anne Marie *social sciences educator*

West Seneca
Wolfgang, Jerald Ira *economic development educator*

Westbury
Kremin, Daniel Paul *clinical forensic psychologist*

White Plains
Bloom, Adam I. *psychologist*
Kaushik, Surendra Kumar *economist*
†Osman, Betty Barshad *psychologist, author*
Rapp, Richard Tilden *economist, consultant*
Rembar, James Carlson *psychologist*

Whitestone
Caputo, Daniel Vincent *psychologist*

Woodbury
Agresti, Miriam Monell *psychologist*

Woodstock
Lieberman, Josefa Nina *psychologist, educator, writer*

Yonkers
Lupiani, Donald Anthony *psychologist*
Monegro, Francisco *psychology educator, alternative medicine consultant*

NORTH CAROLINA

Apex
Brunet, James Robert *public administration educator*

Asheville
Carr, L(ewis) Charles *clinical psychologist*
Dickens, Charles Henderson *retired social scientist, consultant*
Sgro, Joseph Anthony *retired psychologist, educator*

Black Mountain
Proctor, Jesse Harris, Jr., *political science educator*

Boone
Hoffman, Marvin Kenneth *political science educator*
Jones, Dan Lewis *psychologist*

Carolina Beach
Brown, Barry Stephen *research psychologist*

Cary
†Johnson, Lillian Beatrice *sociologist, educator, counselor*

Cashiers
O'Connell, Edward James, Jr., *psychology educator, computer applications and data analysis consultant*

Chapel Hill
Baroff, George Stanley *psychologist, educator*
Barton, Allen Hoisington *sociologist, educator*
Black, Stanley Warren, III, *economics educator*
Brockington, Donald Leslie *anthropologist, archaeologist, educator*
Brown, Frank *social science educator*
Fieleke, Norman Siegfried *economist, educator*
Fox, Ronald Ernest *psychologist*
Friedman, James Winstein *economist, educator*
Gottlieb, Gilbert *psychobiologist, educator*
Graham, George Adams *political scientist, emeritus educator*
Gray, Virginia Hickman *political science educator*
Hartlyn, Jonathan *political scientist, educator*
Hausman, Gary J. *social sciences educator*
Hernandez, Jeanne Taylor *psychologist, human services researcher, personal/professional coach*
Ingram, James Carlton *economist, educator*
Jones, Lyle Vincent *psychologist, educator*
†Leserman, Jane *medical sociologist, educator*
Lowman, Robert Paul *psychology educator, academic administrator*
Lunde, Anders Steen *demographer*
†Magness, Jodi *archaeologist, educator*
†Ornstein, Peter Arnold *psychologist, educator*
Pfouts, Ralph William *economist, consultant*
Rindfuss, Ronald Richard *sociology educator*
Rosefielde, Steven Shelley *economics educator*
Salemi, Michael Kerry *economist, educator*
Schoultz, Lars *political scientist, educator*
Simpson, Richard Lee *sociologist, educator*
Smith, James Finley *economist, educator*
Snyder, Glenn Herald *political science educator, writer*
Stenberg, Carl W., III, *public administration educator, dean*
Steponaitis, Vincas Petras *archaeologist, anthropologist, educator*
Tarascio, Vincent Joseph *economist, educator*
Treml, Vladimir Guy *economist, educator*
†Wasik, Barbara Hanna *psychologist, educator*
Wilson, Glenn *economist, educator*
Wright, Deil Spencer *political science educator*

Charlotte
Brandon, William Pew, Jr., *social sciences educator*
Brazeal, Donna Smith *psychologist*

Zanesville
Shatz, Mark Allen *psychologist, educator*
Workman, James E. *retired school psychologist*

OKLAHOMA

Edmond
Necco, E(dna) Joanne *school psychologist*
Smock, Donald Joe *governmental liaison, political consultant*

Noble
Watrous, Naoma Dicksion *retired clinical psychologist*

Norman
Affleck, Marilyn *sociology educator*
Barwick-Snell, Katherine Lane *family human relations and women's studies educator, home economics consultant*
Bell, Robert Eugene *anthropologist educator*
Hassig, Ross *anthropologist*
Henderson, George *educational sociologist, educator*
Hufnagel, Glenda Ann Lewin *human relations educator and administrator*
Kenney, Charles Dennison *political science educator*
Kondonassis, Alexander John *economist, educator*
Logue, Dennis Emhardt *financial economics educator, consultant*

Oklahoma City
Allbright, Karan Elizabeth *psychologist, consultant*
Craig, George Dennis *economics educator, consultant*
Heath, Paul A. *psychologist*
Morgan, Catherine Marie *psychologist, writer*
Rundell, Orvis Herman, Jr., *psychologist, educator*

Stillwater
Darcy, Robert Emmett *political scientist, educator, statistician*
Jadlow, Joseph Martin *economics educator*
Moomaw, Ronald Lee *economics educator*
Poole, Richard William *economics educator*
Steindl, Frank George *economist, educator*

Tulsa
†Bailey, Garrick Alan *anthropologist, educator*
†Brooker, Timothy Douglas *social studies educator*
Cooke, Marvin Lee *sociologist, consultant, urban planner*
Dugger, William Mayfield *economics educator*
†Ferraro, Jay *psychologist, consultant*
Kemp, Sarah (Sally Leech) *developmental psychologist, neuropsychologist*

Weatherford
Albaugh, Bernard John, II, *social science researcher*

OREGON

Beaverton
Ricks, Mary F(rances) *archaeologist, anthropologist, consultant*

Corvallis
Bernieri, Frank John *social psychology educator*
Clinton, Richard Lee *international relations educator*
Ray, Edward John *economics educator, administrator*

Eugene
Aikens, C(lyde) Melvin *anthropology educator, archaeologist, museum director*
Burris, Vallon Leon, Jr., *sociologist, educator*
Davis, Richard Malone *economics educator*
Evans, George William *economics educator*
Goldman, Marion Sherman *sociology and religious studies educator, consultant on cults*
Gwartney, Patricia Anne *sociology educator*
Khang, Chulsoon *economics educator*
Littman, Richard Anton *psychologist, educator*
Mikesell, Raymond Frech *economics educator*
Novkov, Julie Lavonne *political scientist*
Peterson, Donna Rae *gerontologist*
Upham, Steadman *anthropology educator, university dean, academic administrator*
Wilson, Wesley Warren *economics educator*
Wolcott, Harry F *anthropologist, educator*

Fairview
Blodgett, Forrest Clinton *economics educator*

Florence
Marble, Duane Francis *geography educator, researcher*

Lake Oswego
Tammen, Ronald *international politics educator*

Monmouth
†Winningham, Robert Gunder *psychologist, educator*

Newberg
Adams, Wayne Verdun *pediatric psychologist, educator*

Pendleton
Reeder, Clinton Bruce *economist, public policy consultant, farmer*

Portland
Broughton, Ray Monroe *economic consultant*
Davis, James Allan *gerontologist, educator*
Kristof, Ladis Kris Donabed *political scientist, writer*
Matarazzo, Joseph Dominic *psychologist, educator*
†Matarazzo, Ruth Gadbois *psychologist, educator*
Mersereau, Susan S. *clinical psychologist*
†Parajuli, Pramod *anthropologist, researcher*
Rufolo, Anthony Michael *economics educator*
Shapiro, Yanina *psychology educator*
Wiens, Arthur Nicholai *psychology educator*

Sandy
Silvey, Murl L. *psychologist*

Tigard
Yesilada, Birol Ali *political science educator*

West Linn
Schmall, Vicki Louise *gerontologist*

PENNSYLVANIA

Abington
Schwartz, Lita Linzer *psychologist, educator*

Alburtis
Stafford, William Butler *retired psychology educator*

Allentown
Graham, Kenneth Robert *psychologist, educator*
Raymond, Arthur Joseph *economics educator*

Annville
Cullari, Salvatore Santino *clinical psychologist, educator, writer*

Bala Cynwyd
Bersh, Philip Joseph *psychologist, educator*

Berwyn
Lee, Chong-Sik *political scientist, educator*

Bethlehem
Aronson, Jay Richard *economics educator, researcher, academic administrator*
†Distler, Megan J. *economist*
Frankel, Barbara Brown *cultural anthropologist*
Heath, Douglas Edwin *geography educator*
Scanlon, Edward Charles *clinical psychologist*
†Scheirer, William Kenneth *economist, consultant*
Schwartz, Eli *economics educator, writer*
Smolansky, Bettie Moretz *sociology educator*
Thornton, Robert James, Sr., *economics educator, author*
Williamson, Robert Clifford *sociology educator*
Wittreich, Warren James *psychologist, consultant*

Bloomsburg
†Holloway, Sybil Lymorise *psychologist, writer*

Bridgeville
Moore, Daniel Edmund *psychologist, educator, retired educational administrator*

Bryn Mawr
Anderson, Eric Edward *psychologist, consultant*
Hoffman, Howard Stanley *experimental psychologist, educator*
†Osirim, Mary Johnson *sociology educator*
Porter, Judith Deborah Revitch *sociologist, educator*

Carbondale
Willis, Ellen Debora *psychiatric nurse*

Carlisle
Jacobs, Norman G(abriel) *sociologist, educator*
Jones, Oliver Hastings *consulting economist*
Strong, Sara Dougherty *psychologist, marriage and family therapist, mediator*

Carlisle Barracks
Terrill, W(allace) Andrew *researcher, educator*

Chester
Waldauer, Charles *economics educator*

Coopersburg
Bednar, Charles Sokol *political scientist, educator*

Coraopolis
Stage, Ginger Rooks *psychologist*

Coudersport
Kysor, Daniel Francis *psychologist*

Cranberry Township
†Fitzpatrick, Robert *psychologist*

Doylestown
Ginsberg, Barry Gavrille *psychologist, consultant, trainer*

East Stroudsburg
Bunjun, Seewoonundun *economics educator*
Crotty, Patricia McGee *political science educator*

Easton
Kincaid, John *political science educator, editor*
Murphy, Bruce Allen *government and law educator, author*

Edinboro
Cocco, Karen Jean *school psychologist*

Elizabethtown
Selcher, Wayne A. *political science educator*

Elkins Park
Eisman, Audrey Waldo *psychologist*
Goode, Paul *psychologist, educator, consultant*

Erie
Adovasio, J. M. *anthropologist, archeologist, educator*
Bennett, Charles Andrew *economics educator*
Gupta, Srabana *economist, researcher*

Exton
Ma, Jinpeng *economics and business educator*

Fairless Hills
Rosella, John Daniel *clinical psychologist, educator*

Fort Washington
Manfredi, Deanna Ann *psychologist*

Friendsville
Babb, Harold *psychologist, educator*

Grantham
Eby, John Wilmer *sociology educator*

Greensburg
Gribschaw, Victoria Marie *social sciences educator, department chairman*
Ramm, Douglas Robert *psychologist*
†Spurlock, John *social studies educator, social sciences educator*

Grove City
†Campbell, George Van Pelt *sociology and religion educator*
Coulter, Michael L *political scientist, educator*

Haverford
de Laguna, Frederica *anthropology educator emeritus, writer, publisher*
Maller, Owen *clinical psychologist*
Mellink, Machteld Johanna *archaeologist, educator*
Northrup, Herbert Roof *economist, business executive*

Hazleton
Tseo, George Kuang Yu *geography educator*

Indiana
Garvin, C(larence) Alexander, Jr., *economics educator*
Mc Cauley, R. Paul *criminologist, educator*
Miller, Vincent Paul, Jr., *geography and regional planning educator*
Stern, T. Noel *political scientist, educator*
Tobin, Lois Moore *home economist, educator, retired*
Walker, Donald Anthony *economist, educator*

Jenkintown
†Spergel, Philip *psychologist*

Johnstown
Teich, Alan Harvey *psychology educator, clinical psychologist*

Kutztown
Dougherty, Percy H. *geographer, educator, politician, planner*

Lancaster
Auster, Carol Jean *sociology educator*
Stephenson, Donald Grier, Jr., *government studies educator*

Langhorne
†Spreat, Scott *psychologist*

Latrobe
Watson, Bradley Charles Stephen *political science educator, lawyer, writer*

Lewisburg
Bannon, George *retired economics educator, department chairman*

Lincoln University
†Nwachuku, Levi Akalazu *social sciences and behavioral studies educator*

Lock Haven
†Forbes, Edward John, III, *developmental psychologist, educator*

Loretto
Melusky, Joseph Anthony *political science educator*

Meadville
Adams, Earl William, Jr., *economics educator*

Media
†Cimbala, Stephen Joseph *political science educator*
Gordon, Lisa Diane *psychologist*
Lewandowski, Theodore Charles *psychology educator*
Smith, David Gilbert *political science educator*

Middletown
†Plant, Jeremy Francis *political scientist, educator*

Milford
Rosenblum, Jeffrey Ira *consulting economist*

Millersville
Bookmiller, Robert James *political science educator*

Mont Alto
Hill, Elizabeth Trezise *economics educator*

New Castle
Grzebieniak, John Francis *psychologist*

Newtown
Buermann, Peter Bruce *psychologist, program administrator*
Richard, James Thomas *retired psychologist, educator*

Norristown
Gaber, Robert *psychologist*

Philadelphia
†Allison, Paul David *sociologist, educator, sociologist, consultant*
Bailey, Elizabeth Ellery *economics educator*
Berg, Ivar Elis, Jr., *social science educator*
Broder, Michael S. *psychologist*
Buerkle, Jack Vincent *sociologist, educator*
†Cass, David *economist, educator*
Clark, John J. *economist, educator, finance educator*
Coché, Judith *psychologist, educator*
†Collins, Lynn H. *psychologist, educator, web site designer*
Coraza, Mary Catherine *psychologist*
†Cummins, John David *economics educator, consultant*
Dean-Zubritsky, Cynthia Marian *psychologist, researcher*
Diebold, Francis X. *economist, educator*
Donaldson, Thomas *ethicist, educator*
†Dowdall, George William *sociology educator*
Erdmann, James Bernard *educational psychologist*
Evan, William Martin *sociologist, educator*
Flubacher, Joseph Francis *retired economics educator*
Fox, Renée Claire *sociology educator*
Frankel, Francine Ruth *political science educator*
Gelles, Richard James *sociology and psychology educator, academic administrator*
Goodenough, Ward Hunt *anthropologist, educator*
Hall, Charles P(otter), Jr., *educator consultant*
Harvey, John Adriance *psychology and pharmacology educator, researcher, consultant*
Hurvich, Leo Maurice *experimental psychologist, educator, vision researcher*
Jeon, Bang Nam *economist, researcher*
Katsenelinboigen, Aron Josef *economist*
Katz, Elihu *sociologist, communications educator*
Klausner, Samuel Zundel *sociologist, educator*
Klein, Lawrence Robert *economist, educator*
Kurzban, Robert Owen *psychologist, researcher*
Lester, Bijou Yang *economist, educator*
Logue, John J(oseph) *psychologist*
McCord, Joan *sociologist, educator, rsearcher*
Meyer, Marshall Warner *management and sociology educator*
Michael, Henry N. *geographer, anthropologist*
Miller, Ronald Eugene *regional science educator*
Newman, Cory Frank *clinical psychologist*
†O'Leary, Brendan (Denis O'Leary) *political science educator, journalist*
Orne, Emily Carota *research psychologist*
†Orr, Nancy A. *educational psychologist*
Peasnall, Brian Lee *archaeologist, educator*
Phelps, Charlotte DeMonte *retired economics educator*
Preston, Samuel Hulse *demographer*
Raff, Daniel Martin Gorodetsky *economist, economic and business historian, educator*
Rescorla, Robert Arthur *psychology educator*
Rima, Ingrid Hahne *economics educator*
Rosenberg, Robert Allen *psychologist, educator, optometrist*
Sabloff, Jeremy Arac *archaeologist*
Schuyler, Robert L. *anthropologist, archaeologist*
Sherman, Lawrence William *criminologist*
Summers, Anita Arrow *public policy and management educator*
Summers, Robert *economics educator*
Szewczyk, Samuel Hideyo *financial economist, educator*
Tokar, Bette Lewis *economics educator*
Van De Walle, Etienne *demographer*
Wadden, Thomas Anthony *psychologist, educator*
Wallace, Anthony Francis Clarke *anthropologist, educator*
Weiss, Mary Alice *insurance economics educator*

Pittsburgh
Baldwin, Carla Suzann *psychologist*
Barry, Herbert, III, *psychologist, educator*
Blumstein, Alfred *urban and public affairs educator*
Bobrow, Davis Bernard *public policy educator*
Brustein, William Irving *sociology educator*
Cohen, Jacqueline *university researcher, sociology educator*
Davis, Otto Anderson *economics educator*
Dawes, Robyn Mason *psychology educator*
Doreian, Patrick *sociologist, educator*
Drennan, Robert D. *archeology educator, researcher*
Eaton, Joseph W. *sociology educator*
Fararo, Thomas John *sociologist, educator*
Fischhoff, Baruch *psychologist, educator*
Gaynor, Martin Scott *economist*
Ginsburg, Mark Barry *comparative sociology of education educator*
Hammond, Paul Young *political scientist, educator*
Haney, Edward Francis *social studies educator, educator*
Harper, Douglas Albert *sociologist, researcher*
Holzner, Burkart *sociologist, educator*
Keefe, William Joseph *political science educator*
Kenkel, James Lawrence *economics educator*
Lave, Judith Rice *economics educator*
†McCallum, Bennett Tarlton *economist, educator*
McClelland, James Lloyd *psychology educator, cognitive neuroscientist*
Meltzer, Allan H. *economist, educator*
†Morrow, Lisa A. *neuropsychologist, researcher*
Ogul, Morris Samuel *political science educator, consultant*
Olson, Josephine Eva *economics educator*
Peele, Pamela Bonifay *economics educator*

PROFESSIONAL INDEX 6665 SOCIAL SCIENCE

Perlman, Mark *economist, educator*
Perloff, Robert *psychologist, educator*
Schaub, Gary John, Jr., *political scientist*
Schorr-Ribera, Hilda Keren *psychologist*
Shadel, William Gustav *psychologist, educator*
Strauss, Robert Philip *economics educator*
Strick, Sadie Elaine *psychologist*
Sussna, Edward *economist, educator*

Polk
Hall, Richard Clayton *retired psychologist*

Reading
Millar, Robert James *social science educator*

Rydal
Heebner, Albert Gilbert *economist, educator, bank executive*

Scranton
Cannon, J. Timothy *psychology educator, neuroscientist*
Giunta, Agatino John *economist, educator*
Parente, William Joseph *political science educator*
Sebastianelli, Carl Thomas *clinical psychologist*
†Yamanouchi-Rynn, Midori *social sciences educator*

Shippensburg
Bej, Emil *economics educator, researcher, journalist*
France, Olin Kenneth, Jr., *psychologist*
Kaluger, George *clinical psychologist, educator*
Kaluger, Meriem Fair *psychologist, educator*

Spring Grove
Butler, Raymond Archibald *cartographer*

State College
Day, David Vaughan *psychology educator*
Day, Lee Monroe *agriculture economics educator*
Gordon, Richard Lewis *mineral economics educator*
Schaie, K(laus) Warner *human development and psychology educator*
Wyand, Martin Judd *economics educator, retired military officer*

Swarthmore
Hollister, Robinson Gill, Jr., *economics educator*
Hopkins, Raymond Frederick *political science educator*
Keith, Jennie *anthropology educator and administrator, writer*
Pryor, Frederic L. *economist, educator*

Tarentum
McGuire, Timothy William *economics and management educator, dean, management executive*

University Park
Epp, Donald James *economist, educator*
Firebaugh, Glenn Allen *sociology educator*
Ford, Donald Herbert *psychologist, educator*
Friedman, Robert Sidney *political science educator*
†Humphrey, Craig Reed *social studies educator*
Klein, Philip Alexander *economist*
Messer, Andrea Elyse *anthropologist, archaeologist, science writer*
†Newsome, Lee Ann *anthropologist, educator*
Ray, William Jackson *psychologist*
†Rose, Adam Zachary *economist, educator*
Snow, Dean Richard *anthropology educator, archaeologist*
Ulmer, Jeffery Todd *sociology educator*
Walden, Daniel *humanities and social sciences educator*
Walker, Alan C. *anthropologist, educator*

Valley Forge
Guttentag, Jack Mark *economist, educator*

Villanova
Johannes, John Roland *political science educator, academic administrator*
Redding, Richard Ellsworth *psychologist, lawyer*

Wallingford
Scherer, Frederic Michael *economics educator*

Wayne
MacNeal, Edward Arthur *economic consultant*
Zlotowski, Martin *psychologist*

West Chester
Benzing, Cynthia Dell *economics educator*
Green, Andrew Wilson *lawyer*

Wynnewood
Phillips, Almarin *economics educator, consultant*

Yardley
Brick, John *biological psychologist, educator, researcher*

York
Kulbicki, Melvin Andrew *political science educator*
McMillan, Wendell Marlin *agricultural economist*

RHODE ISLAND

Barrington
Paolino, Ronald Mario *clinical psychologist, consultant, psychopharmacologist, pharmacist*

Kingston
Alexander, Lewis McElwain *geographer, educator*
†Biller, Henry Burt *psychologist, educator*
Burkett, John Philip *economics educator*
Cunnigen, Donald *sociologist, educator*
†Felner, Robert David *psychology educator, researcher, consultant*
†Molloy, David Scott, Jr., *labor relations educator*
Newman, Barbara Miller *psychologist, educator*
Seifer, Marc Jeffrey *psychology educator*
Turnbaugh, William Arthur *archaeologist, educator*

Newport
Brown, David William *economist, educator, consultant*
†Delaney, Robert Finley *columnist, political sociologist, lecturer*
Lawber, Harold Ernest, Jr., *economist, educator*

Peace Dale
Brennan, Noel-Anne Gerson *anthropologist, educator, writer*

Providence
Anton, Thomas Julius *political science and public policy educator, consultant*
Church, Russell Miller *psychology educator*
Feldman, Allan Maurice *economist*
Goldstein, Sidney *sociology educator, demographer*
Goodman, Elliot Raymond *political scientist, educator*
Goulder, Caroljean Hempstead *retired psychologist, consultant*
Groden, Gerald *psychologist*
Grossman, Herschel I. *economics educator*
Heath, Dwight Braley *anthropologist, educator*
Herz, Rachel Sarah *research psychologist*
Holloway, Robert Ross *archaeologist, educator*
Jones, Ferdinand Taylor, Jr., *psychologist, educator*
†Kates, Robert William *geographer, educator*
†Liu, Jianhong *sociologist, educator*
Marsh, Robert Mortimer *sociologist, educator*
†Orr, Marion *political scientist, educator*
Perkins, Whitney Trow *political science educator emeritus*
Riordan, Cornelius *sociology educator, writer, consultant*
Rueschemeyer, Marilyn Schattner *sociology educator*
Siqueland, Einar *psychology educator*
Stein, Jerome Leon *economist, educator*
Stultz, Newell Maynard *retired political science educator*

Smithfield
Morahan-Martin, Janet May *psychologist, educator*

Wakefield
Newman, Philip Robert *psychologist*

SOUTH CAROLINA

Abbeville
Cellura, A(ngele) Raymond *psychologist*

Cayce
Sheldon, Jeffrey Andrew *social sciences researcher*

Charleston
Bowman, Daniel Oliver *psychologist*
Hittner, James Bryant *psychologist, educator*
Jacobs, Walter Darnell *political scientist, educator*
Kimmel, Herbert David *psychology educator*
†Kitner, Kathi R. *anthropologist*
Lovinger, Sophie Lehner *child psychologist*
Moore, William Vincent *political science educator*
Sharpe, Kathryn Moye *psychologist*
Smedley, Charles Vincent *sociology educator*

Clemson
†Cawthon, Tony W. *social sciences educator*
Melton, Gary Bentley *psychology and law educator*

Columbia
Cohn, Elchanan *economics educator*
Davis, Keith Eugene *psychologist, educator, consultant*
Kiker, Billy Frazier *economics educator*
Logan, Sandra Jean *retired economics and business educator*
Markovsky, Barry Neil *sociology educator*
Martin, Robert William *econometrician*
Powell, Donald Ashmore *clinical research psychologist*
Rippeteau, Bruce Estes *archaeologist, administrator*
†Songer, Donald Raymond *political science educator*
Starr, Harvey *political scientist, educator*
Wilder, Ronald Parker *economics educator*
Wood, Oliver Gillan, Jr., *economist, educator*
Zaepfel, Glenn P. *psychologist*

Fort Mill
Park, John *finance, investment consultant*

Greenville
†Abrams, Douglas Carl *social studies educator*
Trevillian, Wallace Dabney *economics educator, retired dean*
Westrope, Martha Randolph *psychologist, consultant*

Lancaster
Garris, William Ralph *criminal justice educator*

Laurens
Chandler, Margaret McNeill *home economist, educator*

Mc Cormick
Zeller, Michael James *psychologist, educator*

Orangeburg
Onunkwo, Emmanuel Nwafor *economics educator*

Rock Hill
†Pantuosco, Louis J., Jr., *economist, educator*

Spartanburg
McAbee, Thomas Allen *psychologist*
Reid, Alliston King *psychology educator, researcher*

SOUTH DAKOTA

Aberdeen
Hedges, Mark Stephen *clinical psychologist*

Brookings
Gilbert, Howard Alden *economics educator*
Lundeen, Ardelle Anne *retired economist*
Tolle, Gordon J. *political science educator*

Buffalo Gap
Pengra, Lilah *anthropologist, consultant*

Canton
Perkinson, Robert Ronald *psychologist, consultant*

Keystone
Wagner, Mary Kathryn *sociology educator, former state legislator*

Lennox
Brendtro, Larry Kay *psychologist*

Madison
Talley, Daniel Alfred *economics educator*

Rapid City
Hughes, Stella Platt *sociology educator*

Vermillion
Carlson, Loren Merle *political science educator*
Clem, Alan Leland *political scientist, educator*
Wang, X. T. (Xiaotian Wang) *psychologist, educator*

Yankton
Ferris, Alan Russel *psychology educator*

TENNESSEE

Alcoa
†Lyon, Terri L. *industrial and organizational psychologist*

Chattanooga
Clark, Jeff Ray *economist*
Drennon-Gala, Donney Thomas *sociologist, educational consultant, writer*
Guo, Zibin *medical anthropologist*
Rabin, Alan A. *economics educator*
Wilson, Richard Lee *political science educator*

Clarksville
†Baldwin, Kathryn Leigh *psychologist, educator, consultant*

Cleveland
Metallo, Thomas Joseph *international studies and political science educator*

Franklin
Sybinsky, Estrella Besinga *political science educator*

Germantown
Depperschmidt, Thomas Orlando *economist, consultant*

Hermitage
Fulmer, Douglas Alan *political consultant, journalist*

Kingsport
Everett, Michael David *economist, educator*

Knoxville
Bell, Corinne Reed *psychologist*
Blanton, Priscilla White *social sciences educator, psychologist, researcher*
†Cole, William Edward *economics educator, consultant*
Harris, Diana Koffman *sociologist, educator*
†Hopko, Derek Richard *psychologist, consultant*
†Stephens, Otis Hammond, Jr., *political science and law educator*

Memphis
Daniel, Coldwell, III, *economist, educator*
†Jones, Effie L. *social sciences educator*
Kamery, Rob Herlong *economics educator, management consultant*
Papachristou, Patricia Towne *economics educator*
Pohlmann, Marcus D. *political science educator*
Rubin, Rose Mohr *economics educator*
†Sherman, Janann Margaret *history educator, writer*

Milligan College
Mills, Lori Lynne *psychologist, educator*

Murfreesboro
Breault, Kevin D. *sociology educator, research scientist*
Klein, Christopher Carnahan *economist*
Littlepage, Glenn E. *social psychology educator*
Zietz, Joachim *economics educator*

Nashville
Benbow, Camilla Persson *psychology educator, researcher*
†Blasi, Anthony Joseph *sociology educator, writer*
Buckles, Stephen Gary *economist, educator*
Fels, Rendigs *economist, educator*
Gove, Walter R. *sociology educator*
Graham, George J., Jr., *political scientist, educator*
Guinsburg, Philip Fried *alcohol and substance abuse counselor*
†Hancock, Terry Blackmon *psychologist, educator*
Hargrove, Erwin Charles, Jr., *political science educator*
Havens, Murray Clark *political scientist, educator*
Joyner, John Wesley *psychologist, educator*
Lazar, Irving *psychologist*
McCarty, Richard Charles *psychology educator, university dean*
Ridley, Carolyn Fludd *retired social studies educator*
Russell, Clifford Springer *economics and public policy educator*
Schoggen, Phil H(oward) *psychologist, educator*
Smith, Dani Allred *sociologist, educator*
Strupp, Hans Hermann *psychologist, educator*
Westfield, Fred M. *economics educator*

Oak Ridge
Das, Sujit *policy analyst*

Sewanee
Mohiuddin, Yasmeen Niaz *economics educator*

TEXAS

Abilene
Hennig, Charles William *psychology educator*

Alamo
Reese, Norma Carol *clinical psychologist*

Alpine
Sechrest, Larry J. *economist, educator*

Amarillo
Ayad, Joseph Magdy *retired psychologist*

Arlington
Cole, Richard Louis *political scientist, educator*
Depken, Craig A., II, *economics educator*
Farrar-Myers, Victoria Anne *political scientist*
Ramsey, Charles Eugene *sociologist, educator*

Austin
Blodgett, Warren Terrell *public affairs educator*
†Boretz, Avron A. *anthropologist, educator*
Buchanan, Bruce, II, *political science educator*
Burnham, Walter Dean *political science educator*
Cleland, Charles Carr *psychologist, educator*
Drake, Stephen Douglas *clinical psychologist, health facility administrator*
Dusansky, Richard *economist, educator*
Eldredge, Linda Gaile *psychologist*
Epstein, Jeremiah Fain *anthropologist, educator*
Firey, Walter Irving, Jr., *retired sociologist, educator*
†Gesn, Paul Randall *social psychologist, researcher*
Glade, William Patton, Jr., *economics educator*
†Glenn, Norval Dwight *sociologist, educator*
Grangaard, Daniel Robert *psychologist*
Griffin, Alan Nash *psychologist*
Hamermesh, Daniel Selim *economics educator*
Hansen, Niles Maurice *economics educator*
Hinich, Melvin Jay *government and economics educator*
Holtzman, Wayne Harold *psychologist, educator*
Holz, Robert Kenneth *retired geography educator*
Huff, David L. *geography educator*
Iscoe, Ira *psychology educator*
Jordan-Bychkov, Terry Gilbert *geography educator*
Keith, Timothy Zook *psychology educator*
Kendrick, David Andrew *economist, educator*
Lariviere, Richard Wilfred *university administrator, educator, consultant*
Loehlin, John Clinton *psychologist, educator*
Lopreato, Joseph *sociologist, writer*
Mc Donald, Stephen Lee *economics educator*
McFadden, Dennis *experimental psychology educator*
†Meston, Cindy M(ay) *psychologist, educator*
Pingree, Dianne *psychotherapist*
Reid, Jackson Brock *psychologist, educator*
†Rentfrow, Peter J *psychologist*
Roach, James Robert *retired political science educator*
Rostow, Elspeth Davies *political science educator*
Schmandt, Jurgen A. *public affairs educator*
Schmitt, Karl Michael *retired political scientist*
Smith, Alfred Goud *anthropologist, educator*
Smith, Todd Malcolm *political consultant*
Thiessen, Delbert Duane *psychologist*
Walter, Virginia Lee *psychologist, educator*
†Warr, Eric Mark *sociologist, educator*

Bedford
Walther, Richard Ernest *psychology educator, library administrator*

Bellaire
Mayo, Clyde Calvin *organizational psychologist, educator*

Brooks AFB
Caldwell, John Alvis, Jr., *experimental psychologist*
†Patterson, John C. *clinical psychology researcher*

Bryan
Branson, Robert Earl *marketing economist*

Luepnitz, Roy Robert *psychologist, consultant, small business owner, entrepreneur*

Canyon
†Thoman, Roy Edward *political scientist, educator*
Welch, Reed Lynn *political scientist, educator*

Cedar Park
Fuller, Mitchell Franklin, II, *political scientist, educator*

College Station
Arnold, J(ames) Barto, III, *marine archaeologist*
Bass, George Fletcher *retired archaeology educator*
Bond, Jon Roy *political science educator*
Burk, James Steven *sociologist*
Edwards, George Charles, III, *political science educator, writer*
Furubotn, Eirik Grundtvig *economics educator*
Greenhut, Melvin Leonard *economist, educator*
Knutson, Ronald Dale *economist, educator, academic administrator*
Maret, Elizabeth Gardner *sociology educator*
Meier, Kenneth John *political scientist*
†Moroney, John Rodgers *economist, educator*
†Nederman, Cary Joseph *political scientist, director*
Saving, Thomas Robert *economics educator, consultant*
Steffy, John Richard *nautical archaeologist, educator*
Van Riper, Paul Pritchard *political science educator*

Corpus Christi
Cutlip, Randall Brower *retired psychologist, university president emeritus*
Lee, Jim *economist, educator*
Long, Ralph Stewart *clinical psychologist*
Rios, Jo Marie *political science educator*

Dallas
Betts, Dianne Connally *economist, educator*
Cochran, Kendall Pinney *economics educator*
Cochran, Mona Sheinfeld *economics educator, consultant*
Fomby, Thomas Blake *economist, educator, consultant, researcher*
Free, Mary Moore *biological and medical anthropologist*
Gibby, Mabel Enid Kunce *psychologist*
†Humphreys, Jean Surratt *social sciences educator*
Kemper, Robert Van *anthropologist, educator, minister*
Stanley, Harold Watkins *political science educator*
Wendorf, Denver Fred, Jr., *anthropology educator*

Denton
Belfiglio, Valentine John *political science educator, pharmacist*
Gibbs, Tyson *chairman anthropology department*
Leung, Paul *psychologist, rehabilitation educator*
McKee, William Lee *economist, arbitrator, mediator*
Naylor, Larry Lee *anthropologist, educator*
Schumacker, Randall *educational psychologist*

Edinburg
Jou, Jerwen *psychology educator*

El Paso
Armitage, Shelley Sue *American studies educator*
Coronado, Irasema *political scientist, educator*
Fullerton, Thomas Mankin, Jr., *economist*
Gilmer, Robert William, III, *economist*
Penley, Julie Anne *psychologist, educator*

Euless
Mabry, Philip T. *political consultant*

Fort Sam Houston
†Mangelsdorff, Arthur David *psychologist, educator*

Fort Worth
Dees, Sandra Kay Martin *psychologist, research scientist*
Durham, Floyd Wesley, Jr., *economist, educator*
†Fleshman, Linda Eilene Scalf *private investigator, writer, columnist, consultant, communications and marketing executive*
Guderjan, Thomas Harold *archaeologist, educator*
Jackson, Donald Wilson *political science educator, lawyer*
Mullendore, Walter Edward *retired economist*
Simpson, Dennis Dwayne *psychologist, educator*

Galveston
Barratt, Ernest Stoelting *psychologist, educator*
Fisher, Seymour *psychologist, educator*
Markides, Kyriakos Socrates *gerontology educator*
†Rosenthal, Susan Leslie *psychologist*

Georgetown
Howe, Thomas Noble *archaeologist, educator, architect*
Neville, Gwen Kennedy *anthropology educator*

Houston
Brito, Dagobert Llanos *economics educator*
Bryant, John Bradbury *economics educator, consultant*
Clearwater, John Murray *political analyst*
Condit, Linda Faulkner *economist*
Cuthbertson, Gilbert Morris *political science educator*
Davidson, Chandler *sociologist, educator*
†Dawson, Harry (Terry) Samuel, Jr., *policy analyst/advisor, consultant*
DeGregori, Thomas Roger *economics educator, consultant*
Dworkin, Anthony Gary *sociologist, educator*
Ewoh, Andrew Ikeh Emmanuel *political science educator*
Foster, Dale Warren *political scientist, educator, management consultant, real estate broker, accountant*
Grossett, Deborah Lou *psychologist, consultant*
†Hartgrove-Freile, Janice Lynn *psychologist, educator, writer*
Haymond, Paula J. *psychologist, diagnostician, hypnotherapist*
Huddle, Donald Leroy *economist, educator*
Hunt, Michael Allen *psychologist, educator*
Justice, Blair (David Blair Justice) *psychology educator, author*
Lachar, David *psychologist, educator*
Martin, Randi Christine *psychology educator*
Martin, William C. *sociology educator, writer*
†Mazas, Carlos Adalberto *psychologist, researcher*
Miller, Janel Howell *psychologist*
Rosin, Lindsay Zweig *clinical psychologist*
†Rubenzer, Steven James *foresnic psychologist*
†Sickles, Robin C. *economics and statistics educator, consultant*
White, Nancy Elizabeth *psychologist, artist*

Hurst
Hurley, Linda Kay *psychologist*

Kerrville
Ference, L.W. *psychologist*

Lubbock
Gilliam, John Charles *economist, educator*
Willingham, Welborn Kiefer *psychologist, educator*

Midland
Sherpa, Fran Magruder *geography educator, animal scientist, small business owner*

Nacogdoches
Tkacik, Michael Patrick *political science educator, lawyer*

Olney
Timmons, Gordon David *economics educator*

Pflugerville
Munzer, Annette Elizabeth *cultural affairs consultant*

Post
Earl, Lewis Harold *economics and management consultant, lawyer*

Prairie VIew
French, Laurence Armand *social science educator, psychology educator*

Richardson
Andrews, Melinda Wilson *human development researcher*
Beron, Kurt James *economics educator*
Berry, Brian Joe Lobley *geographer, political economist, urban planner*
Harpham, Edward John *political science educator, dean, writer, research*
†Holmes, Jennifer Smith *political scientist, educator*
†Leaf, Murray John *anthropologist, consultant*
†Scotch, Richard K. *sociologist, educator*
Vijverberg, Wim Petrus Maria *economics educator*

San Angelo
Butler, Michael Ward *economics educator*

San Antonio
Anderson, Kathryn B. *psychology educator*
Bellows, Thomas John *political scientist, educator*
Benz, George Albert *economist, consultant , retired economist educator*
Breit, William *economist, educator, writer*
Brooks, Franklin Ramon *psychologist, army officer*
Celmer, Virginia *psychologist*
Crockett, David Anthony *political science educator*
Furino, Antonio *economist, educator*
Gambitta, Richard Anthony *political science educator*
Garb, Howard Neil *clinical psychologist, educator*
Henington, C. Dayle *retired economist*
Hermann, John Robert *political science educator*
Hirsch, Barry T. *economist, educator*
†Lien, Donald *economist, educator*
Mathews, Jennifer Pauline *anthropologist, educator, archaeologist*
†McDonald, James H. *anthropologist, educator*
Mott, Peggy Laverne *sociologist, educator*
†Petersen, Rebecca D *criminologist, educator*
†Raiford, Susan Engi *psychologist, education educator*
Ribble, Ronald George *retired psychologist, educator, writer*
Rogers, William *psychologist, behavior specialist, writer, lecturer, journalist*
Spiro, Herbert John *political scientist, politician, educator, ambassador*
Spraggins, Johnnie David *social studies educator*
†Stedman, James Murphy *psychologist, educator*
Truett, Dale Brian *economics/finance educator, consultant*
Truett, Lila Flory *economics educator*

San Marcos
Boehm, Richard Glennon *geography educator, writer*
Fletcher, John Lynn *psychology educator*
Mullins, Wayman C. *educator, consultant*
†Ogletree, Shirley Matile *psychologist, educator*

Sherman
Han, Lori Cox *political science educator*
Parker, Harry John *retired psychologist, educator*

Stafford
Gonzalez, Larry Justin *political scientist, educator*
Krenek, Mary Louise *political scientist, researcher*

Stephenville
Stanley-Stevens, Leslie *sociology educator*

Sugar Land
Harribance, Sean Lalsingh *parapsychologist*

The Woodlands
Dougan, Deborah Rae *neuropsychology professional*

Tyler
Martin, William Allen *sociology educator*

Waco
Achor, Louis Joseph Merlin *psychology and neuroscience educator*
McKinney, Joseph Arthur *economist, educator*
Osborne, Harold Wayne *sociology educator, consultant*
Sharp, Ronald Arvell *sociology educator*

Weatherford
Buckner-Reitman, Joyce *psychologist, educator*

UTAH

Bountiful
Mangum, Garth Leroy *economist, educator*

Logan
Fifield, Marvin G. *psychologist, educator*
†Hartman, Cathy *economist, educator*

North Salt Lake
Barden, Robert Christopher *lawyer, psychologist, educator, legislative analyst, speaker, writer*

Ogden
Julander, Roydon O. *political science educator, lobyist*

Orem
†Kazemzadeh, Masoud *political scientist, educator*

Provo
Bahr, Howard Miner *sociologist, educator*
Ballif-Spanvill, Bonnie *psychologist, educator*
Creer, Thomas Laselle *psychologist, educator*
Fry, Earl Howard *political scientist, educator*
Kunz, Phillip Ray *sociologist, educator*
McDonald, James Bott *economics educator*
Porter, Blaine Robert Milton *sociology and psychology educator*
Pritchett, B(ruce) Michael, Sr., *economics educator, consultant*
Slife, Brent Donald *psychologist, educator, author*
Snow, Karl Nelson, Jr., *public management educator, university administrator, former state senator*
Wilson, Ramon B. *educator*

Salt Lake City
Benjamin, Lorna Smith *psychologist*
Girton, Lance *economics educator*
Hilke, John Coryell *economist*
Huefner, Robert P. *political science educator*
†Korbanka, Juergen Erich *psychologist, educator*
Kumpfer, Karol Linda *research psychologist*
Lien, Pei-te *political scientist, educator*

Sandy
Park, William Laird *agricultural economics educator, consultant, college associate dean*
Smith, Willard Grant *psychologist*

South Jordan
Rowley, Maxine Lewis *home economics and consumer educator, writer*

VERMONT

Barre
Black, Percy *psychology educator*

Brandon
Farnsworth, Frank Albert *retired economics educator*

Brattleboro
Kotkov, Benjamin *clinical psychologist*

Burlington
†Berkowitz, Stephen David *sociologist, educator*
Cutler, Stephen Joel *sociologist, educator*
Dinitz, Jeffrey H. *mathematics educator*
Hilberg, Raul *political science educator*
Lawson, Robert Bernard *psychology educator*
Sampson, Samuel Franklin *sociology educator*
†Stout, Neil Ralph *retired history educator*

Charlotte
Naylor, Thomas Herbert *economist, educator, consultant*

Essex Junction
Dietzel, Louise Alverta *psychologist*

Middlebury
Davis, Eric Lyle *political scientist, educator, college administrator*
Robison, Olin Clyde *political science educator, former college president*

Norwich
Foster, Michael Kirk *anthropologist, linguist*

Poultney
Edwards, Edgar O. *economist*

Shelburne
Little, George Thomas *international relations educator, retired*
Smallwood, Franklin *political science educator*

VIRGINIA

Alexandria
†Boudon, Henry Lawrence *social sciences educator, editor*
Carleson, Robert Bazil *public policy consultant, corporation executive*
Carvalho, Julie Ann *psychologist*
Cavin, Edward Scott *economist, consultant*
Garcia, Gillian Glenys *economist*
Guerra, Gonzalo Enrique *economist*
Hinkle, Wade P. *political scientist*
Johnson, Edgar McCarthy *psychologist*
Kollander, Mel *social scientist, statistician*
Krueger, Gerald Peter *psychologist*
Lytle, Michael Allen *criminologist, consultant*
Mann, Seymour Zalmon *political science and public administration educator emeritus, union official*
Oh, Kongdan *international policy analyst, consultant*
Reinl, Harry Charles *economist*
Roof, Michael Kitching *demographer, researcher*

Annandale
Wood, John Thurston *cartographer, jazz musician*
Wunderlich, Gene Lee *economist*

Arlington
Angell, Wayne D. *economist, banker*
Bradburn, Norman M. *behavioral science educator*
Brown, Robert Lyle *retired foreign affairs consultant*
†Buckley, F.H. *economist, educator*
Burkhart, Jennifer Ellen *business psychologist*
Chipman, Susan Elizabeth *psychologist, researcher*
Clare, Kenneth Guilford *economist, consultant*
Coats, Warren L., Jr., *economist*
Cobble, Steven Bruce *political consultant, strategist*
Coleman, Rodney Albert *government affairs consultant*
Davis, Lynn Etheridge *political scientist, educator*
Fuchs, Roland John *geography educator, university science official*
Gunn, Joseph Ridgeway, III, *consulting economist*
Howenstine, E. Jay *housing economist*
Kerns, Wilmer Lee *social science researcher*
Preeg, Ernest Henry *manufacturers alliance executive*
Siddayao, Corazón Morales *economist, educator, consultant*
Sundquist, James Lloyd *retired political scientist*
Taddesse, Samuel *economist, consultant*
Thompson, Robert Lee *agricultural economist, retired nonprofit executive*
Weidemann, Celia Jean *social scientist, international business and financial development consultant*

Blacksburg
Bryant, Clifton Dow *sociologist, educator*
Connerley, Mary L. *psychologist, educator*
Cook, Samuel Robert *anthropologist, educator*
Jannuzi, F. Tomasson *economics educator*
Mandelstamm, Allan Beryle *economics educator, consultant*
Morgan, George Emir, III, *financial economics educator*
Shepard, Jon Max *sociologist, educator*
Taylor, Charles Lewis *political science educator*
Walcott, Charles Eliot *political science educator*

Bluemont
Kobetz, Richard William *criminologist, consultant*

Burke
Bermant, Gordon *psychologist, lawyer, consultant, writer*

Charlottesville
Abraham, Henry Julian *political science educator*
†Allen, Joseph P. *psychologist, educator*
†Dienstag, Joshua Foa *political scientist, educator*
†Elzinga, Kenneth Gerald *economics educator*
Feigert, Frank Brook *retired political science educator, writer*
Goeree, Jacob Klaas *economist, educator*
Handler, Jerome Sidney *anthropology educator*
Henry, Laurin Luther *public affairs educator*
Hetherington, Eileen Mavis *psychologist, educator*
Holt, Charles Asbury *economics educator*
Hymes, Dell Hathaway *anthropologist, educator*
Kiewra, Gustave Paul *psychologist, educator*
McLaren, John Edward *economics educator*
Meiburg, Charles Owen *business administration educator*
Moreno, Zerka Toeman *psychodrama educator*
Olsen, Edgar Oliver *economics educator*
Perdue, Charles L., Jr., *social sciences educator, language educator*
Quandt, William Bauer *political scientist*
Reppucci, Nicholas Dickon *psychologist, educator*
Rhoads, Steven Eric *political science educator*
Stern, Steven Neal *economics educator*

Nichols, Donald Arthur *economist, educator*
Rice, Joy Katharine *psychologist, educational policy studies and women's studies educator*
Robinson, Arthur Howard *geography educator*
Schmidt, John Richard *agricultural economics educator*
Slesinger, Doris Peyser *sociology educator*
Strier, Karen Barbara *anthropologist, educator*
Thiesenhusen, William Charles *agricultural economist, educator*
Weimer, David Leo *political science educator*
West, Kenneth D. *economist, educator*
Wilson, Franklin D. *sociology educator*
Wolfe, Barbara L. *economics educator, researcher*
Young, Merwin Crawford *political science educator*

Menasha
†Peter, Gregory A. *sociology educator*
†Taheri, Abbas Ali *economist, educator*

Menomonee Falls
Griswold, Paul Michael *clinical psychologist, consultant*

Menomonie
Eggert, James Edward *economics educator, writer*

Middleton
†Caldwell, Michael Francis *psychologist*
Dorner, Peter Paul *retired economist, educator*
Taylor, Fannie Turnbull *social education and arts administration educator*

Milwaukee
Bibby, John Franklin *political science educator, writer*
†Carter, Charlene Ann *psychologist*
†Delwiche, William Arthur *economist, researcher*
Friman, H. Richard *political science educator*
Heo, Uk *political scientist, educator*
Kupst, Mary Jo *psychologist, researcher*
LaMalfa, Joachim Jack *retired clinical psychologist*
Mamalakis, Markos John *economics educator*
Moberg, David Oscar *sociology educator*
Perlman, Richard Wilfred *economist, educator*
Qureshi, Mohammed Younus *psychology educator, consultant*
Warren, Richard M. *experimental psychologist, educator*
Wei, Yehua Dennis *geography educator*
Wolfe, Christopher *political science educator*

New Berlin
Bielke, Patricia Ann *psychologist*
Marsh, Clare Teitgen *retired school psychologist*

Oshkosh
Gruberg, Martin *political science educator*
Liu, Baodong *political scientist, consultant*

Prescott
Kees, Mary Adele *school psychologist*

Racine
Hamberger, Larry Kevin *clinical psychologist, educator*
Keehn, Richard H. *economics educator emeritus*

Ripon
Steinbring, John Henry (Jack Steinbring) *archaeologist*

River Falls
LeCapitaine, John Edward *counseling psychology professor, researcher, writer*
Potts, Glenn Thomas *economics educator*

Schofield
Gontarz, Michael Joseph *school psychologist*

Stevens Point
†Blakeman, John Charles *political science educator*
Doherty, Patricia Anne *psychologist*
Wang, Jin *economics educator*

Waukesha
Graham, George Andrew, Jr., *psychologist, consultant*

Wausau
Ament, Richard Rand *psychologist*

Whitefish Bay
Hawkins, Brett William *political science educator*

Whitewater
Laurent, Jerome King *economics educator*
Marks, Louis Denton, Jr., *economist, educator, researcher*

WYOMING

Laramie
Allen, John Logan *geographer, department chairman*
Barbier, Edward B. *economist, educator*
Chai, Winberg *political science educator*
Crocker, Thomas Dunstan *economics educator*
Gill, George Wilhelm *anthropologist*
Shaffer, Sherrill Lynn *economist*
St Clair, James Sheldon *agricultural economics educator*

Powell
Brophy, Dennis Richard *psychology and philosophy educator, administrator, clergyman*

Wilson
Breitenbach, Mary Louise McGraw *psychologist, chemical dependency counselor*

TERRITORIES OF THE UNITED STATES

GUAM

Mangilao
Iverson, Thomas John *economist, educator*

PUERTO RICO

Bayamon
Herrans-Perez, Laura Leticia *psychologist, educator, research consultant*

Hormigueros
Acosta, Ursula *psychologist*

San Juan
Prevor, Ruth Claire *psychologist*
Rivera-Urrutia, Beatriz Dalila *psychology and rehabilitation counseling educator*

MILITARY ADDRESSES OF THE UNITED STATES

ATLANTIC

Apo
†Linares, Olga F. *anthropologist, researcher*

CANADA

ALBERTA

Calgary
Stebbins, Robert Alan *sociology educator*

Edmonton
Freeman, Milton Malcolm Roland *anthropology educator*
Krotki, Karol Jozef *sociology educator, demographer*
Mardon, Austin Albert *geographer, writer, researcher*

Saint Albert
Randhawa, Bikkar Singh *psychologist, educator*

BRITISH COLUMBIA

Burnaby
Brantingham, Paul Jeffrey *criminology educator*
Copes, Parzival *economist, researcher*
Kimura, Doreen *psychology educator, researcher*

Vancouver
Aberle, David Friend *anthropologist, educator*
Cynader, Max Sigmund *psychology, physiology, brain research educator, researcher*
†Eckbo, Bjorn Espen Espen *economics educator*
Ericson, Richard Victor *sociologist, educator, law educator, academic administrator*
Feaver, George Arthur *political science educator*
Holsti, Kalevi Jacque *political scientist, educator*
Jones, Lawrence Donald *economics educator*
Kesselman, Jonathan Rhys *economics educator, public policy researcher*
Langdon, Frank Corriston *political science educator, researcher*
Laponce, Jean Antoine *political scientist, educator*
Lipsey, Richard George *economist, educator*
Marchak, Maureen Patricia *anthropology and sociology educator*
Nemetz, Peter Newman *economics researcher, policy analysis educator*
Olsen, Inger Anna *psychologist, educator*
Robinson, John Lewis *geography educator*
Shearer, Ronald Alexander *economics educator*
Slaymaker, Olav *geography educator*
Suedfeld, Peter *psychologist, educator*
Tees, Richard Chisholm *psychology educator, researcher*

NEW BRUNSWICK

Fredericton
Kenyon, Gary Michael *gerontology educator, researcher*

NOVA SCOTIA

Chester Basin
Parr-Johnston, Elizabeth *economy and policy consultant*

Halifax
Lenzer, Irmingard Isolde *psychology educator*
Stairs, Denis Winfield *political science educator*
†Winham, Gilbert Rathbone *political science educator*

ONTARIO

Ajax
Mills, Jon K. *psychologist, educator, philosopher*

Hamilton
George, Peter James *economist, educator*
Ryan, Ellen Bouchard *psychology educator, gerontologist*

Kingston
Kaliski, Stephan Felix *economics educator*
MacKinnon, James Gordon
Meisel, John *political scientist*

Lindsay
Montgomery, Tommie Sue *political scientist, educator*

London
Laidler, David Ernest William *economics educator*
Wonnacott, Ronald Johnston *economics educator*

Niagara-on-the-Lake
Olley, Robert Edward *economist, educator*

North York
Flock, Howard *psychology educator*

Ottawa
Brigaldino, Glenn *social scientist, consultant*
Brooks, David Barry *resource economist*
Cappe, Melvin Samuel *economist*
Cornell, Peter McCaul *economic consultant, former government official*
Dagum, Camilo *economist, educator*
Griller, David *economics and technology consultant*
†Leth-Steensen, Craig *psychologist, educator*

Saint Catharines
Stevenson, Garth *social sciences educator*

Toronto
Bird, Richard Miller *economics educator*
Carr, Jack Leslie *economics educator, economic consultant*
Dobson, Wendy Kathleen *economics educator*
Ferguson, Kingsley George *retired psychologist*
Floyd, John Earl *economics educator*
Fuss, Melvyn Allan *educator, researcher*
Goldfarb, Martin *sociologist, researcher*
Grayson, Albert Kirk *Near Eastern studies educator*
Helleiner, Gerald Karl *economics educator*
Kingston, Rebecca Edith Dawson *political science educator*
Moggridge, Donald Edward *economics educator, author*
Munro, John Henry Alexander *economics educator, writer*
Pratt, Robert Cranford *political scientist, educator*
Rapoport, Anatol *peace studies educator, mathematical biologist*
Rose, Jeffrey Raymond *economist, educator, negotiator*
Smith, Lawrence Berk *economist, educator*
Tulving, Endel *psychologist, educator*
Wilson, Thomas Arthur *economics educator*

Waterloo
Fallding, Harold Joseph *sociology educator*
Nelson, J. Gordon *geography educator*
Stewart, Max Douglas *economics educator, consultant*
Vogel-Sprott, Muriel Doris *psychology educator, researcher*

Windsor
Auld, Frank *psychologist, educator*

QUEBEC

Ile des Soeurs
Dagenais, Marcel Gilles *economist, educator*

Montreal
Brecher, Irving *economics educator*
Brecher, Michael *political science educator*
Butler, Susan Ruth *clinical psychologist*
Dufour, Jean-Marie *economics researcher, educator*
Ikawa-Smith, Fumiko *anthropologist, educator*
Matziorinis, Kenneth N. *economics educator*
Melzack, Ronald *psychology educator*
Milner, Brenda Atkinson Langford *neuropsychologist*
Milner, Peter Marshall *psychology educator*
Nayar, Baldev Raj *political science educator*
Normandeau, Andre Gabriel *criminologist, educator*
Raynauld, Andre *economist, educator*
Stewart, Jane *psychology educator*
Szabo, Denis *criminologist, educator*
Trigger, Bruce Graham *anthropology educator*
Vaillancourt, Jean-Guy *sociology researcher and educator*
Waller, Harold Myron *political science educator*

Quebec
Belanger, Gerard *economics educator*
Tremblay, Marc Adélard *anthropologist, educator*

Saskatoon
Zhao, Jingang *economist, educator*

MEXICO

Mexico DF
Gonzalez-Sanchez, Enrique *economist*

Puebla
Creuheras, Santiago *social scientist*

ARGENTINA

Buenos Aires
Berardi, Jorge Enrique *economist*
†Lopez-Murphy, Ricardo Hipolito *economist*

AUSTRALIA

Canberra
Snooks, Graeme Donald *political economist, stratologist*

Melbourne
Corden, Warner Max *economics educator*

Victoria Armadale
†Neil, Sandra Eilleen Silverberg *psychologist*

AUSTRIA

Graz
Prisching, Manfred *sociology educator*

Vienna
Matzner, Egon *economics educator*
Swięcicki, Marcin *politician, economist*

BELGIUM

Brussels
Prodi, Romano *economist, educator, researcher, former prime minister of Italy*

Leuven
Buyst, Erik Cesar *economic history educator*

BERMUDA

Saint Georges
Jackson, Hermoine Prestine *psychologist*

BRAZIL

Rio de Janeiro
Resende, Marcelo *economist, educator*

CHINA

Beijing
Banister, Judith *demographer, educator*
Zhao, Ren Wei *economist, educator*

CZECH REPUBLIC

Prague
Manas, Miroslav *economics educator, researcher*

DENMARK

Aarhus
Vastrup, Claus *economist*

Aarhus V
Smith, Nina *economics educator*

Copenhagen
Joergensen, Per Bay *economist, insurance executive*
Olgaard, Anders *economics educator*

Gentofte
Egsmose, Ragna Kopp *cultural sociologist, researcher*

EGYPT

Cairo
Sullivan, Earl Le Roy *political science educator, academic administrator*

ENGLAND

Aldwych London
O'Brien, Patrick Karl *economic history educator*

Cambridge
Mirrlees, Sir James Alexander *economics educator*
Renfrew, Andrew Colin (Lord Renfrew of Kaimsthorn) *archaeologist, academic administrator*
Richard, Alison Fettes *anthropology educator*
Sen, Amartya Kumar *economist, educator*
Singh, Ajit *economist*

Devon
Rossmiller, George Eddie *agricultural economist*

Durham
Moberly, Elizabeth Rosamund *archaeologist, educator*
Spooner, Frank Clyffurde *economic history educator*

Guildford
Bulmer, Martin *sociologist, educator*

London
Blundell, Richard William *economics educator*
Cornelius, Peter Klaus *economist*
Dahrendorf, Lord Ralf Gustav *social scientist, educator*
Foldes, Lucien Paul *economics educator*
Gomulka, Stanislaw *economist, educator*
Hakim, Catherine *sociologist*
Junz, Helen B. *economist*

King, Mervyn Allister *economist, educator*
Kuper, Adam Jonathan *anthropologist, educator*
Portes, Richard David *economics educator*
Shaw, Timothy Milton *political science educator*
†Steele, Howard L. *psychology educator*

Norwich
Smith, Richard David *economics educator*

Oxford
Halsey, Albert Henry *sociologist*
Kaser, Michael Charles *economist, educator*

York
Williams, Alan Harold *economics educator*

ESTONIA

Tallinn
Köörna, Arno *economist, educator*

FINLAND

Turku
Dunlap, Riley Eugene *sociologist*

FRANCE

Epinay Sur Orge
Naszályi, Baron Philippe Jacques *economics educator, publication director*

Fontainebleau
Ayres, Robert Underwood *environmental economics and technology educator*

Guyancourt
Dubar, Claude Roger *sociologist*

Lyon
Naaoush, Sabah Faraj *economist, consultant*

Paris
Allais, Maurice Felix *economist*
Fitoussi, Jean-Paul Samuel *economist, educator*
Garnier, Olivier Pierre *economist*
Jenny, Frederic Yves *economist, educator*
Memmi, Albert *sociologist, educator*

Paris
Couteau, Marie-José *sociologist*

GERMANY

Berlin
Blankart, Charles Beat *economics educator*
Ollenburg, Guenter Wilhelm *retired economics educator, tax consultant*
Weiss, Dieter Waldemar *economics educator, consultant*

Bochum
Folkers, Cay *economics educator*

Bonn
Albach, Horst *economist*
Krelle, Wilhelm Ernst *emeritus economics educator*
Selten, Reinhard *retired economist, educator*

Cologne
Fels, Gerhard *economist*

Düsseldorf
Lüschen, Günther Rudolf Friedo *sociology educator*

Frankfurt
Glatzer, Wolfgang P. W. *sociology educator*

Frankfurt am Main
Tietz, Reinhard *economics educator*

Goettingen
Kucera, Gustav *economics educator*

Göttingen
Achtenhagen, Frank *economics educator*

Hamburg
Holler, Manfred Joseph *economics educator*

Kiel
Clausen, Lars *social scientist*
Siebert, Horst *economics educator, institute administrator*

Leipzig
Mancke, Richard Bell *economist, educator, investor*

Munich
Reimann, Helga Luise *sociologist*
Whetten, Lawrence L. *international relations educator*

Siegen
Buhr, Walter Heinrich Wilhelm *economics educator*

Wuppertal
Vaitkus, Steven Anthony *sociologist, researcher, educator*

GREECE

Athens
Kalamotousakis, George John *economist, merchant banker, educator*

Koulourianos, Dimitri Theodore *economist*

HONG KONG

Kowloon
Cheng, Joseph Yu-shek *political scientist, educator*
Qiu, Larry Dongxiao *economics educator*

HUNGARY

Budapest
Forgó, Ferenc *economics educator*
Hámori, Éva Lydia *economist*
Simai, Mihaly *economics and business educator*

INDIA

Baner Pune
Ohri, Sangeeta Jean Mary *social educator*

INDONESIA

Jakarta
Colfer, Carol Jean Pierce *anthropologist, researcher*

ISRAEL

Arad
Hollander, Samuel *economist, educator*

Beer Sheva
Hare, A(lexander) Paul *sociology educator*
Justman, Moshe *economics educator*

Jerusalem
Kessler, Avraham Albert *economist, researcher*
Pomerantz, Sherwin Bernard *economic development consultant*

Metar
Lithwick, Norman Harvey *economics educator*

Ramat-Gan
Rier, David Alan *sociologist, educator*

Tel Aviv
Bahiri, Simcha *economist*

ITALY

Pisa
Settis, Salvatore *archaeologist, art historian*

Rome
Scognamiglio, Carlo *economics and finance educator, Italian government senator*
Westley, John Richard *economist*

Torino
Antonelli, Cristiano *economist, educator*

Turin
Gros-Pietro, Gian Maria *economics educator*

JAPAN

Higashi-Osaka
Kazuya, Tetsuji *business educator*

Ibaraki
Kawano, Toshiaki *retired economics educator*

Inagi Tokyo
Iinuma, Hiroichi *international economics and trade educator, researcher*

Izumisano Shi
Ando, Seiichi *economics, Japanese history educator*

Mie
Isshiki, Masayuki *sociologist, educator, dean*

Nagoya
Kajitani, Motohisa *sociology educator*
Senda, Jun-ichi *economics educator*
Yamori, Nobuyoshi *economist*

Osaka
Horioka, Charles Yuji *economics educator*

Sakai
Fujita, Sei *political economist, educator*

Tokyo
Fukushima, Kiyohiko *economist*
Gyohten, Toyoo *economist*
Kato, Yoshiki *international economics educator*
Lo, Fu-chen *economist, educator, ambassador*
Maki, Atsushi *economics educator*
Miyazaki, Koichi *economics educator*
Nishiyama, Chiaki *economics educator*
Van Ginkel, Johannes Auguste *geographer, educator*

Yokohama
Kuroda, Yasumasa *political science educator, researcher*

MALTA

Valletta
†Bonello, Michael C. *economist*

NETHERLANDS

Zoetermeer
†Ritzen, Jozef Maria Mathias *economist*

NIGERIA

Abuja
Kouyaté, Lansana *economist, international official, diplomat*

Ijebu Ode
Adedeji, Adebayo *economist, former government official*

NORWAY

Oslo
Nyborg, Karine *economist, researcher*

PHILIPPINES

Makati
Thompson, Willard Scott (W. Scott Thompson) *social sciences educator*

Quezon City
Bunyi, Milagros Calderon *economics and marketing research executive*

POLAND

Jelenia Gora
Dziedzic, Zuzanna *economist*

Lodz
Mortimer-Szymczak, Halina Barbara *economics educator*

Lublin
Orlowski, Ryszard *economist, educator*

Poznan
Buchowski, Michal Janusz *anthropologist*

REPUBLIC OF KOREA

Kwangju
Kim, Kyou Yung *economist, educator*
Lee, Jung-Koo *economist, educator*

Seoul
†Ahn, Choong Yong *economics educator*

Suwon
Lee, Tong Hun *economics educator*

ROMANIA

Iasi
Tarca, Mihai *economist, educator*

RUSSIA

Moscow
Saltykov, Boris Georgievich *economist, politician*

SCOTLAND

Edinburgh
MacKenzie, Donald Angus *sociology educator*

SOUTH AFRICA

Bellville
Tapscott, Christopher Peter *sociologist*

SPAIN

Castellon
Georgantzis, Nikolaos *economist*

Madrid
Albi, Emilio *economist*
Merino, Fernando *economist, researcher, educator*

SRI LANKA

Colombo
Spain, James William *political scientist, writer, investor*

SWEDEN

Lund
Bauhn, Per Roald *sociology educator*

Saltsjo-Duvnas
Lundgren, Nils Gustav Herman *economist*

Stockholm
Blomström, Magnus Conrad *economics educator*
Wanden, Stig *economist, researcher*

Uppsala
Himmelstrand, J. Ulf I. *sociology educator, writer*

SWITZERLAND

Aarau
Rich, Georg *economist, bank executive*

Geneva
†Sidjanski, Dusan *economist, educator*
Twarog, Sophia Nora *economist, international civil servant*

Geneva
Jovanovic, Miroslav N. *economics educator*

TAIWAN

Taichung
Yen, Gili *economics researcher*

THAILAND

Bangkok
Kornell, Ronald Frank *economist*

UKRAINE

Mariupol
Vasiljev, Alexander Valerjovich *metallurgical engineer, economist*

ADDRESS UNPUBLISHED

Adams, Robert McCormick *anthropologist, educator*
Adelman, Richard Charles *gerontologist, educator*
Ahmed, Syed Z. *anthropologist*
Aiken, Lewis Roscoe, Jr., *psychologist, educator*
Alker, Hayward Rose *political scientist, educator*
Allen, Leatrice Delorice *psychologist*
Allen, William Sheridan *retired social sciences educator*
Alpher, Victor Seth *consultant, clinical psychologist*
Altman, Irwin *psychology educator*
Altshuler, Alan Anthony *political scientist, educator*
Amuzegar, Jahangir *economic consultant*
Ancoli-Israel, Sonia *psychologist, researcher*
Anderson, Bernard E. *economist*
†Anderson, James Allen *psychologist, writer*
Anderson, James George *sociologist, educator*
†Anderson, Odin Waldemar *sociologist, writer, artist*
Andrain, Charles Franklin *political science educator*
Andreatta, Susan L. *anthropologist*
Archer, Stephen Hunt *economist, educator*
Arditti, Fred D. *economist, educator*
Axilrod, Stephen Harvey *global economic consultant, economist*
Baba, Marietta Lynn *business anthropologist, university administrator*
Bach, Jonathan P.G. *political scientist*
Baker, Edward Martin *engineering and industrial psychologist*
Bambrick, James Joseph *labor economist, labor relations executive*
Bandopadhyaya, Amitava (Amit Bando) *economist, consultant, educator*
†Barber, Clarence Lyle *economics educator*
Barnes, Samuel Henry *political scientist, educator*
Batson, Raymond Milner *retired cartographer*
Bauer, Bernard Oswald *geography educator*
Bayack, Patricia Elaine *psychotherapist, social welfare administrator, social worker*
Beahm, Donald Lee *political science educator*
Beal, Wanda Elnora *psychologist, writer, artist*
Becker, Charles McVey *economics and finance educator*
Bell, Linda Green *psychology educator, therapist*
Benbow, Richard Addison *psychological counselor*
Bergin, Allen Eric *clinical psychologist, educator*
Bernstein, Phyliss Louise *psychologist*
†Berry, Cynthia Joan *psychologist, consultant*
†Beyle, Thad Lewis *political science educator*
Blank, Rebecca Margaret *economist*
Blaszczynski, Andre Boguslaw *economist, educator*
Blick, Robert Howard *economist, consultant*
Bluestone, Barry Alan *economics educator*
Bohannan, Paul James *anthropologist, writer, former university administrator*
Bohn, Marsha J. *anthropologist, researcher*
†Bonnell, Victoria Eileen *sociologist, educator*
Bostain, Nancy S. *psychologist, educator*
Bourguignon, Erika Eichhorn *anthropologist, educator*
Bowman, Larry Wayne *investigator, English and criminal justice educator*
Boyce, David Edward *transportation and regional science educator*
Bracey, Earnest Norton *political science educator*
Braddock, Walter David, III, *economist*
Brandl, John Edward *public affairs educator*

Bredfeldt, John Creighton *economist, financial analyst, retired air force officer*
Briggs, Philip James *political science educator, author, lecturer, reviewer*
Brint, Steven Gregory *sociologist, educator*
Broberg, Merle *retired social worker*
Brown, Donald McCarty *economic development specialist*
Buchanan, Scott Eugene *political science educator*
Buchin, Jean *psychologist, educator*
Buck, Jane Louise *psychology educator*
†Bullard, Judith Eve *psychologist, systems engineer*
Burns, Joseph M. *economist*
†Cantril, Albert H(adley) *public opinion analyst*
Carlsen, Mary Baird *clinical psychologist*
Carlson, Gustav Gunnar *anthropology educator*
Carlson, Janet Frances *psychologist, educator*
†Carlson, Roger David *psychologist, clergyman, educator*
†Carpentieri, Sarah C. *neuropsychologist, researcher, clinical psychologist*
†Cast, Alicia DeAnne *social sciences educator*
Cattell, Heather Birkett *psychologist*
Cavin, Susan Elizabeth *sociologist, writer*
Chang, Gene Hsin *economics educator, humanities educator*
Chang, Winston Wen-tsuen *economist, educator*
Chapman, Hope Horan *psychologist*
Chapman, Richard LeRoy *public policy researcher*
Chase, Clinton Irvin *psychologist, educator, business executive*
Chatterji, Angana P. *anthropologist*
Chirinko, Robert S. *economics educator*
Christian, James Wayne *economist*
Ciullo, Rosemary *psychologist*
Clark, Caleb Morgan *political scientist, educator*
Clark, Jere Walton *economics educator, researcher*
Cochran, John P. *economics educator*
Cohen, Jerome *psychology educator, electrophysiologist*
Collins, Harker *economist, manufacturing executive, publisher, marketing, financial, business and legal consultant*
Colosimo, Mary Lynn Sukurs *psychology educator*
Cotten, Annie Laura *psychologist, educator*
Cox, Gary Walter *political science educator*
Crawford, Edward E. *retired psychologist*
Crozier, Prudence Slitor *economist*
Cutting, Laurie E. *psychology educator, researcher*
Dailey, Victoria Ann *economist, policy analyst*
Daniels, Arlene Kaplan *sociology educator*
Danielsen, Albert Leroy *economics educator, energy and utilities consultant, energy executive, consultant*
Deacon, Sharon Rae *clinical psychologist*
Dean, Edwin Robinson *economist, educator, consultant*
†Deater-Deckard, Kirby *psychology educator, researcher*
Debreu, Gerard *economics and mathematics educator*
Dellere, Diana Marie *school psychologist*
Denevan, William Maxfield *geographer, prehistorian, ecologist*
DeVaris, Jeannette Mary *psychologist*
Dewald, William Guenthner *economist*
d'Heurle, Adma Jeha *psychology educator*
†Diem, Richard A. *social studies educator, educational consultant*
†Di Natale, Marisa Lyn *economist*
†Disch, William Burton *psychologist, researcher*
Dixon, Denise *psychologist, educator*
Dobriansky, Lev Eugene *economist, educator, diplomat*
Dole, Arthur Alexander *psychology educator*
Dominowski, Roger L. *psychologist, educator*
Donaldson, Loraine *economics educator*
Dorman, Patricia M. *sociologist, educator*
Dowd, Morgan Daniel *political science educator*
Downen, Robert Lynn *international affairs analyst and political consultant, editor, writer*
Downs, Amy Louise *psychologist*
Drummond, Dorothy Weitz *geography education consultant, educator, author*
†Dunn, Marija Gavrilova *psychologist, educator*
Dwyer, Gerald Paul, Jr., *economist, bank executive*
†Dzindolet, Mary Teresa *psychology educator*
Earle, Timothy Keese *anthropology educator*
Ebben, Joy Marie *human factors/ergonomics psychologist*
Ebert, Viola Roth *neuropsychologist, entrepreneur*
Egnor, Joanne McClellan *psychology educator*
Eikleberry, Carol *psychologist, writer*
Eley, Lynn W. *political science educator, former mayor*
Elgin, Gita *psychologist*
Elmendorf, Douglas William *economist*
Engel, Bernard Theodore *psychologist, educator*
Evans, Lance *psychology educator*
Everly, George Stotelmyer, Jr., *psychologist, psychophysiologist, educator, mathematician*
Feldman, David Henry *psychologist, educator*
Feldman, Douglas A. *anthropologist*
Finn, Daniel Kevin *economics and theology educator, former dean*
Finnberg, Elaine Agnes *psychologist, editor*
Fischer, Lucy Rose *gerontologist, researcher, artist*
Flood, Patrick James *political scientist, writer, retired diplomat*
†Foley, Paul E. *political scientist, educator*
Follingstad, Carol C. *psychologist, consultant, educator*
†Forbes, Thais R. *anthropologist, consultant*
†Foy, Edward Joseph *sociologist, educator, social worker*
†Fraga, Mike A. *history educator, accountant*
Frankel, Judith Jennifer Mariasha *clinical psychologist, consultant*

Franklin, Margery Bodansky *psychology educator, researcher*
Frazier, Lois E. *business and economics educator*
Fred-Mensah, Ben Kwame *international development educator, consultant*
Freilich, Morris *anthropologist, educator*
†Freshman, Brenda Lee *psychologist, educator, psychologist, researcher*
†Friedman, Martin Philip *applied behavior sciences specialist, education educator*
Fritz, Jan Marie *planning educator, mediator, clinical sociologist*
Fromlet, K. Hubert *banking economist*
Frost, Ellen Louise *political economist*
Funseth, Robert Lloyd Eric Martin *international consultant, lecturer, retired senior foreign service officer, foundation administrator*
Gabel, Creighton *retired anthropologist, educator*
Gardner, Bruce Lynn *agricultural economist*
Gay, David Edward Ryan *economist*
Geake, Raymond Robert *psychologist*
Geertz, Hildred Storey *anthropology educator*
†Gimbel, David Nelson *archaeologist*
Gleach, Frederic Wright *anthropologist, educator*
Glendening, Terry Sky *psychologist*
Goldston, Stephen Eugene *community psychologist, educator, consultant*
†Gomis Porqueras, Pedro *economics eduator*
Gracias, Maurice *economist*
Graham, Norma Van Surdam *psychologist, educator*
†Gray, Lori Ann *psychologist, researcher, educator*
Greeley, Andrew Moran *sociologist, author*
Greenwood, Janet Kae Daly *psychologist, educational administrator, marketing professional*
Gribben, Monica Anne *social scientist, researcher*
Grimm, Larry Leon *psychologist*
Grow, Robert Theodore *economist, association executive*
Guinn, Janet Martin *psychologist, consultant*
Guthrie, Robert Val *retired psychologist and educator*
Gutmann, David Leo *psychology educator*
Haber, Ralph Norman *psychology consultant, researcher, educator*
Hahn, Frank Horace *economics educator*
Haining, Jeane *psychologist*
Hall, Ella Taylor *clinical school psychologist*
Hall, Jay *social psychologist*
Hanks, Gary Arlin *psychology educator*
Hanushek, Eric Alan *economics educator*
Hardin, Joan Rothchild *psychologist, artist*
Harkness, S. Suzan Jane *political scientist, educator*
Harshbarger, Richard B. *economics educator*
Hartzell, Irene Janofsky *psychologist*
†Harvey, James Cardwell *political science educator, consultant*
Hawes, Bess Lomax *retired anthropologist*
Haywood, H(erbert) Carl(ton) *psychologist, educator*
Heart, Tracy *therapist, counselor, human resources specialist*
Hefferan, Colien Joan *economist*
Helfgott, Roy B. *economist, educator*
Henry, Lois Hollender *psychologist*
Hewitt, Benjamin Attmore *psychologist, consultant*
Hiler, Monica Jean *reading and sociology educator*
Hilliard, Sam Bowers *geography educator*
Hires, William Leland *psychologist, consultant*
†Hirsh-Pasek, Kathryn Ann *psychology educator*
Hockings, Paul Edward *anthropologist, editor*
†Hodge, David R. *social science researcher*
†Hodgson, Dorothy L. *social studies educator*
Holmes, Paul Luther *political scientist, educational consultant*
†Hoobler, Elizabeth Dressel *anthropologist, educator*
Hopkins, Jeffrey Willard *economist, researcher*
Hosek, James Robert *economist*
Huckstead, Charlotte Van Horn *retired home economist, artist*
Hughes, Ann Hightower *retired economist, international trade consultant*
Hull, Elaine Mangelsdorf *psychology educator*
Hume, Susan Rachel *finance and economics educator*
Ioffe, Grigory *geography educator, researcher*
Isaacs, Kenneth S(idney) *psychoanalyst, educator*
Isserman, Nancy *political scientist, researcher*
Jacobs, Grace Gaines *retired gerontologist, adult education educator*
Jacobsen, Diane DeMell *business executive and foreign policy specialist*
James, Estelle *economist, educator*
Jayne, Cynthia Elizabeth *psychologist*
Jett, Stephen Clinton *geography and textiles educator, researcher*
Johnson, Albert Wesley *retired advisor on governance*
†Johnson, Daniel Milo *sociology educator, university dean*
Johnson, J(anet) Susan *psychologist*
Jones, Edward Douglass, III, *economist*
Jones, Joan Megan *anthropologist*
Jones-Johnson, Gloria *sociologist, educator, consultant*
Jordan, Robert Smith *political science educator*
Juviler, Peter Henry *political scientist, educator*
Kahana, Eva Frost *sociology educator*
†Kalinina, Olga *economist*
Kaliski, Mary *psychologist*
Kalkhoff, William Webster *sociologist, educator*
Karczmar, Mieczyslaw *economist*
Karson, Samuel *psychologist, educator*
Kaslow, Florence Whiteman *psychologist, educator, family business consultant*
†Kassinove, Jeffrey Ian *psychologist, educator, research scientist*

Kay, Sean I. *politics and government educator*
†Kelley, Dana Lyn *social studies educator, consultant*
Kendrick, Budd Leroy *psychologist*
Kennedy, Marla Catherine *psychologist*
Kennedy-Minott, Rodney *international relations educator, former ambassador*
Kenyon, Daphne Anne *economics educator*
Keyes, Margaret Naumann *home economics educator*
Khavari, Khalil Akhtar *psychology educator*
Kisselev, Kate *economist*
Kohan, Dennis Lynn *international trade educator, consultant*
Koo, Shou-Eng *economics educator*
Korey, John L. *political scientist, educator*
†Korrasik, Jason J. *social sciences educator, researcher*
Kostere, Kim Martin *psychologist, consultant*
Kottler, Raymond George Michael *economist, researcher*
†Kottraba, Carin *psychologist*
†Kovacs, Malcolm *sociology educator, religious studies educator*
Kramer, Karen Sue *mind-body psychologist*
†Kreimer, Osvaldo N. *sociologist, consultant, lawyer*
Kreps, Juanita Morris *economics educator, former government official*
†Kubisch, Anne Christine *political scientist*
†Lague, Michael Robert *biological anthropologist*
Landon, William J. *intelligence officer*
Lanzillotti, Robert Franklin *economist, educator*
Lasky, Richard Donald *psychoanalyst, educator*
Laughlin, Louis Gene *economic analyst, consultant*
†Laws, Eric Laban *psychologist, educator*
LeBlanc, Hugh Linus *political science educator, consultant*
Lee, Aldora G. *social psychologist*
Levi, Maurice David *economics educator*
Lewis, Charles Leonard *psychologist*
Lewis, Robert Turner *former psychologist*
Lewis Mill, Barbara Jean *school psychologist, educator*
Lichtenberg, Byron K. *futurist, manufacturing executive, space flight consultant, pilot*
Liebman, Nina R. *economic developer*
Lief, Thomas Parrish *sociologist, educator*
Lindsey, Lawrence Benjamin *economist*
Linz, Gerhard David *psychologist, consultant*
Lipsitt, Lewis Paeff *psychology educator*
Lobao, Linda Mary *sociologist, educator*
Locke, Edwin Allen, III, *psychologist, educator, retired*
Lockheed, Marlaine Elizabeth *sociologist, World Bank official*
Loftus, Elizabeth F. *psychology educator*
Lombard, Karen Virginia *economist*
Lonergan, Thomas Francis, III, *criminal justice consultant*
Lucas, Wayne Lee *sociologist, educator*
Ludden, John Franklin *retired financial economist*
Lueptow, Lloyd Benjamin *retired sociology educator*
Lurensky, Robert Lee *economist, educator*
Lurie, Daphne *clinical psychologist, lecturer, educator*
MacDougall, Sir Donald (Sir George Donald Alastair MacDougall) *economist*
MacLennan, Beryce Winifred *psychologist*
Maehr, Martin Louis *psychology educator*
†Mair, Charles *social studies educator*
Maple, Opal Lucille *school psychologist*
Mark, Jonathan Greenfield *political scientist, educator, writer*
Markovich, Patricia Helen *economist*
†Marks, Mitchell Lee *organizational psychologist*
Martinson, Elizabeth Ann *archaeologist*
Marx, Gary T. *sociologist, writer*
Massa, Salvatore Peter *psychologist*
Matema, Zsun-nee Kimball (Annette K. Miller) *social sciences educator*
Matheny, Adam Pence, Jr., *child psychologist, educator, consultant, researcher*
Matthews, Wendy Schempp *psychologist, researcher*
†McArthur, John William *economist, researcher*
McCann, Lee I. *psychology educator*
Mc Clellan, Catharine *anthropologist, educator*
†McClure, Jennifer Bonner *psychologist, researcher*
McDougal, Marie Patricia *retired educator, freelance writer and editor*
McEvoy, Michael Joseph *economist*
McGough, Duane Theodore *economist, consultant, retired government official*
†McGreevy, Mary Sharron *former psychology educator*
†McLennan, Conor Thomas *cognitive psychologist, researcher*
Mesa-Lago, Carmelo *economist, educator*
Migue, Jean Luc *economics educator*
Montgomery, Edward Bruce *economics educator, university dean*
Moore, John Runyan *agricultural and resource economics educator*
Morris, Dolores Orinskia *psychologist, psychoanalyst*
Morris, Jane Elizabeth *home economics educator*
Mortimer, Robert Amsden *political science educator*
Moss, Michael *economist*
†Mullen, Brian *psychology educator*
Mutalipassi, Louis Richard *psychologist, educator*
Nas, Tevfik Fikret *economics educator*
Natani, Kirmach *forensic psychologist*
†Nepstad, Sharon Erickson *sociologist, educator*
Newborn, Jud *anthropologist, writer, curator, educator*
Ni, Shawn *economics educator*
Noll, Richard Dean, Jr., *psychologist, educator, historian*
Norman, Donald Arthur *cognitive scientist*

Nuechterlein, Donald Edwin *political scientist, educator, writer*
Obligacion, Freddie Rabelas *sociology educator, researcher*
O'Brien, John Wilfrid *economist, emeritus university president, educator*
Olson, William Clinton *anthologist, international affairs specialist*
Pace, Charles Robert *psychologist, educator*
Palisi, Anthony Thomas *psychologist, educator*
†Pannell, Clifton Wyndham *geography educator, writer*
Papaioannou, Evangelia-Lilly *psychologist, researcher*
Parker, Ronald Carlyle *transpersonal psychologist*
†Partridge, Charles Robert *program evaluator*
Pattanaik, Prasanta Kumar *economics educator*
Paupp, Terrence Edward *research associate, educator*
Pearson, Richard Joseph *archaeologist, educator*
Peattie, Lisa Redfield *urban anthropology educator*
Pedersen, Knud George *economics educator, academic administrator*
Pedersen, Paul Bodholdt *psychologist, educator*
Peleg, Ilan *political science educator*
†Peregrine, Peter Neal *archaeologist, writer*
Perez, Luz Lillian *psychologist*
†Pérez-Monforti, Jessica L. *social sciences educator, researcher*
†Peterson, Christopher *psychologist*
Petri, Peter Alexander *economist, educator, director*
Phelps, Gerry Charlotte *economist, minister*
Pilisuk, Marc *community psychology educator*
Pinilla, Ana Rita *neuropsychologist, researcher*
†Plank, Stephen Brandt *sociologist*
Polage, Danielle Cristi *psychology educator*
Pollack, Gerald Alexander *economist, government official*
†Pollard, Stephen Randall *social sciences educator*
Pomerantz, James Robert *psychology educator, academic administrator*
Prewitt, Kenneth *political science educator, foundation executive*
Ragan, James Francis *economics educator*
Ragusea, Stephen Anthony *psychologist, educator*
Rakove, Jack Norman *history educator*
Randall, Richard Rainier *geographer*
Raphaelson, Arnold Herbert *economist educator*
Reed, Diane Marie *psychologist*
Reese, Hayne Waring *psychologist, educator*
Reider, Richard Gary *geographer, educator*
Renard, Deborah Elaine *psychologist, counselor, educator*
Revankar, Nagesh Subray *economics educator*
Revere, Virginia Lehr *clinical psychologist*
Reynolds, Clark Winton *economist, educator*
Richards, Ruth *psychiatrist, educational psychologist*
Richmond, Anthony Henry *sociologist, emeritus educator*
Richstone, Beverly June *psychologist, writer*
Rickel, Annette Urso *psychology and psychiatry researcher, educator*
Riecken, Henry William *psychologist, research director*
Ringler, Lenore *educational psychologist, educator*
Risley, Todd Robert *psychologist, educator*
Roberts, Ray Crouse, Jr., *retired economics educator*
Robinson, James Arthur *policy scientist*
Robinson, Marguerite Stern *anthropologist, educator, consultant*
Robinson, Marshall Alan *economics educator, foundation executive*
Roche de Coppens, Peter George *sociologist, educator*
Rosen, Lawrence *anthropology educator*
†Rosenkrans, Amy Lynn *social studies educator*
Roskamp, Karl Wilhelm *economics educator*
Ross, William Dee, Jr., *economist*
Rossi, Peter Henry *sociology educator*
Ruback, Richard Barry *psychologist, educator*
Rubin, Zick *psychology educator, lawyer, writer*
Ruchelman, Leonard Isadore *urban studies and public administration educator*
Ruderman, Armand Peter *health economics educator, consultant, volunteer*
Salovey, Peter *psychology educator*
Salzmann, Zdenek *anthropology educator*
Sameroff, Arnold Joshua *developmental psychologist, educator, research scientist*
†Santuzzi, Alecia Marie *psychologist, educator, psychologist, researcher*
Sargent, Thomas Andrew *retired political science educator*
†Saunders, Mari Pittman *psychologist*
†Schacter, John Lawrence *educational psychologist, researcher*
†Schaler, Jeffrey Alfred *psychologist, educator*
Schenkel, Susan *psychologist, educator, author*
†Schlichting, Kimberly Sue *psychologist, educator, health facility administrator*
Schmandt-Besserat, Denise *archaeologist, educator*
Schmidt, Harvey Martin *economic forecaster, educator, financial consultant*
†Schnuriger, Sarah *social sciences educator, historian*
Schubert, Glendon *political scientist, educator*
Schwartz, Teri J. *clinical psychologist, educator*
Scully, Gerald William *economics educator*
Sebastian, Peter *international affairs consultant, former ambassador*
Seltzer, Vivian Center *psychologist, educator*
Shakow, Alexander *economist, government official*
Shapiro, Leo J. *social researcher*
Sharpe, William Forsyth *economics educator*
Shepard, Roger Newland *psychologist, educator*
Shepp, Bryan Eugene *psychologist, educator*
Shulman, David George *economist*

UNCLASSIFIED

UNITED STATES

CALIFORNIA

Arcadia
†Tressel, Violet Manooshaq

Palm Desert
Joseph, Jerry

COLORADO

Thornton
Johnson, Carole Jean

ILLINOIS

Rockford
†Sherman, Deborah Lynn

KENTUCKY

Elizabethtown
†Paparinov, Rafael Raytchev

OHIO

Wright Patterson Afb
Amend, Joseph H., III,

TEXAS

Kaufman
Teagle, David Bryan

WEST VIRGINIA

Princeton
Worrell, Mason Dewey

WISCONSIN

Madison
†Stotsky, David M.

ADDRESS UNPUBLISHED

†Stableford, Karen P.

Retiree Index

The index below lists the names of those individuals whose biographical sketches last appeared in the 55th, 56th or 57th Edition of *Who's Who in America*. The latest volume containing a full sketch is indicated by 55, 56 or 57 following each name. The listees have since retired from active participation in their respective occupations.

A

Abels, Robert Frederick, *57*
Allen, James Henry, Sr., *57*
Andrews, James E., *56*

B

Baird, Haynes Wallace, *57*
Baker, Roy E., *57*
Barnard, Morton John, *57*
Bauer, Dietrich Charles, *57*
Beach, Lee Roy, *55*
Beltran, Violeta Centeno, *57*
Bergen, Robert Ludlum, Jr., *57*
Blackwell, Cecil, *57*
Bossman, Sandra Lou, *56*
Boston, Leona, *57*
Bragg, Albert Forsey, *55*
Buck, Alfred Andreas, *57*
Burkhardt, Charles Henry, *57*
Burns, Jacqueline Mary, *57*
Burton, John Jacob, *57*
Butler, Stephen Gregory, *57*
Butterfield, Samuel Hale, *57*

C

Carroll, Bonnie, *56*
Chase, Norman Eli, *55*
Cheney, William D., *57*
Church, Avery Grenfell, *57*
Clark, Marcia Rachel, *57*
Cleberg, Harry C., *55*
Colburn, Richard Dunton, *57*
Conerly, Albert Wallace, *57*
Conger, Bob Vernon, *57*
Cooper, Francis Loren, *56*
Copeland, James E., Jr., *57*
Copley, Helen Kinney, *57*
Craft, James Pressley, Jr., *55*
Cruze, Alvin M., *56*
Curry, Thomas James, *57*

D

Daly, Simeon, *57*
Debas, Haile T., *57*

De Hoff, John Burling, *57*
Dickey, John Sloan, Jr., *57*
Drakulich, Martha, *57*
Drezdzon, William Lawrence, *56*
Driscoll, Lee Francis, Jr., *57*
Duke, Miriam D. Wansley, *57*
Durham, Barbara, *56*

E

Ederer, Grace Mary, *55*
Estep, Sarah Virginia, *55*
Evans, Ralph Aiken, *55*

F

Ferguson, Charlotte Brainard, *55*
Ferguson, Robert Bruce, *57*
Flood, A. L. (Al Flood), *56*
Florence, Sally Ann, *57*
Frederick, Lloyd Randall, *57*
Fritz, Cecil Morgan, *56*

G

Gandrud, Robert P., *55*
Garvey, John Leo, *55*
Gary, James Frederick, *57*
Geck, Francis Joseph, *57*
Gerhard, Harry E., Jr., *57*
Giuffrida, Matthew Roland, *57*
Gnant, Randall, *57*
Grafton, W. Robert, *55*
Grant, Robert James, *57*
Green, Bruce, *55*
Griffin, Villard Stuart, Jr., *55*
Grundy, Roy Rawsthorne, *57*
Grunska, Gerald P(aul), *57*

H

Hackett, Louise, *55*
Hager, John Patrick, *57*
Halford, Rick, *57*
Hall, Carl Loren, *57*
Halvorsen, Morrie Edward, *55*
Handler, Alan B., *56*

Harding, Enoch, Jr., *57*
Harris, Miles Fitzgerald, *57*
Harte, Houston Harriman, *57*
Hash, John Frank, *55*
Horton, Sherman D., Jr., *57*
Hummel, Charles Frederick, *57*

I

Imbembo, Anthony Louis, *57*

J

Jennings, A. Drue, *56*
Jones, Gordon Edwin, *57*
Jones, Lawrence David, *57*

K

Kasten, Paul Rudolph, *55*
Kastner, Cynthia, *56*
Keith, Alexander Macdonald, *57*
Kirkland, John Leonard, *57*
Kitchin, Kate Parks, *57*
Kogan, Gerald, *56*
Kolb, John, *56*
Kondo, Edward Shinichi, *55*
Kraus, Eileen S., *57*

L

Laskawy, Philip Alan, *57*
Lear, Robert William, *57*
Leimkuhler, Ferdinand Francis, *57*
Lemmon, Jean Marie, *57*
Lewis, Clyde A., *57*
Lindsay, James Wiley, *57*
Lynch, Neil L(awrence), *57*
Lyon, Wayne Barton, *57*

M

Mancel, Claude Paul, *57*
Marco, Guy Anthony, *57*
Masubuchi, Koichi, *57*

Mazza, Thomas Carmen, *57*
McCarthy, Lynn Cowan, *57*
McCoy, Helen Thomas, *55*
McDonald, Mary M., *57*
McFarland, Jon Weldon, *57*
Mc Farlane, Karen Elizabeth, *57*
McLean, James, *56*
Medeiros, Prisca Bicoy Daniel, *57*
Moore, George S., Jr., *55*
Morello, Josephine A., *57*
Morris, M(ary) Rosalind, *55*
Moursund, Kenneth Carroll, *57*
Muller, Frederick Arthur, *57*
Muresanu, Violeta Ana, *57*

N

Nairn, Charles Edward, *57*
Narath, Albert, *57*
Nihart, Franklin Brooke, *57*
Nishitani, Martha, *57*
Noto, Lucio A., *57*

O

Olesen, Douglas Eugene, *57*
Oscarson, Kathleen Dale, *57*
Ownbey, Lenore F. Daly, *57*

P

Porter, Brian Stanley, *57*
Pritzker, Robert Alan, *57*

R

Rahn, Saundra L., *56*
Rakowski, Dennis Thomas, *56*
Randolph, Kenneth E., *55*
Rázim, William Wendell, *57*
Richards, Robert Wadsworth, *55*
Royalty, Kenneth Marvin, *56*
Rusnack, William C., *57*
Rynear, Nina Cox, *57*

S

Sayre, E(noch) Phillip, *57*
Schreiber, Averil Elspeth, *57*
Scott, Joyce M. C., *57*
Seegmiller, Jarvis Edwin, *57*
Seward, Grace Evangeline, *57*
Shaffer, Frances, *57*
Sharp, Thomas B., *57*
Skromme, Arnold Burton, *57*
Sorensen, W. Robert, *57*
Spinks, John Lee, *57*
Steele, Clarence Hart, *57*
Stormont, Clyde Junior, *56*
Strong, Roger Lee, *56*
Summers, James Irvin, *57*

T

Tanner, Candace JoAnn, *57*
Thomas, Carmen Christine, *57*

U

Ungerer, Walter John, *57*
Ursu, John Joseph, *57*

V

Van Alstyne, Judith Sturges, *57*

W

Wadler, Arnold L., *57*
Wallach, Philip C(harles), *57*
Weiss, William, *56*
Whitehead, Marvin Delbert, *55*
Whiting, Henry H., *57*
Wilson, Sonja Mary, *57*
Woglom, James Russell, *57*
Wynne, John Oliver, *56*

Y

Yancey, Eleanor Garrett, *53*
Yates, Robert Doyle, *57*

Necrology Index

Biographees of the 58th Edition of *Who's Who in America* whose deaths have been reported to the editors prior to the close of compilation of this edition are listed below. For those individuals whose deaths were reported prior to May 2003, complete biographical information, including date of death and place of interment, can be found in Volume XV of *Who Was Who in America*.

A

Abadi, Fritzie
Abrams, Herbert E.
Abul-Haj, Elizabeth
Acheson, Roy Malcolm
Adam, Orval Michael
Adams, Algalee Pool
Adams, Clinton
Adams, Perry Ronald
Adams, Walter
Adaskin, Murray
Agnelli, Giovanni
Ahmann, Mathew Hall
Albinski, Henry Stephen
Alcock, Charles Benjamin
Allen, Ivan, Jr.
Aller, Lawrence Hugh
Almond, Gabriel Abraham
Almy, Thomas Pattison
Alonso, Antonio Enrique
Alvarado, Ricardo Raphael
Amarel, Saul
Amon, William Frederick, Jr.
Anderson, Duwayne Marlo
Anderson, Michael P.
Andrews, Robert Vincent
Antupit, Samuel Nathaniel
App, James Leonard
Aptheker, Herbert
Arends, Wendell Leonard
Arnett, Foster Deaver
Ash, Philip
Atherton, Alfred Leroy, Jr.
Auchincloss, Kenneth
Austin, Tom Al

B

Bagby, William Rardin
Bailar, Benjamin Franklin
Bailey, Martin Jean
Baillie, Charles Douglas
Baird, Mellon Campbell, Jr.
Baker, Edward George
Baker, Louis Coombs Weller
Baker, Walter Louis
Baldwin, Garza, Jr.
Ballard, John William, Jr.
Baney, John Edward
Bangs, John Wesley, III
Bareiss, Erwin Hans
Barnes, John Wadsworth
Barnett, Lester Alfred
Baron, Martin Raymond
Barratt, Raymond William
Barriskill, Maudanne Kidd
Barton, Peter Richard
Barton, Russell William
Batavia, Andrew I.
Batscha, Robert Michael
Bauman, George Duncan
Baumgartner, Rudolf
Beach, Edward Latimer
Beatty, William Louis
Beck, Earl Ray
Beck, John Roland
Beckley, Donald Kauffman
Beetham, Stanley Williams
Beglarian, Grant
Behnke, Richard Frederick
Behrend, William Louis
Belin, Gaspard d'Andelot
Bell, William Jack
Benham, Priscilla Carla
Bennett, Harold Clark
Benton, Robert Dean
Berg, David
Bergholz, Richard Cady
Bergson, Abram
Berliner, Robert William
Berne, Robert Matthew
Bernfield, Merton Ronald
Bernstein, Elliot Louis
Berrey, Bedford Hudson
Berry, William Wells

Bertram, Frederic Amos
Beverett, Andrew Jackson
Biller, Morris (Moe Biller)
Billingsley, Charles Edward
Binns, Walter Gordon, Jr.
Blackburn, Robert McGrady
Blackey, Edwin Arthur, Jr.
Blair, Robert Noel
Block, Herbert Lawrence (Herblock)
Blumenthal, Fritz
Bober, Phyllis Pray
Boeker, Paul Harold
Boettcher, Harold Paul
Boger, Lawrence Leroy
Bonner, Thomas Neville
Bookout, John G.
Booth, Taylor Lockwood
Borel, Armand
Bosse, Malcolm Joseph, Jr.
Bourcier, John Paul
Bower, Marvin
Bowers, John Zimmerman
Boyce, Alfred Warne
Boyd, William, Jr.
Bozorth, Squire Newland
Braden, Samuel Edward
Bradford, Richard Roark
Brady, Frank Benton
Brakhage, James Stanley
Branch, Charles Hendrix
Bray, Absalom Francis, Jr.
Bray, R(obert) Bruce
Breines, Simon
Brierley, John E. C.
Brinkhous, Kenneth Merle
Bro, Kenneth Arthur
Brodhead, Quita
Bross, Steward, Jr.
Brown, David M.
Brown, Dee Alexander
Brown, Fred Elmore
Brown, James Isaac
Brown, John Carter
Brown, Paul Bradley
Brown, Robert Thorson
Browner, Julius Harvey
Brundidge, Nancy Corinne
Brzustowicz, Richard John
Buck, Anne Marie
Budge, Hamer Harold
Burack, Sylvia Kamerman
Burke, B. Meredith
Burke, Mary Thomas
Burr, Gray
Burton, Daniel G.
Bush, Richard James
Bushnell, George Edward, Jr.
Bussman, John Wood
Butts, Virginia
Bye, Arthur Edwin, Jr.
Byrne, Frank Loyola

C

Cahan, William George
Calderwood, Stanford Matson
Calkins, Gary Nathan
Cameron, Ken
Campbell, Donald Alfred
Cannon, Helen Loura Harrelson
Cannon, Isabella Walton
Canter, Ralph Raymond
Capehart, Harriet Jane Holmes
Carbone, Paul Peter
Carey, Thomas Devore
Carleton, Richard Allyn
Carmichael, Virgil Wesly
Carpenter, Donald Blodgett
Carter, Gerald Emmett
Carter, Ruth B. (Mrs. Joseph C. Carter)
Cashman, Edmund Joseph, Jr.
Cassill, Ronald Verlin
Cates, Nelia Barletta de
Catts, Frances Austin
Chait, William
Chang, David Ping-Chung

Chapanis, Alphonse
Chaplin, George
Chargaff, Erwin
Charp, Sylvia
Cheniae, George Maurice
Chestnut, Harold
Childs, James William
Ching, Julia
Chook, Edward Kongyen
Chou, Shelley Nien-chun
Chrisman, O. Donald
Christensen, Ila Snyder
Christian, Sherril D.
Churchill, Allen Delos
Citron, David Sanford
Clark, Laurel Blair Salton
Clarke, Richard Alan
Cleary, John Washington
Clements, James David
Coale, Ansley Johnson
Cobean, Richard Winfield
Coffield, Mary Eleanor
Cohen, Sylvan M.
Cohn, Jess Victor
Cohn, Leonard Allan
Cole, Benjamin Richason
Cole, Jack Westley
Coleman, John Edward
Coleman, Robert Elliott
Collins, Philip Reilly
Collins, Vincent Patrick
Colvin, Burton Houston
Connell, William Francis
Conniff, Ray
Connolly, Thomas Edmund
Connor, Paul Eugene
Cook, Chauncey William Wallace
Cook, James
Cook, James Fielder
Cooper, Arthur Martin
Cooper, James Clinton
Cooper, William Eugene
Coplans, John Rivers
Corbett, Jack Elliott
Cordasco, Francesco
Corey, Jeff
Cornell, David Roger
Coser, Lewis Alfred
Cox, Dallas Wendell, Jr.
Cox, J. William
Cox, Paul
Coxeter, Harold Scott Macdonald
Craighead, Frank Cooper, Jr.
Crawford, William Rex, Jr.
Crews, Grasty, II
Crisona, James Joseph
Cromwell, Edwin Boykin
Cronyn, Hume
Crosby, John O'Hea
Cross, Ralph Emerson
Crump, Spencer
Culberson, William Louis
Cummings, Ralph Waldo
Curtis, Chester Harris
Cutler, Cassius Chapin
Czorniak, Andrew

D

Dahl, Arthur Ernest
Dahlsten, Donald Lee
Daniel, Richard Nicholas
Daniels, Doral Lee
D'Arms, John Haughton
Davidson, Donald Herbert
Davis, Charles Hargis
Davis, Mattie Belle Edwards
Davis, Raymond Gilbert
Davis, True
Davis, Vincent
Davis, Walter Stewart
Dawson, John Myrick
Day, Chon
Dazey, William Boyd
Dean, Francis Hill
Deere, Cyril Thomas

De Hartog, Jan
Deiter, Newton Elliott
DeLay, Dorothy (Mrs. Edward Newhouse)
Del Re, Robert
DeMarco, Roland R.
Denfarest, Daniel Anthony
Dembo, Lawrence Sanford
Deming, Frederick Lewis
Demola, James, Sr.
Dennis, Walter Decoster
Densen-Gerber, Judianne
Dent, Ernest DuBose, Jr.
De Shazor, Ashley Dunn
Dewhurst, William George
Diamond, Irene (Irene Diamond)
Di Biasi, Eleanor S.
Diehl, William Henry S.
Dillon, Clarence Douglas
Dodge, Harry Leon
D'Oench, Russell Grace, Jr.
Donohue, Carroll John
Donovan, Robert John
Dorfman, Robert
Douglass, Malcolm Paul
Dowdy, Homer Earl
Downing, William H.
Drahmann, Brother Theodore Robert
Dressner, Howard Roy
Drickamer, Harry George
Droessler, Earl George
Drown, Eugene Ardent
Duberg, John Edward
Dubnick, Bernard
Dunn, James Joseph
Dunn, Parker Southerland
Durbin, Enoch Job
Duval, Michael Raoul
Dwyer, William L.
Dyer, John Martin

E

Easterbrook, James Arthur
Ebert, James David
Eckdahl, Donald Edward
Ecker, Peder Kaloides
Edwards, Ian Keith
Edwards, James Edwin
Edwardson, John Richard
Eforo, John Francis
Eggertsen, Paul Fred
Ehrlich, Lawrence
Ehrlich, Paul
Eisenpreis, Alfred
Elliott, Holly Hall
Ellis, Elizabeth Mueller
Ellmann, William Marshall
Elrod, John William
Endler, Norman Solomon
Engel, Charles Robert
Epstein, David Mayer
Erskine, Harold Lester
Estle, Thomas Leo
Etzwiler, Donnell Dencil
Evans, Roger Lynwood

F

Falcone, Alfonso Benjamin
Farley, Jennie Tiffany Towle
Farrell, John Stanislaus
Fast, Howard Melvin
Faul, George Johnson
Feeley, John Paul
Feinstein, Alvan Richard
Feldman, Robert George
Feller, David E.
Felts, William Robert, Jr.
Fendler, Oscar
Ferris, Frederick Joseph
Ferson, Lu Ann
Feuvrel, Sidney Leo, Jr.
Fiedler, Leslie Aaron
Filby, Percy William

Filipos, Xenia Elizabeth Lychos
Fisch, Charles
Fisher, Charles Worley
Fisher, Chester Lewis, Jr.
Fitzgerald, Dorothea Marguerite
Fitzpatrick, Thomas Bernard
Flaschen, Steward Samuel
Fleck, Stephen
Flygaard, Ole
Forbes, Gilbert Burnett
Ford, Donald Hainline
Ford, Franklin Lewis
Forester, Russell
Forward, Robert L(ull)
Foster, Catherine Rierson
Fouchard, Joseph James
Frank, John Paul
Fraser, David A.
Fraser, Robert Gordon
Fredrickson, Donald Sharp
Freeman, Mark
Freeman, Orville Lothrop
Freestone, Barbara Seaman
Freiwald, David Allen
Fried, Burton David
Friedheim, Eric Arthur
Friedman, Ronald Marvin
Fromm, Erika (Mrs. Paul Fromm)
Fromm, Hanna
Frumkin, Allan
Frye, Judith Eleen Minor
Furimsky, Stephen, Jr.

G

Gaines, Howard Clarke
Gallagher, John Jerome
Garance, Dominick (D. G. Garan)
Garcés, Ramón
Gardner, Richard Alan
Gardner, Robert Joseph
Gardner, Warner Winslow
Garland, James Boyce
Garner, Alto Luther
Gaucher, Donald Holman
Gaudry, Roger
Gay, Elisabeth Feitler
Gaylord, Edward Lewis
Gellermann, Marian DeBelle
Gellis, Sydney Saul
Georges, Maurice Ostrow
Georgiade, Nicholas George
Gessow, Alfred
Gibbs, Jordan Smith
Gibson, Eleanor Jack (Mrs. James J. Gibson)
Gibson, James John
Giddens, Charles Edwin
Ginsberg, Harold Samuel
Ginzberg, Eli
Giroux, Paul Henry
Gladstone, Richard Bennett
Glazer, Tom (Thomas Zacariah Glazer)
Gleckner, Robert Francis
Gliedman, Marvin L.
Goldberg, Joseph Philip
Goldsmith, Werner
Good, Robert Alan
Goode, William Josiah
Goodman, David Barry Poliakoff
Gordon, Eugene Andrew
Gould, James Spencer
Gould, R. Martin (Richard Martin Goldman)
Gowens, Verneeta Viola
Goz, Harry G.
Grabemann, Karl W.
Graham, Hugh Davis
Grant, James Deneale
Graves, Fred Hill
Green, Adolph
Green, Sedgwick William
Greenberg, Joseph H.
Greene, Ralph Vernon
Greer, Joseph Epps
Gregory, Norman Wayne

Griggs, Ruth Marie
Griswold, Idawease Johnson
Grodberg, Marcus Gordon
Grold, L. James
Gross, Hal Raymond
Grossweiner, Leonard Irwin
Guerin, John Joseph
Gumb, Raymond Daniel
Gunther, Gerald
Gustavson, Brandt
Guth, Paul C.
Guyton, Arthur Clifton

H

Haas, Merrill Wilber
Haensel, Vladimir
Halaby, Najeeb E.
Hamburg, Joseph
Hamilton, Howard Laverne
Hanchett, Charles Emery
Handy, Nixeon Civille
Hansen, Wendell Jay
Hanson, David Gordon
Happel, John
Harari, Hananiah
Hare, Frederick Kenneth
Hargroder, Charles Merlin
Harkarvy, Benjamin
Harris, Gwen Moyers
Harris, Leon Abraham, Jr.
Harris, Neison
Hart, Jay Albert Charles
Harvey, Edmund Lukens
Haslam, Charles Linn
Haus, Hermann Anton
Hawkins, Merrill Morris, Sr.
Hawthorne, Frank Howard
Haydanek, Ronald Edward
Haynes, Jean Reed
Hecht, Donn
Hein, John William
Heit, Raymond Anthony
Helms, Richard McGarrah
Heming, Charles E.
Henderson, Sarah Cothran
Henschel, Milton G.
Hepburn, Katharine Houghton
Herkness, Lindsay Coates, III
Hersey, David Floyd
Hershcopf, Berta Ruth
Herskowitz, Ira
Hess, Donald F.
Hewitt, Frankie Lea
Heyer, Anna Harriet
Higham, John
Hildreth, R(oland) James
Hill, George Roy
Hill, Samuel Richardson, Jr.
Hintz, Robert Louis
Hirschfeld, Albert
Hoadley, Walter Evans
Hodgetts, Richard Michael
Holloway, Edgar Austin
Holloway, Marvin Lawrence
Holmes, Darrell
Hopkins, Jack Walker
Hopkins, Thomas Matthews
Hoppel, Robert Gerald, Jr.
Horton, Kenneth
Howe, Harold, II
Howells, Muriel Gurdon Seabury (Mrs. William White Howells)
Howie, John Robert
Hoyt, Don, Sr.
Hudson, Herbert Alexander
Hughes, Monica
Hughes, Sue Evans
Hunt, Peter Roger
Hunter, Kim (Janet Cole)
Hurd, John Gavin
Hyman, Sigmund M.

I

Iachetti, Rose Maria Anne
Iglehart, T. D.
Illich, Ivan
Ingram, William Austin
Iverson, Francis Kenneth
Izenour, Steven

J

Jackson, Daniel Wyer
Jacobsen, Thomas H(erbert)
Jacobson, Harold Karan
James, Daniel J.
Jamplis, Robert Warren
Jenner, William Alexander
Jensen, Helen
Jervey, Harold Edward, Jr.
Johns, Varner Jay, Jr.
Johnson, David Gale
Johnson, Paul Owen
Johnson, Richard Vernon
Johnson, Robert Eugene
Johnston, Waldo Cory Melrose
Jones, Anne Macfarlane
Jones, James Rees
Jones, Nancy Gale
Joppa, Robert Glenn
Jordan, Richard Charles
Joy, La Verne Gough

K

Kachadoorian, Zubel
Kagan, Sioma
Kain, John Forrest
Kamm, Herbert
Kanade, Ashok
Kapnick, Harvey Edward, Jr.
Kaskey, Baylen
Katayama, Arthur Shoji
Katz, Sir Bernard
Katz, Israel
Keable, Doreen Marie
Keach, Stacy, Sr.
Keane, Gustave Robert
Keen, Noel Thomas
Keim, Robert Phillip
Keller, Barbara Lynn
Kelley, William
Kelly, James
Kendig, Edwin Lawrence, Jr.
Kendrick, Joseph Trotwood
Kennedy, Harvey John, Jr.
Kennedy, John Edward
Kesey, Ken
Kethley, Lancelot Imre
Kienzle, William Xavier
Kilgore, Carolyn Harrell (Carolyn Lawton Harrell)
Kimerer, Neil Banard, Sr.
Kindleberger, Charles P., II
King, Charles Thomas
King, Robert Augustin
King Hookham, Eleanor
Kismaric, Carole Lee
Kitchin, Kate Parks
Klauber, Julie B.
Klaw, Barbara Van Doren
Klein, Morton
Klein, Samuel Edwin
Kline, Jacob
Knight, V. C.
Knotts, Glenn R(ichard)
Knowler, Faith Marion
Koch, Charles Joseph
Koch, Robert
Koger, Frank Williams
Kohn, James Paul
Konvitz, Milton Ridbaz
Koppett, Leonard
Kovach, Barbara Ellen
Kraft, C. William, Jr.
Kramer, Charles Henry
Kramer, Ferdinand
Krieg, Dorothy Linden
Krinsky, Mary McInerney
Krueger, Alan Douglas
Kullberg, John Francis
Kupferman, Theodore R.
Kupsch, Walter Oscar
Kushner, Donn Jean

L

Laatsch, Audrey Frieda
Labalme, Patricia Hochschild
Lacombe, Michael
Lair, Robert Louis
Laitin, Joseph
Lambert, Robert Lowell
Lams, Edmond George
Lamson, George Herbert
Landahl, Herbert Daniel
Landar, Herbert Jay
Landgren, George Lawrence
Langlinais, Joseph Willis
Langum, W. Sue
Larsen, Ethel Paulson
Lasagna, Louis Cesare
Lasker, Gabriel Ward
Lazarus, Richard Stanley
Leach, Gordon L.
Leach, Russell
Lechay, James
Lecours, Michel
Ledebur, Linas Vockroth, Jr.
Lederberg, Victoria
Leedy, Daniel Loney
Leeper, Harold Harris
LeFrak, Samuel Jayson
Lehne, Pascal Horst
Leis, Henry Patrick, Jr.
Leiser, Ernest Stern
Leisure, George Stanley, Jr.
Leith, John Haddon
Lenga, J. Thomas
Lerner, Alfred
Levin, Carl
Levine, Israel E.
Levine, Ruth Rothenberg
Lewis, Richard Stanley
Light, James Forest
Lind, James Forest
Lindsay, George Edmund
Lions, Jacques Louis
Lipman, Bernard
Lippold, Richard
Lipton, Clifford Carwood
Longmire, William Polk, Jr.
Lucker, Raymond Alphonse
Ludgin, Chester Hall
Lundy, Robert Fielden
Luther, Darlene
Lynt, Richard King

M

Ma, Fengchow Clarence
Macdonald, Donald Arthur
MacDonald, Gordon James Fraser
Mackey, Leonard Bruce
MacLeod, Robert Fredric
Mac Rae, Herbert Farquhar
Madden, Bartley Joseph
Magliochetti, Joseph M.
Maletz, Herbert Naaman
Malvern, Lawrence Earl
Manning, Jack
Mansmann, Carol Los
Marcus, Dorothy Mann
Marke, Julius Jay
Marks, Edwin S.
Marsh, Robert Charles
Marshall, Burke
Marshall, Susan Lockwood
Marth, Fritz Ludwig
Martin, Keith
Massey, Donald Wayne
Mather, John Russell
Mathews, Kenneth Pine
Mathis, William Lowrey
Mayberry, Herbert Sylvester
McAnally, Johnnie Sue
McBay, Arthur John
McCall, Billy Gene
Mc Carthy, D. Justin
McCauley, Helen Nora
McCool, William C.
McCormack, Mark Hume
McCully, Bruce Calvin
McDaniel, Boyce Dawkins
McDermid, Alice Marguerite Connell (Mrs. Ralph Manewal McDermid)
Mc Elroy, William Theodore
McGary, Betty Winstead
McGrath, J. Nicholas
Mc Kitrick, Eric Louis
Mc Lucas, John Luther
Mc Mullen, Edwin Wallace, Jr.
McNabb, Talmadge Ford
Medearis, Roger Norman
Meehl, Paul Everett
Mehring, Clinton Warren
Meier, Marianne Marlyn
Melmon, Kenneth Lloyd
Meloan, Taylor Wells
Merchant, Donald Joseph
Meredith, Howard Lynn
Merton, Robert K.
Metz, Ronald Irwin
Metzler, Dwight Fox
Miceli, Mother Ignatius
Middleton, John Albert
Miller, Israel
Miller, Rene Harcourt
Mills, Liston Oury
Milner, Max
Minahan, John English
Mink, Patsy Takemoto
Mintz, Kenneth Andrew
Miracle, Robert Warren
Mitchell, Robert Everitt
Modigliani, Franco
Mogabgab, William Joseph
Moll, Clarence Russel
Moore, Paul, Jr.
Moore, Thomas Carrol
Morath, Inge
Morgan, Lewis Render
Morris, John Theodore
Mortola, Edward Joseph
Moynihan, Daniel Patrick
Mueller, William Martin
Mulligan, James Francis
Murphy, Francis Seward
Murray, Leonard Hugh
Murray, Peter Bryant
Murtagh, John Edward
Myers, Minor, Jr.

N

Nakamura, Kazuo
Navalkar, Ramchandra Govindrao
Neilson, Elizabeth Anastasia
Nelkin, Dorothy
Nelson, Richard Philip
Newman, Harry Rudolph
Newman, James Wilson
Newman, Richard Alan
Newton, James Quigg, Jr.
Nichols, Sandra Lee
Nickford, Juan
Nicol, Jessie Thompson
Niehaus-Kleinman, Agnes
Nissenbaum, Gerald
Noble, Richard Lloyd
Noelke, Paul
Norling, Irwin Denison
Nowstrup, Eldon Inor
Nye, John Calvin

O

Oakes, John Bertram
O'Bannon, Frank Lewis
O'Donohue, Walter John, Jr.
O'Hara, Thomas Edwin
O'Hare, Marilynn Ryan
Olayan, Suliman Saleh
Oldham, Lea Leever
Olsen, Jack
Olson, Robert Leonard
Orban, Edmond Henry
Otteson, Holly Carol Harvick-Ward

P

Pachman, Daniel J.
Paddock, Austin Joseph
Paganucci, Paul Donnelly
Palmer, Robert Roswell
Pan, Huo-Hsi
Pane, Michael Anthony
Papper, Emanuel Martin
Parker, Fred I.
Parker, Harold Talbot
Parker, Warren Andrew
Parmer, Edgar Alan
Parmley, Loren Francis, Jr.
Paul, Courtland Price
Pearlstein, Stephanie Lilienthal
Pearson, Nathan Williams
Pearson, Phillip Theodore
Pease, John Alan
Perkins, James Winslow
Petacque, Arthur M.
Peterson, Leroy
Peterson, Leslie Ernest
Phibbs, Harry Albert
Phillips, Spencer Kleckner
Pickett, Doyle C.
Pickett, George Bibb, Jr.
Pierce, Samuel Riley, Jr.
Pike, Douglas Eugene
Pilchik, Ely Emanuel
Pittman, David Joshua
Plano, Jack Charles
Platthy, Jeno
Plimpton, George Ames
Ploger, Robert Riis
Politz, Henry Anthony
Pollitzer, William Sprott
Pomeroy, Harlan
Poor, Anne
Poulsen, Lawrence LeRoy
Povish, Kenneth Joseph
Powers, Edward Latell
Prevoznik, Stephen Joseph
Pribble, Easton
Price, Lucile Brickner Brown
Prigogine, Ilya
Purdy, John Edgar
Putnam, Joanne White

Q

Queen, Daniel

R

Rabb, Maxwell Milton
Rada, Alexander
Radcliff, William Franklin
Radway, Laurence Ingram
Randall, William B.
Rankin, Helen Cross
Reagan, Barbara Benton
Rector, Margaret Hayden
Redstone, Louis Gordon
Regan, Donald Thomas
Reinemund, John Adam
Remick, Oscar Eugene
Reynolds, H. Gerald
Reynolds, Harry Lincoln
Reynolds, Jack W.
Reynolds, John W.
Rhoads, Jonathan Evans
Rhodes, John Jacob
Rhyne, Charles Sylvanus
Riach, Douglas Alexander
Rice, Ross R(ichard)
Rice, Stan, Jr.
Richler, Mordecai
Rick, Charles Madeira, Jr.
Ricker, William Edwin
Riegert, Robert Adolf
Riemer, Neal
Riley, Anthony William
Riley, William Franklin
Rinsch, Charles Emil
Rizer, Franklin Morris
Roach, John Robert
Roach, William Russell
Robbins, Frederick Chapman
Roberts, James Gordon
Robinson, Theodore Curtis, Jr.
Robson, John Edwin
Rochlis, James Joseph
Rogers, Fred McFeely
Rohlena, Robert Charles
Rollhaus, Philip Edward, Jr.
Romanoff, Elijah Brauman
Rose, Reginald
Rose, Ruth Ormsby
Rosen, Charles Abraham
Rosenthal, Harold Leslie
Rosow, Jerome Morris
Ross, Charles Robert
Rostow, Walt Whitman
Rothenberg, Robert Edward
Rothing, Frank John
Rotman, Morris Bernard
Rowe, Joseph Everett
Rudd, Eldon
Rueger, Lauren John
Rusoff, Irving Isadore

S

Sabaroff, Rose Epstein
Saffels, Dale Emerson
Sager, Roderick Cooper
Said, Edward W.
Saine, Betty Boston
St. Landau, Norman
Sakita, Bunji
Samuel, Howard David
Saunders, Dero Ames
Sauvey, Donald (Donald Robert Sauvey)
Schaap, Richard Jay
Schaefer, Jacob Wernli
Scheer, Julian Weisel
Schenken, Jerald Rudolph
Schooley, Dolores Harter
Schorr, Martin Mark
Schroeder, David Harold
Schutz, Herbert Dietrich
Schwab, Glenn Orville
Schwartz, Allen G.
Schwartz, William A(llen)
Schwarz, J(ames) Conrad
Schwed, Peter
Scurlock, Arch Chilton
Segal, George
Segal, Geraldine Rosenbaum
Segal, Irving Randall
Seiler, Wallace Urban
Selby, Roy Clifton, Jr.
Seton, Fenmore Roger
Sevier, Ernest Youle
Sewell, William Hamilton
Shannon, James Patrick
Shatan, Chaim Felix
Shatzkin, Leonard
Shaw, John Arthur
Shen, Jerome Tseng Yung
Sher, Norman
Shields, Carol Ann
Shine, Mary Tonissen
Shirley, Glenn Dean
Short, Earl DeGrey, Jr.
Sickels, Robert Judd
Sidransky, Herschel
Siegel, Melvyn Harry
Silverman, Herbert R.
Simmons, Miriam Quinn
Simnad, Massoud T.
Simon, Julian Lincoln
Sims, Thomas Auburn
Singer, Merton
Singletary, Otis Arnold, Jr.
Sisson, Robert F.
Skinner, David Bernt
Slade, Winton Lee
Slater, Joseph Elliott
Slepian, Paul
Sloane, Robert Malcolm
Smalley, Eugene Byron
Smith, Alexander Goudy
Smith, Bennett Walker
Smith, Bruce David
Smith, Charles Lewis
Smith, Howard McQueen
Smith, Jerome Hazen
Smith, Leonard Bingley
Smith, Ruth Lillian Schluchter
Smith, Samuel Boyd
Snell, John Raymond
Sokolow, Maurice
Solberg, Myron
Soldo, John J.
Solender, Sanford
Sollid, Faye Eising
Solomon, Ezra
Solomon, George Freeman
Sorrel, William Edwin
Spector, Louis
Spedale, Vincent John
Spencer, Donald Clayton
Spirtos, Nicholas George
Sprague, James Mather
Stannett, Vivian Thomas
Stare, Fredrick John
Staver, Leroy Baldwin
Sternberg, Harry
Stevenson, Earl, Jr.
Stewart, Harris Bates, Jr.
Stiver, William Earl
Stokes, Charles Junius
Stolper, Wolfgang Friedrich
Stone, Elizabeth Wenger
Stone, Franz Theodore
Stone, Peter
Stoner, Gerald Lee
Storer, Thomas Perry
Strandjord, Paul Edphil
Strandness, Donald Eugene, Jr.
Strosahl, William Austin
Stump, Robert Lee
Sturrock, Thomas Tracy
Sugarman, Samuel Louis
Summersell, Frances Sharpley
Sumner, James DuPre, Jr.
Sundberg, Alan Carl
Sunderman, Frederick William, Sr.
Sunia, Tauese Tuailemafua Pita Fiti
Sutcliffe, Marion Shea
Sutherland, Donald James
Sutton, Willis Anderson, Jr.
Sweeney, George Bernard
Szabad, George Michael
Szoverffy, Joseph
Szulc, Tad

T

Takano, Masaharu
Taplin, Frank E., Jr.
Tapper, David
Taylor, Barbara Jo Anne Harris
Taylor, Kenneth J.
Teclaff, Ludwik Andrzej
Temple, Wick
Tener, George E.
Terry, John Hart
Terzian, Shohig Garine Sherry
Thielsch, Helmut John
Thomas, Harold Allen, Jr.
Thompson, William Benbow, Jr.
Throckmorton, Joan Helen
Throdahl, Monte Corden
Thuillier, Richard Howard
Thurmond, Strom
Timberg, Sigmund
Timberlake, Marshall
Timpte, Robert Nelson
Tombaugh, Richard Lee
Tomlinson, Warren Leon
Townsend, Frank Marion
Trezise, Philip Harold
Trippe, Kenneth Alvin Battershill
Triska, Jan Francis
Troy, Joseph Freed
Truman, David Bicknell
Tuck, Edward Hallam
Tunnessen, Walter William, Jr.
Turner, Arthur Edward
Tuttle, Arthur Norman, Jr.

V

Vance, Robert Mercer
Van Cleve, William Moore
Varnedoe, John Kirk Train

Vazsonyi, Balint
Velde, John Ernest, Jr.
Ventry, Paul Guerin
Vermeule, Emily Townsend (Mrs. Cornelius C. Vermeule III)
Vernon, David Harvey
Villars, Felix Marc Hermann
Vogel, Ronald Bruce
Vollmer, Richard Wade
Voris, David Clarence
Vorwerk, Etta Charlsie

W

Walker, Harold Blake
Walker, Richard Louis
Walker, Warren Stanley

Walklet, John James, Jr.
Wallace, Virginia Barton
Walsh, George William
Walters, Raymond, Jr.
Ward, Hiram Hamilton
Ward, Robert Joseph
Warner, Harry Backer, Jr.
Watkins, John Cletis
Webb, Howard William, Jr.
Webb, Robert Kiefer
Wechter, Vivienne Thaul
Weil, Gilbert Harry
Weinhouse, Sidney
Weir, Thomas Charles
Weisbrot, Marvin Myron
Weiss, Donald L(ogan)
Weiss, Theodore Russell

Wells, Fay Gillis
Wellstone, Paul
Wentworth, Michael Justin
Wertheimer, Franc
Wertz, Dorothy Corbett
West, Arthur James, II
Wester, Keith Albert
Whipple, David Doty
Whitford, Albert Edward
Whitney, Robert Michael
Whitten, C. G.
Widiss, Alan I.
Wiener, Jerry M.
Wieschenberg, Klaus
Wiesner, Louis Arnold
Wilbur, Stephen
Wiley, Don Craig

Willey, Gordon Randolph
Williams, George Howard
Williams, Harold Anthony
Williams, Hiram Draper
Wilson, Arthur Jess
Wilson, John
Wilson, Robert Neal
Wilzig, Siggi Bert
Winks, Robin William
Wise, Sybil Zulalian
Wohl, Ronald Gene
Work, William
Wray, John Lawrence
Wronski, Stanley Paul
Wu, Nelson Ikon
Wurzburger, Walter Samuel
Wyman, Louis Crosby

Y

Yardley, John Finley
York, Richard Travis
Young, John Byron

Z

Zachmann, Milo
Zeleny, Marjorie Pfeiffer (Mrs. Charles Ellingson Zeleny)
Zick, Leonard Otto
Ziegler, Ronald Louis
Ziff, Paul
Zimmerman, Everett Lee